O31
W92w
1977

Late News, Addenda, Changes

Population

U.S. Population: The Census Bureau estimated the total U.S. population, including Armed Forces overseas, as of Aug. 1, 1976, at 215,276,000; total resident in U.S. at 214,808,000 (P. 227).

Wilkes County, Ga.: The 1970 Census population should read 10,184 (P. 268).

U.S. Public Officials

The new Army chief of staff is Gen. Bernard W Rogers (P. 321).

Secretary of Agriculture Earl L. Butz resigned Oct. 4 (Pp. 289, 301).

Julius L. Katz was confirmed as an assistant secretary of state Sept. 15, 1976 (P. 288).

The new U.S. Commissioner of Education is Edward Aguirre (P. 290).

Military Pay Scales

U.S. military pay scales were raised Oct. 1, 1976, an overall average 4.85%, allocated as follows: basic pay, 3.62%; allowance for quarters, 9.64% to 16.33%, depending on grade; subsistence, 4.83% (Pp. 328-329).

Heads of States, Prime Ministers (Pp. 593-595)

Barbados: J.M.G. Adams, Labor party, succeeded Errol W. Barrow, Democratic Labor, as prime minister Sept. 3, 1976, after an election.

Ireland: Pres. Cearbhall O. Dalaigh resigned Oct. 22, 1976. A presidential commission took over pending a new election.

Kuwait: Prime Minister Crown Prince Jaber al-Ahmed al-Sabah resigned Aug. 29.

Lebanon: Elias Sarkis, a Maronite Christian, was inaugurated president Sept. 23, 1976.

Madagascar: Justin Rakotoniaina succeeded Joel Rakotomalala, killed in a helicopter crash, as prime minister Aug. 21, 1976.

Sweden: Thorbjorn Falldin, Center party, was elected Sweden's first non-Socialist prime minister in 44 years, Oct. 7, 1976, succeeding Olof Palme.

Thailand: Adm. Sa-ngad Chaloryu, defense minister, took over the government as head of an Administrative Reform Committee, ousting the government of Prime Minister Seni Pramoj, in a military coup, Oct. 6, 1976.

North American Cities

El Paso: The area of El Paso should read 160,742 sq. mi. (P. 619).

Hartford, Conn.: The Hartford Times went out of

(Continued on Page 41)

The World Almanac

and Book of Facts for 1977

The Ten Top Stories of 1976

Muddle and mediocrity marked the most lackluster **presidential campaign** in a generation. It was enlivened only by the novelty of debates between **Carter and Ford** and by a series of minor blunders by both candidates. There was little attempt to discuss the issues. The public was noticeably unenthusiastic about either candidate.

Yielding to pressure from Saudi Arabia, left-wing Palestinians and Syrian forces **fighting in Lebanon** agreed to a ceasefire, thus bringing relative peace to that country for the first time in 18 months of civil war and Syrian intervention.

Rhodesian isolation epitomized extensive changes in **southern African affairs.** As leftist governments consolidated their holds on Angola and Mozambique, South Africa and the U.S. pressured Rhodesia into accepting black majority rule by 1978. South Africa itself showed some sign of accommodation to black demands after the most violent black rioting in the country's history.

Ninety-one hostages and twelve Air France crewmen were rescued in a daring night **raid on Entebee** airport, Uganda, by Israeli airborne commandos. The brilliant military operation killed the Arab terrorists who had taken the hostages captive. Also dead were several Ugandan soldiers whose leader, Uganda President Idi Amin, apparently collaborated with the terrorists.

After nearly 30 years of strong leadership by Chairman Mao Tse-tung and Premier Chou En-lai, **Communist China** faced an uncertain future when these two men died within months of each other.

Lawless **FBI and CIA activities** were thoroughly documented by Senate and House investigating committees which recommended extensive changes in the ways both organizations were overseen by Congress and the executive branch.

Economic news, which had been cautiously promising in the first half of the year, turned sour in July as **economic growth slowed,** unemployment rose, and the Dow Jones industrial average once again fell below 1,000.

Battling down to the wire, President Ford's and challenger Ronald Reagan's **fight for the Republican nomination** brought suspense and excitement to the usually humdrum process of nominating an incumbent president.

Offering love and honesty, former Georgia Governor Jimmy **Carter's nomination race** stunned the Democratic party and a field of contending stalwarts as he burst from obscurity to capture the party's prize on the first ballot.

Viking landers I and II became the first man-made objects to be soft-landed successfully on another planet, Mars. U.S. scientists were still puzzled over remote experiment reports from the landers which left undecided the question of life on Mars.

Carter Wins With Old Democratic Coalition

In a climactic finish to a presidential race termed "too close to call" by political pollsters, Democrat Jimmy Carter, Nov. 2, won an extremely narrow victory over Pres. Gerald R. Ford.

Pulling together a 297 to 241 electoral vote edge, Carter swept his native south and gathered enough support in the industrial north to give him the strength to win a close electoral vote majority.

In the popular vote contest, where almost 80 million votes were cast, Carter topped Ford by 1.75 million votes for a 51%-48% margin, the closest since 1968 when Richard M. Nixon won by 510,000 votes.

Carter became the first man from the deep south to win the presidency since Zachary Taylor was elected a century and a quarter ago. Ford, the first appointed president in the nation's history, was the first incumbent since Herbert Hoover to lose a presidential election.

South, Northeast Decisive

When the final results were in, Carter had won in 23 states and the District of Columbia. In his sweep of

the south, Carter carried all 11 states of the old Confederacy, except Virginia, as well as the border states of Kentucky, Tennessee, West Virginia, Maryland, and Delaware. The chief factors in the president-elect's solid southern showing were the support of blacks and the party organizations, with support in some black precincts running 20-to-one. Carter's victories in New York, Pennsylvania, Texas, Ohio and Massachusetts solidified his election as he got heavy backing from labor, and black, hispanic, and urban voters.

President Ford won heavily in the western and Rocky Mountain states to take a total of 27 states, including New Jersey, Michigan, Indiana, and Virginia. His victories were not large enough to offset Carter's southern and eastern strength. Most of the president's support came from white-collar and upper-income voters.

Carter Loses Early Lead

The presidential race that ended in a dead heat on election day looked much different in July when

Carter, after emerging from the Democratic National Convention with a solid first-ballot victory, led Ford by a 33% margin according to one poll. Ford gained strength following his defeat of Ronald Reagan and slowly began to whittle down Carter's lead as the campaign progressed. Ford's advisers had urged him to stay in the White House and play the role of the incumbent during the outset of the campaign. That strategy seemed to work.

Meanwhile, Carter, who had waged a brilliant primary campaign against some dozen opponents, found the general election campaign much harder going. At the beginning, he ran into militant anti-abortion demonstrations that gave a frivolous look to the campaign. An interview with Playboy magazine, in which he used lusty language, and an uninspiring performance in the first presidential debate further lowered Carter's stock with the electorate. Although he went on the attack in the 2d debate to emerge the winner, his virulent attacks on Ford for his Eastern European gaffe also brought criticism.

Ford often re-emphasized his image as a bumbler, especially when he inadvertently liberated Eastern Europe from Soviet domination or couldn't remember where he was on the campaign trail. Although Ford had promised to run on his record, time and again during the campaign, the president and his running mate Kansas Sen. Robert J. Dole made Carter the issue, calling him "weird" and dangerously inexperienced.

Perhaps the most significant aspect of the campaign as it progressed was the unusually high number of voters undecided up to the last days of the campaign. Political observers attributed the indecision to voter apathy in face of a choice between 2 uninspiring candidates. However, the undecided voters, contrary to projections, flocked to the polls in respectable numbers.

Mondale Helps Democrats

Carter's running mate, Minnesota Sen. Walter F. Mondale, played a significant role in the Democratic victory, perhaps supplying the strength Carter needed to win the election. An earnest, sincere campaigner, Mondale consistently ran about 3% ahead of Dole in polls, who was burdened by the reputation of being a hatchet man and Nixon apologist.

Another potential factor in the election was the 3d party candidacy of former Minnesota Sen. Eugene McCarthy. Fears that he would siphon away enough Carter votes to lose the election for the Democrats did not materialize, although McCarthy probably did cost Carter several close states.

Democratic Congress

The Democrats maintained their dominance of the Congress, assuring control of both the legislative and executive branches of government by the same party for the first time since the 1964-1968 Lyndon B. Johnson administration. The make-up of the new Congress seemed to assure President-elect Carter of support he would need to carry out his pledges to lower unemployment, reform government bureaucracy, and reform the nation's tax system.

In the Senate, the Democrats and Republicans ran neck-and-neck in the 33 seats in contention, each taking seats previously held by the other party. The Democrats would maintain a 62-38 margin over the Republicans. Virginia Sen. Harry F. Byrd Jr., runs as an independent but votes with the Democrats in the Senate.

Freshmen Stay On in House

In the House of representatives, despite a flurry of scandals involving Democrats and fears for the fate of their 75 freshman members, the Democrats increased their majority control by as many as 3 seats.

Of the 75 freshmen lawmakers, many of whom had come into office in the wake of the Watergate scandal, only 3 lost their seats, including Utah's Howe. All 17 Republican first-termers won re-election. Of other incumbents in both parties, only 9 lost their seats. The return of incumbents was the major trend in the election.

Women Add to House

In a controversial race in Kansas, incumbent Democrat Martha Keyes, a divorcee heavily criticized for her marriage last January to Indiana Democratic Rep. Andrew Jacobs, won re-election. Jacobs, who had received no criticism for the marriage, easily won his 6th term in Indiana. The victory of Keyes, who had outlasted a very close primary battle, was seen as a victory for women's rights.

Among 17 other women elected to the House, only 2 were newcomers. The newly-elected legislators were both Democratic councilwomen: Barbara Mikulski of Baltimore and Mary Rose Oakar of Cleveland.

More Democratic Governors

In races for state governorships, the Democrats increased their historically high domination of state executives by one, winning 9 out of 14 races for a 37 to 12 nationwide edge. As Democrats and Republicans swapped state control in half the races, the most stunning change came in Missouri with Democrat Joseph P. Teasdale's upset victory over the Republican incumbent, Gov. Christopher S. Bond. The Democrats also wrested state houses from Republicans in West Virginia, Washington, and North Carolina, while the Republicans retaliated in vermont, Delaware, and Illinois.

In the biggest Republican victory, in Illinois, the Republican candidate, James R. Thompson, the U.S. Attorney who had successfully prosecuted former Gov. Otto Kerner, defeated Secretary of State Michael J. Howlett, the hand-picked candidate of Chicago Mayor Richard Daley.

In Puerto Rico, San Juan Mayor Carlos Romero Barcelo, running on the pro-statehood New Progressive Party ticket, staged a staggering upset over the incumbent, Gov. Rafael Hernandez Colon. The loss was only the 2d since 1940 for Colon's Popular Democratic party.

Nuclear Power Favored

On the controversial issue of nucler power expansion, voters in 6 out of 7 states defeated proposals that would have restricted or controlled nuclear power plant development. Only in Missouri did voters strongly approve a measure that could block 2 nuclear plants and upset other electric utility construction plans. However, in Arizona, Colorado, Montana, Ohio, Oregon, and Washington, voters rejected anti-nuclear propositions that generally would have required legislative approval of new plants and eliminated federal restrictions on atomic power plant financial liability.

In other controversial state issues, the California electorate defeated Proposition 14, the proposal which, according to its backers, would have assured new rights for farm workers. In Arkansas, attempted repeal of the state's "right to work" law was rejected almost 2 to 1. The Arkansas contest had been considered a test of the possibility of abolishing elsewhere laws which forbid requiring workers to join unions as a condition of employment.

Biographies of the Principal Candidates in 1976

Pres. Gerald R. Ford — for biography, see Page 317.

James Earl "Jimmy" Carter Jr., first major-party nominee for president from the Deep South since before the Civil War, was born Oct. 1, 1924, at Plains, Ga., where his parents, 5th generation Georgians, had a farm and store. After studying at Georgia Tech, he fulfilled a boyhood dream by going to Annapolis; on graduating from the Naval Academy he entered the Navy's nuclear submarine program, working as a staff aide to Adm. Hyman Rickover, and studied nuclear physics at Union College, Schenectady.

His father died in 1953 and Carter left the Navy to take over the family businesses — seed-peanut raising, warehousing, and cotton-ginning — continuing their successful growth. He became a Baptist Church deacon, Sunday school teacher, and public school board member, was elected to the Georgia state Senate, was defeated for governor in 1966, and was elected in 1970.

At his inauguration in 1971 he declared: "No poor, rural, weak, or black person should ever have to bear the additional burden of being deprived of the opportunity of an education, a job, or simple justice." He appointed blacks to high state positions and, in 1972, hung a portrait of the Rev. Dr. Martin Luther King Jr. in the State Capitol.

As governor, he believed his main achievement was his government reorganization program; 300 government agencies and departments were consolidated into 22; he said he had saved the state $50 million a year, a figure representing a reduction in projected spending, not past spending. His administration spent more on "needed services," but was able to claim credit for a $166 million surplus when he left office.

In his campaign Carter said the cure for government ills was abolition of government secrecy, a return to majority control and "a government as good as the American people."

Viewed as a representative of the "new South," Carter was also an unusual candidate as an outspokenly religious man. And, he was the first nuclear physicist to run for the White House.

He married Rosalynn Smith, a neighbor, in 1946. They have 3 sons and a daughter. Carter described his father as a conservative, a foe of racial integration. His mother, the former Lillian Gordy, who had been a nurse, he called a liberal; at age 68, she joined the Peace Corps and spent 2 years in India.

Sen. Robert Joseph Dole of Kansas, Pres. Ford's choice for his vice-presidential running mate, was born in Russell, Kan., July 22, 1923. He planned to study medicine but joined the Army in World War II; he was severely wounded by a bursting shell in combat in Italy. His life was saved by an experimental dose of the new drug, streptomycin, but his wounds left him with a withered right arm.

He became a lawyer and launched a successful political career, never losing an election for legislator, county prosecutor, congressman, and senator. His voting record was strongly conservative except for his support of civil rights and food stamp legislation, which critics ascribed to lack of a major Negro rights problem in mostly-white Kansas and to the boost food stamps gave to the sale of Kansas wheat. Despite his conservative stance he had also been a staunch supporter of Ford in the latter's long battle with conservative Ronald Reagan for the Republican nomination.

Dole's aggressive speaking style won him a reputation as a strongly partisan "gut fighter." He had been a longtime supporter of Richard Nixon, who made him chairman of the GOP National Committee in 1971 but dropped him from the post a year later, apparently for displaying too much independence. Dole's defense of Nixon against Watergate charges in the Senate cost him support in his own reelection campaign in 1974; he scored a come-from-behind victory only after dissociating himself from Nixon and Watergate.

Dole's first wife, Phyllis Holden, whom he married in 1948 and divorced in 1972, was the physiotherapist who helped him overcome the effects of his wounds. They had a daughter, Robin, his only child. In 1975 he married Mary Elizabeth Hanford, a member of the Federal Trade Commission.

Sen. Walter Frederick "Fritz" Mondale of Minnesota, Jimmy Carter's choice for his vice-presidential running mate, was born Jan. 5, 1928, in Ceylon, Minn. One of 7 children of a Methodist minister, he was a high-ranking student at the University of Minnesota Law School, served 2 years in the Army in Korea, married Joan Adams, daughter of a Presbyterian minister, and got into politics as a protege of Hubert Humphrey.

Appointed Minnesota attorney general in 1960 by Gov. Orville L. Freeman, in whose law office he was working, Mondale a few months later became the youngest ever elected to the office. In 1962, he won re-election by an even larger margin. He achieved recognition for prosecuting charity frauds and illegal price fixing, and for battling for consumer protection.

Picked by his Democratic-Farmer-Labor party to succeed Humphrey as senator, Mondale proved a hard-working liberal who played major roles in the passage of anti-poverty legislation, the $35 individual income tax credit, and liberalization of the Senate cloture rule against filibusters. He also fought for greater spending on domestic needs and less on defense and space programs, higher taxes on the wealthy and on oil companies, and strong civil rights laws.

In 1974, he made a try at the presidential nomination himself, campaigning across the country, but dropped out in 1975 saying he preferred attending to his Senate duties and family obligations and felt he had no real chance of winning anyway. The Mondales have 2 sons and a daughter.

Republicans Nominate Ford and Dole

The Republican national convention, Aug. 16-19, 1976, brought to a dramatic windup a sharply-fought, 6-month, nationwide, running battle between Pres. Gerald R. Ford and ex-Gov. Ronald Reagan of California for the GOP presidential nomination.

Incumbent Ford, first unelected president in the nation's history, won a narrow victory over his conservative challenger at the Kansas City, Mo., showdown, 1,187 votes (1,130 needed to win) to 1,070 for Reagan, a 117-vote margin.

Apparently seeking to restore party harmony, rent in the long, abrasive fight for delegate votes, Ford conferred with Reagan immediately after the late-night convention vote, and announced the next day that Sen. Robert J. Dole, a conservative from Kansas, was his choice for vice-presidential nominee. The convention approved Dole by 1,921 votes of the total 2,259. The other 338 included votes for 31 seemingly random choices plus 103 abstentions, mostly protests against the Dole selection but including some irreconcilable Reaganites.

The naming of Dole was not Reagan's only success; his backers had forced the adoption of a conservative party platform, viewed by many as critical of the Ford administration's own foreign policies but apparently accepted by Ford forces to mollify the conservatives.

Just prior to the convention, several surprise moves topped off the long, hot campaign. Most astonishing was Reagan's announcement July 26 that Sen.

Richard S. Schweiker of Pennsylvania would be his running-mate should he win the nomination. Schweiker was one of the most liberal and pro-labor Republicans in Congress and the move came as a shock to the GOP conservatives who formed the hard core of Reagan backers. The choice brought a small flurry of switches among delegates but the main result seemed to be an increase in the number of those in the uncommitted column.

In apparent reply from the Ford camp, John B. Connally, former Texas governor, former Treasury secretary, and former Democrat, appeared with Ford at the White House the next day to announce he had finally jumped off his fence and was endorsing Ford's candidacy.

On June 30, Sen. Barry Goldwater of Arizona, the party's standard-bearer in 1964 and Reagan's conservative spiritual godfather, endorsed Ford — solely, he said, to avoid months of government reorganization if the incumbent lost.

The next unexpected maneuver came Aug. 11 when Sen. James L. Buckley, Conservative-Republican of New York, announced that conservative supporters had urged him to enter the presidential race as a "compromise candidate"; he said he had not said yes but that he would not "slam the door" on the possibility.

Ford campaign officials charged it was a ploy by Reagan backers to siphon votes from the president on the first ballot and force a second roll call, when many delegates would be freed to switch their votes.

Sen. Jesse Helms (N.C.), a conservative, said he suggested it to Buckley in hopes it would stop Ford and convince Reagan to let the convention make the vice-presidential choice. He was displeased at the Schweiker selection.

Buckley put an end to his "boomlet" on the first day of the convention, announcing that he would not seek the nomination and urging that no one vote for him. A draft-Buckley leader said he had been able to round up only 12 "solid" commitments of support from delegates.

The fierce intraparty rivalry, which would not be decided until the convention-floor vote, got under way with the early February primaries. The lead seesawed dramatically; much of the time it was indeterminable, clouded by conflicting claims from the 2 camps.

Ford won the first primaries, narrowly in New Hampshire, strongly in Massachusetts, Florida, and Illinois. Reagan captured North Carolina, Mar. 23, lost in Wisconsin, but smashed Ford in Texas May 1 and took Indiana, Georgia, and Alabama May 4, topped with a Nebraska landslide May 11. Reagan now had the lead in total delegates.

As May wore on, Ford took West Virginia, Michigan (by 2 to one), and Maryland. On one day, May 25, Ford swept Oregon, Kentucky, and Tennessee while Reagan reaped Arkansas, Idaho, and Nevada. A day earlier, Vice President Nelson A. Rockefeller swung 119 votes in his home state, New York, to the president and this gave Ford a strong lead in delegate strength.

June started with Ford getting Rhode Island while Reagan won South Dakota and Montana. A week later, the president swept Ohio and New Jersey, but Reagan followers delivered him his home state, California.

By convention time, Ford was apparently almost 100 delegates in the lead. But, according to various news media sources — newspapers, wire services, TV networks — which had been trying to keep accurate counts, neither candidate had enough votes for a first ballot victory.

But spokesman for both camps claimed they had more than enough. The Ford men said they had 1,134 votes (4 more than needed), and Reagan's manager was "certain" of 1,140.

Two leading newspapers were close in their tallies: 1,115 counted by each for Ford; 1,033 and 1,035 for Reagan; 109 and 111 still uncommitted.

But after the votes were counted, Ford called Reagan to the speaker's podium and the defeated candidate urged the party to go forth "united" against the Democrats. "There is no substitute for victory," he declared. He reminded the delegates, nearly half of whom had backed his conservative banner, that they had had great influence in shaping the platform on which the party would seek victory.

Ford, in his acceptance speech, called also for party reunification and introduced a new note in such addresses, issuing a challenge to Jimmy Carter, his next opponent, to meet him in a series of televised, "face to face" debates.

Democrats Nominate Carter and Mondale

Georgia's Jimmy Carter, far-out-front leader in the Democratic presidential primaries, went to his party's national convention in New York City, July 12-15, a sure winner. Victory in the important Ohio primary in June brought him pledges of sufficient delegate support from conceding rivals to take the nomination on the first ballot.

Carter proceeded to do it overwhelmingly with 2,238.5 votes (1,505 needed for nomination), to 329.5 for Rep. Morris K. Udall of Arizona, 300.5 for Gov. Edmund G. Brown Jr. of California, 22 for anti-abortion candidate Ellen McCormack, and 117.5 for others.

The major suspense at the conclave was provided by the question of Carter's vice-presidential choice, a secret he held leakproof until he announced, on the final convention day, it was Sen. Walter F. Mondale of Minnesota, whom the convention promptly approved by 2,817 of the 3,008 votes cast.

Convention Highlights

Highlights of the convention included a rousing keynote speech, July 12, by Rep. Barbara C. Jordan of Texas, the party's first black and first woman to be a keynoter. Her own role, she declared, went to show "that the American dream need not forever be deferred."

The varied backgrounds of convention speakers showed the wide coalition the Democrats were seeking to create: Sen. George McGovern, the 1972 nominee; Alabama Gov. George Wallace; Chicago Mayor Richard J. Daley; Coretta Scott King, widow of the Rev. Dr. Martin Luther King Jr.; Jerry Wurf, president of the State, County, and Municipal Employees; Adm. Elmo R. Zumwalt; and Cesar Chavez, United Farm Workers president.

Carter himself staged important meetings during but outside the convention; one with black leaders who declared afterward they would support him "without reservation." It took 2 meetings with women leaders to reach agreement, Carter promising to appoint women to high posts, to back passage of the Equal Rights Amendment, and to give them increased participation at the 1980 convention.

Ohio Is the Clincher

It was Ohio, where the primary vote had been so important to Carter's pre-convention strength, whose delegates cast the votes putting him over the 1,505 needed on the first ballot on July 14. It was followed by a welter of confusing vote-switches from other states to the Carter bandwagon, during which Gov. Brown, who had hung in for the vote along with Udall and McCormack, rose to tell his California delegation to give their votes to Carter "to begin a Democratic sweep across the country."

Mondale was chosen by Carter from among 6 senators and Rep. Peter Rodino of New Jersey, with each of whom he held pre-convention meetings. They included Henry Jackson (Wash.), Frank Church (Ida.), Adlai Stevenson 3d (Ill.), Edmund Muskie (Me.), and John Glenn (Oh.).

In accepting the nomination, Carter decried "lack of leadership . . . moral decay . . . lack of goals and values" and declared "a time for healing" has come.

He saw a need for love and peace; "love," he said, "must be aggressively translated into simple justice, while peace should be "the unceasing effort to preserve human rights."

Mondale accepted with a declaration that the American people want "a government that would restore honesty and decency and hope in American public life."

1976 Platforms of Major Parties

The party platforms adopted by the Democrats in July 1976 and by the Republicans in August contrasted sharply and offered American voters unusually clear choices between opposing views on a range of issues, most especially domestic. On foreign affairs, the Republican planks were not so different from the Democratic, the result of compromises by Pres. Ford's forces with the critical views of conservative Ronald Reagan's backers. The Democratic platform was in most part a reflection of the views of candidate Jimmy Carter.

Platform Preambles — The Democrats promised "an alternative to the failures of previous administrations" and pledged "a government that will be committed to a fairer distribution of wealth, income, and power." The Republicans called for less government, less spending, less inflation — "we want you to retain more of your own money, to use as you see fit for the necessities and the conveniences of life."

Jobs — The Democrats promised "every responsible effort to reduce adult unemployment to 3% in 4 years." The Republicans denounced "massive, federally-funded programs" such as the Humphrey-Hawkins jobs guarantee bill.

Taxes — The Republicans promised expanded tax cuts for the oil industry, for businesses, for investors, and for parents of college students. The Democrats pledged tax reforms to ease the burden for the poor and increase it for the rich.

Voting Procedure — The Democrats supported a federal law to permit voters to register by mail. The Republicans opposed such a law.

Busing — The Republicans said that should Congress fail to take action, they would favor a Constitutional amendment barring assignments of students to schools "on the basis of race." The Democrats declared that busing pupils to schools beyond their neighborhoods "remains a judicial tool of last resort," endorsing it.

Health Insurance — The Democrats suggested "a

comprehensive national system with universal and mandatory coverage." The Republicans said they opposed "compulsory national health insurance."

Abortion — The Republicans said they supported "the efforts of those who seek enactment of a Constitutional amendment to restore protection of the right to life of unborn children." The Democratic plank said that while some persons found abortions morally objectionable, the party opposed an amendment that would prohibit abortion.

Defense Spending — The Republicans urged a "superior" national defense and "a period of sustained growth in our defense efforts." The Democrats said they wanted to reduce current defense spending by $5 billion to $7 billion.

Gun Control — The Republicans opposed federal registration of firearms, but advocated mandatory sentences for crimes committed "with a lethal weapon." The Democrats similarly supported mandatory sentences for committing a felony with a gun, but urged stronger controls over handguns.

New Weapons — The Republicans urged development of a new intercontinental ballistic missile, the B-1 strategic bomber, a new missile-launching submarine force, and "a major shipbuilding program" for the Navy. The Democrats proposed a "tough-minded" attitude toward proposed new weapons which would add "only marginal military value" and postponement of B-1 production until next February, while urging a Navy that was "the foremost fleet in the world."

China — The Republicans declared that while normalizing relations with China, the U.S. should continue to support Taiwan's freedom and independence and remain committed to its mutual defense treaty with Taiwan. The Democrats said relations with China should include "early movement toward normalizing diplomatic relations in the context of a peaceful resolution of the future of Taiwan."

(Continued on page 40)

Voter Turnout in Presidential Elections, 1960-1972*
Source: League of Women Voters

National Average

1960....63%	1968....60%
1964....62%	1972....55.4%

1972 by State (%)

Alabama.	44	Kentucky.	48	North Dakota.	70
Alaska.	48	Louisiana.	45	Ohio.	57
Arizona.	52	Maine.	63	Oklahoma.	57
Arkansas.	49	Maryland.	50	Oregon.	62
California.	60	Massachusetts.	62	Pennsylvania.	56
Colorado.	61	Michigan.	59	Rhode Island.	62
Connecticut.	66	Minnesota.	68	South Carolina.	40
Delaware.	64	Mississippi.	46	South Dakota.	71
Dist. of Col.	32	Missouri.	57	Tennessee.	44
Florida.	51	Montana.	69	Texas.	45
Georgia.	38	Nebraska.	56	Utah.	70
Hawaii.	51	Nevada.	52	Vermont.	61
Idaho.	65	New Hampshire.	64	Virginia.	46
Illinois.	63	New Jersey.	60	Washington.	62
Indiana.	61	New Mexico.	61	West Virginia.	65
Iowa.	64	New York.	56	Wisconsin.	63
Kansas.	59	North Carolina.	44	Wyoming.	65

*Percentage of eligible population voting. The sharp drop in 1972 reflects the expansion of eligibility with the enfranchisement of 18 to 21 year olds.

Soviet Union — The Republicans said U.S. policy should be "based upon a realistic assessment of the Communist challenge in the world" and that the U.S. should remain "firm in the face of pressure" but willing to work on new reciprocal agreements toward peace and stability.' The Democrats urged establishment of relations on "a stable basis, avoiding excesses of both hope and fear," while negotiating with increased firmness.

Middle East — Democrats and Republicans both pledged support for peace in the area and continued U.S. support for Israel; both declared their opposition to boycotts. The Republicans said they had improved relations with the "more moderate" Arab nations. The Democrats said "the special relationships" with Israel did not prejudice improved relations with other nations.

Panama Canal — The Republicans said any negotiations on the canal's future must not cede any rights or jurisdiction "necessary for the protection and security of the U.S. and the entire Western Hemisphere." The Democrats promised support for a new Panama Canal treaty that "insures the interests of the U.S., "recognizes the interests of canal workers, and has "wide hemispheric support."

Other Issues — The Democratic platform committee rejected proposals favoring decriminalization of marijuana and endorsing homosexual rights. The Republicans deleted, in late action requested by a Ford delegate, the only mention of former Pres. Richard M. Nixon, which appeared in the plank on Chinese relations.

Electoral Votes for President, 1956-72

The Constitution, Article 2, Section 1 (consult index), provides for the appointment of electors, the counting of the electoral ballots and the procedure in the event of a tie. *(See Electoral College.)*

State	1956 R...	D.	1960 R.	D.	1964 R.	D.	1968 R.	D.	3d	1972 R.	D.
Ala.		'11		²5	10			10	9		
Alas.			³3		3			3			
Ariz.	4		4		5		5			6	
Ark.		8		8		6		6		6	
Cal.	32		32		40	40		40		45	
Col.	6		6		6	6				7	
Conn.	8		8		8		8			8	
Del.	3		3		3	3			3		
D.C.			³3			3			3		3
Fla.	10		10		14	14			17		
Ga.		12		12	12			12	12		
Ha.			³3		4	4			4		4
Ida.	4		4		4	4			4		4
Ill.	27		27		26	26			26		26
Ind.	13		13		13	13			13		13
Ia.	10		10		9	9			8		
Kan.	8		8		7	7			7		
Ky.	10		20		9	9			9		
La.	10			10	10			10	10		
Me.	5		5		4	4			4		
Md.	9		9		10	10			10		
Mass.	16		16		14	14			14		14
Mich.	20		20		21	21			21		
Minn.	11		11		10	10			10		
Miss.		8	(²)	7		7	7			7	
Mo.		13		13	12	12			12		
Mon.	4		4		4	4			4		

State	1956 R...	D.	1960 R.	D.	1964 R.	D.	1968 R.	D.	3d	1972 R.	D.
Neb.	6		6		5	5			5		
Nev.	3		3		3	3			3		
N.H.	4		4		4	4			4		
N.J.	16		16		17	17			17		
N.M.	4		4		4	4			4		
N.Y.	45		45		43	43		43		41	
N.C.		14		14	13	12		⁴1	13		
N.D.	4		4		4	4			3		
Oh.	25		25		26	26			25		
Okla.	8		²7		8	8			8		
Ore.	6		6		6	6			6		
Pa.	32		32		29	29			27		
R.I.	4		4		4	4			4		
S.C.	8		8	8		8			8		
S.D.	4		4		4	4			4		
Tenn.	11		11		11	11			10		
Tex.	24		24		25		25		26		
Ut.	4		4		4	4			4		
Vt.	3		3		3	3			3		
Va.	12		12		12	12			⁵11		
Wash.	9		9		9	9			9		
W. Va.	8		8		7	7			6		
Wis.	12		12		12	12			11		
Wy.	3		3		3	3			3		
Totals.	457	'74	219	303	52	486	301	191	46	520	17
Plurality.	383	...	...	²84	...	434	110	...	...	²503	...

(1.) In 1956 in Alabama one Democratic elector refused to vote for Stevenson and cast his ballot for Walter B. Jones, making the Democratic total actually 73.

(2.) In 1960 Sen. Harry F. Byrd (D.-Va.) got 15 electoral votes including those of 8 unpledged Mississippi Democratic electors, 6 unpledged Alabama Democrats, and one Oklahoma Republican.

(3.) First Presidential election.

(4.) In 1968 in North Carolina one Republican elector cast his ballot for Wallace.

(5.) In 1972 one Republican elector in Virginia cast his ballot for John Hospers.

Party Nominees for President and Vice President

Asterisk (*) denotes winning ticket

	Democratic		Republican	
Year	President	Vice President	President	Vice President
1900	William J. Bryan	Adlai E. Stevenson	William McKinley*	Theodore Roosevelt
1904	Alton B. Parker	Henry G. Davis	Theodore Roosevelt*	Charles W. Fairbanks
1908	William J. Bryan	John W. Kern	William H. Taft*	James S. Sherman
1912	Woodrow Wilson*	Thomas R. Marshall	William H. Taft	James S. Sherman(1)
1916	Woodrow Wilson*	Thomas R. Marshall	Charles E. Hughes	Charles W. Fairbanks
1920	James M. Cox	Franklin D. Roosevelt	Warren G. Harding*	Calvin Coolidge
1924	John W. Davis	Charles W. Bryan	Calvin Coolidge*	Charles G. Dawes
1928	Alfred E. Smith	Joseph T. Robinson	Herbert Hoover*	Charles Curtis
1932	Franklin D. Roosevelt*	John N. Garner	Herbert Hoover	Charles Curtis
1936	Franklin D. Roosevelt*	John N. Garner	Alfred M. Landon	Frank Knox
1940	Franklin D. Roosevelt*	Henry A. Wallace	Wendell L. Willkie	Charles McNary
1944	Franklin D. Roosevelt*	Harry S. Truman	Thomas E. Dewey	John W. Bricker
1948	Harry S. Truman*	Alben W. Barkley	Thomas E. Dewey	Earl Warren
1952	Adlai E. Stevenson	John J. Sparkman	Dwight D. Eisenhower*	Richard M. Nixon
1956	Adlai E. Stevenson	Estes Kefauver	Dwight D. Eisenhower*	Richard M. Nixon
1960	John F. Kennedy*	Lyndon B. Johnson	Richard M. Nixon	Henry Cabot Lodge
1964	Lyndon B. Johnson*	Hubert H. Humphrey	Barry M. Goldwater	William E. Miller
1968	Hubert H. Humphrey	Edmund S. Muskie	Richard M. Nixon*	Spiro T. Agnew
1972	George S. McGovern	R. Sargent Shriver Jr.	Richard M. Nixon*	Spiro T. Agnew

(1) Died Oct. 30 and the Republican National Committee named Nicholas Murray Butler.

business Oct. 20, 1976 (P. 622-623).

Miami: The new executive editor of the Miami Herald is John McMullan (P. 631).

New York: The new treasurer of the New York News is Robert Schneider (P. 634-635).

Sports (Pp. 825-918)

Team Canada won the Canada Cup, defeating Czechoslovakia for the "world title" of hockey Sept. 15, 1976.

James Hunt, Britain, won the World Grand Prix auto driving championship in Gotemba, Japan, Oct. 24, 1976.

Nations of the World

Botswana: A new monetary unit was introduced Aug. 23, 1976, the pula (divided into 100 thebe), replacing the South African rand (P. 517).

China: Hua Kuo-feng was proclaimed chairman of the Chinese Communist party Oct. 24, 1976, succeeding the late Mao Tse-tung (P. 523).

Ambassadors (Pp. 596-597)

The Senate confirmed the nominations of 8 ambassadors Sept. 15, 1976. The ambassadors and their posts were:

Walter J. Stoessel Jr., West Germany.
David Eugene Boster, Guatemala.
Francois M. Dickman, United Arab Emirates.
Frank Crigler, Rwanda.
Charles A. James, Niger.
Patricia M. Byrne, Mali.
Ronald D. Palmer, Togo.
Melissa F. Wells, Guinea-Bissau.

Colleges and Universities

Dr. Joseph S. Murphy, president of Queens College, N.Y., (P. 202), became president of Bennington College in Vermont (P. 195).

Dr. Howard R. Swearer, president of Carleton College, Northfield, Minn. (P. 196), became president of Brown University (P. 195).

Msgr. Thomas G. Fahy, president of Seton Hall University, died Oct. 27, 1976 (P. 206).

1976 Awards, Prizes (Pp. 404-416)

The United States scored a clean sweep of the 1976 Nobel Prizes in the sciences, literature, and economics, the first time citizens of a single nation won all prizes awarded. The Nobel Peace Prize was not awarded in 1976.

Nobel Prize in Literature: Saul Bellow, born in Canada but grew up and lives in Chicago; $160,000.

Nobel Prize in Chemistry: Prof. William N. Lipscomb of Harvard University for studies on the structure of boranes or boron hydrides; $160,000.

Nobel Prize in Physics: Shared by Prof. Burton Richter of Stanford University and Prof. Samuel C.C. Ting of Massachusetts Institute of Technology for the discovery of a new type of elementary particle known as psi or J; $160,000 shared.

Nobel Prize in Medicine: Shared by Dr. Baruch S. Blumber, University of Pennsylvania Medical School, and Dr. D. Carleton Gajdusek, National Institute for Neurological Disease at Bethesda, Md., for discoveries concerning new mechanisms for the origin and dissemination of infectious diseases; $160,000 shared.

Nobel Memorial Prize in Economics: Dr. Milton Friedman, University of Chicago, for achievements in the fields of consumption analysis, monetary history, and stabilization policy; $160,000.

Louisa Gross Horwitz Prize: Two research biologists — Dr. Seymour Benzer, California Institute of Technology, and Dr. Charles Yanofsky, Stanford University, for studies on genetic structure and function; $20,000 shared.

Pulitzer Prizes: The name of the 1975 Editorial Cartoon Prize winner should be spelled Garry Trudeau (P. 408).

Gallatin Medal: Awarded by New York University to Alice Tully, musician and philanthropist for "contributions of lasting significance to society."

Miss America 1977: Dorothy Kathleen Benham, 20,

of Edina, Minn., a student majoring in vocal performance at Macalester College, St. Paul.

National Medal of Science: For distinguished scientific achievement, awarded by Pres. Ford to 15 scientists. They were: John W. Backus of I.B.M.; Manson Benedict, of Massachusetts Institute of Technology; Hans A. Bethe, Cornell University; Shiing-Shen Chern, University of California at Berkeley; George B. Dantzig, Stanford University; Hallowell Davis, Washington University; Paul Gyorgy, late of the University of Pennsylvania School of Medicine; Sterling Brown Hendricks, formerly of the Dept. of Agriculture; Joseph O. Hirschfelder, University of Wisconsin; William H. Pickering, California Institute of Technology's Jet Propulsion Lab; Lewis H. Sarett, Merck & Co.; Frederick E. Terman, Stanford University; Orville Alvin Vogel, Dept. of Agriculture and Washington State University; E. Bright Wilson Jr., Harvard University; Chien-Hsiung Wu, Columbia University.

Maria Moors Cabot Prizes: A gold medal and $1,000 awarded by Columbia University for journalism advancing inter-American understanding to each of 2 persons: Bernard Diederich, Time-Life News Service; Jorge S. Remonda-Ruibal, La Voz del Interior, Cordoba, Argentina. Special citations to: Robert U. Brown, Editor & Publisher, and German E. Ornes, El Caribe, Santo Domingo.

ZIP Codes (P. 264)

Rose Hill, Va.: the ZIP Code should be 22310.

Noted Personalities

American Writers of the Past: The correct spelling is James K. Paulding (P. 365).

Roman Catholic Hierarchy (P. 358)

Giacomo Cardinal Lercaro died Oct. 18, 1976.

Women (P. 285)

Judges who selected America's 25 most influential women should include (names not available at deadline): Vernon Jordan, executive director, National Urban League; Matina Horner, president, Radcliffe College; Eleanor Holmes Norton, N.Y. City commissioner for human rights.

Among the 25 most influential women, the name should be spelled Joan Ganz Cooney.

Aircraft Disasters (P. 749)

A Czechoslovak Ilyushin 18, Soviet-made, turboprop airliner crashed into a lake near Bratislava, July 28, 1976; 76 died.

A Venezuelan Air Force transport, a Lockheed Hercules C-130, crashed at a U.S. Air Force base in the Azores Sept. 4, while carrying a university choir; 68 died.

A British Airways Trident 3 jet and a Yugoslav-chartered DC-9 jet, collided near Zagreb, Yugoslavia, Sept. 10; all 176 died in aviation's worst collision disaster.

A Turkish Airlines Boeing 727 crashed into a mountain near Isparta, Turkey, Sept. 20; all 146 aboard died.

A Cuban DC-8 crashed into the sea off Barbados Oct. 6, apparently after an explosion; all 73 aboard died.

An Indian Airlines Caravelle jet crashed after takeoff at Bombay's Santa Cruz Airport Oct. 12; 95 were reported dead.

A Boeing 707 cargo jet, leased by Lloyd Aereo Boliviano, crashed in downtown Santa Cruz, Bolivia, Oct. 14, killing an estimated 100, in the plane and on the ground.

Hurricanes, Other Storms (P. 747)

Typhoon Olga caused tremendous floods on Luzon Is. in the Philippines May 23, 1976, killing at least 60 and leaving 630,000 homeless.

A typhoon struck Japan's southern island of Kyushu Sept. 13, leaving at least 84 dead and 41 missing.

Hurricane Liza struck La Paz, in Mexico's Baja California, Oct. 1, leaving at least 650 dead; authorities estimated the final count might be 1,000.

Election Statistics[1]

Popular and Electoral Vote for President 1976

States	1972 Election Vote Nixon	McGovern	Republican Nixon	Democrat McGovern	Electoral Vote Carter	Ford	Popular Vote Democrat Carter	Republican Ford	Indep. McCarthy	Am. Indep. Maddox
Ala.....	9		728,701	256,923	9		644,579	495,318		9,536
Alas.....	3		55,349	32,967		3	22,994	39,008		
Ariz.....	6		402,812	198,540		6	294,668	417,413	19,148	
Ark.....	6		445,751	198,899	6		495,909	266,713		
Cal.....	45		4,602,096	3,475,847	45		3,709,715	3,837,202		50,606
Col.....	7		597,189	329,980		7	446,807	566,870	25,062	
Conn. ...	8		810,763	555,498		8	646,760	715,235		6,818
Del.....	3		140,357	92,298	3		122,610	109,926	2,426	
D.C.....		3	35,226	127,627	3		127,562	25,184		
Fla.....	17		1,857,759	718,117	17		1,561,383	1,375,296	22,457	
Ga.....	12		881,496	289,529	12		955,191	470,530		
Ha.....	4		168,865	101,409	4		147,375	140,003		
Ida.....	4		199,384	80,826		4	126,362	204,188		5,747
Ill.......	26		2,788,179	1,913,472	26		2,223,107	2,324,669	50,129	
Ind.....	13		1,405,154	708,568	13		1,006,636	1,169,144		
Ia.......	8		706,207	496,206	8		619,710	632,486	18,602	
Kan.....	7		619,812	270,287		7	429,008	501,759		5,521
Ky.......	9		676,446	371,159	9		610,017	525,607	6,665	2,869
La.....	10		686,852	298,142	10		683,512	606,204	7,981	11,187
Me.....	4		256,458	160,584		4	231,283	234,434	11,423	
Md.....	10		829,305	505,781	10		735,618	648,980		
Mass....		14	1,112,078	1,332,540	14		1,425,476	1,027,883	65,561	
Mich.....	21		1,961,721	1,459,435		21	1,694,288	1,884,752	46,030	
Minn.....	10		898,269	802,346	10		1,067,894	818,120	34,682	
Miss.....	7		505,125	126,872	7		373,917	362,056	3,405	5,161
Mo.....	12		1,154,058	698,531	12		986,185	918,620	23,534	
Mont.....	4		183,976	120,197		4	146,696	170,156		
Neb.....	5		406,298	169,991		5	230,152	349,736	8,984	3,321
Nev.....	3		115,750	66,016		3	92,088	100,926		1,465
N.H.....	4		213,724	116,435		4	147,618	185,472.	4,892	
N.J.....	17		1,845,502	1,102,211	17		1,420,668	1,477,858	28,846	5,572
N.M.....	4		235,606	141,084		4	199,225	207,718		
N.Y.....	41		4,192,778	2,951,084	41		3,336,665	3,060,695	249	
N.C.....	13		1,054,889	438,705	13		923,533	738,545		
N.D.....	3		174,109	100,384		3	134,503	151,515	2,671	275
Oh.....	25		2,441,827	1,558,889	25		2,000,035	1,992,460	58,292	16,057
Okla.....	8		759,025	247,147		8	530,242	543,221	14,040	
Ore.....	6		486,686	392,760		6	484,643	485,305	39,980	
Pa.....	27		2,714,521	1,796,951	27		2,315,494	2,187,038	47,580	26,142
R.I.....	4		218,290	191,981	4		216,991	172,138		
S.C.....	8		477,044	186,824	8		443,901	342,409		2,073
S.D.....	4		166,476	139,945		4	146,153	151,619		
Tenn.....	10		813,147	357,293	10		822,250	633,228	4,785	2,368
Tex.....	26		2,298,896	1,154,289	26		2,036,484	1,880,581		
Ut.....	4		323,643	126,284		4	180,974	335,144	3,871	1,162
Vt.....	3		117,149	68,174		3	63,346	101,504	3,085	
Va.....	11*		988,493	438,887		12	810,696	834,605		
Wash....	9		837,135	568,334		9	643,333	679,631	32,621	7,377
W.Va....	6		484,964	277,435	6		430,404	311,012		
Wis.....	11		989,430	810,174	11		1,037,056	1,003,039	34,412	8,588
Wyo.....	3		100,464	44,358		3	62,267	92,831		
TOTAL[2]..	**520**	**17**	**47,165,234**	**28,168,110**	**297**	**241**	**40,276,040**	**38,532,630**	**657,785**	**168,724**

*One elector in Virginia for John Hospers and Theodora Nathan.
[1]1976 figures preliminary and unofficial.
[2]Totals may not add because they reflect later figures.

Presidential Election Returns by States

Compiled from official and unofficial returns by the World Almanac. (Preliminary)

Some County figures may not add to total shown.

Alabama

County	1972 McGovern (D)	Nixon (R)	1976 Carter (D)	Ford (R)
Autauga	1,593	5,367	4,640	4,512
Baldwin	2,923	15,104	9,191	13,256
Barbour	1,846	4,985	4,729	3,758
Bibb	837	3,332	2,850	1,591
Blount	1,582	6,486	6,665	4,223
Bullock	2,321	2,178	3,536	1,482
Butler	1,401	4,685	4,310	2,901
Calhoun	5,832	20,364	20,122	11,636
Chambers	2,076	8,716	6,164	5,488
Cherokee	1,182	3,179	4,533	1,603
Chilton	1,356	7,349	5,182	4,640
Choctaw	1,934	3,055	3,937	3,060
Clarke	2,031	5,256	4,730	4,126
Clay	507	3,948	2,946	1,885
Cleburne	581	3,420	2,490	1,436
Coffee	2,160	9,076	7,837	4,783
Colbert	4,811	11,215	11,861	4,373
Conecuh	1,042	3,214	2,835	1,640
Coosa	773	2,872	2,533	1,196
Covington	1,547	9,278	7,081	4,977
Crenshaw	1,085	3,129	3,372	1,801
Cullman	3,571	14,390	12,908	6,872
Dale	1,594	8,346	6,446	4,996
Dallas	5,427	8,644	8,866	7,144
DeKalb	3,759	9,434	6,295	4,207
Elmore	1,891	8,461	6,646	6,551
Escambia	1,598	8,883	6,654	4,840
Etowah	7,372	20,851	25,009	10,333
Fayette	836	4,240	4,076	2,165
Franklin	1,840	5,877	6,231	3,305
Geneva	1,049	5,851	5,805	3,101
Greene	3,235	1,404	2,900	903
Hale	1,779	2,859	3,735	2,503
Henry	853	3,414	3,144	2,052
Houston	2,358	12,622	8,754	10,597
Jackson	2,985	6,202	10,144	3,682
Jefferson	57,288	135,095	96,615	105,193
Lamar	766	3,283	3,860	1,739
Lauderdale	5,112	14,410	14,511	6,406
Lawrence	1,416	4,433	7,221	1,490
Lee	3,622	11,571	8,427	9,833
Limestone	2,079	6,188	8,703	2,994
Lowndes	2,559	1,990	3,731	1,620
Macon	3,636	1,931	5,915	1,387
Madison	13,108	38,899	36,235	21,150
Marengo	2,645	5,156	4,528	3,741
Marion	986	5,927	6,102	2,994
Marshall	3,894	12,090	13,174	5,751
Mobile	20,694	62,639	48,086	59,115
Monroe	1,636	5,159	3,669	3,476
Montgomery	12,723	35,353	24,515	29,265
Morgan	5,004	18,100	16,724	9,216
Perry	2,718	2,800	4,526	2,164
Pickens	1,933	4,071	3,777	2,968
Pike	1,624	5,690	5,386	4,363
Randolph	1,330	4,427	3,419	2,284
Russell	2,644	6,034	8,028	4,150
St. Clair	1,859	6,952	758	679
Shelby	1,538	9,390	7,200	9,025
Sumter	2,737	2,686	3,457	2,191
Talladega	4,567	12,763	10,538	6,345
Tallapoosa	2,113	8,535	7,603	5,240
Tuscaloosa	8,272	21,172	20,275	16,021
Walker	3,724	14,581	12,759	5,900
Washington	1,096	3,282	3,471	2,269
Wilcox	3,254	2,641	3,708	1,799
Winston	779	4,971	3,945	3,553
Totals	**256,923**	**728,701**	**644,579**	**495,318**

Alabama Vote Since 1932

1932 (Pres.), Roosevelt, Dem., 207,910; Hoover, Rep., 34,675; Foster, Com., 406; Thomas, Soc., 2,030; Upshaw, Proh., 13.

1936 (Pres.), Roosevelt, Dem., 238,195; Landon, Rep., 35,358; Colvin, Proh., 719; Browder, Com., 679; Lemke, Union, 549; Thomas, Soc., 242.

1940 (Pres.), Roosevelt, Dem., 250,726; Willkie, Rep., 42,174; Babson, Proh., 698; Browder, Com., 509; Thomas, Soc., 100.

1944 (Pres.), Roosevelt, Dem., 198,918; Dewey, Rep., 44,540; Watson, Proh., 1,095; Thomas, Soc., 190.

1948 (Pres.), Thurmond, States' Rights, 171,443; Dewey, Rep., 40,930; Wallace, Prog., 1.522; Watson,

Proh., 1,085.

1952 (Pres.), Eisenhower, Rep., 149,231; Stevenson, Dem., 275,075; Hamblen, Proh., 1,814.

1956 (Pres.), Stevenson, Dem., 290,844; Eisenhower, Rep., 195,694; Independent electors, 20,323.

1960 (Pres.), Kennedy, Dem., 324,050; Nixon, Rep., 237,981; Faubus, States' Rights, 4,367; Decker, Proh., 2,106; King, Afro-Americans, 1,485; scattering, 236.

1964 (Pres.), Dem., 209,848 (electors unpledged); Goldwater, Rep., 479,085; scattering, 105.

1968 (Pres.), Nixon, Rep., 146,923; Humphrey, Dem., 196,579; Wallace, 3d party, 691,425; Munn, Proh., 4,022.

1972 (Pres.), Nixon, Rep., 728,701; McGovern, Dem. 219,108 plus 37,815 Natl. Demo. Party of Alabama; Schmitz, Conservative, 11,918; Munn, Proh., 8,551.

Alaska

Election District	1972 McGovern (D)	Nixon (R)	1976 Carter (D)	Ford (R)
No. 1	1,526	2,529	1,150	1,958
No. 2	967	1,386	491	831
No. 3	1,393	1,549	917	1,362
No. 4	2,968	4,277	2,550	4,386
No. 5	903	1,689	444	797
No. 6	849	2,384	837	1,725
No. 7	2,854	4,527	2,446	3,460
No. 8	2,454	5,275	2,822	5,106
No. 9	2,501	6,759	1,422	2,196
No. 10	2,854	6,882	2,422	5,973
No. 11	1,337	2,686	3,081	5,781
No. 12	727	1,117	2,279	5,513
No. 13	178	293	1,758	3,493
No. 14	843	1,042	550	877
No. 15	1,235	919	312	449
No. 16	1,004	902	209	236
No. 17	5,535	7,672	389	384
No. 18	640	1,202	363	385
No. 19	1,155	1,114	619	894
No. 20	...	...	5,160	8,638
No. 21	...	...	646	373
No. 22	...	...	921	966
Totals	**32,967**	**55,349**	**31,788**	**55,783**

Alaska Vote Since 1960

1960 (Pres.), Kennedy, Dem., 29,809; Nixon, Rep., 30,-953.

1964 (Pres.), Johnson, Dem., 44,329; Goldwater, Rep., 22,930.

1968 (Pres.), Nixon, Rep., 37,600; Humphrey, Dem., 35,411; Wallace, 3d party, 10,024.

1972 (Pres.), Nixon, Rep., 55,349; McGovern, Dem., 32,967; Schmitz, American, 6,906.

Arizona

County	1972 McGovern (D)	Nixon (R)	1976 Carter (D)	Ford (R)
Apache	3,145	3,394	6,503	3,424
Cochise	6,023	11,706	9,316	9,981
Coconino	6,250	10,611	9,470	11,054
Gila	4,295	5,673	6,440	5,136
Graham	1,863	3,575	3,050	3,659
Greenlee	2,013	1,758	2,601	1,532
Maricopa	95,135	244,593	144,326	257,751
Mohave	2,588	6,755	6,173	7,166
Navajo	4,003	6,999	7,264	6,745
Pima	56,223	73,154	70,987	76,982
Pinal	6,404	10,584	10,595	9,354
Santa Cruz	1,866	2,137	2,265	2,312
Yavapai	3,977	12,277	7,685	12,998
Yuma	4,755	9,596	7,993	9,319
Totals	**198,540**	**402,812**	**294,668**	**417,413**

Arizona Vote Since 1932

1932 (Pres.), Roosevelt, Dem., 79,264; Hoover, Rep., 36,104; Thomas, Soc., 2,030; Foster, Com., 406.

1936 (Pres.), Roosevelt, Dem., 86,722; Landon, Rep., 33,433; Lemke, Union, 3,307; Colvin, Proh., 384;

Thomas, Soc., 317.
1940 (Pres.), Roosevelt, Dem., 95,267; Willkie, Rep., 54,030; Babson, Proh., 742.
1944 (Pres.), Roosevelt, Dem., 80,826; Dewey, Rep., 56,287; Watson, Proh., 421.
1948 (Pres.), Truman, Dem., 95,251; Dewey, Rep., 77,-597; Wallace, Prog., 3,310; Watson, Proh., 786; Teichert, Soc. Lab., 121.
1952 (Pres.), Eisenhower, Rep., 152,042; Stevenson, Dem., 108,528.
1956 (Pres.), Eisenhower, Rep., 176,990; Stevenson, Dem., 112,880; Andrews, Ind. 303.
1960 (Pres.), Kennedy, Dem., 176,781; Nixon, Rep., 221,241; Haas, Soc. Lab., 469.
1964 (Pres.), Johnson, Dem., 237,753; Goldwater, Rep., 242,535; Haas, Soc. Labor, 482.
1968 (Pres.), Nixon, Rep., 266,721; Humphrey, Dem., 170,514; Wallace, 3d party, 46,573; McCarthy, New Party, 2,751; Halstead, Soc. Worker, 85; Cleaver, Peace and Freedom, 217; Bloman, Soc. Labor, 75.
1972 (Pres.), Nixon, Rep., 402,812; McGovern, Dem., 198,540; Schmitz, American, 21,208; Soc. Worker, 30,945. (Due to ballot peculiarities in 3 counties (particularly Pima), thousands of voters cast ballots for the Socialist Workers Party and one of the major candidates. Court ordered both votes counted as official.

Arkansas

County	1972 McGovern (D)	Nixon (R)	1976 Carter (D)	Ford (R)
Arkansas	1,849	5,225	5,204	2,291
Ashley	1,680	5,506	5,253	3,092
Baxter	2,677	6,754	5,816	5,822
Benton	4,083	14,621	11,246	12,560
Boone	1,862	5,484	5,388	3,959
Bradley	1,368	3,218	3,374	1,076
Calhoun	707	1,298	2,014	495
Carroll	1,401	3,565	3,791	2,804
Chicot	1,469	2,858	3,868	1,621
Clark	2,741	4,173	6,641	1,816
Clay	1,933	4,381	5,664	1,893
Cleburne	1,400	2,870	5,617	1,892
Cleveland	734	1,837	2,320	646
Columbia	2,193	5,801	4,868	4,287
Conway	3,009	4,187	6,443	2,177
Craighead	5,843	11,312	13,840	6,213
Crawford	1,520	6,974	5,946	4,764
Crittenden	3,246	7,971	8,249	5,202
Cross	1,221	3,743	4,198	1,909
Dallas	1,402	2,152	3,266	1,012
Desha	1,665	3,385	4,412	1,372
Drew	1,168	3,334	3,750	1,730
Faulkner	4,604	6,746	11,118	3,822
Franklin	1,252	3,678	3,703	1,973
Fulton	960	2,030	2,670	1,038
Garland	5,207	15,602	15,607	10,394
Grant	1,147	2,414	3,797	1,047
Greene	2,263	6,128	7,495	2,690
Hempstead	2,047	4,963	5,397	2,859
Hot Spring	2,872	5,378	7,677	2,148
Howard	1,069	2,682	3,210	1,575
Independence	2,630	5,076	7,116	2,878
Izard	1,108	2,001	3,311	1,394
Jackson	2,092	4,196	6,456	1,783
Jefferson*	10,346	16,888	20,827	8,034
Johnson	2,045	4,107	5,044	2,173
Lafayette	952	2,460	2,342	1,467
Lawrence	1,751	3,981	5,167	1,708
Lee	1,907	3,540	3,463	1,574
Lincoln	1,115	2,318	3,045	699
Little River	1,091	2,550	3,142	1,431
Logan	1,956	4,964	5,313	2,909
Lonoke	2,504	5,298	7,761	2,522
Madison	1,889	3,372	2,926	2,502
Marion	1,108	2,331	2,979	2,052
Miller	2,855	8,355	6,828	4,735
Mississippi	3,544	10,931	10,135	5,800
Monroe	1,578	2,897	3,357	1,230
Montgomery	688	1,555	2,420	924
Nevada	1,179	2,513	3,101	1,163
Newton	831	1,924	1,840	1,611
Ouachita	3,931	6,620	8,946	2,753
Perry	810	1,445	2,310	832
Phillips	4,283	6,235	7,774	3,342
Pike	798	2,316	2,847	1,234
Poinsett	1,908	7,010	6,835	2,726
Polk	1,120	3,609	3,505	2,432
Pope	3,302	6,917	8,354	4,358
Prairie	873	2,186	2,479	733
Pulaski	33,611	57,576	63,541	37,690

Randolph	1,525	2,578	4,571	1,591
St. Francis	2,674	5,692	6,851	3,639
Saline	4,503	7,972	12,008	4,123
Scott	771	2,424	2,880	1,427
Searcy	853	3,163	2,067	1,767
Sebastian	5,770	25,219	15,698	17,661
Sevier	1,048	2,526	3,391	1,468
Sharp	1,154	2,677	3,378	2,151
Stone	958	1,989	2,718	1,014
Union	3,53†	11,925	8,257	7,918
Van Buren	1,594	2,622	3,868	1,605
Washington	7,108	17,523	15,610	14,132
White	4,161	8,701	11,132	4,677
Woodruff	1,183	1,989	3,044	867
Yell	1,669	3,310	5,417	1,805
Totals	**198,899**	**445,751**	**495,909**	**266,713**

*Official vote only. Actual vote was higher.

Arkansas Vote Since 1932

1932 (Pres.), Roosevelt, Dem., 189,602; Hoover, Rep., 28,467; Thomas, Soc., 1,269; Harvey, Ind., 1,049; Foster, Com., 175.
1936 (Pres.), Roosevelt, Dem., 146,765; Landon, Rep., 32,039; Thomas, Soc., 446; Browder, Com., 164; Lemke, Union, 4.
1940 (Pres.), Roosevelt, Dem., 158,622; Willkie, Rep.,42,121; Babson, Proh., 793; Thomas, Soc., 305.
1944 (Pres.), Roosevelt, Dem., 148,965; Dewey, Rep., 63,551; Thomas, Soc. 438.
1948 (Pres.), Truman, Dem., 149,659; Dewey, Rep., 50,959; Thurmond, States' Rights, 40,068; Thomas, Soc., 1,037; Wallace, Prog., 751; Watson, Proh., 1.
1952 (Pres.), Eisenhower, Rep., 177,155; Stevenson, Dem., 226,300; Hamblen, Proh., 886; MacArthur, Christian Nationalist, 458; Haas, Soc. Lab. 1.
1956 (Pres.), Stevenson, Dem., 213,277; Eisenhower, Rep., 186,287; Andrews, Ind., 7,008.
1960 (Pres.), Kennedy, Dem., 215,049; Nixon, Rep., 184,508; National States' Rights, 28,952.
1964 (Pres.), Johnson, Dem., 314,197; Goldwater, Rep., 243,264; Kasper, Nat'l. States Rights, 2,965.
1968 (Pres.), Nixon, Rep., 189,062; Humphrey, Dem., 184,901; Wallace, 3d party, 235,627.
1972 (Pres.), Nixon, Rep. 445,751; McGovern, Dem., 198,899; Schmitz, Amer. Party, 3,016.

California

County	1972 McGovern (D)	Nixon (R)	1976 Carter (D)	Ford (R)
Alameda	259,254	201,862	233,780	153,212
Alpine	195	366	189	225
Amador	2,705	3,533	4,036	3,698
Butte	18,401	28,819	24,133	28,306
Calaveras	2,268	4,119	3,602	3,691
Colusa	1,810	2,715	2,334	2,732
Contra Costa	111,718	139,044	123,182	125,846
Del Norte	2,156	2,927	2,785	2,466
El Dorado	8,654	11,330	12,750	12,442
Fresno	72,682	79,051	74,077	71,699
Glenn	2,681	4,569	3,500	4,090
Humboldt	21,132	22,345	23,433	18,002
Imperial	7,982	14,178	10,247	10,618
Inyo	2,006	4,873	2,635	3,906
Kern	41,937	71,686	50,514	57,937
Kings	7,274	10,509	8,061	8,263
Lake	4,715	6,477	6,350	5,428
Lassen	3,134	3,618	3,798	3,060
Los Angeles	1,189,977	1,549,717	1,208,798	1,159,186
Madera	6,580	7,835	9,363	6,833
Marin	47,414	54,123	43,545	53,346
Mariposa	1,487	2,122	2,093	2,010
Mendocino	9,435	11,128	10,602	9,613
Merced	13,914	17,737	16,537	14,836
Modoc	1,271	2,085	1,732	1,917
Mono	828	1,872	1,025	1,598
Monterey	32,545	47,004	36,615	40,634
Napa	14,529	23,403	17,945	20,706
Nevada	5,693	8,004	7,918	8,163
Orange	176,847	448,291	227,472	397,917
Placer	16,911	18,597	21,037	18,261
Plumas	3,057	2,952	3,429	2,884
Riverside	71,591	108,120	95,589	97,080
Sacramento	137,287	141,218	142,803	121,755
San Benito	2,582	3,961	2,802	3,398
San Bernardino	85,986	144,689	109,385	112,984
San Diego	206,455	371,627	259,298	246,552
San Francisco	170,882	127,461	132,966	103,213
San Joaquin	44,062	61,646	48,425	50,002
San Luis Obispo	20,779	28,566	24,830	27,660
San Mateo	109,745	135,377	102,239	116,475

	1972		1976	
	(D)	(R)	(D)	(R)
Santa Barbara.......	50,609	67,075	54,726	60,557
Santa Clara.........	208,506	237,334	206,818	217,817
Santa Cruz.........	32,336	34,799	37,521	31,594
Shasta............	17,214	16,618	18,428	16,630
Sierra.............	658	629	841	680
Siskiyou...........	6,434	7,563	7,057	7,062
Solano............	24,766	31,314	33,641	26,105
Sonoma...........	43,746	57,697	50,302	50,482
Stanislaus.........	35,005	39,521	38,190	32,744
Sutter.............	5,409	10,224	6,930	8,767
Tehama...........	5,175	6,054	6,990	6,110
Trinity.............	1,621	1,868	2,171	1,989
Tulare	21,775	36,048	25,527	31,826
Tuolumne..........	4,596	5,894	6,482	6,092
Ventura...........	49,307	95,310	68,323	82,345
Yolo..............	23,694	17,969	23,474	18,329
Yuba.............	4,435	6,623	6,440	5,487
Totals...........	**3,475,847**	**4,602,096**	**3,709,715**	**3,837,202**

California Vote Since 1932

1932 (pres.), Roosevelt, Dem., 1,324,157; Hoover, Rep., 847,902; Thomas, Soc., 63,299; Upshaw, Proh., 20,637; Harvey, Liberty, 9,827; Foster, Com., 1,023.

1936 (pres.), Roosevelt, Dem., 1,766,836; Landon, Rep., 836,431; Colvin, Proh., 12,917; Thomas, Soc., 11,325; Browder, Com., 10,877.

1940 (pres.), Roosevelt, Dem., 1,877,618; Willkie, Rep., 1,351,419; Thomas, Prog., 16,506; Browder, Com., 13,586; Babson, Proh., 9,400.

1944 (pres.), Roosevelt, Dem., 1,988,564; Dewey, Rep., 1,512,965; Watson, Proh., 14,770; Thomas, Soc., 3,923; Teichert, Soc. Lab., 327.

1948 (pres.), Truman, Dem., 1,913,134; Dewey, Rep., 1,895,269; Wallace, Prog., 190,381; Watson, Proh., 16,926; Thomas, Soc., 3,459; Thurmond, States' Rights, 1,228; Teichert, Soc. Lab., 195; Dobbs, Soc. Wkr., 133.

1952 (pres.), Eisenhower, Rep., 2,897,310; Stevenson, Dem., 2,197,548; Hallinan, Prog., 24,106; Hamblen, Proh., 15,653; MacArthur, (Tenny Ticket), 3,326; (Kellems Ticket) 178; Haas, Soc. Lab., 273; Hoopes, Soc., 206; Scattered, 3,249.

1956 (pres.), Eisenhower, Rep., 3,027,668; Stevenson, Dem., 2,420,136; Holtwick, Proh., 11,119; Andrews, Constitution, 6,087; Haas, Soc. Lab., 300; Hoopes, Soc., 123; Dobbs, Soc. Workers, 96; Smith, Christian Nat'l., 8.

1960 (pres.), Kennedy, Dem., 3,224,099; Nixon, Rep., 3,259,722; Decker, Proh., 21,706; Haas, Soc. Lab., 1,051.

1964 (pres.), Johnson, Dem., 4,171,877; Goldwater, Rep., 2,879,108; Haas, Soc. Labor, 489; DeBerry, Soc. Worker, 378; Munn, Proh., 305; Hensley, Universal, 19.

1968 (pres.), Nixon, Rep., 3,467,664; Humphrey, Dem., 3,244,318; Wallace, 3d party, 487,270; Peace and Freedom party, 27,707; McCarthy, Alternative, 20,721; Gregory, write-in, 3,230; Mitchell, Communist, 260; Munn, Prohibition, 59; Blomen, Socialist, 341; Soeters, Defense, 17.

1972 (pres.), Nixon, Rep., 4,602,096; McGovern, Dem., 3,475,847; Schmitz, Amer., 232,554; Spock, Peace and Freedom, 55,167; Hall, Communist, 373; Hospers,·Libertarian, 980; Munn, Prohibition, 53; Fisher, Soc. Labor, 197; Jenness, Soc. Workers, 574; Green, Universal, 21.

Colorado

	1972		1976	
	McGovern	Nixon	Carter	Ford
County	(D)	(R)	(D)	(R)
Adams.............	24,170	40,372	40,512	35,352
Alamosa...........	1,540	2,916	2,052	2,599
Arapahoe..........	18,631	52,283	33,675	63,154
Archuleta..........	300	606	652	778
Baca.............	527	1,645	1,164	1,303
Bent..............	787	1,525	1,268	1,156
Boulder...........	29,494	40,766	26,456	33,929
Chaffee...........	1,354	2,859	1,954	2,925
Cheyenne..........	400	815	625	910
Clear Creek........	815	1,557	1,069	1,477
Conejos...........	1,140	1,658	1,346	1,280
Costilla...........	744	602	1,032	392

	1972	1976		
Crowley............	414	1,094	667	834
Custer.............	154	495	259	491
Delta..............	1,903	4,890	3,242	4,980
Denver............	98,062	121,995	112,229	105,960
Dolores............	166	498	374	343
Douglas...........	1,048	3,625	2,469	5,083
Eagle.............	1,306	1,920	1,502	2,963
Elbert.............	451	1,416	1,058	1,279
El Paso...........	21,234	53,892	32,510	50,356
Fremont...........	2,813	6,701	4,886	5,647
Garfield...........	2,088	4,452	2,852	4,379
Gilpin.............	362	516	563	451
Grand.............	685	1,721	910	1,703
Gunnison..........	1,187	2,231	1,250	2,568
Hinsdale...........	44	172	83	189
Huerfano..........	1,341	1,620	1,932	1,182
Jackson...........	178	623	279	455
Jefferson..........	31,555	80,082	52,782	87,080
Kiowa.............	372	849	529	598
Kit Carson.........	824	2,316	1,647	1,888
Lake..............	1,263	1,556	240	232
La Plata...........	2,830	5,691	3,843	6,225
Larimer...........	13,731	27,462	18,972	32,110
Las Animas........	3,222	3,659	4,456	2,607
Lincoln............	685	1,678	1,059	1,276
Logan.............	2,426	5,352	3,541	4,254
Mesa.............	6,358	15,527	7,568	15,657
Mineral............	96	247	167	235
Moffat.............	591	1,928	1,451	2,099
Montezuma.........	1,223	3,391	1,993	3,007
Montrose..........	1,870	4,571	3,164	4,831
Morgan............	2,081	5,365	3,798	4,603
Otero.............	2,929	6,016	4,018	4,597
Ouray.............	186	669	333	645
Park..............	386	1,001	751	1,034
Philips.............	687	1,480	1,172	1,142
Pitkin.............	2,531	2,064	2,494	2,954
Prowers...........	1,860	3,272	2,860	2,578
Pueblo............	19,620	25,607	25,866	18,482
Rio Blanco.........	414	1,586	627	1,439
Rio Grande........	1,029	2,787	1,475	2,627
Routt.............	1,613	2,629	2,140	2,832
Saguache..........	578	1,062	1,059	1,094
San Juan..........	140	238	167	221
San Miguel........	426	583	674	622
Sedgwick..........	588	4,129	773	902
Summit............	707	1,082	1,088	1,835
Teller.............	535	1,440	986	1,410
Washington........	643	1,837	1,211	1,440
Weld..............	11,690	24,695	10,510	14,521
Yuma.............	1,066	2,873	2,035	2,365
Total............	**329,980**	**597,189**	**446,807**	**566,870**

Colorado Vote Since 1932

1932 (Pres.), Roosevelt, Dem., 250,877; Hoover, Rep., 189,617; Thomas, Soc., 14,018; Upshaw, Proh., 1,928.

1936 (Pres.), Roosevelt, Dem., 295,081; Landon, Rep., 18,267; Lemke, Union, 9,962; Thomas, Soc., 1,593; Browder, Com., 497; Aiken, Soc. Labor, 336.

1940 (Pres.), Roosevelt, Dem., 265,554; Willkie, Rep., 279,576; Thomas, Soc., 1,899; Babson, Proh., 1,597; Browder, Com., 378.

1944 (Pres.), Roosevelt, Dem., 234,331; Dewey, Rep., 268,731; Thomas, Soc., 1,977.

1948 (Pres.), Truman, Dem., 267,288; Dewey, Rep., 239,714; Wallace, Prog., 6,115; Thomas, Soc., 1,678; Dobbs, Soc. Workers, 229; Teichert, Soc. Lab., 214.

1952 (Pres.), Eisenhower, Rep., 379,782; Stevenson, Dem., 245,504; MacArthur, Constitution, 2,181; Hallinan, Prog., 1,919; Hoopes, Soc., 365; Haas, Soc. Lab., 352.

1956 (Pres.), Eisenhower, Rep., 394,479; Stevenson, Dem., 263,997; Haas, Soc. Lab., 3,308; Andrews, Ind., 759; Hoopes, Soc., 531.

1960 (Pres.), Kennedy, Dem., 330,629; Nixon, Rep., 402,242; Haas, Soc. Lab., 2,803; Dobbs, Soc. Workers, 572.

1964 (Pres.), Johnson, Dem., 476,024; Goldwater, Rep., 296,767; Haas, Soc. Labor, 302; DeBerry, Soc. Worker, 2,537; Munn, Proh., 1,356.

1968 (Pres.), Nixon, Rep., 409,345; Humphrey, Dem., 335,174; Wallace, 3d party, 60,813; Blomen, Soc., 3,016; Gregory, New-party, 1,393; Munn, Proh., 275; Halstead, Soc. Work., 235.

1972 (Pres.), Nixon, Rep., 597,189; McGovern, Dem., 329,980; Fisher, Soc. Labor, 4,361; Hospers, Libertarian, 1,111; Hall, Com., 432; Jenness, Soc. Wrks., 555; Munn, Proh., 467; Schmitz, American, 17,269; Spock, Peoples, 2,403.

Connecticut

County	1972 McGovern (D)	Nixon (R)	1976 Carter (D)	Ford (R)
Fairfield	125,128	233,188	142,813	200,656
Hartford	174,837	194,095	189,922	152,695
Litchfield	27,929	43,478	32,458	40,732
Middlesex	23,573	33,249	29,067	31,141
New Haven	135,132	200,818	158,311	176,722
New London	32,935	58,516	44,951	46,058
Tolland	19,505	25,798	23,079	23,711
Windham	16,459	21,621	19,617	18,200
Totals	**555,498**	**810,763**	**640,218**	**712,000**

Connecticut Vote Since 1932

1932 (Pres.), Roosevelt, Dem., 281,632; Hoover, Rep., 288,420; Thomas, Soc., 22,767.

1936 (Pres.), Roosevelt, Dem., 382,129; Landon, Rep., 278,685; Lemke, Union, 21,805; Thomas, Soc., 5,683; Browder, Com., 1,193.

1940 (Pres.), Roosevelt, Dem., 417,621; Willkie, Rep., 361,021; Browder, Com., 1,091; Aiken, Soc. Lab., 971; Willkie, Union, 798.

1944 (Pres.), Roosevelt, Dem., 435,146; Dewey, Rep., 390,527; Thomas, Soc., 5,097; Teichert, Soc. Lab., 1,220.

1948 (Pres.), Truman, Dem., 423,297; Dewey, Rep., 437,754; Wallace, Prog., 13,713; Thomas, Soc., 6,964; Teichert, Soc. Lab., 1,184; Dobbs, Soc. Workers, 606.

1952 (Pres.), Eisenhower, Rep., 611,012; Stevenson, Dem., 481,649; Hoopes, Soc., 2,244; Hallinan, Peoples, 1,466; Haas, Soc. Lab., 535; write-in, 5.

1956 (Pres.), Eisenhower, Rep., 711,837; Stevenson, Dem., 405,079; scattered, 205.

1960 (Pres.), Kennedy, Dem., 657,055; Nixon, Rep., 565,813.

1964 (Pres.), Johnson, Dem., 826,269; Goldwater, Rep., 390,996; scattered, 1,313.

1968 (Pres.), Nixon, Rep., 556,721; Humphrey, Dem., 621,561; Wallace, 3d party, 76,650; scattered, 1,300.

1972 (Pres.), Nixon, Rep., 810,763; McGovern, Dem., 555,498; Schmitz, Amer. Party, 17,239; scattered, 777.

Delaware

County	1972 McGovern (D)	Nixon (R)	1976 Carter (D)	Ford (R)
New Castle	70,190	100,681	16,669	12,614
Kent	10,463	17,712	87,479	80,159
Sussex	11,630	21,964	18,464	17,153
Totals	**92,283**	**140,357**	**122,610**	**109,926**

Delaware Vote Since 1932

1932 (Pres.), Hoover, Rep., 57,074; Roosevelt, Dem., 54,319; Thomas, Soc., 1,376; Foster, Com., 133.

1936 (Pres.), Roosevelt, Dem., 69,702; Landon, Rep. 54,014; Lemke, Union, 442; Thomas, Soc., 179; Browder, Com., 52.

1940 (Pres.), Roosevelt, Dem., 74,559; Willkie, Rep., 61,440; Babson, Proh., 220; Thomas, Soc., 115.

1944 (Pres.), Roosevelt, Dem., 68,166; Dewey, Rep., 56,747; Watson, Proh., 294; Thomas, Soc., 154.

1948 (Pres.), Truman, Dem., 67,813; Dewey, Rep., 69,-688; Wallace, Prog., 1,050; Watson, Proh., 343; Thomas, Soc., 250; Teichert, Soc. Lab., 29.

1952 (Pres.), Eisenhower, Rep., 90,059; Stevenson, Dem., 83,315; Haas, Soc. Lab., 242; Hamblen, Proh., 234; Hallinan, Prog., 155; Hoopes, Soc., 20.

1956 (Pres.), Eisenhower, Rep., 98,057; Stevenson, Dem., 79,421; Oltwick, Proh., 400; Haas, Soc. Lab., 110.

1960 (Pres.), Kennedy, Dem., 99,590; Nixon, Rep., 96,-373; Faubus, States' Rights, 354; Decker, Proh., 284; Haas, Soc. Lab., 82.

1964 (Pres.), Johnson, Dem., 122,704; Goldwater, Rep., 78,078; Haas, Soc. Lab., 113; Munn, Proh., 425.

1968 (Pres.), Nixon, Rep., 96,714; Humphrey, Dem., 89,194; Wallace, 3d party, 28,459.

1972 (Pres.), Nixon, Rep., 140,357; McGovern, Dem., 92,283; Schmitz, Amer. Party, 2,638; Munn, Proh., 238.

District of Columbia

County	1972 McGovern (D)	Nixon (R)	1976 Carter (D)	Ford (R)
Dist. of C	127,627	35,226	127,562	25,184
Totals	**127,627**	**35,226**	**127,562**	**25.184**

District of Columbia Vote Since 1964

1964 (Pres.), Johnson, Dem., 169,796; Goldwater, Rep., 28,801.

1968 (Pres.), Nixon, Rep., 31,012; Humphrey, Dem., 139,566.

1972 (Pres.), Nixon, Rep., 35,226; McGovern, Dem., 127,627; Reed, Soc. Worker, 316; Hall, Communist, 252.

Florida

County	1972 McGovern (D)	Nixon (R)	1976 Carter (D)	Ford (R)
Alachua	17,245	22,536	26,634	14,483
Baker	379	1,943	2,206	847
Bay	3,914	20,245	2,459	2,814
Bradford	1,217	3,652	3,719	1,566
Brevard	16,854	62,773	34,135	30,255
Broward	74,127	196,528	168,919	152,046
Calhoun	461	2,069	2,360	1,085
Charlotte	3,874	12,888	9,060	10,710
Citrus	2,607	8,848	7,744	6,471
Clay	1,748	10,467	7,753	7,347
Collier	3,201	13,501	8,235	13,328
Columbia	1,664	6,723	6,413	3,653
Dade	177,693	256,529	240,141	176,694
De Soto	852	2,958	2,590	1,895
Dixie	367	1,628	2,096	511
Duval	46,530	122,154	94,758	64,307
Escambia	14,078	56,071	31,699	33,306
Flagler	493	1,409	1,956	1,135
Franklin	490	2,277	1,707	935
Gadsden	3,829	5,995	3,429	2,126
Gilchrist	247	1,306	1,705	487
Glades	253	1,019	1,311	624
Gulf	713	2,628	2,492	1,467
Hamilton	626	1,741	1,923	729
Hardee	647	3,563	2,512	2,038
Hendry	739	2,763	2,008	1,475
Hernando	2,110	6,296	1,810	1,144
Highlands	2,458	9,645	6,228	6,689
Hillsborough	45,305	106,956	91,327	74,255
Holmes	309	3,819	2,338	1,392
Indian River	3,316	11,741	2,914	3,134
Jackson	2,220	8,904	7,360	4,886
Jefferson	1,049	2,108	2,182	1,283
Lafayette	173	1,060	1,126	523
Lake	4,803	23,079	13,686	18,760
Lee	9,404	36,738	29,216	35,613
Leon	15,555	27,479	12,631	12,165
Levy	862	3,273	1,915	934
Liberty	222	1,199	875	429
Madison	1,187	3,236	3,083	1,651
Manatee	8,058	32,664	15,792	20,404
Marion	5,397	19,505	10,813	10,363
Martin	2,946	11,296	2,988	3,482
Monroe	4,469	11,688	10,284	7,262
Nassau	1,293	5,078	5,679	2,920
Okaloosa	2,843	23,303	10,783	12,349
Okeechobee	621	2,581	2,982	1,496
Orange	23,840	94,516	55,219	65,046
Osceola	1,875	9,320	3,792	4,042
Palm Beach	40,825	108,670	63,146	68,122
Pasco	11,330	29,249	32,447	26,816
Pinellas	77,197	179,541	135,888	139,532
Polk	16,419	60,748	36,701	32,655
Putnam	2,901	8,741	7,346	3,712
St. Johns	2,549	8,919	6,659	5,820
St. Lucie	4,593	14,258	7,885	6,649
Santa Rosa	1,491	12,669	3,664	3,620
Sarasota	12,235	48,939	24,728	40,915
Seminole	6,503	27,658	14,774	18,274
Sumter	1,107	3,695	4,541	2,101
Suwannee	1,027	4,435	4,431	2,232
Taylor	754	4,109	3,130	1,773
Union	253	1,314	1,405	509
Volusia	21,637	52,656	34,828	23,229
Wakulla	539	2,466	1,801	1,223
Walton	988	6,217	4,607	2,407
Washington	606	3,777	3,331	2,106
Totals	**718,117**	**1,857,759**	**1,561,383**	**1,375,296**

Florida Vote Since 1932

1932 (Pres.), Roosevelt, Dem., 206,307; Hoover, Rep., 69,170; Thomas, Soc., 775.

1936 (Pres.), Roosevelt, Dem., 249,117; Landon, Rep., 78,248; Thomas, Soc., 775.

1940 (Pres.), Roosevelt, Dem., 359,334; Willkie, Rep., 126,158.

1944 (Pres.), Roosevelt, Dem., 339,377; Dewey, Rep., 143,215.

1948 (Pres.), Truman, Dem., 281,988; Dewey, Rep., 194,280; Thurmond, States' Rights, 89,755; Wallace, Prog., 11,620.

1952 (Pres.), Eisenhower, Rep., 544,036; Stevenson, Dem., 444,950; scattered, 351.

1956 (Pres.), Eisenhower, Rep., 643,849; Stevenson, Dem., 480,371.

1960 (Pres.), Kennedy, Dem., 748,700; Nixon, Rep., 795,476.

1964 (Pres.), Johnson, Dem., 948,540; Goldwater, Rep., 905,941.

1968 (Pres.), Nixon, Rep., 886,804; Humphrey, Dem., 676,794; Wallace, 3d party, 624,207.

1972 (Pres.), Nixon, Rep., 1,857,759; McGovern, Dem., 718,117; scattered 7,407.

Georgia

County	1972 McGovern (D)	1972 Nixon (R)	1976 Carter (D)	1976 Ford (R)
Appling	512	2,755	3,585	961
Atkinson	309	924	1,552	343
Bacon	192	1,771	1,574	459
Baker	345	965	1,162	305
Baldwin	1,435	4,826	4,674	3,577
Banks	356	1,336	2,181	312
Barrow	867	3,423	4,757	1,364
Bartow	1,590	4,836	7,947	1,821
Ben Hill	703	2,104	2,449	814
Berrien	371	2,285	3,758	1,209
Bibb	10,201	27,402	31,902	12,819
Bleckley	377	2,308	2,446	713
Brantley	338	1,587	2,294	358
Brooks	643	2,430	2,653	1,102
Bryan	263	1,409	2,010	741
Bulloch	1,524	5,683	5,199	3,156
Burke	1,058	2,846	2,727	1,378
Butts	727	1,968	2,898	819
Calhoun	495	892	1,389	434
Camden	753	2,380	2,887	944
Candler	238	1,427	1,342	614
Carroll	2,158	8,296	10,050	3,640
Catoosa	894	6,008	4,501	2,619
Charlton	310	1,244	1,750	452
Chatham	15,566	38,079	25,913	15,953
Chattahoochee	121	345	478	162
Chattooga	923	3,188	4,615	1,068
Cherokee	1,159	5,509	5,543	2,042
Clarke	6,090	11,465	10,743	6,157
Clay	283	632	948	289
Clayton	3,740	23,681	21,432	12,905
Clinch	239	1,127	1,414	383
Cobb	7,688	43,977	45,002	34,324
Coffee	607	3,934	4,601	1,417
Colquitt	930	6,900	6,928	2,181
Columbia	946	4,839	4,771	2,774
Cook	525	2,135	2,882	670
Coweta	1,560	5,751	6,195	3,044
Crawford	512	1,167	1,842	378
Crisp	682	3,623	3,747	1,328
Dade	148	2,110	2,161	1,340
Daswon	230	828	1,384	370
Decatur	1,196	4,292	3,736	2,501
DeKalb	30,671	104,750	81,138	63,661
Dodge	884	4,346	4,042	658
Dooly	590	1,904	2,344	628
Dougherty	3,625	12,878	11,461	9,337
Douglas	982	6,610	7,584	3,823
Early	513	2,396	2,405	1,157
Echols	68	404	585	111
Effingham	497	3,175	2,906	1,654
Elbert	884	2,875	4,495	877
Emanuel	916	3,684	4,181	1,370
Evans	375	1,666	1,595	693
Fannin	949	3,873	3,118	2,419
Fayette	450	3,401	3,230	2,466
Floyd	3,372	15,485	12,260	6,258
Forsyth	549	2,968	3,318	1,144
Franklin	435	2,022	4,192	684
Fulton	74,329	96,256	129,760	61,525
Gilmer	768	2,729	900	608
Glascock	41	578	777	422
Glynn	3,002	9,443	8,837	4,956
Gordon	870	4,344	6,052	1,698
Grady	874	3,732	3,614	1,151
Greene	919	1,679	2,542	656
Gwinnett	2,986	18,181	20,845	13,969
Habersham	172	971	5,120	1,315
Hall	2,440	10,686	12,269	4,724
Hancock	1,502	1,595	2,117	651
Haralson	767	3,460	4,394	1,229

County	1972 McGovern (D)	1972 Nixon (R)	1976 Carter (D)	1976 Ford (R)
Harris	701	2,617	2,761	1,544
Hart	784	2,308	4,351	775
Heard	276	1,239	1,593	433
Henry	1,460	5,155	5,436	2,456
Houston	2,556	13,576	12,597	5,088
Irwin	335	1,851	1,291	370
Jackson	1,055	4,124	5,931	1,239
Jasper	463	12,289	1,741	618
Jeff Davis	302	1,857	2,330	587
Jefferson	1,184	2,777	3,156	1,289
Jenkins	484	1,769	1,820	563
Johnson	417	2,201	2,210	698
Jones	861	2,483	3,530	1,332
Lamar	666	1,844	2,600	785
Lanier	193	850	1,269	207
Laurens	2,130	7,350	8,617	3,281
Lee	390	1,441	1,727	1,110
Liberty	1,217	2,337	3,328	979
Lincoln	340	1,246	1,583	576
Long	236	764	1,189	213
Lowndes	2,015	7,812	8,830	4,512
Lumpkin	38ᴱ	1,477	2,225	513
Macon	83,	2,005	2,875	579
Madison	572	2,600	3,367	1,115
Marion	164	850	1,314	291
McDuffie	996	2,990	3,024	1,694
McIntosh	833	1,367	1,978	535
Meriwether	1,213	3,420	3,991	1,155
Miller	118	1,269	1,457	415
Mitchell	1,120	2,400	4,489	1,566
Monroe	789	2,181	2,048	725
Montgomery	337	1,370	1,610	626
Morgan	668	2,007	2,274	904
Murray	644	2,643	3,511	889
Muscogee	18,234	28,449	23,121	12,753
Newton	1,380	4,647	6,258	2,108
Oconee	464	2,029	2,228	1,184
Oglethorpe	326	1,712	1,146	511
Paulding	1,004	2,814	5,420	1,432
Peach	2,413	3,747	3,713	1,035
Pickens	520	2,101	2,571	973
Pierce	269	1,982	2,628	544
Pike	423	1,432	1,903	776
Polk	1,317	4,929	6,115	1,944
Pulaski	444	1,966	2,318	485
Putnam	604	1,963	2,040	835
Quitman	140	502	513	158
Rabun	366	1,477	2,242	542
Randolph	798	1,603	2,172	748
Richmond	9,219	24,362	24,042	17,893
Rockdale	791	3,560	4,577	2,941
Schley	162	694	783	268
Screven	575	2,402	2,168	1,176
Seminole	376	1,851	2,073	685
Spalding	1,702	7,183	7,593	3,739
Stephens	871	3,773	5,560	1,340
Stewart	353	1,020	1,483	385
Sumter	1,268	4,533	5,008	1,920
Talbot	508	990	779	221
Taliaferro	372	585	748	236
Tattnall	492	2,892	3,498	1,299
Taylor	514	1,580	1,962	504
Telfair	687	2,245	3,534	637
Terrell	686	2,057	2,358	1,168
Thomas	2,171	6,668	6,147	3,263
Tift	816	4,591	5,185	2,162
Toombs	675	4,080	4,047	2,122
Towns	404	1,573	1,786	1,175
Treutlen	210	1,346	1,567	465
Troup	2,056	8,350	7,699	4,422
Turner	437	2,120	2,265	416
Twiggs	1,113	1,363	2,515	513
Union	742	2,317	2,615	1,049
Upson	896	4,892	4,119	2,900
Walker	1,574	8,728	8,003	4,808
Walton	1,140	3,994	5,402	1,687
Ware	1,724	6,578	7,719	2,661
Warren	475	1,175	1,335	720
Washington	1,246	3,901	3,468	1,457
Wayne	733	3,677	4,489	1,496
Webster	108	483	504	126
Wheeler	294	1,093	1,378	344
White	343	1,537	3,580	2,673
Whitfield	1,955	8,591	10,041	4,466
Wilcox	315	1,863	1,599	256
Wilkes	646	2,195	2,461	1,067
Wilkinson	751	2,196	2,652	837
Worth	542	2,942	2,790	1,156
Totals	**289,529**	**881,496**	**955,191**	**470,530**

Georgia Vote Since 1932

1932 (Pres.), Roosevelt, Dem., 234,118; Hoover, Rep., 19,863; Upshaw, Proh., 1,125; Thomas, Soc., 461; Foster, Com., 23.

1936 (Pres.), Roosevelt, Dem., 255,364; Landon, Rep., 36,942; Colvin, Proh., 660; Lemke, Union, 141; Thomas, Soc., 68.

1940 (Pres.), Roosevelt, Dem., 265,194; Willkie, Rep.,

23,934; Ind. Dem., 22,428; total, 46,362; Babson, Proh., 983.

1944 (Pres.), Roosevelt, Dem., 268,187; Dewey, Rep., 56,506; Watson, Proh., 36.

1948 (Pres.), Truman, Dem., 254,646; Dewey, Rep., 76,691; Thurmond, States' Rights, 85,055; Wallace, Prog., 1,636; Watson, Proh., 732.

1952 (Pres.), Eisenhower, Rep., 198,979; Stevenson, Dem., 456,823; Liberty Party, 1.

1956 (Pres.), Stevenson, Dem., 444,388; Eisenhower, Rep., 222,778; Andrews, Ind., write-in, 1,754.

1960 (Pres.), Kennedy, Dem., 458,638; Nixon, Rep., 274,472; write-in 239.

1964 (Pres.), Johnson, Dem., 522,557; Goldwater, Rep., 616,600.

1968 (Pres.), Nixon, Rep., 380,111; Humphrey, Dem., 334,440; Wallace, 3d party, 535,550; write-in vote, 162.

1972 (Pres.), Nixon, Rep., 881,496; McGovern, Dem., 289,529; Schmitz, Amer. Party, 2,288; scattered.

Hawaii

County	1972 McGovern (D)	Nixon (R)	1976 Carter (D)	Ford (R)
Hawaii	11,652	16,832	15,960	15,366
Honolulu	76,957	132,844	110,820	107,441
Kauai	5,401	7,571	8,105	6,278
Maui	7,339	11,618	11,921	10,318
Totals	**101,409**	**168,865**	**147,375**	**140,003**

Hawaii Vote Since 1960

1960 (Pres.), Kennedy, Dem., 92,410; Nixon, Rep., 92,295.

1964 (Pres.), Johnson, Dem., 163,249; Goldwater, Rep., 44,022.

1968 (Pres.), Nixon, Rep., 91,425; Humphrey, Dem., 141,324; Wallace, 3d party, 3,469.

Idaho

County	1972 McGovern (D)	Nixon (R)	1976 Carter (D)	Ford (R)
Ada	12,687	36,665	21,118	41,120
Adams	293	963	639	809
Bannock	7,840	12,856	10,130	13,000
Bear Lake	716	2,213	960	2,094
Benewah	1,062	1,494	1,549	1,458
Bingham	2,476	6,886	4,347	7,327
Blaine	1,240	2,113	1,604	2,178
Boise	256	676	432	684
Bonner	2,599	4,405	4,085	4,549
Bonneville	4,199	13,134	7,230	15,794
Boundary	860	1,587	1,217	1,459
Butte	387	788	663	751
Camas	95	344	160	288
Canyon	5,630	18,383	9,460	17,263
Caribou	614	2,069	1,110	2,252
Cassia	1,080	4,576	1,879	4,575
Clark	64	339	169	334
Clearwater	1,412	1,590	1,752	1,469
Custer	274	989	516	850
Elmore	1,153	3,078	2,279	3,085
Franklin	611	2,787	1,157	2,720
Freemont	819	2,621	1,445	2,581
Gem	1,069	2,717	1,978	2,401
Gooding	1,030	3,124	1,923	2,909
Idaho	1,622	3,235	2,313	3,185
Jefferson	715	2,983	1,745	3,599
Jerome	888	3,661	1,800	3,188
Kootenai	5,162	9,958	7,225	10,493
Latah	4,548	6,043	5,020	6,373
Lemhi	526	1,812	1,158	1,684
Lewis	635	961	897	824
Lincoln	313	1,120	728	1,011
Madison	710	3,606	1,320	4,190
Minidoka	1,423	4,097	2,511	3,822
Nez Perce	5,081	6,232	6,324	6151
Oneida	402	1,204	637	1,065
Owyhee	463	1,630	1,054	1,519
Payette	1,113	3,577	2,195	3,115
Power	625	1,405	1,286	1,374
Shoshone	3,020	3,868	3,216	3,570
Teton	298	932	514	904
Twin Falls	3,344	13,075	6,027	12,753
Valley	537	1,324	897	1,374
Washington	935	2,264	1,693	2,044
Totals	**80,826**	**199,384**	**126,362**	**204,188**

Idaho Vote Since 1932

1932 (Pres.), Roosevelt, Dem., 109,479; Hoover, Rep., 71,312; Harvey, Lib., 4,712; Thomas, Soc., 526; Foster, Com., 491.

1936 (Pres.), Roosevelt, Dem., 125,683; Landon, Rep., 66,256; Lemke, Union, 7,684.

1940 (Pres.), Roosevelt, Dem., 127,842; Willkie, Rep., 106,553; Thomas, Soc., 497; Browder, Com., 276.

1944 (Pres.), Roosevelt, Dem., 107,399; Dewey, Rep., 100,137; Watson, Proh., 503; Thomas, Soc., 282.

1948 (Pres.), Truman, Dem., 107,370; Dewey, Rep., 101,514; Wallace, Prog., 4,972; Watson, Proh., 628; Thomas, Soc., 332.

1952 (Pres.), Eisenhower, Rep., 180,707; Stevenson, Dem., 95,081; Hallinan, Prog., 443; write-in, 23.

1956 (Pres.), Eisenhower, Rep., 166,979; Stevenson, Dem., 105,868; Andrews, Ind., 126; write-in, 16.

1960 (Pres.), Kennedy, Dem., 138,853; Nixon, Rep., 161,597.

1964 (Pres.), Johnson, Dem., 148,920; Goldwater, Rep., 143,557.

1968 (Pres.), Nixon, Rep., 165,369; Humphrey, Dem., 89,273; Wallace, 3d party, 36,541.

1972 (Pres.), Nixon, Rep., 199,384; McGovern, Dem., 80,826; Schmitz, American, 28,869; Spock, Peoples.

Illinois

County	1972 McGovern (D)	Nixon (R)	1976 Carter (D)	Ford (R)
Adams	9,055	20,731	11,918	18,177
Alexander	2,482	3,669	3,246	2,349
Bond	2,704	4,475	3,682	3,716
Boone	3,131	7,003	4,458	3,470
Brown	1,203	1,780	1,553	1,379
Bureau	6,133	12,786	7,542	10,800
Calhoun	1,299	1,705	1,549	1,364
Carroll	2,571	6,041	3,372	5,059
Cass	2,803	4,414	3,589	3,527
Champaign	24,743	33,700	26,840	34,530
Christian	7,556	10,072	9,306	7,445
Clark	2,965	5,706	4,071	4,506
Clay	2,844	5,283	3,838	3,860
Clinton	4,756	7,931	6,275	7,295
Coles	7,988	13,681	8,560	10,926
Cook	1,063,268	1,234,307	1,144,578	968,068
Crawford	3,477	6,568	5,007	5,572
Cumberland	2,083	3,257	2,752	2,518
DeKalb	12,375	18,910	11,535	18,193
DeWitt	2,672	5,025	3,477	4,137
Douglas	2,656	5,840	3,827	4,635
DuPage	57,043	172,341	72,063	174,877
Edgar	3,889	7,195	5,055	5,842
Edwards	1,055	3,017	1,648	2,379
Effingham	4,431	8,752	5,950	7,248
Fayette	4,192	6,574	5,127	5,059
Ford	1,934	5,656	2,689	4,801
Franklin	8,545	10,121	12,274	6,399
Fulton	7,529	12,328	9,314	9,588
Gallatin	1,844	2,148	2,611	1,499
Greene	2,824	4,673	4,057	3,706
Grundy	3,584	8,725	5,534	7,581
Hamilton	2,006	3,282	3,036	2,433
Hancock	3,592	7,519	4,730	6,133
Hardin	1,140	1,915	1,602	1,393
Henderson	1,744	2,689	9,815	12,848
Henry	6,368	14,796	8,288	10,463
Iroquois	3,723	11,995	5,167	10,126
Jackson	13,146	12,393	12,940	10,152
Jasper	2,114	3,461	2,772	2,794
Jefferson	6,396	9,448	8,989	7,437
Jersey	3,317	5,164	4,621	4,273
JoDaviess	3,318	5,763	2,802	4,275
Johnson	1,293	2,826	2,182	2,417
Kane	27,525	64,546	34,033	59,219
Kankakee	13,434	26,866	18,400	22,998
Kendall	2,525	9,373	4,202	9,011
Knox	9,333	17,315	11,525	14,123
Lake	47,416	92,052	57,781	92,312
LaSalle	21,405	31,190	23,105	25,114
Lawrence	2,818	5,347	4,038	4,345
Lee	4,788	10,636	6,081	8,206
Livingston	5,110	13,217	3,832	7,947
Logan	4,395	10,277	5,689	8,623
Macon	20,296	29,596	28,243	24,893
Macoupin	9,662	13,583	11,910	10,242
Madison	43,289	55,385	56,360	43,993
Marion	6,968	10,755	9,834	8,729

| | 1972 | | 1976 | |
| | McGov-ern | Nixon | Carter | Ford |
County	(D)	(R)	(D)	(R)
Marshall	2,141	4,452	2,570	4,017
Mason	2,901	4,897	3,952	3,847
Massac	1,831	4,313	3,762	3,133
McDonough	5,143	10,573	5,464	9,683
McHenry	12,090	36,114	16,799	37,115
McLean	14,824	31,060	16,660	28,489
Menard	1,587	3,657	2,308	3,143
Mercer	3,477	5,452	4,090	4,816
Monroe	2,958	6,479	3,984	5,602
Montgomery	6,858	9,025	8,622	7,379
Morgan	5,674	11,103	7,403	8,885
Moultrie	2,350	3,143	3,332	2,803
Ogle	4,743	13,512	6,459	11,206
Peoria	27,264	50,324	27,291	36,633
Perry	4,084	6,968	5,980	5,286
Piatt	2,394	5,057	3,510	4,442
Pike	3,883	5,940	5,006	5,055
Pope	773	1,440	1,070	1,187
Pulaski	1,683	2,485	2,489	1,836
Putnam	1,112	1,665	1,344	1,572
Randolph	6,440	9,761	8,693	8,190
Richland	2,553	5,558	3,169	3,937
Rock Island	32,529	37,548	35,330	33,102
St. Clair	46,636	50,519	59,079	40,106
Saline	5,226	7,660	7,472	5,690
Sangamon	25,720	50,458	38,017	43,309
Schuyler	1,534	2,994	2,014	2,635
Scott	1,145	2,228	1,424	1,789
Shelby	4,389	7,217	5,772	5,153
Stark	993	2,529	1,146	2,191
Stephenson	6,404	13,584	7,192	11,678
Tazewell	15,576	31,937	22,784	28,918
Union	3,428	5,034	4,863	3,433
Vermilion	14,413	24,863	18,427	19,737
Wabash	1,985	4,310	2,781	3,388
Warren	2,969	7,021	3,751	5,822
Washington	2,327	5,179	3,222	4,485
Wayne	2,763	6,400	4,303	5,208
White	3,678	6,052	5,306	4,600
Whiteside	7,909	17,305	11,255	14,308
Will	33,633	65,155	51,097	61,772
Williamson	9,202	14,101	13,579	10,703
Winnebago	35,937	57,682	42,399	52,736
Woodford	3,558	9,622	4,819	8,899
Totals	**1,913,472**	**2,788,179**	**2,223,107**	**2,324,669**

Illinois Vote Since 1932

1932 (Pres.), Roosevelt, Dem., 1,882,304; Hoover, Rep., 1,432,756; Thomas, Soc., 67,258; Foster, Com., 15,582; Upshaw, Proh., 6,388; Reynolds, Soc. Lab., 3,638.

1936 (Pres.), Roosevelt, Dem., 2,282,999; Landon, Rep., 1,570,393; Lemke, Union, 89,439; Thomas, Soc., 7,530; Colvin, Proh., 3,439; Aiken, Soc. Lab., 1,921.

1940 (Pres.), Roosevelt, Dem., 2,149,934; Willkie, Rep., 2,047,240; Thomas, Soc., 10,914; Babson, Proh., 9,190.

1944 (Pres.), Roosevelt, Dem., 2,079,479; Dewey, Rep., 1,939,314; Teichert, Soc. Lab., 9,677; Watson, Proh., 7,411; Thomas, Soc., 180.

1948 (Pres.), Truman, Dem., 1,994,715; Dewey, Rep., 1,961,103; Watson, Proh., 11,959; Thomas, Soc., 11,-522; Teichert, Soc. Lab., 3,118.

1952 (Pres.), Eisenhower, Rep., 2,457,327; Stevenson, Dem., 2,013,920; Haas, Soc. Lab., 9,363; write-in, 448.

1956 (Pres.), Eisenhower, Rep., 2,623,327; Stevenson, Dem., 1,775,682; Haas, Soc. Lab., 8,342; write-in, 56.

1960 (Pres.), Kennedy, Dem., 2,377,846; Nixon, Rep., 2,368,988; Haas, Soc. Lab., 10,560; write-in, 15.

1964 (Pres.), Johnson, Dem., 2,796,833; Goldwater, Rep., 1,905,946; write-in, 62.

1968 (Pres.), Nixon, Rep., 2,174,774; Humphrey, Dem., 2,039,814; Wallace, 3d party, 390,958; Blomen, Soc. Labor, 13,878; write-in, 325.

1972 (Pres.), Nixon, Rep., 2,788,179; McGovern, Dem., 1,913,472; Fisher, Soc. Labor, 12,344; Schmitz, Amer., 2,471; Hall, Communist, 4,541; others, 2.229.

Indiana

| | 1972 | | 1976 | |
| | McGov-ern | Nixon | Carter | Ford |
County	(D)	(R)	(D)	(R)
Adams	3,971	7,549	4,908	6,280

Allen	38,621	76,924	43,518	68,982
Bartholomew	6,974	17,365	11,203	14,777
Benton	1,566	3,703	2,071	3,093
Blackford	2,311	3,876	3,174	2,886
Boone	3,235	9,874	5,686	9,214
Brown	1,443	2,737	2,098	2,199
Carroll	2,214	5,885	3,606	4,797
Cass	5,317	12,681	7,610	10,342
Clark	10,838	16,111	16,670	12,732
Clay	3,742	7,146	5,433	5,674
Clinton	4,283	9,849	6,828	8,199
Crawford	1,801	2,623	2,721	2,181
Daviess	3,538	8,490	4,952	6,829
Dearborn	4,137	7,689	6,348	6,176
Decatur	2,994	6,761	4,365	5,555
Dekalb	4,354	8,834	6,151	7,860
Delaware	17,936	32,468	25,151	26,413
Dubois	6,365	6,637	7,385	6,383
Elkhart	12,659	31,009	16,313	25,797
Fayette	3,519	7,273	5,519	5,704
Floyd	9,243	13,198	12,574	10,993
Fountain	2,977	5,979	4,089	4,903
Franklin	2,131	4,324	3,115	3,557
Fulton	2,150	6,170	3,488	5,083
Gibson	5,633	9,115	8,442	7,105
Grant	7,912	20,969	13,470	16,847
Greene	4,450	8,453	7,263	6,473
Hamilton	4,151	20,247	7,885	21,789
Hancock	3,069	11,019	6,191	10,072
Harrison	3,927	5,910	5,685	4,911
Hendricks	4,384	17,699	9,003	16,725
Henry	5,610	14,538	9,230	10,646
Howard	8,083	23,089	14,815	19,571
Huntington	4,908	10,858	6,515	9,182
Jackson	4,984	9,546	7,610	7,615
Jasper	1,920	6,369	3,424	5,530
Jay	3,349	6,090	4,124	4,606
Jefferson	4,267	6,722	6,142	5,593
Jennings	2,903	5,156	4,430	4,505
Johnson	5,067	17,537	10,075	16,414
Knox	6,089	11,940	9,612	9,108
Kosciusko	4,233	16,216	7,328	14,505
LaGrange	1,658	4,152	2,369	4,161
Lake	88,510	115,480	120,700	90,119
LaPorte	13,222	26,243	18,217	21,989
Lawrence	4,278	10,936	7,908	9,278
Madison	20,921	39,036	29,811	32,437
Marion	102,166	206,065	139,877	166,800
Marshall	4,349	11,908	7,541	10,978
Martin	2,021	3,470	2,827	2,702
Miami	3,889	9,477	6,257	8,263
Monroe	15,241	19,953	16,458	18,803
Montgomery	3,431	10,997	5,320	9,509
Morgan	3,390	11,980	7,377	10,983
Newton	1,252	3,771	2,236	3,204
Noble	4,250	7,916	5,868	6,879
Ohio	922	1,368	1,300	1,027
Orange	2,932	5,715	4,031	4,399
Owen	1,708	3,896	3,103	2,896
Parke	2,207	5,014	3,158	3,929
Perry	4,277	5,204	5,620	4,088
Pike	2,648	4,252	3,938	3,138
Porter	8,943	26,877	16,468	25,489
Posey	3,586	6,771	5,296	5,136
Pulaski	1,863	4,243	2,652	3,182
Putnam	3,339	7,879	5,116	6,063
Randolph	3,409	8,754	5,140	6,581
Ripley	3,601	6,594	4,992	5,253
Rush	1,764	5,985	3,052	4,723
St. Joseph	41,629	64,808	45,339	46,578
Scott	2,785	3,564	4,229	2,657
Shelby	4,028	10,794	7,098	8,918
Spencer	3,867	5,518	4,796	4,166
Starke	2,994	5,520	4,753	4,354
Steuben	2,401	5,636	3,323	5,079
Sullivan	3,624	5,338	5,198	3,747
Switzerland	1,612	1,872	2,150	1,329
Tippecanoe	14,598	31,565	17,850	29,186
Tipton	2,095	5,674	3,428	4,676
Union	765	2,043	1,160	1,631
Vanderburgh	22,163	47,806	34,895	37,920
Vermillion	3,515	4,764	4,971	3,674
Vigo	18,898	29,730	24,684	23,555
Wabash	4,601	10,011	5,686	8,448
Warren	1,164	2,746	1,906	2,377
Warrick	4,296	8,520	7,804	7,200
Washington	3,086	4,758	4,409	3,794
Wayne	7,655	21,610	12,306	16,697
Wells	3,244	6,425	4,250	5,596
White	2,675	7,419	3,963	6,287
Whitley	3,838	7,489	5,445	6,761
Totals	**708,568**	**1,405,154**	**1,006,636**	**1,169,144**

Indiana Vote Since 1932

1932 (Pres.), Roosevelt, Dem., 862,054; Hoover, Rep., 677,184; Thomas, Soc., 21,388; Upshaw, Proh., 10,-399; Foster, Com., 2,187; Reynolds, Soc. Lab., 2,070.

1936 (Pres.), Roosevelt, Dem., 943,974; Landon, Rep., 691,570; Lemke, Union, 19,407; Thomas, Soc., 3,856; Browder, Com., 1,090.

1940 (Pres.), Roosevelt, Dem., 874,063; Willkie, Rep., 899,466; Babson, Proh., 6,437; Thomas, Soc., 2,075; Aiken, Soc. Lab., 706.

1944 (Pres.), Roosevelt, Dem., 781,403; Dewey, Rep., 875,891; Watson, Proh., 12,574; Thomas, Soc., 2,223.

1948 (Pres.), Truman, Dem., 807,833; Dewey, Rep., 821,079; Watson, Proh., 14,711; Wallace, Prog., 9,649; Thomas, Soc., 2,179; Teichert, Soc. Lab., 763.

1952 (Pres.), Eisenhower, Rep., 1,136,259; Stevenson, Dem., 801,530; Hamblen, Proh., 15,335; Hallinan, Prog., 1,222; Haas, Soc. Lab., 979.

1956 (Pres.), Eisenhower, Rep., 1,182,811; Stevenson, Dem., 783,908; Holtwick, Proh., 6,554; Haas, 1,334.

1960 (Pres.), Kennedy, Dem., 952,358; Nixon, Rep., 1,175,120; Decker, Proh., 6,746; Haas, Soc. Lab., 1,136.

1964 (Pres.), Johnson, Dem., 1,170,848; Goldwater, Rep., 911,118; Munn, Proh., 8,266; Haas, Soc. Lab., 1,374.

1968 (Pres.), Nixon, Rep., 1,067,885; Humphrey, Dem., 806,659; Wallace, 3d party, 243,108; Munn,-Prohibition, 4,616; Halstead, Soc. Worker, 1,293; Gregory, 36.

1972 (Pres.), Nixon, Rep., 1,405,154; McGovern, Dem., 708,568; Reed, Soc. Worker, 5,575; Fisher, Soc. Labor, 1,688; Spock, Peace & Freedom, 4,544.

Iowa

County	1972 McGovern (D)	Nixon (R)	1976 Carter (D)	Ford (R)
Adair	1,642	3,041	2,294	2,326
Adams	1,161	1,814	1,507	1,388
Allamakee	2,271	4,150	2,566	3,647
Appanoose	2,283	4,321	3,424	3,036
Audubon	1,533	2,515	2,104	1,967
Benton	4,282	5,273	5,513	5,013
Black Hawk	21,721	30,929	29,478	31,669
Boone	5,057	6,271	6,639	5,359
Bremer	3,122	6,333	4,203	6,247
Buchanan	3,609	5,277	4,257	4,892
Buena Vista	3,460	5,685	4,188	5,084
Butler	1,682	4,615	2,503	4,207
Calhoun	2,446	3,821	3,001	3,215
Carroll	4,608	4,415	5,316	4,081
Cass	1,923	5,234	2,867	4,589
Cedar	2,465	4,452	3,353	4,328
Cerro Gordo	9,460	11,856	11,168	10,592
Cherokee	2,780	4,726	3,356	3,993
Chickasaw	3,134	3,836	3,503	3,432
Clarke	1,590	2,241	2,333	1,737
Clay	2,887	4,564	3,775	4,548
Clayton	3,366	5,447	3,803	4,824
Clinton	9,895	12,768	11,743	12,398
Crawford	3,018	4,493	3,903	3,873
Dallas	5,085	6,143	6,722	5,308
Davis	1,806	2,287	2,426	1,631
Decatur	1,880	2,638	2,698	1,932
Delaware	2,944	4,848	3,167	4,161
Des Moines	8,869	10,216	11,272	9,020
Dickinson	2,373	3,739	3,704	3,795
Dubuque	18,417	17,272	20,522	17,540
Emmet	1,970	3,436	2,720	2,872
Fayette	4,413	7,263	5,265	6,692
Floyd	3,338	4,726	4,639	4,357
Franklin	1,986	3,643	2,680	3,055
Fremont	1,210	2,642	1,964	2,167
Greene	2,152	3,371	3,094	2,811
Grundy	1,844	4,706	2,407	4,160
Guthrie	2,258	3,655	2,859	2,633
Hamilton	2,913	4,803	3,953	3,928
Hancock	2,349	3,706	2,975	3,127
Hardin	3,516	5,969	4,481	4,681
Harrison	2,369	4,721	3,228	3,489
Henry	2,721	5,066	3,879	3,848
Howard	2,439	2,980	2,923	2,616
Humboldt	2,062	3,622	2,677	3,074
Ida	1,490	2,819	1,868	2,589
Iowa	2,578	4,202	3,367	3,925
Jackson	3,704	4,975	4,465	4,221
Jasper	7,007	9,133	8,783	7,728
Jefferson	2,362	4,628	3,377	3,746
Johnson	20,922	14,823	20,269	16,077
Jones	3,468	4,962	4,250	4,463
Keokuk	2,619	3,831	3,499	3,020
Kossuth	4,393	5,841	5,187	4,649
Lee	7,510	9,748	8,992	8,484
Linn	31,370	36,503	38,248	36,515
Louisa	1,707	2,806	2,088	2,284
Lucas	1,759	2,851	2,738	2,075
Lyon	1,407	3,788	1,868	3,547
Madison	2,234	3,480	3,107	2,681
Mahaska	3,382	6,374	4,836	5,264

County	1972 McGovern (D)	Nixon (R)	1976 Carter (D)	Ford (R)
Marion	4,643	6,583	6,214	5,424
Marshall	6,618	10,798	8,686	9,554
Mills	1,060	3,531	1,906	2,722
Mitchell	2,449	3,395	2,883	2,838
Monona	2,189	3,237	2,651	2,635
Monroe	1,736	2,357	2,360	1,581
Montgomery	1,559	4,391	2,229	3,673
Muscatine	4,917	8,436	6,559	7,678
O'Brien	2,224	5,159	2,811	4,642
Osceola	1,317	2,262	1,309	1,955
Page	1,790	6,200	2,864	5,342
Palo Alto	2,845	3,141	3,181	2,618
Plymouth	4,033	6,339	4,287	5,586
Pocahontas	2,241	3,138	3,052	2,700
Polk	59,169	70,245	71,652	62,283
Pottawattamie	8,074	19,722	14,729	17,244
Poweshiek	3,718	4,785	4,357	4,193
Ringgold	1,003	2,264	1,738	1,493
Sac	2,452	4,017	2,994	3,346
Scott	23,810	34,135	29,629	34,897
Shelby	2,259	4,052	2,851	3,301
Sioux	2,867	10,721	3,322	9,448
Story	13,972	16,617	15,560	18,302
Tama	3,693	5,058	4,584	4,379
Taylor	1,247	3,042	1,947	2,059
Union	2,112	3,734	2,955	2,872
Van Buren	1,268	2,272	1,805	1,802
Wapello	8,348	9,301	10,345	6,785
Warren	5,143	7,332	7,653	6,098
Washington	2,784	5,187	3,448	4,217
Wayne	1,574	2,681	2,145	1,781
Webster	8,358	11,133	10,289	8,939
Winnebago	2,324	4,300	2,935	3,308
Winneshiek	4,401	5,877	4,160	4,765
Woodbury	16,974	23,757	19,590	21,908
Worth	2,034	2,564	2,399	1,964
Wright	2,780	4,278	3,637	3,544
Total	496,206	706,207	619,710	632,486

Iowa Vote Since 1932

1932 (Pres.), Roosevelt, Dem., 598,019; Hoover, Rep., 414,433; Thomas, Soc., 20,467; Upshaw, Proh., 2,111; Coxey, Farm-Lab., 1,094; Foster, Com., 559. (Pres.),

1936 (Pres.), Roosevelt, Dem., 621,756; Landon, Rep., 487,977; Lemke, Union, 29,687; Thomas, Soc., 1,373; Colvin, Proh., 1,182; Browder, C., 506; Aiken, Soc. Lab., 252.

1940 (Pres.), Roosevelt, Dem., 578,800; Willkie, Rep., 632,370; Babson, Proh., 2,284; Browder, Com., 1,524; Aiken, Soc. Lab., 452.

1944 (Pres.), Roosevelt, Dem., 499,876; Dewey, Rep., 547,267; Watson, Proh., 3,752; Thomas, Soc., 1,511; Teichert, Soc. Lab., 193.

1948 (Pres.), Truman, Dem., 522,380; Dewey, Rep., 494,018; Wallace, Prog., 12,125; Teichert, Soc. Lab., 4,274; Watson, Proh., 3,382; Thomas, Soc., 1,829; Dobbs, Soc. Workers, 26.

1952 (Pres.), Eisenhower, Rep., 808,906; Stevenson, Dem., 451,513; Hallinan, Prog., 5,085; Hamblen, Proh., 2,882; Hoopes, Soc., 219; Haas, Soc. Lab., 139; scattering 29.

1956 (Pres.), Eisenhower, Rep., 729,187; Stevenson, Dem., 501,858; Andrews (A.C.P. of Iowa), 3,202; Hoopes, Soc., 192; Haas, Soc. Lab., 125.

1960 (Pres.), Kennedy, Dem., 550,565; Nixon, Rep., 722,381; Haas, Soc. Lab., 230; write-in, 634.

1964 (Pres.), Johnson, Dem., 733,030; Goldwater, Rep., 449,148; Haas, S. L., 182; DeBerry, S. W., 159; Munn, P., 1,902.

1968 (Pres.), Nixon, Rep., 619,106; Humphrey, Dem., 476,699; Wallace, 3d party, 66,422; Munn, Proh., 362; Halstead, Soc. Worker, 3,377; Cleaver, Peace and Freedom, 1,332; Blomen, S. L., 241.

1972 (Pres.), Nixon, Rep., 706,207; McGovern, Dem., 496,206; Schmitz, American, 22,056; Jenness, Soc. Worker, 488; Fisher, Soc. Labor, 195; Hall, Communist, 272; Green, Universal, 199; scattered, 321.

Kansas

County	1972 McGovern (D)	Nixon (R)	1976 Carter (D)	Ford (R)
Allen	1,610	3,938	2,746	3,269
Anderson	1,035	2,718	1,886	1,872
Atchison	2,404	5,471	4,107	4,029
Barber	727	2,308	1,491	1,568
Barton	3,481	8,479	5,497	7,311
Bourbon	1,912	4,776	3,235	3,589
Brown	1,038	4,314	1,745	3,407

	1972		1976	
	(D)	(R)	(D)	(R)
Butler	4,669	11,045	8,540	8,390
Chase	315	1,184	642	921
Chautauqua	378	1,546	866	1,159
Cherokee	2,806	6,019	5,154	3,957
Cheyenne	399	1,440	758	1,008
Clark	311	1,142	680	761
Clay	887	3,562	1,609	3,084
Cloud	1,806	3,832	2,969	2,952
Coffey	782	2,667	1,549	2,145
Comanche	281	1,052	630	719
Cowley	3,592	10,332	7,091	7,609
Crawford	6,683	9,652	9,021	7,225
Decatur	616	1,707	1,011	1,237
Dickinson	1,957	6,515	3,572	4,759
Doniphan	690	2,856	1,428	2,469
Douglas	11,646	15,316	11,922	14,277
Edwards	757	1,534	1,304	1,001
Elk	428	1,522	865	1,087
Ellis	4,113	5,463	6,061	4,466
Ellsworth	1,028	2,087	1,578	1,473
Finney	2,062	4,335	3,813	3,711
Ford	2,804	6,232	4,934	4,679
Franklin	2,056	6,011	3,607	4,758
Geary	1,708	4,299	2,843	3,230
Gove	466	1,226	848	860
Graham	488	1,440	936	1,112
Grant	476	1,469	1,116	1,140
Gray	511	1,235	1,111	837
Greeley	212	639	479	389
Greenwood	951	3,157	1,737	2,319
Hamilton	394	941	432	282
Harper	729	2,628	1,681	1,777
Harvey	3,555	8,287	6,003	6,624
Haskell	383	1,036	676	761
Hodgeman	331	853	541	422
Jackson	1,191	3,363	2,128	2,722
Jefferson	1,237	3,679	2,470	3,224
Jewell	716	2,242	666	942
Johnson	24,324	76,161	30,032	65,443
Kearny	325	876	658	674
Kingman	1,107	2,756	2,138	1,839
Kiowa	406	1,559	764	1,180
Labette	3,210	6,399	3,137	3,029
Lane	294	943	651	651
Leavenworth	4,727	10,762	7,709	7,839
Lincoln	476	1,649	36	61
Linn	876	2,593	643	711
Logan	428	1,164	473	629
Lyon	3,720	9,157	632	861
Marion	1,478	4,373	2,482	3,518
Marshall	1,823	4,127	2,814	3,010
McPherson	2,858	7,457	5,366	6,187
Meade	526	1,712	963	1,109
Miami	2,140	5,234	4,000	3,999
Mitchell	1,030	2,830	1,910	2,095
Montgomery	3,685	11,717	7,157	8,864
Morris	704	2,471	895	1,221
Morton	363	1,165	735	738
Nemaha	1,777	3,422	2,584	2,757
Neosho	2,559	5,034	3,842	4,038
Ness	652	1,539	1,111	1,016
Norton	776	2,688	572	746
Osage	1,522	4,073	2,762	2,945
Osborne	724	2,182	356	377
Ottawa	705	2,065	1,393	1,629
Pawnee	1,110	2,370	826	819
Phillips	827	2,919	1,264	2,317
Pottawatomie	1,298	3,947	495	613
Pratt	1,214	3,253	2,307	2,427
Rawlins	560	1,553	72	303
Reno	8,183	15,714	14,621	11,222
Republic	1,059	2,421	1,617	2,294
Rice	1,825	3,843	3,056	2,584
Riley	5,333	11,120	6,540	9,518
Rooks	904	2,457	1,412	1,664
Rush	806	1,629	1,351	1,170
Russell	1,011	3,168	1,453	3,165
Saline	5,406	12,592	8,476	11,218
Scott	449	1,547	1,119	1,195
Sedgwick	39,220	83,949	63,851	69,886
Seward	989	3,866	1,876	3,576
Shawnee	20,383	43,727	27,710	35,281
Sheridan	552	1,134	793	846
Sherman	785	2,225	1,573	1,671
Smith	818	2,600	1,333	2,004
Stafford	844	2,200	1,659	1,430
Stanton	259	754	489	510
Stevens	408	1,392	901	1,262
Summer	2,685	6,941	5,161	4,394
Thomas	943	2,300	1,802	2,246
Trego	621	1,369	1,003	1,025
Wabaunsee	622	2,461	1,354	1,920
Wallace	214	782	486	600
Washington	996	3,301	1,564	2,543
Wichita	288	794	179	146
Wilson	1,043	3,568	1,957	2,541
Woodson	550	1,592	904	1,104
Wyandotte	28,206	34,157	32,943	19,887
Totals	**270,287**	**619,812**	**429,008**	**501,759**

Kansas Vote Since 1932

1932 (Pres.), Roosevelt, Dem., 424,204; Hoover, Rep., 349,498; Thomas, Soc., 18,276.

1936 (Pres.), Roosevelt, Dem., 464,520; Landon, Rep., 397,727; Thomas, Soc., 2,766; Lemke, Union, 494.

1940 (Pres.), Roosevelt, Dem., 364,725; Willkie, Rep., 489,169; Babson, Proh., 4,056; Thomas, Soc., 2,347.

1944 (Pres.), Roosevelt, Dem., 287,458; Dewey, Rep., 442,096; Watson, Proh., 2,609; Thomas, Soc., 1,613.

1948 (Pres.), Truman, Dem., 351,902; Dewey, Rep., 423,039; Watson, Proh., 6,468; Wallace, Prog., 4,603; Thomas, Soc., 2,807.

1952 (Pres.), Eisenhower, Rep., 616,302; Stevenson, Dem., 273,296; Hamblen, Proh., 6,038; Hoopes, Soc., 530.

1956 (Pres.), Eisenhower, Rep., 566,878; Stevenson, Dem., 296,317; Holtwick, Proh., 3,048.

1960 (Pres.), Kennedy, Dem., 363,213; Nixon, Rep., 561,474; Decker, Proh., 4,138.

1964 (Pres.), Johnson, Dem., 464,028; Goldwater, Rep., 386,579; Munn, Proh., 5,393; Haas, Soc. Labor, 1,901.

1968 (Pres.), Nixon, Rep., 478,674; Humphrey, Dem., 302,996; Wallace, 3d, 88,921; Munn, Proh., 2,192.

1972 (Pres.), Nixon, Rep., 619,812; McGovern, Dem., 270,287; Schmitz, Cons. 21,808; Munn, Proh. 4,188.

Kentucky

	1972		1976	
	McGovern	Nixon	Carter	Ford
County	(D)	(R)	(D)	(R)
Adair	1,610	3,859	2,366	3,201
Allen	1,259	3,025	2,231	2,508
Anderson	1,302	2,298	2,387	1,682
Ballard	1,411	1,542	2,794	649
Barren	3,384	6,070	5,878	3,797
Bath	1,347	1,919	2,113	938
Bell	3,219	6,518	5,284	5,035
Boone	2,595	7,355	5,602	5,602
Bourbon	1,860	3,180	3,504	2,260
Boyd	6,434	12,812	11,142	9,106
Boyle	2,395	4,317	4,089	3,511
Bracken	873	1,628	1,577	879
Breathitt	2,677	1,346	3,521	1,005
Breckinridge	1,921	3,574	3,255	2,591
Bullitt	2,827	4,517	5,263	3,639
Butler	835	2,941	1,539	2,256
Caldwell	1,345	2,952	3,016	1,808
Calloway	3,468	5,167	8,089	3,084
Campbell	8,585	20,025	12,423	15,798
Carlisle	872	1,169	1,985	435
Carroll	1,308	1,228	2,251	805
Carter	2,591	4,082	3,915	3,185
Casey	913	3,727	1,602	3,379
Christian	4,063	7,414	7,745	4,964
Clark	2,020	4,506	4,575	3,011
Clay	1,709	4,046	1,674	3,652
Clinton	659	2,632	987	2,354
Crittenden	859	2,248	1,715.	1,596
Cumberland	686	2,294	853	1,653
Daviess	8,168	17,234	8,577	7,367
Edmonson	722	2,327	939	1,550
Elliott	1,499	782	1,987	365
Estill	1,322	3,054	2,034	2,250
Fayette	19,828	42,362	28,012	35,170
Fleming	1,455	2,484	2,317	1,647
Floyd	7,544	6,099	10,151	3,108
Franklin	5,601	7,781	10,475	5,536
Fulton	1,024	1,807	2,367	1,043
Gallatin	612	719	1,164	436
Garrard	1,441	3,143	1,187	2,045
Grant	1,054	2,086	2,336	1,212
Graves	3,701	6,098	8,982	3,195
Grayson	1,839	4,155	2,313	2,829
Green	1,209	2,755	2,085	2,397
Greenup	4,491	6,828	6,880	5,062
Hancock	791	1,583	1,558	1,124
Hardin	4,060	8,740	7,977	6,965
Harlan	4,349	6,527	7,300	4,624
Harrison	1,780	2,732	3,582	1,911
Hart	2,307	3,582	3,132	1,987
Henderson	3,889	6,231	7,916	4,053
Henry	1,688	1,919	2,985	1,192
Hickman	976	1,430	2,035	585
Hopkins	3,129	7,133	7,586	4,964
Jackson	436	5,303	680	2,766
Jefferson	88,143	142,436	119,698	126,541
Jessamine	1,269	3,819	2,795	3,081
Johnson	1,840	4,907	2,981	4,282
Kenton	12,872	28,076	17,977	21,046
Knott	2,774	1,479	1,001	238
Knox	1,805	5,017	3,642	4,931
Larue	1,483	2,449	2,207	1,409

	1972		1976	
	(D)	(R)	(D)	(R)
Laurel.	2,274	7,276	3,813	6,186
Lawrence.	1,529	2,392	2,402	1,838
Lee.	744	1,629	1,091	1,449
Leslie	913	3,299	1,478	3,770
Letcher.	2,908	4,213	4,829	3,249
Lewis	1,200	3,124	1,887	1,942
Lincoln.	1,882	3,623	3,198	2,685
Livingston	1,065	1,673	2,455	869
Logan.	2,459	3,573	4,850	2,430
Lyon.	687	1,030	1,606	585
McCracken	7,567	11,260	14,956	6,997
McCreary.	684	3,203	1,381	2,400
McLean.	1,191	2,298	2,346	1,212
Madison.	4,328	8,659	7,299	6,581
Magoffin.	2,024	2,243	2,451	1,793
Marion.	2,351	2,370	3,520	1,723
Marshall.	2,806	4,290	6,812	2,517
Martin.	661	2,495	1,267	2,120
Mason.	2,459	3,529	3,397	2,529
Meade.	1,541	2,492	3,030	1,755
Menifee.	732	596	1,041	304
Mercer.	1,707	3,575	3,411	2,451
Metcalfe.	1,308	1,896	1,877	1,356
Monroe	768	3,770	1,287	2,901
Montgomery.	1,657	2,868	3,141	2,032
Morgan	1,815	1,535	2,897	973
Muhlenberg.	3,246	5,596	7,058	4,292
Nelson	2,828	3,495	4,454	2,804
Nicholas.	804	1,076	1,582	738
Ohio.	906	2,392	3,608	3,764
Oldham	1,311	3,041	2,819	3,695
Owen	1,161	1,456	2,332	676
Owsley.	251	1,328	305	1,053
Pendleton	909	1,966	2,147	1,230
Perry	3,601	5,373	5,633	4,434
Pike.	9,513	12,535	14,320	9,178
Powell	1,230	1,766	1,859	1,148
Pulaski	3,080	10,602	5,752	9,226
Robertson	421	456	546	275
Rockcastle	968	3,437	1,408	2,583
Rowan	2,169	3,245	3,541	2,244
Russell	1,169	3,992	1,803	2,882
Scott	1,642	3,255	3,118	2,408
Shelby	2,074	3,893	3,841	2,916
Simpson	1,325	2,285	2,782	1,481
Spencer	481	1,120	1,209	742
Taylor.	1,859	4,035	828	854
Todd	1,222	1,964	2,336	1,095
Trigg	1,514	1,767	2,727	991
Trimble.	757	935	1,568	517
Union	1,855	2,701	3,540	1,716
Warren	5,934	12,481	9,657	9,439
Washington.	1,552	2,378	2,376	1,765
Wayne	1,853	3,514	2,537	3,243
Webster	1,712	2,396	3,523	1,402
Whitley.	2,199	6,788	4,211	6,100
Wolfe	957	936	1,720	632
Woodford	1,268	3,363	2,689	2,646
Totals	**371,159**	**676,446**	**610,017**	**525,607**

Kentucky Vote Since 1932

1932 (Pres.), Roosevelt, Dem., 580,574; Hoover, Rep., 394,716; Upshaw, Proh., 2,252; Thomas, Soc., 3,853; Reynolds, Soc. Lab., 1,396; Foster, Com., 272.

1936 (Pres.), Roosevelt, Dem., 541,944; Landon, Rep., 369,702; Lemke, Union, 12,501; Colvin, Proh., 929; Thomas, S., 627; Aiken, S. L., 294; Browder, Com., 204.

1940 (Pres.), Roosevelt, Dem., 557,222; Willkie, Rep., 410,384; Babson, Proh., 1,443; Thomas, Soc., 1,014.

1944 (Pres.), Roosevelt, Dem., 472,589; Dewey, Rep., 392,448; Watson, Proh., 2,023; Thomas, Soc., 535; Teichert, Soc. Lab., 326.

1948 (Pres.), Truman, Dem., 466,756; Dewey, Rep., 341,210; Thurmond, States' Rights, 10,411; Wallace, Prog., 1,567; Thomas, Soc., 1,284; Watson, Proh., 1,245; Teichert, Soc. Lab., 185.

1952 (Pres.), Eisenhower, Rep., 495,029; Stevenson, Dem., 495,729; Hamblen, Proh., 1,161; Haas, Soc. Lab., 893; Hallinan, Proh., 336.

1956 (Pres.), Eisenhower, Rep., 572,192; Stevenson, Dem., 476,453; Byrd, States' Rights, 2,657; Holtwick, Proh., 2,145; Haas, Soc. Lab., 358.

1960 (Pres.), Kennedy, Dem., 521,855; Nixon, Rep., 602,607.

1964 (Pres.), Johnson, Dem., 669,659; Goldwater, Rep., 372,977; John Kasper, Nat'l. States Rights, 3,469.

1968 (Pres.), Nixon, Rep., 462,411; Humphrey, Dem., 397,547; Wallace, 3d p., 193,098; Halstead, S. W., 2,843.

1972 (Pres.), Nixon, Rep., 676,446; McGovern, Dem., 371,159; Schmitz, Amer., 17,627; Jenness, Soc. Worker, 685; Hall, Comm., 464; Spock, Peoples, 1,118.

Louisiana

	1972		1976	
	McGovern	Nixon	Carter	Ford
Parish	(D)	(R)	(D)	(R)
Acadia.	4,406	9,698	10,005	5,463
Allen.	2,029	3,581	5,365	2,086
Ascension.	3,324	5,187	9,100	4,320
Assumption.	2,065	3,751	1,258	1,130
Avoyelles.	3,395	6,225	8,104	4,574
Beauregard.	1,728	4,955	5,322	3,106
Bienville.	1,890	3,384	3,402	2,499
Bossier.	2,914	12,856	8,031	12,067
Caddo.	15,649	40,157	30,462	42,757
Calcasieu.	15,330	24,778	33,957	16,955
Caldwell.	508	2,306	1,827	1,882
Cameron.	739	1,391	2,431	819
Catahoula.	823	2,683	2,543	2,079
Claiborne.	1,551	3,432	1,555	2,118
Concordia.	2,142	4,521	3,891	3,849
DeSoto.	2,596	4,017	4,628	3,601
E. Baton Rouge. .	23,617	52,648	51,113	54,204
East Carroll. . . .	1,661	1,736	2,367	1,677
East Feliciana. . .	1,603	1,992	3,486	1,668
Evangeline.	2,919	5,523	6,669	3,680
Franklin.	1,272	4,967	3,824	3,947
Grant.	859	3,626	3,670	2,279
Iberia.	5,143	11,812	10,392	9,984
Iberville.	3,650	3,972	7,148	3,797
Jackson.	1,477	4,152	3,193	3,591
Jefferson.	20,981	75,348	53,230	71,732
Jefferson Davis. .	2,551	5,903	6,376	3,603
Lafayette.	8,740	22,939	19,918	22,806
Lafourche.	5,713	13,936	14,072	11,322
LaSalle.	651	3,858	2,393	2,632
Lincoln.	2,589	6,736	6,828	4,971
Livingston.	1,898	7,481	9,875	5,555
Madison.	2,249	2,420	3,222	2,096
Morehouse.	2,355	5,770	4,917	5,418
Natchitoches. . . .	3,180	6,994	6,692	5,243
Orleans.	60,790	88,075	118,395	90,539
Ouachita.	6,920	24,860	15,738	23,940
Plaquemines. . . .	990	6,595	2,614	6,054
Pointe Coupee. . .	3,133	3,192	5,147	2,567
Rapides.	8,422	22,306	20,842	17,757
Red River.	957	2,245	1,837	1,708
Richland.	1,335	4,304	3,486	3,602
Sabine.	1,332	4,935	4,565	3,511
St. Bernard. . . .	3,189	15,198	12,959	12,707
St. Charles.	2,788	5,469	6,872	4,270
St. Helena.	943	1,446	2,622	1,046
St. James.	2,633	3,112	4,531	2,749
St. John.	2,815	3,525	5,683	3,585
St. Landry.	7,421	12,510	15,613	9,947
St. Martin.	3,202	6,337	7,798	4,112
St. Mary.	4,435	11,117	9,401	8,919
St. Tammany. . . .	3,949	15,438	14,191	15,347
Tangipahoa. . . .	5,227	11,607	14,342	9,244
Tensas.	1,568	1,729	1,831	1,443
Terrebonne.	4,415	13,753	10,623	12,832
Union	1,465	4,322	775	1,006
Vermillion.	3,876	8,909	11,639	6,114
Vernon.	1,345	6,225	6,202	3,970
Washington. . . .	2,947	8,162	10,005	5,677
Webster.	2,859	8,829	7,234	7,506
W. Baton Rouge. .	1,849	2,626	3,809	1,901
West Carroll. . . .	571	2,997	2,607	2,370
West Feliciana . . .	1,079	1,001	1,890	990
Winn	1,490	4,235	3,558	3,188
Totals	**298,142**	**686,852**	**683,512**	**606,204**

Louisiana Vote Since 1932

1932 (Pres.), Roosevelt, Dem., 249,418; Hoover, Rep., 18,863.

1936 (Pres.), Roosevelt, Dem., 292,894; Landon, Rep., 36,791.

1940 (Pres.), Roosevelt, Dem., 319,751; Willkie, Rep., 52,446.

1944 (Pres.), Roosevelt, Dem., 281,564; Dewey, Rep., 67,750.

1948 (Pres.), Thurmond, States' Rights, 204,290; Truman, Dem., 136,344; Dewey, Rep., 72,657; Wallace, Prog., 3,035.

1952 (Pres.), Eisenhower, Rep., 306,925; Stevenson, Dem., 345,027.

1956 (Pres.), Eisenhower, Rep., 329,047; Stevenson, Dem., 243,977; Andrews, States' Rights, 44,520.

1960 (Pres.), Kennedy, Dem., 407,339; Nixon, Rep., 230,890; States' Rights (unpledged) 169,572.

1964 (Pres.), Johnson, Dem., 387,068; Goldwater,

Rep., 509,225.

1968 (Pres.), Nixon, Rep., 257,535; Humphrey, Dem., 309,615; Wallace, 3d party, 530,300.

1972 (Pres.), Nixon, Rep., 686,852; McGovern, Dem., 298,142; Schmitz, American, 52,099; Jenness, Soc. Worker, 14,398.

Maine

| | 1972 | | 1976 | |
| | McGovern | Nixon | Carter | Ford |
County	(D)	(R)	(D)	(R)
Androscoggin	19,509	19,406	26,484	16,330
Aroostook	11,474	19,051	15,552	15,760
Cumberland	33,326	51,268	46,578	48,856
Franklin	2,988	5,958	5,146	5,799
Hancock	4,191	11,889	6,723	12,064
Kennebec	16,379	24,617	21,136	21,151
Knox	3,601	8,478	5,922	8,315
Lincoln	2,903	7,580	4,818	6,754
Oxford	6,661	12,114	10,340	10,551
Penobscot	18,552	30,186	23,782	27,887
Piscataquis	2,518	4,617	3,727	4,088
Sagadahoc	3,414	6,463	5,257	5,652
Somerset	5,921	10,079	9,465	8,862
Waldo	2,941	6,480	4,853	6,283
Washington	3,742	7,820	6,664	7,038
York	22,464	30,452	31,996	27,380
Totals	**160,584**	**256,458**	**228,437**	**232,770**

Maine Vote Since 1932

1932 (Pres.), Roosevelt, Dem., 128,907; Hoover, Rep., 166,631; Thomas, Soc., 2,439; Reynolds, Soc. Lab., 255; Foster, Com., 162.

1936 (Pres.), Landon, Rep., 168,823; Roosevelt, Dem., 126,333; Lemke, Union, 7,581; Thomas, Soc., 783; Colvin, Proh., 334; Browder, Com., 257; Aiken, Soc. Lab., 129.

1940 (Pres.), Roosevelt, Dem., 156,478; Willkie, Rep., 165,951; Browder, Com., 411.

1944 (Pres.), Roosevelt, Dem., 140,631; Dewey, Rep., 155,434; Teichert, Soc. Lab., 335.

1948 (Pres.), Truman, Dem., 111,916; Dewey, Rep., 150,234; Wallace, Prog., 1,884; Thomas, Soc., 547; Teichert, Soc. Lab., 206.

1952 (Pres.), Eisenhower, Rep., 232,353; Stevenson, Dem., 118,806; Hallinan, Prog., 332; Haas, Soc. Lab., 156; Hoopes, Soc., 138; scattered, 1.

1956 (Pres.), Eisenhower, Rep., 249,238; Stevenson, Dem., 102,468.

1960 (Pres.), Kennedy, Dem., 181,159; Nixon, Rep., 240,608.

1964 (Pres.), Johnson, Dem., 262,264; Goldwater, Rep., 118,701.

1968 (Pres.), Nixon, Rep., 169,254; Humphrey, Dem., 217,312; Wallace, 3d party, 6,370.

1972 (Pres.), Nixon, Rep., 256,458; McGovern, Dem., 160,584; scattered, 229.

Maryland

| | 1972 | | 1976 | |
| | McGovern | Nixon | Carter | Ford |
County	(D)	(R)	(D)	(R)
Allegany	10,808	20,687	15,686	14,940
Anne Rundel	26,082	71,707	53,103	59,220
Baltimore	70,309	175,897	115,717	139,137
Calvert	2,232	4,024	4,535	3,321
Caroline	1,567	4,325	2,946	3,030
Carroll	4,408	16,847	9,665	15,263
Cecil	4,113	10,759	8,695	7,535
Charles	4,502	9,665	9,334	7,547
Dorchester	2,136	6,859	4,461	4,671
Frederick	8,235	19,907	14,389	17,638
Garrett	1,510	5,480	3,205	4,465
Hartford	8,737	25,141	18,020	22,364
Howard	10,668	19,265	19,936	20,448
Kent	2,168	4,036	2,930	2,689
Montgomery	100,228	133,090	123,705	116,478
Prince George's	79,914	116,166	109,616	78,752
Queen Anne's	1,712	4,380	3,414	3,334
St. Mary's	3,571	7,689	7,054	5,432
Somerset	2,036	4,342	3,401	3,059
Talbot	2,181	6,620	3,583	5,581
Washinton	10,039	24,234	15,480	19,427
Wicomico	5,510	13,115	9,116	10,141
Worcester	1,792	5,584	3,952	4,477
BALTIMORE CITY	141,323	119,486	173,675	79,971
Totals	**505,781**	**829,305**	**735,618**	**648,980**

Maryland Vote Since 1932

1932 (Pres.), Roosevelt, Dem., 314,314; Hoover, Rep., 184,184; Thomas, Soc., 10,489; Reynolds, Soc. Lab., 1,036; Foster, Com., 1,031.

1936 (Pres.), Roosevelt, Dem., 389,612; Landon, Rep., 231,435; Thomas, Soc., 1,629; Aiken, Soc. Lab., 1,305; Browder, Com.,915.

1940 (Pres.), Roosevelt, Dem., 384,546; Wilkie, Rep., 269,534; Thomas, Soc., 4,093; Browder, Com., 1,274; Aiken, Soc. Lab., 657.

1944 (Pres.), Roosevelt, Dem., 315,490; Dewey, Rep., 292,949.

1948 (Pres.), Truman, Dem., 286,521; Dewey, Rep., 294,814; Wallace, Prog., 9,983; Thomas, Soc., 2,941; Thurmond, States' Rights, 2,476; Wright, write-in, 2,294.

1952 (Pres.), Eisenhower, Rep., 499,424; Stevenson, Dem., 395,337; Hallinan, Prog., 7,313.

1956 (Pres.), Eisenhower, Rep., 559,738; Stevenson, Dem., 372,613.

1960 (Pres.), Kennedy, Dem., 565,800; Nixon, Rep., 489,538.

1964 (Pres.), Johnson, Dem., 730,912; Goldwater, Rep., 385,495; write-in, 50.

1968 (Pres.), Nixon, Rep., 517,995; Humphrey, Dem., 538,310; Wallace, 3d party, 178,734.

1972 (Pres.), Nixon, Rep., 829,305; McGovern, Dem., 505,781; Schmitz, American Party, 18,726.

Massachusetts

| | 1972 | | 1976 | |
| | McGovern | Nixon | Carter | Ford |
County	(D)	(R)	(D)	(R)
Barnstable	22,636	36,340	31,268	39,295
Berkshire	35,391	30,380	41,505	28,792
Bristol	103,163	84,390	111,546	69,832
Dukes	2,001	2,312	2,513	2,365
Essex	157,324	138,040	164,153	124,919
Franklin	11,968	16,088	150,103	14,857
Hampden	94,945	86,164	109,977	69,835
Hampshire	28,572	24,529	34,987	22,219
Middlesex	345,343	269,064	356,556	255,392
Nantucket	952	1,418	1,115	1,399
Norfolk	150,232	134,459	140,748	140,238
Plymouth	69,124	76,062	83,250	74,230
Suffolk	166,250	85,272	141,093	80,159
Worcester	144,139	127,560	168,752	103,286
Totals	**1,332,540**	**1,112,078**	**1,402,466**	**1,026,818**

Massachusetts Vote Since 1932

1932 (Pres.), Roosevelt, Dem., 800,148; Hoover, Rep., 736,959; Thomas, Soc., 34,305; Foster, Com., 4,821; Reynolds, Soc. Lab., 2,668; Upshaw, Proh., 1,142.

1936 (Pres.), Roosevelt, Dem., 942,716; Landon, Rep., 768,613; Lemke, Union, 118,639; Thomas, Soc., 5,111; Browder, Com., 2,930; Aiken, Soc. Lab., 1,305; Colvin, Proh., 1,032.

1940 (Pres.), Roosevelt, Dem., 1,076,522; Willkie, Rep., 939,700; Thomas, Soc., 4,091; Browder, Com., 3,806; Aiken, Soc. Lab., 1,492; Babson, Proh., 1,370.

1944 (Pres.), Roosevelt, Dem., 1,035,296; Dewey, Rep., 921,350; Teichert, Soc. Lab., 2,780; Watson, Proh., 973.

1948 (Pres.), Truman, Dem., 1,151,788; Dewey, Rep., 909,370; Wallace, Prog., 38,157; Teichert, Soc. Lab., 5,535; Watson, Proh., 1,663.

1952 (Pres.), Eisenhower, Rep., 1,292,325; Stevenson, Dem., 1,083,525; Hallinan, Prog., 4,636; Hass, Soc. Lab., 1,957; Hamblen, Proh., 886; scattered, 69; blanks, 41,150.

1956 (Pres.), Eisenhower, Rep., 1,393,197; Stevenson, Dem., 948,190; Haas, Soc. Lab., 5,573; Holtwick, Proh., 1,205; others, 341.

1960 (Pres.), Kennedy, Dem., 1,487,174; Nixon, Rep., 976,750; Haas, Soc. Lab., 3,892; Decker, Proh., 1,633; others, 31; blank and void, 26,024.

1964 (Pres.), Johnson, Dem., 1,786,422; Goldwater, Rep., 549,727; Haas, Soc. Lab., 4,755; Munn, Proh., 3,735; scattered, 159; blank, 48,104.

1968 (Pres.), Nixon, Rep., 766,844; Humphrey, Dem., 1,469,218; Wallace, 3d party, 87,088; Blomen, Soc. Labor, 6,180; Munn, Prohibition, 2,369; scattered,

53; blanks, 25,394.

1972 (Pres.), Nixon, Rep., 1,112,078; McGovern, Dem., 1,332,540; Jenness, Soc. Worker, 10,600; Fisher, Soc. Labor, 129; Schmitz, American, 2,877; Spock, Peoples, 101; Hall, Communist, 46; Hospers, Libertarian, 43; scattered, 342.

Michigan

County	1972 McGovern (D)	1972 Nixon (R)	1976 Carter (D)	1976 Ford (R)
Alcona	1,195	2,434	2,038	2,338
Alger	1,803	2,035	2,379	1,722
Allegan	7,883	18,407	9,794	19,330
Alpena	5,104	6,513	6,500	6,656
Antrim	2,000	4,068	3,031	4,368
Arenac	1,829	2,588	2,695	2,687
Baraga	1,517	1,905	1,778	1,788
Barry	5,484	10,393	7,703	11,178
Bay	21,712	23,094	25,900	23,042
Benzie	1,310	2,686	1,891	3,085
Berrien	18,597	43,047	25,163	40,944
Branch	4,887	8,388	6,301	8,251
Calhoun	22,154	32,531	25,227	30,389
Cass	4,982	10,398	7,844	9,905
Charlevoix	2,831	4,522	3,953	5,145
Cheboygan	2,985	4,529	3,870	4,894
Chippewa	4,744	7,028	6,036	7,025
Clare	2,434	4,402	4,173	4,897
Clinton	5,770	13,438	7,508	13,454
Crawford	1,143	1,953	1,889	2,359
Delta	8,003	7,647	8,927	7,809
Dickinson	5,339	5,989	6,134	5,922
Eaton	8,986	20,413	12,083	22,120
Emmet	3,081	4,288	4,014	5,911
Genesee	73,896	85,747	88,967	80,004
Gladwin	2,016	3,484	3,719	3,794
Gogebic	4,984	5,631	6,341	3,963
Grand Traverse	5,810	11,421	7,262	13,325
Gratiot	4,370	9,904	5,429	9,426
Hillsdale	3,942	9,261	5,444	9,348
Houghton	6,402	9,053	7,234	7,713
Huron	4,456	9,832	5,717	9,297
Ingham	53,458	63,376	48,444	67,308
Ionia	6,240	10,898	6,820	11,733
Iosco	3,065	5,750	4,875	5,500
Iron	3,512	3,630	4,401	3,224
Isabella	7,446	9,682	7,281	10,577
Jackson	19,350	34,220	24,826	32,972
Kalamazoo	33,324	50,405	33,384	51,458
Kalkaska	924	1,855	1,957	2,280
Kent	67,587	104,041	58,973	126,635
Keweenaw	456	715	658	626
Lake	1,548	1,532	2,179	1,598
Lapeer	5,531	11,615	9,503	12,349
Leelanau	1,855	3,809	2,437	4,245
Lenawee	11,018	19,125	14,550	18,406
Livingston	7,634	16,856	12,399	19,393
Luce	862	1,579	1,099	1,379
Mackinac	1,937	3,096	2,452	3,107
Macomb	82,346	147,777	121,177	132,410
Manistee	3,625	5,070	4,489	5,325
Marquette	11,555	13,249	8,725	8,067
Mason	3,697	6,811	4,540	6,812
Mecosta	3,799	7,158	4,747	7,279
Menominee	4,657	6,060	5,596	5,633
Midland	9,504	16,473	11,959	17,631
Missaukee	924	2,647	1,688	2,943
Monroe	17,726	23,263	23,076	20,688
Montcalm	5,402	9,591	6,684	10,439
Montmorency	914	1,798	1,684	1,882
Muskegon	22,804	36,428	27,014	35,488
Newaygo	3,978	8,254	5,622	8,258
Oakland	129,400	241,613	170,934	246,486
Oceana	2,525	4,992	3,427	4,161
Ogemaw	2,056	3,367	3,545	3,212
Ontonagon	2,140	3,040	3,105	2,462
Osceola	1,706	4,441	2,586	4,422
Oscoda	678	1,561	1,108	1,541
Otsego	1,912	2,854	2,724	3,154
Ottawa	15,119	42,169	16,681	48,675
Presque Isle	2,440	3,372	3,334	3,545
Roscommon	2,187	4,136	3,688	4,608
Saginaw	29,424	47,920	36,138	46,652
St. Clair	15,712	23,471	21,204	24,779
St. Joseph	5,119	18,438	7,305	11,784
Sanilac	3,780	11,031	5,963	10,409
Schoolcraft	1,759	2,310	2,157	1,933
Shiawassee	3,932	15,489	12,202	15,111
Tuscola	5,449	12,198	7,932	12,058
Van Buren	7,159	13,903	9,558	13,343
Washtenaw	55,350	50,535	49,931	54,954
Wayne	514,913	435,877	546,064	348,059
Wexford	3,048	5,221	4,519	5,670
Totals	**1,459,435**	**1,961,721**	**1,694,288**	**1,884,752**

Michigan Vote Since 1932

1932 (Pres.), Roosevelt, Dem., 871,700; Hoover, Rep., 739,894; Thomas, Soc., 39,025; Foster, Com., 9,318; Upshaw, Proh., 2,893; Reynolds, Soc. Lab., 1,041; Harvey, Lib., 217.

1936 (Pres.), Roosevelt, Dem., 1,016,794; Landon, Rep., 699,733; Lemke, Union, 75,795; Thomas, Soc., 8,208; Browder, Com., 3,384; Aiken, Soc. Lab., 600; Colvin, Proh., 579.

1940 (Pres.), Roosevelt, Dem., 1,032,991; Willkie, Rep., 1,039,917; Thomas, Soc., 7,593; Browder, Com., 2,834; Babson, Proh., 1,795; Aiken, Soc. Lab., 795.

1944 (Pres.), Roosevelt, Dem., 1,106,899; Dewey, Rep., 1,084,423; Watson, Proh., 6,503; Thomas, Soc., 4,598; Smith, America First, 1,530; Teichert, Soc. Lab., 1,264.

1948 (Pres.), Truman, Dem., 1,003,448; Dewey, Rep., 1,038,595; Wallace, Prog., 46,515; Watson, Proh., 13,052; Thomas, Soc., 6,063; Teichert, Soc. Lab., 1,263; Dobbs, Soc. Workers, 672.

1952 (Pres.), Eisenhower, Rep., 1,551,529; Stevenson, Dem., 1,230,657; Hamblen, Proh., 10,331; Hallinan, Prog., 3,922; Haas, Soc. Lab., 1,495; Dobbs, Soc. Workers, 655; scattered, 3.

1956 (Pres.), Eisenhower, Rep., 1,713,647; Stevenson, Dem., 1,359,898; Holtwick, Proh., 6,923.

1960 (Pres.), Kennedy, Dem., 1,687,269; Nixon, Rep., 1,620,428; Dobbs, Soc. Workers, 4,347; Decker, Proh., 2,029; Daly, Tax Cut, 1,767; Haas, Soc. Lab., 1,718; Ind. American 539.

1964 (Pres.), Johnson, Dem., 2,136,615; Goldwater, Rep., 1,060,152; DeBerry, Soc. Workers, 3,817; Haas, Soc. Lab., 1,704; Proh. (no candidate listed), 699; scattering, 145.

1968 (Pres.), Nixon, Rep., 1,370,665; Humphrey, Dem., 1,593,082; Wallace, 3d party, 331,968; Halstead, Soc. Worker, 4,099; Blomen, Soc. Labor, 1,762; Cleaver, New Politics, 4,585; Munn, Prohib., 60; scattering, 29.

1972 (Pres.), Nixon, Rep., 1,961,721; McGovern, Dem., 1,459,435; Schmitz, Amer., 63,321; Fisher, Soc. Labor, 2,437; Jenness, Soc. Worker, 1,603; Hall, Communist, 1,210.

Minnesota

County	1972 McGovern (D)	1972 Nixon (R)	1976 Carter (D)	1976 Ford (R)
Aitkin	2,687	3,241	4,325	2,477
Anoka	28,031	29,546	47,571	27,681
Becker	4,695	6,033	6,597	5,610
Beltrami	5,194	5,947	7,540	5,214
Benton	4,282	4,652	6,235	4,099
Big Stone	2,185	1,748	2,580	1,332
Blue Earth	10,638	12,702	12,930	11,998
Brown	4,347	7,791	5,792	7,479
Carlton	7,116	5,445	9,247	4,371
Carver	4,852	8,546	7,362	8,079
Cass	3,347	4,906	5,424	4,403
Chippewa	3,630	3,787	4,648	3,254
Chisago	4,174	4,718	6,619	3,872
Clay	9,076	11,089	10,877	10,323
Clearwater	1,751	1,819	2,437	1,374
Cook	742	1,047	1,018	1,033
Cottonwood	2,802	4,396	3,813	3,906
Crow Wing	7,328	8,774	10,443	8,072
Dakota	28,479	34,967	44,253	37,542
Dodge	1,921	3,863	3,009	3,446
Douglas	5,501	6,678	7,094	5,910
Faribault	3,519	6,503	5,049	5,577
Fillmore	3,155	7,107	4,758	5,984
Freeborn	7,163	9,797	9,470	8,220
Goodhue	6,147	11,107	8,926	9,967
Grant	2,085	1,899	2,624	1,635
Hennepin	205,943	228,951	255,755	211,401
Houston	2,467	5,186	3,861	4,853
Hubbard	2,136	3,294	3,196	2,980
Isanti	3,660	3,715	6,013	3,159
Itasca	8,683	7,558	13,009	6,646
Jackson	3,304	3,599	4,311	2,870
Kanabec	1,979	2,395	3,188	1,943
Kandiyohi	7,241	6,624	9,992	6,664
Kittson	1,584	1,832	2,008	1,555
Koochiching	3,396	3,681	4,846	2,896
LacQuiParle	2,845	2,773	3,647	2,292
Lake	3,640	2,575	3,973	2,313
Lake O' Woods	672	877	1,105	757

	1972		1976	
	(D)	(R)	(D)	(R)
Le Sueur	4,725	5,388	6,556	4,565
Lincoln	2,148	1,881	2,594	1,599
Lyon	5,614	5,820	7,124	5,033
McLeod	4,538	7,820	6,249	6,513
Mahnomen	1,397	1,246	1,595	905
Marshall	2,790	3,264	3,744	2,560
Martin	3,816	7,569	5,672	6,484
Meeker	3,601	5,097	5,295	4,096
Mille Lacs	3,221	4,291	5,172	3,212
Morrison	5,993	5,714	8,176	4,590
Mower	10,286	9,929	12,866	8,179
Murray	2,893	2,959	3,684	2,605
Nicollet	4,680	6,230	5,777	6,071
Nobles	5,464	4,951	6,034	4,503
Norman	2,444	2,536	2,946	1,983
Olmsted	9,817	23,806	14,518	23,749
Otter Tail	7,881	13,519	11,881	12,113
Pennington	2,892	3,548	3,797	3,023
Pine	3,794	3,881	5,442	3,057
Pipestone	2,758	3,543	3,272	3,018
Polk	7,366	8,139	9,065	6,553
Pope	2,910	2,610	3,746	2,251
Ramsey	108,392	95,716	133,614	86,430
Red Lake	1,409	1,052	1,748	737
Redwood	3,177	5,776	4,525	4,926
Renville	4,499	5,329	5,762	4,482
Rice	8,065	9,195	10,590	8,311
Rock	2,089	3,470	2,769	2,892
Roseau	2,396	2,844	3,148	2,449
St. Louis	61,103	41,435	74,883	35,270
Scott	6,745	7,310	9,912	7,154
Sherburne	4,070	4,332	6,678	4,361
Sibley	2,433	4,543	3,752	3,871
Stearns	19,315	18,951	25,027	19,578
Steele	4,010	7,678	6,263	7,051
Stevens	2,870	2,830	3,171	2,484
Swift	3,823	2,673	4,392	2,226
Todd	4,270	5,387	6,533	4,278
Traverse	1,744	1,276	2,020	1,130
Wabasha	3,017	5,158	4,286	4,484
Wadena	2,430	3,408	3,164	3,148
Waseca	2,767	5,064	3,544	4,040
Washington	16,102	19,142	26,349	20,316
Watonwan	2,229	3,960	3,177	3,351
Wilkin	1,739	2,292	2,103	1,882
Winona	8,080	10,910	10,959	10,436
Wright	8,695	9,996	13,379	9,314
Yellow Med	3,462	3,683	4,337	2,946
Totals	**802,346**	**898,269**	**1,067,894**	**818,120**

Minnesota Vote Since 1932

1932 (Pres.), Roosevelt, Dem., 600,806; Hoover, Rep., 363,959; Thomas, Soc., 25,476; Foster, Com., 6,101; Coxey, Farm.-Lab., 5,731; Reynolds, Ind., 770.

1936 (Pres.), Roosevelt, Dem., 698,811; Landon, Rep., 350,461; Lemke, Union, 74,296; Thomas, Soc., 2,872; Browder, Com., 2,574; Aiken, Soc., 961.

1940 (Pres.), Roosevelt, Dem., 644,196; Willkie, Rep., 596,274; Thomas, Soc., 5,454; Browder, Com., 2,711; Aiken, Ind., 2,553.

1944 (Pres.), Roosevelt, Dem., 589,864; Dewey, Rep., 527,416; Thomas, Soc., 5,073; Teichert, Ind. Gov't., 3,176.

1948 (Pres.), Truman, Dem., 692,966; Dewey, Rep., 483,617; Wallace, Prog., 27,866; Thomas, Soc., 4,646; Teichert, Soc. Lab., 2,525; Dobbs, Soc. Workers, 606.

1952 (Pres.), Eisenhower, Rep., 763,211; Stevenson, Dem., 608,458; Hallinan, Prog., 2,666; Haas, Soc. Lab., 2,383; Hamblen, Proh., 2,147; Dobbs, Soc. Workers, 618.

1956 (Pres.), Eisenhower, Rep., 719,302; Stevenson Dem., 617,525; Haas, Soc. Lab. (Ind. Gov.), 2,080; Dobbs, Soc. Workers, 1,098.

1960 (Pres.), Kennedy, Dem., 779,933; Nixon, Rep., 757,915; Dobbs, Soc. Workers, 3,077; Industrial Gov., 962.

1964 (Pres.), Johnson, Dem., 991,117; Goldwater, Rep., 559,624; DeBerry, Soc. Workers, 1,177; Haas, Industrial Gov., 2,544.

1968 (Pres.), Nixon, Rep., 658,643; Humphrey, Dem., 857,738; Wallace, 3d party, 68,931; scattered, 2,443; Halstead, Soc. Worker, 808; Blomen, Ind. Gov't., 285; Mitchell, Communist, 415; Cleaver, Peace, 935; McCarthy, write-in, 585; scattered 170.

1972 (Pres.), Nixon, Rep. 898,269; McGovern, Dem., 802,346; Schmitz, American, 31,407; Spock, Peoples, 2,805; Fisher, Soc. Labor, 4,261; Jenness, Soc. Worker, 940; Hall, Communist, 662; scattered 962.

Mississippi

	1972		1976	
	McGovern	Nixon	Carter	Ford
County	(D)	(R)	(D)	(R)
Adams	3,697	8,500	6,400	5,920
Alcorn	982	5,732	7,022	3,468
Amite	1,185	2,846	2,577	2,263
Attala	1,103	4,738	4,062	3,145
Benton	701	1,483	2,335	790
Bolivar	3,616	7,397	7,556	5,133
Calhoun	245	3,023	2,709	1,872
Carroll	580	1,777	1,577	1,567
Chickasaw	579	3,753	2,813	2,513
Choctaw	326	2,301	1,527	1,569
Claiborne	2,076	1,521	2,517	960
Clarke	954	4,561	2,814	2,935
Clay	1,410	4,035	2,829	2,441
Coahoma	3,708	6,602	6,372	4,250
Copiah	1,803	5,498	4,314	3,778
Covington	642	3,842	2,828	2,560
DeSoto	1,557	7,917	4,480	3,981
Forrest	2,933	14,418	7,793	10,572
Franklin	561	2,361	1,554	1,710
George	270	3,979	3,068	1,910
Greene	513	2,884	2,127	1,538
Grenada	1,471	4,800	3,272	3,592
Hancock	745	5,133	3,776	3,855
Harrison	4,761	28,962	16,569	19,294
Hinds	12,679	49,877	27,769	44,342
Holmes	3,459	3,158	4,616	2,438
Humphreys	892	2,334	1,429	2,157
Issaquena	395	701	567	325
Itawamba	509	4,419	4,474	2,142
Jackson	2,534	22,204	12,308	17,039
Jasper	935	3,597	3,107	2,362
Jefferson	1,457	1,131	2,504	766
Jefferson Davis	1,005	2,830	2,604	1,820
Jones	2,790	16,489	10,055	11,177
Kemper	837	2,748	2,452	1,720
Lafayette	1,545	5,391	4,323	3,708
Lamar	493	5,022	3,048	3,939
Lauderdale	3,453	18,337	9,861	14,132
Lawrence	709	3,294	2,227	2,097
Leake	1,053	4,217	3,251	2,792
Lee	1,632	10,730	8,504	7,369
Leflore	2,038	6,779	6,136	5,863
Lincoln	1,070	7,593	3,828	5,801
Lowndes	2,398	10,098	6,272	7,811
Madison	3,464	5,047	5,501	4,473
Marion	1,693	6,805	5,286	5,300
Marshall	1,875	3,326	6,462	2,526
Monroe	1,279	7,273	6,097	4,736
Montgomery	925	3,210	2,388	2,277
Neshoba	812	6,815	4,255	3,859
Newton	597	5,585	2,741	3,813
Noxubee	1,052	2,239	2,064	1,866
Oktibbeha	1,880	6,160	4,305	5,095
Panola	2,091	5,284	5,119	3,060
Pearl River	901	7,487	3,414	3,100
Perry	446	2,689	1,958	1,606
Pike	2,332	6,542	5,749	5,659
Pontotoc	488	4,476	4,069	2,217
Prentiss	398	4,607	4,390	2,335
Quitman	790	2,524	1,889	1,012
Rankin	1,913	12,187	6,937	11,507
Scott	1,213	5,244	3,607	3,716
Sharkey	655	1,426	1,283	1,024
Simpson	871	5,669	2,938	3,442
Smith	329	4,419	2,444	3,166
Stone	293	2,467	1,648	1,575
Sunflower	1,874	5,389	4,315	3,457
Tallahatchie	835	3,442	2,787	2,146
Tate	1,151	3,966	3,747	2,592
Tippah	569	3,937	4,242	1,890
Tishomingo	443	4,177	3,734	1,969
Tunica	858	1,446	1,668	905
Union	658	5,477	3,155	1,486
Walthall	747	3,110	2,609	2,063
Warren	3,480	10,420	6,293	8,692
Washington	4,623	9,634	9,828	7,582
Wayne	975	4,648	2,870	2,635
Webster	403	3,624	2,202	1,925
Wilkinson	1,409	1,608	2,315	1,284
Winston	1,354	5,155	118	88
Yalobusha	797	2,944	2,599	1,799
Yazoo	2,008	5,555	3,953	4,246
Totals	**126,782**	**505,125**	**373,917**	**362,056**

Mississippi Vote Since 1932

1932 (Pres.), Roosevelt, Dem., 140,168; Hoover, Rep., 5,180; Thomas, Soc., 686.

1936 (Pres.), Roosevelt, Dem., 157,318; Landon, Rep., Howard faction, 2,760; Rowlands faction, 1,675 total, 4,435; Thomas, Soc., 329.

1940 (Pres.), Roosevelt, Dem., 168,252; Willkie, Ind. Rep., 4,550; Rep., 2,814; total, 7,364; Thomas, Soc., 103.

1944 (Pres.), Roosevelt, Dem., 158,515; Dewey, Rep., 3,742; Reg. Dem., 9,964; Ind. Rep., 7,859.

1948 (Pres.), Thurmond, States' Rights, 167,538; Truman, Dem., 19,384; Dewey, Rep., 5,043; Wallace, Prog., 225.

1952 (Pres.), Eisenhower, Ind. vote pledged to Rep. candidate, 112,966; Stevenson, Dem., 172,566.

1956 (Pres.), Stevenson, Dem., 144,498; Eisenhower, Rep., 56,372; Black and Tan Grand Old Party, 4,313; total, 60,685; Byrd, Independent, 42,966.

1960 (Pres.), Democratic unpledged electors, 116,248; Kennedy, Dem., 108,362; Nixon, Rep., 73,561. Mississippi's victorious slate of 8 unpledged Democratic electors cast their votes for Sen. Harry F. Byrd (D-Va.).

1964 (Pres.), Johnson, Dem., 52,618; Goldwater, Rep., 356,528.

1968 (Pres.), Nixon, Rep., 88,516; Humphrey, Dem., 150,644; Wallace, 3d party, 415,349.

1972 (Pres.), Nixon, Rep., 505,125; McGovern, Dem., 126,782; Schmitz, American, 11,598; Jenness, Soc. Worker, 2,458.

Missouri

	1972		1976	
	McGovern	Nixon	Carter	Ford
County	(D)	(R)	(D)	(R)
Adair	2,286	6,157	3,684	5,250
Andrew	1,686	4,180	3,042	3,130
Atchison	1,509	2,927	1,926	1,960
Audrain	3,706	7,197	5,600	5,378
Barry	3,167	7,295	5,146	5,053
Barton	1,140	4,026	2,279	2,638
Bates	3,020	5,314	4,288	3,350
Benton	1,423	3,537	2,684	2,875
Bollinger	1,818	3,069	2,603	2,010
Boone	13,666	17,488	17,513	16,027
Buchanan	11,395	21,850	17,407	16,506
Butler	3,466	9,198	5,635	4,633
Caldwell	1,231	3,167	1,540	1,532
Callaway	3,036	6,313	4,818	5,067
Camden	1,761	4,996	4,005	4,469
Cape Girardeau	6,280	15,693	10,210	12,607
Carroll	1,927	4,100	2,060	1,786
Carter	565	1,257	1,154	842
Cass	3,731	9,242	6,535	6,743
Cedar	1,152	3,520	2,092	2,752
Chariton	1,999	2,812	3,055	2,128
Christian	1,945	6,305	3,830	4,553
Clark	1,403	2,499	1,240	1,005
Clay	14,538	33,017	25,807	23,836
Clinton	1,944	3,924	3,415	2,790
Cole	4,754	16,685	7,949	14,370
Cooper	2,332	5,172	3,087	3,694
Crawford	2,248	4,595	3,565	3,224
Dade	747	2,624	1,681	2,149
Dallas	1,085	3,120	2,448	2,430
Daviess	1,430	2,840	2,131	1,794
DeKalb	1,339	2,766	2,023	1,759
Dent	1,710	3,024	2,156	1,774
Douglas	1,209	3,773	1,725	2,352
Dunklin	2,776	5,926	7,107	3,314
Franklin	7,464	13,785	11,629	12,138
Gasconade	1,226	4,944	1,702	3,924
Gentry	1,642	2,984	2,249	1,772
Greene	20,155	48,348	33,824	37,691
Grundy	1,428	3,969	2,597	2,646
Harrison	1,383	3,574	2,304	2,478
Henry	3,125	5,802	4,417	3,470
Hickory	622	1,851	1,398	1,403
Holt	1,011	2,578	1,529	1,777
Howard	2,041	2,613	1,664	865
Howell	2,795	7,253	5,304	4,692
Iron	1,346	2,203	2,645	1,765
Jackson	92,830	129,989	129,302	100,977
Jasper	7,652	22,482	14,909	16,996
Jefferson	13,787	21,947	24,129	18,231
Johnson	3,044	7,228	5,463	5,429
Knox	1,031	1,986	1,319	1,216
Laclede	2,186	6,152	4,381	4,066
Lafayette	4,063	9,187	6,410	6,823
Lawrence	3,130	8,445	5,315	5,784
Lewis	1,695	2,738	1,812	1,370
Lincoln	2,784	5,127	4,473	3,581
Linn	3,073	4,595	4,092	3,114
Livingston	2,662	5,253	3,819	3,010
McDonald	1,787	4,339	3,236	2,954
Macon	2,844	4,538	3,366	2,684
Madison	1,451	2,837	2,230	1,740
Maries	1,219	2,082	1,796	1,485
Marion	4,171	7,197	6,121	5,501
Mercer	607	1,592	1,117	949
Miller	1,598	5,682	2,739	4,095

Mississippi	1,470	2,727	3,406	1,734
Moniteau	1,395	3,963	1,327	1,491
Monroe	2,299	2,141	3,014	1,388
Montgomery	1,691	3,707	2,535	2,665
Morgan	1,685	4,021	2,738	2,821
New Madrid	3,500	4,735	3,769	1,715
Newton	4,291	10,701	7,045	7,276
Nodaway	3,322	5,942	4,955	4,558
Oregon	1,352	2,118	2,564	1,122
Osage	1,485	4,266	2,015	3,224
Ozark	625	2,119	888	1,000
Pemiscot	2,017	4,697	4,681	2,543
Perry	1,953	4,736	2,801	4,086
Pettis	5,016	10,065	7,892	7,344
Phelps	3,567	7,598	6,261	6,153
Pike	2,659	4,452	3,770	3,355
Platte	4,183	8,764	8,651	8,103
Polk	2,245	5,409	3,663	3,893
Pulaski	1,903	4,243	3,802	2,432
Putnam	571	2,112	1,242	1,595
Ralls	1,371	1,827	1,289	776
Randolph	3,814	5,195	5,490	3,533
Ray	2,844	4,205	5,535	2,883
Reynolds	1,031	1,541	2,143	879
Ripley	1,361	2,810	2,577	1,637
St. Charles	11,034	25,677	22,196	26,116
St. Clair	1,410	2,847	2,271	1,808
St. Francois	4,658	8,812	8,452	7,002
Ste. Genevieve	2,247	2,900	3,091	2,241
St. Louis	160,801	264,147	195,920	245,586
Saline	3,460	6,641	4,113	3,545
Schuyler	991	1,495	1,417	1,193
Scotland	1,269	1,918	785	619
Scott	3,646	7,316	8,077	5,202
Shannon	1,134	1,623	1,990	1,019
Shelby	1,569	2,057	2,264	1,452
Stoddard	2,636	6,282	6,097	3,989
Stone	1,094	4,180	2,359	3,442
Sullivan	1,588	2,611	2,313	2,223
Taney	1,435	4,982	3,626	4,696
Texas	2,737	5,104	4,638	3,338
Vernon	3,057	4,892	4,638	3,246
Warren	1,225	3,530	2,164	3,214
Washington	2,229	3,818	3,286	2,345
Wayne	1,746	3,091	2,989	1,963
Webster	2,343	5,095	3,757	3,509
Worth	727	1,170	771	969
Wright	1,368	4,350	2,456	2,922
ST. LOUIS CITY	119,817	72,402	82,850	52,047
Write-in Vote	1,384	206	0,000	0,000
Totals	**698,531**	**1,154,058**	**986,185**	**918,620**

Missouri Vote Since 1932

1932 (Pres.), Roosevelt, Dem., 1,025,406; Hoover, Rep., 564,713; Thomas, Soc., 16,374; Upshaw, Proh., 2,429; Foster, Com., 568; Reynolds, Soc. Lab., 404.

1936 (Pres.), Roosevelt, Dem., 1,111,403; Landon, Rep., 697,891; Lemke, Union, 14,630; Thomas, Soc., 3,454; Colvin, Proh., 908; Browder, Com., 417; Aiken, Soc. Lab., 292.

1940 (Pres.), Roosevelt, Dem., 958,476; Willkie, Rep., 871,009; Thomas, Soc., 2,226; Babson, Proh., 1,809; Aiken, Soc. Lab., 209.

1944 (Pres.), Roosevelt, Dem., 807,357; Dewey, Rep., 761,175; Thomas, Soc., 1,750; Watson, Proh., 1,175; Teichert, Soc. Lab., 221.

1948 (Pres.), Truman, Dem., 917,315; Dewey, Rep., 655,039; Wallace, Prog., 3,998; Thomas, Soc., 2,222.

1952 (Pres.), Eisenhower, Rep., 959,429; Stevenson, Dem., 929,830; Hallinan, Prog., 987; Hamblen, Proh., 885; MacArthur, Christian Nationalist, 302; America First, 233; Hoopes, Soc. 227; Haas, Soc.-Lab., 169.

1956 (Pres.), Stevenson, Dem., 918,273; Eisenhower, Rep., 914,299.

1960 (Pres.), Kennedy, Dem., 972,201; Nixon, Rep., 962,221.

1964 (Pres.), Johnson, Dem., 1,164,344; Goldwater, Rep., 653,535.

1968 (Pres.), Nixon, Rep., 811,932; Humphrey, Dem., 791,444; Wallace, 3d party, 206,126.

1972 (Pres.), Nixon, Rep., 1,154,058; McGovern, Dem., 698,531.

Montana

	1972		1976	
	McGovern	Nixon	Carter	Ford
County	(D)	(R)	(D)	(R)
Beaverhead	775	2,460	913	2,261
Big Horn	1,552	2,148	1,974	1,603

	1972 (D)	1972 (R)	1976 (D)	1976 (R)
Blaine	1,151	1,513	1,356	1,349
Broadwater	411	916	557	820
Carbon	1,292	2,378	1,853	2,111
Carter	218	726	344	558
Cascade	12,899	16,159	13,484	13,692
Chouteau	1,149	2,027	1,568	1,814
Custer	1,875	3,486	2,426	3,120
Daniels	570	973	797	816
Dawson	1,685	3,207	2,201	2,639
Deer Lodge	3,979	2,373	3,871	2,197
Fallon	531	1,034	847	934
Fergus	1,652	4,082	2,470	3,556
Flathead	5,412	10,417	7,784	10,451
Gallatin	5,096	10,663	6,213	11,062
Garfield	173	695	273	625
Glacier	1,469	2,143	1,755	1,892
Golden Valley	170	359	255	302
Granite	422	804	509	746
Hill	3,061	3,759	3,576	3,168
Jefferson	904	1,281	1,210	1,387
Judith Basin	557	961	771	809
Lake	2,260	4,172	3,253	3,810
Lewis & Clark	6,081	10,719	8,117	10,315
Liberty	365	808	506	638
Lincoln	2,402	3,276	3,146	3,018
Madison	669	1,780	427	799
McCone	562	854	749	730
Meagher	230	674	364	486
Mineral	659	706	819	679
Missoula	13,784	15,557	14,824	15,933
Musselshell	689	1,202	922	1,117
Park	1,923	3,771	2,364	3,281
Petroleum	87	232	110	211
Phillips	828	1,659	1,117	1,347
Pondera	1,215	1,890	1,413	1,666
Powder River	267	844	429	683
Powell	1,050	1,720	1,302	1,610
Prairie	303	685	415	597
Ravalli	2,480	4,611	3,213	4,560
Richland	1,438	2,645	2,000	2,150
Roosevelt	1,464	2,304	2,110	1,926
Rosebud	777	1,486	1,411	1,534
Sanders	1,197	1,779	1,725	1,738
Sheridan	1,197	1,500	1,560	1,114
Silver Bow	11,704	7,967	11,377	7,506
Stillwater	716	1,698	1,143	1,446
Sweet Grass	350	1,260	502	1,135
Teton	1,121	1,991	1,506	1,725
Toole	897	1,679	1,080	1,469
Treasure	176	377	239	315
Valley	1,973	3,210	2,352	2,520
Wheatland	445	761	535	755
Wibaux	283	390	352	308
Yellowstone	13,602	25,205	18,307	25,123
Totals	**120,197**	**183,976**	**146,696**	**170,156**

Montana Vote Since 1932

1932 (Pres.), Roosevelt, Dem., 127,286; Hoover, Rep., 78,078; Thomas, Soc., 7,891; Foster, Com., 1,775; Harvey, Lib., 1,449.

1936 (Pres.), Roosevelt, Dem., 159,690; Landon, Rep., 63,598; Lemke, Union, 5,549; Thomas, Soc., 1,066; Browder, Com., 385; Colvin, Proh., 224.

1940 (Pres.), Roosevelt, Dem., 145,698; Willkie, Rep., 99,579; Thomas, Soc., 1,443; Babson, Proh., 664; Browder, Com., 489.

1944 (Pres.), Roosevelt, Dem., 112,556; Dewey, Rep., 93,163; Thomas, Soc., 1,296; Watson, Proh., 340.

1948 (Pres.), Truman, Dem., 119,071; Dewey, Rep., 96,770; Wallace, Prog., 7,313; Thomas, Soc., 695; Watson, Proh., 429.

1952 (Pres.), Eisenhower, Rep., 157,394; Stevenson, Dem., 106,213; Hallinan, Prog., 723; Hamblen, Proh., 548; Hoopes, Soc., 159.

1956 (Pres.), Eisenhower, Rep., 154,933; Stevenson, Dem., 116,238.

1960 (Pres.), Kennedy, Dem., 134,891; Nixon, Rep., 141,841; Decker, Proh., 456; Dobbs, Soc. Workers, 391.

1964 (Pres.), Johnson, Dem., 164,246; Goldwater, Rep., 113,032; Kasper, Nat'l States Rights, 519; Munn, Proh., 499; DeBerry, Soc. Worker, 332.

1968 (Pres.), Nixon, Rep., 138,835; Humphrey, Dem., 114,117; Wallace, 3d party, 20,015; Halstead, Soc. Worker, 457; Munn, Prohibition 510; Caton, New Reform, 470.

1972 (Pres.), Nixon, Rep., 183,976; McGovern, Dem., 120,197; Schmitz, American, 13,430.

Nebraska

	1972 McGovern (D)	1972 Nixon (R)	1976 Carter (D)	1976 Ford (R)
County				
Adams	3,359	8,841	7,562	4,932
Antelope	851	3,228	2,109	1,164
Arthur	45	236	64	192
Banner	96	404	210	277
Blaine	56	343	122	271
Boone	883	2,406	1,273	1,920
Box Butte	960	3,431	1,412	2,714
Boyd	506	1,419	787	1,002
Brown	330	1,462	554	1,214
Buffalo	2,988	8,587	4,170	7,740
Burt	900	2,937	1,470	2,492
Butler	1,812	2,301	2,349	1,783
Cass	1,805	4,503	3,190	3,781
Cedar	1,807	2,995	2,151	2,308
Chase	307	1,318	683	1,068
Cherry	483	2,610	898	2,247
Cheyenne	950	3,120	1,656	2,230
Clay	861	2,542	1,358	2,227
Colfax	1,107	2,799	1,657	2,347
Cuming	1,019	3,810	3,115	1,288
Custer	1,147	4,836	1,955	3,881
Dakota	1,748	2,879	2,276	2,611
Dawes	711	2,987	1,272	2,424
Dawson	1,424	6,211	2,307	5,085
Deuel	224	1,001	397	768
Dixon	941	2,299	1,283	1,974
Dodge	3,826	9,837	5,247	8,860
Douglas	48,201	101,579	59,895	89,092
Dundy	221	1,003	238	723
Fillmore	1,270	2,511	1,479	2,092
Franklin	599	1,510	935	1,162
Frontier	324	1,315	534	917
Furnas	676	2,282	1,097	1,744
Gage	3,588	6,298	4,487	5,173
Garden	204	1,161	443	919
Garfield	209	903	343	723
Gosper	242	829	329	646
Grant	69	376	115	309
Greeley	760	1,005	873	763
Hall	4,218	10,987	5,938	10,636
Hamilton	907	2,960	1,276	2,572
Harlan	539	1,549	865	1,301
Hayes	123	486	264	406
Hitchcock	364	1,339	781	893
Holt	1,053	4,147	1,737	3,370
Hooker	52	394	96	325
Howard	945	1,691	1,303	1,344
Jefferson	1,476	3,008	2,063	2,607
Johnson	917	1,637	1,114	1,294
Kearney	759	2,203	1,140	1,724
Keith	665	2,513	1,129	2,466
Keya Paha	146	563	245	401
Kimball	437	1,650	685	1,236
Knox	1,289	3,318	1,918	2,588
Lancaster	25,924	42,573	28,067	38,661
Lincoln	3,220	7,502	5,325	7,030
Logan	73	320	195	283
Loup	58	345	140	299
McPherson	42	247	104	220
Madison	2,224	8,580	3,319	7,943
Merrick	887	2,418	1,346	2,166
Morrill	520	1,740	962	1,342
Nance	641	1,413	933	1,097
Nemaha	909	2,600	1,322	1,988
Nuckolls	999	2,089	1,417	1,747
Otoe	1,718	4,815	2,431	4,476
Pawnee	524	1,299	839	980
Perkins	354	1,165	581	918
Phelps	735	3,356	1,159	3,197
Pierce	653	2,451	994	2,165
Platte	2,855	7,871	3,557	6,878
Polk	827	2,050	1,183	1,792
Red Willow	931	3,701	1,709	2,930
Richardson	1,508	3,662	2,310	2,948
Rock	138	937	252	728
Saline	2,654	2,828	3,100	2,228
Sarpy	3,904	11,514	7,352	11,821
Saunders	2,501	4,492	3,499	3,822
Scotts Bluff	2,764	8,649	4,265	6,830
Seward	2,087	3,707	2,543	3,102
Sheridan	481	2,386	806	1,983
Sherman	811	1,099	1,074	931
Sioux	129	639	328	529
Stanton	478	1,662	756	1,456
Thayer	978	2,274	1,310	1,971
Thomas	73	397	102	343
Thurston	840	1,565	1,018	1,288
Valley	771	2,011	997	1,481
Washington	1,401	4,290	2,233	3,780
Wayne	902	2,659	1,086	2,506
Webster	696	1,631	1,030	1,261
Wheeler	84	361	146	273
York	1,318	4,651	1,646	4,171
Totals	**169,991**	**406,298**	**230,152**	**349,736**

Nebraska Vote Since 1932

1932 (Pres.), Roosevelt, Dem., 359,082; Hoover, Rep., 201,177; Thomas, Soc., 9,876.
1936 (Pres.), Roosevelt, Dem., 347,454; Landon, Rep., 248,731; Lemke, Union, 12,847.
1940 (Pres.), Roosevelt, Dem., 263,677; Willkie, Rep., 352,201.
1944 (Pres.), Roosevelt, Dem., 233,246; Dewey, Rep., 329,880.
1948 (Pres.), Truman, Dem., 224,165; Dewey, Rep., 264,774.
1952 (Pres.), Eisenhower, Rep., 421,603; Stevenson, Dem., 188,057.
1956 (Pres.), Eisenhower, Rep., 378,108; Stevenson, Dem., 199,029.
1960 (Pres.), Kennedy, Dem., 232,542; Nixon, Rep., 380,553.
1964 (Pres.), Johnson, Dem., 307,307; Goldwater, Rep., 276,847.
1968 (Pres.), Nixon, Rep., 321,163; Humphrey, Dem., 170,784; Wallace, 3d party, 44,904.
1972 (Pres.), Nixon, Rep., 406,298; McGovern, Dem., 169,991; scattered 817.

Nevada

| | 1972 | | 1976 | |
| | McGovern | Nixon | Carter | Ford |
County	(D)	(R)	(D)	(R)
Churchill	1,038	2,970	1,800	2,358
Clark	36,807	53,101	51,158	48,204
Douglas	983	2,898	1,934	3,095
Elko	1,467	3,886	1,955	3,293
Esmeralda	127	273	213	180
Eureka	139	371	163	272
Humboldt	713	1,659	1,074	1,380
Lander	468	798	458	561
Lincoln	382	841	642	700
Lyon	959	2,813	1,866	2,068
Mineral	768	2,111	1,361	1,104
Nye	802	1,287	997	792
Pershing	365	853	633	635
Storey	226	508	310	274
Washoe	17,106	33,539	21,687	29,264
White Pine	1,546	2,446	1,963	1,464
CARSON CITY	2,120	5,396	3,874	5,282
Totals	66,016	115,750	92,088	100,926

Nevada Vote Since 1932

1932 (Pres.), Roosevelt, Dem., 28,756; Hoover, Rep., 12,674.
1936 (Pres.), Roosevelt, Dem., 31,925; Landon, Rep., 11,923.
1940 (Pres.), Roosevelt, Dem., 31,945; Willkie, Rep., 21,229.
1944 (Pres.), Roosevelt, Dem., 29,623; Dewey, Rep., 24,611.
1948 (Pres.), Truman, Dem., 31,291; Dewey, Rep., 29,-357; Wallace, Prog., 1,469.
1952 (Pres.), Eisenhower, Rep., 50,502; Stevenson, Dem., 31,688.
1956 (Pres.), Eisenhower, Rep., 56,049; Stevenson, Dem., 40,640.
1960 (Pres.), Kennedy, Dem., 54,880; Nixon, Rep., 52,387.
1964 (Pres.), Johnson, Dem., 79,339; Goldwater, Rep., 56,094.
1968 (Pres.), Nixon, Rep., 73,188; Humphrey, Dem., 60,598; Wallace, 3d party, 20,432.
1972 (Pres.), Nixon, Rep., 115,750; McGovern, Dem. 66,016.

New Hampshire

| | 1972 | | 1976 | |
| | McGovern | Nixon | Carter | Ford |
County	(D)	(R)	(D)	(R)
Belknap	4,610	11,536	5,981	9,661
Carroll	2,395	8,525	3,374	8,561
Cheshire	9,157	13,390	6,726	8,055
Coos	5,829	9,468	7,380	7,087
Grafton	8,888	16,605	8,464	13,720
Hillsborough	34,739	65,274	45,083	53,159
Merrimack	11,737	25,354	14,605	21,516
Rockingham	21,998	38,825	29,956	36,480
Strafford	12,028	16,846	11,204	11,315
Sullivan	5,554	7,901	4,444	5,021
Totals	116,435	213,724	137,399	174,575

New Hampshire Vote Since 1932

1932 (Pres.), Roosevelt, Dem., 100,680; Hoover, Rep., 103,629; Thomas, Soc., 947; Foster, Com., 264.
1936 (Pres.), Roosevelt, Dem., 108,640; Landon, Rep., 104,642; Lemke, Union, 4,819; Browder, Com., 193.
1940 (Pres.), Roosevelt, Dem., 125,292; Willkie, Rep., 110,127.
1944 (Pres.), Roosevelt, Dem., 119,663; Dewey, Rep., 109,916; Thomas, Soc., 46.
1948 (Pres.), Truman, Dem., 107,995; Dewey, Rep., 121,299; Wallace, Prog., 1,970; Thomas, Soc., 86; Teichert, Soc. Lab., 83; Thurmond, States' Rights, 7.
1952 (Pres.), Eisenhower, Rep., 166,287; Stevenson, Dem., 106,663.
1956 (Pres.), Eisenhower, Rep., 176,519; Stevenson, Dem., 90,364; Andrews, Const., 111.
1960 (Pres.), Kennedy, Dem., 137,772; Nixon, Rep., 157,989.
1964 (Pres.), Johnson, Dem., 182,065; Goldwater, Rep., 104,029.
1968 (Pres.), Nixon, Rep., 154,903; Humphrey, Dem., 130,589; Wallace, 3d party, 11,173; New Party, 421; Halstead, Soc. Worker, 104.
1972 (Pres.), Nixon, Rep., 213,724; McGovern, Dem., 116,435; Schmitz, American, 3,386; Jenness, Soc. Worker, 368; scattered, 142.

New Jersey

| | 1972 | | 1976 | |
| | McGovern | Nixon | Carter | Ford |
County	(D)	(R)	(D)	(R)
Atlantic	28,203	45,667	40,898	35,295
Bergen	147,155	285,458	180,661	237,262
Burlington	41,520	70,805	35,238	33,813
Camden	75,202	111,935	105,971	79,164
Cape May	8,729	22,621	9,364	11,052
Cumberland	18,692	26,409	29,065	20,535
Essex	161,270	170,036	54,657	41,578
Gloucester	25,509	44,806	38,726	34,888
Hudson	89,977	136,895	116,238	92,621
Hunterdon	9,031	21,282	12,303	19,287
Mercer	62,180	69,303	25,892	25,176
Middlesex	88,397	149,033	122,805	113,539
Monmouth	63,176	124,830	32,371	38,507
Morris	50,937	113,469	39,394	65,836
Ocean	27,710	77,979	54,641	74,499
Passaic	63,302	108,511	76,184	85,101
Salem	8,609	16,371	12,624	11,637
Somerset	26,537	56,524	36,258	51,260
Sussex	8,585	25,977	14,759	23,613
Union	90,482	148,290	102,245	112,794
Warren	10,008	19,301	14,238	15,254
Totals	1,102,211	1,845,502	1,420,668	1,477,858

New Jersey Vote Since 1932

1932 (Pres.) Roosevelt, Dem., 806,630; Hoover, Rep., 775,684; Thomas, Soc., 42,998; Foster, Com., 2,915; Reynolds, Soc. Lab., 1,062; Upshaw, Proh., 774.
1936 (Pres.) Roosevelt, Dem., 1,083,549; Landon, Rep., 719,421; Lemke, Union, 9,405; Thomas, Soc., 3,895; Browder, Com., 1,590; Colvin, Proh., 916; Aiken, Soc. Lab., 346.
1940 (Pres.) Roosevelt, Dem., 1,016,404; Willkie, Rep., 944,876; Browder, Com., 8,814; Thomas, Soc., 2,823; Babson, Proh., 851; Aiken, Soc. Lab., 446.
1944 (Pres.) Roosevelt, Dem., 987,874; Dewey, Rep., 961,335; Teichert, Soc. Lab., 6,939; Watson, Nat'l Proh., 4,255; Thomas, Soc., 3,385.
1948 (Pres.) Truman, Dem., 895,455; Dewey, Rep., 981,124; Wallace, Prog., 42,683; Watson, Proh., 10,-593; Thomas, Soc., 10,521; Dobbs, Soc. Workers, 5,825; Teichert, Soc. Lab., 3,354.
1952 (Pres.) Eisenhower, Rep., 1,373,613; Stevenson, Dem., 1,015,902; Hoopes, Soc., 8,593; Haas, Soc. Lab., 5,815; Hallinan, Prog., 5,589; Krajewski, Poor Man's, 4,203; Dobbs, Soc. Workers, 3,850; Hamblen, Proh., 989.
1956 (Pres.) Eisenhower, Rep., 1,606,942; Stevenson,

Dem., 850,337; Holtwick, Proh., 9,147; Haas, Soc. Lab., 6,736; Andrews, Conservative, 5,317; Dobbs, Soc. Workers, 4,004; Krajewski, American Third Party, 1,829.

1960 (Pres.) Kennedy, Dem., 1,385,415; Nixon, Rep., 1,363,324; Dobbs, Soc. Workers, 11,402; Lee, Conservative, 8,708; Haas, Soc. Lab., 4,262.

1964 (Pres.) Johnson, Dem., 1,867,671; Goldwater, Rep., 963,843; DeBerry, Soc. Workers, 8,181; Haas, Soc. Labor, 7,075,

1968 (Pres.) Nixon, Rep., 1,325,467; Humphrey, Dem., 1,264,206; Wallace, 3d party, 262,187; Halstead, Soc. Worker, 8,667; Gregory, Peace Freedom, 8,084; Blomen, Soc. Labor, 6,784.

1972 (Pres.) Nixon, Rep., 1,845,502; McGovern, Dem., 1,102,211; Schmitz, American, 34,378; Spock, Peoples, 5,355; Fisher, Soc. Labor, 4,544; Jenness, Soc. Worker, 2,233; Mahalchik, Amer. First, 1,743; Hall, Communist, 1,263.

New Mexico

County	1972		1976	
	McGovern (D)	Nixon (R)	Carter (D)	Ford (R)
Bernalillo	48,753	79,993	62,412	74,063
Catron	271	829	517	602
Chaves	4,296	11,493	7,419	10,633
Colfax	1,855	2,663	2,718	2,259
Curry	2,416	8,392	5,003	6,232
De Baca	270	752	597	556
Dona Ana	9,416	14,562	11,912	13,682
Eddy	5,040	9,921	9,097	7,698
Grant	4,081	4,431	4,780	4,095
Guadalupe	1,202	1,297	1,379	1,047
Harding	220	522	285	387
Hidalgo	562	1,051	702	449
Lea	3,429	12,478	6,533	8,773
Lincoln	696	2,528	1,395	2,320
Los Alamos	2,435	5,039	2,890	5,383
Luna	1,560	2,958	2,872	2,966
McKinley	5,124	5,366	6,827	4,601
Mora	1,135	1,165	1,438	904
Otero	2,981	7,033	5,235	5,916
Quay	1,161	3,224	2,095	2,059
Rio Arriba	5,642	4,351	7,181	3,206
Roosevelt	1,612	4,727	3,111	3,269
Sandoval	3,293	3,507	5,063	4,100
San Juan	4,296	30,788	8,743	10,514
San Miguel	4,663	4,434	4,968	3,000
Santa Fe	10,761	12,211	14,022	11,221
Sierra	934	2,074	1,564	1,665
Socorro	1,994	2,658	2,606	2,265
Taos	3,472	3,617	4,412	3,012
Torrance	908	1,758	1,526	1,462
Union	496	1,545	975	1,146
Valencia	6,110	8,239	8,730	7,791
Totals	**141,084**	**235,606**	**199,225**	**207,718**

New Mexico Vote Since 1932

1932 (Pres.), Roosevelt, Dem., 95,089; Hoover, Rep., 54,217; Thomas, Soc., 11,776; Harvey, Lib., 389; Foster, Com., 135.

1936 (Pres.), Roosevelt, Dem., 105,838; Landon, Rep., 61,710; Lemke, Union, 942; Thomas, Soc., 343; Browder, Com., 43.

1940 (Pres.), Roosevelt, Dem., 103,699; Willkie, Rep., 79,315.

1944 (Pres.), Roosevelt, Dem., 81,389; Dewey, Rep., 70,688; Watson, Proh., 148.

1948 (Pres.), Truman, Dem., 105,464; Dewey, Rep., 80,303; Wallace, Prog., 1,037; Watson, Proh., 127; Thomas, Soc., 83; Teichert, Soc. Lab., 49.

1952 (Pres.), Eisenhower, Rep., 132,170; Stevenson, Dem., 105,661; Hamblen, Proh., 297; Hallinan, Ind. Prog., 225; MacArthur, Christian National, 220; Haas, Soc. Lab., 35.

1956 (Pres.), Eisenhower, Rep., 146,788; Stevenson, Dem., 106,098; Holtwick, Proh., 607; Andrews, Ind., 364; Haas, Soc. Lab., 69.

1960 (Pres.), Kennedy, Dem., 156,027; Nixon, Rep., 153,733; Decker, Proh., 777; Haas, Soc. Lab., 570.

1964 (Pres.), Johnson, Dem., 194,017; Goldwater, Rep., 131,838; Haas, Soc. Labor, 1,217; Munn, Proh., 543.

1968 (Pres.), Nixon, Rep., 169,692; Humphrey, Dem., 130,081; Wallace, 3d party, 25,737; Chavez, 1,519; Halstead, Soc. Worker, 252.

1972 (Pres.), Nixon, Rep., 235,606; McGovern, Dem., 141,084; Schmitz, Amer., 8,767; Jenness, Soc. Worker, 474.

New York

County	1972		1976	
	McGovern (D-L*)	Nixon (R-C**)	Carter (D)	Ford (R)
Albany	67,297	81,848	66,011	65,307
Allegany	4,812	13,426	6,036	11,473
Broome	37,154	55,736	38,524	51,557
Cattaraugus	10,909	21,906	13,214	18,785
Cayuga	11,907	22,774	13,330	19,761
Chatauqua	26,253	37,158	26,205	32,069
Chemung	12,650	26,200	16,964	20,258
Chenango	5,695	13,770	6,986	11,750
Clinton	9,703	17,048	11,542	15,148
Columbia	7,558	17,995	10,362	15,887
Cortland	5,234	12,885	6,655	10,816
Delaware	5,243	15,136	7,222	12,407
Dutchess	27,872	68,864	37,032	50,111
Erie	218,105	256,462	226,831	218,248
Essex	4,955	11,763	6,302	9,690
Franklin	5,266	10,959	7,045	8,555
Fulton	7,303	15,200	9,290	12,075
Genesee	8,631	17,107	10,450	14,317
Greene	5,260	14,213	7,397	10,914
Hamilton	731	2,597	1,145	2,286
Herkimer	9,487	20,194	12,337	14,546
Jefferson	11,629	23,123	12,935	19,388
Lewis	2,987	6,591	4,142	6,760
Livingston	7,031	15,886	9,489	13,782
Madison	6,241	18,392	8,773	15,443
Monroe	120,031	196,579	132,331	163,977
Montgomery	9,460	16,640	11,244	12,996
Niagara	38,991	54,777	42,987	44,807
Oneida	33,642	78,549	43,967	53,501
Onondaga	61,895	140,039	73,953	111,918
Ontario	11,012	23,828	14,443	19,899
Orange	25,778	63,556	40,056	48,885
Orleans	4,371	10,938	5,904	8,945
Oswego	11,317	29,109	16,700	25,248
Otsego	7,898	17,364	9,657	14,567
Putnam	7,747	21,673	11,403	17,835
Rensselaer	24,019	48,864	28,372	39,349
Rockland	35,771	64,753	48,240	51,578
St. Lawrence	15,286	26,145	17,992	22,571
Saratoga	17,899	40,582	22,530	36,227
Schenectady	29,619	47,529	32,499	43,939
Schoharie	3,730	8,664	5,125	6,884
Schuyler	1,937	4,945	2,811	4,000
Seneca	4,441	9,368	5,522	7,120
Steuben	9,462	28,708	14,532	23,361
Sullivan	9,847	17,035	12,537	12,142
Tioga	5,470	13,396	6,966	11,919
Tompkins	12,344	17,605	12,104	14,802
Ulster	21,371	46,883	28,999	33,857
Warren	5,760	16,649	8,278	15,752
Washington	5,677	16,136	5,779	11,056
Wayne	8,203	23,379	11,727	18,651
Wyoming	4,365	11,184	5,698	9,651
Yates	1,958	6,639	2,876	5,750
Outside				
N.Y. Metro	1,068,404	1,914,829	1,251,551	1,572,490
Nassau	252,831	438,723	301,382	328,190
Suffolk	132,441	316,452	206,382	246,422
Westchester	154,412	262,901	170,476	204,564
N.Y.				
Suburban	539,684	1,018,076	678,140	779,176
Bronx	243,345	196,754	236,484	97,075
Kings	387,768	373,903	415,960	192,452
New York	354,326	178,515	331,881	118,114
Queens	328,316	426,015	376,674	245,495
Richmond	29,241	84,688	45,975	55,893
Greater				
N.Y.Metro	1,342,996	1,259,873	2,085,114	1,488,205
D/R total	2,767,956	3,824,642	3,190,358	2,778,620
2d Party				
(Lib/Con)	83,128	368,136	146,307	282,075
Totals	**2,951,084**	**4,192,778**	**3,336,665**	**3,060,695**

*Democratic and Liberal **Republican and Conservative

New York Vote Since 1932

1932 (Pres.), Roosevelt, Dem., 2,534,959; Hoover, Rep., 1,937,963; Thomas, Soc., 177,397; Foster, Com., 27,956; Reynolds, Soc. Lab., 10,339.

1936 (Pres.), Roosevelt, Dem., 3,018,298; American Lab., 274,924; total, 3,293,222; Landon, Rep., 2,180,-670; Thomas, Soc., 86,879; Browder, Com., 35,609.

1940 (Pres.), Roosevelt, Dem., 2,834,500; American Lab., 417,418; total 3,251,918; Willkie, Rep., 3,027,-478; Thomas, Soc., 18,950; Babson, Proh., 3,250.

1944 (Pres.), Roosevelt, Dem., 2,478,598; American Lab., 496,405; Liberal, 329,325; total, 3,304,238;

Dewey, Rep., 2,987,647; Teichert, Ind. Gov't., 14,-352; Thomas, Soc., 10,553.

1948 (Pres.), Truman, Dem., 2,557,642; Liberal, 222,-562; total, 2,780,204; Dewey, Rep., 2,841,163; Wallace, Amer. Lab., 509,559; Thomas, Soc., 40,879; Teichert, Ind. Gov't., 2,729; Dobbs, Soc. Workers, 2,675.

1952 (Pres.), Eisenhower, Rep., 3,952,815; Stevenson, Dem., 2,687,890, Liberal, 416,711; total, 3,104,601; Hallinan, American Lab., 64,211; Hoopes, Soc., 2,664; Dobbs, Soc. Workers, 2,212; Haas, Ind. Gov't., 1,560; scattering, 178; blank and void, 87,813.

1956 (Pres.), Eisenhower, Rep., 4,340,340; Stevenson, Dem., 2,458,212; Liberal, 292,557; total, 2,750,769; write-in votes for Andrews, 1,027; Werdel, 492; Haas, 150; Hoopes, 82; others, 476.

1960 (Pres.), Kennedy, Dem., 3,423,909; Liberal, 406,-176; total, 3,830,085; Nixon, Rep., 3,446,419; Dobbs, Soc. Workers, 14,319; scattering, 256; blank and void, 88,896.

1964 (Pres.), Johnson, Dem., 4,913,156; Goldwater, Rep., 2,243,559; Haas, Soc. Labor, 6,085; DeBerry, Soc. Workers, 3,215; scattering, 188; blank and void, 151,383.

1968 (Pres.), Nixon, Rep., 3,007,932; Humphrey, Dem., 3,378,470; Wallace, 3d party, 358,864; Blomen, Soc. Labor, 8,432; Halstead, Soc. Worker, 11,851; Gregory, Freedom and Peace, 24,517; blank, void, and scattering, 171,624.

1972 (Pres.), Nixon, Rep., 3,824,642; Conservative, 368,136; McGovern, Dem., 2,767,956; Liberal, 183,-128; Reed, Soc. Worker, 7,797; Fisher, Soc. Labor, 4,530; Hall, Communist, 5,641; blank, void, or scattered, 161,641.

North Carolina

County	1972 McGovern (D)	Nixon (R)	1976 Carter (D)	Ford (R)
Alamance	6,833	22,046	17,371	12,680
Alexander	2,468	5,865	5,246	4,625
Alleghany	1,304	2,158	2,550	1,532
Anson	2,188	3,551	4,796	1,608
Ashe	3,313	5,784	5,193	4,936
Avery	627	3,510	5,193	4,936
Beaufort	2,901	6,915	5,728	4,677
Bertie	1,819	2,874	4,117	1,332
Bladen	2,201	4,205	6,009	1,600
Brunswick	2,500	6,153	6,365	3,185
Buncombe	12,626	32,091	26,641	22,456
Burke	6,197	14,447	14,251	10,070
Cabarrus	5,336	18,384	11,599	11,799
Caldwell	4,886	12,976	11,894	9,872
Camden	556	909	1,231	562
Carteret	2,805	8,463	6,790	5,510
Caswell	1,922	2,983	2,398	1,277
Catawba	7,744	24,106	16,766	18,532
Chatham	3,624	6,175	6,397	4,278
Cherokee	2,411	4,113	2,859	2,624
Chowan	936	1,906	1,862	1,019
Clay	797	1,545	1,551	1,411
Cleveland	4,994	13,726	14,399	8,020
Columbus	3,305	8,468	10,708	3,184
Craven	2,384	9,372	7,443	5,881
Cumberland	9,853	24,376	24,112	14,223
Currituck	718	1,578	1,999	954
Dare	634	1,986	2,191	1,680
Davidson	7,691	24,875	17,832	18,913
Davie	1,578	5,613	1,817	2,319
Duplin	2,857	7,153	7,697	3,912
Durham	15,566	25,576	18,433	17,675
Edgecombe	4,635	8,244	8,001	4,850
Forsyth	20,928	46,415	33,467	34,706
Franklin	2,341	5,431	5,396	2,629
Gaston	8,462	27,956	22,878	19,727
Gates	1,177	1,264	2,291	722
Graham	1,057	1,699	1,792	1,621
Granville	2,918	6,037	5,244	2,955
Greene	847	2,788	2,740	1,356
Guilford	25,800	61,381	47,413	45,539
Halifax	4,241	8,908	7,892	5,257
Harnett	3,347	10,259	8,965	9,935
Haywood	4,515	8,903	10,671	5,948
Henderson	2,701	12,134	7,939	10,397
Hertford	1,928	2,794	2,521	735
Hoke	1,466	1,927	3,186	920
Hyde	403	1,112	1,084	672
Iredell	5,088	16,736	13,296	11,573
Jackson	3,169	4,709	5,228	3,536
Johnston	3,488	14,272	10,301	8,511
Jones	1,093	1,650	2,015	948
Lee	2,024	5,836	5,104	3,491
Lenoir	3,672	11,065	7,650	7,715
Lincoln	5,100	8,597	9,463	6,684
Macon	1,749	4,134	3,703	3,067
Madison	2,039	3,273	3,433	2,446
Martin	1,840	4,188	3,279	1,331
McDowell	2,348	6,570	6,246	4,685
Mecklenburg	33,730	77,546	60,000	58,198
Mitchell	800	4,240	1,961	3,620
Montgomery	2,175	4,417	4,305	2,867
Moore	3,627	9,406	7,373	7,557
Nash	4,503	12,679	8,937	8,477
New Hanover	5,984	19,060	14,452	13,653
Northampton	3,233	2,997	2,709	680
Onslow	2,424	10,343	7,676	5,827
Orange	12,634	11,632	15,755	9,329
Pamlico	919	1,847	2,113	1,068
Pasquotank	2,115	3,906	3,438	2,730
Pender	1,415	3,327	4,422	2,063
Perquimans	723	1,299	1,650	904
Person	2,246	5,941	3,803	2,946
Pitt	5,858	14,406	10,885	9,097
Polk	1,416	3,121	3,145	2,592
Randolph	5,346	18,724	12,714	14,337
Richmond	3,508	5,692	8,793	2,848
Robeson	7,391	11,362	20,705	4,907
Rockingham	5,530	14,519	13,413	9,362
Rowan	6,834	20,735	15,801	14,972
Rutherford	4,140	9,506	10,262	6,717
Sampson	4,888	9,684	8,869	6,965
Scotland	1,938	3,485	4,430	1,932
Stanly	5,218	12,459	9,260	8,840
Stokes	3,254	7,118	6,647	6,030
Surry	4,706	10,497	9,874	7,420
Swain	1,101	2,052	2,151	1,608
Transylvania	2,321	5,860	3,860	3,240
Tyrrell	459	676	900	403
Union	3,886	10,264	10,578	6,384
Vance	3,117	6,491	5,620	3,808
Wake	22,807	56,808	44,003	44,249
Warren	1,698	2,603	3,193	1,428
Washington	1,546	2,559	2,799	1,481
Watauga	3,451	6,017	5,358	5,390
Wayne	5,234	14,352	9,265	9,607
Wilkes	4,634	13,105	10,176	11,768
Wilson	4,166	12,060	5,883	5,575
Yadkin	1,592	6,824	4,497	5,915
Yancey	2,278	3,106	3,932	2,687
Totals	**438,705**	**1,054,889**	**923,533**	**738,545**

North Carolina Vote Since 1932

1932 (Pres.), Roosevelt, Dem., 497,566; Hoover, Rep., 208,344; Thomas, Soc., 5,591.

1936 (Pres.), Roosevelt, Dem., 616,141; Landon, Rep., 223,283; Thomas, Soc., 21; Browder, Com., 11; Lemke, Union, 2.

1940 (Pres.), Roosevelt, Dem., 609,015; Willkie, Rep., 213,633.

1944 (Pres.), Roosevelt, Dem., 527,399; Dewey, Rep., 263,155.

1948 (Pres.), Truman, Dem., 459,070; Dewey, Rep., 258,572; Thurmond, States' Rights, 69,652; Wallace, Prog., 3,915.

1952 (Pres.), Eisenhower, Rep., 558,107; Stevenson, Dem., 652,803.

1956 (Pres.), Eisenhower, Rep., 575,062; Stevenson, Dem., 590,530.

1960 (Pres.), Kennedy, Dem., 713,136; Nixon, Rep., 655,420.

1964 (Pres.), Johnson, Dem., 800,139; Goldwater, Rep., 624,844.

1968 (Pres.), Nixon, Rep., 627,192; Humphrey, Dem., 464,113; Wallace, 3d party, 496,188.

1972 (Pres.), Nixon, Rep., 1,054,889; McGovern, Dem., 438,705; Schmitz, American, 25,018.

North Dakota

County	1972 McGovern (D)	Nixon (R)	1976 Carter (D)	Ford (R)
Adams	665	1,177	955	932
Barnes	2,804	4,518	3,293	3,995
Benson	1,635	2,050	1,966	1,685
Billings	192	509	275	350
Bottineau	1,369	3,263	2,080	2,747
Bowman	643	1,111	901	1,028
Burke	651	1,446	897	1,084
Burleigh	5,841	13,909	9,170	13,637
Cass	14,073	21,770	17,850	22,544
Cavalier	1,867	2,898	2,091	1,980
Dickey	1,266	2,277	1,605	2,021

	1972		1976	
	(D)	(R)	(D)	(R)
Divide	774	1,230	818	576
Dunn	644	1,438	1,049	1,040
Eddy	911	1,022	1,119	884
Emmons	1,115	2,194	1,455	1,369
Foster	861	1,352	1,146	1,117
Golden Val.	362	774	479	633
Grand Forks	9,416	13,361	11,229	13,235
Grant	596	1,569	943	1,203
Griggs	901	1,312	1,131	1,091
Hettinger	726	1,511	1,094	1,134
Kidder	557	1,315	935	950
La Moure	1,399	2,110	1,717	1,734
Logan	554	1,408	809	941
McHenry	1,554	2,765	1,983	2,035
McIntosh	521	2,440	910	1,781
McKenzie	937	1,913	1,321	1,591
McLean	1,703	3,575	2,799	2,724
Mercer	784	2,567	1,297	1,664
Morton	3,312	5,494	3,048	3,075
Mountrail	1,391	2,038	2,161	1,411
Nelson	1,358	1,625	1,594	1,161
Oliver	293	669	528	571
Pembina	1,801	3,317	2,191	2,644
Pierce	973	1,970	1,433	1,393
Ramsey	2,384	3,954	3,102	3,302
Ransom	1,355	2,056	1,712	1,696
Renville	702	1,121	1,007	812
Richland	3,367	5,194	4,580	5,011
Rolette	1,803	1,713	2,215	1,042
Sargent	1,331	1,616	1,644	1,340
Sheridan	334	1,460	569	935
Sioux	557	561	696	354
Slope	249	413	345	355
Stark	2,636	5,115	4,071	4,364
Steele	892	1,063	1,064	838
Stutsman	3,589	6,269	4,864	5,628
Towner	944	1,349	1,216	990
Traill	1,892	3,118	2,351	2,800
Walsh	2,908	3,991	3,559	3,524
Ward	6,706	13,900	9,468	12,713
Wells	1,297	2,519	1,740	1,936
Williams	2,989	4,800	4,178	4,125
Totals	**100,384**	**174,109**	**134,503**	**151,515**

North Dakota Vote Since 1932

1932 (Pres.), Roosevelt, Dem., 178,350; Hoover, Rep., 71,772; Harvey, Lib., 1,817; Thomas, Soc., 3,521; Foster, Com., 830.

1936 (Pres.), Roosevelt, Dem., 163,148; Landon, Rep., 72,751; Lemke, Union, 36,708; Thomas, Soc., 552; Browder, Com., 360; Colvin, Proh., 197.

1940 (Pres.), Roosevelt, Dem., 124,036; Willkie, Rep., 154,590; Thomas, Soc., 1,279; Knuttson, Com., 545; Babson, Proh., 325.

1944 (Pres.), Roosevelt, Dem., 100,144; Dewey, Rep., 118,535; Thomas, Soc., 943; Watson, Proh., 549.

1948 (Pres.), Truman, Dem., 95,812; Dewey, Rep., 115,139; Wallace, Prog., 8,391; Thomas, Soc., 1,000; Thurmond, States' Rights, 374.

1952 (Pres.), Eisenhower, Rep., 191,712; Stevenson, Dem., 76,694; MacArthur, Christian Nationalist, 1,075; Hallinan, Prog., 344; Hamblen, Proh., 302.

1956 (Pres.), Eisenhower, Rep., 156,766; Stevenson, Dem., 96,742; Andrews, American, 483.

1960 (Pres.), Kennedy, Dem., 123,963; Nixon, Rep., 154,310; Dobbs, Soc. Workers, 158.

1964 (Pres.), Johnson, Dem., 149,784; Goldwater, Rep., 108,207; DeBerry, Soc. Worker, 224; Munn, Proh., 174.

1968 (Pres.), Nixon, Rep., 138,669; Humphrey, Dem., 94,769; Wallace, 3d party, 14,244; Halstead, Soc. Worker, 128; Munn, Prohibition, 38; Troxell, Ind., 34.

1972 (Pres.), Nixon, Rep., 174,109; McGovern, Dem., 100,384; Jenness, Soc. Worker, 288; Hall, Communist, 87; Schmitz, American, 5,646.

Ohio

	1972		1976	
	McGovern	Nixon	Carter	Ford
County	(D)	(R)	(D)	(R)
Adams	2,709	4,980	4,159	3,928
Allen	10,184	26,966	14,627	23,726
Ashland	4,302	12,470	7,104	9,762
Ashtabula	15,052	22,762	20,911	16,882
Athens	9,977	9,735	9,207	7,858
Auglaize	4,617	11,900	5,844	9,774
Belmont	14,800	17,628	21,239	13,518
Brown	3,770	6,772	5,439	4,520
Butler	21,194	50,380	35,087	49,577
Carroll	2,755	5,984	5,007	5,090
Champaign	3,626	8,756	4,747	6,526
Clark	19,725	34,447	25,963	26,706
Clermont	8,276	22,936	14,857	19,618
Clinton	2,709	8,140	4,958	6,597
Columbiana	15,683	27,308	23,103	22,422
Coshocton	3,790	8,082	5,827	6,352
Crawford	5,518	14,632	7,560	10,799
Cuyahoga	317,670	329,493	346,227	254,906
Darke	6,534	13,862	9,762	11,472
Defiance	4,377	8,914	5,849	7,522
Delaware	4,452	12,950	7,056	12,275
Erie	10,889	16,714	13,847	14,733
Fairfield	7,746	21,909	13,355	19,096
Fayette	2,344	6,970	4,465	5,740
Franklin	117,562	219,771	141,008	189,316
Fulton	3,615	8,387	4,836	7,892
Gallia	2,341	6,506	4,939	5,141
Geauga	7,329	15,624	10,437	14,979
Greene	12,736	25,349	20,245	22,598
Guernsey	4,757	9,648	7,434	7,753
Hamilton	119,054	239,212	135,292	210,791
Hancock	6,084	18,111	8,548	15,981
Hardin	3,535	8,713	5,600	6,116
Harrison	2,388	4,554	4,072	3,516
Henry	3,145	8,099	4,569	7,556
Highland	3,464	8,524	6,322	6,871
Hocking	2,874	5,407	5,136	4,114
Holmes	1,507	3,752	2,223	2,846
Huron	5,491	10,942	7,741	9,396
Jackson	3,410	7,351	6,708	6,000
Jefferson	16,198	21,531	22,388	14,821
Knox	5,370	10,705	7,400	9,290
Lake	27,523	42,488	40,850	36,408
Lawrence	7,112	15,125	12,071	10,624
Licking	12,460	28,070	19,247	23,514
Logan	3,786	10,938	5,948	9,093
Lorain	36,634	51,102	50,043	38,060
Lucas	90,142	88,401	103,495	75,615
Madison	2,484	8,372	5,523	6,380
Mahoning	62,428	64,144	75,842	46,327
Marion	7,970	17,197	10,878	12,995
Medina	10,643	21,010	16,249	19,064
Meigs	2,335	5,961	5,079	4,645
Mercer	5,798	8,587	6,717	7,672
Miami	9,121	21,226	13,076	18,685
Monroe	2,483	3,721	4,222	2,809
Montgomery	82,231	120,998	105,625	99,881
Morgan	1,554	3,679	2,796	3,011
Morrow	2,527	6,886	4,875	5,816
Muskingum	10,313	19,897	14,228	15,380
Noble	1,449	3,274	2,617	3,005
Ottawa	6,465	9,772	9,658	8,422
Paulding	2,283	4,553	3,228	3,595
Perry	3,728	6,716	6,285	5,647
Pickaway	2,978	9,661	5,907	7,694
Pike	3,531	5,037	5,739	3,725
Portage	20,769	23,294	24,409	17,919
Preble	3,472	8,993	5,845	6,650
Putnam	3,729	8,185	5,100	7,301
Richland	13,468	31,117	22,980	24,289
Ross	5,879	15,573	10,745	11,478
Sandusky	8,308	15,489	11,196	13,091
Scioto	11,008	19,998	18,015	13,016
Seneca	8,180	13,939	10,078	12,251
Shelby	4,721	9,089	6,406	8,033
Stark	51,565	92,110	69,464	71,989
Summit	108,534	112,419	120,583	78,214
Trumbull	35,278	47,680	53,611	36,571
Tuscarawas	12,255	18,413	16,530	13,994
Union	2,447	8,389	4,400	7,499
Van Wert	3,644	9,545	5,690	8,348
Vinton	1,537	2,725	2,620	2,150
Warren	6,941	20,210	13,348	16,113
Washington	5,814	14,023	8,911	11,505
Wayne	9,260	20,368	13,085	16,977
Williams	4,278	9,083	4,918	7,600
Wood	13,494	21,080	16,740	19,368
Wyandot	2,771	6,414	4,066	5,661
Totals	**1,558,889**	**2,441,827**	**2,000,035**	**1,992,460**

Ohio Vote Since 1932

1932 (Pres.), Roosevelt, Dem., 1,301,695; Hoover, Rep., 1,227,679; Thomas, Soc., 64,094; Upshaw, Proh., 7,421; Foster, Com., 7,221; Reynolds, Soc. Lab., 1,968.

1936 (Pres.), Roosevelt, Dem., 1,747,122; Landon, Rep., 1,127,709; Lemke, Union, 132,212; Browder, Com., 5,251; Thomas, Soc., 117; Aiken, Soc. Lab., 14.

1940 (Pres.), Roosevelt, Dem., 1,733,139; Willkie, Rep., 1,586,773.

1944 (Pres.), Roosevelt, Dem., 1,570,763; Dewey, Rep., 1,582,293.

1948 (Pres.), Truman, Dem., 1,452,791; Dewey, Rep.,

1,445,684; Wallace, Prog., 37,596.

1952 (Pres.), Eisenhower, Rep., 2,100,391; Stevenson, Dem., 1,600,367.

1956 (Pres.), Eisenhower, Rep., 2,262,610; Stevenson, Dem., 1,439,655.

1960 (Pres.), Kennedy, Dem., 1,944,248; Nixon, Rep., 2,217,611.

1964 (Pres.), Johnson, Dem., 2,498,331; Goldwater, Rep., 1,470,865.

1968 (Pres.), Nixon, Rep., 1,791,014; Humphrey, Dem., 1,700,586; Wallace, 3d party, 467,495; Gregory, 372; Munn, Prohibition, 19; Blomen, Soc. Labor, 120; Halstead, Soc. Worker, 69; Mitchell, Communist, 23.

1972 (Pres.), Nixon, Rep., 2,441,827; McGovern, Dem., 1,558,889; Fisher, Soc. Labor, 7,107; Hall, Communist, 6,437; Schmitz, American, 80,067; Wallace, Ind., 460.

Oklahoma

| County | 1972 | | 1976 | |
	McGovern (D)	Nixon (R)	Carter (D)	Ford (R)
Adair	1,601	4,720	3,183	3,013
Alfalfa	641	3,208	1,728	2,113
Atoka	993	2,905	3,276	1,098
Beaver	522	2,562	1,213	1,801
Beckham	1,608	4,472	4,530	2,351
Blaine	963	3,958	2,297	2,682
Bryan	3,144	5,397	7,410	2,848
Caddo	2,921	7,683	7,382	3,854
Canadian	2,751	11,400	7,288	9,766
Carter	4,577	9,368	7,210	6,650
Cherokee	2,899	7,080	6,006	4,443
Choctaw	1,798	3,399	4,269	1,821
Cimarron	323	1,350	962	872
Cleveland	11,126	25,777	20,054	22,098
Coal	680	1,461	1,774	818
Comanche	4,559	19,759	12,504	12,530
Cotton	798	2,050	1,903	1,127
Craig	1,642	4,163	3,577	2,540
Creek	3,705	12,396	8,964	8,458
Custer	2,298	7,267	4,597	4,847
Delaware	2,135	5,476	4,924	3,642
Dewey	626	2,106	1,540	1,230
Ellis	473	2,059	1,256	1,428
Garfield	4,557	19,348	8,969	14,202
Garvin	2,685	7,245	6,797	3,905
Grady	3,440	7,762	7,155	4,686
Grant	805	2,829	1,853	1,685
Greer	1,004	2,154	2,113	1,164
Harmon	568	1,319	1,371	666
Harper	385	1,976	978	1,303
Haskell	1,408	2,815	3,414	1,401
Hughes	1,787	3,497	4,077	1,666
Jackson	2,054	5,519	4,914	3,189
Jefferson	969	1,709	2,303	956
Johnston	983	2,205	2,760	1,127
Kay	4,246	17,244	9,371	12,441
Kingfisher	912	4,861	2,368	3,247
Kiowa	1,495	3,711	3,403	1,971
Latimer	1,239	2,520	2,661	1,312
Le Flore	3,433	7,932	8,115	4,907
Lincoln	1,919	6,512	4,998	4,429
Logan	2,760	6,543	4,594	4,302
Love	671	1,407	1,923	846
McClain	1,350	4,241	4,048	2,444
McCurtain	2,568	6,441	7,560	3,423
McIntosh	1,686	3,216	4,145	1,822
Major	512	3,203	1,347	2,282
Marshall	1,113	2,273	2,939	1,358
Mayes	2,656	7,535	6,298	5,040
Murray	1,294	2,983	2,932	1,563
Muskogee	7,380	15,161	14,678	10,287
Noble	999	4,085	2,278	2,634
Nowata	1,096	3,293	2,196	2,077
Okfuskee	1,328	2,862	2,663	1,630
Oklahoma	46,986	156,437	86,654	117,418
Okmulgee	4,494	8,706	8,499	5,333
Osage	2,968	9,288	6,832	6,398
Ottawa	3,657	8,348	7,446	4,985
Pawnee	1,135	4,280	3,031	3,111
Payne	5,644	17,019	9,987	13,481
Pittsburg	4,748	9,989	10,743	4,807
Pontotoc	3,160	8,762	7,466	4,895
Pottawatomie	4,822	13,308	11,255	9,091
Pushmataha	1,016	2,456	2,987	1,360
Roger Mills	420	1,696	1,346	873
Rogers	2,607	9,697	7,310	7,376
Seminole	2,746	6,879	5,874	4,237
Sequoyah	2,519	6,842	5,873	3,938
Stephens	3,623	10,309	9,795	7,099
Texas	924	5,726	2,591	3,919
Tillman	1,256	3,331	2,857	1,802
Tulsa	32,779	125,278	65,298	108,653
Wagoner	2,257	6,569	5,879	5,071
Washington	3,658	16,347	6,898	14,560
Washita	1,305	3,578	3,304	2,165
Woods	1,234	4,413	2,530	2,788
Woodward	1,104	5,350	2,729	3,866
Totals	**247,147**	**759,025**	**530,242**	**543,221**

Oklahoma Vote Since 1932

1932 (Pres.), Roosevelt, Dem., 515,468; Hoover, Rep., 188,165.

1936 (Pres.), Roosevelt, Dem., 501,069; Landon, Rep., 245,122; Thomas, Soc., 2,221; Colvin, Proh., 1,328.

1940 (Pres.), Roosevelt, Dem., 474,313; Willkie, Rep., 348,872; Babson, Proh., 3,027.

1944 (Pres.), Roosevelt, Dem., 401,549; Dewey, Rep., 319,424; Watson, Proh., 1,663.

1948 (Pres.), Truman, Dem., 452,782; Dewey, Rep., 268,817.

1952 (Pres.), Eisenhower, Rep., 518,045; Stevenson, Dem., 430,939.

1956 (Pres.), Eisenhower, Rep., 473,769; Stevenson, Dem., 385,581.

1960 (Pres.), Kennedy, Dem., 370,111; Nixon, Rep., 533,039.

1964 (Pres.), Johnson, Dem., 519,834; Goldwater, Rep., 412,665.

1968 (Pres.), Nixon, Rep., 449,697; Humphrey, Dem., 301,658; Wallace, 3d party, 191,731.

1972 (Pres.), Nixon, Rep., 759,025; McGovern, Dem., 247,147; Schmitz, American, 23,728.

Oregon

| County | 1972 | | 1976 | |
	McGovern (D)	Nixon (R)	Carter (D)	Ford (R)
Baker	2,047	3,441	3,305	3,336
Benton	10,842	14,906	11,661	15,361
Clackamas	32,540	41,767	42,499	47,662
Clatsop	6,017	5,998	6,679	6,613
Columbia	5,997	5,348	7,992	5,348
Coos	11,778	10,370	14,015	9,393
Crook	1,743	2,167	2,506	2,096
Curry	2,108	2,832	3,051	2,748
Deschutes	6,319	7,747	8,649	8,144
Douglas	9,009	15,881	14,940	16,462
Gilliam	335	665	509	611
Grant	932	1,781	1,392	1,643
Harney	1,004	1,693	1,573	1,648
Hood River	2,330	3,152	3,107	3,207
Jackson	14,529	24,003	23,370	24,230
Jefferson	1,229	1,816	1,777	1,814
Josephine	5,009	9,911	9,063	10,724
Klamath	5,719	11,169	9,715	11,711
Lake	777	1,619	1,393	1,563
Lane	46,177	47,739	56,478	46,241
Lincoln	5,117	6,112	6,525	5,569
Linn	11,178	15,079	15,779	14,127
Malheur	1,870	5,908	3,429	5,565
Marion	23,908	36,441	33,339	34,941
Morrow	718	1,059	1,167	1,095
Multnomah	125,470	118,219	127,582	111,127
Polk	5,908	8,985	8,137	8,522
Sherman	330	677	491	567
Tillamook	3,544	4,120	4,149	4,042
Umatilla	6,090	10,470	7,903	9,224
Union	3,272	5,073	4,064	4,750
Wallowa	899	1,909	1,303	1,686
Wasco	3,749	4,331	4,556	4,252
Washington	27,890	43,958	33,334	49,584
Wheeler	267	474	402	355
Yamhill	6,008	9,660	8,809	9,794
Totals	**392,760**	**486,686**	**485,305**	**484,643**

Oregon Vote Since 1932

1932 (Pres.), Roosevelt, Dem., 213,871; Hoover, Rep., 136,019; Thomas, Soc., 15,450; Reynolds, Soc. Lab., 1,730; Foster, Com., 1,681.

1936 (Pres.), Roosevelt, Dem., 266,733; Landon, Rep., 122,706; Lemke, Union, 21,831; Thomas, Soc., 2,143; Aiken, Soc. Lab., 500; Browder, Com., 104; Colvin, Proh., 4.

1940 (Pres.), Roosevelt, Dem., 258,415; Willkie, Rep., 219,555; Aiken, Soc. Lab., 2,487; Thomas, Soc., 398; Browder, Com., 191; Babson, Proh., 154.

1944 (Pres.), Roosevelt, Dem., 248,635; Dewey, Rep.,
225,365; Thomas, Soc., 3,785; Watson, Proh., 2,362.

1948 (Pres.), Truman, Dem., 243,147; Dewey, Rep.,
260,904; Wallace, Prog., 14,978; Thomas, Soc.,
5,051.

1952 (Pres.), Eisenhower, Rep., 420,815; Stevenson,
Dem., 270,579; Hallinan, Ind., 3,665.

1956 (Pres.), Eisenhower, Rep., 406,393; Stevenson,
Dem., 329,204.

1960 (Pres.), Kennedy, Dem., 367,402; Nixon, Rep.,
408,060.

1964 (Pres.), Johnson, Dem., 501,017; Goldwater,
Rep., 282,779; write-in, 2,509.

1968 (Pres.), Nixon, Rep., 408,433; Humphrey, Dem.,
358,866; Wallace, 3d party, 49,683; write-in,
McCarthy, 1,496; N. Rockefeller, 69; others, 1,075.

1972 (Pres.), Nixon, Rep., 486,686; McGovern, Dem.,
392,760; Schmitz, American, 46,211; write-in,
2,289.

Pennsylvania

County	1972 McGovern (D)	1972 Nixon (R)	1976 Carter (D)	1976 Ford (R)
Adams............	5,529	13,593	8,793	12,116
Allegheny.........	282,496	371,737	327,089	301,878
Armstrong.........	10,490	17,557	15,185	13,372
Beaver...........	31,570	43,637	46,148	33,614
Bedford...........	3,836	11,243	6,654	9,345
Berks............	36,563	66,172	50,989	54,551
Blair.............	10,023	33,126	18,486	28,230
Bradford..........	5,204	15,050	7,757	12,613
Bucks............	56,784	99,684	79,212	84,949
Butler............	14,695	29,665	22,610	26,361
Cambria...........	27,950	43,825	38,820	32,498
Cameron..........	828	1,935	1,319	1,616
Carbon...........	7,774	11,639	10,764	8,837
Centre...........	13,194	20,683	17,336	20,543
Chester..........	31,118	72,726	44,961	67,637
Clarion...........	4,509	10,073	6,543	8,146
Clearfield.........	9,246	16,780	13,648	14,463
Clinton...........	4,772	8,205	6,516	5,836
Columbia.........	7,222	14,187	12,116	11,505
Crawford..........	9,371	18,393	14,712	15,338
Cumberland.......	14,562	42,099	23,119	37,919
Dauphin..........	22,587	54,307	34,766	47,683
Delaware.........	94,144	175,414	117,492	149,139
Elk..............	4,710	7,900	6,705	6,248
Erie..............	42,022	61,542	55,385	49,641
Fayette...........	22,475	27,288	32,089	19,953
Forest...........	509	1,374	1,010	1,325
Franklin..........	9,456	24,093	12,525	16,935
Fulton............	1,192	2,515	1,747	2,229
Greene...........	5,562	7,890	8,767	5,285
Huntingdon........	3,394	9,606	5,410	7,843
Indiana...........	10,833	18,122	14,210	15,218
Jefferson.........	5,024	11,631	7,551	8,372
Juniata...........	2,156	4,412	3,129	4,026
Lackawanna.......	45,465	58,838	57,695	43,364
Lancaster.........	24,223	81,036	35,455	71,874
Lawrence.........	17,595	23,712	23,295	18,446
Lebanon..........	6,683	25,008	11,717	20,828
Lehigh...........	33,325	58,023	46,524	46,632
Luzerne..........	51,128	81,358	74,591	59,908
Lycoming.........	11,999	28,913	14,722	17,168
McKean..........	4,513	11,958	6,361	10,478
Mercer...........	18,087	27,961	24,669	22,292
Mifflin...........	3,667	9,989	6,007	7,729
Monroe..........	5,619	12,701	9,542	10,216
Montgomery.......	91,959	173,662	112,672	155,826
Montour..........	1,755	4,386	2,727	3,259
Northampton......	32,335	41,822	42,419	32,807
Northumberland....	13,885	25,912	18,781	19,173
Perry............	2,731	8,082	4,600	7,442
Philadelphia.......	431,736	344,096	480,843	231,073
Pike.............	1,385	4,568	2,775	4,241
Potter............	1,710	4,422	2,859	3,828
Schuylkill.........	26,077	44,071	33,760	31,874
Snyder...........	1,834	7,308	3,160	6,564
Somerset.........	8,743	19,739	13,397	15,734
Sullivan..........	885	1,886	1,357	1,583
Susquehanna......	4,154	9,476	6,075	8,331
Tioga............	3,733	10,028	5,793	8,420
Union............	2,278	6,905	3,395	6,290
Venango..........	6,302	13,991	8,611	12,155
Warren...........	4,877	10,018	7,364	8,592
Washington........	34,781	42,587	49,140	32,653
Wayne...........	2,733	8,948	4,325	7,737
Westmoreland.....	59,322	75,085	73,994	58,934
Wyoming..........	2,112	6,423	3,628	5,704
York.............	27,520	63,606	41,235	56,811
Totals..........	**1,796,951**	**2,714,521**	**2,315,494**	**2,187,036**

Pennsylvania Vote Since 1932

1932 (Pres.), Roosevelt, Dem., 1,295,948; Hoover,
Rep., 1,453,540; Thomas, Soc., 91,119; Upshaw,
Proh., 11,319; Foster, Com., 5,658; Cox, Jobless,
725; Reynolds, Indust., 659.

1936 (Pres.), Roosevelt, Dem., 2,353,788; Landon,
Rep., 1,690,300; Lemke, Royal Oak, 67,467;
Thomas, Soc., 14,375; Colvin, Proh., 6,691; Browd-
er, Com., 4,060; Aiken, Ind., Lab., 1,424.

1940 (Pres.), Roosevelt, Dem., 2,171,035; Willkie,
Rep., 1,889,848; Thomas, Soc., 10,967; Browder,
Com., 4,519; Aiken, Ind. Gov., 1,518.

1944 (Pres.), Roosevelt, Dem., 1,940,479; Dewey, Rep.,
1,835,054; Thomas, Soc., 11,721; Watson, Proh.,
5,750; Teichert, Ind. Gov., 1,789.

1948 (Pres.), Truman, Dem., 1,752,426; Dewey, Rep.,
1,902,197; Wallace, Prog., 55,161; Thomas, Soc., 11,-
325; Watson, Proh., 10,338; Dobbs, Militant
Workers, 2,133; Teichert, Ind. Gov., 1,461.

1952 (Pres.), Eisenhower, Rep., 2,415,789; Stevenson,
Dem., 2,146,269; Hamblen, Proh., 8,771; Hallinan,
Prog., 4,200; Hoopes, Soc., 2,684; Dobbs, Militant
Workers, 1,502; Haas, Ind. Gov., 1,347; scattered,
155.

1956 (Pres.), Eisenhower, Rep., 2,585,252; Stevenson,
Dem., 1,981,769; Haas, Soc. Lab., 7,447; Dobbs, Militant Workers, 2,035.

1960 (Pres.), Kennedy, Dem., 2,556,282; Nixon, Rep.,
2,439,956; Haas, Soc. Lab., 7,185; Dobbs, Soc. Workers, 2,678; scattering, 440.

1964 (Pres.), Johnson, Dem., 3,130,954; Goldwater,
Rep., 1,673,657; DeBerry, Soc. Worker, 10,456;
Haas, Soc. Labor, 5,092; scattering, 2,531.

1968 (Pres.), Nixon, Rep., 2,090,017; Humphrey,
Dem., 2,259,405; Wallace, 3d party, 378,582;
Blomen, Soc. Labor, 4,977; Halstead, Soc. Worker,
4,862; Gregory, 7,821; others, 2,264.

1972 (Pres.), Nixon, Rep., 2,714,521; McGovern, Dem.,
1,796,951; Schmitz, American, 70,593; Jenness, Soc.
Worker, 4,639; Hall, Communist, 2,686; others
2,715.

Rhode Island

County	1972 McGovern (D)	1972 Nixon (R)	1976 Carter (D)	1976 Ford (R)
Bristol............	9,928	12,009	10,692	9,584
Kent.............	29,004	40,534	34,584	32,319
Newport..........	12,844	19,142	16,591	13,706
Providence........	129,232	129,418	138,028	99,512
Washington........	13,637	19,280	17,136	17,017
Totals..........	**194,645**	**220,383**	**207,031**	**172,138**

Rhode Island Vote Since 1932

1932 (Pres.), Roosevelt, Dem., 146,604; Hoover, Rep.,
115,266; Thomas, Soc., 3,138; Foster, Com., 546;
Reynolds, Soc. Lab., 433; Upshaw, Proh., 183.

1936 (Pres.), Roosevelt, Dem., 165,238; Landon, Rep.,
125,031; Lemke, Union, 19,569; Aiken, Soc. Lab.,
929; Browder, Com., 411.

1940 (Pres.), Roosevelt, Dem., 182,182; Willkie, Rep.,
138,653; Browder, Com., 239; Babson, Proh., 74.

1944 (Pres.), Roosevelt, Dem., 175,356; Dewey, Rep.,
123,487; Watson, Proh., 433.

1948 (Pres.), Truman, Dem., 188,736; Dewey, Rep.,
135,787; Wallace, Prog., 2,619; Thomas, Soc., 429;
Teichert, Soc. Lab., 131.

1952 (Pres.), Eisenhower, Rep., 210,935; Stevenson,
Dem., 203,293; Hallinan, Prog., 187; Haas, Soc.
Lab., 83.

1956 (Pres.), Eisenhower, Rep., 225,819; Stevenson,
Dem., 161,790.

1960 (Pres.), Kennedy, Dem., 258,032; Nixon, Rep.,
147,502.

1964 (Pres.), Johnson, Dem., 315,463; Goldwater,
Rep., 74,615.

1968 (Pres.), Nixon, Rep., 122,359; Humphrey, Dem.,
246,518; Wallace, 3d party, 15,678; Halstead, Soc.
Worker, 383.

1972 (Pres.), Nixon, Rep., 220,383; McGovern, Dem., 194,645; Jenness, Soc. Worker, 729.

South Carolina

	1972		1976	
	McGovern	Nixon	Carter	Ford
County	(D)	(R)	(D)	(R)
Abbeville	1,347	3,265	1,817	791
Aiken	5,745	21,117	14,824	15,930
Allendale	1,383	1,740	957	417
Anderson	5,241	17,514	19,964	10,109
Bamberg	1,680	2,537	3,313	1,847
Barnwell	1,560	3,955	4,082	2,568
Beaufort	3,237	5,929	5,811	5,743
Berkeley	4,497	9,345	8,641	6,736
Calhoun	1,148	1,867	2,040	1,379
Charleston	16,856	39,832	32,730	33,430
Cherokee	2,107	7,570	7,151	3,629
Chester	2,352	4,724	7,669	2,517
Chesterfield	2,938	5,230	4,360	1,452
Clarendon	3,276	3,958	5,446	3,023
Colleton	2,376	5,738	4,404	2,346
Darlington	4,414	11,758	10,164	6,680
Dillon	1,604	4,364	4,246	2,501
Dorchester	3,606	8,095	7,662	6,552
Edgefield	1,326	2,812	3,219	1,884
Fairfield	2,491	2,608	4,265	1,969
Florence	7,451	18,107	15,989	13,123
Georgetown	4,448	6,114	7,116	4,075
Greenville	10,163	46,360	35,904	39,068
Greenwood	3,400	9,370	9,976	5,937
Hampton	2,086	2,891	3,017	1,521
Horry	4,437	15,324	15,571	9,339
Jasper	1,203	1,650	2,059	805
Kershaw	2,531	8,035	5,282	5,031
Lancaster	2,461	9,016	8,212	4,949
Laurens	2,650	8,141	5,625	3,901
Lee	1,996	3,076	3,114	1,926
Lexington	4,069	25,327	14,194	21,315
Marion	844	1,302	1,357	483
Marlboro	2,535	4,719	1,106	395
McCormick	2,999	3,838	1,152	491
Newberry	2,035	7,325	1,862	1,875
Oconee	1,739	6,825	3,004	1,775
Orangeburg	7,652	11,711	13,652	8,694
Pickens	2,255	11,776	5,681	4,514
Richland	20,875	38,500	36,545	32,970
Saluda	1,022	3,095	2,715	2,032
Spartanburg	9,723	31,187	27,612	20,735
Sumter	5,795	10,892	10,369	9,292
Union	2,676	8,337	3,970	2,380
Williamsburg	5,213	5,729	8,709	5,270
York	6,374	14,441	11,843	8,686
Totals	**186,824**	**477,044**	**443,901**	**342,409**

South Carolina Vote Since 1932

1932 (Pres.), Roosevelt, Dem., 102,347; Hoover, Rep., 1,978; Thomas, Soc., 82.

1936 (Pres.), Roosevelt, Dem., 113,791; Landon, Rep., Tolbert faction 953, Hambright faction 693, total, 1,646.

1940 (Pres.), Roosevelt, Dem., 95,470; Willkie, Rep., 1,727.

1944 (Pres.), Roosevelt, Dem., 90,601; Dewey, Rep., 4,547; Southern Democrats, 7,799; Watson, Proh., 365; Rep. Tolbert faction, 63.

1948 (Pres.), Thurmond, States' Rights, 102,607; Truman, Dem., 34,423; Dewey, Rep., 5,386; Wallace, Prog., 154; Thomas, Soc., 1.

1952 (Pres.), Eisenhower ran on two tickets. Under State law vote cast for two Eisenhower slates of electors could not be combined. Eisenhower, Ind., 158,289; Rep., 9,793; total 168,082; Stevenson, Dem., 173,004; Hamblen, Proh., 1.

1956 (Pres.), Stevenson, Dem., 136,372; Byrd., Ind., 88,509; Eisenhower, Rep., 75,700; Andrews, Ind., 2.

1960 (Pres.), Kennedy, Dem., 198,129; Nixon, Rep., 188,558; write-in, 1.

1964 (Pres.), Johnson, Dem., 215,700; Goldwater, Rep., 309,048; write-ins: Nixon, 1; Wallace, 5; Powell, 1; Thurmond, 1.

1968 (Pres.), Nixon, Rep., 254,062; Humphrey, Dem., 197,486; Wallace, 3d party, 215,430.

1972 (Pres.), Nixon, Rep., 477,044; McGovern, Dem., 184,559; United Citizens, 2,265; Schmitz, American, 10,075; write-in, 17.

South Dakota

	1972		1976	
	McGovern	Nixon	Carter	Ford
County	(D)	(R)	(D)	(R)
Aurora	1,257	1,075	1,269	831
Beadle	4,297	5,922	4,846	4,756
Bennett	476	808	482	609
Bon Homme	2,368	2,116	2,154	1,897
Brookings	4,701	5,182	4,685	5,278
Brown	8,216	8,134	8,888	7,596
Brule	1,665	1,421	1,534	1,175
Buffalo	275	221	240	194
Butte	1,085	2,452	1,366	2,055
Campbell	361	1,169	490	897
Chas. Mix	2,691	2,020	2,583	1,779
Clark	1,336	1,617	1,376	1,449
Clay	2,821	2,518	2,592	2,647
Codington	4,601	4,936	4,680	4,504
Corson	689	975	1,067	846
Custer	798	1,476	995	1,373
Davison	4,710	3,796	4,419	3,753
Day	2,719	1,971	2,611	1,617
Deuel	1,370	1,357	1,464	1,178
Dewey	699	1,008	706	820
Douglas	887	1,434	975	1,315
Edmunds	1,646	1,567	1,629	1,294
Fall River	1,107	2,374	1,644	2,154
Faulk	986	1,004	1,063	869
Grant	2,231	2,247	2,399	2,051
Gregory	1,555	1,670	1,658	1,475
Haakon	366	1,021	477	812
Hamlin	1,276	1,693	1,402	1,452
Hand	1,307	1,806	1,477	1,510
Hanson	1,022	876	1,005	693
Harding	253	637	459	470
Hughes	2,037	4,231	2,506	3,997
Hutchinson	2,248	3,092	2,062	2,822
Hyde	533	789	572	687
Jackson	261	581	313	532
Jerauld	829	988	847	821
Jones	346	642	374	515
Kingsbury	1,632	2,320	1,762	1,844
Lake	2,886	2,919	2,930	2,530
Lawrence	2,533	4,795	3,102	4,206
Lincoln	2,617	3,201	2,957	3,105
Lyman	744	1,166	831	892
Marshall	1,646	1,500	1,721	1,233
McCook	1,993	1,963	1,822	1,744
McPherson	579	1,950	693	1,662
Meade	1,633	3,146	2,478	3,096
Mellette	433	637	429	508
Miner	1,337	1,059	1,289	839
Minnehaha	22,386	22,447	21,310	22,891
Moody	1,895	1,648	1,942	1,500
Pennington	8,592	13,654	10,058	13,354
Perkins	900	1,691	1,251	1,288
Potter	858	1,389	908	1,198
Roberts	2,976	2,187	2,879	1,926
Sanborn	1,074	1,064	1,025	881
Shannon	1,246	356	756	301
Spink	2,321	2,547	2,652	2,003
Stanley	492	779	548	637
Sully	414	773	505	630
Todd	907	806	583	826
Tripp	1,538	2,592	1,822	1,980
Turner	1,993	3,007	1,906	2,694
Union	2,554	2,271	2,540	2,297
Walworth	1,287	2,416	1,516	2,186
Washabaugh	211	245	276	229
Yankton	3,835	4,366	3,977	4,109
Ziebach	378	486	376	369
Totals	**139,945**	**166,476**	**146,153**	**151,619**

South Dakota Vote Since 1932

1932 (Pres.), Roosevelt, Dem., 183,515; Hoover, Rep., 99,212; Harvey, Lib., 3,333; Thomas, Soc., 1,551; Upshaw, Proh., 463; Foster, Com., 364.

1936 (Pres.), Roosevelt, Dem., 160,137; Landon, Rep., 125,977; Lemke, Union, 10,338.

1940 (Pres.), Roosevelt, Dem., 131,862; Willkie, Rep., 177,065.

1944 (Pres.), Roosevelt, Dem., 96,711; Dewey, Rep., 135,365.

1948 (Pres.), Truman, Dem., 117,653; Dewey, Rep., 129,651; Wallace, Prog., 2,801.

1952 (Pres.), Eisenhower, Rep., 203,857; Stevenson, Dem., 90,426.

1956 (Pres.), Eisenhower, Rep., 171,569; Stevenson, Dem., 122,288.

1960 (Pres.), Kennedy, Dem., 128,070; Nixon, Rep., 178,417.

1964 (Pres.), Johnson, Dem., 163,010; Goldwater, Rep., 130,108.

1968 (Pres.), Nixon, Rep., 149,841; Humphrey, Dem.,

118,023; Wallace, 3d party, 13,400.
1972 (Pres.), Nixon, Rep., 166,476; McGovern, Dem., 139,945; Jenness, Soc. Worker, 994.

	McGovern (D)	Nixon (R)	Carter (D)	Ford (R)
Warren	2,118	3,565	6,666	2,170
Washington	5,284	17,343	12,245	12,733
Wayne	673	2,898	1,068	1,467
Weakley	2,027	5,836	6,605	2,875
White	1,392	2,252	2,770	951
Williamson	2,616	7,556	1,019	516
Wilson	3,096	6,486	1,386	516
Totals	357,293	813,147	822,250	633,228

Tennessee Vote Since 1932

1932 (Pres.), Roosevelt, Dem., 259,817; Hoover, Rep., 126,806; Upshaw, Proh., 1,995; Thomas, Soc., 1,786; Foster, Com., 234.

1936 (Pres.), Roosevelt, Dem., 327,083; Landon, Rep., 146,516; Thomas, Soc., 685; Colvin, Proh., 632; Browder, Com., 319; Lemke, Union, 296.

1940 (Pres.), Roosevelt, Dem., 351,601; Willkie, Rep., 169,153; Babson, Proh., 1,606; Thomas, Soc., 463.

1944 (Pres.), Roosevelt, Dem., 308,707; Dewey, Rep., 200,311; Watson, Proh., 882; Thomas, Soc., 892.

1948 (Pres.), Truman, Dem., 270,402; Dewey, Rep., 202,914; Thurmond, States' Rights, 73,815; Wallace, Prog., 1,864; Thomas, Soc., 1,288.

1952 (Pres.), Eisenhower, Rep., 446,147; Stevenson, Dem., 443,710; Hamblen, Proh., 1,432; Hallinan, Prog., 885; MacArthur, Christian Nationalist, 379.

1956 (Pres.), Eisenhower, Rep., 462,288; Stevenson, Dem., 456,507; Andrews, Ind., 19,820; Holtwick, Proh., 789.

1960 (Pres.), Kennedy, Dem., 481,453; Nixon, Rep., 556,577; Faubus, States' Rights, 11,304; Decker, Proh., 2,458.

1964 (Pres.), Johnson, Dem., 635,047; Goldwater, Rep., 508,965; write-in, 34.

1968 (Pres.), Nixon, Rep., 472,592; Humphrey, Dem., 351,233; Wallace, 3d party, 424,792.

1972 (Pres.), Nixon, Rep., 813,147; McGovern, Dem., 357,293; Schmitz, American, 30,373; write-in, 369.

Tennessee

	1972		1976	
	McGovern	Nixon	Carter	Ford
County	(D)	(R)	(D)	(R)
Anderson	6,713	13,865	13,401	11,495
Bedford	2,565	4,262	4,666	1,918
Benton	1,479	2,614	2,517	1,031
Bledsoe	899	1,952	1,757	1,620
Blount	5,303	16,078	12,086	13,852
Bradley	2,804	10,440	8,780	9,143
Campbell	1,629	4,909	4,930	4,045
Cannon	911	1,615	1,182	462
Carroll	2,290	5,784	4,519	3,333
Carter	2,191	11,102	5,714	7,007
Cheatham	1,321	2,235	4,225	1,376
Chester	961	2,787	1,742	1,087
Claiborne	1,230	3,632	3,461	3,227
Clay	648	982	1,247	710
Cocke	805	5,268	3,041	5,344
Coffee	2,973	6,416	8,576	4,069
Crockett	735	2,642	2,959	1,694
Cumberland	1,482	4,593	4,539	4,118
Davidson	48,869	82,636	67,460	43,706
Decatur	1,187	2,368	2,432	1,637
De Kalb	1,243	2,014	3,223	1,443
Dickson	2,619	3,645	5,811	2,285
Dyer	1,600	6,066	5,639	4,086
Fayette	2,067	3,264	3,853	2,113
Fentress	665	2,154	1,953	1,767
Franklin	2,896	4,136	1,500	527
Gibson	3,625	9,900	10,356	5,563
Giles	1,875	2,914	5,252	1,962
Grainger	828	2,842	1,161	1,756
Greene	2,764	9,772	6,220	7,522
Grundy	1,005	1,364	2,849	850
Hamblen	2,563	8,879	7,404	6,989
Hamilton	20,657	58,469	3,192	2,474
Hancock	393	1,813	764	1,312
Hardeman	1,550	3,494	3,934	2,254
Hardin	1,202	4,401	2,780	2,625
Hawkins	2,608	7,791	5,790	6,207
Haywood	1,966	3,123	3,681	1,952
Henderson	1,313	5,122	1,648	2,832
Henry	2,694	4,613	7,162	2,585
Hickman	1,393	1,943	2,408	726
Houston	870	800	771	180
Humphreys	1,973	2,263	3,502	1,225
Jackson	1,085	956	2,082	523
Jefferson	1,357	5,925	3,194	4,569
Johnson	450	3,362	1,464	2,986
Knox	24,076	64,747	17,312	17,798
Lake	536	1,147	1,808	539
Lauderdale	1,771	3,597	4,747	2,105
Lawrence	2,824	6,438	7,140	4,967
Lewis	1,138	1,056	2,391	617
Lincoln	1,867	3,266	5,732	1,724
Loudon	1,604	5,357	4,683	4,458
McMinn	2,838	7,423	5,357	5,175
McNairy	1,610	4,774	1,173	936
Macon	653	2,295	1,951	2,063
Madison	5,203	15,481	5,491	3,957
Marion	1,929	3,711	1,043	704
Marshall	1,526	2,593	4,452	1,684
Maury	3,262	7,371	8,875	5,816
Meigs	539	1,052	1,254	975
Monroe	2,870	5,657	5,368	5,335
Montgomery	5,691	7,839	12,310	5,923
Moore	356	608	1,105	331
Morgan	1,084	2,531	2,953	1,945
Obion	2,243	5,800	6,787	3,179
Overton	1,573	1,947	3,897	115
Perry	937	900	1,650	516
Pickett	357	957	948	986
Polk	1,431	2,285	3,284	1,835
Putnam	3,738	6,038	8,485	4,079
Rhea	1,312	3,842	3,387	3,189
Roane	3,433	8,742	9,172	7,121
Robertson	2,985	4,175	7,547	2,585
Rutherford	5,811	11,256	15,350	7,921
Scott	679	2,775	2,260	2,432
Sequatchie	629	1,298	1,733	1,069
Sevier	1,128	8,273	3,993	7,608
Shelby	81,089	161,922	137,121	108,269
Smith	1,260	1,812	3,753	1,332
Stewart	1,098	790	2,442	510
Sullivan	10,007	27,593	17,218	16,351
Sumner	4,596	10,020	13,848	7,938
Tipton	1,853	5,542	5,691	3,340
Trousdale	539	663	1,385	333
Unicoi	822	3,877	2,317	2,964
Union	570	1,927	1,631	1,801
Van Buren	364	629	1,085	346

Texas

	1972		1976	
	McGovern	Nixon	Carter	Ford
County	(D)	(R)	(D)	(R)
Anderson	2,233	5,826	5,078	3,319
Andrews	677	2,615	1,777	2,127
Angelina	4,970	11,453	9,750	7,227
Aransas	844	2,037	2,136	1,985
Archer	632	1,494	1,577	966
Armstrong	177	768	513	520
Atascosa	1,804	3,400	3,627	2,189
Austin	1,043	3,084	2,323	2,696
Bailey	465	1,837	1,356	1,255
Bandera	434	1,796	1,183	1554
Bastrop	1,906	3,097	4,788	2,383
Baylor	598	1,190	1,335	783
Bee	2,067	3,779	3,690	2,953
Bell	6,848	17,525	17,496	15,226
Bexar	91,662	137,572	145,201	109,024
Blanco	460	1,215	924	1,002
Borden	96	330	234	150
Bosque	1,014	2,947	2,951	1,912
Bowie	5,227	14,722	12,445	9,590
Brazoria	11,350	21,045	21,711	19,475
Brazos	5,692	14,243	10,628	15,685
Brewster	904	1,524	1,227	1,368
Briscoe	349	642	823	285
Brooks	1,657	1,117	2,782	641
Brown	2,171	5,990	5,580	4,492
Burleson	1,361	1,762	2,919	1,142
Burnet	1,227	3,438	3,818	2,777
Caldwell	1,974	3,171	3,647	2,235
Calhoun	1,936	3,614	3,642	2,377
Callahan	665	2,223	2,236	1,581
Cameron	13,340	20,816	24,768	15,339
Camp	1,041	1,599	2,146	1,134
Carson	561	1,868	1,542	1,269
Cass	1,981	5,303	5,179	3,795
Castro	751	1,685	2,033	1,007
Chambers	1,206	2,390	2,927	1,835
Cherokee	2,467	5,743	6,505	3,921
Childress	729	1,716	1,578	1,043
Clay	1,023	1,893	2,504	1,197
Cochran	415	1,106	1,031	701
Coke	358	761	844	517
Coleman	721	2,368	2,264	1,689
Collin	4,783	17,667	14,039	21,609
Collingsworth	501	1,250	1,169	629

	1972 (D)	1972 (R)	1976 (D)	1976 (R)		1972 (D)	1972 (R)	1976 (D)	1976 (R)
Colorado	1,502	3,495	3,028	2,991	Lee	920	1,877	1,937	1,348
Comal	1,823	6,761	4,078	6,377	Leon	863	1,699	2,085	1,162
Comanche	1,176	2,608	3,470	1,297	Liberty	3,311	6,111	7,086	4,552
Concho	350	709	715	525	Limestone	1,452	2,949	3,584	2,040
Cooke	1,702	6,317	4,123	4,737	Lipscomb	156	1,226	644	858
Coryell	1,235	5,077	4,710	4,140	Live Oak	610	1,745	1,656	1,287
Cottle	571	564	1,047	311	Llano	766	2,164	1,693	1,489
Crane	349	1,123	664	963	Loving	7	55	35	47
Crockett	329	851	804	802	Lubbock	15,353	43,564	23,900	36,241
Crosby	1,021	1,503	2,176	897	Lynn	697	1,766	1,575	1,166
Culberson	238	555	407	373	Madison	561	1,540	1,885	1,062
Dallam	327	1,271	1,029	936	Marion	1,106	1,680	1,860	1,293
Dallas	129,662	305,112	188,313	244,170	Martin	287	935	905	703
Dawson	846	3,247	1,578	1,274	Mason	369	1,096	814	805
Deaf Smith	1,240	3,690	2,613	2,776	Matagorda	2,473	5,003	4,973	3,679
Delta	581	957	1,559	421	Maverick	1,710	1,477	2,840	924
Denton	9,720	19,138	19,081	20,096	McCulloch	753	1,769	1,688	1,113
DeWitt	1,357	3,755	2,540	2,754	McLennan	15,947	33,377	30,061	25,370
Dickens	534	708	1,222	343	McMullen	88	304	194	217
Dimmit	1,078	1,172	1,721	890	Medina	1,507	4,059	3,681	3,252
Donley	350	1,229	895	704	Menard	273	644	543	441
Duval	3,729	623	2,423	203	Midland	4,388	18,905	7,725	19,178
Eastland	1,630	4,106	4,320	2,340	Milam	2,159	3,554	4,871	2,404
Ector	5,449	21,386	10,802	18,973	Mills	388	1,089	1,012	684
Edwards	109	520	258	412	Mitchell	699	1,790	1,730	1,004
Ellis	3,839	8,779	9,994	7,019	Montague	1,286	3,463	4,087	2,182
El Paso	32,435	49,981	45,477	42,697	Montgomery	4,358	15,067	8,051	7,671
Erath	1,648	4,777	4,949	2,939	Moore	863	3,620	2,767	2,759
Falls	1,825	3,017	4,277	2,261	Morris	1,162	2,699	3,081	1,843
Fannin	2,295	3,826	5,745	2,102	Motley	230	657	522	428
Fayette	1,400	3,882	3,541	3,094	Nacogdoches	3,656	8,757	6,655	7,360
Fisher	933	1,207	1,993	573	Navarro	3,246	6,039	6,689	3,922
Floyd	841	2,181	1,991	1,402	Newton	1,636	1,946	3,364	1,011
Foard	312	369	711	241	Nolan	1,338	3,634	3,094	2,431
Fort Bend	4,541	10,475	4,267	5,962	Nueces	33,277	41,682	52,754	32,797
Franklin	546	1,059	1,641	754	Ochiltree	298	2,861	1,084	2,471
Freestone	1,283	2,459	2,652	1,596	Oldham	173	666	554	364
Frio	1,588	1,904	2,598	1,280	Orange	7,172	13,234	15,179	9,147
Gaines	669	1,923	1,880	1,643	Palo Pinto	2,181	5,058	5,170	2,684
Galveston	22,565	30,936	36,252	23,597	Panola	1,511	4,324	3,731	3,218
Garza	446	1,153	957	755	Parker	3,184	7,152	8,186	5,288
Gillespie	526	3,490	1,260	3,541	Parmer	495	2,304	1,914	1,487
Glasscock	75	288	190	218	Pecos	847	2,419	1,970	2,234
Goliad	464	1,018	875	840	Polk	1,760	3,048	4,384	2,529
Gonzales	1,164	2,707	3,219	1,789	Potter	6,264	18,891	11,917	13,819
Gray	1,367	7,968	3,876	6,012	Presidio	674	785	1,232	687
Grayson	6,952	16,769	17,015	11,981	Rains	532	865	1,339	510
Gregg	5,325	19,927	9,827	17,582	Randall	3,470	18,557	9,074	17,115
Grimes	1,116	2,243	2,650	1,473	Reagan	244	703	553	666
Guadalupe	3,404	8,287	5,177	5,769	Real	150	483	510	448
Hale	2,135	7,051	5,580	5,390	Red River	1,361	3,112	3,772	1,854
Hall	607	1,303	1,633	671	Reeves	1,510	2,427	2,623	1,711
Hamilton	685	1,931	1,981	1,176	Refugio	1,060	1,937	2,218	1,537
Hansford	202	1,947	983	1,401	Roberts	71	467	202	350
Hardeman	614	1,357	1,403	805	Robertson	1,976	1,977	884	226
Hardin	2,952	5,190	6,558	4,046	Rockwall	610	1,890	1,828	2,087
Harris	215,916	365,672	317,929	352,402	Runnels	739	2,752	2,134	2,162
Harrison	4,333	9,600	7,796	7,787	Rusk	2,867	8,179	6,722	5,876
Hartley	206	946	774	811	Sabine	936	1,333	2,391	904
Haskell	950	1,744	2,512	843	San Augustine	753	1,508	1,816	1,047
Hays	4,068	5,406	6,702	5,288	San Jacinto	1,020	1,296	2,263	1,015
Hemphill	214	942	707	858	San Patricio	5,097	7,179	9,539	5,843
Henderson	2,741	6,263	8,365	4,663	San Saba	567	1,106	1,508	582
Hidalgo	18,366	22,920	34,666	17,024	Schleicher	250	630	468	516
Hill	1,882	4,481	5,327	2,680	Scurry	1,223	3,777	2,654	2,797
Hockley	1,625	4,084	3,956	3,187	Shackelford	331	909	764	748
Hood	949	1,743	3,228	1,892	Shelby	1,792	4,292	4,992	2,859
Hopkins	1,710	3,903	4,993	2,556	Sherman	169	996	718	679
Houston	1,844	3,317	3,179	2,229	Smith	8,041	23,671	16,856	23,450
Howard	2,714	7,343	6,984	4,899	Somervell	284	703	1,209	430
Hudspeth	250	467	479	395	Starr	3,320	2,389	4,646	664
Hunt	3,655	9,535	8,137	6,676	Stephens	678	2,259	1,796	1,621
Hutchinson	1,405	7,411	3,691	6,135	Sterling	94	286	174	202
Irion	111	363	297	302	Stonewall	394	662	812	252
Jack	775	1,719	1,814	1,049	Sutton	245	705	768	830
Jackson	1,163	2,743	2,524	1,884	Swisher	1,300	1,790	2,811	753
Jasper	2,746	4,575	5,422	3,157	Tarrant	69,187	151,586	122,218	124,473
Jeff Davis	202	382	309	288	Taylor	6,024	22,417	14,110	18,909
Jefferson	29,909	45,819	47,581	32,451	Terrell	124	467	321	317
Jim Hogg	848	765	1,655	429	Terry	1,099	3,057	2,113	2,859
Jim Wells	4,404	5,283	7,777	3,580	Throckmorton	348	568	658	356
Johnson	3,968	10,042	10,864	7,194	Titus	1,703	3,671	4,205	2,603
Jones	1,050	3,202	2,510	1,459	Tom Green	6,082	15,784	11,064	12,316
Karnes	1,780	2,639	2,996	1,677	Travis	54,147	70,561	78,585	71,031
Kaufman	2,795	5,100	5,896	3,630	Trinity	826	1,467	2,100	1,042
Kendall	484	2,681	1,190	2,543	Tyler	1,321	2,955	3,322	1,965
Kenedy	88	124	139	65	Upshur	1,879	4,736	4,902	3,272
Kent	223	465	474	171	Upton	256	1,186	686	869
Kerr	1,511	6,039	3,767	6,021	Uvalde	1,438	3,883	2,225	3,048
Kimble	266	971	759	846	Val Verde	2,049	4,052	4,029	2,485
King	75	143	100	96	Van Zandt	1,939	4,839	6,461	3,388
Kinney	234	425	438	311	Victoria	4,226	11,246	7,325	9,594
Kleberg	4,481	5,312	5,803	3,771	Walker	2,940	5,082	2,860	2,877
Knox	638	1,148	1,498	551	Waller	1,538	2,263	2,766	1,984
Lamar	2,865	7,736	8,595	4,436	Ward	1,049	2,687	2,046	2,123
Lamb	1,350	3,981	3,374	2,413	Washington	1,323	3,862	2,635	3,820
Lampasas	688	2,251	2,396	1,563	Webb	8,435	6,011	8,050	3,472
LaSalle	567	1,073	1,294	677	Wharton	3,481	6,271	5,914	4,692
Lavaca	1,429	3,288	3,740	2,466	Wheeler	502	1,766	1,598	1,273

	1972		1976	
	(D)	(R)	(D)	(R)
Wichita	10,948	25,197	22,264	19,096
Wilbarger	1,139	3,183	3,280	2,145
Willacy	1,384	2,317	2,984	1,542
Williamson	3,806	6,998	9,355	7,489
Wilson	2,072	2,953	3,417	1,784
Winkler	602	2,467	1,382	1,842
Wise	1,741	4,230	5,133	2,856
Wood	1,842	4,746	4,107	3,076
Yoakum	457	1,952	1,181	1,477
Young	1,486	3,353	3,473	2,652
Zapata	768	695	1,186	461
Zavala	1,122	1,288	1,822	735
Totals	1,154,289	2,298,896	2,036,484	1,880,581

Texas Vote Since 1932

1932 (Pres.), Roosevelt, Dem., 760,348; Hoover, Rep., 97,959; Thomas, Soc., 4,450; Harvey, Lib., 324; Foster, Com., 207; Jackson Party, 104.

1936 (Pres.), Roosevelt, Dem., 734,485; Landon, Rep., 103,874; Lemke, Union, 3,281; Thomas, Soc., 1,075; Colvin, Proh., 514; Browder, Com., 253.

1940 (Pres.), Roosevelt, Dem., 840,151; Willkie, Rep., 199,152; Babson, Proh., 925; Thomas, Soc., 728; Browder, Com., 212.

1944 (Pres.), Roosevelt, Dem., 821,605; Dewey, Rep., 191,425; Texas Regulars, 135,439; Watson, Proh., 1,017; Thomas, Soc., 594; America First, 250.

1948 (Pres.), Truman, Dem., 750,700; Dewey, Rep., 282,240; Thurmond, States' Rights, 106,909; Wallace, Prog., 3,764; Watson, Proh., 2,758; Thomas, Soc., 874.

1952 (Pres.), Eisenhower, Rep., 1,102,878; Stevenson, Dem., 969,228; Hamblen, Proh., 1,983; MacArthur, Christian Nationalist, 833; MacArthur, Constitution, 730; Hallinan, Prog., 294.

1956 (Pres.), Eisenhower, Rep., 1,080,619; Stevenson, Dem., 859,958; Andrews, Ind., 14,591.

1960 (Pres.), Kennedy, Dem., 1,167,932; Nixon, Rep., 1,121,699; Sullivan, Constitution, 18,169; Decker, Proh., 3,870; write-in, 15.

1964 (Pres.), Johnson, Dem., 1,663,185; Goldwater, Rep., 958,566; Lightburn, Constitution, 5,060.

1968 (Pres.), Nixon, Rep., 1,227,844; Humphrey, Dem., 1,266,804; Wallace, 3d party, 584,269; write-in, 489.

1972 (Pres.), Nixon, Rep., 2,298,896; McGovern, Dem., 1,154,289; Schmitz, American, 6,039; Jenness, Soc. Worker, 8,664; others, 3,393.

Utah

	1972		1976	
	McGov-ern	Nixon	Carter	Ford
County	(D)	(R)	(D)	(R)
Beaver	682	1,332	961	1,087
Box Elder	2,134	9,880	3,372	9,275
Cache	4,018	16,538	5,363	16,330
Carbon	3,335	3,956	5,157	3,263
Daggett	50	204	130	216
Davis	7,954	29,706	14,071	31,145
Duchesne	629	2,183	1,110	2,612
Emery	769	1,666	1,764	1,717
Garfield	242	1,290	536	1,154
Grand	560	1,837	936	1,776
Iron	1,098	5,085	1,697	4,733
Juab	691	1,629	1,145	1,287
Kane	218	1,146	330	1,094
Millard	777	2,689	1,223	2,477
Morgan	363	1,456	701	1,356
Piute	102	475	265	375
Rich	120	604	248	541
Salt Lake	64,489	132,066	85,403	142,389
San Juan	677	1,893	1,180	1,838
Sanpete	1,220	3,995	2,009	3,836
Sevier	820	3,700	1,560	3,677
Summit	836	2,209	1,278	2,310
Tooele	2,621	5,641	4,356	4,617
Unitah	716	4,712	1,331	3,996
Utah	10,828	42,179	18,647	49,309
Wasatch	693	2,046	1,090	1,931
Washington	956	5,176	1,889	5,927

Wayne	183	597	334	553
Weber	14,503	37,753	22,888	34,323
Totals	126,284	323,643	180,974	335,144

Utah Vote Since 1932

1932 (Pres.), Roosevelt, Dem., 116,750; Hoover, Rep., 84,795; Thomas, Soc., 4,087; Foster, Com., 947.

1936 (Pres.), Roosevelt, Dem., 150,246; Landon, Rep., 64,555; Lemke, Union, 1,121; Thomas, Soc., 432; Browder, Com., 280; Colvin, Proh., 43.

1940 (Pres.), Roosevelt, Dem., 154,277; Willkie, Rep., 93,151; Thomas, Soc., 200; Browder, Com., 191.

1944 (Pres.), Roosevelt, Dem., 150,088; Dewey, Rep., 97,891; Thomas, Soc., 340.

1948 (Pres.), Truman, Dem., 149,151; Dewey, Rep., 124,402; Wallace, Prog., 2,679; Dobbs, Soc. Workers, 73.

1952 (Pres.), Eisenhower, Rep., 194,190; Stevenson, Dem., 135,364.

1956 (Pres.), Eisenhower, Rep., 215,631; Stevenson, Dem., 118,364.

1960 (Pres.), Kennedy, Dem., 169,248; Nixon, Rep., 205,361; Dobbs, Soc. Workers, 100.

1964 (Pres.), Johnson, Dem., 219,628; Goldwater, Rep., 181,785.

1968 (Pres.), Nixon, Rep., 238,728; Humphrey, Dem., 156,665; Wallace, 3d party, 26,906; Halstead, Soc. Worker, 89; Peace and Freedom, 180.

1972 (Pres.), Nixon, Rep., 323,643; McGovern, Dem., 126,284; Schmitz, American, 28,549.

Vermont

	1972		1976	
	McGov-ern	Nixon	Carter	Ford
County	(D)	(R)	(D)	(R)
Addison	3,262	6,467	4,144	5,717
Bennington	4,804	7,542	5,322	6,708
Caledonia	3,094	6,762	3,510	5,461
Chittenden	16,163	23,063	17,846	21,930
Essex	655	1,441	990	1,162
Franklin	3,898	8,109	5,565	6,190
Grand Isle	743	1,259	868	1,005
Lamoille	1,659	4,164	2,003	3,529
Orange	2,332	5,389	3,115	4,759
Orleans	2,793	4,906	3,545	4,059
Rutland	8,261	14,143	9,885	11,571
Washington	7,596	12,421	8,760	10,859
Windham	5,925	9,062	6,653	7,883
Windsor	6,989	12,421	8,140	10,671
Totals	68,174	117,149	63,346	101,504

Vermont Vote Since 1932

1932 (Pres.), Roosevelt, Dem., 56,266; Hoover, Rep., 78,984; Thomas, Soc., 1,533; Foster, Com., 195.

1936 (Pres.), Landon, Rep., 81,023; Roosevelt, Dem., 62,124; Browder. Com., 405.

1940 (Pres.), Roosevelt, Dem., 64,269, Willkie, Rep.,78,371; Browder, Com., 411.

1944 (Pres.), Roosevelt, Dem., 53,820; Dewey, Rep., 71,527.

1948 (Pres.), Truman, Dem., 45,557; Dewey, Rep., 75,-926; Wallace, Prog., 1,279; Thomas, Soc., 585.

1952 (Pres.), Eisenhower, Rep., 109,717; Stevenson, Dem., 43,355; Hallinan, Prog., 282; Hoopes, Soc., 185.

1956 (Pres.), Eisenhower, Rep., 110,390; Stevenson, Dem., 42,549; scattered, 39.

1960 (Pres.), Kennedy, Dem., 69,186; Nixon, Rep., 98,131.

1964 (Pres.), Johnson, Dem., 107,674; Goldwater, Rep., 54,868.

1968 (Pres.), Nixon, Rep., 85,142; Humphrey, Dem., 70,255; Wallace, 3d party, 5,104; Halstead, Soc.

Worker, 295; Gregory, New Party, 579.
1972 (Pres.), Nixon, Rep., 117,149; McGovern, Dem., 68,174; Spock, Liberty Union, 1010; Jenness, Soc. Worker, 296; scattered, 318.

Virginia

County	1972 McGovern (D)	Nixon (R)	1976 Carter (D)	Ford (R)
Accomack	2,406	6,496	4,807	4,494
Albemarle	4,303	8,447	7,310	9,084
Alleghany	1,069	2,584	2,462	1,756
Amelia	778	1,606	1,715	1,634
Amherst	1,512	4,909	3,675	3,956
Appomattox	684	2,788	1,702	2,064
Arlington	25,877	39,406	32,503	30,876
Augusta	1,766	9,106	5,626	8,452
Bath	462	1,127	1,029	888
Bedford	1,501	5,286	4,772	4,189
Bland	527	1,352	961	1,047
Botetourt	1,519	3,806	4,032	3,359
Brunswick	2,130	3,072	3,070	2,661
Buchanan	3,566	4,801	5,786	3,840
Buckingham	1,186	2,107	2,179	1,486
Campbell	2,055	11,676	4,354	7,442
Caroline	1,814	2,086	3,276	1,648
Carroll	1,583	5,247	4,010	4,820
Charles City	1,177	535	1,455	439
Charlotte	1,182	2,501	2,312	2,023
Chesterfield	3,823	24,934	14,144	27,811
Clarke	715	1,816	1,276	1,440
Craig	425	774	1,103	546
Culpeper	1,316	3,707	2,892	3,659
Cumberland	969	1,371	1,302	1,284
Dickenson	2,711	3,633	4,582	3,470
Dinwiddie	1,901	3,314	3,873	2,422
Essex	808	1,482	1,305	1,375
Fairfax	54,844	112,135	92,017	110,411
Fauquier	2,039	4,654	4,001	4,712
Floyd	708	2,444	390	314
Fluvanna	637	1,438	1,415	1,296
Franklin	2,273	4,674	6,438	3,532
Frederick	1,604	5,367	3,389	5,162
Giles	1,869	3,671	3,779	2,731
Gloucester	1,292	3,642	3,155	3,025
Goochland	1,254	2,127	2,259	2,104
Grayson	1,603	3,565	3,145	3,018
Greene	318	1,208	895	1,095
Greensville	1,197	1,608	2,413	1,136
Halifax	2,384	5,469	4,352	4,045
Hanover	2,200	11,095	6,069	11,555
Henrico	8,420	52,536	21,503	45,572
Henry	4,042	7,556	9,717	5,612
Highland	206	774	493	928
Isle of Wight	2,305	3,555	4,139	2,712
James City	1,992	3,372	2,999	3,184
King George	658	1,675	1,513	1,383
King and Queen	708	1,033	1,111	778
King William	797	1,839	1,501	1,597
Lancaster	1,009	2,683	1,573	2,381
Lee	2,825	4,957	5,249	4,544
Loudoun	3,941	9,417	7,992	9,190
Louisa	1,338	2,545	2,856	2,150
Lunenburg	1,044	2,464	1,735	1,809
Madison	639	1,864	1,462	1,708
Mathews	730	2,164	1,309	1,908
Mecklenburg	2,804	6,381	4,084	4,394
Middlesex	724	1,697	1,309	1,606
Montgomery	3,692	9,348	7,540	7,971
Nelson	954	2,145	2,426	1,516
New Kent	633	1,370	1,337	1,259
Northampton	1,246	2,587	2,459	2,043
Northumberland	884	2,332	1,184	2,167
Nottoway	1,308	2,979	2,557	2,506
Orange	1,032	2,758	2,308	2,549
Page	1,585	4,326	3,401	3,780
Patrick	942	2,951	2,247	1,989
Pittsylvania	4,429	12,108	7,962	9,172
Powhatan	810	1,751	1,528	2,010
Prince Edward	1,585	3,199	2,448	2,734
Prince George	1,084	2,405	2,630	2,252
Prince William	7,266	20,149	15,215	15,446
Pulaski	2,311	6,281	5,546	4,764
Rappahannock	471	1,055	1,071	881
Richmond	435	1,565	864	1,391
Roanoke	5,318	19,920	13,120	13,586
Rockbridge	956	3,009	2,525	2,157
Rockingham	2,026	10,025	5,353	9,777
Russell	3,367	5,010	6,008	4,277
Scott	2,474	5,125	4,486	4,305
Shenandoah	1,422	7,128	3,364	6,296
Smyth	2,280	6,409	5,245	5,031
Southampton	1,498	3,225	3,398	2,366
Spotsylvania	1,775	3,577	4,231	3,180
Stafford	1,901	5,222	4,900	4,446
Surry	988	1,067	1,829	929
Sussex	1,645	2,120	2,487	1,370
Tazewell	3,181	7,233	7,565	5,554
Warren	1,508	3,718	3,259	3,014
Washington	3,028	8,805	6,177	7,568
Westmoreland	1,113	2,331	2,355	1,909
Wise	4,402	6,739	7,108	5,693
Wythe	1,431	4,553	3,578	4,231
York	2,302	7,745	4,735	5,603
Total	251,451	621,848	488,228	539,479
CITIES				
Alexandria	15,409	20,235	19,857	16,879
Bedford	529	1,407	1,122	1,043
Bristol	1,157	2,665	3,249	2,895
Buena Vista	373	990	993	771
Charlottesville	5,240	7,935	6,843	6,670
Chesapeake	7,289	17,722	17,651	12,851
Clifton Forge	575	1,127	993	770
Colonial Heights	541	5,304	2,409	4,291
Covington	948	1,910	1,820	1,173
Danville	4,148	12,463	6,425	10,233
Emporia	565	1,340	899	1,055
Fairfax	2,274	5,063	3,464	4,173
Falls Church	1,895	2,967	2,202	2,323
Franklin	738	1,419	1,116	1,127
Fredericksburg	1,702	3,211	2,550	2,527
Galax	524	1,497	1,218	1,258
Hampton	10,648	21,897	18,632	14,251
Harrisonburg	992	3,626	1,803	3,376
Hopewell	1,485	5,229	3,691	3,764
Lexington	695	1,345	945	1,026
Lynchburg	4,208	13,259	8207	14,562
Manassas	N.A.	N.A.	1,645	1,992
Manassas Park	N.A.	N.A.	709	444
Martinsville	2,292	3,879	3,491	3,146
Newport News	12,233	27,169	22,959	20,916
Norfolk	25,737	38,385	39,305	28,099
Norton	463	823	811	577
Petersburg	5,156	6,710	7,852	5,044
Poquosin	N.A.	N.A.	1,140	1,461
Portsmouth	13,124	20,090	22,812	12,868
Radford	1,121	2,577	2,240	1,843
Richmond	33,055	46,244	44,748	37,176
Roanoke	9,498	18,541	20,696	14,738
Salem	1,744	5,649	4,394	4,196
South Boston	709	1,865	1,001	1,389
Staunton	1,416	5,531	2,951	4,681
Suffolk	4,827	7,502	9,245	6,066
Virginia Beach	10,373	38,074	25,239	34,345
Waynesboro	1,061	4,163	2,209	3,528
Williamsburg	1,274	1,786	1,468	1,654
Winchester	1,418	4,647	2,364	4,075
Total	187,436	366,645	322,468	295,126
Aggregate	438,887	988,493	810,696	834,605

Virginia Vote Since 1932

1932 (Pres.), Roosevelt, Dem., 203,979; Hoover, Rep., 89,637; Thomas, Soc., 2,382; Upshaw, Proh., 1,843; Foster, Com., 86; Cox, Ind., 15.

1936 (Pres.), Roosevelt, Dem., 234,980; Landon, Rep., 98,366; Colvin, Proh., 594; Thomas, Soc., 313; Lemke, Union, 233; Browder, Com., 98.

1940 (Pres.), Roosevelt, Dem., 235,961; Willkie, Rep., 109,363; Babson, Proh., 882; Thomas, Soc., 282; Browder, Com., 71; Aiken, Soc. Lab., 48.

1944 (Pres.), Roosevelt, Dem., 242,276; Dewey, Rep., 145,243; Watson, Proh., 459; Thomas, Soc., 417; Teichert, Soc. Lab., 90.

1948 (Pres.), Truman, Dem., 200,786; Dewey, Rep., 172,070; Thurmond, States' Rights, 43,393; Wallace, Prog., 2,047; Thomas, Soc., 726; Teichert, Soc. Lab., 234.

1952 (Pres.), Eisenhower, Rep., 349,037; Stevenson, Dem., 268,677; Haas, Soc. Lab., 1,160; Hoopes, Social Dem., 504; Hallinan, Prog., 311.

1956 (Pres.), Eisenhower, Rep., 386,459; Stevenson, Dem., 267,760; Andrews, States' Rights, 42,964; Hoopes, Soc. Dem., 444; Haas, Soc. Lab., 351.

1960 (Pres.), Kennedy, Dem., 362,327; Nixon, Rep., 404,521; Coiner, Conservative, 4,204; Haas, Soc. Lab., 397.

1964 (Pres.), Johnson, Dem., 558,038; Goldwater, Rep., 481,334; Haas, Soc. Lab., 2,895.

1968 (Pres.), Nixon, Rep., 590,319; Humphrey, Dem., 442,387; Wallace, 3d party, *320,272; Blomen, Soc. Labor, 4,671; Munn, Prohibition, 601; Gregory, Peace and Freedom, 1,680.
*10,561 votes for Wallace were omitted in the count.

1972 (Pres.), Nixon. Rep., 988,493; McGovern, Dem.,

438,887; Schmitz, American, 19,721; Fisher, Soc. Labor, 9,918.

1972 (Pres.), Nixon, Rep., 837,135; McGovern, Dem., 568,334; Schmitz, American, 58,906; Spock, Ind., 2,644; Fisher, Soc. Labor, 1,102; Jenness, Soc. Worker, 623; Hall, Communist, 566; Hospers, Libertarian, 1,537.

Washington

County	1972 McGovern (D)	1972 Nixon (R)	1976 Carter (D)	1976 Ford (R)
Adams	1,110	3,083	1,618	2,458
Asotin	2,559	2,911	2,614	2,395
Benton	9,824	18,517	9,809	19,386
Chelan	5,889	10,470	6,802	9,015
Clallam	5,620	9,372	7,958	8,682
Clark	27,179	28,775	29,518	26,184
Columbia	533	1,445	719	952
Cowlitz	12,682	14,431	13,486	11,120
Douglas	2,420	4,512	3,443	3,972
Ferry	560	815	736	693
Franklin	3,867	5,972	3,684	4,817
Garfield	481	1,004	486	678
Grant	5,487	9,370	6,659	7,650
Grays Harbor	11,786	10,839	11,798	8,021
Island	3,149	7,495	4,896	6,474
Jefferson	2,096	2,770	2,273	2,172
King	212,509	298,707	227,852	248,758
Kitsap	17,011	25,831	24,491	21,540
Kittitas	4,299	5,464	4,191	4,021
Klickitat	2,293	3,061	2,584	2,228
Lewis	6,946	12,071	8,064	9,635
Lincoln	1,453	3,647	1,762	2,501
Mason	3,907	4,873	5,727	4,465
Okanogan	3,835	5,796	4,845	4,696
Pacific	3,585	3,349	4,189	2,685
Pend Oreille	1,071	1,746	1,195	1,161
Pierce	56,933	84,265	63,664	58,239
San Juan	906	1,786	1,118	1,475
Skagit	9,233	14,212	11,210	11,291
Skamania	1,153	1,288	1,309	946
Snohomish	39,471	60,032	50,802	50,027
Spokane	44,337	74,320	50,201	59,112
Stevens	2,390	4,839	3,343	4,010
Thurston	14,596	22,297	19,308	18,847
Wahkiakum	796	818	878	639
Walla Walla	5,364	12,579	5,805	9,023
Whatcom	15,027	22,585	16,965	16,586
Whitman	6,248	9,548	5,974	7,904
Yakima	19,729	32,240	21,357	25,173
Totals	**568,334**	**837,135**	**643,333**	**679,631**

Washington Vote Since 1932

1932 (Pres.), Roosevelt, Dem., 353,260; Hoover, Rep., 208,645; Harvey, Lib., 30,308; Thomas, Soc., 17,080; Foster, Com., 2,972; Upshaw, Proh., 1,540; Reynolds, Soc. Lab., 1,009.

1936 (Pres.), Roosevelt, Dem., 459,579; Landon, Rep., 206,892; Lemke, Union, 17,463; Thomas, Soc., 3,496; Browder, Com., 1,907; Pellsy, Christian, 1,598; Colvin, Proh., 1,041; Aiken, Soc. Lab., 362.

1940 (Pres.), Roosevelt, Dem., 462,145; Willkie, Rep., 322,123; Thomas, Soc., 4,586; Browder, Com., 2,626; Babson, Proh., 1,686; Aiken, Soc. Lab., 667.

1944 (Pres.), Roosevelt, Dem., 486,774; Dewey, Rep., 361,689; Thomas, Soc., 3,824; Watson, Proh., 2,396; Teichert, Soc. Lab., 1,645.

1948 (Pres.), Truman, Dem., 476,165; Dewey, Rep., 386,315; Wallace, Prog., 31,692; Watson, Proh., 6,117; Thomas, Soc., 3,534; Teichert, Soc. Lab., 1,133; Dobbs, Soc. Workers, 103.

1952 (Pres.), Eisenhower, Rep., 599,107; Stevenson, Dem., 492,845; MacArthur, Christian Nationalist, 7,290; Hallinan, Prog., 2,460; Haas, Soc. Lab., 633; Hoopes, Soc., 254; Dobbs, Soc. Workers, 119.

1956 (Pres.), Eisenhower, Rep., 620,430; Stevenson, Dem., 523,002; Haas, Soc. Lab., 7,457.

1960 (Pres.), Kennedy, Dem., 599,298; Nixon, Rep., 629,273; Haas, Soc. Lab., 10,895; Curtis, Constitution, 1,401; Dobbs, Soc. Workers, 705.

1964 (Pres.), Johnson, Dem., 779,699; Goldwater, Rep., 470,366; Haas, Soc. Labor, 7,772; DeBerry, Freedom Soc., 537.

1968 (Pres.), Nixon, Rep., 588,510; Humphrey, Dem., 616,037; Wallace, 3d party, 96,990; Blomen, Soc. Labor, 488; Cleaver, Peace and Freedom, 1,609; Halstead, Soc. Worker, 270; Mitchell, Free Ballot, 377.

West Virginia

County	1972 McGovern (D)	1972 Nixon (R)	1976 Carter (D)	1976 Ford (R)
Barbour	2,258	4,432	3,635	3,229
Berkeley	4,523	10,954	7,831	8,274
Boone	5,342	5,985	8,205	3,042
Braxton	2,771	3,155	3,993	1,899
Brooke	5,226	7,544	8,189	4,796
Cabell	14,312	29,582	20,678	19,543
Calhoun	1,528	1,992	1,861	1,056
Clay	1,830	2,168	2,657	1,281
Doddridge	645	2,284	1,241	1,803
Fayette	9,966	11,876	15,085	5,354
Gilmer	1,359	2,056	2,245	1,371
Grant	614	3,556	1,323	2,969
Greenbrier	4,423	8,827	8,291	5,861
Hampshire	1,637	3,084	3,104	2,097
Hancock	6,727	10,634	10,542	6,758
Hardy	1,510	2,690	2,373	1,898
Harrison	12,910	22,196	21,444	15,138
Jackson	3,007	7,226	5,321	5,351
Jefferson	2,782	4,822	4,849	3,642
Kanawha	38,032	65,021	53,352	42,232
Lewis	2,062	5,778	3,953	3,744
Lincoln	3,876	4,673	4,988	2,929
Logan	10,045	9,533	13,033	4,071
Marion	11,864	16,095	10,506	4,073
Marshall	6,378	10,966	17,694	10,312
Mason	4,008	7,129	8,552	6,652
McDowell	7,826	17,846	6,761	5,201
Mercer	3,276	7,157	14,524	10,879
Mineral	5,585	7,484	5,890	5,136
Mingo	10,721	16,758	8,345	3,008
Monongalia	2,114	3,716	15,385	11,248
Monroe	1,118	3,014	3,293	2,752
Morgan	6,811	8,942	1,913	2,359
Nicholas	3,628	5,907	6,227	3,458
Ohio	10,491	18,435	11,779	12,441
Pendleton	1,248	2,207	2,093	1,554
Pleasants	1,207	2,025	1,727	1,621
Pocahontas	1,635	2,391	2,329	1,738
Preston	2,977	7,807	5,591	5,712
Putnam	4,771	8,265	8,210	6,416
Raleigh	10,586	19,150	18,184	10,085
Randolph	3,809	6,923	7,256	4,818
Ritchie	990	3,635	1,940	2,864
Roane	2,386	4,253	3,146	2,837
Summers	2,518	3,895	3,943	2,254
Taylor	2,085	4,385	3,902	2,890
Tucker	1,457	2,163	2,320	1,395
Tyler	1,125	3,362	2,508	1,811
Upshur	1,795	6,449	3,503	4,784
Wayne	6,251	9,775	9,947	6,013
Webster	2,069	2,114	2,922	965
Wetzel	3,276	6,046	5,034	3,785
Wirt	691	1,442	1,182	1,042
Wood	10,886	27,315	17,025	18,348
Wyoming	4,468	7,926	8,580	4,223
Totals	**277,435**	**484,964**	**430,404**	**311,012**

West Virginia Vote Since 1932

1932 (Pres.), Roosevelt, Dem., 405,124; Hoover, Rep., 330,731; Thomas, Soc., 5,133; Upshaw, Proh., 2,342; Foster, Com., 444.

1936 (Pres.), Roosevelt, Dem., 502,582; Landon, Rep., 325,358; Colvin, Prog., 1,173; Thomas, Soc., 832.

1940 (Pres.), Roosevelt, Dem., 495,662; Willkie, Rep., 372,414.

1944 (Pres.), Roosevelt, Dem., 392,777; Dewey, Rep., 322,819.

1948 (Pres.), Truman, Dem., 429,188; Dewey, Rep., 316,251; Wallace, Prog., 3,311.

1952 (Pres.), Eisenhower, Rep., 419,970; Stevenson, Dem., 453,578.

1956 (Pres.), Eisenhower, Rep., 449,297; Stevenson, Dem., 381,534.

1960 (Pres.), Kennedy, Dem., 441,786; Nixon, Rep., 395,995.

1964 (Pres.), Johnson, Dem., 538,087; Goldwater, Rep., 253,953.

1968 (Pres.), Nixon, Rep., 307,555; Humphrey, Dem., 374,091; Wallace, 3d party, 72,560.
1972 (Pres.), Nixon, Rep., 484,964; McGovern, Dem., 277,435.

Wisconsin

County	1972		1976	
	McGovern	Nixon	Carter	Ford
	(D)	(R)	(D)	(R)
Adams	1,833	2,200	3,089	2,377
Ashland	3,771	3,478	3,880	3,035
Barron	5,376	8,418	8,782	7,385
Bayfield	2,736	3,045	3,885	2,724
Brown	26,511	37,101	33,572	36,571
Buffalo	2,461	3,079	3,448	2,844
Burnett	2,389	2,972	3,720	2,573
Calumet	4,804	6,446	6,241	6,589
Chippewa	8,210	8,451	11,638	8,137
Clark	4,617	7,138	7,238	6,695
Columbia	7,083	10,122	9,457	10,085
Crawford	2,487	3,705	3,629	3,393
Dane	79,567	56,020	82,112	63,480
Dodge	9,898	17,068	13,653	17,245
Door	3,430	6,503	4,553	6,560
Douglas	11,054	8,419	13,478	6,999
Dunn	5,681	6,660	7,882	6,751
Eau Claire	14,300	15,883	18,263	16,387
Florence	757	971	965	922
Fond du Lac	N.A.	N.A.	16,571	22,226
Forest	1,678	1,856	2,574	1,604
Grant	6,915	11,873	9,637	12,016
Green	3,634	7,422	5,632	7,085
Green Lake	2,174	5,046	3,411	5,021
Iowa	3,131	4,387	4,278	4,195
Iron	1,648	1,723	2,399	1,213
Jackson	2,445	3,937	3,409	3,735
Jefferson	9,303	14,621	12,576	15,527
Juneau	2,943	4,833	4,511	4,242
Kenosha	19,441	24,041	27,590	22,449
Kewaunee	3,360	4,802	4,447	4,607
La Crosse	12,152	21,992	16,674	24,188
La Fayette	2,804	4,898	3,906	4,131
Langlade	3,011	4,368	4,134	4,630
Lincoln	4,175	6,206	5,808	5,672
Manitowoc	16,489	16,599	19,819	16,039
Marathon	18,500	21,454	24,932	21,898
Marinette	5,900	8,740	8,482	9,591
Marquette	1,537	2,682	2,511	2,607
Menominee	608	355	766	324
Milwaukee	210,802	191,874	247,764	189,056
Monroe	3,640	7,625	6,466	7,242
Oconto	4,041	6,511	6,541	6,232
Oneida	4,262	6,811	6,921	7,347
Outagamie	17,477	27,533	22,979	28,365
Ozaukee	8,503	15,759	11,271	19,817
Pepin	1,409	1,458	1,955	1,312
Pierce	5,611	5,899	8,044	5,676
Polk	5,738	6,567	8,476	6,159
Portage	13,564	9,346	15,912	9,520
Price	2,831	3,694	4,028	3,204
Racine	27,778	38,490	37,089	36,747
Richland	2,492	5,062	3,642	4,476
Rock	21,053	30,361	28,052	28,269
Rusk	3,075	3,007	4,061	2,724
St. Croix	7,488	8,553	10,604	7,685
Sauk	6,980	10,285	9,204	9,577
Sawyer	1,765	3,081	3,055	2,720
Shawano	3,940	8,807	6,752	8,515
Sheboygan	21,114	21,500	24,226	22,332
Taylor	2,934	4,125	4,106	3,591
Trempealeau	4,232	5,723	6,220	5,303
Vernon	3,407	6,836	5,542	6,133
Vilas	1,907	4,422	3,277	4,761
Walworth	8,598	17,823	12,417	18,094
Washburn	2,336	3,220	3,503	2,792
Washington	10,434	15,338	14,420	18,796
Waukesha	34,573	59,399	47,522	70,016
Waupaca	4,418	11,040	6,857	10,849
Waushara	2,094	4,466	3,485	4,449
Winnebago	20,450	29,488	24,485	32,149
Wood	10,415	14,806	14,628	15,379
Totals	**810,174**	**989,430**	**1,037,056**	**1,003,039**

Wisconsin Vote Since 1932

1932 (Pres.), Roosevelt, Dem., 707,410; Hoover, Rep., 347,741; Thomas, Soc., 53,379; Foster, Com., 3,112; Upshaw, Proh., 2,672; Reynolds, Soc. Lab., 494.
1936 (Pres.), Roosevelt, Dem., 802,984; Landon, Rep., 380,828; Lemke, Union, 60,297; Thomas, Soc., 10,-626; Browder, Com., 2,197; Colvin, Proh., 1,071; Aiken, Soc. Lab., 557.
1940 (Pres.), Roosevelt, Dem., 704,821; Willkie, Rep., 679,260; Thomas, Soc., 15,071; Browder, Com., 2,394; Babson, Proh., 2,148; Aiken, Soc. Lab., 1,882.

1944 (Pres.), Roosevelt, Dem., 650,413; Dewey, Rep., 674,532; Thomas, Soc., 13,205; Teichert, Soc. Lab., 1,002.
1948 (Pres.), Truman, Dem., 647,310; Dewey, Rep., 590,959; Wallace, Prog., 25,282; Thomas, Soc., 12,-547; Teichert, Soc. Lab., 399; Dobbs, Soc. Workers, 303.
1952 (Pres.), Eisenhower, Rep., 979,744; Stevenson, Dem., 622,175; Hallinan, Ind., 2,174; Dobbs, Ind., 1,350; Hoopes, Ind., 1,157; Haas, Ind., 770.
1956 (Pres.), Eisenhower, Rep., 954,844; Stevenson, Dem., 586,768; Andrews, Ind., 6,918; Hoopes, Soc., 754; Haas, Soc. Lab., 710; Dobbs, Soc. Workers, 564.
1960 (Pres.), Kennedy, Dem., 830,805; Nixon, Rep., 895,175; Dobbs, Soc. Workers, 1,792; Haas, Soc. Lab., 1,310.
1964 (Pres.), Johnson, Dem., 1,050,424; Goldwater, Rep., 638,495; DeBerry, Soc. Worker, 1,692; Haas, Soc. Lab., 1,204.
1968 (Pres.), Nixon, Rep., 809,997; Humphrey, Dem., 748,804; Wallace, 3d party, 127,835; Blomen, Soc. Labor, 1,338; Halstead, Soc. Worker, 1,222; scattered, 2,342.
1972 (Pres.), Nixon, Rep., 989,430; McGovern, Dem., 810,174; Schmitz, American, 47,525; Spock, Ind., 2,701; Fisher, Soc. Labor, 998; Hall, Communist, 663; Reed, Ind., 506; scattered, 893.

Wyoming

County	1972		1976	
	McGovern	Nixon	Carter	Ford
	(D)	(R)	(D)	(R)
Albany	4,873	7,021	4,663	6,734
Big Horn	1,049	3,244	1,618	3,117
Campbell	783	2,953	1,620	3,306
Carbon	2,292	4,037	3,011	3,556
Converse	682	2,312	1,160	2,178
Crook	339	1,760	661	1,538
Fremont	3,248	7,359	4,433	6,584
Goshen	1,515	3,629	2,262	2,764
Hot Springs	689	1,678	958	1,413
Johnson	436	2,203	797	2,042
Laramie	7,791	15,010	12,040	14,061
Lincoln	969	2,459	1,555	2,464
Natrona	6,514	15,849	8,640	13,761
Niobrara	289	1,245	427	1,057
Park	1,950	5,890	2,656	5,879
Platte	925	2,200	1,593	1,844
Sheridan	2,874	6,432	3,206	5,383
Sublette	304	1,348	528	1,284
Sweetwater	3,713	5,175	4,637	4,319
Teton	810	2,182	1,204	2,668
Uinta	968	2,011	1,559	2,129
Washakie	825	2,604	1,168	2,361
Weston	520	2,063	934	1,771
Totals	**44,358**	**100,464**	**62,267**	**92,831**

Wyoming Vote Since 1932

1932 (Pres.), Roosevelt, Dem., 54,370; Hoover, Rep., 39,583; Thomas, Soc. 2,829; Foster, Com., 180.
1936 (Pres.), Roosevelt, Dem., 62,624; Landon, Rep., 38,739; Lemke, Union, 1,653; Thoms, Soc., 200; Browder, Com., 91; Colvin, Proh., 75.
1940 (Pres.), Roosevelt, Dem., 59,287; Willkie, Rep., 52,633; Babson, Proh., 172; Thomas, Soc., 148.
1944 (Pres.), Roosevelt, Dem., 49,419; Dewey, Rep., 51,921.
1948 (Pres.), Truman, Dem., 52,354; Dewey, Rep., 47,-947; Wallace, Prog., 931; Thomas, Soc., 137; Teichert, Soc. Lab., 56.
1952 (Pres.), Eisenhower, Rep., 81,047; Stevenson, Dem., 47,934; Hamblen, Proh., 194; Hoopes, Soc., 40; Haas, Soc. Lab., 36.
1956 (Pres.), Eisenhower, Rep., 74,573; Stevenson, Dem., 49,554.
1960 (Pres.), Kennedy, Dem., 63,331; Nixon, Rep., 77,451.
1964 (Pres.), Johnson, Dem., 80,718; Goldwater, Rep., 61,998.
1968 (Pres.), Nixon, Rep., 70,927; Humphrey, Dem., 45,173; Wallace, 3d party, 11,105.
1972 (Pres.), Nixon, Rep., 100,464; McGovern, Dem., 44,358; Schmitz, American, 748.

Major Parties' Popular and Electoral Vote for President

(F) Federalist; (D) Democrat; (R) Republican; (DR) Democrat Republican; (NR) National Republican;
(W) Whig; (P) People's; (PR) Progressive; (SR) States' Rights; (LR) Liberal Republican; Asterisk (*)—See notes
below.

Year	President Elected	Popular	Elec.	Losing Candidate	Popular	Elec.
1789	George Washington (F)	Unknown	69	No opposition		
1792	George Washington (F)	Unknown	132	No opposition		
1796	John Adams (F)	Unknown	71	Thomas Jefferson (DR)	Unknown	68
1800	Thomas Jefferson (DR)	Unknown	73	Aaron Burr (DR)	Unknown	73
	Elected by House of Representatives (due to tie vote)					
1804	Thomas Jefferson (DR)	Unknown	162	Charles Pinckney (F)	Unknown	14
1808	James Madison (DR)	Unknown	122	Charles Pinckney (F)	Unknown	47
1812	James Madison (DR)	Unknown	128	DeWitt Clinton (F)	Unknown	89
1816	James Monroe (DR)	Unknown	183	Rufus King (F)	Unknown	34
1820	James Monroe (DR)	Unknown	231	John Quincy Adams (DR)	Unknown	1
1824	John Quincy Adams (NR)	105,321	84	Andrew Jackson (D)	155,872	99
	Elected by House of Representatives (no			Henry Clay (DR)	46,587	37
	candidate having polled a majority)			William H. Crawford (DR)	44,282	41
1828	Andrew Jackson (D)	647,231	178	John Quincy Adams (NR)	509,097	83
1832	Andrew Jackson (D)	687,502	219	Henry Clay (DR)	530,189	49
	First national Presidential convention					
1836	Martin Van Buren (D)	762,678	170	William H. Harrison (W)	548,007	73
1840	William H. Harrison (W)	1,275,017	234	Martin Van Buren (D)	1,128,702	60
1844	James K. Polk (D)	1,337,243	170	Henry Clay (W)	1,299,068	105
1848	Zachary Taylor (W)	1,360,101	163	Lewis Cass (D)	1,220,544	127
1852	Franklin Pierce (D)	1,601,474	254	Winfield Scott (W)	1,386,578	42
1856	James C. Buchanan (D)	1,927,995	174	John C. Fremont (R)	1,391,555	114
1860	Abraham Lincoln (R)	1,866,352	180	Stephen A. Douglas (D)	1,375,157	12
				John C. Breckinridge (D)	845,763	72
				John Bell (Const. Union)	589,581	39
1864	Abraham Lincoln (R)	2,216,067	212	George McClellan (D)	1,808,725	21
1868	Ulysses S. Grant (R)	3,015,071	214	Horatio Seymour (D)	2,709,615	80
1872*	Ulysses S. Grant (R)	3,597,070	286	Horace Greeley (D-LR)	2,834,079	....
1876*	Rutherford B. Hayes (R)	4,033,950	185	Samuel J. Tilden (D)	4,284,757	184
1880	James A. Garfield (R)	4,449,053	214	Winfield S. Hancock (D)	4,442,030	155
1884	Grover Cleveland (D)	4,911,017	219	James G. Blaine (R)	4,848,334	182
1888*	Benjamin Harrison (R)	5,444,337	233	Grover Cleveland (D)	5,540,050	168
1892	Grover Cleveland (D)	5,554,414	277	Benjamin Harrison (R)	5,190,802	145
				James Weaver (P)	1,027,329	22
1896	William McKinley (R)	7,035,638	271	William J. Bryan (D-P)	6,467,946	176
1900	William McKinley (R)	7,219,530	292	William J. Bryan (D)	6,358,071	155
1904	Theodore Roosevelt (R)	7,628,834	336	Alton B. Parker (D)	5,084,491	140
1908	William H. Taft (R)	7,679,006	321	William J. Bryan (D)	6,409,106	162
1912	Woodrow Wilson (D)	6,286,214	435	Theodore Roosevelt (PR)	4,216,020	88
				William H. Taft (R)	3,483,922	8
1916	Woodrow Wilson (D)	9,129,606	277	Charles E. Hughes (R)	8,538,221	254
1920	Warren G. Harding (R)	16,152,200	404	James M. Cox (D)	9,147,353	127
1924	Calvin Coolidge (R)	15,725,016	382	John W. Davis (D)	8,385,586	136
				Robert M. LaFollette (PR)	4,822,856	13
1928	Herbert Hoover (R)	21,392,190	444	Alfred E. Smith (D)	15,016,443	87
1932	Franklin D. Roosevelt (D)	22,821,857	472	Herbert Hoover (R)	15,761,841	59
				Norman Thomas (Socialist)	884,781	....
1936	Franklin D. Roosevelt (D)	27,751,597	523	Alfred Landon (R)	16,679,583	8
1940	Franklin D. Roosevelt (D)	27,243,466	449	Wendell Willkie (R)	22,304,755	82
1944	Franklin D. Roosevelt (D)	25,602,505	432	Thomas E. Dewey (R)	22,006,278	99
1948	Harry S. Truman (D)	24,105,812	303	Thomas E. Dewey (R)	21,970,065	189
				J. Strom Thurmond (SR)	1,169,021	39
				Henry A. Wallace (PR)	1,157,172	....
1952	Dwight D. Eisenhower (R)	33,936,252	442	Adlai E. Stevenson (D)	27,314,992	89
1956*	Dwight D. Eisenhower (R)	35,585,316	457	Adlai E. Stevenson (D)	26,031,322	73
1960*	John F. Kennedy (D)	34,227,096	303	Richard M. Nixon (R)	34,108,546	219
1964	Lyndon B. Johnson (D)	43,126,506	486	Barry M. Goldwater (R)	27,176,799	52
1968	Richard M. Nixon (R)	31,785,480	301	Hubert H. Humphrey (D)	31,275,166	191
				George C. Wallace (3d party)	9,906,473	46
1972*	Richard M. Nixon (R)	47,165,234	520	George S. McGovern (D)	29,168,110	17

1872 — Greeley died Nov. 29, 1872. His electoral votes were split among 4 individuals.
1876 — Fla., La., Ore., and S. C. election returns were disputed. Congress in joint session (Mar. 2, 1877) declared Hayes and Wheeler elected President and Vice-President.
1888 — Cleveland had more votes than Harrison but the 233 electoral votes cast for Harrison against the 168 for Cleveland elected Harrison President.
1956 — Democrats elected 74 electors but one from Alabama refused to vote for Stevenson.
1960 — Sen. Harry F. Byrd (D-Va.) received 15 electoral votes.
1972 — John Hospers of Cal. and Theodora Nathan of Ore. received one vote from an elector of Virginia.

The Ninety-Fifth Congress
With Unofficial 1976 Election Results

The Senate

Terms are for 6 years and end January 3 of the year preceding name. Annual salary $44,625. To be eligible for the U.S. Senate a person must be at least 30 years of age, a citizen of the United States for at least 9 years, and a resident of the state from which he is chosen. The Congress must meet annually on Jan. 3, unless it has, by law, appointed a different day.

Senate officials: Pres. Pro Tempore, James O. Eastland; Secretary, Francis R. Valeo; Sgt. at Arms, William H. Wannall; Chaplain, the Rev. Edward L. R. Elson, S.T.D.

Dem., 61; Rep., 38; Ind., 1; Total, 100. *Star designates senior senator.

Term Ends	Senator (Party, Home)	1976 Election	Term Ends	Senator (Party, Home)	1976 Election
	Alabama			**Indiana**	
1979	John Sparkman* (D, Huntsville)........		1981	Birch Bayh* (D, Indianapolis).........	
1981	James B. Allen (D, Gadsden)..........		1983	Richard G. Lugar (R, Indianapolis)......	1,255,175
				Vance Hartke* (D, Evansville)..........	871,379
	Alaska			**Iowa**	
1979	Ted Stevens* (R, Anchorage).........				
1981	Mike Gravel (D, Anchorage)..........		1979	Dick Clark* (D, Marion)..............	
			1981	C. Culver (D, Cedar Rapids)...........	
	Arizona			**Kansas**	
1981	Barry M. Goldwater* (R, Scottsdale).....		1979	James B. Pearson* (R, Prairie Village)...	
1983	Dennis DeConcini (D, Tucson)........	399,097	1981	Robert J. Dole (R, Russell)...........	
	Sam Steiger (R, Prescott)............	320,231			
	Arkansas			**Kentucky**	
			1979	Walter Huddleston* (D, Elizabethtown)...	
1979	John L. McClellan* (D, Little Rock)......		1981	Wendell H. Ford (D, Owensboro).......	
1981	Dale Bumpers (D, Charleston)........				
	California			**Louisiana**	
			1979	J. Bennett Johnston Jr. (D, Shreveport)..	
1981	Alan Cranston* (D, Palm Springs).......		1981	Russell B. Long* (D, Baton Rouge)......	
	S. I. (Sam) Hayakawa (R, Mill Valley)....	3,701,024			
1983	John V. Tunney (D, Beverly Hills).......	3,464,583		**Maine**	
			1979	William D. Hathaway (D, Auburn).......	
	Colorado		1983	Edmund S. Muskie* (D, Waterville)......	292,140
1979	Floyd K. Haskell* (D, Denver).........			Robert A. G. Monks (R, Cape Elizabeth)..	192,118
1981	Gary Hart (D, Denver)...............				
				Maryland	
	Connecticut		1981	Charles C. Mathias* (R, Frederick)......	
1981	Abraham R. Ribicoff* (D, Hartford)......		1983	Paul S. Sarbanes (D, Baltimore)........	747,869
1983	Lowell P. Weicker Jr. (R, Greenwich)....	779,280		J. Glenn Beall Jr. (R, Frostburg)........	510,825
	Gloria Schaffer (D, Woodbridge)........	557,613			
				Massachusetts	
	Delaware		1979	Edward W. Brooke (R, Newton Center)...	
1979	Joseph R. Biden Jr. (D, Faulkland)......		1983	Edward M. Kennedy* (D, Boston).......	1,724,642
1983	William V. Roth Jr.* (R, Wilmington).....	125,496		Michael S. Robertson (R, Berkley)......	722,777
	Thomas C. Maloney (D, Wilmington).....	97,758			
				Michigan	
	Florida		1979	Robert P. Griffin* (R, Traverse City).....	
1981	Richard Stone (D, Tallahassee)........		1983	Donald W. Riegle Jr. (D, Flint)..........	1,817,927
1983	Lawton Chiles* (D, Lakeland)..........	1,693,869		Marvin L. Esch (R, Ann Arbor)..........	1,622,626
	John Grady (R, Belle Glade)..........	1,018,288			
				Minnesota	
	Georgia		1979	(To be named.)....................	
			1983	Hubert H. Humphrey (D, Waverly).......	1,288,753
1979	Sam Nunn (D, Perry)................			Jerry Brekke (R)...................	477,670
1981	Herman E. Talmadge* (D, Lovejoy).....				
				Mississippi	
	Hawaii		1979	James O. Eastland* (D, Doddsville).....	
1981	Daniel K. Inouye* (D, Honolulu)........		1983	John C. Stennis (D, DeKalb)...........	
1983	Spark M. Matsunaga (D, Honolulu)......	162,305		Unopposed	
	William Quinn (R, Honolulu)...........	122,724			
				Missouri	
	Idaho		1981	Thomas F. Eagleton* (D, St. Louis).....	
			1983	John C. Danforth (R, Jefferson City).....	1,079,158
1979	James A. McClure (R, Payette)........			Warren E. Hearnes (D, Charleston).....	803,629
1981	Frank Church* (D, Boise)............				
				Montana	
	Illinois		1979	Lee Metcalf* (D, Helena).............	
			1983	John Melcher (D, Forsyth)............	202,668
1979	Charles H. Percy* (R, Kenilworth).......			Stanley C. Burger (R, Bozeman)........	112,700
1981	Adlai E. Stevenson 3d (D, Chicago).....				

Term Ends	Senator (Party, Home)	1976 Election	Term Ends	Senator (Party, Home)	1976 Election
	Nebraska			**Rhode Island**	
1979	Carl T. Curtis* (R, Minden)		1979	Claiborne Pell* (D, Newport)	
	Edward Zorinsky (D, Omaha)	307,913	1983	John H. Chafee, (R, Warwick)	222,646
1983	John Y. McCollister (R, Omaha)	277,761		Richard P. Lorber (D, Providence)	162,837
	Nevada			**South Carolina**	
1981	Paul Laxalt (R, Carson City)		1979	Strom Thurmond* (R, Aiken)	
1983	Howard W. Cannon* (D, Las Vegas)	126,715	1981	Ernest F. Hollings (D, Columbia)	
	David Towell (R, Minden)	63,256			
				South Dakota	
	New Hampshire		1979	James Abourezk (D, Rapid City)	
1979	Thomas J. McIntyre* (D, Laconia)		1981	George McGovern* (D, Mitchell)	
1981	John A. Durkin (D, Manchester)				
				Tennessee	
	New Jersey		1979	Howard H. Baker Jr.* (R, Knoxville)	
1979	Clifford P. Case* (R, Rahway)		1983	James R. Sasser (D, Nashville)	748,429
1983	Harrison A. Williams Jr. (D, Bedminister) .	1,667,037		Bill Brock (R, Lookout Mountain)	667,256
	David F. Norcross (R, Morristown)	1,025,611			
				Texas	
	New Mexico		1979	John G. Tower* (R, Wichita Falls)	
1979	Pete V. Domenici* (R, Albuquerque)		1983	Lloyd Bentsen (D, Houston)	2,155,553
1983	Harrison "Jack" Schmitt (R, Silver City) . .	231,515		Alan Steelman (R, Dallas)	1,589,497
	Joseph M. Montoya* (D, Santa Fe)	174,308			
				Utah	
	New York		1981	Jake Garn* (R, Salt Lake City)	
			1983	Orrin G. Hatch (R, Salt Lake City)	239,633
1981	Jacob K. Javits* (R,L, New York)			Frank E. Moss (D, Salt Lake City)	
1983	Daniel Patrick Moynihan (D, New York) . .	3,365,134			
	James L. Buckley (R,C, New York)	2,791,301		**Vermont**	
			1981	Patrick J. Leahy (D, Burlington)	
	North Carolina		1983	Robert T. Stafford* (R, Rutland)	
1979	Jesse A. Helms* (R, Raleigh)			Thomas P. Salmon (D, Rockingham)	82,048
1981	Robert Morgan (D, Lillington)				
				Virginia	
	North Dakota		1979	William Lloyd Scott (R, Fairfax)	
1981	Milton R. Young* (R, LaMoure)		1983	Harry F. Byrd Jr.* (I, Winchester)	878,519
1983	Quentin N. Burdick (D, Fargo)	172,194		E. R. (Bud) Zumwalt (D, Arlington)	589,794
	Robert Stroup (R, Hazen)	102,873			
				Washington	
	Ohio		1981	Warren G. Magnuson* (D, Seattle)	
1981	John Glenn* (D, Columbia)		1983	Henry M. Jackson (D, Everett)	948,568
1983	Howard M. Metzenbaum (D, Shaker Heights)	1,924,749		George M. Brown (R, Renton)	314,231
	Robert Taft Jr. (R, Indian Hill)	1,806,344			
				West Virginia	
	Oklahoma		1979	Jennings Randolph* (D, Elkins)	
1979	Dewey F. Bartlett (R, Tulsa)		1983	Robert C. Byrd (D, Sophia)	
1981	Henry Bellmon* (R, Red Rock)			Unopposed	
	Oregon			**Wisconsin**	
			1981	Gaylord A. Nelson (D, Madison)	
1979	Mark O. Hatfield* (R, Salem)		1983	William Proxmire* (D, Madison)	1,393,272
1981	Robert W. Packwood (R, Lake Oswego) . .			Stanley York (R, Madison)	519,564
	Pennsylvania			**Wyoming**	
1981	Richard S. Schweiker* (R, Worcester) . . .		1979	Clifford P. Hansen* (R, Jackson)	
1983	H. John Heinz III (R, Pittsburgh)	2,367,942	1983	Malcolm Wallop (R, Big Horn)	84,824
	William J. Green (D, Philadelphia)	2,103,094		Gale McGee (D, Laramie)	70,464

The House of Representatives

Members' terms to Jan. 3, 1979. Annual salary $44,625; House Speaker $62,500 and $10,000 expenses, all taxable. To be eligible for membership, a person must be at least 25, a U.S. citizen for at least 7 years, and a resident of the state from which he is chosen.

Parliamentarian, William Brown; chaplain, Rev. Edward G. Latch; sergeant at arms, Kenneth Harding; clerk, Edmund Lee Henshaw Jr.; doorkeeper, William M. Miller; postmaster, Robert V. Rota.

Democrats, 291, Republicans, 142, 2 races undecided at press time. Total 435.

(Those marked * served in the 94th Congress.)

Dist.	Representative (Party, Home)	1976 Election
	Alabama	
1.	Bill Davenport (D, Citronelle)	57,610
	Jack Edwards* (R, Mobile)	103,191
2.	J. Carole Keahey (D, Ozark)	66,519
	William L. "Bill" Dickinson* (R,Montgomery)	89,974
3.	Bill Nichols* (D, Sylac Aula)	Unopposed
4.	Tom Bevill* (D.Jasper)	132,585
	Leonard Wilson (R. Jasper)	31,685
5.	Ronnie G. Flippo (D, Florence)	Unopposed
6.	Mel Bailey (D, Birmingham)	67,397
	John H. Buchanan Jr.* (R, Birmingham)	85,166
7.	Walter Flowers* (D, Tuscaloosa)	Unopposed
	Alaska - At Large	
	Eben Hopson (D, Barrow)	17,628
	Don Young* (R, Fort Yukon)	45,464
	Arizona	
1.	Patricia M. Fullinwider (D, Tempe)	68,285
	John J. Rhodes* (R, Mesa)	96,307
2.	Morris K. Udall* (D, Tucson)	105,791
	Laird Guttersen (R, Tucson)	71,609
3.	Bob Stump (D, Tolleson)	88,417
	Fred Koory Jr. (R, Glendale)	78,744
4.	Tony Mason (D, Phoenix)	92,113
	Eldon Rudd (R, Scottsdale)	92,823
	Arkansas	
1.	Bill Alexander* (D, Osceola)	116,004
	Harlan "Bo" Holleman (R, Wynne)	52,115
2.	Jim Guy Tucker (D, Little Rock)	142,795
	James J. Kelley (R, North Little Rock)	22,607
3.	John Paul Hammerschmidt* (R, Harrison)	Unopposed
4.	Ray Thornton* (D, Sheridan)	Unopposed
	California	
1.	Harold T. (Bizz) Johnson* (D, Roseville)	159,090
	James E. Taylor (R, Auburn)	56,040
2.	Oscar Klee (D, Ukiah)	88,200
	Don H. Clausen* (R, Cresent City)	120,840
3.	John E. Moss* (D, Sacramento)	138,367
	George R. Marsh Jr. (R, Sacramento)	51,434
4.	Robert L. Leggett* (D, Suisun City)	75,626
	Albert Dehr (R, Citrus Heights)	74,909
5.	John L. Burton* (D, San Francisco)	103,223
	Branwell Fanning (R, Tiburon)	63,865
6.	Phillip Burton* (D, San Francisco)	85,752
	Tom Spinosa (R, San Francisco)	35,124
7.	George Miller* (D, Martinez)	146,314
	Robert L. Vickers (R, Concord)	45,538
8.	Ronald V. Dellums* (D, Berkeley)	119,666
	Philip Stiles Breck Jr. (R, Berkeley)	67,455
9.	Fortney H. (Pete) Stark* (D, Oakland)	114,036
	James K. Mills (R, Livermore)	43,552
10.	Don Edwards* (D, San Jose)	110,806
	Herb Smith (R, San Jose)	37,746
11.	Leo J. Ryan* (D, Belmont)	107,193
	Bob Jones (R, Belmont)	62,088
12.	David Harris (D, Menlo Park)	60,701
	Paul N. "Pete" McClosksy Jr.* (R, Menlo Park)	128,839
13.	Norman Y. Mineta* (D, San Jose)	134,734
	Ernest L. Konnyu (R, Saratoga)	62,888
14.	John J. McFall* (D, Manteca)	122,349
	Roger A. Blain (R, Stockton)	46,323

Dist.	Representative (Party, Home)	1976 Election
15.	B.F. Sisk* (D, Fresno)	92,200
	Carol Harner (R, Mariposa)	36,851
16.	Leon E. Panetta (D, Carmel Valley)	103,872
	Burt Talcott* (R, Salinas)	90,490
17.	John Krebs* (D, Fresno)	102,521
	Henry J. Andreas (R, Sanger)	53,609
18.	Dean Close (D, Bakersfield)	56,431
	William M. Ketchum* (R, Bakersfield)	101,093
19.	Dan Sisson (D, Santa Barbara)	68,399
	Robert J. Lagomarsino* (R, Ventura)	123,598
20.	Patti Lear Corman (D, Encino)	70,420
	Barry Goldwater Jr.*(R, Woodland Hills)	144,748
21.	James C. Corman* (D, Van Nuys)	100,628
	Erwin "Ed" Hogan (R, Panorama City)	43,536
22.	Robert L. Salley (D, Altadena)	67,543
	Carlos J. Moorhead* (R, Glendale)	112,885
23.	Anthony C. Beilenson (D, Los Angeles)	128,742
	Thomas F. Bartman (R, Sherman Oaks)	85,252
24.	Henry A. Waxman* (D, Los Angeles)	106,676
	David Irving Simmons (R, Los Angeles)	50,449
25.	Edward R. Roybal* (D, Los Angeles)	57,257
	Jim Madrid (R, Los Angeles)	17,368
26.	John H. Rousselot* (R, San Marino)	111,179
	Lotta (Dem.)	58,472
27.	Gary Familian (D, Marina Del Rey)	93,414
	Robert K. Dornan (R, Los Angeles)	112,675
28.	Yvonne Brathwaite Burke* (D, Los Angeles)	113,390
	Edward S. Skinner (R, El Monte)	27,894
29.	Augustus F. "Gus" Hawkins* (D, Los Angeles)	81,688
	Michael D. Germonprez (R, Los Angeles)	10,684
30.	George E. Danielson* (D, Monterey Park)	81,966
	Harry Couch (R, Monterey Park)	28,167
31.	Charles H. Wilson* (D, Hawthorne)	Unopposed
32.	Glenn M. Anderson* (D, Harbor City)	91,163
	Clifford C. Young (R, Carson)	34,937
33.	Ted Snyder (D, Whittier)	77,037
	Del Clawson* (R, Downey)	94,310
34.	Mark W. Hannaford* (D, Lakewood)	99,858
	Daniel E. Lungren (R, Long Beach)	96,992
35.	Jim Lloyd* (D, West Covina)	86,858
	Louis Brutocao (R, Covina)	76,110
36.	George E. Brown Jr.* (D, Colton)	90,415
	Grant Carner (R, Riverside)	49,075
37.	Douglas C. Nilson Jr. (D, Mentone)	48,768
	Shirley N. Pettis* (R, Loma Linda)	132,997
38.	Jerry Patterson* (D, Buena Park)	101,962
	James (Jim) Combs (R, Costa Mesa)	58,279
39.	William E. "Bill" Farris (D, Orange)	84,855
	Charles E. Wiggins* (R, Fullerton)	119,338
40.	Vivian Hall (D, Irvine)	99,042
	Robert E. Badham (R, Newport Beach)	143,336
41.	King Golden Jr. (D, San Diego)	93,178
	Bob C. Wilson* (R, San Diego)	126,609
42.	Lionel Van Deerlin*(D,Chula Vista)	101,364
	Wes Marden (R, Chula Vista)	31,850
43.	Pat Kelly (D, Vista)	92,300
	Clair W. Burgener* (R, La Jolla)	170,749
	Colorado	
1.	Patricia Schroeder* (D, Denver)	103,038
	Don Friedman (R, Denver)	89,384
2.	Timothy E. Wirth* (D, Denver)	118,520
	Ed Scott (R, Lakewood)	116,631
3.	Frank E. Evans* (D, Beulah)	92,334
	Melvin H. Takaki (R, Pueblo)	81,015

Dist.	Representative (Party, Home)	1976 Election
4.	Daniel M. Ogden Jr. (D, Fort Collins)	73,846
	James P. Johnson* (R, Fort Collins)	**111,892**
5.	Dorothy Hores (D, Littleton)	63,942
	William L. Armstrong* (R, Aurora)	**126,669**

Connecticut

1.	William R. Cotter* (D, Hartford)	**128,052**
	Lucien P. Di Fazior Jr. (R, Hartford)	93,768
2.	Christopher J. Dodd* (D, North Stonington)	**139,095**
	Richard M. Jackson (R, Willimantic)	73,521
3.	Robert N. Giaimo* (D, North Haven)	**121,154**
	John G. Pucciano (R, Orange)	97,019
4.	Geoffrey N. Peterson (D, Westport)	76,601
	Stewart B. McKinney* (R, Fairfield)	**126,311**
5.	Michael J. Adanti (D, Ansonia)	77,166
	Ronald A. Sarasin* (R, Beacon Falls)	**149,812**
6.	Anthony Tobe Moffett** (D, Unionville)	**130,997**
	Thomas F. Upson (R, Watertown)	100,236

Delaware - At Large

	Samuel L. Shipley (D, Wilmington)	102,229
	Thomas B. Evans Jr. (R, Wilmington)	**110,700**

Florida

1.	Robert L. F. Sikes* (D, Crestview)	**Unopposed**
2.	Don Fuqua* (D, Altha)	**Unopposed**
3.	Charles E. Bennett* (D, Jacksonville)	**Unopposed**
4.	Bill Chappell Jr.* (D, Ocala)	**Unopposed**
5.	Jo Ann Saunders (D, Orlando)	92,903
	Richard Kelly* (R, Holiday)	**130,326**
6.	Gabriel Cazares (D, Clearwater)	78,131
	C.W. Bill Young* (R, St. Petersburg)	**142,487**
7.	Sam Gibbons* (D, Tampa)	**98,232**
	Dusty Owens (R, Temple Terrace)	51,421
8.	Andy Ireland (D, Winter Haven)	**98,952**
	Bob Johnson (R, Sarasota)	69,918
9.	Joseph A. Rosier (D, Winter Park)	34,077
	Louis Frey Jr.* (R, Winter Park)	**121,564**
10.	Bill Sikes (D, Clewiston)	81,065
	L.A. (Skip) Bafalis*, (R, Fort Myers Beach)	**158,413**
11.	Paul G. Rogers* (D, West Palm Beach)	**188,106**
	Adams (A)	17,490
12.	Charlie Friedman (D, Hollywood)	87,606
	J. Herbert Burke* (R, Hollywood)	**101,292**
13.	William Lehman* (D, North Miami Beach)	**122,580**
	Lee Arnold Spiegelman (R, Miami Shores)	33,891
14.	Claude Pepper* (D, Miami)	**78,544**
	Evelio S. Estrella (R, Miami)	29,678
15.	Dante B. Fascell* (D, Miami)	**114,507**
	Paul R. Cobb (R, Miami)	47,576

Georgia

1.	Bo Ginn* (D, Millen)	**Unopposed**
2.	Dawson Mathis* (D, Albany)	**Unopposed**
3.	Jack Brinkley* (D, Columbus)	**88,612**
	Steven Dugan (R, Warner Robins)	11,088
4.	Elliott H. Levitas* (D, Atlanta)	**102,837**
	George T. Warren II (R, Decatur)	47,965
5.	Andrew Young* (D, Atlanta)	**95,955**
	Edward W. Gadrix (R, Atlanta)	47,965
6.	John J. Flynt Jr. (D, Griffin)	**76,831**
	Newt Gingrich (R, Carrollton)	71,844
7.	Larry P. McDonald* (D, Marietta)	**83,275**
	Quincy Collins (R, Marietta)	68,221
8.	Bill Lee Evans (D, Macon)	**87,767**
	Billy Adams (R, Macon)	38,859
9.	Ed Jenkins (D, Jaspar)	**105,310**
	Louise Wofford (R, Gainesville)	26,784
10.	Doug Barnard (D, Augusta)	**Unopposed**

Hawaii

1.	Cecil L. Heftel (D, Honolulu)	**60,050**
	Frederick Rohlfing (R, Honolulu)	53,745

Dist.	Representative (Party, Home)	1976 Election
2.	Daniel K. Akaka (D, Honolulu)	**124,116**
	Hank Inouye (R, Honolulu)	23,917

Idaho

1.	Ken Pursley (D, Boise)	79,194
	Steven D. Symms* (R, Caldwell)	**95,371**
2.	Stan Kress (D, Firth)	82,240
	George Hansen* (R, Pocatello)	**84,442**

Illinois

1.	Ralph H. Metcalfe* (D, Chicago)	**124,924**
	A.A. Rayner Jr. (R, Chicago)	10,137
2.	Morgan F. Murphy* (D, Chicago)	**122,808**
	Spencer Leak (R, Chicago)	22,476
3.	Martin A. Russo* (D, S. Holland)	**113,945**
	Ronald Buikema (R, S. Holland)	79,313
4.	Ronald A. Rodger (D, Tinley Park)	62,513
	Edward Derwinski* (R, Flossmoor)	**120,560**
5.	John G. Fary* (D, Chicago)	**116,650**
	Vincent Krok (R, Chicago)	35,661
6.	Marilyn D. Clancy (D, Oak Park)	68,258
	Henry J. Hyde* (R, Park Ridge)	**104,165**
7.	Cardiss Collins* (D, Chicago)	**84,749**
	Newell Ward (R, Chicago)	15,536
8.	Daniel D. Rostenkowski* (D, Chicago)	**103,418**
	John F. Urbaszewski (R, Chicago)	25,909
9.	Sidney R. Yates* (D, Chicago)	**120,346**
	Thomas J. Wajerski (R, Chicago)	46,443
10.	Abner J. Mikva* (D, Evanston)	105,487
	Samuel H. Young (R, Glenview)	105,280
11.	Frank Annunzio* (D, Chicago)	**133,017**
	Daniel C. Reber (R, Chicago)	64,190
12.	Edwin L. Frank (D, Hoffman Estates)	54,720
	Philip M. Crane* (R, Mount Prospect)	**146,894**
13.	James J. Cummings (D, Barrington)	49,762
	Robert McClory* (R, Lake Bluff)	**109,682**
14.	Marie Agnes Fese (D, Elmhurst)	60,433
	John Erlenborn* (R, Glen Ellyn)	**175,889**
15.	Tim L. Hall* (D, Dwight)	87,677
	Tom Corcoran (R, Ottawa)	**102,538**
16.	Stephen Eytalis (D, Rockford)	53,125
	John B. Anderson* (R, Rockford)	**112,208**
17.	Merlin Karlock (D, Momence)	81,090
	George M. O'Brien* (R, Joliet)	**112,570**
18.	Matthew Ryan (D, Washington)	71,432
	Robert H. Michel* (R, Peoria)	**98,013**
19.	John Craver (D, London Mills)	60,753
	Tom Railsback* (R, Moline)	**130,219**
20.	Peter Mack (D, Springfield)	78,063
	Paul Findley* (R, Pittsfield)	**136,190**
21.	Anna Wall Scott (D, Urbana)	46,982
	Edward R. Madigan* (R, Lincoln)	**137,074**
22.	George E. Shipley* (D, Olney)	**127,635**
	Ralph Y. McGinnis (R, Charleston)	79,869
23.	Melvin Price* (D, E. St. Louis)	**126,122**
	Sam P. Drenovac (R, Granite City)	35,044
24.	Paul Simon (D, Carbondale)	**146,657**
	Peter G. Prineas (R, Carbondale)	72,162

Indiana

1.	Adam Benjamin Jr. (D, Hobart)	**121,155**
	Robert J. Billings (R, Dyer)	48,756
2.	Floyd J. Fithian* (D, Lafayette)	**117,592**
	William W. Erwin (R, Bourbon)	95,920
3.	John Brademas* (D, South Bend)	**99,264**
	Thomas L. Thorson (R, LaPorte)	75,914
4.	J. Edward Roush* (D, Huntington)	86,265
	J. Danforth Quayle (R, Huntington)	**105,516**
5.	William C. Stout (D, Rochester)	77,723
	Elwood Hillis* (R, Kokomo)	**125,897**
6.	David W. Evans* (D, Indianapolis)	**103,453**
	David G. Crane (R, Martinsville)	85,061
7.	John E. Tipton (D, Jasonville)	74,441
	John T. Myers* (R, Covington)	**126,344**

Dist.	Representative (Party, Home)	1976 Election
8.	David L. Cornwell (D, Paoli)	108,997
	Belden Bell (R, Evansville)	106,974
9.	Lee H. Hamilton* (D, Columbus)	**Unopposed**
10.	Philip R. Sharp* (D, Muncie)	114,277
	William G. Frazier (R, Muncie)	76,649
11.	Andrew Jacobs Jr.* (D, Indianapolis)	110,588
	Lawrence L. Buell (R, Indianapolis)	70,212

Iowa

Dist.	Representative (Party, Home)	1976 Election
1.	Edward Mezvinsky* (D, Iowa City)	99,970
	James A.S. Leach (R, Bettendorf)	108,762
2.	Michael T. Blouin* (D, Dubuque)	102,960
	Tom Riley (R, Cedar Rapids)	100,468
3.	Stephen J. Rapp (D, Waterloo)	90,774
	Charles E. Grassley* (R, Clear Lake)	118,287
4.	Neal Smith* (D, Altoona)	144,820
	Charles E. Minor (R, Mitchellville)	64,894
5.	Tom Harkin* (D, Ames)	135,509
	Kenneth R. Fulk (R, Clarinda)	71,394
6.	Berkley Bedell* (D, Spirit Lake)	133,343
	Joanne D. Soper (R, Sioux City)	62,233

Kansas

Dist.	Representative (Party, Home)	1976 Election
1.	Randy Yowell (D, Hays)	52,588
	Keith G. Sebelius* (R, Norton)	141,635
2.	Martha Keys* (D, Manhattan)	88,451
	Ross Freeman (R, Topeka)	82,400
3.	Philip S. Rhoads (D, Kansas City)	52,076
	Larry Winn Jr.* (R, Overland Park)	122,757
4.	Dan Glickman (D, Wichita)	89,855
	Garner E. Shriver* (R, Wichita)	86,726
5.	Virgil Leon Olson (D, Chanute)	65,082
	Joe Skubitz* (R, Pittsburg)	108,848

Kentucky

Dist.	Representative (Party, Home)	1976 Election
1.	Carroll Hubbard Jr.*(D, Mayfield)	118,101
	Bob Bersky (R, Sturgis)	26,086
2.	William H. Natcher* (D, Bowling Green)	64,389
	Walter A. Baker (R, Glasgow)	40,967
3.	Romano L. Mazzoli* (D, Louisville)	77,440
	Denzil J. Ramsey (R, Louisville)	56,868
4.	Edward J. Winterberg (D, Covington)	76,152
	Gene Snyder* (R, Brownsboro Farms)	95,536
5.	Charles C. Smith (D, Williamsburg)	76,152
	Tim Lee Carter* (R, Tomkinsville)	101,810
6.	John B. Breckinridge* (D, Lexington)	90,616
7.	Carl D. Perkins* (D, Hindman)	110,369
	Granville Thomas (R, London)	40,429

Louisiana

Dist.	Representative (Party, Home)	1976 Election
1.	Richard A. Tonry (D, Arabi)	59,745
	Robert L. Livingston (R, Algiers)	54,724
2.	Lindy (Mrs. Hale) Boggs* (D, New Orleans)	83,914
3.	David H. "Pro" Scheuermann Jr. Jr. (D, Metairie)	39,779
	David C. Treen* (R, Metairie)	106,666
4.	Joe D. Waggonner Jr.* (D, Plain Dealing)	**Unopposed**
5.	Jerry Huckaby (D, Ringgold)	81,669
	Frank Spooner (R, Monroe)	74,336
6.	J.D. De-Blieux (D, Baton Rouge)	52,829
	W. Henson Moore* (R, Baton Rouge)	97,833
7.	John B. Breaux* (D, Crowley)	116,338
	Charles F. "Chuck" Huff, (R, Lafayette)	23,518
8.	Gillis W. Long* (D, Alexandria)	105,684
	Courtney (I)	6,574

Maine

Dist.	Representative (Party, Home)	1976 Election
1.	Frederick D. Barton (D, Portland)	107,863
	David F. Emery* (R, Augusta)	142,579
2.	Leighton Cooney (D, Sabattus)	42,955
	William S. Cohen* (R, Bangor)	168,932

Maryland

Dist.	Representative (Party, Home)	1976 Election
1.	Roy Dyson (D, Great Mills)	69,791
	Robert E. Bauman* (R, Easton)	80,812
2.	Clarence D. Long* (D, Ruxton)	135,025
	John M. Seney (R, Towson)	34,226
3.	Barbara A. Mikulski (D, Baltimore)	104,168
	Samuel A. Culotta (R, Baltimore)	35,503
4.	Werner Fornos (D, Davidsonville)	68,233
	Marjorie S. Holt* (R, Severna Park)	92,250
5.	Gladys Noon Spellman* (D, Laurel)	75,910
	John Burcham (R, Lanham)	55,956
6.	Goodloe E. Byron* (D, Frederick)	124,493
	Arthur T. Bond (R, Frostburg)	50,269
7.	Parren J. Mitchell* (D, Baltimore)	92,760
8.	Lanny Davis (D, Silver Spring)	93,973
	Newton I. Steers Jr. (R, Bethesda)	105,650

Massachusetts

Dist.	Representative (Party, Home)	1976 Election
1.	Edward A. McColgan (D, Easthampton)	77,406
	Silvio O. Conte* (R, Pittsfield)	136,788
2.	Edward P. Boland* (D, Springfield)	135,827
	Thomas P. Swank (R, Springfield)	41,765
3.	Joseph D. Early* (D, Worchester)	**Unopposed**
4.	Robert F. Drinan* (D, Newton)	108,687
	Arthur D. Mason (R, Brookline)	100,275
5.	Paul E. Tsongas* (D, Lowell)	121,832
	Roger P. Durkin (R, Lowell)	58,173
6.	Michael Harrington* (D, Beverly)	120,583
	William E. Bronson (R, Manchester)	91,164
7.	Edward J. Markey (D, Malden)	156,421
	Richard W. Daly (R, Melrose)	35,574
8.	Thomas P. O'Neill Jr. * (D, Cambridge)	122,764
	William A. Barnstead (R, Arlington)	28,741
9.	Joe Moakley* (D, Boston)	102,981
	Robert G. Cunningham (R, Westwood)	34,584
10.	Margaret M. Heckler* (R, Wellesley)	**Unopposed**
11.	James A. Burke* (D, Milton)	129,697
12.	Gerry E. Studds* (D, Cohasset)	Unopposed

Michigan

Dist.	Representative (Party, Home)	1976 Election
1.	John Conyers Jr.* (D, Detroit)	124,672
	Isaac Hood (R, Detroit)	8,967
2.	Edward C. Pierce (D, Ann Arbor)	93,934
	Carl D. Pursell (R, Plymouth)	93,419
3.	Howard Wolpe (D, Kalamazoo)	95,235
	Garry Brown* (R, Schoolcraft)	99,125
4.	Richard E. Daugherty (D, Dowagiac)	68,534
	Dave Stockman (R, St. Joseph)	107,191
5.	Richard F. Vander Veen* (D, Grand Rapids)	95,707
	Harold S. Sawyer (R, Rockford)	110,559
6.	Bob Carr* (D, East Lansing)	108,882
	Clifford W. Taylor (R, East Lansing)	95,983
7.	Dale E. Kildee (D, Flint)	124,260
	Robin Widgery (R, Flint)	50,401
8.	Bob Traxler* (D, Bay City)	106,739
	E. Brady Denton (R, Saginaw)	75,019
9.	Stephen E. Fawley (D, Hudsonville)	61,790
	Guy A. Vander Jagt* (R, Luther)	146,710
10.	Donald J. Albosta (D, Charles)	89,905
	Elford A. Cederberg* (R, Midland)	118,945
11.	Francis Brouillette (D, Iron Mountain)	93,952
	Philip E. Ruppe* (R, Houghton)	112,167
12.	David E. Bonior (D, Clemens)	91,966
	David M. Serotkin (R, Clemens)	83,896
13.	Charles C. Diggs Jr.* (D, Detroit)	82,594
	Richard A. Golden (R, Detroit)	9,084
14.	Lucien N. Nedzi* (D, Detroit)	107,373
	John Edward Getz (R, Grosse Pointe Farms)	52,967
15.	William D. Ford* (D, Taylor)	100,903
	James D. Walaskey (R, Plymouth)	34,390
16.	John D. Dingell* (D, Trenton)	121,128
	William E. Rostron (R, Detroit)	36,044
17.	William M. Brodhead* (D, Detroit)	94,289
	James W. Burdick (R, Southfield)	50,241

Dist.	Representative (Party, Home)	1976 Election
18.	James J. Blanchard* (D, Pleasant Ridge) . . .	123,113
	John E. Olsen (R, Huntington Woods)	61,005
19.	Dorthea Becker (D, Birmingham).	64,462
	William S. Broomfield* (R, Birmingham). . : . .	131,487

Minnesota

Dist.	Representative (Party, Home)	1976 Election
1.	Robert C. "Bob" Olson Jr. (D, Kasson)	70,463
	Albert H. Quie* (R, Dennison)	158,697
2.	Gloria Griffin (D, Excelsior).	96,973
	Tom Hagedorn* (R, Truman).	148,669
3.	Jerome W. Coughlin (D, Brooklyn Park)	71,624
	Bill Frenzel* (R, Golden Valley).	148,694
4.	Bruce F. Vento (D, St. Paul).	132,333
	Andrew Engerbretson (R, St. Paul).	59,627
5.	Donald M. Fraser* (D, Minneapolis)	143,438
	Richard M. Erdall (R, Minneapolis)	50,348
6.	Richard Nolan* (D, Waite Park).	147,224
	James "Jim" Anderson (R, Marshall).	99,120
7.	Bob Bergland* (D, Roseau).	173,818
	Bob Leiseth (R, Lake Park).	64,477
8.	James L. Oberstar* (D, Chisholm).	Unopposed

Mississippi

Dist.	Representative (Party, Home)	1976 Election
1.	Jamie L. Whitten* (D, Charleston).	Unopposed
2.	David R. Bowen* (D, Cleveland).	70,111
	Roland Byrd (R, Louisville)	42,095
3.	G. V. (Sonny) Montgomery* (D, Meridian). . .	127,240
	Dorothy Colby Cleveland (R, Union).	13,258
4.	Sterling P. Davis (D, Vicksburg).	27,611
	Thad Cochran* (R, Jackson).	101,808
5.	Gerald Blessey (D, Biloxi).	48,698
	Trent Lott* (R, Pascagoula).	104,597

Missouri

Dist.	Representative (Party, Home)	1976 Election
1.	William (Bill) Clay* (D, St. Louis).	85,456
	Robert L. Witherspoon (R, St. Louis)	45,321
2.	Robert A. Young (D, St. Ann).	111,366
	Robert O. Snyder (R, Kirkwood).	106,571
3.	Richard A. Gephardt (D, St. Louis)·.	111,807
	Joseph L. Badaracco (R, St. Louis)	64,069
4.	Ike Skelton (D, Lexington)	115,364
	Richard A. King (R, Independence)	91,700
5.	Richard Bolling* (D, Kansas City)	99,778
	Joanne M. Collins (R, Kansas City)	41,216
6.	Morgan Maxfield (D, Kansas City)	83,197
	E. Thomas Coleman (R, Kansas City)	119,521
7.	Dolan G. Hawkins (D, Springfield)	80,077
	Gene Taylor* (R, Sarcoxie).	130,636
8.	Richard H. Ichord* (D, Houston).	131,052
	Charles R. Leick (R, Davisville)	59,591
9.	Harold L. Volkmer (D, Hannibal).	120,192
	Joe Frappier (R, Forissant).	94,630
10.	Bill D. Burlison* (D, Cape Girardeau)	129,425
	Joe Carron (R, Arnold).	50,441

Montana

Dist.	Representative (Party, Home)	1976 Election
1.	Max Baucus* (D, Missoula).	109,511
	W. D. "Bill" Diehl (R, Helena).	54,985
2.	Thomas E. "Tom" Towe (D, Billings)	67,044
	Ron Marlenee (R, Scobey)	82,418

Nebraska

Dist.	Representative (Party, Home)	1976 Election
1.	Pauline F. Anderson (D, Lincoln)	53,127
	Charles Thone* (R, Lincoln).	144,589
2.	John J. Cavanaugh (D, Omaha).	103,313
	Lee Terry (R, Omaha).	85,149
3.	James Thomas Hansen (D, Gering)	49,724
	Virginia Smith* (R, Chappell).	147,121

Nevada — At Large

Dist.	Representative (Party, Home)	1976 Election
	Jim Santini* (D, Las Vegas).	153,201
	Walden Charles Earhart (R, Carson City)	24,005

New Hampshire

Dist.	Representative (Party, Home)	1976 Election
1.	Norman E. D'Amours* (D, Manchester)	108,563
	John Adams (R, Exeter)	48,207
2.	J. Joseph Grandmaison (D, Nashua).	64,577
	James C. Cleveland* (R, New London)	98,966

New Jersey

Dist.	Representative (Party, Home)	1976 Election
1.	James J. Florio* (D, Camden)	134,918
	Joseph I. McCullough Jr. (R, Haddon Heights).	55,161
2.	William J. Hughes* (D, Ocean City)	138,120
	James R. Hurley (R, Millville).	84,834
3.	James J. Howard* (D, Spring Lake Heights) .	121,407
	Ralph A. Siciliano (R, Red Bank)	72,396
4.	Frank Thompson Jr.* (D. Trenton).	111,176
	Joseph S. Indyk (R, Jamesburg).	55,403
5.	Frank R. Nero (D, North Plainfield).	63,861
	Millicent H. Fenwick* (R, Bernardsville).	136,647
6.	Catherine A. Costa (D, Willingboro).	81,470
	Edwin B. Forsythe* (R, Morristown)	120,095
7.	Andrew Maguire* (D, Ridgewood).	120,475
	James J. Sheehan (R, Wyckoff)	92,589
8.	Robert A. Roe* (D, Wayne)	108,714
	Bessie Doty (R, Haskell).	44,775
9.	Henry Helstoski* (D, Rutherford).	89,728
	Harold C. Hollenbeck (R, E. Rutherford). . . .	107,413
10.	Peter W. Rodino Jr.* (D, Newark).	89,647
	Tony Grandison (R, Newark).	16,678
11.	Joseph G. Minish* (D, West Orange).	119,326
	Charles A. Poekel Jr. (R. Essex Fells)	58,266
12.	Richard A. Buggelli (D, Union).	47,159
	Matthew J. Rinaldo* (R, Union).	130,060
13.	Helen S. Meyner* (D, Phillipsburg).	104,443
	William E. Schluter (R, Pennington).	99,231
14.	Joseph A. Le Fante (D, Bayonne).	73,177
	Anthony Louis Campenni (R, Bayonne).	66,312
15.	Edward J. Patten* (D, Perth Amboy).	104,702
	Charles W. Wiley (R, Sayreville).	54,298

New Mexico

Dist.	Representative (Party, Home)	1976 Election
1.	Raymond Garcia (D, Albuquerque)	60,577
	Manuel Lujan Jr.* (R, Albuquerque).	158,732
2.	Harold Runnels* (D, Lovington).	123,180
	Donald W. Trubey (R, Portales).	52,286

New York

Dist.	Representative (Party, Home)	1976 Election
1.	Otis G. Pike* (D, L, Riverhead).	127,692
	Salvatore Nicosia (R, Holbrook).	58,867
	Seth C. Morgan (C, Manorville)	9,610
2.	Thomas J. Downey* (D, West Islip)	90,260
	Peter F. Cohalan (R, C, Bayport).	67,040
	Rochelle Davidson (L, Deer Park)	993
3.	Jerome A. Ambro Jr.* (D, East Northport) . . .	91,843
	Howard T. Hogan Jr. (R, Lattingtown).	83,899
	Hy York (L, Jericho).	2,413
4.	Gerald P. Halpern (D, L, Freeport).	83,323
	Norman F. Lent* (R, C, East Rockaway)	105,202
5.	Allard K. Lowenstein (D, L, Long Beach)	87,977
	John W. Wydler* (R, C, Garden City)	110,932
6.	Lester L. Wolff* (D, L, Great Neck).	111,684
	Vincent R. Balletta Jr. (R, Port Washington) . .	60,921
	Nelson J. Gammans (C, Oyster Bay).	8,880
7.	Joseph P. Addabbo* (D, R, L, Ozone Park) . .	96,136
	William H. Whitman (C, Ozone Park)	9,421
8.	Benjamin S. Rosenthal* (D, L, Elmhurst). . . .	105,755
	Albert Lemishow (R, C, Flushing).	30,584
9.	James J. Delaney* (D, R, C, Long Island City)	107,788
	Alan M. Kluger (L, Flushing).	6,243
10.	Mario Biaggi* (D, Bronx).	102,931
	John P. Hagan (L, Bronx)	4,026
	Joanne S. Fuchs (C, Bronx).	7,100
11.	James H. Scheuer* (D, Neponsit)	83,073
	Arthur Cuccia (R, Brooklyn)	19,101
	Joseph Rothenberg (L, Rockaway Park)	4,203
	Bryan F. Levinson (C, Howard Beach).	6,291

Dist.	Representative (Party, Home)	1976 Election
12.	Shirley Chisholm* (D, L, Brooklyn)	41,790
	Horace L. Morancie (R, Brooklyn)	5,291
	Martin S. Shepherd Jr. (C, Brooklyn)	1,090
13.	Stephen J. Solarz* (D, L, Brooklyn)	107,595
	Jack Dobosh (R, C, Brooklyn)	21,235
14.	Frederick W. Richmond* (D, L, Brooklyn)	51,832
	Frank X. Gargiulo (R, C, Brooklyn)	8,789
15.	Leo C. Zeferetti* (D, C, Brooklyn)	69,019
	Ronald J. D'Angelo (R, Brooklyn)	33,935
16.	Elizabeth Holtzman* (D, L, Brooklyn)	89,910
	Gladys Pemberton (R, C, Brooklyn)	18,019
17.	John M. Murphy* (D, L, Staten Island)	85,030
	Kenneth J. Grossberger (R, New York)	26,518
	John M. Peters (C, Staten Island)	9,940
	Ned Schneier (L, New York)	8,404
18.	Edward I. Koch* (D, L, New York)	110,466
	Sonia Landau (R, New York)	29,673
	James W. McConnell (C, New York)	6,454
19.	Charles B. Rangel* (D, R, L, New York)	84,466
	Benton Cole (C, New York)	5,795
20.	Theodore S. Weiss (D, L, New York)	87,697
	Denise T. Wiseman (R, New York)	14,162
	Herman Dinsmore (C, New York)	3,490
21.	Herman Badillo* (D, L, Bronx)	40,691
	Lawrence W. Lindsley Sr. (C, Bronx)	615
22.	Jonathan B. Bingham* (D, L, Bronx)	89,074
	Paul Slotkin (R, Bronx)	10,732
	Patrick J. Bonner (C, Bronx)	3,616
23.	J. Edward Meyer (D, L, New Castle)	75,079
	Bruce F. Caputo (R, C, Yonkers)	82,651
24.	Richard L. Ottinger* (D, Pleasantville)	95,246
	David V. Hicks (R, C, Briarcliff Manor)	78,658
	Edmund J. Assante (L, New Rochelle)	2,153
25.	Minna Post Peyser (D, L, Putnam Valley)	55,524
	Hamilton Fish Jr.* (R, Millbrook)	133,381
26.	John R. Maloney (D, Nanuet)	60,070
	Benjamin A. Gilman* (R, C, Middletown)	117,568
	Eugene R. Victor (L,)	3,299
27.	Matthew F. McHugh* (D, L, Ithaca)	122,083
	William H. Harter (R, C, Margaretville)	62,009
28.	Samuel S. Stratton* (D, L, Amsterdam)	160,722
	Mary A. Bradt (R, C, Schenectady)	42,582
29.	Edward W. Pattison* (D, L, West Sand Lake)	98,150
	Joesph A. Martino (R, C, Ballston Lake)	92,805
	James E. De Young (C,)	15,017
30.	Norma A. Bartle (D, L, Oswego)	72,283
	Robert C. McEwen* (R, C, Ogdensburg)	92,976
31.	Anita Maxwell (D, L, Newport)	58,649
	Donald J. Mitchell* (R, C, Herkimer)	138,620
32.	James M. Hanley* (D, Syracuse)	100,121
	George C. Wortley (R, C, Manlius)	79,797
	Earl W. Colvin (L, Syracuse)	2,107
33.	Charles R. Welch (D, Camillus)	49,186
	William F. Walsh* (R, Syracuse)	120,431
	Lillian Reiner (L, Syracuse)	2,576
	William C. Elkins (C, Burdett)	6,121
34.	William C. Larsen (D, L, Pittsford)	57,148
	Frank J. Horton* (R, Rochester)	122,650
	Thomas D. Cook (C, Pittsford)	7,185
35.	Michael Macaluso Sr. (D, L, Rochester)	66,650
	Barber B. Conable Jr.* (R, C, Alexander)	115,344
36.	John J. La Falce* (D, L, Kenmore)	121,459
	Ralph J. Argen (R, C, Eggertsville)	60,544
37.	Henry J. Nowak* (D, L, Buffalo)	98,321
	Calvin Kimbrough (R, Grand Island)	23,571
	Stephen Grimm (C, Buffalo)	4,293
38.	Peter J. Geraci (D, L, N. Tonawanda)	45,715
	Jack F. Kemp* (R, C, Hamburg)	163,278
39.	Stanley N. Lundine* (D, L, Jamestown)	106,858
	Richard A. Snowden (R, C, Olean)	66,092

North Carolina

Dist.	Representative (Party, Home)	1976 Election
1.	Walter B. Jones* (D, Farmville)	92,576
	Joseph M. Ward (R, Greenville)	26,099
2.	L. H. Fountain* (D, Tarboro)	Unopposed
3.	Charles Whitley (D, Mt. Olive)	77,193
	Willard J. (Jack) Blanchard (R, Salemburg)	35,386
4.	Ike Andrews* (D, Siler City)	95,543
	Johnnie L. Gallemore, Jr. (R, Durham)	56,086

Dist.	Representative (Party, Home)	1976 Election
5.	Stephen L. (Steve) Neal* (D, Winston-Salem)	97,887
	Wilmer (Vinegar Bend) Mizell (R, Winston-Salem)	82,746
6.	Richardson Preyer* (D, Greensboro)	101,273
	Wagle, LB.	2,060
7.	Charles G. Rose* (D, Fayetteville)	95,485
	M. H. (Mike) Vaughan (R, Wilmington)	21,842
8.	W. G. (Bill) Hefner* (D, Concord)	97,293
	Carl Eagle (R, Salisbury)	47,422
9.	Arthur Goodman Jr. (D. Charlotte)	70,969
	James G. Martin* (R, Davidson)	82,480
10.	John J. (Jack) Hunt (D, Lattimore)	67,168
	James T. (Jim) Broyhill* (R, Lenoir)	99,918
11.	Lamar Gudger (D, Asheville)	93,666
	Bruce Briggs (R, Mars Hill)	88,483

North Dakota - At Large

Lloyd B. Omdahl (D, Grand Forks)		100,897
Mark Andrews* (R, Mapleton)		175,611

Ohio

Dist.	Representative (Party, Home)	1976 Election
1.	William F. Bowen (D, Cincinnati)	56,936
	Willis D. Gradison Jr.* (R. Cincinnati)	109,674
2.	Thomas A. Luken (D, Cincinnati)	87,876
	Donald D. Clancy* (R, Cincinnati)	83,218
3.	Leonard E. Stubbs Jr. (D, Dayton)	34,008
	Charles W. Whalen Jr.* (R, Dayton)	100,812
4.	Clinton G. Dorsey (D, Troy)	52,013
	Tennyson Guyer* (R, Findlay)	121,039
5.	Bruce Edwards (D, Bowling Green)	60,254
	Delbert L. Latta* (R, Bowling Green)	124,919
6.	Ted Strickland (D, Lucasville)	66,479
	William H. Harsha* (R, Portsmouth)	106,185
7.	Dorothy Franke (D, Lucasville)	53,864
	Clarence J. Brown (R, Urbana)	98,820
8.	John W. Griffin (D, Miamisburg)	45,311
	Thomas N. Kindness* (R, Hamilton)	107,237
9.	Thomas Ludlow Ashley* (D, Maumee)	91,042
	Carleton S. Finkbeiner (R, Toledo)	73,857
10.	James A. Plummer (D, Jackson)	54,213
	Clarence E. Miller* (R, Lancaster)	121,374
11.	Thomas R. West Jr. (D, Hubbard)	46,743
	J. William Stanton* (R, Painesville)	116,992
12.	Francine Ryan (D, Columbus)	89,271
	Samuel L. Devine* (R, Columbus)	91,181
13.	Donald J. Pease (D, Oberlin)	105,085
	Woodrow W. Mathna (R, Lorain)	49,219
14.	John F. Seiberling* (D, Akron)	118,684
	James E. Houston (R, Akron)	39,129
15.	Mike McGee (D, Columbus)	57,565
	Chalmers P. Wylie* (R, Worthington)	108,772
16.	John G. Freedom (D, North Canton)	55,312
	Ralph Regula* (R, Navarre)	115,579
17.	John C. McDonald (D, Newark)	72,134
	John M. Ashbrook* (R, Johnstown)	94,860
18.	Douglas Appelgate (D, Steubenville)	116,797
	Ralph R. McCoy (R, Woodsfield)	45,597
19.	Charles J. Carney* (D, Youngstown)	90,538
	Jack C. Hunter (R, Youngstown)	85,864
20.	Mary Rose Oakar (D, Cleveland)	98,128
	Grabow (D)	20,450
21.	Louis Stokes* (D, Warrensville Heights)	91,203
	Barbara Sparks (R, Shaker Heights)	12,433
22.	Charles A. Vanik* (D, Euclid)	126,446
	Harry A. Hanna (R, Shaker Heights)	41,443
23.	Ronald M. Mottl* (D, Parma)	130,591
	Michael T. Scanlon (R, North Olmsted)	47,764

Oklahoma

Dist.	Representative (Party, Home)	1976 Election
1.	James R. Jones* (D, Tulsa)	100,501
	James J. Inhofe (R, Tulsa)	84,141
2.	Theodore M. (Ted) Risenhoover* (D, Tahlequah)	102,303
	Bud Stewart (R, Muskogee)	87,314
3.	Wes Watkins (D, Ada)	150,953
	Gerald Beasley Jr. (R, Duncan)	31,758
4.	Tom Steed* (D, Shawnee)	114,692
	M. C. Stanley (R, Midwest City)	33,172

Dist.	Representative (Party, Home)	1976 Election
5.	Tom Dunlap (D, Oklahoma City)	73,146
	Mickey Edwards (R, Oklahoma City)	75,398
6.	Glenn English* (D, Cordell)	136,265
	Carol McCurley (R, Yukon)	56,120

Oregon

1.	Les AuCoin* (D, Forest Grove)	151,774
	Phil Bladine (R, McMinnville)	106,777
2.	Al Ullman,* (D, Baker)	167,851
	Thomas H. Mercer (R, Bend)	64,947
3.	Robert B. Duncan* (D, Portland)	147,031
	Simon (I)	27,897
4.	James Weaver (D, Eugene)	124,737
	Jerry Lausmann (R, Medford)	85,647

Pennsylvania

1.	Michael O. Myers (D, Philadelphia)	115,755
	Samuel N. Fanelli (R, Philadelphia)	40,362
2.	Robert N. C. Nix* (D, Philadelphia)	108,384
	Jesse W. Woods Jr. (R, Philadelphia)	37,173
3.	Raymond F. Lederer (D, Philadelphia)	98,055
	Terence J. Schade (R, Philadelphia)	35,407
4.	Joshua Eilberg* (D, Philadelphia)	143,291
	James E. Mugford (R, Philadelphia)	68,179
5.	Anthony Campolo (D, St. Davids)	76,721
	Richard T. Schulze* (R, Malvern)	119,353
6.	Gus Yatron* (D, Reading)	133,583
	Stephen Postupack (R, Tamaqua)	46,251
7.	Robert W. Edgar* (D, Bromall)	106,769
	John M. Kenney (R, Swarthmore)	90,922
8.	Peter H. Kostmayer (D, Solebury)	93,156
	John S. Renninger (R, Newton)	91,884
9.	Bud Shuster* (R, Everett)	Unopposed
10.	Edward Mitchell (D, Scranton)	74,753
	Joseph M. McDade* (R, Scranton)	125,209
11.	Daniel J. Flood* (D, Wilkes-Barre)	129,800
	Howard G. Williams (R, Wilkes-Barre)	53,289
12.	John P. Murtha* (D, Johnstown)	121,824
	Theodore L. Humes (R, Johnstown)	57,902
13.	Gertrude Strick (D, Jenkintown)	75,704
	Lawrence Coughlin* (R, Villanova)	131,182
14.	William S. Moorhead* (D, Pittsburgh)	113,428
	John F. Bradley (R, Pittsburgh)	43,090
15.	Fred B. Rooney* (D, Bethlehem)	70,873
	Alica B. Sullivan (R, Easton)	37,829
16.	Michael J. Minney (D, Lancaster)	56,289
	Robert S. Walker (R, East Petersburg)	96,151
17.	Allen E. Ertel (D, Montoursville)	86,461
	H. J. Hepford (R, Harrisburg)	82,799
18.	Douglas Walgren (D, Pittsburgh)	113,253
	Robert J. Casey (R, Pittsburgh)	77,420
19.	Richard P. Noll (D, York)	51,563
	William F. Goodling* (R, Jacobus)	123,685
20.	Joesph M. Gaydos* (D, McKeesport)	134,361
	Joseph P. Kostelac (R, White Oak)	44,688
21.	John H. Dent* (D, Greensburg)	99,097
	Robert H. Miller (R, Greensburg)	67,731
22.	Austin J. Murphy (D, Monongahela)	92,585
	Roger R. Fischer (R, Washington)	74,823
23.	Joseph S. Ammerman (D, Curwensville)	96,054
	Albert W. Johnson* (R, Smethport)	73,220
24.	Joseph P. Vigorito* (D, Erie)	79,566
	Marc L. Marks (R, Sharon)	100,764
25.	Eugene V. Atkinson (D, Aliquippa)	78,356
	Gary A. Myers* (R, Butler)	102,583

Rhode Island

1.	Fernand J. St. Germain* (d, Woonsocket)	112,771
	John J. Slocum Jr. (R, Newport)	65,215
2.	Edward P. Beard* (D, Cranston)	150,636
	Thomas V. Iannitfi (R, West Warwick)	43,815

South Carolina

1.	Mendel J. Davis* (D, Charleston)	85,934
	Lonnie Rowell (R, Summerville)	39,262
2.	Clyde Burns Livingston (D, Orangeburg)	59,989
	Floyd D. Spence* (R, Lexington)	83,136
3.	Butler C. Derrick* (D, Edgefield)	Unopposed

Dist.	Representative (Party, Home)	1976 Election
4.	James R. Mann* (D, Greenville)	92,249
	Robert L. Watkins (R, Greenville)	33,165
5.	Kenneth L. Holland* (D, Camden)	64,538
	Robert C. Richardson Jr. (R, Sumter)	60,164
6.	John W. Jenrette Jr.*(D, North Myrtle Beach)	74,980
	Edward L. Young (R, Florence)	59,798

South Dakota

1.	James V. Guffey (D, Watertown)	29,090
	Larry Pressler* (R, Humboldt)	120,314
2.	Grace Mickelson (D, Rapid City)	43,663
	James Abdnor* (R, Kennebec)	99,426

Tennessee

1.	Lloyd H. Blevins (D, Kingsport)	59,535
	James H. (Jimmy) Quillen* (R, Kingsport)	82,954
2.	Mike Rowland (D, Knoxville)	68,775
	John J. Duncan* (R, Knoxville)	116,149
3.	Marilyn Lloyd* (D, Chattanooga)	124,690
	Lamar Baker (R, Chattanooga)	57,524
4.	Albert Gore Jr. (D, Carthage)	115,297
	McGlamery (I)	7,083
5.	Clifford Allen* (D, Nashville)	125,447
	Bissell (I)	10,259
6.	Ross Bass (D, Pulaski)	63,833
	Robin L. Beard Jr.* (R, Brentwood)	121,976
7.	Ed Jones * (D, Yorkville)	Unopposed
8.	Harold E. Ford* (D, Memphis)	100,693
	A. D. (Andy) Allissandratos (R, Memphis)	63,698

Texas

1.	Sam B. Hall Jr.*(D, Marshall)	132,141
	James Hogan (R, Atlanta)	25,758
2.	Charles Wilson* (D, Lufkin)	116,165
3.	Les Shackerord Jr. (D, Dallas)	56,809
	James M. Collins* (R, Dallas)	159,155
4.	Ray Roberts* (D, McKinney)	104,478
	Frank S. Glenn (R, Flint)	62,598
5.	Jim Mattox (D, Dallas)	65,266
	Nancy Judy (R, Dallas)	52,122
6.	Olin E. Teague* (D, College Station)	120,521
	Wes Mowery (R, Fort Worth)	59,680
7.	Bill Archer* (R, Houston)	Unopposed
8.	Bob Eckhardt* (D, Houston)	84,404
	Nick Gearhart (R, Houston)	54,666
9.	Jack Brooks* (D, Beaumont)	Unopposed
10.	J. J. Pickle* (D, Austin)	158,334
	Paul MClure (R, Austin)	47,980
11.	W. R. Poage* (D, Waco)	92,689
	Jack Burgess (R, Waco)	68,199
12.	Jim Wright* (D, Fort Worth)	97,751
	W. R. Durham (R, Fort Worth)	33,582
13.	Jack Hightower* (D, Vernon)	94,847
	Bob Price (R, Pampa)	67,725
14.	John Young* (D, Corpus Christi)	93,705
	I. Dean Holford (R, Port Lavaca)	58,683
15.	E. (Kika) de la Garza* (D, Mission)	92,860
	R. L. (Lendy) McDonald (R, Los Fresnos)	33,940
16.	Richard C. White* (D, El Paso)	71,868
	Vic Shackelford (R, Odessa)	52,499
17.	Omar Burleson* (D, Abilene)	Unopposed
18.	Barbara Jordan* (D, Houston)	86,738
	Sam H. Wright (R, Houston)	15,626
19.	George Mahon* (D, Lubbock)	85,904
	Jim Reese (R, Odessa)	72,114
20.	Henry B. Gonzalez* (D, San Antonio)	Unopposed
21.	Robert (Bob) Krueger* (D, New Braunfels)	145,920
	Bobby A. Locke (R, San Antonio)	55.467
22.	Bob Gammage (D, Houston)	96,422
	Ron Paul* (R, Lake Jackson)	96,328
23.	Abraham (Chick) Kazen Jr.* (D, Laredo)	Unopposed
24.	Dale Milford* (D, Grand Prairie)	83,221
	Leo Berman (R, Arlington)	45,749

Utah

1.	Gunn McKay* (D, Huntsville)	147,255
	Joe H. Ferguson (R, American Fork)	106,009
	Gerlach (A)	4,400
2.	Allan T. Howe* (D, Salt Lake City)	103,295
	Dan Marriott (R, Salt Lake City)	142,638
	McC,arty (I)	20,506

Dist.	Representative (Party, Home)	1976 Election
Vermont — At Large		
	John A. Burgess (D, Montpelier).	60,044
	James M. Jeffords* (R, Rutland)	**122,722**
Virginia		
1.	Robert E. Quinn (D, Hampton).	69,769
	Paul S. Trible Jr. (R, Tappahannock).	72,124
2.	Robert E. (Bob) Washington (D, Norfolk). . . .	41,244
	G. William Whitehurst* (R, Virginia Beach). . .	**77,945**
3.	David E. Satterfield III* (D, Richmond)	**116,987**
	Alan R. Ogden (I, Richmond).	16,448
4.	J. W. "Billy" O'Brien (D, Chesapeake).	66,019
	Robert W. "Bob" Daniel Jr.* (R, Spring Grove).	**74,341**
5.	W. C. (Dan) Daniel* (D, Danville)	Unopposed
6.	M. Caldwell Butler* (R, Roanoke).	**90,636**
	Warren D. Saunders (I, Moneta).	55,385
7.	J. Kenneth Robinson* (R, Winchester).	**114,447**
	James B. Hutt Jr. (I, Warrenton)	26,011
8.	Herbert E. Harris II* (D, Alexandria)	**83,787**
	James R. Tate (R, Fairfax).	69,187
9.	Charles J. Horne (D, Abingdon).	70,995
	William C. Wampler* (R, Bristol).	**95,608**
10.	Joseph L. Fisher* (D, Arlington)	**104,460**
	Vincent C. Callahan Jr. (R, McLean).	74,166
	E. Stanley Rittenhouse (I, Dunn Loring).	12,323
Washington		
1.	Dave Wood (D, Seattle).	54,369
	Joel Pritchard* (R, Seattle).	**146,673**
2.	Lloyd Meeds* (D, Lake Stevens).	94,193
	John Nance Garner (R, Everett).	94,061
3.	Don Bonker*(D, Olympia).	**129,315**
	chuck Elhart (R, Lacey).	50,254
4.	Mike McCormack* (D, Richland).	**101,349**
	dick Granger (R, Vancouver).	72,316
5.	Thomas S. Foley* (D, Spokane).	**105,004**
	Duane Alton (R, Spokane).	74,511
6.	Norman D. Dicks (D, Port Orchard).	**117,446**
	Robert M. Reynolds (R, Racoma).	37,421
7.	Brock Adams* (D, Seattle).	**119,544**
	Raymond Pritchard (R, Seattle).	40,635

Dist.	Representative (Party, Home)	1976 Election
West Virginia		
1.	Robert H. Mollohan* (D, Fairmont).	**107,829**
	John F. McCuskey (R, Bridgeport).	77,978
2.	Harley O. Staggers* (D, Keyser)	**133,027**
	Jim Sloan (R, Beverly).	50,553
3.	John M. Slack* (D, Charleston)	**Unopposed**
4.	Nick Joe Rahall II (D, Beckley).	**73,616**
	E. S. (Steve) Goodman (R, Huntington).	29,692
	Hechler (Ind.).	36,169
Wisconsin		
1.	Les Apsin* (D, Racine).	**136,057**
	William W. Petrie (R, Waterford).	71,414
2.	Robert W. Kastenmeier* (D, Sun Prairie). . . .	**154,819**
	Elizabeth T. Miller (R, Portage).	81,516
3.	Alvin J. Baldus*(D, Menomonie).	**138,424**
	Adolf L. Gundersen (R, LaCrosse).	99,721
4.	Clement J. Zablocki* (D, Milwaukee).	**Unopposed**
5.	Henry S. Reuss* (D, Milwaukee).	**133,806**
	Robert L. Hicks (R, Milwaukee).	37,157
6.	Joseph C. Smith (D, Oshkosh)	80,624
	William A. Steiger* (R, Oshkosh).	**139,705**
7.	David R. Obey* (D, Wausau).	**171,101**
	Frank A. Savino (R, Schofield).	61,001
8.	Robert J. Cornell* (D, DePere).	**115,771**
	Harold V. Froehlich (R, Appleton).	106,888
9.	Lynn M. McDonald (D, Whitefish Bay)	83,706
	Robert W. Kasten Jr.* (R, Theinsville).	**160,833**
Wyoming At Large		
	Teno Roncalio* (D, Cheyenne)	**85,725**
	Larry Hart (R, Powell)	66,178

Non-Voting Delegates

District of Columbia	Walter E. Fauntroy* (D, D.C.)
Guam	Antonio Borja Won Pat* (D, Agana)
Virgin Islands	Ron De Lugo* (D, Christiansted)

Puerto Rico

Jaime Benitez* (Pop. D, Cayey)
Baltasar Corrada del Rio (New Prog., San Juan)
Baltasar Quinones Elias (P.R. Indep.)

Longevity of Male Government Officials to End of 1968

By period of initial entry into office (Compared to white males in U.S. population)
Source: Statistical Bulletin, Metropolitan Life Ins. Co.

Period of 1st Entry to Office	Number at Entry	Avg. Age at Entry	No. Died By End of 1968	Avg. Years Lived From Entry to End '68 or Prior Death	Differ-entials
Representatives					
1861-1900	2,434	45.4	2,434	23.8	0.1
1901-1930	1,582	46.1	1,520	24.6	0.4
1931-1968	1,659	45.7	585	17.0	0.2
Senators					
1861-1900	392	49.5	392	21.7	0.8
1901-1930	319	52.3	310	21.0	1.1
1931-1968	339	51.5	148	15.7	0.4
State Governors					
1901-1930	415	49.5	412	22.1	0.7
1931-1968	441	49.6	179	15.5	0.5
Cabinet Officers					
1789-1860	118	47.8	118	21.4	−0.2
1861-1900	108	53.1	108	20.0	1.4
1901-1930	73	52.9	73	21.1	1.8
1931-1968	92	52.7	38	12.2	−0.7
Supreme Court Justices					
1789-1900	57	51.2	57	20.2	0.2
1901-1968	39	54.3	25	17.2	1.4

*The difference between (a) the average number of years actually lived from entry into office to end of 1968 or prior death and (b) the average life expectancy of contemporaneous cohorts of white males in the general population of the United States observed for the same periods.

Political Divisions of the U.S. Senate and House of Representatives from 1855 (34th Cong.) to 1975-77 (94th Cong.)

Source: Clerk of the House of Representatives

Congress	Years	Senate					House of Representatives				
		Number of Senators	Democrats	Republicans	Other parties	Vacant	Number of Representatives	Democrats	Republicans	Other parties	Vacant
34th	1855-57	62	42	15	5		234	83	108	43	
35th	1857-59	64	39	20	5		237	131	92	14	
36th	1859-61	66	38	26	2		237	101	113	23	
37th	1861-63	50	11	31	7	1	178	42	106	28	2
38th	1863-65	51	12	39			183	80	103		
39th	1865-67	52	10	42			191	46	145		
40th	1867-69	53	11	42			193	49	143		1
41st	1869-71	74	11	61		2	243	73	170		
42d	1871-73	74	17	57			243	104	139		
43d	1873-75	74	19	54		1	293	88	203		2
44th	1875-77	76	29	46		1	293	71	107	3	2
45th	1877-79	76	36	39	1		293	156	137		
46th	1879-81	76	43	33			293	150	128	14	1
47th	1881-83	76	37	37	2		293	130	152	11	
48th	1883-85	76	36	40			325	200	119	6	
49th	1885-87	76	34	41		1	325	182	140	2	1
50th	1887-89	76	37	39			325	170	151	4	
51st	1889-91	84	37	47			330	156	173	1	
52d	1891-93	88	39	47	2		333	231	88	14	
53d	1893-95	88	44	38	3	3	356	220	126	10	
54th	1895-97	88	39	44	5		357	104	246	7	
55th	1897-99	90	34	46	10		357	134	206	16	1
56th	1899-1901	90	26	53	11		357	163	185	9	
57th	1901-3	90	29	56	3	2	357	153	198	5	1
58th	1903-5	90	32	58			386	178	207		1
59th	1905-7	90	32	58			386	136	250		
60th	1907-9	92	29	61		2	386	164	222		
61st	1909-11	92	32	59		1	391	172	219		
62d	1911-13	92	42	49		1	391	228	162	1	
63d	1913-15	96	51	44	1		435	290	127	18	
64th	1915-17	96	56	39	1		435	231	193	8	3
65th	1917-19	96	53	42	1		435	¹210	216	9	
66th	1919-21	96	47	48	1		435	191	237	7	
67th	1921-23	96	37	59			435	132	300	1	2
68th	1923-25	96	43	51	2		435	207	225	3	
69th	1925-27	96	40	54	1	1	435	183	247	5	
70th	1927-29	96	47	48	1		435	195	237	3	
71st	1929-31	96	39	56	1		435	163	267	1	4
72d	1931-33	96	47	48	1		435	²216	218	1	
73d	1933-35	96	59	36	1		435	313	117	5	
74th	1935-37	96	69	25	2		435	322	103	10	
75th	1937-39	96	75	17	4		435	333	89	13	
76th	1939-41	96	69	23	4		435	262	169	4	
77th	1941-43	96	66	28	2		435	267	162	6	
78th	1943-45	96	57	38	1		435	222	209	4	
79th	1945-47	96	57	38	1		435	243	190	1	
80th	1947-49	96	45	51			435	188	246	1	
81st	1949-51	96	54	42			435	263	171	1	
82d	1951-53	96	48	47	1		435	234	199	2	
83d	1953-55	96	46	48	2		435	213	221	1	
84th	1955-57	96	48	47	1		435	232	203		
85th	1957-59	96	49	47			435	234	201		
86th	1959-61	98	64	34			³436	283	153		
87th	1961-63	100	64	36			⁴437	262	175		
88th	1963-65	100	67	33			435	258	176		1
89th	1965-67	100	68	32			435	295	140		
90th	1967-69	100	64	36			435	248	187		
91st	1969-71	100	58	42			435	243	192		
92d	1971-73	100	54	44	2		435	255	180		
93d	1973-75	100	56	42	2		435	242	192	1	
94th	1975-77	100	61	37	2		435	291	144		

¹Democrats organized House with help of other parties. ²Democrats organized House due to Republican deaths. ³Proclamation declaring Alaska a State issued Jan. 3, 1959. ⁴ Proclamation declaring Hawaii a State issued Aug. 21, 1959.

Governors of States and Possessions

Reflecting Nov. 2, 1976 election

State	Capital	Governor	Party	Term Years	Term Expires	Annual Salary
Alabama	Montgomery	George C. Wallace	Dem.	4	Jan. 1979	$25,000
Alaska	Juneau	Jay Hammond	Rep.	4	Dec. 1978	40,000
Arizona	Phoenix	Raul Castro	Dem.	4	Jan. 1979	35,000
Arkansas	Little Rock	David Pryor	Dem.	2	Jan. 1979	10,000
California	Sacramento	Edmund G. Brown Jr.	Dem.	4	Jan. 1979	49,100
Colorado	Denver	Richard D. Lamm	Dem.	4	Jan. 1979	40,000
Connecticut	Hartford	Ella T. Grasso	Dem.	4	Jan. 1979	35,000
Delaware	Dover	Pierre S. du Pont	Rep.	4	Jan. 1981	35,000
Florida	Tallahassee	Reubin Askew	Dem.	4	Jan. 1979	40,000
Georgia	Atlanta	George Busbee	Dem.	4	Jan. 1979	50,000
Hawaii	Honolulu	George R. Ariyoshi	Dem.	4	Dec. 1978	42,000
Idaho	Boise	Cecil D. Andrus	Dem.	4	Jan. 1979	30,000
Illinois	Springfield	James R. Thompson	Rep.	4	Jan. 1981	50,000
Indiana	Indianapolis	Otis R. Bowen	Rep.	4	Jan. 1981	36,000
Iowa	Des Moines	Robert D. Ray	Rep.	4	Jan. 1979	40,000
Kansas	Topeka	Robert F. Bennett	Rep.	4	Jan. 1979	20,000
Kentucky	Frankfort	Julian Carroll	Dem.	4	Dec. 1979	30,000
Louisiana	Baton Rouge	Edwin W. Edwards	Dem.	4	May 1980	28,374
Maine	Augusta	James Longley	Ind.	4	Jan. 1979	35,000
Maryland	Annapolis	Marvin Mandel	Dem.	4	Jan. 1979	25,000
Massachusetts	Boson	Michael S. Dukakis	Dem.	4	Jan. 1979	40,000
Michigan	Lansing	William G. Milliken	Rep.	4	Jan. 1979	45,000
Minnesota	St. Paul	Wendell R. Anderson	Dem.	4	Jan. 1979	41,000
Mississipi	Jackson	Charles C. Finch	Dem.	4	Jan. 1980	35,000
Missouri	Jefferson City	Joseph P. Teasdale	Dem.	4	Jan. 1981	37,500
Montana	Helena	Thomas L. Judge	Dem.	4	Jan. 1981	25,000
Nebraska	Lincoln	J. James Exon	Dem.	4	Jan. 1979	25,000
Nevada	Carson City	Mike O'Callaghan	Dem.	4	Jan. 1979	30,000
New Hampshire	Concord	Meldrim Thomson Jr.	Rep.	2	Jan. 1979	32,760
New Jersey	Trenton	Brendan T. Byrne	Dem.	4	Jan. 1978	50,000
New Mexico	Santa Fe	Jerry Apodaca	Dem.	4	Jan. 1979	26,000
New York	Albany	Hugh L. Carey	Dem.	4	Jan. 1979	85,000
North Carolina	Raleigh	James B. Hunt Jr.	Dem.	4	Jan. 1981	35,000
North Dakota	Bismarck	Arthur A. Link	Dem.	4	Jan. 1981	18,000
Ohio	Columbus	James A. Rhodes	Rep.	4	Jan. 1979	50,000
Oklahoma	Oklahoma City	David Boren	Dem.	4	Jan. 1979	35,000
Oregon	Salem	Robert Straub	Dem.	4	Jan. 1979	35,000
Pennsylvania	Harrisburg	Milton J. Shapp	Dem.	4	Jan. 1979	45,000
Rhode Island	Providence	J. Joseph Garrahy	Dem.	2	Jan. 1979	42,500
South Carolina	Columbia	James B. Edwards	Rep.	4	Jan. 1979	35,000
South Dakota	Pierre	Richard F. Kneip	Dem.	4	Jan. 1979	25,000
Tennessee	Nashville	Ray Blanton	Dem.	4	Jan. 1979	50,000
Texas	Austin	Dolph Briscoe	Dem.	4	Jan. 1979	63,000
Utah	Salt Lake City	Scott M. Matheson	Dem.	4	Jan. 1981	33,000
Vermont	Montpelier	Richard A. Snelling	Rep.	2	Jan. 1979	35,000
Virginia	Richmond	Mills E. Godwin Jr.	Rep.	4	Jan. 1978	35,000
Washington	Olympia	Dixy Lee Ray	Dem.	4	Jan. 1981	34,300
West Virginia	Charleston	John D. Rockefeller 4th	Dem.	4	Jan. 1981	35,000
Wisconsin	Madison	Patrick J. Lucey	Dem.	4	Jan. 1979	25,000
Wyoming	Cheyenne	Ed Herschler	Dem.	4	Jan. 1979	37,500

Possessions

State	Capital	Governor	Party	Term Years	Term Expires	Annual Salary
Guam	Agana	Ricardo J. Bordallo	Rep.	4	Jan. 1981	35,000
Puerto Rico	San Juan	Carlos Romero Barcelo	N.P.	4	Jan. 1981	35,000
Virgin Isls.	Charlotte Amalie	Cyril E. King	ICM	4	Jan. 1979	35,505

The Races for Governor[1]

In 1976, there were 36 Democratic and 13 Republican governors. As result of the November 2 election, the roster became 37 Democrats to 12 Republicans. There is one independent governor, in Maine.

State	Democrats	Vote	Republicans	Vote
Arkansas	**David Pryor***	**599,722**	Leon Griffith	122,495
Delaware	Sherman W. Tribbitt*	97,514	**Pierre S. du Pont**	**130,566**
Illinois	Michael J. Howlett*	1,573,463	**James R. Thompson**	**2,948,335**
Indiana	Larry Conrad	915,418	**Otis R. Bowen***	**1,216,816**
Missouri	**Joseph P. Teasdale**	**958,218**	Christopher S. Bond*	945,695
Montana	**Thomas L. Judge***	**191,419**	Robert Woodahl	112,409
New Hampshire	Harry V. Spanos	144,504	**Meldrim Thomson Jr.***	**197,033**
No. Carolina	**James B. Hunt Jr.**	**1,076,454**	David T. Flaherty	561,468
N. Dakota	**Arthur A. Link***	**148,210**	Richard Elkin	134,468
Rhode Island	**J. Joseph Garrahy**	**211,770**	James L. Taft Jr.	172,252
Utah	**Scott M. Matheson**	**277,875**	Vernon B. Romney	245,368
Vermont	Stella B. Hackel	74,028	**Richard A. Snelling**	**96,235**
Washington	**Dixy Lee Ray**	**732,697**	John Spellman	602,990
West Virginia	**John D. Rockefeller 4th**	**489,949**	Cecil H. Underwood	251,754

*Incumbent. **Bold face type** denotes the winner. ([1])Preliminary unofficial returns.

Mayors and City Managers of Larger North American Cities
as of Nov. 2 elections, 1976

*Asterisk before name denotes city manager. All others are mayors. For mayors, dates are those of expiration of term, for city managers, they are dates of appointment.

D., Democrat: R., Republican; N-P, Non-Partisan

City	Name	Term
Abilene, Tex.	*Fred Sandlin	1974, May
Abington, Pa.	*Fred Schaefer	1967, Jan.
Akron, Ohio	John S. Ballard, R.	1979, Dec.
Alameda, Cal.	*John Goss	1973, Dec.
Albany, Ga.	*S. A. Roos	1961, Aug.
Albany, N.Y.	Erastus Corning, 2d, D.	1977, Dec.
Albuquerque, N.M.	Harry Kinney, R.	1977, Dec.
Alexandria, La.	John K. Snyder, D	1977, June
Alexandria, Va.	*Douglas Harman	1976, Jan.
Alhambra, Cal.	*Donald L. Russell	1976, July
Allen Park, Mich.	Frank J. Lada, D.	1977, Nov.
Allentown, Pa.	Joseph Daddona, D.	1978, Dec.
Alton, Ill.	Paul A. Lenz, N-P.	1977, Apr.
Altoona, Pa.	William C. Stouffer, R.	1979, Dec.
Amarillo, Tex.	*John S. Stiff.	1963, Sept.
Ames, Iowa	*Terry Sprenkel	1976, Apr.
Anaheim, Cal.	*Keith A. Murdoch	1958, Nov.
Anchorage, Alas.	*Douglas G. Weiford.	1974, May
Anderson, Ind.	Robert Rock, D.	1900, Jan.
Anderson, S.C.	*Charles B. Martin	1973, Mar.
Ann Arbor, Mich.	*Sylvester Murray	1973, July
Appleton, Wis.	James P. Sutherland, N-P.	1980, Apr.
Arcadia, Cal.	*Lyman H. Cozad	1966, July
Arlington, Mass.	*Donald R. Marquis	1966, Nov.
Arlington, Tex.	*Ross Calhoun	1973, Mar.
Arlington, Va.	*W. V. Ford.	1976, Feb.
Arlington Hts., Ill.	*L.A. Hanson	1959, June
Arvada, Col.	*Capp F. Shanks Jr.	1973, Aug.
Asheville, N.C.	*Ernest J. Ward	1972, Sept
Athens, Ga.	Upshaw Bentley, D.	1979, Nov.
Atlanta, Ga.	Maynard Jackson, D.	1978, Jan.
Atlantic City, N.J.	Joseph Lazarow, R.	1980, May
Auburn, N.Y.	*Bruce L. Clifford	1966, Aug.
Augusta, Ga.	Lewis A. Newman	1977, Dec.
Aurora, Col.	*W. Robert Semple	1972, Feb.
Aurora, Ill.	Albert D. McCoy, N-P.	1977, Apr.
Austin, Tex.	*Dan H. Davidson	1972, Aug.
Bakersfield, Cal.	*Harold E. Bergen.	1966, July
Baldwin Park, Cal.	*James Sexton, Act.	1976, Mar.
Baltimore, Md.	William Schaefer, D.	1979, Jan.
Bangor, Me.	*Vacant.	
Baton Rouge, La.	W. W. Dumas, D.	1980, Dec.
Battle Creek, Mich.	*Gordon Jaeger.	1976, Mar.
Bay City, Mich.	*Carlton Laird	1975, July
Baytown, Tex.	*Fritz Lanham	1972, May
Beaumont, Tex.	*Howard McDaniel (act.)	1975, June
Belleville, Ill.	Charles E. Nichols, N-P.	1977, Apr.
Belleville, N.J.	Michael Marotti, D.	1979, May
Bellevue, Wash.	*L. Joe Miller.	1961, Jan.
Bellflower, Cal.	*Peter B. Feenstra.	1968, Oct.
Beloit, Wis.	*H. Herbert Holt	1970, Mar.
Berkeley, Cal.	*Elijah B. Rogers	1976, July
Berwyn, Ill.	Emil Vacin, D.	1977, Apr.
Bessemer, Ala.	Ed Porter, D.	1978, Oct.
Bethlehem, Pa.	Gordon Mowrer, D.	1977, Nov.
Billings, Mont.	Joseph Leone, D.	1977, May
Biloxi, Miss.	Jerry O'Keefe, D.	1977, July
Binghamton, N.Y.	Alfred J. Libous, D.	1977, Dec.
Birmingham, Ala.	David Vann, D.	1979, Nov.
Bismarck, N.D.	Robert Heskin, N-P.	1978, Apr.
Bloomfield, N.J.	*H. Joseph North	1967, Oct.
Bloomington, Ill.	*Vacant.	
Bloomington, Ind.	Francis X. McCloskey, D.	1979, Dec.
Bloomington, Minn.	*John Pidgeon.	1967, Dec.
Boise, Idaho.	Dick Eardley, N-P.	1977, Dec.
Bossier City, La.	James Cathey, D.	1977, June
Boston, Mass.	Kevin White, D.	1979, Dec.
Boulder, Col.	*Robert Westdyke	1976, Aug.
Bowie, Md.	*G. C. Moore.	1976, Mar.
Bowling Green, Ky.	*Paul McCauley	1973, Jan.
Bridgeport, Conn.	John Mandanici, D.	1977, Nov.
Bristol, Conn.	Henry Wojtusik, D.	1977, Nov.
Brockton, Mass.	David L. Crosby, D.	1977, Dec.
Brookfield, Wis.	William Mitchell Jr.	1978, Apr.
Brookline, Mass.	Board of Selectmen	
Brooklyn Center, Minn.	*Donald G. Poss.	1966, Dec.
Brownsville, Tex.	*J. W. Sloss	1974, Nov.
Bryan, Tex.	*J. Louis Odle	1974, May
Buffalo, N.Y.	Stanley M. Makowsky, D.	1977, Dec.
Burbank, Cal.	*Joseph N. Baker.	1968, Mar.
Burlington, Vt.	Gordon H. Paquette, D.	1977, Apr.
Calumet City, Ill.	Robert C. Stefaniak, D.	1977, Apr.
Cambridge, Mass.	*James L. Sullivan.	1974, Apr.
Camden, N.J.	Angelo Errichetti, D.	1977, July
Canton, Ohio	Stanley A. Cmich, R.	1979, Dec.
Cape Girardeau, Mo.	*W. G. Lawley.	1970, July
Carson, Cal.	*E. Frederick Bien.	1968, June
Casper, Wyo.	*Kenneth Erickson.	1969, Oct.
Cedar Rapids, Iowa	Donald J. Canney, N-P.	1977, Dec.
Champaign, Ill.	*Eugene Miller.	1974, Sept.
Charleston, S.C.	Joseph P. Riley Jr., D.	1979, Dec.
Chaleston, W. Va.	*Hugh Bosely.	1973, Apr.
Charlotte, N.C.	*David A. Burkhalter.	1971, May
Charlottesville, Va.	*Cole Hendrix	1971, Jan.
Chattanooga, Tenn.	Charles A. Rose, N-P.	1979, Apr.
Chesapeake, Va.	*Durwood S. Curling.	1971, Jan.
Chester, Pa.	John Nacrelli, R.	1980, Jan.
Cheyenne, Wyo.	Donald Erickson, N-P.	1980, Dec.
Chicago, Ill.	Richard J. Daley, D.	1979, Apr.
Chicago Hts., Ill.	Charles Panici, R.	1979, Apr.
Chicopee, Mass.	Howard Redfern Jr.	1977, Dec.
Chula Vista, Cal.	*Lane F. Cole.	1975, Feb.
Cicero, Ill.	Christy Berkos.	1980, Apr.
Cincinnati, Ohio	*William V. Donaldson.	1975, June
Clarksville, Tenn.	Charles W. Crow, D.	1979, Jan.
Clearwater, Fla.	*Picot B. Floyd.	1973, Oct.
Cleveland, Ohio.	Ralph J. Perk, R.	1977, Nov.
Cleveland Heights	*Robert A. Edwards.	1975, June
Clifton, N.J.	*William Holster.	1957, Jan.
Col. Spgs., Col.	*George H. Fellows	1966, July
Columbia, Mo.	*Terry Novak.	1974, Feb.
Columbia, S.C.	*Graydon V. Olive Jr.	1970, Mar.
Columbus, Ga.	*Franklyn Lambert.	1971, Jan.
Columbus, Ohio.	Tom Moody, R.	1980, Jan.
Commerce, Cal.	*Robert Hinderliter.	1973, Aug.
Compton, Cal.	*Allen Parker.	1975, Dec.
Concord, Cal.	*F. A. Stewart	1960, Apr.
Concord, N.H.	*John E. Henchey.	1968, Jan.
Coon Rapids, Minn.	*John K. Cottingham.	1969, Dec.
Coral Gables, Fla.	*J. Martin Gainer.	1975, Jan.
Corpus Christi, Tex.	*R. Marvin Townsend.	1968, Jan.
Corvallis, Ore.	*C. Dean Smith.	1968, Jan.
Costa Mesa, Cal.	*Fred Sorsable.	1970, Nov.
Council Bluffs, Ia.	*M. Don Harmon.	1968, Feb.
Covington, Ky.	George Wermeling, D.	1979, Dec.
Cranston, R. I.	James L. Taft Jr., R.	1978, Dec.
Crystal, Minn.	*John Irving.	1964, Jan.
Culver City, Cal.	*H. Dale Jones.	1969, June
Cuyahoga Falls. O.	Robert Quirk, D.	1977, Dec.
Dallas, Tex.	*George R. Schrader	1972, Dec.
Daly City, Cal.	*David R. Rowe	1969, Aug.
Danbury, Conn.	Charles A. Ducibella, D.	1977, Dec.
Danville, Ill.	David S. Palmer, D.	1979, Apr.
Danville, Va.	*James W. Lord.	1971, Nov.
Davenport, Ia.	Robert Duax, R.	1977, Dec.
Dayton, Ohio.	*James Alloway	1974, Feb.
Daytona Bch., Fla.	*Russell C. Smith.	1970, Apr.
Dearborn, Mich.	Orville L. Hubbard, N-P.	1978, Jan.
Decatur, Ala.	Bill Dukes, D.	1980, Oct.
Decatur, Ill.	*Leslie T. Allen.	1972, Sept.
Denton, Tex.	*Jim White	1968, May
Denver, Col.	William H. McNichols, D.	1979, July
Des Moines, Ia.	*Richard A. Wilkey.	1974, Mar.
Des Plaines, Ill.	Charles Bolek, N-P.	1977, Apr.
Detroit, Mich.	Coleman A. Young, N-P.	1978, Jan.
Dotham, Ala.	*Christian P. Morris.	1974, Mar.
Downers Grove, Ill.	*James R. Griesemer.	1972, Sept.
Dubuque, Ia.	*Gilbert D. Chavenelle.	1960, July
Duluth, Minn.	Robert Beaudin, D.	1977, Dec.
Durham, N.C.	*I. Harding Hughes Jr.	1963, Feb.

City	Name	Term
E. Chicago, Ind.	Robert A. Pastrick, D.	1979, Dec.
E. Cleveland, Oh.	*Edwin M. Robinson	1976, Sept.
E. Detroit, Mich.	*W. Larry Collins	1975, Mar.
E. Hartford, Conn.	Richard H. Blackstone, D.	1977, Nov.
E. Lansing, Mich.	*Vacant.	
E. Orange, N.J.	William S. Hart, D.	1977, Dec.
E. Providence, R.I.	*Paul A. Flynn.	1972, Aug.
E. St. Louis, Ill.	William Mason, D.	1979, May
Eau Claire, Wis.	*Ray E. Wachs	1970, June
Edina, Minn.	*Warren Hyde	1955, May
Edison, N.J.	Thomas Paterniti, D.	1977, Dec.
El Cajon, Cal.	*Robert M. Applegate	1958, Sept.
Elgin, Ill.	*Leo Nelson.	1972, Dec.
Elizabeth, N.J.		1980, Dec.
Elkhart, Ind.	Peter Sarantos, R.	1979, Dec.
Elmhurst, Ill.	*Robert T. Palmer.	1953, June
Elmira, N.Y.	*Joseph E. Sartori.	1972, June
El Monte, Cal.	*Kenneth Botts	1969, Aug.
El Paso, Tex.	Don Henderson, N-P.	1977, Apr.
Elyria, Ohio.	Marguerite Bowman, R.	1979, Dec.
Enfield, Conn.	*William L. McDivitt.	1975, July
Enid, Okla.	*Tom Sailors Jr.	1969, Oct.
Erie, Pa.	Louis J. Tullio, D.	1977, Dec.
Escondido, Cal.	*Kenneth Lounsbery.	1976, Aug.
Euclid, Oh.	Anthony Sustarsic, N-P.	1979, Dec.
Eugene, Ore.	*Charles T. Henry.	1975, July
Evanston, Ill.	*Edward A. Martin.	1971, Jan.
Evansville, Ind.	Russell Lloyd, R.	1980, Jan.
Everett, Mass.	George R. McCarthy, D.	1977, Dec.
Everett, Wash.	Robert C. Anderson, D.	1978, Jan.
Fairborn, Ohio	*Vacant.	
Fairfield, Cal.	*B. Gale Wilson	1956, Mar.
Fairfield, Conn.	John J. Sullivan, D.	1977, Nov.
Fair Lawn, N.J.	*Frank Vanore	1975, Oct.
Fall River, Mass.	Wilfred C. Driscoll, D.	1979, Dec.
Fayetteville, Ark.	*Donald Grimes	1972, Apr.
Fayetteville, N.C.	*J. Guy Smith.	1971, Jan.
Fitchburg, Mass.	Hedley Bray, D.	1978, Jan.
Flagstaff, Ariz.	*Charles McClain.	1973, Nov.
Flint, Mich.	*Peter Kleinpell.	1976, Jan.
Florissant, Mo.	James J. Eagan, D.	1979, Apr.
Fond du Lac, Wis.	*Myron J. Medin Jr.	1967, Nov.
Ft. Collins, Col.	*Robert L. Brunton.	1972, Oct.
Ft. Lauderdale, Fla.	*Richard E. Anderson.	1975, July
Ft. Lee, N.J.	*James J. Mulcare.	1973, Jan.
Ft. Smith, Ark.	*Ray A. Riley.	1972, Dec.
Ft. Wayne, Ind.	Robert Armstrong, D.	1979, Dec.
Ft. Worth, Tex.	*Rodger Line	1971, Apr.
Fremont, Cal.	*Don Driggs.	1967, Jan.
Fresno, Cal.	*Ralph W. Hanley	1973, Sept.
Fullerton, Cal.	*Leslie R. White.	1976, July
Gadsden, Ala.	Steve Means, D.	1978, Oct.
Gainesville, Fla.	*B. Harold Farmer.	1968, Nov.
Galesburg, Ill.	*Thomas B. Herring.	1960, Nov.
Galveston, Tex.	*Jack Nichols.	1975, June
Gardena, Cal.	*Craig McDowell.	1973, Dec.
Garden Grove, Cal.	*Richard R. Powers.	1972, Apr.
Garfield Hts., Ohio	Raymond Stachewicz, D.	1977, Dec.
Garland, Tex.	*C. E. Duckworth	1965, Jan.
Gary, Ind.	R. G. Hatcher, D.	1979, Nov.
Gastonia, N.C.	*Gary Hicks	1973, Dec.
Glendale, Ariz.	*S. F. Van de Putte	1960, Aug.
Glendale, Cal.	*J. Keithley	1972, Sept.
Grand Forks, N.D.	Cyril P. O'Neill, D.	1978, Apr.
Gr. Island, Neb.	*John M. Carpenter	1964, Aug.
Gr. Prairie, Tex	*Clifford A. Johnson.	1962, Oct.
Gr. Rapids, Mich.	*Joseph G. Zainea.	1976, Oct.
Granite City, Ill.	Paul Schuler, D.	1978, Apr.
Great Falls, Mont.	*Richard D. Thomas	1973, May
Green Bay, Wis.	Michael Monfils, N-P.	1979, Apr.
Greensboro, N.C.	*Thomas Z. Osborne	1973, Jan.
Greensville, S.C.	*John J. Dullea	1971, Oct.
Greenwich, Conn.	Ruppert Vernon, R.	1977, Dec.
Groton, Conn.	Donald Sweet, N-P.	1977, May
Gulfport, Miss.	Arthur W. Long Jr., D.	1977, July
Hackensack, N.J.	*Joseph J. Squillace	1964, Oct.
Hagerstown, Md.	Varner L. Paddack, R.	1977, Apr.
Hamden, Conn.	Lucien A. DiMeo, R.	1977, Nov.
Hamilton, Ohio.	*Edward C. Smith	1971, June
Hammond, Ind.	Edward J. Raskowsky, D.	1979, Dec.
Hampton, Va.	*C. E. Johnson.	1958, May
Harlingen, Tex.	*W.T. Snyder Jr.	1974, Dec.
Harrisburg, Pa.	Harold Swenson, D.	1978, Jan.

City	Name	Term
Hartford, Conn.	*James B. Daken.	1976, Oct.
Harvey, Ill.	James A. Haines, R.	1979, Apr.
Hattiesburg, Miss.	A. L. Gerrard Jr., D.	1977, July
Haverhill, Mass.	Louis C. Burton, D.	1977, Dec.
Hawthorne, Cal.	*Donald W. Mansfield.	1972, Jan.
Hayward, Cal.	*William C. Hanley.	1972, Feb.
Hempstead, N.Y.	Dalton R. Miller, R.	1977, Apr.
Hialeah, Fla.	Dale Bennett, D.	1977, Dec.
High Point, N.C.	*Cyrus L. Brooks.	1976, Aug.
Highland Pk., Ill.	*Larry Rice.	1975, Jan.
Hoboken, N.J.	Steve Cappiello, D.	1977, July
Holyoke, Mass.	Ernest Proulx, D.	1978, Jan.
Hollywood, Fla.	*Tony M. Reasons.	1974, Dec.
Honolulu, Hawaii.	Frank F. Fasi, D.	1981, Jan.
Hot Springs, Ark.	Tom Ellsworth, N-P.	1978, Dec.
Houston, Tex.	Fred Hofheinz, D.	1978, Jan.
Huntington, W. Va.	*Barry R. Evans.	1973, Mar.
Huntington Beach, Cal.	*David D. Rowlands.	1972, Feb.
Huntsville, Ala.	Joe W. Davis, N-P.	1980, Oct.
Hutchinson, Kan.	*George W. Pyle.	1967, Sept.
Independence, Mo.	*Lyle Alberg.	1968, Sept.
Indianapolis, Ind.	William Hudnut, R.	1979, Dec.
Inglewood, Cal.	*Douglas W. Ayres.	1968, Apr.
Inkster, Mich.	*David S. Williams.	1973, Oct.
Iowa City, Iowa	*Neal Berlin.	1975, Mar.
Irving, Tex.	*Jack Huffman.	1973, Dec.
Irvington, N.J.	Robert Miller, R.	1978. July
Jackson, Mich.	*S. W. McAllister Jr.	1974, Mar.
Jackson, Miss.	Russell C. Davis, D.	1977, July
Jackson, Tenn.	Bob Conger, D.	1979, July
Jacksonville, Fla.	Hans Tanzler Jr., D.	1979, July
Jamestown, N.Y.	Stanley Macowski, D.	1977, Dec.
Janesville, Wis.	*Philip L. Deaton.	1976, Mar.
Jefferson City, Mo.	Robert Hyder, D.	1979, Apr.
Jersey City, N.J.	Paul Jordan, D.	1977, July
Johnson City, Tenn.	*William Ricker.	1971, Oct.
Johnstown, Pa.	Herbert Pfuhl, R.	1978, Jan.
Joliet, Ill.	*Lynn Neuhart	1972, Feb.
Joplin, Mo.	*Robert E. Metzinger.	1968, Mar.
LaCrosse, Wis.	Patrick Zielke, N-P.	1977, Apr.
Lafayette, Ind.	James Riehle, D.	1979, Dec.
Lafayette, La.	Kenneth Bowen, D.	1980, July
La Habra, Cal.	*Lee Risner.	1970, Nov.
La Mesa, Cal.	*Gayle T. Martin.	1975, June
La Mirada, Cal.	*Claude J. Klug.	1971, Aug.
Lake Charles, La.	William E. Boyer, D.	1977, June
Lakeland, Fla.	*Robert V. Youkey.	1960, Jan.
Lakewood, Cal.	*Howard L. Chambers.	1976, June
Lakewood, Col.	*Ray Wells.	1974, Sept.
Lakewood, Oh.	Robert M. Lawther, R.	1979, Dec.
Lancaster, Pa.	Richard M. Scott, R.	1978, Jan.
Lansing, Mich.	Gerald Graves, N-P.	1977, Dec.
Laredo, Tex.	J. C. Martin Jr., N-P.	1978, May
Las Cruces, N.M.	*Harold Yungmeyer.	1975, Jan.
Las Vegas, Nev.	*William E. Adams.	1976, Mar.
Lawrence, Kan.	*Buford M. Watson Jr.	1970, Jan.
Lawrence, Mass.	John J. Buckley, D.	1977, Dec.
Lawton, Okla.	*Vacant.	
Lewiston, Me.	Lillian L. Caron, D.	1978, Jan.
Lexington, Ky.	H. Foster Pettit, D.	1978, Jan.
Lima, Oh.	Harry Moyer, R.	1977, Nov.
Lincoln, Neb.	Helen Boosalis, D.	1979, May
Lincoln Pk., Mich.	Melvin L. Gish, N-P.	1977, Dec.
Linden, N.J.	John Gregorio, D.	1978, Dec.
Little Rock, Ark.	*Carleton E. McMullin.	1973, Oct.
Livermore, Cal.	*William H. Parness.	1957, Oct.
Livonia, Mich.	E. H. McNamara, D.	1978, Jan.
Lombard, Ill.	*Warren Browning.	1975, Sept.
Long Beach, Cal.	*Robert Creighton, act.	1976, June
Long Beach, N.Y.	*Laurence P. Farbstein.	1976, June
Longview Tex.	*Harry G. Mosley.	1952, July
Kalamazoo, Mich.	*Bruce Brown.	1975, Jan.
Kansas City, Kan.	John Reardon, D.	1979, Apr.
Kansas City, Mo.	*Robert A. Kipp.	1974, Jan.
Kenosha, Wis.	Paul Saftig, N-P.	1980, Apr.
Kettering, Oh.	*John W. Laney.	1976, Mar.
Key West, Fla.	*Robert J. Stack.	1974, June
Killeen, Tex.	*Mike Eastland.	1976, Apr.
Knoxville, Tenn.	Randell L. Tyree, D.	1979, Dec.
Kokomo, Ind.	Arthur LaDow, R.	1980, Jan.

City	Name	Term
Los Angeles, Cal.	Thomas Bradley, D.	1977, June
Louisville, Ky.	Harvey Sloane, D.	1977, Nov.
Lowell, Mass.	*William Taupier.	1975, Oct.
L. Merion, Pa.	*Thomas B. Fulweiler.	1968, Jan.
Lubbock, Tex.	*Larry Cunningham.	1976, Aug.
Lynchburg, Va.	*David B. Norman.	1970, Nov.
Lynn, Mass.	Anthony J. Marino, N-P.	1978, Jan.
Lynwood, Cal.	*Stephen Wright.	1973, Feb.
Macon, Ga.	Buckner Melton, D.	1979, Nov.
Madison, Wis.	Paul Soglin, N-P.	1977, Apr.
Madison Heights, Mich.	Virginia Solberg, N-P.	1977, Apr.
Malden, Mass.	James Conway, D.	1978, Jan.
Manchester, Conn.	*Robert B. Weiss.	1966, Jan.
Manchester, N.H.	Charles Stanton, D.	1977, Dec.
Manitowoc, Wis.	Anthony V. Dufek, N-P.	1977, Apr.
Mansfield, Oh.	Richard A. Porter, R.	1979, Dec.
Marion, Ind.	Anthony Maidenberg, D.	1979, Dec.
McKeesport, Pa.	Thomas Fullard, R.	1980, Jan.
Medford, Mass.	*James Nicholson.	1970, Oct.
Melbourne, Fla.	*Ernest E. Watkins.	1969, July
Memphis, Tenn.	Wyeth Chandler, N-P.	1979, Dec.
Mentor, Oh.	*Arthur V. Dickard.	1969, Sept.
Meridian, Miss.	*Joel W. Forrester.	1959, July
Mesa, Ariz.	*J.A. Petrie.	1952, June
Mesquite, Tex.	*C. K. Duggins.	1976, Feb.
Miami, Fla.	*Joseph Grassie.	1976, July
Miami Beach, Fla.	*Frank Spence.	1972, Nov.
Middletown, Oh.	*Dale F. Helsel.	1970, Oct.
Midland, Tex.	*James W. Brown.	1964, Nov.
Midwest City, Okla.	*Jerry Wade.	1976, Jan.
Milford, Conn.	Joel Baldwin, D.	1977, Nov.
Milwaukee, Wis.	Henry W. Maier, D.	1980, Apr.
Minneapolis	Charles Stenvig, N-P.	1978, Jan.
Minnetonka, Minn.	*Carsten D. Leikvold.	1973, Dec.
Minot, N.D.	*John Arnold.	1972, Oct.
Mobile, Ala.	Lambert C. Mims, N-P.	1978, Sept.
Modesto, Cal.	*Garth Lipsky.	1974, Jan.
Moline, Ill.	Earl Wendt, R.	1977, May
Monroe, La.	W. L. Howard, D.	1980, June
Montclair, N.J.	Grant M. Gille, N-P.	1980, May
Montebello, Cal.	*Roy Pederson.	1969, Jan.
Monterey Park, Cal.	*Lloyd De Llamas.	1976, Sept.
Montgomery, Ala.	Jim Robinson, R.	1979, Nov.
Mt. Prospect, Ill.	*Robert J. Eppley.	1971, Aug.
Mt. Vernon, N.Y.	August Petrillo, R.	1979, Dec.
Mountain View, Cal.	*Bruce Liedstrand.	1976, Aug.
Muncie, Ind.	Robert Cunningham, D.	1979, Dec.
Mundelein, Ill.	Maurice A. Noll, N-P.	1977, Apr.
Muskegon, Mich.	*Paul F. Frederick.	1970, June
Muskogee, Okla.	*Bob Hill.	1975, Dec.
Napa, Cal.	*Lee M. Roberts.	1953, Aug.
Nashua, N.H.	Dennis Sullivan, N-P.	1980, Jan.
Nashville, Tenn.	Richard Fulton, D.	1979, Sept.
National City, Cal.	*Cleo Osburn.	1965, July
New Bedford, Mass.	John Markey, N-P.	1978, Jan.
New Britain, Conn.	Matthew Avitable, D.	1977, Nov.
New Brunswick, N.J.	*Paul Abdalla.	1975, Sept.
New Castle, Pa.	Francis J. Rogan, D.	1979, Dec.
New Haven, Conn.	Frank Logue, D.	1977, Dec.
New Kensington, Pa.	Verle N. Bevan, D.	1977, Dec.
New Orleans, La.	Moon Landrieu, D.	1978, Apr.
New Rochelle, N.Y.	*C. Samuel Kissinger.	1975, Jan.
New York, N.Y.	Abraham Beame, D.	1977, Dec.
Newark, N.J.	Kenneth Gibson, D.	1978, July
Newport, R.I.	*Paul Steinbrenner.	1976, May
Newport Beach, Cal.	*Robert L. Wynn.	1971, Aug.
Newport News, Va.	*Frank Smiley.	1976, Oct.
Newton, Mass.	Theodore Mann, R.	1977, Dec.
Niagara Falls, N.Y.	*Donald J. O'Hara.	1976, May
Niles, Ill.	*Kenneth Scheel.	1973, May
Norfolk, Va.	*Julian Hirst.	1975, July
Norma, Okla.	*James D. Crosby.	1976, Feb.
North Charleston, S.C.	John Bourne, R.	1978, June
North Chicago, Ill.	Leo F. Kukla, D.	1977, Apr.
No. Little Rock, Ark.	Eddie Powell, D.	1980, Dec.
Norwalk, Cal.	*William H. Kraus.	1973, May
Norwalk, Conn.	Jennie Cave, N-P.	1977, Nov.
Norwich, Conn.	*Charles Whitty.	1973, June
Novato, Cal.	*Phillip J. Brown.	1974, May
Oak Lawn, Ill.	*Richard E. O'Neill.	1976, Sept.
Oak Park, Ill.	*Jack Gruber, act.	1976, June
Oak Park, Mich.	*James B. Thompson.	1970, Aug.

City	Name	Term
Oak Ridge, Tenn.	*William N. Haddock.	1974, Dec.
Oakland, Cal.	*Cecil S. Riley.	1972, Sept.
Oceanside, Cal.	*Daniel E. Stone.	1975, Dec.
Odessa, Tex.	*Ronald J. Neighbors.	1968, Nov.
Ogden, Utah	*R. L. Larsen.	1972, Feb.
Oklahoma City, Okla.	*James J. Cook.	1976, Apr.
Omaha, Neb.	Edward Zorinsky, D.	1977, May
Ontario, Cal.	*Roger Hughbanks.	1975, July
Orange, Cal.	*Gifford Miller.	1968, Dec.
Orange, N.J.	Carmine Capone, N-P.	1980, July
Orlando, Fla.	Carl Langford, D.	1980, Oct.
Oshkosh, Wis.	*W. O. Frueh.	1976, Aug.
Overland Park, Kan.	Jack Walker.	1977, Apr.
Owensboro, Ky.	*Max N. Rhoads.	1959, Sept.
Oxnard, Cal.	*Paul E. Wolven.	1953, Feb.
Pacifica, Cal.	*Donald Weidner.	1974, Oct.
Palm Springs, Cal.	William Foster, R.	1977, Mar.
Palo Alto, Cal.	*George Sipel.	1972, Feb.
Parkersburg, W. Va.	William Nicely, R.	1977, Dec.
Parma, Ohio	John Petruska, D.	1979, Dec.
Pasadena, Cal.	*Donald F. McIntyre.	1973, June
Pasadena, Tex.	John Ray Harrison, D.	1977, May
Passaic, N.J.	Gerald Goldman, R.	1977, June
Paterson, N.J.	*Larry Worth.	1974, Sept.
Pawtucket, R.I.	Dennis Lynch, D.	1978, Jan.
Pekin, Ill.	William L. Waldmeier, D.	1979, Apr.
Pensacola, Fla.	*Frank A. Faison.	1971, Mar.
Peoria, Ill.	*Robert O. Wright.	1970, Oct.
Perth Amboy, N.J.	*Richard Pucci.	1976, July
Petersburg, Va.	*William Cook.	1976, July
Philadelphia, Pa.	Frank L. Rizzo, D.	1980, Jan.
Phoenix, Ariz.	*Marvin Andrews, act.	1976, Aug.
Pico Rivera, Cal.	*Howard Schroyer.	1970, July
Pine Bluff, Ark.	Charles Moore, D.	1980, Dec.
Pittsburgh, Pa.	Peter Flaherty, D.	1977, Dec.
Pittsfield, Mass.	Evan S. Dobelle, N-P.	1978, Jan.
Plainfield, N.J.	*Lawrence Bashe.	1974, Mar.
Pocatello, Idaho	*Charles W. Moss.	1970, Sept.
Pomona, Cal.	*Jerrold R. Gonce.	1973, Oct.
Pompano Bch., Fla.	*John Schoeberlein.	1975, Oct.
Pontiac, Mich.	*Vacant.	
Portage, Mich.	*Donald P. Ziemke.	1974, Aug.
Port Arthur, Tex.	*George E. Dibrell.	1962, Oct.
Port Huron, Mich.	*Gerald R. Bouchard.	1965, June
Portland, Me.	*A. J. Wilson Jr.	1976, May
Portland, Ore.	Neil Goldschmidt, N-P.	1980, Dec.
Portsmouth, Ohio.	*C. Scott Johnson.	1974, Feb.
Portsmouth, Va.	*Robert T. Williams.	1975, Apr.
Poughkeepsie, N.Y.	*Vacant.	
Prichard, Ala.	A.J. Cooper Jr.	1980, Oct.
Providence, R.I.	Vincent Cianci, R.	1979, Jan.
Provo, Utah.	Russell D. Grange, N-P.	1977, Dec.
Pueblo, Col.	*Fred E. Weisbroad.	1967, Feb.
Quincy, Ill.	Don Nicholson, D.	1977, May
Quincy, Mass.	Joseph J. LaRaia, D.	1978, Jan.
Racine, Wis.	Stephen Olson, N-P.	1977, Apr.
Raleigh, N.C.	*L. P. Zachary Jr.	1973, Nov.
Rapid City, S.D.	Arthur La Croix, N-P.	1977, May
Raytown, Mo.	Willard H. Ross, R.	1977, Apr.
Reading, Pa.	Joseph Kuzminski, D.	1980, Jan.
Redlands, Cal.	*Robert Mitchell, act.	1976, Apr.
Redondo Beach, Cal.	*Joseph P. Leach.	1973, Feb.
Redwood City, Cal.	*James M. Fales Jr.	1971, Aug.
Reno, Nev.	*Robert H. Oldland.	1975, Jan.
Revere, Mass.	William Reinstein, D.	1980, Jan.
Richardson, Tex.	*Bob Hughey.	1974, Jan.
Richfield, Minn.	*Wayne Burggraaff.	1968, Dec.
Richmond, Cal.	*Kenneth Smith.	1967, Sept.
Richmond, Ind.	Clifford Dickman, R.	1979, Dec.
Richmond, Va.	*William J. Leidinger.	1972, June
Riverside, Cal.	*William F. Cornett.	1976, Jan.
Roanoke, Va.	*Byron E. Haner.	1973, Jan.
Rochester, Minn.	*Robert W. Freson.	1974, Sept.
Rochester, N.Y.	*Elisha Freedman.	1974, Jan.
Rock Hill, S.C.	*Max Holland.	1965, Mar.
Rock Island, Ill.	*Raymond P. Botch.	1961, Feb.
Rockford, Ill.	Robert McGaw, D.	1977, May
Rockville, Md.	*Larry N. Blick.	1972, Nov.
Rome, N.Y.	William A. Valentine, R.	1978, Dec.
Rosemead, Cal.	*Frank Trippei.	1974, Oct.
Roseville, Mich.	*Harvey Weatherwax.	1974, Dec.
Roseville, Minn.	*James Andre.	1974, May
Roswell, N.M.	*Robert J. Owen.	1973, Oct.
Royal Oak, Mich.	*William Baldridge.	1975, Sept.

City	Name	Term
Sacramento, Cal.	*Walter J. Slipe	1976, Mar.
Saginaw, Mich.	*E. H Potthoff Jr.	1961, July
St. Clair Shores, Mich.	*Donald J. Harm	1962, Jan.
St. Cloud, Minn.	Alcuin Loehr N-P.	1980, Apr.
St. Joseph, Mo.	W. J. Bennett, D.	1978, Apr.
St. Louis, Mo.	John Poelker, D.	1977, Apr.
St. Louis Pk., Minn.	*Chris Cherches	1968, Dec.
St. Paul, Minn.	George Latimer, D.	1978, June
St. Petersburg, Fla.	*R. E. Harbaugh	1970, May
Salem, Mass.	Jean Levesque, D.	1978, Jan.
Salem, Ore.	*Robert S. Moore.	1968, Aug.
Salina, Kan.	*Norris D. Olson.	1964, May
Salinas, Cal.	*Robert Christofferson.	1972, Dec.
Salt Lake City, Utah	Ted Wilson, D.	1980, Jan.
San Angelo, Tex.	*H. D. Howard.	1958, May
San Antonio, Tex.	*Sam Granata Jr.	1973, Mar.
San Bernardino, Cal.	*Marshall Julian.	1971, Nov.
San Buenaventura, Cal.	*Edward McCombs.	1970, Feb.
San Diego, Cal.	*Hugh McKinley.	1975, Apr.
San Francisco, Cal.	George Moscone, D.	1980, Jan.
San Jose, Cal.	*Ted Tedesco.	1973, Feb.
San Leandro, Cal.	*Leroy Riordan.	1976, Jan.
San Mateo, Cal.	*Richard Delong.	1976, Sept.
San Rafael, Cal.	*William J. Bielser.	1973, Jan.
Sandusky, Ohio.	*Frank Link.	1972, Jan.
Santa Ana, Cal.	*Bruce C. Spragg.	1972, Sept.
Santa Barbara, Cal.	*John L. Scott.	1973, Mar.
Santa Cruz, Cal.	*David C. Koester.	1962, Oct.
Santa Fe, N.M.	*Philip Baca.	1972, Aug.
Santa Maria, Cal.	*Robert Grogan.	1963, Jan.
Santa Monica, Cal.	*James D. Williams.	1973, Oct.
Santa Rosa, Cal.	*Kenneth R. Blackman.	1970, July
Sarasota, Fla.	*Kenneth Thompson.	1950, Feb.
Savannah, Ga.	*Arthur A. Mendonsa.	1971, Sept.
Schenectady, N.Y.	*Peter Caputo.	1973, Oct.
Scottsdale, Ariz.	*Frank Aleshire.	1975, July
Scranton, Pa.	Eugene J. Peters, R.	1977, Dec.
Seattle, Wash.	Wesley C. Uhlman, D.	1977, Dec.
Shaker Heights, Oh.	Walter C. Kelley, N-P.	1979, Dec.
Sheboygan, Wis.	Richard Suscha, R.	1977, Apr.
Shreveport, La.	L. Calhoun Allen Jr., D.	1978, Nov.
Simi Valley, Cal.	*Richard Malcolm.	1974, May
Sioux City, Ia.	*Gary F. Pokorny.	1974, Jan.
Sioux Falls, S.D.	Rick Knobe, R.	1979, May
Skokie, Ill.	*John N. Matzer Jr.	1970, Jan.
Somerville, Mass.	S. Lester Ralph, D.	1978, Jan.
South Bend, Ind.	Peter J. Nemeth, D.	1979, Dec.
So. Gate, Cal.	John Murdock, D.	1977, Mar.
So. S. F., Cal.	*Vacant.	
Southfield, Mich.	*Peter Cristiano	1968, July
Southgate, Mich.	*William Valusek.	1972, Feb.
Spartanburg, S.C.	*W. H. Carstarphen	1975, Mar.
Spokane, Wash.	*F. Sylvin Fulwiler.	1963, Aug.
Springfield, Ill.	William C. Telford, N-P.	1979, Apr.
Springfield, Mass.	William Sullivan, D.	1978, Jan.
Springfield, Mo.	*Don G. Busch.	1971, Oct.
Springfield, Ohio.	*Alfred Strozdas.	1968, Nov.
Stamford, Conn.	Louis Clapes, R.	1977, Nov.
Sterling Hts., Mich.	*Leonard Hendricks, .	1975, Jan.
Stillwater, Okla.	*Lawrence Gish.	1966, Aug.
Stockton, Cal.	*Elder Gunter.	1969, July
Stratford, Conn.	*H. B. Ewert.	1976, Aug.
Sunnyvale, Cal.	*John E. Dever.	1967, Aug.
Syracuse, N.Y.	Lee Alexander, D.	1977, Dec.
Tacoma, Wash.	*Erling O. Mork.	1975, June
Tallahassee, Fla.	*Daniel A. Kleman.	1974, Aug.
Tampa, Fla.	William Poe, N-P.	1979, Sept.
Taunton, Mass.	Benjamin Friedman, D.	1977, Dec.
Taylor, Mich.	S. Richard Marshall, D.	1977, Nov.
Teaneck, N.J.	*Werner H. Schmid.	1959, Mar.
Tempe, Ariz.	*Kenneth A. McDonald	1968, June
Temple, Tex.	William Courtney.	1978, Apr.
Terre Haute, Ind.	William Brighton, D.	1979, Dec.
Thousand Oaks, Cal.	*Glenn Kendall	1966
Titusville, Fla.	*Norman Hickey.	1974, June
Toledo, Ohio.	*Frank Pizza, act.	1976, Sept.
Topeka, Kan.	William McCormick, N-P.	1977, Apr.
Torrance, Cal.	*Edward J. Ferraro.	1964, Mar.
Trenton, N.J.	Arthur Holland, N-P.	1978, July
Troy, Mich.	*Frank Gerstenecker.	1970, Feb.
Troy, N.Y.	*John P. Buckley.	1972, June
Tucson, Ariz.	*Joel Valdez.	1974, Apr.
Tulsa, Okla.	Robert La Fortune, R.	1978, May
Tuscaloosa, Ala.	C. Snow Hinton, D.	1977, Oct.
Tyler, Tex.	*R. D. Brockman.	1976, Feb.

City	Name	Term
Univ. City, Mo.	*Victor Ellman.	1975, Dec.
Upland, Cal.	*S. Lee Travers.	1974, June
Upper Arlington, O.	*H. W. Hyrne.	1968, May
Urbana, Ill.	Hiram Paley, D.	1977, May
Utica, N.Y.	Edward Hanna, N-P.	1977, Dec.
Vallejo, Cal.	*Gerald R. Davis.	1973, Aug.
Vancouver, Wash.	*Alan Harvey	1969, May
Ventura, Cal.	*Edward E. McCombs.	1970, Mar.
Victoria, Tex.	*John Lee.	1959, Sept.
Vineland, N.J.	Patrick R. Fiorilli, N-P.	1980, July
Virginia Beach, Va.	*George L. Hanbury.	1974, Nov.
Waco, Tex.	*David F. Smith Jr.	1971, Sept.
Walnut Creek, Cal.	*Thomas G. Dunne.	1972, May
Waltham, Mass.	Arthur J. Clarke.	1980, Jan.
Warren, Mich.	Ted Bates, N-P.	1977, Nov.
Warwick, R. I.	Joseph Walsh, D.	1979, Jan.
Wash., D.C.	Walter Washington, D.	1979, Jan.
Waterbury, Conn.	Edward Bergin, D.	1977, Dec.
Waterloo, Ia.	Leo Rooff, N-P.	1978, Jan.
Waukegan, Ill.	Robert Sabonjian, R.	1977, Apr.
Waukesha, Wis.	Paul Vrakas, N-P.	1978, Apr.
Wauwatosa, Wis.	James A. Benz.	1980, Apr.
West Allis, Wis.	Jack Barlich, N-P.	1980, Apr.
W. Covina, Cal.	*Herman Fast.	1976, Aug.
W. Hartford, Conn.	*Richard H. Custer.	1972, Sept.
W. Haven Conn.	Robert A. Johnson, D.	1977, Dec.
W. New York, N.J.	Anthony De Fino, D.	1979, May
W. Orange, N.J.	William F. Cuozzi, D.	1978, June
W. Palm Beach, Fla.	*Richard Simmons.	1969, Aug.
Westland, Mich.	Thomas Taylor, N-P.	1977, Dec.
Westminster, Cal.	*Robert J. Huntley.	1967, July
Weymouth, Mass.	Board of Selectmen.	
Wheaton, Ill.	*William Kirchhoff.	1973, May
Wheeling, W. Va.	*Jack Maloney.	1976, June
White Plains, N.Y.	Alfred Del Vecchio, R.	1978, Jan.
Wichita, Kan.	*E. H. Denton.	1976, July
Wichita Falls, Tex.	*Gerald G. Fox.	1969, Feb.
Wilkes-Barre, Pa.	Walter Lisman, D.	1980, Jan.
Williamsport, Pa.	Daniel Kirby, D.	1980, Jan.
Wilmington, Del.	William T. McLaughlin, D.	1981, Jan.
Wilmington, N.C.	*John A. Jones.	1971, Sept.
Winston-Salem, N.C.	*Orville W. Powell.	1972, Nov.
Woonsocket, R.I.	Gerard Bouley, D.	1977, Nov.
Worcester, Mass.	*Francis J. McGrath.	1951, May
Wyandotte, Mich.	*William Sullivan, D.	1977, Apr.
Wyoming, Mich.	*Vacant.	
Yakima, Wash.	*Craig McMicken.	1967, Sept.
Yonkers, N.Y.	*J.E. Casey.	1974, July
Youngstown, Oh.	Jack Hunter, R.	1977, Dec.
York, Pa.	John D. Krout, R.	1978, Jan.
Zanesville, Oh.	*Frank Patrizio.	1974, Sept.

Canadian Cities

City	Name	Term
Calgary, Alta.	Rod Sykes.	1976, Oct.
Dartmouth, N.S.	Eileen Stubbs.	1977, Dec.
Edmonton, Alta.	T. J. Cavanagh.	1977, Oct.
Guelph, Ont.	N. Jary.	1976, Dec.
Halifax, N.S.	Edmund L. Morris.	1977, Oct.
Hamilton, Ont.	Victor K. Copps.	1976, Dec.
Hull, Que.	Gilles Rocheleau.	1979, Nov.
Kingston, Ont.	George N. Speal.	1976, Dec.
Kitchener, Ont.	Edith MacIntosh.	1976, Dec.
Lachine, Que.	Guy Descary.	1977, Nov.
La Salle, Que.	Gerald Raymond.	1979, Nov.
Laval, Que.	Lucien Paliement.	1977, Nov.
London, Ont.	Mrs. Jane Bigelow.	1976, Dec.
Moncton, N.B.	G.D. Wheeler.	1977, June
Montreal, Que.	Jean Drapeau.	1978, Nov.
Oshawa, Ont.	J. H. Potticary.	1976, Dec.
Ottawa, Ont.	Lorry Greenberg.	1976, Dec.
Peterborough, Ont.	James J. Behan.	1976, Dec.
Quebec, Que.	J. Gilles Lamontagne.	1977, Nov.
Regina, Sask.	Henry H.P. Baker.	1976, Oct.
St. John, N.B.	E. Flewwelling.	
Saskatoon, Sask.	Herbert S. Sears.	1976, Oct.
Sault Ste. Marie, Ont.	Nicholas Trbovich.	1976, Dec.
Sherbrooke, Que.	J. O'Brady.	1977, Nov.
Sudbury, Ont.	J. Gordon.	1976, Dec.
Toronto, Ont.	David Crombie.	1976, Dec.
Vancouver, B.C.	Art Phillips.	1976, Nov.
Victoria, B.C.	M. Young.	1976, Nov.
Waterloo, Ont.	D. P. Meston.	1976, Dec.
Windsor, Ont.	Bert Weeks.	1976, Dec.
Winnipeg, Man.	Stephen Juba.	1977, Oct.

PERSONAL FINANCE

Using The Consumer Price Index

To measure the impact of inflation, the indispensable tool is the Consumer Price Index (CPI) published monthly by the Bureau of Labor Statistics. The index has been specifically designed to apply to a worker family's pattern of purchases. Unless your own budget is markedly different from this norm, you should be able to employ the CPI to interpret your own affairs. The index is reported each month by most of the news media, often specifically for your own city, and what follows tells, step by step, how to employ the figures to analyze your own financial affairs.

The CPI emerges each month as a single number. In June 1976 it stood at 170.1, meaning that all the goods and services it measured cost 70.1% more that month than they did in the base year 1967. It can be considered this way: the 1967 value was 100.0%; by June 1976 another 70.1% had been added to living costs. The total comes to 170.1, the term "index" having the same sense as percent, merely omitting the percent sign.

The change in the price level for consumer goods and services can be calculated by comparing the CPI readings in one period against another. The June 1976 CPI of 170.1 may be compared to the June reading for 1975 of 160.6. Dividing 170.1 by 160.6, the excess over 1 is the percentage increase over the 12-month period: in this case, 5.91%. A similar year-to-year comparison may be made each month — indeed, these percentage changes often figure in the news releases when the month's CPI is announced.

We determined above that the CPI increased by 5.91% between June 1975 and June 1976. Did your income do the same? To make the comparison you might dig out your paycheck stubs for the same months and follow the arithmetic below.

The comparison can be made in terms of your base

Average Consumer Price Indexes

Source: Bureau of Labor Statistics, United States Department of Labor

The Consumer Price Index measures the average change in prices of goods and services purchased by urban wage-earner and clerical-worker families and single workers living alone. Data for 56 large, medium size, and small cities are combined for the all-city average.

(1967 — 100)

Year and month	All items	Food	Housing Total	Rent	Gas and electricity	Fuel and utilities	Household furnishings & operation	Apparel and upkeep	Transportation	Medical care	Personal care	Reading and recreation	Other goods and services
1970.	116.3	114.9	118.9	110.1	107.3	107.6	113.4	116.1	112.7	120.6	113.2	113.4	116.0
1971.	121.3	118.4	124.3	115.2	114.7	115.1	118.1	119.8	118.6	128.4	116.8	119.3	120.9
1972.	125.3	123.5	129.2	119.2	120.5	120.1	121.0	122.3	119.9	132.5	119.8	122.8	125.5
1973.	133.1	141.4	135.0	124.2	126.4	126.9	124.9	126.8	123.8	137.7	125.2	125.9	129.0
1974.	147.7	161.7	150.6	130.6	145.8	150.2	140.5	136.2	137.7	150.5	137.3	133.8	137.2
1975.	161.2	175.4	166.8	137.3	169.6	167.8	158.1	142.3	150.6	168.6	150.7	144.4	147.4
1976 Jan.	166.7	180.8	173.2	141.2	179.5	176.3	163.7	143.3	158.1	176.6	155.7	148.2	150.5
Feb.	167.1	180.0	173.8	142.1	181.9	177.9	165.2	144.0	158.5	178.8	157.0	148.5	151.3
Mar.	167.5	178.7	174.5	142.7	183.7	178.9	166.6	145.0	159.8	180.6	157.4	149.0	151.8
Apr.	168.2	179.2	174.9	143.2	184.4	179.3	167.4	145.7	161.3	181.6	158.3	149.5	152.5
May. . . .	169.2	180.0	175.6	143.8	186.1	180.2	167.9	146.8	163.5	182.6	158.9	150.3	152.9
June. . . .	170.1	180.9	176.5	144.4	188.5	181.7	168.5	146.9	165.9	183.7	159.8	150.9	153.2

Indexes of Retail Prices of Foods

Source: Bureau of Labor Statistics, U. S. Department of Labor (1967=100)

Year and Month	All food	Food away from home	Food prepared at home Food at home	Cereals, bakery	Beef, veal	Pork	Other meats	Poultry	Fish	Dairy products	Fruits, vegetables	Other foods	Nonalcoholic beverages
1969.	108.9		108.2	103.3						106.7	109.3	107.9	
1970.	114.9		113.7	108.9						111.8	113.4	114.1	
1971.	118.4	126.1	116.4	113.9	124.9	105.0	115.6	109.0	130.2	115.3	119.1	115.9	121.6
1972.	123.5	131.1	121.6	114.7	136.6	121.6	124.0	110.4	141.9	117.1	125.0	116.7	121.3
1973.	141.4	141.4	141.4	127.7	161.1	161.7	154.4	154.8	162.8	127.9	142.5	130.3	130.2
1974.	161.7	159.4	162.4	166.1	168.5	161.0	159.2	146.9	187.7	151.9	165.8	162.8	155.6
1975.	175.4	174.3	175.8	184.8	170.0	196.9	168.5	162.4	203.3	156.6	171.0	184.8	178.9
1976 Jan. . . .	180.8	180.9	180.8	182.0	174.9	210.1	180.3	164.5	216.1	168.2	173.3	186.7	191.1
Feb.	180.0	181.9	179.6	181.1	168.3	208.5	178.8	159.8	219.2	168.5	173.2	186.6	191.7
Mar.	178.7	182.8	177.7	180.6	164.7	204.3	177.7	157.7	219.3	167.9	173.6	182.9	193.0
Apr.	179.2	183.8	178.1	180.2	160.0	200.0	178.4	158.0	222.3	167.9	179.0	183.9	198.0
May. . .	180.0	184.8	178.8	180.8	167.1	201.9	180.2	155.3	225.1	167.4	176.4	184.1	203.3
June. . .	180.9	185.6	179.7	181.3	166.5	205.0	181.9	160.7	226.3	167.9	176.7	185.2	208.7

pay — your basic rate of earnings — or in terms of what you actually take home after standard deductions. Both gross and takehome comparisons are likely to be of interest to you, but take care to compare equals. Overtime pay should be omitted. When dealing with takehome pay, look out for changes in deductions which are unrelated to inflation, such as added exemptions, credit union deductions, payroll bonds, and the like.

Measuring Your Paycheck

A To compare the year-to-year earnings in percent form, divide your June 1976 earnings by your June 1975 earnings and express the result as a percent. If you earned the wage of the average U.S. worker, for example, your paycheck showed $175.81 per week in June 1976 as compared with $163.71 in June of 1975, an increase of 7.39%. Since prices rose by 5.91% during the same 12-month period, the average worker made a slight gain in real income that year.

B. Another way of dealing with the same figures takes a dollar form. For this calculation, assume your wage in June 1975 was $163.71 per week. Prices increased by 5.91%, according to the CPI. To match that pace, your wage should have gone to $173.38 ($163.71 times 1.0591) by June of 1976. If your earnings did not go up by that amount, you lost money to inflation, while the average worker gained.

Single readings on a weekly or monthly basis could be misleading; the inflation rate changes rapidly, earnings are affected by special situations unrelated to inflation. Repeated readings over a period of months provide a broader look. For this purpose you may consider an entire year as the appropriate period for measuring the total impact of inflation on your earnings.

The CPI provides us with an index of 161.2 for the year 1975 as a whole and 147.7 for 1974. Dividing 161.2 by 147.7, we get 1.0914; the excess over 1 shows price increases of 9.14% over the year. If you compare your earnings for the same years by the methods we have described, your shortfall due to or gain over inflation can be ascertained in percent or dollar form. You can readily determine your annual earnings on your income tax return or from your W-2 statements.

The figures cited above measure an individual's progress as compared with the rate of inflation, as if matching the rate were the sole target. Nothing is said about your personal capacity for advancement. Figuring your loss to inflation is only the first step of the reckoning, a way to true up your income figures so you can check your real progress and advancement.

Savings

Less visible to the average individual than the loss on earnings is the attrition inflation brings to his savings. Narrowly considered, savings are the funds salted away in some savings institution. Although such funds earn interest, it is clear that during double-digit inflation of 10% to 12%, interest rates of 5% to 8% cause a real loss in the value of the savings.

The apparent loss in the value of savings — the

Consumer Price Indexes by Cities
(1967=100)

City	All Items 1974	All Items 1975	Food 1974	Food 1975	City	All Items 1974	All Items 1975	Food 1974	Food 1975
U.S. City Average	147.7	161.2	161.7	175.4	Los Angeles, Calif.	142.5	157.6	156.3	170.1
Atlanta, Georgia	148.5	161.7	165.6	181.8	Milwaukee, Wis.	144.1	157.0	158.1	171.9
Baltimore, Maryland	152.4	165.2	164.4	178.2	Minneapolis, Minn.	148.3	160.9	163.6	178.9
Boston, Mass.	148.7	162.1	161.3	175.2	New York, N. Y.	154.8	166.6	166.1	179.6
Buffalo, N. Y.	149.5	161.8	160.1	173.6	Philadelphia, Pa.	151.6	164.2	165.2	179.6
Chicago, Illinois	146.1	157.6	161.6	175.1	Pittsburgh, Pa.	147.3	160.0	164.2	177.4
Cincinnati, Ohio	146.3	160.3	163.6	177.4	Portland, Ore.	142.8	156.5	154.4	168.4
Cleveland, Ohio	147.8	160.9	161.1	175.8	St. Louis, Mo.	142.2	156.1	159.7	174.3
Dallas, Texas	145.3	158.2	157.9	172.5	San Diego, Calif.	147.2	160.8	159.6	173.9
Detroit, Michigan	149.1	160.3	164.1	171.6	San Francisco, Calif.	144.4	159.1	155.6	171.2
Honolulu, Hawaii	141.8	154.4	158.7	176.7	Scranton, Pa.	151.1	164.7	161.7	172.9
Houston, Texas	147.8	164.9	164.9	181.2	Seattle, Wash.	141.5	155.8	155.8	169.6
Kansas City, Mo.	144.2	157.9	162.5	177.8	Washington, D.C.	150.0	161.6	166.9	180.7

Latest Month, 1976[1]

City	All Items (Month)	Food (June)	City	All Items (Month)	Food (June)
U.S. City Average	170.1 (6)	180.9	Los Angeles, Calif.	167.0(6)	173.1
Atlanta, Georgia	168.5 (6)	184.5	Milwaukee, Wis.	165.9(5)	180.1
Baltimore, Maryland	173.7 (6)	185.2	Minneapolis, Minn.	168.7(4)	186.3
Boston, Mass.	172.5 (4)	183.4	New York, N. Y.	176.0(6)	185.7
Buffalo, N. Y.	169.1 (5)	178.9	Philadelphia, Pa.	171.9(6)	186.3
Chicago, Illinois	164.9(6)	180.3	Pittsburgh, Pa.	166.7(4)	181.4
Cincinnati, Ohio	169.9 (6)	184.1	Portland, Ore.	166.4(4)	[2]175.5
Cleveland, Ohio	166.9 (5)	186.9	St. Louis, Mo.	165.2(6)	180.5
Dallas, Texas	166.2 (5)	177.4	San Diego, Calif.	169.3(5)	179.6
Detroit, Michigan	168.1 (6)	175.7	San Francisco, Calif.	166.9(6)	172.8
Honolulu, Hawaii	162.3 (6)	182.9	Scranton, Pa.	170.0(5)	[3]177.1
Houston, Texas	174.1 (4)	187.5	Seattle, Wash.	162.6(5)	173.4
Kansas City, Mo.	165.9 (6)	178.9	Washington, D.C.	170.0(5)	186.9

[1] All items indexes are computed monthly in 5 areas and on a rotating cycle in other areas: (6)=June, (5)=May, (4)=April.
[2] In April.   [3] In May.

amount of goods and services the funds will ultimately buy — should be considered in terms of a broadened view of savings. In addition to funds placed at interest, savings would include the paid-up value of a home or insurance policy and the value of savings bonds.

Purchasing Power of the Dollar

Source: U.S. Department of Labor, Bureau of Labor Statistics

1967=$1.00

Beginning 1961, wholesale prices include data for Alaska and Hawaii; and, beginning 1964, consumer prices include them. Obtained by dividing the average price index for 1967 base period (100.0) by the price index for given period and expressing the result in dollars and cents.

Year	Monthly average as measured by— Wholesale prices	Consumer prices	Year	Monthly average as measured by— Wholesale prices	Consumer prices
1940	$2.469	$2.381	1966	$1.002	$1.029
1950	1.222	1.387	1967	1.000	1.000
1955	1.139	1.247	1968	.976	.960
1957	1.072	1.186	1969	.939	.911
1958	1.057	1.155	1970	.906	.860
1959	1.055	1.145	1971	.878	.824
1960	1.054	1.127	1972	.840	.799
1961	1.058	1.116	1973	.744	.752
1962	1.055	1.104	1974	.625	.677
1963	1.058	1.091	1975	.572	.620
1964	1.056	1.076	1976, June	.546	.588
1965	1,035	1,058			

Average Weekly Earnings of Production Workers[1]

Source: Bureau of Labor Statistics

Year and month	Private nonagricultural workers						Manufacturing workers					
	Gross average weekly earnings		Spendable average weekly earnings[2]				Gross average weekly earnings		Spendable average weekly earnings[2]			
			Worker with no dependents		Worker with 3 dependents				Worker with no dependents		Worker with 3 dependents	
	Current dollars	1967 dollars	Current dollars	1967 dollars	Current dollars	1967 dollars	Current dollars	1967 dollars	Current dollars	1967 dollars	Current dollars	1967 dollars
1969	114.61	104.38	90.96	82.84	99.99	91.07	129.51	117.95	101.90	92.81	111.44	101.49
1970	119.46	102.72	95.94	82.49	104.61	89.95	133.73	114.99	106.62	91.68	115.90	99.66
1971	127.28	104.93	103.78	85.56	112.41	92.67	142.44	117.43	114.97	94.78	124.24	102.42
1972	136.16	108.67	111.65	89.11	121.09	96.64	154.69	123.46	125.32	100.02	135.56	108.19
1973	145.43	109.26	117.54	88.31	127.41	95.73	165.65	124.46	132.00	99.17	142.90	107.36
1974	154.45	104.57	124.14	84.05	134.37	90.97	176.00	119.16	139.80	94.52	150.94	102.19
1975	163.89	101.67	132.74	82.34	145.93	90.53	189.51	117.56	150.71	93.49	165.33	102.56
1976: January	169.92	101.93	139.31	83.57	151.61	90.95	200.30	120.16	161.23	96.72	174.55	104.71
February	170.64	102.12	139.83	83.68	152.17	91.07	201.10	120.35	161.80	96.83	175.15	104.82
March	170.53	101.81	139.75	83.43	152.08	90.79	202.40	120.84	162.73	97.32	176.12	105.15
April	171.24	101.81	140.26	83.39	152.63	90.74	198.74	118.16	160.10	95.18	173.37	103.07
May	174.48	103.12	142.60	84.28	155.13	91.68	205.82	121.64	165.22	97.65	178.69	105.61
June	175.81	103.36	143.56	84.40	156.14	91.79	208.06	122.32	166.89	98.11	180.38	106.04

[1]Data relate to production workers in mining and manufacturing; to construction workers in contract construction; and to nonsupervisory workers in transportation and public utilities; wholesale and retail trade; finance, insurance, and real estate; and services.
[2]Spendable average weekly earnings are based on gross average weekly earnings less the estimated amount of the worker's Federal, social security, and income taxes. (p)—preliminary.

Annual Percent Change in Productivity and Related Data, 1965-75

Source: Bureau of Labor Statistics

Item	1965	1966	1967	1968	1969	1970	1971	1972	1973	1974	1975
Total private:											
Output per hour of all persons	3.0	3.5	2.0	2.7	0.1	1.1	3.7	3.3	2.2	-2.6	1.3
Real compensation per hour	2.3	4.1	2.6	3.3	1.7	1.2	2.5	2.7	1.7	-1.4	0.
Unit labor cost	1.0	3.4	3.4	4.8	7.1	6.0	3.1	2.7	5.7	12.3	7.7
Unit non-labor payments	3.7	2.5	1.7	2.9	1.2	2.4	7.4	4.9	5.5	5.3	12.2
Implicit price deflator	2.0	3.1	2.8	4.1	4.9	4.7	4.6	3.5	5.6	9.7	9.3
Private nonfarm:											
Output per hour of all persons	2.6	1.0	1.7	2.6	-.4	.6	3.5	3.4	2.0	-2.5	.9
Real compensation per hour	1.9	3.2	2.7	3.1	1.3	.8	2.5	2.9	1.5	-1.4	-.1
Unit labor cost	1.0	3.1	1.3	4.7	7.1	6.1	3.3	2.7	5.7	12.2	8.1
Unit non-labor payments	2.9	2.3	1.9	3.2	.7	2.8	7.4	3.7	1.5	6.2	13.5
Implicit price deflator	1.7	2.8	3.1	4.1	4.7	4.9	4.7	3.1	4.2	10.1	9.9
Manufacturing:											
Output per hour of all persons	3.1	1.6	.3	3.6	1.2	-.4	5.6	5.1	1.7	-4.0	-.7
Real compensation per hour	.5	1.7	2.2	2.7	1.1	.8	2.2	2.2	.8	-1.0	1.1
Unit labor cost	.9	3.0	4.8	3.3	5.2	7.2	1.0	.4	5.2	14.5	11.1
Unit non-labor payments	5.2	-.7	-2.3	3.7	-4.2	-3.5	8.9	2.2	-3.5	-8.5	(¹)
Implicit price deflator	.8	1.8	2.5	3.5	2.3	4.2	3.1	1.0	2.7	8.4	(¹)

[1]Not available.

Federal Individual Income Tax
Source: Internal Revenue Service, Treasury Dept.

Who Must File
Every individual under 65 years of age who resided in the United States and had a gross income of $2,450 or more during the year must file a Federal income tax return. Anyone 65 or older on the last day of the tax year is not required to file a return unless he had gross income of $3,200 or more during the year. A married couple both 65 or older, need not file unless their gross income exceeds $5,100.

A taxpayer with gross income of less than $2,450 (or less than $3,200 if 65 or older) should file a return to claim the refund of any taxes withheld, even if he is listed as a dependent by another taxpayer.

Forms to Use
A taxpayer may, at his election, use form 1040 or Form 1040A. However, those taxpayers who choose to itemize deductions must use the longer form 1040.

Deductions
A taxpayer may either itemize deductions or choose one of the two types of standard deduction — the percentage standard deduction or the low-income allowance. For taxpayers with adjusted gross income of $15,000 or more, the percentage standard deduction is 16% of adjusted gross income up to a maximum of $2,800. ($1,400 for married persons filing separate returns). The low-income allowance for 1976 is $2,100. For single people, the percentage standard deduction is $2,400; the low income allowance is $1,700.

Dates For Filing Returns
For individuals using the calendar year, Apr. 15 is final date (unless it falls on a Saturday, Sunday or a legal holiday) for filing income tax returns and for payment of any tax due, and the first quarterly installment of the estimated tax. Other installments of estimated tax to be paid June 15, Sept. 15 and Jan. 15.

Apr. 15 is final date for filing declaration of estimated tax. Amended declarations may be filed June 15, Sept. 15, and Jan. 15.

Instead of paying the 4th installment a final income return may be filed Jan. 31. Farmers may file a final return Mar. 1 to satisfy estimated tax requirements.

Joint Return
A husband and wife may make a return jointly, even if one has no income personally. Their tax will be twice the tax imposed if the income were cut in half and taxed at the married filing separate rate.

One provision stipulates that if one spouse dies, the survivor may compute his tax using joint return rates for the first two taxable years following, provided he or she also was entitled to file a joint return the year of the death, and furnishes over half the cost of maintaining in his household a home for a dependent child or stepchild. If the taxpayer remarries before the end of the taxable year these privileges are lost but he is permitted to file a joint return with his new spouse. An individual legally separated or divorced is not considered married.

Estimated Tax
If total tax exceeds withheld tax by at least $100, declarations of estimated tax are required from (1) single individuals, heads of a household or surviving spouses, or a married person entitled to file a joint return whose spouse does not receive wages, who expects a gross income over $20,000; (2) married individuals with over $10,000 where both spouses receive wages; (3) married individuals with over $5,000 not entitled to file a joint return; and (4) individuals whose gross income can reasonably be expected to include more than $500 from sources other than wages subject to withholdings.

Exemptions
Personal exemption is $750.

Every individual has an exemption of $750, to be deducted from gross income. A husband and a wife are each entitled to a $750 exemption. A taxpayer 65 or over on the last day of the year gets another exemption of $750. A person blind on the last day of the year gets another exemption of $750.

Exemption for dependents, over one-half of whose total support comes from the taxpayer and for whom the other dependency tests have been met, is $750. This applies to a child, stepchild or adopted child as well as certain other relatives with less than $750 gross income; also to a child, stepchild, or adopted child of the taxpayer who is under 19 at the end of the year or was a full-time student during 5 months of the year even if he makes $750 or more. A dependent can be a non-relative if a member of the taxpayer's household and living there all year. There is a special $35 tax credit per dependent for 1976 or 2% of the first $9,000 of taxable income, whichever is greater.

Taxpayer gets the exemption for his child who is a student regardless of the student's age or earnings, provided the taxpayer provides over half of the student's total support. If the student gets a scholarship, this is not counted as support.

Child and Disabled Dependent Care
To qualify, a taxpayer must be employed and provide over one-half the cost of maintaining a household for a dependent child under 15, a disabled dependent of any age, or a disabled spouse.

Taxpayers may be allowed a credit of an amount equal to 20% of employment related expenses.

For further information consult your local IRS office or the instructional material attached to your return form.

Life Insurance
Life insurance paid to survivors is not taxed as income. Interest on life insurance left with the insurance company and paid to survivors at intervals is taxable when available. Surviving spouse has an exclusion of the prorata amount of principal payable at death plus up to $1,000 per year of interest earned when life insurance proceeds are payable in installments.

Regular payments under the Railroad Retirement Act, and those received as social security, are exempt.

Dividends
The first $100 in dividends can be excluded from income. If husband and wife both receive $100 on their joint return they can exclude $200.

The exclusion does not apply to dividends from tax-exempt corporations, mutual savings banks, building and loan associations and several others.

Dividends paid in stock or in stock rights are generally exempt from tax, except when paid in place of preferred stock dividends of the current or preceding year, or when the stockholder has an option to take stock or property or when the stock distribution is disproportionate.

Deductible Medical Expenses
Expenses for medical care, not compensated for by insurance or other payment for taxpayer, spouse, and dependents, in excess of 3% of adjusted gross income are deductible. This rule also applies to taxpayers 65 or over and dependent parents 65 or over, previously these persons were not subject to the percentage limitations. There is no limit to the maximum amount of medical expense that can be deducted.

Medical care includes diagnosis, treatment and prevention of disease or for the purpose of affecting any structure or function of the body, and amounts paid for insurance to reimburse for hospitalization, surgical fees and other medical expenses.

Only medicine and drugs in excess of 1% of adjusted gross income may be included in medical expenses.

One-half the cost of medical care insurance premiums up to $150 can be deducted without regard to the 3% limitation. The other half plus any excess over $150 is included with other medical expenses subject to the 3% limit.

Medical expenses for a decedent paid by his estate within one year after his death may be treated as expenses of the decedent taxpayer.

Medical and hospital benefits provided by the employer may be exempt from individual income tax. Wages paid as "sick day" are exempt up to $100 a week after a certain waiting period.

Deductions For Contributions

Deductions up to 50% of taxpayers' adjusted gross income may be taken for contribution to most publicly supported charitable organizations, including churches or associations of churches, tax-exempt educational institutions, tax-exempt hospitals, and medical research organizations associated with a hospital. The deduction is generally limited to 20% for such organizations as private nonoperating foundations, and certain organizations that do not qualify for the 50% limitation.

Taxpayers also are permitted to carry over for five years certain contributions, generally to publicly supported organizations, which exceed the 50% allowable deduction the year the contribution was made.

Also permissible is the deduction as a charitable contribution of unreimbursed amounts up to $50 a school month spent to maintain an elementary or high school student, other than a dependent or relative, in taxpayer's home. There must be a written agreement between you and a qualified organization.

Deductions for Interest Paid

Interest paid by the taxpayer is deductible.

If personal property is bought under a contract providing for payment by installments, and in which carrying charges are stated but interest is not ascertainable, then subject to limitation payments are held to include interest equal to 6% on average unpaid balance.

However, the amount charged to a customer's revolving charge account is solely for the privilege of deferring payment and is interest.

Prizes and Awards

All prizes and awards must be reported in gross income, except when received without action by the recipient. To be exempt, awards must be received primarily in recognition of religious, charitable, scientific, educational, artistic, literary, or civic achievement. (Nobel and Pulitzer prizes exempt.)

Deductions for Employees

An employee may take the standard deduction and deduct as well the following if in connection with his employment: transportation, except commuting; automobile expense, including gas, oil, and depreciation; however, meals and lodging are deductible as

traveling expense only if the employee is away from home overnight.

An outside salesman—a salesman who works full-time outside the office, using the latter only for incidentals—may deduct both the standard deduction and all his business expenses.

An employee who is reimbursed and is required to account to his employer for his business expenses will not be required to report either the reimbursement or the expenses on his tax return. Any allowance to the employee in excess of his expenses must be included in gross income. If he claims a deduction for an excess of expenses over reimbursement he will have to report the reimbursement and claim actual expenses.

An employee who is not required to account to his employer must report on his return the total amounts of reimbursements and expenses for travel, transportation, entertainment, etc., that he incurs under a reimbursement arrangement with his employer.

The expense of moving to a new place of employment may be deducted under certain circumstances regardless of whether the taxpayer is a new or continuing employee, or whether he pays his own expenses or is reimbursed by his employer. Reimbursement must be reported as income.

Tax Credit For the Elderly

Subject to certain rules or exclusions, taxpayers 65 or older may claim a credit which varies according to filing status. Taxpayers should read IRS instructions carefully for full details.

The credit is limited to 15% of $2,500 for single taxpayers; 15% of $2,500 for married taxpayers filing a joint return when only one taxpayer is 65 or older; 15% of $3,750 for married taxpayers both 65 or older filing a joint return; and 15% of $1,875 for a married taxpayer filing a separate return.

Net Capital Losses

An individual taxpayer may deduct capital losses up to $2,000 against his ordinary income. However, it takes $2 of net long-term capital loss to get $1 of offset against other income. He may carry the rest over to subsequent years at the same rate, no legal limit on the number of years.

Income Averaging

Individuals with large fluctuations in their annual income may be able to take advantage of averaging provisions available to taxpayers whose income for a particular year exceeds 120% of their average income for the prior 4 years, if the excess is more than $3,000.

Major Federal Tax Expenditures (Loopholes)

Source: Office of Management and Budget
(Estimates for fiscal year 1975)

Income tax provisions resulting in tax expenditures are defined as exceptions to the "normal structure" of individual and corporate income tax. They reduce tax liabilities for particular groups of taxpayers. The normal structure is nowhere defined in the tax code. Existing rates are accepted as "normal"; when the rate structure is changed, for whatever reason, the new rate structure becomes the new norm.

The following features of the tax system are defined as part of the normal tax structure and therefore do not result in tax expenditures: progres-

sive rate schedules for individual income tax; personal exemptions and the minimum standard deduction; separate schedules for single and married persons, married persons filing separately, and heads of households, deduction of business expenses; exclusion of unrealized capital gains and losses; exclusion of gifts and bequests received; exclusion of the value of government services received in kind (e.g., food stamps); foreign tax credits; treatment of individuals and corporations as separate tax paying entities.

Item	Amount (in millions) Individual	Corporate
State and local tax deduction	$8,490	$ —
Investment credit	950	4,860
Capital gains, lower tax on	5,090	695
Home mortgage interest deduction	5,405	—
Employer pension contribution exclusion	5,225	—
Charitable contributions deduction	4,385	385
Home property tax deduction	4,510	—
Interest on state and local bonds exclusion	1,130	2,675
Corporate profits, lower tax on first $50,000	—	3,345
Employer medical care and insurance payments exclusion	3,275	—

Item	Amount (in millions) Individual	Corporate
Social security retirement benefits exclusion	2,740	—
Percentage depletion allowance	465	2,010
Medical expense deduction	2,315	—
Unemployment insurance benefits exclusion	2,300	—
Interest on life insurance savings exclusion	1,545	—
Expensing of construction period interest and taxes	525	985
Excess of percentage standard deduction over low income allowance	1,385	—
Consumer credit interest deduction	1,185	—
Deferral for domestic international sales corporations	—	1,130
Additional exemption for over 65	1,100	—

Individual Income Tax Returns for 1974

Source: Internal Revenue Service
(Money amounts in thousands of dollars.)

Size of Adj. Gross Income	All returns Returns Number	Percent of total	Adjusted gross income Amount	Average (dollars)	Taxable returns Returns Number	Percent of total	Adjusted gross income Amount
Total	83,343,345	100.0	908,082,336	10,872	67,248,148	100.0	880,179,247
No adjusted gross income	540,949	0.6	−4,831,895	−8,932	2,152	(1)	−201,880
$1 under $1,000	5,517,576	6.6	3,037,085	550	10,322	(1)	9,677
$1,000 under $2,000	5,627,476	6.8	8,368,042	1,487	122,715	0.2	198,334
$2,000 under $3,000	5,209,580	6.3	12,901,965	2,477	3,399,354	5.1	8,511,025
$3,000 under $4,000	4,862,157	5.8	17,035,870	3,504	3,794,113	5.6	13,329,724
$4,000 under $5,000	5,067,058	6.1	22,864,235	4,512	4,381,046	6.5	19,804,763
$5,000 under $6,000	4,619,456	5.5	25,310,418	5,479	4,276,583	6.4	23,440,380
$6,000 under $7,000	4,286,741	5.1	27,868,517	6,501	4,083,170	6.1	26,554,357
$7,000 under $8,000	4,051,628	4.9	30,347,801	7,490	3,917,036	5.8	29,342,730
$8,000 under $9,000	3,873,616	4.6	32,888,337	8,490	3,786,759	5.6	32,142,873
$9,000 under $10,000	3,728,111	4.5	35,404,919	9,497	3,676,683	5.5	34,920,400
$10,000 under $11,000	3,385,754	4.1	35,531,585	10,494	3,348,513	5.0	35,141,300
$11,000 under $12,000	3,332,260	4.0	38,317,821	11,499	3,306,235	4.9	38,017,648
$12,000 under $13,000	3,106,085	3.7	38,797,222	12,491	3,085,963	4.6	38,547,143
$13,000 under $14,000	3,078,196	3.7	41,531,326	13,492	3,085,252	4.6	41,356,522
$14,000 under $15,000	2,743,108	3.3	39,771,418	14,499	2,732,989	4.1	39,626,309
$15,000 under $20,000	10,059,049	12.1	173,358,707	17,234	10,033,177	14.9	172,923,345
$20,000 under $25,000	4,920,640	5.9	109,165,668	22,185	4,910,367	7.3	108,944,715
$25,000 under $30,000	2,272,480	2.7	61,704,926	27,153	2,267,487	3.4	61,569,873
$30,000 under $50,000	2,193,723	2.6	80,848,105	36,854	2,183,803	3.2	80,474,554
$50,000 under $100,000	700,900	0.8	46,258,207	65,998	698,500	1.0	46,098,303
$100,000 under $200,000	135,405	0.2	17,666,518	130,472	134,752	0.2	17,580,808
$200,000 under $500,000	26,991	(1)	7,559,184	280,063	26,805	(1)	7,506,779
$500,000 under $1,000,000	3,278	(1)	2,170,918	662,269	3,249	(1)	2,149,877
$1,000,000 or more	1,128	(1)	2,205,437	1,955,174	1,123	(1)	2,189,688

Taxable returns—continued

Size of Adjusted Gross Income	Taxable income Amount	Income tax after credits Number of returns	Amount	Total income tax Amount	Percent of adjusted gross income	Average (dollars)
Total	572,447,144	67,243,440	123,560,278	123,690,314	14.1	1,839
No adjusted gross income	—	—	—	13,952	—	6,483
$1 under $1,000	1,458	10,218	204	434	4.5	45
$1,000 under $2,000	44,683	122,679	6,316	6,550	3.3	53
$2,000 under $3,000	1,519,244	3,399,267	216,459	216,812	2.5	64
$3,000 under $4,000	4,537,965	3,794,085	673,701	673,894	5.1	178
$4,000 under $5,000	8,532,627	4,381,020	1,332,580	1,332,825	6.7	304
$5,000 under $6,000	11,296,620	4,276,526	1,821,963	1,822,233	7.8	426
$6,000 under $7,000	13,885,442	4,083,147	2,289,546	2,289,701	8.6	561
$7,000 under $8,000	16,234,961	3,916,965	2,737,336	2,737,623	9.3	699
$8,000 under $9,000	18,632,336	3,786,761	3,214,915	3,215,388	10.0	849
$9,000 under $10,000	20,558,745	3,676,590	3,581,134	3,581,403	10.3	974
$10,000 under $11,000	21,059,082	3,348,492	3,729,334	3,729,613	10.6	1,114
$11,000 under $12,000	22,885,057	3,306,189	4,065,013	4,065,338	10.7	1,230
$12,000 under $13,000	23,858,301	3,085,956	4,279,604	4,279,810	11.1	1,387
$13,000 under $14,000	25,966,037	3,065,151	4,724,730	4,725,178	11.4	1,542
$14,000 under $15,000	25,377,537	2,732,784	4,649,449	4,649,658	11.7	1,701
$15,000 under $20,000	115,482,636	10,032,995	22,045,402	22,046,916	12.7	2,197
$20,000 under $25,000	77,047,360	4,910,254	15,766,031	15,767,780	14.5	3,211
$25,000 under $30,000	44,858,564	2,267,407	9,797,106	9,798,247	15.9	4,321
$30,000 under $50,000	60,841,076	2,183,420	15,190,793	15,197,010	18.9	6,959
$50,000 under $100,000	36,455,064	697,966	12,210,657	12,228,277	26.5	17,506
$100,000 under $200,000	14,144,973	134,481	6,118,933	6,141,712	34.9	45,578
$200,000 under $500,000	5,936,916	26,699	3,087,172	3,111,971	41.5	116,097
$500,000 under $1,000,000	1,633,580	3,206	964,247	980,403	45.6	301,755
$1,000,000 or more	1,656,880	1,112	1,057,650	1,077,586	49.2	959,560

(1) Less than 0.05 per cent.

Returns with Itemized Deductions for 1974
Source: Internal Revenue Service

Adjusted Gross Income (thsds.)	Total Deductions		Standard Deduction		Itemized Deductions		
	No. of Returns	Amount (thousands)	No. of Returns	Amount (thousands)	No. of Returns	%²	Amount (thousands)
Total, all returns¹	82,802,396	$195,532,260	53,076,473	$75,834,602	29,725,923	35.9	$119,697,658
$1.00 to $1,000	5,517,576	7,086,271	5,486,588	7,001,314	30,988	0.6	84,957
1,000 to 2,000	5,627,476	7,208,663	5,560,338	7,063,797	67,138	1.2	144,867
2,000 to 3,000	5,209,580	6,750,557	5,051,876	6,425,020	157,704	3.0	325,537
3,000 to 4,000	4,862,157	6,543,613	4,467,170	5,654,709	394,987	8.1	888,903
4,000 to 5,000	5,067,058	7,137,421	4,407,864	5,615,201	659,194	13.0	1,522,220
5,000 to 6,000	4,619,456	6,712,966	3,858,660	4,927,984	760,796	16.5	1,784,982
6,000 to 7,000	4,286,741	6,664,159	3,293,425	4,241,006	993,316	23.2	2,423,153
7,000 to 8,000	4,051,628	6,695,305	2,934,232	3,770,729	1,117,396	27.6	2,929,576
8,000 to 9,000	3,873,616	6,664,743	2,611,778	3,392,558	1,254,838	32.4	3,272,185
9,000 to 10,000	3,728,111	7,046,927	2,288,418	3,232,291	1,439,693	38.6	3,814,636
10,000 to 11,000	3,385,754	7,076,277	1,987,273	3,091,494	1,398,481	41.3	3,984,783
11,000 to 12,000	3,332,260	7,719,954	1,800,113	3,077,026	1,532,147	46.0	4,642,928
12,000 to 13,000	3,106,085	7,600,598	1,667,453	3,092,133	1,438,632	46.3	4,508,465
13,000 to 14,000	3,078,196	8,125,014	1,572,793	3,122,530	1,505,403	48.9	5,002,483
14,000 to 15,000	2,743,108	7,551,598	1,285,035	2,557,334	1,458,073	53.2	4,994,264
15,000 to 20,000	10,059,049	31,745,785	3,909,933	6,603,573	6,749,116	67.1	25,142,213
20,000 to 25,000	4,920,640	19,013,808	960,662	1,916,857	3,959,978	80.5	17,096,950
25,000 to 30,000	2,272,480	10,711,939	294,730	589,039	1,977,750	87.0	10,122,900
30,000 to 50,000	2,193,723	13,895,567	191,665	381,205	2,002,058	91.3	13,514,362
50,000 to 100,000	700,900	7,779,773	34,799	69,504	666,101	95.0	7,710,269
100,000 to 200,000	135,405	3,151,914	4,079	8,155	131,326	97.0	3,143,760
200,000 to 500,000	26,991	1,560,784	553	1,072	26,438	98.0	1,559,712
500,000 to 1,000,000	3,278	539,849	27	53	3,251	99.2	539,796
1,000,000 or more	1,128	548,775	9	18	1,119	99.2	548,757

Adjusted Gross Income (thousands)	Medical and Dental		Taxes Paid		Contributions	
	No. of Returns	Amount (thousands)	No. of Returns	Amount (thousands)	No. of Returns	Amount (thousands)
Total, all returns¹	22,354,671	$11,542,508	29,601,379	$43,579,844	27,984,800	$14,960,838
$1 to $1,000	21,609	37,289	25,999	16,525	16,640	5,633
1,000 to 2,000	46,044	30,546	58,767	52,789	40,548	10,021
2,000 to 3,000	135,839	104,922	153,883	92,056	121,543	34,618
3,000 to 4,000	337,437	301,127	387,686	246,611	349,457	104,803
4,000 to 5,000	597,527	525,547	649,022	394,537	569,178	160,635
5,000 to 6,000	628,489	471,975	759,006	479,289	665,211	207,485
6,000 to 7,000	840,714	584,143	985,748	685,776	894,162	288,385
7,000 to 8,000	920,100	641,988	1,114,694	855,500	1,007,995	309,350
8,000 to 9,000	1,033,181	635,607	1,244,729	970,751	1,156,170	366,637
9,000 to 10,000	1,181,792	629,385	1,428,050	1,129,055	1,284,314	418,383
10,000 to 11,000	1,080,126	639,779	1,386,512	1,208,858	1,271,103	416,790
11,000 to 12,000	1,218,020	624,399	1,528,269	1,431,292	1,417,076	507,999
12,000 to 13,000	1,110,660	521,125	1,435,194	1,438,987	1,338,360	489,391
13,000 to 14,000	1,132,660	531,466	1,498,137	1,622,545	1,417,100	527,329
14,000 to 15,000	1,007,714	491,388	1,448,662	1,693,445	1,387,828	546,689
15,000 to 20,000	4,859,020	1,961,673	6,739,153	9,171,620	6,484,890	2,696,307
20,000 to 25,000	2,803,207	1,145,176	3,957,289	6,814,961	3,861,434	1,996,571
25,000 to 30,000	1,447,510	581,980	1,976,884	4,197,074	1,934,528	1,243,469
30,000 to 50,000	1,435,224	713,612	1,996,875	5,784,369	1,960,044	1,804,395
50,000 to 100,000	421,980	274,629	664,964	3,293,083	648,823	1,300,597
100,000 to 200,000	77,936	72,651	131,121	1,220,881	128,340	643,386
200,000 to 500,000	15,439	18,763	26,373	505,899	25,776	436,017
500,000 to 1,000,000	1,861	2,813	2,243	146,705	3,184	188,686
1,000,000 or more	582	525	1,119	127,236	1,096	257,262

Adjusted Gross Income (thsds.)	Miscellaneous³		Taxable Returns			
	No. of Returns	Amount (thousands)	No. of Returns	Total Adjusted Gross Income (thousands)	Total Tax (thousands)	Total tax as % of Total A.G.I.
Total, all returns¹	24,992,220	$12,453,280	28,461,844	$538,303,327	$82,103,368	15.3
$1 to $1,000	16,505	7,416	—⁴	—⁴	—⁴	—⁴
1,000 to 2,000	39,297	25,094	8,764	13,910	960	6.9
2,000 to 3,000	102,832	23,003	46,195	120,760	4,663	3.9
3,000 to 4,000	270,848	54,499	185,325	667,293	17,957	2.7
4,000 to 5,000	487,677	161,525	416,640	1,904,991	72,075	3.8
5,000 to 6,000	566,166	186,335	594,483	3,285,959	155,642	4.7
6,000 to 7,000	781,964	257,757	870,288	5,670,952	324,462	5.7
7,000 to 8,000	874,047	291,560	1,019,999	7,643,931	497,532	6.5
8,000 to 9,000	1,016,323	355,314	1,196,786	10,167,466	741,940	7.3
9,000 to 10,000	1,223,739	482,013	1,400,249	13,302,202	1,077,885	8.1
10,000 to 11,000	1,171,915	445,909	1,368,814	14,377,883	1,248,743	8.7
11,000 to 12,000	1,337,376	558,454	1,512,117	17,396,167	1,548,692	8.9
12,000 to 13,000	1,244,368	521,597	1,421,047	17,773,893	1,672,898	9.4
13,000 to 14,000	1,323,794	583,854	1,493,949	20,156,257	1,990,799	9.9
14,000 to 15,000	1,261,275	568,013	1,450,135	21,037,605	2,177,334	10.3
15,000 to 20,000	5,924,853	2,696,051	6,730,436	116,860,672	13,753,380	11.8
20,000 to 25,000	3,404,624	1,586,426	3,953,037	87,935,330	12,192,792	13.9
25,000 to 30,000	1,669,039	914,962	1,973,669	53,667,510	8,299,623	15.5
30,000 to 50,000	1,623,104	1,316,263	1,994,837	73,717,108	13,727,331	18.6
50,000 to 100,000	517,578	768,029	663,775	43,881,540	11,587,165	26.4
100,000 to 200,000	108,284	351,774	130,680	17,058,371	5,936,236	34.8
200,000 to 500,000	22,708	184,183	26,256	7,354,666	3,035,901	41.3
500,000 to 1,000,000	2,895	64,082	3,222	2,130,610	969,279	45.5
1,000,000 or more	1,009	50,167	1,114	2,178,238	1,069,893	49.1

(1) Not including 540,949 returns with no adjusted gross income. (2) Percent of returns, in each income category, which are itemized. (3) All other deductions except those for interest paid. (4) Estimate not shown because sample base is too small.

Social Security Programs

Source: Office of Research and Statistics, Social Security Administration, Dept. of Health, Education and Welfare

Medicare; Old-Age, Survivors and Disability Insurance: Supplemental Security Income

Medicare provisions of the legislation enacted in 1976 amended the Social Security Act to continue until Oct. 1, 1977, to reimburse teaching physicians in hospitals for program services on a cost basis if certain conditions are met, to update reasonable charge screens on July 1, rather than October 1, the beginning of the new Federal fiscal year, and to provide that the prevailing charge for a physician service for any period after fiscal year 1976 may not be lower than the charge in effect in fiscal year 1975. Supplemental security income (SSI) legislation provides food stamp eligibility, through June 30, 1977, for most persons receiving SSI payments, and excludes from income for SSI purposes certain emergency support and maintenance rendered as a result of a declared disaster occurring from June 1 through December 31, 1976.

The second cost-of-living increase in social security benefits — amounting to 6.4% — went into effect in June 1976 and was reflected in monthly checks received in July by all persons on the rolls in May except those affected by the special minimum benefit provision. Since Federal SSI payments administered by the Social Security Administration are also affected by the automatic provisions, they rose at the same rate, effective for July. The next automatic cost-of-living increase will be based on the rise in the consumer price index from the first quarter of 1976 (if there is no legislated increase) to the first quarter of 1977; if the index rises 3% or more, the benefit level will be raised as of June 1977 by the same percentage.

The 1976 benefit increase made necessary two other automatic adjustments, effective for 1977: (1) The maximum taxable and creditable earnings base was raised from $15,300 to $16,500, and (2) the annual exempt earnings amount for social security beneficiaries was increased from $2,760 to $3,000 (or $250 in a month).

In Medicare, following the required annual review of hospital costs under the program, increases were made in the hospital insurance deductible amount (what the patient must pay for hospital services before reimbursement can begin) and in the cost-sharing for days above the number specified in the law.

The Commissioner of Social Security is James B. Cardwell. There are 632 district offices (with 506 branches), 173 metropolitan branch offices, and 29 teleservice centers where the public may obtain information about benefit rights.

Medicare
Health Insurance for Aged and Disabled

Under Medicare, protection against the costs of hospital care is provided for social security and railroad retirement beneficiaries aged 65 and over (beginning July 1966) and, effective July 1973, for persons entitled for 24 months to receive a social security disability benefit, certain persons with chronic kidney disease and their dependents, and, on a voluntary basis with payment of a special premium, persons aged 65 and over not otherwise eligible for hospital benefits; all those eligible for hospital benefits may enroll for medical benefits and pay a monthly premium and so may persons aged 65 and over who are not eligible for hospital benefits.

Persons eligible for both hospital and medical insurance or for medical insurance only may choose to have their covered services provided through a Health Maintenance Organization (a prepaid group health or other capitation plan that meets prescribed standards).

Hospital insurance. — In the 10th year of operation (July 1975 - June 1976) about $12.4 billion was withdrawn from the hospital insurance trust fund for hospital and related benefits. About 24,640,500 persons were enrolled under the program as of July 1975

— 2,168,400 of them disabled beneficiaries under age 65.

The hospital insurance program pays the cost of covered services for hospital and posthospital care as follows:

- Up to 90 days of hospital care during a benefit period (spell of illness) starting the first day that care as a bed-patient is received in a hospital or skilled-nursing facility and ending when the individual has not been a bed-patient for 60 consecutive days. For the first 60 days, the hospital insurance pays for all but the first $124 of expenses; for the 61st day to 90th day, the program pays all but $31 a day for covered services. In addition, each person has a 60-day lifetime reserve that can be used after the 90 days of hospital care in a benefit period are exhausted, and all but $62 a day of expenses during the reserve days are paid. Once used, the reserve days are not replaced. (Payment for care in a mental hospital is limited to 190 days.)
- Up to 100 days' care in a skilled-nursing facility (skilled-nursing home) in each benefit period. Hospital insurance pays for all covered services for the first 20 days and all but $15.50 daily for the next 80 days. At least 3 days' hospital stay must precede these services, and the skilled-nursing facility must be entered within 14 days after leaving the hospital. (The 1972 law permits more than 14 days in certain circumstances.)
- Up to 100 visits by nurses or other health workers (not doctors) from a home health agency in the 365 days after release from a hospital or extended-care facility.

Money to pay these benefits comes from special contributions paid by workers, their employers, and the self-employed. The 1976 rate was 0.9% on earnings up to $15,300 (the maximum taxable for that year). It is 0.9% on earnings up to $16,500 for 1977.

Medical insurance—Aged persons can receive benefits under this supplementary program only if they sign up for them and agree to a monthly premium ($7.20 to July 1977). The Federal Government pays the rest of the cost. In December of each year the Secretary of Health, Education, and Welfare announces the amount of the premium payable starting in July of the following year. The premiums are to be increased only when there is a general benefit increase in the year and it will rise no more than the percent by which the cash benefits have been increased since the last premium increase.

About 80.9 million bills were reimbursed under the medical insurance program in fiscal year 1976 for a total of $4.7 billion. As of July 1975, 23,904,500 persons were enrolled — 1,959,250 of them disabled persons under age 65.

The medical insurance program pays 80% of the reasonable charges (after the first $60 in each calendar year) for the following services:

- Physicians' and surgeons' services, whether in the doctor's office, a clinic, or hospital or at home (but physician's charges for X-ray or clinical laboratory services for hospital bed-patients are paid in full and without meeting the deductible).
- Other medical and health services, such as diagnostic tests, surgical dressings and splints, and rental or purchase of medical equipment. Beginning July 1, 1973, services of a physical therapist in independent practice, furnished in his office or the patient's home. Beginning Jan. 1, 1973, a hospital or extended-care facility may provide covered outpatient physical therapy services under the medical insurance program to its patients who have exhausted their hospital insurance coverage.
- Physical therapy services furnished under the supervision of a practicing hospital, clinic, skilled nursing facility, or agency.
- Certain services by podiatrists.
- All outpatient services of a participating hospital (including diagnostic tests).

- Outpatient speech pathology services, under the same requirements as physical therapy.
- Services of licensed chiropractors who meet uniform standards, but only for treatment by means of manual manipulation of the spine and treatment of subluxation of the spine demonstrated by X-ray.
- Supplies related to colostomies are considered prosthetic devices and payable under the program.
- Home health services even without a hospital stay (up to 100 visits a year) are paid up to 100%.

To get medical insurance protection, persons approaching age 65 may enroll in the 7-month period that includes 3 months before the 65th birthday, the month of the birthday, and 3 months after the birthday, but if they wish coverage to begin in the month they reach 65 they must enroll in the 3 months **before** their birthday. Persons not enrolling within their first enrollment period may enroll later, during the first 3 months of each year but their premium is 10% higher for each 12-month period elapsed since they first could have enrolled.

The monthly premium is deducted from the cash benefit for persons receiving social security, railroad retirement, or civil service retirement benefits. Income from the medical premiums and the Federal matching payments are put in a Supplementary Medical Insurance Trust Fund, from which benefits and administrative expenses are paid.

Medicare card. Persons qualifying for hospital insurance under social security receive a health insurance card similar to cards now used by Blue Cross and other health agencies. The card indicates whether the individual has taken out medical insurance protection. It is to be shown to the hospital, skilled nursing facility, home health agency, doctor, or whoever provides the covered services.

Payments are made only in the 50 States, Puerto Rico, the Virgin Islands, Guam, and American Samoa, except that hospital services may be provided in border areas immediately outside the U.S. if comparable services are not accessible in the U.S. for a beneficiary who becomes ill or is injured in the U.S.

Old-Age Survivors, and Disability Insurance

Retired and disabled workers and their families and the survivors of deceased workers received $70.8 billion in social security cash benefits in the 12 months ended in June 1976. In that month the average benefit being received by a retired worker was about $222; for retired workers just coming on the rolls, the average benefit award was about $236. For a disabled worker, the average June check was $243 and new disabled-worker beneficiaries were awarded $269, on the average.

Old-age, survivors, and disability insurance covers almost all jobs in which people work for wages or salaries, as well as most work of self-employed persons, whether in a city job, or in business, or on a farm.

Old-age, survivors, and disability insurance is paid for by a tax on earnings (for 1976 up to $15,300 and for 1977 up to $16,500; the taxable earnings base is now subject to adjustment when cost-of-living benefit increases have been made). The employed worker and his employer share the tax equally (cash tips count as covered wages if they amount to $20 or more from one place of employment. The worker reports them to his employer, who includes them in his social security tax reports, but only the worker pays contributions on the amount of the tips).

The employer deducts the tax each payday and sends it, with an equal amount as his own share, to the District Director of Internal Revenue. The collected taxes are deposited in the Federal Old-Age and Survivors Insurance Trust Fund and the Federal Disability Insurance Trust Fund; they can be used only to pay benefits, the costs of rehabilitation services, and administrative expenses.

Amount of Work Required

To qualify for benefits for himself and his family, the worker must have been in covered employment long enough to become insured. Just how long depends on his date of birth (or if he dies or becomes disabled, the date of his death or disability).

A person is fully covered if he has one quarter of coverage for every year after 1950 (or year he reaches age 21) up to but not including the year in which he reaches age 62 or dies.

Certain provisions in the law permit special monthly payments under the social security program to persons aged 72 and over who are not eligible for regular social security benefits since they had little or no opportunity to earn social security work credits during their working lifetime.

To get disability benefits, the worker must also have credit for 5 out of 10 years before he becomes disabled. Persons disabled before age 31 can qualify with a briefer period of coverage.

Work Years Required

The following table shows the number of work years required to be fully insured for old-age or survivors benefits, according to the year worker reaches retirement age or dies.

Work credit for retirement benefits

If you reach 62 in	Years you need	If you reach 62 in	Years you need
1974	6*	1979	7
1975	6	1981	7½
1976	6¼	1983	8
1977	6½	1987	9
1978	6¾	1991 or later	10

*For 1974 a woman needs only 5¾ years.

Work credit for survivors checks

Born after 1929, die at	Born before 1930, die before age 62	Years you need
28 or younger		1½
30		2
32		2½
34		3
36		3½
38		4
40		4½
42		5
44	1973	5½
45	1974	5¾
46	1975	6
48	1977	6½
50	1979	7
52	1981	7½
54	1983	8
56	1985	8½
58	1987	9
60	1989	9½
62 or older	1991 or later	10

Self-Employed

A self-employed person who has earnings of $400 or more in a year must report his earnings for income tax and social security tax purposes. If he is not a farmer he reports only net returns from his business. He need not add income from real estate, savings, dividends, loans, pensions or insurance policies if these are not part of his business.

A self-employed person who has net earnings of $400 or more in a year gets 4 quarters of coverage for that year. If his earnings are less than $400 in a year they do not count toward social security credits. The nonfarm self-employed person must make estimated payments of his social security taxes, on a quarterly basis, for taxable years after 1966, if combined estimated income tax and social security tax amount to at least $40.

The self-employed now have the option, comparable to that for farm workers, of reporting their earnings as ⅔ of their gross income from self-employment but not more than $1,600 a year. This option can be used only if actual net earnings from self-employment income is less than $1,600 and less than ⅔ of gross income and may be used only 5 times.

When a person has both taxable wages and earnings from self-employment, only as much of the self-employment income as will bring total earnings up to the current taxable maximum is subject to tax for social security purposes. A self-employed person pays the tax at a lower rate than the combined rate for an employee and his employer — about 1 1/2 times what the employee alone pays.

Farm Owners and Hands

Self-employed farmers whose gross annual earnings from farming are under $2,400 may report ²/₃ of their gross earnings instead of net earnings for social security purposes. Cash or crop shares received from a tenant or share farmer count if the owner participated materially in production or management. The self-employed farmer pays contributions at the same rate as other self-employed, but he may make his tax returns annually.

Farm Workers. Earnings from farm work count toward benefits (1) if the employer pays $150 or more in cash during the year; (2) if the employee works on 20 or more days for cash pay figured on a time basis. Under these rules a person gets credit for one calendar quarter for each $100 in cash pay in a year but no more than four quarters in any one year.

Foreign farm workers admitted to the United States on a temporary basis are not covered.

Household Workers

Anyone working as maid, cook, laundress, nursemaid, baby-sitter, chauffeur, gardener and at other household tasks in the house of another, is covered by social security if he or she earns $50 or more in cash in three months from any one employer. Room and board do not count, but carfare counts if paid in cash. The job does not have to be regular or fulltime. The employee should get a card at the social security office and show it to the employer.

The employer deducts the amount of the social security tax from the worker's pay, adds an identical amount as his own tax and sends the total amount to the Federal Government, with the number of the employee's social security card.

What Aged Workers Get

When a person has enough work in covered employment and reaches retirement age (65 for full benefit, 62 for reduced benefit), he may retire and get monthly old-age benefits. If he continues to work and has earnings of more than $3,000, $1 in benefits will be withheld for every $2 above $3,000. The amount that can be earned in a month without loss of any benefits is $250. The annual exempt amount and the monthly test will be raised automatically in the future, according to the rise in general earnings levels. The eligible worker who is 72 receives the full amount of benefit, regardless of earnings.

A worker's benefit will be raised by 1% for each year after 1970 for which the worker between 65 and 72 did not receive benefits because of earnings from work. No increases are to be paid to the worker's dependents or survivors under this provision.

A special minimum benefit is payable to persons who worked 20 or more years under social security as an alternative to the regular minimum of $101.40 if a higher amount results. The highest minimum under this provision would be $180 a month for a person ($270 for a couple) with 30 or more years of coverage.

When a person receives old-age benefits, payments can also be made to certain of his dependents, including a wife 62 or over, dependent children under 18 or who became totally disabled before age 22 or who are full-time students not yet aged 22, a wife (regardless of age) if caring for an eligible child, and a dependent husband 62 or over.

The special benefit for persons aged 72 or over who do not meet the regular coverage requirements is $74.10 a month ($111.20 for a couple if both members are eligible). Like the monthly benefits, these payments are subject to cost-of-living increases, beginning June 1975. The special payment is not made to

persons on the public assistance or supplemental security income rolls.

Social Security benefits are not subject to income taxes.

A woman worker is eligible for a full old-age benefit at age 65, but she may retire at 62 and get 80% of her full benefit for the rest of her life; the nearer she is to 65 when she begins collecting her benefit, the larger it will be. (Benefits for men retiring before 65 are reduced at the same rate as benefits for women retiring before 65.)

A child can get benefits based on his mother's earnings on the same conditions as those entitling a child to benefits based on his father's earnings record.

Benefits for Worker's Wife (or Husband)

The wife of a man who is getting social security retirement or disability payments may become entitled to wife's insurance benefits in a reduced amount when she reaches 62, or she may wait until she reaches 65 and get the entire amount of the wife's benefit, which is one-half of the husband's benefit. Benefits are also payable to the divorced wife of an insured worker if she was married to him for at least 20 years and he was contributing to or was ordered by a court to contribute to her support.

If a woman worker entitled to an old-age benefit has a dependent husband aged 65 or over, he may draw a benefit similar to a wife's benefit at 65 (or a reduced benefit at age 62).

Benefits for Children of Retired or Disabled Workers

If a worker has children under 18 when he retires for age or disability they will get a benefit that is half his benefit, and so will his wife, even if she is under 62. Total benefits paid on a worker's earnings record are subject to a maximum and if the total paid to a family exceeds that maximum, the individual dependents' benefits are adjusted downward. (Total benefits paid to the family of a worker who retired in 1974 at age 65 with average yearly earnings of $5,838 could be no higher than $541.)

When his children reach 18, their benefits will stop, except that a child permanently and totally disabled before 22 may get a benefit as long as his disability meets the definition in the law. In addition, child's benefits are payable until the child reaches his 22nd birthday if he is attending school as a full-time student. Benefits may now be paid to a grandchild or step-grandchild of a worker or of his spouse, in special circumstances.

What Disabled Workers Get

If a worker becomes so severely disabled that he is unable to work, he may be eligible to receive a monthly disability benefit that is the same amount he would receive as an old-age benefit if he were 65 at the start of his disability. When he reaches 65, his disability benefit becomes an old-age benefit.

Benefits like those provided for dependents of retired-worker beneficiaries may be paid to dependents of disabled beneficiaries.

Survivor Benefits

If a worker should die while insured, one or more types of benefits would be payable to survivors.

1. A cash payment to cover burial expenses that amounts to 3 times the basic benefit but not more than $255, paid at the death of every insured worker.

2. A benefit for each child until the child reaches 18 (or up to age 22, if he is attending school). The monthly benefit of each child of a worker who has died is three-quarters of the amount the worker would have received if he had lived and drawn retirement benefits. A child with a permanent disability that began before age 22 may receive his benefit after that age.

3. A mother's benefit for the widow, if children under 18 are left in her care. Her benefit is 75% of the basic benefit and she draws it until the youngest child reaches 18. Payments stop then even if the

child's benefit continues because he is attending school. They will start again when she is 62 (or 60), unless she marries. If she marries and the marriage is ended, she regains benefit rights. If she has a disabled child beneficiary aged 18 or over in her care, her benefits also continue.

Disabled widows and widowers qualify for benefits at age 50 at reduced rates that depend on age at entitlement. The widow or widower must have become totally disabled before or within 7 years after the spouse's death.

4. If there are no children entitled to receive benefits, the widow will receive a benefit that is 100% of the husband's basic amount, if it is first payable when she is 65. She may choose to get her benefit when she is 60; her benefit is then reduced by 19/40 of 1% for each month it is paid before she is 65. However, for widows aged 62 and over whose husbands claimed their benefits before 65, the benefit is the reduced amount he would be getting if he were alive but not less than 82 1/2% of his basic benefit. Dependent widowers aged 60 or over are entitled to survivor benefits on same basis as widows.

5. Dependent parents may be eligible for benefits, if they have been receiving at least half their support from the worker before his death, have reached age 62, and (except in certain circumstances) have not remarried since the worker's death. Each parent gets 75% of the basic benefit except that if only one parent survives the benefit is 82½%.

The survivors of a woman worker receive benefits on the same basis as those of men workers.

Maximum Benefits Payable

The illustrative table below shows a column heading for average earnings of $12,000, but the benefit amounts shown in the column are not in general payable yet, since it will be some time before workers can have an average that high (years when the maximum creditable amount of earnings was lower than $13,200 — the 1974 maximum — must currently be included when the average is figured). Benefit amounts larger than those shown in the table will eventually be payable to persons who raise their average yearly earnings for social security purposes by earning, for a sufficient period, the highest creditable amount in years with the higher maximums specified in the law — $15,300 in 1976 and $16,500 in 1977 (higher amounts in the future whenever the base is raised under the automatic adjustment procedure).

Examples of Monthly OASDI Cash Payments
Average yearly earnings after 1950

Benefits can be paid to:	$923 or less	$3,000	$4,000	$5,000	$6,000	$8,000	$10,000	$12,000
Worker:								
Retired at 65	107.90	223.20	262.60	304.50	344.10	427.80	474.00	516.10
Under 65 and disabled	107.90	223.20	262.60	304.50	344.10	427.80	474.00	516.10
Retired at 62	86.40	178.60	210.10	243.60	275.30	342.30	379.20	412.90
Wife:								
at 65	54.00	111.60	131.30	152.30	172.10	213.90	237.00	258.10
at 62, with no child	40.50	83.70	98.50	114.30	129.10	160.50	177.80	193.60
Under 65 and one child in her care	54.00	118.00	186.20	257.40	287.20	321.00	355.60	387.00
Widow:								
At 65 (if worker never received reduced retirement benefits)	107.90	223.20	262.60	304.50	344.10	427.80	474.00	516.10
at 60 (if sole survivor)	77.20	159.60	187.80	217.80	246.10	305.90	339.00	369.10
at 50 and disabled (if sole survivor)	56.80	111.70	131.40	152.40	172.20	214.00	237.10	258.20
Widowed mother (or father) caring for one child	161.90	334.80	394.00	456.80	516.20	641.80	711.00	774.20
Maximum family payment	161.90	341.20	448.80	561.90	631.30	748.70	829.50	903.10

*Generally, average earnings are figured over the period from 1951 until the worker reaches retirement age, becomes disabled, or dies. Up to 5 years of low earnings or no earnings can be excluded. The maximum earnings creditable for social security are $3,600 for 1951-1954; $4,200 for 1955-1958; $4,800 for 1959-65; $6,600 for 1966-67; $7,800 for 1968-71; $9,000 for 1972; $10,800 for 1973; $13,200 for 1974; $14,100 for 1975; $15,300 for 1976; and $16,500 for 1977. As the text under the heading "Maximum Benefits Payable" explains, amounts shown in the last column will generally not be payable until later. When a person is entitled to more than one benefit, the amount actually payable is limited to the larger of the benefits.

Contribution Rate for Employees, Employers, and Self-Employed
Percent of Covered Earnings

Years	Employees and employers			Self-employed		
	OASDI Benefits	Hospital Insurance	Total	OASDI Benefits	Hospital Insurance	Total
1974-77	4.95	0.90	5.85	7.0	0.90	7.90
1978-80	4.95	1.10	6.05	7.0	1.10	8.10
1981-85	4.95	1.35	6.30	7.0	1.35	8.35
1986-97	4.95	1.50	6.45	7.0	.50	8.50
1998-2010*	4.95	(1.50)	(6.45)	7.0	(1.50)	(8.50)
2011 and thereafter	5.95	(1.50)	(7.45)	7.0	(1.50)	(8.50)

*Costs of hospital insurance estimated only through 1997.

Supplemental Security Income

On Jan. 1, 1974, the supplemental security income program established by the 1972 Social Security Act amendments replaced the former Federal grants to States for aid to the needy aged, blind, and disabled in the 50 States and the District of Columbia. The program provides both for Federal payments based on uniform national standards and eligibility requirements and for State supplementary payments varying from State to State. The Social Security Administration administers the Federal payments financed from general funds of the Treasury — and the State supplements as well, if the State elects to have its supplementary program federally administered. The States may supplement the Federal payment for all recipients and must supplement it for persons otherwise adversely affected by the transition from the former public assistance programs. In June 1976, the number of persons receiving Federal payments and federally administered State payments was 4,308,000, and the amount of these payments was $489,581,000. The average amount of combined federal payments and federally administered state payments was $114 for that month.

As a result of the 6.4 percent cost-of-living increase in social security benefits in June, 1976, the Federal SSI payment levels were raised in July, 1976, from $157.70 per month for an individual and $236.60 for a couple to $167.80 and $251, respectively.

Social Security Trust Funds
Old-Age and Survivors and Disability Insurance Trust Funds, 1937-1976
(In thousands)

| Period and fiscal year | Receipts | | Expenditures | | | |
	Net contrib. inc., transfers, and reimb. from gen. rev.	Net interest received	Cash benefit payments and rehab. services	Transfers to R.R. acct.	Adminis-trative expenses	Total assets at end of period
1937.	$ 265,000	$ 2,262	$ 27	. . . .	$ 26,840	$ 267,235
1940.	550,000	42,489	15,805	. . . .	12,288	1,744,698
1945.	1,309,919	123,854	239,834	. . . .	26,950	6,613,381
1950.	2,109,992	256,778	727,266	. . . .	56,841	12,892,612
1955.	5,087,154	438,029	4,333,147	-9,551	103,202	21,141,001
1960.	10,829,764	564,040	10,798,013	573,606	234,291	22,995,939
1965.	17,032,456	648,372	16,618,084	459,253	379,145	22,187,184
1970.	34,554,182	1,572,375	29,064,972	589,257	623,055	37,719,951
1973.	47,305,791	2,281,098	47,373,415	802,457	913,984	44,285,368
1974.	55,182,906	2,521,043	54,060,950	930,912	877,581	46,119,873
1975.	63,872,883	2,803,838	62,547,281	1,010,299	1,100,693	48,138,321
1976[1].	67,867,099	2,816,383	71,462,416	1,238,669	1,200,326	44,920,393
Cumulative to June 1976*	595,831,416	28,821,407	557,427,260	10,619,221	11,685,950	44,920,393

(1.) Preliminary. *Cumulative totals are not totals of columns since several years are omitted.

Hospital Insurance Trust Fund: Status, 1966-76
(In thousands)

| Period | Receipts | | | | Expenditures | | Total assets |
	Net contribution income[1]	Transfers from general revenues[2]	Transfers from rail-road retirement account[3]	Net interest[4]	Net hospital and related service benefits[5]	Adminis-trative expenses[6]	
July 1966-June 1976[7]	$68,049,062	$5,561,889	$716,971	$2,658,432	$64,335,701	$1,814,939	$10,835,714
Fiscal year:							
1966.	908,797			5,970		63,564	851,204
1967.	2,688,684	337,850	16,200	45,903	2,507,773	88,848	1,343,221
1968.	3,514,049	283,631	43,613	61,091	3,736,322	78,647	1,430,636
1969.	4,423,236	770,968	53,776	96,063	4,653,976	104,182	2,016,521
1970.	4,784,789	628,262	61,307	139,423	4,804,242	148,660	2,677,401
1971.	4,897,979	873,849	63,255	183,027	5,442,971	149,434	3,103,106
1972.	5,225,891	551,351	63,782	190,105	6,109,139	166,370	2,858,725
1973.	7,663,119	429,415	61,222	197,844	6,648,819	192,839	4,368,666
1974.	10,606,551	498,780	96,163	408,273	7,785,596	258,066	7,934,772
1975.	11,296,773	529,353	126,749	614,989	10,355,390	256,134	9,870,039
1976[7].	12,039,194	658,430	130,904	715,744	12,270,382	308,215	10,835,714

(1.)Represents amounts appropriated (estimated tax collections with suitable subsequent adjustments), after deductions for refund of estimated amount of employee-tax overpayment. (2.)Represents Federal Government transfers from general funds appropriations to meet costs of benefits for persons not insured for cash benefits under OASDHI or railroad retirement and for costs of benefits arising from military wage credits. (3.)Represents receipts under the financial interchange with railroad retirement account with respect to contributions for hospital insurance coverage of railroad workers. (4.)Represents interest and profit on investments after transfers of interest on administrative expenses reimbursed to the OASI trust fund and on amounts transferred from railroad accounts. (5.)Represents (1) payment vouchers on letters of credit issued to fiscal intermediaries under sec. 1816 and (2) direct payments to providers of services under sec. 1815 of the Social Security Act. (6.)Subject to subsequent adjustment among all 4 social security trust funds, for allocated cost of each operation. (7.)Preliminary.

Supplementary Medical Insurance Trust Fund: Status, 1966-76
(In thousands)

| Period | Receipts | | | Expenditures | | Total assets |
	Premium income[1]	Transfers from general revenues[2]	Net interest[3]	Net medical service benefits[4]	Adminis-trative expenses[5]	
July 1966-June 1976[6]	$12,746,117	$14,508,318	$446,149	$23,670,206	$2,811,823	$1,218,555
Fiscal year:						
1967.	646,682	623,000	14,052	664,261	133,682	485,791
1968.	698,465	634,000	20,677	1,389,622	142,608	306,703
1969.	902,821	984,287	23,466	1,644,842	194,660	377,774
1970.	36,000	928,151	11,536	1,979,287	216,993	57,181
1972.	1,340,052	1,365,295	28,993	2,255,069	288,619	480,709
1973.	1,462,607	1,430,451	45,049	2,391,232	245,861	745,722
1974.	1,703,189	2,028,926	75,924	2,869,132	409,146	1,275,483
1975.	1,886,962	2,329,590	105,539	3,765,397	404,458	1,424,413
1976[6].	1,951,221	2,939,338	103,645	4,671,847	528,214	1,218,555

(1.)Represents voluntary premium payments from and in behalf of insured persons. (2.)Represents Federal Government transfers from general funds appropriations to match aggregate premiums paid. (3.) Represents interest and profit on investments after transfer of interest on administrative expenses reimbursed to the OASI trust fund (see footnote 5). (4.)Represents payment vouchers on letters of credit issued to carriers under section 1842 of the Social Security Act. (5.)Subject to subsequent adjustment among all 4 social security trust funds for allocated cost of each operation. (6.)Preliminary.

Employment and Training Services and Unemployment Insurance

Source: Employment and Training Administration, U.S. Department of Labor

Employment Service

The Federal-State Employment Service consists of the U.S. Employment Service and affiliated state employment services with their network of about 2,400 local offices. During fiscal year 1976, these offices made a total of 5.2 million placements, of which 4.6 million were in nonagricultural and 600,000 agricultural industries. Overall, 3-4 million different individuals were placed in employment.

The employment service works to refer employable applicants to job openings that use their highest skills and helps the unemployed obtain services or training to make them employable. It also provides special attention to help meet the needs of older workers, youth, minorities, the poor, handicapped workers, migrants, seasonal farmworkers, and workers who lose their jobs because of foreign trade competition. Special efforts are being made to improve services in rural areas.

The employment service helps employers find needed workers and offers many employer services, including job-related personnel assistance. To give employers a wider choice of workers and applicants access to more job openings, it has developed job banks, which provide computerized daily lists of all available jobs in a city or area. Statewide networks of job banks now serve about 85% of the nation's population. Other activities include enforcing standards on housing, transportation, and other conditions for farm and woods workers recruited for jobs in other states.

Special Veterans Service

Veterans receive special services and absolute preference in placements at all employment service offices. During the year, these offices placed nearly 600,000 veterans in jobs, two-thirds of them veterans of the Vietnam era. The requirement that Federal contractors list job openings with the employment service continues to prove of particular benefit to veterans. During the fiscal year 1976, these listings accounted for nearly one-fifth of the jobs in which veterans were placed. Other efforts included counseling on education, training, and job opportunities, given to 188,000 veterans.

Community Manpower System

The Comprehensive Employment and Training Act of 1973 sets up a community manpower system to give people training and job-related services and place them in jobs. Under this system, which replaces certain Federal manpower programs, all states and cities, counties, and combinations of local units with populations of 100,000 or more receive Federal grants to plan and run comprehensive manpower programs in their localities. The job-related services provided are much the same as those formerly offered by national programs, but they vary from one area to another, according to local decisions on the needs of the area's workers and the demands of its labor market. Among them are work experience, classroom and on-the-job training, education, job referral, and needed services such as child care and medical aid.

A major part of the community manpower system is transitional public service employment. Besides supporting public jobs provided by comprehensive manpower programs and public employment programs for areas with high jobless rates, CETA subsidizes public jobs authorized under emergency legislation enacted in December 1974. During the year, these programs created jobs for substantial numbers of unemployed workers across the country.

National Activities

The Federal role under the system is to provide support and technical assistance to local programs; insure proper use of Federal money; and serve Indians, migrant and seasonal farmworkers, and others with particular job disadvantages. In addition, subsidized jobs for older workers are funded under the Older American Community Service Employment Act of 1973. The Federal Government also continues to administer some programs and act as the Federal partner in the employment service system and the unemployment insurance program. These responsibilities are carried out by the Department of Labor's Employment and Training Administration. Continuing national activities include apprenticeship, Job Corps, and the Work Incentive Program. Apprenticeship is conducted by employers, often jointly with labor unions, to train workers in a skilled trade on the job and in related classroom instruction. During the year, the Federal Government continued activities to guide, assist, and improve apprenticeship and give more minority members and women a chance to become apprentices. Job Corps, which trains disadvantaged youth largely at residential centers, conducted nontraditional training for women, including programs leading to union apprenticeship jobs in the construction trades. The Work Incentive Program provides manpower, placement, and other services to help people on Aid to Families with Dependent Children get and keep jobs. During the year, 211,000 WIN registrants were placed in unsubsidized jobs.

Unemployment Insurance

Unlike old-age and survivors insurance, entirely a Federal program, the unemployment insurance program is a Federal-State system which provides insured wage earners with partial replacement of wages lost during involuntary unemployment. The program protects most workers in industry, but few in agriculture. Some 71.8 million jobs in commerce, industry, and government, including the Armed Forces, were covered under the Federal-State system during calendar year 1975. In addition, 594,250 railroad workers were insured against unemployment under a system administered by the Railroad Retirement Board.

Each state, as well as the District of Columbia and Puerto Rico, has its own law and operates its own program. The amount and duration of the weekly benefits are determined by state laws, based on prior wages and length of employment. States are required to extend the duration of benefits when unemployment rises to and remains above specified state or national levels; costs of extended benefits are shared by the state and Federal governments.

Under the Federal Unemployment Tax Act, as amended in 1970, the tax rate is 3.2% on the first $4,200 paid to each employee of employers with one or more employees in 20 weeks of the year or a quarterly payroll of $1,500. A credit of up to 2.7% is allowed for taxes paid under state unemployment insurance laws that meet certain criteria, leaving the Federal share at 0.5% of taxable wages, from which the Federal government pays its share of the cost of extended benefits and makes grants to the states to cover the administrative costs of the unemployment insurance and employment service programs. Grants from this source for employment service administrative costs are limited to that proportion of total employment service costs that is attributable to the covered work force.

Social Security Requirement

The Social Security Act requires, as a condition of such grants, prompt payment of due benefits. The Federal Unemployment Tax Act provides safeguards for workers' right to benefits if they refuse jobs that fail to meet certain labor standards. Through the Unemployment Insurance Service of the Employment and Training Administration, the Secretary of Labor determines whether states qualify for grants and for tax offset credit for employers.

Benefits are financed solely by employer contributions, except in Alaska, Alabama, and New Jersey, where employees also contribute. Benefits are paid through the public employment offices, at which unemployed workers must register for work and to which they must report regularly for referral to a possible job during the time when they are drawing weekly benefit payments. During the 1975 calendar year, $11.8 billion in benefits were paid under the state unemployment insurance programs to 11,160,000 beneficiaries, representing compensation for 207,580,200 weeks of unemployment. They received an average weekly payment of $70.23 for total unemployment for an average of 15.7 weeks.

Federal Worker Benefits

Title 5, chapter 85 of the U.S. Code provided unemployment insurance protection during calendar year 1975 to about 2,735,000 Federal civilian employees

and about 2,180,000 members of the Armed Forces. Benefits for unemployed Federal workers and exservicemen are financed through direct Federal appropriations but are paid by the state agencies as agents of the Federal government.

During calendar year 1975, a total of $277,297,600 was paid to 120,100 unemployed Federal civilian workers for a total of 2,332,930 weeks of unemployment. The average weekly payment was $69.55 and was paid for an average of 19.0 weeks. A total of $528,467,600 was paid to 303,300 unemployed exservicemen for 5,191,650 weeks of unemployment. The average weekly benefit was $73.71 and was paid for an average of 17.3 weeks.

Employment Security

Source: Employment and Training Administration, U.S. Dept. of Labor

Selected Unemployment Insurance Data by State

Fiscal year 1976, State Programs Only

State	Insured claimants[1] (1,000)	Beneficiaries[2] (1,000)	Exhaustions[3] (1,000)	Benefits paid initial claims[4] (1,000)	Total[5] (1,000)	Avg. weekly benefit for total unemp'ment (dollars)	Funds available for benefits June 30, 1976 (millions)	Employers subject to state law March 31, 1976 (1,000)
Alabama	159	144	59	299	$ 120,067	$65.84	19	56
Alaska	39	35	6	64	41,023	79.74	83	9
Arizona	80	76	43	182	88,768	72.13	42	49
Arkansas	101	75	35	201	63,671	61.55	11	42
California	1,492	1,108	474	2,584	1,184,302	68.87	478	442
Colorado	82	63	32	163	62,946	83.18	37	55
Connecticut	[7]272	[7]253	[7]93	489	(8)	[7]76.41	(8)	69
Delaware	29	25	13	59	36,064	[7]76.83	8	12
District of Columbia	40	33	17	52	56,923	95.90	16	16
Florida	301	264	167	586	262,263	63.27	51	164
Georgia	263	206	118	428	155,279	65.34	231	86
Hawaii	52	44	18	70	57,956	81.85	—11	18
Idaho	38	34	11	83	23,373	68.09	49	19
Illinois	530	482	233	982	743,413	89.51	—315	196
Indiana	[7]238	166	97	476	150,172	63.63	198	84
Iowa	95	81	36	159	100,367	82.94	39	61
Kansas	65	59	23	109	51,094	66.59	142	47
Kentucky	140	118	49	267	106,348	66.00	129	57
Louisiana	175	100	41	201	97,901	64.86	160	62
Maine	60	69	26	174	43,389	59.90	8	22
Maryland	93	130	46	306	150,523	73.48	—6	69
Massachusetts	338	280	144	605	394,819	75.28	118	116
Michigan	624	476	240	1,354	590,995	91.89	217	148
Minnesota	158	155	81	248	169,487	76.48	29	74
Mississippi	73	53	24	130	37,464	48.82	93	36
Missouri	237	182	92	546	179,934	72.44	82	85
Montana	35	27	11	67	23,665	62.78	2	20
Nebraska	54	42	21	82	38,890	67.46	29	33
Nevada	34	39	18	113	39,538	71.79	9	15
New Hampshire	50	40	8	83	31,346	64.21	29	19
New Jersey	466	401	221	788	550,788	76.86	70	146
New Mexico	30	26	11	67	24,983	57.73	32	23
New York	971	700	378	2,061	1,076,351	73.55	399	382
North Carolina	299	271	101	673	192,634	62.32	295	94
North Dakota	16	14	4	31	12,700	66.73	19	15
Ohio	411	333	166	931	458,805	81.33	235	180
Oklahoma	80	70	37	152	61,059	58.62	19	50
Oregon	145	126	42	350	118,069	67.30	28	52
Pennsylvania	733	619	223	1,601	888,530	85.29	106	191
Puerto Rico	135	127	95	272	96,167	41.60	12	41
Rhode Island	84	59	33	166	67,960	70.95	—50	22
South Carolina	143	118	51	258	94,590	62.33	83	44
South Dakota	12	12	4	23	8,732	62.83	17	15
Tennessee	235	154	75	320	135,503	59.90	183	66
Texas	262	199	101	444	144,792	54.46	218	210
Utah	45	40	15	76	36,817	72.22	24	24
Vermont	63	22	9	51	24,082	67.76	2	12
Virginia	136	106	47	237	99,733	67.25	101	78
Washington	178	177	79	558	192,849	73.69	—92	76
West Virginia	83	72	19	139	52,146	59.35	74	28
Wisconsin	231	160	72	427	202,565	81.43	118	85
Wyoming	121	10	3	14	7,440	68.55	32	11
Total	**10,719**	**8,675**	**4,064**	**20,804**	**$9,649,275**	**$73.61**	**$3,902**	**4,025**

(1) Claimants whose base-period earnings or whose employment — covered by the unemployment insurance program — was sufficient to make them eligible for unemployment insurance benefits as provided by State law. (2) Based on number of first payments. (3) Based on final payments. Some claimants shown, therefore, actually experienced their final week of compensable unemployment toward the end of the previous fiscal year but received their final payments in the current fiscal year. Similarly, some claimants who served their last week of compensable unemployment toward the end of the current fiscal year did not receive their final payment in this fiscal year and hence are not shown. A final week of compensable unemployment in a benefit year results in the exhaustion of benefit rights for the benefit year. Claimants who exhaust their benefit rights in one benefit year may be entitled to further benefits in the following benefit year. (4) Excludes intrastate transitional claims to reflect more nearly instances of new unemployment. Includes claims filed by interstate claimants in the Virgin Islands. (5) Adjusted for voided benefit checks and transfers under interstate combined wage plan. (6) SUM OF BALANCE IN State clearing accounts, benefit payment accounts, and unemployment trust fund accounts maintained in the U.S. Treasury. (7) Preliminary. (8) Information not available.

Canada: Taxable Returns by Income, 1973

Source: Taxation Statistics

Total income $ 1973	Number	%	Total income (millions)	%	Taxed income (millions)	Federal Tax[1] (millions	%
0–1,000	636,580	5.79	359.6	.46	1.9	0.1	.00
1,000–2,000	1,154,135	10.49	1,711.1	2.20.	27.4	0.9	.01
2,000–3,000	1,018,850	9.26	2,536.0	3.26	443.1	13.8	.16
3,000–4,000	970,745	8.82	3,397.8	4.37	1,136.8	98.1	1.11
4,000–5,000	966,767	8.79	4,346.9	5.59	1,913.6	224.1	2.54
5,000–10,000	3,676,872	33.41	26,818.4	34.49	15,905.2	2,498.5	28.28
10,000–15,000	1,677,129	15.24	20,164.5	25.93	13,763.6	2,582.2	29.23
15,000–20,000	455,197	4.14	7,731.5	9.94	5,602.2	1,163.1	13.17
20,000–25,000	148,075	1.35	3,269.3	4.20	2,447.8	549.8	6.22
25,000–50,000	143,534	1.30	4,715.7	6.07	3,712.1	937.8	10.62
50,000–100,000	29,576	.27	1,941.9	2.50	1,645.6	502.3	5.69
100,000–200,000	4,710	.04	609.5	.78	530.1	185.4	2.10
200,000–& over	792	.01	253.3	.33	214.5	77.1	.87
Total	11,003,862	100.00	77,751.8	100.00	47,344.5	8,834.0	100.00

(1) Federal taxes include income taxes, social development tax, and old age security tax.

Federal Taxes in Major Canadian Cities, 1973*

Source: Taxation Statistics

City	Rank[1]	No. of Returns[2]	Average Income	Avg. Tax	City	Rank[1]	No. of Returns[2]	Average Income	Avg. Tax
Barrie	36	17,524	$8,707	$1,112	New Westminister	26	21,965	8,902	1,197
Belleville	65	18,640	8,226	1,018	Niagara Falls	66	28,466	8,216	1,006
Brantford	54	33,089	8,396	1,055	North Bay	57	20,920	8,305	1,015
Brockville	70	10,844	8,146	989	Oakville	1	27,890	10,922	1,673
Calgary	21	188,166	9,086	1,200	Oshawa	5	43,557	9,817	1,381
Cambridge	85	31,938	7,865	952	Ottawa	4	208,427	9,982	1,423
Charlottetown	96	10,029	7,421	832	Peterborough	47	29,143	8,496	1,068
Chatham	17	18,132	9,187	1,226	Prince George	11	24,620	9,451	1,276
Chicoutimi	33	22,268	8,754	773	Quebec	18	151,407	9,142	888
Cornwall	68	18,001	8,210	973	Regina	64	60,690	8,229	993
Dartmouth	46	29,819	8,500	1,022	St. Catharines	29	58,633	8,834	1,121
Dawson Creek	63	5,939	8,233	972	Saint John, N.B.	92	34,822	7,624	861
Drummondville	88	15,075	7,743	675	St. John's, Nfld.	80	41,081	7,924	968
Edmonton	37	225,600	8,691	1,123	Sarnia	8	32,541	9,667	1,301
Fredericton	61	18,345	8,265	1,000	Saskatoon	59	52,972	8,294	972
Guelph	48	30,550	8,494	1,073	Saulte Ste. Marie	13	32,727	9,255	1,195
Halifax	39	60,597	8,597	1,079	Sherbrooke	51	31,693	8,431	775
Hamilton	23	220,727	9,040	1,219	Sudbury	19	54,928	9,139	1,195
Hull	32	50,271	8,782	840	Sydney-Glace Bay.	100	39,456	7,234	743
Kamloops	22	22,334	9,083	1,176	Thunder Bay	35	47,234	8,719	1,117
Kingston	25	40,385	8,937	1,173	Timmins	72	15,552	8,078	951
Kitchener-Waterloo	38	82,660	8,633	1,124	Toronto	12	1,115,434	9,315	1,330
Lethbridge	62	19,055	8,242	992	Trois-Rivieres	49	20,735	8,481	774
Levis	60	19,652	8,283	726	Vancouver	16	477,477	9,195	1,264
London	24	116,397	8,964	1,185	Victoria	30	98,126	8,803	1,100
Longueuil	58	41,403	8,297	723	Welland	43	20,883	8,528	1,083
Mississauga	3	84,672	10,284	1,513	Windsor	9	106,852	9,598	1,294
Moncton	95	27,015	7,525	824	Winnipeg	71	250,199	8,126	975
Montreal	15	801,865	9,212	921					

*Cities arranged alphabetically and selected from top 100 Canadian cities. [1] Rank refers to position in order of average income. [2] Taxable returns only.

City Income Tax in Cities Over 50,000

Compiled by Tax Foundation from Commerce Clearing House data and other sources.

City	Rates% 1976	Orig.	Year Start	City	Rates% 1976	Orig.	Year Start
Cities with 500,000 or more inhabitants				Scranton, Pa.	2.0	1.0	1948
Baltimore, Md. (50% of state tax)	1.0		1966	Toledo, Oh.	1.5	1.0	1946
Cleveland, Oh.	1.0	0.5	1967	Youngstown, Oh.	1.5	0.3	1948
Columbus, Oh.	1.5	0.5	1947	**Cities with 50,000 to 99,000 inhabitants**			
Detroit, Mich.	2.0	1.0	1965	Altoona, Pa.	1.0	1.0	1948
Kansas City, Mo.	1.0	0.5	1964	Bethlehem, Pa.	1.0	1.0	1957
New York, N.Y.	0.9–4.3	.4–2.0	1966	Chester, Pa.	1.0	1.0	1956
Philadelphia, Pa.	4.3125	1.5	1939	Covington, Ky.	2.5	1.0	1956
Pittsburgh, Pa.	1.0	1.0	1954	Euclid, Oh.	1.0	0.5	1967
St. Louis, Mo.	1.0	.25	1948	Gadsden, Ala.	2.0	1.0	1956
Cities with 100,000 to 499,000 inhabitants				Hamilton, Oh.	1.5	0.8	1960
Akron, Oh.	1.5	1.0	1963	Harrisburg, Pa.	1.0	1.0	1966
Allentown, Pa.	1.0	1.0	1958	Lakewood, Oh.	1.0	1.0	1968
Birmingham, Ala.	1.0	1.0	1970	Lancaster, Pa.	1.0	0.5	1959
Canton, Oh.	1.5	0.6	1954	Lima, Oh.	1.0	.75	1959
Cincinnati, Oh.	2.0	1.0	1954	Lorain, Oh.	1.0	0.5	1967
Dayton, Oh.	1.75	0.5	1949	Pontiac, Mich.	1.0	1.0	1968
Erie, Pa.	1.0	1.0	1948	Reading, Pa.	1.0	1.0	1975
Flint, Mich.	1.0	1.0	1965	Saginaw, Mich.	1.0	1.0	1965
Grand Rapids, Mich.	1.0	1.0	1967	Springfield, Oh.	2.0	1.0	1948
Lansing, Mich.	1.0	1.0	1968	Warren, Oh.	1.0	0.5	1952
Lexington, Ky.	2.0	1.0	1952	Wilkes-Barre, Pa.	1.0	1.0	1966
Louisville, Ky.	2.0	1.0	1948	York, Pa.	1.0	1.0	1965
Parma, Oh.	1.0	0.5	1967	Wilmington, Del.	1.25	0.5	1970

State Individual Income Taxes: Rates, Exemptions

Source: Tax Foundation Inc. Data as of July 1, 1976

State	Net income after pers'l. exemption	Percentage rates	Net income after pers'l. exemption	Percentage rates	Personal Exemp. Single	Married family head	Credit Depends.
Alabama[1]	First $1,000 1,001- 3,000	1.5 3	$3,001-$5,000 Over 5,000	4.5 5	$1,500	$3,000	$300
Alaska	Rates range from 3% on first $4,000 to 14¹/₂% over $300,000				Federal exemptions		
Arizona[1 2]	First 1,000 1,001- 2,000 2,001- 3,000	2 3 4	3,001- 4,000 4,001- 5,000 5,001- 6,000	5 6 7	1,000 Over 6,000 8	2,000	600
Arkansas[3]	First 3,000 3,001- 6,000 6,001- 9,000	1 2.5 3.5	9,001-15,000 15,001-25,000 Over 25,000	4.5 6 7	17.50 (tax credit)	35	6
California[1 2]	First 2,000 2,001- 3,500 3,501- 5,000 5,001- 6,500 6,501- 8,000	1 2 3 4 5	8,001- 9,500 9,501-11,000 11,001-12,500 12,501-14,000 14,001-15,500	6 7 8 9 10	(tax credit) 25 Heads of households have slightly lower tax rates. Over 15,500 11	50	8
Colorado[1 4]	First 1,000 1,001- 2,000 2,001- 3,000 3,001- 4,000 4,001- 5,000 5,001- 6,000	3 3.5 4 4.5 5 5.5	6,001- 7,000 7,001- 8,000 8,001- 9,000 9,001-10,000 Over 10,000	6 6.5 7 7.5 8	750 Surtax on intangible income over $5,000, 2%. A credit equal to ¹/₂ of 1% of net taxable income is allowed for income under $9,000.	1,500	750
Connecticut	Capital gains	7					
Delaware[3]	First 1,000 1,001- 2,000 2,001- 3,000 3,001- 4,000 4,001- 5,000 5,001- 6,000	1.6 2.2 3.3 4.4 5.5 6.6	6,001- 8,000 8,001-20,000 20,001-25,000 25,001-30,000 30,001-40,000 40,001-50,000	7.7 8.8 9.3 9.9 12.1 13.2	600	1,200 50,001- 75,000 75,001-100,000 Over 100,000	600 15.4 16.5 19.8
Dist. of Col.[1 4]	First 1,000 1,001-2,000 2,001-3,000 3,001-4,000 4,001-5,000	2 3 4 5 6	5,001-10,000 10,001-13,000 13,001-17,000 17,001-25,000 Over 25,000	7 8 9 10 11	1,000 A tax credit is provided for low-income taxpayers (adjusted gross not over $6,000) for increased sales tax on food ($2 to $6 credit per exemption). A refund is allowed if the credit exceeds tax liability.	2,000	500
Georgia[3 5]	First 750 751- 2,250 2,251- 3,750 3,751- 5,250	1 2 3 4	5,251- 7,000 Over 7,000	5 6	1,500 For married persons filing separately, rates range from 1% on the first $500 to 6% on $5,000 or more. For married couples filing jointly and heads of households, rates range from 1% on the first $1,000 to 6% on $10,000 or more.	3,000	700
Hawaii[1]	First 500 501- 1,000 1,001- 1,500 1,501- 2,000 2,001- 3,000 3,001- 5,000	2.25 3.25 4.5 5 6.5 7.5	5,001-10,000 10,001-14,000 14,001-20,000 20,001-30,000 Over 30,000	8.5 9.5 10 10.5 11	750 Special tax rates for heads of households.	1,500	750
Idaho[2 3 4]	First 1,000 1,001- 2,000 2,001- 3,000	2 4 4.5	3,001- 4,000 4,001- 5,000 Over 5,000	5.5 6.5 7.5	Federal exemptions Plus tax credit of $15 for each exemption.		
Illinois	Total net income	2.5			1,000	2,000	1,000
Indiana[4]	Adjusted gross	2			1,000	*2,000	500
	*Lesser of $1,000 or adjusted gross income of each spouse, but not less than $500.						
Iowa[1]	First 1,000 1,001- 2,000 2,001- 3,000	0.5 1.25 2.75	3,001- 4,000 4,001- 7,000 7,001- 9,000	3.5 5 6	(tax credit) 15 Incomes $4,000 or less are exempt. Up to 13% over $75,000	30	10
Kansas[1 4]	First 2,000 2,001- 3,000 3,001- 5,000	2 3.5 4	5,001- 7,000 Over 7,000	5 6.5	600	1,200	600
Kentucky[1]	First 3,000 3,001- 4,000	2 3	4,001- 5,000 5,001- 8,000	4 5	(tax credit) 20 Over 8,000 6	40	20

State	Net income after pers'l. exemption	Percentage rates	Net income after pers'l. exemption	Per-centage rates	Personal Exemp.		
					Single	Married family head	Credit Depends.
Louisiana[2] [3]	First 10,000 10,001-50,000	2 4	Over 50,000	6	2,500	5,000	400
Credits are allowed new income which is taxed at 2%; additional $1,000 exemp. for blindness allowed for dependents.							
Maine.........	First 2,000 2,001-4,000 4,001-5,000	1 2 3	5,001-6,000 6,001-8,000 8,001-12,000	3.5 4.5 5	1,000 on up to 8% over 50,000	2,000	1,000
Maryland[1] [4]	First 1,000 1,001- 2,000	2 3	2,001- 3,000 Over 3,000	4 5	800	1,600	800
An additional exemption of $800 is allowed for each dependent 65 or over.							
Massachusetts[4]	Earned and business income: Interest, divs., capital gains on intangibles:	5* 9*	The exemptions shown are those allowed against business income, including salaries and wages. A specific exemption of $2,000 is allowed for each taxpayer. In addition, a dependency exemption of $600 is allowed for a dependent spouse who has income from all sources of less than $2,000. In the case of a		2,000	2,600-4,600	600
joint return, the exemption is the smaller of (1) $4,600 or (2) $2,600 plus the income of the spouse having the smaller income. *Plus 7.5% surtax.							
Michigan[4]......			All taxable income	4.6	1,500	3,000	1,500
Minnesota[1] [4] ...	First 500 501- 1,000 1,001- 2,000 2,001- 3,000 3,001- 4,000 4,001- 5,000	1.6 2.2 3.5 5.8 7.3 8.8	5,001- 7,000 7,001- 9,000 9,001-12,500 12,501-20,000 Over 20,000	10.2 11.5 12.8 14 15	21 An additional tax credit of $21 is allowed for each taxpayer 65 years old.	42	21
Mississippi[3]....	First 5,000	3	Over 5,000	4	4,500	6,500	750
Missouri[1].......	First 1,000 1,001- 2,000 2,001- 3,000 3,001- 4,000 4,001- 5,000	1.5 2 2.5 3 3.5	5,001- 6,000 6,001- 7,000 7,001- 8,000 8,001- 9,000 Over 9,000	4 4.5 5 5.5 6	1,200 An additional $800 exemption is allowed unmarried head of household.	2,400	400
Montana[3]......	First 1,000 1,001-2,000 2,001-4,000 4,001-6,000 6,001-8,000	2 3 4 5 6	8,001-10,000 10,001-14,000 14,001-20,000 20,001-35,000 Over 35,000	7 8 9 10 11	650	1,300	650
Nebraska[3] [4] The tax is imposed as a % of the taxpayer's Fed. income tax liability (not including surtax) before credits, with limited adjustments. For the year 1976 the rate was set at 15% by State Board of Equalization and Assessment.					Federal exemptions		
New Hampshire.	Interest and dividends (except interest on savings accounts).	4.25	4% commuter tax		600	600-1,200	
Joint returns are not permitted; each spouse with taxable income is allowed a $600 exemption.							
New Jersey[3]	First 20,000 Over 20,000	2 2.5			1,000	1,000	1,000
New Mexico[2] [3] ...	First 500 501-1,000 1,001-1,500 1,501-2,000 2,001-3,000 3,001-4,000 4,001-5,000 5,001-6,000	0.9 1.1 1.3 1.5 1.6 1.9 2.3 2.4	6,001-7,000 7,001-8,000 8,001-10,000 10,001-12,000 12,001-20,000 20,001-50,000 50,001-100,000 Over 100,000	3.0 3.3 3.6 4.3 6.1 8.0 8.5 9.0	Federal exemptions The income classes reported are for individuals. For joint returns and heads of households, a separate rate schedule is provided. A credit is allowed for state and local taxes for gross income of less than $6,000.		
New York[1]......	First 1,000 1,001- 3,000 3,001- 5,000 5,001- 7,000 7,001- 9,000 9,001-11,000 11,001-13,000	2 3 4 5 6 7 8	13,001-15,000 15,001-17,000 17,001-19,000 19,001-21,000 21,001-23,000 23,001-25,000 Over 25,000	9 10 11 12 13 14 15	650 Tax credits of $12.50 for single persons, $12.50 for married persons filing separately, and $25 for married persons filing jointly and heads of households are allowed. Income from unincorporated business is taxed at 5¹/₂%. The following credit is al-	1,300	650

lowed: $110 or less, full amount; $110 to $550, difference between $137.50 and 25% of amount of tax; $550 or more, no credit. A 2.5% surtax is imposed.

State	Net Income after pers'l. exemption	Percentage rates	Net Income after pers'l. exemption	Per-centage rates	Personal Exemp. Single	Married family head	Credit Depends.
North Carolina[3]	First 2,000	3	6,001-10,000	6	1,000	2,000	600
	2,001-4,000	4	Over 10,000	7			
	4,001-6,000	5					

An additional exemption of $1,000 is allowed a married woman with a separate income; joint returns are not permitted.

State							
North Dakota[3]	First 1,000	1	6,001-8,000	7.5	750	1.500	750
	1,001-3,000	2	Over 8,000	10			
	3,001-5,000	3					
	5,001-6,000	5					

An additional 1% tax is imposed on net incomes of individuals, estates, trusts and corporations (minimum $20). A credit of 25% of income tax liability is allowed

State							
Ohio[4]	First 5,000	0.5	15,001-20,000	2.5	650	1,300	650
	5,001-10,000	1	20,001-40,000	3			
	10,001-15,000	2	Over 40,000	3.5			

Maximum personal exemption is $3,000 per return. Taxpayers age 65 or older are allowed a $25 credit, or if they have received a lump sum distribution from a pension, retirement or profit sharing plan during the tax year, they are allowed a credit equal to $25 times the taxpayer's expected remaining life. Credit may not exceed tax otherwise due. Credit is also allowed for an amount paid during the school year for elementary and secondary education or instruction or training of dependents who do not have a high school diploma.

State							
Oklahoma[1]	First 1,000	0.5	5,001-6,250	4	750	1,500	750
	1,001-2,500	1	6,251-7,500	5			
	2,501-3,750	2	Over 7,500	6			
	3,751-5,000	3					

For joint returns the rates shown apply to income classes twice as large. Rates of heads of households range from $1/2%$ on the first $1,500 to 6% on taxable income over $11,250. Non-residents are taxed at a flat rate of 6% of Oklahoma taxable income.

State							
Oregon[1]	First $500	4	3,001-4,000	8	750	1,500	750
	501-1,000	5	4,001-5,000	9			
	1,001-2,000	6	Over 5,000	10			
	2,001-3,000	7					

A credit is provided in an amount equal to 25% of the Federal retirement income tax credit to the extent that such a credit is based on Oregon taxable income.

State							
Pennsylvania	All taxable income	2					

Pennsylvania residents working in New Jersey are subject to a flat 2.3% commuter's tax on their New Jersey income.

State							
Rhode Island	Federal income tax liability 17						Federal Exemptions.

State							
South Carolina[1]	First 2,000	2	6,001-8,000	5	800	1,600	800
	2,001-4,000	3	8,001-10,000	6			
	4,001-6,000	4	Over 10,000	7			

State							
Tennessee	Interest and dividends	6					

Dividends from corporations, 75% of whose property is taxable in Tenn., are taxed at 4%.

State							
Utah[3]	First 750	2.25	2,251-3,000	5.25			Federal exemptions
	751-1,500	3.25	3,001-3,750	6.25	Over 4,500	7.75	
	1,501-2,250	4.25	3,751-4,500	7.25			

State							
Vermont							Federal Exemptions.

The tax is imposed at a rate of 25% of the Fed. income tax liability of the taxpayer for the taxable year after certain credits (retirement income, investment, foreign tax and tax-free covenant bonds) but before any surtax on Fed. liability, reduced by a % equal to the % of the taxpayer's adjusted gross income for the taxable year which is not Vermont income. A 9% surcharge is imposed for 1974, and thereafter

State							
Virginia[3]	First 3,000	2	5,001-12,000	5	600	1,200	600
	3,001-5,000	3	Over 12,000	5.75			

State							
West Virginia[1]	First 2,000	2.1	26,001-32,000	6.5	600	1,200	600
	2,001-4,000	2.3	32,001-38,000	6.8			
	4,001-6,000	2.8	38,001-44,000	7.2			
	6,001-8,000	3.2	44,001-50,000	7.5			
	8,001-10,000	3.5	50,001-60,000	7.9			
	10,001-12,000	4	60,001-70,000	8.2			
	12,001-14,000	4.6	70,001-80,000	8.6			
	14,001-16,000	4.9	80,001-90,000	8.8			
	16,001-18,000	5.3	90,001-100,000	9.1			
	18,001-20,000	5.4	100,001-150,000	9.3			
	20,001-22,000	6	150,001-200,000	9.5			
	22,001-26,000	6.1	Over 200,000	9.6			

For joint returns and a return of a surviving spouse, a separate rate schedule is provided.

State							
Wisconsin[1 4]	First 1,000	3.1	8,001-9,000	8.2	(Tax Credit) 20	40	20
	1,001-2,000	3.4	9,001-10,000	8.8			
	2,001-3,000	3.6	10,001-11,000	9.3			
	3,001-4,000	4.8	11,001-12,000	9.9			
	4,001-5,000	5.4	12,001-13,000	10.5			
	5,001-6,000	5.9	13,001-14,000	11.1			
	6,001-7,000	6.5	Over 14,000	11.4			
	7,001-8,000	7.6					

(1) A standard deduction and optional tax table are provided.
(2) Community property state in which, in general, one-half of the community income is taxable to each spouse.
(3) A standard deduction is allowed.
(4) A limited tax credit is allowed for sales taxes in Colorado, Idaho, Indiana, Massachusetts, Nebraska, and Vermont; for property taxes on homesteads of the elderly in Arizona, Colorado, Kansas, Michigan, Minnesota, Missouri, New Jersey, Oklahoma, Vermont, and Wisconsin; for property taxes and city income taxes in Michigan; and for personal property taxes in Maryland.
(5) Tax credits are allowed: $15 for single person or married person filing separately if AGI is $3,000 or less. (For each dollar by which the Federal AGI exceeds $3,000, the credit is reduced by $1 until no credit is allowed if Federal AGI is $3,015 or more.) $30 for heads of households or married persons filing jointly with $6,000 or less AGI. (For each dollar by which Federal AGI exceeds $6,000, credit is reduced by $1 until no credit is allowed if Federal AGI is $6,030 or more.)

State Retail Sales Taxes; Types and Rates

Source: Tax Foundation Inc. Data as of July 1, 1976

State	Tangible Personal Property	Admissions	Rest. Meals	Transient Lodging	Public Utilities	Rates on other services and nonretail business
Alabama[2]	4%[3] agric., mining and mfg. mach., 1.5%.	4%	4%	4%	...	Gross rcpts of amus't operators, 4%;
Arizona[2]	4	4	4	3	4	Timbering, 1.5%; storage, apt., office rental, 3%.
Arkansas[2]	3 from coin-operated dev.; repair services incl. auto and elect., 3%.	3	3	3	3	Printing, photographic services; rcpts.
California[2]	4.75[5] processing, printing, 4.75%.	...	4.75	...	[14]	Renting, leasing, producing, fabricating,
Colorado[2]	3	...	3	3[10]	3	
Connecticut	7 property items. 7%.		7[7]	7[10]	7[13]	Storing for use or consumption of personal
D. of C.	5[3] lic stenographic services, 5%; sales of food for off-premise consumption, nonprescription medicines, 2%.	5	6	6	5	Duplicating, mailing, addressing and pub-
Florida	4	4	4	4	...	Rental income of amus't. mach., 4%.
Georgia	3	3	3	3	3	Levies on amus't dev., 3%.
Hawaii[1]	4 selected businesses, ¹/₂%; insur. solicitors, 2%; contractors, sales rep., professions, radio stations, 4% .	4	4	4	...	Sugar processors, pineapple farmers and
Idaho[6]	3	3	3	3	...	Closed circuit tv boxing, wrestling, 5%.
Illinois[2]	4 service, 4%; remodeling, repairing and reconditioning of tangible personal property, 4%.	...	4	4	...	Property sold in connection with a sale of
Indiana	4	...	4	4	4	
Iowa	3 cold storage, photography, printing, repairs, barber and beauty parlor services, advt., dry cleaning equip. rentals and gross rcpts. from amus't dev., 3%.	3	3	3	3	Laundry, dry cleaning, automobile and
Kansas[2]	3 ated devices; commer. amus't, 3%.	3	3	3	3	Gross rcpts. from operation of coin-oper-
Kentucky[2]	5 photo fin., 5%; ticket sales to boxing or wrestling on closed circuit tv, 5% of gross rcpts; tax also applies to pay'ts for right to broadcast matches.	5	5	5	5	Storage, sewer services, photog. and
Louisiana[2]	3	3	3	3	...	Food and prescpt'n. drugs, exempt.
Maine	5	...	5	5	5	Proceeds from closed circuit tv, 5%.
Maryland[2]	4[3] that used in generation of electricity or in R.&S. sold to mfrs., 2%; watercraft, 3%.	[11]	4[7]	4	4	Farm equip., 2%; mfg. equip., including
Mass.	5	...	[7]	5.7[9]	...	
Michigan	4	...	4	4	4	
Minnesota[2]	4[3] coin-operated vending mach., 3% of gross sales.	4	4	4	4	Food, medicines and clothing are exempt;
Mississippi[1]	5[3] sales of meat for human consumption; 5% on beer, alc. bevs., soft drinks and motor fuel); extracting or mining of minerals, specified miscellaneous bus. incl. bowling, pool halls, warehouses, laundry and dry cleaning, pest control services, specified repair services, 5%; cotton ginning, 15c per bale; sales of materials to railroads for use in track structures, 3%; tractors, indust. fuel and mfg. mach. sales over $500, 1%.	...	5	5	5	Wholesaling, ¹/₈% (one-half of 1% on
Missouri[2]	3	3	3	3	3	
Nebraska[2]	2.5	2.5	2.5	2.5	2.5	
Nevada[2]	3[10]	...	3	...	...	

State	Tangible Personal Property	Admissions	Selected Service			Rates on other services and nonretail business
			Rest. Meals	Transient Lodging	Public Utilities	
N.J.[1][2]	5	5[11]	5	5[9]	...	
N.M.[1-2]	4[3]	4	4	4	4	
N.Y.[2]	4	4[11]	4[7]	4[9]	4	Safe deposit rentals, 4%.
N.C.[2]	3[3]	...	3	3	...	Farm and industrial machinery, 1% ($80 max.); airplanes, boats and locomotives, 2% ($120 max.); sales of horses and mules, 1%.
N.D.	4[3]	4	4	4	4	Severance of sand or gravel from the soil, 4%.
Ohio[2]	4	...	4	4	...	
Okla.[2]	2[3]	2	2	2	2	Advert. (exclusive of newspapers, periodicals, billboards), printing, auto storage, gross proceeds from amusement dev., 2%.
Penn.[2]	6	...	6[7]	6	6	Cleaning, polishing, lubr. and insp. motor vehicles, rental income of coin-operated amuse. dev., 6%.
R.I.	6	...	6	6	6	
S.C.	4	...	4	4	4	
S.D.[1][2]	4[3]	4	4	3	3	Farm mach. and agric. irrigation equip., 2%; gross rcpts. from professions (other than medical), 4%.
Tenn.[2]	4.5	...	4.5	4.5	4.5	Vending machines, 1.5% (except tobacco products, 2.5%); industrial. farm equipment and machinery, 1%.
Texas[2]	4[3]	...	4	...	4	
Utah[2]	4	4	4	4	4	
Vt.	3	3	3[12]	3[12]	3	
Va.[2]	3[3]	...	3	3	3	
Wash.[1][2]	4.6	4.6	4.6	4.6	...	Rentals, auto, parking, other specified services, amusements, recreations, 4.5% (unless subject to county or city adm. taxes, when they remain taxable under the state business, occupation levy, 1%).
W. Va.[1]	3[3]	3	3	3	...	All services except public util. and pers., prof., 3%.
Wis.[2]	4	4[11]	4	4	4	
Wyo.[2]	3	3	3	3	3	

(1) All but a few States levy sales taxes of the single-stage retail type. Ha. and Miss. levy multiple-stage sales taxes. The N.M. and S.D. taxes have broad bases with respect to taxable services but, they are not multiple-stage taxes. Wash. and W.Va. levy gross receipts taxes on all business, distinct from their sales taxes. Alaska also levies a gross receipts tax on businesses. The rates applicable to retailers, with exceptions, under these gross receipts taxes are as follows: Alaska, 1/2% on gross receipts of $20,000-$100,000 and 1/4% on gross receipts in excess of $100,000; Wash., 44/100% plus a 6% surtax; and W. Va.. 55/100% N.J. imposes a tax of 1/20 of 1% on retail stores with income in excess of $150,000, and an unincorporated business tax at the rate of 1/4 of 1% if gross receipts exceed $5,000.

(2) In addition to the State tax, sales taxes are also levied by certain cities and/or counties.

(3) Motor vehicles are taxed at the general sales tax rates with the following exceptions: Ala., 1 1/2%; Miss., 3%; and N.C., 2% ($120 maximum) Motor vehicles are exempt from the general sales and use taxes but are taxed under motor vehicle tax laws in Md., 4%; Minn., 4%; N.M., 2%; N.D. 4%; Okla., 2%; S.D. and W.Va., 3%; Tex., 4%; Va., 2%; and the D.C., 4%.

(4) Ariz. and Miss. also tax the transportation of oil and gas by pipeline. Ga., Mo., Okla. and Utah do not tax transportation of property. Miss. taxes taxicab transportation at the rate of 2%. Okla. does not tax fares of 15c or less on local transportation. Utah does not tax street railway fares.

(5) "Lease" excludes the use of tangible personal property for a period of less than one day for a charge of less than $10 when the privilege of using the property is restricted to use on the premises or at a business location of the grantor.

(6) A limited credit (or refund) in the form of a flat dollar amount per personal exemption is allowed against the personal income tax to compensate for (1) sales taxes paid on food in Colo., D.C. and Neb.; and (2) all sales taxes paid in Idaho, Mass. and Vt. Low-income taxpayers (adjusted gross income not over $6,000) are allowed a credit against D.C. tax liability ranging from $2 to $6 per personal exemption, depending on taxpayer's income bracket. A refund is allowed if credit exceeds tax liability.

(7) Restaurant meals below a specified price are exempt: Conn. and Md. less than $1; N.Y. less than $1 (when alcoholic beverages are sold, meals are taxable regardless of price); and Penn., 50c or less. In Mass., restaurant meals ($1 or more) which are taxed at 8% under the meals excise tax are exempt.

(8) Conn., exempts clothing for children under 10 years of age. Penn. and Wisc. exempt clothing with certain exceptions.

(9) In Colo. and Conn., the first 30 consecutive days of rental or occupancy of rooms is taxable. Over 30 days is exempt. In Mass., transient lodging (in excess of $2 a day) is subject to a 5.7% (5% plus 14% surtax) room occupancy excise tax. In N.J. and N.Y., rooms which rent for $2 a day or less are exempt.

(10) Includes a statewide mandatory 1% county sales tax collected by the state and paid to the counties for support of local school districts.

(11) Md. taxes at 1/2 of 1% gross receipts derived from charges for rentals of sporting or recreational equipment, and admissions, cover charges for tables, services or merchandise at any roof garden or cabaret. In N.J., admissions to a place of amusement are taxable if the charge is in excess of 75c. N.Y. taxes admissions when the charge is over 10c; exempt are participating sports (such as bowling and swimming), motion picture theaters, race tracks, boxing, wrestling, and live dramatic or musical performances. In Wisc., sales of admissions to motion picture theaters costing 75c or less are exempt.

(12) Meals and rooms are exempt from sales tax, but are subject to a special excise tax of 5%.

(13) Gas, water, electricity, telephone and telegraph services provided to consumers through mains, lines or pipes are exempt. Gas and electric energy used for domestic heating are exempt. Interstate telephone calls are exempt, as are calls from coin-operated telephones.

(14) Beginning Jan. 1, 1975 a surcharge for efficiency is imposed at the rate of 1/10th mill ($0.0001) per kwh.

State Inheritance Tax Rates and Exemptions

Source: Compiled by Tax Foundation from Commerce Clearing House data. As of Sept. 1, 1976

State (a)	Rates (per cent) (b)			Max. Rate applies above ($1,000)	Exemptions (c) ($1,000)			
	Spouse Child or parent	Brother or sister	Other than relative		spouse	Child or parent	Brother or sister	Other than relative
California	3-14	6-20	10-24	$400	$60 (d)	$5 (e)	$2	$.3
Colorado (f)	2-8	3-10	10-19	500	30	10 (e)	2	.5 (g)
Connecticut (i)	2-8	4-10	8-14	1,000	50	10	3	.5
Delaware	1-6	5-10	10-16	200	20 (i)	3	1	None
Dist. of Col.	1-8	5-23	5-23	1,000	5	5	1	1
Hawaii	1.5-7.5	3.5-9	3.5-9	250	20	5	.5	.5
Idaho	2-15	4-20	8-30	500	30 (d)	15	10	10
Illinois	2-14	2-14	10-30	500	20	20	10	.1
Indiana	1-10	5-15	7-20	1,500	15	2 (e)	.5	.1
Iowa	1-8	5-10	10-15	150	80	10 (e)	None	None
Kansas	.5-5	3-12.5	10-15	500	75	15	5	.2 (g)
Kentucky	2-10	4-16	6-16	500 (j)	20	5 (e)	1	.5
Louisiana	2-3	5-7	5-10	25	5 (d)	5	1	.5
Maine	5-10	8-14	14-18	250	50	25	1	1
Maryland (k)	1	10	10	(l)	.15 (g)	.15 (g)	.15 (g)	.15 (g)
Massachusetts (m)	1.8-11.8	5.5-19.3	8-19.3	1,000	30 (n)	15 (n)	5 (n)	5 (n)
Michigan	2-8(o)	2-8 (o)	10-15 (o)	750	30 (e)	5	5	none
Minnesota	1.5-10	6-25	8-30	1,000	60	9 (e)	1.5	.5
Missouri	1-6	3-18	5-30	400	20 (p)	5 (e)	.5	.1 (g)
Montana	2-8	4-16	8-32	100	25	2 (e)	.5	None
Nebraska	1	1	6-18	60	10	10	10	.5
New Hampshire	(q)	15	15	(1)	(q)	(q)	None	None
New Jersey	1-16	11-16	15-16	3,200	5	5	.5 (g)	.5 (g)
North Carolina	1-12	4-16	8-17	3,000	10	2 (e)	None	None
Oregon	3-12	3-12 (r)	3-12 (r)	500	(r, s)	(r, s)	3	.5
Pennsylvania	6	15	15	(l)	None (t)	None (t)	None	None
Rhode Island	2-9	3-10	8-15	1,000 (u)	10	10	5	1
South Dakota (a)	(v)	4-16	6-24	100	60 (v)	3 (e)	.5	.1
Tennessee	5.5-9.5	6.5-20	6.5-20	500	60	60	1	1
Texas	1-6	3-10	5-20	1,000	25 (d)	25	10	.5
Virginia	1-5	2-10	5-15	1,000	5	5	2	1
Washington	1-10	3-20	10-25	500	5 (d)	5	1	None
West Virginia (a)	3-13	4-18	10-30	1,000	30	10	10	None
Wisconsin	1.25-12.5	5-25	10-30 (w)	500	50	4	1	.5
Wyoming	2	2	6	(l)	60	10	10	None

(a) In addition to an inheritance tax, all states listed also levy an estate tax, generally to assure full absorption of the Federal credit. Exceptions are S. D., and W. Va.

(b) Rates generally apply to excess above graduated absolute amounts.

(c) Generally, transfers to governments or to solely charitable, educational, scientific, religious, literary, public, and other similar organizations in the U.S. are wholly exempt. Some states grant additional exemptions either for insurance, homestead, joint deposits, support allowance, disinherited minor children, orphaned, incompetent or blind children, and for previously or later taxed transfers. In many states, exemptions are deducted from the first bracket only. Adopted children generally receive the same consideration as natural children.

(d) Community property state in which, in general, either all community property to the surviving spouse is exempt, or only one-half of the community property is taxable on the death of either spouse.

(e) Exemption for child (in thousands); $15 in Iowa; and $10 in S. D. Exemption for minor child is (in thousands): $12 in Calif.; $15 in Col.; $30 in Idaho; $5 in Ind.; $10 in Ky.; $30 in Minn.; $5 in Mont.; $15 in N.C. In Mo. the exemption for an insane, blind or otherwise incapacitated lineal descendant is (thousands) $15. In Mich. a widow receives $5,000 for every minor child to whom no property is transferred in addition to the normal exemption for a spouse.

(f) Colo. imposes an additional tax of 10% upon the amount of tax computed at above rates.

(g) No exemption if share exceeds amount stated.

(h) On estates an additional inheritance tax equal to 30% of the basic tax is imposed.

(i) Eff. 1/1/77 exemption increases to $70.

(j) Estates over $3,000,000 are not subject to the inheritance tax but are subject to an estate tax equal to the amount of the Federal credit.

(k) Where property of a decedent subject to administration in Md. is $5,000 or less, no inheritance taxes are due.

(l) Rate applies to entire share.

(m) Mass. imposes a 14% surtax in addition to the inheritance tax on all property or interests. This tax is suspended with respect to estates of decedents dying on or after 1/1/76.

(n) No exemption if share exceeds amount stated except that the tax shall not reduce the share below the amount of the exemption. In addition there are certain exemptions for the spouse's home.

(o) There is no tax on the share of any beneficiary if the value of the share is less than $100.

(p) In addition, an exemption of one-half of the decedent's estate, or one-third if decedent is survived by lineal descendants.

(q) Spouses, minor children and minor adopted children in the decedent's line of succession are entirely exempt. Parents have no exemption and are taxable at the flat rate of 15%.

(r) An additional tax of 3-25% is levied on all beneficiaries other than grandparents, parents, spouse, children, stepchildren or lineal descendants. These categories of beneficiaries are exempt from the additional taxes.

(s) A credit of $300,000 is allowed against the tax base for spouse, minor child, or child incapable of self-support.

(t) However, the $2,000 family exemption is specifically allowed as a deduction.

(u) Estates of $250,000 or more are taxed at rates from 8-15% in addition to the rates above.

(v) The rates range from 1.5-6% for a spouse or a child and from 3-12% for parents.

(w) Maximum rate applies above $50,000.

Federal Estate Tax

Source: Tax Foundation

An estate tax return must be filed for every citizen or resident of the United States whose gross estate exceeds $60,000 in value at the time of his death. In general, the tax must be paid within 9 mos. from the date of death. Extensions may be granted in hardship cases. A return must be filed for a non-resident, not a citizen, if his gross estate in the U.S. exceeds $30,000 in value.

An estate gets credit for state death taxes, according to a graduated table; also deductions for funeral expenses, administration, claims, and bequests to religious, charitable and fraternal organizations or government welfare agencies.

Life insurance payable to named beneficiaries is not to be included in the gross estate if the insured retained no incidents of ownership in the policy. A reversionary inter-est which exceeds 5 per cent of the value of the policy is considered an incident of ownership in the policy.

The marital deduction provides that the value of the taxable estate "shall be determined by deducting from the value of the gross estate an amount equal to the value of any interest in property which passes or has passed from the decedent to his surviving spouse." Thus the deduction applies when the surviving spouse has a right to the income for life from all or only a part of the property, as well as power to appoint all, or the part in which the survivor has income rights, whether or not the property is held in trust. If the spouse has control only over part, the deduction is limited proportionately. The deduction is limited, however, to the value of one-half of the adjusted gross estate.

Estate Tax Rate

The tax is computed under the rates listed below on the net taxable estate of the decedent, citizen or resident of the United States after allowing for the specific exemption of $60,000 and deduction for debts, expenses, charitable, marital deductions. There is a credit allowance for state death taxes.

If the taxable estate is:			The tax shall be:	
Not over $5,000.			3% of the taxable estate	
Over	$5,000	but not over	$10,000	$150, plus 7% of excess over	$5,000
Over	$10,000	but not over	$20,000	$500, plus 11% of excess over	$10,000
Over	$20,000	but not over	$30,000	$1,600, plus 14% of excess over	$20,000
Over	$30,000	but not over	$40,000	$3,000, plus 18% of excess over	$30,000
Over	$40,000	but not over	$50,000	$4,800, plus 22% of excess over	$40,000
Over	$50,000	but not over	$60,000	$7,000, plus 25% of excess over	$50,000
Over	$60,000	but not over	$100,000	$9,500, plus 28% of excess over	$60,000
Over	$100,000	but not over	$250,000	$20,700, plus 30% of excess over	$100,000
Over	$250,000	but not over	$500,000	$65,700, plus 32% of excess over	$250,000
Over	$500,000	but not over	$750,000	$145,700, plus 35% of excess over	$500,000
Over	$750,000	but not over	$1,000,000	$233,200, plus 37% of excess over	$750,000
Over	$1,000,000	but not over	$1,250,000	$325,700, plus 39% of excess over	$1,000,000
Over	$1,250,000	but not over	$1,500,000	$423,200, plus 42% of excess over	$1,250,000
Over	$1,500,000	but not over	$2,000,000	$528,200, plus 45% of excess over	$1,500,000
Over	$2,000,000	but not over	$2,500,000	$753,200, plus 49% of excess over	$2,000,000
Over	$2,500,000	but not over	$3,000,000	$998,200, plus 53% of excess over	$2,500,000
Over	$3,000,000	but not over	$3,500,000	$1,263,200, plus 56% of excess over	$3,000,000
Over	$3,500,000	but not over	$4,000,000	$1,543,200, plus 59% of excess over	$3,500,000
Over	$4,000,000	but not over	$5,000,000	$1,838,200, plus 63% of excess over	$4,000,000
Over	$5,000,000	but not over	$6,000,000	$2,468,200, plus 67% of excess over	$5,000,000
Over	$6,000,000	but not over	$7,000,000	$3,138,200, plus 70% of excess over	$6,000,000
Over	$7,000,000	but not over	$8,000,000	$3,838,200, plus 73% of excess over	$7,000,000
Over	$8,000,000	but not over	$10,000,000	$4,568,200, plus 76% of excess over	$8,000,000
Over	$10,000,000			$6,088,200, plus 77% of excess over	$10,000,000

State Estate Tax Rates and Exemptions*

Source: Compiled by Tax Foundation from Commerce Clearing House Data
As of Sept. 1, 1976. *See index for state inheritance tax rates and exemptions.

State (a)	Rates (on net estate after exemptions) (b)	Maximum rate applies above	Exemption	
Alabama	Maximum federal credit (c, d).	$10,040,000	$60,000	
Alaska	Maximum federal credit (c, d).	10,040,000	60,000	
Arizona	0.8% on first $50,000 to 16% (e).	10,000,000	100,000	(f, g)
Arkansas	Maximum federal credit (c, d).	10,040,000	60,000	(g)
Florida	Maximum federal credit (c, d).	10,040,000	60,000	
Georgia	Maximum federal credit (c, d).	10,040,000	60,000	
Massachusetts	5% on first $50,000 to 16%.	4,000,000	30,000	(h)
Mississippi	1% on first $60,000 to 16%.	10,000,000	60,000	(f, g)
New Mexico	Maximum federal credit (c, d).	10,040,000	60,000	
New York	2% on first $50,000 to 21% (e,i).	10,100,000	60,000	(f, g, j)
North Dakota	2% on first $30,000 to 20%.	1,500,000	60,000	(g)
Ohio	2% on first $40,000 to 7% (e).	500,000	5,000	(g, k)
Oklahoma	1% on first $10,000 to 10% (e).	10,000,000	60,000	(g, l, m)
South Carolina	4% on first $40,000 to 6%.	100,000	60,000	(g)
Utah	5% of first $35,000 to 10% (e).	85,000	60,000	(g)
Vermont	Maximum federal credit (e, n).	10,040,000	60,000	(g)

(a) Excludes states shown in table on page 107 which levy an estate tax, in addition to their inheritance taxes, to assure full absorption of the Federal credit.

(b) The rates generally are in addition to graduated absolute amounts.

(c) Maximum Federal credit allowed under the 1954 code for state estate taxes paid is expressed as a percentage of the taxable estate (after $60,000 exemption) in excess of $40,000, plus a graduated absolute amount.

(d) A tax on nonresident estates is imposed on the proportionate share of the net estate which the property located in the state bears to the entire estate wherever situated.

(e) An additional estate tax is imposed to assure full absorption of the Federal credit.

(f) Insurance receives special treatment.

(g) Transfers to religious, charitable, educational, and municipal corporations are fully exempt. Limited in Mississippi to those located in U.S. or its possessions.

(h) Applies to net estates above $60,000.

(i) On net estate before exemption.

(j) The specific exemptions ($20,000 of the net estate transferred to spouse and $5,000 to lineal ancestors and descendants and certain other named relatives) are allowed in an amount equal to 2% of the first $50,000 and 3% of the next $100,000.

(k) Property is exempt to the extent transferred to surviving spouse not exceeding $30,000; for a child under 18, $7,000 and for each child 18 or over, $3,000.

(l) An estate valued at $100 or less is exempt.

(m) Exemption is a total aggregate of $60,000 for father, mother, child, and other named relatives.

(n) The tax is 30% of the federal estate tax liability.

Savings by Individuals in the U. S.

Source: Federal Reserve System
*Indicates less than $50 million. Seasonally adjusted annual rates (Billions of Dollars).

	1970	1971	1972	1973	1974	1975	1976¹
Inc. in financial assets	80.6	105.3	123.6	139.3	143.3	168.8	178.8
Currency and demand deposits	8.9	9.1	10.8	8.9	9.1	11.3	8.0
Savings acounts	43.6	67.8	71.0	67.9	57.9	86.7	90.7
Securities	-1.4	-4.8	1.3	21.0	31.8	16.8	19.9
U.S. Savings Bonds	.3	2.3	3.3	2.7	3.0	4.0	4.1
Other U.S. Treasury sec.	-9.1	-9.5	-.2	12.3	7.8	-1.7	-.4
U.S.G. agency securities	4.6	-2.3	-3.5	-.7	-2.0	-3.1	-1.0
State & local obligations	-.8	-.3	2.2	7.2	11.2	8.4	8.5
Corporation & foreign bonds	9.5	8.3	4.2	.9	5.3	10.1	11.8
Commercial paper	-5.2	.3	*	5.4	7.9	1.2	-.6
Investment company shares	2.8	1.3	-.5	-1.2	-.5	.8	-1.4
Other corporate stock	-3.5	-5.0	-4.0	-5.7	-.7	-2.8	-1.0
Private life insurance reserves	5.1	6.1	6.5	7.2	6.4	7.6	11.0
Private insured pension reserves	3.3	4.5	4.3	5.5	6.2	8.7	9.7
Private noninsured pension reserves	7.1	7.3	6.9	8.5	10.9	12.8	13.2
Government ins. & pension reserves	8.9	9.5	11.6	11.7	12.5	14.7	10.6
Miscellaneous financial assets	5.1	5.9	11.3	8.6	8.4	10.2	15.8
Gross investment in tangible assets	142.1	167.5	194.8	217.5	202.1	211.4	249.4
Nonfarm homes	25.2	32.6	40.6	45.0	42.8	42.4	55.5
Noncorporate business construction & equipment	31.6	35.1	41.1	44.2	36.9	35.5	38.9
Consumer durables	84.9	97.1	111.2	123.7	121.6	131.7	153.2
Inventories	.4	2.7	1.9	4.6	-1.3	1.8	1.7
Capital consumption allowances	113.1	121.7	130.1	144.7	164.4	184.6	200.0
Nonfarm homes	12.8	13.7	14.7	17.1	19.5	22.0	23.8
Noncorporate business plant and equipment	23.2	24.9	25.7	29.3	34.4	39.4	42.8
Consumer durables	77.0	83.2	89.7	98.3	110.6	123.2	133.4
Net investment in tangible assets	29.1	45.8	64.7	72.8	37.6	26.8	49.4
Nonfarm homes	12.4	18.9	25.9	27.9	23.2	20.4	31.7
Noncorporate business construction and equipment	8.4	10.3	15.4	14.8	4.6	-3.9	-3.8
Consumer durables	7.9	13.9	21.5	25.4	11.1	8.5	19.8
Inventories	.4	2.7	1.9	4.6	-1.3	1.8	1.7
Increase in debt	32.9	58.6	90.2	94.1	59.9	63.3	96.4
Mortgage debt on nonfarm homes	14.6	27.0	41.4	47.0	35.3	40.0	54.6
Noncorporate business mortgage debt	7.4	12.1	15.9	15.7	12.4	7.3	10.4
Consumer credit	5.9	11.6	18.6	21.7	9.8	8.5	19.4
Security credit	-1.8	2.7	4.5	-4.3	-1.8	2.2	5.9
Policy loans	2.3	1.0	1.0	2.2	2.7	1.6	1.4
Other debt	4.6	4.1	8.8	11.9	1.6	3.6	4.7
Individual saving	76.8	92.5	09.0	117.9	121.0	132.3	131.9
Less-Govt. ins. & pen. reserves	8.9	9.5	11.6	11.7	12.5	14.7	10.6
Net inv. in cons. dur.	7.9	13.9	21.5	25.4	11.1	8.5	19.8
Capital gains dividends from invest. cos.	.9	.8	1.4	.9	.5	.2	-.2
Net savings by farm crops	-.1	-.1	.1	.4	-.1	-.1	-.1
Equals pers. saving, F/F basis	59.1	68.4	63.4	79.5	97.0	108.9	101.8
Personal saving, NIA basis	50.6	57.3	49.4	70.3	72.2	84.0	81.2
Difference	8.6	11.1	14.0	9.2	24.8	25.0	20.6

(1.) First quarter, 1976.

Federal Gift Tax
Source: Tax Foundation

Any citizen or resident who within the calendar year makes gifts in excess of $3,000 to any one individual, or any gift of a future interest regardless of value, must file a gift tax return. Since 1971, the tax has been levied quarterly on a return due one and one-half months after the end of the quarter. In addition to the annual $3,000 exclusion for each person to whom gifts are made, each donor also has a

specific lifetime exemption of $30,000, and this may be taken all at one time or spread over years.

When a husband or wife transfers by gift an interest in property to his or her spouse a deduction in computing gift tax will be allowed to the extent of one-half of the value of the gift. Also gifts to a third party by either husband or wife may be treated as made one-half by each.

If the taxable gifts are:		The tax will be: 2 1/4% of the taxable gifts	
Not over $5,000			
Over $5,000 but not over	$10,000	$112.50, plus 5 1/4% of excess over	$5,000
Over $10,000 but not over	$20,000	$375, plus 8 1/4% of excess over	$10,000
Over $20,000 but not over	$30,000	$1,200, plus 10 1/2% of excess over	$20,000
Over $30,000 but not over	$40,000	$2,250, plus 13 1/2% of excess over	$30,000
Over $40,000 but not over	$50,000	$3,600, plus 16 1/2% of excess over	$40,000
Over $50,000 but not over	$60,000	$5,250, plus 18 3/4% of excess over	$50,000
Over $60,000 but not over	$100,000	$7,125, plus 21 % of excess over	$60,000
Over $100,000 but not over	$250,000	$15,525, plus 22 1/2% of excess over	$100,000
Over $250,000 but not over	$500,000	$49,275, plus 24 % of excess over	$250,000
Over $500,000 but not over	$750,000	$109,275, plus 26 1/4% of excess over	$500,000
Over $750,000 but not over	$1,000,000	$174,900, plus 27 3/4% of excess over	$750,000
Over $1,000,000 but not over	$1,250,000	$244,275, plus 29 1/4% of excess over	$1,000,000
Over $1,250,000 but not over	$1,500,000	$317,400, plus 31 1/2% of excess over	$1,250,000
Over $1,500,000 but not over	$2,000,000	$396,150, plus 33 3/4% of excess over	$1,500,000
Over $2,000,000 but not over	$2,500,000	$564,900, plus 36 3/4% of excess over	$2,000,000
Over $2,500,000 but not over	$3,000,000	$748,650, plus 39 3/4% of excess over	$2,500,000
Over $3,000,000 but not over	$3,500,000	$947,400, plus 42 % of excess over	$3,000,000
Over $3,500,000 but not over	$4,000,000	$1,157,400, plus 44 1/4% of excess over	$3,500,000
Over $4,000,000 but not over	$5,000,000	$1,378,650, plus 47 1/4% of excess over	$4,000,000
Over $5,000,000 but not over	$6,000,000	$1,851,150, plus 50 1/4% of excess over	$5,000,000
Over $6,000,000 but not over	$7,000,000	$2,353,650, plus 52 1/2% of excess over	$6,000,000
Over $7,000,000 but not over	$8,000,000	$2,878,650, plus 54 3/4% of excess over	$7,000,000
Over $8,000,000 but not over	$10,000,000	$3,426,150, plus 57 % of excess over	$8,000,000
Over $10,000,000		$4,566,150, plus 57 3/4% of excess over	$10,000,000

How and Where to Get Help on Consumer Complaints
by Kenneth C. Johnston

While Congress again failed, in 1975-76, to approve creation of a federal consumer protection agency, there were many other places to which a customer dissatisfied with faulty merchandise or shoddy repair work could turn for help.

Many big businesses now provide phone numbers (some toll-free) or addresses where complainants can receive courteous consideration and have some hope of action.

Among government agencies, the Federal Trade Commission has been given new powers on behalf of consumers; it may now force manufacturers to repair or replace guaranteed products "within a reasonable time."

The range of services open to consumers includes Better Business Bureaus, government prosecutors, small claims courts, and local government consumer agencies.

There are also industry and trade associations and those newspapers and radio stations which intercede for readers or listeners.

What Corporations Provide

Here's what some big companies suggest you do if you can't get satisfaction from your local dealer:

Ford: Phone or write Ford Parts & Service Div., district office (see phone book or ask local Ford dealer); or phone 800 648-4848 (free call) for all vehicles made by Ford (from Nevada, phone 800-992-5777).

Chrysler: Phone or write Chrysler Corp., Customer Service (ask dealer or see phone book); or write to: Consumer Affairs, Chrysler Corp., P.M. Box 856, Detroit, Mich. 48231; include your own phone no.

General Motors: Phone or write Divisional Owner Relations Office (listed in owner's manual), or GM Owner Relations, Central Office, 3044 Grand Boulevard, Detroit, Mich. 48202.

American Motors: Contact zone office (see owner's manual); then write Harry Allen, Owner Relations Manager, AMC, 14250 Plymouth Rd., Detroit, Mich. 48232.

Volkswagen: Try Customer Assistance Dept. at Volkswagen regional office (see owner's manual); or write Customer Assistance, Volkswagen of America, Englewood Cliffs, N.J. 07632.

General Electric: Write to Manager of Customer Relations, General Electric Co., 3135 Easton Turnpike, Fairfield, Conn. 06431. But, on appliances, the warranty tells customer where to write.

RCA: On any RCA product, phone 212 598-4921 or write Consumer Relations, RCA Corp., 30 Rockefeller Plaza, New York, N.Y. 10020.

Panasonic: Write nearest regional office listed on card accompanying product.

Admiral Corporation: Write Frank Williamson, Consumer Relations, Admiral Corp., 200 Murray Hill Parkway, East Rutherford, N.J. 07073

Whirlpool: Round-the-clock, toll-free service through 800 253-1301.

Union Carbide: The product or the guarantee has address to write to: or write Union Carbide Corp., Consumer Information, 270 Park Ave., New York, N.Y. 10017.

Exxon: Write to John B. Boatwright, Marketing Dept., Exxon, Box 2180, Houston, Tex. 77001, on product, service, or credit card complaints.

Gulf Oil: See phone book or dealer for nearest Gulf Oil district office or write Gulf Oil Corp., 439 7th Ave., Pittsburgh, Pa. 15230 on products or service; for credit card troubles, see address on bill.

Mobil Oil: See dealer or write or call local district sales office or regional marketing offices in Los Angeles, Scarsdale, N.Y.; Valley Forge, Pa., or Woodfield, Ill. For credit card troubles, write, call, or wire Mobil Oil Credit Corp., 210 W. 10th St., Kansas City, Mo. 64105.

Texaco: See retailer or phone book for nearest Texaco, Inc., division office; otherwise, write Texaco, Assistant General Manager (Resale), Marketing Dept. —U.S., 135 E. 42d St., New York, N.Y. 10017.

ARCO: See phone book or dealer for Atlantic Richfield district office or write to Atlantic Richfield Co., Consumer Relations, P.O. Box 2679 T.A., Los Angeles, Cal. 90051. On credit cards, use free "800" phone no. shown on bill.

Goodyear: See dealer or phone book for Goodyear Tire & Rubber Co. customer service representative at district office, or write Director of Consumer Affairs, Goodyear Tire & Rubber Co., 1144 E. Market St., Akron, Ohio 44316.

Firestone: See dealer or phone book, under Firestone Tire & Rubber Co., for district office, contact consumer affairs representative there (in some 35 cities); or phone 800 321-9638 (free call).

Sears, Roebuck: Ask for Customer Service at the store; then, the store manager; finally, write Sears, Roebuck & Co., Customer Relations, Sears Tower, Chicago, Ill. 60684.

J. C. Penney: See store manager; if unsatisfied, write Patricia Ludorf, Customer Relations Dept., J. C. Penney Co., 1301 Avenue of the Americas, New York, N.Y. 10019.

Woolworth's: See store manager; if not satisfied, write F.W. Woolworth Co., 233 Broadway, New York, N.Y. 10007; Attention Consumer Relations Dept.

Kresge's: See section supervisor; then, store manager; finally, get from manager address of S.S. Kresge Co. regional office, write to Customer Relations there.

Kodak: See phone book under Eastman Kodak Co. for Kodak Consumer Center (in some 35 cities) for free minor adjustments and advice; write Eastman Kodak Co., 343 State St., Rochester, N.Y. 14650, attention—Dept. 841.

A & P: See store manager or phone book under A & P Food Stores or Great Atlantic & Pacific Tea Co. for Customer Relations Dept. (in 28 cities); finally, write Executive Office, A & P Food Stores. 2 Paragon Dr., Montvale N.J. 07645.

DuPont: See dealer or phone book under duPont de Nemours, Product Information (in 8 major cities), or write duPont Co., Wilmington, Del. 19898.

General Foods: Write to General Foods Corp., 250 North St., White Plains, N.Y. 10625.

Procter & Gamble: Write Consumer Services, P.O. Box 599, Cincinnati, Ohio 45201. If possible, include your phone number, times you can be reached and name and serial number from the product package.

United Van Lines: Call toll-free 800-325-3870, ask for Bette Malone.

Avis: Write Customer Service Dep't., Avis Rent A Car System, World Headquarters, 900 Old Country Road, Garden City, N.Y. 11530.

Hertz: Phone 212 598-4921 or write Consumer Relations, RCA Corp., 30 Rockefeller Plaza, New York, N.Y. 10020.

Government Agencies

There are numerous government agencies which can be helpful:

Cities: Some have Offices of Consumer Complaints or Depts. of Consumer Affairs (see phone book). In N.Y. City, for example, the department will investigate the complaint, then may try to work out a settlement; it may sue on behalf of a consumer, issue violation notices, hold hearings and fine a company or revoke or suspend a company's license to operate in the city.

Many **towns** and **counties** also have consumer protection agencies.

States likewise offer aid to the unhappy consumer.

Usually, it is a part of the Attorney General's office.

Write or phone the Attorney General, Attention Consumer Protection Office, in your state.

Nationally, one may write to the Bureau of Consumer Protection, Federal Trade Commission, Washington, D.C. 20580, or the nearest FTC regional office.

The Consumer Product Safety Commission, a federal agency created in 1973, offers a toll-free number, 800 638-2666, where you can find out if a particular product has been declared unsafe or complain about one you believe is hazardous. If enough complaints are received, the commission will investigate and can order the product banned.

For a complaint against an airline (fares, baggage, service, delays), write Office of the Consumer Advocate, Civil Aeronautics Board, Washington, D.C. 20428.

In **Canada,** one may write the Director, Trade Practices Branch, Dept. of Consumer and Corporate Affairs, 219 Laurier Ave. West, Ottawa, Ontario.

Other Industry Aids

Within industry groups there are industry and trade associations which may be helpful. One which claims an excellent record in handling a large number of complaints is MACAP, the **Major Appliance Consumer Action Panel,** 20 North Wacker Drive, Chicago, Ill. 60606. You may write or make a free, collect phone call to 312 236-3165, if you don't get satisfaction from a manufacturer of home laundry equipment, range, refrigerator, freezer, room air conditioner, water heater, dehumidifier, dishwasher, disposer, gas incinerator, or humidifier. Give full details.

A similar organization is CRICAP, the **Carpet and Rug Industry Consumer Action Panel,** Box 1568, Dalton, Ga. 30720. Write them, if the dealer and maker won't cooperate, giving full details and your phone number. They will recommend appropriate action to the company involved; they claim good results, especially among firms that are members of the Carpet & Rug Institute.

Among industry complaint centers sponsored by the U.S. Chamber of Commerce are:

American Apparel Manufacturers Assn., 1611 N. Kent St., Arlington, Va. 22209.

American Footwear Manufacturers Assn., 342 Madison Ave., N.Y. 10017.

Direct Mail Advertising Assn., 230 Park Ave., New York, N.Y. 10017.

Direct Selling Assn., 1730 M St. N.W., Washington, D.C. 20036. (On door-to-door sales.)

Master Photo Dealers and Finishers Assn., 603 Lansing Ave., Jackson, Mich. 49202.

Mobile Homes Manufacturing Assn., 14650 Lee Rd., Chantilly, Va. 22021.

National Assn. of Furniture Manufacturers, 8401 Connecticut Ave., Suite 911, Washington, D.C. 20015.

National Employment Assn., 2000 K St. N.W., Washington, D. C. 20006. (For employment agencies.)

National Automobile Dealers Assn., 2000 K St. Connecticut Ave., Suite 911, Washington, D.C. 20015.

National Consumer Finance Assn., 1000 16th St. N.W., Washington, D.C. 20036.

National Employment Assn., 2000 K St. N.W., Washington, D.C. 20006. (On employment agencies.)

National Institute of Drycleaning, 909 Burlington Ave., Silver Spring, Md. 20910.

The Council of Better Business Bureaus has a central office; complaints about nationwide products, especially, may be sent to it: Council of Better Business Bureaus, Trade Practices Dept., 1150 17th St. N.W., Washington, D.C. 20036. The council will seek solutions for complaints.

Don't Forget

As a complaining consumer you will find it helpful to provide whatever agency you appeal to with copies of receipts and guarantees (not the actual receipts). Be as specific as possible about the dealer's name and address, purchase date, price, name, and serial number (if any) of the product, places you may already have sought relief, with dates. Don't forget your name, address, and phone number (some companies or agencies may want to serve you as rapidly as possible and may need further information).

The consumer may even return the favor in some cases and help the manufacturer: as a Procter & Gamble spokesman points out, some manufacturers will want the consumer to hold on to the offending product so that the maker can analyze it, find out what went wrong, and try to prevent its happening again.

Consumers' Association of Canada

The Consumers' Association of Canada, CAC, is a voluntary, non-profit organization, founded in 1947. The National Office is located at 801-251 Laurier Avenue West, Ottawa, Ontario, K1P 5A7. CAC's aims are:
(a) to unite the strength of consumers,
(b) to study consumer problems and make recommendations for their solutions,
(c) to enunciate the views and concerns of consumers,
(d) to establish a two-way channel of communication between governments, trade and industry, regulatory bodies, and the consumer,
(e) to provide information on consumer legislation, to

research and test consumer goods and services, encourage conservation and to inform and monitor the metric conversion.

CAC publishes bi-monthly, bilingual magazines, CANADIAN CONSUMER and LE CONSOMMATEUR CANADIEN; circulation 93,000. Across Canada there are 10 provincial and 2 territorial branches and 93 English and 26 French local associations and consumer committees.

CAC has attained notable achievements in implementing better packaging and labelling, improved safety standards and selling practices and updating food and drug regulations.

Consumer Credit Statistics

Source: Federal Reserve System (Estimated amounts outstanding. In millions of dollars)

End of year or month	Total	Installment credit					Noninstallment credit			
		Total	Automobile paper	Mobile homes paper	Home improvement loans	All other	Total	Single payment loans	Charge Accounts	Service credit
1970......	126,997	101,898	35,060	2,462	5,010	59,377	25,099	9,675	7,968	7,456
1971......	138,640	111,195	38,536	7,189	5,239	60,232	27,445	10,931	8,350	8,164
1972......	157,247	126,756	44,097	9,321	5,915	67,421	30,491	12,636	8,881	8,974
1973......	178,964	146,434	50,065	11,698	6,950	77,721	32,530	13,353	9,198	9,979
1974......	188,740	155,384	50,392	12,496	7,754	84,742	33,356	12,966	9,506	10,884
1975......	197,276	162,237	53,028	12,155	8,004	89,049	35,039	13,072	9,940	12,027
1976 June...	NA	166,664	56,667	11,733	8,367	89,897	NA	NA	NA	NA

NA—not available. Note—Details do not add to totals because of rounding.

Interest Laws and Consumer Finance Loan Rates

Source: Revised by Christian T. Jones of Chicago, Editor Consumer Finance Law Bulletin

Most states have laws regulating interest rates. These laws fix a legal or conventional rate which applies when there is no contract for interest. They also fix a general maximum contract rate, but in many states there are so many exceptions that the general contract maximum actually applies only to exceptional cases.

1. Legal rate of interest. The legal or conventional rate of interest applies to money obligations when no interest rate is contracted for and also to judgments. The rate is usually 6% a year; 5% or 7% in some states.

2. General maximum contract rates. General interest laws in most states set the maximum rate between 8% and 12% per year. The general maximum is fixed by the State Constitution rather than by statute at 10% per year in Arkansas, California, Tennessee, and Texas. Loans to corporations are frequently exempted or subject to a higher maximum. In recent years, it has also been common to provide special rates for home mortgage loans. Courts generally hold that installment sale charges are not interest, but installment sale charges are limited by laws in many states.

3. Specific enabling acts. In many states special statutes permit industrial loan companies and banks to charge interest and fees without regard to installment payments which yield 1 1/2% a month or more.

Laws regulating charge accounts and credit cards generally limit charges to 1 1/2% per month. Credit unions may generally charge 1% a month. Pawnbrokers' rates vary widely. Building and loan associations, and loans insured by the F.H.A., are also specially regulated.

4. Consumer finance loan statutes. Most consumer finance loan statutes are based on early models drafted by the Russell Sage Foundation (1916-42) to provide small loans to wage earners under license and other protective regulations. Since 1969, however, the model has frequently been the Uniform Consumer Credit Code which applies to credit sales and loans for consumer purposes up to $25,000. In general, licensed lenders may charge 2 1/2% or 3% a month for $300 or less and reduced rates for additional amounts up to $2,000 or more. A number of states permit add-on rates of 17% to 20% ($17 to $20 per $100) a year of the original principal for $300 and lower rates for additional amounts. An add-on of 17% ($17 per $100) per year yields about 2 1/2% per month when the loan is paid in equal monthly installments. In the table below unless otherwise stated, monthly and annual rates are based on reducing principal balances, annual add-on rates are based on the original principal for the full term, and two or more rates apply to different portions of balance or original principal.

The states with consumer finance loan laws and the rates of charge as of Oct. 1, 1976, are as follows:

Maximum rate	Monthly unless otherwise stated	Maximum rate

Ala.... Annual add-on: 15% to $500, 10% to $1,000, 8% to $2,000. Over $2,000, 8% add-on entire balance. Higher rates for loans up to $300.

Alas.... 3% to $400, 2% to $800, 1% to $1,500. 5% to $50.

Ariz.... 3% to $300, 2% to $600, 1¹/₂% to $1,500, 1% to $2,500.

Cal.... 2¹/₂% to $225, 2% to $625, 1¹/₂% to $1,650, 1% to $10,000 (1¹/₂% min.).

Colo... .36% per annum to $300, 21% to $1,000, 15% to $25,-000 (18% min.).

Conn... Annual Add-on: 17% to $300, 11% to $5,000.

Del.... Annual Discount: 9% for 1st 36 mos., 6% for remaining months; plus 2% fee.

Fla.... 30% per annum to $500, 24% to $1,000, 16% to $2,500.

Haw.... 3¹/₂% to $100, 2¹/₂% to $300.

Idaho.. .36% per annum to $480, 21% to $1,600, 15% to $40,-000 (18% min.).

Ill.... . 2¹/₂% to $300, 2% to $600, 1¹/₂% to $1,500.

Ind.... .36% per annum to $390, 21% to $1,300, 15% to $32,-500 (18% min.).

Ia.... 3% to $250, 2% to $400, 1¹/₂% to $1,000.

Kan... : 36% per year to $300, 21% to $1,000, 14.45% to $25,000. (18% min.)

Ky.... .3% to $500, 2% to $1,200, 1¹/₂% to $1,500.

La.... .36% per annum to $800, 27% to $2,000, 21% to $3,500, 15% to $25,000 (18% min.).

Me.... 30% per annum to $300, 21% to $1,000, 15% to $25,-000 (18% min.).

Md.... 3% to $300, 2% to $500.

Mass... 2¹/₂% to $200, 2% to $600, 1³/₄% to $1,000, ³/₄% to $3,000.

Mich... .2¹/₂% to $400, 1¹/₄% to $1,500.

Minn... .2³/₄% to $300, 1¹/₂% to $600, 1¹/₄% to $1,200 plus fee of $1 per $100.

Miss.. .36% per annum to $600, 33% to $1,800, 24% to $4,500, 12% over $4,500.

Mo.... 2.218% to $500, 10% per annum on any remainder.

Mont... .Annual add-on: 20% to $300, 16% to $500, 12% to $1,000, 10% to $7,500. Special rate to $90.

Neb.... 30% per annum to $300, 24% to $500, 18% to $1,000, 12% to $3,000.

Nev.... Annual add-on: 9% to $1,000, 8% to $2,500; monthly fee of 1% on first $200 and ¹/₂% on next $200; over $2,500 to $10,000 annual interest is 17.74%.

N.H.... .2% to $600, 1¹/₂% to $1,500; 1¹/₂% on entire amount over $1,500 to $5,000.

N.J.... .24% per annum to $500, 22% to $1,500, 18% to $2,500.

N.M.... 3% to $150, 2¹/₂% to $300, 1% to $2,500 (1¹/₂% min.).

N.Y.... .2¹/₂% to $100, 2% to $300, 1¹/₂% to $900, 1¹/₄% to $2,500.

N.C.... .3% to $300, 1¹/₂% to $1,500. Special rate up to $95.

N.D.... .2¹/₂% to $250, 2% to $500, 1³/₄% to $750, 1¹/₂% to $1,000; 1¹/₂% on entire amount over $1,000 to $2,500.

Ohio... Annual add-on: 16% to $750, 11% to $1,500, 9% to $3,000; or equivalent simple interest rate.

Okla... .30% per annum to $300, 21% to $1,000, 15% to $25,-000. (18% min.). Special rates to $100.

Ore.... .3% to $300, 1³/₄% to $1,000, 1¹/₄% to $5,000. Over $5,000, 1¹/₂%.

Pa.... 3% to $150, 2% to $300, 1% to $600.

P.R.... Annual Add-on: 20% to $300, 7% to $600.

R.I.... 3% to $300, 2¹/₂% for loans between $300 and $800; 2% for larger loans to $2,500.

S.C.... .36% per annum to $300, 21% to $1,000, 15% to $25,-000 (18% min.). Special rate to $150.

S.D.... .2¹/₂% to $300, 2% to $1,000, 1¹/₂% to $1,500, 1% to $2,500; 1¹/₂% on entire amount to $5,000. $2 minimum.

Tenn... .7¹/₂% per annum discount plus fees; no size limit.

Texas.. Annual add-on: 18% to $300, 8% to $2,500. Special rates to $100.

Utah... 36% per annum to $480, 21% to $1,600, 15% to $40,-000 (18% min.).

Vt.... .Annual add-on of 14% to $1,500.

Va.... 2¹/₂% to $300, 1¹/₂% to $1,500; annual add-on of 17% to $500, 13% to $1,000, 11% to $1,500.

Wash.. 3% to $300, 1¹/₂% to $500, 1% to $1,000; $1 minimum.

W.Va.. 36% per year to $200, 24% to $600, 18% to $1,200.

Wis.... Annual Discount: 9¹/₄% on first $1,000, 8% to $3,000 up to 36 months; 18% per annum for larger loans.

Wyo.... 36% per annum to $300, 21% to $1,000, 15% to $25,-000 (18% min.).

ECONOMICS
U.S. Budget Receipts and Outlays—1975-1976

Source: Treasury Department; each fiscal year ends June 30
(thousands of dollars)

Classification	Fiscal 1975	Fiscal 1976
Net Receipts		
Individual income taxes	122,385,980	131,602,555
Corporation income taxes	40,621,179	41,408,703
Social insurance taxes and contributions:		
Federal old-age and survivors insurance	55,207,343	58,702,690
Federal disability insurance	7,250,217	7,686,092
Federal hospital insurance	11,257,522	11,995,098
Railroad retirement taxes	1,489,333	1,525,144
Total employment taxes and contributions	75,204,416	79,909,024
Other insurance and retirement:		
Unemployment	6,770,706	8,053,658
Federal supplementary medical insurance	1,900,887	1,937,296
Federal employees retirement	2,512,548	2,760,167
Civil service retirement and disability	52,434	54,231
Total social insurance taxes and contributions	86,440,989	92,714,377
Excise taxes	16,550,686	16,962,582
Estate and gift taxes	4,611,125	5,216,229
Customs duties	3,675,532	4,074,176
Deposits of earnings-Federal Reserve Banks	5,776,550	5,450,824
Petroleum import license fees	442,615	1,890,326
All other miscellaneous receipts	532,810	685,305
Net Budget Receipts	281,037,466	300,005,077
Net Outlays		
Legislative Branch	726,199	779,052
The Judiciary	283,754	325,021
Executive Office of the President:		
The White House Office	15,294	15,791
Office of Management and Budget	21,736	23,591
Special Office for Drug Abuse Prevention	33,794	12,826
Total Executive Office	92,939	79,224
Funds appropriated to the President:		
Appalachian regional development	311,374	319,283
Disaster relief	205,858	291,137
Foreign Assistance-security	1,394,870	1,101,398
Foreign assistance-development-multilateral	684,699	1,045,829
Foreign assistance-development-bilateral	870,462	623,516
Miscellaneous	519,014	143,530
Total funds appropriated to the President	3,986,277	3,524,692
Agriculture Department:		
Food stamp program	4,598,956	5,774,500
Child Nutrition Program	1,452,267	1,801,566
Total Agriculture Department	9,727,716	12,796,311
Commerce Department	1,582,752	2,020,005
Defense Department:		
Military personnel	24,967,611	25,063,518
Retired military personnel	6,241,772	7,295,679
Operation and maintenance	26,329,633	27,901,590
Procurement	16,041,841	15,963,849
Research and development	8,866,499	8,923,023
Military construction	1,461,767	2,018,627
Family housing	1,124,297	1,191,772
Civil defense	86,404	79,835
Corps of Engineers and other civil	2,050,662	2,124,252
Total Defense Department	87,017,373	90,160,407
Health, Education and Welfare Department:		
National Institutes of Health	1,889,343	2,349,289
Old-age and survivors benefits	54,838,818	62,164,263
Public assistance (including health care and social services)	14,009,701	16,675,438
Education Division	6,514,748	6,903,749
Total HEW	112,409,704	128,784,967
Housing and Urban Development Department	7,488,207	7,079,133
Interior Department	2,171,404	2,293,480
Justice Department:		
Federal Bureau of Investigation	438,501	468,764
Total Justice Department	2,066,769	2,241,574
Labor Department:		
Unemployment Trust Fund	13,211,123	17,920,413
Total Labor Department	17,648,632	25,742,379
State Department	828,694	1,061,820
Transportation Department	9,246,454	11,936,056
Treasury Department:		
Internal Revenue Service	1,959,041	2,924,389
Interest on the public debt	32,665,008	37,063,211
General revenue sharing	6,137,917	6,242,926
Total Treasury Department	41,173,936	44,335,468
Energy Research and Development Agency	3,198,973	3,759,025
Environmental Protection Agency	2,530,466	3,117,746
General Services Administration	−621,448	−92,142
National Aeronautics and Space Administration	3,329,924	3,669,502
Veterans Administration	16,571,969	18,414,835

Classification	Fiscal 1975	Fiscal 1976
Net Outlays (cont'd)		
Independent agencies:		
Action.	178,166	177,011
Arms Control and Disarmament Agency.	9,726	10,704
Board for International Broadcasting.	49,858	59,340
Civil Aeronautics Board.	80,884	90,939
Civil Service Commission.	7,036,236	8,320,440
Commission on Civil Rights.	6,920	7,863
Community Services Administration.	546,314	448,733
Consumer Product Safety Commission.	34,212	38,351
Corporation for Public Broadcasting.	62,000	70,000
District of Columbia.	429,312	464,738
Emergency Loan Guarantee Board.	—7,144	—5,570
Equal Employment Opportunity Commission.	56,120	56,143
Federal Communications Commission.	47,938	52,486
Federal Deposit Insurance Corporation.	—407,682	—478,330
Federal Energy Administration.	120,672	140,603
Federal Home Loan Bank Board.	924,200	—78,853
Federal Maritime Commission.	7,229	7,784
Federal Mediation and Conciliation Service.	15,497	17,908
Federal Power Commission.	34,407	35,704
Federal Trade Commission.	38,703	43,729
Historical and Memorial Commissions.	11,581	12,788
Intergovernmental Agencies.	177,663	174,099
International Trade Commission.	8,296	9,715
Interstate Commerce Commission.	43,962	47,440
Legal Services Corporation.	—	84,634
National Credit Union Administration.	—13,537	—19,896
National Foundation on the Arts and Humanities.	128,082	151,860
National Labor Relations Board.	60,889	67,466
National Science Foundation.	662,161	731,905
Nuclear Regulatory Commission.	52,792	179,956
Postal Service.	1,877,112	1,719,650
Railroad Retirement Board.	3,083,036	3,482,102
Securities and Exchange Commission.	44,395	50,618
Selective Service System.	48,544	37,493
Small Business Administration.	617,893	436,164
Smithsonian Institution.	102,852	112,772
Temporary Study Commissions.	12,239	13,602
Tennessee Valley Authority.	767,225	980,318
U.S. Information Agency.	239,806	257,034
U.S. Railway Association.	22,700	329,020
Water Resources Council.	9,415	10,943
Other independent agencies.	37,339	52,031
Total independent agencies.	**17,258,013**	**18,285,947**
Undistributed offsetting receipts.	—14,077,119	—14,704,375
Net Budget Outlays.	**324,641,586**	**365,610,129**
Less net receipts.	281,037,466	300,005,077
Deficit.	**—43,604,120**	**—65,605,052**

U.S. Net Receipts and Outlays

Source: Treasury Department; annual statements for year ending June 30

Yearly average	Receipts $1,000	Expenditures $1,000	Yearly average	Receipts $1,000	Expenditures $1,000	Yearly average	Receipts $1,000	Expenditures $1,000
1789-1800[1]	5,717	5,776	1871-1875	336,830	287,460	1911-1915	710,227	720,252
1801-1810[2]	13,056	9,086	1876-1880	288,124	255,598	1916-1920[6]	3,483,652	8,065,333
1811-1820[2]	21,032	23,943	1881-1885	366,961	257,691	1921-1925	4,306,673	3,578,989
1821-1830[2]	21,928	16,162	1886-1890	375,448	279,134	1926-1930	4,069,138	3,182,807
1831-1840[2]	30,461	24,495	1891-1895	352,891	363,599	1931-1935[4]	2,770,973	5,214,874
1841-1850[2]	28,545	34,097	1896-1900	434,877	457,451	1936-1040[4]	4,960,614	10,192,367
1851-1860	60,237	60,163	1901-1905	559,481	535,559	1941-1945[4]	25,951,137	66,037,928
1861-1865	160,907	683,785	1906-1910	628,507	639,178	1946-1950[678]	39,047,243	42,334,534
1866-1870	447,301	377,642						

Fiscal Year	Receipts	Expenditures	Fiscal Year	Receipts	Expenditures
1955.	60,389,743,895	64,569,972,817	1968.	153,675,705,000	172,803,186,000
1959.	67,915,348,624	80,342,335,375	1970.	193,843,791,000	194,968,258,000
1960.	77,763,460,220	76,539,412,798	1971.	188,332,129,000	210,652,667,000
1961.	77,659,424,905	81,515,167,453	1972[9]	215,262,638,670	238,285,906,846
1962.	81,409,092,072	87,786,766,580	1973.	232,191,842,000	246,603,359,000
1963.	86,357,020,251	92,589,764,029	1974.	264,847,484,000	268,342,952,000
1964.	89,458,664,071	97,684,374,794	1975.	281,037,466,000	324,641,586,000
1965.	93,071,796,891	96,506,904,210	1976.	300,005,077,000	365,610,129,000

(1) Average for period March 4, 1789, to Dec. 31, 1800.
(2) Years ended Dec. 31, 1801, to 1842; average for 1841-1850 is for the period Jan. 1, 1841, to June 30, 1850.
(3) Receipts from 1937 on have deducted appropriations to Federal old-age and survivors insurance trust fund.
(4) Expenditures for years 1932 through 1946 have been revised to include Government Corps. (wholly owned) etc. (net).
(5) Effective January 3, 1949, amounts refunded by the Government, principally for the overpayment of taxes, are being reported as deductis from total receipts rather than as expenditures. Also, effective July 1, 1948, payments to the Treasury, principally by wholly owned Government corporations for retirement of capital stock and for disposition of earnings, are excluded in reporting both budget receipts and expenditures. Neither of these changes affects the size of the budget surplus or deficit. Beginning 1931 figures in each case have been adjusted accordingly for comparative purposes.
(6) Figures for 1918 through 1946 are revised to exclude statutory debt retirement (sinking fund, etc.).
(7) Excludes $3 billion transferred to Foreign Economics Corporation Trust Fund.
(8) Includes $3 billion representing expenditures made from the FEC Trust Fund.
(9) Effective fiscal year 1972 loan repayments and loan disbursements will be netted against expenditures and known as outlays.

Summary of U.S. Receipts by Source and Outlays by Function

Source: U.S. Treasury Department (June 30, 1976)

(in thousands)

Net Receipts	Fiscal Year	1976	1975	1974
Individual income taxes		$131,602,555	$122,385,980	$118,750,071
Corporation income taxes . . . .∴. . .		41,408,703	40,621,179	38,664,197
Social insurance taxes and contributions:				
Employment taxes and contributions		79,909,024	75,204,416	65,893,961
Unemployment insurance		8,053,658	6,770,706	6,906,711
Contributions for other insurance and retirement . . .		4,751,695	4,465,868	4,048,681
Excise taxes		16,962,582	16,550,686	16,885,403
Estate and gift taxes		5,216,229	4,611,125	5,009,320
Customs		4,074,176	3,675,532	3,334,127
Miscellaneous		8,026,454	6,751,975	5,355,013
Total		**300,005,077**	**281,037,466**	**264,847,484**
Outlays				
National defense		90,215,930	86,532,996	78,792,890
International affairs		4,461,848	4,356,420	4,175,456
General science, space, and technology		4,196,683	4,048,164	3,228,146
Natural resources, environment, and energy		11,674,436	9,567,201	-989,552
Agriculture		1,994,004	1,666,548	5,182,770
Commerce and transportation		17,238,524	16,010,079	12,549,002
Community and regional development		5,022,863	4,431,128	5,129,221
Education, training, employment and social services . .		17,678,274	15,248,690	10,574,715
Health		33,600,713	27,646,689	21,501,547
Income security		126,895,958	108,605,000	84,075,160
Veterans benefits and services		18,444,339	16,594,399	13,369,846
Law enforcement and justice		3,325,494	2,942,316	
General government		2,951,242	3,086,581	6,485,062
Revenue sharing and general purpose				
fiscal assistance		7,114,160	7,005,543	6,105,922
Interest		35,500,036	30,974,951	28,101,163
Undistributed offsetting receipts		-14,704,375	-14,075,119	-9,938,397
Total		**365,610,129**	**324,641,586**	**268,342,952**

U. S. Customs and Internal Revenue Receipts

Gross. Not reduced by appropriations to Federal old-age and survivors insurance trust fund or refunds or receipts. Data are for fiscal years.

Year	Customs	Internal Revenue	Year	Customs	Internal Revenue	Year	Customs	Internal Revenue
1930	$587,000,903	$3,039,295,014	1955	606,396,634	66,288,691,586	1972	3,284,922,000	208,595,814,000
1935	343,353,034	3,277,690,028	1960	1,123,037,579	91,774,802,823	1973	3,175,268,000	232,191,842,000
1940	348,590,635	5,303,133,988	1965	1,477,548,820	114,428,991,753	1974	3,334,127,000	264,847,484,000
1945	354,775,542	43,902,001,929	1970	2,429,799,000	193,743,251,000	1975	3,665,929,000	277,255,054,000
1950	422,650,329	39,448,607,109	1971	2,589,973,339	188,332,129,000	1976	4,074,176,000	295,930,901,000

U.S. Direct Investments Abroad, Countries and Industries

Source: Bureau of Economic Analysis, U.S. Dept. of Commerce

(Millions of Dollars)

	Direct investment position		Net capital outflows		Reinvested earnings		Balance of payments income		Earnings	
	1974	1975	1974	1975	1974	1975	1974	1975	1974	1975
Bulk all areas	118,819	133,168	7,653	6,307	7,777	8,184	17,849	9,456	25,612	17,473
Developed countries	83,025	91,139	5,273	2,883	5,526	5,149	4,892	4,576	10,383	9,683
Canada	28,404	31,155	643	482	2,214	2,227	1,180	1,218	3,344	3,399
Petroleum . . . . ·	5,731	6,209	-110	-54	530	*534	252	311	796	865
Manufacturing . . . . ·.	13,450	14,718	410	125	1,298	1,138	506	532	1,811	1,684
Other	9,223	10,228	344	411	385	555	423	375	738	850
Europe	44,782	49,621	3,793	2,265	2,768	2,525	2,945	2,628	5,738	5,164
Petroleum	9,960	11,381	1,023	1,262	434	179	360	376	693	502
Manufacturing	23,990	26,136	1,602	756	1,586	1,396	1,534	1,332	3,188	2,772
Other	10,832	12,104	1,169	247	748	950	1,051	920	1,857	1,890
Other	9,839	10,363	836	137	544	397	767	730	1,301	1,119
Petroleum	2,642	2,746	425	-24	151	127	165	142	284	253
Manufacturing	4,533	4,747	179	26	290	194	288	248	598	460
Other	2,664	2,670	231	135	103	75	315	341	419	406
Developing countries . . . . : . .	28,459	34,874	1,676	3,713	1,841	2,928	12,556	4,540	14,468	7,382
Latin America	19,491	22,223	2,208	1,347	1,109	1,462	2,036	1,603	3,065	3,002
Petroleum	3,564	3,370	418	-233	95	89	667	255	765	348
Manufacturing	7,541	8,553	565	265	568	773	343	353	907	1,117
Other	8,386	10,300	1,225	1,315	446	601	1,026	995	1,393	1,536
Other	8,968	12,651	-532	2,366	732	1,466	10,520	2,937	11,403	4,380
Petroleum	4,693	7,776	-1,014	2,136	329	1,068	10,033	2,491	10,516	3,564
Manufacturing	1,658	1,885	105	128	194	103	77	94	271	199
Other	2,616	2,989	377	102	209	294	410	351	617	617
International and unallocated	7,335	7,155	704	-288	410	107	401	339	761	408

Gross National Product, National Income, and Personal Income

Source: Department of Commerce. Office of Economic Analysis
(In millions of dollars) Includes Alaska and Hawaii beginning in 1960

	1950	1960	1970	1973	1974	1975
Gross national product.....................	284,769	503,734	977,080	1,306,554	1,413,206	1,516,338
Less: Capital consumption allowances..........	18,342	43,408	87,254	117,652	137,700	161,382
Equals: Net national product...............	266,427	460,326	889,826	1,188,902	1,275,506	1,354,956
Less: Indirect business tax and nontax liability.....	23,334	45,200	93,461	120,193	128,358	138,690
Business transfer payments................	778	1,878	3,989	5,375	5,613	6,277
Statistical discrepancy..................	1,488	—1,031	—6,392	2,629	6,624	4,419
Plus: Subsidies minus current surplus of government enterprises...................	247	243	1,694	3,872	838	2,014
Equals: National income.................	241,074	414,522	800,462	1,064,577	1,135,749	1,207,584
Less: Corporate profits and inventory valuation adjustment................	37,669	49,904	69,240	99,064	84,847	91,604
Contributions for social insurance...........	6,870	20,672	57,708	91,524	103,416	109,657
Wage accruals less disbursement...........	24	0	0	—56	—530	...
Plus: Government transfer payment to persons...	14,294	26,609	75,119	113,511	134,643	168,933
Personal income interest..................	7,198	15,083	30,998	84,051	101,392	110,663
Dividends........................	8,838	13,437	24,680	27,792	30,756	32,105
Business transfer payments...............	778	1,878	3,989	5,375	5,613	6,277
Equals: Personal income..................	227,619	400,953	808,290	1,052,440	1,153,293	1,249,673

National Income by Type of Income

(Millions of dollars)

	1960	1965	1970	1973	1974	1975
Compensation of employees...............	294,226	393,844	603,869	799,194	875,823	928,871
Wage and salaries.....................	270,844	358,885	541,976	701,214	764,486	806,663
Private.........................	222,108	289,621	426,875	552,630	604,126	630,830
Government.......................	48,736	69,264	115,101	148,584	160,360	175,833
Supplements to wages, salary.............	23,382	34,959	61,893	97,980	111,337	122,118
Empl. contrib. soc. ins...............	11,380	16,217	29,717	49,289	55,838	59,658
Other labor income.................	12,002	18,742	32,176	48,691	55,499	62,460
Proprietors' income.....................	46,209	57,253	66,919	92,421	86,930	90,168
Business and professional...............	34,244	42,416	50,017	60,418	61,105	65,304
Inventory valuation adj..............	—19	—380	—706	—1,749	—3,625	—1,140
Farm..........................	11,965	14,837	16,902	32,003	25,825	24,864
Rental income of persons.................	15,822	18,952	23,938	31,322	33,302	36,961
Corp. prof., inv. adjust.................	49,904	76,070	69,240	99,064	84,847	91,604
Corp. profits before tax...............	49,712	77,787	74,041	115,758	127,620	114,549
Corp. profits tax liability.............	23,032	31,326	34,789	48,702	52,434	49,245
Corp. profits after tax................	26,680	46,461	39,252	67,056	75,186	65,304
Dividends......................	13,437	19,808	24,680	27,792	30,756	32,105
Undistributed profits...............	13,243	26,653	14,572	39,264	44,430	33,199
Inventory valuation adj...............	192	—1,717	—4,801	—18,584	—39,782	—11,415
Net interest.........................	8,361	18,217	36,496	52,334	67,127	74,628
National income......................	414,522	564,336	800,462	1,064,577	1,135,749	1,207,584

Public Debt of the U. S.

Source: Treasury Department

Fiscal Year	Gross Debt Dollars	Per Cap. Dollars	Fiscal Year	Gross Debt Dollars	Per Cap. Dollars	Fiscal Year	Gross Debt Dollars	Per Cap. Dollars
1870..	2,436,453,269	61.06	1930..	16,185,309,831	131.51	1971..	398,129,744,455	1,923.12
1880..	2,090,908,872	41.60	1940..	42,967,531,038	367.48	1972..	427,260,460,940	2,046.00
1890..	1,132,396,584	17.80	1950..	257,357,352,351	1,696.67	1973..	458,141,605,312	2,177.30
1900..	1,263,416,913	16.60	1960..	286,330,760,848	1,584.70	1974..	475,059,815,732	2,241.81
1910..	1,146,939,969	12.41	1965..	317,273,898,984	1,630.46	1975..	533,188,263,000	2,495.84
1920..	24,299,321,467	228.23	1970..	370,918,706,950	1,811.12	1976..	620,432,257,000	2,893.86

Appropriations by the Federal Government

Source: Treasury Department (Fiscal Year)

Year	Appropriations	Year	Appropriations	Year	Appropriations	Year	Appropriations
1890..	$395,430\,284.26	1940..	$13,349,202,681.73	1953..	$94,916,821,231.67	1963..	$102,149,886,566.52
1895..	492,477,759.97	1944..	118,411,173,965.24	1954..	74,744,844,304.88	1965..	107,555,087,622.62
1900..	698,912,982.83	1945..	73,067,712,071.39	1955..	54,761,172,461.58	1967..	140,861,235,376.56
1905..	781,288,21'.95	1946..	76,597,999,662.67	1956..	63,857,731,203.86	1968[1].	195,908,743,535.65
1910..	1,044,433,62 6'	1947..	40,823,734,061.18	1957..	70,717,305,080.55	1969..	203,049,351,090.91
1915..	1,122,471,91 12	1948..	42,098,608,820.42	1958..	77,145,934,082.25	1970..	222,200,021,901.52
1920..	6,454,596,6 56	1949..	47,357,993,957.59	1959..	82,055,863,758.58	1971..	247,623,820,964.75
1925..	3,748,651,750.35	1950..	52,867,672,466.21	1960..	80,169,728,902.87	1972..	247,638,104,722.57
1930..	4,665,236,673.04	1951..	67,966,083,088.46	1961..	89,229,575,129.94	1973..	275,554,945,383.88
1935..	7,527,559,327.66	1952..	127,788,153,262.97	1962..	91,447,827,731.00	1974..	311,728,034,120.95

(1.) This appropriation for 1968 incorporates for the first time the changes in the President's Budget for 1969, in consonance with those recommendations of the President's Commission on Budget Concepts which were adopted and implemented during fiscal year 1968.

National Income by Industry

Source: Department of Commerce, Bureau of Economic Analysis

(Millions of dollars)

	1960	1965	1968	1970	1973	1974	1975
Agricul., forestry, fisheries	16,852	21,017	22,080	25,582	47,003	42,716	44,386
Farms	15,857	19,630	20,425	23,639	43,835	39,204	40,600
Agri. services, forestry, fisheries	995	1,417	1,655	1,943	3,168	3,512	3,786
Mining	5,732	6,116	6,702	7,682	10,149	15,406	18,804
Metal mining	817	908	888	1,177	1,489	1,539	1,693
Coal mining	1,253	1,332	1,429	2,157	2,869	5,189	6,732
Crude petroleum, natural gas	2,734	2,754	3,153	3,048	3,908	6,602	8,180
Nonmetallic min. & quar.	928	1,122	1,232	1,300	1,883	2,076	2,199
Contract construction	20,810	29,116	36,270	42,791	58,442	61,240	60,366
Manufacturing	125,822	172,572	212,672	217,505	283,540	298,150	309,941
Nondurable goods	52,208	66,482	82,069	88,902	107,183	119,275	126,695
Food, kindred products	12,225	14,495	17,130	19,530	20,958	23,104	28,083
Tobacco manufactures	1,017	1,111	1,359	1,738	1,775	2,194	2,665
Textile mill products	4,488	5,837	7,123	7,419	8,704	10,164	8,787
Appa'l, other fabric prod.	4,953	6,556	8,307	8,634	10,287	10,496	10,736
Paper, allied products	4,707	5,929	7,338	7,970	10,910	11,770	11,908
Ptg., pub., allied indust.	6,655	8,746	10,766	11,929	14,873	15,080	16,356
Chemicals, allied products	9,159	12,648	15,614	16,342	20,345	21,672	23,772
Petroleum refining, related ind.	4,586	5,381	6,680	7,342	8,535	14,053	13,778
Rubber, misc. plastic products	2,809	3,949	5,477	5,776	8,430	8,258	8,312
Leather, leather products	1,609	1,830	2,275	2,222	2,366	2,484	2,298
Durable goods	73,614	106,090	130,603	128,603	176,357	178,875	183,246
Lumber, wood, except furn.	3,255	4,212	5,035	5,135	9,550	9,961	8,173
Furniture and fixtures	2,092	2,870	3,485	3,657	4,917	5,025	4,719
Stone, clay, glass products	4,640	5,713	6,329	6,894	9,750	9,680	9,451
Primary metal industries	11,103	14,735	15,871	15,961	21,876	27,966	26,032
Fabricated metal products	8,113	11,518	14,354	14,635	20,687	21,265	22,729
Machinery, except electrical	11,861	18,357	22,891	24,296	32,107	33,429	36,918
Electrical equip. and supplies	10,469	14,850	19,772	20,327	26,612	26,444	25,756
Trans. equip. exc. autos	8,270	11,361	16,435	14,347	15,661	15,418	17,491
Motor vehicles equipment	8,532	15,432	17,156	13,801	23,095	17,678	18,516
Instruments	2,954	4,170	5,742	5,843	7,230	7,309	8,272
Misc. manufacturing	2,325	2,872	3,533	3,707	4,872	4,700	5,189
Transportation	18,177	23,150	26,909	29,824	41,056	44,983	44,754
Railroad	6,718	7,047	6,992	7,358	9,712	10,436	9,906
Local suburban highway pass.	1,639	1,897	2,210	2,285	2,503	2,771	2,941
Motor freight trans., warehous'g.	5,840	8,317	10,326	11,632	17,544	18,765	18,431
Water transportation	1,654	1,990	2,476	2,502	2,771	3,002	3,189
Air transportation	1,400	2,697	3,556	4,374	6,412	7,038	7,106
Pipeline transportation	355	401	414	518	412	433	482
Transportation service	571	801	935	1,155	1,702	2,538	2,699
Communication	8,237	11,241	14,131	16,787	22,648	24,250	26,391
Telephone and telegraph	7,304	9,991	12,594	15,074	20,374	21,926	23,574
Radio broadcasting, television	933	1,250	1,537	1,713	2,274	2,324	2,817
Electric, gas, sanitary services	8,934	11,447	13,391	14,718	18,759	18,414	22,873
Wholesale and retail trade	64,396	84,302	106,069	121,274	161,583	174,248	195,621
Wholesale trade	23,126	30,341	38,394	44,430	62,999	73,588	80,047
Retail trade	41,270	53,961	67,675	76,844	98,584	100,660	115,574
Finance, ins. and real estate	45,940	61,857	77,755	89,948	117,964	126,827	137,649
Banking	7,276	8,989	12,258	16,437	18,368	19,281	19,318
Credit agencies, holding, other investment co.	−435	−505	−1,209	−1,873	−6,368	−6,082	−5,748
Security, commodity brokers	1,243	1,903	4,023	2,675	3,198	3,191	4,145
Insurance carriers	4,641	5,186	6,520	8,544	12,767	12,192	12,395
Insurance agents, brokers, service	1,948	2,671	3,299	3,871	5,665	5,864	6,574
Real estate	31,267	43,613	52,864	60,294	84,334	92,381	100,965
Services	44,371	64,076	85,721	102,876	136,842	150,613	165,056
Hotels, other lodging places	2,111	2,788	3,744	4,236	6,113	6,493	6,999
Personal services	4,608	5,993	7,265	7,433	7,720	8,076	8,315
Misc. business services	5,093	8,413	11,490	13,984	19,349	20,884	22,163
Automobile repair, serv., garages	1,762	2,450	3,106	3,628	5,154	5,461	5,782
Misc. repair services	1,105	1,501	1,866	2,117	2,862	3,321	3,494
Motion pictures	894	1,205	1,535	1,565	1,700	1,666	1,942
Amusement, recreation services	1,661	2,221	2,783	2,344	4,320	4,605	5,108
Medical, other health services	10,724	16,256	23,250	29,942	41,014	46,649	53,471
Legal services	2,636	4,069	5,114	6,443	9,672	10,769	11,819
Education services	2,402	4,191	5,975	7,231	8,948	9,940	11,118
Nonprofit membership org.	3,815	5,306	6,955	8,376	11,450	12,441	13,392
Misc. professional services	3,761	5,719	8,009	9,847	13,138	14,723	15,650
Private households	3,799	3,964	4,629	4,830	5,402	5,585	5,803
Govt., govt. enterprises	52,891	75,233	104,704	126,850	165,785	180,620	199,737
Federal	21,868	33,458	46,058	53,414	62,407	66,732	72,302
General Govt.	25,524	28,450	39,496	45,164	51,923	54,924	59,300
Govt. enterprises	3,656	5,008	6,562	8,250	10,484	11,808	13,002
State & local	25,615	41,775	58,646	73,436	103,378	113,888	127,435
General Govt.	27,367	39,345	55,434	69,553	97,139	106,688	119,230
Government enterprises	1,752	2,430	3,212	3,883	6,239	7,200	8,205
Rest of the world	2,360	4,179	4,736	4,625	9,058	14,535	10,597
All industries, total	414,522	564,336	711,140	800,462	1,072,829	1,152,002	1,236,175

State Finances

Revenues, Expenditures, Debts, Taxes, U.S. Aid, Military Contracts

For fiscal 1975 (year ending June 30, 1975, except: Alabama, Sept. 30; New York, Mar. 31; Texas, Aug. 31).

Sources: Census Bureau, Treasury and Defense Depts. *Military prime contracts. All figures in dollars.

State	Receipts (add 000)	Outlays (add 000)	Total Debt (add 000)	Per Cap Debt	Per Cap Taxes	Per Cap U.S. Aid	*Mltry Cntrcts (add 000)
Alabama	$2,317,561	$2,332,629	$895,835	$247.88	$307.50	$256.03	$416,596
Alaska	696,085	833,911	709,821	2,016.54	576.27	776.20	131,818
Arizona	1,622,386	1,597,045	87,359	39.28	421.94	236.24	- 667,745
Arkansas	1,231,020	1,240,596	122,922	58.09	308.43	276.28	48,149
California	18,801,572	17,712,038	6,470,355	305.42	451.48	250.63	7,907,977
Colorado	1,863,502	1,740,582	122,859	48.48	341.92	256.10	293,803
Connecticut	1,972,518	2,283,697	2,922,230	944.18	342.12	229.22	2,348,567
Delaware	550,565	568,653	592,920	1,024.04	580.99	221.21	50,012
Florida	4,666,797	4,901,551	1,597,560	191.16	334.00	138.56	1,030,015
Georgia	2,932,388	3,036,002	1.148,785	233.21	314.21	265.72	630,005
Hawaii	1,113,975	1,166,897	1,164,873	1,346.67	665.37	315.14	298,601
Idaho	616,837	599,781	39,583	48.27	363.50	270.29	10,104
Illinois	7,488,996	7,842,927	2,798,172	251.07	395.65	222.12	493,964
Indiana	3,099,901	3,002,409	615,210	115.84	349.08	163.58	811,702
Iowa	2,003.254	1,936,194	127,209	44.32	370.02	204.66	174,989
Kansas	1,386,715	1,311,417	306,294	135.11	339.23	202.89	504,566
Kentucky	2,394,647	2,231,044	1,965,352	578.73	378.01	288.18	166,756
Louisiana	2,882,584	2,796,126	1,224,700	323.05	403.24	271.88	477,482
Maine	801,433	863,261	460,035	434.41	348.46	306.47	55,511
Maryland	3,053,387	3,410,574	2,095,020	511.23	422.33	268.54	802,254
Massachusetts	4,104,904	4,939,813	3,940,953	676.21	380.67	264.95	1,770,288
Michigan	6,938,098	7,688,334	1,663,997	181.72	380.69	245.04	766,063
Minnesota	3,484,007	3,139,168	875,590	223.02	515.09	240.43	437,566
Mississippi	1,623,648	1,578,478	613,341	261.44	339.89	319.30	972,801
Missouri	2,420,558	2,452,721	277,455	58.25	273.56	209.44	1,361,409
Montana	614,475	554,721	81,399	108.82	311.11	321.24	5,100
Nebraska	826,055	866,032	68,673	44.42	274.78	227.87	49,060
Nevada	570,665	499,259	51,804	87.51	450.71	255.05	44,875
New Hampshire	512,162	559,338	248,790	304.14	210.77	223.70	188,920
New Jersey	4,795,353	5,217,884	3,886,307	531.21	287.17	222.86	990,929
New Mexico	1,092,985	907,961	152,723	133.15	452.97	384.52	93,612
New York	17,206,113	17,405,591	14,635,017	807.67	493.33	326.37	3,743,942
North Carolina	3,604,808	3,562,338	616,529	113.10	348.64	215.40	398,752
North Dakota	589,826	490,614	63,308	99.70	415.18	276.74	175,671
Ohio	6,796,066	6,824,242	2,661,620	247.39	282.48	196.45	1,013,876
Oklahoma	1,747,090	1,637,444	945,800	348.75	325.86	279.22	170,083
Oregon	1,941,187	1,783,168	1,676,559	732.76	346.60	286.29	58,866
Pennsylvania	8,723,817	9,475,515	5,359,575	453.16	400.22	244.02	1,066,737
Rhode Island	750,736	782,772	459,545	495.73	377.73	288.19	73,525
South Carolina	1,884,803	2,033,096	931,844	330.68	339.45	246.87	203,800
South Dakota	424,938	419,241	67,619	99.00	250.55	323.93	18,867
Tennessee	2,234,018	2,417,217	775,156	185.09	275.08	246.39	359,580
Texas	6,709,260	6,106,543	1,943,212	158.80	297.23	206.54	2,023,746
Utah	907,865	895,403	88,924	73.73	330.68	253.44	140,736
Vermont	452,957	471,815	461,606	980.06	397.02	348.58	122,962
Virginia	3,281,811	3,374,150	691,367	139.19	334.74	215.29	1,206,616
Washington	3,306,685	3,195,846	1,272,036	358.93	438.51	245.61	1,637,012
West Virginia	1,555,099	1,459,362	1,062,648	589.38	412.02	337.29	73,888
Wisconsin	3,647,105	3,695,146	1,009,601	219.41	464.69	206.34	236,794
Wyoming	389,247	330,849	77,285	206.64	412.48	360.65	28,968
Total or Average	$154,632,464	$156,171,395	$72,127,377	$339.57	$377.37	......	$37,319,429

U.S. Money in Circulation, by Denominations

Source: U.S. Mint
Outside Treasury and Federal Reserve Banks. (In millions of dollars)

End of year	Total in circulation	Coin and small denomination							Large denomination currency						
		Total	Coin	$1	$2	$5	$10	$20	Total	$50	$100	$500	$1,000	$5,000	$10,000
1950	27,741	19,305	1,554	1,113	64	2,049	5,998	8,529	8,438	2,422	5,043	368	588	4	12
1960	32,869	23,521	2,427	1,533	88	2,246	6,691	10,536	9,348	2,815	5,954	249	316	3	10
1970	57,093	39,639	6,281	2,310	136	3,161	9,170	18,581	17,454	4,896	12,084	215	252	3	4
1973	72,497	48,288	7,759	2,639	135	3,614	10,226	23,915	24,210	6,514	17,288	185	216	2	4
1974	79,743	51,604	8,331	2,720	135	3,718	10,503	26,197	28,136	7,444	20,298	179	209	2	4
1975	86,547	54,866	8,959	2,809	135	3,841	10,777	28,344	31,681	8,157	23,139	175	204	2	4

Bureau of the Mint
Source: Bureau of the Mint

The first United States Mint was established in Philadelphia, Pa., then the nation's capital, by the Act of April 2, 1792, which provided for gold, silver, and copper coinage. Originally, supervision of the Mint was a function of the Secretary of State, but it became (1799) an independent agency reporting directly to the president. When the Coinage Act of 1873 was passed, all mint and assay office activities were placed under a newly organized Bureau of the Mint in the Department of the Treasury.

The Bureau of the Mint manufactures all U.S. coins and distributes them through the Federal Reserve banks and branches. The Mint also maintains physical custody of the Treasury's monetary stocks of gold and silver, and refines and processes silver bullion. Functions performed by the Mint on a reimbursable basis include: the manufacture and sale of medals of a national character, the production and sale of numismatic coins and coin sets, and, as scheduling permits, the manufacture of foreign coins.

Amendments to the Coinage Act of 1965 (Public Law 91-607, Dec 31, 1970) authorized the production of dollar coins and provided that the dollar and half dollar coins for general circulation be of the same nonsilver clad composition as the quarter dollars and dimes. The cladding is an alloy of 75 percent copper and 25 percent nickel, bonded to a core of pure copper. The coins were first minted in calendar year 1971. The legislation authorized the Secretary of the Treasury to mint and issue not more than 150 million one dollar pieces containing 40-percent silver for sale to the public at premium prices. The dollar coins which bore the likeness of the late U.S. President Eisenhower and a reverse design emblematic of the Apollo 11 moon landing were minted and issued from 1971 until early in 1975.

Public Law 93-127, Oct. 18, 1973, authorized the minting for issue after July 4, 1975, of dollar, half dollar, and quarter dollar coins with reverse designs emblematic of the Bicentennial and the obverse dates 1776-1976, for general issue; and the production of 45 million numismatic 40-percent silver coins of the same designs and denominations to be sold to the public at premium prices.

The composition of the five cent coin continues to be 75 percent copper, 25 percent nickel, while the one cent coins are 95 percent copper and 5 percent zinc.

Calendar year 1975 coinage production follows:

Domestic Coinage Executed During Calendar Year 1975

Denomination Dollars - non-silver	Philadelphia	Denver	San Francisco	Total Value	Total Pieces
1974 Dated	-0-	$ 10,051,000.00	-0-	$ 10,051,000.00	10,051,000
Bicentennial	$ 83,008,000.00	78,672,710.00	-0-	161,680,710.00	161,680,710
Total Dollars	**$ 83,008,000.00**	**$ 88,723,710.00**	**-0-**	**$171,731,710.00**	**171,731,710**
Subsidiary					
Half-Dollars - 1974 Dated	$ 37,495,000.00	$ 7,220,650.00	-0-	$ 44,715,650.00	89,431,300
Half-Dollars - Bicentennial	81,534,000.00	107,723,000.00	-0-	189,257,000.00	378,514,000
Quarters - 1974 Dated	109,003,000.00	33,483,825.00	-0-	142,486,825.00	569,947,300
Quarters - Bicentennial	109,680,000.00	94,462,000.00	-0-	204,142,000.00	816,568,000
Dimes	51,368,200.00	31,370,530.00	$7,199,190.00	89,937,920.00	899,379,200
Total Subsidiary	**$389,080,200.00**	**$274,260,005.00**	**$7,199,190.00**	**$670,539,395.00**	**2,753,839,800**
Minor					
Five-cent Pieces	$ 9,088,600.00	$ 20,093,765.00	-0-	$ 29,182,365.00	583,647,300
One-cent Pieces	54,514,761.42	45,052,753.00	-0-	99,567,514.42	9,956,751,442
Total Minor	**$ 63,603,361.42**	**$ 65,146,518.00**	**-0-**	**$128,749,879.42**	**10,540,398,742**
Total Domestic Coinage	**$535,691,561.42**	**$428,130,233.00**	**$7,199,190.00**	**$971,020,984.42**	**13,465,970,252**

Manufactured at San Francisco Assay Office
1975 Proof Coin Sets - 2,909,369
40% Silver Bicentennial Proof Coin Sets - 2,250,302
40% Silver Bicentennial Uncirculated Sets - 2,841,522
'Includes $15,772,941.42 in one-cent coins manufactured at West Point Depository.

Coinage Executed for Foreign Governments	
Country	No. of Pieces
Haiti	33,200,000
Liberia	13,909,678
Nepal	73,801
Panama	29,317,237
Peru	309,697,810
Philippines	375,927,837
Total	**762,126,363**

Large Denominations of U.S. Currency Discontinued

The largest denomination of United States currency now being issued is the $100 bill. Issuance of currency in denominations of $500, $1,000, $5,000 and $10,000 has been discontinued because their use has declined sharply over the past two decades.

As large denomination bills reach the Federal Reserve Bank they are removed from circulation.

Because some of the discontinued currency is expected to be in the hands of holders for many years, the descriptions of the various denominations below is continued:

Portraits on U.S. Currency

Amt.	Portrait	Embellishment on Back	Amt.	Portrait	Embellishment on Back
$ 1	Washington	Great Seal of U.S.	$ 100	Franklin	Independence Hall
2	Jefferson	Signers of Declaration	* 500	McKinley	Ornate denominational marking
5	Lincoln	Lincoln Memorial	* 1,000	Cleveland	Ornate denominational marking
10	Hamilton	U.S. Treasury	* 5,000	Madison	Ornate denominational marking
20	Jackson	White House	* 10,000	Chase	Ornate denominational marking
50	Grant	U.S. Capitol	*100,000	Wilson	Ornate denominational marking

*For use only in transactions between Federal Reserve System and Treasury Department.

Portraits on U.S. Treasury Bills, Bonds, Notes and Savings Bonds

Denomination	Savings bonds	Treas. bills	Treas. bonds	Treas. notes
25	Washington			
50	Jefferson		Jefferson	
75	Kennedy			
100	Cleveland		Jackson	
200	F.D. Roosevelt			
500	Wilson		Washington	
1,000	Lincoln	H.McCulloch	Lincoln	Lincoln
5,000		J.G. Carlisle	Monroe	Monroe
10,000	T. Roosevelt	J. Sherman	Cleveland	Cleveland
50,000		C. Glass		
100,000		A. Gallatin	Grant	Grant
1,000,000		O. Wolcott	T. Roosevelt	T. Roosevelt
100,000,000				Madison
500,000,000				McKinley

U. S. Currency and Coin — June 30, 1976

Source: Treasury Department

Amounts Outstanding and in Circulation

	Total Currency and Coin	Total Coin	Coin[a] Dollars	Fractional Coin
Amounts outstanding	$94,551,376,975	$9,952,681,898	[b]$1,052,268,898	$8,900,413,000
Less amounts held by:				
The Treasury	480,064,882	372,434,999	74,753,596	297,681,403
The Federal Reserve banks. . . .	5,193,645,455	335,700,022	36,716,338	298,983,684
Amounts in circulation	88,877,666,638	9,244,546,877	940,798,964	8,303,747,913

Currency[c]

	Total	Federal Reserve Notes[d]	United States Notes	Currency No Longer Issued
Amounts outstanding	$84,598,695,077	$83,993,338,695	$322,539,016	$282,817,366
Less amounts held by:				
The Treasury	107,629,883	106,725,462	800,039	104,382
The Federal Reserve banks. . . .	4,857,945,433	4,857,899,088	34,460	11,885
Amounts in circulation	79,633,119,761	79,028,714,145	321,704,517	282,701,099

Currency by Denominations, and Coin, in Circulation

Denomination	Total	Federal Reserve Notes[d]	United States Notes	Currency No Longer Issued
1 Dollar	$2,705,910,503	$2,549,453,212	$144,025	$156,313,266
2 Dollars	619,328,106	484,051,618	135,263,082	13,406
5 Dollars	3,688,532,436	3,529,826,665	116,741,060	41,964,711
10 Dollars	10,363,444,150	10,336,852,490	10,585	26,581,075
20 Dollars	28,700,978,404	28,680,401,360	3,890	20,573,154
50 Dollars	8,447,403,225	8,434,990,700	25	12,412,500
100 Dollars	24,726,496,450	24,632,754,100	69,539,850	24,202,500
500 Dollars	173,693,000	173,483,000	2,000	208,000
1,000 Dollars	201,678,000	201,441,000.		237,000
5,000 Dollars	1,925,000	1,860,000.		65,000
10,000 Dollars	3,730,000	3,600,000.		130,000
Fractional parts	487.			487
Total currency	79,633,119,761	79,028,714,145	321,704,517	282,701,099
Total coin	9,244,546,877			
Total currency and coin	88,877,666,638			

Comparative Totals of Money in Circulation — Selected Dates

Date	Amounts (in millions)	Per Capita[e]	Date	Amounts (in millions)	Per Capita[e]	Date	Amounts (in millions)	Per Capita[e]
June 30, 1976	[f]$88,887.7	$413.17	June 30, 1955	30,229.3	182.90	June 30, 1930	4,522.0	36.74
June 30, 1975	81,196.4	380.07	June 30, 1950	27,156.3	179.03	June 30, 1925	4,815.2	41.56
June 30, 1970	54,351.0	265.39	June 30, 1945	26,746.4	191.14	June 30, 1920	5,467.6	51.36
June 30, 1965	39,719.8	204.14	June 30, 1940	7,847.5	59.40	June 30, 1915	3,319.6	33.01
June 30, 1960	32,064.6	177.47	June 30, 1935	5,567.1	43.75	June 30, 1910	3,148.7	34.07

[a]Excludes coin sold to collectors at premium prices. [b]Includes $481,781,898 in standard silver dollars. [c]Excludes gold certificates, Series of 1934, which are issued only to Federal Reserve banks and do not appear in circulation. [d]Issued on and after July 1, 1929. [e]Based on Bureau of the Census estimates of population. [f]Highest amount to date. [g]Revised.

The requirement for a gold reserve against U.S. notes was repealed by Public Law 90-269 approved Mar. 18, 1968. Silver certificates issued on and after July 1, 1929 became redeemable from the general fund on June 24, 1968. The amount of security after those dates has been reduced accordingly.

*Seigniorage on Coin and Silver Bullion

Source: Fiscal Service, Dept. of Treasury
(Jan. 1, 1935 to June 30, 1975)

	Total	Potential[1]
Fiscal Year Jan. 1, 1935–June 30, 1965, cumulative.	$2,525,927,763.84	[2]$ 6,560,393.72
1968.	[r]383,141,339.00	759,844,047.56
1969.	250,170,276.34	700,000,000.00
1970.	274,217,884.01.	
1971.	399,652,811.18.	
1972.	580,586,683.00.	
1973.	399,799,682.00.	
1974.	320,706,638.49.	
1975.	660,898,070.69.	
Cumulative Jan. 1, 1935–June 30, 1975.	7,280,639,514.69.	

*Seigniorage is the profit from coining money; it is the difference between the monetary value of coins and their cost, including the manufacturing expense.
(r.) Revised to include seigniorage on clad coins.
(1.) Not cumulative, as coinage metals held by the Treasurer of the United States changes, the potential seigniorage changes. Potential seigniorage also changes depending on the denomination of the coins manufactured.
(2.) Represents potential seigniorage as of June 30, 1965.

World Gold Production

Source: Federal Reserve Board. In millions of dollars at $35 per fine troy ounce through 1971, at $38 for 1972.

| Year | estimated world prod. | Africa | | | North and South America | | | | | Other | | | | |
		South Africa	Ghana	Zaire	United States	Canada	Mexico	Nicaragua	Colombia	Australia	India	Japan	Phil-ippines	All other
1960	1,175.0	748.4	30.8	11.1	58.8	162.0	10.5	7.0	15.2	38.0	5.6	11.8	14.4	61.4
1965	1,440.0	1,069.4	26.4	2.3	58.6	125.6	7.6	5.4	11.2	30.7	4.6	18.1	15.3	64.8
1966	1,445.0	1,080.8	24.0	5.6	63.1	114.6	7.5	5.2	9.8	32.1	4.2	19.4	15.8	62.9
1967	1,410.0	1,068.7	26.7	5.4	53.4	103.7	5.8	5.2	9.0	28.4	3.4	23.7	17.2	59.4
1968	1,420.0	1,088.0	25.4	5.9	53.9	94.1	6.2	4.9	8.4	27.6	4.0	21.5	18.5	61.6
1969	1,420.0	1,090.7	24.8	6.0	60.1	89.1	6.3	3.7	7.7	24.5	3.4	23.7	20.0	60.0
1970	1,450.0	1,128.0	24.8	6.2	63.5	84.3	6.9	4.0	7.1	21.7	3.7	24.8	21.1	54.1
1971p		1,098.7	24.4	6.0	52.3	79.1	5.3	3.7	6.6	23.5	4.1	27.0	22.2	
1972p		1,109.8			54.3	77.2			7.1		4.0	32.2	23.0	

(p) Preliminary.

Gold Reserves of Central Banks and Governments

Source: Federal Reserve Board

Millions of dollars; valued at $35 per ounce through 1971, at $38 for 1972, and $42.22 thereafter.

Dec.	(Est.) total world[1]	Int'l Mone-tary Fund	United States	Canada	(Est.) rest of world	Bel-gium	France	Ger-many Fed. Rep. of	Italy	Neth-er-lands	Swit-zer-land	United King-dom
1960	40,540	2,439	17,804	885	20,295	1,170	1,641	2,971	2,203	1,451	2,185	2,800
1965	43,230	1,869	13,806	1,151	27,285	1,558	4,706	4,410	2,404	1,756	3,042	2,265
1970	41,275	4,339	11,072	791	25,865	1,470	3,532	3,980	2,887	1,787	2,732	1,349
1971	41,175	4,732	10,206	792	26,235	1,544	3,523	4,077	2,884	1,909	2,909	775
1972	44,890	5,830	10,487	834	28,575	1,638	3,826	4,459	3,130	2,059	3,158	800
1973	49,850	6,478	11,652	927	30,793	1,781	4,261	4,966	3,483	2,294	3,513	886
1974	49,800	6,478	11,652	927	30,733	1,781	4,262	4,966	3,483	2,294	3,513	888
1975	49,740	6,478	11,599	927	30,738	1,781	4,262	4,966	3,483	2,294	3,513	888

(1.) Excludes USSR, other Eastern European countries, and People's Republic of China.

Reserves not listed above, Dec. 1975. Algeria 231, Argentina 312, Austria 882, Republic of China (Taiwan) 97, Denmark 76, Egypt 103, Greece 153, India 293, Iran 158, Iraq 173, Japan 891, Kuwait 169, Lebanon 389, Libya 103, Mexico 154, Pakistan 67, Portugal 1,170, Saudi Arabia 129, South Africa 749, Spain 602, Sweden 244, Thailand 99, Turkey 151, Uruguay 135, Venezuela 472, Bank for International Settlements (net) 246.

U.S. and World Silver Production

Source: Bureau of Mines

Largest production of silver in the United States in 1915—74,961,075 fine ounces. (r) revised (p) preliminary.

| | United States | | World | Year | United States | | World |
	Fine ozs.	Value	Fine ozs.	(Cal.)	Fine ozs.	Value	Fine ozs.
1930	50,748,127	$19,538,000	248,708,426	1960	36,000,000	$33,305,858	241,300,000
1935	45,924,454	33,008,000	220,704,231	1965r	39,806,033	51,469,201	257,415,000
1940	69,585,734	49,483,000	275,387,000	1970r	45,006,000	79,697,000	310,891,000
1945	29,063,255	20,667,200	162,000,000	1973r	37,484,000	95,883,000	307,974,000
1950	43,308,739	38,291,545	203,300,000	1974p	33,762,000	159,018,000	294,935,000
1955	36,469,610	33,006,839	224,000,000	1975p	34,938,000	154,424,000	293,452,000

Bank Rates on Short-Term Business Loans

Source: Federal Reserve System

% per annum. Estimates based on reports from banks in 35 centers. Short-term loans mature within one year.

| | All size loans | | | | | | | Size of loan in $1,000 | | | |
	Avg. 35 Cities	N.Y. C.	7 Other N.E.	8 No. Cent.	7 S.E.	8 S.W.	4 West	1-9	10-99	100 to 499	500 to 999	1,000 and Over
1967 Aug. 1-15	5.95	5.66	6.29	5.92	5.92	6.01	6.02	6.58	6.46	6.16	5.89	5.72
Nov. 1-15	5.96	5.71	6.29	5.91	5.94	6.03	6.03	6.60	6.48	6.17	5.90	5.73
1970 Aug. 1-15	8.50	8.24	8.89	8.47	8.49	8.53	8.54	9.15	9.07	8.75	8.46	8.25
Nov. 1-15	8.07	7.74	8.47	8.05	8.15	8.08	8.16	8.89	8.79	8.34	8.09	7.74
1971 Aug.	6.51	6.25	6.77	6.46	6.77	6.64	6.54	7.68	7.27	6.88	6.58	6.27
Nov.	6.18	5.86	6.40	6.13	6.47	6.43	6.21	7.51	7.05	6.51	6.26	5.93
1973 Aug.	9.24	9.08	9.49	9.24	9.25	9.16	9.25	8.95	9.25	9.50	9.31	9.14
Nov.	10.08	9.90	10.51	10.02	9.96	10.08	10.04	9.80	10.14	10.43	10.18	9.95
1974 Feb.	9.91	9.68	10.28	9.98	9.80	9.93	9.78	9.86	10.09	10.28	10.06	9.75
May	11.15	11.08	11.65	11.09	10.88	10.82	11.19	10.90	11.06	11.41	11.32	11.06
1975 Feb.	9.94	9.61	10.31	9.87	10.24	10.01	9.99	10.94	10.73	10.25	9.93	9.73
May	8.16	7.88	8.37	8.00	8.70	8.34	8.33	9.57	9.10	8.52	8.18	7.90
1976 Feb.	7.54	7.14	7.93	7.50	7.86	7.56	7.77	9.03	8.44	7.80	7.55	7.33
May	7.44	6.99	7.99	7.44	7.66	7.51	7.75	8.91	8.38	7.78	7.52	7.18

NOTE:—The Quarterly Survey of Interest Rates Charged by Banks on Business Loans has been revised beginning with the survey period of February 1971. The revision incorporates a number of technical changes in coverage, sampling, and interest rate calculations. These include elimination of accounts receivable loans from the survey, shortening the sample period for respondent banks in most districts, and calculation of effective annual interest rates on discounted loans using a revised formula based on annual rather than quarterly compounding of interest. As a result of the above changes, new weights derived from this survey have been used to calculate the weighted average rates.

U. S. Commercial Banks With Deposits Over $1 Billion

A compilation of the 300 largest commercial banks in the United States is made twice a year by the American Banker, daily banking newspaper, 525 W. 42 St., New York, N. Y. 10036. Of these the first 89 banks had deposits of more than $1 billion on June 30, 1976. They are listed below. (Copyright 1976, by American Banker)

Rank 6/30/74	Deposits	Rank 6/30/74	Deposits
1 Bank of America NT&SA, San Francisco . .	$56,586,753,000	46 European-American B&T Co., New York. .	1,964,951,000
2 Citibank NA, New York.	45,912,506,000	47 First Wisconsin National Bank, Milwaukee.	1,912,130,388
3 Chase Manhattan Bank NA, New York. . . .	35,196,619,919	48 California First Bank, San Francisco	1,870,516,318
4 Manufacturers Hanover Trust Co., N. Y. . .	23,454,514,000	49 First National Bank of Arizona, Phoenix. . .	1,848,884,000
5 Chemical Bank, New York.	19,179,237,000	50 Bank of Tokyo Trust Co., New York.	1,838,251,955
6 Morgan Guaranty Trust Co., New York . . .	18,936,312,346	51 First Union NB of North Car., Charlotte . . .	1,538,358,000
7 Continental Illinois NB&T Co., Chicago. .	15,648,352,000	52 Virginia National Bank, Norfolk.	1,519,803,535
8 Bankers Trust Co., New York.	15,519,728,000	53 Hartford National Bk., & Trust Co., Conn. .	1,512,184,000
9 First National Bank, Chicago.	13,379,295,000	54 National City Bank, Cleveland.	1,498,797,000
10 Security Pacific Nat'l Bank, Los Angeles. .	12,442,318,000	55 Industrial NB of Rhode Island, Providence.	1,470,566,000
11 Wells Fargo Bank NA, San Francisco . . .	10,221,255,000	56 American Fletcher NB&T Co., Indianpls. . .	1,438,536,000
12 Marine Midland Bank, Buffalo, N.Y.	9,224,961,000	57 Riggs National Bank, Washington, D. C. . .	1,398,127,976
13 Crocker National Bank, San Francisco. . .	9,022,383,000	58 Connecticut Bank & Trust Co., Hartford . . .	1,391,808,880
14 United California Bank, Los Angeles.	7,712,395,796	59 Republic National Bank of New York.	1,389,805,124
15 Irving Trust Co., New York	7,384,866,202	60 Equibank NA, Pittsburgh.	1,382,363,000
16 Mellon Bank NA, Pittsburgh.	6,517,184,000	61 Michigan National Bank, Lansing.	1,359,144,907
17 First National Bank, Boston.	5,992,185,000	62 Central National Bank, Cleveland	1,336,390,000
18 National Bank of Detroit	5,992,157,727	63 First National Bank, Atlanta, Ga.	1,327,180,555
19 First Pennsylvania Bank NA, Philadelphia .	4,224,701,000	64 Southeast First National Bank, Miami	1,307,231,679
20 Bank of New York.	4,137,741,058	65 American National B&T Co., Chicago	1,304,139,883
21 First National Bank, Dallas.	3,654,923,000	66 Indiana National Bank, Indianapolis.	1,287,860,486
22 Seattle-First National Bank	3,654,377,234	67 Manuf. & Traders Trust Co., Buffalo, N. Y. .	1,263,924,092
23 Republic National Bank, Dallas	3,357,654,000	68 Mercantile Trust Co. NA, St. Louis, Mo.. . .	1,242,473,000
24 Harris Trust & Savings Bank, Chicago . . .	3,148,298,737	69 Lloyds Bank California, Los Angeles	1,241,617,105
25 Union Bank, Los Angeles	3,104,982,000	70 Trust Co. Bank, Atlanta, Ga.	1,235,336,000
26 Cleveland Trust Co.	2,900,591,000	71 Northwestern NB, Minneapolis, Minn.	1,226,954,934
27 Northern Trust Co., Chicago'.	2,777,167,000	72 First National Bank, St. Louis, Mo.	1,193,060,300
28 Philadelphia National Bank.	2,771,558,000	73 Provident National Bank, Philadelphia	1,181,467,000
29 Valley National Bank, Phoenix, Ariz.	2,760,709,785	74 State Street Bank & Trust Co., Boston	1,169,132,615
30 First City National Bank, Houston, Tex. . . .	2,731,684,000	75 Shawmut Bank of Boston NA	1,152,236,000
31 Detroit Bank & Trust Co.	2,727,450,000	76 Bank of Hawaii, Honolulu.	1,122,379,343
32 Girard Bank, Philadelphia	2,714,304,000	77 First National Bank, Minneapolis, Minn. . . .	1,118,591,000
33 Wachovia B&T Co. NA, Wnstn-Sal., N. C. .	2,653,215,848	78 First American Nat'l Bank, Nshvle., Tenn. .	1,074,876,166
34 North Carolina National Bank, Charlotte . .	2,607,409,000	79 New England Merchants NB, Boston	1,071,040,601
35 Manufacturers National Bank, Detroit	2,503,317,000	80 Bank for Svgs. & Loan Assocs., Chicago . .	1,067,615,750
36 Bank of California NA, San Francisco	2,499,892,000	81 Equitable Trust Co., Baltimore, Md..	1,047,380,000
37 National Bank of North America, N. Y.	2,416,658,000	82 First National State Bank of N. J., Newark. .	1,032,097,000
38 Texas Commerce Bank NA, Houston.	2,394,005,000	83 Continental Bank, Norristown, Pa.	1,018,313,924
39 First National Bank of Oregon, Portland. . .	2,369,079,000	84 American Bank & Trust Co., Reading, Pa.. .	1,013,868,000
40 United States NB of Oregon, Portland. . . .	2,356,327,804	85 Whitney National Bank, New Orleans, La.. .	1,012,747,938
41 Citizens & Southern NB, Atlanta, Ga.	2,348,482,000	86 BancOhio/Ohio National Bank, Columbus. .	1,012,689,921
42 Rainier National Bank, Seattle	2,300,640,804	87 First-Citizens B&T Co., Raleigh, N.C.	1,006,750,910
43 Pittsburgh National Bank.	2,240,925,387	88 First National Bank, St. Paul, Minn.'.	1,002,889,000
44 Fidelity Bank, Philadelphia	2,153,758,000	89 Northwestern Bk, North Wilkesboro, N. C. .	1,002,551,000
45 Maryland National Bank, Baltimore	1,999,248,891		

Largest Bank in Each of 38 Foreign Countries

Source 500 Largest Banks in the Free World, compiled by the American Banker, New York. (Copyright 1976) Based on deposits Jan. 1, 1976, or nearest fiscal year-end. For Canada, see Index.
(in thousands)

Banks and Country	Deposits in U.S. $	Banks and Country	Deposits in U.S. $
Argentina, Banco de la Nacion.	1,083,302	Kuwait, National Bank of.	1,399,531
Australia, Commonwealth Bkng. Corp.	12,129,333	Luxembourg, Cie, Luxembourgeoise.	4,249,746
Austria, Creditanstalt-Bankverein.	5,458,346	Mexico, Banco de Comercio.	2,500,939
Belgium, Societe Generale de Banque	11,972,934	Netherlands, Cooperatieve Centrale	
Brazil, Banco do Brasil.	17,796,335	Raiffeisen-Boerenleenbank.	16,300,932
Denmark, Copenhagen Handelsbank.	2,790,676	New Zealand, Bank of.	1,485,364
Egypt, National Bank of Egypt.	4,695,035	No. Ireland, Northern Bank Ltd.	972,839
England, Barclay's Bank.	29,332,036	Norway, Norske Creditbank.	1,608,821
Finland, Kansallis-Osake Pankki	2,699,225	Pakistan, Habib Bank Ltd.	1,170,812
France, Banque Nationale de Paris	37,522,146	Peru, Banco de la Nacion	2,352,017
Germany, Deutsche Bank.	32,388,680	Portugal, Banco Pinto & Sotto Mayor.	1,612,082
Greece, National Bank of Greece	4,706,304	Scotland, Bank of.	2,784,529
Hong Kong, Hongkong & Shanghai	8,242,039	South Africa, Standard Bank of.	2,519,423
India, State Bank of India.	4,968,216	Spain, Banco Espanol de Credito	8,431,296
Iran, Bank Melli Iran.	5,289,840	Sweden, Post-Och Kreditbanken	8,517,748
Ireland, Bank of Ireland.	2,789,458	Switzerland, Swiss Bank Corp.	17,148,533
Israel, Bank Leumi le-Israel.	7,070,122	Taiwan, Bank of.	2,237,013
Italy, Banca Nazionale del Lavoro.	20,657,798	Thailand, Bangkok Bank Ltd.	1,703,413
Japan, Dai-Ichi Kangyo Bank Ltd.	23,765,734	Turkey, Turkiye Is Bankasi.	2,592,552
Korea, Korea First Bank.	972,387		

Federal Deposit Insurance Corporation (FDIC)

The primary purpose of the Federal Deposit Insurance Corporation (FDIC) is to insure the deposits of all banks entitled to insurance benefits under the Federal Deposit Insurance Act. The major functions of the FDIC are to pay off depositors of insured banks closed without adequate provision having been made to pay depositors' claims, to act as receiver for all national banks placed in receivership and for state banks placed in receivership when appointed receiver by state authorities, and to prevent the continuance or development of unsafe and unsound banking practices. The FDIC's entire income consists of assessments on insured banks and income from investments; it receives no appropriations from Congress. It may borrow from the U.S. Treasury not to exceed $3 billion outstanding at any one time, but has made no such borrowings since it was organized in 1933. The FDIC surplus (Deposit Insurance Fund) as of Dec. 31, 1975, was $6.7 billion.

Corporations and Stocks
Stock Exchanges Trade Record 6.24 Billion Shares in U.S. Firms

The Securities and Exchange Commission reported in 1976 that a record 6.24 billion shares of stock were traded on the New York, American, and other U.S. stock exchanges in 1975.

The N.Y. Stock Exchange listed 2,138 issues of 1,563 companies for a total of 23.9 billion shares, valued on Aug. 31, 1976, at $810 billion. Average daily trading was 21,706,140 through Aug. 31, 1976, compared to 13,365,138 in 1974.

The American Stock Exchange listed 1,277 issues of 1,175 companies, totaling 3.2 billion shares, valued Aug. 31, 1976, at $34.2 billion. Average daily volume through Aug. 31 was 2.07 million shares.

A 1975 count indicated that 25.3 million persons owned shares in American corporations.

50 U.S. Companies with Largest Annual Sales or Revenues

Top listed companies on N.Y. Stock Exchange for 1975 as shown by its Research Dep't.

Company	Sales or revenues (in millions)	Net profit (or *loss) (in millions)	Company	Sales or revenues (in millions)	Net profit (or *loss) (in millions)
Exxon Corp.	$47,795.5	$2,503.0	Westinghouse Electric	5,862.7	165.2
General Motors Corp.	35,724.9	1,253.1	Englehard Mins. & Chems.	5,672.5	114.7
American Tel. & Tel.	28,957.2	3,147.7	Union Carbide Corp.	5,665.0	381.7
Texaco Inc.	24,507.5	830.6	Tenneco Inc.	5,630.3	342.9
Ford Motor Co.	24,009.1	227.5	Goodyear Tire & Rubber	5,452.5	161.6
Mobil Oil Corp.	22,135.3	809.9			
			Union Oil Co. of Cal.	5,437.3	232.8
Standard Oil Co. of Cal.	17,523.6	772.5	Occidental Petroleum	5,345.9	174.6
Gulf Oil Corp.	15,838.0	700.0	Kroger Co.	5,339.2	34.4
Int'l Business Machines	14,436.5	1,989.9	Int'l Harvester Co.	5,246.0	115.9
Sears, Roebuck & Co.	13,639.9	522.6	Phillips Petroleum	5,133.6	342.6
General Electric Co.	13,399.1	580.8	Bethlehem Steel Corp.	4,977.2	242.0
Chrysler Corp.	11,598.4	*207.2	Caterpillar Tractor Co.	4,963.7	398.7
Int'l Tel. & Tel. Corp.	11,338.1	398.2	Eastman Kodak Co.	4,958.5	613.7
Standard Oil Co. (Ind.)	11,034.2	787.0	Rockwell International	4,943.4	101.6
Safeway Stores, Inc.	9,716.9	148.6	Dow Chemical Co.	4,888.1	615.7
Shell Oil Co.	8,876.2	514.8	Kraftco Corp.	4,857.4	139.6
U.S. Steel Corp.	8,167.2	559.6	Reynolds (R.J.) Inds.	4,837.6	338.7
Atlantic Richfield Co.	7,746.5	350.4	Marcor Inc.	4,822.3	135.2
Penney (J.C.) Company	7,678.6	189.6	RCA Corp.	4,789.5	110.0
Continental Oil Co.	7,500.3	330.9	Esmark Inc.	4,730.7	79.7
du Pont de Nemours (E.I.)	7,221.5	271.8	Beatrice Foods Co.	4,690.6	153.1
Kresge (S.S.) Co.	6,798.1	200.8	Woolworth (F.W.) Co.	4,650.3	99.5
Great A. & P. Tea Co.	6,537.9	2.5	Sun Co., Inc.	4,389.1	220.1
Procter & Gamble Co.	6,081.7	333.9	LTV Corp.	4,312.5	13.1
General Tel. & Electronics	5,948.4	388.2	Halliburton Co.	4,209.6	222.5

30 Largest Industrial Companies Outside the U.S.

Reprinted by special permission from the Fortune Directory, as listed for 1975; copyright 1976, Time Inc.

Company	Sales (add 000)	Net profit (Or *loss) (add 000)	Company	Sales (add 000)	Net profit (Or *loss) (add 000)
Royal Dutch Shell, N-B.	$32,105,096	$2,110,927	Bayer, G.	7,223,302	128,229
National Iranian Oil, Ir	18,854,547	16,947,071	Toyota Motor, J.	7,104,139	250,848
British Petroleum, B.	17,285,854	369,202	ELF-Aquitaine, F.	7,165,390	199,875
Unilever, B-N.	15,015,994	322,108	Nestle, S.	7,080,160	309,365
Philips Gloeilampenfab, N	10,746,485	11,186,804	ICI (Imp Chem Inds), B.	6,884,219	424,294
Cie Francaise des Petroles, F.	9,145,778	8,036,813	Petrobras (Brazil Oil), Br.	6,625,516	703,586
Nippon Steel, J.	8,796,902	111,935	British American Tobacco, B.	6,145,979	314,041
August Thyssen-Hutte, G.	8,764,899	99,926	Hitachi, J.	5,916,135	94,084
Hoechst, G.	8,462,322	100,972	Mitsubishi Heavy Inds, J.	5,693,994	40,699
ENI, I.	8,334,432	*134,869	Nissan Motor, J.	5,479,562	115,532
Daimler-Benz, G.	8,194,271	125,768	Montedison, I.	5,417,741	*183,912
BASF (Badische Anilin), G.	8,152,318	152,831	British Steel, B.	5,340,183	171,867
Renault, F.	7,831,330	*128,702	Mannesmann, G.	5,333,142	288,833
Siemens, G.	7,759,909	201,275	AEG-Telefunken, G.	5,187,098	*36,149
Volkswagenwerk, G.	7,680,786	*63,971	St. Gobain-Pont-a-Mousson, F.	4,941,803	28,025

Nation of hqs: B, Britain; Br, Brazil; F, France; G, West Germany; Ir, Iran; It, Italy; J, Japan, N, Netherlands; S, Switzerland.

Stocks Most Widely Held by Investment Cos., Insurance Cos., Trust Funds

As listed in 1976 by the N.Y. Stock Exchange
(In order of number of institutions, etc., which held shares, 1976)

Int'l. Bus. Machs.	Minn. Mng. Mfg.	Burroughs Corp.	Phillip Morris	Weyerhaeuser Co.
Exxon Corp.	Dow Chemical	Phillips Petroleum	Pfizer Inc.	Southern Co.
Eastman Kodak	Merck & Co.	Union Carbide	Goodyear Rub.	Inco Ltd.
Amer. Tel. & Tel.	Standard Oil (Ind.)	Kresge (S.S.)	Warner-Lambert	Schering-Plough
General Motors	Atlantic Richfield	Gulf Oil	Halliburton Co.	Int'l. Tel. & Tel.
General Electric	Ford Motor	Caterpillar Tractor	Intern'l Paper	Commonwealth Ed.
Xerox Corp.	Mobil Oil	Texas Utilities	Johns'n & Johns'n	Coca-Cola Co.
Texaco Inc.	duPont (E.I.)	Procter & Gamble	Continental Oil	Federated Stores
Sears, Roebuck	General Tel. & Elec.	Standard Oil of Cal.	Penney (J.C.)	Lilly (Eli)
Citicorp	American Home Prod.	Monsanto Co.	Schlumberger Ltd.	Avon Products

N.Y. Stock Exchange Transactions and Seat Prices
Source: New York Stock Exchange

Year	Yearly Volumes Stock Shares	Yearly Volumes Bonds Par Values	Seat Price High	Seat Price Low	Year	Yearly Volumes Stock Shares	Yearly Volumes Bonds Par Values	Seat Price High	Seat Price Low
1900	138,981,000	$579,293,000	$47,500	$37,500	1940	207,599,749	$1,669,438,000	$60,000	$33,000
1905	260,569,000	1,026,254,000	85,000	72,000	1945	377,563,575	2,261,985,110	95,000	49,000
1910	163,705,000	634,863,000	94,000	65,000	1950	524,799,621	1,112,425,170	54,000	46,000
1915	172,497,000	961,700,000	74,000	38,000	1960	766,693,818	1,346,419,750	162,000	135,000
1920	227,636,000	3,868,422,000	115,000	85,000	1970	2,937,359,448	4,494,864,600	320,000	130,000
1925	459,717,623	3,427,042,210	150,000	99,000	1972	4,138,187,706	5,444,117,100	250,000	150,000
1929	1,124,800,410	2,996,398,000	625,000	550,000	1973	4,053,201,306	4,424,671,800	170,000	72,000
1930	810,632,546	2,720,301,800	480,000	205,000	1974	3,821,942,000	4,052,123,000	105,000	65,000
1935	381,635,752	3,339,458,000	140,000	65,000	1975	*4,693,427,000	5,178,300,000	138,000	55,000

*Record high for trading in stocks and bonds.

American Stock Exchange Transactions and Seat Prices
Source: American Stock Exchange

Year	Yearly Volumes Stock Shares	Yearly Volumes Bonds Par Values	Seat Price High	Seat Price Low	Year	Yearly Volumes Stock Shares	Yearly Volumes Bonds Par Values	Seat Price High	Seat Price Low
1929	476,140,375	$513,551,000	$254,000	$150,000	1965	534,221,999	$146,927,000	$80,000	$55,000
1930	222,270,065	863,541,000	225,000	70,000	1970	843,116,260	641,270,000	180,000	70,000
1940	42,928,337	303,902,000	7,250	6,900	1972	1,117,989,153	728,524,000	145,000	70,000
1945	143,309,392	167,333,000	32,000	12,000	1973	759,840,245	457,940,000	100,000	27,000
1950	107,792,340	47,549,000	11,000	6,500	1974	475,297,000	256,865,000	60,000	27,000
1960	286,039,982	32,670,000	60,000	51,000	1975	457,610,360	259,128,000	72,000	34,000

U.S. Business Indexes
Source: Federal Reserve System (1967 = 100, except as noted)

Period	Industrial production Total	Market Products Total	Market Products Final Total	Market Products Final Consumer goods	Market Products Final Equipment	Intermediate	Materials	Manufacturing	Industry Capacity utilization in mfg. (1967 output =100)	Construction contracts	Nonagricultural employment— Total[1]	Manufacturing Employment	Manufacturing Payrolls	Total retail sales	Prices Consumer	Prices Wholesale commodity
1963..	76.5	76.4	75.5	81.3	67.5	79.9	76.7	75.8	83.0	86.1	86.1	87.8	76.0	79	91.7	94.5
1965..	89.8	88.2	87.6	92.6	80.7	90.6	92.4	89.7	89.0	93.2	92.3	93.9	88.1	90	94.5	96.6
1968..	106.3	106.2	106.2	105.9	106.5	106.3	106.5	106.4	87.7	113.2	103.2	101.4	108.3	109	104.2	102.5
1969..	111.1	110.3	109.6	109.8	109.3	112.9	112.5	111.0	86.5	123.7	106.9	103.2	116.6	114	109.8	106.5
1970..	107.8	106.9	105.3	109.0	100.1	112.9	109.2	106.4	78.3	123.1	107.7	98.1	114.1	119	116.3	110.4
1971..	109.6	108.5	106.3	114.7	94.7	116.7	111.3	108.2	75.0	145.4	108.1	94.2	116.7	130	121.2	113.9
1972..	119.7	118.0	115.7	124.4	103.8	126.5	122.3	118.9	78.6	165.3	111.9	97.6	131.5	142	125.3	119.8
1973..	129.8	127.1	124.4	131.5	114.5	137.2	133.9	129.8	83.0	179.5	116.8	103.2	149.2	160	133.1	134.7
1974..	129.3	127.3	125.1	128.9	120.0	135.3	132.4	129.4	78.9	169.7	119.1	102.1	157.1	171	147.7	160.1
1975..	117.8	119.3	118.2	124.0	110.2	123.1	115.5	116.3	68.7	166.0	116.9	91.4	151.0	186	161.2	174.9
1976 June	129.9	129.0	·127.2	136.6	144.4	135.4	131.4	129.7	......	......	119.9	94.9	170.7	......	......	183.1

(1) Employees only; excludes personnel in the Armed Forces. (2) Production workers only. Revised back to 1973. (3) F.R. index based on Census Bureau figures. (4) Prices are not seasonally adjusted. Latest figure is final.
NOTE.—All series: Data are seasonally adjusted unless otherwise noted.

Wholesale Price Indexes
Source: Bureau of Labor Statistics, U. S. Department of Labor

The Wholesale Primary Market Price Index is designed to show the rate and direction of the composite of price movements, and to measure price changes not influenced by quality, quantity, terms of sale, etc. Wholesale refers to sales in quantities, not to prices received or paid by wholesalers.

Commodity group (1967 = 100)	1976 June	1976 Jan.	1975 Avg.	1974 Avg.
All commodities	183.1	179.3	174.9	160.1
Farm products, processed foods, and feeds	187.5	184.6	184.2	177.4
Farm products	196.5	192.8	186.7	187.7
Processed foods and feeds	181.8	179.4	182.6	170.9
All commodities except farm products	181.4	177.6	173.4	156.8
Industrial commodities	181.3	177.3	171.5	153.8
Textile products and apparel	148.1	145.1	137.9	139.1
Hides, skins, leathers, and related products	167.4	157.5	148.5	145.1
Fuels and related products and power	260.3	257.3	245.1	208.3
Chemicals and allied products	187.1	184.2	181.3	146.8
Rubber and plastic products	157.2	152.4	150.2	136.2
Lumber and wood products	199.8	190.5	176.9	183.6
Pulp, paper, and allied products	179.5	174.8	170.4	151.7
Metals and metal products	196.4	187.7	185.6	171.9
Machinery and equipment	170.2	167.0	161.4	139.4
Furniture and household durables	145.3	143.1	139.7	127.9
Nonmetallic mineral products	186.0	181.1	174.0	153.2
Transportation equipment (Dec. 1968 = 100)	149.1	148.7	141.5	125.5
Miscellaneous products	154.4	151.8	147.7	133.1

Assets and Liabilities of Insured Commercial Banks

Source: Federal Reserve System, Federal Deposit Insurance Corp., Comptroller of the Currency.
As of December 31, 1975 (In thousands of dollars)

State	Loans and Securities	Total Assets	Total Deposits	Total Liabilities	Reserves and Cap.Accts.	State	Loans and Securities	Total Assets	Total Deposits	Total Liabilities	Reserves and Cap.Accts.
Ala...	9,166,179	10,858,894	9,164,081	9,935,555	923,320	Neb...	6,073,620	7,256,703	6,250,829	6,642,002	614,701
Alas...	1,106,101	1,437,048	1,250,032	1,331,402	105,646	Nev...	1,755,520	2,136,249	1,884,940	1,959,669	176,580
Ariz...	6,329,003	7,597,214	6,018,265	7,092,919	504,295	N.H...	1,632,263	1,901,941	1,638,839	1,727,661	174,280
Ark...	5,772,469	6,944,113	6,018,265	6,372,666	571,447	N.J...	21,363,506	25,332,597	21,784,457	23,214,974	2,117,623
Cal...	79,348,060	104,277,054	85,317,024	97,445,056	6,831,825	N.M...	2,764,951	3,408,282	2,986,616	3,139,063	269,219
Col...	7,148,268	8,765,211	7,392,596	8,036,332	728,767	N.Y...	120,792,244	164,252,859	126,411,776	149,509,533	14,743,300
Conn...	6,776,157	8,705,062	7,392,759	7,995,107	709,955	N.C...	12,461,173	15,282,324	12,698,816	13,995,566	1,286,727
Del...	2,149,724	2,453,428	1,955,536	2,261,852	191,576	N.D...	2,610,752	2,950,073	2,611,619	2,708,189	241,884
D.C...	3,511,541	4,427,445	3,672,571	4,012,842	414,603	Oh...	31,496,083	37,774,671	31,134,757	34,362,658	3,411,849
Fla...	23,717,852	28,773,146	24,885,339	26,248,406	2,524,740	Okla...	9,634,969	11,801,124	10,201,853	10,793,470	1,007,561
Ga...	12,410,013	15,783,295	12,356,701	14,358,307	1,424,988	Ore...	6,163,302	7,748,097	6,014,750	7,147,233	600,852
Ha...	2,450,310	2,954,367	2,599,156	2,719,173	235,194	Pa...	46,368,573	55,541,802	44,485,826	50,779,989	4,760,993
Ida...	2,532,474	3,027,698	2,625,581	2,811,972	215,726	R.I...	3,266,884	3,852,378	3,222,913	3,546,456	305,922
Ill...	63,862,716	74,493,005	59,445,585	68,611,747	5,881,215	S.C...	3,971,498	4,872,998	4,123,916	4,431,486	441,512
Ind...	18,151,295	21,311,092	17,909,682	19,679,636	1,631,437	S.D...	2,870,525	3,271,281	2,913,576	3,006,696	264,585
Ia...	11,564,817	13,370,366	11,799,129	12,285,023	1,085,042	Tenn...	12,633,327	15,434,298	13,097,519	14,192,819	1,241,252
Kan...	8,692,753	10,199,760	8,790,678	9,298,193	900,996	Tex...	45,317,048	56,878,991	47,282,132	52,356,967	4,521,037
Ky...	9,630,530	11,463,611	9,798,326	10,521,461	942,150	Ut...	3,178,585	3,918,446	3,372,847	3,628,580	289,724
La...	11,881,473	14,224,684	11,938,616	13,071,212	1,153,468	Vt...	1,338,714	1,520,992	1,353,412	1,395,987	125,005
Me...	1,970,963	2,283,234	1,978,571	2,087,520	195,714	Va...	13,625,635	16,082,933	13,720,895	14,739,903	1,342,808
Md...	8,635,653	10,323,294	8,734,945	9,451,135	872,159	Wash...	9,318,329	11,883,529	9,673,765	11,062,439	821,089
Mass...	14,304,601	18,524,373	14,934,707	16,930,630	1,593,743	W. Va...	5,695,653	6,551,626	5,505,941	5,969,678	581,948
Mich...	29,178,822	34,584,799	29,447,566	31,730,872	2,853,910	Wis...	15,029,738	17,531,905	15,007,562	16,113,900	1,417,917
Minn...	15,195,669	17,776,795	14,738,504	16,312,731	1,464,064	Wy...	1,588,136	1,870,411	1,633,588	1,717,850	152,561
Miss...	5,441,289	6,500,629	5,653,988	5,946,775	553,462	*Others	5,082,382	7,796,824	5,539,548	7,516,033	280,791
Mo...	17,644,409	21,190,689	17,259,643	19,422,689	1,767,994	U.S.	762,399,707	944,654,187	775,209,120	867,203,599	77,446,118
Mon...	2,875,408	3,347,371	2,910,524	3,089,618	257,753						

*Includes American Samoa, Guam, Puerto Rico, and Virgin Islands.

Bank Suspensions

Source: Federal Deposit Insurance Corp. The figures for bank suspensions represent banks which, during the periods shown, closed temporarily or permanently on account of financial difficulties; does not include banks whose deposit liabilities were assumed by other banks at the time of closing (in some instances with Federal Deposit Insurance Corp. loans). Deposits in thousands of dollars.

Year	Suspensions	Depo	Year	Suspensions	Depo	Year	Suspensions	Depo	Year	Suspensions	Depo
1929...	659	230,643	1936...	42	11,241	1959...	3	2,593	1967...	4	10,878
1930..	1,352	853,363	1937...	50	14,960	1960...	1	6,930	1969...	4	9,011
1931..	2,294	1,690,669	1938...	50	10,296	1961...	5	8,936	1970...	4	34,040
1932..	1,456	715,626	1939...	32	32,738	1963...	2	23,444	1971...	5	74,605
1933*.	4,004	3,598,975	1940...	19	5,657	1964...	7	23,438	1972...	1	20,482
1934...	9	1,968	1955(a)..	4	6,503	1965...	3	42,889	1973...	3	25,811
1935...	24	9,091	1958...	3	4,156	1966...	1	774	1975...	1	18,248

*Figures for 1933 comprise 628 banks with deposits of $360,413,000 suspended before or after the banking holiday (the holiday began March 6 and closed March 15) or placed in receivership during the holiday; 2,124 banks with deposits of $2,520,391,000 which were not licensed following the banking holiday and were placed in liquidation or receivership; and 1,252 Banks with deposits of $718,171,000 which had not been licensed by June 30, 1933, (a) No suspensions in years 1945-1954, 1962, 1968, 1974.

Federal Reserve System

The Federal Reserve System, central banking system of the United States, was established Dec. 23, 1913, by an Act of Congress to give the country an elastic currency, to provide facilities for discounting commercial paper, and to improve supervision of banking. Today it is generally recognized that the primary function of the System is to foster a flow of credit and money that will facilitate orderly economic growth, a stable dollar, and a long-run balance in international payments.

The Federal Reserve System consists of the (1) Board of Governors of the Federal Reserve System; (2) Federal Open Market Committee; (3) 12 Fed. Reserve Banks and 25 branches; (4) member banks; (5) Fed. Advisory Council, and (6) the Consumer Advisory Council.

The 7 members of the Board of Governors in Washington are appointed by the President with the advice and consent of the Senate; Dr. Arthur F. Burns is chairman. One of the Board's principal functions is in the area of monetary policy. The Board has authority to approve changes in discount rates, to change member bank reserve requirements within specified limits, to set margin requirements for certain kinds of stock transactions, and to set maximum interest rates payable on member banks' savings and time deposits. Another important duty of the Board relates to supervision of Federal Reserve Banks, member banks, and bank holding companies. Expenses of the Board of Governors are paid out of assessments upon the Reserve Banks. The Federal Reserve has also been given responsibility by Congress for regulating the use of credit in securities markets and for rule writing and enforcement of a number of consumer credit protection laws.

The Federal Open Market Committee is composed of the 7 members of the Board of Governors and 5 Federal Reserve Bank presidents elected annually. The Committee establishes System open market policy for the purchases and sales of securities and for operations in foreign currencies.

Rather than having one central bank in the political capital, as in central banking systems of most countries, the Federal Reserve System is divided into 12 districts, each with a Federal Reserve Bank—in Boston, New York, Philadelphia, Cleveland, Richmond, Atlanta, Chicago, St. Louis, Minneapolis, Kansas City, Dallas, and San Francisco. Reserve Banks are operated for public service. By statute, their stock is held entirely by member banks, which include all national banks and such state banks and trust companies as have been admitted to membership. Ownership of Reserve Bank stock is in the nature of an obligation incident to membership in the System and does not carry with it the attributes of control and financial interest ordinarily attached to stock ownership in corporations that are operated for profit. The amount of stock that member banks own is specified by law and dividends are limited to 6% per annum. In case of the liquidation of any Reserve Bank, its surplus would be paid entirely to the United States. Each Reserve Bank has 9 directors, 6 of whom are chosen by member banks and 3 by the Board of Governors.

The 12-member Federal Advisory Council is composed of one member selected annually by the directors of each Federal Reserve Bank. The Council meets in Washington at least 4 times a year and advises the Board of Governors on matters within the Board's jurisdiction.

The Consumer Advisory Council was established by Congress in connection with the 1975 amendments to the Equal Credit Opportunity Act, to advise the Board on its responsibilities under various consumer protection laws.

U.S. Balance of International Payments

Source: Bureau of Economic Analysis, Dept. of Commerce

(In millions of dollars.)

	1955	1960	1965	1970	1972	1973	1974	1975
Exports of goods and services	19,948	27,595	39,548	62,483	72,664	102,154	144,773	148,410
Merchandise, adjusted	14,424	19,650	26,461	42,469	49,381	71,410	98,310	107,133
Transfers under U.S. military agency sales contracts	200	335	830	1,501	1,163	2,342	2,952	3,897
Receipts of income on U.S. investments abroad	2,817	3,350	5,899	8,575	10,161	13,997	26,233	18,219
Other services	2,507	4,261	6,359	9,938	11,959	14,405	17,278	19,162
Imports of goods and services	−17,795	−23,555	−32,443	−59,545	−78,618	−98,249	−141,187	−132,141
Merchandise, adjusted	−11,527	−14,758	−21,510	−39,866	−55,797	−70,499	−103,679	−98,150
Direct defense expenditures	−2,901	−3,087	−2,952	−4,855	−4,784	−4,629	−5,035	−4,780
Payments of income on foreign investments in the U.S.	−520	−1,063	−1,730	−5,056	−5,841	−8,819	−16,006	−12,212
Other services	−2,847	−4,646	−6,252	−9,771	−12,198	−14,303	−16,466	−16,999
Unilateral transfers, net	−2,498	−2,308	−2,854	−3,294	−3,848	−3,883	−7,184	−4,620
U.S. official reserve assets, net	182	2,145	1,222	2,477	32	209	−1,434	−607
U.S. Government assets, other than official reserve assets, net	−310	−1,100	−1,605	−1,589	−1,568	−2,645	365	−3,463
U.S. private assets, net	−1,255	−3,878	−3,793	−6,920	−8,708	−13,998	−32,323	−27,061
Foreign official assets in the United States, net	{1,357	1,473	¶32	6,907	10,705	6,299	10,981	6,336
Other foreign assets in the United States, net		647	249	−984	10,422	12,220	21,452	8,544
Allocations of special drawing rights	—	—	—	—	867	710	—	—
Statistical discrepancy	371	−1,019	−457	−402	−1,790	−2,107	4,557	4,602
Memoranda:								
Balance on merchandise trade	2,897	4,892	4,951	2,603	−6,416	911	−5,369	8,983
Balance on goods and services	2,153	4,040	7,105	2,938	−5,954	3,905	3,586	16,269
Balance on goods, services, and remittances	1,556	3,404	6,059	1,380	−7,629	1,960	1,877	14,542
Balance on current account	−345	1,732	4,251	−356	−9,802	22	−3,598	11,650

Note. — Details may not add to totals because of rounding.

All Banks in U. S.—Number, Deposits

Source: Federal Reserve System

Comprises all national banks in the United States and all state commercial banks, trust companies, mutual and stock savings banks, private and industrial banks, and special types of institutions that are treated as banks by the Federal bank supervisory agencies.

		Number of Banks					Total Deposits (Millions of Dollars)				
			Member Banks		Nonmember			Member			Nonmember
Date June 30	Total All Banks	Total	Nat'l	State	Mutual Savings	Other	Total All Banks	Total	Nat'l	State	Mutual Savings	Other
1925	26,479	9,538	8,066	1,472	621	18,320	51,641	32,457	19,912	12,546	7,089	12,095
1930	23,855	8,315	7,247	1,068	604	14,936	59,828	38,069	23,235	14,834	9,117	12,642
1935	16,047	6,410	5,425	985	569	9,068	51,149	34,938	22,477	12,461	9,830	6,381
1940	14,955	6,398	5,164	1,234	551	8,008	70,770	51,729	33,014	18,715	10,631	8,410
1945	14,542	6,840	5,015	1,825	539	7,163	151,033	118,378	76,534	41,844	14,413	18,242
1950	14,674	6,885	4,971	1,914	527	7,262	163,770	122,707	82,430	40,277	19,927	21,137
1955	14,309	6,611	4,744	1,867	525	7,173	208,850	154,670	98,636	56,034	27,310	26,870
1960	14,006	6,217	4,542	1,675	513	7,276	249,163	179,519	116,178	63,341	35,316	34,328
1965	14,295	6,235	4,803	1,432	504	7,556	362,611	259,743	171,528	88,215	50,980	51,889
1970	14,167	5,803	4,637	1,166	496	7,868	502,658	346,229	254,261	91,967	69,285	87,145
1974,Dec.31	14,944	5,780	4,706	1,074	479	8,685	847,663	575,838	431,039	144,799	99,371	172,454
1975,Dec.31	15,108	5,787	4,741	1,046	475	8,846	897,101	590,999	447,590	143,409	110,569	195,533

Bank Clearings in Major U.S. Cities

Source: Dun & Bradstreet, Inc.

Year (Cal.)	New York $1,000	Chicago $1,000	Phila. $1,000	Los Ang. $1,000	Boston $1,000	San Fran. $1,000	Detroit $1,000	Dallas $1,000
1935	181,551,008	13,194,988	16,909,000	5,852,244	10,645,822	6,478,835	4,523,167	1,969,290
1940	160,878,038	16,684,672	21,455,000	7,543,880	11,943,665	6,773,877	6,312,233	2,986,774
1945	334,432,654	27,279,588	34,710,000	17,144,078	19,589,725	15,743,086	16,472,971	6,634,514
1950	399,308,634	40,674,983	51,102,000	26,504,731	25,348,336	21,982,689	22,855,273	14,451,332
1955	530,883,498	52,818,527	59,962,000	42,818,633	32,472,726	31,492,157	36,364,754	21,678,567
1960	738,604,276	66,651,600	56,716,000	53,635,826	40,759,040	39,787,147	39,101,854	27,811,939
1965	1,280,402,568	82,507,560	69,116,728	111,587,481	60,318,717	87,095,481	56,068,833	42,414,327
1970	3,752,515,518	110,219,418	94,003,896	174,153,125	125,033,163	122,929,389	136,965,556	51,886,403
1973	11,266,959,408	143,210,068	120,093,097	238,642,471	105,641,315	172,693,995	188,512,471	67,794,226
1974	13,163,126,958	148,493,173	129,756,288	254,091,476	117,527,838	188,674,386	212,028,019	74,039,017
1975	13,189,673,325	153,368,143	129,025,579	274,825,654	100,151,380	200,376,308	195,847,574	76,064,440

Year (Cal.)	Kan. City $1,000	Houston $1,000	Pittsburgh $1,000	Cleveland $1,000	St. Louis $1,000	Minneap. $1,000	Baltimore $1,000	Atlanta $1,000
1935	4,348,113	1,420,404	5,245,718	3,417,055	3,940,654	3,044,735	2,910,637	2,204,500
1940	4,997,593	2,568,518	7,074,775	5,734,407	4,822,016	3,787,088	4,201,985	3,430,900
1945	10,856,497	5,982,318	12,978,668	11,529,428	9,723,815	8,196,279	8,315,468	8,263,900
1950	16,707,120	11,922,307	16,782,419	17,683,829	14,896,444	14,113,814	12,154,904	12,910,100
1955	20,057,800	19,199,929	21,142,527	26,426,614	18,481,105	18,496,868	17,071,914	18,597,100
1960	24,967,583	21,887,889	23,913,706	32,364,009	21,138,861	25,129,318	20,423,684	22,993,200
1965	33,936,377	33,938,170	29,070,474	44,600,090	28,399,392	34,029,120	25,893,740	34,371,000
1970	53,509,523	39,855,427	42,418,973	52,690,067	33,611,932	43,112,445	29,964,761	53,784,237
1973	52,973,946	67,188,692	66,898,891	61,478,321	44,130,125	55,880,907	35,622,338	77,755,923
1974	51,771,171	80,517,773	87,752,769	69,231,013	37,993,730	61,765,880	34,858,768	80,579,538
1975	52,692,225	88,375,890	93,419,382	66,424,707	35,009,485	62,917,478	37,954,018	78,791,721

Per Capita Personal Income, by States and Regions

Source: Department of Commerce, Bureau of Economic Analysis. (DOLLARS)

State and Region	1970	1972r	1973r	1974r	1975r
United States	3,966	4,537	5,049	5,486	5,902
New England	4,300	4,783	5,227	5,668	6,098
Connecticut	4,917	5,382	5,929	6,487	6,973
Maine	3,302	3,693	4,158	4,536	4,786
Massachusetts	4,340	4,854	5,262	5,667	6,114
New Hampshire	3,737	4,183	4,633	4,986	5,315
Rhode Island	3,959	4,509	4,873	5,355	5,841
Vermont	3,468	3,884	4,296	4,602	4,960
Mideast	4,471	5,044	5,479	5,968	6,433
Delaware	4,524	5,225	5,846	6,284	6,748
Dist. of Columbia	5,079	5,924	6,420	7,043	7,742
Maryland	4,309	4,970	5,453	5,973	6,474
New Jersey	4,701	5,303	5,718	6,242	6,722
New York	4,712	5,248	5,657	6,120	6,564
Pennsylvania	3,971	4,530	4,989	5,485	5,943
Great Lakes	4,135	4,751	5,311	5,731	6,121
Illinois	4,507	5,131	5,750	6,268	6,789
Indiana	3,772	4,370	4,959	5,295	5,653
Michigan	4,180	4,950	5,509	5,846	6,173
Ohio	4,020	4,568	5,063	5,481	5,810
Wisconsin	3,812	4,290	4,831	5,281	5,669
Plains	3,751	4,318	5,115	5,364	5,785
Iowa	3,751	4,297	5,344	5,561	6,077
Kansas	3,853	4,540	5,276	5,615	6,023
Minnesota	3,859	4,328	5,112	5,469	5,807
Missouri	3,781	4,293	4,794	5,065	5,510
Nebraska	3,789	4,441	5,251	5,379	6,087
North Dakota	3,086	4,015	5,768	5,698	5,737
South Dakota	3,123	3,790	4,957	4,860	4,924
Southeast	3,257	3,859	4,346	4,740	5,055
Alabama	2,948	3,472	3,905	4,284	4,643
Arkansas	2,878	3,343	3,952	4,379	4,620
Florida	3,738	4,510	5,107	5,406	5,638
Georgia	3,354	3,968	4,441	4,798	5,086
Kentucky	3,112	3,608	4,048	4,565	4,871
Louisiana	3,090	3,573	3,961	4,456	4,904
Mississippi	2,626	3,186	3,579	3,837	4,052
North Carolina	3,252	3,853	4,300	4,649	4,952
South Carolina	2,990	3,507	3,972	4,390	4,618
Tennessee	3,119	3,708	4,206	4,567	4,895
Virginia	3,712	4,400	4,902	5,377	5,785
West Virginia	3,061	3,602	3,989	4,480	4,918
Southwest	3,546	4,051	4,567	5,019	5,487
Arizona	3,665	4,333	4,833	5,152	5,355
New Mexico	3,077	3,518	3,927	4,299	4,775
Oklahoma	3,387	3,834	4,336	4,823	5,250
Texas	3,606	4,102	4,632	5,106	5,631
Rocky Mountain	3,590	4,214	4,785	5,222	5,576
Colorado	3,855	4,610	5,137	5,549	5,985
Idaho	3,290	3,786	4,489	5,140	5,159
Montana	3,500	4,070	4,781	5,079	5,422
Utah	3,227	3,741	4,186	4,539	4,923
Wyoming	3,815	4,276	4,945	5,644	6,131
Far West	4,374	4,924	5,403	5,976	6,481
California	4,493	5,044	5,497	6,089	6,593
Nevada	4,563	5,138	5,742	6,161	6,647
Oregon	3,719	4,328	4,848	5,398	5,769
Washington	4,053	4,558	5,146	5,646	6,247
Alaska	4,644	5,192	6,005	7,037	9,448
Hawaii	4,623	5,123	5,570	6,010	6,658

r Revised. Per capita personal income for each state is derived by dividing total personal income for the calendar year by resident population (as estimated by the Bureau of the Census) as of July 1. Personal income consists of wage and salary disbursements, other labor income, proprietors' income, less personal contributions for social insurance plus a residence adjustment, plus property income (dividends, interest and rent), plus transfer payments (disbursements made to individuals by government and business for which no services are rendered currently, such as unemployment benefits and relief, welfare, and social insurance payments).

Average Percent Increase in Earnings

Period and area Feb. 1973 to Feb. 1974	All Industries				Manufacturing			
	Office Clerical	Industrial nurses	Skilled maintenance	Unskilled plant	Office Clerical	Industrial nurses	Skilled maintenance	Unskilled plant
United States	6.2	7.2	7.7	7.1	6.3	6.8	7.5	7.7
Northeast	6.2	6.9	7.2	6.4	6.3	6.7	6.9	6.9
South	6.2	6.9	7.5	7.3	6.1	6.9	7.2	8.0
North Central	6.3	7.5	8.1	7.5	6.4	7.0	8.1	8.4
West	5.8	6.8	7.3	6.8	6.0	6.5	7.1	5.8

Indexes of Manufacturing, Industrial Countries

Source: U.S. Bureau of Labor Statistics (1967=100.0)

Output per Hour

Country	1960	1965	1970	1971	1972	1973	1974	1975
United States	78.8	98.2	104.5	110.3	116.0	119.3	114.7	114.9
11 foreign countries	68.4	89.9	123.8	129.9	138.8	148.9	153.6	NA
Canada	75.5	94.4	115.2	122.9	126.9	131.1	131.0	133.0
Japan	52.6	79.1	146.5	151.7	163.9	184.3	187.5	181.9
Belgium	70.5	88.0	129.2	136.3	152.6	164.2	174.0	NA
Denmark	66.6	86.7	129.3	138.8	150.7	161.0	167.4	NA
France	68.7	88.5	121.2	127.5	135.9	142.2	146.1	139.7
Germany	66.4	90.4	116.6	122.5	130.3	138.6	145.6	150.4
Italy	65.1	91.6	117.8	123.5	133.1	147.8	155.5	149.5
Netherlands	68.1	87.8	132.2	140.6	152.0	163.9	173.3	NA
Sweden	63.1	88.5	124.5	129.0	137.9	147.4	154.7	154.7
Switzerland	80.4	90.5	125.5	131.3	137.9	147.7	150.7	NA
United Kingdom	76.8	92.4	109.1	114.3	121.2	127.9	127.1	125.4
9 European countries	69.1	90.7	119.2	125.7	134.3	142.6	147.5	NA
Original EEC	67.9	90.8	120.0	126.3	135.1	144.0	150.0	NA

Unit Labor Costs in U.S. Dollars

Country	1960	1965	1970	1971	1972	1973	1974	1975
United States	97.7	92.6	116.5	117.6	118.1	123.2	140.9	156.4
11 foreign countries	82.6	97.5	111.8	124.9	142.9	172.3	196.1	NA
Canada	106.3	91.3	111.5	115.6	122.3	127.0	144.6	158.4
Japan	82.5	102.5	113.3	130.7	160.1	194.3	233.4	272.9
Belgium	74.2	93.6	101.5	112.4	128.5	155.2	176.5	NA
Denmark	74.7	91.8	104.4	112.4	123.2	157.1	179.7	NA
France	81.7	98.3	98.9	105.5	120.8	148.1	162.0	224.2
Germany	78.1	95.7	124.6	141.8	162.5	208.3	235.2	267.3
Italy	76.5	97.1	119.2	135.6	151.9	172.5	183.4	243.5
Netherlands	65.4	91.8	108.4	120.3	138.9	174.1	202.8	NA
Sweden	80.5	93.3	105.4	116.1	132.6	149.2	163.6	208.9
Switzerland	71.1	95.6	99.7	113.1	129.5	165.2	194.9	NA
United Kingdom	85.7	98.7	106.0	117.9	127.7	134.9	153.9	187.9
9 European countries	79.3	96.4	112.6	125.7	142.3	173.4	194.2	NA
Original EEC	77.8	96.2	115.6	129.2	147.3	183.7	204.6	NA

NA=Not available.

U. S. Labor Force, Employment and Unemployment

Source: Bureau of the Census, U. S. Dept. of Commerce; Bureau of Labor Statistics, U. S. Dept. of Labor
(Unemployment by sex, age, race and other characteristics)

	1973	1974	1975	Jan.	Feb.	Mar.	Apr.	May	June
						1976			
				(Numbers in thousands)					
U.S. Pop. (incl. armed forces overseas)	210,410[1]	211,894[1]	213,631[1]	214,435	214,550	214,647	214,756	214,864	214,988
Labor Force[2]									
Labor force, persons 16 years of age and over ...	91,040	93,240	94,793	94,805	94,944	95,260	95,618	95,724	98,251
Civilian labor force	88,714	91,011	92,613	92,665	92,798	93,112	93,474	93,582	96,114
Employed total	84,409	85,935	84,783	84,491	84,764	85,588	86,584	87,278	88,460
Agriculture	3,452	3,492	3,380	2,853	2,802	2,897	3,273	3,415	3,780
Nonagricultural industries	80,957	82,443	81,403	81,638	81,963	82,961	83,311	83,863	84,680
Unemployed, total	4,304	5,076	7,830	8,174	8,033	7,525	6,890	6,304	7,655
Long term, 15 weeks and over	812	937	2,483	2,754	2,294	2,961	2,729	2,310	2,297
Seasonally adjusted									
Civilian labor force	.....	.....	.....	93,484	93,455	93,719	94,439	94,557	94,643
Employed, total	.....	.....	.....	86,194	86,319	86,692	87,399	87,697	87,500
Agriculture	.....	.....	.....	3,343	3,170	3,179	3,417	3,329	3,294
Nonagricultural industries	.....	.....	.....	82,851	83,149	83,513	83,982	84,368	84,206
Unemployed, total	.....	.....	.....	7,290	7,136	7,027	7,040	6,860	7,143
Long term, 15 weeks and over	.....	.....	.....	2,785	2,515	2,294	2,035	1,998	2,215
Rates (unemployed in each group as percent of total in the group):									
All civilian workers	4.9	5.6	8.5	7.8	7.6	7.5	7.5	7.3	7.5
Males, 20 years and over	3.2	3.8	6.7	5.8	5.7	5.6	5.4	5.6	6.0
Females, 20 years and over	4.8	5.5	8.0	7.5	7.5	7.3	7.3	6.8	7.1
Both sexes, 16-19 years	14.5	16.0	19.9	19.9	19.2	19.1	19.2	18.5	18.4
White	4.3	5.0	7.8	7.1	6.8	6.8	6.7	6.6	6.8
Black and other races	8.9	9.9	13.9	13.2	13.7	12.5	13.0	12.2	13.3
Household heads	2.9	3.3	5.8	5.1	4.9	5.0	4.8	4.8	5.1
Married men	2.3	2.7	5.1	4.1	4.1	4.1	3.9	4.0	4.4
Occupation:									
White-collar workers	2.9	3.3	4.7	4.7	4.6	4.6	4.8	4.6	4.4
Blue-collar workers	5.3	6.7	11.7	9.4	9.3	9.1	9.0	9.0	9.3
Industry of last job (nonagricultural)									
Private wage and salary workers	4.8	5.7	9.2	8.1	8.0	7.7	7.6	7.6	7.8
Construction	8.8	10.6	18.1	15.4	15.5	16.0	15.3	14.1	17.0
Manufacturing	4.3	5.7	10.9	8.1	8.0	7.3	7.6	7.3	7.6
Durable goods	3.9	5.4	11.3	8.2	8.0	7.4	7.7	7.4	7.5

(1) As of July 1. (2) Effective January 1972, data reflect adjustment to the 1970 Census of Population. For example the civilian labor force and employment totals were increased by a little more than 300,000; unemployment levels and rates were essentially unchanged. A subsequent census adjustment, primarily affecting whites and black and other groups, was introduced into the survey for March 1973. As a result, the white labor force and employment levels were lowered by about 150,000, while black levels were raised by 210,000. Consequently, the overall labor force and employment showed a net increase of about 60,000. Unemployment levels and rates were not affected significantly. Comparisons with data prior to these two dates should take these adjustments into account.

Employed Persons by Major Occupational Groups and Sex

Source: Bureau of Labor Statistics

Annual Averages 1975

	Thousands of persons			Percent Distribution		
Occupational Group	Both sexes	Males	Females	Both sexes	Males	Females
Total employed	84,783	51,230	33,553	100.0	100.0	100.0
White-collar workers	42,227	21,134	21,092	49.8	41.3	62.9
Professional and technical	12,748	7,481	5,267	15.0	14.6	15.7
Managers and administrators, except farm	8,891	7,162	1,729	10.5	14.0	5.2
Sales workers	5,460	3,137	2,323	6.4	6.1	6.9
Clerical workers	15,128	3,355	11,773	17.8	6.5	35.1
Blue-collar workers	27,962	23,220	4,742	33.0	45.3	14.1
Craft and kindred workers	10,972	10,472	501	12.9	20.4	1.5
Operatives, except transport	9,637	5,934	3,703	11.4	11.6	11.0
Transport equipment operatives	3,219	3,037	182	3.8	5.9	.5
Nonfarm laborers	4,134	3,777	357	4.9	7.4	1.1
Service workers	11,657	4,400	7,258	13.7	8.6	21.6
Private household workers	1,171	30	1,141	1.4	.1	3.4
Other service workers	10,486	4,370	6,116	12.4	8.5	18.2
Farm workers	2,936	2,476	460	3.5	4.8	1.4
Farmers and farm managers	1,593	1,492	102	1.9	2.9	.3
Farm laborers and supervisors	1,343	985	358	1.6	1.9	1.1

Employment and Unemployment in the U.S.

Civilian Labor Force, Persons 16 Years of Age and Over (in thousands)

Year	Civilian Labor Force	Employed	Unemployed	Year	Civilian Labor Force	Employed	Unemployed
						First Half Average	
1970	82,715	78,627	4,088	1970	81,907	78,151	3,756
1971	84,113	79,120	4,993	1971	83,165	78,064	5,101
1972	86,542	81,702	4,840	1972	85,616	80,524	5,090
1973	88,714	84,409	4,304	1974	90,022	85,234	4,788
1974	91,011	85,936	5,076	1975	91,768	83,625	8,143
1975	92,613	84,783	7,830	1976	93,624	86,194	7,430

Civilian Employment of the Federal Government

Source: United States Civil Service Commission, Manpower Statistics Division, data as of June 30, 1976

Agency	All Areas	United States Total	Full-Time	Part-Time & Intermittent	Outside United States Total	Territories	Foreign Countries
Total, All Agencies (a).............	2,881,864	2,758,482	2,538,926	219,556	123,382	33,511	89,871
Percent distribution........	100	96	88	8	4	1	3
Legislative Branch.................	39,404	39,328	38,500	828	76	...	76
Congress.....................	18,019	18,019	18,019	...	...	...	...
United States Senate............	6,733	6,733	6,733	...	...	...	...
House of Representatives.........	11,286	11,286	11,286	...	...	...	...
Architect of the Capitol...........	2,103	2,103	1,975	128	...	...	...
General Accounting Office..........	5,417	5,348	5,253	95	69	...	69
Government Printing Office.........	8,260	8,260	7.944	316	...	...	...
Library of Congress...............	4,930	4,923	4,667	256	7	...	7
United States Tax Court...........	200	200	192	8	...	...	...
Judicial Branch....................	11,259	11,149	10,604	545	110	110	...
United States Courts..............	10,956	10,846	10,326	520	110	110	...
Supreme Court..................	303	303	278	25	...	...	...
Executive Branch..................	2,831,201	2,708,005	2,489,822	218,183	123,196	33,401	89,795
Executive Office of the President.....	1,848	1,848	1,735	113	...	...	...
White House Office..............	541	541	499	42	...	...	...
Office of the Vice President........	24	24	23	1	...	...	...
Office of Management and Budget..	724	724	705	19	...	...	...
Council of Economic Advisors.....	39	39	39	...	...	...	...
Council on Internt'l Economic Policy.	34	34	29	5	...	...	...
Citizens' Advisory Committee on Environmental Quality..........	1	1	1	...	...	...	...
Council on Environmental Quality...	59	59	59	...	...	...	...
Council on Wage and Price Stability.	55	55	52	3	...	...	...
Domestic Council................	49	49	48	1	...	...	...
Executive Mansion and Grounds...	83	83	82	1	...	...	...
National Security Council..........	95	95	67	28	...	...	...
Office of Special Representative for Trade Negotiations............	48	48	45	3	...	...	...
Office of Telecommunications Policy	96	96	86	10	...	...	...
Executive Departments............	1,732,177	1,634,655	1,572,204	62,451	97,522	14,417	83,105
State (b)......................	30,457	10,848	10,235	613	19,609	...	19,609
Treasury......................	125,600	124,671	120,953	3,718	929	582	347
Defense......................	1,008,981	936,678	925,794	10,884	72,303	10,736	61,567
Department of the Army........	369,465	336,159	331,856	4,303	33,306	3,827	29,479
Department of the Navy........	315,440	292,090	288,818	3,272	23,350	4,791	18,559
Department of the Air Force.....	252,687	238,213	235,443	2,770	14,474	1,961	12,513
Defense Supply Agency........	50,651	50,117	49,925	192	534	58	476
Other Defense Activities........	20,738	20,099	19,752	347	639	99	540
Justice........................	53,982	53,116	51,733	1,383	866	365	501
Interior.......................	81,844	81,448	74,985	6,463	396	336	60
Agriculture....................	128,052	126,709	102,124	24,585	1,343	710	633
Commerce.....................	37,569	37,300	31,665	5,635	269	82	187
Labor........................	16,730	16,640	15,872	768	90	89	1
Health, Education, and Welfare....	155,096	154,376	147,390	6,986	720	671	49
Housing and Urban Development...	16,579	16,397	16,192	205	182	182	...
Transportation.................	77,287	76,472	75,261	1,211	815	664	151
Independent agencies.............	1,097,176	1,071,502	915,883	155,619	25,674	18,984	6,690
ACTION.......................	1,932	1,372	1,332	40	560	29	531
Board of Governors, Fed. Res. Sys....	1,481	1,481	1,448	33	...	...	...
Canal Zone Government...........	3,215	...	...	...	3,215	3,215	...
Civil Service Commission..........	8,131	8,110	6,884	1,226	21	21	...
Community Service Administration....	1,099	1,099	1,087	12	...	...	...
Energy Res. and Dev. Admin.........	9,038	9,027	8,758	269	11	...	11
Environmental Protection Agency.....	11,089	11,077	10,294	783	12	11	1
Federal Communication Comm.......	2,094	2,087	2,082	5	7	7	...
Federal Energy Administration.......	3,478	3,478	3,425	53	...	...	...
Federal Power Commission.........	1,365	1,365	1,356	9	...	...	...
Federal Trade Commission..........	1,739	1,739	1,693	46	...	...	...
General Services Administration......	38,857	38,776	37,548	1,228	81	74	7
Information Agency...............	8,732	3,294	3,264	30	5,438	...	5,438
Interstate Commerce Commission....	2,178	2,178	2,168	10	...	...	...
Natl. Aero. & Space Admin.........	26,244	26,225	26,063	162	19	1	18
National Labor Relations Board......	2,642	2,620	2,593	27	22	22	...
Nuclear Regulatory Commission.....	2,639	2,639	2,560	79	...	...	...
Panama Canal Company...........	10,597	89	89	...	10,508	10,508	...
Securities & Exchange Comm........	1,943	1,943	1,913	30	...	...	...
Selective Service System...........	208	204	171	33	4	4	...
Small Business Administration.......	4,741	4,631	4,528	103	110	110	...
Tennessee Valley Authority.........	31,302	31,297	30,930	367	5	...	5
U. S. Postal Service...............	675,653	672,794	540,471	132,323	2,859	2,859	...
Veterans Administration............	222,313	220,034	202,483	17,551	2,279	1,994	285
a-All other agencies...............	24,466	23,943	22,743	1,200	523	129	394

(a) Excludes employees of Central Intelligence Agency, National Security Agency (not reported to the Civil Service Commission) and uncompensated employees. June 1976 total includes 42,864 employees exempted from personnel ceilings in the Youth Programs and Worker Trainee Opportunities Program. (b) Includes 6,198 employees in Agency for International Development (2,841 in the Washington, D.C. metropolitan area): employees in foreign countries include 577 paid from local currency trust funds established by foreign governments.

Foreign Direct Investment in the U.S.

Source: U.S. Dept. of Commerce

The foreign direct investment position in the United States increased $4.3 billion in 1975 to $26.7 billion at year-end. The increase resulted from reinvested earnings of $1.9 billion and net capital inflows of $2.4 billion. *Interest, dividends, and branch profits account for most of the income received by foreign owners from direct investments in the U.S.

(Millions of dollars)	Book Value	Net Cap. inflows	Earnings Total	Int.* Div.	Reinv'd.
1974	22,421	2,745	7,082	5,495	1,581
1975 Total (prelim.)	26,740	2,437	3,992	2,127	1,881
By country:					
Canada	5,146	−56	467	182	272
United Kingdom	6,669	239	647	425	242
Netherlands	3,649	608	331	128	201
Switzerland	2,455	55	250	122	149
Other	8,822	1,592	2,297	1,270	1,018

Canadian Labor Force

Source: Statistics Canada (Apr., 1975, seasonally adjusted)
(thousands of workers)

	Can.	Nfld.	P.E.I.	N.S.	N.B.	Que.	Ont.	Man.	Sask.	Alta.	B.C.
Labor Force	9,925	189	44	302	256	2,677	3,768	425	379	778	1,109
Employed	9,208	156	40	277	227	2,435	3,540	405	369	746	1,019
Unemployed	717	33	...	25	29	242	228	20	10	32	90
Percent unemployed	7.2	17.5	...	8.3	11.3	9.0	6.1	4.7	2.6	4.1	8.1

Canada: Labor Force Characteristics

Source: Statistics Canada

	Labor force (000)	Employed (thousands)					Unemployed (000)	Unemployed %
		All workers			Paid workers			
		Total	Agriculture	Non-Agriculture	Total	Non-Agriculture		
1950	5,163	4,976	1,018	3,958	3,522	3,411	186	3.6
1955	5,610	5,364	819	4,546	4,133	4,027	245	4.4
1960	6,411	5,965	683	5,282	4,843	4,732	446	7.0
1965	7,141	6,862	594	6,268	5,760	5,655	280	3.9
1970	8,374	7,879	511	7,368	6,839	6,740	495	5.9
1971	8,631	8,079	510	7,569	7,029	6,927	552	6.4
1972	8,891	8,329	481	7,848	7,310	7,211	562	6.3
1973	9,279	8,759	467	8,292	7,757	7,661	520	5.6
1974	9,662	9,137	473	8,664	8,105	8,006	525	5.4

Average Weekly Canadian Wages and Salaries, by Province (C$)

Source: Canadian Statistical Review, Apr. 1976

Year & Month	Canada	Nfld.	P.E.I.	N.S.	N.B.	Que.	Ont.	Man.	Sask.	Alta.	B.C.
1960	117.63	106.00	80.87	94.51	96.80	114.24	121.55	107.67	107.90	117.95	129.35
1970	126.82	117.70	83.82	104.21	104.01	122.38	131.52	115.88	114.87	128.15	137.97
1974	178.09	168.48	126.92	149.99	154.58	172.89	181.43	162.70	160.93	160.99	200.50
1975 Jan.	192.08	188.74	144.67	164.46	174.41	187.85	193.97	174.28	175.17	184.43	216.16
Apr.	197.44	190.93	145.08	169.51	181.24	194.16	199.56	180.99	183.43	200.85	223.31
Jul.	205.25	198.37	153.80	173.33	182.15	200.86	206.77	190.56	190.32	210.14	231.69
Oct.	211.85	205.87	155.53	176.11	189.89	207.76	213.65	193.54	198.05	217.22	237.98

Activities of the Unemployment Insurance Commission — Canada

Source: Canadian Statistical Review — Apr., 1976

Benefits Paid (thousand dollars)

Year and Month	Claims Data Claimants[1][2]	Claims received (000)	Weeks paid (000)	Total[3] Paid	Benefits Paid				
					Regular	Sickness	Maternity	Retirement	Fishing
1972	804	2,470	30,462	1,871,802	1,764,030	58,855	36,431	2,440	20,404
1973	828	2,239	29,537	2,004,211	1,850,928	80,179	66,750	3,690	20,296
1974	828	2,411	28,460	2,119,213	1,924,543	98,319	81,710	4,165	22,676
Jan.	981	278	3,368	247,603	226,850	8,481	6,752	396	6,076
1975 Jan.	1,134	356	3,725	306,501	281,638	10,600	8,777	578	5,839

[1] Persons who have applied for or are in receipt of unemployment insurance benefit at the end of the month.
[2] Annual figures are average of 12 months.
[3] Includes adjustments for cancellation of warrants and collection of overpayments.

Canada: Provincial Unemployment Rates, 1971-1974

Source: Statistics Canada

Year	Can.	Nfld.	P.E.I.	N.S.	N.B.	Que.	Ont.	Man.	Sask.	Alta.	B.C.
1971	6.4	11.4	...	7.6	7.4	8.2	5.2	4.9	3.7	4.7	7.0
1972	6.3	12.1	...	7.5	8.4	8.3	4.8	4.5	4.3	4.4	7.6
1973	5.6	12.8	...	6.8	9.2	7.4	4.0	3.9	3.6	4.0	6.5
1974	5.4	16.7	...	6.7	9.2	7.3	4.1	3.1	2.8	2.7	6.0

Total Value of Construction Work Performed in Canada

(thousand dollars)
Source: Statistics Canada

Province	1974 New	1974 Repair	1974 Total	1975 New	1975 Repair	1975 Total
Canada	19,589,685	3,563,661	23,153,346	23,079,028	4,170,158	27,249,186
Newfoundland	452,945	60,820	513,765	531,759	73,945	605,704
Prince Edward Island	98,231	20,371	118,602	90,842	17,965	108,807
Nova Scotia	601,208	108,044	709,252	617,199	128,281	745,480
New Brunswick	517,301	103,365	602,666	714,376	121,133	838,509
Quebec	4,315,028	748,593	5,063,621	5,491,243	847,464	6,338,707
Ontario	6,989,776	1,290,548	8,280,324	7,822,176	1,547,297	9,369,473
Manitoba	800,910	169,008	969,918	822,315	199,133	1,021,448
Saskatchewan	590,104	189,215	779,319	838,754	237,005	1,075,759
Alberta	2,265,339	390,105	2,655,444	2,805,099	460,535	3,265,634
British Columbia	2,958,843	483,592	3,442,435	3,345,265	537,400	3,882,665

Includes residential, commercial, institutional, marine, road, highway and aerodrome, waterworks and sewage systems, and all other construction.

Pulpwood, Wood Pulp, and Newsprint—Canada

(thousand tons)
Source: Canadian Statistical Review, Apr. 1976

Year and Month	Pulpwood Production (thousand Units[1])	Wood Pulp Production[2] Total	Wood Pulp Production[2] Mechanical	Wood Pulp Production[2] Chemical	Wood pulp Exports[3]	News-Print Production	Newsprint Total	Newsprint Shipments Domestic	Export[4]
1972	18,805	18,593.3	7,520.8	11,033.9	6,071.2	8,660.8	8,739.4	779.7	7,959.8
1974	2,640	21,168	7,870	12,001	7,057	9,548	9,597	886	8,711
1975	2,112	15,660	6,827	9,698	5,389	7,679	7,723	864	6,863
1976 Jan.	709	986.7	312.1	673.0	525.3	369.5	339.4	52.4	287.0
Feb.		123.5	453.0	781.5	. . .	552.1	483.7	58.8	424.9

(1) 100 cu. ft. of solid wood; pulpwood produced for domestic use and excluding exports, but including receipts of purchased round-wood.
(2) Total pulp production covers "screenings" which are already included in exports. "Screenings" are excluded throughout from mechanical and chemical pulp.
(3) Customs exports.
(4) Mill shipments destined for export.

Telephones in North American Cities with Over 100,000 Telephones

Source: American Telephone and Telegraph Co., and Trans-Canada Telephone Systems (Jan. 1, 1975)

City	Number	City	Number	City	Number	City	Number
Akron	334,130	Springfield, Ore.	123,084	Memphis	533,789	Saginaw, Mich.	115,754
Albany, N.Y.	162,779	Evansville	116,271	Mexico City	1,255,297	St. Louis	567,793
Albuquerque	250,167	Fayetteville	116,073	Miami	943,340	St. Petersburg	272,780
Alexandria, Va.	217,443	Flint	202,052	Milwaukee	791,978	Salt Lake City	409,963
Allentown, Pa.	135,433	Ft. Lauderdale	337,670	Minn.-St. Paul.	1,486,400	San Antonio	381,555
Amarillo	115,131	Fort Wayne	166,638	Mobile	194,710	San Diego (Area)	919,547
Anaheim, Cal.	197,440	Fort Worth	309,255	Monterrey, Mex.	149,423	San Francisco	763,170
Ann Arbor, Mich.	113,526	Fremont City	107,384	Montgomery	133,406	San Jose	506,315
Atlanta, Ga.	833,868	Fresno	218,952	Montreal	1,158,708	San Mateo	114,205
Augusta, Ga.	123,608	Gary	124,688	Mt. Vernon, N.Y.	118,530	Santa Ana	350,082
Austin, Tex.	261,241	Grand Rapids	266,702	Nashville	357,427	Santa Barbara	120,257
Bakersfield, Cal.	144,002	Greensboro	169,532	New Haven	255,333	Savannah	126,631
Baltimore	1,203,137	Greenville, N.C.	153,980	New Orleans	631,407	Schenectady	125,814
Baton Rouge	229,506	Guadalajara, Mex.	143,134	New York	5,913,942	Seattle	577,720
Birmingham	390,363	Halifax	131,698	Newark	315,746	Shreveport	183,344
Boston	515,447	Hamilton	192,307	Newport News	187,766	Skokie, Ill.	142,372
Bridgeport	171,953	Harrisburg	192,880	Norfolk (Area)	409,463	South Bend	130,819
Buffalo	432,469	Hartford	307,738	Oklahoma City	528,767	Spokane	193,731
Calgary	337,463	Hayward, Cal.	128,982	Omaha	400,800	Springfield, Ill.	132,664
Cambridge	109,484	Hollywood, Fla.	192,638	Orlando	225,427	Springfield, Mass.	145,416
Canton	124,454	Honolulu	323,844	Ottawa	395,189	Springfield, Mo.	111,588
Cedar Rapids	112,900	Houston	1,165,823	Palo Alto	141,637	Stamford, Conn.	105,881
Charleston, S.C.	175,945	Huntington Beach	109,592	Passaic	133,022	Stockton, Cal.	122,763
Charlotte	304,899	Huntsville, Ala.	128,964	Paterson	117,363	Syracuse	255,986
Chattanooga	220,040	Indianapolis	624,813	Pensacola	133,223	Tacoma	212,564
Chicago	2,454,624	Jackson, Miss.	172,589	Peoria	174,346	Tampa	356,990
Cincinnati	689,894	Jacksonville	393,619	Philadelphia	1,622,069	Toledo	293,409
Cleveland	892,052	Jersey City	171,275	Phoenix	790,738	Topeka	106,808
Colorado Springs	185,561	Kalamazoo	134,355	Pittsburgh	770,670	Toronto	1,538,577
Columbia, S.C.	233,722	Kansas City, Kan.	156,357	Pomona	155,740	Tucson	268,770
Columbus, Ga.	123,597	Kansas City, Mo.	337,057	Pompano Beach	142,443	Tulsa	350,879
Columbus, Oh.	467,694	Kitchener	104,754	Pontiac	108,153	Union City, N.J.	117,285
Corpus Christi	128,620	Knoxville	188,197	Portland, Ore.	451,082	Vancouver	401,306
Covington	108,760	Lansing	199,828	Providence	254,738	Victoria	124,010
Dallas	742,724	Las Vegas	273,000	Quebec City	234,230	Warren, Mich.	280,386
Davenport	106,100	Lexington	142,644	Raleigh	166,557	Washington, D.C.	981,443
Dayton	366,304	Lincoln	142,700	Reading, Pa.	152,098	West Palm Beach	251,045
Denver	1,021,448	Little Rock	193,854	Reno	112,123	Wichita	208,472
Des Moines	252,500	Livonia, Mich.	161,196	Richmond, Va.	352,523	Wilmington, Del.	194,970
Detroit	1,451,549	London	158,254	Riverside, Cal.	135,500	Windsor	116,924
East Orange, N.J.	128,552	Los Angeles (Area)	5,333,005	Roanoke, Va.	117,538	Winnipeg	355,565
Edmonton	304,700	Louisville	504,354	Rochester, N.Y.	361,971	Winston-Salem	149,643
El Paso	230,044	Lubbock, Tex.	136,527	Rockford, Ill.	168,740	Winter Park	109,968
Erie	132,988	Madison, Wis.	175,577	Royal Oak, Mich.	185,172	Worcester	132,999
Eugene-				Sacramento	442,174	Youngstown	180,563

ENERGY
Nuclear Power Reactors in U.S.
Source: U. S. Energy Research and Development Administration (June 30, 1976)

State	Site	Plant Name	Capacity (kilowatts)	Utility	Commercial Operation
Alabama	Decatur	Browns Ferry Unit 1	1,067,000	Tennessee Valley Authority	1974
	Decatur	Browns Ferry Unit 2	1,067,000	Tennessee Valley Authority	1975
	Decatur	Browns Ferry Unit 3	1,067,000	Tennessee Valley Authority	1976
	Dothan	Joseph M. Farley Unit 1	829,000	Alabama Power Co.	1976
	Dothan	Joseph M. Farley Unit 2	829,000	Alabama Power Co.	1977
Arkansas	Russellville	Arkansas Unit 1	850,000	Ark. Power & Light Co.	1974
	Russellville	Arkansas Unit 2	912,000	Ark. Power & Light Co.	1978
California	Eureka	Humboldt Bay Unit 3	65,000	Pacific Gas & Electric Co.	1963
	San Clemente	San Onofre Unit 1	430,000	So. Calif. Ed. & San Diego Gas & El. Co.	1968
	Diabolo Canyon	Diabolo Canyon Unit 1	1,084,000	Pacific Gas & Electric Co.	1976
	Diabolo Canyon	Diabolo Canyon Unit 2	1,106,000	Pacific Gas & Electric Co.	1977
	Clay Station	Rancho Seco Station	913,000	Sacramento Munic. Utility District	1975
Colorado	Platteville	Ft. St. Vrain Station	330,000	Public Service Co. of Colorado	1976
Connecticut	Haddam Neck	Haddam Neck	575,000	Conn. Yankee Atomic Power Co.	1968
	Waterford	Millstone Unit 1	652,100	Northeast Nuclear Energy Co.	1971
	Waterford	Millstone Unit 2	828,000	Northeast Nuclear Energy Co.	1975
Florida	Florida City	Turkey Point Unit 3	666,000	Fla. Power & Light Co.	1972
	Florida City	Turkey Point Unit 4	666,000	Fla. Power & Light Co.	1973
	Red Level	Crystal River Unit 3	825,000	Florida Power Corp.	1976
	Ft. Pierce	St. Lucie Unit 1	810,000	Fla. Power & Light Co.	1976
Georgia	Baxley	Edwin I. Hatch Unit 1	786,000	Georgia Power Co.	1975
Illinois	Morris	Dresden Unit 1	200,000	Commonwealth Edison Co.	1960
	Morris	Dresden Unit 2	809,000	Commonwealth Edison Co.	1970
	Morris	Dresden Unit 3	809,000	Commonwealth Edison Co.	1971
	Zion	Zion Unit 1	1,050,000	Commonwealth Edison Co.	1973
	Zion	Zion Unit 2	1,050,000	Commonwealth Edison Co.	1974
	Cordova	Quad-Cities Unit 1	800,000	Comm. Ed. Co.-Ia.-Ill. Gas & Elec. Co.	1972
	Cordova	Quad-Cities Unit 2	800,000	Comm. Ed. Co.-Ia.-Ill. Gas & Elec. Co.	1972
	Seneca	LaSalle County Unit 1	1,078,000	Commonwealth Edison Co.	1978
Iowa	Palo	Duane Arnold Unit 1	535,000	Iowa Electric Light and Power Co.	1975
Maine	Wiscasset	Maine Yankee	790,000	Me. Yankee Atomic Power Co.	1972
Maryland	Lusby	Calvert Cliffs Unit 1	845,000	Baltimore Gas & Electric Co.	1975
	Lusby	Calvert Cliffs Unit 2	845,000	Baltimore Gas & Electric Co.	1977
Massachusetts	Rowe	Yankee Station	175,000	Yankee Atomic Electric Co.	1961
	Plymouth	Pilgrim Unit 1	670,000	Boston Edison Co.	1972
Michigan	Big Rock Point	Big Rock Point	75,000	Consumers Power Co.	1965
	South Haven	Palisades Station	700,000	Consumers Power Co.	1971
	Bridgman	Donald C. Cook Unit 1	1,060,000	Ind. & Michigan Electric Co.	1975
	Bridgman	Donald C. Cook Unit 2	1,060,000	Ind. & Michigan Electric Co.	1978
Minnesota	Monticello	Monticello	545,000	Northern States Power Co.	1971
	Red Wing	Prairie Island Unit 1	530,000	Northern States Power Co.	1973
	Red Wing	Prairie Island Unit 2	530,000	Northern States Power Co.	1974
Nebraska	Fort Calhoun	Ft. Calhoun Unit 1	457,400	Omaha Public Power District	1973
	Brownville	Cooper Station	778,000	Neb. Pub. Power Dist.-Ia. Power & Light Co.	1974
New Jersey	Forked River	Oyster Creek Unit 1	640,000	Jersey Central Power & Light Co.	1969
	Salem	Salem Unit 1	1,090,000	Public Service Electric & Gas Co.	1976
New York	Indian Point	Indian Point Unit 1	265,000	Consolidated Edison Co.	1962
	Indian Point	Indian Point Unit 2	873,000	Consolidated Edison Co.	1973
	Indian Point	Indian Point Unit 3	965,000	Power Authority of State of N.Y.	1975
	Scriba	Nine Mile Point Unit 1	610,000	Niagara Mohawk Power Co.	1969
	Ontario	R.E. Ginna Unit 1	490,000	Rochester Gas & Electric Co.	1970
	Brookhaven	Shoreham Station	819,000	Long Island Lighting Co.	1978
	Scriba	James A. FitzPatrick	821,000	Power Authority of State of N.Y.	1975
North Carolina	Southport	Brunswick Steam Unit 1	821,000	Carolina Power & Light Co.	1977
	Southport	Brunswick Steam Unit 2	821,000	Carolina Power & Light Co.	1975
	Cowans Ford Dam	Wm. B. McGuire Unit 1	1,180,000	Duke Power Co.	1978
Ohio	Oak Harbor	Davis-Besse Unit 1	906,000	Toledo Edison-Cleveland El. Illum. Co.	1976
Oregon	Prescott	Trojan Unit 1	1,130,000	Portland Gen. Electric Co.	1976
Pennsylvania	Peach Bottom	Peach Bottom Unit 2	1,065,000	Philadelphia Electric Co.	1974
	Peach Bottom	Peach Bottom Unit 3	1,065,000	Philadelphia Electric Co.	1974
	Shippingport	Shippingport Station	90,000	U.S. Energy Research & Devel. Admin.	1957
	Shippingport	Beaver Valley Unit 1	852,000	Duquesne Light Co.-Ohio Edison Co.	1976
	Goldsboro	Three Mile Island Unit 1	819,000	Metropolitan Edison Co.	1974
	Goldsboro	Three Mile Island Unit 2	906,000	Jersey Central Power & Light Co.	1978
South Carolina	Hartsville	H. B. Robinson Unit 2	700,000	Carolina Power & Light Co.	1971
	Seneca	Oconee Unit 1	871,000	Duke Power Co.	1973
	Seneca	Oconee Unit 2	871,000	Duke Power Co.	1974
	Seneca	Oconee Unit 3	871,000	Duke Power Co.	1974
Tennessee	Daisy	Sequoyah Unit 1	1,148,000	Tennessee Valley Authority	1978
Vermont	Vernon	Vermont Yankee Station	513,900	Vt. Yankee Nuclear Power Corp.	1972
Virginia	Gravel Neck	Surry Unit 1	788,000	Va. Electric & Power Co.	1972
	Gravel Neck	Surry Unit 2	788,000	Va. Electric & Power Co.	1973
	Mineral	North Anna Unit 1	898,000	Va. Electric & Power Co.	1977
	Mineral	North Anna Unit 2	898,000	Va. Electric & Power Co.	1977
Washington	Richland	N-Reactor/WPPSS Steam	850,000	U.S. Energy Research & Devel. Admin.	1966
Wisconsin	Genoa	Genoa Station	50,000	Dairyland Power Cooperative	1971
	Two Creeks	Point Beach Unit 1	497,000	Wis. Mich. Power Co.	1970
	Two Creeks	Point Beach Unit 2	497,000	Wis. Mich. Power Co.	1972
	Carlton	Kewaunee Unit 1	541,000	Wis. Public Service Corp.	1974

Nuclear plant capacity (kilowatts): operable 41,257,400; being built 97,421,200; planned 98,294,000; total 236,972,600.

World Nuclear Power
Source: Federal Energy Administration

Country	Operational reactors	Capacity[1]	Generation[2] April 1976	Country	Operational reactors	Capacity[1]	Generation[2] April 1976
Canada	5	2,380	1.34	Japan	12	6,600	2.88
France	10	3,070	1.50	Spain	3	1,120	0.46
Germany, West	7	3,450	1.93	Sweden	5	3,310	1.64
Great Britain	29	6,140	2.66[3]	Switzerland	3	1,050	0.74
India	3	620	0.21	United States	55	39,370	11.58
Italy	3	620	0.19	Total	135	67,730	25.13

[1]Megawatts. [2]Billion kilowatt-hours. [3]Four-week operating period.

Gasoline Economy, Comparative Miles per Gallon

New 1977 model cars averaged 6% better fuel economy than 1976 cars and 34% better than 1974 cars, accordcording to tests by the U. S. Environmental Protection Agency. Average for all cars tested was 18.6 miles per gallon.

Cars were tested on a dynamometer, simulating varied driving conditions for both city (at average 20 miles per hour) and highway (49 m.p.h.). The tests showed that substantial reductions in exhaust emissions accompanied the improved economy, the EPA reported.

Make & Model	Cu. In. Displcmt.	Cylinders	City mpg	Hwy mpg	Make & Model	Cu. In. Displcmt.	Cylinders	City mpg	Hwy mpg	Make & Model	Cu.In. Displcmt.	Cylinders	City mpg	Hwy mpg
AMC Gremlin	258	6	17	26	Datsun B-210, F-10	85	4	29	41	Oldsmobile Cutlass	403	8	15	21
AMC Gremlin	232	6	20	27	Dodge Celeste, Colt	98	4	26	35	Oldsmobile Delta 88	231	6	17	25
AMC Pacer	232	6	18	23	Dodge Aspen	225	6	20	29	Oldsmobile Delta 88	403	8	15	21
AMC Hornet	232	6	18	23	Dodge Aspen	360	8	14	19	Oldsmobile 98	403	8	15	21
AMC Matador	304	8	13	17	Dodge Charger	360	8	14	20	Oldsmobile Omega	225	6	16	21
Audi Fox	97	4	24	36	Dodge Monaco	440	8	9	17	Oldsmobile Starfire	140	4	21	28
Audi 100	114	4	18	27	Dodge Monaco	225	6	17	22	Oldsmobile Toronado	403	8	13	19
Buick Opel	111	4	23	36	Dodge Monaco	400	8	11	19	Plym. Arrow	98	4	26	39
Buick Skylark	231	6	18	25	Dodge Monaco	440	8	9	17	Plym. Cricket	98	4	28	42
Buick Apollo, Skylark	301	8	17	23	Ford Pinto	140	4	23	32	Plym. Volare	225	6	20	29
Buick Skyhawk	231	6	18	29	Ford Pinto	171	6	18	23	Plym. Volare	360	8	11	17
Buick Century, Regl	231	6	17	25	Ford Mustang II	140	4	23	33	Plymouth Fury	225	6	17	22
Buick Century, Regl	350	8	15	22	Ford Mustang II	171	6	20	27	Plymouth Fury	318	8	14	23
Buick LeSabre	350	8	16	22	Ford Mustang II	302	8	16	21	Plymouth Fury	400	8	11	19
Chevrolet Vega, Monza	140	4	24	33	Ford Maverick	250	6	21	28	Plymouth Fury	440	8	9	17
Cadillac Seville	350	8	14	19	Ford Maverick	302	8	17	22	Pontiac Astre, Sunbird	151	4	26	37
Cadillac Eldorado	425	8	11	18	Ford Granada	250	6	18	23	Pontiac Firebird	231	6	17	25
Chevrolet Vega, Monza	140	4	24	33	Ford Granada	302	8	16	22	Pontiac Firebird	400	8	12	19
Chevrolet Chevette	98	4	31	43	Ford	351	8	13	19	Pontiac Ventura	151	4	22	34
Chevrolet Monza	305	8	16	22	Ford	460	8	11	16	Pontiac Ventura	305	8	16	22
Chevrolet Nova	250	6	19	27	Lincoln Contntl	400	8	13	18	Pontiac Grand Prix	301	8	16	23
Chevrolet Nova	350	8	15	20	Mercury Bobcat	171	6	18	23	Pontiac Grand Prix	400	8	14	21
Chevrolet Camaro	250	6	18	25	Mazda 808	78	4	35	42	Pontiac LeMans	225	6	16	26
Chev. Malibu Wgn	350	8	13	17	Mercury Bobcat	140	4	26	37	Pontiac LeMans	400	8	14	21
Chevrolet Monte Carlo	305	8	16	20	Mercury Bobcat	171	6	18	23	Porsche 2-Seater 924	121	4	17	31
Chevrolet Malibu	350	8	14	19	Mercury Comet	200	6	21	28	Subaru	97	4	28	41
Chev. Malibu Wgn	350	8	13	17	Mercury Comet	302	8	17	22	Toyota Corolla	71	4	36	49
Chevrolet	305	8	16	21	Mercury Monarch	200	6	21	28	Toyota Corolla	97	4	25	31
Chevrolet	350	8	15	20	Merucry Monarch	351	8	16	24	Toyota Corona	134	4	21	35
Chevrolet Corvette	350	8	15	20	Merc. Cougar XR-7	302	8	15	19	Toyota Celica	133	4	22	29
Chrysler Cordoba	360	8	14	20	Merc. Cougar XR-7	400	8	13	18	Volkswgn Diesl Rabt	90	4	39	52
Datsun 2-Seater 280Z	168	6	18	27	Oldsmobile Omega	231	6	16	27	Volkswgn Diesl Dashr	90	4	35	47
Chrysler	360	8	12	18	Oldsmobile Omega	305	8	16	21	Volkswgn Rabt, Scirocco	97	4	29	43
Chrysler	440	8	10	16	Oldsmobile Cutlass	231	6	17	26	Volkswgn Beetle	97	4	23	33
Datsun 2-Seater 280Z	168	6	18	27	Oldsmobile Cutlass	260	8	16	21					

U.S. Petroleum and Natural Gas Production

Source: Bureau of Mines

Year	Crude oil Production 1,000 bbls.	Value $1,000	Natural gas liquids Production 1,000 bbls.	Value $1,000	Total 1,000 bbls.	Natural gas Marketed Mil. Cu. ft.	Value $1,000
1945	1,713,655	2,094,250	112,004	187,564	1,828,539	3,944,021	191,006
1950	1,973,574	4,963,380	181,961	419,605	2,155,693	6,282,060	408,521
1955	2,484,428	6,870,380	281,371	619,006	2,766,325	9,405,351	978,357
1960	2,574,933	7,420,181	340,157	808,385	2,915,365	12,771,038	1,789,970
1965	2,848,514	8,158,298	441,556	911,603	3,290,083	16,042,753	2,494,542
1970	3,517,450	11,173,726	605,916	1,275,112	4,123,366	21,920,642	3,745,680
1971	3,453,914	11,692,998	617,815	1,386,054	4,071,729	22,493,012	4,085,482
1972	3,455,368	11,706,510	638,216	1,452,233	4,093,584	22,531,698	4,180,462
1973	3,360,903	13,057,905	634,423	1,857,073	3,995,326	22,647,549	4,894,072
1974	3,202,585	21,580,549	616,098	3,087,927	3,818,683	21,600,522	6,573,402
1975	3,056,779	23,116,059	595,958	2,772,588	3,652,737	20,108,661	8,945,062

U. S. Crude Petroleum Production by Chief States

Source: Bureau of Mines (Figures in thousands of 42-gallon barrels)

Year	Ark.	Cal.	Ill.	Kans.	La.	Miss.	N.M.	N.D.	Okla.	Tex.	Wyo.
1950	31,108	327,607	62,028	107,586	208,965	38,236	47,367	....	164,599	829,874	61,631
1960	30,117	305,352	77,341	113,453	400,832	51,673	107,380	21,992	192,913	927,479	133,910
1965	25,930	316,428	63,708	104,733	594,853	56,183	119,166	26,350	203,441	1,000,749	138,314
1970	18,035	372,191	43,747	84,853	906,907	65,119	128,184	21,998	223,574	1,249,697	160,345
1972	18,519	347,022	34,874	73,744	891,827	61,100	110,525	20,624	207,633	1,301,685	140,011
1973	18,016	336,075	30,669	66,227	831,524	56,102	100,986	20,235	191,204	1,294,671	141,914
1974	16,527	323,003	27,553	61,691	737,324	50,779	98,695	19,697	177,785	1,262,126	139,997
1975	16,133	322,199	26,067	59,106	650,840	46,614	95,063	20,452	163,123	1,221,929	135,943

World Production of Crude Petroleum[1]

Source: Bureau of Mines
(thousands of 42-gallon barrels)

Country	1974	1975	Percent of change	Country	1974	1975	Percent of change
North America:				**Africa:**			
Canada	616,532	518,878	−15.8	Algeria	368,139	350,753	−4.7
Mexico[1]	238,271	294,190	+23.5	Angola	61,392	57,943	−5.6
United States[1] .	3,202,585	3,052,048	−4.7	Congo[2]	22,434	12,410	−44.7
Cuba (E)	775	775		Egypt[2]	53,715	81,069	+50.9
Total	**4,058,163**	**3,865,891**	**−4.7**	Gabon	73,548	81,948	+11.4
South America:				Libya	555,291	551,150	−0.8
Argentina	151,110	144,364	−4.5	Morocco	191	171	−10.5
Barbados	48	123	+156.3	Nigeria	823,347	651,890	−20.8
Bolivia	16,603	14,732	−11.3	Tunisia	31,841	34,567	+8.6
Brazil	64,751	62,766	−3.1	Zaire	51	—	
Chile	10,055	8,946	−11.0	**Total . . . . .**	**1,989,898**	**1,821,952**	**−8.4**
Colombia	60,867	57,685	−5.2	**Asiatic Area:**			
Ecuador	63,678	58,753	−7.7	Australia	140,396	149,873	+6.8
Peru	28,069	26,384	−6.0	Brunei	70,338	65,932	−6.3
Trinidad	68,131	78,613	+15.4	Burma	7,581	6,700	−11.6
Venezuela	1,086,332	856,364	−21.2	India	55,733	61,611	+10.6
Total	**1,549,644**	**1,308,730**	**−15.6**	Indonesia	501,838	477,055	−4.9
Western Europe:				Japan	4,936	4,378	−11.3
Austria	15,609	14,205	−9.0	Malaysia	29,537	35,774	+21.1
Denmark	689	1,327	+92.6	New Zealand[1] .	1,385	1,423	+2.7
France	7,863	7,460	−5.1	Pakistan	2,923	2,190	−25.1
Germany, West	44,718	40,900	−8.5	Taiwan	1,321	1,351	+2.3
Italy	6,956	6,743	−3.1	Thailand (E) . .	42	42	0.0
Netherlands . .	10,227	9,676	−5.4	**Total . . . . .**	**816,030**	**806,329**	**−1.2**
Norway	12,707	68,900	+442.2	**East Europe and Peoples'**			
Spain	14,334	14,822	+3.4	**Rep. of China:**			
United Kingdom	3,289	8,000	+143.2	Albania	15,045	15,012	−0.2
Yugoslavia . . .	25,613	27,347	+6.8	Bulgaria	1,095	913	−16.6
Total	**142,005**	**199,380**	**+40.4**	Czech	1,085	1,017	−6.3
Middle East:				Germany,			
Bahrain	24,597	20,805	−15.4	East (E)	2,500	2,500	0.0
Iran	2,197,901	1,952,650	−11.2	Hungary	15,237	15,306	+0.5
Iraq	720,729	808,840	+12.2	Peoples' Rep. of			
Israel[2] (E)	36,500	27,345	−25.1	China	474,500	571,590	+20.5
Kuwait	830,580	670,918	−19.2	Poland (E)	4,080	4,200	+2.9
Neutral Zone . .	198,195	181,040	−8.7	Romania	107,964	108,739	+0.7
Oman	106,046	124,600	+17.5	U.S.S.R.[1]	3,373,650	3,608,850	+7.0
Qatar	189,348	159,482	−15.8	**Total . . . . .**	**3,995,156**	**4,328,127**	**+8.3**
Saudi Arabia . .	2,996,543	2,491,855	−16.8	**Total World.**	**20,537,727**	**19,473,903**	**−5.2**
Syria	45,352	65,930	+45.4				
Turkey	24,555	21,719	−11.6				
United Arab Emirates	616,485	618,310	+0.3				
Total	**7,986,831**	**7,143,494**	**−10.6**				

(E) Estimate.
[1] Crude oil and field condensate. [2] Israeli production from Sinai peninsula oilfields included with Israel rather than Egypt.

U.S. Motor Fuel Supply[1] and Demand

Source: Bureau of Mines (Figures in thousands of 42-gallon barrels)

Year	Supply Production	Supply Daily average	Demand Domestic	Demand Export	Year	Supply Production	Supply Daily average	Demand Domestic	Demand Export
1945	793,431	2,174	696,333	88,059	1970	2,135,838	5,852	2,162,642	2,956
1950	1,024,481	2,806	994,290	24,721	1971 (rev.) .	2,231,157	6,113	2,242,921	3,104
1955	1,373,950	3,764	1,329,788	34,521	1972	2,352,310	6,427	2,382,569	2,165
1960*	1,522,479	4,160	1,511,670	13,456	1973	2,434,943	6,671	2,484,262	3,318
1965	1,733,258	4,749	1,750,028	6,391	1974	2,371,004	6,496	2,434,368	2,313
1969	2,057,041	5,636	2,072,144	4,468	1975	2,420,962	6,633	2,477,812	2,071

*Beginning with 1960 Alaska and Hawaii are included. (1.) Includes special naptha.

U. S. Total Fuel Supply and Demand[1]

In thousands of 42-gallon barrels. *Includes special naphtha production. †Includes kerosene type jet fuel.

Year	Gasoline* Production	Gasoline* Total Demand	Kerosene† Production	Kerosene† Total Demand	Distillate fuel oil Production	Distillate fuel oil Total Demand	Residual fuel oil Production	Residual fuel oil Total Demand
1950[2]	1,024,181	1,019,011	118,512	119,922	398,912	75,435	425,217	570,021
1960	1,522,497	1,525,126	136,842	133,188	667,050	695,165	332,147	577,934
1965	1,733,258	1,756,419	201,788	219,932	765,430	779,644	268,567	601,893
1970	2,135,838	2,165,598	313,544	358,146	897,097	928,109	257,510	824,073
1971	2,231,157	2,246,025	306,847	365,308	912,097	974,077	274,684	851,262
1972	2,352,310	2,384,734	313,554	379,984	963,625	1,067,321	292,519	937,707
1973	2,434,943	2,487,580	327,818	384,063	1,030,178	1,127,548	354,597	1,029,165
1974	2,371,004	2,436,681	290,780	346,706	974,025	1,076,771	390,491	968,185
1975[3]	2,420,962	2,479,883	308,034	347,399	968,650	1,040,108	450,957	893,305

(1) Demand usually exceeds the production; the difference is made up by dipping into stocks or by imports. (2) 1950 figures are on a 48-state basis. (3) Preliminary.

U.S. Petroleum and Natural Gas Resources

(onshore and offshore to water depth of 200 meters)
Source: U. S. Geological Survey
Crude Oil — billions of barrels

Area	Cumulative[1] Production	Demonstrated Resources Measured	Demonstrated Resources Indicated	Inferred[2] Reserves	Undiscovered Recoverable Resources Statistical Mean	Undiscovered Recoverable Resources Estimated Range[3] (95%-5%)
Alaska onshore	0.154	9.944	0.013	6.1	12	6- 19
48 states onshore	99.892	21.086	4.315	14.3	44	29- 64
Total onshore	100.046	31.030	4.328	20.4	56	37- 81
Alaska offshore	0.456	0.150	—[4]	0.1	15	3- 31
Pacific offshore	1.499	0.858	0.258	0.2	3	2- 5
Gulf of Mexico	4.135	2.212	0.050	2.4	5	3- 8
Atlantic offshore	0.000	0.000	0.000	0.0	3	2- 4[5]
Total offshore	6.090	3.220	0.308	2.7	26	10- 49
Total U.S.	106.136	34.250	4.636	23.1	82	50-127
Subeconomic[6]				120 — 140		44-111

Natural Gas — trillion cubic feet

Area	Cumulative[1] Production	Measured Reserves	Inferred[2] Reserves	Undiscovered Recoverable Reserves Statistical Mean	Undiscovered Recoverable Reserves Estimated Range[3] (95%-5%)
Alaska onshore	0.482	31.722	14.7	32	16- 57
48 states onshore	446.366	169.454	119.4	345	246-453
Total onshore	446.848	201.176	134.1	377	264-506
Alaska offshore	0.423	0.145	0.1	44	8- 80
Pacific offshore	1.415	0.463	0.4	3	2- 6
Gulf of Mexico	32.138	35.348	67.0	50	18- 91
Atlantic offshore	0.000	0.000	0.0	10	5- 14[6]
Total offshore	33.976	35.956	67.5	107	42-181
Total U.S.	480.824	237.132	201.6	484	322-655
Subeconomic[6]		90 — 115			40- 82

[1] To Dec. 31, 1974. [2] Based on historical data. [3] The low value of the range is associated with a 95% probability that there is at least this amount; the high value has a 5% probability that there is at least this amount. [4] Less than one million barrels. [5] Based on 75%-25% probability. [6] Recoverable with improved technology or higher prices.

U.S. Fuel Consumption—Past, Present, Future

Source: Joint Congressional Committee on Atomic Energy report, Understanding the "National Energy Dilemma," published by The Center for Strategic and International Studies, 1973.
(millions of barrels per day of oil equivalent[1])

Energy Source and Use....	1950	1960	1970	1980[2]
Natural Gas	2.9	5.9	10.7	12.2
(imported)	—	(0.1)	(0.4)	(1.9)
(from coal and oil gassification)	—	—	—	(0.3)
Electricity generation	0.3	0.8	1.9	1.6
Residential and commercial	0.8	2.0	3.5	5.0
Industrial	1.6	2.8	4.6	4.7
Transportation	0.1	0.2	0.3	0.4
Non-energy	0.2	0.2	0.3	0.5
Coal	6.5	5.3	7.4	10.5
Electricity generation	1.1	2.0	3.7	5.2
Residential and commercial	1.4	0.5	0.2	0.1
Industrial	2.8	2.3	2.5	3.5
Transportation	0.8	0.1	—	—
Non-energy	0.1	0.1	0.1	0.1
Exports	0.4	0.5	0.9	1.4
Gassification	—	—	—	0.2
Oil	6.5	9.7	13.9	21.5
(Imported)	(0.9)	(1.9)	(3.5)	(10.0)
Electricity generation	0.3	0.3	1.0	2.0
Residential and commercial	1.2	2.0	2.5	2.0
Industrial	1.0	1.3	1.6	2.7
Transportation	3.2	5.0	7.4	11.5
Non-energy	0.4	0.8	1.5	3.1
Exports	0.3	0.2	—	—
Gassification	—	—	—	0.2
Nuclear	—	—	0.1	3.6
Geothermal	—	—	0.003	0.2
Hydroelectric	0.2	0.3	0.4	0.6
TOTAL INPUT	16.1	21.3	32.5	48.3[3]

	1950	1960	1970	1980
Electricity generation				
Input (from above sources)	1.9	3.4	7.1	13.2
Residential and commercial	0.2	0.5	1.3	2.7
Industrial	0.2	0.7	1.2	2.0
Transportation	—	—	0.007	0.5
Conversion losses	1.4	2.3	4.6	8.1
End Use and Loss				
Residential and commercial	3.6	5.0	7.5	9.9
Used	2.7	3.5	5.6	7.3
Lost	0.9	1.5	1.9	2.6
Industrial	5.6	7.1	9.9	13.0
Used	4.2	4.9	7.4	9.6
Lost	1.4	2.1	2.4	3.4
Transportation	4.1	5.3	7.7	12.0
Used	1.0	1.2	1.9	3.0
Lost	3.1	4.0	5.8	9.0
Total Used Energy	7.9	9.6	15.0	19.9
Total lost[4]	6.8	9.9	14.7	23.3
Exports	0.7	0.7	0.9	1.4
Non-energy	0.7	1.1	1.9	3.7
TOTAL OUTPUT	16.1	21.3	32.5	48.3·

[1] All energy sources have been converted to barrels of oil equivalent (B/DOE) by determining their heat value and converting that Btu figure to barrels of oil, viz.: 5,800,000 Btu = one barrel of crude oil; 3,412 Btu = one kilowatt-hour; 1,000 Btu = 1 cu. ft. of natural gas; 26,000,000 Btu = one ton of coal. Figures may not add to totals due to rounding while converting to B/DOE.
[2] "There are many reasons for the high degree of confidence in the predictability of 1980 . . . The Nation has already ordered a large part of the electrical capacity that can be functioning commercially by the year 1980; it has already ordered every major rail-based mass transit system that can be functioning by 1980 . . ." etc.
[3] Corrected for coal and oil gassification.
[4] Including conversion loss in electricity generation and in coal and oil gassification.

Measuring Energy

Source: House Subcommittee on Energy

The following tables of equivalents contain those figures commonly used to compare different types of energy sources and their various measurements.

Btu - a British thermal unit — the amount of heat required to raise one pound of water one degree Fahrenheit. Equivalent to 1,055 joules or about 252 gram calories. A **therm** is usually 100,000 Btu but is sometimes used to refer to other units.

Calorie - the amount of heat required to raise one gram of water one degree centigrade; abbreviated cal.; equivalent to about .003968 Btu. More common is the kilogram calorie, also called a **kilocalorie** and abbreviated **Cal.** or **Kcal**; equivalent to about 3.97 Btu. (One Kcal is equivalent to one food calorie.)

Btu Values of Energy Sources

(These are conventional or average values, not precise equivalents.)

Coal (per 2,000 lb. ton):
Anthracite	= 25.4 x 10^6 Btu
Bituminous	= 26.2 x10^6
Sub-bituminous	= 19.0 x 10^6
Lignite	= 13.4 x 10^6

Average heating value of coal used to generate electricity in 1969 was 27.7 x 10^6 Btu.

Natural Gas (per cubic foot):
Dry	= 1,031 Btu
Wet	= 1,103
Liquid (avg.)	= 4,100

Electricity— 1 kwh = 3,413 Btu.

Petroleum (per barrel)
Crude Oil	= 5.60 x 10^6 Btu
Residual fuel oil	= 6.29 x 10^6
Distillate fuel oil	= 5.83 x 10^6
Gasoline (including av gas)	= 5.25 x 10^6
Jet fuel (kerosene)	= 5.67 x 10^6
Jet fuel (naphtha)	= 5.36 x 10^6
Kerosene	= 5.67 x 10^6

Nuclear
1 gram of fissioned U-235 — 74,000,000 Btu

The Btu. and cal., being small amounts of energy, are usually expressed as follows when large numbers are involved.
1 x 10^3 Btu	=	1,000
1 x 10^6 Btu	=	1,000,000
1 x 10^9 Btu	=	1,000,000,000
1 x 10^{12} Btu	=	1 trillion
1 x 10^{15} Btu	=	1 quadrillion
1 x 10^{18} Btu	=	1 quintillion or 1 Q unit
One Q unit	=	38.46 billion tons of coal
	=	172.4 billion barrels of oil
	=	968.9 trillion cubic ft. of natural gas

Other Conversion Factors

Electricity— 1 kwh =
	=	0.88 lbs. of coal
	=	0.076 gallon of oil
	=	10.4 cu. ft. of natural gas

Natural Gas— 1 tcf (trillion cubic feet) =
	=	39.3x10^6 tons of coal
	=	184x10^6 barrels of oil

Coal— 1 mtce (million tons of coal equivalent =
	=	4.48 x 10^6 barrels of oil
	=	67 tons of oil
	=	25.19 x 10^{12} cu. ft. of natural gas

Oil— 1 million tons (6.65x10^6 barrels) =
	=	4x10^9 kwh of electricity (when used to generate power)
	=	12x10^9 kwh unconverted
	=	1.5 x 10^6 tons of coal
	=	41.2x10^9 cu. ft. of natural gas

Approximate Conversion Factors For Oils

To convert	Barrels to Metric tons	Metric tons to barries	Barrels/ days to tons/year	Tons/year to barrels/day
		Multiply by —		
Crude oil [1]..	0.136	7.33	49.8	0.0201
Gasoline . .	.118	8.45	43.2	.0232
Kerosene...	.128	7.80	46.8	.0214
Diesel fuel. .	.133	7.50	48.7	.0205
Fuel oil	.149	6.70	54.5	.0184

[1] Based on world average gravity (excluding natural gas liquids).

Coal and Coke Production in the U. S.

Source: Bureau of Mines

Year	Penn. Anthracite Production 1,000 net tons	Value $1,000	Bituminous Production 1,000 net tons	Value $1,000	Year	Penn. Anthracite Production 1,000 net tons	Value $1,000	Bituminous Production 1,000 net tons	Value $1,000
1945	54,934	323,944	577,617	1,768,204	1970	9,729	105,341	602,932	3,772,662
1950	44,077	392,398	516,311	2,500,374	1972	7,106	85,251	595,386	4,561,983
1955	26,205	206,097	464,633	2,092,383	1973	6,830	90,260	591,738	5,049,612
1960	18,817	147,116	415,512	1,950,421	1974	6,617	144,695	603,406	9,502,347
1965	14,866	122,021	512,088	2,276,022	1975 est. . . .	6,200	155,000	637,000	11,946,700

Coal Production (1,000 net tons—value in $1,000)—(1968) 63,653, $1,157,359; (1969) 64,757, $1,355,260; (1970) 66,525, $1,849,160; (1971) 57,436, $1,745,693; (1972) 60,507, $2,012,486; (1973) 64,325, $2,442,151; (1974) 61,581, $4,510,150.

Coke Exports (short tons)—(1968) 791,909; (1969) 1,629,000; (1970) 2,478,338; (1971) 1,508,639; (1972) 1,231,633; (1973) 1,394,980; (1974) 1,277,681; (1975) 1,272,906. **Imports**—(1968) 94,085; (1969) 173,052; (1970) 152,879; (1971) 173,914; (1972) 185,023; (1973) 1,077,737; (1974) 3,540,326.

Anthracite exports (net tons)—(1966) 766,025; (1967) 594,797; (1968) 518,159; (1969) 627,492; (1970) 789,499; (1971) 671,024; (1972) 743,451; (1973) 716,546; (1974) 735,173; (1975) 639,601.

Production of Electricity in the U.S. by Source

Source: Federal Power Commission

Amounts include both privately-owned and publicly-owned utilities.

Calendar Year	Net Production Mln. Kwh.	Percentage Coal	Oil	Gas	Produced by Source Nuclear	Hydro	Other[1]	Fuel Consumption Coal 1,000 Sht. Tns.	Oil 1,000 Bbls.	Gas Bln. Cu. Ft.
1972	1,747,323	44.0	15.4	21.6	3.0	15.5	0.3	351,043	493,929	3,978,672
1974	1,864,847	44.5	16.1	17.2	6.0	16.1	0.1	392,361	536,174	3,429,109
1975	1,908,784	44.6	15.1	15.7	8.7	15.7	0.2	404,674	506,371	3,143,295
1976[2]	655,673	46.8	16.2	12.5	8.8	15.5	0.2	145,348	185,365	849,872

(1) Includes electricity produced from geothermal, wood and waste. (2) Four months.

World's Largest Hydroelectric Generating Plants

Source: Bureau of Reclamation
UC—Under construction. NA—Not available. Year—Initial operation.

Name	Present Megawatts	Ultimate Megawatts	Year	Name	Present Megawatts	Ultimate Megawatts	Year
Itaipu, Brazil/Paraguay	—	12,600	U.C.	Chief Joseph, U.S.A.	1,024	2,069	1956
Grand Coulee, U.S.A.	2,161	9,780	1941	Salto Santiago, Brazil	—	2,000	U.C.
Paulo Afonso, Brazil	1,299	6,774	1955	Robert Moses-Niagara, U.S.A.	1,950	1,950	1961
Guri, Venezuela	524	6,500	1967	Salto Grando, Argentina	—	1,890	U.C.
Tucurui, Brazil.	—	6,480	U.C.	Dinorwic', Great Britain.	—	1,880	U.C.
Sayanskaya, U.S.S.R.	—	6,400	U.C.	Ludington', U.S.A.	1,872	1,872	1973
Krasnoyarsk, U.S.S.R.	6,096	6,096	1968	St. Lawrence Power Dam,			
La Grande, Canada	—	5,416	U.C.	U.S.A./ Canada	1,824	1,824	1958
Churchill Falls, Canada.	5,225	5,225	1971	The Dalles, U.S.A.	1,807	1,807	1957
Bratsk, U.S.S.R.	4,100	4,600	1964	Karakaya, Turkey	—	1,800	U.C.
Sukhovo, U.S.S.R.	—	4,500	U.C.	Mica, Canada	—	1,740	U.C.
Ust-Ipirnsk, U.S.S.R.	720	4,320	1974	Beauharnois, Canada.	1,021	1,670	1950
Irha Solteira, Brazil.	3,200	4,100	1973	Kemano, Canada.	813	1,670	1954
Cabora Bassa, Mozambique	2,000	4,000	1975	Blue Ridge', U.S.A.	—	1,600	U.C.
Inga, Zaire	350	3,700	U.C.	Patia, Colombia.	—	1,540	U.C.
Rogunsky, U.S.S.R.	—	3,600	U.C.	Racoon Mountain', U.S.A.	1,530	1,530	1975
Inga, Zaire	350	2,820	U.C.	Kariba, Rhodesia.	600	1,500	1959
John Day, U.S.A.	2,160	2,700	1968	Tumut-3, Australia.	750	1,500	1972
Nurek, U.S.S.R.	—	2,700	U.C.	Marimbondo, Brazil.	1,440	1,440	1975
Sao Simao, Brazil	—	2,680	U.C.	Jupia, Brazil.	1,411	1,411	1966
Volgograd-22nd Congress,				McNary, U.S.A.	980	1,406	1953
U.S.S.R.	2,560	2,560	1958	Cheboksary, U.S.S.R.	1,404	1,404	1972
Chicoasen, Mexico	—	2,400	U.C.	Agua Vermelha, Brazil.	—	1,380	U.C.
Volga-V.I. Lenin, U.S.S.R.	2,300	2,300	1955	Saratov, U.S.S.R.	1,360	1,360	1967
W.A.C. Bennett, Canada	1,816	2,270	1969	Daniel Johnson, Canada	650	1,353	1970
Foz Do Areia, Brazil.	—	2,250	U.C.	Hoover, U.S.A.	1,345	1,345	1936
High Aswan (Sadd-el-Aali),				Wanapum, U.S.A.	831	1,330	1964
Egypt.	2,100	2,100	1967	Inguri, U.S.S.R.	—	1,300	U.C.
Iron Gate, Romania/Yugoslavia	2,100	2,100	1970	Zeya, U.S.S.R.	300	1,290	1975
Bath County', U.S.A.	—	2,100	U.C.	Takase, Japan.	—	1,280	U.C.
Itumbiara, Brazil.	—	2,100	U.C.	Priest Rapids, U.S.A.	789	1,262	1959

(1) Pumped storage installation.

Non-Federal Hydroelectric Plants in U.S.

Capacities of 150,000 Kilowatts or More as of Jan. 1, 1976

Auxiliary and pumped storage units are not included in hydroelectric capacities.
Source: Federal Power Commission, Bureau of Power

Plant	State	Owner	Kilowatts
Robert Moses, (Niagara)	N. Y.	Power Authority State of N. Y.	1,953,900
Rocky Reach	Wash.	Chelan County Dist. No. 1.	1,213,100
Robert Moses, (Massena)	N. Y.	Power Authority State of N. Y.	912,000
Wanapum	Wash.	Grant County Dist. No. 2.	831,250
Priest Rapids	Wash.	Grant County Dist. No. 2.	788,500
Wells	Wash.	Douglas County PUD No. 1.	774,300
Boundary	Wash.	Seattle Dept. of Lighting.	551,000
Conowingo	Md.	Philadelphia Electric Co.	474,480
Hells Canyon	Ore.	Idaho Power Co.	391,500
Brownlee	Idaho	Idaho Power Co.	360,400
Ross	Wash.	Seattle Dept. of Lighting Co.	360,000
Edward Hyatt	Calif.	Calif. Dept. of Water Resources.	351,000
Cowans Ford	N. C.	Duke Power Co.	350,000
Upper Smith Mt.	Va.	Appalachian Power Co.	300,200
Mossyrock	Wash.	City of Tacoma.	300,000
New Colgate	Calif.	Yuba County Water Agency.	284,400
Noxon Rapids	Mont.	The Washington Water Power Co.	282,880
Round Butte	Ore.	Portland Gen. Elec. Co.	247,050
Safe Harbor	Pa.	Safe Harbor Water Power Corp.	226,500
Walter Bouldin	Ala.	Alabama Power Co.	225,000'
Rock Island	Wash.	Chelan Couhty Dist. No. 1.	212,100
Swift No. 1.	Wash.	Pacific Power and Light Co.	204,000
Cabinet Gorge	Idaho	The Washington Water Power Co.	200,000
Saluda	S. C.	So. Carolina Electric and Gas Co.	197,500
Oxbow	Oreg.	Idaho Power Co.	190,000
White Rock	Calif.	Sacramento Mun. Utility Dist.	190,000
Caribou No. 1 & 2.	Calif.	Pacific Gas and Electric Co.	184,800
Gaston	N. C.	Virginia Electric and Power Co.	177,920
Lay Dam	Ala.	Alabama Power Co.	177,000
Osage	Mo.	Union Electric Co. of Mo.	172,000
Kerr	Mont.	The Montana Power Co.	168,000
Lewis Smith	Ala.	Alabama Power Co.	157,500
James B. Black	Calif.	Pacific Gas and Electric Co.	154,800
Martin Dam	Ala.	Alabama Power Co.	154,200

'Units out of service Feb. 1975 in dam failure.

World Electricity Production

Source: United Nations Monthly Bulletin of Statistics, July, 1976

million kilowatt-hours

Country	1975 Production	Country	1975 Production	Country	1975 Production
United States	1,999,680	France	177,480	India²	79,920
USSR	1,038,000	Italy	144,792	Sweden	79,224
Japan'	460,704	China' (E).	112,000	Norway	77,580
West Germany	301,800	Poland	97,164	South Africa	75,612
Canada	272,652	East Germany	84,564	Australia	74,112
United Kingdom	272,232	Spain	82,380	Brazil'	70,476

(E) Estimate. (') 1974. (²) Excluding generation by industrial establishments.

MANUFACTURES AND MINERALS
General Statistics for Major Industry Groups
Source: Bureau of the Census

The estimates for 1973 in the following table are based upon reports from a representative sample of about 70,000 manufacturing establishments.

Industry	All Employees Number (1,000)	All Employees Payroll (Millions)	Production Workers Number (1,000)	Production Workers Man-hours (Millions)	Production Workers Wages (Millions)	Value added by mf'r adj. (Millions)
Food and kindred products	1,560	$13,670	1,081	2,158	$8,471	$39,693
Tobacco manufactures	69	557	59	111	440	2,900
Textile mill products	980	6,605	863	1,751	5,237	13,016
Apparel and other textile products	1,400	7,707	1,228	2,191	5,841	14,648
Lumber and wood products	722	5,471	628	1,214	4,311	12,357
Furniture and fixtures	479	3,532	404	790.5	2,561	6,736
Paper and allied products	645	6,482	509	1,056	4,695	15,166
Printing and publishing	1,084	10,523	649	1,203	5,830	21,871
Chemicals and allied products	852	9,440	535	1,075	5,149	36,239
Petroleum and coal products	137	1,716	96	194	1,110	7,740
Rubber and plastics products	672	5,812	532	1,042	4,080	13,440
Leather and leather products	268	1,595	235	434	1,230	2,962
Stone, clay, and glass products	644	6,079	511	1,028	4,457	13,801
Primary metal industries	1,222	14,148	996	2,028	10,873	28,614
Fabricated metal products	1,567	15,374	1,213	2,440	10,742	30,573
Machinery, except electrical	1,994	21,598	1,400	2,843	13,494	44,559
Electric, electronic equipment	1,797	17,151	1,278	2,505	10,190	34,984
Transportation equipment	1,836	22,572	1,341	2,732	14,834	45,685
Instruments and related products	485	4,801	316	614	2,490	12,224
Miscellaneous manufacturing industries	447	3,351	352	660	2,188	7,166
Administrative and auxiliary[1]	1,040	15,140	—	—	—	—
All industries total	**19,898**	**193,325**	**14,223**	**28,069**	**118,224**	**404,376**

(1) In addition to the employment and payroll for operating manufacturing establishments, manufacturing concerns reported separately for central administrative offices or auxiliary units (e.g., research laboratories, storage warehouses, power plants, garages, repair shops, etc.) which serve the manufacturing establishments of a company rather than the public.

Manufacturing Production Worker Statistics
Source: Bureau of Labor Statistics, U.S. Dept. of Labor (PPreliminary)

Year	All Employees	Production Workers	Payroll Index 1967=100	Avg. Weekly Earnings	Avg. Hourly Earnings	Avg. Hrs. Weekly
1955	16,882,000	13,288,000	61.1	75.70	1.86	40.7
1960	16,796,000	12,586,000	68.9	89.72	2.26	39.7
1965	18,062,000	13,434,000	88.1	107.53	2.61	41.2
1970	19,349,000	14,020,000	114.1	133.73	3.36	39.8
1971	18,572,000	13,467,000	116.7	142.44	3.57	39.9
1972	19,090,000	13,957,000	131.5	159.69	3.81	40.6
1973	20,068,000	14,760,000	149.2	166.06	4.08	40.7
1974	20,046,000	14,613,000	157.1	176.40	4.41	40.0
1975	18,347,000	13,070,000	151.0	189.51	4.81	39.4
1976/Jan.	18,495,000	13,243,000	161.7	200.30	5.02	39.9
Feb.	18,545,000	13,290,000	162.9	201.10	5.04	39.9
March	18,679,000	13,409,000	165.7	202.80	5.07	40.0
April	18,813,000	13,529,000	163.6	198.74	5.07	39.2
May	18,872,000	13,571,000	170.4	205.82	5.12	40.2
June (p)	19,103,000	13,764,000	174.5	208.06	5.15	40.4
July (p)	18,805,000	13,452,000	168.9	206.28	5.17	39.9

Hourly Earnings in Manufacturing Industries
Source: Bureau of Labor Statistics, U.S. Dept. of Labor (P Preliminary)

Year and month (annual average)	Manufacturing Gross	Manufacturing Excluding overtime	Durable goods Gross	Durable goods Excluding overtime	Nondurable goods Gross	Nondurable goods Excluding overtime
1950	$1.440	$1.39	$1.519	$1.46	$1.347	$1.31
1955	1.86	1.79	1.99	1.91	1.67	1.62
1960	2.26	2.20	2.43	2.36	2.05	1.99
1965	2.61	2.51	2.79	2.67	2.36	2.27
1970	3.36	3.24	3.55	3.43	3.08	2.97
1971	3.57	3.44	3.79	3.66	3.26	3.14
1972	3.81	3.66	4.06	3.89	3.47	3.33
1973	4.08	3.89	4.34	4.13	3.68	3.53
1974	4.41	4.24	4.69	4.50	3.99	3.84
1975	4.81	4.66	5.14	4.98	4.35	4.20
1976/Jan.	5.02	4.85	5.38	5.20	4.53	4.37
Feb.	5.04	4.86	5.40	5.21	4.54	4.38
March	5.07	4.88	5.43	5.24	4.56	4.39
April	5.07	4.92	5.41	5.26	4.59	4.44
May	5.12	4.93	5.49	5.28	4.59	4.42
June (p)	5.15	4.96	5.52	5.31	4.62	4.45
July (p)	5.17	4.98	5.52	5.32	4.68	4.51

General Manufacturing Statistics for States

Source: Bureau of the Census, Census of Manufacturers 1973 General Summary

Divisions, Regions, and States	All employees Number (1,000)	Payroll (millions)	Production workers Number (1,000)	Man-hrs. (millions)	Wages (millions)	Value added by mfr. (millions)	Value of shipments. (millions)	Capital expend. (millions)
New England Division.	1,411	$13,131	981	1,919	$7,464	$25,252	$46,052	$1,370
Maine.	100	731	83	160	534	1,567	3,257	112
New Hampshire.	93	736	70	134	453	1,462	2,643	102
Vermont.	38	343	27	53	196	688	1,360	43
Massachusetts.	639	6,028	436	846	3,366	11,718	21,337	669
Rhode Island.	122	977	95	180	620	1,924	3,629	89
Connecticut.	419	4,316	270	546	2,295	7,893	13,826	355
Middle Atlantic Division.	4,029	40,155	2,724	5,264	22,356	78,182	156,160	4,168
New York.	1,712	17,387	1,105	2,126	8,829	33,610	64,649	1,644
New Jersey.	852	8,604	560	1,089	4,662	17,754	35,925	955
Pennsylvania.	1,465	14,164	1,059	2,049	8,865	26,818	55,586	1,569
East North Central Division.	5,227	57,887	3,735	7,562	37,179	114,895	249,353	7,449
Ohio.	1,419	15,510	1,010	2,047	10,056	31,174	64,022	1,939
Indiana.	750	7,850	562	1,119	5,362	16,369	34,176	1,107
Illinois.	1,373	14,383	945	1,876	8,657	29,357	62,582	1,699
Michigan.	1,152	14,768	827	1,736	9,545	27,170	63,411	1,998
Wisconsin.	533	5,376	391	784	3,559	10,825	25,162	706
West North Central Division.	1,282	12,250	893	1,748	7,457	27,597	71,530	1,526
Minnesota.	324	3,203	208	401	1,749	6,704	15,279	331
Iowa.	232	2,377	169	335	1,560	5,647	16,157	327
Missouri.	452	4,284	313	611	2,563	9,121	21,481	436
North Dakota.	12	96	9	18	63	330	773	24
South Dakota.	20	159	15	28	106	420	1,275	32
Nebraska.	89	769	66	133	517	1,990	6,955	109
Kansas.	153	1,362	113	222	899	3,385	9,610	267
South Atlantic Division.	2,861	22,806	2,201	4,355	14,875	50,433	111,003	4,140
Delaware.	71	830	39	75	332	1,448	3,767	114
Maryland.	263	2,630	184	358	1,594	5,257	11,499	317
District of Columbia.	20	237	10	18	107	407	697	23
Virginia.	386	3,097	301	594	2,085	6,875	14,700	615
West Virginia.	128	1,241	98	191	845	2,884	5,609	231
North Carolina.	781	5,459	635	1,249	3,813	12,593	27,441	1,054
South Carolina.	366	2,627	299	606	1,885	5,853	12,472	596
Georgia.	484	3,635	382	761	2,464	8,619	21,092	670
Florida.	362	3,050	253	503	1,750	6,497	13,726	520
East South Central Division.	1,314	10,241	1,050	2,061	7,217	24,562	54,117	1,898
Kentucky.	277	2,457	217	423	1,707	6,471	14,332	504
Tennessee.	493	3,756	389	761	2,582	8,773	18,919	674
Alabama.	335	2,614	272	536	1,905	5,841	13,020	481
Mississippi.	209	1,414	172	341	1,023	3,477	7,846	239
West South Central Division.	1,324	11,464	966	1,907	7,165	28,283	70,122	2,724
Arkansas.	196	1,317	164	319	982	3,153	7,836	232
Louisiana.	184	1,706	138	280	1,152	4,845	12,968	704
Oklahoma.	157	1,375	104	200	754	2,597	6,336	254
Texas.	787	7,066	560	1,108	4,277	17,688	42,982	1,534
Mountain Division.	413	3,828	287	552	2,300	8,671	20,806	830
Montana.	22	195	17	34	146	515	1,794	66
Idaho.	45	385	35	66	268	976	2,345	75
Wyoming.	8	62	6	11	42	171	548	16
Colorado.	135	1,362	91	177	794	2,733	6,473	311
New Mexico.	26	183	19	35	111	416	1,061	59
Arizona.	104	1,003	68	133	551	2,398	4,940	219
Utah.	62	539	43	81	325	1,238	3,125	71
Nevada.	11	99	8	15	63	224	520	13
Pacific Division.	2,110	21,894	1,445	2,797	12,506	47,518	98,045	2,776
Washington.	245	2,626	172	320	1,584	5,734	13,524	446
Oregon.	192	1,863	150	298	1,321	4,284	9,067	333
California.	1,641	17,119	1,098	2,134	9,414	36,759	73,881	1,917
Alaska.	8	90	7	13	69	245	487	43
Hawaii.	24	196	18	32	118	496	1,086	37
Total.	19,971	193,656	14,282	28,165	118,519	405,393	877,188	26,881

Employees in Non-Agricultural Establishments

Source: Bureau of Labor Statistics, U.S. Dept. of Labor (P) Preliminary

Annual Average by Industry Division

(In thousands)

Year	Total	Mining	Contract construc-tion	Manu-factur-ing	Trans. and public utilities	Whole., retail trade	Finance, insur., real estate	Service, miscel-laneous	Govern-ment
1955.	50,675	792	2,802	16,882	4,141	10,535	2,335	6,274	6,914
1960.	54,234	712	2,885	16,796	4,004	11,391	2,669	7,423	8,353
1965.	60,815	632	3,186	18,062	4,036	12,716	3,023	9,087	10,074
1970.	70,920	623	3,536	—	4,504	15,040	3,687	11,621	12,561
1972.	73,714	625	3,831	19,090	4,517	15,975	3,943	12,392	13,340
1973.	76,896	644	4,015	20,068	4,644	16,674	4,091	13,021	13,739
1974.	78,413	694	3,957	20,046	4,696	17,017	4,208	13,617	14,177
1975.	76,985	745	3,457	18,347	4,498	16,947	4,223	13,995	14,773
1976 July (P)	78,817	806	3,568	18,805	4,536	17,468	4,370	14,734	14,530

Profits of Manufacturing Corporations by Industry Groups

Source: Federal Trade Commission

Industry Group (Amounts estimated in millions of dollars)	Before Income Taxes			Profits After Taxes		
	1975	Pct. of sales 1975	1974	1975	Pct. of sales 1975	1974
Durable goods	31,047	6.0	7.7	21,409	4.1	4.7
Transportation equipment	4,132	3.5	4.4	2,968	2.5	2.7
Motor vehicles and qquipment[1]	2,258	3.0	4.1	1,737	2.3	2.7
Electrical and electronic equipment	4,243	5.3	6.7	2,564	3.2	3.9
Machinery, except electrical	8,257	8.4	9.8	6,311	6.4	5.9
Fabricated metal products	4,269	7.0	7.9	2,523	4.2	4.6
Primary iron and steel	3,171	6.9	10.8	2,281	5.0	6.4
Primary nonferrous metals	683	3.2	10.7	663	3.1	7.0
Stone, clay, and glass products	1,449	5.5	7.1	968	3.7	4.4
Instruments and related products	2,569	10.8	14.9	1,823	7.7	9.2
Other durable goods	2,278	4.9	6.0	1,307	2.8	3.5
Nondurable goods	40,439	7.4	9.6	27,725	5.1	6.4
Food and kindred products	8,333	5.1	4.9	5,154	3.2	2.8
Tobacco manufactures	1,396	14.0	15.0	919	9.2	8.9
Textile mill products	860	3.1	4.9	409	1.5	2.5
Paper and allied products	2,538	7.9	12.0	1,801	5.6	7.1
Printing and publishing	2,995	8.3	8.5	1,663	4.6	4.7
Chemicals and allied products	9,668	11.0	13.6	6,703	7.6	8.4
Petroleum and coal products	11,670	9.6	*15.5	9,307	7.6	12.6
Rubber and miscellaneous plastic products	1,180	4.8	8.5	759	3.1	5.0
Other nondurable products	1,800	4.4	4.5	1,010	2.4	2.4
All Manufacturing Corps.	71,486	6.7	8.7	49,135	4.6	5.5

[1] Included in major industry above.

Occupational Earnings in Selected Cities

Source: Bureau of Labor Statistics, Department of Labor

(Average earnings (1) for selected occupations studied in 6 broad industry divisions: Manufacturing; transportation, communication, and other public utilities; wholesale; retail; finance, insurance, and real estate; and services, March-May 1975)

Occupations (men and women combined)	Birmingham Ala.	Fort Lauderdale-Hollywood and West Palm Beach-Boca Raton, Fla.	Houston, Tex.	St. Louis, Mo.-Ill.	San Francisco-Oakland, Calif.	Toledo, O. Mich.	Worcester, Mass.
Office Workers		Average weekly earnings, straight-time					
Accounting clerks[2]	$179.50	$167.50	$183.50	$194.00	$199.00	$192.50	$180.50
Computer operators[2]	205.00	—	245.00	237.00	248.00	211.50	213.00
Computer programmers, business[2]	283.00	—	299.50	285.00	337.00	261.50	324.00
Computer systems analysts, business[2]	343.00	—	386.50	366.00	353.00	339.50	332.00
Drafters[2]	257.50	258.50	292.00	290.00	283.00	295.00	242.50
File clerks[2]	141.00	—	183.50	147.50	165.50	—	—
Keypunch operators[2]	139.50	181.50	164.50	172.00	196.50	186.00	159.00
Messengers	121.00	128.50	120.50	122.50	138.00	132.50	115.00
Nurses, industrial (registered)	210.00	—	227.00	239.00	248.50	240.50	220.50
Secretaries	175.50	167.00	192.00	181.00	203.50	199.00	178.50
Stenographers, general	155.50	165.50	163.50	161.50	179.00	175.50	151.00
Typists[2]	140.50	156.50	151.00	160.00	153.50	156.00	149.50
		Average hourly earnings, straight-time					
Maintenance, custodial, and material movement workers							
Carpenters	$ 6.35	$ 5.74	$ 7.09	$ 6.53	$ 7.70	$ 7.16	$ 5.30
Electricians	6.77	6.29	7.05	7.07	7.76	7.05	5.89
Engineers, stationary	6.66	—	5.62	6.73	7.99	6.62	5.69
Helpers, trades	5.35	4.31	4.48	5.37	5.97	5.53	—
Machinists	6.66	—	7.23	6.95	7.82	7.06	6.09
Mechanics, automotive	5.34	6.02	6.49	6.72	8.08	6.73	5.94
Painters	5.87	—	6.13	6.61	8.25	6.56	—
Guards and watchmen	2.66	2.77	2.84	3.17	3.37	3.22	3.42
Janitors, porters, cleaners	2.65	2.76	2.66	3.63	4.91	4.40	3.83
Laborers, material handling	3.44	3.22	3.70	5.41	6.37	5.79	3.93
Packers, shipping	4.33	3.32	3.71	4.79	5.17	5.32	4.26
Shipping clerks	4.84	—	4.54	5.20	5.84	5.47	4.35
Truck drivers, local	4.31	4.54	4.85	6.52	7.31	6.44	5.49

1. Weekly earnings relate to regular straight-time salaries that are paid for standard workweeks. Hourly earnings exclude premium pay for overtime, weekends, holidays, or late shifts.
2. More than one skill level surveyed. Earnings are for the highest level surveyed.

Annual Rates of Profit on Stockholders' Equity

Source: Federal Trade Commission

(Each rate is the arithmetic mean of 4 quarterly rates, each on an annual basis.)

By industry after taxes: by percent	1950	1960	1965	1969[1]	1970	1973	1974[2]	1975
All manufacturing corporations, except newspapers	15.4	9.2	13.0	11.5	9.3	12.8	14.9	11.6
Durable goods industries	16.8	8.6	13.8	11.4	8.3	13.1	12.6	10.3
Metals and metal fabricating industries	16.9	8.6	14.2	11.2	*	*	*	*
Transportation equipment	21.5	11.7	18.5	12.0	6.3	13.1	8.0	7.5
Motor vehicles and equipment	25.2	13.5	19.5	12.6	6.1	15.1	6.9	6.2
Aircraft and parts	*	7.4	15.1	10.6	6.8	10.3	10.6	11.0
Electrical machinery, equipment and supplies	20.8	9.5	13.5	11.1	9.1	13.1	11.1	9.0
Machinery, except electrical	14.0	7.6	14.1	12.2	9.9	13.4	13.2	13.7
Metalworking machinery and equipment	*	5.3	14.4	11.6	8.3	13.5	*	*
Other fabricated metal products	15.9	5.6	13.2	11.3	8.6	13.9	16.6	13.2
Primary metal industries	14.5	7.2	10.6	9.5	7.0	10.1	16.4	8.6
Blast furnaces, steel works and foundries	14.3	7.2	9.8	7.6	4.3	9.5	16.8	10.9
Nonferrous metals	15.0	7.1	11.9	12.2	10.7	10.8	15.8	5.0
Other durable goods industries	16.3	8.6	12.2	12.4	*	*	*	*
Lumber and wood products, except furniture	17.4	3.6	10.0	13.2	5.9	22.4	*	*
Furniture and fixtures	15.1	6.5	13.3	12.6	7.9	13.2	*	*
Stone, clay and glass products	17.6	9.9	10.2	9.2	6.9	11.2	10.6	8.3
Instruments and related products	16.7	11.6	17.5	15.6	14.2	15.9	16.1	13.5
Miscellaneous manufacturing and ordnance	12.2	9.2	10.7	11.6	10.0	11.5	*	*
Nondurable goods industries	14.0	9.8	12.2	11.5	10.3	12.6	17.2	12.9
Chemicals: petroleum, rubber, and plastics	15.4	10.8	13.0	12.0	*	*	*	*
Chemicals and allied products	17.8	12.2	15.2	12.8	11.5	14.8	18.2	15.2
Basic chemicals and related products	*	11.1	14.3	10.5	8.5	13.0	17.4	13.3
Drugs	*	16.8	20.3	18.4	17.6	19.0	18.8	17.8
Petroleum refining and related industries	13.8	10.1	11.8	11.7	11.0	11.6	21.0	12.5
Petroleum refining	*	10.1	11.8	11.7	11.0	11.6	*	*
Rubber and miscellaneous plastics products	16.7	9.1	11.7	10.4	7.1	12.1	14.4	8.0
Other nondurable goods industries	12.8	8.5	11.1	10.8	*	*	*	*
Food and kindred products	12.3	8.7	10.7	10.9	10.8	12.8	14.0	14.4
Dairy products	*	*	10.6	10.1	10.2	10.8	*	*
Bakery products	*	*	9.3	8.6	8.8	5.8	*	*
Alcoholic beverages	*	7.1	9.3	10.3	10.5	10.8	*	*
Tobacco manufacturers	11.5	13.4	13.5	14.4	15.7	14.8	15.6	15.9
Textile mill products	12.6	5.8	10.8	7.9	5.1	9.0	8.2	4.2
Apparel and other fabricated textile products	10.1	7.7	12.6	9.3	11.9	10.8	*	*
Paper and allied products	16.1	8.5	9.4	10.1	7.0	12.9	17.8	12.6
Printing and publishing, except newspapers	11.5	10.6	14.1	12.6	11.2	12.9	13.2	12.8
Leather and leather products	10.9	6.3	11.6	9.3	9.4	9.4	*	*

*—Not available. (1.) Includes newspapers for the first time. (2.) Profits for 1974 include equity in earnings (net of taxes) of nonconsolidated subsidiaries. In prior years this component was included in adjustment to earned surplus.

Personal Consumption Expenditures for the U.S.

Source: Bureau of Economic Analysis, U.S. Department of Commerce

(In millions of dollars)

	1950	1955	1960	1965	1970	1973	1974	1975
Food and tobacco	58,120	72,236	87,510	107,183	141,181	181,199	203,840	224,286
Clothing, accessories and jewelry	23,709	27,982	33,032	43,318	62,834	71,811	76,148	81,742
Personal care	2,438	3,461	5,324	7,578	10,420	12,613	13,434	14,271
Housing	21,286	33,738	46,305	63,509	90,926	123,173	136,363	150,219
Household operation	29,461	37,322	46,906	61,789	87,360	117,698	130,358	142,190
Medical care	8,788	12,755	19,116	28,082	47,401	68,327	76,142	86,425
Personal business	6,858	10,049	14,974	21,879	35,314	40,553	44,751	50,287
Transportation	24,672	35,574	43,134	58,154	77,776	110,862	115,257	126,037
Recreation	11,147	14,078	18,295	26,298	40,653	55,199	60,765	65,999
Private educ. and research	1,618	2,339	3,718	5,927	10,363	12,600	13,607	14,653
Religious and welfare act	2,282	3,257	4,748	5,972	8,601	10,647	11,578	12,113
Foreign travel and other—net	630	1,590	2,179	3,150	4,815	5,203	5,251	4,994
Total personal consumption expenditures	**191,009**	**254,381**	**325,241**	**432,839**	**617,644**	**809,885**	**887,494**	**973,216**

Work Stoppages (Strikes) in the U.S.

Source: Bureau of Labor Statistics, U. S. Department of Labor

	Number stoppages	Workers involved	Man days idle	Year	Number stoppages	Workers involved	Man days idle
Average 1935 to 1939	2,862	1,130,000	16,900,000	1970	5,716	3,305,000	66,414,000
				1971	5,138	3,280,000	47,589,000
War Period Dec. 8, 1941- Aug. 14, 1945	14,371	6,744,000	36,300,000	1972	5,010	1,714,000	27,066,000
				1973	5,353	2,251,000	27,948,000
Year				1974	6,074	2,778,000	47,991,000
				1975 (p)	5,031	1,746,000	31,237,000
1947-49	3,573	2,380,000	39,700,000	1976 Jan.	278	54,000	1,120,000
1950	4,843	2,410,000	38,800,000	Feb.	288	74,000	726,000
1955	4,320	2,650,000	28,200,000	Mar.	339	143,000	1,398,000
1960	3,333	1,320,000	19,100,000	Apr.	446	493,000	3,222,000
1965	3,963	1,550,000	23,300	May.	653	222,000	4,633,000
1969	5,700	2,481,000	42,869,000	June.	712	276,000	5,463,000

Retail Store Sales, by Kind of Business

Source: Bureau of the Census, U.S. Dept. of Commerce. In millions of dollars

Kinds of business	1974	1975	Kinds of business	1974	1975
All retail stores................	537,800	584,423	Nondurable goods stores .	370,500	403,698
			Apparel group................	24,900	26,749
Durable goods stores.....	167,300	180,725	Men's and boys' wear stores...	5,700	6,085
Automotive group.............	93,100	102,105	Women's apparel, accessory		
Motor vehicle, other			stores..................	9,600	10,396
automotive dealers........	84,800	93,046	Shoe stores	4,000	4,123
Tire, battery, accessory			Food group.................	119,800	131,723
dealers................	8,300	9,055	Grocery stores............	111,300	122,666
Furniture and appliance group...	25,500	26,123	General merchandise group		
Furniture, home furnishings			with non stores...........	89,300	95,402
stores................	15,400	15,283	Department stores, excl.		
Household appliance, radio			mail order...............	55,900	60,719
TV stores...............	8,000	8,420	Mail order (catalog sales).......	5,800	5,995
Lumber, building, hardware			Variety stores.............	8,700	9,120
group................	23,500	23,974	Eating and drinking places......	41,800	47,514
Lumber, building materials			Gasoline service stations.......	39,900	43,895
dealers................	18,300	18,202	Drug and proprietary stores.....	16,800	18,098
Hardware stores............	5,200	5,772	Liquor stores...............	10,300	10,974

Total Retail Stores Sales (In millions of dollars) — (1955) 183,851; (1956) 189,729; (1957) 200,002; (1958) 200,353; (1959) 215,413; (1960) 219,529; (1961) 218,992; (1962) 235,563; (1963) 246,666; (1964) 261,870; (1965) 284,128; (1966) 303,956; (1967) 313,809; (1968) 341,876; (1969) 357,885; (1970) 375,527; (1971) 408,850; (1972) 448,400; (1973) 503,300; (1974) 537,800; (1975) 584,423.

Cotton, Wool, Silk, and Man-Made Fibers Production

Source: Economic Research Service, U.S. Dept. of Agriculture

Cotton and wool from reports of the Dept. of Agriculture; silk, rayon and non-cellulosic man-made fibers from Textile Organon, a publication of the Textile Economics Bureau, Inc.

Year	Cotton[1] U.S. Mil. bales[5]	Cotton[1] World Mil. bales[5]	Wool[2] U.S. Mil. lb.	Wool[2] World Mil. lb.	Silk World Mil. lb.	Man-made fibers[3] Rayon & Acetate U.S. Mil. lb.	Man-made fibers[3] Rayon & Acetate World Mil. lb.	Man-made fibers[3] Non-Cellulosic[4] U.S.[4] Mil. lb.	Man-made fibers[3] Non-Cellulosic[4] World Mil. lb.
1940.........	12.6	31.2	434.0	4,180	130	471.2	2,485.3	4.6	4.6
1950.........	10.0	30.6	249.3	4,000	42	1,259.4	3,552.8	145.9	177.4
1960.........	14.2	46.2	298.9	5,615	68	1,028.5	5,749.1	854.2	1,779.1
1964.........	15.1	52.9	237.4	5,766	71	1,431.8	7,245.4	1,646.2	4,067.3
1965.........	15.0	55.0	224.8	5,836	72	1,527.0	7,359.4	2,062.4	4,928.9
1966.........	9.6	50.6	219.2	5,958	72.	1,519.0	7,364.2	2,415.2	5,227.0[6]
1967.........	7.4	49.5	211.4	6,040	75	1,388.1	7,297.4	2,662.1	6,013.0
1968.........	10.9	54.8	197.9	6,295	82	1,594.3	7,780.2	3,632.1	7,889.0
1969.........	10.0	53.2	182.8	6,261	86	1,576.2	7,835.6	4,029.3	9,207.0
1970.........	10.2	53.8	176.8	6,163	90	1,373.2	7,565.2	4,053.5	10,351.0
1971.........	10.5	59.2	172.2	6,033	90	1,390.9	7,613.8	4,761.0	12,335.0
1972.........	13.7	61.6	168.6	5,631	93	1,394.3	7,833.1	5,927.3	13,994.0
1973[7].......	13.0	62.5	153.2	5,508	97	1,357.0	8,080.0	6,997.4	16,727.0
1974.........	11.5	63.1	138.6	5,758	99	1,198.8	7,700.0	6,908.5	16,400.0

(1.) Year beginning Aug. 1. (2.) Grease basis. (3.) Includes filament yarn and staple and tow fiber. (4.) Includes textile glass fiber. (5.) 480-pound net weight bales, U.S. beginning 1960 and World beginning 1965. (6.) 1966 to date, excludes Olefin. (7.) Preliminary.

World Production of Natural Rubber

Source: Bureau of Domestic Commerce, U.S. Dept. of Commerce

Metric Tons

Year	Far East	Tropical America	Africa	Total	Year	Far East	Tropical America	Africa	Total
1940.....	1,379,000	26,000	16,000	1,421,000	1970.....	2,857,500	32,000	213,000	3,102,500
1945.....	173,000	49,000	54,000	276,000	1971.....	2,847,050	34,200	203,750	3,085,000
1950.....	1,771,500	27,000	55,000	1,853,500	1972.....	2,875,700	40,800	208,500	3,125,000
1955.....	1,798,000	27,500	98,500	1,924,000	1973.....	3,247,600	40,400	224,500	3,512,500
1960.....	1,825,100	29,900	148,000	2,002,000	1974.....	3,178,150	36,600	232,750	3,447,500
1965.....	2,156,950	36,300	159,250	2,352,500	1975.....	3,044,700	39,300	208,500	3,292,500

Full-time and Part-time Status of Civilian Labor Force

Source: Bureau of Labor Statistics, U.S. Dept. of Labor

(Numbers in thousands seasonally adjusted)

Employment Status . . Total, 16 years and over:	1975 July	Aug.	Sept.	Oct.	Nov.	Dec.	1976 Jan.	Feb.	Mar.	April	May	June
Full Time												
Civilian labor force ..	79,004	79,348	79,593	79,790	79,738	79,824	79,801	79,900	80,283	80,633	80,750	79,144
Employed..........	72,311	72,882	72,899	73,032	73,112	73,500	73,962	74,222	74,646	75,024	75,299	73,308
Unemployed.......	6,693	6,466	6,694	6,758	6,626	6,324	5,839	5,678	5,637	5,609	5,451	5,836
Unemployed rate ...	8.5	8.1	8.4	8.5	8.3	7.9	7.3	7.1	7.0	7.0	6.8	7.4
Part Time												
Civilian labor force ..	14,165	13,969	13,743	13,534	13,411	13,295	13,760	13,657	13,480	13,911	13,651	14,150
Employed..........	12,769	12,524	12,389	12,127	12,049	11,893	12,317	12,231	12,098	12,425	12,263	12,875
Unemployed.......	1,396	1,445	1,354	1,407	1,362	1,402	1,442	1,426	1,382	1,486	1,388	1,275
Unemployment rate .	9.9	10.3	9.9	10.4	10.2	10.5	10.5	10.4	10.3	10.7	10.2	9.0

Labor Union Membership

SOURCE: AFL-CIO and Dept. of Labor

AFL-CIO unions with a membership of 25,000 or over (July, 1976)

Union	Members
Actors and Artists of America, Associated	76,000
Air Line Pilots Association	46,000
Aluminum Workers International Union	27,000
Bakery and Confectionery Workers International Union of America	123,000
Barbers, Hairdressers and Cosmetologists' International Union of America, the Journeymen	42,000
Boilermakers, Iron Ship Builders, Blacksmiths, Forgers and Helpers, International Brotherhood of	123,000
Boot and Shoe Workers' Union	34,000
Bricklayers, Masons, and Plasterers International Union of America	143,000
Carpenters and Joiners of America, United Brotherhood of	700,000
Chemical Workers Union, International	58,000
Clothing Workers of America, Amalgamated	232,000
Communications Workers of America	476,000
Dolls, Toys, Playthings, Novelties and Allied Products of the United States and Canada, AFL-CIO, International Union of.	30,000
Electrical, Radio and Machine Workers, International Union of	255,000
Electrical Workers, International Brotherhood of	856,000
Engineers, International Union of Operating	300,000
Fire Fighters, International Association of	123,000
Firemen and Oilers, International Brotherhood of	40,000
Furniture Workers of America, United	28,000
Garment Workers of America, United	32,000
Garment Workers Union, International Ladies'	363,000
Glass and Ceramic Workers of North America, United	28,000
Glass Bottle Blowers' Association of the United States and Canada	75,000
Glass Workers Union, American Flint	35,000
Government Employees, American Federation of	251,000
Grain Millers, American Federation of	29,000
Graphic Arts International Union	93,000
Hotel and Restaurant Employees' and Bartenders' International Union	421,000
Industrial Workers of America, International Union, Allied	93,000
Iron Workers, International Association of Bridge and Structural	160,000
Laborers' International Union of North America	475,000
Leather Goods, Plastics and Novelty Workers Union, International	39,000
Letter Carriers, National Association of	151,000
Longshoremen's Association, International	60,000
Machinists and Aerospace Workers, International Association of	780,000
Maintenance of Way Employees, Brotherhood of	71,000
Maritime Union of America, National	35,000
Meat Cutters and Butcher Workmen of North America, Amalgamated	451,000
Molders and Allied Workers Union, International	50,000
Musicians, American Federation of	215,000
Newspaper Guild, The	26,000
Office and Professional Employees International Union	74,000
Oil, Chemical and Atomic Workers International Union	145,000
Painters & Allied Trades of the United States and Canada, International Brotherhood of	160,000
Paper Workers International Union, United	275,000
Plasterers' & Cement Masons' International Association of the United States and Canada, Operative	55,000
Plumbing and Pipe Fitting Industry of the United States & Canada, United Association of Journeymen & Apprentices of the	228,000
Postal Workers Union, American	249,000
Printing and Graphics Communications Union, International	105,000
Railway, Airline and Steamship Clerks, Freight Handlers, Express & Station Employes, Brotherhood of	160,000
Railway Carmen of the United States & Canada, Brotherhood	56,000
Retail Clerks International Association	602,000
Retail, Wholesale and Department Store Union	118,000

Union	Members
Roofers, Damp & Waterproof Workers Association, United Slate, Tile & Composition	27,000
Rubber, Cork, Linoleum & Plastic Workers of America, United	173,000
Seafarers International Union of North America	80,000
Service Employees International Union, AFL-CIO	480,000
Sheet Metal Workers International Association	120,000
Shoe Workers of America, United	25,000
Stage Employes & Moving Picture Machine Operators of the United States & Canada, International Alliance of Theatrical	50,000
State, County & Municipal Employees, American Federation of	647,000
Steelworkers of America, United	1,062,000
Teachers, American Federation of	396,000
Textile Workers of America, United	36,000
Textile Workers Union of America	105,000
Tobacco Workers International Union	26,000
Transit Union, Amalgamated	90,000
Transport Workers Union of America	95,000
Transportation Union, United	134,000
Typographical Union, International	73,000
Upholsterers' International Union of North America	50,000
Utility Workers Union of America	52,000
Woodworkers of America, International	52,000

Independent Unions

(Sept., 1975)

Automobile, Aerospace and Agricultural Implement Workers of America, Intl. Union, United	1,393,501
Distributive Workers of America	50,000
Education Assn., National	1,165,617
Electrical, Radio, and Machine Workers of America, United	165,000
Federal Employees, Nat'l. Federation of	85,000
Government Employees, Nat'l. Assn. of	100,000
Letter Carriers Assn., Nat'l. Rural	46,300
Locomotive Engineers, Brotherhood of	37,600
Longshoremen's and Warehousemen's Union Int'l.	58,000
Mine Workers of America, United	213,113
Nurses' Assn., American	156,665
Postal Union, National	80,000
Postal and Federal Employees, Nat'l. Alliance of	45,000
Postal Supervisors, Nat'l. Assn. of	32,965
Teamsters, Chauffeurs, Warehousemen and Helpers of America, Int'l. Brotherhood of	1,854,659
Telephone Unions; Alliance of Independent	50,000
Treasury Employees Union, Nat'l.	33,000
University Professors, American Assn. of	85,614

Canadian Unions

Independent Unions (1975)

Government Employees' Union, Quebec	30,112
Teachers' Corporation, Quebec	84,905
Teachers' Federation, Ontario Secondary School	34,407

CNTU Unions (1975)

Public Service Employees Inc., Federation of	29,681
Social Affairs Federation	61,130

CLC Unions (1975)

Automobile, Aerospace and Agricultural Implement Workers of America, International Union, United	117,486
Civil Service Assn. of Alberta, The	26,396
Civil Service Assn. of Ontario, The	55,448
Government Employees' Union, British Columbia	27,622
Paperworkers Union, Canadian	56,000
Public Employees, Canadian Union of	198,872
Public Service Alliance of Canada	135,998
Railway, Transport and General Workers, Canadian Brotherhood of	40,638

Mineral Production in U. S.[1]

Source: Bureau of Mines

Mineral Fuels	1974 Quantity	1974 Value (thousands)	1975p Quantity	1975p Value (thousands)
Asphalt and related bitumens (native):				
Bituminous limestone & sandstone & gilsonite . . . . . . short tons	2,021,165	$16,666	e1,941,000	e$16,490
Carbon dioxide, natural (e). . . . . thousand cubic feet	966,118	237	1,070,024	279
Coal: Bituminous and lignite[2]. . . . . .thousand short tons	603,406	9,502,347	e637,000	e11,900,000
Pennsylvania anthracite. . . . . thousand short tons	6,617	144,695	e6,200	e153,000
Helium: Crude. . . . . million cubic feet	184	2,208	334	4,008
Grade A. . . . . million cubic feet	699	18,128	745	19,915
Natural gas . . . . million cubic feet	21,600,522	6,573,402	20,108,661	8,945,062
Natural gas liquids: Gasoline products. . . . . thousand 42-gal. bbls.	168,152	1,107,158	151,872	878,698
LP gases . . . . thousand 42-gal. bbls.	447,946	1,980,769	444,086	1,893,890
Peat. . . . . thousand short tons	706	10,989	746	12,294
Petroleum (crude). . . . . .thousand 42-gal. bbls.	3,202,585	21,580,549	3,056,779	23,116,059
Total mineral fuels.	XX	40,937,000	XX	e46,940,000

Non Metals (except fuels)

Abrasive stones[3] . . . . short tons	3,134	717	2,953	1,060
Asbestos. . . . . short tons	109,091	13,393	98,654	14,220
Barite . . . . thousand short tons	1,106	16,822	1,287	20,673
Boron minerals. thousand short tons	1,185	128,306	1,172	158,772
Bromine . . . . thousand pounds	432,094	117,715	407,163	113,126
Calcium-magnesium chloride . . . . short tons	867,100	29,189	594,400	29,047
Cement: Portland . . . . thousand short tons	75,983	1,992,695	65,215	2,015,625
Masonry . . . . .thousand short tons	3,371	111,106	2,868	111,801
Natural and slag . . . . .thousand short tons	W	W	—	—
Clays. . . . . .thousand short tons	60,796	422,542	49,047	424,556
Diatomite . . . . short tons	664,303	50,693	573,000	45,812
Feldspar. . . . . short tons	853,702	14,482	684,898	11,893
Fluorspar. . . . . short tons	201,116	14,297	139,913	10,888
Garnet (abrasive). . . . . short tons	24,684	2,550	17,204	1,690
Gem stones (e)	NA	4,583	NA	13,900
Gypsum . . . . thousand short tons	11,999	52,894	9,751	44,654
Lime. . . . . thousand short tons	21,606	473,685	19,133	523,805
Magnesium compounds from sea water and brine				
(except for metals). . . . . short tons, MgO equivalent	907,492	96,742	W	W
Mica: Scrap. . . . . .thousand short tons	137	5,475	135	5,219
Sheet. . . . . : . pounds	15,000	15	W	W
Perlite . . . . short tons	555,000	7,024	512,000	7,282
Phosphate rock. .thousand short tons	45,686	501,429	48,816	1,122,184
Potassium salts. . . . . thousand short tons, K₂0 equivalent	2,552	158,974	2,501	223,098
Pumice. . . . . thousand short tons	3,937	9,121	3,892	11,203
Pyrites. . . . . thousand long tons	424	4,238	625	4,776
Salt . . . . .thousand short tons	46,536	360,763	41,030	368,063
Sand and gravel . . . . thousand short tons	978,754	1,451,071	e861,304	e1,550,000
Sodium carbonate (natural) . . . . thousand short tons	4,059	137,486	4,328	182,620
Sodium sulfate (natural). . . . . thousand short tons	684	16,411	667	27,667
Stone[4]. . . . . .thousand short tons	1,043,542	2,186,155	902,889	2,122,578
Sulfur: Frasch process mines. . . . . .thousand long tons	7,898	241,066	6,077	304,843
Talc, soapstone, and pyrophyllite. . . . . short tons	1,267,633	11,099	e1,106,000	e11,360
Tripoli . . . . short tons	86,000	3,665	80,562	565
Vermiculite. thousand short tons	341	10,120	330	`13,761
Value of items that cannot be disclosed: Aplite, brucite, emery, graphite, iodine, kyanite, lithium minerals, magnesite, greensand marl, olivine, staurolite, wollastonite, and values of nonmetal items indicated by symbol W.		35,763	XX	e161,344
Total nonmetals.	XX	8,682,000	XX	e9,658,000

Metals

Antimony ore concentrate, short tons, antimony content.	661	2,040	886	2,131
Bauxite. . . . . thousands long tons, dried equivalent	1,949	25,663	1,772,268	25,083
Beryllium concentrate . . . . short tons, gross weight	w	w	w	w
Copper (recoverable content of ores, etc.). . . . . short tons	1,597,002	2,468,964	1,413,366	1,814,763
Gold (recoverable content of ores, etc.). . . . . troy ounces	1,126,886	180,009	1,052,252	169,928
Iron ore (excluding iron sinter). . . . . . . thousand long tons, gr. wgt.	84,985	1,388,447	75,695	1,620,599
Lead (recoverable content of ores, etc.). . . . . short tons	663,870	298,742	621,464	267,230
Manganese ore (35% or more Mn). . . . . . . short tons, gross weight	—	—	—	—
Manganiferous ore (5 to 35% Mn). . . . . . . short tons, gross weight	272,908	2,323	158,725	1,412
Mercury. . . . . 76-pound flasks	2,189	617	7,366	1,165
Molybdenum (content of concentrate). . . . . thousand pounds	118,163	234,658	105,170	259,328
Nickel (content of ore and concentrate). . . . . short tons	16,618	W	16,987	W
Rare-earth metal concentrates . . . . short tons	35,218	15,966	W	W
Silver (recoverable content of ores, etc.). . . . . .thousand troy ozs.	33,762	159,018	34,938	154,424
Titanium concentrate, ilmenite. . . . . short tons, gross weight	755,338	22,715	702,252	26,946
Tungsten ore and concentrate. . . . . thousand pounds	7,836	37,413	5,490	29,090
Uranium (Recoverable content U₃O₈). . . . . thousand pounds	23,227	243,884	22,877	281,388
Vanadium (recoverable in ore and concentrate) . . . . . . short tons	4,870	38,266	4,743	49,329
Zinc (recoverable content of ores, etc.). . . . . short tons	499,872	358,908	469,355	366,097
Value of items that cannot be disclosed: symbol W.	XX	74,824	XX	130,796
Total metals.	XX	5,552,000	XX	5,200,000
Grand total mineral production.	XX	55,172,000	XX	61,797,000

(e) Estimate. (NA) Not available. (W) Withheld to avoid disclosing individual company confidential data; included with "Value of items that cannot be disclosed." (XX) Not applicable. (p) Preliminary.
(1) Production as measured by mine shipments, sales, or marketable production (including consumption by producers).
(2) Includes a small quantity of anthracite mined in states other than Pennsylvania.
(3) Grindstones, pulpstones, grinding pebbles, sharpening stones, and tube mill liners.
(4) Excludes abrasive stone, bituminous limestone, bituminous sandstone, and soapstone, all included elsewhere.

Mineral Production in U.S.—Leading States
Source: Bureau of Mines (1974)

State	Value (thousands)	Rank	Percent of U.S. total	Principal minerals, in order of value
Texas	$13,711,144	1	24.25	Petroleum, natural gas, natural gas liquids, cement.
Louisiana	8,146,578	2	14.77	Petroleum, natural gas, natural gas liquids, sulfur.
California	2,797,080	3	5.07	Petroleum, cement, sand and gravel, natural gas.
Kentucky	2,563,210	4	4.65	Coal, stone, petroleum, natural gas.
West Virginia	2,403,177	5	4.36	Coal, natural gas, stone, cement.
Pennsylvania	2,374,512	6	4.30	Coal, cement, stone, lime.
Oklahoma	2,123,690	7	3.85	Petroleum, natural gas, natural gas liquids, cement.
New Mexico	1,941,544	8	3.52	Petroleum, natural gas, copper, natural gas liquids.
Arizona	1,562,234	9	2.83	Copper, molybdenum, sand and gravel, cement.
Wyoming	1,437,200	10	2.60	Petroleum, sodium compounds, coal, uranium.

Value of Mineral Production in the U. S.[2]
Source: Bureau of Mines (r-Revised)
(In millions of dollars)

Year[1]	Fuels	Nonme-tallic	Metals	Total[3]	Year[1]	Fuels	Nonme-tallic	Metals	Total[3]
1930	2,500	973	501	3,980	1969	17,965	5,624	3,333	26,921
1940	2,662	784	752	4,198	1970	20,152	r5,712	3,928	r29,792
1950	8,689	1,882	1,351	11,862	1971	21,247	6,058	r3,406	r30,711
1960	12,142	3,868	2,022	18,032	1972	22,061	6,482	3,642	32,185
1965	14,047	4,933	2,544	21,524	1973	25,012	7,413	4,362	36,787
1967	16,195	5,200	2,327	36,788	1974	40,937	8,682	5,552	55,172
1968	16,820	5,449	2,698	r24,966	1975p	46,940	9,658	5,200	61,798

(1.) Excludes Alaska and Hawaii, 1930-53. (2.) Production as measured by mine shipments sales or marketable production. (3.) Data may not add to total because of rounding figures. (P.) Preliminary.

Copper, Lead, and Zinc Production in the U.S.
Source: Bureau of Mines

Year	Copper Mil. lbs.	Copper $1,000	Lead[1] Short Tons	Lead[1] $1,000	Zinc Short tons	Zinc Mil. dol.	Year	Copper Mil. lbs.	Copper $1,000	Lead[1] Short Tons	Lead[1] $1,000	Zinc Short tons	Zinc Mil. dol.
1950	1,823	379,122	418,809	113,078	591,454	167	1972	3,330	1,704,796	618,915	186,046	478,318	170
1960	2,286	733,708	228,899	53,562	334,101	87	1973	3,436	2,044,346	603,024	196,465	478,850	198
1965	2,703	957,028	301,147	93,959	611,153	178	1974	3,194	2,468,964	668,870	298,742	499,872	359
1970	3,439	1,984,484	571,767	178,609	534,136	164	1975	2,827	1,814,763	621,464	267,230	469,355	366
1971	3,044	1,583,071	578,550	159,679	502,543	162	(1.) Production from domestic ores.						

U.S. Pig Iron and Steel Output
Source: American Iron and Steel Institute; figures show net tons

Year	Total pig iron	Pig iron and ferro-alloys	Raw steel	Year	Total pig iron	Pig iron and ferro-alloys	Raw steel
1940	46,071,666	47,398,529	66,982,686	1970	91,435,000	93,851,000	131,514,000
1945	53,223,169	54,919,029	79,701,648	1971	81,299,000	83,468,000	120,443,000
1950	64,586,907	66,400,311	96,836,075	1972	88,942,000	91,338,000	133,241,000
1955	76,857,417	79,263,865	117,036,085	1973	100,837,000	103,089,000	150,799,000
1960	66,480,648	68,566,384	99,281,601	1974	95,909,000	98,332,000	145,720,000
1965	88,184,901	90,918,040	131,461,601	1975	101,208,000	103,345,000	116,642,000

Steel figures include only that portion of the capacity and production of steel for castings used by foundries which were operated by companies producing steel ingots.

Raw Steel Production
(Thousands of Net Tons)

State	1975	State	1975
New York	3,401	Indiana	19,807
Pennsylvania	25,761	Illinois	9,552
R.I., Conn., N.J., Del., Md.	5,094	Michigan	9,093
Va., W. Va., Ga., Fla., N.C., S.C.	4,795	Minn., Mo., Okla., Texas	5,399
Kentucky	2,081	Ariz., Colo., Utah, Wash., Ore., Hawaii	4,380
Ala., Tenn., Miss., Ark.	4,308	California	3,351
Ohio	19,620	Total	116,642

U.S. Primary Aluminum Production
Source: The Aluminum Association

Year	Short tons	Year	Short tons	Year	Short tons	Year	Short tons
1883-1902	13,981	1930	114,518	1965	2,754,478	1972	4,122,392
1903-1912	108,412	1940	206,280	1969	3,793,062	1973	4,529,117
1913-1923	282,722	1950	718,622	1970	3,976,148	1974	4,903,427
1924-1925	145,340	1960	2,014,498	1971	3,925,224	1975	3,879,000

Shipments by Major Markets (1975)

Market	Millions of lbs.	Percent	Market	Millions of lbs.	Percent
Building & Construction	2,246	22.6	Containers & Packaging	2,001	20.2
Transportation	1,709	17.2	Exports	818	8.2
Consumer Durables	753	7.6	Other	525	5.3
Electrical	1,216	12.2			
Machinery & Equipment	650	6.6	Total industry	9,928	100.0

TRADE AND TRANSPORTATION

Notable Steamships and Motorships

Source: Lloyd's Register of Shipping as of Aug. 2, 1976

Gross tonnage is a measurement of enclosed space (1 gross ton = 100 cu. ft.). Deadweight tonnage is the weight (long tons) of car, fuel, etc., which a vessel is designed to carry safely.

Oil Tankers
350,000 tons deadweight and over

Name-registry	Dwght. ton.	Lgth. Ft.	Bdth. Ft.
Batillus, Fr.	550,000	1312	206
Nissei Maru, Jap.	484,337	1243	203
Globtik London, Br.	483,939	1243	203
Globtik Tokyo, Br.	483,664	1243	203
Andros Petros, Liber.	449,934	1241	223
Homeric, Liber.	446,500	1115	223
Berge Empress, Nor.	423,700	1252	223
Berge Emperor, Nor.	414,000	1285	223
Porthos, Liber.	412,000	1174	209
Coraggio, It.	409,500	1181	226
Hilda Knudson, Nor.	409,500	1240	226
Jinku Maru, Jap.	407,300	1200	229
Aiku Maru, Jap.	407,300	1200	229
Esso Japan, Liber.	402,000	1148	229
Shat-Alarab, Iraq.	386,700	1213	209
Ioannis Colocotronis, Gr.	386,612	1213	210
Brazilian Hope, Liber.	386,600	1213	210
Vassiliki Colocotronis, Gr.	386,600	1213	210
Jarmada, Nor.	380,000	1225	210
Titus, Nor.	380,000	1225	209
Malmros Mariner, Swed.	372,280	1193	208
Hemland, Swed.	372,201	1193	208
Nisseki Maru, Jap.	366,813	1138	179
La Santa Maria, Sp.	362,946	1189	175
Al Andalus, Kuw.	362,946	1188	175
Stavros G.L., Gr.	357,130	1187	196
Tina, Gr.	357,023	1190	200
Sea Symphony, Swed.	356,400	1190	197
Sea Scape, Swed.	356,400	1190	197
Sea Saint, Swed.	356,400	1190	197
Sea Stratus, Swed.	356,400	1190	197
Sea Serenade, Swed.	356,400	1187	196

Bulk, Ore, Bulk Oil & Ore Oil Carriers
169,000 tons deadweight and over

Name-registry	Dwght. ton.	Lgth. Ft.	Bdth. Ft.
Svealand, Swed.	282,450	1109	179
Docecanyon, Liber.	271,235	1113	180
Jose Bonifacio, Braz.	270,358	1106	179
Tarfala, Swed.	265,000	1099	170
Mary R. Koch, Liber.	265,000	1099	170
Torne, Swed.	265,000	1099	170
Usa Maru, Jap.	264,523	1105	179
Nordic Conqueror, Br.	264,485	1101	176
Lauderdale, Br.	260,424	1101	176
Licorne Atlantique, Fr.	258,268	1101	176
La Loma, Br.	245,288	1069	170
Hoegh Hood, Nor.	244,677	1069	170
Hoegh Hill, Nor.	241,447	1069	170
Falkefjell, Nor.	231,045	1075	160
Berge Vanga, Liber.	227,561	1030	164
Berge Adria, Nor.	227,561	1030	164
San Giusto, It.	227,408	1091	149
Havkong, Nor.	227,406	1075	161
Ambrosiana, It.	227,400	1091	149
Berge Brioni, Nor.	227,187	1030	165
Andros Atlas, Gr.	224,074	1061	158
Andros Antares, Liber.	223,808	1061	158
Andros Aries, Gr.	223,808	1061	158
Sysla, Nor.	223,500	1096	149
Alva Bay, Br.	222,331	1091	149
Alva Sea, Br.	221,457	1090	149
Tartar, Nor.	215,621	1075	164
Jarl Malmros, Swed.	215,500	1075	164
Tantalus, Br.	214,592	1075	164
Atsuta Maru, Jap.	214,017	1075	164
Tsurumi Maru, Jap.	213,842	1075	164
Adria Maru, Jap.	183,572	1023	156
Aralura Maru, Jap.	180,626	1023	156
Larina, Liber.	175,927	984	157
Romantic, Liber.	174,107	995	151
Rhetoric, Liber.	173,668	995	151
Sir John Hunter, Br.	171,400	965	145
Cedros, Liber.	170,418	995	142
Cetra Centaurus, Fr.	170,414	981	143
Bunga Mawar, Malaysia	169,623	967	155

Name-registry	Dwght. ton.	Lgth. Ft.	Bdth. Ft.
Cetra Vela, Fr.	169,317	967	155
Champagne, Fr.	169,300	967	155
Garden Green, Liber.	169,147	967	155
Sir Alexander Glen, Br.	169,080	965	144

World's Largest Passenger Ships
30,000 gross tons and over

Name-registry	Gross ton.	Lgth. Ft.	Bdth. Ft.
Queen Elizabeth 2, Br.	66,852	963	105
France, Fr.	66,348	1035	110
Raffaello, It.	45,933	904	101
Michelangelo, It.	45,911	904	101
Canberra, Br.	44,807	818	102
Oriana, Br.	41,910	804	97
United States, U.S.	38,216	990	101
Rotterdam, Neth. Antil.	37,783	748	94
Windsor Castle, Br.	36,277	783	92
Leonardo Da Vinci, It.	33,340	767	92
Eugenio C., It.	30,567	713	96
S.A. Vaal, S. Afr.	30,213	760	90

Container, Liquefied Gas, Misc. Ships
32,700 gross tons and over

Name-registry	Gross ton.	Lgth. Ft.	Bdth. Ft.
Hilli, Liber.	90,000	961	136
Ben Franklin, Fr.	88,071	894	134
LNG Challenger, Br.	76,496	857	131
Norman Lady, Br.	76,416	818	131
El Paso Paul Kayser, Liber.	66,808	920	136
Palace Tokyo, Jap.	64,378	807	131
Cardigan Bay, Br.	58,899	950	106
Kowloon Bay, Br.	58,889	950	106
Liverpool Bay, Br.	58,889	950	106
Tokyo Bay, Br.	58,889	950	106
Osaka Bay, Br.	58,889	950	106
Nedlloyd Delft, Neth.	58,716	941	106
Nedlloyd Dejima, Neth.	58,716	941	106
City of Edinburgh, Br.	58,440	950	106
Benavon, Br.	58,440	950	106
Benalder, Br.	58,440	950	106
Hamburg Express, W. Ger.	58,088	943	105
Tokio Express, W. Ger.	58,082	895	105
Bremen Express, W. Ger.	57,535	941	106
Hongkong Express, W. Ger.	57,525	941	106
Korrigan, Br.	57,249	946	105
Esso Fuji, Panama.	55,896	807	131
Geomitra, Br.	53,128	846	114
Genota, Br.	53,128	846	113
Toyama, Nor.	52,196	902	106
Elbe Maru, Jap.	51,623	882	105
Kitano Maru, Jap.	51,159	856	105
Kurama Maru, Jap.	51,139	856	105
Kamakura Maru, Jap.	51,139	856	105
Rhine Maru, Jap.	51,085	856	105
Nihon, Swed.	50,805	902	105
Selandia, Den.	49,890	900	106
Jutlandia, Den.	49,890	900	106
Gouldia,	48,662	844	114
Gari, Br.	48,662	842	114
Gastrana, Br.	48,662	842	114
Gadila, Br.	48,662	842	114
Gadinia, Br.	48,662	842	114
Yusho Maru, Jap.	47,783	744	114
Sun River, Jap.	45,647	734	106
Polar Alaska, Liber.	44,088	798	111
Artic Tokyo, Liber.	44,088	798	111
Nyhammer, Nor.	43,000	757	105
Remuera, Br.	42,007	824	105
Kanayama Maru, Jap.	41,939	734	113
Sea-Land Exchange, U.S.	41,555	946	105
Sea-Land Commerce, U.S.	41,127	946	105
Sea-Land Trade, U.S.	41,127	946	105
Sea-Land Market, U.S.	41,127	946	105
Sea-Land Resource, U.S.	41,127	946	105
Sea-Land Finance, U.S.	41,127	946	105
Sea-Land Galloway, U.S.	41,127	946	105
Sea-Land Mclean, U.S.	41,127	946	105

Name-registry	Gross ton.	Lgth. Ft.	Bdth. Ft.
Bridgestone Maru V. Jap.	40,934	690	106
World Concord, Liber.	39,500	734	106
Verrazano Bridge, Jap.	39,153	867	105
Seven Seas Bridge, Jap.	39,152	867	105
Tokuho Maru, Jap.	39,117	705	105
Izumisan Maru, Jap.	38,872	705	105
New York Maru, Jap.	38,825	862	105
Kiso Maru, Jap.	38,540	857	105
Svendborg Maersk, Den.	38,540	856	105
Kurobe Maru, Jap.	37,845	854	105
Ogden General, Liber.	37,809	744	113
New Jersey Maru, Jap.	37,799	863	105
World Rainbow, Panama.	36,917	734	113
Amvrosios, Liber.	36,911	734	113
Pine Queen, Liber.	36,905	734	113
Nektar, Liber.	36,902	734	113
Hongkong Container, Liber.	36,885	867	105

Name-registry	Gross ton.	Lgth. Ft.	Bdth. Ft.
World Bridgestone, Panama.	36,556	690	106
Ogden Bridgestone, Panama	36,125	690	106
Tohbei Maru, Jap.	35,491	806	105
Kazutama Maru, Jap.	34,529	656	103
Providence Multina, Fr.	34,341	710	106
Malmros Multina, Swed.	34,241	710	106
Antilla Bay, Neth. Antil.	34,015	710	105
Japan Ambrose, Jap.	33,287	748	105
Descartes, Fr.	32,702	721	104

Nuclear Powered Merchant Ships

Name-registry	Gross ton.	Lgth. Ft.	Bdth. Ft.
Arktika, USSR.	18,172	492	98
Otto Hahn, W. Ger.	16,871	564	76
Savannah, U.S.	15,585	595	78
Lenin, USSR.	14,067	439	90
Mutsu, Jap.	8,214	428	62

U.S. Exports and Imports of Leading Commodities

Source: Bureau of International Commerce, Dept. of Commerce (Value in millions of dollars)

Commodity	Exports 1973	Exports 1974	Exports 1975	Imports 1973	Imports 1974	Imports 1975
Total	$70,223	$98,506	$107,652	$69,121	$100,972	$96,140
Food and live animals	11,931	13,983	15,487	7,986	9,379	8,509
Meat	444	381	528	1,668	1,344	1,141
Dairy products and eggs	56	67	134	...	...	...
Cheese	...	...	...	156	236	165
Fish	242	196	268	1,387	1,499	1,356
Grains and preparations	8,495	10,331	11,643	105	171	180
Wheat and wheat flour	4,151	4,589	5,292	...	...	...
Rice	541	852	858	...	...	...
Corn	2,837	3,772	4,448	...	...	...
Fruit and nuts	662	757	871	577	627	637
Vegetables	307	391	406	409	387	355
Sugar	...	...	...	918	2,256	1,870
Coffee, green	...	...	...	1,566	1,504	1,561
Beverages and tobaccos	1,008	1,247	1,310	1,213	1,321	1,419
Alcoholic Beverages	...	...	...	996	1,028	1,033
Tobacco, unmanufactured	681	832	853	187	255	343
Crude materials, inedible other than fuels	8,384	10,934	9,784	4,988	5,915	5,564
Synthetic rubber	196	290	261	...	...	...
Ores and metal scrap	1,081	1,475	1,355	1,291	1,838	1,977
Coal	1,014	2,436	3,259	...	...	...
Petroleum and products	518	792	907	7,548	24,210	24,814
Animal and vegetable oils and fats	684	1,423	944	255	544	554
Chemicals	5,748	8,822	8,705	2,437	3,991	3,696
Medicinal and Pharmaceutical	626	800	866	164	214	235
Machinery and transport equipment	27,842	38,189	45,710	20,970	24,713	23,465
Automotive engines	578	673	763	983	1,013	1,040
Agricultural machinery	346	545	706	313	440	474
Tractors and parts	339	483	752	292	412	430
Metalworking machinery	489	639	920	188	305	361
Textile and leather machinery	375	528	486	625	609	518
Other nonelectrical machinery	1,300	1,930	2,245	1,052	1,384	1,156
Electrical apparatus	5,031	7,019	7,587	4,471	5,417	4,911
Transport equipment	10,255	13,871	16,495	10,876	12,630	11,495
New motor vehicles	2,666	3,681	5,135	6,479	7,544	7,130
Aircraft and parts	4,124	5,766	6,171	554	510	519
Other manufactured goods	11,112	16,516	16,590	21,382	27,507	23,929
Rubber manufacturers	308	544	544	...	...	...
Paper and manufactures	919	1,522	1,448	1,457	1,831	1,673
Diamonds excluding industrial	314	305	237	827	775	730
Metals and manufactures	1,111	1,665	1,891	6,885	11,383	8,944
Iron and steel-mill products	1,258	2,491	2,382	2,769	5,013	4,037
Nonferrous base metals	951	1,300	1,090	1,994	3,042	2,063
Textiles other than clothing	1,225	1,795	1,625	1,568	1,629	1,219
Clothing	254	372	382	2,154	1,323	2,562
Other transactions	1,844	2,587	3,162	1,790	2,252	2,529

U.S. Merchandise Exports and Imports, by Continent

Source: International Trade Analysis Division, Dept. of Commerce (Value in millions of dollars)

Year	Exports Western Hemisp.	Exports Europe	Exports Asia & Oceania	Exports Africa	General Imports Western Hemisp.	General Imports Europe	General Imports Asia & Oceania	General Imports Africa
1965	9,932	9,397	7,129	1,071	9,257	6,292	4,999	867
1970	15,611	14,817	11,294	1,502	16,928	11,395	10,515	1,090
1971	16,850	14,562	11,086	1,631	18,730	12,881	12,694	1,217
1972	19,694	16,180	12,407	1,500	21,930	15,744	16,279	1,578
1973	25,003	23,157	20,395	2,081	27,229	19,687	19,614	2,552
1974	35,745	30,878	28,129	3,204	40,702	24,636	29,073	6,547
1975	38,873	32,726	31,281	4,267	37,796	21,466	28,591	8,277

U.S. Foreign Trade with Leading Countries

Source: Bureau of International Commerce, Dept. of Commerce
(Value in millions of dollars)

Exports from the U.S. to the following areas and countries and imports into the U.S. from those areas and countries:	Exports			Imports		
	1973	1974	1975	1973	1974	1975
Total	$71,314	$98,506	$107,652	$69,121	$100,972	$96,140
Western Hemisphere	25,003	35,745	38,873	27,229	40,702	37,796
Canada	15,073	19,932	21,759	17,670	22,282	21,747
19 American Republics	8,921	14,504	15,670	7,790	13,678	11,840
Central American Common Market	621	1,033	968	685	788	825
Latin American Free Trade Ass'n	7,708	12,571	. . .	6,668	12,199	. . .
Dominican Republic	229	410	453	307	471	634
Panama	286	364	317	67	108	194
Bahamas	208	253	208	286	958	880
Jamaica	268	337	381	176	233	308
Netherlands Antilles	159	193	228	733	2,018	1,558
Trinidad and Tobago	133	192	256	409	1,273	1,170
Europe	23,157	30,071	32,726	19,687	24,636	21,466
OECD Countries (Excludes depend and Yugo.)	21,094	28,268	29,569	18,994	23,470	20,471
Western Europe	21,361	28,639	29,939	19,167	23,745	20,735
European Economic Community	16,746	22,069	22,862	15,513	19,205	16,610
Belgium and Luxembourg	1,622	2,285	2,427	1,261	1,681	1,190
France	2,263	2,942	3,031	1,717	2,305	2,137
Germany, Federal Republic of	3,756	4,986	5,194	5,318	6,428	5,382
Italy	2,119	2,752	2,867	1,989	2,593	2,397
Netherlands	2,860	3,979	4,183	925	1,453	1,083
United Kingdom	3,563	4,574	4,525	3,642	4,021	3,784
Denmark	404	360	445	458	477	461
Ireland	159	193	190	202	247	176
European Free Trade Association	2,307	2,984	. . .	2,500	3,068	. . .
Austria	118	148	181	228	457	238
Finland	133	201	261	178	212	148
Iceland	26	38	32	77	75	85
Norway	297	498	510	261	307	403
Portugal	232	407	427	192	241	156
Sweden	542	908	925	753	876	877
Switzerland	960	1,150	1,153	811	900	867
Greece	375	488	450	92	158	111
Spain	1,319	1,899	2,161	761	899	831
Turkey	347	463	608	129	141	145
Yugoslavia	236	310	328	167	268	260
Eastern Europe	1,796	1,432	2,787	519	891	731
Asia	18,651	26,239	28,942	18,060	27,570	27,083
Near East	3,041	5,557	8,977	1,370	4,735	5,432
Egypt	225	455	683	26	70	28
Iraq	56	285	310	16	1	19
Iran	771	1,734	3,242	340	2,132	1,400
Israel	961	1,206	1,551	265	282	313
Jordan	79	105	195	. . .	. . .	1
Kuwait	119	209	366	65	13	111
Lebanon	162	287	402	32	30	33
Saudi Arabia	442	835	1,502	507	1,671	2,625
Japan	8,312	10,679	9,565	9,645	12,455	11,268
East and South Asia	6,609	9,196	10,095	6,979	10,264	10,224
China, Republic of (Taiwan)	1,168	1,427	1,660	1,772	2,108	1,938
Hong Kong	740	882	808	1,444	1,637	1,575
India	525	760	1,290	437	561	548
Indonesia	442	531	810	499	1,688	2,221
Korea, Republic of	1,242	1,546	1,761	971	1,460	1,416
Malaysia	162	377	395	417	773	766
Singapore	684	988	994	459	553	532
Pakistan	239	398	372	39	61	49
Philippines	495	747	832	663	1,091	754
Thailand	256	369	357	140	184	217
Vietnam	314	675	213	3	8	6
Oceania	1,744	2,697	2,339	1,554	1,503	1,508
Australia	1,439	2,157	1,816	1,062	1,042	1,147
New Zealand and Western Samoa	249	454	414	410	348	246
Africa	2,081	3,204	4,267	2,552	6,547	8,277
North Africa excluding Egypt	504	826	1,339	565	1,224	2,498
Algeria	160	315	632	215	1,091	1,359
Ethiopia	25	33	70	79	64	49
Libya	104	139	232	216	1	1,046
Morocco	113	184	200	13	20	10
Tunisia	60	87	90	33	21	26
Western and Equatorial Africa	561	827	1,170	1,266	4,287	4,457
Angola	38	62	53	166	378	426
Ghana	63	77	100	90	126	150
Ivory Coast	69	49	78	108	95	160
Liberia	46	70	90	72	96	97
Nigeria	161	286	536	650	3,286	3,282
Central and Southern Africa	1,016	1,552	1,763	721	1,034	2,324
Kenya	39	49	49	26	39	36
South Africa	46	1,160	1,302	374	609	841
Zaire	115	145	188	70	68	67

Important Waterways and Canals

The **St. Lawrence & Great Lakes Waterway**, the largest inland navigation system on the continent, extends from the Atlantic Ocean to Duluth at the western end of Lake Superior, a distance of 2,342 miles. With the deepening of channels and locks to 27 ft., ocean carriers are able to penetrate to ports in the Canadian interior and the American midwest.

The major canals are those of the St. Lawrence-Great Lakes waterway — the 3 new canals of the St. Lawrence Seaway, with their 7 locks, providing navigation for vessels of 26-foot draught from Montreal to Lake Ontario; the Welland Ship Canal by-passing the Niagara River between Lake Ontario and Lake Erie with its 8 locks, and the Sault Ste. Marie Canal and lock between Lake Huron and Lake Superior. These 16 locks overcome a drop of 580 ft. from the head of the lakes to Montreal. From Montreal to Lake Ontario the former bottleneck of narrow, shallow canals and of slow passage through 22 locks has been overcome, giving faster and safer movement for larger vessels. The new locks and linking channels now accommodate all but the largest ocean-going vessels and the upper St. Lawrence and Great Lakes are open to 80% of the world's saltwater fleet.

Subsidiary Canadian canals or branches include the St. Peters Canal between Bras d'Or Lakes and the Atlantic Ocean in Nova Scotia; the St. Ours and Chambly Canals on the Richelieu River, Quebec; the Ste. Anne and Carillon Canals on the Ottawa River; the Rideau Canal between the Ottawa River and Lake Ontario, the Trent and Murray Canals between Lake Ontario and Georgian Bay in Ontario and the St. Andrew's Canal on the Red River. The commercial value of these canals is not great but they are maintained to control water levels and permit the passage of small vessels and pleasure craft. The Canso Canal, completed 1957, permits shipping to pass through the causeway connecting Cape Breton Island with the Nova Scotia mainland.

The 1975 shipping season was the longest in the 17-year history of the Seaway, 271 days. The Seaway closed for the winter Dec. 20.

Cargo tonnage on the Montreal-Lake Ontario Section of the Seaway amounted to 48 million tons, an 8.8% increase over 1974. Bulk cargo was up 12%. A sharp upswing during fall and early winter, spurred by grain sales to the USSR, helped grain movement rise 34%. Wheat tonnage climbed to a record high of 12.4 million tons. Iron ore shipments advanced 1.4%.

St. Lawrence Seaway provides a navigational channel with a minimum water depth of 27 ft. to link the Great Lakes to the Atlantic Ocean. A vessel entering the Great Lakes from the Atlantic ascends 20 ft. above sea level in the 1,000-mile-long reach up the Gulf of St. Lawrence and St. Lawrence River to Montreal, Quebec. At Montreal, the vessel enters the first of 7 new locks, 5 of which are in Canadian waters and 2 within United States waters, which raise or lower shipping a total of 226 ft. in the 182-mile stretch of the St. Lawrence River between Montreal and Lake Ontario. Crossing Lake Ontario, the vessel enters Canada's 28-mile-long Welland Canal, with 8 locks to compensate for the difference in elevation of 326 ft. between Lake Ontario and Lake Erie.

The signing of the Merchant Marine Bill of 1970 removed the major obstacles to the future development of the St. Lawrence Seaway. The bill eliminated interest payments on the Seaway's debt, gave official "fourth seacoast" identity to the Great Lakes-St. Lawrence Waterway, and enabled lake shipbuilders to qualify for federal shipbuilding subsidies.

Addresses: St. Lawrence Seaway Development Corporation (U.S.), P.O. Box 520, Massena, N.Y., David W. Oberlin, Administrator, and St. Lawrence Seaway Authority (Canada), Ottawa, Ont., Mr. Paul D. Normandeau, president.

The **Welland Canal** overcomes the 326-ft. drop of Niagara Falls and the rapids of the Niagara River. It has 8 locks, each 859 ft. long, 80 ft. wide and 30 ft. deep. Regulations permit ships of 730-ft. length and 75-ft. beam to transit.

The Welland Section cargo tonnage totalled 61.5 million in comparison with 51.1 million tons for 1974. The principal commodities carried in the Welland Section in order of tonnage were: iron ore, wheat, coal, corn, manufactured iron and steel, and barley.

Sault Ste. Marie Canal reported 88,829,075 short tons of freight passed through during the season of 1975 compared with 100,673,498 for 1974.

Panama Canal

The Panama Canal is a lock and lake canal, crossing the Isthmus of Panama from the Caribbean Sea in a southeasterly direction to the Bay of Panama of the Pacific Ocean. It is 50 mi. long from deep water to deep water, at least 500 ft. wide at the bottom of excavated channels, 110 ft. wide in lock chambers, which have a usable length of 1,000 ft. Depth varies, but is not less than 40 ft. Time in transit is about 8 hours.

Gatun Dam blocks the Chagres River near its Atlantic mouth, creating Gatun Lake, 23 3/4 mi. long, 85 ft. above sea level, about 45 ft. deep. Ships ascend to the lake by locks and then pass through Gaillard (formerly Culebra) Cut, 8 mi. long.

Cargo tonnage on the Panama Canal in fiscal 1976 amounted to 117.4 million compared with 140.6 million tons in 1975. Transit of oceangoing ships in fiscal 1976 totaled 12,280 compared with 13,786 in fiscal 1975. Toll collections in fiscal 1976 were $135.0 million, $143.3 million in 1975.

Improvements have included the widening of the 8-mile long channel through Gaillard Cut from 300 to 500 ft., costing $60 million; illumination of Gaillard Cut and installation of new towing locomotives at the locks costing $8 million.

Thatcher Ferry Bridge, opened 1962, spans Panama Canal 201 ft. above the water level near Balboa. It is a steel-arch bridge, about one mi. long, with 3 spans and 4 lanes. It cost $20 million authorized by the U.S. Congress in 1956.

Other Foreign Canals

One of the busiest canals in Europe is the Gota, in Sweden, 115 mi. long. Others: Kiel Canal, Germany, connecting the Baltic with the North Sea, 61 mi.; Elbe, Germany, 41 mi.; Amsterdam, Netherlands, 16 mi. Also the Manchester Ship Canal, England, 35.5 mi.

U. S. Foreign Trade, by Economic Classes

Source: International Trade Analysis Div., Dept. of Commerce. (Value in Millions of dollars)

Year (cal.)	Value of domestic exports					Value of imports				
	Crude Mater'ls	Crude Foods	Manu'd Foods	Semi Manuf's	Finish. Manuf's	Crude Mater'ls	Crude Foods	Manu'd Foods	Semi Manuf's	Finish. Manuf's
1965.....	2,887	2,587	1,590	4,114	16,008	3,709	2,008	1,877	4,964	8,871
1970.....	4,492	2,748	1,921	6,866	26,563	4,126	2,579	3,519	7,263	22,464
1973.....	7,826	8,804	3,524	9,250	40,820	7,795	3,552	5,494	13,043	39,238
1974.....	11,150	10,246	4,196	14,913	56,638	19,995	3,720	6,810	22,067	48,380
1975.....	10,883	11,804	4,221	12,815	66,434	23,568	3,642	5,972	17,323	46,435

Total agricultural exports were valued as follows (in millions of dollars): 1965—1,942; 1968—2,177; 1969—2,057; 1970—2,524; 1971—2,884; 1972—3,325; 1973—5,290; 1974—6,981; 1975—5,747. Agricultural imports for consumption (in millions of dollars): 1965—864; 1968—834; 1969—909; 1970—797; 1971—685; 1972—801; 1973—1,080; 1974—1,348; 1975—1,280.

Shortest Navigable Distances Between Ports

Source: Distances Between Ports, 1965. Defense Mapping Agency Hydrographic Center.

Distances shown are in nautical miles (1,852 meters or about 6,076.115 feet).

To get statute miles, multiply by 1.15 (one statute mile equals 5280 feet).

TO	FROM	New York	Montreal	Colon[1]
Algiers, Algeria		3,617	3,600	4,745
Amsterdam, Netherlands		3,438	3,162	4,825
Baltimore, Md.		417	1,769	1,901
Barcelona, Spain		3,714	3,697	4,842
Boston, Mass.		386	1,308	2,157
Buenos Aires, Argentina		5,817	6,455	5,472
Cape Town, S. Africa[2]		6,786	7,118	6,494
Cherbourg, France		3,154	2,878	4,541
Cobh, Ireland		2,901	2,603	4,308
Copenhagen, Denmark		3,846	3,570	5,233
Dakar, Senegal		3,335	3,566	3,694
Galveston, Tex.		1,882	3,165	1,492
Gibraltar[3]		3,204	3,187	4,332
Glasgow, Scotland		3,086	2,691	4,508
Halifax, N.S.		600	895	2,295
Hamburg, W. Germany		3,674	3,398	5,061
Hamilton, Bermuda		697	1,572	1,659
Havana, Cuba		1,186	2,473	998
Helsinki, Finland		4,309	4,033	5,696
Istanbul, Turkey		5,001	4,984	6,129
Kingston, Jamaica		1,474	2,690	551
Lagos, Nigeria		4,883	5,130	5,049
Lisbon, Portugal		2,972	2,943	4,152
Marseille, France		3,891	3,874	5,019
Montreal, Quebec		1,460		3,126
Naples, Italy		4,181	4,164	5,309
Nassau, Bahamas		962	2,274	1,166
New Orleans, La.		1,708	2,991	1,389
New York, N.Y.			1,460	1,974
Norfolk, Va.		294	1,700	1,779
Oslo, Norway		3,827	3,165	5,053
Piraeus, Greece		4,688	4,671	5,816
Port Said, Egypt		5,123	5,106	6,251
Rio de Janeiro, Brazil		4,770	5,354	4,367
St. John's, Nfld.		1,093	1,043	2,695
San Juan, Puerto Rico		1,399	2,445	993
Southampton, England		3,189	2,913	4,576

TO	FROM	San. Fran.	Vancouver	Panama[1]
Acapulco, Mexico		1,833	2,613	1,426
Anchorage, Alas.		1,872	1,444	5,093
Bombay, India		9,794	9,578	12,962
Calcutta, India		8,991	8,728	12,154
Colon, Panama[1]		3,298	4,076	44
Djakarta, Indonesia		7,641	7,360	10,637
Haiphong, Vietnam		6,496	6,231	9,673
Hong Kong		6,044	5,777	9,195
Honolulu, Hawaii		2,091	2,423	4,685
Los Angeles, Cal.		371	1,161	2,913
Manila, Philippines		6,221	5,976	9,347
Melbourne, Australia		6,970	7,343	7,928
Pusan, S. Korea		4,914	4,623	8,074
Saigon, Vietnam		6,878	6,664	10,017
San Francisco, Cal.			812	3,245
Seattle, Wash.		807	126	4,020
Shanghai, China		5,396	5,110	8,566
Singapore		7,353	7,078	10,505
Suva, Fiji		4,749	5,183	6,325
Valparaiso, Chile		5,140	5,915	2,616
Vancouver, B.C.		812		4,032
Vladivostok, USSR		4,563	4,378	7,741
Yokohama, Japan		4,536	4,262	7,682

TO	FROM	Port Said	Cape Town[2]	Singapore
Bombay, India		3,049	4,616	2,441
Calcutta, India		4,695	5,638	1,649
Dar es Salaam, Tanzania		3,238	2,365	4,042
Djakarta, Indonesia		5,293	5,276	525
Hong Kong		6,462	7,006	1,454
Kuwait		3,360	5,176	3,833
Manila, Philippines		6,348	6,777	1,330
Melbourne, Australia		7,842	5,963	3,844
Saigon, Vietnam		5,667	6,263	649
Singapore		5,018	5,614	
Yokohama, Japan		7,907	8,503	2,889

(1) Colon on the Atlantic is 44 nautical miles from Panama (port) on the Pacific. (2) Cape Town is 35 nautical miles northwest of the Cape of Good Hope. (3) Gibraltar (port) is 24 nautical miles east of the Strait of Gibraltar.

Mississippi River System and Gulf Intracoastal Waterway
Source: Corps of Engineers, Department of the Army.

(Note—The Mississippi River System comprises main channels and all tributaries of the Mississippi, Illinois, Missouri and Ohio Rivers. The Gulf Intracoastal Waterway, 1,137 miles long, extends from Apalachee Bay, Florida, to the Mexican border).

Port	1963 Tonnage	1972 Tonnage	1974 Tonnage
Minneapolis	825,429	1,671,323	2,528,968
St. Paul	4,210,106	5,059,621	5,143,251
Metropolitan St. Louis		*22,008,151	21,662,116
Memphis	7,024,509	10,612,101	11,096,770
Helena	1,740,938	2,672,209	3,238,699
Greenville	1,250,608	2,278,634	2,427,011

Port	1963 Tonnage	1972 Tonnage	1974 Tonnage
Lake Providence	Not Compiled	366,387	— —
Vicksburg	1,258,508	2,571,546	2,854,131
Natchez	582,942	898,682	1,162,865
Baton Rouge	30,272,282	52,903,352	59,126,282
New Orleans	79,130,710	125,719,378	144,189,409

*Port limits expanded in 1972

Reach

Port	1963 Tonnage	1972 Tonnage	1974 Tonnage
Mississippi R. System	271,319,518	419,805,850	442,844,560
Minneapolis to the Gulf	157,807,291	271,980,414	302,589,614
Minneapolis to St. Louis	30,943,237	60,746,385	62,013,644
St. Louis to Cairo	35,726,911	67,545,404	69,995,050
Cairo to Baton Rouge	49,370,417	102,698,573	111,381,795

Port	1963 Tonnage	1972 Tonnage	1974 Tonnage
Baton Rouge to N. Orleans	69,913,376	163,345,088	185,988,142
New Orleans to the Gulf	99,554,315	171,370,861	193,370,192
Gulf Intracoastal Waterway	67,320,002	108,999,010	103,076,142

Ton-Mileage of Freight Carried on Inland Waterways
Source: Corps of Engineers, Department of the Army.

System	1971	1972	1974
Atlantic coast waterways	28,619,707,000	29,238,516,000	35,391,955,000
Gulf coast waterways	30,473,095,000	32,513,287,000	33,510,277,000
Pacific coast waterways	8,525,013,000	9,549,062,000	10,253,815,000
Mississippi River system, including Ohio River and tributaries	142,385,476,000	158,453,365,000	168,274,841,000
Great Lakes System, U.S. Commerce	105,027,016,000		107,450,897,000
Total	**315,030,307,000**	**108,938,909,000**	**354,881,785,000**

Commerce at Principal North American Ports

Excluding Great Lakes Shipping
Source: Corps of Engineers, U.S. Army
Calendar Year 1974. Canadian Ports 1970. In tons of 2,000 pounds.

Ports Handling over 7,500,000 Tons

Port of New York, N.Y. and N.J.	195,095,611
New Orleans, La.	144,189,409
Houston, Texas	89,106,389
Philadelphia Harbor, Pa.	59,920,178
Norfolk Harbor, Va.	55,304,017
Baltimore Harbor and Channels, Md.	59,891,068
Baton Rouge, La.	59,126,282
Beaumont, Texas	33,503,880
Tampa Harbor, Fla.	40,918,807
Los Angeles Harbor, Calif.	25,919,367
Corpus Christi, Texas	32,844,400
Port Arthur, Texas	27,799,593
Portland Harbor, Me.	27,606,379
Paulsboro, N.J. and Vicinity	29,593,361
Mobile Harbor, Ala.	33,153,954
Boston, Mass.	25,728,945
Marcus Hook, Pa. and Vicinity	23,446,286
Huntington, W. Va.	12,020,612
Lake Charles, La.	16,564,654
Texas City, Tex.	20,151,777
Richmond Harbor, Calif.	14,763,822
Portland, Ore.	20,770,885
Clairton-Elizabeth, Pa.	9,696,822
Seattle Harbor, Wash.	14,251,989
Port of Newport News, Va.	17,682,465
Long Beach, Calif.	26,893,767
Pascagoula Harbor, Miss.	13,073,153
Penn Manor, Pa. and Vicinity	9,173,896
New Castle, Del. and Vicinity	12,084,268
New Haven Harbor, Conn.	12,054,957
Port of Metropolitan St. Louis	21,662,116
Jacksonville Harbor, Fla.	14,794,938
Cincinnati, Ohio	8,833,459
Providence River and Harbor, R.I.	8,856,218
Pittsburgh, Pa.	9,604,267
Port of Albany, N.Y.	9,610,040
Louisville, Ky.	8,172,141
Memphis, Tenn.	11,096,770
Port Everglades Harbor, Fla.	11,556,518
Vancouver, B.C.	26,517,891
Sept-Iles, P.Q.	24,240,914
Montreal, P.Q.	22,376,281
Thunder Bay, Ont.	20,754,165
Port Cartier, P.Q.	16,017,407
Halifax, N.S.	11,072,468
Quebec, P.Q.	8,552,289
Baie Comeau, P.Q.	7,695,715

Weedon Island, Fla.	339,392
Guntersville, Ala.	1,353,428
Greenville, Miss.	2,427,011
Gulfport Harbor, Miss.	821,024
Natchez, Miss.	1,162,865
Vicksburg, Miss.	2,854,131
Brownsville, Texas	2,836,684
Freeport Harbor, Texas	8,896,947
Galveston, Texas	7,171,226
Harbor Island, Texas	5,406,031
Orange, Texas	1,131,360
Port Isabel, Texas	255,938
Matagorda Ship Channel, Port Lavaca, Tex.	4,930,654
Sabine Pass Harbor, Texas	390,370
Victoria, Texas	3,135,921
Helena, Ark.	3,238,699
Chattanooga, Tenn.	1,796,770
Knoxville, Tenn.	357,812
Nashville, Tenn.	2,946,916
Mount Vernon, Ind.	1,904,916
Kansas City, Mo.	3,562,966
Minneapolis, Minn.	2,528,968
St. Paul, Minn.	5,143,251
Carpinteria, Calif.	344,848
Crescent City Harbor, Calif.	262,309
El Segundo, Calif.	8,504,884
Humboldt Harbor and Bay, Calif.	1,397,567
Moss Landing Harbor, Calif.	713,173
Oakland Harbor, Calif.	6,811,770
Redwood City Harbor, Calif.	447,135
San Diego Harbor, Calif.	2,115,074
San Francisco Harbor, Calif.	3,913,071
San Luis Obispo Harbor, Calif.	1,548,005
Stockton, Calif.	1,476,216
Ventura Harbor, Calif.	1,709,882
Astoria, Ore.	2,233,754
Coos Bay, Ore.	7,632,831
Oregon Slough (No. Portland Hbr.), Ore.	521,221
Anacortes Harbor, Wash.	3,971,825
Bellingham Bay and Harbor, Wash.	1,945,661
Everett Harbor, Wash.	4,321,156
Grays Harbor and Chehalis River, Wash.	3,495,352
Hammersley Inlet, Wash. (Shelton Hbr.).	1,106,472
Longview, Wash.	1,767,611
Olympia Harbor, Wash.	1,216,135
Port Angeles Harbor, Wash.	2,989,619
Port Gamble Harbor, Wash.	495,867
Port Townsend Harbor, Wash.	1,338,391
Tacoma Harbor, Wash.	7,600,036
Vancouver, Wash.	3,142,364

Other Ports, Maine to Washington

Searsport Harbor, Maine	1,216,294
Portsmouth Harbor, N.H.	2,364,290
Burlington Harbor, Vt.	555,953
Beverly Harbor, Mass.	254,136
Fall River Harbor, Mass.	5,122,188
Gloucester Harbor, Mass.	187,766
New Bedford, Fairhaven Harbor, Mass.	340,874
Salem Harbor, Mass.	2,030,773
Bridgeport Harbor, Conn.	3,295,195
New London Harbor, Conn.	4,579,685
Norwalk Harbor, Conn.	799,974
Stamford Harbor, Conn.	989,766
Hempstead Harbor, N.Y.	3,229,077
Huntington Harbor, N.Y.	256,923
Peekskill Harbor, N.Y.	524,402
Plattsburg, N.Y.	524,402
Port Chester Harbor, N.Y.	318,537
Port Jefferson Harbor, N.Y.	4,464,031
Rondout Harbor, N.Y.	650,322
Tarrytown Harbor, N.Y.	669,239
Camden-Gloucester, N.J.	10,852,964
Trenton Harbor, N.J.	1,190,989
Aliquippa-Rochester, Pa.	6,138,449
Chester, Pa.	446,349
Wilmington Harbor, Del.	3,888,848
Washington Harbor, D.C.	1,412,631
Alexandria, Va.	162,993
Port of Hopewell, Va.	1,156,422
Port of Richmond, Va.	1,544,901
Morehead City Harbor, N.C.	1,512,883
Port of Wilmington, N.C.	8,718,081
Charleston Harbor, S.C.	8,992,563
Georgetown Harbor, S.C.	1,619,986
Brunswick Harbor, Ga.	1,965,799
Savannah Harbor, Ga.	9,698,679
Canaveral Harbor, Fla.	3,241,780
Charlotte Harbor, Fla.	2,660,184
Fernandina Harbor, Fla.	372,791
Miami Harbor, Fla.	4,141,407
Palm Beach Harbor, Fla.	1,097,230
Panama City Harbor, Fla.	1,891,204
Pensacola Harbor, Fla.	2,238,582
Port St. Joe Harbor, Fla.	548,797
St. Petersburg Harbor, Fla.	306,854

Alaska, Hawaii, Puerto Rico

Anchorage, Alaska	2,340,181
Iliuliuk Harbor, Alaska	157,477
Juneau Harbor, Alaska	154,329
Ketchikan Harbor, Alaska	2,162,374
Sitka Harbor, Alaska	969,901
Skagway Harbor, Alaska	1,514,744
Whittier Harbor, Alaska	662,315
Wrangell Harbor, Alaska	1,023,323
Barbers Point, Oahu, Hawaii	4,360,221
Hilo Harbor, Hawaii, Hawaii	928,619
Honolulu Harbor, Oahu, Hawaii	7,556,891
Kahului Harbor, Maui, Hawaii	982,110
Kaumalapau Harbor, Lanai, Hawaii	197,910
Kaunakakai Harbor, Molokai, Hawaii	162,010
Kawaihae Harbor, Hawaii, Hawaii	291,036
Nawiliwili Harbor, Kauai, Hawaii	380,495
Pearl Harbor, Oahu, Hawaii	553,273
Wake Island Harbor	None reported
Guanica Harbor, P.R.	179,687
Mayaguez Harbor, P.R.	308,156
Ponce Harbor, P.R.	960,508
San Juan Harbor, P.R.	11,804,869
St. Thomas Harbor, V.I.	371,796
Guam Island, Pacific Ocean	193,841
Comer Brook, Nfld.	1,225,372
St. John's, Nfld.	794,494
Charlottetown, P.E.I.	554,399
Hantsport, N.S.	1,648,191
Sydney, N.S.	1,966,105
Saint John, N.B.	6,400,885
Port Alfred, Que.	4,973,666
Sorel, Que.	6,813,817
Trois Rivieres, Que.	4,954,649
Port Colborne, Ont.	2,259,345
Sarnia, Ont.	7,331,360
Saulte Ste. Marie, Ont.	5,753,245
Toronto, Ont.	5,162,904
Windsor, Ont.	3,550,556
Nanaimo, B.C.	2,492,110
New Westminster, B.C.	4,564,477
Powell River, B.C.	1,783,686
Victoria, B.C.	2,071,342

Commerce at Great Lakes Ports

Source: Corps of Engineers, U.S. Army
Calendar Year 1974, in tons of 2,000 pounds

Duluth-Superior Hbr., Minn. & Wis.	40,344,702	Port Dolomite, Mich.	4,436,981
Silver Bay, Minn.	11,420,140	Port Gypsum, Mich.	273,027
Taconite Harbor, Minn.	12,543,129	Port Huron, Mich.	308,098
Ashland Harbor, Wis.	378,335	Port Inland, Mich.	4,324,129
Green Bay Harbor, Wis.	2,531,487	Port Of Detroit, Mich.	-27,541,167
Kewaunee Harbor, Wis.	1,281,178	Presque Isle Harbor, Mich.	3,118,370
Manitowoc Harbor, Wis.	869,439	St. Clair, Mich.	3,075,056
Milwaukee Harbor, Wis.	4,263,862	St. Ignace, Mich.	119,849
Oak Creek, Wis.	154,837	St. Joseph Harbor, Mich.	433,073
Port Washington Harbor, Wis.	676,362	Sault Ste. Marie, Mich.	87,464
Racine Harbor, Wis.	74,726	Stoneport, Mich.	9,859,217
Sheboygan Harbor, Wis.	182,376	Traverse City Harbor, Mich.	405,158
Two Rivers Harbor, Wis.	31,371	Wells, Mich.	116,662
Alabaster, Mich.	409,239	Port Of Chicago, Ill.	-45,885,579
Alpena Harbor, Mich.	3,082,304	Waukegan Harbor, Ill.	474,335
Calcite, Mich.	14,767,439	Buffington Harbor, Ind.	2,367,775
Cheboygan Harbor, Mich.	117,155	Gary Harbor, Ind.	10,954,691
Detour, Mich.	204,494	Indiana Harbor, Ind.	17,164,765
Drummond Island, Mich.	2,909,592	Michigan City Harbor, Ind.	188
Escanaba, Mich.	9,685,677	Ashtabula Harbor, Ohio	10,852,259
Frankfort Harbor, Mich.	801,645	Cleveland Harbor, Ohio	21,933,874
Gladstone Harbor, Mich.	230,924	Conneaut Harbor, Ohio	16,566,435
Gd. Haven Harbor & Gd. River, Mich.	2,215,873	Fairport Harbor, Ohio	2,937,601
Holland Harbor, Mich.	368,891	Huron Harbor, Ohio	3,325,132
Lime Island, Mich.	37,813	Lorain Harbor, Ohio	9,076,890
Ludington Harbor, Mich.	2,178,835	Marblehead, Ohio	766,496
Mackinaw City, Mich.	90,742	Sandusky Harbor, Ohio	4,220,604
Manistee Harbor, Mich.	506,769	Toledo Harbor, Ohio	21,556,519
Manistique Harbor, Mich.	93	Erie Harbor, Pa.	903,187
Marquette Harbor, Mich.	1,036,070	Ogdensburg Harbor, N.Y.	214,944
Marysville, Mich.	577,663	Oswego Harbor, N.Y.	902,343
Mendminee Harbor, Mich. & Wis.	152,398	Port Of Buffalo, N.Y.	10,442,084
Muskegon Harbor, Mich.	2,508,138	Rochester (Charlotte) Harbor, N.Y.	309,886
Petoskey Penn Dixie Harbor, Mich.	501,509		

Total Exports and Exports Financed by Foreign Aid

Source: Bureau of International Commerce, Dept. of Commerce

(In millions of dollars)	1965	1970	1971	1972	1973	1974	1975
Exports, total.	27,530	43,224	44,130	49,778	71,314	98,506	107,652
Agricultural commodities.	6,306	7,349	7,786	9,505	17,855	22,257	22,097
Nonagricultural commodities.	20,445	35,310	35,763	39,714	52,943	75,650	85,094
Manufactured goods (domestic).	17,439	29,343	30,443	33,742	44,702	63,527	71,005
Military grant—aid.	779	565	581	560	516	599	461
Export financed under P.L. 480.	1,323	1,021	983	1,064	750	760	1,181
Sales for foreign currency.	899	276	174	70	4	—	—
Donations, including disaster relief.	253	255	291	376	209	272	257
Barter for strategic goods.	19	—	—	—	—	—	—
Long-term dollar credit sales.	152	490	518	618	537	488	924

Value of Principal Agricultural Exports

(In millions of dollars)	Avg. 1961-1965	Avg. 1966-1970	1965	1970	1972	1973	1974
Bread grains & preparations	1,268	1,197	1,214	1,144	1,490	4,278	4,678
Coarse grains, except rice	841	1,082	1,162	1,099	1,559	3,598	4,727
Rice	178	311	244	314	389	539	853
Fodders and feeds	179	386	278	496	596	1,266	1,287
Vegetable oils, oilseeds, etc.	774	1,182	1,029	1,642	1,852	3,417	4,865
Cotton, unmanufactured	639	408	495	377	508	940	1,353

Value of U.S. Merchandise Exports and Imports

Source: International Trade Analysis Division, Dept. of Commerce
Value in millions of dollars (revised)

	U.S. exports					U.S. imports		
	Domestic and foreign							
Year	Total	Military aid	Excl. military aid	Domestic merchandise	Foreign merchandise	General	For consumption	Gross merchandise balance[1]
1950. . .	10,279	[2]282	9,997	10,146	133	8,954	8,844	1,043
1955. . .	15,554	1,256	14,298	15,426	128	11,566	11,519	2,732
1960. . .	20,608	949	19,659	20,408	201	15,073	15,069	4,586
1965. . .	27,521	779	26,742	27,178	343	21,427	21,345	5,315
1970. . .	43,224	565	42,659	42,590	634	39,952	39,756	2,707
1972. . .	49,778	560	49,219	48,979	600	55,583	53,310	6,384
1973. . .	71,314	516	70,798	70,223	1,091	69,121	68,656	1,347
1974. . .	98,506	599	97,907	97,143	1,363	100,972	99,391	—3,065
1975. . .	107,652	461	107,191	106,157	1,495	96,140	95,729	11,051

(1.) Balance represents exports excluding military grant-aid valued f.a.s. less imports which are valued generally at the market value in the foreign country. Export values include both commercially-financed shipments and shipments under government-financed programs. (2) Includes data from April when shipments under the program began.

Merchant Fleets of the World

Source: Maritime Administration, U.S. Dept. of Commerce

Oceangoing steam and motor ships of 1,000 gross tons and over as of Dec. 31, 1975; excludes ships operating exclusively on the Great Lakes and inland waterways and special types such as channel ships, icebreakers, cable ships, etc., and merchant ships owned by any military force. Tonnage is in thousands.

Gross tonnage is a volume measurement; each cargo gross ton represents 100 cubic ft. of enclosed space. Deadweight tonnage is the carrying capacity of a ship in long tons (2,240 lbs. ea.)

Country of Registry	Total No.	Gross Tons	Dwt. Tons	Bulk Carriers No.	Bulk Carriers Dwt.	Freighters No.	Freighters Dwt.	Tankers No.	Tankers Dwt.
Total—All Countries	22,872	333,042	556,572	4,272	150,080	11,517	95,197	5,311	302,217
United States[1]	857	12,301	17,694	19	544	505	7,018	267	9,711
Privately owned	580	10,103	15,028	19	544	305	4,959	250	9,475
Government owned	277	2,198	2,666	-	-	200	2,059	17	236
British Commonwealth									
United Kingdom	1,576	33,229	54,913	343	14,508	617	5,935	459	32,869
Australia	90	1,083	1,570	33	728	39	349	18	493
Bangladesh	16	83	122	-	-	14	118	2	4
British Colonies	101	1,887	3,181	31	1,027	33	214	28	1,923
Canada	68	380	524	11	175	21	77	26	260
Cyprus	573	3,252	4,762	48	601	461	3,233	47	860
Ghana	19	127	166	-	-	18	163	-	-
India	308	4,400	6,943	76	3,129	196	2,235	25	1,510
Malaysia	26	360	518	7	304	13	121	4	89
New Zealand	36	154	210	10	36	21	93	2	51
Nigeria	19	127	180	1	15	18	165	-	-
Pakistan	54	478	639	2	30	44	524	1	27
Singapore	403	4,594	7,600	44	1,613	254	1,872	73	3,965
Algeria	27	212	289	3	36	17	84	7	169
Argentina	155	1,296	1,796	14	262	66	581	49	808
Austria	19	74	111	2	34	17	77	-	-
Belgium	79	1,341	2,130	21	997	29	385	21	697
Brazil	260	2,837	4,546	35	1,304	158	1,236	53	1,944
Bulgaria	114	868	1,314	29	384	57	361	20	532
Chile	43	384	585	7	156	27	264	6	160
China (Taiwan)	153	1,401	2,143	29	720	91	703	14	616
*China (People's Rep.)	379	2,913	4,254	46	804	248	2,263	48	1,029
Colombia	36	207	274	1	2	34	243	1	29
*Cuba	64	428	581	4	34	42	435	7	76
Czechoslovakia	13	144	214	5	160	8	54	-	-
Denmark	333	4,480	7,430	40	1,093	212	1,640	59	4,594
Ecuador	17	142	206	-	-	6	53	9	140
Egypt	57	291	405	-	-	36	144	12	215
Finland	187	1,829	2,895	17	288	101	574	51	1,988
France	444	10,319	17,690	57	2,405	189	1,869	154	13,190
Gabon	5	106	183	1	15	3	28	1	140
Germany (West)	611	8,347	13,453	79	3,993	406	3,517	83	5,627
Germany (East)	152	1,217	1,749	18	369	106	777	12	513
Greece	1,804	22,598	37,638	483	13,205	879	8,439	345	15,557
Indonesia	169	629	804	10	49	109	525	20	136
Iran	47	634	1,024	-	-	38	471	8	549
Iraq	17	278	455	-	-	6	71	11	384
Ireland	17	164	247	9	229	5	12	3	6
Israel	49	452	587	9	277	32	234	-	-
Italy	633	10,064	16,081	151	6,541	180	1,312	236	7,953
Ivory Coast	18	135	185	-	-	16	174	-	-
Japan	2,051	37,164	63,238	535	21,270	866	7,586	531	33,950
Korea (South)	163	1,324	2,208	24	380	104	652	30	1,150
Kuwait	42	1,037	1,781	1	9	32	469	8	1,294
Lebanon	46	142	201	3	8	41	189	-	-
Liberia	2,546	70,139	132,694	925	37,243	544	5,594	1,014	89,470
Libya	9	234	425	-	-	3	10	6	415
Maldives	35	96	123	-	-	31	114	-	-
Mexico	49	464	689	3	61	17	138	27	484
Morocco	23	74	112	1	25	12	54	2	6
Netherlands	448	5,457	8,496	35	920	293	2,369	88	5,074
Norway	991	27,167	47,796	318	16,696	289	2,451	332	28,467
Panama	1,556	13,743	22,112	224	4,515	1,017	7,023	238	10,224
Peru	40	347	518	9	216	26	245	4	52
Philippines	154	787	1,139	5	112	93	598	29	366
Poland	291	2,821	4,220	75	1,613	182	1,522	14	1,001
Portugal	104	1,096	1,635	6	125	61	472	24	954
*Romania	96	793	1,197	18	397	65	343	7	433
Saudi Arabia	22	124	233	-	-	12	47	3	170
Somalia	249	1,840	2,683	30	601	199	1,767	14	284
South Africa	55	450	575	4	88	40	333	3	61
Spain	452	4,998	8,450	61	1,943	215	1,043	114	5,257
Sweden	324	7,511	12,723	88	4,785	128	1,165	79	6,524
Switzerland	27	253	375	5	171	18	195	2	6
Thailand	29	150	245	1	2	18	91	10	152
Turkey	107	849	1,231	8	205	61	476	23	518
Uruguay	17	156	240	-	-	8	47	7	180
*USSR[2]	2,404	14,292	18,250	148	1,652	1,434	9,116	462	5,861
Venezuela	43	428	606	3	16	23	166	16	415
Vietnam (N. & S.)	21	80	118	1	3	17	72	3	43
Yugoslavia	226	1,853	2,692	37	888	157	1,348	17	382
Zaire	11	106	153	-	-	8	128	-	-

*Source material limited. (1) Excludes 57 non-merchant type ships which are currently in the National Defense Reserve Fleet. (2) Includes U.S. Government-owned ships transferred to USSR under lend-lease agreements, 38 of which are still under that registry.

Notable Ocean Passages by Ships

Time	From	To	Distance Naut. mi.	Date	Ship
		One Hundred Years of Sailing Vessels			
16d	Liverpool.	New York	3,150	Nov. 1846	Yorkshire
76d 6h	San Francisco. . .	Boston	. . .	1853	Northern Light
12d 6h	Boston Light. . . .	Light Rock.	. . .	1854	James Baines
89d	New York	San Francisco. . .	15,091	1854	Flying Cloud
89d 20h	New York	San Francisco. . .	13,700	1860	Andrew Jackson
63d 18h 15m. .	Liverpool.	Melbourne.		1868-69	Thermopylae
13d 1h 25m. .	New York	Liverpool.	3,150	. . . .	Red Jacket
36d	50 S. Lat.	Golden Gate		. . . .	Starr King
12d 12h	Equator.	San Francisco. . .		. . . .	Golden Fleece
12d 4h 1m. . .	Sandy Hook	England	3,013	1905	Atlantic
23d	England	Sandy Hook	3,013	1928	Atlantic
22d 6h 7m. . .	Bishop's Rock. . .	Boston Light. . . .		1936	Yankee
		Atlantic Crossings by power vessels			
29d 4h	Savannah	Liverpool.	. . .	May 22, 1819	Savannah (Amer.) (a)
15d	Bristol.	New York	. . .	Apr. 1838	Great Western (Br.)
14d 8h	Liverpool.	New York	3,150	July 1840	Britannia (Br.) (b)
9d 13h	Liverpool.	New York	3,054	Aug. 1852	Baltic (Amer.)
8d 1h 45m. . .	Queenstown	New York	2,780	1856	Persia
8d 2h 48m. . .	Queenstown	New York	2,780	1866	Scotia
7d 4h 1m. . . .	Queenstown	New York	. . .	1867	City of Paris (Br.)
7d 22h 3m. . .	Queenstown	New York	2,780	1869	City of Brussels (Br.)
7d 20h 9m. . .	Queenstown	New York	2,780	1873	Baltic (Br.)
7d 15h 48m. .	Queenstown	New York	2,780	1875	City of Berlin (Br.)
7d 11h 37m. .	Queenstown	New York	2,780	1876	Germanic (Br.)
7d 10h 53m. .	Queenstown	New York	2,780	1877	Britannic (Br.)
7d 8h 0m. . .	New York	Queenstown	. . .	1879	Arizona (Br.)
6d 7h 23m. . .	Queenstown	New York	2,780	1880	Arizona (Br.)
6d 18h 37m. .	New York	Queenstown	2,780	1882	Alaska (Br.)
6d 21h 40m. .	Queenstown	New York	2,780	1883	Alaska (Br.)
6d 10h 40m. .	New York	Queenstown	2,780	1884	Oregon (Br.)
6d 4h 34m. . .	Queenstown	New York	2,780	1887	Umbria (Br.)
5d 1h 55m. . .	Queenstown	New York	2,780	1888	Etruria (Br.)
5d 22h 50m. .	New York	Queenstown	2,780	1889	City of Paris (Br.)
5d 16h 31m. .	Queenstown	New York	2,780	1891	Teutonic (Br.)
5d 14h 24m. .	Queenstown	New York	2,780	1892	City of Paris (Br.)
5d 9h 6m. . . .	Queenstown	New York	2,780	1893	Campania (Br.)
5d 7h 23m. . .	Queenstown	New York	2,780	1894	Lucania (Br.)
5d 15h 20m. .	Southampton	New York	3,189	1898	Kaiser Wilhelm Der Grosse (Ger.)
5d 7h 38m. . .	Sandy Hook	Plymouth.	3,082	Sept. 1900	Deutschland (Ger.)
4d 11h 42m. .	Queenstown	New York	2,780	1909	Lusitania (Br.)
4d 10h 41m. .	Queenstown	New York	2,780	1910	Mauretania (Br.)
5d 6h 21m. . .	New York	Cherbourg.	3,227	Oct. 1924	Leviathan (Amer.)
4d 17h 42m. .	Cherbourg.	Ambrose Lt.	3,164	July 1929	Bremen (Ger.)*
4d 14h 30m. .	New York	Plymouth.	3,082	July 1929	Bremen (Ger.)
4d 19h 57m. .	Ambrose Lt.	Cherbourg.	3,196	June 1933	Europa (Ger.)
4d 16h 48m. .	Cherbourg.	New York	3,149	July 1933	Europa (Ger.)
4d 13h 58m. .	Gibraltar.	Ambrose Lt.	3,181	Aug. 1933	Rex (Ital.)
4d 14h 27m. .	Cherbourg.	Ambrose Lt.	3,092	Nov. 1934	Bremen (Ger.)
4d 12h 24m. .	Cherbourg.	Ambrose Lt.	3,158	May-June, 1936	Queen Mary (Br.)*
3d 23h 02m. .	Bishop's Rock. . .	Ambrose Lt.	2,906	July-Aug., 1937	Normandie (Fr.)
3d 22h 07m. .	New York	Southampton	2,936	Aug. 1937	Normandie (Fr.)
3d 20h 42m. .	Ambrose Lt.	Bishop's Rock. . .	3,120	Aug. 10-14, 1938	Queen Mary (Br.)
3d 31h 48m. .	Bishop's Rock. . .	Ambrose Lt.	3,120	Aug. 1948	Queen Mary (Br.)
3d 10h 40m. .	Ambrose Lt.	Bishop's Rock. . .	2,942	July 3-7, 1952	United States (U.S.)* (e)
3d 12h 12m. .	Bishop's Rock. . .	Ambrose Lt.	2,902	July 11-14, 1952	United States (U.S.) (e)
3d 11h 24m. .	Bishop's Rock. . .	Ambrose Lt.	2,912	Aug. 20, 1973	Sea-Land Exchange (U.S.) (j)
		Other Ocean Passages			
3d 00h 36m. .	San Pedro	Honolulu	2,226	June 1928	U.S.S. Lexington
86d	Halifax.	Vancouver	7,295	July-Sept. 1944	St. Roch (Can.) (c)
3d 2h 30m. . .	San Francisco. . .	Oahu, Hawaii. . . .	2,091	July 16-19, 1945	U.S.S. Indianapolis (d)
4d 8h 51m. . .	Gibraltar.	Newport News . . .	3,360	Nov. 26, 1945	U.S.S. Lake Champlain
7d 18h 36m. .	Japan.	San Francisco. . .	5,000	July-Aug. 4, 1950	U.S.S. Boxer
7d 13h	Yokosuka	Alameda	5,000	June 1-9, 1951	U.S.S. Philippine Sea
8d 11h	Nantucket	Portland, Eng. . . .	3,161	Feb. 25-Mar. 4, '58	U.S.S. Skate (f)
7d 5h	Lizard Head	Nantucket, Mass. .	. . .	Mar. 23-29, 1958	U.S.S. Skate (f)
15d	Pearl Harbor	Iceland (via N. Pole)		July 23-Aug. 7, '58	U.S.S. Nautilus (g)
84d	New London	Rehoboth, Del. . . .	41,500	Feb. 16-May 10, '60	U.S.S. Triton (h)
6d	Baffin Bay	NW Passage, Pac	850	Aug. 15-20, 1960	U.S.S. Seadragon (i)
12d 16h 22m.	New York	Cape Town	6,786	Oct. 30-Nov. 11, '62	African Comet*
5d 6h	Kobe	Race Rock, B.C. . .	4,126	Aug. 24, 1973	Sea-Land Trade (U.S.)

*Maiden voyage. (a) The Savannah, a fully rigged sailing vessel with steam auxiliary (over 300 tons, 98.5 ft. long, beam 25.8 ft., depth 12.9 ft.) was launched in the East River in 1818. It was the first ship to use steam in crossing any ocean. It was supplied with engines and detachable paddle wheels. On its famous voyage it used steam 105 hours. (b) First Cunard liner. (c) First ship to complete NW Passage in one season. (d) Carried Hiroshima atomic bomb in World War II. (e) Set world speed record; average speed eastbound on maiden voyage 35.59 knots (about 41 m.p.h.); westbound, 34.51 knots. (f) First atomic submarine to cross Atlantic, both ways submerged. (g) World's first atomic submarine also first to make undersea voyage under polar ice cap, 1,830 mi. from Point Barrow, Alaska, to Atlantic Ocean, Aug. 1-4, 1958, reaching North Pole Aug. 3. Second undersea transit of the North Pole made by submarine USS Skate Aug. 11, 1958, during trip from New London, Conn., and return. (h) World's largest submarine. Nuclear-powered Triton was submerged during nearly all its voyage around the globe. It duplicated the route of Ferdinand Magellan's circuit (1519-1522), 30,708 mi., starting from St. Paul Rocks off the NE coast of Brazil, Feb. 24-Apr. 25, 1960, then sailed to Cadiz, Spain, before returning home. (i) First underwater transit of Northwest Passage. (j) Fastest freighter crossing of Atlantic.

Fastest Scheduled Train Runs in U.S. and Canada

Source: Donald M. Steffee; figures are based on 1976 timetables

Electric Traction-Passenger-(81 mph and over)

Railroad	Train	From	To	Dis.	Time	Speed
Amtrak	Metroliners (5)	Baltimore	Wilmington	68.4	44	93.3
Amtrak	Metroliners (7)	Wilmington	Baltimore	68.4	44	93.3
Amtrak	Metroliners (5)	Baltimore	Wilmington	68.4	45	91.2
Amtrak	Metroliners (5)	Wilmington	Baltimore	68.4	45	91.2
Amtrak	Metroliner	Metro Park	Philadelphia	66.3	44	90.4
Amtrak	Metroliners (2)	Wilmington	Baltimore	68.4	46	89.2
Amtrak	Metroliner	Newark	Trenton	48.1	34	84.9
Amtrak	Metroliner	Metro Park	Trenton	33.9	24	84.7
Amtrak	Metroliner	No. Philadelphia	Newark	76.0	54	84.4
Amtrak	Metroliner	Baltimore	Philadelphia	94.0	67	84.2
Amtrak	Metroliners (3)	Newark	Philadelphia	80.5	58	83.3
Amtrak	Metroliners (3)	Metro Park	Philadelphia	66.3	48	82.9
Amtrak	Metroliners (2)	Trenton	Newark	48.1	35	82.4
Amtrak	Metroliners (5)	Philadelphia	Newark	80.5	59	81.9
Amtrak	Metroliner	Newark	Philadelphia	80.5	59	81.9
Amtrak	Metroliner	New York	No. Philadelphia	86.0	63	81.9
Amtrak	Metroliner	Philadelphia	Baltimore	94.0	69	81.7
Amtrak	Metroliner	Trenton	Metro Park	33.9	25	81.3
Amtrak	Metroliners (2)	Philadelphia	Metro Park	66.3	49	81.2
Amtrak	Metroliner	New York	Trenton	58.1	43	81.1

Diesel Traction-Passenger-(75 mph and over)

Railroad	Train	From	To	Dis.	Time	Speed
Canadian National	Turbotrain	Kingston	Dorval	165.8	109	91.3
Canadian National	Turbotrain	Kingston	Dorval	165.8	110	90.4
Canadian National	Turbotrains (2)	Dorval	Kingston	165.8	113	88.0
Canadian National	Turbotrains (2)	Kingston	Guildwood	145.1	102	85.4
Canadian National	Turbotrains (2)	Guildwood	Kingston	145.1	103	84.7
Canadian National	Ontarian	Cobourg	Trenton	32.3	24	80.7
Amtrak	Southwest Limited	Dodge City	Hutchinson	120.1	90	80.1
Amtrak	Southwest Limited	Garden City	Lamar	99.9	76	78.9
Amtrak	Lone Star	Marceline	Carrollton	39.1	30	78.2
Amtrak	Southwest Limited	Lamar	Garden City	99.9	77	77.8
Canadian National	Rapido	Dorval	Kingston	165.8	128	77.7
Canadian National	Rapido	Dorval	Guildwood	310.9	244	76.4
Canadian National	Rapido	Guildwood	Dorval	310.9	245	76.1
Canadian National	Rapido	Guildwood	Kingston	145.1	115	75.7
Amtrak	San Francisco Zephyr	Akron	McCook	143.0	114	75.3
Amtrak	Flordian	West Palm Beach	Sebring	102.6	82	75.1

Diesel Traction-Freight-(65 mph and over)

Railroad	Train	From	To	Dis.	Time	Speed
Santa Fe	Super C	Gallup	Winslow	127.2	105	72.7
Santa Fe	Super C	Winslow	Gallup	127.2	105	72.7
Santa Fe	Super C	Waynoka	Wellington	106.6	90	71.1
Santa Fe	Super C	Clovis	Belen	240.7	205	70.4
Santa Fe	Super C	Fort Madison	Marceline	111.8	100	67.1
Santa Fe	Super C	Marceline	Fort Madison	111.8	100	67.1
Santa Fe	Super C	Amarillo	Waynoka	205.2	185	66.6
Santa Fe	Super C	Wellington	Waynoka	106.6	96	66.6
Santa Fe	Chief No. 568	Gallup	Winslow	127.2	115	66.4
Santa Fe	No. 991	Kingman	Seligman	88.1	80	66.1
Santa Fe	Super C	Belen	Clovis	240.7	220	65.6

Some Fast Railway Runs in the U. S. and Canada

Date		Railroad	Run	Miles	H.	M.	S.	MPH
May,	1876	Pennsylvania-Chicago & Northwestern-Union Pacific-Central Pacific	Jersey City-Oakland	3310.8	83	45		39.5
July,	1885	New York, West Shore & Buffalo	East Buffalo-Weehawken	422.6	9	23		45.0
Aug.,	1894	Atlantic Coast Line Route	Jacksonville-Washington	780.9	15	49		49.4
Sept.,	1895	New York Central	New York-Buffalo	436.32	6	51	56	66.54
Oct.,	1895	Lake Shore & Michigan Southern	Chicago-Buffalo	510.1	8	1	7	63.61
May,	1905	Atlantic City	Camden-Atlantic City	55.5		42	33	78.3
July,	1905	Atchison, Topeka & Santa Fe	Los Angeles-Chicago	2244.5	44	54		50.0
April,	1911	Lake Shore & Michigan Southern	Toledo-Elkhart	133.0	1	46*		75.28
Nov.,	1925	Canadian National	Montreal-Vancouver	2937.5	67	0	0	43.8
May,	1934	Chicago, Burlington & Quincy	Denver-Chicago	1015.31	13	5	44	77.6
July,	1934	Chicago, Milwaukee, St. Paul & Pac.	Chicago-Milwaukee	85.0	1	7	35	75.46
Oct.,	1934	Union Pacific	Cheyene-Omaha	506.7	6	11	0	81.95
Oct.,	1934	Union Pacific, Chicago & Northwestern, New York Central	Los Angeles-New York	3257.6	56	55		57.2
Jan.,	1935	Pennsylvania	Philadelphia-Washington	134.2	1	50		73.2
April,	1935	New York, New Haven & Hartford	Providence-Boston	43.8		32	35	80.6
Oct.,	1936	Chicago, Burlington & Quincy	Chicago-Denver	1017.23	12	12	27	83.3
May,	1937	Atchison, Topeka & Santa Fe	Los Angeles-Chicago	2228.6	36	49		60.5
July,	1966	New York Central	Bryan, Ohio (MP 350-345)	5.0			39³/₄	181.0*
May,	1967	Pennsylvania	County Tower-Milheim Tower	21.2		11†		115.66†
Jan.,	1968	Atchison, Topeka & Santa Fe	Corwith-Hobart Yards (Super C Frgt.)	2202.1	34	35	40	63.6

*The official speed measured by ground instruments was 183.85 mph on passing mile post 347 + 13 over an accurately measured 300 feet of track. This is the highest speed on rails ever recorded in the United States. The run was made by a single Budd Rail Diesel car fitted with two turbo-jet J-47 aircraft engines mounted on forward end. †Time and speed calculated from standing start at County Tower to passing Milheim Tower (end of test track) at 80-mph, after which the train was gradually braked down on regular track to a stop in Trenton passenger station. Between mileposts 46 and 51, speed was 150 mph or over, a momentary peak of 156 mph, was reached in the vicinity of milepost 47.

Fastest Scheduled Train Runs in European Countries
Passenger

Country	Train	From	To	Dis.	Time	Speed
France	Etendard	St. Perre des Corps	Poitiers	62.7	37	101.5
Great Britain	Six trains	Rugby	Watford	65.1	44	88.8
West Germany	Three trains	Offenburg	Freiburg	39.0	27	86.7
Russia	Aurora*	Moscow	Bologoe	205.5	147	83.9
Italy	Three trains	Rome	Naples	130.3	95	82.3
	Two trains	Naples	Rome	130.3	95	82.3
Sweden	Gotëborgarin	Skovde	Hallsberg	70.8	55	77.2

Freight

Great Britain	Freightliner	Carlisle	Wigan	105.3	95½	66.2
France	Freight Express	Orange	St. Rambert d'Albon	87.6	81	64.9

*Operated during summer months only.

114 Japanese Trains Average over 100 Miles per Hour

Service between Tokyo and Osaka via the standard-gauged New Tokaido Line is headed by 57 "Hikari" superexpress trains daily in each direction which make the 320.1-mile run, inclusive of stops at Nagoya and Kyoto, in 3 hrs. 10 min. at average overall speed of 101.1 mph. Between Tokyo and Nagoya, 212.4 miles are covered in 121 minutes - 105.3 mph. With the extension of the New Sanyo Line westward from Okayama to Hakata in March, 1975, the runs of many "Hikari" trains were extended to provide service over the new line. Fastest time for the 664 mile run between Tokyo and Hakata is 6 hr. 56 min. - at 95.8 mph inclusive of six stops.

French Achieve 90-100 Miles per Hour Speeds on Regular Schedule

Having upgraded about 80% of its Paris to Bordeaux mainline to a 125-mile an hour standard, French National Railways has quickened the times of a number of trains between the two cities. Below are shown the fastest point-to-point timings in current French timetables.

Train	From	To	Time		Speed
L'Etendard..........	St. Pierre des Corps...	Poitiers.......	62.7	37	101.5
L'Etendard..........	Paris...............	St. Pierre des Corps...	143.4	93	92.2
L'Aquitaine.........	Angouleme........	Poitiers.............	70.00	46	91.3

New Canadian Speed Records Set in 1976

During a series of tests of the new LRC (light, rapid, comfortable) train conducted on March 10th on Canadian Pacific's Adirondack subdivision, an average of 124.5 m.p.h. was made over a one mile stretch of track wherein a top speed of 129 m.p.h. was attained.

The above record was broken on April 22 as a nine-car Canadian National Turbotrain accelerated from 95 to 140.6 m.p.h. over a smooth 20-mile stretch of welded rail east of Prescott, Ont. (miles 104 to 84). This run was staged "to attract attention to Canadian National's new passenger service in the Quebec-Ontario Corridor."

American Railway Statistics
Source: Interstate Commerce Commission

Year	Mileage Owned	Miles Built	Locomo.es In Use	Freight Cars In Use	Pass. Cars in Use	Passengers	Freight Carried	Employees	Employees Wages
	Miles	Miles	No.	No.	No.	No.	Tons	No.	Dollars
1960....	217,552	21	31,178	1,690,396	25,746	327,171,745	2,409,039,608	793,071	4,956,902,360
1965....	211,384	59	30,061	1,515,169	20,022	305,825,407	2,741,706,964	654,670	4,886,739,954
1970....	205,782	80	29,122	1,453,708	11,378	289,468,947	2,798,324,161	577,435	5,646,480,859
1974....	200,391	18	30,220	1,369,186	7,080	275,185,000	2,881,030,000	541,649	7,670,980,934

Passenger and Freight Data

Year	Passenger Revenue Dollars	Freight Revenue Dollars	Miles Traveled by Passenger Thousands	Rev. per Pas. Mile Cts.	Ave. Trip per Pas. Miles	Fre. Rev. a ton Mile Cts.	Miles Traveled by Pas. Trains Miles	Miles Traveled by Freight Trains Miles	Casualties Killed No.	Casualties Inj. No.
1960...	641,495,655	8,151,706,391	21,284,084	3.01	65.05	1.42	209,676,995	411,173,556	2,248	19,577
1965...	555,985,653	9,036,540,448	17,453,919	3.19	57.07	1.28	173,579,220	430,716,900	2,399	25,789
1970...	423,190,535	11,124,128,498	10,785,746	3.92	37.26	1.44	93,575,236	434,584,544	2,225	21,327
1974...	540,441,000	15,992,602,000	10,349,227	5.21	37.68	1.88	65,011,000	474,864,000	1,908	20,818

Revenues, Expenses, and Dividends

Year	Total Operating Revenues Dollars	Operating Expenses Dollars	Tax Accruals Dollars	Net Railway Operating Income Dollars	Net Income Dollars	Dividends Declared Dollars	Ratio Oper. Exp. to Oper. Rev. Pct.
1960...	9,641,592,812	7,657,328,712	1,020,471,011	594,618,250	473,174,842	411,649,958	79.42
1965...	10,425,052,359	8,002,684,949	949,215,638	980,065,623	865,898,530	532,649,374	76.76
1970...	12,209,237,323	9,805,555,323	1,103,988,230	505,669,405	*126,429,274	486,132,169	80.31
1974...	17,458,315,000	13,758,455,000	1,872,298,000	538,744,000	*558,418,000	643,538,000	78.81

Values, Stocks, Bonds, and Capital

Year	Investment In Road and Equipment Dollars	Common Stock Outstand.[1] Dollars	Preferred Stock Outstand.[1] Dollars	Funded Debt Outstand.[1] Dollars	Tot. Railway Capital Outstand.[1] Dollars	Amount of Stock Pay Dividends Dollars
1960....	35,513,350,796	6,185,117,735	1,218,060,497	8,730,551,088	16,133,729,320	5,617,239,155
1965....	35,489,328,198	5,579,833,608	1,115,727,381	8,161,792,077	14,857,353,066	4,845,089,946
1970....	37,918,381,770	5,604,882,147	718,205,376	8,015,822,800	14,338,910,323	3,594,834,452
1974....	38,936,610,000	5,136,695,000	733,001,000	7,087,872,000	12,957,568,000	3,297,410,000

(1.) Data for Years prior to 1965 have been revised to represent amounts actually outstanding in order that they may be comparable to those shown for the year 1965. *After extraordinary and prior period time.

Highway Mileage Between Selected Canadian and U.S. Cities

	CALGARY	EDMONTON	HALIFAX	LONDON	MONCTON	MONTREAL	OTTAWA	QUEBEC	REGINA	ST. JOHN	SAULT STE. MARIE	THUNDER BAY	TORONTO	VANCOUVER	WINNIPEG
BANGOR, ME.	2592	2595	450	762	287	310	436	241	2115	188	936	1331	651	3250	1760
BOSTON, MASS.	2620	2639	683	675	520	333	458	390	2142	421	958	1403	564	3168	1812
BUFFALO, N.Y.	2106	2125	1141	142	978	383	350	533	1628	879	532	977	102	2878	1377
BUTTE, MONT.	378	561	2950	1859	2787	2309	2033	2470	629	2739	1533	1303	1972	764	875
CALGARY, ALTA.		183	3073	2246	2910	2282	2202	2432	478	2862	1601	1271	2142	659	832
DETROIT, MICH.	1915	1934	1336	122	1204	576	475	738	1437	1156	246	691	235	2505	1149
DULUTH, MINN.	1240	1243	1842	777	1679	1051	925	1199	763	1631	425	195	865	1898	408
EDMONTON, ALTA.	183		3076	2249	2913	2285	2205	2435	497	2865	1632	1274	2145	842	835
FARGO, N.D.	989	1172	2092	1048	1929	1502	1175	764	511	1881	675	445	1161	1654	233
HALIFAX, N.S.	3073	3076		1243	163	791	917	657	2596	262	1417	1812	1132	3731	2241
LONDON, ONT.	2246	2249	1243		1080	452	359	602	1769	1032	403	985	111	2904	1414
MONCTON, N.B.	2910	2913	163	1080		628	754	494	2433	99	1254	1649	969	3568	2078
MONTREAL, QUE.	2282	2285	791	452	628		126	150	1805	580	626	1021	341	2940	1450
OTTAWA, ONT.	2202	2205	917	359	754	126		274	1725	706	500	941	248	2860	1370
QUEBEC, QUE.	2432	2435	657	602	494	150	274		1955	446	774	1171	491	3090	1600
REGINA, SASK.	478	497	2596	1769	2433	1805	1725	1955		2385	1146	794	1665	1136	355
ST. JOHN, N.B.	2862	2865	262	1032	99	580	706	446	2385		1206	1601	921	3520	2030
SAULT STE. MARIE	1601	1632	1417	403	1254	626	500	774	1146	1206		445	440	2201	797
SEATTLE, WASH.	762	945	3494	2489	3331	2693	2577	2934	1092	3283	2077	1883	2600	146	1444
THUNDER BAY, ONT.	1271	1274	1812	985	1649	1021	941	1171	794	1601	445		881	1929	439
TORONTO, ONT.	2142	2145	1132	111	969	341	248	491	1665	921	440	881		2800	1310
VANCOUVER, B.C.	659	842	3731	2904	3568	2940	2860	3090	1136	3520	2201	1929	2800		1490
WINNIPEG, MAN.	832	835	2241	1414	2078	1450	1370	1600	355	2030	797	439	1310	1490	

Motor Bus Passenger Operations, Intercity Class I Carriers
Source: Interstate Commerce Commission

Year ended December 31	1970	1972	1973	1974	1975
Number of carriers reporting	71	72	71	75	83
Miles of line, regular route	192,130	NA	NA	NA	NA
Regular route intercity service revenue (dollars)	509,753,126	534,611,714	563,466,235	639,750,810	638,630,892
Local and suburban revenue (dollars)	13,894,726	11,652,843	12,018,079	11,945,416	11,651,981
Charter or special service bus (dollars)	80,473,873	93,953,690	103,325,461	122,091,663	145,087,516
Total operating revenue (dollars)	722,174,070	768,055,522	813,396,249	916,315,874	948,596,610
Total expenses (dollars)	638,435,771	682,458,001	735,979,839	842,092,947	888,244,779
Net operating revenue (dollars)	83,738,299	85,597,521	77,416,410	74,222,927	60,351,831
Bus-miles in intercity line service	745,691,295	698,920,436	706,378,742	717,861,566	685,662,326
Bus-miles in local and suburban service	17,869,121	14,499,911	14,800,065	13,974,842	12,962,267
Bus-miles in charter or special service	111,236,118	121,363,601	127,093,013	136,622,201	143,809,320
Intercity revenue passengers carried	132,041,325	120,899,734	118,862,777	119,969,288	117,036,940
Local and suburban revenue passengers carried	21,782,439	5,500,788	14,832,110	13,403,859	13,601,862
Charter or special revenue passengers carried	19,683,951	20,389,118	22,115,336	19,413,151	20,710,034

Intercity Bus Operations
Source: National Association of Motor Bus Owners

	1970	1972	1973	1975[4]
Operating Companies	1,000	1,000	1,000	950
Buses	22,000	21,400	20,800	20,500
Miles of highway served (Dec. 31)[1]	267,000	270,000	270,000	272,000
Employees (Dec. 31)[2]	49,500	49,100	48,400	46,600
Total bus miles	1,209,000,000	1,182,000,000	1,178,000,000	1,120,000,000
Revenue Passengers	401,000,000	393,000,000	381,000,000	354,000,000
Revenue passenger-miles	25,300,000,000	25,600,000,000	84,800,000,000	25,600,000,000
Operating revenue, all services	$901,400,000	974,400,000	1,022,700,000	1,165,400,000
Operating expenses	$812,200,000	882,100,000	937,900,000	1,097,900,000
Net operating rev. before inc. taxes	$89,200,000	92,300,000	84,800,000	67,500,000
Taxes assignable to operations[3]	$76,700,000	84,100,000	89,600,000	95,800,000

(1.) Includes duplication between carriers. (2). Operating companies only. (3). Excludes income taxes. (4). Preliminary.

Minimum Legal Age for Purchase of Alcoholic Beverages
In the U.S. and Canada

	Years		Years		Years		Years
Alabama	19	Indiana	21	New Brunswick	21	Quebec	18
Alaska	19	Iowa	18	Newfoundland	21	Rhode Island	18
Alberta	18	Kansas (c)	21	New Hampshire	18	Saskatchewan	18
Arizona	19	Kentucky	21	New Jersey	18	South Carolina (e)	21
Arkansas	21	Louisiana	18	New Mexico	21	South Dakota (c)	21
British Columbia	19	Maine	18	New York	18	Tennessee	18
California	21	Manitoba	18	North Carolina (b)	21	Texas	18
Colorado (c)	21	Maryland (b)	21	North Dakota	21	Utah	21
Connecticut	18	Massachusetts	18	Northwest Territories	19	Vermont	18
Delaware	20	Michigan	18	Nova Scotia	19	Virginia (c)	21
Dist. of Col. (b)	21	Minnesota	19	Ohio (c)	21	Washington	21
Florida	18	Mississippi (f)	21	Oklahoma (d)	21	West Virginia	18
Georgia	18	Missouri	21	Oregon	21	Wisconsin	18
Hawaii	18	Montana	18	Ontario	18	Wyoming	19
Idaho	19	Nebraska	19	Pennsylvania	21	Yukon Territory	19
Illinois (a)	21	Nevada	21	Prince Edward Island	18		

(a) Wine, beer 19. (b) Light wine, beer 18. (c) 3.2 beer 18. (d) 3.2 beer: male 21; female 18. (e) Beer and wine 18. (f) Beer and wine not over 4% by wt. 18.

Highway Mileage Between Selected Cities

Cities In The East*	ALBANY, N.Y.	ATLANTA, GA.	BALTIMORE, MD.	BANGOR, ME.	BIRMINGHAM, ALA.	BOSTON, MASS.	BUFFALO, N.Y.	CHARLESTON, W. VA.	CHICAGO, ILL.	CINCINNATI, OHIO	CLEVELAND, OHIO	DETROIT, MICH.	INDIANAPOLIS, IND.	JACKSON, MISS.	JACKSONVILLE, FLA.
ALBANY		988	321	366	1091	170	283	712	807	707	466	536	766	1379	1117
ATLANTA	988		671	1315	155	1070	876	519	707	467	692	726	539	400	315
BALTIMORE	321	671		632	800	400	366	391	690	497	348	510	565	998	794
BANGOR	366	1315	632		1407	233	652	1018	1174	1094	827	892	1136	1635	1426
BIRMINGHAM	1091	155	800	1407		1210	932	589	661	499	742	743	492	243	427
BOSTON	170	1070	400	233	1210		458	781	974	861	640	707	931	1446	1201
BUFFALO	283	876	366	652	932	458		439	520	428	186	249	486	1115	1080
CHARLESTON	712	519	391	1018	589	781	439		483	202	268	357	301	786	671
CHICAGO	807	707	690	1174	661	974	520	483		294	345	269	188	747	1017
CINCINNATI	707	467	497	1094	499	861	428	202	294		244	251	104	678	783
CLEVELAND	466	692	348	827	742	640	186	268	345	244		168	300	924	971
DETROIT	536	726	510	892	743	707	249	357	269	251	168		277	931	1039
INDIANAPOLIS	766	539	565	1136	492	931	486	301	188	104	300	277		631	852
JACKSON	1379	400	998	1635	243	1446	1115	786	747	678	924	931	631		597
JACKSONVILLE	1117	315	794	1426	427	1201	1080	671	1017	783	971	1039	852	597	
LOUISVILLE	827	428	602	1198	362	964	537	266	304	108	351	363	114	573	766
MEMPHIS	1217	366	951	1594	247	1340	924	615	548	487	737	726	444	210	672
MIAMI	1468	665	1143	1773	765	1539	1431	1043	1377	1133	1322	1387	1197	920	345
NASHVILLE	1090	251	732	736	201	1126	717	409	452	289	532	544	293	375	577
NEW ORLEANS	1476	517	1153	1747	359	1556	1248	936	929	820	1060	1077	839	182	568
NEW YORK	147	863	192	450	988	211	367	566	828	635	486	626	716	1232	979
NORFOLK	560	592	249	881	753	543	561	397	874	600	531	699	698	996	661
PHILADELPHIA	233	771	99	897	897	303	360	481	758	571	425	578	639	1153	889
PITTSBURGH	457	737	230	819	763	576	220	233	459	278	127	287	355	972	893
PORTLAND, ME.	275	1185	513	128	1325	106	574	895	1089	967	752	817	1037	1552	1293
RICHMOND	472	545	144	773	697	543	473	309	786	512	443	611	620	944	646
ST. LOUIS	1016	553	804	1379	503	1188	723	538	291	338	540	513	239	505	881
TAMPA	1331	464	986	1620	552	1383	1263	884	1187	948	1166	1201	1005	678	194
TRENTON	223	783	128	520	915	289	358	513	780	590	435	594	660	1163	921
WASHINGTON	367	640	39	673	767	440	372	355	687	497	362	516	567	1000	754

	LOUISVILLE, KY.	MEMPHIS, TENN.	MIAMI, FLA.	NASHVILLE, TENN.	NEW ORLEANS, LA.	NEW YORK, N.Y.	NORFOLK, VA.	PHILADELPHIA, PA.	PITTSBURGH, PA.	PORTLAND, ME.	RICHMOND, VA.	ST. LOUIS, MO.	TAMPA, FLA.	TRENTON, N.J.	WASHINGTON, D.C.
ALBANY	827	1217	1468	1090	1476	147	560	233	457	275	472	1016	1331	223	367
ATLANTA	428	366	665	251	517	863	592	771	737	1185	545	553	464	783	640
BALTIMORE	602	951	1143	732	1153	192	249	99	230	513	144	804	986	128	39
BANGOR	1198	1594	1773	736	1747	450	881	541	819	128	773	1379	1620	520	673
BIRMINGHAM	362	247	765	201	359	988	753	897	763	1325	697	503	552	915	767
BOSTON	964	1340	1539	1126	1556	211	543	303	576	106	543	1188	1383	289	440
BUFFALO	537	924	1431	717	1248	367	561	360	220	574	473	723	1263	358	372
CHARLESTON	266	615	1043	409	936	566	397	481	233	895	309	538	884	513	355
CHICAGO	304	548	1377	452	929	828	874	758	459	1089	786	291	1187	780	687
CINCINNATI	108	487	1133	289	820	635	600	571	278	967	512	338	948	590	497
CLEVELAND	351	737	1322	532	1060	486	531	425	127	752	443	540	1166	435	362
DETROIT	363	726	1387	544	1077	626	699	578	287	817	611	513	1201	594	516
INDIANAPOLIS	114	444	1197	293	839	716	698	639	355	1037	620	239	1005	660	567
JACKSON	573	210	920	375	182	1232	996	1153	972	1552	944	505	678	1163	1000
JACKSONVILLE	766	672	345	577	568	979	661	889	893	1293	646	881	194	921	754
LOUISVILLE		365	1078	180	719	759	693	682	398	1070	575	267	865	705	605
MEMPHIS	365		1017	220	399	1142	958	1057	786	1446	845	294	782	1064	917
MIAMI	1078	1017		916	878	1327	1013	1230	1237	1649	994	1222	248	1276	1105
NASHVILLE	180	220	916		536	929	713	838	568	1232	625	295	908	853	697
NEW ORLEANS	719	399	878	536		1353	1101	1239	1113	1655	1057	699	644	1270	1150
NEW YORK	759	1142	1327	929	1353		441	91	363	317	330	961	1176	70	226
NORFOLK	693	958	1013	713	1101	441		348	400	649	88	930	859	359	195
PHILADELPHIA	682	1057	1230	838	1239	91	348		294	409	240	881	1083	32	136
PITTSBURGH	398	786	1237	568	1113	363	400	294		682	312	599	1045	205	229
PORTLAND, ME.	1070	1446	1649	1232	1655	317	649	409	682		649	1294	1488	395	549
RICHMOND	575	845	994	625	1057	330	88	240	312	649		842	842	277	107
ST. LOUIS	267	294	1222	295	699	961	930	881	599	1294	842		1030	897	804
TAMPA	865	782	248	908	644	1176	859	1083	1045	1488	842	1030		1109	947
TRENTON	705	1064	1276	853	1270	70	359	32	205	395	277	897	1109		169
WASHINGTON	605	917	1105	697	1150	226	195	136	229	549	107	804	947	169	

*Directions for Use of Mileage Charts

To measure mileage between the east and west charts there are 5 key cities: Chicago, Jackson (Miss.), Memphis, New Orleans and St. Louis.

Plot your course between the city listed nearest your home town and whichever of the 5 key cities you desire to pass through to the city of your destination. Add the mileage shown and this will give you the approximate total mileage.

For example: The mileage between Cheyenne and Philadelphia through St. Louis: Philadelphia to St. Louis - 881 miles, St. Louis to Cheyenne - 910; the total is 1.791 miles.

Highway Mileage Between Selected Cities

Cities in The West

	ALBUQUERQUE, N.M.	BOISE, IDA.	CHEYENNE, WY.	CHICAGO, ILL.	DALLAS, TEX.	DENVER, COL.	DES MOINES, IA.	FARGO, N.D.	HELENA, MON.	HOUSTON, TEX.	JACKSON, MISS.	KANSAS CITY, MO.	LITTLE ROCK, ARK.	LOS ANGELES, CAL.	MEMPHIS, TENN.
ALBUQUERQUE		980	545	1285	650	432	1032	1310	1111	844	1062	791	901	805	1032
BOISE	980		766	1726	1637	867	1397	1228	494	1825	2063	1446	1833	887	1913
CHEYENNE	545	766		967	880	101	632	823	700	1143	1282	657	1053	1182	1127
CHICAGO	1285	1726	967		936	1018	330	657	1478	1092	747	505	652	2106	548
DALLAS	650	1637	880	936		784	704	1110	1571	245	411	498	330	1410	468
DENVER	432	867	101	1018	784		674	901	792	1028	1219	613	962	1162	1058
DES MOINES	1032	1397	632	330	704	674		491	1162	948	828	207	581	1788	608
FARGO, N.D.	1310	1228	823	657	1110	901	491		822	1364	1271	636	1054	1935	1061
HELENA	1111	494	700	1478	1571	792	1162	822		1813	1922	1261	1666	1234	1720
HOUSTON	844	1825	1143	1092	245	1028	948	1364	1813		433	744	439	1554	572
JACKSON	1062	2063	1282	747	411	1219	828	1271	1922	433		613	257	1864	210
KANSAS CITY	791	1446	657	505	498	613	207	636	1261	744	613		409	1620	467
LITTLE ROCK	901	1833	1053	652	330	962	581	1045	1666	439	257	409		1698	139
LOS ANGELES	805	887	1182	2106	1410	1162	1788	1935	1234	1554	1864	1620	1698		1823
MEMPHIS	1032	1913	1127	548	468	1058	627	1061	1720	572	210	467	139	1823	
MILWAUKEE	1390	1763	1019	87	1063	1039	358	573	1392	1163	826	564	727	2145	632
MINNEAPOLIS	1223	1446	821	418	964	845	254	239	1056	1211	1062	461	833	1996	852
NEW ORLEANS	1145	2140	1376	929	500	1284	1028	1479	2070	358	182	846	434	1916	399
OKLAHOMA CITY	545	1489	702	826	212	566		900	1392	458	587	357	350	1353	482
OMAHA	892	1267	491	465	672	537	139	436	1056	917	882	208	623	1698	671
PHOENIX	449	1020	924	1753	1021	826	1449	1726	1147	1158	1456		1337	389	1470
PORTLAND, ORE.	1461	435	1211	2131	2057	1285	1819	1590	657	2282	2506	1901	2284	994	2367
RENO	1036	427	995	1970	1695	1040	1638	1639	905	1888	2104	1665	2030	476	2083
ST. LOUIS	1057	1701	910	291	651	863	349	812	1498	801	505	254	357	1862	294
SALT LAKE CITY	612	363	457	1443	1262	512	1089	1215	500	1453	1685	1118	1444	730	1570
SAN FRANCISCO	1132	654	1209	2183	1773	1267	1851	1873	1134	1955	2203	1893	2032	403	2162
SEATTLE	1511	529	1279	2031	2136	1377	1766	1505	611	2354	2601	1904	2273	1177	2362
SIOUX FALLS	1082	1295	654	525	844	655	282	230	960	1110	1013	390	799	1817	858
TUCSON	454	1191	999	1739	951	845	1462	1746	1270	1070	1362	1255	1278	512	1417
WICHITA	620	1663	590	711	386	512	403	731	1241	629	733	202	472	1384	549

	MILWAUKEE, WIS.	MINNEAPOLIS, MINN.	NEW ORLEANS, LA.	OKLAHOMA CITY, OKLA.	OMAHA, NEB.	PHOENIX, ARIZ.	PORTLAND, ORE.	RENO, NEV.	ST. LOUIS MO.	SALT LAKE CITY, UTAH	SAN FRANCISCO, CAL.	SEATTLE, WASH.	SIOUX FALLS, S.D.	TUCSON, ARIZ.	WICHITA, KAN.
ALBUQUERQUE	1390	1223	1145	545	892	449	1461	1036	1057	612	1132	1511	1082	454	620
BOISE	1763	1446	2140	1489	1267	1020	435	427	1701	363	654	525	1295	1191	1663
CHEYENNE	1019	821	1376	702	491	924	1211	995	910	457	1209	1279	654	999	590
CHICAGO	87	418	929	826	465	1753	2131	1970	291	1443	2183	2031	525	1739	711
DALLAS	1063	964	500	212	672	1021	2057	1695	651	1262	1773	2136	844	951	386
DENVER	1039	845	1284	616	537	826	1285	1040	863	512	1267	1377	655	845	512
DES MOINES	358	254	1028	566	139	1449	1819	1638	349	1089	1851	1766	282	1462	403
FARGO, N.D.	573	239	1479	900	436	1726	1590	1639	812	1215	1873	1505	230	1746	731
HELENA	1392	1056	2070	1392	1056	1147	657	905	1498	500	1134	611	960	1270	1241
HOUSTON	1163	1211	358	458	917	1158	2282	1888	801	1453	1955	2354	1110	1070	629
JACKSON	826	1062	182	587	882	1456	2506	2104	505	1685	2203	2601	1013	1362	733
KANSAS CITY	564	461	846	357	208	1238	1901	1665	254	1118	1893	1904	390	1255	202
LITTLE ROCK	727	833	434	350	623	1337	2284	2030	357	1444	2032	2273	799	1278	472
LOS ANGELES	2145	1996	1916	1353	1698	389	994	476	1862	730	403	1177	1817	512	1384
MEMPHIS	632	852	399	482	671	1470	2367	2083	294	1570	2162	2362	858	1417	549
MILWAUKEE		334	1034	905	501	1833	2069	2003	371	1502	2203	2045	507	1819	792
MINNEAPOLIS	334		1251	818	364	1671	1721	1797	553	1246	2001	1673	221	1677	650
NEW ORLEANS	1034	1251		684	1065	1527	2591	2199	699	1773	2278	2645	1265	1436	840
OKLAHOMA CITY	905	818	648		477	989	1926	1529	523	1112	1692	1975	644	941	168
OMAHA	1501	364	1065	477		1325	1700	1500	453	955	1720	1657	187	1341	309
PHOENIX	1833	1671	1527	989	1325		1273	762	1492	688	794	1510	1481	123	1040
PORTLAND, ORE.	2069	1721	2591	1926	1700	1273		566	2113	807	669	173	1580	1396	1854
RENO	2003	1797	2199	1529	1500	762	566		1906	531	227	760	1472	912	1542
ST. LOUIS	371	553	699	523	453	1492	2113	1879		1381	2133	2102	632	1457	460
SALT LAKE CITY	1502	1246	1773	1112	953	688	807	531	1381		755	869	941	820	1020
SAN FRANCISCO	2203	2001	2278	1692	1720	794	669	227	2133	755		858	1696	921	1730
SEATTLE	2045	1673	2645	1975	1657	1510	173	760	2102	869	858		1526	1666	1842
SIOUX FALLS	507	221	1265	644	187	1481	1580	1472	632	941	1696	1526		1536	221
TUCSON	1819	1677	1436	941	1341	123	1396	912	1457	820	921	1666	1536		1074
WICHITA	792	650	840	168	309	1040	1854	1542	460	1020	1730	1842	493	1074	

Trucking: Employees, Payroll, Registration

Source: American Trucking Assns.; Dept. of Transportation

1974	Employees	Annual Payroll	Truck Registration 1974	1975	1974	Employees	Annual Payroll	Truck Registration 1974	1975
Alabama...	162,700	$1,417,605,100	527,174	584,074	Nebraska..	91,800	763,225,200	324,133	350,494
Alaska....	14,700	229,555,200	61,392	81,857	Nevada....	42,200	414,868,200	109,052	117,155
Arizona....	115,000	1,103,310,000	374,561	392,025	New Hamp..	28,400	238,872,400	78,545	79,465
Arkansas..	135,200	1,035,226,400	383,167	411,105	New Jersey.	212,300	2,252,715,300	352,412	407,355.
California..	1,188,100	13,922,155,800	2,379,693	2,643,397	New Mexico	56,100	504,170,700	216,881	268,387
Colorado...	146,400	1,395,338,400	445,022	480,369	New York..	408,700	4,535,752,600	728,472	824,934
Connecticut	127,400	1,310,691,200	139,577	148,599	N. Carolina.	312,600	2,485,482,600	718,957	806,999
Delaware..	29,900	308,657,700	55,106	60,424	N. Dakota..	37,300	301,495,900	197,846	218,213
Dist. of Col..	10,900	139,367,400	9,726	16,996	Ohio......	332,200	3,422,988,800	813,243	868,927
Florida....	273,300	2,424,990,900	839,462	878,389	Oklahoma..	167,800	1,466,907,600	616,360	671,959
Georgia....	216,400	1,916,871,200	671,949	688.310	Oregon....	120,500	1,158,848,500	274,373	300,760
Hawaii....	21,100	201,357,300	59,325	65,081	Penna.....	453,300	4,351,226,700	893,047	1,045,387
Idaho.....	49,300	405,739,000	212,873	238,114	R. Island...	35,800	305,803,600	63,597	62,944
Illinois....	341,200	3,674,041,600	853,199	968,908	S. Carolina.	144,800	1,156,517,600	313,976	362,558
Indiana....	322,300	3,184,324,000	693,366	735,754	S. Dakota..	37,800	284,520,600	165,799	187,765
Iowa......	165,000	1,460,745,000	494,619	547,375	Tennessee.	143,300	1,212,747,900	549,627	624,270
Kansas....	148,500	1,253,637,000	511,683	559,182	Texas.....	679,300	6,157,854,500	1,928,529	2,149,675
Kentucky...	154,300	1,368,641,000	514,117	562,631	Utah......	59,800	532,220,000	211,161	256,761
Louisiana..	167,200	1,506,806,400	491,232	510,480	Vermont....	18,600	155,347,200	50,953	52,638
Maine.....	55,200	434,148,000	133,253	146,555	Virginia....	181,300	1,643,665,800	484,835	530,304
Maryland...	122,600	1,207,364,800	322,597	339,336	Washington	194,000	2,003,244,000	580,029	645,386
Mass.....	165,700	1,590,554,300	283,136	321,815	W. Va.....	88,000	838,816,000	222,000	228,981
Michigan...	316,200	3,628,395,000	808,897	903,159	Wisconsin..	156,000	1,473,888,000	411,884	454,936
Minnesota..	191,000	1,785,468,000	553,001	559,696	Wyoming...	25,100	234,183,000	111,606	132,548
Mississippi.	106,300	792,785,400	355,156	378,375	U.S. TOTAL	9,065,300	88,295,403,600	23,462,479	25,775,715
Missouri...	241,700	2,277,297,400	659,561	679,706	1973				
Montana...	50,700	424,967,400	212,318	230,202	Totals.....	9,052,400	82,207,953,100	22,175,645	

Intercity Truck Tonnage

Source: American Trucking Associations
Based on operations of 2,004 Class I & II intercity motor carriers. In tons.

Region	1974	1975	Commodity Class	1974	1975
New England................	20,775,283	17,642,097	General Freight...............	234,848,878	200,067,983
Middle Atlantic...............	143,088,343	124,308,631	Household Goods.............	2,849,034	2,585,466
Central....................	170,894,007	147,490,235	Heavy Machinery.............	9,124,534	7,925,435
Southern...................	106,187,531	96,413,114	Liquid Petroleum.............	174,847,673	161,175,011
Northwestern................	52,207,360	46,668,110	Refrig. Solids & Liquids.......	17,898,013	18,875,227
Midwestern.................	42,263,591	41,926,910	Agricultural Commodities......	11,779,858	11,679,357
Southwestern...............	67,336,437	62,062,040	Motor Vehicles...............	22,141,054	19,939,114
Rocky Mountain..............	20,785,510	19,829,320	Building Materials............	23,343,031	21,351,266
Pacific....................	57,961,601	52,121,032	All Other Classes............	184,667,588	164,862,630
United States...............	681,499,663	608,461,489	All Commodities..............	681,499,663	608,461,489

Automobile Factory Sales

Source: Motor Vehicle Manufacturers Association, Detroit, Mich.—Values, Wholesale

Year	Passenger Cars Number	Value	Motor Trucks, Buses Number	Value	Total Number	Value
1900..........	4,192	$4,899,443	...	...	4,190	$4,899,443
1905..........	24,250	38,670,000	350	$1,330,000	24,600	240,000,000
1910..........	181,000	215,340,000	6,000	9,660,000	187,000	225,000,000
1915..........	895,930	575,978,000	74,000	125,800,000	969,930	701,778,000
1920..........	1,905,560	1,809,170,963	321,789	423,249,410	2,227,349	2,232,420,373
1925..........	3,735,171	2,458,370,026	530,659	458,400,277	4,265,830	2,916,770,303
1930..........	2,787,456	1,644,083,152	575,364	390,752,061	3,362,820	2,034,853,213
1935..........	3,273,874	1,707,836,325	697,367	380,997,330	3,971,241	2,088,833,655
1940..........	3,717,385	2,370,654,083	754,901	567,820,414	4,472,286	2,938,474,497
1945..........	69,532	57,254,655	655,683	1,181,955,532	725,215	1,239,210,187
1950..........	6,665,863	8,468,137,000	1,337,193	1,707,748,000	8,003,056	10,175,885,000
1955..........	7,920,186	12,452,871,000	1,249,106	2,020,973,000	9,169,292	14,473,844,000
1960..........	6,674,796	12,164,234,000	1,194,475	2,350,680,000	7,869,271	14,514,914,000
1965..........	9,305,561	18,380,036,000	1,751,805	3,733,664,000	11,057,366	22,113,700,000
1970..........	6,546,817	14,630,217,000	1,692,440	4,819,752,000	8,239,257	19,449,969,000
1973..........	9,657,647	26,239,996,000	2,979,688	9,544,112,000	12,637,335	35,784,108,000
1974..........	7,331,256	21,653,000	2,727,313	10,163,203,000	10,058,569	31,816,239,000
1975..........	6,712,852	23,400,000*	2,272,160	9,900,000,000*	8,985,012	33,300,000,000*

After July 1, 1964 all tactical vehicles are excluded. Federal excise taxes are excluded in all years. *Preliminary.

Automotive Exports from U.S.

Source: Bureau of Economic Analysis, Dept. of Commerce
(in millions)

	Total Value Vehicles	Automotive*		Total Value Vehicles	Automotive*		Total Value Vehicles	Automotive*
1940......	$147	$259	1965......	$739	$1,929	1972......	$2,008	$5,119
1950......	406	746	1968......	1,414	3,453	1973......	2,678	6,343
1955......	747	1,276	1969......	1,554	3,888	1974......	3,684	8,162
1960......	634	1,266	1970......	1,397	3,652	1975......	4,979	10,077

*Includes new and used passenger cars and trucks, trailers, parts for assembly, and garage equipment.

Passenger Car Production, U.S. Plants

Source: Motor Vehicle Manufacturers Association of the U.S., Inc.

	1974	1975	1976 7 mos.		1974	1975	1976 7 mos.
American Motors Corp.				Total Lincoln	87,569	101,520	71,926
Gremlin	113,776	51,471	22,582	**Total Ford Motor.**	2,205,245	1,808,038	1,342,693
Hornet	127,680	69,557	37,741	**General Motors Corp.**			
Pacer	—	140,996	42,413	Chevrolet	472,292	318,400	198,740
Matador	83,618	61,772	19,782	Corvette	33,869	45,948	28,079
Total American	352,088	323,796	122,788	Monte Carlo	232,410	266,578	215,980
Chrysler Corp.				Chevelle	292,719	246,759	191,965
Voyager (Valiant)	370,316	215,761	44,043	Camaro	157,909	156,400	115,837
Volare	—	33,416	255,969	Nova	386,947	296,493	221,516
Fury	137,636	122,703	66,208	Vega	327,707	193,245	93,266
Gran Fury	90,715	71,670	33,181	Monza Notchback	8	82,954	21,059
Total Plymouth	602,606	443,550	399,401	Chevette	—	80,394	114,959
Chrysler	96,630	102,940	62,113	**Total Chevrolet**	1,903,861	1,687,091	1,201,401
Imperial	13,433	1,930	—	Pontiac	122,037	104,073	86,633
Total Chry.-Plym.	712,669	548,420	461,514	Grand Prix	78,793	112,896	158,173
Sportsman (Dart)	268,323	203,473	56,321	Le Mans	114,786	88,364	57,996
Aspen	—	25,129	192,328	Firebird	78,919	94,198	65,198
Coronet	126,432	72,417	42,794	Ventura	78,701	60,405	47,873
Dodge	63,175	53,463	24,859	Astre	28,847	55,805	28,261
Total Dodge	463,993	354,482	316,302	Sunbird	—	7,728	17,075
Total Chrysler Corp.	1,176,662	902,902	777,816	**Total Pontiac**	502,083	523,469	461,209
Ford Motor Co.				Oldsmobile	166,424	226,845	174,445
Ford	283,961	191,405	158,732	Toronado	19,479	22,535	11,644
Torino	329,607	153,510	136,989	Cutlass	312,004	363,814	320,299
Elite	73,120	90,738	105,989	Omega	50,751	37,261	39,741
Club Wagon	23,745	34,639	24,645	Starfire	—	3,887	8,391
Granada	120,094	336,864	278,819	**Total Oldsmobile**	548,658	654,342	554,520
Maverick	197,531	105,418	62,579	Buick	172,562	227,732	180,558
Pinto	301,707	163,510	70,072	Riviera	17,136	16,759	10,176
Mustang	338,136	187,554	117,047	Century	158,438	212,948	199,835
Thunderbird	49,074	37,776	32,099	Apollo/Skylark	52,126	74,443	76,385
Total Ford	1,716,975	1,301,414	986,971	Skyhawk	—	3,938	11,830
Mercury	71,114	79,507	55,943	**Total Buick**	400,262	535,820	478,784
Montego	85,253	52,751	33,238	Cadillac	192,729	193,444	136,285
Cougar	86,641	57,215	60,605	Eldorado	37,920	48,134	25,157
Monarch	47,900	108,103	89,271	Seville	—	36,826	23,301
Comet	109,793	46,822	19,457	**Total Cadillac**	230,649	278,404	184,743
Bobcat	—	60,706	25,282	**Total Gen. Mts.**	3,585,513	3,679,126	2,880,657
Total Mercury	400,701	405,104	283,796	Checker Motors	4,996	3,181	2,783
Lincoln	37,541	55,499	40,586				
Mark IV	50,028	46,021	31,340	**Total Passenger Cars**	7,324,504	6,717,043	5,126,737

Total Road and Street Mileage in U. S.

Source: Federal Highway Administration, Dept. of Transportation 1974

State	Rural	Urban	Surfaced	Total	State	Rural	Urban	Surfaced	Total
Ala.	68,382	18,033	81,554	86,415	Neb.	90,742	7,016	79,588	97,798
Alas.	8,346	1,502	6,004	9,848	Nev.	47,735	1,920	16,663	49,655
Ariz.	45,085	7,020	24,609	52,105	N.H.	10,262	4,894	12,598	15,156
Ark.	68,015	10,095	64,072	78,110	N.J.	13,738	18,966	30,943	32,704
Cal.	122,242	47,374	125,048	169,616	N.M.	64,977	5,221	21,554	70,198
Colo.	76,134	8,190	54,518	84,324	N.Y.	56,031	51,712	104,034	107,743
Conn.	5,476	13,377	18,752	18,853	N.C.	73,554	15,070	81,955	88,624
Del.	4,359	801	5,146	5,160	N.D.	102,657	3,277	70,885	105,934
Fla.	71,320	26,771	62,329	98,091	Oh.	86,139	24,108	108,720	110,247
Ga.	85,367	15,222	69,702	100,589	Okla.	93,451	15,014	83,825	108,465
Ha.	2,642	1,039	3,534	3,681	Ore.	97,014	6,870	66,123	103,884
Ida.	53,230	3,284	30,927	56,514	Pa.	90,363	24,505	100,176	114,868
Ill.	101,874	29,256	125,054	131,130	R.I.	1,019	4,456	5,221	5,475
Ind.	75,555	15,851	87,839	91,406	S.C.	53,493	7,138	42,705	60,631
Ia.	98,940	13,892	106,905	112,832	S.D.	79,498	3,034	61,741	82,532
Kan.	123,228	11,496	102,115	134,724	Tenn.	68,756	12,286	79,329	81,042
Ky.	63,883	6,050	62,719	69,933	Tex.	198,489	55,306	191,832	253,795
La.	42,662	11,598	50,990	54,260	Ut.	43,724	4,663	23,484	48,387
Me.	18,981	2,563	20,186	21,544	Vt.	12,817	1,019	12,862	13,836
Md.	23,182	4,246	27,370	27,428	Va.	52,817	9,606	61,253	62,423
Mass.	13,648	17,721	31,369	31,369	Wash.	71,308	10,222	65,163	81,530
Mich.	98,675	19,916	101,565	118,591	W. Va.	32,826	3,639	27,197	36,465
Minn.	110,649	17,685	117,760	128,334	Wis.	89,944	14,776	99,167	104,720
Miss.	59,728	7,222	65,033	66,950	Wyo.	30,493	1,364	18,298	31,857
Mo.	99,004	17,720	110,152	116,724	D. C.	—	1,102	1,102	1,102
Mon.	75,658	2,547	45,768	78,205	**Total**	3,178,152	637,655	3,067,438	3,815,807

Car, Truck, and Bus Drivers in the U.S.

Source: Federal Highway Administration, estimated total licenses in force during 1975.

State	No. of drivers	State	No. of drivers	State	No. of drivers	State	No. of drivers
Alabama	1,944,155	Indiana	3,337,783	Nebraska	1,063,910	South Carolina	1,556,027
Alaska	208,397	Iowa	1,883,513	Nevada	418,704	South Dakota	417,698
Arizona	1,326,436	Kansas	1,671,609	New Hampshire	534,094	Tennessee	2,430,363
Arkansas	1,312,403	Kentucky	1,910,041	New Jersey	4,323,242	Texas	7,509,497
California	13,564,000	Louisiana	2,121,973	New Mexico	735,172	Utah	729,193
Colorado	1,689,795	Maine	627,962	New York	8,832,000	Vermont	309,940
Connecticut	1,860,781	Maryland	2,440,554	North Carolina	3,294,096	Virginia	3,017,481
Delaware	373,774	Massachusetts	3,554,287	North Dakota	372,554	Washington	2,176,585
Florida	5,673,691	Michigan	5,949,949	Ohio	7,545,084	West Virginia	1,262,038
Georgia	3,038,079	Minnesota	2,416,869	Oklahoma	1,720,912	Wisconsin	2,721,284
Hawaii	517,667	Mississippi	1,456,039	Oregon	1,551,356	Wyoming	280,057
Idaho	522,944	Missouri	2,971,765	Pennsylvania	6,861,134	Dist. of Col.	335,515
Illinois	6,389,533	Montana	514,426	Rhode Island	528,512	**Total**	129,814,873

Motor Vehicle Registrations, Taxes, Motor Fuel, Drivers' Ages

Source: Federal Highway Adm.

State	Driver's Age Jan. 1 (1) Regular	1976 (2) Juvenile	Registered autos, buses & trucks est. (1975) Number	State Gas Tax per gal. (1975) Cents	Motor Fuel Gross Tax Collections $1,000 (1975)	Motor Fuel consumption (1975) Highway 1,000 Gallons	Non-Highway 1,000 Gallons	Total 1,000 Gallons
Alabama	16		2,492,785	7	147,874	2,055,998	46,725	2,102,723
Alaska	16		225,575	8	16,585	182,517	42,966	225,483
Arizona	16		1,459,492	8	106,722	1,282,931	47,993	1,330,924
Arkansas	16		1,283,321	8.5	108,684	1,288,475	29,019	1,317,494
California	16/18	14	13,890,670	7	766,186	10,768,379	233,678	11,002,057
Colorado	21	16	1,925,198	7	96,769	1,400,773	54,620	1,455,393
Connecticut	16/18		1,949,239	10	141,677	1,404,039	22,815	1,426,854
Delaware	16/18		350,992	9	28,347	311,639	5,515	317,154
Florida	16/18		5,395,372	8	361,194	4,456,610	135,547	4,592,157
Georgia	16		3,210,973	7.5	229,184	3,041,988	49,311	3,091,299
Hawaii	15		462,011	8.5	21,054	290,202	11,472	301,674
Idaho	16	14	647,446	8.5	44,633	484,309	45,307	529,616
Illinois	16/18		6,343,875	7.5	397,035	5,243,371	237,704	5,481,075
Indiana	16/18		3,315,371	8	244,530	3,017,213	84,745	3,101,958
Iowa	16/18	14	2,099,336	7	132,192	1,670,668	190,224	1,860,892
Kansas	16	14	1,805,434	7	104,185	1,370,652	125,186	1,495,838
Kentucky	16		2,245,138	9	176,980	1,843,676	32,725	1,876,401
Louisiana	17	15	2,187,521	8	157,434	1,944,602	50,373	1,994,975
Maine	15/17	15	648,131	9	51,568	565,959	11,219	577,178
Maryland	16/18		2,422,724	9	179,894	1,934,042	31,061	1,965,103
Massachusetts	18	16½	3,107,051	8.5	189,788	2,412,546	26,953	2,439,499
Michigan	16/18	14	5,545,460	9	404,634	4,650,037	182,368	4,832,405
Minnesota	16/18	15	2,524,517	9	175,482	2,053,941	170,850	2,224,791
Mississippi	15		1,376,510	9	119,403	1,280,168	28,686	1,308,854
Missouri	16		2,866,219	7	197,283	2,744,108	145,006	2,889,114
Montana	15/16		601,957	7.75	39,757	477,639	45,256	522,895
Nebraska	16	14	1,177,845	8.5	82,034	902,152	82,736	984,888
Nevada	16	14	463,835	6	26,834	447,272	17,859	465,131
New Hampshire	16/18	16	485,306	9	37,875	407,492	6,183	413,675
New Jersey	17	16	4,654,542	8	285,567	3,475,998	60,904	3,536,902
New Mexico	15/16		826,568	7	56,456	791,551	15,433	806,984
New York	17/18	16	7,591,358	8	492,881	5,727,762	171,059	5,898,821
North Carolina	16/18		3,689,569	9	276,752	3,009,525	77,072	3,086,597
North Dakota	16	14	550,827	7	32,073	372,324	101,200	473,524
Ohio	16/18	14	7,178,933	7	379,540	5,390,402	150,363	5,540,765
Oklahoma	16		2,112,733	6.5	112,308	1,758,817	50,647	1,809,464
Oregon	16	14	1,627,592	7	85,691	1,346,727	50,333	1,397,060
Pennsylvania	17/18	16	7,659,305	9	469,880	5,043,674	128,763	5,172,437
Rhode Island	16/18		562,641	10	38,115	389,815	17,385	407,200
South Carolina	16	15	1,772,362	8	130,969	1,608,738	34,364	1,643,102
South Dakota	16	14	526,896	8	38,491	421,386	75,351	496,737
Tennessee	16		2,725,569	7	175,956	2,485,364	42,715	2,528,079
Texas	16/18	15	8,396,489	5	408,811	8,006,190	166,550	8,172,740
Utah	16		844,974	7	47,797	684,671	27,715	712,386
Vermont	18	16	287,109	9	21,214	254,727	6,680	261,407
Virginia	16/18		3,250,861	9	247,497	2,692,810	52,275	2,745,085
Washington	16/18		2,539,764	9	169,216	1,821,447	59,860	1,881,307
West Virginia	16/18		966,009	8.5	78,150	896,139	9,985	906,124
Wisconsin	16/18	14	2,590,709	7	164,755	2,270,399	108,758	1,379,157
Wyoming	16	14	336,824	7	25,957	344,479	30,931	375,410
District Of Columbia	18		255,472	10	19,425	254,984	4,364	259,348
Total United States			132,950,410		8,543,318	108,984,327	3,642,309	112,626,636

(1) Unrestricted operation of private passenger car. When 2 ages are shown, license is issued at lower age upon completion of approved driver education course. (2) Juvenile license issued for use between home and school in Cal., Iowa, Kan., Me., Mich., Neb., Nev., N.H., N.D., Oreg.; restricted to daylight or curfew hours in Idaho, Ill., La., Mass., Minn., N.Y., Pa., S.C., S.D., Tenn., Wisc.; hardship cases in Ohio and Texas; for agricultural pursuits in N.J. (3) Estimated.

Auto Registrations, Taxes, Gasoline, Drivers' Ages in Canada

Source: Statistics Canada and Digest of Motor Laws, 1976

	Driver's age (1975) Min.	Minor	Registered[1] autos, buses, trucks & motorcycles (1974)	Province gas tax per gal. (1974) cents	Motor fuel gross tax collect's 1,000 (1974)	Fuel consumption 1974 Roads & highways 1,000 gallons	Non-highway 1,000 gallons	Total[3] 1,000 gallons
Newfoundland	17	—	163,975	25	32,606	117,676	15,995	133,670
Prince Edward Island	16	*	53,332	21	7,893	35,264	2,952	38,216
Nova Scotia	16	*	346,392	21	53,475	229,772	10,344	240,116
New Brunswick	18	16-18	274,173	20	44,767	194,551	21,407	215,958
Quebec	17	16	2,799,352	19	392,244	1,663,133	49,439	1,712,572
Ontario	16	—	3,891,603	19	571,601	2,534,024	101,962	2,635,986
Manitoba	16	*	508,751	18	55,255	280,874	51,920	332,794
Saskatchewan	16	—	568,918	12	46,279	275,392	119,760	395,152
Alberta	16	14	1,035,562	10	79,692	610,136	121,816	731,952
British Columbia	19	16	1,333,277	17	146,533	728,139	122,799	850,938
Yukon & Northwest Territories			26,668	14	7,822	11,712	3,162	20,874
Total			11,002,003		1,438,166	6,686,677	621,553	7,308,230

(1) Registrations include: passenger automobiles 8,472,224; motor trucks and tractors 1,980,106; buses 47,459; motorcycles 321,167; other motor vehicles (includes farm tractors) 181,047. (2) Refers to gasoline sales only and exludes aviation and aviation turbo fuels. (3) Gasoline for motive purposes only. Aviation and aviation turbo fuels included but liquefied petroleum gases excluded. *No junior permit.

Memorable Manned Space Flights

Sources: National Aeronautics and Space Administration and The World Almanac.

Crew, Date	Mission Name	Orbits	Duration	Remarks
Yuri A. Gagarin (4/12/61)	Vostok 1	1	1h 48m	First manned orbital flight.
Alan Z. Shepard Jr. (5/5/61)	Mercury-Redstone 3	(2)	15m 22s	First American in space.
Virgil I. Grissom (7/21/61)	Mercury-Redstone 4	(2)	15m 37s	Spacecraft sank, Grissom rescued.
Gherman S. Titov (8/6-7/61)	Vostok 2	16	25h 18m	First space flight of more than 24 hrs.
John H. Glenn Jr. (2/20/62)	Mercury-Atlas 6	3	4h 55m 23s	First American in orbit.
M. Scott Carpenter (5/24/62)	Mercury-Atlas 7	3	4h 56m 05s	Manual retrofire error caused 250 mi. landing overshoot.
Andrian G. Nikolayev (8/11-15/62)	Vostok 3	64	94h 22m	Vostok 3 and 4 made first group flight.
Pavel R. Popovich (8/12-15/62)	Vostok 4	48	70h 57m	On first orbit it came within 3 miles of Vostok 3.
Walter M. Schirra, Jr. (10/3/62)	Mercury-Atlas 8	6	9h 13m 11s	Closest splashdown to target to date (4.5 mi.).
L. Gordon Cooper (5/15-16/63)	Mercury-Atlas 9	22	34h 19m 49s	First U.S. evaluation of effects on man of one day in space.
Valery F. Bykovsky (6/14-6/19/63)	Vostok 5	81	119h 06m	Vostok 5 and 6 made 2d group flight.
Valentina V. Tereshkova (6/16-19/63)	Vostok 6	48	70h 50m	First woman in space.
Vladimir M. Komarov, Konstantin P. Feoktistov, Boris B. Yegorov (10/12/64)	Voskhod 1	16	24h 17m	First 3-man orbital flight; first without space suits.
Pavel I. Belyayev, Aleksei A. Leonov (3/18/65)	Voskhod 2	17	26h 02m	Leonov made first "space walk" (10 min.).
Virgil I. Grissom, John W. Young (3/23/65)	Gemini-Titan 3	3	4h 53m 00s	First manned spacecraft to change its orbital path.
James A. McDivitt, Edward H. White 2d, (6/3-7/65)	Gemini-Titan 4	62	97h 56m 11s	White was first American to "walk in space" (20 min.).
L. Gordon Cooper Jr., Charles Conrad Jr. (8/21-29/65)	Gemini-Titan 5	120	190h 55m 14s	First use of fuel cells for electric power; evaluated guidance and navigation system.
Frank Borman, James A. Lovell Jr. (12/4-18/65)	Gemini-Titan 7	206	330h 35m 31s	Longest duration Gemini flight.
Walter M. Schirra Jr., Thomas P. Stafford (12/15-16/65)	Gemini-Titan 6-A	16	25h 51m 24s	Completed world's first space rendezvous with Gemini 7.
Neil A. Armstrong, David R. Scott (3/16-17/66)	Gemini-Titan 8	6.5	10h 41m 26s	First docking of one space vehicle with another; mission aborted, control malfunction.
John W. Young, Michael Collins (7/18-21/66)	Gemini-Titan 10	43	70h 46m 39s	First use of Agena target vehicle's propulsion systems; rendezvoused with Gemini 8.
Charles Conrad Jr., Richard F. Gordon Jr. (9/12-15/66)	Gemini-Titan 11	44	71h 17m 08s	Docked, made 2 revolutions of earth tethered; set Gemini altitude record (739.2 mi.).
James A. Lovell Jr., Edwin E. Aldrin Jr. (11/11-15/66)	Gemini-Titan 12	59	94h 34m 31s	Final Gemini mission; record 5½ hrs. of extravehicular activity.
Vladimir M. Komarov (4/23/67)	Soyuz 1	17	26h 40m	Crashed after re-entry killing Komarov.
Walter M. Schirra Jr., Donn F. Eisele, R. Walter Cunningham (10/11-22/68)	Apollo-Saturn 7	163	260h 09m 03s	First manned flight of Apollo spacecraft command-service module only.
Georgi T. Beregovoi (10/26-30/68)	Soyuz 3	64	94h 51m	Made rendezvous with unmanned Soyuz 2.
Frank Borman, James A. Lovell Jr., William A. Anders (12/21-27/68)	Apollo-Saturn 8	10^3	147h 00m 42s	First flight to moon (command-service module only); views of lunar surface televised to earth.
Vladimir A. Shatalov (1/14-17/69)	Soyuz 4	45	71h 14m	Docked with Soyuz 5.
Boris V. Volyanov, Aleksei S. Yeliseyev, Yevgeny V. Khrunov (1/15-18/69)	Soyuz 5	46	72h 46m	Docked with Soyuz 4; Yeliseyev and Khrunov transferred to Soyuz 4.

(continued)

Crew, Date	Mission Name	Orbits	Duration	Remarks
James A. McDivitt, David R. Scott, Russell L. Schweickart (3/3-13/69)	Apollo-Saturn 9	151	241h 00m 54s	First manned flight of lunar module.
Thomas P. Stafford, Eugene A. Cernan, John W. Young (5/18-26/69)	Apollo-Saturn 10	31[4]	192h 03m 23s	First lunar module orbit of moon.
Neil A. Armstrong, Edwin E. Aldrin Jr., Michael Collins (7/16-24/69)	Apollo-Saturn 11	30[3]	195h 18m 35s	First lunar landing made by Armstrong and Aldrin; collected 48.5 lbs. of soil, rock samples; lunar stay time 21 h, 36 m, 21 s.
Georgi S. Shonin, Valery N. Kubasov (10/11-16/69)	Soyuz 6	79	118h 42m	First welding of metals in space.
Anatoly V. Filipchenko, Vladislav N. Volkov, Viktor V. Gorbatko (10/12-17/69)	Soyuz 7	79	118h 41m	Space lab construction tests made; Soyuz 6, 7 and 8 — first time 3 spacecraft 7 crew orbited earth at once.
Vladimir A. Shatalov, Aleksei S. Yeliseyev (10/13-18/69)	Soyuz 8	79	118h 41m	Orbiting space laboratory construction tests were made.
Charles Conrad Jr., Richard F. Gordon, Alan L. Bean (11/14-24/69)	Apollo-Saturn 12	45[3]	244h 36m 25s	Conrad and Bean made 2d moon landing; collected 74.7 lbs. of samples, lunar stay time 31 h, 31 m.
James A. Lovell Jr., Fred W. Haise Jr., John L. Swigart Jr. (4/11-17/70)	Apollo-Saturn 13		142h 54m 41s	Aborted after service module oxygen tank ruptured; crew returned safely using lunar module oxygen and power.
Alan B. Shepard Jr., Stuart A. Roosa, Edgar D. Mitchell (1/31-2/9/71)	Apollo-Saturn 14	34[3]	216h 01m 57s	Shepard and Mitchell made 3d moon landing, collected 96 lbs. of lunar samples; lunar stay 33 h, 31 m.
Vladimir A. Shatalov, Aleksei S. Yeliseyev, Nikolai Rukavishnikov (4/22-24/71)	Soyuz 10	32	47h 46m	Docked with prototype Salyut orbiting space station for 5¹/₂ hrs, then mission was aborted.
Georgi T. Dobrovolsky, Vladislav N. Volkov, Viktor I. Patsayev (6/6-30/71)	Soyuz 11	360	569h 40m	Docked with Salyut space station; and orbited in Salyut for 23 days; crew died during re-entry from loss of pressurization.
David R. Scott, Alfred M. Worden, James B. Irwin (7/26-8/7/71)	Apollo-Saturn 15	74[3]	295h 11m 53s	Scott and Irwin made 4th moon landing; first lunar rover use; first deep space walk; 170 lbs. of samples; 66 h, 55 m, stay.
Charles M. Duke Jr., Thomas K. Mattingly, John W. Young (4/16-27/72)	Apollo-Saturn 16	64[3]	265h 51m 05s	Young and Duke made 5th moon landing; collected 213 lbs. of lunar samples; lunar stay time 71 h, 2 m.
Eugene A. Cernan, Ronald E. Evans, Harrison H. Schmitt (12/7-19/72)	Apollo-Saturn 17	75[3]	301h 51m 59s	Cernan and Schmitt made 6th manned lunar landing; collected 243 lbs. of samples; record lunar stay of 75 h.
Charles Conrad Jr., Joseph P. Kerwin, Paul J. Weitz (5/25-6/22/73)	Skylab 2	. .	672h 49m 49s	First American manned orbiting space station; made long-flights tests, crew repaired damage caused during boost.
Alan L. Bean, Jack R. Lousma, Owen K. Garriott (7/28-9/25/73)	Skylab 3	. .	1,427h 09m 04s	Crew systems and operational tests, exceeded pre-mission plans for scientific activities; space walk total 13 h, 44 m.
Gerald P. Carr, Edward G. Gibson, William Pogue (11/16/73-2/8/74)	Skylab 4	. .	2,017h 16m 30s	Final Skylab mission; record space walk of 7 h, 1 m., record space walks total for a mission 22 h, 21 m.
Alexi Leonov, Valeri Kubason (7/15-7/21/75)	Soyuz 19	96	143h 31m	
Vance Brand, Thomas P. Stafford, Donald K. Slayton (7/15-7/24/75)	Apollo 18	136	217h 30m	U.S.-USSR joint flight. Crews linked-up in space, conducted experiments, shared meals, and held a joint news conference.

(1) The Americans measure orbital flights in revolutions while the Soviets use "orbits." (2) suborbital. (3) Moon orbits in command module. (4) Moon orbits.

Fire aboard spacecraft Apollo I on the ground at Cape Kennedy, Fla. killed Virgil I. Grissom, Edward H. White and Roger B. Chaffee on Jan. 27, 1967. They were the only U.S. astronauts killed in space tests.

Notable Ocean and Intercontinental Flights

(Flights approved by FAI as of Jan., 1976)

Pilot, Plane	From	To	Miles	Time	Date
		Dirigible Balloons			
British R-34 (1)........	East Fortune, Scot.......	Mineola, N.Y...........	....	108 hrs.	Jul. 2-6, 1919
	Mineola, N.Y...........	Pulham, Eng...........	....	75 hrs.	Jul. 9-13, 1919
Amundsen-Ellsworth-Nobile expedition....	Spitsbergen...........	Teller, Alaska.......	....	80 hrs.	May 11-14, 1926
Graf Zeppelin..........	Friedrichshafen.......	Lakehurst, N.J......	6,630	4d 15h 46m	Oct. 11-15, 1928
Hindenburg Zeppelin..	Germany.............	Lakehurst, N.J......	....	51h 17m	Jun. 30-Jul. 2, 1936
	Lakehurst, N.J........	Frankfort, Ger......	....	42h 53m	Aug. 9-11, 1936
USN ZPG-2 Blimp.....	S. Weymouth, Mass....	Africa............			
	Africa..............	Key West, Fla.......	7,000	275h	Mar. 4-16, 1957
		Airplanes			
USN NC- 4...........	Rockaway, N.Y........	Lisbon, Port.......	....	....	May 8-27, 1919
John Alcock-A. W. Brown (2)...........	St. John's, Nfld........	Clifden, Ireland....	1,960	16h 12m	Jun. 14-15, 1919
Richard E. Byrd(3).....	Spitsbergen...........	North Pole.........	1,545	15h 30m	May 9, 1926
Charles Lindbergh (4)..	Mineola, N.Y..........	Paris.............	3,610	33h 29m 30s	May 20-21, 1927
C. Levin-Roosevelt Field, C. Chamberlin (5)...	Mineola, N.Y........	Isleben, Germany....	3,911	42h 31m	Jun. 4-6, 1927
Baron G. von Huenefeld, crew (6)........	Dublin..............	Greenly Isl., Lab....	....	37 hrs.	Apr. 12-13, 1928
Sir Hubert Wilkins (9).	Point Barrow, Alaska...	Spitsbergen.........	....	.....	Apr. 16, 1928
Sir Chas. Kingsford-Smith, crew (7)......	Oakland, Cal.........	Brisbane, Aust......	....	....	May 31-Jun. 8, 1928
Amelia Earhart Putnam, W. Stultz, L. Gordon..........	Trepassy, Nfld........	Burry Port, Wales...	....	20h 40m	Jun. 17-18, 1928
Richard E. Byrd (8)....	Bay of Wales.........	South Pole........	....	.....	Nov. 28-29, 1929
D. Coste-M. Bellonte...	Paris................	Valley Stream, N.Y...	4,100	37h 18m 30s	Sept. 1-2, 1930
Wiley Post-Harold Gatty..............	Harbor Grace, Nfld....	England............	2,200	16h 17m	Jun. 23-24, 1931
Clyde Pangborn-Hugh Herndon Jr. (10).....	Tokyo..............	Wenatchee, Wash....	4,458	41h 34m	Oct. 3-5, 1931
Amelia Earhart Putnam (11)........	Harbor Grace, Nfld....	Ireland............	2,026	14h 56m	May 20-21, 1932
James A. Mollison (12).	Portmarnock, Ire......	Pennfield, N.B......	....	....	Aug. 18, 1932
China Clipper (Pan Am. Airways) (13)..	San Francisco........	Manila, P.I........	....	....	Nov. 22-28, 1935
	Manila, P.I.........	San Francisco.......	....	....	Dec. 1-6, 1935
Gromoff, Yumasheff, Danilin (USSR)......	Moscow, USSR........	San Jacinto, Cal....	6,262	62h 02m	Jul. 12-14, 1937
Douglas C. Corrigan....	New York............	Dublin, Ire........	....	28h 13m	Jul. 17-18, 1938
B-29 (C.J. Miller)......	Honolulu...........	Washington, D.C.....	4,640	17h 21m	Sept. 1, 1945
C-54 (Maj. G.E. Cain)...	Tokyo..............	Washington, D.C.....	....	31h 24m	Sept. 3, 1945
Col. David C. Schilling, USAF (14)..........	England.............	Limestone, Me......	3,300	10h 01m	Sept. 22, 1950
Chas. F. Blair Jr.......	New York............	London............	3,500	7h 48m	Jan. 31, 1951
Chas. F. Blair Jr. (15)...	Bardufoss, Norway.....	Fairbanks, Alaska...	3,300	10h 29m	May 29, 1951
Chas. F. Blair Jr.......	Fairbanks, Alaska.....	New York..........	3,450	9h 31m	May 30, 1950
Canberra Bomber.......	England.............	Australia..........	....	20h 20m	Mar. 16, 1952
Two U. S. S-55 Helicopters (16)........	Westover AFB, Mass....	Prestwick, Scotland..	3,410	42h 30m	Jul. 15-31, 1952
Canberra Bomber (17).	Aldergrove, N.Ire......	Gander, Nfld.......	2,073	4h 34m	Aug. 26, 1952
	Gander, Nfld........	Aldergrove, N.Ire....	2,073	3h 25m	Aug. 26, 1952
British Comet........	London-Tokyo........	Tokyo-London.......	20,400	74h 52m	Apr. 3-7, 1953
British Comet........	London.............	Rio de Janeiro......	6,000	12h 30m	Sept. 13-14, 1953
Max Conrad (solo).....	New York............	Paris.............	....	22h 23m	Nov. 7, 1954
	Gander, Nfld........	Aldergrove, N.Ire,...	2,073	3h 25m	Aug. 26, 1952
Canberra Bomber....	London (round trip)...	New York..........	6,920	14h 21m 45.4s	Aug. 23, 1955
Capt. William F. Judd..	New York...........	Paris.............	....	24h 11m	Jan. 29-30, 1956
Three USAF F-100Cs..	London.............	Los Angeles, Cal....	6,710	14h 5m	May 13, 1957
Spirit of St. Louis II (USAF F-100F jet)...	McGuire AFB, N.J......	Le Bourget, Paris....	....	6h 38m	May 21, 1957
USAF KC-135........	Tokyo..............	Lajes AFB, Azores...	10,230	18h 48m	Apr. 7-8, 1958
Max Conrad (solo).....	New York............	Palermo, Sicily.....	4,440	32h 55m	Jun. 22-23, 1958
Capt. Marion Boling...	Manila, P.I..........	Pendleton, Ore......	6,979	45h 42m	Jul. 31-Aug. 1, 1958
USAF KC-135........	Yokota AB, Japan......	Washington, D.C.....	7,100	12h 28m	Sept. 12, 1958
Max Conrad (solo).....	Chicago............	Rome.............	5,000	34 3m	Mar. 5-6, 1959
Max Conrad (solo).....	Casablanca, Africa.....	Los Angeles........	7,700	58h 36m	Jun. 2-4, 1959
USSR TU-114 (18)....	Moscow............	New York..........	5,092	11h 6m	Jun. 28, 1959
Boeing 707 airliner....	San Francisco........	Sydney, Australia....	7,630	16h 10m	Jul. 2, 1959
Boeing 707-320.......	New York...........	Moscow...........	c.5,090	8h 54m	Jul. 23, 1959
Max Conrad (solo).....	Casablanca, Mor......	El Paso, Tex.......	6,911	56h 26m	Nov. 22-26, 1959
Col. J.B. Swindal......	Washington, D.C.......	Moscow...........	5,004	8h 39m 02.2s	May 19, 1963
Mrs. Jerrie Mock (19)...	Columbus, Oh........	Columbus, Oh......	23,206	29d 11h 59m	Mar. 19-Apr. 18, 1964
Joan Merriam (20).....	Oakland, Cal.........	Oakland, Cal.......	27,750	56d	Mar. 17-May 12, 1964
Elgen Long (solo) (21)...	San Francisco........	San Francisco.......	38,896	28d 00h 43m	Nov. 5-Dec. 3, 1971

Notable first flights: 1, Atlantic aerial round trip. **2,** Non-stop transatlantic flight. **3,** Polar flight. **4,** Solo transatlantic flight in the Ryan monoplane the "Spirit of St. Louis." **5,** Transatlantic passenger flight. **6,** East-West transatlantic crossing. **7,** U.S. to Australia flight. **8,** South Pole flight. **9,** Trans-Arctic flight. **10,** Non-Stop Pacific flight. **11,** Woman's transoceanic solo flight. **12,** Westbound transatlantic solo flight. **13,** Pacific airmail and U.S. to Philippines crossing. **14,** Non-stop jet transatlantic flight. **15,** Solo across North Pole. **16,** Transatlantic helicopter flight. **17,** Transatlantic round trip on same day. **18** Non-stop between Moscow and New York. **19,** First woman pilot to circle globe; First woman to fly both North Atlantic and Pacific. **20,** Followed route Amelia Earhart partly completed in 1937. **21,** Speed record around the world over both the earth's poles.

International Aeronautical Records

Source: The National Aeronautic Association, 806 15th St., N.W., Washington, D.C. 20005, representative in the United States of the Federation Aeronautique Internationale, certifying agency for world aviation and space records. The International Aeronautical Federation was formed in 1905 by representatives from Belgium, France, Germany, Great Britain, Spain, Italy, Switzerland, and the United States, with headquarters in Paris. Regulations for the control of official records were signed Oct. 14, 1905. World records are defined as maximum performance, regardless of class or type of aircraft used. Records to June, 1976.

World Air Records—Maximum Performance in Any Class

Speed over a straight course — 3,331,507 kmph. (2,070.101 mph) — Col. R. L. Stephens, USAF, Lockheed YF-12; Edwards Air Force Base, Cal., May 1, 1965.

Speed over a closed circuit — 2,981.5 kmph. (1,850.61 mph) — Mikhail Komarov, USSR; F-266 jet; Oct. 5, 1967.

Distance in a straight line — 20,168.75 kms (12,532.28 mi.) — Maj. Clyde P. Evely, USAF, Boeing B52-H; Kadena, Okinawa, to Madrid, Spain, Jan. 11, 1962.

Distance over a closed course — 18,245.5 kms (11,336.92 mi.) — Capt. William Stevenson, USAF, Boeing B52h; Seymour-Johnson, N.C., June 6-7, 1962.

Altitude — 95.935.99 meters (314,750 feet) — Maj. Robert M. White, USAF, North American X-15-1; Edwards AFB, Cal., July 17, 1962.

Altitude in horizontal flight 24,462,596 meters (80,257.86 ft.) — Col. R. L. Stephens, USAF, Lockheed F1-2A; Edwards Air Force Base, Cal., May 1, 1965.

Manned Space Craft

Duration — 84 days 1 hr. 15 min. 32 sec. — Gerald P. Carr, Edward G. Gibson, William R. Pogue, U.S.; Skylab 3 Nov. 16, 1973-Feb. 8, 1974.

Altitude — 377,668.0 kms (234,672.5 mi.) — Frank Borman, James A. Lovell Jr., William Anders, Spacecraft Apollo 8; Dec. 21-27, 1968.

Greatest mass lifted — 127,980 kgs. (282,197 lbs.) — Frank Borman, James S. Lovell Jr., William Anders, Spacecraft Apollo 8; Dec. 21-27, 1968.

Distance — 55,560,000 kms. (34,523,000 mi.) — Gerald P. Carr, Edward G. Gibson, William R. Pogue, U.S.; Skylab 3; Nov. 16, 1973-Feb. 8, 1974.

World "Class" Records

All other records, international in scope, are termed World "Class" records and are divided into classes: airships, free balloons, airplanes, seaplanes, amphibians, gliders, and rotorplanes. Airplanes (Class C) are sub-divided into four groups: Group I — piston engine aircraft, Group II — turbo-prop aircraft, Group III — Jet aircraft, Group IV — rocket powered aircraft. A partial listing of world records follows:

Airplanes (Class C, Group I — Piston Engine)

Distance, closed circuit — 14,441.26 kms (8,974 mi.) — James R. Bede, U.S.; BD-2, 1 Continental 360-C engine, Columbus, Ohio to Kansas City course, Nov. 7-9, 1969.

Distance in a straight line. Airline (international) — 18,081,990 kms. (11,235.6 miles) — Cmdr. Thomas D. Davies, USN; Cmdr. Eugene P. Rankin, USN; Cmdr. Walter S. Reid, USN, and Lt. Cmdr. Ray A. Tabeling, USN; Lockheed P2V-1; from Pearce Field, Perth, Australia, to Port Columbus, Ohio, Sept. 29-Oct. 1, 1946.

Maximum speed over 3-kilometer measured course — 776.449 kmph. (482.462 mph) — Darryl Greenamyer, U.S., Grumman F8F Bearcat, Edwards AFB, Cal., Aug. 16, 1969. (United States) — 663.054 kmph. (412.002 mph.) Jacqueline Cochran, U.S.; North American F-51, Thermal, Cal., Dec. 17, 1947.

Speed for 100 kilometers (62.137 miles) without payload (international) — 755.668 kmph. (469.549 mph.) — Jacqueline Cochran, U.S.; North American P-51; Coachella Valley, Cal., Dec. 10, 1947.

Speed for 1,000 kilometers (621.369 miles) without payload — 693.78 kph. (431.09 mph.) — Jacqueline Cochran, U.S.; North American P-51; Santa Rosasummit, Cal. — Flagstaff, Arizona course, May 24, 1948.

Speed for 5,000 kilometers (3,106.849 miles) without payload — 544.59 kph. (338.39 mph.) — Capt. James Bauer, USAF, Boeing B-29; Dayton, Ohio, June 28, 1946.

Speed around the world — 326.48 kpmh (202.86 mph) — D.N. Dalton, Australia; Beechcraft Duke, 2 Lycoming T-10-541-E engines; Brisbane, Aust., July 20-25, 1975. Time: 5 days, 2 hours, 17 min.

Light Airplanes—Class C-1.d

Distance in a straight line. Airline (international) — 12,341.26 kms. (7,668.48 miles) — Max Conrad, U.S.; Piper Comanche 250, Lycoming 0540-A1A5 250 hp.; Casablanca, Morocco to Los Angeles, June 2-4, 1959.

Speed for 100 kilometers — (62.137 miles) in a closed circuit (international) — 519.480 kmph. (322.789 mph.) — Miss R. M. Sharpe, Great Britain; Vickers Supermarine Spitfire 5-B; Wolverhampton, June 17, 1950.

Helicopters (Class E-1)

Distance in a straight line — 3,561.55 kms. (2,213.04 miles) — Robert G. Ferry, U.S.; Hughes YOH-6A helicopter; Culver City, Cal., to Daytona, Fla., Apr. 6-7, 1966.

Speed over 3-km. course — 348.971 kmph. (216.839 mph.) — Byron Graham, U.S.; Sikorsky S-67 helicopter; Windsor Locks, Conn., Dec. 14, 1970.

Gliders (Class D—Single-place)

Distance, straight line — 1,460.8 kms. (907.7 miles) — Hans Werner Grosse, West Germany; ASK12 sailplane; Luebeck to Bairritz, Apr. 25, 1972.

Altitude above sea level — 14,102 meters (46,267 feet) — Paul F. Bikle, United States; Sailplane Schweizer SGS 123E; Mojave, Lancaster, Cal., Feb. 25, 1961.

Airplanes (Class C, Group II—Turbo-prop)

Distance in a straight line — 14,052.95 kms. (8,732.09 miles) — Lt. Col. Edgar L. Allison Jr., U.S. Lockheed HC-130 Hercules aircraft; Feb. 20, 1972.

Speed over a 15-25 km. course — Cmdr. D.H. Lilienthal, USN, Lockheed P3 C Orion aircraft; 806 kmph. (501 mph.); Jan. 27, 1971.

Altitude — 15.549 meters (51,014 ft.) — Donald R. Wilson, Greenville, Tex., LTV L450F aircraft; Mar. 27, 1972.

Speed for 1,000 kilometers (621.369 miles) without payload (international) — 871.38 kmph. (541.449 mph.) — Ivan Soukhomline, Boris Timochok, and crew, USSR; TU-114 swept wing monoplane, 4 turbo-prop TB-12 engines; Sternbeng Course; Mar. 24, 1960.

Speed for 5,000 kilometers (3,106.849 miles) without payload (international) — 877.212 kmph. (545.072 mph.) — Ivan Soukhomline, K. Sapielkine, and crew, USSR; TU-114 swept wing monoplane, 4 turbo-prop TB-12 engines; Sternberg-Svierdlovsk-Sebastopol-Sternberg; Apr. 9, 1960.

Airplanes (Class C, Group III—Jet-powered)

Distance in a straight line — 20.168.78 kms. (12.532.28 mi.) — Maj. Clyde P. Evely, USAF, Boeing B52-H, 8 Pratt & Whitney TF-33P-3 engines; Kadena, Okinawa, to Madrid, Spain, Jan. 10-11, 1962.

Distance in a closed circuit — 18.245.05 kms. (11.326.92 miles) — Capt. William Stevenson, USAF, Boeing B52H, 8 Pratt & Whitney TF-33P-3 engines; terminal: Seymour-Johnson, N.C., June 6-7, 1962.

Altitude — 36.240 meters (118.893 ft.) — Alexander Fedotov, USSR; E-266 Airplane; Podmoskovnoye, USSR, July 25, 1973.

Speed over a 3-kilometer course — 1.452.777 kmph. (902.769 mph) — Lt. Hunt Hardisty, USN; McDonnell F4H Phantom, 2 G e J-79 Jet engines; White Sands, N.M., Aug. 29, 1961.

Speed for 100 kilometers — 2.600 kmph. (1.615 mph.) — Alexander Fedotov, USSR; E-266 airplane, 2 RD jet engines, Apr. 8, 1973.

Speed for 500 kilometers in a closed circuit — 2.981.5 kmph. (1.852.61 mph.) — Mikhail Komarov, USSR; E-266 airplane, 2 RD jet engines, Oct. 5, 1967.

Speed for 1.000 kilometers in a closed circuit — 2.920.67 kmph. (1.814.81 mph.) — Pyotr Ostapenko, USSR; E-266 airplane, 2 RD jet engines, Oct. 27, 1967.

Speed for 2.000 kilometers in closed circuit — 1.708.817 kmph. (1.061.808 mph.) — Maj. H. J. Deutchendorf Jr., USAF, Convair B-58 Hustler Bomber; Desert, Stoval, Boundary, Morris, Desert. Edwards AFB. Cal. course, Jan. 12, 1961.

Sustained altitude — 24.462.596 meters (80.257.86 ft) — Col. R. L. Stephens, USAF; Lockheed YF-12A, 2 Pratt & Whitney J 58 engines; Edwards AFB, Cal., May 1, 1965.

Free Balloons (Tenth category, 4001 cu. meters or more)

Altitude — 34,668 meters (113,739.9 feet) — Cmdr. Malcolm D. Ross, USNR; Lee Lewis Memorial Winzen Research Balloon; Gulf of Mexico, May 4, 1961.

FAI Course Records

Los Angeles to New York — 1,954.79 kmph (1,214.65 mph)—Capt. Robert G. Sowers, USAF; Convair B58 Hustler, 4 GEj79-5B engines; Elapsed time: 2 hrs. 58.71 sec., Mar. 5, 1962.

New York to Los Angeles — 1,741 kmph (1,081.80 mph)—Capt. Robert G. Sowers, USAF; Convair B58 Hustler: Elapsed time: 2 hrs. 15 min. 50.08 sec., Mar. 5, 1962.

Los Angeles-New York-Los Angeles — 1,681.71 kmph (1,044.46 mph)—Capt. Robert G. Sowers, USAF; Convair B58 Hustler. Elapsed time: 4 hrs. 41 min. 14.98 sec., Mar. 5, 1962.

New York to Paris — 1,753.068 kmph (1,089.36 mph)—Maj. W. R. Payne, United States; Convair B58 Hustler. Elapsed time: 3 hrs. 10 min. 58 sec., May 26, 1961.

London to New York (international) — 945.423 kmph (587.457 mph)—Maj. Burl B. Davenport, Lt. James J. Jones and crew USAF; Boeing KC-135 Stratotanker; London International Airport to Idlewild International Airport, New York, June 27, 1958. Elapsed time: 5 hrs. 29 min. 14.64 sec.

Baltimore to Moscow, USSR — 906.64 kmph (563.36 mph)—Col. James B. Swindal, USAF; Boeing VC-137 (707). Elapsed time: 9 hrs. 54 min. 48.5 sec. May 20-21, 1963.

Belfast to Gander, Newfoundland (international) — 774.255 kmph (481.099 mph)—Wing Commander R. P. Beamont and crew, Great Britain; Camberra bomber, two Rolls-Royce turbo-jet engines, Aug. 31, 1951. Elapsed time: 4 hrs. 18 min. 24.4 sec.

New York to London (international) — 2,914.3 kmph (1,810.9 mph)—Maj. James V. Sullivan, USAF; Lockheed SR-71. Elapsed time 1 hr. 55 min. 32 sec., Sept. 1, 1974.

London to Los Angeles (international) — 2,394.39 kmph (1,487.81 mph)—Capt. Harold B. Adams, USAF; Lockheed SR-71. Elapsed time: 3 hrs. 47 min. 39 sec., Sept. 13, 1974.

Aviation Hall of Fame

The Aviation Hall of Fame at Dayton, Oh., is dedicated to honoring aviation's outstanding pioneers. It operates as a non-profit privately supported organization under a charter granted in 1964 by the Congress of the U.S.

1962
Orville Wright
Wilbur Wright
1963
Octave Chanute
Samuel Pierpont Langley
Frank Purdy Lahm
Benjamin Delahauf Foulois
1964
Thomas Scott Baldwin
Theodore Gordon Ellyson
Henry W. Walden
Glenn Hammond Curtiss
Calbraith Perry Rodgers
John Joseph Montgomery
1965
Alexander Graham Bell
Alfred Austell Cunningham
Albert Cushing Read
Eugene Burton Ely
A. Roy Knabenshue
Thomas Etholen Selfridge

Charles Edward Taylor
Edward Vernon Rickenbacker
1966
Lincoln Beachey
William Edward Boeing
Robert Hutchings Goddard
Glenn Luther Martin
William "Billy" Mitchell
John Henry Towers
1967
Henry Harley "Hap" Arnold
James Harold Doolittle
Charles Augustus Lindbergh
Carl Andrew Spaatz
1968
Richard Evelyn Byrd
Amelia Earhart Putnam
John Arthur MacReady
Igor Ivan Sikorsky
1969
Donald Wills Douglas

Grover Cleveland Loening
Wiley Hardeman Post
Juan Terry Trippe
1970
Alexander P. deSeversky
Ira Clarence Eaker
Robert Ellsworth Gross
1971
William McPherson Allen
Jacqueline Cochran (Odlum)
Harry Frank Guggenheim
George Churchill Kenney
1972
Claire Lee Chennault
Leroy Randle Grumman
J.H. "Dutch" Kindelberger
Curtis Emerson LeMay
1973
Bernt Balchen
Howard Robard Hughes
Elmer Ambrose Sperry Sr.

Charles Elwood Yeager
1974
C.L. "Kelly" Johnson
John K. Northrop
Cyrus R. Smith
T. Claude Ryan
Leigh Wade
1975
Reuben H. Fleet
Frank Luke Jr.
Robert C. Reeve
Roscoe Turner
1976
Clarence F. Chamberlin
John Glenn
George Goddard
Albert F. Hegenberger
Edwin A. Link
Sanford A. Moss
William A. Patterson
Nathan F. Twining

Consolidated Airline Traffic

Source: Air Transport Assn. of America. (in thousands)

	1973	1974	1975
Passenger Traffic			
Revenue passengers enplaned	202,208	207,458	205,062
Revenue passenger miles	161,957,307	162,918,594	162,810,057
Available seat miles	310,597,107	297,006,062	303,006,243
Cargo Traffic (Ton Miles)	6,034,200	6,121,752	5,892,605
Freight	4,736,729	4,890,026	4,766,118
Express	100,497	80,845	29,190
U.S. Mail	1,197,974	1,150,881	1,097,297
Overall Traffic and Service			
Nonscheduled traffic — total ton miles	1,685,782	1,474,597	1,346,765
Total revenue ton miles—all services	23,927,657	23,900,208	23,532,302
Total available ton miles—all services	51,443,758	48,941,526	49,286,148

Fastest Trips Around the World
(Flights approved by FAI as of Jan., 1976)

Fast circuits of the earth have been a subject of wide interest since Jules Verne, French novelist, described an imaginary trip by Phileas Fogg in Around the World in 80 Days, assertedly occurring Oct. 2 to Dec. 20, 1872. Notable actual such events follow:

Craft, pilot	Terminal	Miles	Time	Date
Nellie Bly	New York, N.Y.		72d 06h 11m	1889
George Francis Train	New York, N.Y.		67d 12h 03m	1890
Charles Fitzmorris	Chicago.		60d 13h 29m	1901
J. W. Willis Sayre.	Seattle		54d 09h 42m	1903
Henry Frederick			54d 07h 02m	1903
Col. Burnlay-Campbell			40d 19h 30m	1907
Andre Jaeger-Schmidt			39d 19h 42m 38s	1911
John Henry Mears			35d 21h 36m	1913
Two U.S. Army airplanes	Seattle (57 hops, 21 countries).	26,103	35d 1h 11m	1924
Edward S. Evans and Linton Wells (New York World) (1).	New York.	18,400	28d 14h 36m 05s	June 16-July 14, 1926
John H. Mears and Capt. C. B. D. Collyer.	New York.		23d 15h 21m 03s	June 29-July 22, 1928
Graf Zeppelin	Friedrichshafen, Ger. via Tokyo, Los Angeles, Lakehurst, N.J.	21,700	20d 04h	Aug. 14-Sept. 4, 1929
Wiley Post and Harold Gatty (Monoplane Winnie Mae)	Roosevelt Field, via Arctic Circle.	15,474	08d 15h 51m	June 23-July 1, 1931
Wiley Post (Monoplane Winnie Mae) (2)	Floyd Bennett Field, via Arctic Circle.	15,596	115h 36m 30s	July 15-22, 1933
H. R. Ekins (Scripps-Howard Newspapers in race) (Zeppelin Hindenburg to Germany, airplanes from Frankfurt)	Lakehurst, N.J., via Frankfurt, Germany.	25,654	18d 11h 14m 33s	Sept. 30-Oct. 19, 1936
Howard Hughes and 4 assistants	New York, Paris, Moscow, Siberia, Fairbanks, Alaska.	14,824	03d 19h 08m 10s	July 10-13, 1938
Mrs. Clara Adams (Pan American Clipper).	Port Washington, N.Y., return Newark, N.J.		16d 19h 04m	June 28-July 15, 1939
Globester, U.S. Air Transport Command	Washington, D.C.	23,279	149h 44m	Sept. 28-Oct. 4, 1945
Capt. William P. Odom (A-26 Reynolds Bombshell)	New York, via Paris, Cairo, Tokyo, Alaska.	20,000	78h 55m 12s	Apr. 12-16, 1947
America, Pan American 4-engine Lockheed Constellation (3)	New York, eastward	22,219	101h 32m	June 17-30, 1947
Col. Edward P. F. Eagan	New York.	20,559	147h 15m	Dec. 13, 1948
USAF B-50 Lucky Lady II (Capt. James Gallagher) (4)	Fort Worth, Texas.	23,452	94h 01m	Feb. 26-Mar. 2, 1949
Jean-Marie Audibert	Paris.		04d 19h 38m	Dec. 11-15, 1952
Pamela Martin	Midway Airport, Chicago		90h 59m	Dec. 5-8, 1953
Three USAF B-52 Stratofortresses (5)	Merced, Cal., via Nfld., Morocco, Saudi Arabia, India, Ceylon, P.I., Guam	24,325	45h 19m	Jan. 15-18, 1957
Joseph Cavoli.	Cleveland, Ohio.		89h 13m 37s	Jan. 31-Feb. 4, 1958
Peter Gluckmann (solo)	San Francisco.	22,800	29d	Aug. 22-Sept. 20,-1959
Milton Reynolds.	San Francisco.		51h 45m 22s	Jan. 12-14, 1960
Sue Snyder.	Chicago.	21,219	62h 59m	June 22-24, 1960
Max Conrad (solo).	Miami, Fla.	25,946	08d 18h 35m 57s	Feb. 28-Mar. 8,-1961
Sam Miller & Louis Fodor	New York.		46h 28m	Aug. 3-4, 1963
Henry G. Beaird	Wichita, Kan.	22,992	65h 38m 49s	May 23-26, 1966
Robert & Joan Wallick (6).	Manila, Philippines	23,129	05d 6h 17m 10s	June 2-7, 1966
Arthur Godfrey, Richard Merrill Fred Austin, Karl Keller	New York.	23,333	86h 9m 1s	June 4-7, 1966
Trevor K. Brougham.	Darwin, Australia.	24,800	05d 05h 57m	Aug. 5-10, 1972

1. Mileage by train and auto, 4,110; by plane, 6,300; by steamship, 8,000. 2. First to fly solo around northern circumference of the world, also first to fly twice around the world. 3. Inception of regular commercial global air service. 4. First non-stop round-the-world flight, refueled 4 times in flight. 5. First non-stop global flight by jet planes; refueled in flight by KC-97 aerial tankers; average speed approx. 525 mph. 6. Official world record for light planes.

The Busiest Airports, 1975
(Total take-offs and landings)

United States
Source: Dept. of Transportation

O'Hare (Chicago).	668,368	(1)
Santa Ana, Cal.	618,889	
Van Nuys, Cal.	588,098	
Long Beach, Cal.	538,230	
Atlanta.	469,499	(2)
Los Angeles.	455,836	(3)
Phoenix.	430,363	
San Jose, Cal.	430,040	
Poa Locka, Fla.	425,783	
Torrance, Cal.	409,858	
Dallas-Ft. Worth.	342,370	(4)
J.F. Kennedy, N.Y.	337,089	(5)

Canada
Source Ministry of Transport

St. Hubert, Que.	292,929	
Pitt Meadows, B.C.	275,691	
Edmonton Municipal, Atla.	265,568	
Toronto International, Ont.	238,197	(1)
Buttonville, Ont.	221,688	
Ottawa International, Ont.	207,440	
Springbank, Alta.	203,747	
Hamilton City, Ont.	203,461	
Vancouver International, B.C.	203,253	(3)
St. Andrews, Man.	199,608	
Montreal International, P.Q.	192,657	(2)
Langley, B.C.	192,381	

Numbers in parentheses indicate top 5 in air carrier operations only.

Air Line Distances Between Selected Cities of the World

Source: Defense Mapping Agency Aerospace Center (Statute Miles)
Point-to-point measurements are usually from City Hall

	Bangkok	Berlin	Cairo	Capetown	Caracas	Chicago	Hong Kong	Honolulu	Lima	London
Bangkok	....	5,352	4,523	6,300	10,555	8,570	1,077	6,609	12,244	5,944
Berlin	5,352	....	1,797	5,961	5,238	4,414	5,443	7,320	6,896	583
Cairo	4,523	1,797	....	4,480	6,342	6,141	5,066	8,848	7,726	2,185
Capetown	6,300	5,961	4,480	....	6,366	8,491	7,376	11,535	6,072	5,989
Caracas	10,555	5,238	6,342	6,366	....	2,495	10,165	6,021	1,707	4,655
Chicago	8,570	4,414	6,141	8,491	2,495	....	7,797	4,256	3,775	3,958
Hong Kong	1,077	5,443	5,066	7,376	10,165	7,797	....	5,556	11,418	5,990
Honolulu	6,609	7,320	8,848	11,535	6,021	4,256	5,556	....	5,947	7,240
London	5,933	583	2,185	5,989	4,655	3,958	5,990	7,240	6,316	....
Madrid	6,337	1,165	2,087	5,308	4,346	4,189	6,558	7,872	5,907	785
Melbourne	4,568	9,918	8,675	6,425	9,717	9,673	4,595	5,505	8,059	10,500
Mexico City	9,793	6,056	7,700	8,519	2,234	1,690	8,788	3,789	2,639	5,558
Montreal	8,338	3,740	5,427	7,922	2,438	745	7,736	4,918	3,970	3,254
Moscow	4,389	1,006	1,803	6,279	6,177	4,987	4,437	7,047	7,862	1,564
New Delhi	1,813	3,598	2,758	5,769	8,833	7,486	2,339	7,412	10,432	4,181
New York	8,669	3,979	5,619	7,803	2,120	714	8,060	4,969	3,639	3,469
Paris	5,877	548	1,998	5,786	4,732	4,143	5,990	7,449	6,370	214
Peking	2,046	4,584	4,698	8,044	8,950	6,604	1,217	5,077	10,349	5,750
Rio de Janeiro	9,994	6,209	6,143	3,781	2,804	5,282	11,009	8,288	2,342	5,750
San Francisco	7,931	5,672	7,466	10,248	3,902	1,859	6,905	2,398	4,518	5,367
Singapore	883	6,164	5,137	6,008	11,402	9,372	1,605	6,726	11,689	6,747
Stockholm	5,089	528	2,096	6,423	5,471	4,331	5,063	6,875	7,166	942
Tokyo	2,865	5,557	5,958	9,154	8,808	6,314	1,791	3,859	9,631	5,959
Warsaw	5,033	322	1,619	5,935	5,559	4,679	5,147	7,366	7,215	905
Washington	8,807	4,181	5,822	7,895	2,047	596	8,155	4,838	3,509	3,674

	Madrid	Melbourne	Mexico City	Montreal	Moscow	Nairobi	New Delhi	New York	Paris	Peking
Bangkok	6,337	4,568	9,793	8,338	4,389	4,483	1,813	8,669	5,877	2,046
Berlin	1,165	9,918	6,056	3,740	1,006	3,949	3,598	3,979	548	4,584
Cairo	2,087	8,675	7,700	5,427	1,803	2,186	2,758	5,619	1,998	4,698
Capetown	5,308	6,425	8,519	7,922	6,279	2,540	5,769	7,803	5,786	8,044
Caracas	4,346	9,717	2,234	2,438	6,177	7,178	8,833	2,120	4,732	8,950
Chicago	4,189	9,673	1,690	745	4,987	8,011	7,486	714	4,143	6,604
Hong Kong	6,558	4,595	8,788	7,736	4,437	5,449	2,339	8,060	5,990	1,217
Honolulu	7,872	5,505	3,789	4,918	7,047	10,741	7,412	4,969	7,449	5,077
London	785	10,500	5,558	3,254	1,564	4,231	4,181	3,469	214	5,074
Madrid	....	10,758	5,643	3,448	2,147	3,841	4,530	3,593	655	5,745
Melbourne	10,758	....	8,426	10,395	8,950	7,153	6,329	10,359	10,430	5,643
Mexico City	5,643	8,426	....	2,317	6,676	9,219	9,120	2,090	5,725	7,753
Montreal	3,448	10,395	2,317	....	4,401	7,267	7,012	331	3,432	6,519
Moscow	2,147	8,950	6,676	4,401	....	3,930	2,698	4,683	1,554	3,607
New Delhi	4,530	6,329	9,120	7,012	2,698	3,374	....	7,318	4,102	2,353
New York	3,593	10,359	2,090	331	4,683	7,364	7,318	....	3,636	6,844
Paris	655	10,430	5,725	3,432	1,554	4,022	4,102	3,636	....	5,120
Peking	5,745	5,643	7,753	6,519	3,607	5,727	2,353	6,844	5,120	....
Rio de Janeiro	5,045	8,226	4,764	5,078	7,170	5,560	8,753	4,801	5,684	10,768
Rome	851	9,929	6,377	4,104	1,483	3,339	3,684	4,293	690	5,063
San Francisco	5,803	7,856	1,887	2,543	5,885	9,597	7,691	2,572	5,577	5,918
Singapore	7,080	3,759	10,327	9,203	5,228	4,638	2,571	9,534	6,673	2,771
Stockholm	1,653	9,630	6,012	3,714	716	4,281	3,414	3,986	1,003	4,133
Tokyo	6,706	5,062	7,035	6,471	4,660	6,999	3,638	6,757	6,053	1,307
Warsaw	1,427	9,598	6,337	4,022	721	3,801	3,277	4,270	852	4,325
Washington	3,792	10,180	1,885	489	4,876	7,551	7,500	205	3,840	6,942

	Rio de Janiero	Rome	San Francisco	Singapore	Stockholm	Teheran	Tokyo	Vienna	Warsaw	Wash. D.C.
Bangkok	9,994	5,494	7,931	883	5,089	3,391	2,865	5,252	5,033	8,807
Berlin	6,209	737	5,672	6,164	528	2,185	5,557	326	322	4,181
Cairo	6,143	1,326	7,466	5,137	2,096	1,234	5,958	1,481	1,619	5,822
Capetown	3,781	5,231	10,248	6,008	6,423	5,241	9,154	5,656	5,935	7,895
Caracas	2,804	5,195	3,902	11,402	5,471	7,320	8,808	5,372	5,559	2,047
Chicago	5,282	4,824	1,859	9,372	4,331	6,502	6,314	4,698	4,679	596
Hong Kong	11,009	5,774	6,905	1,605	5,063	3,843	1,791	5,431	5,147	8,155
Honolulu	8,288	8,040	2,398	6,726	6,875	8,070	3,859	7,632	7,366	4,838
London	5,750	895	5,367	6,747	942	2,743	5,959	771	905	3,674
Madrid	5,045	851	5,803	7,080	1,653	2,978	6,706	1,128	1,427	3,792
Melbourne	8,226	9,929	7,856	3,759	9,630	7,826	5,062	9,790	9,598	10,180
Mexico City	4,764	6,377	1,887	10,327	6,012	8,184	7,035	6,320	6,337	1,885
Montreal	5,078	4,104	2,543	9,203	3,714	5,880	6,471	4,009	4,022	489
Moscow	7,170	1,483	5,885	5,228	716	1,532	4,660	1,043	721	4,876
New Delhi	8,753	3,684	7,691	2,571	3,414	1,583	3,638	3,465	3,277	7,500
New York	4,801	4,293	2,572	9,534	3,986	6,141	6,757	4,234	4,270	205
Paris	5,684	690	5,577	6,673	1,003	2,625	6,053	645	852	3,840
Peking	10,768	5,063	5,918	2,771	4,133	3,490	1,307	4,648	4,325	6,942
Rio de Janeiro	....	5,707	6,613	9,785	6,683	7,374	11,532	6,127	6,455	4,779
Rome	5,707	....	6,259	6,229	1,245	2,127	6,142	477	820	4,497
San Francisco	6,613	6,259	....	8,448	5,399	7,362	5,150	5,994	5,854	2,441
Singapore	9,785	6,229	8,448	....	5,936	4,103	3,300	6,035	5,843	9,662
Stockholm	6,683	1,245	5,399	5,936	....	2,173	5,053	780	494	4,183
Tokyo	11,532	6,142	5,150	3,300	5,053	4,775	....	5,689	5,347	6,791
Warsaw	6,455	820	5,854	5,843	494	1,879	5,689	347	....	4,472
Washington	4,779	4,497	2,441	9,662	4,183	6,341	6,791	4,438	4,472	....

AGRICULTURE

World and Regional Food and Agricultural Production, 1971 to 1975

(Source: Food and Agriculture Organization)

Region	Total 1971	1972	1973	1974	1975	Change 1974 to 1975 %	Per capita 1971	1972	1973	1974	1975	Change 1974 to 1975 %
			1961-65 = 100						1961-65 = 100			
Food production												
Developed market economies²	123	122	125	129	132	+2	114	111	114	116	117	+1
Western Europe	121	119	125	131	127	-3	114	112	116	121	118	-2
North America	124	122	124	125	133	+6	113	110	111	111	117	+5
Oceania	126	126	140	133	142	+7	109	107	117	110	115	+5
Eastern Europe and the USSR	127	126	147	140	135	-4	118	115	134	126	121	-4
Total developed countries	124	123	132	132	133	+1	115	113	120	119	118	-1
Developing market economies²	125	125	129	132	138	+5	102	99	100	99	102	+3
Latin America	125	126	128	134	137	+2	101	99	99	99	99	—
Far East	125	121	132	129	140	+9	102	99	97	99	99	—
Near East	128	140	133	143	153	+7	103	110	103	106	109	+6
Africa	124	124	121	127	127	—	101	99	94	96	93	-3
Asian centrally planned economies	125	124	130	133	137	+3	110	107	110	110	112	+2
Total developing countries	125	125	129	132	138	+5	104	102	103	103	105	+2
World	125	124	131	132	135	+2	107	104	108	107	108	+1
Agricultural production												
Developed market economies²	120	119	122	125	127	+2	111	109	111	112	114	+2
Western Europe	120	119	124	130	127	-2	114	112	116	121	117	-3
North America	119	118	120	120	126	+5	108	106	107	107	111	+4
Oceania	123	122	127	121	130	+7	106	104	107	100	105	+5
Eastern Europe and the USSR	127	126	146	140	135	-4	118	116	133	126	121	-4
Total developed countries	122	121	129	129	130	+1	113	111	117	116	116	—
Developing market economies²	124	125	129	131	137	+5	101	99	100	99	101	+2
Latin America	122	124	125	132	134	+2	99	97	96	98	97	-1
Far East	125	122	132	129	138	+7	102	97	103	98	103	+5
Near East	128	140	132	142	150	+6	104	110	101	106	109	+3
Africa	123	124	121	127	127	—	101	99	94	96	93	-3
Asian centrally planned economies	126	125	132	135	138	+2	110	107	111	112	113	+1
Total developing countries	125	125	130	132	137	+4	104	102	103	103	104	+1
World	123	123	129	131	133	+2	106	104	107	106	106	—

Note: The indices above are based on net production as amounts used for feed and seed have been deducted from total production figures. However, for eastern Europe and the USSR, the indices are based on gross production.
¹Preliminary.
²Including countries in other regions not specified.

Europe: Wheat and Coarse Grain Production

(1976 revised forecast following severe European drought¹)

(Source: Food and Agriculture Organization)

	Wheat 1975	1976 June forecast	1976 July forecast	Coarse Grains 1975	1976 June forecast	1976 July forecast	Total 1975	1976 June forecast	1976 July forecast
	(					million tons			)
Western Europe	53.0	60.2	54.7	92.1	93.9	84.1	145.1	154.1	138.8
EEC	38.1	43.6	38.3	58.9	60.6	51.7	97.0	104.2	90.0
Spain	4.4	4.8	4.1	9.7	9.5	7.6	14.1	14.3	11.7
Sweden	1.5	1.6	1.8	3.8	3.9	3.9	5.3	5.5	5.7
Yugoslavia	4.4	5.1	5.4	10.6	10.2	11.2	15.0	15.3	16.6
Others	4.6	5.1	5.1	9.1	9.7	9.7	13.7	14.8	14.8
Eastern Europe	24.5	28.6	27.2	47.5	51.8	51.4	72.0	80.4	78.6
Germany D.R.	3.2	3.2	3.0	5.5	6.3	6.1	8.7	9.5	9.1
Hungary	4.0	5.0	4.5	8.1	8.1	8.1	12.1	13.1	12.6
Poland	5.2	6.6	6.5	14.4	16.2	16.2	19.6	22.8	22.7
Romania	4.9	5.7	5.6	10.5	11.1	11.1	15.4	16.8	16.7
Others	7.2	8.1	7.6	9.0	10.1	9.9	16.2	18.2	17.5
Total Europe	77.5	88.8	81.9	139.6	145.7	135.5	217.1	234.5	217.4

¹Beginning in April 1976, a prolonged and severe drought, combined with unusually high temperatures, affected most of Europe, with the exception of Scandinavia and southern Italy. Beginning in southern England and western Europe, by June the drought spread eastward to central and eastern Europe.

World Cereal Production

(**Source:** Food and Agriculture Organization)

	1974	1975	1976 Trend value (1960-1975)	1976 July Forecast	Change 1976 over 1975
	(........................ in million tons ....)				(percent)
Wheat	360	355	386	389	+10
Coarse grains	653	660	696	704	+7
Total above	1,013	1,015	1,082	1,093	+8
Rice	214	229	226	...	
Total cereals	1,227	1,244	1,308	...	

World Cereal Production by Regions

(**Source:** Food and Agriculture Organization)

	Rice (milled)			Wheat			Coarse Grains		
	1974	1975 Prelim.	1976 Fore-cast	1974	1975 Prelim.	1976 Fore-cast	1974	1975 Prelim.	1976 Fore-cast
	(........................ million tons ....)								
Far East	193.9	207.3		67.7	74.3	78.9	120.0	128.1	131
Bangladesh	11.3	12.7		0.1	0.1	0.4	0.1	0.1	
Burma	5.7	5.8		—	—		0.1	0.1	
China	76.8	77.7		37.0	41.0	42.0	77.8	81.0	
India	40.0	47.0		21.8	24.2	27.0	25.4	29.1	
Indonesia	15.2	15.4		—	—	—	3.0	^.9	
Japan	10.4	11.4		0.2	0.2	0.2	0.3	∪.3	
Pakistan	2.2	2.5		7.6	7.7	8.3	1.4	1.6	
Philippines	3.8	4.2		—	—	—	2.6	2.9	
Thailand	8.9	10.1		—	—	—	2.8	3.3	
Others	19.6	20.5		1.0	1.1	1.0	6.5	6.8	
Near East	2.9	3.1		24.1	28.6	32.1	16.7	20.4	22
Egypt	1.5	1.6		1.9	2.0	2.1	3.6	3.8	
Iran	0.9	0.9		4.7	5.5	6.0	0.9	1.5	
Turkey	0.2	0.2		11.1	14.8	16.5	5.7	7.0	
Others	0.3	0.4		6.4	6.3	7.5	6.5	8.1	
Africa	3.4	3.5	3.4	6.2	5.8	8.4	46.2	42.5	43
Madagascar	1.3	1.4		—	—	—	0.1	0.1	
Morocco	—	—	—	1.9	1.3	2.1	3.0	1.8	
Nigeria	0.2	0.2		—	—	—	7.5	7.7	
South Africa	—	—	—	1.6	1.8	1.8	12.0	9.7	
Others	1.9	1.9		2.7	2.7	4.5	23.6	23.2	
Latin America	7.8	8.7	10.0	13.4	15.0	17.4	53.9	52.0	53
Argentina	0.2	0.2	0.2	6.0	8.6	8.0	17.3	14.2	
Brazil	4.3	4.8	6.0	2.9	1.8	4.6	18.0	16.9	
Mexico	0.3	0.4	0.4	2.7	2.7	3.1	11.2	13.1	
Others	3.0	3.3	3.4	1.8	1.9	1.7	7.4	7.8	
North America	3.4	3.9	3.3	62.2	75.2	74.5	167.9	204.1	221
Canada	—	—		13.3	17.1	19.0	17.4	20.0	
U.S.A.	3.4	3.9	3.3	48.9	58.1	55.5	150.5	184.1	
Western Europe	1.1	1.2		62.9	53.0	54.7	94.4	92.1	84
EC	0.7	0.7		45.3	38.1	38.3	62.9	58.9	
Spain	0.2	0.3		4.5	4.4	4.1	8.4	9.7	
Sweden	—	—	—	1.8	1.5	1.8	4.8	3.8	
Yugoslavia	—	—	—	6.3	4.4	5.4	9.3	10.6	
Others	0.2	0.2		5.0	4.6	5.1	9.0	9.1	
Eastern Europe	0.1	0.1	0.1	27.7	24.5	27.2	48.0	47.5	51
Hungary	—	—	—	5.0	4.0	4.5	7.4	8.1	
Poland	—	—	—	6.4	5.2	6.5	16.6	14.4	
Romania	—	—	—	5.0	4.9	5.6	8.5	10.5	
Others	—	—	—	11.3	10.4	10.6	15.5	14.5	
USSR	1.3	1.3	83.9	66.1	87.0	101.2	67.2	93	
Oceania	0.3	0.3	0.3	11.6	12.2	9.0	5.1	6.1	6
Australia	0.3	0.3	0.3	11.3	12.0	8.5	4.6	5.5	
World	214.2	229.4		359.7	354.7	389	653.4	660.0	704
Developing countries	115.6	128.2		71.9	80.0	92	143.4	148.6	154
Developed countries	15.3	16.7		138.8	142.6	140	279.8	312.4	319
Centrally planned economies	83.3	84.5		149.0	132.1	157	230.2	199.0	231

Forecast for 1976 as of July 20, 1976.

World Trade in Wheat and Coarse Grains

(Source: Food and Agriculture Organization)

	Wheat			Coarse Grains		
Exports	1974/75	1975/76 preliminary	1976/77[2] projected		1975/76 preliminary	1976/77[2] projected
	(.......................... million tons............................)					
Far East	0.2			2.2	2.8	2.6
Thailand	0.1			2.1	2.6	
Near East					0.1	0.3
Africa	0.1			4.0	3.6	2.5
South Africa Rep.				3.4	3.2	
Latin America	2.2	3.3	3.0	10.2	6.6	6.5
Argentina	2.2	3.3		8.6	5.3	
North America	39.5	43.7	39.0-43.0	37.3	50.4	47.1-49.1
Canada	11.2	12.2		2.8	4.2	
U.S.	28.3	31.5		34.5	46.2	
Western Europe	8.3	8.5	8.0	2.4	2.8	2.5
EEC[1]	7.1	7.5		1.6	2.3	1.3
Eastern Europe	1.0	1.0	1.0	1.3	2.0	2.0
USSR	4.0	1.0	1.5	1.0	0.2	0.5
Oceania	8.2	7.5	7.5	2.9	3.0	3.0
Australia	8.2	7.5		2.9	3.0	
World	63.5	65.0	60.0-64.0	61.3	71.5	67.0-69.0
Imports						
Far East	25.4	21.3	21.0-23.0	19.4	19.7	20.0
China	5.7	2.5		0.5	0.1	
India	5.4	5.7		0.4	0.8	
Japan	5.4	5.5		13.2	13.3	
Near East	9.9	7.5	8.5	0.8	0.5	0.5
Egypt	4.0	3.8		0.7	0.4	
Africa	4.8	5.4	5.0	1.2	1.0	1.0
Latin America	7.3	8.5	8.0	5.5	4.7	4.5
Brazil	1.7			0.1	0.1	
Mexico	0.8	3.4		3.0	2.2	
North America				1.5	1.1	1.0
Western Europe	6.9	7.0	7.0	25.7	26.2	28.0
EEC[1]	5.3	5.5		16.2	18.5	
Eastern Europe	4.5	4.5	4.5	6.2	6.8	6.0
USSR	2.8	10.5	6.0-8.0	2.7	11.5	6.0-8.0
Oceania	0.3	0.3		0.1		
World	61.9	65.0	60.0-64.0	63.1	71.5	67.0-69.0

[1] Excluding EEC intra-trade. [2] As of June/July 1976.

Dietary Energy Supplies for Selected Developing Countries[1]

(per capita in relation to nutritional requirements)

(Source: Food and Agriculture Organization)

	Average 1969-71	Average 1970-74	1971	1972	1973	1974
	.....................Percentage of requirements.....................					
Far East	94	93	95	93	90	93
Bangladesh	88	88	85	86	87	92
Bhutan	94	94	94	94	94	94
Burma	101	100	101	93	100	103
Cambodia	99	96	99	99	98	85
India	92	91	94	93	85	89
Indonesia	91	93	91	88	96	98
Lao People's Dem. Rep.	95	94	93	92	94	93
Nepal	93	92	90	87	93	95
Pakistan	93	93	94	94	92	93
Philippines	86	86	85	86	88	87
Sri Lanka	103	97	99	94	94	91
Latin America	106	107	106	106	107	107
Bolivia	76	77	77	79	77	77
Colombia	93	93	94	93	92	94
Dominican Republic	90	93	90	94	95	98
Ecuador	90	90	88	90	91	93
El Salvador	80	82	82	82	81	84
Guatemala	92	91	91	91	91	91
Haiti	87	89	87	90	90	90
Honduras	96	93	94	92	90	90
Peru	98	99	98	98	99	100
Venezuela	97	97	97	96	97	98
Africa						
Ethiopia	93	90	93	92	89	82
Ghana	99	99	99	100	99	100
Kenya	97	95	99	93	92	91
Near East						
Turkey	112	112	114	112	112	113

[1] In the Far East and Latin America, countries where available supplies were below requirements in 1969-71 or 1970-74; in Africa and the Near East, countries for which data are so far available for 1970-74.

Estimated World Carryover Stocks of Cereals
(Source: Food and Agriculture Organization estimates) Millions of Tons

Commodity	1972	1973	Crop year ending in: 1974	1975	1976	1977
Wheat Stocks	66	43	40	47	55	60
Rice Stocks	21	13	14	13	16	. . .
Coarse Grains Stocks	73	59	50	44	45	57
Total Cereals	160	115	104	104	116	. . .
Proportion of Total Consumption	19%	13%	12%	12%	13%	. . .

Excluding China and USSR. Forecast Projected FAO estimates a minimum ratio of 17-18% to assure world food security.

Grain, Hay, Potato, Cotton, Tobacco Production
Source: Economic Research Service: Department of Agriculture

1974 State	Barley 1,000 bushels	Corn; grain 1,000 bushels	Cotton' lint 1,000 bales	All Hay 1,000 tons	Oats 1,000 bushels	Potatoes 1,000 cwt.	Rye 1,000 bushels	Tobacco 1,000 pounds	All Wheat 1,000 bushels
Alabama	—	29,900	522	1,044	816	3,336	—	1,140	2,990
Alaska	—	—	—	—	—	—	—	—	—
Arizona	7,100	340	995	1,511	—	2,236	—	—	15,510
Arkansas	—	1,012	920	1,170	3,774	—	—	—	10,400
California	45,604	25,787	2,595	7,695	5,000	24,716	—	—	38,994
Colorado	10,000	49,490	—	2,718	1,426	10,655	114	—	67,725
Connecticut	—	—	—	173	—	598	—	7,915	—
Delaware	792	12,416	—	51	—	1,530	198	—	1,120
Florida	—	19,104	12.7	414	420	5,533	—	27,805	600
Georgia	360	105,280	419	1,069	4,180	—	2,070	161,402	3,680
Hawaii	—	—	—	—	—	—	—	—	—
Idaho	31,970	2,408	—	4,427	2,850	81,195	—	—	61,860
Illinois	540	821,700	.3	3,196	24,480	248	361	—	51,900
Indiana	516	387,660	—	2,017	10,750	1,375	216	16,660	50,040
Iowa	—	960,000	—	6,391	82,500	660	115	—	1,860
Kansas	1,550	131,480	—	4,229	6,665	—	380	—	319,000,
Kentucky	1,824	95,200	2.6	2,996	370	—	63	452,008	12,285
Louisiana	—	3,672	560	752	429	252	—	125	600
Maine	—	—	—	371	2,480	36,400	—	—	—
Maryland	4,500	44,940	—	621	1,378	294	253	30,240	5,328
Massachusetts	—	—	—	241	—	800	—	2,419	—
Michigan	1,020	110,410	—	2,906	19,250	9,926	625	—	37,600
Minnesota	29,564	359,900	—	7,496	96,960	17,425	1,800	—	80,862
Mississippi	—	5,904	1,595	1,128	880	190	—	—	3,888
Missouri	297	149,050	230	5,491	4,340	—	170	5,748	37,990
Montana	37,120	910	—	4,261	8,820	1,750	—	—	120,108
Nebraska	945	387,600	—	6,270	25,145	1,542	1,100	—	98,600
Nevada	700	—	2.1	913	100	3,188	—	—	946.
New Hampshire	—	—	—	168	—	144	—	—	—
New Jersey	988	7,743	—	271	343	2,430	243	—	2,214
New Mexico	940	3,157	148	915	—	840	—	—	2,916
New York	528	35,200	—	5,333	21,240	13,718	416	—	8,400
North Carolina	2,760	116,180	133	530	4,505	2,753	400	789,220	9,900
North Dakota	53,265	7,301	—	4,580	40,600	22,950	2,756	—	210,752
Ohio	598	266,450	—	3,151	29,400	2,641	168	23,130	64,680
Oklahoma	3,360	8,008	310	3,087	3,920	—	765	—	134,400
Oregon	8,740	828	—	2,491	4,200	17,482	300	—	52,950
Pennsylvania	8,690	89,100	—	4,292	20,145	7,360	512	26,000	12,600
Rhode Island	—	—	—	17	—	1,034	—	—	—
South Carolina	960	31,262	274	440	3,234	—	780	172,000	3,950
South Dakota	12,800	76,890	—	5,189	81,120	371	4,242	—	57,020
Tennessee	465	34,770	308	1,818	1,110	540	54	110,945	9,425
Texas	1,350	73,600	2,465	5,106	8,100	3,206	200	—	52,800
Utah	7,205	1,680	—	1,695	636	1,481	—	—	7,982
Vermont	—	—	—	844	—	220	—	—	—
Virginia	5,250	43,320	1.2	1,737	1,848	4,030	416	141,577	10,175
Washington	13,950	2,970	—	2,577	2,499	41,160	200	—	122,220
West Virginia	500	5,016	—	1,007	799	323	—	2,923	561
Wisconsin	893	154,360	—	10,600	85,400	14,000	240	18,471	2,853
Wyoming	6,468	1,633	—	1,644	1,665	1,528	136	—	6,503
Total U.S.	304,112	4,663,631	11,449.9	127,143	613,777	342,060	19,293	1,989,728	1,796,187

Equiv. 480 lbs.

Grain Receipts at Western Grain Centers
Source: Canadian Grain Commission (in thousands of bushels)

Crop Year 1973-74 Province	Wheat	Oats	Barley	Rye	Flaxseed	Rapeseed	Total
Western Canada	536,328	39,812	235,051	7,447	15,404	43,802	877,844
Manitoba	61,349	14,057	46,065	1,391	6,158	6,402	135,423
Saskatchewan	358,594	12,488	103,352	2,464	7,046	20,005	503,949
Alberta	116,385	13,266	85,364	3,592	2,200	17,395	238,471

Production of Chief U. S. Crops

Source: Economic Research Service: Department of Agriculture

Year	Corn grain 1,000 bushels	Oats 1,000 bushels	Barley 1,000 bushels	Sorghums for grain 1,000 bushels	All Wheat 1,000 bushels	Rye 1,000 bushels	Flax-seed 1,000 bushels	Cotton Lint 1,000 bales	Cotton Seed 1,000 tons
1965	4,102,867	929,554	393,055	672,698	1,315,603	33,307	35,402	14,938	6,087
1970	4,151,938	917,159	416,139	683,571	1,351,558	36,840	29,548	10,192	4,068
1971	5,641,112	881,227	463,601	875,752	1,617,789	49,288	18,198	10,477	4,240
1972	5,573,320	691,973	423,461	809,264	1,544,936	29,183	13,909	13,704	5,393
1973	5,646,806	666,867	421,527	930,012	1,705,167	26,263	16,091	12,974	5,016
1974	4,663,631	613,777	304,112	629,222	1,796,187	19,293	13,541	11,540	4,556
1975	5,766,991	656,862	382,980	758,454	2,133,803	17,875	14,557	8,326	3,260

Year	Tobacco 1,000 lbs.	All Hay 1,000 tons	Beans dry edible 1,000 cwt.	Peas dry field 1,000 cwt.	Peanuts 1,000 lbs.	Soybeans 1,000 bushels	Potatoes 1,000 cwt.	Sweet Potatoes 1,000 cwt.	Five seed crops* 1,000 lbs.
1965	1,854,568	125,610	16,457	3,031	2,389,596	845,608	291,109	15,469	302,592
1970	1,906,453	126,971	17,399	3,315	2,979,465	1,127,100	325,752	13,409	254,429
1971	1,704,884	129,119	15,917	3,930	3,005,118	1,175,989	319,354	11,718	220,059
1972	1,749,085	128,614	18,118	2,103	3,274,761	1,270,630	295,955	12,453	165,876*
1973	1,742,105	134,751	16,389	1,665	3,473,837	1,547,165	299,410	12,534	172,957
1974	1,989,728	127,143	20,343	3,228	3,667,604	1,214,802	342,060	13,921	177,400
1975	2,184,075	132,917	17,196	2,731	3,866,615	1,521,370	315,647	13,642	158,947

*Five seed crops include alfalfa, red clover, sweet clover, lespedeza, and timothy. Beginning 1972 sweet clover was discontinued.

Year	Sugar and seed 1,000 tons	Syrup 1,000 gallons	Sugar beets 1,000 tons	Pecans 1,000 tons	Almonds 1,000 tons	Walnuts 1,000 tons	Filberts 1,000 tons	Oranges and tangerines 1,000 boxes	Grapefruit 1,000 boxes
1965	23,663	2,923	20,918	125.6	72.9	80.3	7.7	139,650	46,695
1970	23,996	...	26,427	77.6	124.0	111.8	9.3	194,790	60,560
1971	24,172	...	27,096	123.6	134.0	136.4	11.4	196,480	64,140
1972	28,332	...	28,410	91.6	125.0	116.8	10.2	229,790	65,640
1973	25,827	...	24,499	137.9	134.0	175.0	12.3	221,050	5,500
1974	24,812	...	22,123	68.6	189.0	156.5	6.7	243,160	61,370
1975	28,499	...	29,270	115.1	159.0	196.2	10.5	NA	NA

(NA) Not available.

Production of Principal Field Crops in Canada

Source: Statistic Canada

1975	Wheats 1,000 bushels	Oats 1,000 bushels	Barley 1,000 bushels	Ryes 1,000 bushels	Flaxseed 1,000 bushels
Canada[1]	627,515	289,619	437,251	20,585	17,500
Prince Edward Island	341	2,350	840	—	—
Nova Scotia	112	747	232	—	—
New Brunswick	146	2,310	354	—	—
Quebec	2,626	25,062	2,063	45	—
Ontario	22,790	25,950	18,062	1,910	—
Manitoba	78,000	50,000	51,000	2,500	8,400
Saskatchewan	387,000	86,000	130,000	7,500	5,900
Alberta	135,000	94,000	228,000	8,500	3,200
British Columbia	1,500	3,200	6,700	130	—

	Mixed Grains 1,000 bushels	Corn Grain 1,000 bushels	Soybeans 1,000 bushels	Rapeseed 1,000 bushels	Potatoes 1,000 c.w.t.
Canada[1]	89,807	142,648	13,478	72,100	46,432
Prince Edward Island	4,050	—	—	—	8,878
Nova Scotia	318	—	—	—	636
New Brunswick	212	—	—	—	9,952
Quebec	5,325	11,266	—	—	7,128
Ontario	46,102	130,632	13,478	—	8,913
Manitoba	7,500	750	—	11,000	4,500
Saskatchewan	6,900	—	—	33,000	525
Alberta	19,000	—	—	27,000	3,400
British Columbia	400	—	—	1,100	2,500

	Mustard seed 1,000 pounds	Sunflower seed 1,000 pounds	Tame hay 1,000 tons	Fodder corn 1,000 tons	Sugar beets 1,000 tons
Canada[1]	110,500	66,000	25,933	13,202	1,039
Prince Edward Island	—	—	238	—	—
Nova Scotia	—	—	281	—	—
New Brunswick	—	—	304	—	—
Quebec	—	—	5,238	2,688	155
Ontario	—	—	6,472	9,864	—
Manitoba	14,500	66,000	2,500	290	396
Saskatchewan	50,000	—	3,400	—	—
Alberta	46,000	—	5,800	—	488
British Columbia	—	—	1,700	360	—

(1) Excluding Newfoundland

Harvested Acreage of Principal Crops

Source: Economic Research Service: Department of Agriculture. In thousands of acres

State	1973	1974	1975	State	1973	1974	1975
Alabama	3,104	3,345	3,551	Nebraska	17,298	17,548	17,707
Arizona	1,098	1,211	1,208	Nevada	479	492	503
Arkansas	7,517	7,531	8,007	New Hampshire	108	108	110
California	5,911	6,284	6,416	New Jersey	390	417	423
Colorado	5,826	5,762	5,695	New Mexico	1,204	966	1,243
Connecticut	146	152	154	New York	3,872	4,057	4,078
Delaware	465	495	502	North Carolina	4,522	4,755	4,748
Florida	1,249	1,340	1,382	North Dakota	19,107	19,436	18,963
Georgia	4,544	4,896	4,873	Ohio	9,745	10,661	10,730
Hawaii	116	101	112	Oklahoma	9,521	10,162	10,381
Idaho	4,078	4,277	4,291	Oregon	2,476	2,664	2,640
Illinois	21,769	22,270	22,825	Pennsylvania	4,329	4,465	4,476
Indiana	11,642	12,192	12,260	Rhode Island	17	17	17
Iowa	23,606	24,057	24,164	South Carolina	2,599	2,781	2,741
Kansas	20,731	21,467	21,661	South Dakota	15,140	15,669	15,395
Kentucky	4,259	4,635	4,700	Tennessee	4,256	4,462	4,606
Louisiana	3,600	3,951	3,660	Texas	21,935	19,581	23,145
Maine	448	438	422	Utah	1,114	1,147	1,155
Maryland	1,383	1,502	1,530	Vermont	566	574	580
Massachusetts	151	153	153	Virginia	2,700	2,834	2,854
Michigan	5,785	6,188	6,272	Washington	4,431	4,772	4,819
Minnesota	19,746	20,256	20,033	West Virginia	764	755	759
Mississippi	5,223	5,438	5,558	Wisconsin	8,843	9,148	9,164
Missouri	12,302	12,872	13,240	Wyoming	1,755	1,713	1,808
Montana	8,935	8,949	9,094	**Total U. S.**	**310,805**	**318,946**	**324,808**

Crop acreages included are corn, sorghum, oats, barley, wheat, rice, rye, soybeans, flaxseed, peanuts, popcorn, cotton, all hay, dry edible beans, dry edible peas, potatoes, sweet potatoes, tobacco, sugarcane and sugar beets.

Livestock on Farms in the U.S.

Source: Economic Research Service: Dept. of Agriculture (in 1,000)

Year (On Jan. 1)	All Cattle	Milk Cows	All Sheep	Hogs	Horses* and Mules	Year (On Jan. 1)	All Cattle	Milk Cows	All Sheep*	Hogs
1890	60,014	15,000	44,518	48,130	18,054	1965‡	109,000	²15,380	25,127	57,030
1900	59,739	16,544	48,105	51,055	21,004	1966‡	108,862	14,490	24,734	³50,519
1910	58,993	19,450	50,239	48,072	24,211	1967‡	108,783	13,725	23,953	³57,125
1920	70,400	21,455	40,743	60,159	25,742	1968‡	109,371	13,115	22,223	³58,818
1925	63,373	22,575	38,543	55,770	22,569	1969‡	110,015	12,550	21,350	³60,829
1930	61,003	23,032	51,565	55,705	19,124	1970‡	112,369	12,091	20,423	³57,046
1935	68,846	26,082	51,808	39,066	16,683	1971‡	114,578	11,909	19,686	³67,433
1940	68,039	24,940	52,107	61,165	14,478	1972‡	117,862	11,778	18,710	³62,507
1945	85,573	27,770	46,520	59,373	11,950	1973‡	121,534	11,624	17,724	³59,180
1950	77,963	23,853	29,826	58,937	7,781	1974	127,540	11,286	16,394	61,106
1955	96,592	23,462	31,582	50,474	4,309	1975¹	131,826	11,217	14,538	55,062
1960	96,236	19,527	33,170	59,026	3,089	1976	127,976	11,092	13,346	49,602

*Discontinued in 1960. ‡Revised. (1) Total estimated value on farms as of Jan. 1, 1975, was as follows (avg. value per head in parentheses): cattle and calves $20,963,981 ($159.00); sheep and lambs $442,271 ($30.40); hogs $2,481,644 ($45.10); chickens $652,799 ($1.71); turkeys $29,223,000 ($9.84) (2) New series, milk cows and heifers that have calved beginning 1965. (3) Dec. 1, preceding year.

Egg Production in the U.S.

Source: USDA, Statistical Reporting Service. (in millions of eggs)

State	1973	1974	1975	State	1973	1974	1975	State	1973	1974	1975	State	1973	1974	1975
Ala.	2,853	2,945	2,951	Ind.	2,770	2,639	2,609	Neb.	775	723	782	S.C.	1,319	1,301	1,385
Alas.	7	6.4	5.0	Ia.	2,141	2,069	2,006	Nev.	4	5	4.3	S.D.	785	770	702
Ariz.	154	149	159	Kan.	673	601	599	N.H.	320	275	283	Tenn.	1,088	1,026	949
Ark.	3,695	3,601	3,594	Ky.	515	527	518	N.J.	756	736	620	Tex.	2,496	2,292	2,360
Cal.	7,680	8,485	8,467	La.	665	664	658	N.M.	208	197	234	Ut.	306	311	321
Col.	317	385	473	Me.	1,549	1,656	1,650	N.Y.	2,052	2,030	1,984	Vt.	150	131	105
Conn.	932	864	798	Md.	327	335	331	N.C.	3,213	3,037	2,802	Va.	789	760	765
Del.	128	134	115	Mass.	522	509	541	N.D.	153	151	132	Wash.	1,063	1,089	1,068
Fla.	2,806	2,852	2,779	Mich.	1,539	1,375	1,303	Oh.	2,060	2,057	1,999	W.Va.	242	248	256
Ga.	5,534	5,827	5,284	Minn.	2,474	2,385	2,209	Okla.	446	428	430	Wis.	1,267	1,183	1,194
Ha.	208	207	209	Miss.	1,981	1,908	1,707	Ore.	535	543	519	Wy.	31	30	29.7
Ida.	197	186	184	Mo.	1,347	1,149	1,241	Pa.	3,576	3,490	3,299	**Total**			
Ill.	1,664	1,543	1,483	Mon.	215	202	197	R.I.	52	65.4	69.5	**U.S.**	**66,579**	**66,083**	**64,362**

Gross income from farm eggs 1973, $2,912,454,000; 1974, $2,935,998,000; 1975, $2,813,412,000. Prices received by farmers per dozen eggs 1973, 52.5c; 1974, 53.3c; 1975, 52.3c. Gross income from farm chickens 1973, $174,098,000; 1974, $122,904,000; 1975 $108,705,000. Commercial broilers produced 1973, 3,008,667,000 ($2,690,362,000); 1974, 2,992,334,000 ($2,435,861,000); 1975, 2,932,711,000 ($2,899,183,000). Gross income from eggs and chickens 1973, $5,776,914,000; 1974, $5,500,000,000; 1975, $5,800,000,000.

Production and Consumption of Meat and Lard

Source: Economic Research Service: Department of Agriculture (in million lbs.)

Year	Beef Production	Beef Consumption	Veal Production	Veal Consumption	Lamb and Mutton Production	Lamb and Mutton Consumption	Pork (exclud. Lard) Production	Pork (exclud. Lard) Consumption	All Meats Production	All Meats Consumption	Lard Production	Lard Consumption
1940	7,175	7,257	981	981	876	873	10,044	9,701	19,076	18,812	2,288	1,901
1950	9,534	9,529	1,230	1,206	597	596	10,714	10,390	22,075	21,721	2,631	1,891
1960	14,753	15,147	1,109	1,093	768	852	11,607	11,566	28,237	28,658	2,562	1,358
1965	18,727	19,060	1,020	992	651	716	11,141	11,235	31,539	32,003	2,045	1,225
1970	21,685	22,926	588	581	551	657	13,436	13,391	36,260	37,555	1,913	939
1973	21,277	22,812	357	376	514	557	12,751	12,820	34,899	36,565	1,254	733
1974	23,017	24,372	471	476	470	489	13,688	13,845	37,646	39,182	1,350	690
1975p	23.976	25,397	873	878	410	431	11,503	11,573	36,762	38,279	995	615

Grain Storage Capacity at Principal Grain Centers in U.S. and Canada

Source: Chicago Board of Trade

U.S.

Cities	Capacity Bushels	Cities	Capacity Bushels
Atlantic Coast	35,500,000	Texas High Plains	97,800,000
Great Lakes		Enid	66,000,000
Toledo	32,200,000	**Gulf Points**	
Buffalo	16,710,000	South Mississippi	48,700,000
Chicago	62,803,000	North Texas Gulf	37,700,000
Milwaukee	5,600,000	South Texas Gulf	14,000,000
Duluth	67,000,000	**Plains**	
River Points		Wichita	57,600,000
Minneapolis	114,400,000	Topeka	61,000,000
Peoria	6,560,000	Salina	26,300,000
St. Louis	25,375,000	Hutchinson	42,000,000
Sioux City	13,800,000	Hastings-Grand Island	21,969,000
Omaha-Council Bluffs	35,300,000	Lincoln	39,600,000
Atchinson	24,500,000	Des Moines	9,640,000
St. Joseph	20,600,000	**Pacific N.W.**	
Kansas City	81,300,000	Puget Sound	12,500,000
Southwest		Portland	31,600,000
Fort Worth	57,600,000	California Ports	16,500,000

Canada

Cities	Capacity Bushels	Cities	Capacity Bushels
Bae Comeau, Que.	13,778,000	Port Colbourne, Ont.	5,250,000
Calgary, Alta.	2,500,000	Port McNicoll, Ont.	6,500,000
Churchill, Man.	5,000,000	Prescott, Ont.	5,500,000
Collingwood, Ont.	2,000,000	Prince Rupert, B.C.	2,250,000
Edmonton, Alta.	2,350,000	Quebec, Que.	8,000,000
Goderich, Ont.	4,600,000	Saint John, N.B.	500,000
Halifax, N.S.	5,152,000	Sarnia, Ont.	5,400,000
Kingston, Ontario	2,350,000	Saskatoon, Sask.	5,500,000
Lethbridge, Alta.	1,250,000	Sorel, Que.	5,230,000
Midland, Ont.	11,550,000	Three Rivers, Que.	5,880,000
Montreal, Que.	19,600,000	Thunder Bay, B.C.	90,397,210
Moose Jaw, Sask.	5,500,000	Toronto, Ont.	4,000,000
North Vancouver, B.C.	6,972,000	Vancouver, B.C.	18,056,000
Owen Sound, Ont.	4,000,000	Victoria, B.C.	1,040,000
Port Cartier, Que.	10,462,000	West St. John, N.B.	2,576,000

Atlantic Coast — Albany, N.Y., Philadelphia, Pa., Baltimore, Md., Norfolk, Va., North Charleston, S.C. Gulf Points: S. Miss. — New Orleans, Baton Rouge, AMA, Belle Chasse, La., Mobile, Ala., Pascagoula, Miss.; N. Texas Gulf — Houston, Galveston, Beaumont, Port Arthur, Texas; S. Texas Gulf — Corpus Christi, Brownsville, Texas. Pacific N.W. — Seattle, Tacoma, Wash., Portland, Oreg., Columbia River. Calif. Ports — San Francisco, Stockton, Sacremento, Los Angeles. Texas High Plains — Amarillo, Lubbock, Hereford, Plainview, Texas.

Grain Receipts at Western Grain Centers

Source: Chicago Board of Trade (in thousands bushels)

1975	Wheat	Corn	Oats	Rye	Barley	Soybeans	Total
Chicago	31,181	106,839	755	201	196	27,592	166,764
Duluth	182,351	13,427	11,596	2,534	19,799	.....	229,707
Enid	88,378	.....	.....	.....	6	.....	88,384
Hutchinson	1,074	24	.....	.....	.....	.....	1,098
Kansas City	82,965	41,715	702	4	6	10,689	136,081
Milwaukee	509	18,372	189	.....	15,563	501	35,134
Minneapolis	117,143	86,501	36,815	3,429	37,526	27,771	309,185
Omaha	17,198	28,287	1,072	36	4	3,866	50,483
Peoria	137	21,641	30	99	.....	138	22,045
Sioux City	2,093	9,343	6,741	.....	14	16,285	34,476
St. Joseph	1,555	4,882	1,421	.....	.....	1,471	9,329
St. Louis	34,094	21,681	642	.....	.....	17,826	74,243
Toledo	35,965	71,069	3,084	2	5	40,367	150,492
Witchita	51,801	4,440	3	.....	216	14,604	71,064
Total	**646,444**	**428,221**	**63,050**	**6,305**	**73,335**	**161,130**	**1,378,485**

Egg Production in Canada

Source: Statistics Canada
(thousand dozens)

Province	1973	1974	1975	Province	1973	1974	1975
Newfoundland	6,835	7,857	6,740	Ontario	190,718	189,323	175,966
Prince Edward Island	2,410	2,363	2,373	Manitoba	52,008	50,498	49,757
Nova Scotia	18,228	19,297	17,756	Saskatchewan	22,444	21,019	20,722
New Brunswick	10,340	8,770	8,852	Alberta	41,437	40,769	42,039
Quebec	58,518	64,613	67,419	British Columbia	56,872	54,942	53,301
				Total	**461,695**	**459,451**	**444,925**

Realized gross farm income from eggs (1973) $255,302,000; (1974) $283,871,000; (1975) $272,660,000. Average price of eggs sold for consumption taking the month of February (1973) $.45; (1974) $.63; (1975) $.56. Realized gross farm income from chickens (1973) $324,992,000; (1974) $344,839,000; (1975) $310,941,000. Fowl produced (1973) 23,965, $13,567; (1974) 23,764, $9,412; (1975) 23,117, $6,657. Realized gross farm income from eggs, chicken and fowl (1973) $580,294,000; (1974) $628,710,000; (1975) $583,601,000.

Canada — Production of Sawn Lumber[1]

Source: Canadian Statistical Review (April, 1976)
(million feet, board measure)

Year	Canada	N.S.	N.B.	Que.	Ont.	Sask.	Alta.	B.C.
1971	12,723.0	157.9	298.8	1,808.6	960.7	111.0	470.0	8,916.0
1972	13,887.5	179.2	313.6	2,146.9	1,082.9	135.6	580.0	9,446.9
1974	13,499	188	342	2,210	1,260	139	618	8,755
1975	11,151	144	256	1,929	948	127	360	7,477

(1)Excludes Newfoundland, P.E.I., Manitoba, the Yukon and the Northwest Territories which, together, account for less than 1% of the total.

Farms in U.S. by State — Number, Acreage, and Value

Source: Bureau of the Census (Census of 1970)

State	Farms No.	Average Acreage	$ Value per Acre	2,000 Acres or more	10-49 Acres	Total Acreage
Alabama	72,491	188.3	$199.60	629	21,439	13,654,215
Alaska	322	4,831.9	12.73	35	32	1,604,211
Arizona	5,890	6,486.0	69.72	897	1,229	38,202,667
Arkansas	60,433	259.7	260.03	625	10,935	15,694,527
California	77,875	458.7	474.65	2,926	28,915	35,722,348
Colorado	27,950	1,312.9	94.58	4,166	3,048	36,697,132
Connecticut	4,490	120.5	921.19	6	1,245	541,372
Delaware	3,710	181.6	498.96	14	872	673,895
Florida	35,586	394.3	354.58	1,062	12,413	14,031,998
Georgia	67,431	234.4	234.00	693	13,737	15,805,892
Hawaii	3,896	528.2	296.82	79	1,281	2,058,087
Idaho	25,475	565.9	176.55	1,218	4,382	14,416,521
Illinois	123,565	242.0	489.52	145	13,487	29,913,190
Indiana	101,479	173.1	406.05	65	19,522	17,572,865
Iowa	140,354	239.1	391.73	84	9,586	33,569,629
Kansas	86,057	573.9	158.78	3,341	5,231	49,390,369
Kentucky	125,069	127.6	253.05	114	26,761	15,968,243
Louisiana	42,269	231.5	321.33	536	13,610	9,788,662
Maine	7,971	220.7	160.79	25	948	1,759,700
Maryland	17,181	163.1	639.63	41	3,733	2,803,442
Massachusetts	5,703	122.8	564.63	7	1,622	700,578
Michigan	77,946	152.7	326.31	43	14,334	11,900,689
Minnesota	110,747	260.4	225.76	305	6,459	28,845,240
Mississippi	72,577	221.0	233.53	894	17,060	16,039,665
Missouri	137,067	236.5	224.22	396	16,823	32,420,284
Montana	24,951	2,521.6	59.57	7,596	1,485	62,918,247
Nebraska	72,257	677.4	154.38	3,509	3,113	48,949,376
Nevada	2,112	5,070.2	53.35	333	305	10,708,346
New Hampshire	2,902	211.1	238.78	6	443	612,750
New Jersey	8,493	121.9	1,092.31	13	2,471	1,035,678
New Mexico	11,641	4,019.6	41.87	2,660	1,704	46,792,302
New York	51,909	195.5	273.13	50	6,589	10,148,359
North Carolina	119,386	106.6	333.31	205	42,911	12,733,751
North Dakota	46,381	929.6	93.82	3,157	721	43,117,831
Ohio	111,332	153.6	398.51	53	19,729	17,111,459
Oklahoma	83,037	433.6	172.58	2,024	7,655	36,007,719
Oregon	29,063	619.9	150.22	1,739	9,000	18,017,850
Pennsylvania	62,824	141.6	372.88	38	10,428	8,900,767
Rhode Island	700	98.1	733.75	...	235	68,720
South Carolina	39,559	176.7	261.23	286	12,129	6,991,718
South Dakota	45,726	996.9	83.69	4,148	1,402	45,584,164
Tennessee	121,406	124.0	267.50	212	35,117	15,056,907
Texas	213,550	667.6	148.49	9,941	27,315	142,566,826
Utah	13,045	867.2	91.90	849	3,159	11,312,951
Vermont	6,874	278.6	223.73	17	465	1,915,520
Virginia	64,572	164.9	286.13	206	15,169	10,649,862
Washington	34,033	515.9	223.83	1,693	10,817	17,559,187
West Virginia	23,142	187.5	135.69	67	3,808	4,340,554
Wisconsin	98,973	182.9	231.98	81	8,118	18,109,273
Wyoming	8,838	4,014.0	40.73	2,689	473	35,476,374
Total	**2,730,242**	**390.5**	**—**	**59,909**	**473,465**	**1,066,218,650**

Total Net Income per Farm by States

Source: U.S. Department of Agriculture, Economic Research Service

State	1966	1967	1968	1969	1970	1971	1972	1973
Alabama	$ 2,296	$ 2,003	$ 2,303	$ 2,909	$ 2,703	$ 3,134	$ 4,171	$ 6,722
Alaska	2,315	1,921	4,172	2,681	4,169	3,203	3,494	1,042
Arizona	13,664	16,850	21,880	22,965	17,482	22,226	24,489	38,672
Arkansas	4,293	3,380	3,752	3,643	4,460	4,195	5,463	11,234
California	14,299	13,690	17,222	16,436	15,149	17,257	22,877	37,296
Colorado	5,184	4,384	6,114	6,442	7,570	8,491	10,158	16,052
Connecticut	7,712	5,895	7,918	8,224	9,632	9,149	8,495	12,247
Delaware	5,257	6,793	5,937	12,413	6,886	8,259	11,837	28,352
Florida	8,453	9,190	10,183	12,417	10,664	14,697	19,075	24,307
Georgia	4,017	3,845	3,477	4,528	4,215	5,126	5,508	8,818
Hawaii	12,644	9,613	11,879	9,967	10,963	14,277	17,097	16,546
Idaho	3,869	4,676	4,093	6,806	7,044	6,755	9,444	16,273
Illinois	6,337	6,029	4,457	6,159	4,644	5,756	6,172	13,224
Indiana	4,023	3,811	3,930	4,852	3,170	5,228	4,127	11,282
Iowa	7,485	6,011	5,771	7,443	7,245	5,744	8,814	19,685
Kansas	4,351	3,564	3,408	4,334	6,014	6,961	10,271	17,018
Kentucky	2,363	2,379	2,471	3,004	2,787	2,870	3,732	4,400
Louisiana	3,272	3,742	4,308	3,339	4,159	4,911	5,709	11,044
Maine	6,962	2,836	3,127	5,561	5,968	5,514	5,917	20,211
Maryland	3,108	3,938	3,725	6,015	5,575	4,316	6,505	11,552
Massachusetts	6,437	4,371	5,741	6,217	6,365	5,967	6,103	7,702
Michigan	3,240	2,561	2,719	3,377	3,185	2,862	4,365	6,171
Minnesota	4,867	4,363	4,607	5,250	6,624	5,957	7,593	19,456
Mississippi	2,920	3,308	3,232	3,127	3,489	3,907	4,806	7,606
Missouri	2,411	2,254	2,709	2,557	2,867	3,029	4,223	7,921
Montana	6,893	5,160	5,376	7,245	8,890	7,169	13,448	22,063
Nebraska	6,194	5,198	4,524	6,986	6,176	6,566	9,687	17,790
Nevada	5,251	2,892	3,944	11,739	11,300	12,197	17,353	26,853
New Hampshire	4,397	3,201	4,062	4,832	4,860	5,178	6,789	8,901
New Jersey	7,591	6,684	6,458	7,535	6,571	6,057	5,314	10,823
New Mexico	5,761	4,894	5,961	6,797	8,866	8,893	9,999	16,265
New York	5,346	4,870	5,037	5,953	5,668	5,443	4,744	7,019
North Carolina	2,997	3,003	2,643	3,696	3,768	3,688	4,860	8,288
North Dakota	5,646	4,966	4,319	6,796	5,262	7,952	13,665	35,631
Ohio	3,710	2,558	3,046	3,105	3,152	2,993	3,720	5,212
Oklahoma	2,554	2,477	1,829	2,483	3,159	2,868	3,831	7,564
Oregon	3,562	3,515	3,349	4,424	3,921	3,703	5,572	11,027
Pennsylvania	2,719	3,649	3,163	4,011	4,122	3,613	3,937	5,939
Rhode Island	6,031	3,800	5,210	6,502	8,769	7,755	7,719	5,547
South Carolina	2,677	2,789	2,146	2,733	2,710	3,036	3,670	5,766
South Dakota	6,728	5,767	6,153	6,364	6,742	7,449	11,331	22,928
Tennessee	1,653	1,459	1,477	1,704	1,730	1,686	2,188	3,426
Texas	3,390	2,505	3,094	3,182	4,114	3,300	4,605	10,235
Utah	2,293	3,071	3,315	3,829	4,171	4,472	5,892	10,408
Vermont	5,346	4,317	5,161	5,978	6,671	6,906	8,466	9,028
Virginia	1,649	2,139	1,804	2,128	2,222	1,907	2,890	4,784
Washington	5,993	5,788	5,959	7,467	5,472	7,024	10,578	19,144
West Virginia	414	769	553	773	617	596	923	1,427
Wisconsin	5,012	4,199	4,858	5,051	5,160	5,796	6,240	8,562
Wyoming	5,053	5,590	4,116	4,832	5,530	5,906	11,105	14,292
Total U.S.	**4,266**	**3,867**	**3,949**	**4,672**	**4,667**	**4,879**	**6,332**	**11,639**

Farm Income—Cash Receipts from Marketings (in $1,000)

1975 State	Crops	Live-stock	Gov't Pay'ts	Total	1975 State	Crops	Live-stock	Gov't Pay'ts	Total
Alabama	545,223	839,508	12,320	1,397,051	Nebraska	1,717,717	2,158,214	71,671	3,947,602
Alaska	4,079	3,723	84	7,886	Nevada	37,102	94,968	821	132,891
Arizona	564,110	488,274	5,753	1,058,137	New Hampshire	19,921	54,130	634	74,685
Arkansas	1,226,305	991,728	16,028	2,234,061	New Jersey	216,899	101,834	668	319,401
California	5,696,870	2,788,225	15,831	8,500,926	New Mexico	184,201	544,953	11,346	740,500
Colorado	608,202	1,339,666	17,994	1,965,862	New York	494,259	1,051,888	5,921	1,552,068
Connecticut	96,455	118,221	373	215,049	North Carolina	1,676,989	996,316	8,879	2,682,184
Delaware	101,550	167,787	222	269,559	North Dakota	1,530,897	452,808	24,883	2,008,588
Florida	1,809,078	624,191	12,875	2,446,144	Ohio	1,632,648	1,125,965	8,822	2,767,435
Georgia	1,102,527	1,116,402	10,771	2,229,700	Oklahoma	825,562	1,074,896	18,777	1,919,235
Hawaii	314,565	57,706	8,620	380,891	Oregon	705,805	325,458	4,644	1,035,907
Idaho	819,327	495,430	8,660	1,323,417	Pennsylvania	475,866	1,146,306	5,310	1,627,482
Illinois	3,513,362	1,891,545	38,933	5,443,840	Rhode Island	15,559	11,786	67	27,412
Indiana	1,774,250	1,222,001	16,783	3,013,034	South Carolina	558,451	270,580	6,745	835,776
Iowa	2,711,698	3,902,547	53,121	6,667,366	South Dakota	559,461	1,256,308	32,815	1,848,584
Kansas	1,857,063	1,508,243	38,394	3,403,700	Tennessee	514,093	581,109	16,601	1,111,803
Kentucky	798,220	669,416	7,278	1,474,914	Texas	2,785,683	3,060,908	146,562	5,993,153
Louisiana	769,784	313,808	18,663	1,102,255	Utah	95,877	232,941	3,299	332,117
Maine	124,402	246,090	2,192	372,684	Vermont	16,953	202,908	1,257	221,118
Maryland	260,853	405,490	1,204	667,547	Virginia	483,481	524,725	5,824	1,014,030
Massachusetts	95,497	106,735	593	202,825	Washington	1,449,733	442,182	6,923	1,898,838
Michigan	943,417	712,801	13,276	1,669,494	West Virginia	43,868	100,703	1,934	146,505
Minnesota	1,812,357	2,042,937	33,877	3,889,171	Wisconsin	538,860	2,112,795	14,083	2,665,738
Mississippi	707,749	666,963	20,107	1,394,809	Wyoming	96,206	250,257	5,333	351,796
Missouri	1,070,797	1,586,666	39,960	2,697,423	Total U.S.	46,661,480	42,901,711	807,081	90,370,272
Montana	657,649	420,680	9,350	1,087,679					

Average Prices Received by U.S. Farmers

Source: Statistical Reporting Service; Department of Agriculture

The figures represent dollars per 100 lbs. for hogs, beef cattle, veal calves, sheep, lamb and, milk (wholesale), dollars per head for milk cows; cents per lb. for milk fat (in cream), chickens, broilers, turkeys, and wool; cents for eggs per dozen. *Revised.

Year[1]	Hogs	Cattle (beef)	Calves (veal)	Sheep	Lambs	Cows (milk)	Milk (wholesale)	Milk fat (in cream)	Chickens (excl. broilers)	Broilers	Turkeys	Eggs	Wool
1930	8.84	7.71	9.68	4.74	7.76	74.20	2.21	34.5	...	...	20.2	23.7	19.5
1940	5.39	7.56	8.83	3.95	8.10	61.00	1.82	28.0	13.0	17.3	15.2	18.0	28.4
1950	18.00	23.30	26.30	11.60	25.10	198.00	3.89	62.0	22.0	27.4	32.9	36.3	62.1
1960	15.30	20.40	22.90	5.61	17.90	223.00	4.21	60.5	12.2	16.9	25.4	36.1	42.0
1965*	19.60	19.90	22.00	6.34	22.80	212.00	4.23	61.1	8.9	15.0	22.2	33.7	47.1
1970	22.70	27.10	34.50	7.51	26.40	332.00	5.71	70.0	9.1	13.6	22.6	39.1	35.5
1971	17.50	29.00	36.40	6.59	25.90	358.00	5.87	69.1	7.7	13.7	22.1	31.4	19.4
1972	25.10	33.50	44.70	7.28	29.10	397.00	6.07	67.5	8.9	14.1	22.2	30.9	35.0
1973	38.40	42.80	56.60	12.70	35.10	496.00	7.14	67.2	15.1	24.0	38.2	52.5	82.7
1974	34.20	35.60	35.20	11.30	37.00	500.00	8.33	63.5	9.7	21.5	28.0	53.3	59.1
1975	46.10	32.30	27.20	11.20	42.10	412.00	8.71	67.0	9.9	26.3	34.8	52.5	44.7

The figures represent cents per lb. for cotton, apples, and peanuts; dollars per bushel for oats, wheat, corn, barley, and soybeans; dollars per 100 lbs. for rice, sorghum, and potatoes; dollars per ton for cottonseed and baled hay.

Crop Year[2]	Corn	Wheat	Upland Cotton[3]	Oats	Barley	Rice	Soybeans	Sorghum	Peanuts	Cottonseed	Hay	Potatoes	Apples
1930	.663	.550	9.46	31.1	.420	1.74	1.34	1.02	3.46	22.00	11.00	1.47	...
1940	.674	.601	9.83	29.8	.393	1.80	.892	.873	3.33	21.70	9.78	.850	...
1950	2.00	1.52	39.90	78.8	1.19	5.09	2.47	1.88	10.9	86.60	21.10	1.50	...
1960	1.74	.997	30.08	59.8	.838	4.55	2.13	1.49	10.0	52.50	21.70	2.00	4.79
1965	1.35	1.16	29.26	62.2	1.02	4.93	2.54	1.76	11.4	46.70	23.20	2.53	4.32
1970	1.33	1.33	22.81	62.3	.973	5.17	2.85	2.04	12.8	56.50	26.10	1.21	4.54
1971	1.08	1.34	28.07	60.5	.993	5.34	3.03	1.88	13.6	56.80	28.10	1.90	4.92
1972	1.57	1.76	27.20	72.5	1.21	6.73	4.37	2.45	14.5	49.50	31.30	3.01	6.43
1973	2.55	3.95	44.40	118.0	2.13	13.80	5.68	3.82	16.2	100.10	41.60	4.89	8.80
1974	3.03	4.09	42.70	153.0	2.80	11.20	6.64	4.96	17.9	135.50	50.90	4.00	8.40
1975	2.46	3.52	49.90	144.0	2.42	7.93	4.60	4.21	19.6	97.50	53.00	4.80	8.30

(1) Weighted calendar year prices for livestock and livestock products other than wool. 1943 through 1963, wool prices are weighted on marketing year basis. The marketing year has been changed (1964) from a calendar year to a Dec.-Nov. basis for hogs, chickens, broilers and eggs. (2) Weighted crop year prices. Crop years are as follows: apples, June-May; wheat, oats, barley, hay and potatoes, July-June; cotton, rice peanuts and cottonseed, August-July; soybeans, September-August; and corn and sorghum grain, October-September. (3) Beginning 1964, 480 lb. net weight bales.

Index Numbers of Prices Received by Farmers

Source: Statistical Reporting Service; Department of Agriculture index (1910-14=100 per cent)

Year	All Farm Products	All Crops	Livestock[1]	Food Grains	Feed Grains and Hay	Feed Grains	Cotton	Tobacco	Oil-bearing Crops	Fruit	Commercial Vegetables[2]	Potatoes Sweetpot	Meat Animals	Dairy Products	Poultry and Eggs	Wool
1910	104	105	102	109	96	97	118	84	120	100	...	83	101	100	104	117
1920	211	235	190	249	202	209	262	233	208	188	...	294	171	202	222	214
1930	125	115	134	93	106	109	104	140	111	149	128	162	133	142	128	119
1940	100	90	109	84	85	86	83	134	103	81	122	89	108	120	98	160
1950	258	233	280	224	193	198	282	402	276	194	211	166	340	249	186	341
1960	239	222	253	203	152	151	254	500	214	244	230	203	296	259	160	235
1965	245	230	260	163	174	—	245	513	265	240	262	293	315	260	144	—
1970	274	225	325	162	179	—	183	604	265	217	292	218	405	350	147	—
1973	447	394	502	379	283	—	274	718	608	312	379	385	664	440	231	—
1974	481	504	454	529	423	—	433	821	625	319	403	543	553	510	214	—
1975	464	453	473	427	400	—	348	899	525	318	465	400	567	535	235	—

(1.) Livestock and livestock products. (2.) For fresh market and processing beg. 1952. (3.) Including dry edible beans.

Average Farm Wages

Calendar year	Per month		Per week		Per day			Per hour	
	With house	With board & room	With board & room	Without board or room	With house	With board & room	Without board or room	With house	Without board or room
1950	$121.00	$99.00	$23.50	$31.00	$3.50	$4.45	$4.50	$.62	$.69
1955	154.00	123.00	29.75	38.00	4.20	5.40	5.30	.74	.82
1960	192.00	149.00	35.50	45.75	5.30	6.50	6.60	.88	.97
1965	223.00	171.00	40.25	51.50	6.20	7.40	7.60	1.03	1.14
1970	328.00	251.00	60.75	78.00	9.80	10.70	11.70	1.50	1.64
1971	340.00	263.00	64.50	81.00	10.30	11.20	12.20	1.56	1.73
1972	361.00	280.00	67.80	85.50	11.20	12.00	13.20	1.65	1.84
1973	393.00	309.00	74.00	94.75	12.30	13.10	14.50	1.81	2.00
1974	423.00	334.00	80.50	102.75	13.60	14.60	16.10	2.01	2.24

Government Payments by Programs, by States

Source: Economic Research Service: Department of Agriculture (in $1,000)

1973 State	Conservation[1]	Sugar Act	Wool Act	Feed Grain Program	Wheat Program	Cotton	Cropland Adjustment	Other[2]	Total
Alabama	1,835	—	8	8,260	320	38,740	2,287	69	51,519
Alaska	21	—	54	—	—	—	—	—	75
Arizona	1,305	501	1,333	3,058	642	34,963	122	1,137	43,061
Arkansas	252	—	11	1,798	831	64,920	242	174	68,228
California	2,745	15,159	4,841	10,162	3,349	68,173	111	967	105,507
Colorado	1,471	4,998	3,401	14,725	17,406	—	795	1,257	44,053
Connecticut	150	—	9	143	1	—	67	3	373
Delaware	95	—	2	811	173	—	43	—	1,124
Florida	877	8,798	5	3,605	96	1,125	967	13	15,486
Georgia	2,643	—	12	19,837	956	29,863	3,614	154	57,079
Hawaii	99	9,154	—	—	—	—	—	—	9,253
Idaho	743	6,420	2,822	4,348	17,338	—	39	221	31,931
Illinois	2,020	—	728	121,174	13,216	87	943	—	138,168
Indiana	1,863	—	476	63,539	9,293	—	1,055	29	76,255
Iowa	1,729	61	1,820	180,649	758	—	960	212	186,189
Kansas	967	1,430	954	71,771	73,646	—	966	711	150,445
Kentucky	1,188	—	170	15,023	1,301	320	1,326	—	19,328
Louisiana	546	9,590	25	1,530	210	31,167	93	186	43,347
Maine	417	—	37	50	1	—	43	12	560
Maryland	711	—	54	4,000	917	—	80	1	5,763
Massachusetts	147	—	18	48	—	—	40	10	263
Michigan	1,018	3,394	595	21,646	9,488	—	2,530	217	38,888
Minnesota	2,142	3,472	1,353	84,337	11,221	—	2,406	133	105,044
Mississippi	817	—	13	5,137	389	94,269	538	100	101,263
Missouri	2,038	—	647	59,391	11,514	18,399	2,202	—3	94,188
Montana	2,129	1,640	3,667	10,397	45,986	—	161	1,010	64,990
Nebraska	1,124	3,647	1,018	113,107	29,679	—	2,018	1,200	151,793
Nevada	591	—	529	108	259	203	—	—	1,690
New Hampshire	157	—	13	38	—	—	2	1	211
New Jersey	195	—	23	1,375	346	—	133	2	2,074
New Mexico	1,294	28	2,282	7,173	4,635	10,519	2,852	582	29,365
New York	4,342	—	226	6,061	3,094	—	851	3	14,577
North Carolina	1,119	—	34	16,858	3,522	13,133	1,196	4	35,866
North Dakota	316	2,073	1,220	34,508	78,702	—	1,273	1,339	119,431
Ohio	1,720	1,568	1,735	37,759	11,518	—	1,528	10	55,838
Oklahoma	796	—	383	13,712	31,345	18,778	791	1,064	66,869
Oregon	1,429	1,054	2,172	2,472	7,840	—	45	272	15,284
Pennsylvania	2,740	—	426	8,249	2,722	—	953	203	15,293
Rhode Island	21	—	3	2	—	—	—	—	26
South Carolina	531	—	2	7,045	1,685	25,137	1,905	77	36,382
South Dakota	717	—	4,723	38,205	25,136	—	1,307	1,265	71,353
Tennessee	1,417	—	74	10,229	1,127	27,244	1,254	—	41,345
Texas	3,280	1,112	15,814	92,299	23,820	241,181	5,950	3,098	386,554
Utah	554	858	3,002	1,167	2,358	—	45	25	8,007
Vermont	742	—	15	90	1	—	16	26	890
Virginia	2,426	—	546	6,633	2,418	195	509	4	12,731
Washington	1,497	4,480	717	4,818	22,695	—	54	876	35,137
West Virginia	506	—	473	454	104	—	34	—	1,571
Wisconsin	2,745	—	314	33,194	332	—	2,986	223	39,794
Wyoming	715	2,246	6,160	1,053	1,924	—	52	578	12,728
Total U. S.	60,942	81,683	64,959	1,142,048	474,294	718,416	47,384	17,465	2,607,191

(1) Includes amounts paid under other similar programs not listed separately.
(2). Includes Milk Indemnity Program, Bee Keepers Indemnity Program, Hay Transportation Assistance Program, Water Bank Program, and Public Access.

Cooperative Farm Credit System

Loans outstanding to farmers and farmer's co-ops from banks and associations supervised by the Farm Credit Admin.

Year ended Dec. 31	Farm mortgage loans Federal land banks	Farm production loans Production Credit ass'ns	Loans to co-operatives by banks for cooperatives	FICB loans and discounts other than interagency	Total
1950	946,469,000	455,472,000	344,979,000	70,020,000	1,816,940,000
1955	1,497,165,000	653,478,000	370,683,000	70,785,000	2,592,111,000
1960	2,563,772,000	1,490,138,000	648,859,000	91,951,000	4,794,720,000
1965	4,280,675,000	2,598,460,000	1,055,163,000	146,091,000	8,080,389,000
1970	7,187,140,000	5,334,495,000	2,029,864,000	222,099,000	14,773,598,000
1973	11,073,276,000	7,859,554,000	2,576,748,000	333,207,000	21,842,785,000
1974	13,863,752,000	9,560,649,000	3,575,483,000	403,402,000	27,403,286,000
1975	16,563,886,000	10,825,963,000	3,978,861,000	372,860,000	31,741,570,000

Farm Employment—Annual Averages

Source: Economic Research Service; Department of Agriculture

Yr.	Total Aver. No. (1,000)	Index %	Family Aver. No. (1,000)	Index %	Hired Aver. No. (1,000)	Index %	Yr.	Family Aver. No. (1,000)	Index %	Total Aver. No. (1,000)	Index %	Hired Aver. No. (1,000)	Index %
1920	13,432	99	10,041	99	3,391	100	1960	7,057	52	5,172	52	1,885	55
1930	12,497	92	9,307	92	3,190	94	1970	4,523	34	3,348	33	1,175	35
1940	10,979	82	8,300	81	2,679	79	1974	4,389	32	3,075	31	1,314	35
1950	9,926	75	7,597	73	2,329	69	1975	4,357	32	3,034	30	1,324	36

Index (1910-14 = 100 per cent)

Farm-Mortgage Debt Outstanding by Lender Groups

Source: National Economic Analysis Division, U.S. Department of Agriculture

Year	Total farm-mortgage debt[1]	Amounts held by principal lender groups				
		Federal land banks[1]	Farmers home adminis-tration[2]	Life in-surance com-panies[3]	All commer-cial banks[4]	Other[4]
	$1,000	$1,000	$1,000	$1,000	$1,000	$1,000
1951	6,112,286	991,439	256,724	1,352,635	985,954	2,525,534
1952	6,662,327	1,026,906	290,529	1,541,874	1,017,360	2,785,658
1953	7,240,937	1,095,257	330,087	1,716,022	1,069,398	3,030,173
1954	7,930,931	1,187,046	352,199	1,892,773	1,091,949	3,215,964
1955	8,245,278	1,279,787	378,108	2,051,784	1,161,308	3,374,291
1956	9,012,016	1,480,204	412,670	2,271,784	1,275,429	3,571,929
1957	9,821,525	1,722,381	462,942	2,476,543	1,298,113	3,861,546
1958	10,382,475	1,897,187	540,762	2,578,958	1,315,530	4,050,038
1959	11,091,390	2,065,372	608,101	2,661,229	1,407,548	4,349,140
1960	12,082,409	2,335,124	676,224	2,819,542	1,523,051	4,728,468
1961	12,820,304	2,539,044	722,870	2,974,609	1,591,762	4,992,019
1962	13,899,105	2,803,103	948,346	3,161,757	1,640,790	5,345,109
1963	15,167,821	3,024,013	1,057,923	3,391,183	1,870,216	5,824,486
1964	16,803,505	3,281,797	1,171,373	3,780,537	2,136,571	6,433,227
1965	18,894,240	3,686,755	1,284,913	4,287,671	2,416,634	7,218,267
1966	21,186,886	4,240,227	1,497,313	4,801,677	2,607,404	8,040,265
1967	23,077,186	4,914,522	1,663,067	5,213,587	2,770,010	8,516,000
1968	25,142,401	5,563,204	1,844,046	5,539,600	3,060,551	9,135,000
1969	27,397,370	6,081,229	2,054,382	5,763,500	3,333,259	10,165,000
1970	29,182,766	6,671,222	2,279,620	5,733,900	3,545,024	10,953,000
1971	30,346,083	7,145,363	2,440,043	5,610,300	3,772,377	11,378,000
1972	32,207,666	6,879,753	2,618,131	5,564,300	4,218,482	11,927,000
1973	35,757,754	9,050,067	2,835,202	5,643,300	4,792,185	13,437,000
1974	41,252,870	10,901,352	3,013,440	5,964,800	5,458,278	15,915,000
1975	46,288,419	13,402,441	3,214,657	6,297,400	5,966,282	17,407,639
1976[6]	50,876,417	15,949,720	3,369,126	6,533,092	6,296,286	18,728,196

(1.) Includes data for joint stock land banks and Federal Farm Mortgage Corporations. (2.) Includes both direct and insured loans. (3.) Taken from Life Insurance Institute Tally sheet. (4.) FDIC number after 1973 prior to 1973 estimates reflect shift of FHA Insured loans to FHA. (5.) Estimated by ERS, USDA 1965-73 revised June, 1974. (6.) Preliminary.

Canadian Farm Cash Receipts[1]

Source: Canadian Statistical Review (April, 1976)
(in millions of dollars)

Crops

Year and quarter	Total cash receipts	Total crops	Wheat[2]	Oats[2]	Barley[2]	C.W.B. Advance pay-ments[3]	Other grains[4]	Sugar beets	Pota-toes	Fruits	Vege-tables	Tobacco	Other crops[5]
1972	5,307.43	2,081.89	948.20	31.85	221.41	—27.46	312.59	20.89	86.58	84.61	115.04	150.03	138.12
1973	6,828.42	2,672.70	1,201.26	43.59	330.27	6.47	539.99	88.28	159.97	137.42	172.39	142.81	231.38
1974	8,836.54	4,150.46	2,033.30	54.17	554.30	11.43	728.30	43.80	213.94	195.49	191.64	207.68	207.55
1975 1	3,157.56	2,057.54	944.75	38.80	216.69	—8.68	59.44	12.77	29.80	10.73	22.86	120.29	43.72
2	2,059.12	712.04	377.61	13.74	121.94	—9.60	87.34	3.54	21.42	11.38	18.69	34.54	31.45

Livestock and Products

Year & Quarter	Total	Cattle	Hogs	Sheep	Dairy Products	Poultry	Eggs	Other	Total forest and maple products	Dairy sup-plementary payments	Deficiency payments
1972	3,076.56	1,195.84	575.71	9.06	778.82	295.85	163.77	57.31	24.46	101.41	23.10
1973	2,969.58	1,479.51	825.49	10.67	849.46	437.94	243.79	74.73	42.63	181.02	60.49
1974	4,328.01	1,620.58	787.72	12.87	1,087.74	472.15	269.09	77.85	40.96	131.02	36.04
1975 1	1,051.02	416.49	203.48	3.64	258.47	84.13	65.30	19.51	6.14	42.86	—0.01
2	1,273.39	523.85	213.55	2.50	373.46	89.08	58.96	11.98	22.44	51.24	—

[1]Cash receipts from farming operations excluding supplementary payments. Excludes Newfoundland. [2]Including participion payments made by the Canadian Wheat Board direct to producers on crops delivered in previous years. [3]Net cash. [4]Includes rye, flaxseed, rapeseed, soybeans, and corn. [5]Includes clover and grass seed, hay, clover, greenhouse products, mustard seed, sunflower seed, hops, dry beans and dry peas and miscellaneous products.

Canada-Farm Cash Receipts from Farming Operations

Source: Statistics Canada
(thousands of dollars)

Province	1971	1972	1973	1974	1975
Prince Edward Island	38,868	44,758	71,923	84,418	81,925
Nova Scotia	65,618	73,734	95,659	104,311	115,784
New Brunswick	52,801	64,953	95,546	103,571	99,052
Quebec	691,515	776,398	977,289	1,159,932	1,336,468
Ontario	1,427,965	1,623,173	1,970,950	2,413,583	2,531,117
Manitoba	367,841	487,883	618,297	842,437	905,954
Saskatchewan	901,408	1,202,870	1,466,242	2,054,638	2,387,226
Alberta	775,443	917,464	1,199,051	1,702,630	1,933,448
British Columbia	224,448	248,479	333,464	371,008	399,135
Total	4,545,907	5,349,712	6,828,421	8,836,528	9,790,109

Farmers' Marketing, Farm Supply, Related Service Cooperatives

Source: Farmer Cooperative Service, U.S. Dept. of Agriculture (Marketing Season 1972-73[1])

A marketing season includes the period during which the farm products of a specified year are moved into the channels of trade. Marketing seasons overlap.

State	Cooperatives No.	Memberships	Net business[2] ($1,000)	State	Cooperatives No.	Memberships	Net business[2] ($1,000)
Alabama	71	80,010	239,750	Nebraska	345	263,870	841,790
Alaska	2	350	2,664	Nevada	4	925	10,656
Arizona	17	85,140	165,161	New Hampshire	7	3,765	45,286
Arkansas	168	108,320	572,737	New Jersey	38	16,985	159,834
California	294	91,850	2,655,901	New Mexico	24	7,360	66,597
Colorado	86	50,220	434,215	New York	287	135,900	1,238,710
Connecticut	11	5,375	101,228	North Carolina	34	146,410	407,576
Delaware	8	13,350	26,639	North Dakota	671	262,445	543,434
Florida	93	54,290	689,948	Ohio	205	217,630	929,699
Georgia	90	177,100	514,131	Oklahoma	154	139,885	439,542
Hawaii	19	2,385	18,649	Oregon	73	58,100	402,248
Idaho	69	47,850	247,742	Pennsylvania	108	77,955	748,554
Illinois	313	318,285	1,427,847	Rhode Island	1	860	18,647
Indiana	114	413,490	847,118	South Carolina	23	40,920	138,522
Iowa	467	373,385	1,827,430	South Dakota	323	175,845	330,323
Kansas	269	202,980	959,004	Tennessee	110	152,605	322,331
Kentucky	82	202,620	338,314	Texas	462	142,630	964,329
Louisiana	99	17,385	199,792	Utah	43	26,650	237,084
Maine	10	9,975	85,245	Vermont	10	6,865	170,489
Maryland	39	44,380	237,086	Virginia	118	179,630	415,567
Massachusetts	18	10,275	143,850	Washington	152	103,465	639,334
Michigan	146	124,465	748,554	West Virginia	64	49,015	71,925
Minnesota	1,092	591,990	1,766,161	Wisconsin	520	422,040	1,783,497
Mississippi	138	126,000	444,870	Wyoming	31	11,265	42,622
Missouri	165	250,155	695,276				
Montana	227	82,105	159,834	**United States**	7,854	6,126,750	26,497,742

(1) Preliminary. (2) The volume of a Hawaiian sugar co-op based in Calif. is included in the dollar volume of Calif.

Food Stamps—Costs and Benefits

Source: U.S. Department of Agriculture

Fiscal Year	Average No. Persons participating per month	Value per year		Avg. bonus per participant per month	
		Total purchase	Bonus	Current $	1967 $
1962	142,817	35,202,266	13,152,695	7.67	8.47
1965	424,652	85,471,989	32,505,096	6.38	6.75
1968	2,211,474	451,800,893	173,142,015	6.52	6.26
1969	2,878,113	603,351,143	228,818,622	6.63	6.04
1970	4,340,030	1,089,960,761	549,663,811	10.55	9.07
1971	9,367,908	2,713,273,217	1,522,749,091	13.55	11.17
1973	12,165,682	3,883,952,103	2,131,404,604	14.60	11.67
1975	17,063,224	7,259,134,365	4,381,389,037	21.40	13.49
1976(p)	18,498,674	8,663,658,669	5,303,484,576	23.89	—

The Food Stamp Program enables low income families to buy more food of greater variety to improve their diets. If a household meets eligibility requirements (a family of 4 must have a net income lower than $553 per month), it is assigned an allotment of stamps based on the number of people in the household ($166 worth of stamps per month for 4 people). The family must pay a portion of the value of the stamps; the amount paid is based on family income and size, but must not exceed 30% of the net income. The value of the stamps in excess of the amount paid is the "bonus," the value of the free food.

Federal Food Program Costs

Source: U.S. Department of Agriculture, Food and Nutrition Service (millions of dollars)

Year	Food Stamps		Food Distribution[2]				Child Nutrition				Total
	Total Issued	Bonus Stamps[1]	Needy Families	Supp. Food	Schools	Institutions	School Lunch	School Bkfst.	Special Food	Special Milk	
1971	3,105	1,699	318	13	296	26	647	22	34	92	3,147
1973	4,046	2,208	224	14	337	27	962	44	52	63	3,913
1974	5,868	3,498	114	16	393	21	1,164	70	101	89	5,466
1975[3]	8,308	5,063	12	18	364	15	1,376	99	121	134	7,202
1976 1st Qtr.[3]	2,544	1,390	3	4	186	0.8	494	51	24	47	2,200
2d Qtr.[3]	2,161	1,328	2	4	108	1	396	29	34	35	1,937

[1]Includes Food Certificate Program. [2]Cost of food delivered to state distribution centers. [3]Preliminary.

Canadian Harvested Acreage

Source: Statistics Canada

Principal Crops[1] (in thousands of acres)

Province	1972	1973	1974	1975	Province	1972	1973	1974	1975
Prince Edward Island	315	328	333	344	Manitoba	8,923	12,619	12,129	12,108
Nova Scotia	189	191	192	193	Saskatchewan	25,147	42,768	41,860	40,917
New Brunswick	282	288	291	290	Alberta	17,302	22,937	22,167	22,245
Quebec	3,889	3,910	3,941	3,984	British Columbia	933	976	1,031	1,042
Ontario	7,798	7,970	8,058	8,115	**Total[2]**	85,803	92,211	90,199	89,453

[1]Crops included are winter wheat, spring wheat, oats, barley, fall rye, spring rye, flaxseed, mixed grains, corn for grain, buckwheat, peas, dry beans, soybeans, rapeseed, potatoes, mustard seed, sunflower seed, tame hay, fodder corn, field roots, and sugar beets. [2]Excluding Newfoundland.

Agricultural Products — U. S. and World Production and Exports

Source: Foreign Agricultural Service, Dept. of Agriculture

Commodity[1]	Unit	Production U.S.	Production World	Production % U.S.	Exports U.S.	Exports World	Exports % U.S.
Wheat, grain only	Mil M.T.	48.9	356.6	13.7	[2][3]27.5	[2][3]68.0	40.4
Oats	Mil. M.T.	8.9	49.3	18.1	[2]0.2	[2]1.1	18.2
Corn	Mil. M.T.	146.5	317.8	46.1	[2]28.4	[2]46.7	60.8
Barley	Mil. M.T.	6.6	160.0	4.1	[2]0.9	[2]11.2	8.0
Soybeans	Mil. M.T.	41.4	65.8	62.9	12.5	16.3	76.6
Rice	Mil. M.T.	[4]5.1	[3]352.2	1.4	[5]2.2	[5]7.7	28.5
Lard[6]	1,000 M.T.	459.0	3,924.1	11.7	39.8	516.3	7.7
Tallow and grease[6]	1,000 M.T.	2,410.4	4,598.6	52.4	891.0	1,437.0	62.0
Tobacco, unmftd[6]	1,000 M.T.	994.6	5,292.4	18.8	255.4	1,226.7	20.8
Edible Veg. Oils[7]	Mil. M.T.	6.8	30.9	22.0	[8]3,119	[9]10,035	31.1
Cotton	1,000 Bales	[10]11,540	64,896	17.7	3,926	17,109	22.9

[1] Crop 1974-75 as follows: Wheat, oats and barley year beginning July 1; corn, October 1; soybeans, September 1; rice and cotton, August 1. Excludes Alaska, Hawaii and Puerto Rico except for exports. [2] Fiscal year 1974-75. [3] Includes wheat flour in grain equivalent. [4] Calendar year. [5] Milled rice. [6] Calendar year 1975. [7] Includes palm oils. [8] Includes oil equivalent of exported oilseeds. [9] Exports from producing countries. [10] Bales of 480 pounds, net weight.

Civilian Consumption of Major Food Commodities per Person

Source: Economic Research Service: Department of Agriculture

Commodity[1]	Avg. (lbs.) 1957-59	1973	1974	Commodity[1]	Avg. (lbs.) 1957-59	1973	1974
Meats (carcass wt.)	156.6	175.7	187.3	Other (exc. melons)	40.5	33.8	35.5
Beef	82.1	109.6	116.3	Processed:			
Veal	7.1	1.8	2.3	Canned fruit	22.4	21.3	19.4
Lamb and mutton	4.4	2.7	2.4	Canned juice	13.5	16.3	14.6
Pork (excl. lard)	63.0	61.6	66.3	Frozen (inc. Juices)	8.6	11.2	11.9
Fish (edible wt.)	10.5	12.7	12.0	Dried	3.3	2.8	3.0
Poultry products				**Vegetables**			
Eggs (farm Basis), No.	356	294	286	Fresh[2]	104.1	99.9	100.4
Chicken (ready to cook)	27.5	41.5	41.7	Canned, excl. potatoes	43.3	54.3	52.3
Turkey (ready to cook)	6.0	8.7	9.0	Frozen, excl. pot.	6.6	10.7	10.1
Dairy products				Potatoes, fresh equiv.	106.9	116.5	117.5
Cheese	7.9	13.7	14.5	**Sweet potatoes**, fresh	8.3	5.1	5.5
Cond. and evap. milk	14.8	6.0	5.3	**Grains**			
Fluid milk and cream	337	257	244	Cornmeal and flour	7.4	7.5	7.6
Ice Cream (prod. wt.)	18.4	17.5	17.6	Corn syrup	9.4	21.7	23.0
Fats and Oils-Total,				Corn sugar	3.6	5.2	5.3
fat content	45.3	54.0	52.5	Wheat flour[3]	120	109	106
Butter (actual wt.)	8.2	4.8	4.5	Wheat cereals	2.8	2.9	2.9
Margarine (act. wt.)	8.9	11.3	11.3	Rice, milled	5.4	7.0	7.3
Lard	9.3	3.4	3.2	**Other**			
Shortening	11.4	17.3	16.5	Coffee (green beans)	15.7	13.7	12.8
Other edible fats and oils	10.8	21.3	20.2	Tea	.58	.79	.80
Fruits				Cocoa Beans	3.5	4.2	3.7
Fresh	95.5	75.6	80.0	Peanuts (shelled)	4.6	6.6	6.4
Citrus	34.0	27.3	28.8	Melons	25.1	21.8	19.1
Apples (com.)	21.0	14.5	15.7	Sugar (refined)	96.1	102.1	97.0

[1] Quantity in pounds except for eggs. Data on calendar year basis except for dried fruits, which are on pack-year basis, fresh citrus fruits and peanuts on a crop-year basis, and rice on August 1 year. Fresh citrus year begins in previous October and rice year begins in previous August. [2] Commercial production for sale as fresh produce. [3] Includes white, whole wheat, and semolina flour.

Recommended Daily Dietary Allowances

The Recommended Daily Dietary Allowances are amounts of nutrients recommended by the Food and Nutrition Board of the National Research council as adequate for maintenance of good nutrition in healthy persons in the U.S. The minimum daily requirements for the adult man are: Vitamin A, 4,000 I.U.; thiamin 1 milligram; riboflavin 1.2 mg.; niacin 10 mg.; ascorbic acid 30 mg.; Calcium 750 mg.; iron 10 mg.

	Years From-up to	Wgt. (lbs.)	Hgt. (in.)	Calories	Protein (grams)	Calcium (grams)	Iron (mg.)	Vit A (IU)	Thia-min (mg.)	Ribo-flavin (mg.)	Niacin (mg.)	Ascorbic acid (mg.)
Infants	0-1/6	9	22	lb. x 54.5	lb. x 1.0	0.4	6	1,500	0.2	0.4	5	35
...	1/6-1/2	15	25	lb. x 50.0	lb. x .09	0.5	10	1,500	0.4	0.5	7	35
...	1/2-1	20	28	lb. x 45.5	lb. x .8	0.6	15	1,500	0.5	0.6	8	35
Children	1-2	26	32	1,100	25	0.7	15	2,000	0.6	0.6	8	40
...	2-3	31	36	1,250	25	0.8	15	2,000	0.6	0.7	8	40
...	3-4	35	39	1,400	30	0.8	10	2,500	0.7	0.8	9	40
...	4-6	42	43	1,600	30	0.8	10	2,500	0.8	0.9	11	40
...	6-8	51	48	2,000	35	0.9	10	3,500	1.0	1.1	13	40
...	8-10	62	52	2,200	40	1.0	10	3,500	1.1	1.2	15	40
Boys	10-12	77	55	2,500	45	1.2	10	4,500	1.3	1.3	17	40
...	12-14	95	59	2,700	50	1.4	18	5,000	1.4	1.4	18	45
...	14-18	130	67	3,000	60	1.4	18	5,000	1.5	1.5	20	55
Men	18-22	147	69	2,800	60	0.8	10	5,000	1.4	1.6	18	60
...	22-35	154	69	2,800	65	0.8	10	5,000	1.4	1.7	18	60
...	35-55	154	68	2,600	65	0.8	10	5,000	1.3	1.7	17	60
...	55-75x	154	67	2,400	65	0.8	10	5,000	1.2	1.7	14	60
Girls	10-12	77	57	2,250	50	1.2	18	4,500	1.1	1.3	15	40
...	12-14	97	61	2,300	50	1.3	18	5,000	1.1	1.4	15	45
...	14-16	114	62	2,400	55	1.3	18	5,000	1.2	1.4	16	50
...	16-18	119	63	2,300	55	1.3	18	5,000	1.2	1.5	15	50
Women	18-22	128	64	2,000	55	0.8	18	5,000	1.0	1.5	13	44
...	22-35	128	64	2,000	55	0.8	18	5,000	1.0	1.5	13	44
...	35-55	128	63	1,850	55	0.8	18	5,000	1.0	1.5	13	55
...	55-75x	128	62	1,700	55	0.8	10	5,000	1.0	1.5	13	55
Pregnant	...	...	...	...	65	.04	18	6,000	x0.1	1.8	15	60
Lactating	...	...	...	...	75	x0.5	18	8,000	x0.5	2.0	20	60

Nutritive Value of Foods (Calories, Proteins, etc.)

Source: Home and Garden Bulletin No. 72, U. S. Department of Agriculture

Available for 75c from Supt. of Documents, U. S. Government Printing Office, Washington, D. C. 20402

Food	Measure	Water %	Food Energy (calories)	Protein (grams)	Fat (grams)	Carbohydrate (grams)	Calcium (mg)	Iron (mg)	Vit. A (I.U.)	Thiamin (mg)	Riboflavin (mg)	Niacin (mg)	Ascorbic acid (mg)
Milk, Cream, Cheese													
Milk, fluid, whole, 3.5% fat	1 cup	87	160	9	9	12	288	0.1	350	0.07	0.41	0.2	2
Milk, fluid nonfat (skim)	1 cup	90	90	9	T	12	296	.1	10	.09	.44	.2	2
Buttermilk, fluid, cultured, made from skim milk	1 cup	90	90	9	T	12	296	.1	10	.10	.44	.2	2
Cheese, Roquefort type	1 oz.	40	105	6	9	1	.89	.1	350	.01	.17	.3	0
Cheese, Cottage, creamed	12 oz.	78	360	46	14	10	320	1.0	580	.10	.85	.3	0
Cream, half-and-half	1 cup	80	325	8	28	11	261	.1	1,160	.07	.39	.1	2
Cream, heavy	1 cup	57	840	5	90	7	179	.1	3,670	.05	.26	.1	2
Custard, baked	1 cup	77	305	14	15	29	297	1.1	930	.11	.50	.3	1
Yoghurt, whole milk	1 cup	88	150	7	8	12	272	.1	340	.07	.39	.2	2
Eggs (large)													
Raw	1 egg	74	80	6	6	T	27	1.1	590	.05	.15	T	0
Scrambled (milk and fat)	1 egg	72	110	7	8	1	51	1.1	690	.05	.18	T	0
Meat, Poultry													
Bacon	2 sli.	8	90	5	8	1	2	.5	0	.08	.05	.8	...
Beef, lean and fat	3 oz.	53	245	23	16	0	10	2.9	30	.04	.18	3.5	...
Hamburger, regular	3 oz.	54	245	21	17	0	9	2.7	30	.07	.18	4.6	...
Steak, broiled, lean and fat	3 oz.	44	330	20	27	0	9	2.5	50	.05	.16	4.0	...
Corned beef	3 oz.	59	185	22	10	0	17	3.7	20	.01	.20	2.9	...
Chicken, cooked:													
Flesh only, broiled	3 oz.	71	115	20	3	0	8	1.4	80	.05	.16	7.4	...
With bone, 1/2 breast, fried	3.3 oz.	58	155	25	5	1	9	1.3	70	.04	.17	11.2	...
Chicken, potpie, baked	8 oz.	57	535	23	31	42	68	3.0	3,020	.25	.26	4.1	5
Lamb chop, thick with bone	4.8 oz.	47	400	25	33	0	10	1.5	...	.14	.25	5.6	...
Lamb, lean and fat	3 oz.	54	235	22	16	0	9	1.4	...	.13	.23	4.7	...
Liver, beef, fried	2 oz.	57	130	15	6	3	6	5.0	30,280	.15	2.37	9.4	15
Ham, light cure, lean	3 oz.	54	245	18	19	0	8	2.2	0	.40	.16	3.1	...
Boiled ham, sliced	2 oz.	59	135	11	10	0	6	1.6	0	.25	.09	1.5	...
Pork roast, lean and fat	3 oz.	46	310	21	24	0	9	2.7	0	.78	.22	4.7	...
Frankfurter, heated	2 oz.	57	170	7	15	1	3	.8	...	.08	.11	1.4	...
Veal cutlet	3 oz.	60	185	23	9	...	9	2.7	...	.06	.21	4.6	...
Veal roast	3 oz.	55	230	23	14	0	10	2.9	...	.11	.26	6.6	...
Fish													
Bluefish, baked with fat	3 oz.	68	135	22	4	0	25	.6	40	.09	.08	1.6	...
Clams, raw, meat only	3 oz.	82	65	11	1	2	59	5.2	90	.08	.15	1.1	8
Crabmeat, canned	3 oz.	77	85	15	2	1	38	.7	...	.07	.07	1.6	...
Oyster, raw, meat	1 cup	85	160	20	4	8	226	13.2	740	.33	.43	6.0	...
Salmon, pink, canned	3 oz.	71	120	17	5	0	167	.7	60	.03	.16	6.8	...
Shrimp, canned, meat	3 oz.	70	100	21	1	1	98	2.6	50	.01	.03	1.5	...
Swordfish, broiled with butter	3 oz.	65	150	24	5	0	23	1.1	1,750	.03	.04	9.3	...
Tuna, canned in oil	3 oz.	61	170	24	7	0	7	1.6	70	.04	.10	10.1	...
Nuts													
Almonds, shelled, whole	1 cup	5	850	26	77	28	332	6.7	0	.34	1.31	5.0	T
Cashew nuts, roasted	1 cup	5	785	24	64	41	53	5.3	140	.60	.35	2.5	...
Peanuts, roasted	1 cup	2	840	37	72	27	107	3.0	...	.46	.19	24.7	0
Pecans, halves	1 cup	3	740	10	77	16	79	2.6	140	.93	.14	1.0	2
Walnuts, black or native, chopped	1 cup	3	790	26	75	19	T	7.6	380	.28	.14	.9	...
Vegetables & Products													
Asparagus, cooked, spears	4 sp.	94	10	1	T	2	13	.4	540	.10	.11	.8	16
Asparagus, canned	1 cup	94	45	5	1	7	44	4.1	1,240	.15	.22	2.0	37
Beans, lima, immature, cooked	1 cup	71	190	13	1	34	80	4.3	480	.31	.17	2.2	29
Beans, snap, green, cooked	1 cup	92	30	2	T	7	63	.8	680	.09	.11	.6	15
Beans, snap, canned, green	1 cup	94	45	2	T	10	81	2.9	690	.07	.10	.7	10
Beans, snap, yellow or wax	1 cup	93	30	2	1	6	63	0.8	290	.09	.11	.6	16
Beans, sprouted mung, cooked	1 cup	91	35	4	T	7	21	1.1	30	.11	.13	.9	8
Beets, cooked	2 beets	91	30	1	T	7	14	.5	20	.03	.04	.3	6
Broccoli, cooked	1 stalk	91	45	6	1	8	158	1.4	4,500	.16	.36	1.4	162
Brussels sprouts, cooked	1 cup	88	55	7	1	10	50	1.7	810	12	.22	1.2	135
Cabbage, raw, shredded	1 cup	92	15	1	T	4	34	.3	90	.04	.04	.2	33
Cabbage, cooked	1 cup	94	30	2	T	6	64	.4	190	.06	.06	.4	48
Carrot, raw 5 1/2 by 1 in.	1	88	20	1	T	5	18	.4	5,500	.03	.03	.3	4
Carrots, cooked, diced	1 cup	91	45	1	T	10	48	.9	15,220	.08	.07	.7	9
Cauliflower, cooked, flower buds	1 cup	93	25	3	T	5	25	.8	70	.11	.10	.7	66
Celery, raw, stalk, large	1 stalk	94	5	T	T	2	16	.1	100	.01	.01	.1	4
Corn, cooked, ear 5 x 1 3/4 in.	1 ear	74	70	3	1	16	2	.5	310	.09	.08	1.0	7
Corn, canned	1 cup	81	170	5	2	40	10	1.0	690	.07	.12	2.3	13
Cucumbers, raw, pared	10 oz.	96	30	1	T	7	35	.6	T	.07	.09	.4	23
Lettuce, Boston type	1 head	95	30	3	T	6	77	4.4	2,130	.14	.13	.6	18
Mushrooms, canned	1 cup	93	40	5	T	6	15	1.2	T	.04	.60	4.8	4
Onion, mature, raw, 2 1/2 in.	1	89	40	2	T	10	30	.6	40	.04	.04	.2	11
Peas, green, cooked	1 cup	82	115	9	1	19	37	2.9	860	.44	.17	3.7	33
Peas, green, canned	1 cup	83	165	9	1	31	50	4.2	1,120	.23	.13	2.2	22
Potato, medium, baked	1	75	90	3	T	21	9	.7	T	.10	.04	1.7	20
Potato, medium, boiled in skin	1	80	105	3	T	23	10	.8	T	.13	.05	2.0	22
Potatoes, mashed, milk added	1 cup	83	125	4	1	25	47	.8	50	.16	.10	2.0	19
Potato chips, medium	10 chips	2	115	1	8	10	8	.4	T	.04	.01	1.0	3
Sauerkraut, canned	1 cup	93	45	2	T	9	85	1.2	120	.07	.09	.4	33
Spinach, cooked	1 cup	92	40	5	1	6	167	4.0	14,580	.13	.25	1.0	50
Squash, summer, diced, cooked	1 cup	96	30	2	T	7	52	.8	820	.10	.16	1.6	21
Squash, winter, baked, mashed	1 cup	81	130	4	1	32	57	1.6	8,610	.10	.27	1.4	27
Sweet potato, baked	1	64	155	2	1	36	44	1.0	8,910	.10	.07	.7	24

Food	Measure	Water %	Food Energy (Calories)	Protein (grams)	Fat (grams)	Carbohydrate (grams)	Calcium (mg)	Iron (mg)	Vit. A (I.U.)	Thiamin (mg)	Riboflavin (mg)	Niacin (mg)	Ascorbic Acid (mg)
Sweet potato, candied 3½ by 2¼ in.	1	60	295	2	6	60	65	1.6	11,030	.10	.08	.8	17
Tomato, raw, medium	1	94	40	2	T	9	24	.9	1,640	.11	.07	1.3	42
Tomato catsup, tablespoon	1 tbsp.	69	15	T	T	4	3	.1	210	.01	.01	.2	2
Tomato juice, canned	1 cup	94	45	2	T	10	17	2.2	1,940	.12	.07	1.9	39
Fruits and Fruit Products													
Apple, medium, raw	1	85	70	T	T	18	8	.4	50	.04	.02	.1	3
Apple juice, bottled or canned	1 cup	88	120	T	T	30	15	1.5		.02	.05	.2	2
Applesauce, canned, sweetened	1 cup	76	230	1	T	61	10	1.3	100	.05	.03	.1	3
Banana, raw 6 by 1½ in.	1	76	100	1	T	26	10	.8	230	.06	.07	.8	12
Blueberries, raw	1 cup	83	85	1	1	21	21	1.4	140	.04	.08	.6	20
Cantaloupe, raw, medium	½ melon	91	60	1	T	14	27	.8	6,540	.08	.06	1.2	63
Cranberry sauce, sweetened, canned	1 cup	62	405	T	1	104	17	.6	60	.03	.03	.1	6
Grapefruit, raw, medium, white	½	89	45	1	T	12	19	.5	10	.05	.02	.2	44
Grapefruit juice, canned, unsweetened	1 cup	89	100	1	T	24	20	1.0	20	.07	.04	.4	84
Grapes, raw, American type	1 cup	82	65	1	1	15	15	.4	100	.05	.03	.2	3
Grapejuice, canned	1 cup	83	165	1	T	42	28	.8		.10	.05	.5	T
Lemon, raw, medium	1	90	20	1	T	6	19	.4	10	.03	.01	.1	39
Lemon juice, raw	1 cup	91	60	1	T	20	17	.5	50	.07	.02	.2	112
Lime juice, fresh	1 cup	90	65	1	T	22	22	.5	20	.05	.02	.2	79
Orange, raw, 2⅝ in. diam.	1	86	65	1	T	16	54	.5	260	.13	.05	.5	66
Orange juice, frozen, undiluted	6 oz. can	55	360	5	T	87	75	.9	1,620	.68	.11	2.8	360
Peach, raw, whole, medium	1	89	35	1	T	10	9	.5	1,320	.02	.05	1.0	7
Peaches, canned, halves or sliced	1 cup	79	200	1	T	52	10	.8	1,100	.02	.06	1.4	7
Pear, raw, 3 by 2½ in.	1	83	100	1	1	25	13	.5	30	.04	.07	.2	7
Pineapple, canned, sliced	Large sli.	80	90	T	T	24	13	.4	50	.09	.03	.2	8
Plums, raw, 2 in. diam.	1 plum	87	25	T	T	7	7	.3	140	.02	.02	.3	3
Prune juice, canned	1 cup	80	200	1	T	49	36	10.5		.03	.03	1.0	5
Raisins, seedless, pkged. ½ oz.	1 pkg.	18	40	T	T	11	9	.5	T	.02	.01	.1	T
Strawberries, raw, capped	1 cup	90	55	1	1	13	31	1.5	90	.04	.10	1.0	88
Watermelon, raw, wedge	1 wedge	93	115	2	1	27	30	2.1	2,510	.13	.13	.7	30
Grain Products													
Bagel, 3 in. diam. egg.	1	32	165	6	2	28	9	1.2	30	.14	.10	1.2	0
Biscuit, baking powder	1	27	105	2	5	13	34	.4	T	.06	.06	.1	T
Bran flakes (40% bran)	1 cup	3	105	4	1	28	25	12.3	0	.14	.06	2.2	0
Bread, cracked wheat	1 loaf	35	1,190	40	10	236	399	5.0	T	.53	.41	5.9	T
Bread, enriched, French	1 loaf	31	1,315	41	14	251	195	10.0	T	1.27	1.00	11.3	0
Bread, enriched, Italian	1 loaf	32	1,250	41	4	256	77	10.0	0	1.32	.91	11.8	0
Bread, raisin, loaf	1	35	1,190	30	13	243	322	5.9	T	.23	.41	3.2	T
Bread, American, rye	1 loaf	36	1,100	41	5	236	340	7.3	0	.82	.32	6.4	0
Bread, white, enriched	1 loaf	36	1,225	39	15	229	381	11.3	T	1.13	.95	10.9	T
Cake, angel food	1 cake	34	1,645	36	1	377	603	1.9	0	.03	.70	.6	0
Cupcake, small, choc. icing.	1 cake	22	130	2	5	21	47	.3	60	.01	.04	.1	T
Cake, Boston cream pie	1 pce.	35	210	4	6	34	46	.3	140	.02	.08	.1	T
Cake, pound	1 loaf	17	2,430	29	152	242	108	4.1	1,440	.15	.46	1.0	0
Saltines	4	4	50	1	1	8	2	.1	0	T	T	.1	0
Danish Pastry, round piece	1 pastry	22	275	5	15	30	33	.6	200	.05	.10	.5	T
Doughnut, cake type	1	24	125	2	6	16	13	.4	30	.05	.05	.4	T
Macaroni, enriched, cooked.	1 cup	64	190	6	1	39	14	1.4	0	.23	.14	1.8	0
Noodles, enriched	1 cup	70	200	7	2	37	16	1.4	110	.22	.13	1.9	0
Oatmeal, or rolled oats, cooked	1 cup	87	130	5	2	23	22	1.4	0	.19	.05	.2	0
Pie, apple, ⅐ of 9-in. pie.	1 sector	48	350	3	15	51	11	.4	40	.03	.03	.5	1
Pie, custard, ⅐ of 9-in. pie	1 sector	58	285	8	14	30	125	.8	300	.07	.21	.4	0
Pie, lemon meringue, ⅐ of 9-in. pie	1 sector	47	305	4	12	45	17	.6	200	.04	.10	.2	4
Pie, mince, ⅐ of 9-in. pie	1 sector	43	365	3	16	56	38	1.4	T	.09	.05	.5	1
Pie, pumpkin, ⅐ of 9-in. pie	1 sector	59	275	5	15	32	66	.7	3,210	.04	.13	.7	T
Pizza, (cheese) ⅛ of 14 in. diam..	1 sector	45	185	7	6	27	107	.7	290	.04	.12	.7	4
Popcorn, plain.	1 cup	4	25	1	T	5	1	.2			.01	.1	0
Roll, home recipe	1 roll	26	120	3	3	20	16	.7	30	.09	.09	.8	T
Spaghetti, enriched, cooked	1 cup	72	155	5	1	32	11	1.3	0	.20	.11	1.5	0
Fats and Oils													
Butter, regular	½ cup	16	810	1	92	1	23	0	3,750				0
Lard	1 cup	0	1,850	0	205	0	0	0	0	0	0	0	0
Vegetable fats	1 cup	0	1,770	0	200	0	0	0		0	0	0	0
Margarine	½ cup	16	815	1	92	1	23	0	3,750				0
Salad dressing, French, regular	1 tbsp.	39	65	T	6	3	2	.1					
Salad dressing, mayonnaise	1 tbsp.	15	100	T	11	T	3	.1	40	T	.01	T	
Salad dressing, 1,000 island	1 tbsp.	32	80	T	8	3	2	.1	50	T	T	T	T
Sugars, Sweets													
Candy, milk chocolate, sweetened.	1 oz.	1	145	2	9	16	65	.3	80	.01	.10	.1	T
Candy, plain fudge	1 oz.	8	115	1	4	21	22	.3	T	.01	.03	.1	T
Chocolate syrup, fudge type	1 oz.	25	125	2	5	20	48	.5	60	.02	.08	.2	T
Honey, strained or extracted	1 tbsp.	17	65	T	0	17	1	.1	0	T	.01	.1	T
Jellies	1 tbsp.	29	50	T	T	13	4	.3	T	0	T	T	1
Sugar, brown	1 cup	2	820	0	0	212	187	7.5	0	.02	.07	4	0
Sugar, granulated	1 cup	T	770	0	0	199	0	.2	0	0	0	0	0
Miscellaneous													
Barbecue sauce	1 cup	81	230	4	17	20	53	2.0	900	.03	.03	.8	13
Beer	12 oz.	92	150	1	0	14	18	T		.01	.11	2.2	
Alcoholic beverage, 86-proof.	1½ fl. oz.	64	105			T							
Cola-type beverage	12 fl. oz.	90	145	0	0	37			0	0	0	0	0
Ginger ale	12 fl. oz.	92	115	0	0	29			0	0	0	0	0
Soup, cream of chicken	1 cup	85	180	7	10	15	172	.5	610	.05	.27	.7	2
Soup, tomato	1 cup	84	175	7	7	23	168	.8	1,200	.10	.25	1.3	15
Beans with pork	1 cup	84	170	8	6	22	63	2.3	650	.13	.08	1.0	3
Clam chowder	1 cup	92	80	2	3	12	34	1.0	880	.02	.02	1.0	

T indicates a trace.

Giant Trees of the United States

Source: The American Forestry Association

There are approximately 1,180 different species of trees native to the continental U.S., including a few imports that have become naturalized to the extent of reproducing themselves in the wild state.

The oldest living trees in the world are reputed to be the bristlecone pines, the majority of which are found growing on the arid crags of California's White Mts. Some of them are estimated to be more than 4,600 years old. The largest known bristlecone pine is the "Patriarch," believed to be 1,500 years old. The oldest known redwoods are about 3,500 years old.

Recognition as the National Champion of each species is determined by total mass of each tree, based on this formula: the circumference in inches as measured at a point 4 1/2 feet above the ground plus the total height of the tree, plus 1/4 of the average crown spread in feet. In case of a tie the Champion is determined on the basis of circumference. It is not possible, due to lack of space, to list all the 865 trees registered with the American Forestry Assn.

(Figure in parentheses is last year tree was reported)

Species	Height (Ft.)	Location
Acacia, Koa (1969)	140	Kau, Ha.
Ailanthus, Tree-of-Heaven (1972)	60	Long Island, N.Y.
Alder, European (1974)	68	Princeton, Ill.
Apple, Southern Crab (1976)	46	Williamsburg, Va.
Ash, Blue (1972)	86	Danville, Ky.
Aspen, Bigtooth (1963)	95	Walker, N.Y.
Bald Cypress, Common (1954)	122	nr. Sharon, Tenn.
Basswood, American (1971)	115	Grand Traverse Cty., Mich.
Bayberry, Pacific (1972)	38	Siuslaw Natl. Forest, Ore.
Beech, American (1976)	161	Three Oaks, Mich.
Birch, River (1974)	95	Cumberland For., Va.
Blackbead, Catclaw (1976)	88	Sarasota, Fla.
Blackhaw, Rusty (1961)	25	nr. Washington, Ark.
Bladdernut, American (1972)	36	nr. Utica, Mich.
Boxelder (1976)	110	Adrian, Mich.
Buckeye, Painted (1972)	144	Union County, Ga.
Buckthorn, Cascara (1975)	35	North Bend, Ore.
Buckwheat tree (1967)	30	nr. Crooked Creek, Fla.
Buffaloberry, Silver (1975)	22	Malheur Co., Ore.
Bumelia, Gum (1972)	52	nr. Fairfield, Tex.
Butternut (1968)	100	Portland, Ore.
Buttonbush, Common (1976)	29	Oakland Co., Mich.
Button-Mangrove (1974)	52	Palm Beach, Fla.
Cajeput (1975)	66	Sarasota, Fla.
Camphor-tree (1974)	65	Mulberry, Fla.
Casuarina, Horsetail (1968)	89	Olowalo, Maui, Ha.
Catalpa, Northern (1972)	94	Lansing, Mich.
Cedar, Port-Orford (1972)	219	Siskiyou Natl. Forest, Ore.
Cercocarpus, Birchleaf (1972)	34	Central Point, Ore.
Cherry, Black (1972)	114	Lawrence, Mich.
Chestnut, American (1972)	78	Oregon City, Ore.
Chinaberry (1967)	75	Kaohe, S. Kona, Ha.
Chinkapin, Golden (1954)	127	nr. Annapolis, Cal.
Chokecherry, Common (1972)	66	Ada, Mich.
Coconut (1968)	94	Hilo, Ha.
Coffeetree, Kentucky (1976)	110	Van Buren Co., Mich.
Cottonwood, Black (1969)	147	Unionville, Ore.
Cypress, Monterey (1975)	97	Brookings, Ore.
Dahoon (1975)	72	Osceola For., Fla.
Desertwillow (1972)	40	Gila Natl. Forest, N.M.
Devil's-walkingstick (1976)	51	San Felasco Hammock, Fla.
Devilwood (1972)	37	Mayo, Fla.
Dogwood, Pacific (1975)	50	nr. Clatskanie, Ore.
Douglas Fir (1975)	302	Coos Bay, Ore.
Doveplum (1965)	45	Miami, Fla.
Elder, Blackbead (1954)	30	nr. Prescott, Ore.
Elm, American (1974)	92	White Creek, N.Y.
False-Mastic (1975)	70	Lignumvitae Key, Fla.
Fig, Florida Strangler (1973)	80	Old Cutler Hammock, Fla.
Fir, Noble (1972)	278	Gifford Pinchot Natl. Forest, Wash.
Franklinia (1973)	38	McLean, Va.
Grapefruit (1972)	38	Ellenton, Fla.
Gumbo-limbo (1973)	50	Homestead, Fla.
Hackberry, Common (1972)	118	Wayland, Mich.
Hawthorn (1967)	50	Glenview, Ill.
Hemlock, Western (1972)	163	Olympic Natl. Pk., Wash.
Hercules-club (1961)	38	Little Rock, Ark.
Hickory, Pignut (1972)	146	nr. Brunswick, Ga.
Holly, Tawnyberry (1973)	55	Homestead, Fla.
Honeylocust,		
Thornless (1976)	130	Washtenaw Co., Mich.
Hophornbeam, Eastern (1972)	78	nr. Winthrop, Me.
Hoptree, Common (1972)	31	Ada, Mich.
Hornbeam, American (1975)	65	Milton, N.Y.
Joshua-tree (1967)	32	San Bernardino Natl. Forest, Cal.
Juniper, Western (1954)	87	Stanislaus Natl. Forest, Cal.
Larch, Western (1972)	177	nr. Kootenai Natl. Forest, Mont.
Laurelcherry, Carolina (1972)	44	Dellwood, Fla.
Lebbek (1968)	65	Lahina, Maui, Ha.
Loblolly-Bay (1972)	84	Hugh's Island, Fla.
Locust, Black (1974)	96	Dansville, N.Y.
Lysiloma, Bahama (1973)	79	Homestead, Fla.
Madrone, Pacific (1955)	80	Humboldt Co., Cal.
Magnolia, Cucumber tree (1974)	92	Bel Air, Md.
Mangrove, Red (1973)	60	North Miami, Fla.
Maple, Red (1972)	125	nr. Armada, Mich.
Mesquite, Velvet (1972)	55	Coronado Natl. Forest, Ariz.
Mountain-Ash, Showy (1972)	58	nr. Gould City, Mich.
Mountain-Laurel (1972)	20	Chattahoochee Natl. Forest, Ga.
Mulberry, White (1976)	82	Battle Creek, Mich.
Oak, California white (1967)	120	nr. Gridley, Cal.
Oleander, Common (1963)	22	Phoenix, Ariz.
Osage-Orange (1972)	51	Charlotte Co., Va.
Palmetto, Cabbage (1972)	90	Highlands Hammock State Pk., Fla.
Paloverde, Blue (1967)	52	Ajo, Ariz.
Paulownia, Royal (1969)	105	Philadelphia Co., Pa.
Pawpaw, Blue (1972)	41	nr. Smith Mills, Ky.
Pear (1976)	57	Clawson, Mich.
(1972)	74	Leslie Co., Ky.
Pecan (1973)	124	Mer Rouge, La.
Peppertree (1972)	47	San Juan Capistrano, Cal.
Pinckneya (1972)	21	nr. Mt. Pleasant, Fla.
Pine, Ponderosa (1974)	223	Plumas, Cal.
Plum, American (1972)	35	Oakland Co., Mich.
Poison Sumac (1972)	20	Robin's Island, N.Y.
Pondcypress (1972)	135	nr. Newton, Ga.
Poplar, Balsam (1976)	128	Champion, Mich.
Possumhaw (1976)	30	Congaree Swamp, S.C.
Redbay (1972)	58	Randolph Co., Ga.
Redwood, Coast (1972)	362	Humboldt Redwoods State Park, Cal.
Royalpalm, Florida (1973)	80	Homestead, Fla.
Sassafras (1972)	100	Owensboro, Ky.
Seagrape (1972)	57	Miami, Fla.
Sequoia, Giant (1961)	272	Sequoia Natl. Pk., Cal.
Serviceberry, Downy (1975)	50	New Philadelphia, Oh.
Silk-oak (1972)	78	nr. La Belle, Fla.
Silktree (1971)	41	Gilmer, Tex.
Silverbell, Two-wing (1971)	55	Tallahassee, Fla.
Smoketree, American (1974)	47	Lewiston, Ida.
Soapberry, Western (1972)	67	Newton County, Tex.
Sourwood (1972)	118	nr. Robbinsville, N.C.
Sparkleberry Tree (1972)	29	Keltys, Tex.
Spruce, Sitka (1973)	216	Seaside, Ore.

(Continued)

Species	Height (Ft.)	Location	Species	Height (Ft.)	Location
Sugarberry (1974)	133	Darlington Co., S.C.	(1971)	139	nr. Houston, Tex.
Sumac, Shining (1974)	55	Grenada Co., Miss.	Wahoo, Eastern (1974)	20	Warrensburg, Mo.
Sweetleaf, Common (1972)	55	Tallahassee, Fla.	Walnut, Cal. (1973)	116	Santa Rosa, Cal.
Sycamore, Cal. (1945)	116	nr. Santa Barbara, Cal.	Willow, Crack (1972)	112	nr. Utica, Mich.
Tamarack (1972)	95	Jay, Me.	Winterberry, Common (1971)	40	Wildwood, Fla.
Tamarisk, Five-Stamen (1972)	37	Albuquerque, N.M.	Witch-Hazel, Common (1976)	43	Muskegon, Mich.
Tanoak (1969)	100	Kneeland, Cal.	Yaupon (1972)	45	nr. Devers, Tex.
Tesota (1972)	31.6	nr. Quartzsite, Ariz.	Yellow-Poplar (1972)	124	Bedford, Va.
Torreya, Cal. (1945)	141	nr. Mendocino, Cal.	Yellowwood (1967)	58	Morrisville, Pa.
Trifoliate-Orange (1968)	26	Harrisburg, Pa.	Yew, Pacific (1959)	60	nr. Mineral, Wash.
Tupelo, Black (1969)	117	Harrison Co., Tex.	Yucca, Aloe (1975)	29	Ormond By The Sea, Fla.

The 1974-1975 Wildfire Season

Source: Forest Service, U.S. Dept. of Agriculture
Federal, State and Private Protected Area

In 1975 two of the Nation's major forest fires were on the Angeles National Forest, California. They spread out of control for 8 days, damaging some 69,-000 acres of watershed and damaging or destroying over 40 structures.

Over 96 percent of all fires were controlled at 10 acres or less in size on the 201 million acres of Forest Service protected lands. Less than one percent were large fires burning over 300 acres. Forest fires burned .66 acres for each 1,000 acres protected.

All fires decreased 20 percent over previous years. However, 10,804 fires burned only 133,198 acres. Aggressive prevention measures followed by hard-hitting attack forces reduced the potential for major conflagrations on national forests.

On all Federal, State and private forest and nonforested watershed lands during 1975, a total of 134,872 fires were reported, a decrease of 10,996 below the 145,868 reported during 1974. However, acreage burned on all lands totaled 1,791,327 — a decrease of 1,087,768 below the 2,879,095 burned during 1974.

Through carelessness or incendiarism, man is blamed for the largest portion of wildfires. During 1975 some 93,936 or 91 percent of the 103,298 reported as having burned on protected land were man-caused. Lightning-started fires amounted to 9,362 or 9 percent of the protected area fires. Causes of the 31,574 fires which occurred on unprotected lands are not known.

More than 726,356,000 acres of State and private forest and nonforested watershed lands are protected under the Federal-State cooperative Forest Fire Control Program. Since the area qualifying for protection under the program is 797,204,000 acres, the goal of the program is to bring protection to the more than 70,848,000 acres not now receiving protection. All States participate in the cooperative forest fire protection effort. The record on State and private protected lands for 1975 follows:

Group	Number of Fires	Acres Burned
Rocky Mountain	9,827	187,150
Pacific	13,993	150,727
North Central	7,591	102,356
Southern	45,297	632,168
Eastern	17,296	47,026
Total	91,026	1,119,427

The record on State and private unprotected lands is:

Group	Number of Fires	Acres Burned
Rocky Mountain	170	1,655
Pacific	1,500	no data
North Central	3,000	60,000
Southern	2,904	147,561
Eastern	24,000	no data
Total	31,574	264,016

Total Fires and Acres Burned — National Forest Protection

Calendar Year	Lightning	Man Caused	Total	Acres Burned	Calendar Year	Lightning	Man Caused	Total	Acres Burned
1970	7,804	7,172	14,976	519,978	1974	6,601	6,937	13,538	208,721
1971	5,876	6,363	12,239	171,867	1975	4,891	5,913	10,804	133,198
1972	8,406	5,748	14,154	116,703	Average				
1973	6,376	6,048	12,424	168,692	1970-75	7,013	6,454	13,467	237,192

National Forest Areas

Source: Forest Service, Dept. of Agriculture.
(In Acres) Data as of June 30, 1975

States	Area	States	Area	States	Area	States	Area
Alabama	638,900	Kansas	107,906	N. Hampshire	683,637	Tennessee	619,219
Alaska	20,715,489	Kentucky	647,994	N. Mexico	9,219,378	Texas	780,135
Arizona	11,271,618	Louisiana	595,589	New York	13,232	Utah	8,047,568
Arkansas	2,462,548	Maine	50,103	N. Carolina	1,143,637	Vermont	254,025
California	20,234,337	Michigan	2,697,677	N. Dakota	1,105,585	Virgin Islands	147
Colorado	14,364,726	Minnesota	2,808,975	Ohio	163,817	Virginia	1,598,561
Connecticut	10	Mississippi	1,137,245	Oklahoma	290,849	Washington	9,071,424
Florida	1,082,173	Missouri	1,452,138	Oregon	15,577,825	W. Virginia	958,049
Georgia	855,134	Montana	16,731,092	Pennsylvania	506,211	Wisconsin	1,491,765
Idaho	20,375,388	Nebraska	351,509	Puerto Rico	27,846	Wyoming	9,251,127
Illinois	254,167	Nevada	5,112,567	S. Carolina	607,020	Total	
Indiana	178,553			S. Dakota	1,994,711	Acreage	187,531,606

National Forest System

Administered by the Forest Service, U. S. Dept. of Agriculture, the National Forest System is made up of 155 national forests, 19 national grasslands, 17 land utilization projects, and other minor acreages which total 187,101,120 acres in 44 states, Puerto Rico, and the Virgin Islands. All lands within the National Forest System are managed under two guiding principles; multiple use — the management of lands to make each area yield the combination of uses best suited to public needs; and sustained yield — maintenance of a continuous supply of all forest resources through wise use, management, and protection.

National forest lands which supply water for agriculture, industry, recreation, and domestic use, for example, also are managed to prevent erosion and help control floods, yet there also may be camping, skiing, and timber harvesting on the same land.

The scenic beauty and recreation opportunities available on national forests yearly draw millions of Americans to these lands to hunt, fish, camp, picnic, boat, recreational play, swim, hike, ski, and to make pack trips into the wilderness. Use reached 192,915,800 visitor days during calendar year 1974.

Giant Trees of Canada

Source: Native Trees of Canada by R. C. Hosie

(Canadian Forestry Service, Dept. of Fisheries & Forestry)

There are nearly 140 species of trees native to Canada on which information is easily available. A "native" tree is defined as a single-stemmed perennial woody plant growing to a height of more than 10 feet, and which is indigenous to Canada. Most of the "giant" trees in Canada are to be found in the forest regions. These regions reflect differences caused by terrain, soil, and climate. The 9 forest regions are: The Grassland, Boreal, Great Lakes-St. Lawrence, Columbia, Deciduous, Coast, Subalpine, Acadian, and Montane.

It is difficult to obtain precise records of single trees of outstanding heights. Given below are several common species of trees native to Canada showing the usual or normal height of the species. But many exceptions have been noted. For example, the Douglas Fir, whose average range in height is given at 150 to 200 ft. with diameters of up to 9 ft., occasionally may attain heights above 300 ft. and diameters of 15 ft. or more. The Sitka Spruce is also known to have reached heights of at least 280 ft., and the Western White Pine is recorded as having attained 200 ft.

Species	Height (Ft.)	Forest Region
Alpine Fir	65-100	Subalpine; N.W. Boreal
Amabilis Fir	80-125	Coast & coastal parts of Subalpine
Balsam Poplar	60-80	Boreal, Great Lakes-St. Lawrence & Acadian
Black Cottonwood	80-125	Throughout B.C. and western Alberta
Black Maple	80-90	Ontario to Montreal Is.
Douglas Fir	150-200	Coast
Eastern Cottonwood	75-100	Gt. Lakes-St. Lawrence
Eastern White Pine	100-175	Through east Canada
Engelmann Spruce	100-120	Southern Subalpine
Grand Fir	100-125	S. Coast & Columbia
Mockernut Hickory	75-90	Deciduous
Silver Maple	80-90	S.E. parts of G. Lakes-St. Lawrence

Species	Height (Ft.)	Forest Region
Sitka Spruce	125-175	Coast
Sugar Maple	80-90	Gt. Lakes-St. Lawrence
Sycamore	Up to 150	Deciduous
Western Hemlock	120-160	Coast & Columbia
Western Larch	100-180	Southern part of Columbia & Montane, B.C.
Western Red Cedar	150-200	Coast & Columbia
Western White Pine	90-110	S. Coast & Columbia
White Birch	Med.-80	Throughout Canada
White Elm	60-80	G. Lakes-St. Lawrence & Acadian
White Oak	Med.-100	Southern Ontario
White Spruce	80-120	Boreal
Yellow Cypress	60-80	Coast & in coastal parts of Subalpine

The 1973 Forest Fire Season in Canada

Source: Environment Canada (Canadian Forestry Service)

Forest fire activity in 1973 was mainly concentrated in western Canada. British Columbia experienced by far the busiest fire season of any region with some 2,862 fires reported in that province alone (37% of the national total) and the Northwest Territories accounted for 2,114,595 acres or 72% of the total area burned in Canada.

However, for the second consecutive year, the total number of forest fires reported in Canada was substantially below the near record established in 1971. Indeed, there were 7,605 fire starts in 1973, compared with 8,263 in 1972 and 9,205 the previous year.

Over the years, whether through negligence or

incendiarism, man has generally been blamed for the largest portion of wildland fires. This remained true in 1973, with 5,524 or 73% of all fires in Canada being of human origin. It must be pointed out, however, that man-caused fires in 1973 only accounted for 141,525 acres or less than 5% of the total area burned. Lightning — the only unpreventable cause of forest fires — was responsible for 27% of the fires but accounted for 2,785,185 acres burned or an increase of one million acres over the previous 5-year average.

The total area afforded some form of organized protection in 1973 amounted to approximately 1,689,-000 square miles.

Forest Fires on Provincial and Federal Protected Lands, 1973

Provincial Lands	No. of Fires	Acres Burned
Newfoundland	102	21,704
Nova Scotia	457	5,884
Prince Edward Island	40	387
New Brunswick	299	889
Quebec	506	7,492
Ontario	1,111	8,913
Manitoba	615	57,784
Saskatchewan	432	589,611
Alberta	478	26,418
British Columbia	2,862	82,508
Federal Lands		
Yukon	109	3,588
Northwest Territories	492	2,114,595
National Parks	90	6,899
Other Federal Lands	12	38
Total all lands	7,605	2,926,710

Total Fires and Acres Burned, by Causes

Year	Man-Caused No. of Fires	Man-Caused Acres Burned	Lightning No. of Fires	Lightning Acres Burned	Year	Man-Caused No. of Fires	Man-Caused Acres Burned	Lightning No. of Fires	Lightning Acres Burned
1968	5,917	1,904,476	1,384	307,129	1972	5,739	716,932	2,524	1,211,000
1969	5,003	809,063	1,658	1,522,641	Average				
1970	6,014	400,447	3,299	2,217,690	'68-'72	5,792	906,179	2,357	1,741,479
1971	6,287	699,978	2,918	3,448,933	1973	5,524	141,525	2,081	2,785,185

Environment

Controlling Pollution
Federal Outlays Rise

The federal government spent nearly $7 billion on protecting the environment and controlling pollution in 1976, an increase of $500 million over 1975. Private nonfarm businesses spent a further $6.5 billion in 1975 for environmental capital investments alone, much of it in response to federal law.

These programs have begun to pay dividends. The pace of environmental decay has slowed, according to various indices. Some forms of pollution have even been reduced, as can be seen in the table below, "Nationwide Air Pollution Emissions."

Federal costs fell into three categories: understanding, describing and predicting the environment, $1,309 billion; protection and enhancement activities, $1,069 billion; pollution control and abatement (excluding construction grants), $2.102 billion; Construction grants for control and abatement came to $2.440 billion (mostly for water systems).

Inflation and more thorough research have driven up future cost estimates. Pollution control itself causes some inflation by adding to the cost of producing goods, but the Environmental Protection Agency (EPA) says this factor will increase prices by only 0.3% to 0.5% a year. Even so, total costs should be well within the reach of government and industry, given a productive economy.

These enormous environmental outlays are expected to yield financial returns on an equal or greater scale, apart from immeasurable benefits to physical and esthetic well-being. The President's Council on Environmental Quality estimates that by 1977, air pollution alone would be causing nearly $25 billion a year in damages to health, residential property, materials and vegetation, if no controls were enforced. Water pollution already takes a toll of over $12 billion a year, according to the EPA.

These figures do not include the benefits of an improved environment to property values, commercial fishing and recreation. In addition, billions would be saved in avoidance costs—those that people incur when they try to avoid or reduce damages, for instance, by traveling to more distant resorts to avoid polluted beaches.

Apart from financial considerations, it has been estimated by the National Academy of Sciences that 15,000 Americans die each year as a result of air pollution, while 7 million days are spent in bed by people whose chronic illnesses were aggravated by air pollution.

In sum, the balance sheet of costs and benefits of a vigorous program of environmental enhancement still points to a strong net gain.

Estimated Total Pollution Control Expenditures
(in billions of 1974 dollars)   Source: Council on Environmental Quality
Does not include land reclamation, or research, conservation, and enhancement programs.

Pollutant/ medium	1974			1983			Cumulative—1974-83		
	O&M[1]	Capital costs[2]	Total annual costs[3]	O&M[1]	Capital costs[2]	Total annual costs[3]	O&M[1]	Capital costs[2]	Total costs[3]
Air pollution									
Public	0.1	0.1	0.2	0.6	0.2	0.8	4.2	1.8	6.0
Private									
Mobile	4.1	1.0	5.1	2.7	6.1	8.8	32.7	37.5	70.2
Industrial	1.0	0.8	1.8	4.6	3.8	8.4	30.4	25.2	55.6
Utilities	0.6	0.4	1.0	3.4	2.5	5.9	19.7	14.6	34.3
Total	5.8	2.3	8.1	11.3	12.6	23.9	87.0	79.1	166.1
Water pollution									
Public									
Federal	0.2	0.05	0.2	0.2	0.05	0.2	2.0	0.3	2.3
State and local	1.6	5.6	7.2	3.2	9.4	12.6	19.4	78.4	97.8
Private									
Industrial	1.3	1.0	2.3	6.7	4.5	11.2	33.5	23.6	57.1
Utilities	0.1	0.1	0.2	0.7	0.6	1.3	4.4	3.7	8.1
Total	3.2	6.7	9.9	10.8	14.5	25.3	59.3	106.0	165.3
Radiation									
Nuclear powerplants	NA	NA	NA	0.02	0.03	0.05	0.1	0.1	0.2
Solid waste									
Public	1.2	0.3	1.5	2.1	0.6	2.7	17.1	4.2	21.3
Private	2.1	0.05	2.1	3.3	0.1	3.4	27.7	0.4	28.1
Total	3.3	0.3	3.6	5.4	0.7	6.1	44.8	4.6	49.4
Noise	NA	NA	NA	NA	NA	NA	NA	NA	NA
Grand total	12.3	9.3	21.6	27.5	27.8	55.3	191.2	189.8	381.0

(1) Operating and maintenance costs. (2) Interest and depreciation. (3) O&M plus capital costs. (NA) Not available.

Nationwide Air Pollution Emissions
Source: Environmental Protection Agency
Estimates. In millions of tons per year.

Pollutants and sources	1970	1971	1972	1973	1974
Particulates					
Transportation[1]	1.2	1.2	1.3	1.3	1.3
Fuel combustion, stationary	8.3	7.5	7.1	6.4	5.9
Industrial processes[2]	15.7	14.5	13.1	11.9	11.0
Solid waste disposal	1.1	0.8	0.7	0.6	0.5

Pollutants and sources	1970	1971	1972	1973	1974
Miscellaneous[3]	1.2	1.2	1.0	0.8	0.8
Total	27.5	25.2	23.2	21.0	19.5
Sulfur oxides					
Transportation[1]	0.7	0.7	0.7	0.8	0.8

Continued

Pollutants and sources	1970	1971	1972	1973	1974
Fuel combustion, stationary	27.0	26.7	25.2	25.6	24.3
Industrial processes[2]	6.4	6.0	6.6	6.7	6.2
Solid waste disposal	0.1	0.0	0.0	0.0	0.0
Miscellaneous[3]	0.1	0.1	0.1	0.1	0.1
Total	34.3	33.5	32.6	33.2	31.4
Carbon monoxide					
Transportation[1]	82.3	80.9	83.4	79.3	73.5
Fuel combustion, stationary	1.1	1.0	1.0	1.0	0.9
Industrial processes[2]	11.8	11.6	12.0	13.0	12.7
Solid waste disposal	5.5	3.9	3.2	2.8	2.4
Miscellaneous[3]	6.6	7.5	5.3	4.8	5.1
Total	107.3	104.9	104.9	100.9	94.6

Pollutants and sources	1970	1971	1972	1973	1974
Hydrocarbons					
Transportation[1]	14.7	14.3	14.1	13.7	12.8
Fuel combustion, stationary	1.6	1.7	1.7	1.7	1.7
Industrial processes[2]	2.9	2.7	2.9	3.1	3.1
Solid waste disposal	1.4	1.0	0.8	0.7	0.6
Miscellaneous[3]	11.5	11.7	11.8	12.1	12.2
Total	32.1	31.4	31.3	31.3	30.4
Nitrogen oxides					
Transportation[1]	9.3	9.8	10.5	11.0	10.7
Fuel combustion, stationary	10.1	10.1	10.8	11.2	11.0
Industrial processes[2]	0.6	0.6	0.6	0.6	0.6
Solid waste disposal	0.3	0.2	0.2	0.1	0.1
Miscellaneous[3]	0.1	0.1	0.1	0.1	0.1
Total	20.4	20.8	22.2	23.0	22.5

(1) Motor vehicles, aircraft, railroads, vessels, and agricultural, industrial, and construction machinery. (2) Emissions for over 80 industrial processes/products were computed, including all major operations known to emit more than 10,000-20,000 tons per year nationally. (3) Including forest fires, coal refuse burning, organic solvents, oil and gasoline production, and other sources.

Total National Pollution Control Expenditures, 1972

(in millions of dollars) **Source:** U.S. Department of Commerce

Preliminary figures. Details may not add to totals due to rounding. Totals do not include spending in agriculture, real estate, or in medical, legal, educational, and cultural activities. Includes capital and operational costs.

	Total	Air	Water	Solid waste	Other and unallo-cated[1]
1 Natl. expend. for abatement and control (2,16,-19)	18,738	6,537	8,590	2,718	893
2 Abatement (3,6,12)	16,802	6,279	8,365	2,691	—533
3 Personal consumption (4,5)	1,922	1,922	—	—	—
4 Durable goods	477	477	—	—	—
5 Nondurable goods, services	1,445	1,445	—	—	—
6 Business (7,8)[2]	8,999	4,233	4,244	1,059	—536
7 Capital account	4,982	2,426	2,411	145	—
8 Current account (9,10,11)	4,017	1,806	1,833	914	—536
9 Private	3,370	1,716	726	914	14
10 Gov. enterprise	1,198	91	1,107	—	—
11 Costs recovered	—550	—	—	—	—550

	Total	Air	Water	Solid waste	
12 Government (13,14,15)	5,880	124	4,121	1,632	3
13 Federal	452	45	401	4	3
14 State and local	1,880	—	252	1,628	1
15 Government enterprise purchases of fixed capital	3,547	80	3,468	—	—
16 Regulation and monitoring (17,18)	351	139	133	13	67
17 Federal	201	48	79	9	65
18 State and local	150	91	55	3	2
19 Research and devel. (20,21,22)	1,585	119	92	15	1,359
20 Private	1,279	—	—	—	1,279
21 Federal	208	114	34	5	55
22 State and local	98	5	58	9	25

(1) Other includes noise, radiation, and pesticide control. 'Unallocated' includes business expenditures for air, water, and solid waste pollution control not assigned to media. (2) Business includes current account spending by government enterprises and all spending by homeowners.

Gestation, Longevity, and Incubation of Animals

Longevity figures were supplied by Ronald T. Reuther, of the Zoological Society of Philadelphia. They refer to animals in captivity; the potential life span of animals is rarely attained in nature. Maximum longevity figures are from the Biology Data Book, 1972. Figures on gestation and incubation are averages based on estimates by leading authorities.

Animal	Gestation (Days)	Average Longevity (Years)	Maximum Longevity (Yrs., mos.)
Ass	365	12	35-10
Baboon	187	20	35-7
Badger	60	12	23-8
Bat	50	6	24
Bear			
Black	219	18	36-10
Grizzly	225	25	—
Polar	240	20	34-8
Beaver	122	5	20-6
Buffalo (African)	—	15	26-6
Buffalo (American)	278	15	—
Arabian Camel	406	12	28-4
Bactrian Camel	406	12	29-5
Cat (domestic)	63	12	28
Chimpanzee	231	20	44-6
Chipmunk	31	6	8
Cow	284	15	30
Deer (white-tailed)	201	8	17-6
Dog (domestic)	61	12	20
Elephant (African)	—	35	60
Elephant (Asian)	645	40	70
Elk	250	15	26-6
Fox (red)	52	7	14
Giraffe	425	10	33-7
Goat (domestic)	151	8	18
Gorilla	257	20	39-4
Guinea pig	68	4	7-6
Hippopotamus	238	25	—
Horse	330	20	46
Kangaroo	42	7	—
Leopard	98	12	19-4
Lion	100	15	25-1
Monkey (rhesus)	164	15	—
Moose	240	12	—
Mouse (meadow)	21	3	—
Mouse (dom. white)	19	3	3-6
Opossum (American)	14-17	1	—
Pig (domestic)	112	10	27
Puma	90	12	19
Rabbit (domestic)	37	5	13
Rhinocerous (black)	450	15	—
Rhinocerous (white)	—	20	—
Sea Lion (California)	350	12	28
Sheep (domestic)	154	12	20
Squirrel (gray)	44	10	—
Tiger	105	16	26-3
Wolf (maned)	63	5	—
Zebra (Grant's)	365	15	—

	Incubation Time (Days)
Chicken	21
Duck	30
Goose	30
Pigeon	18
Turkey	26

Speeds of Animals

Source: *Natural History* Magazine, March 1974.
Copyright© The American Museum of Natural History, 1974.

Animals	Speeds in mph	Animals	Speeds in mph	Animals	Speeds in mph
Cheetah	70	Mongolian wild ass	40	Human	27.89
Proghorn antelope	61	Greyhound	39.35	Elephant	25
Wildebeest	50	Whippet	35.50	Black mamba snake	20
Lion	50	Rabbit (domestic)	35	Six-lined race runner	18
Thomson's gazelle	50	Mule Deer	35	Wild Turkey	15
Quarter horse	47.5	Jackal	35	Squirrel	12
Elk	45	Reindeer	32	Pig (domestic)	11
Cape hunting dog	45	Giraffe	32	Chicken	9
Coyote	43	White-tailed deer	30	Spider (Tegenaria atrica)	1.17
Gray fox	42	Wart hog	30	Giant tortoise	0.17
Hyena	40	Grizzly bear	30	Three-toed sloth	0.15
Zebra	40	Cat (domestic)	30	Garden snail	0.03

Most of these measurements are for maximum speeds over approximate quarter-mile distances. Exceptions — which are included to give a wide range of animals — are the lion and elephant, whose speeds were clocked in the act of charging; the whippet, which was timed over a 200-yard course; the cheetah over a 100-yard distance; man for a 15-yard segment of a 100-yard run (of 13.6 seconds); and the black mamba, six-lined race runner, spider, giant tortoise, three-toed sloth, and garden snail, which were measured over various small distances.

A Collection of Animal Collectives

The English language boasts an abundance of nouns used to describe groups of things, particularly pairs or aggregations of animals. Some of these words have fallen into comparative disuse, but many of them are still in service, helping to enrich the vocabularies of those who like their language to be precise, who tire of hearing a group referred to as "a bunch of," or who simply don't want their ears overworked.

Here is a lexicon of some of these "collectives":

band of gorillas
bed of clams, oysters
bevy of quail, swans
brace of ducks
brood of chicks
cast of hawks
cete of badgers
charm of goldfinches
chattering of choughs
cloud of gnats
clowder of cats
clutch of chicks
clutter of cats
colony of ants
congregation of plovers
covert of coots
covey of quail, partridge

cry of hounds
down of hares
draught of fish
drift of swine
drove of cattle, sheep
exaltation of larks
flight of birds
flock of sheep, geese
gaggle of geese
gam of whales
gang of elks
grist of bees
herd of curlews, elephants
hive of bees
horde of gnats
husk of hares

kindle or **kendle** of kittens
knot of toads
leap of leopards
leash of greyhounds, foxes
litter of pigs
mob of kangaroos
murder of crows
muster of peacocks
mute of hounds
nest of vipers
nest, nide of pheasants
pack of hounds, wolves
pair of horses
pod of whales, seals
pride of lions
school of fish
sedge or **siege** of cranes

shoal of fish, pilchards
skein of geese
skulk of foxes
sleuth of bears
sounder of boars, swine
span of mules
spring of teals
swarm of bees
team of ducks, horses
tribe of goats
trip of goats
troop of kangaroos, monkeys
volery of birds
watch of nightingales
wing of plovers
yoke of oxen

Young of Animals Have Special Names

The young of many animals, birds and fish have come to be called by special names. A young eel, for example, is an elver. Many young animals, of course, are often referred to simply as infants or babies. Some of the more distinctive names. and the animals, fish, or birds of which these young are the offspring, follow.

bunny: rabbit.
calf: cattle, elephant, antelope, rhino, hippo, whale, etc.
cheeper: grouse, partridge, quail.
chick, chicken: fowl.
cockerel: rooster.
codling, sprag: codfish.
colt: horse (male).
cub: lion, bear, shark, fox, etc.
cygnet: swan.
duckling: duck.
eaglet: eagle.
elver: eel.
eyas: hawk, others.
fawn: deer.

filly: horse (female).
fingerling: fish generally.
flapper: wild fowl.
fledgling: birds generally.
foal: horse, zebra, others.
fry: fish generally.
gosling: goose.
heifer: cow.
joey: kangaroo, others.
kid: goat.
kit: fox, beaver, rabbit, cat.
kitten, kitty, catling: cats, other fur-bearers.
lamb, lambkin, cosset, hog: sheep.
leveret: hare.
nestling: birds generally.

owlet: owl.
parr, smolt, grilse: salmon.
piglet, shoat, farrow, suckling: pig.
polliwog, tadpole: frog.
poult: turkey.
pullet: hen.
pup: dog, seal, sea lion, fox.
puss, pussy: cat.
spike, blinker, tinker: mackerel.
squab: pigeon.
squeaker: pigeon, others.
whelp: dog, tiger, beasts of prey.
yearling: cattle, sheep, horse, etc.
younglet, youngling: animals generally.

Some Endangered Species in North America

Source: U.S. Fish and Wildlife Service

Common Name	Scientific Name	Range
Mammals		
Wood Bison	Bison bison athabascae	Alberta, Canada
Black-Footed Ferret	Mustela nigripes	U.S., Canada
Northern Kit Fox	Vulpus velox hebes	Canada

West Indian (Florida) Manatee	Trichechus inunguis	Caribbean (once U.S.)
Sonoran Pronghorn	Antilocapra americana sonoriensis	U.S., Mexico
Eastern Timber Wolf	Canis lupus lycaon	(endangered in U.S. only)
Northern Rocky Mountain Wolf	Canis lupus irremotus	U.S., Canada
Red Wolf	Canis rufus	U.S.
Eastern Cougar	Felis concolor cougar	U.S., Canada

Birds

Bald Eagle	Haliaetus leucocephalus	(endangered in U.S. only)
Masked Bobwhite	Colinus virginianus ridgwayi	U.S., Mexico
California Condor	Gymnogyps californianus	Southern California
Whooping Crane	Grus americana	Canada, U.S.
Eskimo Curlew	Numenius borealis	Canada to Argentina
American Peregrine Falcon	Falco peregrinus anatum	Canada to Mexico
Arctic Peregrine Falcon	Falco peregrinus tundrius	Canada to Mexico
Aleutian Canada Goose	Branta canadensis leucopareia	U.S. to Japan
Brown Pelican	Pelecanus occidentalis	Canada to Panama
Attwater's Greater Prairie Chicken	Tympanuchus cupido attwateri	U.S.
Bachman's Warbler	Vermivora bachmani	Southeast U.S., Cuba
Kirtland's Warbler	Dendroica kirtlandi	Michigan, Bahamas
Ivory-Billed Woodpecker	Campephilus principalis	Southeast U.S., Cuba

Some Other Endangered Species in the World

Source: U.S. Fish and Wildlife Service

Common Name	Scientific Name	Range
Mammals		
Asiatic Wild Ass	Equus hemionus	Iran to Mongolia
Dugong	Dugong dugon	East Africa to Okinawa
Slender-Horned Gazelle	Gazella leptoceros	North Africa, Arabia
Mountain Gorilla	Gorilla gorilla beringei	Central Africa
Orang Utan	Pongo pygmaeus	Indonesia, Malaysia
Great Indian Rhinoceros	Rhinoceros unicornus	India, Nepal
Javan Rhinoceros	Rhinoceros sondaicus	Indonesia
Sumatran Rhinoceros	Didermocerus sumatrensis	Bangladesh to Vietnam, Indonesia
Northern White Rhinoceros	Ceratotherium simum cottoni	Sudan, Zaire, Uganda
Blue Whale	Balaenoptera musculus musculus	Oceanic
Humpback Whale	Megaptera novaeangliae	Oceanic
Birds		
Great Indian Bustard (largest land bird)	Choriotis nigriceps	India, Pakistan
Japanese Crane	Grus japonicus	Japan (once all north Asia)
Chinese Egret	Egretta eulophotes	China (once all east Asia)
Japanese Crested Ibis	Nipponia nippon	Japan (once all north Asia)

Major Public Zoological Parks In U.S.

Prepared by Ronald T. Reuther, President, Zoological Society of Philadelphia. Figures are for 1975.

Zoo	Budget (Dollars)	Attendance	Major Attractions
San Diego	9,000,000	3,240,000	Bus tours, primate pavillion, walk-through bird cages.
National (Washington, D.C.)	5,600,000	3,750,000E	Giant pandas, flight cage, great Indian rhinocerous.
Bronx	4,270,000+	2,400,000	World of Darkness, World of Birds.
Brookfield (Chicago)	5,148,000	2,000,000	Porpoise show, Tropical World.
San Diego Wild Animal Park	5,000,000	900,000	5 1/2-mile monorail, Nairobi Village.
Los Angeles	4,500,000	1,600,000	Zoogeographic design, Bird World.
St. Louis	3,600,000	2,000,000E	Cat Country, aquatic house.
Detroit	3,266,000	1,600,000	Penguinarium, great ape house.
Philadelphia	3,181,000	1,136,092	Reptile House, African Plains.
Milwaukee	3,127,437	1,139,000	Zoogeographic design, bird house.
San Francisco	2,000,000+	966,117	Great apes, Monkey Island, bears.
Lincoln Park (Chicago)	2,000,000+	4,000,000E	Small mammal house, great ape house, sea lions.
Memphis	1,600,000	550,000	Great ape house, aquarium.
Cincinnati	1,400,000	750,000	Walk-through cat exhibit, great apes, aquarium.
Baltimore	1,300,000	341,352	Pachyderm building, children's zoo.
Portland, Ore.	1,300,000	524,028	Steam train, primates, elephant herd.
Cleveland	1,214,330	510,773	Children's farm, pachyderm building, hoofed animals.
Columbia, S.C.	1,200,000	550,000	Underwater viewing of polar bear.
Pittsburgh	1,125,000+	579,872	Underground zoo, Aquazoo, children's zoo.
San Antonio	1,123,150	804,238	Hoofed animals.
Houston	1,000,000	1,598,796	Small mammals, reptiles, great apes, bird house.
Denver	963,100	920,953	Walk-through bird house, primates, hoofed animals, cat building.
Columbus, O.	870,700	448,153	Reptiles, great apes.
Phoenix	850,000	614,000	Safari train, Arizona wildlife display, children's zoo.
Dallas	737,492	549,424	Bird and reptile house, hoofed animals, primates, pachyderms.

(E) Estimate.

Environmental Quality Index

Source: National Wildlife Federation.
Adapted from the Feb.-Mar., 1976 issue of National Wildlife Magazine.

In 1969, the National Wildlife Federation began to record an index of environmental quality which measures progress or decline in 7 environmental areas. The index represents the rough judgment of environmental protection experts and advocates influenced by very high standards of environmental quality. While their judgment is, in part, subjective and open to dispute, it does provide a relative indication of success and failure in achieving one set of goals.

Wildlife: The continued conversion of over a million acres a year of land from rural to urban use remains the greatest threat to the preservation of wildlife in its present numbers and diversity. The Interior Department expanded its endangered species list to 126 animals; 170 other animals, and thousands of plant species, are under review. But some species are staging recoveries — there are more deer and wild turkeys than ever before in our history; DDT residues in migratory songbirds are down 90% from 1969.

Living Space: Seventeen states passed land use laws in 1975, and 10 others have bills pending. Several seacoast states have developed plans to control coastal development near offshore oil exploration areas. But the federal government has been slow to add new land for parks and wildlife refuges. The birth rate decline has apparently ended.

Soil: Our farmers produced huge bumper crops in 1975 to help meet critical world food needs. In the process, 9 million acres of soil bank reserves, grasslands, and woodlands were ploughed up. One-half of U.S. cropland is now protected against erosion — but 3.5 billion tons of soil are still lost to erosion each year. Single-crop farming, and intensive use of chemical fertilizers and pesticides, pose threats to soil quality.

Timber: The U.S. Forest Service unveiled a proposal last year for a master plan to reconcile timbering, preservation, and recreation on the 92 million acres of federal forestland. More timber is being grown, more land reforested. But debate over the practice of clearcutting continued.

Minerals: The U.S. still lacks a comprehensive energy policy, to conserve and recycle our shrinking resources, safeguard the environment, and develop solar, geothermal, and nuclear fusion energy technologies. Americans still use energy wastefully and fail to recover usable minerals from wastes. With only 5% of the world's population, we use 1/3 of its energy output. But auto makers are switching to gas-efficient small cars; vast new U.S. coal reserves have been confirmed; and Congress has been funding more energy research.

Air: Air quality continued its recent improving trend in 1975. Compared with 1970, when the Clean Air Act was passed, pollution from sulfur dioxide had declined 25%, from carbon monoxide, over 50%, from suspended particulates, 14%. Nearly 80% of major stationary sources of air pollution were either in compliance with emission limits, or on their way to compliance. The number of air quality monitoring stations had increased to 6,500 nationally. But far more inspectors are needed to monitor and enforce existing federal and state laws, especially because 65% of all regions still report substandard air quality, and dangerous levels of smog have now been shown to exist even in rural areas. Air pollution cleanup would cost $12.3 billion a year — but $12.3 billion in annual health, property, and crop damage would be avoided.

Water: Despite increased efforts at water cleanup, the goals recede as the dimensions of the problem, and the costs of control, continue to increase. Surveys have determined that non-point sources (run-off from farm chemicals, mines, urban areas) account for 50% of water pollution. Potentially dangerous traces of organic chemicals have been found in all tested drinking water systems. Two out of 3 plants in spot checks were found to have violated their waste discharge permits. But impounded federal sewer-treatment funds were released by the Supreme Court in 1975. Bacteria and organic wastes in water declined; nitrogen and phosphate levels rose.

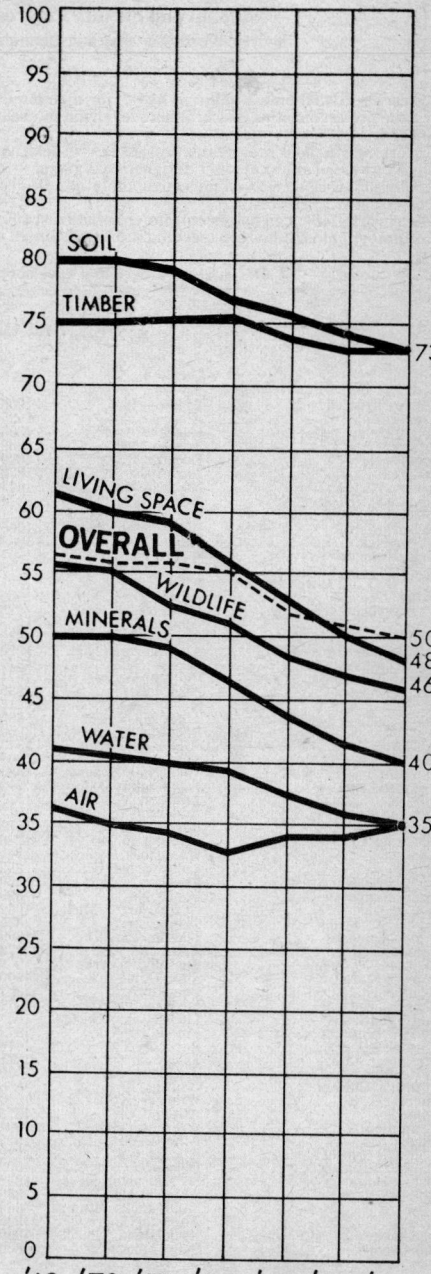

EDUCATION

American Colleges and Universities

For Canadian Colleges and Universities see Index

Student and Faculty Figures for Spring Term, 1976

Source: World Almanac questionnaires and U.S. Office of Education

All coeducational unless followed by (M) for men only, or (W) for women only. Even though marked (M) or (W) some are coeducational at graduate level and in evening and summer divisions. Asterisk (*) denotes land-grant college.

Governing official is president unless otherwise designated. Year is that of founding. The word college is part of the name listed unless another designation is given.

Affiliation: C-county; D-religious denomination; Di-district; F-federal; Mu-municipal; P-private; S-state; T-territorial govt.; Y-YMCA.

Each institution listed has an enrollment of at least 200 students of college grade. Number of teachers is the total number of individuals on teaching staff. Enrollment and faculty in italics all branches and campuses.

(A) Designates colleges that have not provided up-to-date information.
(See Index for typical tuition fees)

SENIOR COLLEGES

Name	Location	Year	Governing Official and Affiliation		Students	Teachers
Abilene Christian	Abilene, Tex.	1906	John C. Stevens	P	4,410	222
Adams State	Alamosa, Col.	1925	John A. Marvel	S	3,000	144
Adelphi Univ.	Garden City, N.Y.	1896	Timothy Costello	P	10,500	373
Adrian	Adrian, Mich.	1859	John H. Dawson	P	1,010	89
Agnes Scott	Decatur, Ga.	1889	Marvin Perry Jr.	P	600	75
Akron, Univ. of	Akron, Oh.	1870	Dominic J. Guzzetta	S	22,453	798
Alabama A&M Univ.	Normal, Ala.	1875	Richard D. Morrison	S	3,413	265
Alabama State Univ.	Montgomery, Ala.	1874	Levi Watkins	S	3,567	186
Alabama, Univ. of	University, Ala.	1831	David Mathews	S	15,460	1,177
at Birmingham	Birmingham, Ala.	1966	J.F. Volker	S	10,365	902
at Huntsville	Huntsville, Ala.	1969	Benjamin B. Graves	S	3,421	200
Alaska Methodist Univ. (A)	Anchorage, Alas.	1957	John O. Picton	P	1,283	62
Alaska, Univ. of*	Fairbanks, Alas.	1917	Robert W. Hiatt	S	18,254	422
Albany Coll. of Pharmacy	Albany, N.Y.	1881	Dean Walter Singer	P	588	36
Albany State	Albany, Ga.	1903	Charles Hays	S	2,026	127
Albertus Magnus (W)	New Haven, Conn.	1925	Sr. Francis Hefferman	D	456	60
Albion	Albion, Mich.	1835	Bernard Tagg Lomas	P,D	1,710	118
Albright	Reading, Pa.	1856	Arthur Schultz	D	1,571	97
Albuquerque, Univ. of	Albuquerque, N.M.	1920	Gil Cordova, Act.	P,D	3,049	173
Alcorn State Univ.	Lorman, Miss.	1871	Walter Washington	S	3,091	134
Alderson-Broaddus	Philippi, W. Va.	1871	Richard E. Shearer	P	891	78
Alfred Univ.	Alfred, N.Y.	1836	M. Richard Rose	P	2,100	180
Allegheny	Meadville, Pa.	1815	Lawrence L. Pelletier	P	1,970	127
Alma	Alma, Mich.	1886	Robert D. Swanson	P	1,145	88
Alvernia	Reading, Pa.	1958	Sister Mary Victorine	P,D	729	54
Alverno (W)	Milwaukee, Wis.	1940	Sister Joel Read	D	910	93
American Cons. of Music	Chicago, Ill.	1886	Leo Heim	P	1,993	144
American International	Springfield, Mass.	1885	Harry J. Courniotes	P	2,213	98
American Univ.	Washington, D.C.	1893	Joseph J. Sisco	D	13,881	763
Amherst	Amherst, Mass.	1821	John William Ward	P	1,332	141
Anderson	Anderson, Ind.	1917	Robert H. Reardon	P,D	1,876	155
Andrews Univ.	Berrien Springs, Mich.	1874	Richard Hammill	D	1,932	194
Angelo State Univ.	San Angelo, Tex.	1928	Lloyd Vincent	S	4,721	176
Annhurst	Woodstock, Conn.	1941	Sister Marie Janelle	D	382	55
Antioch	Yellow Spgs., Oh.	1852	James P. Dixon	P	4,876	432
Appalachian Bible Inst.	Bradley, W. Va.	1950	Lester E. Pipkin	P,D	274	17
Appalachian State Univ.	Boone, N.C.	1899	Herbert W. Wey	S	8,014	146
Aquinas	Grand Rapids, Mich.	1922	Norbert J. Hruby	P,D	1,800	85
Arizona State Univ.	Tempe, Ariz.	1885	John W. Schwada	S	36,441	1,342
Arizona, Univ. of*	Tucson, Ariz.	1885	John Paul Schaefer	S	30,737	1,862
Arkansas College	Batesville, Ark.	1872	Dan C. West	D	464	33
Arkansas Polytechnic	Russellville, Ark.	1909	Kenneth Kersh	S	2,400	130
Arkansas State Univ.	State Univ., Ark.	1909	Ross Pritchard	S	7,989	353
Arkansas State Coll. of	Conway, Ark.	1907	Jefferson Farris	S	5,280	212
Arkansas, Univ. of*	Fayetteville, Ark.	1871	Charles Bishop	S	28,120	1,587
at Little Rock	Little Rock, Ark.	1927	G. Robert Ross, Chan.	S	8,400	278
at Pine Bluff (A)	Pine Bluff, Ark.	1873	Herman Smith Jr.	S	2,656	149
Armstrong	Berkeley, Cal.	1918	John E. Armstrong	P	600	45
Armstrong State	Savannah, Ga.	1935	Henry L. Ashmore	S	3,719	165
Art Center Coll. of Design	Pasadena, Cal.	1930	Donald R. Kubly	P	875	180
Art Inst. of Chicago	Chicago, Ill.	1866	Donald Irving, Dir.	P	1,517	134
Asbury	Wilmore, Ky.	1890	Dennis F. Kinlaw	P	1,179	89
Ashland	Ashland, Oh.	1878	Glenn L. Clayton	D,P	2,075	140
Assumption	Worcester, Mass.	1904	Pasquale DiPasquale Jr.	D	1,182	131
Athens	Athens, Ala.	1822	Sidney Sandridge	S	903	52
Atlanta College of Art	Atlanta, Ga.	1928	William Voos	P	750	45
Atlantic Christian	Wilson, N.C.	1902	Arthur D. Wenger	D	1,710	117
Atlantic Union	So. Lancaster, Mass.	1882	W.G. Nelson	D	748	71
Auburn Univ.*	Auburn, Ala.	1856	Harry Philpott	S	20,821	1,180
Augsburg	Minneapolis, Minn.	1869	Oscar A. Anderson	D	1,762	171
Augusta	Augusta, Ga.	1925	George A. Christenberry	S	3,546	150
Augustana	Rock Island, Ill.	1860	J. Thomas Tredway	D	2,262	135
Augustana	Sioux Falls, S.D.	1860	Charles L. Balcer	P	2,243	178

Name	Location	Year	Governing Official and Affiliation		Stu-dents	Teach-ers
Aurora	Aurora, Ill.	1897	Lloyd Richardson	D	1,056	96
Austin	Sherman, Tex.	1849	John D. Moseley	D,P	1,216	93
Austin Peay State Univ.	Clarksville, Tenn.	1927	Robert O. Riggs	S	4,168	172
Averett	Danville, Va.	1859	Conwell A. Anderson	P,D	1,086	50
Avila	Kansas City, Mo.	1916	Sister Olive Dallavis	D,P	1,703	167
Azusa Pacific	Azusa, Cal.	1899	Cornelius Haggard	P	2,110	76
Babson	Babson Park, Mass.	1919	Ralph Sorenson	P	2,634	123
Baker Univ.	Baldwin City, Kan.	1858	Jerald C. Walker	D	876	66
Baldwin-Wallace	Berea, Oh.	1845	A. B. Bonds, Jr.	D	2,869	181
Ball State Univ.	Muncie, Ind.	1918	John J. Pruis	S	18,972	889
Baltimore, Univ. of.	Baltimore, Md.	1925	H. Mebane Turner	S	5,974	265
Baptist Bible College of Pa.	Clarks Summit, Pa.	1932	Ernest Pickering	D	811	45
Baptist Coll. at Charleston (A)	Charleston, S.C.	1965	John Hamrick	D	2,241	106
Barat (W)	Lake Forest, Ill.	1919	Sister Margaret Burke	P	853	80
Barber-Scotia	Concord, N.C.	1867	Mable McLean	P	480	41
Bard	Annandale, N.Y.	1934	Leon Botstein	P	648	77
Barnard (W)	New York, N.Y.	1889	Jacquelyn Mattfeld	P	1,930	150
Barrington	Barrington, R.I.	1900	Harold Fickett Jr.	P	597	60
Barry	Miami Shores, Fla.	1940	Sister M. Trinita Flood	P	1,425	75
Bates	Lewiston, Me.	1864	Thomas H. Reynolds	P	1,286	104
Baylor Univ.	Waco, Tex.	1845	Abner V. McCall	D	8,633	425
Beaver	Glenside, Pa.	1853	Edward D. Gates	P	1,696	87
Belhaven	Jackson, Miss.	1883	Howard J. Cleland	D	878	45
Bellarmine	Louisville, Ky.	1950	Eugene Petrick	P	1,561	85
Bellevue	Bellevue, Neb.	1966	Richard Winchell	P	1,836	39
Belmont	Nashville, Tenn.	1951	Herbert C. Gabhart	D	1,115	70
Belmont Abbey	Belmont, N.C.	1876	Rev. John Bradley	D,P	750	50
Beloit	Beloit, Wis.	1846	Martha Peterson	P	1,418	108
Bemidji State	Bemidji, Minn.	1919	Robert Decker	S	4,208	222
Benedict	Columbia, S.C.	1870	Henry Ponder	P	1,667	86
Benedictine	Atchison, Kan.	1971	Rev. Gerard Senecal	D,P	979	85
Benjamin Franklin Univ.	Washington, D.C.	1925	Mrs. John Kennedy	P	1,000	40
Bennett (W)	Greensboro, N.C.	1863	Isaac H. Miller	D	563	65
Bennington	Bennington, Vt.	1925	Joseph Iseman, Act.	P	588	76
Bentley	Waltham, Mass.	1917	Gregory Adamian	P	4,097	181
Berea	Berea, Ky.	1855	W.D. Weatherford.	P	1,504	129
Berry	Mount Berry, Ga.	1902	John R. Bertrand	D	1,692	108
Bethany	Lindsborg, Kan.	1881	Arvin Hahn	D	750	71
Bethany	Bethany, W.Va.	1840	Orville Wake, Act.	P,D	1,108	65
Bethany Bible	Santa Cruz, Cal.	1919	C. Morse Ward	D,P	573	26
Bethany Nazarene	Bethany, Okla.	1899	Stephen Nease	P	1,208	66
Bethel	Mishawaka, Ind.	1947	Albert Beutler	P	448	31
Bethel	North Newton, Kan.	1887	Harold Schultz	D	629	44
Bethel	McKenzie, Tenn.	1842	William L. Odom	Mu	319	25
Bethel	St. Paul, Minn.	1947	Carl Lundquist	P	1,467	99
Biola	La Mirada, Cal.	1908	J. Richard Chase	P	2,605	182
Birmingham Southern	Birmingham, Ala.	1856	Neal R. Berte	P	840	65
Biscayne	Miami, Fla.	1962	Rev. John McDonnell	D	14,974	83
Bishop	Dallas, Tex.	1881	Milton K. Curry Jr.	P	1,832	97
Black Hills State	Spearfish, S.D.	1883	M. Fitzgerald, Act.	S	3,090	123
Blackburn	Carlinville, Ill.	1837	John Alberti	P	545	49
Bloomfield	Bloomfield, N.J.	1868	Merle F. Allshouse	D	1,590	74
Bloomsburg State	Bloomsburg, Pa.	1839	James McCormick	S	2,963	281
Blue Mountain (W)	Blue Mountain, Miss.	1873	E. Harold Fisher	D,P	301	35
Bluefield State	Bluefield, W.Va.	1895	J. Wade Gilley	S	1,523	103
Bluffton	Bluffton, Oh.	1899	Benjamin Sprunger	P	690	58
Bob Jones Univ.	Greenville, S.C.	1927	Bob Jones, Chan.	P	4,587	304
Boca Raton	Boca Raton, Fla.	1963	Thomas Carlin	P	432	33
Boise State	Boise, Ida.	1932	John Barnes	S	9,757	463
Boston	Chestnut Hill, Mass.	1863	Rev. J. Donald Monan	D	9,844	745
Boston State	Boston, Mass.	1852	Kermit C. Merrissey	S	5,805	295
Boston Conserv. of Music	Boston, Mass.	1867	George Brambilla	P	506	97
Boston Univ.	Boston, Mass.	1869	John Silber	P	24,292	2,000
Bowdoin	Brunswick, Me.	1794	Roger Howell, Jr.	P	1,340	110
Bowie State	Bowie, Md.	1865	Samuel L. Myers	S	3,098	169
Bowling Green State Univ.	Bowling Green, Oh.	1910	Hollis A. Moore Jr.	S	17,277	740
Bradley Univ.	Peoria, Ill.	1897	Martin G. Abegg	P	5,025	320
Brandeis Univ.	Waltham, Mass.	1948	Marver Bernstein	P	2,968	365
Brenau	Gainesville, Ga.	1878	James T. Rogers	P	596	45
Brescia	Owensboro, Ky.	1950	Sister Geo. Ann Cecil	P	1,008	81
Briar Cliff	Sioux City, Ia.	1930	Kasper Marking	D,P	764	61
Briarcliff	Briarcliff Manor, N.Y.	1903	Josiah Bunting	P	400	58
Bridgeport Engineering Inst.	Bridgeport, Conn.	1924	William J. Owens	P	366	54
Bridgeport, Univ. of.	Bridgeport, Conn.	1927	Leland Miles	P	7,200	548
Bridgewater	Bridgewater, Va.	1880	Wayne F. Geisert	D	804	60
Bridgewater State	Bridgewater, Mass.	1840	Adrian Rondileau	S	7,850	280
Brigham Young Univ.	Provo, Ut.	1875	Dallin U. Oaks	P,D	26,470	1,259
Brooklyn Law School	Brooklyn, N.Y.	1901	Raymond Lisle, Dean	P	1,036	55
Brown Univ.	Providence, R.I.	1764	Donald F. Hornig	P	5,275	485
Bryan	Dayton, Tenn.	1930	Theodore Mercer	P	582	42
Bryant	Smithfield, R.I.	1863	Harry Evarts	P	4,600	142
Bryn Mawr (W)	Bryn Mawr, Pa.	1885	Harris L. Wofford, Jr.	P	1,526	177
Bucknell Univ.	Lewisburg, Pa.	1846	C. H. Watts, 2d	P	3,148	239
Buena Vista	Storm Lake, Ia.	1891	Keith G. Briscoe	D	879	47
Butler Univ.	Indianapolis, Ind.	1855	Alexander E. Jones	P	4,300	235
Caldwell	Caldwell, N.J.	1939	Sr. M. Anne John O'Laughlin	D,P	850	73
California Baptist	Riverside, Cal.	1950	James R. Staples	D	814	55
Calif. Coll. of Arts and Crafts	Oakland, Cal.	1907	Harry Xavier Ford	P	1,132	125
Calif. College of Podiatric Med.	San Francisco, Cal.	1914	H. D. Bailey	P	338	45
Calif. Inst. of the Arts	Valencia, Cal.	1961	Robert Fitzpatrick	P	700	66
Calif. Inst. of Tech	Pasadena, Cal.	1891	Harold Brown	P	1,595	275
Calif. Lutheran	Thousand Oaks, Cal.	1959	Mark Mathews	P	6,156	195
Calif. Maritime Academy	Vallejo, Cal.	1929	R. Adm. Joseph Rizza	S	349	24
Calif. State Polytechnic	San Luis Obispo, Cal.	1901	Robert Kennedy	S	15,158	800
Calif. State	Bakersfield, Cal.	1965	Jacob Frankel	S	3,000	160

Name	Location	Year	Governing Official and Affiliation		Stu-dents	Teach-ers
Calif. State	California, Pa.	1859	George Roadman	S	5,193	304
Calif. State	Dominguez Hills, Cal.	1960	Leo Cain	S	6,800	239
Calif. State	Rohnert Park, Cal.	1960	Marjorie Wagner	S	6,000	385
Calif. State	San Bernardino, Cal.	1962	John Pfau	S	4,000	180
Calif. State	Turlock, Cal.	1957	Walter Olson	S	5,200	180
Calif. State Polytechnic Univ.	Pomona, Cal.	1938	Robert C. Kramer	S	12,064	660
Calif. State Univ.	Northridge, Cal.	1958	James W. Cleary	S	26,000	1,385
Calif. State Univ.	Chico, Cal.	1887	Stanford Cazier	S	13,383	933
Calif. State Univ.	Fresno, Cal.	1911	Norman Baxter	S	15,526	966
Calif. State Univ.	Fullerton, Cal.	1959	Donald Shields	S	21,400	773
Calif. State Univ.	Hayward, Cal.	1957	Ellis McCune	S	11,771	675
Calif. State Univ.	Long Beach, Cal.	1949	Stephen Horn	S	31,785	1,809
Calif. State Univ.	Los Angeles, Cal.	1947	J. A. Greenlee	S	26,400	1,510
Calif. State Univ.	Sacramento, Cal.	1947	James Bond	S	19,800	864
Calif. State Univ.	San Francisco, Cal.	1899	Paul F. Romberg	S	23,409	1,500
Calif. Univ. of*	Berkeley, Cal.	1868	David S. Saxon	S	128,000	12,500
Berkeley Campus	Berkeley, Cal.	1873	Albert H. Bowker, Chan.	S	30,001	2,429
Davis Campus	Davis, Cal.	1905	James Meyer, Chan.	S	17,231	1,269
Irvine Campus	Irvine, Cal.	1965	D.G. Aldrich, Chan.	S	9,361	724
Los Angeles Campus	Los Angeles, Cal.	1919	Charles Young, Chan.	S	33,228	2,200
Riverside Campus	Riverside, Cal.	1907	Ivan Hinderaker, Chan.	S	5,058	766
San Diego Campus	La Jolla, Cal.	1912	William D. McElroy, Chan.	S	8,875	946
San Francisco Campus	San Francisco, Cal.	1873	F. A. Sooy, Chan.	S	3,295	1,414
Santa Barbara Campus	Santa Barbara, Cal.	1898	Vernon Cheadle, Chan.	S	14,584	947
Santa Cruz Campus	Santa Cruz, Cal.	1965	A.E. Taylor, Act. Chan.	S	6,093	421
Calumet	E. Chicago, Ind.	1951	Rev. James McCabe	D,P	1,800	100
Calvary Bible	Kansas City, Mo.	1932	Leslie Madison	P	295	25
Calvin	Grand Rapids, Mich.	1876	William Spoelhof	Mu	3,414	202
Cameron	Lawton, Okla.	1907	Don Owen	S	6,000	235
Campbell	Buies Creek, N.C.	1887	Norman A. Wiggins	D,P	2,024	106
Campbellsville	Campbellsville, Ky.	1906	William R. Davenport	P,D	711	44
Canisius	Buffalo, N.Y.	1870	V. Rev. James Demske	D	4,274	207
Capital Univ.	Columbus, Oh.	1850	Thomas H. Langevin	D	2,667	167
Capitol Inst. of Tech.	Kensington, Md.	1964	E.L. Fleckenstein	D	275	15
Cardinal Stritch	Milwaukee, Wis.	1937	Sister M. Kliebhan	D	1,300	101
Carleton	Northfield, Minn.	1866	Howard R. Swearer	P	1,648	120
Carlow	Pittsburgh, Pa.	1929	Sister Jane Scully	D,P	943	75
Carnegie-Mellon Univ.	Pittsburgh, Pa.	1900	Richard M. Cyert	P	4,842	416
Carroll	Helena, Mon.	1909	Francis Kerius	D,P	1,400	105
Carroll	Waukesha, Wis.	1846	Robert V. Cramer	P	1,267	100
Carson-Newman	Jefferson City, Tenn.	1851	John A. Fincher	P,D	1,559	115
Carthage	Kenosha, Wis.	1847	Harold H. Lentz	P	1,645	103
Case Western Reserve Univ.	Cleveland, Oh.	1826	L. A. Toepfer	P	8,843	1,500
Castleton State	Castleton, Vt.	1787	Dorothy Burns, Act.	P	1,837	121
Catawba	Salisbury, N.C.	1851	M.L. Shotzberger	P	981	78
Cathedral (M)	Douglaston, N.Y.	1914	Rev. Thomas Gradilone	D	213	56
Catholic Univ. of America	Washington, D.C.	1887	Clarence C. Walton	P	7,133	562
Cath. Univ. of Puerto Rico	Ponce, Puerto Rico	1948	F.J. Carreras	D	9,856	400
Cedar Crest (W)	Allentown, Pa.	1867	Pauline Tompkins	P,D	668	72
Cedarville	Cedarville, Oh.	1887	James Jeremiah	D	1,050	66
Central Bible	Springfield, Mo.	1922	Rev. Philip Crouch	D	1,109	52
Central	Pella, Ia.	1853	Kenneth J. Weller	P	1,350	92
Central Connecticut State	New Britain, Conn.	1849	F. Don James	S	5,143	522
Central Methodist	Fayette, Mo.	1854	Harold Hamilton	D	685	58
Central Mich. Univ.	Mt. Pleasant, Mich.	1892	Harold Abel	S	15,708	700
Central Missouri State Univ.	Warrensburg, Mo.	1871	Warren C. Lovinger	S	9,678	414
Central State Univ.	Edmond, Okla.	1890	Bill Lillard	S	11,299	390
Central State Univ.	Wilberforce, Oh.	1887	Lionel H. Newsom	S	2,335	120
Central Washington State	Ellensburg, Wash.	1891	James E. Brooks	S	8,012	380
Central Wesleyan	Central S.C.	1906	Claude Rickman	D,P	386	30
Chadron State	Chadron, Neb.	1911	Edwin Nelson	S	2,020	95
Chaminade Col. of Honolulu	Honolulu, Ha.	1955	Rev. Charles Lees.	D	1,600	181
Charleston, Coll. of	Charleston, S.C.	1770	Theodore Stern	S	4,562	215
Chatham (W)	Pittsburgh, Pa.	1889	Edward D. Eddy	P	642	65
Chestnut Hill (W)	Philadelphia, Pa.	1924	Sister Mary Xavier	D	857	83
Cheyney State (A)	Cheyney, Pa.	1837	Wade Wilson	S	2,400	230
Chicago Academy of Fine Arts	Chicago, Ill.	1902	Richard Hamper	P	359	40
Chicago Coll. (Osteopathic)	Chicago, Ill.	1900	Thaddeus Kawalek	S	380	150
Chicago State Univ.	Chicago, Ill.	1869	Benjamin Alexander	P	6,600	260
Chicago Technical	Chicago, Ill.	1904	Leslie Morey	P	451	16
Chicago, Univ. of	Chicago, Ill.	1891	John Wilson	P	8,000	1,050
Christian Brothers	Memphis, Tenn.	1871	Bro. Bernard LoCoco	P,D	813	78
Cincinnati, Univ. of	Cincinnati, Oh.	1870	Warren G. Bennis	S,Mu	38,841	3,161
Citadel, The (Military) (M)	Charleston, S.C.	1842	Gen. George Seignious	S	3,281	220
Claflin	Orangeburg, S.C.	1869	Hubert V. Manning	D	895	56
Claremont Men's	Claremont, Cal.	1946	Jack Lee Stark	P	802	94
Clarion State	Clarion, Pa.	1867	James Gemmell	S	4,864	304
Clark	Atlanta, Ga.	1869	Chas. Knight, Act.	P,D	1,658	112
Clark Univ.	Worcester, Mass.	1887	Mortimer Appley	P	2,983	189
Clarkson Coll. of Tech.	Potsdam, N.Y.	1896	Robert A. Plane	P	2,957	190
Clemson Univ.	Clemson, S.C.	1889	Robert C. Edwards	S	11,361	700
Cleveland Inst. of Art	Cleveland, Oh.	1882	Joseph McCullough	P	988	81
Cleveland Inst. of Music	Cleveland, Oh.	1920	Grant Johannesen	P	275	160
Cleveland State Univ.	Cleveland, Oh.	1964	Walter Waetjen	S	16,974	715
Coe	Cedar Rapids, Ia.	1851	Leo Nussbaum	P,D	1,100	103
Colby	Waterville, Me.	1813	Robert E.L. Strider	P	1,620	135
Colby-Sawyer	New London, N.H.	1837	Louis Vaccard	P	731	63
Colgate Univ.	Hamilton, N.Y.	1819	Thomas Bartlett	P	2,289	214
Colorado	Colo. Spgs. Col.	1874	Lloyd E. Worner	P	1,925	146
Colorado Sch. of Mines	Golden, Col.	1874	Guy McBride, Jr.	S	2,204	133
Colorado State Univ.*	Fort Collins, Col.	1879	A.R. Chamberlain	S	16,809	1,035
Colorado, Univ. of (A)	Boulder, Col.	1876	Frederick P. Thieme	S	30,428	2,729
Colorado Springs	Colorado Springs, Col.	1965	Lawrence Silverman	S	3,344	130
Colorado Women's (W)	Denver, Col.	1888	Dumont F. Kenny	P	750	60
Columbia (W)	Columbia, S.C.	1854	R. Wright Spears	P,D	850	64
Columbia	Columbia, Mo.	1851	W. Merle Hill	P	1,400	71
Columbia Bible	Columbia, S.C.	1923	J. Robertson McQuilkin	P	736	35
Columbia Union	Takoma Park. Md.	1904	Colin Standish	Mu	890	84

Name	Location	Year	Governing Official and Affiliation		Stu-dents	Teach-ers
Columbia Univ.	New York, N.Y.	1754	William McGill	P	14,475	6,000
Teachers College (A)	New York, N.Y.	1888	John H. Fischer	P	5,199	403
Columbus	Columbus, Ga.	1958	Thomas Y. Whitley	S	5,674	213
Columbus Coll. of Art & Design	Columbus, Oh.	1870	Joseph Canzani, Dean.	P	593	54
Concord	Athens, W.Va.	1872	Billy Coffindaffer	S	1,537	96
Concordia	Bronxville, N.Y.	1881	Robert Schnabel	D	625	58
Concordia	Moorhead, Minn.	1891	Paul Dover	D	2,402	200
Concordia	St. Paul, Minn.	1893	Luther Mueller, Act.	D	684	56
Concordia Teachers	River Forest, Ill.	1864	Paul A. Zimmerman	D	1,204	93
Concordia Teachers	Seward, Neb.	1894	W. T. Janzow.	D	1,061	107
Connecticut	New London, Conn.	1911	Oakes Ames	P	1,980	183
Connecticut Univ. of*	Storrs, Conn.	1939	Glenn Ferguson	S	22,450	1,375
Converse (W)	Spartanburg, S.C.	1889	Robert T. Coleman, Jr.	P	805	83
Cooper Union	New York, N.Y.	1859	John White.	P	908	140
Coppin State	Baltimore, Md.	1900	Calvin Burnett.	S	2,897	217
Cornell	Mt. Vernon, Ia.	1853	Philip Secor	P	895	87
Cornell Univ.*	Ithaca, N.Y.	1865	Dale R. Corson.	P	17,407	1,763
Creighton Univ.	Omaha, Neb.	1878	Rev. Joseph Labaj	D,P	2,771	781
Culver-Stockton	Canton, Mo.	1853	Harold Doster.	D	481	44
Cumberland	Williamsburg, Ky.	1889	J.M. Boswell.	D	1,600	110
Curry	Milton, Mass.	1879	John S. Hafer.	P	940	75
Dakota State	Madison, S.D.	1881	Dr. Clyde Brashier, Dean	S	996	54
Dakota Wesleyan Univ.	Mitchell, S.D.	1885	Donald E. Messer	D	517	54
Dallas Baptist.	Dallas, Tex.	1965	W.E. Thorn.	D	1,268	69
Dallas, Univ. of	Irving, Tex.	1956	Donald A. Cowan.	P	1,708	125
Dana	Blair, Neb.	1884	Earl Mezoff	D	583	48
Dartmouth	Hanover, N.H.	1769	John George Kemeny	P	3,887	305
David Lipscomb	Nashville, Tenn.	1891	Athens C. Pullias	D,P	2,187	105
Davidson	Davidson, N.C.	1837	Samuel R. Spencer, Jr.	P,D	1,250	94
Dayton, Univ. of.	Dayton, Oh.	1850	Rev. R. A. Roesch.	D	8,370	425
Defiance	Defiance, Oh.	1850	M. Ludwig.	P	800	60
Delaware State	Dover, Del.	1891	Luna I. Mishoe.	S	2,184	114
Delaware, Univ. of*	Newark, Del.	1833	E.A. Trabant.	P	19,000	758
Del. Valley Coll. of S&A.	Doylestown, Pa.	1896	Joshua Feldstein.	P	1,423	82
Delta State Univ.	Cleveland, Miss.	1925	Kent Wyatt.	S	2,259	172
Denison Univ.	Granville, Oh.	1831	Robert C. Good.	P	2,177	147
Denver, Univ. of	Denver, Col.	1864	Maurice B. Mitchell.	P	7,800	454
DePaul Univ	Chicago, Ill.	1898	Rev. J. R. Cortelyou.	P	10,915	329
DePauw Univ.	Greencastle, Ind.	1837	William E. Kerstetter.	P	2,412	170
Detroit Bible	Detroit, Mich.	1945	Wendell Johnston.	P	291	23
Detroit Coll. of Business	Dearborn, Mich.	1932	Robert Sneden.	P	2,917	101
Detroit Coll. of Law.	Detroit, Mich.	1891	G. Cameron Buchanan.	P	990	46
Detroit Inst. of Technology.	Detroit, Mich.	1891	Dewey F. Barich, Chan.	P	1,712	145
Detroit, Univ. of*.	Detroit, Mich.	1877	Rev. M. Carron	P	7,911	561
DeVry Inst. of Tech.	Atlanta, Ga.	1969	Harry Overton Jr.	P	737	35
DeVry Inst. of Tech.	Dallas, Tex.	1969	Douglas Kerr	P	752	42
DeVry Inst. of Tech.	Chicago, Ill.	1931	Samuel Edmonds	P	2,907	100
DeVry Inst. of Tech.	Phoenix, Ariz.	1967	F. Roger Hess.	P	2,220	89
DeVry Inst. of Tech.	Woodbridge, N.J.	1969	Robert Bocchino.	P	1,090	43
Dickinson (A)	Carlisle, Pa.	1773	Howard L. Rubendal.	P	1,660	120
Dickinson School of Law.	Carlisle, Pa.	1834	Dale F. Shughart	P	450	31
Dickinson State.	Dickinson, N.D.	1918	R. C. Gilluind	S	1,001	62
Dillard Univ.	New Orleans, La.	1869	Samuel Cook.	Mu	1,117	93
District of Col. Teachers.	Washington, D.C.	1851	Wendell Russell.	Mu	1,542	137
Doane.	Crete, Neb.	1872	Philip C. Heckman	P	625	37
Dr. Martin Luther.	New Ulm, Minn.	1884	Rev. Conrad Frey	D	715	70
Dominican Coll. of Blauvelt.	Blauvelt, N.Y.	1952	Sister Natalie Casey	P	1,137	70
Dominican Coll. of S. Rafael.	San Rafael, Cal.	1890	Sister M. Samuel Conlan	D	734	111
Dordt	Sioux Center, Ia.	1955	B. J. Haan.	D	990	50
Dowling	Oakdale, N.Y.	1968	Allyn Robinson.	P	1,473	176
Drake Univ.	Des Moines, Ia.	1881	Wilbur C. Miller.	P	6,836	326
Drew Univ.	Madison, N.J.	1866	Paul Hardin	P	1,531	191
Drexel Univ.	Philadelphia, Pa.	1891	William W. Hagerty.	P	8,919	544
Drury	Springfield, Mo.	1873	William Everheart.	P	2,214	156
Dubuque Univ. of (A)	Dubuque, Ia.	1852	Walter F. Peterson.	P	1,004	66
Duke Univ.	Durham, N.C.	1838	Terry Sanford.	P	10,047	1,210
Duquesne Univ.	Pittsburgh, Pa.	1878	Rev. J. McAnulty.	P	7,795	470
Dyke	Cleveland, Oh.	1848	John Corfias.	P	1,104	54
D'Youville	Buffalo, N.Y.	1908	Sister Mary C. Barton	P	1,143	80
Earlham	Richmond, Ind.	1847	Franklin Wallin	D,P	1,164	120
East Central Univ.	Ada, Okla.	1909	Stanley Wagner	S	3,212	144
East Stroudsburg State	E. Stroudsburg, Pa.	1893	Darrell Holmes	S	3,940	195
East Tennessee State Univ.	Johnson City, Tenn.	1911	Delos Culp	S	10,288	426
East Texas Baptist.	Marshall, Tex.	1912	Howard C. Bennett	Mu	788	43
East Texas State Univ.	Commerce, Tex.	1889	F. H. McDowell	S	11,084	375
Eastern.	St. Davids, Pa.	1952	Daniel E. Weiss.	D,P	658	63
Eastern Conn. State	Willimantic, Conn.	1889	Charles Richard Webb	S	1,996	210
Eastern Illinois Univ.	Charleston, Ill.	1895	Gilbert C. Fite	S	9,879	501
Eastern Kentucky Univ.	Richmond, Ky.	1906	Robert R. Martin	S	13,430	528
Eastern Mennonite	Harrisonburg, Va.	1917	Myron S. Augsburger.	P,D	969	67
Eastern Michigan Univ.	Ypsilanti, Mich.	1849	James Brickley.	S	18,931	752
Eastern Montana	Billings, Mon.	1927	Stanley Heywood.	S	3,055	170
Eastern Nazarene	Quincy, Mass.	1918	Donald Irwin	D	825	46
Eastern New Mexico Univ.	Portales, N.M.	1934	Warren Armstrong.	S	3,730	210
Eastern Oregon State.	LaGrande, Ore.	1929	Rodney A. Briggs.	S	1,437	105
Eastern Washington State	Cheney, Wash.	1890	P. Marshall, V.P.	S	6,634	374
Eckerd.	Cincinnati, Oh.	1935	Sr. M.A. Molitor.	S	851	72
Edgewood.	Madison, Wis.	1927	Sister Cecilia Carey.	P,D	624	60
Edinboro State.	Edinboro, Pa.	1861	Chester T. McNerney.	S	7,041	422
Eisenhower.	Seneca Falls, N.Y.	1965	Joseph Coffee Jr.	P	550	61
Elizabeth City State Univ.	Eliz. City, N.C.	1891	Marion Thorpe, Chan.	S	1,629	114
Elizabethtown.	Elizabethtown, Pa.	1899	Morely J. Mays.	P	2,041	133
Elmhurst.	Elmhurst, Ill.	1871	Ivan Frick.	P	2,630	167

Name	Location	Year	Governing Official and Affiliation		Students	Teachers
Elmira	Elmira, N.Y.	1855	Leonard Grant	P	3,320	157
Elon	Elon College, N.C.	1889	J. F. Young	P	2,175	94
Embry-Riddle Aero. Univ.	Daytona Beach, Fla.	1926	Jack R. Hunt	P	1,886	146
Emerson	Boston, Mass.	1880	Gus Turbeville	P	1,435	125
Emmanuel (W)	Boston, Mass.	1919	Sister Mary McCarthy	D	1,276	96
Emory & Henry	Emory, Va.	1836	Thomas F. Chilcote	D	818	62
Emory Univ.	Atlanta, Ga.	1836	S. S. Atwood	D	7,180	2,208
Emporia Kansas State	Emporia, Kan.	1863	John Visser	S	6,511	269
Erskine	Due West, S.C.	1839	M. S. Bell	D	771	52
Eureka	Eureka, Ill.	1855	Ira W. Langston	P	451	42
Evangel	Springville, Mo.	1955	Robert Spence	P	1,133	72
Evansville, Univ. of	Evansville, Ind.	1854	Wallace B. Graves	D	5,169	283
Evergreen State Coll.	Olympia, Wash.	1967	Charles McCann	S	2,507	130
Fairfield Univ.	Fairfield, Conn.	1942	Rev. Thomas Fitzgerald	P	5,107	304
Fairleigh Dickinson Univ.	Rutherford, N.J.	1942	Jerome Pollack	P	17,594	1,999
Fairmont State	Fairmont, W. Va.	1867	Eston K. Feaster	S	5,072	180
Faith Baptist Bible	Ankeny, Ia.	1924	David Nettleton	P	600	29
Federal City	Washington, D.C.	1968	Wendell P. Russell	Mu	7,774	701
Felician	Lodi, N.J.	1942	Sr. Mary Justitia	P,D	595	712
Ferris State	Big Rapids, Mich.	1884	Robert Ewigleben	S	9,264	427
Findlay	Findlay, Oh.	1882	Glen R. Rasmussen	P	975	74
Fisk Univ.	Nashville, Tenn.	1867	J. R. Lawson	P	1,489	107
Fitchburg State	Fitchburg, Mass.	1894	James Hammond	P	7,408	250
Flagler	St. Augustine, Fla.	1968	William L. Proctor	P	635	49
Florence State Univ. (A)	Florence, Ala.	1872	Robert M. Guillot	S	3,642	162
Florida Atlantic Univ.	Boca Raton, Fla.	1961	G. L. Creech	S	7,200	281
Florida A.&M. Univ.*	Tallahassee, Fla.	1887	Benjamin Luther Perry Jr.	S	5,600	421
Florida Inst. of Tech.	Melbourne, Fla.	1958	Jerome P. Keuper	P	2,400	218
Florida Southern	Lakeland, Fla.	1885	Robert Davis	D	1,440	82
Florida State Univ.	Tallahassee, Fla.	1857	Stanley Marshall	S	21,414	1,100
Florida Technological Univ.	Orlando, Fla.	1963	Charles N. Millican	S	10,500	380
Florida Univ. of*	Gainesville, Fla.	1853	Robert Marston	S	27,738	2,600
Fontbonne	St. Louis, Mo.	1917	Sister Jane Hassett	P	880	81
Fordham Univ.	Bronx, N.Y.	1841	Rev. James C. Finley	P	14,211	799
Ft. Hays Kansas State	Hays, Kan.	1902	John W. Gustad	S	5,062	257
Ft. Lauderdale Coll.	Ft. Lauderdale, Fla.	1940	Lyle E. Anderson	P	1,176	54
Ft. Lewis	Durango, Col.	1911	Rexer Berndt	S	3,100	148
Fort Valley State*	Fort Valley, Ga.	1895	Cleveland W. Pettigrew	S	1,800	151
Ft. Wayne Art Inst.	Fort Wayne, Ind.	1921	William McNagny	P	204	11
Fort Wayne Bible	Fort Wayne, Ind.	1904	Timothy Warner	D,P	596	39
Ft. Wright	Spokane, Wash.	1907	Helen Volkommer	D,P	435	53
Framingham State	Framingham, Mass.	1839	D. Justin McCarthy	S	3,500	160
Francis Marion	Florence, S.C.	1970	Walter D. Smith	S	2,115	113
Franklin	Franklin, Ind.	1834	Edwin A. Penn	P,D	690	50
Franklin Univ.	Columbus, Oh.	1902	Joseph Frasch	P	3,850	144
Franklin and Marshall	Lancaster, Pa.	1787	Keith Spalding	P	2,700	136
Franklin Pierce	Rindge, N.H.	1962	Walter Peterson	P	1,102	53
Freed-Hardeman	Henderson, Tenn.	1908	E. Claude Gardner	D	1,437	80
Free Will Baptist Bible	Nashville, Tenn.	1942	L. C. Johnson	D	541	23
Friends Univ.	Wichita, Kan.	1898	Harold C. Cope	D,P	886	65
Frostburg State	Frostburg, Md.	1902	Nelson Guild	S	3,172	174
Furman Univ.	Greenville, S.C.	1826	Gordon W. Blackwell	D,P	2,732	167
Gallaudet	Washington, D.C.	1864	Edward C. Merrill Jr.	P	943	126
Gannon	Erie, Pa.	1944	Rev. W. J. Nash	D	2,558	195
Gardner-Webb	Boiling Springs, NC	1905	Thomas McGraw, Act.	D,P	1,325	80
General Motors Institute	Flint, Mich.	1919	Harold P. Rodes	P	2,447	138
Geneva	Beaver Falls, Pa.	1848	Edwin C. Clarke	D	1,445	95
George Fox	Newberg, Ore.	1891	David La Shana	D,P	607	42
George Mason Univ.	Fairfax, Va.	1957	V. H. Dykstra	P	7,893	481
George Peabody Coll. for Teachers	Nashville, Tenn.	1875	John Dunworth	P	2,000	150
Geo. Washington Univ.	Washington, D.C.	1821	Lloyd H. Elliott	P	15,200	1,225
George Williams	Downers Grove, Ill	1890	Richard E. Hamlin	P	1,700	94
Georgetown	Georgetown, Ky.	1829	Robert L. Mills	P	1,057	75
Georgetown Univ. (A)	Washington, D.C.	1789	Rev. Timothy Healy	D	10,359	1,013
Georgia	Milledgeville, Ga.	1889	J. Whitney Bunting	S	3,770	166
Georgia Inst. Of Technology	Atlanta, Ga.	1885	Joseph M. Pettit	S	12,000	804
Georgia State Univ.	Statesboro, Ga.	1906	Pope A. Duncan	S	6,125	328
Georgia Southwestern	Americus, Ga.	1908	William B. King	S	2,648	120
Georgia State Univ.	Atlanta, Ga.	1913	Noah N. Langdale Jr.	S	20,876	821
Georgia, Univ. of*	Athens, Ga.	1785	Fred C. Davison	S	21,442	1,694
Georgian Court (W)	Lakewood, N.J.	1908	Sister Maria Cordis	P	753	80
Gettysburg	Gettysburg, Pa.	1832	Carl Arnold Hanson	P	1,897	160
Glassboro State	Glassboro, N.J.	1923	Mark Chamberlain	S	11,790	419
Glenville State	Glenville, W.Va.	1872	D. Banks Wilburn	S	1,622	75
Goddard	Plainfield, Vt.	1864	Richard Graham	P	1,652	85
Golden Gate Univ.	San Francisco, Cal.	1901	Otto Butz	P	9,000	500
Gonzaga Univ.	Spokane, Wash.	1887	Bernard Coughlin	P	3,200	250
Gordon	Wenham, Mass.	1889	Richard Gross	P	1,050	60
Goshen	Goshen, Ind.	1894	J. Lawrence Burkholder	D,P	1,265	100
Goucher (W)	Towson, Md.	1885	Rhoda Dorsey	P	1,039	118
Governors State Univ.	Park Forest South, Ill.	1969	William Engbretson	S	4,583	150
Grace Coll. of the Bible	Omaha, Neb.	1943	Robert Benton	P	551	29
Graceland	Lamoni, Ia.	1895	Gerald Knutson	P	1,451	97
Grambling State Univ.	Grambling, La.	1901	Ralph W. E. Jones	S	3,749	208
Grand Canyon	Phoenix, Ariz.	1949	William R. Hintze	P	1,211	73
Grand Valley State	Allendale, Mich.	1963	Arend Lubbers	S	7,340	340
Grand View	Des Moines, Ia.	1896	Karl F. Langrock	P	967	62
Great Falls, Coll. of	Great Falls, Mon.	1932	Msgr. A. M. Brown	P	1,231	74
Green Mountain	Poultney, Vt.	1834	Raymond Withey	P	475	43
Grinnell	Grinnell, Ia.	1846	A. Richard Turner	P	1,157	115
Grove City	Grove City, Pa.	1876	Charles S. MacKenzie	P,D	2,139	118
Gulford	Greensboro, N.C.	1837	Grimsley T. Hobbs	D	1,590	100

Name	Location	Year	Governing Official and Affiliation		Stu-dents	Teach-ers
Gulf-Coast Bible	Houston, Tex.	1953	John Conley	D,P	351	23
Gustavus Adolphus	St. Peter, Minn.	1862	Edward Lindell	D,P	2,096	132
Gwynedd-Mercy	Gwynedd Valley, Pa.	1948	Sister Isabelle Keiss	D,P	917	93
Hahnemann Medical	Philadelphia, Pa.	1848	Wharton R. Shober	P	1,550	363
Hamilton (M)	Clinton, N.Y.	1812	J. M. Carovano	P	965	85
Hamline Univ.	St. Paul, Minn.	1854	Jerry E. Hudson	D	1,200	121
Hampden-Sydney (M)	Hampden-Sydney, Va.	1776	W. Taylor Reveley	D	746	55
Hampshire (A)	Amherst, Mass.	1965	Charles Longsworth	P	1,000	90
Hampton Institute	Hampton, Va.	1868	Roy D. Hudson	P	2,796	214
Hanover	Hanover, Ind.	1827	John E. Horner	D	932	72
Hardin-Simmons Univ.	Abilene, Tex.	1891	Elwin L. Skiles	D	1,772	113
Harding	Searcy, Ark.	1924	Clinton L. Ganus, Jr.	D	2,843	146
Harris Teachers	St. Louis, Mo.	1857	Richard Stumpe	Mu	950	80
Hartford, Univ. of	W. Hartford, Conn.	1877	A. M. Woodruff	P	8,939	550
Hartwick	Oneonta, N.Y.	1928	Adolph G. Anderson	P	1,698	114
Harvard Univ.**(1)	Cambridge, Mass.	1636	Derek Curtis Bok	P	20,498	3,860(2)
Harvey Mudd	Claremont, Cal.	1957	Joseph B. Platt	P	450	54
Hastings	Hastings, Neb.	1882	Clyde B. Matters	P,D	684	60
Haverford (M)	Haverford, Pa.	1833	John R. Coleman	P	800	101
Hawaii, The Church Coll. of (A)	Laie, Ha.	1955	Stephen Brower	P	1,008	75
Hawaii, Univ. of	Honolulu, Ha.	1907	Fujio Matsuda	S	47,214	2,302
Heald Engineering	San Francisco, Cal.	1863	James Dietz	P	1,000	70
Heidelberg	Tiffin, Oh.	1850	Leslie H. Fishel, Jr.	P	1,133	109
Henderson State	Arkadelphia, Ark.	1890	Martin Garrison	S	3,650	175
Hendrix	Conway, Ark.	1884	Roy Shilling, Jr.	D	1,058	54
High Point	High Point, N.C.	1924	Wendell M. Patton	P	1,132	60
Hillsdale	Hillsdale, Mich.	1844	George C. Roche	P	953	70
Hiram	Hiram, Oh.	1850	Elmer Jagow	P,D	1,184	95
Hobart & William Smith	Geneva, N.Y.	1822	Allan A. Kuusisto	P	1,795	143
Hofstra Univ.	Hempstead, N.Y.	1935	Robert J. Payton	P	10,798	500
Hollins (W)	Hollins Coll., Va.	1852	Carroll Brewster	P	1,033	99
Holy Cross, Coll. of the	Worcester, Mass.	1843	Rev. John Brooks	D	2,400	169
Holy Family	Philadelphia, Pa.	1954	Sister Mary Lillian	D,P	945	77
Holy Names	Oakland, Cal.	1868	Sister M. Irene Woodward	P	675	108
Hood	Frederick, Md.	1893	Martha Church	P	1,001	125
Hope	Holland, Mich.	1866	Gordon Van Wylen	P	2,275	150
Houghton	Houghton, N.Y.	1883	Wilber T. Dayton	P	1,284	93
Houston Baptist Univ.	Houston, Tex.	1963	William Hinton	D	1,206	87
Houston, Univ. of	Houston, Tex.	1927	Philip G. Hoffman	S	38,500	1,750
Downtown College	Houston, Tex.	1948	J. Don Boney, Chan.	S	4,475	174
Howard Payne	Brownwood, Tex.	1889	Roger L. Brooks	P	1,422	90
Howard Univ.	Washington, D.C.	1867	James E. Cheek	P	9,031	1,600
Humboldt State Univ.	Arcata, Cal.	1913	Alistair McCrone	S	7,700	450
Huntingdon	Montgomery, Ala.	1854	Allen Jackson	D	584	53
Huntington	Huntington, Ind.	1897	E. DeWitt Baker	P,D	576	58
Husson	Bangor, Me.	1898	Franklin Peters	P	1,030	89
Huston-Tillotson	Austin, Tex.	1876	John T. King	D	725	44
Idaho, Coll. of	Caldwell, Ida.	1891	William Cassell	P	849	63
Idaho State Univ.	Pocatello, Ida.	1901	Charles Kegel	S	9,412	325
Idaho, Univ. of*	Moscow, Ida.	1889	Ernest W. Hartung	S	8,170	650
Illinois	Jacksonville, Ill.	1829	Donald Mundinger	P	800	63
Illinois Benedictine	Lisle, Ill.	1887	Rev. Daniel Kucera	P	1,301	85
Illinois Coll. of Optometry	Chicago, Ill.	1872	Alfred Rosenbloom	P	570	50
Illinois Inst. of Technology	Chicago, Ill.	1940	Thomas L. Martin	P	6,459	735
Illinois State Univ.	Normal, Ill.	1857	Gene Budig	S	21,031	1,250
Illinois, Univ. of*	Urbana; Champaign.	1867	John E. Corbally	S	64,531	7,558
Chicago Circle	Chicago, Ill.	1965	Donald Riddle, Chan.	S	20,693	1,222
Medical Center	Chicago, Ill.	1896	Joseph Begando, Chan.	S	4,537	3,812
Urbana — Champaign	Urbana, Ill.	1867	Jack W. Peltason, Chan.	S	35,117	2,590
Illinois Wesleyan Univ.	Bloomington, Ill.	1850	Robert Eckley	P,D	1,679	145
Immaculata	Immaculata, Pa.	1920	Sister Mary Antione	P,D	1,079	143
Immaculate Heart	Los Angeles, Cal.	1916	Sister Helen Kelley	P	729	79
Incarnate Word College	San Antonio, Tex.	1881	Sr. Margaret Slattery	D	1,440	114
Indiana Central	Indianapolis, Ind.	1902	Gene Sease	P,D	3,100	168
Indiana Inst. of Tech.	Ft. Wayne, Ind.	1930	Charles W. Terrell	P	358	32
Indiana State Univ.	Terre Haute, Ind.	1865	Richard Landini	S	11,012	750
Indiana Univ.	Bloomington, Ind.	1820	John W. Ryan	S	76,905	2,878
Indiana Univ. of Penn.	Indiana, Pa.	1875	Robert C. Wilburn	S	11,119	557
Insurance, Coll. of	New York, N.Y.	1962	A. Leslie Leonard	P	1,559	142
Inter American Univ. of P.R.	San Juan, P.R.	1912	Sol Luis Descartes	P	23,300	1,042
Iona	New Rochelle, N.Y.	1940	Rev. Bro. John Driscoll	P	5,000	280
Iowa State Univ.*	Ames, Ia.	1868	W. Robert Parks	S	19,321	1,682
Iowa, Univ. of	Iowa City, Ia.	1847	Willard L. Boyd	S	21,271	1,193
Iowa Wesleyan	Mt. Pleasant, Ia.	1842	Louis Haselmayer	P	651	45
Ithaca	Ithaca, N.Y.	1892	James J. Whalen	P	4,200	370
Jackson State Univ.	Jackson, Miss.	1877	John A. Peoples, Jr.	S	7,718	359
Jacksonville State Univ.	Jacksonville, Ala.	1883	Ernest Stone	S	6,500	250
Jacksonville Univ.	Jacksonville, Fla.	1934	Robert H. Spiro	P	2,308	150
Jamestown	Jamestown, N.D.	1886	J. N. Anderson	P	470	58
Jarvis Christian	Hawkins, Tex.	1912	John Paul Jones	P	398	45
Jersey City State	Jersey City, N.J.	1926	William Maxwell	S	9,000	300
John Brown Univ.	Siloam Springs, Ark.	1919	John E. Brown, Jr.	P	591	45
John Carroll Univ.	Cleveland, Oh.	1886	Rev. Henry Birkenhauer	P	3,621	265
John F. Kennedy Univ.	Orinda, Cal.	1964	Robert Fisher	P	550	85
John Marshall Law School	Chicago, Ill.	1899	F. Herzog, Dean.	P	1,450	75
John Wesley	Owosso, Mich.	1909	Kenneth Armstrong	P	600	24
Johns Hopkins Univ.	Baltimore, Md.	1876	Steven Muller	P	9,685	756
Johnson C. Smith Univ.	Charlotte, N.C.	1867	Wilbert Greenfield	P,D	1,350	93

(1) Includes Radcliffe College (2) Includes teaching fellows.
**oldest college in the United States.

Name	Location	Year	Governing Official and Affiliation		Students	Teachers
Johnson State	Johnston, Vt.	1866	E. Elmendorf	S	1,253	100
Johnson & Wales	Providence, R.I.	1914	Morris J. Gaebe	P	8,341	450
Jones	Ft. Pierce, Fla.	1918	Delores C. Jones	P	432	16
	Jacksonville, Fla.	1918	Delores C. Jones	P	1,840	58
	Orlando, Fla.	1918	Delores C. Jones	P	1,902	67
Norfolk Extension	Norfolk, Va.	1918	Delores C. Jones	P	389	31
Juilliard School, The	New York, N.Y.	1906	Peter Mennin	P	1,191	180
Juniata	Huntingdon, Pa.	1876	Frederick M. Binder	P	1,074	90
Kalamazoo (A)	Kalamazoo, Mich.	1833	George N. Rainsford	D	1,356	74
Kan. City Art Inst	Kansas City, Mo.	1885	John W. Lottes	P	727	59
Kan. City Coll. of Osteop. Med.	Kansas City, Mo.	1916	Rudolph Bremen	P	578	117
Kansas Newman	Wichita, Kan.	1933	Rev. Roman S. Galiardi	D	659	51
Kansas State	Pittsburg, Kan.	1903	George F. Budd	S	4,646	250
Kansas State Univ.*	Manhattan, Kan.	1863	Duane Acker	S	17,901	1,360
Kansas, Univ. of	Lawrence, Kan.	1865	Archie R. Dykes	S	23,541	1,975
Kansas Wesleyan	Salina, Kan.	1886	Daniel Bratton	D	497	40
Kean Coll. of New Jersey	Union, N.J.	1855	Nathan Weiss	S	14,103	720
Kearney State	Kearney, Neb.	1903	Brendan McDonald	S	5,322	219
Keene State	Keene, N.H.	1909	Leo Redfern	S	2,998	147
Kent State Univ.	Kent, Oh.	1910	Glenn A. Olds	S	24,850	836
Kentucky State Univ.*	Frankfort, Ky.	1886	W. A. Butts	S	2,123	208
Kentucky, Univ. of*	Lexington, Ky.	1865	Otis A. Singletary	S	22,154	977
Kentucky Wesleyan (A)	Owensboro, Ky.	1783	William James	P	933	71
Kenyon	Gambier, Oh.	1824	Philip Jordan, Jr.	P	1,456	125
Keuka (W)	Keuka Park, N.Y.	1890	William Boyle, Jr.	P	600	52
King	Bristol, Tenn.	1867	Powell A. Fraser	P	282	37
King's	Briarcliff Manor, N.Y.	1938	Robert A. Cook	D	850	67
King's	Wilkes-Barre, Pa.	1946	Rev. Charles Sherrer	D	2,139	140
Kirksville Coll. of Osteop. Med.	Kirksville, Mo.	1892	H. C. Moore	P	491	85
Knox	Galesburg, Ill.	1837	E. Inman Fox	P	1,187	91
Knoxville	Knoxville, Tenn.	1875	Robert Harvey, Act.	D,P	950	73
Kutztown State	Kutztown, Pa.	1866	Lawrence M. Stratton	S	5,506	283
Ladycliff	Highland Falls, N.Y.	1933	Rev. Francis J. Breidenbach	P	512	51
Lafayette	Easton, Pa.	1826	K. R. Bergethon	P,D	2,308	182
LaGrange	LaGrange, Ga.	1831	Waights Henry, Jr.	D	757	45
Lake Erie (W)	Painesville, Oh.	1856	Paul Weaver	P	849	80
Lake Forest	Lake Forest, Ill.	1857	Eugene Hotchkiss III	P,D	1,100	80
Lakeland	Sheboygan, Wis.	1862	Ralph Mirse	D	485	36
Lake Superior State	Sault Ste. Marie, Mich.	1946	Kenneth Shouldice	S	2,371	115
Lamar Univ.	Beaumont, Tex.	1923	John E. Gray	S	12,723	414
Lander	Greenwood, S.C.	1872	Larry Jackson	S	1,570	85
Langston Univ.*	Langston, Okla.	1897	James Mosley, Act.	S	1,024	74
LaRoche	Pittsburgh, Pa.	1963	Sister Mary Coultas	D,P	729	74
La Salle	Philadelphia, Pa.	1863	Bro. Daniel Burke	D,P	5,600	375
La Verne	La Verne, Cal.	1891	Leland Newcomer	P	1,046	80
Lawrence Inst. Of Tech.	Southfield, Mich.	1932	W. H. Buell	P	4,413	216
Lawrence Univ.	Appleton, Wis.	1847	Thomas S. Smith	P	1,378	108
Lebanon Valley	Annville, Pa.	1866	Frederick Sample	P	1,100	110
Lee	Cleveland, Tenn.	1918	Charles Conn	D	1,180	55
Lehigh Univ.	Bethlehem, Pa.	1865	W. Deming Lewis	P	6,261	605
Leland Stanford Univ.	Stanford, Col.	1891	Richard W. Lyman	P	11,123	1,097
Le Moyne	Syracuse, N.Y.	1946	Rev. William L. Reilly	P	1,787	125
Le Moyne-Owen	Memphis, Tenn.	1870	Walter Walker	P	1,107	60
Lenoir Rhyne	Hickory, N.C.	1891	Raymond Bost	D,P	1,300	120
Lesley (W)	Cambridge, Mass.	1909	Don A. Orton	P	1,311	109
Lewis Univ.	Lockport, Ill.	1932	Lester Carr	P	4,003	241
Lewis & Clark	Portland, Ore.	1867	John R. Howard	P	2,977	199
Limestone	Gaffney, S.C.	1845	Jack Jones Early	P	690	55
Lincoln Christian	Lincoln, Ill.	1944	Robert Phillips	P	870	50
Lincoln Memorial Univ.	Harrogate, Tenn.	1897	Frank W. Welch	P	860	51
Lincoln Univ.	Jefferson City, Mo.	1866	James Frank	S	2,400	165
Lincoln Univ.	Lincoln Univ., Pa.	1854	Herman Branson	S	1,103	103
Lincoln Univ.	San Francisco, Cal.	1919	T. Kong Lee, Chan.	P	1,100	62
Lindenwood	St. Charles, Mo.	1827	William Spencer	P	1,572	113
Linfield	McMinnville, Ore.	1849	Charles Walker	P	1,049	76
Livingston Univ.	Livingston, Ala.	1839	Asa Green	S	1,450	75
Livingstone	Salisbury, N.C.	1879	F. George Shipman	D	857	65
Lock Haven State	Lock Haven, Pa.	1870	Francis Hamblin	S	2,400	180
Loma Linda Univ.	Loma Linda, Cal.	1905	V. Norskov Olsen	Mu	4,396	1,416
Lone Mountain	San Francisco, Cal.	1898	Sister Gertrude Patch	P	892	47
Long Island Univ.	Brooklyn, N.Y.	1926	Edward Clark	P	7,000	418
C. W. Post (A)	Greenvale, N.Y.	1954	Vacant	P	9,700	331
Longwood	Farmville, Va.	1839	Henry I. Willett, Jr.	S	2,150	150
Loras	Dubuque, Ia.	1839	Msgr. Francis P. Friedl	D	1,391	92
Los Angeles Baptist	Newhall, Cal.	1927	John Dunkin	D	317	16
Louisiana	Pineville, La.	1906	Robert Lynn	P	1,170	56
Louisiana St. Univ.*	Baton Rouge, La.	1860	Martin Woodin	S	45,824	4,034
Baton Rouge Campus	Baton Rouge, La.	1860	Paul Murrill, Chan.	S	24,791	1,171
Medical Center	New Orleans, La.	1931	Allen Copping, Chan.	S	1,967	1,830
New Orleans Campus	New Orleans, La.	1956	Homer L. Hitt, Chan.	S	13,705	446
Shreveport Campus	Shreveport, La.	1965	Donald Shipp, Chan.	S	3,001	132
Louisiana Tech. Univ.	Ruston, La.	1894	F.J. Taylor	S	8,868	410
Louisville, Univ. of	Louisville, Ky.	1798	James G. Miller	S	15,781	1,718
Lowell Univ.	Lowell, Mass.	1894	John B. Duff	S	10,000	480
Loyola	Baltimore, Md.	1852	Rev. J. A. Sellinger	D	4,000	203
Loyola Univ.	Chicago, Ill.	1870	Rev. R.C. Baumhart	D	14,567	629
Loyola Univ.	New Orleans, La.	1912	Rev. James Carter	D	4,324	302
Loyola Marymount Univ.	Los Angeles, Cal.	1911	Rev. D. P. Merrifield	D	5,303	335
Lubbock Christian	Lubbock, Tex.	1957	W. Joe Hacker Jr.	P	1,355	104
Luther	Decorah, Ia.	1861	Elwin D. Farwell	D	1,872	121
Lycoming	Williamsport, Pa.	1812	Harold Hutson	D	1,400	75
Lynchburg	Lynchburg, Va.	1903	Carey Brewer	P	2,020	126
Lyndon State	Lyndonville, Vt.	1911	Edward Stevens	S	974	91

Name	Location	Year	Governing Official and Affiliation		Stu-dents	Teach-ers
Macalester	St. Paul, Minn.	1874	John B. Davis, Jr.	P	1,600	155
MacMurray	Jacksonville, Ill.	1846	John Wittich	P,D	749	61
Madison	Harrisonburg, Va.	1908	Ronald Carrier	S	7,345	440
Madonna	Livonia, Mich.	1947	Sister Mary Danatha	P,D	2,021	95
Maine Maritime Academy	Castine, Me.	1941	E.A. Rodgers (Supt.)	S	622	55
Maine System, Univ. of (A)	Bangor, Me.	1968	Stanley Freeman, Act. Chan.	S	25,696	1,115
at Augusta	Augusta, Me.	1968	Lloyd Jewett	S	2,595	51
at Farmington	Farmington, Me.	1864	Einar Olsen	S	1,898	95
at Ft. Kent	Ft. Kent, Me.	1878	Richard J. Spath	S	520	26
at Machias	Machias, Me.	1909	Arthur Buswell	S	638	36
at Orono, Me.	Orono, Me.	1865	Howard Nevill	S	10,576	579
at Portland-Gorham	Portland, Me.	1970	E. Miller	S	8,080	263
at Presque Isle	Presque Isle, Me.	1903	Stanley Salwak	S	1,389	65
Malone	Canton, Oh.	1892	Lon D. Randall	D	891	58
Manchester	N. Manchester, Ind.	1889	Alfred B. Helman	D	1,171	91
Manhattan	Riverdale, N.Y.	1853	Brother Stephen Sullivan	P	4,590	272
Manhattan Sch. of Music	New York, N.Y.	1917	George Schick	P	1,000	200
Manhattanville	Purchase, N.Y.	1841	Barbara K. Debs	P	2,498	153
Mankato State	Mankato, Minn.	1867	Douglas Moore	S	13,000	550
Mansfield State	Mansfield, Pa.	1857	Lawrence Park	S	3,014	215
Marian	Indianapolis, Ind.	1851	Louis C. Gatto	D	801	80
Marian Coll. of Fond du Lac	Fon du Lac, Wis.	1936	James Hanlon	P	517	63
Marietta	Marietta, Oh.	1835	Sherrill Cleland	P	1,647	115
Marion	Marion, Ind.	1920	Woodrow Goodman	D	775	64
Marist	Poughkeepsie, N.Y.	1946	Linus Richard Foy	P	1,909	118
Marlboro	Marlboro, Vt.	1946	Thomas B. Ragle	P	210	37
Marquette Univ.	Milwaukee, Wis.	1881	Rev. J.P. Raynor	P	12,001	720
Mars Hill	Mars Hill, N.C.	1856	Fred Blake Bentley	D	1,910	106
Marshall Univ.	Huntington, W. Va.	1837	Robert B. Hayes	S	10,847	410
Mary Baldwin	Staunton, Va.	1842	Patrician Menk. Act.	D	700	60
Mary Hardin Baylor	Belton, Tex.	1845	Bobby E. Parker	D	1,091	63
Mary Washington	Fredericksburg, Va.	1908	Prince B. Woodward	S	2,040	137
Marycrest	Davenport, Ia.	1939	Ron Van Ryswyk	P	949	95
Marygrove	Detroit, Mich.	1910	Raymond Fleck	D	1,700	164
Maryland Inst. of Art	Baltimore, Md.	1826	William J. Finn	P	1,566	95
Maryland, Univ. of*	College Park, Md.	1859	Wilson Elkins	S	35,890	3,454
Eastern Shore	Princess Anne, Md.	1886	William P. Hytche, Act.	S	1,100	83
Marylhurst	Marylhurst, Ore.	1893	Sr. Marian D. Robinson	D	603	46
Marymount	Salina, Kan.	1922	Sr. Mary Buser	D	717	56
Marymount (W)	Tarrytown, N.Y.	1917	Robert Christin	P	958	114
Marymount Coll. of Va.	Arlington, Va.	1950	Sr. M. Matella Berg	D	615	43
Marymount Manhattan	New York, N.Y.	1947	Colette Mahoney	P	1,740	142
Maryville	Maryville, Tenn.	1819	Joseph J. Copeland	D,P	690	56
Maryville	St. Louis, Mo.	1872	Sister Harriet Switzer	P	1,041	90
Marywood	Scranton, Pa.	1915	Sister M. Coleman Nee	P	2,600	214
Massachusetts Coll. Of Art	Boston, Mass.	1873	John Nolan	S	1,547	108
Mass. Coll. of Pharmacy	Boston, Mass.	1823	Raymond A. Gosselin	P	1,325	130
Mass. Institute of Tech.*	Cambridge, Mass.	1861	Jerome Wiesner	P	7,972	972
Mass. Maritime Academy (M)	Buzzards Bay, Mass.	1891	Lee Harrington	S	1,560	99
Massachusetts, Univ. of*	Boston, Mass.	1863	Robert C. Wood	S	33,589	2,381
Boston Campus	Boston, Mass.	1964	Carlo L. Golino, Chan.	S	6,600	500
Mayville State	Mayville, N.D	1889	James Schobel	S	675	41
McKendree	Lebanon, Ill.	1828	Julian Murphy	D	702	39
McMurry	Abilene, Tex.	1923	Tom K. Kim	D	1,330	84
McNeese State Univ.	Lake Charles, La.	1939	Thomas S. Leary	S	6,010	344
McPherson	McPherson, Kan.	1887	Galen Snell	P	485	48
Medaille	Buffalo, N.Y.	1875	Robert Hesse	P	681	75
Medical Coll. of Ga.	Augusta, Ga.	1828	William Moretz	S	2,224	440
Medical Univ. of S.C.	Charleston, S.C.	1824	William McCord	S	2,020	630
Meharry Medical	Nashville, Tenn.	1876	Lloyd C. Elam	P	790	240
Memphis Academy of Arts	Memphis, Tenn.	1936	Jameson Jones	P	240	24
Medical Coll. of Pa.	Philadelphia, Pa.	1850	Robert J. Slater	P	836	423
Memphis State Univ.	Memphis Tenn.	1912	Billy Jones	S	22,695	707
Menlo	Menlo Park, Cal.	1915	Richard O'Brien	P	540	50
Mercer Univ.	Macon, Ga.	1833	Rufus C. Harris	P	3,611	125
Mercy	Dobbs Ferry, N.Y.	1950	Donald Grunewald	P	2,676	172
Mercy Coll. of Detroit	Detroit, Mich.	1941	Sister Agnes Mary Mansour	D	1,936	120
Mercyhurst	Erie, Pa.	1926	Marion Shane	P	1,349	95
Meredith (W)	Raleigh, N.C.	1891	John Edgar Weems	D,P	1,400	135
Merrimack	No. Andover, Mass.	1947	Rev. John Aherne	P	2,450	182
Mesa College	Grand Junction Col.	1925	John Tomlinson	S	2,716	163
Messiah	Grantham, Pa.	1909	D. Ray Hostetter	P	1,081	92
Methodist	Fayetteville, N.C.	1956	Richard-Pearce	P	671	45
Metropolitan State	Denver, Col.	1963	James D. Palmer	S	12,651	301
Miami Univ.	Oxford, Oh.	1809	Phillip R. Shriver	S	17,555	824
Miami, Univ. of	Coral Gables, Fla.	1925	Henry K. Stanford	P	13,213	1,279
Michigan State Univ.*	East Lansing, Mich.	1855	Clifton R. Wharton, Jr.	S	43,459	2,687
Michigan Tech. Univ.	Houghton, Mich.	1885	Raymond L. Smith	S	5,958	300
Michigan, Univ. of	Ann Arbor, Mich.	1817	Robben W. Fleming	S	44,372	5,362
Mid-America Nazarene	Olathe, Kan.	1968	R. Curtis Smith	D	1,057	61
Middle Tenn. State Univ.	Murfreesboro, Tenn.	1911	M.G. Scarlett	S	10,514	570
Middlebury	Middlebury, Vt.	1800	Olin Robinson	P	1,917	155
Midland Lutheran	Fremont, Neb.	1883	L. Dale Lund	D	802	70
Midwestern Univ.	Wichita Falls, Tex.	1922	John Barker	S	4,586	155
Miles	Birmingham, Ala.	1905	W. Clyde Williams	D	1,245	89
Millersville State	Millersville, Pa.	1855	William Duncan	S	6,179	294
Milligan	Milligan Coll., Tenn.	1881	Jess W. Johnson	D	810	54
Millikin Univ.	Decatur, Ill.	1901	J. Roger Miller	P,D	1,786	181
Mills (W)	Oakland, Cal.	1885	Robert J. Wert	P	913	107
Milsaps	Jackson, Miss.	1890	Edward Collins	D	955	77
Milton	Milton, Wis.	1867	Joseph Kipper	P	500	45
Milwaukee Sch. of Eng.	Milwaukee, Wis.	1903	Karl O. Werwath	P	2,185	154
Minneapolis Coll. of Art & Design	Minneapolis, Minn.	1886	J. Hausman	P	960	78
Minnesota, Univ. of*	Minneapolis, Minn.	1851	C.P. Magrath	S	55,114	5,767
Duluth Campus	Duluth, Minn.	1947	R.W. Darland (Prov.)	S	7,200	362
Morris Campus	Morris, Minn.	1960	John Imholte (Prov.)	S	2,150	89
Minot State	Minot, N.D.	1913	Gordon Olson	S	2,150	139
Misericordia	Dallas, Pa.	1924	Sister Ann Gallagher	D	943	71

Name	Location	Year	Governing Official and Affiliation		Students	Teachers
Mississippi	Clinton, Miss.	1826	Lewis Nobles	D	3,514	173
Mississippi Industrial	Holly Springs, Miss.	1905	E.E. Rankin	D	401	20
Miss. Univ. for Women (W)	Columbus, Miss.	1884	Charles P. Hogarth	S	2,986	170
Mississippi State Univ.*	Miss. State, Miss.	1878	William L. Giles	S	12,011	900
Mississippi Univ. of	University, Miss.	1848	P.L. Fortune, Jr. (Chan.)	S	11,000	500
Mississippi Valley State Univ.	Itta Bena, Miss.	1950	E.A. Boykins	S	3,042	145
Missouri Baptist College	St. Louis, Mo.	1968	R. Sutherland Act.	D	405	20
Missouri Inst. of Tech.	Kansas City, Mo.	1931	C.R. LeValley	P	624	29
Missouri Southern State	Joplin, Mo.	1937	Leon Billingsley	S	3,700	185
Missouri Univ. of*	Columbia, Mo.	1839	C. Brice Ratchford	S	51,100	2,722
at Columbia	Columbia, Mo.	1839	H.W. Schooling, Chan.	S	23,500	3,515
at Kansas City	Kansas City, Mo.	1933	James Olson, Chan.	S	12,000	1,500
at Rolla	Rolla, Mo.	1870	R. Bisplinghoff, Chan.	S	4,350	670
at St. Louis	St. Louis, Mo.	1963	A. Grobman, Chan.	S	11,863	535
Missouri Valley	Marshall, Mo.	1889	Donald Ziemke	P	493	44
Missouri Western State	St. Joseph, Mo.	1915	Marvin Looney	S	3,187	170
Mobile	Mobile, Ala.	1961	William K. Weaver, Jr.	P	1,000	70
Molloy	Rockville Ctre, N.Y.	1955	Sister Janet Fitzgerald	D	1,188	117
Monmouth	Monmouth, Ill.	1853	DeBow Freed	P	750	70
Monmouth College	W. Long Branch, N.J.	1933	Richard Stonesifer	P	3,957	208
Montana Coll. of Mineral Science and Technology	Butte, Mon.	1893	Fred W. DeMoney	S	933	52
Montana State Univ.	Bozeman, Mon.	1893	Carl McIntosh	S	9,000	500
Montana, Univ. of	Missoula, Mon.	1893	Richard Bowers	S	8,826	508
Montclair State	Upper Montclair, N.J.	1908	David W.D. Dickson	S	15,640	515
Monterey Inst. of Foreign Studies	Monterey, Cal.	1955	Stuart McIntyre	P	424	60
Montevallo, Univ. of (A)	Montevallo, Ala.	1896	Kermit Johnson	S	3,600	160
Moody Bible Institute	Chicago, Ill.	1886	George Sweeting	P,D	2,955	98
Moore Coll. of Art (W)	Philadelphia Pa.	1844	M.B. Allen	P	685	81
Moorehead State	Moorehead, Minn.	1885	Roland Dille	S	4,916	319
Moravian	Bethlehem, Pa.	1807	Herman E. Collier	D,P	1,497	144
Morehead State Univ.	Morehead, Ky.	1922	Adron Doran	S	7,318	306
Morehouse (M)	Atlanta, Ga.	1867	Hugh Gloster	P	1,350	101
Morgan State	Baltimore, Md.	1867	A. Billingsley	S	6,361	286
Morningside	Sioux City, Ia.	1894	Thomas S. Thompson	D,P	1,502	101
Morris Brown	Atlanta, Ga.	1881	Robert Threatt	P	1,643	103
Morris Harvey	Charleston, W. Va.	1888	Robert L. Bliss	P	2,134	146
Mt. Holyoke (W)	S. Hadley, Mass.	1837	David Bicknell Truman	P	1,964	178
Mt. Marty	Yankston, S.D.	1936	Bruce Weier	D,P	617	65
Mt. Mary (W)	Milwaukee, Wis.	1913	Sister Mary Nora Barber	P	1,278	127
Mt. Mercy	Cedar Rapids, Ia.	1928	Sister Mary Hennessey	P	900	76
Mt. St. Joseph (W)	Mt. St. Joseph, Oh.	1920	Robert Wolverton	P,D	894	104
Mt. St. Mary (M)	Hooksett, N.H.	1934	Sister Amy Hoey	P,D	205	42
Mt. St. Mary	Newburgh, N.Y.	1959	William O'Hara	P,D	960	88
Mt. St. Mary's	Los Angeles, Cal.	1925	Sister Cecilia Louise Moore	D,P	1,077	112
Mt. St. Mary's	Emmitsburg, Md.	1808	John J. Dillon	P	1,216	84
Mt. St. Vincent, Coll. of	Riverdale, N.Y.	1847	Sister Doris Smith	P	1,106	84
Mt. Senario	Ladysmith, Wis.	1962	Robert Lovett	P	410	35
Mt. Union	Alliance, Oh.	1846	Ronald Weber	P	1,101	84
Mt. Vernon	Washington, D.C.	1875	Peter Pelham	P	430	48
Mt. Vernon Nazarene	Mount Vernon, Oh.	1966	L. Guy Nees	D	819	56
Muhlenberg	Allentown, Pa.	1848	John H. Morey	P,D	1,825	118
Multnomah Sch. of the Bible	Portland, Ore.	1936	Willard M. Aldrich	P	804	42
Mundelein	Chicago, Ill.	1930	Susan Rink	D	1,375	136
Murray State Univ.	Murray, Ky.	1922	C. Curris	S	7,355	355
Muskingum	New Concord, Oh.	1837	John A. Brown	P,D	1,025	99
National Coll. of Business	Rapid City, S.D.	1941	John Hauer	P	1,199	65
National Coll. of Chiropractic	Lombard, Ill.	1906	Joseph Janse	P	811	55
National Coll. of Education	Evanston, Ill.	1886	Calvin Gross	P	3,610	144
Nazareth Coll. at Kalamazoo	Nazareth, Mich	1924	John S. Lore	P,D	472	71
Nazareth Coll. of Rochester	Rochester, N.Y.	1924	Alice Foley	P	2,590	142
Nebraska, Univ. of*	Lincoln, Neb.	1869	Durward Varner	S	38,923	2,465
at Omaha	Omaha, Neb.	1908	Ronald Roskens	S	14,294	581
Nebraska Wesleyan Univ.	Lincoln, Neb.	1887	Vance Rogers	S	1,169	92
Nevada Univ. of*	Reno, Nev.	1864	Max Milam	S	8,225	617
at Las Vegas	Las Vegas, Nev.	1955	Donald Baepler	S	8,382	422
New	Sarasota, Fla.	1960	George Mayer, Provost.	S	450	43
New England	Henniker, N.H.	1946	J.K. Cummiskey	P	1,466	129
New England Cons. of Music	Boston, Mass.	1867	Gunther Schuller	P	759	135
New Hampshire	Manchester, N.H.	1,932	Edward Shapiro	P	3,512	124
New Hampshire, Univ. of*	Durham, N.H.	1866	Eugene Mills	S	11,993	634
New Haven, Univ. of*	New Haven, Conn.	1920	Phillip Kaplan	P	6,453	125
New Jersey Inst. of Tech.	Newark, N.J.	1881	Paul H. Newell, Jr.	S	5,377	240
New Mexico Highlands Univ.	Las Vegas N.M.	1893	John Aragon	S	2,045	144
N. Mexico Inst. of Min. & Tech.	Socorro, N.M.	1889	Kenneth Ford	S	920	79
New Mexico State Univ.*	Las Cruces, N.M.	1888	Gerald W. Thomas	S	13,539	460
New Mexico, Univ. of	Albuquerque, N.M.	1889	William Davis	S	20,032	1,419
New Rochelle, Coll. of (W)	New Rochelle, N.Y.	1904	Sister Dorothy Ann Kelly	P	2,979	230
New School for Social Research	New York, N.Y.	1919	John R. Everett	P	25,000	1,050
New York, City Univ. of.		1847	Robert J. Kibbee, Chan.	Mu	269,929	15,116
Bernard M. Baruch	New York, N.Y.	1919	Clyde J. Wingfield	Mu	17,271	980
Brooklyn	Brooklyn, N.Y.	1930	John W. Kneller	Mu	36,947	2,019
City	New York, N.Y.	1847	Robert E. Marshak	Mu	20,388	1,392
Medgar Evers**	Brooklyn, N.Y.	1968	Richard D. Trent	Mu	3,506	278
**Will become a 2 yr. College in Sept. 1976						
Hunter	New York, N.Y.	1870	Jacqueline G. Wexler	Mu	25,677	1,327
John Jay Coll. of Criminal Just.	New York, N.Y.	1964	Gerald Lynch, Act.	Mu	9,812	423
Herbert H. Lehman	Bronx, N.Y.	1931	Leonard Lief	Mu	16,306	1,023
Queens	Flushing, N.Y.	1937	Joseph Murphy	Mu	28,735	1,612
Richmond**	Staten Island, N.Y.	1965	Edmond Volpe	Mu	3,741	215
**Federated with Staten Island Comm. on Sept. 1, 1976.						
York	Jamaica, N.Y.	1966	Milton G. Bassin	Mu	6,771	419
N.Y. Inst. of Technology	Old Westbury, N.Y.	1957	Alexander Schure	P	20,000	600
New York Law School	New York, N.Y.	1891	E. Shapiro	P	850	56
New York Medical (A)	New York, N.Y.	1860	Frederick L. Stone	P	613	1,200

Name	Location	Year	Governing Official and Affiliation		Students	Teachers
New York, State Univ. of	Albany, N.Y.	1948	Ernest L. Boyer, (Chan.)	S	171,570	9,345
State Univ.	Albany, N.Y.	1844	Emmet B. Fields.	S	15,414	790
" "	Buffalo, N.Y.	1846	Robert Ketter.	S	24,025	947
" "	Binghampton, N.Y.	1946	Clifford D. Clark.	S	9,695	463
" "	Stony Brook, N.Y.	1957	John Toll.	S	14,849	630
State Univ. Colleges.	Brockport, N.Y.	1867	Albert W. Brown.	S	11,696	541
" " "	Buffalo, N.Y.	1867	Elbert K. Fretwell.	S	12,604	587
" " "	Cortland, N.Y.	1866	Richard Jones.	S	6,075	321
" " "	Fredonia, N.Y.	1867	Dallas Beal.	S	5,233	272
" " "	Geneseo, N.Y.	1867	Robert Mac Vittie.	S	6,374	295
" " "	New Paltz, N.Y.	1885	Stanley K. Coffman.	S	8,892	396
" " "	Oneonta, N.Y.	1887	Clifford Craven.	S	6,344	368
" " "	Oswego, N.Y.	1861	James E. Perdue.	S	9,764	417
" " "	Old Westbury, N.Y.	1965	John Maguire.	S	1,875	84
" " "	Plattsburgh, N.Y.	1889	Joseph C. Burke.	S	6,709	312
" " "	Potsdam, N.Y.	1867	Thomas Barrington.	S	5,021	290
" " "	Purchase, N.Y.	1965	Abbott Kaplan.	S	2,778	97
" " "	Utica, N.Y.	1966	William Kunsela.	S	2,928	101
" " Empire State.	Saratoga Spgs., N.Y.	1971	James Hall.	S	3,537	98
Buffalo Health Sciences Ctr.	Buffalo, N.Y.	1846	F.C. Pannill, V.P.	S	3,009	403
College of Ceramics.	Alfred, N.Y.	1900	W.G. Lawrence, Dean.	S	570	43
Env'm'nt'l Sci. & Forestry.	Syracuse, N.Y.	1911	Edward Palmer.	S	2,487	95
Downstate Medical Center	Brooklyn, N.Y.	1858	Calvin H. Plimpton.	S	1,468	505
Health Sciences Center	Stony Brook, N.Y.	1957	James H. Oaks, V.P.	S	1,261	222
Maritime College (M).	Bronx, N.Y.	1874	Sheldon Kinney.	S	1,004	56
Upstate Medical Center	Syracuse, N.Y.	1834	Richard P. Schmidt.	S	1,005	267
New York Univ.	New York, N.Y.	1831	John Sawhill.	P	41,000	5,500
Newark Coll. of Engineering (A)	Newark, N.J.	1881	William Hazell.	S	4,200	291
Newberry.	Newberry, S.C.	1856	Glenn Whitesides.	D,P	860	57
Newcomb Coll.	New Orleans, La.	1886	James Davidson, Dean.	P	1,622	112
Niagara Univ.	Niagara Univ., N.Y.	1856	Rev. K.F. Slattery.	D	4,123	270
Nicholls State Univ.	Thibodaux, La.	1948	Vernon Galliano.	S	6,410	262
Nichols.	Dudley, Mass.	1815	Darcy C. Coyle.	P	579	37
Norfolk State.	Norfolk, Va.	1935	Lyman Brooks.	S	6,260	405
North Adams State.	North Adams, Mass.	1894	James Amsler.	S	2,671	130
North Carolina, Univ. of.	Chapel Hill, N.C.	1972	William Friday.	S	104,786	6,325
A&T State Univ.	Greensboro, N.C.	1891	Lewis Dowdy, Chan.	S	5,345	310
Appalachian State Univ.	Boone, N.C.	1899	Herbert Wey.	S	7,989	520
at Asheville.	Asheville, N.C.	1927	William Highsmith.	S	1,455	80
at Chapel Hill.	Chapel Hill, N.C.	1789	N.F.Taylor.	S	19,400	2,600
at Charlotte.	Charlotte, N.C.	1946	D.W. Colvard.	S	7,570	474
E. Carolina Univ.	Greenville, N.C.	1907	Leo W. Jenkins, Chan.	S	2,852	679
Elizabeth City State Univ.	Elizabeth City, N.C.	1891	Marion Thorpe, Chan.	S	1,629	114
Fayetteville State Univ.	Fayetteville, N.C.	1877	Charles A. Lyons Jr.	S	3,593	271
at Greensboro.	Greensboro, N.C.	1892	J.S. Ferguson, Chan.	S	9,459	494
North Carolina Central Univ.	Durham, N.C.	1910	Albert N. Whiting.	S	4,730	258
N.C. School of the Arts.	Winston-Salem, N.C.	1965	Robert Suderburg, Chan.	S	320	93
Pembroke State Univ.	Pembroke, N.C.	1887	English E. Jones.	S	1,784	112
at Raleigh State Univ.	Raleigh, N.C.	1887	Joab L. Thomas.	S	17,500	1,200
Western Carolina Univ.	Cullowhee, N.C.	1889	H.F. Robinson, Chan.	S	6,084	296
at Wilmington	Wilmington, N.C.	1947	Wm. H. Wagoner, Chan.	S	3,309	187
Winston-Salem State Univ.	Winston-Salem, N.C.	1892	Kenneth Williams, Chan.	S	2,055	135
North Carolina Wesleyan	Rocky Mount, N.C.	1956	S. Bruce Petteway.	D,P	481	30
North Central Bible	Minneapolis, Minn.	1932	Rev. E.M. Clark.	S	557	25
North Central	Naperville, Ill.	1861	Gael D. Swing.	P	987	65
North Dakota State Univ.	Fargo, N.D.	1890	L.D. Loftsgard.	S	6,600	475
North Dakota, Univ. of.	Grand Forks, N.D.	1883	Thomas Clifford.	S	8,171	428
North Georgia.	Dahlonega, Ga.	1873	John H. Owen.	S	1,754	92
North Park.	Chicago, Ill.	1891	Lloyd Ahlem.	D	1,313	109
North Texas State Univ.	Denton, Tex.	1890	C.C. Nolen.	S	16,879	606
Northeast Louisiana Univ.	Monroe, La.	1931	Dwight Vines.	S	9,718	400
Northeast Missouri St. Univ.	Kirksville, Mo.	1867	Charles T. McClain.	S	5,495	313
Northeastern Illinois Univ.	Chicago, Ill.	1961	James Mullen.	S	10,179	438
Northeastern Okla. State	Tahlequah, Okla.	1846	Robert Collier	S	6,102	225
Northeastern Univ. (A).	Boston, Mass.	1898	Asa S. Knowles	P	33,557	1,889
Northern Arizona Univ.	Flagstaff, Ariz.	1899	J. Lawrence Walkup.	S	10,165	480
Northern Colorado, Univ. of	Greeley, Col.	1889	Richard R. Bond	S	10,879	604
Northern Ill. Univ.	DeKalb, Ill.	1895	Richard Nelson.	S	21,269	1,017
Northern Iowa, Univ. of.	Cedar Falls, Ia.	1876	John Kamerick.	S	8,700	540
Northern Michigan Univ.	Marquette, Mich.	1899	John X. Jamrich.	S	8,800	399
Northern Montana	Havre, Mon.	1929	Joseph R. Crowley.	S	1,020	62
Northern State.	Aberdeen, S.D.	1901	Norbert Baumgart.	S	2,369	115
Northland.	Ashland, Wis.	1892	Malcolm McLean.	D	715	59
Northrop Univ.	Inglewood, Cal.	1942	B.J. Shell.	P	1,448	108
Northwest.	Kirkland, Wash.	1934	D.V. Hurst.	D	627	44
Northwest Christian	Eugene, Ore.	1895	Barton A. Dowdy.	D	481	23
Northwest Missouri State Univ.	Maryville, Mo.	1905	Robert P. Foster.	S	4,503	240
Northwest Nazarene.	Nampa, Ida.	1913	Kenneth Pearsall.	D,P	1,112	81
Northwestern	Orange City, Ia.	1882	H.V. Rowenhorst.	D	755	45
Northwestern State Univ	Natchitoches. La.	1884	Arnold R. Kilpatrick.	S	6,685	313
Northwestern State.	Alva, Okla.	1897	Joe Struckle.	S	1,868	90
Northwestern Univ.	Evanston, Ill.	1851	Robert Henry Strotz.	P	15,390	2,748
Norwich Univ.	Northfield, Vt.	1819	Loring Hart.	P	1,425	105
Northwood Institute	Midland, Mich.	1959	Arthur Turner, Chairman.	P	1,250	47
Notre Dame, Coll. of.	Belmont, Cal.	1868	Sr. Catharine Cunningham.	P	990	91
Notre Dame.	St. Louis, Mo.	1896	Sister Barbara Brumleve.	D, P	381	34
Notre Dame.	Manchester, N.H.	1950	Jeannette Vezeau.	P, D	442	42
Notre Dame (W).	Cleveland, Oh.	1922	Sister Mary Marthe.	D, P	606	40
Notre Dame of Maryland.	Baltimore, Md.	1873	Sister Kathleen Feeley.	D	838	79
Notre Dame, Univ. Of.	Notre Dame, Ind.	1842	Rev. T.M. Hesburgh.	D	6,847	661
Nova Univ.	Ft. Lauderdale, Fla.	1964	Abraham Fischler.	P	4,516	260
Nyack.	Nyack, N.Y.	1882	Thomas Bailey.	D P	682	55
Oakland Univ.	Rochester, Mich.	1957	Donald D. O'Dowd.	S	10,526	508
Oakwood.	Huntsville, Ala.	1896	C.B. Rock.	D	1,013	60
Oberlin.	Oberlin, Oh.	1833	E. Danenberg.	P	2,700	226
Occidental.	Los Angeles, Cal.	1887	Richard C. Gilman	P	1,625	120

Name	Location	Year	Governing Official and Affiliation		Stu-dents	Teach-ers
Oglethorpe Univ.	Atlanta, Ga.	1835	Manning Pattillo Jr.	P	900	51
Ohio Dominican	Columbus, Oh.	1911	Sister M. Suzanne Uhrhane.	P	1,010	67
Ohio Coll. of Podiatric Med.	Cleveland, Oh.	1916	Abe Rubin	P	469	72
Ohio Inst. of Technology	Columbus, Oh.	1952	Richard A. Czerniak	P	2,569	108
Ohio Northern Univ.	Ada, Oh.	1871	Samuel L. Meyer	D,P	2,759	163
Ohio State Univ.*	Columbus, Oh.	1870	Harold L. Enarson.	S	54,640	3,600
Ohio Univ.	Athens, Oh.	1804	Harry Crewson	S	17,552	1,095
Ohio Wesleyan Univ.	Delaware, Oh.	1842	Thomas Wenzlau	D	2,280	150
Oklahoma Baptist Univ.	Shawnee, Okla.	1910	William G. Tanner	P	1,818	125
Oklahoma Christian	Oklahoma City, Okla.	1950	J. Johnson.	P,D	1,322	56
Oklahoma City Univ.	Oklahoma City, Okla.	1904	Dolphus Whitten, Jr.	D	2,754	205
Okla. Coll. of Liberal Arts	Chickasha, Okla.	1909	Roy Troutt	S	1,396	75
Oklahoma Panhandle State	Goodwell, Okla.	1909	Thomas L. Palmer.	S	1,115	74
Oklahoma State Univ.*	Stillwater, Okla.	1890	Robert B. Kamm.	S	23,079	1,747
Oklahoma, Univ. of	Norman, Okla.	1890	Paul F. Sharp.	S	26,252	1,168
Old Dominion Univ.	Norfolk, Va.	1930	James Bugg.	S	13,160	617
Olivet	Olivet, Mich.	1844	Ray B. Loeschner	P	850	67
Olivet Nazarene.	Kankakee, Ill.	1907	Leslie Parrott.	P	1,853	89
Oral Roberts Univ.	Tulsa, Okla.	1966	Oral Roberts.	P	3,500	180
Orangeburg-Calhoun Tech.	Orangeburg, S.C.	1966	M. Rudy Groomes.	S	1,502	112
Oregon College of Education	Monmouth, Ore.	1856	Leonard Rice.	S	3,291	250
Oregon Inst. of Technology	Klamath Falls, Ore.	1947	Winston Purvine.	S	2,309	150
Oregon State Univ.*	Corvallis, Ore.	1868	R. MacVicar.	S	16,500	2,686
Oregon, Univ. of.	Eugene, Ore.	1876	William Boyd.	S	17,384	1,062
Ottawa Univ.	Ottawa, Kan.	1865	Peter H. Armacost.	P,D	680	72
Otterbein.	Westerville, Oh.	1847	Thomas Jefferson Kerr.	D,P	1,250	82
Ouachita Baptist Univ.	Arkadelphia, Ark.	1886	Daniel R. Grant.	D,S	1,588	104
Our Lady of Angels.	Aslon, Pa.	1965	Sr. Marie Cunningham.	D	516	55
Our Lady of Elms, Col. of (W)	Chicopee, Mass.	1928	Edward D'Alessio	D,P	410	60
Our Lady of the Lake	San Antonio, Tex.	1911	Gerald Burns.	D	2,083	134
Ozarks, Coll. of the	Clarksville, Ark.	1834	Robert Qualls.	D,P	448	38
Ozarks, School of the.	Pt. Lookout, Mo.	1906	M. Graham Clark	P	1,150	81
Pace Univ.	New York, N.Y.	1906	Edward J. Mortola.	P	14,575	789
Pacific.	Fresno, Cal.	1944	Edmund Janzen.	P	437	27
Pacific Christian.	Fullerton, Cal.	1928	Medford Jones.	D,P	468	36
Pacific Lutheran Univ.	Tacoma, Wash.	1890	William Rieke.	P,D	3,428	238
Pacific States Univ.	Los Angeles, Cal.	1928	Steven Kase.	P	650	50
Pacific Union	Angwin, Cal.	1882	J. W. Cassel, Jr.	P	2,140	150
Pacific Univ.	Forest Grove, Ore.	1849	James Miller.	P,D	1,063	129
Pacific, Univ. of the	Stockton, Cal.	1851	Stanley McCaffrey.	P	5,571	486
Palm Beach Atlantic	W. Palm Beach, Fla.	1968	Warner Fusselle.	P	458	53
Palmer Coll. of Chiropractic (A)	Davenport, Ia.	1895	David Palmer.	P	1,370	26
Pan American Univ.	Edinburg, Tex.	1927	Ralph Schilling.	S	7,183	321
Park	Kansas City, Mo.	1875	Gerald Knutson.	P	920	66
Parsons School of Design.	New York, N.Y.	1896	John R. Everett.	D	1,000	200
Paul Quinn	Waco, Tex.	1872	S. E. Rutland.	D	481	45
Peabody Cons. of Music.	Baltimore, Md.	1868	Richard F. Goldman.	P	482	88
Penn Col. of Optometry	Philadelphia, Pa.	1919	Norman F. Wallis.	P	555	80
Penn. State Univ.	University Park, Pa.	1855	John W. Oswald.	S	68,223	3,386
Pennsylvania, Univ. of.	Philadelphia, Pa.	1740	Martin Meyerson.	P	8,262	1,700
Pepperdine Univ.	Malibu, Cal.	1937	William S. Banowsky.	D	6,412	716
Peru State (A)	Peru, Neb.	1867	Douglas Pearson.	P	685	46
Pfeiffer	Misenheimer, N.C.	1885	Douglas Reid Sasser.	D	1,036	68
Phila. College of Art.	Philadelphia, Pa.	1876	Thomas Schutte.	P	1,650	135
Phila. Coll. of Bible.	Philadelphia, Pa.	1913	D. B. MacCorkle	P	762	53
Phila. Coll. of Osteopathic Med.	Philadelphia, Pa.	1898	Thomas Rowland, Jr.	P	798	217
Phila. Coll. of Pharm. & Science.	Philadelphia, Pa.	1821	John Bergen.	P	1,047	85
Phila. Coll. of Textiles & Science.	Philadelphia, Pa.	1884	Lawson A. Pendleton.	P	2,051	64
Philander Smith.	Little Rock, Ark.	1868	Walter Hazzard.	D	701	52
Phillips Univ.	Enid, Okla.	1907	R. Justice.	P	1,485	89
Piedmont.	Demerest, Ga.	1897	James E. Walter.	P	400	24
Piedmont Bible.	Winston-Salem, N.C.	1946	Donald Drake.	D	488	26
Pikeville	Pikeville, Ky.	1889	Jackson Hall	D,P	650	50
Pittsburgh, Univ. of.	Pittsburgh, Pa.	1787	Wesley W. Posvar.	S	26,626	2,153
Pitzer	Claremont, Cal.	1963	Robert Atwell.	P	730	55
Plymouth State.	Plymouth, N.H.	1871	Harold E. Hyde.	S	3,014	124
Point Park.	Pittsburgh, Pa.	1960	John Hopkins.	P	1,638	109
Polytechnic Institute (A).	Brooklyn, N.Y.	1854	George Bugliarello.	P	4,500	230
Pomona.	Claremont, Cal.	1887	David Alexander.	P	1,300	130
Portland State Univ.	Portland, Ore.	1946	Joseph Blumel.	S	15,320	742
Portland, Univ. of.	Portland, Ore.	1901	Rev. P. E. Waldschmidt.	P	2,247	95
Pratt Institute.	Brooklyn, N.Y.	1887	Richardson Pratt, Jr.	P	4,089	488
Presbyterian.	Clinton, S.C.	1880	Marc C. Weersing.	D	850	62
Princeton Univ.	Princeton, N.J.	1746	William G. Bowen	P	5,798	690
Principia.	Elsah, Ill.	1910	David K. Andrews.	P	849	67
Providence.	Providence, R.I.	1917	Rev. T. R. Peterson.	P	5,123	207
Puerto Rico, Univ. of*	Rio Piedras, P.R.	1903	A. Carrion.	S	51,061	3,337
Puget Sound, Univ. of.	Tacoma, Wash.	1888	Philip M. Phibbs.	P	5,017	253
Purdue Univ.*	W. Lafayette, Ind.	1869	Arthur G. Hansen.	S	40,284	2,475
Queens (W)	Charlotte, N.C.	1857	Alfred Canon.	D,P	550	72
Quincy	Quincy, Ill.	1859	Rev. Titus Ludes.	D	1,527	88
Quinnipiac.	Hamden, Conn.	1929	Leonard Kent.	P	2,800	225
Radcliffe (W).	Cambridge, Mass.	1879	Matina Souretia Horner	P	(a)	(a)
(a) See Harvard University.						
Radford.	Radford, Va.	1913	Donald N. Dedmon.	S	4,443	277
Ramapo College of New Jersey	Mahwah, N.J.	1969	George T. Potter.	S	3,862	167
Randolph-Macon.	Ashland, Va.	1830	Luther W. White III.	P,D	811	72
Randolph-Macon Woman's (W)	Lynchburg, Va.	1891	William F. Quillian, Jr.	D,P	725	76
Redlands, Univ. of.	Redlands, Cal.	1907	Eugene Dawson.	P	2,598	205
Reed.	Portland, Ore.	1909	Paul Bragdon.	P	1,184	115

Name	Location	Year	Governing Official and Affiliation		Students	Teachers
Regis	Denver, Col.	1877	Rev. David M. Clarke	D,P	1,017	80
Regis (W)	Weston, Mass.	1927	Sister Therese Higgins	P	753	72
Rensselaer Poly. Inst.	Troy, N.Y.	1824	George M. Low	P	5,183	324
Rhode Island	Providence, R.I.	1854	Charles B. Willard	S	8,714	364
R.I. School of Design	Providence, R.I.	1877	Lee Hall	S	1,829	196
Rhode Island, Univ. of	Kingston, R.I.	1888	Frank Newman	P	16,527	846
Rice Univ.	Houston, Tex.	1891	Norman Hackerman	P	3,475	408
Richmond, Univ. of	Richmond, Va.	1830	E. Bruce Heilman	P	6,176	292
Ricker	Houlton, Me.	1848	W. Abbott	P	802	31
Rider	Trenton, N.J.	1865	Frank N. Elliott	P	5,781	310
Ripon	Ripon, Wis.	1951	Bernard S. Adams	P	923	70
Rivier	Nashua, N.H.	1933	Sister Doris Benoit	P	1,494	45
Roanoke	Salem, Va.	1842	Norman Fintel	P,D	1,252	64
Robert Morris	Pittsburgh, Pa.	1921	Charles Sewall	P	3,574	143
Roberts Wesleyan	Rochester, N.Y.	1866	Paul L. Adams	D	660	76
Rochester Inst. of Tech.	Rochester, N.Y.	1829	Paul A. Miller	P	12,671	1,028
Rochester, Univ. of	Rochester, N.Y.	1850	Robert Sproull	P	8,558	2,348
Rockford	Rockford, Ill.	1847	John A. Howard	P	1,269	87
Rockhurst	Kansas City, Mo.	1910	Rev. M.E. Van Ackeren	P,D	3,038	210
Rocky Mountain	Billings, Mon.	1878	B. Alton	D,P	450	50
Roger Williams	Bristol, R.I.	1948	Ralph Gauvey	P	2,661	69
Rollins	Winter Park, Fla.	1885	Jack Critchfield	P	4,227	286
Roosevelt Univ.	Chicago, Ill.	1945	Rolf A. Weil	P	7,400	250
Rosary	River Forest, Ill.	1901	Sister Candida Lund	P	1,315	143
Rosary Hill	Buffalo, N.Y.	1948	Robert S. Marshall	P	1,200	115
Rose-Hulman Inst. of Tech.	Terre Haute, Ind.	1874	John Logan	P	1,050	62
Rosemont	Rosemont, Pa.	1921	Sister Ann Marie Durst	D	694	80
Russell Sage (A)	Troy, N.Y.	1916	William Kahl	P	3,671	259
Rust	Holly Spgs., Miss.	1866	W.A. McMillan	D,P	785	46
Rutgers Univ.*	New Brunswick, N.J.	1766	Edward J. Bloustein	S	46,305	2,445
Sacred Heart, Coll. of the (A)	San Juan, P.R.	1935	Pedro Gonzalez Ramos	D	2,201	147
Sacred Heart Univ.	Bridgeport, Conn.	1963	Robert Kidera	P	2,481	139
Saginaw Valley State	Univ. Center, Mich.	1963	Jack Ryder	S	3,232	79
St. Ambrose	Davenport, Ia.	1882	William Bakrow	D,P	1,454	112
St. Andrews Presbyterian	Laurinburg, N.C.	1958	Donald J. Hart	P	637	53
St. Anselm's	Manchester, N.H.	1889	Rev. B. P. Donnelly	D	1,894	135
St. Augustine's	Raleigh, N.C.	1867	Prezell R. Robinson	D	1,579	78
St. Benedict, Coll. of (W)	St. Joseph, Minn.	1927	Beverly Miller	P	1,560	107
St. Bernard	St. Bernard, Ala.	1891	Robert Kaffer	P	450	52
St. Bonaventure Univ.	St. Bonaventure, N.Y.	1856	V. Rev. M. Doyle	P	2,546	160
St. Catherine, Coll. of (W)	St. Paul, Minn.	1905	Sister Alberta Huber	P,D	1,833	134
St. Cloud State	St. Cloud, Minn.	1869	Charles J. Graham	S	10,945	437
St. Edward's Univ.	Austin, Tex.	1885	Bro. Stephen Walsh	P	1,645	82
St. Elizabeth, Coll. of (W)	Convent Station, N.J.	1899	Sister Eliz. Ann Maloney	D,P	632	76
St. Francis	Fort Wayne, Ind.	1890	Sister M. Jo Ellen Scheetz	D	1,329	75
St. Francis	Biddeford, Me.	1953	Jack S. Ketchum	P	400	30
St. Francis	Brooklyn, N.Y.	1858	Rev. Donald Sullivan	P	3,041	156
St. Francis	Loretto, Pa.	1847	Rev. Sean Sullivan	D,P	1,573	87
St. Francis, Coll. of	Joliet, Ill.	1930	John Orr	P,D	1,756	74
St. John Coll. of Cleveland	Cleveland, Oh.	1928	Rev. James McManamon	D	732	76
St. John Fisher	Rochester, N.Y.	1948	Rev. C. J. Lavery	P,D	1,782	110
St. John's	Annapolis, Md.	1696	Richard D. Weigle	P	640	95
St. John's Univ. (M)	Collegeville, Minn.	1883	Rev. Michael P. Blecker	D,P	1,837	130
St. John's Univ.	Jamaica, N.Y.	1870	V. Rev. Joseph T. Cahill	P,D	14,759	707
St. Joseph	West Hartford, Conn.	1932	Sr. Mary O'Connor	P	1,027	60
St. Joseph's	Rensselaer, Ind.	1889	Rev. Charles Banet	D	1,091	68
St. Joseph's	North Windham, Me.	1912	Bernard Currier	P	507	35
St. Joseph's	Philadelphia, Pa.	1851	Rev. Terrence Toland	D	5,716	250
St. Lawrence Univ.	Canton, N.Y.	1856	Frank Peter Piskor	P	2,200	150
St. Leo	St. Leo, Fla.	1963	Thomas Southard	P,D	940	67
St. Louis Coll. of Pharmacy	St. Louis, Mo.	1864	Charles C. Rabe	P	720	33
St. Louis Univ.	St. Louis, Mo.	1818	Rev. D. O'Connell	P	10,406	1,642
Parks Coll.	Cahokia, Ill.	1927	Leon Z. Seltzer (Dean)	D	767	56
St. Martin's	Olympia, Wash.	1895	Fr. John C. Scott	D	740	77
St. Mary, Coll. of	Omaha, Neb.	1923	Sister Mary A. Costello	D	549	50
St. Mary (W)	Leavenworth, Kan.	1868	Sr. Mary J. McGilley	D	511	60
St. Mary-of-the-Woods (W)	St. Mary-of-Woods, Ind.	1840	Sister Jeanne Knoerle	D,P	572	60
St. Mary's	Notre Dame, Ind.	1844	John Duggan	P	1,738	151
St. Mary's	Winona, Minn.	1912	Brother Peter Clifford	D,P	1,031	85
St. Mary's Coll. of Cal.	Moraga, Cal.	1863	Bro. Mel Anderson	P,D	1,104	105
St. Mary's Coll. of Maryland	St. Mary's City, Md.	1839	J. Renwick Jackson, Jr.	S	1,212	99
St. Mary's Dominican (W)	New Orleans, La.	1910	Sr. Mary Eugene Cazayoux	D,P	830	76
St. Mary's Univ.	San Antonio, Tex.	1852	Rev. James Young	D,P	3,376	155
St. Michael's	Winooski, Vt.	1904	Rev. F. Moriarty	P	1,523	95
St. Norbert	DePere, Wis.	1898	Neil Webb	P	1,461	100
St. Olaf	Northfield, Minn.	1874	Sidney A. Rand	D,P	2,818	242
St. Paul Bible	Bible College, Minn.	1916	Francis W. Grubbs	D,P	462	33
St. Paul's	Lawrenceville, Va.	1888	James Alvin Russell, Jr.	D	600	38
St. Peter's	Jersey City, N.J.	1872	V. Rev. V. R. Yanitelli	D	4,586	350
St. Rose, Coll. of	Albany, N.Y.	1920	Thomas Manion	P	2,076	147
St. Scholastica, Coll. of	Duluth, Minn.	1912	Bruce Stender	D,P	1,192	114
St. Theresa, Coll. of (W)	Winona, Minn.	1907	Sister Joyce Rowland	D	1,161	134
St. Thomas Aquinas	Sparkill, N.Y.	1952	D. McNelis	P	970	65
St. Thomas, Coll. of	St. Paul, Minn.	1885	Msgr. Terrence Murphy	P	2,105	150
St. Thomas, Univ. of	Houston, Tex.	1947	Rev. Patrick Braden	D	1,585	101
St. Vincent (M)	Latrobe, Pa.	1846	Rev. Cecil Diethrich	D	1,031	79
St. Xavier	Chicago, Ill.	1847	Sr. M. Chekouras	D	1,450	141
Salem (W) (A)	Winston-Salem, N.C.	1772	John H. Chandler	P	617	72
Salem	Salem, W. Va.	1888	Dallas Bailey	P	1,290	75
Salem State	Salem, Mass.	1854	Vincent Mara	S	7,910	294
Salisbury State	Salisbury, Md.	1925	Norman Crawford	S	3,840	145
Salve Regina	Newport, R.I.	1934	Sister Lucille McKillop	D	1,485	98
Sam Houston State Univ.	Huntsville, Tex.	1879	E. T. Bowers	S	9,864	365
Samford Univ.	Birmingham, Ala.	1841	Leslie S. Wright	D,P	3,697	224
San Diego, Univ. of	San Diego, Cal.	1949	Author E. Hughes	P	3,100	150
San Diego State	San Diego, Cal.	1897	Brage Golding	S	30,543	1,996

Name	Location	Year	Governing Official and Affiliation		Students	Teachers
San Francisco Art Inst.	San Francisco, Cal.	1871	A. Herstand	P	907	65
San Francisco, Univ. of	San Francisco, Cal.	1855	William McInnes	P	5,500	340
Sangamon State Univ.	Springfield, Ill.	1969	Robert Spencer	S	3,977	202
San Jose State Univ.	San Jose, Cal.	1857	John H. Bunzel	S	26,000	1,600
Santa Clara, Univ. of	Santa Clara, Cal.	1851	Rev. Thomas Terry	D,P	6,796	297
Sante Fe, Coll. of	Sante Fe, N.M.	1947	Bro. Cyprian Luke Roney	D,P	1,273	80
Sarah Lawrence	Bronxville, N.Y.	1926	Charles DeCarlo	P	863	149
Savannah State	Savannah, Ga.	1890	Prince Jackson	S	2,412	136
Scranton, Univ. of	Scranton, Pa.	1888	Rev. William Byron	D	4,333	210
Scripps (W)	Claremont, Cal.	1926	Mark H. Curtis	P	565	65
Seattle Pacific	Seattle, Wash.	1891	David L. McKenna	D	2,408	170
Seattle Univ.	Seattle, Wash.	1891	Fr. William Sullivan	P,D	3,459	185
Selma Univ. (A)	Selma, Ala.	1878	Marshall C. Cleveland	D	321	23
Seton Hall Univ.	S. Orange, N.J.	1856	Msgr. Thomas G. Fahy	D	9,880	305
Seton Hill (W)	Greensburg, Pa.	1883	Sister Mary Schmidt	D	841	78
Shaw Coll. at Detroit	Detroit, Mich.	1970	Romallus Murphy	P	1,332	84
Shaw Univ.	Raleigh, N.C.	1875	J. Archie Hargraves	D	1,625	149
Shenandoah Coll. of Music	Winchester, Va.	1875	Robert P. Parker	D	722	85
Shepherd	Shepherdstown, W. Va.	1871	James Butcher	S	2,399	115
Shippensburg State	Shippensburg, Pa.	1871	Gilmore B. Seavers	S	5,700	272
Shorter	Rome, Ga.	1873	Randall H. Minor	P	729	57
Siena	Loundonville, N.Y.	1938	Rev. Hugh F. Hines	P	2,238	136
Siena Heights	Adrian, Mich.	1919	Hugh L. Thompson	D,P	1,063	85
Simmons (W)	Boston, Mass.	1902	William J. Holmes, Jr.	P	2,695	205
Simpson	Indianola, Ia.	1860	Richard Lancaster	P	835	77
Simpson	San Francisco, Cal.	1921	Mark W. Lee	P	418	26
Sioux Falls	Sioux Falls, S.D.	1883	Owen Halleen	D,P	715	60
Skidmore	Saratoga Spgs., N.Y.	1922	Joseph C. Palamountain, Jr.	P	2,110	166
Slippery Rock State (A)	Slippery Rock, Pa.	1893	Albert A. Watrel	S	5,500	346
Smith (W)	Northampton, Mass.	1875	Thomas C. Mendenhall	P	2,518	240
South, Univ. of the	Sewanee, Tenn.	1857	James J. Bennett, V. Chan.	D	992	91
South Alabama. Univ. of	Mobile, Ala.	1963	Frederick Whiddon	S	6,443	461
S. Carolina, Med. Coll. of	Charleston, S.C.	1824	William H. Knisely	S	2,216	675
South Carolina St.*	Orangeburg, S.C.	1896	M. M. Nance, Jr.	S	3,519	224
South Carolina, Univ. of	Columbia, S.C.	1801	William Patterson	S	32,259	1,484
S.D. Sch. of Mines & Tech.	Rapid City, S.D.	1885	Richard Schleusener	S	1,624	92
South Dakota State Univ.*	Brookings, S.D.	1881	H. M. Briggs	S	6,217	569
South Dakota, Univ. of	Vermillion, S.D.	1862	Richard E. Bowen	S	5,601	475
South Eastern Bible	Lakeland, Fla.	1935	Cyril Homer	D	957	25
South Florida, Univ. of	Tampa, Fla.	1956	Maruice Mackey, Jr.	S	20,236	972
Southeast Missouri State Univ.	Cape Girardeau, Mo.	1873	Robert Leestamper	S	8,269	352
Southeastern Louisiana Univ.	Hammond, La.	1925	Clea E. Parker	S	6,696	327
Southeastern Mass. Univ.	N. Dartmouth, Mass.	1895	Donald E. Walker	S	7,768	330
Southeastern Okla. State Univ.	Durant, Okla.	1909	Leon Hibbs	S	4,267	133
Southern California	Costa Mesa, Cal.	1920	Emil Balliet	D	645	53
Southern Cal., Univ. of	Los Angeles, Cal.	1880	John R. Hubbard	P	28,074	2,038
S. Cal. College of Optometry	Fullerton, Cal.	1904	Richard Hopping	P	300	79
Southern Coll. of Optometry	Memphis, Tenn.	1932	Spurgeon B. Eure	P	616	49
Southern Colorado State	Pueblo, Col.	1961	Harry P. Bowes	S	5,770	327
Southern Conn. State	New Haven, Conn.	1893	Manson Van B. Jennings	S	11,977	611
Southern Illinois Univ.	Edwardsville, Ill.	1965	Andrew Kochman, Act.	S	12,212	610
Southern Illinois Univ.	Carbondale, Ill.	1869	David Derge	S	21,214	3,076
Southern Methodist Univ.	Dallas, Tex.	1911	Willis Tate, Chan.	D	9,643	662
Southern Missionary	Collegedale, Tenn.	1892	Frank Knittel	D	1,682	120
Southern Mississippi, U. of	Hattiesburg, Miss.	1910	Aubrey Lucas	S	11,707	576
Southern Oregon State	Ashland, Ore.	1925	James K. Sours	S	4,300	220
Southern State	Magnolia, Ark.	1909	Harold T. Brinson	S	1,970	114
Southern Tech. Inst.	Marietta, Ga.	1948	Joseph Pettit	S	2,134	82
Southern Univ.	Baton Rouge, La.	1880	Jesse Stone, Jr.	S	8,685	397
Southern Utah State	Cedar City, Ut.	1897	R. C. Braithwaite	S	1,850	129
Southwest Baptist	Bolivar, Mo.	1878	James L. Sells	P	1,435	75
Southwest Minnesota State	Marshall, Minn.	1963	Jay Jones	S	2,011	141
Southwest Missouri St. U.	Springfield, Mo.	1906	Duane Meyer	S	12,153	644
Southwest Texas State Unv.	San Marcos, Tex.	1899	Lee Smith	S	13,011	503
Southwestern	Winfield, Kan.	1885	Donald Ruthenberg	D,P	900	54
Southwestern La., Univ. of	Lafayette, La.	1898	Ray Authement	S	13,078	493
Southwestern at Memphis	Memphis, Tenn.	1848	James Daughdrill	D	1,082	103
Southwestern Okla. State, Univ. of	Weatherford, Okla.	1901	Leonard Campbell	S	4,027	211
Southwestern Union	Keene, Tex.	1893	Donald McAdams	D	800	46
Southwestern Univ.	Georgetown, Tex.	1840	Durwood Fleming	D	927	75
Spalding	Louisville, Ky.	1920	Sister Eileen Egan	P	1,141	92
Spelman (W)	Atlanta, Ga.	1881	Albert E. Manley	P	1,155	100
Spring Arbor	Spring Arbor, Mich.	1873	E. A. Voller	D	833	70
Spring Garden	Philadelphia, Pa.	1850	Robert H. Thompson	P	850	60
Spring Hill	Mobile, Ala.	1830	Rev. Paul S. Tipton	P	790	62
Springfield	Springfield, Mass.	1885	Wilbert Locklin	P	2,400	128
Stanford Univ.	Stanford, Cal.	1891	Richard W. Lyman	P	11,484	1,599
Stephen F. Austin State U.	Nacogdoches, Tex.	1923	Ralph W. Steen	S	11,293	420
Stephens (W)	Columbia, Mo.	1833	Arland Christ-Janer	P	1,850	154
Sterling	Sterling, Kan.	1887	C. Schoenherr	P	492	44
Stetson Univ.	De Land, Fla.	1883	John E. Johns	P	2,720	163
Steubenville, Coll. of	Steubenville, Oh.	1946	Rev. M. Scanlon	D,P	890	46
Stevens Inst. of Tech.	Hoboken, N.J.	1870	Kenneth C. Rogers	P	2,050	130
Stillman	Tuscaloosa, Ala.	1876	Harold N. Stinson	D,P	785	41
Stockton State	Pomona, N.J.	1971	Richard Bjork	S	3,900	170
Stonehill	N. Easton, Mass.	1948	Rev. Ernest Bartell	D	2,170	127
Strayer	Washington, D.C.	1904	Murray Donoho	P	1,550	65
Suffolk Univ.	Boston, Mass.	1906	Thomas Fulham	P	4,722	232
Sul Ross State Univ.	Alpine, Tex.	1917	Hugh Meredith	S	2,730	90
Susquehanna Univ.	Selinsgrove, Pa.	1858	Gustave W. Weber	P	1,750	110
Swarthmore	Swarthmore, Pa.	1864	Theodore Friend	P	1,260	142
Sweet Briar	Sweet Briar, Va.	1901	Harold B. Whiteman, Jr.	P	687	81
Syracuse Univ.	Syracuse, N.Y.	1870	M. A. Eggers (Chan.)	P	10,539	848
Tabor	Hillsboro, Kan.	1908	Roy Just	P,D	521	55
Talladega	Talladega, Ala.	1867	Herman H. Long	P	465	54
Tampa College	Tampa, Fla.	1890	Delores C. Jones	S	1,699	72

Name	Location	Year	Governing Official and Affiliation		Stu-dents	Teach-ers
Tampa, Univ. of	Tampa, Fla.	1931	B. D. Owens	P	2,000	105
Tarkio	Tarkio, Mo.	1883	Eldon E. Breazier	P,D	450	34
Taylor Univ.	Upland, Ind.	1846	Robert Baptista	P	1,467	72
Temple Univ.	Philadelphia, Pa.	1888	Marvin Wachman	S	33,967	2,018
Tennessee State Univ.	Nashville, Tenn.	1912	F. Humphries	S	5,186	260
Tennessee System, Univ. of	Knoxville, Tenn.	1968	Edward Boling	S	49,082	3,257
at Nashville	Nashville, Tenn.	1971	Charles Smith, Act. Chan.	S	5,493	130
at Chattanooga	Chattanooga, Tenn.	1886	James Drinnon, Jr., Chan.	S	5,808	327
at Knoxville	Knoxville, Tenn.	1794	Jack Reese, Chan.	S	29,999	1,668
at Martin	Martin, Tenn.	1900	Larry T. McGhee, Chan.	S	5,188	265
Ctr. for Health Sci.	Memphis, Tenn.	1911	T. Farmer, Chan.	S	2,594	866
Tennessee Tech. Univ.	Cookeville, Tenn.	1915	Arliss Roaden	S	7,120	339
Tennessee Temple	Chattanooga, Tenn.	1946	Lee Roberson	P	1,834	88
Tennessee Wesleyan	Athens, Tenn.	1857	Vacant	D	425	40
Texas	Tyler, Tex.	1894	Allen C. Hancock	P	592	37
Texas A & I Univ.	Kingsville, Tex.	1925	Gerald Robins	S	7,441	344
Tex. A. & M.	College Station, Tex.	1876	Jack K. Williams	S	25,000	2,500
Prairie View A. & M. Univ.	Prairie View, Tex.	1876	Alvin Thomas	S	5,500	248
Tarleton State Univ.	Stephenville, Tex.	1899	William O. Trogden	S	2,853	150
Texas Christian Univ.	Fort Worth, Tex.	1873	J. M. Moudy (Chan.)	P,D	5,803	401
Texas Eastern Univ.	Tyler, Tex.	1971	James Stewart Jr.	S	1,229	57
Texas Lutheran	Seguin, Tex.	1891	Joe Menn	D	1,097	71
Texas Southern Univ.	Houston, Tex.	1947	Granville Sawyer	S	8,485	366
Texas System, Univ. of	Austin, Tex.	1883	Charles A. LeMaistre, Chan.	S	87,516	7709
at Arlington	Arlington, Tex.	1895	Wendell Nedderman	S	16,309	854
at Austin	Austin, Tex.	1883	L. Rogers, Act.	S	42,958	1,624
at Corpus Christi (A)	Corpus Christi, Tex.	1973	D. W. Halliday	S	1,249	68
at Dallas	Dallas, Tex.	1969	Bryce Jordan	S	3,586	250
El Paso	El Paso, Tex.	1913	Alkeigh Templeton	S	13,441	442
Health Science Center	Houston, Tex.	1905	Charles Berry	S	1,440	485
Medical Branch	Galveston, Tex.	1891	William Levin	S	1,108	379
at San Antonio	San Antonio, Tex.	1969	Peter Flawn	S	4,437	197
Health Science Center	Dallas, Tex.	1943	Charles Sprague	S	1,113	682
at Odessa	Odessa, Tex.	1969	V. Cardozier, Act.	S	1,475	85
at San Antonio	San Antonio, Tex.	1959	Frank Harrison	S	810	364
Texas Tech. Univ. Sch. of Med.	Lubbock, Tex.	1969	Grover Murray	S	132	145
Texas Wesleyan	Fort Worth, Tex.	1891	William Pearce	D	1,876	72
Texas Woman's Univ. (W)	Denton, Tex.	1901	Mary B. Huey, Act.	S	8,086	479
Thiel	Greenville, Pa.	1866	Frank Bretz	D	1,025	69
Thomas	Waterville, Me.	1894	John L. Thomas, Jr.	P	900	36
Thomas Jefferson Univ.	Philadelphia, Pa.	1824	Vacant	P	1,800	1,240
Thomas More	Covington, Ky.	1921	Richard A. DeGraff	D,P	1,358	98
Tiffin Univ.	Tiffin, Oh.	1918	Richard Pfeiffer	P	1,060	35
Tift (W)	Forsyth, Ga.	1847	Robert W. Jackson	P	680	35
Toledo, Univ. of	Toledo, Oh.	1872	Glen R. Driscoll	S	15,742	700
Tougaloo	Tougaloo, Miss.	1869	George A. Owens	P	1,001	62
Towson State	Baltimore, Md.	1866	James L. Fisher	S	13,041	525
Transylvania Univ.	Lexington, Ky.	1780	William Kelly	P	722	59
Trenton State	Trenton, N.J.	1855	C. B. Brower	S	8,800	546
Trevecca Nazarene	Nashville, Tenn.	1901	Mark Moore	D,P	856	59
Trinity	Hartford, Conn.	1823	Theodore Lockwood	P	2,099	148
Trinity	Deerfield, Ill.	1897	Harry Evans	P	875	60
Trinity	Burlington, Vt.	1925	Sister Elizabeth Candon	D	500	62
Trinity	Washington, D.C.	1897	Sr. Roseanne Fleming	D	900	109
Trinity Univ.	San Antonio, Tex.	1869	Duncan Wimpress	P	3,546	225
Tri-State	Angola, Ind.	1884	Carl Elliott	P	1,129	86
Troy State Univ.	Troy, Ala.	1887	Ralph W. Adams	S	10,136	450
Tufts Univ.	Medford, Mass.	1852	Jean Mayer	P	6,500	500
Tulane Univ.	New Orleans, La.	1834	Sheldon Hackney	P	9,191	804
Tulsa, Univ. of	Tulsa, Okla.	1894	J. Paschal Twyman	P,D	6,540	362
Tusculum	Greenville, Tenn.	1794	Thomas Voss	P	427	35
Tuskegee Institute	Tuskegee Inst., Ala.	1881	Luther H. Foster	P	3,460	357
Union	Barbourville, Ky.	1879	Mahlon A. Miller	P	1,038	69
Union	Lincoln, Neb.	1891	Myrl O. Manley	D	957	87
Union	Schenectady, N.Y.	1795	Thomas Bonner	P	3,152	189
Union Univ.	Jackson, Tenn.	1825	Robert E. Craig	D,P	924	61
U.S. Air Force Academy	Col. Springs, Col.	1955	Lt. Gen. J. Allen, Supt.	F	4,000	550
U.S. Coast Guard Acad.	New London, Conn.	1876	Rear Adm. W. Jenkins, Supt.	F	1,134	122
U.S. International Univ.	San Diego, Cal.	1952	William Rust	P	3,000	146
U.S. Merch. Marine Acad.	Kings Point, N.Y.	1938	Rear Adm. A. Engel, Supt.	F	1,028	88
U.S. Military Academy	West Point, N.Y.	1802	Lt. Gen. S. Berry, Supt.	F	4,000	626
U.S. Naval Academy	Annapolis, Md.	1845	Kinnaird McKee, Supt.	F	4,200	550
Unity	Unity, Me.	1966	Allan Karstetter	P	394	29
Upper Iowa	Fayette, Ia.	1857	Aldrich Paul	P	509	40
Upsala (A)	E. Orange, N.J.	1893	Carl J. Fiellman	D	1,611	114
Urbana	Urbana, Oh.	1850	Roland Patzer	P,D	411	21
Ursinus	Collegeville, Pa.	1869	William Pettit	P	1,698	100
Ursuline	Cleveland, Oh.	1871	Sister M. Kenan	D,P	800	95
Utah State Univ.*	Logan, Ut.	1888	Glen L. Taggart	S	9,113	436
Utah, Univ. of	Salt Lake City, Ut.	1850	David P. Gardner	S	22,575	1,225
Valdosta State	Valdosta, Ga.	1913	S. Walter Martin	S	5,012	237
Valley City State	Valley City, N.D.	1890	Ted DeVries	S	861	60
Valparaiso Univ.	Valparaiso, Ind.	1859	Albert Huegli	P	3,517	339
Vanderbilt Univ.	Nashville, Tenn.	1873	Alexander Heard, Chan.	P	6,731	1,616
Vassar	Poughkeepsie, N.Y.	1861	Alan Simpson	P	2,200	223
Vermont, Univ. of*	Burlington, Vt.	1791	Lattie Coor	S	8,200	673
Villa Maria (W)	Erie, Pa.	1925	Sr. M. Lawrence Antoun	P	550	64
Villanova Univ.	Villanova, Pa.	1842	Rev. John M. Driscoll	P	9,619	572
Virgin Islands, Coll. of the	St. Thomas, V.I.	1962	L. C. Wanlass	D,P	2,079	83
Virginia Commonwealth Univ.	Richmond, Va.	1838	T. Temple	S	18,053	1,727
Virginia Intermont	Bristol, Va.	1884	Floyd Turner	D,P	535	44
Virginia Military Inst. (M)	Lexington, Va.	1839	Lt. Gen. R. Irby	S	1,298	106
Virginia Poly. Inst. & Univ.*	Blacksburg, Va.	1872	William Lavery	S	18,477	1,493

Name	Location	Year	Governing Official and Affiliation		Students	Teachers
Virginia State*	Petersburg, Va.	1882	Thomas Law	S	4,559	226
Virginia Union Univ.	Richmond, Va.	1865	Allix B. James	P	1,318	123
Virginia Univ. of.	Charlottesville, Va.	1819	F. Hereford, Jr.	S	15,179	1,532
Virginia Wesleyan	Norfolk, Va.	1961	Lambuth M. Clarke	P,D	650	42
Viterbo	La Crosse, Wis.	1931	Rev. J. Thomas Finucan	P	893	107
Voorhees	Denmark, S.C.	1897	Harry Graham	D,P	1,018	59
Wabash (M)	Crawfordsville, Ind.	1832	Thaddeus Seymour	P	850	90
Wagner	Staten Island, N.Y.	1883	John Satterfield	P	2,690	230
Wake Forest Univ.	Winston-Salem, N.C.	1834	James R. Scales	D	4,442	728
Walla Walla	College Place, Wash.	1892	Robert Reynolds	P	1,919	140
Walsh	Canton, Oh.	1960	Bro. Robert Francoeur	D,P	704	63
Walsh Coll. of Accounting	Troy, Mich	1922	Jeffrey Barry	P	1,057	47
Warner Pacific	Portland, Ore.	1937	E. J. Gilliam	D,P	406	40
Warren Wilson	Swannanoa, N.C.	1894	Reuben H. Holden	P,D	461	57
Wartburg	Waverly, Ia.	1852	W. Jellema	P,D	1,202	75
Washburn Univ. of Topeka	Topeka, Kan.	1865	John W. Henderson	Mu	5,590	313
Washington	Chestertown, Md.	1782	Joseph McLain	P	731	68
Washington and Jefferson	Washington, Pa.	1781	Howard J. Burnett	P	1,220	95
Washington and Lee Univ.	Lexington, Va.	1749	Robert Huntley	P	1,600	126
Washington State Univ.	Pullman, Wash.	1890	Glenn Terrell	S	16,184	918
Washington Tech. Inst.*	Washington, D.C.	1968	Cleveland Dennard	F	4,022	187
Washington Univ.	St. Louis, Mo.	1853	W. H. Danforth(Chan.)	P	10,917	2,063
Washington, Univ. of.	Seattle, Wash.	1861	John R. Hogness	S	34,504	2,052
Way Coll. of Emporia, The.	Emporia, Kan.	1882	V. P. Wierwille	P	346	29
Wayland Baptist	Plainview, Tex.	1908	Roy C. McClung	D	1,070	60
Wayne State	Wayne, Neb.	1910	Lyle Seymour	S	2,232	92
Wayne State Univ.	Detroit, Mich.	1868	George Gullen	D	34,706	2,142
Waynesburg	Waynesburg, Pa.	1849	Joseph Marsh	D	802	61
Weber State	Ogden, Ut.	1889	Joseph Bishop	S	9,458	425
Webster	St. Louis, Mo.	1915	Leigh Gerdine	P	4,207	506
Wellesley (W)	Wellesley, Mass.	1875	Barbara W. Newell	P	2,045	254
Wells (W)	Aurora, N.Y.	1868	Frances Farenthold	P	500	75
Wesleyan (W)	Macon, Ga.	1836	W. Earl Strickland	D	570	53
Wesleyan Univ.	Middletown, Conn.	1831	Colin G. Campbell	P	2,302	313
West Chester State	West Chester, Pa.	1871	Charles Mayo	S	9,295	520
West Coast Univ.	Los Angeles, Cal.	1909	Victor Elconin	P	1,192	137
West Florida, Univ. of.	Pensacola, Fla.	1963	James Robinson	S	4,787	247
West Georgia	Carrollton, Ga.	1933	Maurice Townsend	S	5,803	265
West Liberty State	West Liberty, W. Va.	1837	James L. Chapman	S	2,680	168
West Texas State Univ.	Canyon, Tex.	1910	Lloyd Watkins	S	6,701	313
W. Va. Inst. of Technology	Montgomery, W. Va.	1895	Leonard C. Nelson	S	2,712	145
West Virginia State(A)	Institute, W. Va.	1891	Harold M. McNeill	S	3,677	167
West Virginia Univ.*	Morgantown, W. Va.	1867	James G. Harlow	S	20,007	1,780
W. Virginia Wesleyan	Buckhannon, W. Va.	1890	John D. Rockefeller IV	D	1,800	114
Western Baptist Bible	Salem, Ore.	1935	W. T. Younger	D	474	30
Western Conn. State	Danbury, Conn.	1903	Robert Bersi	S	4,981	251
Western Illinois Univ.	Macomb, Ill.	1899	L. Malpass	S	15,357	771
Western Kentucky Univ.	Bowling Green, Ky.	1907	Dero Downing	P	12,769	468
Western Maryland	Westminster, Md.	1868	Ralph C. John	P	1,726	163
Western Mich. Univ.	Kalamazoo, Mich.	1903	John T. Bernhard	S	21,361	1,150
Western Montana	Dillon, Mon.	1893	James E. Short	S	759	36
Western New England	Springfield, Mass.	1915	Beaumont A. Herman	P	3,792	121
Western New Mexico Univ.	Silver City, N.M.	1893	John Snedeker	S	1,830	72
Western State Col. of Colo.	Gunnison, Col.	1911	John Mellon	S	3,100	130
Western Washington State	Bellingham, Wash.	1899	Paul Olscamp	S	8,697	439
Westfield State	Westfield, Mass.	1839	Robert L. Randolph	S	3,900	155
Westmar	Le Mars, Ia.	1890	Laurence Smith	P	729	46
Westminster	Fulton, Mo.	1851	Dale Purcell	P	709	63
Westminster	New Wilmington, Pa.	1852	Earland I. Carlson	P	1,489	125
Westminster	Salt Lake City, Ut.	1875	Helmut Hofmann	P	1,250	75
Westminster Choir Coll.	Princeton, N.J.	1926	Ray E. Robinson	P	450	27
Westmont	Santa Barbara, Cal.	1940	Ernest Ettlich, Act.	P	936	86
Wheaton	Wheaton, Ill.	1860	Hudson T. Armerding	P	2,210	143
Wheaton (W)	Norton, Mass.	1834	William C. H. Prentice	P	1,112	117
Wheeling	Wheeling, W. Va.	1954	Rev. Charles Currie	D	726	54
Wheelock	Boston, Mass.	1939	Gordon L. Marshall	P	755	81
White Plains, College of	White Plains, N.Y.	1923	Katherine Restaino	P	675	49
Whitman	Walla Walla, Wash.	1859	Robert Skotheim	P	1,055	92
Whittier	Whittier, Cal.	1901	W. R. Newsom	P	1,972	130
Whitworth	Spokane, Wash.	1890	Edward B. Lindaman	P	1,821	152
Wichita State Univ.	Wichita, Kan.	1895	Clark Ahlberg	S	15,714	814
Widener	Chester, Pa.	1821	Clarence R. Moll	P	3,231	210
Wilberforce Univ.	Wilberforce, Oh.	1856	Rembert E. Stokes	D,P	1,159	58
Wiley	Marshall, Tex.	1873	Robert Hayes Sr.	D	612	39
Wilkes	Wilkes-Barre, Pa.	1933	Robert Capin, Act.	P	2,377	150
Willamette Univ.	Salem, Ore.	1842	Robert Lisensky	P	1,724	154
William Carey	Hattiesburg, Miss.	1906	J. Ralph Noonkester	P	1,749	86
William Jewell	Liberty, Mo.	1849	Thomas Field	P,D	1,653	124
Wm. and Mary, College of	Williamsburg, Va.	1693	Thomas A. Graves Jr.	S	5,947	458
Wm. Mitchell Coll. of Law	St. Paul, Minn.	1900	William H. Abbott	P	840	50
Wm. Paterson Coll. of N.J.	Wayne, N.J.	1855	William McKeefery	S	12,999	443
William Penn	Oskaloosa, Ia.	1873	Duane Moon	P	650	40
William Woods (W)	Fulton, Mo.	1870	Randall B. Cutlip	P	910	88
Williams	Williamstown, Mass.	1793	John W. Chandler	P	1,863	160
Wilmington	Wilmington, Oh.	1870	Robert E. Lucas	D	849	60
Wilmington	New Castle, Del.	1968	Donald E. Ross	P	800	50
Wilson (W)	Chambersburg, Pa.	1869	Margaret Waggoner	P,D	362	53
Winona State	Winona, Minn.	1858	Robt. DuFresne	S	4,776	183
Winthrop	Rock Hill, S.C.	1886	Charles Vail	S	3,501	274
Wisconsin, Univ. of*	Madison, Wis.	1971	John Weaver	S	143,740	7,459
Eau Claire	Eau Claire, Wis.	1916	Leonard Haas, Chan.	S	9,920	491
Green Bay	Green Bay, Wis.	1968	Edward W. Wiedner, Chan.	S	3,874	155
La Crosse	La Crosse, Wis.	1909	Kenneth Lindner, Chan.	S	7,734	344
Madison	Madison, Wis.	1849	Edwin Young, Chan.	S	38,545	2,284
Marinette	Marinette, Wis.	1965	Edward Fort, Chan.	S	407	17
Milwaukee	Milwaukee, Wis.	1885	Werner Baum. Chan.	S	24,961	809

Name	Location	Year	Governing Official and Affiliation	Students	Teachers
(Continued)					
Oshkosh	Oshkosh, Wis.	1871	Robert Birnbaum, Chan. S	10,555	520
Parkside	Kenosha, Wis.	1968	Alan Guskin, Chan. S	5,404	165
Platteville	Platteville, Wis.	1866	Warren Carrier, Chan. S	4,285	242
River Falls	River Falls, Wis.	1874	George Field, Chan. S	4,433	236
Stevens Point	Stevens Point, Wis.	1894	Lee S. Dreyfus, Chan. S	8,220	432
Stout	Menomonie, Wis.	1893	Robert Swanson, Chan. S	5,609	333
Superior	Superior, Wis.	1896	Karl W. Meyer, Chan. S	2,610	157
Whitewater	Whitewater, Wis.	1868	James Connor, Chan. S	8,727	403
Wittenberg Univ.	Springfield, Oh.	1845	W. A. Kinnison, Act. P,D	2,333	150
Wofford	Spartanburg, S. C.	1854	J. M. Lesesne Jr. P,D	930	73
Woodbury	Los Angeles, Cal.	1884	Dora E. Kirby P	1,419	62
Wooster, Coll. of	Wooster, Oh.	1866	J. G. Drushal. P	1,800	134
Worcester Polytechnic Inst.	Worcester, Mass.	1865	George W. Hazzard P	2,761	180
Worcester State	Worcester, Mass.	1874	Joseph Orze S	5,786	209
Wright State Univ.	Dayton, Oh.	1964	R. J. Kegerreis. S	14,403	592
Wyoming Univ. of*	Laramie, Wy.	1886	William Carlson S	8,043	856
Xavier Univ. of Louisiana	New Orleans, La.	1925	Norman C. Francis. D	1,700	158
Xavier Univ.	Cincinnati, Oh.	1831	Rev. Robert Mulligan P	6,265	285
Yale Univ.	New Haven, Conn.	1701	Kingman Brewster Jr. P	9,661	1,261
Yankton	Yankton, S.D.	1881	Alfred M. Gibbens. P	820	41
Yeshiva Univ.	New York N.Y.	1886	Vacant P	6,264	2,500
York College of Pa.	York, Pa.	1942	Ray A. Miller. P	3,110	78
Youngstown State Univ.	Youngstown, Oh.	1908	John J. Coffelt. S	13,917	760

Community and Junior Colleges

Enrollment and faculty figures in italics include all branches and campuses

Name	Location	Year	Governing Official and Affiliation	Students	Teachers
Abraham Baldwin Agric.	Tifton, Ga.	1908	Stanley Anderson. S	2,431	111
Adirondacks Community	Glens Falls, N.Y.	1960	Charles R. Eisenhart. S	3,518	58
Aeronautics, Academy of	Flushing, N.Y.	1932	Walter M. Hartung. P	800	42
Aims.	Greeley, Col.	1968	Richard Laughlin. C	4,000	200
Alabama Christian	Montgomery, Ala.	1942	E.R. Brannan. D,P	1,546	83
Alamance, Tech. Inst. of	Burlington, N.C.	1959	William Taylor. S	1,169	150
Alameda, Coll. of.	Alameda, Cal.	1963	Jeanette Poore. C	6,930	150
Albany Junior	Albany, Ga.	1966	B.R. Tilley. S	2,148	100
Albany, Junior Coll. of.	Albany, N.Y.	1957	William Kahl. P	1,045	42
Albemarle, Coll. of the.	Elizabeth City, N.C.	1960	S. Bruce Petteway. S	1,006	60
Alexander City State Junior	Alexander City, Ala.	1965	W. Byron Causey. S	1,550	85
Allen Co. Comm. Jr.	Iola, Kan.	1923	Bill R. Spencer. C	747	52
Alice Lloyd.	Pippa Passes, Ky.	1923	Will Hayes. P	222	20
Allan Hancock Joint Comm.	Santa Maria, Cal.	1920	Walter E. Conrad. Di.	8,941	528
Allegany Community	Cumberland, Md.	1961	W. Ardell Haines. C	1,750	110
Allegheny Co., Comm. College of.	Pittsburgh, Pa.	1966	John B. Hirt. C	14,399	1,356
Alpena Community	Alpena, Mich.	1952	Herbert N. Stoutenberg. C	1,850	110
Alvin Comm.	Alvin, Tex.	1949	Thomas Jenkins. C	2,387	156
Amarillo.	Amarillo, Tex.	1929	Charles Lutz, Jr. Mu	4,069	197
American International.	Springfield, Mass.	1885	Harry Courniotes. P	2,231	154
American River.	Sacramento, Cal.	1955	Kenneth Boettcher. Di	17,364	497
Anderson.	Anderson, S.C.	1911	J. Cordell Maddox. D	1,231	63
Andrew.	Cuthbert, Ga.	1854	J.C. Martinson Jr. P	250	21
Angelina.	Lufkin, Tex.	1968	Jack W. Hudgins. S	1,475	88
Anne Arundel Community	Arnold, Md.	1961	Robert P. Ludlum. CS	5,766	265
Anoka-Ramsey Comm.	Coon Rapids, Minn.	1965	H. B. Monroe. S	2,000	72
Anson Tech. Inst.	Ansonville, N.C.	1962	H. B. Monroe. S	576	61
Antelope Valley	Lancaster, Cal.	1929	Clinton Stine. S	4,665	200
Aquinas Junior	Milton, Mass.	1956	Sr. Mary Morgan. D	350	23
Aquinas Junior	Nashville, Tenn.	1961	Sister Henry Suso Fletcher. D	399	45
Arapahoe Community	Littleton, Col.	1968	Joseph K. Bailey. S	4,800	174
Arizona Western.	Yuma, Ariz.	1963	Robert Garin. S	4,300	70
Asheville Buncombe Tech. Inst.	Asheville, N.C.	1959	Harvey Haynes. S	1,019	119
Ashland Community	Ashland, Ky.	1957	Robert Goodpaster. S	1,253	62
Atlantic Comm.	Mays Landing, N.J.	1964	L. R. Winchell Jr. C,S	4,215	211
Auburn Community	Auburn, N.Y.	1953	Albert T. Skinner. S	3,306	83
Austin Comm.	Austin, Minn.	1940	Arlan Burmeister. S	900	50
Bacone.	Muskogee, Okla.	1880	Charles D. Holleyman. P.D	557	37
Bakersfield	Bakersfield, Cal.	1913	John J. Collins. S	12,000	475
Baltimore, Com. Col. of.	Baltimore, Md.	1947	Harry Bard. Mu	11,700	350
Barstow Community	Barstow, Cal.	1960	Wm. R. Graham. Mu	2,019	82
Barton County Comm.	Great Bend, Kan.	1969	Jimmie Downing. C	1,000	53
Bay de Noc Community	Escanaba, Mich.	1962	Edwin E. Wuehle. C	1,320	64
Bay Path Junior	Longmeadow, Mass.	1897	Randle Elliott. P	510	33
Beal.	Bangor, Me.	1891	David Tibbetts. P	380	30
Beaufort County Tech. Inst.	Washington, N.C.	1968	James P. Blanton. S	700	41
Beaver County, Com. Col. of	Monaca, Pa.	1967	Richard Adams. C	2,000	97
Becker Junior.	Worcester, Mass.	1887	Lloyd H. Van Buskirk. P	1,010	44
Beckley.	Beckley, W.Va.	1933	John Saunders. P	1,155	35
Bee County	Beeville, Tex.	1965	Grady C. Hogue. C	2,440	100
Bell and Howell Schools (A)	Chicago, Ill.	1969	George Doherty. P	7,200	350
Belleville Area.	Belleville, Ill.	1946	William Keel. S	9,364	666
Bellevue Community	Bellevue, Wash.	1966	Merle Landerholm. S	7,580	347
Belmont Technical	St. Clairsville, Oh.	1971	Paul Tien. S	850	70
Bend Lake	Ina, Ill.	1967	W.T. Martin Jr. S	3,000	163
Bennett.	Millbrook, N.Y.	1891	J. William Nystrom. P	223	29

Name	Location	Year	Governing Official and Affiliation		Students	Teachers
Bergen Community	Paramus, N.J.	1965	Sidney Silverman	C	9,261	508
Berkeley School, The	E. Orange, N.J.	1931	Larry Luing	S	2,050	65
Berkshire Community	Pittsfield, Mass.	1960	T. E. O'Connell	S	3,000	150
Big Bend Community	Moses Lake, Wash.	1962	Robert J. Wallenstein	S	2,600	117
Biscayne Southern	Charlotte, N.C.	1948	Delores C. Jones	P	1,556	57
Bismarck Junior (A)	Bismarck, N.D.	1939	Ralph Werner	Mu	1,900	85
Black Hawk	Moline, Ill.	1946	Alban E. Reid	S,C	9,257	698
Blackhawk Technical Inst.	Janesville, Wis.	1968	O. L. Johnson (Dir.)	Di	1,562	265
Blinn	Brenham, Tex.	1883	James H. Atkinson	C	2,100	70
Bliss	Columbus, Oh.	1899	Gerald J. Wickham	P	525	25
Bluefield	Bluefield, Va.	1922	Charles L. Tyer	D	435	28
Blue Mountain Community	Pendleton, Ore.	1962	Ronald L. Daniels	C,S	2,500	77
Blue Ridge Comm.	Weyers Cave, Va.	1966	James A. Armstrong	S	1,967	62
Brandywine	Wilmington, Del.	1966	W. Polishook	P	2,099	56
Brazosport	Lake Jackson, Tex.	1968	J. R. Jackson	S	2,941	88
Brevard Community (A)	Cocoa, Fla.	1960	Maxwell King	S	7,600	300
Brewton Parker	Mt. Vernon, Ga.	1904	J. Theodore Phillips	D	1,042	52
Bristol Community	Fall River, Mass.	1957	Jack Hudnall	S	5,501	200
Bronx Community	Bronx, N.Y.	1957	M. Rosenstock, Act.	Mu	17,754	945
Brookdale Community	Lincroft, N.J.	1967	Donald H. Smith	C	7,683	198
Broome Community	Binghamton, N.Y.	1946	Peter Blomerly	S	4,753	164
Broward Community	Ft. Lauderdale, Fla.	1960	Hugh Adams	S	16,000	275
Brunswick Junior	Brunswick, Ga.	1961	John W. Teel	S	1,068	54
Bucks County Comm.	Newtown, Pa.	1965	Charles Rollins	C	7,368	181
Butler County Comm.	Butler, Pa.	1965	Thomas Ten Hoeve Jr.	C	1,410	110
Butler County Comm.	El Dorado, Kan.	1927	Edwin J. Walbourn	C	1,509	85
Butte Community	Durham, Cal.	1968	Albert Schlueter	C	7,161	400
Cabrillo Comm. (A)	Aptos, Cal.	1959	Robert E. Swenson	Di	7,102	241
Caldwell Comm. & Tech.	Lenoir, N.C.	1964	H. Edwin Beam	C	1,832	108
Camden County	Blackwood, N.J.	1967	Otto R. Mauke	C	6,890	328
Canada	Redwood City, Cal.	1968	J.W. Wenrich	D	8,788	305
Canyons, Coll. of the	Valencia, Cal.	1969	Robert Rockwell	D	3,324	98
Cape Cod Comm.	W. Barnstable, Mass.	1960	James F. Hall	S	3,400	163
Cape Fear Tech. Inst.	Wilmington, N.C.	1964	M. J. McLeod	S	732	51
Carl Albert Junior	Poteau, Okla.	1934	Joe E. White	S	1,973	55
Carl Sandburg	Galesburg, Ill.	1967	Eltis Henson	S,C	3,226	158
Carteret Tech. Inst.	Morehead City, N.C.	1964	Donald Bryant	S	984	69
Casper	Casper, Wy.	1945	Tilghman Aley	C	4,001	172
Catawba Valley Tech Inst.	Hickory, N.C.	1960	Robert E. Paap	S	2,000	100
Catonsville Community	Baltimore, Md.	1957	Robert Barringer	C,S	8,881	413
Cazenovia (W)	Cazenovia, N.Y.	1824	Stephen Schneeweiss	P	350	38
Cecil Community	No. East, Md.	1968	William O'Connor	S	1,506	150
Centenary Coll. for Women (W)	Hackettstown, N.J.	1867	Charles H. Dick	P	485	44
Central Arizona	Coolidge, Ariz.	1969	Don Pence	C	4,200	50
Central Carolina Tech. Inst.	Sanford, N.C.	1963	James F. Hockaday	S	1,780	122
Central College	McPherson, Kan.	1884	Bruce L. Kline	P	232	22
Central Florida Community	Ocala, Fla.	1958	Henry E. Goodlett	S	2,168	95
Central Oregon Community	Bend, Ore.	1949	Frederick Boyle	S	1,348	65
Central Piedmont Comm.	Charlotte, N.C.	1963	Richard H. Hagemeyer	S	18,947	692
Central Nebr. Tech. Comm.	Grand Island, Neb.	1973	Chester Gausman	C	3,520	132
Central Texas	Killeen, Tex.	1967	L. M. Morton Jr.	S	5,000	125
Central Virginia Comm.	Lynchburg, Va.	1966	Donald Puyear	S	3,003	121
Central Wyoming	Riverton, Wy.	1966	William Day	C	1,806	92
Central YMCA Comm.	Chicago, Ill.	1960	Donald A. Canar	P	3,873	233
Centralia	Centralia, Wash.	1925	Nels W. Hanson	S	4,182	200
Cerritos Community	Norwalk, Cal.	1955	Wilford Michael	S	23,536	724
Cerro Coso Comm.	Ridgecrest, Cal.	1973	Richard Meyers	S	4,400	218
Chabot	Hayward, Cal.	1961	Reed L. Buffington	Di	19,348	900
Chaffey	Alta Loma, Cal.	1883	T. Stanley Warburton	Di	10,750	348
Champlain	Burlington, Vt.	1878	C. Bader Brouilette	P	1,100	68
Charles Co. Community	La Plata, Md.	1958	J. N. Carsey	S	2,146	115
Charles S. Mott Comm.	Flint, Mich.	1923	Charles Pappas	C	9,710	430
Chattanooga St. Tech. Inst.	Chattanooga, Tenn.	1965	Charles W. Branch	S	3,137	151
Chemeketa Comm.	Salem, Ore.	1969	Donald Newport	Di	25,881	553
Chicago, City Colleges of	Chicago, Ill.	1911	Oscar Shabat, Chan.	Mu	105,401	1,400
Kennedy-King Coll.	Chicago, Ill.	1935	Maceo T. Bowie	S	11,236	229
Loop College	Chicago, Ill.	1962	David H. Heller	S	15,925	209
Malcolm X Coll.	Chicago, Ill.	1911	Ewen M. Akin Jr.	S	6,280	156
Olive-Harvey Coll.	Chicago, Ill.	1957	Eugene T. Speller	S	6,818	184
Southwest Coll.	Chicago, Ill.	1960	Virginia R. Keehan	S	8,210	140
Wright Coll.	Chicago, Ill.	1935	Ernest Clements	S	17,139	227
Chipola Junior	Marianna, Fla.	1947	Raymond M. Deming	S	1,957	87
Chowan	Murfreesboro, N.C.	1848	Bruce E. Whitaker	P	1,015	62
Cisco Junior	Cisco, Tex.	1935	Norman Wallace	S	2,038	85
Citrus Community	Azusa, Cal.	1915	Robert Haugh	S	9,081	335
Clackamas Comm.	Oregon City, Ore.	1966	John Hakanson	D	9,647	392
Claremore Junior	Claremore, Okla.	1971	Richard Mosier	S	1,646	60
Clarendon	Clarendon, Tex.	1898	Kenneth D. Vaughan	S	557	37
Clark	Vancouver, Wash.	1933	I. S. Hakanson	S	5,755	225
Clark Tech.	Springfield, Oh.	1966	Richard Brinkman	S	1,900	97
Clarke	Newton, Miss.	1908	W. L. Compere	D	255	20
Clatsop Community	Astoria, Ore.	1962	Philip Bainer	S	2,976	192
Clayton Junior	Morrow, Ga.	1965	Harry S. Downs	S	3,095	128
Cleveland Co. Tech. Inst.	Shelby, N.C.	1965	James Petty	S	1,810	130
Cleveland State Comm.	Cleveland, Tenn.	1967	D. F. Adkisson	S	3,583	80
Clinton Community	Clinton, Ia.	1946	G. Clemmensen	D	900	50
Clinton Community	Plattsburgh, N.Y.	1966	Albert B. Light	S	1,276	31
Cloud County Comm.	Concordia, Kan.	1965	James P. Ihrig	C,S	1,073	54
Coahoma Junior	Clarksdale, Miss.	1949	James Earl Miller	S,C	1,546	59
Coastal Carolina Community	Jacksonville, N.C.	1963	James Henderson, Jr.	S,C	1,876	95
Cochise	Douglas, Ariz.	1964	John R. Edwards	C	3,612	217
Coffeyville Comm. Junior	Coffeyville, Kan.	1923	Russell Graham	S	744	49
Colby Comm.	Colby, Kan.	1964	James Tangeman	C	1,508	85
Colorado Mountain	Glenwood Spgs., Col.	1967	Elbie L. Gann	C	4,918	313
Colorado Northwestern Comm.	Rangely, Col.	1962	James H. Bos	Di	1,100	50
Columbia Greene Comm.	Athens, N.Y.	1966	Edward J. Owens	S	1,022	27

Name	Location	Year	Governing Official and Affiliation		Stu-dents	Teach-ers
Columbia Junior	Columbia, Cal.	1968	Harvey Rhodes	S	3,020	150
Columbia State Comm.	Columbia, Tenn.	1966	Harold S. Pryor	S	2,156	91
Columbus Tech. Inst.	Columbus, Oh.	1963	Clarence Schauer	S	4,966	264
Compton Comm.	Compton, Cal.	1927	Abel B. Sykes, Jr.	S	6,465	212
Concordia	Portland, Ore.	1950	E.P. Weber	D	201	19
Concordia	Milwaukee, Wis.	1881	Walter W. Stuenkel	D	561	71
Concordia Lutheran	Austin, Tex.	1926	Ray F. Martens	P	317	26
Connors State	Warner, Okla.	1908	Melvin Self	S	1,957	72
Cooke County	Gainesville, Tex.	1924	Alton Laird	S,C	1,750	66
Copiah-Lincoln Junior	Wesson, Miss.	1928	Billy Thames	S	1,365	98
Corning Community	Corning, N.Y.	1956	Robert W. Frederick, Jr.	S	2,849	98
Cottey (W)	Nevada, Mo.	1884	Evelyn Milam	P	351	34
Cowley County Comm.	Arkansas City, Kan.	1922	Owen Nelson	C	1,221	60
Crafton Hills	Yucaipa, Cal.	1972	Roger Anton	S	3,176	110
Craven Comm.	New Bern, N.C.	1965	Thurman E. Brock	S,C	1,400	55
Crowder	Neosho, Mo.	1964	Dell Reed	S	1,000	53
Cuesta (A)	San Luis Obispo, Cal.	1965	Merlin Eisenbise	C	4,254	149
Cumberland County	Vineland, N.J.	1965	John Humes	C,S	1,774	55
Curry	Milton, Mass.	1879	John S. Hafer	P	1,027	54
Cuyahoga Community	Cleveland, Oh.	1963	Nolen Ellison	C	27,500	455
Cypress	Cypress, Cal.	1966	Omar Scheidt	S	12,500	350
Dabney S. Lancaster Comm.	Clifton Forge, Va.	1964	John F. Backels	S	1,000	50
Dallas Co. Comm. Col. System	Dallas, Tex.	1965	Bill J. Priest	C	33,000	617
Dalton Jr.	Dalton, Ga.	1967	Derrell Roberts	S	1,813	86
Danville Junior	Danville, Ill.	1946	William Langas	S	4,300	100
Davenport Coll. of Business	Grand Rapids, Mich.	1866	Robert W. Sneden	P	1,311	46
Davidson County Comm.	Lexington, N.C.	1959	Grady Love	S	2,597	198
Davis Junior Coll. of Business	Toledo, Oh.	1858	Ruth L. Davis	P	1,150	72
Dawson	Glendive, Mon.	1940	James Hoffman	C,S	1,800	50
Daytona Beach Comm. (A)	Daytona Beach, Fla.	1958	Roy F. Bergengren	S	3,527	144
Dean Junior	Franklin, Mass.	1865	Richard Crockford	P	1,500	78
De Anza	Cupertino, Cal.	1967	A. Robert DeHart	S	15,364	652
DeKalb Community	Clarkston, Ga.	1964	James H. Hinson, Jr.	C	10,454	256
Delgado Junior	New Orleans, La.	1921	Marvin E. Thames	S	8,903	275
Del Mar	Corpus Christi, Tex.	1935	Jean Richardson	S	7,158	358
Delaware County Comm.	Media, Pa.	1967	Douglas Libby, Jr.	S	4,800	250
Delta	University Ctr., Mich.	1961	Donald Carlyon	S	9,700	400
Denver, Comm. Coll. of.	Denver, Col.	1968	Leland Luchsinger	S	12,500	700
Des Moines Area Comm.	Ankeny, Ia.	1966	Paul Lowery (Supt.)	S	4,200	300
Desert, Coll. of the.	Palm Desert, Cal.	1958	F.D. Stout	S	8,790	267
Diablo Valley	Pleasant Hill, Cal.	1949	William P. Niland	Di	18,606	500
District One Tech. Inst.	Eau Claire, Wis.	1912	Norbert Wurtzel, Dir.	S	2,147	120
Dixie	St. George, Ut.	1911	Ferron C. Losee	S	1,260	70
Dodge City Community	Dodge City, Kan.	1935	Charles M. Barnes	C	1,200	73
Donnelly	Kansas City, Mo.	1949	Rev. Raymond Davern	D	890	41
Dundalk Community	Baltimore, Md.	1969	John E. Ravekes	C	2,200	65
Du Page, Coll. of	Glen Ellyn, Ill.	1966	Rodney Berg	S	12,344	594
Durham Tech. Inst.	Durham, N.C.	1965	John Crumpton Jr.	S, C	2,000	130
Dutchess Community	Poughkeepsie, N.Y.	1957	John J. Connolly	S	5,423	135
Dyersburg State Comm.	Dyersburg, Tenn.	1969	Edward Eller	S	944	55
East Central Junior	Decatur, Miss.	1928	Charles V. Wright	S	1,335	55
East Central Junior	Union, Mo.	1968	Donald D. Shook	Di	1,452	42
East Los Angeles	Los Angeles, Cal.	1946	A. Rodriguez	D	18,544	680
East Mississippi Junior	Scooba, Miss.	1927	William Reeves	S	987	58
Eastern Arizona	Thatcher, Ariz.	1888	Dean Curtis	S, C	2,675	174
Eastern Iowa Comm.	Davenport, Ia.	1965	Gerald Clemmensen (Supt.)	S, Di	2,889	152
Eastern Maine Voc. Tech.	Bangor, Me.	1966	Francis Sprague, Dir.	S	2,280	100
Eastern Oklahoma State	Wilburton, Okla.	1909	James Miller	S	1,879	89
Eastern Utah, Coll. Of.	Price, Ut.	1938	Dean McDonald	S	525	44
Eastern Wyoming	Torrington, Wy.	1948	Charles Rogers	S	677	70
Eastfield	Mesquite, Tex.	1970	Byron McClenney	C	11,800	402
Edgecombe Tech. Inst.	Tarboro, N.C.	1968	Charles McIntyre	S	1,000	50
Edison Community	Ft. Myers, Fla.	1961	David G. Robinson	S	2,756	92
Edmonds Community	Lynnwood, Wash.	1966	James Warren	S	4,560	180
El Camino	Torrance, Cal.	1947	Stuart E. Marsee	Di	28,398	675
El Centro	Dallas, Tex.	1966	Ruby H. Herd	S	7,811	368
El Paso Comm.	Colorado Springs, Col.	1968	D. Sieck, Act.	C	5,200	259
El Paso Community	El Paso, Tex.	1971	Ray Salazan	C	9,800	347
El Reno	El Reno, Okla.	1938	Bill S. Cole	S	765	37
Elgin Community	Elgin, Ill.	1949	Mark L. Hopkins	S	5,435	263
Elizabeth Seton	Yonkers, N.Y.	1960	Sr. Mary Ellen Brosnan	P	699	63
Elizabethtown Community	Elizabethtown, Ky.	1964	James Owen, Dir.	S	1,346	78
Ellsworth Comm.	Iowa Falls, Ia.	1890	G. P. Warford (Dean)	S	900	57
Emmanuel	Franklin Spgs., Ga.	1919	C. Y. Melton	P	410	23
Endicott Junior (W)	Beverly, Mass.	1939	Eleanor Tupper	P	740	54
Erie Community	Buffalo, N.Y.	1946	Robert H. Stauffer	S	11,105	304
Essex Community	Baltimore, Md.	1957	Vernon Wanty	C	8,900	285
Essex County	Newark, N.J.	1966	J. Harry Smith	C	7,080	490
Everett Comm.	Everett, Wash.	1941	Norman Clark	S	6,887	250
Fashion Inst. of Technology	New York, N.Y.	1944	Marvin J. Feldman	S	6,575	153
Faulkner State Jr.	Bay Minette, Ala.	1963	L. Sibert	S	2,347	78
Fayetteville Tech. Inst.	Fayetteville, N.C.	1961	Howard Boudreau	S	4,249	225
Feather River	Quincy, Cal.	1968	Dale P. Wren	S	1,837	53
Fergus Falls Comm.	Fergus Falls, Minn.	1960	W. A. Waage	S	542	34
Ferrum	Ferrum, Va.	1913	Joseph T. Hart	D	1,301	63
Finger Lakes, Comm. Coll. of	Canandaigua, N.Y.	1965	Charles Meder	S	2,170	55
Fisher Junior	Boston, Mass.	1903	Scott Fisher	P	2,700	105
Flathead Valley Comm.	Kalispell, Mon.	1967	John Bartlett	S	1,861	120
Florida	Temple Terrace, Fla.	1946	James R. Cope	P	471	33
Florida Jr. Coll. at Jacksonville	Jacksonville, Fla.	1966	Benjamin R. Wygal	S	75,158	1,590
Florida Keys Comm.	Key West, Fla.	1965	John S. Smith	S	1,267	55
Florissant Valley Community(A)	St. Louis, Mo.	1962	Raymond J. Stith	Di	6,869	350
Floyd Junior	Rome, Ga.	1970	David McCorkle	S	1,646	103
Foothill	Los Altos Hills, Cal.	1958	James Fitzgerald	Di	15,314	559
Forest Park Community (A)	St. Louis, Mo.	1962	Ralph H. Lee	Di	5,828	367
Forsyth Tech. Inst.	Winston-Salem, N.C.	1963	Harley Affeldt	S	2,200	125

Name	Location	Year	Governing Official and Affiliation		Students	Teachers
Ft. Steilacoom Comm.	Tacoma, Wash.	1967	Marion O. Oppelt.	S	7,500	350
Fox Valley Tech. Inst.	Appleton, Wis.	1967	William Sirek (Dir.)	D	23,575	747
Franklin Inst. of Boston	Boston, Mass.	1908	Michael Mazzola (Dir.)	P	910	55
Fresno City	Fresno, Cal.	1910	Clyde McCully	Di	17,061	525
Fullerton (A)	Fullerton, Cal.	1913	John Casey.	S	17,999	510
Fulton-Montgomery Community	Johnstown, N.Y.	1963	Hadley S. DePuy.	S	1,701	50
Gadsden State Junior.	E. Gadsden, Ala.	1965	A. D. Naylor.	S	9,627	215
Gainesville Junior	Gainesville, Ga.	1964	Hugh Mills, Jr.	S	1,655	65
Galveston (A)	Galveston, Tex.	1967	Melvin M. Plexco.	S	1,700	100
Garden City Community Junior	Garden City, Kan.	1919	Raymond Wamsley	C,S	1,464	64
Gaston.	Dallas, N.C.	1963	Joseph L. Mills.	S	2,870	90
Gateway Tech. Inst.	Kenosha, Wis.	1912	Keith Stoehr, Dir.	C,S	45,400	920
Gavilan	Gilroy, Cal.	1919	Rudy Melone.	S	2,000	113
Genesee Community	Batavia, N.Y.	1966	Cornelius V. Robbins	S	2,800	88
George C. Wallace State Comm.	Dothan, Ala.	1965	Phillip J. Hamm	S	2,239	96
Germanna Comm.	Locust Grove, Va.	1970	Arnold E. Wirtala.	S	1,000	60
Glen Oaks Comm.	Centreville, Mich.	1965	Justus Sundermann.	S	900	66
Glendale.	Glendale, Cal.	1927	John Grande.	Mu	7,587	307
Gloucester County.	Sewell, N.J.	1968	William Apetz.	C	2,316	104
Gogebic Community	Ironwood, Mich.	1932	James Perry.	S	1,244	65
Golden West.	Huntgtn. Bch., Cal.	1965	R. Dudley Boyce	S	23,063	555
Goldey Beacom.	Wilmington, Del.	1886	Paul R. Brown.	P	2,350	150
Gordon Junior	Barnesville, Ga.	1852	Jerry M. Williamson	P	1,104	53
Grahm Junior	Boston, Mass.	1950	Arthur Griffin	P	831	72
Grand Rapids Junior.	Grand Rapids, Mich.	1914	Richard Calkins.	Mu	7,301	230
Grand View.	Des Moines, Ia.	1896	K. F. Langrock.	P	858	40
Grays Harbor.	Aberdeen, Wash.	1930	Joseph Malik.	S	3,300	182
Grayson County Junior.	Denison, Tex.	1964	Truman Wester.	S,C	4,900	183
Greater Hartford Comm.	Hartford, Conn.	1967	Arthur C. Banks Jr.	S	2,396	89
Green River Comm.	Auburn, Wash.	1964	Melvin Lindbloom.	S	6,990	215
Greenfield Comm.	Greenfield, Mass.	1962	Lewis Turner.	S	1,480	99
Greenville Tech.	Greenville, S.C.	1962	Thomas Barton Jr.	S	9,012	200
Grossmont.	El Cajon, Cal.	1961	Erv. F. Metzgar.	S	16,301	553
Guilford Tech. Inst.	Jamestown, N.C.	1958	Woodrow Sugg.	C	3,300	240
Gulf Coast Community	Panama City, Fla.	1957	Lawrence Tyree.	S	2,805	128
Hagerstown Junior.	Hagerstown, Md.	1946	Atlee Kepler.	C	1,924	105
Halifax County Tech. Inst.	Weldon, N.C.	1967	Philip W. Taylor.	S,C	771	54
Harcum Junior	Bryn Mawr, Pa.	1915	Michael A. Duzy.	P	850	52
Harrisburg Area Comm.	Harrisburg, Pa.	1964	S. James Manilla	Di	4,400	157
Hartford Community.	Bel Air, Md.	1957	Kenneth Oosting	C	2,818	146
Hartford Col. for Wm. (W).	Hartford, Conn.	1939	Laura A. Johnson	P	228	25
Hartford State Tech.	Hartford, Conn.	1948	L. Barrell	S	1,800	80
Hartnell.	Salinas, Cal.	1920	Gibb R. Madsen	C	7,035	310
Haskell Indian Junior	Lawrence, Kan.	1884	Wallace Galluzzi	F	1,086	81
Hawkeye Inst. of Technology	Waterloo, Ia.	1966	John Hawse	S	21,642	442
Haywood Tech. Inst.	Clyde, N.C.	1965	M. C. Nix	S	1,000	90
Hazard Community	Hazard, Ky.	1968	Marvin Jolly.	S	222	22
Henderson Community	Henderson, Ky.	1960	Marshall Arnold	S	639	57
Henderson County Junior	Athens, Tex.	1946	T. M. Harvey.	C	1,786	95
Henry Ford Community	Dearborn, Mich.	1938	Stuart M. Bundy.	Mu	14,856	609
Herkimer County Comm.	Herkimer, N.Y.	1966	Robert McLaughlin.	S	1,439	48
Hesston.	Hesston, Kan.	1909	Laban Peachey.	D	625	78
Hibbing Comm.	Hibbing, Minn.	1916	Jennis Bapst.	S	704	34
Highland Comm.	Freeport, Ill.	1961	Howard Sims.	S	1,814	101
Highland Community Junior	Highland, Kan.	1858	Jack D. Nutt.	S	996	33
Highline Comm.	Midway, Wash.	1961	Orville Carnahan.	S	8,100	384
Hilbert.	Hamburg, N.Y.	1967	Sister Edmunette.	P	600	50
Hill Junior.	Hillsboro, Tex.	1962	Oran Bailey.	S	700	51
Hillsborough Comm.	Tampa, Fla.	1968	Morton S. Shanberg.	S	13,000	492
Hinds Junior.	Raymond, Miss.	1917	Robert Mayo.	C,S	8,516	337
Hiwassee	Madisonville, Tenn.	1849	Horace N. Barker.	D	650	33
Hocking Technical.	Nelsonville, Oh.	1968	John J. Light.	S	1,750	123
Holding Tech. Inst.	Raleigh, N.C.	1963	R. LeMay Jr.	S	1,362	83
Holmes Junior.	Goodman, Miss.	1925	Frank Branch.	S	1,338	68
Holy Cross Junior.	Notre Dame, Ind.	1966	Bro. John Driscoll.	D	275	23
Holyoke Community.	Holyoke, Mass.	1946	George Frost.	S	4,340	250
Honolulu Comm.	Honolulu, Ha.	1920	C. Yoshioka.	S	3,547	119
Hopkinsville Community	Hopkinsville, Ky.	1965	Thomas Riley.	S	1,345	65
Horry — Georgetown Tech.	Conway, S.C.	1966	W. F. Anderson.	S	1,100	53
Hostos Community	Bronx, N.Y.	1968	Candido De Leon.	C	2,871	202
Housatonic Comm.	Bridgeport, Conn.	1966	V. Darnowski.	S	2,829	110
Houston Community	Houston, Tex.	1971	J. B. Whiteley.	S	23,000	2,655
Howard Community	Columbia, Md.	1970	Alfred Smith Jr.	C	1,450	69
Howard County Jr.	Big Spring, Tex.	1946	Charles Hays	SC	1,448	98
Hudson Valley Community	Troy, N.Y.	1953	J. Fitzgibbons	S	7,006	257
Humphreys.	Stockton, Cal.	1896	John Humphreys.	P	416	21
Hutchinson Community Jr.	Hutchinson, Kan.	1928	A. H. Elland.	S	2,416	174
Illinois Central.	E. Peoria, Ill.	1967	Leon Perley.	S	23,000	700
Illinois Eastern Comm.	Olney, Ill.	1968	James Spencer, Chan.	C	5,262	88
Illinois Valley Comm.	Oglesby, Ill.	1924	Alfred Wisgoski.	Mu	3,100	150
Imperial Valley	Imperial, Cal.	1922	Terrell Spencer.	S	4,565	213
Independence Comm. Jr.	Independence, Kan.	1925	Neil Edds.	C,S	891	31
Indian Hills Community	Ottumwa, Ia.	1966	Lyle A. Hellyer.	S	1,095	93
Indian Hills Comm.	Centerville, Ia.	1930	Lyle Hellyer.	S	1,228	96
Indian River Comm.	Ft. Pierce, Fla.	1960	Herman Heise	S	2,751	78
Indian Valley	Novato, Cal.	1971	Ernest H. Berg.	C	3,064	145
Indiana Vocational Tech.	Indianapolis, Ind.	1963	Glenn W. Sample.	S	11,341	701
Inver Hills Comm.	Inver Hills Hts., Minn.	1970	Curtis Johnson	S	2,161	90
Iowa Central Comm.	Ft. Dodge, Ia.	1966	Edwin Barbour.	C	2,500	130
Iowa Lakes Comm.	Estherville, Ia.	1967	Richard Blacker, Supt.	S	1,755	139
Iowa Western Comm.	Council Bluffs, Ia.	1966	R. Looft.	S	1,703	121
Isothermal Comm.	Spindale, N.C.	1965	Fred J. Eason.	S	1,029	50
Itasca Comm.	Grand Rapids, Minn.	1922	Bruce M. Bauer	S	513	37
Itawamba Junior	Fulton, Miss.	1948	W. O. Benjamin	S	2,172	106

Name	Location	Year	Governing Official and Affiliation		Students	Teachers
Jackson Comm.	Jackson, Mich.	1928	Harold Sheffer	C,S	10,500	441
Jackson State Comm.	Jackson, Tenn.	1965	F. E. Wright	S	2,634	81
Jamestown Community	Jamestown, N.Y.	1950	Roger Seager	S	3,267	91
Jeff Davis State Jr.	Brewton, Ala.	1965	W. P. Patterson	S	1,200	43
Jefferson Community	Louisville, Ky.	1968	Ronald Horvath, Dir.	S	6,056	320
Jefferson Comm.	Hillsboro, Mo.	1963	B.R. Henry	Di	4,300	236
Jefferson Community	Watertown, N.Y.	1961	James McVean	C	1,524	46
Jefferson State Jr.	Birmingham, Ala.	1965	George Layton	S	8,900	275
John A. Logan	Carterville, Ill.	1967	Robert Tarvin	S	3,147	71
John C. Calhoun St. Comm.	Decatur, Ala.	1965	Carlton Kelley	S	3,495	197
John Tyler Comm.	Chester, Va.	1967	James Walpole	S	909	83
Johnson County Comm.	Overland Park, Kan.	1968	John E. Cleek	C	5,085	204
Joliet Junior	Joliet, Ill.	1901	H. D. McAninch	S	7,702	127
Jones County Junior	Ellisville, Miss.	1911	Terrell Tisdale	S	2,035	128
Kalamazoo Valley Comm. (A)	Kalamazoo, Mich.	1966	Dale B. Lake	C	4,300	150
Kankakee Comm.	Kankakee, Ill.	1966	John Samlin	S	5,436	210
Kan. City Kan. Comm. Junior	Kansas City, Kan.	1923	Jack M. Platt	S	2,985	100
Kapiolani Comm. (A)	Honolulu, Ha.	1964	Frederick Haehnlen, Prov.	S	3,545	154
Kaskaskia	Centralia, Ill.	1965	Ray Searby	S	3,024	49
Katherine Gibbs School	New York, N.Y.	1917	Vacant	P	1,000	25
Kauai Community	Lihue, Ha.	1965	Edward White, Provost	S	1,128	54
Kellogg Community	Battle Creek, Mich.	1956	Richard F. Whitmore	S	8,389	263
Kendall	Evanston, Ill.	1934	Andrew Cothran	P	838	35
Kennesaw Junior	Marietta, Ga.	1966	Horace W. Sturgis	S	2,241	85
Kettering Coll. of Medical Arts	Kettering, Oh.	1967	Winton Beaven, Dean	D	368	45
Keystone Junior	La Plume, Pa.	1868	John B. Hibbard	P	852	32
Kilgore	Kilgore, Tex.	1935	Randolph C. Watson	S	4,000	165
Kingsborough Community	Brooklyn, N.Y.	1963	Leon M. Goldstein	Mu	10,165	569
Kirtland Comm.	Roscommon, Mich.	1966	Robert A. Stenger	S	1,100	75
Kirkwood Comm.	Cedar Rapids, Ia.	1966	Selby Ballantyne (Supt.)	S	4,128	266
Kishwaukee	Malta, Ill.	1967	W. Lamar Fly	S	3,410	210
Labette Community Jr.	Parsons, Kan.	1923	James J. Altendorf	C,S	723	40
La Guardia Community	Long Island City, N.Y.	1968	Joseph Shenker	Mu	6,120	315
Lake City Comm.	Lake City, Fla.	1947	Herbert E. Phillips	S	2,712	155
Lake County, Coll. of	Grayslake, Ill.	1968	Richard Erzen	S	8,401	405
Lakeland	Mentor, Oh.	1966	Wayne Rodehorst	C	5,859	108
Lake Michigan (A)	Benton Harbor, Mich.	1946	James Lehman	S	2,800	60
Lake Region Jr.	Devils Lake, N.D.	1941	Merril Berg	S	933	45
Lake Sumter Comm.	Leesburg, Fla.	1962	Paul P. Williams	Di	2,231	77
Lakeshore Tech Inst.	Cleveland, Wis.	1912	Frederick Nierode	Mu	1,136	342
Lakewood Comm.	White Bear L., Minn.	1967	N. Christenson, Act.	S	2,474	93
Lamar Community (A)	Lamar, Col.	1937	Carl Westbrook	S	510	46
Lane Community (A)	Eugene, Ore.	1965	Eldon G. Schafer	Di	6,276	343
Lansing Community	Lansing, Mich.	1957	Philip Gannon	S	15,901	816
Laramie County Community	Cheyenne, Wy.	1968	Harlan L. Heglar	S,C	3,133	166
Laredo Junior	Laredo, Tex.	1946	D. Archiga	Di	4,642	93
Lasell Junior (W)	Newton, Mass.	1851	Arthur Griffin	P	573	70
Lassen	Susanville, Cal.	1924	Robert Theiler	Di	2,666	182
Lee	Baytown, Tex.	1934	Jim Sturgeon	Di	5,009	169
Lees-McRae	Banner Elk, N.C.	1900	H. C. Evans Jr.	P	691	45
Lehigh County Comm.	Schnecksville, Pa.	1966	John G. Bernier	S,Di	2,808	137
Leicester Jr.	Leicester, Mass.	1784	L. Van Burkirk	P	209	26
Lenoir Comm.	Kinston, N.C.	1958	Jesse L. McDaniel	S	2,132	102
Lewis and Clark Community	Godfrey, Ill.	1971	Wilbur R. L. Trimpe	S	4,153	184
Lexington Technical Inst.	Lexington, Ky.	1965	William Price	S	1,600	85
Lima Technical	Lima, Oh.	1971	James S. Biddle	S	915	50
Lincoln Land Comm.	Springfield, Ill.	1967	Robert L. Poorman	S,C	5,972	255
Lincoln	Lincoln, Ill.	1865	J. Richard Stoltz	P	450	43
Lincoln Trail	Robinson, Ill.	1969	Joseph Piland	S	2,000	103
Linn-Benton Comm.	Albany, Ore.	1967	Raymond J. Needham	S	6,333	552
Long Beach City	Long Beach, Cal.	1927	Frank Pearce	Mu	29,343	1,312
Longview Community	Lee's Summit, Mo.	1969	William D. Hatley	Di	5,138	229
Lorain County Comm.	Elyria, Oh.	1964	Omar Olson	C	5,277	231
Los Angeles City	Los Angeles, Cal.	1929	John Anthony	C	23,000	650
Los Angeles Harbor	Wilmington, Cal.	1949	Eugene A. Pimentel	S	12,349	459
Los Angeles Pierce	Woodland Hills, Cal.	1947	Edward Liston	S	23,500	750
Los Angeles Southwest	Los Angeles, Cal.	1967	Franklin Turner	S	4,777	197
L.A. Trade Technical	Los Angeles, Cal.	1949	Fred Brinkman	Mu	18,528	945
Los Angeles Valley	Van Nuys, Cal.	1949	Alice Thurston	Mu	23,707	669
Louisburg	Louisburg, N.C.	1787	J. Allen Norris Jr.	D	576	39
Louisiana State Univ. at Alexandria	Alexandria, La.	1960	James DeLee, Act. Dean	S	1,261	66
at Eunice	Eunice, La.	1967	Anthony Mumphrey	S	939	42
Lower Columbia	Longview, Wash.	1934	David Story	S	3,765	158
Lurleen B. Wallace State Jr.	Andalusia, Ala.	1969	W. H. McWhorter	S	1,072	50
Luzerne County Comm.	Nanticoke, Pa.	1966	Byron Rinehimer	C	1,800	120
Macomb County Community	Warren, Mich.	1962	R. F. Roelofs	C	25,700	861
MacCormac Junior	Chicago, Ill.	1904	Gordon Borchardt	P	327	16
Macon Junior	Macon, Ga.	1968	William Wright	S	2,790	71
Madison Area Technical	Madison, Wis.	1912	Norman P. Mitby, Dir.	Di	7,383	220
Madison Business	Madison, Wis.	1856	Otto J. Madland	P	229	20
Maine, Univ. of at Augusta, Me.	Augusta, Me.	1965	Lloyd J. Jewett	S	3,269	180
Mainland, Coll. of the	Texas City, Tex.	1966	Fred Taylor	Di	1,891	91
Manatee Junior	Bradenton, Fla.	1957	Samuel R. Neel Jr.	S	3,672	175
Manhattan Comm.	New York, N.Y.	1963	Edgar Draper	Mu	10,909	457
Manor Jr.	Jenkintown, Pa.	1947	Mother M. Olga	D	295	43
Maple Woods Community	Kansas City, Mo.	1969	John M. Gazda	S	2,500	108
Maria	Albany, N.Y.	1958	Sr. Mary B. Mahoney	D	479	48
Maricopa Tech. County Comm.	Phoenix, Ariz.	1968	N. Bruemmer, Dean	C	7,000	400
Marion Institute	Marion, Ala.	1842	R. Adm. Draper Kauffman	P	350	37
Marshalltown Community	Marshalltown, Ia.	1927	James McKinstry, Dean.	Di	1,053	52
Martin	Pulaski, Tenn.	1870	Bill Starns	D,P	487	38
Martin	Williamston, N.C.	1968	Joseph B. Carter	S,C	1,250	65
Massachusetts Bay Comm.	Watertown, Mass.	1961	John McKenzie	S	4,208	269
Massasoit Comm.	Brockton, Mass.	1966	John Musselman	S	5,158	187

Name	Location	Year	Governing Official and Affiliation		Students	Teachers
Mater Dei	Ogdensburg, N.Y.	1960	Sr. Patricia Burke	D	313	55
Mattatuck Community	Waterbury, Conn.	1967	Charles B. Kinney	S	3,062	122
Maui Community	Kahului, Ha.	1965	Sanae Moikeha, Provost	S	1,615	82
McCook	McCook, Neb.	1926	John N. Harms	C	769	44
McDowell Tech. Inst.	Marion, N.C.	1964	John Price	S	544	20
McHenry County	Crystal Lake, Ill.	1967	James Davis	Di	3,000	102
McLennan Comm.	Waco, Tex.	1966	Wilbur Ball	C	3,455	172
Medgar Evers Coll. **	Brooklyn, N.Y.	1968	Richard D. Trent	Mu	3,506	278
**Will become a 2 yr. college in Sept. 1976						
Meramec Community	St. Louis, Mo.	1962	Glynn E. Clark	Di	7,070	378
Merced	Merced, Cal.	1962	Lowell Barker	S	8,231	275
Mercer County Comm.	Trenton, N.J.	1966	John P. Hanley	D	7,274	158
Mercy	Dobbs Ferry, N.Y.	1950	Donald Grunewald	P	4,300	275
Meridian Jr.	Meridian, Miss.	1937	William F. Scaggs	Mu	2,900	241
Merrit	Oakland, Cal.	1964	Donald Godbold	Mu	11,000	350
Mesa (A)	Gd. Junction, Col.	1925	Theodore E. Albers	S	3,573	125
Mesabi Comm.	Virginia, Minn.	1918	Gilbert Staupe	S	850	37
Metropolitan Comm.	Minneapolis, Minn.	1965	Rafael Cortada	S	2,200	140
Metropolitan Comm.	Kansas City, Mo.	1916	Ervin Harlacher, Chan.	S	15,329	277
Miami-Dade Comm.	Miami, Fla.	1960	Peter Masiko Jr.	S	40,099	1,535
Miami-Jacobs Jr. Coll. of Bus.	Dayton, Oh.	1860	Charles P. Harbottle	P	1,500	53
Michael J. Owens Tech.	Perrysburg, Oh.	1967	Jacob H. See	S	3,000	120
Michigan Christian Jr.	Rochester, Mich.	1959	Don. E. Gardner	D,P	343	27
Midland	Midland, Tex.	1972	Al G. Langford	S	1,600	101
Mid Michigan Community	Harrison, Mich.	1965	Eugene W. Gillaspy	S	1,500	100
Mid-Plains Comm.	No. Platte, Neb.	1967	Kenneth L. Aten	C	1,433	60
Mid-State Tech. Inst.	Wis. Rapids, Wis.	1967	Earl F. Jaeger	Di,S	1,500	250
Middle Georgia	Cochran, Ga.	1884	Louis C. Alderman Jr.	S	1,904	100
Middlesex Comm.	Middletown, Conn.	1966	Philip Wheaton	S	2,166	45
Middlesex County	Edison, N.J.	1964	Robert Harris	C	10,082	414
Midlands Tech.	Columbia S.C.	1974	Robert Grigsby Jr.	S,C	8,500	250
Miles Comm.	Miles City, Mon.	1939	Vernon R. Railey	Di	850	35
Milwaukee Area Technical	Milwaukee, Wis.	1911	William Ramsey (Dir.)	Di	42,291	1,870
Mineral Area.	Flat River, Mo.	1922	Richard Caster	Di	917	53
Mira Costa	Oceanside, Cal.	1934	John MacDonald	S	5,400	190
Mississippi Delta Jr.	Moorhead, Miss.	1926	J. T. Hall.	S,C	1,900	101
Mississippi Gulf Coast Jr.	Perkinston, Miss.	1925	J. J. Hayden Jr.	S	10,102	353
Mitchell	New London, Conn.	1938	Robert C. Weller	P	799	42
Mitchell Comm.	Statesville, N.C.	1856	Charles Poindexter.	S	1,063	74
Moberly Area Junior.	Moberly, Mo	1972	Henry T. Norris.	S	750	85
Modesto Junior	Modesto, Cal.	1921	Kenneth Griffin	S	14,057	601
Mohawk Valley Community	Utica, N.Y.	1946	G. H. Robertson	S	6,586	143
Mohegan Comm.	Norwich, Conn.	1970	Robert N. Rue.	S	2,000	72
Monroe Community	Rochester, N.Y.	1961	Moses Kock	S	10,306	293
Monroe County Comm.	Monroe, Mich.	1964	Ronald Campbell	C	1,704	67
Montcalm Comm.	Sidney, Mich.	1965	C. J. Bedore	C	1,050	27
Monterey Peninsula	Monterey, Cal.	1947	George J. Faul	C	12,000	425
Montgomery Community	Rockville, Md.	1946	William Strasser	C	13,907	684
Montgomery County Comm. (A)	Blue Bell, Pa.	1964	Leroy Brendlinger	C	5,000	250
Montreat-Anderson.	Montreat, N.C.	1916	Silas M. Vaughn.	D	427	27
Moorpark	Moorpark, Cal.	1967	W. Ray Hearon	S	10,000	525
Moraine Valley Comm.	Palos Hills, Ill.	1968	James Koeller	S	11,000	400
Morgan Comm.	Ft. Morgan, Col.	1970	Robert W. Johnson.	S	1,000	16
Morris, County College of.	Dover, N.J.	1965	Sherman H. Masten	C	8,411	350
Morristown	Morristown, Tenn.	1881	Raymond White.	D	233	18
Morse Sch. of Bus. Inc.	Hartford, Conn.	1860	Michael Taub.	P	350	30
Morton (A)	Cicero, Ill.	1924	Vincent A. Guarna	Di	1,757	103
Motlow State Comm.	Tullahoma, Tenn.	1969	Harry D. Wagner.	S	1,140	46
Mt. Aloysius Junior	Cresson, Pa.	1939	Sr. Mary Cecilia Meighan	P	504	50
Mt. Hood Comm.	Gresham, Ore.	1966	Earl L. Klapstein	Di	12,500	700
Mt. Ida Junior	Newton, Mass.	1899	F. Roy Carlson	P	700	58
Mt. Olive	Mt. Olive, N.C.	1951	Williams B. Raper.	D	408	23
Mt. San Antonio	Walnut, Cal	1946	Eldon Pearce	Di	19,489	655
Mt. San Jacinto	San Jacinto, Cal.	1963	Milo P. Johnson.	S	2,500	47
Mt. St. Clare	Clinton, Ia.	1928	Sr. Eileen Smith.	D	230	30
Mt. Wachusett Comm.	Gardner, Mass.	1963	Arthur F. Haley.	S	2,956	149
Murray State.	Tishomingo, Okla.	1908	Clyde Kindell.	S	1,459	34
Muskegon Community	Muskegon, Mich.	1926	Charles Greene.	C	5,701	200
Napa	Napa, Cal.	1942	George Clark	C	5,478	243
Nash Tech. Inst.	Rocky Mount, N.C.	1968	Jack D. Ballard.	S	813	35
Nassau Community	Garden City, N.Y.	1959	George Chambers	C	17,555	435
Navarro.	Corsicana, Tex.	1946	Kenneth Walker.	C	2,081	85
Nebraska Western	Scottsbluff, Neb.	1928	Alex Easton.	Mu	761	51
Neosho County Comm. Jr.	Chanute, Kan.	1936	J. C. Sanders.	C	613	43
New Hampshire Tech. Inst.	Concord, N.H.	1965	D. Larrabee Sr.	S	2,700	90
New Hampshire Voc. Tech.	Manchester, N.H.	1945	George C. Knox, Dir.	S	815	54
New Mexico Junior	Hobbs, N.M.	1965	Jodie Smith.	S	1,154	58
New Mexico Military Inst. (M).	Roswell, N.M.	1891	Robert Kemble.	S	525	22
New River Community.	Dublin, Va.	1969	W. Robert Sullins.	S	1,752	85
N.Y. City Community Coll.	Brooklyn, N.Y.	1946	Herbert M. Sussman.	Mu	18,367	1,440
New York, State Univ. of						
Agric. & Tech. Inst.	Alfred, N.Y.	1908	David H. Huntington.	S	4,386	221
" " "	Canton, N.Y.	1906	Earl MacArthur.	S	2,834	127
" " "	Cobleskill, N.Y.	1911	Walton A. Brown.	S	2,761	140
" " "	Delhi, N.Y.	1913	Francis Hennessy	S	2,755	137
" " "	Farmingdale, N.Y.	1912	Charles W. Laffin.	S	13,642	338
" " "	Morrisville, N.Y.	1908	Royson N. Whipple.	S	3,051	135
Niagara County Community	Sanborn, N.Y.	1962	Jack C. Watson	S	4,651	133
Normandale Comm.	Bloomington, Minn.	1968	Dale Lorenz	S	4,277	196
North Central Michigan	Petoskey, Mich.	1958	A. D. Shankland.	S,C	1,569	90
North Central Tech. Inst.	Wausau, Wis.	1912	L. B. Hoyt (Dir.)	C	2,502	445
North Country Comm.	Saranac Lake, N.Y.	1967	George Hodson.	S	1,275	42
N. Dak. St. Sch. of Science	Wahpeton, N.D.	1903	Clair I. Blikre	S	3,118	168
North Florida Junior	Madison, Fla.	1958	Stephen McMahon.	S	870	53
North Greenville.	Tigerville, S.C.	1892	George Silver	D	599	50
North Harris County	Houston, Tex.	1972	W. W. Thorne.	S	1,500	75
North Hennepin Comm.	Brooklyn Pk., Minn.	1966	John F. Helling.	S	3,330	147
North Idaho.	Coeur d' Alene, Ida.	1933	Barry Schuler.	Di	1,600	107

Name	Location	Year	Governing Official and Affiliation		Stu-dents	Teach-ers
North Iowa Area Comm.	Mason City, Ia.	1918	David Randall Pierce.	S	2,014	90
North Shore Community.	Beverly, Mass.	1965	George Traicoff.	S	6,392	358
Northampton Co. Area Comm. (A).	Bethlehem, Pa.	1966	Richard Richardson Jr.	C	3,008	215
Northeast Alabama State Jr.	Rainsville, Ala.	1965	E.R. Knox.	S	2,978	148
Northeast Miss. Junior.	Booneville, Miss.	1948	Harold T. White.	S	1,556	95
Northeast Neb. Tech. Comm.	Norfolk, Neb.	1973	Robert P. Cox.	S	1,166	91
Northeast Wisconsin Tech. Inst.	Green Bay, Wis.	1910	K. W. Hanbenschild (Dir.)	Mu	17,776	732
Northeastern Junior.	Sterling, Col.	1941	Ervin S. French.	C,S	1,800	90
Northeastern Okla. A&M	Miami, Okla.	1919	D. D. Creech.	S	2,730	120
Northern Essex Comm.	Haverhill, Mass.	1960	Harold Bentley.	S	6,899	336
Northern Oklahoma.	Tonkawa, Okla.	1901	Edwin Vineyard.	S	1,258	64
Northern Virginia Comm.	No. Springfield, Va.	1965	Richard Ernst.	S	27,198	1,229
Northland Comm.	Thief R. Falls, Minn.	1965	Theodore A. Easton.	S	700	28
Northwest Community.	Powell, Wy.	1946	Sinclair Orendorff.	S	1,053	89
Northwest Miss. Junior.	Senatobia, Miss.	1927	Henry B. Koon.	S	2,743	130
Northwestern Conn. Comm.	Winsted, Conn.	1965	Regina Duffy.	S	1,906	65
Northwestern Michigan.	Traverse City, Mich.	1951	William J. Yankee.	S	4,135	172
Norwalk Community.	Norwalk, Conn.	1961	E. I. L. Baker.	S	2,866	93
Norwalk State Tech.	Norwalk, Conn.	1961	Frank Juszli.	S	2,052	102
Oakland Community.	Bloomfield Hills, Mich.	1965	Joseph Hill.	C	18,873	292
Oakton Comm. (A).	Morton Grove, Ill.	1969	William Koehnline.	S	15,371	671
Ocean County.	Toms River, N.J.	1964	Andrews S. Moreland.	C	4,426	153
Odessa.	Odessa, Tex.	1946	Philip Speegle.	S	3,224	188
Ohlone.	Fremont, Cal.	1966	W. B. Richter.	Di	9,000	385
Okaloosa-Walton Jr.	Niceville, Fla.	1963	J. E. McCracken.	S	2,866	155
Oklahoma City Southwestern.	Oklahoma City, Okla.	1945	Hugh H. Morgan.	D	1,500	75
Oklahoma Sch. of Business Accountancy, Law & Finance.	Tulsa, Okla.	1919	H. Everett Pope Jr.	P	525	23
Olney Central.	Olney, Ill.	1963	Paul Thompson.	S	1,576	63
Olympic.	Brennerton, Wash.	1946	Henry Milander.	S	7,500	350
Onondaga Community.	Syracuse, N.Y.	1961	Roger J. Manges.	S	5,815	180
Orange Coast.	Costa Mesa, Cal.	1948	Robert Moore.	C	31,261	780
Orange County Community.	Middletown, N.Y.	1950	Robert T. Novak.	S	5,253	136
Orangeburg Calhoun Tech (A).	Orangeburg, S.C.	1968	M. Rudy Groomes.	S	1,800	111
Oscar Rose Junior.	Midwest City, Okla.	1971	Joe Leone.	S	7,818	251
Otero Junior.	La Junta, Col.	1941	William L. McDivitt.	S	977	42
Ottumwa Heights.	Ottumwa, Ia.	1925	Jerry Solloway.	P	364	31
Paducah Comm.	Paducah, Ky.	1932	Donald J. Clemens.	S	1,300	71
Palm Beach Junior.	Lake Worth, Fla.	1933	Harold C. Manor.	S	7,642	330
Palomar, Comm.	San Marcos, Cal.	1946	Frederick R. Huber.	Mu	11,172	400
Palo Verde.	Blythe, Cal.	1947	George W. Pennell.	S	900	45
Panola Junior.	Carthage, Tex.	1947	Arthur Johnson.	S	849	38
Paris Junior.	Paris, Tex.	1924	Louis B. Williams.	Di	2,300	103
Parkersburg Community.	Parkersburg, W.Va.	1971	Jerry Jones.	S	5,149	83
Parkland.	Champaign, Ill.	1966	William M. Staerkel.	Di	6,451	200
Pasadena City.	Pasadena, Cal.	1924	E. H. Floyd.	S	20,700	712
Pasco Hernando Comm.	Dade City, Fla.	1972	Milton O. Jones.	S	1,700	174
Passaic Co. Comm.	Paterson, N.J.	1968	Gustavo Mellander.	C	1,344	91
Patrick Henry State Jr.	Monroeville, Ala.	1965	Cecil Murphy.	S	1,013	57
Paul D. Camp Comm.	Franklin, Va.	1971	Perry Adams.	S	1,232	50
Paul Smith's.	Paul Smiths, N.Y.	1946	Gray Twombly, Act.	P	1,216	81
Peace (W).	Raleigh, N.C.	1857	S. David Frazier.	D	521	33
Pearl River Junior.	Poplarville, Miss.	1921	M. R. White.	S	2,500	106
Peirce Junior.	Philadelphia, Pa.	1865	Thomas M. Peirce III.	P	1,407	71
Peninsula.	Port Angeles, Wash.	1961	Paul G. Cornaby.	S	2,800	120
Penn Valley Community.	Kansas City, Mo.	1915	Thomas M. Law.	S	5,459	306
Pensacola Jr.	Pensacola, Fla.	1948	T. Felton Harrison.	S	17,000	340
Philadelphia, Comm. Coll. of.	Philadelphia, Pa.	1964	Allen T. Bonnell.	Mu	11,000	617
Phillips County Comm.	Helena, Ark.	1965	John Easley.	S	1,713	54
Phoenix.	Phoenix, Ariz.	1920	William Berry.	C	14,000	180
Piedmont Tech.	Greenwood, S.C.	1966	Lex Walters.	S	3,300	200
Piedmont Tech. Inst.	Roxboro, N.C.	1970	Edward W. Cox.	S	877	59
Piedmont Virginia Comm.	Charlottesville, Va.	1969	James Walpole.	S	2,016	102
Pima Comm.	Tucson, Ariz.	1967	Irwin Spector.	S	20,166	1,029
Pine Manor Junior (W).	Chestnut Hill, Mass.	1911	Rosemary Ashby.	P	475	40
Pitt Tech. Inst.	Greenville, N.C.	1961	W. E. Fulford Jr.	S,C	1,605	80
Polk Comm.	Winter Haven, Fla.	1964	Frederick T. Lenfestey.	S	4,200	150
Porterville.	Porterville, Cal.	1927	O. H. Shires.	S	2,443	143
Portland Community.	Portland, Ore.	1961	Amo De Bernardis.	C	31,201	2,056
Post Junior.	Waterbury, Conn.	1890	Harold Harlow, Act.	P	1,220	72
Potomac State.	Keyser, W. Va.	1901	A. G. Slonaker (Dean).	S	943	43
Prairie State.	Chicago Hts., Ill.	1958	Richard Creal.	Di	6,200	289
Pratt Community.	Pratt, Kan.	1938	Norman Myers.	C	1,350	97
Prince George's Community.	Largo, Md.	1958	Robert Bickford.	C	11,430	249
Puerto Rico Jr.	Rio Piedras, P.R.	1949	Federico J. Modesto.	P	5,691	218
Queensborough Community.	Bayside, N.Y.	1958	Kurt R. Schmeller.	Mu	16,051	837
Quincy Jr.	Quincy, Mass.	1958	Edward Pierce.	Mu	4,201	150
Quinebaug Valley Comm.	Danielson, Conn.	1971	Robert E. Miller.	S	604	30
Quinsigamond Comm.	Worcester, Mass.	1963	Paul Preus.	S	5,107	309
Randolph Tech. Inst.	Asheboro, N.C.	1962	M. H. Branson.	S	702	49
Ranger Junior.	Ranger, Tex.	1926	Jack Elsom.	S	550	32
Rangley (A).	Rangley, Col.	1962	James H. Bos.	Di	726	35
Reading Area Comm.	Reading, Pa.	1971	Lewis Ogle.	S	950	65
Redwoods, Coll. of the.	Eureka, Cal.	1964	Donald Weichert.	S,C	8,600	465
Reedley.	Reedley, Cal.	1926	Clifford M. Boyer.	S	3,471	156
Reinhardt.	Waleska, Ga.	1893	Allen O. Jernigan.	D	797	44
Rend Lake (A).	Ina, Ill.	1956	James Snyder.	S	1,302	76
Rhode Island Jr. (A).	Warwick, R.I.	1964	William F. Flanagan.	S	4,470	286
Richland.	Dallas, Tex.	1972	Ed Bidgerstaff.	C,S	10,531	440
Richland Comm.	Decatur, Ill.	1971	Murray Deutsch.	Di	2,604	101
Richmond Tech. Inst.	Hamlet, N.C.	1965	Joseph Nanney.	S	881	52
Ricks.	Rexburg, Ida.	1888	Henry B. Evring.	D	5,300	206
Rio Hondo.	Whittier, Cal.	1961	Walter Garcia.	S	14,576	543
Riverside City.	Riverside, Cal.	1916	Foster Davidoff.	S	14,064	469
Robeson Tech. Inst.	Lumberton, N.C.	1965	R. Craig Allen.	S	1,800	103
Rochester Comm.	Rochester, Minn.	1915	Charles Hill.	S	2,400	140

Name	Location	Year	Governing Official and Affiliation		Students	Teachers
Rockland Community	Suffern, N.Y.	1957	Seymour Eskow	S	8,281	145
Rock Valley	Rockford, Ill.	1964	Karl Jacobs	S	9,563	451
Rockingham Comm.	Wentworth, N.C.	1966	Gerald B. James	S	1,300	60
Rogue Comm.	Grants Pass, Ore.	1970	Henry O. Pete	C,S	2,000	90
Sacramento City	Sacramento, Cal.	1916	Sam Kipp	S,C	14,125	575
Saddleback	Mission Viejo, Cal.	1967	R. A. Lombardi	S	10,867	553
St. Clair County Comm.	Pt. Huron, Mich.	1923	Richard L. Norris	C	4,494	91
St. John's	Winfield, Kan.	1893	Rev. M. J. Stelmachowicz	D	291	30
St. John's River Junior	Palatka, Fla.	1958	Robert L. McLendon	S	1,388	44
St. Louis Community						
at Florissant Valley	St. Louis, Mo.	1962	Raymond Smith	Di	9,337	473
at Forest Park	St. Louis, Mo.	1962	Ralph H. Lee	Di	9,616	500
at Meramec	St. Louis, Mo.	1962	Glynn Clark	Di	9,039	433
St. Mary's Jr.	Minneapolis, Minn.	1964	Sr. Anne Joachim Moore	D,P	788	88
St. Mary's (W)	Raleigh, N.C.	1847	Rev. Frank W. Pisam	D	516	50
St. Petersburg Junior (A)	St. Petersburg, Fla.	1927	Michael Bennett	S	9,759	306
Salem Community	Penns Grove, N.J.	1972	Herbert C. Donaghay	C	923	56
Sampson Tech Inst.	Clinton, N.C.	1965	Bruce Howell	S	745	87
San Antonio	San Antonio, Tex.	1925	Jerome Weynand	S	21,402	1,199
San Bernardino Valley	San Bernardino, Cal.	1926	Arthur Jensen	S	15,797	692
San Diego City	San Diego, Cal.	1914	Allen Repashy	S	5,250	144
San Diego, Mesa	San Diego, Cal.	1962	Ellis Benson	Mu	10,114	240
San Francisco, City Coll. of	San Francisco, Cal.	1935	K.S. Washington	C,Mu	27,000	1,038
San Jacinto	Pasadena, Tex.	1960	Thomas M. Spencer	S	8,443	336
San Joaquin Delta Comm.	Stockton, Cal.	1935	Joseph Blanchard	S,Di	16,136	544
San Jose City	San Jose, Cal.	1921	Theodore Murguia	C	15,735	705
San Luis Obispo Co. Comm.	San Luis Obispo, Cal.	1965	Merlin Eisenbise	C	5,504	200
San Mateo, Coll. of	San Mateo, Cal.	1922	David H. Mertes	C	14,654	610
Sandhills Comm.	Southern Pines, N.C.	1964	Raymond A. Stone	S	1,622	109
Santa Ana (A)	Santa Ana, Cal.	1915	John E. Johnson	S	10,985	344
Santa Barbara City	Santa Barbara, Cal.	1908	Glenn Gooder	Di,S	9,078	329
Santa Fe Community	Gainesville, Fla.	1965	Alan Robertson	S	6,171	350
Santa Monica	Santa Monica, Cal.	1917	Richard Moore	Mu	22,000	750
Santa Rosa Junior	Santa Rosa, Cal.	1918	Roy Mikalson	C	15,861	560
Sauk Valley	Dixon, Ill.	1965	George Cole	S	2,989	68
Schenectady County Comm.	Schenectady, N.Y.	1967	Robert Larsson	S	2,924	39
Schoolcraft	Livonia, Mich.	1964	C. Nelson Grote	S	6,816	914
Schreiner	Kerrville, Tex.	1923	Sam Junkin	D,P	450	25
Scottsdale Community	Scottsdale, Ariz.	1970	Ray Cattan, Exec. Dean	C	5,100	200
S. D. Bishop State Jr.	Mobile, Ala.	1965	Sanford Bishop	S	1,993	71
Seattle Central Community	Seattle, Wash.	1967	Roy G. Phillips	S	8,694	329
Selma Univ.	Selma, Ala.	1878	Rev. M. Cleveland, Jr.	D,P	603	32
Seminole Comm.	Sanford, Fla.	1965	E.S. Weldon	S	3,425	235
Sequoias, Coll. of the	Visalia, Cal.	1925	Ivan Crookshanks	Di	6,592	331
Seward County Comm.	Liberal, Kan.	1967	Wade Kirk	C,S	960	28
Shasta	Redding, Cal.	1950	Dale Miller	C	12,800	482
Shelby State Comm.	Memphis, Tenn.	1972	Jess Parrish	S	4,326	236
Sheldon Jackson	Sitka, Alas.	1878	Merton Munn	D	433	38
Sheridan	Sheridan, Wy.	1948	Gordon Ward	S	817	49
Shoreline Community	Seattle, Wash.	1964	Richard S. White	S	8,000	320
Sierra	Rocklin, Cal.	1914	Marion Akers, Act.	S	7,500	270
Sinclair Community	Dayton, Oh.	1887	David Ponitz	C	11,323	543
Siskiyous, Coll. of the	Weed, Cal.	1957	Eugene Schumacher	Di	3,500	163
Skagit Valley	Mt. Vernon, Wash.	1926	Norwood Cole	S	5,560	223
Snead State Jr.	Boaz, Ala.	1935	Virgil McCain Jr.	S	2,323	100
Snow	Ephraim, Ut.	1888	J.M. Higbee	S	893	55
Solano Comm.	Suisun City, Cal.	1946	William Wilson, Act.	S	9,500	350
Somerset Community	Somerset, Ky.	1965	Roscoe Kelley	S	760	61
Somerset County	Somerville, N.J.	1966	Joseph Fink	S	2,500	134
South Central Community	New Haven, Conn.	1968	W. De Homer Waller	S	1,679	37
South Florida Jr.	Avon Park, Fla.	1965	William Stallard	S	675	86
South Georgia	Douglas, Ga.	1906	Denton Coker	S	1,342	58
South Oklahoma City Junior	Oklahoma City, Okla.	1972	Dale L. Gibson	S	3,605	101
South Plains	Levelland, Tex.	1957	Marvin L. Baker	Di	2,500	150
South Texas Junior (A)	Houston, Tex.	1948	David Royce Reagan	P	2,609	103
Southeast Comm.	Fairbury, Neb.	1941	Eugene Marcy	C	358	37
Southeastern Comm.	Burlington, Ia.	1967	C.W. Callison, Supt.	S	2,005	123
Southeastern Community	Keokuk, Ia.	1953	C.W. Callison	C	414	30
Southeastern Community	Whiteville, N.C.	1965	W.R. McCarter	S	1,666	105
Southeastern Illinois	Harrisburg, Ill.	1960	Harry Abell	S	1,706	38
Southern Baptist	Walnut Ridge, Ark.	1941	D.W. Nicholas	P	602	41
Southern Idaho, Coll. of	Twin Falls, Ida.	1965	James L. Taylor	S	3,250	110
Southern Ohio	Cincinnati, Oh.	1927	Clyde Tidwell	P	900	40
Southern Seminary Jr.	Buena Vista, Va.	1867	R.L. Strickland Jr.	P	249	31
Southern Union State Jr.	Wadley, Ala.	1922	L. Ray Jones	S	1,527	85
Southwest Mississippi Junior	Summit, Miss.	1929	Horace Holmes	S	1,105	59
Southwest Texas Junior	Uvalde, Tex.	1946	Wayne Matthews	S	2,147	142
Southwest Virginia Comm.	Richlands, Va.	1967	Charles King	S	2,183	110
Southwestern	Chula Vista, Cal.	1961	C.S. DeVore	S	11,761	400
Southwestern Comm.	Creston, Ia.	1966	John A. Smith	S	585	42
Southwestern Michigan	Dowagiac, Mich.	1966	R.M. Owens	C	1,260	87
Southwestern Oregon Comm.	Coos Bay, Ore.	1961	Jack E. Brookins	S	3,500	190
Spartanburg Junior (A)	Spartanburg, S.C.	1911	James S. Barrett	D	1,008	66
Spokane Comm.	Spokane, Wash.	1963	Lloyd Stannard	S	3,600	343
Spokane Falls Community	Spokane, Wash.	1970	Gerald Saling	S	3,904	131
Spoon River	Canton, Ill.	1959	Hearl C. Bishop	S	1,415	40
Springfield Tech. Comm.	Springfield, Mass.	1964	Robert Geitz	S	8,183	321
Springfield Coll. in Illinois	Springfield, Ill.	1929	Sr. Mary Ann Luth	D	606	48
State Fair Comm.	Sedalia, Mo.	1968	Fred E. Davis	Di	1,295	108
State Tech. Inst.	Memphis, Tenn.	1967	Charles Whitehead	S	4,332	217
Staten Island Community**	Staten Island, N.Y.	1955	William M. Birenbaum	Mu	12,325	540
**Federated with Richmond Coll. on Sept. 1, 1976						
Sue Bennett	London, Ky.	1896	Earl F. Hays	D	215	27
Suffolk County Community	Selden, N.Y.	1959	Albert M. Ammerman	S	18,537	371
Sullivan County Community	Loch Sheldrake, N.Y.	1962	Richard F. Grego	S	1,740	66
Sumter Area Tech.	Sumter, S.C.	1963	James M. Morris Jr.	S	4,600	125

Name	Location	Year	Governing Official and Affiliation		Students	Teachers
Suomi	Hancock, Mich.	1896	Ralph J. Jalkanen	P,D	382	25
Surry Community	Dobson, N.C.	1974	Swanson Richards	S	1,650	81
Tacoma Comm.	Tacoma, Wash.	1965	Thronton Ford	S	5,400	251
Taft	Taft, Cal.	1922	Wendell Reeder	Di	1,026	46
Tallahassee Community	Tallahassee, Fla.	1966	Fred W. Turner	S	2,800	99
Tarrant County Junior	Ft. Worth, Tex.	1965	Joe B. Rushing	S,C	19,338	785
Tech. Career Institutes	New York, N.Y.	1909	Samuel Steinman	P	2,200	80
Tech. Inst. of Alamance	Haw River, N.C.	1959	William Taylor	S	9,000	150
Temple Junior	Temple, Tex.	1926	Marvin Felder	S	1,896	90
Texarkana	Texarkana, Tex.	1927	Carl M. Nelson	S	2,946	128
Texas Southmost	Brownsville, Tex.	1926	A.L. Oliveira	Mu	4,600	95
Thames Valley St. Tech (A)	Norwich, Conn.	1963	Donald Welter	S	1,100	43
Thomas Nelson Comm. (A).	Hampton, Va.	1968	Gerald O. Cannon	S	3,082	189
Thornton Comm.	So. Holland, Ill.	1927	J. Philip Dalby	Di	11,736	490
Three Rivers Community	Poplar Bluff, Mo.	1966	H. Tudor Westover	S	1,485	51
Tidewater Comm.	Portsmouth, Va.	1968	George Pass	S	11,250	216
Tomkins-Courtland Comm.	Groton, N.Y.	1967	Hushang Bahar	S	2,802	47
Treasure Valley Comm.	Ontario, Ore.	1962	Emery Skinner	Di	1,441	52
Tri-County Tech. Inst.	Murphy, N.C.	1964	Vincent W. Crisp	S	694	46
Tri-County Tech	Pendleton, S.C.	1962	Don Garrison	S	2,362	250
Trident Tech	Charleston, S.C.	1964	Richard Waldroup Jr.	S	7,356	241
Trinidad State Junior	Trinidad, Col.	1925	Thomas Sullivan	S	1,410	87
Triton	River Grove, Ill.	1964	Herbert Zeitlin	Di	19,799	1,027
Truett McConnell	Cleveland, Ga.	1946	Ronald Weitman	Di	730	49
Tulsa Junior (A)	Tulsa, Okla.	1968	Alfred M. Phillips	D	5,002	225
Tunxis Community	Farmington, Conn.	1970	Benjamin G. Davis	S	3,263	153
Tyler Junior	Tyler, Tex.	1926	Harry E. Jenkins	S	9,114	291
Ulster County Community	Stone Ridge, N.Y.	1961	Robert T. Brown	S	2,803	89
Umpqua Comm.	Roseburg, Ore.	1964	I. S. Hakanson	C	7,500	165
Union	Cranford, N.J.	1933	Saul Orkin	P	5,019	238
Union County Tech. Inst.	Scotch Plains, N.J.	1960	Harvey Charles	C	3,297	150
Utica Junior	Utica, Miss.	1903	J. Louis Stokes	S	1,215	75
Valencia Community (A)	Orlando, Fla.	1967	James F. Gollattscheck	S	5,432	222
Ventura	Ventura, Cal.	1925	Richard A. Glenn	S	12,723	655
Vermillion Comm.	Ely, Minn.	1922	C. Donald Miller	S	421	20
Vermont, Comm. Coll. of	Montpelier, Vt.	1970	Peter Smith	S	2,000	455
Vermont Technical	Randolph Center, Vt.	1957	Pierre Kieffer	S	654	45
Victor Valley	Victorville, Cal.	1961	B. W. Wadsworth	Di	3,197	141
Victoria	Victoria, Tex.	1925	Roland E. Bing	C	2,258	85
Villa Julie	Stevenson, Md.	1952	Sister Mary Stephen	P	452	54
Vincennes Univ.	Vincennes, Ind.	1801	Isaac K. Beckes	S	4,518	250
Virginia Highlands Comm.	Abingdon, Va.	1969	Emma Schulken	S	1,333	66
Virginia Western Comm.	Roanoke, Va.	1966	Harold H. Hopper	S	4,002	166
Wabash Valley	Mt. Carmel, Ill.	1961	John Cox	Di	1,589	33
Wake Tech. Inst.	Raleigh, N.C.	1963	Robert LeMay Jr.	S	1,500	89
Waldorf	Forest City, Ia.	1903	Paul Mork	S	492	33
Walker	Jasper, Ala.	1938	David J. Rowland	P	710	44
Walla Walla Comm.	Walla Walla, Wash.	1967	Eldon Dietrich	S	3,800	100
Walters State Community	Morristown, Tenn.	1970	Jack E. Campbell	S	2,877	80
Washington State Comm.	Spokane, Wash.	1963	Max M. Snyder	S	19,803	584
Washtenaw Comm.	Ann Arbor, Mich.	1965	Gunder Myran	C	6,338	341
Waterbury State Technical	Waterbury, Conn.	1964	Kenneth Fogg	S	1,234	76
Waubonsee Comm.	Sugar Grove, Ill.	1966	F. D. Etheredge	C	6,021	251
Wayne Community	Goldsboro, N.C.	1957	Clyde Erwin Jr.	S	2,213	127
Wayne County Comm.	Detroit, Mich.	1969	Reginald Wilson	S	14,000	700
Weatherford	Weatherford, Tex.	1869	E. W. Mince	C	1,521	58
Wenatchee Valley	Wenatchee, Wash.	1939	William Steward	S	3,873	206
Wentworth Institute	Boston, Mass.	1904	Edward I. Kirkpatrick	P	1,658	151
Wesley	Dover, Del.	1873	William W. Hassler	D	784	55
West Hills	Coalinga, Cal.	1932	Robert A. Annand	S,C	1,100	95
West Los Angeles	Culver City, Cal.	1968	Morris Heldman	Di	7,200	250
West Shore Comm.	Scottville, Mich	1967	John Eaton	C,S	950	57
West Valley Comm.	Saratoga, Cal.	1963	James P. Hardy	S	23,000	750
West Virginia North, Comm.	Wheeling, W. Va.	1972	Daniel B. Crowder	S	3,633	113
Westlark Comm. (A).	Ft. Smith, Ark.	1928	Shelby Breedlove	S	4,809	80
Westbrook	Portland, Me.	1831	James F. Dickinson	P	869	79
Westchester Community	Valhalla, N.Y.	1946	Joseph N. Hankin	S	8,558	177
Western Iowa Tech. Comm.	Sioux City, Ia.	1967	Robert Kiser	S	938	77
Western Okla. State	Altus, Okla.	1926	W. C. Burris	S	1,450	48
Western Piedmount Comm.	Morganton, N.C.	1964	Gordon Blank	S	1,750	56
Western Texas	Snyder, Tex.	1969	Robert Clinton	C,S	1,187	80
Western Wisc. Tech. Inst.	La Crosse, Wis.	1912	Charles Richardson, Dir.	C,Mu	3,584	175
Wharton County Junior	Wharton, Tex.	1946	Theodore Nicksick Jr.	S	2,011	96
Wilkes Community	Wilkesboro, N.C.	1964	Howard Thompson	S	2,225	101
William Rainey Harper (A)	Palatine, Ill.	1967	Robert E. Lahti	S	13,400	325
Williamsport Area Comm.	Williamsport, Pa.	1965	William Fedderson	S,C	2,198	155
Willmar Comm.	Willmar, Minn.	1962	John Torgelson	S	765	47
Wingate	Wingate, N.C.	1896	Thomas Corts	D	1,226	70
Wisconsin Center, Univ. of						
at Barron	Rice Lake, Wis.	1966	Edward B. Fort, Chan.	S	552	28
at Manitowoc	Manitowoc, Wis.	1933	Edward B. Fort, Chan.	S	272	15
at Marathon	Wausau, Wis.	1947	W. R. Peters, Dean	S	840	47
at Marshfield/Wood	Marshfield, Wis.	1964	Norbert Koopman, Dean.	S	471	28
at Richland	Richland Ctr., Wis.	1967	Edward Fort	S	300	22
at Rock County	Janesville, Wis.	1966	T. Walterman	S	670	38
at Sheboygan	Sheboygan, Wis.	1933	K. M. Bailey, Dean.	S	640	38
at Washington	West Bend, Wis.	1968	R. O. Thompson, Dean	S	543	37
Worcester Junior	Worcester, Mass.	1905	Ross Dixon	P	1,250	75
Worthington Comm.	Worthington, Minn.	1936	Leon Flancher	S	476	36
Yakima Valley (A)	Yakima, Wash.	1929	William Russell	S	4,505	140
Yavapai	Prescott, Ariz.	1969	Joseph Russo	C	4,442	221
York	York, Neb.	1890	Dale Larsen	D,P	324	25
York Technical	Rock Hill, S.C.	1965	Baxter Hood, Dir.	S	1,700	110
Young Harris	Young Harris, Ga.	1886	Ray Farley	D,P	528	29
Yuba Comm.	Marysville, Cal.	1927	Daniel G. Walker	C,S	7,047	223

Degree-Granting Canadian Colleges and Universities

All coeducational unless followed by (M) for men only. Governing official is president unless otherwise designated. Year is that of founding. The word college is part of the name listed unless another designation is given. Each institution listed has an enrollment of at least 200 students of college grade. Number of teachers is the total number of individuals on teaching staff. Enrollment and faculty in italics include all branches and campuses.

Name	Location	Year	Governing Official	Students	Teachers
Acadia Univ.	Wolfville, Nova Scotia	1838	J.M.R. Beveridge	2,553	171
Alberta, Univ. of	Edmonton, Calgary, Alb.	1906	Harry E. Gunning	18,525	1,512
Bishop's Univ.	Lennoxville, Que.	1843	D. Healy	720	75
Brandon Univ.	Brandon, Man.	1899	A. L. Dulmage	933	130
British Columbia, Univ. of.	Vancouver, B.C.	1908	Douglas T. Kenny	23,185	1,653
Brock Univ.	St. Catharines, Ont.	1964	A. J. Earp	2,247	201
Calgary, Univ. of	Calgary, Alberta	1945	W. A. Cochrane	9,279	798
Carleton, Univ.	Ottawa, Ont.	1942	Michael Oliver	8,241	588
Concordia Univ.	Montreal, Que.	1974	John O'Brien, Rector	5,409	624
Dalhousie Univ.	Halifax, Nova Scotia	1818	Henry D. Hicks	6,645	624
Guelph, Univ. of	Guelph, Ont.	1964	Donald F. Forster	8,622	738
King's Coll., Univ. of.	Halifax, Nova Scotia	1789	J. Graham Morgan	263	9
Lakehead Univ.	Thunder Bay, Ont.	1965	A. D. Booth	2,358	225
Laurentian Univ.	Sudbury, Ont.	1960	Edward J. Monahan	1,893	240
Laval Universite	Quebec, Que.	1852	Larkin Kerwin	10,959	1,233
Lethbridge, Univ. of.	Lethbridge, Alberta	1967	W. E. Beckel	1,086	135
Manitoba, Univ. of.	Winnipeg, Man.	1877	Ernest Sirluck	13,350	1,173
McGill Univ.	Montreal, Que.	1821	Robert E. Bell, Prin.	15,993	1,246
McMaster Univ.	Hamilton, Ont.	1887	A. N. Bourns	8,622	747
Moncton, Univ. of.	Moncton, N.B.	1963	M. Jean Cadieux, Rector	3,120	252
Montreal, Universite de	Montreal, Que.	1920	M. Paul Lacoste, Rector	23,055	1,191
Mount Allison Univ.	Sackville, N.B.	1840	W. S. H. Crawford	1,356	120
Mount St. Vincent Univ.	Halifax, Nova Scotia	1925	Sr. Mary Albertus	1,729	75
New Brunswick, Univ. of	Fredericton, N.B.	1785	John M. Anderson	5,097	501
Newfoundland, Mem. Univ. of.	St. John's, Newfdld.	1925	M. O. Morgan	6,420	705
Notre Dame Univ.	Nelson, B.C.	1963	Hugh Farguhar	381	39
Nova Scotia Coll. of Arts & Design	Halifax, Nova Scotia	1887	Garry Neill Kennedy	381	36
Nova Scotia Technical.	Halifax, Nova Scotia	1907	Allison E. Steeves	426	66
Ontario Inst. for Studies in Education	Toronto, Ont.	1965	Clifford C. Pitt	2,161	135
Ottawa, Univ. of	Ottawa, Ont.	1848	Rev. Roger Guindon	9,423	888
Prince Edward Island, Univ. of	Charlottetown, P.E.I.	1834	Ronald J. Baker	1,410	123
Quebec, Universite de	Montreal, Que.	1969	M. Robert Despres	9,021	1,008
Queen's Univ.	Kingston, Ont.	1841	R. L. Watts	9,183	828
Regina, Univ. of	Regina, Sask.	1974	Lloyd I. Barber	2,931	396
Royal Military Coll. of Can. (M)	Kingston, Ont.	1876	J. R. Dacey	627	111
Ryerson Polytechnical	Toronto, Ont.	1948	Walter G. Pitman	8,277	500
St. Francis Xavier Univ.	Antigonish, Nova Scotia	1853	Rev. M. MacDonell	2,118	207
St. Mary's Univ.	Halifax, Nova Scotia	1802	D. Owen Carrigan	2,394	171
St. Paul Univ.	Ottawa, Ont.	1866	Rev. Marcel Patry	288	27
Saskatchewan, Univ. of	Saskatoon, Sask.	1907	R. W. Begg	8,916	885
Sherbrooke, Univ. of.	Sherbrooke, Que.	1954	Yves Martin	4,677	561
Simon Fraser Univ.	Burnaby, B.C.	1965	Pauline Jewett	6,215	378
Toronto, Univ. of	Toronto, Ont.	1827	John Robert Evans	29,289	2,166
Trent Univ.	Peterborough, Ont.	1963	T. E. W. Nind	1,830	174
Victoria Univ.	Toronto, Ont.	1841	G. S. French	2,534	99
Victoria, Univ. of.	Victoria, B.C.	1963	Howard E. Petch	6,968	396
Waterloo, Univ. of	Waterloo, Ont.	1959	B. C. Matthews	12,933	729
Western Ontario, Univ. of.	London, Ont.	1878	D. Carlton Williams	13,785	1,206
Wilfrid Laurier Univ.	Waterloo, Ont.	1973	W. H. Tayler	2,517	144
Windsor, Univ. of.	Windsor, Ont.	1857	John Francis Leddy	5,706	492
Winnipeg, Univ. of.	Winnipeg, Man.	1871	Henry E. Duckworth	2,382	159
York Univ.	Downsview, Ont.	1959	H. Ian Macdonald	10,038	1,008

Typical Tuition Fees at Selected Canadian Colleges and Universities*

Source: Statistics Canada

Institution	Cost Range	Institution	Cost Range
Alberta, The University of	$400-600	McMaster University	$580-645
British Columbia, The Univ. of	428-644	New Brunswick, University of	581-611
Calgary, The University of	200(2)	Ottawa, University of	565-640
Carleton University, Ottawa	580-640	Queen's University of Kingston	600-725
Concordia University	450-540	Quebec, Universite du	250(1)
Dalhousie University	680-725	Ryerson Polytechnical Institute	424
Guelph, University of	288-323(1)	Saskatchewan, University of	460-555
Laval, Universite	260-335(3)	Toronto, University of	603-1,123
Manitoba, The University of	425-550	Victoria, University of	428
Montreal, Universite de	250-463(2)	Waterloo, University of	625-780
Memorial University of Newfoundland	250(1)	Western Ontario, The University of	580-774
McGill University	570	Windsor, University of	580-645
		York University	660

*Undergraduate tuition fees at Universities and Colleges with enrollment of 5,000 full day-time students or more. Fee is for 1975-76 academic year.
(1) Per semester
(2) Per session
(3) Per trimester

Typical Tuition Fees at Selected Colleges and Universities

Source: World Almanac Questionnaire

The College Entrance Examination Board has estimated that the average cost in a private college in the fall of 1976 was $4,568, a 6% increase over the previous year. The cost at a public college averaged $2,790.

Fees for tuition charged per year by colleges and universities for courses, use of libraries, laboratories and other facilities, are a major part of student expenses. Tuition varies considerably, depending on the type of institution, its control and location. The lowest tuition fees are those of state-controlled or other public-controlled institutions for residents of their state, city, etc. Students from other states or areas have to pay more. In the following list, such state or other public institutions are shown with two figures. The lower one is the tuition fee for residents, the higher one the tuition fee for students from other states or areas.

(Tuition does not include room, board or other expenses)

School	Tuition	School	Tuition	School	Tuition
Akron, Univ. of	$780-1,740	Hampton Inst.	2,455	Pennsylvania State Univ.	1,095-2,295
Alabama, Univ. of	618-1,236	Harvard Univ.	3,740	Pittsburgh, Univ. of	1,164-2,304
Allegheny	3,050	Haverford	3,880	Portland, Univ. of	2,442
Amherst	3,725	Holy Cross	3,450	Princeton Univ.	4,400
Anderson	2,200	Houston, Univ. of	400-1,400	Purdue Univ.	750-1,700
Arizona, Univ. of	450-1,640	Idaho, Univ. of	400-1,400	Radcliffe	3,740
Arkansas, Univ. of	400-930	Idaho State Univ.	410-1,260	Redlands, Univ. of	3,545
Auburn	732-1,432	Illinois Inst. of Tech.	2,800	Rhode Island, Univ. of	895-1,935
Avila	1,700	Indiana Univ.	722-1,640	Richmond, Univ. of	2,600
Baldwin-Wallace	2,829	Indiana State Univ.	744-1,302	Roger Williams	2,096
Ball State	720-1,440	Jacksonville Univ.	1,980	Rutgers Univ.	928-1,288
Baylor	1,282	John Carroll Univ.	2,200	St. Bonaventure Univ.	2,550
Black Hills State	676-1,245	Kansas, Univ. of	576-1,366	St. Olaf	2,800
Bob Jones	1,101	Kansas State Univ.	558-1,348	St. Paul Bible	1,120
Boston	3,580	Kentucky, Univ. of	1,260	Santa Clara, Univ. of	2,718
Bowdoin	3,880	Lawrence Univ.	3,754	Sarah Lawrence	4,450
Bowling Green State	858-2,058	Lehigh Univ.	3,550	Seattle Univ.	2,380
Brigham Young (a)	720	Louisville, Univ. of	780-1,980	Selma Univ.	964
Brown	3,900	Loyola Marymount	2,800	South Carolina, Univ. of	654-1,414
Canisius	2,500	Maine, Univ. of	675-1,850	South Florida, Univ. of	1,317-3,021
Carleton	4,600	Miami, Univ. of	3,300	Southern Calif., Univ. of	3,626
Carnegie-Mellon	3,125	Marquette Univ.	2,650	Southern Methodist Univ.	2,510
Case Western Reserve Univ.	3,300	Memphis State Univ.	448-1,288	Stanford Univ.	4,275
Chicago, Univ. of	3,630	Minnesota, Univ. of	825-2,065	Temple Univ.	1,300-2,400
Clemson Univ.	660-1,360	Mississippi State Univ.	561-700	Texas A & M Univ.	400-1,480
Columbia Univ.	3,990	Mississippi, Univ. of	603-1,305	Tufts Univ.	3,600
Dakota State	665-1,233	Montana, Univ. of	541-1,513	Tulane Univ.	3,300
Dallas, Univ. of	2,080	Montana State Univ.	510-1,482	Utah, Univ. of	525-1,335
Dana	2,270	Morgan State	701-1,151	Valdosta State	435-1,236
Dartmouth Univ.	4,230	Muskingum	2,810	Vanderbilt Univ.	3,400
Dayton, Univ. of	2,140	New Hampshire, Univ. of	982-2,682	Vassar	3,735
Delaware, Univ. of	795-1,930	New Mexico, Univ. of	520-1,516	Vermont, Univ. of	1,248-3,082
Denver, Univ. of	3,375	New York State Univ.	750-1,275	Virginia, Univ. of	465-1,465
Doane	2,160	New York Univ.	3,550	Wake Forest Univ.	2,500
Drake Univ.	2,930	Niagara Univ.	2,290	Washburn Univ. of Topeka	680-1,080
Duke Univ.	3,230	North Carolina State Univ.	524-2,070	Wellesley	3,600
Duquesne Univ.	2,830	North Carolina, Univ. of	490-2,156	Wheaton College	2,610
Evansville, Univ. of	2,199	Notre Dame, Univ. of	2,982	Williams College	3,750
Fordham Univ.	2,700	Oberlin	3,841	Wyoming, Univ. of	435-1,400
Furman Univ.	2,392	Ohio State Univ.	810-1,860	Yale Univ.	4,400
George Washington	2,600	Oklahoma State Univ.	474-1,254		
Georgia, Univ. of	555-1,506	Old Dominion Univ.	620-1,240	(a) Non-members of Mormon Church $1,080	
Gonzaga Univ.	2,100	Oral Roberts Univ.	1,454		

Federal Funds for Education

Source: Office of Education, Dept. of Health, Education and Welfare
(In thousands of dollars. Includes grants, loans, and directly administered services. Estimated.)

Type of support, level, and program	1976
Total grants and loans	$16,211,901
Grants, total	15,752,353
Elementary-secondary education	4,873,870
School asst.—federally affected areas	364,369
Economic Opportunity Programs	879,161
National Defense Education Act	28,475
Supporting services	411,709
Asst. for educationally deprived children	2,088,233
Teacher Corps	36,383
Vocational education	263,973
Dependents' schools abroad	233,903
Public lands revenue for schools	156,954
Assistance in special areas	124,141
Veterans' education	79,810
Emergency school asst.	152,810
Other	53,949
Higher education	7,271,864
Basic research	1,412,000
Research facilities	199,000
Training grants, fellowships and traineeships	1,000,181

Facilities and equipment	122,023
Other institutional support	419,691
Other student assistance	4,118,969
Vocational-tech. and continuing ed.	3,606,619
Vocational-technical education	2,675,500
Veterans' education	773,462
General continuing education	145,746
Training State and local personnel	11,911
Loans, total	459,548
Student loan program, Nat. Def. Ed. Act.	486,943
College facilities loans	-27,395
Other federal funds, total	5,578,189
Applied research and development	1,770,000
School lunch and milk programs	1,463,364
Training of federal personnel	1,148,159
U.S. Academies	295,678
Professional training, military	808,352
Civilian education and training in non-federal facilities	44,129
Library services	265,072
Grants to public libraries	41,266

(Continued)

National library services	223,806	Agricultural extension service	219,785
International education	**209,613**	Educational television facilities	41,766
Educational exchange program	38,568	Education in federal correctional inst.	12,784
AID Projects	152,950	Other education and training	155,646
ACTION (previously Peace Corps)	16,411	Value of surplus property transferred:	
Other international educ. and training	1,684	acquisition cost of personal property	266,000
Other	**721,981**	Fair value of real property	26,000

Fall Enrollment and Teachers in Full-Time Day Schools
Public Elementary and Secondary Day Schools Fall 1975

Source: United States Office of Education

	Pupils Enrolled[1]		Teachers[2]	1974 High School Graduates[1]	
	Elementary	Secondary		Male	Female
United States	30,400,000	14,300,000	12,394,000	1,364,000	1,398,000
Alabama	518,000	239,000	38,060	22,861	22,641
Alaska	60,000	26,000	4,170	2,190	2,058
Arizona	341,000	142,000	22,650	12,525	12,399
Arkansas	312,000	139,000	21,330	12,298	12,086
California	2,969,000	1,425,000	218,830	131,532	136,961
Colorado	381,000	182,000	29,170	17,177	17,176
Connecticut	452,000	203,000	41,190	18,567	20,604
Delaware	86,000	43,000	7,310	3,970	4,195
District of Columbia	96,000	34,000	8,240	2,206	3,334
Florida	1,059,000	485,000	76,510	37,041	37,789
Georgia	755,000	317,000	48,510	27,697	30,329
Hawaii	120,000	55,000	8,810	5,704	5,722
Idaho	123,000	63,000	8,860	6,327	6,449
Illinois	1,545,000	733,000	130,920	68,599	70,505
Indiana	799,000	378,000	54,140	36,653	36,724
Iowa	410,000	206,000	36,190	21,659	21,849
Kansas	293,000	153,000	27,280	16,865	16,509
Kentucky	477,000	218,000	34,800	20,295	21,056
Louisiana	580,000	253,000	48,190	22,345	24,463
Maine	171,000	77,000	13,200	7,075	7,416
Maryland	611,000	276,000	48,240	26,075	28,053
Massachusetts	822,000	378,000	77,140	39,000	39,000
Michigan	1,423,000	698,000	101,710	66,422	67,914
Minnesota	577,000	307,000	49,640	31,953	32,028
Mississippi	355,000	154,000	26,890	12,306	13,358
Missouri	669,000	325,000	52,100	30,886	31,297
Montana	113,000	58,000	9,600	6,075	6,060
Nebraska	211,000	105,000	19,540	11,123	11,153
Nevada	94,000	42,000	5,740	3,563	3,397
New Hampshire	118,000	53,000	10,880	4,926	5,006
New Jersey	1,004,000	454,000	90,360	45,113	46,825
New Mexico	185,000	95,000	13,420	8,418	8,946
New York	2,282,000	1,129,000	220,860	102,669	104,744
North Carolina	805,000	364,000	53,010	33,679	35,383
North Dakota	84,000	48,000	8,180	5,408	5,416
Ohio	1,559,000	755,000	117,610	76,373	77,501
Oklahoma	404,000	187,000	29,870	18,560	18,210
Oregon	316,000	157,000	23,640	15,130	15,676
Pennsylvania	1,484,000	777,000	130,500	82,400	78,200
Rhode Island	122,000	55,000	11,060	5,426	5,691
South Carolina	439,000	183,000	29,610	18,692	20,145
South Dakota	101,000	52,000	8,810	5,985	5,909
Tennessee	607,000	258,000	41,490	23,681	25,960
Texas	1,955,000	807,000	140,740	78,125	78,859
Utah	207,000	97,000	12,790	9,612	9,286
Vermont	73,000	31,000	7,050	3,169	3,147
Virginia	743,000	341,000	57,510	30,085	33,761
Washington	524,000	255,000	36,020	25,862	26,006
West Virginia	278,000	123,000	19,640	12,506	12,895
Wisconsin	630,000	338,000	56,860	34,242	35,099
Wyoming	58,000	27,000	5,130	2,950	2,810
Outlying areas	**606,000**	**177,000**	**32,330**	**12,031**	**14,840**
American Samoa	8,000	2,000	710	237	211
Canal Zone	8,000	3,000	630	333	393
Guam	21,000	7,000	1,500	506	496
Puerto Rico	550,000	160,000	27,940	10,648	13,433
Virgin Islands	19,000	5,000	1,550	307	307

[1]Estimated. [2]Full and part-time classroom teachers.

National Spelling Bee Champions

The National Spelling Bee, conducted by Scripps-Howard Newspapers and other newspapers since 1939, was instituted by the Louisville (Ky.) Courier-Journal in 1925. Children under 16 years of age sponsored by participating newspapers are eligible to compete for the cash prizes and prize trips.

Recent winners are:

1976—1. Tim Kneale, 13, Nedrow, N.Y. (Syracuse Herald-Journal-American). 2. Rachel Wachtel, 13, Shreve, Oh. (Akron Beacon Journal). 3. William M. Mulhern, 13, Beattie, Kan. (Topeka Daily Capital).

1975—1. Hugh C. Tosteson, 14, San German, Puerto Rico (San Juan Star). 2. Mark Ogle, 14, Greenwood, Ind. (Indianapolis News). 3. Diane Bryan, 14, Lubbock, Tex. (Lubbock Avalanche-Journal).

Public School Attendance, Teachers, Expenditures

Source: National Center for Education Statistics; Salaries cover supervisors, principals, and teachers

School Year	Pop. 5 to 17 yrs.	Pupils Enrolled	Pupils Av. daily attend.	Teachers' Male	Teachers' Female	Teachers' Total	Teachers' Salary[2]	Total Expend.
1900........	21,404,322	15,503,110	10,632,772	126,588	296,474	423,062	$325	$214,964,618
1910........	24,239,948	17,813,852	12,827,307	110,481	412,729	523,210	485	426,250,434
1920........	27,728,788	21,578,316	16,150,035	95,654	583,648	679,302	871	1,036,151,209
1930........	31,571,322	25,678,015	21,264,886	141,771	712,492	854,263	1,420	2,316,790,384
1940........	29,805,259	25,433,542	22,042,151	194,725	680,752	875,477	1,441	2,344,048,927
1950........	30,788,000	25,111,427	22,283,845	194,968	718,703	913,671	3,010	5,837,643,000
1960........	43,881,000	36,086,771	32,477,440	392,700	962,300	1,355,000	5,174	15,613,255,000
1968 (Fall)....	52,288,000	44,961,662	41,157,000	617,805	1,324,980	1,942,785	8,200	35,511,170,000
1970 (Fall)....	52,435,000	45,909,088	42,495,346	649,250	1,411,865	2,061,115	9,570	44,423,865,000
1971 (Fall)....	52,133,000	46,081,000	42,544,000	668,000	1,395,000	2,063,000	10,100	48,513,986,000
1972 (Fall).....	51,637,000	45,744,000	42,408,000	702,000	1,400,000	2,102,000	10,608	51,905,025,000
1974........	51,485,000	46,441,189	41,438,054	722,868	1,432,580	2,155,448	11,185	56,970,355,000
1975 (Fall) (P)..	50,364,000	44,838,490	41,373,473	748,000	1,455,000	2,203,000	13,967	67,102,569,000

(1.) Prior to 1954 includes other nonsupervisory instructional staff (librarians and guidance and psychological personnel)
(2.) Average annual salary per member of instructional staff. (P) Preliminary.

Cost per Pupil by State

Source: Office of Education, Dept. HEW

Estimated expenditures per pupil in average daily attendance in public elementary and secondary day schools, by state 1974-75.

State	Expenditure per pupil Total	Current	Capital outlay	Interest on school debt
United States	$1,431	$1,255	$133	$43
Alabama..........	933	871	56	6
Alaska...........	2,228	1,624	491	113
Arizona..........	1,546	1,176	328	42
Arkansas.........	1,087	896	164	27
California........	1,373	1,210	116	47
Colorado.........	1,423	1,188	188	47
Connecticut.......	1,596	1,507	46	43
Delaware.........	1,723	1,485	169	69
District of Columbia..	1,957	1,814	143	..
Florida...........	1,392	1,147	222	23
Georgia..........	1,087	1,000	53	34
Hawaii...........	1,600	1,384	210	6
Idaho............	1,232	910	299	23
Illinois...........	1,637	1,376	218	43
Indiana..........	1,298	1,074	181	43
Iowa.............	1,400	1,240	132	28
Kansas..........	1,607	1,444	137	26
Kentucky.........	960	864	60	36
Louisiana........	1,637	1,376	218	43
Maine...........	1,130	1,007	92	31
Maryland.........	1,771	1,369	354	47
Massachusetts.....	1,504	1,356	87	62
Michigan.........	1,770	1,547	164	56
Minnesota........	1,635	1,423	159	53
Mississippi.......	921	834	77	10
Missouri..........	1,203	1,078	97	28
Montana.........	1,392	1,269	101	23
Nebraska........	$1,378	$1,211	$137	$30
Nevada..........	1,308	1,101	135	72

State	Expenditure per pupil Total	Current	Capital outlay	Interest on school debt
New Hampshire....	1,173	1,095	42	36
New Jersey........	1,713	1,565	94	54
New Mexico.......	1,282	1,052	216	14
New York.........	2,241	2,005	165	71
North Carolina.....	1,151	1,052	86	13
North Dakota......	1,199	1,032	140	27
Ohio.............	1,270	1,144	93	33
Oklahoma........	1,131	1,009	108	14
Oregon..........	1,642	1,425	188	29
Pennsylvania......	1,587	1,446	53	88
Rhode Island......	1,665	1,493	98	74
South Carolina.....	1,125	984	113	28
South Dakota......	1,062	973	77	12
Tennessee........	997	903	59	35
Texas............	1,073	894	128	51
Utah.............	1,265	942	301	22
Vermont.........	1,267	1,095	127	45
Virginia..........	1,231	1,054	139	38
Washington.......	1,339	1,199	109	31
West Virginia......	1,020	910	94	16
Wisconsin........	1,452	1,323	91	38
Wyoming.........	1,404	1,322	61	21
Outlying Areas				
American Samoa...	891	880	11	..
Canal Zone........	1,603	1,560	43	..
Guam...........	1,114	1,114	..	..
Puerto Rico[1]......	483	453	30	..
Virgin Islands......	2,149	1,572	677	..
[1]Estimated.				

Fall Enrollment and Teachers in Full-time Day Schools — Canada

Public Elementary and Secondary Day Schools — 1974-1975

Source: Statistics Canada

	1974-75 Enrollment[p] Elementary Kdgn-Gr. 8	Secondary Gr. 9 and up	Total	1974-75 Teachers Elementary Kdgn-Gr. 8[e]	Secondary Gr. 9 and up[e]	Total[p]
Canada.................	3,694,594	1,724,260	5,418,854	158,095	102,645	260,740
Newfoundland..........	124,493	33,521	158,014	4,930	1,860	6,790
Prince Edward Island......	20,699	7,450	28,149	1,000	550	1,550
Nova Scotia.............	149,848	54,432	204,280	6,360	3,630	9,990
New Brunswick..........	116,760	49,790	166,550	5,000	2,790	7,790[e]
Quebec................	896,887	525,598	1,422,485	40,950	31,850	72,800[e]
Ontario................	1,376,971	617,518	1,994,489	55,574	35,336	90,910
Manitoba..............	163,020	66,532	229,552	7,310	4,460	11,770
Saskatchewan..........	157,715	66,461	224,176	7,010	3,610	10,620[e]
Alberta................	297,638	134,539	432,177	13,371	8,609	21,980
British Columbia.........	376,382	165,193	541,575	15,855	9,720	25,575
Yukon.................	3,698	1,205	4,903	185	100	285
Northwest Territories.......	10,483	2,021	12,504	550	130	680

e-estimate   p-preliminary

Public Libraries in Selected North American Cities

Source: World Almanac Questionnaire

Figure in parentheses denotes number of branches; asterisk (*) indicates county library jurisdiction; **(A) Designates libraries have not provided up-to-date information.**

City	No. of Volumes	Circulation	Cost of Operation
Akron, Oh.* (17)	832,650	2,022,684	$ 2,954,894
Albany, N.Y. (6)	264,024	521,121	N/A
Albuquerque, N.M. (6)A	306,885	1,073,422	686,400
Atlanta, Ga. (19)A	784,613	2,223,977	3,757,494
Augusta, Ga.* (5)	318,670	725,360	765,148
Baltimore, Md. (19)A	2,253,775	2,880,360	5,978,856
Baton Rouge, La.* (9)	315,466	886,265	1,029,479
Birmingham, Ala. (16)A	895,823	3,337,200	1,518,042
Boston, Mass. (26)	3,863,786	2,624,352	8,936,136
Bridgeport, Conn. (4)	482,000	517,570	1,122,548
Buffalo, N.Y.* (58)	2,931,233	6,198,903	9,186,756
Calgary, Alb. (13)	562,180	2,385,973	2,926,858
Charleston, W.V.* (5)	412,812	857,005	826,979
Charlotte, N.C.* (15)	627,441	1,374,890	1,966,614
Chattanooga, Tenn.* (1)	261,758	564,723	817,859
Chicago, Ill. (77)	5,796,461	678,151	25,000,000
Cincinnati, Oh.* (36)	3,055,231	5,752,429	7,208,060
Cleveland, Oh. (35)	3,598,824	3,142,016	8,148,812
Columbus, Oh. (21)	1,167,912	3,170,647	3,460,555
Corpus Christi, Tex. (3)	319,540	677,280	665,708
Dallas, Tex. (17)	1,637,004	4,019,643	5,078,549
Dayton, Oh.* (19)	1,221,653	4,242,475	3,254,490
Denver, Col. (21)	1,561,033	3,180,893	6,025,362
Des Moines, Ia. (5)	393,634	1,210,579	1,299,108
Detroit, Mich. (26)	2,325,146	2,644,164	10,865,834
El Paso, Tex. (6)A	428,046	949,394	878,950
Erie, Pa.* (7)	390,000	1,000,000	1,350,000
Evansville, Ind.* (7)	475,000	1,031,955	1,011,436
Halifax, N.S.* (1)	204,017	616,797	740,604
Hamilton, Ont. (10)	723,113	1,923,660	3,394,735
Hartford, Conn. (8)	466,653	548,000	1,362,972
Honolulu, Ha.* (10)	228,023	622,027	702,993
Houston, Tex. (24)	1,707,851	4,707,045	5,449,495
Jacksonville, Fla. (10)	965,811	1,944,402	1,982,707
Kansas City, Mo. (12)	1,159,653	1,206,562	2,560,000
Kitchener, Ont. (2)	334,677	853,851	1,271,712
Knoxville, Tenn.* (19)	512,382	1,426,983	1,422,611
Little Rock, Ark.* (4)	399,458	699,607	579,123
Los Angeles, Cal.* (95)	3,730,765	10,615,932	19,325,122
Louisville, Ky. (30)A	946,009	1,542,270	N/A
Memphis, Tenn.* (18)	1,347,015	2,531,677	3,790,611
Miami, Fla.* (18)	869,000	2,590,753	7,339,072
Milwaukee, Wis. (12)	2,388,907	3,488,280	7,513,319
Minneapolis, Minn. (15)	1,380,968	2,652,696	$4,938,415
Montreal, Ont. (27)	1,133,000	1,910,812	2,205,234
Nashville, Tenn.* (14)	496,966	1,399,573	2,338,006
New Orleans, La. (11)	703,932	1,383,186	2,574,079
New York	5,412,568	None	16,463,000
N.Y. branches	3,485,795	10,630,426	24,153,000
Brooklyn* (57)	3,662,188	7,696,280	N/A
Queens* (55)	3,073,715	6,481,352	16,256,039
Norfolk, Va. (10)	553,208	1,224,975	1,758,556
Okla. City, Okla.* (12)	600,000	1,540,842	2,031,074
Orlando, Fla. (12)	483,077	177,551	3,222,309
Ottawa, Ont. (7)	545,228	2,157,406	3,657,691
Philadelphia, Pa. (46)	2,973,594	5,397,217	14,737,866
Phoenix, Ariz. (9)	998,012	2,997,859	3,809,260
Pittsburgh, Pa. (19)	2,085,985	3,509,648	6,842,188
Portland, Me. (4)	245,321	403,157	653,845
Portland, Ore. (16)	1,076,470	2,793,079	3,591,669
Providence, R.I. (9)	688,884	790,606	1,765,468
Regina, Sask. (4)	254,829	1,038,934	1,996,484
Richmond, Va. (4)	521,594	1,028,063	1,247,718
Roanoke, Va. (5)A	271,455	364,516	486,386
Rochester, N.Y. (12)	829,651	1,606,580	3,670,000
Sacramento, Cal. (29)	944,575	3,897,945	4,285,933
St. Louis, Mo. (21)	1,372,530	2,556,567	4,273,037
St. Paul, Minn. (10)A	705,677	1,945,433	1,692,178
St. Petersburg, Fla. (3)	352,286	1,240,901	910,657
Salt Lake City, Ut. (3)	462,898	907,778	1,284,908
San Antonio, Tex. (8)	869,388	2,317,104	2,212,445
San Diego, Cal. (25)	1,246,322	4,376,688	4,630,899
San Francisco, Ca. (26)A	1,443,848	3,195,475	5,501,847
San Jose, Cal.* (13)	914,633	3,587,114	3,608,449
Saskatoon, Sask. (4)A	279,847	1,005,827	1,042,608
Seattle, Wash. (15)	1,500,000	4,000,000	6,000,000
Syracuse, N.Y.* (8)	434,029	1,057,169	2,347,636
Tallahassee, Fla.* (2)	180,000	499,990	511,565
Tampa, Fla. (7)A	395,316	1,498,497	1,942,107
Toledo, Oh.* (17)	1,260,094	2,846,081	3,744,346
Tucson, Ariz. (6)	577,072	2,312,847	4,985,275
Tulsa, Okla.* (18)	660,000	1,945,205	2,239,945
Vancouver, B.C. (15)	754,787	3,889,383	5,375,066
Washington, D.C. (23)	1,989,045	2,031,195	8,466,063
Wichita, Kan. (8)	360,000	1,245,000	1,369,870
Winnipeg, Man. (7)	457,651	1,395,175	1,735,910
Winston-Salem, N.C.* (8)	298,900	1,068,145	1,200,000

Major American Academic Libraries

Source: World Almanac Questionnaire

Institution	No. of Volumes	Microfilm Units	Enrollment	Staff Prof.	Staff Total	Expenditures
Harvard University	9,206,670	1,208,064	15,823	230	873	$14,015,162
Yale University	6,158,848	893,165	10,081	185	602	10,773,000
Univ. of Illinois, Urbana-Champaign	5,226,951	1,252,817	33,508	165	495	6,232,062
Univ. Of Michigan	4,668,188	1,055,673	36,335	148	577	7,578,835
Columbia University	4,661,913	1,304,093	15,201	143	538	7,601,966
Univ. of California, Berkeley	4,649,533	896,481	29,950	165	543	8,928,051
Cornell University	4,272,959	1,382,680	16,208	124	363	6,817,428
Stanford University	4,092,362	1,258,485	11,774	144	461	8,581,139
Univ. of Texas at Austin	3,726,134	1,228,272	42,598	121	476	5,403,149
Univ. of California, Los Angeles	3,643,000	1,386,769	29,729	160	420	9,899,954
Univ. of Chicago	3,622,000	458,750	10,000	70	431	5,001,000
Univ. of Minnesota	3,559,511	1,005,487	55,079	150	359	7,080,882
Princeton University	3,000,000	1,000,000	5,700	90	305	6,000,000
Univ. of Wisconsin, Madison	2,973,300	1,002,733	38,545	105	402	6,348,883
Ohio State University	2,911,839	977,990	54,640	115	473	5,015,530
Indiana University, Bloomington	2,762,582	628,919	28,869	100	248	4,258,640
Univ. of Pennsylvania	2,640,013	602,694	20,538	90	277	5,293,838
Duke University	2,622,124	218,799	8,653	84	228	4,040,000
Northwestern University	2,474,852	556,786	12,767	100	323	4,796,486
Univ. of No. Carolina, Chapel Hill	2,125,640	1,039,265	19,952	84	293	4,628,324
Johns Hopkins University	2,030,152	872,250	6,178	65	164	923,269

105 Years of Public Schools

Source: National Center for Education Statistics, Dept. of Health, Education and Welfare

Pupils and teachers (in thousands)	1869-70	1899-1900	1909-10	1919-20	1929-30	1939-40	1949-50	1959-60	1969-70	1973-74
Total U.S. population	39,818	75,995	90,492	104,512	121,770	130,880	148,665	179,323	203,212	209,843
Population 5-17 years of age	12,055	21,573	24,009	27,556	31,417	30,150	30,168	43,881	52,490	51,485
Percent aged 5-17 years.	30.3	28.4	26.5	26.4	25.8	23.0	20.3	24.5	25.8	24.5
Enrollment:										
Elementary and Secondary	6,872	15,503	17,814	21,578	25,678	25,434	25,111	36,087	45,619	45,409
Percent pop. 5-17 enrolled	57.0	71.9	74.2	78.3	81.7	84.4	83.2	82.2	86.9	88.2
Percent in high schools	1.2	3.3	5.1	10.2	17.1	26.0	22.7	23.5	28.5	31.0
High school graduates.	. . . .	62	111	231	592	1,143	1,063	1,627	2,589	2,762
Average school term (in days).	132.2	144.3	157.5	161.9	172.7	175.0	177.9	178.0	178.9	178.7
Total instructional staff	. . . .	. . . .	. . . .	678	880	912	962	1,464	2,253	2,425
Teachers, Librarians: Men	78	127	110	93	140	195	195	402	691	766
Women	123	296	413	565	703	681	719	985	1,440	1,521
Percent men	38.7	29.9	21.1	14.1	16.6	22.2	21.3	29.0	33.4	33.5
Receipts & Expenditures (in millions)										
Total receipts	$219	$433	$970	$2,088	$2,260	$5,437	$14,746	$40,227	$58,231	
Total expenditures	$63	214	426	1,036	2,316	2,344	5,837	15,613[1]	40,683	56,970
Current, elem. and secondary . . .	. . . .	179	356	861	1,843	1,941	4,687	12,329	34,218	50,025
Capital outlay	. . . .	35	69	153	370	257	1,014	2,661	4,659	4,979
Interest on school debt	. . . .	. . . .	. . . .	18	92	130	100	489	1,171	1,514
Other	. . . .	. . . .	. . . .	3	9	13	35	132	636	453

Salaries and Pupil Cost	Data in unadjusted dollars				Data in adjusted dollars					
Average annual teacher salary[2]	$189	$325	$485	$1,554	$3,869	$3,894	$5,928	$8,213	$10,917	$11,185
Expenditure per capital total pop. . . .	1.59	2.83	4.71	17.68	51.85	48.40	77.34	138.21	247.23	271.49
Current expenditure per pupil ADA[3] .	. . . .	16.67	27.85	95.15	236.25	238.05	411.29	595.50	1,007.65	1,207.21

(1) Because of a modification of the scope, "current expenditures for elementary and secondary schools" data for 1959-60 and later years are not entirely comparable with data for prior years. (2) Includes supervisors, principals, teachers and other non-supervisory instructional staff. (3) "ADA" means average daily attendance in elementary and secondary day schools.

Income Discrimination: Male and Female, Black and White

Source: Bureau of the Census

Total Money Income (Includes full and part-time workers, 25 and over, Mar. 1975)		Years of Schooling					
	Total	7 or less	8	9-11	12	13-15	18 or more
White Males with Income (1,000)	48,925	5,071	5,127	6,848	16,196	6,654	9,019
Percent	100.0	100.0	100.0	100.0	100.0	100.0	100.0
Loss to $2,999	9.3	28.8	16.9	10.0	5.5	5.5	4.3
$3,000 to $5,999	14.8	31.8	27.4	17.0	10.8	10.0	7.3
$6,000 to $7,999	10.3	13.2	14.6	12.9	10.0	8.2	6.1
$8,000 to $9,999	11.2	8.9	11.9	14.6	13.3	9.5	7.2
$10,000 to $14,999	27.8	12.3	19.7	29.1	34.8	32.9	23.8
$15,000 and over	26.4	5.1	9.6	16.4	25.8	33.8	51.3
Mean Income	$11,902	$6,114	$7,816	$9,987	$12,010	$13,591	$17,499
Black Males with Income (1,000)	4,787	1,451	377	964	1,216	457	322
Percent	100.0	100.0	100.0	100.0	100.0	100.0	100.0
Loss to $2,999	22.6	44.0	24.7	16.1	11.4	9.1	7.1
$3,000 to $5,999	23.4	27.8	36.5	25.5	17.2	17.1	14.2
$6,000 to $7,999	14.4	11.8	17.0	18.4	15.4	11.6	11.9
$8,000 to $9,999	12.2	8.0	9.3	15.3	15.1	14.1	11.1
$10,000 to $14,999	19.9	7.0	9.5	20.4	31.1	31.7	30.2
$15,000 and over	7.5	1.3	5.0	4.3	9.8	16.4	25.6
Mean Income	$7,240	$4,595	$5,957	$7,146	$8,877	$9,631	$11,360
Mean Income, Full-Time Males	$14,119	$8,829	$10,334	$11,751	$13,299	$15,134	$20,582
White Females with Income (1,000)	39,235	3,912	4,312	5,975	15,344	4,834	4,860
Percent	100.0	100.0	100.0	100.0	100.0	100.0	100.0
Loss to $2,999	43.3	68.6	60.8	47.5	38.3	34.8	26.6
$3,000 to $5,999	26.6	24.6	27.7	32.6	28.4	24.4	16.7
$6,000 to $7,999	11.9	4.8	6.3	9.8	15.3	15.0	11.5
$8,000 to $9,999	7.9	1.2	2.5	5.2	9.3	11.1	13.8
$10,000 to $14,999	7.8	0.9	2.1	3.9	7.1	11.3	22.0
$15,000 and over	2.5	0.3	0.5	0.9	1.7	3.5	9.3
Mean Income	$4,692	$2,730	$3,150	$3,908	$4,760	$5,541	$7,546
Black Females with Income (1,000)	5,174	1,250	451	1,215	1,451	456	352
Percent	100.0	100.0	100.0	100.0	100.0	100.0	100.0
Loss to $2,999	47.6	77.5	66.0	45.7	32.9	29.8	7.7
$3,000 to $5,999	28.2	18.6	26.6	37.3	33.4	25.7	13.6
$6,000 to $7,999	10.5	2.6	4.4	10.3	16.2	14.8	17.8
$8,000 to $9,999	7.2	1.1	1.8	3.5	10.7	15.5	22.9
$10,000 to $14,999	5.5	—	1.3	2.4	6.4	11.9	29.9
$15,000 and over	1.1	0.2	—	0.7	0.5	2.3	8.2
Mean Income	$4,129	$2,277	$2,669	$3,748	$4,787	$5,909	$8,874
Mean Income, Full-time Females	$7,794	NA	NA	$5,605	$7,070	$8,087	$9,757

(Percentages may not add to 100.0 due to rounding;—represents zero or rounds to zero.)

Explanation: The tables above demonstrate that while income tends to rise with educational attainment, it rises far less for women and blacks than for white men. For every year of schooling, the black man tends to gain less than his white counterpart. (Black women appear to improve their incomes in comparison with white women, but this is probably because more black women tend to work full-time.)

Looking at the mean incomes for full-time workers, we can see that all women tend to make only a little more than half the earnings of men with the same educational attainments.

Educational Attainment by Age, Race, and Sex

Source: Bureau of the Census   (Number of Persons in thousands)

1974 Age, Race and Sex	Total Pop.	Elementary 5 years	Elementary 6 & 7 years	Elementary 8 years	High School 1 year	High School 2 years	High School 3 years	High School 4 years	College 1 year	College 2 years	College 3 years	College 4 years	College 5 or more
White													
Total, 14 years and over	138,798	1,507	7,743	15,561	9,232	10,402	7,913	48,267	7,200	7,879	3,355	9,872	6,108
14 and 15 years	7,133	33	1,816	3,287	1,855	104	12	6	-	-	-	-	-
16 and 17 years	7,026	4	107	439	1,741	2,887	1,646	157	9	6	1	-	-
18 and 19 years	6,676	3	67	119	257	451	1,319	3,541	799	74	14	4	1
20 and 21 years	6,441	6	70	125	207	238	267	2,835	1,040	1,025	508	81	2
22 to 24 years	8,998	26	123	174	232	353	356	3,692	786	929	684	1,291	296
25 years and over	102,524	1,435	5,560	11,417	4,941	6,369	4,313	38,037	4,566	5,845	2,147	8,496	5,809
Male, 14 years and over	66,550	735	3,970	7,651	4,326	4,798	3,710	20,690	3,573	4,025	1,751	5,267	4,155
14 and 15 years	3,635	21	1,061	1,701	800	33	5	-	-	-	-	-	-
16 and 17 years	3,564	2	74	264	953	1,434	767	50	5	2	-	-	-
18 and 19 years	3,264	3	30	59	126	252	726	1,642	375	28	3	3	1
20 and 21 years	3,135	3	24	50	89	118	119	1,342	578	516	256	23	2
22 to 24 years	4,417	12	67	81	124	171	177	1,628	417	527	399	606	181
25 years and over	48,534	694	2,714	5,496	2,235	2,790	1,916	16,028	2,198	2,952	1,092	4,635	3,971
25 to 29 years	6,870	27	118	230	181	245	210	2,595	544	604	295	1,060	680
30 to 34 years	5,752	34	132	214	182	266	225	2,269	332	464	152	657	741
35 to 44 years	9,772	97	400	616	416	538	399	3,666	447	628	235	1,071	1,045
45 to 54 years	10,201	122	469	1,020	523	660	476	3,659	463	583	194	949	788
55 to 64 years	8,212	129	635	1,415	473	623	410	2,486	246	440	110	471	434
65 to 74 years	5,134	162	617	1,266	332	336	141	1,012	109	174	72	312	225
75 years and over	2,593	124	343	736	128	123	55	340	56	60	35	116	58
Female, 14 years and over	72,248	772	3,773	7,910	4,906	5,604	4,203	27,577	3,628	3,854	1,604	4,605	1,953
14 and 15 years	3,498	12	755	1,586	1,055	71	8	6	-	-	-	-	-
16 and 17 years	3,462	3	33	174	787	1,454	879	107	4	5	1	-	-
18 and 19 years	3,412	-	37	60	131	199	593	1,898	424	46	11	1	-
20 and 21 years	3,306	3	47	75	118	120	148	1,493	462	508	252	57	-
22 to 24 years	4,584	14	56	93	108	182	179	2,064	369	403	284	685	115
25 years and over	53,990	740	2,846	5,922	2,706	3,578	2,397	22,009	2,368	2,892	1,055	3,862	1,838
25 to 29 years	6,966	17	125	164	232	331	268	3,181	493	561	219	961	347
30 to 34 years	5,838	26	110	199	205	348	288	2,894	331	350	139	597	301
35 to 44 years	10,081	76	324	476	491	681	501	4,978	503	524	193	785	386
45 to 54 years	10,893	114	447	935	530	789	580	5,148	429	555	201	610	325
55 to 64 years	9,185	130	609	1,445	560	721	444	3,376	341	404	156	455	249
65 to 74 years	6,734	192	702	1,483	479	492	199	1,671	184	313	84	317	170
75 years and over	4,293	185	528	1,220	209	218	118	760	87	185	64	136	60
Negro & Other Races													
Total, 14 years and over	18,486	472	1,838	1,819	1,706	1,823	1,399	4,944	733	751	294	717	431
14 and 15 years	1,276	19	426	485	302	24	3	3	-	-	-	-	-
16 and 17 years	1,230	7	50	156	378	407	206	20	-	-	-	-	-
18 and 19 years	1,096	-	20	57	63	141	252	467	80	9	2	-	-
20 and 21 years	1,001	-	17	19	52	85	93	427	144	102	45	12	2
22 to 24 years	1,401	2	38	45	80	113	79	604	86	131	72	113	27
25 years and over	12,481	445	1,287	1,057	831	1,053	767	3,423	423	509	175	593	403
Male, 14 years and over	8,490	216	907	890	753	747	622	2,100	334	341	137	346	249
14 and 15 years	638	9	253	221	135	9	3	1	-	-	-	-	-
16 and 17 years	613	5	33	110	179	195	82	5	-	-	-	-	-
18 and 19 years	510	-	10	40	32	69	134	185	33	-	2	-	-
20 and 21 years	455	-	9	9	34	42	47	186	65	38	19	2	-
22 to 24 years	640	1	16	15	43	53	39	262	38	63	39	51	13
25 years and over	5,633	201	586	494	330	378	316	1,459	198	240	76	293	236
25 to 29 years	854	2	18	27	32	55	57	374	71	68	25	66	37
30 to 34 years	746	7	30	21	44	58	62	254	55	37	25	65	66
35 to 44 years	1,235	31	104	92	86	116	84	401	31	65	16	77	65
45 to 54 years	1,159	41	150	143	92	71	72	278	24	39	5	47	41
55 to 64 years	839	43	144	131	44	63	26	109	11	14	4	30	12
65 to 74 years	546	43	94	57	24	16	12	33	3	11	-	9	9
75 years and over	255	34	46	24	8	-	2	11	1	5	1	-	6
Female, 14 years and over	9,996	256	931	930	952	1,077	778	2,844	399	411	157	372	182
14 and 15 years	638	9	173	264	168	16	-	2	-	-	-	-	-
16 and 17 years	617	1	17	47	200	212	124	15	-	-	-	-	-
18 and 19 years	586	-	10	17	31	72	118	281	47	9	-	-	-
20 and 21 years	546	-	8	10	18	43	45	241	79	65	25	10	2
22 to 24 years	761	2	22	30	37	59	40	342	48	68	33	62	14
25 years and over	6,848	243	701	563	500	675	451	1,964	225	269	99	299	167
25 to 29 years	1,042	4	36	36	49	115	82	438	61	67	40	73	31
30 to 34 years	904	6	39	35	56	105	67	359	52	54	17	71	31
35 to 44 years	1,527	28	106	117	125	184	112	528	63	72	25	73	44
45 to 54 years	1,349	49	151	135	122	144	106	378	30	44	8	31	36
55 to 64 years	979	62	163	115	77	83	49	170	14	21	3	36	15
65 to 74 years	678	56	142	93	51	33	28	57	3	7	4	7	9
75 years and over	369	39	65	32	19	11	7	34	2	4	3	8	-

Education Pays—Black or White
Source: Bureau of the Census
(— represents zero or rounds to zero. B means base less than 75,000.)

Race, Age, Income, Occupation (1973)	Total (1,000)	Percent Distribution, Years of Schooling						Median Years
		0-8	9-11	12	13-15	16	16+	
White employed males, age 25-44	20,336	934	2,399	7,797	3,333	2,599	2,290	12.8
Under $3,000	844	57	123	243	138	85	69	12.5
$3,000-$5,999	1,835	171	333	564	238	136	136	12.3
$6,000-$9,999	5,086	335	771	2,107	795	458	259	12.5
$10,000-$14,999	7,236	262	852	3,253	1,231	809	641	12.7
$15,000 & over	5,334	109	320	1,630	931	1,111	1,186	14.8
White-collar workers	9,523	103	391	2,526	1,962	2,269	2,200	15.6
Under $6,000	791	13	58	196	183	139	178	14.7
$6,000 & over	8,732	90	333	2,330	1,779	2,130	2,022	14.8
Blue-collar workers	9,099	718	1,820	4,483	1,081	221	57	12.3
Under $6,000	1,366	154	325	446	135	55	9	12.1
$6,000 & over	7,733	564	1,495	4,037	946	166	48	12.4
Service workers	1,077	49	119	518	227	67	24	12.6
Under $6,000	237	15	37	74	35	17	14	12.1
$6,000 & over	840	34	82	444	192	50	10	12.7
Farm workers	637	63	70	270	63	42	9	12.2
Under $6,000	285	46	36	92	22	9	5	10.2
$6,000 & over	352	17	34	178	41	33	4	12.5
Black employed males, age 25-44	1,970	99	482	754	261	98	55	12.2
Under $3,000	197	15	61	49	19	—	2	10.6
$3,000-$5,999	418	36	136	118	34	8	4	11.0
$6,000-$9,999	712	40	179	305	91	36	10	12.3
$10,000-$14,999	506	7	84	241	86	33	24	12.5
$15,000 & over	137	2	22	41	31	21	15	13.0
White-collar workers	487	6	11	172	114	84	55	13.3
Under $6,000	79	—	8	38	20	5	6	(B)
$6,000 & over	409	6	33	124	94	79	49	13.3
Blue-collar workers	1,220	68	376	491	112	14	—	12.0
Under $6,000	406	35	148	100	21	3	—	10.4
$6,000 & over	814	33	228	391	91	11	—	12.3
Service workers	217	17	49	88	35	—	—	12.2
Under $6,000	84	7	25	26	14	—	—	12.2
$6,000 & over	133	10	24	62	21	—	—	12.2
Farm workers	46	8	16	3	—	—	—	(B)
Under $6,000	46	8	16	3	—	—	—	(B)
$6,000 & over	—	—	—	—	—	—	—	(B)
White employed males, age 45-64	15,524	1,878	2,620	5,395	1,806	1,278	1,159	12.3
Under $3,000	647	126	123	152	49	22	19	10.0
$3,000-$5,999	1,359	253	259	366	85	44	43	10.4
$6,000-$9,999	3,595	629	794	1,176	265	126	78	11.4
$10,000-$14,999	5,086	592	953	2,116	575	304	228	12.3
$15,000 & over	4,866	279	493	1,585	831	782	791	13.0
White-collar workers	6,958	293	622	2,340	1,290	1,161	1,126	13.2
Under $6,000	517	51	84	161	89	50	59	12.7
$6,000 & over	6,441	242	538	2,179	1,201	1,111	1,067	12.8
Blue-collar workers	6,680	1,201	1,602	2,420	402	76	21	11.2
Under $6,000	849	190	173	189	28	8	2	8.9
$6,000 & over	5,831	1,011	1,429	2,231	374	68	19	12.2
Service workers	1,028	184	242	363	71	17	2	11.2
Under $6,000	253	50	52	67	11	1	—	9.8
$6,000 & over	775	134	190	296	60	16	2	12.2
Farm workers	888	201	155	272	43	23	10	10.2
Under $6,000	387	89	73	100	6	7	2	8.9
$6,000 & over	501	112	82	172	37	16	8	12.1
Black employed males, age 45-64	1,347	192	270	252	65	42	29	8.9
Under $3,000	162	21	14	30	3	4	—	7.4
$3,000-$5,999	369	63	63	36	6	1	—	7.6
$6,000-$9,999	432	68	110	79	18	12	8	9.3
$10,000-$14,999	273	25	70	86	18	9	9	11.4
$15,000 & over	111	14	13	22	21	16	12	12.7
White-collar workers	211	19	23	72	27	27	27	12.7
Under $6,000	40	5	7	16	2	2	—	(B)
$6,000 & over	171	14	16	56	25	25	27	(B)
Blue-collar workers	782	131	166	126	31	10	—	8.6
Under $6,000	298	61	34	26	6	1	—	7.0
$6,000 & over	484	70	132	100	25	9	—	10.6
Service workers	287	38	77	49	7	6	2	8.9
Under $6,000	136	17	33	18	1	2	—	7.9
$6,000 & over	151	21	44	31	6	4	2	9.5
Farm workers	67	4	3	4	—	—	—	(B)
Under $6,000	58	2	3	4	—	—	—	(B)
$6,000 & over	9	2	—	—	—	—	—	(B)

The Principal Languages of the World

Source: Sidney S. Culbert, Assoc. Professor of Psychology, University of Washington

Total number of speakers of languages spoken by at least one million persons (Midyear 1976)
Parenthesized numbers after names of languages refer to notes below table.

Language	Millions
Afrikaans (S. Africa)	6
Albanian	3
Amharic (Ethiopia)	9
Arabic	130
Armenian	4
Assamese (1) (India)	13
Aymara (Bolivia; Peru)	1
Azerbaijani (USSR; Iran)	8
Bahasa (See Malay-Indonesian)	
Balinese	3
Baluchi (Pakistan; Iran)	3
Batak (Indonesia)	2
Bemba (S. Central Africa)	2
Bengali (1) (Bangladesh; India)	127
Berber (2) (N. Africa)	
Bhili (India)	4
Bihari (India)	22
Bikol (Philippines)	2
Bisaya (see Cebuano, Panay-Hiligaynon, and Samar-Leyte)	
Bugi (Indonesia)	2
Bulgarian	9
Burmese	23
Byelorussian (mainly USSR)	9
Cambodian (Cambodia; Asia)	7
Canarese (see Kannada)	
Cantonese (China)	48
Catalan (Spain; France; Andorra)	6
Cebuano (Philippines)	8
Chinese (3)	
Chuang (7) (China)	
Chuvash (USSR)	2
Czech	11
Danish	5
Dayak (Borneo)	1
Dutch (see Netherlandish)	
Edo (W. Africa)	1
Efik	2
English	363
Esperanto	1
Estonian	1
Ewe (W. Africa)	3
Fang-Bulu (W. Africa)	1
Finnish	5
Flemish (see Netherlandish)	
French	92
Fula (W. Africa)	8
Galician (Spain)	3
Galla (Ethiopia)	7
Ganda (or Luganda) (E. Africa)	3
Georgian (USSR)	3
German	120
Gilaki (Iran)	1
Gondi (India)	2
Greek	10
Guarani (mainly Paraguay)	3
Gujarati (1) (India)	30
Hakka (China)	21
Hausa (W. and Central Africa)	19
Hebrew	3
Hindi (1) (4)	213
Hindustani (4)	
Hungarian (or Magyar)	13
Ibibio (see Efik)	
Ibo (or Igbo) (W. Africa)	10
Ijaw (W. Africa)	1
Ilocano (Philippines)	4
Iloko (see Ilocano)	

Language	Millions
Indonesian (see Malay-Indonesian)	……
Italian	60
Japanese	112
Javanese	45
Kamba (E. Africa)	1
Kanarese (see Kannada)	
Kannada (1) (India)	29
Kanuri (W. and Cent. Africa)	3
Kashmiri (1)	3
Kazakh (USSR)	6
Khalkha (Mongolia)	2
Kikongo (see Kongo)	
Kikuyu (or Gekoyo) (Kenya)	3
Kimbundu (see Mbundu-Kim.)	
Kirghiz (USSR)	2
Kituba (Congo River)	2
Kongo (Congo River)	2
Konkani (India)	2
Korean	53
Kumauni (India)	1
Kurdish (S.W. of Caspian Sea)	7
Kurukh (or Oraon) (India)	1
Lao (5) (Laos, Asia)	3
Latvian (or Lettish)	2
Lingala (see Ngala)	
Lithuanian	3
Luba-Lulua (Zaire)	3
Luganda (see Ganda)	
Luhya (or Luhia) (Kenya)	1
Luo (Kenya)	2
Luri (Iran)	1
Macedonian (Yugoslavia)	1
Madurese (Indonesia)	8
Makua (S.E. Africa)	3
Malagasy (Madagascar)	8
Malay-Indonesian	98
Malayalam (1) (India)	25
Malinke-Bambara-Dyula (Africa)	6
Mandarin (China)	660
Mazandarani (Iran)	1
Marathi (1) (India)	52
Mbundu (Umbundu group) (S. Angola)	3
Mbundu (Kimbundu group) (Angola)	2
Mende (Sierra Leone)	1
Meo (see Miao)	
Miao (and Meo) (S.E. Asia)	3
Min (China)	39
Moldavian (inc. W/Rumanian)	
Mongolian (see Khalkha)	
Mordvin (USSR)	1
More (see Mossi)	
Mossi (W. Africa)	3
Ndongo (see Mbundu-Kimbundu)	
Nepali (Nepal; India)	10
Netherlandish (Dutch and Flem.)	20
Ngala (or Lingala) (Africa)	2
Norwegian	5
Nyamwezi-Sukuma (S.E. Africa)	2
Nyanja (S.E. Africa)	3
Oraon (see Kurukh)	
Oriya (1) (India)	24
Panay-Hiligaynon (Philippines)	4
Panjabi (see Punjabi)	

Language	Millions
Pashto (see Pushtu)	
Pedi (see Sotho. Northern)	
Persian	25
Polish	36
Portuguese	129
Provencal (Southern France)	6
Punjabi (1) (India; Pakistan)	57
Pushtu (mainly Afghanistan)	16
Quechua (S. America)	7
Rajasthani (India)	21
Romanian	22
Ruanda (S. Central Africa)	6
Rundi (S. Central Africa)	4
Russian (Great Russian only)	240
Samar-Leyte (Philippines)	1
Sango (Central Africa)	2
Santali (India)	4
Sepedi (see Sotho, Northern)	
Serbo-Croatian (Yugoslavia)	19
Shan (Burma)	2
Shona (S.E. Africa)	4
Siamese (see Thai)	
Sindhi (India; Pakistan)	9
Sinhalese (Sri Lanka)	10
Slovak	5
Slovene (Yugoslavia)	2
Somali (E. Africa)	5
Sotho, Northern (S. Africa)	2
Sotho, Southern (S. Africa)	3
Spanish	219
Sundanese (Indonesia)	15
Swahili (E. Africa)	21
Swedish	10
Tagalog (Philippines)	21
Tajiki (USSR)	3
Tamil (1) (India; Sri Lanka)	54
Tatar (or Kazan-Turkic) (USSR)	6
Telugu (1) India	54
Thai (5)	31
Thonga (S.E. Africa)	1
Tibetan	6
Tigrinya (Ethiopia)	4
Tiv (E. Central Nigeria)	1
Tswana (S. Africa)	2
Tulu (India)	1
Turkish	40
Turkoman (USSR)	2
Twi-Fante (or Akan) (W. Africa)	4
Uighur-(Sinkiang, China)	4
Ukrainian (mainly USSR)	42
Umbundu (see Mbundu-Umbundu)	
Urdu (1) (Pakistan; India)	58
Uzbek (USSR)	9
Vietnamese	37
Visayan (see Cebuano, Panay-Hiligaynon, and Samar-Leyte)	
White Russian (see Byelorussian)	
Wolof (W. Africa)	3
Wu (China)	43
Xhosa (S. Africa)	4
Yi (China)	3
Yiddish (6)	
Yoruba (W. Africa)	12
Zhuang (7) (China)	
Zulu (S. Africa)	4

(1.) One of the fourteen languages of the Constitution of India. (2.) Here considered a group of dialects. 3.) See Mandarin, Cantonese, Wu, Min, and Hakka. The "national language" (Guoyu) is a standardized form of Mandarin as spoken in the area of Peking. (4.) Hindi and Urdu are essentially the same language, Hindustani. As the official language of India it is written in the Devanagari script and called Hindi. As the official language of Pakistan it is written in a modified Arabic script and called Urdu. (5.) Thai includes Central, Southwestern, Northern, and Northeastern Thai. The distinction between Northeastern Thai and Lao is political rather than linguistic. (6.) Yiddish is usually considered a variant of German, though it has its own standard grammar, dictionaries, a highly developed literature, and is written-in Hebrew characters. Speakers number about 3,000,000. (7.) A group of Thai-like dialects with about 9 million speakers.

UNITED STATES POPULATION

Fertility Rate at New Low

By Vincent P. Barabba
Director, U.S. Bureau of the Census

On January 1, 1976, the population of the United States including Armed Forces overseas was estimated at 214.5 million.

During 1975, the Nation's population increased by 1.7 million, the result of 3.1 million births, 1.9 million deaths, and 494,000 added by net immigration. This compares with a net gain of 1.6 million in 1974.

Fertility

In 1975, as in each successive year since 1972, the total fertility rate reached a new record low in the history of the United States. The total fertility rate — the number of births 1,000 women would have in their life-times based upon the birth rates occurring in a given calendar year — was estimated in 1975 to be 1.80. This compares with 1.86 in 1974.

Although the present age structure of the population is such that even at present low birth rates it would be many years before the United States attained zero population growth, the current total fertility rate is nevertheless well below the rate of 2.1 children per woman required for the natural replacement of the population.

Results of a 1975 survey of birth expectations regarding future births and total lifetime fertility show that pronounced differences exist between women 18 to 24 years old and women 35 to 39 years old with respect to average numbers of lifetime births expected. Among currently married women of all races, the younger group expects to have an average of 2.2 children per woman, whereas the average for the older group is about 3.1.

Marriages and Divorces

In 1975, for the first time in U.S. history, the annual number of divorces passed the one million mark. Data show that the number of divorces in 1975 was 1,026,000 and the number of marriages 2,126,000. Corresponding 1974 figures were 970,000 divorces and 2,223,000 marriages. The divorce rate per 1,000 population was 4.8 in 1975, 3.5 in 1970, and 2.2 in 1960. The marriage rate per 1,000 population was 10.0 in 1975, down from a peak of 11.0 in 1972. In 1970 it was 10.6 and in 1960, 8.5.

The proportion of adults in the United States who had never married increased substantially during the decade of the 1960's and has continued to increase during the first half of the 1970's. Particularly notable has been the continued increase in the percent single at those ages when most men and women have traditionally married. The proportion single among persons 20 to 24 years old — the range of years in which the median age at first marriage for both men and women falls — increased from 28 percent in 1960 to 40 percent in 1975 for women, and from 53 percent in 1960 to 60 percent in 1975 for men. The figures may reflect the development of a trend toward a larger proportion of persons remaining single throughout their entire lives.

Education

In the fall of 1975, 61 million students 3 to 34 years old were enrolled in school. In addition, 1.2 million 35 years old and over were enrolled in college. The number of students enrolled in nursery school increased by 60 percent between 1970 and 1975, whereas the number enrolled in kindergarten rose by 6 percent. The number in elementary school decreased by 10 percent during these 5 years because of the declining birth rate over the last two decades. The number in high school increased by 6 percent, and college attendance rose by 31 percent in the 5 year period. Although a larger number of males than females under 35 years old were enrolled in college, the rise in attendance since 1970 was much greater for females than for males (45 percent versus 21 percent).

The largest percent gains in college enrollment have occurred among persons who are above the traditional age for college attendance. The number of persons enrolled in college rose between 1970 and 1975 by 72 percent for those 25 to 29 years old and by 108 percent for those 30 to 34 years old. In 1975, over one-third of all college students were 25 years old or over. A large majority of these students were attending college on a part-time basis.

As the population of college students was becoming older between 1970 and 1975, the composition of the student population was also changing. Female college students constituted 41 percent of the college enrollees in 1970, but this proportion rose to 45 percent in 1975. During this 5-year period the number of women enrolled in college increased by twice as much as did enrollment of men. The increase from 1970 to 1975 in the number of persons who were enrolled in college amounted to 82 percent for blacks as compared with 26 percent for whites. As a result, the proportion of college students who were black rose from 7 percent in 1970 to 10 percent in 1975.

In 1975 a majority (63 percent) of the adult population 25 years old and over in the United States had completed at least 4 years of high school. Only among those 65 years old and over were less than half of the persons not high school graduates.

A total of 18.2 million persons in the United States in 1975 had completed 4 or more years of college. This number includes 2.0 million under 25 years of age as well as the 16.2 million 25 years old and over. Although, in 1975, 6 out of 10 adults 25 years old and over had graduated from high school, only 14 percent had completed a 4-year college degree. About one-fifth of the youngest persons but only 8 percent of the oldest were college graduates in 1975.

Metropolitan Areas

Since 1970 an important change has taken place in one of the most clearly established patterns of population redistribution in the United States. The growth rate of metropolitan areas — the larger cities with their suburbs — has fallen below the growth rate of the remainder of the country. In 1975 over two-thirds of the population lived in standard metropolitan statistical areas (SMSA's), which are comprised essentially of counties with cities of 50,000 or more inhabitants together with neighboring counties that are closely associated with them by daily commuting ties. Between 1970 and 1975, the population of SMSA's increased by nearly 5 million persons, or 3.6 percent. During the same period, nonmetropolitan population increased by nearly 4 million persons, or 6.3 percent. The numerical growth of the metropolitan areas is still larger than that of nonmetropolitan areas, but the latter are growing at a considerably faster rate.

The larger metropolitan areas have shown the least growth since 1970. Of the eight metropolitan areas with more than 3 million population, only two grew by as much as 3 percent between the 1970 census and July 1, 1974 (the Washington, D.C. SMSA and the San Francisco-Oakland-San Jose Standard Consolidated Statistical Area). The central cities of metropolitan areas have lost population since 1970. This loss is accounted for entirely by a decline in white population.

Between 1970 and 1975 the population of black and other races has decreased in nonmetropolitan areas and increased in metropolitan areas. The increase of black and other races in central cities has averaged 1.9 percent per year since 1970, a lower annual increase than in the 1960's. At the same time, the population of black and other races living in the balance of SMSA's outside central cities (mostly suburban areas) grew by 5.2 percent per year from 1970 to 1975, an annual gain considerably greater than in the 1960's. Even so, only 26 percent of the metropolitan population of black and other races lived outside central cities in 1975, as compared with 62 percent of their white counterparts.

Employment

The civilian labor force in 1975 averaged 92.6 million persons or 61.2 percent of the civilian noninstitutional population 16 years old and over. Between 1960 and 1970, the labor force grew by about 13.1 million persons. Since 1970 it has increased by another 9.9 million persons. Over the entire 15-year period, women accounted for 13.7 million or 60 percent of the labor force growth. The labor force participation rate for women has risen from 37.7 percent in 1960 to 43.3 percent in 1970 and to 46.3 percent in 1975, representing 37 million women in the labor force. Men in the civilian labor force numbered approximately 55.6 million in 1975 for a labor force participation rate of 77.9 percent. This represents a continuation of the decline in male participation rates from 83.3 percent in 1960 to 79.7 percent in 1970.

There were slight decreases from 1960 to 1970 and from 1970 to 1975 in the labor force participation rates for men 25 to 54 years of age. For men aged 55 and over the drop in the percent in the labor force was more pronounced, reflecting the trend toward earlier retirement.

The civilian labor force continued its long-term growth in 1975. However, the growth in the number of employed declined for the first time since 1961. Thus, with more people looking for jobs, and the number of people with jobs decreasing, there was a 54.3 percent increase in the number of unemployed.

The downturn in the economy during late 1974 and 1975 resulted in increased unemployment among all major demographic groups. Overall, the unemployment rate averaged 5.1 percent during the first half of 1974, began to rise during the last half of 1974, and peaked during the second quarter (April-June) of 1975. These trends were generally the same for adult men and women, teenagers, whites, blacks and other races, household heads, and married men. Throughout 1974 and 1975 the unemployment rates for teenagers were the highest of all the population groups. Adult women had higher rates than adult men. And blacks and other races had higher rates than whites. However, the largest relative increases in unemployment rates were for adult men, household heads, and married men. The second quarter 1975 rates for these population groups were double or more the rates of early 1974.

U.S. Area and Population: 1790 to 1970

Source: Bureau of the Census

Area figures represent area on indicated date including in some cases considerable areas not then organized or settled, and not covered by the census. Area figures have been adjusted to bring them into agreement with remeasurements made in 1940. Changes in land and water area between 1960 and 1970 due to construction of dams and reservoirs. Also total area of Texas reduced approximately one square mile in the Chamizal agreement between U.S. and Mexico.

| Census Date | Area (square miles) | | | Population | | | |
	Gross	Land	Water	Number	Per sq. mile of land	Increase over preceding census No.	%
1790 (Aug. 2)	888,811	864,746	24,065	3,929,214	4.5	(X)	(X)
1800 (Aug. 4)	888,811	864,746	24,065	5,308,483	6.1	1,379,269	35.1
1810 (Aug. 6)	1,716,003	1,681,828	34,175	7,239,881	4.3	1,931,398	36.4
1820 (Aug. 7)	1,788,006	1,749,462	38,544	9,638,453	5.5	2,398,572	33.1
1830 (June 1)	1,788,006	1,749,462	38,544	12,866,020	7.4	3,227,567	33.5
1840 (June 1)	1,788,006	1,749,462	38,544	17,069,453	9.8	4,203,433	32.7
1850 (June 1)	2,992,747	2,940,042	52,705	23,191,876	7.9	6,122,423	35.9
1860 (June 1)	3,022,387	2,969,640	52,747	31,443,321	10.6	8,251,445	35.6
1870 (June 1)	3,022,387	2,969,640	52,747	'39,818,449	'13.4	8,375,128	26.6
1880 (June 1)	3,022,387	2,969,640	52,747	50,155,783	16.9	10,337,334	26.0
1890 (June 1)	3,022,387	2,969,640	52,747	62,947,714	21.2	12,791,931	25.5
1900 (June 1)	3,022,387	2,969,834	52,553	75,994,575	25.6	13,046,861	20.7
1910 (Apr. 15)	3,022,387	2,969,565	52,822	91,972,266	31.0	15,977,691	21.0
1920 (Jan. 1)	3,022,387	2,969,451	52,936	105,710,620	35.6	13,738,354	14.9
1930 (Apr. 1)	3,022,387	2,977,128	45,259	122,775,046	41.2	17,064,426	16.1
1940 (Apr. 1)	3,022,387	2,977,128	45,259	131,669,275	44.2	8,894,229	7.2
1950 (Apr. 1)²	3,615,211	3,552,206	63,005	151,325,798	42.6	19,161,229	14.5
1960 (Apr. 1)²	3,615,123	3,540,911	74,212	179,323,175	50.5	27,997,377	18.5
1970* (Apr. 1)²	3,615,122	3,536,855	78,267	203,211,926	57.5	23,888,751	13.3

(X) Not applicable. (1) Revised to include adjustments for underenumeration in Southern States; unrevised number is 38,558,371. (2) Includes Alaska and Hawaii.

Population, Urban and Rural, by Race: 1960 and 1970

Source: Bureau of the Census

In thousands. An urbanized area comprises at least one city of 50,000 inhabitants (central city) plus contiguous, closely settled areas (urban fringe)

| YEAR AND AREA | 1960 | | | 1970 | | |
	Total	White	Negro and other	Total	White	Negro and other
Population, total	179,823	158,832	20,491	¹203,212	177,749	25,463
Urban	125,269	110,428	14,840	149,325	128,773	20,552
Inside urbanized areas	95,848	83,770	12,070	118,447	100,952	17,495
Central cities	57,975	47,627	10,348	63,922	49,547	14,375
Urban fringe	37,873	36,143	1,731	54,525	51,405	3,120
Outside urbanized areas	29,420	26,658	2,762	30,878	27,822	3,057
Rural	54,054	48,403	5,651	53,887	48,976	4,911

Population of the U.S., 1960-70

Region, Division, and State	1970 Census	1960 Census	Pct. + or -	1970 Urban	Rural	Pct. Urban	Rank 1970	1960
United States................	203,235,298	179,323,175	13.3	149,324,930	53,886,996	73.5	...	...
Regions:								
Northeast..................	48,999,999	44,677,819	9.7	39,449,818	9,590,885	80.4	...	...
North Central..............	56,577,067	51,619,139	9.6	40,480,760	16,090,903	71.6	...	...
South.....................	62,798,347	54,973,113	14.2	40,539,961	22,255,406	64.6	...	...
West......................	34,809,359	28,053,104	24.1	28,854,391	5,949,802	82.9	...	...
New England............	11,847,186	10,509,367	12.7	9,043,517	2,798,146	76.4	...	...
Maine.....................	993,663	969,265	2.5	504,157	487,891	50.8	38	36
New Hampshire............	737,681	606,921	21.5	416,040	321,641	56.4	42	45
Vermont...................	444,732	389,881	14.1	142,889	301,441	32.2	49	47
Massachusetts.............	5,689,170	5,148,578	10.5	4,810,449	878,721	84.6	10	9
Rhode Island..............	949,723	859,488	10.5	824,930	121,795	87.1	39	39
Connecticut...............	3,032,217	2,535,234	19.6	2,345,052	686,657	77.4	24	25
Middle Atlantic........	37,152,813	34,168,452	8.7	30,406,301	6,792,739	81.7	...	...
New York..................	18,241,266	16,782,304	8.4	15,602,486	2,634,481	85.6	2	1
New Jersey................	7,168,164	6,066,782	18.2	6,373,405	794,759	88.9	8	8
Pennsylvania..............	11,793,909	11,319,366	4.2	8,430,410	3,363,499	71.5	3	3
East North Central......	40,252,678	36,225,024	11.1	30,091,847	10,160,629	74.8	...	...
Ohio......................	10,652,017	9,706,397	9.7	8,025,775	2,625,242	75.3	6	5
Indiana...................	5,193,669	4,662,498	11.4	3,372,060	1,821,609	64.9	11	11
Illinois..................	11,113,976	10,081,158	10.2	9,229,821	1,884,155	83.0	5	4
Michigan..................	8,875,083	7,823,194	13.4	6,553,773	2,321,310	73.8	7	7
Wisconsin.................	4,417,933	3,951,777	11.8	2,910,418	1,507,313	65.9	16	15
West North Central......	16,324,389	15,394,115	6.0	10,388,913	5,930,274	63.7	...	...
Minnesota.................	3,805,069	3,413,864	11.5	2,527,308	1,277,663	66.4	19	18
Iowa......................	2,825,041	2,757,537	2.4	1,616,405	1,207,971	57.2	25	24
Missouri..................	4,677,399	4,319,813	8.3	3,277,662	1,398,839	70.1	13	13
North Dakota..............	617,761	632,446	-2.3	273,442	344,319	44.3	46	44
South Dakota..............	666,257	680,514	-2.1	296,628	368,879	44.6	45	40
Nebraska..................	1,483,791	1,411,330	5.1	912,598	570,895	61.5	35	34
Kansas....................	2,249,071	2,178,611	3.2	1,484,870	761,708	66.1	28	28
South Atlantic..........	30,671,337	25,971,732	18.1	19,523,920	11,147,417	63.7	...	...
Delaware..................	548,104	446,292	22.8	395,569	152,535	72.2	47	46
Maryland..................	3,922,399	3,100,689	26.5	3,003,935	918,464	76.6	18	21
District of Columbia......	756,510	763,956	-1.0	756,510	...	100.0	41	...
Virginia..................	4,648,494	3,966,949	17.2	2,934,841	1,713,653	63.1	14	14
West Virginia.............	1,744,237	1,860,421	-6.2	679,491	1,064,746	39.0	34	30
North Carolina............	5,082,059	4,556,155	11.5	2,285,168	2,796,891	45.0	12	12
South Carolina............	2,590,516	2,382,594	8.7	1,232,195	1,358,321	47.6	26	26
Georgia...................	4,589,575	3,943,116	16.4	2,768,074	1,821,501	60.3	15	16
Florida...................	6,789,443	4,951,560	37.1	5,468,137	1,321,306	80.5	9	10
East South Central......	12,804,552	12,050,126	6.3	6,987,943	5,815,527	54.6	...	...
Kentucky..................	3,219,311	3,038,156	6.0	1,684,053	1,534,653	52.3	23	22
Tennessee.................	3,924,164	3,567,089	10.0	2,305,307	1,618,380	58.7	17	17
Alabama...................	3,444,165	3,266,740	5.4	2,011,941	1,432,224	58.4	21	19
Mississippi...............	2,216,912	2,178,141	1.8	986,642	1,230,270	44.5	29	29
West South Central......	19,322,458	16,951,255	14.0	14,028,098	5,292,462	72.6	...	...
Arkansas..................	1,923,295	1,786,272	7.7	960,865	962,430	50.0	32	31
Louisiana.................	3,643,180	3,257,022	11.9	2,406,150	1,235,156	66.1	20	20
Oklahoma..................	2,559,253	2,328,284	9.9	1,740,137	819,092	68.0	27	27
Texas.....................	11,196,730	9,579,677	16.9	8,920,946	2,275,784	79.7	4	6
Mountain................	8,283,585	6,855,060	20.8	6,054,979	2,226,583	73.1	...	...
Montana...................	694,409	674,767	2.9	370,676	323,733	53.4	44	41
Idaho.....................	713,008	667,191	6.9	385,434	327,133	54.1	43	42
Wyoming...................	332,416	330,066	0.7	201,111	131,305	60.5	50	48
Colorado..................	2,207,259	1,753,947	25.8	1,733,311	473,948	78.5	30	33
New Mexico................	1,016,000	951,023	6.8	708,775	307,225	69.8	37	37
Arizona...................	1,772,482	1,302,161	36.1	1,408,864	362,036	79.6	33	35
Utah......................	1,059,273	890,627	18.9	851,472	207,801	80.4	36	38
Nevada....................	488,738	285,278	71.3	395,336	93,402	80.9	48	49
Pacific.................	26,525,774	21,198,044	25.1	22,799,412	3,723,219	86.0	...	...
Washington................	3,409,169	2,853,214	19.5	2,476,468	932,701	72.6	22	23
Oregon....................	2,091,385	1,768,687	18.2	1,402,704	688,681	67.1	31	32
California................	19,953,134	15,717,204	27.0	18,136,045	1,817,089	90.9	1	2
Alaska....................	302,173	226,167	33.6	145,512	154,870	48.4	51	50
Hawaii....................	769,913	632,772	21.7	638,683	128,878	83.1	40	43

Urban and rural figures do not equal total 1970 population because of errors discovered by Census Bureau after tabulation.

Congressional Apportionment

State	1970 Census	1960 Census	State	1970 Census	1960 Census	State	1970 Census	1960 Census	State	1970 Census	1960 Census	State	1970 Census	1960 Census
Ala....	7	8	Ida....	2	2	Minn..	8	8	N.D....	1	2	Vt.....	1	1
Alas...	1	1	Ill.....	24	24	Miss...	5	5	Oh.....	23	24	Va.....	10	10
Ariz...	4	3	Ind.....	11	11	Mo.....	10	10	Okla...	6	6	Wash...	7	7
Ark....	4	4	Ia......	6	7	Mon....	2	2	Ore....	4	4	W. Va..	4	5
Cal....	43	38	Kan....	5	5	Neb....	3	3	Pa.....	25	27	Wis....	9	10
Col....	5	4	Ky.....	7	7	Nev....	1	1	R.I....	2	2	Wy.....	1	1
Conn...	6	6	La.....	8	8	N.H....	2	2	S.C....	6	6			
Del....	1	1	Me.....	2	2	N.J....	15	15	S.D....	2	2			
Fla....	15	12	Md.....	8	8	N.M....	2	2	Tenn...	8	9	Totals .	435	435
Ga.....	10	10	Mass...	12	12	N.Y....	39	41	Tex....	24	23			
Ha.....	2	2	Mich...	19	19	N.C....	11	11	Ut.....	2	2			

The chief reason why the Constitution provided for a census of the population every 10 years was to give a basis for apportionment of representatives among the states. This apportionment has largely determined the number of electoral votes allotted to each state.

The number of representatives of each state in Congress is determined by the state's population, except that each state is entitled to one representative regardless of population. A Congressional apportionment has been made after each decennial census except that of 1920.

Under provisions of a law that became effective Nov. 15, 1941, apportionment of representatives is made by the method of equal proportions. In the application of this method, the apportionment is made so that the average population per representative has the least possible variation between one state and any other. The first House of Representatives, in 1790, had 65 members, or one representative for each 30,000 of the estimated population, as provided by the Constitution. As the population grew, the number of representatives was increased but the total membership has been fixed at 435 since 1912.

U.S. Population (Official Census), 1790-1880 . . .

Source: Bureau of the Census

State	1790	1800	1810	1820	1830¹	1840¹	1850	1860	1870	1880
Ala.....	.....	1,250	9,046	127,901	309,527	590,756	771,623	964,201	996,992	1,262,505
Ariz.....	.....	.....	.....	.....	.....	.....	.....	.....	9,658	40,440
Ark.....	.....	.....	1,062	14,273	30,388	97,574	209,897	435,450	484,471	802,525
Cal.....	.....	.....	.....	.....	.....	.....	92,597	379,994	560,247	864,694
Col.....	.....	.....	.....	.....	.....	.....	.....	34,277	39,864	194,327
Conn....	237,946	251,002	261,942	275,248	297,675	309,978	370,792	460,147	537,454	622,700
Del.....	59,096	64,273	72,674	72,749	76,748	78,085	91,532	112,216	125,015	146,608
D.C.....	.....	14,093	24,023	33,039	39,834	43,712	51,687	75,080	131,700	177,624
Fla.....	.....	.....	.....	.....	34,730	54,477	87,445	140,424	187,748	269,493
Ga.....	82,548	162,686	252,433	340,989	516,823	691,392	906,185	1,057,286	1,184,109	1,542,180
Ida.....	.....	.....	.....	.....	.....	.....	.....	.....	14,999	32,610
Ill.....	.....	.....	12,282	55,211	157,445	476,183	851,470	1,711,951	2,539,891	3,077,871
Ind.....	.....	5,641	24,520	147,178	343,031	685,866	988,416	1,350,428	1,680,637	1,978,301
Iowa....	.....	.....	.....	.....	.....	43,112	192,214	674,913	1,194,020	1,624,615
Kan.....	.....	.....	.....	.....	.....	.....	.....	107,206	364,399	996,096
Ky.....	73,677	220,995	406,511	564,317	687,917	779,828	982,405	1,155,684	1,321,011	1,648,690
La.....	.....	.....	76,556	153,407	215,739	352,411	517,762	708,002	726,915	939,946
Me.....	96,540	151,719	228,705	298,335	399,455	501,793	583,169	628,279	626,915	648,936
Md.....	319,728	341,548	380,546	407,350	447,040	470,019	583,034	687,049	780,894	934,943
Mass....	378,787	422,845	472,040	523,287	610,408	737,699	994,514	1,231,066	1,457,351	1,783,085
Mich....	.....	.....	4,762	8,896	31,639	212,267	397,654	749,113	1,184,059	1,636,937
Minn....	.....	.....	.....	.....	.....	.....	6,077	172,023	439,706	780,773
Miss....	.....	8,850	40,352	75,448	136,621	375,651	606,526	791,305	827,922	1,131,597
Mo.....	.....	.....	19,783	66,586	140,455	383,702	682,044	1,182,012	1,721,295	2,168,380
Mon.....	.....	.....	.....	.....	.....	.....	.....	.....	20,595	39,159
Neb.....	.....	.....	.....	.....	.....	.....	.....	28,841	122,993	452,402
Nev.....	.....	.....	.....	.....	.....	.....	.....	6,857	42,491	62,266
N. H....	141,885	183,858	214,460	244,161	269,328	284,574	317,976	326,073	318,300	346,991
N. J....	184,139	211,149	245,562	277,575	320,823	373,306	489,555	672,035	906,096	1,131,116
N. M....	.....	.....	.....	.....	.....	.....	61,547	93,516	91,874	119,565
N. Y....	340,120	589,051	959,049	1,372,812	1,918,608	2,428,921	3,097,394	3,880,735	4,382,759	5,082,871
N. C....	393,751	478,103	555,500	638,829	737,987	753,419	869,039	992,622	1,071,361	1,399,750
N. D....	.....	.....	.....	.....	.....	.....	.....	.....	*2,405	36,909
Oh.....	.....	45,365	230,760	581,434	937,903	1,519,467	1,980,329	2,339,511	2,665,260	3,198,062
Okla.....	.....	.....	.....	.....	.....	.....	.....	.....	.....	.....
Ore.....	.....	.....	.....	.....	.....	.....	13,294	52,465	90,923	174,768
Pa.....	434,373	602,365	810,091	1,049,458	1,348,233	1,724,033	2,311,786	2,906,215	3,521,951	4,282,891
R. I.....	68,825	69,122	76,931	83,059	97,199	108,830	147,545	174,620	217,353	276,531
S. C.....	249,073	345,591	415,115	502,741	581,185	594,398	668,507	703,708	705,606	995,577
S. D.....	.....	.....	.....	.....	.....	.....	.....	*4,837	*11,776	98,268
Tenn....	35,691	105,602	261,727	422,823	681,904	829,210	1,002,717	1,109,801	1,258,520	1,542,359
Tex.....	.....	.....	.....	.....	.....	.....	212,592	604,215	818,579	1,591,749
Ut.....	.....	.....	.....	.....	.....	.....	11,380	40,273	86,786	143,963
Vt.....	85,425	154,465	217,895	235,981	280,652	291,948	314,120	315,098	330,551	332,286
Va.....	821,287	880,200	974,600	1,065,366	1,211,405	1,239,797	1,421,661	1,596,318	1,225,163	1,512,565
Wash....	.....	.....	.....	.....	.....	.....	1,201	11,594	23,955	75,116
W. Va....	.....	.....	.....	.....	.....	.....	.....	.....	442,014	618,457
Wis.....	.....	.....	.....	.....	.....	30,945	305,391	775,881	1,054,670	1,315,497
Wy.....	.....	.....	.....	.....	.....	.....	.....	.....	9,118	20,789
U.S.....	3,929,214	5,308,483	7,239,881	9,638,453	12,866,020	17,069,453	23,191,876	31,443,321	38,558,371	50,155,783

*1860 figure is for Dakota Territory; 1870 figures are for parts of Dakota Territory.

(1.) U.S. total includes persons (5,318 in 1830 and 6,100 in 1840) on public ships in the service of the United States not credited to any region, division, or state.

Density of Population by States

By Square Mile, Land Area Only

State	1920	1960	1970	State	1920	1960	1970	State	1920	1960	1970
Ala........	45.8	64.2	67.9	Ky........	60.1	76.2	81.2	N. D........	9.2	9.1	8.9
Alas.*.....	0.1	0.4	0.5	La.........	39.6	72.2	81.0	Oh.........	141.4	236.8	260.0
Ariz.......	2.9	11.5	15.6	Me.........	25.7	31.3	32.1	Okla.......	29.2	33.8	37.2
Ark.......	33.4	34.2	37.0	Md.........	145.8	313.5	396.6	Ore........	8.2	18.4	21.7
Cal.......	22.0	100.4	127.6	Mass......	479.2	657.3	727.0	Pa.........	194.5	251.4	262.3
Col.......	9.1	16.9	21.3	Mich......	63.8	137.6	156.2	R. I.......	566.4	819.3	905.5
Conn......	286.4	520.6	623.7	Minn......	29.5	43.0	48.0	S. C.......	55.2	78.7	85.7
Del.......	113.5	225.2	276.5	Miss......	38.6	46.0	46.9	S. D.......	8.3	9.0	8.8
D.C.......	7,292.9	12,523.9	12,401.8	Mo.........	49.5	62.6	67.8	Tenn.......	56.1	86.2	94.9
Fla.......	17.7	91.5	125.5	Mon.......	3.8	4.6	4.8	Tex........	17.8	36.4	42.7
Ga........	49.3	67.8	79.0	Neb.......	16.9	18.4	19.4	Ut.........	5.5	10.8	12.9
Ha.*......	39.9	98.5	119.8	Nev.......	.7	2.6	4.4	Vt.........	38.6	42.0	47.9
Ida.......	5.2	8.1	8.6	N. H.......	49.1	67.2	81.7	Va.........	57.4	99.5	116.9
Ill.......	115.7	180.4	199.4	N. J.......	420.0	805.5	953.1	Wash.......	20.3	42.8	51.2
Ind........	81.3	128.8	143.9	N. M.......	2.9	7.8	8.4	W. Va......	60.9	77.2	72.5
Ia.........	43.2	49.2	50.5	N. Y.......	217.9	350.6	381.3	Wis........	47.6	72.6	81.1
Kan.......	21.6	26.6	27.5	N. C.......	52.5	93.2	104.1	Wy........	2.0	3.4	3.4
								U.S........	*29.9	50.6	57.5

*For purposes of comparison, Alaska and Hawaii included in above tabulation for 1920, even though not states then.

Number of inhabitants per sq. mi. of land area in U.S. (1790) 4.5; (1800) 6.1; (1810) 4.3; (1820) 5.5; (1830) 7.4; (1840) 9.8; (1850) 7.9; (1860) 10.6; (1870) 13.0; (1880) 16.9; (1890) 21.2; (1900) 25.6; (1910) 31.0; (1920) 35.5; (1930) 41.2; (1940) 44.2; (1950) 50.7; (1960) 50.6; (1970) 57.5. (Alaska and Hawaii included in 1960 and 1970.)

. . . U.S. Population (Official Census) 1890-1970

Source: Bureau of the Census

State	1890	1900	1910	1920	1930	1940	1950	1960	1970
Ala.	1,513,401	1,828,697	2,138,093	2,348,174	2,646,248	2,832,961	3,061,743	3,266,740	3,444,164
Alaska.								226,167	302,173
Ariz.	88,243	122,931	204,354	334,162	435,573	499,261	749,587	1,302,161	1,772,482
Ark.	1,128,211	1,311,564	1,574,449	1,752,204	1,854,482	1,949,387	1,909,511	1,786,272	1,923,295
Cal.	1,213,398	1,485,053	2,377,549	3,426,861	5,677,251	6,907,387	10,586,223	15,717,204	19,953,134
Col.	413,249	539,700	799,024	939,629	1,035,791	1,123,296	1,325,089	1,753,947	2,207,259
Conn.	746,258	908,420	1,114,756	1,380,631	1,606,903	1,709,242	2,007,280	2,535,234	3,032,217
Del.	168,493	184,735	202,322	223,003	238,380	266,505	318,085	446,292	548,104
D.C.	230,392	278,718	331,069	437,571	486,869	663,091	802,178	763,956	756,510
Fla.	391,422	528,542	752,619	968,470	1,468,211	1,897,414	2,771,305	4,951,560	6,789,443
Ga.	1,837,353	2,216,331	2,609,121	2,895,832	2,908,506	3,123,723	3,444,578	3,943,116	4,589,575
Ha.								632,772	769,913
Ida.	88,548	161,772	325,594	431,866	445,032	524,873	588,637	667,191	713,008
Ill.	3,826,352	4,821,550	5,638,591	6,485,280	7,630,654	7,897,241	8,712,176	10,081,158	11,113,976
Ind.	2,192,404	2,516,462	2,700,876	2,930,390	3,238,503	3,427,796	3,934,224	4,662,498	5,193,669
Iowa.	1,912,297	2,231,853	2,224,771	2,404,021	2,470,939	2,538,268	2,621,073	2,757,537	2,825,041
Kan.	1,428,108	1,470,495	1,690,949	1,769,257	1,880,999	1,801,028	1,905,299	2,178,611	2,249,071
Ky.	1,858,635	2,147,174	2,289,905	2,416,630	2,614,589	2,845,627	2,944,806	3,038,156	3,219,311
La.	1,118,588	1,381,625	1,656,388	1,798,509	2,101,593	2,363,880	2,683,516	3,257,022	3,643,180
Me.	661,086	694,466	742,371	768,014	797,423	847,226	913,774	969,265	993,663
Md.	1,042,390	1,188,044	1,295,346	1,449,661	1,631,526	1,821,244	2,343,001	3,100,689	3,922,399
Mass.	2,238,947	2,805,346	3,366,416	3,852,356	4,249,614	4,316,721	4,690,514	5,148,578	5,689,170
Mich.	2,093,890	2,420,982	2,810,173	3,668,412	4,842,325	5,256,106	6,371,766	7,823,194	8,875,083
Minn.	1,310,283	1,751,394	2,075,708	2,387,125	2,563,953	2,792,300	2,982,483	3,413,864	3,805,069
Miss.	1,289,600	1,551,270	1,797,114	1,790,618	2,009,821	2,183,796	2,178,914	2,178,141	2,216,912
Mo.	2,679,185	3,106,665	3,293,335	3,404,055	3,629,367	3,784,664	3,954,653	4,319,813	4,677,399
Mon.	142,924	243,329	376,053	548,889	537,606	559,456	591,024	674,767	694,409
Neb.	1,062,656	1,066,300	1,192,214	1,296,372	1,377,963	1,315,834	1,325,510	1,411,330	1,483,791
Nev.	47,355	42,335	81,875	77,407	91,058	110,247	160,083	285,278	488,738
N.H.	376,530	411,588	430,572	443,083	465,293	491,524	533,242	606,921	737,681
N.J.	1,444,933	1,883,669	2,537,167	3,155,900	4,041,334	4,160,165	4,835,329	6,066,782	7,168,164
N.M.	160,282	195,310	327,301	360,350	423,317	531,818	681,187	951,023	1,016,000
N.Y.	6,003,174	7,268,894	9,113,614	10,385,227	12,588,066	13,479,142	14,830,192	16,782,304	18,241,266
N.C.	1,617,949	1,893,810	2,206,287	2,559,123	3,170,276	3,571,623	4,061,929	4,556,155	5,082,059
N.D.	190,983	319,146	577,056	646,872	680,845	641,935	619,636	632,446	617,761
Oh.	3,672,329	4,157,545	4,767,121	5,759,394	6,646,697	6,907,612	7,946,627	9,706,397	10,652,017
Okla.	258,657	790,391	1,657,155	2,028,283	2,396,040	2,336,434	2,233,351	2,328,284	2,559,253
Ore.	317,704	413,536	672,765	783,389	953,786	1,089,684	1,521,341	1,768,687	2,091,385
Pa.	5,258,113	6,302,115	7,665,111	8,720,017	9,631,350	9,900,180	10,498,012	11,319,366	11,793,909
R.I.	345,506	428,556	542,610	604,397	687,497	713,346	791,896	859,488	949,723
S.C.	1,151,149	1,340,316	1,515,400	1,683,724	1,738,765	1,899,804	2,117,027	2,382,594	2,509,516
S.D.	348,600	401,570	583,888	636,547	692,849	642,961	652,740	680,514	666,257
Tenn.	1,767,518	2,020,616	2,184,789	2,337,885	2,616,556	2,915,841	3,291,718	3,567,089	3,924,164
Tex.	2,235,527	3,048,710	3,896,542	4,663,228	5,824,715	6,414,824	7,711,194	9,579,677	11,196,730
Ut.	210,779	276,749	373,351	449,396	507,847	550,310	688,862	890,627	1,059,273
Vt.	332,422	343,641	355,956	352,428	359,611	359,231	377,747	389,881	444,732
Va.	1,655,980	1,854,184	2,061,612	2,309,187	2,421,851	2,677,773	3,318,680	3,966,949	4,648,494
Wash.	357,232	518,103	1,141,990	1,356,621	1,563,396	1,736,191	3,378,962	2,853,214	3,409,169
W. Va.	762,794	958,800	1,221,119	1,463,701	1,729,205	1,901,974	2,005,553	1,860,421	1,744,237
Wis.	1,693,330	2,069,042	2,333,860	2,632,067	2,939,006	3,137,583	3,434,575	3,951,777	4,417,933
Wy.	62,555	92,531	145,965	194,402	225,565	250,742	290,529	330,066	332,416
Tot. U.S.	62,947,714	75,994,575	91,972,266	105,710,620	122,775,046	131,669,275	150,697,361	179,323,175	203,235,298

Members of the Armed Forces overseas or other U.S. nationals overseas are not included.

U.S. Center of Population, 1790-1970

Center of population is that point which may be considered as center of population gravity of the U.S. or that point upon which the U.S. would balance if it were a rigid plane without weight and the population distributed thereon with each individual being assumed to have equal weight and to exert an influence on a central point proportional to his distance from that point.

Year	N.Lat. ° ' "			W.Long. ° ' "			Approximate location
1790	39	16	30	76	11	12	23 miles east of Baltimore, Md.
1800	39	16	6	76	56	30	18 miles west of Baltimore, Md.
1810	39	11	30	77	37	12	40 miles northwest by west of Washington, D.C. (in Va.)
1820	39	5	42	78	33	0	16 miles east of Moorefield, W. Va.[1]
1830	38	57	54	79	16	54	19 miles west-southwest of Moorefield, W. Va.[1]
1840	39	2	0	80	18	0	16 miles south of Clarksburg, W. Va.[1]
1850	38	59	0	81	19	0	23 miles southeast of Parkersburg, W. Va.[1]
1860	39	0	24	82	48	48	20 miles south by east of Chillicothe, Oh.
1870	39	12	0	83	35	42	48 miles east by north of Cincinnati, Oh.
1880	39	4	8	84	39	40	8 miles west by south of Cincinnati, Oh. (in Ky.)
1890	39	11	56	85	32	53	20 miles east of Columbus, Ind.
1900	39	9	36	85	48	54	6 miles southeast of Columbus, Ind.
1910	39	10	12	86	32	20	In the city of Bloomington, Ind.
1920	39	10	21	86	43	15	8 miles south-southeast of Spencer, Owen County, Ind.
1930	39	3	45	87	8	6	3 miles northeast of Linton, Greene County, Ind.
1940	38	56	54	87	22	35	2 miles southeast by east of Carlisle, Haddon township, Sullivan County, Ind.
1950 (Inc. Alaska & Hawaii)	38	48	15	88	22	8	3 miles northeast of Louisville, Clay County, Ill.
1960 (Inc. Alaska & Hawaii)	38	35	58	89	12	35	6 1/2 miles northwest of Centralia, Ill.
1970 (Inc. Alaska & Hawaii)	38	27	47	89	42	22	5 miles east southeast of Mascoutah, St. Clair County, Ill.

(1) West Virginia was set off from Virginia Dec. 31, 1862, and admitted as a State June 20,1863.

Rankings of U.S. Standard Metropolitan Statistical Areas

Source: Bureau of the Census

Metropolitan areas are ranked by 1974 provisional population size based on new SMSA definitions and compared with a ranking of areas as defined in the 1970 census. Included are 259 of the 272 Standard Metropolitan Statistical Areas (SMSA's) as defined through December 1975 by the Office of Management and Budget, excluding 4 areas in Puerto Rico not covered in the report.

Asterisk (*) indicates 13 New England County Metropolitan Areas comprised of 26 New England SMSA's.

SMSA	1974 (P) Rank	Pop.	1970 Rank	Pop.
New York, N.Y.-N.J.	1	9,634,400	1	9,973,716
Chicago, Ill.	2	6,971,200	3	6,977,611
Los Angeles-Long Beach, Cal.	3	6,926,100	2	7,041,980
Philadelphia, Pa.-N.J.	4	4,809,900	4	4,824,110
Detroit, Mich.	5	4,434,300	5	4,435,051
Boston-Lowell-Brockton-Lawrence-Haverhill, Mass.-N.H.*	6	3,918,400	6	3,848,593
San Francisco-Oakland, Cal.	7	3,135,900	7	3,108,782
Washington, D.C.-Md.-Va.	8	3,015,300	8	2,910,111
Nassau-Suffolk, N.Y.[1]	9	2,620,700	9	2,555,868
Dallas-Ft. Worth, Tex.[3]	10	2,498,500	12	2,378,353
St. Louis, Mo.-Ill.	11	2,371,400	10	2,410,492
Pittsburgh, Pa.	12	2,333,600	11	2,401,362
Houston, Tex.	13	2,222,700	16	1,999,316
Baltimore, Md.	14	2,140,400	13	2,071,016
Newark, N.J.	15	2,019,200	15	2,057,468
Minneapolis-St. Paul, Minn.-Wis.	16	2,010,800	17	1,965,391
Cleveland, Oh.	17	1,984,100	14	2,063,729
Atlanta, Ga.	18	1,776,000	18	1,595,517
Anaheim-Santa Ana-Garden Grove, Cal.	19	1,660,900	20	1,421,233
San Diego, Cal.	20	1,518,000	23	1,357,854
Miami, Fla.	21	1,415,900	26	1,267,792
Milwaukee, Wis.	22	1,415,400	21	1,403,884
Seattle-Everett, Wash.	23	1,396,400	19	1,424,605
Denver-Boulder, Col.	24	1,391,100	27	1,239,477
Cincinnati, Oh.-Ky.-Ind.	25	1,375,800	22	1,385,103
Tampa-St. Petersburg, Fla.	26	1,332,900	30	1,088,549
Buffalo, N.Y.	27	1,330,700	24	1,349,211
Kansas City, Mo.-Kans.	28	1,301,600	25	1,273,926
Riverside-San Bernardino-Ontario, Cal.	29	1,213,900	28	1,141,307
San Jose, Cal.	30	1,181,600	31	1,065,313
Phoenix, Ariz.	31	1,172,200	36	969,425
Indianapolis, Ind.	32	1,143,700	29	1,111,352
New Orleans, La.	33	1,090,200	32	1,046,470
Portland, Ore.-Wash.	34	1,079,700	34	1,007,130
Columbus, Oh.	35	1,067,000	33	1,017,847
Hartford-New Britain-Bristol, Conn.*	36	1,058,700	35	1,035,195
San Antonio, Tex.	37	979,900	38	888,179
Rochester, N.Y.	38	966,400	37	961,516
Louisville, Ky.-Ind.	39	892,500	39	867,330
Sacramento, Cal.	40	882,600	42	803,793
Providence-Warwick-Pawtucket, R.I.*	41	854,400	45	855,495
Memphis, Tenn.-Ark.-Miss.	42	853,100	41	834,103
Dayton, Oh.	43	844,800	40	852,531
Fort Lauderdale-Hollywood, Fla.	44	806,800	61	620,100
Albany-Schenectady-Troy, N.Y.	45	799,400	44	777,977
Bridgeport-Stamford-Norwalk-Danbury, Conn.*	46	791,000	43	792,814
Birmingham, Ala.	47	785,000	46	767,230
Toledo, Ohio-Mich.	48	781,000	47	762,658
Oklahoma City, Okla.	49	766,200	53	699,092
Norfolk-Virginia Beach-Portsmouth, Va.-N.C.	50	766,000	49	732,600
Salt Lake City-Ogden Ut.[3]	51	765,500	51	705,458
New Haven-West Haven-Waterbury-Meriden, Conn.*	52	759,700	48	744,948
Greensboro-Winston-Salem-High Point, N.C.	53	759,500	50	724,129
Nashville-Davidson, Tenn.	54	744,600	52	699,271
Honolulu, Hawaii.	55	691,200	58	630,528
Jacksonville, Fla.	56	674,900	60	621,827
Akron, Ohio.	57	671,300	54	679,239
Worcester-Fitchburg-Leominster, Mass.*	58	648,400	55	637,037
Syracuse, N.Y.	59	645,800	56	636,596
Gary-Hammond-East Chicago, Ind.	60	643,900	57	633,367
Northeast Pennsylvania[3].	61	633,100	59	621,882
Allentown-Bethlehem-Easton, Pa.-N.J.	62	616,600	63	594,382
New Brunswick-Perth Amboy-Sayreville, N.J.[1].	63	590,200	64	583,813
Springfield-Chicopee-Holyoke, Mass.*	64	589,700	65	583,031
Charlotte-Gastonia, N.C.	65	589,300	66	557,785
Jersey City, N.J.	66	583,000	62	607,839
Orlando, Fla.	67	578,600	77	453,270
Tulsa, Okla.	68	576,100	67	549,154
Omaha, Nebr.-Ia.	69	575,100	68	542,646
Richmond, Va.	70	569,500	69	542,242
Grand Rapids, Mich.	71	558,700	70	539,225
Youngstown-Warren, Oh.	72	542,900	71	537,124
Greenville-Spartanburg, S. C.	73	522,200	74	473,454
Flint, Mich.	74	522,200	72	508,664
Wilmington, Del.-N.J.-Md.	75	513,300	73	499,493
Long Branch-Asbury Park, N.J.[1]	76	485,700	75	461,849
New Bedford/Fall River, Mass.*	77	463,700	78	444,301
Raleigh/Durham, N.C.[3].	78	462,300	80	419,394
Paterson/Clifton-Passaic, N.J.	79	456,200	76	460,782
West Palm Beach-Boca Raton, Fla.	80	433,600	96	348,993
Lansing-East Lansing, Mich.	81	440,600	79	424,271
Fresno, Cal.	82	439,400	81	413,329
Tucson, Ariz.	83	433,500	95	351,667
Oxnard-Simi Valley-Ventura, Cal.	84	430,200	87	378,497
Knoxville, Tenn.	85	427,700	84	409,409
Harrisburg, Pa.	86	425,500	83	410,505
El Paso, Tex.	87	410,000	94	359,291
Baton Rouge, La.	88	407,200	89	375,628
Canton, Oh.	89	404,500	85	393,789
Tacoma, Wash.	90	397,600	82	412,344
Mobile, Ala.	91	396,400	88	476,690
Johnson City-Kingsport-Bristol, Tenn.-Va.[1].	92	391,700	90	373,591
Chattanooga, Tenn.-Ga.	93	390,300	91	370,857
Austin, Tex.	94	388,600	107	323,158
Wichita, Kans.	95	379,000	86	389,352
Albuquerque, N.M.	96	378,900	102	333,266
Fort Wayne, Ind.	97	373,200	93	361,984
Davenport-Rock Island-Moline, Ia.-Ill.	98	364,400	92	362,638
Charleston-North Charleston, S. C.	99	362,000	100	336,125
Columbia, S.C.	100	360,800	108	322,880
Little Rock-North Little Rock, Ark.	101	356,100	106	323,296
Peoria, Ill.	102	352,000	98	341,979
Newport News-Hampton, Va.	103	346,800	103	333,140
York, Pa.	104	345,900	105	329,540
Beaumont-Port Arthur-Orange, Tex.	105	344,600	97	347,568
Shreveport, La.	106	343,400	101	333,826
Utica-Rome, N.Y.	107	337,900	99	340,670
Lancaster, Pa.	108	337,900	109	320,079
Bakersfield, Cal.	109	337,600	104	330,234
Des Moines, Ia.	110	328,400	110	313,562
Las Vegas, Nev.	111	319,600	124	273,288
Trenton, N.J.	112	319,100	111	304,116
Reading, Pa.	113	304,500	113	296,382
Spokane, Wash.	114	303,800	116	287,487
Madison, Wis.	115	303,000	115	290,272
Binghamton, N. Y.-Pa.	116	300,400	112	302,672
Stockton, Cal.	117	299,200	114	291,073
Corpus Christi, Tex.	118	295,100	119	284,832
Colorado Springs, Col.	119	293,200	138	239,288

SMSA	1974(P) Rank	Pop.	1970 Rank	Pop.
Huntington-Ashland, W. Va.-Ky.-Oh.	120	290,400	117	286,935
Evansville, Ind.-Ky.	121	288,600	118	284,959
Lexington-Fayette, Ky.	122	286,300	126	266,701
Huntsville, Ala.	123	285,200	120	282,450
Appleton-Oshkosh, Wis.	124	281,800	122	276,948
Santa Barbara-Santa Maria-Lompoc, Cal.	125	281,800	128	264,324
South Bend, Ind.	126	280,400	121	280,031
Jackson, Miss.	127	278,600	131	258,906
Augusta, Ga.-S. C.	128	273,900	123	275.787
Erie, Pa.	129	273,700	129	263,654
Rockford, Ill.	130	270,300	125	272,063
Vallejo-Fairfield-Napa, Cal.	131	267,700	135	251,129
Johnstown, Pa.	132	266,000	130	262,822
Lorain-Elyria, Oh.	133	265,800	134	156,843
Pensacola, Fla.	134	263,600	137	243,075
Lakeland-Winter Haven, Fla.[1]	135	263,200	143	228,515
Duluth-Superior, Minn.-Wis.	136	262,200	127	265,350
Kalamazoo-Portage, Mich.	137	261,600	132	257,723
Salinas-Seaside-Monterey, Cal.	138	260,600	136	247,450
Charlestown, W. Va.	139	253,700	133	257,140
Ann Arbor, Mich.	140	250,100	140	234,103
Montgomery, Ala.	141	248,400	146	225,911
Santa Rosa, Cal.	142	242,600	154	204,885
Hamilton-Middletown, Oh.	143	242,300	145	226,207
New London-Norwich, Conn.[*]	144	239,700	141	230,654
Manchester-Nashua, N.H.[*]	145	238,500	147	223,941
Eugene-Springfield, Ore.	146	236,600	150	215,401
Macon, Ga.	147	235,500	144	226,782
Poughkeepsie, N.Y.[1]	148	233,300	148	222,295
Melbourne-Titusville-Cocoa, Fla.[1]	149	229,400	142	230,006
Portland, Me.[*]	150	227,300	157	225,386
Saginaw, Mich.	151	226,900	149	219,743
Fayetteville, N.C.	152	223,100	151	212,042
Columbus, Ga.-Ala.	153	218,000	139	238,584
McAllen-Pharr-Edinburg, Tex.	154	217,600	161	181,535
Roanoke, Va.	155	212,200	155	203,153
Modesto, Cal.	156	211,100	156	194,506
Lima, Ohio	157	210,800	152	210,074
Killeen-Temple, Tex.[1]	158	202,200	180	159,794
Salem, Ore.	159	201,800	159	186,658
Daytona Beach, Fla.[1]	160	199,600	171	169,487
Savannah, Ga.	161	199,100	153	207,987
Lubbock, Tex.	162	194,500	164	179,295
Atlantic City, N.J.	163	190,000	167	175,043
Springfield, Mo.	164	187,500	158	187,606
Springfield, Mo.	165	187,400	172	168,053
Wheeling, W. Va.-Oh.	166	182,900	160	181,954
Lincoln, Nebr.	167	182,200	173	167,972
Battle Creek, Mich.	168	181,900	163	180,129
Topeka, Kans.	169	179,500	162	180,619
Galveston-Texas City, Tex.	170	179,100	170	169,812
Springfield, Ill.	171	177,500	168	171,020
Muskegon-Norton Shores-Muskegon Heights, Mich.[1]	172	176,700	165	175,410
Terre Haute, Ind.	173	173,700	166	175,143
Racine, Wis.	174	173,500	169	170,838
Biloxi-Gulfport, Miss.	175	173,200	179	160,070
Fort Smith, Ark.-Okla.	176	172,700	178	160,421
Brownsville-Harlingen-San Benito, Tex.	177	168,300	189	140,368
Steubenville-Weirton, Oh.-W. Va.	178	166,800	174	165,627
Green Bay, Wis.	179	166,600	181	158,244
Asheville, N.C.	180	166,300	177	161,059
Cedar Rapids, Ia.	181	164,600	176	163,213
Provo-Orem, Ut.	182	163,000	191	137,776
Champaign-Urbana-Ranroul, Ill.	183	163,000	175	163,281
Sarasota, Fla.[1]	184	158,900	209	120,413
Waco, Tex.	185	154,400	184	147,553
Fort Myers, Fla.[1]	186	154,100	228	105,216
Yakima, Wash.[1]	187	151,200	186	145,212
Pittsfield, Mass.[*]	188	150,500	182	149,402
Amarillo, Tex.	189	150,200	187	144,396
Parkersburg-Marietta, W. Va.-Oh.[2]	190	150,000	183	148,132
Lake Charles, La.	191	149,300	185	145,415
Anchorage, Alas.	192	148,800	202	126,385

SMSA	1974 (P) Rank	Pop.	1970 Rank	Pop.
St. Cloud, Minn.[1]	193	148,300	193	134,585
Santa Cruz, Cal.[1]	194	147,200	204	123,790
Jackson, Mich.	195	145,000	188	143,274
Fayetteville-Springdale, Ark.[1]	196	144,900	201	127,846
Reno, Nev.[1]	197	142,700	207	121,068
Lynchburg, Va.	198	141,500	194	133,258
Clarksville-Hopkinsville, Tenn.-Ky.[1]	199	140,000	211	118,945
Anderson, Ind.	200	139,400	190	138,522
Alexandria, La.[2]	201	136,100	196	131,749
Altoona, Pa.	202	135,600	192	135,356
Tallahassee, Fla.	203	132,700	225	109,355
Waterloo-Cedar Falls, Ia.	204	132,300	195	132,916
Boise City, Ida.	205	131,500	222	112,230
Vineland-Millville-Bridgeton, N.J.	206	131,400	206	121,374
Mansfield, Oh.	207	131,200	197	129,997
Muncie, Ind.	208	130,600	198	129,219
Abilene, Tex.	209	128,400	205	122,164
Wichita Falls, Tex.	210	127,300	200	128,642
Wilmington, N.C.	211	126,900	227	107,219
Fargo-Moorhead, N. Dak.-Minn.	212	125,600	210	120,261
Decatur, Ill.	213	125,200	203	125,010
Petersburg-Colonial Heights-Hopewell, Va.	214	124,300	199	128,809
Pueblo, Col.	215	124,300	212	118,238
Longview, Tex.	216	124,200	208	120,770
Gainesville, Fla.	217	124,000	229	104,764
Eau Claire, Wis.	218	123,700	219	114,936
Monroe, La.	219	122,600	218	115,387
Tuscaloosa, Ala.	220	122,500	217	116,029
Lafayette, La.	221	122,200	223	111,643
Kenosha, Wis.	222	122,100	213	117,917
Florence, Ala.[1]	223	120,900	214	117,743
Bay City, Mich.	224	119,400	215	117,339
Sioux City, Ia.-Neb.	225	118,500	216	116,189
Williamsport, Pa.[1]	226	116,400	221	113,296
Fort Collins, Col.	227	114,900	244	89,900
Bloomington-Normal, Ill.	228	114,400	230	104,389
Texarkana, Tex.-Ark.	229	114,200	226	113,488
Lafayette-West Lafayette, Ind.	230	112,200	224	109,378
Greeley, Col.	231	106,600	245	89,297
Anniston, Ala.[1]	232	105,900	231	103,092
Tyler, Tex.	233	105,700	235	97,096
Lawton, Okla.	234	105,400	226	108,144
Pascagoula-Moss Point, Miss.	235	104,200	246	87,975
Albany, Ga.	236	100,700	236	96,683
St. Joseph, Mo.	237	99,400	233	98,828
Burlington, N.C.[1]	238	99,400	237	96,362
Elmira, N.Y.[1]	239	99,300	232	101,537
Sioux Falls, S. D.	240	98,400	238	95,209
Richland-Kennewick, Wash.[1]	241	97,100	240	93,356
Kankakee, Ill.[1]	242	95,900	234	97,250
Lewiston-Auburn, Me.[*]	243	94,700	242	91,279
Gadsden, Ala.	244	94,700	239	94,144
Billings, Mont.	245	94,500	247	87,367
Odessa, Tex.	246	93,900	241	92,660
Dubuque, Ia.	247	91,600	243	90,609
Bloomington, Ind.	248	89,100	249	85,221
Rochester, Minn.	249	88,600	250	84,104
Columbia, Mo.	250	86,400	253	80,935
Great Falls, Mont.	251	84,400	252	81,804
Pine Bluff, Ark.	252	84,000	248	85,329
La Crosse, Wis.	253	83,300	254	80,468
Owensboro, Ky.	254	81,000	255	79,486
Laredo, Tex.	255	78,100	256	72,859
Sherman-Denison, Tex.	256	77,500	251	83,225
San Angelo, Tex.	257	74,600	257	71,047
Bryan-College Station, Tex.	258	67,900	259	47,978
Midland, Tex.	259	66,000	258	65,433

(1) New SMSA established since 1970 census.
(2) New SMSA established in Nov. 1971, and area definition changed in Apr. 1973.
(3) Merger of two existing SMSAs since 1970 census; rank and population given for 1970 definition refer to the larger of the two merged SMSAs.

How the Cities Grew
Source: Bureau of the Census
(Cities over 100,000 ranked by 1973 population estimates)

Rank	City	1973 Est.	1970	1960	1950	1900	1850	1790
1	New York, N.Y.	7,646,818	7,895,563	7,781,984	7,891,957	3,437,202	¹696,115	¹49,401
	Bronx boro.	1,424,327	1,471,701	1,424,815	1,451,277	200,507	8,032	1,781
	Brooklyn boro.	2,485,477	2,602,012	2,627,319	2,738,175	1,166,582	138,882	4,495
	Manhattan boro.	1,456,362	1,539,233	1,698,281	1,960,101	1,850,093	515,547	33,131
	Queens boro.	1,965,912	1,986,473	1,809,578	1,550,849	152,999	18,593	6,159
	Staten Is. boro	314,740	295,443	221,991	191,555	67,021	15,061	3,835
2	Chicago, Ill.	3,172,929	3,369,357	3,550,404	3,620,962	1,698,575	29,963	. . .
3	Los Angeles, Cal.	2,746,854	2,809,813	2,479,015	1,970,358	102,479	1,610	. . .
4	Philadelphia, Pa.	1,861,719	1,949,996	2,002,512	2,071,605	1,293,697	121,376	28,522
5	Detroit, Mich.	1,386,817	1,514,063	1,670,144	1,849,568	285,704	21,019	. . .
6	Houston, Tex.	1,320,018	1,233,535	938,219	596,163	44,633	2,396	. . .
7	Baltimore, Md.	877,838	905,787	939,024	949,708	508,957	169,054	13,603
8	Dallas, Tex.	815,866	844,401	679,684	434,462	42,638	. . .	. . .
9	San Diego, Cal.	757,148	697,027	573,224	334,387	17,700	. . .	. . .
10	San Antonio, Tex.	756,226	707,503	587,718	408,442	53,321	3,488	. . .
11	Indianapolis, Ind.	738,657	742,674	476,258	427,173	169,164	8,091	. . .
12	Washington, D.C.	733,801	756,668	763,956	802,178	278,718	40,001	. . .
13	Milwaukee, Wis.	690,685	717,372	741,324	637,392	285,315	20,061	. . .
14	San Francisco, Cal.	687,450	715,674	740,316	775,357	342,782	²34,776	. . .
15	Cleveland, Oh.	678,615	750,879	876,050	914,808	381,768	17,034	. . .
16	Memphis, Tenn.	658,868	623,530	497,524	396,000	102,320	8,841	. . .
17	Phoenix, Ariz.	637,121	587,213	439,170	106,818	5,544	. . .	. . .
18	Boston, Mass.	618,275	641,071	697,197	801,444	560,892	136,881	18,320
19	New Orleans, La.	573,479	593,471	627,525	570,445	287,104	116,375	. . .
20	St. Louis, Mo.	558,000	622,236	750,026	856,796	575,238	77,860	. . .
21	Jacksonville, Fla.	548,007	528,865	201,030	204,517	28,429	1,045	. . .
22	Columbus, Oh.	540,933	540,025	471,316	375,901	125,560	17,832	. . .
23	San Jose, Cal.	523,116	459,913	204,196	95,280	21,500	. . .	. . .
24	Denver, Col.	515,593	514,678	493,887	415,786	133,859	. . .	. . .
25	Seattle, Wash.	503,073	530,831	557,087	467,591	80,671	. . .	. . .
26	Kansas City, Mo.	487,799	507,330	475,539	456,622	163,752	. . .	. . .
27	Pittsburgh, Pa.	479,276	520,089	604,332	676,806	321,616	46,601	. . .
28	Atlanta, Ga.	451,123	495,039	487,455	331,314	89,872	2,572	. . .
29	Nashville, Tenn.³	449,109	447,877	170,874	174,307	80,865	10,165	. . .
30	Cincinnati, Oh.	426,245	451,410	502,550	503,998	325,902	115,435	. . .
31	Buffalo, N.Y.	425,101	462,768	532,759	580,132	352,387	42,261	. . .
32	Minneapolis, Minn.	382,423	434,400	482,872	521,718	202,718	. . .	. . .
33	Portland, Ore.	378,134	379,967	372,676	373,628	90,426	. . .	. . .
34	Toledo, Oh.	377,423	383,062	318,003	303,616	131,822	3,829	. . .
35	Omaha, Neb.	377,292	354,389	301,598	251,117	102,555	. . .	. . .
36	Oklahoma City, Okla.	373,717	368,164	324,253	243,504	10,037	. . .	. . .
37	Newark, N.J.	367,683	381,930	405,220	438,776	246,070	38,894	. . .
38	Fort Worth, Tex.	359,542	393,476	356,263	278,778	26,688	. . .	. . .
39	Miami, Fla.	353,984	334,859	291,688	249,276	1,681	. . .	. . .
40	El Paso, Tex.	353,226	322,261	276,687	130,435	15,906	. . .	. . .
41	Long Beach, Cal.	346,793	358,879	344,168	250,767	2,252	. . .	. . .
42	Oakland, Cal.	345,880	361,561	367,548	384,575	66,960	. . .	. . .
43	Honolulu, Ha.	338,148	324,871	294,194	248,034	39,306	. . .	. . .
44	Louisville, Ky.	335,696	361,706	390,639	369,129	204,731	43,194	200
45	Tulsa, Okla.	335,444	330,350	261,685	182,740	1,390	. . .	. . .
46	Tucson, Ariz.	307,551	265,799	212,892	45,454	7,531	. . .	. . .
47	Birmingham, Ala.	295,686	300,910	340,887	326,037	38,415	. . .	. . .
48	Austin, Tex.	291,214	251,808	186,545	132,459	22,258	629	. . .
49	St. Paul, Minn.	287,305	309,866	313,411	311,349	163,065	1,112	. . .
50	Charlotte, N.C.	284,738	274,640	201,564	134,042	18,091	1,065	. . .
51	Norfolk, Va.	283,064	307,951	304,869	213,513	46,624	14,326	2,959
52	Rochester, N.Y.	276,796	295,011	318,611	332,488	162,608	36,403	. . .
53	Tampa, Fla.	275,643	277,714	274,970	124,681	15,839	. . .	. . .
54	Albuquerque, N.M.	273,902	243,751	201,189	96,815	6,238	. . .	. . .
55	Sacramento, Cal.	267,483	257,105	191,667	137,572	29,282	6,820	. . .
56	Akron, Oh.	261,520	275,425	290,351	274,605	42,728	3,266	. . .
57	Wichita, Kan.	261,231	276,554	254,698	168,279	24,671	. . .	. . .
58	Jersey City, N.J.	255,030	260,350	276,101	299,017	206,433	6,856	. . .
59	Richmond, Va.	238,087	249,431	219,958	230,310	85,050	27,570	3,761
60	St. Petersburg, Fla.	234,284	216,159	181,298	96,738	1,575	. . .	. . .
61	Dayton, Oh.	214,377	242,917	262,332	243,872	85,333	10,977	. . .
62	Corpus Christi, Tex.	212,431	204,525	167,690	108,287	4,703	. . .	. . .
63	Virginia Beach, Va.	199,613	172,106	8,091	5,390	. . .	. . .	. . .
64	Des Moines, Ia.	199,145	201,404	208,982	177,965	62,139	. . .	. . .
65	Yonkers, N.Y.	195,542	204,297	190,634	152,798	47,931	. . .	. . .
66	Grand Rapids, Mich.	190,696	197,649	177,313	176,515	87,565	2,686	. . .
67	Mobile, Ala.	188,531	190,026	194,856	129,009	38,469	20,515	. . .
68	Anaheim, Cal.	186,842	166,408	104,184	14,566	1,456	. . .	. . .
69	Fort Wayne, Ind.	185,488	178,021	161,776	133,607	45,115	4,282	. . .
70	Syracuse, N.Y.	184,710	197,297	216,038	220,583	103,374	22,271	. . .
71	Lexington, Ky.	184,603	174,323	62,810	55,534	26,369	8,159	834
72	Shreveport, La.	184,030	182,064	164,372	127,206	16,013	1,728	. . .
73	Knoxville, Tenn.	182,276	174,587	111,827	124,769	32,637	2,076	. . .
74	Flint, Mich.	181,684	193,317	196,940	163,143	13,103	. . .	. . .
75	Gary, Ind.	177,925	188,398	178,320	133,911	. . .	. . .	. . .
76	Warren, Mich.	175,927	179,260	89,246	727	350	. . .	. . .
77	Colorado Springs, Col.	175,745	135,060	70,194	45,472	21,083	. . .	. . .
78	Fresno, Cal.	174,882	165,655	133,929	91,669	12,470	. . .	. . .
79	Spokane, Wash.	173,971	170,516	181,608	161,721	36,848	. . .	. . .

Rank	City	1973 Est.	1970	1960	1950	1900	1850	1790
80	Baton Rouge, La.	173,872	165,921	152,419	125,629	11,269	3,905	. . .
81	Kansas City, Kans.	172,994	178,561	121,901	129,553	51,418	. . .	. . .
82	Worcester, Mass.	170,730	176,572	186,587	203,486	118,421	17,049	2,095
83	Providence, R.I.	169,931	179,116	207,493	248,674	175,597	41,513	6,380
84	Madison, Wis.	169,749	171,809	126,706	96,056	19,164	1,525	. . .
85	Salt Lake City, Ut.	169,234	175,885	189,454	182,121	53,531	. . .	. . .
86	Santa Ana, Cal.	167,905	155,710	100,350	45,533	4,933	. . .	. . .
87	Jackson, Miss.	163,924	162,380	144,422	98,271	7,816	1,881	. . .
88	Lincoln, Neb.	163,440	149,518	128,521	98,884	40,169	. . .	. . .
89	Columbus, Ga.	161,208	167,377	116,779	79,611	17,614	5,942	. . .
90	Springfield, Mass.	160,358	163,905	174,463	162,399	62,059	11,766	1,574
91	Fort Lauderdale, Fla.	155,605	139,590	83,648	36,328	. . .	. . .	. . .
92	Greensboro, N.C.	155,514	144,076	119,574	74,389	10,035	. . .	. . .
93	Riverside, Cal.	154,618	140,089	84,332	46,764	7,973	. . .	. . .
94	Lubbock, Tex.	153,752	149,101	128,691	71,747	. . .	. . .	. . .
95	Montgomery, Ala.	153,013	140,102	134,393	106,525	30,346	8,728	. . .
96	Tacoma, Wash.	149,420	154,407	147,979	143,673	37,714	. . .	. . .
97	Hartford, Conn.	148,526	158,017	162,178	177,397	72,850	13,555	2,683
98	Bridgeport, Conn.	148,337	156,542	156,748	158,709	70,996	6,080	. . .
99	Las Vegas, Nev.	144,333	125,787	64,405	24,624	. . .	. . .	. . .
100	Paterson, N.J.	143,372	144,824	143,663	139,336	105,171	11,334	. . .
101	Rockford, Ill.	142,173	147,370	126,706	92,927	31,051	. . .	. . .
102	Little Rock, Ark.	142,065	132,483	107,813	102,213	38,307	2,167	. . .
103	Huntington Bch., Cal.	140,706	115,960	11,492	5,237	. . .	. . .	. . .
104	Winston-Salem, N.C.	139,711	133,683	111,135	87,811	13,650	. . .	. . .
105	Chattanooga, Tenn.	137,957	141,904	130,009	131,041	30,154	. . .	. . .
106	Newport News, Va.	137,827	138,177	113,662	42,358	19,635	. . .	. . .
107	Huntsville, Ala.	137,750	139,282	72,365	16,437	8,068	2,863	. . .
108	Evansville, Ind.	136,165	138,764	141,543	128,635	59,007	3,235	. . .
109	Topeka, Kan.	136,059	132,952	119,484	76,791	33,608	. . .	. . .
110	Youngstown, Oh.	133,452	140,909	166,689	168,330	44,885	. . .	. . .
111	Torrance, Cal.	133,318	134,968	100,991	22,241	. . .	. . .	. . .
112	Raleigh, N.C.	133,050	123,793	93,931	65,679	13,643	4,518	. . .
113	New Haven, Conn.	131,262	137,707	152,048	164,443	108,027	20,345	4,487
114	Erie, Pa.	130,084	129,231	138,440	130,803	52,733	5,858	. . .
115	Amarillo, Tex.	129,808	127,010	137,969	74,246	1,442	. . .	. . .
116	Lansing, Mich.	129,186	131,403	107,807	92,129	16,485	. . .	. . .
117	Glendale, Cal.	128,338	132,664	119,442	95,702	. . .	. . .	. . .
118	Springfield, Mo.	128,310	120,096	95,865	66,731	23,267	415	. . .
119	Hampton, Va.	128,119	120,779	89,258	5,966	2,764	. . .	. . .
120	Peoria, Ill.	127,898	126,963	103,162	111,856	56,100	5,095	. . .
121	South Bend, Ind.	122,004	127,328	132,445	115,911	35,999	1,652	. . .
122	Macon, Ga.	121,714	122,423	69,764	70,252	23,272	5,720	. . .
123	Hialeah, Fla.	120,809	102,452	66,972	19,676	. . .	. . .	. . .
124	Garden Grove, Cal.	118,622	121,155	84,238	. . .			
125	Fremont, Cal.	116,950	100,869	43,790	. . .			
126	Hollywood, Fla.	116,864	106,873	35,237	14,351	. . .	. . .	. . .
127	Livonia, Mich.	114,922	110,109	66,702	17,534	. . .	. . .	. . .
128	Independence, Mo.	114,272	111,630	62,328	36,963	6,974	. . .	. . .
129	Stockton, Cal.	114,159	109,963	86,321	70,853	17,506	. . .	. . .
130	Beaumont, Tex.	112,620	117,548	119,175	94,014	9,427	. . .	. . .
131	Columbia, S.C.	112,164	113,542	97,433	86,914	21,103	6,060	. . .
132	Berkeley, Cal.	111,637	114,091	111,268	113,805	13,214	. . .	. . .
133	Albany, N.Y.	111,373	115,781	129,726	134,995	94,151	50,763	3,498
134	San Bernardino, Cal.	110,987	106,869	91,992	63,058	6,150	. . .	. . .
135	Waterbury, Conn.	110,698	108,033	107,130	104,477	45,859	. . .	. . .
136	Elizabeth, N.J.	110,303	112,654	107,698	112,817	52,130	5,583	. . .
137	Cedar Rapids, Ia.	109,897	110,642	92,035	72,296	25,656	. . .	. . .
138	Orlando, Fla.	109,818	99,006	88,135	52,367	2,481	. . .	. . .
139	Portsmouth, Va.	109,295	110,963	114,773	80,039	17,427	8,626	. . .
140	Pasadena, Cal.	109,241	112,951	116,407	104,577	3,117	. . .	. . .
141	Alexandria, Va.	108,758	110,927	91,023	61,787	14,528	8,734	2,748
142	Allentown, Pa.	108,655	109,871	108,347	106,756	35,416	3,779	. . .
143	Canton, Oh.	106,897	110,053	113,631	118,912	30,667	2,603	. . .
144	Lakewood, Col.	106,476	92,473	. . .				
145	Hammond, Ind.	106,383	107,983	111,698	87,594	12,376	. . .	. . .
146	Sunnyvale, Cal.	106,179	95,976	52,898	9,829	. . .	. . .	. . .
147	Savannah, Ga.	105,768	118,349	149,245	119,638	54,244	15,312	. . .
148	Ann Arbor, Mich.	104,791	100,035	67,340	48,251	14,509	. . .	. . .
149	Stamford, Conn.	104,651	108,798	92,713	74,293	15,997	. . .	. . .
150	Trenton, N.J.	104,156	104,786	114,167	128,009	73,307	6,461	. . .
151	Pueblo, Col.	103,163	97,774	91,181	63,685	28,157	. . .	. . .
152	Durham, N.C.	102,328	95,438	78,302	71,311	6,679	. . .	. . .
153	Arlington, Tex.	102,228	90,032	44,775	7,692	1,079	. . .	. . .
154	Irving, Tex.	101,716	98,961	45,985	2,621	. . .	. . .	. . .
155	Parma, Oh.	101,482	100,216	82,845	28,897	. . .		
156	Garland, Tex.	101,099	81,437	38,501	10,571	819	. . .	. . .
157	Dearborn, Mich.	100,767	104,199	112,007	94,994	844	. . .	. . .
158	Camden, N.J.	100,171	102,551	117,159	124,555	75,935	9,479	. . .
	San Juan, P.R.	N/A	452,749	432,377	224,767	32,048	. . .	. . .
	Bayamon, P.R.	N/A	147,552	13,109	20,171	2,218	. . .	. . .
	Ponce, P.R.	N/A	128,233	114,286	99,492	27,952	. . .	. . .

(1) Population shown for years prior to 1900 is for New York and its boroughs as constituted under the act of consolidation in 1898. (2) Population shown is for 1862 as given in State census for that year; 1850 returns for San Francisco were destroyed by fire. (3) Figure for 1970 is for the Metropolitan Government of Nashville and Davidson County; figures for previous years are for Nashville city. (4) Winston city and Salem town consolidated as Winston-Salem city between 1910 and 1920. Figure for 1900 represents combined population of Winston and Salem.

Foreign Born and 2d Generation in U.S.; Countries of Origin
Source: Bureau of the Census

The table below shows, state by state, the country of origin of U.S. residents who were either foreign born or had at least one foreign-born parent. "Mixed" means one native and one foreign-born parent.

In the table, Germany includes both East and West Germany; West Asia includes European Turkey; and China includes both the mainland and Taiwan.

	Ala.	Alaska	Ariz.	Ark.	Cal.	Col.	Conn.	Del.	D.C.	Fla.
Mixed parents..	47,742	24,842	219,830	29,269	3,234,089	219,579	708,193	48,710	39,340	695,699
Foreign born...	15,988	7,763	76,570	8,287	1,757,990	60,311	261,614	15,648	33,562	540,284
U.K........	8,944	3,081	19,866	3,797	373,495	26,377	71,532	7,949	5,638	114,870
Ireland........	1,912	804	5,670	1,056	109,888	7,804	60,366	4,244	3,553	36,389
Norway........	643	2,501	4,745	408	69,278	4,787	5,513	510	504	12,288
Sweden.......	678	1,565	6,903	1,100	103,913	13,193	23,427	676	773	26,944
Denmark......	555	632	3,180	559	61,757	5,508	5,471	231	426	9,944
Netherlands...	526	215	2,947	537	63,772	3,609	3,586	485	408	10,800
Switzerland....	408	201	1,629	989	44,483	2,419	4,291	309	533	6,909
France........	1,799	630	2,972	1,010	63,449	3,695	8,388	686	1,881	14,833
Germany......	12,074	3,526	25,653	9,806	360,656	43,172	60,290	5,991	5,642	123,429
Poland.......	2,097	765	7,930	1,331	115,833	7,882	103,820	7,263	2,787	50,591
Czech........	989	536	3,483	1,170	44,964	5,074	19,871	865	804	16,222
Austria.......	1,556	603	5,370	1,027	77,382	9,242	24,595	1,819	1,612	35,896
Hungary......	819	169	3,144	310	58,097	3,035	21,641	952	847	23,054
Yugo.........	421	361	2,592	198	53,868	6,079	3,447	331	474	5,728
USSR........	1,854	679	8,812	912	221,198	28,023	48,150	3,523	5,597	81,833
Lithuania......	415	169	1,591	355	22,063	1,146	20,469	487	953	8,938
Greece.......	2,092	208	2,009	500	43,645	3,111	10,933	1,117	1,716	11,637
Italy.........	5,771	866	12,498	2,284	340,675	21,411	227,782	12,112	4,657	84,881
Other Europe..	1,358	1,208	6,952	854	189,979	7,252	32,304	1,648	2,368	47,368
Western Asia..	1,753	103	2,501	672	64,565	2,272	8,655	457	1,614	13,755
China........	554	282	3,162	661	136,860	1,697	2,195	523	2,099	3,110
Japan........	1,392	1,203	2,310	625	144,335	6,005	1,492	516	602	4,843
Other Asia.....	1,797	1,808	3,488	945	222,709	4,418	6,008	1,690	4,084	10,963
Canada.......	5,232	6,499	26,136	3,016	439,862	21,580	126,305	4,047	3,914	114,615
Mexico.......	975	766	113,816	862	1,112,008	24,759	1,220	246	611	11,047
Cuba........	680	56	505	86	47,699	945	5,772	483	902	252,520
Other Amer....	2,146	576	3,586	572	176,586	3,519	18,844	1,239	11,514	44,411

	Ga.	Ha.	Ida.	Ill.	Ind.	Iowa	Kan.	Ky.	La.	Me.
Mixed parents..	78,528	180,577	60,972	1,572,843	268,060	257,342	147,206	56,080	100,221	149,746
Foreign born...	32,988	75,595	12,572	628,898	83,198	40,217	27,842	16,553	39,542	43,014
U.K........	14,517	5,114	10,406	115,891	30,039	22,008	15,986	7,619	9,252	12,073
Ireland........	3,461	1,056	1,653	101,856	9,931	9,441	4,853	3,156	3,240	6,528
Norway........	933	664	3,534	34,922	2,934	20,418	1,920	457	1,331	1,234
Sweden.......	1,641	841	5,333	98,254	8,274	21,108	9,622	817	1,284	2,740
Denmark......	759	532	3,627	22,021	2,269	20,024	3,200	473	729	1,050
Netherlands...	971	355	1,568	27,189	6,760	19,213	1,692	555	1,005	448
Switzerland....	517	275	1,736	11,827	3,710	3,476	3,256	1,650	608	222
France........	2,684	811	865	19,266	5,372	2,911	2,775	1,848	5,420	1,052
Germany......	20,951	5,112	9,894	312,070	64,883	101,974	43,252	21,438	14,237	4,488
Poland.......	4,574	775	684	299,316	34,590	3,323	4,046	2,147	2,771	2,532
Czech........	1,456	385	1,118	88,259	13,681	10,995	4,978	857	977	741
Austria.......	2,646	746	1,091	65,026	10,441	3,347	5,581	1,626	1,751	826
Hungary......	1,286	342	357	35,822	14,108	1,007	938	1,103	1,267	240
Yugo.........	824	198	421	59,280	14,410	2,202	3,815	451	1,412	133
USSR........	5,831	828	3,136	110,321	9,933	4,563	17,664	2,531	3,073	2,878
Lithuania......	798	207	151	58,285	4,265	1,226	507	545	358	1,172
Greece.......	2,984	371	657	48,669	7,852	2,085	965	861	1,560	1,281
Italy.........	5,220	1,656	1,595	228,984	17,935	7,683	4,552	4,499	29,031	6,083
Other Europe..	3,668	8,318	3,966	67,143	15,478	6,160	3,810	2,092	4,149	2,986
Western Asia..	2,457	344	177	18,270	4,098	1,670	1,738	1,523	2,758	1,079
China........	1,278	20,939	456	11,833	1,976	1,073	786	539	1,117	284
Japan........	1,775	105,223	1,322	12,948	1,888	787	2,435	1,056	1,308	226
Other Asia.....	4,068	79,410	571	28,637	4,948	2,448	3,066	2,324	3,109	922
Canada.......	10,021	5,865	10,452	80,611	21,920	13,297	10,425	4,823	6,090	136,801
Mexico.......	1,562	1,159	5,669	117,268	18,325	4,546	13,728	692	4,865	277
Cuba........	3,816	235	73	19,649	1,690	382	796	556	6,711	223
Other Amer....	3,880	1,371	371	31,276	4,208	1,538	2,011	1,998	18,235	808

	Md.	Mass.	Mich.	Minn.	Miss.	Mo.	Mon.	Neb.	Nev.	N.H.
Mixed parents..	329,813	1,397,064	1,259,961	609,218	22,862	245,948	101,688	175,556	50,274	133,502
Foreign born...	124,345	494,660	424,309	98,056	8,125	65,744	19,634	28,796	18,179	37,048
U.K........	40,291	152,741	148,612	25,672	3,910	23,080	11,293	11,083	6,969	14,040
Ireland........	18,267	218,798	28,667	11,900	816	15,470	5,274	4,846	1,991	8,436
Norway........	3,385	8,969	12,899	114,221	347	2,257	14,595	3,183	1,163	1,219
Sweden.......	4,546	38,753	33,639	114,512	445	6,274	6,177	17,099	1,670	2,774
Denmark......	2,461	5,163	11,951	22,762	294	2,879	4,302	13,202	1,485	593
Netherlands...	3,312	5,656	72,763	13,166	237	2,425	2,731	1,754	796	616
Switzerland....	2,437	3,845	5,442	4,282	160	5,204	1,225	2,054	1,103	422
France........	6,519	12,342	12,149	3,766	733	5,297	1,160	1,296	1,959	1,265
Germany......	59,680	54,846	184,192	137,442	4,960	77,748	15,593	62,726	7,023	6,308
Poland.......	39,334	117,992	214,085	26,931	730	15,469	1,781	8,333	1,578	6,886
Czech........	11,111	6,434	32,176	17,905	377	7,504	2,171	19,551	796	428
Austria.......	13,516	16,898	40,730	17,266	576	11,755	3,464	3,612	1,483	1,297
Hungary......	7,817	5,583	39,202	3,741	266	5,861	828	1,060	751	481
Yugo.........	3,148	1,776	30,375	12,266	574	6,517	3,020	1,599	957	229
USSR........	46,332	104,223	65,606	18,666	534	19,127	11,365	14,160	2,247	2,982
Lithuania......	9,090	32,617	16,908	2,445	152	2,168	242	1,428	282	1,929
Greece.......	12,508	39,669	19,519	2,833	471	4,209	541	859	1,205	5,040

Continued

Continued from previous page

	Md.	Mass.	Mich.	Minn.	Miss.	Mo.	Mon.	Neb.	Nev.	N.H.
Italy	49,619	294,318	117,064	12,910	3,957	30,114	3,415	6,414	7,927	6,465
Other Europe	15,069	117,653	94,603	41,228	954	9,085	4,157	3,823	3,645	3,952
Western Asia	8,124	27,159	31,579	2,411	1,249	3,279	377	771	633	1,281
China	5,975	11,324	5,725	1,998	1,078	2,337	245	543	811	541
Japan	3,784	3,390	4,952	2,206	394	2,618	675	1,106	1,084	370
Other Asia	13,832	10,897	12,925	4,749	945	5,301	746	1,428	2,148	662
Canada	25,300	466,942	353,154	57,604	2,496	15,532	21,106	8,247	7,587	96,834
Mexico	2,714	2,136	31,067	4,575	783	8,353	1,485	5,552	5,760	209
Cuba	4,931	6,915	3,231	765	241	1,131	45	608	1,306	195
Other Amer	19,309	27,299	13,339	3,390	1,427	3,857	426	1,017	1,147	728

	NJ.	N.M.	N.Y.	N.C.	N.D.	Ohio	Okla.	Ore.	Pa.	R.I.
Mixed parents	1,521,045	66,170	3,885,445	65,661	127,689	994,850	72,713	229,357	1,687,145	237,233
Foreign born	634,818	22,510	2,109,776	28,620	18,437	316,496	20,160	66,149	445,895	74,374
U.K.	172,308	6,000	334,424	12,826	3,537	108,027	9,812	28,525	198,190	34,178
Ireland	122,600	1,718	386,403	2,506	1,248	37,941	2,386	7,175	118,174	21,041
Norway	17,474	872	47,605	773	38,722	4,382	901	18,085	5,251	1,093
Sweden	19,366	1,681	52,058	1,401	8,434	12,539	1,962	17,830	20,370	6,669
Denmark	11,000	721	20,911	728	3,442	4,492	1,396	8,792	4,935	574
Netherlands	28,440	655	32,043	1,444	1,120	6,539	1,101	4,776	5,691	749
Switzerland	13,219	557	23,773	678	426	12,337	1,200	6,816	8,039	522
France	22,152	1,219	56,861	1,820	402	13,640	1,669	3,263	18,484	3,261
Germany	219,178	7,438	516,216	16,614	21,004	188,386	21,475	40,242	202,611	768
Poland	217,509	1,422	557,478	3,037	1,952	116,262	2,670	4,855	243,752	13,389
Czech	51,599	763	90,641	1,132	2,473	93,187	3,411	4,144	118,855	763
Austria	83,165	1,483	237,836	1,664	2,254	62,829	1,893	5,294	145,815	2,896
Hungary	70,424	687	115,474	1,190	1,590	82,944	793	2,298	62,014	589
Yugo	16,202	899	41,756	449	194	73,843	400	3,220	54,424	278
USSR	143,234	1,725	569,813	2,928	33,177	54,520	5,463	15,709	15,348	11,198
Lithuania	22,658	371	42,863	545	117	13,979	559	778	43,183	1,459
Greece	25,703	747	90,886	3,883	168	22,210	667	3,480	23,198	2,242
Italy	515,889	3,916	1,330,057	4,658	485	166,629	3,531	9,644	444,841	73,255
Other Europe	69,176	1,725	197,966	2,764	4,076	48,002	2,584	13,752	52,748	33,222
Western Asia	23,415	865	87,036	2,536	770	18,246	2,488	2,348	20,191	4,211
China	7,748	506	66,407	1,178	150	4,987	758	4,423	6,010	1,069
Japan	6,064	1,029	17,304	2,988	391	5,169	1,810	3,983	4,480	783
Other Asia	16,085	1,137	51,785	3,583	555	14,066	2,539	5,345	15,248	2,278
Canada	58,720	5,663	286,047	10,334	15,630	63,258	7,811	53,002	47,827	66,003
Mexico	3,301	37,822	12,249	1,770	276	13,349	6,071	7,739	4,707	407
Cuba	71,233	418	98,479	1,330	46	3,593	352	689	5,195	516
Other Amer	54,867	1,484	415,906	3,012	378	11,679	2,114	2,887	20,183	2,788

	S.C.	S.D.	Tenn.	Tex.	Ut.	Vt.	Va.	Wash.	W.Va.	Wis.
Mixed parents	35,436	98,147	49,368	889,246	102,036	62,680	179,518	481,586	57,358	617,479
Foreign born	14,364	10,899	19,024	309,772	29,573	18,482	72,281	156,020	16,662	130,669
U.K.	7,779	4,562	8,682	49,185	28,531	3,071	10,162	13,266	1,742	9,433
Ireland	1,336	1,980	2,087	12,143						
Norway	392	18,898	600	5,442	4,113	651	3,077	60,427	191	52,681
Sweden	686	7,790	1,081	10,873	7,477	1,142	4,144	45,251	601	27,352
Denmark	325	6,584	630	4,801	10,464	476	2,195	14,422	170	18,959
Netherlands	516	5,126	698	4,722	7,617	518	2,690	13,297	223	15,315
Switzerland	576	950	802	4,314	3,392	529	1,640	7,675	762	14,316
France	1,069	399	1,333	8,992	1,014	759	6,210	6,145	881	4,457
Germany	9,193	26,792	11,675	104,726	14,179	4,195	32,596	71,353	6,960	234,767
Poland	1,701	1,052	2,789	16,328	904	2,797	9,423	9,821	6,360	71,534
Czech	704	3,507	776	29,536	668	393	4,675	6,137	2,996	26,465
Austria	935	1,305	1,354	13,397	1,436	614	6,827	10,332	2,572	27,343
Hungary	479	503	995	4,852	394	602	3,814	4,269	2,931	12,448
Yugo	391	280	376	2,992	1,337	84	1,775	7,580	2,549	19,873
USSR	1,661	14,041	3,649	16,149	1,151	1,171	11,129	23,466	1,996	24,246
Lithuania	228	140	388	2,069	112	211	2,040	1,436	602	5,796
Greece	2,188	284	1,563	6,168	3,372	504	5,712	4,061	1,894	4,746
Italy	2,653	616	6,054	26,886	4,688	4,982	18,026	21,422	17,906	30,513
Other Europe	1,658	2,659	1,678	15,713	2,396	1,707	8,005	24,907	2,564	22,142
Western Asia	1,382	523	1,579	9,219	672	652	6,248	3,411	2,522	3,388
China	408	270	1,032	7,606	983	165	2,936	8,107	135	2,141
Japan	892	273	1,352	8,388	2,834	66	4,691	15,777	433	1,871
Other Asia	2,106	403	2,726	12,465	1,533	449	14,060	18,701	1,704	4,928
Canada	4,805	6,617	6,213	35,900	11,194	46,176	24,048	136,546	2,492	36,888
Mexico	668	472	1,036	711,058	7,710	111	3,167	17,892	513	9,160
Cuba	860	58	894	7,749	116	7	4,479	570	110	787
Other Amer	1,405	303	1,593	21,300	1,593	356	10,538	5,173	772	3,834

Wyoming

Mixed parents	31,014	Germany	5,721	Other Europe	1,194
Foreign born	6,989	Poland	1,033	Western Asia	177
U.K.	5,367	Czech	824	China	177
Ireland	1,066	Austria	1,300	Japan	341
Norway	1,257	Hungary	250	Other Asia	385
Sweden	2,156	Yugo	1,263	Canada	3,069
Denmark	1,505	USSR	2,913	Mexico	2,638
Netherlands	332	Lithuania	82	Cuba	
Switzerland	563	Greece	728	Other Amer	277
France	504	Italy	1,750		

The Poor, 1971-1974, by Family Status, Sex, and Race

Source: Bureau of the Census
(numbers in thousands)

	1974 No.	%*	1973 No.	%*	1972 No.	%*	1971 No.	%*
Total Poor....................	24,260	11.6	22,973	11.1	24,460	11.9	25,559	12.5
In families..................	19,440	10.2	18,299	9.7	19,577	10.3	20,405	10.8
Head........................	5,109	9.2	4,828	8.8	5,075	9.3	5,303	10.0
Related children............	10,196	15.5	9,453	14.2	10,082	14.9	10,344	15.1
Other relatives.............	4,135	6.0	4,018	5.9	4,420	6.6	4,757	7.2
Unrelated individuals........	4,820	25.5	4,674	25.6	4,883	29.0	5,154	31.6
In male-head families.........	10,877	6.5	10,121	6.0	11,463	6.8	12,608	7.5
Head........................	2,757	5.7	2,635	5.5	2,917	6.1	3,203	6.8
Related children............	4,809	8.7	4,282	7.6	4,988	8.6	5,494	9.3
Other relatives.............	3,310	5.2	3,204	5.1	3,558	5.7	3,910	6.3
Unrelated male individuals.......	1,607	20.4	1,495	19.8	1,410	21.1	1,543	23.9
In female-head families.......	8,563	36.8	8,178	37.5	8,114	38.2	7,797	38.7
Head........................	2,351	32.5	2,193	32.2	2,158	32.7	2,100	33.9
Related children............	5,387	51.5	5,171	52.1	5,094	53.1	4,850	53.1
Other relatives.............	825	14.9	814	16.0	862	17.0	847	17.5
Unrelated female individuals.....	3,212	29.3	3,179	29.7	3,473	34.3	3,611	36.6
Total White Poor..............	16,290	8.9	15,142	8.4	16,203	9.0	17,780	9.9
In families..................	12,517	7.5	11,412	6.9	12,268	7.4	13,566	8.2
Head........................	3,482	7.0	3,219	6.6	3,441	7.1	3,751	7.9
Female......................	1,297	24.9	1,190	24.5	1,135	24.3	1,191	26.5
Related children............	6,180	11.2	5,462	9.7	5,784	10.1	6,341	10.9
Other relatives.............	2,855	4.7	2,731	4.5	3,043	5.1	3,474	5.8
Unrelated individuals........	3,773	23.2	3,730	23.7	3,935	27.1	4,214	29.6
Total Black Poor..............	7,467	31.4	7,388	31.4	7,710	33.3	7,396	32.5
In families..................	6,506	30.3	6,560	30.8	6,841	32.4	6,530	31.2
Head........................	1,530	27.8	1,527	28.1	1,529	29.0	1,484	28.8
Female......................	1,024	52.8	974	52.7	972	53.3	879	53.5
Related children............	3,819	40.7	3,822	40.6	4,025	42.7	3,836	40.7
Other relatives.............	1,157	17.6	1,211	18.7	1,287	20.0	1,210	19.1
Unrelated individuals........	961	41.0	828	37.9	870	42.9	866	46.0

*Per cent of total individuals in that classification who were poor. For example, of all black female heads of households in 1974, 52.8 per cent were poor.

Poverty Level, 1974, by Family Size and Sex of Head

Number of family members...................	Total	Non-Farm Total	Male	Female	Farm Total	Male	Female
1 member........................	$2,487	$2,495	$2,610	$2,413	$2,092	$2,158	$2,029
Under 65 yrs...................	2,557	2,562	2,658	2,458	2,197	2,258	2,089
65 years and over..............	2,352	2,364	2,387	2,357	2,013	2,030	2,002
2 members.......................	3,191	3,211	3,220	3,167	2,707	2,711	2,632
Head under 65 yrs...............	3,294	3,312	3,329	3,230	2,819	2,824	2,706
Head 65 & over.................	2,958	2,982	2,984	2,966	2,535	2,535	2,533
3 members.......................	3,910	3,936	3,957	3,822	3,331	3,345	3,133
4 members.......................	5,008	5,038	5,040	5,014	4,302	4,303	4,262
5 members.......................	5,912	5,950	5,957	5,882	5,057	5,057	5,072
6 members.......................	6,651	6,699	6,706	6,642	5,700	5,700	5,702
7 or more members...............	8,165	8,253	8,278	8,079	7,018	7,017	7,066

Poverty by Age, Race and Sex

(in thousands)

Age and Sex (March, 1975)	Total	White Number Of Poor	% Of Total	Total	Black Number Of Poor	% Of Total
Both sexes, total....................	182,355	16,310	8.9	23,705	7,456	31.5
Under 3 years..................	7,624	1,020	13.4	1,364	544	39.9
3 to 5 years...................	8,575	1,061	12.4	1,533	604	30.4
6 to 13 years..................	25,189	2,921	11.6	4,251	1,817	42.8
14 and 15 years................	7,142	707	9.9	1,164	461	39.6
16 to 21 years.................	20,512	1,822	8.9	3,079	1,069	34.7
22 to 44 years.................	55,439	3,640	6.6	6,687	1,409	21.1
45 to 54 years.................	21,045	1,102	5.2	2,218	506	22.8
55 to 59 years.................	9,380	704	7.5	866	203	23.5
60 to 64 years.................	8,243	692	8.4	819	217	26.5
65 years and over..............	19,206	2,642	13.8	1,722	626	36.4
Male, total over 16...............	64,015	4,016	6.3	6,926	1,390	20.1
16 to 21 years.................	10,193	801	7.9	1,448	496	34.3
22 to 44 years.................	27,410	1,449	5.3	2,966	370	12.5
45 to 54 years.................	10,194	434	4.3	1,017	165	16.2
55 to 59 years.................	4,477	267	6.0	388	70	18.0
60 to 64 years.................	3,848	268	7.0	379	80	21.1
65 years and over..............	7,893	797	10.1	728	209	28.7
Female, total over 16..............	69,812	6,583	9.4	8,466	2,466	31.2
16 to 21 years.................	10,319	1,020	9.9	1,630	573	35.2
22 to 44 years.................	28,030	2,190	7.8	3,722	1,039	27.9
45 to 54 years.................	10,851	668	6.2	1,201	341	28.4
55 to 59 years.... '...........	4,903	436	8.9	479	134	28.0
60 to 64 years.................	4,396	424	9.6	439	136	31.0
65 years and over..............	11,313	1,845	16.3	995	417	41.9

Aid to Families with Dependent Children

(February 1976)

Source: Social and Rehabilitation Service, Department of Health Education and Welfare

State	Number Of Families	Number of Recipients Total (a)	Number of Recipients Children	Payments to Recipients Total Amount	Payments to Recipients Average Per Family	Payments to Recipients Average Per Recipient	% Change From Feb. 1975 In No. of Recip.	% Change From Feb. 1975 In Amount
Alabama	52,779	167,775	124,375	$5,268,342	$99.82	$31.48	2.9	9.3
Alaska	3,725	10,121	7,505	1,044,108	280.30	103.16	-15.6	-5.8
Arizona	20,307	67,018	50,303	2,733,143	134.59	40.78	-6.0	4.4
Arkansas	34,657	108,514	80,330	4,079,412	117.71	37.59	5.4	1.5
California	469,023	1,444,850	993,341	123,013,824	262.28	85.14	2.9	17.1
Colorado	33,311	99,457	69,472	6,871,972	206.30	69.09	1.0	10.7
Connecticut	41,982	134,144	96,843	11,194,036	266.64	83.45	6.1	8.5
Delaware	10,284	31,432	22,757	2,005,571	195.02	63.81	-3.4	19.8
Dist. of Columbia	32,061	102,344	73,687	7,523,170	234.65	73.51	-2.2	-2.4
Florida	81,388	250,918	186,833	10,108,100	124.20	40.28	-5.1	5.4
Georgia	100,477	299,738	222,311	9,686,809	96.41	32.32	-16.3	-16.6
Guam	824	3,366	2,637	167,233	202.95	49.68	4.9	10.9
Hawaii	16,647	54,505	37,547	5,649,970	339.40	103.66	12.1	26.2
Idaho	6,694	19,892	13,979	1,652,569	246.87	83.08	1.5	23.5
Illinois	232,729	811,042	583,013	63,255,773	271.80	77.99	3.6	-10.0
Indiana	58,262	178,352	130,073	9,939,145	170.59	55.73	9.3	28.1
Iowa	30,415	96,080	65,580	8,305,182	273.06	86.44	11.7	10.5
Kansas	26,213	77,955	56,846	6,178,994	235.72	79.26	16.4	34.5
Kentucky	63,889	201,411	140,590	11,387,335	178.24	56.54	24.3	24.5
Louisiana	67,807	231,225	174,031	8,248,033	121.64	35.67	-1.5	3.8
Maine	(b) 20,517	65,962	47,255	3,672,153	178.98	55.67	-20.8	-13.1
Maryland	70,403	219,332	156,376	12,973,083	184.27	59.15	0.4	13.1
Massachusetts	114,707	361,768	251,123	31,702,657	276.38	87.63	1.7	3.5
Michigan	218,665	685,432	476,653	61,062,491	289.86	89.09	4.6	14.0
Minnesota	45,055	131,533	92,173	11,967,852	265.63	90.99	3.2	10.6
Mississippi	55,054	185,718	143,103	2,669,767	48.49	14.38	-0.5	-0.3
Missouri	88,059	274,998	197,687	12,664,697	143.82	46.05	5.5	25.6
Montana	6,507	18,905	13,712	1,099,340	168.95	58.15	-14.1	-8.8
Nebraska	11,741	36,346	26,011	2,411,286	205.37	66.34	-4.9	12.4
Nevada	5,306	15,559	11,250	873,081	164.55	56.11	9.0	27.6
New Hampshire	8,739	26,882	18,671	1,976,469	226.17	73.52	0.9	-1.6
New Jersey	136,080	451,508	322,622	37,512,633	275.67	83.08	1.8	5.4
New Mexico	18,836	59,940	43,866	2,618,747	139.03	43.69	-2.8	1.3
New York	369,153	1,226,347	856,565	127,119,324	344.35	103.66	2.0	11.8
North Carolina	68,084	191,225	138,870	10,572,697	155.29	55.29	8.2	11.4
North Dakota	4,583	13,717	9,946	995,415	217.20	72.57	1.6	10.5
Ohio	188,775	590,288	404,461	38,518,588	204.04	65.25	6.9	28.2
Oklahoma	28,141	89,617	67,729	5,341,387	189.81	59.60	-10.1	-4.5
Oregon	39,483	116,565	78,772	9,731,537	246.47	83.49	9.6	34.4
Pennsylvania	196,022	643,947	440,301	55,597,498	283.63	86.34	0.6	12.8
Puerto Rico	(b) 44,496	(b) 204,568	(b) 149,202	(b) 2,009,471	45.16	9.82	-11.8	-7.9
Rhode Island	17,167	54,811	38,148	4,216,415	245.61	76.93	3.5	7.7
South Carolina	45,001	139,774	102,685	3,876,893	86.15	27.74	1.6	3.5
South Dakota	8,327	25,239	18,563	1,725,958	207.27	68.38	2.3	8.1
Tennessee	69,779	211,397	155,108	7,249,026	103.89	34.29	1.9	6.9
Texas	106,622	353,274	262,337	11,251,549	105.53	31.85	-9.7	-8.0
Utah	12,734	37,494	26,116	3,061,756	240.44	81.66	6.3	14.3
Vermont	7,409	25,179	16,420	1,932,311	260.81	76.74	13.1	15.7
Virgin Islands	(b) 1,124	(b) 3,857	(b) 3,169	(b) 145,169	129.15	37.64	-7.4	-5.2
Virginia	59,979	179,413	128,759	11,616,116	193.67	64.75	1.4	6.5
Washington	50,462	151,631	98,912	13,049,210	258.59	86.06	1.4	13.9
West Virginia	22,881	74,406	50,891	4,105,866	179.44	55.18	1.0	9.6
Wisconsin (e)	61,501	185,658	131,002	18,898,354	307.29	101.79	11.9	21.7
Wyoming	2,347	6,604	4,801	422,836	180.16	64.03	-4.7	19.1
Total (b)	3,579,213	11,449,033	8,115,312	$812,954,393	$227.13	$71.01	1.6	10.0

(e) Estimated. (a) Includes as recipients the children and one or both parents or one caretaker relative other than a parent in families in which the requirements of such adults were considered in determining the amount of assistance. (b) Incomplete. Data for foster care not reported by Puerto Rico and the Virgin Islands; case data for foster care not reported by Maine.

Recipients and Payments, 1945-1975

	Category	1945 Dec.	1950, Dec.	1955, Dec.	1960, Dec.	1965, Dec.	1970, Dec.	1975, Dec.
Old-age:	Recipients	2,056,000	2,786,000	2,538,000	2,305,000	2,087,000	2,082,000	(B)
	Total amt	$63,489,000	$119,955,000	$127,003,000	$135,759,000	$131,674,000	$161,642,000	"
	Avg. amt	$30.90	$43.05	$50.05	$58.90	$63.10	$77.65	"
	(A) Avg. real $	56.70	57.50	62.25	65.95	66.15	65.20	"
AFDC:	Recipients	943,000	2,233,000	2,192,000	3,073,000	4,396,000	9,659,000	11,389,000
	Total amt	$14,278,000	$46,529,000	$51,472,000	$87,051,000	$144,355,000	$485,877,000	$824,648,000
	Avg. amt	$15.15	$20.85	$23.50	$28.35	$32.85	$50.30	$72.40
	(A) Avg. real $	27.80	27.85	29.25	31.75	34.45	42.25	43.55
Blind	Recipients	71,500	97,500	104,000	107,000	85,100	81,000	(B)
	Total amt	$2,395,000	$4,481,000	$5,803,000	$7,215,000	$6,922,000	$8,446,000	"
	Avg. amt	$33.50	$46.00	$55.55	$67.45	$81.35	$104.35	"
	(A) Avg. real$	61.45	61.40	69.10	75.55	85.25	87.60	"
Disabled	Recipients	—	68,800	241,000	369,000	557,000	935,000	(B)
	Total amt	—	$3,033,000	$11,750,000	$20,711,000	$37,035,000	$91,325,000	"
	Avg. amt	—	$44.10	$48.75	$56.15	$66.50	$97.65	"
	(A) Avg. real $	—	58.90	60.65	62.90	69.70	82.00	"

(A) Dollar amounts adjusted to represent actual purchasing power in terms of average value of dollar during 1967 based on the consumer's price index for moderate-income families in large cities.

(B) Administration of the public assistance programs of Old-age Assistance, Aid to the Blind, and Aid to the Disabled was transferred to the Social Security Administration by Public Law 92-603 effective 1/1/74.

Jewish Population by Countries and Cities

Source: Jewish Statistical Bureau, Dr. H. S. Linfield, Exec. Secy. Figures are latest estimates

North America	6,145,500	Australia and New Zealand	77,000
Central and South America	756,685	Africa	185,200
Europe	4,142,750		
Asia	3,001,210	**World Total**	14,308,345

Europe

Albania	300
Austria	12,000
Belgium	41,000
Bulgaria	7,000
Czechoslovakia	14,000
Denmark	6,500
Finland	1,300
France	550,000
Germany	32,000
Gibraltar	600
Great Britain	450,000
Greece	6,500
Hungary	80,000
Irish Free State	4,000
Italy	35,000
Luxembourg	1,000
Malta	50
Netherlands	30,000
Norway	900
Poland	8,000
Portugal	600
Romania	80,000
Soviet Union	2,700,000
Spain	9,000
Sweden	15,000
Switzerland	21,000
Turkey	30,000
Yugoslavia	7,000

North America

Canada	308,000
United States	5,800,000
Mexico	37,500

Central and South America

Argentina	475,000
Barbados	85
Bolivia	2,000
Brazil	155,000
Chile	30,000
Colombia	12,000
Costa Rica	1,500
Cuba	1,500
Curacao	700
Dominican Rep.	200
Surinam	650
Ecuador	1,000
El Salvador	300
Guatemala	1,900
Haiti	150
Honduras	200
Jamaica	500
Nicaragua	200
Panama	2,000
Paraguay	1,200
Peru	5,300
Trinidad	300
Uruguay	50,000
Venezuela	15,000

Asia

Afghanistan	200
Burma	200
Cyprus	30
China	30
Hong Kong	200
India	12,000
Indonesia	100
Iran	80,000
Iraq	500
Israel	3,400,000[1]
Japan	500
Lebanon	2,000
Pakistan	250
Philippines	200
Singapore	500
Syria	4,000
Yemen	500

Africa

Algeria	1,000
Congo	250
Egypt	500
Ethiopia	20,000
Kenya	200
Libya	50
Morocco	30,000
Rhodesia	4,800
Tunisia	8,000
Rep. of South Africa	120,000
Zambia	400

Australia and New Zealand

Australia	72,000
New Zealand	5,000

(1.) Includes about 500,000 Christians and Mohammedans.

Estimated Jewish Population in Foreign Cities

Amsterdam	20,000
Antwerp	13,000
Ascalon[1]	46,700
Ashdod[1]	48,200
Athens	2,800
Basle	2,500
Beersheba[1]	93,400
Belgrade	1,500
Berlin	6,000
Bet Shean[1]	12,000
Birmingham	6,000
B'nai B'rak	81,000
Bordeaux	6,400
Brussels	24,500
Bucharest	40,000
Budapest	65,000
Buenos Aires	350,000
Casablanca	30,000
Copenhagen	6,000
Czernowitz	70,000[1]
Elat[1]	4,000
Glasgow	13,000
Haifa[1]	210,000
Istanbul	22,000
Jerusalem[1]	284,500
Johannesburg	63,000
Kharkov	80,000
Kiev	170,000
Kovno (Lith.)	8,000
Leeds	18,000
Leningrad	165,000
Liverpool	6,500
Lod (Lydda)[1]	30,200
London (Gr.)	280,000
Lvov (Poland)	40,000
Lyons	20,000
Marseilles	65,000
Manchester and Salford	35,000
Melbourne	34,000
Milan	10,000
Minsk (Poland)	47,000
Montreal	114,000
Moscow	285,000
Nazareth[1]	35,400
Nazareth Illet[1]	18,000
Nice	20,000
Odessa	120,000
Ottawa	7,000
Paris	300,000
Petach Tikvah	107,000
Ramath Gan[1]	121,000
Rehovoth	46,400
Riga (Poland)	40,000
Rio de Janeiro	50,000
Rome	15,000
Safed	14,400
Santiago	25,000
Sao Paulo	65,000
Stockholm	8,000
Strasbourg	12,000
Sydney	28,000
Teheran	50,000
Tel Aviv-Jaffa[1]	394,000
Tiberias[1]	35,300
Toronto	110,000
Toulouse	18,000
Vancouver	11,500
Vienna	9,000
Warsaw	5,000
Winnipeg	20,000
Zurich	6,150

(1.) Includes some Christians, Mohammedans

Estimated Jewish Population in Large U. S. Cities

Albany	13,500
Alexandria Arlington & Fairfax cos., Va.	15,000
Atlanta	18,000
Atlantic City	10,000
Baltimore	94,000
Bergen County	100,000
Boston	180,000
Bridgeport	14,500
Buffalo	23,500
Camden	26,000
Chicago	253,000
Cincinnati	30,000
Cleveland	80,000
Columbus	13,000
Dallas	20,000
Denver	26,000
Detroit	80,000
Elizabeth*	50,000
Hartford	23,000
Hollywood, Fla.	25,000
Houston	22,000
Jersey City	10,000
Kansas City	22,000
Long Beach, Cal.	16,000
Los Angeles*	463,000
Lynn	19,000
Miami*	225,000
Milwaukee	23,900
Minneapolis	22,085
Montg'y Co., Md.	50,000
New B'nswick*	18,000
New Haven	20,000
New Orleans	10,500
New York City	1,228,000
Manhattan	171,000
Bronx	143,000
Brooklyn	514,000
Queens	379,000
Richmond	21,000
N.Y. City environs:	
Nassau Co. and Suffolk Co.	605,000
Westchester Co.	165,000
Newark:	
Essex Co.	95,000
Oakland:	
Alameda and Contra Costa Cos.*	21,000
Orange Co. Calif.	37,500
Passaic	9,200
Paterson*	28,000
Philadelphia*	350,000
Phoenix*	14,000
Pittsburgh	52,000
Prince George County, Md.	15,000
Providence*	22,000
Richmond, Va.	10,000
Rochester	21,500
Rockland Co., N.Y.	25,000
St. Louis	60,000
St. Paul	10,000
San Diego	15,000
San Francisco*	75,000
Seattle	13,000
Springfield, Mass.	11,000
Stanford	10,800
Syracuse	11,000
Trenton, N.J.	9,900
Washington	112,500
Worcester*	10,000

*Indicates greater area.

Black Population by States

Source: Bureau of the Census (1970)

Ala.	903,467	Ill.	1,425,674	Mon.	1,995	R. I.	25,338
Alaska	8,911	Ind.	357,464	Neb.	39,911	S. C.	789,041
Ariz.	53,344	Iowa	32,596	Nev.	27,762	S. D.	1,627
Ark.	352,445	Kan.	106,977	N. H.	2,505	Tenn.	621,261
Cal.	1,400,143	Ky.	230,793	N. J.	770,292	Tex.	1,399,005
Col.	66,411	La.	1,086,832	N. M.	19,555	Ut.	6,617
Conn.	181,177	Me.	2,800	N. Y.	2,168,949	Vt.	761
Del.	78,276	Md.	699,479	N. C.	1,126,478	Va.	861,368
D.C.	537,712	Mass.	175,817	N. D.	2,494	Wash.	71,308
Fla.	1,401,651	Mich.	991,066	Oh.	970,477	W. Va.	67,342
Ga.	1,187,149	Minn.	34,868	Okla.	171,892	Wis.	128,224
Ha.	7,573	Miss.	815,770	Ore.	26,308	Wy.	2,568
Ida.	2,130	Mo.	480,172	Pa.	1,016,514	**Total**	22,580,289

U.S. Places of 5,000 or More Population—with ZIP Codes
Source: U.S. Bureau of the Census; U.S. Postal Service

The listings below show the official urban population of the United States. "Urban population" is defined as all persons living in (a) places of 5,000 inhabitants or more, incorporated as cities, villages, boroughs (except Alaska), and towns (except in New England, New York, New Jersey, Pennsylvania and Wisconsin), but excluding those persons living in the rural portions of extended cities; (b) unincorporated places of 5,000 inhabitants or more; and (c) other territory, incorporated or unincorporated, included in urbanized areas.

The non-urban portion of an extended city contains one or more areas, each at least 5 square miles in extent and with a population density of less than 100 persons per square mile. The area or areas constitute at least 25 percent of the legal city's land area of a total of 25 square miles or more.

In New England, New York, New Jersey, Pennsylvania, and Wisconsin, minor civil divisions called "towns" often include rural areas and one or more urban areas. Only the urban areas of these "towns" are included here, except in the case of New England where entire town populations, which may include some rural population, are shown in italics. Boroughs in Alaska may contain one or more urban areas which are included here.

(u) means place is unincorporated.

Where special censuses were taken after April 1, 1970, the year appears after the name of the place.

The ZIP Code of each place appears before the name of that place, if it is obtainable.

CAUTION—Where an asterisk (*) appears before the ZIP Code, ask your local postmaster for the correct ZIP Code for a specific address within the place listed.

Zip Code	Place	1970	1960
	Alabama		
35950	Albertville	9,963	8,250
35010	Alexander City	12,358	13,140
36420	Andalusia	10,092	10,263
36201	Anniston	31,533	33,657
.....	Anniston Northwest(u)	6,609	.....
35611	Athens	14,360	9,330
36502	Atmore	8,293	8,173
35954	Attalla	7,510	8,257
36830	Auburn	22,767	16,261
36507	Bay Minette	6,727	5,197
35020	Bessemer	33,428	33,052
*35203	Birmingham	300,910	340,887
35226	Bluff Park(u)	12,431	.....
35957	Boaz	5,635	4,654
36426	Brewton	6,747	6,309
35215	Center Point(u)	15,675	.....
36611	Chickasaw	8,447	10,002
35045	Clanton	5,868	5,683
35055	Cullman	12,601	10,883
36322	Daleville	5,182	693
35601	Decatur	38,044	29,217
36732	Demopolis	7,651	7,377
36301	Dothan	36,733	31,440
36330	Enterprise	15,591	11,410
36027	Eufaula	9,102	8,357
35064	Fairfield	14,369	15,316
36532	Fairhope	5,720	4,858
35630	Florence	34,031	31,649
35214	Forestdale(u)	6,091	.....
35967	Fort Payne	8,435	7,029
36201	Fort McClellan(u)	5,334	.....
36360	Fort Rucker(u)	14,242	.....
35068	Fultondale	5,163	2,001
*35901	Gadsden	53,928	58,088
35071	Gardendale	6,537	4,712
36037	Greenville	8,033	6,894
35976	Guntersville	6,491	6,592
35640	Hartselle	7,355	5,000
35209	Homewood	21,137	20,289
35020	Hueytown	8,174	5,997
*35804	Huntsville	139,282	72,365
36545	Jackson	5,957	4,959
36265	Jacksonville	7,715	5,678
35501	Jasper	10,798	10,799
36863	Lanett	6,908	7,674
35094	Leeds	6,991	6,162
35228	Midfield	6,340	3,556
*36601	Mobile	190,026	194,856
*36104	Montgomery	133,386	134,393
35223	Mountain Brook	19,509	12,680
35660	Muscle Shoals	6,907	4,084
35476	Northport	9,435	5,245
36801	Opelika	19,027	15,678
36467	Opp	6,493	5,535
36360	Ozark	13,555	9,534
35125	Pell City	5,602	4,165
36867	Phenix City	25,281	27,630
36272	Piedmont	5,063	4,794
35127	Pleasant Grove	5,090	3,097
36067	Prattville	13,116	6,616
36610	Prichard	41,578	47,371
36274	Roanoke	5,251	5,288
35653	Russellville	7,814	6,628
36571	Saraland	7,840	4,595
35768	Scottsboro	9,324	6,449
35701	Selma	27,379	28,385
35660	Sheffield	13,115	13,491
35150	Sylacauga	12,255	12,857
35160	Talladega	17,662	17,742
35217	Tarrant City	6,835	7,810
36081	Troy	11,482	10,234
35401	Tuscaloosa	65,773	63,370
35674	Tuscumbia	8,828	8,994
36083	Tuskegee	11,028	7,240
35216	Vestavia Hills 1975	14,199	4,029
36201	West End—Cobb(u)	5,515	5,485
	Alaska		
*99502	Anchorage	48,081	44,237
99702	Eielson(u)	6,149	.....
99506	Elmendorf(u)	6,018	.....
99701	Fairbanks	14,771	13,311
99505	Fort Richardson(u)	10,751	.....
99703	Fort Wainwright(u)	9,097	.....
99801	Juneau	6,050	6,797
99901	Ketchikan	6,994	6,483
99503	Spenard(u)	18,089	9,074
	Arizona		
85321	Ajo(u)	5,881	7,049
85323	Avondale	6,626	6,151
85603	Bisbee	8,328	9,914
85222	Casa Grande	10,536	8,311
85224	Chandler	13,763	9,531
85533	Clifton	5,087	4,191
85228	Coolidge 1975	6,711	4,990
85607	Douglas 1975	12,422	11,925
85231	Eloy 1975	6,493	4,899
86001	Flagstaff	26,117	18,214
85613	Fort Huachuca(u)	6,659	.....
*85301	Glendale	36,228	15,893
85501	Globe	7,333	6,217
86401	Kingman 1974	7,202	4,525
85501	Luke(u)	5,047	.....
*85201	Mesa	62,853	33,772
85621	Nogales	8,946	7,286
86040	Page(u) 1975	5,892	2,960
85253	Paradise Valley	7,155	.....
*85026	Phoenix	582,500	439,170
86301	Prescott	13,283	12,861
85546	Safford 1975	5,947	4,648
*85251	Scottsdale	67,823	10,026
85635	Sierra Vista 1975	20,121	3,121
85713	South Tucson	6,220	7,004
85351	Sun City(u)	13,670	.....
*85282	Tempe	63,550	24,897
*85726	Tucson	262,933	212,892
85364	West Yuma(u)	5,552	2,781
86047	Winslow	8,066	8,862
85364	Yuma	29,007	23,974
	Arkansas		
71923	Arkadelphia	9,841	8,069
72501	Batesville 1974	7,085	6,207
72015	Benton	16,499	10,399
72712	Bentonville 1972	6,391	3,649
72315	Blytheville	24,752	20,797
72021	Brinkley	5,275	4,636
71701	Camden	15,147	15,823
72032	Conway 1973	16,772	9,791
71635	Crossett	6,191	5,370
71639	Dumas 1974	5,290	3,540
71730	El Dorado	25,283	25,292
72701	Fayetteville 1972	31,915	20,274
72335	Forrest City	12,521	10,544
72901	Fort Smith 1973	65,393	52,991
72601	Harrison	7,239	6,580
72342	Helena 1971	10,201	11,500
71801	Hope	8,830	8,399
71901	Hot Springs	35,631	28,337
72076	Jacksonville 1972	22,392	14,488

ZIP Code	Place	1970	1960
72401	Jonesboro 1974	28,962	21,418
*72201	Little Rock 1974	139,703	107,813
71753	Magnolia 1973	11,527	10,651
72104	Malvern 1974	9,848	9,566
72360	Marianna	6,196	5,134
71655	Monticello 1972	7,034	4,412
72110	Morrilton	6,814	5,997
72653	Mountain Home 1973	5,028	2,105
72112	Newport	7,725	7,007
*72114	North Little Rock	60,040	58,032
72370	Osceola	7,204	6,189
72450	Paragould	10,639	9,947
72455	Pocahantas 1974	5,448	3,665
71601	Pine Bluff	57,389	44,037
72756	Rogers 1974	13,189	5,700
72801	Russellville	11,750	8,921
72143	Searcy 1973	10,867	7,272
72761	Siloam Springs 1975	6,433	3,953
72204	Southwest Little Rock (u).	13,231	......
72764	Springdale 1974	19,962	10,076
72160	Stuttgart	10,477	9,661
75501	Texarkana	21,682	19,788
72472	Trumann 1974	6,402	4,511
72956	Van Buren 1975	9,452	6,787
71671	Warren	6,433	6,752
72390	West Helena 1973	10,838	8,385
72301	West Memphis 1973	28,236	19,374
72396	Wynne 1974	7,292	4,922

California

ZIP Code	Place	1970	1960
94501	Alameda	70,968	63,855
94507	Alamo-Danville (u)	14,059	......
94706	Albany	14,674	14,804
*91802	Alhambra	62,125	54,807
90249	Alondra Park (u)	12,193	......
91001	Altadena (u).	42,415	40,568
95116	Alum Rock (u).	18,355	18,942
*92803	Anaheim	166,408	104,184
96007	Anderson	5,492	4,492
94509	Antioch	28,060	17,305
92307	Apple Valley (u)	6,702	......
95003	Aptos (u).	8,704	......
91006	Arcadia	45,138	41,005
95521	Arcata	8,985	5,235
95825	Arden-Arcade (u)	82,492	73,352
93420	Arroyo Grande.	7,454	3,291
90701	Artesia	14,757	9,993
93203	Arvin 1975	6,014	......
94577	Ashland (u).	14,810	......
93422	Atascadero (u).	10,290	5,983
94025	Atherton	8,085	7,717
95301	Atwater	11,640	7,318
95603	Auburn	6,570	5,586
92505	August School Area (u)	6,735	......
91746	Avocado Heights (u).	9,810	......
91702	Azusa	25,217	20,497
*93302	Bakersfield	69,515	56,848
91706	Baldwin Park	47,285	33,951
92220	Banning	12,034	10,250
92311	Barstow 1975	16,812	11,644
95903	Beale East (u).	7,029	......
92223	Beaumont.	5,484	4,288
90201	Bell	21,836	19,450
90706	Bellflower	51,454	45,909
90201	Bell Gardens	29,308	......
94002	Belmont.	23,538	15,996
94510	Benicia	7,349	6,070
*94704	Berkeley	116,716	111,268
*90213	Beverly Hills	33,416	30,817
92314	Big Bear (u)	5,268	1,562
92316	Bloomington (u).	11,957	......
92225	Blythe	7,047	6,023
92227	Brawley 1974	13,940	12,703
92621	Brea	18,447	8,487
95605	Broderick-Bryte (u).	12,782	......
*90620	Buena Park	63,646	46,401
*91505	Burbank	88,871	90,155
94010	Burlingame.	27,320	24,036
92231	Calexico 1974	12,829	7,992
93725	Calwa (u).	5,191	......
93010	Camarillo	19,219	......
93010	Camarillo Heights (u).	5,892	1,704
95124	Cambrian Park (u)	5,316	......
95008	Campbell	24,770	11,863
95010	Capitola.	5,080	2,021
92007	Cardiff-by-the-Sea (u).	5,724	3,149
92008	Carlsbad.	14,944	9,253
95608	Carmichael (u).	37,625	20,455
93013	Carpinteria	6,982	......
90744	Carson.	71,150	......
94546	Castro Valley (u).	44,760	37,120
95307	Ceres	6,029	4,406
90701	Cerritos	15,856	3,508
94541	Cherryland (u).	9,969	......
95926	Chico.	19,580	14,757
95926	Chico North (u).	6,656	......
93555	China Lake (u).	11,105	......
91710	Chino 1975.	27,490	10,305

ZIP Code	Place	1970	1960
*92010	Chula Vista.	67,901	42,034
95610	Citrus Heights (u)	21,760	......
91711	Claremont.	23,464	12,633
93612	Clovis.	13,856	5,546
92236	Coachella.	8,353	4,854
93210	Coalinga.	6,161	5,965
92324	Colton 1975.	18,686	18,666
90022	Commerce.	10,536	9,555
*90220	Compton.	78,547	71,812
*94520	Concord.	85,164	36,000
93212	Corcoran.	5,249	4,976
91720	Corona.	27,519	13,336
92118	Coronado.	20,020	18,039
94925	Corte Madera.	8,464	5,962
*92626	Costa Mesa.	72,660	37,550
*91722	Covina.	30,395	20,124
91730	Cucamonga (u).	5,796	......
90201	Cudahy.	16,998	......
90230	Culver City.	34,451	32,163
95014	Cupertino.	18,216	3,664
90630	Cypress.	31,569	1,753
*94017	Daly City.	66,922	44,791
95616	Davis.	23,488	8,910
90250	Del Aire (u).	11,930	......
93215	Delano.	14,559	11,913
91765	Diamond Bar (u).	10,576	......
93618	Dinuba.	7,917	6,103
90810	Dominguez (u).	5,980	......
*90241	Downey.	88,445	82,505
91010	Duarte.	14,981	13,962
94566	Dublin (u).	13,641	......
90220	East Compton (u).	5,853	......
90638	East La Mirada (u).	12,339	......
90022	East Los Angeles (u).	105,033	104,270
94303	East Palo Alto (u).	18,099	......
93523	Edwards (u).	10,331	......
*92020	El Cajon.	52,273	37,618
92243	El Centro 1973	21,134	16,811
94530	El Cerrito.	25,190	25,437
93017	El Encanto Heights (u).	6,225	......
*91734	El Monte.	69,892	13,163
93446	El Paso de Robles.	7,168	6,677
93030	El Rio (u).	6,173	6,966
90245	El Segundo.	15,620	14,219
92630	El Toro (u).	8,654	......
92709	El Toro Station (u).	6,970	......
92024	Encinitas (u).	5,375	2,786
96001	Enterprise (u).	11,486	4,946
*92025	Escondido.	36,792	16,377
95501	Eureka.	24,337	28,137
94930	Fairfax.	7,661	5,813
94533	Fairfield.	44,146	14,968
95628	Fair Oaks (u).	11,256	......
92028	Fallbrook (u).	6,945	4,814
93015	Fillmore.	6,285	4,808
90001	Florence-Graham (u).	42,895	38,164
95828	Florin (u).	9,646	......
95630	Folsom.	5,810	3,925
92335	Fontana 1975.	23,629	14,659
94404	Foster City (u).	9,522	......
92708	Fountain Valley.	31,886	2,068
95019	Freedom (u).	5,563	4,206
*94536	Fremont.	100,869	43,790
*93706	Fresno.	165,972	133,929
*92631	Fullerton.	85,987	56,180
*90247	Gardena.	41,021	35,943
95205	Garden Acres (u).	7,870	......
*92640	Garden Grove.	120,967	84,238
92392	George (u).	7,404	......
95020	Gilroy.	12,665	7,348
92509	Glen Avon (u).	5,759	3,416
*91209	Glendale.	132,664	119,442
91740	Glendora.	31,380	20,752
92324	Grand Terrace (u).	5,901	......
95945	Grass Valley.	5,149	4,876
92041	Grossmont-Mt. Helix (u).	8,723	......
93433	Grover City.	5,939	5,210
91745	Hacienda Heights (u).	35,969	......
93230	Hanford.	15,179	10,133
90716	Hawaiian Gardens.	9,052	......
90250	Hawthorne.	53,304	33,035
*94544	Hayward.	93,058	72,700
95448	Healdsburg.	5,438	4,816
92343	Hemet.	12,252	5,416
92343	Hemet East (u).	8,598	1,936
90254	Hermosa Beach.	17,412	16,115
92346	Highland (u).	12,669	......
94010	Hillsborough.	8,753	7,554
95023	Hollister.	7,663	6,071
91720	Home Gardens (u).	5,116	1,541
*92647	Huntington Beach.	115,960	11,492
90255	Huntington Park.	33,744	29,920
92032	Imperial Beach.	20,244	17,773
92201	Indio.	14,459	9,745
*90306	Inglewood.	89,985	63,390
93017	Isla Vista (u).	13,441	......
94707	Kensington (u).	5,823	......
91011	La Canada-Flintridge (u)	20,652	18,338

ZIP Code	Place	1970	1960
91214	La Crescenta-Montrose(u)......	19,620	
90045	Ladera Heights(u)	6,535	
94549	Lafayette	20,484	7,114
*92651	Laguna Beach	14,550	9,288
92653	Laguna Hills(u)	13,676	
90631	La Habra	41,350	25,136
92040	Lakeside(u)	11,991	
*90714	Lakewood	83,025	67,126
92041	La Mesa	39,178	30,441
90638	La Mirada	30,808	22,444
93241	Lamont(u)	7,007	6,177
93534	Lancaster(u)	32,728	26,012
90624	La Palma	9,687	622
*91747	La Puente	31,092	24,723
94939	Larkspur	10,487	5,710
91750	La Verne	12,965	6,516
90260	Lawndale	24,825	21,740
92045	Lemon Grove(u)	19,690	19,348
93245	Lemoore Station(u)	9,210	
90304	Lennox(u)	16,121	31,224
95207	Lincoln Village(u)	6,112	
95901	Linda(u)	7,731	6,129
93247	Lindsay	5,206	5,397
95062	Live Oak(u) (Santa Cruz)	6,443	3,518
94550	Livermore	37,703	16,058
95240	Lodi	28,691	22,229
92354	Loma Linda 1975	7,651	
90717	Lomita	19,784	
93436	Lompoc	25,284	14,415
*90801	Long Beach	358,879	344,168
90720	Los Alamitos	11,346	4,312
94022	Los Altos	24,726	19,696
94022	Los Altos Hills	6,865	3,412
*90052	Los Angeles	2,809,813	2,479,015
93635	Los Banos	9,188	5,272
95030	Los Gatos	23,735	9,036
90262	Lynwood	43,354	31,614
93637	Madera	16,044	14,430
90266	Manhattan Beach	35,352	33,934
95336	Manteca	13,845	8,242
93933	Marina(u)	8,343	3,310
94553	Martinez	16,506	9,604
95901	Marysville	9,353	9,553
95655	Mather(u)	7,027	
90270	Maywood	16,996	14,588
93023	Meiners Oaks-Mira Monte(u)	7,025	
94025	Menlo Park	26,826	26,957
95340	Merced	22,670	20,068
94030	Millbrae	20,792	15,873
94941	Mill Valley	12,942	10,411
95035	Milpitas	27,149	6,572
91752	Mira Loma(u)	8,482	3,982
92675	Mission Viejo(u)	11,933	
*95350	Modesto	61,712	36,585
91016	Monrovia	30,562	27,079
91763	Montclair 1975	21,072	13,546
90640	Montebello	42,807	32,097
93940	Monterey	26,302	22,618
91754	Monterey Park	49,166	37,821
94556	Moraga(u)	14,205	
95037	Morgan Hill	6,485	3,151
93442	Morro Bay	7,109	
*94042	Mountain View	54,304	30,889
92405	Muscoy(u)	7,091	
94558	Napa	35,978	22,170
92050	National City	43,184	32,771
94560	Newark	27,153	9,884
91321	Newhall(u)	9,651	4,705
*92660	Newport Beach	49,422	26,564
91760	Norco	14,511	
94025	North Fair Oaks(u)	9,740	
95660	North Highlands(u)	31,854	21,271
92135	North Island(u)	6,892	
90650	Norwalk	91,827	88,739
94947	Novato	31,006	17,881
95361	Oakdale	6,594	4,980
*94615	Oakland	361,561	367,548
92054	Oceanside	40,494	24,971
93308	Oildale(u)	20,879	
93023	Ojai	5,591	4,495
95961	Olivehurst(u)	8,100	4,835
*91761	Ontario 1975	63,186	46,617
95060	Opal Cliffs(u)	5,425	3,825
*92667	Orange	77,365	26,444
95662	Orangevale(u)	16,493	
93454	Orcutt(u)	8,500	1,414
94563	Orinda Village(u)	6,790	5,568
95965	Oroville	7,536	6,115
92010	Otay-Castle Park(u)	15,445	
93030	Oxnard	71,225	40,265
94044	Pacifica	36,020	20,995
93950	Pacific Grove	13,505	12,121
93550	Palmdale	8,511	
92260	Palm Desert(u)	6,171	1,295
92262	Palm Springs	20,936	13,468
*94302	Palo Alto	55,835	52,287
90274	Palos Verdes Estates	13,631	9,564
90274	Palos Verdes Peninsula(u)	38,918	
95969	Paradise(u)	14,539	8,268

ZIP Code	Place	1970	1960
90723	Paramount	34,734	27,249
95823	Parkway-Sacramento So.(u)	28,574	
*91109	Pasadena	112,951	116,407
92055	Pendleton North(u)	11,803	
92055	Pendleton South(u)	13,692	
94952	Petaluma	24,870	14,035
90660	Pico Rivera	54,170	49,150
94611	Piedmont	10,917	11,117
94564	Pinole	13,266	6,064
94565	Pittsburg	20,651	19,062
92670	Placentia	21,948	5,861
95667	Placerville	5,416	4,439
94523	Pleasant Hill	24,610	23,844
94546	Pleasanton	18,328	4,203
*91766	Pomona	87,384	67,157
93257	Porterville	12,602	7,991
93257	Porterville West(u)	6,200	
93041	Port Hueneme	14,295	11,067
92064	Poway(u)	9,422	1,921
95670	Rancho Cordova(u)	30,451	7,429
95014	Rancho Rinconada(u)	5,149	
96080	Red Bluff	7,676	7,202
96001	Redding	16,659	12,773
92373	Redlands 1975	36,566	26,829
*90277	Redondo Beach	57,451	46,986
*94064	Redwood City	55,686	46,290
93654	Reedley	8,131	5,850
92376	Rialto 1975	31,069	18,567
*94802	Richmond	79,043	71,854
93555	Ridgecrest	7,629	
95673	Rio Linda(u)	7,524	2,189
*92502	Riverside	140,089	84,332
94572	Rodeo(u)	5,356	
94928	Rohnert Park	6,133	
90274	Rolling Hills Estates	6,735	3,941
95401	Roseland(u)	5,105	4,510
91770	Rosemead	40,972	15,476
95678	Roseville	18,221	13,421
90720	Rossmoor(u)	12,922	
91745	Rowland Heights(u)	16,881	
92509	Rubidoux(u)	13,969	
*95813	Sacramento	257,105	191,667
93901	Salinas	58,896	28,957
94960	San Anselmo	13,031	11,584
*92403	San Bernardino 1975	102,303	91,922
94066	San Bruno	36,254	29,063
	San Buenaventura (See Ventura)		
94070	San Carlos	26,053	21,370
92672	San Clemente	17,063	8,527
*92109	San Diego	697,027	573,224
91773	San Dimas	15,692	
*91340	San Fernando	16,571	16,093
*94101	San Francisco	715,674	740,316
91776	San Gabriel	29,336	22,561
93657	Sanger	10,088	8,072
*95101	San Jose	445,779	204,196
*94577	San Leandro	68,698	65,962
94580	San Lorenzo(u)	24,633	23,773
93401	San Luis Obispo	28,036	20,437
91108	San Marino	14,177	13,658
*94402	San Mateo	78,991	69,870
94806	San Pablo	21,461	19,687
*94901	San Rafael	38,977	20,460
*92711	Santa Ana	155,762	100,350
*93102	Santa Barbara	70,215	58,768
*95050	Santa Clara	87,717	58,880
95060	Santa Cruz	32,076	25,596
90670	Santa Fe Springs	14,750	16,342
93454	Santa Maria	32,749	20,027
93454	Santa Maria South(u)	7,129	
*90406	Santa Monica	88,289	83,249
93060	Santa Paula	18,001	13,279
*95402	Santa Rosa	50,006	31,027
92071	Santee(u)	21,107	
95070	Saratoga	27,110	14,861
94965	Sausalito	6,158	5,331
90740	Seal Beach	24,441	6,994
93955	Seaside	35,935	19,353
93662	Selma	7,459	6,934
93263	Shafter	5,327	4,576
91024	Sierra Madre	12,140	9,732
93461	Signal Hill	5,588	4,627
*93065	Simi Valley	59,832	
92075	Solana Beach(u)	5,023	
95073	Soquel(u)	5,795	
91733	South El Monte	13,443	4,850
90280	South Gate	56,909	53,831
95705	South Lake Tahoe	12,921	
95350	South Modesto(u)	7,889	5,465
91030	South Pasadena	22,979	19,706
94080	South San Francisco	46,646	39,418
91770	South San Gabriel(u)	5,051	
91744	South San Jose Hills(u)	12,386	
90605	South Whittier(u)	46,641	
95991	South Yuba(u)	5,352	3,200
*92077	Spring Valley(u)	29,742	
94305	Stanford(u)	8,691	
90680	Stanton	18,186	11,163
*95204	Stockton	109,963	86,321

ZIP Code	Place	1970	1960
92381	Sun City(u)	5,519	
92388	Sunnymead(u)	6,708	3,404
*94086	Sunnyvale	95,408	52,898
96130	Susanville	6,608	5,598
91780	Temple City	31,034	......
*91360	Thousand Oaks	35,873	......
94920	Tiburon	6,209	......
*90510	Torrance	134,968	100,991
95376	Tracy	14,724	11,289
93274	Tulare	16,235	13,824
95380	Turlock	13,992	9,116
92680	Tustin	21,180	2,006
92705	Tustin-Foothills(u)	26,598	......
92277	Twentynine Palms(u)	5,667	......
92278	Twentynine Palms Base(u)	5,647	......
95482	Ukiah	10,095	9,900
94587	Union City	14,724	6,618
91786	Upland 1975	37,253	15,918
95688	Vacaville	21,690	10,898
91744	Valinda(u)	18,837	......
94590	Vallejo	71,710	60,877
93437	Vandenburg(u)	13,193	......
*93001	Ventura	57,964	29,114
92392	Victorville 1975	12,344	......
90043	View Park-Windsor Hills(u)	12,268	......
93277	Visalia	27,268	15,791
92083	Vista	24,688	......
91793	Walnut	5,992	934
*94596	Walnut Creek	39,844	9,903
94596	Walnut Creek West(u)	8,330	......
90255	Walnut Park(u)	8,925	......
93280	Wasco	8,269	6,841
95076	Watsonville	14,569	13,293
90044	West Athens(u)	13,311	......
90502	West Carson(u)	15,918	......
90247	West Compton(u)	5,605	......
*91793	West Covina	68,034	50,645
90069	West Hollywood(u)	34,622	28,870
92683	Westminster	59,874	25,750
95351	West Modesto(u)	6,135	1,897
90047	Westmont(u)	29,310	......
94565	West Pittsburg(u)	5,969	5,188
91746	West Puente Valley(u)	20,733	......
95691	West Sacramento(u)	12,002	......
*90606	West Whittier-Los Nietos(u)	20,845	......
*90605	Whittier	72,863	33,663
90222	Willowbrook(u)	32,328	......
95695	Woodland	20,677	13,524
92686	Yorba Linda	11,856	......
96097	Yreka City	5,394	4,759
95991	Yuba City	13,986	11,507
92399	Yucaipa(u)	19,284	......

Colorado

ZIP Code	Place	1970	1960
81101	Alamosa	6,985	6,205
80401	Applewood(u)	8,214	......
*80001	Arvada	49,083	19,242
80010	Aurora	74,974	48,548
*80302	Boulder	66,870	37,718
80601	Brighton	8,309	7,055
80020	Broomfield	7,261	......
81212	Canon City	9,206	8,973
*80901	Colorado Springs	135,060	70,194
80022	Commerce City	17,407	8,970
81321	Cortez	6,032	6,764
*80202	Denver	514,678	493,887
80022	Derby(u)	10,206	10,124
81301	Durango	10,333	10,530
80110	Englewood	33,695	33,398
80913	Fort Carson(u)	19,399	......
80521	Fort Collins	43,337	25,027
80701	Fort Morgan	7,594	7,379
80401	Golden	9,817	7,118
81501	Grand Junction	20,170	18,694
80631	Greeley	38,902	26,314
81050	La Junta	7,938	8,026
80215	Lakewood	92,743	......
81052	Lamar	7,797	7,369
80120	Littleton	26,466	13,670
80120	Littleton Southeast(u)	22,899	......
80501	Longmont	23,209	11,489
80537	Loveland	16,220	9,734
81401	Montrose	6,496	5,044
80233	North Glenn	27,937	......
81501	Orchard Mesa(u)	5,824	4,956
*81003	Pueblo	97,453	91,181
80911	Security-Widefield(u)	15,297	9,017
80221	Sherrelwood(u)	18,868	......
80751	Sterling	10,636	10,751
80906	Stratton Meadows(u)	6,223	......
80229	Thornton	13,326	11,353
81082	Trinidad	9,901	10,691
80229	Welby(u)	6,875	......
80030	Westminster	19,432	13,850
80221	Westminster East(u)	7,576	......
80033	Wheat Ridge	29,778	......

ZIP Code	Place	1970	1960
	Connecticut		
	See Note on Page 241		
06401	Ansonia	21,160	19,819
06001	Avon	8,352	5,273
06037	Berlin	14,149	11,250
06801	Bethel	10,945	8,200
06002	Bloomfield	18,301	13,613
06405	Branford	20,444	16,610
*06602	Bridgeport	156,542	156,748
06010	Bristol	55,487	45,499
06804	Brookfield	9,688	3,405
06019	Canton	6,868	4,783
06410	Cheshire	19,051	13,383
06413	Clinton	10,267	4,166
06413	Clinton Center(u)	5,957	2,693
06415	Colchester	6,603	4,648
06340	Conning Towers-Nautilus Park(u)	9,791	3,457
06238	Coventry	8,140	6,356
06416	Cromwell	7,400	6,780
06810	Danbury	50,781	22,928
06820	Darien	20,411	18,437
06418	Derby	12,599	12,132
06424	East Hampton	7,078	5,403
06108	East Hartford	57,583	43,977
06512	East Haven	25,120	21,388
06333	East Lyme	11,399	6,782
06016	East Windsor	8,513	7,500
06029	Ellington	7,707	5,580
06082	Enfield	46,189	31,464
06430	Fairfield	56,487	46,183
06032	Farmington	14,390	10,813
06033	Glastonbury	20,651	14,497
06035	Granby	6,150	4,968
06830	Greenwich	59,755	53,793
06351	Griswold	7,763	6,472
06340	Groton	38,244	29,937
06340	Groton Borough	8,933	10,111
06437	Guilford	12,033	7,913
06514	Hamden	49,357	41,056
*06101	Hartford	158,017	162,178
06239	Killingly	13,573	11,298
06339	Ledyard	14,837	5,395
06759	Litchfield	7,399	6,264
06443	Madison	9,768	4,567
06040	Manchester	47,994	42,102
06250	Mansfield	19,994	14,638
06450	Meriden	55,959	51,850
06762	Middlebury	5,542	4,785
06457	Middletown	36,924	33,250
06460	Milford	50,858	41,662
06468	Monroe	12,047	6,402
06353	Montville	15,662	7,759
06770	Naugatuck	23,034	19,511
*06050	New Britain	83,441	82,201
06840	New Canaan	17,455	13,466
06810	New Fairfield	6,991	3,355
*06510	New Haven	137,707	152,048
06111	Newington	26,037	17,664
06320	New London	31,630	34,182
06776	New Milford	14,601	8,318
06470	Newtown	16,942	11,373
06471	North Branford	10,778	6,771
06473	North Haven	22,194	15,935
06856	Norwalk	79,113	67,775
06360	Norwich	41,739	38,506
06475	Old Saybrook	8,468	5,274
06477	Orange	13,524	8,547
02891	Pawcatuck(u)	5,255	4,389
06374	Plainfield	11,957	8,884
06062	Plainville	16,733	13,149
06782	Plymouth	10,321	8,981
06480	Portland	8,812	7,496
06712	Prospect	6,543	4,367
06260	Putnam	6,918	6,952
	Putnam	8,598	8,412
06875	Redding	5,590	3,359
06877	Ridgefield Center(u)	5,878	2,954
	Ridgefield	18,188	8,165
06067	Rocky Hill	11,103	7,404
06483	Seymour	12,776	10,100
06484	Shelton	27,165	18,190
06070	Simsbury	17,475	10,138
06071	Somers	6,893	3,702
06488	Southbury	7,852	5,186
06489	Southington	30,946	22,797
06074	South Windsor	15,553	9,460
06075	Stafford	8,680	7,476
*06904	Stamford	108,798	92,713
06378	Stonington	15,940	13,969
06268	Storrs(u)	10,691	6,054
06497	Stratford	49,775	45,012
06078	Suffield	8,634	6,779
06787	Thomaston	6,233	5,850
06277	Thompson	7,580	6,217
06084	Tolland	7,857	2,950
06790	Torrington	31,952	30,045
06611	Trumbull	31,394	20,379

ZIP Code	Place	1970	1960
06060	Vernon	27,237	16,961
06492	Wallingford	35,714	29,920
*06701	Waterbury	108,033	107,130
06385	Waterford	17,227	15,391
06795	Watertown	18,610	14,837
06107	West Hartford	68,031	62,382
06516	West Haven	52,851	43,002
06880	Weston	7,417	4,039
06880	Westport	27,414	20,955
06109	Wethersfield	26,662	20,561
06226	Willimantic	14,402	13,881
06897	Wilton	13,572	8,026
06094	Winchester	11,106	10,496
06280	Windham	19,626	16,973
06095	Windsor	22,502	19,467
06096	Windsor Locks	15,080	11,411
06098	Winsted	8,954	8,136
06716	Wolcott	12,495	8,889
06525	Woodbridge	7,673	5,182
06798	Woodbury	5,869	3,910

Delaware

ZIP Code	Place	1970	1960
19711	Brookside Park(u)	7,856	
19703	Claymont(u)	6,584	
19901	Dover	17,488	7,250
19901	Dover Base(u)	8,106	
19805	Elsmere	8,415	7,319
19963	Milford	5,314	5,795
19711	Newark	21,298	11,404
19973	Seaford	5,537	4,430
*19899	Wilmington	80,386	95,827
19720	Wilmington Manor —Chelsea—Leedom	10,134	

District of Columbia

ZIP Code	Place	1970	1960
*20013	Washington	756,510	763,956
	Northeast	184,439	197,536
	Northwest	347,337	374,165
	Southeast	194,365	173,988
	Southwest	30,369	18,267

Florida

ZIP Code	Place	1970	1960
33821	Arcadia	5,658	5,889
33823	Auburndale	5,386	5,595
33825	Avon Park	6,712	6,073
32807	Azalea Park(u)	7,367	
33830	Bartow	12,891	12,849
33505	Bayshore Gardens(u)	9,255	2,297
33430	Belle Glade	15,949	11,273
33432	Boca Raton	28,506	6,961
33435	Boynton Beach	18,115	10,467
*33506	Bradenton	21,040	19,380
33511	Brandon(u)	12,749	1,665
33314	Broadview Park-Rock Hill(u)	6,049	
33311	Browardale(u)	17,444	
33142	Browns Village(u)	23,442	
33054	Bunche Park(u)	5,773	
33904	Cape Coral(u)	10,193	
33055	Carol City(u)	27,361	21,749
33023	Carver Ranch Estates(u)	5,515	
32707	Casselberry	9,438	2,463
33505	Cedar Hammock- Bradenton South(u)	10,820	
32324	Chattahoochee	7,944	9,699
*33515	Clearwater	52,074	34,653
32922	Cocoa	16,110	12,294
32931	Cocoa Beach	9,952	3,475
32922	Cocoa West(u)	5,779	3,975
33064	Collier Manor-Cresthaven(u)	7,202	
32809	Conway(u)	8,642	
33134	Coral Gables	42,494	34,793
32536	Crestview	7,952	7,467
33157	Cutler Ridge(u)	17,441	7,005
33004	Dania	9,013	7,065
33314	Davie	5,859	
*32015	Daytona Beach	45,327	37,395
33441	Deerfield Beach	16,662	9,573
32720	De Land	11,641	10,775
33444	Delray Beach	19,915	12,230
33528	Dunedin	17,639	8,444
33610	East Lake-Orient Park(u)	5,711	
33940	East Naples(u)	6,152	
32542	Eglin(u)	7,769	
33614	Egypt Lake(u)	7,556	
33533	Englewood(u)	5,108	2,877
32726	Eustis	6,722	6,189
32034	Fernandina Beach	6,955	7,276
33030	Florida City	5,133	4,114
*33310	Fort Lauderdale	139,590	82,648
33902	Fort Myers	27,351	22,523
33901	Fort Myers Southwest(u)	5,086	
33450	Fort Pierce	29,721	25,256
32548	Fort Walton Beach	19,994	12,147
*32601	Gainesville	64,510	29,701

ZIP Code	Place	1970	1960
32960	Gifford(u)	5,772	3,509
33170	Goulds(u)	6,690	5,121
33581	Gulf Gate Estates(u)	5,874	
33737	Gulfport	9,976	9,730
33844	Haines City	8,956	9,135
33009	Hallandale	23,849	10,483
*33010	Hialeah	102,452	66,972
32805	Holden Heights(u)	6,206	
32017	Holly Hill	8,191	4,182
*33022	Hollywood	106,873	35,237
33030	Homestead	13,674	9,152
33030	Homestead Base(u)	8,257	
32937	Indian Harbour Beach	5,371	
*32201	Jacksonville	528,865	201,030
33156	Kendall(u)	35,497	
33040	Key West	29,312	33,956
32741	Kissimmee	7,119	6,845
33618	Lake Carroll(u)	5,577	
32055	Lake City	10,575	9,465
32208	Lake Forest(u)	5,216	
33803	Lake Holloway(u)	6,227	3,172
*33802	Lakeland	41,550	41,350
33612	Lake Magdalene(u)	9,266	
33403	Lake Park	6,993	3,589
33853	Lake Wales	8,240	8,346
33460	Lake Worth	23,714	20,758
33460	Lantana	7,126	5,021
33540	Largo	22,031	5,302
33313	Lauderdale Lakes	10,577	
33313	Lauderhill	8,465	132
32748	Leesburg	11,869	11,172
33614	Leto(u)	8,458	
33064	Lighthouse Point	9,071	2,453
32060	Live Oak	6,830	6,544
32810	Lockhart(u)	5,809	
32751	Maitland	7,157	3,570
33063	Margate	8,867	2,646
32446	Marianna	6,741	7,152
*32901	Melbourne	40,236	11,982
33314	Melrose Park(u)	6,111	
32952	Merritt Island(u)	29,233	3,554
*33152	Miami	334,859	291,688
33139	Miami Beach	87,072	63,145
33153	Miami Shores	9,425	8,865
33166	Miami Springs	13,279	11,229
32570	Milton	5,360	4,108
32754	Mims(u)	8,309	1,307
33023	Miramar	23,997	5,485
32506	Myrtle Grove(u)	16,186	
33940	Naples	12,042	4,655
33552	New Port Richey 1973	7,137	3,520
32069	New Smyrna Beach	10,580	8,781
33308	North Andrews Terrace(u)	7,082	
33903	North Fort Myers(u)	8,798	
33314	North Lauderdale 1974	9,285	
33161	North Miami	34,767	28,708
33160	North Miami Beach	30,544	21,405
33408	North Palm Beach	9,035	2,684
33169	Norwood(u)	14,973	
33308	Oakland Park	16,261	5,331
32670	Ocala	22,583	13,598
32548	Ocean City(u)	5,267	
33054	Opa-Locka	11,902	9,810
32073	Orange Park	7,619	2,624
*32802	Orlando	99,006	88,135
32074	Ormond Beach	14,063	8,658
32074	Ormond By-The-Sea(u)	6,002	3,476
33476	Pahokee	5,663	4,709
32077	Palatka	9,444	11,028
32905	Palm Bay	7,176	2,808
33480	Palm Beach	9,086	6,055
33403	Palm Beach Gardens	6,102	1
33561	Palmetto	7,422	5,556
33619	Palm River-Clair Mel(u)	8,536	
32401	Panama City	32,096	33,275
33023	Pembroke Pines	15,496	1,429
*32502	Pensacola	59,507	56,752
33157	Perrine(u)	10,257	6,424
32347	Perry	7,701	8,030
32808	Pine Hills(u)	13,882	
33565	Pinellas Park	22,287	10,848
33566	Plant City	15,451	15,711
33314	Plantation	23,523	4,772
*33060	Pompano Beach	38,587	15,992
33064	Pompano Beach Highlands(u)	5,014	
33950	Port Charlotte(u)	10,769	3,197
32351	Quincy	8,334	8,874
33156	Richmond Heights(u)	6,663	4,311
33312	Riverland Village- Lauderdale Isles(u)	5,512	
33404	Riviera Beach	21,401	13,046
32955	Rockledge	10,523	3,481
32084	St. Augustine	12,352	14,734
32769	St. Cloud	5,041	4,353
*33730	St. Petersburg	216,159	181,298
33706	St. Petersburg Beach	8,024	6,268
32771	Sanford	17,393	19,175
*33578	Sarasota	40,237	34,083
33579	Sarasota Southeast(u)	6,885	

ZIP Code	Place	1970	1960
32937	Satellite Beach	6,558	825
33870	Sebring	7,223	6,939
33143	South Miami	11,780	9,846
33157	South Miami Heights(u)	10,395	
32937	South Patrick Shores(u)	10,313	
32401	Springfield	5,949	4,628
33304	Sunrise 1972	11,693	
33614	Sweetwater Creek(u)	19,453	
*32303	Tallahassee	72,624	48,174
33313	Tamarac 1975	22,614	
*33602	Tampa	277,753	274,970
33589	Tarpon Springs	7,118	6,768
33617	Temple Terrace	7,347	3,812
33905	Tice(u)	7,254	4,377
32780	Titusville	30,515	6,410
33740	Treasure Island	6,120	3,506
33620	University (Hillsborough)(u)	10,039	
32580	Valparaiso	6,504	5,975
33595	Venice	6,648	3,444
32960	Vero Beach	11,908	8,849
32960	Vero Beach South(u)	7,330	
32507	Warrington(u)	15,848	16,752
33505	West Bradenton(u)	6,162	
32446	West End(u)	5,289	3,124
33144	West Miami	5,494	5,296
*33401	West Palm Beach	57,375	56,208
32505	West Pensacola(u)	20,924	
33880	West Winter Haven(u)	7,716	5,050
33165	Westwood Lakes(u)	12,811	22,517
33305	Wilton Manors	10,948	8,257
32787	Winter Garden	5,153	5,513
33880	Winter Haven	16,136	16,277
32789	Winter Park	21,895	17,162

Georgia

ZIP Code	Place	1970	1960
*31701	Albany	72,623	55,890
31709	Americus	16,091	13,472
30601	Athens	44,342	31,355
*30304	Atlanta	497,421	487,455
*30901	Augusta	59,864	70,626
31717	Bainbridge	10,887	12,714
31723	Blakely	5,267	3,580
31520	Brunswick	19,585	21,703
31728	Cairo	8,061	7,427
30117	Carrollton	13,520	10,973
30120	Cartersville	10,138	8,668
30125	Cedartown	9,253	9,340
30341	Chamblee	9,127	6,635
31014	Cochran	5,161	4,714
30337	College Park	18,203	23,469
*31902	Columbus	155,028	116,779
31015	Cordele	10,733	10,609
30209	Covington	10,267	8,167
30720	Dalton	18,872	17,868
31742	Dawson	5,383	5,062
*30030	Decatur	21,943	22,026
31520	Dock Junction(u)	6,009	5,417
30340	Doraville	9,157	4,437
31533	Douglas	10,195	8,736
30134	Douglasville	5,472	4,462
31021	Dublin	15,143	13,814
31023	Eastman	5,416	5,118
30344	East Point	39,315	35,633
30635	Elberton	6,438	7,107
31750	Fitzgerald	8,187	8,781
30050	Forest Park	19,994	14,201
31905	Fort Benning(u)	27,495	
30905	Fort Gordon(u)	15,589	
30741	Fort Oglethorpe 1974	5,083	2,251
31030	Fort Valley	9,251	8,310
30501	Gainesville	15,459	16,523
31408	Garden City	5,790	5,451
30223	Griffin	22,734	21,735
30354	Hapeville	9,567	10,082
31545	Jesup	9,091	7,304
30728	La Fayette	6,044	5,588
30240	La Grange	23,301	23,632
30245	Lawrenceville	5,115	3,804
*31201	Macon	122,423	69,764
30060	Marietta	27,216	25,565
31034	Midway-Hardwick(u)	14,047	16,909
31061	Milledgeville	11,601	11,117
30655	Monroe	8,071	6,826
31768	Moultrie	14,400	15,764
30263	Newnan	11,205	12,169
31069	Perry	7,771	6,032
30161	Rome	30,759	32,226
30075	Roswell	5,430	2,983
31522	St. Simons(u)	5,346	3,199
31082	Sandersville	5,546	5,425
*31401	Savannah	118,349	149,245
30080	Smyrna	19,157	10,157
30458	Statesboro	14,616	8,356
30747	Summerville	5,043	4,706
30401	Swainsboro	7,325	5,943
30286	Thomaston	10,024	9,336
31792	Thomasville	18,155	18,246
30824	Thomson	6,503	4,522

ZIP Code	Place	1970	1960
31794	Tifton	12,179	9,903
30577	Toccoa	6,971	7,303
31601	Valdosta	32,303	30,652
30474	Vidalia	9,507	7,569
31093	Warner Robins	33,491	18,633
31501	Waycross	18,996	20,944
30830	Waynesboro	5,530	5,359
30680	Winder	6,605	5,555
31406	Windsor Forest(u)	7,288	

Hawaii

ZIP Code	Place	1970	1960
96701	Aiea	12,560	11,826
96706	Ewa Beach	7,765	4,627
96701	Halawa Heights	5,809	
96824	Hickam Housing	7,352	
96720	Hilo	26,353	25,966
*96813	Honolulu	324,871	294,194
96732	Kahului	8,280	4,223
96734	Kailua	33,783	25,622
96744	Kaneohe	29,903	14,414
96734	Maunawili	5,303	
96734	Mokapu	7,860	
96792	Nanakuli	6,506	2,745
96782	Pacific Palisades	7,846	
96782	Pearl City	19,552	
96786	Schofield Barracks	13,516	
96786	Wahiawa	17,598	15,512
96793	Wailuku	7,979	6,969
96797	Waipahu	24,150	

Idaho

ZIP Code	Place	1970	1960
83221	Blackfoot	8,716	7,378
*83708	Boise City	74,990	34,481
83318	Burley	8,279	7,508
83605	Caldwell	14,219	12,230
83814	Coeur D'Alene	16,228	14,291
83401	Idaho Falls	35,776	33,161
83338	Jerome 1974	5,625	4,761
83501	Lewiston	26,068	12,691
83843	Moscow	14,146	11,183
83647	Mountain Home 1974	6,755	5,984
83648	Mountain Home Base (u)	6,038	
83651	Nampa	20,768	18,897
83661	Payette 1975	5,235	4,451
83201	Pocatello	40,036	28,534
83440	Rexburg 1973	9,761	4,767
83301	Twin Falls	21,914	20,126

Illinois

ZIP Code	Place	1970	1960
60101	Addison 1973	25,645	6,741
60658	Alsip 1974	15,694	3,770
62002	Alton	39,700	43,047
*60004	Arlington Heights 1972	69,204	27,878
*60507	Aurora	74,182	63,715
60010	Barrington	8,674	5,434
61607	Bartonville	7,221	7,253
60510	Batavia 1974	10,816	7,496
62618	Beardstown	6,222	6,294
*62220	Belleville	41,699	37,264
60104	Bellwood 1971	21,473	20,729
61008	Belvidere	14,061	11,223
60106	Bensenville	12,956	9,141
62812	Benton	6,833	7,023
60162	Berkeley	6,152	5,792
60402	Berwyn	52,502	54,224
62010	Bethalto 1974	8,001	3,235
60108	Bloomingdale 1975	8,788	1,262
61701	Bloomington 1975	41,409	36,271
60406	Blue Island	22,958	19,618
60439	Bolingbrook 1974	25,519	
60914	Bourbonnais 1974	8,390	3,336
60915	Bradley 1972	10,631	8,082
60455	Bridgeview 1972	13,495	7,334
60153	Broadview 1971	9,470	8,588
60513	Brookfield	20,284	20,429
60090	Buffalo Grove 1974	18,390	1,492
60459	Burbank	29,900	
62206	Cahokia	20,649	15,829
62914	Cairo	6,277	9,348
60409	Calumet City 1972	35,808	25,000
60643	Calumet Park	10,069	8,448
61520	Canton	14,217	13,588
62901	Carbondale	22,816	14,670
62626	Carlinville	5,675	5,440
62821	Carmi	6,033	6,152
60187	Carol Stream 1973	7,519	836
60110	Carpentersville 1975	24,869	17,424
62801	Centralia	15,217	13,904
62206	Centreville	11,378	12,769
61820	Champaign	56,532	49,583
61920	Charleston	16,421	10,505
62233	Chester	5,310	4,460
*60607	Chicago	3,366,957	3,550,404
60411	Chicago Heights	40,900	34,331
60415	Chicago Ridge 1974	12,576	5,748
61523	Chillicothe	6,052	3,054
60650	Cicero	67,058	69,130

ZIP Code	Place	1970	1960
60514	Clarendon Hills.............	6,750	5,885
61727	Clinton.............	7,570	7,355
62234	Collinsville.............	17,992	14,217
60477	Country Club Hills 1975...........	12,239	3,421
60525	Countryside 1973...........	5,434	......
60435	Crest Hill 1973.............	8,322	5,887
60445	Crestwood 1973...........	7,557	1,213
61611	Creve Coeur 1973...........	6,594	6,684
60014	Crystal Lake 1975...........	16,797	8,314
61832	Danville.............	42,570	41,856
60559	Darien 1973...........	9,770	......
*62521	Decatur.............	90,397	78,004
60015	Deerfield 1972.............	18,867	11,786
60115	De Kalb.............	32,949	18,486
*60016	Des Plaines 1973.............	55,594	34,886
61021	Dixon.............	18,147	19,565
60419	Dolton 1974.............	26,321	18,746
60515	Downers Grove.............	32,751	21,154
62832	Du Quoin.............	6,691	6,558
62024	East Alton.............	7,309	7,630
60411	East Chicago Heights 1973...........	6,405	3,270
60064	North Chicago.............	47,275	22,938
61611	East Peoria.............	18,455	12,310
*62201	East St. Louis.............	69,996	81,712
62025	Edwardsville.............	11,070	9,996
62401	Effingham.............	9,458	8,172
60120	Elgin 1972.............	56,937	49,447
60007	Elk Grove Village 1974...........	25,303	6,608
60126	Elmhurst.............	48,887	36,991
60635	Elmwood Park.............	26,160	23,866
*60201	Evanston.............	80,113	79,283
60642	Evergreen Park 1971...........	25,981	24,178
62837	Fairfield.............	5,897	6,362
62208	Fairview Heights.............	8,625	......
62839	Flora.............	5,283	5,331
60422	Flossmoor 1975...........	8,310	4,624
60130	Forest Park.............	15,472	14,452
60131	Franklin Park.............	20,348	18,322
61032	Freeport.............	27,736	26,628
60030	Gages Lake-Wildwood(u)...........	5,337	......
61401	Galesburg 1971...........	34,501	37,243
61254	Geneseo.............	5,840	5,169
60134	Geneva 1974...........	9,140	7,646
60022	Glencoe.............	10,675	10,472
60137	Glendale Heights 1975...........	15,528	173
60137	Glen Ellyn.............	21,909	15,972
60025	Glenview.............	24,880	18,132
60425	Glenwood 1975...........	10,409	882
62040	Granite City.............	40,685	40,073
60030	Grayslake 1974...........	5,062	3,762
60103	Hanover Park 1972...........	19,609	451
62946	Harrisburg.............	9,535	9,171
60033	Harvard.............	5,177	4,248
60426	Harvey.............	34,636	29,071
60656	Harwood Heights 1971...........	8,837	5,688
60429	Hazel Crest 1974...........	13,229	6,205
62948	Herrin.............	9,623	9,474
60457	Hickory Hills 1974...........	13,951	2,707
62249	Highland.............	5,981	4,943
60035	Highland Park.............	32,263	25,532
60162	Hillside 1971.............	9,466	7,794
60521	Hinsdale.............	15,918	12,859
60172	Hoffman Estates 1974...........	31,549	8,296
60456	Hometown.............	6,729	7,479
60430	Homewood 1973...........	20,074	13,371
60942	Hoopeston.............	6,461	6,806
62650	Jacksonville.............	20,553	21,690
62052	Jerseyville.............	7,446	7,420
*60431	Joliet.............	78,887	66,780
60458	Justice.............	9,473	2,803
60901	Kankakee.............	30,944	27,666
61109	Ken Rock(u).............	5,945	......
61443	Kewanee.............	15,762	16,324
60525	La Grange.............	17,814	15,285
60525	La Grange Highlands(u)...........	6,842	......
60525	La Grange Park.............	15,459	13,793
60044	Lake Bluff.............	5,008	3,494
60045	Lake Forest.............	15,642	10,687
60047	Lake Zurich 1975...........	6,789	3,458
60438	Lansing 1973...........	28,232	18,098
61301	La Salle.............	10,736	11,897
62439	Lawrenceville.............	5,863	5,492
60439	Lemont.............	5,080	3,397
60048	Libertyville 1974...........	13,396	8,560
62656	Lincoln.............	17,582	16,890
60645	Lincolnwood.............	12,929	11,744
60532	Lisle 1974.............	8,428	4,219
62056	Litchfield.............	7,190	7,330
60441	Lockport.............	9,985	7,560
60148	Lombard 1974...........	36,839	22,561
61111	Loves Park.............	12,390	9,086
60534	Lyons.............	11,124	9,936
60050	McHenry 1972...........	7,680	3,336
61455	Macomb 1973...........	22,304	12,135
62060	Madison.............	7,042	6,861
62959	Marion 1972...........	12,899	11,274
60426	Markham.............	15,987	11,704
62258	Mascoutah.............	5,045	3,625
60443	Matteson 1974...........	6,086	3,225

ZIP Code	Place	1970	1960
61938	Mattoon 1972.............	19,270	19,088
60153	Maywood.............	29,019	27,330
*60160	Melrose Park.............	22,716	22,291
61342	Mendota.............	6,902	6,154
62960	Metropolis.............	6,940	7,339
60445	Midlothian 1974...........	14,241	6,605
61264	Milan 1972...........	5,053	3,065
61265	Moline.............	46,237	42,705
61462	Monmouth.............	11,022	10,372
60450	Morris 1972...........	8,435	7,935
61550	Morton 1973...........	12,217	5,325
60053	Morton Grove.............	26,369	20,533
62863	Mount Carmel.............	8,096	8,594
60056	Mount Prospect 1973...........	46,525	18,906
62864	Mount Vernon.............	16,382	15,566
60060	Mundelein 1974...........	17,315	10,526
62966	Murphysboro.............	10,013	8,673
60540	Naperville 1973...........	27,837	12,933
60648	Niles 1971.............	32,432	20,393
61761	Normal 1975...........	32,091	13,357
60656	Norridge 1971...........	18,043	14,087
60542	North Aurora 1974...........	5,344	2,088
60062	Northbrook 1974...........	27,681	11,635
60064	North Chicago.............	47,275	22,938
60093	Northfield.............	5,010	4,005
60164	Northlake.............	14,212	12,318
61111	North Park(u).............	15,679	......
60546	North Riverside 1971...........	7,849	7,989
60452	Oak Forest 1972...........	20,903	3,724
*60454	Oak Lawn 1974...........	62,245	27,471
*60301	Oak Park.............	62,511	61,093
62269	O'Fallon 1973...........	10,045	4,018
62450	Olney.............	8,974	8,780
60462	Orland Park 1973...........	11,219	2,592
61350	Ottawa.............	18,716	19,408
60067	Palatine 1973...........	28,807	11,504
60463	Palos Heights 1973...........	9,879	3,775
60465	Palos Hills 1972...........	9,778	3,766
62557	Pana.............	6,326	6,432
61944	Paris.............	9,971	9,823
60466	Park Forest.............	30,638	29,993
60068	Park Ridge.............	42,614	32,659
61554	Pekin 1974...........	32,315	28,146
*61601	Peoria.............	126,963	103,162
61614	Peoria Heights 1975...........	8,239	7,064
61354	Peru.............	11,772	10,460
61764	Pontiac.............	10,595	8,435
60469	Posen.............	5,498	4,517
61356	Princeton.............	6,959	6,250
60070	Prospect Heights(u)...........	13,333	......
62301	Quincy.............	45,288	43,793
61866	Rantoul.............	25,562	22,116
60471	Richton Park 1973...........	6,551	933
60627	Riverdale.............	15,806	12,008
60305	River Forest.............	13,402	12,695
60171	River Grove.............	11,465	8,464
60546	Riverside.............	10,432	9,750
60472	Robbins.............	9,641	7,511
62454	Robinson.............	7,178	7,226
61068	Rochelle 1974...........	8,850	7,008
61071	Rock Falls.............	10,287	10,261
*61125	Rockford.............	147,370	126,706
61201	Rock Island.............	50,166	51,863
60008	Rolling Meadows 1974...........	19,785	10,879
60441	Romeoville 1971...........	15,336	3,574
60172	Roselle 1973...........	7,986	3,581
60073	Round Lake Beach 1974...........	10,525	5,011
60174	St. Charles 1974...........	15,144	9,269
62881	Salem 1973...........	6,359	6,165
60548	Sandwich.............	5,056	3,842
60411	Sauk Village 1974...........	9,956	4,687
60172	Schaumburg 1974...........	36,944	986
60176	Schiller Park.............	12,712	5,687
62225	Scott(u).............	7,871	......
61282	Silvis.............	5,907	3,973
60076	Skokie 1971...........	68,911	59,364
60473	South Holland 1972...........	25,220	10,412
60459	South Stickney(u) (see Burbank)		
*62703	Springfield.............	91,753	83,271
61362	Spring Valley.............	5,605	5,371
60475	Steger 1973...........	9,285	6,432
61081	Sterling.............	16,113	15,688
60402	Stickney.............	6,601	6,239
60103	Streamwood.............	18,176	4,821
61364	Streator.............	15,600	16,868
60501	Summit.............	11,569	10,374
62221	Swansea 1975...........	5,473	3,018
60178	Sycamore.............	7,843	6,961
62568	Taylorville.............	10,927	8,801
60477	Tinley Park 1974...........	20,782	6,392
61801	Urbana.............	32,800	27,294
62471	Vandalia.............	5,160	5,537
60181	Villa Park 1971...........	25,546	20,391
61571	Washington 1973...........	9,466	5,919
62204	Washington Park.............	9,524	6,601
60970	Watseka.............	5,294	5,219
60084	Wauconda 1974...........	5,662	3,227
60085	Waukegan 1975...........	65,133	55,719
60153	Westchester.............	20,033	18,092

ZIP Code	Place	1970	1960
60185	West Chicago 1972	11,624	6,854
61120	West End(u)	7,554	
60558	Western Springs 1974	13,728	10,838
62896	West Frankfort	8,854	9,027
60559	Westmont	8,920	5,997
61604	West Peoria(u)	6,873	
60187	Wheaton 1973	36,148	24,312
60090	Wheeling 1974	18,106	7,169
60091	Wilmette	32,134	28,268
60093	Winnetka	13,998	13,368
60191	Wood Dale 1973	10,494	3,071
60515	Woodridge 1974	16,827	542
62095	Wood River	13,186	11,694
60098	Woodstock	10,226	8,897
60482	Worth 1971	12,153	8,196
60099	Zion	17,268	11,941

Indiana

ZIP Code	Place	1970	1960
46001	Alexandria	5,600	5,582
*46011	Anderson	70,787	49,061
46703	Angola	5,117	4,746
46706	Auburn	7,388	6,350
47421	Bedford	13,087	13,024
46107	Beech Grove 1973	14,651	10,973
46408	Black Oak(u)	9,624	
47401	Bloomington	43,262	31,357
46714	Bluffton	8,297	6,238
47601	Boonville	5,736	4,801
47834	Brazil	8,163	8,853
46112	Brownsburg	5,751	4,478
46032	Carmel 1974	13,484	1,442
46303	Cedar Lake	7,589	
47111	Charlestown	5,933	5,726
46304	Chesterton	6,177	4,335
47130	Clarksville 1974	14,117	8,088
47842	Clinton	5,340	5,843
47201	Columbus	26,457	20,778
47331	Connersville	17,604	17,698
47933	Crawfordsville	13,842	14,231
46307	Crown Point 1973	13,420	8,443
46733	Decatur	8,445	8,327
46312	East Chicago	46,982	57,669
46405	East Gary	9,858	9,309
46514	Elkhart	43,152	40,274
46036	Elwood	11,196	11,793
*47708	Evansville	138,764	141,543
*46802	Fort Wayne	178,021	161,776
46041	Frankfort	14,956	15,302
46131	Franklin	11,477	9,453
*46401	Gary	175,415	178,320
46933	Gas City	5,742	4,469
46526	Goshen	17,871	13,718
46135	Greencastle	8,852	8,506
46140	Greenfield 1973	10,808	9,049
47240	Greensburg	8,620	7,492
46142	Greenwood	11,408	7,169
46319	Griffith 1974	17,681	9,483
*46320	Hammond	107,885	111,698
47348	Hartford City	8,207	8,053
46322	Highland	24,947	16,284
46342	Hobart	21,485	18,680
46750	Huntington	16,217	16,185
*46206	Indianapolis	746,302	476,258
47546	Jasper	8,641	6,737
47130	Jeffersonville	20,008	19,522
46755	Kendallville	6,838	6,765
46901	Kokomo	44,042	47,197
*47901	Lafayette	44,955	42,330
46350	La Porte	22,140	21,157
46226	Lawrence	16,917	10,103
46052	Lebanon	9,766	9,523
47441	Linton	5,450	5,736
46947	Logansport	19,255	21,106
47250	Madison	13,081	10,488
46952	Marion	39,607	37,854
46151	Martinsville	9,723	7,525
46410	Merrillville 1973	25,978	
46360	Michigan City	39,369	36,653
46544	Mishawaka	35,517	33,361
46158	Mooresville	5,800	3,856
47620	Mount Vernon 1974	7,092	5,970
*47302	Muncie	69,082	68,603
46321	Munster 1973	18,894	10,313
47150	New Albany	38,402	37,812
47362	New Castle	21,215	20,349
46774	New Haven	5,728	3,396
46060	Noblesville	7,548	7,664
46962	North Manchester	5,791	4,377
46970	Peru	14,139	14,453
46168	Plainfield	8,211	5,460
46563	Plymouth	7,661	7,558
46368	Portage 1973	20,624	11,822
47371	Portland	7,115	6,999
47670	Princeton	7,431	7,906
47374	Richmond	43,999	44,149
46173	Rushville	6,686	7,264
47167	Salem	5,041	4,546
47274	Seymour	13,352	11,629

Iowa

ZIP Code	Place	1970	1960
46176	Shelbyville	15,094	14,317
*46624	South Bend	125,580	132,445
46224	Speedway	14,649	9,624
47586	Tell City 1974	8,515	6,609
*47808	Terre Haute	70,335	72,500
46072	Tipton	5,313	5,604
46383	Valparaiso 1974	20,544	15,227
47591	Vincennes	19,867	18,046
46992	Wabash	13,379	12,621
46580	Warsaw 1974	9,679	7,234
47501	Washington	11,358	10,846
46408	West Glen Park(u)	5,940	
47906	West Lafayette	19,157	12,680
46394	Whiting	7,152	8,137
47394	Winchester	5,493	5,742

Iowa

ZIP Code	Place	1970	1960
50511	Algona	6,032	5,702
50010	Ames	39,505	27,003
50021	Ankeny	9,151	2,964
50022	Atlantic	7,306	6,890
52722	Bettendorf 1975	24,290	11,534
50036	Boone	12,468	12,468
52601	Burlington	32,366	32,430
51401	Carroll	8,716	7,682
50613	Cedar Falls 1974	33,154	21,195
*52401	Cedar Rapids	110,642	92,035
52544	Centerville	6,531	6,629
50049	Chariton	5,009	5,042
50616	Charles City 1974	9,119	9,964
51012	Cherokee	7,272	7,724
51632	Clarinda	5,420	5,901
50428	Clear Lake City 1973	6,876	6,158
52732	Clinton	34,719	33,589
52240	Coralville	6,130	2,357
51501	Council Bluffs	60,348	55,641
50801	Creston	8,234	7,667
*52802	Davenport 1975	99,836	88,981
52101	Decorah	7,458	6,435
51442	Denison	6,218	4,930
*50318	Des Moines	201,404	208,982
52001	Dubuque	62,309	56,606
51334	Estherville	8,108	7,927
50707	Evansdale	5,038	5,738
52556	Fairfield	8,715	8,054
50501	Fort Dodge	31,263	28,399
52627	Fort Madison	13,996	15,247
50112	Grinnell	8,402	7,367
51537	Harlan	5,049	4,350
50644	Independence	5,910	5,498
50125	Indianola 1975	9,611	7,062
52240	Iowa City 1974	47,744	33,443
50126	Iowa Falls	6,454	5,565
52632	Keokuk	14,631	16,316
50138	Knoxville	7,755	7,817
51031	Le Mars	8,159	6,767
52060	Maquoketa	5,677	5,909
52302	Marion 1974	18,190	10,882
50158	Marshalltown 1975	26,506	22,521
50401	Mason City	30,379	30,642
52641	Mount Pleasant	7,007	7,339
52761	Muscatine	22,405	20,997
50208	Newton	15,619	15,381
50662	Oelwein	7,735	8,282
52577	Oskaloosa	11,224	11,053
52501	Ottumwa	29,610	33,871
50219	Pella	6,668	5,198
50220	Perry	6,906	6,442
51566	Red Oak	6,210	6,421
51601	Shenandoah	5,968	6,567
*51101	Sioux City	85,925	89,159
51301	Spencer	10,278	8,864
50588	Storm Lake	8,591	7,728
50322	Urbandale	14,434	5,821
52353	Washington	6,317	6,037
*50701	Waterloo	75,533	71,755
50677	Waverly	7,205	6,357
50595	Webster City	8,488	8,520
50265	West Des Moines 1975	20,712	11,949
50311	Windsor Heights	6,303	4,715

Kansas

ZIP Code	Place	1970	1960
67410	Abilene	6,661	6,746
67005	Arkansas City	13,216	14,262
66002	Atchison	12,565	12,529
67010	Augusta	5,977	6,434
66720	Chanute	10,341	10,849
67337	Coffeyville	15,116	17,382
66901	Concordia	7,221	7,022
67037	Derby	7,947	6,458
67801	Dodge City	14,127	13,520
67042	El Dorado	12,308	12,523
66801	Emporia	23,327	18,190
66205	Fairway	5,133	5,398
66027	Fort Leavenworth(u)	8,060	
66701	Fort Scott	8,967	9,410

ZIP Code	Place	1970	1960
67846	Garden City	14,790	11,811
67735	Goodland	5,510	4,459
67530	Great Bend	16,133	16,670
67601	Hays	15,396	11,947
67060	Haysville	6,483	5,836
67501	Hutchinson	36,885	37,574
67301	Independence	10,347	11,222
66749	Iola	6,493	6,885
66441	Junction City	19,018	18,700
*66110	Kansas City	168,213	121,901
66044	Lawrence	45,698	32,858
66048	Leavenworth	25,147	22,052
66206	Leawood	10,349	7,466
66215	Lenexa	5,242	2,487
67901	Liberal	13,789	13,813
67460	McPherson	10,851	9,996
66502	Manhattan	27,575	22,993
66203	Merriam	10,851	5,084
66222	Mission	8,376	4,626
67114	Newton	15,439	14,877
66442	North Fort Riley(u)	12,469	......
66061	Olathe	17,917	10,987
66067	Ottawa	11,036	10,673
66204	Overland Park	79,034	......
67357	Parsons	13,015	13,929
66762	Pittsburg	20,171	18,678
66208	Prairie Village	28,138	25,356
67124	Pratt	6,736	8,156
66203	Roeland Park	9,974	8,949
67665	Russell	5,371	6,113
67401	Salina	37,714	43,202
*66203	Shawnee	20,482	9,072
*66603	Topeka	125,011	119,484
67152	Wellington	8,072	8,809
*67202	Wichita	276,554	254,698
67156	Winfield	11,405	11,117

Kentucky

ZIP Code	Place	1970	1960
41101	Ashland	29,245	31,283
40004	Bardstown	5,816	4,798
41073	Bellevue	8,847	9,336
40403	Berea	6,956	4,302
42101	Bowling Green	36,705	28,338
40218	Buechel(u)	5,359	......
42718	Campbellsville	7,598	6,966
42330	Central City	5,450	3,694
40701	Corbin	7,317	7,119
*41011	Covington	52,535	60,376
41031	Cynthiana	6,356	5,641
40422	Danville	11,542	9,010
41074	Dayton	8,751	9,050
42701	Elizabethtown	11,748	9,641
41018	Elsmere	5,161	4,607
41018	Erlanger	12,676	7,072
41139	Flatwoods	7,380	3,741
41042	Florence	11,661	5,837
42223	Fort Campbell North(u)	13,616	......
40121	Fort Knox(u)	37,608	......
41017	Fort Mitchell	6,982	525
41075	Fort Thomas	16,338	14,896
40601	Frankfort	21,902	18,365
42134	Franklin	6,553	5,319
40324	Georgetown	8,629	6,986
42141	Glasgow	11,301	10,069
40330	Harrodsburg	6,741	6,061
41701	Hazard	5,459	5,958
42420	Henderson	22,976	16,892
42240	Hopkinsville	21,250	19,465
40299	Jeffersontown	9,701	3,431
40033	Lebanon	5,528	4,813
*40511	Lexington	108,137	62,810
*40201	Louisville	361,706	390,639
41016	Ludlow	5,815	6,233
42431	Madisonville	15,332	13,110
42066	Mayfield	10,724	10,762
41056	Maysville	7,411	8,484
40965	Middlesborough	11,878	12,607
40351	Morehead	7,191	4,170
40353	Mount Sterling	5,083	5,370
42071	Murray	13,537	9,303
*41071	Newport	25,998	30,070
40356	Nicholasville	5,829	4,275
40219	Okolona(u)	17,643	......
42301	Owensboro	50,329	42,471
42001	Paducah	31,627	34,479
40361	Paris	7,823	7,791
41501	Pikeville	5,205	4,754
40258	Pleasure Ridge Park(u)	28,566	10,612
42445	Princeton	6,292	5,618
40160	Radcliff	7,881	3,384
40475	Richmond	16,861	12,168
42276	Russellville	6,456	5,861
40207	St. Matthews	13,152	8,738
40216	Shively	19,139	15,155
42501	Somerset	10,436	7,112
40272	Valley Station(u)	24,471	10,533

ZIP Code	Place	1970	1960
40383	Versailles	5,679	4,060
40391	Winchester	13,402	10,187

Louisiana

ZIP Code	Place	1970	1960
70510	Abbeville	10,996	10,414
71301	Alexandria	41,557	40,279
70714	Baker	8,281	4,823
71220	Bastrop	14,713	15,193
*70821	Baton Rouge	165,963	152,419
70360	Bayou Cane(u)	9,077	3,173
70380	Bayou Vista(u)	5,121	......
70427	Bogalusa	18,412	21,423
71010	Bossier City	41,595	32,776
71322	Bunkie	5,395	5,188
71101	Cooper Road(u)	9,034	......
70433	Covington	7,170	6,754
70526	Crowley	16,104	15,617
70726	Denham Springs	6,752	5,991
70634	De Ridder	8,030	7,188
70346	Donaldsonville	7,367	6,082
70535	Eunice	11,390	11,326
71334	Ferriday	5,239	4,563
70538	Franklin	9,325	8,673
70053	Gretna	24,875	21,967
70401	Hammond	12,487	10,563
70123	Harahan	13,037	9,275
70058	Harvey(u)	6,347	......
70360	Houma	30,922	22,561
70544	Jeanerette	6,322	5,568
70121	Jefferson Heights(u)	16,489	19,353
70546	Jenning	11,783	11,887
71251	Jonesboro	5,072	3,848
70548	Kaplan	5,540	5,267
70062	Kenner	29,858	17,037
70501	Lafayette	68,908	40,400
70501	Lafayette Southwest	5,396	6,682
70601	Lake Charles	77,998	63,392
71254	Lake Providence	6,183	5,781
70068	Laplace(u)	5,953	3,541
71446	Leesville	8,928	4,689
70123	Little Farms(u)	15,713	......
71052	Mansfield	6,432	5,839
70072	Marrero(u)	29,015	......
*70004	Metairie(u)	136,477	......
71055	Minden	13,996	12,785
71201	Monroe	56,374	52,219
70380	Morgan City	16,586	13,540
71457	Natchitoches	15,974	13,924
70560	New Iberia	30,147	29,062
*70113	New Orleans	593,471	627,525
71459	North Fort Polk(u)	7,955	......
71463	Oakdale	7,301	6,618
70570	Opelousas	20,387	17,417
71360	Pineville	8,951	8,636
70764	Plaquemine	7,739	7,689
70767	Port Allen	5,728	5,026
70578	Rayne	9,510	8,634
70084	Reserve(u)	6,381	5,297
71270	Ruston	17,365	13,991
70582	St. Martinville	7,153	6,468
70807	Scotlandville(u)	22,557	......
*71102	Shreveport	182,064	164,372
70458	Slidell	16,101	6,356
71459	South Fort Polk(u)	15,600	......
71075	Springhill	6,496	6,437
70663	Sulphur	14,959	11,429
71282	Tallulah	9,643	9,413
71285	Terry(u)	13,382	......
70301	Thibodaux	15,028	13,403
71373	Vidalia	5,538	4,313
70586	Ville Platte	9,692	7,512
71291	West Monroe	14,868	15,215
70094	Westwego	11,402	9,815
71483	Winnfield	7,142	7,022
71295	Winnsboro	5,349	4,437

Maine

See Note on Page 241

ZIP Code	Place	1970	1960
04210	Auburn	24,151	24,449
04330	Augusta	21,945	21,680
04401	Bangor	33,168	38,912
04530	Bath	9,679	10,717
04005	Belfast	5,957	6,140
04005	Biddeford	19,983	19,255
04412	Brewer	9,300	9,009
04011	Brunswick Center(u)	10,867	9,444
......	Brunswick	16,195	15,797
04107	Cape Elizabeth	7,873	5,505
04736	Caribou	10,419	12,464
......	Fairfield	5,684	5,829
04105	Falmouth	6,291	5,976
......	Farmington	5,657	5,001
04345	Gardiner	6,685	6,897
......	Gorham	7,839	5,767
04730	Houlton Center(u)	6,760	5,976
......	Houlton	8,111	8,289

ZIP Code	Place	1970	1960
....	Kennebunk.................	5,646	551
03904	Kittery Center(u)...........	7,363	8,051
....	Kittery.....................	11,028	10,689
04240	Lewiston..................	41,779	40,804
04750	Limestone................	10,360	13,102
04250	Lisbon....................	6,544	5,042
04750	Loring(u).................	7,881	....
....	Madawaska................	5,585	5,507
04462	Millinocket Center(u).......	7,558	7,318
....	Millinocket................	7,742	7,453
04064	Old Orchard Beach Ctr.(u)..	5,273	4,431
....	Old Orchard Beach.........	5,404	4,580
04468	Old Town.................	9,057	8,626
04473	Orono Center(u)...........	9,146	3,234
....	Orono.....................	9,989	8,341
*04101	Portland..................	65,116	72,566
04769	Presque Isle..............	11,452	12,886
04841	Rockland.................	8,505	8,769
04276	Rumford Compact(u).......	6,198	7,233
....	Rumford..................	9,363	10,005
04072	Saco.....................	11,678	10,515
04073	Sanford Center(u).........	10,457	10,936
....	Sanford...................	15,812	14,962
04074	Scarborough..............	7,845	6,418
04976	Skowhegan Center(u)......	6,571	6,667
....	Skowhegan................	7,601	7,661
04106	South Portland............	23,267	22,788
....	Topsham..................	5,022	3,818
04901	Waterville................	18,192	19,001
04092	Westbrook................	14,444	13,820
04082	Windham..................	6,593	4,498
04901	Winslow Center(u).........	5,389	3,640
....	Winslow...................	7,299	5,891
03909	York......................	5,690	4,663

Maryland

ZIP Code	Place	1970	1960
21001	Aberdeen.................	12,375	9,679
21005	Aberdeen Proving Ground(u).	7,403	....
20331	Andrews(u)................	6,418	....
*21401	Annapolis.................	30,095	23,385
21227	Arbutus(u)................	22,745	22,402
20853	Aspen Hill(u).............	16,823	....
20783	Avenel-Hilandale(u).......	19,520	....
21905	Bainbridge Center(u)......	5,257	....
*21233	Baltimore.................	905,759	939,024
21014	Bel Air...................	6,307	4,300
20705	Beltsville(u)..............	8,912	....
20014	Bethesda(u)..............	71,621	56,527
20021	Birchwood City(u).........	13,514	....
20710	Bladensburg..............	7,488	3,103
20715	Bowie....................	35,028	1,072
21225	Brooklyn(u)...............	13,896	....
20705	Calverton(u)..............	6,543	....
21613	Cambridge................	11,595	12,239
20031	Camp Springs(u)..........	22,776	....
20027	Carmody Hills-Pepper Mill(u).	6,335	....
21228	Catonsville(u)............	54,812	37,372
20027	Chapel Oaks-Cedar Heights(u).	6,049	....
20785	Cheverly(u)...............	6,808	5,223
20015	Chevy Chase(u)...........	16,424	....
20783	Chillum(u)................	35,656	....
20904	Colesville(u)..............	9,455	....
20740	College Park..............	26,156	18,482
21043	Columbia(u)...............	8,815	....
20027	Coral Hills(u).............	9,058	....
21502	Cumberland...............	29,724	33,415
22222	Defense Heights(u)........	6,775	....
20028	District Heights...........	7,659	7,524
21222	Dundalk(u)................	85,377	82,428
21601	Easton...................	6,809	6,337
21219	Edgemere(u)..............	10,352	11,775
21040	Edgewood(u)..............	8,551	1,670
21921	Elkton....................	5,362	5,989
*21043	Ellicott(u)................	9,435	....
21221	Essex(u)..................	38,193	35,205
21061	Ferndale(u)...............	9,929	....
20028	Forestville(u).............	16,188	....
20755	Fort Meade(u)............	16,699	....
21701	Frederick.................	23,641	21,744
21532	Frostburg................	7,327	6,722
20760	Gaithersburg..............	8,344	3,847
21061	Glen Burnie(u)............	38,608	....
20801	Good Luck(u).............	10,584	....
20770	Greenbelt................	18,199	7,479
21740	Hagerstown...............	35,862	36,660
21740	Halfway(u)................	6,106	4,256
20852	Halpine(u)................	6,118	....
21078	Havre De Grace...........	9,791	8,510
20031	Hillcrest Heights.........	24,037	15,295
*20780	Hyattsville...............	14,998	15,168
21085	Joppatowne(u)............	9,092	....
20904	Kemp Mill(u)..............	10,037	....
20785	Kentland(u)...............	9,649	....
20785	Landover(u)...............	5,597	....
20787	Langley Park(u)...........	11,564	11,510
20801	Lanham-Seabrook(u).......	13,244	....

ZIP Code	Place	1970	1960
21227	Lansdowne-Baltimore Highlands(u)	17,770	13,134
20810	Laurel....................	10,525	8,503
20653	Lexington Pk.-Patuxent R.(u).....	9,136	....
21090	Linthicum(u)..............	9,775	....
21093	Lutherville-Timonium(u).........	24,055	12,265
20810	Maryland City(u)..........	7,102	....
21220	Middle River(u)...........	19,935	10,825
20852	Montrose(u)...............	5,902	....
20822	Mount Rainier.............	8,180	9,855
20784	New Carrollton............	14,870	3,385
20854	North Potomac(u)..........	12,784	....
20012	North Takoma Park(u)......	7,373	....
21113	Odenton(u)...............	5,989	1,914
21206	Overlea(u)................	13,124	10,795
21117	Owings Mills(u)...........	7,360	3,810
20021	Oxon Hill(u)..............	11,974	....
20785	Palmer Park(u)............	8,172	....
21234	Parkville(u)...............	33,589	27,236
21128	Perry Hall(u)..............	5,446	....
21208	Pikesville(u)..............	25,395	18,737
20016	Potomac Valley(u).........	5,122	....
21227	Pumphrey(u)..............	6,425	....
21133	Randallstown(u)...........	33,683	....
20853	Randolph(u)...............	13,215	....
21136	Reisterstown(u)...........	12,568	4,216
20840	Riverdale.................	5,724	4,389
20840	Riverdale Hgts.-E. Pines(u)..	8,941	....
21122	Riviera Beach(u)..........	7,464	4,902
*20850	Rockville.................	41,821	26,090
21237	Rosedale(u)...............	19,417	....
21801	Salisbury.................	15,252	16,302
20027	Seat Pleasant.............	7,217	5,365
21146	Severna Park(u)...........	16,358	3,728
*20907	Silver Spring(u)...........	77,411	66,348
21061	South Gate(u).............	9,356	....
20795	South Kensington(u).......	10,289	....
20810	South Laurel(u)...........	13,345	....
20023	Suitland-Silver Hills(u)......	30,355	10,300
20012	Takoma Park..............	18,507	16,799
21204	Towson(u)................	77,768	19,090
20601	Waldorf(u)................	7,368	1,048
20028	Walker Mill(u).............	7,103	....
21157	Westminster..............	7,207	6,123
20902	Wheaton(u)...............	66,280	54,635
20903	White Oak(u)..............	19,769	....
21207	Woodlawn-Woodmoor(u).....	28,821	....

Massachusetts
See Note on Page 241

ZIP Code	Place	1970	1960
02351	Abington..................	12,334	10,607
01720	Acton....................	14,770	7,238
02743	Acushnet.................	7,767	5,755
01220	Adams Center(u)..........	11,256	11,949
....	Adams....................	11,772	12,391
01001	Agawam..................	21,717	15,718
01913	Amesbury Center(u).......	10,088	9,625
....	Amesbury.................	11,388	10,787
01002	Amherst Center...........	17,926	10,306
....	Amherst..................	26,331	13,718
01810	Andover..................	23,695	17,134
02174	Arlington.................	53,534	49,953
01721	Ashland..................	8,882	7,779
01331	Athol Center(u)...........	9,723	10,161
....	Athol.....................	11,185	11,637
02703	Attleboro.................	32,907	27,118
01501	Auburn...................	15,347	14,047
02322	Avon.....................	5,295	4,301
*01432	Ayer.....................	7,393	14,927
02630	Barnstable................	19,842	13,465
01730	Bedford..................	13,513	10,969
01007	Belchertown..............	5,936	5,186
02019	Bellingham...............	13,967	6,774
02178	Belmont..................	28,285	28,715
01915	Beverly..................	38,348	36,108
01821	Billerica.................	31,648	17,867
01504	Blackstone...............	6,566	5,130
*02109	Boston...................	641,071	697,197
02532	Bourne...................	12,636	14,011
02184	Braintree.................	35,050	31,069
02324	Bridgewater...............	11,829	10,276
*02403	Brockton.................	89,040	72,813
02146	Brookline.................	58,886	54,044
01803	Burlington................	21,980	12,852
*02138	Cambridge................	100,361	107,716
02021	Canton...................	17,100	12,771
01824	Chelmsford...............	31,432	15,130
02150	Chelsea..................	30,625	33,749
*01021	Chicopee.................	66,676	61,553
01510	Clinton...................	13,383	12,848
02025	Cohasset.................	6,954	5,840
01742	Concord..................	16,148	12,517
01226	Dalton...................	7,505	6,436
01923	Danvers..................	26,151	21,926
02714	Dartmouth................	18,800	14,607
02026	Dedham..................	25,938	23,869
02638	Dennis...................	6,454	3,727

ZIP Code	Place	1970	1960	ZIP Code	Place	1970	1960
01826	Dracut	18,214	13,674	02062	Norwood	30,815	24,898
01570	Dudley	8,087	6,510	01364	Orange	6,104	6,154
02332	Duxbury	7,636	4,727	01253	Otis(u)	5,596	
02333	East Bridgewater	8,347	6,139	01540	Oxford Center(u)	6,109	6,985
01027	Easthampton	13,012	12,326		Oxford	10,345	9,282
01028	East Longmeadow	13,029	10,294	01069	Palmer	11,680	10,358
02334	Easton	12,157	9,078	01960	Peabody	48,080	32,202
02149	Everett	42,485	43,544	02359	Pembroke	11,193	4,919
02719	Fairhaven	16,332	14,339	01463	Pepperell	5,887	4,336
*02722	Fall River	96,898	99,942	01866	Pinehurst	5,681	1,991
*02540	Falmouth Center(u)	5,806	3,308	01201	Pittsfield	57,020	57,879
	Falmouth	15,942	13,037	*02360	Plymouth Center(u)	6,940	6,488
01420	Fitchburg	43,343	43,021		Plymouth	18,606	14,445
01433	Fort Devens(u)	12,019		02169	Quincy	87,966	87,409
02035	Foxborough	14,218	10,136	02368	Randolph	27,035	18,900
01701	Framingham	64,048	44,526	02767	Raynham	6,705	4,150
02038	Franklin Center(u)	8,863	6,391	01867	Reading	22,539	19,259
	Franklin	17,830	10,530	02769	Rehoboth	6,512	4,953
01440	Gardner	19,748	19,038	02151	Revere	43,159	40,080
01833	Georgetown	5,290	3,755	02370	Rockland	15,674	13,119
01930	Gloucester	27,941	25,789	01966	Rockport	5,636	4,616
01519	Grafton	11,659	10,627	01970	Salem	40,556	39,211
01033	Granby	5,473	4,221	02563	Sandwich	5,239	2,082
01230	Great Barrington	7,537	6,624	01906	Saugus	25,110	20,666
01301	Greenfield Center(u)	14,642	14,389	02066	Scituate	16,973	11,214
	Greenfield	18,116	17,690	02771	Seekonk	11,116	8,399
01450	Groton	5,109	3,904	02067	Sharon	12,367	10,070
01834	Groveland	5,382	3,297	01545	Shrewsbury	19,196	16,622
01936	Hamilton	6,373	5,488	02725	Somerset	18,088	12,196
02339	Hanover	10,107	5,923	02143	Somerville	88,779	94,697
02341	Hanson	7,148	4,370	01772	Southborough	5,798	3,996
01451	Harvard	12,494	2,563	01550	Southbridge Center(u)	14,261	15,889
02645	Harwich	5,892	3,747		Southbridge	17,057	16,523
01830	Haverhill	46,120	46,346	01075	South Hadley	17,033	14,956
02043	Hingham	18,845	15,378	01077	Southwick	6,330	5,139
02343	Holbrook	11,775	10,104	02664	South Yarmouth(u)	5,380	2,029
01520	Holden	12,564	10,117	01562	Spencer Center	5,895	5,593
01746	Holliston	12,069	6,222		Spencer	8,779	7,838
01040	Holyoke	50,112	52,689	*01101	Springfield	163,905	174,463
01748	Hopkinton	5,981	4,932	02180	Stoneham	20,725	17,821
01749	Hudson Center(u)	14,283	7,987	02072	Stoughton	23,459	16,328
	Hudson	16,084	9,666	01776	Sudbury	13,506	7,447
02045	Hull	9,961	7,055	01907	Swampscott	13,578	13,294
02601	Hyannis(u)	6,847	5,139	02777	Swansea	12,640	9,916
01938	Ipswich(u)	5,022	4,617	02780	Taunton	43,756	41,132
	Ipswich	10,750	8,544	01468	Templeton	5,863	5,371
02364	Kingston	5,999	4,302	01876	Tewksbury	22,755	15,902
01523	Lancaster	6,095	3,958	01983	Topsfield	5,225	3,351
*01842	Lawrence	66,915	70,933	01376	Turners Falls(u)	5,168	4,917
01238	Lee	6,426	5,271	01569	Uxbridge	8,253	7,789
01524	Leicester	9,140	8,177	01880	Wakefield	25,402	24,295
01240	Lenox	5,804	4,253	02081	Walpole	18,149	14,068
01453	Leominster	32,939	27,929	02154	Waltham	61,582	55,413
02173	Lexington	31,886	27,691	01082	Ware Center(u)	6,509	6,650
01773	Lincoln	7,567	5,613		Ware	8,187	7,517
01460	Littleton	6,380	5,109	02571	Wareham	11,492	9,461
01106	Longmeadow	15,630	10,565	02172	Watertown	39,307	39,092
*01853	Lowell	94,239	92,107	01778	Wayland	13,461	10,444
01056	Ludlow	17,580	13,805	01570	Webster Center(u)	12,432	12,072
01462	Lunenburg	7,419	6,334		Webster	14,917	13,680
*01901	Lynn	90,294	94,478	02181	Wellesley	28,051	26,071
01940	Lynnfield	10,826	8,398	01581	Westborough	12,594	9,599
02148	Malden	56,127	57,676	01583	West Boylston	6,369	5,526
01944	Manchester	5,151	3,932	02379	West Bridgewater	7,152	5,061
02048	Mansfield	9,939	7,773	01085	Westfield	31,433	26,302
01945	Marblehead	21,295	18,521	01886	Westford	10,368	6,261
01752	Marlborough	27,936	18,819	02193	Weston	10,870	8,261
02050	Marshfield	15,223	6,748	02790	Westport	9,791	6,641
01754	Maynard	9,710	7,695	01089	West Springfield	28,461	24,924
02052	Medfield	9,821	6,021	02090	Westwood	12,750	10,354
02155	Medford	64,397	64,971	02188	Weymouth	54,610	48,177
02053	Medway	7,938	5,168	01588	Whitinsville(u)	5,210	5,102
02176	Melrose	33,180	29,619	02382	Whitman	13,059	10,485
01844	Methuen	35,456	28,114	01095	Wilbraham	11,984	7,387
02346	Middleborough Center(u)	6,259	6,003	01267	Williamstown	8,454	7,322
	Middleborough	13,607	11,065	01887	Wilmington	17,102	12,475
01757	Milford Center(u)	13,740	13,722	01475	Winchendon	6,635	6,237
	Milford	19,352	15,749	01890	Winchester	22,269	19,376
01527	Millbury	11,987	9,623	02152	Winthrop	20,335	20,303
02054	Millis	5,686	4,374	01801	Woburn	37,406	31,214
02186	Milton	27,190	26,375	*01613	Worcester	176,572	186,587
01057	Monson	7,355	6,712	02093	Wrentham	7,315	6,685
01351	Montague	8,451	7,836	02675	Yarmouth	12,033	5,504
01760	Natick	31,057	28,831				
02192	Needham	29,748	25,793		**Michigan**		
*02741	New Bedford	101,777	102,477				
01950	Newburyport	15,807	14,004	49221	Adrian	20,382	20,347
02158	Newton	91,066	92,384	49224	Albion	12,112	12,749
01247	North Adams	19,195	19,905	48101	Allen Park	40,747	37,494
01060	Northampton	29,664	30,058	48801	Alma	9,611	8,978
01845	North Andover	16,284	10,908	49707	Alpena	13,805	14,682
*02760	North Attleborough	18,665	14,777	*48106	Ann Arbor	99,797	67,340
01532	Northborough	9,218	6,687	*49016	Battle Creek	38,931	44,169
01534	Northbridge	11,795	10,800	48706	Bay City	49,449	53,604
01864	North Reading	11,264	8,331	48809	Belding	5,121	4,887
02060	North Scituate(u)	5,507	3,421	49022	Benton Central(u)	8,067	
02766	Norton	9,487	6,818	49022	Benton Harbor	16,481	19,136
02061	Norwell	7,796	5,207	48072	Berkley	21,879	23,275

ZIP Code	Place	1970	1960
48009	Beverly Hills	13,598	8,633
49307	Big Rapids	11,995	8,686
*48012	Birmingham	26,170	25,525
49601	Cadillac	9,990	10,112
48724	Carrollton(u)	7,300	......
48015	Center Line	10,379	10,164
48813	Charlotte	8,244	7,657
49721	Cheboygan	5,553	5,859
48017	Clawson	17,617	14,795
49036	Coldwater	9,155	8,880
49041	Comstock(u)	5,003	......
49321	Comstock Park(u)	5,766	......
49508	Cutlerville(u)	6,267	......
48423	Davison	5,259	3,761
*48120	Dearborn	104,199	112,007
48127	Dearborn Heights	80,069	......
*48233	Detroit	1,513,601	1,670,144
49047	Dowagiac	6,583	7,208
48020	Drayton Plains(u)	16,462	......
48021	East Detroit	45,920	45,756
49506	East Grand Rapids	12,565	10,924
48823	East Lansing	47,540	30,198
49001	Eastwood(u)	9,682	......
48229	Ecorse	17,515	17,328
49829	Escanaba	15,368	15,391
48024	Farmington	10,329	6,881
48430	Fenton	8,284	6,142
48220	Ferndale	30,850	31,347
48134	Flat Rock	5,643	4,696
*48502	Flint	193,317	196,940
48433	Flushing	7,190	3,761
48026	Fraser	11,868	7,027
48135	Garden City	41,864	38,017
49837	Gladstone	5,237	5,267
48439	Grand Blanc	5,132	1,565
49417	Grand Haven	11,844	11,066
48837	Grand Ledge	6,032	5,165
*49501	Grand Rapids	197,649	177,313
49418	Grandville	10,764	7,975
48838	Greenville	7,493	7,440
48138	Grosse Ile(u)	8,306	......
48236	Grosse Pointe	6,637	6,631
48236	Grosse Pointe Farms	11,701	12,172
48236	Grosse Pointe Park	15,641	15,457
48236	Grosse Pointe Woods	21,878	18,580
48212	Hamtramck	27,245	34,137
48236	Harper Woods	20,186	19,995
49058	Hastings	6,501	6,375
48030	Hazel Park	23,784	25,631
48203	Highland Park	35,444	38,063
49242	Hillsdale	7,728	7,629
49423	Holland	26,479	24,777
48842	Holt(u)	6,980	4,818
48931	Houghton	6,067	3,393
48843	Howell	5,224	4,861
48070	Huntington Woods	8,536	8,746
48141	Inkster	38,595	39,097
48846	Ionia	6,361	6,754
49801	Iron Mountain	8,702	9,299
49938	Ironwood	8,711	10,265
49849	Ishpeming	8,245	8,857
*49201	Jackson	45,484	50,720
49428	Jenison(u)	11,266	......
*49001	Kalamazoo	85,555	82,089
49508	Kentwood	20,310	......
49788	Kincheloe(u)	6,331	......
49801	Kingsford	5,276	5,084
49843	K.I. Sawyer(u)	8,224	......
49015	Lakeview(u)	11,391	10,384
48144	Lambertville(u)	5,711	1,168
*48924	Lansing	131,403	107,807
48446	Lapeer	6,314	6,160
48503	Lapeer Heights(u)	7,130	......
48146	Lincoln Park	52,984	53,933
*48150	Livonia	110,109	66,702
49431	Ludington	9,021	9,421
48071	Madison Heights	38,599	33,343
49660	Manistee	7,723	8,324
49855	Marquette	21,967	19,824
49068	Marshall	7,253	6,736
48040	Marysville	5,610	4,065
48854	Mason	5,468	4,522
48122	Melvindale	13,862	13,089
49858	Menominee	10,748	11,289
48640	Midland	35,176	27,779
48161	Monroe	23,894	22,968
48043	Mount Clemens	20,476	21,016
48858	Mount Pleasant	20,524	14,875
*49440	Muskegon	44,631	46,485
49444	Muskegon Heights	17,304	19,552
49866	Negaunee	5,248	6,126
49120	Niles	12,988	13,842
48167	Northville	5,400	3,967
49441	Norton Shores	22,271	......
48050	Novi	9,668	6,390
48237	Oak Park	36,762	36,632
48864	Okemos(u)	7,770	......
48867	Owosso	17,179	17,006
49770	Petoskey	6,342	6,138

ZIP Code	Place	1970	1960
48170	Plymouth	11,758	8,766
*48053	Pontiac	85,279	82,233
49081	Portage	33,590	......
48060	Port Huron	35,794	36,084
48024	Quakertown North(u)	7,101	......
48218	River Rouge	15,947	18,147
48192	Riverview	11,342	7,237
48063	Rochester	7,054	5,431
48066	Roseville	60,529	50,195
*48068	Royal Oak	86,238	80,612
48605	Saginaw	91,849	98,265
*48083	St. Clair Shores	88,093	76,657
48879	St. Johns	6,672	5,629
49085	St. Joseph	11,042	11,755
48176	Saline 1974	6,050	2,334
49783	Sault Ste. Marie	15,136	18,722
48075	Southfield	69,285	31,501
48198	Southgate	33,909	29,404
49090	South Haven	6,471	6,149
*48078	Sterling Heights	61,365	......
49091	Sturgis	9,295	8,915
48180	Taylor	70,020	......
49286	Tecumseh	7,120	7,045
49093	Three Rivers	7,355	7,092
49684	Traverse City	18,048	18,432
48183	Trenton	24,127	18,439
48084	Troy	39,419	19,402
49504	Walker	11,492	......
*48089	Warren	179,260	89,246
48184	Wayne	21,054	16,034
48185	Westland	86,749	......
49007	Westwood(u)	9,143	......
48753	Wurtsmith(u)	6,932	......
*48192	Wyandotte	41,061	43,519
49509	Wyoming	56,560	45,829
48197	Ypsilanti	29,538	20,957

Minnesota

ZIP Code	Place	1970	1960
56007	Albert Lea	19,418	17,108
56308	Alexandria	6,973	6,713
55303	Anoka	13,295	10,562
55068	Apple Valley	8,502	......
55112	Arden Hills	5,149	3,930
55912	Austin	25,074	27,908
56601	Bemidji	11,490	9,958
55433	Blaine	20,625	7,570
55420	Bloomington	81,970	50,498
56401	Brainerd	11,667	12,898
55429	Brooklyn Center	35,173	24,356
55429	Brooklyn Park 1972	29,945	10,197
55337	Burnsville	19,940	......
55316	Champlin 1972	6,298	1,271
55317	Chanhassen 1971	5,054	244
55318	Chaska 1972	5,398	2,501
55719	Chisholm	5,913	7,144
55720	Cloquet	8,699	9,013
55421	Columbia Heights	23,837	17,533
55433	Coon Rapids	30,505	14,931
55016	Cottage Grove	13,419	......
56716	Crookston	8,312	8,546
55428	Crystal	30,925	24,283
56501	Detroit Lakes	5,797	5,633
*55806	Duluth	100,578	106,884
56721	East Grand Forks	7,607	6,998
55343	Eden Prairie	6,938	......
55424	Edina	44,046	28,501
56031	Fairmont	10,751	9,745
55113	Falcon Heights	5,641	5,927
55021	Fairbault	16,595	16,926
56537	Fergus Falls	12,443	13,733
55421	Fridley	29,233	15,173
55427	Golden Valley	24,246	14,559
55744	Grand Rapids	7,247	7,265
55033	Hastings	12,195	8,965
55746	Hibbing	16,104	17,731
55343	Hopkins	13,428	11,370
55350	Hutchinson	8,031	6,207
56649	International Falls	6,439	6,778
55075	Inver Grove Heights	12,148	......
55044	Lakeville	7,556	924
55355	Litchfield	5,262	5,078
55110	Little Canada 1974	5,977	3,512
56345	Little Falls	7,467	7,551
56001	Mankato	30,895	23,797
55369	Maple Grove	6,275	2,213
55109	Maplewood	25,222	18,519
56258	Marshall	9,886	6,681
55118	Mendota Heights	6,165	5,028
*55401	Minneapolis	434,400	482,872
55343	Minnetonka	35,737	25,037
56265	Montevideo	5,661	5,693
56560	Moorhead	29,687	22,934
56267	Morris	5,366	4,199
55364	Mound	7,572	5,440
55112	Mounds View	10,641	6,146
55112	New Brighton	19,507	6,448
54428	New Hope	23,180	3,552
56073	New Ulm	13,051	11,114

ZIP Code	Place	1970	1960
55057	Northfield	10,235	8,707
56001	North Mankato	7,347	5,927
55109	North St. Paul	11,950	8,520
55119	Oakdale	7,304	.....
55391	Orono	6,787	5,643
55060	Owatonna	15,341	13,409
56164	Pipestone	5,328	5,324
55427	Plymouth	18,077	9,576
55066	Red Wing	10,441	10,528
55423	Richfield	47,231	42,523
55422	Robbinsdale	16,845	16,381
55901	Rochester	53,766	40,663
55113	Roseville	34,438	23,997
55418	St. Anthony	9,239	5,084
56301	St. Cloud 1975	40,715	33,815
55426	St. Louis Park	48,922	43,310
*55101	St. Paul	309,714	313,411
55071	St. Paul Park	5,587	3,267
56082	St. Peter	8,339	8,484
56379	Sauk Rapids	5,051	4,038
55379	Shakopee	6,876	5,201
55112	Shoreview	10,995	7,157
55075	South St. Paul	25,016	22,032
55432	Spring Lake Park	6,417	3,260
55082	Stillwater	10,191	8,310
56701	Thief River Falls	8,618	7,151
55792	Virginia	12,450	14,034
56093	Waseca	6,789	5,898
55118	West St. Paul	18,799	13,101
55110	White Bear Lake	23,313	12,849
56201	Willmar	12,869	10,417
55987	Winona	26,438	24,895
55119	Woodbury	6,184	.....
56187	Worthington	9,916	9,015

Mississippi

ZIP Code	Place	1970	1960
39730	Aberdeen	6,507	6,450
38821	Amory	7,236	6,474
39520	Bay St. Louis	6,752	5,073
*39530	Biloxi 1975	46,497	44,053
38829	Booneville	5,895	3,480
39601	Brookhaven	10,700	9,885
39046	Canton	10,503	9,707
38614	Clarksdale	21,673	21,105
38732	Cleveland	13,327	10,172
39056	Clinton	7,289	3,438
39429	Columbia	7,587	7,117
39701	Columbus	25,795	24,771
38834	Corinth	11,581	11,453
39532	D'Iberville(u)	7,288	3,005
38701	Greenville	39,648	41,502
38930	Greenwood	22,400	20,436
38901	Grenada	9,944	7,914
39501	Gulfport	40,791	30,204
39401	Hattiesburg	38,277	34,989
38635	Holly Springs	5,728	5,621
38751	Indianola	8,947	6,714
*39205	Jackson	153,968	144,422
39090	Kosciusko	7,266	6,800
39440	Laurel	24,145	27,889
38756	Leland	6,000	6,295
39560	Long Beach 1975	7,113	4,770
39339	Louisville	6,626	5,066
39648	McComb	11,969	12,020
39301	Meridian 1974	46,087	49,374
39563	Moss Point	19,321	6,631
39120	Natchez	19,704	23,791
38652	New Albany	6,426	5,151
39564	Ocean Springs	9,580	5,025
38655	Oxford City	13,846	5,283
39567	Pascagoula	27,264	17,155
39208	Pearl(u)	9,623	5,081
39465	Petal(u)	6,986	4,007
39350	Philadelphia	6,274	5,017
39466	Picayune	10,467	7,834
38671	Southaven(u)	8,931	.....
39759	Starkville	11,369	9,041
38801	Tupelo	20,471	17,221
39180	Vicksburg	25,478	29,143
39501	West Gulfport(u)	6,996	3,323
39773	West Point	8,714	8,550
38967	Winona	5,521	4,282
39194	Yazoo City	11,688	11,236

Missouri

ZIP Code	Place	1970	1960
63123	Affton(u)	24,264	.....
65605	Aurora	5,359	4,683
63011	Ballwin	10,656	5,710
63137	Bellefontaine Neighbors	14,084	13,650
63133	Bel-Ridge	5,346	4,395
64012	Belton	12,179	4,897
63134	Berkeley	19,743	18,676
64015	Blue Springs	6,779	2,555
65233	Boonville	7,514	7,090
63114	Breckenridge Hills	7,011	6,299
63144	Brentwood	11,248	12,250
63044	Bridgeton	19,992	7,820

ZIP Code	Place	1970	1960
64628	Brookfield	5,491	5,694
63701	Cape Girardeau	31,282	24,947
64836	Carthage	11,035	11,264
63830	Caruthersville	7,350	8,643
63834	Charleston	5,131	5,911
64601	Chillicothe	9,519	9,236
63105	Clayton	16,100	15,245
64735	Clinton	7,504	6,925
65201	Columbia	58,812	36,650
63128	Concord(u)	21,217	.....
63126	Crestwood	15,123	11,106
63141	Creve Coeur	8,967	5,122
63136	Dellwood	7,137	4,720
63020	De Soto	5,984	5,804
63131	Des Peres	5,333	4,362
63841	Dexter	6,024	5,519
64024	Excelsior Springs	9,411	6,473
63640	Farmington	6,590	5,618
63135	Ferguson	28,759	22,149
63028	Festus	7,530	7,021
*63033	Florissant	65,908	38,166
65473	Fort Leonard Wood(u)	33,799	.....
63251	Fulton	12,248	11,131
64118	Gladstone	23,422	14,502
63122	Glendale	6,981	7,048
64030	Grandview	17,456	6,027
63401	Hannibal	18,698	20,028
64701	Harrisonville	5,052	3,510
*63042	Hazelwood	14,082	6,045
*64051	Independence	111,630	62,328
63755	Jackson	5,896	4,875
65101	Jefferson City	32,407	28,228
63136	Jennings	19,379	19,965
64801	Joplin	39,256	38,958
*64108	Kansas City	507,330	475,539
63857	Kennett	10,090	9,098
63140	Kinloch	5,629	6,501
63501	Kirksville	15,560	13,123
63122	Kirkwood	31,679	29,421
63124	Ladue	10,359	9,466
65536	Lebanon	8,616	8,220
64063	Lee's Summit	16,230	8,267
63125	Lemay(u)	40,516	.....
64067	Lexington	5,388	4,845
64068	Liberty	13,704	8,909
63552	Macon	5,301	4,547
63863	Malden	5,374	5,007
63011	Manchester	5,031	2,021
63143	Maplewood	12,785	12,552
65340	Marshall	12,051	9,572
63043	Maryland Heights(u)	8,805	.....
64468	Maryville	9,970	7,807
65265	Mexico	11,807	12,889
65270	Moberly	12,988	13,170
65708	Monett	5,937	5,359
64850	Neosho	7,517	7,452
64772	Nevada	9,736	8,416
63121	Normandy	6,236	4,452
64116	North Kansas City 1974	5,046	5,657
63366	O'Fallon	7,018	3,770
63124	Olivette	9,156	8,257
63114	Overland	24,819	22,763
63133	Pagedale	5,044	5,106
63775	Perryville	5,149	5,117
63120	Pine Lawn	5,745	5,943
63901	Poplar Bluff	16,653	15,926
64133	Raytown	33,306	17,083
63117	Richmond Heights	13,802	15,622
63124	Rock Hill	6,815	6,523
65401	Rolla	13,571	11,132
63074	St. Ann	18,215	12,155
63301	St. Charles	31,834	21,189
63114	St. John	8,960	7,342
*64501	St. Joseph	72,691	79,673
*63155	St. Louis	622,236	750,026
63126	Sappington(u)	10,603	.....
65301	Sedalia	22,847	23,874
63119	Shrewsbury	5,896	4,730
63801	Sikeston	14,699	13,765
63138	Spanish Lake(u)	15,647	.....
*65901	Springfield	120,096	95,865
63080	Sullivan	5,111	4,098
64683	Trenton	6,063	6,262
63084	Union	5,183	3,897
63130	University City	47,527	51,249
64093	Warrensburg	13,125	9,689
63090	Washington	8,499	7,961
64870	Webb City	6,923	6,740
63119	Webster Groves	27,457	28,990
63112	Wellston	7,050	7,979
65775	West Plains	6,893	5,836
65301	Whiteman	5,040	.....
63134	Woodson Terrace	5,880	6,048

Montana

ZIP Code	Place	1970	1960
59711	Anaconda	9,771	12,054
*59101	Billings	61,581	52,851
59715	Bozeman	18,670	13,361

ZIP Code	Place	1970	1960
59701	Butte	23,368	27,877
59701	Floral Park(u)	5,113	4,079
59330	Glendive	6,305	7,058
*59401	Great Falls	60,091	55,244
59501	Havre	10,558	10,740
59601	Helena	22,730	20,227
59901	Kalispell	10,526	10,151
59457	Lewistown	6,437	7,408
59047	Livingston	6,883	8,229
59402	Malmstrom(u)	8,374	
59301	Miles City	9,023	9,665
59801	Missoula	29,497	27,090
59801	Missoula West(u)	9,148	
59701	Silver Bow Park(u)	5,524	4,798

Nebraska

ZIP Code	Place	1970	1960
69301	Alliance	6,862	7,845
68310	Beatrice	12,389	12,132
68005	Bellevue 1974	21,145	8,831
68008	Blair	6,106	4,931
69337	Chadron	5,921	5,079
68601	Columbus	15,471	12,476
68352	Fairbury	5,265	5,572
68355	Falls City	5,444	5,598
68025	Fremont	22,962	19,698
69341	Gering	5,639	4,585
68801	Grand Island	31,269	25,742
68901	Hastings	23,580	21,412
68949	Holdrege	5,635	5,226
68847	Kearney	19,181	14,210
68128	La Vista 1974	7,840	1,004
68850	Lexington	5,654	5,572
*68501	Lincoln	149,518	128,521
69001	McCook	8,285	8,301
68137	Millard	7,460	1,014
68410	Nebraska City	7,441	7,252
68701	Norfolk	16,607	13,640
69101	North Platte	19,447	17,184
68113	Offutt East(u)	5,195	
68113	Offutt West(u)	8,445	
*68108	Omaha	346,929	301,598
68046	Papillion 1974	6,493	2,235
68048	Plattsmouth	6,371	6,244
69361	Scottsbluff	14,507	13,377
68434	Seward	5,294	4,208
69162	Sidney	6,403	8,004
68776	South Sioux City	7,920	7,200
68787	Wayne	5,379	4,217
68467	York	6,778	6,173

Nevada

ZIP Code	Place	1970	1960
89005	Boulder City	5,223	4,059
89701	Carson City	15,468	5,163
89112	East Las Vegas(u)	6,501	
89801	Elko	7,621	6,298
89015	Henderson	16,395	12,525
*89114	Las Vegas	125,787	64,405
89110	Nellis(u)	6,449	
89030	North Las Vegas	36,216	18,422
89109	Paradise(u)	24,477	
*89501	Reno	72,863	51,470
89431	Sparks	24,187	16,618
89110	Sunrise Manor(u)	10,886	
89109	Vegas Creek(u)	8,970	
89101	Winchester(u)	13,981	

New Hampshire
See note on page 241

ZIP Code	Place	1970	1960
03102	Bedford	5,859	3,636
03570	Berlin	15,256	17,821
03743	Claremont	14,221	13,563
03301	Concord	30,022	28,991
03038	Derry Compact(u)	6,090	4,468
03038	Derry	11,712	6,987
03820	Dover	20,850	19,131
03824	Durham Compact(u)	7,221	4,688
	Durham	8,869	5,504
03833	Exeter Compact(u)	6,439	5,896
	Exeter	8,892	7,243
03235	Franklin	7,292	6,742
03045	Goffstown	9,284	7,230
03842	Hampton Compact(u)	5,407	3,281
	Hampton	8,011	5,379
03755	Hanover Compact(u)	6,147	5,649
	Hanover	8,494	7,329
03106	Hooksett	5,564	3,713
03051	Hudson	10,638	5,876
03431	Keene	20,467	17,562
03246	Laconia	14,888	15,288
03766	Lebanon	9,725	9,299
03516	Littleton	5,290	5,003
03053	Londonderry	5,346	2,457
*03101	Manchester	87,754	88,282
03054	Merrimack	8,595	2,989
03055	Milford	6,622	4,863

ZIP Code	Place	1970	1960
03060	Nashua	55,820	39,096
03773	Newport	5,899	5,458
03076	Pelham	5,408	2,605
03801	Portsmouth	25,717	26,900
03867	Rochester	17,938	15,927
03079	Salem	20,142	9,210
03874	Seabrook 1974	5,128	2,209
03878	Somersworth	9,026	8,529

New Jersey

ZIP Code	Place	1970	1960
08201	Absecon	6,094	4,320
07401	Allendale	6,240	4,092
07712	Asbury Park	16,533	17,366
*08401	Atlantic City	47,859	59,544
07716	Atlantic Highlands	5,102	4,119
08106	Audubon	10,802	10,440
08007	Barrington	8,409	7,943
07002	Bayonne	72,743	74,215
07109	Belleville	37,629	35,005
08030	Bellmawr	15,618	11,853
07719	Belmar	5,782	5,190
07621	Bergenfield	29,000	27,203
07922	Berkeley Hts. Twp.	13,078	8,721
07924	Bernardsville	6,652	5,515
07003	Bloomfield	52,029	51,867
07403	Bloomingdale	7,797	5,293
07603	Bogota	8,960	7,965
07005	Boonton	9,261	7,981
08805	Bound Brook	10,450	10,263
08723	Brick Twp.	35,057	16,299
08302	Bridgeton	20,435	20,966
08203	Brigantine	6,741	4,201
08015	Browns Mills(u)	7,144	
08016	Burlington	11,991	12,687
07405	Butler	7,051	5,414
07006	Caldwell	8,677	6,942
*08101	Camden	102,551	117,159
08701	Candlewood(u)	5,629	
07072	Carlstadt	6,724	6,042
07008	Carteret	23,137	20,502
07009	Cedar Grove Twp.	15,582	14,603
07928	Chatham	9,566	9,517
*08002	Cherry Hill Twp.	64,395	31,522
08077	Cinnaminson Twp.	16,962	8,302
07066	Clark Twp.	18,829	12,195
08312	Clayton	5,193	4,711
07010	Cliffside Park	18,891	17,642
07721	Cliffwood-Cliffwood Beach(u)	7,056	
*07015	Clifton	82,437	82,084
07624	Closter	8,604	7,767
08108	Collingswood	17,422	17,370
07016	Cranford Twp.	27,391	26,424
07626	Cresskill	8,298	7,290
08075	Delran Twp.	10,065	5,327
07627	Demarest	5,133	4,231
07834	Denville Twp.	14,045	10,632
08096	Deptford Twp.	24,232	17,878
07801	Dover	15,039	13,034
07628	Dumont	20,155	18,882
08812	Dunellen	7,072	6,840
08816	East Brunswick Twp.	34,166	19,965
*07019	East Orange	75,471	77,259
07407	East Paterson	20,511	19,344
07073	East Rutherford	8,536	7,769
08520	East Windsor Twp. 1974	19,788	2,298
07724	Eatontown	14,619	10,334
08817	Edison Twp.	67,120	44,799
*07207	Elizabeth	112,654	107,698
07630	Emerson	8,428	6,849
*07631	Englewood	24,985	26,057
07632	Englewood Cliffs	5,938	2,913
08053	Evesham Twp.	13,477	4,548
08618	Ewing Twp.	32,831	26,628
07006	Fairfield	6,884	
07701	Fair Haven	6,142	5,678
07410	Fair Lawn	37,975	36,421
07022	Fairview	10,698	9,399
07023	Fanwood	8,920	7,963
08518	Florence-Roebling(u)	7,551	
07932	Florham Park	8,094	7,222
08640	Fort Dix(u)	26,290	
07024	Fort Lee	30,631	21,815
07417	Franklin Lakes	7,550	3,316
07728	Freehold	10,545	9,140
07026	Garfield	30,797	29,253
07027	Garwood	5,260	5,426
08028	Glassboro	12,938	10,253
07028	Glen Ridge	8,518	8,322
07452	Glen Rock	13,011	12,896
08030	Gloucester City	14,707	15,511
07093	Guttenberg	5,754	5,118
*07602	Hackensack	36,008	30,521
07840	Hackettstown	9,472	5,276
08108	Haddon Twp.	18,192	17,099
08033	Haddonfield	13,118	13,201
08035	Haddon Heights	9,365	9,260
07508	Haledon	6,767	6,161

ZIP Code	Place	1970	1960
08037	Hammonton	11,464	9,854
07981	Hanover Twp.	10,700	9,329
07029	Harrison	11,811	11,743
07604	Hasbrouck Heights	13,651	13,046
07506	Hawthorne	19,173	17,735
07730	Hazlet Twp.	22,239	15,334
08904	Highland Park	14,385	11,049
08520	Hightstown	5,431	4,317
07642	Hillsdale	11,768	8,734
07205	Hillside Twp.	21,636	22,304
07030	Hoboken	45,380	48,441
07843	Hopatcong	9,052	3,391
08560	Hopewell Twp. (Mercer)	10,030	7,818
07111	Irvington	59,743	59,379
08527	Jackson Twp.	18,276	5,939
*07303	Jersey City	260,350	276,101
07734	Keansburg	9,720	6,854
07032	Kearny	37,585	37,472
08824	Kendall Park(u)	7,412	....
07033	Kenilworth	9,165	8,379
07735	Keyport	7,205	6,440
07405	Kinnelon	7,600	4,431
07034	Lake Hiawatha(u)	11,389	....
07871	Lake Mohawk(u)	6,262	4,647
07054	Lake Parsippany(u)	7,488	....
08701	Lakewood(u)	17,874	13,004
08879	Laurence Harbor(u)	6,715	....
07605	Leonia	8,847	8,384
07035	Lincoln Park	9,034	6,048
07036	Linden	41,409	39,931
08021	Lindenwold 1973	16,265	7,335
08221	Linwood	6,159	3,847
07424	Little Falls Twp.	11,727	9,730
07643	Little Ferry	9,064	6,176
07739	Little Silver	6,010	5,202
07039	Livingston Twp.	30,127	23,124
07644	Lodi	25,163	23,502
07740	Long Branch	31,774	26,228
07071	Lyndhurst Twp.	22,729	21,867
07940	Madison	16,710	15,122
08049	Magnolia	5,893	4,199
07430	Mahwah Twp.	10,800	7,376
08835	Manville	13,029	10,995
08052	Maple Shade Twp.	16,464	12,947
07040	Maplewood Twp.	24,932	23,977
08402	Margate City	10,576	9,474
07746	Marlboro Twp.	12,273	8,038
08053	Marlton(u)	10,180	....
07747	Matawan	9,136	5,097
07607	Maywood	11,087	11,460
08641	McGuire(u)	10,933	....
08619	Mercerville-Hamilton Sq.(u)	24,465	....
08840	Metuchen	16,031	14,041
08846	Middlesex	15,038	10,520
07748	Middletown Twp.	54,623	39,675
07432	Midland Park	8,159	7,543
07041	Millburn Twp.	21,089	18,799
08850	Milltown	6,470	5,435
08332	Millville	21,366	19,096
07434	Monroe Twp. (Gloucester)	14,071	9,396
*07042	Montclair	44,043	43,129
07645	Montvale	7,327	3,699
07045	Montville Twp.	11,846	6,772
08057	Moorestown-Lenola(u)	14,179	....
07950	Morris Plains	5,540	4,703
07960	Morristown	17,662	17,712
07092	Mountainside	7,520	6,325
08059	Mount Ephraim	5,625	5,447
08060	Mount Holly Twp.	12,713	13,271
07753	Neptune Twp.	27,863	21,487
07753	Neptune City	5,502	4,013
*07102	Newark	381,930	405,220
*08901	New Brunswick	41,885	40,139
08511	New Hanover	27,410	28,528
07646	New Milford	19,149	18,810
07974	New Providence	13,796	10,243
07724	New Shrewsbury	8,395	7,313
07860	Newton	7,297	6,563
07032	North Arlington	18,096	17,477
07047	North Bergen Twp.	47,751	42,387
08902	North Brunswick Twp.	16,691	10,099
07006	North Caldwell	6,733	4,163
08225	Northfield	8,875	5,849
07508	North Haledon	7,614	6,020
07060	North Plainfield	21,796	16,993
07647	Northvale	5,177	2,892
07110	Nutley	31,913	29,513
07755	Oakhurst(u)	5,558	4,374
07436	Oakland	14,420	9,446
08226	Ocean City	10,575	7,618
07757	Oceanport	7,503	4,937
08857	Old Bridge(u)	25,176	....
07649	Oradell	8,903	7,487
*07050	Orange	32,566	35,789
07650	Palisades Park	13,351	11,943
08065	Palmyra	6,969	7,036
07652	Paramus	28,381	23,238
07656	Park Ridge	8,709	6,389
*07055	Passaic	55,124	53,963

ZIP Code	Place	1970	1960
*07510	Paterson	144,824	143,663
08066	Paulsboro	8,084	8,121
08110	Pennsauken Twp.	36,394	33,771
08069	Penns Grove	5,727	6,176
08070	Pennsville Center(u)	11,014	....
07440	Pequannock Twp.	14,350	10,553
*08861	Perth Amboy	38,798	38,007
08865	Phillipsburg	17,849	18,502
08021	Pine Hill	5,132	3,939
08854	Piscataway Twp.	36,418	19,890
08071	Pitman	10,257	8,644
*07061	Plainfield	46,862	45,330
08232	Pleasantville	13,778	15,172
08742	Point Pleasant	15,968	10,182
07442	Pompton Lakes	11,397	9,445
08540	Princeton	12,331	11,890
08540	Princeton North(u)	5,488	4,506
07508	Prospect Park	5,176	5,201
*07065	Rahway	29,114	27,699
08057	Ramblewood(u)	5,556	....
07446	Ramsey	12,571	9,527
07970	Randolph Twp.	13,296	7,295
08869	Raritan	6,691	6,137
07701	Red Bank	12,847	12,482
07657	Ridgefield	11,308	10,788
07660	Ridgefield Park	13,990	12,701
*07451	Ridgewood	27,547	25,391
07456	Ringwood	10,393	4,182
07661	River Edge	12,850	13,264
08075	Riverside Twp.	8,591	8,474
07662	Rochell Park Twp.	6,380	6,119
07866	Rockaway	6,383	5,413
07203	Roselle	22,585	21,032
07204	Roselle Park	14,227	12,546
07760	Rumson	7,421	6,405
08078	Runnemede	10,475	6,396
*07070	Rutherford	20,802	20,473
07662	Saddle Brook Twp.	15,975	13,834
08079	Salem	7,648	8,941
08872	Sayreville	32,508	22,553
07076	Scotch Plains Twp.	22,279	18,491
07094	Secaucus	13,228	12,154
08083	Somerdale	6,510	4,839
08244	Somers Point	7,919	4,504
08876	Somerville	13,652	12,458
08879	South Amboy	9,338	8,422
07079	South Orange	16,971	16,175
07080	South Plainfield	21,142	17,879
08882	South River	15,428	13,397
07871	Sparta Twp.	10,819	6,717
08884	Spotswood	7,891	5,788
07081	Springfield Twp.	15,740	14,467
08084	Stratford	9,801	4,308
07747	Strathmore	7,674	....
07901	Summit	23,620	23,677
07666	Teaneck Twp.	42,355	42,085
07670	Tenafly	14,827	14,264
08753	Toms River	7,303	6,062
07512	Totowa	11,580	10,897
*08608	Trenton	104,786	114,167
07083	Union Twp.	53,077	51,499
07735	Union Beach	6,472	5,862
07087	Union City	57,305	52,180
07458	Upper Saddle River	7,949	3,570
08406	Ventnor City	10,385	8,688
07044	Verona	15,067	13,782
08360	Vineland	47,399	37,685
07463	Waldwick	12,313	10,495
07057	Wallington	10,284	9,261
07465	Wanaque	8,636	7,126
07882	Washington	5,943	5,723
07675	Washington Twp. (Bergen)	10,557	6,654
07470	Wayne Twp.	49,141	29,353
07087	Weehawken Twp.	13,383	13,504
07006	West Caldwell	11,913	8,314
*07091	Westfield	33,720	31,447
07764	West Long Branch	6,845	5,337
07480	West Milford Twp.	17,304	8,157
07093	West New York	40,627	35,547
07052	West Orange	43,715	39,895
07424	West Paterson	11,692	7,602
08093	Westville	5,170	4,951
07675	Westwood	11,105	9,046
07885	Wharton	5,535	5,006
08610	White Horse-Yardville(u)	18,680	....
07886	White Meadow Lake(u)	8,499	....
08046	Willingboro Twp. 1973	44,607	11,861
08095	Winslow Twp.	11,202	9,142
07095	Woodbridge Twp.	98,944	78,846
08096	Woodbury	12,408	12,453
07675	Woodcliff Lake	5,506	2,742
07075	Wood-Ridge	8,311	7,964
07481	Wyckoff Twp.	16,039	11,205

New Mexico

ZIP Code	Place	1970	1960
88310	Alamogordo	23,035	21,723
*87101	Albuquerque	243,751	201,189
88210	Artesia	10,315	12,000

ZIP Code	Place	1970	1960
88101	Cannon(u)	5,461	
88220	Carlsbad	21,297	25,541
88101	Clovis	28,495	23,713
88030	Deming	8,343	6,764
87401	Farmington	21,979	23,786
87301	Gallup	14,596	14,089
87020	Grants	8,768	10,274
88240	Hobbs	26,025	26,275
88330	Holloman(u)	8,001	
88001	Las Cruces	37,857	29,367
87701	Las Vegas (city)	7,528	7,790
87701	Las Vegas (town)	6,307	6,028
87544	Los Alamos(u)	11,310	12,584
88260	Lovington	8,915	9,660
87107	North Valley(u)	10,366	
88130	Portales	10,554	9,695
88740	Raton	6,962	8,146
88201	Roswell	33,908	39,593
87115	Sandia(u)	6,867	
87501	Santa Fe	41,167	33,394
88061	Silver City	8,557	6,972
87801	Socorro	5,849	5,271
87105	South Valley(u)	29,389	
88401	Tucumcari	7,189	8,143

New York

ZIP Code	Place	1970	1960
*12207	Albany	115,781	129,726
11507	Albertson(u)	6,825	
14411	Albion	5,122	5,182
11701	Amityville	9,794	8,318
12010	Amsterdam	25,524	28,772
12603	Arlington(u)	11,203	8,317
13021	Auburn	34,599	35,249
*11702	Babylon	12,897	11,062
11510	Baldwin(u)	34,525	30,204
13027	Baldwinsville	6,298	5,985
14020	Batavia	17,338	18,210
14810	Bath	6,053	6,166
11705	Bayport(u)	8,232	
11706	Bay Shore(u)	11,119	
11709	Bayville	6,147	3,962
12508	Beacon	13,255	13,922
11710	Bellmore(u)	18,431	12,784
11714	Bethpage(u)	18,555	
*13902	Binghamton	64,123	75,941
10913	Blauvelt(u)	5,426	
11716	Bohemia(u)	8,926	
11717	Brentwood(u)	28,327	15,387
10510	Briarcliff Manor	7,878	5,105
14420	Brockport	6,251	5,256
10708	Bronxville	6,674	6,744
*14240	Buffalo	462,768	532,759
14424	Canadaigua 1971	10,753	9,370
13032	Canastota	5,033	4,896
13617	Canton	6,398	5,046
11514	Carle Place(u)	6,326	
12414	Catskill	5,317	5,825
11516	Cedarhurst	6,941	6,954
11720	Centereach(u)	9,427	8,524
11722	Central Islip(u)	36,391	
12065	Clifton Knolls(u)	5,771	
12047	Cohoes	18,653	20,129
11724	Cold Spring Harbor(u)	5,450	1,705
12205	Colonie	8,701	6,992
11725	Commack(u)	24,138	9,613
10920	Congers(u)	5,928	
11726	Copiague(u)	19,632	14,081
14830	Corning	15,792	17,085
13045	Cortland	19,621	19,181
10520	Croton-on-Hudson	7,523	6,812
14437	Dansville	5,436	5,460
11729	Deer Park(u)	32,274	16,726
14043	Depew	22,158	13,580
13214	DeWitt(u)	10,032	
11746	Dix Hills(u)	10,050	
10522	Dobbs Ferry	10,353	9,260
14048	Dunkirk	16,855	18,205
14052	East Aurora	7,033	6,791
10709	Eastchester(u)	23,750	
12302	East Glenville(u)	5,898	
11746	East Half Hollow Hills(u)	9,691	
11576	East Hills	8,624	7,184
11730	East Islip(u)	6,861	
11758	East Massapequa(u)	15,926	14,779
11554	East Meadow(u)	46,290	46,036
11743	East Neck(u)	5,221	3,789
11731	East Northport(u)	12,392	8,381
11772	East Patchogue(u)	8,092	
14445	East Rochester	8,347	8,152
11518	East Rockaway	11,795	10,721
13902	East Vestal(u)	10,472	
*14901	Elmira	39,945	46,517
11003	Elmont(u)	29,363	30,138
11731	Elwood(u)	15,031	
13760	Endicott	16,556	18,775

ZIP Code	Place	1970	1960
13760	Endwell(u)	15,999	
13219	Fairmount(u)	15,317	
14450	Fairport	6,474	5,507
12601	Fairview(u)	8,517	8,626
11735	Farmingdale	9,297	6,128
*11001	Floral Park	18,466	17,499
11010	Franklin Square(u)	32,156	32,483
14063	Fredonia	10,326	8,477
11520	Freeport	40,374	34,419
13069	Fulton	14,003	14,261
11530	Garden City	25,373	23,948
11040	Garden City Park(u)	7,488	
14454	Geneseo	5,714	3,284
14456	Geneva	16,793	17,286
11542	Glen Cove	25,770	23,817
12801	Glens Falls	17,222	18,580
12078	Gloversville	19,677	21,741
*11022	Great Neck	10,798	10,171
11020	Great Neck Plaza	6,043	4,948
11740	Greenlawn(u)	8,493	5,422
11746	Half Hollow Hills(u)	12,081	
14075	Hamburg	10,215	9,145
10528	Harrison Town(u)	21,544	19,201
10530	Hartsdale(u)	12,026	
10706	Hastings-on-Hudson	9,479	8,979
11787	Hauppauge(u)	13,957	
10927	Haverstraw	8,198	5,771
*11551	Hempstead	39,411	34,641
13350	Herkimer	8,960	9,396
11040	Herricks(u)	9,112	
11557	Hewlett(u)	6,796	
*11802	Hicksville(u)	49,820	50,405
10977	Hillcrest(u)	5,357	
11741	Holbrook-Holtsville(u)	10,103	
14843	Hornell	12,144	13,907
14845	Horseheads Village	7,989	7,207
12534	Hudson	8,940	11,075
12839	Hudson Falls	7,917	7,752
11743	Huntington(u)	12,601	11,255
11746	Huntington Station(u)	28,817	23,438
13357	Ilion	9,808	10,199
11696	Inwood(u)	8,433	10,362
10533	Irvington	5,878	5,494
11558	Island Park	5,396	3,846
11751	Islip(u)	7,692	
14850	Ithaca	26,226	28,799
14701	Jamestown	39,795	41,818
10535	Jefferson Valley-Yorktown(u)	9,008	
11753	Jericho(u)	14,010	10,795
13790	Johnson City	18,025	19,118
12095	Johnstown	10,045	10,390
14217	Kenmore	20,980	21,261
11754	Kings Park(u)	5,555	4,949
11024	Kings Point	5,614	5,410
12401	Kingston	25,544	29,260
14218	Lackawanna	28,657	29,564
11755	Lake Grove 1975	9,359	
14086	Lancaster	13,365	12,254
10538	Larchmont	7,203	6,789
12110	Latham(u)	9,661	
11559	Lawrence	6,566	5,907
14482	Le Roy	5,118	4,662
11756	Levittown(u)	65,440	65,276
11757	Lindenhurst	28,359	20,905
13365	Little Falls	7,629	8,935
14094	Lockport	25,399	26,443
11791	Locust Grove(u)	11,626	11,558
11561	Long Beach(u)	33,127	26,473
12211	Loudonville(u)	9,299	
11563	Lynbrook	23,151	19,881
10541	Mahopac(u)	5,265	1,337
12953	Malone	6,048	8,737
11565	Malverne	10,036	9,968
10543	Mamaroneck	18,909	17,673
11030	Manhasset(u)	8,541	
11050	Manorhaven	5,488	3,566
11758	Massapequa(u)	26,821	32,900
11762	Massapequa Park	22,112	19,904
13662	Massena	14,042	15,478
13211	Mattydale(u)	8,292	
12118	Mechanicville	6,247	6,831
14103	Medina	6,415	6,681
11746	Melville(u)	6,641	
11566	Merrick(u)	25,904	18,789
10940	Middletown	22,607	23,475
11501	Mineola	21,744	20,519
10952	Monsey(u)	8,797	
12701	Monticello	5,991	5,222
10549	Mt. Kisco	8,172	6,805
*10551	Mount Vernon	72,788	76,010
10954	Nanuet(u)	10,447	
11767	Nesconset(u)	10,048	1,964
14513	Newark 1975	10,717	12,868
12550	Newburgh	26,219	30,979
11590	New Cassel(u)	8,721	
10956	New City(u)	27,344	
11040	New Hyde Park	10,116	10,808

ZIP Code	Place	1970	1960
*10802	New Rochelle	75,385	76,812
*12550	New Windsor	8,803	4,041
*10001	New York	7,895,563	7,781,984
*10451	Bronx	1,471,701	1,424,815
*11201	Brooklyn	2,602,012	2,627,319
*10001	Manhattan	1,539,233	1,698,281
*(Q)	Queens	1,987,174	1,809,578

(Q) There are 4 Zip Codes for Queens: 11101 for L. I. City; 11690 Far Rockaway; 11351 Flushing and 11431 Jamaica.

ZIP Code	Place	1970	1960
*10314	Staten Island	295,443	221,991
*14302	Niagara Falls	85,615	102,394
13745	Nimmonsburg-Chenango Br.(u)	5,059	....
12309	Niskayuna(u)	6,186	....
11701	North Amityville(u)	11,936	....
11703	North Babylon(u)	39,526	....
11710	North Bellmore(u)	22,893	19,639
11713	North Bellport(u)	5,903	....
11752	North Great River(u)	12,080	....
11757	North Lindenhurst(u)	11,117	....
11758	North Massapequa(u)	23,123	....
11566	North Merrick(u)	13,650	12,976
11040	North New Hyde Park(u)	18,154	17,929
11772	North Patchogue(u)	5,232	....
10803	North Pelham	5,184	5,326
11768	Northport	7,494	5,972
13212	North Syracuse	8,687	7,412
10591	North Tarrytown	8,334	8,818
14120	North Tonawanda	36,012	34,757
11580	North Valley Stream(u)	14,881	17,239
11793	North Wantagh(u)	15,053	....
13815	Norwich	8,843	9,175
10960	Nyack	6,659	6,062
11769	Oakdale(u)	7,334	....
11572	Oceanside(u)	35,372	30,448
13669	Ogdensburg	14,554	16,122
11804	Old Bethpage(u)	7,084	....
14760	Olean	19,169	21,868
13421	Oneida	11,658	11,677
13820	Oneonta	16,030	13,412
10562	Ossining	21,659	18,662
13126	Oswego	20,913	22,155
11771	Oyster Bay(u)	6,822	....
11772	Patchogue 1975	11,283	8,838
10965	Pearl River(u)	17,146	....
10566	Peekskill	19,283	18,737
10803	Pelham Manor	6,673	6,114
14527	Penn Yan	5,293	5,770
11714	Plainedge(u)	10,759	21,973
11803	Plainview(u)	31,695	27,710
12901	Plattsburgh	18,715	20,172
12903	Plattsburgh Base(u)	7,078	....
10570	Pleasantville	7,110	5,877
10573	Port Chester	25,803	24,960
11777	Port Jefferson 1975	5,800	....
11776	Port Jefferson Station(u)	7,403	1,041
12771	Port Jervis	8,852	9,268*
11050	Port Washington(u)	15,923	15,657
13676	Potsdam	10,303	7,765
*12601	Poughkeepsie	32,029	38,330
12144	Rensselaer	10,136	10,506
11901	Riverhead(u)	7,585	5,830
*14603	Rochester	296,233	318,611
*11570	Rockville Centre	27,444	26,355
12205	Roessleville(u)	5,476	....
13440	Rome	50,148	51,646
11779	Ronkonkoma(u)	7,284	4,220
11575	Roosevelt(u)	15,008	12,883
11577	Roslyn Heights(u)	7,242	....
12303	Rotterdam(u)	25,214	16,871
10580	Rye	15,869	14,225
11780	St. James(u)	10,500	3,524
14779	Salamanca	7,877	8,480
11754	San Remo(u)	8,302	3,160
12983	Saranac Lake	6,086	6,421
12866	Saratoga Springs	18,845	16,630
11782	Sayville(u)	11,680	....
10583	Scarsdale	19,229	17,968
*12301	Schenectady	77,958	81,682
12302	Scotia	7,370	7,625
11579	Sea Cliff	5,890	5,669
11783	Seaford(u)	17,379	14,718
11784	Selden(u)	11,613	1,604
13148	Seneca Falls	7,794	7,439
11733	Setauket-South Setauket(u)	6,857	....
11967	Shirley(u)	6,280	....
14225	Sloan	5,216	5,803
13209	Solvay	8,280	9,732
11735	South Farmingdale(u)	20,464	16,318
11741	South Holbrook(u)	6,700	....
11746	South Huntington(u)	9,115	7,084
14904	Southport(u)	8,685	6,698
11790	South Stony Brook(u)	15,329	....
11581	South Valley Stream(u)	6,595	....
11590	South Westbury(u)	10,978	11,977
10977	Spring Valley	18,112	6,538

ZIP Code	Place	1970	1960
11790	Stony Brook(u)	6,391	3,548
10980	Stony Point(u)	8,270	3,330
10901	Suffern	8,273	5,094
11791	Syosset(u)	10,084	....
*13201	Syracuse	197,297	216,038
10983	Tappan(u)	7,424	....
10591	Tarrytown	11,115	11,109
10594	Thornwood(u)	6,874	....
14150	Tonawanda	21,898	21,561
*12180	Troy	62,918	67,492
10707	Tuckahoe	6,236	6,423
11553	Uniondale(u)	22,077	20,041
*13503	Utica	91,340	100,410
10989	Valley Cottage(u)	6,007	....
*11580	Valley Stream	40,413	38,629
11731	Vernon Valley(u)	7,925	5,998
13850	Vestal-Twin Orchards(u)	8,303	....
10901	Viola(u)	5,136	....
12586	Walden	5,277	4,851
11793	Wantagh(u)	21,873	34,172
12590	Wappingers Falls	5,607	4,447
13165	Waterloo	5,418	5,098
13601	Watertown	30,787	33,306
12189	Watervliet	12,404	13,917
14892	Waverly	5,261	5,950
14580	Webster	5,037	3,060
14895	Wellsville	5,815	5,967
11758	West Amityville(u)	6,424	....
11704	West Babylon(u)	12,893	....
11590	Westbury	15,362	14,757
14905	West Elmira(u)	5,901	5,763
10993	West Haverstraw	8,558	5,020
11552	West Hempstead(u)	20,375	....
11795	West Islip(u)	17,374	....
12203	Westmere(u)	6,364	....
10994	West Nyack(u)	5,510	....
11796	West Sayville(u)	7,386	....
13219	Westvale(u)	7,253	....
*10602	White Plains	50,346	50,485
14221	Williamsville	6,835	6,316
11596	Williston Park	9,154	8,255
11598	Woodmere(u)	19,831	14,011
11798	Wyandanch(u)	15,716	....
11980	Yaphank(u)	5,460	....
*10701	Yonkers	204,297	190,634
10598	Yorktown Heights(u)	6,805	2,478

North Carolina

ZIP Code	Place	1970	1960
27910	Ahoskie	5,105	4,583
28001	Albemarle	11,126	12,261
27203	Asheboro	10,797	9,449
*28801	Asheville	57,681	60,192
28012	Belmont	5,054	5,007
28607	Boone	8,754	3,686
28712	Brevard	5,243	4,857
27215	Burlington	35,930	33,199
28542	Camp Le Jeune Central(u)	34,549	....
28716	Canton	5,158	5,068
27510	Carrboro	5,058	1,997
27511	Cary 1975	14,677	3,356
27514	Chapel Hill	25,537	12,573
*28202	Charlotte	241,178	201,564
28533	Cherry Point(u)	12,029	....
28021	Cherryville	5,258	3,607
28328	Clinton	7,157	7,461
28025	Concord	18,464	17,799
28334	Dunn	8,302	7,566
*27701	Durham	95,438	78,302
27288	Eden	15,871	....
27909	Elizabeth City	14,381	14,062
*28302	Fayetteville	53,510	47,106
28043	Forest City	7,179	6,556
28307	Fort Bragg(u)	46,995	....
28052	Gastonia	47,142	37,276
27530	Goldsboro	26,810	28,873
27253	Graham	8,172	7,723
*27420	Greensboro	144,076	119,574
27834	Greenville	29,063	22,860
28532	Havelock	5,283	2,433
27536	Henderson	13,896	12,740
28739	Hendersonville	6,443	5,911
28601	Hickory	20,569	19,328
*27260	High Point	63,259	62,063
28540	Jacksonville	16,289	13,491
28081	Kannapolis(u)	36,293	34,647
28086	Kings Mountain	8,465	8,008
28501	Kinston	23,020	24,819
28352	Laurinburg	8,859	8,242
28645	Lenoir	14,705	10,257
27292	Lexington	17,205	16,093
28092	Lincolnton	5,293	5,699
28358	Lumberton	16,961	15,305
28110	Monroe	11,282	10,882
28115	Mooresville	8,808	6,918
28557	Morehead City	5,233	5,583
28655	Morganton	13,625	9,186
27030	Mount Airy	7,325	7,055

ZIP Code	Place	1970	1960
28120	Mount Holly	5,107	4,037
28560	New Bern	14,660	15,717
28540	New River Gieger(u)	8,699	......
28658	Newton	7,857	6,658
28012	North Belmont(u)	10,672	8,328
27565	Oxford	7,178	6,978
*27611	Raleigh	123,793	93,931
27320	Reidsville	13,636	14,267
27870	Roanoke Rapids	13,508	13,320
28379	Rockingham	5,852	5,512
27801	Rocky Mount	34,284	32,147
27573	Roxboro	5,370	5,147
28144	Salisbury	22,515	21,297
27330	Sanford	11,716	12,253
27530	Seymour-Johnson(u)	8,172	......
28150	Shelby	16,328	17,698
27577	Smithfield	6,677	6,117
28387	Southern Pines	5,937	5,198
28677	Statesville	20,007	19,844
27886	Tarboro	9,425	8,411
27360	Thomasville	15,230	15,190
27889	Washington	8,961	9,339
28786	Waynesville	6,488	6,159
28025	West Concord(u)	5,347	5,510
27892	Williamston	6,570	6,924
28401	Wilmington	46,169	44,013
27893	Wilson	29,347	28,753
*27102	Winston-Salem	133,683	111,135

North Dakota

ZIP Code	Place	1970	1960
58501	Bismarck 1975	38,123	27,670
58301	Devils Lake 1974	7,354	6,299
58601	Dickinson	12,405	9,971
58102	Fargo	53,365	46,662
58237	Grafton 1973	5,931	5,885
58201	Grand Forks(u) 1971	40,060	34,451
58201	Grand Forks Base(u)	10,474	......
58401	Jamestown 1971	15,078	15,163
58554	Mandan 1973	11,400	10,525
58701	Minot	32,290	30,604
58701	Minot Base(u)	12,077	......
58072	Valley City	7,843	7,809
58075	Wahpeton	7,076	5,876
58078	West Fargo 1972	6,437	3,328
58801	Williston	11,280	11,866

Ohio

ZIP Code	Place	1970	1960
45810	Ada	5,309	3,918
*44309	Akron	275,425	290,351
44601	Alliance	26,547	28,362
44001	Amherst	9,902	6,750
44805	Ashland	19,872	17,419
44004	Ashtabula	24,313	24,559
45701	Athens	24,168	16,470
44202	Aurora	6,549	4,049
44515	Austintown(u)	29,393	......
44011	Avon	7,214	6,002
45404	Avondale(u)	5,240	......
44012	Avon Lake	12,261	9,403
44203	Barberton	33,052	33,805
44140	Bay Village	18,163	14,489
44122	Beachwood	9,631	6,089
44146	Bedford	17,552	15,223
44146	Bedford Heights	13,063	5,275
43906	Bellaire	9,655	11,502
44311	Bellefontaine	11,255	11,424
44811	Bellevue	8,604	8,286
45714	Belpre	7,189	5,418
44017	Berea	22,465	16,592
43209	Bexley	14,888	14,319
43004	Blacklick Estates(u)	8,351	......
45242	Blue Ash	8,324	8,341
44512	Boardman(u)	30,852	......
43402	Bowling Green	21,760	13,574
44141	Brecksville	9,137	5,435
45211	Bridgetown(u)	13,352	......
44141	Broadview Heights	11,463	6,209
44144	Brooklyn	13,142	10,733
44142	Brook Park	30,774	12,856
44212	Brunswick	15,852	11,725
43506	Bryan	7,008	7,361
44820	Bucyrus	13,111	12,276
43725	Cambridge	13,656	14,562
44405	Campbell	12,577	13,406
*44711	Canton	110,053	113,631
45822	Celina	8,072	7,659
45459	Centerville	10,333	3,490
45211	Cheviot	11,135	10,701
45601	Chillicothe	24,842	24,957
44505	Churchill(u)	7,457	......
*45234	Cincinnati	451,455	502,550
43113	Circleville	11,687	11,059
*44101	Cleveland	750,879	876,050
44118	Cleveland Heights	60,767	61,813

ZIP Code	Place	1970	1960
43410	Clyde	5,503	4,826
*43216	Columbus	540,025	471,316
44030	Conneaut	14,552	10,557
43812	Coshocton	13,747	13,106
45238	Covedale(u)	6,639	......
44827	Crestline	5,947	5,521
45341	Crystal Lakes(u)	5,851	1,569
*44222	Cuyahoga Falls	49,678	47,922
45401	Dayton	242,917	262,332
45236	Deer Park	7,415	8,423
43512	Defiance	16,281	14,553
43015	Delaware	15,008	13,282
45833	Delphos	7,608	6,961
44622	Dover	11,516	11,300
44112	East Cleveland	39,600	37,991
44094	Eastlake	19,690	12,467
43920	East Liverpool(u)	20,020	22,306
43920	East Liverpool North	6,223	......
44413	East Palestine	5,604	5,232
45320	Eaton	6,020	5,034
*44035	Elyria	53,427	43,782
45322	Englewood	7,885	1,515
44117	Euclid	71,552	62,998
45324	Fairborn	32,267	19,453
45014	Fairfield	14,680	9,734
44313	Fairlawn	6,102	......
44126	Fairview Park	21,681	14,624
45840	Findlay	35,800	30,344
45405	Forest Park	15,139	......
45426	Fort McKinley(u)	11,536	......
44830	Fostoria	16,037	15,732
45005	Franklin	10,075	7,917
43420	Fremont	18,490	18,767
43230	Gahanna	12,400	2,717
44833	Galion	13,123	12,650
45631	Gallipolis	7,490	8,775
44125	Garfield Heights	41,417	38,455
44041	Geneva	6,449	5,677
44420	Girard	14,119	12,997
45237	Golf Manor	5,170	4,848
43212	Grandview Heights	8,460	8,270
45218	Greenhills	6,092	5,407
45331	Greenville	12,380	10,585
43123	Grove City	13,911	8,107
*45012	Hamilton	67,865	72,354
43055	Heath	6,768	2,426
44124	Highland Heights	5,926	2,929
43026	Hilliard	8,369	5,633
45133	Hillsboro	5,584	5,474
44425	Hubbard	8,583	7,137
45424	Huber Heights(u)	18,943	......
44839	Huron	6,896	5,197
44131	Independence	7,034	6,868
45243	Indian Hill	5,651	4,526
45638	Ironton	15,030	15,745
45640	Jackson	6,843	6,980
44240	Kent	28,183	17,836
43326	Kenton	8,315	8,747
45236	Kenwood(u)	15,789	......
45429	Kettering	71,864	54,462
44094	Kirtland	5,530	......
45432	Knollwood(u)	5,353	......
44107	Lakewood	70,173	66,154
43130	Lancaster	32,911	29,916
45036	Lebanon	7,934	5,993
*45802	Lima	53,734	51,037
45215	Lincoln Heights	6,099	7,798
43228	Lincoln Village(u)	11,215	......
45215	Lockland	5,288	5,292
43138	Logan	6,269	6,417
43140	London	6,481	6,379
*44052	Lorain	78,185	68,932
44641	Louisville	6,298	5,116
45140	Loveland	7,144	5,008
44124	Lyndhurst	19,749	16,805
44056	Macedonia	6,375	......
45243	Madeira	6,713	6,744
44057	Madison North(u)	6,882	......
*44901	Mansfield	55,047	47,325
44137	Maple Heights	34,093	31,667
45750	Marietta	16,861	16,847
43302	Marion	38,646	37,079
43935	Martins Ferry	10,757	11,919
43040	Marysville	5,744	4,952
45040	Mason	5,677	4,727
44646	Massillon	32,539	31,236
45537	Maumee	15,937	12,063
44124	Mayfield Heights	22,139	13,478
44256	Medina	10,913	8,235
44060	Mentor	36,912	4,354
44060	Mentor-on-the-Lake	6,517	3,290
45342	Miamisburg	14,797	9,893
44017	Middleburg Heights	12,367	7,282
45042	Middletown	48,767	42,115
43938	Mingo Junction	5,278	4,987
45242	Montgomery	5,683	3,075
45231	Mount Healthy	7,446	6,553
43050	Mount Vernon	13,373	13,284
43545	Napoleon	7,791	6,739

ZIP Code	Place	1970	1960
43055	Newark	41,836	41,790
45344	New Carlisle	6,112	4,107
44663	New Philadelphia	15,184	14,241
44444	Newton Falls	5,378	5,038
44446	Niles	21,581	19,545
44720	North Canton	15,228	7,727
45239	North College Hill	12,363	12,035
44070	North Olmsted	34,861	16,290
45414	Northridge(u)	10,084	
44039	North Ridgeville	13,152	8,057
44133	North Royalton	12,807	9,290
44203	Norton	12,308	
44857	Norwalk	13,386	12,900
45212	Norwood	30,420	34,580
45419	Oakwood City	10,095	10,493
44074	Oberlin	8,761	8,198
44667	Orrville	7,408	6,511
43616	Oregon	16,563	13,319
45431	Overlook-Page Manor(u)	19,719	
45056	Oxford	15,868	7,828
44077	Painesville	16,536	16,116
44077	Painesville Southwest(u)	5,461	
44129	Parma	100,216	82,845
44130	Parma Heights	27,192	18,100
44124	Pepper Pike	5,382	3,217
43551	Perrysburg	7,693	5,373
45356	Piqua	20,741	19,219
43452	Port Clinton	7,202	6,870
45662	Portsmouth	27,633	33,637
44266	Ravenna	11,780	10,918
45215	Reading	14,617	12,832
43068	Reynoldsburg	13,921	7,793
44143	Richmond Heights	9,220	5,068
43217	Rickenbacker Base(u)	5,623	
44270	Rittman	6,308	5,410
44116	Rocky River	22,958	18,097
43460	Rossford	5,302	4,406
45217	St. Bernard	6,080	6,778
45885	St. Marys	7,699	7,737
44460	Salem	14,186	13,854
44870	Sandusky	32,674	31,989
44870	Sandusky South(u)	8,501	4,724
44131	Seven Hills	12,700	5,708
43947	Shadyside	5,070	5,028
44120	Shaker Heights	36,306	36,460
45241	Sharonville	11,393	3,890
44054	Sheffield Lake	8,734	6,884
44875	Shelby	9,847	9,106
45415	Shiloh(u)	11,368	
45365	Sidney	16,332	14,663
45236	Silverton	6,588	6,682
44139	Solon	11,519	6,333
44121	South Euclid	29,579	27,569
45246	Springdale	8,127	3,556
*45501	Springfield	81,941	82,723
43952	Steubenville	30,771	32,495
44224	Stow	19,847	12,194
44240	Streetsboro	7,966	
44136	Strongsville	15,182	8,504
44471	Struthers	15,343	15,631
43560	Sylvania	12,031	5,187
44278	Tallmadge	15,274	10,246
44883	Tiffin	21,596	21,478
45371	Tipp City	5,090	4,267
*43601	Toledo	383,105	318,003
43964	Toronto	7,705	7,780
45067	Trenton	5,278	3,064
45426	Trotwood	6,997	4,992
45373	Troy	17,186	13,685
44087	Twinsburg	6,432	4,098
44683	Uhrichsville	5,731	6,201
44118	University Heights	17,055	16,641
43221	Upper Arlington	38,727	28,486
43351	Upper Sandusky	5,645	4,941
43078	Urbana	11,237	10,461
45377	Vandalia	10,796	6,342
45891	Van Wert	11,320	11,323
44089	Vermilion	9,872	4,785
44281	Wadsworth	13,142	10,635
45895	Wapakoneta	7,324	6,756
*44481	Warren	63,494	59,648
44122	Warrensville Heights	18,925	10,609
43160	Washington	12,495	12,388
45692	Wellston	5,410	5,728
43968	Wellsville	5,891	7,117
45449	West Carrollton	10,748	4,749
43081	Westerville	12,530	7,011
44145	Westlake	15,689	12,906
43213	Whitehall	25,263	20,818
44092	Wickliffe	21,354	15,760
44890	Willard	5,510	5,457
44094	Willoughby	18,634	15,058
44094	Willoughby Hills	5,247	4,241
44094	Willowick	21,237	18,749
45177	Wilmington	10,051	8,915
44691	Wooster	18,703	17,046
43085	Worthington	15,326	9,239
45433	Wright-Patterson(u)	10,151	
45215	Wyoming	9,089	7,736

ZIP Code	Place	1970	1960
45385	Xenia	25,373	20,445
*44501	Youngstown	140,909	166,689
43701	Zanesville	33,045	39,077

Oklahoma

ZIP Code	Place	1970	1960
74820	Ada	14,859	14,347
73521	Altus	23,302	21,225
73717	Alva	7,440	6,258
73005	Anadarko	6,682	6,299
73401	Ardmore	20,881	20,184
74003	Bartlesville	29,683	27,893
73008	Bethany	22,694	12,342
74631	Blackwell	8,645	9,588
74012	Broken Arrow	11,787	5,928
74018	Chickasha	14,194	14,866
74017	Claremore	9,084	6,639
73601	Clinton	8,513	9,617
74023	Cushing	7,529	8,619
73115	Del City	27,133	12,934
73533	Duncan	19,718	20,009
74701	Durant	11,118	10,467
73034	Edmond	16,633	8,577
73644	Elk City	7,323	8,196
73036	El Reno	14,510	11,015
73701	Enid	44,986	38,859
73503	Fort Sill(u)	21,217	
73542	Frederick	6,132	5,879
73044	Guthrie	9,575	9,502
73942	Guymon	7,674	5,760
74437	Henryetta	6,430	6,551
74848	Holdenville	5,181	5,712
74743	Hugo	6,585	6,287
74745	Idabel	5,946	4,967
73501	Lawton	74,470	61,697
74501	McAlester	18,802	17,419
74354	Miami	13,880	12,869
73110	Midwest City	48,212	36,058
73060	Moore	18,761	1,783
74401	Muskogee	37,331	38,059
73069	Norman	52,117	33,412
*73125	Oklahoma City	368,377	324,253
74447	Okmulgee	15,180	15,951
73075	Pauls Valley	5,769	6,856
73077	Perry	5,341	5,210
74601	Ponca City	25,940	24,411
74953	Poteau	5,500	4,428
74361	Pryor	7,057	6,476
74063	Sand Springs	10,565	7,754
74066	Sapulpa	15,159	14,282
74868	Seminole	7,878	11,464
74801	Shawnee	25,075	24,326
74074	Stillwater	31,126	23,965
73086	Sulphur	5,158	4,737
74464	Tahlequah	9,254	5,840
73120	The Village	13,695	12,118
*74101	Tulsa	330,350	261,685
74301	Vinita	5,847	6,027
73132	Warr Acres	9,887	7,135
73096	Weatherford	7,959	4,499
74884	Wewoka	5,284	5,954
73801	Woodward	9,412	7,747
73099	Yukon 1975	12,980	3,076

Oregon

ZIP Code	Place	1970	1960
97321	Albany	18,181	12,926
97601	Altamont(u)	15,746	10,811
97520	Ashland	12,342	9,119
97103	Astoria	10,244	11,239
97814	Baker	9,354	9,986
97005	Beaverton	18,577	5,937
97701	Bend	13,710	11,936
97420	Coos Bay	13,466	7,084
97330	Corvallis	35,056	20,669
97424	Cottage Grove	6,004	3,895
97338	Dallas	6,361	5,072
*97401	Eugene	79,028	50,977
97116	Forest Grove	8,275	5,628
97301	Four Corners(u)	5,823	4,743
97027	Gladstone	6,254	3,854
97526	Grants Pass	12,455	10,118
97030	Gresham	10,030	3,944
97303	Hayesville(u)	5,518	4,568
97123	Hillsboro	14,675	8,232
97303	Keizer(u)	11,405	5,288
97601	Klamath Falls	15,775	16,949
97850	La Grande	9,645	9,014
97034	Lake Oswego	14,615	8,906
97355	Lebanon	6,636	5,858
97128	McMinnville	10,125	7,656
97501	Medford	28,454	24,425
97222	Milwaukie	16,444	9,099
97361	Monmouth	5,237	2,229
97132	Newberg	6,507	4,204
97365	Newport	5,188	5,344

ZIP Code	Place	1970	1960
97459	North Bend	8,553	7,512
97914	Ontario	6,523	5,101
97045	Oregon City	9,176	7,996
97801	Pendleton	13,197	14,434
*97208	Portland	379,967	372,676
97470	Roseburg	14,461	11,467
97051	St. Helens	6,212	5,022
*97301	Salem	68,480	49,142
97477	Springfield	26,874	19,616
97058	The Dalles	10,423	10,493
97223	Tigard	5,302	......
97068	West Linn	7,091	3,933
97071	Woodburn	7,495	3,120

Pennsylvania

ZIP Code	Place	1970	1960
19001	Abington(u)	8,594	......
19018	Aldan	5,001	4,324
15001	Aliquippa	22,277	26,369
*18101	Allentown	109,527	108,347
*16603	Altoona	63,115	69,407
19002	Ambler	7,800	6,765
15003	Ambridge	11,324	13,865
18403	Archbald	6,118	5,642
19003	Ardmore(u)	5,131	......
15068	Arnold	8,174	9,437
15202	Avalon	7,010	6,859
15005	Baden	5,536	6,109
19004	Bala-Cynwyd(u)	6,403	......
15234	Baldwin	26,729	24,489
18013	Bangor	5,425	5,766
15009	Beaver	6,100	6,160
15010	Beaver Falls	14,375	16,240
16823	Bellefonte	6,828	6,088
15202	Bellevue	11,586	11,412
18603	Berwick	12,274	13,353
15102	Bethel Park	34,791	23,650
*18016	Bethlehem	72,686	75,408
18447	Blakely	6,391	6,374
17815	Bloomsburg	11,652	10,655
15104	Braddock	8,795	12,337
16701	Bradford	12,672	15,061
19406	Brandywine Village(u)	11,411	......
15227	Brentwood	13,732	13,706
19405	Bridgeport	5,630	5,306
15017	Bridgeville	6,717	7,112
19007	Bristol	12,085	12,364
19015	Brookhaven 1973	7,262	5,280
19010	Bryn Mawr(u)	5,815	......
16001	Butler	18,691	20,975
15419	California	6,635	5,978
17011	Camp Hill	9,931	8,559
15317	Canonsburg	11,439	11,877
18407	Carbondale	12,808	13,595
17013	Carlisle	18,079	16,623
15106	Carnegie	10,864	11,887
15108	Carnot-Moon(u)	13,093	......
15234	Castle Shannon	11,899	11,836
18032	Catasauqua	5,702	5,062
19095	Cedarbrook-Melrose Park (u)	9,980	......
19428	Cedar Heights(u)	6,326	......
17201	Chambersburg	17,315	17,670
15022	Charleroi	6,723	8,148
19380	Chatwood(u)	7,168	3,621
*19003	Chester	56,331	63,658
15025	Clairton	15,051	18,389
16214	Clarion	6,095	4,958
18411	Clarks Summit	5,376	3,693
16830	Clearfield	8,176	9,270
19018	Clifton Heights	8,348	8,005
19320	Coatesville	12,331	12,971
19023	Collingdale	10,605	10,268
17512	Columbia	11,237	12,075
15425	Connellsville	11,643	12,814
19428	Conshohocken	10,195	10,259
15108	Coraopolis	8,435	9,643
16407	Corry	7,435	7,744
15205	Crafton	8,233	8,418
17821	Danville	6,176	6,889
19023	Darby	13,729	14,059
18519	Dickson City	7,698	7,738
15033	Donora	8,825	11,131
15216	Dormont	12,856	13,098
19335	Downingtown	7,437	5,598
18901	Doylestown	8,270	5,917
15801	Du Bois	10,112	10,667
18512	Dunmore	17,300	18,917
15110	Duquesne	11,410	15,019
18642	Duryea	5,264	5,626
18042	Easton	29,450	31,955
18301	East Stroudsburg	7,894	7,674
15005	Economy 1973	7,605	5,925
15218	Edgewood	5,138	5,124
18704	Edwardsville	5,633	5,711
17022	Elizabethtown	8,072	6,780
16117	Ellwood City	10,857	12,413
18049	Emmaus	11,511	10,262
17522	Ephrata	9,662	7,688

ZIP Code	Place	1970	1960
*16501	Erie	129,231	138,440
15223	Etna	5,819	5,519
16121	Farrell	11,022	13,793
19031	Flourtown(u)	9,149	......
19032	Folcroft	9,610	7,013
15221	Forest Hills	9,561	8,796
18704	Forty Fort	6,114	6,431
18015	Fountain Hill	5,384	5,428
17931	Frackville	5,445	5,654
16323	Franklin	8,629	9,586
15143	Franklin Park	5,310	......
18052	Fullerton(u)	7,908	......
19004	General Wayne(u)	5,368	......
17325	Gettysburg	7,275	7,960
19045	Glassport	7,450	8,418
19036	Glenolden	8,697	7,249
19038	Glenside(u)	17,353	......
15601	Greensburg	17,077	17,383
15220	Green Tree	6,441	5,226
16125	Greenville	8,704	8,765
16127	Grove City	8,312	8,368
17331	Hanover	15,623	15,538
*17105	Harrisburg	68,061	79,697
19040	Hatboro	8,880	7,315
19044	Hatboro West(u)	13,542	......
18201	Hazelton	30,426	32,056
18055	Hellertown	6,615	6,716
17033	Hershey(u)	7,407	6,851
18042	Highland Park (Northampton)(u)	5,500	......
16648	Hollidaysburg	6,262	6,475
16001	Homeacre-Lyndora(u)	8,415	......
15120	Homestead	6,309	7,502
18431	Honesdale	5,224	5,569
16652	Huntingdon	6,987	7,234
15701	Indiana	16,100	13,005
15644	Jeannette	15,209	16,565
15344	Jefferson	8,512	8,280
19401	Jefferson-Trooper(u)	13,022	......
19046	Jenkintown	5,990	5,017
17740	Jersey Shore	5,322	5,613
18229	Jim Thorpe	5,456	5,945
*15901	Johnstown	42,476	53,949
16735	Kane	5,001	5,380
18704	Kingston	18,325	20,261
16201	Kittanning	6,231	6,793
19444	Lafayette Hills-Plymouth Meeting(u)	8,275	......
*17604	Lancaster	57,690	61,055
19446	Lansdale	18,451	12,612
19050	Lansdowne	14,090	12,601
18232	Lansford	5,168	5,958
15650	Latrobe	11,749	11,932
17042	Lebanon	28,572	30,045
18235	Lehighton	6,095	6,318
17837	Lewisburg	6,376	5,523
17044	Lewistown	11,098	12,640
17543	Lititz	7,072	5,987
17745	Lock Haven	11,427	11,748
15068	Lower Burrell	13,654	11,952
*15134	McKeesport	37,977	45,489
15136	McKees Rocks	11,901	13,185
17948	Mahanoy City	7,257	8,536
17545	Manheim	5,434	4,790
16335	Meadville	16,573	16,671
17055	Mechanicsburg	9,385	8,123
*19063	Media	6,444	5,803
19066	Merion(u)	5,686	......
17057	Middletown	9,080	11,182
15059	Midland	5,271	6,425
17551	Millersville	6,396	3,883
15209	Millvale	5,815	6,624
17847	Milton	7,723	7,972
17954	Minersville	6,012	6,606
15061	Monaca	7,486	8,394
15062	Monessen	15,216	18,424
15063	Monongahela	7,113	8,388
15146	Monroeville	29,011	22,446
17754	Montoursville	5,985	5,211
19067	Morrisville	11,309	7,790
17851	Mount Carmel	9,317	10,760
17552	Mount Joy	5,041	3,292
15210	Mount Oliver	5,487	5,980
15666	Mount Pleasant	5,895	6,107
15120	Munhall	16,574	17,312
18634	Nanticoke	14,632	15,601
19072	Narberth	5,151	5,209
18064	Nazareth	5,815	6,209
15066	New Brighton	7,637	8,397
*16101	New Castle	38,559	44,790
17070	New Cumberland	9,803	9,257
15068	New Kensington	20,312	23,485
*19401	Norristown	38,169	38,925
18067	Northampton	8,389	8,866
19003	North Ardmore(u)	5,856	......
15104	North Braddock	10,838	13,204
19038	North Hills-Ardsley(u)	13,096	......
19074	Norwood	7,229	6,729
19126	Oak Lane(u)	6,192	......

ZIP Code	Place	1970	1960
15139	Oakmont	7,550	7,504
19117	Ogontz(u)	5,463	2,254
16301	Oil City	15,033	17,692
18518	Old Forge	9,522	8,928
18447	Olyphant	5,422	5,864
19075	Oreland(u)	9,261	......
18071	Palmerton	5,620	5,942
17078	Palmyra	7,615	6,999
19301	Paoli(u)	5,835	......
17331	Parkville(u)	5,120	4,516
19004	Pencoyo(u)	6,650	......
19401	Penn Sq.-Plymouth Valley(u)	20,238	......
19151	Penn Wynne(u)	6,038	......
18944	Perkasie	5,451	4,650
*19104	Philadelphia	1,949,996	2,002,512
19460	Phoenixville	14,823	13,797
*15219	Pittsburgh	520,117	604,332
*18640	Pittston	11,113	12,407
18705	Plains(u)	6,606	......
15236	Pleasant Hills	10,409	8,573
15239	Plum	21,932	10,241
18651	Plymouth	9,536	10,401
15133	Port Vue	5,862	6,635
19464	Pottstown	25,355	26,144
17901	Pottsville	19,715	21,659
19076	Prospect Park	7,250	6,596
15767	Punxsutawney	7,792	8,805
18951	Quakertown	7,276	6,305
*19603	Reading	87,643	98,177
17356	Red Lion	5,645	5,594
15853	Ridgway	6,022	6,387
19078	Ridley Park	9,025	7,387
19001	Roslyn(u)	18,380	......
19046	Rydal(u)	5,083	......
15857	St. Marys	7,470	8,065
18840	Sayre	7,473	7,917
17972	Schuylkill Haven	6,125	6,470
15683	Scottdale	5,818	6,244
*18503	Scranton	103,564	111,443
17870	Selinsgrove	5,116	3,948
15143	Sewickley	5,660	6,157
17872	Shamokin	11,719	13,674
16146	Sharon	22,653	25,267
19079	Sharon Hill	7,464	7,123
15215	Sharpsburg	5,453	6,096
16150	Sharpsville	6,126	6,061
17976	Shenandoah	8,287	11,073
19607	Shillington	6,249	5,639
17257	Shippensburg	6,536	6,138
15501	Somerset	6,269	6,347
18964	Souderton	6,366	5,381
17701	South Williamsport	7,153	6,972
15144	Springdale	5,202	5,602
16801	State College	33,778	22,409
17113	Steelton	8,556	11,266
18360	Stroudsburg	5,451	6,070
16323	Sugar Creek	5,944	......
17801	Sunbury	13,025	13,687
19081	Swarthmore	6,156	5,753
15218	Swissvale	13,819	15,089
18704	Swoyersville	6,786	6,751
18252	Tamaqua	9,246	10,173
15084	Tarentum	7,379	8,232
18517	Taylor	6,977	6,148
16354	Titusville	7,331	8,356
15145	Turtle Creek	8,308	10,607
16686	Tyrone	7,072	7,792
15401	Uniontown	16,282	17,942
15690	Vandergrift	7,889	8,742
16365	Warren	12,998	14,505
15301	Washington	19,827	23,545
17268	Waynesboro	10,011	10,427
15370	Waynesburg	5,152	5,188
19380	West Chester	19,301	15,705
18201	West Hazleton	6,059	6,278
15122	West Mifflin	28,070	27,289
15905	Westmont	6,673	6,573
18643	West Pittston	7,074	6,998
15229	West View	8,312	8,079
17404	West York	5,314	5,526
18052	Whitehall	16,551	16,075
15131	White Oak	9,304	9,047
*18701	Wilkes-Barre	58,856	63,551
15221	Wilkinsburg	26,780	30,066
17701	Williamsport	37,918	41,967
19090	Willow Grove(u)	16,494	......
15025	Wilson	8,406	8,465
15963	Windber	6,332	6,994
19610	Wyomissing	7,136	5,044
19050	Yeadon	12,136	11,610
*17405	York	50,335	54,504

Rhode Island

See Note on Page 241

ZIP Code	Place	1970	1960
02806	Barrington	17,554	13,826
02809	Bristol	17,860	14,570
02830	Burrillville	10,087	9,119
02863	Central Falls	18,716	19,858
02816	Coventry	22,947	15,432
02910	Cranston	74,287	66,766
02864	Cumberland	26,605	18,792
02818	East Greenwich	9,577	6,100
02914	East Providence	48,207	41,955
02814	Glocester	5,160	3,397
02833	Hopkinton	5,392	4,174
02919	Johnston	22,037	17,160
02881	Kingston(u)	5,601	2,616
02865	Lincoln	16,182	13,551
02840	Middletown	29,290	12,675
02882	Narragansett	7,138	3,444
02840	Newport	34,562	47,049
02843	Newport East(u)	10,285	2,643
02852	North Kingstown	29,793	18,977
02908	North Providence	24,337	18,220
02876	North Smithfield	9,349	7,632
*02860	Pawtucket	76,984	81,001
02871	Portsmouth	12,521	8,251
*02904	Providence	179,116	207,498
02857	Scituate	7,489	5,210
02917	Smithfield	13,468	9,442
02879	South Kingstown	16,913	11,942
02878	Tiverton	12,559	9,461
02880	Wakefield-Peacedale(u)	6,331	5,569
02885	Warren	10,523	8,750
*02887	Warwick	83,694	68,504
02891	Westerly Center(u)	13,654	9,698
02891	Westerly	17,248	14,267
02893	West Warwick	24,323	21,414
02895	Woonsocket	46,820	47,080

South Carolina

ZIP Code	Place	1970	1960
29620	Abbeville	5,515	5,436
29801	Aiken	13,436	11,243
29621	Anderson	27,556	41,316
29407	Avondale-Moorland(u)	5,236	......
29902	Beaufort	9,434	6,298
29627	Belton	5,257	5,106
29512	Bennettsville	7,468	6,963
29611	Berea	7,186	......
29020	Camden	8,532	6,842
29033	Cayce	9,967	8,517
*29401	Charleston	66,945	65,925
29404	Charleston Base(u)	6,238	......
29408	Charleston Yard(u)	13,565	......
29520	Cheraw	5,627	5,171
29706	Chester	7,045	6,906
29631	Clemson	5,578	1,587
29325	Clinton	8,138	7,937
*29201	Columbia	113,542	97,433
29526	Conway	8,151	8,563
29532	Darlington	6,990	6,710
29536	Dillon	6,391	6,173
29640	Easley	11,175	8,283
29501	Florence	25,997	24,722
29206	Forest Acres	6,808	3,842
29340	Gaffney	13,253	10,435
29605	Gantt(u)	11,386	......
29440	Georgetown	10,449	12,261
*29602	Greenville	61,436	66,188
29646	Greenwood	21,069	16,644
29651	Greer	10,642	8,967
29410	Hanahan(u) 1974	11,518	......
29550	Hartsville	8,017	6,392
29560	Lake City	6,247	6,059
29720	Lancaster	9,186	7,999
29360	Laurens	10,298	9,598
29571	Marion	7,435	7,174
29662	Mauldin 1973	5,480	1,462
29464	Mount Pleasant	6,879	5,116
29574	Mullins	6,006	6,299
29577	Myrtle Beach	9,035	7,834
29108	Newberry	9,218	8,208
29841	North Augusta	12,883	10,348
29115	Orangeburg	13,252	13,852
29905	Parris Island(u)	8,868	......
29730	Rock Hill	33,846	29,404
29407	St. Andrews(u)	9,202	......
29678	Seneca	6,382	5,227
29150	Shannontown(u)	7,491	7,064
29152	Shaw(u)	5,819	......
29681	Simpsonville 1974	6,209	2,282
*29301	Spartanburg	44,546	44,352
29150	Sumter	24,555	23,062
29687	Taylors(u)	6,831	1,071
29379	Union	10,775	10,191
29607	Wade-Hampton(u)	17,152	......
29488	Walterboro	6,257	5,417
29169	West Columbia	7,838	6,410
29745	York	5,081	4,758

ZIP Code	Place	1970	1960
	South Dakota		
57401	Aberdeen	26,476	23,073
57006	Brookings	13,717	10,558
57706	Ellsworth(u)	6,207	
57350	Huron	14,299	14,180
57754	Lead	5,420	6,211
57042	Madison	6,315	5,420
57301	Mitchell	13,425	12,555
57501	Pierre	9,699	10,088
57701	Rapid City	43,836	42,399
*57101	Sioux Falls	72,488	65,466
57785	Sturgis 1974	5,162	4,639
57069	Vermillion	9,128	6,102
57201	Watertown	13,388	14,077
57078	Yankton	11,919	9,279
	Tennessee		
37701	Alcoa	7,739	6,395
37303	Athens	11,790	12,103
38008	Bolivar	6,674	3,338
37620	Bristol	20,064	17,582
38012	Brownsville	7,011	5,424
*37401	Chattanooga	119,923	130,009
37040	Clarksville	31,719	22,021
37311	Cleveland	20,651	16,196
38401	Columbia	21,471	17,624
38501	Cookeville	14,270	7,805
38019	Covington	5,801	5,298
38555	Crossville	5,381	4,668
37055	Dickson	5,665	5,028
38024	Dyersburg	14,523	12,499
37801	Eagleton Village(u)	5,345	5,068
37412	East Ridge	21,799	19,570
37643	Elizabethton	12,269	10,896
37334	Fayetteville	7,030	6,804
42223	Fort Campbell South(u)	9,279	
37064	Franklin 1974	11,298	6,977
37066	Gallatin	13,253	7,901
37075	Greater Hendersonville(u)	11,996	
37743	Greeneville	13,722	11,759
37748	Harriman	8,734	5,931
37343	Hixson(u)	6,188	
38343	Humboldt	10,066	8,482
38301	Jackson	39,996	34,376
37760	Jefferson City	5,124	4,550
37601	Johnson City	33,770	31,187
*37662	Kingsport	31,938	26,314
37665	Kingsport North(u)	13,118	
*37901	Knoxville	174,587	111,827
37766	La Follette	6,902	6,204
37416	Lake Hills-Murray Hills(u)	7,806	
38464	Lawrenceburg	8,889	8,042
37087	Lebanon	12,492	10,512
37771	Lenoir City	5,324	4,979
37091	Lewisburg	7,207	6,338
38351	Lexington	5,024	3,943
37110	Mc Minnville	10,662	9,013
37355	Manchester	6,208	3,930
38237	Martin	7,781	4,750
37801	Maryville	13,808	10,348
*38101	Memphis	623,530	497,524
38358	Milan	7,313	5,208
38053	Millington	21,177	6,059
37814	Morristown	20,318	21,267
37130	Murfreesboro	26,360	18,991
*37202	Nashville-Davidson	**447,877	170,874
37821	Newport	7,328	6,448
37830	Oak Ridge	28,319	27,169
38242	Paris	9,892	9,325
38478	Pulaski	6,989	8,616
37415	Red Bank	12,715	10,777
37854	Rockwood	5,259	5,345
38372	Savannah	5,576	4,315
37160	Shelbyville	12,262	10,466
37167	Smyrna	5,698	3,612
37379	Soddy-Daisy	7,569	
37311	South Cleveland(u)	5,070	1,512
37172	Springfield	9,720	9,221
37388	Tullahoma	15,311	12,242
38261	Union City	11,925	8,837
37398	Winchester	5,256	4,760

**Comprises the Metropolitan Government of Nashville and Davidson County.

ZIP Code	Place	1970	1960
	Texas		
*79604	Abilene	89,653	90,368
78209	Alamo Heights	6,933	7,552
78332	Alice	20,121	20,861
79830	Alpine	5,971	4,740
77511	Alvin	10,671	5,643
*79105	Amarillo	127,010	137,969

ZIP Code	Place	1970	1960
79714	Andrews	8,625	11,135
77515	Angleton	9,770	7,312
78336	Aransas Pass	5,813	6,956
*76010	Arlington	90,032	44,775
75751	Athens	9,582	7,086
75551	Atlanta	5,007	4,076
*78710	Austin	251,808	186,545
75149	Balch Springs	10,464	6,821
77414	Bay City	13,445	11,656
77520	Baytown	43,980	28,159
*77704	Beaumont	117,548	119,175
76021	Bedford	10,049	2,706
78102	Beeville	13,506	13,811
77401	Bellaire	19,009	19,872
76704	Bellmead	7,698	5,127
76513	Belton	8,696	8,163
76126	Benbrook	8,169	3,254
79720	Big Spring	28,735	31,230
75418	Bonham	7,698	7,357
79007	Borger	14,195	20,911
76230	Bowie	5,185	4,566
76825	Brady	5,557	5,338
76024	Breckenridge	5,944	6,273
77833	Brenham	8,922	7,740
77611	Bridge City(u)	8,164	4,677
79316	Brownfield	9,647	10,286
78520	Brownsville	52,522	48,040
76801	Brownwood	17,368	16,974
77801	Bryan	33,719	27,542
76354	Burkburnett	9,230	7,621
76028	Burleson	7,713	2,345
76520	Cameron	5,546	5,640
79015	Canyon	8,333	5,864
78834	Carrizo Springs	5,374	5,699
75006	Carrollton	13,855	4,242
75633	Carthage	5,392	5,262
78213	Castle Hills	5,311	2,622
79201	Childress	5,408	6,399
76031	Cleburne	16,015	15,381
77327	Cleveland	5,627	5,838
77531	Clute City	6,023	4,501
76834	Coleman	5,608	6,371
77840	College Station	17,676	11,396
79512	Colorado City	5,227	6,457
75428	Commerce	9,534	5,789
77301	Conroe	11,969	9,192
76522	Copperas Cove	10,818	4,567
*78408	Corpus Christi	204,525	167,690
75110	Corsicana	19,972	20,344
75835	Crockett	6,616	5,356
78839	Crystal City	8,104	9,101
77954	Cuero	6,956	7,338
79022	Dalhart	5,705	5,160
*75260	Dallas	844,401	679,684
77536	Deer Park	12,773	4,865
78840	Del Rio	21,330	18,612
75020	Denison	24,923	22,748
76201	Denton	39,874	26,844
75115	De Soto	6,617	1,969
77539	Dickinson(u)	10,776	4,715
78537	Donna	7,365	7,522
79029	Dumas	9,771	8,477
75116	Duncanville	14,105	3,774
78852	Eagle Pass	15,364	12,094
78539	Edinburg	17,163	18,706
77957	Edna	5,332	5,038
77437	El Campo	9,332	7,700
*79910	El Paso	322,261	276,687
75119	Ennis	11,046	9,347
76039	Euless	19,316	4,263
78355	Falfurrias	6,355	6,515
75234	Farmers Branch	27,492	13,441
76119	Forest Hill	8,236	3,221
79906	Fort Bliss(u)	13,288	
76544	Fort Hood(u)	32,597	
78234	Fort Sam Houston(u)	10,553	
79735	Fort Stockton	8,283	6,373
*76101	Fort Worth	393,476	356,268
78624	Fredericksburg	5,326	4,629
77541	Freeport	11,997	11,619
77546	Friendswood	5,675	
76240	Gainesville	13,830	13,083
77547	Galena Park	10,479	10,852
77550	Galveston	61,809	67,175
*75040	Garland	81,437	38,501
78626	Georgetown	6,395	5,218
75647	Gladewater	5,574	5,742
78629	Gonzales	5,854	5,829
76046	Graham	7,477	8,505
75050	Grand Prairie	50,904	30,386
76051	Grapevine	7,023	2,821
75401	Greenville	22,043	19,087
77619	Groves	18,067	17,304
76117	Haltom City	28,127	23,133
78550	Harlingen	33,503	41,207
75652	Henderson	10,187	9,666
79045	Hereford	13,414	7,652

ZIP Code	Place	1970	1960
75205	Highland Park	10,133	10,411
76645	Hillsboro	7,224	7,402
77563	Hitchcock	5,565	5,216
78861	Hondo	5,487	4,992
*77013	Houston	1,232,802	938,219
77340	Huntsville	17,610	11,999
76053	Hurst	27,215	10,165
76367	Iowa Park	5,796	3,295
*75061	Irving	97,260	45,985
77029	Jacinto City	9,563	9,547
75766	Jacksonville	9,734	9,590
75951	Jasper	6,251	4,889
79745	Kermit	7,884	10,465
78028	Kerrville	12,672	8,901
75662	Kilgore	9,495	10,092
76541	Killeen	35,507	23,377
78363	Kingsville	28,915	25,297
78236	Lackland(u)	19,141	......
77566	Lake Jackson	13,376	9,651
77568	La Marque	16,131	13,969
79331	Lamesa	11,559	12,438
76550	Lampasas	5,922	5,061
75146	Lancaster	10,522	7,501
77571	La Porte	7,149	4,512
78040	Laredo	69,024	60,678
77573	League City	10,818	......
79336	Levelland	11,445	10,153
75067	Lewisville	9,264	3,956
77575	Liberty	5,591	6,127
79339	Littlefield	6,738	7,236
78644	Lockhart	6,489	6,084
75601	Longview 1975	51,953	40,050
*79408	Lubbock	149,101	128,691
75901	Lufkin	23,049	17,641
78501	McAllen	37,636	32,728
75069	McKinney	15,193	13,763
76661	Marlin	6,351	6,918
75670	Marshall	22,937	23,846
76368	Mathis	5,351	6,075
78570	Mercedes	9,355	10,943
75149	Mesquite	55,131	27,526
76667	Mexia	5,943	6,121
79701	Midland	59,463	62,625
76067	Mineral Wells	18,411	11,053
78572	Mission	13,043	14,081
79756	Monahans	8,333	8,567
75455	Mount Pleasant	9,459	8,027
75961	Nacogdoches	22,544	12,674
77868	Navasota	5,111	4,937
77627	Nederland	16,810	12,036
78130	New Braunfels	17,859	15,631
76118	North Richland Hills	16,514	8,662
*79760	Odessa	78,380	80,338
77630	Orange	24,457	25,605
75801	Palestine	14,525	13,974
79065	Pampa	21,726	24,664
75460	Paris	23,441	20,977
*77501	Pasadena	89,277	58,737
77581	Pearland	6,444	1,497
78061	Pearsall	5,545	4,957
79772	Pecos	12,682	12,728
79070	Perryton	7,810	7,903
78577	Pharr	15,829	14,106
79072	Plainview	19,096	18,735
75074	Plano	17,872	3,695
78064	Pleasanton	5,407	3,467
77640	Port Arthur	57,371	66,676
78374	Portland	7,302	2,538
77979	Port Lavaca	10,491	8,864
77651	Port Neches	10,894	8,696
75475	Randolph(u)	5,329	......
75080	Raymondville	7,987	9,385
75080	Richardson	48,582	16,810
76118	Richland Hills	8,865	7,804
77469	Richmond	5,777	3,668
78582	Rio Grande City(u)	5,676	5,835
77019	River Oaks	8,193	8,444
78380	Robstown	11,217	10,266
77471	Rosenberg	12,098	9,698
76901	San Angelo	63,884	58,815
*78284	San Antonio	654,153	587,718
78586	San Benito	15,176	16,422
78589	San Juan	5,070	4,371
78666	San Marcos	18,860	12,713
78155	Seguin	15,934	14,299
79360	Seminole	5,007	5,737
75090	Sherman	29,061	24,988
77656	Silsbee	7,271	6,277
78387	Sinton	5,563	6,008
79364	Slaton	6,583	6,568
79549	Snyder	11,171	13,850
77587	South Houston	11,527	7,523
76401	Stephenville	9,277	7,359
75482	Sulphur Springs	10,642	9,160
79556	Sweetwater	12,020	13,914
76574	Taylor	9,616	9,434
76501	Temple	33,431	30,419
75160	Terrell	14,182	13,803

ZIP Code	Place	1970	1960
78209	Terrell Hills	5,225	5,572
75501	Texarkana	30,497	30,218
77590	Texas City	38,908	32,065
79088	Tulia	5,294	4,410
75701	Tyler	57,770	51,230
78148	Universal City	7,613	......
76308	University Park	23,498	23,202
78801	Uvalde	10,764	10,293
76384	Vernon	11,454	12,141
77901	Victoria	41,349	33,047
77662	Vidor	9,738	......
*76701	Waco	95,326	97,808
75165	Waxahachie	13,452	12,749
76086	Weatherford	11,750	9,759
78596	Weslaco	15,313	15,649
77005	West University Place	13,317	14,628
77488	Wharton	7,881	5,734
76108	White Settlement	13,449	11,513
*76307	Wichita Falls	96,265	101,724
77995	Yoakum	5,755	5,761

Utah

ZIP Code	Place	1970	1960
84003	American Fork	7,713	6,373
84010	Bountiful	27,751	17,039
84302	Brigham City	14,007	11,728
84720	Cedar City	8,946	7,543
84015	Clearfield	13,316	8,833
84121	Cottonwood(u)	8,431	......
84109	East Millcreek(u)	26,579	......
84119	Granger-Hunter(u)	9,029	......
84106	Granite Park(u)	9,573	......
84117	Holladay(u)	23,014	......
84037	Kaysville	6,192	3,608
84118	Kearns(u)	17,247	17,172
84041	Layton	13,603	9,027
84321	Logan	22,333	18,731
84044	Magna(u)	5,509	6,442
84047	Midvale	7,840	5,802
84117	Mount Olympus(u)	5,909	......
84107	Murray	21,206	16,806
84404	North Ogden	5,257	2,621
*84401	Ogden	69,478	70,197
84057	Orem	25,729	18,394
84062	Pleasant Grove	5,327	4,772
84501	Price	6,218	6,802
84601	Provo	53,131	36,047
84067	Roy	14,356	9,239
84770	St. George	7,097	5,130
*84101	Salt Lake City	175,885	189,454
84070	Sandy City	6,438	3,322
84403	South Ogden	9,991	7,405
84115	South Salt Lake	7,810	9,520
84660	Spanish Fork	7,284	6,472
84663	Springville	8,790	7,913
84015	Sunset	6,268	4,235
84074	Tooele	12,539	9,133
84403	Washington Terrace	7,241	6,441
74070	White City(u)	6,402	......

Vermont

See Note on Page 241

ZIP Code	Place	1970	1960
05641	Barre	10,209	10,387
......	Barre	6,509	4,580
05201	Bennington	14,586	13,002
......	Bennington	7,950	8,023
05301	Brattleboro Center(u)	9,055	9,315
......	Brattleboro	12,239	11,734
05401	Burlington	38,633	35,531
05446	Colchester	8,776	4,718
05451	Essex	10,951	7,090
05452	Essex Junction	6,511	5,340
05047	Hartford	6,477	6,355
05753	Middlebury	6,532	5,305
05602	Montpelier	8,609	8,782
05101	Rockingham	5,501	5,704
05701	Rutland	19,293	18,325
05478	St. Albans	8,082	8,806
05819	St. Johnsbury	8,409	8,869
05401	South Burlington	10,032	6,903
05156	Springfield Center(u)	5,632	6,600
......	Springfield	10,063	9,934
05401	Williston Road Section(u)	5,376	3,259
05404	Winooski	7,309	7,420

Virginia

ZIP Code	Place	1970	1960
*22313	Alexandria	110,927	91,023
22003	Annandale(u)	27,405	......
*22210	Arlington(u)	174,284	163,401
22041	Bailey's Crossroads(u)	7,295	......
24523	Bedford	6,011	5,921
22307	Belleview(u)	8,299	......
24060	Blacksburg	9,384	7,070
24605	Bluefield	5,286	4,235
23235	Bon Air(u)	10,771	......

ZIP Code	Place	1970	1960
24201	Bristol	14,857	17,144
24416	Buena Vista	6,425	6,300
*22906	Charlottesville	38,880	29,427
*23320	Chesapeake	89,580	......
23831	Chester(u)	5,556	1,290
24073	Christiansburg	7,857	3,653
24422	Clifton Forge	5,501	5,268
24078	Collinsville(u)	6,015	3,586
23834	Colonial Heights	15,097	9,587
24426	Covington	10,060	11,062
22701	Culpeper	6,056	2,412
22191	Dale City(u)	13,857	......
24541	Danville	46,391	46,577
23847	Emporia	5,300	5,535
22030	Fairfax	21,970	13,585
*22046	Falls Church	10,772	10,192
22060	Fort Belvoir(u)	14,591	......
22308	Fort Hunt(u)	10,415	......
22801	Fort Lee(u)	12,435	......
23851	Franklin	6,880	7,264
22401	Fredericksburg	14,450	13,639
22630	Front Royal	8,211	7,949
24333	Galax	6,278	5,254
22306	Groveton(u)	11,761	......
*23360	Hampton	120,779	89,258
22801	Harrisonburg	14,605	11,916
23075	Highland Springs(u)	7,345	......
23860	Hopewell	23,471	17,895
22303	Huntington(u)	5,559	......
22042	Jefferson(u)	25,432	......
22041	Lake Barcroft(u)	11,605	......
23228	Lakeside(u)	11,137	......
24450	Lexington	7,597	7,537
22312	Lincolnia(u)	10,761	......
22030	Long Branch(u)	21,634	......
*24505	Lynchburg	54,083	54,790
22110	Manassas	9,164	3,555
22110	Manassas Park	6,844	5,342
22030	Mantua(u)	6,911	......
24354	Marion	8,158	8,385
24112	Martinsville	19,653	18,798
22101	McLean(u)	17,698	......
23111	Mechanicsville(u)	5,189	......
*23607	Newport News	138,177	113,662
*23501	Norfolk	307,951	304,869
22151	North Springfield(u)	8,631	......
23803	Petersburg	36,103	36,750
23662	Poquoson	5,441	4,278
*23705	Portsmouth	110,963	114,773
24301	Pulaski	10,279	10,469
22134	Quantico Station(u)	6,213	......
24141	Radford	11,596	9,371
22070	Reston(u)	5,723	......
*23232	Richmond	249,431	219,958
*24001	Roanoke	92,115	97,110
24281	Rose Hill(u)	14,492	......
24153	Salem	21,982	16,058
22044	Seven Corners(u)	5,590	......
24592	South Boston	6,889	5,974
*22150	Springfield(u)	11,613	10,783
24401	Staunton	24,504	22,232
22170	Sterling Park(u)	8,321	......
23434	Suffolk	9,858	12,609
22180	Vienna	17,146	11,440
24179	Vinton	6,347	3,432
*23458	Virginia Beach	172,106	8,091
22980	Waynesboro	16,707	15,694
22152	West Springfield(u)	14,143	......
23185	Williamsburg	9,069	6,832
22601	Winchester	14,643	15,110
22191	Woodbridge-Marumsco(u)	25,412	......
24382	Wytheville	6,069	5,634

Washington

ZIP Code	Place	1970	1960
98520	Aberdeen	18,489	18,741
98221	Anacortes	7,701	8,414
98002	Auburn	21,653	11,933
*98009	Bellevue	61,196	12,809
98225	Bellingham	39,375	34,688
98011	Bothell	5,420	2,237
98310	Bremerton	35,307	28,922
98607	Camas	5,790	5,666
98531	Centralia	10,054	8,586
98532	Chehalis	5,727	5,199
99004	Cheney	6,358	3,173
99403	Clarkston	6,312	6,209
99213	Dishman(u)	9,079	......
98020	Edmonds	23,998	8,016
98926	Ellensburg	13,568	8,625
98823	Ephrata	5,255	6,548
*98201	Everett	53,622	40,304
99011	Fairchild(u)	6,754	......
98466	Fircrest	5,651	3,565
98433	Fort Lewis(u)	38,054	......
98550	Hoquiam	10,466	10,762
98626	Kelso	10,296	8,379
99336	Kennewick	15,212	14,244

ZIP Code	Place	1970	1960
98031	Kent	16,596	9,017
98033	Kirkland	14,970	6,025
98503	Lacey	9,696	......
98499	Lakes District(u)	48,195	......
98632	Longview	28,373	23,349
98036	Lynwood	16,919	7,207
98438	McChord(u)	6,515	......
98040	Mercer Island	19,047	......
98837	Moses Lake	10,310	11,299
98273	Mount Vernon	8,804	7,921
98277	Oak Harbor	9,167	3,942
*98501	Olympia	23,296	18,273
99214	Opportunity(u)	16,604	12,465
98444	Parkland(u)	21,012	......
99301	Pasco	13,920	14,522
98362	Port Angeles	16,367	12,653
98368	Port Townsend	5,241	5,074
99163	Pullman	20,509	12,957
98371	Puyallup	14,742	12,063
98052	Redmond	11,020	1,426
98055	Renton	25,878	18,453
99352	Richland	26,290	23,548
*98109	Seattle	530,831	557,087
98584	Shelton	6,515	5,651
98290	Snohomish	5,174	3,894
98387	Spanaway(u)	5,768	......
*99210	Spokane	170,516	181,608
98944	Sunnyside	6,751	6,208
*98402	Tacoma	154,407	147,979
98948	Toppenish	5,744	5,667
99268	Town and Country(u)	6,484	......
98502	Tumwater	5,373	3,885
98406	University Place(u)	13,230	......
*98660	Vancouver	41,859	32,464
99362	Walla Walla	23,619	24,536
98801	Wenatchee	16,912	16,726
*98901	Yakima	45,588	43,284

West Virginia

ZIP Code	Place	1970	1960
25801	Beckley	19,884	18,642
24701	Bluefield	15,921	19,256
26201	Buckhannon	7,261	6,386
*25301	Charleston	71,505	85,796
26301	Clarksburg	24,864	28,112
25064	Dunbar	9,151	11,006
26241	Elkins	8,287	8,307
26554	Fairmont	26,093	27,477
26354	Grafton	6,433	5,791
*25701	Huntington	74,315	83,627
26726	Keyser	6,586	6,192
25401	Martinsburg	14,626	15,179
26505	Morgantown	29,431	22,487
26041	Moundsville	13,560	15,163
26155	New Martinsville	6,528	5,607
25143	Nitro	8,019	6,894
26105	Parkersburg	44,208	44,797
25550	Point Pleasant	6,122	5,785
24740	Princeton	7,253	8,393
25177	St. Albans	14,356	15,103
25303	South Charleston	16,333	19,180
26101	Vienna	11,549	9,381
26062	Weirton	27,131	28,201
26452	Weston	7,323	8,754
26505	Westover	5,086	4,749
26003	Wheeling	48,188	53,400
25661	Williamson	5,831	6,746

Wisconsin

ZIP Code	Place	1970	1960
54301	Allouez(u)	13,753	......
54409	Antigo	9,005	9,691
54911	Appleton	56,377	48,411
54806	Ashland	9,615	10,132
54304	Ashwaubenor(u)	9,323	......
53913	Baraboo	7,931	7,660
53916	Beaver Dam	14,265	13,118
53511	Beloit 1974	35,957	32,846
54923	Berlin	5,338	4,838
53005	Brookfield 1974	33,371	19,812
53209	Brown Deer	12,582	11,280
53105	Burlington	7,479	5,856
53012	Cedarburg	7,697	5,191
54729	Chippewa Falls	12,351	11,708
53110	Cudahy	22,078	17,975
53115	Delavan	5,526	4,846
54115	De Pere	13,309	10,045
54701	Eau Claire	44,619	37,987
53122	Elm Grove	7,201	4,994
54935	Fond du Lac	35,515	32,719
53538	Fort Atkinson	9,164	7,908
53217	Fox Point	7,939	7,315
53132	Franklin	12,247	10,006
53022	Germantown 1974	8,219	622
53209	Glendale	13,426	9,537
53024	Grafton 1973	7,169	3,748
*54305	Green Bay	87,809	62,888
53220	Greenfield	24,424	17,636

ZIP Code	Place	1970	1960
53130	Hales Corners	7,771	5,549
53027	Hartford	6,499	5,627
54016	Hudson 1973	5,322	4,325
53545	Janesville	46,426	35,164
53549	Jefferson	5,429	4,548
54130	Kaukauna	11,308	10,096
53140	Kenosha	78,805	67,899
54136	Kimberly	6,131	5,322
54601	La Crosse	51,153	47,575
54140	Little Chute	5,522	5,099
*53701	Madison 1974	168,671	126,706
53701	Madison town 1975	5,995	4,925
54220	Manitowoc	33,430	32,275
54143	Marinette	12,696	13,329
54449	Marshfield	15,619	14,153
54952	Menasha	14,836	14,647
53051	Menomonee Falls	31,697	18,276
54751	Menomonie	11,275	8,624
53092	Mequon	12,150	8,543
54452	Merrill	9,502	9,451
53562	Middleton	8,286	4,410
*53203	Milwaukee 1975	669,022	741,324
53716	Monona	10,420	8,178
53566	Monroe	8,654	8,050
53150	Muskego	11,573	
54956	Neenah	22,902	18,057
53151	New Berlin	26,910	15,788
54961	New London	5,801	5,288
53154	Oak Creek	13,928	9,372
53066	Oconomowoc	8,741	6,682
54901	Oshkosh	53,082	45,110
53511	Perry Go Place(u)	5,912	4,475
53818	Platteville	9,599	6,957
53073	Plymouth	5,810	5,128
53901	Portage	7,821	7,822
53074	Port Washington	8,752	5,984
53821	Prairie Du Chien	5,540	5,649
*53401	Racine	95,162	89,144
54501	Rhinelander	8,218	8,790
54868	Rice Lake	7,278	7,303
53581	Richland Center	5,086	4,746

ZIP Code	Place	1970	1960
54971	Ripon	7,053	6,163
54022	River Falls	7,238	4,857
53207	St. Francis 1974	9,951	10,065
54166	Shawano	6,488	6,103
53081	Sheboygan	48,484	45,747
53211	Shorewood	15,576	15,990
53172	South Milwaukee	23,297	20,307
54656	Sparta	6,258	6,080
54481	Stevens Point	23,479	17,837
53589	Stoughton	6,096	5,555
54235	Sturgeon Bay 1973	7,202	7,353
53590	Sun Prairie	9,935	4,008
54880	Superior	32,237	33,563
54660	Tomah	5,647	5,321
54241	Two Rivers 1974	13,243	12,393
53094	Watertown	15,683	13,943
53186	Waukesha	39,695	30,004
53963	Waupun	7,946	7,935
54401	Wausau	32,806	31,943
54401	Wausau West(u)	6,399	4,105
53213	Wauwatosa	58,676	56,923
53214	West Allis	71,649	68,157
53095	West Bend	16,555	9,969
53217	Whitefish Bay	17,402	18,390
53190	Whitewater	12,038	6,380
54494	Wisconsin Rapids 1975	18,134	15,042

Wyoming

ZIP Code	Place	1970	1960
82601	Casper	39,361	38,930
82001	Cheyenne	40,914	43,505
82414	Cody	5,161	4,838
82716	Gillette	7,194	3,580
82520	Lander	7,125	4,182
82070	Laramie	23,143	17,520
82301	Rawlins	7,855	8,968
82501	Riverton	7,995	6,845
82901	Rock Springs	11,657	10,371
82801	Sheridan	10,856	11,651
82401	Worland	5,055	5,806

1970 Census & Areas of Counties and States

WITH NAMES OF COUNTY SEATS OR COURT HOUSES; LAND AREA IN SQUARE MILES
Source: Bureau of the Census

County	Pop. Apr. 1 1970	County Seat or Court House	Land Area Sq. Mi.

Alabama

(67 counties, 50,708 sq. mi. land; pop., 3,444,165)

County	Pop. Apr. 1 1970	County Seat or Court House	Land Area Sq. Mi.
Autauga	24,460	Prattville	599
Baldwin	59,382	Bay Minette	1,578
Barbour	22,543	Clayton	891
Bibb	13,812	Centreville	625
Blount	26,853	Oneonta	639
Bullock	11,824	Union Springs	615
Butler	22,007	Greenville	773
Calhoun	103,092	Anniston	611
Chambers	36,356	Lafayette	597
Cherokee	15,606	Centre	556
Chilton	25,180	Clanton	699
Choctaw	16,589	Butler	911
Clarke	26,724	Grove Hill	1,232
Clay	12,636	Ashland	603
Cleburne	10,996	Heflin	574
Coffee	34,872	Elba	677
Colbert	49,632	Tuscumbia	596
Conecuh	15,645	Evergreen	850
Coosa	10,662	Rockford	650
Covington	34,079	Andalusia	984
Crenshaw	13,188	Luverne	611
Cullman	52,445	Cullman	730
Dale	52,938	Ozark	559
Dallas	55,296	Selma	976
De Kalb	41,981	Fort Payne	778
Elmore	33,661	Wetumpka	624
Escambia	34,912	Brewton	962
Etowah	94,144	Gadsden	555
Fayette	16,252	Fayette	627
Franklin	23,933	Russellville	644
Geneva	21,924	Geneva	577
Greene	10,650	Eutaw	649
Hale	15,888	Greensboro	662
Henry	13,254	Abbeville	554
Houston	56,574	Dothan	575
Jackson	39,202	Scottsboro	1,079
Jefferson	644,991	Birmingham	1,115
Lamar	14,335	Vernon	605
Lauderdale	68,111	Florence	662
Lawrence	27,281	Moulton	685
Lee	61,268	Opelika	612
Limestone	41,699	Athens	546
Lowndes	12,897	Hayneville	715
Macon	24,841	Tuskegee	616
Madison	186,540	Huntsville	803
Marengo	23,819	Linden	978
Marion	23,788	Hamilton	743
Marshall	54,211	Guntersville	571
Mobile	317,308	Mobile	1,240
Monroe	20,883	Monroeville	1,032
Montgomery	167,790	Montgomery	790
Morgan	77,306	Decatur	570
Perry	15,388	Marion	734
Pickens	20,326	Carrollton	887
Pike	25,038	Troy	673
Randolph	18,331	Wedowee	581
Russell	45,394	Phenix City	627
St. Clair	27,956	Ashville & Pell City	640
Shelby	38,037	Columbiana	798
Sumter	16,974	Livingston	915
Talladega	65,280	Talladega	750
Tallapoosa	33,840	Dadeville	704
Tuscaloosa	116,029	Tuscaloosa	1,333
Walker	56,246	Jasper	805
Washington	16,241	Chatom	1,066
Wilcox	16,303	Camden	899
Winston	16,654	Double Springs	615

Alaska

(29 divisions, 566,432 sq. mi. land; pop., 302,173)

Census Division	Pop. Apr. 1, 1970	Land Area Sq. Mi.
Aleutian Islands	8,057	14,583
Anchorage	126,385	927
Angoon	503	2,825
Barrow	2,663	57,587

Census Division	Pop. Apr. 1 1970	Land Area Sq. Mi.
Bethel	7,767	19,642
Bristol Bay Borough	1,147	531
Bristol Bay	3,485	36,565
Cordova-McCarthy	1,857	15,481
Fairbanks	45,864	7,074
Haines	1,504	2,128
Juneau	13,556	1,286
Kenai-Cook Inlet	14,250	12,474
Ketchikan	10,041	1,345
Kobuk	4,434	42,978
Kodiak	9,409	5,375
Kuskokwim	2,306	56,562
Matanuska-Susitna	6,509	25,730
Nome	5,749	24,968
Outer Ketchikan	1,676	3,762
Prince of Wales	2,106	3,485
Seward	2,336	3,727
Sitka	6,106	2,296
Skagway-Yakutat	2,157	8,646
Southeast Fairbanks	4,179	17,713
Upper Yukon	1,684	84,142
Valdez-Chitina-Whittier	3,098	18,619
Wade Hampton	3,917	16,770
Wrangell-Petersburg	4,913	6,178
Yukon-Koyukuk	4,758	73,053

Arizona

(14 counties, 113,417 sq. mi. land; pop. 1,772,482)

County	Pop. Apr. 1, 1970	County Seat or Court House	Land Area Sq. Mi.
Apache	32,304	Saint Johns	11,171
Cochise	61,918	Bisbee	6,256
Coconino	48,326	Flagstaff	18,540
Gila	29,255	Globe	4,748
Graham	16,578	Safford	4,618
Greenlee	10,330	Clifton	1,879
Maricopa	968,487	Phoenix	9,155
Mohave	35,714	Kingman	13,217
Navajo	47,559	Holbrook	9,910
Pima	351,667	Tucson	9,240
Pinal	68,579	Florence	5,364
Santa Cruz	13,966	Nogales	1,246
Yavapai	37,005	Prescott	8,091
Yuma	60,827	Yuma	9,983

Arkansas

(75 counties, 51,945 sq. mi. land; pop. 1,923,295)

County	Pop. Apr. 1, 1970	County Seat or Court House	Land Area Sq. Mi.
Arkansas	23,347	DeWitt & Stuttgart	1,015
Ashley	24,976	Hamburg	928
Baxter	15,319	Mountain Home	537
Benton	50,476	Bentonville	851
Boone	19,073	Harrison	586
Bradley	12,778	Warren	651
Calhoun	5,573	Hampton	629
Carroll	12,301	Berryville and Eureka Sprg.	626
Chicot	18,164	Lake Village	643
Clark	21,537	Arkadelphia	878
Clay	18,771	Corning; Piggott	639
Cleburne	10,349	Heber Springs	554
Cleveland	6,605	Rison	601
Columbia	25,952	Magnolia	768
Conway	16,805	Morrilton	561
Craighead	52,068	Jonesboro and Lake City	716
Crawford	25,677	Van Buren	596
Crittenden	48,106	Marion	608
Cross	19,783	Wynne	625
Dallas	10,022	Fordyce	672
Desha	18,761	Arkansas City	736
Drew	15,157	Monticello	832
Faulkner	31,578	Conway	641
Franklin	11,301	Charleston and Ozark	613
Fulton	7,699	Salem	608
Garland	54,131	Hot Spgs. Nat'l Pk.	658
Grant	9,711	Sheridan	631
Greene	24,765	Paragould	579
Hempstead	19,308	Hope	726
Hot Spring	21,963	Malvern	621
Howard	11,412	Nashville	569
Independence	22,723	Batesville	752
Izard	7,381	Melbourne	574
Jackson	20,452	Newport	629
Jefferson	85,329	Pine Bluff	873
Johnson	13,630	Clarksville	673
Lafayette	10,018	Lewisville	523
Lawrence	16,320	Walnut Ridge	590
Lee	18,884	Marianna	608

County	Pop. Apr. 1 1970	County Seat or Court House	Land Area Sq. Mi.
Lincoln	12,913	Star City	563
Little River	11,194	Ashdown	486
Logan	16,789	Booneville & Paris	718
Lonoke	26,249	Lonoke	796
Madison	9,453	Huntsville	832
Marion	7,000	Yellville	584
Miller	33,385	Texarkana	623
Mississippi	62,060	Blytheville and Osceola	904
Monroe	15,657	Clarendon	607
Montgomery	5,821	Mount Ida	775
Nevada	10,111	Prescott	616
Newton	5,844	Jasper	822
Ouachita	30,896	Camden	736
Perry	5,634	Perryville	551
Phillips	40,046	Helena	686
Pike	8,711	Murfreesboro	600
Poinsett	26,843	Harrisburg	760
Polk	13,297	Mena	859
Pope	28,607	Russellville	812
Prairie	10,249	Des Arc and De Valls Bluff	661
Pulaski	287,189	Little Rock	765
Randolph	12,645	Pocohontas	647
St. Francis	30,799	Forest City	635
Saline	36,107	Benton	724
Scott	8,207	Waldron	898
Searcy	7,731	Marshall	664
Sebastian	79,237	Fort Smith; Greenwood	527
Sevier	11,272	De Queen	522
Sharp	8,233	Ash Flat	581
Stone	6,838	Mountain View	608
Union	45,428	El Dorado	1,050
Van Buren	8,275	Clinton	699
Washington	77,370	Fayetteville	958
White	39,253	Searcy	1,041
Woodruff	11,566	Augusta	591
Yell	14,208	Danville and Dardanelle	929

California

(58 counties, 156,361 sq. mi. land; pop. 19,953,134)

County	Pop. Apr. 1 1970	County Seat or Court House	Land Area Sq. Mi.
Alameda	1,073,184	Oakland	733
Alpine	484	Markleeville	727
Amador	11,821	Jackson	583
Butte	101,969	Oroville	1,645
Calaveras	13,585	San Andreas	1,024
Colusa	12,430	Colusa	1,152
Contra Costa	555,805	Martinez	735
Del Norte	14,580	Crescent City	1,007
El Dorado	43,833	Placerville	1,715
Fresno	413,329	Fresno	5,966
Glenn	17,521	Willows	1,314
Humboldt	99,692	Eureka	3,586
Imperial	74,492	El Centro	4,241
Inyo	15,571	Independence	10,130
Kern	329,281	Bakersfield	8,152
Kings	66,717	Hanford	1,396
Lake	19,548	Lakeport	1,261
Lassen	16,796	Susanville	4,561
Los Angeles	7,040,697	Los Angeles	4,069
Madera	41,519	Madera	2,145
Marin	206,758	San Rafael	520
Mariposa	6,015	Mariposa	1,453
Mendocino	51,101	Ukiah	3,511
Merced	104,629	Merced	1,958
Modoc	7,469	Alturas	4,097
Mono	4,016	Bridgeport	3,027
Monterey	247,450	Salinas	3,324
Napa	79,140	Napa	787
Nevada	26,346	Nevada City	973
Orange	1,420,676	Santa Ana	782
Placer	77,632	Auburn	1,431
Plumas	11,707	Quincy	2,566
Riverside	459,074	Riverside	7,176
Sacramento	634,190	Sacramento	975
San Benito	18,226	Hollister	1,396
San Bernardino	682,233	San Bernardino	20,117
San Diego	1,357,854	San Diego	4,261
San Francisco	715,674	San Francisco	45
San Joaquin	289,564	Stockton	1,412
San Luis Obispo	105,690	San Luis Obispo	3,183
San Mateo	556,605	Redwood City	447
Santa Barbara	264,324	Santa Barbara	2,737
Santa Clara	1,066,174	San Jose	1,300
Santa Cruz	123,790	Santa Cruz	440
Shasta	77,640	Redding	3,788
Sierra	2,365	Downieville	958
Siskiyou	33,225	Yreka	6,262
Solano	171,989	Fairfield	823
Sonoma	204,885	Santa Rosa	1,604
Stanislaus	194,506	Modesto	1,511

County	Pop. Apr. 1 1970	County Seat or Court House	Land Area Sq. Mi.
Sutter	41,935	Yuba City	603
Tehama	29,517	Red Bluff	2,982
Trinity	7,615	Weaverville	3,173
Tulare	188,322	Visalia	4,812
Tuolumne	22,169	Sonora	2,252
Ventura	378,497	Ventura	1,863
Yolo	91,788	Woodland	1,028
Yuba	44,736	Marysville	639

County	Pop. Apr. 1 1970	County Seat or Court House	Land Area Sq. Mi.
New Castle	385,856	Wilmington	438
Sussex	80,356	Georgetown	950

District of Columbia

(61 sq. mi. land; pop. 756,510)

Colorado

(63 counties, 103,766 sq. mi. land; pop. 2,207,259)

County	Pop. Apr. 1 1970	County Seat or Court House	Land Area Sq. Mi.
Adams	185,789	Brighton	1,237
Alamosa	11,422	Alamosa	719
Arapahoe	162,142	Littleton	797
Archuleta	2,733	Pagosa Springs	1,364
Baca	5,674	Springfield	2,563
Bent	6,493	Las Animas	1,519
Boulder	131,889	Boulder	748
Chaffee	10,162	Salida	1,038
Cheyenne	2,396	Cheyenne Wells	1,772
Clear Creek	4,819	Georgetown	394
Conejos	7,846	Conejos	1,268
Costilla	3,091	San Luis	1,213
Crowley	3,086	Ordway	802
Custer	1,120	Westcliffe	737
Delta	15,286	Delta	1,154
Denver	514,678	Denver	95
Dolores	1,641	Dove Creek	1,026
Douglas	8,407	Castle Rock	843
Eagle	7,498	Eagle	1,681
Elbert	3,903	Kiowa	1,864
El Paso	235,972	Colorado Springs	2,157
Fremont	21,942	Canon City	1,561
Garfield	14,821	Glenwood Springs	2,996
Gilpin	1,272	Central City	148
Grand	4,107	Hot Sulphur Springs	1,854
Gunnison	7,578	Gunnison	3,220
Hinsdale	202	Lake City	1,054
Huerfano	6,590	Walsenburg	1,574
Jackson	1,811	Walden	1,622
Jefferson	235,300	Golden	783
Kiowa	2,029	Eads	1,767
Kit Carson	7,530	Burlington	2,171
Lake	8,282	Leadville	379
La Plata	19,199	Durango	1,683
Larimer	89,900	Fort Collins	2,611
Las Animas	15,744	Trinidad	4,794
Lincoln	4,836	Hugo	2,593
Logan	18,852	Sterling	1,822
Mesa	54,374	Grand Junction	3,301
Mineral	786	Creede	921
Moffat	6,525	Craig	4,743
Montezuma	12,952	Cortez	2,094
Montrose	18,366	Montrose	2,238
Morgan	20,105	Fort Morgan	1,278
Otero	23,523	LaJunta	1,254
Ouray	1,546	Ouray	540
Park	2,185	Fairplay	2,162
Phillips	4,131	Holyoke	680
Pitkin	6,185	Aspen	973
Prowers	13,258	Lamar	1,621
Pueblo	118,238	Pueblo	2,405
Rio Blanco	4,842	Meeker	3,263
Rio Grande	10,494	Del Norte	915
Routt	6,592	Steamboat Spgs.	2,330
Saguache	3,827	Saguache	3,144
San Juan	831	Silverton	391
San Miguel	1,949	Telluride	1,283
Sedgwick	3,405	Julesburg	544
Summit	2,665	Breckenridge	604
Teller	3,316	Cripple Creek	553
Washington	5,550	Akron	2,526
Weld	89,297	Greeley	4,002
Yuma	8,544	Wray	2,379

Connecticut

(8 counties, 4,862 sq. mi. land; pop. 3,032,217)

County	Pop. Apr. 1 1970	County Seat or Court House	Land Area Sq. Mi.
Fairfield	792,814	Bridgeport	626
Hartford	816,737	Hartford	739
Litchfield	144,091	Litchfield	925
Middlesex	115,018	Middletown	372
New Haven	744,948	New Haven	604
New London	230,654	Norwich	667
Tolland	103,440	Rockville	416
Windham	84,515	Putnam	514

Delaware

(3 counties, 1,982 sq. mi. land; pop. 548,104)

County	Pop. Apr. 1 1970	County Seat or Court House	Land Area Sq. Mi.
Kent	81,892	Dover	594

Florida

(67 counties, 54,090 sq. mi. land; pop. 6,789,443)

County	Pop. Apr. 1 1970	County Seat or Court House	Land Area Sq. Mi.
Alachua	104,764	Gainesville	916
Baker	9,242	Macclenny	585
Bay	75,283	Panama City	747
Bradford	14,625	Starke	294
Brevard	230,006	Titusville	1,011
Broward	620,100	Fort Lauderdale	1,219
Calhoun	7,624	Blountstown	561
Charlotte	27,559	Punta Gorda	703
Citrus	19,196	Inverness	560
Clay	32,059	Green Cove Spgs.	593
Collier	38,040	Naples	2,006
Columbia	25,250	Lake City	784
Dade	1,267,792	Miami	2,042
De Soto	13,060	Arcadia	648
Dixie	5,480	Cross City	692
Duval	528,865	Jacksonville	766
Escambia	205,334	Pensacola	665
Flagler	4,454	Bunnell	487
Franklin	7,065	Apalachicola	536
Gadsden	39,184	Quincy	512
Gilchrist	3,551	Trenton	346
Glades	3,669	Moore Haven	753
Gulf	10,096	Port St. Joe	565
Hamilton	7,787	Jasper	514
Hardee	14,889	Wauchula	829
Hendry	11,859	La Belle	1,187
Hernando	17,004	Brooksville	484
Highlands	29,507	Sebring	997
Hillsborough	490,265	Tampa	1,038
Holmes	10,720	Bonifay	482
Indian River	35,992	Vero Beach	506
Jackson	34,434	Marianna	935
Jefferson	8,778	Monticello	605
Lafayette	2,892	Mayo	549
Lake	69,305	Tavares	961
Lee	105,216	Fort Myers	785
Leon	103,047	Tallahassee	670
Levy	12,756	Bronson	1,083
Liberty	3,379	Bristol	839
Madison	13,481	Madison	703
Manatee	97,115	Bradenton	739
Marion	69,030	Ocala	1,600
Martin	28,035	Stuart	556
Monroe	52,586	Key West	1,034
Nassau	20,626	Fernandina Beach	650
Okaloosa	88,187	Crestview	944
Okeechobee	11,233	Okeechobee	777
Orange	344,311	Orlando	910
Osceola	25,267	Kissimmee	1,313
Palm Beach	348,993	West Palm Beach	2,023
Pasco	75,955	Dade City	742
Pinellas	522,329	Clearwater	265
Polk	228,026	Bartow	1,858
Putnam	36,424	Palatka	779
St. Johns	31,035	Saint Augustine	605
St. Lucie	50,836	Fort Pierce	584
Santa Rosa	37,741	Milton	1,032
Sarasota	120,413	Sarasota	587
Seminole	83,692	Sanford	305
Sumter	14,839	Bushnell	555
Suwannee	15,559	Live Oak	686
Taylor	13,641	Perry	1,051
Union	8,112	Lake Butler	241
Volusia	169,487	De Land	1,062
Wakulla	6,308	Crawfordville	601
Walton	16,087	De Funiak Springs	1,053
Washington	11,453	Chipley	585

Georgia

(159 counties, 58,073 sq. mi. land; pop. 4,589,575)

County	Pop. Apr. 1 1970	County Seat or Court House	Land Area Sq. Mi.
Appling	12,726	Baxley	513
Atkinson	5,879	Pearson	318
Bacon	8,233	Alma	293
Baker	3,875	Newton	355
Baldwin	34,240	Milledgeville	255
Banks	6,833	Homer	231
Barrow	16,859	Winder	171
Bartow	32,911	Cartersville	461
Ben Hill	13,171	Fitzgerald	255
Berrien	11,556	Nashville	468

County	Pop. Apr. 1 1970	County Seat or Court House	Land Area Sq. Mi.
Bibb	143,418	Macon	254
Bleckley	10,291	Cochran	219
Brantley	5,940	Nahunta	447
Brooks	13,743	Quitman	491
Bryan	6,539	Pembroke	443
Bulloch	31,585	Statesboro	685
Burke	18,255	Waynesboro	831
Butts	10,560	Jackson	185
Calhoun	6,606	Morgan	289
Camden	11,334	Woodbine	653
Candler	6,412	Metter	250
Carroll	45,404	Carrollton	495
Catoosa	28,271	Ringgold	167
Charlton	5,680	Folkston	796
Chatham	187,816	Savannah	445
Chattahoochee	25,813	Cusseta	253
Chattooga	20,541	Summerville	317
Cherokee	31,059	Canton	415
Clarke	65,177	Athens	116
Clay	3,636	Fort Gaines	200
Clayton	98,126	Jonesboro	149
Clinch	6,405	Homerville	797
Cobb	196,793	Marietta	343
Coffee	22,828	Douglas	612
Colquitt	32,298	Moultrie	563
Columbia	22,327	Appling	290
Cook	12,129	Adel	233
Coweta	32,310	Newnan	442
Crawford	5,748	Knoxville	315
Crisp	18,087	Cordele	292
Dade	9,910	Trenton	168
Dawson	3,639	Dawsonville	211
Decatur	22,310	Bainbridge	575
De Kalb	415,387	Decatur	269
Dodge	15,658	Eastman	498
Dooly	10,404	Vienna	395
Dougherty	89,639	Albany	324
Douglas	28,659	Douglasville	202
Early	12,682	Blakely	524
Echols	1,924	Statenville	425
Effingham	13,632	Springfield	480
Elbert	17,262	Elberton	358
Emanuel	18,357	Swainsboro	686
Evans	7,290	Claxton	186
Fannin	13,357	Blue Ridge	394
Fayette	11,364	Fayetteville	199
Floyd	73,742	Rome	514
Forsyth	16,928	Cumming	219
Franklin	12,784	Carnesville	263
Fulton	607,592	Atlanta	530
Gilmer	8,956	Ellijay	439
Glascock	2,280	Gibson	143
Glynn	50,528	Brunswick	412
Gordon	23,570	Calhoun	358
Grady	17,826	Cairo	466
Greene	10,212	Greensboro	403
Gwinnett	72,349	Lawrenceville	437
Habersham	20,691	Clarkesville	282
Hall	59,405	Gainesville	378
Hancock	9,019	Sparta	478
Haralson	15,927	Buchanan	285
Harris	11,520	Hamilton	465
Hart	15,814	Hartwell	231
Heard	5,354	Franklin	297
Henry	23,724	McDonough	331
Houston	62,924	Perry	380
Irwin	8,036	Ocilla	372
Jackson	21,093	Jefferson	346
Jasper	5,760	Monticello	373
Jeff Davis	9,425	Hazlehurst	331
Jefferson	17,174	Louisville	530
Jenkins	8,332	Millen	351
Johnson	7,727	Wrightsville	313
Jones	12,218	Gray	402
Lamar	10,688	Barnesville	181
Lanier	5,031	Lakeland	177
Laurens	32,738	Dublin	810
Lee	7,044	Leesburg	355
Liberty	17,569	Hinesville	514
Lincoln	5,895	Lincolnton	193
Long	3,746	Ludowici	402
Lowndes	55,112	Valdosta	508
Lumpkin	8,728	Dahlonega	292
McDuffie	15,276	Thomson	253
McIntosh	7,371	Darien	426
Macon	12,933	Oglethorpe	403
Madison	13,517	Danielsville	281
Marion	5,099	Buena Vista	365
Meriwether	19,461	Greenville	499
Miller	6,424	Colquitt	287
Mitchell	18,956	Camilla	510
Monroe	10,991	Forsyth	398
Montgomery	6,099	Mount Vernon	237
Morgan	9,904	Madison	356
Murray	12,986	Chatsworth	342
Muscogee	167,377	Columbus	220
Newton	26,282	Covington	271

County	Pop. Apr. 1 1970	County Seat or Court House	Land Area Sq. Mi.
Oconee	7,915	Watkinsville	186
Oglethorpe	7,598	Lexington	435
Paulding	17,520	Dallas	318
Peach	15,990	Fort Valley	151
Pickens	9,620	Jasper	225
Pierce	9,281	Blackshear	342
Pike	7,316	Zebulon	230
Polk	29,656	Cedartown	312
Pulaski	8,066	Hawkinsville	253
Putnam	9,394	Eatonton	339
Quitman	2,180	Georgetown	156
Rabun	8,327	Clayton	368
Randolph	8,734	Cuthbert	436
Richmond	162,437	Augusta	323
Rockdale	18,152	Conyers	128
Schley	3,097	Ellaville	162
Screven	12,591	Sylvania	651
Seminole	7,059	Donalsonville	246
Spalding	39,514	Griffin	201
Stephens	20,331	Toccoa	173
Stewart	6,511	Lumpkin	452
Sumter	26,931	Americus	488
Talbot	6,625	Talbotton	390
Taliaferro	2,423	Crawfordville	195
Tattnall	16,557	Reidsville	490
Taylor	7,865	Butler	403
Telfair	11,394	McRae	440
Terrell	11,416	Dawson	329
Thomas	34,562	Thomasville	541
Tift	27,288	Tifton	266
Toombs	19,151	Lyons	368
Towns	4,565	Hiawassee	166
Treutlen	5,647	Soperton	194
Troup	44,466	La Grange	415
Turner	8,790	Ashburn	293
Twiggs	8,222	Jeffersonville	364
Union	6,811	Blairsville	309
Upson	23,505	Thomaston	334
Walker	50,691	La Fayette	445
Walton	23,404	Monroe	330
Ware	33,525	Waycross	912
Warren	6,669	Warrenton	284
Washington	17,480	Sandersville	674
Wayne	17,858	Jesup	645
Webster	2,362	Preston	195
Wheeler	4,596	Alamo	306
White	7,742	Cleveland	243
Whitfield	55,108	Dalton	281
Wilcox	6,998	Abbeville	383
Wilkes	18,184	Washington	468
Wilkinson	9,393	Irwinton	458
Worth	14,770	Sylvester	579

Hawaii

(4 counties, 6,425 sq. mi. land; pop. 769,913)

County	Pop. Apr. 1 1970	County Seat or Court House	Land Area Sq. Mi.
Hawaii	63,468	Hilo	4,037
Honolulu	630,528	Honolulu	596
Kauai	29,761	Lihue	619
Maui*	46,156	Wailuku	1,173

*Includes population of Kalawao County (279) shown separately in 1960 but included with Maui County in 1970.

Idaho

(44 counties, 82,677 sq. mi. land; pop. 713,008)

County	Pop. Apr. 1 1970	County Seat or Court House	Land Area Sq. Mi.
Ada	112,230	Boise	1,043
Adams	2,877	Council	1,371
Bannock	52,200	Pocatello	1,122
Bear Lake	5,801	Paris	984
Benewah	6,230	Saint Maries	788
Bingham	29,167	Blackfoot	2,084
Blaine	5,749	Hailey	2,647
Boise	1,763	Idaho City	1,910
Bonner	15,560	Sandpoint	1,733
Bonneville	52,457	Idaho Falls	1,836
Boundary	5,484	Bonners Ferry	1,275
Butte	2,925	Arco	2,239
Camas	728	Fairfield	1,054
Canyon	61,288	Caldwell	578
Caribou	6,534	Soda Springs	1,746
Cassia	17,017	Burley	2,544
Clark	741	Dubois	1,751
Clearwater	10,871	Orofino	2,521
Custer	2,967	Challis	4,929
Elmore	17,479	Mountain Home	3,048
Franklin	7,373	Preston	664
Fremont	8,710	Saint Anthony	1,864
Gem	9,387	Emmett	555
Gooding	8,645	Gooding	720
Idaho	12,891	Grangeville	8,516
Jefferson	11,740	Rigby	1,096
Jerome	10,253	Jerome	595

County	Pop. Apr. 1 1970	County Seat or Court House	Land Area Sq. Mi.
Kootenai	35,332	Coeur d'Alene	1,249
Latah	24,898	Moscow	1,090
Lemhi	5,566	Salmon	4,580
Lewis	3,867	Nezperce	476
Lincoln	3,057	Shoshone	1,203
Madison	13,452	Rexburg	473
Minidoka	15,731	Rupert	750
Nez Perce	30,376	Lewiston	844
Oneida	2,864	Malad City	1,191
Owyhee	6,422	Murphy	7,641
Payette	12,401	Payette	402
Power	4,864	American Falls	1,413
Shoshone	19,718	Wallace	2,609
Teton	2,351	Driggs	457
Twin Falls	41,807	Twin Falls	1,947
Valley	3,609	Cascade	3,676
Washington	7,633	Weiser	1,462

Illinois

(102 counties, 55,748 sq. mi. land; pop. 11,113,976)

County	Pop. Apr. 1 1970	County Seat or Court House	Land Area Sq. Mi.
Adams	70,861	Quincy	862
Alexander	12,015	Cairo	229
Bond	14,012	Greenville	378
Boone	25,440	Belvidere	283
Brown	5,586	Mount Sterling	306
Bureau	38,541	Princeton	866
Calhoun	5,675	Hardin	247
Carroll	19,276	Mount Carroll	456
Cass	14,219	Virginia	371
Champaign	163,281	Urbana	1,000
Christian	35,948	Taylorville	709
Clark	16,216	Marshall	505
Clay	14,735	Louisville	464
Clinton	28,315	Carlyle	434
Coles	47,815	Charleston	506
Cook	5,493,766	Chicago	954
Crawford	19,824	Robinson	443
Cumberland	9,772	Toledo	347
De Kalb	71,654	Sycamore	636
De Witt	16,975	Clinton	399
Douglas	18,997	Tuscola	420
Du Page	490,822	Wheaton	331
Edgar	21,591	Paris	628
Edwards	7,090	Albion	225
Effingham	24,608	Effingham	481
Fayette	20,752	Vandalia	703
Ford	16,382	Paxton	488
Franklin	38,329	Benton	434
Fulton	41,900	Lewistown	877
Gallatin	7,418	Shawneetown	328
Greene	17,014	Carrollton	543
Grundy	26,535	Morris	432
Hamilton	8,665	McLeansboro	435
Hancock	23,664	Carthage	797
Hardin	4,914	Elizabethtown	183
Henderson	8,451	Oquawka	376
Henry	53,217	Cambridge	826
Iroquois	33,532	Watseka	1,122
Jackson	55,008	Murphysboro	605
Jasper	10,741	Newton	495
Jefferson	31,848	Mount Vernon	573
Jersey	18,492	Jerseyville	376
Jo Daviess	21,766	Galena	606
Johnson	7,550	Vienna	345
Kane	251,005	Geneva	520
Kankakee	97,250	Kankakee	678
Kendall	26,374	Yorkville	320
Knox	60,939	Galesburg	728
Lake	382,638	Waukegan	457
La Salle	111,409	Ottawa	1,150
Lawrence	17,522	Lawrenceville	374
Lee	37,947	Dixon	728
Livingston	40,690	Pontiac	1,043
Logan	33,538	Lincoln	622
Mc Donough	36,653	Macomb	582
Mc Henry	111,555	Woodstock	610
Mc Lean	104,389	Bloomington	1,173
Macon	125,010	Decatur	578
Macoupin	44,557	Carlinville	872
Madison	250,911	Edwardsville	733
Marion	38,986	Salem	579
Marshall	13,302	Lacon	391
Mason	16,180	Havana	541
Massac	13,889	Metropolis	245
Menard	9,685	Petersburg	312
Mercer	17,294	Aledo	556
Monroe	18,831	Waterloo	382
Montgomery	30,260	Hillsboro	705
Morgan	36,174	Jacksonville	561
Moultrie	13,263	Sullivan	326
Ogle	42,867	Oregon	758
Peoria	195,318	Peoria	623
Perry	19,757	Pinckneyville	439
Piatt	15,509	Monticello	437
Pike	19,185	Pittsfield	828
Pope	3,857	Golconda	381
Pulaski	8,741	Mound City	204
Putnam	5,007	Hennepin	160
Randolph	31,379	Chester	594
Richland	16,829	Olney	364
Rock Island	166,734	Rock Island	424
St. Clair	285,199	Belleville	673
Saline	25,721	Harrisburg	383
Sangamon	161,335	Springfield	879
Schuyler	8,135	Rushville	434
Scott	6,096	Winchester	251
Shelby	22,589	Shelbyville	752
Stark	7,510	Toulon	291
Stephenson	48,861	Freeport	568
Tazewell	118,649	Pekin	652
Union	16,071	Jonesboro	416
Vermilion	97,047	Danville	899
Wabash	12,841	Mt. Carmel	222
Warren	21,595	Monmouth	541
Washington	13,780	Nashville	564
Wayne	17,004	Fairfield	715
White	17,312	Carmi	502
Whiteside	62,877	Morrison	687
Will	247,825	Joliet	847
Williamson	49,021	Marion	429
Winnebago	246,623	Rockford	519
Woodford	28,012	Eureka	528

Indiana

(92 counties, 36,097 sq. mi. land; pop. 5,193,669)

County	Pop. Apr. 1 1970	County Seat or Court House	Land Area Sq. Mi.
Adams	26,871	Decatur	345
Allen	280,455	Fort Wayne	671
Bartholomew	57,022	Columbus	402
Benton	11,262	Fowler	409
Blackford	15,888	Hartford City	167
Boone	30,870	Lebanon	427
Brown	9,057	Nashville	319
Carroll	17,734	Delphi	374
Cass	40,456	Logansport	415
Clark	75,876	Jeffersonville	384
Clay	23,933	Brazil	364
Clinton	30,547	Frankfort	407
Crawford	8,033	English	312
Daviess	26,602	Washington	430
Dearborn	29,430	Lawrenceburg	306
Decatur	22,738	Greensburg	370
De Kalb	30,837	Auburn	366
Delaware	129,219	Muncie	396
Dubois	30,934	Jasper	433
Elkhart	126,529	Goshen	468
Fayette	26,216	Connersville	215
Floyd	55,622	New Albany	149
Fountain	18,257	Covington	397
Franklin	16,943	Brookville	394
Fulton	16,984	Rochester	368
Gibson	30,444	Princeton	498
Grant	83,955	Marion	421
Greene	26,894	Bloomfield	549
Hamilton	54,532	Noblesville	401
Hancock	35,096	Greenfield	305
Harrison	20,423	Corydon	479
Hendricks	53,974	Danville	417
Henry	52,603	New Castle	400
Howard	83,198	Kokomo	293
Huntington	34,970	Huntington	369
Jackson	33,187	Brownstown	520
Jasper	20,429	Rensselaer	562
Jay	23,575	Portland	386
Jefferson	27,006	Madison	366
Jennings	19,454	Vernon	377
Johnson	61,138	Franklin	315
Knox	41,546	Vincennes	516
Kosciusko	48,127	Warsaw	540
Lagrange	20,890	Lagrange	381
Lake	546,253	Crown Point	513
La Porte	105,342	La Porte	607
Lawrence	38,038	Bedford	459
Madison	138,522	Anderson	453
Marion	793,769	Indianapolis	392
Marshall	34,986	Plymouth	443
Martin	10,969	Shoals	345
Miami	39,246	Peru	377
Monroe	85,221	Bloomington	386
Montgomery	33,930	Crawfordsville	507
Morgan	44,176	Martinsville	406
Newton	11,606	Kentland	413
Noble	31,382	Albion	412
Ohio	4,289	Rising Sun	87
Orange	16,968	Paoli	405
Owen	12,163	Spencer	390
Parke	14,600	Rockville	445
Perry	19,075	Cannelton	384
Pike	12,281	Petersburg	335
Porter	87,114	Valparaiso	425
Posey	21,740	Mount Vernon	412

County	Pop. Apr. 1 1970	County Seat or Court House	Land Area Sq. Ml.	County	Pop. Apr. 1 1970	County Seat or Court House	Land Area Sq. Ml.
Pulaski	12,534	Winamac	433	Mills	11,832	Glenwood	447
Putnam	26,932	Greencastle	490	Mitchell	13,108	Osage	467
Randolph	28,915	Winchester	457	Monona	12,069	Onawa	699
Ripley	21,138	Versailles	442	Monroe	9,357	Albia	435
Rush	20,352	Rushville	409	Montgomery	12,781	Red Oak	422
St. Joseph	245,045	South Bend	466	Muscatine	37,181	Muscatine	443
Scott	17,144	Scottsburg	193	O'Brien	17,522	Primghar	575
Shelby	37,797	Shelbyville	409	Osceola	8,555	Sibley	398
Spencer	17,134	Rockport	396	Page	18,537	Clarinda	535
Starke	19,280	Knox	310	Palo Alto	13,289	Emmetsburg	561
Steuben	20,159	Angola	309	Plymouth	24,322	Le Mars	863
Sullivan	19,889	Sullivan	457	Pocahontas	12,793	Pocahontas	581
Switzerland	6,306	Vevay	221	Polk	286,130	Des Moines	578
Tippecanoe	109,378	Lafayette	500	Pottawattamie	86,991	Council Bluffs	963
Tipton	16,650	Tipton	261	Poweshiek	18,803	Montezuma	589
Union	6,582	Liberty	168	Ringgold	6,373	Mount Ayr	538
Vanderburgh	168,772	Evansville	241	Sac	15,573	Sac City	578
Vermillion	16,793	Newport	263	Scott	142,687	Davenport	454
Vigo	114,528	Terre Haute	415	Shelby	15,528	Harlan	587
Wabash	35,553	Wabash	398	Sioux	27,996	Orange City	766
Warren	8,705	Williamsport	368	Story	62,783	Nevada	568
Warrick	27,972	Boonville	391	Tama	20,147	Toledo	720
Washington	19,278	Salem	516	Taylor	8,790	Bedford	528
Wayne	79,109	Richmond	405	Union	13,557	Creston	425
Wells	23,821	Bluffton	368	Van Buren	8,643	Keosauqua	487
White	20,995	Monticello	497	Wapello	42,149	Ottumwa	437
Whitley	23,395	Columbia City	337	Warren	27,432	Indianola	558
				Washington	18,967	Washington	568
				Wayne	8,405	Corydon	532
				Webster	48,391	Fort Dodge	718
				Winnebago	12,990	Forest City	401
				Winneshiek	21,758	Decorah	688
				Woodbury	103,052	Sioux City	871
				Worth	8,984	Northwood	400
				Wright	17,294	Clarion	577

Iowa

(99 counties; 55,941 sq. mi. land; pop. 2,825,041)

County	Pop. Apr. 1 1970	County Seat or Court House	Land Area Sq. Ml.
Adair	9,487	Greenfield	569
Adams	6,322	Corning	426
Allamakee	14,968	Waukon	636
Appanoose	15,007	Centerville	523
Audubon	9,595	Audubon	448
Benton	22,885	Vinton	718
Black Hawk	132,916	Waterloo	568
Boone	26,470	Boone	573
Bremer	22,737	Waverly	439
Buchanan	21,762	Independence	568
Buena Vista	20,693	Storm Lake	572
Butler	16,953	Allison	582
Calhoun	14,292	Rockwell City	571
Carroll	22,912	Carroll	574
Cass	17,007	Atlantic	569
Cedar	17,655	Tipton	585
Cerro Gordo	49,223	Mason City	575
Cherokee	17,269	Cherokee	573
Chickasaw	14,969	New Hampton	505
Clarke	7,581	Oscea	429
Clay	18,464	Spencer	580
Clayton	20,606	Elkader	779
Clinton	56,749	Clinton	693
Crawford	19,116	Denison	716
Dallas	26,085	Adel	597
Davis	8,207	Bloomfield	509
Decatur	9,737	Leon	530
Delaware	18,770	Manchester	572
Des Moines	46,982	Burlington	408
Dickinson	12,565	Spirit Lake	380
Dubuque	90,609	Dubuque	612
Emmet	14,009	Estherville	394
Fayette	26,898	West Union	728
Floyd	19,860	Charles City	503
Franklin	13,255	Hampton	586
Fremont	9,282	Sidney	524
Greene	12,716	Jefferson	569
Grundy	14,119	Grundy Center	501
Guthrie	12,243	Guthrie Center	596
Hamilton	18,383	Webster City	577
Hancock	13,506	Garner	570
Hardin	22,248	Eldora	574
Harrison	16,240	Logan	696
Henry	18,114	Mount Pleasant	440
Howard	11,442	Cresco	471
Humboldt	12,519	Dakota City	435
Ida	9,283	Ida Grove	431
Iowa	15,419	Marengo	584
Jackson	20,839	Maquoketa	644
Jasper	35,425	Newton	731
Jefferson	15,774	Fairfield	436
Johnson 1974	75,025	Iowa City	619
Jones	19,868	Anamosa	585
Keokuk	13,943	Sigourney	579
Kossuth	22,937	Algona	979
Lee	42,996	Fort Madison and Keokuk	527
Linn	163,213	Cedar Rapids	717
Louisa	10,682	Wapello	403
Lucas	10,163	Chariton	434
Lyon	13,340	Rock Rapids	588
Madison	11,558	Winterset	564
Mahaska	22,177	Oskaloosa	572
Marion	26,352	Knoxville	498
Marshall	41,076	Marshalltown	574

Kansas

(105 counties, 81,787 sq. mi. land; pop. 2,249,071)

County	Pop. Apr. 1 1970	County Seat or Court House	Land Area Sq. Ml.
Allen	15,043	Iola	505
Anderson	8,501	Garnett	577
Atchison	19,165	Atchison	427
Barber	7,016	Medicine Lodge	1,146
Barton	30,663	Great Bend	894
Bourbon	15,215	Fort Scott	639
Brown	11,685	Hiawatha	577
Butler	38,658	El Dorado	1,442
Chase	3,408	Cottonwood Falls	774
Chautauqua	4,642	Sedan	647
Cherokee	21,549	Columbus	586
Cheyenne	4,256	Saint Francis	1,027
Clark	2,896	Ashland	983
Clay	9,890	Clay Center	635
Cloud	13,466	Concordia	711
Coffey	7,397	Burlington	617
Comanche	2,702	Coldwater	800
Cowley	35,012	Winfield	1,136
Crawford	37,850	Girard	598
Decatur	4,988	Oberlin	899
Dickinson	19,993	Abilene	855
Doniphan	9,107	Troy	388
Douglas	57,932	Lawrence	471
Edwards	4,581	Kinsley	617
Elk	3,858	Howard	647
Ellis	24,730	Hays	900
Ellsworth	6,146	Ellsworth	717
Finney	19,029	Garden City	1,301
Ford	22,587	Dodge City	1,091
Franklin	20,007	Ottawa	577
Geary	28,111	Junction City	374
Gove	2,940	Gove	1,070
Graham	4,751	Hill City	891
Grant	5,961	Ulysses	571
Gray	4,516	Cimarron	872
Greeley	1,819	Tribune	783
Greenwood	9,141	Eureka	1,133
Hamilton	2,747	Syracuse	992
Harper	7,871	Anthony	801
Harvey	27,236	Newton	540
Haskell	3,672	Sublette	580
Hodgeman	2,662	Jetmore	860
Jackson	10,342	Holton	656
Jefferson	11,945	Oskaloosa	510
Jewell	6,099	Mankato	910
Johnson	220,073	Olathe	476
Kearny	3,047	Lakin	855
Kingman	8,886	Kingman	864
Kiowa	4,088	Greensburg	720
Labette	25,775	Oswego	654
Lane	2,707	Dighton	720
Leavenworth	53,340	Leavenworth	466
Lincoln	4,582	Lincoln	725
Linn	7,770	Mound City	606
Logan	3,814	Oakley	1,073
Lyon	32,071	Emporia	841
McPherson	24,778	McPherson	896

County	Pop. Apr. 1 1970	County Seat or Court House	Land Area Sq. Mi.
Marion	13,935	Marion	945
Marshall	13,139	Marysville	883
Meade	4,912	Meade	979
Miami	19,254	Paola	592
Mitchell	8,010	Beloit	714
Montgomery	39,949	Independence	628
Morris	6,432	Council Grove	697
Morton	3,576	Elkhart	728
Nemaha	11,825	Seneca	708
Neosho	18,812	Erie	587
Ness	4,791	Ness City	1,081
Norton	7,279	Norton	872
Osage	13,352	Lyndon	707
Osborne	6,416	Osborne	886
Ottawa	6,183	Minneapolis	723
Pawnee	8,484	Larned	755
Phillips	7,888	Phillipsburg	897
Pottawatomie	11,755	Westmoreland	820
Pratt	10,056	Pratt	729
Rawlins	4,393	Atwood	1,078
Reno	60,765	Hutchinson	1,260
Republic	8,498	Belleville	718
Rice	12,320	Lyons	725
Riley	56,788	Manhattan	597
Rooks	7,628	Stockton	888
Rush	5,117	LaCrosse	724
Russell	9,428	Russell	867
Saline	46,592	Salina	720
Scott	5,606	Scott City	724
Sedgwick	350,694	Wichita	1,007
Seward	16,062	Liberal	646
Shawnee	155,322	Topeka	548
Sheridan	3,859	Hoxie	893
Sherman	7,792	Goodland	1,055
Smith	6,757	Smith Center	893
Stafford	5,943	Saint John	795
Stanton	2,287	Johnson	676
Stevens	4,198	Hugoton	731
Sumner	23,553	Wellington	1,186
Thomas	7,501	Colby	1,070
Trego	4,436	Wakeeney	901
Wabaunsee	6,397	Alma	792
Wallace	2,215	Sharon Springs	911
Washington	9,249	Washington	891
Wichita	3,274	Leoti	724
Wilson	11,317	Fredonia	574
Woodson	4,789	Yates Center	497
Wyandotte	186,845	Kansas City	152

Kentucky

(120 counties, 39,650 sq. mi. land; pop. 3,219,311)

County	Pop. Apr. 1 1970	County Seat or Court House	Land Area Sq. Mi.
Adair	13,037	Columbia	370
Allen	12,598	Scottsville	351
Anderson	9,358	Lawrenceburg	206
Ballard	8,276	Wickliffe	259
Barren	28,677	Glasgow	468
Bath	9,235	Owingsville	287
Bell	31,121	Pineville	370
Boone	32,812	Burlington	249
Bourbon	18,476	Paris	300
Boyd	52,376	Catlettsburg	159
Boyle	21,861	Danville	183
Bracken	7,227	Brooksville	204
Breathitt	14,221	Jackson	494
Breckinridge	14,789	Hardinsburg	554
Bullitt	26,090	Shepherdsville	300
Butler	9,723	Morgantown	443
Caldwell	13,179	Princeton	357
Calloway	27,692	Murray	384
Campbell	88,704	Alexandria	149
Carlisle	5,354	Bardwell	195
Carroll	8,523	Carrollton	130
Carter	19,850	Grayson	397
Casey	12,930	Liberty	435
Christian	56,224	Hopkinsville	725
Clark	24,090	Winchester	259
Clay	18,481	Manchester	474
Clinton	8,174	Albany	190
Crittenden	8,493	Marion	365
Cumberland	6,850	Burkesville	310
Daviess	79,486	Owensboro	462
Edmonson	8,751	Brownsville	298
Elliott	5,933	Sandy Hook	240
Estill	12,752	Irvine	260
Fayette	174,323	Lexington	280
Fleming	11,366	Flemingsburg	350
Floyd	35,889	Prestonsburg	399
Franklin	34,481	Frankfort	211
Fulton	10,183	Hickman	203
Gallatin	4,134	Warsaw	100
Garrard	9,457	Lancaster	236
Grant	9,999	Williamstown	249
Graves	30,939	Mayfield	60

County	Pop. Apr. 1 1970	County Seat or Court House	Land Area Sq. Mi.
Grayson	16,445	Leitchfield	496
Green	10,350	Greensburg	282
Greenup	33,192	Greenup	351
Hancock	7,080	Hawesville	187
Hardin	78,421	Elizabethtown	616
Harlan	37,370	Harlan	469
Harrison	14,158	Cynthiana	308
Hart	13,980	Munfordville	420
Henderson	36,031	Henderson	433
Henry	10,910	New Castle	289
Hickman	6,264	Clinton	246
Hopkins	38,167	Madisonville	553
Jackson	10,005	McKee	337
Jefferson	695,055	Louisville	375
Jessamine	17,430	Nicholasville	177
Johnson	17,539	Paintsville	264
Kenton	129,440	Independence	165
Knott	14,698	Hindman	356
Knox	23,689	Barbourville	373
Larue	10,672	Hodgenville	260
Laurel	27,386	London	446
Lawrence	10,726	Louisa	425
Lee	6,587	Beattyville	210
Leslie	11,623	Hyden	409
Letcher	23,165	Whitesburg	339
Lewis	12,355	Vanceburg	486
Lincoln	16,663	Stanford	340
Livingston	7,596	Smithland	311
Logan	21,793	Russellville	563
Lyon	5,562	Eddyville	216
McCracken	58,281	Paducah	250
McCreary	12,548	Whitley City	418
McLean	9,062	Calhoun	257
Madison	42,730	Richmond	446
Magoffin	10,443	Salyersville	303
Marion	16,714	Lebanon	343
Marshall	20,381	Benton	303
Martin	9,377	Inez	231
Mason	17,273	Maysville	238
Meade	18,796	Brandenburg	305
Menifee	4,050	Frenchburg	210
Mercer	15,960	Harrodsburg	256
Metcalfe	8,177	Edmonton	296
Monroe	11,642	Tompkinsville	334
Montgomery	15,364	Mount Sterling	204
Morgan	10,019	West Liberty	369
Muhlenberg	27,537	Greenville	481
Nelson	23,477	Bardstown	437
Nicholas	6,508	Carlisle	204
Ohio	18,790	Hartford	596
Oldham	14,687	La Grange	184
Owen	7,470	Owenton	351
Owsley	5,023	Booneville	197
Pendleton	9,949	Falmouth	279
Perry	26,259	Hazard	341
Pike	61,059	Pikeville	782
Powell	7,704	Stanton	173
Pulaski	35,234	Somerset	653
Robertson	2,163	Mount Olivet	101
Rockcastle	12,305	Mount Vernon	311
Rowan	17,010	Morehead	290
Russell	10,542	Jamestown	254
Scott	17,948	Georgetown	284
Shelby	18,999	Shelbyville	383
Simpson	13,054	Franklin	239
Spencer	5,488	Taylorsville	193
Taylor	17,138	Campbellsville	277
Todd	10,823	Elkton	376
Trigg	8,620	Cadiz	408
Trimble	5,349	Bedford	146
Union	15,882	Morganfield	340
Warren	57,884	Bowling Green	546
Washington	10,728	Springfield	307
Wayne	14,268	Monticello	440
Webster	13,282	Dixon	339
Whitley	24,145	Williamsburg	459
Wolfe	5,669	Campton	227
Woodford	14,434	Versailles	193

Louisiana

(64 parishes, 44,930 sq. mi. land; pop. 3,643,180)

County	Pop. Apr. 1 1970	County Seat or Court House	Land Area Sq. Mi.
Acadia	52,109	Crowley	663
Allen	20,794	Oberlin	774
Ascension	37,086	Donaldsonville	301
Assumption	19,654	Napoleonville	356
Avoyelles	37,751	Marksville	832
Beauregard	22,888	De Ridder	1,181
Bienville	16,024	Arcadia	832
Bossier	63,703	Benton	849
Caddo	230,184	Shreveport	899
Calcasieu	145,415	Lake Charles	1,105
Caldwell	9,354	Columbia	551
Cameron	8,149	Cameron	1,441
Catahoula	11,769	Harrisonburg	742
Claiborne	17,024	Homer	763

County	Pop. Apr. 1 1970	County Seat or Court House	Land Area Sq. Mi.
Concordia	22,578	Vidalia	718
De Soto	22,764	Mansfield	894
East Baton Rouge	285,167	Baton Rouge	459
East Carroll	12,884	Lake Providence	436
East Feliciana	17,657	Clinton	454
Evangeline	31,932	Ville Platte	669
Franklin	23,946	Winnsboro	648
Grant	13,671	Colfax	670
Iberia	57,397	New Iberia	589
Iberville	30,746	Plaquemine	627
Jackson	15,963	Jonesboro	582
Jefferson	338,229	Gretna	369
Jefferson Davis	29,554	Jennings	658
Lafayette	111,643	Lafayette	283
Lafourche	68,941	Thibodaux	1,141
La Salle	13,295	Jena	643
Lincoln	33,800	Ruston	469
Livingston	36,511	Livingston	654
Madison	15,065	Tallulah	661
Morehouse	32,463	Bastrop	804
Natchitoches	35,219	Natchitoches	1,292
Orleans	593,471	New Orleans	197
Ouachita	115,387	Monroe	638
Plaquemines	25,225	Pointe a la Hache	1,030
Pointe Coupee	22,002	New Roads	563
Rapides	118,078	Alexandria	1,318
Red River	9,226	Coushatta	406
Richland	21,774	Rayville	576
Sabine	18,638	Many	873
St. Bernard	51,185	Chalmette	514
St. Charles	29,550	Hahnville	294
St. Helena	9,937	Greensburg	420
St. James	19,733	Convent	253
St. John The Baptist	23,813	Edgard	227
St. Landry	80,364	Opelousas	932
St. Martin	32,453	Saint Martinville	736
St. Mary	60,752	Franklin	624
St. Tammany	63,585	Covington	887
Tangipahoa	65,875	Amite	808
Tensas	9,732	Saint Joseph	626
Terrebonne	76,049	Houma	1,368
Union	18,447	Farmerville	885
Vermilion	43,071	Abbeville	1,205
Vernon	53,794	Leesville	1,351
Washington	41,987	Franklinton	665
Webster	39,939	Minden	615
West Baton Rouge	16,864	Port Allen	203
West Carroll	13,028	Oak Grove	356
West Feliciana	11,376	Saint Francisville	405
Winn	16,369	Winnfield	950

Maine

(16 counties, 30,920 sq. mi. land; pop. 993,663)

County	Pop. Apr. 1 1970	County Seat or Court House	Land Area Sq. Mi.
Androscoggin	91,279	Auburn	474
Aroostook	94,078	Houlton	6,821
Cumberland	192,528	Portland	879
Franklin	22,444	Farmington	1,709
Hancock	34,598	Ellsworth	1,536
Kennebec	95,306	Augusta	872
Knox	29,013	Rockland	369
Lincoln	20,537	Wiscasset	454
Oxford	43,457	South Paris	2,080
Penobscot	125,393	Bangor	3,390
Piscataquis	16,285	Dover-Foxcroft	3,892
Sagadahoc	23,452	Bath	257
Somerset	40,597	Skowhegan	3,894
Waldo	23,328	Belfast	737
Washington	29,859	Machias	2,554
York	111,576	Alfred	1,001

Maryland

(23 cos., 1 ind. city, 9,891 sq. mi. land; pop. 3,922,399)

County	Pop. Apr. 1 1970	County Seat or Court House	Land Area Sq. Mi.
Allegany	84,044	Cumberland	428
Anne Arundel	298,042	Annapolis	423
Baltimore	620,409	Towson	598
Calvert	20,682	Prince Frederick	217
Caroline	19,781	Denton	321
Carroll	69,006	Westminster	456
Cecil	53,291	Elkton	362
Charles	47,678	La Plata	459
Dorchester	29,405	Cambridge	594
Frederick	84,927	Frederick	665
Garrett	21,476	Oakland	659
Harford	115,378	Bel Air	453
Howard	62,394	Ellicott City	251
Kent	16,146	Chestertown	281
Montgomery	522,809	Rockville	495
Prince Georges	661,082	Upper Marlboro	485
Queen Annes	18,422	Centreville	375
St. Marys	47,388	Leonardtown	373
Somerset	18,924	Princess Anne	339

County	Pop. Apr. 1 1970	County Seat or Court House	Land Area Sq. Mi.
Talbot	23,682	Easton	261
Washington	103,829	Hagerstown	459
Wicomico	54,236	Salisbury	381
Worcester	24,442	Snow Hill	479
Independent City.			
Baltimore	905,787		78

Massachusetts

(14 counties; 7,826 sq. mi. land; pop. 5,689,170)

County	Pop. Apr. 1 1970	County Seat or Court House	Land Area Sq. Mi.
Barnstable	96,656	Barnstable	393
Berkshire	149,402	Pittsfield	941
Bristol	444,301	Taunton	554
Dukes	6,117	Edgartown	104
Essex	637,887	Salem	494
Franklin	59,210	Greenfield	708
Hampden	459,050	Springfield	619
Hampshire	123,981	Northampton	529
Middlesex	1,397,465	Cambridge	825
Nantucket	3,774	Nantucket	46
Norfolk	604,854	Dedham	394
Plymouth	333,314	Plymouth	654
Suffolk	735,190	Boston	56
Worcester	637,037	Worcester	1,509

Michigan

(83 counties; 56,817 sq. mi. land; pop. 8,875,083)

County	Pop. Apr. 1 1970	County Seat or Court House	Land Area Sq. Mi.
Alcona	7,113	Harrisville	678
Alger	8,568	Munising	905
Allegan	66,575	Allegan	826
Alpena	30,708	Alpena	565
Antrim	12,612	Bellaire	476
Arenac	11,149	Standish	367
Baraga	7,789	L'Anse	901
Barry	38,166	Hastings	554
Bay	117,339	Bay City	447
Benzie	8,593	Beulah	316
Berrien	163,940	Saint Joseph	580
Branch	37,906	Coldwater	506
Calhoun	141,963	Marshall	709
Cass	43,312	Cassopolis	491
Charlevoix	16,541	Charlevoix	414
Cheboygan	16,573	Cheboygan	721
Chippewa	32,412	Sault Sainte Marie	1,590
Clare	16,695	Harrison	571
Clinton	48,492	Saint Johns	572
Crawford	6,482	Grayling	561
Delta	35,924	Escanaba	1,177
Dickinson	23,753	Iron Mountain	757
Eaton	68,892	Charlotte	571
Emmet	18,331	Petoskey	461
Genesee	445,589	Flint	642
Gladwin	13,471	Gladwin	503
Gogebic	20,676	Bessemer	1,107
Grand Traverse	39,175	Traverse City	462
Gratiot	39,246	Ithaca	566
Hillsdale	37,171	Hillsdale	600
Houghton	34,652	Houghton	1,017
Huron	34,083	Bad Axe	819
Ingham	261,039	Mason	559
Ionia	45,848	Ionia	575
Iosco	24,905	Iowas City	544
Iron	13,813	Crystal Falls	1,171
Isabella	44,594	Mount Pleasant	572
Jackson	143,274	Jackson	698
Kalamazoo	201,550	Kalamazoo	562
Kalkaska	5,272	Kalkaska	566
Kent	411,044	Grand Rapids	857
Keweenaw	2,264	Eagle River	538
Lake	5,661	Baldwin	571
Lapeer	52,361	Lapeer	658
Leelanau	10,872	Leland	345
Lenawee	81,951	Adrian	753
Livingston	58,967	Howell	572
Luce	6,789	Newberry	906
Mackinac	9,660	Saint Ignace	1,014
Macomb	625,309	Mount Clemens	480
Manistee	20,393	Manistee	553
Marquette	64,686	Marquette	1,828
Mason	22,612	Ludington	490
Mecosta	27,992	Big Rapids	560
Menominee	24,587	Menominee	1,038
Midland	63,769	Midland	520
Missaukee	7,126	Lake City	565
Monroe	119,172	Monroe	557
Montcalm	39,660	Stanton	712
Montmorency	5,247	Atlanta	555
Muskegon	157,426	Muskegon	501
Newaygo	27,992	White Cloud	849
Oakland	907,871	Pontiac	867
Oceana	17,984	Hart	536
Ogemaw	11,903	West Branch	571
Ontonagon	10,548	Ontonagon	1,316

County	Pop. Apr. 1 1970	County Seat or Court House	Land Area Sq. Mi.
Osceola	14,838	Reed City	581
Oscoda	4,726	Mio	563
Otsego	10,422	Gaylord	527
Ottawa	128,181	Grand Haven	563
Presque Isle	12,836	Rogers City	648
Roscommon	9,892	Roscommon	521
Saginaw	219,743	Saginaw	814
St. Clair	120,175	Port Huron	734
St. Joseph	47,392	Centreville	506
Sanilac	35,181	Sandusky	961
Schoolcraft	8,226	Manistique	1,181
Shiawassee	63,075	Corunna	540
Tuscola	48,603	Caro	815
Van Buren	56,173	Paw Paw	603
Washtenaw	234,103	Ann Arbor	711
Wayne	2,670,368	Detroit	605
Wexford	19,717	Cadillac	559

Minnesota

(87 counties; 79,289 sq. mi. land; pop. 3,805,069)

County	Pop. Apr. 1 1970	County Seat or Court House	Land Area Sq. Mi.
Aitkin	11,403	Aitkin	1,828
Anoka	154,401	Anoka	424
Becker	24,372	Detroit Lakes	1,297
Beltrami	26,373	Bemidji	2,507
Benton	20,841	Foley	402
Big Stone	7,941	Ortonville	490
Blue Earth	52,322	Mankato	737
Brown	28,887	New Ulm	610
Carlton	28,072	Carlton	862
Carver	28,331	Chaska	359
Cass	17,323	Walker	1,998
Chippewa	15,109	Montevideo	582
Chisago	17,492	Center City	419
Clay	46,608	Moorhead	1,045
Clearwater	8,013	Bagley	1,000
Cook	3,423	Grand Marais	1,346
Cottonwood	14,887	Windom	636
Crow Wing	34,826	Brainerd	995
Dakota	139,808	Hastings	576
Dodge	13,037	Mantorville	435
Douglas	22,910	Alexandria	647
Faribault	20,896	Blue Earth	711
Fillmore	21,916	Preston	859
Freeborn	38,064	Albert Lea	701
Goodhue	34,804	Red Wing	753
Grant	7,462	Elbow Lake	546
Hennepin	960,080	Minneapolis	567
Houston	17,556	Caledonia	565
Hubbard	10,983	Park Rapids	932
Isanti	16,560	Cambridge	438
Itasca	35,530	Grand Rapids	2,633
Jackson	14,352	Jackson	696
Kanabec	9,775	Mora	524
Kandiyohi	30,548	Willmar	783
Kittson	6,853	Hallock	1,123
Koochiching	17,131	International Falls	3,127
Lac Qui Parle	11,164	Madison	768
Lake	13,351	Two Harbors	2,062
Lake of the Woods 1974	4,196	Baudette	1,311
Le Sueur	21,332	Le Center	440
Lincoln	8,143	Ivanhoe	531
Lyon	24,273	Marshall	709
McLeod	27,662	Glencoe	488
Mahnomen	5,638	Mahnomen	563
Marshall	13,060	Warren	1,789
Martin	24,316	Fairmont	703
Meeker	18,387	Litchfield	619
Mille Lacs	15,703	Milaca	571
Morrison	26,949	Little Falls	1,127
Mower	43,783	Austin	703
Murray	12,508	Slayton	703
Nicollet	24,518	Saint Peter	432
Nobles	23,208	Worthington	712
Norman	10,008	Ada	885
Olmstead	84,104	Rochester	656
Otter Tail	46,097	Fergus Falls	1,962
Pennington	13,266	Thief River Falls	622
Pine	16,821	Pine City	1,414
Pipestone	12,791	Pipestone	464
Polk	34,435	Crookston	2,013
Pope	11,107	Glenwood	669
Ramsey	476,350	Saint Paul	155
Red Lake	5,388	Red Lake Falls	432
Redwood	20,024	Redwood Falls	874
Renville	21,139	Olivia	979
Rice	41,582	Faribault	496
Rock	11,346	Luverne	485
Roseau	11,569	Roseau	1,676
St. Louis	220,693	Duluth	6,092
Scott	32,423	Shakopee	353
Sherburne	18,344	Elk River	431
Sibley	15,845	Gaylord	583
Stearns	95,400	Saint Cloud	1,342
Steele	26,931	Owatonna	425
Stevens	11,218	Morris	558

County	Pop. Apr. 1 1970	County Seat or Court House	Land Area Sq. Mi.
Swift	13,177	Benson	739
Todd	22,114	Long Prairie	942
Traverse	6,254	Wheaton	568
Wabasha	17,224	Wabasha	522
Wadena	12,412	Wadena	536
Waseca	16,663	Waseca	415
Washington	82,948	Stillwater	386
Watonwan	13,298	Saint James	433
Wilkin	9,389	Breckenridge	752
Winona	44,409	Winona	620
Wright	38,933	Buffalo	674
Yellow Medicine	14,523	Granite Falls	753

Mississippi

(82 counties, 47,296 sq. mi. land; pop. 2,216,912)

County	Pop. Apr. 1 1970	County Seat or Court House	Land Area Sq. Mi.
Adams	37,293	Natchez	449
Alcorn	27,179	Corinth	405
Amite	13,763	Liberty	729
Attala	19,570	Kosciusko	724
Benton	7,505	Ashland	412
Bolivar	49,409	Cleveland & Rosedale	923
Calhoun	14,623	Pittsboro	575
Carroll	9,397	Carrollton & Vaiden	637
Chickasaw	16,805	Houston & Okolona	506
Choctaw	8,440	Ackerman	417
Claiborne	10,086	Port Gibson	489
Clarke	15,049	Quitman	697
Clay	18,840	West Point	414
Coahoma	40,447	Clarksdale	569
Copiah	24,764	Hazlehurst	780
Covington	14,002	Collins	416
De Soto	35,885	Hernando	476
Forrest	57,849	Hattiesburg	468
Franklin	8,011	Meadville	568
George	12,459	Lucedale	481
Greene	8,545	Leakesville	728
Grenada	19,854	Grenada	431
Hancock	17,387	Bay Saint Louis	482
Harrison	134,582	Gulfport	585
Hinds	214,973	Jackson & Raymond	876
Holmes	23,120	Lexington	769
Humphreys	14,601	Belzoni	421
Issaquena	2,737	Mayersville	414
Itawamba	16,847	Fulton	541
Jackson	87,975	Pascagoula	736
Jasper	15,994	Bat Springs & Paulding	683
Jefferson	9,295	Fayette	521
Jefferson Davis	12,936	Prentiss	414
Jones	56,357	Ellisville & Laurel	702
Kemper	10,233	De Kalb	757
Lafayette	24,181	Oxford	668
Lamar	15,209	Purvis	500
Lauderdale	67,087	Meridian	708
Lawrence	11,137	Monticello	433
Leake	17,075	Carthage	586
Lee	46,148	Tupelo	455
Leflore	42,111	Greenwood	592
Lincoln	26,198	Brookhaven	586
Lowndes	49,700	Columbus	508
Madison	29,737	Canton	727
Marion	22,871	Columbia	550
Marshall	24,027	Holly Springs	710
Monroe	34,043	Aberdeen	769
Montgomery	12,918	Winona	403
Neshoba	20,802	Philadelphia	568
Newton	18,983	Decatur	580
Noxubee	14,288	Macon	695
Oktibbeha	28,752	Starkville	454
Panola	26,829	Batesville & Sardis	693
Pearl River	27,802	Poplarville	828
Perry	9,065	New Augusta	653
Pike	31,813	Magnolia	409
Pontotoc	17,363	Pontotoc	501
Prentiss	20,133	Booneville	418
Quitman	15,888	Marks	412
Rankin	43,933	Brandon	775
Scott	21,369	Forest	615
Sharkey	9,937	Rolling Fork	436
Simpson	19,947	Mendenhall	587
Smith	13,561	Raleigh	642
Stone	8,101	Wiggins	448
Sunflower	37,047	Indianola	694
Tallahatchie	19,338	Charleston & Sumner	644
Tate	18,544	Senatobia	405
Tippah	15,852	Ripley	464
Tishomingo	14,940	Iuka	443
Tunica	11,854	Tunica	458
Union	19,096	New Albany	422
Walthall	12,500	Tylertown	403

County	Pop. Apr. 1 1970	County Seat or Court House	Land Area Sq. Mi.
Warren	44,981	Vicksburg	581
Washington	70,581	Greenville	734
Wayne	16,650	Waynesboro	827
Webster	10,047	Walthall	416
Wilkinson	11,099	Woodville	674
Winston	18,406	Louisville	606
Yalobusha	11,915	Coffeeville & Water Valley	488
Yazoo	27,314	Yazoo City	938

Missouri

(114 cos., 1 ind. city, 68,995 sq. mi. land; pop., 4,677,399)

County	Pop. Apr. 1 1970	County Seat or Court House	Land Area Sq. Mi.
Adair	22,472	Kirksville	572
Andrew	11,913	Savannah	436
Atchison	9,240	Rockport	549
Audrain	25,362	Mexico	692
Barry	19,597	Cassville	783
Barton	10,431	Lamar	594
Bates	15,468	Butler	841
Benton	9,695	Warsaw	735
Bollinger	8,820	Marble Hill	621
Boone	80,935	Columbia	685
Buchanan	86,915	Saint Joseph	404
Butler	33,529	Poplar Bluff	715
Caldwell	8,351	Kingston	430
Callaway	25,991	Fulton	835
Camden	13,315	Camdenton	640
Cape Girardeau	49,350	Jackson	574
Carroll	12,565	Carrollton	697
Carter	3,878	Van Buren	506
Cass	39,448	Harrisonville	698
Cedar	9,424	Stockton	496
Chariton	11,084	Keytesville	754
Christian	15,124	Ozark	567
Clark	8,260	Kahoka	506
Clay	123,702	Liberty	412
Clinton	12,462	Plattsburg	420
Cole	46,228	Jefferson City	384
Cooper	14,732	Boonville	566
Crawford	14,828	Steelville	760
Dade	6,850	Greenfield	504
Dallas	10,054	Buffalo	537
Daviess	8,420	Gallatin	563
De Kalb	7,305	Maysville	423
Dent	11,457	Salem	756
Douglas	9,268	Ava	809
Dunklin	33,742	Kennett	543
Franklin	55,127	Union	934
Gasconade	11,878	Hermann	519
Gentry	8,060	Albany	488
Greene	152,929	Springfield	677
Grundy	11,819	Trenton	435
Harrison	10,257	Bethany	720
Henry	18,451	Clinton	734
Hickory	4,481	Hermitage	377
Holt	6,654	Oregon	458
Howard	10,561	Fayette	472
Howell	23,521	West Plains	920
Iron	9,529	Ironton	554
Jackson	654,178	Independence	603
Jasper	79,852	Carthage	642
Jefferson	105,248	Hillsboro	668
Johnson	34,172	Warrensburg	826
Knox	5,692	Edina	512
Laclede	19,944	Lebanon	770
Lafayette	26,626	Lexington	632
Lawrence	24,585	Mount Vernon	619
Lewis	10,993	Monticello	508
Lincoln	18,041	Troy	625
Linn	15,125	Linneus	622
Livingston	15,368	Chillicothe	530
McDonald	12,357	Pineville	540
Macon	15,432	Macon	798
Madison	8,641	Fredericktown	496
Maries	6,851	Vienna	525
Marion	28,121	Palmyra	438
Mercer	4,910	Princeton	455
Miller	15,026	Tuscumbia	600
Mississippi	16,647	Charleston	415
Moniteau	10,742	California	419
Monroe	9,542	Paris	669
Montgomery	11,000	Montgomery City	534
Morgan	10,083	Versailles	592
New Madrid	23,420	New Madrid	679
Newton	32,981	Neosho	629
Nodaway	22,467	Maryville	877
Oregon	9,180	Alton	784
Osage	10,994	Linn	608
Ozark	6,226	Gainesville	732
Pemiscot	26,373	Caruthersville	493
Perry	14,393	Perryville	471
Pettis	34,137	Sedalia	679
Phelps	29,567	Rolla	677
Pike	16,928	Bowling Green	681
Platte	32,081	Platte City	427
Polk	15,415	Bolivar	637
Pulaski	53,967	Waynesville	551
Putnam	5,916	Unionville	518
Ralls	7,764	New London	478
Randolph	22,434	Huntsville	473
Ray	17,599	Richmond	573
Reynolds	6,106	Centerville	817
Ripley	9,803	Doniphan	639
St. Charles	92,954	St. Charles	551
St. Clair	7,667	Osceola	697
St. Francois	36,875	Farmington	457
St. Louis	951,671	Clayton	499
Ste. Genevieve	12,867	Ste. Genevieve	499
Saline	24,837	Marshall	757
Schuyler	4,665	Lancaster	306
Scotland	5,499	Memphis	441
Scott	33,250	Benton	421
Shannon	7,196	Eminence	999
Shelby	7,906	Shelbyville	501
Stoddard	25,771	Bloomfield	823
Stone	9,921	Galena	449
Sullivan	7,572	Milan	654
Taney	13,023	Forsyth	615
Texas	18,320	Houston	1,183
Vernon	19,065	Nevada	838
Warren	9,699	Warrenton	426
Washington	15,086	Potosi	760
Wayne	8,546	Greenville	766
Webster	15,562	Marshfield	590
Worth	3,359	Grant City	267
Wright	13,667	Hartville	684
Independent City St. Louis	623,236		61

Montana

(57 counties, 145,587 sq. mi. land; pop., 694,409)

County	Pop. Apr. 1 1970	County Seat or Court House	Land Area Sq. Mi.
Beaverhead	8,187	Dillon	5,551
Big Horn	10,057	Hardin	5,023
Blaine	6,727	Chinook	4,275
Broadwater	2,526	Townsend	1,193
Carbon	7,080	Red Lodge	2,066
Carter	1,956	Ekalaka	3,313
Cascade	81,804	Great Falls	2,661
Chouteau	6,473	Fort Benton	3,927
Custer	12,174	Miles City	3,756
Daniels	3,083	Scobey	1,443
Dawson	11,269	Glendive	2,370
Deer Lodge	15,652	Anaconda	740
Fallon	4,050	Baker	1,633
Fergus	12,611	Lewistown	4,242
Flathead	39,460	Kalispell	5,137
Gallatin	32,505	Bozeman	2,517
Garfield	1,796	Jordan	4,455
Glacier	10,783	Cut Bank	2,964
Golden Valley	931	Ryegate	1,176
Granite	2,737	Philipsburg	1,733
Hill	17,358	Havre	2,927
Jefferson	5,238	Boulder	1,652
Judith Basin	2,667	Stanford	1,880
Lake	14,445	Polson	1,494
Lewis & Clark	33,281	Helena	3,476
Liberty	2,359	Chester	1,439
Lincoln	18,063	Libby	3,714
McCone	2,875	Circle	2,607
Madison	5,014	Virginia City	3,528
Meagher	2,122	White Sulphur Springs	2,354
Mineral	2,958	Superior	1,222
Missoula	58,263	Missoula	2,612
Musselshell	3,734	Roundup	1,887
Park	11,197	Livingston	2,626
Petroleum	675	Winnett	1,655
Phillips	5,386	Malta	5,213
Pondera	6,611	Conrad	1,645
Powder River	2,862	Broadus	3,288
Powell	6,660	Deer Lodge	2,336
Prairie	1,752	Terry	1,730
Ravalli	14,409	Hamilton	2,382
Richland	9,837	Sidney	2,079
Roosevelt	10,365	Wolf Point	2,385
Rosebud	6,032	Forsyth	5,037
Sanders	7,093	Thompson Falls	2,778
Sheridan	5,779	Plentywood	1,694
Silver Bow	41,981	Butte	715
Stillwater	4,632	Columbus	1,794
Sweet Grass	2,980	Big Timber	1,840
Teton	6,116	Choteau	2,294
Toole	5,839	Shelby	1,950
Treasure	1,069	Hysham	985
Valley	11,471	Glasgow	4,974
Wheatland	2,529	Harlowton	1,420
Wibaux	1,465	Wibaux	890
Yellowstone	87,367	Billings	2,642
Yellowstone Nat. Park	64		269

Nebraska

(93 counties, 76,483 sq. mi. land; pop. 1,483,791)

County	Pop. Apr. 1 1970	County Seat or Court House	Land Area Sq. Mi.
Adams	30,553	Hastings	562
Antelope	9,047	Neligh	853
Arthur	606	Arthur	704
Banner	1,034	Harrisburg	738
Blaine	847	Brewster	710
Boone	8,190	Albion	683
Box Butte	10,094	Alliance	1,065
Boyd	3,752	Butte	538
Brown	4,021	Ainsworth	1,216
Buffalo	31,222	Kearney	949
Burt	9,247	Tekamah	483
Butler	9,461	David City	582
Cass	18,076	Plattsmouth	555
Cedar	12,192	Hartington	742
Chase	4,129	Imperial	890
Cherry	6,846	Valentine	5,966
Cheyenne	10,778	Sidney	1,186
Clay	8,266	Clay Center	570
Colfax	9,498	Schuyler	406
Cuming	12,034	West Point	571
Custer	14,092	Broken Bow	2,558
Dakota	13,137	Dakota City	255
Dawes	9,761	Chadron	1,386
Dawson	19,771	Lexington	975
Deuel	2,717	Chappell	436
Dixon	7,453	Ponca	475
Dodge	34,782	Fremont	528
Douglas	389,455	Omaha	335
Dundy	2,926	Benkelman	921
Fillmore	8,137	Geneva	577
Franklin	4,566	Franklin	578
Frontier	3,982	Stockville	962
Furnas	6,897	Beaver City	722
Gage	25,731	Beatrice	858
Garden	2,929	Oshkosh	1,678
Garfield	2,411	Burwell	569
Gosper	2,178	Elwood	464
Grant	1,019	Hyannis	764
Greeley	4,000	Greeley	570
Hall	42,851	Grand Island	537
Hamilton	8,867	Aurora	537
Harlan	4,357	Alma	556
Hayes	1,530	Hayes Center	711
Hitchcock	4,051	Trenton	712
Holt	12,933	O'Neil	2,405
Hooker	939	Mullen	722
Howard	6,807	Saint Paul	564
Jefferson	10,436	Fairbury	577
Johnson	5,743	Tecumseh	377
Kearney	6,707	Minden	512
Keith	8,487	Ogallala	1,032
Keya Paha	1,340	Springview	768
Kimball	6,009	Kimball	953
Knox	11,723	Center	1,107
Lancaster	167,972	Lincoln	845
Lincoln	29,538	North Platte	2,522
Logan	991	Stapleton	570
Loup	854	Taylor	574
McPherson	623	Tryon	856
Madison	27,402	Madison	572
Merrick	8,751	Central City	480
Morrill	5,813	Bridgeport	1,402
Nance	5,142	Fullerton	439
Nemaha	8,976	Auburn	400
Nuckolls	7,404	Nelson	579
Otoe	15,576	Nebraska City	619
Pawnee	4,473	Pawnee City	433
Perkins	3,423	Grant	885
Phelps	9,553	Holdrege	544
Pierce	8,493	Pierce	573
Platte	26,544	Columbus	667
Polk	6,468	Osceola	432
Red Willow	12,191	McCook	686
Richardson	12,277	Falls City	550
Rock	2,231	Bassett	1,009
Saline	12,809	Wilber	575
Sarpy	66,200	Papillion	239
Saunders	17,108	Wahoo	759
Scotts Bluff	36,432	Gering	726
Seward	14,460	Seward	571
Sheridan	7,285	Rushville	2,462
Sherman	4,725	Loup City	567
Sioux	2,034	Harrison	2,063
Stanton	5,758	Stanton	431
Thayer	7,779	Hebron	577
Thomas	954	Thedford	716
Thurston	6,942	Pender	388
Valley	5,783	Ord	569
Washington	13,310	Blair	386
Wayne	10,400	Wayne	443
Webster	5,396	Red Cloud	575
Wheeler	1,051	Bartlett	576
York	13,685	York	577

Nevada

(16 cos., 1 ind. city, 109,889 sq. mi. land; pop. 488,738)

County	Pop. Apr. 1 1970	County Seat or Court House	Land Area Sq. Mi.
Churchill	10,513	Fallon	4,883
Clark	273,288	Las Vegas	7,874
Douglas	6,882	Minden	703
Elko	13,958	Elko	17,162
Esmeralda	629	Goldfield	3,570
Eureka	948	Eureka	4,182
Humboldt	6,375	Winnemucca	9,702
Lander	2,666	Austin	5,621
Lincoln	2,557	Pioche	10,649
Lyon	8,221	Yerington	2,030
Mineral	7,051	Hawthorne	3,765
Nye	5,599	Tonopah	18,064
Pershing	2,670	Lovelock	6,001
Storey	695	Virginia City	262
Washoe	121,068	Reno	6,366
White Pine	10,150	Ely	8,904
Independent City			
Carson City	15,468	Carson City	150

New Hampshire

(10 counties, 9,027 sq. mi. land; pop. 737,681)

County	Pop. Apr. 1 1970	County Seat or Court House	Land Area Sq. Mi.
Belknap	32,367	Laconia	400
Carroll	18,548	Ossipee	938
Cheshire	52,364	Keene	715
Coos	34,291	Lancaster	1,820
Grafton	54,914	Woodsville	1,732
Hillsborough	223,941	Nashua	887
Merrimack	80,925	Concord	930
Rockingham	138,951	Exeter	691
Strafford	70,431	Dover	376
Sullivan	30,949	Newport	539

New Jersey

(21 counties, 7,521 sq. mi. land; pop. 7,168,164)

County	Pop. Apr. 1 1970	County Seat or Court House	Land Area Sq. Mi.
Atlantic	175,043	Mays Landing	569
Bergen	897,148	Hackensack	234
Burlington	323,132	Mount Holly	819
Camden	456,291	Camden	221
Cape May	59,554	Cape May Court House	267
Cumberland	121,374	Bridgeton	500
Essex	932,526	Newark	130
Gloucester	172,681	Woodbury	329
Hudson	607,839	Jersey City	47
Hunterdon	69,718	Flemington	423
Mercer	304,116	Trenton	228
Middlesex	583,813	New Brunswick	312
Monmouth	461,849	Freehold	476
Morris	383,454	Morristown	468
Ocean	208,470	Toms River	642
Passaic	460,782	Paterson	192
Salem	60,346	Salem	365
Somerset	198,372	Somerville	307
Sussex	77,528	Newton	527
Union	543,116	Elizabeth	103
Warren	73,960	Belvidere	362

New Mexico

(32 counties, 121,412 sq. mi. land; pop. 1,016,000)

County	Pop. Apr. 1 1970	County Seat or Court House	Land Area Sq. Mi.
Bernalillo	315,774	Albuquerque	1,169
Catron	2,198	Reserve	6,897
Chaves	43,335	Roswell	6,084
Colfax	12,170	Raton	3,764
Curry	39,517	Clovis	1,403
De Baca	2,547	Fort Sumner	2,356
Dona Ana	69,773	Las Cruces	3,804
Eddy	41,119	Carlsbad	4,167
Grant	22,030	Silver City	3,970
Guadalupe	4,969	Santa Rosa	2,998
Harding	1,348	Mosquero	2,134
Hidalgo	4,734	Lordsburg	3,447
Lea	49,554	Lovington	4,393
Lincoln	7,560	Carrizozo	4,858
Los Alamos	15,198	Los Alamos	108
Luna	11,706	Deming	2,957
McKinley	43,208	Gallup	5,454
Mora	4,673	Mora	1,940
Otero	41,097	Alamogordo	6,638
Quay	10,903	Tucumcari	2,875
Rio Arriba	25,170	Tierra Amarilla	5,843
Roosevelt	16,479	Portales	2,454
Sandoval	17,492	Bernalillo	3,714
San Juan	52,517	Aztec	5,500
San Miguel	21,951	Las Vegas	4,741
Santa Fe	54,774	Santa Fe	1,902
Sierra	7,189	Truth or Consequences	4,166
Socorro	9,763	Socorro	6,603
Taos	17,516	Taos	2,256

County	Pop. Apr. 1 1970	County Seat or Court House	Land Area Sq. Mi.
Torrance	5,290	Estancia	3,346
Union	4,925	Clayton	3,816
Valencia	40,576	Los Lunas	5,656

New York
(62 counties, 47,831 sq. mi. land; pop., 18,241,266)

County	Pop. Apr. 1 1970	County Seat or Court House	Land Area Sq. Mi.
Albany	286,742	Albany	526
Allegany	46,458	Belmont	1,047
Bronx	1,471,701	Bronx	41
Broome	221,815	Binghamton	714
Cattaraugus	81,666	Little Valley	1,318
Cayuga	77,439	Auburn	698
Chautauqua	147,305	Mayville	1,081
Chemung	101,537	Elmira	415
Chenango	46,368	Norwich	903
Clinton	72,934	Plattsburgh	1,059
Columbia	51,519	Hudson	645
Cortland	45,894	Cortland	502
Delaware	44,718	Delhi	1,443
Dutchess	222,295	Poughkeepsie	813
Erie	1,113,491	Buffalo	1,058
Essex	34,631	Elizabethtown	1,823
Franklin	43,931	Malone	1,674
Fulton	52,637	Johnstown	498
Genesee	58,722	Batavia	501
Greene	33,136	Catskill	653
Hamilton	4,714	Lake Pleasant	1,735
Herkimer	67,633	Herkimer	1,435
Jefferson	88,508	Watertown	1,294
Kings	2,602,012	Brooklyn	70
Lewis	23,644	Lowville	1,291
Livingston	54,041	Geneseo	638
Madison	62,864	Wampsville	661
Monroe	711,917	Rochester	675
Montgomery	55,883	Fonda	408
Nassau	1,428,838	Mineola	289
New York	1,539,233	New York	23
Niagara	235,720	Lockport	532
Oneida	273,037	Utica	1,223
Onondaga	472,835	Syracuse	794
Ontario	78,849	Canandaigua	651
Orange	221,657	Goshen	833
Orleans	37,305	Albion	396
Oswego	100,897	Oswego	964
Otsego	56,181	Cooperstown	1,013
Putnam	56,696	Carmel	231
Queens	1,987,174	Jamaica	108
Rensselaer	152,510	Troy	665
Richmond	295,443	Saint George	58
Rockland	229,903	New City	176
St. Lawrence	112,309	Canton	2,768
Saratoga	121,764	Ballston Spa	818
Schenectady	161,078	Schenectady	207
Schoharie	24,750	Schoharie	624
Schuyler	16,737	Watkins Glen	330
Seneca	35,083	Ovid & Waterloo	330
Steuben	99,546	Bath	1,410
Suffolk	1,127,030	Riverhead	929
Sullivan	52,580	Monticello	980
Tioga	46,513	Owego	524
Tompkins	77,064	Ithaca	482
Ulster	141,241	Kingston	1,141
Warren	49,402	Lake George	887
Washington	52,725	Hudson Falls	836
Wayne	79,404	Lyons	606
Westchester	894,406	White Plains	443
Wyoming	37,688	Warsaw	598
Yates	19,831	Penn Yan	343

North Carolina
(100 counties, 48,798 sq. mi. land; pop., 5,082,059)

County	Pop. Apr. 1 1970	County Seat or Court House	Land Area Sq. Mi.
Alamance	96,362	Graham	428
Alexander	19,466	Taylorsville	259
Alleghany	8,134	Sparta	225
Anson	23,488	Wadesboro	533
Ashe	19,571	Jefferson	426
Avery	12,655	Newland	245
Beaufort	35,980	Washington	826
Bertie	20,528	Windsor	698
Bladen	26,477	Elizabethtown	883
Brunswick	24,223	Southport	856
Buncombe	145,056	Asheville	657
Burke	60,364	Morganton	511
Cabarrus	74,629	Concord	363
Caldwell	56,699	Lenoir	469
Camden	5,453	Camden	239
Carteret	31,603	Beaufort	536
Caswell	19,055	Yanceyville	428
Catawba	90,873	Newton	394
Chatham	29,554	Pittsboro	709
Cherokee	16,330	Murphy	452
Chowan	10,764	Edenton	173
Clay	5,180	Hayesville	209

County	Pop. Apr. 1 1970	County Seat or Court House	Land Area Sq. Mi.
Cleveland	72,556	Shelby	468
Columbus	46,937	Whiteville	945
Craven	62,554	New Bern	699
Cumberland	212,042	Fayetteville	654
Currituck	6,976	Currituck	246
Dare	6,995	Manteo	391
Davidson	95,627	Lexington	549
Davie	18,855	Mocksville	265
Duplin	38,015	Kenansville	815
Durham	132,681	Durham	295
Edgecombe	52,341	Tarboro	510
Forsyth	215,118	Winston-Salem	419
Franklin	26,820	Louisburg	491
Gaston	148,415	Gastonia	356
Gates	8,524	Gatesville	337
Graham	6,562	Robbinsville	292
Granville	32,762	Oxford	537
Greene	14,967	Snow Hill	267
Guilford	288,645	Greensboro	655
Halifax	53,884	Halifax	734
Harnett	49,667	Lillington	603
Haywood	41,710	Waynesville	551
Henderson	42,804	Hendersonville	378
Hertford	23,529	Winton	353
Hoke	16,436	Raeford	389
Hyde	5,571	Swanquarter	613
Iredell	72,197	Statesville	572
Jackson	21,593	Sylva	491
Johnston	61,737	Smithfield	797
Jones	9,779	Trenton	467
Lee	30,467	Sanford	256
Lenoir	55,204	Kinston	400
Lincoln	32,682	Lincolnton	297
McDowell	30,648	Marion	436
Macon	15,788	Franklin	513
Madison	16,003	Marshall	450
Martin	24,730	Williamston	455
Mecklenburg	354,656	Charlotte	530
Mitchell	13,447	Bakersville	215
Montgomery	19,267	Troy	488
Moore	39,048	Carthage	704
Nash	59,122	Nashville	544
New Hanover	82,996	Wilmington	185
Northampton	24,009	Jackson	536
Onslow	103,126	Jacksonville	765
Orange	57,707	Hillsboro	400
Pamlico	9,467	Bayboro	338
Pasquotank	26,824	Elizabeth City	228
Pender	18,149	Burgaw	871
Perquimans	8,351	Hertford	246
Person	25,914	Roxboro	401
Pitt	73,900	Greenville	655
Polk	11,735	Columbus	239
Randolph	76,358	Asheboro	798
Richmond	39,889	Rockingham	475
Robeson	84,842	Lumberton	949
Rockingham	72,402	Wentworth	569
Rowan	90,035	Salisbury	523
Rutherford	47,337	Rutherfordton	563
Sampson	44,954	Clinton	945
Scotland	26,929	Laurinburg	319
Stanly	42,822	Albemarle	398
Stokes	23,782	Danbury	457
Surry	51,415	Dobson	536
Swain	8,835	Bryson City	524
Transylvania	19,713	Brevard	382
Tyrrell	3,806	Columbia	390
Union	54,714	Monroe	639
Vance	32,691	Henderson	249
Wake	229,006	Raleigh	858
Warren	15,810	Warrenton	424
Washington	14,038	Plymouth	343
Watauga	23,404	Boone	317
Wayne	85,408	Goldsboro	557
Wilkes	49,524	Wilkesboro	757
Wilson	57,486	Wilson	375
Yadkin	24,599	Yadkinville	336
Yancey	12,629	Burnsville	312

North Dakota
(53 counties, 69,273 sq. mi. land; pop., 617,761)

County	Pop. Apr. 1 1970	County Seat or Court House	Land Area Sq. Mi.
Adams	3,832	Hettinger	989
Barnes	14,669	Valley City	1,479
Benson	8,245	Minnewaukan	1,403
Billings	1,198	Medora	1,139
Bottineau	9,496	Bottineau	1,677
Bowman	3,901	Bowman	1,170
Burke	4,739	Bowbells	1,119
Burleigh	40,714	Bismarck	1,625
Cass	73,653	Fargo	1,749
Cavalier (1973)	10,977	Langdon	1,512
Dickey	6,976	Ellendale	1,143
Divide	4,564	Crosby	1,300
Dunn	4,895	Manning	1,992

County	Pop. Apr. 1 1970	County Seat or Court House	Land Area Sq. Mi.
Eddy	4,103	New Rockford	635
Emmons	7,200	Linton	1,503
Foster	4,832	Carrington	645
Golden Valley	2,611	Beach	1,014
Grand Forks	61,102	Grand Forks	1,438
Grant	5,009	Carson	1,666
Griggs	4,184	Cooperstown	710
Hettinger	5,075	Mott	1,134
Kidder	4,362	Steele	1,358
La Moure	7,117	La Moure	1,136
Logan	4,245	Napoleon	1,001
McHenry	8,977	Towner	1,879
McIntosh	5,545	Ashley	992
McKenzie	6,127	Watford City	2,735
McLean	11,251	Washburn	2,065
Mercer	6,175	Stanton	1,042
Morton	20,310	Mandan	1,920
Mountrail	8,437	Stanley	1,819
Nelson	5,807	Lakota	995
Oliver	2,322	Center	721
Pembina	10,728	Cavalier	1,124
Pierce	6,323	Rugby	1,038
Ramsey	12,915	Devils Lake	1,248
Ransom	7,102	Lisbon	861
Renville	3,828	Mohall	886
Richland	18,089	Wahpeton	1,449
Rolette	11,549	Rolla	913
Sargent	5,937	Forman	853
Sheridan	3,232	McClusky	989
Sioux	3,632	Fort Yates	1,103
Slope	1,484	Amidon	1,225
Stark	19,613	Dickinson	1,316
Steele	3,749	Finley	710
Stutsman	23,550	Jamestown	2,264
Towner	4,645	Cando	1,043
Traill	9,571	Hillsboro	861
Walsh	16,251	Grafton	1,286
Ward	58,560	Minot	2,044
Wells	7,847	Fessenden	1,299
Williams	19,301	Williston	2,064

Ohio

(88 counties, 40,975 sq. mi. land; pop., 10,652,017)

County	Pop. Apr. 1 1970	County Seat or Court House	Land Area Sq. Mi.
Adams	18,957	West Union	587
Allen	111,144	Lima	410
Ashland	43,303	Ashland	424
Ashtabula	98,237	Jefferson	700
Athens	55,747	Athens	504
Auglaize	38,602	Wapakoneta	400
Belmont	80,917	Saint Clairsville	534
Brown	26,635	Georgetown	490
Butler	226,207	Hamilton	471
Carroll	21,579	Carrollton	390
Champaign	30,491	Urbana	432
Clark	157,115	Springfield	402
Clermont	95,887	Batavia	458
Clinton	31,464	Wilmington	410
Columbiana	108,310	Lisbon	534
Coshocton	33,486	Coshocton	562
Crawford	50,364	Bucyrus	404
Cuyahoga	1,720,835	Cleveland	456
Darke	49,141	Greenville	605
Defiance	36,949	Defiance	412
Delaware	42,908	Delaware	450
Erie	75,909	Sandusky	264
Fairfield	73,301	Lancaster	505
Fayette	25,461	Washington, C. H.	404
Franklin	833,249	Columbus	538
Fulton	33,071	Wauseon	407
Gallia	25,239	Gallipolis	471
Geauga	62,977	Chardon	407
Greene	125,057	Xenia	415
Guernsey	37,665	Cambridge	528
Hamilton	923,205	Cincinnati	414
Hancock	61,217	Findlay	532
Hardin	30,813	Kenton	467
Harrison	17,013	Cadiz	401
Henry	27,058	Napoleon	416
Highland	28,996	Hillsboro	549
Hocking	20,322	Logan	421
Holmes	23,024	Millersburg	424
Huron	49,587	Norwalk	497
Jackson	27,174	Jackson	419
Jefferson	96,193	Steubenville	411
Knox	41,795	Mount Vernon	531
Lake	197,200	Painesville	231
Lawrence	56,868	Ironton	456
Licking	107,799	Newark	686
Logan	35,072	Bellefontaine	460
Lorain	256,843	Elyria	495
Lucas	483,594	Toledo	343
Madison	28,318	London	463
Mahoning	304,545	Youngstown	415
Marion	64,724	Marion	405
Medina	82,717	Medina	425
Meigs	19,799	Pomeroy	436
Mercer	35,558	Celina	444
Miami	84,342	Troy	407
Monroe	15,739	Woodsfield	456
Montgomery	608,413	Dayton	459
Morgan	12,375	McConnelsville	420
Morrow	21,348	Mount Gilead	403
Muskingum	77,826	Zanesville	651
Noble	10,428	Caldwell	398
Ottawa	37,099	Port Clinton	261
Paulding	19,329	Paulding	417
Perry	27,434	New Lexington	410
Pickaway	40,071	Circleville	504
Pike	19,114	Waverly	443
Portage	125,868	Ravenna	495
Preble	34,719	Eaton	427
Putnam	31,134	Ottawa	486
Richland	129,997	Mansfield	496
Ross	61,211	Chillicothe	687
Sandusky	60,983	Fremont	409
Scioto	76,951	Portsmouth	608
Seneca	60,696	Tiffin	551
Shelby	37,748	Sidney	408
Stark	372,210	Canton	576
Summit	553,371	Akron	408
Trumbull	232,579	Warren	608
Tuscarawas	77,211	New Philadelphia	569
Union	23,786	Marysville	434
Van Wert	29,194	Van Wert	409
Vinton	9,420	McArthur	411
Warren	85,505	Lebanon	408
Washington	57,160	Marietta	641
Wayne	87,123	Wooster	561
Williams	33,669	Bryan	421
Wood	89,722	Bowling Green	619
Wyandot	21,826	Upper Sandusky	406

Oklahoma

(77 counties, 68,782 sq. mi. land; pop., 2,559,253)

County	Pop. Apr. 1 1970	County Seat or Court House	Land Area Sq. Mi.
Adair	15,141	Stilwell	570
Alfalfa	7,224	Cherokee	868
Atoka	10,972	Atoka	991
Beaver	6,282	Beaver	1,790
Beckham	15,754	Sayre	907
Blaine	11,794	Watonga	917
Bryan	25,552	Durant	889
Caddo	28,931	Anadarko	1,272
Canadian	32,245	El Reno	897
Carter	37,349	Ardmore	830
Cherokee	23,174	Tahlequah	756
Choctaw	15,141	Hugo	778
Cimarron	4,145	Boise City	1,843
Cleveland	81,839	Norman	527
Coal	5,525	Coalgate	526
Comanche	108,144	Lawton	1,084
Cotton	6,832	Walters	651
Craig	14,722	Vinita	764
Creek	45,532	Sapulpa	936
Custer	22,665	Arapaho	980
Delaware	17,767	Jay	707
Dewey	5,656	Taloga	1,018
Ellis	5,129	Arnett	1,242
Garfield	56,343	Enid	1,054
Garvin	24,874	Pauls Valley	814
Grady	29,354	Chickasha	1,096
Grant	7,117	Medford	1,007
Greer	7,979	Mangum	633
Harmon	5,136	Hollis	545
Harper	5,151	Buffalo	1,041
Haskell	9,578	Stigler	602
Hughes	13,228	Holdenville	807
Jackson	30,902	Altus	810
Jefferson	7,125	Waurika	780
Johnston	7,870	Tishomingo	638
Kay	48,791	Newkirk	950
Kingfisher	12,857	Kingfisher	904
Kiowa	12,532	Hobart	1,027
Latimer	8,601	Wilburton	737
Le Flore	32,137	Poteau	1,560
Lincoln	19,482	Chandler	973
Logan	19,645	Guthrie	751
Love	5,637	Marietta	513
McClain	14,157	Purcell	573
McCurtain	28,642	Idabel	1,800
McIntosh	12,472	Eufaula	608
Major	7,529	Fairview	963
Marshall	7,682	Madill	366
Mayes	23,302	Pryor	648
Murray	10,669	Sulphur	423
Muskogee	59,542	Muskogee	818
Noble	10,043	Perry	743
Nowata	9,773	Nowata	537
Okfuskee	10,683	Okemah	637
Oklahoma	527,717	Oklahoma City	700

County	Pop. Apr. 1 1970	County Seat or Court House	Land Area Sq. Mi.
Okmulgee	35,358	Okmulgee	700
Osage	29,750	Pawhuska	2,272
Ottawa	29,800	Miami	464
Pawnee	11,338	Pawnee	61
Payne	50,654	Stillwater	694
Pittsburg	37,521	McAlester	1,241
Pontotoc	27,867	Ada	714
Pottawatomie	43,134	Shawnee	794
Pushmataha	9,385	Antlers	1,420
Roger Mills	4,452	Cheyenne	1,140
Rogers	28,425	Claremore	685
Seminole	25,144	Wewoka	630
Sequoyah	23,370	Sallisaw	696
Stephens	35,902	Duncan	891
Texas	16,352	Guymon	2,062
Tillman	12,901	Frederick	901
Tulsa	399,982	Tulsa	573
Wagoner	22,163	Wagoner	563
Washington	42,302	Bartlesville	424
Washita	12,141	Cordell	1,009
Woods	11,920	Alva	1,298
Woodward	15,537	Woodward	1,251

Oregon

(36 counties, 96,184 sq. mi. land; pop., 2,091,385)

County	Pop. Apr. 1 1970	County Seat or Court House	Land Area Sq. Mi.
Baker	14,919	Baker	3,068
Benton	53,776	Corvallis	668
Clackamas	166,088	Oregon City	1,884
Clatsop	28,473	Astoria	805
Columbia	28,790	Saint Helens	639
Coos	56,515	Coquille	1,604
Crook	9,985	Prineville	2,975
Curry	13,006	Gold Beach	1,627
Deschutes	30,442	Bend	3,031
Douglas	71,743	Roseburg	5,063
Gilliam	2,342	Condon	1,208
Grant	6,996	Canyon City	4,530
Harney	7,215	Burns	10,166
Hood River	13,187	Hood River	523
Jackson	94,533	Medford	2,812
Jefferson	8,548	Madras	1,793
Josephine	35,746	Grants Pass	1,625
Klamath	50,021	Klamath Falls	5,970
Lake	6,343	Lakeview	8,231
Lane	215,401	Eugene	4,552
Lincoln	25,755	Newport	986
Linn	71,914	Albany	2,283
Malheur	23,169	Vale	9,859
Marion	151,309	Salem	1,166
Morrow	4,465	Heppner	2,060
Multnomah	554,668	Portland	423
Polk	35,349	Dallas	736
Sherman	2,139	Moro	830
Tillamook	18,034	Tillamook	1,115
Umatilla	44,923	Pendleton	3,227
Union	19,377	La Grande	2,032
Wallowa	6,247	Enterprise	3,178
Wasco	20,133	The Dalles	2,381
Washington	157,920	Hillsboro	716
Wheeler	1,849	Fossil	1,707
Yamhill	40,213	McMinnville	711

Pennsylvania

(67 counties, 44,966 sq. mi. land; pop., 11,793,909)

County	Pop. Apr. 1 1970	County Seat or Court House	Land Area Sq. Mi.
Adams	56,937	Gettysburg	526
Allegheny	1,605,133	Pittsburgh	728
Armstrong	75,590	Kittanning	652
Beaver	208,418	Beaver	440
Bedford (1973)	43,278	Bedford	1,018
Berks	296,382	Reading	862
Blair	135,356	Hollidaysburg	530
Bradford	57,962	Towanda	1,148
Bucks	416,728	Doylestown	614
Butler	127,941	Butler	794
Cambria	186,785	Ebensburg	692
Cameron	7,096	Emporium	401
Carbon	50,573	Jim Thorpe	404
Centre	99,267	Bellefonte	1,115
Chester	277,746	West Chester	761
Clarion	38,414	Clarion	597
Clearfield	74,619	Clearfield	1,139
Clinton	37,721	Lock Haven	899
Columbia	55,114	Bloomsburg	484
Crawford	81,342	Meadville	1,012
Cumberland	158,177	Carlisle	555
Dauphin	223,713	Harrisburg	518
Delaware	601,715	Media	184
Elk	37,770	Ridgeway	807
Erie	263,654	Erie	813
Fayette	154,667	Uniontown	802
Forest	4,926	Tionesta	419
Franklin	100,833	Chambersburg	754
Fulton	10,776	McConnellsburg	435
Greene	36,090	Waynesburg	578
Huntingdon	39,108	Huntingdon	895
Indiana	79,451	Indiana	825
Jefferson	43,695	Brookville	652
Juniata	16,712	Mifflintown	386
Lackawanna	234,107	Scranton	454
Lancaster	320,079	Lancaster	946
Lawrence	107,374	New Castle	367
Lebanon	99,665	Lebanon	363
Lehigh	255,304	Allentown	348
Luzerne	342,329	Wilkes-Barre	886
Lycoming	113,296	Williamsport	1,216
McKean	51,915	Smethport	992
Mercer	127,225	Mercer	670
Mifflin	45,268	Lewistown	431
Monroe	45,422	Stroudsburg	611
Montgomery	623,956	Norristown	496
Montour	16,508	Danville	130
Northampton	214,545	Easton	376
Northumberland	99,190	Sunbury	453
Perry	28,615	New Bloomfield	551
Philadelphia	1,949,996	Philadelphia	129
Pike	11,818	Milford	542
Potter	16,395	Coudersport	1,092
Schuylkill	160,089	Pottsville	784
Snyder	29,269	Middleburg	327
Somerset	76,037	Somerset	1,078
Sullivan	5,961	Laporte	478
Susquehanna	34,344	Montrose	833
Tioga	39,691	Wellsboro	1,146
Union	28,603	Lewisburg	318
Venango	62,353	Franklin	678
Warren	47,682	Warren	905
Washington	210,876	Washington	857
Wayne	29,581	Honesdale	741
Westmoreland	376,935	Greensburg	1,024
Wyoming	19,082	Tunkhannock	398
York	272,603	York	909

Rhode Island

(5 counties, 1,049 sq. mi. land; pop., 949,723)

County	Pop. Apr. 1 1970	County Seat or Court House	Land Area Sq. Mi.
Bristol	45,937	Bristol	25
Kent	142,382	East Greenwich	173
Newport	94,228	Newport	115
Providence	581,470	Providence	416
Washington	85,706	West Kingston	321

South Carolina

(46 counties, 30,225 sq. mi. land; pop., 2,590,516)

County	Pop. Apr. 1 1970	County Seat or Court House	Land Area Sq. Mi.
Abbeville	21,112	Abbeville	506
Aiken	91,023	Aiken	1,087
Allendale	9,783	Allendale	418
Anderson	105,474	Anderson	749
Bamberg	15,950	Bamberg	395
Barnwell	17,176	Barnwell	553
Beaufort	51,136	Beaufort	579
Berkeley	56,199	Moncks Corner	1,110
Calhoun	10,780	Saint Matthews	377
Charleston	247,650	Charleston	939
Cherokee	36,791	Gaffney	394
Chester	29,811	Chester	584
Chesterfield	33,667	Chesterfield	790
Clarendon	25,604	Manning	599
Colleton	27,622	Walterboro	1,049
Darlington	53,442	Darlington	543
Dillon	28,838	Dillon	407
Dorchester	32,276	Saint George	569
Edgefield	15,692	Edgefield	482
Fairfield	19,999	Winnsboro	696
Florence	89,636	Florence	805
Georgetown	33,500	Georgetown	812
Greenville	240,774	Greenville	792
Greenwood	49,686	Greenwood	446
Hampton	15,878	Hampton	562
Horry	69,992	Conway	1,154
Jasper	11,885	Ridgeland	652
Kershaw	34,727	Camden	781
Lancaster	43,328	Lancaster	502
Laurens	49,713	Laurens	711
Lee	18,323	Bishopville	409
Lexington	89,012	Lexington	717
McCormick	7,955	McCormick	360
Marion	30,270	Marion	487
Marlboro	27,151	Bennettsville	483
Newberry	29,273	Newberry	635
Oconee	40,728	Walhalla	654
Orangeburg	69,789	Orangeburg	1,106
Pickens	58,956	Pickens	492
Richland	233,868	Columbia	748
Saluda	14,528	Saluda	458
Spartanburg	173,724	Spartanburg	831
Sumter	79,425	Sumter	672
Union	29,230	Union	514
Williamsburg	34,243	Kingstree	935
York	85,216	York	684

South Dakota

(67 counties, 75,955 sq. mi. land; pop., 666,257)

County	Pop. Apr. 1 1970	County Seat or Court House	Land Area Sq. Mi.
Aurora	4,183	Plankinton	709
Beadle	20,877	Huron	1,259
Bennett	3,088	Martin	1,181
Bon Homme	8,577	Tyndall	560
Brookings	22,158	Brookings	800
Brown	36,920	Aberdeen	1,674
Brule	5,870	Chamberlain	818
Buffalo	1,739	Gannvalley	482
Butte	7,825	Belle Fourche	2,250
Campbell	2,866	Mound City	732
Charles Mix	9,994	Lake Andes	1,097
Clark	5,515	Clark	964
Clay	12,923	Vermillion	405
Codington	19,140	Watertown	687
Corson	4,994	McIntosh	2,470
Custer	4,698	Custer	1,557
Davison	17,319	Mitchell	432
Day	8,713	Webster	1,030
Deuel	5,686	Clear Lake	639
Dewey	5,170	Timber Lake	2,351
Douglas	4,569	Armour	435
Edmunds	5,548	Ipswich	1,154
Fall River	7,505	Hot Springs	1,743
Faulk	3,893	Faulkton	996
Grant	9,005	Milbank	681
Gregory	6,710	Burke	997
Haakon	2,802	Philip	1,816
Hamlin	5,520	Hayti	511
Hand	5,883	Miller	1,432
Hanson	3,781	Alexandria	430
Harding	1,855	Buffalo	2,682
Hughes	11,632	Pierre	748
Hutchinson	10,379	Olivet	815
Hyde	2,515	Highmore	863
Jackson	1,531	Kadoka	808
Jerauld	3,310	Wessington Spgs.	527
Jones	1,882	Murdo	973
Kingsbury	7,657	De Smet	818
Lake	11,456	Madison	567
Lawrence	17,453	Deadwood	800
Lincoln	11,761	Canton	576
Lyman	4,060	Kennebec	1,683
McCook	7,246	Salem	575
McPherson	5,022	Leola	1,147
Marshall	5,965	Britton	848
Meade	17,020	Sturgis	3,465
Mellette	2,420	White River	1,306
Miner	4,454	Howard	570
Minnehaha	95,209	Sioux Falls	813
Moody	7,622	Flandreau	523
Pennington	59,349	Rapid City	2,779
Perkins	4,769	Bison	2,860
Potter	4,449	Gettysburg	869
Roberts	11,678	Sisseton	1,108
Sanborn	3,697	Woonsocket	570
Shannon	8,198	(Attached to Fall River)	2,100
Spink	10,595	Redfield	1,505
Stanley	2,457	Fort Pierre	1,414
Sully	2,362	Onida	1,004
Todd	6,606	(Attached to Tripp)	1,388
Tripp	8,171	Winner	1,620
Turner	9,872	Parker	612
Union	9,643	Elk Point	452
Walworth	7,842	Selby	718
Washabaugh	1,389	(Attached to Jackson)	1,061
Yankton	19,039	Yankton	519
Zeibach	2,221	Dupree	1,981

Tennessee

(95 counties, 41,328 sq. mi. land; pop., 3,924,164)

County	Pop. Apr. 1 1970	County Seat or Court House	Land Area Sq. Mi.
Anderson	60,300	Clinton	335
Bedford	25,039	Shelbyville	482
Benton	12,126	Camden	392
Bledsoe	7,643	Pikeville	404
Blount	63,744	Maryville	575
Bradley	50,686	Cleveland	334
Campbell	26,045	Jacksboro	451
Cannon	8,467	Woodbury	271
Carroll	25,741	Huntingdon	596
Carter	42,259	Elizabethton	348
Cheatham	13,199	Ashland City	305
Chester	9,927	Henderson	285
Claiborne	19,420	Tazewell	444
Clay	6,624	Celina	233
Cocke	25,283	Newport	424
Coffee	32,572	Manchester	434
Crockett	14,402	Alamo	269
Cumberland	20,733	Crossville	678
Davidson	447,877	Nashville	508
Decatur	9,457	Decaturville	337
De Kalb	11,151	Smithville	278
Dickson	21,977	Charlotte	485
Dyer	30,427	Dyersburg	529
Fayette	22,692	Somerville	704
Fentress	12,593	Jamestown	498
Franklin	27,289	Winchester	553
Gibson	47,871	Trenton	607
Giles	22,138	Pulaski	619
Grainger	13,948	Rutledge	282
Greene	47,630	Greeneville	613
Grundy	10,631	Altamont	358
Hamblen	38,696	Morristown	155
Hamilton	255,077	Chattanooga	550
Hancock	6,719	Sneedville	230
Hardeman	22,435	Bolivar	656
Hardin	18,212	Savannah	587
Hawkins	33,757	Rogersville	480
Haywood	19,596	Brownsville	519
Henderson	17,360	Lexington	515
Henry	23,749	Paris	567
Hickman	12,096	Centerville	610
Houston	5,853	Erin	201
Humphreys	13,560	Waverly	530
Jackson	8,141	Gainesboro	323
Jefferson	24,940	Dandridge	274
Johnson	11,569	Mountain City	293
Knox	276,293	Knoxville	508
Lake	8,074	Tiptonville	167
Lauderdale	20,271	Ripley	477
Lawrence	29,097	Lawrenceburg	634
Lewis	6,761	Hohenwald	285
Lincoln	24,318	Fayetteville	580
Loudon	24,266	Loudon	237
McMinn	35,462	Athens	432
McNairy	18,369	Selmer	569
Macon	12,315	Lafayette	304
Madison	65,774	Jackson	560
Marion	20,577	Jasper	506
Marshall	17,319	Lewisburg	377
Maury	44,028	Columbia	614
Meigs	5,219	Decatur	191
Monroe	23,475	Madisonville	660
Montgomery	62,721	Clarksville	539
Moore	3,568	Lynchburg	124
Morgan	13,619	Wartburg	539
Obion	30,247	Union City	556
Overton	14,866	Livingston	441
Perry	5,238	Linden	411
Pickett	3,774	Byrdstown	158
Polk	11,669	Benton	434
Putnam	35,487	Cookeville	405
Rhea	17,202	Dayton	312
Roane	38,881	Kingston	350
Robertson	29,102	Springfield	476
Rutherford	59,428	Murfreesboro	612
Scott	14,762	Huntsville	544
Sequatchie	6,331	Dunlap	273
Sevier	28,241	Sevierville	597
Shelby	722,111	Memphis	755
Smith	12,509	Carthage	323
Stewart	7,319	Dover	470
Sullivan	127,329	Blountville	413
Sumner	56,266	Gallatin	534
Tipton	28,001	Covington	459
Trousdale	5,155	Hartsville	114
Unicoi	15,254	Erwin	185
Union	9,072	Maynardville	212
Van Buren	3,758	Spencer	254
Warren	26,972	McMinnville	439
Washington	73,924	Jonesboro	323
Wayne	12,365	Waynesboro	739
Weakley	28,827	Dresden	576
White	16,329	Sparta	382
Williamson	34,423	Franklin	593
Wilson	36,999	Lebanon	567

Texas

(254 counties, 262,134 sq. mi. land; pop., 11,196,730)

County	Pop. Apr. 1 1970	County Seat or Court House	Land Area Sq. Mi.
Anderson	27,789	Palestine	1,072
Andrews	10,372	Andrews	1,504
Angelina	49,349	Lufkin	738
Aransas	8,902	Rockport	275
Archer	5,759	Archer City	913
Armstrong	1,895	Claude	907
Atascosa	18,696	Jourdanton	1,206
Austin	13,831	Bellville	663
Bailey	8,487	Muleshoe	835
Bandera	4,747	Bandera	763
Bastrop	17,297	Bastrop	890
Baylor	5,221	Seymour	845
Bee	22,737	Beeville	842
Bell	124,483	Belton	1,047
Bexar	830,460	San Antonio	1,246

County	Pop. Apr. 1 1970	County Seat or Court House	Land Area Sq. Mi.	County	Pop. Apr. 1 1970	County Seat or Court House	Land Area Sq. Mi.
Blanco	3,567	Johnson City	719	Houston	17,855	Crockett	1,237
Borden	888	Gail	907	Howard	37,796	Big Spring	911
Bosque	10,966	Meridian	990	Hudspeth	2,392	Sierra Blanca	4,554
Bowie	67,813	Boston	891	Hunt	47,948	Greenville	826
Brazoria	108,312	Angleton	1,423	Hutchinson	24,443	Stinnett	875
Brazos	57,978	Bryan	586	Irion	1,070	Mertzon	1,073
Brewster	7,780	Alpine	6,204	Jack	6,711	Jacksboro	945
Briscoe	2,794	Silverton	874	Jackson	12,975	Edna	850
Brooks	8,005	Falfurrias	904	Jasper	24,692	Jasper	907
Brown	25,877	Brownwood	938	Jeff Davis	1,527	Fort Davis	2,259
Burleson	9,999	Caldwell	670	Jefferson	246,402	Beaumont	951
Burnet	11,420	Burnet	996	Jim Hogg	4,654	Hebbronville	1,143
Caldwell	21,178	Lockhart	544	Jim Wells	33,032	Alice	845
Calhoun	17,831	Port Lavanca	527	Johnson	45,769	Cleburne	740
Callahan	8,205	Baird	856	Jones	16,106	Anson	956
Cameron	140,368	Brownsville	896	Karnes	13,462	Karnes City	758
Camp	8,005	Pittsburg	192	Kaufman	32,392	Kaufman	815
Carson	6,358	Panhandle	900	Kendall	6,964	Boerne	670
Cass	24,133	Linden	941	Kenedy	678	Sarita	1,394
Castro	10,394	Dimmitt	880	Kent	1,434	Jayton	880
Chambers	12,187	Anahuac	616	Kerr	19,454	Kerrville	1,101*
Cherokee	32,008	Rusk	1,049	Kimble	3,904	Junction	1,274
Childress	6,605	Childress	699	King	464	Guthrie	944
Clay	8,079	Henrietta	1,102	Kinney	2,006	Brackettville	1,393
Cochran	5,326	Morton	783	Kleberg	33,166	Kingsville	851
Coke	3,087	Robert Lee	911	Knox	5,972	Benjamin	851
Coleman	10,288	Coleman	1,280	Lamar	36,062	Paris	984
Collin	66,920	McKinney	836	Lamb	17,770	Littlefield	1,022
Collingsworth	4,755	Wellington	894	Lampasas	9,323	Lampasas	726
Colorado	17,638	Columbus	949	La Salle	5,014	Cotulla	1,500
Comal	24,165	New Braunfels	567	Lavaca	17,903	Hallettsville	975
Comanche	11,898	Comanche	944	Lee	8,048	Giddings	637
Concho	2,937	Paint Rock	1,004	Leon	8,738	Centerville	1,102
Cooke	23,471	Gainesville	985	Liberty	33,014	Liberty	1,180
Coryell	35,311	Gatesville	1,043	Limestone	18,100	Groesbeck	931
Cottle	3,204	Paducah	900	Lipscomb	3,486	Lipscomb	934
Crane	4,172	Crane	795	Live Oak	6,697	George West	1,055
Crockett	3,885	Ozona	2,794	Llano	6,979	Llano	941
Crosby	9,085	Crosbyton	911	Loving	164	Mentone	648
Culberson	3,429	Van Horn	3,851	Lubbock	179,295	Lubbock	893
Dallam	6,012	Dalhart	1,494	Lynn	9,107	Tahoka	915
Dallas	1,327,695	Dallas	859	McCulloch	8,571	Brady	1,066
Dawson	16,604	Lamesa	902	McLennan	147,553	Waco	1,000
Deaf Smith	18,999	Hereford	1,510	McMullen	1,095	Tilden	1,159
Delta	4,927	Cooper	276	Madison	7,693	Madisonville	480
Denton	75,633	Denton	911	Marion	8,517	Jefferson	380
Dewitt	18,660	Cuero	910	Martin	4,774	Stanton	911
Dickens	3,737	Dickens	931	Mason	3,356	Mason	935
Dimmit	9,039	Carrizo Springs	1,344	Matagorda	27,913	Bay City	1,157
Donley	3,641	Clarendon	905	Maverick	18,093	Eagle Pass	1,289
Duval	11,722	San Diego	1,814	Medina	20,249	Hondo	1,352
Eastland	18,092	Eastland	952	Menard	2,646	Menard	914
Ector	91,805	Odessa	907	Midland	65,433	Midland	939
Edwards	2,107	Rocksprings	2,076	Milam	20,028	Cameron	1,028
Ellis	46,638	Waxahachie	940	Mills	4,212	Goldthwaite	734
El Paso	359,291	El Paso	1,057	Mitchell	9,073	Colorado City	920
Erath	18,141	Stephenville	1,085	Montague	15,326	Montague	932
Falls	17,300	Marlin	764	Montgomery	49,479	Conroe	1,090
Fannin	22,705	Bonham	905	Moore	14,060	Dumas	909
Fayette	17,650	La Grange	934	Morris	12,310	Daingerfield	260
Fisher	6,344	Roby	904	Motley	2,178	Matador	980
Floyd	11,044	Floydada	993	Nacogdoches	36,362	Nacogdoches	902
Foard	2,211	Crowell	676	Navarro	31,150	Corsicana	1,070
Fort Bend	52,314	Richmond	869	Newton	11,657	Newton	949
Franklin	5,291	Mount Vernon	293	Nolan	16,220	Sweetwater	922
Freestone	11,116	Fairfield	865	Nueces	237,544	Corpus Christi	841
Frio	11,159	Pearsall	1,116	Ochiltree	9,704	Perryton	907
Gaines	11,593	Seminole	1,489	Oldham	2,258	Vega	1,478
Galveston	169,812	Galveston	399	Orange	71,170	Orange	359
Garza	5,289	Post	914	Palo Pinto	28,962	Palo Pinto	948
Gillespie	10,553	Fredericksburg	1,055	Panola	15,894	Carthage	869
Glasscock	1,155	Garden City	863	Parker	33,888	Weatherford	903
Goliad	4,869	Goliad	871	Parmer	10,509	Farwell	859
Gonzales	16,375	Gonzales	1,056	Pecos	13,748	Fort Stockton	4,740
Gray	26,949	Pampa	934	Polk	14,457	Livingston	1,100
Grayson	83,225	Sherman	940	Potter	90,511	Amarillo	898
Gregg	75,929	Longview	282	Presidio	4,842	Marfa	3,892
Grimes	11,855	Anderson	801	Rains	3,752	Emory	210
Guadalupe	33,554	Seguin	714	Randall	53,885	Canyon	914
Hale	34,137	Plainview	979	Reagan	3,239	Big Lake	1,132
Hall	6,015	Memphis	885	Real	2,013	Leakey	622
Hamilton	7,198	Hamilton	844	Red River	14,298	Clarksville	1,033
Hansford	6,351	Spearman	907	Reeves	16,526	Pecos	2,608
Hardeman	6,795	Quanah	687	Refugio	9,494	Refugio	774
Hardin	29,996	Kountze	897	Roberts	967	Miami	899
Harris	1,741,912	Houston	1,723	Robertson	14,389	Franklin	877
Harrison	44,841	Marshall	894	Rockwall	7,046	Rockwall	147
Hartley	2,782	Channing	1,488	Runnels	12,108	Ballinger	1,058
Haskell	8,512	Haskell	877	Rusk	34,102	Henderson	939
Hays	27,642	San Marcos	650	Sabine	7,187	Hemphill	456
Hemphill	3,084	Canadian	904	San Augustine	7,858	San Augustine	473
Henderson	26,466	Athens	943	San Jacinto	6,702	Coldspring	624
Hidalgo	181,535	Edinburg	1,543	San Patricio	47,288	Sinton	685
Hill	22,596	Hillsboro	1,010	San Saba	5,540	San Saba	1,120
Hockley	20,396	Levelland	908	Schleicher	2,277	Eldorado	1,331
Hood	6,368	Granbury	426	Scurry	15,760	Snyder	904
Hopkins	20,710	Sulphur Springs	793	Shackelford	3,323	Albany	887

County	Pop. Apr. 1 1970	County Seat or Court House	Land Area Sq. MI.
Shelby	19,672	Center	778
Sherman	3,657	Stratford	916
Smith	97,096	Tyler	934
Somervell	2,793	Glen Rose	197
Starr	17,707	Rio Grande City	1,211
Stephens	8,414	Breckenridge	899
Sterling	1,056	Sterling City	914
Stonewall	2,397	Aspermont	926
Sutton	3,175	Sonora	1,493
Swisher	10,373	Tulia	896
Tarrant	716,317	Fort Worth	861
Taylor	97,853	Abilene	912
Terrell	1,940	Sanderson	2,391
Terry	14,118	Brownfield	899
Throckmorton	2,205	Throckmorton	920
Titus	16,702	Mount Pleasant	418
Tom Green	71,047	San Angelo	1,500
Travis	295,516	Austin	1,012
Trinity	7,628	Groveton	707
Tyler	12,417	Woodville	919
Upshur	20,976	Gilmer	584
Upton	4,697	Rankin	1,312
Uvalde	17,348	Uvalde	1,588
Val Verde	27,471	Del Rio	3,241
Van Zandt	22,155	Canton	845
Victoria	53,766	Victoria	892
Walker	27,680	Huntsville	790
Waller	14,285	Hempstead	509
Ward	13,019	Monahans	827
Washington	18,842	Brenham	594
Webb	72,859	Laredo	3,306
Wharton	36,729	Wharton	1,076
Wheeler	6,434	Wheeler	914
Wichita	120,563	Wichita Falls	611
Wilbarger	15,355	Vernon	952
Willacy	15,570	Raymondville	591
Williamson	37,305	Georgetown	1,104
Wilson	13,041	Floresville	802
Winkler	9,640	Kermit	887
Wise	19,687	Decatur	922
Wood	18,589	Quitman	721
Yoakum	7,344	Plains	830
Young	15,400	Graham	888
Zapata	4,352	Zapata	957
Zavala	11,370	Crystal City	1,291

Utah

(29 counties, 82,096 sq. mi. land; pop. 1,059,273)

County	Pop. Apr. 1 1970	County Seat or Court House	Land Area Sq. MI.
Beaver	3,800	Beaver	2,584
Box Elder	28,129	Brigham City,	5,603
Cache	42,331	Logan	1,174
Carbon	15,647	Price	1,476
Daggett	666	Manila	682
Davis	99,028	Farmington	297
Duchesne	7,299	Duchesne	3,255
Emery	5,137	Castle Dale	4,439
Garfield	3,157	Panguitch	5,158
Grand	6,688	Moab	3,682
Iron	12,177	Parowan	3,300
Juab	4,574	Nephi	3,412
Kane	2,421	Kanab	3,904
Millard	6,988	Fillmore	6,793
Morgan	3,983	Morgan	603
Piute	1,164	Junction	754
Rich	1,615	Randolph	1,023
Salt Lake	458,607	Salt Lake City	764
San Juan	9,606	Monticello	7,707
Sanpete	10,976	Manti	1,597
Sevier	10,103	Richfield	1,929
Summit	5,879	Coalville	1,849
Tooele	21,545	Tooele	6,923
Uintah	12,684	Vernal	4,487
Utah	137,776	Provo	2,014
Wasatch	5,863	Heber City	1,191
Washington	13,669	Saint George	2,427
Wayne	1,483	Loa	2,486
Weber	126,278	Ogden	581

Vermont

(14 counties, 9,267 sq. mi. land; pop. 444,732)

County	Pop. Apr. 1 1970	County Seat or Court House	Land Area Sq. MI.
Addison	24,266	Middlebury	784
Bennington	29,282	Bennington	672
Caledonia	22,789	Saint Johnsbury	612
Chittenden	99,131	Burlington	533
Essex	5,416	Guildhall	663
Franklin	31,282	Saint Albans	660
Grand Isle	3,574	North Hero	83
Lamoille	13,309	Hyde Park	474
Orange	17,676	Chelsea	690
Orleans	20,153	Newport	715
Rutland	52,637	Rutland	927
Washington	47,659	Montpelier	707
Windham	33,476	Newfane	784
Windsor	44,082	Woodstock	962

Virginia

(96 cos., 38 ind. cities, 39,780 sq. mi. land; pop. 4,648,494)

County	Pop. Apr. 1 1970	County Seat or Court House	Land Area Sq. MI.
Accomack	29,004	Accomac	476
Albemarle	37,780	Charlottesville	740
Alleghany	12,461	Covington	444
Amelia	7,592	Amelia, C. H.	366
Amherst	26,072	Amherst	470
Appomattox	9,784	Appomattox	345
Arlington	174,284	Arlington	26
Augusta	44,220	Staunton	986
Bath	5,192	Warm Springs	540
Bedford	26,728	Bedford	727
Bland	5,423	Bland	369
Botetourt	18,193	Fincastle	548
Brunswick	16,172	Lawrenceville	579
Buchanan	32,071	Grundy	508
Buckingham	10,597	Buckingham	582
Campbell	43,319	Rustburg	529
Caroline	13,925	Bowling Green	545
Carroll	23,092	Hillsville	494
Charles City	6,158	Charles City	181
Charlotte	12,366	Charlotte Courthouse	470
Chesterfield	77,045	Chesterfield	442
Clarke	8,102	Berryville	174
Craig	3,524	New Castle	336
Culpeper	18,218	Culpeper	389
Cumberland	6,179	Cumberland	291
Dickenson	16,077	Clintwood	332
Dinwiddie	25,046	Dinwiddie	507
Essex	7,099	Tappahannock	250
Fairfax	455,032	Fairfax	399
Fauquier	26,375	Warrenton	660
Floyd	9,775	Floyd	383
Fluvanna	7,621	Palmyra	288
Franklin	28,163	Rocky Mount	716
Frederick	28,893	Winchester	405
Giles	16,741	Pearisburg	363
Gloucester	14,059	Gloucester	228
Goochland	10,069	Goochland	289
Grayson	15,439	Independence	452
Greene	5,248	Stanardsville	153
Greensville	9,604	Emporia	299
Halifax	30,076	Halifax	796
Hanover	37,479	Hanover	465
Henrico	154,364	Richmond	229
Henry	50,901	Martinsville	381
Highland	2,529	Monterey	416
Isle of Wight	18,285	Isle of Wight	317
James City	17,853	Williamsburg	152
King and Queen	5,491	King and Queen	318
King George	8,039	King George	176
King William	7,497	King William	278
Lancaster	9,126	Lancaster	137
Lee	20,321	Jonesville	438
Loudoun	37,150	Leesburg	517
Louisa	14,004	Louisa	517
Lunenburg	11,687	Lunenburg	442
Madison	8,638	Madison	327
Mathews	7,168	Mathews	89
Mecklenburg	29,426	Boydton	612
Middlesex	6,295	Saluda	130
Montgomery	47,157	Christiansburg	394
*Nansemond	35,166	Suffolk	408
Nelson	11,702	Lovingston	471
New Kent	5,300	New Kent	210
Northampton	14,442	Eastville	220
Northumberland	9,239	Heathsville	190
Nottoway	14,260	Nottoway	308
Orange	13,792	Orange	355
Page	16,581	Luray	316
Patrick	15,282	Stuart	464
Pittsylvania	58,789	Chatham	1,001
Powhatan	7,696	Powhatan	269
Prince Edward	14,379	Farmville	357
Prince George	29,092	Prince George	276
Prince William	111,102	Manassas	347
Pulaski	29,564	Pulaski	328
Rappahannock	5,199	Washington	267
Richmond	6,504	Warsaw	190
Roanoke	67,339	Salem	262
Rockbridge	16,637	Lexington	601
Rockingham	47,890	Harrisonburg	865
Russell	24,533	Lebanon	483
Scott	24,376	Gate City	539
Shenandoah	22,852	Woodstock	507
Smyth	31,349	Marion	435
Southampton	18,582	Courtland	602
Spotsylvania	16,424	Spotsylvania	409
Stafford	24,587	Stafford	270
Surry	5,882	Surry	277
Sussex	11,464	Sussex	494
Tazewell	39,816	Tazewell	522

County	Pop. Apr. 1 1970	County Seat or Court House	Land Area Sq. Mi.
Warren	15,301	Front Royal	219
Washington	40,835	Abingdon	574
Westmoreland	12,142	Montross	229
Wise	35,947	Wise	412
Wythe	22,139	Wytheville	460
York	33,203	Yorktown	129

*1/1/74 merged with ind. city of Suffolk.

Independent Cities

County	Pop. Apr. 1 1970	County Seat or Court House	Land Area Sq. Mi.
Alexandria	110,927		15
Bedford	6,011		7
Bristol	14,857		4
Buena Vista	6,425		3
Charlottesville	38,880		10
Chesapeake	89,580		341
Clifton Forge	5,501		4
Colonial Heights	15,097		8
Covington	10,060		4
Danville	46,391		17
Emporia	5,300		2
Fairfax	21,970		6
Falls Church	10,772		2
Franklin	6,880		4
Fredericksburg	14,450		6
Galax	6,278		7
Hampton	120,779		55
Harrisonburg	14,605		6
Hopewell	23,471		9
Lexington	7,597		3
Lynchburg	54,083		25
Martinsville	19,653		11
Newport News	138,177		69
Norfolk	307,951		53
Norton	4,172		4
Petersburg	36,103		8
Portsmouth	110,963		29
Radford	11,596		5
Richmond	249,431		60
Roanoke	92,115		27
Salem	21,982		14
South Boston	6,889		5
Staunton	24,504		9
Suffolk	9,858		2
Virginia Beach	172,106		259
Waynesboro	16,707		7
Williamsburg	9,069		5
Winchester	14,643		3

Washington

(39 counties, 66,570 sq. mi. land; pop., 3,409,169)

County	Pop. Apr. 1 1970	County Seat or Court House	Land Area Sq. Mi.
Adams	12,014	Ritzville	1,894
Asotin	13,799	Asotin	633
Benton	67,540	Prosser	1,722
Chelan	41,103	Wenatchee	2,918
Clallam	34,770	Port Angeles	1,753
Clark	128,454	Vancouver	627
Columbia	4,439	Dayton	853
Cowlitz	68,616	Kelso	1,144
Douglas	16,787	Waterville	1,831
Ferry	3,655	Republic	2,202
Franklin	25,816	Pasco	1,253
Garfield	2,911	Pomeroy	709
Grant	41,881	Ephrata	2,675
Grays Harbor	59,553	Montesano	1,910
Island	27,011	Coupeville	212
Jefferson	10,661	Port Townsend	1,805
King	1,159,375	Seattle	2,128
Kitsap	101,732	Port Orchard	393
Kittitas	25,039	Ellensburg	2,317
Klickitat	12,138	Goldendale	1,908
Lewis	45,467	Chehalis	2,423
Lincoln	9,572	Davenport	2,306
Mason	20,918	Shelton	962
Okanogan	25,867	Okanogan	5,301
Pacific	15,796	South Bend	908
Pend Oreille	6,025	Newport	1,402
Pierce	411,027	Tacoma	1,676
San Juan	3,856	Friday Harbor	179
Skagit	52,381	Mount Vernon	1,735
Skamania	5,845	Stevenson	1,672
Snohomish	265,236	Everett	2,098
Spokane	287,487	Spokane	1,758
Stevens	17,405	Colville	2,481
Thurston	76,894	Olympia	714
Wahkiakum	3,592	Cathlamet	261
Walla Walla	42,176	Walla Walla	1,262
Whatcom	81,950	Bellingham	2,126
Whitman	37,900	Colfax	2,153
Yakima	144,971	Yakima	4,268

West Virginia

(55 counties, 24,070 sq. mi. land; pop., 1,744,237)

County	Pop. Apr. 1 1970	County Seat or Court House	Land Area Sq. Mi.
Barbour	14,030	Philippi	341
Berkeley	36,356	Martinsburg	316
Boone	2,118	Madison	501
Braxton	12,666	Sutton	511
Brooke	29,685	Wellsburg	88
Cabell	106,918	Huntington	279
Calhoun	7,046	Grantsville	281
Clay	9,330	Clay	343
Doddridge	6,389	West Union	319
Fayette	49,332	Fayetteville	663
Gilmer	7,782	Glenville	339
Grant	8,607	Petersburg	478
Greenbrier	32,090	Lewisburg	1,026
Hampshire	11,710	Romney	639
Hancock	39,749	New Cumberland	83
Hardy	8,855	Moorefield	585
Harrison	73,028	Clarksburg	418
Jackson	20,903	Ripley	461
Jefferson	21,280	Charles Town	211
Kanawha	229,515	Charleston	907
Lewis	17,847	Weston	392
Lincoln	18,912	Hamlin	438
Logan	46,269	Logan	456
McDowell	50,666	Welch	533
Marion	61,356	Fairmont	311
Marshall	37,598	Moundsville	304
Mason	24,306	Point Pleasant	433
Mercer	63,206	Princeton	417
Mineral	23,109	Keyser	330
Mingo	32,780	Williamson	423
Monongalia	63,714	Morgantown	365
Monroe	11,272	Union	473
Morgan	8,547	Berkeley Springs	233
Nicholas	22,552	Summersville	642
Ohio	64,197	Wheeling	106
Pendleton	7,031	Franklin	695
Pleasants	7,274	St. Marys	129
Pocahontas	8,870	Marlinton	943
Preston	25,455	Kingwood	645
Putnam	27,625	Winfield	348
Raleigh	70,080	Beckley	605
Randolph	24,596	Elkins	1,036
Ritchie	10,145	Harrisville	452
Roane	14,111	Spencer	486
Summers	13,213	Hinton	350
Taylor	13,878	Grafton	174
Tucker	7,447	Parsons	421
Tyler	9,929	Middlebourne	256
Upshur	19,092	Buckhannon	352
Wayne	37,581	Wayne	513
Webster	9,809	Webster Springs	551
Wetzel	20,314	New Martinsville	363
Wirt	4,154	Elizabeth	235
Wood	86,818	Parkersburg	368
Wyoming	30,095	Pineville	504

Wisconsin

(72 counties, 54,464 sq. mi. land, pop., 4,417,933)

County	Pop. Apr. 1 1970	County Seat or Court House	Land Area Sq. Mi.
Adams	9,234	Friendship	646
Ashland	16,743	Ashland	1,038
Barron	33,955	Barron	864
Bayfield	11,683	Washburn	1,460
Brown	158,244	Green Bay	524
Buffalo	13,743	Alma	711
Burnett	9,276	Grantsburg	840
Calumet	27,604	Chilton	322
Chippewa	47,717	Chippewa Falls	1,018
Clark	30,361	Neillsville	1,221
Columbia	40,150	Portage	776
Crawford	15,252	Prairie du Chien	568
Dane	290,272	Madison	1,198
Dodge	69,004	Juneau	889
Door	20,106	Sturgeon Bay	492
Douglas	44,657	Superior	1,305
Dunn	29,154	Menomonie	853
Eau Claire	67,219	Eau Claire	647
Florence	3,298	Florence	487
Fond Du Lac	84,567	Fond du Lac	725
Forest (1973)	8,265	Crandon	1,007
Grant	48,398	Lancaster	1,147
Green	26,714	Monroe	585
Green Lake	16,878	Green Lake	354
Iowa	19,306	Dodgeville	762
Iron	6,533	Hurley	747
Jackson	15,325	Black River Falls	999
Jefferson	60,060	Jefferson	564
Juneau	18,455	Mauston	774
Kenosha	117,917	Kenosha	272
Kewaunee	18,961	Kewaunee	330
La Crosse	80,468	La Crosse	451
Lafayette	17,456	Darlington	643
Langlade	19,220	Antigo	856
Lincoln	23,499	Merrill	892
Manitowoc	82,294	Manitowoc	590
Marathon	97,457	Wausau	1,586
Marinette	35,810	Marinette	1,378

County	Pop. Apr. 1 1970	County Seat or Court House	Land Area Sq. Mi.	County	Pop. Apr. 1 1970	County Seat or Court House	Land Area Sq. Mi.
Marquette	8,865	Montello	455	Waushara	14,795	Wautoma	627
Menominee	2,607	Keshena	360	Winnebago	129,946	Oshkosh	448
Milwaukee	1,054,249	Milwaukee	237	Wood	65,362	Wisconsin Rapids	807
Monroe	31,610	Sparta	915				
Oconto	25,553	Oconto	1,001				
Oneida	24,427	Rhinelander	1,112				
Outaramie	119,398	Appleton	634				

Wyoming
(23 counties, 97,203 sq. mi. land; pop., 332,416)

County	Pop. Apr. 1 1970	County Seat or Court House	Land Area Sq. Mi.
Ozaukee	54,461	Port Washington	236				

County	Pop. Apr. 1 1970	County Seat or Court House	Land Area Sq. Mi.
Pepin	7,319	Durand	235	Albany	26,431	Laramie	4,248
Pierce	26,652	Ellsworth	590	Big Horn	10,202	Basin	3,157
Polk	26,666	Balsam Lake	931	Campbell	12,957	Gillette	4,756
Portage	47,541	Stevens Point	806	Carbon	13,354	Rawlins	7,905
Price	14,520	Phillips	1,260	Converse	5,938	Douglas	4,281
Racine	170,838	Racine	337	Crook	4,535	Sundance	2,882
Richland	17,079	Richland Center	583	Fremont	28,352	Lander	9,106
Rock	131,970	Janesville	721	Goshen	10,885	Torrington	2,228
Rusk	14,238	Ladysmith	906	Hot Springs	4,952	Thermopolis	2,022
St. Croix	34,354	Hudson	734	Johnson	5,587	Buffalo	4,175
Sauk	39,057	Baraboo	841	Laramie	56,360	Cheyenne	2,703
Sawyer	9,670	Hayward	1,259	Lincoln	8,640	Kemmerer	4,085
Shawano	32,650	Shawano	919	Natrona	51,264	Casper	5,342
Sheboygan	96,660	Sheboygan	505	Niobrara	2,924	Lusk	2,614
Taylor	16,958	Medford	975	Park	17,752	Cody	6,959
Trempealeau	23,344	Whitehall	735	Platte	6,486	Wheatland	2,086
Vernon	24,557	Viroqua	802	Sheridan	17,852	Sheridan	2,532
Vilas	10,958	Eagle River	867	Sublette	3,755	Pinedale	4,851
Walworth	63,444	Elkhorn	557	Sweetwater	18,391	Green River	10,429
Washburn	10,601	Shell Lake	817	Teton	4,823	Jackson	4,000
Washington	63,839	West Bend	429	Uinta	7,100	Evanston	2,086
Waukesha	231,338	Waukesha	554	Washakie	7,569	Worland	2,262
Waupaca	37,780	Waupaca	751	Weston	6,307	Newcastle	2,407

1970 Population of Outlying Areas
Source: Bureau of the Census

Puerto Rico

Zip Code	Municipios	Pop. April 1	Land Area Sq. Mile	Zip Code	Municipios	Pop. April 1	Land Area Sq. Mile	Zip Code	Municipios	Pop. April 1	Land Area Sq. Mile
00601	Adjuntas	18,691	66	00653	Guanica	14,889	37	00720	Orocovis	20,201	63
00602	Aguada	25,658	30	00654	Guayama	36,249	65	00723	Patillas	17,828	48
00603	Aguadilla	51,355	36	00656	Guayanilla	18,144	42	00724	Penuelas	15,973	44
00607	Aguas Buenas	18,600	30	00657	Guaynabo	67,042	27	00731	Ponce	158,981	116
00609	Aibonito	20,044	31	00658	Gurabo	18,289	28	00742	Quebradillas	15,582	23
00610	Anasco	19,416	40	00659	Hatillo	21,913	42	00743	Rincon	9,094	14
00612	Arecibo	73,468	127	00660	Hormigueros	10,827	11	00745	Rio Grande	22,032	61
00615	Arroyo	13,033	15	00661	Humacao	36,023	45	00747	Sabana Grande	16,343	37
00617	Barceloneta	20,792	34	00662	Isabela	30,430	56	00751	Salinas	21,837	69
00618	Barranquitas	20,118	33	00664	Jayuya	13,588	39	00753	San German	27,990	54
00619	Bayamon	156,192	44	00665	Juana Diaz	36,270	61	00936	San Juan	463,242	47
00623	Cabo Rojo	26,060	72	00666	Juncos	21,814	26	00754	San Lorenzo	27,755	53
00625	Caguas	95,661	58	00667	Lajas	16,545	60	00755	San Sebastian	30,157	71
00627	Camuy	19,922	46	00669	Lares	25,263	62	00757	Santa Isabel	16,056	34
00630	Carolina	107,643	48	00670	Las Marias	7,841	44	00758	Toa Alta	18,964	27
00632	Catano	26,459	5	00671	Las Piedras	18,112	33	00759	Toa Baja	46,384	24
00633	Cayey	38,432	50	00672	Loiza	39,062	53	00760	Tujillo Alto	30,669	21
00635	Ceiba	18,312	27	00673	Luquillo	10,390	26	00761	Utuado	35,494	115
00638	Ciales	15,595	66	00701	Manati	30,559	46	00762	Vega Alta	22,810	28
00639	Cidra	23,892	36	00706	Maricao	5,991	37	00763	Vega Baja	35,327	47
00640	Coamo	26,468	77	00707	Maunabo	10,792	21	00765	Vieques	7,767	52
00642	Comerio	18,819	28	00708	Mayaguez	85,857	77	00766	Villalba	18,733	37
00643	Corozal	24,545	42	00716	Moca	22,361	51	00767	Yabucoa	30,165	55
00645	Culebra	732	10	00717	Morovix	19,059	39	00768	Yauco	35,103	68
00646	Dorado	17,388	23	00718	Naguabo	17,996	52				
00648	Faiardo	23,032	31	00719	Naranjito	19,913	28	**Total**		**2,712,033**	**3,421**

Zip Code	Area	Pop. April 1	Land Area Sq. Mile	Zip Code	Area	Pop. April 1	Land Area Sq. Mile	Zip Code	Area	Pop. April 1	Land Area Sq. Mile
	American Samoa				Dededo	10,780	30		**Virgin Islands**		
96920	American Samoa	27,159	76		Inarajan	1,897	19		St. Croix	31,779	80
					Mangilao	3,228	10	00830	St. John	1,729	20
	Canal Zone				Merizo	1,529	6	00801	St. Thomas	28,960	32
	Canal Zone	44,198	362		Mongmong-Too-Maite	6,057	2	00801	Charlotte Amalie	12,220	
	Balboa	32,552	222		Piti	1,284	7	00820	Christiansted	3,020	
	Cristobal	11,646	140		Santa Rita	8,109	17	00840	Frederiksted	1,531	
					Sinajana	3,506	1		**Total**	**62,468**	**132**
	Guam				Talofofo	1,935	17				
96910	Guam	84,996	209		Tamuning	10,218	6		**Trust Territory of Pacific Islands**		
	Agana	2,119	1		Umatac	813	6		Mariana district	9,640	184
	Agana Hts.	3,156	1		Yigo	11,542	35		Marshall district	22,888	70
	Agat	4,308	10		Yona	2,599	20		Palau district	11,210	192
	Asan	2,629	6						Ponape district	18,536	176
	Barrigada	6,356	9						Truk district	21,041	49
	Chalan-Pago-Ordot	2,931	6						Yap district	7,625	46
									Total	**90,940**	**717**

Women in 1976: Progress (?) Report

By Hana Umlauf

When television personality Barbara Walters accepted an offer from ABC to be the first woman to co-anchor an evening network news program, she also became the highest paid newscaster in the world, earning $1,000,000 per year. Her ability to draw such a formidable salary, however, is hardly typical of the American woman worker. Despite some conspicuous gains for women in employment, the gap between the average income of full-time working women and men continues to grow.

Although the number of women working has doubled since 1950, the Census Bureau reports that in 1974 the median income for women was $6,957 or only 57% of the average take-home pay of the typical American male worker, $12,152. Just four years earlier, in 1970, the average working woman earned $5,440 or 59% of the median income for men, $9,184.

The Census Bureau, however, took an optimistic view of the statistics in its report, "A Statistical Portrait of Women in the U.S.," issued in April 1976. It states that the decline was "probably" due to the dramatic increase in the number of women working. Bureau officials predicted that the gap would gradually close as women increased their educational and vocational skills and, consequently, move into higher-paying positions. Currently, most women entering the job market take lower-paying clerical and service positions. This tends to pull the median wage down. Women in these lower-paying positions still comprise over half of the female work force today.

Statistical Portrait of Women

Beyond income data, the Census Bureau's report drew a comprehensive statistical portrait of women in the United States. As of July 1975, females outnumbered males — 109.4 million to 103.8 million — in the U.S. Projections estimated that the female majority will increase to a range of 6.9 to 7.9 million by the year 2000. This numerical superiority is partly explained by women's greater life expectancy. Women live an average of 75.3 years, exceeding the average lifespan of men by almost 8 years.

The report also indicated that the relationship between employment and traditional variables, such as marital status and the presence and age of children, has changed dramatically. While in 1950 only 12% of working women were married with preschool children, 35% of women workers fell into that category in 1975. In 1975, 13% of all families were headed by women. Below the poverty level, 46% of all families were headed by women in 1974.

An increasing proportion of young women in the U.S. remain single or are divorced. Reflecting recent trends in marriage and divorce, the percentage of women aged 20 to 24 who were single rose from 28% to 40% from 1950 to 1975.

New Approach for Women

This statistical portrait, characterized by some profound changes in the traditional social and economic role of women, supports the basic thesis of feminist Betty Friedan. That thesis states that the rapid entry of women into the job market during the last decade was bound to force further changes in the lifestyle of both American men and women. Although the women's liberation movement played a crucial role during the past decade, Friedan believes women must now change course in order to achieve further economic gains. "The women's movement was only a way station," Friedan told a Ford Foundation-sponsored conference on "Women and the American Economy" at Harrison, N. Y., in November 1975. She added, "The questions we face cannot be solved by women alone." Friedan urged women to turn to the rest of society to find new allies and to develop innovative ideas to reform fundamental social institutions.

Friedan also expressed concern about the apparent collision between the aspirations of an increasingly larger number of women and an "erosion" in support for affirmative action programs and equal rights. This erosion is laid to the attempt of anti-feminist groups to use the nation's high unemployment rate to persuade women to leave the labor force. For more than half of working women, Friedan stressed, there simply is no alternative — they must remain in the work force to support themselves and their families. The conference of academicians, businessmen, lawyers, and public officials, specifically recommended that "highest priority" be given to a national policy to achieve full employment. The conference also stated that it was time for society to accept financial responsibility for educating preschool children just as it does school-age children.

Major Bias Suits Settled

The recent settlement of several major antidiscrimination suits lodged by women and minority group workers boded well for closing the income gap in some important areas.

In early June 1976, the nation's largest brokerage concern, Merrill Lynch, Pierce, Fenner and Smith, agreed to settle two suits brought by the Equal Employment Opportunity Commission (EEOC). In the first — which charged the firm had followed a "practice and pattern" of discrimination in its recruitment, hiring, job assignment, promotion, testing, and maternal leave policies — Merrill Lynch agreed to pay $1.9 million to individuals it had wrongfully failed to hire or promote. The firm also agreed to establish a $1.3 million 5-year affirmative action program to employ more women and minority group members and to change maternity leave policies. In the second suit, Helen B. O'Bannon, currently a member of the Pennsylvania Public Utility Commission, was awarded $10,000 in compensation for being unlawfully refused a job as an account executive, the highest category of brokerage salesperson. Her lawyer was awarded $182,000 for fees and expenses. EEOC general counsel Abner W. Sibal was optimistic that the decisions would have a "constructive impact" on other companies in the securities industry that "have yet to institute affirmative measures toward complying with equal opportunity law."

In February 1976, Rogers and Wells, a major New York City law firm, settled a sex-discrimination suit by agreeing to a quota system. The system requires the firm to offer jobs to women based on the percentages of women in graduating classes of law schools from which they recruit new lawyers. Specifically, according to the settlement, in the next 3 years, the percentage of women receiving job offers must be at least 20% higher than the percentage of women in the graduating classes of law schools. Rogers and Wells also agreed to offer the same terms to similarly qualified men and women and to assign work without regard to sex, stating that "sex is not permissible criterion in determining remuneration and advancement."

Affirmative Action in Education Lagging

Unlike the law and securities fields, there is not encouraging news to report from the nation's colleges and universities. Five years after the beginning of the federal government's affirmative action program to hire more women and minority faculty members, the U.S. Civil Rights Office has approved affirmative action programs for only 31 of the nation's eligible colleges and universities. Nor has any institution lost its federal funding — as the law provides — for failing to comply with the law. Nor is there any competent monitoring system of approved plans to assure compliance.

In fact, according to the U.S. Office of Education, women faculty members lost ground in both salary increases and rank in 1975. "The average salaries of men continue to exceed the average salaries of women at every rank and at every institutional level, in both publicly and privately controlled institutions," the education office stated. The average women's salary at a public institution was $14,710, while the average male faculty member's salary was $17,558. At private colleges and universities, the average salaries were $12,968 for women and $16,676 for men.

Walter J. Leonard, the affirmative action coordinator at Harvard University, feels the problem lies with the federal government: "There is clearly a retreat in Washington from affirmative action." Dr. Bernice Sandler, director of the Project on the Status of Women for the Association of American Colleges, feels there has been progress in attitudes if not in numbers. "A lot of overt discriminatory policies and practices are pretty much going by the boards," she stated.

More encouraging is the news that in 1976-77, Rhodes Scholarships will be offered to women for the first time. Also, in February 1976, the Harvard Law Review, one of the most influential legal journals in the U.S., elected its first woman president, Susan Estrich. Although she believes she was chosen on merit alone, Estrich said her election reflected a "long process" at Harvard of breaking down sexual stereotypes. As president, she has final editorial responsibility for anything published in the journal.

Few Women Office Holders

Women hold less than 5% of all elective offices in the United States, according to a study by the Center for the American Woman and Politics at Rutgers University, the study, the first complete count of all elected women officials in the U.S., also indicated that women even hold only a small portion of those offices generally believed to be more open to women. For instance, women comprised only 13% of elected school board officials, 4% of state senators, and 9% of the members of the lower houses of state legislatures.

In January 1976, more than 500 women from the Washington, D.C., area met at a conference sponsored by the Washington Institute for Women in Politics to debate the problem of involving more women in the political process. A majority of the participants felt that women could not become influential in politics unless they worked long hours. Ann Lewis, the deputy campaign manager for Birch Bayh, commented that political decisions "aren't made until night when the telephones quiet down" and "to the extent that people get to seeing you at night, the more they accept you."

One woman, Mary King, Jimmy Carter's chief adviser on women, has taken a very positive approach to introducing more women into public office. She is director of the newly formed "Committee of 51.3%" (the percentage of women in the U.S. population), a group of women officials and leaders who, if Carter wins the presidency, will advise him on national issues and help him search for qualified women to fill government posts. King is using the "ice-pick" system, that is, reducing thousands of resumes to computerized cards because, she says, "I want to make sure that for every appointment Carter makes as President he will have the resume of at least one completely qualified woman."

America's 25 Most Influential Women

The following women, listed alphabetically, were chosen by: Jane O'Reilly, syndicated columnist for the Washington Star and NEA; Jacqueline Wexler, president of Hunter College; Otto Zausmer, associate editor of The Boston Globe; Clayton Kirkpatrick, editor of The Chicago Tribune; Helen Thomas, UPI White House Correspondent; Mike Grehl, editor of the Memphis Commercial-Appeal; Pia Lindstrom, NBC News correspondent; Walt Friedenberg, editor of The Cincinnati Post; Paul Conroy, editor of The San Jose Mercury; and Hana Umlauf, associate editor of The World Almanac.

Bella Abzug, Democratic Congresswoman from New York City since 1970, has become a national figure in Congress.

Carla Anderson Hills, secretary of Housing and Urban Development, also served as an assistant attorney general in charge of the Justice Department's civil division.

Anne Armstrong, U.S. Ambassador to Great Britain, a Texas Republican, was Republican National Committee co-chairman and a White House Counselor.

Helen Gurley Brown, editor of Cosmopolitan since 1965, was an advertising copywriter when she wrote the bestseller, "Sex and the Single Girl."

Shirley Chisholm, Congresswoman (D., N.Y.) was the first major party black woman presidential candidate in 1972.

Joan Ganz Cooley, head of the Children's Television Workshop, with "Sesame Street" and "The Electric Company," brought a fresh concept to children's television.

Charlotte Curtis, Op-Ed page editor of The New York Times since 1973, joined The Times in 1961 where, as family/style editor, she broke the mold of society writing.

Betty Ford, as First Lady, has spoken out on her interest in the arts and in underprivileged and retarded children.

Betty Friedan, author of "The Feminine Mystique," was a founding member of the National Organization for Women and the National Woman's Caucus.

Katherine Graham, publisher of The Washington Post, also controls the parent company which owns Newsweek and radio and television stations.

Ella Grasso, Democratic Governor of Connecticut, has served Connecticut as a state representative and secretary of state, and in the U.S. Congress.

Nancy Hanks, chairman of the National Endowment for the Arts and National Council for the Arts since 1969. also directed a socio-economic study of the arts in America.

Lenore Hershey, editor of the Ladies' Home Journal, was influential in the creation of the federal government's Advisory Committee on the Economic Role of Women.

Lady Bird Johnson, former First Lady, has been active in environmental and national beautification projects.

Barbara Jordan, Congresswoman (D., Tex.), serves on the Judiciary Committee and, in 1976, ignited the Democratic National Convention with her keynote address.

Billie Jean King, tennis star and 5-time Wimbledon champion, has boosted interest in women's tennis and helped build purses on the women's tour to near those of men.

Coretta King, civil rights leader, has become increasingly prominent since the assassination of her husband, Rev. Dr. Martin Luther King Jr.

Mary Wells Lawrence, chairman of the board of Wells, Rich, Greene, a New York City advertising agency, has won wide acclaim for her achievements in advertising.

Margaret Mead, anthropologist, has studied 7 cultures, written 17 books, and is a major intellectual force.

Mary McGrory, a nationally-syndicated political columnist for The Washington Star, won a Pulitzer Prize in 1975.

Sylvia Porter, financial and consumer columnist since 1939, today appears in more than 340 newspapers.

Gloria Steinem, feminist, an articulate spokeswoman for the rights of women and blacks, helped found Ms magazine and the National Women's Political Caucus.

Helen Thomas, White House Correspondent for United Press International, joined UPI as a wire service reporter in 1943.

Abigail Van Buren, personal advice columnist, has written "Dear Abby" since 1956 and now appears in newspapers all over the world.

Barbara Walters, television anchorwoman, became the first woman to anchor a national evening news program.

Federal and State Indian Reservations

Source: U. S. Dept. of Commerce (data as of circa Dec., 1972)

State	No. of Reservations	Tribally-owned Acreage[1]	Alloted Acreage[1]	No. of Tribes[3]	No. of Persons[4]	Avg. Unemp. Rate%[5]	Major Tribes
Alaska	13[2]	(2)	(2)	6	35,817	NA	Eskimo, Tlingit, Haida, Aleut, Athapascan[6]
Arizona	17	23,467,727	892,917	13	173,412	41	Navaho, Apache, Papago, Hopi, Pima
California	76	386,954	67,390	(7)	6,905	45	Quechan, Hoopa, Paiute, mission bands[7]
Colorado	2	888,155	14,425	1	2,144	37	Ute
Connecticut	4	795	—	3	25	NA	Pequot, Mohegan[8]
Florida	5	183,319	—	2	1,511	31	Seminole, Miccosukee[9]
Idaho	4	274,428	36,723	5	4,849	36	Shoshone, Bannock, Nez Perce
Iowa	1	3,476	—	1	561	35	Sac and Fox[10]
Kansas	4	2,436	24,030	5	3,009	10	Potawatomi, Kickapoo, Iowa
Louisiana	1	262	—	1	268	NA	Chitimacha
Maine	3	27,546	—	2	1,077	45	Passamaquoddy, Penobscot
Massachusetts	1	12	—	1	1	0	Hassanamisco-Nipmuk[11]
Michigan	5	4,425	12,210	2	2,069	38	Chippewa, Potawatami
Minnesota	11	682,534	50,935	2	10,739	40	Chippewa, Sioux
Mississippi	1	17,381	209	1	3,294	10	Choctaw
Montana	7	1,792,383	3,279,926	10	24,137	38	Blackfeet, Sioux, Crow, Assiniboine, Cheyenne
Nebraska	3	27,193	45,467	3	2,601	62	Omaha, Winnebago, Santee Sioux
Nevada	23	1,133,529	32,691	3	4,784	46	Paiute, Shoshone, Washoe
New Mexico	24	3,329,270	119,877	7	30,125	43	Keresan, Zuni, Apache, Tanoan, Navajo[12]
New York	9	88,158	—	7	11,616	27	Seneca, Mohawk, Onondaga, Oneida[13]
North Carolina	1	56,573	—	1	4,880	21	Cherokee
North Dakota	4	375,936	996,744	5	16,735	41	Chippewa, Sioux, Mandan, Arikara, Hidatsa
Oklahoma[14]	(14)	56,741	991,715	27	80,994	24	Cherokee, Creek, Choctaw, Chicasaw, Cheyenne, Arapaho[14]
Oregon	4	495,842	165,778	8	2,718	41	Warm Springs, Wasco, Paiute, Umatilla
South Dakota	8	1,807,623	2,371,427	1	29,119	37	Sioux
Texas	2	4,400	—	3	1,000	30	Tigua (Pueblo), Alabama, Coushatta
Utah	4	1,095,531	48,095	3	1,961	36	Ute, Southern Paiute, Goshute
Virginia	2	925	—	1	110	NA	Algonquian
Washington	22	1,920,850	537,876	20	18,138	45	Yakima, Confederated, Lummi, Quinault
Wisconsin	10	61,911	82,977	6	7,497	38	Chippewa, Oneida, Winnegabo
Wyoming	1	1,776,136	109,344	2	4,435	47	Shoshone, Arapaho

[1]Approximations. Ownership of reservation land is very complex. Most tribally-owned land listed here is owned by tribal organizations, but some of it is held in trust by the government and some is leased to or occupied by non-Indians. Government-owned land, even that held for the exclusive use of Indians, and non-Indian land formally included in reservations is not counted here.
Allotted land was land held by Indian individuals or families. The Department of Commerce data is not clear on whether all land listed as alloted is still securely held by Indians.

[2]Alaskan Indian affairs are handled under the Native Claims Settlement Act (Dec. 18, 1971). The act provides for the establishment of regional and village corporations to conduct business for profit. There are 12 regional corporations. Within each regional corporation, village corporations must be organized. These village corporations then receive title to lands previously held in reservations. There were approximately 2.5 million acres in reservations subject to the Settlement Act. Another 86,471 acres remain outside the Act in the Annette Island Reserve. Latest figures show that 5,687 acres have been assigned to village corporations, while an additional 13,490 acres have been surveyed but not yet assigned.

[3]The concept of "tribe" is, in many cases, a white man's invention and, at first, was used to define loosely associated Indians with cultural similarities. Today, "tribe" is a formal status of Indians organized by law. Some present day "tribes", such as the Blackfeet are really confederacies of smaller groups. The Alaskan natives are organized, on paper, into general linguistic groups.

[4]Unemployment rate of Indians living on or adjacent to reservations. When these figures are compared to 1970 census figures, it appears that nearly 64% of Indians are living on or near reservations.

[5]Unemployment rate of Indian labor force living on or adjacent to reservations.

[6]Aleuts and Eskimos are racially and linguistically related. Athapascans are related to the Navaho and Apache Indians.

[7]Many California Indians are historically associated with groups which settled near Spanish missions where much of the traditional culture was destroyed. Many of these bands, however, still retain some of their Indian language and customs. Excluding the bands, there are 22 tribes represented on California reservations.

[8]The Mohegan or Mohican are a branch of the Pequot.

[9]"Seminole" means "runaways" and these Indians from various tribes were originally refugees from whites in the Carolinas and Georgia. Later joined by runaway slaves, the Seminole were united by their hostility to the United States. Formal peace with the Seminoles in Florida was not achieved until 1934. The Miccosukee are a branch of the Seminole; they retain their Indian religion and have not made formal peace with the U.S.

[10]Once two tribes, the Sac and Fox formed a political alliance in 1734.

[11]Reservation prior to 1728 consisted of 8,000 acres. The land was sold to whites who put the Indians' money in a bank. Over the years the money was "lost" or "borrowed." In 1848, the state granted 11.9 acres to one Indian family of which there are about 20 direct descendants today.

[12]Tanoan, Keresan, and Zuni are all pueblo-dwelling Indians.

[13]These 4 tribes along with the Cayuga and Tuscarora made up the Iroquois League, which ruled large portions of New York, New England, and Pennsylvania and ranged into the Mid-West and South. The Onondaga, who traditionally provide the president of the League, maintain that they are a foreign nation within New York and the U.S.

[14]Indian land status in Oklahoma is unique and there are no reservations in the sense that the term is used elsewhere in the U.S. Likewise, many of the Oklahoma tribes are unique in their high degree of assimilation to the white culture.

Off-Beat News Stories of 1976

In 1976, the Soviet Union contributed, as usual, its share, or more than its share, of off-beat, zany news.

One Russian citizen copped what must surely be the all-time nepotism championship, putting more relatives on the payroll of the Ukraine Agricultural Academy than most folks have. Dean V. Yruchishin, investigation showed, hired no fewer than 160 of his relatives on his teaching staff. He was also accused of "borrowing" works from other scientists for his doctorate thesis and permitting widespread cheating. The Communist party paper Pravda reported his punishment: he was expelled from the Communist party.

Truly hairy troubles were encountered by Mrs. Lidia Pavlova of Orsk, who now wears a wig. On a visit to far-off Alma Ata, near the Chinese border, she dropped into the "beauty" parlor at the railway station to have her waves restored after her long train trip. The Kazakhstan edition of Pravda reported that when she woke the next day she had neither curls nor half her hair. When she stepped into the street, the rest of her hair blew away with the breeze. The head cosmetician told her it wasn't unusual, it was a matter of chance whether his "special chemical treatment" produced a head of beautiful curls or a bald one. "Don't worry," he added, "it will grow back again in 6 months."

The rest of the world strove to keep up with the interesting pace set by the Soviets.

Love Letters Pay Off

A young man in Taipei, Taiwan, wrote 700 letters to his girl during the past 2 years, proposing marriage. His persistence brought results.

A Taipei newspaper reported that the woman became engaged to the postman who faithfully delivered all the letters.

Another surprise ending hit John Gunset of Omaha, Neb., who was stranded on Interstate 74 near Crawfordsville, Ind., after his car stalled. He broadcast a citizen band radio call for help. A driver stopped on the other side of the highway, walked across, pulled a knife and robbed Gunset of $54.

Bedford, England, contributed the story of Judge Robert Lymbery, who also suffered a surprise. The judge overruled a lower court's order that a 168-lb. Great Dane be destroyed. Then he gave the dog a friendly pat. The big beast promptly bit the judge's hand.

Bathtub Suds

Customs officials in Munich, West Germany, nabbed 5 students brewing English beer in a university bathtub. They charged them with violating a medieval law guarding the purity of German beer.

Mixed-up Medics. A Miami jury awarded $125,000 to Mrs. Evelyn Kazdan, who charged that a team of physicians at a local hospital performed surgery on her right knee, when it was her left knee that needed it.

Medical Mixup. The Seattle Fire Department computer, in its yearly report, said department personnel had delivered 6 babies: 5 to women and one to a man. "Either the computer goofed or one delivery made medical history," the department newsletter said.

Staggering Statistics

Women nabbed for drunken driving got some advice from Rutgers University researchers. Never argue with the cop, they said. Their statistics showed most intoxicated drivers arrested were men, but they found indications that this might only be because police were reluctant to arrest women — except when they aggravated the situation by arguing or becoming abusive.

"Helping" the Odds. The Philadelphia Flyers hockey team had Kate Smith; when she sang "God Bless America" the team always won. The Boston Red Sox had a witch to cast spells on other teams. Both "assistants" had successful but brief runs. In Tanzania, the National Soccer Assn. hired a witch doctor to accompany the team on out-of-town games. When the government, which takes such things seriously, found out, it fired the whole committee.

Sportsmanship. Hockey player Dan Maloney of the Detroit Red Wings was arrested and tried on a charge of assault for brawling with a Maple Leafs player during a game. The jury found him not guilty but added: "While our verdict was based on the evidence and the law . . . we hope these actions do not continue in future." Translation: "not guilty but don't do it again."

Living Junkyard. That's what surgeons called the man they operated on at New York's Metropolitan Hospital. They suspected an abdominal tumor; what they found was over 500 metal objects, including 300 quarters, pennies, and subway tokens, can openers, parts of knives, forks, spoons, nuts, bolts, a chain and keys, and a broken thermometer. The doctors reported the 38-year-old human vacuum cleaner suffered no internal damage.

Animal Absurdities

A berserk bunny bugged service on London's central subway when he jumped into a cab and bit, clawed and scratched the driver. It happened on an elevated suburban stretch of track and tied up 6 trains.

Calcutta police had to kill a 14-ft. python which was swallowing an owl (always a slow business) on an airport runway and delaying an Air India plane waiting to land.

Rats with high blood pressure were warned by Long Island University scientists not to ride New York's subways. The noise, vibration and crowding could kill them before their time, said the good doctors, after exhaustive testing. New York people rose in wrath (no pun). Said one: "At least rats don't have to pay for this abuse. And they probably don't mind riding in the dark — a frequent occurrence. How about someone worrying about us?"

Out of their skulls. UCLA researchers wondered why woodpeckers don't get headaches from bashing their beaks into trees all day and "why the countryside is not littered with dazed and dying woodpeckers." The birds' skulls, they found, are of dense, spongy bone surrounded by shock-absorbing muscles. They said football etc. helmets might be made similarly and be safer.

Snake breaks leg. In Atlanta, a woman seeing a snake in her kitchen, screamed. Her husband, taking a shower, ran in dripping, stepped on their dog, who howled. The snake slithered under a cabinet, the husband knelt down to look for it; the dog touched the husband with its cold nose; the husband, thinking it was the snake, passed out cold. The wife phoned an ambulance, the husband said he was OK; the ambulance men insisted he might have had a heart attack and put him on a stretcher; as they lifted it, the snake came out again, one ambulance man dropped the stretcher, the husband fell out and broke his leg. Snakes are supposed to bite legs, not break them.

Crazy Crime

Making like Robin Hood, a Staten Island, N.Y., housewife repulsed an intruder with her husband's trusty bow and arrow. Husband John, a huntsman, was away when Mrs. Grace Lisk heard a prowler in the cellar. She grabbed one of John's bows, fitted an arrow, and let fly. The steel-tipped shaft hit the man in the shoulder, he yelled "Ouch," and fled. Mrs. Lisk ran to a neighbor who told police: "She was real excited."

A bumbling bank robber was nabbed when he fled from a Bowery bank in N.Y. City and tried to stash his loot in a trash can behind a building. It turned out to be Police Headquarters and one of the men spotted and grabbed the robber . . . and the loot.

UNITED STATES GOVERNMENT

The Ford Administration
As of June 11, 1976

Terms of office of the president and vice president, from Jan. 20, 1973 to Jan. 20, 1977. No person may be elected president of the United States for more than 2 4-year terms.

PRESIDENT — Gerald R. Ford of Michigan. Receives salary of $200,000 a year taxable, and in addition an expense allowance, also taxable, of $50,000 to assist in defraying expenses resulting from his official duties. Also there may be expended not exceeding $100,000, non-taxable, a year for travel expenses and official entertainment. Congress has provided lifetime pensions of $60,000 a year, free mailing privileges, free office space, and up to $90,000 a year for office help for ex-Presidents and $20,000 annually for their widows.

VICE PRESIDENT — Nelson A. Rockefeller, N. Y., salary $65,625 a year and $10,000 for expenses, all of which is taxable.

For succession to presidency, see Succession in Index.

The Cabinet
(Salaries $63,000 each)

Secretary of State — Henry A. Kissinger, Wash., D.C.
Secretary of Treasury — William E. Simon, N.J.
Secretary of Defense — Donald H. Rumsfeld, Ill.
Attorney General — Edward H. Levi, Ill.
Secretary of Interior — Thomas S. Kleppe, N.D.
Secretary of Agriculture — Earl L. Butz, Ind.
Secretary of Commerce — Elliot L. Richardson, Mass.
Secretary of Labor — W. J. Usery Jr., Ga.
Secretary of Health, Education, and Welfare — Forrest D. Mathews, Ala.
Secretary of Housing and Urban Development — Carla Anderson Hills, Cal.
Secretary of Transportation — William T. Coleman Jr., Pa.

The White House Staff
1600 Pennsylvania Ave. NW 20500

Counselor to the President — Robert Hartmann.
Assistant to the President — Richard Cheney.
Press Secretary to the President — Ronald H. Nessen.
Counsel to the President — Philip Buchen.
Personal Assistant to the President — Mildred Leonard.
Press Secretary to the First Lady — Sheila Weidenfeld.
Physician to the President — Rear Adm. William M. Lukash, USN.
Chief Usher — Rex W. Scouten.

Executive Agencies

National Security Council — Assistant to the President for Natl. Security Affairs—Brent Scowcroft.
Council of Economic Advisers—Alan Greenspan.
Council on Environmental Quality—Dr. Russell W. Peterson, chairman.
Central Intelligence Agency—George Bush, director.
Office of Management and Budget—James T. Lynn, director.
Special Representative for Trade Negotiations—Frederick B. Dent.

Department of State
2201 C St. NW 20520

Secretary of State — Henry A. Kissinger.
Deputy Secretary — Charles W. Robinson.
Under Sec. for Political Affairs — Joseph J. Sisco.
Under Sec. for Security Assistance — Carlysle E. Maw.
Deputy Under Secretaries — vacant (for economic affairs), Lawrence S. Eagleburger (for management).
Ambassadors at Large — U. Alexis Johnson, Ellsworth Bunker, Robert J. McCloskey, T. Vincent Learson.
Counselor — Helmut Sonnenfeldt.
Legal Advisor — Monroe Leigh.
Director of Policy Planning Staff — Winston Lord.
Assistant Secretaries for:
  Administration — John M. Thomas.
  African Affairs — William E. Schaufele Jr.
  Congressional Relations — Robert J. McCloskey.
  Economic Affairs — Jose A. Greenwald.
  Educational & Cultural Affairs — John Richardson.
  European Affairs — Arthur A. Hartman.
  East Asian & Pacific Affairs — Philip C. Habib.
  Internatl. Organization Affairs — Saul W. Lewis.
  Inter-American Affairs — William D. Rogers.
  Near-Eastern & S. Asian Affairs — Alfred L. Atherton Jr.
  Public Affairs — John E. Reinhardt.
Bureau of Security & Consular Affairs — Leonard F. Walentynowicz, administrator.
Inspector General, Foreign Assistance — John A. Shaw.
Chief of Protocol — Shirley Temple Black (nominee).
Dir. General, Foreign Service — Carol C. Laise.
Dir. of Intelligence & Research — Harold H. Saunders.
Bureau of Oceans and Internatl Environmental and Scientific Affairs — Assistant Sec. Frederick Irving.
Dir. of Politico-Military Affairs — George S. Vest.
Insp. Gen. Foreign Service — Robert M. Sayre.
Foreign Service Inst. — Howard E. Sollenberger, director.
Agency for Internatl. Development — Daniel Parker, administrator.
ACTION — Michael P. Balzano.
U.S. Rep. to the UN and Rep. in the Security Council — William Scranton, ambassador.

Treasury Department
15th St. & Pennsylvania Ave. NW 20220

Secretary of the Treasury — William E. Simon.
Deputy Sec. of the Treasury — George H. Dixon.
Under Sec. for Monetary Affairs — Edwin H. Yeo.
Under Sec. — Jerry Thomas.
General Counsel — Richard Albrecht.
Assistant Secretaries: David R. Macdonald, Warren F. Brecht, Gerald L. Parsky, Sidney L. Jones, Harold F. Eberle, Charles M. Walker, David Mosso.
Special Assistants to the Secretary: William F. Rhatican (public affairs), William N. Morell (national security).
Bureaus:
  Alcohol, Tobacco, and Firearms — Rex D. Davis, director.
  Consolidated Federal Law Enforcement Training Center — Arthur F. Brandstatter, director.
  Comptroller of the Currency — James E. Smith.
  Customs — Vernon D. Acree, commissioner.
  Engraving & Printing — James A. Conlon, director.
  Internal Revenue Service — Donald C. Alexander, commissioner.
  Mint — Mrs. Mary T. Brooks, director.
  Public Debt — H. J. Hintgen, commissioner.
  Treasurer of the U. S. — Francine I. Neff.
  U. S. Savings Bonds — Francine I. Neff, national director.
  U. S. Secret Service — H. Stuart Knight, director.

Department of Defense
The Pentagon 20301

Secretary of Defense — Donald H. Rumsfeld.
Principal Deputy Sec. — William P. Clements Jr.
Deputy Sec. — Robert Ellsworth.
Dir. of Def. Research and Engineering — Dr. Malcolm R. Currie.
Asst. Secretaries of Defense:
  Comptroller — Terrence E. McClary.
  Installations & Logistics — Frank Schrontz.
  Intelligence — Vacant.
  Internatl. Security — Eugene McAuliffe.
  Legislative Affairs — Vacant.
  Manpower & Reserve — William K. Brehm.
  Public Affairs — William I. Greener Jr.
  General Counsel — Richard Wiley.
Joint Chiefs of Staff, chairman — Gen. George S. Brown, USAF.

Department of the Army
The Pentagon 20310

Secretary of the Army — Martin R. Hoffmann.
Under Secretary — Norman R. Augustine.
Assistant Secretaries for:
  Finance Management — Hadlai A. Hull.
  Civil Works — Victor V. Veysey.
  Installations & Logistics — Harold L. Browman.
  Research & Development — Edward A. Miller.

Manpower & Reserve Affairs — Daniel G. Brotzman.
Chief of Public Information — Maj. Gen. L. Gordon Hill Jr.
Chief of Staff — Gen. Fred C. Weyand.
Comptroller of the Army — Lt. Gen. John A. Kjellstrom.
Surgeon General — Lt. Gen. Richard R. Taylor.
Adjutant General — Maj. Gen. Paul T. Smith.
Inspector General & Auditor General — Lt. Gen. Herron N. Maples.
Judge Advocate General — Maj. Gen. Wilton B. Persons Jr.
Deputy Chiefs of Staff:
  'Logistics — Lt. Gen. Jack C. Fuson.
  Operations & Plans — Lt. Gen. John W. Vessey Jr.
  Research, Development, Acquisition — Lt. Gen. Howard H. Cooksey.
  Personnel — Lt. Gen. Harold G. Moore.
Ass't. Chief of Staff, Intelligence — Maj. Gen. Harold R. Aaron.
Chief of Engineers — Lt. Gen. W.C. Gribble Jr.
Director, Women's Army Corps. — Brig. Gen. Mary E. Clarke.
Nat. Guard Bureau — Maj. Gen. LaVern E. Weber.
Chief Army Reserve — Maj. Gen. Henry Mohr.
U.S. Army Materiel Command — Gen. John R. Deane Jr.
U.S. Army Forces Command — Gen. Bernard W. Rogers.
U.S. Army Training and Doctrine Command — Gen. William E. DePuy.
Commanding Generals, U. S. Armies:
  1st, Fort Meade Md. — Lt. Gen. Jeffrey G. Smith.
  5th, Ft. Sam Houston Tex. — Lt. Gen. Allen M. Burdette.
  6th, Presidio of San Francisco Cal. — Lt. Gen. Edward M. Flanagan Jr.
  Military Dist. of Washington — Maj. Gen. Robert G. Yerks.
  XVIII Airborne Corps. Ft. Bragg, N.C. — Lt. Gen. Henry E. Emerson.
  III Corps, Ft. Hood, Tex. — Lt. Gen. Robert M. Shoemaker.

Department of the Navy
The Pentagon 20360

Secretary of the Navy — J. William Middendorf 2d.
Under Secretary — vacant.
Assistant Secretaries for:
  Financial Management — Gary D. Penisten.
  Installations & Logistics — Jack L. Bowers.
  Manpower & Reserve Affairs — Joseph T. McCullen Jr.
  Research & Development — H. Tyler Marcy.
Judge Advocate General — R. Adm. H. B. Robertson Jr.
Chief of Naval Operations — Adm. James L. Holloway 3d.
Chief of Naval Materiel — Adm. F. H. Michaelis.
Bureau Chiefs:
  Medicine & Surgery — V. Adm. Donald Custis.
  Naval Personnel — V. Adm. J. D. Watkins.
Military Sealift Command — R. Adm. Sam H. Moore.
U. S. Marine Corps:
  Commandant — Gen. Louis H. Wilson.
  Asst. Commandant — Gen. Samuel Jaskilka.
  Chief of Staff — Lt. Gen. Leslie E. Brown.
Dir. of Women Marines — Col. Margaret A. Brewer.
Commandants, Naval Districts:
  1st, Boston — R. Adm. Roy D. Snyder Jr.
  3d, New York — R. Adm. Frank D. Guest.
  4th, Philadelphia — R. Adm. W. D. Tolle.
  5th, Norfolk — R. Adm. W. H. Ellis.
  6th, Charleston — R. Adm. Julian T. Burke Jr.
  8th, New Orleans — R. Adm. George L. Cassel.
  9th, Great Lakes — R. Adm. A. M. Sackett.
  11th, San Diego — R. Adm. Samuel L. Gravely Jr.
  12th, San Francisco — R. Adm. J. T. Coughlin.
  13th, Seattle — R. Adm. Lando W. Zech Jr.
  14th, San Francisco — R. Adm. R. S. Wentworth Jr.
Naval District, Wash., D. C. — R. Adm. R. H. Carnahan.

Department of the Air Force
The Pentagon 20330

Secretary of the Air Force — Thomas C. Reed.
Under Secretary of the Air Force — James W. Plummer.
Deputy Under Secretary for Space Systems — Dr. Charles W. Cook.
Assistant Secretaries for:
  Financial Management — Francis Hughes.
  Research and Development — John J. Martin (acting).
  Installations and Logistics — Gordon Knapp.
  Manpower and Reserve Affairs — David P. Taylor.
General Counsel — Jack L. Stempler.
Director of Information — Brig. Gen. H. J. Dalton Jr.
Director of Space Systems — Brig. Gen. W. L. Shields Jr.
Chief of Staff — Gen. David C. Jones.
Vice Chief of Staff — Gen. William V. McBride.
Chief, National Guard Bureau — Maj. Gen. LaVern Weber (U. S. Army).
Chief of Air Force Reserves — Maj. Gen. William Lyon.
Surgeon General — Lt. Gen. George E. Schafer.
Judge Advocate — Maj. Gen. H. R. Vague.
Inspector General — Lt. Gen. Donald G. Nunn.
Deputy Chiefs of Staff:
  Systems and Logistics — Lt. Gen. Robert E. Hails.
  Programs and Resources — Lt. Gen. James A. Hill.
  Personnel — Lt. Gen. Kenneth L. Tallman
  Research and Development — Lt. Gen. Alton D. Slay.
  Plans and Operations — Lt. Gen. John W. Pauly.
Major Air Commands:
  NORAD/ADCOM — Gen. Daniel James Jr.
  AF Logistics Command — Gen. F. Michael Rogers.
  AF Systems Command — Gen. William J. Evans.
  Air Training Command — Lt. Gen. John W. Roberts
  Air University — Lt. Gen Raymond B. Furlong.
  Headquarters Command — Gen. William C. Norris.
  Military Airlift Command — Gen. Paul K. Carlton.
  Strategic Air Command — Gen. Russell E. Dougherty
  Tactical Air Command — Gen. Robert J. Dixon.
  Alaskan Air Command — Lt. Gen. James E. Hill.
  USAF Southern Command — Maj. Gen. James M. Breedlove
  Pacific Air Forces — Gen. Louis L. Wilson Jr.
  USAF Europe — Gen. Richard H. Ellis.
  USAF Security Service — Brig. Gen. Kenneth D. Burns.
  AF Communications Service — Maj. Gen. Rupert H. Burris.

Department of Justice
Constitution Ave. & 10th St. NW 20530

Attorney General — Edward H. Levi.
Deputy Attorney General — Harold R. Tyler Jr.
Solicitor General — Robert H. Bork.
Assistant Attorneys General:
  Antitrust Division — Thomas E. Kauper.
  Civil Division — Rex E. Lee.
  Civil Rights Division — J. Stanley Pottinger.
  Criminal Division — Richard L. Thornburgh.
  Drug Enforcement Admin. — Peter G. Bensinger.
  Land & Natural Resources Division — Peter R. Taft.
  Legal Counsel — Antonin Scalia.
  Office of Legislative Affairs — Michael L. M. Uhlmann.
  Office of Management & Finance — Glen E. Pommerening.
  Public Information — Robert Havel, director.
  Tax Division — Scott P. Crampton.
Fed. Bureau of Investigation — Clarence M. Kelley.
Board of Immigration Appeals — David L. Mil-Hollan, chairman.
Board of Parole — Maurice H. Sigler.
Bureau of Prisons — Norman A. Carlson.
Community Relations Ser. — Benjamin Holman, dir.
Immigration and Naturalization Service — Leonard F. Chapman Jr., commissioner.
Law Enforcement Assistance Admin. — Richard W. Velde.
Pardon Attorney — Lawrence M. Traylor.

Department of the Interior
C St. between 18th & 19th Sts. NW 20240

Secretary of the Interior — Thomas S. Kleppe.
Under Secretary — Kent Frizzell.
Assistant Secretaries for:
  Fish, Wildlife and Parks — Nathaniel P. Reed.
  Energy & Minerals — William L. Fisher.
  Land and Water Resources — Jack O. Horton.
  Program Development & Budget — Ronald G. Coleman.
  Management — Albert Zapanta (nominee).
  Congressional & Legislative Affairs — John H. Kyl.
Commissioner of Indian Affairs — Morris Thompson.
Bureau of Land Management — Curtis J. Berklund.
Bureau of Mines — Dr. Thomas V. Falkie.
Bureau of Outdoor Recreation — John Crutcher.
Bureau of Reclamation — Gilbert G. Stamm.
Bureau of Sport Fisheries & Wildlife — Lynn Greenwalt.
Geological Survey — V.E. McKelvey.
National Park Service — Gary E. Everhardt.
Office of Public Affairs — L. J. Churchville, director.
Office of Water Research and Technology — William S. Butcher, director.
Office of Solicitor — H. Gregory Austin.

Department of Agriculture
14th St. & Independence Ave. SW 20250

Secretary of Agriculture — Earl L. Butz.
Under Secretary — John A. Knebel.
Conservation, Research, & Education — Robert W. Long.

Internatl. Affairs & Commodity Programs — Richard E. Bell.
Marketing & Consumer Services — Richard L. Feltner.
Rural Development — William H. Walker 3d.
Agricultural Economics — Don Paarlberg.
Congressional & Public Affairs — Paul A. Theis.
Intergovernmental Affairs — R. B. Wilson.
Agric. Mktg. Service — Donald Wilkinson.
Agric. Stabilization & Conserv. Service — Kenneth Frick, administrator.
Animal & Plant Health Inspection Ser. — F. J. Mulhern.
Cooperative State Research Ser. — R. L. Lovvorn.
Econ. Research Service — Quentin M. West, admin.
Extension Service — Edward Kirby, admin.
Farmer Coop. Service — Randall Torgerson, admin.
Farmers Home Admin. — Frank B. Elliott, admin.
Fed. Crop Insurance Corp. — Melvin R. Peterson.
Food & Nutrition Ser. — Edward J. Hekman, admin.
Foreign Agric. Service — David L. Hume.
Forest Service — John R. McGuire, chief.
General Counsel — James D. Keast.
Office of Investigations — John V. Graziano, dir.
Packers & Stockyards Admin — Marvin McLain.
Rural Electrific. Admin. — David Hamil, admin.
Soil Conservation Service — Ronello M. Davis, admin.
Statistical Reporting Service — William Kibler.

Department of Commerce
14th St. between Constitution & E St. NW 20230
Secretary of Commerce — Elliot L. Richardson.
Under Secretary — vacant.
Asst Secretaries — Robert J. Blackwell, Betsy Ancker-Johnson, James L. Pate.
General Counsel — John T. Smith 2d.
Maritime Affairs — Robert J. Blackwell.
Science & Technology — Betsy Ancker-Johnson.
Bureau of the Census — Vincent R. Barabba.
Bureau of Economic Analysis — George Jaszi.
Bureau of Internatl. Commerce — Charles W. Hostler.
Bureau of East-West Trade — Arthur Downey.
Bureau of Domestic Commerce — Samuel B. Sherwin.
Natl. Oceanic & Atmospheric Admin. — Robert M. White, administrator.
Natl. Technical Info. Service — William T. Knox, director.
Economic Develop. Admin. — John Eden (acting).
Natl. Bureau of Standards — Ernest Ambler (acting).
Office of Minority Business Enterprise — Alex M. Armendaris, director.
Office of Product Standards — Howard I. Forman.
Office of Telecommunications — John M. Richardson, acting director.
Office of Textiles — Arthur Garel, director.
U.S. Patent Office — C. Marshall Dann.
U.S. Travel Service — Creighton Holden.

Department of Labor
200 Constitution Ave. NW 20210
Secretary of Labor — W. J. Usery Jr.
Under Secretary — Michael H. Moscow.
Executive Assistant-Counselor — James Hogue.
Assistant Secretaries for:
  Employment and Training — William H. Kolberg.
  Labor-Management Relations — Bernard E. DeLury.
  Occupational Safety & Health — Morton Corn.
  Employment Standards — John C. Read.
Women's Bureau — Carmen R. Maymi, director.
Asst. Secretary for Policy, Evaluation & Research — Abraham Weiss.
Solicitor of Labor — William J. Kilberg.
Bureau of Labor Statistics — Julius Shiskin.
Dep. Under Secy. for Internatl. Affairs — Joel Segall.
Dep. Under Secy. for Legislative Affairs — Timothy Smith (acting).
Asst. Secretary for Admin. & Management — Fred G. Clark.
Director of Public Affairs & Counselor — Richard Lukstat.
Office of Information, Publications, & Reports — John W. Leslie, director.

Department of Health, Education, and Welfare
330 Independence Ave. SW 20201
Secretary of HEW — F. David Mathews.
Under Secretary — Marjorie W. Lynch.
Assistant Secretaries for:
  Administration and Management — John R. Ottina.
  Public Affairs — Edward J. McVeigh (acting).
  Health — Dr. Theodore Cooper.
  Planning and Evaluation — William Morrill.
  Education — Virginia Y. Trotter.
  Human Development — Stanley B. Thomas.
  Legislation — Stephen Kurzman.
  Comptroller — John D. Young.
General Counsel — William Howard Taft.
Surgeon General, Public Health Ser. — Dr. S. Paul Ehrlich (acting).
Center for Disease Control — Dr. David J. Sencer, dir.
Alcohol, Drug Abuse, and Mental Health Admin. — James D. Isbister (acting).
Health Resources Admin. — Dr. Kenneth Endicott.
Health Services Admin. — Dr. Louis M. Wellman.
Office for Civil Rights — Martin Gerry, director.
Social and Rehabilitation Serv. — Don I. Wortman (acting).
Commissioners of:
  Education — Vacant.
  Social Security — James B. Cardwell.
  Food and Drug Admin. — Dr. Alexander M. Schmidt.
National Institutes of Health — Dr. Donald S. Frederickson.
National Institute of Education — Harold L. Hodgkinson.

Department of Housing and Urban Development
451 7th St. SW 20410
Secretary of Housing & Urban Development — Carla Anderson Hills.
Under Secretary — John B. Rhinelander.
Assistant Secretaries:
  Administration — Thomas G. Cody.
  Community Planning & Development — David O. Meeker Jr.
  Fair Housing and Equal Opportunity — James H. Blair.
  Housing Management — James L. Young.
  Housing Production & Mortgage Credit — David S. Cook.
  Policy Development & Research — Charles J. Orlebeke.
  Consumer Affairs & Regulatory Functions — Constance B. Newman.
  Legislative Affairs — Sol Mosher.
President, Govt. Natl. Mortgage Assn. — David M. DeWilde.
Office of Public Affairs — Grace Bassett.
Office of International Affairs, — Donald Stegall.
General Counsel — Robert R. Elliott.
Federal Insurance Administrator — J. Robert Hunter Jr. (acting).
Fed. Disaster Assistance Admin. — Thomas P. Dunne.
New Communities Admin. — James F. Dausch.
Inspector General — James B. Thomas Jr.

Department of Transportation
400 7th St. SW 20590
Secretary — William T. Coleman Jr.
Deputy Secretary — John W. Barnum.
Assistant Secretaries — William S. Heffelfinger, Judith T. Connor, Robert H. Binder, Hamilton Herman, Roger W. Hooker Jr.
General Counsel — John Hart Ely.
National Highway Traffic Safety Admin. — Dr. James B. Gregory.
U. S. Coast Guard Commandant — Adm. Owen W. Siler.
Federal Aviation Admin. — Dr. John L. McLucas.
Federal Highway Admin. — Norbert T. Tiemann.
Federal Railroad Admin. — Asph H. Hall (acting).
Urban Mass Transportation Admin. — Robert E. Patricelli.
St. Lawrence Seaway Development Corp. — David W. Oberlin, administrator.

(continued from page 297)
court's decision and end the case there. But it can also send the case back to the lower court for retrial or for other proceedings that may be appropriate.

Ultimately, all decisions of these courts can be reviewed by the U.S. Supreme Court, which is also the first court of appeal from the U.S. Court of Claims. Besides reviewing federal court decisions, the Supreme Court is empowered to hear suits between the states and to review state supreme court decisions if an issue of federal law or the Constitution is involved.

State Officials, Salaries, Party Membership

Compiled by the World Almanac from statistics supplied by the Secretaries of State.

ALABAMA
Governor — George C. Wallace, D., $28,955.
Lt. Gov. — Jere Beasley, D., $50 per legislative day, plus annual salary of $300 per month.
Sec. of State — Mrs. Agnes Baggett, D., $22,959.
Atty. Gen. — Bill Baxley, D., $33,500.
Treasurer — Mrs. Melba Till Allen, D., $22,959.
Auditor — Bettye Frink, D., $22,959.
Legislature
Meets annually, first Tuesday in May, at Montgomery. Members receive $50 per day during legislative sessions, limited to 30 days, plus annual salary of $300 per month.
Senate — Dem., 35; Rep., 0. Total, 35.
House — Dem., 105; Rep., 0. Total, 105.

ALASKA
Governor — Jay S. Hammond, R., $50,000.
Lt. Gov. — Lowell Thomas Jr., R., $44,000.
Atty. General — Avrum M. Gross, D., $48,000.
Comm. of Educ. — Marshall L. Lind.
Legislature
Meets annually, in January, at Juneau, for as long as may be necessary. First session in odd years. Members receive $14,720 per year plus $48 per day if from out of town, $35 if from Juneau, while in session. Also, $4,000 for stenographic services and other expenses.
Senate — Rep., 7; Dem., 13. Total, 20.
House — Rep., 9; Dem., 30; Non-partisan, 1. Total, 40.

ARIZONA
Governor — Raul H. Castro, D., $40,000.
Sec. of State — Wesley Bolin, D., $22,000.
Atty. Gen. — Bruce Babbitt, D., $35,000.
Treasurer — Bart Fleming, R., $22,500.
Supt. Public Instr. — Carolyn Warner, D., $27,500.
Legislature
Meets annually, in January, at Phoenix. Each member receives an annual salary of $6,000.
Senate — Dem., 18; Rep., 12. Total 30.
House — Dem., 27; Rep., 33. Total, 60.

ARKANSAS
Governor — David Pryor, D., $10,000.
Lt. Gov. — Joe Purcell, D., $2,500.
Sec. of State — George O. Jarnigan, D., $5,000.
Auditor — Jimmy Jones, D., $5,000.
Atty. Gen. — Jim Guy Tucker, D., $6,000.
Treasurer — Mrs. Nancy J. Hall, D., $5,000.
Dir. of Public Instr. — A. W. Ford.
General Assembly
Meets odd years, in January, at Little Rock. Members receive $1,200 per year, $20 a day in regular session, $6 a day in special session, plus 5c a mile travel expense.
Senate — Dem., 34; Rep., 1. Total, 35.
House — Dem., 97; Rep., 3. Total, 100.

CALIFORNIA
Governor — Edmund G. Brown Jr., D., $49,100.
Lt. Gov. — Mervyn M. Dymally, D., $35,000.
Sec. of State — March Fong Eu, D., $35,000.
Comptroller — Kenneth Cory, D., $35,000.
Atty. Gen. — Evelle J. Younger, R., $42,500.
Treasurer — Jesse M. Unruh, D., $35,000.
Supt. Public Instr. — Wilson Riles, NP, $35,000.
Legislature
Meets at Sacramento, in biennial general sessions, unlimited as to duration. Members receive $23,232 per year plus mileage and $30 daily expenses while in session. Daily expenses on interim business: $30.
Senate — Dem., 24; Rep., 15; 1 vacancy. Total, 40.
Assembly — Dem., 55; Rep., 25. Total, 80.

COLORADO
Governor — Dick Lamb, D., $40,000.
Lt. Gov. — George Brown, D., $25,000.
Secy. of State — Mary Estill Buchanan, R., $25,000.
Atty. Gen. — J. D. MacFarlane, D., $32,500.
Treasurer — Palmer Burch, R., $20,000.
General Assembly
Meets annually, in January, at Denver. Members receive $7,600 annually, plus $35 per day for non-session meetings up to a maximum of $1,050 in any calendar year.
Senate — Dem., 16; Rep., 19. Total, 35.
House — Dem., 39; Rep., 26. Total, 65.

CONNECTICUT
Governor — Ella T. Grasso, D., $42,000.
Lt. Gov. — Robert K. Killian, D., $18,000.
Sec. of State — Gloria Schaffer, D., $20,000.
Treasurer — Robert I. Berdon, R., $20,000.
Comptroller — J. Edward Caldwell, D., $20,000.
Atty. Gen. — Carl R. Ajello Jr., D., $30,000.
General Assembly
Meets annually odd years in January and even years in February at Hartford. Salary $11,000 per 2-year term plus $2,000 per 2-year term for expenses and 10c per mile travel allowance.
Senate — Dem., 29; Rep., 7. Total, 36.
House — Dem., 118; Rep., 33. Total, 151.

DELAWARE
Governor — Sherman W. Tribbitt, D., $35,000.
Lt. Gov. — Eugene D. Bookhammer, R., $12,000.
Sec. of State — Robert H. Reed, D., $18,720.
Auditor — Richard T. Collins, R., $18,000.
Atty. Gen. — Richard R. Wier Jr., D., $30,000..
Treasurer — Mary D. Jornlin, R., $18,000.
General Assembly
Meets annually at Dover, from the 2d Tuesday in January to midnight June 30. Members receive $9,000 per year.
Senate — Dem., 13; Rep., 8. Total, 21.
House — Dem., 25; Rep., 16. Total, 41.

FLORIDA
Governor — Reubin Askew, D., $50,000.
Lt. Gov. — J. H. Williams, D., $36,000.
Sec. of State — Bruce A. Smathers, D., $40,000.
Comptroller — Gerald Lewis, D., $40,000.
Atty. Gen. — Robert L. Shevin, D., $40,000.
Treasurer — Philip F. Ashlev, D., $40,000.
Comm. of Publ. Educ. — Ralph D. Turlington, $40,000.
Legislature
Meets annually, in April, at Tallahassee. Members receive $12,000 per year plus expense allowance while on official business.
Senate — Dem., 27; Rep., 12; Ind., 1. Total, 40.
House — Dem., 86; Rep., 34. Total, 120.

GEORGIA
Governor — George Busbee, D., $50,000.
Lt. Gov. — Zell Miller, D., $25,000.
Sec. of State — Ben W. Fortson Jr., D., $35,000.
Comptroller General — Johnnie L. Caldwell, D., $35,000.
Atty. Gen. — Arthur K. Bolton, D., $40,000.
Auditor — Ernest Davis, $32,000.
Supt. of Schools — Jack P. Nix, D., $35,000.
General Assembly
Meets annually at Atlanta. Members receive $4,200 per year. During session $25 per day for expenses.
Senate — Dem., 51; Rep., 5. Total, 56.
House — Dem., 154; Rep., 25; Ind., 1. Total, 180.

HAWAII
Governor — George R. Ariyoshi, D., $50,000.
Lt. Gov. — Nelson K. Doi, D., $45,000.
Dir., Budg. & Finance — Eileen Anderson, D., $42,500.
Atty. Gen. — Ronald Amemiya, D., $42,500.
Supt. Educ. Dept. — George Clark, D., $42,500.
Comptroller — Hideo Murakami, D., $42,500.
Legislature
Meets annually, in January, at Honolulu. Members receive $12,000 per year plus allowance for expenses.
Senate — Dem., 18. Rep., 7. Total, 25.
House — Dem., 35. Rep., 16. Total, 51.

IDAHO
Governor—Cecil D. Andrus, D., $30,000.
Lt. Gov.—John V. Evans, D., $8,000.
Sec. of State—Pete T. Cenarrusa, R., $21,500.
Treasurer—Marjorie Ruth Moon, D., $21,500.
Atty. Gen.—Wayne L. Kidwell, R., $25,000.
Auditor—Joe R. Williams, D., $21,500.
Supt. Publ. Instr.—Roy Truby, D., $23,000.
Legislature
Meets on the Monday after the first day in January, at Boise. Members receive $10 per day served, plus $25 per day expenses, plus travel allowances.
Senate—Dem., 14; Rep., 21. Total, 35.
House—Dem., 27; Rep., 43. Total, 70.

ILLINOIS
Governor—Daniel Walker, D., $50,000.
Lt. Gov.—Neil F. Hartigan, D., $37,500.
Sec. of State—Michael J. Howlett, D., $42,500.
Comptroller—George W. Lindberg, R., $40,000.
Atty. Gen.—William J. Scott, R., $42,500.
Treasurer—Alan J. Dixon, D., $40,000.

General Assembly
Meets each year in January, at Springfield. Members receive $20,000 per annum.
Senate—Dem., 34; Rep., 25. Total, 59.
House—Dem., 101; Rep., 76. Total, 177.

INDIANA
Governor—Otis R. Bowen, R., $36,000 plus discretionary expenses.
Lt. Gov.—Robert Orr, R., $23,500; also $6,000 per year as president of Senate, plus $25 per day during legislative sessions.
Sec. of State—Larry Conrad, D., $23,500.
Auditor—Mary Aikins Currie, D., $23,500.
Atty. Gen.—Theodore L. Sendak, R., $27,000.
Treasurer—Jack L. New, D., $23,500.
Supt. Publ. Instr.—Harold Negley, R., $25,000.
General Assembly
Meets annually in January. Members receive $6,000 per year, plus $100 each month not in session, plus $25 per day expense allowance when in session. Also, 8c a mile for round trip each week.
Senate—Dem., 23; Rep., 27. Total, 50.
House—Dem., 56; Rep., 44. Total, 100.

IOWA
Governor—Robert D. Ray, R., $40,000, plus $5,000 expenses.
Lt. Gov.—Arthur A. Neu, R., $12,000 plus personal expenses and travel allowances at same rate as for a senator.
Sec. of State—Melvin D. Synhorst, R., $22,500.
Auditor—Lloyd R. Smith, R., $22,500.
Atty. Gen.—Richard C. Turner, R., $28,000.
Treasurer—Maurice E. Baringer, R., $22,500.
Supt. Public Instr.—Robert Benton.
General Assembly
Meets annually in January, at Des Moines. Members receive $8,000, plus maximum expense allowance of $15 per day 5 days a week during session, mileage expenses at 15c a mile.
Senate—Dem., 26; Rep., 24. Total, 50.
House—Dem., 62; Rep., 38. Total, 100.

KANSAS
Governor—Robert F. Bennett, R., $35,000.
Lt. Gov.—Shelby Smith, R., $10,400.
Sec. of State—Mrs. E.M. Shanahan, R., $18,500.
Atty. Gen.—Curt Schneider, D., $32,500.
Treasurer—Joan Finney, D., $18,500.
Legislature
Meets annually in January, at Topeka. Members receive $25 a day plus $44 a day expenses, plus $200 per month while not in session.
Senate—Rep., 26; Dem., 14. Total, 40.
House—Rep., 78; Dem., 47. Total, 125.

KENTUCKY
Governor—Julian Carroll, D., $35,000.
Lt. Gov.—Thelma Stovall, D., $27,900.
Sec. of State—Drexel Davis, D., $27,900.
Auditor—George Adkins, D., $27,900.
Atty. Gen.—Robert Stephens, D., $27,900.
Treasurer—Francis Mills, D., $27,900.
Supt. Public Instr.—Robert Graham, $27,900.
General Assembly
Meets even years, in January, at Frankfort. Members receive $50 per day during session; officers, $70-$75. All members also receive $65 per day for expenses.
Senate—Dem., 31; Rep., 7. Total, 38.
House—Dem., 78; Rep., 22. Total, 100.

LOUISIANA
Governor—Edwin W. Edwards, D., $50,000.
Lt. Gov.—James E. Fitzmorris Jr., D., $40,000.
Sec. of State—Paul Hardy, D., $35,000.
Atty. Gen.—William J. Guste Jr., D., $35,000.
Treasurer—Mary Evelyn Parker, D., $35,000.
Supt. of Education—Kelly Nix, D., $35,000.
Legislature
Meets annually for 60 legislative days, commencing on 3d Monday in April. Members receive $50 per day and mileage at 16 cents a mile for 8 round trips, plus $500 per month expense allowance.
Senate—Dem., 39; Rep., 0. Total, 39.
House—Dem., 102; Rep., 3. Total, 105.

MAINE
Governor—James B. Longley, I., $35,000.
Sec. of State—Markham L. Gartley, D., $20,000.
Atty. Gen.—Joseph E. Brennan, D., $25,500.
Auditor—Raymond M. Rideout Jr., R., $17,500.
Treasurer—Rodney L. Scribner, $15,000.
Comm. of Education H. Sawin Millett Jr., $25,500.

Legislature
Meets biennially in January, at Augusta. Members receive $4,500 for regular session, $2,500 for special session; presiding officers receive 50% more.
Senate—R., 19; D., 14. Total, 33.
House—R., 59; D., 91. Total, 151.

MARYLAND
Governor—Marvin Mandel, D., $25,000.
Lt. Gov.—Blair Lee 3d, R., $24,000.
Comptroller—Louis L. Goldstein, D., $20,000.
Atty. Gen.—Francis B. Burch, D., $20,000.
Treasurer—William S. James, D., $2,500.
Supt. of Education—James A. Sensenbaugh.
General Assembly
Meets 90 days annually on the 3rd Wednesday in January, at Annapolis. Members receive $11,000 per year.
Senate—Dem., 39; Rep., 8. Total, 47.
House—Dem., 126; Rep., 15. Total, 141.

MASSACHUSETTS
Governor—Michael S. Dukakis, D., $40,000.
Lt. Gov.—Thomas P. O'Neill 3d, D., $25,000.
Sec. of the Commonwealth—Paul Guzzi, D., $25,000.
Atty. Gen.—Francis X. Belloti, D., $30,000.
Auditor—Thaddeus Buczko, D., $25,000.
Treasurer—Robert Q. Crane, D., $25,000.
General Court (Legislature)
Meets each January in Boston. Salaries $11,400 per annum.
Senate—Dem., 33; Rep., 7. Total, 40.
House—Dem. 189; Rep., 46; Ind., 3; vacancies, 2. Total, 240.

MICHIGAN
Governor—William G. Milliken, R., $47,250.
Lt. Gov.—James J. Damman, R., $27,500.
Sec. of State—Richard H. Austin, D., $45,000.
Atty. Gen.—Frank J. Kelley, D., $45,000.
Auditor—Albert Lee, $36,000.
Treasurer—Allison Green, $33,950.
Supt. Public Instr.—John Porter, $40,875.
Legislature
Meets annually in January, at Lansing. Members receive $19,000 per year plus $3,500 expense allowance.
Senate—Dem., 24; Rep., 14. Total, 38.
House—Dem., 66; Rep., 44. Total, 110.

MINNESOTA
Governor—Wendell R. Anderson, DFL., $41,000.
Lt. Gov.—Rudy Perpich, DFL., $30,000.
Sec. of State—Joan Anderson Growe, DFL., $25,000.
Auditor—Robert W. Mattson, DFL., $26,000.
Atty. Gen.—Warren Spannaus, DFL., $36,500.
Treasurer—Jim Lord, DFL., $25,000.
(DFL means Democratic-Farmer-Labor. IR means Independent Republican.)
Legislature
Meets for a total of 120 days within every 2 years, at St. Paul. Members receive $8,400 per year plus expense allowance during session.
Senate—DFL., 38; IR, 28; Ind., 1. Total, 67.
House—DFL., 103; IR, 31. Total, 134.

MISSISSIPPI
Governor—Cliff Finch, D., $43,000.
Lt. Gov.—Evelyn Gandy, D., $15,000 per regular legislative session, plus expense allowance.
Sec. of State—Heber Ladner, D., $28,000.
Auditor—W.H. (Hamp) King, D., $26,000.
Atty. Gen.—A.L. Summer, D., $30,000.
Treasurer—Edwin Lloyd Pittman, D., $26,000.
Supt. Public Educ.—Charles E. Holladay, D., $26,000.
Legislature
Meets annually in January, at Jackson. Members receive $8,100 per regular session, plus travel allowance and $210 per month while not in session.
Senate—Dem., 50; Rep., 2. Total, 52.
House—Dem., 119; Rep., 3. Total, 122.

MISSOURI
Governor — Christopher S. Bond, R., $37,500.
Lt. Gov. — William C. Phelps, R., $16,000.
Sec. of State — James C. Kirkpatrick, D., $25,000.
Atty. Gen. —John C. Danforth, R., $25,000.
Treasurer James I. Spainhower, D., $20,000.
Comm. of Educ. — Arthur L. Mallory.
General Assembly
Meets in Jefferson City annually, first Wednesday after first Monday in January; adjournment in odd-numbered years by June 30, in even-numbered years by May 15. Members receive $8,400 per annum.
Senate — Dem., 23; Rep., 11. Total, 34.

House — Dem., 113; Rep., 50. Total, 163.

MONTANA
Governor — Thomas L. Judge, D., $30,000.
Lt. Gov. — Bill Christiansen, D., $20,500.
Sec. of State — Frank Murray, D., $18,000.
Auditor — E. V. (Sonny) Omholt, R., $18,000.
Atty. Gen. — Bob Woodahl, R., $25,000.
Treasurer — Hollis G. Connors, R., $18,000.
Supt. Public Instr. — Dolores Colburg, D., $17,500.

Legislative Assembly
Meets biennially in January, at Helena. Members receive $68.18 per month plus $40 per day for expenses while in session.
Senate — Dem., 30; Rep., 20. Total, 50.
House — Dem., 67; Rep., 33. Total, 100.

NEBRASKA
Governor — J. James Exon, D., $25,000.
Lt. Gov. — Gerald T. Whelan, D., $25,000.
Sec. of State — Allen J. Beermann, R., $25,000.
Auditor — Ray A. C. Johnson, R., $16,000.
Atty. Gen. — Paul Douglas, R., $24,000.
Treasurer — Wayne Swanson, R., $15,000.

Legislature
Meets annually in January, at Lincoln. Members receive salary of $4,800 annually plus travelling expenses for one round trip to and from session.
Unicameral body composed of 49 members who are elected on a nonpartisan ballot and are classed as Senators.

NEVADA
Governor — Mike O'Callaghan, D., $40,000.
Lt. Gov. — Harry M. Reid, D., $6,000, plus $40 per day when acting as Governor and president of the Senate during legislative sessions.
Sec. of State — William D. Swackhamer, D., $25,000.
Comptroller — Wilson McGowen, R., $22,500.
Atty. Gen. — Robert List, R., $30,000.
Treasurer — Michael Mirabelli, D., $22,500.
Supt. Public Instr. — Burnell Larson.

Legislature
Meets odd years in January, at Carson City. All members receive $40 per day for 60 days (20 days for special sessions). All members receive per diem of $25 per day for 60 days (20 days special session). Travel allowance of 10c per mile.
Senate — Dem., 17; Rep., 3. Total, 20.
Assembly — Dem., 31; Rep., 9. Total, 40.

NEW HAMPSHIRE
Governor — Meldrim Thomson, Jr., R., $34,070.
Sec. of State — Robert L. Stark, R., $25,216.
Atty. Gen. — David H. Souter, $28,846.
Comptroller — Arthur H. Fowler.
Comm. of Education — Newell J. Paire.
Dir. of Accounts — Donald Bernier.
Treasurer — Robert W. Flanders, R., $25,216.

General Court (Legislature)
Meets odd years, in January, at Concord. Members receive $200; presiding officers $250.
Senate — Rep., 12; Dem., 12. Total, 24.
House — Rep., 232; Dem., 165; Vacancies, 3. Total, 400.

NEW JERSEY
Governor — Brendan Byrne, D., $55,000.
Sec. of State — J. Edward Crabiel, D., $43,000.
Atty. Gen. — William F. Hyland, $43,000.
Treasurer — Richard C. Leone, $43,000.
Auditor — George B. Harper, $21,000.
Comm. of Education — Fred G. Burke, $43,000.

Legislature
Meets annually, in January, at Trenton. Members receive $10,000 per year, except president of Senate and speaker of Assembly who receive ⅛ more by virtue of their office.
Senate — Dem., 29; Rep., 10; Ind., 1. Total, 40.
Assembly — Dem., 49; Rep. 31, Total, 80.

NEW MEXICO
Governor — Jerry Apodaca, D., $35,000.
Lt. Gov. — Robert E. Ferguson, D., $60 per day when presiding over Senate. Acting governor, $75 per day.
Sec. of State — Ernestine D. Evans, D., $24,000.
Auditor — Max Sanchez, D., $24,000.
Atty. Gen. — Tony Anaya, D., $30,000.
Treasurer — Edward Murphy, D., $24,000.

Legislature
Meets in January, at Sante Fe, odd years for 60 days, even years for 30 days. Members receive $24 per day while in session.
Senate — Dem., 30; Rep., 12. Total, 42.
House — Dem., 51; Rep., 19. Total, 70.

NEW YORK
Governor — Hugh L. Carey, D., $85,000.
Lt. Gov. — Mary Anne Krupsak, D., $60,000.
Sec. of State — Mario M. Cuomo, D., $47,800.
Comptroller — Arthur Levitt, D., $60,000.
Atty. Gen. — Louis J. Lefkowitz, R., $60,000.
Comm. of Education — Ewald B. Nyquist.

Legislature
Meets annually, in January, at Albany. Members receive $23,500 per year.
Senate — Dem., 25; Rep., 34; Vacancy, 1. Total, 60.
Assembly — Dem., 87; Rep., 62; Vacancy, 1. Total, 150.

NORTH CAROLINA
Governor — James E. Holshouser Jr., R., $38,500.
Lt. Gov. — James B. Hunt, D., $30,000 per year, plus $20 per day not to exceed 120 days per regular session; $4,000 per year expense allowance.
Sec. of State — Thad Eure, D., $31,000.
Auditor — Henry L. Bridges, D., $31,000.
Atty. Gen. — Rufus L. Edmisten, D., $35,000.
Treasurer — Edwin Gill, D., $31,000.
Supt. Public Inst. — Craig Phillips, D., $33,500.

General Assembly
Meets odd years in January, at Raleigh. Members receive $4,800 annual salary and $1,200 annual expense allowance plus subsistence and travel allowance while in session.
Senate — Dem., 49; Rep., 1. Total, 50.
House — Dem., 111; Rep., 9. Total, 120.

NORTH DAKOTA
Governor — Arthur A. Link, D., $18,000 plus $22,000 per year expense allowance.
Lt. Gov. — Wayne Sanstead, D., $2,500 plus $4,500.
Sec. of State — Ben Meier, R., $11,000.
Auditor — Robert W. Peterson, R., $11,000 plus $16,000.
Atty. Gen. — Allen I. Olson, R., $13,000 plus $19,000.
Treasurer — Walter Christensen, D., $11,000 plus $16,000.
Supt. Public Instruction — M. F. Peterson, N-P., $12,000 plus $16,000.

Legislative Assembly
Meets odd years, in January at Bismarck. Members receive $60 per day during session, plus $75 per month.
Senate — Rep., 41; Dem., 10. Total, 51.
House — Rep., 79; Dem., 23. Total, 102.

OHIO
Governor — James A. Rhodes, R., $50,000.
Lt. Gov. — Richard F. Celeste, D., $30,000.
Sec. of State — Ted W. Brown, R., $38,000.
Atty. Gen. — William J. Brown, D., $25,000.
Auditor — Thomas E. Ferguson, D., $38,000.
Treasurer — Gertrude W. Donahey, D., $38,000.

General Assembly
Meets at Columbus on first Monday in January in odd-numbered years; no later than Mar. 15 of following year for 2d session. Members receive $17,500 per annum.
Senate — Dem., 21; Rep., 12. Total, 33.
House — Dem., 40; Rep., 59. Total, 99.

OKLAHOMA
Governor — David L. Boren, D., $42,500.
Lt. Gov. — George Nigh, D., $24,000.
Sec. of State — Jerome W. Byrd, D., $18,500.
Auditor — Joe Bailey Cobb, D., $18,500.
Atty. Gen. — Larry Derryberry, D., $27,000.
Treasurer — Leo Winters, D., $22,000.
Supt. Public Instr. — Leslie R. Fisher, D., $30,000.

Legislature
Meets each year in January, at Oklahoma City. Members receive the sum of $9,960 per annum.
Senate — Dem., 39; Rep., 9. Total, 48.
House — Dem., 76; Rep., 25. Total, 101.

OREGON
Governor — Robert W. Straub, D., $38,500, plus $1,000 monthly expenses.
Sec. of State — Clay Myers, R., $31,900.
Atty. Gen. — Lee Johnson, R., $31,900.
Treasurer — James A. Redden, D., $31,900.
Supt. Public Instr. — Verne A. Duncan, N-P, $31,900.

Legislative Assembly
Meets odd years, in January, at Salem. Members receive $440 monthly and $35 expenses per day while in session; $175 per month while not in session.
Senate — Dem., 22; Rep., 7; Ind., 1. Total, 30.
House — Dem., 38; Rep., 22. Total, 60.

PENNSYLVANIA
Governor — Milton J. Shapp, D., $60,000.
Lt. Gov. — Ernest P. Kline, D., $45,000.
Sec. of State — C. DeLores Tucker, D., $35,000.

Atty. Gen. — Robert Kane, D., $40,000.
Treasurer — Grace M. Sloan, D., $35,000.

General Assembly
Meets annually, in January, at Harrisburg. Members receive $15,800 per year plus $5,000 for expenses. Legislators elected in this year's election will receive salaries of $15,600 plus expenses of $2,500.
Senate — Dem., 30; Rep., 20. Total, 50.
House — Dem., 111; Rep., 89. Total, 200.

RHODE ISLAND
Governor — Philip W. Noel, D., $42,500.
Lt. Gov. — J. Joseph Garrahy, D., $25,500.
Sec. of State — Robert F. Burns, D., $25,500.
Atty. Gen. — Julius C. Michaelson, D., $31,875.
Treasurer — Raymond H. Hawksley, D., $25,500.

General Assembly
Meets annually, in January, at Providence. Members receive $5 per day for 60 days (the Speaker, $10), also travel allowance of 8¢ per mile.
Senate — Dem., 46; Rep., 4. Total, 50.
House — Dem., 82; Rep., 18. Total, 100.

SOUTH CAROLINA
Governor — James B. Edwards, R., $39,000.
Lt. Gov. — W. Brantley Harvey Jr., D., $16,250.
Sec. of State — O. Frank Thornton, D., $34,000.
Comptroller Gen. — John Henry Mills, D., $34,000.
Atty. Gen. — Daniel R. McLeod, D., $34,000.
Treasurer — G. L. Patterson Jr., D., $34,000.
Supt. of Educ. — Cyril B. Busbee, D., $34,000.

General Assembly
Meets annually in January, at Columbia. Members receive $7,000 per year plus expense allowance of $25 per day and travel and postage allowance.
Senate — Dem., 43; Rep., 3. Total, 46.
House — Dem. 107; Rep., 17. Total, 124.

SOUTH DAKOTA
Governor — Richard F. Kneip, D., $27,500.
Lt. Gov. — Harvey Wollman, D., $4,500 plus $25 per legislative day.
Sec. of State — Lorna B. Herseth, D., $17,500.
Treasurer — David Volk, R., $17,500.
Atty. Gen. — William J. Janklow, R., $23,000.
Auditor — Alice Kundert, R., $17,500.

Legislature
Meets annually in January, at Pierre. Members receive $3,000 for 45 day session in odd-numbered years, and $2,000 for 30 day session in even-numbered years, plus $25 per legislative day.
Senate — Dem., 19; Rep., 16. Total, 35.
House — Dem., 33; Rep., 37. Total, 70.

TENNESSEE
Governor — Ray Blanton, D., $50,000.
Lt. Gov. — John S. Wilder, D.
Sec. of State — Joe C. Carr, D., $34,000.
Comptroller — William Snodgrass, D., $38,000.
Atty. Gen. — R. A. Ashley, D., $34,000.
Comm. of Education — Sam Ingram, D.

General Assembly
Meets annually in January, at Nashville. Members receive $6,000 yearly plus expenses for each day in session (not to exceed 105 days).
Senate — Dem., 20; Rep., 12; I., 1. Total, 33.
House — Dem., 63; Rep., 35; I., 1. Total, 99.

TEXAS
Governor — Dolph Briscoe, D., $66,800.
Lt. Gov. — Bill Hobby, D., same salary as state senator while presiding over Senate, plus living quarters. Governor's salary when acting as governor.
Sec. of State — Mark W. White, D., $39,900.
Comptroller — Bob Bullock, D., $42,300.
Atty. Gen. — John L. Hill, D., $42,300.
Treasurer — Jesse James, D., $42,300.

Legislature
Meets odd years in January, at Austin. Members receive annual salary not exceeding $4,800 plus per diem while in session and travel allowance.
Senate — Dem., 28; Rep., 3. Total, 31.
House — Dem., 135; Rep., 16. Total, 150.

UTAH
Governor — Calvin L. Rampton, D., $35,000.
Sec. of State — Clyde L. Miller, D., $22,000.
Auditor — David S. Monson, R., $21,000.
Atty. Gen. — Vernon B. Romney, R., $25,000.
Treasurer — David L. Duncan, R., $21,000.

Legislature
Meets annually in January at Salt Lake City. While in session members receive $25 per diem. expenses of $15 per diem, plus mileage.
Senate — Dem., 15; Rep., 14. Total, 29.
House — Dem., 40; Rep., 35. Total, 75.

VERMONT
Governor — Thomas P. Salmon, D., $36,100.
Lt. Gov. — Brian D. Burns, D., $15,500.
Sec. of State — Richard C. Thomas, R., $19,600.
Auditor — Alexander V. Acebo, R., $19,600.
Atty. Gen. — M. Jerome Diamond, D., $24,700.
Treasurer — Stella B. Hackel, D., $19,600.

General Assembly
Meets odd years, in January, at Montpelier. Members receive $150 weekly, while in session, with a limit of $4,500 for a regular session and $30 per day for special session, with specified expenses.
Senate — Dem., 17; Dem., 11; R-D, 1; D-I, 1. Total, 30.
House — Rep., 74; Dem., 65; R-D, 4; D-R, 2; I, 2; I-D, 2; D-I, 1. Total, 150.

VIRGINIA
Governor — Mills E. Godwin Jr., R., $50,000.
Lt. Gov. — John M. Dalton, R., $10,525.
Atty. Gen. — Andrew P. Miller, D., $37,500.
Sec. of the Commonwealth — Patricia R. Perkinson, I., $17,400.
Treasurer — Robert C. Watts Jr., R., $31,800.
Auditor — Charles K. Trible, $27,700.
Supt. Public Instr. — Dr. Walter E. Campbell.

General Assembly
Meets every year in January, at Richmond. Members receive $5,475 per year.
Senate — Dem., 35; Rep., 5. Total, 40.
House — Dem., 78; Rep., 17. Ind., 5. Total, 100.

WASHINGTON
Governor — Daniel J. Evans, R., $42,150.
Lt. Gov. — John A. Cherberg, D., $17,800.
Sec. of State — Bruce K. Chapman, R., $21,400.
Auditor — R. V. Graham, D., $24,950.
Atty. Gen. — Slade Gorton, R., $31,500.
Treasurer — Robert S. O'Brien, D., $24,150.
Supt. of Public Instr. — Dr. Frank Brouillet, NP, $31,500.

Legislature
Meets odd years in January, at Olympia. Members receive $7,200 annually, plus $40 per day while in session for subsistence and lodging.
Senate — Dem., 30; Rep., 19. Total, 49.
House — Dem., 62; Rep., 36. Total, 98.

WEST VIRGINIA
Governor — Arch A. Moore Jr., R., $35,000.
Sec. of State — James R. McCartney, R., $22,500.
Auditor — John M. Gates, R., $22,500.
Atty. Gen. — Chauncey Browning Jr., D., $22,500.
Treasurer — Ronald D. Pearson, R., $22,500.
Comm. of Agric. — Gus R. Douglas, D., $22,500.

Legislature
Meets annually in January, at Charleston. Members receive compensation fixed by citizens' commission.
Senate — Dem., 26; Rep., 8. Total, 34.
House — Dem., 86; Rep., 14. Total, 100.

WISCONSIN
Governor — Patrick J. Lucey, D., $44,292.
Lt. Gov. — Martin J. Schreiber, D., $28,668.
Sec. of State — Douglas La Follette, D., $13,500.
Treasurer — Charles P. Smith, D., $22,140.
Atty. Gen. — Bronson C. LaFollette, D., $36,450.
Supt. of Public Instr. — Barbara Thompson, NP, $36,450.

Legislature.
Meets in January, at Madison. Members receive $15,678 annually plus $25 per day expenses.
Senate — Dem., 19; Rep., 14. Total, 33.
Assembly — Dem., 64; Rep., 35. Total, 99.

WYOMING
Governor — Ed Herschler, D., $37,500.
Sec. of State — Mrs. Thyra Thompson, R., $23,000.
Auditor — James B. Griffith, R., $23,000.
Atty. Gen. — V. Frank Mendicino, D., $24,000.
Treasurer — Edwin J. Wirtzenburger, R., $23,000.
Supt. of Public Instr. — Robert G. Schrader, R., $23,000.

Legislature
Meets odd years in January, even years in February, at Cheyenne. Members receive $15 per day while in session, plus $36 per day for expenses.
Senate — Rep., 15; Dem., 15. Total, 30.
House — Rep., 32; Dem., 29; Ind., 1. Total, 62.

PUERTO RICO
Governor — Rafael-Hernandez Colon, $35,000.
Secretaries:
Agric. — Antonio Gonzalez Chapel, $25,000.
Commerce — Damian Folch, $25,000.

Educ. — Ramon Cruz, $25,000.
Health — Jose Alvarez de Choudens, $25,000.
Justice — Carlos Rios, $25,000.
Labor — Luis Silva Recio, $25,000.
Public Works — Rafael Ignacio.
Social Services — Ramon Garcia Santiago, $25,000.
State — Juan Albors, $25,500.

Treasury — Salvador Cassellas, $25,000.
All officials belong to the Popular Democratic Party.

Legislative Assembly

Composed of a Senate of 26 members and a House of Representatives of 51 members. Meets annually, in January, at San Juan. Members receive $9,600 plus expenses and travel allowances.

Judiciary of the U.S.

Data as of July 15, 1976
Justices of the United States Supreme Court

The Supreme Court comprises the chief justice of the United States and 8 associate justices, all appointed by the president with advice and consent of the Senate. Salaries: chief justice $65,600 annually, associate justice $63,000.

Name; apptd from Chief Justices in italics	Service Term	Yrs.	Born	Died
John Jay, N. Y.	1789-1795	5	1745	1829
John Rutledge, S. C.	1789-1791	1	1739	1800
William Cushing, Mass.	1789-1810	20	1732	1810
James Wilson, Pa.	1789-1798	8	1742	1798
John Blair, Va.	1789-1796	6	1732	1800
James Iredell, N. C.	1790-1799	9	1751	1799
Thomas Johnson, Md.	1791-1793	1	1732	1819
William Paterson, N. J.	1793-1806	13	1745	1806
John Rutledge, S. C.	1795(a)	—	1739	1800
Samuel Chase, Md.	1796-1811	15	1741	1811
Oliver Ellsworth, Conn.	1796-1800	4	1745	1807
Bushrod Washington, Va.	1798-1829	31	1762	1829
Alfred Moore, N. C.	1799-1804	4	1755	1810
John Marshall, Va.	1801-1835	34	1755	1835
William Johnson, S. C.	1804-1834	30	1771	1834
Henry B. Livingston, N.Y.	1806-1823	16	1757	1823
Thomas Todd, Ky.	1807-1826	18	1765	1826
Joseph Story, Mass.	1811-1845	33	1779	1845
Gabriel Duval, Md.	1811-1835	22	1752	1844
Smith Thompson, N. Y.	1823-1843	20	1768	1843
Robert Trimble, Ky.	1826-1828	2	1777	1828
John McLean, Oh.	1829-1861	32	1785	1861
Henry Baldwin, Pa.	1830-1844	14	1780	1844
James M. Wayne, Ga.	1835-1867	32	1790	1867
Roger B. Taney, Md.	1836-1864	28	1777	1864
Philip P. Barbour, Va.	1836-1841	4	1783	1841
John Catron, Tenn.	1837-1865	28	1786	1865
John McKinley, Ala.	1837-1852	15	1780	1852
Peter V. Daniel, Va.	1841-1860	19	1784	1860
Samuel Nelson, N. Y.	1845-1872	27	1792	1873
Levi Woodbury, N. H.	1845-1851	5	1789	1851
Robert C. Grier, Pa.	1846-1870	23	1794	1870
Benjamin R. Curtis, Mass.	1851-1857	6	1809	1874
John A. Campbell, Ala.	1853-1861	8	1811	1889
Nathan Clifford, Me.	1858-1881	23	1803	1881
Noah H. Swayne, Oh.	1862-1881	18	1804	1884
Samuel F. Miller, Ia.	1862-1890	28	1816	1890
David Davis, Ill.	1862-1877	14	1815	1886
Stephen J. Field, Cal.	1863-1897	34	1816	1899
Salmon P. Chase, Oh.	1864-1873	8	1808	1873
William Strong, Pa.	1870-1880	10	1808	1895
Joseph P. Bradley, N. J.	1870-1892	21	1813	1892
Ward Hunt, N. Y.	1872-1882	9	1810	1886
Morrison R. Waite, Oh.	1874-1888	14	1816	1888
John M. Harlan, Ky.	1877-1911	34	1833	1911
William B. Woods, Ga.	1880-1887	6	1824	1887
Stanley Matthews, Oh.	1881-1889	7	1824	1889
Horace Gray, Mass.	1881-1902	20	1828	1902
Samuel Blatchford, N.Y.	1882-1893	11	1820	1893
Lucius Q.C. Lamar, Miss.	1888-1893	5	1825	1893
Melville W. Fuller, Ill.	1888-1910	21	1833	1910
David J. Brewer, Kan.	1889-1910	20	1837	1910
Henry B. Brown, Mich.	1890-1906	15	1836	1913
George Shiras Jr., Pa.	1892-1903	10	1832	1924
Howell E. Jackson, Tenn.	1893-1895	2	1832	1895
Edward D. White, La.	1894-1910	16	1845	1921

Name; apptd from Chief Justices in italics	Service Term	Yrs.	Born	Died
Rufus W. Peckham, N.Y.	1895-1909	13	1838	1909
Joseph McKenna, Cal.	1898-1925	26	1843	1926
Oliver W. Holmes, Mass.	1902-1932	29	1841	1935
William R. Day, Oh.	1903-1922	19	1849	1923
William H. Moody, Mass.	1906-1910	3	1853	1917
Horace H. Lurton, Tenn.	1909-1914	4	1844	1914
Charles E. Hughes, N.Y.	1910-1916	5	1862	1948
Willis Van Devanter, Wy.	1910-1937	26	1859	1941
Joseph R. Lamar, Ga.	1910-1916	5	1857	1916
Edward D. White, La.	1910-1921	10	1845	1921
Mahlon Pitney, N. J.	1912-1922	10	1858	1924
Jas. C. McReynolds, Tenn.	1914-1941	26	1862	1946
Louis D. Brandeis, Mass.	1916-1939	22	1856	1941
John H. Clarke, Oh.	1916-1922	5	1857	1945
William H. Taft, Conn.	1921-1930	8	1857	1930
George Sutherland, Ut.	1922-1938	15	1862	1942
Pierce Butler, Minn.	1922-1939	16	1866	1939
Edward T. Sanford, Tenn.	1923-1930	7	1865	1930
Harlan F. Stone, N. Y.	1925-1941	16	1872	1946
Charles E. Hughes, N.Y.	1930-1941	11	1862	1948
Owen J. Roberts, Pa.	1930-1945	15	1875	1955
Benjamin N. Cardozo, N.Y.	1932-1938	6	1870	1938
Hugo L. Black, Ala.	1937-1971	34	1886	1971
Stanley F. Reed, Ky.	1938-1957	19	1884	—
Felix Frankfurter, Mass.	1939-1962	23	1882	1965
William O. Douglas, Conn.	1939-1975	—	1898	—
Frank Murphy, Mich.	1940-1949	9	1890	1949
Harlan F. Stone, N.Y.	1941-1946	5	1872	1946
James F. Byrnes, S. C.	1941-1942	1	1879	1972
Robert H. Jackson, N.Y.	1941-1954	12	1892	1954
Wiley B. Rutledge, Ia.	1943-1949	6	1894	1949
Harold H. Burton, Oh.	1945-1958	13	1888	1964
Fred M. Vinson, Ky.	1946-1953	7	1890	1953
Tom C. Clark, Tex.	1949-1967	18	1899	—
Sherman Minton, Ind.	1949-1956	7	1890	1965
Earl Warren, Cal.	1953-1969	16	1891	1974
John Marshall Harlan, N. Y.	1955-1971	16	1899	1971
William J. Brennan Jr., N.J.	1956 —	—	1906	—
Charles E. Whittaker, Mo.	1957-1962	5	1901	1973
Potter Stewart, Oh.	1958 —	—	1915	—
Byron R. White, Col.	1962 —	—	1917	—
Arthur J. Goldberg, Ill.	1962-1965	3	1908	—
Abe Fortas, Tenn.	1965-1969	4	1910	—
Thurgood Marshall, N.Y.	1967 —	—	1908	—
Warren E. Burger, Va.	1969 —	—	1907	—
Harry A. Blackmun, Minn.	1970 —	—	1908	—
Lewis F. Powell Jr., Va.	1971 —	—	1907	—
William H. Rehnquist, Ariz.	1971 —	—	1924	—
John Paul Stevens	1975 —	—	1920	—

(a) Rejected Dec. 15, 1795.

U.S. Court of Customs and Patent Appeals

Washington, D.C. 20439 (Salaries, $44,600)

Chief Judge — Howard T. Markey.
Associate Judges — Giles S. Rich, Phillip B. Baldwin, Donald E. Lane, Jack R. Miller.

U. S. Customs Court

New York, N.Y. 10007 (Salaries, $42,000)
Chief Judge — Nils A. Boe.
Judges — Morgan Ford, Scovel Richardson, Frederick Landis, James L. Watson, Herbert N. Maletz, Bernard Newman, Edward D. Re, Paul P. Rao.

U. S. Court of Claims
Washington, D.C. 20005 (Salaries, $44,600)
Chief Judge — Wilson Cowen.
Associate Judges — Oscar H. Davis, Shiro Kashiwa, Robert L. Kunzig, Marion T. Bennett, Byron G. Skelton, Philip Nichols Jr.

U. S. Tax Court
Washington, D.C. 20217 (Salaries, $42,000)
Chief Judge — Howard A. Dawson Jr.
Judges — Arnold Raum, Irene F. Scott, William M. Fay, William M. Drennen, Theodore Tannenwald Jr., Charles R. Simpson, C. Moxley Featherston, Leo H. Irwin, Samuel B. Sterrett, William Quealy, William A. Goffe, Cynthia H. Hall, Darrell D. Wiles, Richard C. Wilbur.

U.S. Courts of Appeals
(Salaries, $44,600. CJ means Chief Judge)
District of Columbia — David L. Bazelon, CJ; J. Skelly Wright, Carl McGowan, Edward Allen Tamm, Harold Leventhal, Spottswood W. Robinson III, Roger Robb, George E. MacKinnon, Malcolm Richard Wilkey; Clerk's office, Washington, D.C. 20001.
First Circuit (Me., Mass., N.H., R.I., Puerto Rico) — Frank M. Coffin, CJ; Edward M. McEntee, Levin H. Campbell; Clerk's Office, Boston, Mass. 02109.
Second Circuit (Conn., N.Y., Vt.) — Irving R. Kaufman, CJ; Wilfred Feinberg, Walter R. Mansfield, William H. Mulligan, James L. Oakes, William H. Timbers, Murray I. Gurfein, Ellsworth Van Graafeiland, Thomas J. Meskill; Clerk's Office, New York, N.Y. 10007.
Third Circuit (Del., N.J., Pa., Virgin Is.) — Collins J. Seitz, CJ; Francis L. Van Dusen, Ruggero J. Aldisert, Arlin M. Adams, John J. Gibbons, Max Rosenn, James Hunter 3d, Joseph F. Weis Jr., Leonard I. Garth; Clerk's Office, Philadelphia, Pa. 19106.
Fourth Circuit (Md., N.C., S.C., Va., W.Va.) — Clement F. Haynsworth Jr., CJ; Harrison L. Winter, J. Braxton Craven Jr., John D. Butzner Jr., Donald Stuart Russell, John A. Field Jr., H. Emory Widener Jr.; Clerk's Office, Richmond, Va. 23219.
Fifth Circuit (Ala., Fla., Ga., La., Miss., Tex., Canal Zone) — John R. Brown, CJ; John Minor Wisdom, Walter Pettus Gewin, Homer Thornberry, James P. Coleman, Irving L. Goldberg, Robert A. Ainsworth Jr., John C. Godbold, David W. Dyer, Lewis R. Morgan, Charles Clark, Thomas G. Gee, Paul H. Roney, Gerald B. Tjoflat; Clerk's Office, New Orleans, La. 70130.
Sixth Circuit (Ky., Mich., Ohio, Tenn.) — Harry Phillips, CJ; Paul C. Weick, George Clifton Edwards Jr., Anthony J. Celebrezze, John W. Peck, Wade H. McCree Jr., William E. Miller, Albert J. Engel, Pierce Lively; Clerk's Office, Cincinnati, Oh. 45202.
Seventh Circuit (Ill., Ind., Wis.) — Thomas E. Fairchild, CJ; Luther M. Swygert, Walter J. Cummings, Wilbur F. Pell Jr., Robert A. Sprecher, Philip W. Tone, William J. Bauer; Clerk's Office, Chicago 60604.
Eighth Circuit (Ark., Ia., Minn., Mo., Neb., N.D., S.D.) — Floyd R. Gibson, CJ; Donald P. Lay, Gerald W. Heaney, Myron H. Bright, Donald R. Ross, Roy L. Stephenson, William H. Webster, J. Smith Hanley; Clerk's Office, St. Louis 63101.
Ninth Circuit (Ariz., Cal., Ida., Mont., Nev., Ore., Wash., Alaska, Ha., Guam) — Richard H. Chambers, CJ; James R. Browning, Ben Cushing Duniway, Walter Ely, Shirley M. Hufstedler, Eugene A. Wright, Ozell M. Trask, Joseph T. Sneed, Herbert Y. C. Choy, J. Clifford Wallace, Alfred T. Goodwin; Clerk's Office, San Francisco 94101.
Tenth Circuit (Col., Kan., N.M., Okla., Ut., Wy.) — David T. Lewis, CJ; Delmas C. Hill, Oliver Seth, William J. Holloway Jr., Robert H. McWilliams, James E. Barrett, William E. Doyle; Clerk's Office, Denver, Col. 80202.
Temporary Emergency Court of Appeals —Edward Allen Tamm, CJ; Clerk's Office, Washington, D.C. 20001.

U. S. District Courts
(Salaries, $42,000. CJ means Chief Judge)
Alabama — **Northern:** Frank H. McFadden, CJ; Sam C. Pointer Jr., James Hughes Hancock, J. Foy Guin Jr.; Clerk's Office, Birmingham 35203. **Middle:** Frank M. Johnson Jr., CJ; Robert E. Varner; Clerk's Office, Montgomery 36101. **Southern:** Virgil Pittman, CJ; William Brevard Hand; Clerk's Office, Mobile 36602.
Alaska — James A. Von der Heydt, CJ; James M. Fitzgerald; Clerk's Office, Anchorage 99510.
Arizona — Walter Early Craig, CJ; James A. Walsh, C. A. Muecke, William P. Copple, William C. Frey; Clerk's Office, Phoenix 85025.
Arkansas — **Eastern:** Garnett Thomas Eisele, CJ; Terry L. Shell; Clerk's Office, Little Rock 72203. **Western:** Paul X.

Williams, CJ; Terry L. Shell; Clerk's Office, Fort Smith 72901.
California—Northern: Oliver J. Carter, CJ; Lloyd H. Burke, Stanley A. Weigel, Robert F. Peckham, Robert H. Schnacke, Samuel Conti, Spencer M. Williams, Charles B. Renfrew; William H. Orrick Jr.; Clerk's Office, San Francisco 94102. **Eastern:** Thomas J. MacBride, CJ; M. D. Crocker, Philip C. Wilkins; Clerk's Office, Sacramento 95814. **Central:** Albert Lee Stephens Jr., CJ; Francis C. Whelan, Irving Hill, A. Andrew Hauk, William P. Gray, Warren J. Ferguson, Manuel L. Real, Harry Pregerson, David W. Williams, Robert J. Kelleher, Wm. Matthew Byrne Jr., Lawrence T. Lydick, Malcolm M. Lucas, Robert Firth; Clerk's Office, Los Angeles 90012. **Southern:** Edward J. Schwartz, CJ; Howard B. Turrentine, Gordon Thompson Jr., Leland C. Nielsen, William B. Enright; Clerk's Office, San Diego 92101.
Colorado — Alfred A. Arraj, CJ; Fred M. Winner, Sherman G. Finesilver, Richard P. Matsch; Clerk's Office, Denver 80202.
Connecticut —T. Emmet Clarie, CJ; M. Joseph Blumenfeld; Robert C. Zampano, Jon O. Newman; Clerk's Office, New Haven 06505.
Delaware — James L. Latchum, CJ; Walter K. Stapleton, Murray M. Schwartz; Clerk's Office, Wilmington 19801.
District of Columbia —William B. Jones, CJ; George L. Hart Jr., John J. Sirica, William B. Jones, Howard F. Corcoran, Oliver Gasch, William B. Bryant, John Lewis Smith Jr., Aubrey E. Robinson Jr., Joseph C. Waddy, Gerhard A. Gesell, John H. Pratt, June L. Green, Barrington D. Parker, Charles R. Richey, Thomas A. Flannery; Clerk's Office, Washington 20001.
Florida—Northern: Winston E. Arnow, CJ; William H. Stafford Jr.; Clerk's Office, Tallahassee 32302. **Middle:** George C. Young, CJ; Charles R. Scott, Ben Krentzman, Gerald B. Tjoflat, William Terrell Hodges, John A. Reed Jr.; Clerk's Office, Jacksonville 32201. **Southern:** Charles B. Fulton, CJ; C. Clyde Atkins, Joe Eaton, Peter T. Fay, James Lawrence King, Norman C. Roettger Jr.; Clerk's Office, Miami 33101.
Georgia — **Northern:** Newell Edenfield, CJ; Albert J. Henderson Jr., William C. O'Kelley, Charles A. Moye Jr., Richard C. Freeman, James C. Hill; Clerk's Office, Atlanta 30303. **Middle:** J. Robert Elliott, CJ; Wilbur D. Owens Jr.; Clerk's Office, Macon 31202. **Southern:** Alexander A. Lawrence, CJ; Anthony A. Alaimo; Clerk's Office, Savannah 31402.
Hawaii — Samuel P. King, CJ; Dick Yin Wong; Clerk's Office, Honolulu 96801.
Idaho — Ray McNichols, CJ; J. Blaine Anderson; Clerk's Office, Boise 83724.
Illinois — **Northern:** James B. Parsons, CJ; Hubert L. Will, Bernard M. Decker, William J. Lynch, Frank J. McGarr, Thomas R. McMillen, Prentice H. Marshall, Joel M. Flaum, Alfred Y. Kirkland, John F. Grady, George N. Leighton; Clerk's Office, Chicago 60604. **Eastern:** Henry S. Wise, CJ; James L. Foreman; Clerk's Office, Danville 61832. **Southern:** Robert D. Morgan, CJ; Harlington Wood Jr.; Clerk's Office, Peoria 61601.
Indiana — **Northern:** Jesse E. Eschbach, CJ; Allen Sharp; Clerk's Office, Hammond 46325. **Southern:** William E. Steckler, CJ; Cale J. Holder, S. Hugh Dillin, James E. Noland; Clerk's Office, Indianapolis 46204.
Iowa — **Northern:** Edward J. McManus, CJ; William C. Hanson; Clerk's Office, Cedar Rapids 52407. **Southern:** William C. Hanson, CJ; William C. Stuart; Clerk's Office, Des Moines 50309.
Kansas — Wesley E. Brown, CJ; Frank G. Theis, Earl E. O'Connor, Richard Dean Rodgers; Clerk's Office, Wichita 67201.
Kentucky — **Eastern:** Bernard T. Moynahan Jr., CJ; Howard David Hermansdorfer, Eugene E. Siler Jr.; Clerk's Office, Lexington 40501. **Western:** Rhodes Bratcher, CJ; Charles M. Allen, Eugene E. Siler Jr.; Clerk's Office, Louisville 40202.
Louisiana — **Eastern:** Frederick J. R. Heebe, CJ; Edward J. Boyle Sr., Lansing L. Mitchell, Fred J. Cassibry, Alvin B. Rubin, R. Blake West, Jack M. Gordon; Clerk's Office, New Orleans 70130. **Middle:** E. Gordon West; Clerk's Office, Baton Rouge 70801. **Western:** Nauman S. Scott, CJ; Tom Stagg; Clerk's Office, Shreveport 71161.
Maine — Edward Thaxter Gignoux; Clerk's Office, Portland 04112.
Maryland — Edward S. Northrop, CJ; Frank A. Kaufman, Alexander Harvey 2d, James R. Miller Jr., Joseph H. Young, Herbert F. Murray, C. Stanley Blair; Clerk's Office, Baltimore 21202.
Massachusetts — Andrew A. Caffrey, CJ; W. Arthur Garrity Jr., Frank J. Murray, Frank H. Freedman, Joseph L. Tauro, Walter Jay Skinner; Clerk's Office, Boston 02109.

Michigan — Eastern: Damon J. Keith, CJ; Lawrence Gubow, Cornelia G. Kennedy, John Feikens, Philip Pratt, Robert E. DeMascio, Charles W. Joiner, James Harvey, James P. Churchill; Clerk's Office, Detroit 48226. **Western:** Noel P. Fox, CJ; Wendell A. Miles; Clerk's Office, Grand Rapids 49502.

Minnesota — Edward J. Devitt, CJ; Earl R. Larson, Miles W. Lord, Donald D. Alsop; Clerk's Office, St. Paul 55101.

Mississippi — Northern: William C. Keady, CJ; Orma R. Smith; Clerk's Office, Oxford 38655. **Southern:** Dan M. Russell Jr., CJ; William Harold Cox, Walter L. Nixon Jr.; Clerk's Office, Jackson 39205.

Missouri — Eastern: James H. Meredith, CJ; John K. Regan, William R. Collinson, H. Kenneth Wangelin, John F. Nangle; Clerk's Office, St. Louis 63101. **Western:** William H. Becker, CJ; John W. Oliver, William R. Collinson, Elmo B. Hunter, H. Kenneth Wangelin; Clerk's Office, Kansas City 64106.

Montana — Russell E. Smith, CJ; James F. Battin; Clerk's Office, Great Falls 59401.

Nebraska — Warren K. Urbom, CJ; Robert V. Denney, Albert G. Schatz; Clerk's Office, Omaha 68101.

Nevada — Roger D. Foley, CJ; Bruce R. Thompson; Clerk's Office, Las Vegas 89101.

New Hampshire — Hugh H. Bownes; Clerk's Office, Concord 03301.

New Jersey — Lawrence A. Whipple, CJ; George H. Barlow, Clarkson S. Fisher, Frederick B. Lacey, Vincent P. Biunno, Herbert J. Stern, H. Curtis Meanor, John F. Gerry, Stanley S. Brotman; Clerk's Office, Trenton 08605.

New Mexico — H. Vearle Payne, CJ; Howard C. Bratton, Edwin L. Mechem; Clerk's Office, Albuquerque 87103.

New York — Northern: James T. Foley; Clerk's Office, Albany 12201. **Eastern:** Jacob Mishler, CJ; John F. Dooling Jr., Jack B. Weinstein, Orrin G. Judd, Mark A. Costantino, Edward R. Neaher, Thomas C. Platt Jr., Henry Bramwell; Clerk's Office, Brooklyn 11201. **Southern:** David N. Edelstein, CJ; Edward Weinfeld, Charles M. Metzner, Lloyd F. MacMahon, Dudley B. Bonsal, Inzer B. Wyatt, John M. Cannella, Charles H. Tenney, Marvin E. Frankel, Constance Baker Motley, Milton Pollack, Morris E. Lasker, Lawrence W. Pierce, Lee P. Gagliardi, Charles L. Brieant Jr., Whitman Knapp, Charles E. Stewart Jr., Thomas P. Griesa, Robert L. Carter, Robert J. Ward, Kevin Thomas Duffy, William C. Conner, Richard Owen, Henry F. Werker; Clerk's Office, N.Y. City 10007. **Western:** John T. Curtin, CJ; Harold P. Burke, John T. Elfvin; Clerk's Office, Buffalo 14202.

North Carolina — Eastern: John D. Larkins Jr., CJ; Franklin T. Dupree Jr.; Clerk's Office, Raleigh 27611. **Middle:** Eugene A. Gordon, CJ; Hiram H. Ward; Clerk's Office, Greensboro 27402. **Western:** Woodrow Wilson Jones, CJ; James B. McMillan; Clerk's Office, Asheville 28802.

North Dakota — Paul Benson, CJ; Bruce M. Van Sickle; Clerk's Office, Bismarck 58501.

Ohio — Northern: Frank J. Battisti, CJ; Don J. Young, William K. Thomas, Thomas D. Lambros, Robert B. Krupansky, Nicholas J. Walinski, Leroy J. Contie Jr.; Clerk's Office, Cleveland 44114. **Southern:** Timothy S. Hogan, CJ; Joseph P. Kinneary, Davis S. Porter, Carl B. Rubin, Robert M. Duncan; Clerk's Office, Columbus 43215.

Oklahoma — Northern: Allen E. Barrow, CJ; Frederick A. Daugherty, H. Dale Cook; Clerk's Office, Tulsa 74103. **Eastern:** Joseph W. Morris, CJ; Frederick A. Daugherty, H. Dale Cook; Clerk's Office, Muskogee 74402 **Western:** Frederick A. Daugherty, CJ; Luther B. Eubanks, H. Dale Cook, Ralph G. Thompson; Clerk's Office, Oklahoma City 73102.

Oregon — Robert C. Belloni, CJ; James M. Burns, Otto R. Skopil Jr.; Clerk's Office, Portland 97207.

Pennsylvania — Eastern: John S. Lord 3d, CJ; Alfred L.

Luongo, A. Leon Higginbotham Jr., John P. Fullam, Charles R. Weiner, E. Mac Troutman, John B. Hannum, Daniel H. Huyett 3d, Donald W. VanArtsdalen, J. William Ditter Jr., Edward R. Becker, James H. Gorbey, Raymond J. Broderick, Clarence C. Newcomer, Clifford Scott Green, Louis Charles Bechtle, Herbert A. Fogel, Joseph L. McGlynn Jr., Edward N. Cahn; Clerk's Office, Philadelphia 19107. **Middle:** Michael H. Sheridan, CJ; William J. Nealon Jr., R. Dixon Herman, Malcolm Muir; Clerk's Office, Scranton 18501. **Western:** Herbert P. Sorg, CJ; Rabe Ferguson Marsh, Edward Dumbauld, Gerald J. Weber, William W. Knox, Hubert I. Teitelbaum, Barron P. McCune, Ralph F. Scalera, Daniel J. Snyder Jr.; Clerk's Office, Pittsburgh 15230.

Rhode Island — Raymond J. Pettine, CJ; Edward William Day; Clerk's Office, Providence 02901.

South Carolina — J. Robert Martin Jr., CJ; Robert W. Hemphill, Charles E. Simons Jr., Solomon Blatt Jr., Robert F. Chapman; Clerk's Office, Columbia 29202.

South Dakota — Fred J. Nichol, CJ; Andrew W. Bogue; Clerk's Office, Sioux Falls 57102.

Tennessee — Eastern: Frank W. Wilson, CJ; Robert L. Taylor, C. G. Neese; Clerk's Office, Knoxville 37901. **Middle:** Frank Gray Jr., CJ; L. Clure Morton; Clerk's Office, Nashville 37203. **Western:** Bailey Brown, CJ; Robert M. McRae Jr., Harry W. Wellford; Clerk's Office, Memphis 38103.

Texas — Northern: William M. Taylor Jr., CJ; Halbert O. Woodward, Eldon B. Mahon, Robert M. Hill, Robert W. Porter, Eldon D. Mahon, Patrick E. Higginbotham; Clerk's Office, Dallas 75242. **Southern:** Reynaldo G. Garza, CJ; James Noel Jr., John V. Singleton Jr., Woodrow B. Seals, Carl O. Bue Jr., Owen D. Cox, Robert O'Conor Jr.; Clerk's Office, Houston 77208. **Eastern:** Joe J. Fisher, CJ; William Wayne Justice, William M. Steger; Clerk's Office, Beaumont 77704. **Western:** Adrian A. Spears, CJ; Dorwin W. Suttle, Jack Roberts, William S. Sessions, John H. Wood Jr.; Clerk's Office, San Antonio 78206.

Utah — Willis W. Ritter, CJ; Aldon J. Anderson; Clerk's Office, Salt Lake City 84101.

Vermont — James S. Holden, CJ; Albert W. Coffrin; Clerk's Office, Burlington 05401.

Virginia — Eastern: Richard B. Kellam, CJ; Robert R. Merhige Jr., John A. MacKenzie, Albert V. Bryan Jr., D. Dortch Warriner, J. Calvitt Clarke; Clerk's Office, Norfolk 23502. **Western:** James C. Turk, CJ; Ted Dalton; Clerk's Office, Roanoke 24006.

Washington — Eastern: Marshall A. Neill, CJ; Clerk's Office, Spokane 99210. **Western:** Walter T. McGovern; Morell E. Sharp, Donald S. Voorhees; Clerk's Office, Seattle 98104.

West Virginia — Northern: Robert Earl Maxwell, CJ; Charles H. Haden 2d; Clerk's Office, Elkins 26241. **Southern:** Dennis Raymond Knapp, CJ; Kenneth K. Hall, Charles H. Haden 2d; Clerk's Office, Charleston 25329.

Wisconsin — Eastern: John W. Reynolds, CJ; Myron L. Gordon, Robert W. Warren; Clerk's Office, Milwaukee 53202. **Western:** James E. Doyle; Clerk's Office, Madison 53701.

Wyoming — Clarence A. Brimmer; Clerk's Office, Cheyenne 82001.

U.S. Territorial District Courts

Canal Zone — Guthrie F. Crowe; Clerk's Office, Balboa Heights.

Guam — Cristobal C. Duenas; Clerk's Office, Agana, 96910.

Puerto Rico — Jose V. Toledo, CJ; Hernan G. Pesquera, Juan R. Torruella; Clerk's Office, San Juan 00904.

Virgin Islands — Almeric L. Christian, CJ; Warren H. Young; Clerk's Office, Charlotte Amalie, St. Thomas 00801.

The Federal Judicial System

The federal judicial system begins with the District Court. There are 94 of these courts, at least one in each state, in Washington, D.C., and in certain territories. Called courts of general jurisdiction, they have power to determine the facts and pass judgment in criminal cases involving violations of federal law and in civil cases where the amount of the suit is $10,000 or more and the contending parties reside in different states. Other types of cases handled by District Courts include suits in admiralty (maritime matters involving navigational waters), bankruptcy, patents, trademarks, and copyrights.

Equal to the District Courts are special courts which handle only certain issues: the U.S. Customs Court, the Tax Court, and the Court of Claims, which hears suits against the U.S. government.

These trial courts are responsible for finding the facts in

a case and for applying the law to the facts found.

The District Courts and special courts are trial courts. Above them are several levels of appellate courts. The U.S. Courts of Appeals, often called circuit courts, sit in 10 judicial circuits and Washington, D.C. They hear appeals from the District Courts and the Tax Court, and will review decisions of federal administrative agencies if it appears that such decisions may be unreasonable or arbitrary. The U.S. Court of Customs and Patent Appeals hears appeals from the Customs Court.

Appellate courts, theoretically, do not review the trial court's findings of fact. The job of the appellate court is to decide whether the trial judge applied the law properly. If an appellate court decides that there was error in the application of the law, it can simply reverse the lower

continued on page 290

Presidents of the U. S.

No.	Name	Politics	Native State	Date Born	Inaug. at Age	Date of Death	Age at Death
1.	George Washington	Fed.	Va.	1732, Feb. 22	1789 . . . 57	1799, Dec. 14	67
2.	John Adams	Fed.	Mass.	1735, Oct. 30	1797 . . . 61	1826, July 4	90
3.	Thomas Jefferson	Dem.-Rep.	Va.	1743, Apr. 13	1801 . . . 57	1826, July 4	83
4.	James Madison	Dem.-Rep.	Va.	1751, Mar. 16	1809 . . . 57	1836, June 28	85
5.	James Monroe	Dem.-Rep.	Va.	1758, Apr. 28	1817 . . . 58	1831, July 4	73
6.	John Quincy Adams	Dem.-Rep.	Mass.	1767, July 11	1825 . . . 57	1848, Feb. 23	80
7.	Andrew Jackson	Dem.	S.C.	1767, Mar. 15	1829 . . . 61	1845, June 8	78
8.	Martin Van Buren	Dem.	N.Y.	1782,Dec. 5	1837 . . . 54	1862, July 24	79
9.	William Henry Harrison	Whig	Va.	1773, Feb. 9	1841 . . . 68	1841, Apr. 4	68
10.	John Tyler	Whig	Va.	1790, Mar. 29	1841 . . . 51	1862, Jan. 18	71
11.	James Knox Polk	Dem.	N.C.	1795, Nov. 2	184 . . . 49	1849, June 15	53
12.	Zachary Taylor	Whig	Va.	1784, Nov. 24	1849 . . . 64	1850, July 9	65
13.	Millard Fillmore	Whig	N.Y.	1800, Jan. 7	1850 . . . 50	1874, Mar. 8	74
14.	Franklin Pierce	Dem.	N.H.	1804, Nov. 23	1853 . . . 48	1869, Oct. 8	64
15.	James Buchanan	Dem.	Pa.	1791, Apr. 23	1857 . . . 65	1868, June 1	77
16.	Abraham Lincoln	Rep.	Ky.	1809, Feb. 12	1861 . . . 52	1865, Apr. 15	56
17.	Andrew Johnson	(see note)*	N.C.	1808, Dec. 29	1865 . . . 56	1875, Jul. 31	66
18.	Ulysses Simpson Grant	Rep.	Oh.	1822, Apr. 27	1869 . . . 46	1885, Jul. 23	63
19.	Rutherford Birchard Hayes	Rep.	Oh.	1822, Oct. 4	1877 . . . 54	1893, Jan. 17	70
20.	James Abram Garfield	Rep.	Oh.	1831, Nov. 19	1881 . . . 49	1881, Sept. 19	49
21.	Chester Alan Arthur	Rep.	Vt.	1829, Oct. 5	1881 . . . 50	1886, Nov. 18	56
22.	Grover Cleveland	Dem.	N.J.	1837, Mar. 18	1885 . . . 47	1908, June24	71
23.	Benjamin Harrison	Rep.	Oh.	1833, Aug. 20	1889 . . . 55	1901, Mar. 13	67
24.	Grover Cleveland	Dem.	N.J.	1837, Mar. 18	1893 . . . 55	1908, June 24	71
25.	William McKinley	Rep.	Oh.	1843, Jan. 29	1897 . . . 54	1901, Sept. 14	58
26.	Theodore Roosevelt	Rep.	N.Y.	1858, Oct. 27	1901 . . . 42	1919, Jan. 6	60
27.	William Howard Taft	Rep.	Oh.	1857, Sept. 15	1909 . . . 51	1930, Mar. 8	72
28.	Woodrow Wilson	Dem.	Va.	1856, Dec. 28	1913 . . . 56	1924, Feb. 3	67
29.	Warren Gamaliel Harding	Rep.	Oh.	1865, Nov. 2	1921 . . . 55	1923, Aug. 2	57
30.	Calvin Coolidge	Rep.	Vt.	1872, July 4	1923 . . . 51	1933, Jan. 5	60
31.	Herbert Clark Hoover	Rep.	Ia.	1874, Aug. 10	1929 . . . 54	1964, Oct. 20	90
32.	Franklin Delano Roosevelt	Dem.	N.Y.	1882, Jan. 30	1933 . . . 51	1945, Apr. 12	63
33.	Harry S. Truman	Dem.	Mo.	1884, May 8	1945 . . . 60	1972, Dec. 26	88
34.	Dwight David Eisenhower	Rep.	Tex.	1890, Oct. 14	1953 . . . 62	1969, Mar. 28	78
35.	John F. Kennedy	Dem.	Mass.	1917, May 29	1961 . . . 43	1963, Nov. 22	46
36.	Lyndon Baines Johnson	Dem.	Tex.	1908, Aug. 27	1963 . . . 55	1973, Jan. 22	64
37.	Richard Milhous Nixon**	Rep.	Cal.	1913, Jan 9	1969 . . . 56	. . . .	. . .
38.	Gerald R. Ford	Rep.	Neb.	1913, July 14	1974 . . . 61	. . . .	. . .

*Andrew Johnson — a Democrat, nominated vice president by Republicans and elected with Lincoln on National Union ticket. **Resigned Aug. 9, 1974.*

Presidents, Vice Presidents, Congresses

President	Service				Vice President	Congress
1 George Washington	Apr.	30,	1789-Mar.	3, 1797	1 John Adams	1, 2, 3, 4
2 John Adams	Mar.	4,	1797-Mar.	3, 1801	2 Thomas Jefferson	5, 6
3 Thomas Jefferson	Mar.	4,	1801-Mar.	3, 1805	3 Aaron Burr	7, 8
"	Mar.	4,	1805-Mar.	3, 1809	4 George Clinton	9, 10
4 James Madison	Mar.	4,	1809-Mar.	3, 1813	"(1)	11, 12
"	Mar.	4,	1813-Mar.	3, 1817	5 Elbridge Gerry(2)	13, 14
5 James Monroe	Mar.	4,	1817-Mar.	3, 1825	6 Daniel D. Tompkins	15, 16, 17, 18
6 John Quincy Adams	Mar.	4,	1825-Mar.	3, 1829	7 John C. Calhoun	19, 20
7 Andrew Jackson	Mar.	4,	1829-Mar.	3, 1833	"(3)	21, 22
"	Mar.	4,	1833-Mar.	3, 1837	8 Martin Van Buren	23, 24
8 Martin Van Buren	Mar.	4,	1837-Mar.	3, 1841	9 Richard M. Johnson	25, 26
9 William Henry Harrison (4)	Mar.	4,	1841-Apr.	4, 1841	10 John Tyler	27
10 John Tyler	Apr.	6,	1841-Mar.	3, 1845		27, 28
11 James K. Polk	Mar.	4,	1845-Mar.	3, 1849	11 George M. Dallas	29, 30
12 Zachary Taylor (4)	Mar.	4,	1849-July	9, 1850	12 Millard Fillmore	31
13 Millard Fillmore	July	10,	1850-Mar.	3, 1853		31, 32
14 Franklin Pierce	Mar.	4,	1853-Mar.	3, 1857	13 William R. King (5)	33, 34
15 James Buchanan	Mar.	4,	1857-Mar.	3, 1861	14 John C. Breckinridge	35, 36
16 Abraham Lincoln	Mar.	4,	1861-Mar.	3, 1865	15 Hannibal Hamlin	37, 38
"(4)	Mar.	4,	1865-Apr.	15, 1865	16 Andrew Johnson	39
17 Andrew Johnson	Apr.	15,	1865-Mar.	3, 1869		39, 40
18 Ulysses S. Grant	Mar.	4,	1869-Mar.	3, 1873	17 Schuyler Colfax	41, 42
"	Mar.	4,	1873-Mar.	3, 1877	18 Henry Wilson (6)	43, 44
19 Rutherford B. Hayes	Mar.	4,	1877-Mar.	3, 1881	19 William A. Wheeler	45, 46
20 James A. Garfield (4)	Mar.	4,	1881-Sept.	19, 1881	20 Chester A. Arthur	47
21 Chester A. Arthur	Sept.	20,	1881-Mar.	3, 1885		47, 48
22 Grover Cleveland (7)	Mar.	4,	1885-Mar.	3, 1889	21 Thomas A. Hendricks (8)	49, 50
23 Benjamin Harrison	Mar.	4,	1889-Mar.	3, 1893	22 Levi P. Morton	51, 52
24 Grover Cleveland (7)	Mar.	4,	1893-Mar.	3, 1897	23 Adlai E. Stevenson	53, 54
25 William McKinley	Mar.	4,	1897-Mar.	3, 1901	24 Garret A. Hobart (9)	55, 56
"(4)	Mar.	4,	1901-Sept.	14, 1901	25 Theodore Roosevelt	57
26 Theodore Roosevelt	Sept.	14,	1901-Mar.	3, 1905		57, 58
"	Mar.	4,	1905-Mar.	3, 1909	26 Charles W. Fairbanks	59, 60
27 William H. Taft	Mar.	4,	1909-Mar.	3, 1913	27 James S. Sherman (10)	61, 62
28 Woodrow Wilson	Mar.	4,	1913-Mar.	3, 1921	28 Thomas R. Marshall	63, 64, 65, 66
29 Warren G. Harding (4)	Mar.	4,	1921-Aug.	2, 1923	29 Calvin Coolidge	67
30 Calvin Coolidge	Aug.	3,	1923-Mar.	3, 1925		68
"	Mar.	4,	1925-Mar.	3, 1929	30 Charles G. Dawes	69, 70
31 Herbert C. Hoover	Mar.	4,	1929-Mar.	3, 1933	31 Charles Curtis	71, 72

(Continued)

32	Franklin D. Roosevelt.......	Mar.	4,	1933-Jan.	20,	1941	32	John N. Garner..............	73, 74, 75, 76
	"		Jan.	20,	1941-Jan.	20,	1945	33	Henry A. Wallace............	77, 78
	"(4)................		Jan.	20,	1945-Apr.	12,	1945	34	Harry S. Truman............	79
33	Harry S. Truman...........	Apr.	12,	1945-Jan.	20,	1949		....	79,80
	"		Jan.	20,	1949-Jan.	20,	1953	35	Alben W. Barkley...........	81, 82
34	Dwight D. Eisenhower......	Jan.	20,	1953-Jan.	20,	1961	36	Richard M. Nixon...........	83, 84, 85, 86
35	John F. Kennedy (4)........	Jan.	20,	1961-Nov.	22,	1963	37	Lyndon B. Johnson.........	87, 88
36	Lyndon B. Johnson.........	Nov.	22,	1963-Jan.	20,	1965		....	88
	"		Jan.	20,	1965-Jan.	20,	1969	38	Hubert H. Humphrey........	89, 90
37	Richard M. Nixon...........	Jan.	20,	1969-Jan.	20,	1973	39	Spiro T. Agnew (11).........	91, 92 93
	"(12)...............		Jan.	20,	1973-Aug.	9,	1974	40	Gerald R. Ford (13)..........	93
38	Gerald R. Ford (14)........	Aug.	9,	1974			41	Nelson A. Rockefeller (15)....	93, 94

(1) Died Apr. 20, 1812. (2) Died Nov. 23, 1814. (3) Resigned Dec. 28, 1832, to become U. S. Senator. (4) Died in office. (5) Died Apr. 18, 1853. (6) Died Nov. 22, 1875. (7) Terms not consecutive. (8) Died Nov. 25, 1885. (8) Died Nov. 21, 1899. (10) Died Oct. 30, 1912. (11) Resigned Oct. 10, 1973. (12) Resigned Aug. 9, 1974. (13) First non-elected vice president, chosen under 25th amendment procedure. (14) First non-elected president. (15) 2d non-elected vice president, sworn in Dec. 19, 1974.

Vice Presidents of the U.S.

The numerals given vice presidents do not coincide with those given presidents, because some presidents had none and some had more than one.

	Name	Birthplace	Year	Residence	Inaug.	Politics	Place of Death	Yr.	Age
1	John Adams...........	Quincy, Mass...........	1735	Mass......	1789	Fed....	Quincy, Mass....	1826	90
2	Thomas Jefferson......	Shadwell, Va...........	1743	Va......	1797	Rep...	Monticello, Va...	1826	83
3	Aaron Burr...........	Newark, N.J...........	1756	N.Y......	1801	Rep...	Staten Island, N.Y.....	1836	80
4	George Clinton.......	Ulster Co., N.Y........	1739	N.Y......	1805	Rep...	Washington, D. C.	1812	73
5	Elbridge Gerry.......	Marblehead, Mass...	1744	Mass....	1813	Rep...	Washington, D. C.	1814	70
6	Daniel D. Tompkins....	Scarsdale, N. Y.	1774	N. Y......	1817	Rep...	Staten Island, N. Y.....	1825	51
7	*John C. Calhoun......	Abbeville, S. C.	1782	S.C......	1825	Rep...	Washington, D. C.	1850	68
8	Martin Van Buren.....	Kinderhook, N. Y. ...	1782	N.Y......	1833	Dem...	Kinderhook, N. Y.	1862	79
9	Richard M. Johnson...	Louisville, Ky..........	1780	Ky.......	1837	Dem...	Frankfort, Ky.......	1850	70
10	John Tyler............	Greenway, Va.........	1790	Va......	1841	Whig..	Richmond, Va.......	1862	71
11	George M. Dallas......	Philadelphia, Pa.......	1792	Pa......	1845	Dem...	Philadelphia, Pa.	1864	72
12	Millard Fillmore.......	Summerhill, N.Y.......	1800	N.Y......	1849	Whig..	Buffalo, N. Y.........	1874	74
13	William R. King.......	Sampson Co., N. C. ..	1786	Ala......	1853	Dem...	Dallas Co., Ala.......	1853	67
14	John C. Breckinridge...	Lexington, Ky.........	1821	Ky.......	1857	Dem...	Lexington, Ky........	1875	54
15	Hannibal Hamlin......	Paris, Me.............	1809	Me.......	1861	Rep...	Bangor, Me..........	1891	81
16	Andrew Johnson......	Raleigh, N.C..........	1808	Tenn.....	1865	(x).....	Carter Co., Tenn......	1875	66
17	Schuyler Colfax.......	New York City, N.Y...	1823	Ind......	1869	Rep...	Makato, Minn........	1885	62
18	Henry Wilson........	Farmington, N.H......	1812	Mass....	1873	Rep...	Washington, D.C......	1875	63
19	William A. Wheeler....	Malone, N.Y..........	1819	N.Y......	1877	Rep...	Malone, N.Y.........	1887	68
20	Chester A. Arthur.....	Fairfield, Vt..........	1830	N.Y......	1881	Rep...	New York City, N.Y. ..	1886	56
21	Thomas A. Hendricks..	Muskingum Co., Ohio..	1819	Ind......	1885	Dem...	Indianapolis, Ind......	1885	66
22	Levi P. Morton.......	Shoreham, Vt.........	1824	N.Y......	1889	Rep...	Rhinebeck, N.Y.......	1920	96
23	Adlai E. Stevenson.....	Christian Co., Ky......	1835	Ill.......	1893	Dem...	Chicago, Ill..........	1914	78
24	Garret A. Hobart......	Long Branch, N.J......	1844	N.J.......	1897	Rep...	Paterson, N.J.	1899	55
25	Theodore Roosevelt....	New York City, N.Y...	1858	N.Y......	1901	Rep...	Oyster Bay, N.Y.	1919	60
26	Charles W. Fairbanks..	Unionville Centre, Ohio.	1852	Ind......	1905	Rep...	Indianapolis, Ind......	1918	66
27	James S. Sherman.....	Utica, N.Y............	1855	N.Y......	1909	Rep...	Utica, N.Y...........	1912	57
28	Thomas R. Marshall...	N. Manchester, Ind....	1854	Ind......	1913	Dem...	Washington, D.C.......	1925	71
29	Calvin Coolidge.......	Plymouth, Vt.........	1872	Mass....	1921	Rep...	Northampton, Mass. ...	1933	60
30	Charles G. Dawes......	Marietta, Ohio........	1865	Ill.......	1925	Rep...	Evanston, Ill.	1951	85
31	Charles Curtis........	Topeka, Kan..........	1860	Kan......	1929	Rep...	Washington, D.C.......	1936	76
32	John Nance Garner....	Red River Co., Tex....	1868	Tex......	1933	Dem...	Uvalde, Tex..........	1967	98
33	Henry Agard Wallace..	Adair County, Ia.......	1888	Iowa.....	1941	Dem...	Danbury, Conn.......	1965	77
34	Harry S. Truman......	Lamar, Mo............	1884	Mo.......	1945	Dem...	Kansas City, Mo.	1972	88
35	Alben W. Barkley......	Graves County, Ky.....	1877	Ky.......	1949	Dem...	Lexington, Va........	1956	78
36	Richard M. Nixon.....	Yorba Linda, Cal......	1913	Calif.....	1953	Rep....			
37	Lyndon B. Johnson....	Johnson City, Tex.....	1908	Tex......	1961	Dem...	San Antonio, Tex......	1973	64
38	Hubert H. Humphrey...	Wallace, S.D..........	1911	Minn.....	1965	Dem...			
39	Spiro T. Agnew.......	Baltimore, Md.........	1918	Md.......	1969	Rep....			
40	Gerald R. Ford.......	Omaha, Neb..........	1913	Mich.....	1973	Rep....			
41	Nelson A. Rockefeller...	Bar Harbor, Me.......	1908	N.Y......	1974	Rep....			

(*) John C. Calhoun resigned Dec. 28, 1832, having been elected to the Senate to fill a vacancy. (x) Andrew Johnson—a Democrat nominated by Republicans and elected with Lincoln on the National Union Ticket. (1) Adlai E. Stevenson, 23rd vice president, was grandfather of Democratic candidate for president, 1952 and 1956.

The Continental Congress: Meetings, Presidents

Meeting Places	Dates of Meetings	Congress Presidents	Date Elected
Philadelphia	Sept. 5 to Oct. 26, 1774	Peyton Randolph, Va. (1).....	Sept. 5, 1774
"		Henry Middleton, S.C........	Oct. 22, 1774
Philadelphia	May 10, 1775 to Dec. 12, 1776	Peyton Randolph, Va........	May 10, 1775
"		John Hancock, Mass.........	May 24, 1775
Baltimore	Dec. 20, 1776 to Mar. 4, 1777	"	
Philadelphia	Mar. 5 to Sept. 18, 1777	"	
Lancaster, Pa.	Sept. 27, 1777 (one day)	"	
York, Pa.	Sept. 30, 1777 to June 27, 1778	Henry Laurens, S.C..........	Nov. 1, 1777(4)
Philadelphia	July 2, 1778 to June 21, 1783	John Jay, N.Y..............	Dec. 10, 1778
"	"	Samuel Huntington, Conn....	Sept. 28, 1779
"	"	Thomas McKean, Del........	July 10, 1781
"	"	John Hanson, Md. (2)........	Nov. 5, 1781
"	"	Elias Boudinot, N.J..........	Nov. 4, 1782
Princeton, N.J.	June 30 to Nov. 4, 1783	Thomas Mifflin, Pa..........	Nov. 3, 1783
Annapolis, Md.	Nov. 26, 1783 to June 3, 1784	"	
Trenton, N.J.	Nov. 1 to Dec. 24, 1784	Richard Henry Lee, Va.......	Nov. 30, 1784
New York City	Jan. 11 to Nov. 4, 1785	"	
"	Nov. 7, 1785 to Nov. 3, 1786	John Hancock, Mass. (3).....	Nov. 23, 1785
		Nathaniel Gorman, Mass.....	June 6, 1786

"	Nov. 6, 1786 to Oct. 30, 1787	Arthur St. Clair, Pa.........	Feb. 2, 1787
"	Nov. 5, 1787 to Oct. 21, 1788	Cyrus Griffin, Va...........	Jan. 22, 1788
"	Nov. 3, 1788 to Mar. 2, 1789	"	

(1) Resigned Oct. 22, 1774.
(2) Titled "President of the United States in Congress Assembled," John Hanson is considered by some to be the first U.S. President as he was the first to serve under the Articles of Confederation. He was, however, little more than presiding officer of the Congress, which retained full executive power. He could be considered the head of government, but not head of state.
(3) Resigned May 29, 1786, without serving, because of illness.
(4) Articles of Confederation agreed upon, Nov. 15, 1777; last ratification from Maryland, Mar. 1, 1781.

Cabinets of the U. S.

Secretaries of State

The Department of Foreign Affairs was created by act of Congress July 27, 1789, and the name changed to Department of State on Sept. 15.

President	Secretary	Home	Apptd.	President	Secretary	Home	Apptd.
Washington....	Thomas Jefferson...	Va..	1789	Arthur.........	James G. Blaine......	Me...	1881
"	Edmund Randolph...	"	1794	"	F. T. Frelinghuysen....	N. J...	1881
"	Timothy Pickering....	Pa..	1795	Cleveland......	"	"	1885
J. Adams......	"	"	1795	"	Thomas F. Bayard...	Del...	1885
"	John Marshall.........	Va..	1800	B. Harrison....	"	"	1889
Jefferson......	James Madison.........	"	1801	F12"	James G. Blaine......	Me..	1889
Madison.......	Robert Smith.........	Md..	1809	"	John W. Foster......	Ind..	1892
"	James Monroe.........	Va..	1811	Cleveland.....	Walter Q. Gresham..	Ill...	1893
Monroe.......	John Quincy Adams....	Mass..	1817	"	Richard Olney......	Mass..	1895
J. Q. Adams...	Henry Clay.........	Ky..	1825	McKinley.....	"	"	1897
Jackson......	Martin Van Buren....	N.Y..	1829	"	John Sherman......	Oh..	1897
"	Edward Livingston....	La..	1831	"	William R. Day......	"	1898
"	Louis McLane......	Del..	1833	"	John Hay.........	D. C...	1898
"	John Forsyth.......	Ga..	1834	T. Roosevelt...	"	"	1901
Van Buren.....	"	"	1837	"	Elihu Root.......	N. Y..	1905
W. H. Harrison.	Daniel Webster......	Mass..	1841	"	Robert Bacon......	"	1909
Tyler.........	"	"	1841	Taft.........	"	"	1909
"	Abel P. Upshur.......	Va..	1843	"	Philander C. Knox...	Pa..	1909
"	John C. Calhoun......	S. C..	1844	Wilson........	"	"	1913
Polk.........	"	"	1845	"	William J. Bryan....	Neb..	1913
"	James Buchanan......	Pa..	1845	"	Robert Lansing....	N. Y..	1915
Taylor........	"	"	1849	"	Bainbridge Colby....	"	1920
"	John M. Clayton......	Del..	1849	Harding......	Charles E. Hughes....	"	1921
Fillmore......	"	"	1850	Coolidge......	"	"	1923
"	Daniel Webster......	Mass..	1850	"	Frank B. Kellogg....	Minn..	1925
"	Edward Everett......	"	1852	Hoover.......	"	"	1929
Pierce.......	William L. Marcy....	N. Y..	1853	"	Henry L. Stimson....	N. Y..	1929
Buchanan.....	"	"	1857	F. D. Roosevelt.	Cordell Hull......	Tenn..	1933
"	Lewis Cass.........	Mich..	1857	"	E. R. Stettinius Jr....	Va..	1944
"	Jeremiah S. Black...	Pa..	1860	Truman.......	"	"	1945
Lincoln.......	"	"	1861	"	James F. Byrnes....	S. C..	1945
"	William H. Seward....	N. Y..	1861	"	George C. Marshall...	Pa..	1947
Johnson, A....	"	"	1865	"	Dean G. Acheson....	Conn..	1949
Grant........	Elihu B. Washburne...	Ill..	1869	Eisenhower....	John Foster Dulles...	N. Y..	1953
"	Hamilton Fish.......	N. Y..	1869	"	Christian A. Herter...	Mass..	1959
Hayes........	"	"	1877	Kennedy.....	Dean Rusk........	N. Y..	1961
"	William M. Evarts.....	"	1877	Johnson, L. B...	"	"	1963
Garfield......	"	"	1881	Nixon........	William P. Rogers....	N. Y..	1969
"	James G. Blaine......	Me..	1881	"	Henry A. Kissinger....	D. C...	1973
				Ford.........	"	"	1974

Secretaries of the Treasury

The Treasury Department was organized by act of Congress on Sept. 2, 1789.

President	Secretary	Home	Apptd.	President	Secretary	Home	Appta.
Washington....	Alexander Hamilton..	N. Y..	1789	Pierce........	James Guthrie........	Ky..	1853
"	Oliver Wolcott.........	Conn..	1795	Buchanan......	Howell Cobb........	Ga..	1857
J. Adams.....	"	"	1797	"	Phillip F. Thomas....	Md..	1860
"	Samuel Dexter........	Mass..	1801	"	John A. Dix........	N. Y..	1861
Jefferson......	"	"	1801	Lincoln......	Salmon P. Chase.....	Oh..	1861
"	Albert Gallatin........	Pa..	1801	"	William P. Fessenden..	Me..	1864
Madison.......	"	Pa..	1809	"	Hugh McCulloch.....	Ind..	1865
"	George W. Campbell..	Tenn..	1814	Johnson, A....	"	"	1865
"	Alexander J. Dallas...	Pa..	1814	Grant........	George S. Boutwell....	Mass..	1869
"	William H. Crawford..	Ga..	1816	"	William A. Richardson.	Mass..	1873
Monroe.......	"	"	1817	"	Benjamin H. Bristow...	Ky..	1874
J. Q. Adams...	Richard Rush........	Pa..	1825	"	Lot M. Morrill......	Me..	1876
Jackson.......	Samuel D. Ingham....	"	1829	Hayes........	John Sherman.......	Oh..	1877
"	Louis McLane......	Del..	1831	Garfield......	William Windom.....	Minn..	1881
"	William J. Duane.....	Pa..	1833	Arthur.......	Charles J. Folger....	N. Y..	1881
"	Roger B. Taney......	Md..	1833	"	Walter Q. Gresham..	Ind..	1884
"	Levi Woodbury......	N. H..	1834	"	Hugh McCulloch.....	"	1884
Van Buren.....	"	"	1837	Cleveland.....	Daniel Manning......	N. Y..	1885
W. H. Harrison.	Thomas Ewing.......	Oh..	1841	"	Charles S. Fairchild...	"	1887
Tyler.........	"	"	1841	B. Harrison....	William Windom.....	Minn..	1889
"	Walter Forward......	Pa..	1841	"	Charles Foster......	Oh..	1891
"	John C. Spencer......	N. Y..	1843	Cleveland.....	John G. Carlisle......	Ky..	1893
"	George M. Bibb......	Ky..	1844	McKinley.....	Lyman J. Gage.....	Ill..	1897
Polk.........	Robert J. Walker....	Miss..	1845	T. Roosevelt...	"	"	1901
Taylor........	William M. Meredith..	Pa..	1849	"	Leslie M. Shaw......	Iowa..	1902
Fillmore......	Thomas Corwin......	Oh..	1850	"	George B. Cortelyou....	N. Y..	1907

President	Secretary	Home	Apptd.
Taft	Franklin MacVeagh	Ill.	1909
Wilson	William G. McAdoo	N.Y.	1913
"	Carter Glass	Va.	1918
"	David F. Houston	Mo.	1920
Harding	Andrew W. Mellon	Pa.	1921
Coolidge	"	"	1923
Hoover	"	"	1929
"	Ogden L. Mills	N.Y.	1932
F. D. Roosevelt	William H. Woodin	"	1933
"	Henry Morgenthau Jr.	"	1934
Truman	Fred M. Vinson	Ky.	1945
"	John W. Snyder	Mo.	1946
Eisenhower	George M. Humphrey	Oh.	1953
"	Robert B. Anderson	Conn.	1957
Kennedy	C. Douglas Dillon	N.J.	1961
Johnson, L. B.	"	"	1963
"	Henry H. Fowler	Va.	1965
"	Joseph W. Barr	Ind.	1968
Nixon	David M. Kennedy	Ill.	1969
"	John B. Connally	Tex.	1970
"	George P. Shultz	Ill.	1972
"	William E. Simon	N.J.	1974
Ford	"	"	1974

Attorneys General

The office of attorney general was organized by act of Congress Sept. 24, 1789. The attorney general was made a member of the cabinet in 1814. The Dept. of Justice was created June 22, 1870.

President	Attorney General	Home	Apptd.
Washington	Edmund Randolph	Va.	1789
"	William Bradford	Pa.	1794
"	Charles Lee	Va.	1795
J. Adams	Charles Lee	Va.	1797
Jefferson	Levi Lincoln	Mass.	1801
"	John Breckenridge	Ky.	1805
Jefferson	Caesar A. Rodney	Del.	1807
Madison	"	"	1809
"	William Pinkney	Md.	1811
"	Richard Rush	Pa.	1814
Monroe	"	"	1817
"	William Wirt	Va.	1817
J. Q. Adams	"	"	1825
Jackson	John McP. Berrien	Ga.	1829
"	Roger B. Taney	Md.	1831
"	Benjamin F. Butler	N. Y.	1833
Van Buren	"	"	1837
"	Felix Grundy	Tenn.	1838
"	Henry D. Gilpin	Pa.	1840
W. H. Harrison	John J. Crittenden	Ky.	1841
Tyler	"	"	1841
"	Hugh S. Legare	S. C.	1841
"	John Nelson	Md.	1843
Polk	John Y. Mason	Va.	1845
"	Nathan Clifford	Me.	1846
"	Isaac Toucey	Conn.	1848
Taylor	Reverdy Johnson	Md.	1849
Fillmore	John J. Crittenden	Ky.	1850
Pierce	Caleb Cushing	Mass.	1853
Buchanan	Jeremiah S. Black	Pa.	1857
"	Edwin M. Stanton	Pa.	1860
Lincoln	Edward Bates	Mo.	1861
"	James Speed	Ky.	1864
A. Johnson	"	Ky.	1865
"	Henry Stanbery	Oh.	1866
"	William M. Evarts	N. Y.	1868
Grant	Ebenezer R. Hoar	Mass.	1869
"	Amos T. Akerman	Ga.	1870
"	George H. Williams	Ore.	1871
"	Edwards Pierrepont	N. Y.	1875
"	Alphonso Taft	Oh.	1876
Hayes	Charles Devens	Mass.	1877
Garfield	Wayne MacVeagh	Pa.	1881
Arthur	Benjamin H. Brewster	"	1881
Cleveland	Augustus Garland	Ark.	1885
B. Harrison	William H. H. Miller	Ind.	1889
Cleveland	Richard Olney	Mass.	1893
"	Judson Harmon	Oh.	1895
McKinley	Joseph McKenna	Cal.	1897
"	John W. Griggs	N. J.	1898
"	Philander C. Knox	Pa.	1901
T. Roosevelt	"	"	1901
"	William H. Moody	Mass.	1904
"	Charles J. Bonaparte	Md.	1906
Taft	George W. Wickersham	N. Y.	1909
Wilson	J. C. McReynolds	Tenn.	1913
"	Thomas W. Gregory	Tex.	1914
"	A. Mitchell Palmer	Pa.	1919
Harding	Harry M. Daugherty	Oh.	1921
Coolidge	"	"	1923
"	Harlan F. Stone	N. Y.	1924
"	John G. Sargent	Vt.	1925
Hoover	William D. Mitchell	Minn.	1929
F. D. Roosevelt	Homer S. Cummings	Conn.	1933
"	Frank Murphy	Mich.	1939
"	Robert H. Jackson	N. Y.	1940
"	Francis Biddle	Pa.	1941
Truman	Tom C. Clark	Tex.	1945
"	J. Howard McGrath	R. I.	1949
"	J. P. McGranery	Pa.	1952
Eisenhower	H. Brownell Jr.	N. Y.	1953
"	William P. Rogers	Md.	1957
Kennedy	Robert F. Kennedy	Mass.	1961
L. B. Johnson	"	"	1963
"	N. de B. Katzenbach	Ill.	1965
"	Ramsey Clark	Tex.	1967
Nixon	John N. Mitchell	N. Y.	1969
"	Richard G. Kleindienst	Ariz.	1972
"	Elliot L. Richardson	Mass.	1973
"	William B. Saxbe	Oh.	1974
Ford	"	"	1974
"	Edward H. Levi	Ill.	1975

Secretaries of Agriculture

The Department of Agriculture was created by act of Congress May 15, 1862. On Feb. 8, 1889, its commissioner was renamed secretary of agriculture and became a member of the cabinet.

President	Secretary	Home	Apptd.
Cleveland	Norman J. Colman	Mo.	1889
B. Harrison	Jeremiah M. Rusk	Wis.	1889
Cleveland	J. Sterling Morton	Neb.	1893
McKinley	James Wilson	Ia.	1897
T. Roosevelt	"	"	1901
Taft	"	"	1909
Wilson	David F. Houston	Mo.	1913
"	Edward T. Meredith	Ia.	1920
Harding	Henry C. Wallace	Ia.	1921
Coolidge	"	"	1923
"	Howard M. Gore	W. Va.	1924
"	W. M. Jardine	Kan.	1925
Hoover	Arthur M. Hyde	Mo.	1929
F. D. Roosevelt	Henry A. Wallace	Ia.	1933
"	Claude R. Wickard	Ind.	1940
Truman	Clinton P. Anderson	N. M.	1945
"	Charles F. Brannan	Col.	1948
Eisenhower	Ezra Taft Benson	Ut.	1953
Kennedy	Orville L. Freeman	Minn.	1961
L. B. Johnson	"	"	1963
Nixon	Clifford M. Hardin	Ind.	1969
"	Earl L. Butz	Ind.	1971
Ford	"	"	1974

Secretaries of the Interior

The Department of Interior was created by act of Congress Mar. 3, 1849

President	Secretary	Home	Apptd.
Taylor	Thomas Ewing	Oh.	1849
Fillmore	Thomas M. T. McKennan	Pa.	1850
"	Alex H. H. Stuart	Va.	1850
Pierce	Robert McClelland	Mich.	1853
Buchanan	Jacob Thompson	Miss.	1857
Lincoln	Caleb B. Smith	Ind.	1861
"	John P. Usher		1863
A. Johnson	John P. Usher	Ind.	1865
"	James Harlan	Ia.	1865
"	Orville H. Browning	Ill.	1866
Grant	Jacob D. Cox	Oh.	1869
"	Columbus Delano		1870
"	Zachariah Chandler	Mich.	1875
Hayes	Carl Schurz	Mo.	1877

President	Secretary	Home	Apptd.	President	Secretary	Home	Apptd.
Garfield	Sam. J. Kirkwood	Ia.	1881	Harding	Hubert Work	Col.	1923
Arthur	Henry M. Teller	Col.	1882	Coolidge	"	"	1923
Cleveland	Lucius Q. C. Lamar	Miss.	1885	"	Roy O. West	Ill.	1929
"	William F. Vilas	Wis.	1888	Hoover	Ray Lyman Wilbur	Cal.	1929
B. Harrison	John W. Noble	Mo.	1889	F. D. Roosevelt	Harold L. Ickes	Ill.	1933
Cleveland	Hoke Smith	Ga.	1893	"	"	Ill.	1943
"	David R. Francis	Mo.	1896	Truman	"	Ill.	1945
McKinley	Cornelius N. Bliss	N. Y.	1897	"	Julius A. Krug	Wis.	1946
"	Ethan A. Hitchcock	Mo.	1898	"	Oscar L. Chapman	Col.	1950
T. Roosevelt	Ethan A. Hitchcock	Mo.	1901	Eisenhower	Douglas McKay	Ore.	1953
"	James R. Garfield	Oh.	1907	"	Fred A. Seaton	Neb.	1956
Taft	Richard A. Ballinger	Wash.	1909	Kennedy	Stewart L. Udall	Ariz.	1961
"	Walter L. Fisher	Ill.	1911	L.B. Johnson	"	"	1963
Wilson	Franklin K. Lane	Cal.	1913	Nixon	Walter J. Hickel	Alas.	1969
"	John B. Payne	Ill.	1920	"	Rogers C. B. Morton	Md.	1971
Harding	Albert B. Fall	N. M.	1921	Ford	"	"	1974
				"	Thomas S. Kleppe	N. D.	1975

Secretaries of Health, Education, and Welfare

The Department of Health, Education, and Welfare was created by act of Congress Apr. 11, 1953.

President	Secretary	Home	Apptd.	President	Secretary	Home	Apptd.
Eisenhower	Oveta Culp Hobby	Tex.	1953	Johnson, L. B.	Wilbur J. Cohen	Mich.	1968
"	Marion B. Folsom	N. Y.	1955	Nixon	Robert H. Finch	Cal.	1969
"	Arthur S. Flemming	Oh.	1958	"	Elliot L. Richardson	Mass.	1970
Kennedy	Abraham A. Ribicoff	Conn.	1961	"	Caspar W. Weinberger	Cal.	1973
"	Anthony J. Celebrezze	Oh.	1962	Ford	"	"	1974
Johnson, L.B.	"	"	1963	"	Forrest D. Mathews	Ala.	1975
"	John W. Gardner	N. Y.	1965				

Secretaries of Housing and Urban Development

The Department of Housing and Urban Development was created by act of Congress Sept. 9, 1965.

President	Secretary	Home	Apptd.	President	Secretary	Home	Apptd.
Johnson, L. B.	Robert C. Weaver	Wash.	1966	Nixon	James T. Lynn	Oh.	1973
"	Robert C. Wood	Mass.	1968	Ford	"	"	1974
Nixon	George W. Romney	Mich.	1969	"	Carla Anderson Hills	Cal.	1975

Secretaries of Defense

The Department of Defense, originally designated the National Military Establishment, was created Sept. 18, 1947. It is headed by the secretary of defense, who is a member of the president's cabinet.

The departments of the army, of the navy, and of the air force function within the Department of Defense, and their respective secretaries are no longer members of the president's cabinet.

President	Secretary	Home	Apptd.	President	Secretary	Home	Apptd.
Truman	James V. Forrestal	N. Y.	1947	Kennedy	Robert S. McNamara	Mich.	1961
"	Louis A. Johnson	W. Va.	1949	Johnson, L. B.	"	"	1963
"	George C. Marshall	Pa.	1950	"	Clark M. Clifford	Md.	1968
"	Robert A. Lovett	N. Y.	1951	Nixon	Melvin R. Laird	Wis.	1969
Eisenhower	Charles E. Wilson	Mich.	1953	"	Elliot L. Richardson	Mass.	1973
"	Neil H. McElroy	Oh.	1957	"	James R. Schlesinger	Va.	1973
"	Thomas S. Gates Jr.	Pa.	1959	Ford	"	"	1974
				"	Donald H. Rumsfeld	Ill.	1975

Not Members of the President's Cabinet

The Dept. of Defense, created Sept. 18, 1947, consolidated the navy, army, air force into a single department.

Secretary of the Air Force	Appointed
W. Stuart Symington	Sept. 18, 1947
Thomas K. Finletter	Apr. 24, 1950
Harold E. Talbot	Feb. 4, 1953
Donald A. Quarles	Aug. 12, 1965
James H. Douglas	Mar. 26, 1957
Dudley C. Sharpe	Dec. 10, 1959
Eugene M. Zuckert	Jan. 23, 1961
Dr. Harold Brown	July 10, 1965
Robert C. Seamans Jr.	Jan. 20, 1969
John L. McLucas	July 19, 1973
Thomas C. Reed	Jan. 2, 1976

Secretary of the Army	
Kenneth C. Royall	Sept. 18, 1947
Gordon Gray*	June 20, 1949
Frank Pace Jr.	Apr. 12, 1950
Earl D. Johnson (Acting)	Jan. 20, 1953
Robert T. Stevens	Feb. 4, 1953
Wilber M. Brucker	July 21, 1955
Elvis J. Stahr Jr.	Jan. 23, 1961
Cyrus R. Vance	May 21, 1962
Stephen Ailes	Jan. 20, 1964
Stanley R. Resor	June 17, 1965

Robert F. Froehlke	June 15, 1971
Howard H. Callaway	May 2, 1973
Norman R. Augustine (acting)	July 3, 1975
Martin R. Hoffman	Aug. 5, 1975

*In addition, Gordon Gray was acting secretary of the army from Apr. 28, 1949, and under secretary from May 25, 1949, until June 20, 1949.

Secretary of the Navy	Appointed
John L. Sullivan	Sept. 18, 1947
Francis P. Matthews	May 25, 1949
Dan A. Kimball	July 31, 1951
Robert B. Anderson	Feb. 4, 1953
Charles S. Thomas	May 3, 1954
Thomas S. Gates Jr.	Apr. 1, 1957
William B. Franke	June 1, 1959
John B. Connally Jr.	Jan. 23, 1961
Fred Korth	Dec. 11, 1961
Paul H. Nitze	Oct. 14, 1963
John T. McNaughton	June 6, 1967
Paul R. Ignatius	Aug. 4, 1967
John H. Chafee	Jan. 20, 1969
John W. Warner	Apr. 7, 1972
J. William Middendorf 2d	June 10, 1974

Secretaries of War

The War (and Navy) Department was created by act of Congress Aug. 7, 1789, and Gen. Henry Knox was commissioned secretary of war under that act Sept. 12, 1789.

President	Secretary	Home	Apptd.	President	Secretary	Home	Apptd.
Washington	Henry Knox	Mass.	1789	J. Adams	Samuel Dexter	Mass.	1800
"	Timothy Pickering	Pa.	1795	Jefferson	Henry Dearborn	"	1801
"	James McHenry	Md.	1796	Madison	William Eustis	Mass.	1809
J. Adams	"	"	1797	"	John Armstrong	N. Y.	1813

President	Secretary	Home	Apptd.
Madison	James Monroe	Va.	1814
"	William H. Crawford	Ga.	1815
Monroe	John C. Calhoun	S.C.	1817
J. Q. Adams	James Barbour	Va.	1825
"	Peter B. Porter	N.Y.	1828
Jackson	John H. Eaton	Tenn.	1829
"	Lewis Cass	Oh.	1831
"	Benjamin F. Butler	N.Y.	1837
Van Buren	Joel R. Poinsett	S.C.	1837
W. H. Harrison	John Bell	Tenn.	1841
Tyler	"	"	1841
Tyler	John C. Spencer	N.Y.	1841
"	James M. Porter	Pa.	1843
"	William Wilkins	"	1844
Polk	William L. Marcy	N.Y.	1845
Taylor	George W. Crawford	Ga.	1849
Fillmore	Charles M. Conrad	La.	1850
Pierce	Jefferson Davis	Miss.	1853
Buchanan	John B. Floyd	Va.	1857
"	Joseph Holt	Ky.	1861
Lincoln	Simon Cameron	Pa.	1861
"	Edwin M. Stanton	Pa.	1862
Johnson, A.	"	"	1865
"	John M. Schofield	Ill.	1868
Grant	John A. Rawlins	Ill.	1869
"	William T. Sherman	Oh.	1869
"	William W. Belknap	Ia.	1869
"	Alphonso Taft	Oh.	1876
Grant	James D. Cameron	Pa.	1876
Hayes	George W. McCrary	Ia.	1877
"	Alexander Ramsey	Minn.	1879
Garfield	Robert T. Lincoln	Ill.	1881
Arthur	"	"	1881
Cleveland	William C. Endicott	Mass.	1885
B. Harrison	Redfield Proctor	Vt.	1890
"	Stephen B. Elkins	W. Va.	1891
Cleveland	Daniel S. Lamont	N.Y.	1893
McKinley	Russel A. Alger	Mich.	1897
"	Elihu Root	N.Y.	1899
T. Roosevelt	"	"	1901
"	William H. Taft	Oh.	1904
"	Luke E. Wright	Tenn.	1908
Taft	Jacob M. Dickinson	"	1909
"	Henry L. Stimson	N.Y.	1911
Wilson	Lindley M. Garrison	N.J.	1913
"	Newton D. Baker	Oh.	1916
Harding	John W. Weeks	Mass.	1921
Coolidge	"	"	1923
"	Dwight F. Davis	Mo.	1925
Hoover	James W. Good	Ill.	1929
"	Patrick J. Hurley	Okla.	1929
F. D. Roosevelt	George H. Dern	Ut.	1933
"	Harry H. Woodring	Kan.	1937
"	Henry L. Stimson	N.Y.	1940
Truman	Robert P. Patterson	N.Y.	1945
"	*Kenneth C. Royall	N.C.	1947

Secretaries of the Navy

The Navy Department was created by act of Congress Apr. 30, 1798.

President	Secretary	Home	Apptd.
J. Adams	Benjamin Stoddert	Md.	1798
Jefferson	"	"	1801
"	Robert Smith	"	1801
Madison	Paul Hamilton	S.C.	1809
"	William Jones	Pa.	1813
"	Benjamin Williams Crowninshield	Mass.	1814
Monroe	"	"	1817
"	Smith Thompson	N.Y.	1818
"	Samuel L. Southard	N.J.	1823
J. Q. Adams	"	"	1825
Jackson	John Branch	N.C.	1829
"	Levi Woodbury	N.H.	1831
"	Mahlon Dickerson	N.J.	1834
Van Buren	"	"	1837
"	James K. Paulding	N.Y.	1838
W. H. Harrison	George E. Badger	N.C.	1841
Tyler	"	"	1841
"	Abel P. Upshur	Va.	1841
"	David Henshaw	Mass.	1843
"	Thomas W. Gilmer	Va.	1844
"	John Y. Mason	"	1844
Polk	George Bancroft	Mass.	1845
"	John Y. Mason	Va.	1846
Taylor	William B. Preston	Va.	1849
Fillmore	William A. Graham	N.C.	1850
"	John P. Kennedy	Md.	1852
Pierce	James C. Dobbin	N.C.	1853
Buchanan	Isaac Toucey	Conn.	1857
Lincoln	Gideon Welles	Conn.	1861
Johnson, A.	"	"	1865
Grant	Adolph E. Borie	Pa.	1869
"	George M. Robeson	N.J.	1869
Hayes	Richard W. Thompson	Ind.	1877
"	Nathan Goff Jr.	W. Va.	1881
Garfield	William H. Hunt	La.	1881
Arthur	William E. Chandler	N.H.	1882
Cleveland	William C. Whitney	N.Y.	1885
B. Harrison	Benjamin F. Tracy	N.Y.	1889
Cleveland	Hilary A. Herbert	Ala.	1893
McKinley	John D. Long	Mass.	1897
T. Roosevelt	"	"	1901
"	William H. Moody	Ill.	1902
"	Paul Morton	Ill.	1904
"	Charles J. Bonaparte	Md.	1905
"	Victor H. Metcalf	Cal.	1906
"	Truman H. Newberry	Mich.	1908
Taft	George von L. Meyer	Mass.	1909
Wilson	Josephus Daniels	N.C.	1913
Harding	Edwin Denby	Mich.	1921
Coolidge	"	"	1923
"	Curtis D. Wilbur	Cal.	1924
Hoover	Charles Francis Adams	Mass.	1929
F. D. Roosevelt	Claude A. Swanson	Va.	1933
"	Charles Edison	N.J.	1940
"	Frank Knox	Ill.	1940
"	*James V. Forrestal	N.Y.	1944
Truman	"	"	1945

*Last members of Cabinet. The War Dept. became the Dept. of the Army and it and the Navy Dept. became branches of the Dept. of Defense, created Sept. 18, 1947.

Secretaries of Commerce and Labor

The Dept. of Commerce & Labor, created by Congress Feb. 14, 1903, was divided by Congress Mar. 4, 1913, into separate Depts. of Commerce and Labor. The secretary of each was made a cabinet member.

Secretaries of Commerce and Labor

President	Secretary	Home	Apptd.
T. Roosevelt	Geo. B. Cortelyou	N.Y.	1903
"	Victor H. Metcalf	Cal.	1904
"	Oscar S. Straus	N.Y.	1906
Taft	Charles Nagel	Mo.	1909

Secretaries of Labor

President	Secretary	Home	Apptd.
Wilson	William B. Wilson	Pa.	1913
Harding	James J. Davis	Pa.	1921
Coolidge	"	"	1923
Hoover	"	"	1929
"	William N. Doak	Va.	1930
F. D. Roosevelt	Frances Perkins	N.Y.	1933
Truman	L. B. Schwellenbach	Wash.	1945
"	Maurice J. Tobin	Mass.	1949
Eisenhower	Martin P. Durkin	Ill.	1953
"	James P. Mitchell	N.J.	1953
Kennedy	Arthur J. Goldberg	Ill.	1961
"	W. Willard Wirtz	Ill.	1962
Johnson, L. B.	W. Willard Wirtz	Ill.	1963
Nixon	George P. Shultz	Ill.	1969
"	James D. Hodgson	Cal.	1970
"	Peter J. Brennan	N.Y.	1973
Ford	"	"	1974
"	John T. Dunlop	Cal.	1975
"	W. J. Usery Jr.	Ga.	1976

Secretaries of Commerce

President	Secretary	Home	Apptd.
Wilson	William C. Redfield	N.Y.	1913
"	Josh. W. Alexander	Mo.	1919
Harding	Herbert C. Hoover	Cal.	1921
Coolidge	"	"	1923
"	William F. Whiting	Mass.	1928
Hoover	Robert P. Lamont	Ill.	1929
"	Roy D. Chapin	Mich.	1932
F. D. Roosevelt	Daniel C. Roper	S.C.	1933
"	Harry L. Hopkins	N.Y.	1939
"	Jesse Jones	Tex.	1940
"	Henry A. Wallace	Ia.	1945
Truman	"	"	1945
Truman	W. Averell Harriman	N.Y.	1947
"	Charles Sawyer	Oh.	1948
Eisenhower	Sinclair Weeks	Mass.	1953
"	Lewis L. Strauss	N.Y.	1958
"	Frederick H. Mueller	Mich.	1959
Kennedy	Luther H. Hodges	N.C.	1961
Johnson, L. B.	John T. Connor	N.J.	1965
"	Alex B. Trowbridge	N.J.	1967
"	C. R. Smith	N.Y.	1968
Nixon	Maurice H. Stans	Minn.	1969
"	Peter G. Peterson	Ill.	1972
"	Frederick B. Dent	S.C.	1973
Ford	"	"	1974
"	Rogers C. B. Morton	Md.	1975
"	Elliot L. Richardson	Mass.	1976

Secretaries of Transportation
The Department of Transportation was created by act of Congress Oct. 15, 1966.

President	Secretary	Home	Apptd.	President	Secretary	Home	Apptd.
Johnson, L. B..	Alan S. Boyd	Fla.	1966	Ford	Claude S. Brinegar	Cal.	1974
Nixon	John A. Volpe	Mass.	1969	"	William T. Coleman Jr.	Pa.	1975
"	Claude S. Brinegar	Cal.	1973				

Postmasters General
Postmasters general were made members of the cabinet Mar. 9, 1829, and 53 men held the position before the organization of the U.S. Postal Service, as an independent agency, July 1, 1971. The Postal Service is not a department and its head is not a cabinet member. (For a full list of postmasters general, see 1974 World Almanac.)

Wives and Children of the Presidents

President*	Wife's Name	State	Born	Married	Died	Sons	Daughters
Washington	Martha (Dandridge) Custis	Va.	1732	1759	1802		
John Adams	Abigail Smith	Mass.	1744	1764	1818	3	2
Jefferson	Martha (Wayles) Skelton	Va.	1748	1772	1782	1	5
Madison	Dorothea "Dolley" (Payne) Todd	N. C.	1768	1794	1849		
Monroe	Elizabeth Kortright (1)	N. Y.	1768	1786	1830		
J. Q. Adams	Louisa Catherine Johnson (2)	Md.	1775	1797	1852	3	1
Jackson	Rachel (Donelson) Robards	Va.	1767	1791	1828		
Van Buren	Hannah Hoes	N. Y.	1783	1807	1819	4	
William H. Harrison	Anna Symmes	N. J.	1775	1795	1864	6	4
Tyler	Letitia Christian	Va.	1790	1813	1842	3	4
"	Julia Gardiner	N. Y.	1820	1844	1889	5	2
Polk	Sarah Childress	Tenn.	1803	1824	1891		
Taylor	Margaret Smith	Md.	1788	1810	1852	1	5
Fillmore	Abigail Powers	N. Y.	1798	1826	1853	1	1
"	Caroline (Carmichael) McIntosh	N. J.	1813	1858	1881		
Pierce	Jane Means Appleton	N. H.	1806	1834	1863	3	
Lincoln	Mary Todd	Ky.	1818	1842	1882	4	
Johnson, Andrew	Eliza McCardle	Tenn.	1810	1827	1876	3	2
Grant	Julia Dent	Mo.	1826	1848	1902	3	1
Hayes	Lucy Ware Webb	Oh.	1831	1852	1889	7	1
Garfield	Lucretia Rudolph	Oh.	1832	1858	1918	4	1
Arthur	Ellen Lewis Herndon	Va.	1837	1859	1880	2	1
Cleveland	Frances Folsom	N. Y.	1864	1886	1947	2	3
Benjamin Harrison	Caroline Lavinia Scott	Oh.	1832	1853	1892	1	1
"	Mary Scott (Lord) Dimmick	Pa.	1858	1896	1948		1
McKinley	Ida Saxton	Oh.	1847	1871	1907		2
Theodore Roosevelt	Alice Hathaway Lee	Mass.	1861	1880	1884		1
"	Edith Kermit Carow	Conn.	1861	1886	1948	4	1
Taft	Helen Herron	Oh.	1861	1886	1943	2	1
Wilson	Ellen Louise Axson	Ga.	1860	1885	1914		3
"	Edith (Bolling) Galt	Va.	1872	1915	1961		
Harding	Florence (Kling) De Wolfe	Oh.	1860	1891	1924		
Coolidge	Grace Anna Goodhue	Vt.	1879	1905	1957	2	
Hoover	Lou Henry	Ia.	1875	1899	1944	2	
F. D. Roosevelt	Anna Eleanor Roosevelt (1)	N. Y.	1884	1905	1962	4	1
Truman	Bess Wallace	Mo.	1885	1919			1
Eisenhower	Mamie Geneva Doud (1)	Ia.	1896	1916		1	
Kennedy	Jacqueline Lee Bouvier (1)	N. Y.	1929	1953		1	1
Johnson, Lyndon	Claudia Alta Taylor	Tex.	1912	1934			2
Nixon	Thelma Catherine Patricia Ryan	Nev.	1912	1940			2
Ford	Elizabeth Bloomer Warren	Ill.	1918	1948		3	1

*James Buchanan, 15th president, was unmarried. (1) plus one infant, deceased. (2) Born London, father a Md. citizen.

Law on Succession to the Presidency

If by reason of death, resignation, removal from office, inability, or failure to qualify there is neither a president nor vice president to discharge the powers and duties of the office of president, then the speaker of the House of Representatives shall upon his resignation as speaker and as representative, act as president. The same rule shall apply in the case of the death, resignation, removal from office, or inability of an individual acting as president.

If at the time when a speaker is to begin the discharge of the powers and duties of the office of president there is no speaker, or the speaker fails to qualify as acting president, then the president pro tempore of the Senate, upon his resignation as president pro tempore and as senator, shall act as president.

An individual acting as president shall continue to act until the expiration of the then current presidential term, except that (1) if his discharge of the powers and duties of the office is founded in whole or in part in the failure of both the president-elect and the vice president-elect to qualify, then he shall act only until a president or vice president qualifies, and (2) if his discharge of the powers and duties of the office is founded in whole or in part on the inability of the president or vice president, then he shall act only until the removal of the disability of one of such individuals.

If, by reason of death, resignation, removal from office, or failure to qualify, there is no president pro tempore to act as president, then the officer of the United States who is highest on the following list, and who is not under disability to discharge the powers and duties of president, shall act as president: the secretaries of state, treasury, defense; attorney general; secretaries of interior, agriculture, commerce, labor; health, education and welfare; housing and urban development; transportation.

(Legislation approved July 18, 1947; amended Sept. 9, 1965, and Oct. 15, 1966. See also Constitutional Amendment XXV.)

Presidents' Original Paternal Ancestry

Dutch: Van Buren, Theodore Roosevelt, Franklin D. Roosevelt. **German:** Eisenhower. **Swiss and Palatinate German:** Hoover.

English: Washington, John Adams, Madison, John Quincy Adams, William Henry Harrison, Tyler, Taylor, Fillmore, Pierce, Lincoln, Andrew Johnson, Grant, Garfield, Cleveland, Benjamin Harrison, Taft, Harding, Coolidge. **English-French-German:** L. B. Johnson. **English-Scottish-Irish:** Truman.

Irish: Jackson, Arthur, Wilson, Kennedy, Nixon. **Scottish:** Monroe, Hayes. **Scottish-Irish:** Polk, Buchanan, McKinley. **Welsh:** Jefferson (according to family tradition).

Religious Background of Presidents

Baptist: Harding, Truman.
Christian Church (Disciples of Christ): Garfield, Lyndon B. Johnson.
Congregationalist: Coolidge.
Episcopalian: Washington, Madison, Monroe, William Henry Harrison, Tyler, Taylor, Pierce, Arthur, Franklin D. Roosevelt, Ford.
Jefferson, an Episcopal Church member, later became a deist, said he was a "disciple of the doctrines of Jesus," and commended Unitarianism.
Friends (Quakers): Hoover, Nixon.

Methodist: Polk, Andrew Johnson, Grant, McKinley. Hayes attended the Methodist Church, but never joined.
Presbyterian: Jackson, Buchanan, Cleveland, Benjamin Harrison, Wilson, Eisenhower.
Lincoln attended Presbyterian services in Washington but was not a member.
Reformed Dutch: Van Buren, Theodore Roosevelt.
Roman Catholic: Kennedy.
Unitarian: John Adams, John Quincy Adams, Fillmore, Taft.

Burial Places of the Presidents

G. Washington....	1732-1799	Mt. Vernon, Va.
John Adams......	1735-1826	Quincy, Mass.
T. Jefferson.....	1743-1826	Charlottesville, Va.
James Madison...	1751-1836	Montpelier Station, Va.
James Monroe....	1758-1831	Richmond, Va.
John Q. Adams...	1767-1848	Quincy, Mass.
Andrew Jackson..	1767-1845	Nashville, Tenn.
M. Van Buren....	1782-1862	Kinderhook, N.Y.
W. H. Harrison..	1773-1841	North Bend, Oh.
John Tyler......	1790-1862	Richmond, Va.
James Knox Polk.	1795-1849	Nashville, Tenn.
Zachary Taylor..	1784-1850	Louisville, Ky.
Millard Fillmore..	1800-1874	Buffalo, N.Y.
Franklin Pierce..	1804-1869	Concord, N.H.
James Buchanan..	1791-1868	Lancaster, Pa.
A. Lincoln......	1809-1865	Springfield, Ill.
Andrew Johnson..	1808-1875	Greeneville, Tenn.
Ulysses S. Grant..	1822-1885	New York City
R. B. Hayes.......	1822-1893	Fremont, Oh.
J. A. Garfield.....	1831-1881	Cleveland, Oh.
C. A. Arthur......	1829-1886	Albany, N. Y.
Grover Cleveland .	1837-1908	Princeton, N.J.
B. Harrison.......	1833-1901	Indianapolis, Ind.
W. McKinley.....	1843-1901	Canton, Oh.
T. Roosevelt......	1858-1919	Oyster Bay, N.Y.
William H. Taft...	1857-1930	Arlington Nat'l. Cem'y.
Woodrow Wilson...	1856-1924	Washington Cathedral
W. G. Harding....	1865-1923	Marion, Oh.
Calvin Coolidge...	1872-1933	Plymouth, Vt.
Herbert Hoover..	1874-1964	West Branch, Ia.
F. D. Roosevelt ...	1882-1945	Hyde Park, N.Y.
Harry S. Truman..	1884-1972	Independence, Mo.
D. D. Eisenhower..	1890-1969	Abilene, Kan.
J. F. Kennedy.....	1917-1963	Arlington Nat'l. Cem'y.
Lyndon B. Johnson	1908-1973	Stonewall, Tex.

Longevity of Presidents of the U. S.

Source: Statistical Bulletin, Metropolitan Life

	Year of Birth	Age, 1st Inauguration	Age at Death	Expectancy After 1st Inaugural	Years Lived After 1st Inaugural		
					Actual	Above Expected	Below Expected
George Washington............	1732	57	67	17.1	10.6		6.5
John Adams...................	1735	61	90	14.4	29.3	15.0	
Thomas Jefferson.............	1743	57	83	16.4	25.3	8.9	
James Madison...............	1751	57	85	16.3	27.3	11.0	
James Monroe................	1758	58	73	15.6	14.3		1.3
John Quincy Adams...........	1767	57	80	16.3	23.0	6.7	
Andrew Jackson..............	1767	61	78	13.5	16.3	2.7	
Martin Van Buren............	1782	54	79	17.2	25.4	8.2	
William H. Harrison†..........	1773	68	68	9.4	.1		9.3
John Tyler...................	1790	51	71	19.2	20.8	1.6	
James K. Polk................	1795	49	53	21.5	4.3		17.2
Zachary Taylor†..............	1784	64	65	12.8	1.3		11.5
Millard Fillmore..............	1800	50	74	20.7	23.7	2.9	
Franklin Pierce..............	1804	48	64	22.0	16.6		5.4
James Buchanan..............	1791	65	77	11.9	11.3		.6
Abraham Lincoln‡............	1809	52	56	19.8	4.1		15.6
Andrew Johnson.............	1808	56	66	17.2	10.3		6.9
Ulysses S. Grant.............	1822	46	63	22.8	16.4		6.4
Rutherford B. Hayes..........	1822	54	70	18.0	15.9		2.1
James A. Garfield‡...........	1831	49	49	21.2	.5		20.7
Chester A. Arthur...........	1829	51	57	20.1	5.2		15.0
Grover Cleveland............	1837	47	71	22.1	23.3	1.2	
Benjamin Harrison...........	1833	55	67	17.2	12.0		5.2
William McKinley‡...........	1843	54	58	18.2	4.5		13.6
Theodore Roosevelt..........	1858	42	60	26.1	17.3		8.8
William H. Taft..............	1851	51	72	20.2	21.0	.8	
Woodrow Wilson.............	1856	56	67	17.2	10.9		6.2
Warren G. Harding†..........	1865	55	57	18.0	2.4		15.6
Calvin Coolidge..............	1872	51	60	21.3	9.4		11.9
Herbert C. Hoover..........	1874	54	90	18.9	35.6	16.7	
Franklin D. Roosevelt†........	1882	51	63	21.7	12.1		9.6
Harry S. Truman............	1884	60	88	15.0	27.7	12.7	
Dwight D. Eisenhower........	1890	62	78	14.4	16.2	1.7	
John F. Kennedy‡............	1917	43	46	28.4	2.8		25.6
Lyndon B. Johnson...........	1908	55	64	19.2	9.2		10.1
Richard M. Nixon	1913	56		18.7			
Gerald R. Ford...............	1913	61		15.3			

†Died during tenure. ‡Assassinated.

BIOGRAPHIES OF U.S. PRESIDENTS

George Washington

George Washington, first president, was born Friday, Feb. 22, 1732 (Feb. 11, 1731, Old Style), the son of Augustine Washington and Mary Ball, at Wakefield on Pope's Creek, Westmoreland Co., Va. Col. John Washington, George's great-grandfather, came from Northamptonshire in 1657 or 1658; in 1665 he and an associate named Spencer bought 5,000 acres on the Potomac. George's father took the north 2,500 acres near Hunting Creek in 1735 and built a house in which George lived from 3 to 6 years of age; then the family moved to Ferry farm, near Fredericksburg. His father died in 1743 when George was 11. He studied mathematics and surveying and when 16 went to live with his half brother Lawrence, who had inherited the Potomac farm and built Mount Vernon, the original house having burned. George surveyed the lands of William Fairfax on the Shenandoah, keeping a diary. He accompanied Lawrence to Barbados, West Indies, contracted small pox, and was deeply scarred. Lawrence died in 1752 and George acquired his property by inheritance and purchase and added the 2,500 acres held by the Spencers. He valued land and when he died owned 70,000 acres in Virginia and 40,000 acres on the Great Kanawha in what is now West Virginia.

Washington's military service began in 1753 when Gov. Dinwiddie of Virginia made him lieutenant-colonel of militia. He clashed with the French and had to surrender Fort Necessity July 3, 1754. He was an aide to Braddock and helped organize the retreat after the fatal ambuscade of July 9, 1755. He helped take Fort DuQuesne from the French in 1758.

After his marriage to Martha Dandridge Custis, a widow, in 1759, Washington lived at Mount Vernon, bred horses and cattle, raised fruit and practiced crop rotation. During the Stamp Act agitation, 1765, he supported the protesting Virginians. Although not at first for independence, he stood out against British exactions and took charge of the Virginia troops before war broke out. He was made commander-in-chief by the Continental Congress June 15, 1775, and took command at Cambridge July 3.

The successful issue of a war filled with hardships was largely due to his leadership. He was resourceful, a stern disciplinarian, and the one strong, dependable force for unity. He favored a federal government and became chairman of the Constitutional Convention of 1787. He helped get the Constitution ratified and was unanimously elected president by the Electoral College and inaugurated, Apr. 30, 1789, on the balcony of New York's Federal Hall at Broad and Wall Sts., now marked by his statue. His pew in St. Paul's Chapel is preserved. He was reelected, again unanimously, in 1792.

His birthplace, Wakefield, was burned in 1780. On Feb. 22, 1932, a new Wakefield, built by donations, was dedicated as the George Washington Birthplace Monument, administered by the National Parks Service. The older Washingtons are buried there. It is 34 mi. from Fredericksburg, Va., and 5 mi. from Stratford Hall, birthplace of Robert E. Lee.

Although a Federalist, Washington made Thomas Jefferson secretary of state. He was reelected 1792, but refused to consider a 3d term and retired to Mount Vernon, 1797. He suffered acute laryngitis after a ride in snow and rain around his estate, was bled profusely (an 18th Century medical practice), and died Dec. 14, 1799, aged 67. He was mourned here and abroad as one of the great men of his time. He was buried in a vault at Mount Vernon. (See article on Mount Vernon.)

John Adams

John Adams, 2d president, Federalist, was born in Braintree (Quincy), Mass., Oct. 30, 1735 (Oct. 19, O.S.), the son of John Adams, a farmer, and Susanna Boylston of Brookline. He was a great-grandson of Henry Adams who came from England in 1636. He was graduated from Harvard, 1755, taught school, studied law. In 1765 he argued against taxation without representation before the royal governor. In 1770 he defended the British soldiers, who fired on civilians in the "Boston Massacre." He took part in the Provincial Congress of Massachusetts and the Continental Congress, seconded the independence resolution presented by Richard Henry Lee and with his cousin, Samuel Adams, signed the Declaration of Independence. He was a commissioner to France, 1778, with Benjamin Franklin and Arthur Lee; won recognition of the United States by The Hague, 1782; was first American minister to England, 1785-1788, and elected vice president with Washington, 1788 and 1792.

In 1796 Adams was chosen president by the electors, 71 to 68, so that opponents called him "president by 3 votes." The candidate with the second highest number of votes became vice president; this was Thomas Jefferson, his opponent. Intense antagonism to America by France caused agitation for war, led by Alexander Hamilton. Adams, breaking with Hamilton, opposed war but put the navy on a fighting basis. The U.S.S. Constitution, the United States, both 44 guns, and the Constellation, 36 guns, and armed merchantmen bagged 84 French ships in an undeclared war. To fight alien influence and muzzle criticism Adams supported the Alien and Sedition laws of 1798, which led to his defeat for reelection. He died July 4, 1826, on the same day as Jefferson (the 50th anniversary of the Declaration of Independence), and is buried in the First Parish Church in Quincy, Mass.

Adams married Abigail Smith, 1764. They had 2 daughters and 3 sons, one of whom, John Quincy Adams, became the 6th president.

Thomas Jefferson

Thomas Jefferson, 3d president, was born Apr. 13, 1743 (Apr. 2, O. S.), at Shadwell, Va., the son of Peter Jefferson, a civil engineer of Welsh descent who raised tobacco, and Jane Randolph. Jefferson was an agrarian and an expansionist. Because he opposed the Federalists and centralization he was called a Republican, the equivalent of a Democrat in later years. His father died when he was 14, leaving him 2,750 acres and his slaves. Jefferson attended the college of William and Mary, 1760-1762, read classics in Greek and Latin and played the violin. In 1769 he was elected to the House of Burgesses. In 1770 he began building Monticello, near Charlottesville. He was a member of the Virginia Committee of Correspondence and the Continental Congress and denied Britain's right to tax. Named a member of the committee to draw up a Declaration of Independence, he wrote the basic draft, 1776. He was a member of the Virginia House of Delegates, 1776-79, elected governor to succeed Patrick Henry, 1779, reelected 1780, resigned June 1781, amid charges of ineffectual military preparation. During his term he wrote the statute on religious freedom. In the Continental Congress, 1783, he drew up an ordinance for the Northwest Territory, forbidding slavery after 1800; its terms were put into the Ordinance of 1787. He was sent to Paris with Benjamin Franklin and John Adams to negotiate treaties of commerce, 1784; made minister to France, 1785. He made treaties with France and Prussia, studied architecture, gardening, and the French Revolution, whose leaders consulted him.

Washington appointed him secretary of state, 1789. Jefferson's strong faith in the consent of the governed, as opposed to executive control favored by Hamilton, secretary of the treasury, often led to conflict:

Dec. 31, 1793, he resigned. He was the Republican candidate for president in 1796; beaten by John Adams, he became vice president. He opposed Adams' alien and sedition laws with the Kentucky and Virginia resolutions, reiterating the basic rights of states. In 1800 Jefferson and Aaron Burr received equal Electoral College votes for president, so the House of Representatives, with Hamilton's help, elected Jefferson, the first president to be inaugurated in Washington. Adams left town before the ceremony, but when Jefferson was reelected in 1804 he voted for him. Jefferson canceled levees and titles and ignored diplomatic precedence. He turned Federalists out of office. He opposed a strong navy. By fighting those who feared to give power to the people he made democracy work. He considered John Marshall's Supreme Court reactionary. Big events of his administration were the Louisiana Purchase, 1803, and the Lewis and Clark Expedition. He established the University of Virginia and designed its buildings. After the Library of Congress was burned by the British he sold Congress some 6,000 vols. for $23,950. He was 6 ft. 2, temperate in debate, a deist in religion. He died July 4, 1826, on the same day as John Adams and was buried at Monticello, which, after various vicissitudes, passed to the Thomas Jefferson Memorial Foundation in 1923.

He married Martha Wayles Skelton, a widow, Jan. 1, 1772. They had one son and 5 daughters.

James Madison

James Madison, 4th president, Republican, was born Mar. 16, 1751 (Mar. 5, 1750, O. S.) at Port Conway, King George Co., Va., the eldest of 12 children of James Madison and Eleanor Rose Conway. His great-grandfather, James Taylor (1674-1729), was also the great-grandfather of Zachary Taylor. Madison was graduated from Princeton, 1771; studied theology, 1772; sat in the Virginia Constitutional Convention, 1776, where his resolution on religious freedom was voted down. He was a member of the Continental Congress and of the Annapolis Convention, 1786, where he and Alexander Hamilton proposed the Constitutional Convention. He was chief recorder at that convention in 1787, and supported ratification in the Federalist papers, written with Hamilton and John Jay. In 1785 he carried Jefferson's statute on religious liberty through the Virginia Assembly. He was elected to the House of Representatives in 1789, helped adopt the Bill of Rights and fought John Adams' alien and sedition laws. He favored agrarian policies with Jefferson, and in 1801 became Jefferson's secretary of state. In 1803, when the Louisiana Purchase was consummated, he insisted on free navigation of the Mississippi, which he had already urged on Jay in 1780.

Elected president in 1808, Madison was a "strict constructionist," opposed to the free interpretation of the Constitution by the Federalists. He vetoed federal funds for state improvements, but changed in his second term. Madison inherited the conflict with Britain over its orders in council and its impressment of American seamen, which had led to Jefferson's embargo act and injured American commerce. He was reelected in 1812 by the votes of the agrarian South and recently admitted western states. Caught between British and French maritime restrictions, Madison drifted into war, declared June 18, 1812, unaware that Britain had canceled the orders 2 days before. While the war was inconclusive, it opened the way to peaceful negotiations. Madison successfully advocated a tariff to protect industry, a national system of roads and canals and a strong military organization. Reelected in 1812, he retired in 1817 to his estate at Montpelier in Orange County, Va., built 1760, with a portico suggested by Jefferson. There he edited his famous papers on the Constitutional Convention. He became rector of the University of Vir-

ginia, 1826. He died June 28, 1836, and was buried near his home.

Madison married Dorothea "Dolley" Payne Todd, a widow, Sept. 15, 1794.

James Monroe

James Monroe, 5th president, Republican, was born Apr. 28, 1758, in Westmoreland Co., Va., the son of Spence Monroe and Eliza Jones, who were of Scottish and Welsh descent, respectively. He attended the College of William and Mary, fought in the 3d Virginia Regiment at White Plains, Brandywine, Monmouth, and was wounded at Trenton. He studied law with Thomas Jefferson, 1780, was a member of the Virginia House of Delegates and of Congress, 1783-86. He opposed ratification of the Constitution because it lacked a bill of rights; was U.S. senator, 1790; minister to France, 1794-96, during which he improved relations with France, Spain, and Algiers; 4 times governor of Virginia, 1799-1802, and 1811. Jefferson sent him to France as minister, 1803, to join R. R. Livingston in buying the Isle of New Orleans from France and East and West Florida from Spain. Exceeding instructions, he signed a treaty for all of Louisiana. He was also sent to Madrid, 1804, and London, 1805, to settle disputes. He ran against Madison for president in 1808. He was elected to the Virginia Assembly, 1810-1811; was secretary of state under Madison, 1811-1817; also secretary of war, Sept. 1814-Mar. 1815.

In 1816 Monroe was elected president; in 1820 reelected with all but one Electoral College vote, this being cast for John Quincy Adams by William Plumer Sr. of New Hampshire. Although many historians have held that Plumer withheld his vote from Monroe so that only Washington would have been elected unanimously, Plumer himself said he voted for Adams because he had "discovered a want of foresight" in Monroe. Monroe's administration became the "Era of Good Feeling." He obtained the Floridas from Spain and suppressed the Seminoles; settled boundaries with Canada and eliminated border forts; supported the anti-slavery position that led to the Missouri Compromise. (In 1801 he had proposed settling Negro slaves in Africa. Monrovia, Liberia, was named for him.) In July, 1823, the U.S. served notice on Russia that it would oppose any Russian colony on this continent, after Russia had prohibited fishing on the northwest coasts. On Dec. 2, 1823, Monroe announced the doctrine that the U. S. would consider its safety endangered if European powers had authority on this hemisphere or attempted colonization. First half had been suggested by George Canning, British foreign minister, to curb Spain; U. S., rejecting proposal for joint declaration, issued it also as warning to Russia. Monroe owned Ash Lawn, 5 mi. from Charlottesville, Va., 1799-1825; inherited Oak Hill, Loudon Co., Va., from his uncle Joseph Jones, 1806. The mansion, replacing Jones' cottage, was designed by Jefferson and executed by James Hoban, White House architect.

Monroe married Elizabeth Kortright in 1786. They had a son who died in infancy and 2 daughters. Mrs. Monroe died in 1830 and he and the daughters moved to New York, where he died July 4, 1831.

John Quincy Adams

John Quincy Adams, 6th president, independent Federalist, was born July 11, 1767, at Braintree (Quincy), Mass., the son of John and Abigail Adams. His father was the 2d president. He was educated in Paris, Leyden, and Harvard, graduating in 1787. He served as American minister in the Netherlands, Berlin, St. Petersburg, and London and helped draft the War of 1812 peace treaty, signed Dec. 24, 1814. He had served as senator from 1803 to 1808 and his support of the Republican administration alienated the Federalists. President Monroe made him secretary of state, 1817, and he negotiated the cession of the Floridas from Spain, supported exclusion of slavery in the Missouri Compromise, and laid the base for the Monroe Doctrine, of which he, as much as Monroe, was the creator. In 1824 he was elected president by the House after he failed to win an Electoral College majority over Henry Clay and Andrew Jackson. His expansion of executive powers was strongly opposed and he was beaten in 1828 by Jackson. In 1831 he was sent to Congress as representative and served 9 terms with distinction and independence. He fought slavery, opposed the annexation of Texas and the war with Mexico; was responsible for the Smithsonian Institution. He had a stroke in the House and died in the Speaker's Room, Feb. 23, 1848.

Adams married Louise Catherine Johnson on July 26, 1797. They had 3 sons and a daughter.

Andrew Jackson

Andrew Jackson, 7th president, was originally a Jeffersonian-Republican, later a Democrat. He was born in the Waxhaws district, New Lancaster Co., S. C., Mar. 15, 1767, the posthumous son of Andrew Jackson, who came from County Antrim, Ireland, with his wife, Elizabeth Hutchinson, and 2 sons, in 1765. At 13 young Andrew joined the militia in the Revolution and was captured; a British officer struck him with his sword when the boy refused to shine his boots. He read law in Salisbury, N. C., moved to Nashville, Tenn., speculated in land, married, and raised cotton at the Hermitage, originally a log house. In 1796 he helped draft the Constitution of Tennessee and for one year occupied its one seat in the national House. He was in the Senate in 1797, and again in 1823. He defeated the Creek Indians at Horseshoe Bend, Ala., 1814, and, as major general, drove the British out of Pensacola. With 6,000 backwoods fighters he defeated Packenham's 12,000 British troops at Chalmette, outside New Orleans, Jan. 8, 1815, losing only 7 to the British loss of 2,000. In 1818 he briefly invaded Spanish Florida to quell Seminoles and outlaws who harassed frontier settlements. In 1824 he ran for president against John Quincy Adams and won the most votes in the Electoral College, but not a majority; the election was decided by the House, which chose Adams. In 1828 he carried everything, the West rising to support "Old Hickory" and a liberal land policy. He was a noisy debater and a duelist and introduced rotation in office called the "spoils system." He was suspicious of privilege; ruined the Bank of the United States by depositing federal funds with state banks. Though "Let the people rule" was his slogan, he at times supported strict constructionist policies against the expansionist West. He killed the Congressional caucus for nominating presidential candidates and substituted the national convention, 1832, when he was reelected, with Martin Van Buren vice president. When South Carolina refused to collect imports under his protective tariff he ordered army and naval forces to Charleston. At the Jefferson Day dinner, 1830, he offered the toast: "Our Federal Union; it must be preserved." Vice President John C. Calhoun, exponent of state sovereignty, gave in reply the toast: "The Union — next to our liberty, most dear." Jackson recognized the Republic of Texas, 1836.

In 1791 Jackson married Rachel Donelson Robards who believed she had been divorced by Capt. Lewis Robards. But he did not actually obtain a divorce until 1793, after which the Jacksons were remarried. Mrs. Jackson died in 1828, shortly after Jackson's first election. He died at the Hermitage, June 8, 1845, and is buried there.

Martin Van Buren

Martin Van Buren, 8th president, Democrat, was born Dec. 5, 1782, at Kinderhook, N. Y., the son of Abraham Van Buren, a Dutch farmer, and Mary Hoes. He was surrogate of Columbia County, N.Y., state senator and attorney general and a law partner of Benjamin F. Butler in Albany. He was U. S. senator 1821, reelected, 1827, elected governor of New York, 1828. He helped swing eastern support to Andrew Jackson in 1828 and was his secretary of state 1829-31. In 1832 he was elected vice president. He was a consummate politician, known as "the little magician," and influenced Jackson's policies. In 1836 he defeated William Henry Harrison for president by 170 to 73 electoral votes. He inaugurated the independent treasury system, and was the first advocate of mutual insurance of deposits by banks. He urged tariffs for revenue only and opposed internal improvements at national expense. His refusal to spend land revenues led to his defeat by Harrison in 1840. He lost the Democratic nomination of 1844 to Polk because he opposed annexation of Texas. In 1848 he ran for president on the Free Soil ticket and lost. He died July 24, 1862, at Kinderhook.

Van Buren married Hannah Hoes, a cousin, in 1807; she died in 1819. One of their sons, Abraham, was secretary to the president. Abraham's wife Angelica Singleton, a cousin of "Dolley" Madison, was White House hostess during Van Buren's term.

William Henry Harrison

William Henry, Harrison, 9th president, Whig, who served only 31 days, was born in Berkeley, Charles City Co., Va., Feb. 9, 1773, the third son of Benjamin Harrison, signer of the Declaration of Independence. Educated at Hampden Sydney College, he later studied medicine under Dr. Benjamin Rush. Commissioned by Washington, he fought under Gen. Anthony Wayne at Fallen Timbers, 1794. He was secretary of the Northwest Territory, 1798; its delegate in Congress, 1799; first governor of Indiana Territory, and superintendent of Indian affairs. With 900 men he routed Tecumseh's Indians at Tippecanoe, Nov. 7, 1811. A major general, he defeated British and Indians at Battle of the Thames, Oct. 5, 1813. He served Ohio in Congress, 1816; as senator, 1824; was minister to Colombia. In 1840, when 68, he was elected president with John Tyler, 234 to 60, on a "log cabin and hard cider" slogan. He caught pneumonia during the inauguration and died Apr. 4, 1841. He was buried in North Bend, Oh.

Harrison married Anna Symmes in 1795. They had 6 sons. A grandson, Benjamin Harrison, became the 23d president.

John Tyler

John Tyler, 10th president, Independent Whig, was born Mar. 29, 1790, in Greenway, Charles City Co., Va., son of John Tyler and Mary Armistead. His father was governor of Virginia, 1808-11. Tyler was graduated from William and Mary, 1807; member of the House of Delegates, 1811; in Congress, 1816-21; in Virginia legislature, 1823-25; governor of Virginia, 1825-26; U. S. senator, 1827-36. In 1840 he was elected vice president and, on President Harrison's death, succeeded him. He favored pre-emption, allowing settlers to get government land; rejected a new bank bill and thus alienated Whig supporters except Daniel Webster, his secretary of state; refused to honor the spoils system. He signed the resolution annexing Texas, Mar. 1, 1845. He accepted renomination, 1844, but withdrew before election. He condemned South Carolina's nullification and secession and, as Virginia's commissioner to Buchanan, tried to keep Fort Sumter neutralized. He was president of the peace congress called in Washington by Virginia, 1861. After its failure he supported secession, sat in the provisional Confederate Congress, became a member of the Confederate House, but died, Jan. 18, 1862, before it met. He was buried in Richmond.

Tyler first married Letitia Christian, in 1813; they

had 3 sons and 4 daughters; she died in 1842. He married Julia Gardiner, of Gardiner's Is., N.Y., in 1844. They had 5 sons and 2 daughters.

James Knox Polk

⸗ James Knox Polk, 11th president, Democrat, was born in Mecklenburg Co., N. C., Nov. 2, 1795, the son of Samuel Polk, farmer and surveyor of Scotch-Irish descent, and Jane Knox. He went to Maury Co., Tenn., 1806; was graduated from the University of North Carolina, 1818; member of the Tennessee state legislature, 1823-25, known as "Napoleon of the Stump." He served in Congress 1825-39 and as speaker 1835-39. He supported Jackson and Van Buren, but was always expansionist. He was governor of Tennessee 1839-41, being defeated 1841 and 1843. In 1844, when both Clay and Van Buren announced opposition to annexing Texas, the Democrats made Polk the first dark horse nominee because he demanded control of all Oregon and annexation of Texas. James Buchanan was his secretary of state. Polk re-established the independent treasury system originated by Van Buren. His expansionist policy was opposed by Clay, Webster, Calhoun; sent Zachary Taylor and an army to the Mexican border and, when Mexicans attacked, declared war existed. Abraham Lincoln, a Whig in Congress, opposed his war policy. Polk approved the acquisition of California, Utah and New Mexico (522,-568 square miles) as part of America's "manifest destiny," but opposed retaining Mexico by force. He compromised on the Oregon boundary ("54-40 or fight!") by accepting the 49th parallel and giving Vancouver to the British. The Wilmot Proviso, outlawing slavery in new states, was debated in his term. Polk died in Nashville, June 15,1849, and was buried on the capitol grounds there.

Polk married Sarah Childress Jan. 1, 1824. They had no children.

Zachary Taylor

Zachary Taylor, 12th president, Whig, who served only 16 months, was born Nov. 24, 1784, in Orange Co., Va., the son of Richard Taylor, later collector of the port of Louisville, Ky. His grandfather and James Madison's paternal grandmother were brother and sister. Taylor enlisted 1806; was commissioned lieutenant by Jefferson, 1808; fought in the War of 1812, the Black Hawk War, 1832, and the Seminole war, 1837. He became known as Old Rough and Ready. He settled on a plantation near Baton Rouge, La. In 1845 Polk sent him with an army to the Rio Grande. When the Mexicans attacked him, Polk declared war. Taylor was successful at Palo Alto and Resaca de la Palma, May 8 and 9, 1846; occupied Monterey. Polk made him major general but gave many of his troops to Gen. Winfield Scott at Veracruz. Taylor, with 5,000 men, defeated Santa Anna's 20,000 at Buena Vista, Feb. 22, 1847. He defeated Scott at the Whig convention, 1848; was elected president, over Martin Van Buren, with Millard Fillmore vice president. He resumed the spoils system and though once a slaveholder worked to have California admitted as a free state. He died of typhus July 9, 1850, and was buried near Louisville.

Taylor married Margaret Smith in 1810. They had one son and 5 daughters, one of whom, Sarah, married Jefferson Davis in 1835. She died a few months later.

Millard Fillmore

Millard Fillmore, 13th president, Whig, was born Jan. 7, 1800, in a log cabin on a Cayuga Co., N. Y., farm cleared in 1795 by his father, Nathaniel. He was apprenticed to a fuller and dyer; bought his freedom for $30 to study and became a teacher and postmaster in Buffalo, N. Y. He was counselor of the state Supreme Court, 1829; in the state Assembly, 1829-32; in Congress, 1833-35 and again 1837-43. He opposed the entrance of Texas as slave territory and voted for a protective tariff. He supported the appropriation of $30,000 for Morse's telegraph. In 1844 he was defeated for governor of New York. In 1848 he was elected vice president and succeeded as president July 10, 1850, after Taylor's death. Fillmore favored the Compromise of 1850 and signed the Fugitive Slave Law. His policies pleased neither expansionists nor slaveholders and he was not renominated in 1852. In 1856 he was nominated by the American (Know-Nothing) party and accepted by the Whigs, but defeated by Buchanan. He was chancellor of the University of Buffalo. He died in Buffalo, Mar. 8, 1874.

Fillmore first married Abigail Powers, in 1826 and they had one son and one daughter. Abigail died in 1853 and Fillmore married Caroline Carmichael McIntosh, a widow, in 1858. They had no children.

Franklin Pierce

Franklin Pierce, 14th president, Democrat, was born in Hillsboro, N. H., Nov. 23, 1804, the son of Benjamin Pierce, veteran of the Revolution and governor of New Hampshire, 1827. He attended Exeter and was graduated from Bowdoin, 1824. A lawyer, he served in the New Hampshire House, 1829-32; in Congress, supporting Jackson, 1833; U.S. senator, 1837-42. He enlisted in the Mexican War, became brigadier general of volunteers and was wounded at Contreras. In 1852 Pierce was nominated on the 49th ballot over the leading candidates: Lewis Cass, Stephen A. Douglas, and James Buchanan, and defeated Gen. Winfield Scott,-Whig. Though against slavery, Pierce was influenced by southern pro-slavery men (Jefferson Davis was his secretary of war) but he ignored the Ostend Manifesto that the U.S. either buy or take Cuba. He approved the Kansas-Nebraska Act, leaving slavery to popular vote ("squatter sovereignty"), 1854, and appointed a pro-slavery governor to Kansas. He signed a reciprocity treaty with Canada and approved the Gadsden Purchase from Mexico, 1853. He supported Commodore Matthew Perry's opening of Japan, 1854. Pierce died at Concord, N.H., Oct. 8, 1869.

Pierce married Jane Means Appleton in 1834. They had 3 children who all died in childhood.

James Buchanan

James Buchanan, 15th president, Federalist, later Democrat, was born of Scottish descent near Mercersburg, Pa., Apr. 23, 1791. He was a volunteer in the War of 1812; graduated from Dickinson, 1809; member, Pennsylvania legislature, 1814-16, Congress, 1820-31; Jackson's minister to Russia, 1831-33; U.S. senator 1834-45. As Polk's secretary of state, 1845-49, he ended the Oregon dispute with Britain, supported the Mexican War and annexation of Texas. As minister to Britain, 1853, he signed the Ostend Manifesto, 1854, urging the U. S. to take Cuba. Nominated by Democrats over Pierce and Stephen A. Douglas, he was elected, 1856, over John C. Fremont (Republican) and Millard Fillmore (American Know-Nothing and Whig tickets). On slavery he favored popular sovereignty and choice by state constitutions; he accepted the pro-slavery Dred Scott decision as binding. His support of the pro-slavery Lecompton constitution for Kansas caused a break with Douglas Democrats. He denied the right of states to secede but wanted U. S. constitutional recognition of property rights in slaves and Federal action against fugitives. Buchanan refused demands of South Carolina for Federal property, but also refused to reinforce forts there until too late to help Fort Sumter. A strict constructionist, he desired to keep peace and found no authority for using force. He died at Wheatland, near Lancaster, Pa., June 1, 1868, at age 77.

Buchanan was a bachelor. The mistress of the White House was the daughter of Buchanan's sister

Jane, Harriet Lane, whose parents had died when she was a child.

Abraham Lincoln

Abraham Lincoln, 16th president, Republican, was born Feb. 12, 1809, in a log cabin on a farm then in Hardin Co., Ky., now in Larue. He was the son of Thomas Lincoln (1778-1851), a descendant of Samuel Lincoln, who came from Hingham, England, 1637, settled at Salem and Hingham, Mass., and had 11 children. Thomas Lincoln, a carpenter, married Nancy Hanks, June 12, 1806. Nancy has been long believed to have been illegitimate, the "natural" daughter of Lucy Hanks. Recent research, however, strongly suggests that Nancy was not illegitimate. Experts disagree on her parentage (one says Mary Berry and Thomas Hanks, others say Lucy Shipley and James Hanks), but most agree that the charge of bastardy arose from a confusion of names and political spite during Abraham Lincoln's life.

Abraham had a sister, Sarah, born 1807, died 1828, and a brother Thomas, who died in infancy.

The Lincolns moved to Spencer Co., Ind., near Gentryville, when Abe was 7. Nancy died Oct. 5, 1818, aged 35. His father married Mrs. Sarah Bush Johnston, 1819; she had a favorable influence on Abe. In 1830 the family moved to Macon Co., Ill., where Abe and a cousin split 3,000 fence rails. In 1831 they moved to Coles Co. In New Salem, 1831-1837, Lincoln lost election to the Illinois General Assembly, 1832, but later won 4 times, beginning in 1834. He enlisted in the militia for the Black Hawk War, 1832. In New Salem he ran a store, 1833; surveyed land, 1834-36, and was postmaster, 1833-36.

In 1837 Lincoln was admitted to the bar and became partner in a Springfield, Ill., law office. He began practice in the 8th Judicial Circuit, 1839. He was a presidential elector, 1839, 1844, 1852, 1856. He failed of nomination for representative, 1843, but was elected to the 30th Congress, 1847. He opposed the Mexican War. He stumped New England for Zachary Taylor, 1848. He refused offices of secretary and governor of Oregon Territory, 1849. He opposed the Kansas-Nebraska Act and extension of slavery, 1854. When elected to the Illinois legislature, 1854, he declined in order to try for the Senate, but failed of election, 1855. He was proposed but not chosen for vice president at the first Republican convention, 1856, and he made 50 speeches for John C. Fremont, presidential nominee.

In 1858 Lincoln had Republican support in the Illinois legislature for the Senate but was defeated by Stephen A. Douglas, Dem., who had sponsored the Kansas-Nebraska Act. The issues were debated by Lincoln and Douglas Aug. 21-Oct. 15 at Ottawa, Freeport, Jonesboro, Charleston, Galesburg, Quincy, and Alton, Ill.

Lincoln was nominated for president by the Republican party on an anti-slavery platform, at Chicago, May 18, 1860. He ran against Stephen A. Douglas, northern Democrat; John C. Breckinridge, southern pro-slavery Democrat; John Bell, Constitutional Union party. Lincoln got only 40% of the votes, but 180 electoral votes; Breckenridge, 72; Bell, 39; Douglas, 12. South Carolina seceded from the Union Dec. 20, 1860, followed in 1861 by 10 southern states.

Lincoln was inaugurated Mar. 4, 1861. Fort Sumter was attacked Apr. 12-14, and surrendered. Lincoln called for 75,000 volunteers Apr. 15, and 500,000 May 3. On Sept. 22, 1862, 5 days after the battle of Antietam, he annnounced that slaves in territory then in rebellion would be free Jan. 1, 1863, date of the Emancipation Proclamation. He reached high degrees of moving eloquence in his Gettysburg and Inaugural Addresses and other speeches.

Lincoln was reelected, 1864, over Gen. Geo. B. McClellan, Democrat. Lee surrendered Apr. 9, 1865. On Apr. 14 (Good Friday) Lincoln was shot by actor John Wilkes Booth in Ford's Theatre, Washington. He died the next day. His body lay in state in New York,

Chicago, and other cities before burial in Springfield, Ill. His estate reached $110,974, most of it saved from his annual salary of $25,000. His humanity, lofty concept of office and generous spirit made him the hero of the common man the world over.

Lincoln married Mary Todd in Springfield, Nov. 4, 1842; they had 4 sons.

Andrew Johnson

Andrew Johnson, 17th president, Democrat, was born in Raleigh, N. C., Dec. 29, 1808, the son of Jacob Johnson, porter at an inn and church sexton, and Mary McDonough Johnson, who had been a maid at the inn. His father died when he was 5. At 10 he was apprenticed to a tailor. At 16 he ran off to Greenville, Tenn. He became an alderman, 1828; mayor, 1830; state representative and senator, 1835-43; member of Congress, 1843-53; governor of Tennessee, 1853-57; U.S. senator, 1857-62. He supported John C. Breckinridge against Lincoln in 1860. He had held slaves, but opposed secession and refused to follow Tennessee out of the Union. In Mar. 1862, Lincoln appointed him military governor of occupied Tennessee. In 1864 he was nominated for vice president with Lincoln on the National Union ticket to win Democratic support. He succeeded Lincoln as president April 15, 1865. In a controversy with Congress over the president's power over the South, he proclaimed, May 26, 1865, an amnesty to all Confederates except certain leaders if they would abolish slavery and ratify the 13th Amendment. States doing so added anti-Negro provisions that enraged Congress, which intended to enfranchise all Negroes and disenfranchise former Confederates. Congress restored military control over the South. When Johnson removed Edwin M. Stanton, secretary of war, without notifying the Senate, thus repudiating the Tenure of Office Act, the House impeached him for this and other reasons. He was tried by the Senate, which voted 35 for conviction, 19 for acquittal, lacking by one the two-thirds necessary to convict, May 26, 1868. He was a candidate before the next Democratic convention, but not nominated. He returned to the Senate in 1875, and in a strong speech defended his course. He supported the Lincoln policies, but his conciliatory attitude toward the South was fought by the radical Republicans. Johnson died July 31, 1875, and was buried at Greenville (now Greeneville), where his log cabin tailor shop and home are museums.

Johnson married Eliza McArdle in 1827. They had 3 sons and 2 daughters.

Ulysses S. Grant

Ulysses Simpson Grant, 18th president, Republican, was born at Point Pleasant, Oh., Apr. 27, 1822, son of Jesse R. Grant, a tanner, and Hannah Simpson Grant. The next year the family moved to Georgetown, Oh. Grant was named Hiram Ulysses, but on entering West Point, 1839, his name was entered as Ulysses Simpson and he adopted it. He was graduated in 1843; and was first lieutenant and captain under Gens. Taylor and Scott in the Mexican War; resigned, 1854; worked in St. Louis until 1860, then went to Galena, Ill., where his father sold leather and hardware. With the start of the Civil War, he was named colonel of the 21st Illinois Vols., 1861, then brigadier general; took Forts Henry and Donelson; was made major general of volunteers; fought at Shiloh. Took Vicksburg, became major general USA, and in March 1864, lieutenant general. He accepted Lee's surrender at Appomattox. In 1866 he was named a full general. President Johnson appointed Grant secretary of war when he suspended Stanton in defiance of the Senate, but Grant was not confirmed. He was nominated for president on the first ballot, May 30, 1868, and elected over Horatio Seymour, Democrat, 214 to 80 electoral votes. The 15th Amendment, amnesty bill, and civil service reform were events of his administration. The Liberal Republicans opposed him with Horace Greeley, also Democratic nominee, 1872, but he was reelected. An attempt by the Stalwarts (Old Guard) to nominate him in 1880 failed. In 1884 the collapse of Grant & Ward, investment house, left him penniless. He began his Personal Memoirs, writing while ill of cancer and completing them 4 days before his death at Mt. McGregor, N.Y., July 23, 1885. The book realized over $450,000. Grant was buried in an imposing tomb on Riverside Drive, New York, where his wife also lies.

Grant married Julia Dent in 1848. They had 3 sons and one daughter.

Rutherford Birchard Hayes

Rutherford Birchard Hayes, 19th president, Republican, was born in Delaware, Oh., Oct. 4, 1822, the posthumous son of Rutherford Hayes, a farmer, and Sophia Birchard. He was descended from George Hayes, a Scot, who reached Windsor, Conn., in 1680. He was raised by his uncle Sardis Birchard, educated in Norwalk, Oh., and Middletown, Conn., and graduated from Kenyon College, 1842, and Harvard Law School, 1845. He practiced law in Lower Sandusky, Oh., now Fremont; was city solicitor of Cincinnati, 1858-61. In the Civil War, he was major of the 23d Ohio Vols., wounded at South Mountain; became brigadier general and major general by brevet, 1864. He served in Congress 1864-67, supporting Reconstruction and Johnson's impeachment. He was elected governor of Ohio, 1867 and 1869; beaten in the race for Congress, 1872; reelected governor, 1875. He supported the merit principle in appointments, economics, prison reform, and public libraries. In 1876 he was nominated for president over James G. Blaine and believed he had lost to Samuel J. Tilden, Democrat, 184 to 163 electoral votes. But Zachariah Chandler, chairman of the Republican National Committee, relying on Republican domination of the South, urged the validity of contesting 22 electoral returns from Florida, South Carolina, Louisiana, and Oregon. Frauds in Louisiana injuring Tilden were permitted to stand. Promises to withdraw troops from the South were reportedly used to suborn Democrats. An Electoral Commission, appointed by Congress, 8 Republicans and 7 Democrats, awarded all disputed votes to Hayes. The Electoral College vote then became 185 for Hayes, 184 for Tilden. The withdrawal of troops followed, but handicapped Republican rule, and as Hayes proceeded to reform the civil service he alienated political spoilsmen. He advocated repeal of the Tenure of Office Act that had led to Johnson's impeachment. He supported sound money and specie payments. Hayes died in Fremont, Oh., Jan. 17, 1893.

Hayes married Lucy Webb in 1852. They had 7 sons and one daughter.

James Abram Garfield

James A. Garfield, 20th president, Republican, was born Nov. 19, 1831, in a log cabin at Orange, Cuyahoga Co., Oh., the son of Abram and Eliza Ballou Garfield. His father, a canal contractor and farmer from New York, was descended from Edward Garfield, who reached Massachusetts Bay Colony in 1630 and helped found Watertown, Mass. James was the youngest of 4 children. His father died in 1833 and his mother supported them. He worked as a canal bargeman, farmer, and carpenter; attended Western Reserve Eclectic, later Hiram College, and was graduated from Williams in 1856. He became professor of ancient languages and literature at Hiram, then principal. He was in the Ohio Senate in 1859. Anti-slavery and anti-secession, he volunteered for the war, became colonel of the 42d Ohio Infantry and brigadier in 1862. He fought at Shiloh, was chief of staff for Rosecrans and was made major general for gallantry at Chickamauga. He entered Congress as a radical Republican in 1863; supported specie payment as against paper money (greenbacks). On the electoral commission in 1876 he voted for Hayes against Tilden on strict party lines. He was senator-elect in 1880 when he became the Republican nomi-

nee for president. He was chosen on the 36th ballot as a compromise over Gen. Grant, James G. Blaine, and John Sherman. This alienated the Grant following but Garfield was elected and Blaine became his secretary of state. On July 2, 1881, Garfield was shot by an unbalanced office-seeker, Charles J. Guiteau, while entering the old Baltimore & Potomac station in Washington. He died Sept. 19, 1881, at Elberon, N.J., and was buried in Cleveland, Oh. Guiteau was hanged June 30, 1882.

Garfield married Lucretia Rudolph in 1858. They had 4 sons and one daughter.

Chester Alan Arthur

Chester A. Arthur, 21st president, Republican, was born at Fairfield, Vt., Oct. 5, 1829, the son of the Rev. William Arthur, from County Antrim, Ireland, and Malvina Stone Arthur, member of a New Hampshire family. He graduated at Union College, 1848, taught school at Pownall, Vt., studied law in New York. In 1853 he argued in a fugitive slave case that slaves transported through N.Y. State were thereby freed; in 1855 he obtained a ruling that Negroes were to be treated the same as whites on street cars. He helped organize the N.Y. State Militia, 1861, was made quartermaster general and equipped troops for the front. He was made collector of the Port of New York, 1871. In 1877 President Hayes, reforming the civil service, ordered Arthur's resignation. He refused because he was not personally culpable, but was removed, 1879. This made Senators Conkling, Platt, and the New York machine stalwarts enemies of Hayes. Arthur and the stalwarts tried to nominate Grant, for a third term in 1880. When Garfield was nominated, Arthur received second place in the interests of harmony. On Sept. 19, 1881, Garfield died and Arthur became president. He supported civil service reform and the tariff of 1883; arranged an unratified canal treaty with Nicaragua. He was defeated for renomination by James G. Blaine, 1884, but supported Blaine. He died Nov. 18, 1886, and was buried in Albany, N. Y.

Arthur married Ellen Lewis Herndon in 1859. They had 2 sons and one daughter.

Grover Cleveland

(According to a ruling of the State Dept. Grover Cleveland is both the 22d and the 24th president, because his 2 terms were not consecutive. By individuals, he is only the 22d.)

Grover Cleveland, 22d and 24th president, Democrat, was born in Caldwell, N. J., Mar. 18, 1837, the son of Richard F. Cleveland, a Presbyterian minister, and Ann Neale, daughter of a Baltimore merchant who had come from Ireland. The future president was named Stephen Grover, but dropped the Stephen. He clerked in Clinton and Buffalo, N. Y., taught in the N.Y. City Institution for the Blind; was admitted to the bar in Buffalo, 1859; became assistant district attorney 1863; sheriff 1869; mayor, 1881; governor of New York, 1882. He was an independent, honest administrator who hated corruption. He was nominated for president over Tammany Hall opposition, 1884, defeating Republican James G. Blaine, 219 to 182 Electoral College votes. He enlarged the civil service, vetoed many pension raids on the Treasury. In 1888 he was defeated by Benjamin Harrison, although his popular vote was larger. Reelected over Harrison, 1892, by 277 to 145, electoral votes, he faced a money crisis brought about by lowering of the gold reserve, circulation of paper and exorbitant silver purchases under the Sherman Act; obtained a repeal of the latter and a reduced tariff. An income tax was passed but declared unconstitutional by the Supreme Court, 1895. A severe depression and labor troubles racked his administration but he refused to interfere in business matters and rejected, as crackpot theory, Jacob Coxey's demand for work relief of $20 million monthly. He broke the Pullman strike with troops to move the mail, 1894. He rejected the platform of William Jennings Bryan's silver Democrats, 1896, and supported the gold Democrats. He died in Princeton, N.J., June 24, 1908.

Cleveland married Frances Folsom in the White House, June 2, 1886. They had 2 sons and 3 daughters.

Benjamin Harrison

Benjamin Harrison, 23d president, Republican, was born at North Bend, Oh., Aug. 20, 1833. His great-grandfather, Benjamin Harrison, was a signer of the Declaration of Independence; his grandfather, William Henry Harrison, was 9th president; his father, John Scott Harrison, was a member of Congress, 1853-57. His mother was Elizabeth F. Irwin. He attended school in a log cabin on his father's farm; graduated from Miami University, 1852; was admitted to the bar, 1853, and practiced in Indianapolis, Ind. As a second lieutenant in the Civil War, he raised recruits and became colonel of the 70th Indiana Volunteer Infantry. He fought at Kenesaw Mountain, Peachtree Creek, Nashville, and in the Atlanta campaign. In 1865 he was made a brigadier general by brevet. He failed to be elected governor of Indiana, 1876; but became senator, 1881, and worked for the G. A. R. pensions vetoed by Cleveland. In 1888 he defeated Cleveland for president 233 to 168 Electoral College votes. He expanded the pension list greatly; suppressed the Louisiana lottery; signed the McKinley high tariff bill and the Sherman silver purchase act. He helped the admission of North and South Dakota, Montana, Washington, Idaho, and Wyoming, Republican states. He was defeated for reelection, 1892. He represented Venezuela in arbitration with Great Britain in Paris, 1899. He died at Indianapolis, Mar. 13, 1901, and was buried there.

Harrison married Caroline Lavinia Scott in 1853; they had one son and one daughter. The first Mrs. Harrison died in 1892 and in 1896 Harrison married her niece, Mary Scott Lord Dimmick, a widow. They had one daughter.

William McKinley

William McKinley, 25th president, Republican, was born in Niles, Oh., Jan. 29, 1843, the son of William McKinley, an iron manufacturer, and Nancy Allison McKinley, and was the 7th of 9 children. His father's family was Scotch-Irish from County Antrim, Ireland; his great-grandfather fought in the American Revolution. McKinley attended school in Poland, Oh., and Allegheny College, Meadville, Pa., and enlisted for the Civil War at 18 in the 23d Ohio, in which Rutherford B. Hayes was a major. He was a commissary sergeant at Antietam. He rose to captain and in 1865 was made major by brevet. He studied law in the Albany, N.Y., law school; opened an office in Canton, Oh., in 1867, and campaigned for Grant and Hayes. From 1876 to 1890, excepting 1882, he served in the House of Representatives and led the fight for a high tariff to protect "infant industries" and reciprocal trade agreements (McKinley bill, enacted Oct. 1, 1890). Defeated on the issue in 1890, he was elected governor of Ohio, 1891 and 1893. He received 182 ballots for president in the Republican convention that nominated Benjamin Harrison in 1892. In 1896 he was elected president on a protective tariff, sound money (gold standard) platform over William Jennings Bryan, Democratic proponent of free silver. Chief factor was astute campaign management by GOP leader Marcus (Mark) Hanna. McKinley was reluctant to intervene in Cuba on grounds of humanity, but the loss of the battleship Maine at Havana crystallized opinion. He demanded Spain's withdrawal from Cuba; Spain agreed to arbitration and armistice but Congress announced state of war as of Apr. 21. (Peace signed Dec. 10). He was reelected in the 1900 campaign, defeating Bryan's anti-imperialist arguments with the prestige of prosperity, "the full dinner pail" and the vigorous campaigning of Theo-

dore Roosevelt, vice presidential nominee. McKinley was a Methodist, beloved for his conciliatory nature, but conservative on business issues. He abhorred violence. On Sept. 6, 1901, while welcoming citizens at the Pan-American Exposition, Buffalo, N.Y., he was shot by Leon Czolgosz, an anarchist. He died Sept. 14. His last words were: "It is God's way. His will, not ours, be done." McKinley, his wife, and infant daughters rest in an imposing tomb in Canton. His favorite flower, the red carnation, was made the state flower.

McKinley married Ida Saxton in 1871. They had 2 daughters; both died in childhood.

Theodore Roosevelt

Theodore Roosevelt, 26th president, Republican, was born in N.Y. City, Oct. 27, 1858, the son of Theodore Roosevelt, collector of the port, and Martha Bulloch, daughter of Maj. J. S. Bulloch, Roswell, Ga. Roosevelt was descended from Claes Martenszan van Rosenvelt, and his wife Janett, who reached New Netherland from Holland about 1650. Theodore was a fifth cousin of Franklin D. Roosevelt and an uncle of Mrs. Eleanor Roosevelt. His mother was of Scotch-Irish, Huguenot stock and a southern sympathizer. Roosevelt was graduated from Harvard, 1880, attended Columbia Law School briefly; sat in the N.Y. State Assembly, 1882-84; ranched in North Dakota, 1884-86; failed election as mayor of N.Y. City, 1886; member of U.S. Civil Service Commission, 1889; president, N.Y. Police Board, 1895, supporting the merit system; assistant secretary of the Navy under McKinley, Apr. 19, 1897 — May 10, 1898, during which he instituted naval target practice and instructed Commodore George Dewey to take Manila in the event of war with Spain. He organized the 1st U.S. Volunteer Cavalry (Rough Riders) as lieutenant colonel; led the charge up Kettle Hill at San Juan and was made colonel by brevet. Elected governor, New York, 1898-1900, he fought the spoils system and achieved taxation of corporation franchises. Drafted for vice president, 1900, he became nation's youngest president at 42 years, 10 mos., 18 days, when McKinley died at Buffalo, Sept. 14, 1901. As president he fought corruption of politics by big business; dissolved Northern Securities Co. and others for violating anti-trust laws; intervened in coal strike on behalf of the public, 1902; instituted the old Dept. of Commerce and Labor; obtained Elkins Law forbidding rebates to favored corporations, 1903; Hepburn Law regulating railroad rates, 1906; Pure Food and Drugs Act, 1906, Reclamation Act and employers' liability laws. He organized conservation, mediated the peace between Japan and Russia, 1905; won the Nobel Peace Prize. He was the first to use the Hague Court of International Arbitration. By recognizing the new Republic of Panama he made Panama Canal possible, appointed Col. George W. Goethals head commissioner and began canal. He was reelected 1904, with 336 electoral votes. vs. 140.

In 1908 he obtained the nomination of William H. Taft, who was elected. Later, considering Taft inimical to liberal policies, he organized the Progressive Party, June 22, 1912, and ran for president against Taft and Woodrow Wilson, splitting the Republicans and insuring Wilson's election. He was shot during the campaign but recovered. He advocated recall of elected officials, referendum on legislation, and recall of judicial decisions, which alienated conservatives. In 1916 he left the Progressives and supported Charles E. Hughes, Republican. A strong friend of Britain, he fought American isolation. In 1917 President Wilson refused to let him organize a division. He wrote on many topics—his Winning of the West is best known—was a naturalist and hunter and traced the River of Doubt in Brazil, 1913-14, now Rio Roosevelt. He died Jan. 6, 1919, at Sagamore Hill, Oyster Bay, N. Y., now a national shrine, and was buried near the Roosevelt bird refuge there.

Roosevelt's first marriage, in 1880, was to Alice

Hathaway Lee, who died in 1884; they had one daughter. In 1886, he married Edith Kermit Carow; they had one daughter and 4 sons. All 4 served in World War I; one was killed and 2 wounded. The 3 left all served in World War II; 2 died of natural causes while on active duty.

William Howard Taft

William Howard Taft, 27th president, Republican, was born in Cincinnati, Oh., Sept. 15, 1857, the son of Alphonso Taft and Louisa Maria Torrey. His father was secretary of war and attorney general in Grant's cabinet; minister to Austria and Russia under Arthur. Taft was graduated from Yale, 1878; Cincinnati Law School, 1880; became law reporter for Cincinnati newspapers; was assistant prosecuting attorney, 1881-83; assistant county solicitor, 1885; judge, Superior Court, 1887; U.S. solicitor-general, 1890; federal circuit judge, 1892. In 1900 he became head of the U.S. Philippines Commission and was first civil governor of the Philippines, 1901-04; secretary of war, 1904; provisional governor of Cuba, 1906. He was groomed for president by Theodore Roosevelt as an exemplary public servant and elected over William Jennings Bryan, 1908. His administration dissolved Standard Oil and tobacco trusts; instituted Department of Labor; drafted direct election of senators and income tax amendments. His tariff and conservation policies angered progressives; though renominated he was fought by Theodore Roosevelt; the result was Democrat Woodrow Wilson's election. Taft was president of the League to Enforce Peace, supporting the League of Nations. He was professor of constitutional law, Yale, 1913-21; Chief Justice of the United States, 1921-30; illness forced him to resign. He died in Washington, Mar. 8, 1930, and was buried in Arlington National Cemetery.

Taft married Helen Herron in 1886; they had 2 sons and a daughter.

Woodrow Wilson

Woodrow Wilson, 28th president, Democrat, was born at Staunton, Va., Dec. 28, 1856, as Thomas Woodrow Wilson, son of a Presbyterian minister, the Rev. Joseph Ruggles Wilson and Janet (Jessie) Woodrow, daughter of a Presbyterian minister. He was a grandson of James Wilson, a Presbyterian of Ulster who reached Philadelphia in 1807, became a printer and in 1808 married an Ulster Presbyterian girl, a shipmate. In his youth Wilson lived in Augusta, Ga., Columbia, S.C., and Wilmington, N.C. He attended Davidson College, 1873-74; was graduated from Princeton, A.B., 1879; A.M., 1882; read law at the University of Virginia, 1881; practiced law, Atlanta, 1882-83; Ph.D., Johns Hopkins, 1886. He taught history and political economy at Bryn Mawr, 1885-88; at Wesleyan, 1888-90; was professor of jurisprudence and political economy at Princeton, 1890-1910; president of Princeton, 1902-1910, during which he tried to introduce innovations of organization that were fought by the graduate dean and alumni; governor of New Jersey, 1911-13, during which he obtained a primary election law, an employers' liability law and other reforms. In 1912 he was nominated for president with the aid of William Jennings Bryan, who sought to block James "Champ" Clark and Tammany Hall. Wilson won the election because the Republican vote for Taft was split by the Progressives under Theodore Roosevelt.

Wilson protected American interests in revolutionary Mexico and fought for American rights on the high seas as the first World War opened. His sharp warnings to Germany led to the resignation of his secretary of state, Bryan, a pacifist, while his protests against British interference with American ships disturbed the Allies. In 1916 he was reelected by a slim margin with the slogan, "He kept us out of war," over Charles Evans Hughes, who was strongly supported by Theodore Roosevelt. Wilson's attempts to mediate in the war failed, Dec. 1916 - Jan. 1917. When the Germans started unrestricted submarine warfare, contrary to pledges, he broke diplomatic relations. After 4 American ships had been sunk he asked a declaration of war against Germany; it was voted Apr. 6, 1917.

Wilson kept tight personal control over all phases of diplomatic and military activity. He relied more on reports of his confidential agent in Europe, Col. E. M. House, than on Secretary of State Robert Lansing and the U.S. ambassadors. However, he backed Gen. John J. Pershing, U.S. commander in chief, Herbert Hoover, food administrator, and others who had his confidence.

Wilson proposed peace Jan. 8, 1918, on the basis of his Fourteen Points, a state paper with worldwide influence. Basic was his doctrine of self-determination, or consent of the governed, in which he opposed handing peoples from one sovereignty to another. He also demanded a league to enforce peace. The Germans overturned their monarchy and a new republic accepted his terms and an armistice, Nov. 11. But at the November elections, the Democrats lost control of Congress.

Wilson went to Paris to help negotiate the peace treaty, the crux of which he considered the League of Nations, also urged by ex-President Taft and Elihu Root. In the U.S. Senate, Henry Cabot Lodge, William E. Borah, and Hiram Johnson demanded reservations that would not make the United States subordinate to the votes of other nations in case of war. Wilson refused to consider any reservations and toured the country to get support. At Pueblo, Col., Sept. 25, 1919, he broke down and several days later suffered a stroke. An invalid for months, he clung to his executive powers while his wife and doctor sought to shield him from affairs which would tire him.

He was awarded the 1919 Nobel Peace Prize, but the treaty, embodying the League of Nations, was rejected by the Senate, Mar. 1920, by 49 to 35 (29 being sufficient to kill it). He made a public appearance on the day of Harding's inauguration in 1921, and formed a law partnership with Bainbridge Colby, but did not practice. He died Feb. 3, 1924, and was buried in Washington Cathedral.

Wilson's first marriage, in 1885, was to Ellen Louise Axson, who died in 1914. They had 3 daughters. Wilson married Edith Bolling Galt, a widow, in 1915; they had no children.

Warren Gamaliel Harding

Warren Gamaliel Harding, 29th president, Republican, was born near Corsica, now Blooming Grove, Oh., Nov. 2, 1865, the son of Dr. George Tyron Harding, a country physician, and Phoebe Elizabeth Dickerson. He attended Ohio Central College, Iberia, Oh., 1879-82; worked on the Star, Marion, Oh., 1884 and a few years later bought the paper with a friend's help for a reported $300. He was state senator, 1900-04; lieutenant governor, 1904-06; defeated for governor, 1910; chosen U. S. senator, 1915. He was a regular, "Old Guard" Republican; supported Taft, opposed federal control of food and fuel; voted for anti-strike legislation, woman's suffrage, and the Volstead prohibition enforcement act over President Wilson's veto, and opposed the League of Nations. In 1920 he was nominated for president on the 10th ballot; Calvin Coolidge was named for vice president. The Republicans capitalized on war weariness and fear that Wilson's League of Nations would curtail U.S. sovereignty. They defeated the Democrats, James M. Cox and Franklin D. Roosevelt, 16,152,200 to 9,147,-353. Harding stressed a return to "normalcy"; worked for tariff revision and repeal of excess profits and high income taxes. He obtained a Congressional resolution declaring peace with Germany, Austria, and Hungary July 2, 1921; peace treaties with the 3 were signed in Aug. 1921. His cabinet included Charles Evans Hughes (state); Herbert Hoover (commerce); Andrew S. Mellon (treasury). Two appointees, Albert

B. Fall (interior) and Harry Daugherty (attorney general), became involved in the Teapot Dome scandal that embittered Harding's last days. He called the International Conference on Limitation of Armaments, 1921-22. Returning from a trip to Alaska he became ill and died in San Francisco, Aug. 2, 1923. He was buried in Marion, Oh.

In 1891 Harding married Florence Kling De Wolfe, who had divorced her first husband. The Hardings had no children.

Calvin Coolidge

Calvin Coolidge, 30th president, Republican, was born in Plymouth, Vt., July 4, 1872, the son of John Calvin Coolidge, a storekeeper, and Victoria J. Moor, and named John Calvin Coolidge. His paternal ancestors came from England to Watertown, later Cambridge, Massachusetts Bay Colony, in 1630. Coolidge was graduated at Amherst, 1895; admitted to the bar in Northampton, Mass., 1897; became city councilman, 1889; city solicitor, 1900-01; clerk of the courts, 1904; member of the lower Massachusetts house, 1907-08; mayor of Northampton, 1910-11; state senator, 1912-15; and Senate president, 1914-15; lieutenant governor, 19 5-18; governor, 1919; reelected, 1920. In Sept., 1 19, Coolidge attained national prominence by hi action in the Boston police strike du ing which he d clared: "There is no right to strike against the public safety by anybody, anywhere, any time." This brought his name before the Republican convention of 1920, where he received 34 votes for president and was nominated for vice president by 674 votes. He succeeded to the presidency on Harding's death, Aug. 2, 1923, the oath being administered by his father, a justice of the peace, in his home in Plymouth, Aug. 3, and again Aug. 17 before Justice A. A. Hoehling of the Supreme Court of the District of Columbia. He opposed the League of Nations; approved the World Court; vetoed the soldiers' bonus bill, which was passed over his veto. In 1924 he was reelected by a huge majority with 15,725,016 over John W. Davis, Democrat, 8,385,586, and Robert M. LaFollette, Progressive, 4,822,856. He reduced the national debt by $2 billion in 3 years. He opposed the McNary-Haugen farm bill, and supported his secretary of state, Frank B. Kellogg, in the Kellogg-Briand treaties outlawing war. His dry, laconic remarks are often quoted. Opposing cuts in Europe's war debt, he said: "They hired the money, didn't they?" With Republicans eager to renominate him he announced, Aug. 2, 1927: "I do not choose to run for president in 1928." He became a life insurance director and wrote syndicated articles. He died of a heart attack in Northampton, Jan. 5, 1933. He was buried on a Plymouth hillside.

Coolidge married Grace Anna Goodhue in 1905. They had 2 sons.

Herbert Hoover

Herbert Clark Hoover, 31st president, Republican, was born at West Branch, Ia., Aug. 10, 1874, son of Jesse Clark Hoover, a blacksmith (1847-1880), and Hulda Randall Minthorn (1848-83). Ancestor Andrew Hoover came to Pennsylvania from the West German Palatinate, 1738. Hoover grew up in Indian Territory and Oregon, won his A.B. in engineering at Stanford, 1891. Briefly with U.S. Geological Survey and western mines; then mining engineer in Australia, Asia, Europe, Africa, America. While chief engineer, imperial mines, China, he directed food relief for victims of Boxer Rebellion, 1900. He became a world figure in relief work, distributing over $5 billion worth during 1914-1923. He directed American Relief Committee, London, 1914-15; U.S. Comm. for Relief in Belgium, 1915-1919; was U.S. Food Administrator, 1917-1919; American Relief Administrator, 1918-1923, feeding children in defeated nations; Russian Relief, 1918-1923; Interallied Food Council; Supreme Economic Council. As secretary of commerce, 1921-28, he began regulation of radio and aviation, pushed research program for National Academy of Science; organized 7-state pact for Colorado River irrigation and Hoover (Boulder) Dam. Elected president over Alfred E. Smith, 1928, he started White House Conferences on child health and protection, and housing; supported conservation of forests, oil, resources; initiated Naval Conference, 1930; organized Reconstruction Finance Corp., Home Loan Banks; expanded Farm Loan Banks. He gave his official salary to charities and to underpaid help. President Truman made him coordinator of European Food Program, 1947, chairman of the Commission for Reorganization of the Executive Branch, 1947-49, and chairman of the 2d Commission on Reorganization, 1953-55. He founded the Hoover Institution on War, Revolution, and Peace at Stanford University. He died in N.Y. City, Oct. 20, 1964, and was buried at West Branch, Ia., where his birthplace is now a memorial.

Hoover married Lou Henry in 1899. They had 2 sons.

Franklin D. Roosevelt

Franklin Delano Roosevelt, 32d president, Democrat, was born near Hyde Park, N.Y., Jan. 30, 1882, the son of James Roosevelt (died 1900) and Sara Delano (died 1941). His ancestor, Claes Martenszan van Rosenvelt, came to New Amsterdam from Holland about 1650. Claes' son Nicholas, a New York alderman in 1700 and 1715, had a son Johannes, from whom Theodore Roosevelt was descended, and a son Jacobus, from whom Franklin D. Roosevelt was descended. Franklin was graduated at Harvard, 1904; attended Columbia Law School; was admitted to the bar. He went to the New York Senate from his Dutchess County district, 1910 and 1913. He voted for Woodrow Wilson at the 1912 Democratic convention. In 1913 Wilson made him assistant secretary of the navy.

Roosevelt ran for vice president, 1920, with James Cox and was defeated. From 1920 to 1928 he was a New York lawyer and vice president of Fidelity & Deposit Co. In Aug., 1921, polio paralyzed his legs. He learned to walk with leg braces and a cane and established the Warm Springs, Ga., Foundation, for helping other victims.

Roosevelt presented the name of Alfred E. Smith to the Democratic conventions of 1924 in New York and 1928 in Houston, calling Smith the Happy Warrior. Smith was nominated in 1928 and defeated. Roosevelt was elected governor of New York, 1928 and 1930. In 1932 at Chicago W. G. McAdoo, pledged to John N. Garner, threw his votes to Roosevelt, who was nominated, alienating Smith. The financial crash, unemployment, and the Democratic promise to repeal prohibition made his victory inevitable. He asked emergency powers, proclaimed the New Deal, and put into effect a vast number of administrative changes. Foremost was "pump priming," or use of public funds for relief and public works, resulting in deficit financing. He greatly expanded the controls of the central government over business, and by an excess profits tax and pyramiding income taxes produced a redistribution of earnings on an unprecedented scale. The Wagner Act gave labor many advantages in organizing and collective bargaining. He was the last president inaugurated on Mar. 4 (1933) and the first inaugurated on Jan. 20 (1937).

Roosevelt was a tremendous worker and traveler despite physical handicaps. He was the first President to use radio for "fireside chats." When the Supreme Court nullified some New Deal laws, he sought power to "pack" the court with additional justices, but Congress refused to give him the authority. Court resignations soon enabled him to replace conservatives who had opposed him. He was the first president to break the "no 3d term" tradition and was elected to a 4th term, 1944, despite failing health.

The culminating event of his career was World War II. He was openly hostile to fascist governments before the war and gave Britain substantial support, such as exchanging 50 destroyers for air bases, before Pearl Harbor made the U.S. a belligerent. He wrote the principles of fair dealing into the Atlantic Charter, Aug. 14, 1941 (with Winston Churchill), and urged the Four Freedoms (freedom of speech, of worship, from want, from fear) Jan. 6, 1941. He conferred with allied heads of state at Casablanca, Jan., 1943; Quebec, Aug., 1943; Teheran, Nov.-Dec., 1943; Cairo, Dec., 1943; Yalta, Feb., 1945. He died at Warm Springs, Ga., Apr. 12, 1945, aged 63, and was buried on his Hyde Park estate, where his house and library are in the national care.

Roosevelt married Anna Eleanor Roosevelt (a 5th cousin who was a niece of Theodore Roosevelt) in 1905. They had 4 sons and one daughter and a child that died in infancy.

Harry S. Truman

Harry S. Truman, 33d president, Democrat, was born at Lamar, Mo., May 8, 1884, the son of John Anderson Truman and Martha Ellen Young. His 4 grandparents were born in Kentucky and moved to Missouri in the 1840s. The Trumans came from England, the president's grandmother from Northern Ireland, while an ancestor of his maternal grandfather, Solomon Young, came from Germany. A family disagreement on whether Harry Truman's middle name was Shippe or Solomon, after names of two grandfathers, resulted in his using only the middle initial S.

He attended public schools in Independence, Mo., worked for the Kansas City Star, 1901, and as railroad timekeeper, and helper in Kansas City banks up to 1905. He joined the Missouri National Guard, 1905, and was rejected by West Point for defective eyesight. He ran his family's farm, 1906-17. He entered the Field Artillery School at Fort Sill, Okla., 1917; became first lieutenant, Battery F, and captain, Battery D, 129th Field Artillery, 35th Div., AEF. He served in the Vosges, Meuse-Argonne, and St. Mihiel actions in World War I and was discharged as major, 1919. After the war he ran a haberdashery, became judge of Jackson Co. Court, 1922-24; attended Kansas City School of Law, 1923-25. He was defeated, then elected presiding judge.

Truman was elected U.S. senator in 1934; reelected 1940. In 1944 with President Roosevelt's approval he was nominated for vice president and elected. On Roosevelt's death Apr. 12,1945, Truman was sworn in as president by Chief Justice Harlan F. Stone. In 1948 he was elected president although polls had predicted his defeat.

Truman authorized the first uses of the atomic bomb (Hiroshima and Nagasaki, Aug. 6 and 9, 1945), bringing World War II to a rapid end. He was responsible for creating NATO, the Marshall Plan (to restore Western Europe economically) and for what came to be called the Truman Doctrine (to aid nations such as Greece and Turkey, threatened by Russian or other communist takeover). He broke a Russian blockade of East Berlin with a massive airlift, 1948-49. When communist North Korea invaded South Korea, June 1950, he won UN approval for a "police action" and sent in forces under Gen. Douglas MacArthur. When MacArthur sought to pursue North Koreans into communist China, Truman removed him from command.

On the domestic front, Truman was responsible for higher-minimum-wage, increased-social-security, and aide-for-housing laws. His 1952 seizure of the nation's steel mills to avert a strike was ruled illegal by the Supreme Court; a strike followed but was settled in 3 weeks. Truman died Dec. 26, 1972, at his Independence, Mo., home at the age of 88.

He married Elizabeth Virginia Wallace in 1919. They had one daughter, Margaret.

Dwight David Eisenhower

Dwight David Eisenhower, 34th president, Republican, was born Oct. 14, 1890, at Denison, Tex., the son of David Jacob Eisenhower and Ida Elizabeth Stover Eisenhower. His paternal grandfather was descended from German Mennonites who left the Rhineland for Pennsylvania in the 1730s, moved to Kansas in 1878. His father met his mother at Lane University, a United Brethren college at Lecompton, Kan. When Dwight was one year old his parents moved to Abilene, Kan. He attended high school and in 1915 was graduated at West Point. He was a lieutenant colonel in charge of a tank corps at Camp Colt, Gettysburg, Pa., in 1918. He was in the office of the chief of staff, 1933-35. He was on the American Military Mission to the Philippines, 1935-39 and during 4 of those years on the staff of Gen. MacArthur. He was chief of staff, 3d Army, 1941, as brigadier general. After the Louisiana maneuvers he was made chief of the War Plans Div., War Dept. General Staff, and then became assistant chief of staff, Operations Div., and in June, 1942, lieutenant general. He was made commander of allied forces landing in North Africa Nov. 8, 1942, and advanced to full general in Feb., 1943, and commander in chief of allied forces in North Africa. He became supreme commander, allied expeditionary forces Dec. 31, 1943, and as such led the Normandy invasion June 6, 1944. He was given the temporary rank of general of the army Dec. 19, 1944, which was made permanent in 1946. On May 7, 1945, he received the surrender of the Germans at Rheims. He was in command of the U.S. Occupation Force in Germany in 1945, and returned to the U.S. to serve as chief of staff, Nov. 19, 1945, to Feb. 7, 1948. From June 7, 1948, to Jan. 19, 1953, he was president of Columbia University, but he took leave of absence Dec. 16, 1950, to serve as supreme allied commander in Europe to organize NATO forces.

Eisenhower resigned from the army in June, 1952, and was nominated for president by the Republicans at Chicago, July 11, 1952. He defeated Adlai E. Stevenson by 442 to 89 electoral votes, was inaugurated Jan. 20, 1953. He was renominated unanimously in San Francisco, Aug. 22, 1956, and defeated Stevenson by 457 to 74. He called himself a moderate, favored "free market system" vs. government price and wage controls; kept government out of labor disputes; reorganized defense establishment; promoted missile programs, including Polaris. With strong aid of John Foster Dulles, his secretary of state, he continued foreign aid; demanded unification of Germany by free elections; sped end of Korean fighting; supplied planes to anti-communist Guatemalan government; endorsed Taiwan and SE Asia defense treaties; backed UN in condemning Anglo-French raid on Egypt; advocated "open skies" policy of mutual inspection to USSR. He sent U.S. troops into Little Rock, Ark., Sept., 1957, during the segregation crisis and ordered Marines into Lebanon July-Aug., 1958.

In 1948, Eisenhower published Crusade in Europe, his war memoirs, which quickly became a best seller. He was an enthusiastic golfer and painter.

During his retirement at his farm near Gettysburg, Pa., Eisenhower took up the role of elder statesman, counseling his 3 successors in the White House. He was hospitalized in early 1968 after his 4th heart attack and died Mar. 28, 1969, in Washington. He was buried in Abilene, Kan.

Eisenhower married Mamie Geneva Doud, July 1, 1916. They had 2 sons; the first died at age 4.

John F. Kennedy

John Fitzgerald Kennedy, 35th president, Democrat, was born May 29, 1917, in Brookline, Mass., the 2d of 9 children of Joseph P. Kennedy, financier, who later became ambassador to Great Britain, and Rose Fitzgerald Kennedy. He entered Harvard, attended the London School of Economics briefly in 1935, received a B.S., *cum laude* from Harvard in 1940. He served in the U. S. Navy, 1941-1945, commanded a PT boat in the Solomons and won the Navy and Marine Corps medal and Purple Heart. He covered the Potsdam Conference and the start of the UN at San Francisco for International News Service. He served as representative in Congress from Massachusetts, 1947-1953, defeated Henry Cabot Lodge for the Senate in 1952, was reelected 1958. He nearly won the vice presidential nomination in 1956.

Kennedy won the Democratic nomination for president at Los Angeles, July 14, 1960; Sen. Lyndon B. Johnson (Tex.), was named for vice president. Kennedy defeated Richard M. Nixon, Republican, by the slim margin of 118,550 popular votes and an electoral vote of 303 to 219. He was the first Roman Catholic to be elected president.

President Kennedy's most important act was his successful demand Oct. 22, 1962, that the Soviet Union dismantle all missile bases in Cuba. He established a quarantine of arms shipments to Cuba and continued surveillance by air. He defied Soviet attempts to force the Allies out of Berlin. He made the steel industry rescind a price rise. He backed civil rights, a mental health program, arbitration of railroad disputes, and expanded medical care for the aged. Astronaut flights and satellite orbiting were greatly developed during his less than 3 years tenure. He wrote *Profiles in Courage*, which won a Pulitzer Prize, and *Why England Slept*. He turned the White House spotlight on the cultural arts.

On Nov. 22, 1963, Kennedy was assassinated in Dallas, Tex. On Nov. 25, a day of national mourning, he was buried in Arlington National Cemetery.

Kennedy married Jacqueline Lee Bouvier Sept. 12, 1953. They had one daughter and one son; a second son died a few hours after birth.

Lyndon Baines Johnson

Lyndon Baines Johnson, 36th president, Democrat, was born on a farm near Stonewall, Tex., Aug. 27, 1908, son of Sam Ealy and Rebekah Baines Johnson. His father and grandfather had served in the Texas legislature. His family moved to Johnson City in 1913, where he was graduated from the high school in 1924. He received a B.S. degree at Southwest Texas State Teachers College, 1930, attended Georgetown Univ. Law School, Washington, 1935. He taught public speaking in Houston High School, 1930-32; served as secretary to Rep. R. M. Kleberg, 1932-35. In 1935 President Roosevelt appointed Johnson Texas state administrator of the National Youth Administration. In 1937 Johnson won a contest to fill the vacancy caused by the death of a representative and in 1938 was elected to the full term, after which he returned for 4 terms. A member of the naval reserve, he was a lieutenant commander, U.S. Navy, 1941-42, winning the Silver Star for a flight over Japanese positions at New Guinea. He was elected U.S. senator in 1948 by Texas and in 1954 he was reelected by a large majority. He became Democratic whip, 1951, and leader, 1953. Johnson was Texas' favorite son for the Democratic presidential nomination in 1956 and had strong support in the 1960 convention, where the nominee, John F. Kennedy, asked him to run for vice president. His campaigning helped overcome religious bias against Kennedy in the South.

Johnson took the oath of office as president at 2:30 p.m., CST, on Nov. 22, 1963, 99 min. after the death of President Kennedy. In filling out the Kennedy term Johnson worked hard for welfare legislation and signed civil rights, anti-poverty, and tax reduction laws, and averted strikes on railroads. He was nominated for president and elected Nov. 3, 1964, by 486 electoral votes to 52. Overshadowing other developments during Johnson's first full term in the White House were the expansion of the war in Vietnam, the committing of more than 500,000 American servicemen to conflict, intensive bombing by U.S. planes, and mounting U.S. casualties.

In the face of increasing division in the nation and his own party over his conductance of the war, Johnson announced, on Mar. 31, 1968, "I shall not seek, and I will not accept the nomination of my party for another term as your president." Near the end of his tenure, he indicated that he felt his greatest achievement was the passage of the Voting Rights Act of 1965. His biggest disappointment was: "peace has eluded me."

Retiring to his LBJ Ranch near Johnson City, Tex., the former president wrote his memoirs, *The Vantage Point* (1971), and oversaw the construction of the Lyndon Baines Johnson Library on the campus of the University of Texas in Austin. Johnson died of a heart attack on Jan. 22, 1973. He was buried on his ranch near the Pedernales River.

Johnson married Claudia Alta (Lady Bird) Taylor on Nov. 17, 1934. They had 2 daughters.

Richard Milhous Nixon

Richard Milhous Nixon, 37th president, Republican, was the only president to voluntarily resign without completing his elected term. He was born in the small farming community of Yorba Linda, Cal., Jan. 9, 1913, the 2d of the 5 sons of Francis Anthony and Hannah Milhous Nixon. In 1922, the family moved to Whittier, Cal., where the future president graduated from Whittier College in 1934. He attended Duke University Law School. After practicing law in Whittier and serving briefly in the Office of Price Administration in 1942, he entered the navy, serving in the South Pacific, and was discharged as a lieutenant commander.

Nixon was elected to the House of Representatives from California's 12th Congressional District in 1946 and reelected in 1948. He achieved prominence as the House Un-American Activities Committee member who forced the showdown that resulted in the Alger Hiss perjury conviction. In 1950 Nixon moved to the Senate by defeating Democrat Helen Gahagan Douglas in a bitter campaign in which he accused her of being "soft on communism."

Elected vice president in the Eisenhower landslides of 1952 and 1956, Nixon achieved more prominence in that position than had his predecessors.

With Eisenhower's endorsement, Nixon won the Republican presidential nomination in 1960. He was defeated by Democrat John F. Kennedy, returned to California, and 2 years later was defeated in his race for governor against Democratic incumbent Pat Brown.

Taking the "long hard road" of the presidential primaries in 1968, he won the presidential nomination easily on the first ballot and went on to defeat Democrat Hubert H. Humphrey.

The 1969-73 Nixon Administration saw remarkable developments in international affairs as Nixon became the first U.S. president to visit China and Russia. He and his foreign affairs advisor, Dr. Henry A. Kissinger, achieved a detente with China and a partial strategic arms limitation agreement with the Soviet Union. In addition, Nixon brought an end to the U.S. ground combat role in South Vietnam.

These diplomatic triumphs did not, however, overshadow the serious economic difficulties which confronted the nation. In Aug., 1971, faced with alarming trade and balance of payments deficits and continuing inflation, Nixon announced a "new economic policy," with wage and price controls at home and negotiations abroad leading to the devaluation of the dollar.

Nixon appointed 4 new Supreme Court justices, including the chief justice, thus altering the court's balance in favor of a more conservative view. A conservative trend on issues of public order was also observed.

By the summer of 1972, the peace movement had cooled, the economy showed signs of healthy growth, and a period of normal relations among the superpowers seemed at hand. On Aug. 22, a confident Republican party nominated Nixon for election to a 2d term as president.

Reelected in a massive landslide in 1972, Nixon soon secured a cease-fire agreement in Vietnam and completed the withdrawal of all U.S. troops in spite of heavy fighting and U.S. bombing in Cambodia and continued sporadic conflict in South Vietnam.

On, Jan. 11, 1973, the Nixon administration ended most mandatory wage and price controls and on Feb. 12 announced a further devaluation of the dollar. Inflation, however, continued at peak levels and the dollar came under heavy pressure in the world's gold markets.

Nixon's 2d term was cut short by "The Watergate Affair," a series of scandals beginning with the espionage burglary of Democratic party national headquarters in the Watergate office complex on June 17, 1972. The break-in was led by employees of Nixon's reelection campaign committee and former White House staff members. Investigations and press revelations exposed the existence of secret wiretapping and political espionage by White House aides dating back to May 1969, as well as an organized attempt to frustrate any investigation of these activities or of the Watergate break-in.

From the beginning, Nixon denied any White House involvement in the Watergate break-in. When White House personnel were implicated in the spring of 1973, Nixon denied personal knowledge of either that involvement or of the subsequent cover-up.

On July 16, 1973, a White House aide, under questioning by the Senate Select Committee on Presidential Campaign Activities, revealed that most of Nixon's office conversations and telephone calls had been recorded by an automatic taping system. The ensuing year saw the most severe constitutional confrontation in the nation's history as the president claimed executive privilege to keep the tapes secret and the courts and Congress sought the tapes for the prosecution of criminal indictments against former White House aides and for a House inquiry into possible impeachment proceedings against Nixon.

The confrontation reached its first climax Oct. 10, 1973, in the "Saturday Night Massacre" when Nixon fired the special prosecutor assigned to Watergate matters and accepted the resignations of the attorney general and his deputy when they refused to go along with the firing. The public outcry which followed caused Nixon to appoint a new special prosecutor and to turn over to the courts a number of subpoenaed tape recordings. Public reaction also brought the initiation of a formal inquiry into possible impeachment by the House of Representatives.

The second climax came on July 24, 1974, when the Supreme Court ruled unanimously that Nixon's claim of executive privilege must fall before the special prosecutor's subpoenas of tapes relevant to criminal trial proceedings. At the same time, the court refused to rule on Nixon's claim that a grand jury erred in naming him an "unindicted co-conspirator" in the Watergate cover-up.

Later the same day, the House Judiciary Committee opened a public, televised debate on whether to recommend that the full House impeach the president. By July 30, the 38-member committee had recommended House adoption of 3 articles charging obstruction of justice (21 Dems., 6 Reps. voting in favor), abuse of power (21 Dems., 7 Reps.), and contempt of Congress for refusing to respond to committee subpoenas (19 Dems., 2 Reps.).

On Aug. 5, under pressure from his special legal counsel, Nixon released transcripts of 3 recordings of conversations held on June 23, 1972, 6 days after the Watergate break-in. These transcripts showed that Nixon had known of, approved, and directed Watergate cover-up activities.

As his defenders in the House and Senate withdrew their support, Nixon's aides and top Republican leaders publicly and privately urged him to resign. He announced his resignation on nationwide television on Aug. 8 and left office at noon on Aug. 9. He retired to San Clemente, Cal. One month later, Sept. 8, his chosen successor, Gerald Ford, granted Nixon an unconditional pardon for all federal crimes he "committed or may have committed" while president.

Nixon married Thelma Catherine Patricia "Pat" Ryan on June 21, 1940. They had 2 daughters.

(See Chronology for further developments.)

Gerald Rudolph Ford

Gerald Rudolph Ford, 38th president, Republican, was born July 14, 1913, in Omaha, Neb., son of Leslie and Dorothy Gardner King, and was named Leslie Jr. When he was 2, his parents were divorced and his mother moved with the boy to Grand Rapids, Mich. There she met and married Gerald R. Ford, head of a paint company, who formally adopted the boy and gave him his own name.

In high school, young Gerald became a star football center, named to all-city and all-state teams. At the University of Michigan he played on the undefeated 1932 and 1933 teams and was named most valuable player on the 1934 team. He turned down a Green Bay Packers professional football bid and went to Yale Law School, working part-time as assistant football coach, boxing coach, and professional model. He graduated in the top third of the 1941 law class.

He began practicing law in Grand Rapids, but in 1942, shortly after U.S. entry into World War II, he joined the navy and served 47 months in the Pacific, leaving the service in 1946 as a lieutenant commander.

Back in Grand Rapids, he resumed his law practice and won several Chamber of Commerce awards for community work. Entering the 1948 GOP primary, he upset the incumbent congressman in Michigan's 5th District and won the November election. He continued to win elections, spending 25 years in the House of Representatives, 8 of them as Republican leader. He also served on the Warren Commission, which investigated the assassination of President Kennedy, and was co-author of a book on the commission's work.

As congressman and GOP leader, he was consistently conservative, opposing much social welfare legislation but giving support to final passage of civil rights bills. His colleagues described him as dogged, sincere, a man of modest tastes.

On Oct. 12, 1973, after Vice President Spiro T. Agnew pleaded "no contest" to charges of income tax fraud and resigned his high office, House Minority Leader Ford was nominated by President Nixon to become the new vice president. It was the first use of the procedures set out in the 25th Amendment. The Senate approved the appointment Nov. 27 by a 92-3 vote; The House followed suit, 387-35, on Dec. 6 and Ford was sworn in as the nation's 40th vice president that same day. As vice president, he spent much of his time on speaking tours, seeking to soothe the divisiveness which gripped the nation in the wake of the Watergate scandals.

When President Nixon, facing probable impeachment, resigned Aug. 9, 1974, Ford was sworn in as president, the first to serve without being chosen by the American people in a national election. On Sept. 8 he pardoned Nixon for any federal crimes he might have committed as president. Ford vetoed 48 bills in his first 21 months in office, including aid bills for housing, schools, health, day care, and farms; strip mining curbs, jobs creation, and tax cuts extension, saying most would prove too costly. He sought to solve the energy crisis by urging an end to oil and natural gas price controls. He visited China. The Democratic controlled Congress overrode 8 of the vetoes.

On Oct. 15, 1948, Ford married Elizabeth Bloomer Warren, whose first marriage had ended in divorce. The Fords had 3 sons and one daughter.

(See Chronology for further developments.)

Presidents Pro Tempore of the Senate

Until 1890, presidents "pro tem" were named "for the occasion only." Beginning with that year, they have served "until the Senate otherwise ordered." Sen. John J. Ingalls, chosen under the old rule in 1887, was again elected, under the new rule, in 1890. Party designations are D, Democrat; R, Republican.

Name	Party	State	Elected	Name	Party	State	Elected
John J. Ingalls	R	Kan.	Apr. 3, 1890	George H. Moses	R	N.H.	Mar. 6, 1925
Charles F. Manderson	R	Neb.	Mar. 2, 1891	Key Pittman	D	Nev.	Mar. 9, 1933
Isham G. Harris	D	Tenn.	Mar. 22, 1893	William H. King	D	Ut.	Nov. 19, 1940
Matt W. Ransom	D	N.C.	Jan. 7, 1895	Pat Harrison	D	Miss.	Jan. 6, 1941
Isham G. Harris	D	Tenn.	Jan. 10, 1895	Carter Glass	D	Va.	July 10, 1941
William P. Frye	R	Me.	Feb. 7, 1896	Kenneth McKellar	D	Tenn.	Jan. 6, 1945
Charles Curtis	R	Kan.	Dec. 4, 1911	Arthur H. Vandeberg	R	Mich.	Jan. 4, 1947
Augustus O. Bacon	D	Ga.	Jan. 15, 1912	Kenneth McKellar	D	Tenn.	Jan. 3, 1949
Jacob H. Gallinger	R	N.H.	Feb. 12, 1912	Styles Bridges	R	N.H.	Jan. 3, 1953
Henry Cabot Lodge	D	Mass.	Mar. 25, 1912	Walter F. George	D	Ga.	Jan. 5, 1955
Frank R. Brandegee	R	Conn.	May 25, 1912	Carl Hayden	D	Ariz.	Jan. 3, 1957
James P. Clarke	D	Ark.	Mar. 23, 1915	Richard B. Russell	D	Ga.	Jan. 3, 1969
Willard Saulsbury	D	Del.	Dec. 14, 1916	Allen J. Ellender	D	La.	Jan. 22, 1971
Albert B. Cummins	R	Ia.	May 19, 1919	James O. Eastland	D	Miss.	July 28, 1972

Speakers of the House of Representatives

Party designations: A, American; D, Democratic; DR, Democratic Republican; F, Federalist; R, Republican; W, Whig. *Served only one day.

Name	Party, State	Tenure	Name	Party, State	Tenure
Frederick A. C. Muhlenberg	F, Pa.	1789-1791	Galusha A. Grow	R, Pa.	1861-1863
Jonathan Trumbull	F, Conn.	1791-1793	Schuyler Colfax	R, Ind.	1863-1869
Frederick A. C. Muhlenberg	F, Pa.	1793-1795	*Theodore M. Pomeroy	R, N.Y.	1869-1869
Jonathan Dayton	F, N.J.	1795-1799	James G. Blaine	R, Me.	1869-1875
Theodore Sedgwick	F, Mass.	1799-1801	Michael C. Kerr	D, Ind.	1875-1876
Nathaniel Macon	DR, N.C.	1801-1807	Samuel J. Randall	D, Pa.	1876-1881
Joseph B. Varnum	DR, Mass.	1807-1811	Joseph W. Keifer	R, Oh.	1881-1883
Henry Clay	DR, Ky.	1811-1814	John G. Carlisle	D, Ky.	1883-1889
Langdon Cheves	DR, S.C.	1814-1815	Thomas B. Reed	R, Me.	1889-1891
Henry Clay	DR, Ky.	1815-1820	Charles F. Crisp	D, Ga.	1891-1895
John W. Taylor	DR, N.Y.	1820-1821	Thomas B. Reed	R, Me.	1895-1899
Philip P. Barbour	DR, Va.	1821-1823	David B. Henderson	R, Ia.	1899-1903
Henry Clay	DR, Ky.	1823-1825	Joseph G. Cannon	R, Ill.	1903-1911
John W. Taylor	D, N.Y.	1825-1827	Champ Clark	D, Mo.	1911-1919
Andrew Stevenson	D, Va.	1827-1834	Frederick H. Gillett	R, Mass.	1919-1925
John Bell	D, Tenn.	1834-1835	Nicholas Longworth	R, Oh.	1925-1931
James K. Polk	D, Tenn.	1835-1839	John N. Garner	D, Tex.	1931-1933
Robert M. T. Hunter	D, Va.	1839-1841	Henry T. Rainey	D, Ill.	1933-1935
John White	W, Ky.	1841-1843	Joseph W. Byrns	D, Tenn.	1935-1936
John W. Jones	D, Va.	1843-1845	William B. Bankhead	D, Ala.	1936-1940
John W. Davis	D, Ind.	1845-1847	Sam Rayburn	D, Tex.	1940-1947
Robert C. Winthrop	W, Mass.	1847-1849	Joseph W. Martin Jr.	R, Mass.	1947-1949
Howell Cobb	D, Ga.	1849-1851	Sam Rayburn	D, Tex.	1949-1953
Linn Boyd	D, Ky.	1851-1855	Joseph W. Martin Jr.	R, Mass.	1953-1955
Nathaniel P. Banks	A, Mass.	1856-1857	Sam Rayburn	D, Tex.	1955-1961
James L. Orr	D, S.C.	1857-1859	John W. McCormack	D, Mass.	1962-1971
William Pennington	R, N.J.	1860-1861	Carl Albert	D, Okla.	1971-

National Political Parties

As of June, 1976

Democratic Party Officers

Chairman—Robert S. Strauss.
Vice Chairmen—Basil Paterson, Caroline Wilkins.
Secretary—Dorothy V. Bush.
Treasurer—Edward Bennett Williams.
Finance Chairman
S. Lee Kling.—
National Headquarters—1625 Massachusetts Ave., N.W., Washington, D.C. 20036.

Republican Party Officers

Chairman—Mrs. Mary Louise Smith.

Co-Chairman—Robert S. Carter.
Vice Chairmen—Ray C. Bliss, Mrs. Hope McCormick, Bernard M. Shanley, Mrs. J. Willard Marriott, Fred J. Agonich, Mrs. Paula F. Hawkins, George P. Stadelman, Mrs. Isabel C. Moberly.
Secretary—Mrs. Estelle Stacy Carrier.
Treasurer—William T. McManus.
General Counsel—William C. Cramer.
Finance Chairman—Jeremiah Milbank.
National Headquarters—310 First St., S.E., Washington, D.C. 20003.

America's Third Parties

Since 1860, there have been only 4 presidential elections in which all third parties together polled more than 10% of the vote: the Populists (James Baird Weaver) in 1892, the National Progressives (Theodore Roosevelt) in 1912, the La Follette Progressives in 1924, and George Wallace's American Party in 1968. In 1948, the combined third parties (Henry Wallace's Progressives, Strom Thurmond's States' Rights party or Dixiecrats, Prohibition, Socialists, and others) received only 5.75% of the vote. In most elections since 1860, fewer than one vote in 20 has been cast for a third party. The only successful third party in American history was the Republican party in the election of Abraham Lincoln in 1860.

Major Third Parties

Party	Presidential Nominee	Election	Issues	Strength in
Anti-Masonic	William Wirt	1832	Against secret societies and oaths	Pennsylvania, Vermont
Free Soil	Martin Van Buren	1848	Anti-slavery	New York, Ohio
American (Know Nothing)	Millard Fillmore	1856	Anti-immigrant	Northeast, South
Greenback	Peter Cooper	1876	For "cheap money," labor rights	National
Greenback	James B. Weaver	1880		
Prohibition	(numerous)	1872	Anti-liquor	National
Populist	James B. Weaver	1892	For "cheap money," end of national banks	South, West
Socialist	Eugene V. Debs	1900-20	For public ownership	National
Socialist	Norman Thomas	1928-48	Liberal reforms	
Progressive (Bull Moose)	Theodore Roosevelt	1912	Against high tariffs	Midwest, West
Progressive	Robert M. LaFollette	1924	Farmer & labor rights	Midwest, West
States' Rights	Strom Thurmond	1948	For segregation	South
Progressive	Henry Wallace	1948	Anti-cold war	New York, California
American	George Wallace	1968	For states' rights	South
American	John G. Schmitz	1972	For "law and order"	California, Ohio

Other Major Political Organizations

American Party
(PO Box 1098, Pigeon Forge, TN 37863)
Chairman—Thomas J. Anderson.

Americans For Democratic Action
(1424 16th St., N.W., Washington, DC 20036)
President—Donald M. Fraser.
National Director—Leon Shull.
Chairperson Exec. Comm.—Cushing Dolbeare.

Comm. on Political Education, AFL-CIO
(AFL-CIO Building, 815 16th St., Wash., DC 20006)
Chairman—George Meany.
Secretary-Treasurer—Lane Kirkland.
National Director—Alexander E. Barken.

Conservative Party of the State of N.Y.
(468 Park Ave. So., New York, NY 10016)
Chairman—J. Daniel Mahoney.
Executive Director—Serphin R. Maltese.
Secretary—Henry S. Jorin Jr.
Treasurer—James E. O'Doherty.

Liberal Party of New York State
(1560 Broadway, New York, NY 10036)
Chairman—Donald S. Harrington.
First Vice Chairman—David Dubinsky.
Secretary & Exec. Director—Ben Davidson.
Treasurer—Bernice Benedick.

Libertarian Party
(1516 P St., N.W., Washington, DC 20005)
Chairman—Edward Crane 3d.
Vice-Chairwoman—Andrea Millen.
Secretary—Gregory Clark.
Treasurer—Francine Youngstein.
Director—Robert Meier.

National States' Rights Party
(P.O. Box 1211, Marietta, GA 30061)
Chairman—J. B. Stoner.
Secretary—Edward R. Fields.
Treasurer—Peter Xavier.

Prohibition National Committee
(P.O. Box 2635, Denver, CO 80201)
National Chairman—Charles Wesley Ewing.
Executive Secretary—Earl F. Dodge.
National Secretary—Roger C. Storms.

Socialist Labor Party
In Minnesota: Industrial Gov't. Party
(914 Industrial Ave., Palo Alto, CA 94303)
National Secretary—Nathan Karp.

Socialist Workers Party
(14 Charles Lane, New York, NY 10014)
National Secretary—Jack Barnes.
Organization Secretary—Barry Sheppard

The Electoral College

The president and the vice president of the United States are the only elective federal officials not elected by direct vote of the people. They are elected by the members of the Electoral College, an institution that has survived since the founding of the nation despite repeated attempts in Congress to alter or abolish it. In the elections of 1824, 1876 and 1888 the presidential candidate receiving the largest popular vote failed to win a majority of the electoral votes.

On presidential election day, the first Tuesday after the first Monday in November of every 4th year, each state chooses as many electors as it has senators and representatives in Congress. In 1964, for the first time, as provided by the 23d Amendment to the Constitution, the District of Columbia voted for 3 electors. Thus, with 100 senators and 435 representatives, there are 538 members of the Electoral College, with a majority of 270 electoral votes needed to elect the president and vice president.

Political parties customarily nominate their lists of electors at their respective state conventions. An elector cannot be a member of Congress or any person holding federal office.

Some states print the names of the candidates for president and vice president at the top of the November ballot while others list only the names of the electors. In either case, the electors of the party receiving the highest vote are elected. The electors meet on the first Monday after the 2d Wednesday in December in their respective state capitals or in some other place prescribed by state legislatures. By long-established custom they vote for their party nominee, thus giving all the state's electoral votes to him, although the Constitution does not require them to do so. The only Constitutional requirement is that at least one of the persons each elector votes for shall not be an inhabitant of that elector's home state.

Certified and sealed lists of the votes of the electors in each state are mailed to the president of the U.S. Senate. He opens them in the presence of the members of the Senate and House of Representatives in a joint session held on Jan. 6 (the next day if that falls on a Sunday), and the electoral votes of all the states are then counted. If no candidate for president has a majority, the House of Representatives chooses a president from among the 3 highest candidates, with all representatives from each state combining to cast one vote for that state. If no candidate for vice president has a majority, the Senate chooses from the top 2, senators voting as individuals.

U.S. Government Independent Agencies
Source: General Services Administration
Address: Washington, D.C. Location and zip codes of agencies in parentheses, as of July 1, 1976

ACTION — Director: Michael P. Balzano, Jr. (806 Connecticut Ave., NW, 20525).

Administrative Conference of the United States — Chmn. Robert A. Anthony (2120 L St., NW, 20037).

American Battle Monuments Commission — Chmn., Mark W. Clark (Forrestal Bldg., 20314).

American Revolution Bicentennial Administration — Administrator: John W. Warner (2401 E St. NW, 20276).

Appalachian Regional Commission — Federal co-chairman: Donald W. Whitehead, states co-chairman: Gov. Milton J. Shapp (1666 Connecticut Ave. NW. 20235).

Arms Control & Disarmament Agency — Director: Fred C. Ikle (Department of State Bldg. 20451).

Central Intelligence Agency — William Colby, director (Wash., D.C. 20505).

Civil Aeronautics Board — Chairman: John E. Robson (1825 Connecticut Ave. NW, 20428).

Civil Service Commission — Robert E. Hampton, chmn., Georginia H. Sheldon, vice chmn. (1900 E. St. NW, 20415).

Commission on Civil Rights — Chmn.: Arthur S. Flemming (1121 Vermont Ave., NW, 20425).

Commission of Fine Arts — J. Carter Brown, chmn. (708 Jackson Pl., NW, 20006).

Community Services Administration — Director: Samuel R. Martinez (1200 19th St. NW, 20506).

Consumer Product Safety Commission — Chairman: Richard O. Simpson (1750 K St. NW, 20207).

Energy Research and Development Administration — Administrator: Robert C. Seamans, Jr. (Washington, D. C. 20545).

Environmental Protection Agency — Administrator: Russell E. Train (401 M St., SW, 20460).

Equal Employment Opportunity Commission — Lowell Perry, chmn. (2401 E NW, 20506).

Export-Import Bank of the United States — Stephen M. DuBrul Jr., pres. and chmn. (811 Vermont Ave. NW, 20571).

Farm Credit Administration — Earl S. Smittcamp, chmn. (490 L'Enfant Plaza East, SW 20578).

Federal Communications Commission — Richard Wiley, chmn. (1919 M St. NW, 20554).

Federal Deposit Insurance Corporation — Chairman: Robert E. Barnett (550 17th St., NW 20429).

Federal Election Commission — Chairman: William L. Spinger (1325 K St. NW, 20461).

Federal Energy Administration — Administrator: Frank G. Zarb (12th St. and Pennsylvania Ave. NW, 20461).

Federal Home Loan Bank Board — Chairman: J. Ralph Stone (320 First St. NW, 20552).

Federal Maritime Commission — Karl E. Bakke, chmn. (1100 L St. NW, 20573).

Federal Mediation and Conciliation Service — Director: James F. Scearce (210 K St. NW, 20427).

Federal Power Commission — Richard L. Dunham, chmn., John Holloman 3d, vice chmn. (825 N. Capital St., NW, 20426).

Federal Reserve System — Chairman, board of governors: Arthur F. Burns. (20th St. & Constitution Ave., NW, 20551).

Federal Trade Commission — Commissioners: Calvin J. Collier, chmn., Paul Rand Dixon, Charles A. Tobin, Elizabeth Hanford Dole, Stephen Nye. (Pennsylvania Ave. at 6th St., NW. 20580).

Foreign Claims Settlement Comm. of the U.S. — J. Raymond Bell, chmn. (1111 20th St., NW, 20579).

General Accounting Office — Comptroller general of the U.S.; Elmer B. Staats. (441 G St., NW, 20548).

General Services Administration — Administrator: Jack Eckerd (18th & F Sts., NW, 20405).

Government Printing Office — Public printer:

Thomas F. McCormick (North Capitol and H Sts., NW, 20401).

Indian Claims Commission — Jerome K. Kuykendall, chmn. (1730 K St., NW, 20006).

Inter-American Foundation — Chmn., Augustin S. Hart, Jr. (1515 Wilson Blvd., Rosslyn, Va., 22209).

Interstate Commerce Commission — George M. Stafford, chmn. (12th St. and Constitution Ave., NW, 20423).

Library of Congress — Daniel J. Boorstin, Librarian (10 First St., SE, 20540).

National Academy of Sciences — National Academy of Engineering — National Research Council — Institute of Medicine — Presidents: Philip Handler (NAS), Courtland D. Perkins (NA of Eng.), David A. Hamburg, M.D. (Inst. of Med.) (2101 Constitution Ave., NW, 20418).

National Aeronautics and Space Administration — Administrator, James C. Fletcher. (Washington, D.C. 20546).

National Credit Union Administration — C. Austin Montgomery, administrator. (2025 M. St., NW, 20456).

National Foundation on the Arts and Humanities — Nancy Hanks, chmn. (arts). Ronald S. Berman, chmn. (humanities) (806 15th St., NW, 20506).

National Labor Relations Board — Chairman: Betty Southard Murphy. (1717 Pennsylvania Ave., NW, 20570).

National Mediation Board — David H. Stowe, chmn. (1425 K St. NW, 20572).

National Science Foundation — Director: Norman Hackerman. (1800 G St., NW, 20550).

National Transportation Safety Board — Chairman: Walter B. Todd Jr. (800 Independence Ave. SW, 20594).

Nuclear Regulatory Commission — Chairman: William A. Anders (Washington, D.C. 20555).

Occupational Safety and Health Review Commission — Chmn., Frank R. Barnako (1825 K St., NW, 20006).

Overseas Private Investment Corporation — President, Marshall T. Mays. (1129 20th St., NW, 20527).

Pension Benefit Guaranty Corporation — Executive Director: Kenneth L. Houck (2020 K St. NW, 20006).

Postal Rate Commission — Chairman: Clyde S. DuPont (2000 L St., NW, 20268).

Railroad Retirement Board — Chairman: James L. Cowen. (Rm. 444, 425 13th St. NW, 20004), Main Office (844 Rush St., Chicago, Ill. 60611).

Renegotiation Board — Chairman: Richard C. Holmquist (2000 M St., NW, 20446).

Securities and Exchange Commission — Commissioners: Roderick M. Hills, chmn.; Irving R. Pollack, Philip Loomis Jr., John R. Evans, one vacancy. (500 N. Capitol St., 20549).

Selective Service System — Director: Byron V. Pepitone. (1724 F St., NW, 20435).

Small Business Administration — Administrator: Mitchell P. Kobelinski (1441 L St., NW, 20416).

Smithsonian Institution — S. Dillon Ripley, secy. (1000 Jefferson Drive, SW, 20560).

Tennessee Valley Authority — Chairman, board of directors: Aubrey J. Wagner. (Commercial Realty Bldg., Knoxville, Tenn. 37902 and Woodward Bldg. 15th and H Sts., NW, Washington, D.C. 20444).

United States Information Agency — Director: James Keogh. (1750 Pennsylvania Ave., NW, 20547).

United States International Trade Commission — Chairman: Will E. Leonard (8th and E Sts. NW, 20436).

United States Postal Service — Benjamin F. Bailar, postmaster general (475 L'Enfant Plaza West, SW 20260).

Veterans Adminstration — Administrator: Richard L. Roudebush. (810 Vermont Ave. NW, 20420).

NATIONAL DEFENSE

Chairman, Joint Chiefs of Staff
George S. Brown (USAF)

Army
General of the Army
Bradley, Omar N. . . . . Sept. 20, 1950
Date of Rank

Chief of Staff—Frederick C. Weyand

Generals

Blanchard, George S.	July	1, 1975
Deane Jr., John R.	Feb.	12, 1975
DePuy, William E.	July	1, 1973
Haig Jr., Alexander M.	Mar.	18, 1974
Hennessey, John J.	Nov.	8, 1974
Kerwin Jr., Walter T.	Feb.	1, 1973
Knowlton, William A.	June	1, 1976
Rogers, Bernard W.	Nov.	7, 1974
Stilwell, Richard G.	July	31, 1973
Weyand, Frederick C.	Oct.	31, 1970

Air Force
Chief of Staff—David C. Jones
Generals

Brown, George S.	Aug.	1, 1968
Carlton, Paul K.	Oct.	9, 1972
Dixon, Robert J.	Oct.	1, 1973
Dougherty, Russell E.	May	5, 1972
Ellis, Richard H.	Sept.	30, 1973
Evans, William J.	Aug.	30, 1975
Huyser, Robert E.	Sept.	1, 1975
James, Daniel	Aug.	29, 1975
McBride, William V.	Sept.	1, 1974

Rogers, Felix M.	Aug.	31, 1975
Seith, Louis T.	Aug.	1, 1974
Wilson Jr., Louis L.	July	1, 1974

Navy
Chief of Naval Operations
Admiral James L. Holloway III (Aviation)

Admirals

Bagley, David H.	May	21, 1975
Gayler, Noel A.M. (Aviation)	Sept.	1, 1972
Kidd, Isaac C.	Dec.	1, 1971
Michaelis, Frederick H. (Aviation) . .	Apr.	19, 1975
Shear, Harold E.	May	24, 1974
Turner, Stansfield	Sept.	1, 1975
Weinel, John P.	Aug.	2, 1974
Weisner, Maurice F. (Aviation)	Sept.	1, 1972

Marine
Corps Commandant, with rank of General
Louis H. Wilson. . . . . July 1, 1975

Asst. Commandant with rank of General
Samuel Jaskilka . . . . July 1, 1975

Coast Guard
Commandant, with rank of Admiral
Owen W. Siler . . . . June 1, 1974

Vice Commandant, with rank of Vice Admiral
Ellis L. Perry . . . . July 1, 1974

United States Unified and Specified Commands

Alaskan Command — Lt. Gen. James E. Hill, USAF.

Atlantic Command — Adm. Isaac C. Kidd, USN.

North American Aerospace Defense Command — Gen. Daniel James, USAF.

U.S. European Command — Gen. Alexander Haig Jr., USA.

Pacific Command — Adm. Noel A. M. Gayler, USN.

U.S. Southern Command — Gen. Dennis P. McAuliffe, USA.

Strategic Air Command — Gen. Russell E. Dougherty, USAF

U.S. Readiness Command — Gen. John J. Hennessey, USA.

North Atlantic Treaty Organization International Commands

Supr. Allied Commander, Europe (SACEUR) — Gen. Alexander Haig Jr., USA.

Deputy SACEUR — Gen. Sir John Mogg (UK).

C-in-C, Allied Forces, Northern Europe — Gen. Sir John Sharp (UK).

C-in-C, Allied Forces, Central Europe — Dr. Gen. Karl Schnell (Germany).

C-in-C, Allied Forces, Southern Europe — Adm. Stanfield Turner, USN.

Cmdr. Naval Forces, Southern Europe — Adm. L. Tomasulo (Italy).

Supr. Allied Cmdr. Atlantic (SACLANT) — Adm. Isaac Kidd, USN.

Deputy SACLANT — Adm. James Jungius (UK).

Cmdr. Striking Fleet Atlantic — V. Adm. John J. Shanahan, USN.

Allied Cmdr. in Chief, Channel — Adm. Sir Edward Ashmore (UK).

Primary U.S. Military Training Centers

Army

Name, P.O. Address	Zip	Nearest City	Name, P.O. Address	Zip	Nearest City
Aberdeen Proving Ground, MD.	21005	Aberdeen	Fort Huachuca, AZ.	85613	Sierra Vista
Carlisle Barracks, PA.	17013	Carlisle	Fort Jackson, SC.	29207	Columbia
Fort Belvoir, VA.	22060	Alexandria	Fort Knox, KY.	40121	Louisville
Fort Benning, GA.	31905	Columbus	Fort Leavenworth, KS.	66027	Leavenworth
Fort Bliss, TX.	79906	El Paso	Fort Lee, VA.	23801	Petersburg
Fort Bragg, NC.	28307	Fayetteville	Fort McClellan, AL.	36201	Anniston
Fort Devens, MA.	01433	Ayer	Fort Monmouth, NJ.	07703	Red Bank
Fort Dix, NJ.	08640	Trenton	Fort Rucker, AL.	36362	Dothan
Fort Eustis, VA.	23604	Newport News	Fort Sill, OK.	73503	Lawton
			Fort Leonard Wood, MO.	65473	Rolla
Fort Gordon, GA.	30905	Augusta	Redstone Arsenal, AL.	35809	Huntsville
Fort Wadsworth, NY.	10305	Staten Island	Rock Island Arsenal, IL.	61202	Rock Island
Fort Benjamin Harrison, IN. . . .	46216	Indianapolis	The Judge Advocate.		Charlottes-
Fort Sam Houston, TX.	78234	San Antonio	General School, VA.	22901	ville

Navy

Great Lakes, IL.	60088	Waukegan	Orlando, FL.	32813	Orlando
San Diego, CA.	92133	San Diego			

Marine Corps

Name, P.O. Address	Zip	Nearest City	Name, P.O. Address	Zip	Nearest City
MCB Camp Lejeune, N.C.	28542	Jacksonville	MCAS (Helo) New River, N.C.	28540	Jacksonville
MCB Camp Pendleton, Cal.	92055	Oceanside	MCAS Iwakuni, Japan	FPO Seattle	Iwakuni
MCB Camp Butler, Okinawa	FPO Seattle	Futenma,		98764	
	98773	Okinawa	MCAS Kaneohe Bay,		
MCB Twentynine Palms, Cal.	92278	Palm Springs	Oahu, Ha.	FPO San Francisco	Kailua
MCDEC Quantico, Va.	22134	Quantico		96615	
MCRD Parris Island, S.C.	29905	Beaufort	MCAS (Helo) Futenma,		
MCRD San Diego, Cal.	92140	San Diego	Okinawa.	FPO Seattle	Futenma
MCAS Cherry Point, N.C.	28533	Cherry Point		98764	
MCAS El Toro (Santa Ana), Cal.	92709	Santa Ana	MCAS Beaufort, S.C.	29902	Beaufort
MCAS (Helo) Santa Ana, Cal.	92709	Santa Ana	MCAS Yuma, Ariz.	85364	Yuma

MCB = Marine Corps Base. MCDEC = Marine Corps Development & Education Command. MCAS = Marine Corps Air Station. Helo = Helicopter.

Air Force

Chanute AFB, Ill.	61866	Rantoul	Maxwell AFB, Ala.	36112	Montgomery
Columbus AFB, Miss.	39701	Columbus	Moody AFB, Ga.	31601	Valdosta
Craig AFB, Ala.	36701	Selma	Nellis AFB, Nev.	89191	Las Vegas
Fairchild AFB, Wash.	99011	Spokane	Randolph AFB, Texas	78148	San Antonio
Keesler AFB, Miss.	39534	Biloxi	Reese AFB, Tex.	79401	Lubbock
Lackland AFB, Texas	78236	San Antonio	Sheppard AFB, Tex.	76311	Wichita Falls
Laughlin AFB, Tex.	78840	Del Rio	Vance AFB, Okla.	73701	Enid
Lowry AFB, Colo.	80230	Denver	Webb AFB, Texas	79720	Big Spring
Mather AFB, Calif.	95655	Sacramento	Williams AFB, Ariz.	85224	Chandler

Personal Salutes and Honors

The United States national salute, 21 guns, is also the salute to a national flag. The independence of the United States is commemorated by the salute to the union — one gun for each state — fired at noon on July 4 at all military posts provided with suitable artillery.

A 21-gun salute on arrival and departure, with 4 ruffles and flourishes, is rendered to the President of the United States, to an ex-President and to a President-elect. The national anthem or *Hail to the Chief*, as appropriate, is played for the President, and the national anthem for the others. A 21-gun salute on arrival and departure, with 4 ruffles and flourishes, also is rendered to the sovereign or chief of state of a foreign country or a member of a reigning royal family; the national anthem of his or her country is played. The music is considered an inseparable part of the salute and will immediately follow the ruffles and flourishes without pause.

Rank	Salute—guns Arrive—Leave		Ruffles flourishes	Music
Vice President of United States	19		4	Hail Columbia
Speaker of House	19		4	March
American or foreign ambassador	19		4	Nat. anthem of official
Premier or prime minister	19		4	Nat. anthem of official
Secretary of Defense, Army, Navy or Air Force	19	19	4	March
Other Cabinet members, Senate President pro tempore, Governor, or Chief Justice of U.S.	19		4	March
Chairman, Joint Chiefs of Staff	19	19	4	
Army Chief of Staff, Chief of Naval Operations, Air Force Chief of Staff, Marine Commandant	19	19	4	General's or Admiral's March
General of the Army, General of the Air Force, Fleet Admiral	19	19	4	
Generals, Admirals	17	17	4	
Assistant Secretaries of Defense, Army, Navy or Air Force	17	17	4	March
Chairman of a Committee of Congress	17		4	March

Other salutes (on arrival only) include 15 guns for American envoys or ministers and foreign envoys or ministers accredited to the United States; 15 guns for a lieutenant general or vice admiral; 13 guns for a major general or rear admiral (upper half); 13 guns for American ministers resident and ministers resident accredited to the U.S.; 11 guns for a brigadier general or rear admiral (lower half); 11 guns for American charges d'affaires and like officials accredited to U.S.; and 11 guns for consuls general accredited to U.S.

Military Units, U.S. Army and Air Force

Army units. Squad. In infantry usually ten men under a staff sergeant. **Platoon.** In infantry 4 squads under a lieutenant. **Company.** Headquarters section and 4 platoons under a captain. (Company in the artillery is a battery; in the cavalry, a troop.) **Battalion.** Hdqts. and 4 or more companies under a lieutenant colonel. (Battalion size unit in the cavalry is a squadron.) **Brigade.** Hdqts. and 3 or more battalions under a colonel. **Division.** Hdqts. and 3 brigades with artillery, combat support and combat service support units under a major general. **Army Corps.** Two or more divisions with corps troops under a lieutenant general. **Field Army.** Hdqts. and two or more corps with field Army troops under a general.

Air Force Units. Flight. Small components of a squadron organized for special purpose such as medical evacuation flights. **Squadron.** The basic organized unit of the Air Force, used by operational as well as support forces but not limited by numbers of personnel assigned; two to three tactical squadrons are assigned to a tactical wing. **Group.** Terminologyy used for special tactical forces and for many support elements. They do not necessarily have subordinate units assigned. **Wing.** Used for tactical and support forces. A tactical wing usually has two to three operational squadrons assigned. **Division.** An organizational component of operational numbered Air Forces consisting of two to three wings, also used to designate numerous support and research components. **Air Force.** An intermediate echelon of command directly under the headquarters of a large operational command, usually with four to seven subordinate divisions. **Major command.** A major subdivision of the Air Force that is assigned a major segment of the USAF mission, usually two or four subordinate Air Force elements.

U. S. Army Insignia and Chevrons

Source: Department of the Army

Grade	Insignia

General of the Armies

(General John J. Pershing, the only person to have held this rank, was authorized to prescribe his own insignia, but never wore in excess of four stars. The rank originally was established by Congress for George Washington in 1799, but no record has been found to show that the appointment was made.)

General of the Army . . . Five silver stars fastened together in a circle and the coat of arms of the United States in gold color metal with shield and crest enameled.

General . . . . Four silver stars
Lieutenant General . . . . Three silver stars
Major General . . . . Two silver stars
Brigadier General . . . . One silver star
Colonel . . . . Silver eagle
Lieutenant Colonel . . . . Silver oak leaf
Major . . . . Gold oak leaf
Captain . . . . Two silver bars
First Lieutenant . . . . One silver bar
Second Lieutenant . . . . One gold bar

Warrant officers

Grade Four—Silver bar with 4 enamel black bands.
Grade Three—Silver bar with 3 enamel black bands.
Grade Two—Silver bar with 2 enamel black bands.
Grade One—Silver bar with 1 enamel black band.

Non-Commissioned officers

Sergeant Major of the Army (E-9). Same as Command Sergeant Major (below). Also wears distinctive red and white shield on lapel.

Command Sergeant Major (E-9). Three chevrons above three arcs with a 5-pointed star with a wreath around the star between the chevrons and arcs.

Sergeant Major (E-9). Three chevrons above three arcs with a five-pointed star between the chevrons and arcs.

First Sergeant (E-8). Three chevrons above three arcs with a lozenge between the chevrons and arcs.

Master Sergeant (E-8). Three chevrons above three arcs.

Platoon Sergeant or Sergeant First Class (E-7). Three chevrons above two arcs.

Staff Sergeant E-6). Three chevrons above one arc.

Sergeant (E-5). Three chevrons.

Corporal (E-4). Two chevrons.

Specialists

Specialist Seven (E-7). Three arcs above the eagle device.
Specialist Six (E-6). Two arcs above the eagle device.
Specialist Five (E-5). One arc above the eagle device.
Specialist Four (E-4). Eagle device only.

Other Enlisted

Private First Class (E-3). One chevron above one arc.
Private (E-2). One chevron.
Private (E-1). None.

U.S. Army

Source: Department of the Army

Army Military Personnel on Active Duty (a)

June 30 (b)	Total strength	Commissioned officers				Warrant officers			Enlisted personnel		
		Total	Male	Female (c)	Male (d)	Female	Total	Male	Female	
1940	267,767	17,563	16,624	939	763	—		249,441	249,441	
1942	3,074,184	203,137	190,662	12,475	3,285	—		2,867,762	2,867,762	———
1943	6,993,102	557,657	521,435	36,222	21,919	0		6,413,526	6,358,200	55,325
1944	7,992,868	740,077	692,351	47,726	36,893	10		7,215,888	7,144,601	71,287
1945	8,266,373	835,403	772,511	62,892	56,216	44		7,374,710	7,283,930	90,780
1946	1,889,690	257,300	240,643	16,657	9,826	18		1,622,546	1,605,847	16,699
1950	591,487	67,784	63,375	4,409	4,760	22		518,921	512,370	6,551
1955	1,107,606	111,347	106,173	5,174	10,552	48		985,659	977,943	7,716
1960	871,348	91,056	86,832	4,224	10,141	39		770,112	761,833	8,279
1965	967,049	101,812	98,029	3,783	10,285	23		854,929	846,409	8,520
1966	1,197,468	106,468	102,347	4,121	11,296	22		1,079,682	1,070,503	9,179
1967	1,440,120	127,393	122,685	4,708	16,090	34		1,296,603	1,286,862	9,741
1968	1,567,900	145,988	140,919	5,069	20,158	27		1,401,727	1,391,016	10,711
1969	1,509,637	148,836	143,699	5,137	23,734	20		1,337,047	1,316,326	10,721
1970	1,319,735	143,704	138,469	5,235	23,005	13		1,153,013	1,141,537	11,476
1971	1,120,822	130,261	125,240	5,021	18,670	19		971,872	960,047	11,825
1972	807,985	105,364	100,961	4,403	15,907	19		686,695	674,346	12,349
1973	798,177	101,194	96,936	4,258	14,990	21		681,972	665,515	16,457
1974	780,464	91,873	87,504	4,369	14,106	19		674,466	648,138	26,328
1975	781,316	89,756	85,184	4,572	13,214	22		678,324	640,621	37,703
1976 (Apr. 30) . .	766,979	85,515	80,588	4,927	12,748	30		668,686	625,792	42,894

(a)Represents strength of the active Army, including Philippine Scouts, retired Regular Army personnel on extended active duty, and National Guard and Reserve personnel on extended active duty; excludes U. S. Military Academy cadets, contract surgeons, and National Guard and Reserve personnel not on extended active duty.

(b)Data for 1940 to 1947 include personnel in the Army Air Forces and its predecessors (Air Service and Air Corps).

(c)Includes: Women Doctors, Dentists and Medical Service Corps Officers for 1946 and subsequent years, women in the Army Nurse Corps for all years, and the Women's Army Corps and Women's Medical Specialists Corps (dieticians, physical therapists and occupational specialists) for 1943 and subsequent years.

(d)Act of Congress approved April 27, 1926, directed the appointment as warrant officers, of field clerks still in active service. Includes Flight Officers as follows: 1943, 5,700, 1944, 13,615, 1945, 31,117, 1946, 2,580.

Army Expenditures for Military Functions (1)

(in millions of dollars)

Fiscal Year	Amount	Fiscal Year	Amount	Fiscal Year	Amount	Fiscal Year	Amount
1942	14,805	1953	16,337	1962	11,427	1969	25,035
1943	42,573	1954	12,910	1963	11,499	1970	24,794
1944	49,289	1955	8,899	1964	12,050	1971	23,077
1945	49,750	1958	9,051	1965	11,600	1972	22,596
1946	27,176	1959	9,468	1966	14,832	1973	20,185
1947	8,027	1960	9,392	1967	21,010	1974	21,395
1950	3,985	1961	10,131	1968	25,223	1975	21,920

(1)Excludes expenditures for all civil functions as defined in "The Budget of the United States Government.' Data for fiscal years to 1947 include all Army Air Force expenditures.

U.S. Navy Insignia

Navy
Stripes and corps device are of gold embroidery.

Stripes

Fleet Admiral	1 two inch with 4 one-half inch.
Admiral	1 two inch with 3 one-half inch.
Vice Admiral	1 two inch with 2 one-half inch.
Rear Admiral	1 two inch with 1 one-half inch.
Commodore (war time only)	1 two inch.
Captain	4 one-half inch.
Commander	3 one-half inch.
Lieut. Commander	2 one-half inch, with 1 one-quarter inch between.
Lieutenant	2 one-half inch.
Lieutenant (j.g.)	1 one-half inch with 1 one-quarter inch above.
Ensign	1 one-half inch.

Warrant Officers—One 1/2'' (1/2'' for Warrant officer W-1) broken with 1/2'' intervals of blue as follows:
Chief Warrant Officer W-4—1 break
Chief Warrant Officer W-3—2 breaks, 2'' apart
Chief Warrant Officer W-2—3 breaks, 2'' apart
The breaks are symmetrically centered on outer face of the sleeve.
Enlisted personnel (non-commissioned petty officers) . . . A rating badge worn on the upper left arm, consisting of a spread eagle, appropriate number of chevrons, and centered specialty mark.

Marine Corps
Marine Corps and Army officer insignia are similar. Marine Corps and Army enlisted insignia, although basically similar, differ in color, design, and fewer Marine Corps subdivisions. The Marine Corps' distinctive cap and collar ornament is a combination of the American eagle, globe, and anchor.

Coast Guard
Coast Guard insignia follow Navy custom, with certain minor changes such as the officer cap insignia. The Coast Guard shield is worn on both sleeves of officers and on the right sleeve of all enlisted men.

U. S. Naval Budget Outlays
Source: Department of the Navy

Fiscal year	Total amount expended	Shipbuilding conversion and modernizations	Aircraft and missile procurement	Military construction	All other expenditures
1940	$885,769	$328,819,394	$24,011,998	$72,503,151	$460,435,251
1945	29,380,421,832	7,228,192,871	3,541,009,589	1,576,096,922	17,035,122,450
1950	4,065,484,778	281,328,056	452,723,233	86,054,932	3,245,378,557
1955	9,637,835	903,303,717	1,834,511,038	238,631,005	6,661,192,075
1960	11,848,690,002	1,380,031,231	2,027,098,025	284,928,383	8,228,632,362
1968	22,106,320,837	1,355,850,877	3,642,007,920	92,966,944	17,015,495,096
1970	2,501,628,282	2,065,660,211	3,183,464,921	333,271,852	16,919,231,298
1971	22,046,000,000	2,592,000,000	3,273,000,000	327,000,000	15,854,000,000
1972	24,100,000,000	3,010,000,000	3,983,000,000	353,000,000	16,754,000,000
1973	25,425,000,000	2,962,000,000	3,673,000,000	486,000,000	18,122,000,000
1974	26,800,000,000	3,509,000,000	3,744,000,000	612,000,000	18,935,000,000
1975	27,934,000,000	3,111,000,000	3,516,000,000	578,000,000	20,730,000,000
1976 (Plan)	31,628,000	3,928,000	4,142,000	810,000,000	22,749,000,000

U.S. Navy Personnel on Active Duty
Source: DOD Comptroller

June 30	Officers[1]	Nurses	Enlisted[2]	Off. Cand.	Total
1940	13,162	442	144,824	2,569	160,997
1945	320,293	11,086	2,988,207	61,231	3,380,817
1950	42,687	1,964	331,860	5,037	381,538
1955	72,423	2,104	579,864	6,304	660,695
1960	67,456	2,103	544,040	4,385	617,984
1965	75,996	1,870	587,183	6,399	671,448
1970	78,488	2,273	605,899	6,000	692,660
1973	68,432	2,134	490,009	3,959	564,534
1974	67,200	—	478,700	—	545,900
1975	65,900	—	483,500	—	549,400
1976	63,871	—	457,637	—	521,508

(1). Nurses are included after 1973.   (2). Officer candidates are included after 1973.

Marine Corps Personnel On Active Duty
Source: DOD Comptroller

Yr.	Officers	Enl.	Total	Yr.	Officers	Enl.	Total	Yr.	Officers	Enl.	Total
1955	18,417	186,753	205,170	1965	17,258	172,955	190,213	1975	18,100	174,100	192,200
1960	16,203	154,408	170,621	1970	24,941	234,796	259,737	1976	18,000	175,000	193,000

The Federal Service Academies

U.S. Military Academy, West Point, N.Y. Founded 1802. Awards B.S. degree and Army commission for a 5-year service obligation. For admissions information, write Admissions Office, USMA, West Point, N.Y. 10996.

U.S. Naval Academy, Annapolis, Md. Founded 1845. Awards B.S. degree and Navy or Marine Corps commission for a 5-year service obligation. For admissions information, write Dean of Admissions, Naval Academy, Annapolis, Md. 21402.

U.S. Air Force Academy, Colorado Springs, Colo. Founded 1954. Awards B.S. degree and Air Force commission for a 5-year service obligation. For admissions information, write Registrar, U.S. Air Force Academy, Colo. 80840.

U.S. Coast Guard Academy, New London, Conn. Founded 1876. Awards B.S. degree and Coast Guard commission for a 5-year service obligation. For admissions information, write Admissions Office, Coast Guard Academy, New London, Conn. 06320.

U.S. Merchant Marine Academy, Kings Point, N.Y. Founded 1943. Awards B.S. degree, a license as a deck or engineer officer, and a U.S. Naval Reserve commission. Service obligations vary according to options taken by the graduating ensign. For admissions information, write Admission Office, U.S. Merchant Marine Academy, Kings Point, N.Y. 11024.

United States Air Force
Source: Department of the Air Force

The Army Air forces were started Aug. 1, 1907, as the Aeronautical Division of the Signal Corps, U.S. Army. The division consisted of one officer and two enlisted men, and it was more than a year before it carried out its first mission in an airplane of its own. When the U.S. entered World War I (April 6, 1917), the Aviation Service, as it was called then, had 55 planes and 65 officers, only 35 of whom were fliers. On the day the Japanese struck at Pearl Harbor

(Dec. 7, 1941), the Army Air Forces, as they had been renamed six months previously, had 10,329 planes, of which only 2,846 were suited for combat service. But when the Army's air arm reached its peak during World War II (in July, 1944), it had 79,908 of all types of aircraft and (in May, 1945) 43,248 combat aircraft and (in March, 1944) 2,411,294 officers and enlisted men. The Air Force was established under the Armed Services Unification Act of July 26, 1947.

USAF Personnel at Home and Overseas — Officers and Enlisted Men

June 30	Continental U. S.	Overseas	Total	June 30	Continental U.S.	Overseas	Total
1940	40,229	10,936	51,165	1969	566,475	291,936	858,411
1945	1,153,373	1,128,886	2,282,259	1970	531,386	255,819	787,205
1950	317,816	93,461	411,277	1971	528,493	222,586	751,079
1955	689,635	270,311	959,946	1972	529,672	191,776	721,449
1957*	651,674	268,161	919,835	1973	515,439	171,399	686,838
1960	607,383	207,369	814,752	1974	472,415	171,380	643,795
1965	635,430	189,232	824,662	1975	457,484	150,853	608,337

*Since 1957 continental U.S. includes Air Force Academy Cadets as follows: (1957) 504; (1960) 1,949; (1963) 2,660; (1946) 2,838; (1965) 2,907; (1966) 3,152; (1967) 3,361; (1968) 3,652; (1969) 3,941; (1970) 4,144; (1971) 2,997; (1972) 2,885; (1973) 4,356; (1974) 4,412; (1975) 4,414.

(1.) Since 1960 Overseas includes Alaska and Hawaii. All figures include Mobilized Personnel.

USAF Military Personnel

June 30	Officers & Airmen	Male Commissioned Officers USAF (Reg.) & RA	USAFR & ORC	ANG & NG	AFUS & AUS	Total Warrant Officers
1950	411,277	19,735	33,585	14	55	2,085
1955	959,946	23,463	105,587	984	2	3,961
1960	814,752	49,584	72,115	248	3	4,069
1965	824,662	62,076	62,537	280	54	2,532
1970	787,205	63,678	65,852	168	105	639
1973	686,838	60,456	49,568	146	37	114
1974	643,795[1]	60,835	9,425[2]	....	27	67
1975	603,317	57,854	42,131	128	28	39

(1.) Includes 4,412 USAF Academy cadets. (2.) Selected Reserves only.

Female Commissioned Officers, and Enlisted Personnel

June 30	Female commissioned officers Total	WAF	Nurses	WMSC	Female WO	Enlisted personnel Total	Male	Female
1950	1,525	303	1,143	79	7	354,271	350,489	3,782
1960	3,858	679	3,020	159	5	685,063	679,412	5,651
1965	4,099	708	3,185	206	1	690,177	685,436	4,741
1970	4,667	1,072	3,407	188	....	657,402	648,415	8,987
1973	4,727	1,241	3,304	182	....	571,790	556,767	15,023
1974	4,767	1,488	3,083	196	....	533,479	514,014	19,465
1975	4,981	1,542	3,236	203	0	503,176	477,944	25,232

Those Who Served in U.S. Wars
Source: Veterans Administration

Revolution (1775-1784)
Participants	290,000
Deaths in Service	4,000
Last Veteran Died April 5, 1869	Age 109

War of 1812 (1812-1815)
Participants	287,000
Deaths in Service	2,000
Last Veteran Died May 13, 1905	Age 105

Mexican War (1846-1848)
Participants	79,000
Deaths in Service	13,000
Last Veteran Died September 3, 1929	Age 98

Civil War (1861-1865) (Union Forces Only)
Participants	2,213,000
Deaths in Service	364,511
Last Veteran Died August 2, 1956	Age 109

Indian Wars (Approx. 1817-1898)
Participants	106,000
Deaths in Service	1,000
Last Veteran Died June 18, 1973	Age 101

Spanish-American War (1898-1902)
Participants	392,000
Deaths in Service	11,000
Living Veterans	854

World War I (1917-1918)
Participants	4,744,00
Deaths in Service	116,000
Living Veterans	910,000

World War II (1940-1947)
Participants	[1]16,535,000
Deaths in Service	406,000
Living Veterans	13,478,000

Korean Conflict (June 27, 1950-Jan. 31, 1955)
Participants	[2]6,807,000
Deaths in Service	55,000
Living Veterans	5,968,000

Service Between Korean Conflict and Vietnam Era (Jan. 31, 1955 — Aug. 5, 1964)
Participants	3,195,000
Deaths in Service	20,000
Living Veterans	3,088,000

Vietnam Era (Active duty service after Aug. 4, 1964)
Participants	[2]9,834,000
On Active Duty	1,761,000

America's Wars
Total through January 1, 1976
Participants*	44,482,000
Deaths in Service	1,096,000
Living Veterans	29,559,000

*Persons who served in more than one war period are counted as participants in each.

1. Includes 1,476,000 who served in both World War II and the Korean Conflict.
2. Includes 1,252,000 who served in both the Vietnam Era and the Korean Conflict.

The Medal of Honor

The Medal of Honor is the highest military award for bravery that can be given to any individual in the United States. The first Army Medals were awarded on March 25, 1863, and the first Navy Medals went to sailors and Marines on April 3, 1863.

The Medal of Honor, established by Joint Resolution of Congress, 12 July 1862 (amended by Act of 9 July 1918 and Act of 25 July 1963) is awarded in the name of Congress to a person who, while a member of the Armed Forces, distinguishes himself conspicuously by gallantry and intrepidity at the risk of his life above and beyond the call of duty while engaged in an action against any enemy of the United States; while engaged in military operations involving conflict with an opposing foreign force; or while serving with friendly foreign forces engaged in an armed conflict against an opposing armed force in which the United States is not a belligerent party. The deed performed must have been one of personal bravery or self-sacrifice so conspicuous as to clearly distinguish the individual above his comrades and must have involved risk of life. Incontestable proof of the performance of service is exacted and each recommendation for award of this decoration is considered on the standard of extraordinary merit.

Prior to World War I, the 2,625 Army Medal of Honor awards up to that time were reviewed to determine which past awards met new stringent criteria. The Army removed 911 names from the list, most of them former members of a volunteer infantry group during the Civil War who had been induced to extend their enlistments when they were promised the Medal.

Since that review Medals of Honor have been awarded in the following numbers:

World War I 124   Korean War 131
World War II 431   Vietnam (to date) 235

(For names of Vietnam winners of the Medal of Honor, see the 1972 and 1973 editions of the World Almanac.)

American Military Action, 1900-1973

1900—Occupation of Puerto Rico (ceded to U.S., 1899).
1900—500 Marines, 1,500 Army troops help relieve Peking in Boxer Rebellion.
1900-1902—Occupation of Cuba.
1900-1902—Guerrilla war in Philippines.
1903—Sailors and Marines from U.S.S. Nashville stop Colombian Army at Panama.
1904—Brief intervention in Dominican Republic.
1906-1909—Intervention in Cuba.
1909—Brief intervention in Honduras.
1910,1912-1913—Intervention in Nicaragua.
1911—Intervention (to collect customs) in Honduras, Nicaragua, Dominican Republic.
1912-1917—Intervention in Cuba.
1914—Intervention in Dominican Republic.
1914—April 21 to Nov. 23. Marines in Vera Cruz; also Atlantic fleet and Brig. Gen. Fredk. Funston.
1914—Navy and Marines enter Haiti, stay until 1934.
1916—Gen. John J. Pershing and 10,000 into Northern Mexico to stop raids by Villa, Mar. 15-Nov. 24.
1916-1924—Marines in Dominican Republic.
1917—Apr. 6 to Nov. 11, 1918. War with Germany, Austria-Hungary.
1918-1920—Expeditions into North Russia, Siberia.
1918-1923—Occupation of Germany.
1922-24—Marines in Nicaragua.
1926-33—Marines in Nicaragua.
1927—1,000 U.S. Marines in China.
1941-1945—War with Japan, Germany, Italy and allies.

Army units posted in Japan and West Germany.
1950-1953—U.S. and other UN countries aid the Republic of Korea to repel North Korean invaders; U.S. Navy protects Taiwan.
1956—U.S. Fleet evacuates U.S. nationals during Suez crisis.
1957—U.S. Fleet to Near East during Jordan crisis.
1958—Navy, Marines and Army units support Lebanon.
1960—Navy patrol in Caribbean to protect Guatemala and Nicaragua.
1961—Army units to Vietnam.
1962—Units of U.S. Navy on Cuban quarantine duty. Marines in Thailand.
1962-65—U.S. Military Assistance Command, Vietnam; units of U.S. Army, Navy, Air Force, Marine Corps, Coast Guard.
1965—Navy, Marines, U.S. Army units to Dominican Republic.
1965—American commanders in Vietnam authorized to send U.S. Armed Force into combat.
1969—President Nixon announces, June 8, first phase of withdrawal of U.S. troops from Vietnam.
1970—Army units participate in Cambodian sanctuary operations, Apr. 29-June 30.
1973—Last U.S. troops leave Vietnam, U.S. Military Assistance Command deactivated, March 29.
1973—End of all U.S. bombing operations over Indochina, Aug. 15

Adjutant General's Figures of Civil War Deaths

Figures reported from the Adjutant General's Office previous to the above revision, and accepted for many years, are as follows:

Union Army, according to records in the office of the Adjutant General of the War Department in Washington — killed or died of wounds, 110,070 (6,365 officers, 103,705 men); Died of disease, 224,586 (2,795 officers, 221,791 men); other deaths, 24,872 (424 officers, 24,448 men). Totals, 359,528 (9,584 officers, 349,944 men).

Confederate Army, estimated, no official records in the office of the Adjutant General of the War Department in Washington — killed in battle, 52,954 (2,086 officers, 50,868 men); died of wounds, 21,570 (1,246 officers, 20,324 men); died of disease, 59,297 (1,294 officers, 58,003 men). Total, 133,821 (4,626 officers, 129,195 men).

World War II Merchant Marine Casualties
Source: U. S. Coast Guard

Died from direct causes while serving on American flag ships, 845; died in prisoner-of-war camps, 37; listed as missing, 4,780.

There were 572 released prisoners of war, and one prisoner unaccounted for. Another 500 men died while serving on foreign flag ships under U. S. control.

The number of U. S. flag ships lost was 605 of 6,000,000 deadweight tons.

How the Military Hand Salute Originated

Hand-raising as a formal greeting originated with the cavemen, who wanted to prove to one another that they carried no weapons, according to the National Geographic Society. Later an armored knight raised his right arm to lift his helmet visor and to show friendship by keeping his sword hand away from the weapon. Before the 19th Century, British soldiers saluted by tipping their hats. In the modern U.S. military salute the right hand is raised smartly so the forefinger touches the forehead just above and to the right of the right eye, thumb and fingers extended, forearm and wrist at a 45-degree angle. This salute, with variations, is common among military forces around the world.

Strategic Nuclear Armaments: U.S. and USSR

Source: International Institute for Strategic Services, London

United States

Land-based missiles[1], Sea-based missiles

Type		Range[2] (statute miles)	Estimated warhead yield[3]	Deployed (July 1975)
Land-based missiles[1]				
ICBM	Titan 2	7,250	5-10 MT	54
	Minuteman 2	8,000	1-2 MT	450
	Minuteman 3	8,000	3x170 KT	550
Sea-based missiles				
SLBM	UGM-27C			
(nuclear	Polaris A3	2,880	3x200 KT	256
subs)	UGM-73A			
	Poseidon	2,880	10x50 KT	400

Type		Range[7] (statute miles)	Weapons load (lb)	Deployed (July 1975)
Aircraft[6]				
Long-range	B-52D-F	11,500	60,000	432[8]
	B-52G/H	12,500	75,000	
Medium range	FB-111A	3,800	37,500	66
Strike aircraft;	F-105D	2,100	16,500	
land-based	F-4	2,300	16,000	1,500[9]
	F-111A/E	3,800	25,000	
	A-7D	3,400	15,000	
	F-15A	2,500	12,000	
Strike aircraft	A-4	2,055	10,000	
carrier-based	A-6A	3,225	18,000	1,000[9]
	A-7A/B/E	3,400	15,000	
	F-4	1,997	1,600	

Soviet Union

Type		Range[2] (statute miles)	Estimated warhead yield[3]	Deployed (July 1975)
Land-based missiles[1]				
ICBM	SS-7 Saddler	6,900	5 MT	190
	SS-8 Sasin	6,900	5 MT	19
	SS-9 Scarp	7,500	20-25 MT[4]	288
	SS-11	6,500	1-2 MT[5]	991
	SS-13 Savage	5,000	1 MT	60
	SS-17	6,500	4x KT	10
	SS-18	7,500	18&25 MT	10
	SS-19	6,500	6x KT	50
Sea-based missiles				
SLBM	SS-N-5 Serb	750	MT	24
(nuclear	SS-N-6-Sawfly	1,750	MT	544
subs)	SS-N-8	4,800	MT	156
SLBM				
(diesel	SS-N-4 Sark	350	MT	27
subs)	SS-N-5 Serb	750	MT	33
SLCM	SS-N-3 Shaddock	450	KT	312

Type		Range[7] (statute miles)	Weapons load (lb)	Deployed (July 1975)
Aircraft[6]				
	Tu-95 Bear	7,800	40,000	100
	Mya-4 Bison	6,050	20,000	35
	Tu-16 Badger	4,000	20,000	755
	Backfire B	3,600	20,000	25
	Il-28 Beagle	2,500	4,850	
	Su-7 Fitter	900	4,500	
	Tu-22 Blinder	1,400	12,000	
	Yak-28 Brewer	1,750	4,400	2,500[9]
	MiG-21 Fishbed J	1,150	2,000	
	MiG-23 Flogger	1,800	2,800	
	Su-19A Fencer	1,800	8,000	
	Su-17/20 Fitter C	1,100	5,000	

(1) ICBM = intercontinental ballistic missile. IRBM = intermediate-range ballistic missile. MRBM = medium-range missile. SLBM = submarine-launched ballistic missile. SLCM = sub-launched cruise missile. (2) Operation range depends upon the payload carried; use of maximum payload may reduce missile range by up to 25%. (3) MT = megaton range = 1,000,000 tons of TNT equivalent or over; KT = kiloton range = 1,000 tons of TNT equivalent or more, but less than 1 MT. (4) Some SS-9 missiles carry 3 warheads of 4-5 MT each. (5) Some SS-11 missiles may carry 3xKT warheads. (6) All aircraft listed are dual-capable and many, especially in the categories of strike aircraft, would be more likely to carry conventional than nuclear weapons. (7) Theoretical maximum range, with internal fuel only, at optimum altitude and speed. Ranges for strike aircraft assume no weapons load. Especially in the case of strike aircraft, therefore, range falls sharply for flights at lower altitude, at higher speed, or with full weapons load. (8) Including approximately 40 B-52 D-F aircraft in active storage. (9) These aircraft are nuclear capable but may not have a nuclear role. Strike craft numbers are estimates.

Women in the Armed Forces

Expansion of military women's programs began in the Department of Defense in fiscal year 1973. The planned end strength for fiscal year 1988 is approximately 204,300 which is 6.2 per cent of the planned end strength of the active forces.

Although women are prohibited by law and directives based on law from serving in combat positions, policy changes in the department have resulted in making possible the assignment of women to almost all other career fields. Career progression for women is now comparable to that for male personnel. Women are routinely assigned to overseas locations formerly closed to female personnel. Test programs have been initiated to place women in pilot training and in command of activities and units which have missions other than administration of women.

Admission of women to the service academies will begin in 1976 and will further the goal of increased numbers of women officers. The Academies will provide single track education, allowing only for minor variations in the cadet program based on physiological differences between men and women.

Women's Army Corps —Brig. Gen. M. E. Clark, WAC Director, Dept. of Army, Washington, D.C. 20310; 2,029 officers, 41,095 enlisted women; wide variety of assignments, world-wide; subsidizes some college training.

Army Nurse Corps — Brig. M. N. Parks, Chief, Army Nurse Corps, Office of the Surgeon General, Dept. of Army, Washington, D.C. 20310; 2,748 female officers; nursing and supervision assignments, world-wide; subsidizes some training; corps includes men.

Navy — Fully integrated, no director for women. For information: Commander, Naval Recruiting, Dept. of Navy, Washington, D.C. 22203; 1,428 officers, 18,437 enlisted women; variety of assignments, world-wide.

Navy Nurse Corps — Rear Adm. Maxine Conder, Director, Navy Nurse Corps, Bureau of Medicine and Surgery, Dept. of Navy, Washington, D.C. 20372; 2,163 female officers; nursing and supervision assignments at U.S. and foreign bases, and shipboard; subsidizes some training; corps includes men.

Air Force — Fully integrated, no director for women. For information: USAF Recruiting Service, Randolph Air Force Base, Tex. 78148; 1,616 officers, 29,034 enlisted women; variety of assignments, world-wide.

Air Force Nurse Corps — Brig. Gen. Claire M. Garrecht, Chief, Air Force Nurse Corps, Office of the Surgeon General, USAF, Washington, D.C. 20314; 3,194 women nurses, 254 other medical officers; nursing and supervision assignments, world-wide; subsidizes training; corps includes men.

Women Marines — Col. Margaret A. Brewer, Director, Women Marines, Headquarters, Marine Corps, Washington, D.C. 20380; 396 officers, 3,068 enlisted women.

Coast Guard Women — Fully integrated, no commander. U.S. Coast Guard, Washington, D.C. 20590; 38 officers, 374 enlisted women.

Monthly Pay Scale of the

Commissioned Officers

					Cumulative years of service			
Pay grade	Army or Air Force rank	Navy rank	Under 2	Over 2	Over 3	Over 4	Over 6	Over 8
0-10[1]	General*	Admiral	$2,841.00	$2,940.90	$2,940.90	$2,940.90	$2,940.90	$3,053.70
0-9	Lieutenant General	Vice Admiral	2,517.90	2,584.20	2,639.10	2,639.10	2,639.10	2,706.00
0-8	Major General	Rear Admiral (up. half)	2,280.60	2,349.00	2,404.80	2,404.80	2,404.80	2,584.20
0-7	Brigadier General	Rear Admiral (low.-half)	1,894.80	2,024.10	2,024.10	2,024.10	2,114.40	2,114.40
0-6	Colonel	Captain	1,404.60	1,543.50	1,644.00	1,644.00	1,644.00	1,644.00
0-5	Lieutenant Colonel	Commander	1,123.20	1,319.40	1,410.30	1,410.30	1,410.30	1,410.30
0-4	Major	Lieutenant Comdr	947.10	1,152.60	1,230.30	1,230.30	1,252.50	1,308.30
0-3	Captain	Lieutenant	880.20	983.70	1,051.50	1,163.70	1,219.20	1,263.30
0-2	First Lieutenant	Lieutenant (J.G.)	767.10	838.20	1,006.80	1,040.40	1,062.30	1,062.30
0-1	Second Lieutenant	Ensign	666.00	693.30	838.20	838.20	838.20	838.20

Commissioned officers with over 4 years service as enlisted members

0-3	Captain	Lieutenant				1,163.70	1,219.20	1,263.30
0-2	First Lieutenant	Lieutenant (J.G.)				1,040.40	1,062.30	1,095.90
0-1	Second Lieutenant	Ensign				838.20	894.90	928.20

Warrant Officer

W-4	Chief Warrant	Comm. Warrant	896.40	961.80	961.80	983.70	1,028.70	1,073.70
W-3	Chief Warrant	Comm. Warrant	815.10	884.10	884.10	894.90	905.70	972.00
W-2	Chief Warrant	Comm. Warrant	713.70	771.90	771.90	794.40	838.20	884.10
W-1	Warrant Officer	Warrant Officer	594.60	681.90	681.90	738.60	771.90	805.50

Enlisted Personnel[2]

E-9[3]	Sergeant Major**	Master C. P. O.						
E-8[3]	Master Sergeant	Senior C.P.O.						854.70
E-7	Sgt. 1st Class	Chief Petty Officer	596.70	643.80	667.80	691.20	715.20	737.40
E-6	Staff Sergeant	Petty Officer 1st Class	515.40	561.90	585.30	609.60	632.70	656.10
E-5	Sergeant	Petty Officer 2nd Cl	452.40	492.60	516.30	538.80	573.90	597.30
E-4	Corporal	Petty Officer 3rd Cl	435.00	459.30	486.00	524.10	544.50	544.50
E-3	Private 1st Class	Seaman	418.20	441.30	459.00	477.00	477.00	477.00
E-2	Private	Seaman Apprentice	402.60	402.60	402.60	402.60	402.60	402.60
E-1	Private	Seaman Recruit	361.20	361.20	361.20	361.20	361.20	361.20

The pay scale also applies to: Coast Guard and Marine Corps, Coast and Geodetic Survey, Public Health Service, National Guard, and the Organized Reserves.

*Basic pay is limited to $3,150.00 by Level V of the Executive Schedule. Four star General or Admiral—personal money allowances of $2,200 per annum, or $4,000 if Chief of Staff or Chief of Naval Operations. Three star General or Admiral—personal money allowance of $500 per annum.

**A new title of Chief Master Sergeant created in 1965 rates E-9 classification.

(1) While serving as Chairman of Joint Chiefs of Staff, Chief of Staff of the Army, Chief of Naval Operations, Chief of Staff of the Air Forces, or Commandant of the Marine Corps, basic pay for this grade is $4,405.50 regardless of years of service.

(2) Air Force enlisted personnel pay grades, E-9, Chief Master Sergeant; E-8, Sr. Master Sergeant; E-7, Master Sergeant; E-6, Technical Sergeant; E-5, Staff Sergeant; E-4, Sergeant; E-3, Airman 1st Class; E-2, Airman; E-1, Basic Airman.

Marine Corps enlisted ranks are as follows: E-9, Sergeant Major and Master Gunnery Sergeant; E-8, First Sergeant and Master Sergeant; E-7, Gunnery Sergeant; E-6, Staff Sergeant; E-5, Sergeant; E-4, Corporal; E-3, Lance Corporal; E-2, Private, First Class Marine; E-1, Private.

Marine Corps officer ranks are same as Army and AF.

(3) While serving as Sergeant Major of the Army, Master Chief Petty Officer of the Navy, Chief Master Sergeant of the Air Force, or Sergeant Major of the Marine Corps, basic pay for this grade is $1,594.50 regardless of years of service.

Hazardous Duty

Flying Duty (enlisted crew member) and Submarine Duty Additional Monthly Pay

	Under 2 yrs.	Over 2 yrs.	Maximum Over—Amt.
O-10	$165	$165	$165
O-9	165	165	165
O-8	155	155	165
O-7	150	150	160
O-6	200	200	18 yrs. —245
O-5	190	190	18 " —245
O-4	170	170	18 " —240
O-3	145	145	14 " —205
O-2	115	125	14 " —185
O-1	100	105	14 " —170
W-4	115	*	18 " —165
W-3	110	115	14 " —140
W-2	105	110	14 " —135
W-1	100	105	12 " —130
E-9	105	105	105
E-8	105	105	105
E-7	80	85	12 yrs. —105
E-6	70	75	14 " —100
E-5	60	70	12 " — 95
E-4	55	65	8 " — 80
E-3	55	60	2 " — 60
E-2	50	60	2 " — 60
E-1	50	55	2 " — 55

Aviation Cadet under 2 years $50.
*W-4 Under 6 years receives $115.

Incentive Pay

Officers and Warrant Officers ... $110.00
Enlisted men ... 55.00

Types of duties for which these flat rates are payable are as follows—(1) Frequent and regular aerial flights not as a crew member. (2) Parachute jumping as an essential part of military duty. (3) Duty involving intimate contact with leprosy. (4) Duty involving demolition of explosives. (5, 6) Special pay is authorized for diving duty. Pay varies with rank and type of duty. (7) Human acceleration or deceleration duty. (8) High-or-low pressure chamber duty. (9) Thermal stress duty. (10) Training for assignment to submarines of advanced design or for positions of increased responsibility aboard a submarine. Rates payable for this category are the same as those paid flying crew members listed under Hazardous Duty. (11) Flight Deck Duty.

Sea and Foreign Duty

Defense Secretary designates places where special duty pay may be awarded.

E-9	$22.50	E-4	13.00
E-8	22.50	E-3	9.00
E-7	22.50	E-2	8.00
E-6	20.00	E-1	8.00
E-5	16.00		

Uniformed Services (1976)

Commissioned Officers

| Cumulative years of service | | | | | | | | Basic allowances for quarters | |
Over 10	Over 12	Over 14	Over 16	Over 18	Over 20	Over 22	Over 26	Without Dependents	With Dependents
3,053.70	3,287.70*	3,287.70*	3,522.90*	3,522.90*	3,758.40*	3,758.40*	3,992.70*	255.30	319.20
2,706.00	2,818.20	2,818.20	3,053.70	3,053.70	3,287.70*	3,287.70*	3,522.90*	255.30	319.20
2,584.20	2,706.00	2,706.00	2,818.20	2,940.90	3,053.70	3,176.10*	3,176.10*	255.30	319.20
2,237.40	2,237.40	2,349.00	2,584.20	2,761.80	2,761.80	2,761.80	2,761.80	255.30	319.20
1,644.00	1,644.00	1,699.80	1,968.90	2,069.70	2,114.40	2,237.40	2,426.10	234.60	286.20
1,453.50	1,530.90	1,633.20	1,755.90	1,856.70	1,912.50	1,979.70	1,979.70	219.60	264.60
1,397.10	1,476.00	1,543.50	1,610.70	1,655.40	1,655.40	1,655.40	1,655.40	198.00	238.80
1,330.80	1,397.10	1,431.30	1,431.30	1,431.30	1,431.30	1,431.30	1,431.30	175.50	216.60
1,062.30	1,062.30	1,062.30	1,062.30	1,062.30	1,062.30	1,062.30	1,062.30	153.60	194.70
838.20	838.20	838.20	838.20	838.20	838.20	838.20	838.20	120.60	156.90
1,330.80	1,397.10	1,453.50	1,453.50	1,453.50	1,453.50	1,453.50	1,453.50	175.50	216.60
1,152.60	1,197.30	1,230.30	1,230.30	1,230.30	1,230.30	1,230.30	1,230.30	153.60	194.70
961.80	995.40	1,040.40	1,040.40	1,040.40	1,040.40	1,040.40	1,040.40	120.60	156.90

Warrant Officers

Over 10	Over 12	Over 14	Over 16	Over 18	Over 20	Over 22	Over 26	Without Dependents	With Dependents
1,118.70	1,197.30	1,252.50	1,296.90	1,330.80	1,374.90	1,420.80	1,530.90	191.10	230.40
1,028.70	1,062.30	1,095.90	1,128.60	1,163.70	1,208.40	1,252.50	1,296.90	172.20	212.40
917.40	950.70	983.70	1,018.20	1,051.50	1,084.80	1,128.60	1,128.60	151.80	192.60
838.20	872.70	905.70	939.30	972.00	1,006.80	1,006.80	1,006.80	137.40	178.20

Enlisted Personnel

Over 10	Over 12	Over 14	Over 16	Over 18	Over 20	Over 22	Over 26	Without Dependents	With Dependents
1,018.50	1,041.60	1,065.30	1,089.90	1,113.90	1,135.80	1,195.80	1,311.60	144.90	204.00
878.40	901.80	925.50	949.50	971.70	995.70	1,053.90	1,171.80	135.00	190.80
760.80	784.80	820.20	843.30	867.00	878.40	937.50	1,053.90	115.80	178.80
679.80	715.20	737.40	760.80	772.80	772.80	772.80	772.80	106.20	166.20
621.30	643.80	656.10	656.10	656.10	656.10	656.10	656.10	102.60	153.60
544.50	544.50	544.50	544.50	544.50	544.50	544.50	544.50	90.30	134.40
477.00	477.00	477.00	477.00	477.00	477.00	477.00	477.00	80.10	116.10
402.60	402.60	402.60	402.60	402.60	402.60	402.60	402.60	70.80	116.10
361.20	361.20	361.20	361.20	361.20	361.20	361.20	361.20	66.60	116.10

*Limited under existing law to $3,150

Basic Allowances for Subsistence

This allowance, the quarters allowance, and any other allowance are not subject to income tax.

Officers — Subsistence (food) is paid to all officers regardless of rank.................................53.05 per month
Enlisted members: When rations in kind are not available...2.85 per day
When assigned to duty under emergency conditions where
no government messing facilities are available.....................3.79 per day (maximum rate)

Family Separation Allowance

Under certain conditions of family separation of more than 30 days, a member in Pay Grades E-4 (with over 4 years' service) and above will be allowed $30 a month in addition to any other allowances to which he is entitled. When separated from family and required to maintain a home for his family and one for himself, the member is entitled to an additional monthly basic allowance for quarters at the "without dependents" rate for his grade.

Uniform Allowance

Enlisted personnel receive an initial uniform allowance valued at about $250, with variations among services. After 6 months and up to the 36th month maintenance allowance of $5.70 is paid. After 36 months the monthly allowance is $8.40. An officer is entitled to an initial allowance of not more than $300.00.

Enlistment Bonus

DOD currently authorizes a bonus of up to $2,500 for a four-year enlistment in certain skills designated as critical.

Reenlistment Bonuses

All reenlistees who were on active duty on June 1, 1974, are entitled to a bonus for reenlisting (Regular Reenlistment Bonus, Selective Reenlistment Bonus, or a combination thereof) of at least $2,000 during a 20-year career. A member who is eligible for both the Regular Reenlistment Bonus and the Selective Reenlistment Bonus may elect to receive either bonus. However, once an individual receives $2,000 in reenlistment bonuses, his entitlement to the Regular Bonus terminates.

Members serving in critical military specialties may, as a special incentive, receive the Selective Reenlistment Bonus. This retention incentive is paid to individuals designated as having a critical military specialty who reenlist for at least 3 years between 21 months and 10 years of service. Maximum allowable Selective Reenlistment Bonus is $15,000 based upon multiples (1 through 6) of monthly basic pay multiplied by years (not to exceed 6) of additional obligated service.

Special Pay

Members of the uniformed services entitled to receive basic pay shall, in addition thereto, be entitled to receive incentive pay for the performance of hazardous duty required by competent orders. The President may, in time of war, suspend the payment of hazardous duty incentive pay. Officers receive no additional pay for overseas or sea duty.

Duty Subject to Hostile Fire

Except in time of war declared by the Congress, a special pay of $65 a month is authorized for any member of the Uniformed Services during any month in which he was subject to hostile fire.

Medical and Dental Corps

Commissioned officers in the Medical and Dental Corps of the Army, Navy and Air Force and commissioned medical, dental, and veterinary officers of the Regular Corps of the Public Health Service receive special pay based on cumulative years of service (0-2 years, $100; 2 to 6 years, $150; 6 to 10 years, $250; over 10 years, $350 for dental officers; and 0-2 years, $100; 2 or more years, $350 for medical officers). In addition to basic pay and allowance Optometrists and Veterinary Corps Officers receive $100 per month extra.

Casualties in Principal Wars of the U. S.

Data on Revolutionary War casualties is from **The Toll of Independence**, Howard H. Peckham, ed., U. of Chicago Press, 1974.

Data prior to World War I are based upon incomplete records in many cases. Casualty data are confined to dead and wounded personnel and therefore exclude personnel captured or missing in action who were subsequently returned to military control. Dash (—) indicates information is not available.

Wars	Branch of service	Number serving	Battle deaths	Other deaths	Casualties Wounds not mortal	Total
Revolutionary War	**Total**	—	**6,824**	**18,500**	**8,445**	**33,769**
1775-1783	Army	184,000	5,992	—	7,988	13,980
	Navy &	to	—	—	—	—
	Marines	250,000	832	—	457	1,289
War of 1812	**Total**	**⁹286,730**	**2,260**	—	**4,505**	**6,765**
1812-1815	Army	—	1,950	—	4,000	5,950
	Navy	—	265	—	439	704
	Marines	—	45	—	66	111
Mexican War	**Total**	**⁹78,718**	**1,733**	**11,550**	**4,152**	**17,435**
1846-1848	Army	—	1,721	11,550	4,102	17,373
	Navy	—	1	—	3	4
	Marines	—	11	—	47	58
Civil War	**Total**	**⁹2,213,363**	**140,414**	**224,097**	**281,881**	**646,392**
(Union forces only)	Army	2,128,948	138,154	221,374	280,040	639,568
1861-1865	Navy	—	2,112	2,411	1,710	6,233
	Marines	84,415	148	312	131	591
Confederate forces	**Total**	—	**74,524**	**59,297**	—	**133,821**
(estimate)[1]	Army	600,000	—	—	—	—
1863-1866	Navy	to	—	—	—	—
	Marines	1,500,000	—	—	—	—
Spanish-American	**Total**	**306,760**	**385**	**2,061**	**1,662**	**4,108**
War	Army[4]	280,564	369	2,061	1,594	4,024
1898	Navy	22,875	10	0	47	57
	Marines	3,321	6	0	21	27
World War I	**Total**	**4,743,826**	**53,513**	**63,195**	**204,002**	**320,710**
April 6, 1917-	Army[5]	4,057,101	50,510	55,868	193,663	300,041
Nov. 11, 1918	Navy	599,051	431	6,856	819	8,106
	Marines	78,839	2,461	390	9,520	12,371
	Coast Gd.	8,835	111	81	—	192
World War II	**Total**	**16,353,659**	**292,131**	**115,185**	**670,846**	**1,078,162**
Dec. 7, 1941-	Army[6]	11,260,000	234,874	83,400	565,861	884,135
Dec. 31, 1946[2]	Navy[7]	4,183,466	36,950	25,664	37,778	100,392
	Marines	669,100	19,733	4,778	67,207	91,718
	Coast Gd.	241,093	574	1,343	—	1,917
Korean War	**Total**	**5,764,143**	**33,629**	**20,617**	**103,284**	**157,530**
June 25, 1950-	Army	2,834,000	27,704	9,429	77,596	114,729
July 27, 1953[3]	Navy	1,177,000	458	4,043	1,576	6,077
	Marines	424,000	4,267	1,261	23,744	29,272
	Air Force	1,285,000	1,200	5,884	368	7,452
	Coast Gd.	44,143	—	—	—	—
Vietnam (preliminary)[10]	**Total**	**8,744,000**	**46,498**	**10,388**	**153,329**	**210,215**
Aug. 4, 1964-	Army	4,368,000	30,684	7,191	96,811	134,686
Jan. 27, 1973	Navy	1,842,000	1,523	910	4,180	6,613
	Marines	794,000	13,009	1,684	51,399	66,092
	Air Force	1,740,000	1,282	603	939	2,824

[1]Authoritative statistics for the Confederate Forces are not available. An estimated 26,000-31,000 Confederate personnel died in Union prisons.

[2]Data are for the period Dec. 1, 1941 through Dec. 31, 1946 when hostilities were officially terminated by Presidential Proclamation, but few battle deaths or wounds not mortal were incurred after the Japanese acceptance of Allied peace terms on Aug. 14, 1945. Numbers serving from Dec. 1, 1941-Aug. 31, 1945 were: Total—14,903,213; Army—10,420,-000; Navy—3,883,520; and Marine Corps—599,693.

[3]Tentative final data based upon information available as of Sept. 30, 1954, at which time 24 persons were still carried as missing in action.

[4]Number serving covers the period April 21-Aug. 13, 1898, while dead and wounded data are for the period May 1-Aug. 31, 1898. Active hostilities ceased on Aug. 13, 1898, but ratifications of the treaty of peace were not exchanged between the United States and Spain until April 11, 1899.

[5]Includes Air Service. Battle deaths and wounds not mortal include casualties suffered by American forces in Northern Russia to Aug. 25, 1919 and in Siberia to April 1, 1920. Other deaths covered the period April 1, 1917-Dec. 31, 1918.

[6]Includes Army Air Forces.

[7]Battle deaths and wounds not mortal include casualties incurred in Oct. 1941 due to hostile action.

[8]Marine Corps data for World War II, the Spanish-American War and prior wars represent the number of individuals wounded, whereas all other data in this column represent the total number (incidence) of wounds.

[9]As reported by the Commissioner of Pensions in his Annual Report for Fiscal Year 1903.

[10]Number serving covers the period 4 August 1964-27 January 1973 (date of ceasefire). Number of casualties incurred in connection with the conflict in Vietnam from 1 January 1961-31 March 1976. Includes casualties incurred in Mayaguez Incident. Wounds not mortal exclude 150,332 persons not requiring hospital care.

Veterans Administration Role Changes

Source: Veterans Administration, Richard L. Roudebush, Administrator, Washington, D. C.

As the enrollment in GI Bill school and training programs peaked and began to fall in 1976, the number of WW II GIs reaching age 65 increased dramatically. Although the VA will continue to provide billions of dollars in GI schooling benefits, there will be a subtle change in orientation to assure that the health and pension needs of the growing number of older veterans will be effectively met.

There are an estimated 29.6 million American veterans living today. Combined with more than 60 million living members of their families and nearly 4 million survivors of deceased veterans, they comprise nearly half of the population of the United States.

The $18.4 billion FY 1977 VA budget has a vast impact on millions of Americans in the implementation of numerous programs which have been enacted by Congress. The VA medical system provides inpatient hospital, nursing home, domiciliary care for 1.4 million veterans patients treated and outpatient care totaling 15.6 million medical visits. The budget contains a construction request of $478.9 million, most of which is for medical facilities, making it the highest construction budget in VA history. This budget permits VA to pay $5.2 billion in compensation benefits to 2.6 million veterans with service-connected disabilities and to survivors of deceased veterans. In addition, VA will send more than $2.8 billion in pension checks to 2.2 million veterans and survivors in financial need. This budget will assist some 2.9 million veterans, their wives or widows and their children with $4.9 billion for education programs. The 1977 budget will also guaranty home loans for over 361,000 veterans, most of whom served their country during the Vietnam Era. VA also administers $101.3 billion in life insurance protection for 8.6 million veterans and service people on active duty. Although it employs 212,000 persons, VA's operating expenses are held to 2.6% of the entire budget.

The GI Bill education and training program has increased for each successive fall and spring enrollment period since it began in June 1966. In the spring of this year, presumably due to the impending delimiting date (10 years after the date of discharge or June 1, 1966, whichever is later), the number of veterans and service personnel in training declined from the fall peak of 1.826 million. Of the 6.437 million veterans and service personnel who had trained under the GI bill through April 30, 1976, nearly 56 percent had taken college training.

The VA's Department of Medicine and Surgery (DM&S) cared for a record number of veterans in 1976, serving 1,289,000 inpatients in its 171 hospitals. Veteran visits to the VA's 220 outpatient clinics totaled 14,630,000.

DM&S education and training activities were at record levels, with more than 82,000 doctors, dentists, nurses and health workers in a total of 40 specialty fields receiving training. The VA increased affiliations to include 102 medical schools for training students in 128 VA hospitals, and to 58 dental schools (all U.S. schools) with 78 hospitals.

The Department sponsored 6,246 individual and 24 multi-hospital cooperative research projects with a total budget of $97.4 million.

DM&S operated 18 Spinal Cord Injury Centers for care of paralyzed veterans, 126 Alcohol and Drug Dependence Treatment Centers, and eight Geriatric Research, Education and Clinical Centers during the year.

The VA's Vet Reps are continuing their mission on campus to facilitate the timely delivery of GI Bill checks to veterans and their dependents. Since the Vet Rep program was instituted in 1974, an increasing number of veterans have received personal service from the on-campus force.

Many full-time educational benefits recipients are assisting in VA's other outreach activities as part of the work-study program. These students contact their peers to encourage them to take advantage of VA benefits and services. Other work-study students assist Vet Reps on campus and perform varied duties in VA offices and centers across the Nation.

Nearly 1.1 million Vietnam Era veterans have received VA-guaranteed home loans valued at almost $28 billion. Since 1944, when the VA home loan program began, 9.25 million loans with a face value of $119.2 billion have been guaranteed or insured by VA. Currently the guaranty amount is $17,500 which can be used by veterans and service personnel to buy, construct, improve, alter or repair a home or farm residence, or to purchase a condominium or mobile home and/or lot.

Veteran Population

May 1976

1.	Veterans in civil life, end of month — Total	29,573,000
2.	War Veterans — Total	26,488,000
3.	Vietnam Era — Total (a)	8,034,000
4.	And service in Korean Conflict	516,000
5.	No service in Korean Conflict	7,518,000
6.	Korean Conflict — Total (includes line 4)(b)	5,954,000
7.	And service in WW II	1,239,000
8.	No service in WW II	4,715,000
9.	World War II (includes line 7)	13,386,000
10.	World War I	868,000
11.	Spanish-American War	1,000
12.	Service between Korean Conflict (January 31, 1955) and Vietnam (August 5, 1964) Only (c)	3,085,000

(a) Service after Aug. 4, 1964; (b) includes 2,385,000 veterans who also served after the end of the Korean Conflict Jan. 31, 1955); (c) excludes men who served on active duty for training only.

Pension Cases and Compensation Payments

Fiscal year	Living veteran cases No.	Deceased veteran cases No.	Total cases No.	Total disbursement Dollars	Fiscal year	Living veteran cases No.	Deceased veteran cases No.	Total cases No.	Total disbursement Dollars
1890	415,654	122,290	537,944	106,093,850	1965	3,204,275	1,277,009	4,481,284	3,901,598,010
1900	752,510	241,019	993,529	138,462,130	1968	3,112,038	1,389,379	4,501,417	4,406,319,385
1910	602,622	318,461	921,083	159,974,056	1969	3,107,162	1,443,367	4,550,529	4,722,489,826
1920	419,627	349,916	769,543	316,418,029	1970	3,127,338	1,487,176	4,614,514	5,113,649,490
1930	542,610	298,223	840,833	418,432,808	1971	3,222,394	1,584,167	4,806,561	5,726,485,000
1940	610,122	239,176	849,298	429,138,465	1972	3,268,826	1,641,370	4,910,196	6,045,214,000
1950	2,368,238	658,123	3,026,361	2,009,462,298	1973	3,256,746	1,654,287	4,911,033	6,426,647,000
1955	2,668,786	808,303	3,477,089	2,634,292,537	1974	3,241,263	1,627,482	4,868,745	6,615,599,000
1960	3,008,935	950,802	3,959,737	3,314,761,383	1975	3,226,701	1,628,146	4,854,847	7,600,000,000

American Military Cemeteries and Memorials on Foreign Soil

Administered by the American Battle Monuments Commission, Washington, D.C. 20314
(Numbers of graves, and numbers of commemorated missing, in parentheses)

World War I Cemeteries

Aisne-Marne, near Belleau (Aisne) France (2,288-1,060)
Brookwood (Surrey) England (468-563)
Flanders Field, Waregem, Belgium (368-43)
Meuse-Argonne, Romagne (Meuse), France (14,246-954)
Oise-Aisne, Seringes (Aisne), near Fere-en-Tardenois (Aisne), France (6,012-241)
St. Mihiel, Thiaucourt (M. et M.), France (4,153-284)
Somme, Bony (Aisne), France (1,844-284)
Suresnes (Seine), France (1,541-974). In this cemetery rest also 24 of our unknown dead of World War II. The World War I chapel was, by the addition of two loggias, converted into a shrine to commemorate our dead of both wars. Senior representatives of the American and French governments assemble here on ceremonial occasions to pay homage to our military dead of these wars.

World War I Monuments

Audenarde, Belgium.
Bellicourt (Aisne), France.
Brest (Finistere), France.
Cantigny (Somme), France.
Chateau-Thierry (Aisne), Fr. Gibraltar.
Kemmel, near Ypres, Belgium.
Montfaucon (Meuse), France.
Montsec (Meuse), France.
Sommepy (Marne), France.
Tours (Indre et Loire), France.

World War II Cemetery Memorials

Ardennes, near Neuville-en-Condroz, Belgium (5,313-462)
Brittany, near St. James (Manche), France (4,410-498)
Cambridge, near Cambridge, England, (3,811-5,125)
Epinal, near Epinal (Vosges), France (5,255-424)
Florence, near Florence (Tuscany), Italy (4,402-1,409)

Henri-Chapelle, near Henri-Chapelle, Belgium (7,989-450)
Lorraine, St. Avold (Moselle), France (10,489-444)
Luxembourg, Hamm, Luxembourg (5,076-370)
Manila, near Manila, Rep. of the Philippines (17,208-36,279)
Netherlands, Margraten, Holland (8,301-1,722)
Normandy, near St. Laurent (Calvados), Fr. (9,386-1,557)
North Africa, Carthage, Tunisia (2,840-3,724)
Rhone, Draguignan (Var), France (861-293)
Sicily-Rome, Nettuno, Italy (7,862-3,094)

World War II Memorials

To commemorate those who met their deaths in the American coastal waters of the Atlantic and Pacific Oceans the commission has erected a memorial in Battery Park, New York City, on which are inscribed 4,596 names, and at the Presidio of San Francisco, California, which carries 412 names. At the Honolulu Cemetery a memorial was erected which records the names of 18,093 missing of World War II and 8,194 missing resulting from the Korean operations.

The commission also maintains a cemetery in Mexico City where the remains of 750 Americans who gave their lives in the Mexican War (1846-1848) are buried.

Services

The commission provides the following services: exact location and other information concerning place of interment or memorialization; best routes and modes of travel in-country to the cemeteries and memorials; escort service within the cemetery memorials for next-of-kin and members of their immediate families; letters authorizing "non-fee" passports for members of the immediate families; color lithographs of World War I and II cemeteries together with black-and-white photographs of the appropriate gravesite or section of the Tablets of the Missing; and arrangements for floral decorations of gravesites or the Tablets of the Missing.

Veterans Administration National Cemeteries (with ZIP Code)

Alabama
Mobile Natl. Cemetery
  Mobile 36604
Arizona
Prescott Natl. Cemetery
  Prescott 86301
Arkansas
Fayetteville Natl. Cemetery
  Fayetteville 72701
Fort Smith Natl. Cemetery
  Fort Smith 72901
Little Rock Natl. Cemetery
  Little Rock 72206
California
Fort Rosecrans Natl. Cemetery
  San Diego 92106
Golden Gate Natl. Cemetery
  San Bruno 94066
Los Angeles Natl. Cemetery
  Los Angeles 90049
San Francisco Natl. Cemetery
  Presidio 94129
Colorado
Fort Logan Natl. Cemetery
  Denver 80235
Fort Lyon Natl. Cemetery
  Fort Lyon 81038
Florida
Barrancas Natl. Cemetery
  Pensacola 32508
Bay Pines Natl. Cemetery
  Bay Pines 33504
St. Augustine Natl. Cemetery
  St. Augustine 32084
Georgia
Marietta Natl. Cemetery
  Marietta 30060
Hawaii
Natl. Memorial Cemetery

of the Pacific
  Honolulu 96813
Illinois
Alton Natl. Cemetery
  Alton 62003
Camp Butler Natl. Cemetery
  Springfield 62707
Danville Natl. Cemetery
  Danville 61832
Mound City Natl. Cemetery
  Mound City 62963
Quincy Natl. Cemetery
  Quincy 62301
Rock Island Natl. Cemetery
  Rock Island 61201
Indiana
Crown Hill Natl. Cemetery
  Indianapolis 46208
Marion Natl. Cemetery
  Marion, 46952
New Albany Natl. Cemetery
  New Albany 47150
Iowa
Keokuk Natl. Cemetery
  Keokuk 52632
Kansas
Fort Leavenworth Natl. Cemetery
  Fort Leavenworth 66027
Fort Scott Natl. Cemetery
  Fort Scott 66701
Leavenworth Natl. Cemetery
  Leavenworth 66048
Kentucky
Camp Nelson Natl. Cemetery
  Nicholasville 40356
Cave Hill Natl. Cemetery
  Louisville 40204
Danville Natl. Cemetery
  Danville 40442
Lebanon Natl. Cemetery
  Lebanon 40033

Lexington Natl. Cemetery
  Lexington 40508
Mill Springs Natl. Cemetery
  Nancy 42544
Perryville Natl. Cemetery
  Perryville 40468
Zachary Taylor Natl. Cemetery
  Louisville 40207
Louisiana
Alexandria Natl. Cemetery
  Pineville 71360
Baton Rouge Natl. Cemetery
  Baton Rouge 70806
Port Hudson Natl. Cemetery
  Zachary 70791
Maine
Togus Natl. Cemetery
  Togus 04330
Maryland
Annapolis Natl. Cemetery
  Annapolis 21401
Baltimore Natl. Cemetery
  Baltimore 21228
Loudon Park Natl. Cemetery
  Baltimore 21229
Minnesota
Fort Snelling Natl. Cemetery
  St. Paul 55111
Mississippi
Biloxi Natl. Cemetery
  Biloxi 39531
Corinth Natl. Cemetery
  Corinth 38834
Natchez Natl. Cemetery
  Natchez 39120
Missouri
Jefferson Barracks Natl. Cemetery
  St. Louis 63125
Jefferson City Natl.

Cemetery
  Jefferson City 65101
Springfield Natl. Cemetery
  Springfield 65804
Nebraska
Fort McPherson Natl. Cemetery
  Maxwell 69151
New Jersey
Beverly Natl. Cemetery
  Beverly 08010
Finn's Point Natl. Cemetery
  Salem 08079
New Mexico
Fort Bayard Natl. Cemetery
  Fort Bayard 88036
Santa Fe Natl. Cemetery
  Santa Fe 87501
New York
Bath Natl. Cemetery
  Bath 14810
Cypress Hills Natl. Cemetery
  Brooklyn 11208
Long Island Natl. Cemetery
  Farmingdale 11735
Woodlawn Natl. Cemetery
  Elmira 14901
North Carolina
New Bern Natl. Cemetery
  New Bern 28560
Raleigh Natl. Cemetery
  Raleigh 27610
Salisbury Natl. Cemetery
  Salisbury 28144
Wilmington Natl. Cemetery
  Wilmington 28401
Ohio
Dayton Natl. Cemetery
  Dayton 45428
Oklahoma
Fort Gibson Natl. Cemetery
  Fort Gibson 74434
Oregon
Roseburg Natl. Cemetery

Roseburg 97470
White City Natl. Cemetery
White City 97501
Willamette Natl.
Cemetery
Portland 97266
Pennsylvania
Philadelphia Natl.
Cemetery
Philadelphia 19138
Puerto Rico
Puerto Rico Natl. Cemetery
Bayamon 00619
South Carolina
Beaufort Natl. Cemetery
Beaufort 29902
Florence Natl. Cemetery
Florence 29501
South Dakota
Black Hills Natl. Cemetery
Sturgis 57785
Fort Meade Natl. Cemetery

Fort Meade 57741
Hot Springs Natl. Cemetery
Hot Springs 57747
Tennessee
Chattanooga Natl.
Cemetery
Chattanooga 37404
Knoxville Natl. Cemetery
Knoxville 37917
Memphis Natl. Cemetery
Memphis 38122
Mountain Home Natl.
Cemetery
Mountain Home 37684
Nashville Natl. Cemetery
Madison 37115
Texas
Fort Bliss Natl. Cemetery
Fort Bliss 79906
Fort Sam Houston Natl.
Cemetery
San Antonio 78209

Houston Natl. Cemetery
Houston 77088
Kerryville Natl. Cemetery
Kerryville 78028
San Antonio Natl. Ceme-
tery
San Antonio 78202

Virginia
Alexandria Natl. Cemetery
Alexandria 22314
Balls Bluff Natl. Cemetery
Leesburg 22075
City Point Natl. Cemetery
Hopewell 23860
Cold Harbor Natl.
Cemetery
Mechanicsville 23111
Culpeper Natl. Cemetery
Culpeper 22701
Danville Natl. Cemetery
Danville 24541
Fort Harrison Natl.

Cemetery
Richmond 23231
Glendale Natl. Cemetery
Richmond 23231
Hampton Natl. Cemetery
Hampton 23369
Richmond Natl. Cemetery
Richmond 23231
Seven Pines Natl.
Cemetery
Sandston 23150
Staunton Natl. Cemetery
Staunton 24401
Winchester Natl. Cemetery
Winchester 22601

West Virginia
Grafton Natl. Cemetery
Grafton 26354

Wisconsin
Wood Natl. Cemetery
Wood 53193

Department of the Army

District of Columbia
Soldiers Home National
Cemetery
Washington, D. C. 20011

Virginia
Arlington National Ceme-
tery
Arlington 22211

Department of the Interior

District of Columbia
Battleground National
Cemetery
Washington, D. C. 20012
Georgia
Andersonville National
Historic Site
Andersonville 31711
Louisiana
Chalmette National Histor-

ical Park
Arabi 70032
Maryland
Antietam National Battle-
field Site and Cemetery
Sharpsburg 21782
Mississippi
Vicksburg National
Military Park and Ceme-
tery

Vicksburg 39180
Montana
Custer Battlefield National
Monument
Crow Agency 59022
Pennsylvania
Gettysburg National Mili-
tary Park and Cemetery
Gettysburg 17325
Tennessee
Andrew Johnson National
Historic Site
Greeneville 37743
Fort Donelson National
Military Park and Ceme-
tery
Dover 37058
Shiloh National Military
Park and Cemetery

Shiloh 38376
Stones River National Bat-
tlefield and Cemetery
Murfreesboro 37131
Virginia
Fredericksburg and Spot-
sylvania County Battle
Memorial
National Military Park
and Cemetery
Fredericksburg 22401
Poplar Grove National
Cemetery
Petersburg National Bat-
tlefield
Petersburg 23803
Yorktown Battlefield
Colonial National Histor-
ical Park
Yorktown 23490

Debts Owed U.S. Arising from World War I

Source: Treasury Department (June 30, 1975)

Country	Original Indebtedness	Interest thru June 30, 1975	Cumulative Payments Principal	Principal and Interest	Unmatured Principal	Interest due and unpaid
Armenia	$11,959,917.49	$33,371,030.27	$32.49	. . . .	. . . .	$45,330,915.27
Austria[1]	26,843,148.66	44,058.93	862,668.00			26,024,539.59
Belgium	419,837,630.37	385,412,720.47	19,157,630.37	$33,033,642.87	$133,580,000.00	619,479,077.60
Cuba	10,000,000.00	2,286,751.58	10,000,000.00	2,286,751.58	. . . .	. . . .
Czechoslovakia	185,071,023.07	147,455,801.64	19,829,914.17	304,178.09	56,960,000.00	255,432,732.45
Estonia	16,466,012.87	26,450,020.01	10.66	1,248,432.07	5,680,000.00	35,987,590.15
Finland	8,999,999.97	12,562,090.96	[5]6,030,999.97	[5]12,562,090.96	2,969,000.00	. . . .
France	4,089,689,588.18	4,315,988,357.14	226,039,588.18	260,036,302.82	1,203,068,636.33	6,716,533,417.99
Great Britain	4,802,181,641.56	8,195,331,958.11	434,181,641.56	1,590,672,656.18	1,539,000,000.00	9,433,659,301.93
Greece	34,319,843.67	5,553,381.77	1,548,506.93	5,209,733.24	[6]19,565,975.33	13,549,009.94
Hungary[3]	1,982,555.50	3,306,099.96	73,995.50	482,924.26	719,355.00	4,012,699.70
Italy	2,042,364,319.28	484,310,220.22	37,464,319.28	63,365,560.88	794,400,000.00	1,631,444,659.34
Latvia	6,888,664.20	11,164,404.91	9,200.00	752,349.07	2,402,900.00	14,888,620.04
Liberia	26,000.00	10,471.56	26,000.00	10,471.56	. . . .	. . . .
Lithuania	6,432,465.00	10,336,652.80	234,783.00	1,003,173.58	2,131,972.00	13,399,189.22
Nicaragua[4]	141,950.36	26,625.48	141,950.36	26,625.48	. . . .	. . . .
Poland	207,344,297.37	336,768,424.38	[5]1,287,297.37	21,359,000.18	65,124,000.00	456,342,424.20
Romania	68,359,192.45	65,782,621.66	[6]64,498,632.07	[2]292,375.20	22,114,000.00	107,236,806.84
Russia	192,601,297.37	553,130,198.39	. . . .	[7]8,750,311.88	. . . .	736,981,183.88
Yugoslavia	63,577,712.55	43,080,277.92	1,952,712.55	696,509.14	24,063,000.00	80,006,218.78
Totals	**12,195,087,259.92**	**14,632,372,478.16**	**763,339,882.46**	**2,002,032,639.04**	**3,871,778,838.66**	**20,190,308,377.92**

(1.) The Federal Republic of Germany has recognized liability for securities falling due between Mar. 12, 1938 and May 8, 1945.
(2.) $8,480,090.26 has been made available for educational exchange programs with Finland pursuant to 22 U.S.C. 2455 (e).
(3.) Interest payments from Dec. 15, 1932 to June 15, 1937 were paid in pengo equivalent.
(4.) The indebtedness of Nicaragua was canceled pursuant to the agreement of Apr. 14, 1938.
(5.) Excludes claim allowance of $1,813,428.69 dated Dec. 15, 1969.
(6.) Excludes payment of $100,000.00 on June 14, 1940 as a token of good faith.
(7.) Principally proceeds from liquidation of Russian assets in the United States.
(8.) Includes $12,813,601.32 on agreement of May 28, 1964.

ASSOCIATIONS AND SOCIETIES

Source: World-Almanac Questionnaire

Arranged according to key words in titles. Last figure indicates membership.

—A—

Aaron Burr Assn. (1946), TremonT, Inca Rd., Linden, VA 22642: 600.

Abortion, Assn. for the Study of (1964), 120 W. 57th St., N.Y., NY 10019; 22,500.

Abortion Rights Action League, Natl. (1969), 706 Seventh St. SE, Wash., DC 20003; 13,000.

Accountants, Amer. Institute of Certified Public (1887), 1211 Ave. of the Americas, N.Y., NY 10036; 103,863.

Accountants, Natl. Assn. of (1919), 919 Third Ave., N.Y., NY 10022; 80,000.

Accountants, Natl. Society of Public (1945), 1717 Pennsylvania Ave., NW, Wash., DC 20006; 16,000.

Acoustical Society of America (1929), 335 E. 45 St., N.Y., NY 10017; 5,000.

Actors' Equity Assn. (1913), 1500 Broadway, N.Y., NY 10036; 19,500.

Actors' Fund of America (1882), 1501 Broadway, N.Y., NY 10036; 3,017.

Actuaries, Society of (1949), 208 S. La Salle St., Chicago, IL 60604; 5,404.

Acupuncture Foundation of America (1972), Box 1424, Nantucket, MA 02554.

Adirondack Mountain Club (1922), 172 Ridge St., Glens Falls, NY 12801; 9,000.

Administrative Management Society (1919), Maryland Rd., Willow Grove, PA 19090; 12,000.

Adult Education Assn. of the U.S.A. (1951), Office of Education, 810 18th St., NW, Wash., DC 20006; 6,500.

Advertisers, Assn. of Natl. (1910), 155 E. 44th St., N.Y., NY 10017; 450 cos.

Advertising Agencies, Amer. Assn. of (1917), 200 Park Ave., N.Y., NY 10017; 420 agencies.

Aeronautic Assn. of the U.S.A., Natl. (1922), 806 15th St., NW, Wash., DC 20005; 150,000.

Aeronautics and Astronautics, Amer. Institute of (1932), 1290 Ave. of the Americas, N. Y., NY 10019.

Aerospace Industries Assn. of America (1919), 1725 DeSales St., NW, Wash., DC 20036; 65 cos.

Aerospace Medical Assn. (1929), Washington National Airport, Wash., DC 20001; 3,632.

African Violet Society of America (1946), 706 Hamilton Bank Blvd., Knoxville, TN 37901; 14,000.

Afro-American Life and History, Assn. for the Study of (1915), 1401 14th St., Wash., DC 20005; 1,200.

Aging Assn., Amer. (1970), Univ. of Neb. Medical Cntr., 42d & Dewey Ave., Omaha, NE 68105; 500.

Agricultural Chemicals Assn., Natl. (1933), 1155 15th St., NW, Wash., DC 20005; 121 cos.

Agricultural Economics Assn., Amer. (1919), Univ. of Kentucky, Lexington, KY 40506; 4,100.

Agricultural Engineers, Amer. Society of (1907), 2950 Niles Rd., St. Joseph, MI 49085; 8,500.

Agricultural History Society (1919), U. S. Dept. of Agriculture, 500 12th St., SW, Wash., DC 20250; 800.

Agronomy, Amer. Society of (1907), 677 S. Segoe Rd., Madison, WI 53711; 8,500.

Ahepa, Order of (1922), 1422 K St., NW, Wash., DC 20005; 26,000.

Air, Citizens for Clean (1965), 25 Broad St., N.Y., NY 10004; 3,000.

Air Force Aid Society (1942), 1117 N. 19th St., Arlington, VA 22209; 23,500.

Air Force Assn. (1946), 1750 Pennsylvania Ave., NW, Wash., DC 20006; 140,000.

Air Force Sergeants Assn. (1961), 4235 28th Ave., Marlow Heights, MD 20031; 51,000.

Air Line Employees Assn. (1952), 5600 S. Central Ave., Chicago, IL 60638; 10,000.

Air Line Pilots Assn. (1931), 1625 Massachusetts Ave., NW, Wash., DC 20036; 30,000.

Air Pollution Control Assn. (1907), 4400 Fifth Ave., Pittsburgh, PA 15213; 6,600.

Air Transport Assn. of America (1936), 1709 New York Ave., NW, Wash., DC 20006; 26 airlines.

Air Transport Assn., Internatl. (1945), P.O. Box 550, Internatl. Aviation Sq., Montreal P. O., Canada H3A2R4; 110 airlines.

Aircraft Assn., Experimental (1953), P.O. Box 229, Hales Corners, WI 53130; 45,000.

Aircraft Owners and Pilots Assn. (1939), 7315 Wisconsin Ave., Bethesda, MD 20014; 180,000.

Airport Operators Council Internatl. (1948) 1700 K St., NW, Wash. DC 20006; 156.

Albert Schweitzer Fellowship (1939) 866 UN Plaza, N.Y., NY 10017.

Albert Schweitzer Friendship House (1967), Hurlburt Rd., Great Barrington, MA 01230.

Alcohol Problems, Amer. Council on (1964), 119 Constitution Ave., NE, Wash., DC 20002.

Alcoholics Anonymous, P.O. Box 459, Grand Central Sta., N.Y., NY 10017; 800,000.

Alcoholism, Natl. Council on (1944), 2 Park Ave., N.Y., NY 10016; 180 affiliates.

Allergy, Amer. Academy of (1943), 225 E. Michigan St., Milwaukee, WI 53202; 2,400.

Allied Youth (1936), 933 N. Kenmore St., Arlington, VA 22201; 10,000.

Alpine Club, Amer. (1902), 113 E. 90th St., N.Y., NY 10028; 1,200.

Altrusa Internatl. (1917), 332 S. Michigan Ave., Chicago, IL 60604; 19,100.

Aluminum Assn. (1933), 750 Third Ave., N.Y., NY 10017; 77 companies.

American Federation of Labor & Congress of Industrial Organizations (AFL-CIO) (1955), by merging **American Federation of Labor** estab. 1881 and **Congress of Industrial Organizations** estab. 1935; 815 16th St. N.W. Wash,, DC 20006; 14,300,000.

Amer. Field Service (1947), 313 E. 43d St., N.Y., NY 10017; 110,000.

Amer. Indian Affairs, Assn. on (1923), 432 Park Ave. S., N.Y., NY 10016; 55,000.

American Legion, The (1919), 700 N. Pennsylvania St., Indianapolis, IN 46204; 2,600,000. **American Legion Auxiliary** (1919), 777 N. Meridian St., Indianapolis, IN 46204; 954,100.

Amer. Veterans of World War II, Korea & Vietnam (AMVETS), (1947), 1710 Rhode Island Ave. NW, Wash., DC 20036; 200,000. **AMVETS Auxiliary** (1946), Saco Rd., Old Orchard Beach, ME 04064; 25,000.

Amputation Foundation, Natl. (1919), 12-45 150th St., Whitestone, NY 11357; 2,000.

Animal Protection Institute of America (1968), 5894 S. Land Park Dr., Sacramento, CA 95822; 75,000.

Animal Welfare Institute (1951), P.O. Box 3650, Wash., DC 20007; 4,000.

Animals, Amer. Society for Prevention of Cruelty to (ASPCA) (1866), 441 E. 92d St., N.Y., NY 10028; 3,000.

Animals, Friends of (1957), 11 W. 60th St., N.Y., NY 10023; 80,000.

Animals, The Fund for (1967), 140 W. 57th St., N.Y., NY 10019; 70,000.

Anthropological Assn., Amer. (1904), 1703 New Hampshire Ave. NW, Wash., DC 20009; 10,030.

Anti-Vivisection Society, Amer. (1883), 1903 Chestnut St., Phila., PA 19103; 15,000.

Antiquarian Society, Amer. (1812), 185 Salisbury St., Worcester, MA 01609; 282.

Antique Automobile Club of America (1935), 501 W. Governor Rd., Hershey, PA 17033; 40,000.

Appalachian Mountain Club (1876), 5 Joy St., Boston, MA 02108; 22,500.

Appalachian Trail Conference (1925), Box 236, Harpers Ferry, WV 25425; 10,002.

Appraisers, Amer. Society of (1952), P.O. Box 17265, Dulles Internatl. Airport, Wash., DC 20041; 4,800.

Arbitration Assn., Amer. (1926), 140 W. 51st St., N.Y., NY 10020; 3,000.

Arboriculture, Internatl. Society of (1924), P.O. Box 71, 3 Lincoln Sq., Urbana, IL 61801; 3,000.

Archaeological Institute of America (1879), 260 W. Broadway, N.Y., NY 10013; 5,752.

Archers Assn., Professional (1961), P.O. Box 7609, Flint, MI 48507; 300.

Archery Assn. of the U.S., Natl. (1879), 1951 Geraldson Dr., Lancaster, PA 17601; 4,000.

Architects, Amer. Institute of (1857), 1735 New York Ave. NW, Wash., DC 20006; 25,000.

Architectural Historians, Society of (1940), 1700 Walnut St., Phila., PA 19103; 4,300.

Archivists, Society of Amer. (1936), P.O. Box 8198, Univ. of Illinois, Chicago, IL. 60680; 2,700.

Armed Forces Communications and Electronics Assn. (1946), 5205 Leesburg Pike, Falls Church, VA C22041; 11,500.

Army and Navy Union U.S.A. (1886), 1391 Main St., Lakemore, OH 44250; 5,700.

Art. Natl. Assn. of Schools of (1944), 11250 Roger Bacon Dr., No. 5, Reston, VA 22090; 80 schools.

Arthritis Foundation (1948), 475 Riverside Dr., N.Y., NY 10027; 73 chapters.

Artists of America, Allied (1914), 1083 Fifth Ave., N.Y., NY 10028; 350.

Arts, Amer. Federation of (1909), 41 E. 65th St., N.Y., NY 10021; 3,000.

Arts Associated Councils of the (1961), 1564 Broadway, N.Y., NY 10036; 964 organizations.

Arts, Natl. Endowment for the (1965), 2401 E. St. NW, Wash., DC 20506.

Arts and Letters, Amer. Academy of (1904), 633 W. 155th St., N.Y., NY 10032; 49.

Arts and Letters, Natl. Institute of (1898), 633 W. 155th St., N.Y., NY 10032; 242.

Arts & Psychology, Assn. for the (1976), P.O. Box 160371, Sacramento, CA 95816.

Arts and Sciences, Amer. Academy of (1780), 165 Allandale St., Jamaica Plain Sta., Boston, MA 02130; 2,500.

Assistance League, Natl. (1935), 5627 Fernwood Ave., Hollywood, CA 90028; 11,000.

Associated Press (1848), 50 Rockefeller Plaza, N.Y., NY 10020; 1,265 newspapers & 3,400 broadcast stations.

Astrologers, Amer. Federation of (1938), 6 Library Ct., SE, Wash., DC 20003; 3,000.

Astronautical Society, Amer. (1953), 6060 Duke St., Alexandria, VA 22304; 700.

Astronomical Society, Amer. (1899), 211 FitzRandolph Rd., Princeton, NJ 08540; 3,300.

Atheist Assn. (1925), Box 2832, San Diego, CA 92112; 200.

Athletic Associations, Natl. Federation of State High School (1920), 400 Leslie St., Elgin, IL 60120; 50 states.

Athletic Conference, Eastern College (1938), 1311 Craigville Beach Rd., Centerville, MA 02632; 212 schools.

Athletic Union of the U.S., Amateur (1888), 3400 W. 86th St., Indianapolis, IN 46268; 235,000 athletes.

Attorneys General, Natl. Assn. of (1907), P.O. Box 11910, Iron Works Pike, Lexington, KY 40511; 55.

Audubon Society, Natl. (1905), 950 Third Ave., N.Y., NY 10022; 335,000.

Authors and Composers, Amer. Guild of (1931), 40 W. 57th St., N.Y., NY 10019; 2,500.

Authors League of America (1912), 234 W. 44th St., N.Y., NY 10036; 6,500.

Automobile Assn., Amer. (1902), 8111 Gatehouse Rd., Falls Church, VA 22042; 17,600,000.

Automobile Club, Natl. (1924), 65 Battery St., San Francisco, CA 94111; 358,000.

Automobile Dealers Assn., Natl. (1917), 8400 Westpark Dr., McLean, VA 22101; 20,000.

Automobile License Plate Collectors' Assn. (1954), Box 399, Brattleboro, VT 05301; 1022.

Automotive Booster Clubs (1921), 605 E. Algonquin Rd., Arlington Heights, IL 60005; 3,000.

Automotive Organization Team (1939), P.O. Box 1742, Midland, MI 48640; 2,600.

Aviation Historical Society, Amer. (1956), P.O. Box 99, Garden Grove, CA 92642; 4,500.

— B —

Badminton Assn., Amer. (1936), 1330 Alexandria Dr., San Diego, CA 92107; 4,000.

Banker Assn., Internatl. (1968), 422 Washington Bldg., Wash., DC 20005; 1,500.

Bankers Assn., Amer. (1875), 1120 Connecticut Ave. NW, Wash., DC 20036; 14,000 banks.

Bankers Assn. of America, Independent (1930), 1168 S. Main St., Sauk Centre, MN 56378; 7,243 banks.

Bar Assn. Amer. (1878), 1155 E. 60th St., Chicago, IL 60637; 205,000.

Bar Assn., Federal (1920), 1815 H Street NW., Wash., DC 20006; 13,614.

Barber Shop Quartet Singing in America, Society for the Preservation & Encouragement of (1938), 6315 Third Ave., Kenosha, WI 53141; 35,508.

Barbers & Beauticians of America Associated Master (1924), 219 Greenwich Rd., Charlotte, NC 28211; 10,000

Baseball Congress, Amer. Amateur (1935), 212 Plaza Bldg., 2855 W. Market St., P.O. Box 5332 Akron, OH 44313.

Baseball Congress of America, Natl. (1931), 338 S. Sycamore, Wichita, KS 67213; 15,000.

Baseball Players of America, Assn. of Professional (1924), 530 E. Wardlow Rd., Long Beach, CA 90807; 5,000.

Basketball Assn., Natl. (1946), 2 Penn Plaza, N.Y., NY 10001; 18 teams.

Baton Twirling Assn. of America & Abroad, Intl. (1967), Box 234, Waldwick, NJ 07463; 1,800.

Battleship Assn., Amer. (1963), P.O. Box 11247, San Diego, CA 92111; 3,000.

Beta Sigma Phi (1931), 1800 W. 91st Pl., Kansas City, MO 64114; 244,639.

Bible Society, Amer. (1816), 1865 Broadway, N.Y., NY 10023; 588,000.

Biblical Literature, Society of (1880), Harvard Divinity School, 45 Francis Ave., Cambridge, MA 02138; 3,200.

Bibliographical Society of America (1904), P.O. Box 397, Grand Central Sta., N.Y., NY 10017; 1,625.

Bicycle Manufacturers Assn. (1965), 1101 15th St. NW, Wash., DC 20005; 6.

Bide-A-Wee Home Assn. (1903), 410 E. 38th St., N.Y., NY 10016; 8,000.

Big Brothers of America (1946), 220 Suburban Station Bldg., Phila., PA 19103; 301 agencies.

Billiard Congress of America (1948), 717 N. Michigan Ave., Chicago, IL 60611; 625.

Biological Chemists, Amer. Society of (1906), 9650 Rockville Pike, Bethesda, MD 20014; 4,100.

Biological Sciences, Amer. Institute of (1948), 1401 Wilson Blvd., Arlington, VA 22209; 10,000.

Blind, Amer. Foundation for the (1921), 15 W. 16th St., N.Y., NY 10011.

Blind, Natl. Federation of the (1940), 218 Randolph Hotel, Des Moines, IA 50309; 50,000.

Blind & Visually Handicapped, Natl. Accreditation Council for Agencies Serving the (1967), 79 Madison Ave., N.Y., NY 10016; 59 agencies and schools.

Blinded Veterans Assn. (1945), 1735 DeSales St. NW, Wash., DC 20036; 2,300.

Blindness, Natl. Society for the Prevention of (1908), 79 Madison Ave., N.Y., NY 10016; 315.

Blindness, Research to Prevent (1960), 598 Madison Ave., N.Y., NY 10022; 1,500.

Blizzard Club, January 12th, 1888 (1940), c/o Historian, 4827 Hillside Ave., Lincoln, NE 68506; 92.

Blood Banks, Amer. Assn. of (1947), 1828 L St. NW, Wash., DC 20036; 4,800.

Blue Cross Assn. (1948), 840 N. Lake Shore Dr., Chicago, IL 60611; 74 plans.

Blue Shield Plans, Natl. Assn. of (1946), 211 E. Chicago Ave., Chicago, IL 60611; 72 plans.

Blueberry Council, No. Amer. (1966), P.O. Box 166, Marmora, NJ 08223; 32 organizations.

B'nai B'rith (1843), 1640 Rhode Island Ave. NW, Wash., DC 20036; 500,000.

Boat Owners Assn. of the U.S. (1966), 5261 Port Royal Rd., Springfield, VA 22151; 33,000.

Book Manufacturers' Institute (1933), 904 Ethan Allen Hwy., Ridgefield, CT 06877; 100 companies.

Booksellers Assn., Amer. (1900), 800 Second Ave., N.Y., NY 10017; 4,200.

Botanical Gardens & Arboretums, Amer. Assn. of (1940), P.O. Box 3530, Dept. of Horticulture, New Mexico State Univ., Las Cruces, NM 88003; 750.

Botanical Society of America (1906), Dept. of Botany, Univ. of Texas, Austin, TX 78703; 4,000.

Bottle Clubs, Federation of Historical (1969), c/o Corresponding Secty., 5001 Queen Avenue N., Minneapolis, MN 55430; 125 clubs.

Bowling Congress, Amer. (1895), 5301 S. 76th St., Greendale, WI 53129; 4.3 million.

Bowling Congress, Women's Internatl. (1916), 5301 S. 76th St., Greendale, WI 53129; 3,695,073.

Boy Scouts of America (1910), N. Brunswick, NJ 08902; 5,318,070.

Boys' Brigades of America, United (1893), P.O. Box 8406, Baltimore, MD 21234.

Boys' Clubs of America (1906), 771 First Ave., N.Y., NY 10017; 1,100,000.

Brand Names Foundation (1947), 477 Madison Ave., N.Y., NY 10022; 300.

Brewers Assn., U.S. (1862), 1750 K St., Wash., DC 20006.

Brick Institute of America (1934), 1750 Old Meadow Rd., McLean, VA 22101; 100 companies.

Brith Sholom (1905), 1235 Chestnut Street, Phila., PA 19107; 20,000.

Broadcasters, Natl. Assn. of (1922), 1771 N St. NW, Wash., DC 20036; 5,000.

Burroughs Bibliophiles, The (1960), 454 Elaine Dr., Pittsburgh, PA 15236; 480.

Business Bureaus, Council on Better (1970), 845 Third Ave., N.Y., NY 10022; 137.

Business Clubs, Natl. Assn. of Amer. (1922), 3315 No. Main St., High Point, NC 27260; 5,000.

Business Communication Assn., Amer. (1935), 317-B David Kinley Hall, Univ. of Illinois, Urbana, IL 61801; 1,150.

Business Education Assn., Natl. (1892), 1906 Association Dr., Reston, VA 22091; 22,000.

Business Law Assn., Amer. (1923), Colorado State Univ., Ft. Collins, CO 80521; 700.

Business Press Editors, Amer. Society of (1949), 2550 Green Bay Rd., Evanston, IL 60201; 300.

Business Professional Advertising Assn. (1922), 205 E. 42d St., N.Y., NY 10017; 3,000.

Button Society, Natl. (1938), 353 Stockton St., Hightstown, NJ 08520; 2,250.

—C—

Camp Fire Girls (1910), 1740 Broadway, N.Y., NY 10019; 500,000.

Campers & Hikers Assn., Natl. (1954), 7172 Transit Rd., Buffalo, NY 14221; 53,000 families.

Camping Assn., Amer. (1910), Bradford Woods, Martinsville, IN 46151; 6000.

Cancer Council, United (1963), 1803 N. Meridian St., Indianapolis, IN 46202; serves 27,500,000 people.

Cancer Society, Amer. (1913), 777 Third Ave., N.Y., NY 10017; 231.

Candy Brokers Assn. of America (1956), P.O. Box 28325 Wash., DC 20005; 300.

Canners Assn., Natl. (1909), 1133 20th St. NW, Wash., DC 20036; 500 companies.

Captive European Nations, Assembly of (1954), 29 W. 57th St., N.Y., NY 10019; 9 national committees.

CARE (Cooperative For American Relief Everywhere) (1946), 660 First Ave., N.Y., NY 10016; 25 agencies.

Carillonneurs in No. America, Guild of (1936), c/o Secty., 3718 Settle Rd., Cincinnati, OH 45227; 308.

Carnegie Hero Fund Commission (1904), 1932 Oliver Bldg., Pittsburgh, PA 15222.

Cartoonists Society, Natl. (1946), 9 Ebony Court, Brooklyn, NY 11229; 480.

Cat Fanciers' Assn. (1906), 11 Globe Ct., P.O. Box 430, Red Bank, NJ 07701; 510 clubs.

Catch Society (1968), Dept. of English, SUNY—Fredonia; Fredonia, NY 14063; 400.

Catholic Bishops, Natl. Conference of—U.S. Catholic Conference (1966), 1312 Massachusetts Ave. NW, Wash., DC 20005; 300.

Catholic Charities, Natl. Conference of (1910), 1346 Connecticut Ave, NW, Wash., DC 20036; 4,500.

Catholic Church Extension Society of the U.S.A. (1905), 1307 S. Wabash Ave., Chicago, IL 60605; 34,000.

Catholic Daughters of America (1903), 10 W. 71st St., N.Y., NY 10023; 182,000.

Catholic Educational Assn., Natl. (1904), One Dupont Circle NW, Wash., DC 20036; 14,000.

Catholic Press Assn. (1911), 119 N. Park Ave., Rockville Centre, NY 11570; 410.

Catholic Rural Life Conference, Natl. (1923), 3801 Grand Ave., Des Moines, IA 50312; 4,000.

Catholic War Veterans, U.S.A. (1935), 2 Massachusetts Ave. NW, Wash., DC 20001; 50,000.

Cemetery Assn., Amer. (1887), 250 E. Broad St., Columbus, OH 43215; 1,200.

Ceramic Society, Amer. (1899), 65 Ceramic Drive, Columbus, OH 43214; 7,300.

Cerebral Palsy Assn., United (1948), 66 E. 34th St., N.Y., NY 10016; 307.

Chamber of Commerce of the U.S.A. (1912), 1615 H St. NW, Wash., DC 20006; 36,000.

Chartered Life Underwriters, Amer. Society of (1928), 270 Bryn Mawr Ave., Bryn Mawr, PA 19010; 20,100.

Chartered Property & Casualty Underwriters, Society of (1944), P.O. Box 556, Media, PA 19063; 7,500.

Chautauqua Institution (1874), Box 28, Chautauqua, NY 14722.

Chemical Society, Amer. (1876), 1155 16th St. NW, Wash. DC 20036; 107,000.

Chemists, Amer. Institute of (1923), 7315 Wisconsin Ave., Washington, DC 20014; 5,800.

Chemists and Chemical Engineers, Assn. of Consulting (1928), 50 E. 41st St., N.Y., NY 10017; 120.

Chess Federation, U.S. (1939), 186 Rte 9W, New Windsor, NY 12550; 51,000.

Chief Warrant and Warrant Officers' Assn., USCG (1929), 955 L'Enfant Plaza N., SW, Wash., DC 20024; 3,033.

Child Study Assn. of America (1888), 50 Madison Ave., N.Y., NY 10010; 1,866.

Child Welfare League of America (1920), 67 Irving Place. N.Y., NY 10003; 400 agencies.

Childbirth Without Pain League (1964), P.O. Box 233, Dana Point, CA 92629; 200.

Children of the Amer. Revolution, Natl. Society (1895), 1776 D St., NW, Wash., DC 20006; 13,000.

Children's Aid Society (1853), 105 E. 22d St., N.Y., NY 10010.

Children's Book Council (1945), 67 Irving Place, N.Y., NY 10003; 63.

Chinese Women's Assn. (1932), 13541 Emperor Dr., Santa Ana, CA 92705; 520.

Chiropractic Assn., Amer. (1964), 2200 Grand Ave., Des Moines, IA 50312; 11,315.

Chiropractors Assn., Internatl. (1926), 741 Brady St., Davenport, IA 52808; 6,100.

Christian Culture Society (1974), P.O. Box 325, Kokomo, IN, 46901; 10,000.

Christian Laymans Counseling Board (1970), 5901 Plainfield Drive, Charlotte, NC 28215; 3,248,389.

Christians and Jews, Natl. Conference of (1928), 43 W. 57th St., N.Y., NY 10019; 200,000.

Cincinnati, Society of the (1783), 2118 Massachusetts Ave. NW, Wash., DC 20008; 2,700.

Circulations, Audit Bureau of (1914), 123 N. Wacker Dr., Chicago, IL 60606; 3,965.

Circus Fans Assn. of America (1926), P.O. Box 605, Aurora, IL 60507; 2,000.

Circus Historical Society (1939), 1325 Commercial St., Atchison, KS 66002; 1,300.

Cities, Natl. League of (1924), 1620 Eye St. NW, Wash., DC 20006; 15,000 municipalities.

City Management Assn., Internatl. (1914), 1140 Connecticut Ave. NW, Wash., DC 20036; 5,821.

Civil Engineers, Amer. Society of (1852), 345 E. 47th St., N.Y., NY 10017; 72,194.

Civil Liberties Union, Amer. (1920), 22 E. 40th St., N.Y., NY 10016; 250,000.

Civil Service League, Natl. (1881), 917 15th St., NW, Wash., DC 20005; 1,200.

Civitan Internatl. (1920), P.O. Box 2102, Birmingham, AL 35201; 55,000.

Classical League, Amer. (1919), Miami Univ., Oxford, OH 45056; 2,800.

Clinical Pastoral Education, Assn. for (1967), 475 Riverside Drive, N.Y., NY 10027; 4,000.

Clinical Pathologists, Amer. Society of (1922), 2100 W. Harrison St., Chicago, IL 60612; 20,000.

Coal Assn., Natl. (1917), 1130 17th St., NW, Wash., DC 20036; 200 companies.

Cocoa Exchange, New York (1925), 127 John St., N.Y., NY 10038; 183.

Coffee and Tea Exchange, New York (1882), 79 Pine St., N.Y., NY 10005; 342.

Collectors Assn., Amer. (1939), 4040 W. 70th St., Minneapolis, MN 55435; 2,575.

College Entrance Examination Board (1900), 888 Seventh Ave., N.Y., NY 10019; 2,347 institutions.

College Physical Education Assn. for Men, Natl. (1897), 108 Cooke Hall, Univ. of Minn., Minneapolis, MN 55455; 1,100.

College Placement Council (1941), 65 E. Elizabeth Ave., Bethlehem, PA 18018; 1,700.

Colleges, Assn. of Amer. (1915), 1818 R St. NW, Wash., DC 20009; 700 institutions.

Collegiate Athletic Assn., Natl. (1906), Highway 50 & Nall Ave., Mission, KS 66222; 829.

Collegiate Schools of Business, Amer. Assembly of (1916), 760 Office Parkway, St. Louis, MO 63141; 627 schools.

Colonial Dames of America (1890), 421 E. 61 St., N.Y., NY 10021; 2,000.

Colonial Dames XVII Century, Natl. Society (1915), 1300 New Hampshire Ave. NW, Wash., DC 20036; 8,500.

Colonial Wars, General Society of (1892), c/o Lawson Whitesides, 840 Woodbine Ave., Glendale, OH 45246; 4,200.

Colored Women's Clubs, Natl. Assn. of (1896), 5808 16th St., NW. Wash., DC 20011; 40,000.

Columbia Assns. in Civil Service, Grand Council of (1938), 299 Broadway, N.Y., NY 10007; 80,000.

Commercial Law League of America (1895), 222 W. Adams St., Chicago, IL 60806; 6,000.

Commercial Travelers of America, United (1888), 632 N. Park St., Columbus, OH 43215; 250,000.

Common Cause (1970), 2030 M St., NW Wash., DC 20036; 300,000

Composers-USA, Natl. Assn. of (1932), P.O. Box 49652, Barrington Sta., Los Angeles, CA 90049; 850.

Composers, Authors & Publishers, Amer. Society of (AS-CAP) (1914), One Lincoln Plaza, N.Y., NY 10023, 20,000.

Computing Machinery, Assn. for (1947), 1133 Ave. of Americas, N.Y., NY 10036; 32,000.

Concrete Institute, Amer. (1905), P.O. Box 19150, Detroit, MI 48219, 15,000.

Conference Board (1916), 845 Third Ave., N.Y., NY 10022; 4,000.

Congress of Racial Equality (1942), 200 W. 135th St., N.Y., NY 10030.

Conscientious Objectors, Central Committee for (1948), 2016 Walnut St., Phila., PA 19103.

Conservation Engineers, Assn. of (1961), Mo. Dept. of Conservation, P.O. Box 180, Jefferson City, MO 65101; 161.

Conservation Foundation (1949), 1717 Massachusetts Ave., NW, Wash., DC 20036.

Construction Industry Manufacturers Assn. (1922), 111 E. Wisconsin Ave., Milwaukee, WI 53202; 200 companies.

Construction Specifications Institute (1948), 1150 17th St., NW, Wash., DC 20036; 11,000.

Consumer Credit Assn., Internatl. (1912), 375 Jackson Ave., St. Louis, MO 63130; 50,000.

Consumer Federation of America (1968), 1012 14th St., NW, Wash., DC 20005; 208 organizations.

Consumer Interests, Amer. Council on (1953), 162 Stanley Hall, Univ. of Mo., Columbia, MO 65201; 3,240.

Consumer Protection Council, Natl. Student (1971), Villanova Univ., Bartley Hall, Villanova, PA 19085; 500.

Consumers League, Natl. (1899), 1785 Massachusetts Ave., NW, Wash., DC 20036; 20,000.

Consumers Union of the U.S. (1936), 256 Washington St., Mount Vernon, NY 10550; 2,000,000

Consumers Unions, Internatl. Organization of (1960), 9 Emmastraat, The Hague, Netherlands; 100 org.

Contract Bridge League, Amer. (1937), 2200 Democrat Rd., Memphis, TN; 38138; 195,000.

Cooperative League of the U.S.A. (1916), 1828 L St. NW, Wash., DC 20036; 140 co-ops.

Correctional Assn., Amer. (1870), 4321 Hartwick Rd., College Park, MD 20740; 10,000.

Cosmopolitan Internatl. (1933), 7341 W. 80th St., Overland Park, KS 68204; 3,700.

Cotton Council of America, Natl. (1938), 1918 North Parkway, Memphis, TN 38112; 282.

Country Music Assn. (1958), 7 Music Circle, N., Nashville, TN 37203; 4,500.

Credit Management, Nat. Assn. of (1896), 475 Park Ave. S., N.Y., NY 10016; 39,000.

Credit Unions, World Council of (1958), 1617 Sherman Ave., Madison, WI 53701; 52,000,000.

Crime and Delinquency, Natl. Council on (1907), 411 Hackensack Ave., Hackensack, NJ 07601; 60,000.

Criminology, Amer. Assn. of (1953), P.O. Box 321, Harvard-Sq. Sta., Cambridge, MA 02138; 2,500.

Crop Science Society of America (1955), 677 S. Segoe Rd., Madison, WI 53711; 3,517.

Cryptogram Assn., Amer. (1932), 9504 Forest Rd., Bethesda, MD 20014; 1,000.

Cyprus, Sovereign Order of (1192; in U.S. 1964), 853 Seventh Ave., N.Y., NY 10019; 417.

—D—

Dairy Council, Natl. (1915), 6300 No. River Rd., Rosemont, IL 60018; 700.

Dairy and Food Industries Supply Assn. (1919), 5530 Wisconsin Ave., Wash., DC 20015; 400 organizations.

Dairy Goat Assn., Amer. (1904), 209 W. Main St., Spindale, NC 28160; 7,500.

Dairy Science Assn., Amer. (1906), 113 N. Neil St., Champaign, IL 61820; 2,761.

Dairylea Cooperative (1919), One Blue Hill Plaza, Pearl River, NY 10965; 6,900.

Data Processing Management Assn. (1951), 505 Busse Highway, Park Ridge, IL 60068; 22,185.

Daughters of the American Revolution, Natl. Society (1890), 1776 D St., NW, Wash., DC 20006; 200,000.

Daughters of the Confederacy, United (1894), 328 North Blvd., Richmond, VA 23220; 35,000.

Daughters of the Union Veterans of the War, 1861-1865 (1885), 503 S. Walnut St., Springfield, IL 62704; 10,000.

Deaf, Alexander Graham Bell Assn. for the (1890), 3417 Volta Place, NW, Wash., DC 20007; 8,000.

Deaf, Conference of Executives of Amer. Schools for the (1868), 5034 Wisconsin Ave., NW, Wash., DC 20016; 300.

Deaf, Convention of Amer. Instructors of the (1850), 5034 Wisconsin Ave., NW, Wash., DC 20016; 3,500.

Deaf, Natl. Assn. of the (1880), 814 Thayer Ave., Silver Spring, MD 20910; 17,000.

Defense Preparedness Assn., Amer. (1919), 740 15th St., NW, Wash., DC 20005; 33,000.

Delta Kappa Gamma Society Internatl. (1929), 416 W. 12th St., Austin, TX 78701; 134,000.

Deltiologists of America (1960), 3709 Gradyville Rd., Newton Square, PA 19073; 2,200.

DeMoley, Order of (1919), 201 E. Armour Blvd., Kansas City, MO 64111; 2,800,000.

Dental Assn., Amer. (1859), 211 E. Chicago Ave., Chicago, IL 60611; 122,000.

Dental Assn., Natl. (1913), P.O. Box 197, Charlottesville, VA 22902; 1,500.

Descendants of the Colonial Clergy, Society of the (1933), 255 Madison St., Dedham, MA 02026; 1,000.

Descendants of the Signers of the Declaration of Independence (1907), 1300 Locust St., Phila., PA 19107; 932.

Desert Protective Council (1954), Box 4294, Palm Springs, CA 92262; 450.

Diabetes Assn., Amer. (1940), One W. 48th St., N.Y., NY 10020; 3,147.

Dialect Society, Amer. (1889), 1611 N. Kent St., Arlington, VA 22209; 900.

Dietetic Assn., Amer. (1917), 620 N. Michigan Ave., Chicago, IL 60611; 28,839.

Direct Mail-Marketing Assn. (1917), 6 E. 43d St., N.Y., NY 10017; 1,600 companies.

Directors Guild of America (1936), 9750 Sunset Blvd., Los Angeles, CA 90046; 4,200.

Disabled Amer. Veterans (1921), P.O. Box 14301, Cincinnati, OH 45214; 510,000.

Disabled Officers Assn. (1919), 1612 K St. NW, Wash., DC 20006; 5,500.

Divorce Reform, U.S. (1961), P.O. Box 243, Kenwood, CA 95452; 6,000.

Dowsers, Amer. Society of (1961), 957 Norwood Ave., Schenectady, NY 12303; 1,400.

Drug, Chemical and Allied Trades Assn. (1890), 350 Fifth Ave., N.Y., NY 10001; 500 firms.

Drum Corps Internatl. (1971), 53 E. Charles Rd., Villa Park, IL 60181.

Ducks Unlimited (1937), P.O. Box 66300, Chicago, IL 60666; 160,203.

Dulcimer Assn., Southern Appalachian (1974), Rte. 1, Box 473, Helena, AL 35080; 60.

Duodecimal Society of America (1944), 4728 Cielo Dr., Huntington Beach, CA 92649; 120.

Dutch Setters Soc. of Albany (1924), 1088 Cortland St., Albany, NY 12203; 325.

—E—

Eagles, Fraternal Order of (1898), 2401 W. Wisconsin Ave., Milwaukee, WI 53233; 850,000.

Earth, Friends of the (1969), 529 Commercial St., San Francisco, CA 94111; 20,000.

Easter Seal Society for Crippled Children and Adults, Natl. (1921), 2023 W. Ogden Ave., Chicago, IL 60612.

Eastern Star, Order of the (1876), 1618 New Hampshire Ave., Wash., DC 20009; 3,000,000.

Ecological Society of America (1915), c/o Frank McCormick, Univ. of N.C., Chapel Hill, N.C 27514; 5,000.

Economic Assn., Amer. (1885), 1313 21st Ave. S., Nashville, TN 37212; 25,000.

Economic Development, Committee for (1942), 477 Madison Ave., N.Y., NY 10022; 200.

Edison Electric Institute (1933), 90 Park Ave., N.Y., NY 10016.

Education, Amer. Council on (1918), One DuPont Circle NW, Wash., DC 20036; 1,600 schools.

Education, Council for Advancement & Support of (1974), One Dupont Circle NW, Wash., DC 20036; 1,800 schools.

Education, Council for Basic (1956), 725 15th St. NW, Wash., DC 20005; 5,325.

Education, Natl. Society for the Study of (1902), 5835 Kimbark Ave., Chicago, IL 60637; 4,600.

Education, Society for the Advancement of (1939), 1860 Broadway, N.Y., NY 10023; 1,500.

Education Assn., Natl. (1857), 1201 16th St. NW, Wash., DC 20036; 1,800,000.

Education Society, Comparative and Internatl. (1956) Grad. School of Education, Univ. of Calif. at Los Angeles, Los Angeles, CA 90024; 2,450.

Education of Young Children, Natl. Assn. for the (1926), 1834 Connecticut Ave. NW, Wash., DC 20009; 26,000.

Educational Broadcasters, Natl. Assn. of (1925), 1346 Connecticut Ave. NW, Wash., DC 20036; 3,000.

Educational Exchange, Council of Internatl. (1947), 777

UN Plaza, N.Y., NY 10017; 196 schools.

Educational Research Assn., Amer. (1915), 1126 16th St. NW, Wash., DC 20036; 12,000.

Educators for World Peace, Internatl. Assn. of (1969), P.O. Box 3282, Blue Springs Sta., Huntsville, AL 35810; 8,850.

Electric Railroaders Assn. (1934), 145 Greenwich St., N.Y., NY 10006; 4,592.

Electrical and Electronics Engineers, Institute of (1884), 345 E. 47th St., N.Y., NY 10017; 170,000.

Electrical Manufacturers Assn., Natl. (1926), 155 E. 44th St., N.Y., NY 10017; 550 companies.

Electrochemical Society (1902), P.O. Box 2071, Princeton, NJ 08540; 4,000.

Electronic Industries Assn. (1924), 2001 Eye St. NW, Wash., DC 20006; 280 firms.

Electronics Technicians, Internatl. Society of Certified (1970), 1715 Expo Lane, Indianapolis, IN 46224; 1,000.

Elks, Benevolent and Protective Order of (1868), 2750 N. Lake View Ave., Chicago, IL 60614; 1,582,735.

Elks, Improved Benevolent Protective Order of (1898), 1522 N. 16th St., Phila., PA 19121; 450,000.

Engine and Boat Manufacturers, Natl. Assn. of (1904), 666 Third Ave., N.Y., NY 10017; 345 firms.

Engineering, Natl. Academy of (1964), 2101 Constitution Ave. NW, Wash., DC 20418; 685.

Engineering Technicians, Amer. Society of Certified (1964), 2029 K St. NW, Wash., DC 20006; 7,300.

Engineering Trustees, United (1904), 345 E. 47th St., N.Y., NY 10017.

Engineers, Natl. Society of Professional (1934), 2029 K St. NW, Wash., DC 20006; 71,000.

Engineers Joint Council (1945), 345 E. 47th St., N.Y., NY 10017; 500,000.

English Assn., College (1939), Oakland Univ., Rochester, MI 48063; 3,000.

English-Speaking Union (1920), 16 E. 69th St., N.Y., NY 10021; 32,500.

Entomological Society of America (1889), 4603 Calvert Rd., College Park, MD 20740; 7,200.

Environmental Defense Fund (1967), 162 Old Town Rd., Setauket, NY 11733; 40,000.

Epilepsy Foundation of America (1968), 1828 L St. NW, Wash., DC 20036; 161 chapters.

Epsilon Pi Tau (1929), Technology Bldg., Bowling Green State Univ., Bowling Green, OH 43403; 25,000.

Esperanto Assn., Internatl. Catholic (1910), Limbiate, Italy; U.S. Rep., 7605 Winona Ln., Sebastopol, CA 95472; 1,600.

Esperanto Assn. of North America (1905), 1837 NE 49th Ave., Portland, OR 97213; 306.

Esperanto League for North America (1952), P.O. Box 508, Burlingame, CA 94010; 750.

Evangelicals, Natl. Assn. of (1942), 350 S. Main Pl., Wheaton, IL 60187; 3,500,000.

Evangelism Crusades, Internatl. (1959), 7970 Woodman Ave., Van Nuys, CA 91402; 125,000.

Exchange Club, Natl. (1911), 3050 Central Ave., Toledo, OH 43606; 50,000.

Experiment in Internatl. Living (1932), Kipling Rd., Brattleboro, VT 05301; 55,000.

Eye-Bank Assn. of America (1961), 3195 Maplewood Ave., Winston-Salem, NC 27103; 64.

Eye-Bank for Sight Restoration (1945), 3195 Maplewood Ave., Winston-Salem, NC 27103.

— F —

Fairs & Expositions, Internatl. Assn. of (1919), 500 Ashland Ave., Chicago Heights, IL 60411.

Family Physicians, Amer. Academy of (1947), 1740 W. 92d St., Kansas City, MO 64114; 37,000.

Family Service Assn. of America (1911), 44 E. 23d St., N.Y., NY 10010; 310 agencies.

Farm Bureau Federation, Amer. (1919), 225 Touhy Ave., Park Ridge, IL 60068; 2,505,258 families.

Farmer Cooperatives, Natl. Council of (1929), 1129 20th St. NW, Wash., DC 20036; 152 co-ops.

Farmers of America, Future (1928), 5630 Mt. Vernon Hwy., Alexandria, VA 22309; 465,180.

Farmers Educational and Co-Operative Union of America (1902), 12025 E. 45th Ave., Denver, CO 80201; 250,000 families.

Federal Employees, Natl. Federation of (1917), 1016 16th St. NW, Wash., DC 20036; 85,000.

Federal Employes Veterans Assn. (1957), 124 Union Ave., Bala Cynwyd, PA 19004; 540.

Federally Employed Women (1968), 1249 Natl. Press Bldg., Wash., DC 20045; 6,000.

Feline Society, Amer. (1938), 41 Union Sq. W., N.Y., NY 10003; 450.

Feminists for Life (1972), P.O. Box 5631, Columbus, OH 43221; 7,000.

Fencers League of America, Amateur (1891), 249 Eton Pl., Westfield, NJ 07090; 6,000.

Film Library Assn., Educational (1943), 17 W. 60 St., N.Y., NY 10023; 1,800.

Financial Analysts Federation (1947), 219 E. 42d St., N.Y., NY 10017; 14,000.

Financial Executives Institute (1931), 633 Third Ave., N.Y., NY 10017; 9,200.

Fire Chiefs, Internatl. Assn. of (1873), 1329 18th St. NW, Wash., DC 20036; 8,000.

Fire Marshals Assn. of No. America (1906), 470 Atlantic Ave., Boston, MA 02210; 937.

Fire Protection Assn., Natl. (1896), 470 Atlantic Ave., Boston MA 02210; 33,000.

Fire Protection Engineers, Society of (1950), 60 Batterymarch St., Boston, MA 02110; 2,025

Fisheries Society, Amer. (1870), 5410 Grosvenor Ln., Bethesda, MD 20014; 7,088.

Fishing Institute, Sport (1949), 608 13th St. NW, Wash., DC 20005; 24,500.

Fishing Tackle Manufacturers Assn., Amer. (1933), 20 No. Wacker Dr. Chicago, IL 60606; 400 companies.

Flag Day Assn., Amer. (1888), P.O. Box 1121, Denver, CO 80201.

Florists, Society of Amer. (1884), 901 N. Washington St., Alexandria, VA 22314; 6,100.

Fluid Power Society (1956), 432 E. Kilbourn Ave., Milwaukee, WI 53202; 3,500.

Folklore Society, Amer. (1888), Ctr. for Folklore & Ethnomusicology—SWB 306, Univ. of Texas, Austin, TX 78712; 2,800.

Food Processing Machinery and Supplies Assn. (1885), 7758 Wisconsin Ave., Wash., DC 20014; 250 firms.

Footwear Industries Assn., Amer. (1869), 1611 N. Kent St., Arlington, VA 22209; 338.

Foreign Policy Assn. (1918), 345 E. 46th St., N.Y., NY 10017.

Foreign Press Assn. (1918), 866 Second Ave., N.Y., NY 10017; 350.

Foreign Relations, Council on (1921), 58 E. 68th St., N.Y., NY 10021; 1,701.

Foreign Student Affairs, Natl. Assn. for (1948), 1860 19th St. NW, Wash., DC 20009; 2,500.

Foreign Study, Amer. Institute for (1964), 102 Greenwich Ave., Greenwich, CT 06830; 80,000.

Foreign Trade Council, Natl. (1914), 10 Rockefeller Plaza, N.Y., NY 10020; 600 companies.

Forensic Sciences, Amer. Academy of (1948), 11400 Rockville Pike, Rockville, MD 20852; 1,700.

Forest Institute, Amer. (1941), 1619 Massachusetts Ave. NW, Wash., DC 20036; 200.

Forest Products Assn., Natl. (1902), 1619 Massachusetts Ave. NW, Wash, DC 20036.

Forest Products Research Society (1947), 2801 Marshall Ct., Madison, WI 53705; 4,500.

Foresters, Society of Amer. (1900), 1010 16th St. NW, Wash., DC 20036; 20,000.

Forestry Assn., Amer. (1875), 1319 18th St. NW, Wash., DC 20036; 80,000.

Foster Parents Plan (1937), 170 Service Road, Warwick, RI 02886; 30,000.

Founders & Patriots of America, Order of the (1896), 53 State St., Boston, MA 02109; 1,000.

Foundrymen's Society, Amer. (1896), Golf & Wolf Rds., Des Plaines, IL 60016; 15,684.

4-H Clubs (1901-05), Extension Service, U.S. Dept. Agriculture, Wash., DC 20250; 5,500,000.

French Institute (1911), 22 E. 60th St., N.Y., NY 10022; 7,200.

French Legion of Honor, Amer. Society of the (1922), 22 E. 60th St., N.Y., NY 10022; 440.

Friends Service Committee, Amer. (1917), 1501 Cherry St., Phila., PA 19102; 557.

— G —

Game Fish Assn., Internatl. (1939), 3000 E. Las Olas Blvd., Ft. Lauderdale, FL 33316; 10,000.

Garden Club of America (1913), 598 Madison Ave., N.Y., NY 10022; 13,000.

Garden Clubs of America, Men's (1932), 5560 Merle Hay Rd., Des Moines, IA 50323; 10,100.

Garden Clubs, Natl. Council of State (1929), 4401 Magnolia Ave., St. Louis, MO 63110; 500,000.

Gas Appliance Manufacturers Assn. (1935), 1901 N. Ft.

Myer Dr., Arlington, VA 22209; 306 companies.

Gas Assn., Amer. (1918), 1515 Wilson Blvd., Arlington, VA 22209; 5,000.

Gay Task Force, Natl. (1973), 80 Fifth Ave., N.Y., NY 10011; 3,000.

Genealogical Society, Natl. (1903), 1921 Sunderland Pl. NW, Wash., DC 20036; 2,700.

General Contractors of America, Associated (1918), 1957 E St. NW, Wash., DC 20006; 8,400.

Genetic Assn., Amer. (1903), 1028 Connecticut Ave. NW, Wash., DC 20036; 1,483.

Geographers, Assn. of Amer. (1904), 1710 16th St. NW, Wash., DC 20009; 6,200.

Geographic Education, Natl. Council for (1914), 115 N. Marion St., Oak Park, IL 60301; 5,000.

Geographic Society, Natl. (1888), 17th & M Sts. NW, Wash., DC 20036; 9,000,000.

Geographical Society, Amer. (1852), Broadway at 156th St., N.Y., NY 10032; 2,500.

Geolinguistics, Amer. Society of (1964), Bronx Community Coll., 120 E. 184th St., Bronx, NY 10468; 120.

Geological Institute, Amer. (1942), 5205 Leesburg Pike, Falls Church, VA 22041; 18 societies.

Geological Society of America (1888), 3300 Penrose Place, Boulder, CO 80301; 11,901.

Geologists, Assn. of Engineering (1957), 8310 San Fernando Way, Dallas, TX 75218; 2,500.

Geophysical Union, Amer. (1919), 1707 L St. NW, Wash., DC 20036; 11,000.

Geophysicists, Society of Exploration (1930), 3707 E. 51st St., Tulsa, OK 74135; 8,173.

Geriatrics Society, Amer. (1942), 10 Columbus Circle, N.Y., NY 10019; 7,500.

Gideons Internatl. (1899), 2900 Lebanon Rd., Nashville, TN 37214; 51,500.

Gifted Children, Amer. Assn. for (1946), 15 Gramercy Park, N.Y., NY 10003; 200.

Gifted Children, Natl. Assn. for (1954), 217 Gregory Dr., Hot Springs, AR 71901; 2,500.

Girl Scouts of the U.S.A. (1912), 830 Third Ave., N.Y., NY 10022; 3,234,000.

Girls Clubs of America (1945), 133 E. 62d St., N.Y., NY 10021; 205,000.

Gladiolus Council, No. Amer. (1945), 11345 Moreno Ave., Lakeside, CA 92040; 2,000.

Gold Star Mothers, Amer. (1928), 2128 Leroy Pl. NW, Wash., DC 20008; 15,000.

Golf Association, U.S. (1894), Golf House, Far Hills, NJ 07928; 4,500 clubs & courses.

Golf Assn., Natl. Amputee (1949), 24 Lakeview Ter., Watchung, NJ 07060; 450.

Goose Island Bird & Girl Watching Society (1960), 301 Arthur Ave., Park Ridge, IL 60068; 889.

Gospel Music Assn. (1964), 38 Music Sq. W., Nashville, TN 37203; 2,000.

Governmental Research Assn. (1914), P.O. Box 387, Ocean Gate, NJ 08740; 450.

Graduate Schools in the U.S., Council of (1961), One Dupont Circle NW, Wash., DC 20036; 343 institutions.

Grandmother Clubs of America, Natl. Federation of (1938), 203 N. Wabash Ave., Chicago, IL 60601; 18,000.

Grange, Natl. (1867), 1616 H St. NW, Wash., DC 20006; 500,000.

Graphic Artists, Society of Amer. (1915), 1083 Fifth Ave., N.Y., NY 10028; 235.

Graphic Arts, Amer. Institute of (1914), 1059 Third Ave., N.Y., NY 10021; 1,750.

Grocery Manufacturers of America (1908), 1425 K St. NW, Wash., DC 20005; 150 firms.

Guide Dog Foundation for the Blind (1946), 109-19 72d Ave., Forest Hills, NY 11375; 25,000.

Gyro Internatl. (1912), P.O. Box 489, 1096 Mentor Ave., Painesville, OH 44077; 5,500.

—H—

Hadassah (1912), 50 W. 58th St., N.Y., NY 10019; 350,000.

Handball Assn., U.S. (1951), 4101 Dempster St., Skokie, Il 60076; 15,000.

Handicapped, Federation of the (1935), 211 W. 14th St., N.Y., NY 10011; 1,000.

Handicapped, Natl. Assn. of the Physically (1958), 76 Elm St., London, OH 43140; 1,400.

Hang Gliding Assn., U.S. (1971), P.O. Box 66306, 11312¹/₂ Venice Blvd., Los Angeles, CA 90066; 16,350.

Health Council, Natl. (1921), 1740 Broadway, N.Y., NY 10019; 70 agencies.

Health Insurance Assn. of America (1956), 1701 K St. NW, Wash., DC 20006; 325 companies.

Health Insurance Institute (1956), 277 Park Ave., N.Y., NY 10017; 322 companies.

Health, Physical Education, & Recreation, Amer. Alliance for (1885), 1201 16th St. NW, Wash., DC 20036; 45,000.

Hearing Aid Society, Natl. (1951), 20361 Middlebelt Rd., Livonia, MI 48152; 3,600.

Hearing and Speech Action, Natl. Assn. for (1919), 814 Thayer Ave., Silver Spring MD 20910; 12,000.

Heart Assn., Amer. (1924), 7320 Greenville Ave., Dallas, TX 75231; 115,000.

Heating, Refrigerating & Air Conditioning Engineers, Amer. Society of (1894), 345 E. 47th St., N.Y., NY 10017; 30,000.

Helicopter Assn. of America (1948), 1156 15th St. NW, Wash., DC 20005; 508.

Helicopter Society, Amer. (1943), 1325 18th St. NW, Wash., DC 20036; 3,000.

HIAS (Hebrew Immigrant Aid Society) (1884), 200 Park Ave. S, N.Y., NY 10003; 15,000.

High Twelve Internatl. (1921), 3681 Lindell Blvd., St. Louis, MO 63108; 20,100.

Historians, Organization of Amer. (1907), 112 N. Bryan St., Bloomington, IN 47401; 12,000.

Historians, The Society of Amer. (1939), 610 Fayerweather Hall, Columbia Univ., N.Y., NY 10027; 200.

Historic Preservation, Natl. Trust for (1948), 740-748 Jackson Pl. NW, Wash., DC 20006; 75,000.

Historical Assn., Amer. (1884), 400 A St. SE, Wash., DC 20003; 15,000

Historical Research Associates, Western (1971), 415 5th Road N., Nampa, ID 83651; 115.

Hockey Assn. of the U.S., Amateur (1937), 10 Lake Circle, Colorado Springs, CO 80906; 10,844 teams.

Hockey League, Natl. (1917), 920 Sun Life Bldg., Montreal, Quebec, Canada H3B 2W2; 18 clubs.

Holiday Institute of Yonkers (1969), 82 BorcherAve., Yonkers, NY 10704; 32.

Holy Cross of Jerusalem, Order of (1965), 853 Seventh Ave., N.Y., NY 10019; 1,055.

Home Builders, Natl. Assn. of (1942), 15th & M Sts. NW, Wash., DC 20005; 75,000 firms.

Home Economics Assn., Amer. (1909), 2010 Massachusetts Ave. NW, Wash., DC 20036; 56,500.

Home Improvement Council, Natl. (1956), 11 E. 44th St., N.Y., NY 10017; 1,800.

Homemakers of America, Future (1945), 2010 Massachusetts Ave. NW, Wash., DC 20036; 450,000.

Homemakers Council, Natl. Extension (1936), Rte. 7, Box 516, Kinston, NC 28501; 570,000.

Horatio Alger Society (1961), 4907 Allison Dr., Lansing, MI 48910; 225.

Horse Show Assn. of America Ltd., Natl. (1883), 527 Madison Ave., N.Y., NY 10022.

Horse Shows Assn., Amer. (1917), 527 Madison Ave., N.Y., NY 10022; 19,000.

Hospital Assn., Amer. (1898), 840 N. Lake Shore Dr., Chicago, IL 60611; 20,000.

Hospital Public Relations of the AHA, Amer. Society for (1965), 840 N. Lake Shore Dr., Chicago, IL 60611; 1,000.

Hot Rod Assn., Natl. (1951), 10639 Riverside Dr., N. Hollywood, CA 91602; 35,000.

Hotel & Motel Assn., Amer. (1911), 888 Seventh Ave., N.Y., NY 10019; 8,000 hotels & motels.

Humane Legislation, Committee for (1967), 910 16th St. NW, Wash., DC 20024; 60,000.

Humane Society of the U.S. (1955), 2100 L St. NW, Wash., DC 20037; 40,000.

Humanics, Amer. (1948), 912 Baltimore Ave., Kansas City, MO 64105; 950.

Humanist Assn., Amer. (1941), 602 Third St., San Francisco, CA 94107; 5,500.

Humanities, Natl. Endowment for the (1965), 806 15th St., NW, Wash., DC 20506.

—I—

Iceland Veterans (1948), 2101 Walnut St., Phila., PA 19103; 1,600.

Identification, Internatl. Assn. for (1915), P.O. Box 139, Utica, NY 13503; 2,000.

Illuminating Engineering Society (1906), 345 E. 47th St.,

N.Y., NY 10017; 10,000.

Illustrators, Society of (1901), 128 E. 63d St., N.Y., NY 10021; 650.

Immigration and Nationality Lawyers, Assn. of (1946), 50 Court St., Brooklyn, NY 11201: 650.

Imperial Order of the Dragon (1900-1901), Temple of Agriculture, P.O. Box 1707, San Francisco, CA 94101.

Indian Rights Assn. (1882), 1505 Race St., Phila., PA 19102; ·2,500.

Indoor Sports Club (1930), 1145 Highland St., Napoleon, OH 43545; 2,300.

Industrial Democracy, League for (1905), 112 E. 19th St., N.Y., NY 10003; 2,000.

Industrial Engineers, Amer. Institute of (1948), 25 Technology Park, Norcross, GA 30071; 20,000.

Industrial Health Foundation (1935), 5231 Centre Ave., Pittsburgh, PA 15232; 140 companies.

Industrial Management Society (1935), 570 Northwest Hwy., Des Plaines, IL 60016; 12,000.

Infant Death Syndrome (SIDS) Foundation, Natl. Sudden (1962), 310 S. Michigan Ave., Chicago, IL 60604; 20,000.

Infant Survival, Internatl. Council for (1964), 1515 Reisterstown Rd., Baltimore, MD 21208; 750 families.

Information Industry Assn. (1969), 4720 Montgomery Ln., Bethesda, MD 20014; 70 companies.

Instrument Society of America (1945), 400 Stanwix St., Pittsburgh, PA 15222; 20,136.

Insurance Assn., Amer. (1866), 85 John St., N.Y., NY 10038; 127 companies.

Intercollegiate Athletics, Natl. Assn. of (1940), 1205 Baltimore St., Kansas City, MO 64105; 555 schools.

Interfraternity Conference, Natl. (1909), P.O. Box 40368, Indianapolis, IN 46240; 47 fraternities.

Interior Designers, Amer. Society of (1975), 730 5th Ave., N.Y., NY 10019; 10,000.

International Education, Institute of (1919), 809 United Nations Plaza, N.Y., NY 10017.

International Law, Amer. Society of (1906), 2223 Massachusetts Ave. NW, Wash., DC 20008; 5,500.

Investment Clubs, Natl. Assn. of (1951), 1515 E. Eleven Mile Rd., Royal Oak, MI 48067; 125,601.

Iron Founders' Society, Gray and Ductile (1928), 20611 Center Ridge Rd., Rocky River, OH 44116; 220 firms.

Iron and Steel Engineers, Assn. of (1907), Three Gateway .Center, Pittsburgh, PA 15222; 12,200.

Italian Historical Society of America (1949), 111 Columbia Heights, Bklyn., NY 11201; 2,300. .

Italy-America Chamber of Commerce (1887), 350 Fifth Ave., N.Y., NY 10001; 950.

Izaak Walton League of America (1922), 1800 N. Kent St., Arlington, VA 22304; 56,000·

—J—

Jamestowne Society (1936), P.O. Box 7389, Richmond, VA 23221; 1,850.

Japanese Amer. Citizens League (1930), 1765 Sutter St., San Francisco, CA 94115; 29,000.

Jaycees, U. S. (1920), P.O. Box 7, 4 W. 21st St., Tulsa, OK 74102; 325,000.

Jewish Appeal, United (1939), 1290 Ave. of the Americas, N.Y., NY 10019.

Jewish Center Workers, Assn. of (1918), 15 E. 26th St., N.Y., NY 10010; 900.

Jewish Committee, Amer. (1906), 165 E. 56th St., N.Y., NY 10022; 40,000.

Jewish Congress, Amer. (1918), 15 E. 84th St., N.Y., NY 10028.

Jewish Federations and Welfare Funds, Council of (1932), 315 Park Ave. S., N.Y., NY 10010; 225 agencies.

Jewish Historical Society, Amer. (1892), 2 Thornton Rd., Waltham, MA 02154; 3,200.

Jewish War Veterans of the U.S.A. (1896), 1712 New Hampshire Ave. NW, Wash., DC 20009; 105,000.

Jewish Welfare Board, Natl. (1917), 15 E. 26th St., N.Y., NY 10010; serves 1,000,000.

Jewish Women, Natl. Council of (1893), 1 W. 47th St., N.Y., NY 10036; 100,000.

Job's Daughters, Internatl. Order of (1921), 1820 Douglas, Masonic Temple, Omaha, NE 68102; 88,000.

Jockey Club (1894), 300 Park Ave. N.Y., NY 10022; 76.

John Birch Society (1958), 395 Concord Ave., Belmont, MA 02178; 60,000 to 100,000.

Journalists, Society of Professional; Sigma Delta Chi (1909), 35 E. Wacker Dr., Chicago, IL 60601; 65,000.

Journalists and Authors, Amer. Society of (1948), 123 W. 43d St., N.Y., NY 10036; 400.

Judaism, Amer. Council for (1943), 309 Fifth Ave., N.Y., NY 10016; 8,500.

Judicature Society, Amer. (1913), 200 W. Monroe, Chicago, IL 60606; 33,152.

Junior Achievement (1919), 550 Summer St., Stamford, CT 06901; 200,000.

Junior College Athletic Assn., Natl. (1938), 12 E. 2d St., Hutchinson, KS 67501; 879.

Junior Colleges, Amer. Assn. of Community and (1920), One Dupont Circle NW, Wash., DC 20036; 1,536.

Junior Leagues, Assn. of (1921), 825 Third Ave., N.Y., NY 10022; 113,000.

Jurists, Amer. Justinian Society of (1966), 31 Chambers St., N.Y., NY 10009; 685.

—K—

Kailtone Adventure Society (1907), P.O. Box 233, Dayton, NV 89403; 106.

Kennel Club, Amer. (1884), 51 Madison Ave., N.Y., NY 10010; 400 clubs.

Key-Club Internatl. (1925), 101 E. Erie St., Chicago, IL 60611; 78,000.

Kitefliers Assn., Internatl. (1960), 321 E. 48th St., N.Y., NY 10017; 30,000.

Kiwanis Internatl. (1915), 101 E. Erie St., Chicago, IL 60611; 282,000.

Knights of Columbus (1882), One Columbus Plaza, New Haven, CT 06510; 1,227,830.

Knights of Equity (1895), 16 Southern Pkwy., Rochester, NY 14618; 1,500.

Knights of Pythias, Supreme Lodge, (1864), 47 N. Grant St., Stockton, CA 95202; 195,865.

Knights Templar U.S.A., Grand Encampment, (1816), 14 E. Jackson Blvd., Chicago, IL 60604; 365,000.

—L—

La Leche League Internatl. (1956), 9616 Minneapolis Ave., Franklin Park, IL 60131; 100,000.

Lacrosse Foundation (1959), Newton H. White Athletic Ctr., Homewood, Baltimore, MD 21218.

Lambs, The (1874), 131 W. 56th St., N.Y., NY 10019; 400.

Landscape Architects, Amer. Society of (1899), 1750 Old Meadow Rd., McLean, VA 22101; 4,500.

Language Teachers Associations, Natl. Federation of Modern (1916), 400 Wilkeson Quad., SUNY-Buffalo, Buffalo, NY 14261.

Law Institute, Amer. (1923), 4025 Chestnut St., Phila., PA 19104; 2,043.

Law Libraries, Amer. Assn. of (1906), 53 W. Jackson Blvd., Chicago, IL 60604; 2,230.

Law and Social Policy, Center for (1969), 1751 N St. NW, Wash., DC 20036.

Lawn Bowls Assn., Amer. (1915), 1033 Cheryl Dr., Sun City, AZ 85351; 9,500.

Learned Societies, Amer. Council of (1919), 345 E. 46th St., N.Y., NY 10017; 42 societies.

Legal Secretaries, Natl. Assn of (1950), 3005 E. Skelly Dr., Tulsa, OK 74105; 22,000.

Legion of Valor of the U.S.A. (1890), 621 S. Taylor St., Arlington, VA 22204; 890.

Leonard Wood Memorial for the Eradication of Leprosy (1928), 2430 Pennsylvania Ave., NW, Wash., DC 20037.

Leprosy Missions, Amer. (1906), 297 Park Ave. S., N.Y., NY 10010; 45,000.

Letter Carriers, Natl. Assn. of (1889), 100 Indiana Ave. NW, Wash., DC 20001; 230,353.

Leukemia Society of America (1949), 211 E. 43d St., N.Y., NY 10017; 1,267 trustees.

Liberty Lobby (1955), 300 Independence Ave. SE, Wash., DC 20003; 25,000.

Libraries Assn., Special (1909), 235 Park Ave. S., N.Y., NY 10003; 10,000.

Library Assn., Amer. (1876), 50 E. Huron St., Chicago, IL 60611; 35,000.

Library Assn., Home and School (1938), 500 Wallace Ave., Covington, KY 41014.

Library Assn., Medical (1898), 919 N. Michigan Ave., Chicago, IL 60611; 3,900.

Life Insurance, Amer. Council of (1976, by merger governing the **Amer. Life Insurance Assn.** and the **Institute of Life Insurance**), 1730 Pennsylvania Ave. NW, Wash., DC 20006; 427 companies.

Life Insurance Marketing & Research Assn. (1916), 170 Sigourney St., Hartford, CT 06105; 546.

Life Office Management Assn. (1923), 100 Park Ave., N.Y., NY 10017; 423.

Life Underwriters, Natl. Assn. of (1890), 1922 F St. NW, Wash., DC 20006; 135,000.

Lifespan (1970), 4274 N. Woodward, Royal Oak, MI 48073; 15,000.

Lighter-Than-Air Society (1952), 1800 Triplett Blvd., Akron, OH 44306; 1,200.

Lions Clubs, Internatl. Assn. of (1917), York & Cermak Rds., Oak Brook, IL 60521; 1,036,802.

Little League Baseball (1939), P. O. Box 1127, Williamsport, PA 17701; 10,423 teams.

Log Rolling Assn., Internatl. (1926), R.R. No. 1, Shawnigan Lake, British Columbia, V0R 2W0, Canada; 180.

Lone Indian Fellowship (1926), 1010 Huron Ave., Sheboygan WI 53081; 850.

Lubrication Engineers, Amer. Society of (1945), 838 Busse Hwy., Park Ridge, IL 60068; 2,700.

Lung Assn., Amer. (formerly **Natl. Tuberculosis & Respiratory Disease Assn.**) (1904), 1740 Broadway, N.Y., NY 10019; 2,000.

Lutheran Education Assn. (1942), 7300 Augusta St., River Forest, IL 60305; 2,750.

—M—

Macaroni Manufacturers Assn., Natl. (1904), 19 S. Bothwell, Box 336, Palatine, IL 60067; 130 firms.

Magazine Publishers Assn. (1919), 575 Lexington Ave., N.Y., NY 10022; 130 companies.

Magicians, Internatl. Brotherhood of (1926), 28 N. Main St., Kenton, OH 44326; 10,000.

Magicians, Society of Amer. (1902), 66 Marked Tree Rd., Needham, MA 02192; 4,500

Magicians Guild of America (1941), 20 W. 40th St., N.Y., NY 10018; 78.

Mammalogists, Amer. Society of (1919), c/o Museum, Oklahoma State Univ., Stillwater, OK 74074; 4,000.

Management, Amer. Institute of (1948), 125 E. 38th St., N.Y., NY 10016; 5,000.

Management Assn., Amer. (1923), 135 W. 50th St., N.Y., NY 10020; 50,000.

Management Consultants, Institute of (1968), 347 Madison Ave., N. Y., NY 10017; 750.

Management Engineers, Assn. of Consulting (1933), 347 Madison Ave., N.Y. NY 10017; 50 firms.

Management Systems Information, Society for (1969), 10 W. 31st St., Chicago, IL 60616; 686.

Manufacturers, Natl. Assn. of (1895), 1776 F St. NW, Wash., DC 20006; 12,100.

Manufacturers' Agents Natl. Assn. (1947), 3130 Wilshire Blvd., Los Angeles, CA 90010; 4,500.

Manufacturing Chemists Assn. (1872), 1825 Connecticut Ave. NW, Wash., DC 20009; 200 companies.

Manufacturing Engineers, Society of (1932), 20501 Ford Rd., Dearborn, MI 48128; 42,000.

March of Dimes, Natl. Foundation (1938), 1275 Mamaroneck Ave., White Plains, NY 10605; 2,100 chapters.

Marine Corps League (1923), 933 N. Kenmore St., Arlington, VA 22201; 20,000.

Marine Surveyors, Natl. Assn. of (1960), P. O. Box 55, Peck Slip Sta., N. Y., NY 10038; 299.

Marine Technology Society (1963), 1730 M St. NW, Wash., DC 20036; 3,500.

Marine Underwriters, Amer. Institute of (1898), 99 John St., N. Y. NY 10038; 296.

Marketing Assn., Amer. (1937), 222 S. Riverside Plaza, Chicago, IL 60606; 17,969.

Masonic Relief Assn. of U. S. and Canada (1885), 415 S. Main Ave., Sioux Falls, SD 57102; 2,956,585.

Masonic Service Assn. of the U. S. (1919), 8120 Fenton St. Silver Spring, MD 20910; 44 lodges.

Masons, Supreme Council 33°, Ancient and Accepted Scottish Rite, Northern Masonic Jurisdiction, (1813), 33 Marrett Rd., Lexington, MA 02173; 507,940.

Masons, Ancient and Accepted Scottish Rite, Southern Jurisdiction, Supreme Council (1801), 1733 16th St. NW, Wash., DC 20009; 637,000.

Masons, Royal Arch, General Grand Chapter (1797), 1084 New Circle Rd., N.E., Lexington KY 40505; 500,000.

Masons of the State of N.Y., Grand Lodge of Free & Accepted (1781), 71 W. 23d St., N.Y., NY 10010; 210,000.

Mathematical Assn. of America (1915), 1225 Connecticut Ave., Wash., DC 20036; 19,000.

Mathematical Society, Amer. (1888), 201 Charles St., Providence, RI 02904; 15,907.

Mathematical Statistics, Institute of (1937), 1367 Laurel, San Carlos, CA 94070; 3,000.

Mathematics, Society for Industrial and Applied (1952), 33 S. 17th St., Phila., PA 19103; 4,250.

Mattachine Society (1953), 59 Christopher St., N.Y., NY 10014; 500.

Mayflower Descendants, General Society of (1897), P.O. Box 297, Plymouth, MA 02360; 16,192.

Mayors, U.S. Conference of (1933), 1620 Eye St. NW, Wash., DC 20006; 750.

Mechanical Engineers, Amer. Society of (1880), 345 E. 47th St., N.Y., NY 10017; 65,795.

Mechanics, Assn. of Chairmen of Departments of (1970), Virginia Polytechnic Institute, Blackburg, VA 24061; 120.

Mechanics, Junior Order of United Amer. (1853), 170 Railway Rd., Grafton, VA 23692; 1,020.

Mediaeval Academy of America (1926), 1430 Massachusetts Ave., Cambridge, MA 02138; 3,990.

Medical Assn., Amer. (1847), 535 N. Dearborn St., Chicago, IL 60610; 210,000.

Medical Assn., Natl. (1895), 2109 E. St. NW, Wash., DC 20037; 3,000.

Medical Colleges, Assn. of Amer. (1876), One Dupont Circle NW, Wash., DC 20036; 2,149.

Medical Record Assn., Amer. (1928), 875 N. Michigan Ave., Chicago IL 60611; 17,700.

Medical Technologists, Amer. (1939), 710 Higgins Rd., Park Ridge, IL 60068; 12,057.

Medical Technologists, Amer. College of (1942), 5608 Lane, Raytown, MO 64133; 368.

Medical Women's Assn., Amer. (1915), 1740 Broadway, N.Y., NY 10019; 6,000.

Medicine, New York Academy of (1847), 2 E. 103d St., N.Y., NY 10029.

Men Voters of the U. S., League of (1969), 88 Arbol, Oroville, CA 95965.

Mensa, Amer. (1945), 1701 W. 3d St., Bklyn., NY 11223; 22,000.

Mental Health, Natl. Assn. for (1909), 1800 N. Kent St., Arlington, VA 22209; 1,000,000.

Mental Health Program Directors, Natl. Assn. of State (1964), 1001 3d St. SW, Wash., DC 20024; 54.

Merchant Marine Library Assn., Amer. (1921), One World Trade Center, Suite 2601, N. Y., NY 10048; 4,160.

Metal Finishers, Natl. Assn. of (1955), 22 S. Park St., Montclair, NJ 07042; 979 firms.

Metals, Amer. Society for (1913), Metals Park, OH 44073; 36,059.

Meteorological Society, Amer. (1919), 45 Beacon St., Boston, MA 02108; 9,000.

Metric Assn., U.S. (1916), Sugarloaf Star Rte., Boulder, CO 80302; 4,800.

Microbiology, Amer. Society for (1899), 1913 Eye St. NW, wash., DC 20006; 24,000.

Micrographics Assn., Natl. (1943), 8728 Colesville Rd., Silver Spring, MD 20910; 7,000.

Middle East, Amer. Friends of the (1951), 1717 Massachusetts Ave. NW, Wash., DC 20036; 400.

Military Chaplains Assn. of the U.S.A. (1925), 7758 Wisconsin Ave. NW, Wash., DC 20014; 2,800.

Military Engineers, Society of Amer. (1920), 740 15th St. NW, Wash., DC 20005; 22,000.

Military Institute, Amer. (1933), P. O. Box 568, Benj. Franklin Sta., Wash., DC 20044; 950.

Military Order of the Loyal Legion of the U.S.A. (1865), 1307 New Hampshire Ave. NW, Wash., DC 20036.

Military Order of the Purple Heart (1782, by Gen. George Washington; reactivated Feb. 22, 1932, by President Herbert Hoover and Chief of Staff Douglas MacArthur), P. O. Box 1901; Wash., DC 20013; 15,000.

Military Order of the World Wars (1920), 1100 17th St. NW, Wash., DC 20036; 11,000.

Military Surgeons of the U.S., Assn. of (1891), 10605 Concord St., Kensington, MD 20795; 10,000.

Mining, Metallurgical and Petroleum Engineers, Amer. Institute of (1871), 345 E. 47th St., N.Y., NY 10017; 49, 726.

Mining and Metallurgical Society of America (1908), 299 Park Ave., N.Y., NY 10017; 330.

Ministerial Assn., Amer. (1929), 446 Salem Ave*, P.O. Box 1252, York, PA 17405; 7,802.

Model Railroad Assn., Natl. (1935), 7061 Twin Oaks Dr., Indianapolis, IN 46226.

Modern Language Assn. of America (1883), 62 Fifth Ave., N.Y., NY 10011; 30,000.

Moose, Loyal Order of (1888), Moosehart, IL 60539; 1,478,672.

Mothers Committee, Amer. (1935), Waldorf Astoria, 301 Park Ave., N.Y., NY 10022; 2,000.

Motion Picture Arts & Sciences, Academy of (1927), 8949 Wilshire Blvd., Beverly Hills, CA 90211; 3,925.

Motion Picture Assn. of America (1922), 522 Fifth Ave., N.Y., NY 10036.

Motion Picture & Television Engineers, Society of (1916), 862 Scarsdale Ave., Scarsdale, NY 10583; 8,000.

Motion Pictures, Natl. Board of Review of (1909), 210 E. 68th St., N.Y., NY 10021.

Motor Bus Owners, Natl. Assn. of (1926), 1025 Connecticut Ave. NW, Wash., DC 20036; 450.

Motor Vehicle Administrators, Amer. Assn. of (1933), 1201 Connecticut Ave. NW, Wash., DC 20036; 130.

Motor Vehicle Manufacturers Assn. (1913), 320 New Center Building, Detroit MI 48202; 125.

Motorcycle Assn., Amer. (1924), P.O. Box 141, 33 Collegeview Ave., Westerville, OH 43081; 140,000.

Motoress Aid (1970), 28671 Northwestern Hwy., Southfield, MI 48025; 5,000.

Multiple Sclerosis Society, Natl. (1946), 257 Park Ave. S., N.Y., NY 10010; 182,000.

Municipal Finance Officers Assn. of the U.S. & Canada (1906), 1313 E. 60th St., Chicago, IL 60637; 5,500.

Municipal League, Natl. (1894), 47 E. 68th St., N.Y., NY 10021; 6,300.

Mural Painters, Natl. Society of (1895), 41 E. 65th St., N.Y., NY 10021; 150.

Muscular Dystrophy Assn. (1950), 810 Seventh Ave., N.Y., NY 10019; 81 corporate members.

Museums, Amer. Assn. of (1906), 2233 Wisconsin Ave. NW, Wash., DC 20007; 5,970.

Music, Natl. Assn. of Schools of (1924), 11250 Roger Bacon Dr., Reston, VA 22090; 437 institutions.

Music Center, Amer. (1940), 250 W. 57th St., N.Y., NY 10019; 1,000.

Music Clubs, Natl. Federation of (1898), 310 S. Michigan Ave., Chicago, IL 60604; 600,000.

Music Conference, Amer. (1947), 150 E. Huron St., Chicago, IL 60611; 300.

Music Council, Natl. (1940), 250 W. 57th St., N.Y., NY 10019; 60 org.

Music Educators Natl. Conference (1907), 1902 Association Dr., Reston, VA 22091; 62,000.

Music Players, Amateur Chamber (1947), Box 547, Vienna, VA 22180; 5,000.

Music Publishers' Assn., Natl. (1917), 110 E. 59th St., N.Y., NY 10022; 102.

Music Scholarship Assn., Amer. (1957), 1926 Carew Tower, Cincinnati, OH 45202; 1,000.

Music Teachers Natl. Assn. (1876), 408 Carew Tower, Cincinnati, OH 45202; 15,000.

Musicians, Amer. Federation of (1896), 1500 Broadway, N.Y., NY 10036; 330,000.

Musicological Society, Amer. (1934), 201 S. 34th St., Phila., PA 19174; 3,071.

Mutual Savings Banks, Natl. Assn. of (1920), 200 Park Ave., N.Y., NY 10017; 475 banks.

Muzzle Loading Rifle Assn. (1933), P.O. Box 67, Friendship, IN 47021; 19,500.

Mystic Seaport (1929), 30 Greenmanville Ave., Mystic, CT 06355; 14,000.

—N—

NAACP (Natl. Assn. for the Advancement of Colored People) (1909), 1790 Broadway, N.Y., NY 10019; 409,018.

NAAFA (Natl. Assn. to Aid Fat Americans) (1969), P. O. Box 475, Westbury, NY 11590; 1,000.

Name Society, Amer. (1951), English Dept., SUNY-Potsdam, Potsdam, NY 13676; 980.

NASCAR (Natl. Assn. for Stock Car Auto Racing) (1948), P.O. Box K, Daytona Beach, FL 32015; 16,000.

National Guard Assn. of the U.S. (1878), One Massachusetts Ave. NW, Wash., DC 20001; 49,000.

Nationalities Service, Amer. Council for (1921), 20 W. 40th St., N.Y., 10018; 28 agencies.

Natural Science for Youth Foundation (1961), 763 Silvermine Rd., New Canaan, CT 06840; 500.

Naturalists, Assn. of Interpretive (1961), 6700 Needwood Rd., Derwood, MD 20855; 1,000.

Nature Conservancy (1951), 1800 N. Kent St., Arlington, VA 22209; 23,000.

Nature & Natural Resources, Internatl. Union for Conservation of (1948), 1110 Morges, Switzerland; 42 countries.

Nature Study Society, Amer. (1908), R.D. 1, Homer, NY 13077; 850.

Naval Architects & Marine Engineers, Society of (1893), 74 Trinity Pl., N.Y., NY 10006; 10,700.

Naval Engineers, Amer. Society of (1888), 1012 14th St. NW, Wash., DC 20005; 4,018.

Naval Institute, U.S. (1873), U.S. Naval Academy, Annapolis, MD 21402; 64,374.

Naval Reserve Assn. (1954), 1913 Eye St. NW, Wash., DC 20006; 17,000.

Navigation, Institute of (1945), 815 15th St. NW, Wash., DC 20005; 3,000.

Navy Club of the U.S.A. (1940), 1602 Wells St., Fort Wayne, IN 46801; 3,000. **Navy Club of the U.S.A. Auxiliary** (1940), 216 W. Suttenfield, Fort Wayne, IN 46807; 1,000.

Navy League of the U.S. (1902), 818 18th St. NW, Wash., DC 20006; 45,000.

Navy Wives Clubs of America (1936), P.O. Box 6971, Wash., DC 20032; 3,000.

Needlework Guild of America (1885), 1736 Pine St., Phila., PA 19103; 400,000.

Negro Business and Professional Women's Clubs, Natl. Assn. of (1935), 3411 Lynchester Rd., Baltimore, MD 21215; 2,000.

Negro College Fund, United (1944), 500 E. 62d St., N.Y., NY 10021; 41 colleges.

Newspaper Editors, Amer. Society of (1922), 1350 Sullivan Trail, Easton, PA 18042; 817.

Newspaper Promotion Assn., Internatl. (1931), 11600 Sunrise Valley Dr., Reston, VA 22091; 1,200.

Newspaper Publishers Assn., Amer. (1887), 11600 Sunrise Valley Dr., Reston, VA 22091; 1,160 newspapers.

Newspaper Publishers Assn., Natl. (1940), 770 National Press Bldg., Wash., DC 20045; 300.

Ninety-Nines (1929), P.O. Box 59964; Will Rogers World Airport, Oklahoma City, OK 73159; 5,000.

Non-Commissioned Officers Assn. of the U.S.A. (1960) 10635 IH 35 No., San Antonio, TX 78233; 150,000.

Notaries, Amer. Society of (1965), 810 18th St. NW, Wash , DC 20006; 6,183.

Nuclear Society, Amer. (1954), 244 E. Ogden Ave., Hinsdale, IL 60521; 12,000.

Numismatic Assn., Amer. (1891), 818 N. Cascade, Colorado Springs, CO 80903; 31,457.

Numismatic Society, Amer. (1858), Broadway bet. 155th & 156 Sts., N.Y., NY 10032; 1,789.

Nurse Education and Service, Natl. Assn. for Practical (1941), 122 E. 42d St., N.Y., NY 10017; 34,212.

Nurses, Natl. Federation of Licensed Practical (1949), 250 W. 57th St., N.Y., NY 10019; 28,000.

Nurses' Assn., Amer. (1896), 2420 Pershing Rd., Kansas City, MO 64108; 200,000.

Nursing, Natl. League for (1952), 10 Columbus Circle, N.Y., NY 10019; 15,000.

Nutrition, Amer. Institute of (1928), 9650 Rockville Pike, Bethesda, MD 20014; 1,600.

—O—

Occupational Therapy Assn., Amer. (1917), 6000 Executive Blvd., Rockville, MD 20852; 25,841.

Odd Fellows, Independent Order of (1819), 16 W. Chase St., Baltimore, MD 21201; 1,100,000.

Old Crows, Assn. of (1964), 2361 S. Jefferson Davis Hwy., Arlington, VA 22202; 8,000.

Olympic Committee, U.S. (1921), 57 Park Ave., N.Y., NY 10016.

Optical Society of America (1916), 2000 L St. NW, Wash., DC 20036; 7,260.

Optimist Internatl. (1919), 4494 Lindell Blvd., St. Louis, MO 63108; 118,000.

Optometric Assn., Amer. (1898), 7000 Chippewa St., St. Louis, MO 63119; 19,100.

Oral Surgeons, Amer. Society of (1918), 211 E. Chicago Ave., Chicago, IL 60611; 3,129.

Order of the Rainbow for Girls, Supreme Assembly Internatl. (1922), 315 E. Carl Albert Pkwy., McAlester, OK 74501; 175,000.

Organists, Amer. Guild of (1896), 630 Fifth Ave., N.Y., NY 10020; 16,000.

Organization of Amer. States (1890), Pan American Union, 17th & Constitution Ave. NW, Wash., DC 20006; 24 nations.

Oriental Society, Amer. (1840), 329 Sterling Memorial Library, Yale Sta., New Haven, CT 06520.

Ornithologists' Union, Amer. (1883), c/o National Museum of Natural History, Smithsonian Institution, Wash., DC 20560; 4,000.

ORT Federation, Amer. (Organization for Rehabilitation through Training) (1972), 817 Broadway, N.Y., NY 10013; 140,000.

Osteopathic Assn., Amer. (1897), 212 E. Ohio St., Chicago, IL 60611; 12,356.

Ostomy Assn., United (1962), 1111 Wilshire Blvd., Los Angeles, CA 90017; 25,200.

Over-the-Counter Cos., Natl. Assn. of (1973), Box 110, Jenkintown, PA 19046; 170 companies.

Overeaters Anonymous (1960), 3730 Motor Ave., Los Angeles, CA 90034; 40,000.

—P—

Paleontological Research Institution (1932), 1259 Trumansburg Rd., Ithaca, NY 14850; 500.

Paper Converters Assn. (1934), 1619 Massachusetts Ave. NW, Wash., DC 20036; 24.

Paper Institute, Amer. (1964), 260 Madison Ave., N.Y., NY 10016; 200 companies.

Parasitologists, Amer. Society of (1924), 1041 New Hampshire St., Box 368, Lawrence, KS 66044; 1,850.

Parents & Teachers, Natl. Congress of (1897), 700 N. Rush St., Chicago, IL 60611; 7,000,000.

Parents Without Partners (1957), 7910 Woodmont Ave. NW, Wash., DC 20016; 130,000.

Parking Assn., Natl. (1951), 1101 17th St. NW, Wash., DC 20036; 1,400.

Parkinson's Disease Foundation (1957), Wm. Black Research Bldg., 640 W. 168th St., N.Y., NY 10032.

Parks & Conservation Assn., Natl. (1919), 1701 18th St. NW, Wash., DC 20009; 45,000.

Pathologists & Bacteriologists, Amer. Assn. of (1900), Dept. of Pathology, Box 3712, Duke Univ. Medical Center, Durham, NC 27710; 1,271.

Pay Toilets in America, Committee to End (1969), Box 71, 118 W. Third St., Dayton, OH 45402; 1,600.

Pearl Harbor Survivors Assn. (1958), 8920 SE Clay St., Portland, OR 97216.

Pedestrian Assn., Amer. (1973), 170 Broadway, N.Y., NY 10038; 180.

P.E.N. Amer. Center (1922), 156 Fifth Ave., N.Y., NY 10010; 1,600.

Pen Women, Natl. League of Amer. (1897), 1300 17th St. NW, Wash., DC 20036; 6,000.

Pennsylvania Society (1899), Suite 594, Waldorf-Astoria Hotel, 301 Park Ave., N.Y., NY 10022; 2,450.

P.E.O. Sisterhood (1869), 3700 Grand Ave., Des Moines, IA 50312; 187,000.

Performance Improvement, Amer. Society for (1966), 790 Broad St., Newark, NJ 07102; 250.

Personnel Administration, Amer. Society for (1948), 19 Church St., Berea, OH 44017; 16,000.

Personnel & Guidance Assn., Amer. (1952), 1607 New Hampshire Ave. NW, Wash., DC 20009; 34,000.

Petroleum Geologists, Amer. Assn. of (1917), Box 979, 1444 S. Boulder, Tulsa, OK 74101; 16,983.

Petroleum Institute, Amer. (1919), 2101 L St. NW, Wash., DC 20037; 7,600.

Petroleum Landmen, Amer. Assn. of (1955), 2404 Continental Life Bldg., Fort Worth, TX 76102; 4,200.

Pharmaceutical Assn., Amer. (1852), 2215 Constitution Ave. NW, Wash., DC 20037; 54,000.

Philatelic Americans, Society of (1894), 58 W. Salisbury Dr., Wilmington, DE 19809; 7,830.

Philatelic Society, Amer. (1886), P.O. Box 300, 336 S. Fraser St., State College, PA 16801; 40,000.

Philaticians, Society of (1972), P.O. Box 150, Salt Point Tpke., Clinton Corners, NY 12514; 212.

Philharmonic Symphony Society of New York (1928), Avery Fisher Hall, Lincoln Center, N.Y., NY 10023; 5,000.

Philological Assn., Amer. (1869), 431-432 N. Burrowes, Penn. State Univ., University Park, PA 16802; 2,900.

Philosophical Assn., Amer. (1900), Univ. of Delaware, Newark, DE 19711; 6,000.

Philosophical Society, Amer. (1743), 104 S. 5th St., Phila., PA 19106; 600.

Phonemic Spelling Council (1971), 525 W. 120th St., N.Y., NY 10027; 100.

Photographers of America, Professional (1880), 1090 Executive Way, Des Plaines, IL 60018; 16,000.

Photographic Society of Amer. (1934), 2005 Walnut St., Phila., PA 19103; 19,000.

Physical Society, Amer. (1899), 335 E. 45th St., N.Y., NY 10017; 29,000

Physical Therapy Assn., Amer. (1921), 1156 15th St. NW, Wash., DC 20005; 25,000.

Physicians, Amer. College of (1915), 4200 Pine St., Phila., PA 19104; 20,000.

Physics, Amer. Institute of (1931), 335 E. 45th St., N.Y., NY 10017; 60,000.

Physiological Society, Amer. (1887), 9650 Rockville Pike, Bethesda, MD 20014; 5,000.

Pilgrim Society (1820), 75 Court St., Plymouth, MA 20360; 700.

Pilgrims of the U.S. (1903), 74 Trinity Pl., N.Y., NY 10006; 1,000.

Pilot Club Internatl. (1921), 244 College St., Macon, GA 31201; 18,000.

Pioneer Women (1925), 315 Fifth Ave., N.Y., NY 10016; 50,000.

Planned Parenthood Federation of America (1922), 810 Seventh Ave., N.Y., NY 10019; 189 affiliates.

Planners, Amer. Institute of (1917), 1776 Massachusetts Ave. NW, Wash., DC 20036; 11,118.

Planning Officials, Amer. Society of (1934), 1313 E. 60th St., Chicago, IL 60637; 11,000.

Plastics Engineers, Society of (1942), 656 W. Putnam Ave., Greenwich, CT 06830; 18,000.

Plastics Industry, Society of (1937) 355 Lexington Ave., N.Y., NY 10017; 1,200 companies.

Platform Assn., Internatl. (1826), 2564 Berkshire Rd., Cleveland Heights, OH 44106; 11,000.

Podiatry Assn., Amer. (1912), 20 Chevy Chase Circle, NW, Wash., DC 20015; 6,400.

Poetry Day Committee, Natl. (1947), 1110 N. Venetian Dr., Miami Beach, FL 33139; 10,000.

Poetry Society of America (1910), 15 Gramercy Park S., N.Y., NY 10003; 725.

Poets, Academy of Amer. (1934), 1078 Madison Ave., N.Y., NY 10028; 86.

Polar Society, Amer. (1934), c/o Secretary, 98-20 62d Dr., Apt. 7H, Rego Park, NY 11374; 2,500.

Police, Amer. Federation of (1966), 1100 NE 125th St. N., Miami FL 33161; 52,000.

Police, Internatl. Assn. of Chiefs of (1893), 11 Firstfield Rd., Gaithersburg, MD 20760; 10,500.

Police, Natl. Assn. of Special and Reserve (1965), Box 45, Bay Sta., Bklyn., NY 11235; 1,000.

Police Reserve Officers Assn., Natl. (1967), 14600 Tamiami Trail N.P., Venice, FL 33595; 17,400.

Polish Army Veterans Assn. of America (1921), 17 Irving Pl., N.Y., NY 10003; 9,762.

Polish Cultural Society of America (1940), 55 W. 42d St., N.Y., NY 10036; 21,651.

Polish Legion of American Veterans (1920), 3024 N. Laramie Ave., Chicago, IL 60641; 20,000.

Political Items Collectors. Amer. (1945), 66 Golf St., Newington, CT 06111; 2,000.

Political Science, Academy of (1880), 2852 Broadway, N.Y., NY 10025; 11,000.

Political Science Assn., Amer. (1903), 1527 New Hampshire Ave. NW, Wash., DC 20036; 12,000.

Political & Social Science, Amer. Academy of (1889), 3937 Chestnut St., Phila., PA 19104; 18,000.

Polo Assn., U.S. (1890), 1301 W. 22d St., Oak Brook, IL 60521; 1,662.

Population Assn. of America (1932), Box 14182, Benj. Franklin Sta., Wash., DC 20044; 2,700.

Portuguese Continental Union of the U.S.A. (1925), 899 Boylston St., Boston, MA 02115; 9,000.

Postmasters of the U.S., Natl. Assn. of (1936), 490 L'Enfant Plaza E., SW, Wash., DC 20024; 33,797.

Postmasters of the U.S., Natl. League of (1904), 955 L'Enfant Plaza SW, Wash., DC 20024; 17,000.

Poultry Science Assn. (1908), c/o Dr. C. B. Ryan, Texas A &

M Univ., College Station, TX 77843; 1,495.

Power Boat Assn., Amer. (1903), 22811 Greater Mack, St. Clair Shores, MI 48080; 6,500.

Power Squadron, U.S. (1914), P.O. Box 30423, Raleigh, NC 27612; 70,000.

Precancel Collectors, Natl. Assn. of (1950), 5121 Park Blvd., Wildwood, NJ 08260; 5,500.

Press Club, Natl. (1908), 529 14th St. NW, Wash., DC 20045; 4,600.

Press Institute, Internatl. (1951), Munstergasse 9, CH-8001 Zurich, Switzerland; 1,900.

Press and Radio Club (1948), P.O.Box 7023, Montgomery, AL 36107; 707.

Press Women, Natl. Federation of (1937), 1105 Main St., Blue Springs, MD 64015; 3,800.

Production & Inventory Control Society, Amer. (1957), 2600 Virginia Ave. NW, Wash., DC 20037; 14,750.

Propeller Club of the U.S. (1927), 1730 M St. NW, Wash., DC 20036; 13,000.

Psychiatric Assn., Amer. (1844), 1700 18th St. NW, Wash., DC 20009; 22,426.

Psychological Research, Amer. Society for (1885), 5 W. 73d St., N.Y., NY 10023; 2,500.

Psychoanalytic Assn., Amer. (1911), One E. 57th St., N.Y., NY 10022; 2,269.

Psychological Assn., Amer. (1892), 1200 17th St. NW, Wash., DC 20036; 42,000.

Psychological Assn. for Psychoanalysis, Natl. (1946), 150 W. 13th St., N.Y., NY 10011; 174.

Psychological Minorities, Society for the Aid of (1953), 4225 Hampton St., Elmhurst, NY 11373; 500.

Psychotherapy Assn., Amer. Group (1942), 1865 Broadway, N.Y., NY 10023; 3,000.

Public Health Assn., Amer. (1872), 1015 18th St. NW, Wash., DC 20036; 23,691.

Public Relations Society of America (1947), 845 Third Ave., N.Y., NY 10022; 7,700.

Public Welfare Assn., Amer. (1930), 1155 16th St. NW, Wash, DC 20036; 7,000.

Publishers, Assn. of Amer. (1970), One Park Ave., N.Y., NY 10016; 260 companies.

— Q & R —

Quality Control, Amer. Society for (1946), 161 W. Wisconsin Ave., Milwaukee, WI 53203; 23,000.

Quint-A (1954), 23219 Lincolnshire Dr., Bay Village, OH 44140; 7,003.

Racing Commissioners, Natl. Assn. of State (1934), P.O. Box 4216, Lexington, KY 40504; 650.

Racquetball Assn., U.S. (1974), 4101 Dempster St., Skokie, IL 60076; 10,000.

Radio Free Europe (1949), 2 Park Ave., N.Y., NY 10016.

Radio Relay League, Amer. (1914), 225 Main St., Newington, CT 06111; 126,000.

Radio and Television Society, Internatl. (1939), 420 Lexington Ave., N.Y., NY 10017; 1,200.

Radio Union, Internatl. Amateur (1925), 225 Main St., Newington, CT 06111; 86 societies.

Radiological Society of No. America (1915), One MONY-Plaza, Syracuse, NY 13202; 7,560.

Railroad Passenger, Natl. Assn. of (1967), 417 New Jersey Ave. SE, Wash., DC 20003; 4,500.

Railroads, Assn. of Amer. (1934), 1920 L St. NW, Wash., DC 20036; 158.

Railway Engineering Assn., Amer. (1899), 59 E. Van Buren St., Chicago, IL 60605; 3,400.

Railway Historical Society, Natl. (1935), P.O. Box 2051, Phila., PA 19103; 10,078.

Railway Progress Institute (1908), 801 N. Fairfax St., Alexandria, VA 22314; 145 companies.

Range Management, Society for (1948), 2120 S. Birch St., Denver, CO 80222; 4,600.

Real Estate Appraisers, Natl. Assn. of (1967), 853 Broadway, N.Y., NY 10003; 1,000.

Real Estate Investment Funds, Natl. Assn. of (1960), 1101 17th St. NW, Wash., DC 20036; 310.

Realtors[R], Natl. Assn. of (1908), 430 N. Michigan Ave., Chicago, IL 60611; 433,182.

Reconciliation, Fellowship of (1915), 523 N. Broadway, Nyack, NY 10960; 23,500.

Recording Industry Assn. of America (1952), One E. 57th St., N.Y., NY 10022; 52 firms.

Records Managers & Administrators, Assn. of (1975), P.O. Box 281, Bradford, RI 02808; 3,900.

Recreation and Park Assn., Natl. (1965), 1601 N. Kent St., Arlington, VA 22209; 16,097.

Red Cross, Amer. Natl. (1881), 17th & D Sts. NW, Wash., DC 20006; 30,945,344.

Red Men, Improved Order of (1765), 1525 West Ave., P.O. Box 683, Waco, TX 76707; 67,000.

Redwoods League, Save-the- (1918), 114 Sansome St., San Francisco, CA 94104; 50,000.

Regional Plan Assn. (1929), 235 E. 45th St., N.Y., NY 10017; 1,500.

Rehabilitation Assn., Natl. (1925), 1522 K St. NW, Wash., DC 20005; 35,000.

Religion, Amer. Academy of (1896), Dept. of Religion, Florida State Univ., Tallahassee, FL 32306; 4,058.

Renaissance Society of America (1954), 1161 Amsterdam Ave., N.Y., NY 10027; 3,200.

Rescue Committee, Internatl. (1933), 386 Park Ave. S., N.Y., NY 10016; 70.

Reserve Officers Assn. (1922), One Constitution Ave. NE, Wash., DC 20002; 100,000.

Responsible Patriotism, Natl. Committee for (1967), Commodore Hotel, 109 E. 42d St., N.Y., NY 10017; 150.

Restaurant Assn., Natl. (1919), IBM Plaza, Chicago, IL 60611; 12,255.

Retail Druggists, Natl. Assn. of (1898), One E. Wacker Dr., Chicago, IL 60601; 32,000.

Retail Grocers, Natl. Assn. of, 2000 Spring Rd., Oak Brook, IL 60521; 38,000.

Retail Merch., Assn., Natl. (1911), 100 W. 31st St., N.Y., NY 10001; 30,000.

Retarded Citizens, Natl. Assn. for (1953), P.O. Box 6109, 2709 Ave. E East., Arlington, TX 76011; 300,000.

Retired Assn. for the Uniformed Services (1970), 1701 21st Ave. S., Nashville, TN 37212; 24,788.

Retired Federal Employees, Natl. Assn. of (1921), 1533 New Hampshire Ave. NW, Wash., DC 20036; 216,000.

Retired Officers Assn. (1929), 1625 Eye St. NW, Wash., DC 20006; 210,000.

Retired Persons, Amer. Assn. of (1958), 1909 K St. NW, Wash., DC 20049; 8,500,000.

Retired Teachers Assn., Natl. (1947), 1909 K St. NW, Wash., DC 20049; 500,000.

Retreads (of World War I & II) (1947), 40-07 154th St., Flushing, NY 11354; 1,500.

Revolver Assn., U.S. (1900), 59 Alvin St., Springfield MA 01104; 1,350.

Rhodes Scholars, Assn. of Amer. (1907), 1100 Philadelphia Natl. Bank Bldg., Phila., PA 19107; 1,493.

Rifle Assn. of America, Natl. (1871), 1600 Rhode Island Ave. NW, Wash., DC 20036; 1,000,000.

Road Builders' Assn., Amer. (1902), 525 School St. SW, Wash., DC 20024; 8,000.

Rodeo Cowboys Assn., Professional (1954), 2929 W. 19th Ave., Denver, CO 80204; 8,000

Roller Skating Confederation, U.S.A. (1973), 7700 A St., Lincoln, NE 68510; 25,000.

Roller Skating Rink Operators Assn. (1937), 7700 A St., Lincoln, NE 68510; 1,100.

Rose Society, Amer. (1889), P.O. Box 30,000, Shreveport, LA 71130; 18,000.

Rosicrucian Fraternity (1614, Germany, 1861 in U.S.), R.D. No. 3; Clymer Rd., Quakertown, PA 18951.

Rosicrucian Order, AMORC (1915), Rosicrucian Park, San Jose, CA 95151; 120,000.

Rosicrucians, Society of (1909), 321 W. 101st St., N.Y., NY 10025.

Rotary Internatl. (1905), 1600 Ridge Ave., Evanston, IL 60201; 785,400.

Round Table Internatl., Knights of the (1911), 61 E. Colorado Blvd., Pasadena, CA 91101; 1,900.

Ruritan Natl. (1928), P.O. Box 487, Dublin, VA 24084; 37,500.

Russian Orthodox Clubs, Federated (1927), 10 Downs Dr. (Plains), Wilkes-Barre, PA 18705; 5,000.

— S —

Safety Council, Natl. (1913), 425 N. Michigan Ave., Chicago, IL 60611; 16,000.

Safety Engineers, Amer. Society of (1911), 850 Busse Hwy., Park Ridge, IL 60068; 14,072.

St. Paul, Natl. Guild of (1937), 601 Hill 'N Dale, Lexington, KY 40503.

Salt Institute (1914), 206 N. Washington St., Alexandria, VA 22314; 27.

Salvation Army, The (1865, England, 1880 in U.S.), 120 W. 14th St., N.Y., NY 10011; 366,471.

Sane World, A Citizen's Organization for a (1957), 318 Massachusetts Ave. NE, Wash., DC 20002; 20,000.

Savings & Loan League, Natl. (1943), 1101 15th St. NW, Wash., DC 20005; 500.

School Administrators, Amer. Assn. of (1865), 1801 N. Moore St., Arlington, VA 22209; 19,000.

School Boards Assn., Natl. (1940), State Natl. Bank Plaza, P.O. Box 1496, Evanston, IL 60204; 53 assns.

School Counselor Assn., Amer. (1953), 1607 New Hampshire Ave. NW, Wash., DC 20009; 14,322.

School Principals, Natl. Assn. of Secondary (1917), 1904 Association Dr., Heston, VA 22091; 35,000.

Schools & Colleges, Amer. Council on (1927), 446 Salem Ave., P.O. Box 1252, York, PA 17405; 127 institutions.

Science, Amer. Assn. for the Advancement of (1848), 1515 Massachusetts Ave. NW, Wash., DC 20005; 118,000.

Science Service (1921), 1719 N St. NW, Wash., DC 20036.

Science Teachers Assn., Natl. (1944), 1742 Connecticut Ave. NW, Wash., DC 20009; 40,000.

Science Writers, Natl. Assn. of (1934), Box H, Sea Cliff, NY 11579; 950.

Sciences, Natl. Academy of (1863), 2101 Constitution Ave. NW, Wash., DC 20418; 1,135.

Sciences, New York Academy of (1818), 2 E. 63d St., N.Y., NY 10021; 25,000.

Scientific Apparatus Makers Assn. (1918), 1140 Connecticut Ave. NW, Wash., DC 20036; 222 companies.

Scientists, Federation of Amer. (1946), 307 Massachusetts Ave. NE, Wash., DC 20002; 8,000

Scottish Clans, Order of (1878), 111 Washington St., Brookline, MA 02146; 10,000.

Screen Actors Guild (1933), 7750 Sunset Blvd., Hollywood, CA 90046; 32,000.

Sculpture Society, Natl. (1893), 75 Rockefeller Plaza, N.Y., NY 10019; 350.

Seamen's Service, United (1942), One World Trade Ctr., N.Y., NY 10048.

Secularists of America, United (1947), 377 Vernon St., Oakland, CA 94610; 900.

Securities Industry Assn. (1972), 20 Broad St., N.Y., NY 10005; 647 firms.

Security Industrial Assn., Natl. (1944), 740 15th St. NW, Wash., DC 20005; 250 corporations.

Seeing Eye, The (1929), Morristown, NJ 07960; 26,000.

Semantics, Institute of General (1938), White Hollow Rd., Lakeville, CT 06039; 800.

Separation of Church & State, Americans United for (1947), 8120 Fenton St., Silver Spring, MD 20910; 125,000.

Separationists, Society of (1963), 4408 Medical Pkwy., Austin, TX 78756; 70,000 families.

Sertoma Internatl. (1912), 1900 E. Meyer Blvd., Kansas City, MO 64132; 33,000.

Settlements & Neighborhood Centers, Natl. Federation of (1911), 232 Madison Ave., N.Y., NY 10016; 175 agencies.

Sex Information & Education Council of the U.S. (SIECUS) (1964), 122 E. 42d St., N.Y., NY 10017.

Shakespeare Assn. of America, 4215 Harding Rd., Nashville, TN 37205; 600.

Sheriff's Assn., Natl. (1940), 1250 Connecticut Ave. NW, Wash., DC 20036; 50,000.

Shipbuilders Council of America (1921), Watergate, 600 New Hampshire Ave. NW, Wash., DC 20037; 40 companies.

Shoe Retailers Assn., Natl. (1912), 200 Madison Ave., N.Y., NY 10016; 3,500.

Shore & Beach Preservation Assn., Amer. (1926), 412 O'-Brien Hall, Univ. of California, Berkeley, CA 94720; 1,500.

Shorthand Reporters Assn., Natl. (1899), 2361 S. Jefferson Davis Hwy., Arlington, VA 22202; 10,500.

Showmen's League of America (1913), 300 W. Randolph St., Chicago, IL 60606; 1,650.

Shrine, Imperial Council of the A. A. Order of Nobles of the Mystic (1878), 323 N. Michigan Ave., Chicago, IL 60601; 928,385.

Shut-In Day Society, Natl. (1970), 237 Franklin St., Reading, PA 19602; 5,000.

Sierra Club (1892), 530 Bush St., San Francisco, CA 94108; 157,000.

Silurians, Society of the (1924), 45 John St., N.Y., NY 10038; 756.

Skating Union of the U.S., Amateur (1927), 4423 W. Deming Pl., Chicago, IL 60639; 2,675.

Skeet Shooting Assn., Natl. (1946), P.O. Box 28188, San Antonio, TX 78238; 19,063.

Ski Assn., U.S. (1904), 1726 Champa St., Denver, CO 80202; 100,000.

Small Business, Amer. Federation of (1963), 407 S. Dearborn St., Chicago, IL 60605; 5,000.

Small Business Assn., Natl. (1937), 1225 19th St. NW, Wash., DC 20036; 40,000.

Smoking & Health, Natl. Clearinghouse for (1965), Ctr. for Disease Control, 1600 Clifton Road NE, Atlanta, GA 30333.

Soaring Society of America (1932), 3200 Airport Ave., Santa Monica, CA 90405; 12,830.

Soccer Federation, U.S. (1913), 350 Fifth Ave., N.Y., NY 10001; 40 assns.

Social Biology, Society for the Study of (1926), c/o Social-Science Research Council, 605 3d Ave., N.Y., NY 10016; 750.

Social Science Research Council (1924), 605 Third Ave., N.Y., NY 10016; 30.

Social Sciences, Natl. Institute of (1912), 622 3d Ave., N.Y., NY 10017; 750.

Social Welfare, Internatl. Council on (1928), 345 E. 46th St., N.Y., NY 10017; 70 natl. committees.

Social Welfare, Natl. Conference on (1873), 22 W. Gay St., Columbus, OH 43215; 5,000.

Social Work Education, Council on (1952), 345 E. 46th St., N.Y., NY 10017; 4,500.

Social Workers, Natl. Assn. of (1955), 1425 H St. NW, Wash., DC 20005; 68,000.

Sociological Assn., Amer. (1905), 1722 N St. NW, Wash., DC 20036; 14,000.

Soft Drink Assn., Natl. (1919), 1101 16th St. NW, Wash., DC 20036; 1,896.

Softball Assn., Amateur (1933), 2801 N.E. 50th St., Oklahoma City, OK 73111; 1,500,000.

Softball League, Cinderella (1958), 34 E. Market St., Corning, NY 14830; 50,000.

Soil Conservation Society of America (1946), 7515 N.E. Ankeny Rd., Ankeny, IA 50021; 13,989.

Sojourners, Natl. (1919), 4600 Duke St., Alexandria, VA 22304; 9,000.

Soldier's, Sailor's and Airmen's Club (1919), 283 Lexington Ave., N.Y., NY 10016.

Sons of the Amer. Legion (1932), P.O. Box 1055, Indianapolis, IN 46206; 24,688.

Sons of the American Revolution, Natl. Society (1889), 2412 Massachusetts Ave. NW, Wash., DC 20008; 20,000.

Sons of Confederate Veterans (1896), Southern Sta., P.O. Box 1, Hattiesburg, MS 39401; 4,000.

Sons of Norway (1895), 1455 W. Lake St., Minneapolis, MN 55408; 100,127.

Sons of Poland, Assn. of the (1903), 655 Newark Ave., Jersey City, NJ 07306; 18,000.

Sons of the Revolution in the State of New York (1876), Fraunces Tavern, 54 Pearl St., N.Y., NY 10004; 1,500.

Sons of St. Patrick, Society of the Friendly (1784), 80 Wall St., N.Y., NY 10005; 1,300.

Sons of Union Veterans of the Civil War (1881), P.O. Box 24, Federal Bldg., Gettysburg, PA 18325; 3,500.

Soroptimist Federation of the Americas (1921), 1616 Walnut St., Phila., PA 19103; 30,000.

Southern Christian Leadership Conference (1957), 334 Auburn Ave., NE, Atlanta, GA 30303; 243 affiliate orgs.

Southern Regional Council (1944), 52 Fairlie St., NW, Atlanta, GA 30303; 110.

Spanish War Veterans, United (1904), 810 Vermont Ave. NW, Wash., DC 20420; 372.

Speech Communication Assn. (1914), 5205 Leesburg Pike, Falls Church, VA 22041; 6,500.

Speech & Hearing Assn., Amer. (1925), 9030 Old Georgetown Rd., Wash., DC 20014; 20,000.

Speleological Society, Natl. (1941), Cave Ave., Huntsville, AL 35810; 4,600.

Speleological Society of America (1964), 1124 100th Ave. NE, Bellevue, WA 98004; 2,195.

Sports Car Club of America (1944), 1562 S. Parker Rd., Denver, CO 80231; 20,000.

Sports Philatelists Internatl. (1962), 3604 S. Home Ave., Berwyn, IL 60402; 300.

Stamp Dealers' Assn., Amer. (1914), 595 Madison Ave., N.Y., NY 10022; 1,000.

Standards Institute, Amer. Natl. (1918), 1430 Broadway, N.Y., NY 10018; 1,000.

State Communities Aid Assn. (1872), 105 E. 22d St., N.Y., NY 10010; 285.

State Governments, Council of (1933), Iron Works Pike, Lexington, KY 40511; 50 states.

State High School Assns., Natl. Federation of (1920), 400

Leslie St., Elgin IL 60120; 50 states, 9 provinces.

State & Local History, Amer. Assn. for (1940), 1400 8th Ave. So., Nashville, TN 37203; 4,750.

Statistical Assn., Amer. (1839), 806 15th St. NW, Wash., DC 20005; 12,000.

Steamship Historical Society of America (1935), 414 Pelton Ave., Staten Island, NY 10310; 2,200.

Steel Construction, Amer. Institute of (1921), 1221 Ave. of the Americas, N.Y., NY 10020; 873.

Steel Founders' Society of America (1903), 20611 Center Ridge Rd., Rocky River. OH 44116; 120 companies.

Steeplechase and Hunt Assn., Natl. (1895), Box 308, Elmont, NY 11003; 3,000.

Sterilization, Assn. for Voluntary (1943), 708 Third Ave., N.Y., NY 10017; 5,000.

Steuben Society of America (1919), 369 Lexington Ave., N.Y., NY 10017.

Stock Exchange, Amer. (1911), 86 Trinity Pl., N.Y., NY 10006; 650.

Stock Exchange, New York (1792), 11 Wall St., N.Y., NY 10005; 1,366.

Stock Exchange, Philadelphia-Baltimore-Washington (1790), 17th St., Stock Exchange Pl., Phila., PA 19103; 448.

Student Assn., U.S. Natl. (1947), 2115 S St. NW, Wash., DC 20008; 500 schools.

Student Councils, Natl. Assn. of (1931), 1904 Association Dr.. Reston, VA 22091; 7,000 secondary schools.

Students of German, Natl. Federation of (1968), 339 Walnut St., Phila., PA 19106; 25,000.

Sugar Brokers Assn., Natl. (1903), 76 Beaver St., N.Y., NY 10005; 255.

Sunbathing Assn., Amer. (1929), 810 N. Mills Ave., Orlando, FL 32803; 16,000.

Sunday League (1933), 279 Highland Ave., Newark, NJ 07104; 25,000.

Surgeons, Amer. College of (1913), 55 E. Erie St., Chicago IL 60611; 38,500

Surgeons, Internatl. College of (1937), 1516 N. Lake Shore Dr., Chicago, IL 60610; 12,000.

Surveying & Mapping, Amer. Congress on (1941), 210 Little Falls, Falls Church, VA 22046; 6,700.

Symphony Orchestra League, Amer. (1942), P.O. Box 66, Vienna, VA 22180; 2,563.

Systems Management, Assn. for (1948), 24587 Bagley Rd., Cleveland, OH 44138; 10,000.

—T—

Table Tennis Assn., U.S. (1933), Box 815, Orange, CT 06477; 5,000.

Tattoo Club of America (1974), 112 W. First St., Mt. Vernon, NY 10550; 5,000.

Tax Accountants, Natl. Assn. of Enrolled Federal (1960), 6108 N. Harding Ave., Chicago, IL 60659; 500.

Tax Administrators, Federation of (1937), 1313 E. 60th St., Chicago, IL 60637.

Tax Assn., Natl. Tax Institute of America (1907), 21 E. State St., Columbus, OH 43215; 2,600.

Tax Foundation (1937), 50 Rockefeller Plaza, N.Y., NY 10020; 1,350.

Tea Assn. of the U.S.A. (1899), 230 Park Ave., N.Y., NY 10017; 250.

Teachers, Amer. Federation of (1916), 11 Dupont Circle NW, Wash., DC 20036; 473,000.

Teachers of English, Natl. Council of (1911), 1111 Kenyon Rd., Urbana, IL 61801; 100,000.

Teachers of French, Amer. Assn. of (1927), 57 E. Armory Ave., Champaign, IL 61820; 11,000.

Teachers of German, Amer. Assn. of (1930), 339 Walnut St., Phila., PA 19106; 8,500.

Teachers of Singing, Natl. Assn. of (1944), 250 W. 57th St., N.Y., NY 10019; 3,000.

Teachers of Spanish & Portuguese, Amer. Assn. of (1917), Holy Cross Coll., Worcester, MA 01610; 13,500.

Technical Communication, Society for (1957), 1010 Vermont Ave. NW, Wash., DC 20005; 3,000.

Television Arts & Sciences, Natl. Academy of (1955), 291 S. La Cienega, Beverly Hills, CA 90211; 10,000.

Television & Radio Artists, Amer. Federation of (1937), 1350 Ave. of Americas, N.Y., NY 10019; 30,000.

Telluride Assn. (1911), 217 West Ave., Ithaca, NY 14850; 70.

Tennis Assn., U. S. (1881), 51 E. 42d St., N.Y., NY 10017; 100,000.

Tennis League, Youth (1968), 1701 Vandalia, Collinsville, IL 62234; 850.

Testing & Materials, Amer. Society for (1898), 1916 Race St., Phila., PA 19103; 24,000.

Textile Assn., Northern (1854), 211 Congress St., Boston, MA 02110; 80 companies.

Textile Manufacturers Institute, Amer. (1949), 2124 Wachovia Ctr., Charlotte, NC 28285; 250 companies.

Theatre & Academy, Amer. Natl. (1935), 245 W. 52d St., N.Y., NY 10019; 800.

Theatre Assn., Amer. (1936), 1317 F St. NW, Wash., DC 20004; 6,000.

Theatre Organ Society, Amer. (1955), P.O. Box 1002, Middleburg, VA 22117; 6,000.

Theatre Owners, Natl. Assn. of (1924), 1501 Broadway, N.Y., NY 10036; 8,000.

Theorore Roosevelt Assn. (1919), P.O. Box 720, Oyster Bay, NY 11771; 500.

Theological Library Assn., Amer. (1947), Lutheran Theological Seminary, 7301 Germantown Ave., Phila., PA 19119; 571.

Theological Schools, Amer. Assn. of (1936), P.O. Box 396, Vandalia, OH 45377; 198 schools.

Theosophical Society (1875), 1926 N. Main St., Wheaton, IL 60187; 5,500.

Thoreau Society (1941), SUNY-Geneseo, Geneseo, NY 14454; 1,200.

Thoroughbred Racing Assn. (1942), 522 Fifth Ave., N.Y., NY 10036; 55 racetracks.

Titanic Historical Society (1963), P.O. Box 53, Indian Orchard, MA 01151; 1,273.

Toastmasters Internatl. (1924), 2200 N. Grand Ave., Santa Ana, CA 92711; 60,000.

Toastmistress Clubs, Internatl. (1938), 9068 E. Firestone Blvd., Downey, CA 90241; 27,998.

Topical Assn., Amer. (1949), 3306 N. 50th St., Milwaukee, WI 53216; 10,000.

Torch Clubs, Internatl. Assn. of (1924), Box 8670, University Sta., Knoxville, TN 37916; 5,000.

Toy Manufacturers of America (1916), 200 5th Ave., N.Y., NY 10010; 250.

Trade Relations Council (1885), 1001 Connecticut Ave. NW, Wash., DC 20036; 50 companies.

Traffic and Transportation, Amer. Society of (1946), 547 W. Jackson Blvd., Chicago, IL 60606; 2,800.

Transportation Engineers, Institute of (1930), 1815 N. Ft. Meyer Dr., Arlington, VA 22209; 5,713.

Training Corps, Amer. (1961), 107-12 Jamaica Ave., Richmond Hill, NY 11418; 300.

Training & Development, Amer. Society for (1943), P.O. Box 5307, Madison, WI 53711; 10,000.

Transit Assn., Amer. Public (1974), 1100 17th St. NW, Wash., DC 20036; 600.

Transportation Assn. of America (1935), 1100 17th St. NW, Wash., DC 20036; 600 companies.

Trapshooting Assn., Amateur (1923), 601 W. National Rd., Vandalia, OH 45377; 69,900.

Travel Agents, Amer. Society of (1931), 711 Fifth Ave., N.Y., NY 10022; 14,200.

Travel Organizations, Discover America (1969), 1100 Connecticut Ave. NW, Wash., DC 20036; 950.

Travelers Aid-Internatl. Social Service of America (1972), 345 E. 46th St., N.Y., NY 10017; 1,010 U.S. & foreign agencies.

Trucking Assn., Amer. (1933), 1616 P St. NW, Wash., DC 20036; 51 assns.

True Sisters, United Order (1846), 150 W. 85th St., N.Y., NY 10024; 12,000.

Turners, Amer. (1848), 1550 Clinton Ave. N., Rochester, NY 14621; 17,000.

—U—

UNICEF, U.S. Committee for (1947), 331 E. 38th St., N.Y., NY 10016; 3,000,000 volunteers.

Unidentified Flying Objects, Natl. Investigations Committee on (1967), 7970 Woodman Ave., Van Nuys, CA 91402; 5,000.

Uniformed Services, Natl. Assn. for (1968), 956 N. Monroe St., Arlington, VA 22201; 26,000.

United Nations, U. S. People for (1967), 777 United Nations Pl. N.Y., NY 10017; 30,000.

United Nations Assn. of the U.S.A. (1923, as **League of Nations Assn.**) 345 E. 46th St., N.Y., NY 10017; 40,000.

United Press Internatl. (1907), 220 E. 42d St., N.Y., NY 10017.

United Service Organizations (USO) (1941), 237 E. 52d St., N.Y., NY 10022

United States Army, Assn. of the (1950) 1529 18th St. NW, Wash., DC 20036; 84,513.

United Way of America (1918), 801 N. Fairfax St., Alexandria, VA 22314; 2,289.

Universities, Assn. of Amer. (1900), One Dupont Circle NW, Wash., DC 20036; 50 institutions.

Universities & Colleges, Assn. of Governing Boards of (1963), One Dupont Circle NW, Wash., DC 20036; 14,000.

University Extension Assn., Natl. (1915), One Dupont Circle NW, Wash., DC 20036; 230 institutions.

University Foundation Internatl. (1973), 501 E. Armour Blvd., Kansas City, MO 64109; 227.

University Professors, Amer. Assn. of (1915), One Dupont Circle NW, Wash., DC 20036; 72,200.

University Women, Amer. Assn. of (1882), 2401 Virginia Ave. NW, Wash., DC 20037; 190.000.

Up With People (1965), 3103 N. Campbell, Tucson, AZ 85719.

Urban Coalition, Natl. (1968), 1201 Connecticut Ave. NW, Wash., DC 20036.

Urban League, Natl. (1910), 500 E. 62d St., N.Y., NY 10021.

Utility Commissioners, Natl. Assn. of Regulatory (1889), P.O. Box 684, Wash., DC 20044; 78 agencies.

—V—

Variety Clubs Internatl. (1928), 7210 Red Rd., S. Miami, FL 33143; 10,000.

Veteran Motor Car Club of America (1938), Museum of Transportation, 15 Newton St., Brookline, MA 02146; 4075.

Veterans Committee, Amer. (1944), 1333 Connecticut Ave. NW, Wash., DC 20036; 25,000.

Veterans of Foreign Wars of the U.S. (1899) **& Ladies Auxiliary** (1914), 406 W. 34th St., Kansas City, MO 64111; 2,300,-000 & 540,000.

Veterans of World War I of the U.S.A. (1949), 916 Prince St., Alexandria, VA 22314; 136,000.

Veterinary Medical Assn., Amer. (1863), 930 N. Meacham Rd., Schaumburg, IL 60172; 25,136.

Victorian Society in America (1966), East Washington Sq., Phila., PA 19106; 2,200.

Vocational Assn., Amer. (1925), 1510 H St. NW, Wash., DC 20005; 57,000.

Volleyball Assn., U.S. (1928), 557 Fourth St., San Francisco, CA 94107; 10,000.

—W—

Walther League (1893), 119 W. Locust St., Chicago, IL 60610.

War of 1812, General Society of (1814), 1307 New Hampshire Ave. NW, Wash., DC 20036; 1,000.

War Mothers, Amer. (1917), 2615 Woodley Pl. NW. Wash., DC 20008; 14,000.

Watch & Clock Collectors, Natl. Assn. of (1943), 514 Poplar St., Columbia, PA 17512; 42,000.

Water Pollution Control Federation (1928), 2626 Pennsylvania Ave. NW, Wash., DC 20037.

Water Resources Assn., Amer. (1964), Mississippi River at 3d Ave. SE, Minneapolis, MN 55414; 1,591.

Water Ski Assn., Amer. (1939), 7th St. & Ave. G, SW, Winter Haven, FL 33880; 12,000.

Water Well Assn., Natl. (1947), 500 W. Bridge Rd., Worthington, OH 43085; 5,000.

Water Works Assn., Amer. (1881), 6666 W. Quincy Ave., Denver, CO 80235; 25,000.

Watercolor Society, Amer. (1866), 1083 5th Ave., N.Y., NY 10028; 550.

Welding Society, Amer. (1919), 2501 NW 7th St., Miami, FL 33125; 28,300.

Wheelchair Athletic Assn., Natl. (1962), 40-24 62d St., Woodside, NY 11377; 2,000.

Wilderness Society (1935), 1901 Pennsylvania Ave. NW, Wash., DC 20006; 90,000.

Wildlife, Defenders of (1925), 1244 19th St. NW, Wash., DC 20036; 35,000.

Wildlife Federation, Natl. (1936), 1412 16th St. NW, Wash., DC 20036; 3,500,000.

Wildlife Foundation, No. Amer. (1935), 709 Wire Bldg., 100 Vermont Ave. NW, Wash., DC 20005.

Wildlife Fund, World (1961), 910 17th St. NW, Wash., DC 20006; 28 national chapters.

Wildlife Management Institute (1946), 1000 Vermont Ave. NW, Wash., DC 20005.

Wildlife Society (1937), S-176, 3900 Wisconsin Ave. NW, Wash., DC 20016; 7,732.

William Penn Assn. (1886), 429 Forbes Ave., Pittsburgh, PA 15219; 69,058.

Wireless Pioneers, Society of (1967), P.O. Box 530, 3366 Mendocino Ave., Santa Rosa, CA 95402; 2,814.

Woman's Assn., Amer. (1914), 1271 Ave. of the Americas, N.Y., NY 10020; 250.

Woman's Christian Temperance Union, Natl. (1874), 1730 Chicago Ave., Evanston, IL 60201; 250,000.

Women, Natl. Organization for (NOW) (1966), 5 S. Wabash, Chicago, IL 60603; 52,000.

Women Artists, Natl. Assn. of (1889), 156 Fifth Ave., N.Y., NY 10010; 700.

Women Engineers, Society of (1950), 345 E. 47th St., N.Y., NY 10017; 3,800.

Women Geographers, Society of (1925), 1619 New Hampshire Ave. NW, Wash., DC 20009; 450.

Women Marines Assn. (1960), 1415 Springdale Ave., McLean, VA 22101; 2,800.

Women Strike for Peace (1961), 145 S. 13th St., Phila., PA 19107; 50,000.

Women of the U.S., Natl. Council of (1888), 345 E. 46th St., N.Y., NY 10017; 1,500.

Women Voters of the U.S., League of (1920), 1730 M St. NW, Wash., DC 20036; 140,000.

Women World War Veterans (1919), 237 Madison Ave., N.Y., NY 10016; 160,000.

Women's Army Corps Veterans Assn. (1946), 6049 Amboy Rd., Dearborn Heights, MI 48127; 1,500.

Women's Clubs, General Federation of (1890), 1734 N St. NW, Wash., DC 20036; 10,000,000.

Women's Clubs, Natl. Federation of Business & Professional (1919), 2012 Massachusetts Ave. NW, Wash., DC 20036; 170,000.

Women's Educational & Industrial Union (1877), 356 Boylston St., Boston, MA 02116; 2,300.

Women's Internatl. League for Peace & Freedom (1915), 1213 Race St., Phila., PA 19107; 10,000.

Women's Overseas Service League (1921), P.O. Box 39033, Friendship Sta., Wash., DC 20016; 1,140.

Women's Veterinary Medical Assn. (1947), c/o Dr. Judith Spurling, 6246 S. Ash Circle E., Littleton, CO 81001.

Woodmen of America, Modern (1883), 1701 First Ave., Rock Island, IL 61201; 495,000.

Woodmen of the World (1890), 1450 Speer Blvd., Denver, CO 80204; 28,954.

Wool Growers Assn., Natl. (1865), 336 Southern Bldg., 805 15th St. NW, Wash., DC 20005; 24 state assns.

Workmen's Circle (1900), 45 E. 33d St., N.Y., NY 10016; 55,000.

World Federalists, World Assn. of (1946), Leliegracht 21, Amsterdam, Netherlands; 40,000.

World Future Society (1966), 4916 St. Elmo Ave., Wash., DC 20014; 18,000.

World Health Organization, U.S. Committee (1951), 777 United Nations Plaza, N.Y., NY 10017; 1,234.

World Ship Society (1946), 3319 Sweet Dr., Lafayette, CA 94549; 3,700.

Writers Assn. of America, Outdoor (1927), 4141 W. Bradley Rd., Milwaukee, WI 53209; 1,396.

—Y & Z—

Yeomen F. Natl. (1926), 223 El Camino Real, Vallejo, CA 94590; 800.

Young Americans for Freedom (1960), Woodland Rd., Sterling, VA 22170; 55,000.

Young Men's Christian Assns., Natl. Council of (1854), 291 Broadway, N.Y., NY 10007; 8,670,000.

YM-YWHAs of Greater New York, Assoc. (1957), 130 E. 59th St., N.Y., NY 10022; 55,000.

Young Women's Christian Assn. of the U.S.A. (1858), 600 Lexington Ave., N.Y., NY 10022; 2,456,000.

Youth Hostels, Amer. (1934), Natl. Campus, Delaplane, VA 22025; 60,000.

Zero Population Growth (1968), 1346 Connecticut Ave.NW, Wash., DC 20036; 10,000.

Ziegfeld Club (1936), 55 W. 42d St., N.Y., NY 10036; 350 women.

Zionist Organization of America (1897), 4 E. 34th St., N.Y., NY 10016; 120,000.

Zonta Internatl. (1919), 59 E. Van Buren St., Chicago, IL 60605; 25,000.

Zoological Parks & Aquariums, Amer. Assn. of (1924), Oglebay Park, Wheeling, WV 26003; 2,000.

Zoologists, Amer. Society of (1890), Box 2739 California Lutheran College, Thousand Oaks, CA 91360; 4,100.

RELIGIOUS INFORMATION
Census of Religious Bodies in the U.S.

Source: World Almanac questionnaire and 1976 Yearbook of American Churches

Membership figures in the following table are the latest available. Some denominations submitted carefully compiled data while others approached the task more casually. The number of churches is given in parentheses.

Denomination	Members
Adventist Bodies:	**511,386**
Advent Christian Church (381)	31,057
Primitive Advent Christian Ch. (10)	530
Seventh-day Adventists (3,333)	479,799
Amana Church Society (7)	**735**
American Rescue Workers (25)	**2,700**
Anglican Orthodox Church (37)	**2,630**
Apostolic Faith (45)	**4,100**
Armenian Church of America (58)	**372,000**
Assemblies of God (9,019)	**1,239,197**
Baptist Bodies:	**26,969,726**
American Baptist Assn. (3,570)	1,071,000
American Baptist Churches in U.S.A. (6,005)	1,579,029
Baptist General Conference (632)	111,093
Baptist Missionary Assn. of Amer. (1,457)	211,000
Christian Unity Baptist Assn. (5)	345
Conserv. Baptist Assn. of Amer. (1,120)	300,000
Duck River (and Kindred) Assns. of Baptists (86)	8,909
Free Will Baptists, Natl. Assn. of (2,350)	215,000
Gen. Assn. of General Baptists (800)	70,000
Gen. Assn. of Regular Baptist Chs. (1,503)	250,000
General Six-Principle Baptist (8)	308
Natl. Baptist Conv. of Amer. (11,398)	2,668,799
Natl. Baptist Conv., U.S.A. (26,000)	5,500,000
Natl. Primitive Baptist Convention (2,198)	1,645,000
N. Amer. Baptist Gen. Conf. (245)	41,437
Progressive Natl. Baptist Conv. (655)	521,692
Regular Bap. Chs., Gen. Assn. of (1,503)	250,000
Separate Baptists in Christ (84)	7,496
Seventh Day Bapt. Gen. Conf. (73)	5,230
Southern Baptist Convention (34,710)	12,513,378
Berean Fundamental Church (50)	**2,350**
Bethel Ministerial Association (25)	**4,000**
Bible Protestant Church (42)	**2,254**
Bible Way Church of Our Lord Jesus Christ World Wide (350)	**30,000**
Brethren (German Baptists):	**233,405**
Brethren Ch. (Ashland, Oh.) (119)	16,279
Brethren Churches, Natl. Fellowship of (243)	33,514
Church of the Brethren (1,038)	179,387
Old German Baptist Brethren (54)	4,225
Brethren, Plymouth (690)	**40,000**
Brethren (River):	**11,132**
Brethren in Christ Church (157)	10,255
United Zion Church (16)	877
Buddhist Churches of America (60)	**60,000**
Christadelphians (850)	**15,800**
Christian & Missionary Alliance (1,094)	**144,245**
Christian Catholic Church (6)	**2,000**
Christian Church (Disciples of Christ) (4,524)	**1,312,326**
Christian Church of N. Amer., Gen. Council (110)	**8,500**
Christian Nation Church, U.S.A. (16)	**2,000**
Christian Union (108)	**5,301**
Church of Christ (Holiness) U.S.A. (159)	**9,289**
Church of Christ, Scientist (2,350) (membership not recorded)	
Church of Christ (32)	**2,400**
The Church of God (2,035)	**75,890**
Church of God in Christ (4,500)	**425,000**
Church of Illumination (14)	**9,000**
Church of the Nazarene (4,727)	**430,128**
Church of Revelation (10)	**750**
Churches of Christ (18,000)	**2,400,000**
Chs. of Christ in Christian Union (245)	**9,786**
Churches of God:	**698,066**
Ch. of God (Anderson, Ind.) (2,239)	161,401
Ch. of God (Cleveland, Tenn.) (4,392)	328,892
Church of God of Prophecy (1,755)	62,743

Denomination	Members
Ch. of God, Seventh Day (7)	2,000
Ch. of God, Seventh Day (Denver) (98)	5,600
Churches of God, Gen. Conference (351)	37,040
The Church of God (2,035)	75,890
The (Original) Ch. of God (70)	20,000
The Church of God by Faith (105)	4,500
Churches of the Living God:	**47,670**
Church of the Living God (276)	45,320
House of God, Which is the Church of the Living God, the Pillar and Ground of the Truth (107)	2,350
Church of New Jerusalem, Gen. (33)	**2,143**
Congregational Christian Churches, Natl. Assn. of (360)	**90,000**
Congregational Holiness Church (147)	**4,859**
Conversative Cong. Christian Conf. (127)	**21,975**
Eastern Orthodox Churches:	**4,193,040**
Albanian Orthodox Archdio. in Amer. (15)	40,000
Albanian Orthodox Diocese of Amer. (10)	5,240
American Carpatho-Russian Orthodox Greek Catholic Church (70)	100,000
American Catholic Church (Syro-Antiochian) (3)	495
Antiochian Orthodox Christian Archdio. of North America (108)	130,000
Armenian Apostolic Ch. of America (29)	125,000
Armenian Church of Amer., Diocese of the (58)	372,000
Bulgarian Eastern Orthodox Ch. (13)	86,000
Greek Orthodox Archdio. of N. and S. America (502)	1,950,000
Holy Orthodox Church in America (Eastern Cath. & Apostolic) (4)	260
Holy Ukrainian Autocephalic Orthodox Ch. in Exile (15)	4,800
Orthodox Church in America (483)	1,000,000
Romanian Orthod. Episcopate of Amer. (40)	40,000
Russian Orthodox Church in the U.S.A., Patriarchal Parishes (41)	51,500
Russian Orthodox Church Outside Russia (81)	55,000
Serbian Eastern Orthodox Church (52)	65,000
Syrian Orthodox Church of Antioch (Archdio. of the U.S.A. & Canada) (10)	50,000
Ukrainian Orthodox Ch. in the U.S.A. (107)	87,745
Ukrainian Orthodox Church in Amer. (Ecumenical Patriarchate) (23)	30,000
Ethical Union, American (25)	**5,000**
Evangelical Congregational Ch. (161)	**29,636**
Evangelical Covenant Ch. of America (508)	**69,960**
Evangelical Free Ch. of America (562)	**70,490**
Evangelistic Associations:	**78,200**
Apostolic Christian Chs. of Amer. (78)	9,500
Apostolic Christian Ch. (Nazarean) (39)	4,000
The Christian Congregation (495)	59,600
Pillar of Fire (61)	5,100
Free Christian Zion Ch. of Christ (742)	**22,260**
Friends:	**125,432**
Evangelical Friends Alliance (254)	27,206
Friends General Conference (233)	26,184
Friends United Meeting (515)	67,431
Religious Society of Friends (Conservative) (26)	1,840
Religious Society of Friends (unaffiliated) (72)	2,771
Holiness Church of God (28)	**927**
Independent Fundamental Churches of Amer. (614)	**87,852**
Internatl. Church of the Foursquare Gospel (741)	**89,215**

Denomination	Members
Jehovah's Witnesses (6,542)	**539,262**
Jewish Congregations:	**3,700,000**
Union of Amer. Hebrew Cong. (715)	1,200,000
Union of Orthodox Jewish Cong. of Amer. (1,000)	1,000,000
United Synagogue of Amer. (820)	1,500,000
Latter-Day Saints:	**2,842,723**
Church of Jesus Christ (Bickertonites) (50)	2,463
Church of Jesus Christ of Latter-Day Saints (Mormon) (5,401)	2,683,573
Reorganized Church of Jesus Christ of Latter-Day Saints (1,039)	156,687
Lutheran Bodies:	**8,194,426**
The Lutheran Ch. in America (5,733)	2,986,970
Lutheran Church-Mo. Synod (5,813)	2,769,594
The American Lutheran Church (4,809)	2,437,862
Other Lutheran Churches:	**443,982**
Church of the Lutheran Brethren of Amer. (100)	9,000
Church of the Lutheran Confession (68)	9,667
Evangelical Lutheran Church in America (Eielsen) (9)	2,500
Evangelical Lutheran Synod (Norwegian Synod) (98)	17,804
Free Lutheran Congregations, Assn. of (125)	13,471
Protestant Conference (Lutheran) (7)	2,675
Wis. Evangelical Lutheran Synod (1,031)	388,865
Mennonite Bodies:	**172,055**
Beachy Amish Mennonite Ch. (72)	4,297
Ch. of God in Christ (Mennonite) (38)	6,204
Evangelical Mennonite Brethren (32)	3,874
Evangelical Mennonite Church (20)	3,131
Gen. Conference Mennonite Ch. (188)	35,534
Hutterian Brethren (29)	3,405
Mennonite Church (1,063)	92,390
Old Order Amish Church (368)	14,720
Old Order (Wisler) Mennonite Ch. (38)	8,000
Reformed Mennonite Church (12)	500
Methodist Bodies:	**12,857,737**
African Meth. Episcopal Ch. (5,878)	1,166,301
African M.E. Zion Church (5,994)	1,024,974
Christian Meth. Episcopal Ch. (2,598)	466,718
Evangelical Methodist Church (139)	10,502
Free Methodist Ch. of N. Amer. (1,046)	65,210
Fundamental Methodist Church (14)	692
The United Methodist Church (39,195)	10,063,046
Primitive Method. Ch. U.S.A. (85)	11,024
Reformed Meth. Union Episc. Ch. (18)	2,192
Reformed Zion Union Apostolic Ch. (50)	16,000
Southern Methodist Church (174)	11,000
Missionary Church, The (273)	20,078
Moravian Bodies:	**61,034**
Moravian Ch. in Amer., North Prov. (98)	33,343
Moravian Ch. in Amer., South Prov. (51)	21,549
Unity of the Brethren (32)	6,142
New Apostolic Church of N. Amer. (298)	**22,563**

Denomination	Members
Old Catholic Churches:	**84,333**
American Catholic Church, N.Y. Archdio. (7)	700
N. Amer. Old R.C. Church (121)	60,098
N. Amer. Old R.C. Church (5)	972
Open Bible Standard Churches (275)	**25,000**
Pentecostal Assemblies:	**506,088**
Elim Fellowship (70)	5,000
Internatl. Pentecostal Assemblies (55)	10,000
Pentecostal Church of Christ (45)	1,435
Pentecostal Ch. of God of Amer. (1,300)	135,000
Pentecostal Fire-Baptized Holiness Ch. (41)	545
Pentecostal Free Will Baptist Ch. (128)	10,000
Pentecostal Holiness Church (1,340)	74,108
United Pentecostal Church (2,775)	270,000
Polish Natl. Catholic Ch. of Amer. (162)	**282,411**
Presbyterian Bodies:	**3,828,870**
Associate Reformed Presbyt. Church (General Synod) (153)	31,154
Cumberland Presbyterian Ch. (854)	93,948
Orthodox Presbyterian Ch. (123)	14,871
Presbyterian Church in America (260)	41,232
Presbyterian Ch. in the U.S. (4,117)	896,203
Reformed Presbyterian Ch., Evangelical Synod (140)	22,452
Reformed Presbyterian Church of N. Amer. (69)	5,445
United Presbyt. Ch. in the U.S.A. (8,675)	2,723,565
Protestant Episcopal Church (7,087)	**2,907,293**
Reformed Bodies:	**232,155**
Christian Reformed Church (527)	206,000
Hungarian Reformed Ch. in Am. (28)	11,679
Reformed Church in America (902)	354,004
Reformed Church in the U.S. (24)	3,940
Reformed Episcopal Church (64)	**6,532**
Roman Catholic Church (18,531)	**48,881,872**
Salvation Army (1,184)	**366,471**
The Schwenkfelder Church (5)	**2,250**
Social Brethren (34)	**1,722**
Spiritualists:	**172,302**
Int. Gen. Assembly of Spiritualists (209)	164,072
Natl. Spiritual Alliance of the U.S.A. (34)	3,230
Natl. Spiritualist Assn. of Chs. (200)	5,000
Triumph the Church and Kingdom of God in Christ (475)	**54,307**
Unitarian Universalist Assn. (946)	**192,510**
United Brethren:	**26,757**
United Brethren in Christ (276)	26,335
United Christian Church (12)	422
United Church of Christ (6,581)	**1,841,312**
United Holy Ch. of America (470)	**28,980**
Vedanta Society of New York (13)	**1,000**
Volunteers of America (583)	**30,740**
Wesleyan Church, The (1,828)	**94,215**

Religious Population of the World

Source: The 1976 Encyclopedia Britannica Book of the Year.

Religion	N. America[1]	S. America	Europe[2]	Asia	Africa	Oceania[3]	Total
Total Christian	229,006,000	164,884,000	354,894,600	87,683,000	101,144,100	17,155,000	954,766,700
Roman Catholic	131,596,500	154,067,000	174,141,000	45,285,000	32,314,500	3,200,000	540,704,000
Eastern Christian	4,120,000	55,000	63,900,600	1,781,000	16,442,000	355,000	86,653,600
Protestant[4]	93,289,500	10,762,000	116,833,000	40,617,000	52,367,600	13,600,000	327,509,100
Jewish	6,653,725	686,700	3,489,750	3,089,150	359,465	75,000	14,353,790
Muslim	242,100	195,300	8,370,000	430,267,000	99,073,500	66,000	538,213,900
Zoroastian	250	—	—	229,650	480	—	230,380
Shinto	60,000	92,000	—	60,004,000	—	—	60,156,000
Taoist[5]	16,000	12,000	—	30,375,700	—	—	30,403,700
Confucian[5]	96,000	85,000	30,000	185,850,700	500	42,000	186,104,300
Buddhist	150,500	190,300	222,000	249,296,500	2,000	16,000	249,877,300
Hindu	75,000	533,000	350,000	522,184,500	490,550	640,000	524,273,050
Totals	**236,299,675**	**166,678,300**	**367,356,350**	**1,568,980,200**	**201,070,595**	**17,994,000**	**2,558,379,120**

(1) Includes Central America and the West Indies. (2) Includes the USSR where it is difficult to determine religious affiliation. (3) Includes Australia, New Zealand, and islands of the South Pacific. (4) Protestant figures include "full members" rather than all baptized persons and are not comparable to those of ethnic religions or churches counting all adherents. (5) Statistics for Confucianism and Taoism are undeterminable in China since the Maoist-Marxist revolution.

Headquarters of U.S. Religious Bodies

(Year organized in parentheses)

Advent Christian Church (1854)—Pres., Rev. Joe Tom Tate. Exec. V.P., Rev. Adrian B. Shepard, Box 23152, Charlotte, NC 28212.

Adventists, Seventh-day, General Conference of, (1863)—Pres., Robert H. Pierson. Sec., C.O. Franz, 6840 Eastern Ave. NW, Takoma Park, Wash., DC 20012.

African Methodist Episcopal Zion Church (1796)—Senior Bishop, Herbert Shaw. Sec., Board of Bishops, Bishop Charles H. Foggie, 1200 Windermere Dr., Pittsburgh, PA 15218.

Antiochian Orthodox Archdiocese of Toledo, Ohio (1936)—Archbishop Metropolitan, Michael G. Shaheen, 2656 Pemberton Dr., Toledo, OH 43606.

Antiochian Orthodox Christian Archdiocese (formerly **Syrian Antiochian Orthodox Church**) (1894)—Head of Archdiocese Metropolitan, Archbishop Philip (Saliba), 358 Mountain Rd., Englewood, NJ 07631.

Armenian Church of America, Diocese of The (1889)—Primate, Most Rev. Archbishop Torkom Manoogian. Sec., Very Rev. Zaven Arzoumanian, 630 Second Ave., N.Y., NY 10016.

Assemblies of God (1914)—Gen. Supt., Thomas F. Zimmerman. Gen. Sec., Joseph R. Flower, 1445 Boonville Ave., Springfield, MO 65802.

Augustana Evangelical Lutheran Church. *See The Lutheran Church in America.*

Baha'i Faith —About 5,500 communities, groups and isolated centers in the U.S. Sec., Natl. Spiritual Assembly, Glenford E. Mitchell, 536 Sheridan Rd., Wilmette, IL 60091.

Baptist Association, American (1905)—Pres., Dr. Roy M. Reed. Sec., Dr. L. Chester Guinn, 4605 N. State Line, Texarkana, TX 75501.

Baptist Association of America, Conservative (1947)—Pres., Rev. Robert P. Dugan Jr. Sec., Rev. Carl E. Abrahamsen Jr., P.O. Box 66, Wheaton, IL 60187.

Baptist Churches in the U.S.A., American (1907)—Pres., Dr. Charles Z. Smith. Gen. Sec., Rev. Dr. Robert Campbell, Valley Forge, PA 19481.

Baptist Churches, Unified Free Will (1964)—Pres., Bishop Caldwell Thomas. Exec. Sec., Ernest Leonard, P.O. Box 4255, Newark, N.J. 07112.

Baptist Convention, Southern (1845)—Pres., Jaroy Weber. Exec. Sec., Dr. Porter Routh, 460 James Robertson Parkway, Nashville, TN 37219.

Baptists, General (1611)—Moderator, Rev. Harlen Webber. Clerk, Vern Whitten, 1629 Stinson Ave., Evansville, IN 47712.

Baptist General Conference (1879)—Gen. Sec., Warren Magnuson, 1233 Central St., Evanston, IL 60201.

Baptist General Conference, North American (1865)—Moderator, Delmar Wesseler. Exec. Sec., Dr. G. K. Zimmerman, 1 So. 210 Summit Ave., Oakbrook Terrace, Villa Park IL 60181.

Baptist, Natl. Assn. of Free Will (1727)—Moderator, Dr. J. D. O'Donnell. Exec. Sec., Rufus Coffey, P.O. Box 1088, Nashville, TN 37202.

Baptist, National, Convention of America (1880)—Pres., Dr. James C. Sams, 1724 Jefferson St., Jacksonville, FL.

Baptist Missionary Assn. of America (formerly **North American Baptist Assn.**) (1950)—Pres., Rev. Kenneth Bobo. Gen. Sec., Craig Branham, 720 Main St., Little Rock, AR 72201.

Buddhist Churches of America (1914)—Bishop Kenryu Takashi Tsuji, 1710 Octavia St., San Francisco, CA 94109.

Bulgarian Eastern Orthodox Church (1909)—Most Rev. Joseph, Metropolitan, 312 W. 101st St., N.Y., NY 10025.

Calvary Grace Christian Churches of Faith (1898)—Internatl. Gen. Supt., Rev. Dr. Herman Keck Jr., P.O. Box 14576, Ft. Lauderdale, FL 33302.

Calvary Grace Church of Faith (1874)—Rev. A. C. Spern, Internatl. Gen. Supt., P.O. Box 333, Rillton, PA 15678.

Christian and Missionary Alliance (1887)—Pres., Dr. Nathan Bailey. Sec., Dr. R. W. Battles, 350 N. Highland Ave., Nyack, NY 10960.

Christian Church (Disciples of Christ) (1809)—Gen. Minister and Pres., Dr. Kenneth L. Teegarden, Box 1986, Indianapolis, IN 46206.

Christian Endeavor, International Society of (1881)—Pres., Dr. LaVerne H. Boss. Gen. Sec., Rev. Charles W. Barner, 1221 East Broad St., P.O. Box 1110, Columbus, OH 43216.

Christian Reformed Church (1857)—Stated Clerk, Rev. William P. Brink, 2850 Kalamazoo Ave., SE, Grand Rapids, MI 49508.

Church of Christ, Scientist (1879)—The Mother Church, The First Church of Christ, Scientist, in Boston, Mass. Pres.,

Mrs. Naomi Price. First Reader, Clem W. Collins. Second Reader, Jane O. Robbins. Clerk, George W. Ledbetter. Christian Science Center, Boston, MA 02115.

Church of God (Anderson, Ind.) (1880)—Exec. Sec., W. E. Reed, Box 2420, Anderson, IN 46011.

Church of God, The (1903)—General Overseer, Bishop Voy M. Bullen, 2504 Arrow Wood Dr., SE, Huntsville, AL 35803.

Church of Jesus Christ of Latter-Day Saints (Mormon) (1830)—Pres., Spencer W. Kimball. Pres. of the Council of Twelve Apostles, Ezra Taft Benson, 47 E. South Temple St., Salt Lake City, UT 84111.

Church of Jesus Christ of Latter-Day Saints, Reorganized (1830)—Pres., W. Wallace Smith. Commissioner of Communications, Elroy Hanton, Saints Auditorium, Independence, MO 64051.

Church of the Brethren (1719)—Gen. Sec., General Board, S. Loren Bowman, 1451 Dundee Ave., Elgin, IL 60120.

Church of the Nazarene (1908)—Gen. Sec., B. Edgar Johnson, 6401 The Paseo, Kansas City, MO 64131.

Churches of Christ —No central organization. B. C. Goodpasture, editor, the Gospel Advocate, 1006 Elm Hill Rd., Nashville, TN 37210.

Churches of God, Gen. Conference (1825)—Pres., Dr. K. E. Boldosser. Sec., Rev. Harry G. Cadamore, 1934 Candlewick Dr., Findlay, OH 45840.

Congregational Christian Churches, General Council. *See United Church of Christ.*

Congregational Christian Churches, Natl. Assn. of (1955)—Moderator, Alexander S. Irvine. Exec. Sec., Rev. Dr. Erwin A. Britton, P.O. Box 1620, Oak Creek, WI 53154.

Ethical Union, American (Ethical Culture Movement) —Pres., Paul Gellert. Exec. Dir., Jean S. Kotkin, 2 W. 64th St., N.Y., NY 10023. Member of Internatl. Humanist and Ethical Union.

Evangelical Christian Churches (1966)—Pres., Dr. Kenneth T. Giles, P.O. Box 174, Jacksonville, FL 32219.

Evangelical Christian Churches, California Synod (1966)—Pres.-Treas., Dr. Richard W. Hart Sr., P.O. Box 399, Huntington Park, CA 90255.

Evangelical Lutheran Synod (Norwegian Synod) (1918)—Pres., Rev. G. M. Orvick. Sec., Rev. Alf Merseth, 106 13th St., S., Northwood, IA 50459.

Evangelical Methodist Church (1946)—Gen. Sec., Rev. R. D. Driggers, 3036 N. Meridan, Wichita, KS 67204.

Evangelical and Reformed Church. *See United Church of Christ.*

Finnish Evangelical Lutheran Church (Suomi Synod). *See Lutheran Church in America.*

Foursquare Gospel, International Church of the (1927)—Pres., Dr. Rolf K. McPherson. Sec., Dr. Leland B. Edwards, 1100 Glendale Blvd., Los Angeles, CA 90026.

Free Methodist Church of North America (1860)—Sec., Board of Bishops, 901 College, Winona Lake, IN 46590.

Friends, General Conference of the Religious Society of (1900)—Chmn., C. Lloyd Bailey. Gen. Sec., Howard W. Bartram, 1520 Race St., Philadelphia, PA 19102.

Friends United Meeting (formerly **Five Years Meeting of Friends**) (1902)—Presiding Clerk, J. Binford Farlow. Gen. Sec., Lorton G. Heusel, 101 Quaker Hill Dr., Richmond, IN 47374.

Greek Orthodox Church of North and South America (1864)—Primate, the Most Rev. Archbishop Iakovos. Chan., Very Rev. George J. Bacopulos, 10 E. 79th St., N.Y., NY 10021.

Hebrew Congregations, Union of American —Pres., Rabbi Alexander M. Schindler, 838 Fifth Ave., N.Y., NY 10021.

Holy Church on the Rock —Pres., Elder F.R. Willis, Pactolus, N.C. 27834.

Independent Fundamental Churches of America (1930)—Pres., Rev. Donald Hurlburt. Exec. Dir., Rev. Bryan J. Jones, Box 242, Westchester, IL 60153.

Jehovah's Witnesses (1884)—Chairmanship (rotating) of Governing Body. Watch Tower Bible and Tract Society; Pres., Nathan H. Knorr, 124 Columbia Heights, Brooklyn, NY 11201.

Jewish Congregations of America, Union of Orthodox —Pres., Harold M. Jacobs. Natl. Dir., Rabbi David Cohen, 116 East 27th St., N.Y., NY 10016.

Latter-Day Saints. *See Church of Jesus Christ.*

Lutheran Brethren of America, Church of The (1900)—Pres., Rev. Everald H. Strom, Box 655, Fergus Falls, MN 56537.

Lutheran Church, The American (1961) — Pres., Dr.

David W. Preus. Sec., Dr. A. R. Mickelson, 422 S. 5th St., Minneapolis, MN 55415.

Lutheran Church in America, The (estab. 1962 by consolidation of Amer. Evangelical Lutheran Ch. (1874), Augustana Evangelical Lutheran Ch. (1860), Finnish Evangelical Lutheran Ch. (1890) and The United Lutheran Ch. in Amer. (1918) — Pres., Rev. Robert J. Marshall. Sec., Rev. James R. Crumley Jr., 231 Madison Ave., N.Y., NY 10016.

Lutheran Church-Missouri Synod (1847)—Pres., Dr. J. A. O. Preus. Sec., Rev. Herbert A. Mueller, 500 N. Broadway, St. Louis, MO 63102.

Lutheran Confession, Church of The (1961)—Pres., Rev. Egbert Albrecht, 213 Spring St., Mankata, MN 56001.

Lutheran World Federation, U.S.A. National Committee of the (formed Jan. 1, 1967, former National Lutheran Council)—Gen. Sec., Rev. Paul A. Wee, 315 Park Ave. South, N.Y., NY 10010.

Mennonite Church (1690)—Moderator, Edward B. Stoltzfus. Sec., Paul N. Kraybill, 528 East Madison St., Lombard, IL 60148.

Methodist Church, The United formed 1968 from union of The Methodist Church (1784) and the Evangelical United Brethren Church (1767)—Council of Bishops Pres., Bishop W. Ralph Ward. Sec., Bishop Ralph T. Alton, 1100 W. 42nd St., Indianapolis, IN 46208.

Moravian Church (Unitas Fratrum) (1740)—**Northern Province:** Hq., 69 West Church St., P.O. Box 1245, Bethlehem, PA 18018; Pres., Provincial Elders' Conf., Dr. J. S. Groenfeldt. **Southern Province:** Hq., 459 S. Church St., Winston-Salem, NC 27101; Pres., Provincial Elders' Conf., Dr. Richard F. Amos.

New Jerusalem in the U.S.A., General Convention of the (1782)—Pres., Rev. Eric J. Zacharias. Rec. Sec., Mrs. Wilfred G. Rice, 983 Fellsway, Apt. 8, Medford MA 02155.

Open Bible Standard Churches (1919)—Gen. Supt., Raymond E. Smith. Sec.-Treas., O. Ralph Isbill, 2020 Bell Ave., Des Moines, IA 50315.

Orthodox Church in America (formerly Russian Orthodox Catholic Ch. of Amer.) (1794)—Primate, Metropolitan Archbishop Ireney. Chancellor, Very Rev. Daniel Hubiak, Rte. 25A, P.O. Box 675, Syosset, NY 11791.

Pentecostal Church of God of America (1919)—Gen. Supt., Dr. R. D. Heard, 211 Main St., Joplin, MO 64801.

Pentecostal Church, United (1945)—Gen. Supt., Stanley W. Chambers. Gen. Sec., Robert L. McFarland, 8855 Dunn Rd., Hazelwood, MO 63042.

Presbyterian Church, Cumberland (1810)—Moderator, Roy E. Blakeburn, Stated Clerk, T.V. Warnick, Memphis, TN 38104.

Presbyterian Church in the U.S. (1861)—Moderator, Rev. Paul M. Edris. Stated Clerk, Rev. James E. Andrews, 341 Ponce de Leon Ave., NE, Atlanta, GA 30308.

Presbyterian Church in the U.S.A., The United (formed 1958 through merger of the Presbyterian Ch. in the U.S.A. (1706) and the United Presbyt. Ch. of N. America (1858)—Moderator, Robert C. Lamar. Stated Clerk, Ruling Elder William P. Thompson, 475 Riverside Dr., N.Y., NY 10027.

Protestant Episcopal Church, The (1789)—Presiding Bishop, Pres. of Exec. Council, Rt. Rev. John M. Allin, 815 Second Ave., N.Y., NY 10017.

Rabbinical Alliance of America—Pres., Rabbi David B. Hollander, 156 5th Ave., N.Y., NY 10010.

Rabbinical Assembly, The—Pres., Rabbi Stanley Rabinowitz. Exec. V.P., Rabbi W. Kelman, 3080 Broadway, N.Y., NY 10027.

Rabbinical Council of America—Pres., Rabbi Fabian Schonfeld. Exec. V.P., Rabbi Israel Klavan, 220 Park Ave. South, N.Y., NY 10003.

Rabbis, Central Conference of American—Pres., Rabbi Arthur J. Lelyveld. Exec. V.P., Rabbi Joseph B. Glaser, 790 Madison Ave., N.Y., NY 10021.

Reformed Church in America (1628)—Pres., Rev. Bert Van Soest. Gen. Sec., Rev. Marion de Velder, D.D., 475 Riverside Dr., N.Y., NY 10027.

Reformed Episcopal Church (1873)—Pres. and Presiding

Bishop, Rev. Theophilus J. Herter. Sec., Rev. D. Ellsworth Raudenbush, 560 Fountain St., Havre de Grace, MD 21078.

Reformed Presbyterian Church, Evangelical Synod (Apr. 6, 1965, union of the Reformed Presbyterian Ch., General Synod and the Evangelical Presbyterian Ch.)—Moderator, Rev. Paul H. Alexander. Stated Clerk, Dr. Paul R. Gilchrist, 107 Hardy Rd., Lookout Mountain, TN 37350.

Regular Baptist Churches, General Assn. of (1932)—Natl. Rep., Dr. Joseph M. Stowell, 180 Oakton Boulevard, Des Plaines, IL 60018.

Roman Catholic Church—National Conference of Catholic Bishops. Pres., Archbishop Joseph J. Bernardin. Sec., Bishop James S. Rausch, 1312 Massachusetts Ave. NW, Washington, D.C. 20005.

Romanian Orthodox Episcopate of America (1929)—Archbishop Valerian D. Trifa. Sec., Rev. Lawrence C. Lazar, 2522 Grey Tower Rd., Jackson, MI 49201.

Russian Orthodox Church Outside Russia (1920)—Pres., Council of Bishops, Most Rev. Metropolitan Philaret, 75 East 93rd St., N.Y., NY 10028.

Salvation Army, The (1865 in Eng., 1880 in America)—Natl. Cmdr., William E. Chamberlain. Natl. Chief Sec., Col. George Nelting. Natl. Hq., 120-130 W. 14th St., N.Y., NY 10011.

Seamen's Church Institute of N.Y. (1834)—Dir., Rev. John M. Mulligan. Sec., Alfred Lee Loomis 3d, 15 State St., N.Y., NY 10004.

Serbian Eastern Orthodox Church —Diocese for U.S., Canada and Europe. Bishops: Most Rev. Dionisije and Iriney. Sec., Very Rev. Aleksandar Ivanovich, St. Sava Monastery, Libertyville, IL 60048.

Serbian Eastern Orthodox Church in U.S. and Canada—Bishops: Rt. Rev. Bishop Firmilian, Midwest Diocese, 5701 N. Redwood Dr., Chicago, IL 60631. Rt. Rev. Gregory, Western Diocese, 2511 W. Garvey Ave., Alhambra, CA 91803. Rev. Sava, Eastern U.S. and Canadian Diocese, Way Hollow Rd., Edgeworth, PA 15143.

Synagogue Council of America—Pres., Joseph H. Lookstein. Exec. V.P., Rabbi Henry Siegman, 432 Park Ave. South, N.Y., NY 10016.

Ukrainian Orthodox Church of the U.S.A. (1919)—Metropolitan Most Rev. Mstyslav S. Skrypnyk, Box 495, South Bound Brook, NJ 08880.

Unitarian Universalist Assn. (formed 1961 by merger of the American Unitarian Assn. (1825) and the Universalist Church of America (1793)—Pres., Rev. Robert Nelson West. Moderator, Dr. Joseph L. Fisher. Sec., Russell F. Benson, 25 Beacon St., Boston, MA 02108

United Church of Christ (formed 1957 through union of the General Council of the Congregational Christian Churches with the Evangelical and Reformed Ch.)—Pres., Rev. Dr. Robert V. Moss Jr. Sec., Rev. Dr. Joseph H. Evans, 297 Park Ave. South, N.Y., NY 10010.

United Sons & Daughters of True Holiness Assn. (1912)—Gen. Sec., Elder B.W. Shoffner, 109 Daniel St., Greensboro, NC 27401.

United Synagogue of America—Pres., Arthur Levine. Exec. Vice Pres., Dr. Benjamin Z. Kreitman, 3080 Broadway, N.Y., NY 10027.

Volunteers of America (1896)—Commander-in-chief, Gen. John F. McMahon. Natl. Field Sec., Lt. Colonel Belle Leach. Hq., 340 West 85th St., N.Y., NY 10024.

Wesleyan Church, The (1968) (organized through the merger of the Pilgrim Holiness Ch. (1897) and the Wesleyan Methodist Ch. of America (1943)—Gen. Superintendents, Dr. Robert W. McIntyre, Dr. M.H. Snyder, Dr. J.D. Abbott, Dr. V.A. Mitchell. Sec., D. Wayne Brown, Box 2000, Marion, IN 46952.

Wisconsin Evangelical Lutheran Synod (1850)—Pres., Rev. Oscar Naumann, 3512 W. North Ave., Milwaukee, WI 53208. Sec., Prof. Heinrich J. Vogel, 11757 N. Seminary Drive 65W, Mequon, WI 53092.

World Council of Churches, U.S. Conference for the—Chmn., Dr. Robert J. Marshall. Exec. Sec., Rev. Charles H. Long Jr. 475 Riverside Dr., N.Y., NY 10027.

National Council of Churches

The National Council of the Churches of Christ in the U.S.A. is a cooperative federation of 30 Protestant and Orthodox churches which seeks to advance programs and policies of mutual interest to its members. The NCC was formed in 1950 by the merger of 12 inter-denominational agencies. The Council's member churches now have an aggregate membership totaling approximately 40 million. The NCC is not a governing body and has no control over the policies or operations of any church belonging to it. The work of the Council is divided into 3 divisions — Church and Society, Education and Ministry, Overseas Ministries, and 5 commissions on Faith and Order, Regional and Local Ecumenism, Communication, Stewardship, and Justice, Liberation, and Human Fulfillment. The chief administrative officer of the NCC is Dr. Claire Randall, 475 Riverside Drive, N.Y., NY 10027.

Leading Protestant Bodies in the U.S.

(For number of churches and total members, and address of headquarters, see preceding 4 pages)

Baptists

The Baptist church was formed in England in 1609 as part of the separatist movement from the Church of England.

The first Baptist Church in America was founded in 1638 in Providence, R.I., by Roger Williams. National organization began in 1814, and a Missionary Convention was formed to permit followers to express themselves in terms of missionary activities.

American Baptist Churches in the U.S.A. (formerly Northern Baptist Convention, renamed American Baptist Convention in 1950, and renamed American Baptist Churches in the U.S.A. in 1973) was organized in 1907. Agencies operating under this convention of Baptists include the American Baptist Board of International Ministries, American Baptist Board of National Ministries, American Baptist Board of Educational Ministries, and the Ministers and Missionaries Benefit Board, all at Valley Forge, Pa. 19481.

National Baptist Convention of America, organized 1880. Consists of the General Organization and 9 others; 1724 Jefferson St., Jacksonville, Fla. 32290.

National Baptist Convention, U.S.A., Inc., founded in 1880, in Montgomery, Ala., is the oldest and parent convention of Negro Baptists; 915 Spain St., Baton Rouge, La. 70802.

Southern Baptist Convention. In 1845 Southern Baptists withdrew from the General Missionary Convention over the question of slavery and other matters and formed the Southern Baptist Convention, largest of Baptist bodies. Churches in all 50 states are related to the Convention; 2,534 missionaries serve in 77 countries. Boards include Sunday Board, Nashville, Tenn.; Foreign Mission Board, Richmond, Va.; Home Mission Board, Atlanta, Ga.; Annuity Board, Dallas, Tex.

Church of Christ, Scientist

First organized in 1879, under the direction of Mary Baker Eddy, the Christian Science Church took its present form in 1892 as the Mother Church, the First Church of Christ, Scientist, in Boston, Mass. Today there are about 3,200 branches in 54 countries. There are 2,350 Christian Science churches in the U.S. Membership figures are not recorded. Christian Science regards the Bible as its ultimate authority and includes spiritual healing as part of its teachings.

The denomination supports radio and television programs, charitable institutions, and a world-wide Board of Lectureship. It also maintains the Christian Science Publishing Society which publishes the Christian Science Monitor and various religious periodicals. The affairs of the denomination are administered by the Christian Science Board of Directors, Christian Science Center, Boston, Mass. 02115.

Disciples of Christ

The Christian Church (Disciples of Christ) is an American communion arising out of a concern for Christian unity expressed by Barton W. Stone in 1804 and by Thomas Campbell and his son Alexander in 1809. The first churches were Cane Ridge in Kentucky and Brush Run near Washington, Pa. The "Christians" of Kentucky and the "Disciples" of Pennsylvania and Virginia united in 1832. The first General Convention was held in 1849. The church is thoroughly ecumenical in stance, and is congregational in government. Congregations in the U.S. and Canada number 4,524; membership is 1,312,326. The communion is served by the General Office of the Christian Church (Disciples of Christ), 17 general units, 37 regional bodies, and 32 educational institutions.

Evangelical Churches

The Evangelical and Reformed Church. See *United Church of Christ.*

The Evangelical United Brethren Church. See *United Methodist Church.*

Latter-Day Saints

The churches of the Latter-Day Saints do not consider themselves Protestants because they had no part in the 16th century Protestant Reformation and consider themselves to be the "restored" Church of Jesus Christ.

The Church of Jesus Christ of Latter-Day Saints, often called the "Mormon" church, regards the Bible, the Book of Mormon, the Doctrine and Covenants, and the Pearl of Great Price as the word of God. The church was organized Apr. 6, 1830, at Fayette, N.Y., by Joseph Smith, first president. After settling in Kirtland, Oh., and Independence, Mo., the members located in Nauvoo, Ill., in 1839 to escape persecution. Attacks by a mob led to the fatal shooting of Joseph Smith and his brother Hyrum while they were in the Carthage, Ill., jail for protection from the mob, Jun. 27, 1844. Beginning in 1847 most members, under the leadership of Brigham Young, moved by covered wagons across the Great Plains to Utah.

The church is divided into stakes, wards, branches, and missions. Highest authority is the First Presidency, consisting of the president and 2 counselors, assisted by 12 apostles. Spencer W. Kimball is the 12th and current president.

The Reorganized Church of Jesus Christ of Latter-Day Saints was founded Apr. 6, 1830, by Joseph Smith Jr. and reorganized under the leadership of the founder's son, Joseph Smith 3d, in 1860. The church is established in 25 countries, the U.S., and Canada.

Lutherans

The church was started in Europe during the Protestant Reformation by the followers of Martin Luther.

Lutheranism was introduced into the U.S. by Dutch colonists on Manhattan, later by Swedes on the Delaware, by Palatines in Pennsylvania and New York, and by Salzburgers in Georgia.

The American Lutheran Church was organized during a constituting convention at Minneapolis, Minn., in Apr. 1960, merging the American Lutheran Church, The Evangelical Lutheran Church, and United Evangelical Lutheran Church. The merger brought together Lutherans of Danish, German, and Norwegian heritage. A fourth body, The Lutheran Free Church, joined with The American Lutheran Church in Feb. 1963. The 4,822 congregations are divided territorially into districts in the U.S. The foreign mission program involves 424 missionaries (including wives) on 13 fields in South America, Africa, and Asia. The church's Board of Publication operates the Augsburg Publishing House, 422 S. 5th St., Minneapolis, Minn. 55415.

Augustana Evangelical Lutheran Church. See *The Lutheran Church in America.*

The Lutheran Church-Missouri Synod was organized in 1847. It is the leader in the conservative group among the Lutherans. The Synod is divided into 40 districts (35 in the U.S., 3 in Canada, 2 in South America). The Synod conducts a world-wide mission program and fosters a system of 16 ministerial and teacher training colleges to staff its congregations and its 1,239 parochial schools. Affiliated are the Lutheran Laymen's League, Lutheran Women's Missionary League, and Walther League (a young people's organization). Valparaiso University, Valparaiso, Ind., is supported and controlled by the Lutheran University Assn. Hq. for the Synod: 500 N. Broadway, St. Louis, Mo. 63102.

The **Lutheran Church in America** was organized Jun. 28, 1962, by the consolidation of the American Evangelical Lutheran Church, the Augustana Evangelical Lutheran Church, the Finnish Evangelical Lutheran Church and the United Lutheran Church in America. The body is the largest of the Lutheran churches in the U.S. The Lutheran Church in America is organized in 33 synods in the U.S., Canada, Puerto Rico, and the Virgin Islands. Several agencies are located at 2900 Queen Lane, Philadelphia, Pa.; 327 South LaSalle St., Chicago, Ill.; and 608 Second Ave. S., 2d floor, Minneapolis, Minn.

Wisconsin Evangelical Lutheran Synod was organized in 1850. Formerly the second largest body of the Synodical conference, Wisconsin withdrew from the Conference in Aug. 1963.

Methodists

The name Methodist was originally given to Charles and John Wesley and several other Oxford students in 1729. It is thought that the term was selected due to the exact and "methodical" manner in which they performed various engagements which a sense of Christian duty induced them to undertake. The Methodist movement was carried to America in 1760, by emigrants from Ireland.

The United Methodist Church was formed Apr. 23, 1968, in Dallas, Tex., by the union of The Methodist Church and The Evangelical United Brethren Church. The two churches shared a common historical and spiritual heritage. The Methodist Church resulted in 1939 from the unification of 3 branches of Methodism — the Methodist Episcopal Church, the Methodist Episcopal Church, South, and the Methodist Protestant Church. The Methodist movement began in 18th century England under the preaching of John Wesley, but the so-called Christmas Conference of 1784 in Baltimore is regarded as the date on which the organized Methodist Church was founded as an ecclesiastical organization. It was there that Francis Asbury was elected the first bishop in this country. The Evangelical United Brethren Church was formed in 1946 with the merger of the Evangelical Church and the Church of the United Brethren in Christ, both of which had their beginnings in Pennsylvania in the evangelistic movement of the 18th and early 19th centuries. Philip William Otterbein and Jacob Albright were early leaders of this movement among German-speaking settlers of the Middle Colonies.

The supreme policy-making body of The United Methodist Church is the quadrennial General Conference. Principal agencies are in the following cities: New York, N.Y.; Evanston, Ill.; Nashville, Tenn.; Washington, D. C.; Dayton, Oh.; and Lake Janaluska, N.C.

African Methodist Episcopal Church, incorporated 1816 under Pennsylvania laws, is second largest of the Methodist bodies. Churches, 4,500, membership, 1,500,000. Pres., Board of Bishops, Bishop Hubert N. Robinson, 951 Old Grove Manor, Jacksonville, Fla. 32207.

Presbyterians

Presbyterianism is a system of representative churches governed by presbyters, or elders. John Calvin (1509-1564) has been regarded as the founder of Presbyterianism. Presbyterians were among the earliest colonists of America. Their first church was established about 1640 and the first presbytery in 1706.

The United Presbyterian Church in the U.S.A., largest of the Presbyterian bodies, was formed on May 28, 1958, by a merger of the Presbyterian Church in the U.S.A. and the United Presbyterian Church of North America. Offices of the General assembly, General Assembly's Mission Council, Support Agency, Program Agency, and Vocations Agency are at 475 Riverside Dr., N.Y., N.Y. 10027.

Presbyterian Church in the United States, which established a separate existence in 1861, is sometimes miscalled the Southern church.

Protestant Episcopal Church

An American religious denomination directly descended from the Church of England. Brought to America by the Jamestown colonists in 1607. Separated from English Church and adopted present name in 1789. Alternate name, "The Episcopal Church," was adopted in 1967.

United Church of Christ

Formed in 1957 by a union of the General Council of the Congregational Christian Church and the Evangelical and Reformed Church. It was the first union in the United States of churches with different forms of church government — congregational and modified presbyterian — and different historical backgrounds. Congregationalism was brought to America by both the Pilgrims of the "Mayflower" and the Puritans of the Massachusetts Bay Colony. Eventually it became the dominant form of church organization in New England. The Evangelical and Reformed Church was started in 1934 with the union of the Evangelical Synod of North America and the Reformed Church in the U.S.

A constitution for the United Church of Christ was declared in force in July 1961. The United Church Board of World Ministries has 251 missionaries and other personnel at work in 30 countries. In the U. S., the United Church of Christ is active in Christian education, church extension, health and welfare, mass communication, race relations, and social action. United Church Board for Homeland Ministries, 287 Park Ave., S., N.Y., N.Y. 10010. United Church Board for World Ministries, 475 Riverside Dr., N.Y., N.Y. 10027.

Leading Protestant Denominations in Canada

Source: Yearbook of American and Canadian Churches and Ontario Bible College

Anglicans

The Anglican Church of Canada was established in the early 1700s, and its first bishop Charles Inglis was appointed in 1787. The General Synod, created in 1893, acts to co-ordinate the various activities of the Church, and usually meets biennially. It is made up of the Church's archbishops and bishops together with the elected clerical and lay representatives from the 28 dioceses and one Episcopal district. The Anglican Church has 1,704 churches, and an inclusive membership of 1,063,199 (1972).

Baptists

The two largest Baptist churches are the Federation of Canada and the Fellowship of Evangelical Baptist Churches. The Federation has about 667,245 (1971) members in 4 subdivisions: the Baptist Convention of Ontario and Quebec; the Baptist Union of Western Canada; the United Baptist Convention of the Atlantic Provinces; and the French Baptist Union. Other large Baptist organizations are the Baptist General Conference, the North American Baptist Conference, and the Canadian Southern Baptist Conference.

Lutherans

The first large settlement of Lutherans in Canada was in Halifax in 1749. There are 3 main Lutheran bodies: the Evangelical Lutheran Church of Canada, the Lutheran Church-Canada (Missouri Synod), and the Lutheran Church in America-Canada Section. These bodies cooperate through the Lutheran Council in Canada. The Lutheran churches of Canada have 715,740 (1971) members.

Presbyterians

The Presbyterian Church in Canada is connected historically to the Church of Scotland. It is organized into 8 synods and 44 presbyteries, and has a membership of 872,335 (1971).

United Church

The United Church of Canada is the largest Protestant denomination in Canada with an inclusive membership of 962,163. It was established in 1925 as a result of a merger among the Methodist Church, the Congregational Churches, and 70% of the Presbyterian Church. The Canada Conference of the Evangelical United Brethren Church joined this union in 1968. The highest policy-making body of the United Church of Canada is the General Council which meets biennially.

Headquarters of Religious Bodies in Canada

Source: The 1976 Corpus Almanac of Canada and The 1976 Canadian Almanac and Directory.
(Year organized in parentheses)

Anglican Church of Canada (creation of General Synod 1893) — Primate, Most Rev. E. W. Scott, Gen. Sec. of the General Synod, The Ven. E.S. Light, 600 Jarvis St., Toronto, Ontario, M4Y 216.

Antiochian Orthodox Christian Church (Syrian) — Rev. Father E. Hanna, 555-575 Jean Talon E., Montreal H2R 1T8.

Apostolic Church in Canada — H. O. 27 Castlefield Avenue, Toronto, Ontario M4R 1G3, Pres., Rev. D.S. Morris, 388 Gerald St., La Salle, P.Q.

Apostolic Church of Pentecost of Canada (Inc. 1921) — H.O. 4-3026 Taylor St., E., Saskatoon, Saskatchewan S7J 4J2. Mod. Rev. D.W. Breen, 14447-104A Ave., Surrey B.C.

Associated Gospel Churches (1922) — Pres., Rev. L.K. Redinger, Sec.-Treas., Rev. J.L. Hockney, 280 Plains Rd. W., Burlington, Ontario L7T 1G4.

Association of Regular Baptist Churches (Canada) — Pres., Dr. H.C. Slade, 337 Jarvis St., Toronto, Ont. M5B 2C7.

Baha'is of Canada, The National Spiritual Assembly of the (1949) — Gen. Sec. J.D. Martin, 7200 Leslie St., Thornhill, Ont. L3T 2A1.

Baptist Federation of Canada — Pres. David Simmonds, Gen. Sec.-Treasurer, Rev. R. Fred Bullen, 91 Queen St., Box 1298, Brantford, Ontario, N3T 3B7.

Bible Holiness Movement, The (1949) — Pres. Evangelist Wesley H. Wakefield, Box 223, Stn. A, Vancouver V6C 2M3.

Brethren in Christ Church, Canada Conference — Mod. Bishop R.V. Sider, Box 65, Sherkston, Ontario.

British Israel World Federation — Office Manager and Secretary, Mrs. S. Cunningham, 313 Sherbourne St., Toronto 2, Ontario.

Buddhist Churches of Canada (1945) — Bishop, Rev. Newton Ishiura, 918 Bathurst St., Toronto, Ontario.

Byelorussian Autocephalic Orthodox Church Abroad — Rt. Rev. Bishop Mikalay, 524 St. Clarens Ave., Toronto M6H 3W7, Ontario.

Canadian Council of Churches, The (1938) — Pres. Rev. Dr. Norman Berner, 40 St. Clair Ave. E., Toronto M4T 1M9.

Canadian Jewish Congress (1919) — Exec. Vice-Pres., Saul Hayes, Q.C., 1590 McGregor Ave., Montreal 109, Quebec.

Canadian Unitarian Church (1842) — Pres. Mrs. Elaine Royer. Admin. Sec. Ms. B.C. Arnott, Canadian Unitarian Council, 175 St. Clair Ave. West, Toronto M4V 1P7.

Christian and Missionary Alliance in Canada, The (1889) — 2026 Yonge St., Toronto, Ontario, M4S 1Z9; Pres., Rev. W.J. Newell, 125 Panin Rd., Burlington, Ontario L7T 1N0.

Christian Church (Disciples of Christ) (All Canada Committee formed 1922) — Pres. Mervin Bailey, Exc. Min. Robert K. Leland; 39 Arkell Rd., R.R. 2, Guelph, Ont., N1H 6H8.

Christian Reformed Churches, The Canadian Council of — Rev. John Van Harmelen, R.R. 8, London, Ont.

Christian Science in Canada — Mr. J.D. Fulton, 696 Yonge St., Ste. 403, Toronto, Ont. M4Y 2A7.

Church Army in Canada, The — Dir. Capt. R.A. Taylor, 397 Brunswick Ave., Toronto, Ont. M5R 2Z2.

Church of Jesus Christ of Latter Day Saints (Mormons), (1830) — Pres. Calgary Stake, L.D. Hanks, 531 Willowbrook Dr. S.E., Calgary, Alta. Pres., Edmonton Stake, Warren S. Wilde, 5108-112 St. Edmonton, Alta. T6H 3J2. Pres., Toronto Stake, J.B. Smith, 79 Alpaca Dr., Scarborough, Ont. Pres., Vancouver Stake, F.E. Berrett, 606 Hawstead Pl., West Vancouver, B.C.

Church of the Nazarene (1902) — Dist. Superintendent of Canada Central District, Rev. N. Hightower, 38 Riverhead Drive, Rexdale, Ont.; Chairman of Exec. Board, Dr. Herman L.G. Smith, 2236 Capitol Hill Crescent, N.W., Calgary, Alta. T2M 4B9.

Evangelical Mennonite Brethren Conference — Mod., Rev. Sam Hepp, 33573 Lynn Ave., Abbotsford, B.C., Mod., H. Kornelsen, R.R. 1, Giroux, Man. R0A 0N0.

Fellowship of Evangelical Baptist Churches in Canada (merging of Union of Regular Baptist Churches of Ontario and Quebec, and Fellowship of Independent Baptist Churches) (1953) — Gen. Sec., Dr. J.H. Watt, 74 Sheppard Ave. W., Willowdale, Ontario.

Free Methodist Church in Canada (1880) — Pres., Bishop D.N. Bastian. Sec., Rev. E.A. Bull, 40 Glen Rd., Belleville, Ont. K8P 4G1.

Gospel Missionary Union of Canada — Sec., Rev. John Harder, 132 High Park Ave., Toronto, Ont. M6P 2S4.

Greek Orthodox Church — Ninth Archdiocese District, Canada, Titular Bishop of Constantia, His Grace Sotirios, 27 Teddington Park Ave., Toronto M4N 2C4.

Independent Holiness Church (merger of former Holiness Movement of Canada with The Free Methodist Church in 1958) — Pres., Rev. R.E. Votary. H.O. 72 Queen St. E., Wellesley, Ontario N0B 2T0.

Italian Pentecostal Church of Canada, The (Incorp. 1959) — Gen. Supt. Rev. D. Ippolito, 384 Sunnyside Ave., Toronto M6R ZS1.

Jehovah's Witnesses (Branch Office established in Winnipeg 1918) — Branch Overseer, Mr. Kenneth A. Little, 150 Bridgeland Ave., Toronto, Ontario M6A 1Z5.

Lutheran Church of Canada, The Evangelical — Pres., Dr. S.T. Jacobson, 212 Wiggins Ave., Saskatoon, Sask. S7N 1K4.

Lutheran Church-Canada (1959) — Pres., Rev. Louis Scholl, 3500 Askin, Windsor, Ont. N9E 3J9.

Lutheran Church in America — Canada Section — Pres., Rev. Donald W. Stoberg, 9901 - 107 St., Edmonton, Alberta T5K 1G4.

Lutheran Council in Canada — a joint body of the three main churches, Pres. Roger Nostibakken, Gen. Sec. Rev. Earl J. Treusch, 500-365 Hargrave St., Winnipeg R3B 2K3.

Mennonite Brethren Churches of North America, Canadian Conference (Inc. 1945) — 159 Henderson Hwy., Winnipeg, Manitoba R2L 1L4; Mod. Herbert J.

Brandt, 1020 No. 5 Rd., Richmond, B.C.

Mennonites in Canada, Conference of — Moderator, Jake Harms, 767 Buckingham Rd., Winnipeg, Man. R3R 1C3.

Mennonite Church, The (Old) — First Mennonite Church, Chmn., Newton L. Gingrich, Tavistock, Ont. N0B.

Missionary Church, The — (an Anabaptist body) — Dist. Supt. (Ontario) Rev. Grant Sloss, Ste. 203, Frederick St. Plaza, Kitchener, Ont. N2H 2P2.

Moravian Church in America, Northern Province, Canadian District of the — Pres., and Corr. Sec., D.H. Laverty, 5719-114A St., Edmonton, Alberta T6H 3M8.

Old German Baptist Brethren in Canada — c/o Elder Amos Baker, Gormley, Ont.

Northern Canada Evangelical Mission — 58 18th St., Prince Albert, Sask.

Overseas Missionary Fellowship (1865) — Gen. Dr., Mr. Michael C. Griffiths, 1058 Avenue Road, Toronto M5N 2C6, Ontario.

Pentecostal Assemblies of Canada, The (incorporated 1919) — Gen. Supt., Rev. Robert W. Taitinger, 10 Overlea Blvd., Toronto, Ontario M4H 1A5.

Pentecostal Holiness Church in Canada — Gen. Supt., Rev. G.H. Nunn, 4 Hobart Dr. S., Willowdale, Ont. M2J 2J5.

Polish National Catholic Church of Canada (1967) — The Rt. Rev. Joseph Nieminski, Bishop of the Canadian Diocese, 186 Cowan Ave., Toronto, Ont. M6K 2N6.

Presbyterian Church in Canada, The (1875) — 50 Wynford Dr., Don Mills, Ont.; Moderator, Rev. David W. Hay. Treasurer, R. R. Merifield, Q.C. Victoria and Grey Trust, 197 Bay St., Toronto, Ont. Clerks of the Gen. Assembly; Rev. D.C. MacDonald, Rev. E.H. Bean, Rev. D.B. Lowry.

Religious Society of Friends (Quakers), (Canadian Yearly Meeting of the Religious Society of Friends formed 1955) — Presiding Clerk, Burton Hill, Box 33, Rockwood, Ont.; Secretary of Yearly Meeting, Ms. Dorothy Muma, 60 Lowther Ave., Toronto M5R 1C7, Ont.

Reorganized Church of Jesus Christ of Latter Day Saints, The (1830) — P.O. Box 38, Guelph, Ontario N1H 6J6.

Roman Catholic Church in Canada — Apostolic Pro Nuncio, His Excellency the Most Reverend Guido Del Mestri, Apostolic Nunciature, 724 Manor Ave., Rockcliffe Park, Ottawa, Ontario K1M 0E3.

Salvation Army, The (1882) — Territorial Commander, Commissioner Arnold Brown, 20 Albert St., Toronto, Ontario M5G 1A6.

Seventh-day Adventist Church in Canada — Pres., L.L. Reile, 1148 King St. E., Oshawa, Ontario L1H 1H8.

Ukrainian Greek Orthodox Church in Canada — Primate, Rev. Archbishop Andrew Presidium, Chmn., V. Rev. D. Luchak, 9 St. John's Ave., Winnipeg, Manitoba R2W 0T9.

Union of Spiritual Communities of Christ (Orthodox Doukhobors in Canada) (1938) — Honorary Chmn. of the Exec. Comm., John J. Verigin, Box 760, Grand Forks, B.C.

Unitarian Church, Canadian (1842) — Pres. Mrs. Elaine Royer; Admin. Sec. Ms. Barbara C. Arnott, Canadian Unitarian Council, 175 St. Clair Ave. W., Toronto M4V 1P7.

United Church of Canada, The (1925) — Mod. Rt. Rev. Wilbur K. Howard; Sec. of General Council, Rev. G. Morrison, 85 St. Clair Ave. E., Toronto, Ontario M4T 1M8.

Protestant Episcopal Calendar and Altar Colors

White — from the First Service (First Vespers) of Christmas Day to the Octave of Epiphany, inclusive (except on the Feasts of Martyrs); on Maundy Thursday (for the celebration); from the First Service of Easter Day to the Vigil of Pentecost (except on Feasts of Martyrs and Rogation Days); on Trinity Sunday, Conversion of St. Paul, Purification, Annunciation, St. John Baptist, St. Michael, All Saints, Saints not Martyrs, and Patron Saints (Transfiguration and Dedication of Church).

Red — from First Vespers of Pentecost to the First Vespers of Trinity Sunday (which includes Ember Days); Holy Innocents, and Feasts of all Martyrs, Apostles and Evangelists.

Violet — from Septuagesima to Maundy Thursday; Easter Even; Advent Sunday to Christmas Eve, Vigils, Ember Days (except in Whitsun Week); and Rogation Days.

An alternate Lenten color scheme: **Violet** — from Septuagesima to the Tuesday before Ash Wednesday; **Lenten White** — from Ash Wednesday to the Saturday after Fourth Lent; and **Crimson** — from Passion Sunday (Fifth Lent) to Easter Even (all inclusive).

Black — Good Friday and at funerals. **Green** — all other days.

Days, Etc.	1975	1976	1977	1978	1979	1980
Golden Number..............................	0	1	2	3	4	5
Sunday Letter.............................	E	DC	B	A	G	FE
Sundays after Epiphany...................	2	5	4	2	5	3
Septuagesima*.............................	Jan. 26	Feb. 14	Feb. 6	Jan. 22	Feb. 11	Feb. 3
Ash Wednesday............................	Feb. 12	Mar. 3	Feb. 23	Feb. 8	Feb. 28	Feb. 20
First Sunday in Lent......................	Feb. 16	Mar. 7	Feb. 27	Feb. 12	Mar. 4	Feb. 24
Passion Sunday*...........................	Mar. 16	Apr. 4	Mar. 27	Mar. 12	Apr. 1	Mar. 23
Palm Sunday..............................	Mar. 23	Apr. 11	Apr. 3	Mar. 19	Apr. 8	Mar. 30
Good Friday...............................	Mar. 28	Apr. 16	Apr. 8	Mar. 24	Apr. 13	Apr. 4
Easter Day................................	Mar. 30	Apr. 18	Apr. 10	Mar. 26	Apr. 15	Apr. 6
Rogation Sunday*.........................	May 4	May 23	May 15	Apr. 30	May 20	May 11
Ascension Day............................	May 8	May 27	May 19	May 4	May 24	May 15
Whitsunday...............................	May 18	Jun. 6	May 29	May 14	Jun. 3	May 18
Trinity Sunday............................	May 25	Jun. 13	Jun. 5	May 21	Jun. 10	May 25
Sundays after Trinity**...................	26	23	24	27	24	25
First Sunday in Advent....................	Nov. 30	Nov. 28	Nov. 27	Dec. 3	Dec. 2	Nov. 30

In the Protestant Episcopal Church the days of fasting are Ash Wednesday and Good Friday. Other days of abstinence are the 40 days of Lent, the Ember Days, and all Fridays of the year except Christmas Day and the Epiphany and any Friday which may fall between them. Ember Days (12 annually at about the beginning of the four seasons) are days of abstinence and prayer for ordinands and the increase of the ministry. They fall on the Wednesday, Friday, and Saturday after the first Sunday in Lent, the Feast of Pentecost (Whitsunday), Sept. 14, and Dec. 13. Rogation Days are the three days from Rogation Sunday (the fifth after Easter) to Ascension Day, and are days of solemn supplication for God's blessing upon the fields and harvests of the world.

The Episcopal Church is studying, and trying out, a revised calendar of the Church Year. If adopted, the following changes in the foregoing list will obtain: *These Sundays will no longer be observed. **This listing will carry the title "Sundays after Pentecost"

Ash Wednesday and Easter Sunday

Year	Ash Wed.	Easter Sunday	Year	Ash Wed.	Easter Sunday	Year	Ash Wed.	Easter Sunday	Year	Ash Wed.	Easter Sunday
1901	Feb. 20	Apr. 7	1951	Feb. 7	Mar. 25	2001	Feb. 28	Apr. 15	2051	Feb. 15	Apr. 2
1902	Feb. 12	Mar. 30	1952	Feb. 27	Apr. 13	2002	Feb. 13	Mar. 31	2052	Mar. 6	Apr. 21
1903	Feb. 25	Apr. 12	1953	Feb. 18	Apr. 5	2003	Mar. 5	Apr. 20	2053	Feb. 19	Apr. 6
1904	Feb. 17	Apr. 3	1954	Mar. 3	Apr. 18	2004	Feb. 25	Apr. 11	2054	Feb. 11	Mar. 29
1905	Mar. 8	Apr. 23	1955	Feb. 23	Apr. 10	2005	Feb. 9	Mar. 27	2055	Mar. 3	Apr. 18
1906	Feb. 28	Apr. 15	1956	Feb. 15	Apr. 1	2006	Mar. 1	Apr. 16	2056	Feb. 16	Apr. 2
1907	Feb. 13	Mar. 31	1957	Mar. 6	Apr. 21	2007	Feb. 21	Apr. 8	2057	Mar. 7	Apr. 22
1908	Mar. 4	Apr. 19	1958	Feb. 19	Apr. 6	2008	Feb. 6	Mar. 23	2058	Feb. 27	Apr. 14
1909	Feb. 24	Apr. 11	1959	Feb. 11	Mar. 29	2009	Feb. 25	Apr. 12	2059	Feb. 12	Mar. 30
1910	Feb. 9	Mar. 27	1960	Mar. 2	Apr. 17	2010	Feb. 17	Apr. 4	2060	Mar. 3	Apr. 18
1911	Mar. 1	Apr. 16	1961	Feb. 15	Apr. 2	2011	Mar. 9	Apr. 24	2061	Feb. 23	Apr. 10
1912	Feb. 21	Apr. 7	1962	Mar. 7	Apr. 22	2012	Feb. 22	Apr. 8	2062	Feb. 8	Mar. 26
1913	Feb. 5	Mar. 23	1963	Feb. 27	Apr. 14	2013	Feb. 13	Mar. 31	2063	Feb. 28	Apr. 15
1914	Feb. 25	Apr. 12	1964	Feb. 12	Mar. 29	2014	Mar. 5	Apr. 20	2064	Feb. 20	Apr. 6
1915	Feb. 17	Apr. 4	1965	Mar. 3	Apr. 18	2015	Feb. 18	Apr. 5	2065	Feb. 11	Mar. 29
1916	Mar. 8	Apr. 23	1966	Feb. 23	Apr. 10	2016	Feb. 10	Mar. 27	2066	Feb. 24	Apr. 11
1917	Feb. 21	Apr. 8	1967	Feb. 8	Mar. 26	2017	Mar. 1	Apr. 16	2067	Feb. 16	Apr. 3
1918	Feb. 13	Mar. 31	1968	Feb. 28	Apr. 14	2018	Feb. 14	Apr. 1	2068	Mar. 7	Apr. 22
1919	Mar. 5	Apr. 20	1969	Feb. 19	Apr. 6	2019	Mar. 6	Apr. 21	2069	Feb. 27	Apr. 14
1920	Feb. 18	Apr. 4	1970	Feb. 11	Mar. 29	2020	Feb. 26	Apr. 12	2070	Feb. 12	Mar. 30
1921	Feb. 9	Mar. 27	1971	Feb. 24	Apr. 11	2021	Feb. 17	Apr. 4	2071	Mar. 4	Apr. 19
1922	Mar. 1	Apr. 16	1972	Feb. 16	Apr. 2	2022	Mar. 2	Apr. 17	2072	Feb. 24	Apr. 10
1923	Feb. 14	Apr. 1	1973	Mar. 7	Apr. 22	2023	Feb. 22	Apr. 9	2073	Mar. 8	Apr. 23
1924	Mar. 5	Apr. 20	1974	Feb. 27	Apr. 14	2024	Feb. 14	Mar. 31	2074	Feb. 28	Apr. 15
1925	Feb. 25	Apr. 12	1975	Feb. 12	Mar. 30	2025	Mar. 5	Apr. 20	2075	Feb. 20	Apr. 7
1926	Feb. 17	Apr. 4	1976	Mar. 3	Apr. 18	2026	Feb. 18	Apr. 5	2076	Mar. 4	Apr. 19
1927	Mar. 2	Apr. 17	1977	Feb. 23	Apr. 10	2027	Feb. 10	Mar. 28	2077	Feb. 24	Apr. 11
1928	Feb. 22	Apr. 8	1978	Feb. 8	Mar. 26	2028	Mar. 1	Apr. 16	2078	Feb. 16	Apr. 3
1929	Feb. 13	Mar. 31	1979	Feb. 28	Apr. 15	2029	Feb. 14	Apr. 1	2079	Mar. 8	Apr. 23
1930	Mar. 5	Apr. 20	1980	Feb. 20	Apr. 6	2030	Mar. 6	Apr. 21	2080	Feb. 21	Apr. 7
1931	Feb. 18	Apr. 5	1981	Mar. 4	Apr. 19	2031	Feb. 26	Apr. 13	2081	Feb. 12	Mar. 30
1932	Feb. 10	Mar. 27	1982	Feb. 24	Apr. 11	2032	Feb. 11	Mar. 28	2082	Mar. 4	Apr. 19
1933	Mar. 1	Apr. 16	1983	Feb. 16	Apr. 3	2033	Mar. 2	Apr. 17	2083	Feb. 17	Apr. 4
1934	Feb. 14	Apr. 1	1984	Mar. 7	Apr. 22	2034	Feb. 22	Apr. 9	2084	Mar. 9	Apr. 24
1935	Mar. 6	Apr. 21	1985	Feb. 20	Apr. 7	2035	Feb. 7	Mar. 25	2085	Feb. 28	Apr. 15
1936	Feb. 26	Apr. 12	1986	Feb. 12	Mar. 30	2036	Feb. 27	Apr. 13	2086	Feb. 13	Mar. 31
1937	Feb. 10	Mar. 28	1987	Mar. 4	Apr. 19	2037	Feb. 18	Apr. 5	2087	Mar. 5	Apr. 20
1938	Mar. 2	Apr. 17	1988	Feb. 17	Apr. 3	2038	Mar. 10	Apr. 25	2088	Feb. 25	Apr. 11
1939	Feb. 22	Apr. 9	1989	Feb. 8	Mar. 26	2039	Feb. 23	Apr. 10	2089	Feb. 16	Apr. 3
1940	Feb. 7	Mar. 24	1990	Feb. 28	Apr. 15	2040	Feb. 15	Apr. 1	2090	Mar. 1	Apr. 16
1941	Feb. 26	Apr. 13	1991	Feb. 13	Mar. 31	2041	Mar. 6	Apr. 21	2091	Feb. 21	Apr. 8
1942	Feb. 18	Apr. 5	1992	Mar. 4	Apr. 19	2042	Feb. 19	Apr. 6	2092	Feb. 13	Mar. 30
1943	Mar. 10	Apr. 25	1993	Feb. 24	Apr. 11	2043	Feb. 11	Mar. 29	2093	Feb. 25	Apr. 12
1944	Feb. 23	Apr. 9	1994	Feb. 16	Apr. 3	2044	Mar. 2	Apr. 17	2094	Feb. 17	Apr. 4
1945	Feb. 14	Apr. 1	1995	Mar. 1	Apr. 16	2045	Feb. 22	Apr. 9	2095	Mar. 9	Apr. 24
1946	Mar. 6	Apr. 21	1996	Feb. 21	Apr. 7	2046	Feb. 7	Mar. 25	2096	Feb. 29	Apr. 15
1947	Feb. 19	Apr. 6	1997	Feb. 12	Mar. 30	2047	Feb. 27	Apr. 14	2097	Feb. 13	Mar. 31
1948	Feb. 11	Mar. 28	1998	Feb. 25	Apr. 12	2048	Feb. 19	Apr. 5	2098	Mar. 5	Apr. 20
1949	Mar. 2	Apr. 17	1999	Feb. 17	Apr. 4	2049	Mar. 3	Apr. 18	2099	Feb. 25	Apr. 12
1950	Feb. 22	Apr. 9	2000	Mar. 8	Apr. 23	2050	Feb. 23	Apr. 10	2100	Feb. 10	Mar. 28

A lengthy dispute over the date for the celebration of Easter was settled by the first Council of the Christian Churches at Nicaea, in Asia Minor, in 325 A.D. The Council ruled that Easter would be observed on the first Sunday following the 14th day of the Paschal Moon, referred to as the Paschal Full Moon. The Paschal Moon is the first moon whose 14th day comes on or after March 21. Dates of the Paschal Full Moon, which are not necessarily the same as those of the real or astronomical full moon, are listed in the table below with an explanation of how to compute the date of Easter.

If the Paschal Full Moon falls on a Sunday, then Easter is the following Sunday. The earliest date on which Easter can fall is March 22; it fell on that date in 1761 and 1818 but will not do so in the 20th or 21st century. The latest possible date for Easter is April 25; it fell on that date in 1943 and will again in 2038.

For western churches Lent begins on Ash Wednesday, which comes about 40 days before Easter Sunday, not counting Sundays. Originally it was a period of but 40 hours. Later it comprised 30 days of fasting, omitting all the Sundays and also all the Saturdays except one. Pope Gregory (590-604), added Ash Wednesday to the fast, together with the remainder of that week.

The last seven days of Lent constitute Holy Week, beginning with Palm Sunday. The last Thursday — Maundy Thursday — commemorates the institution of the Eucharist. The following day, Good Friday, commemorates the day of the Crucifixion.

Easter is the chief festival of the Christian year, commemorating the Resurrection of Christ. It occurs about the same time as the ancient Roman celebration of the Vernal Equinox, the arrival of spring. In the second century, A.D., Easter Day among Christians in Asia Minor was the 14th Nisan, the seventh month of the Jewish calendar. The Christians in Europe observed the nearest Sunday.

Date of Paschal Full Moon, 1900-2199

The Golden Number, used in determining the date of Easter, is greater by unity (one) than the remainder obtained upon dividing the given year by 19. For example, when dividing 1977 by 19, one obtains a remainder of 1. Adding 1 gives 2 as the Golden Number for the year 1977. From the table then the date of the Paschal Full Moon is Apr. 3, 1977. This being a Sunday, the date of Easter is the following Sunday Apr. 10.

Golden Number	Date	Golden Number	Date	Golden Number	Date	Golden Number	Date
1	April 14	6	Apr. 18	11	Mar. 25	16	Mar. 30
2	Apr. 3	7	Apr. 8	12	Apr. 13	17	Apr. 17
3	Mar. 23	8	Mar. 28	13	Apr. 2	18	Apr. 7
4	Apr. 11	9	Apr. 16	14	Mar. 22	19	Mar. 27
5	Mar. 31	10	Apr. 5	15	Apr. 10		

Jewish Holy Days, Festivals, and Fasts

Source: Synagogue Council of America

All Jewish holy days, etc., begin at sunset on the day previous. *Also observed the following day.

+Hebrew date varies to avoid conflict with Sabbath.

Festivals and Fasts	Hebrew Date	1976-1977 (5737)	1977-1978 (5738)	1978-1979 (5739)	1979-1980 (5740)
Rosh Hashana (New Year)*	Tishri 1	Sept. 25 Sa	Sept. 13 Tu	Oct. 2 Mo	Sept. 22 Sa
Fast of Gedalia	Tishri 3	Sept. 27 Mo	Sept. 15 Th	Oct. 4 We	Sept. 24 Mo
Fast of Gedalia	Tishri 4				
Yom Kippur (Day of Atonement)	Tishri 10	Oct. 4 Mo	Sept. 22 Th	Oct. 11 We	Oct. 1 Mo
Sukkoth (Feast of Tabernacles), 1st Day*	Tishri 15	Oct. 9 Sa	Sept. 27 Tu	Oct. 16 Mo	Oct. 6 Sa
Sukkoth, 8th Day (Shemini Atzereth)	Tishri 22	Oct. 16 Sa	Oct. 4 Tu	Oct. 23 Mo	Oct. 13 Sa
Simchat Torah (Rejoicing of the Law)	Tishri 23	Oct. 17 Su	Oct. 5 We	Oct. 24 Tu	Oct. 14 Su
Chanukah (Feast of Lights)	Kislev 25	Dec. 17 Fr	Dec. 5 Mo	Dec. 25 Mo	Dec. 15 Sa
Fast of Tebet+	Tebet 10	Dec. 31 Fr	Dec. 20 Tu	Jan. 9 Tu	Dec. 30 Su
Fast of Esther+	Adar 13	Mar. 3 Th		Mar. 12 Mo	
Fast of Esther+	Adar II 13		Mar. 22 We		Feb. 28 Th
Purium (Feast of Lots)	Adar 14	Mar. 4 Fr		Mar. 13 Tu	Mar. 2 Su
Purim	Adar II 14		Mar. 23 Tu		
Pesach (Passover), 1st Day*	Nisan 15	Apr. 3 Su	Apr. 22 Sa	Apr. 12 Th	Apr. 1 Tu
Pesach, 7th Day*	Nisan 21	Apr. 9 Sa	Apr. 28 Fr	Apr. 18 We	Apr. 7 Mo
Lag B'Omer	Iyar 18	May 6 Fr	May 25 Th	May 15 Tu	May 4 Su
Shavuoth (Feast of Weeks)*	Sivan 6	May 23 Mo	Jun. 11 Su	Jun. 1 Fr	May 21 We
Fast of Tammuz+	Tammuz 17	Jul. 3 Su	Jul. 23 Su	Jul. 12 Th	Jul. 1 Tu
Tisha B'Av (Fast of Av)+	Av 9	Jul. 24 Su	Aug. 13 Su	Aug. 2 Th	Jul. 22 Tu

The months of the Jewish year are: 1 Tishri; 2 Chesvan (also Marchesvan); 3 Kisley; 4 Tebet (also Tebeth); 5 Sebat (also Shebhat); 6 Adar; 6a, added month some years, Adar Sheni (II); 7 Nisan; 8 Iyar; 9 Sivan; 10 Tammuz, 11 Av (also Abh); 12 Elul.

Greek Orthodox Church Calendar, 1977

Date		Holy Days
Jan.	1	The Circumcision of Christ—The Feast day of St. Basil—New Year's Day
Jan.	6	The Epiphany—The Baptism of Jesus Christ—The Sanctification of the Waters
Jan.	7	Feast day of St. John the Baptist
Jan.	30	Feast day of Three Hierarchs; St. Basil, St. Gregory, and St. John Chrysostom
Feb.	2	Presentation of Jesus in the Temple
Feb.	21	Easter Lent begins
Feb.	27	Sunday of Orthodoxy (1st Sun. of Lent)
Mar.	25	The Annunciation of the Virgin Mary
Apr.	3	Palm Sunday
Apr.	3-9	Holy Week
Apr.	8	Good Friday—The Burial of Christ
Apr.	10	Easter Sunday
Apr.	23	Feast day of St. George
May	19	The Ascension

Date		Holy Days
May	29	Sunday of Pentecost
June	29	Feast day of Saints Peter and Paul
June	30	Feast day of the Twelve Holy Apostles
Aug.	6	The Transfiguration
Aug.	15	The Dormition of the Virgin Mary
Aug.	29	Beheading of St. John the Baptist
Sept.	1	Beginning of the Church Year
Sept.	8	Nativity of the Virgin Mary
Sept.	14	The Elevation of the Holy Cross
Oct.	23	The Feast of James (Iakovos)
Oct.	26	Feast day of St. Demetrios the Martyr
Nov.	15	The beginning of the Christmas Lent
Nov.	21	Presentation of Blessed Virgin Mary
Nov.	30	The Feast of St. Andrew, Founder Ecumenical Patriarchate of Constantinople
Dec.	6	Feast day of St. Nicholas, Bishop of Myra
Dec.	25	Christmas Day: The Birth of Jesus Christ

The dates above are according to the Gregorian calendar, adopted by the Greek Church in 1923. First Greek Orthodox church in U. S. founded 1864, in New Orleans, La.

Islamic (Moslem) Calendar 1976-1977

The Islamic calendar, often referred to as Mohammedan, is a lunar reckoning from the year of the Hegira, 622 A.D., when Mohammed moved to Medina from Mecca. It runs in cycles of 30 years, of which the 2d, 5th, 7th, 10th, 13th, 16th, 18th, 21st, 24th,26th and 29th are leap years. Common years have 354 days, leap years 355, the extra day being added to the last month, Zu'lhijjah. Except for this case, the 12 months beginning with Muharram have alternately 30 and 29 days. The month begins at sunset on the day before that given in the tables.

Year	Name of Month	Month Begins	Year	Name of Month	Month Begins
1397	Muharram (New Year)	Dec. 23, 1976	1398	Muharram (New Year)	Dec. 12, 1977
1397	Safar	Jan. 22, 1977	1398	Safar	Jan. 11, 1978
1397	Rabia I	Feb. 20, 1977	1398	Rabia I	Feb. 9, 1978
1397	Rabia II	Mar. 22, 1977	1398	Rabia II	Mar. 11, 1978
1397	Jumada I	Apr. 20, 1977	1398	Jumada I	Apr. 9, 1978
1397	Jumada II	May 20, 1977	1398	Jumada II	May 9, 1978
1397	Rajab	Jun. 18, 1977	1398	Rajab	Jun. 7, 1978
1397	Shaban	Jul. 18, 1977	1398	Shaban	Jul. 7, 1978
1397	Ramadan	Aug. 16, 1977	1398	Ramadan	Aug. 5, 1978
1397	Shawwai	Sept. 15, 1977	1398	Shawai	Sept. 4, 1978
1397	Zu'lkadah	Oct. 14, 1977	1398	Zu'lkadah	Oct. 3, 1978
1397	Zu'lhijjah	Nov. 13, 1977	1398	Zu'lhijjah	Nov. 2, 1978

Roman Catholic Hierarchy

Source: Apostolic Delegation, Washington, D.C.

Supreme Pontiff

At the head of the Roman Catholic Church is the Supreme Pontiff, Paul VI, Giovanni Battista Montini, born at Concesio, Italy, Sept. 26, 1897, ordained priest May 29, 1920, enthroned archbishop of Milan Jan. 6, 1955, proclaimed cardinal Dec. 15, 1958; elected Pope as successor of John XXIII, June 21, 1963; crowned June 30, 1963.

Cardinals

		Nationality	Born	Chosen
Alfrink: Bernard	Archbishop of Utrecht	Dutch	1900	1960
Antonelli: Ferdinando		Italian	1896	1973
Aponte Martinez: Luis	Archbishop of San Juan in Puerto Rico	American	1922	1973
Aramburu: Juan	Archbishop of Buenos Aires	Argentinian	1912	1976
Arns: Paulo	Archbishop of Sao Paulo	Brazilian	1921	1973
Bafile: Corrado	Prefect of the Sacred Congregation for the Causes of Saints	Italian	1903	1976
Baggio: Sebastiano	Prefect of the Sacred Congregation for the Bishops	Italian	1913	1969
Barbieri: Antonio Maria	Archbishop of Montevideo	Uruguayan	1892	1958
Baum: William	Archbishop of Washington	American	1926	1976
Bengsch: Alfred	Archbishop-Bishop of Berlin	German	1921	1967
Beras Rojas: Octavio	Archbishop of Santo Domingo	San Domingan	1906	1976
Bertoli: Paolo		Italian	1908	1969
Biayenda: Emile	Archbishop of Brazzaville	Congolese	1927	1973
Brandao Vilela: Avela	Archbishop of Sao Salvador da Bahia	Brazilian	1912	1973
Bueno y Monreal: Jose M	Archbishop of Seville	Spanish	1904	1958
Caggiano: Antonio	Archbishop of Buenos Aires	Argentinian	1889	1946
Carberry: John	Archbishop of St. Louis	American	1904	1969
Carpino: Francesco		Italian	1905	1967
Casariego: Mario	Archbishop of Guatemala	Guatemalan	1909	1969
Cerejeira: Manuel Goncalves		Portuguese	1888	1929
Cody: John P	Archbishop of Chicago	American	1907	1967
Colombo: Giovanni	Archbishop of Milan	Italian	1902	1965
Confalonieri: Carlo		Italian	1893	1958
Conway: William	Archbishop of Armagh	Irish	1913	1965
Cooke: Terence	Archbishop of New York	American	1921	1969
Cooray: Thomas B	Archbishop of Colombo in Ceylon	Ceylonese	1901	1965
Cordeiro: Joseph	Archbishop of Karachi	Pakistanian	1918	1973
da Costa Nunes: Jose		Portuguese	1880	1962
Darmojuwono: Justin	Archbishop of Semarang	Indonesian	1914	1967
de Araujo Sales: Eugenio	Archbishop of St. Sebastian of Rio de Janeiro	Brazilian	1920	1969
Dearden: John	Archbishop of Detroit	American	1907	1969
de Furstenberg: Maximilian		Belgian	1904	1967
Delargey: Reginald	Archbishop of Wellington	New Zealander	1914	1976
Di Jorio: Alberto		Italian	1884	1958
Doepfner: Julius	Archbishop of Munich	German	1913	1958
Duval: Leon-Etienne	Archbishop of Algiers	Algerian	1903	1965
Ekandem: Dominic	Bishop of Ikot Ekpene	Nigerian	1917	1976
Enrique y Tarancon: Vincenzo	Archbishop of Madrid	Spanish	1907	1969
Felici: Pericle	President of Pontifical Commission for the Revision of Code of Canon Law	Italian	1911	1967
Filipiak: Boleslaw	Dean of the Prelate Auditors of the Tribunal of the Sacred Roman Rota	Polish	1901	1976
Flahiff: George	Archbishop of Winnipeg	Canadian	1905	1969
Florit: Ermenegildo	Archbishop of Florence	Italian	1901	1965
Freeman: James	Archbishop of Sydney	Australian	1907	1973
Frings: Joseph		German	1887	1946
Garrone: Gabriele M	Prefect of the Sacred Congregation for Catholic Education	French	1901	1967
Gilroy: Norman		Australian	1896	1946
Gonzalez Martin: Marcelo	Archbishop of Toledo	Spanish	1918	1973
Gouyon: Paul	Archbishop of Rennes	French	1910	1969
Gracias: Valerian	Archbishop of Bombay	Indian	1900	1953
Gray: Gordon	Archbishop of St. Andrews and Edinburgh	Scottish	1910	1969
Guerri: Sergio	Pro-President of the Pontifical Comm. for Vatican City State	Italian	1905	1969
Guyot: Louis	Archbishop of Toulouse	French	1905	1973
Hoffner: Joseph	Archbishop of Cologne	German	1906	1969
Hume: Basil	Archbishop of Westminster	English	1923	1976
Jubany Arnau: Narciso	Archbishop of Barcelona	Spanish	1913	1973
Kim Sou Hwan: Stephan	Archbishop of Seoul	Korean	1922	1969
Knox: James	Prefect ot the Sacred Congregations of the Sacraments and of Devine Worship	Australian	1914	1973
Koenig: Franz	Archbishop of Vienna	Austrian	1905	1958
Krol: John	Archbishop of Philadelphia	American	1910	1967
Landazuri: Ricketts Juan	Archbishop of Lima	Peruvian	1913	1962
Leger: Paul		Canadian	1904	1953
Lekai: Laszlo	Archbishop of Esztergom	Hungarian	1910	1976
Lercaro: Giacomo		Italian	1891	1953
Lorscheider: Aloisio	Archbishop of Portaleza	Brazilian	1924	1976
Luciani: Albino	Patriarch of Venice	Italian	1912	1973
Malula: Joseph	Archbishop of Kinshasa	Congolese	1917	1969

Cardinals		Nationality	Born	Chosen
Manning: Timothy	Archbishop of Los Angeles.	American	1909	1973
Marella: Paolo.		Italian	1895	1959
Martin: Joseph.		French	1891	1965
Marty: Francis	Archbishop of Paris.	French	1904	1969
Maurer: Jose.	Archbishop of Sucre.	Bolivian	1900	1967
McCann: Owen.	Archbishop of Cape Town.	S. African	1907	1965
McIntyre: James.		American	1886	1953
Medeiros: Humberto.	Archbishop of Boston.	American	1915	1973
Miranda y Gomez: Miguel.	Archbishop of Mexico.	Mexican	1895	1969
Motta: Carlos Carmelo de Vasconcellos	Archbishop of Aparecida.	Brazilian	1890	1946
Mozzoni: Umberto.		Italian	1904	1973
Munoz Duque: Anibal.	Archbishop of Bogota.	Colombian	1908	1973
Munoz Vega: Paolo	Archbishop of Quito.	Ecuadorian	1903	1969
Nasalli Rocca: Mario.		Italian	1903	1969
Nsubuga: Emmanuel	Archbishop of Kampala.	Ugandan	1914	1976
O'Boyle: Patrick.		American	1896	1967
Oddi: Silvio.		Italian	1910	1969
Ottaviani: Alfredo.		Italian	1890	1953
Otunga: Maurice.	Archbishop of Nairobi.	Kenyan	1923	1973
Palazzini: Pietro.		Italian	1912	1973
Pappalardo: Salvatore.	Archbishop of Palermo.	Italian	1918	1973
Parecattil: Joseph.	Archbishop of Ernakulam.	Indian	1912	1969
Parente: Pietro.		Italian	1891	1967
Paupini: Giuseppe.	Grand Penitentiary.	Italian	1907	1969
Pellegrino: Michele.	Archbishop of Turin.	Italian	1903	1967
Philippe: Paul	Prefect of the Sacred Congregation for the Oriental Churches.	French	1905	1973
Picachy: Lawrence	Archbishop of Calcutta.	Indian	1916	1976
Pignedoli: Sergio.	President of the Secretariat for Non-Christians.	Italian	1910	1973
Pironio: Eduardo.	Prefect of the Sacred Congregation for Religious and for Secular Institutes.	Argentinian	1920	1976
Poletti: Ugo.	Vicar General of His Holiness for the City of Rome.	Italian	1914	1973
Poma: Antonio.	Archbishop of Bologna.	Italian	1910	1969
Primatesta: Francisco.	Archbishop of Cordova.	Argentinian	1919	1973
Quintero: Jose	Archbishop of Caracas	Venezuelan	1902	1961
Razafimahatratra: Victor	Archbishop of Tananarive.	Madagascaran	1921	1976
Renard: Alexandre.	Archbishop of Lyon.	French	1906	1967
Ribeiro: Antonio.	Patriarch of Lisbon.	Portuguese	1928	1973
Roberti: Francesco.		Italian	1889	1958
Rosales: Julio.	Archbishop of Cebu.	Filipino	1906	1969
Rossi: Angelo.	Prefect of the Sacred Congregation for the Evangelization of Peoples.	Brazilian	1913	1965
Rossi: Opilio.		Italian	1910	1976
Roy, Maurice.	Archbishop of Quebec.	Canadian	1905	1965
Salazar Lopez: Jose.	Archbishop of Guadalajara.	Mexican	1910	1973
Samore: Antonio.	Archivist of Holy Roman Church.	Italian	1905	1967
Schroffer: Joseph.	Titular Archbishop of Volturnum and Secretary of the Sacred Congregation for Catholic Education.	German	1903	1976
Sensi: Giuseppe.	Titular Archbishop of Sardis.		1907	1976
Seper: Franjo.	Prefect of Sacred Congregation for the Doctrine of the Faith.	Yugoslav	1905	1965
Shehan: Lawrence.		American	1898	1965
Sherer: Alfred.	Archbishop of Porto Alegre.	Brazilian	1903	1969
Sidarouss: Stephanos.	Coptic Patriarch of Alexandria.	United Arab Republic	1904	1965
Silva Henriquez: Raul.	Archbishop of Santiago.	Chilean.	1907	1962
Sin: Jaime.	Archbishop of Manila.	Filipino	1928	1976
Siri: Giuseppe.	Archbishop of Genoa.	Italian	1906	1953
Slipyj: Josyf.	Ukrainian Archbishop of Lwow.	Ukrainian	1892	1965
Staffa: Dino.	Prefect of Supreme Tribunal of Apostolic Signatura.	Italian	1906	1967
Suenens: Leo.	Archbishop of Malines Brussels.	Belgian	1904	1962
Taguchi: Paul.	Archbishop of Osaka.	Japanese	1902	1973
Taofinu'u: Pio.	Bishop of Apia.	Samoan	1923	1973
Thiandoum: Hyacinthe.	Archbishop of Dakar.	Senegalese	1921	1976
Traglia: Luigi.		Italian	1895	1960
Trin Nhu Khue: Joseph.	Archbishop of Hanoi.	Vietnamese	1899	1976
Ursi: Corrado.	Archbishop of Naples.	Italian	1908	1967
Vagnozzi: Egidio.	Pres. of the Prefecture of the Holy See's Economic Affairs.	Italian	1906	1967
Villot: Jean.	Secretary of State of His Holiness.	French	1905	1965
Violardo: Giacomo.		Italian	1898	1969
Volk: Hermann.	Bishop of Mainz.	German	1903	1973
Willebrands: John.	President of Secretariat for the Union of Christians Archbishop of Utrecht.	Dutch	1909	1969
Wojtyla: Karol.	Archbishop of Krakow.	Polish	1920	1967
Wright: John.	Prefect of the Sacred Congregation for the Clergy.	American	1909	1969
Wyszynski: Stefan.	Archbishop of Gniezno-Warsaw.	Polish	1901	1953
Yu Pin: Paul.	Archbishop of Nanking.	Chinese	1901	1969
Zoungrana: Paul.	Archbishop of Ouagadougou.	Upper Volta	1917	1965

NOTED PERSONALITIES

American Statesmen

(Excluding Presidents, Vice Presidents, Sup. Ct. Justices, and most signers of the Declaration of Independence; listed elsewhere.)

Born	Died	Name	Born	Died	Name	Born	Died	Name
1893	1971	Acheson, Dean	1706	1790	Franklin, Benjamin	1757	1824	Pinckney, Charles
1807	1886	Adams, Charles Francis	1761	1849	Gallatin, Albert	1746	1825	Pinckney, Charles C.
1841	1915	Aldrich, Nelson W.	1858	1946	Glass, Carter	1753	1813	Randolph, Edmund
1874	1940	Bankhead, William B.	1757	1804	Hamilton, Alexander	1773	1833	Randolph, John
1870	1965	Baruch, Bernard M.	1737	1793	Hancock, John	1721	1775	Randolph, Peyton
1772	1858	Benton, Thomas Hart	1838	1905	Hay, John	1880	1973	Rankin, Jeannette
1830	1893	Blaine, James G.	1736	1799	Henry, Patrick	1882	1961	Rayburn, Sam
1835	1899	Bland, Richard P.	1895	1972	Hoover, J. Edgar	1872	1937	Robinson, Joseph T.
1865	1940	Borah, William E.	1890	1946	Hopkins, Harry L.	1884	1962	Roosevelt, Eleanor
1821	1875	Breckinridge, John C.	1858	1938	House, Edward M.	1845	1937	Root, Elihu
1860	1925	Bryan, William Jennings	1793	1863	Houston, Samuel	1829	1906	Schurz, Carl
1891	1967	Bullitt, William C.	1871	1955	Hull, Cordell	1733	1804	Schuyler, Philip J.
1904	1971	Bunche, Ralph	1866	1945	Johnson, Hiram W.	1801	1872	Seward, William H.
1887	1966	Byrd, Harry F.	1903	1963	Kefauver, Estes	1873	1944	Smith, Alfred E.
1808	1873	Chase, Salmon P.	1856	1937	Kellogg, Frank B.	1814	1869	Stanton, Edwin M.
1850	1921	Clark, Champ	1925	1968	Kennedy, Robert F.	1812	1883	Stephens, Alexander H.
1777	1852	Clay, Henry	1755	1827	King, Rufus	1900	1949	Stettinius, Edward R. Jr.
1769	1828	Clinton, DeWitt	1874	1944	Knox, Frank	1900	1965	Stevenson, Adlai E.
1829	1888	Conkling, Roscoe	1855	1925	La Follette, Robert M.	1867	1950	Stimson, Henry L.
1877	1963	Connally, Tom	1850	1924	Lodge, Henry Cabot	1889	1953	Taft, Robert A.
1870	1957	Cox, James M.	1786	1857	Marcy, William L.	1884	1968	Thomas, Norman M.
1787	1863	Crittenden, John J.	1880	1959	Marshall, George C.	1814	1886	Tilden, Samuel J.
1808	1889	Davis, Jefferson	1863	1941	McAdoo, William G.	1890	1961	Tydings, Millard E.
1902	1971	Dewey, Thomas E.	1874	1944	McNary, Charles L.	1859	1949	U'Ren, W.S.
1896	1969	Dirksen, Everett M.	1891	1967	Morgenthau, Henry Jr.	1884	1951	Vandenberg, Arthur H.
1813	1861	Douglas, Stephen A.	1752	1816	Morris, Gouverneur	1877	1953	Wagner, Robert F.
1888	1959	Dulles, John Foster	1873	1931	Morrow, Dwight W.	1782	1852	Webster, Daniel
1794	1865	Everett, Edward	1900	1974	Morse, Wayne	1892	1961	Welles, Sumner
1808	1893	Fish, Hamilton	1861	1944	Norris, George W.	1882	1975	Wheeler, Burton K.
1892	1949	Forrestal, James V.				1892	1944	Willkie, Wendell L.

American Reformers, Social-Economic Leaders

Born	Died	Name	Born	Died	Name	Born	Died	Name
1860	1935	Addams, Jane	1839	1897	George, Henry	1801	1877	Owen, Robt. Dale
1909	1972	Alinsky, Saul O.	1837	1927	Gerry, Elbridge T.	1842	1933	Parkhurst, Charles H.
1820	1906	Anthony, Susan B.	1850	1924	Gompers, Samuel	1811	1884	Phillips, Wendell
1891	1969	Arnold, Thurman W.	1873	1952	Green, William	1849	1914	Riis, Jacob A.
1867	1961	Balch, Emily G.	1887	1975	Hansen, Alvin	1883	1967	Sanger, Margaret
1821	1912	Barton, Clara H.	1887	1946	Hillman, Sidney	1797	1874	Smith, Gerrit
1818	1895	Bloomer, Amelia J.	1801	1876	Howe, Samuel G.	1816	1902	Stanton, Eliz. Cady
1809	1890	Brisbane, Albert	1880	1968	Keller, Helen	1818	1893	Stone, Lucy
1800	1859	Brown, John	1929	1968	King, Martin Luther	1867	1960	Townsend, Francis E.
1859	1947	Catt, Carrie Chapman	1855	1925	LaFollette, Robt. M.	1844	1928	Villard, Helen G.
1855	1926	Debs, Eugene	1880	1969	Lewis, John L.	1893	1955	White, Walter
1802	1887	Dix, Dorothea	1793	1880	Mott, Lucretia	1931	1973	Wiley, George
1817	1895	Douglass, Frederick	1886	1952	Murray, Phillip	1839	1898	Willard, Frances E.
1805	1879	Garrison, Wm. L.	1846	1911	Nation, Carry	1921	1971	Young, Whitney M.
			1811	1886	Noyes, John H.			

American Educators and Religious Leaders

Educators

Born	Died	Name
1897	1967	Allport, Gordon
1869	1949	Angell, James R.
1811	1900	Barnard, Henry
1862	1947	Butler, Nich. Murray
1862	1948	Cross, Wilbur
1859	1952	Dewey, John
1851	1931	Dewey, Melvil
1868	1963	DuBois, William E. B.
1834	1926	Eliot, Charles W.
1863	1940	Finley, John H.
1903	1967	Gassner, John W.
1831	1908	Gilman, Daniel C.
1906	1963	Griswold, A. Whitney
1844	1924	Hall, G. Stanley
1856	1906	Harper, William R.
1842	1910	James, William
1882	1974	Kallen, Horace M.
1797	1849	Lyon, Mary
1800	1873	McGuffey, William H.
1796	1859	Mann, Horace
1872	1964	Meiklejohn, Alexander
1818	1901	Muhlenberg, Fred. A.
1869	1946	Neilson, William A.
1827	1908	Norton, Chas. Eliot
1855	1902	Palmer, Alice Freeman
1804	1894	Peabody, Elizabeth P.
1870	1964	Pound, Roscoe

Born	Died	Name
1855	1916	Royce, Josiah
1885	1963	Seymour, Charles
1779	1864	Silliman, Benjamin
1917	1969	Smith, Courtney C.
1840	1910	Sumner, Wm. Graham
1893	1969	Tannenbaum, Frank
1858	1915	Washington, Booker T.
1787	1870	Willard, Emma

Religious Leaders

Born	Died	Name
1835	1922	Abbott, Lyman
1745	1816	Asbury, Francis
1813	1887	Beecher, Henry Ward
1775	1863	Beecher, Lyman
1835	1893	Brooks, Phillips
1780	1842	Channing, Wm. Ellery
1584	1652	Cotton, John
1895	1970	Cushing, Richard
1752	1817	Dwight, Timothy
1821	1910	Eddy, Mary Baker
1703	1758	Edwards, Jonathan
1902	1973	Eisendrath, Maurice N.
1878	1969	Fosdick, Harry E.
1900	1968	Fry, Franklin C.
1834	1921	Gibbons, James
1867	1938	Hayes, Patrick J.
1748	1830	Hicks, Elias

Born	Died	Name
1879	1964	Holmes, John Haynes
1590	1643	Hutchinson, Anne
1883	1968	Jones, Bob
1843	1926	Kohler, Kaufmann
1663	1728	Mather, Cotton
1873	1970	McKay, David O.
1890	1944	McPherson, Aimee Semple
1837	1899	Moody, Dwight L.
1897	1975	Muhammad, Elijah
1711	1787	Muhlenberg, H. M.
1891	1963	Oxnam, G. Bromley
1810	1860	Parker, Theodore
1913	1969	Pike, James A.
1884	1968	Poling, Daniel A.
1729	1796	Seabury, Samuel
1774	1821	Seton, Elizabeth
1886	1969	Sheil, Bernard J.
1882	1968	Shipler, Guy E.
1881	1968	Silver, Eliezer
1805	1844	Smith, Joseph
1876	1972	Smith, Joseph Fielding
1889	1970	Sockman, Ralph W.
1889	1967	Spellman, Francis
1863	1935	Sunday, Wm. (Billy)
1886	1965	Tillich, Paul
1862	1969	Welch, Herbert
1599	1683	Williams, Roger
1874	1949	Wise, Stephen S.
1801	1877	Young, Brigham

360

American Military Leaders
All Army unless marked (N) Navy; (M) Marine; (AF) Air Force.

Born	Died	Name	Born	Died	Name	Born	Died	Name
1914	1974	Abrams, Creighton	1883	1959	Halsey, William F. (N)	1860	1948	Pershing, John J.
1737	1789	Allen, Ethan	1818	1902	Hampton, Wade	1739	1817	Pickens, Andrew
1741	1801	Arnold, Benedict	1728	1777	Herkimer, Nicholas	1825	1875	Pickett, George E.
1886	1950	Arnold, Henry H. (Hap) (AF)	1825	1865	Hill, Ambrose P.	1813	1891	Porter, David D. (N)
1745	1803	Barry, John (N)	1892	1966	Hobbs, Leland	1905	1970	Power, Thomas S. (AF)
1818	1893	Beauregard, Pierre	1870	1937	Hobson, Richmond (N)	1809	1867	Price, Stirling
1853	1930	Bliss, Tasker H.	1887	1966	Hodges, Courtney	1896	1973	Radford, Arthur (N)
1878	1967	Bloch, Claude C. (N)	1814	1879	Hooker, Joseph	1890	1973	Rickenbacker, Edward (AF)
1817	1876	Bragg, Braxton	1831	1879	Hood, John B.	1819	1892	Rodgers, C. R. P. (N)
1775	1828	Brown, Jacob J.	1773	1843	Hull, Isaac (N)	1773	1838	Rodgers, John (N)
1888	1950	Buchanan, Pat (N)	1824	1863	Jackson, Thomas (Stonewall)	1819	1898	Rosecrans, William S.
1823	1914	Buckner, Simon B.				1736	1818	St. Clair, Arthur
1886	1945	Buckner, Simon Jr.	1803	1862	Johnston, Albert S.	1840	1903	Sampson, William T. (N)
1826	1863	Buford, John	1807	1891	Johnston, Joseph	1831	1906	Schofield, John
1861	1947	Bullard, Robert L.	1747	1792	Jones, John Paul (N)	1786	1866	Scott, Winfield
1824	1881	Burnside, Ambrose	1814	1862	Kearny, Philip	1835	1906	Shafter, William R.
1818	1893	Butler, Benjamin F.	1794	1848	Kearny, Stephen	1831	1888	Sheridan, Phillip
1884	1970	Cates, Clifton B. (M)	1879	1956	King, Ernest J. (N)	1820	1891	Sherman, William T.
1772	1840	Chauncey, Isaac (N)	1781	1813	Lawrence, James (N)	1858	1936	Sims, William S. (N)
1842	1914	Chaffee, Adna R.	1843	1899	Lawton, Henry	1882	1967	Smith, Holland M. (M)
1890	1958	Chennault, Claire (AF)	1875	1959	Leahy, William D. (N)	1895	1961	Smith, W. Bedell
1752	1818	Clark, George Rogers	1756	1818	Lee, Henry	1891	1974	Spaatz, Carl A. (AF)
1786	1836	Crockett, David	1807	1870	Lee, Robert E.	1886	1969	Spruance, Raymond (N)
1819	1893	Crittenden, Thomas L.	1907	1975	Lincoln, George A.	1728	1822	Stark, John
1828	1890	Crook, George	1821	1904	Longstreet, James	1883	1946	Stilwell, Joseph W.
1842	1874	Cushing, William B. (N)	1818	1861	Lyon, Nathaniel	1726	1783	Stirling, Lord (Alexander)
1839	1876	Custer, George	1845	1912	MacArthur, Arthur			
1779	1820	Decatur, Stephen (N)	1880	1964	MacArthur, Douglas	1890	1969	Stratemeyer, George (AF)
1837	1917	Dewey, George (N)	1898	1975	McAuliffe, Anthony C.	1833	1864	Stuart, J. E. B.
1857	1927	Dickman, Joseph T.	1733	1795	Marion, Francis	1740	1795	Sullivan, John
1879	1951	Drum, Hugh A.	1826	1885	McClellan, George B.	1822	1880	Sykes, George
1816	1894	Early, Jubal A.	1818	1885	McDowell, Irvin	1784	1850	Taylor, Zachary
1886	1961	Eichelberger, R. L.	1828	1864	McPherson, James	1827	1890	Terry, Alfred H.
1890	1969	Eisenhower, Dwight D.	1815	1872	Meade, George	1816	1870	Thomas, George H.
1846	1912	Evans, Robley D. (N)	1839	1925	Miles, Nelson A.	1884	1955	Towers, John H. (N)
1817	1872	Ewell, Richard	1879	1936	Mitchell, Billy	1899	1954	Vandenberg, Hoyt (AF)
1801	1870	Farragut, David G. (N)	1887	1947	Mitscher, Marc A. (N)	1883	1953	Wainwright, Jonathan
1806	1863	Foote, Andrew (N)	1736	1775	Montgomery, Richard	1732	1799	Washington, George
1821	1877	Forrest, Nathan B.	1736	1802	Morgan, Daniel	1745	1796	Wayne, Anthony
1865	1917	Funston, Frederick	1730	1805	Moultrie, William	1836	1906	Wheeler, Joseph
1728	1806	Gates, Horatio	1885	1966	Nimitz, Chester (N)	1837	1925	Wilson, James H.
1805	1877	Goldsborough, L. M. (N)	1906	1971	O'Donnell, Emmett (Rosy) (AF)	1860	1927	Wood, Leonard
1822	1885	Grant, Ulysses S.	1896	1959	Parks, Floyd L.	1818	1897	Worden, John L. (N)
1742	1786	Greene, Nathanael	1885	1945	Patton, George S.	1820	1899	Wright, Horatio G.
1896	1970	Groves, Leslie R.	1814	1881	Pemberton, J. C.	1898	1969	Wyman, Willard G.
1815	1872	Halleck, Henry	1785	1819	Perry, Oliver H. (N)	1876	1959	Yarnell, Hy. E. (N)

American Explorers, Naturalists

Born	Died	Name	Born	Died	Name	Born	Died	Name
1864	1926	Akeley, Carl Ethan	1809	1868	Carson, Kit	1784	1864	Long, Stephen H.
1884	1960	Andrews, Roy C.	1770	1838	Clark, William	1874	1970	Macmillan, Donald
1778	1838	Ashley, William Henry	1775	1813	Colter, John	1838	1914	Muir, John
1785	1851	Audubon, John J.	1865	1940	Cook, Frederick A.	1799	1877	Palmer, Nathaniel B.
1875	1946	Bartlett, Robert A.	1898	1970	Cruzen, Richard H.	1856	1920	Peary, Robert E.
1850	1941	Beard, Daniel C.	1844	1881	De Long, G. W.	1779	1813	Pike, Zebulon M.
1799	1847	Bent, Charles	1880	1951	Ellsworth, Lincoln	1834	1902	Powell, John W.
1875	1956	Bingham, Hiram	1799	1854	Fitzpatrick, Thomas	1793	1864	Schoolcraft, Henry R.
1796	1878	Bonneville, Benjamin	1813	1890	Fremont, John C.	1849	1892	Schwatka, Frederick
1734	1820	Boone, Daniel	1844	1935	Greely, Adolphus W.	1799	1845	Sublette, William L.
1796	1836	Bowie, James	1884	1937	Johnson, Martin	1817	1862	Thoreau, Henry D.
1804	1881	Bridger, James	1894	1953	Johnson, Osa	1798	1876	Walker, Joseph R.
1849	1926	Burbank, Luther	1820	1857	Kane, Elisha K.	1802	1847	Whitman, Marcus
1837	1921	Burroughs, John	1774	1809	Lewis, Meriwether	1798	1877	Wilkes, Charles
1888	1957	Byrd, Richard E.	1902	1974	Lindbergh, Charles A.	1766	1813	Wilson, Alexander

American Inventors

Born	Died	Name	Born	Died	Name	Born	Died	Name
1891	1954	Armstrong, Edwin	1765	1815	Fulton, Robert	1791	1872	Morse, S. F. B.
1847	1922	Bell, Alex. Graham	1818	1903	Gatling, Richard J.	1811	1861	Otis, Elisha
1890	1970	Bell, Herbert A.	1882	1945	Goddard, Robert H.	1831	1897	Pullman, George M.
1851	1929	Berliner, Emile	1800	1860	Goodyear, Charles	1894	1974	de Seversky, Alexander P.
1857	1898	Burroughs, William	1803	1855	Gorrie, John	1889	1972	Sikorsky, Igor
1906	1968	Carlson, Chester F.	1835	1901	Gray, Elisha	1894	1970	Spencer, Percy L.
1876	1950	Carrier, Willis	1797	1878	Henry, Joseph	1860	1930	Sperry, Elmer A.
1873	1975	Coolidge, William D.	1812	1886	Hoe, Richard M.	1856	1943	Tesla, Nikola
1874	1961	De Forest, Lee	1819	1867	Howe, Elias	1853	1937	Thomson, Elihu
1862	1938	Duryea, Charles E.	1866	1949	Lake, Simon	1846	1914	Westinghouse, George
1870	1967	Duryea, J. Frank	1881	1957	Langmuir, Irving	1900	1975	Williams, David M.
1803	1889	Ericsson, John	1826	1886	Loomis, Mahlon	1871	1948	Wright, Orville
1743	1798	Fitch, John	1854	1899	Mergenthaler, Ottmar	1867	1912	Wright, Wilbur

American Painters

Born	Died	Name	Born	Died	Name	Born	Died	Name
1852	1911	Abbey, Edwin A.	1848	1892	Harnett, William M.	1851	1914	Pearce, Charles S.
1779	1843	Allston, Washington	1868	1933	Hart, George O.	1912	1956	Pollock, Jackson
1785	1851	Audubon, John James	1859	1935	Hassam, Childe	1823	1879	Powell, William H.
1893	1965	Avery, Milton C.	1813	1894	Healy, George P. A.	1861	1924	Prendergast, Maurice B.
1863	1942	Beaux, Cecelia	1865	1929	Henri, Robert	1801	1881	Quidor, John
1882	1925	Bellows, George W.	1780	1849	Hicks, Edward	1861	1909	Remington, Frederic
1889	1975	Benton, Thomas Hart	1880	1966	Hofmann, Hans	1838	1905	Richards, William T.
1885	1974	Biddle, George	1836	1910	Homer, Winslow	1903	1970	Rothko, Mark
1830	1902	Bierstadt, Albert	1882	1967	Hopper, Edward	1847	1917	Ryder, Albert P.
1811	1879	Bingham, George Caleb	1824	1879	Hunt, William M.	1856	1925	Sargent, John Singer
1848	1936	Blashfield, Edwin H.	1801	1846	Inman, Henry	1898	1969	Shahn, Ben
1847	1927	Bridgman, Frederic A.	1825	1894	Inness, George	1883	1965	Sheeler, Charles
1845	1926	Cassatt, Mary	1818	1872	Kensett, John F.	1871	1951	Sloan, John
1796	1872	Catlin, George	1835	1910	La Farge, John	1883	1962	Speicher, Eugene E.
1849	1916	Chase, William M.	1816	1868	Leutze, Emanuel	1880	1946	Stella, Joseph
1826	1900	Church, Frederic	1867	1933	Luks, George B.	1755	1828	Stuart, Gilbert
1801	1848	Cole, Thomas	1866	1912	MacCameron, Robert L.	1783	1872	Sully, Thomas
1737	1815	Copley, John S.	1872	1953	Marin, John	1849	1921	Thayer, Abbott H.
1856	1919	Cox, Kenyon	1898	1954	Marsh, Reginald	1848	1933	Tiffany, Louis C.
1897	1946	Curry, John Steuart	1836	1897	Martin, Homer	1756	1843	Trumbull, John
1862	1928	Davies, Arthur B.	1813	1884	Matteson, Tompkins H.	1849	1925	Tryon, Dwight N.
1894	1964	Davis, Stuart	1832	1932	Maurer, Louis	1853	1902	Twachtman, John H.
1884	1958	duBois, Guy Pene	1860	1932	Melchers, Gari	1775	1852	Vanderlyn, John
1796	1886	Durand, Asher Brown	1858	1925	Metcalf, Willard L.	1836	1923	Vedder, Elihu
1848	1919	Duveneck, Frank	1829	1901	Moran, Edward	1858	1933	Vonnoh, Robert W.
1844	1916	Eakins, Thomas	1837	1926	Moran, Thomas	1843	1929	Walker, Henry Oliver
1751	1801	Earle, Ralph	1860	1961	Moses, Grandma	1881	1961	Weber, Max
1871	1956	Feininger, Lyonel	1807	1868	Mount, William S.	1841	1926	Weir, John F.
1863	1930	Ferris, J. L. G.	1867	1940	Myers, Jerome	1852	1919	Weir, Julian Alden
1822	1884	Fuller, George	1741	1827	Peale, Charles W.	1803	1889	Weir, Robert W.
1904	1948	Gorky, Arshile	1749	1831	Peale, James	1738	1820	West, Benjamin
1866	1946	Guerin, Jules	1774	1825	Peale, Raphaelle	1834	1903	Whistler, James A. M.
1792	1866	Harding, Chester	1778	1860	Peale, Rembrandt	1891	1942	Wood, Grant

American Sculptors

Born	Died	Name	Born	Died	Name	Born	Died	Name
1878	1949	Aitken, Robert I.	1850	1931	French, Daniel C.	1867	1917	Pratt, Bela
1887	1964	Archipenko, Alexander	1805	1852	Greenough, Horatio	1868	1929	Quinn, Edmond T.
1819	1911	Ball, Thomas	1887	1967	Hoffman, Malvina	1816	1879	Rimmer, William
1863	1938	Barnard, George Grey	1830	1908	Hosmer, Harriet	1825	1874	Rinehart, William H.
1865	1925	Bartlett, Paul W.	1847	1914	Hoxie, Vinnie Ream	1829	1904	Rogers, John
1867	1915	Bitter, Karl T.	1825	1879	Jackson, John Adams	1825	1892	Rogers, Randolph
1913	1969	Boehm, Edward M.	1868	1925	Jaegers, Albert	1756	1833	Rush, William
1871	1941	Borglum, Gutzon	1892	1969	Jones, Thomas H.	1848	1907	St.-Gaudens, Augustus
1868	1922	Borglum, Solon H.	1863	1947	Kitson, Henry Hudson	1871	1922	Shrady, Henry M.
1814	1886	Brown, Henry K.	1871	1932	Kitson, Theo Alice	1839	1913	Simmons, Franklin
1870	1945	Calder, Alexander S.	1882	1935	Lachaise, Gaston	1903	1975	Slobodkin, Louis
1814	1857	Crawford, Thomas	1877	1954	Laessle, Albert	1906	1965	Smith, David
1861	1944	Dallin, Cyrus	1877	1963	Lawrie, Lee	1819	1895	Story, William W.
1884	1952	Davidson, Jo	1871	1935	Lukeman, Henry A.	1860	1936	Taft, Lorado
1844	1917	Ezekiel, Moses Jacob	1863	1937	MacMonnies, Fred W.	1830	1910	Ward, J. Q. A.
1869	1943	Farnham, Sally James	1885	1966	Manship, Paul	1870	1952	Weinman, Adolph A.
1895	1942	Flannagan, John	1879	1947	McCartan, Edward	1877	1942	Whitney, Gertrude
1877	1953	Fraser, James E.	1883	1962	Mestrovic, Ivan	1877	1957	Young, Mahonri M.
1790	1852	Frazee, John	1817	1904	Palmer, Erastus Dow	1887	1966	Zorach, William
			1805	1873	Powers, Hiram			

American Scientists, Physicians, Engineers

Born	Died	Name	Born	Died	Name	Born	Died	Name
1838	1916	Abbe, Cleveland	1903	1973	Gibbon, John H.	1866	1945	Morgan, Thomas H.
1872	1973	Abbot, Charles Greeley	1839	1903	Gibbs, Josiah W.	1819	1868	Morton, W. T. G.
1807	1873	Agassiz, Louis	1858	1928	Goethals, George W.	1890	1967	Muller, Hermann J.
1823	1887	Baird, Spencer	1874	1929	Goldberger, Joseph	1904	1967	Oppenheimer, J. Robert
1839	1903	Beard, George Miller	1854	1920	Gorgas, William C.	1883	1962	Papanicolaou, George N.
1785	1853	Beaumont, William	1863	1914	Hall, Charles M.	1903	1967	Pincus, Gregory
1889	1967	Bigelow, Henry B.	1896	1965	Hench, Philip S.	1851	1902	Reed, Walter S.
1899	1964	Blalock, Alfred	1883	1964	Hess, Victor F.	1846	1927	Remsen, Ira
1773	1838	Bowditch, Nath.	1905	1973	Kuiper, Gerard	1871	1910	Ricketts, Howard T.
1882	1961	Bridgman, Percy W.	1834	1906	Langley, Samuel P.	1806	1869	Roebling, John A.
1890	1974	Bush, Vannevar	1881	1957	Langmuir, Irving	1879	1970	Rous, Peyton
1868	1939	Cabot, Richard C.	1884	1964	Lanza, Anthony J.	1745	1813	Rush, Benjamin
1864	1943	Carver, George W.	1901	1958	Lawrence, Ernest O.	1877	1967	Schick, Bela
1887	1968	Cobb, Stanley	1815	1878	Long, Crawford	1885	1972	Shapley, Harlow
1892	1962	Compton, Arthur H.	1855	1916	Lowell, Percival	1813	1883	Sims, James M.
1877	1954	Compton, Karl T.	1806	1873	Maury, Matthew F.	1859	1934	Smith, Theobald
1901	1974	Condon, Edward	1865	1939	Mayo, Charles H.	1865	1923	Steinmetz, Charles
1869	1939	Cushing, Harvey W.	1898	1968	Mayo, Charles W.	1915	1974	Sutherland, Earl W.
1927	1961	Dooley, Thomas	1861	1939	Mayo, William J.	1898	1964	Szilard, Leo
1901	1965	Du Mont, Allen	1845	1913	McBurney, Charles	1899	1972	Theiler, Max
1907	1975	Dunning, John R.	1909	1968	McLean, John Milton	1888	1973	Waksman, Selman
1820	1887	Eads, James P.	1899	1966	Menninger, William C.	1886	1973	White, Paul Dudley
1879	1955	Einstein, Albert	1852	1931	Michelson, Albert A.	1894	1964	Wiener, Norbert
1706	1790	Franklin, Benjamin	1903	1966	Millikan, Clark	1844	1930	Wiley, Harvey W.
1895	1974	Fremont-Smith, Frank	1868	1953	Millikan, Robert	1856	1931	Williams, Daniel Hale
1884	1967	Funk, Casimir				1898	1974	Zwicky, Fritz

American Business Leaders, Philanthropists

Born	Died	Name
1884	1966	Arden, Elizabeth
1832	1901	Armour, Phillip D.
1763	1848	Astor, John Jacob
1894	1968	Bache, Harold L.
1853	1924	Belmont, August
1786	1844	Biddle, Nicholas
1821	1905	Cooke, Jay
1791	1883	Cooper, Peter
1807	1874	Cornell, Ezra
1834	1928	Depew, Chauncey M.
1826	1893	Drexel, Anthony J.
1856	1925	Duke, James B.
1739	1817	duPont, Pierre S.
1890	1962	Fairless, Benjamin F.
1835	1906	Field, Marshall
1860	1937	Filene, Edward A.
1894	1970	Folsom, Frank M.
1846	1927	Gary, Elbert H.
1898	1974	Gerber, Daniel
1885	1966	Gimbel, Bernard F.
1836	1892	Gould, Jay
1834	1916	Green, Henrietta (Hetty)
1828	1905	Guggenheim, Meyer
1874	1940	Harkness, Edward S.
1848	1909	Harriman, Edward H.
1865	1957	Hartford, Geo. L.A.
1882	1975	Hogg, Ima
1795	1873	Hopkins, Johns
1889	1974	Hunt, H.L.
1821	1900	Huntington, C.P.
1882	1967	Kaiser, Henry J.
1888	1969	Kennedy, Joseph P.
1876	1958	Kettering, Charles F.
1879	1948	Knudsen, Wm. S.
1867	1966	Kresge, S. S.
1863	1955	Kress, Samuel H.
1870	1948	Lamont, Thomas W.
1891	1969	Lehman, Robert
1903	1972	Litton, Charles
1831	1902	Mackay, John W.
1855	1937	Mellon, Andrew W.
1899	1970	Mellon, Richard K.
1884	1968	Mennen, William G.
1825	1910	Mills, Darius
1875	1973	Mott, Charles Stewart
1875	1970	Neiman, Abraham
1887	1963	Olds, Irving S.
1795	1869	Peabody, George
1887	1973	Post, Marjorie Merriweather
1906	1975	Revson, Charles
1874	1960	Rockefeller, J. D. Jr.
1862	1932	Rosenwald, Julius
1828	1918	Sage, Margaret Olivia
1740	1785	Salomon, Haym
1847	1920	Schiff, Jacob H.
1845	1912	Straus, Isidor
1848	1931	Straus, Nathan
1839	1903	Swift, Gustavus
1794	1877	Vanderbilt, Cornelius
1843	1899	Vanderbilt, Cornelius
1849	1920	Vanderbilt, Wm. K.
1835	1900	Villard, Henry
1838	1922	Wanamaker, John
1896	1969	Warburg, James P.
1888	1974	Whitney, Richard
1841	1904	Whitney, Wm. C.
1886	1972	Wilson, Charles E.
1890	1961	Wilson, Chas. Erwin
1879	1969	Wood, Robert E.
1852	1919	Woolworth, Frank

Hall of Fame for Business Leadership

Selected by Fortune Magazine for Junior Achievement

1975
William M. Allen, b. 1900
Andrew Carnegie, 1835-1919
George Eastman, 1854-1932
Thomas A. Edison, 1847-1931
Henry Ford, 1863-1947
Amadeo P. Giannini, 1870-1949
J. Erik Jonnson, b. 1901
Royal Little, b. 1896
Cyrus H. McCormick, 1809-1884

J. Pierpont Morgan, 1837-1913
M. J. Rathbone, b. 1900
John D. Rockefeller, 1863-1947
David Sarnoff, 1891-1971
Alfred P. Sloan Jr., 1875-1966
Alexander T. Stewart, 1803-1876
J. Edgar Thomson, 1808-1874
Theodore N. Vail, 1845-1920
George Washington, 1732-1799
Eli Whitney, 1765-1825

1976
Stephen D. Bechtel Sr., b. 1900
Walter E. Disney, 1901-1966
James J. Hill, 1838-1916
Albert D. Lasker, 1880-1952
Charles E. Merrill, 1885-1956
George S. Moore, b. 1905
James C. Penney, 1875-1971
William C. Procter, 1862-1934
Cyrus R. Smith, b. 1899
Thomas J. Watson Jr., b. 1914

The Hall of Fame for Great Americans

The Hall of Fame for Great Americans was a gift to the American people by Mrs. Helen Gould Shepard. New York University acts as Trustee for the Shrine for the nation. Busts and tablets are donated. The Americans honored since 1900 are:

1900
John Adams
John James Audubon
Henry Ward Beecher
William Ellery Channing
Henry Clay
Peter Cooper
Jonathan Edwards
Ralph Waldo Emerson
David Glasgow Farragut
Benjamin Franklin
Robert Fulton
Ulysses Simpson Grant
Asa Gray
Nathaniel Hawthorne
Washington Irving
Thomas Jefferson
James Kent
Robert Edward Lee
Abraham Lincoln
Henry Wadsworth Longfellow
Horace Mann
John Marshall
Samuel Finley Breese Morse
George Peabody
Joseph Story
Gilbert Charles Stuart
George Washington
Daniel Webster
Eli Whitney

1905
John Quincy Adams
James Russell Lowell
Mary Lyon
James Madison
Maria Mitchell
William Tecumseh Sherman
John Greenleaf Whittier
Emma Willard

1910
George Bancroft
Phillips Brooks
William Cullen Bryant
James Fenimore Cooper
Oliver Wendell Holmes
Andrew Jackson
John Lothrop Motley
Edgar Allan Poe
Harriet Beecher Stowe
Frances Elizabeth Willard

1915
Louis Agassiz
Daniel Boone
Rufus Choate
Charlotte Saunders Cushman
Alexander Hamilton
Joseph Henry
Mark Hopkins
Elias Howe
Francis Parkman

1920
Samuel Langhorne Clemens (Mark Twain)
James Buchanan Eads
Patrick Henry
William Thomas Green Morton
Alice Freeman Palmer
Augustus Saint-Gaudens
Roger Williams

1925
Edwin Booth
John Paul Jones

1930
Matthew Fontaine Maury
James Monroe
James Abbott McNeil Whistler
Walt Whitman

1935
Grover Cleveland
Simon Newcomb
William Penn

1940
Stephen Collins Foster

1945
Sidney Lanier
Thomas Paine
Walter Reed
Booker T. Washington

1950
Susan B. Anthony
Alexander Graham Bell
Josiah Willard Gibbs
William Crawford Gorgas
Theodore Roosevelt
Woodrow Wilson

1955
Thomas Jonathan Jackson
George Westinghouse
Wilbur Wright

1960
Thomas A. Edison
Edward A. MacDowell
Henry David Thoreau

1965
Jane Addams
Oliver Wendell Holmes Jr.
Sylvanus Thayer
Orville Wright

1970
Albert Abraham Michelson
Lillian D. Wald

1973
Louis Dembitz Brandeis
George Washington Carver
Franklin Delano Roosevelt
John Philip Sousa

American Writers of the Past

Novelists, Poets, Historians, Biographers

Charles Francis Adams, biographer, diplomat, 1807-1886.
Charles Francis Adams, historian, lawyer, 1835-1915.
Henry Adams, historian, philosopher, 1838-1918.
James Truslow Adams, historian, 1878-1949.
George Ade, humorist, dramatist, 1866-1944.
Conrad Aiken, poet, critic, 1889-1973.
Louisa May Alcott, novelist, 1832-1889. Little Women.
Horatio Alger, author of "rags-to-riches" boys books, 1832-1899.
James Lane Allen, novelist, 1849-1925.
Charlotte Armstrong, mystery writer, 1905-1969.
Gertrude Atherton, novelist, 1857-1948. Black Oxen.
Mary Austin, novelist, playwright, 1868-1934.

Irving Bacheller, novelist, journalist, 1859-1950. Eben Holden.
Ray Stannard Baker, biographer, historian, 1870-1946.
George Bancroft, historian, diplomat, 1800-1891.
Margaret Ayer Barnes, novelist, 1886-1967. Years of Grace.
Bruce Barton, author, businessman, 1875-1967. The Man Nobody Knows.
Charles A. Beard, historian, 1874-1948.
Mary Ritter Beard, historian, 1876-1958.
Edward Bellamy, novelist, 1850-1898. Looking Backward: 2000-1887.
Stephen Vincent Benet, poet, novelist, 1898-1943.
William Rose Benet, poet, novelist, 1886-1950.
John Berryman, poet, 1914-1972.
Ambrose Bierce, short-story writer, journalist, 1842-1914.
Earl Derr Biggers, novelist, 1884-1933. Created Charlie Chan.
Josh Billings (H. W. Shaw), humorist, 1818-1885.
Louise Bogan, lyric poet, 1897-1970.
Gamaliel Bradford, biographer, 1863-1932.
Anne Bradstreet, poet, 1612-1672.
Louis Bromfield, novelist, essayist, 1896-1956.
Van Wyck Brooks, historian, critic, 1886-1963.
Orestes Brownson, author, editor, clergyman, 1803-1876.
Pearl Buck, author, won the Pulitzer and Nobel Prizes, 1892-1973. The Good Earth.
Ned Buntline, wrote dime novels, 1823-1886. Nicknamed "Buffalo Bill" Cody.
Edgar Rice Burroughs, novelist, 1875-1950. Tarzan of the Apes.

George W. Cable, novelist, essayist, 1844-1925.
Will Carleton, poet, journalist, 1845-1912. Over the Hill to the Poorhouse.
Rachel Carson, marine biologist, author, 1907-1964. Silent Spring.
Alice Cary, novelist, 1820-1871.
Phoebe Cary, poet, 1824-1871. One Sweetly Solemn Thought.
Willa Cather, novelist, essayist, 1876-1947. O Pioneers!, My Antonia.
Robert W. Chambers, novelist, artist, 1865-1933. The Rogue's Moon.
Raymond Chandler, wrote detective fiction, 1888-1959. Philip Marlowe series.
Winston Churchill, novelist, 1871-1947. The Crisis.
Walter Van Tilburg Clark, novelist, 1909-1972. The Ox-Bow Incident.
James Fenimore Cooper, novelist, 1789-1851. Leather-Stocking Tales.
Thomas B. Costain, novelist, journalist, 1885-1965. The Black Rose.
Hart Crane, poet, 1899-1932.
Stephen Crane, novelist, 1871-1900. The Red Badge of Courage.
Francis Marion Crawford, novelist, 1854-1909.
Countee Cullen, poet, 1903-1946. The Black Christ.
E. E. Cummings, poet, 1894-1962.

Richard H. Dana, author, lawyer, 1815-1882. Two Years Before the Mast.
Bernard De Voto, historian, editor, 1897-1955.
Emily Dickinson, poet, 1830-1886.
Thomas Dixon, novelist, clergyman, 1865-1946. The Clansman.
J. Frank Dobie, author, educator, 1888-1964.
Hilda Doolittle (H.D.), poet, 1886-1961.
John Dos Passos, author, 1896-1970. U.S.A., Midcentury.
Joseph Rodman Drake, poet, 1795-1820.
Theodore Dreiser, novelist, 1871-1945. An American Tragedy.
Paul L. Dunbar, poet, novelist, 1872-1906.

Edward Eggleston, novelist, clergyman, 1837-1902.
Ralph Waldo Emerson, poet, essayist, 1803-1882.
John Erskine, novelist, educator, 1879-1951. The Private Life of Helen of Troy.

Martha Farquharson, author of juveniles, 1828-1909. Elsie Dinsmore series.
William Faulkner, novelist, 1897-1962. Sanctuary, Light in August.
Edna Ferber, novelist, 1885-1968. Show Boat, Saratoga Trunk, Giant.
Arthur D. Ficke, poet, novelist, 1883-1945.
Eugene Field, poet, journalist, 1850-1895. Little Boy Blue; Wynken, Blynken and Nod.
Louis Fischer, historian, 1896-1970. The Life of Lenin.
Dorothy Canfield Fisher, novelist, writer of juveniles, 1879-1958.
John Fiske, historian, philosopher, 1842-1901.
F. Scott Fitzgerald, novelist, short-story writer, 1896-1940. The Great Gatsby.
John Gould Fletcher, poet, critic, 1886-1950.
Kathryn Forbes, novelist, 1909-1966. Mama's Bank Account.
Paul Leicester Ford, novelist, historian, 1865-1902.
Gene Fowler, journalist, author, 1890-1960. Good Night, Sweet Prince.
John W. Fox Jr., novelist, 1863-1919. The Little Shepherd of Kingdom Come.
Mary E. W. Freeman, short-story writer, 1852-1930.
Philip Freneau, poet, journalist, 1752-1832.
Robert Frost, poet, 1874-1963.

Zona Gale, novelist, dramatist, 1874-1938.
Erle Stanley Gardner, author, lawyer, 1889-1970. Perry Mason series.
Hamlin Garland, novelist, 1860-1940. Main-Traveled Roads.
Ellen Glasgow, novelist, 1873-1945.
Susan Glaspell, novelist, dramatist, 1882-1948.
Zane Grey, writer of western stories, 1875-1939.
Edgar A. Guest, poet, 1881-1959. A Heap of Livin'.
Louis I. Guiney, poet, essayist, 1861-1920.
Arthur Guiterman, poet, 1871-1943.

Edward Everett Hale, author, clergyman, 1822-1909. The Man Without a Country.
James Norman Hall, novelist, 1887-1951. Co-author Mutiny on the Bounty.
Dashiell Hammett, writer of detective fiction, 1894-1961. Created Sam Spade.
Joel Chandler Harris, short-story writer, 1848-1908. Uncle Remus series.
Bret Harte, short-story writer, poet, 1836-1902. The Luck of Roaring Camp.
George B. M. Harvey, journalist, diplomat, 1864-1928.
Cameron Hawley, novelist, 1905-1969. Executive Suite.
Nathaniel Hawthorne, novelist, 1804-1864. The Scarlet Letter.
John M. Hay, historian, diplomat, 1838-1905. Abraham Lincoln: A History.
Lafcadio Hearn, author, 1850-1904.
Ben Hecht, novelist, playwright, journalist, 1894-1964.
Ernest Hemingway, novelist, short-story writer, 1899-1961. A Farewell to Arms.
Burton J. Hendrick, biographer, journalist, 1871-1949.
O. Henry (W. S. Porter), short-story writer, 1862-1910. The Gift of the Magi.
Joseph Hergesheimer, novelist, 1880-1954. Java Head.
Robert Hillyer, poet, novelist, 1895-1962.
Alice Tisdale Hobart, novelist, 1882-1967. Oil for the Lamps of China.
Samuel Hoffenstein, poet, 1890-1947.
Charles Fenno Hoffman, poet, editor, 1806-1884.
Richard Hofstadter, historian, 1916-1970. The Age of Reform.
Oliver Wendell Holmes, poet, novelist, 1809-1894.
Mark DeWolfe Howe, historian, 1906-1967.
Julia Ward Howe, poet, reformer, 1819-1910. The Battle Hymn of the Republic.
William Dean Howells, novelist, critic, 1837-1920.
Elbert Hubbard, author, editor, 1856-1915. A Message to Garcia.
Langston Hughes, poet, playwright, 1902-1967.
Rupert Hughes, novelist, playwright, 1872-1956.
Fannie Hurst, novelist, 1889-1968. Back Street, Lummox.

Washington Irving, essayist, author, 1783-1859. Rip Van Winkle.

Charles Jackson, novelist, 1887-1968. The Lost Weekend.
Henry James, novelist, critic, 1843-1916. Washington Square.
Robinson Jeffers, poet, dramatist, 1887-1962.
Sarah Orne Jewett, novelist, short-story writer, 1849-1909.
James Weldon Johnson, author, poet, 1871-1938.

Clarence Budington Kelland, novelist, short-story writer, 1881-1964.
Jack Kerouac, author, 1922-1969. On the Road.
Francis Scott Key, poet, 1779-1843. The Star-Spangled Banner.
Frances Parkinson Keyes, author, editor, 1885-1970. Dinner at Antoine's.
Joyce Kilmer, poet, 1886-1918. Trees.
Joseph Wood Krutch, author, naturalist, 1885-1970. The Measure of Man.

Oliver La Farge, novelist, 1901-1963. Laughing Boy.
Rose Wilder Lane, novelist, 1887-1968. Let the Hurricane Roar.
Sidney Lanier, poet, critic, 1842-1881.
Ring Lardner, short-story writer, journalist, 1885-1933.
Emma Lazarus, poet, essayist, 1849-1887. The New Colossus.
Margaret Leech, author, historian, 1893-1974.
William Ellery Leonard, poet, 1876-1944.
Oscar Lewis, author, anthropologist, 1914-1970. La Vida.
Sinclair Lewis, novelist, playwright, 1885-1951. Babbitt, Arrowsmith, Dodsworth.
Ludwig Lewisohn, novelist, critic, 1882-1955.
Willy Ley, science writer, 1906-1969.
Vachel Lindsay, poet, 1879-1931.
Louis Lomax, author, 1922-1970. The Negro Revolt.
Jack London, novelist, journalist, 1876-1916. The Call of the Wild.
Henry Wadsworth Longfellow, poet, 1807-1882. The Wreck of the Hesperus, Evangeline, The Song of Hiawatha.
Benson John Lossing, historian, artist, 1813-1891. Pictorial Field Book of the Revolution.
Amy Lowell, poet, critic, 1874-1925.
James Russell Lowell, poet, editor, 1819-1891.

Edwin Markham, poet, 1852-1940. The Man with the Hoe.
John P. Marquand, novelist, 1893-1960. The Late George Apley.
Edgar Lee Masters, poet, biographer, 1869-1950. Spoon River Anthology.
Carson McCullers, novelist, 1917-1967. The Heart is a Lonely Hunter.
John B. McMaster, historian, 1852-1932.
Herman Melville, novelist, poet, 1819-1891. Moby Dick.
Thomas Merton, poet, religious writer, 1915-1968. Seven Storey Mountain.
Edna St. Vincent Millay, poet, 1892-1950.
Joaquin Miller, poet, 1839-1913.
Max Miller, novelist, 1889-1967. I Cover the Waterfront.
Margaret Mitchell, novelist, 1900-1949. Gone With the Wind.
William Vaughn Moody, poet, dramatist, 1869-1910.
Clement C. Moore, poet, educator, 1779-1863. A Visit from Saint Nicholas.
Marianne Moore, poet, 1887-1972.
John L. Motley, historian, diplomat, 1814-1877.
Willard Motley, novelist, 1912-1966. Knock on Any Door.

Ogden Nash, poet, 1902-1971.
Allan Nevins, historian, biographer, 1890-1971.
John G. Nicolay, biographer, 1832-1901. Abraham Lincoln: A History.
Charles B. Nordhoff, novelist, 1887-1947. Co-author Mutiny on the Bounty.
Frank Norris, novelist, journalist, 1870-1902. The Pit.
Kathleen Norris, novelist, 1880-1966.

Edwin G. O'Connor, novelist, 1918-1968. Edge of Sadness, The Last Hurrah.
John O'Hara, novelist, 1905-1970. Butterfield 8, Ten North Frederick.
James Oppenheim, poet, novelist, 1882-1932.

Thomas (Tom) Paine, author, political theorist, 1737-1809. Common Sense.
Dorothy Parker, poet, short-story writer, 1893-1967.
Francis Parkman, historian, 1823-1893.
James K. Pauling, poet, novelist, 1778-1860.
John Howard Payne, poet, dramatist, 1791-1852. Home, Sweet Home.
Josephine P. Peabody, poet, dramatist, 1874-1922.
Egar Allan Poe, poet, short-story writer, critic, 1809-1849. Annabel Lee.
Ernest Poole, journalist, novelist, 1880-1950.
Ezra Pound, poet, 1885-1972.

William H. Prescott, historian, 1796-1859.

James G. Randall, historian, 1881-1953.
Marjorie Kinnan Rawlings, novelist, 1896-1953. The Yearling.
Thomas Buchanan Read, poet, painter, 1822-1872. Sheridan's Ride.
Lizette Woodworth Reese, poet, 1856-1935.
Erich Maria Remarque, novelist, 1898-1970. All Quiet on the Western Front.
James Ford Rhodes, historian, 1848-1927.
Alice Hegan Rice, novelist, 1870-1952. Mrs. Wiggs of the Cabbage Patch.
Cale Young Rice, poet, novelist, 1872-1943.
Conrad M. Richter, novelist, 1890-1968. The Town.
James Whitcomb Riley, poet, 1849-1916.
Mary Roberts Rinehart, mystery writer, 1876-1958. The Circular Staircase, The Bat.
Elizabeth Madox Roberts, poet, novelist, 1886-1941.
Kenneth Roberts, novelist, 1885-1957. Northwest Passage.
Edwin Arlington Robinson, poet, 1869-1935.
Theodore Roethke, poet, 1908-1963.
Damon Runyon, short-story writer, journalist, 1884-1946. Guys and Dolls.
Cornelius Ryan, novelist, 1920-1974. The Longest Day.

Carl Sandburg, poet, biographer, 1878-1967.
George Santayana, poet, essayist, philosopher, 1863-1952.
Lew Sarett, poet, 1888-1954.
Alan Seeger, poet, 1888-1916. I Have a Rendezvous with Death.
Gilbert Seldes, author, critic, 1893-1970. The 7 Lively Arts, The Great Audience.
Ernest Thompson Seton, author, naturalist, 1860-1946. Wild Animals I Have Known.
Anne Sexton, poet, won Pulitzer Prize, 1928-1974.
Frank Dempster Sherman, poet, educator, 1860-1916.
Lydia H. Sigourney, poet, 1791-1865.
Edward Rowland Sill, poet, educator, 1841-1887.
Upton Sinclair, novelist, 1878-1968. The Jungle, Dragon's Teeth.
Betty Smith, novelist, 1896-1972. A Tree Grows in Brooklyn.
Lillian Smith, novelist, 1897-1966. Strange Fruit.
Samuel Francis Smith, poet, clergyman, 1808-1895. America.
Jared Sparks, historian, educator, 1789-1866.
Burt L. Standish (Gilbert Patten), author, 1866-1945. Frank Merriwell series.
Edmund C. Stedman, poet, critic, 1833-1908.
Lincoln Steffens, editor, author, 1866-1936. The Shame of the Cities.
Gertrude Stein, author, 1874-1946. Three Lives.
John Steinbeck, novelist, 1902-1968. Of Mice and Men, The Grapes of Wrath.
George Sterling, poet, 1869-1926.
Wallace Stevens, poet, 1879-1955.
Frank R. Stockton, novelist, short-story writer, 1834-1902. The Lady or the Tiger?
Rex Stout, mystery novelist, 1886-1975. Created Nero Wolfe.
Harriet Beecher Stowe, novelist, 1811-1896. Uncle Tom's Cabin.
Edward Stratemeyer, author, 1862-1930. Creator of such series as the Rover Boys, Bobbsey Twins, Tom Swift.
Gene Stratton-Porter, novelist, 1863-1924. A Girl of the Limberlost.
Mark Sullivan, journalist, author, 1874-1952.
Jacqueline Susann, novelist, 1921-1974. Valley of the Dolls.

John B. Tabb, poet, 1845-1909.
Genevieve Taggard, poet, 1894-1948.
Ida M. Tarbell, editor, author, 1857-1944. The History of the Standard Oil Company.
Booth Tarkington, novelist, 1869-1946. Seventeen, Alice Adams.
Bayard Taylor, poet, novelist, 1825-1878. The Bedouin Love Song.
Edward Taylor, poet, c. 1642-1729.
Sara Teasdale, poet, 1884-1933.
Albert Payson Terhune, novelist, journalist, 1872-1942. Lad: A Dog.
Henry D. Thoreau, essayist, naturalist, 1817-1862. Walden.
James Thurber, humorist, artist, 1894-1961. The New Yorker.
Eunice Tietjens, poet, novelist, 1884-1944.
Ridgely Torrence, poet, dramatist, 1875-1950.
Charles Hanson Towne, poet, editor, 1877-1949.
Frederick J. Turner, historian, educator, 1861-1932.
Mark Twain (Samuel Clemens), novelist, humorist, 1835-1910. The Adventures of Huckleberry Finn, Tom Sawyer.

Carl Van Doren, historian, critic, educator, 1885-1950.
Mark Van Doren, poet, author, critic, 1894-1972.
Henry Van Dyke, poet, educator, essayist, 1852-1933.

Lew Wallace, novelist, diplomat, 1827-1905. Ben Hur.
Artemus Ward (Charles F. Browne), humorist, 1834-1867.
Nathanael West, novelist, 1903-1940.
Edith Wharton, novelist, 1862-1937. The Age of Innocence.
Steward Edward White, novelist, 1873-1946.
Walt Whitman, poet, 1819-1892. Leaves of Grass.
John Greenleaf Whittier, poet, journalist, 1809-1892. Snow-Bound.
Kate Douglas Wiggin, children's author, educator, 1856-1923. Rebecca of Sunnybrook Farm.
Ella Wheeler Wilcox, poet, 1850-1919.

Robert Wilder, novelist, 1901-1974. Written on the Wind.
Ben Ames Williams, novelist, 1889-1953.
William Carlos Williams, poet, physician, 1883-1963.
P.G. Wodehouse, novelist, playwright, 1881-1975.
Thomas Wolfe, novelist, 1900-1938. Look Homeward, Angel.
Samuel Woodworth, poet, dramatist, 1784-1842.
Harold Bell Wright, novelist, 1872-1944. The Shepherd of the Hills.
Richard Wright, novelist, 1908-1960. Native Son.
Elinor Wylie, poet, novelist, 1885-1928.
Philip Wylie, author, 1902-1971. Generation of Vipers.

Journalists, Publishers

Franklin P. Adams, journalist, 1881-1960.
Thomas Bailey Aldrich, author, editor, 1836-1907.
Henry M. Alden, editor, 1836-1919. Harper's Magazine.
Stewart Alsop, political columnist, writer, 1914-1974.
Hamilton Fish Armstrong, journalist, 1893-1973. Editor of Foreign Affairs.

Arthur (Bugs) Baer, humorous columnist, 1886-1969.
John Bartlett, publisher, 1820-1905. Familiar Quotations.
Lucius M. Beebe, journalist, author, 1902-1966. N. Y. Herald Tribune.
Robert C. Benchley, humorist, journalist, 1889-1945.
James Gordon Bennett, journalist, 1795-1872. Founded N. Y. Herald.
James Gordon Bennett Jr., journalist, 1841-1918, N.Y. Herald Evening Telegram.
William Benton, publisher, 1900-1973. Encyclopaedia Britannica.
Ambrose Bierce, short-story writer, journalist, 1842-1914.
Samuel Bowles II, editor, 1826-1878. Springfield Republican.
William Cowper Brann, iconoclast, editor, reformer, 1855-1898.
Arthur Brisbane, journalist, 1864-1936. N. Y. Sun, Evening Sun, World.
Heywood Broun, journalist, 1888-1939. N. Y. Tribune, World.
John Mason Brown, drama, literary critic, 1900-1969.
William Cullen Bryant, poet, editor, 1794-1878.
Henry C. Bunner, journalist, poet, 1855-1896. Editor of Puck.

Henry Seidel Canby, editor, critic, 1878-1961. Saturday Review of Literature.
Jimmy Cannon, sports columnist, 1909-1973.
Raymond Clapper, journalist, 1892-1944.
Irvin S. Cobb, humorist, journalist, 1876-1944.
Bob Considine, journalist, syndicated columnist, 1908-1975. "On the Line."
Royal Cortissoz, journalist, author, 1869-1948. N. Y. Herald Tribune.
Cyrus H.K. Curtis, magazine, newspaper publisher, 1850-1933.
George William Curtis, journalist, author, 1824-1892.

Charles A. Dana, editor, 1819-1897. New York Sun.
Josephus Daniels, journalist, statesman, 1862-1948. Raleigh News & Observer.
Elmer Davis, journalist, radio commentator, 1890-1958.
Richard Harding Davis, journalist, novelist, 1864-1916.
Ludwell Denny, journalist, 1894-1970. Scripps-Howard Newspapers.
Michael H. De Young, newspaper editor, 1849-1925. San Francisco Chronicle.
Orvil E. Dryfoos, newspaper publisher, 1912-1963. New York Times.

John C. Farrar, publisher, editor, 1896-1974.
James T. Fields, editor, author, 1817-1881. Atlantic Monthly.
F.M. Flynn, president, publisher, N.Y. Daily News, 1903-1975.
Douglas S. Freeman, historian, editor, 1886-1953. Richmond News Leader.

Frank E. Gannett, newspaper publisher, 1876-1957. Gannett Newspapers.
Floyd Gibbons, journalist, radio personality, 1887-1939.
Edwin L. Godkin, journalist, 1831-1902. Founded The Nation.
Henry W. Grady, journalist, orator, 1850-1889. Atlanta Constitution.
Horace Greeley, journalist, politician, 1811-1872. N. Y. Tribune.
Abel Green, journalist, editor, 1900-1973. Variety.
Gilbert H. Grosvenor, editor, geographer, 1875-1966. National Geographic.
John Gunther, journalist, author, 1901-1970. Inside U.S.A., Inside Europe.

Norman Hapgood, magazine editor, author, 1868-1937.
George B. M. Harvey, journalist, diplomat, 1864-1928.
Gabriel Heatter, radio commentator, 1890-1972.
William Randolph Hearst, newspaper publisher, 1863-1951.
Burton J. Hendrick, biographer, journalist, 1871-1949.
William M. (Bill) Henry, journalist, radio analyst, 1890-1970. Los Angeles Times.
Ben Hibbs, editor, 1901-1975. Saturday Evening Post.
Marguerite Higgins, journalist, 1920-1966.
Roy W. Howard, newspaper publisher, editor, 1883-1964. Scripps-Howard Newspapers.
Ed Howe, journalist, author, 1853-1937.
Frazier (Spike) Hunt, journalist, war correspondent, 1885-1967.
Chet Huntley, TV newscaster, 1911-1974.

Wallace Irwin, journalist, humorist, 1876-1959.
Will Irwin, journalist, author, 1873-1948.

H. V. Kaltenborn, editor, radio commentator, 1878-1965.
Edward R. Kennedy, publisher, 1923-1975. The World Almanac.
Dorothy Kilgallen, journalist, radio-TV personality, 1913-1965.
Bernard Kilgore, journalist, 1908-1967. Wall Street Journal.
Willard M. Kiplinger, journalist, 1891-1967. Changing Times.
Arthur Krock, journalist, 1887-1974, N. Y. Times.

William M. Laffan, publisher, 1848-1900. New York Sun, N. Y. Evening Sun.
David Lawrence, journalist, founder and editor of U. S. News & World Report, 1888-1973.
Charles Godfrey Leland, author, journalist, 1824-1903.
Fulton Lewis, Jr., radio news commentator, 1903-1966.
Walter Lippmann, dean of American political journalism, 1889-1974.
Elijah P. Lovejoy, journalist, abolitionist, 1802-1837.*
Jim Lucas, journalist, 1914-1970. Scripps-Howard Newspapers.
Henry R. Luce, publisher, 1898-1967. Time, Life, Fortune magazines.

Don Marquis, humorist, journalist, 1878-1937. The Old Soak.
James McClatchy, publisher, editor, 1824-1883. McClatchy Newspapers.
S. S. McClure, editor, publisher, 1857-1949.
Joseph Medill McCormick, journalist, politician, 1887-1925. Chicago Tribune.
Robert R. McCormick, editor, publisher, 1880-1955. Chicago Tribune.
Ralph E. McGill, editor, publisher, 1898-1969. Atlanta Constitution.
Joseph Medill, journalist, 1823-1899. Chicago Tribune.
Henry L. Mencken, editor, author, philologist, 1880-1956. Baltimore Sun, American Mercury.
Christopher Morley, journalist, novelist, 1890-1957. Kitty Foyle.
Edward R. Murrow, radio-TV commentator, 1908-1965.

William Rockhill Nelson, journalist, 1841-1915. Kansas City Star.
Frank B. Noyes, newspaper executive, 1863-1948. Associated Press.

Adolph S. Ochs, newspaper publisher, 1858-1935. The New York Times.
Fremont Older, journalist, 1856-1935. San Francisco Call-Bulletin.

Frederick Palmer, war correspondent, 1873-1958.
Alicia Patterson, journalist, 1906-1963. Newsday.
Eleanor Medill Patterson, journalist, 1884-1948. Washington Times-Herald.
Joseph Medill Patterson, publisher, 1879-1946. Founded N.Y. Daily News.

Drew Pearson, newspaper columnist, 1897-1969.
Westbrook Pegler, newspaper columnist, 1894-1969.
David G. Phillips, journalist, novelist, 1867-1911.
Ernest Poole, journalist, novelist, 1880-1950.
Joseph Pulitzer, journalist, 1847-1911. St. Louis Post-Dispatch, N. Y. World.
Joseph Pulitzer, journalist, 1885-1955. St. Louis Post-Dispatch.
Ralph Pulitzer, journalist, 1879-1939. St. Louis Post-Dispatch, N.Y. World.
Ernie Pyle, journalist, war correspondent, 1900-1945.

Burton Rascoe, journalist, author, 1892-1957.
Ogden M. Reid, journalist, 1882-1947. N. Y. Herald Tribune.
Whitelaw Reid, journalist, diplomat, 1837-1912. N. Y. Tribune.
Quentin Reynolds, journalist, author, 1902-1965.
Grantland Rice, journalist, 1880-1954.
Roy A. Roberts, journalist, 1887-1967. Kansas City Star.
Robert Ruark, journalist, author, 1915-1965. Something of Value.

Max L. Schuster, editor, publisher, 1897-1970. Simon & Schuster.
Edward W. Scripps, newspaper publisher, 1854-1926.
Robert P. Scripps, newspaper publisher, 1895-1938. Scripps-Howard Newspapers.
Vincent Sheean, foreign correspondent, 1899-1975.
Merriman Smith, newspaper correspondent, 1913-1970. UPI.
Frank L. Stanton, poet, journalist, 1857-1927. Mighty Lak'a Rose.
Melville E. Stone, journalist, 1848-1929. Associated Press.

Anna Louise Strong, journalist, 1885-1970.
Mark Sullivan, journalist, author, 1874-1952.
Arthur Hays Sulzberger, publisher, 1891-1968. The New York Times.
Herbert Bayard Swope, journalist, 1882-1958. N. Y. World.

Dorothy Thompson, journalist, author, 1894-1961.
James Thurber, humorist, artist, 1894-1961. The New Yorker.
George A. Townsend, journalist, war correspondent, 1841-1914.

Hendrik Willem van Loon, historian, journalist, 1882-1944.
Carl Van Vechten, music critic, novelist, 1880-1964.
Oswald G. Villard, editor, author, 1872-1949. The Nation.

Henry Watterson, editor, author, 1840-1921. Louisville Courier-Journal.
William Allen White, editor, author, 1868-1944. Emporia (Kan.) Gazette.
Nathaniel P. Willis, journalist, author, 1806-1867.
Edmund Wilson, author, literary and social critic, 1895-1972.
Lyle C. Wilson, journalist, 1899-1967. United Press International.
Walter Winchell, Broadway columnist, 1897-1972.
Frederick E. Woltman, journalist, 1907-1970. N. Y. World-Telegram & Sun.
Alexander Woollcott, journalist, critic, 1887-1943.

John Peter Zenger, journalist, printer, 1697-1746. N. Y. Weekly Journal.

Noted American Cartoonists

Charles Addams, b. 1912. Noted for macabre cartoons.
Peter Arno, 1904-1968. Noted for urban characterizations.
George Baker, 1915-1975. The Sad Sack.
Jim Berry, b. 1932. Berry's World.
Herb Block (Herblock), b. 1909. Leading political cartoonist.
Clare Briggs, 1875-1930. Mr. & Mrs.
Ernie Bushmiller, b. 1905. Nancy.
Milton Caniff, b. 1907. Terry & the Pirates; Steve Canyon.
Al Capp, b. 1909. Li'l Abner.
Roy Crane, b. 1901. Captain Easy; Buz Sawyer.
Jay N. Darling (Ding), 1876-1962. Political cartoonist won 2 Pulitzer Prizes.
Billy DeBeck, 1890-1942. Barnie Google.
Rudolph Dirks, 1877-1968. The Katzenjammer Kids.
Walt Disney, 1901-1966. Producer of animated cartoons created Mickey Mouse & Donald Duck.
Alan Dunn, 1900-1974. Cartoonist for The New Yorker.
Jules Feiffer, b. 1929. Satirical Village Voice cartoonist.
Bud Fisher, 1885-1954. Mutt & Jeff.
Ham Fisher, 1900-1955. Joe Palooka.
James Montgomery Flagg, 1877-1960. Illustrator, created the famous Uncle Sam recruiting poster during WWI.
Hal Foster, b. 1892. Tarzan; Prince Valiant.
Fontaine Fox, 1884-1964. Toonerville Folks.
Rube Goldberg, 1883-1970. Boob McNutt. Famed for cartoons of mechanical contrivances whose humor is derived from their absurd, unnecessary complexity.
Chester Gould, b. 1900. Dick Tracy.
Harold Gray, 1894-1968. Little Orphan Annie.
John Held Jr., 1889-1958. His cartoons epitomized the spirit of the "jazz age" of the 20s.
George Herriman, 1881-1944. Krazy Kat.
Harry Hershfield, 1885-1974. Raconteur; Abie the Agent.
Burne Hogarth, b. 1911. Tarzan.
Helen Hokinson, 1900-1949. Known for satirical drawings of plump, bewildered suburban matrons and clubwomen.

Walt Kelly, 1913-1973. Pogo.
Hank Ketcham, b. 1920. Dennis the Menace.
Ted Key, b. 1912. Hazel.
Frank King, 1883-1969. Gasoline Alley.
Jack Kirby, b. 1917. Captain America.
Rollin Kirby, 1875-1952. Political cartoonist won 3 Pulitzer Prizes.
Bill Mauldin, b. 1921. Depicted squalid life of the G.I. in WW II.
Winsor McCay, 1872-1934. Little Nemo.
John T. McCutcheon, 1870-1949. Noted for cartoons of mid-western rural life.
George McManus, 1884-1954. Bringing Up Father (Maggie & Jiggs).
Dale Messick, b. 1906. Brenda Starr.
Bob Montana, 1920-1975. Archie.
Thomas Nast, 1840-1902. His political cartoons were instrumental in breaking the corrupt Boss Tweed ring in N.Y. Created the donkey and elephant to represent the Democratic and Republican parties.
Frederick Burr Opper, 1857-1937. Happy Hooligan.
Richard Outcault, 1863-1928. Yellow Kid; Buster Brown.
Alex Raymond, 1909-1956. Flash Gordon; Jungle Jim.
Art Sansom, b. 1920. The Born Loser.
Charles Schulz, b. 1922. Peanuts.
Elzie C. Segar, 1894-1938. Popeye.
Sydney Smith, 1887-1935. The Gumps.
Otto Soglow, 1900-1975. The Little King; The Canyon Kiddies.
James Swinnerton, 1875-1974. Little Jimmy.
James Thurber, 1894-1961. New Yorker cartoonist of the smugly childish line coupled with the sophisticated caption.
Mort Walker, b. 1923. Beetle Bailey.
Russ Westover, 1887-1966. Tillie the Toiler.
Frank Willard, 1893-1958. Moon Mullins.
J. R. Williams, 1888-1957. The Willets Family; Out Our Way.
Art Young, 1866-1943. Political radical and satirist.
Chic Young, 1901-1973. Blondie.

Modern American Playwrights and Some of Their Plays

George Abbott, b. 1887. Co-author Three Men on a Horse, The Boys from Syracuse, Damn Yankees.
Edward F. Albee, b. 1928. Who's Afraid of Virginia Woolf?, Tiny Alice, A Delicate Balance, Seascape.
William Alfred, b. 1922. Hogan's Goat.
Maxwell Anderson (1888-1959). What Price Glory?, Winterset, Saturday's Children, High Tor, Key Largo.
Philip Barry (1886-1949). The Animal Kingdom, Holiday, The Philadelphia Story.
Abe Burrows, b. 1910. Co-author Guys and Dolls, How to Succeed in Business Without Really Trying.
Mary C. Chase, b. 1907. Harvey.
Paddy Chayefsky, b. 1923. Middle of the Night, The Tenth Man, Gideon, The Passions of Josef D.
Marc Connelly, b. 1890. The Green Pastures.

Russell Crouse (1893-1966). Co-author State of the Union, Life With Father, Call Me Madam, The Sound of Music.
Edna Ferber (1885-1968). Co-author Dinner at Eight, Stage Door.
Paul Foster, b. 1932. Tom Paine.
Jack Gelber, b. 1932. The Connection, The Cuban Thing,
William Gibson, b. 1914. Two for the Seesaw, The Miracle Worker.
Frank D. Gilroy, b. 1915. The Subject Was Roses, The Only Game in Town.
Charles Gordone, b. 1925. No Place to Be Somebody.
Paul Green, b. 1894. In Abraham's Bosom, Wilderness Road.
William Hanley, b. 1931. Slow Dance on the Killing Ground.
Lorraine Hansberry (1930-1965). A Raisin in the Sun.
Moss Hart (1904-1961). Co-author Once in a Lifetime, You

Can't Take it With You.

Ben Hecht (1884-1964). Co-author The Front Page.

Lillian Hellman, b. 1907. The Children's Hour, The Little Foxes, Watch on the Rhine.

Sidney Howard (1881-1939). The Silver Cord, Yellow Jack, They Knew What They Wanted.

William Inge (1913-1973). Come Back Little Sheba, Picnic, Bus Stop, The Dark at the Top of the Stairs, A Loss of Roses.

LeRoi Jones (Imamu Amini Baraka), b. 1934. Dutchman, The Slave.

George S. Kaufman (1889-1961). Co-author Dinner at Eight, Stage Door, You Can't Take It With You, The Man Who Came to Dinner.

George Kelly (1887-1974). The Show-off, Craig's Wife.

Jean Kerr, b. 1923. Mary, Mary, Poor Richard, Finishing Touches.

Joseph Kesserlring (1902-1967). Arsenic and Old Lace.

Sidney Kingsley, b. 1906. Men in White, The Patriots, Dead End, Darkness at Noon.

Arthur Kopit, b. 1937. Oh Dad, Poor Dad, Mamma's Hung You in a Closet and I'm Feelin' So Sad.

Howard Lindsay (1889-1968). Co-author State of the Union, Life With Father, Call Me Madam, The Sound of Music.

Charles MacArthur (1895-1956). Co-author The Front Page.

Archibald MacLeish, b. 1892. J. B.

Terrence McNally, b. 1939. And Things That Go Bump in the Night, Sweet Eros.

Arthur Miller, b. 1915. All My Sons, Death of a Salesman, Crucible, View from the Bridge, After the Fall, Incident at Vichy, The Price.

Jason Miller, b. 1940. That Championship Season.

Anne Nichols (1891-1966). Abie's Irish Rose.

Clifford Odets (1906-1963). Waiting for Lefty, Awake and Sing, Golden Boy, The Country Girl.

Eugene O'Neill (1888-1953). The Long Voyage Home, The Emperor Jones, Anna Christie, Desire Under the Elms, Strange Interlude, Mourning Becomes Electra, Ah, Wilderness, The Iceman Cometh, Long Day's Journey Into Night.

John Patrick, b. 1905. The Hasty Heart, Teahouse of the August Moon.

Elmer Rice (1892-1967). The Adding Machine, Street Scene, Counsellor-at-Law, Dream Girl.

Howard Sackler, b. 1930. The Great White Hope.

William Saroyan, b. 1908. My Heart's in the Highlands, The Time of Your Life.

Dore Schary, b. 1905. Sunrise at Campobello.

Murray Schisgal, b. 1926. The Typists and the Tiger, Luv.

Robert Sherwood (1896-1955). Reunion in Vienna. The Petrified Forest, Idiot's Delight, There Shall Be No Night, Abe Lincoln in Illinois.

Neil Simon, b. 1927. Sweet Charity, Plaza Suite, The Odd Couple, Barefoot in the Park, Last of the Red Hot Lovers, The Gingerbread Lady, The Prisoner of Second Avenue, The Sunshine Boys, The Good Doctor.

Samuel A. Taylor, b. 1912. The Happy Time, The Pleasure of His Company, co-author Sabrina Fair and No Strings.

John Van Druten (1901-1957). The Voice of the Turtle; I Remember Mama; Bell, Book and Candle; I Am a Camera.

Thornton Wilder, b. 1897. Our Town, The Skin of Our Teeth, The Matchmaker.

Tennessee Williams, b. 1914. The Glass Menagerie, A Streetcar Named Desire, Cat on a Hot Tin Roof, The Night of the Iguana, The Milk Train Doesn't Stop Here Anymore, Camino Real.

American Architects and Some of Their Achievements

Max Abramovitz, b. 1908. Avery Fisher Hall at Lincoln Center, N.Y.C.

Henry Bacon, (1866-1924) Lincoln Memorial.

Pietro Belluschi, b. 1899. Julliard School of Music, Lincoln Center, N.Y.C.

Marcel Breuer, b. 1902. Whitney Museum of American Art, N.Y.C. (with Hamilton Smith).

Charles Bulfinch, (1763-1844) State House, Boston; Capitol, Washington, (part).

Daniel H. Burnham, (1846-1912) Union Station, Washington; Flatiron, N.Y.C.

Ralph Adams Cram, (1863-1942) Cathedral of St. John the Divine, N.Y.C.; U.S. Military Academy (part).

Alexander J. Davis, (1803-1892) Sub-treasury, N.Y.C.; capitols of Ind., N. C., Ill., Ohio.

R. Buckminster Fuller, b. 1895. U.S. Pavilion, Expo 67, Montreal (geodesic domes).

William F. Gibbs, (1886-1967) Designed liner United States.

Cass Gilbert, (1859-1934) Custom House, Woolworth Bldg., N.Y.C.; Capitol, St. Paul.

Bertrand Goldberg, b. 1913. Marina City Towers, Chicago.

Bertram G. Goodhue, (1869-1924) Capitol, Lincoln, Neb.; St. Thomas, St. Bartholomew, N.Y.C.

Walter Gropius, (1883-1969) Pan Am Building, N.Y.C. (with Pietro Belluschi).

Peter Harrison, (1716-1775) Jeshuat Israel Synagogue, Redwood Library, Newport, R.I.

Wallace K. Harrison, b. 1895. Metropolitan Opera House at Lincoln Center, N.Y.C.

Thomas Hastings, (1860-1929) Public Library, Frick Mansion, N.Y.C.

James Hoban, (1762-1831) The White House.

William Holabird (1854-1923) Crerar Library, City Hall, Chicago.

Raymond Hood, (1881-1934) Rockefeller Center, N.Y.C. (part); Daily News, N.Y.C.; Tribune, Chicago.

Richard M. Hunt, (1828-1896) Metropolitan Museum, N.Y.C. (part); The Breakers, Newport.

William Le Baron Jenney, (1832-1907) Home Insurance, Chicago (demolished).

Philip C. Johnson, b. 1906. N.Y. State Theater at Lincoln Center, N.Y.C.

Albert Kahn, (1869-1942) Athletic Club Bldg., General Motors Bldg., N.Y.C.

Louis Kahn, (1901-1974) Salk Laboratory, La Jolla, Cal.; Yale Art Gallery.

Christopher Grant LaFarge, (1862-1938) Chapel, West Point; Cathedral, Seattle.

Benjamin H. Latrobe, (1764-1820) U.S. Capitol (part).

Pierre L'Enfant, (1754-1825) Laid out Washington, D.C.

William Lescaze, (1896-1969) Philadelphia Savings Fund Society; Borg-Warner Bldg., Chicago.

Theodore C. Link, (1850-1923) Union Station, St. Louis.

Charles F. McKim, (1847-1909) Public Library, Boston; Columbia Univ., N.Y.C. (part).

Charles M. McKim, b. 1920. KUHT-TV Transmitter Building, Houston; Lutheran Church of the Redeemer, Houston.

Milton B. Medary, (1874-1929) Bok Carillon Tower, Mountain Lake, Fla.

Ludwig Mies van der Rohe, (1886-1969) Seagram Building, N.Y.C. (with Philip C. Johnson); National Gallery, Berlin.

Robert Mills, (1781-1855) Washington Monument.

Richard J. Neutra, (1892-1970) Mathematics Park, Princeton; Orange Co. Courthouse, Santa Ana, Cal.

Frederick L. Olmsted, (1822-1903) Central Park, N.Y.C.; Fairmount Park, Philadelphia.

Ieoh Ming Pei, b. 1917. Kips Bay Plaza, N.Y.C.; Earth Sciences Building (M.I.T.) Cambridge, Mass.; National Center for Atmospheric Research, Boulder, Col.

John Russell Pope, (1874-1937) National Gallery.

John Portman, b. 1924. Peachtree Center, Atlanta.

James Renwick Jr., (1818-1895) Grace Church, St. Patrick's Cathedral, N.Y.C.; Smithsonian, Corcoran Galleries, Wash., D.C.

Henry H. Richardson, (1838-1886) Trinity, Boston.

Kevin Roche, b. 1922. Oakland Cal. Museum; Fine Arts Center, U. of Mass.

James Gamble Rogers, (1867-1947) Columbia-Presbyterian Medical Center, N.Y.C.; Northwestern Univ., Chicago.

John Weldon Root, b. 1887. Palmolive Building, Chicago; Hotel Statler, Washington; Hotel Tamanaco, Caracas.

Paul Rudolph, b. 1918. Jewitt Art Center, Wellesley College; Art & Architecture Bldg., Yale.

Eero Saarinen, (1910-1961) Gateway to the West Arch, St. Louis; Trans World Flight Center, N.Y.C.

Louis Skidmore, (1897-1962) AEC town site, Oak Ridge, Tenn.; Terrace Plaza Hotel, Cincinnati.

Clarence W. Stein, b. 1882. Temple Emanu-El, N.Y.C.

Edward Durell Stone, b. 1902. U.S. Embassy, New Delhi, India; (H. Hartford) Gallery of Modern Art, N.Y.C.

Louis H. Sullivan, (1856-1924) Auditorium, Chicago.

Richard Upjohn, (1802-1878) Trinity Church, N.Y.C.

Ralph T. Walker, (1889-1973) N.Y. Telephone Hdqrs., N.Y.C.; IBM Research Lab., Poughkeepsie, N.Y.

Roland A. Wank, (1898-1970) Cincinnati Union Terminal; head architect TVA, 1933-44.

Stanford White, (1853-1906) Washington Arch; First Madison Square Garden, N.Y.C.

Frank Lloyd Wright, (1869-1959) Imperial Hotel, Tokyo; Guggenheim Museum, N.Y.C.

William Wurster, b. 1895. Ghirardelli Sq., San Francisco; Cowell College, U. Cal., Berkeley.

Minoru Yamasaki, b. 1912. World Trade Center, N.Y.C.

Noted Black Americans

(Names of black athletes and entertainers are not included here as they are well known and are listed elsewhere in The World Almanac.)

Explorers, Settlers

James P. Beckwourth (1798-c. 1867) western fur-trader, scout, after whom Beckwourth Pass in northern California is named.

Jean Baptiste Point du Sable (c.1750-1818) pioneer trader and first settler of Chicago, 1779.

Estevanico explorer led Spanish expedition of 1538 into Amer. Southwest.

Matthew A. Henson (1866-1955), member of Peary's 1909 expedition to the North Pole; placed U.S. flag at the Pole.

Pedro Alonzo Nino, navigator of the Nina, one of Columbus' 3 ships on his first voyage of discovery to the New World, 1492.

Soldiers, Patriots

Crispus Attucks (c. 1723-1770), agitator led group which precipitated the "Boston Massacre" and slain with 4 others, Mar. 5, 1770.

Lt. Gen. Benjamin O. Davis Jr., b. 1912, West Point (1936), first black Air Force general (1954).

Brig. Gen. Benjamin O. Davis Sr., b. 1877, first black general (1940) in U. S. Army.

Isaiah Dorman (19th century), U. S. Army interpreter, killed with Custer, 1876, at Battle of the Little Big Horn.

Henry O. Flipper, first black to graduate, 1877, from West Point.

Adm. Samuel L. Gravely Jr., b. 1922, first black admiral, 1971, served in World War II, Korea, and Vietnam.

(Of 274,937 blacks who served in the U.S. Armed Forces during the Vietnam conflict (1965-1974), 5,681 were killed in combat.)

Gen. Daniel James Jr., b. 1920, first black 4-star general, 1975; Commander-in-Chief of the North Atlantic Air Defense Command.

Pvt. Henry Johnson (1897-1929) the first American decorated by France in World War I with the Croix de Guerre.

(Of 367,000 blacks in the Armed Forces in World War I, 100,000 served in France.)

Dorie Miller of Waco, Tex., Navy hero of Pearl Harbor attack; awarded the Navy Cross.

(More than 1,000,000 blacks served in the U. S. Armed Forces in World War II; all-black fighter and bomber AAF units and infantry divisions gave distinguished service. In 1954 the policy of all-black units was finally abolished.)

Peter Salem, one of the defenders at the Battle of Bunker Hill, June 17, 1775, shot and killed British commander Maj. John Pitcairn.

(About 5,000 blacks served in the Continental Army, mostly in integrated units, some in all-black combat outfits.)

Harriet Tubman (c. 1820-1913) Underground Railroad conductor served as nurse and spy for Union Army in the Civil War.

(Some 200,000 blacks served in the Union Army during the Civil War; 38,000 gave their lives; 22 won the Medal of Honor, the nation's highest award.)

Scientists, Inventors

Benjamin Banneker (1731-1806), author of annual almanacs, 1791-1802, served on commission which surveyed and helped lay out the future city of Washington, D. C.

Henry Blair (19th century), obtained patents (believed the first issued to a black) for a corn-planter, 1834, and for a cotton-planter, 1836.

George E. Carruthers, b. 1940, physicist developed the Apollo 16 lunar surface ultraviolet camera/spectograph.

George Washington Carver (1861-1943) botanist, chemurgist, and educator; his extensive experiments in soil building and plant diseases revolutionized the economy of the South.

Dr. Charles Richard Drew (1904-1950) pioneer in development of blood banks; director of American Red Cross blood donor project in World War II.

Dr. William A. Hinton (1883-1959) developed the Hinton and Davies-Hinton tests for detection of syphilis; first black professor, 1949, at Harvard Medical School.

Lewis H. Latimer (1848-1928) associate of Thomas Edison; supervised installation of first electric street lighting in New York.

Jan Matzeliger (1852-1889) invented lasting machine which revolutionized the shoe industry.

Norbert Rillieux (1806-1894) invented a vacuum pan evaporator, 1846, which revolutionized the sugar-refining industry.

Dr. Daniel Hale Williams (1856-1931) performed one of first 2 open-heart operations 1893; founded Provident, Chicago's first Negro hospital; first black elected a fellow of the American College of Surgeons.

Granville T. Woods (1856-1910) invented the third-rail system now used in subways and a complex railway telegraph device that helped reduce train accidents.

Writers, Educators

James Baldwin, b. 1924, author, playwright; Another Country, The Fire Next Time, Blues for Mister Charlie.

Imamu Amiri Baraka, b. LeRoi Jones, 1934; poet, playwright, community leader in Newark, N.J.

Edward Bouchet (1852-1918) first black to earn a Ph.D, Yale, 1876, at a U. S. university; first to be elected to Phi Beta Kappa.

Gwendolyn Brooks, b. 1917, poet, novelist; first black to win a Pulitzer Prize, 1950, for Annie Allen.

William Wells Brown (1815-1884) novelist, dramatist; first American black to publish a novel.

Charles Waddell Chestnutt (1858-1932) author known primarily for his short stories, including The Conjure Woman.

Countee Cullen (1903-1946) poet, winner of numerous literary prizes.

Frederick Douglass (1817-1895) author, editor, orator, diplomat; edited the abolitionist weekly, The North Star, in Rochester, N.Y.; became U. S. Minister and Consul General to Haiti.

William Edward Burghardt Du Bois (1868-1963) historian, sociologist; a founder of the NAACP, around 1909, and founding editor of its magazine The Crisis; author, The Souls of Black Folk.

Paul Laurence Dunbar (1872-1906) poet, novelist; won fame with Lyrics of Lowly Life, 1896.

Ralph Ellison b. 1914, novelist, winner of 1952 National Book Award for Invisible Man.

Charles Gordone, b. 1925, won 1970 Pulitzer Prize in Drama with No Place to Be Somebody.

Jupiter Hammon (c.1720-1800) poet; the first black American to have his works published.

Lorraine Hansberry (1930-1965) playwright; won N. Y. Drama Critics Circle Award, 1959, with Raisin in the Sun.

Langston Hughes (1902-1967) poet; also author of stories and song lyrics.

James Weldon Johnson (1871-1938) poet, lyricist, novelist; first black admitted to Florida bar; a U.S. consul in Venezuela and Nicaragua.

Willard Motley (1912-1965) novelist; Knock on Any Door.

Wilson C. Riles, b. 1917, elected, 1970, California State Superintendent of Public Instruction.

John B. Russwurm (1799-1851) with **Samuel E. Cornish** (1793-1858) founded, 1827, the nation's first black newspaper, Freedom's Journal, in N.Y.C.

Booker T. Washington (1856-1915) founder, 1881, and first president of Tuskegee Institute; author; Up From Slavery.

Phillis Wheatley (c. 1753-1784) poet; 2d American woman and first black woman to have her works published.

Dr. Carter G. Woodson (1875-1950) historian; founded Journal of Negro History and Assn. for Study of Negro Life and History, 1915.

Richard Wright (1908-1960) novelist; Native Son, Black Boy.

Frank Yerby, b. 1916, most successful of American black novelists; The Foxes of Harrow, Vixen.

Public Officials

Dr. Mary McCleod Bethune (1875-1955) adviser to Presidents F. D. Roosevelt and Truman; division administrator in National Youth Administration, 1935; founder, president of Bethune-Cookman College.

Julian Bond, b. 1940, civil rights leader first elected to the Georgia state legislature, 1965; helped found Student Nonviolent Coordinating Committee.

Thomas Bradley, b. 1917, elected mayor of Los Angeles, 1973.

Andrew F. Brimmer, b. 1926, first black member, 1966, Federal Reserve Board.

Edward W. Brooke, b. 1919, attorney general, 1962, of Massachusetts; first black elected to U.S. Senate, 1967, since 19th century Reconstruction.

Dr. Ralph Bunche (1904-1971) first black to win the Nobel Peace Prize, 1950; undersecretary of the United Nations, 1950.

Mrs. Shirley Chisholm, b. 1924, first black woman elected to House of Representatives (Brooklyn, N. Y. 1968).

William L. Dawson (1886-1970) Illinois congressman, first black chairman of a major House of Representatives committee.

William H. Hastie, b. 1904, first black federal judge, appointed 1937; Governor of Virgin Islands, 1946-1949; judge, U.S. Circuit Court of Appeals, 1949.

Robert C. Henry, elected mayor of Springfield, Oh., 1965, first black mayor of a moderate-sized city in the 20th century.

Maynard Jackson, elected mayor Atlanta, 1973.

Thurgood Marshall, b. 1908, first black U.S. solicitor general 1965; first black justice of the U. S. Supreme Court, 1967; as a lawyer led the legal battery which won the historic decision from the Supreme Court declaring racial segregation of public schools unconstitutional, 1954.

Adam Clayton Powell (1908-1972) early civil rights leader, congressman, 1945-1969; as head of House Committee on Education and Labor, 1960-1967, was responsible for 48 major pieces of social legislation.

Joseph H. Rainey (1832-1887) first black elected to House of Representatives, 1869, from South Carolina.

Charles Rangel, b. 1930, congressman from N.Y.C. (1970); chairman of the Congressional Black Caucus.

Hiram R. Revels (1822-1901) first black U. S. Senator, elected in Mississippi, served 1870-1871.

Carl R. Towan, b. 1925, prize-winning journalist; director of the U. S. Information Agency, 1964, making him the first black to sit on the National Security Council; U. S. ambassador to Finland, 1963.

Dr. Robert C. Weaver, b. 1907, first black member of the U.S. Cabinet, secretary of the Department of Housing & Urban Development, 1966.

(As of May, 1976, there were 152 black mayors, 1,442 city officials, 355 county officers, 223 state senators, 223 state representatives, one U.S. senator, and 17 U.S. representatives. There are now 3,979 blacks holding elected office in the United States, an increase of 14% over the previous year, according to a survey by the Joint Center for Political Studies, Washington, D.C.)

Labor, Civil Rights Leaders

The Rev. Dr. Ralph David Abernathy, b. 1926, organizer, 1957, and president, 1968, of the Southern Christian Leadership Conference.

James Farmer, b. 1920, a founder of the Congress of Racial Equality, 1942; asst. secretary of H.E.W., 1969.

Marcus Garvey (1887-1940) founded Universal Negro Improvement Assn., 1911, sought to promote a Back to Africa movement.

The Rev. Jesse Jackson, national director, Operation Bread Basket, and major community leader in Chicago.

The Rev. Dr. Martin Luther King Jr. (1929-1968) led 382-day, Montgomery, Ala., boycott which brought 1956 U.S. Supreme Court decision holding segregation on buses unconstitutional; founder, president of the Southern Christian Leadership Conference, 1957; leader of rights marches; won Nobel Peace Prize 1964.

Malcolm X (1925-1965) founded the Organization of Afro-American Unity, 1963, a leading spokesman for black pride.

Elijah Muhammad (1897-1975) founded the Nation of Islam, or Black Muslims, 1931.

A. Philip Randolph, b. 1889, organized the Brotherhood of Sleeping Car Porters, 1925; organizer of 1941 and 1963 March on Washington movements; vice president, AFL-CIO.

Bayard Rustin, b. 1910, organizer of the 1963 March on Washington; executive director of the A. Philip Randolph Institute.

Bishop Stephen Spottswood (1897-1974) board chairman of NAACP from 1966.

Willard Townsend (1895-1957) organized the United Transport Service Employees, 1935 (redcaps, etc.); vice president of AFL-CIO.

Sojourner Truth (1797-1883) born Isabella Baumfree; preacher, abolitionist; raised funds for Union in Civil War; worked for black educational opportunities.

Nat Turner (1800-1831) leader of the most significant of over 200 slave revolts in U.S. history, in Southhampton, Va.; he and 16 others were hanged.

Walter White (1893-1955) executive secretary, NAACP, 1931-1955.

Roy Wilkins, b. 1901, became executive secretary, 1955, NAACP.

Whitney M. Young Jr. (1921-1971) executive director, 1961, of the National Urban League; author, lecturer, newspaper columnist.

Widely Known Americans of the Present

Statesmen, Authors, Military Men, and Other Prominent Persons Not Listed in Other Categories.

Name	Birthplace	Birthdate	Name	Birthplace	Birthdate
Abernathy, Ralph (Linden, Ala.)		3/11/26	Borman, Frank (Gary, Ind.)		3/14/28
Abzug, Bella (New York, N.Y.)		7/24/20	Bowles, Chester (Springfield, Mass.)		4/5/01
Agnew, Spiro (Baltimore, Md.)		11/9/18	Bradley, Omar N. (Clark, Mo.)		2/12/93
Albee, Edward (Washington, D.C.)		3/12/28	Bradley, Thomas (Calvert, Tex.)		12/29/17
Albert, Carl (McAlester, Okla.)		5/10/08	Braun, Wernher von (Wirsitz, Germany)		3/23/12
Aldrin, Edwin E. Jr. (Buzz) (Glen Ridge, N.J.)		1/20/30	Brennan, William J. (Newark, N.J.)		4/25/06
Ali, Muhammad (Louisville, Ky.)		1/18/42	Breslin, Jimmy (Jamaica, L.I., N.Y.)		10/17/30
Alioto, Joseph (San Francisco, Cal.)		2/12/16	Brewster, Kingman (Longmeadow, Mass.)		6/17/19
Alsop, Joseph W. Jr. (Avon, Conn.)		10/11/10	Brinkley, David (Wilmington, N.C.)		7/10/20
Alston, Walter (Butler Co., Oh.)		12/1/11	Brooke, Edward (Washington, D.C.)		10/26/19
Anderson, Jack (Long Beach, Cal.)		10/19/22	Brown, Edmund G. Jr. (San Francisco, Cal.)		4/7/38
Arcaro, Eddie (Cincinnati, Oh.)		2/19/16	Buchwald, Art (Mt. Vernon, N.Y.)		10/20/25
Armstrong, Neil (Wapakoneta, Oh.)		8/5/30	Buckley, James (New York, N.Y.)		3/9/23
Ashe, Arthur (Richmond, Va.)		7/10/43	Buckley, William F. (New York, N.Y.)		11/24/25
Askew, Reubin (Muskogee, Okla.)		9/11/28	Burns, Arthur F. (Stanislau, Aust.)		4/27/04
			Bundy, McGeorge (Boston, Mass.)		3/30/19
Bailey, F. Lee (Waltham, Mass.)		6/10/33	Burger, Warren (St. Paul, Minn.)		9/17/07
Baker, Howard (Huntsville, Tenn.)		11/15/25	Bush, George (Milton, Mass.)		6/12/24
Baker, Russell (Loudoun Co., Va.)		8/14/25	Butz, Earl (Albion, Ind.)		7/3/09
Baldwin, Faith (New Rochelle, N.Y.)		10/1/93	Byrd, Robert (N. Wilkesboro, N.C.)		1/15/18
Baldwin, James (New York, N.Y.)		8/2/24			
Ball, George (Des Moines, Ia.)		12/21/09	Caldwell, Erskine (Coweta Co., Ga.)		12/17/03
Barth, John (Cambridge, Md.)		5/27/30	Capote, Truman (New Orleans, La.)		9/30/24
Bayh, Birch (Terre Haute, Ind.)		1/22/28	Carey, Hugh (Brooklyn, N.Y.)		4/11/19
Beame, Abraham (London, Eng.)		3/20/06	Carter, Jimmy (Plains, Ga.)		10/1/24
Belli, Melvin (Sonora, Cal.)		7/29/07	Case, Clifford (Franklin Park, N.J.)		4/16/04
Bellow, Saul (Quebec, Canada)		7/10/15	Celler, Emmanuel (Brooklyn, N.Y.)		5/6/88
Bentsen, Lloyd (Mission, Tex.)		2/11/21	Chamberlain, Wilt (Philadelphia, Pa.)		8/21/36
Bernstein, Carl (Washington, D.C.)		2/14/44	Chancellor, John (Chicago, Ill.)		7/14/27
Bishop, Jim (Jersey City, N.J.)		11/21/07	Chavez, Cesar (Yuma, Ariz.)		3/31/27
Blackmun, Harry (Nashville, Ill.)		11/12/08	Cheney, Richard B. (Lincoln, Neb.)		1/30/41
Bok, Derek (Ardmore, Pa.)		3/22/30	Chisholm, Shirley (Brooklyn, N.Y.)		11/30/24
Bond, Julian (Nashville, Tenn.)		1/14/40	Church, Frank (Boise, Ida.)		7/25/24

Name	Birthplace	Birthdate
Safire, William (New York, N.Y.)		12/17/29
Salinger, J. D. (New York, N.Y.)		1/1/19
Salinger, Pierre (San Francisco, Cal.)		6/14/25
Salk, Jonas (New York, N.Y.)		10/28/14
Samuelson, Paul A. (Gary, Ind.)		5/15/15
Schlesinger, Arthur Jr. (Columbus, Oh.)		10/15/17
Schlesinger, James (New York, N.Y.)		2/15/29
Scott, Hugh (Fredericksburg, Va.)		11/11/00
Scranton, William W. (Madison, Conn.)		7/19/17
Seaborg, Glenn T. (Ishpeming, Mich.)		4/19/12
Sevareid, Eric (Velva, N.D.)		11/26/12
Sheen, Fulton J. (El Paso, Ill.)		5/8/95
Shirer, William L. (Chicago, Ill.)		2/23/04
Shoemaker, Willie (Fabens, Tex.)		8/19/31
Shor, Toots (Philadelphia, Pa.)		5/6/05
Shriver, R. Sargent (Westminster, Md.)		11/9/15
Shultz, George (New York, N.Y.)		12/13/20
Simon, Neil (New York, N.Y.)		7/4/27
Simon, William (Paterson, N.J.)		1927
Sirica, John J. (Waterbury, Conn.)		3/19/04
Smith, Howard K. (Ferriday, La.)		5/12/14
Smith, Margaret Chase (Skowhegan, Me.)		12/14/97
Snyder, Tom (Milwaukee, Wisc.)		5/12/36
Sorenson, Theodore (Lincoln, Neb.)		5/8/28
Spillane, Mickey (Brooklyn, N.Y.)		3/9/18
Spock, Benjamin (New Haven, Conn.)		5/2/03
Stassen, Harold (West St. Paul, Minn.)		4/13/07
Steinem, Gloria (Toledo, Oh.)		3/25/34
Stevenson 3d, Adlai (Chicago, Ill.)		10/10/30
Stewart, Potter (Jackson, Mich.)		1/23/15
Stokes, Carl (Cleveland, Oh.)		6/21/27
Stone, Irving (San Francisco, Cal.)		7/14/03
Symington, Stuart (Amherst, Mass.)		6/26/01
Taft, Robert Jr. (Cincinnati, Oh.)		2/26/17
Talmadge, Herman (Lovejoy, Ga.)		8/9/13
Taylor, Maxwell D. (Keytesville, Mo.)		8/26/01
Thomas, Helen (Winchester, Ky.)		8/4/20
Thomas, Lowell (Woodington, Oh.)		4/6/92
Thurmond, J. Strom (Edgefield, S.C.)		12/5/02

Name	Birthplace	Birthdate
Tower, John (Houston, Tex.)		9/29/25
Truman, Mrs. Harry (Independence, Mo.)		2/13/85
Truman, Margaret (Mrs. Clifton Daniel) (Independence, Mo.)		2/17/24
Tuchman, Barbara (New York, N.Y.)		1/30/12
Tunney, Gene (New York, N.Y.)		5/25/98
Tunney, John V. (New York, N.Y.)		6/26/34
Udall, Morris K. (St. Johns, Ariz)		6/15/22
Ullman, Al (Great Falls, Mont.)		3/9/14
Unitas, John (Pittsburgh, Pa.)		5/7/33
Vanderbilt, Alfred G. (London, England)		9/22/12
Van Buren, Abigail (Sioux City, Ia.)		7/4/18
Veeck, Bill (Chicago, Ill.)		2/9/14
Vidal, Gore (West Point, N.Y.)		10/3/25
Volpe, John (Wakefield, Mass.)		12/8/08
Vonnegut, Kurt Jr. (Indianapolis, Ind.)		11/11/22
Wagner, Robert F. (New York, N.Y.)		4/20/10
Walcott, Jersey Joe (Merchantville, N.J.)		1/31/14
Wallace, George (Clio, Ala.)		8/25/19
Walters, Barbara (Boston, Mass.)		9/25/31
Wambaugh, Joseph (E. Pittsburgh, Pa.)		1/22/37
Warren, Robert Penn (Guthrie, Ky.)		4/24/05
Weicker, Lowell (Paris, France)		5/16/31
Weinberger, Casper (San Francisco, Cal.)		8/18/17
Westmoreland, William (Spartanburg, S.C.)		3/26/14
White, Byron R. (Ft. Collins, Col.)		6/8/17
White, Theodore (Boston, Mass.)		5/6/15
Wicker, Tom (Hamlet, N.C.)		6/18/26
Wilkins, Roy (St. Louis, Mo.)		8/30/01
Williams, Edward Bennett (Hartford, Conn.)		5/31/20
Williams, Ted (San Diego, Cal.)		8/30/18
Williams, Tennessee (Columbus, Miss.)		3/26/14
Woodcock, Leonard (Providence, R.I.)		2/15/11
Woodward, Bob (Geneva, Ill.)		3/26/43
Wouk, Herman (New York, N.Y.)		5/27/15
Yorty, Sam (Lincoln, Neb.)		10/1/09
Ziegler, Ronald (Covington, Ky.)		5/12/39

British

British Statesmen

Born	Died	Name	Born	Died	Name	Born	Died	Name
1852	1928	Asquith, Herbert H.	1869	1940	Chamberlain, Neville	1863	1935	Henderson, Arthur
1879	1964	Astor, Viscountess	1874	1965	Churchill, Winston	1889	1969	Horsbrugh, Florence
1883	1967	Atlee, Clement	1725	1774	Clive, Robert	1858	1923	Law, Andrew Bonar
1867	1947	Baldwin, Stanley	1889	1952	Cripps, Stafford	1863	1945	Lloyd George, David
1848	1930	Balfour, Arthur J.	1599	1658	Cromwell, Oliver	1866	1937	MacDonald, J. Ramsay
1879	1964	Beaverbrook, Lord	1859	1925	Curzon of Kedleston	1854	1925	Milner, Alfred
1897	1960	Bevan, Aneurin	1804	1881	Disraeli, Benjamin	1732	1792	North, Frederick
1881	1951	Bevin, Ernest	1749	1806	Fox, Charles James	1784	1865	Palmerston, Viscount
1838	1922	Bryce, James	1906	1963	Gaitskell, Hugh	1788	1850	Peel, Robert
1884	1968	Cadogan, Alexander	1809	1898	Gladstone, Wm. E.	1759	1806	Pitt, William (Younger)
1770	1827	Canning, George	1764	1845	Grey, Charles	1708	1778	Pitt, William (Chatham)
1769	1822	Castlereagh, Robert	1862	1933	Grey, Edward	1853	1902	Rhodes, Cecil
1864	1958	Cecil, Edgar	1594	1643	Hampden, John	1792	1878	Russell, John
1863	1937	Chamberlain, Austen	1732	1818	Hastings, Warren	1830	1903	Salisbury, Robert
1836	1914	Chamberlain, Joseph				1676	1745	Walpole, Robert

British Army (A), Navy (N), Air Force (F), Explorers (E)

Born	Died	Name	Born	Died	Name	Born	Died	Name
1891	1969	Alexander, Harold R. (A)	1877	1967	Ellington, Edward (F)	1872	1945	Keyes, Roger (N)
1861	1936	Allenby, Edmund (A)	1841	1920	Fisher, John A. (N)	1850	1916	Kitchener, H. H. (A)
1717	1797	Amherst, Jeffrey (A)	1710	1759	Forbes, John (A)	1888	1935	Lawrence, T. E. (A)
1584	1622	Baffin, William (E)	1786	1847	Franklin, John (E)	1650	1722	Marlborough, Duke of (A)
1871	1936	Beatty, David (N)	1535	1594	Frobisher, Martin (E)	1871	1951	Maurice, Frederick (A)
1873	1967	Boyle, Wm. H. D. (N)	1721	1787	Gage, Thomas (A)	1867	1948	Milne, George (A)
1695	1755	Braddock, Edward (A)	1833	1885	Gordon, Chas. G. (A)	1894	1967	Morgan, Frederick (A)
1839	1908	Buller, Redvers (A)	1541	1591	Grenville, Richard (N)	1782	1853	Napier, Charles J. (A)
1723	1792	Burgoyne, John (A)	1861	1928	Haig, Douglas (A)	1810	1890	Napier, Robert C. (A)
1663	1733	Byng, George (N)	1853	1947	Hamilton, Ian (A)	1758	1805	Nelson, Horatio (N)
1675	1726	Cadogan, Wm. (A)	1795	1857	Havelock, Henry (A)	1696	1785	Oglethorpe, James (A)
1593	1676	Cavendish, Wm. (A)	1745	1792	Hearne, Samuel (E)	1895	1968	Robb, James (F)
1873	1967	Chatfield, Alfred (N)	1536	1624	Howard, Charles (N)	1832	1914	Roberts, Frederick (A)
1738	1795	Clinton, Henry, (A)	1726	1799	Howe, Richard (N)	1719	1792	Rodney, George (N)
1770	1851	Codrington, Ed. (N)	1729	1814	Howe, William (A)	1800	1862	Ross, James C. (E)
1727	1779	Cook, James (E)	1575	1611	Hudson, Henry (E)	1893	1969	Scobie, Ronald M. (A)
1738	1805	Cornwallis, Chas. (A)	1883	1966	Humphrey, Noel (E)	1868	1912	Scott, Robert F. (E)
1550	1605	Davis, John (E)	1880	1959	Ironside, Wm. E. (A)	1874	1922	Shackleton, Ernest (E)
1896	1969	Dempsey, Miles (A)	1859	1935	Jellicoe, John (N)	1891	1970	Slim, Wm. Joseph (A)
1883	1970	Dowding, Hugh C. (F)	1715	1774	Johnson, Wm. (A)	1841	1904	Stanley, Henry M. (E)
1540	1596	Drake, Francis (N)				1869	1951	Swinton, Ernest (A)

Born	Died	Name	Born	Died	Name	Born	Died	Name
1890	1967	Tedder, Arthur W. (F)	1883	1950	Wavell, Archibald (A)	1769	1852	Wellington, Duke of (A)
1757	1798	Vancouver, George (E)	1787	1834	Weddell, James (E)	1727	1759	Wolfe, James (A)

British Scientists, Engineers, Physicians

Born	Died	Name	Born	Died	Name	Born	Died	Name
1813	1898	Bessemer, Henry	1849	1945	Fleming, Ambrose	1642	1727	Newton, Isaac
1897	1974	Blackett, Patrick	1898	1968	Florey, Howard W.	1903	1969	Powell, Cecil F.
1899	1966	Cameron, Roy	1892	1964	Haldane, J. B. S.	1733	1804	Priestley, Joseph
1881	1966	Campbell, Donald F.	1578	1657	Harvey, William	1886	1975	Robinson, Robert
1731	1810	Cavendish, Henry	1792	1871	Herschel, John	1857	1932	Ross, Ronald
1891	1974	Chadwick, James	1738	1822	Herschel, William	1871	1937	Rutherford, Ernest
1905	1967	Cockcroft, John	1897	1967	Hinshelwood, Cyril	1624	1689	Sydenham, Thomas
1832	1919	Crookes, William	1861	1947	Hopkins, Frederick	1892	1975	Thomson, George
1875	1968	Dale, Henry H.	1887	1975	Huxley, Julian	1824	1907	Thomson, Wm. (Kelvin)
1766	1844	Dalton, John	1749	1823	Jenner, Edward	1823	1913	Wallace, Alf. Russell
1809	1882	Darwin, Charles	1815	1898	Jenner, William	1892	1973	Watson-Watt, Robert
1791	1867	Faraday, Michael	1827	1912	Lister, Jos.	1736	1819	Watt, James E.
1881	1955	Fleming, Alexander	1831	1879	Maxwell, James Clerk	1802	1875	Wheatstone, Chas.

British Religious Leaders

Born	Died	Name	Born	Died	Name	Born	Died	Name
1118	1170	Becket, Thomas a	1860	1954	Inge, William Ralph	1613	1667	Taylor, Jeremy
1685	1753	Berkeley, George	1874	1966	Johnson, Hewlett	1492	1536	Tyndale, William
1829	1912	Booth, William B.	1505	1572	Knox, John	1703	1791	Wesley, John
1566	1644	Brewster, William	1485	1555	Latimer, Hugh	1714	1770	Whitefield, Geo.
1489	1556	Cranmer, Thos.	1813	1873	Livingston, David	1802	1865	Wiseman, Nicholas
1624	1691	Fox, George	1808	1892	Manning, Henry E.	1475	1530	Wolsey, Thomas
1554	1600	Hooker, Richard	1801	1890	Newman, John H.	1320	1384	Wycliffe, John

British Painters and Sculptors

Born	Died	Name	Born	Died	Name	Born	Died	Name
1872	1898	Beardsley, Aubrey	1648	1721	Gibbons, Grinling	1834	1896	Morris, William
1757	1827	Blake, William	1903	1975	Hepworth, Barbara	1878	1931	Orpen, William
1833	1898	Burne-Jones, Edward	1697	1764	Hogarth, William	1756	1823	Raeburn, Henry
1896	1967	Charoux, Siegfried	1827	1910	Hunt, W. Holman	1723	1792	Reynolds, Joshua
1776	1837	Constable, John	1646	1723	Kneller, Godfrey	1734	1802	Romney, George
1782	1842	Cotman, John S.	1856	1941	Lavery, John	1828	1882	Rossetti, Dante G.
1793	1865	Eastlake, Charles L.	1769	1830	Lawrence, Thomas	1891	1959	Spencer, Stanley
1880	1959	Epstein, Jacob	1806	1870	Maclise, Daniel	1775	1851	Turner, J. M. W.
1755	1826	Flaxman, John	1829	1896	Millais, John	1817	1904	Watts, George
1727	1788	Gainsborough, Thos.				1785	1841	Wilkie, David

Poets, Dramatists, Essayists, Historians, Novelists

Born	Died	Name	Born	Died	Name	Born	Died	Name
1672	1719	Addison, Joseph	1878	1957	Coppard, A. E.	1709	1784	Johnson, Samuel
1805	1882	Ainsworth, W. H.	1855	1924	Corelli, Marie	1573	1637	Jonson, Ben
1904	1966	Allingham, Margery	1731	1800	Cowper, William	1795	1821	Keats, John
1832	1904	Arnold, Edwin	1908	1973	Creasey, John	1896	1967	Kennedy, Margaret
1822	1888	Arnold, Matthew	1660	1731	Defoe, Daniel	1819	1875	Kingsley, Charles
1775	1817	Austen, Jane	1873	1956	De la Mare, Walter	1865	1936	Kipling, Rudyard
1561	1626	Bacon, Francis	1785	1859	De Quincey, Thomas	1775	1834	Lamb, Charles
1214	1294	Bacon, Roger	1812	1870	Dickens, Charles	1332	1400	Langland, William
1762	1851	Baillie, Joanna	1573	1631	Donne, John	1885	1930	Lawrence, David H.
1860	1937	Barrie, James M.	1868	1952	Douglas, Norman	1838	1903	Lecky, W. E. H.
1584	1616	Beaumont, Francis	1867	1900	Dowson, Ernest	1866	1947	LeGallienne, Richard
673	735	Bede, the Venerable	1859	1930	Doyle, Arthur Conan	1894	1957	Lewis, Wyndham
1872	1956	Beerbohm, Max	1563	1631	Drayton, Michael	1895	1970	Liddell Hart, Basil
1870	1953	Belloc, Hilaire	1631	1700	Dryden, John	1632	1704	Locke, John
1867	1931	Bennett, Arnold	1834	1896	du Maurier, Geo. L.	1800	1859	Macaulay, Thomas B.
1748	1832	Bentham, Jeremy	1819	1880	Eliot, George	1863	1947	Machen, Arthur
1662	1742	Bentley, Richard	1888	1965	Eliot, T. S.	1888	1923	Mansfield, Katherine
1869	1951	Blackwood, Algernon	1620	1706	Evelyn, John	1564	1593	Marlowe, Christopher
1757	1827	Blake, William	1707	1754	Fielding, Henry	1897	1969	Martin, Kingsley
1740	1795	Boswell, James	1809	1883	Fitzgerald, Edward	1878	1967	Masefield, John
1844	1930	Bridges, Robert	1908	1964	Fleming, Ian	1583	1640	Massinger, Phillip
1816	1855	Bronte, Charlotte	1873	1939	Ford, Ford Madox	1874	1965	Maugham, W. Somerset
1818	1848	Bronte, Emily	1889	1966	Forester, C. S.	1828	1909	Meredith, George
1806	1861	Browning, Elizabeth B.	1879	1970	Forster, E. M.	1806	1873	Mill, John Stuart
1812	1889	Browning, Robert	1908	1967	Frankau, Pamela	1882	1956	Milne, A. A.
1628	1688	Bunyan, John	1867	1933	Galsworthy, John	1608	1674	Milton, John
1729	1797	Burke, Edmund	1685	1732	Gay, John	1838	1923	Morley, John
1759	1796	Burns, Robert	1737	1794	Gibbon, Edward	1870	1916	Munro, H. H. (Saki)
1788	1824	Byron, Lord Geo. Gordon	1857	1903	Gissing, George	1880	1958	Noyes, Alfred
1777	1844	Campbell, Thomas	1728	1774	Goldsmith, Oliver	1903	1950	Orwell, George
1795	1881	Carlyle, Thomas	1716	1771	Gray, Thomas	1839	1894	Pater, Walter
1832	1898	Carroll, Lewis	1840	1928	Hardy, Thomas	1785	1866	Peacock, Thomas L.
1888	1957	Cary, Joyce	1831	1923	Harrison, Frederic	1633	1703	Pepys, Samuel
1340	1400	Chaucer, Geoffrey	1778	1830	Hazlitt, William	1688	1744	Pope, Alexander
1694	1773	Chesterfield, Earl of	1849	1903	Henley, Wm. Ernest	1900	1969	Potter, Stephen
1874	1936	Chesterton, G. K.	1591	1674	Herrick, Robert	1664	1721	Prior, Matthew
1911	1968	Churchill, Randolph	1588	1679	Hobbes, Thomas	1863	1944	Quiller-Couch, Arthur T.
1763	1835	Cobbett, William	1770	1835	Hogg, James	1552	1618	Raleigh, Sir Walter
1772	1834	Coleridge, S. T.	1799	1845	Hood, Thomas	1814	1884	Reade, Charles
1824	1889	Collins, Wilkie	1859	1936	Housman, Alfred E.	1689	1761	Richardson, Samuel
1670	1729	Congreve, William	1711	1776	Hume, David	1819	1900	Ruskin, John
1857	1924	Conrad, Joseph	1894	1963	Huxley, Aldous	1872	1970	Russell, Bertrand

Born	Died	Name	Born	Died	Name	Born	Died	Name
1886	1967	Sassoon, Siegfried	1774	1843	Southey, Robert	1876	1962	Trevelyan, Geo. M.
1893	1957	Sayres, Dorothy L.	1552	1599	Spenser, Edmund	1815	1882	Trollope, Anthony
1771	1832	Scott, Sir Walter	1672	1729	Steele, Richard	1884	1941	Walpole, Hugh
1564	1616	Shakespeare, William	1713	1768	Sterne, Laurence	1593	1683	Walton, Izaak
1856	1950	Shaw, G. Bernard	1850	1894	Stevenson, Robert Louis	1851	1920	Ward, Mrs. Humphry
1797	1851	Shelley, Mary W.	1880	1932	Strachey, Lytton	1903	1966	Waugh, Evelyn
1792	1822	Shelley, Percy Bysshe	1667	1745	Swift, Jonathan	1866	1946	Wells, H. G.
1751	1816	Sheridan, Richard B.	1837	1909	Swinburne, Algernon C.	1906	1964	White, T. H.
1554	1586	Sidney, Sir Phillip	1809	1892	Tennyson, Alfred	1861	1947	Whitehead, Alfred N.
1887	1964	Sitwell, Edith	1811	1863	Thackeray, W. M.	1856	1900	Wilde, Oscar
1892	1969	Sitwell, Osbert	1914	1953	Thomas, Dylan	1882	1941	Woolf, Virginia
1771	1845	Smith, Sydney	1892	1973	Tolkien, J.R.R.	1770	1850	Wordsworth, William
1721	1771	Smollett, Tobias	1889	1975	Toynbee, Arnold	1640	1715	Wycherly, William

Poets Laureate of England

There is no authentic record of the origin of the office of Poet Laureate of England. According to Warton, there was a Versificator Regis, or King's Poet, in the reign of Henry III (1216-1272), and he was paid 100 shillings a year. Geoffrey Chaucer (1340-1400) assumed the title of Poet Laureate, and in 1389 got a royal grant of a yearly allowance of wine. In the reign of Edward IV (1461-1483), John Kay held the post. Under Henry VII (1485-1509), Andrew Bernard was the Poet Laureate, and was succeeded under Henry VIII (1509-1547) by John Skelton. Next came Edmund Spenser, who died in 1599; then Samuel Daniel, appointed 1599, and then Ben Jonson, 1619. Sir William D'Avenant was appointed in 1637. He was a godson of William Shakespeare.

Others were John Dryden, 1670; Thomas Shadwell, 1688; Nahum Tate, 1692; Nicholas Rowe, 1715; the Rev. Laurence Eusden, 1718; Colly Cibber, 1730; William Whitehead, 1757, on the refusal of Gray; Rev. Thomas Warton, 1785, on the refusal of Mason; Henry J. Pye, 1790; Robert Southey, 1813, on the refusal of Sir Walter Scott; William Wordsworth, 1843; Alfred, Lord Tennyson, 1850; Alfred Austin, 1896; Robert Bridges, 1913; John Masefield, 1930; Cecil Day Lewis, 1967; Sir John Betjeman, 1972.

Canadian

Born	Died	Name	Born	Died	Name	Born	Died	Name
		Statesmen	1809	1866	Garneau, Francis X.	1888	1951	Trotter, R. G.
			1824	1882	Gerin-Lajoie, Antoine	1856	1926	Weir, R. Stanley
1878	1943	Aberhart, William	1860	1937	Gordon, Chas. W.	1860	1948	Wrong, George M.
1804	1858	Baldwin, Robert			(Ralph Connor)			
1870	1957	Bennett, Richard B.	1878	1967	Groulx, Lionel A.			**Painters and Sculptors**
1833	1912	Blake, Edward	1871	1948	Grove, Frederick			
1854	1937	Borden, Robert	1796	1865	Haliburton, Thos. C.	1759	1830	Baillarge, Francois
1823	1917	Bowell, Mackenzie	1880	1913	Hemon, Louis	1905	1960	Borduas, Paul-Emile
1884	1969	Bracken, John	1766	1844	Heriot, George	1827	1916	Bourassa, Napoleon
1818	1880	Brown, George	1894	1952	Innis, H. A.	1855	1925	Brymner, William
1814	1873	Cartier, Georges	1881	1943	Kennedy, W. P. M.	1871	1945	Carr, Emily
1890	1959	Duplessis, Maurice	1859	1931	Kingsford, William	1866	1934	Cullen, Maurice
1895	1973	Frost, Leslie	1817	1906	Kirby, William	1881	1942	Gagnon, Clarence
1817	1893	Galt, Alexander T.	1862	1913	Johnson, Pauline	1817	1870	Hamel, Theophile
1869	1953	Hepburn, Mitchell F.	1871	1960	Laberge, Albert	1885	1870	Harris, Lawren Stewart
1804	1873	Howe, Joseph	1861	1899	Lampman, Archibald	1849	1919	Harris, Robert
1874	1950	King, W. Mackenzie	1871	1936	Laut, Agnes	1850	1917	Hebert, Louis P.
1841	1919	Laurier, Wilfrid	1869	1944	Leacock, Stephen	1882	1974	Jackson, Alexander Y.
1815	1891	Macdonald, John A.	1909	1957	Lowry, Malcolm	1810	1871	Kane, Paul
1795	1861	Mackenzie, Wm. Lyon	1878	1924	Lozeau, Albert	1815	1872	Krieghoff, Cornelius
1825	1868	McGee, Thomas D'Arcy	1874	1942	Macdonald, Lucy M.	1864	1955	Leduc, Ozias
1874	1960	Meighen, Arthur	1876	1951	Mac Innes, Tom	1795	1855	Legare, Joseph
1897	1972	Pearson, Lester B.	1862	1933	MacMechan, Archibald	1887	1968	Loring, Frances
1904	1968	Robertson, Norman A.	1840	1927	Mair, Charles	1873	1932	MacDonald, J. E. H.
1855	1927	Tupper, Charles H.	1844	1895	Marmette, Joseph	1882	1953	Milne, David
			1864	1936	Marquis, Thomas	1865	1924	Morrice, James Wilson
		Authors	1882	1958	Martin, Chester	1860	1892	Peel, Paul
			1872	1918	McCrae, John	1802	1895	Plamondon, Antoine S.
1850	1931	Beauchemin, Neree	1820	1907	McMullen, John	1869	1937	Suzor-Cote, Aurele de Foy
1861	1924	Blake, W. H.	1865	1944	Miner, John T. (Jack)	1877	1918	Thomson, Tom
1868	1952	Bourassa, Henri	1874	1942	Montgomery, Lucy	1881	1969	Varley, F. H.
1840	1901	Buies, Arthur	1803	1885	Moodie, Susanna	1858	1938	Walker, Horatio
1861	1918	Campbell, W. Wilfred	1889	1963	Morin, Paul	1855	1936	Watson, Homer
1861	1929	Carman, W. Bliss	1879	1941	Nelligan, Emile	1881	1968	Wyle, Florence
1831	1904	Casgrain, Henri R.	1737	1818	Odell, Jonathan			
1858	1946	Chapais, Thomas	1862	1932	Parker, Gilbert			**Science, Industry**
1850	1917	Chapman, William	1887	1970	Phelps, Arthur L.			
1820	1890	Chauveau, Pierre	1883	1922	Pickthall, Marjorie	1859	1942	Adams, Frank D.
1885	1953	Chopin, Rene	1883	1964	Pratt, Edwin J.	1810	1882	Allan, Hugh
1827	1879	Cremazie, Octave	1749	1809	Quesnel, Joseph	1891	1941	Banting, Fredk. G.
1831	1904	Cosgrain, Abbe R.	1796	1852	Richardson, John	1877	1943	Beatty, Edward W.
1866	1944	Dafoe, John Wesley	1860	1943	Roberts, Chas. G. D.	1889	1966	Hilton, Hugh G.
1865	1945	Dantin, Louis	1885	1961	Roche, Mazo de la	1798	1875	Logan, William
1895	1958	Dawson, R. MacGregor	1839	1920	Routhier, Adolphe B.	1849	1919	Osler, William
1848	1917	Dionne, Narcisse	1870	1943	Roy, Camille	1876	1935	Macleod, John J. R.
1860	1936	Doughty, Arthur G.	1858	1913	Roy, Joseph E.	1863	1892	Stairs, Wm. Grant
1854	1907	Drummond, W. H.	1822	1893	Sangster, Charles	1902	1967	Zimmerman, Adam
1862	1932	Duncan, Sara J.	1862	1947	Scott, Duncan C.			
1864	1922	Edwards, Robert (Bob)	1874	1958	Service, Robert W.			**Anthropologists, Geologists, and Naturalists**
1799	1870	Faillon, Etienne	1859	1931	Short, Adam			
1805	1865	Ferland, Jean	1878	1941	Skelton, O. D.	1876	1961	Anderson, Rudolph M.
1839	1908	Frechette, Louis H.	1823	1910	Smith, Goldwin	1883	1969	Barbeau, Charles M.
			1841	1923	Sulte, Benjamin			

Born	Died	Name	Born	Died	Name	Born	Died	Name
1820	1876	Billings, Elkanah	1862	1920	Macoun, James Melville	1867	1937	Saunders, Sir Charles E.
1846	1925	Dionne, Charles Eusibe	1831	1920	Macoun, John	1836	1914	Saunders, William
1817	1896	Hale, Horatio	1869	1933	Macoun, William Tyrell	1872	1940	Smith, Harlan I.
1859	1944	Hill-Tout, Charles	1885	1944	Marie-Victorin, frere	1875	1947	Taverner, Percy A.
1826	1892	Hunt, Thomas Sterry	1867	1947	Massicotte, Edouard Z.	1858	1957	Tyrrell, Joseph Burr
1886	1969	Jenness, Diamond	1820	1892	Provancher, Leon, abbe	1872	1924	Waugh, Fredrick W.
1833	1881	LaRue, Francois A. H.	1905	1970	Rousseau, Jacques	1881	1964	Wilson, Alice Evelyn
1798	1875	Logan, Sir William E.	1891	1957	Rowan, William	1876	1941	Wintemberg, William J.
			1870	1953	Roy, Pierre Georges			

French

French Political Leaders

Born	Died	Name	Born	Died	Name	Born	Died	Name
1884	1966	Auriol, Vincent	1620	1698	Frontenac, Louis de	1905	1975	Mollet, Guy
1872	1950	Blum, Leon	1838	1882	Gambetta, Leon	1860	1934	Poincare, Raymond
1862	1932	Briand, Aristide	1872	1957	Herriot, Edouard	1911	1974	Pompidou, Georges
1841	1929	Clemenceau, Georges	1889	1975	Laniel, Joseph	1884	1970	Queuille, Henri
1619	1683	Colbert, Jean-Bapt.	1883	1945	Laval, Pierre	1878	1966	Reynaud, Paul
1884	1970	Daladier, Edouard	1871	1950	Lebrun, Albert	1585	1642	Richelieu, Cardinal de
1759	1794	Danton, Georges	1744	1793	Marat, Jean-Paul	1758	1794	Robespierre, Max.
1890	1970	DeGaulle, Charles	1602	1661	Mazarin, Jules	1208	1265	Simon de Montfort
1760	1794	Desmoulins, Camille	1749	1791	Mirabeau, Honore	1754	1838	Talleyrand, Chas. de

French Military Leaders and Explorers

Born	Died	Name	Born	Died	Name	Born	Died	Name
1769	1821	Bonaparte, Napoleon	1753	1800	Kleber, Jean-Bapt.	1769	1851	Soult, Nicolas J.
1753	1823	Carnot, Lazare	1757	1834	Lafayette, Marquis de	1611	1675	Turenne, Vicomte de
1877	1969	Catroux, Georges	1902	1947	Leclerc, Jacques P.			**Explorers**
1519	1572	Coligny, Gasp. de	1854	1934	Lyautey, Louis H.	1658	1730	Cadillac, Antoine
1621	1686	Conde, Prince de	1756	1817	Massena, Andre	1491	1557	Cartier, Jacques
1881	1942	Darlan, Jean F.	1712	1759	Montcalm, Louis de	1567	1635	Champlain, Sam'l de
1722	1788	DeGrasse, Francois	1763	1813	Moreau, Jean V.	1867	1936	Charcot, Jean B.
1739	1823	Dumouriez, Chas. F.	1767	1815	Murat, Joachim	1868	1969	David-Neel, Alexandra
1897	1975	Ely, Paul	1769	1815	Ney, Michel	1640	1701	Hennepin, Louis
1851	1929	Foch, Ferdinand	1856	1951	Petain, Henri Philippe	1645	1700	Jolliet, Louis
1849	1916	Gallieni, Jos. S.	1725	1807	Rochambeau, Jean-Bapt.	1643	1687	LaSalle, Robt. de
1879	1949	Giraud, Henri H.	1579	1638	Rohan, Henri	1637	1675	Marquette, Jacques
1852	1931	Joffre, Jos.	1696	1750	Saxe, Maurice de			

French Scientists, Physicians

Born	Died	Name	Born	Died	Name	Born	Died	Name
1775	1836	Ampere, Andre-Marie	1890	1967	Danjon, Andre	1811	1877	LeVerrier, Urbain
1788	1878	Becquerel, A. C.	1678	1761	Fauchard, Pierre	1862	1954	Lumiere, Auguste
1852	1908	Becquerel, H. A.	1842	1925	Flammarion, Camille	1864	1948	Lumiere, Louis
1827	1907	Berthelot, Marcelin	1778	1850	Gay-Lussac, Joseph	1852	1907	Moissan, Henri
1813	1878	Bernard, Claude	1900	1958	Joliot-Curie, Frederic	1807	1873	Nelaton, Auguste
1872	1936	Bleriot, Louis	1897	1956	Joliot-Curie, Irene	1863	1933	Painleve, Paul
1873	1944	Carrel, Alexis	1781	1826	Laennec, Rene	1647	1714	Papin, Denis
1825	1893	Charcot, Jean M.	1736	1813	Lagrange, Joseph	1510	1590	Pare, Ambroise
1746	1823	Charles, Jacques	1744	1829	Lamarck, Jean B.	1822	1895	Pasteur, Louis
1786	1889	Chevreul, Michel	1749	1827	Laplace, Pierre S.	1854	1912	Poincare, Henri
1867	1934	Curie, Marie	1743	1794	Lavoisier, Antoine	1850	1935	Richet, Charles
1859	1906	Curie, Pierre	1822	1900	Lenoir, Etienne	1875	1965	Schweitzer, Albert

French Authors, Dramatists, Historians, Religionists

Born	Died	Name	Born	Died	Name	Born	Died	Name
1079	1142	Abelard, Pierre	1768	1848	Chateaubriand, Francois	1869	1951	Gide, Andre
1717	1783	Alembert, Jean d'	1762	1794	Chenier, Andre	1882	1944	Giraudoux, Jean
1885	1969	Allain, Marcel	1895	1969	Chevallier, Gabriel	1816	1882	Gobineau, Comte de
1880	1918	Apollinaire, Guillaume	1889	1963	Cocteau, Jean	1822	1896	Goncourt, Edmond de
1820	1889	Augier, (Emile)	1873	1954	Colette, Sidonie	1830	1870	Goncourt, Jules de
1902	1967	Ayme, Marcel	1445	1509	Comines, Philippe de	1787	1874	Guizot, Francois
1799	1850	Balzac, Honore de	1798	1857	Comte, Auguste	1842	1905	Heredia, Jose-Maria de
1823	1891	Banville, Theodore de	1743	1794	Condorcet, Marquis de	1857	1915	Hervieu, Paul
1873	1935	Barbusse, Henri	1767	1830	Constant, Benjamin	1802	1885	Hugo, Victor
1862	1923	Barres, Maurice	1842	1908	Coppee, Francois	1848	1907	Huysmans, Joris-Karl
1821	1867	Baudelaire, Charles	1845	1875	Corbiere, Tristan	1876	1944	Jacob, Max
1732	1799	Beaumarchais, Pierre	1606	1684	Corneille, Pierre	1868	1938	Jammes, Francis
1837	1899	Becque, Henry	1854	1928	Curel, Francois de	1412	1431	Joan of Arc
1780	1857	Beranger, Pierre	1840	1897	Daudet, Alphonse	1815	1888	Labiche, Eugene
1859	1941	Bergson, Henri	1596	1650	Descartes, Rene	1645	1696	La Bruyere, Jean de
1888	1948	Bernanos, Georges	1902	1969	De Vilmorin, Louise	1695	1695	La Fontaine, Jean de
1866	1947	Bernard, Tristan	1713	1784	Diderot, Denis	1860	1887	Laforgue, Jules
1876	1953	Bernstein, Henri	1881	1958	Du Gard, Roger M.	1790	1869	Lamartine, Alphonse de
1876	1967	Birot, Pierre A.	1803	1870	Dumas, Alexandre	1846	1870	Lautreamont, Comte de
1636	1711	Boileau, Nicolas	1824	1895	Dumas (Fils), Alexandre	1818	1894	Leconte de Lisle
1627	1704	Bossuet, Jacques	1926	1967	Fall, Bernard B.	1853	1914	Lemaitre, Jules
1852	1935	Bourget, Paul	1651	1715	Fenelon, Francois de	1668	1747	Lesage, Alain-Rene
1858	1932	Brieux, Eugene	1821	1880	Flaubert, Gustave	1850	1923	Loti, Pierre (J. Viaud)
1707	1788	Buffon, Georges	1886	1914	Fournier, Alain	1889	1973	Marcel, Gabriel
1509	1564	Calvin, John	1844	1924	France, Anatole	1842	1898	Mallarme, Stephane
1913	1960	Camus, Albert	1333	1400	Froissart, Jean	1882	1973	Maritain, Jacques
1541	1603	Charron, Pierre	1811	1872	Gautier, Theophile	1688	1763	Marivaux, Pierre

Born	Died	Name	Born	Died	Name	Born	Died	Name
1850	1893	Maupassant, Guy de	1639	1699	Racine, Jean	1626	1696	Sevigne, (Mme. de)
1885	1967	Maurois, Andre	1864	1936	Regnier, Henri de	1875	1959	Siegfried, Andre
1803	1870	Merimee, Prosper	1823	1892	Renan, Ernest	1766	1817	Stael, (Mme. de)
1798	1874	Michelet, Jules	1854	1891	Rimbaud, Arthur	1783	1842	Stendhal, (Beyle)
1622	1673	Moliere, Jean-Baptiste	1866	1944	Rolland, Romain	1839	1907	Sully-Prudhomme, Rene
1533	1592	Montaigne, Michel de	1524	1585	Ronsard, Pierre de	1828	1893	Taine, Hippolyte
1689	1755	Montesquieu, Charles de	1868	1918	Rostand, Edmond	1795	1856	Thierry, Augustin
1810	1857	Musset, Alfred de	1712	1778	Rousseau, Jean-Jacques	1805	1859	Tocqueville, A. C. de
1394	1465	Orleans, Charles d'	1610	1703	Saint-Evremond, de	1871	1945	Valery, Paul
1623	1662	Pascal, Blaise	1900	1944	Saint-Exupery, Ant. de	1844	1896	Verlaine, Paul
1895	1974	Pagnol, Marcel	1675	1755	Saint-Simon, Duc de	1828	1905	Verne, Jules
1873	1914	Peguy, Charles	1804	1869	Sainte-Beuve, Charles A.	1797	1863	Vigny, Alfred de
1887	1975	Perse, St.-John	1567	1622	Sales (Saint Francois de)	1838	1889	Villiers de l'Isle, Adam
1697	1763	Prevost (L'Abbe)	1804	1876	Sand, George (Lucile Dupin)	1431	1484	Villon, Francois
1871	1922	Proust, Marcel	1831	1908	Sardou, Victorien	1694	1778	Voltaire, (Arouet)
1495	1553	Rabelais, Francois	1791	1861	Scribe, Eugene	1840	1902	Zola, Emile

French Painters and Sculptors

Born	Died	Name	Born	Died	Name	Born	Died	Name
1834	1904	Bartholdi, Frederic	1880	1954	Derain, Andre	1884	1920	Modigliani, Amadeo
1848	1884	Bastien-Lepage, Jules	1807	1876	Diaz de la Pana, N. V.	1840	1926	Monet, Claude
1822	1899	Bonheur, Rosa	1877	1953	Dufy, Raoul	1824	1898	Moreau, Gustave
1867	1947	Bonnard, Pierre	1811	1889	Dupre, Jules	1830	1903	Pissarro, Camille
1703	1770	Boucher, Francois	1732	1806	Fragonard, Jean	1594	1665	Poussin, Nicolas
1825	1905	Bouguereau, W.	1820	1876	Fromentin, Eugene	1758	1823	Prudhon, Pierre
1876	1957	Brancusi, Constantin	1848	1903	Gauguin, Paul	1824	1898	Puvis de Chavannes, P. C.
1882	1963	Braque, Georges	1770	1837	Gerard, Francois	1840	1916	Redon, Odilon
1851	1933	Carrier-Belleuse, P.	1791	1824	Gericault, J. L. A. T.	1841	1919	Renoir, Pierre
1839	1906	Cezanne, Paul	1628	1715	Girardon, Fr.	1840	1917	Rodin, Auguste
1699	1779	Chardin, Jean-Bapt.	1725	1805	Greuze, J. B.	1871	1958	Rouault, Georges
1600	1682	Claude Lorrain	1741	1828	Houdon, J. A.	1812	1867	Rousseau, P. E. T.
1796	1875	Corot, J. B. C.	1780	1867	Ingres, J. A. D.	1859	1891	Seurat, Georges
1819	1877	Courbet, Gustave	1887	1965	Le Corbusier	1863	1935	Signac, Paul
1817	1878	Daubigny, C. F.	1891	1973	Lipchitz, Jacques	1839	1899	Sisley, Alfred
1808	1879	Daumier, Honore	1861	1944	Maillol, Aristide	1900	1955	Tanguy, Yves
1748	1825	David, Louis J.	1832	1883	Manet, Edouard	1864	1901	Toulouse-Lautrec
1783	1856	David d'Angers, P. J.	1869	1954	Matisse, Henri	1883	1955	Utrillo, Maurice
1834	1917	Degas, H. G. E.	1815	1891	Meissonier, J. L. E.	1876	1958	Vlaminck, Maurice
1799	1863	Delacroix, Eugene	1815	1875	Millet, J. F.	1868	1940	Vuillard, Edouard
1797	1856	Delaroche, Paul				1684	1721	Watteau, Antoine

German

German Political and Military Leaders, Economists

Born	Died	Name	Born	Died	Name	Born	Died	Name
1876	1967	Adenauer, Konrad	1863	1931	Hipper, Franz v.	1879	1969	Papen, Franz v.
1856	1921	Bethmann-Hollweg, T. v.	1889	1945	Hitler, Adolf	1876	1960	Raeder, Erich
1815	1898	Bismarck, Otto von	1887	1960	Kesselring, Albert	1867	1922	Rathenau, Walter
1742	1819	Bluecher, Gebhart v.	1871	1919	Liebknecht, Karl	1891	1944	Rommel, Erwin
1885	1970	Bruning, Heinrich	1886	1966	Luckner, Felix v.	1876	1953	Rundstedt, Karl v.
1849	1929	Bulow, Bernard v.	1865	1937	Ludendorff, Erich	1877	1970	Schacht, Hjalmar
1780	1831	Clausewitz, Karl v.	1880	1919	Luxemburg, Rosa	1865	1939	Scheidemann, Philipp
1875	1921	Erzberger, Matthias	1849	1945	Machensen, August v.	1833	1913	Schlieffen, Alfred v.
1760	1831	Gneisenau, August	1818	1883	Marx, Karl	1878	1929	Stresemann, Gustav
1893	1946	Goering, Hermann	1800	1891	Moltke, Helmuth von	1849	1930	Tirpitz, Alf. v.
1847	1934	Hindenburg, Paul v.	1848	1916	Moltke, Helmuth von	1893	1973	Ulbricht, Walter

German Engineers, Naturalists, Scientists, Industrialists

Born	Died	Name	Born	Died	Name	Born	Died	Name
1840	1905	Abbe, Ernst	1882	1964	Franck, James	1848	1896	Lilienthal, Otto
1902	1958	Adler, Kurt	1400	1468	Gutenberg, Johannes	1734	1815	Mesmer, Franz
1193	1280	Albertus, Magnus	1834	1919	Haeckel, Ernst	1899	1968	Nordhoff, Heinrich
1844	1929	Benz, Carl	1879	1968	Hahn, Otto	1787	1854	Ohm, Geo. S.
1882	1970	Born, Max	1755	1843	Hahnemann, Samuel	1853	1932	Ostwald, Wilhelm
1874	1940	Bosch, Karl	1821	1894	Helmholz, Hermann v.	1858	1947	Planck, Max
1811	1899	Bunsen, Robert	1857	1894	Hertz, Heinrich	1875	1951	Porsche, Ferdinand
1834	1900	Daimler, Gottlieb	1769	1859	Humboldt, Alex. v.	1632	1694	Pufendorf, Samuel
1858	1913	Diesel, Rudolf	1859	1935	Junkers, Hugo	1845	1923	Roentgen, Wilhelm
1895	1964	Domagk, Gerhard	1571	1630	Kepler, Johannes	1822	1890	Schliemann, Heinrich
1884	1969	Dornier, Claude	1843	1910	Koch, Robert	1816	1892	Siemens, Ernst Werner v.
1861	1935	Duisberg, Carl	1812	1887	Krupp, Alfred	1842	1926	Thyssen, Aug.
1868	1954	Eckener, Hugo	1907	1967	Krupp, Alfred	1821	1902	Virchow, Rudolf
1854	1915	Ehrlich, Paul	1900	1967	Kuhn, Richard	1883	1970	Warburg, Otto
1686	1736	Fahrenheit, Gabriel	1646	1716	Leibnitz, Gottfried v.	1866	1925	Wassermann, Aug. v.
1852	1919	Fischer, Emil	1803	1873	Liebig, Justus v.	1838	1917	Zeppelin, Ferd. v.

German Authors, Dramatists, Essayists, Religionists

Born	Died	Name	Born	Died	Name	Born	Died	Name
1769	1860	Arndt, Ernest Moritz	1740	1815	Claudius, Matthias	1170	1220	Eschenbach, Wolfram v.
1886	1956	Benn, Gottfried	1863	1920	Dehmel, Richard	1884	1958	Feuchtwanger, Lion
1898	1956	Brecht, Bertolt	1788	1857	Eichendorff, Josef v.	1762	1814	Fichte, Johann G.
1778	1842	Brentano, Clemens	1820	1895	Engels, Friedrich	1869	1966	Foerster, Friedrich
1491	1551	Bucer, Martin	1886	1933	Ernst, Paul	1819	1898	Fontane, Theodor

Born	Died	Name	Born	Died	Name	Born	Died	Name
1816	1895	Freytag, Gustav	1724	1803	Klopstock, Friedr	1899	1966	Ropke, Wilhelm
1868	1933	George, Stefan	1875	1967	Kolb, Annette	1788	1866	Rueckert, Friedrich
1749	1832	Goethe, Johann W. v.	1646	1716	Leibnitz, Gottfried	1494	1576	Sachs, Hans
1785	1863	Grimm, Jakob	1729	1781	Lessing, Gotthold	1775	1854	Schelling, Friedrich v.
1786	1859	Grimm, Wilhelm	1844	1909	Liliencron, Detlev v.	1759	1805	Schiller, Friedrich
1890	1941	Hasenclever, Walter	1881	1948	Ludwig, Emil	1767	1845	Schlegel, Aug. W.
1862	1946	Hauptmann, Gerhart	1483	1546	Luther, Martin	1772	1829	Schlegel, Friedrich v.
1813	1863	Hebbel, Friedrich	1871	1950	Mann, Heinrich	1768	1834	Schleiermacher, Friedrich
1770	1831	Hegel, Georg W. F.	1875	1955	Mann, Thomas	1788	1860	Schopenhauer, Arthur
1797	1856	Heine, Heinrich	1804	1875	Moerike, Eduard	1817	1888	Storm, Theodor
1744	1803	Herder, Johann v.	1817	1903	Mommsen, Theodor	1857	1928	Sudermann, Hermann
1877	1962	Hesse, Hermann	1844	1900	Nietzsche, Friedrich	1893	1939	Toller, Ernst
1878	1945	Kaiser, Georg	1796	1835	Platen, August v.	1834	1896	Treitschke, Heinrich v.
1724	1804	Kant, Immanuel	1795	1886	Ranke, Leopold, v.	1787	1862	Uhland, Ludwig
1896	1966	Kasack, Hermann	1810	1874	Reuter, Fritz	1873	1934	Wassermann, Jakob
1777	1811	Kleist, Heinrich v.	1763	1825	Richter, (Jean Paul)	1733	1813	Wieland, Chris. M.
			1875	1926	Rilke, Rainer Maria			

German Painters, Sculptors, Architects

Born	Died	Name	Born	Died	Name	Born	Died	Name
1480	1538	Altdorfer, Albrecht	1829	1880	Feuerbach, Anselm	1847	1935	Liebermann, Max
1476	1545	Baldung, Hans	1774	1840	Friedrich, Caspar	1880	1916	Marc, Franz
1870	1938	Barlach, Ernst	1480	1528	Grunewald, Mathias	1837	1887	Marees, Hans v.
1884	1950	Beckmann, Max	1847	1921	Hildebrand, Adolf von	1815	1905	Menzel, Adolf v.
1726	1801	Chodowiecki, Dan'l	1460	1524	Holbein, Hans (Sr.)	1803	1884	Richter, Ludwig
1858	1925	Corinth, Lovis	1497	1543	Holbein, Hans (Jr.)	1764	1850	Schadow, Johann
1783	1867	Cornelius, Peter	1877	1947	Kolbe, Georg	1781	1841	Schinkel, Karl
1472	1553	Cranach, Lucas	1867	1945	Kollwitz, Kaethe	1839	1924	Thoma, Hans
1471	1528	Durer, Albrecht				1455	1529	Vischer, Peter

Ancient Greeks and Latins

B. C. years are in black type; A. D. years in light, Herodotus believed Homer lived c. 850 B.C.

Greeks

Born	Died	Name	Subj.	Born	Died	Name	Subj.	Born	Died	Name	Subj.
389	314	Aeschines	Orat.	450	...	Empedocles	Philos.	582	500	Pythagoras	Philos.
525	456	Aeschylus	Dram.	55	135	Epictetus	Philos.	600	...	Sappho	Poet
...	550	Aesop	Tales	342	270	Epicurus	Philos.	556	469	Simonides	Poet
563	478	Anacreon	Poet	480	406	Euripides	Dram.	469	399	Socrates	Philos.
500	428	Anaxagoras	Philos.	576	480	Heraclitus	Philos.	495	405	Sophocles	Dram.
287	212	Archimedes	Physt.	484	424	Herodotus	Hist.	63	24	Strabo	Geog.
448	380	Aristophanes	Dram.	...	735	Hesiod	Poet	600	540	Thales	Philos.
384	322	Aristotle	Philos.	460	377	Hippocrates	Medic.	530	460	Themistocles	Polit.
...	194	Atenaeus	Antiq.	...	...	Homer	Poet	...	255	Theocritus	Poet
460	370	Democritus	Philos.	342	292	Menander	Dram.	382	287	Theophrastus	Philos.
310	240	Callimachus	Poet	522	443	Pindar	Poet	471	401	Thucydides	Hist.
382	322	Demosthenes	Orat.	429	347	Plato	Philos.	280	...	Timon	Philos.
50	13	Diodorus	Hist.	49	120	Plutarch	Biog.	430	357	Xenophon	Hist.
...	7	Dionysius	Hist.	207	122	Polybius	Hist.	490	...	Zeno	Philos.

Latins

Born	Died	Name	Subj.	Born	Died	Name	Subj.	Born	Died	Name	Subj.
330	390	Ammianus	Hist.	59	17	Livy	Hist.	35	95	Quintilian	Critic
125	200	Apuleius	Satir.	38	65	Lucan	Poet	86	34	Sallust	Hist.
130	175	Aulus Gellius	Satir.	180	103	Lucilius	Satir.	5	65	Seneca	Moral.
475	524	Boethius	Philos.	96	52	Lucretius	Philos.	25	100	Silius	Poet
100	44	Caesar, Julius	States.	43	104	Martial	Poet	61	96	Statius	Poet
234	149	Cato (Elder!)	Orat.	100	30	Nepos	Hist.	70	150	Suetonius	Biog.
87	54	Catullus	Poet	43	18	Ovid	Poet	55	117	Tacitus	Hist.
107	43	Cicero	Orat.	34	62	Persius	Satir.	185	159	Terence	Dram.
365	408	Claudian	Poet	254	184	Plautus	Dram.	54	18	Tibullus	Poet
65	8	Horace	Poet	23	79	Pliny	Natur.	70	19	Virgil	Poet
60	140	Juvenal	Satir.	62	113	Pliny (Younger)	Letter	70	16	Vitruvius	Arch.

Italian

Italian Painters, Sculptors, and Architects

Born	Died	Name	Born	Died	Name	Born	Died	Name
1404	1472	Alberti, Leon Battista	1697	1768	Canaletto (Canale)	1420	1497	Gozzoli, Benozzo
1512	1572	Alessi, Galeazzo	1757	1822	Canova, Antonio	1902	1975	Levi, Carlo
1447	1522	Amadeo, Giovanni	1570	1610	Caravaggio, Merisi	1406	1469	Lippi, Fra Filippo
1387	1455	Angelico, Fra	1450	1522	Carpaccio, Vittore	1459	1504	Lippi, Filippino
1591	1666	Barbieri, Giovanni	1881	1966	Carra, Carlo	1431	1506	Mantegna, Andrea
1475	1517	Bartolomeo, Fra	1500	1571	Cellini, Benvenuto	1401	1428	Masaccio, Tommaso
1426	1507	Bellini, Gentile	1240	1302	Cimabue, Giovanni	1827	1887	Mengoni, Giuseppe
1428	1516	Bellini, Giovanni	1489	1534	Correggio, Antonio da	1475	1564	Michelangelo Buonarroti
1400	1470	Bellini, Jacopo	1462	1521	Cosimo, Piero di	1826	1901	Morelli, Domenico
1467	1516	Beltraffio, Giovanni	1486	1531	Del Sarto, Andrea	1518	1580	Palladio, Andrea
1562	1629	Bernini, Gian Lor.	1386	1466	Donatello, Donato	1480	1528	Palma, Jacopo
1598	1680	Bernini, Pietro	1378	1455	Ghiberti, Lorenzo	1445	1523	Perugino, Pietro
1445	1510	Botticelli, Sandro	1449	1494	Ghirlandaio, Domenico	1720	1778	Piranesi, Giovanni
1444	1514	Bramante, Donato	1477	1510	Giorgione	1454	1513	Pinturicchio
1377	1446	Brunelleschi, Filippo	1260	1336	Giotto di Bondone	1483	1520	Raphael (Raffaelo)

Born	Died	Name	Born	Died	Name	Born	Died	Name
1575	1642	Reni, Guido	1858	1899	Segantini, Giovanni	1397	1475	Uccello, Paolo
1400	1482	Robbia, Luca della	1883	1966	Severini, Gino	1511	1574	Vasari, Giorgio
1615	1673	Rosa, Salvator	1696	1770	Tiepolo, Giambattista	1528	1588	Veronese, Paolo
1460	1529	Sansovino, Andrea	1518	1594	Tintoretto, Jacopo	1435	1488	Verrocchio, Andrea
1486	1570	Sansovino, Jacopo	1477	1576	Titian (Tiziano)	1452	1519	Vinci, Leonardo da

Authors, Dramatists, Poets, Philosophers, Historians

Born	Died	Name	Born	Died	Name	Born	Died	Name
1749	1803	Alfieri, Vittorio	1863	1938	D'Annunzio, Gabriele	1785	1873	Manzoni, Alessandro
1846	1908	Amicis, Edmond de	1265	1321	Dante, Alighieri	1805	1872	Mazzini, Giuseppe
1227	1274	Aquinas, Thomas	1875	1936	Deledda, Grazia	1698	1782	Metastasio (P. Trapassi)
1492	1556	Aretino, Pietro	1817	1883	De Sanctis, Francesco	1672	1750	Muratori, Ludovico
1474	1533	Ariosto, Ludovico	1909	1967	Emanuelli, Enrico	1848	1923	Pareto, Vilfredo
1829	1907	Ascoli, Graziadio	1842	1911	Fogazzaro, Antonio	1855	1912	Pascoli, Giovanni
1791	1863	Belli, Giuseppe	1778	1827	Foscolo, Ugo	1788	1854	Pellico, Silvio
1313	1375	Boccaccio, Giovanni	1875	1944	Gentile, Giovanni	1304	1374	Petrarca, Francesco
1441	1494	Boiardo, Matteo Maria	1809	1850	Giusti, Giuseppe	1867	1936	Pirandello, Luigi
1548	1599	Bruno, Giordano	1707	1793	Goldoni, Carlo	1432	1484	Pulci, Luigi
1568	1639	Campanella, Tommaso	1713	1786	Gozzi, Gaspare	1901	1968	Quasimodo, Salvatore
1835	1907	Carducci, Giosue	1483	1540	Guicciardini, Francesco	1626	1698	Redi, Francesco
1725	1798	Casanova, Giacomo	1798	1837	Leopardi, Giacomo	1544	1595	Tasso, Torquato
1478	1529	Castiglione, Baldassarre	1836	1909	Lombroso, Cedare	1888	1970	Ungaretti, Giuseppe
1884	1966	Cecchi, Emilio	1469	1527	Machiavelli, Niccolo	1840	1922	Verga, Giovanni
1866	1952	Croce, Benedetto	1898	1957	Malaparte, Curzio	1668	1744	Vico, Giambattista
			1449	1515	Manuzio, Aldo (Aldus)			

Italian Explorers, Scientists, Political Leaders

Born	Died	Name	Born	Died	Name	Born	Died	Name
1776	1856	Avogadro, Amedeo	1847	1897	Ferraris, Galileo	1859	1953	Nitti, Francesco
1738	1794	Beccaria, Cesare	1564	1642	Galileo (G. Galilei)	1254	1324	Polo, Marco
1835	1900	Beltrami, Eugenio	1737	1798	Galvani, Luigi	1626	1698	Redi, Francesco
1476	1507	Borgia, Cesare	1807	1882	Garibaldi, Giuseppe	1878	1970	Ruini, Meuccio
1450	1498	Cabot, John (Caboto)	1882	1955	Graziani, Rodolfo	1835	1910	Schiaparelli, Giovanni
1826	1910	Cannizzaro, Stanislao	1483	1540	Guicciardini, Francesco	1818	1878	Secchi, Angelo
1810	1861	Cavour, Camillo Benso	1628	1694	Malpighi, Marcello	1872	1952	Sforza, Carlo
1451	1506	Columbus, Christopher	1874	1937	Marconi, Guglielmo	1729	1799	Spallanzani, Lazzaro
1830	1903	Cremona, Luigi	1389	1464	Medici, Cosimo de' (1)	1608	1647	Torricelli, Evangelista
1881	1954	De Gasperi, Alcide	1519	1574	Medici, Cosimo de' (2)	1485	1533	Verrazano, Giovanni da
1466	1560	Doria, Andrea	1449	1492	Medici, Lorenzo de'	1454	1512	Vespucci, Amerigo
1901	1954	Fermi, Enrico	1846	1910	Mosso, Angelo	1745	1827	Volta, Alessandro
			1883	1945	Mussolini, Benito			

Russian

Political Leaders

Born	Died	Name
1899	1953	Beria, Lavrenti
1814	1876	Bakunin, Mikhail
1888	1938	Bukharin, Nikolai
1895	1975	Bulganin, Nikolai A.
1875	1946	Kalinin, Mikhail
1883	1936	Kamenev, Lev
1881	1970	Kerensky, Aleksandr
1842	1921	Kropotkin, Pyotr
1870	1924	Lenin, Vladmir
1877	1952	Litvinov, Maxim
1857	1918	Plekhanov, Georgi
1739	1791	Potemkin, Grigori
1772	1839	Speransky, Mikhail
1879	1953	Stalin, Josef
1863	1911	Stolypin, Pyotr
1879	1940	Trotsky, Leon
1849	1915	Witte, Sergei
1883	1936	Zinoviev, Grigori

Military Leaders

Born	Died	Name
1883	1973	Budenny, Semyon
1872	1947	Denikin, Anton
1874	1920	Kolchak, Aleksandr
1897	1973	Konev, Ivan
1870	1918	Kornilov, Lavr
1745	1813	Kutuzov, Mikhail
1902	1974	Kuznetzov, Nikolai
1859	1914	Samsonov, Aleksandr
1729	1800	Suvorov, Aleksandr
1895	1970	Timoshenko, Semyon
1881	1969	Voroshilov, Klimenti Y.

Born	Died	Name
1895	1974	Zhukov, Georgi K.

Scientists

Born	Died	Name
1877	1968	Arbuzov, Aleksandr
1898	1967	Balandin, Aleksei
1857	1927	Bekhterev, Vladmir
1908	1968	Landau, Lev D.
1711	1765	Lomonosov, Mikhail
1909	1967	Maltsev, Anatoli
1834	1907	Mendeleyev, Dmitri
1845	1916	Metchnikov, Elie
1905	1970	Mikoyan, Artem I.
1849	1936	Pavlov, Ivan
1859	1905	Popov, Aleksandr
1907	1966	Sisakian, Norayr M.
1891	1969	Stechkin, Boris S.
1857	1935	Tsiolkovsky, Konstantin E.

Authors—Poets

Born	Died	Name
1888	1966	Akhmatova, Anna A.
1791	1859	Aksakov, Sergei
1878	1927	Artsibashev, Mikhail
1894	1941	Babel, Isaac
1811	1848	Belinsky, Vissarion
1880	1921	Blok, Aleksandr
1891	1940	Bulgakov, Mikhail
1870	1953	Bunin, Ivan
1860	1904	Chekhov, Anton
1821	1881	Dostoyevsky, Fyodor
1891	1967	Ehrenburg, Ilya G.
1809	1852	Gogol, Nicholas V.
1812	1891	Goncharov, Ivan A.

Born	Died	Name
1868	1936	Gorky, Maxim
1886	1921	Gumilev, Nikolai
1812	1870	Herzen, Aleksandr
1853	1921	Korolenko, Vladimir
1768	1844	Krylov, Ivan
1870	1938	Kuprin, Aleksandr
1814	1841	Lermontov, Mikhail
1831	1895	Leskov, Nikolai
1891	1938	Mandelstam, Osip
1893	1930	Mayakovsky, Vladimir
1821	1877	Nekrasov, Nikolai
1823	1886	Ostrovsky, Aleksandr
1890	1960	Pasternak, Boris
1799	1837	Pushkin, Aleksandr
1856	1919	Rozanov, Vasili
1820	1879	Soloviev, Sergei
1883	1945	Tolstoy, Alexei
1828	1910	Tolstoy, Lev
1892	1941	Tsvetaeva, Marina
1818	1883	Turgenev, Ivan
1895	1925	Yesenin, Sergei

Artists

Born	Died	Name
1866	1924	Bakst, Leon S.
1866	1944	Kandinsky, Vasili
1783	1836	Kiprensky, Orest
1878	1927	Kostodiev, Boris
1861	1900	Levitan, Isaak
1844	1918	Repin, Ilya
1865	1911	Serov, Valentin
1842	1904	Vereshchagin, Vasili
1865	1918	Vrubel, Mikhail
1890	1967	Zadkine, Ossip

Additional Foreign Personalities of the Past

S. Y. Agnon, Israeli novelist, 1888-1970.
Emilio Aguinaldo, Filipino revolutionary, 1869-1964.
Roald Amundsen, Norwegian explorer, 1872-1928.
Hans Christian Andersen, Danish writer, 1805-1875.
Tyula Andrassy, Hungarian statesman, 1823-1890.

Ivo Andric, Yugoslav novelist, 1892-1975.
Pedro Aramburu, Argentine statesman, 1903-1970.
Sholem Asch, Polish-born Yiddish writer, 1880-1957.
Miguel Angel Asturias, Guatemalan novelist, 1899-1974.
Vasco Nunez de Balboa, Spanish explorer, 1475-1519.

Karl Barth, Swiss theologian, 1886-1966.
Brendan Behan, Irish playwright, 1923-1964.
Bjarni Benediktson, Icelandic statesman, 1908-1970.
Eduard Benes, Czech. statesman, 1884-1948.
David Ben-Gurion, first Israeli premier, 1886-1973.
Vitus Bering, Danish explorer, 1680-1741.
Folke Bernadotte, Swedish statesman, 1895-1948.
Vicente Blasco-Ibanez, Spanish novelist, 1867-1928.
Niels Bohr, Danish physicist, 1885-1962.
Louis Botha, South African statesman, 1862-1919.
Emil Brunner, Swiss theologian, 1889-1966.
Martin Buber, Austrian-born Jewish philosopher, 1878-1965.

Plutarco Calles, Mexican statesman, 1877-1945.
Karel Capek, Czech. writer, 1890-1938.
Lazaro Cardenas, Mexican statesman, 1895-1970.
Venustiano Carranza, Mexican political leader, 1859-1920.
Roger Casement, Irish revolutionary, 1864-1916.
Humberto Castelo Branco, Brazilian political leader, 1900-1967.
Miguel de Cervantes Saavedra, Spanish novelist, 1547-1616.
Chiang Kai-shek, president of Nationalist China, 1886-1975.
Henri Christophe, Haitian revolutionary, 1767-1820.
Nicholas Copernicus, Polish astronomer, 1473-1543.
Hernando Cortez, Spanish conqueror of Mexico, 1485-1547.

Hernando de Soto, Spanish explorer, 1500-1542.
Eamon de Valera, Irish statesman, 1882-1975.
Jean J. Dessalines, Haitian emperor, 1758-1806.
Porfirio Diaz, Mexican statesman, 1830-1915.
Ngo Dinh Diem, South Vietnamese president, 1901-1963.
Isak Dinesen, Danish author, 1885-1962.
Engelbert Dollfuss, Austrian statesman, 1892-1934.
Christian Doppler, Austrian physicist, 1803-1853.

Robert Emmet, Irish nationalist, 1778-1803.
Enver Pasha, Turkish political leader, 1881-1922.
Desiderius, Erasmus, Dutch scholar, 1466-1536.
Levi Eshkol, Israeli statesman, 1895-1969.

Makik Faisal, King of Saudi Arabia, 1906-1975.
Manuel de Falla, Spanish composer, 1876-1946.
Ragnar Frisch, Norwegian economist, 1895-1973.

Vasco da Gama, Portuguese explorer, 1469-1524.
Mohandas K. Gandhi, Indian political leader, 1869-1948.
Vincent van Gogh, Dutch painter, 1853-1890.
Francisco Goya y Lucientes, Spanish painter, 1746-1828.
El Greco, Greek painter in Spain, 1541-1614.
Lady Augusta Gregory, Irish dramatist, 1859-1932.
Edvard Grieg, Norwegian composer, 1843-1907.

Franz Hals, Dutch painter, 1580-1666.
Dag Hammarskjold, Swedish statesman, 1905-1961.
Theodor Herzl, Austrian founder of modern Zionism, 1860-1904.
Ho Chi Minh, North Vietnamese president, 1890-1969.
Andreas Hofer, Austrian patriot, 1767-1810.
Nicholas Horthy, Hungarian statesman, 1868-1957.
Mykhailo Hrushevsky, Ukrainian historian, 1866-1934.
Jan Hus, Czech. religionist, 1369-1415.

Henrik Ibsen, Norwegian playwright, 1828-1906.

James Joyce, Irish author, 1882-1941.
Benito Juarez, Mexican statesman, 1806-1872.

Franz Kafka, Czech.-born Austrian author, 1883-1924.
Konstantine Kanaris, Greek statesman, 1790-1877.
Joseph Kasavubu, Congolese political leader, 1910-1969.
Abdul Karim Kassem, Iraqi politician, 1914-1963.
Yasunari Kawabata, Japanese novelist, 1899-1972.
Kemal Ataturk, Turkish statesman, 1881-1938.
Elizabeth (Sister) Kenny, Australian nurse, 1886-1952.
Paul Klee, Swiss painter, 1879-1940.
Thaddeus Kosciusko, Polish general, 1746-1817.
Paul Kruger, South African statesman, 1825-1904.
Mykola Kulish, Ukrainian dramatist, 1892-1934.
Frank Kupka, Czech. painter, 1871-1957.

Par Lagerkrist, Swedish novelist, 1891-1974.
Selma Lagerlof, Swedish writer, 1858-1940.
Wanda Landowska, Polish harpsichordist, 1879-1959.
Francisco Largo Caballero, Spanish statesman, 1869-1946.
Trygve Lie, Norwegian statesman, 1896-1968.
Patrice E. Lumumba, Congolese political leader, 1925-1961.

Francisco I. Madera, Mexican statesman, 1873-1913.
Maurice Maeterlinck, Belgian dramatist, 1862-1949.

Ferdinand Magellan, Portuguese explorer, 1480-1521.
Carl Gustav Mannerheim, Finnish statesman, 1867-1951.
Jose Marti, Cuban patriot, 1853-1895.
Jan Masaryk, Czech. statesman, 1886-1948.
Thomas Masaryk, Czech. statesman, 1850-1937.
Tom Mboya, Kenyan political leader, 1930-1969.
Lise Meitner, Austrian mathematician, 1878-1968.
Gregor J. Mendel, Austrian botanist, 1822-1884.
John Metaxas, Greek statesman, 1871-1941.
Klemens W. N. L. Metternich, Austrian statesman, 1773-1859.
Draja Mikhailovich, Yugoslav political leader, 1893-1946.
Carl Milles, Swedish sculptor, 1875-1955.
Jozef Cardinal Mindszenty, Roman Catholic primate of Hungary, 1892-1975.
Yukio Mishima, Japanese author, 1925-1970.
Vilehm Moberg, Swedish novelist, 1898-1973.
Ferenc Molnar, Hungarian dramatist, 1878-1952.
George Moore, Irish novelist, 1852-1933.
Thomas Moore, Irish poet, 1779-1852.
Jose M. Morelos y Pavon, Mexican patriot, 1765-1815.
Mohammed Mossadegh, Iranian statesman, 1880-1967.
Bartolome E. Murillo, Spanish painter, 1617-1682.

Fridtjof Nansen, Norwegian explorer, 1861-1930.
Jawaharlal Nehru, Indian statesman, 1889-1964.
Florence Nightingale, English nurse, 1820-1910.
Alfred Nobel, Swedish philanthropist, 1833-1898.

Alvaro Obregon, Mexican statesman, 1880-1928.
Sean O'Casey, Irish dramatist, 1884-1964.
Daniel O'Connell, Irish political leader, 1775-1847.
Frank O'Connor, Irish writer, 1903-1966.
Thomas P. O'Connor, Irish journalist, 1848-1929.
Aristotle Onassis, Greek shipping magnate, 1900-1975.

George Papandreou, Greek statesman, 1888-1968.
Charles Stewart Parnell, Irish nationalist, 1846-1891.
Juan Peron, president of Argentina, 1895-1974.
Pablo Picasso, Spanish artist & sculptor, 1881-1973.
Joseph Pilsudski, Polish statesman, 1867-1935.
Miguel Primo de Rivera, Spanish dictator, 1870-1930.
Casimir Pulaski, Polish statesman, 1748-1779.

Manuel L. Quezon, Filipino statesman, 1878-1944.

Adam Rapacki, Polish statesman, 1910-1970.
Rembrandt van Rijn, Dutch painter, 1606-1669.
Syngman Rhee, South Korean president, 1875-1965.
Jose Rizal, Filipino patriot, 1861-1896.
Peter Paul Rubens, Flemish painter, 1577-1640.

Antonio de O. Salazar, Portuguese statesman, 1899-1970.
Antonio L. de Santa Anns, Mexican general, 1795-1876.
Eisaku Sato, Japanese statesman, 1901-1975.
Arthur Schnitzler, Austrian dramatist, 1862-1931.
Haile Selassie, Ethiopian emperor, 1891-1975.
Dudley Senanayake, Ceylon statesman, 1911-1973.
David Alfaro Siqueiros, Mexican artist, 1898-1974.
Moshe Sharett, Israeli statesman, 1894-1965.
Taras Shevchenko, Ukrainian poet, 1814-1861.
Frans E. Sillanpaa, Finnish novelist, 1888-1964.
Jan C. Smuts, South African statesman, 1870-1950.
Paul Henri Spaak, Belgian statesman, 1899-1972.
Baruch Spinoza, Dutch philosopher, 1632-1677.
Antonio Stradivari, Italian violin-maker, 1644-1737.
August Strindberg, Swedish writer, 1849-1912.
Sun Yat-Sen, Chinese statesman, 1866-1925.
Otto Sverdrup, Norwegian explorer, 1855-1930.
Emanuel Swedenborg, Swedish scientist, scholar, 1688-1772.
John M. Synge, Irish dramatist, 1871-1909.

Rabindranath Tagore, Indian poet, 1861-1941.
Vaino A. Tanner, Finnish statesman, 1881-1966.
U Thant, Burmese statesman, 1909-1974.
Hideki Tojo, Japanese political & military leader, 1885-1948.
Rafael L. Trujillo Molina, Dominican dictator, 1891-1961.
Moise K. Tshombe, Congolese leader, 1919-1969.

Lesia Ukrainka, Ukrainian poet, 1871-1913.
Sigrid Undset, Norwegian author, 1882-1949.

Anthony Van Dyck, Flemish painter, 1599-1641.
Getulio D. Vargas, Brazilian statesman, 1883-1954.
Diego Velazquez, Spanish painter, 1599-1660.
Eleutherios Venizelos, Greek statesman, 1864-1936.
Jan Vermeer, Dutch painter, 1632-1675.
Hendrik F. Verwoerd, South African prime minister, 1901-1966.
Volodymyr Vynnychenko, Ukrainian novelist, 1880-1951.

Artturi Virtanen, Finnish chemist, 1895-1973.

Franz Werfel, Austrian author, 1890-1945.
Chaim Weizmann, first Israeli president, 1874-1952.

William Butler Yeats, Irish poet, 1865-1939.

Emiliano Zapata, Mexican revolutionary, 1879-1919.
Stefan Zweig, Austrian author, 1881-1942.

Rulers of England and Great Britain

Name	England	Began	Died	Age	Rgd
	Saxons and Danes				
Egbert	King of Wessex, won allegiance of all English	827	839	—	12
Ethelwulf	Son, King of Wessex, Sussex, Kent, Essex	839	858	—	19
Ethelbald	Son of Ethelwulf, displaced father in Wessex	858	860	—	2
Ethelbert	2d son of Ethelwulf, united Kent and Wessex	860	866	—	6
Ethelred	3d son, King of Wessex, defeated Danes	866	871	—	5
Alfred	The Great, 4th son, fought Danes, fortified London	871	901	52	30
Edward	The Elder, Alfred's son, united English, claimed Scotland	901	925	55	24
Athelstan	The Glorious, Edward's son, King of Mercia, Wessex	925	940	45	15
Edmund	3d son of Edward, King of Wessex, Mercia	940	946	25	6
Edred	4th son of Edward	946	955	32	9
Edwy	The Fair, eldest son of Edmund, King of Wessex	955	959	18	3
Edgar	The Peaceful, son of Edmund, ruled all English	959	975	32	17
Edward	The Martyr, son of Edgar, murdered by stepmother	975	978	17	4
Ethelred II	The Unready, son of Edgar, married Emma of Normandy	978	1016	48	37
Edmund	Ironside, son of Ethelred II, King of London	1016	1016	27	0
Canute	The Dane, gave Wessex to Edmund, married Emma	1016	1035	40	19
Harold I	Harefoot, natural son of Canute	1035	1040	—	5
Hardicanute	Son of Canute by Emma, Danish King	1040	1042	24	2
Edward	The Confessor, son of Ethelred II (Canonized 1161)	1042	1066	62	24
Harold II	Edward's brother-in-law, last Saxon King	1066	1066	44	0
	House of Normandy				
William I	The Conqueror, defeated Harold at Hastings	1066	1087	60	21
William II	Rufus, 3d son of William I, killed by arrow	1087	1100	43	13
Henry I	Beauclerc, youngest son of William I	1100	1135	67	35
	House of Blois				
Stephen	Son of Adela, 4th dau. of William I, and Count of Blois	1135	1154	50	19
	House of Plantagenet				
Henry II	Son of Goeffrey Plantagenet (Angevin) by Matilda, dau. of Henry I	1154	1189	56	35
Richard I	Coeur de Lion, son of Henry II, crusader	1189	1199	42	10
John	Lackland, son of Henry II, signed Magna Carta, 1215	1199	1216	50	17
Henry III	Son of John, acceded at 9, under regency until 1227	1216	1272	65	56
Edward I	Longshanks, son of Henry III	1272	1307	68	35
Edward II	Son of Edward I, deposed by Parliament, 1327	1307	1327	43	20
Edward III	Of Windsor, son of Edward II	1327	1377	65	50
Richard II	Grandson of Edw. III, minor until 1389, deposed 1399	1377	1400	34	22
	House of Lancaster				
Henry IV	Son of John of Gaunt, Duke of Lancaster, son of Edw. III	1399	1413	47	13
Henry V	Son of Henry IV, victor of Agincourt	1413	1422	34	9
Henry VI	Son of Henry V, deposed 1461, died in Tower	1422	1471	49	39
	House of York				
Edward IV	Great-great-grandson of Edward III, son of Duke of York	1461	1483	41	22
Edward V	Son of Edward IV, murdered in Tower of London	1483	1483	13	0
Richard III	Crookback, bro. of Edward IV, fell at Bosworth Field	1483	1485	35	2
	House of Tudor				
Henry VII	Son of Edmund Tudor, Earl of Richmond, whose father had married the widow of Henry V; descended from Edward III through his mother, Margaret Beaufort via John of Gaunt. By marriage with dau. of Edward IV he united Lancaster and York	1485	1509	53	24
Henry VIII	Son of Henry VII *See Meorable Dates.*	1509	1547	56	38
Edward VI	Son of Henry VIII, by Jane Seymour, his 3d queen. Ruled under regents. Was forced to name Lady Jane Grey his successor. Council of State proclaimed her queen Jul. 10, 1553. Mary Tudor won Council, was proclaimed queen Jul. 19, 1553. Mary had Lady Jane Grey beheaded for treason, Feb., 1554	1547	1553	16	6
Mary I	Daughter of Henry VIII, by Catherine of Aragon	1553	1558	43	5
Elizabeth I	Daughter of Henry VIII, by Anne Boleyn, *Designated Elizabeth I in 1952*	1558	1603	69	44
	Great Britain				
	House of Stuart				
James I	James VI of Scotland, son of Mary, Queen of Scots. *First to call himself King of Great Britain. This became official with the Act of Union,* 1707	1603	1625	59	22
Charles I	Only surviving son of James I: beheaded Jan. 30, 1649	1625	1649	48	24
	Commonwealth, 1649-1660 Council of State, 1649; Protectorate, 1653				
The Cromwells	Oliver Cromwell, Lord Protector	1653	1658	59	—
	Richard Cromwell, Lord Protector, resigned May 25, 1659	1658	1712	86	—
	House of Stuart (Restored)				
Charles II	Eldest son of Charles I, died without issue	1660	1685	55	25
James II	2d son of Charles I. Deposed 1688. Interregnum Dec. 11, 1688, to Feb. 13, 1689	1685	1701	68	3
William III	Son of William, Prince of Orange, by Mary, dau. of Charles I	1689	1702	51	13
and Mary II	Eldest daughter of James II and wife of William III		1694	33	6
Anne	2d daughter of James	1702	1714	49	12

House of Hanover

George I..........Son of Elector of Hanover, by Sophia, grand-dau. of James I........	1714	1727	67	13
George II......... Only son of George I, married Caroline of Brandenburg...........	1727	1760	77	33
George III.........Grandson of George II, married Charlotte of Mecklenburg..........	1760	1820	81	59
George IV.........Eldest son of George III, Prince Regent, from Feb., 1811..........	1820	1830	67	10
William IV.........3d son of George III, married Adelaide of Saxe-Meiningen...........	1830	1837	71	7
Victoria...........Dau. of Edward, 4th son of George III; married (1840) Prince Albert of Saxe-Coburg and Gotha, who became Prince Consort..........	1837	1901	81	63

House of Saxe-Coburg and Gotha

Edward VII........Eldest son of Victoria, married Alexandria, Princess of Denmark.....	1901	1910	68	9

House of Windsor
Name Adopted Jul. 17, 1917

George V......... 2d son of Edward VII, married Princess Mary of Teck..............	1910	1936	70	25
Edward VIII....... Eldest son of George V; acceded Jan. 20, 1936, abdicated Dec. 11...	1936	1972	77	1
George VI.........2d son of George V; married Lady Elizabeth Bowes-Lyon..........	1936	1952	56	15
Elizabeth II........Elder daughter of George VI, acceded Feb. 6, 1952..............	1952	—	—	—

Rulers of Scotland

The Romans gave the name of Caledonia to present-day Scotland. The Scots, a Celtic race that spoke Gaelic, came from Ireland, then called Scotia.

Kenneth I MacAlpin was the first Scot to rule both Scots and Picts, 843 A. D.

Duncan I was the first general ruler, 1034. Macbeth seized the kingdom 1040, was slain by Duncan's son, Malcolm III Canmore, 1058.

Malcolm married Margaret, Saxon princess who had fled from the Normans. Queen Margaret introduced English language and English monastic customs. She was canonized. Her son Edgar, 1097, moved the court to Edinburgh. His brothers Alexander I and David I succeeded. Malcolm IV, 1153, grandson of David I, was followed by his brother, William the Lion, 1165, whose son was Alexander II, 1214. The latter's son, Alexander III, 1249, defeated the Norse and regained the Hebrides. When he died, 1286, his granddaughter, Margaret, child of Eric of Norway and grandniece of Edward I of England, known as the Maid of Norway, was chosen ruler, but died on the way, 1290.

John Baliol, 1292-1296. (Interregnum, 10 years).

Robert Bruce (The Bruce), 1306-1329, victor at Bannockburn, 1314.

David II, only son of Robert Bruce, ruled 1329-1371.

Robert II, 1371-1390, grandson of Robert Bruce, son of Walter, the Steward of Scotland, was called The Steward, first of the so-called Stuart line.

Robert III, son of Robert II, 1390-1406.

James I, son of Robert III, 1406-1437.

James II, son of James I, 1437-1460.

James III, 1460-1488, eldest son of James II.

James IV, 1488-1513, eldest son of James III.

James V, 1513-1542, eldest son of James IV.

Mary, daughter, born 1542, became queen when 1 week old; was crowned 1543. Married, 1558, Francis, son of Henry II of France, who became king 1559, died 1560. Mary ruled Scots 1561 until abdication, 1567. She also married (2) Henry Stewart, Lord Darnley, and (3) James, Earl of Bothwell. Imprisoned by Elizabeth I; beheaded 1587.

James VI, 1567-1625, son of Mary and Lord Darnley, became King of England on death of Elizabeth in 1603. Although the thrones were thus united, the legislative union of Scotland and England was not effected until the Act of Union, May 1, 1707.

Rulers of France: Kings, Queens, Presidents

Caesar to Charlemagne

Julius Caesar subdued the Gauls, native tribes of Gaul (France) 57 to 52 B. C. The Romans ruled 500 years. The Franks, a Teutonic tribe, reached the Somme from the East ca. 250 A. D. By the 5th century the Merovingian Franks ousted the Romans. In 451 A.D., with the help of Visigoths, Burgundians and others, they defeated Attila and the Huns at Chalons-sur-Marne.

Childeric I became leader of the Merovingians 458 A. D. His son Clovis I (Chlodwig, Ludwig, Louis), crowned 481, founded the dynasty. After defeating the Alemanni (Germans) 496, he was baptized a Christian and made Paris his capital. His line ruled until Childeric III was deposed, 742.

The West Merovingians were called Neustrians, the eastern Austrasians. Pepin of Herstal (687-714) major domus, or head of the palace, of Austrasia, took over Neustria as dux (leader) of the Franks. Pepin's son, Charles, called Martel (the Hammer) defeated the Saracens at Tours-Poitiers, 732; was succeeded by his son, Pepin the Short, 741, who deposed Childeric III and ruled as king until 768.

His son, Charlemagne, or Charles the Great (742-814) became king of the Franks, 768, with his brother Carloman, who died 771. He ruled France, Germany, parts of Italy, Spain, Austria and enforced Christianity. Crowned Emperor of the Romans by Pope Leo III in St. Peter's, Rome, Dec. 25, 800 A. D. Succeeded by son, Louis the Pious, 814. At death, 840, Louis left empire to sons, Lothair (Roman emperor); Pepin I (king of Aquitaine); Louis II of Germany; Charles the Bald (France). They quarreled and by the peace of Verdun, 843, divided the empire.

A.D.   Name and Year of Accession

The Carolingians

840   Charles I (the Bald), Roman Emperor, 875
877   Louis II (the Stammerer), son
879   Louis III (died 882) and Carloman (bro.)
884   Charles II (the Fat), Roman Emperor, 881
888   Eudes (Odo) elected by nobles. Ceded land to
898   Charles III (the Simple), son of Louis II, defeated by
922   Robert, brother of Eudes, killed in war
923   Rodolph (Raoul) Duke of Burgundy
936   Louis IV, son of Charles III
954   Lothair, son, aged 13, defeated by Capet
986   Louis V (the Sluggard), left no heirs

The Capets

987   Hugh Capet, son of Hugh the Great
996   Robert (the Wise), his son
1031 Henry I, his son, last Norman
1060 Philip I (the Fair), son, king at 14
1108 Louis VI (the Fat), son
1137 Louis VII (the Younger), son
1180 Philip II (Augustus), son, crowned at Reims
1223 Louis VIII (the Lion), son
1226 Louis IX, son, crusader; Louis IX (1214-1270) reigned 44 years, arbitrated disputes with English King Henry III; led crusades, 1248 (captured in Egypt 1250) and 1270, when he died of plague in Tunis. Canonized 1297 as St. Louis.
1270 Philip III (the Hardy), son
1285 Philip IV (the Fair), son, king at 17
1314 Louis X (the Headstrong), son. His posthumous son, John I, lived only 7 days
1316 Philip V (the Tall), brother of Louis X
1322 Charles IV (the Fair), brother of Louis X

House of Valois

1328 Philip VI (of Valois), grandson of Philip III
1350 John II (the Good), his son, retired to England
1364 Charles V (the Wise), son
1380 Charles VI (the Beloved), son
1422 Charles VII (the Victorious), son. In 1429 Joan of Arc (Jeanne d'Arc) promised Charles to oust the English, who occupied northern France. Joan won at Orleans and Patay and had Charles crowned at Reims July 17, 1429. Joan was captured May 24, 1430, and executed May 30, 1431, at Rouen for heresy. Charles ordered her rehabilitation, effected 1455.
1461 Louis XI (the Cruel), son, civil reformer
1483 Charles VIII (the Affable), son
1498 Louis XII, great-grandson of Charles V
1515 Francis I, of Angouleme, nephew, son-in-law. Francis I (1494-1547) reigned 32 years, fought 4 big wars, was patron of the arts, aided Cellini, del Sarto, Leonardo da Vinci, Rabelais. Embellished Fontainebleau.
1547 Henry II, son, killed at a joust in a tournament. He was the husband of Catherine de Medici (1519-1589) and the lover of Diane de Poitiers (1499-1566). Catherine was born in Flor-

ence, daughter of Lorenzo de Medici. By her marriage to Henry II she became the mother of Francis II, Charles IX, Henry III and Queen Margaret (Reine Margot) wife of Henry IV. She persuaded Charles IX to order the massacre of Huguenots on the Feast of St. Bartholomew, Aug. 24, 1572, the day her daughter was married to Henry of Navarre.

1559 Francis II, son of Henry II. In 1548, Mary, Queen of Scots since infancy, was betrothed when 6 to Francis, aged 4. They were married 1558. Francis died 1560, aged 16; Mary ruled Scotland, abdicated 1567.

1560 Charles IX, brother of Francis II

1574 Henry III, brother, assassinated

House of Bourbon

1589 Henry IV, of Navarre, assassinated. Henry IV made enemies when he gave tolerance to Protestants by Edict of Nantes, 1598. He was grandson of Queen Margaret of Navarre, literary patron. He married Margaret of Valois, Catherine de Medici's daughter; was divorced; in 1600 married Marie de Medicis, who became Regent of France, 1610-17 for her son, Louis XIII, but was exiled by Richelieu, 1631.

1610 Louis XIII (the Just), son, Louis XIII (1610-1643) married Anne of Austria. His ministers were Cardinals Richelieu and Mazarine.

1643 Louis XIV (The Grand Monarch), son. Louis XIV was king 72 years. He exhausted a prosperous country in wars for thrones and territory. By revoking the Edict of Nantes (1685) he caused the emigration of the Huguenots. He said: "I am the state."

1715 Louis XV, great-grandson. Louis XV married a Polish princess, lost Canada to the English. His favorites, Mme. Pompadour and Mme. Du Barry influenced policies. Noted for saying: Apres moi, le deluge. (After me, the deluge).

1774 Louis XVI, grandson; married Marie Antoinette, daughter of Empress Maria Therese of Austria. King and queen beheaded by Revolution, 1793. Their son, called Louis XVII, died in prison, never ruled.

First Republic

1792 National Convention of the French Revolution

1792 Directory, under Barras and others

1799 Consulate, Napoleon Bonaparte, First Consul. In 1802 elected Consul for life.

First Empire

1804 Napoleon I, Emperor. Josephine (de Beauharnais) Empress, 1804-09; Marie Louise, Empress, 1810-1814. Her son, Fran-

cois (1811-1832) titular King of Rome, later Duke de Reichstadt and "Napoleon II," never ruled. Napoleon abdicated 1814, died 1821.

Bourbons Restored

1814 Louis XVIII king; brother of Louis XVI.

1824 Charles X, brother: reactionary, deposed by the July Revolution, 1830.

House of Orleans

1830 Louis Philippe, the Citizen King.

Second Republic

1848 Louis Napoleon. President, nephew of Napoleon I. He became:

Second Empire

1852 Napoleon III, Emperor, Eugenie (de Montijo) Empress. Lost Franco-Prussian war, deposed 1870. Son, Prince Imperial (1856-79), died in Zulu War. Eugenie died 1920.

Third Republic—Presidents

1871 Thiers, Louis Adolphe (1797-1877)

1873 MacMahon, Marshal Patrice M. (1808-1893)

1879 Grevy, Paul J. (1807-1891), resigned

1887 Sadi-Carnot, M. (1837-1894), assassinated

1894 Casimir-Pernier, Jean P. P. (1847-1907), resigned

1895 Faure, Francois Felix (1841-1899)

1899 Loubet, Emile (1838-1929)

1906 Fallieres, Armand (1841-1931)

1913 Poincare, Raymond (1860-1934)

1920 Deschanel, Paul (1856-1922), resigned

1920 Millerand, Alexandre (1859-1943), resigned

1924 Doumergue, Gaston (1863-1937)

1931 Doumer, Paul (1857-1932), assassinated

1932 Lebrun, Albert (1871-1950), resigned 1940

1940 Vichy govt. under German armistice: Henri Philippe Petan (1856-1951) Chief of State, 1940-1944.
Provisional govt. after liberation: Chas. de Gaulle (1890-1970) Oct. 1944-Jan. 21, 1946; Felix Gouin (1884-   ) Jan. 23, 1946; Georges Bidault (1899-   ) June 24 1946.

Fourth Republic—Presidents

1947 Auriol, Vincent (1884-1966)

1954 Coty, Rene (1882-1962)

Fifth Republic—Presidents

1958 De Gaulle, Charles Andre M. J. (1890-1970)

1969 Pompidou, Georges J. R. (1911-1974)

1974 Giscard d'Estaing, Valery (1926-

Rulers of Middle Europe; Rise and Fall of Dynasties

Carolingian Dynasty

Charles the Great, or Charlemagne, ruled France, Italy, and Middle Europe; established Ostmark (later Austria); crowned Roman emperor by pope in Rome, 800 A. D. Died 814.

Louis I (Ludwig) the Pious, son; crowned by Charlemagne 813, d. 840.

Louis the German, son; succeeded to East Francia (Germany) 843-876.

Charles the Fat, son; inherited East Francia and West Francia (France) 876, reunited empire, crowned emperor by pope, 881, deposed 887.

Arnulf, nephew, 887-899. Partition of empire.

Louis the Child, 900-911, last direct descendant of Charlemagne.

Conrad I, duke of Franconia, first elected German king, 911-918, founded House of Franconia.

Saxon Dynasty; First Reich

Henry I; the Fowler, duke of Saxony, 919-936.

Otto I, the Great, 936-973, son; crowned Holy Roman Emperor by pope, 962.

Otto II, 973-983, son; failed to oust Greeks and Arabs from Sicily.

Otto III, 983-1002, son; crowned emperor at 16.

Henry II, duke of Bavaria, 1002-1024, great-grandson of Henry the Fowler.

House of Franconia

Conrad II, 1024-1039, son-in-law of Otto I.

Henry III, 1039-1056, son; deposed 3 popes; annexed Burgundy.

Henry IV, 1056-1106, son; regency by his mother, Agnes of Poitou. Banned by Pope Gregory VII, he did penance at Canossa.

Henry V, 1106-1125, son; last of Salic House.

Lothair, duke of Saxony, 1125-1137. Crowned emperor in Rome, 1134.

House of Hohenstaufen

Conrad III, duke of Suabia, 1138-1152. In 2d Crusade.

Frederick I, Barbarossa, 1152-1190; son of Conrad's brother; in 3d Crusade.

Henry VI, 1190-1196, took lower Italy from Normans. Son became king of Sicily.

Philip of Suabia, 1198-1208, son of Frederick I.

Otto IV, of House of Welf, 1198-1215; deposed.

Frederick II, 1215-1250, son of Henry VI; king of Sicily; crowned king of Jerusalem; in 5th Crusade.

Conrad IV, 1250-1254, son; lost lower Italy to Charles of Anjou.

Conradin, son, king of Jerusalem and Sicily, beheaded. Last Hohenstaufen.

Interregnum, 1250-1273, Rise of the Electors.

Transition

Rudolph of Hapsburg, 1273-1291, defeated King Ottocar II of Bohemia. Bequeathed duchy of Austria to eldest son, Albert.

Adolphus, count of Nassau, 1291-1298, killed in war with Albert of Austria.

Albert I, German king, 1298-1308.

Henry VII, of Luxemburg, 1308-1313, crowned emperor in Rome. Seized Bohemia, 1310.

Louis IV of Bavaria (Wittelsbach), 1314-1347. Also elected was Frederick of Austria, 1314-1330 (Hapsburg). Abolition of papal sanction for election of Holy Roman Emperor.

Charles IV, of Luxemburg, 1347-1378, grandson of Henry VII, German emperor and king of Bohemia, Lombardy, Burgundy; took Mark of Brandenburg.

Wenceslaus, 1378-1400, deposed.

Rupert, Duke of Palatine, 1400-1410.

Hungary

Stephen I, house of Arpad, 907-1038. Crowned king by Pope Silvester II, 1001 A. D., converted Magyars. After several centuries of feuds Charles Robert of Anjou became Charles I, 1308-1342.

Louis I, the Great, 1342-1382, son; joint ruler of Poland with Casimir III, 1370. Defeated Turks.

Mary, daughter, 1385-1395, ruled with husband. Sigismund of Luxemburg, 1387-1437, also king of Bohemia. As bro. of Wenceslaus he succeeded Rupert as Holy Roman Emperor, 1410.

Albert II, 1438-1439, son-in-law of Sigismund; also Roman emperor. (See under Hapsburg.)

Ulaszlo I of Poland, died in battle, 1444.

Ladislaus V, child. John Hunyadi (Hunyadi Janos) guardian, fought Turks, Czechs; died 1456.

Matthias I (Corvinus) son of Hunyadi, 1458-1490. Shared rule of Bohemia, captured Vienna, 1485, annexed Austria, Styria, Carinthia.

Ulaszlo II (King of Bohemia), 1490-1516.

Louis II, son, aged 10, 1516-1526. Wars with Suleiman, Turk. In 1527 Hungary was split between Ferdinand I, Archduke of Austria, bro.-in-law of Louis II, and John Zapolya of Transylvania. After Turkish invasion, 1547, Hungary was split between Ferdinand, Prince John Sigismund (Transylvania) and the Turks.

House of Hapsburg

Albert V of Austria, Hapsburg, crowned king of Hungary, Jan. 1438, Roman emperor, March, 1438, as Albert II; died 1439.

Frederick III, cousin, 1430-1493. Fought Turks.

Maximilian I, son, 1493-1519. Assumed title of Holy Roman Emperor (German), 1493.

Charles V, grandson, 1519-1556. King of Spain with mother co-regent; crowned Roman emperor at Aix, 1520. Confronted Luther at Worms; attempted church reform and religious conciliation. Abdicated 1556.

Ferdinand I, king of Bohemia, 1526, of Hungary, 1527; disputed. German king, 1531. Crowned Roman emperor on abdication of Charles V, 1556.

Maximilian II, son, 1564-1576; Rudolph II, son, 1576-1612.

Matthias, brother, 1612-1619, king of Bohemia and Hungary.

Ferdinand II of Styria, king of Bohemia, 1617, of Hungary, 1618, Roman emperor, 1619. Bohemian Protestants deposed him, elected Frederick V of Palatine, starting Thirty Years War.

Ferdinand III, son, king of Hungary, 1625, Bohemia, 1627, Roman emperor, 1637. Peace of Westphalia, 1648, ended war. Leopold I, 1658-1705; Joseph I, 1705-1711; Charles VI, 1711-1740.

Maria Theresa, daughter, 1740-1780, Archduchess of Austria, queen of Hungary; ousted pretender, Charles VII, crowned 1742; in 1745 obtained election of her husband Francis I as Roman emperor and co-regent (d. 1765). Fought Seven Years' War with Frederick II (the Great) of Prussia. Mother of Marie Antoinette, Queen of France.

Joseph II, son, 1765-1790, Roman emperor, reformer; powers restricted by Empress Maria Theresa until her death, 1780. First partition of Poland. Leopold II, 1790-1792.

Francis II, 1792-1835. Fought Napoleon. Proclaimed first hereditary emperor of Austria, 1806. Forced to abdicate as Roman emperor, 1806; last use of title. Ferdinand I, son, 1835-1848, abdicated during revolution.

Austro-Hungarian Monarchy

Francis Joseph I, nephew, 1848-1916, emperor of Austria, king of Hungary. Dual monarchy of Austria-Hungary formed, 1867. After assassination of heir, Archduke Francis Ferdinand, June 28, 1914, Austrian diplomacy precipitated World War I.

Charles I, grand-nephew, 1916-1918, last emperor of Austria and king of Hungary. Abdicated Nov. 11-13, 1918, died 1922.

Rulers of Prussia

Nucleus of Prussia was the Mark of Brandenburg. First margrave was Albert the Bear (Albrecht), 1134-1170. First Hohenzollern margrave was Frederick, burggrave of Nuremberg, 1415-1440.

Frederick William, 1640-1688, the Great Elector. Son, Frederick III, 1688-1713, was crowned King Frederick of Prussia, 1701.

Frederick II, the Great, 1740-1786, annexed Silesia part of Austria.

Frederick William II, nephew, 1786-1797.

Frederick William III, 1797-1840. Napoleonic wars.

Frederick William IV, 1840-1861. Uprising of 1848 and first parliament and constitution.

Second and Third Reich

William I, 1861-1888, brother. Annexation of Schleswig and Hanover; Franco-Prussian war, 1870-71, proclamation of German Reich, Jan. 18, 1871, at Versailles; William, German emperor (Deutscher Kaiser), Bismarck, chancellor.

Frederick III, son, 1888.

William II, son, 1888-1918. Led Germany in World War I, abdicated as German emperor and king of Prussia, Nov. 9, 1918. Died in exile in Netherlands June 4, 1941. Minor rulers of Bavaria, Saxony, Wurttemberg also abdicated.

Germany proclaimed a republic at Weimar, July 1, 1919. Presidents: Friedrich Ebert, 1919-1925, Paul von Hindenburg-Beneckendorff, 1925, reelected 1932, d. Aug. 2, 1934. Adolf Hitler, chancellor, chosen successor as Leader-Chancellor (Fuehrer & Reichskanzler) of Third Reich. Annexed Austria, March, 1938. Precipitated World War II, 1939-1945. Committed suicide April 30, 1945.

Rulers of Denmark, Sweden, Norway

Denmark

Earliest rulers invaded Britain; King Canute, who ruled in London 1017-1035, was most famous. The Valdemars furnished kings until the 15th century. In 1282 the Danes won the first national assembly, Danehof, from King Erik.

Most redoubtable medieval character was Margaret, daughter of Valdemar IV, born 1353, married at 10 to King Haakon VI of Norway. In 1375 she had her first infant son Olaf made king of Denmark. After his death, 1387, she was regent of Denmark and Norway. In 1388 Sweden accepted her as sovereign. In 1389 she made her grand-nephew, Duke Erik of Pomerania, titular king of Denmark, Sweden and Norway, with herself as regent. In 1397 she effected the Union of Kalmar of the three kingdoms and had Erik crowned. In 1439 the three kingdoms deposed him and elected Christopher of Bavaria king (Christopher III). On his death, 1448, the union broke up.

Succeeding rulers were unable to enforce their claims as rulers of Sweden until 1520, when Christian II conquered Sweden. He was thrown out 1522, and in 1523 Gustavus Vasa united Sweden. Denmark continued to dominate Norway until the Napoleonic wars, when Frederick VI joined the Napoleonic cause after Britain had destroyed the Danish fleet (1807). In 1814 he was forced to cede Norway to Sweden and Helgoland to Britain, receiving Lauenburg. Successors: 1839—Christian VIII; 1848—Frederick VII; 1863-Christian IX; 1906—Frederick VIII; 1912—Christian X; 1947—Frederick IX; 1972—Queen Margrethe.

Sweden

Early kings ruled at Uppsala, but did not dominate the country. Sverker (1134-1156) united the Swedes and Goths. In 1435 Sweden obtained the Riksdag, or parliament. After the Union of Kalmar, 1379, the Danes either ruled or harried the country until Christian II of Denmark conquered it anew, 1520. This led to a rising under Gustavus Vasa, who ruled Sweden 1523-1560, and established an independent kingdom. Charles IX (1594-1611, crowned 1607), conquered Moscow. Gustavus II Adolphus (1611-1633) was called the Great. Later rulers, 1633—Christina; 1654—Charles X; 1660—Charles XI; 1697—Charles XII (invader of Russia and Poland, defeated at Poltava, June 28, 1709); 1718—his sister, Unrika Eleanora, elected queen; 1720—her husband, Frederick I (of Hesse); 1751—Adolphus—his sister, Unrika Eleanora, elected queen; 1720—her husband, Frederick I (of Hesse); 1751—Adolphus Charles XIV. He was Jean Bernadotte, Napoleon's Prince of Ponte Corvo, elected 1810 to succeed Charles XIII. He founded the present dynasty. 1844—Oscar I; 1859—Charles XV; 1872—Oscar II; 1907—Gustavus V; 1950—Gustav VI Adolf; 1973—Carl XVI Gustaf.

Norway

Overcoming many rivals, Harald Haarfager (872-930) conquered Norway, Orkneys and Shetlands; Olaf, great-grandson (995-1000) brought Christianity into Norway, Iceland and Greenland. In 1035 Magnus the Good also became king of Denmark. Haakon V (1299-1319)had married his daughter to Erik of Sweden. Their son, Magnus, became ruler of Norway and Sweden at 6. His son, Haakon VI, married Margaret of Denmark; their son Olaf became king of Norway and Denmark, followed by Margaret's regency and the Union of Kalmar, 1397.

In 1450 Norway became subservient to Denmark. Christian IV (1588-1648) founded Christiania, now Oslo. After

Napoleonic wars, when Denmark ceded Norway to Sweden, a strong nationalist movement forced recognition of Norway as an independent kingdom united with Sweden under the Swedish kings, 1814-1905. In 1905 the union was dissolved and Prince Carl of Denmark became Haakon VII. He died Sept. 21, 1957, aged 85; succeeded by son, Olav V. b. July 2, 1903.

Rulers of the Netherlands and Belgium

The Netherlands (Holland)

William Frederick, Prince of Orange, led a revolt against French rule, 1813, and was crowned King of the Netherlands, 1815. Belgium seceded Oct. 4, 1830, after a revolt, and formed a separate government. The change was ratified by the two kingdoms by treaty Apr. 19, 1839.

(1840) William II; (1849) William III; (1890) Wilhelmina (daughter of William III and his second wife Princess Emma of Waldeck); Wilhelmina abdicated Sept. 4, 1948, in favor of daughter, Juliana, 39.

Belgium

A national congress elected Prince Leopold of Saxe-Coburg King; he took the throne July 21, 1831, as Leopold I. (1865) Leopold II; (1909) Albert I, nephew of Leopold II; (1934) Leopold III, son of Albert; (1944) Prince Charles, Regent; Leopold returned, 1950, yielded powers to son Baudouin, Prince Royal, Aug. 6, 1950, abdicated July 16, 1951. Baudouin I took throne July 17, 1951.

For political history prior to 1830 see articles on the Netherlands and Belgium.

Roman Rulers

From Romulus to the end of the Empire in the West. Rulers of the Roman Empire in the East sat in Constantinople and for a brief period in Nicaea, until the capture of Constantinople by the Turks in 1453, when Byzantium was succeeded by the Ottoman Empire.

B.C.	Name	A.D.	Name	A.D.	Name
	The Kingdom	79	Titus	314	Constantinus I and Licinius
753	Romulus (Quirinus)	81	Domitianus	324	Constantinus I (the Great)
716	Numa Pompilius	96	Nerva	337	Constantinus II, Constans I,
673	Tullus Hostilius	98	Trajanus		Constantius II
640	Ancus Marcius	117	Hadrianus	340	Constantius II and Constans I
616	L. Tarquinius Priscus	138	Antoninus Pius	350	Constantius II
578	Servius Tullius	161	Marcus Aurelius and Lucius Verus	360	Julianus II (the Apostate)
534	L. Tarquinius Superbus	169	Marcus Aurelius (alone)	363	Jovianus
		180	Commodus		
	The Republic	193	Pertinax; Julianus I		
509	Consulate established	193	Septimius Severus		**West (Rome) and East**
509	Quaestorship instituted	211	Caracalla and Geta		**(Constantinople)**
498	Dictatorship introduced	212	Caracalla (alone)	364	Valentinianus I (West) and Valens
494	Plebeian Tribunate created	217	Macrinus		(East)
494	Plebeian Aedileship created	218	Elagabalus (Heligabalus)	367	Valentinianus I with
444	Consular Tribunate organized	222	Alexander Severus		Gratianus (West) and Valens (East)
443	Censorship instituted	235	Maximinus (the Thracian)	375	Gratianus with Valentinianus
366	Praetorship established	238	Gordianus I and Gordianus II;		II (West) and Valens (East)
366	Curule Aedileship created		Pupienus and Balbinus	378	Gratianus with Valentinianus II
362	Military Tribunate elective	238	Gordianus III		(West) Theodosius I (East)
326	Proconsulate introduced	244	Philippus (the Arabian)	383	Valentinianus II (West) and
311	Naval Duumvirate elective	249	Decius		Theodosius I (East)
217	Dictatorship of Fabius Maximus	251	Gallus and Volusianus	394	Theodosius I (the Great)
133	Tribunate of Tiberius Gracchus	253	Aemilianus	395	Honorius (West) and Arcadius (East)
123	Tribunate of Gaius Gracchus	253	Valerianus and Gallienus	408	Honorius (West) and Theodosius II
82	Dictatorship of Sulla	258	Gallienus (alone)		(East)
60	First Triumvirate formed	268	Claudius II (the Goth)	423	Valentinianus III (West) and
	(Caesar, Pompeius, Crassus)	270	Quintillus		Theodosius II (East)
46	Dictatorship of Caesar	270	Aurelianus	450	Valentinianus III (West)
43	Second Triumvirate formed	275	Tacitus		and Marcianus (East)
	(Octavianus, Antonius, Lepidus)	276	Florianus	455	Maximus (West), Avitus
		276	Probus		(West); Marcianus (East)
		282	Carus	456	Avitus (West), Marcianus (East)
	The Empire	283	Carinus and Numerianus	457	Majorianus (West), Leo I (East)
27	Augustus (Gaius Julius	284	Diocletianus	461	Severus II (West), Leo I (East)
	Caesar Octavianus)	286	Diocletianus and Maximianus	467	Anthemius (West), Leo I (East)
A.D.		305	Galerius and Constantius I	472	Olybrius (West), Leo I (East)
14	Tiberius I	306	Galerius, Maximinus II, Severus I	473	Glycerius (West), Leo I (East)
37	Gaius (Caligula)	307	Galerius, Maximinus	474	Julius Nepos (West), Leo II (East)
41	Claudius I		II, Constantinus I, Licinius,	475	Romulus Augustulus (West) and
54	Nero		Maxentius		Zeno (East)
68	Galba	311	Maximinus II, Constantinus I,	476	End of Empire in West; Odovacar,
69	Galba; Otho; Vitellius		Licinius, Maxentius		King, drops title of Emperor; murdered
69	Vespasianus	314	Maximinus II, Constantinus I,		by King Theodoric of Ostrogoths 493 A. D.
			Licinius		

Rulers of Modern Italy

After the fall of Napoleon in 1814, the Congress of Vienna, 1815, restored Italy as a political patchwork, comprising the Kingdom of Naples and Sicily, the Papal States, and smaller units. Piedmont and Genoa were awarded to Sardinia, ruled by King Victor Emmanuel I of Savoy.

United Italy emerged under the leadership of Camillo, Count di Cavour (1810-1861), Sardinian prime minister. Agitation was led by Giuseppe Mazzini (1805-1872) and Giuseppe Garibaldi (1807-1882), soldier. Victor Emmanuel I abdicated 1821. After a brief regency for a brother, Charles Albert was King 1831-1849, abdicating when defeated by the Austrians at Novara. Succeeded by Victor Emmanuel II (1820-1878).

In 1859 France forced Austria to cede Lombardy to

Sardinia, which gave rights to Savoy and Nice to France. In 1860 Garibaldi led 1,000 volunteers in a spectacular campaign, took Sicily and expelled the King of Naples. In 1860 the House of Savoy annexed Tuscany, Parma, Moderna, Romagna, the Two Sicilies, the Marches, and Umbria. Victor Emmanuel assumed the title of King of Italy at Turin Mar. 17, 1861. In 1866 he joined Prussia and Austria in the Triple Alliance and received Venetia from Austria. On Sept. 20, 1870, his troops under Gen. Raffaele Cardorna entered Rome and took over the Papal States, ending the temporal power of the Roman Catholic Church.

Succession: Humbert I, 1878, assassinated 1900; Victor Emmanuel III, 1900, abdicated 1946, died 1947; Humbert II, 1946, ruled a month. In 1921 Benito Mussolini (1883-

[1945) formed the Fascist party and became prime minister Oct. 31, 1922. He made the King Emperor of Ethiopia, 1937; entered World War II as ally of Hitler. He was deposed Jul. 25, 1943.

At a plebiscite Jun. 2, 1946, Italy voted for a republic, Premier Alcide de Gasperi became Chief of State June 13,

1946. On Jun. 28, 1946, the Constituent Assembly elected Enrico de Nicola, Liberal, Provisional President of the Republic of Italy. Successive presidents: Luigi Einaudi, elected May 11, 1948; Giovanni Gronchi, Apr. 29, 1955; Antonio Segni, May 6, 1962; Giuseppe Saragat Dec. 28, 1964; Giovanni Leone Dec. 29, 1971.

Chronological List of Popes

Source: Annuario Pontifici Table lists year of coronation of each Pope.

The Roman Catholic Church names the Apostle Peter as founder of the Church in Rome. He arrived there c. 42, was martyred there c. 67, and raised to sainthood.

The Pope's temporal title is: Sovereign of the State of Vatican City.

The Pope's spiritual titles are: Bishop of Rome, Vicar of Jesus Christ, Successor of St. Peter, Prince of the Apostles, Supreme Pontiff of the Universal Church, Patriarch of the West, Primate of Italy, Archbishop and Metropolitan of the Roman Province and Sovereign of the State of Vatican City.

Anti-Popes are in *Italics*. Anti-Popes were illegitimate claimants of or pretenders to the papal throne.

Year	Name of Pope	Year	Name of Pope	Year	Name of Pope	Year	Name of Pope
See above.	St. Peter	575	Benedict I	928	Stephen VII	1216	Honorius III
67	St. Linus	579	Pelagius II	931	John XI	1227	Gregory IX
76	St. Anacletus	590	St. Gregory	936	Leo VII	1241	Celestine IV
	or Cletus	604	Sabinian	939	Stephen VIII	1243	Innocent IV
88	St. Clement I	607	Boniface III	942	Marinus II	1254	Alexander IV
97	St. Evaristus	608	St. Boniface IV	946	Agapitus II	1261	Urban IV
105	St. Alexander I	615	St. Deusdedit	955	John XII	1265	Clement IV
115	St. Sixtus I		or Adeodatus I	963	Leo VIII	1271	Gregory X
125	St. Telesphorus	619	Boniface V	964	Benedict V	1276	Innocent V
136	St. Hyginus	625	Honorius I	965	John XIII	1276	Adrian V
140	St. Pius I	640	Severinus	973	Benedict VI	1276	John XXI
155	St. Anicetus	640	John IV	*974*	*Boniface VII*	1277	Nicholas III
166	St. Soter	642	Theodore I	974	Benedict VII	1281	Martin IV
175	St. Eleutherius	649	St. Martin I	983	John XIV	1285	Honorius IV
189	St. Victor I	654	St. Eugene I	985	John XV	1288	Nicholas IV
199	St. Zephyrinus	657	St. Vitalian	996	Gregory V	1294	St. Celestine V
217	St. Callistus I	672	Adeodatus II	*997*	*John XVI*	1294	Boniface VIII
217	*St. Hippolytus*	676	Donus	999	Sylvester II	1303	Benedict XI
222	St. Urban I	678	St. Agatho	1003	John XVII	1305	Clement V
230	St. Pontian	682	St. Leo II	1004	John XVIII	1316	John XXII
235	St. Anterus	684	St. Benedict II	1009	Sergius IV	*1328*	*Nicholas V*
236	St. Fabian	685	John V	1012	Benedict VIII	1334	Benedict XII
251	St. Cornelius	686	Conon	*1012*	*Gregory*	1342	Clement VI
251	*Novatian*	687	Theodore	1024	John XIX	1352	Innocent VI
253	St. Lucius I	687	Paschal	1032	Benedict IX	1362	Urban V
254	St. Stephen I	687	St. Sergius I	1045	Sylvester III	1370	Gregory XI
257	St. Sixtus II	701	John VI	1045	Benedict IX	1378	Urban VI
259	St. Dionysius	705	John VII	1045	Gregory VI	*1378*	*Clement VII*
269	St. Felix I	708	Sisinnius	1046	Clement II	1389	Boniface IX
275	St. Eutychian	708	Constantine	1047	Benedict IX	*1394*	*Benedict XIII*
283	St. Caius	715	St. Gregory II	1048	Damasus II	1404	Innocent VII
296	St. Marcellinus	731	St. Gregory III	1049	St. Leo IX	1406	Gregory XII
308	St. Marcellus I	741	St. Zachary	1055	Victor II	*1409*	*Alexander V*
309	St. Eusebius	752	Stephen II	1057	Stephen IX	*1410*	*John XXIII*
311	St. Melchiades	757	St. Paul I	*1058*	*Benedict X*	1417	Martin V
314	St. Sylvester I	*767*	*Constantine*	1059	Nicholas II	1431	Eugene IV
336	St. Mark	*768*	*Philip*	1061	Alexander II	*1440*	*Felix V*
337	St. Julius I	768	Stephen III	*1061*	*Honorius II*	1447	Nicholas V
352	Liberius	772	Adrian I	1073	St. Gregory VII	1455	Callistus III
355	*Felix II*	795	St. Leo III	*1080*	*Clement III*	1458	Pius II
366	St. Damasus I	816	Stephen IV	1086	Victor III	1464	Paul II
366	*Ursinus*	817	St. Paschal I	1088	Urban II	1471	Sixtus IV
384	St. Siricius	824	Eugene II	1099	Paschal II	1484	Innocent VIII
399	St. Anastasius I	827	Valentine	*1100*	*Theodoric*	1492	Alexander VI
401	St. Innocent I	827	Gregory IV	*1102*	*Albert*	1503	Pius III
417	St. Zozimus	*844*	*John*	*1105*	*Sylvester IV*	1503	Julius II
418	St. Boniface I	844	Sergius II	1118	Gelasius II	1513	Leo X
418	*Eulalius*	847	St. Leo IV	*1118*	*Gregory VIII*	1522	Adrian VI
422	St. Celestine I	855	Benedict III	1119	Callistus II	1523	Clement VII
432	St. Sixtus III	*855*	*Anastasius*	1124	Honorius II	1534	Paul III
440	St. Leo I	858	St. Nicholas I	*1124*	*Celestine II*	1550	Julius III
461	St. Hilary	867	Adrian II	1130	Innocent II	1555	Marcellus II
468	St. Simplicius	872	John VIII	*1130*	*Anacletus II*	1555	Paul IV
483	St. Felix III or II	882	Marinus I	*1138*	*Victor IV*	1559	Pius IV
492	St. Gelasius I	884	St. Adrian III	1143	Celestine II	1566	St. Pius V
496	St. Anastasius II	885	Stephen V	1144	Lucius II	1572	Gregory XIII
498	St. Symmachus	891	Formosus	1145	Eugene III	1585	Sixtus V
498	*Lawrence*	896	Boniface VI	1153	Anastasius IV	1590	Urban VII
	(501-505)	896	Stephen VI	1154	Adrian IV	1590	Gregory XIV
514	St. Hormisdas	897	Romanus	1159	Alexander III	1591	Innocent IX
523	St. John I	897	Theodore II	*1159*	*Victor IV*	1592	Clement VIII
526	St. Felix IV or III	898	John IX	*1164*	*Paschal III*	1605	Leo XI
530	Boniface II	900	Benedict IV	*1168*	*Callistus III*	1605	Paul V
530	*Dioscorus*	903	Leo V	*1179*	*Innocent III*	1621	Gregory XV
533	John II	*903*	*Christopher*	1181	Lucius III	1623	Urban VIII
535	St. Agapitus	904	Sergius III	1185	Urban III	1644	Innocent X
536	St. Silverius	911	Anastasius III	1187	Gregory VIII	1655	Alexander VII
537	Vigilius	913	Landus	1187	Clement III	1667	Clement IX
556	Pelagius I	914	John X	1191	Celestine III	1670	Clement X
561	John III	928	Leo VI	1198	Innocent III	1676	Innocent XI

Year	Name of Pope	Year	Name of Pope	Year	Name of Pope	Year	Name of Pope
1689	Alexander VIII	1740	Benedict XIV	1829	Pius VIII	1922	Pius XI
1691	Innocent XII	1758	Clement XIII	1831	Gregory XVI	1939	Pius XII
1700	Clement XI	1769	Clement XIV	1846	Pius IX	1958	John XXIII
1721	Innocent XIII	1775	Pius VI	1878	Leo XIII	1963	Paul VI
1724	Bennedict XIII	1800	Pius VII	1903	St. Pius X		
1730	Clement XII	1823	Leo XII	1914	Benedict XV		

Rulers of Spain

From 8th to 11th centuries Spain was dominated by the Moors (Arabs and Berbers). The Christian reconquest established small competing kingdoms of the Asturias, Aragon, Castile, Catalonia, Leon, Navarre, and Valencia. In 1474 Isabella (Isabel), b. 1451, became Queen of Castile & Leon. Her husband, Ferdinand, b. 1452, inherited Aragon 1474, with Catalonia, Valcencia, and the Balearic Islands, became Ferdinand V of Castile. By Isabella's request Pope Sixtus IV established the Inquisition, 1478. Last Moorish kingdom, Granada, fell 1492. Columbus opened New World of colonies, 1492. Isabella died 1504, succeeded by her daughter, Juana "the Mad," but Ferdinand ruled until his death 1516.

Charles I, b. 1500, son of Juana and grandson of Ferdinand and Isabella, and of Maximilian I of Hapsburg; succeeded later as Holy Roman Emperor, Charles V, 1520. Abdicated 1556. Philip II, son, 1556-1598, inherited only Spanish throne; conquered Portugal, fought Turks, persecuted non-Catholics, sent Armada vs. England. Was briefly married to Mary I of England, 1554-1558. Succession: Philip III, 1598-1621; Philip IV, 1621-1665; Charles II, 1665-1700; left Spain to Philip of Anjou, grandson of Louis XIV, who as Philip V, 1700-1746, founded Bourbon dynasty. Ferdinand IV, 1746-1759; Charles III, 1759-1788; Charles IV, 1788-1808, abdicated.

Napoleon now dominated politics and made his brother Joseph King of Spain but the Spanish ousted him finally in 1813. Ferdinand VII, 1814-1833, lost American colonies; succeeded by daughter Isabella II, aged 3, with wife Maria Christina of Naples regent

until 1843. Isabella deposed by revolution 1868. Prince Amadeo of Savoy, 1870-1873. First republic, 1873-1874. Alphonso XII 1875-1885. His posthumous son was Alphonso XIII, with his mother, Queen Maria Christina regent; Spanish-American war, Spain lost Cuba, gave up Puerto Rico, Philippines, Sulu Is., Marianas. Alphonso took throne 1902, aged 16, married British Princess Victoria Eugenia of Battenberg. The dictatorship of Primo de Rivera, 1923-30, precipitated the revolution of 1931. Alphonso agreed to leave without formal abdication. The monarchy was abolished and the second republic established, with strong socialist backing. Presidents were Niceto Alcala Zamora, to 1936, when Manuel Anzana was chosen.

In July, 1936, the army in Morocco revolted against the government and General Francisco Franco led the troops into Spain. The revolution succeeded by Feb., 1939, when Anzana resigned. Franco became chief of state, with provisions that if he is incapacitated the Regency Council by two-thirds vote may propose a king to the Cortes, which must have a two-thirds majority to elect him.

Alphonso XIII, died in Rome Feb. 28, 1941, aged 54. His property and citizenship had been restored.

A succession law restoring the monarchy was approved in a 1947 referendum. Prince Juan Carlos, son of the pretender to the throne, was designated by Franco and the Cortes in 1969 as the future king and chief of state. Upon Franco's death, Nov. 20, 1975, Juan Carlos was proclaimed King, Nov. 22, 1975.

Leaders in the South American Wars of Liberation

Simon Bolivar (1783-1830), José Francisco de San Martin (1783-1850), and Francisco Antonio Gabriel Miranda (1750-1816) were among the heroes of the early 19th century struggles of South American nations to free themselves from Spain. All three, and their contemporaries, operated in periods of intense factional strife, during which soldiers and civilians suffered.

Miranda, a Venezuelan, who had served with the French in the American Revolution and commanded parts of the French Revolutionary armies in the Netherlands, attempted to start a revolt in Venezuela in 1806 and failed. In 1810, with British and American backing, he returned and was briefly a dictator, until the British withdrew their support. In 1812 he was overcome by the royalists in Venezuela and taken prisoner, dying in a Spanish prison in 1816.

San Martin was born in Argentina and during 1789-1811 served in campaigns of the Spanish armies in Europe and Africa. He first joined the independence movement in Argentina in 1812 and then in 1817 invaded Chile with 4,000 men over the high mountain passes. Here he and General Bernardo O'Higgins (1778-1842) defeated the Spaniards at Chacabuco, 1817, and O'Higgins was named Liberator and became first dictator of Chile, 1817-1823. In 1821 San Martin occupied Lima and Callao, Peru, and became Protector of Peru.

Bolivar, the greatest leader of South American liberation from Spain, was born in Venezuela, the son of an aristocratic family. His organizing and administrative abilities were superior and he foresaw many of the political difficulties of the future. He first served

under Miranda in 1812 and in 1813 captured Caracas, where he was named Liberator. Forced out next year by civil strife, he led a campaign that captured Bogota in 1814. In 1817 he was again in control of Venezuela and was named dictator. He organized Nueva Granada with the help of General Francisco de Paula Santander (1792-1840). By joining Nueva Granada, Venezuela and the present terrain of Panama and Ecuador, the republic of Colombia was formed with Bolivar president. After numerous setbacks he decisively defeated the Spaniards in the second battle of Carabobo, Venezuela, June 24, 1821.

In May, 1822, Gen. Antonio Jose de Sucre, Bolivar's trusted lieutenant, took Quito. Bolivar went to Guayaquil to confer with San Martin, who resigned as Protector of Peru and withdrew from politics. With a new army of Colombians and Peruvians Bolivar defeated the Spaniards in a saber battle at Juin in 1824 and cleared Peru.

De Sucre organized Charcas (Upper Peru) as Republica Bolivar (now Bolivia) and acted as president in place of Bolivar, who wrote its constitution. De Sucre defeated the Spanish faction of Peru at Ayacucho, Dec. 19, 1824.

Continued civil strife finally caused the Colombian federation to break apart. Santander turned against Bolivar, who in later defeated him and banished him. In 1828 Bolivar gave up the presidency he had held precariously for 14 years. He became ill from tuberculosis and died Dec. 17, 1830. He was honored as the great liberator and is buried in the national pantheon in Caracas.

Rulers of Russia; Premiers of the USSR

First ruler to consolidate Slavic tribes was Rurik, leader of the Russians who established himself at Novgorod, 862 A. D. He and his immediate successors had Scandinavian affiliations. They moved to Kiev after 972 A. D. and ruled as Dukes of Kiev. In 988 Vladimir was converted and adopted the Byzantine Greek Orthodox service, later modified by Slav influences. Important as organizer and lawgiver was Yaroslav, 1018-1054, whose daughters married kings of Norway, Hungary and France. His grandson, Vladimir II (Monomarchos), 1113-1125, was progenitor of several rulers, but in 1169 Andrew Bogolubski overthrew Kiev and began the line known as Grand Dukes of Vladimir.

Of the Grand Dukes of Vladimir, Alexander Nevsky, 1245-1263, had a son, Daniel, first to be called Duke of Muscovy (Moscow) who ruled 1294-1303. His successors became Grand Dukes of Muscovy. After Dmitri III Donskoi defeated the Tartars in 1380, they also became Grand Dukes of all Russia. Independence of the Tartars and

considerable territorial expansion were achieved under Ivan III, 1462-1505.

Czars of Muscovy—Ivan III was referred to in church ritual as Czar. He married Sofia, niece of the last Byzantine emperor. His successor, Basil, died in 1533 when Basil's son Ivan was only 3. He became Ivan IV, "the Terrible," crowned 1547 as Czar of all the Russians, ruled till 1584. Under the weak rule of his son, Feodor, Boris Godunov had control. The dynasty died, and after years of tribal strife and intervention by Polish and Swedish armies, the Russians united under 17-year-old Michael Romanov, distantly related to the first wife of Ivan IV. He ruled 1613-1645 and established the Romanov line. Fourth ruler after Michael was Peter I.

Czars, or Emperors of Russia (Romanovs)—Peter I, 1682-1725, known as Peter the Great, took title of Emperor in 1721. His successors and dates of accession were: Catherine, his widow, 1725, Peter II, his grandson, 1727, d. 1730; Anne, Duchess of Courtland, 1730, daughter of Peter the Great's brother, Czar Ivan; Ivan VI, 1740-1741, great-grandson of Ivan V, child, kept in prison and murdered 1764; Elizabeth, daughter of Peter I, 1741; Peter III, grandson of Peter I, 1761, deposed 1762 for his consort, Catherine II, former princess of Anhalt Zerbst (Germany) who is known as Catherine the Great, 1762-1796; Paul I, her son, 1796, killed 1801, Alexander I, son of Paul, 1801-1825, defeated Napoleon; Nicholas I, his brother, 1825; Alexander II, son of Nicholas, 1855, assassinated 1881 by terrorists; Alexander III, son, 1881-1894.

Nicholas II, son, 1894-1917, last Czar of Russia, was forced to abdicate by the Revolution that followed defeat by Germany. The Czar, the Czarina, the Czarevitch (Crown Prince) and the Czar's 4 daughters were murdered by the Bolsheviks in Ekaterinburg, July 16, 1918.

Provisional Government—Prince Georgi Lvov and Alexander Kerensky, premiers, 1917.

Union of Soviet Socialist Republics

Bolshevik Revolution, Nov. 7, 1917, displaced Kerensky; council of People's Commissars formed, Nicolai Lenin, premier. Lenin died Jan. 21, 1924. Alexei Rykov (executed 1938) and V. M. Molotov held the office, but actual ruler was Joseph Stalin (Joseph Vissarionovich Djugashvili), general secretary of the Central Committee of the Communist Party. Stalin became president of the Council of Ministers (premier) May 7, 1941, died Mar. 5, 1953. Succeeded by Georgi M. Malenkov, as head of the Council and premier and Nikita S. Khrushchev, first secretary of the Central Committee. Malenkov resigned Feb. 8, 1955, became deputy premier, was dropped July 3, 1957. Marshal Nikolai A. Bulganin became premier Feb. 8, 1955; was demoted and Krushchev became premier Mar. 27, 1958. Krushchev was ousted Oct. 14-15, 1964, replaced by Leonid I. Brezhnev as first secretary of the party and by Aleksei N. Kosygin as premier.

The Dynasties of China

(Until 221 B.C. and frequently thereafter, China was not a unified state. Where dynastic dates overlap, the rulers or events referred to appeared in different areas of China.)

Hsia	c.2000B.C.	-c. 1500B.C.
Shang	c.1500B.C.	-c. 1000B.C.
Western Chou	c.1000B.C.	771B.C.
Eastern Chou	770B.C.	256B.C.
Warring States	403B.C.	222B.C.
Ch'in (first unified empire)	221B.C.	206B.C.
Han	202B.C.	220A.D.
Western Han (expanded Chinese state beyond the Yellow and Yangtze River valleys)	202B.C.	9A.D.
Hsin (Wang Mang, usurper)	9A.D.	23A.D.
Eastern Han (expanded Chinese state into Indo-China and Turkestan)	25	220
Three Kingdoms (Wei, Shu, Wu)	220	264
Chin (western)	265	317
(eastern)	317	420
Northern Dynasties (followed several short-lived governments by Turks, Mongols, etc.)	386	581
Southern Dynasties (capital: Nanking)	420	589
Sui (reunified China)	581	618
T'ang (a golden age of Chinese culture; capital: Sian)	618	907
Five Dynasties (Yellow River basin)	907	959
Ten Kingdoms (southern China)	907	979
Liao (Khitan Mongols; capital: Peking)	947	1125
Sung	960	1279
Northern Sung (reunified central and southern China)	960	1127
Western Hsai (non-Chinese rulers in northwest)	990	1227
Chin (Tartars; drove Sung out of central China)	1114	1234
Yuan (Mongols; Kublai Khan made Peking his capital in 1267)	1271	1368
Ming (China reunified under Chinese rule; capital: Nanking, then Peking in 1420)	1368	1644
Ch'ing (Manchus, descendents of Tartars)	1644	1912
Republic (disunity: provincial rulers, warlords)	1912	1949

Composers of the Western World

Carl Philipp Emanuel Bach, 1714-1788. (G.) Prussian and Wurtembergian Sonatas.

Johann Christian Bach, 1735-1782. (G.) Concertos; sonatas.

Johann Sebastian Bach, 1685-1750. (G.) St. Matthew Passion, The Well-Tempered Clavichord.

Samuel Barber, b. 1910 (U.S.) Adagio for Strings, Vanessa.

Bela Bartok, 1881-1945. (Hung.) Concerto for Orchestra, The Miraculous Mandarin.

Ludwig Van Beethoven, 1770-1827. (G.) Concertos (Emperor); sonatas (Moonlight, Pastorale, Pathetique); symphonies (Eroica).

Vincenzo Bellini, 1801-1835. (It.) La Sonnambula, Norma, I Puritani.

Alban Berg, 1885-1935. (Aus.) Wozzeck, Lulu.

Hector Berlioz, 1803-1869. (F.) Damnation of Faust, Symphonie Fantastique, Requiem.

Leonard Bernstein, b. 1918. (U.S.) Jeremiah, West Side Story.

Georges Bizet, 1838-1875. (F.) Carmen, Pearl Fishers.

Ernest Bloch, 1880-1959. (Swiss) Schelomo, Voice in the Wilderness, Sacred Service.

Luigi Boccherini, 1743-1805 (It.) Cello Concerto in B Flat, Symphony in C.

Alexander Borodin, 1834-1887. (R.) Prince Igor, in the Steppes of Central Asia.

Johannes Brahms, 1833-1897. (G.) Liebeslieder Waltzes, Rhapsody in E Flat Major, Opus 119 for Piano, Academic Festival Overture; symphonies; quartets.

Benjamin Britten, b. 1913. (Br.) Peter Grimes, Turn of the Screw, Ceremony of Carols.

Anton Bruckner, 1824-1896, (Aus.) Symphonies (Romantic), Intermezzo for String Quintet.

Ferruccio Busoni, 1866-1924. (It.) Doctor Faust, Comedy Overture.

Dietrich Buxtehude, 1637-1707. (G.) Cantatas, Trio sonatas.

William Byrd, 1543-1623 (Br.) Masses, Sacred Songs.

Alexis Emmanuel Chabrier, 1841-1894. (Fr.) Le Roi Malgre Lui, Espana.

Gustave Charpentier, 1860-1956. (Fr.) Louise.

Frederic Chopin, 1810-1849. (P.) Concertos, Polonaise No. 6 in A Flat Major (Heroic); sonatas.

Aaron Copland, b. 1900. (U.S.) Appalachian Spring.

Claude Achille Debussy, 1862-1918. (F.) Pelleas et Melisande, La Mer, Prelude to the Afternoon of a Faun.

C. P. Leo Delibes, 1836-1891, (F.) Lakme, Coppelia, Sylvia.

Norman Dello Joio, b. 1913. (U.S.), Triumph of St. Joan, Psalm of David.

Gaetano Donizetti, 1797-1848. (It.) Elixir of Love, Lucia de Lammermoor, Daughter of the Regiment.

Paul Dukas, 1865-1935. (Fr.) Sorcerer's Apprentice.

Antonin Dvorak, 1841-1904. (C.) Symphony in E Minor (from the New World).

Edward Elgar, 1857-1934. (Br.) Pomp and Circumstance.

Manuel de Falla, 1876-1946. (Sp.) La Vide Breve, El Amor Brujo.

Gabriel Faure, 1845-1924. (Fr.) Requiem, Ballade.

Friedrich von Flotow, 1812-1883. (G.) Martha.

Cesar Franck, 1822-1890. (Belg.) D Minor Symphony.

George Gershwin, 1898-1937. (U.S.) Rhapsody in Blue, American in Paris, Porgy and Bess.

Umberto Giordano, 1867-1948 (It.) Andrea Chenier.

Alex K. Glazunoff, 1865-1936. (R.) Symphonies, Stenka Razin.

Mikhail Glinka, 1857-1904. (R.) Ruslan & Ludmilla.

Christoph W. Gluck, 1714-1787. (G.) Alceste, Iphigenie en Tauride.

Charles Gounod, 1818-1893. (F.) Faust, Romeo and Juliet.

Edvard Grieg, 1843-1907. (Nor.) Peer Gynt Suite, Concerto in A Minor.

George Frederick Handel, 1685-1759. (G.-Br.) Messiah, Xerxes, Berenice.

Howard Hanson, b. 1896. (U.S.) Symphonies No. 1 (Nordic) and 2 (Romantic).

Roy Harris, b. 1898. (U.S.) Symphonies, Amer. Portraits.

Joseph Haydn, 1732-1809. (Aus.) Symphonies (Clock); oratorios; chamber music.

Paul Hindemith, 1895-1963. (U.S.) Mathis Der Maler.

Gustav Holst, 1874-1934. (Br.) The Planets.

Arthur Honegger, 1892-1955. (Swiss) Judith, Le Roi David, Pacific 231.

Alan Hovhaness, b. 1911. (U.S.) Symphonies, Magnificat.

Engelbert Humperdinck, 1854-1921. (G.) Hansel and Gretel.

Charles Ives, 1874-1954. (U.S.) Third Symphony.

Aram Khachaturian, b. 1903. (R.) Gayane (ballet), symphonies.

Zoltan Kodaly, 1882-1967. (Hung.) Hary Janos, Psalmus Hungaricus.

Fritz Kreisler, 1875-1962. (Aus.) Caprice Viennois, Tambourin Chinois.

Rodolphe Kreutzer, 1766-1831. (F.) 40 etudes for violin.

Edouard V. A. Lalo, 1823-1892. (F.) Symphonie Espagnole.

Ruggiero Leoncavallo, 1858-1919, (It.) I Pagliacci.

Franz Liszt, 1811-1886. (Hung.) 20 Hungarian Rhapsodies; symphonic poems.

Edward MacDowell, 1861-1908. (U.S.) To a Wild Rose.

Gustav Mahler, 1860-1911. (Aus.) Lied von der Erde.

Pietro Mascagni, 1863-1945. (It.) Cavalleria Rusticana.

Jules Massenet, 1842-1912. (F.) Manon, Le Cid, Thais.

Mendelssohn-Bartholdy, 1809-1847. (G.) Midsummer Night's Dream, Songs Without Words.

Gian-Carlo Menotti, b. 1911. (It.-U.S.) The Medium, The Consul, Amahl and the Night Visitors.

Claudio Monteverdi, 1567-1643. (It.) Opera; masses; madrigals.

Wolfgang Amadeus Mozart, 1756-1791. (Aus.) Magic Flute, Marriage of Figaro; concertos; symphonies; etc.

Modest Moussorgsky, 1835-1881. (R.) Boris Godunov, Pictures at an Exhibition.

Jacques Offenbach, 1819-1880. (F.) Tales of Hoffman.

Karl Orff, b. 1895 (G.) Carmina Burana.

Ignace Paderewski, 1860-1941 (P.) Minuet in G.

Giovanni P. da Palestrina, 1524-1594. (It.) Masses; madrigals.

Amilcare Ponchielli, 1834-1886. (It.) La Gioconda.

Francis Poulenc, 1899-1963. (F.) Dialogues des Carmelites.

Serge Prokofiev, 1891-1953. (R.) Love for Three Oranges, Lt. Kije, Peter and the Wolf.

Giacomo Puccini, 1858-1924. (It.) La Boheme, Manon Lescaut, Tosca, Madame Butterfly.

Sergei Rachmaninov, 1873-1943. (R.) Prelude in C Sharp Minor.

Maurice Ravel, 1875-1937. (Fr.) Bolero, Daphne et Chloe, Rapsodie Espagnole.

Nikolai Rimsky-Korsakov, 1844-1908. (R.) Golden Cockerel, Cappriccio Espagnol, Scheherazade, Russian Easter Overture.

Gioacchino Rossini, 1792-1868. (It.) Barber of Seville, Semiramide, William Tell.

Chas. Camille Saint-Saens, 1835-1921. (F.) Samson and Delilah, Danse Macabre.

Alessandro Scarlatti, 1659-1725. (It.) Cantatas; concertos.

Arnold Schoenberg, 1874-1951. (Aus.) Pelleas and Melisande, Transfigured Night, De Profundis.

Franz Schubert, 1797-1828. (A.) Lieder; symphonies (Unfinished); overtures (Rosamunde).

William Schuman, b. 1910. (U.S.) Credendum, New England Triptych.

Robert Schumann, 1810-1856. (G.) Symphonies, songs.

Aleksandr Scriabin, 1872-1915. (R.) Prometheus.

Dimitri Shostakovich, b. 1906-1975. (R.) Symphonies, Lady Macbeth of Minsk, The Nose.

Jean Sibelius, 1865-1957, (Finn.) Finlandia, Karelia.

Bedrich Smetana, 1824-1884. (C.) The Bartered Bride.

Karlheinz Stockhausen, b. 1928. (G.) Kontrapunkte, Kontakte.

Richard Strauss, 1864-1949. (G.) Salome, Elektra, Der Rosenkavalier, Thus Spake Zarathustra.

Igor F. Stravinsky, 1882-1971. (R.-U.S.) Oedipus Rex, Le Sacre du Printemps, Petrushka.

Peter I. Tchaikovsky, 1840-1893. (R.) Nutcracker Suite, Swan Lake, Eugen Onegin.

Ambroise Thomas, 1811-1896. (F.) Mignon.

Ralph Vaughan Williams, 1872-1958, (Br.) Job, London Symphony, Symphony No. 7 (Antarctica).

Giuseppe Verdi, 1813-1901. (It.) Aida, Rigoletto, Don Carlo, Il Trovatore, La Traviata, Falstaff, Macbeth.

Hector Villa Lobos, 1887-1959. (Brazil) Choros.

Antonio Vivaldi, 1669-1741. (It.) Operas and cantatas.

Richard Wagner, 1813-1883. (G.) Rienzi, Tannhauser, Lohengrin, Tristan und Isolde.

Karl Maria von Weber, 1786-1826. (G.) Der Freischutz.

Composers of Operettas, Musicals, and Popular Music

Leroy Anderson, 1908-1975. (U.S.) Syncopated Clock, Typewriter Serenade.

Harold Arlen, b. 1905. (U.S.) Stormy Weather, Over the Rainbow, Blues in the Night, That Old Black Magic.

Burt Bacharach, b. 1928. (U.S.) Raindrops Keep Fallin' on My Head, Walk on By, What the World Needs Now is Love.

Ernest Ball, 1878-1927. (U.S.) Mother Machree, When Irish Eyes are Smiling.

Irving Berlin, b. 1888. (U.S.) This is the Army; Annie Get Your Gun; Call Me Madam; God Bless America; White Christmas.

Jerry Bock, b. 1928. (U.S.) Mr. Wonderful; Fiorello; Fiddler on the Roof; The Rothschilds.

Carrie Jacobs Bond, 1862-1946. (U.S.) I Love You Truly.

George M. Cohan, 1878-1942. (U.S.) Give My Regards to Broadway, You're A Grand Old Flag, Over There.

Sherman Edwards, b. 1919. (U.S.) See You in September; Wonderful! Wonderful!

Stephen Collins Foster, 1826-1864. (U.S.) My Old Kentucky Home, Old Folks At Home.

Rudolf Friml, 1879-1972. (naturalized U.S.) The Firefly; Rose Marie; Vagabond King; Bird of Paradise.

John Gay, 1685-1732. (Br.) The Beggar's Opera.

Edwin F. Goldman, 1878-1956. (U.S.) Marches.

Percy Grainger, 1882-1961. (Br.) Country Gardens.

Ferde Grofe, 1892-1972. (U.S.) Grand Canyon Suite.

W. C. Handy, 1873-1958. (U.S.) St. Louis Blues.

Victor Herbert, 1859-1924. (Ir.-U.S.) Mlle. Modiste; Babes in Toyland; The Red Mill; Naughty Marietta; Sweethearts.

Jerry Herman, b. 1932. (U.S.) Milk and Honey; Hello Dolly; Mame; Dear World.

Scott Joplin, 1868-1917. (U.S.) Treemonisha.

Jerome Kern, 1885-1945. (U.S.) Sally; Sunny; Show Boat; Cat and the Fiddle; Music in the Air; Roberta.

Burton Lane, b. 1912. (U.S.) Three's a Crowd; Finnian's Rainbow; On A Clear Day You Can See Forever.

Franz Lehar, 1870-1948. (Hung.) Merry Widow.

Mitch Leigh, b. 1928. (U.S.) Man of La Mancha.

Frank Loesser, 1910-1969. (U.S.) Guys and Dolls; Where's Charley?; The Most Happy Fella.

Frederick Loewe, b. 1901. (Aust.-U.S.) The Day Before Spring; Brigadoon; Paint Your Wagon; My Fair Lady; Camelot.

Henry Mancini, b. 1924. (U.S.) Moon River, Days of Wine and Roses, Pink Panther Theme.

Cole Porter, 1893-1964. (U.S.) Anything Goes; Jubilee; DuBarry Was a Lady; Panama Hattie; Mexican Hayride; Kiss Me Kate; Can Can; Silk Stockings.

Andre Previn, b. 1929. (U.S.) Coco.

Richard Rodgers, b. 1902. (U.S.) Garrick Gaieties; Connecticut Yankee; America's Sweetheart; On Your Toes; Babes in Arms; The Boys from Syracuse; Oklahoma!; Carousel; South Pacific; The King and I; Flower Drum Song; The Sound of Music.

Sigmund Romberg, 1887-1951. (Hung.) Maytime; The Student Prince; Desert Song; Blossom Time.

Harold Rome, b. 1908. (U.S.) Pins and Needles; Call Me Mister; Wish You Were Here; Fanny; Destry Rides Again.

Harry Ruby, 1895-1974. (U.S.) Three Little Words; Who's Sorry Now?

Arthur Schwartz, b. 1900. (U.S.) The Band Wagon, Inside U.S.A., A Tree Grows in Brooklyn.

Stephen Sondheim, b. 1930. (U.S.) A Little Night Music.

John Philip Sousa, 1854-1932. (U.S.) The Smuggler; Desiree; Queen of Hearts; El Capitan; The Bride-Elect.

Oskar Straus, 1870-1954. (Aus.) Chocolate Soldier.

Johann Strauss, 1825-1899. (Aus.) Gypsy Baron, Die Fledermaus, Waltzes; Blue Danube, Artist's Life.

Charles Strouse, b. 1928. (U.S.) Bye Bye, Birdie; All American; Golden Boy; Applause.

Jule Styne, b. 1905. (b. London-U.S.) Gentlemen Prefer Blondes; Bells Are Ringing; Gypsy; Funny Girl.

Arthur S. Sullivan, 1842-1900. (Br.) H.M.S. Pinafore, Pirates of Penzance, The Mikado (with W. S. Gilbert, 1836-1911, librettist).

Deems Taylor, 1885-1966. (U.S.) Peter Ibbetson.

James Van Heusen, b. 1913. (U.S.) Moonlight Becomes You, Swinging on a Star.

Harry Warren, b. 1893. (U.S.) You're My Everything, We're in the Money, I Only Have Eyes for You, September in the Rain.

Kurt Weill, 1900-1950. (G.-U.S.) Three-Penny Opera; Lady in the Dark; Knickerbocker Holiday; One Touch of Venus.

Meredith Willson, b. 1902. (U.S.) The Music Man.

Vincent Youmans, 1898-1946. (U.S.) Two Little Girls in Blue; Wildflower; No, No, Nanette; Hit the Deck; Rainbow; Smiles.

Noted Jazz Artists

Jazz has been called America's only completely unique contribution to Western culture. The following individuals have made major contributions in this field:

Julian "Cannonball" Adderley, (1928-1975): alto sax.
Henry "Red" Allen, (1908-1967): trumpet.
Albert Ammons, (1907-1949): Boogie-woogie pianist.
Louis "Satchmo" Armstrong, (1900-1971): trumpet, singer; originated the "scat" vocal.
Mildred Bailey, (1907-1951): blues singer.
Count Basie, b. 1904: orchestra leader, piano.
Sidney Bechet, (1897-1959): early innovator on the soprano sax.
Bix Beiderbecke, (1903-1931): cornet, piano, composer.
Bunny Berigan, (1909-1942): trumpet, singer, "I Can't Get Started With You".
Art Blakey, b. 1919: Drums, leader.
Jimmy Blanton, (1921-1942): bass.
Charles "Buddy" Bolden, (1868-1931): cornet; formed the first jazz band in the 1890s.
Big Bill Broonzy, (1893-1958): blues singer, guitar.
Dave Brubeck, b. 1920: piano, combo leader.
Harry Carney, (1910-1975): baritone sax.
Benny Carter, b. 1907: alto sax, trumpet, clarinet.
Sidney Catlett, (1910-1951): a leading drummer of the 30s and 40s.
Charlie Christian, (1919-1942): guitar; often given credit for the term "bebop".
Buck Clayton, b. 1911: trumpet, arranger
Al Cohn, b. 1925: tenor sax, composer.
Cozy Cole, b. 1909: drums.
Ornette Coleman, b. 1930: saxophonist noted for his unorthodox style.
John Coltrane, (1926-1967): tenor sax innovator.
Eddie Condon, (1904-1973): guitar, band leader; promoter of dixieland.
Miles Davis, b. 1926: trumpet; pioneer of cool jazz.
Buddy De Franco, b. 1933: clarinet.
Warren "Baby" Dodds, (1898-1959): dixieland drummer.
Johnny Dodds, (1892-1940): clarinet.
Jimmy Dorsey, (1904-1957): clarinet, alto sax; band leader in the swing era.
Tommy Dorsey, (1905-1956): trombone; band leader in swing era.
Roy Eldridge, b. 1911: trumpet, drums, singer.
Duke Ellington, (1899-1974): piano, orchestra leader, composer.
Bill Evans, b. 1929: piano.
Ella Fitzgerald, b. 1918: singer.
Erroll Garner, b. 1921: piano, composer, "Misty".
Stan Getz, b. 1927: tenor sax.
Terry Gibbs, b. 1924: vibes.
John "Dizzy" Gillespie, b. 1917: trumpet, composer; a developer of bop.
Benny Goodman, b. 1909: clarinet, band and combo leader.
Bobby Hackett, (1915-1976): trumpet, cornet.
Lionel Hampton, b. 1913: vibes, drums, piano, combo leader.
W. C. Handy, (1873-1958): composer, "St. Louis Blues", "Memphis Blues".
Bill Harris, (1916-1973): trombone.
Coleman Hawkins, (1904-1969): tenor sax; 1939 recording of "Body and Soul" a classic.
Fletcher Henderson, (1898-1952): orchestra leader, arranger; first jazz man to use written arrangements pioneering the regimented jazz and dance bands of the 30s.
Woody Herman, b. 1913: clarinet, alto sax, band leader.
Jay C. Higginbotham, (1906-1973): trombone.
Bertha "Chippie" Hill, (1905-1950): blues singer.
Earl "Fatha" Hines, b. 1905: piano, songwriter.
Johnny Hodges, b. 1906: alto sax.
Billie Holiday, (1915-1959): blues singer, "Strange Fruit", "God Bless the child".
Sam "Lightnin'" Hopkins, b. 1912: blues singer, guitar.
Mahalia Jackson, (1911-1972): gospel singer; and example of the link between the religious and secular roots of jazz.
Milt Jackson, b. 1923: vibes, piano, guitar.
Blind Lemon Jefferson, (1897-1930): blues singer, guitar.
Bunk Johnson, (1879-1949): cornet, trumpet.
James P. Johnson, (1891-1955): piano, composer.
J. J. Johnson, b. 1924: trombone, composer.
Quincy Jones, b. 1933: arranger.
Scott Joplin, (1868-1917): ragtime composer, "Maple Leaf Rag".
Stan Kenton, b. 1912: orchestra leader, composer, piano.
Freddie Keppard, (1899-1933): trumpet.
John Kirby, (1908-1952): major combo leader of the 30s.
Lee Konitz, b. 1927: alto sax.
Gene Krupa, (1909-1973): drums, band and combo leader.
Tommy Ladnier, (1900-1939): trumpet.

Eddie Lang, (1904-1933): guitar.
Huddie Ledbetter (Leadbelly), (1888-1949): blues singer, guitar.
John Lewis, b. 1920: composer, piano, combo leader.
Jimmie Lunceford, (1902-1947): band leader, sax.
Shelly Manne, b. 1920: drums.
Jimmy McPartland, b. 1907: trumpet.
Glenn Miller, (1904-1944): trombone, dance band leader.
Charles Mingus, b. 1922: bass, composer, combo leader.
Thelonious Monk, b. 1920: piano, composer, combo leader; a developer of bop.
Wes Montgomery, (1925-1971): guitar.
Ferdinand "Jelly Roll" Morton, (1885-1941): composer, piano, singer.
Bennie Moten, (1894-1935): piano; an early organizer of large jazz orchestras.
Gerry Mulligan, b. 1927: baritone sax, arranger, leader.
Turk Murphy, b. 1915: trombone, band leader.
Theodore "Fats" Navarro, (1923-1950): trumpet.
Red Nichols, (1905-1965): cornet, combo leader.
Jimmie Noone, (1895-1944): clarinet, band leader.
Red Norvo, b. 1908: vibes, band leader.
Anita O'Day, b. 1919: singer.
King Oliver, (1885-1938): cornet, band leader; teacher of Louis Armstrong.
Kid Ory, (1886-1973): trombone, composer, "Muskrat Ramble".
Charlie "Bird" Parker, (1920-1955): alto sax, composer; rated by many as the greatest jazz improviser.
Oscar Peterson, b. 1925: piano, composer, combo leader.
Oscar Pettiford, (1922-1960): a leading bassist in the bop era.
Bud Powell, (1924-1966): piano, composer; modern jazz pioneer.
Gertrude "Ma" Rainey, (1886-1939): first of the great blues singers; teacher of Bessie Smith.
Don Redman, (1900-1964): composer, arranger; pioneer in the evolution of the large orchestra.
Django Reinhardt, (1910-1953): guitar; Belgian gypsy; first European to influence American jazz.
Buddy Rich, b. 1917: drums, band leader.
Max Roach, b. 1925: drums.
Shorty Rogers, b. 1924: composer, trumpet, band leader; a founder of the west coast school of jazz.
Sonny Rollins, b. 1929: tenor sax.
Pete Rugolo, b. 1915: composer, orchestra leader.
Jimmy Rushing, (1903-1972): blues singer.
Pee Wee Russell, (1906-1969): clarinet.
Artie Shaw, b. 1910: clarinet, combo leader; 1939 recording of "Begin the Beguine" a classic.
George Shearing, b. 1919: piano, composer, "Lullaby of Birdland".
Horace Silver, b. 1928: piano, leader.
Zoot Sims, b. 1925: tenor, alto sax; clarinet.
Zutty Singleton, (1898-1975): dixieland drummer.
Bessie Smith, (1894-1937): blues singer.
Clarence "Pinetop" Smith, (1904-1929): piano, singer; pioneer of boogie-woogie.
Joe Smith, (1902-1937): trumpet.
Willie "The Lion" Smith, (1897-1973): stride style pianist.
Muggsy Spanier, (1906-1967): cornet, band leader.
Sonny Stitt, b. 1924: alto, tenor sax.
Art Tatum, (1910-1956): piano; considered one of the great technical virtuosos in jazz.
Billy Taylor, b. 1921: piano.
Jack Teagarden, (1905-1964): trombone, singer.
Dave Tough, (1908-1948): drums.
Lennie Tristano, b. 1919: piano, composer.
Joe Turner, b. 1911: blues singer.
Joe Turner, b. 1907: stride piano.
Sarah Vaughan, b. 1924: singer.
Thomas "Fats" Waller, (1904-1943): piano, singer, composer, "Ain't Misbehavin".
Dinah Washington, (1924-1963): singer.
Teddy Weatherford, (1903-1945): piano.
Chick Webb, (1902-1939): band leader, drums; generally credited with laying the foundations for jazz percussion.
Paul Whiteman, (1890-1967): orchestra leader; a major figure in the introduction of jazz to a large audience.
Charles "Cootie" Williams, b. 1908: trumpet, band leader.
Mary Lou Williams, b. 1910: singer.
Teddy Wilson, b. 1912: piano, composer.
Kai Winding, b. 1922: trombone, composer.
Jimmy Yancey, (1894-1951): piano.
Lester "Pres" Young, (1909-1959): tenor sax, composer; a bop pioneer.

Entertainment Personalities — Where and When Born
Actors, Actresses, Dancers, Musicians, Producers, Radio-TV Performers, Singers

Name	Birthplace	Born	Name	Birthplace	Born
A			Aznavour, Charles	Paris, France	1924
Abbott, George	Forestville, N.Y.	1887	**B**		
Abel, Walter	St. Paul, Minn.	1898	Bacall, Lauren	New York, N.Y.	1924
Abner (Norris Goff)	Cove, Ark.	1906	Backus, Jim	Cleveland, Ohio	1913
Ackermann, Bettye	Cottageville, S.C.	1928	Baddeley, Hermione	Shropshire, Eng.	1906
Acuff, Roy	Maynardsville, Tenn.	1903	Baer, Max Jr.	Oakland, Cal.	1937
Adams, Don	New York, N.Y.	1927	Baez, Joan	Staten Island, N.Y.	1941
Adams, Edie	Kingston, Pa.	1929	Bailey, Pearl	Newport News, Va.	1918
Adams, Joey	New York, N.Y.	1911	Bailey, Raymond	San Francisco, Cal.	1904
Adams, Julie	Waterloo, Iowa	1926	Bain, Barbara	Chicago, Ill.	1934
Addams, Dawn	Suffolk, England.	1930	Baird, Bill	Grand Island, Neb.	1904
Adler, Kurt H.	Vienna, Austria	1905	Baker, Carroll	Johnstown, Pa.	1931
Adler, Larry	Baltimore, Md.	1914	Baker, Diane	Hollywood, Cal.	1938
Adler, Luther	New York, N.Y.	1903	Baker, Kenny	Monrovia, Cal.	1912
Agar, John	Chicago, Ill.	1921	Baker, Stanley	Glamorgan, Wales	1928
Aherne, Brian	Worcestershire, Eng.	1902	Bakewell, William	Hollywood, Cal.	1908
Aimee, Anouk	Paris, France	1932	Balanchine, George	St. Petersburg, Russia	1904
Akins, Claude	Bedford, Ind.	1918	Ball, Lucille	Jamestown, N.Y.	1911
Albanese, Licia	Bari, Italy	1913	Ballard, Kaye	Cleveland, Ohio	1926
Alberghetti, Anna	Pesaro, Italy	1936	Balsam, Martin	New York, N.Y.	1919
Albert, Eddie	Rock Island, Ill.	1908	Bampton, Rose	Cleveland, Ohio	1909
Albert, Edward	Los Angeles, Cal.	1951	Bancroft, Anne	New York, N.Y.	1931
Albertson, Jack	Malden, Mass.	1910	Bannon, Ian	Airdrie, Scotland	1928
Albright, Lola	Akron, Ohio	1925	Barber, Red	Columbus, Miss.	1908
Alda, Alan	New York, N.Y.	1936	Bardot, Brigitte	Paris, France	1934
Alda, Robert	New York, N.Y.	1914	Bari, Lynn	Roanoke, Va.	1917
Alexander, Jane	Boston, Mass.	1939	Barnett, Vincent	Pittsburgh, Pa.	1902
Alexander, Katherine	Arkansas	1901	Barrault, Jean-Louise	Le Vesinet, France	1919
Allan, Elizabeth	England	1910	Barrett, Sheila	Washington, D.C.	1909
Allbritton, Louise	Oklahoma City, Okla.	1920	Barrie, Mona	London, Eng.	1909
Allen, Mel	Birmingham, Ala.	1913	Barrie, Wendy	Hong Kong, China.	1913
Allen, Steve	New York, N.Y.	1921	Barry, Gene	New York, N.Y.	1922
Allen, Woody	Brooklyn, N.Y.	1935	Barry, Jack	Lindenhurst, N.Y.	1918
Allison, Fran	LaPorte City, Ia.	—	Barrymore, John, Jr.	Beverly Hills, Cal.	1932
Allyson, June	Lucerne, N.Y.	1923	Bartholomew, Freddie	London, England.	1924
Alpert, Herb	Los Angeles, Cal.	1935	Bartok, Eva	Budapest, Hungary	1929
Altman, Robert	Kansas City, Mo.	1925	Basehart, Richard	Zanesville, Ohio	1914
Ameche, Don	Kenosha, Wis.	1908	Basie, Count (Wm.)	Red Bank, N.J.	1904
Ames, Ed	Boston, Mass.	1929	Bassey, Shirley	Cardiff, Wales	1937
Ames, Leon	Portland, Ind.	1903	Bates, Alan	Allestree, Eng.	1934
Ames, Nancy	Washington, D.C.	1937	Baum, Kurt	Cologne, Germany.	1908
Amos (F. F. Gosden)	Richmond, Va.	1904	Bavier, Frances	New York, N.Y.	1905
Amos, John	Newark, N.J.	—	Baxter, Anne	Michigan City, Ind.	1923
Amsterdam, Morey	Chicago, Ill.	1914	Beal, John	Joplin, Mo.	1909
Anderson, Judith	Adelaide, Australia.	1898	Bean, Orson	Burlington, Vt.	1928
Anderson, Lynn	Grand Forks, N.D.	1947	Beatty, Robert	Hamilton, Ont.	1909
Anderson, Marian	Philadelphia, Pa.	1902	Beatty, Warren	Richmond, Va.	1938
Anderson, Mary	Birmingham, Ala.	1922	Becker, Sandy	New York, N.Y.	1922
Anderson, Michael Jr.	London, England.	1943	Bedelia, Bonnie	New York, N.Y.	1948
Anderson, Warner	Brooklyn, N.Y.	1911	Beery, Noah, Jr.	New York, N.Y.	1916
Andersson, Bibi	Stockholm, Sweden	1935	Belafonte, Harry	New York, N.Y.	1927
Andress, Ursula	Switzerland	1938	Bel Geddes, Barbara	New York, N.Y.	1922
Andrews, Dana	Collins, Miss.	1909	Bellamy, Ralph	Chicago, Ill.	1904
Andrews, Edward	Griffin, Ga.	1915	Belmondo, Jean-Paul	Neuilly-sur-Seine, Fr.	1933
Andrews, Julie	Walton, England	1935	Benjamin, Dick	New York, N.Y.	1939
Andrews, Maxene	Minneapolis, Minn.	1918	Bennett, Joan	Palisades, N.J.	1910
Andrews, Patty	Minneapolis, Minn.	1920	Bennett, Tony	Astoria, N.Y.	1926
Angel, Heather	Oxford, England.	1909	Bentley, John	Warwickshire, England	1916
Anka, Paul	Ottawa, Canada.	1941	Bergen, Candice	Beverly Hills, Cal.	1946
Ann-Margret	Stockholm, Sweden	1941	Bergen, Edgar	Chicago, Ill.	1903
Annabella	Paris, France	1912	Bergen, Polly	Knoxville, Tenn.	1930
Ansara, Michael	Lowell, Mass.	1927	Berger, Senta	Vienna, Austria	1941
Archer, John	Osceola, Neb.	1915	Bergerac, Jacques	Biarritz, France	1927
Arden, Eve	Mill Valley, Cal.	1912	Bergman, Ingmar	Uppsala, Sweden	1918
Arkin, Alan	New York, N.Y.	1934	Bergman, Ingrid	Stockholm, Sweden	1915
Arnaz, Desi	Santiago, Cuba.	1917	Bergner, Elisabeth	Vienna, Austria	1900
Arnaz, Desi Jr.	Los Angeles, Cal.	1953	Berle, Milton	New York, N.Y.	1908
Arnaz, Lucie	Hollywood, Cal.	1951	Berlinger, Warren	Brooklyn, N.Y.	1937
Arness, James	Minneapolis, Minn.	1923	Berman, Shelley	Chicago, Ill.	1926
Arnold, Eddy	Henderson, Tenn.	1918	Bernardi, Hershel	New York, N.Y.	1923
Arrau, Claudio	Chillau, Chile.	1903	Bernstein, Elmer	New York, N.Y.	1922
Arroyo, Martina	New York, N.Y.	1937	Bernstein, Leonard	Lawrence, Mass.	1918
Arthur, Beatrice	New York, N.Y.	1926	Berry, Chuck	St. Louis, Mo.	1926
Arthur, Jean	New York, N.Y.	1908	Berry, Ken	Moline, Ill.	—
Ashley, Elizabeth	Ocala, Fla.	1941	Bessell, Ted	Flushing, N.Y.	1936
Asner, Edward	Kansas City, Kan.	1929	Bikel, Theodore	Vienna, Austria	1924
Astaire, Fred	Omaha, Neb.	1899	Birney, David	Washington, D.C.	
Astin, John	Baltimore, Md.	1930	Bishop, Joey	Bronx, N.Y.	1918
Astor, Mary	Quincy, Ill.	1906	Bisset, Jacqueline	Weybridge, England	1944
Atkins, Chet	Luttrell, Tenn.	1924	Bixby, Bill	San Francisco, Cal.	1934
Attenborough, Richard.	Cambridge, Eng.	1923	Black, Karen	Park Ridge, Ill.	1942
Aumont, Jean-Pierre	Paris, France	1913	Blaine, Vivian	Newark, N.J.	1924
Autry, Gene	Tioga, Texas.	1907	Blair, Janet	Altoona, Pa.	1921
Avalon, Frankie	Philadelphia, Pa.	1940	Blair, Linda	Westport, Conn.	1959
Ayres, Lew	Minneapolis, Minn.	1908	Blake, Amanda	Buffalo, N.Y.	1931

Name	Birthplace	Born	Name	Birthplace	Born
Blake, Robert	Nutley, N.J.	1938	Cantinflas	Mexico City, Mex.	1917
Blanc, Mel	San Francisco, Cal.	1908	Cantrell, Lana	Sydney, Australia.	1944
Bloch, Ray	Alsace-Lorraine	1902	Capra, Frank	Palermo, Italy.	1897
Blondell, Joan	New York, N.Y.	1912	Cardinale, Claudia	Tunisia.	1939
Bloom, Claire	London, England.	1931	Carey, Macdonald	Sioux City, Ia.	1913
Blyth, Ann	Mt. Kisco, N.Y.	1928	Carey, Phil	Hackensack, N.J.	1925
Boehm, Karl	Graz, Austria.	1894	Carle, Frankie	Providence, R.I.	1903
Bogarde, Dirk	London, England.	1921•	Carlisle, Kitty	New Orleans, La.	1915
Bogdanovich, Peter	Kingston, N.Y.	1939	Carlson, Richard	Alberta Lea, Minn.	1914
Boiger, Ray	Boston, Mass.	1904	Carmichael, Hoagy	Bloomington, Ind.	1899
Bondi, Beulah	Chicago, Ill.	1892	Carmichael, Ian	Hull, England	1920
Bono, Sonny	Detroit, Mich.	1940	Carne, Judy	Northampton, England.	1939
Boone, Pat	Jacksonville, Fla.	1934	Carney, Art	Mt. Vernon, N.Y.	1918
Boone, Richard	Los Angeles, Cal.	1917	Carnovsky, Morris	St. Louis, Mo.	1897
Booth, Shirley	New York, N.Y.	1909	Caron, Leslie	Boulogne, France.	1931
Borge, Victor	Copenhagen, Denmark	1909	Carpenter, Karen	New Haven, Conn.	1950
Borgnine, Ernest	Hamden, Conn.	1917	Carpenter, Richard	New Haven, Conn.	1946
Bosley, Tom	Chicago, Ill.	1927	Carr, Vicki	El Paso, Tex.	1942
Boswell, Connee	New Orleans, La.	—	Carradine, David	Hollywood, Cal.	1940
Bottoms, Timothy	Santa Barbara, Cal.	1951	Carradine, John	New York, N.Y.	1906
Bowman, Lee	Cincinnati, Ohio	1914	Carroll, Diahann	Bronx, N.Y.	1935
Boyd, Stephen	Belfast, Ireland.	1928	Carroll, Madeleine	W. Bromwich, England.	1906
Boyer, Charles	Figeac, France.	1899	Carroll, Pat	Shreveport, La.	1927
Boyle, Peter	Philadelphia, Pa.	1933	Carson, Jeannie	Yorkshire, England	1929
Bracken, Eddie	Astoria, N.Y.	1920	Carson, Johnny	Corning, Ia.	1925
Brand, Neville	Kewanee, Ill.	1921	Carson, Mindy	New York, N.Y.	1927
Brando, Marlon	Omaha, Neb.	1924	Carter, Jack	New York, N.Y.	1923
Brasselle, Keefe	Elyria, Ohio.	1923	Casadesus, Gaby	Marseilles, France	1902
Brazzi, Rossano	Bologna, Italy.	1916	Cash, Johnny	Kingsland, Ark.	1932
Brennan, Eileen	Los Angeles, Cal.	1937	Cass, Peggy	Boston, Mass.	1926
Brent, George	Dublin, Ireland.	1904	Cassavetes, John	New York, N.Y.	1929
Brewer, Teresa	Toledo, Ohio.	1931	Cassidy, David	New York, N.Y.	1950
Brian, David	New York, N.Y.	1914	Cassidy, Jack	New York, N.Y.	1927
Bridges, Beau	Hollywood, Cal.	1941	Cassidy, Ted	Pittsburgh, Pa.	1932
Bridges, Jeff	Los Angeles, Cal.	1950	Castellano, Richard	New York, N.Y.	1934
Bridges, Lloyd	San Leandro, Cal.	1913	Caulfield, Joan	West Orange, N.J.	1922
Britton, Barbara	Long Beach, Cal.	1923	Cavallaro, Carmen	New York, N.Y.	1913
Brolin, James	Los Angeles, Cal.	1942	Cavett, Dick	Gibbon, Neb.	1936
Bronson, Charles	Scooptown, Pa.	1921	Chamberlain, Richard	Beverly Hills, Cal.	1935
Brooks, Louise	Cherryvale, Kansas	1906	Champion, Gower	Geneva, Ill.	1921
Brooks, Mel	New York, N.Y.	1926	Champion, Marge	Los Angeles, Cal.	1923
Brooks, Stephen	Columbus, Ohio.	1942	Channing, Carol	Seattle, Wash.	1923
Brown, James	Augusta, Ga.	1934	Chaplin, Charles	London, England.	1889
Brown, Jimmy	St. Simons Island, Ga.	1936	Chaplin, Geraldine	Santa Monica, Cal.	1944
Brown, Les	Reinerton, Pa.	1912	Chaplin, Sydney	Beverly Hills, Cal.	1926
Brown, Tom	New York, N.Y.	1913	Charisse, Cyd	Amarillo, Tex.	1923
Brown, Vanessa	Vienna, Austria.	1928	Charles, Ray	Albany, Ga.	1930
Bruce, Carol	Great Neck, N.Y.	1919	Chase, Chevy	New York, N.Y.	1943
Bruce, Virginia	Minneapolis, Minn.	1910	Chase, Ilka	New York, N.Y.	1905
Bryant, Anita	Barnsdale, Okla.	1940	Checker, Chubby	Philadelphia, Pa.	1941
Brynner, Yul	Sakhalin, Japan.	1920	Cher	El Centro, Cal.	1946
Bubbles, John	Louisville, Ky.	1903	Christian, Linda	Tampico, Mexico.	1924
Buchanan, Edgar	Humansville, Mo.	1903	Christie, Audrey	Chicago, Ill.	1912
Bucholz, Horst	Berlin, Germany.	1933	Christie, Julie	Chukur, India.	1941
Bujold, Genevieve	Montreal, Que.	1942	Christopher, Jordon	Youngstown, Ohio.	1941
Buono, Victor	Los Angeles, Cal.	1938	Christy, June	Springfield, Ill.	1925
Burke, Paul	New Orleans, La.	1926	Cilento, Diane	Queensland, Australia	1933
Burnett, Carol	San Antonio, Tex.	1936	Claire, Ina	Washington, D.C.	1892
Burns, George	New York, N.Y.	1896	Clark, Dane	New York, N.Y.	1915
Burr, Raymond	New Westminster, B.C.	1917	Clark, Dick	Mt. Vernon, N.Y.	1929
Burrows, Abe	New York, N.Y.	1910	Clark, Petula	Ewell, Surrey, England.	1934
Burstyn, Ellen	Detroit, Mich.	1932	Clark, Roy	Meherrin, Va.	1933
Burton, Richard	South Wales	1925	Clayton, Jan	Tularosa, N. M.	1925
Bushell, Anthony	Kent, England.	1904	Cliburn, Van	Shreveport, La.	1934
Buttons, Red	New York, N.Y.	1919	Clooney, Rosemary	Maysville, Ky.	1928
Buzzell, Eddie	Brooklyn, N.Y.	1897	Coburn, James	Laurel, Neb.	1928
Buzzi, Ruth	Westerly, R.I.	1936	Coca, Imogene	Philadelphia, Pa.	1920
			Coco, James	New York, N.Y.	1929
C			Cohen, Myron	Grodno, Poland.	1902
Caan, James	New York, N.Y.	1939	Colbert, Claudette	Paris, France.	1907
Cabot, Sebastian	London, England.	1918	Cole, Dennis	Detroit, Mich.	1943
Caesar, Sid	Yonkers, N.Y.	1922	Cole, Michael	Madison, Wis.	1945
Cagney, James	New York, N.Y.	1899	Cole, Tina	Hollywood, Cal.	1943
Caine, Michael	London, England.	1933	Collins, Dorothy	Windsor, Ontario.	1926
Caldwell, Zoe	Melbourne, Australia.	1933	Collins, Joan	London, England.	1933
Calhoun, Rory	Los Angeles, Cal.	1922	Collins, Judy	Seattle, Wash.	1939
Callahan, James	Grand Rapids, Mich.	1930	Colonna, Jerry	Boston, Mass.	1903
Callan, Michael	Philadelphia, Pa.	1935	Como, Perry	Canonsburg, Pa.	1912
Callas, Maria	New York, N.Y.	1923	Conklin, Peggy	Dobbs Ferry, N.Y.	1912
Calloway, Cab	Rochester, N.Y.	1907	Conley, Eugene	Lynn, Mass.	1908
Calvert, Phyllis	London, England.	1917	Conner, Nadine	Compton, Cal.	1913
Calvet, Corinne	Paris, France.	1926	Connery, Sean	Edinburgh, Scotland	1930
Cambridge, Godfrey	New York, N.Y.	1933	Conniff, Ray	Attleboro, Mass.	1916
Cameron, Rod	Calgary, Canada.	1912	Connors, Chuck	Brooklyn, N.Y.	1921
Campbell, Glen	Billstown, Ark.	1936	Connors, Michael	Fresno, Cal.	1925
Canary, David	Elwood, Ind.	1938	Conrad, Robert	Chicago, Ill.	1935
Cannon, Dyan	Tacoma, Wash.	1937	Conrad, William	Louisville, Ky.	1920
Canova, Judy	Jacksonville, Fla.	1916	Conried, Hans	Baltimore, Md.	1917
			Considine, Tim	Los Angeles, Cal.	1940

Name	Birthplace	Born
Converse, Frank	St. Louis, Mo.	1938
Conway, Gary	Boston, Mass.	1938
Conway, Shirl	Franklinville, N.Y.	1916
Conway, Tim.	Chagrin Falls, Ohio	1933
Coogan, Jackie.	Los Angeles, Cal.	1914
Cook, Barbara	Atlanta, Ga.	1927
Cooke, Alistair	England	1908
Cooper, Alice	Phoenix, Ariz.	1939
Cooper, Jackie.	Los Angeles, Cal.	1922
Corey, Jeff	New York, N.Y.	1914
Cornell, Don.	New York, N.Y.	1921
Cortez, Ricardo.	Vienna, Austria	1899
Cosby, Bill.	Philadelphia, Pa.	1937
Costello, Dolores	Pittsburgh, Pa.	1905
Cotsworth, Staats	Oak Park, Ill.	1908
Cotten, Joseph	Petersburg, Va.	1905
Courtenay, Tom.	Hull, England	1937
Crabbe, Buster	Oakland, Cal.	1908
Crain, Jeanne	Barstow, Cal.	1925
Crane, Bob	Waterbury, Conn.	1928
Crawford, Broderick.	Philadelphia, Pa.	1911
Crawford, Joan	San Antonio, Tex.	1908
Crawford, Michael.	Salisbury, England.	1942
Crenna, Richard	Los Angeles, Cal.	1927
Cristal, Linda.	Argentina	1936
Cronyn, Hume	London, Ontario	1911
Crosby, Bing (Harry)	Tacoma, Wash.	1904
Crosby, Bob.	Spokane, Wash.	1913
Crowley, Pat	Scranton, Pa.	1929
Cruz, Brandon	Bakersfield, Cal.	1962
Cugat, Xavier.	Barcelona, Spain	1900
Cullen, Bill.	Pittsburgh, Pa.	1920
Cullum, John.	Knoxville, Tenn.	1930
Culp, Robert	Berkeley, Cal.	1930
Cummings, Constance.	Seattle, Wash.	1910
Cummings, Robert.	Joplin, Mo.	1910
Cumminis, Peggy	Prestatyn, N. Wales	1925
Curtin, Phyllis	Clarksburg, W. Va.	1930
Curtis, Ken.	Lamar, Col.	1916
Curtis, Tony	New York, N.Y.	1925
Cusack, Cyril	Durban, So. Africa.	1910
Cushing, Peter.	Surrey, England.	1913

D

Name	Birthplace	Born
Dagmar (Egnor)	Huntington, W.Va.	1926
Dahl, Arlene	Minneapolis, Minn.	1927
Dailey, Dan.	New York, N.Y.	1917
Dalrymple, Jean.	Morristown, N.J.	1910
Dalton, Abby.	Las Vegas, Nev.	1935
Daly, James.	Wisconsin Rapids, Wis.	1918
Daly, John.	Johannesburg, S. Africa.	1914
Damita, Lili.	Paris, France	1907
Damone, Vic.	Brooklyn, N.Y.	1928
Dana, Bill	Quincy, Mass.	1924
Dangerfield, Rodney.	Babylon, N.Y.	1921
Daniels, William.	Brooklyn, N.Y.	1927
Danilova, Alexandra	Peterhof, Russia.	1907
Danton, Ray.	New York, N.Y.	1931
Darby, Kim.	Hollywood, Cal.	1948
Darcel, Denise	Paris, France	1925
Darren, James.	Philadelphia, Pa.	1936
Darrieux, Danielle	Bordeaux, France	1917
Darrow, Henry	New York, N.Y.	1933
Da Silva, Howard	Cleveland, Ohio.	1909
Dassin, Jules	Middletown, Conn.	1911
Dauphin, Claude.	Corbeil, France.	1905
Davidson, John.	Pittsburgh, Pa.	1941
Davis, Ann B.	Schenectady, N.Y.	1926
Davis, Bette.	Lowell, Mass.	1908
Davis, Clifton	Chicago, Ill.	1945
Davis, Ossie	Cogdell, Ga.	1917
Davis, Sammy Jr.	New York, N.Y.	1925
Dawn, Hazel	Ogden, Utah	1898
Day, Dennis	New York, N.Y.	1917
Day, Doris.	Cincinnati, Ohio.	1924
Day, Laraine	Roosevelt, Ut.	1920
Dean, Jimmy.	Plainview, Tex.	1928
De Camp, Rosemary.	Prescott, Ariz.	1913
De Carlo, Yvonne	Vancouver, B. C.	1924
Dee, Frances.	Los Angeles, Cal.	1907
Dee, Joey	Passaic, N.J.	1940
Dee, Ruby.	Cleveland, Ohio.	1924
Dee, Sandra	Bayonne, N.J.	1942
DeFore, Don	Cedar Rapids, Ia.	1917
DeHaven, Gloria	Los Angeles, Cal.	1925
de Havilland, Olivia.	Tokyo, Japan.	1916
Del Rio, Dolores.	Durango, Mexico.	1905
De Niro, Robert.	New York, N.Y.	1945
Dell, Gabriel.	Brooklyn, N.Y.	1921

Name	Birthplace	Born
Della, Chiesa, Vivienne.	Chicago, Ill.	1920
Delon, Alain	France	1935
DeLuise, Dom.	Brooklyn, N.Y.	1933
Demarest, William	St. Paul, Minn.	1892
De Mille, Agnes.	New York, N.Y.	1905
Dempster, Carol	Duluth, Minn.	1901
Deneuve, Catherine.	Paris, France	1943
Denning, Richard.	Poughkeepsie, N.Y.	1914
Dennis, Sandy	Hastings, Neb.	1937
Denver, Bob.	New Rochelle, N.Y.	1935
Denver, John.	Roswell, N.M.	1943
Derek, John.	Hollywood, Cal.	1926
Dern, Bruce	Chicago, Ill.	1936
Desmond, Johnny.	Detroit, Mich.	1921
Devane, William.	Albany, N.Y.	1937
Devine, Andy	Flagstaff, Ariz.	1905
Dewhurst, Colleen	Montreal, Canada.	1926
Diamond, Neil.	Brooklyn, N.Y.	1941
Dickinson, Angie.	Kulm, N. D.	1936
Dietrich, Marlene	Berlin, Germany.	1901
Diller, Phyllis.	Lima, Ohio.	1917
Dillman, Bradford.	San Francisco, Cal.	1930
Dixon, Ivan.	New York, N.Y.	1931
Domino, Fats	New Orleans, La.	1928
Donahue, Troy.	New York, N.Y.	1936
Donald, James.	Aberdeen, Scotland	1917
Donald, Peter.	Bristol, England.	1918
Donnelly, Ruth.	Trenton, N.J.	1896
Donovan.	Glasgow, Scotland.	1946
Dors, Diana.	Swindon, England.	1931
d'Orsay, Fifi	Montreal, Canada.	1908
Douglas, Donna.	Baywood, La.	1939
Douglas, Kirk	Amsterdam, N.Y.	1918
Douglas, Melvyn	Macon, Ga.	1901
Douglas, Michael.	New Brunswick, N.J.	1945
Douglas, Mike.	Chicago, Ill.	1925
Downey, Morton	Wallingford, Conn.	1902
Downs, Hugh.	Akron, Ohio.	1921
Dragonette, Jessica.	Calcutta, India.	—
Drake, Alfred.	Bronx, N.Y.	1914
Drake, Betsy	Paris, France	1923
Drew, Ellen.	Kansas City, Mo.	1915
Dreyfuss, Richard.	Brooklyn, N.Y.	1949
Dru, Joanne.	Logan, W.Va.	1923
Drury, James.	New York, N.Y.	1934
Duchin, Peter.	New York, N.Y.	1937
Duff, Howard.	Bremerton, Wash.	1917
Duke, Patty.	New York, N.Y.	1946
Dullea, Keir.	Cleveland, Ohio.	1936
Dunaway, Faye.	Bascom, Fla.	1941
Duncan, Sandy	Henderson, Texas.	1946
Duncan, Todd.	Danville, Ky.	1900
Duncan, Vivian.	Los Angeles, Cal.	1902
Dunham, Katherine.	Chicago, Ill.	1910
Dunne, Irene.	Louisville, Ky.	1904
Dunnock, Mildred.	Baltimore, Md.	1906
Durante, Jimmy	New York, N.Y.	1893
Durbin, Deanna	Winnipeg, Canada.	1922
Duvall, Robert.	San Diego, Cal.	1931
Dvorak, Ann.	New York, N.Y.	1912
Dylan, Bob.	Duluth, Minn.	1941

E

Name	Birthplace	Born
Eastwood, Clint.	San Francisco, Cal.	1930
Eaton, Shirley	London, England.	1937
Ebsen, Buddy	Belleville, Ill.	1908
Eckstine, Billy	Pittsburgh, Pa.	1914
Edelman, Herb.	Brooklyn, N.Y.	1933
Eden, Barbara	Tucson, Ariz.	1934
Edwards, Ralph	Merino, Col.	1913
Edwards, Vincent.	Brooklyn, N.Y.	1928
Egan, Richard.	San Francisco, Cal.	1923
Eggar, Samantha.	London, England.	1939
Eggerth, Marta.	Budapest, Hungary.	1916
Ekberg, Anita.	Malmo, Sweden.	1931
Ekland, Britt.	Stockholm, Sweden.	1942
Elam, Jack.	Phoenix, Ariz.	—
Eldridge, Florence	Brooklyn, N.Y.	1901
Elgart, Larry.	New London, Conn.	1922
Elgart, Les	New Haven, Conn.	1918
Elliott, Bob.	Boston, Mass.	1923
Emerson, Faye	Elizabeth, La.	1917
Erickson, Leif	Alameda, Cal.	1911
Esmond, Jill.	London, England.	1908
Etting, Ruth.	David City, Neb.	1896
Evans, Dale	Uvalde, Tex.	1912
Evans, Dame Edith.	London, England.	1888
Evans, Maurice.	Dorchester, England.	1901
Everett, Chad.	South Bend, Ind.	1937

Name	Birthplace	Born
Evers, Jason	New York, N.Y.	1927
Ewell, Tom	Owensboro, Ky.	1909

F

Name	Birthplace	Born
Fabares, Shelley	Santa Monica, Cal.	1944
Fabian (Forte)	Philadelphia, Pa.	1943
Fabray, Nanette	San Diego, Cal.	1920
Fadiman, Clifton	Brooklyn, N.Y.	1904
Fairbanks, Doug, Jr.	New York, N.Y.	1909
Falk, Peter	New York, N.Y.	1927
Falkenburg, Jinx	Barcelona, Spain	1919
Farber, Barry	Baltimore, Md.	1930
Farentino, James	Brooklyn, N.Y.	1938
Fargo, Donna	Mt. Airy, N.C.	1945
Farr, Felicia	Westchester, N.Y.	1932
Farrell, Charles	Onset Bay, Mass.	1901
Farrell, Eileen	Willimantic, Conn.	1920
Farrow, Mia	Los Angeles, Cal.	1946
Faye, Alice	New York, N.Y.	1915
Feld, Fritz	Berlin, Germany	1900
Feldon, Barbara	Pittsburgh, Pa.	1941
Feliciano, Jose	Puerto Rico	1945
Fellini, Federico	Rimini, Italy	1920
Fellows, Edith	Boston, Mass.	1923
Feldman, Marty	England	1933
Ferrer, Jose	Santurce, P.R.	1912
Ferrer, Mel	Elberon, N.J.	1917
Ferris, Barbara	London, England.	1942
Fetchit, Stepin	Key West, Fla.	1902
Fiedler, Arthur	Boston, Mass.	1894
Field, Sally	Pasadena, Cal.	1946
Fields, Gracie	Rochdale, England	1898
Fields, Totie	Hartford, Conn.	1931
Finch, Peter	London, England.	1916
Finney, Albert	Salford, England.	1936
Firkusny, Rudolf	Napajedla, Czechoslovakia	1912
Fisher, Eddie	Philadelphia, Pa.	1928
Fisher, Gail	Orange, N.J.	
Fitzgerald, Ella	Newport News, Va.	1918
Fitzgerald, Geraldine	Dublin, Ireland.	1914
Fitzgerald, Pegeen	Norcatur, Kan.	1910
Fix, Paul	Dobbs Ferry, N.Y.	1902
Flack, Roberta	Black Mountain, N.C.	1940
Flatt, Lester	Overton County, Tenn.	1914
Fleming, Rhonda	Hollywood, Cal.	1923
Foch, Nina	Leyden, Netherlands.	1924
Fonda, Henry	Grand Island, Neb.	1905
Fonda, Jane	New York, N.Y.	1937
Fonda, Peter	New York, N.Y.	1939
Fontaine, Frank	Cambridge, Mass.	1920
Fontaine, Joan	Tokyo, Japan	1917
Fontanne, Lynn	London, England.	1887
Fonteyn, Margot	Reigate, England	1919
Foran, Dick	Flemington, N.J.	1910
Forbes, Bryan	London, England.	1926
Ford (Tenn.), Ernie	Bristol, Tenn.	1919
Ford, Glenn	Quebec, Canada.	1916
Ford, Ruth	Hazelhurst, Miss.	1915
Forrest, Steve	Huntsville, Tex.	1925
Forster, Robert	Rochester, N.Y.	1942
Forsythe, John	Penns Grove, N.J.	1918
Fosse, Bob	Chicago, Ill.	1927
Foster, Phil	Brooklyn, N.Y.	1914
Fox, James	London, England.	1939
Foxx, Redd	St. Louis, Mo.	1922
Foy, Eddie, Jr.	New Rochelle, N.Y.	1905
Francescatti, Zino	Marseilles, France	1904
Franciosa, Anthony	New York, N.Y.	1928
Francis, Arlene	Boston, Mass.	1908
Francis, Connie	Newark, N.J.	1938
Franciscus, James	Clayton, Mo.	1934
Frankenheimer, John	Malba, N.Y.	1930
Franklin, Aretha	Memphis, Tenn.	1942
Franklin, Joe	New York, N.Y.	1926
Franz, Arthur	Perth Amboy, N.J.	1920
Freberg, Stan	Pasadena, Cal.	1926
Freed, Bert	New York, N.Y.	1919
Freeman, Mona	Baltimore, Md.	1926
Froman, Jane	St. Louis, Mo.	1911
Frost, David	Tenterden, England.	1939
Frye, David	Brooklyn, N.Y.	1934
Funicello, Annette	Utica, N.Y.	1942
Funt, Allen	New York, N.Y.	1914
Furness, Betty	New York, N.Y.	1916

G

Name	Birthplace	Born
Gabel, Martin	Philadelphia, Pa.	1912
Gabin, Jean	Villette, Paris, France.	1904
Gabor, Eva	Hungary	1921

Name	Birthplace	Born
Gabor, Zsa Zsa	Hungary	1919
Gahagan, Helen	Boonton, N.J.	1900
Galloway, Don	Brooksville, Ky.	1937
Gam, Rita	Pittsburgh, Pa.	1929
Gambling, John	New York, N.Y.	1930
Garagiola, Joe	St. Louis, Mo.	1926
Garbo, Greta	Stockholm, Sweden.	1905
Gardenia, Vincent	Naples, Italy	1922
Gardiner, Reginald	Wimbledon, England.	1903
Gardner, Ava	Smithfield, N.C.	1922
Gargan, William	Brooklyn, N.Y.	1905
Garfunkel, Art	New York, N.Y.	1941
Garland, Beverly	Santa Cruz, Cal.	1930
Garner, Erroll	Pittsburgh, Pa.	1923
Garner, James	Norman, Okla.	1928
Garner, Peggy Ann	Canton, Ohio.	1932
Garrett, Betty	St. Joseph, Mo.	1919
Garroway, Dave	Schenectady, N.Y.	1913
Garson, Greer	Co. Down, N. Ireland.	1908
Garver, Kathy	Long Beach, Cal.	1948
Gary, John	Watertown, N.Y.	1932
Gavin, John	Los Angeles, Cal.	1932
Gaynor, Janet	Philadelphia, Pa.	1906
Gaynor, Mitzi	Chicago, Ill.	1931
Gazzara, Ben	New York, N.Y.	1930
Gedda, Nicolai	Sweden.	1925
Geer, Will	Frankfort, Ind.	1902
Geeson, Judy	Sussex, England.	1948
Genevieve (G. Auger)	Paris, France	1930
Genn, Leo	London, England.	1905
Gennaro, Peter	Metairie, La.	1924
Gentry, Bobby	Chickasaw Co., Miss.	1944
Ghostley, Alice	Eve, Mo.	1926
Gibson, Henry	Germantown, Pa.	1935
Gielgud, John	London, England.	1904
Gifford, Frank	Santa Monica, Cal.	1930
Gilford, Jack	New York, N.Y.	1907
Gillespie, Dizzy	Cheraw, N.C.	1917
Gillette, Anita	Baltimore, Md.	1936
Gingold, Hermione	London, England.	1897
Gish, Lillian	Springfield, Ohio.	1896
Givot, George	Omaha, Neb.	1903
Gleason, Jackie	Brooklyn, N.Y.	1916
Gobel, George	Chicago, Ill.	1919
Godard, Jean Luc	Paris, France	1930
Goddard, Paulette	Great Neck, N.Y.	1911
Godfrey, Arthur	New York, N.Y.	1903
Goldsboro, Bobby	Marianne, Fla.	1941
Goodman, Benny	Chicago, Ill.	1909
Gordon, Gale	New York, N.Y.	1906
Gordon, Max	New York, N.Y.	1892
Gordon, Ruth	Wollaston, Mass.	1896
Gorin, Igor	Ukraine, Russia	1909
Gorme, Eydie	Bronx, N.Y.	1932
Gorshin, Frank	Pittsburgh, Pa.	1935
Gortner, Marjoe	Long Beach, Cal.	1945
Gosden, Freeman (Amos)	Richmond, Va.	1904
Gould, Elliot	Brooklyn, N.Y.	1938
Gould, Morton	Richmond Hill, N.Y.	1913
Goulding, Ray	Lowell, Mass.	1922
Goulet, Robert	Lawrence, Mass.	1933
Gowdy, Curt	Green River, Wy.	1919
Grady, Don	San Diego, Cal.	1944
Graham, Martha	Pittsburgh, Pa.	1902
Graham, Virginia	Chicago, Ill.	1913
Grahame, Gloria	Los Angeles, Cal.	1929
Grahame, Margot	Canterbury, England.	1911
Granger, Farley	San Jose, Cal.	1925
Granger, Stewart	London, England.	1913
Granville, Bonita	New York, N.Y.	1923
Grant, Cary	Bristol, England.	1904
Grant, Kathryn	Houston, Tex.	1933
Grant, Lee	New York, N.Y.	1927
Grauer, Ben	New York, N.Y.	1908
Graves, Peter	Minneapolis, Minn.	1926
Gray, Coleen	Staplehurst, Neb.	1922
Gray, Dolores	Chicago, Ill.	1924
Grayson, Kathryn	Winston-Salem, N.C.	1923
Graziano, Rocky	New York, N.Y.	1922
Greco, Buddy	Philadelphia, Pa.	1926
Greco, Jose	Abruzzi, Italy	1918
Greco, Juliette	Paris, France	—
Greene, Lorne	Ottawa, Canada.	1915
Greenwood, Charlotte	Philadelphia, Pa.	1893
Greenwood, Joan	London, England.	1921
Greer, Jane	Washington, D.C.	1924
Gregory, Dick	St. Louis, Mo.	1933
Grey, Joel	Cleveland, Ohio.	1932

Name	Birthplace	Born
Griffin, Merv	San Mateo, Cal.	1925
Griffith, Andy	Mount Airy, N.C.	1926
Griffith, Hugh	Wales	1912
Grimes, Tammy	Lynn, Mass.	1936
Grizzard, George	Roanoke Rapids, N.C.	1928
Guardino, Harry	New York, N.Y.	1925
Guinness, Alec	London, England	1914
Gunn, Moses	St. Louis, Mo.	1929
Guthrie, Arlo	New York, N.Y.	1947

H

Name	Birthplace	Born
Hackett, Buddy	Brooklyn, N.Y.	1924
Hackett, Joan	New York, N.Y.	1933
Hackman, Gene	San Bernardino, Cal.	1931
Hagen, Uta	Gottingen, Germany	1919
Haggard, Merle	Bakersfield, Cal.	1937
Hagman, Larry	Ft. Worth, Tex.	1931
Hale, Barbara	DeKalb, Ill.	1922
Haley, Jack	Boston, Mass.	1899
Hall, Huntz	New York, N.Y.	1920
Hall, Monty	Winnipeg, Canada	1923
Hall, Tom T.	Olive Hill, Ky.	1936
Hamilton, George	Memphis, Tenn.	1939
Hamilton, Margaret	Cleveland, Ohio	1902
Hamilton, Neil	Lynn, Mass.	1899
Hampshire, Susan	London, England	1941
Hampton, Lionel	Birmingham, Ala.	1914
Hampton, Ruth	Throop, Pa.	1932
Harding, Ann	Ft. Sam Houston, Tex.	1904
Harper, Ron	Turtle Creek, Pa.	1935
Harper, Valerie	Suffern, N.Y.	1940
Harrington, Pat, Jr.	New York, N.Y.	1929
Harris, Barbara	Evanston, Ill.	1935
Harris, Julie	Grosse Pte. Park, Mich.	1925
Harris, Phil	Linton, Ind.	1906
Harris, Richard	Co. Limerick, Ireland	1933
Harris, Rosemary	Ashby, England	1930
Harrison, George	Liverpool, England	1943
Harrison, Noel	London, England	1933
Harrison, Rex	Huyton, England	1908
Hartman, David	Pawtucket, R.I.	1935
Hartman, Elizabeth	Boardman, Ohio	1943
Hartman, Paul	San Francisco, Cal.	1904
Hasso, Signe	Stockholm, Sweden	1915
Haver, June	Rock Island, Ill.	1926
Havoc, June	Vancouver, Canada	1916
Hawn, Goldie	Washington, D.C.	1945
Haworth, Jill	Sussex, England	1945
Hayden, Melissa	Toronto, Canada	1928
Hayden, Russell	Chico, Cal.	1912
Hayden, Sterling	Montclair, N.Y.	1916
Hayes, Helen	Washington, D.C.	1900
Hayes, Isaac	Covington, Tenn.	1942
Hayes, Peter Lind	San Francisco, Cal.	1915
Hayes, Roland	Curryville, Ga.	1887
Haymes, Dick	Buenos Aires, Argentina	1918
Haynes, Lloyd	South Bend, Ind.	1934
Hayward, Louis	Johannesburg, S. Africa	1909
Hayworth, Rita	New York, N.Y.	1918
Healy, Mary	New Orleans, La.	1918
Heatherton, Joey	Rockville Centre, N.Y.	1944
Heckart, Eileen	Columbus, Ohio	1919
Hefner, Hugh	Chicago, Ill.	1926
Heifetz, Jascha	Vilna, Russia	1901
Helmore, Tom	London, England	1912
Helpmann, Robert	Mt. Gambier, Australia	1909
Hemmings, David	Guilford, England	1941
Henderson, Florence	Dale, Ind.	1934
Henderson, Marcia	Andover, Mass.	1932
Henderson, Skitch	Halstad, Minn.	1918
Henning, Linda Kaye	Toluca Lake, Calif.	1944
Henreid, Paul	Trieste, Italy	1908
Hepburn, Audrey	Brussels, Belgium	1929
Hepburn, Katharine	Hartford, Conn.	1909
Herbert, Evelyn	Philadelphia, Pa.	1898
Herlie, Eileen	Glasgow, Scotland	1920
Heston, Charlton	Evanston, Ill.	1924
Heywood, Anne	Birmingham, England	1937
Hickman, Darryl	Los Angeles, Cal.	1931
Hickman, Dwayne	Los Angeles, Cal.	1934
Hildegarde	Adell, Wis.	1906
Hill, Arthur	Melfort, Sask., Canada	1922
Hiller, Wendy	Stockport, England	1912
Hines, Earl (Fatha)	Duquesne, Pa.	1905
Hines, Jerome	Hollywood, Cal.	1921
Hines, Mimi	Vancouver, B.C.	1933
Hingle, Pat	Denver, Col.	1924
Hirt, Al	New Orleans, La.	1922
Hitchcock, Alfred	London, England	1899

Name	Birthplace	Born
Ho, Don	Kakaako, Oahu, Hawaii	1930
Hobart, Rose	New York, N.Y.	1906
Hoffman, Dustin	Los Angeles, Cal.	1937
Holbrook, Hal	Cleveland, Ohio	1925
Holden, William	O'Fallon, Ill.	1918
Holder, Geoffrey	Trinidad	1930
Holloway, Stanley	London, England	1890
Holloway, Sterling	Cedartown, Ga.	1905
Holm, Celeste	New York, N.Y.	1919
Holtz, Lou	San Francisco, Cal.	1893
Homeier, Skip	Chicago, Ill.	1930
Homolka, Oscar	Vienna, Austria	1903
Hooks, Robert	Washington, D.C.	1937
Hope, Bob	London, England	1903
Hopkin, Mary	Wales	1950
Hopper, Dennis	Dodge City, Kan.	1936
Horne, Lena	Brooklyn, N.Y.	1917
Horowitz, Vladimir	Kiev, Russia	1904
Horton, Robert	Los Angeles, Cal.	1924
Howard, Clint	Burbank, Cal.	1959
Howard, Ken	El Centro, Cal.	1944
Howard, Ron	Duncan, Okla.	1954
Howard, Trevor	Kent, England	1916
Howes, Sally Ann	London, England	1934
Hudson, Rock	Winnetka, Ill.	1925
Hull, Henry	Louisville, Ky.	1890
Humperdinck, Engelbert	Madras, India	1936
Hunnicutt, Arthur	Gravelly, Ark.	1911
Hunt, Lois	York, Pa.	1925
Hunt, Marsha	Chicago, Ill.	1917
Hunter, Kim	Detroit, Mich.	1922
Hunter, Ross	Cleveland, Ohio	1924
Hunter, Tab	New York, N.Y.	1931
Hussey, Olivia	Buenos Aires, Argentina	1952
Hussey, Ruth	Providence, R.I.	1917
Huston, John	Nevada, Mo.	1906
Hutchinson, Josephine	Seattle, Wash.	1916
Hutton, Betty	Battle Creek, Mich.	1921
Hutton, Ina Ray	Chicago, Ill.	1918
Hutton, Lauren	Charleston, S.C.	1944
Hyde-White, Wilfrid	England	1903
Hyer, Martha	Fort Worth, Tex.	1929
Hyland, Diana	Cleveland Hts., Ohio	1937
Hyman, Earle	Rocky Mt., N.C.	1926

I

Name	Birthplace	Born
Ian, Janis	New York, N.Y.	1951
Inescort, Frieda	Edinburgh, Scotland	1901
Ingels, Marty	Brooklyn, N.Y.	1936
Ireland, John	Vancouver, B.C.	1915
Iturbi, Jose	Valencia, Spain	1895
Ives, Burl	Hunt, Ill.	1909

J

Name	Birthplace	Born
Jackson, Anne	Allegheny, Pa.	1926
Jackson, Glenda	Cheshire, England	1937
Jaeckel, Richard	Long Beach, Cal.	1926
Jaffe, Sam	New York, N.Y.	1891
Jagger, Dean	Columbus Grove, Ohio	1905
Jagger, Mick	Dartford, England	1944
James, Dennis	Jersey City, N.J.	1917
James, Harry	Albany, Ga.	1916
Janssen, David	Naponee, Neb.	1930
Jason, Rick	New York, N.Y.	1926
Jeanmaire, Renee	Paris, France	1925
Jeffreys, Anne	Goldsboro, N.C.	1923
Jeffries, Fran	San Jose, Cal.	1939
Jeffries, Lionel	England	1926
Jennings, Waylon	Littlefield, Tex.	1937
Jens, Salome	Milwaukee, Wis.	1935
Jepson, Helen	Titusville, Pa.	1907
Jeritza, Maria	Brunn, Austria	1887
Jessel, George	New York, N.Y.	1898
John, Elton	Middlesex, England	1947
Johns, Glynis	Durban, S. Africa	1923
Johnson, Ben	Foraker, Okla.	1918
Johnson, Richard	Essex, England	1927
Johnson, Van	Newport, R.I.	1916
Johnston, Johnny	St. Louis, Mo.	1916
Jones, Allan	Scranton, Pa.	1907
Jones, Anissa	W. Lafayette, Ind.	1958
Jones, Carolyn	Amarillo, Tex.	1933
Jones, Chris	Jackson, Tenn.	1941
Jones, Dean	Morgan Co., Ala.	1935
Jones, Grandpa	Niagara, Ky.	1913
Jones, Henry	Philadelphia, Pa.	1912
Jones, Jack	Hollywood, Cal.	1938
Jones, James Earl	Tate Co., Miss.	1931
Jones, Jennifer	Tulsa, Okla.	1919
Jones, Quincy	Chicago, Ill.	1933

Name	Birthplace	Born	Name	Birthplace	Born
Jones, Shirley	Smithtown, Pa.	1934	Lane, Priscilla	Indianola, Ia.	1917
Jones, Tom	Pontypridd, Wales.	1940	Lane, Sara	New York, N.Y.	1949
Jory, Victor	Dawson, Yukon, Canada	1902	Lange, Hope	Redding Ridge, Conn.	1933
Joslyn, Allyn	Milford, Pa.	1905	Langella, Frank	Bayonne, N.J.	1940
Jourdan, Louis	Marseilles, France	1921	Langford, Frances	Lakeland, Fla.	1913
Jurado, Katy	Guadalajara, Mexico	1927	Lansbury, Angela	London, England.	1925
			Lansing, Robert	San Diego, Calif.	1929
K			Lanson, Snooky (Roy)	Memphis, Tenn.	1919
Kahn, Madeline	New York, N.Y.	—	LaPlante, Laura	St. Louis, Mo.	1904
Kamen, Milt	Harleyville, N.Y.	1924	La Rosa, Julius	Brooklyn, N.Y.	1930
Kaminska, Ida	Odessa, Russia	1899	La Rue, Jack	New York, N.Y.	—
Kaplan, Gabe	Brooklyn, N.Y.	1945	Lasser, Louise	New York, N.Y.	—
Kashi, Aliza	Tel-Aviv, Israel	1940	Laurie, Piper	Detroit, Mich.	1932
Kasznar, Kurt	Vienna, Austria	1913	Law, John Philip	Hollywood, Calif.	1937
Kaye, Danny	Brooklyn, N.Y.	1913	Lawford, Peter	London, England.	1923
Kaye, Sammy	Lakewood, Ohio.	1913	Lawrence, Barbara	Carnegie, Okla.	1930
Kazan, Elia	Constantinople, Turkey	1909	Lawrence, Carol	Melrose Park, Ill.	1934
Kazan, Lainie	New York, N.Y.	1940	Lawrence, Marjorie	Victoria, Australia.	1909
Keach, Stacy	Savannah, Ga.	1941	Lawrence, Steve	Brooklyn, N.Y.	1935
Keaton, Diane	Santa Ana, Cal.	1949	Lawrence, Vicki	Inglewood, Cal.	1949
Keel, Howard	Gillespie, Ill.	1919	Leachman, Cloris	Des Moines, Ia.	1926
Keeler, Ruby	Halifax, N.S., Canada	1910	Lean, David	Croydon, England.	1908
Keeshan, Bob	Lynbrook, N.Y.	1927	Lederer, Francis	Prague, Czechoslovakia	1906
Keitel, Harvey	Brooklyn, N.Y.	1941	Lee, Brenda	Atlanta, Ga.	1944
Keith, Brian	Bayonne, N.J.	1921	Lee, Christopher	London, England.	1922
Kellerman, Sally	Long Beach, Cal.	1937	Lee, Lila	New York, N.Y.	1905
Kelley, DeForrest	Atlanta, Ga.	1920	Lee, Michele	Los Angeles, Cal.	1942
Kelly, Emmett	Sedan, Kan.	1898	Lee, Peggy	Jamestown, N.D.	1920
Kelly, Gene	Pittsburgh, Pa.	1912	Lee, Pinky	St. Paul, Minn.	—
Kelly, Grace	Philadelphia, Pa.	1929	Le Gallienne, Eva	London, England.	1899
Kelly, Jack	Astoria, N.Y.	1927	Legrand, Michel	Paris, France	1932
Kelly, Nancy	Lowell, Mass.	1921	Lehmann, Lotte	Perleberg, Germany	1888
Kelly, Patsy	Brooklyn, N.Y.	1910	Leigh, Janet	Merced, Cal.	1927
Kennedy, Arthur	Worcester, Mass.	1914	Leinsdorf, Erich	Vienna, Austria	1912
Kennedy, George	New York, N.Y.	1926	Lembeck, Harvey	New York, N.Y.	1923
Kennedy, Madge	Chicago, Ill.	—	Lemmon, Jack	Boston, Mass.	1925
Kent, Allegra	Los Angeles, Cal.	1938	Lennon, Dianne	Los Angeles, Cal.	1939
Kenyon, Doris	Syracuse, N.Y.	1897	Lennon, Janet	Culver City, Cal.	1946
Kerr, Deborah	Helensburgh, Scotland	1921	Lennon, John	Liverpool, England	1940
Kerr, John	New York, N.Y.	1931	Lennon, Kathy	Santa Monica, Cal.	1934
Kert, Larry	Los Angeles, Cal.	1930	Lennon, Peggy	Los Angeles, Cal.	1941
Keyes, Evelyn	Port Arthur, Tex.	1925	Leonard, Sheldon	New York, N.Y.	1907
Kiley, Richard	Chicago, Ill.	1922	Leontovich, Eugenie	Moscow, Russia.	1894
Kilian, Victor	Jersey City, N.J.	1898	LeRoy, Mervyn	San Francisco, Cal.	1900
King, Alan	Brooklyn, N.Y.	1927	Leslie, Joan	Detroit, Mich.	1925
King, B. B.	Itta Bena, Miss.	1925	Lester, Jerry	Chicago, Ill.	1911
King, Carole	Brooklyn, N.Y.	1941	Lester, Mark	Richmond, England	1958
King, Henry	Christianburg, Va.	1896	Lester, Tom	Jackson, Miss.	1938
King, Peggy	Greensburg, Pa.	1931	Levene, Sam	Russia.	1905
King, Walter Woolf	San Francisco, Cal.	1899	Levenson, Sam	New York, N.Y.	1911
King, Wayne	Savannah, Ill.	1901	Lewis, Jerry	Newark, N.J.	1926
Kirby, Durward	Covington, Ky.	1912	Lewis, Jerry Lee	Ferriday, La.	1935
Kirby, Michael	Canada.	1925	Lewis, Monica	Chicago, Ill.	1925
Kirk, Lisa	Brownsville, Pa.	1925	Lewis, Robert Q.	New York, N.Y.	1924
Kirk, Phyllis	Plainfield, N.J.	1930	Lewis, Shari	New York, N.Y.	1934
Kirsten, Dorothy	Montclair, N.J.	1919	Liberace	West Allis, Wis.	1919
Kitt, Eartha	North, S.C.	1928	Lillie, Beatrice	Toronto, Canada.	1894
Klemperer, Werner	Cologne, Germany	1920	Lincoln, Abbey	Chicago, Ill.	1930
Klugman, Jack	Philadelphia, Pa.	1922	Linden, Hal	New York, N.Y.	1931
Knight, Gladys	Atlanta, Ga.	1944	Lindfors, Viveca	Uppsala, Sweden.	1920
Knight, Ted	Terryville, Conn.	—	Lindsay, Margaret	Dubuque, Ia.	1910
Knotts, Don	Morgantown, W.Va.	1924	Lindsey, Mort	Newark, N.J.	1923
Knowles, Patric	Horsforth, England.	1911	Linkletter, Art	Saskatchewan, Canada	1912
Knox, Alexander	Strathroy, Canada.	1907	Lipton, Peggy	Lawrence, N.Y.	1948
Korjus, Miliza	Warsaw, Poland.	1912	Lisi, Virna	Italy	1937
Korman, Harvey	Chicago, Ill.	1927	Little, Cleavon	Chickasha, Okla.	1939
Kostelanetz, Andre	St. Petersburg, Russia	1901	Little, Rich	Ottawa, Canada.	1938
Kramer, Stanley	New York, N.Y.	1913	Little Richard	Macon, Ga.	1935
Kristofferson, Kris	Brownsville, Tex.	1936	Livingston, Barry	Los Angeles, Cal.	1953
Kruger, Hardy	Berlin, Germany.	1928	Livingston, Stanley	Los Angeles, Cal.	1950
Kubelik, Rafael	Bychori, Czechoslovakia	1914	Livingstone, Mary	Seattle, Wash.	1909
Kubrick, Stanley	Bronx, N.Y.	1928	Lockhart, June	New York, N.Y.	1925
Kulp, Nancy	Harrisburg, Pa.	1921	Lockwood, Margaret	Karachi, India.	1916
Kwan, Nancy	Hong Kong.	1939	Loden, Barbara	Marion, N.C.	1937
Kyser, Kay	Rocky Mount, N.C.	1905	Loder, John	London, England.	1898
			Logan, Joshua	Texarkana, Tex.	1908
L			Lollobrigida, Gina	Subiaco, Italy.	1929
Laine, Frankie	Chicago, Ill.	1913	Lom, Herbert	Prague, Czechoslovakia	1917
Lamarr, Hedy	Vienna, Austria	1915	Lombardo, Guy	London, Ont., Canada.	1902
Lamas, Fernando	Buenos Aires, Argentina	1915	London, Julie	Santa Rosa, Cal.	1926
Lamb, Gil	Minneapolis, Minn.	1906	Longet, Claudine	France	1942
Lamour, Dorothy	New Orleans, La.	1914	Lopez, Trini	Dallas, Tex.	1937
Lancaster, Burt	New York, N.Y.	1913	Lord, Jack	New York, N.Y.	1930
Lanchester, Elsa	London, England.	1902	Loren, Sophia	Rome, Italy.	1934
Landers, Harry	New York, N.Y.	1921	Loring, Gloria	New York, N.Y.	1946
Landau, Martin	Brooklyn, N.Y.	1934	Loudon, Dorothy	Boston, Mass.	1932
Landon, Michael	Forest Hills, N.Y.	—	Louise, Tina	New York, N.Y.	1934
Lane, Abbe	Brooklyn, N.Y.	1932	Love, Bessie	Midland, Tex.	1898
Lane, Lola	Macy, Ind.	1909	Loy, Myrna	Helena, Mon.	1905

Name	Birthplace	Born
Lucas, Nick	New Jersey	1897
Ludwig, Christa	Berlin, Germany	1928
Luke, Keye	Canton, China	1904
Lulu	Glasgow, Scotland	1948
Lum (Chester Lauck)	Allene, Ark.	1902
Lumet, Sidney	Philadelphia, Pa.	1924
Lund, John	Rochester, N.Y.	1913
Lunt, Alfred	Milwaukee, Wis.	1892
Lupino, Ida	London, England	1918
Lynde, Paul	Mt. Vernon, Ohio	1926
Lynley, Carol	New York, N.Y.	1942
Lynn, Jeffrey	Auburn, Mass.	1909
Lynn, Loretta	Butcher Hollow, Ky.	1932
Lyon, Ben	Atlanta, Ga.	1901
Lyon, Sue	Davenport, Ia.	1946

M

Name	Birthplace	Born
MacArthur, James	Los Angeles, Cal.	1937
MacGraw, Ali	Pound Ridge, N.Y.	1939
MacKenzie, Gisele	Winnipeg, Man., Canada	1927
MacKay, Jim	Philadelphia, Pa.	1921
MacLaine, Shirley	Richmond, Va.	1934
MacMurray, Fred	Kankakee, Ill.	1908
MacRae, Gordon	East Orange, N.J.	1921
MacRae, Meredith	Houston, Tex.	1945
MacRae, Sheila	London, England	1924
Macy, Bill	Revere, Mass.	1922
Madison, Guy	Bakersfield, Cal.	1922
Malbin, Elaine	New York, N.Y.	1932
Malden, Karl	Gary, Ind.	1913
Malone, Dorothy	Chicago, Ill.	1925
Malone, Nancy	New York, N.Y.	1935
Mancini, Henry	Cleveland, Ohio	1924
Mandrell, Barbara	Houston, Tex.	1948
Mann, Herbie	New York, N.Y.	1930
Manning, Irene	Cincinnati, Ohio	1918
Mantovani, Annuzio	Venice, Italy	1905
Marceau, Marcel	France	1923
Marsh, Jean	London, Eng.	1934
Margo	Mexico City, Mexico	1918
Margolin, Janet	New York, N.Y.	1943
Markova, Alicia	London, England	1910
Marlowe, Hugh	Philadelphia, Pa.	1914
Marshall, Brenda	Philippines	1915
Marshall, E. G.	Awatonna, Minn.	1910
Marshall, William	Chicago, Ill.	1917
Martin, Dean	Steubenville, Ohio	1917
Martin, Dick	Detroit, Mich.	1922
Martin, Mary	Weatherford, Tex.	1913
Martin, Ross	Poland	1920
Martin, Strother	Kokomo, Ind.	1919
Martin, Tony	San Francisco, Cal.	1913
Martini, Nino	Verona, Italy	1905
Martino, Al	Philadelphia, Pa.	1927
Marvin, Lee	New York, N.Y.	1924
Marx, Herbert (Zeppo)	New York, N.Y.	1901
Marx, Julius (Groucho)	New York, N.Y.	1890
Mason, Jackie	Sheboygan, Wis.	1931
Mason, James	Huddersfield, England	1909
Mason, Marsha	St. Louis, Mo.	—
Mason, Pamela	Westgate, England	1918
Massey, Curt	Midland, Tex.	—
Massey, Raymond	Toronto, Canada	1896
Massine, Leonide	Moscow, Russia	1896
Mastroianni, Marcello	Italy	1924
Mathieu, Mireille	Avignon, Framsace.	1946
Mathis, Johnny	San Francisco, Cal.	1935
Matthau, Walter	New York, N.Y.	1920
Mature, Victor	Louisville, Ky.	1916
May, Billy	Pittsburgh, Pa.	1916
May, Elaine	Philadelphia, Pa.	1932
Mayehoff, Eddie	Baltimore, Md.	1914
Mayo, Virginia	St. Louis, Mo.	1920
Mazurki, Mike	Austria	1909
McBride, Patricia	Teaneck, N.J.	1942
McCallum, David	Glasgow, Scotland	1933
McCambridge, Mercedes	Joliet, Ill.	1918
McCarthy, Kevin	Seattle, Wash.	1915
McCartney, Paul	Liverpool, England	1942
McClure, Doug.	Glendale, Cal.	1935
McCord, Kent	Los Angeles, Cal.	1942
McCoy, Tim	Saginaw, Mich.	1891
McCrary, Tex (John)	Calvert, Tex.	1910
McCrea, Joel	Los Angeles, Cal.	1905
McDowall, Roddy	London, England	1928
McDowell, Malcolm.	Leeds, England	1943
McEachin, James	Pennert, N.C.	1930

Name	Birthplace	Born
McFarland, George (Spanky)	Dallas, Tex.	1928
McGavin, Darren	San Joaquin, Cal.	1922
McGee, Fibber	Peoria, Ill.	1896
McGoohan, Patrick	Astoria, N.Y.	1928
McGuire Sisters:		
Christine	Middletown, Ohio	1928
Dorothy	Middletown, Ohio	1930
Phyllis	Middletown, Ohio	1931
McGuire, Dorothy	Omaha, Neb.	1919
McHugh, Frank	Homestead, Pa.	1899
McIntire, John	Spokane, Wash.	1907
McKay, Scott	Pleasantville, Ia.	1915
McKenna, Siobhan	Belfast, Ireland	1923
McKuen, Rod	San Francisco, Cal.	1933
McLean, Don	New Rochelle, N.Y.	1945
McLerie, Allyn	Grand Mere, Que., Canada	1926
McMahon, Ed	Detroit, Mich.	1923
McNair, Barbara	Chicago, Ill.	1939
McQueen, Butterfly	Tampa, Fla.	1911
McQueen, Steve	Indianapolis, Ind.	1930
Meadows, Audrey	Wu Chang, China.	1924
Meadows, Jayne	Wu Chang, China.	1926
Meara, Anne	New York, N.Y.	1929
Medford, Kay	New York, N.Y.	1920
Meeker, Ralph	Minneapolis, Minn.	1920
Melton, Sid	Brooklyn, N.Y.	1920
Menuhin, Yehudi	New York, N.Y.	1916
Mercouri, Melina	Athens, Greece	1915
Meredith, Burgess	Cleveland, Ohio	1909
Merkel, Una	Covington, Ky.	1903
Merman, Ethel	Astoria, N.Y.	1909
Merrick, David	Hong Kong.	1911
Merrill, Dina	New York, N.Y.	1925
Merrill, Gary	Hartford, Conn.	1915
Merrill, Robert	Brooklyn, N.Y.	1919
Middleton, Ray	Chicago, Ill.	1907
Midler, Bette	Honolulu, Hawaii.	1945
Milanov, Zinka	Zagreb, Yugoslavia.	1908
Miles, Sarah	Ingatestone, England.	1941
Miles, Vera	near Boise City, Okla.	1930
Milland, Ray	Neath, Wales	1908
Miller, Ann.	Houston, Tex.	1923
Miller, Cheryl.	Sherman Oaks, Cal.	1943
Miller, Jason	Scranton, Pa.	1940
Miller, Mitch	Rochester, N.Y.	1911
Miller, Roger	Erick, Okla.	1936
Mills, Hayley	London, England.	1946
Mills, John	Suffolk, England.	1908
Mills, Juliet	London, England.	1941
Milner, Martin	Detroit, Mich.	1937
Milstein, Nathan	Odessa, Russia	1904
Mimieux, Yvette	Hollywood, Cal.	1942
Minnelli, Liza	Los Angeles, Cal.	1946
Mitchell, Cameron	Dallastown, Pa.	1918
Mitchell, Guy	Detroit, Mich.	1925
Mitchell, Joni	Alberta, Canada.	1943
Mitchum, Robert	Bridgeport, Conn.	1917
Moffo, Anna	Wayne, Pa.	1934
Montalban, Ricardo	Mexico City, Mexico	1920
Montand, Yves	Monsummano, Italy	1921
Montgomery, Elizabeth	Hollywood, Cal.	1933
Montgomery, George.	Brady, Mon.	1916
Montgomery, Robert	Beacon, N.Y.	1904
Moore, Colleen	Port Huron, Mich.	1902
Moore, Constance	Sioux City, Ia.	1922
Moore, Dickie	Los Angeles, Cal.	1925
Moore, Garry	Baltimore, Md.	1915
Moore, Mary Tyler	Brooklyn, N.Y.	1937
Moore, Melba	New York, N.Y.	1945
Moore, Roger	London, England.	1928
Moore, Terry	Los Angeles, Cal.	1932
Moreau, Jeanne	Paris, France	1929
Moreno, Rita	Humacao, P.R.	1931
Morgan, Dennis	Prentice, Wis.	1910
Morgan, Harry	Detroit, Mich.	1915
Morgan, Henry	New York, N.Y.	1915
Morgan, Jane	Boston, Mass.	1920
Morgana, Nina	Buffalo, N.Y.	1895
Moriarty, Michael	Detroit, Mich.	1942
Morini, Erika	Vienna, Austria	1910
Morison, Patricia	New York, N.Y.	1915
Morley, Robert	Wiltshire, England.	1908
Morris, Greg	Cleveland, Ohio	1934
Morris, Howard	New York, N.Y.	1919
Morrow, Vic	Bronx, N.Y.	1932
Morse, Robert	Newton, Mass.	1931
Moss, Arnold	Brooklyn, N.Y.	1911

Name	Birthplace	Born	Name	Birthplace	Born
Mostel, Zero (Sam)	Brooklyn, N.Y.	1915	Ormandy, Eugene	Budapest, Hungary	1899
Muir, Jean	New York, N.Y.	1911	O'Sullivan, Maureen	Boyle, Ireland	1911
Mulhall, Jack	Wappingers Falls, N.Y.	1894	O'Toole, Peter	Connemara, Ireland	1934
Mulhare, Edward	Ireland	1923	Owens, Buck	Sherman, Tex.	1929
Mundy, Meg	London, England	—			
Munsel, Patrice	Spokane, Wash.	1925	**P**		
Murphy, George	New Haven, Conn.	1902	Paar, Jack	Canton, Ohio	1918
Murray, Anne	Springhill, Nova Scotia	—	Pacino, Al	New York, N.Y.	1940
Murray, Arthur	New York, N.Y.	1895	Page, Geraldine	Kirksville, Mo.	1924
Murray, Don	Hollywood, Cal.	1929	Page, Patti	Claremore, Okla.	1927
Murray, Jan	New York	1917	Paige, Janis	Tacoma, Wash.	1923
Murray, Kathryn	Jersey City, N.J.	1906	Paige, Robert	Indianapolis, Ind.	1910
Murray, Ken	New York, N.Y.	1903	Palance, Jack	Lattimer, Pa.	1920
Musante, Tony	Bridgeport, Conn.	1941	Palmer, Betsy	East Chicago, Ind.	1929
			Palmer, Lili	Posen, Germany	1914
N			Papas, Irene	Greece	1926
Nabors, Jim	Sylacauga, Ala.	1933	Papp, Joseph	Brooklyn, N.Y.	1921
Namath, Joe	Beaver Falls, Pa.	1943	Parker, Eleanor	Cedarville, Ohio	1922
Nardini, Tom	Los Angeles, Cal.	1945	Parker, Fess	Ft. Worth, Tex.	1925
Natwick, Mildred	Baltimore, Md.	1908	Parker, Frank	New York, N.Y.	1906
Neal, Patricia	Packard, Ky.	1926	Parker, Jean	Deer Lodge, Mon.	1916
Neff, Hildegarde	Ulm, Germany	1925	Parker, Suzy	New York, N.Y.	1934
Negri, Pola	Lipno, Poland	1899	Parkins, Barbara	Vancouver, Canada	1942
Nelson, Barry	San Francisco, Cal.	1920	Parks, Bert	Atlanta, Ga.	1914
Nelson, David	New York, N.Y.	1936	Parsons, Estelle	Lynn, Mass.	1927
Nelson, Ed	New Orleans, La.	1928	Parton, Dolly	Sevierville, Tenn.	1946
Nelson, Gene	Seattle, Wash.	1920	Pasternak, Joseph	Hungary	1901
Nelson, Harriet (Hilliard)	Des Moines, Ia.	1914	Patterson, Melody	Los Angeles, Cal.	1947
Nelson, Ricky	Teaneck, N.J.	1940	Patterson, Neva	Nevada, Ia.	1922
Nero, Peter	New York, N.Y.	1934	Paulsen, Pat	South Bend, Wash.	—
Nesbit, Cathleen	Cheshire, England	1889	Pavan, Marisa	Cagliari, Sardinia	1932
Newhart, Bob	Oak Park, Ill.	1929	Payne, John	Roanoke, Va.	1912
Newley, Anthony	Hackney, England	1931	Pearl, Jack	New York, N.Y.	1895
Newman, Barry	Boston, Mass.	1938	Pearl, Minnie	Centerville, Tenn.	1912
Newman, Paul	Cleveland, Ohio	1925	Peck, Gregory	La Jolla, Cal.	1916
Newman, Phyllis	Jersey City, N.J.	1935	Peerce, Jan	New York, N.Y.	1904
Newmar, Julie	Los Angeles, Cal.	1935	Penn, Arthur	Philadelphia, Pa.	1922
Newton, Wayne	Roanoke, Va.	1942	Peppard, George	Detroit, Mich.	1928
Newton-John, Olivia	England	1949	Perkins, Anthony	New York, N.Y.	1932
Nicholas, Denise	Detroit, Mich.	—	Persoff, Nehemiah	Jerusalem	1920
Nichols, Mike	Berlin, Germany	1931	Peters, Bernadette	Queens, N.Y.	1944
Nicholson, Jack	Neptune, N.J.	1937	Peters, Brock	New York, N.Y.	1927
Nielsen, Leslie	Regina, Canada	1926	Peters, Jean	Canton, Ohio	1926
Nilsson, Birgit	W. Karop, Sweden	1918	Peters, Roberta	New York, N.Y.	1930
Nimoy, Leonard	Boston, Mass.	1931	Petit, Pascale	France	1937
Niven, David	Kirriemuir, Scotland	1910	Pettet, Joanna	London, England	1944
Noble, Ray	Sussex, England	1908	Piatigorsky, Gregor	Russia	1903
Nolan, Doris	New York, N.Y.	1916	Piazza, Marguerite	New Orleans, La.	1926
Nolan, Jeannette	Los Angeles, Cal.	1911	Pickens, Jane	Macon, Ga.	—
Nolan, Kathy	St. Louis, Mo.	1934	Pickens, Slim	Kingsberg, Cal.	1919
Nolan, Lloyd	San Francisco, Cal.	1902	Pickford, Mary	Toronto, Canada	1894
Nolte, Nick	Omaha, Neb.	1940	Picon, Molly	New York, N.Y.	1898
North, Jay	Hollywood, Cal.	1953	Pidgeon, Walter	E. St. John, N.B.	1898
North, John Ringling	Baraboo, Wis.	1903	Piston, Walter	Rockland, Me.	1894
North, Sheree	Los Angeles, Cal.	1933	Pleasance, Donald	Worksop, England	1919
Norton, Judy	Santa Monica, Cal.	1958	Pleshette, Suzanne	New York, N.Y.	1937
Novak, Kim	Chicago, Ill.	1933	Plimpton, George	New York, N.Y.	1927
Nugent, Edward	New York, N.Y.	1904	Plowright, Joan	Brigg, England	1929
Nugent, Elliott	Dover, Ohio	1899	Plummer, Christopher	Toronto, Canada	1929
Nureyev, Rudolf	Russia	1938	Poitier, Sidney	Miami, Fla.	1927
Nuyen, France	Marseilles, France	1939	Polanski, Roman	Paris, France	1933
			Pollard, Michael	Passaic, N.J.	1939
O			Ponselle, Carmela	Schenectady, N.Y.	1892
Oakie, Jack	Sedalia, Mo.	1903	Ponselle, Rosa	Meriden, Conn.	1897
Oakland, Simon	New York, N.Y.	1922	Ponti, Carlo	Milan, Italy	1913
Oberon, Merle	Tasmania, Australia	1911	Poston, Tom	Columbus, Ohio	1927
O'Brian, Hugh	Rochester, N.Y.	1930	Powell, Eleanor	Springfield, Mass.	1912
O'Brien, Edmond	New York, N.Y.	1915	Powell, Jane	Portland, Ore.	1929
O'Brien, George	San Francisco, Cal.	1900	Powell, William	Pittsburgh, Pa.	1892
O'Brien, Margaret	San Diego, Cal.	1937	Powers, Mala	San Francisco, Cal.	1931
O'Brien, Pat	Milwaukee, Wis.	1899	Powers, Stefanie	Hollywood, Cal.	1942
O'Connell, Arthur	New York, N.Y.	1908	Preminger, Otto	Vienna, Austria	1906
O'Connell, Helen	Lima, Ohio	1920	Prentiss, Paula	San Antonio, Tex.	1939
O'Connor, Carroll	New York, N.Y.	1925	Presley, Elvis	Tupelo, Miss.	1935
O'Connor, Donald	Chicago, Ill.	1925	Preston, Robert	Newton, Mass.	1918
Odetta	Birmingham, Ala.	1930	Previn, Andre	Berlin, Germany	1929
O'Driscoll, Martha	Tulsa, Okla.	1922	Price, Leontyne	Laurel, Miss.	1927
O'Hara, Jill	Warren, Pa.	1947	Price, Ray	Perryville, Tex.	1926
O'Hara, Maureen	Dublin, Ireland	1921	Price, Roger	Charleston, W. Va.	1920
O'Herlihy, Dan	Wexford, Ireland	1919	Price, Vincent	St. Louis, Mo.	1911
O'Keefe, Walter	Hartford, Conn.	1907	Pride, Charlie	Sledge, Miss.	1938
Olivier, Laurence	Dorking, England	1907	Prima, Louis	New Orleans, La.	1912
O'Malley, J. Pat	Burnley, England	1901	Prince, William	Nichols, N.Y.	1913
O'Neal, Patrick	Ocala, Fla.	1927	Prinze, Freddie	New York, N.Y.	1954
O'Neal, Ryan	Los Angeles, Cal.	1941	Provine, Dorothy	Deadwood, S. D.	1937
O'Neill, Jennifer	Brazil	1949	Prowse, Juliet	Bombay, India	1937
Opatoshu, David	New York, N.Y.	1918	Pyle, Denver	Bethune, Col.	1920
Orbach, Jerry	New York, N.Y.	1935			
Orlando, Tony	New York, N.Y.	1944	**Q**		
			Qualen, John	Vancouver, B.C.	1899

Name	Birthplace	Born
Quayle, Anthony	Lancashire, England	1913
Quillan, Eddie	Philadelphia, Pa.	1907
Quinn, Anthony	Chihuahua, Mexico	1916

R

Name	Birthplace	Born
Raffin, Deborah	Los Angeles, Cal.	1953
Raft, George	New York, N.Y.	1895
Rainer, Luise	Vienna, Austria	1912
Raines, Ella	Snoqualmie Falls, Wash.	1921
Raitt, John	Santa Ana, Cal.	1917
Ralston, Esther	Bar Harbor, Me.	1902
Ralston, Vera	Prague, Czechoslovakia	1921
Randall, Tony	Tulsa, Okla.	1920
Rawls, Lou	Chicago, Ill.	1935
Ray, Aldo	Pen Argyl, Pa.	1926
Ray, Johnnie	Dallas, Ore.	1927
Rayburn, Gene	Christopher, Ill.	1917
Raye, Martha	Butte, Mont.	1916
Raymond, Gene	New York, N.Y.	1908
Reddy, Helen	Melbourne, Australia.	1941
Redford, Robert	Santa Monica, Cal.	1937
Redgrave, Lynn	London, England.	1943
Redgrave, Michael	Bristol, England.	1908
Redgrave, Vanessa	London, England.	1937
Redman, Joyce	Co. Mayo, Ireland.	1918
Reed, Donna	Denison, Ia.	1921
Reed, Jerry	Atlanta, Ga.	1937
Reed, Rex	Ft. Worth, Tex.	1940
Reed, Robert	Highland Park, Ill.	1932
Reese, Della	Detroit, Mich.	1932
Regan, Phil	Brooklyn, N.Y.	1906
Reid, Kate	London, England.	1930
Reilly, Charles Nelson	New York, N.Y.	1931
Reiner, Carl	Bronx, N.Y.	1922
Reiner, Rob	Bronx, N.Y.	1945
Remick, Lee	Boston, Mass.	1937
Renaldo, Duncan	Camden, N.J.	1904
Resnik, Regina	New York, N.Y.	1923
Rey, Alejandro	Buenos Aires, Brazil.	1930
Reynolds, Burt	Waycross, Ga.	1936
Reynolds, Debbie	El Paso, Tex.	1932
Reynolds, Marjorie	Buhl, Ida.	1921
Reynolds, William	Los Angeles, Cal.	1931
Rhodes, Hari	Cincinnati, Ohio	1932
Rich, Charlie	Forest City, Ark.	1932
Rich, Irene	Buffalo, N.Y.	1897
Richardson, Ralph	Cheltenham, England	1902
Richardson, Tony	Shipley, England.	1929
Rickles, Don	New York, N.Y.	1926
Riddle, Nelson	Hackensack, N.J.	1921
Rigg, Diana	England	1938
Ritchard, Cyril	Sydney, Australia.	1898
Ritz, Harry	Newark, N.J.	1908
Ritz, Jimmy	Newark, N.J.	1905
Rivers, Joan	Brooklyn, N.Y.	1937
Robards, Jason Jr.	Chicago, Ill.	1922
Robbins, Jerome	New York, N.Y.	1918
Robbins, Marty	Glendale, Ariz.	1925
Robertson, Cliff	La Jolla, Cal.	1925
Robertson, Dale	Oklahoma City, Okla.	1923
Robinson, Jay	New York, N.Y.	1930
Robson, Flora	South Shields, England.	1902
Rochester (E. Anderson)	Oakland, Cal.	1905
Rockwell, Geo. (Doc.)	Providence, R.I.	1889
Rodgers, Jimmie	Camas, Wash.	1933
Rodriquez, Johnny	Sabinal, Tex.	1951
Rogers, Chas. (Buddy)	Olathe, Kan.	1904
Rogers, Ginger	Independence, Mo.	1911
Rogers, Roy	Cincinnati, Ohio	1912
Roland, Gilbert	Juarez, Mexico.	1905
Rolle, Esther	Pompano Beach, Fla.	—
Roman, Ruth	Boston, Mass.	1924
Romero, Cesar	New York, N.Y.	1907
Rooney, Mickey	Brooklyn, N.Y.	1920
Rose Marie	New York, N.Y.	—
Ross, David	St. Paul, Minn.	1924
Ross, Diana	Detroit, Mich.	1944
Ross, Katharine	Hollywood, Cal.	1943
Ross, Lanny	Seattle, Wash.	1906
Roth, Lillian	Boston, Mass.	1910
Roundtree, Richard	New Rochelle, N.Y.	1942
Rowan, Dan	Beggs, Okla.	1922
Rowlands, Gena	Cambria, Wis.	1936
Rubin, Benny	Boston, Mass.	1899
Rubinoff, David	Grodno, Russia.	1897
Rubinstein, Artur	Lodz, Poland.	1889
Rudolf, Max	Frankfurt, Germany.	1902
Rule, Janice	Norwood, Ohio.	1931
Rush, Barbara	Denver, Col.	1930

Name	Birthplace	Born
Russell, Jane	Bemidji, Minn.	1921
Russell, Ken	Southampton, England	1927
Russell, Nipsy	Atlanta, Ga.	1924
Russell, Rosalind	Waterbury, Conn.	1911
Rutherford, Ann	Toronto, Canada.	1924
Ryan, Peggy	Long Beach, Cal.	1924
Rydell, Bobby	Philadelphia, Pa.	1942

S

Name	Birthplace	Born
Sahl, Mort	Montreal, Que., Canada.	1927
Saint, Eva Marie	Newark, N.J.	1924
Sainte-Marie, Buffy	Craven, Sask., Canada.	1941
St. James, Susan	Los Angeles, Cal.	1946
St. John, Jill	Los Angeles, Cal.	1940
Sales, Soupy	Franklinton, N.C.	1926
Sand, Paul	Los Angeles, Cal.	1941
Sands, Tommy	Chicago, Ill.	1937
Sargent, Dick	Carmel, Cal.	1933
Sarnoff, Dorothy	New York, N.Y.	1919
Sarrazin, Michael	Quebec City, Que., Can.	1940
Saunders, Lori	Kansas City, Mo.	1941
Savalas, Telly	Garden City, N.Y.	1927
Saxon, John	Brooklyn, N.Y.	1935
Sayao, Bidu	Rio de Janeiro, Brazil.	1908
Shallert, William	Los Angeles, Cal.	1922
Schary, Dore	Newark, N.J.	1905
Scheider, Roy	Orange, N.J.	1934
Schell, Maria	Vienna, Austria.	1926
Schell, Maximilian	Vienna, Austria	1930
Schenkel, Chris	Bippus, Ind.	1924
Scherman, Thomas	New York, N.Y.	1917
Schippers, Thomas	Kalamazoo, Mich.	1930
Schneider, Alexander	Vilna, Poland.	1908
Schneider, Romy	Austria	1938
Schreiber, Avery	Chicago, Ill.	1935
Schuman, William	New York, N.Y.	1910
Schwarzkopf, Elisabeth	Jarotschin, Poland.	1915
Scofield, Paul	Hurst, Pierpont, England.	1922
Scott, George C.	Wise, Va.	1927
Scott, Hazel	Trinidad.	1920
Scott, Lizabeth	Scranton, Pa.	1923
Scott, Martha	Jamesport, Mo.	1914
Scott, Randolph	Orange Co., Va.	1903
Scourby, Alexander	New York, N.Y.	1913
Sebastian, John	New York, N.Y.	1944
Seberg, Jean	Marshalltown, Ia.	1938
Seeger, Pete	New York, N.Y.	1919
Segal, George	Great Neck, N.Y.	1934
Segal, Vivienne	Philadelphia, Pa.	1897
Sellers, Peter	Southsea, England.	1925
Serkin, Rudolf	Eger, Austria?	1903
Severinsen, Doc	Arlington, Ore.	1927
Shankar, Ravi	India.	1920
Sharif, Omar	Alexandria, Egypt.	1932
Shatner, William	Montreal, Canada.	1931
Shaw, Reta	S. Paris, Me.	1912
Shaw, Robert	Red Bluff, Cal.	1916
Shaw, Robert	West Houghton, England.	1927
Shaw, Winfred	Sari Francisco, Cal.	1899
Shawn, Dick	Buffalo, N.Y.	1929
Shearer, Moira	Scotland.	1926
Shearer, Norma	Montreal, Canada	1904
Sheen, Martin	Dayton, Ohio.	1940
Sheldon, Jack	Jacksonville, Fla.	1931
Shepherd, Cybill	Memphis, Tenn.	1950
Shepherd, Jean	Chicago, Ill.	1929
Sherman, Bobby	Santa Monica, Cal.	1945
Sherwood, Roberta	St. Louis, Mo.	1913
Shirley, Ann	New York, N.Y.	1918
Shore, Dinah	Winchester, Tenn.	1921
Short, Bobby	Danville, Ill.	1936
Sidney, Sylvia	New York, N.Y.	1910
Siepi, Cesare	Milan, Italy.	1923
Signoret, Simone	Wiesbaden, Germany.	1921
Sills, Beverly	Brooklyn, N.Y.	1929
Silvers, Phil	Brooklyn, N.Y.	1912
Sim, Alastair	Edinburgh, Scotland	1900
Simmons, Jean	London, England.	1929
Simon, Paul	New York, N.Y.	1940
Simon, Simone	Marseilles, France	1914
Simone, Nina	Tyron, N.C.	1933
Sinatra, Frank	Hoboken, N.J.	1915
Sinatra Jr., Frank	Jersey City, N.J.	1944
Sinatra, Nancy	Jersey City, N.J.	1940
Skelton, Red (Richard)	Vincennes, Ind.	1913
Skinner, Cornelia Otis	Chicago, Ill.	1903
Slezak, Walter	Vienna, Austria	1902
Slick, Grace	Chicago, Ill.	1939
Smith, Alexis	Penticton, Canada	1921

Name	Birthplace	Born	Name	Birthplace	Born
Smith, Bob	Buffalo, N.Y.	1917	Thaxter, Phillis	Portland, Me.	1921
Smith, Connie	Elkhart, Ind.	1941	Theborn, Blanche	Monessen, Pa.	1919
Smith, Ethel	Pittsburgh, Pa.	1921	Thibault, Conrad	Northbridge, Mass.	1898
Smith, Kate	Greenville, Va.	1909	Thinnes, Roy	Chicago, Ill.	1938
Smith, Keely	Norfolk, Va.	1935	Thomas, B.J.	Houston, Tex.	1942
Smith, Loring	Stratford, Conn.	1900	Thomas, Danny	Deerfield, Mich.	1914
Smith, Maggie	Ilford, England	1934	Thomas, Lowell	Woodrington, Ohio	1892
Smith, Roger	South Gate, Cal.	1934	Thomas, Marlo	Detroit, Mich.	1943
Smothers, Dick	New York, N.Y.	1939	Thomas, Richard	New York, N.Y.	1951
Smothers, Tom	New York, N.Y.	1937	Thompson, Marshall	Peoria, Ill.	1926
Snodgrass, Carrie	Park Ridge, Ill.	1945	Thompson, Sada	Des Moines, Ia.	1929
Snow, Hank	Nova Scotia, Canada	1914	Thulin, Ingrid	Sweden	1929
Somes, Michael	nr. Stroud, England	1917	Tierney, Gene	Brooklyn, N.Y.	1920
Sommer, Elke	Berlin, Germany	1942	Tierney, Lawrence	Brooklyn, N.Y.	1919
Sorvino, Paul	Brooklyn, N.Y.	1939	Tiffin, Pamela	Oklahoma City, Okla.	1942
Sothern, Ann	Valley City, N.D.	1912	Tillstrom, Burr	Chicago, Ill.	1917
Specht, Bobby	Superior, Wis.	1921	Tiny Tim	New York, N.Y.	—
Spewack, Bella	Hungary	1899	Tobias, George	New York, N.Y.	1901
Spivak, Lawrence	Brooklyn, N.Y.	1900	Todd, Richard	Dublin, Ireland	1919
Stack, Robert	Los Angeles, Cal.	1919	Tomlin, Lili	Detroit, Mich.	1939
Stafford, Jo	Coalinga, Cal.	1918	Tomlinson, David	Scotland	1917
Stamp, Terence	London, England	1940	Tompkins, Angel	Albany, Cal.	1943
Stang, Arnold	Chelsea, Mass.	1925	Toomey, Regis	Pittsburgh, Pa.	1902
Stanley, Kim	Tularosa, N.M.	1925	Torme, Mel	Chicago, Ill.	1925
Stanwyck, Barbara	Brooklyn, N.Y.	1907	Torn, Rip	Temple, Tex.	1931
Stapleton, Jean	New York, N.Y.	1923	Totter, Audrey	Joliet, Ill.	1923
Stapleton, Maureen	Troy, N.Y.	1925	Tracy, Arthur	Philadelphia, Pa.	1903
Starr, Kay	Dougherty, Okla.	1924	Travers, Mary	Louisville, Ky.	1936
Starr, Ringo	Liverpool, England	1940	Trevor, Claire	New York, N.Y.	1909
Steber, Eleanor	Wheeling, W. Va.	1916	Truffaut, Francois	Paris, France	1932
Steele, Bob	Pendleton, Ore.	1907	Tryon, Tom	Hartford, Conn.	1926
Steele, Karen	Hawaii	1934	Tucker, Forrest	Plainfield, Ind.	1919
Steele, Tommy	London, England	1937	Tucker, Orrin	St. Louis, Mo.	1911
Steiger, Rod	W. Hampton, N.Y.	1925	Tucker, Tanya	Seminole, Tex.	1958
Steinberg, David	Winnipeg, Canada	1942	Tucker, Tommy	Souris, N.D.	1907
Sterling, Jan	New York, N.Y.	1923	Turner, Lana	Wallace, Ida.	1920
Sterling, Robert	New Castle, Pa.	1917	Tushingham, Rita	Liverpool, England	1942
Stern, Isaac	Kreminisey, Russia	1920	Twiggy (Leslie Hornby)	London, England	1949
Stevens, Cat	London, England	1948	Twitty, Conway	Friar's Point, Miss.	—
Stevens, Connie	Brooklyn, N.Y.	1938	Tyrell, Susan	New Canaan, Conn.	1946
Stevens, Kaye	Pittsburgh, Pa.	1935	Tyson, Cicely	New York, N.Y.	—
Stevens, Mark	Cleveland, Ohio	1922			
Stevens, Onslow	Los Angeles, Cal.	1902		**U**	
Stevens, Rise	New York, N.Y.	1913	Uggams, Leslie	New York, N.Y.	1943
Stevens, Stella	Yazoo City, Miss.	1938	Ullman, Liv	Tokyo, Japan	1939
Stevens, Warren	Clark's Summit, Pa.	1919	Umeki, Miyoshi	Hokkaido, Japan	1929
Stewart, James	Indiana, Pa.	1908	Ustinov, Peter	London, England	1921
Stewart, Rod	London, England	1944			
Stickney, Dorothy	Dickinson, N.D.	1903		**V**	
Stockwell, Dean	Hollywood, Cal.	1936	Vaccaro, Brenda	Brooklyn, N.Y.	1939
Stokowski, Leopold	London, England	1882	Vale, Jerry	New York, N.Y.	1931
Stone, Carol	New York, N.Y.	1916	Valente, Caterina	Italy	1931
Stone, Dorothy	Bensonhurst, N.Y.	1905	Valentine, Karen	Santa Rosa, Cal.	1947
Stone, Ezra	New Bedford, Mass.	1917	Vallee, Rudy	Island Pond, Vt.	1901
Stone, Milburn	Burton, Kan.	1904	Valli, Alida	Pola, Italy	1921
Stone, Paula	New York, N.Y.	1916	Vance, Vivian	Cherryvale, Kan.	1912
Storch, Larry	New York, N.Y.	1925	Van Cleef, Lee	Somerville, N.J.	1925
Storm, Gale	Bloomington, Tex.	1922	Van Doren, Mamie	Rowena, S.D.	1933
Storrs, Suzanne	Salt Lake City, Ut.	1934	Van Dyke, Dick	West Plains, Mo.	1925
Straight, Beatrice	Old Westbury, N.Y.	1918	Van Dyke, Jerry	Danville, Ill.	1932
Strasberg, Susan	New York, N.Y.	1938	Van Fleet, Jo	Oakland, Cal.	1922
Streisand, Barbra	Brooklyn, N.Y.	1942	Van Vooren, Monique	Brussels, Belgium	1933
Stritch, Elaine	Detroit, Mich.	1925	Vandervere, Trish	Tenafly, N.J.	1945
Strode, Woody	Los Angeles, Cal.	1914	Varnay, Astrid	Stockholm, Sweden	1918
Struthers, Sally	Portland, Ore.	1948	Varsi, Diane	San Francisco, Cal.	1938
Sullivan, Barry	New York, N.Y.	1912	Vaughn, Robert	New York, N.Y.	1932
Sumac, Yma	Ichocan, Peru	1928	Vaughn, Sarah	Newark, N.J.	1924
Susskind, David	New York, N.Y.	1920	Venuta, Benay	San Francisco, Cal.	1911
Sutherland, Donald	New Brunswick, Canada	1934	Vera-Ellen	Cincinnati, Ohio	1926
Sutherland, Joan	Sydney, Australia	1926	Verdon, Gwen	Los Angeles, Cal.	1926
Suzuki, Pat	Cressey, Cal.	1931	Vereen, Ben	Miami, Fla.	1946
Swanson, Gloria	Chicago, Ill.	1899	Vernon, Jackie	New York, N.Y.	1929
Sweet, Blanche	Chicago, Ill.	1896	Vidor, King Louis	Galveston, Tex.	1895
Swit, Loretta	Passaic, N.J.	—	Villella, Edward	Long Island, N.Y.	1936
			Vinson, Helen	Beaumont, Tex.	1907
	T		Vinton, Bobby	Canonsburg, Pa.	1935
Talbot, Lyle	Pittsburgh, Pa.	1902	Vogel, Mitch	Alhambra, Cal.	1956
Talbot, Nita	New York, N.Y.	1930	Voight, Jon	Yonkers, N.Y.	1938
Tallchief, Maria	Fairfax, Okla.	1925	Von Furstenberg, Betsy	Westphalia, Germany	1932
Tamblyn, Russ	Los Angeles, Cal.	1935	Von Sydow, Max	Lund, Sweden	1929
Tandy, Jessica	London, England	1909	Von Zell, Harry	Indianapolis, Ind.	1906
Taylor, Elizabeth	London, England	1932	Voorhees, Donald	Allentown, Pa.	1903
Taylor, James	Boston, Mass.	1948			
Taylor, Kent	Nashua, Ia.	1907		**W**	
Taylor, Rod	Sydney, Australia	1930	Waggoner, Lyle	Kansas City, Kan.	1935
Tebaldi, Renata	Pesaro, Italy	1922	Wagner, Robert	Detroit, Mich.	1930
Temple, Shirley	Santa Monica, Cal.	1928	Wagoner, Porter	West Plains, Mo.	1927
Terris, Norma	Columbus, Kan.	1904	Wain, Bea	Bronx, N.Y.	1917
Terry-Thomas	London, England	1911	Waite, Ralph	White Plains, N.Y.	1928

Name	Birthplace	Born	Name	Birthplace	Born
Walker, Clint	Hartford, Ill.	1927	Wilson, Demond	Valdosta, Ga.	—
Walker, Nancy	Philadelphia, Pa.	1922	Wilson, Dolores	Philadelphia, Pa.	1929
Wallace, Mike	Brookline, Mass.	1918	Wilson, Don	Lincoln, Neb.	1900
Wallach, Eli	Brooklyn, N.Y.	1915	Wilson, Flip	Jersey City, N.J.	1933
Wallenstein, Alfred	Chicago, Ill.	1898	Wilson, Julie	Omaha, Neb.	1924
Wallis, Hal	Chicago, Ill.	1899	Wilson, Nancy	Chillicothe, Oh.	1937
Walston, Ray	New Orleans, La.	1918	Winchell, Paul	New York, N.Y.	1922
Ward, Burt	Los Angeles, Cal.	1946	Windom, William	New York, N.Y.	1923
Warden, Jack	Newark, N.J.	1920	Winkler, Henry	New York, N.Y.	1945
Warfield, William	Helena, Ark.	1920	Winters, Jonathan	Dayton, Ohio	1925
Warhol, Andy	Cleveland, Oh.	1931	Winters, Shelley	St. Louis, Mo.	1922
Waring, Fred	Tyrone, Pa.	1900	Winwood, Estelle	Lee, England	1884
Warner, David	Manchester, England	1941	Wiseman, Joseph	Montreal, Canada	1918
Warwicke, Dionne	E. Orange, N.J.	1941	Withers, Jane	Atlanta, Ga.	1927
Waters, Ethel	Chester, Pa.	1900	Wonder, Stevie	Detroit, Mich.	1951
Watts, Andre	Germany	1946	Wood, Helen	Clarksville, Tenn.	1937
Wayne, David	Traverse City, Mich.	1914	Wood, Natalie	San Francisco, Cal.	1938
Wayne, John	Winterset, Ia.	1907	Wood, Peggy	Brooklyn, N.Y.	1892
Weaver, Dennis	Joplin, Mo.	1924	Woodward, Joanne	Thomasville, Ga.	1930
Weaver, Fritz	Pittsburgh, Pa.	1926	Worley, Jo Anne	Lowell, Ind.	1937
Webb, Jack	Santa Monica, Cal.	1920	Worth, Irene	Nebraska	1916
Weissmuller, Johnny	Windber, Pa.	1904	Wray, Fay	Alberta, Canada	1907
Welch, Raquel	Chicago, Ill.	1942	Wright, Martha	Seattle, Wash.	1926
Weld, Tuesday	New York, N.Y.	1943	Wright, Teresa	New York, N.Y.	1919
Welk, Lawrence	nr. Strasburg, N.D.	1903	Wrightson, Earl	Baltimore, Md.	1916
Welles, Orson	Kenosha, Wis.	1915	Wyatt, Jane	Campgaw, N.J.	1912
Wells, Kitty	Nashville, Tenn.	1919	Wyler, William	Mulhouse, France	1902
Werner, Oskar	Vienna, Austria	1922	Wyman, Jane	St. Joseph, Mo.	1914
West, Adam	Walla Walla, Wash.	1929	Wynette, Tammy	Red Bay, Ala.	1942
West, Mae	Brooklyn, N.Y.	1892	Wynn, Keenan	New York, N.Y.	1916
Whitaker, Johnny	Van Nuys, Cal.	1959	Wynter, Dana	London, England	1930
White, Jesse	Buffalo, N.Y.	1919			
Whiting, Margaret	Detroit, Mich.	1924	**Y**		
Whitman, Stuart	San Francisco, Cal.	1936	Yarborough, Glenn	Milwaukee, Wis.	1930
Whitmore, James	White Plains, N.Y.	1921	Yarrow, Peter	New York, N.Y.	1938
Widmark, Richard	Sunrise, Minn.	1914	York, Dick	Ft. Wayne, Ind.	1928
Wilcoxon, Henry	British West Indies	1905	York, Michael	Fulmer, England	1942
Wilde, Cornel	New York, N.Y.	1918	York, Susannah	London, England	1942
Wilder, Billy	Vienna, Austria	1906	Young, Alan	Northumberl'd, England	1919
Wilder, Gene	Milwaukee, Wis.	1935	Young, Gig	St. Cloud, Minn.	1917
Wilding, Michael	Essex, England	1912	Young, Loretta	Salt Lake City, Ut.	1913
Williams, Andy	Wall Lake, Ia.	1930	Young, Robert	Chicago, Ill.	1907
Williams, Clarence	New York, N.Y.	1946	Young, Stephen	Toronto, Canada	1939
Williams, Emlyn	Mostyn, Wales	1905	Youngman, Henny	Liverpool, England	1906
Williams, Esther	Los Angeles, Cal.	1923			
Williams, Joe	Cordele, Ga.	1918	**Z**		
Williams, Mason	Abilene, Tex.	1938	Zanuck, Darryl F.	Wahoo, Neb.	1902
Williams, Paul	Omaha, Neb.	1940	Zimbalist, Efrem	Rostov, Russia	1889
Williams, Roger	Omaha, Neb.	1926	Zimbalist, Efrem Jr.	New York, N.Y.	1923
Williamson, Fred	Gary, Ind.	1937	Zimmer, Norma	Larsen, Ida.	—
Williamson, Nicol	Hamilton, Scotland	1936	Zorina, Vera	Berlin, Germany	1917
Wills, Chill	Seagoville, Tex.	1903			

Entertainment Personalities of the Past

Born	Died	Name	Born	Died	Name	Born	Died	Name
		A	1903	1951	Bailey, Mildred	1894	1974	Benny, Jack
1896	1974	Abbott, Bud	1893	1968	Bainter, Fay	1867	1944	Beresford, Harry
1872	1953	Adams, Maude	1895	1957	Baker, Belle	1899	1966	Berg, Gertrude
1931	1968	Adams, Nick	1906	1975	Baker, Josephine	1895	1976	Berkeley, Busby
1855	1926	Adler, Jacob P.	1898	1963	Baker, Phil	1863	1927	Bernard, Sam
1898	1933	Adoree, Renee	1882	1956	Bancroft, George	1844	1923	Bernhardt, Sarah
1909	1964	Albertson, Frank	1903	1968	Bankhead, Tallulah	1893	1943	Bernie, Ben
1885	1952	Alda, Frances	1890	1952	Banks, Leslie	1889	1967	Bickford, Charles
1894	1956	Allen, Fred	1897	1950	Banks, Monty	1911	1960	Bjoerling, Jussi
1906	1964	Allen, Gracie	1890	1955	Bara, Theda	1898	1973	Blackmer, Sidney
1883	1950	Allgood, Sara	1810	1891	Barnum, Phineas T.	1882	1951	Blaney, Charles E.
1882	1971	Anderson, Gilbert (Bronco Billy)	1879	1959	Barrymore, Ethel	1900	1943	Bledsoe, Jules
1886	1954	Anderson, John Murray	1882	1942	Barrymore, John	1928	1972	Blocker, Dan
1915	1967	Andrews, Laverne	1878	1954	Barrymore, Lionel	1888	1959	Blore, Eric
1933	1971	Angeli, Pier	1848	1905	Barrymore, Maurice	1901	1975	Blue, Ben
1876	1958	Anglin, Margaret	1897	1963	Barthelmess, Richard	1899	1957	Bogart, Humphrey
1887	1933	Arbuckle, Fatty (Roscoe)	1890	1962	Barton, James	1885	1965	Boland, Mary
1900	1976	Arlen, Richard	1873	1951	Bauer, Harold	1897	1969	Boles, John
1868	1946	Arliss, George	1893	1951	Baxter, Warner	1903	1960	Bond, Ward
1900	1971	Armstrong, Louis	1880	1928	Bayes, Nora	1833	1893	Booth, Edwin
1890	1956	Arnold, Edward	1904	1965	Beatty, Clyde	1796	1852	Booth, Junius Brutus
1905	1974	Arquette, Cliff (Charlie Weaver)	1904	1962	Beavers, Louise	1894	1953	Bordoni, Irene
1885	1946	Atwill, Lionel	1887	1955	Beecher, Janet	1888	1960	Bori, Lucrezia
1845	1930	Auer, Leopold	1884	1946	Beery, Noah	1867	1943	Bosworth, Hobart
1905	1967	Auer, Mischa	1889	1949	Beery, Wallace	1905	1965	Bow, Clara
1900	1972	Austin, Gene	1901	1970	Begley, Ed	1874	1946	Bowes, Maj. Edward
1898	1940	Ayres, Agnes	1854	1931	Belasco, David	1895	1972	Boyd, William
		B	1906	1968	Benaderet, Bea	1893	1939	Brady, Alice
1864	1922	Bacon, Frank	1906	1964	Bendix, William	1863	1950	Brady, William A.
			1905	1965	Bennett, Constance	1871	1936	Breese, Edmund
			1924	1970	Benzell, Mimi	1898	1964	Brendel, El
			1873	1944	Bennett, Richard	1901	1948	Breneman, Tom

Born	Died	Name
1894	1974	Brennan, Walter
1875	1948	Brian, Donald
1891	1951	Brice, Fanny
1891	1959	Broderick, Helen
1898	1965	Brokenshire, Norman
1904	1951	Bromberg, J. Edward
1892	1973	Brown, Joe E.
1926	1966	Bruce, Lenny
1895	1953	Bruce, Nigel
1891	1957	Buchanan, Jack
1886	1957	Buck, Gene
1904	1965	Bunce, Alan
1863	1915	Bunny, John
1885	1970	Burke, Billie
1912	1967	Burnette, Smiley
1896	1956	Burns, Bob
1902	1971	Burns, David
1882	1941	Burr, Henry
1883	1966	Bushman, Francis X.
1896	1946	Butterworth, Charles
1893	1971	Byington, Spring

C

Born	Died	Name
1905	1972	Cabot, Bruce
1895	1956	Calhern, Louis
1858	1942	Calve, Emma
1865	1940	Campbell, Mrs. Patrick
1892	1964	Cantor, Eddie
1878	1947	Carey, Harry
1876	1941	Carle, Richard
1897	1954	Carney, "Uncle Don"
1880	1961	Carrillo, Leo
1892	1972	Carroll, Leo G.
1905	1965	Carroll, Nancy
1910	1963	Carson, Jack
1862	1937	Carter, Mrs. Leslie
1873	1921	Caruso, Enrico
1876	1973	Casals, Pablo
1894	1969	Castle, Irene
1887	1918	Castle, Vernon
1889	1960	Catlett, Walter
1874	1944	Cavalieri, Lina
1887	1950	Cavanaugh, Hobart
1873	1938	Chaliapin, Feodor
1919	1961	Chandler, Jeff
1883	1930	Chaney, Lon
1906	1973	Chaney Jr., Lon
1893	1940	Chase, Charlie
1893	1961	Chatterton, Ruth
1888	1971	Chevalier, Maurice
1888	1960	Clark, Bobby
1914	1968	Clark, Fred
1887	1950	Clayton, Lou
1920	1966	Clift, Montgomery
1900	1937	Clive, Colin
1932	1963	Cline, Patsy
1892	1967	Clyde, Andy
1911	1976	Cobb, Lee J.
1877	1961	Coburn, Charles
1887	1934	Cody, Lew
1878	1942	Cohan, George M.
1876	1916	Cohan, Josephine
1919	1965	Cole, Nat (King)
1878	1955	Collier, Constance
1866	1944	Collier, William, Sr.
1890	1965	Collins, Ray
1891	1958	Colman, Ronald
1908	1934	Columbo, Russ
1907	1944	Compton, Betty
1887	1940	Connolly, Walter
1855	1909	Conried, Henrich
1918	1975	Conte, Richard
1904	1967	Conway, Tom
1901	1961	Cook, Donald
1890	1959	Cook, Joe
1893	1958	Cook, Phil
1901	1961	Cooper, Gary
1891	1971	Cooper, Gladys
1896	1973	Cooper, Melville
1914	1968	Corey, Wendell
1893	1974	Cornell, Katherine
1890	1972	Correll, Charles
1876	1951	Cossart, Ernest
1904	1957	Costello, Helene
1906	1959	Costello, Lou
1877	1950	Costello, Maurice
1899	1973	Coward, Noel
1890	1950	Cowl, Jane
1924	1973	Cox, Wally

Born	Died	Name
1847	1924	Crabtree, Lotta
1875	1945	Craven, Frank
1916	1944	Cregar, Laird
1880	1942	Crews, Laura Hope
1880	1974	Crisp, Donald
1943	1973	Croce, Jim
1910	1960	Cromwell, Richard
1897	1975	Cross, Milton
1893	1966	Crouse, Russell
1878	1968	Currie, Finlay
1816	1876	Cushman, Charlotte

D

Born	Died	Name
1924	1965	Dandridge, Dorothy
1869	1941	Danforth, William
1894	1963	Daniell, Henry
1901	1971	Daniels, Bebe
1860	1935	Daniels, Frank
1936	1973	Darin, Bobby
1921	1965	Darnell, Linda
1894	1967	Darwell, Jane
1866	1949	Davenport, Harry
1900	1961	Davies, Marion
1908	1961	Davis, Joan
1931	1955	Dean, James
1881	1950	DeCordoba, Pedro
1905	1968	Dekker, Albert
1898	1965	Demarco, Tony
1881	1959	DeMille, Cecil B.
1891	1967	Denny, Reginald
1902	1974	DeSica, Vittorio
1878	1949	Desmond, William
1878	1930	Destinn, Emmy
1942	1972	De Wilde, Brandon
1907	1974	De Wolfe, Billy
1865	1950	De Wolfe, Elsie
1879	1947	Digges, Dudley
1890	1944	Dinehart, Alan
1901	1966	Disney, Walt
1895	1949	Dix, Richard
1856	1924	Dockstader, Lew
1892	1941	Dolly, Jennie
1892	1970	Dolly, Rosie
1905	1958	Donat, Robert
1903	1972	Donlevy, Brian
1907	1959	Douglas, Paul
1889	1956	Draper, Ruth
1881	1965	Dresser, Louise
1869	1934	Dressler, Marie
1820	1897	Drew, Mrs. John
1853	1927	Drew, John (son)
1879	1920	Drew, Sydney
1909	1951	Duchin, Eddy
1940	1971	Duel, Peter
1890	1965	Dumont, Margaret
1877	1927	Duncan, Isadora
1905	1967	Dunn, James
1873	1947	Dupree, Minnie
1907	1968	Duryea, Dan
1859	1924	Duse, Eleanora

E

Born	Died	Name
1894	1929	Eagles, Jeanne
1896	1930	Eames, Clare
1865	1952	Eames, Emma
1901	1967	Eddy, Nelson
1894	1971	Edwards, Cliff
1879	1945	Edwards, Gus
1899	1974	Ellington, Duke
1941	1974	Elliot, Cass
1871	1940	Elliott, Maxine
1891	1967	Elman, Mischa
1881	1951	Errol, Leon
1903	1967	Erwin, Stuart
1913	1967	Evelyn, Judith

F

Born	Died	Name
1883	1939	Fairbanks, Douglas
1915	1970	Farmer, Frances
1870	1929	Farnum, Dustin
1876	1953	Farnum, William
1882	1967	Farrar, Geraldine
1904	1971	Farrell, Glenda
1868	1940	Faversham, William
1861	1939	Fawcett, George
1897	1960	Fay, Frank
1895	1962	Fazenda, Louise
1903	1971	Fernandel
1918	1973	Field, Betty

Born	Died	Name
1867	1941	Fields, Lew
1879	1946	Fields, W. C.
1902	1975	Fine, Larry
1865	1932	Fiske, Minnie Maddern
1888	1961	Fitzgerald, Barry
1874	1941	Fitzgerald, Cissy
1895	1962	Flagstad, Kirsten
1900	1971	Flippen, Jay C.
1909	1959	Flynn, Errol
1925	1974	Flynn, Joe
1880	1942	Fokine, Michel
1910	1968	Foley, Red
1905	1951	Forbes, Ralph
1853	1937	Forbes-Robertson
1887	1970	Ford, Ed (Senator)
1895	1973	Ford, John
1901	1976	Ford, Paul
1899	1965	Ford, Wallace
1806	1872	Forrest, Edwin
1904	1970	Foster, Preston
1854	1928	Foy, Eddie
1905	1968	Francis, Kay
1893	1966	Frawley, William
1885	1938	Frederick, Pauline
1870	1955	Friganza, Trixie
1890	1958	Frisco, Joe
1860	1915	Frohman, Charles
1851	1940	Frohman, Daniel
1885	1947	Fyffe, Will

G

Born	Died	Name
1901	1960	Gable, Clark
1889	1963	Galli-Curci, Amelita
1877	1967	Garden, Mary
1913	1952	Garfield, John
1922	1969	Garland, Judy
1893	1963	Gaxton, William
1904	1954	George, Gladys
1879	1961	George, Grace
1892	1962	Gibson, Hoot
1890	1957	Gigli, Beniamino
1894	1971	Gilbert, Billy
1897	1936	Gilbert, John
1855	1937	Gillette, William
1867	1943	Gillmore, Frank
1879	1939	Gilpin, Charles
1898	1968	Gish, Dorothy
1886	1959	Gleason, James
1884	1938	Gluck, Alma
1874	1955	Golden, John
1882	1974	Goldwyn, Samuel
1917	1969	Gorcey, Leo
1884	1940	Gordon, C. Henry
1887	1948	Gordon, Vera
1869	1944	Gottschalk, Ferdinand
1829	1869	Gottschalk, Louis
1916	1973	Grable, Betty
1901	1959	Gray, Gilda
1879	1954	Greenstreet, Sydney
1874	1948	Griffith, David Wark
1885	1957	Guitry, Sacha
1912	1967	Guthrie, Woody
1875	1959	Gwenn, Edmund

H

Born	Died	Name
1888	1942	Hackett, Charles
1902	1958	Hackett, Raymond
1870	1943	Haines, Robert T.
1892	1950	Hale, Alan
1847	1919	Hammerstein, Oscar
1895	1960	Hammerstein, Oscar, 2d
1879	1955	Hampden, Walter
1924	1964	Haney, Carol
1893	1964	Hardwicke, Sir Cedric
1892	1957	Hardy, Oliver
1883	1939	Hare, T. E. (Ernie)
1911	1937	Harlow, Jean
1872	1946	Harned, Virginia
1844	1911	Harrigan, Edward
1895	1943	Hart, Lorenz
1870	1946	Hart, William S.
1907	1955	Hartman, Grace
1928	1973	Harvey, Laurence
1876	1945	Harwood, John
1910	1973	Hawkins, Jack
1890	1973	Hayakawa, Sessue
1885	1969	Hayes, Gabby
1902	1971	Hayward, Leland
1919	1975	Hayward, Susan

Born	Died	Name
1896	1937	Healy, Ted
1910	1971	Heflin, Van
1879	1936	Heggie, O. P.
1873	1918	Held, Anna
1903	1947	Hellinger, Mark
1885	1955	Hempel, Frieda
1943	1970	Hendrix, Jimi
1913	1969	Henie, Sonja
1879	1942	Herbert, Henry
1887	1951	Herbert, Hugh
1886	1956	Hersholt, Jean
1895	1942	Hibbard, Edna
1857	1927	Hillard, Robert C.
1865	1929	Hitchcock, Raymond
1914	1955	Hodiak, John
1876	1957	Hofmann, Josef
1894	1973	Holden, Fay
1923	1965	Holliday, Judy
1888	1951	Holt, Jack
1871	1947	Homer, Louise
1902	1973	Hopkins, Miriam
1858	1935	Hopper, DeWolf
1874	1959	Hopper, Edna Wallace
1890	1966	Hopper, Hedda
1916	1970	Hopper, William
1888	1970	Horton, Edward Everett
1874	1926	Houdini, Harry
1881	1965	Howard, Eugene
1867	1961	Howard, Joe
1893	1943	Howard, Leslie
1897	1975	Howard, Moe
1886	1955	Howard, Tom
1886	1949	Howard, Willie
1914	1972	Hudson, Rochelle
1886	1957	Hull, Josephine
1907	1967	Hume, Benita
1895	1958	Humphrey, Doris
1895	1945	Hunter, Glenn
1925	1969	Hunter, Jeffrey
1901	1962	Husing, Ted
1884	1950	Huston, Walter

I

Born	Died	Name
1892	1950	Ingram, Rex
1895	1969	Ingram, Rex
1838	1905	Irving, Henry
1871	1944	Irving, Isabel
1872	1914	Irving, Laurence
1862	1938	Irwin, May

J

Born	Died	Name
1875	1942	Jackson, Joe
1911	1972	Jackson, Mahalia
1889	1956	Janis, Elsie
1886	1950	Jannings, Emil
1829	1905	Jefferson, Joseph
1859	1923	Jefferson, Thomas
1900	1974	Jenkins, Allen
1862	1930	Jewett, Henry
1892	1962	Johnson, Chic
1878	1952	Johnson, Edward
1888	1950	Jolson, Al
1899	1940	Jones, Billy
1889	1942	Jones, Buck
1911	1965	Jones, Spike
1943	1970	Joplin, Janis
1897	1961	Jordan, Marian
		(Molly McGee)
1890	1955	Joyce, Alice

K

Born	Died	Name
1878	1965	Kaltenborn, Hans V.
1910	1966	Kane, Helen
1887	1969	Karloff, Boris
1893	1970	Karns, Roscoe
1811	1868	Kean, Charles
1806	1880	Kean, Mrs. Charles
1787	1833	Kean, Edmund
1895	1966	Keaton, Buster
1858	1929	Keenan, Frank
1830	1873	Keene, Laura
1841	1898	Keene, Thomas W.
1899	1960	Keith, Ian
1894	1973	Kellaway, Cecil
1899	1956	Kelly, Paul
1873	1939	Kelly, Walter C.
1909	1968	Kelton, Pert
1823	1895	Kemble, Agnes

Born	Died	Name
1775	1854	Kemble, Charles
1809	1893	Kemble, Fannie
1848	1935	Kendal, Dame Madge
1843	1917	Kendal, William H.
1926	1959	Kendall, Kay
1890	1948	Kennedy, Edgar
1885	1965	Kennedy, Tom
1886	1945	Kent, William
1880	1947	Kerrigan, J. Warren
1886	1956	Kibbee, Guy
1902	1966	Kiepura, Jan
1888	1964	Kilbride, Percy
1863	1933	Kilgour, Joseph
1894	1964	King, Charles
1897	1971	King, Dennis
1889	1938	Kohler, Fred
1897	1957	Korngold, Erich W.
1919	1962	Kovacs, Ernie
1885	1974	Kruger, Otto
1909	1973	Krupa, Gene

L

Born	Died	Name
1913	1964	Ladd, Alan
1895	1967	Lahr, Bert
1919	1973	Lake, Veronica
1904	1948	Landi, Elissa
1919	1948	Landis, Carole
1904	1972	Landis, Jessie Royce
1884	1944	Langdon, Harry
1856	1929	Langtry, Lillian
1921	1959	Lanza, Mario
1881	1958	Lasky, Jesse L.
1870	1950	Lauder, Harry
1899	1962	Laughton, Charles
1890	1965	Laurel, Stan
1892	1954	Laurie Jr., Joe
1898	1952	Lawrence, Gertrude
1890	1929	Lawrence, Margaret
1907	1952	Lee, Canada
1914	1970	Lee, Gypsy Rose
1848	1929	Lehmann, Lilli
1896	1950	Lehr, Lew
1913	1967	Leigh, Vivien
1852	1908	Leighton, Margaret
1922	1976	Leighton, Margaret
1894	1931	Leitzel, Lillian
1831	1905	Lemoyne, W. J.
1870	1941	Leonard, Eddie
1911	1973	Leonard, Jack E.
1906	1972	Levant, Oscar
1881	1955	Levy, Ethel
1902	1971	Lewis, Joe E.
1891	1971	Lewis, Ted
1874	1944	Lhevinne, Josef
1889	1952	Lincoln, Elmo
1820	1887	Lind, Jenny
1889	1968	Lindsay, Howard
1869	1952	Lipman, Clara
1889	1971	Lloyd, Harold
1876	1922	Lloyd, Marie
1891	1957	Lockhart, Gene
1876	1947	Loftus, Cissie (Marie)
1913	1969	Logan, Ella
1909	1942	Lombard, Carole
1927	1974	Long, Richard
1895	1975	Lopez, Vincent
1890	1950	Lord, Pauline
1888	1968	Lorne, Marion
1904	1964	Lorre, Peter
1917	1970	Louise, Anita
1914	1962	Lovejoy, Frank
1892	1971	Lowe, Edmund
1892	1947	Lubitsch, Ernst
1885	1956	Lugosi, Bela
1895	1971	Lukas, Paul
1853	1932	Lupino, Stanley
1893	1942	Lupino, Stanley
1897	1957	Lyman, Abe
1926	1971	Lynn, Diana
1885	1954	Lytell, Bert
1867	1936	Lytton, Henry

M

Born	Died	Name
1907	1965	MacDonald, Jeanette
1902	1969	MacLane, Barton
1909	1973	Macready, George
1861	1946	Macy, George Carleton
1908	1973	Magnani, Anna
1896	1967	Mahoney, Will

Born	Died	Name
1890	1975	Main, Marjorie
1933	1967	Mansfield, Jayne
1857	1907	Mansfield, Richard
1897	1975	March, Fredric
1920	1970	March, Hal
1865	1950	Marlowe, Julia
1890	1966	Marshall, Herbert
1864	1943	Marshall, Tully
1885	1969	Martinelli, Giovanni
1887	1961	Marx, Leonard (Chico)
1888	1964	Marx, Arthur (Harpo)
1862	1951	Maude, Cyril
1922	1972	Maxwell, Marilyn
1879	1948	May, Edna
1885	1957	Mayer, Louis B.
1895	1973	Maynard, Ken
1884	1945	McCormack, John
1907	1962	McCormick, Myron
1888	1931	McCoy, Bessie
1883	1936	McCullough, Paul
1895	1952	McDaniel, Hattie
1924	1965	McDonald, Marie
1913	1975	McGiver, John
1879	1949	McIntyre, Frank J.
1857	1937	McIntyre, James
1879	1937	McKinley, Mabel
1886	1959	McLaglen, Victor
1907	1971	McMahon, Horace
1880	1946	Meek, Donald
1879	1936	Meighan, Thomas
1861	1931	Melba, Nellie
1890	1973	Melchior, Lauritz
1904	1961	Melton, James
1890	1963	Menjou, Adolphe
1902	1966	Menken, Helen
1882	1939	Mercer, Beryl
1880	1946	Merivale, Phillip
1904	1944	Miller, Glenn
1860	1926	Miller, Henry
1898	1936	Miller, Marilyn
1895	1927	Mills, Florence
1939	1976	Mineo, Sal
1903	1955	Minnevitch, Borrah
1917	1955	Miranda, Carmen
1875	1957	Mitchell, Grant
1892	1962	Mitchell, Thomas
1880	1940	Mix, Tom
1845	1909	Modjeska, Helena
1926	1962	Monroe, Marilyn
1912	1973	Monroe, Vaughn
1875	1964	Monteux, Pierre
1824	1861	Montez, Lola
1919	1951	Montez, Maria
1903	1947	Moore, Grace
1885	1955	Moore, Tom
1876	1962	Moore, Victor
1906	1974	Moorehead, Agnes
1882	1949	Moran, George
1884	1952	Moran, Polly
1890	1949	Morgan, Frank
1900	1941	Morgan, Helen
1888	1956	Morgan, Ralph
1901	1970	Morris, Chester
1849	1925	Morris, Clara
1914	1959	Morris, Wayne
1944	1971	Morrison, Jim
1897	1969	Mowbray, Alan
1897	1967	Muni, Paul
1894	1953	Munn, Frank
1906	1955	Munson, Ona
1924	1971	Murphy, Audie
1885	1965	Murray, Mae

N

Born	Died	Name
1897	1970	Nagel, Conrad
1900	1973	Naish, J. Carrol
1898	1961	Naldi, Nita
1888	1950	Nash, Florence
1865	1945	Nash, George
1879	1945	Nazimova, Alla
1846	1905	Neilson, Ada
1848	1880	Neilson, Adelaide
1907	1975	Nelson, Ozzie
1868	1957	Neilson-Terry, Julia
1885	1967	Nesbit, Evelyn
1870	1951	Nethersole, Olga
1905	1956	Newton, Robert
1874	1948	Niblo, Fred
1890	1950	Nijinsky, Vaslav

Born	Died	Name
1893	1974	Nilsson, Anna Q.
1898	1930	Normand, Mabel
1879	1959	Norworth, Jack
1905	1968	Novarro, Ramon
1893	1951	Novello, Ivor

O

Born	Died	Name
1860	1926	Oakley, Annie
1898	1943	O'Connell, Hugh
1881	1959	O'Connor, Una
1878	1945	O'Hara, Fiske
1908	1968	O'Keefe, Dennis
1880	1938	Oland, Warner
1860	1932	Olcott, Chauncey
1885	1942	Oliver, Edna May
1892	1963	Olsen, Ole
1847	1920	O'Neill, James
1887	1949	Ouspenskaya, Maria
1887	1972	Owen, Reginald

P

Born	Died	Name
1860	1941	Paderewski, Ignace
1889	1954	Pallette, Eugene
1894	1958	Pangborn, Franklin
1914	1975	Parks, Larry
1881	1972	Parsons, Louella
1881	1940	Pasternack, Josef A.
1837	1908	Pastor, Tony
1843	1919	Patti, Adelina
1840	1889	Patti, Carlotta
1885	1931	Pavlova, Anna
1899	1973	Paxinou, Katina
1868	1934	Payton, Corse
1917	1966	Pearce, Alice
1885	1950	Pemberton, Brock
1899	1967	Pendleton, Nat
1904	1941	Penner, Joe
1892	1937	Perkins, Osgood
1893	1956	Peters, Brandon
1915	1963	Piaf, Edith
1893	1957	Pinza, Ezio
1900	1963	Pitts, Zasu
1904	1976	Pons, Lili
1903	1969	Portman, Eric
1904	1963	Powell, Dick
1869	1931	Power, F. Tyrone
1914	1958	Power, Tyrone E.
1872	1935	Powers, Eugene
1900	1964	Price, George E.
1856	1919	Primrose, George
1879	1956	Prouty, Jed
1871	1942	Pryor, Arthur
1925	1970	Pyne, Joe

R

Born	Died	Name
1906	1946	Ragland, John (Rags)
1890	1967	Rains, Claude
1889	1970	Rambeau, Marjorie
1900	1947	Rankin, Arthur
1892	1967	Rathbone, Basil
1897	1960	Ratoff, Gregory
1883	1953	Rawlinson, Herbert
1891	1943	Ray, Charles
1860	1916	Rehan, Ada
1893	1923	Reid, Wallace
1873	1943	Reinhardt, Max
1909	1971	Rennie, Michael
1870	1940	Richman, Charles
1895	1972	Richman, Harry
1872	1961	Ring, Blanche
1888	1958	Risdon, Elizabeth
1907	1974	Ritter, Tex
1905	1969	Ritter, Thelma
1903	1966	Ritz, Al
1898	1976	Robeson, Paul
1878	1949	Robinson, Bill
1893	1973	Robinson, Edward G.
1865	1942	Robson, May
1897	1933	Rodgers, Jimmy
1894	1958	Rodzinsky, Artur
1879	1935	Rogers, Will
1937	1937	Roland, Ruth
1880	1962	Rooney, Pat
1899	1966	Rose, Billy
1882	1936	Rothafel, S. L. (Roxy)
1873	1953	Ruffo, Titta
1892	1970	Ruggles, Charles
1864	1936	Russell, Annie

Born	Died	Name
1924	1961	Russell, Gail
1861	1922	Russell, Lillian
1892	1972	Rutherford, Margaret
1902	1973	Ryan, Irene
1909	1973	Ryan, Robert

S

Born	Died	Name
1877	1968	St. Denis, Ruth
1884	1955	Sakall, S.Z.
1885	1936	Sale (Chic), Charles
1906	1972	Sanders, George
1934	1973	Sands, Diana
1896	1960	Savo, Jimmy
1879	1954	Scheff, Fritzi
1892	1930	Schenck, Joe
1895	1964	Schildkraut, Joseph
1865	1930	Schildkraut, Rudolph
1889	1965	Schipa, Tito
1882	1951	Schnabel, Artur
1910	1949	Schumann, Henrietta
1861	1936	Schumann-Heink, E.
1866	1945	Scott, Cyril
1914	1965	Scott, Zachary
1843	1896	Scott-Siddons, Mrs.
1892	1974	Seeley, Blossom
1902	1965	Selznick, David O.
1858	1935	Sembrick, Marcella
1884	1960	Sennett, Mack
1881	1951	Shattuck, Arthur
1860	1929	Shaw, Mary
1891	1972	Shawn, Ted
1868	1949	Shean, Al
1915	1967	Sheridan, Ann
1924	1973	Sherman, Allan
1885	1934	Sherman, Lowell
1918	1970	Shriner, Herb
1883	1953	Shubert, Lee
1755	1831	Siddons, Mrs. Sarah
1882	1930	Sills, Milton
1914	1970	Silvera, Frank
1878	1946	Sis Hopkins (Melville)
1891	1934	Skelly, Hal
1858	1942	Skinner, Otis
1870	1952	Skipworth, Alison
1892	1970	Skulnik, Menasha
1863	1948	Smith, C. Aubrey
1826	1881	Sothern, Edward A.
1859	1933	Sothern, Edward H.
1884	1957	Sothern, Harry
1854	1932	Sousa, John Philip
1884	1957	Sparks, Ned
1876	1974	Speaks, Oley
1890	1970	Spitalny, Phil
1873	1937	Standing, Guy
1871	1956	Stephenson, Henry
1900	1941	Stephenson, James
1883	1939	Sterling, Ford
1882	1928	Stevens, Emily A.
1934	1970	Stevens, Inger
1896	1961	Stewart, Anita
1873	1959	Stone, Fred
1879	1953	Stone, Lewis
1871	1954	Straus, Oskar
1902	1974	Sullivan, Ed
1911	1960	Sullavan, Margaret
1903	1956	Sullivan, Francis L.
1892	1946	Summerville, Slim
1904	1969	Swarthout, Gladys

T

Born	Died	Name
1897	1957	Talmadge, Norma
1917	1968	Talman, William
1900	1972	Tamiroff, Akim
1878	1947	Tanguay, Eva
1899	1934	Tashman, Lilyan
1885	1966	Taylor, Deems
1899	1958	Taylor, Estelle
1887	1946	Taylor, Laurette
1911	1969	Taylor, Robert
1878	1938	Tearle, Conway
1884	1953	Tearle, Godfrey
1892	1937	Tell, Alma
1881	1934	Tellegen, Lou
1864	1942	Tempest, Marie
1910	1963	Templeton, Alec
1848	1928	Terry, Ellen
1874	1940	Tetrazzini, Luisa

Born	Died	Name
1899	1936	Thalberg, Irving
1857	1914	Thomas, Brandon
1892	1960	Thomas, John Charles
1882	1976	Thorndike, Sybil
1869	1936	Thurston, Howard
1896	1960	Tibbett, Lawrence
1887	1940	Tinney, Frank
1909	1958	Todd, Michael
1906	1935	Todd, Thelma
1874	1947	Toler, Sidney
1905	1968	Tone, Franchot
1878	1933	Torrence, Ernest
1867	1957	Toscanini, Arturo
1898	1968	Tracy, Lee
1900	1967	Tracy, Spencer
1903	1972	Traubel, Helen
1894	1975	Treacher, Arthur
1853	1917	Tree, Herbert Beerbohm
1890	1973	Truex, Ernest
1883	1942	Tucker, Richard
1915	1975	Tucker, Richard
1884	1966	Tucker, Sophie
1911	1970	Tufts, Sonny
1874	1940	Turpin, Ben
1908	1959	Twelvetrees, Helen

U

Born	Died	Name
1894	1970	Ulric, Lenore
1933	1975	Ure, Mary

V

Born	Died	Name
1895	1926	Valentino, Rudolph
1870	1950	Van, Billy B.
1894	1943	Veidt, Conrad
1886	1957	Von Stroheim, Erich

W

Born	Died	Name
1887	1969	Walburn, Raymond
1874	1946	Waldron, Charles D.
1904	1966	Walker, June
1919	1951	Walker, Robert
1876	1962	Walter, Bruno
1878	1936	Walthall, Henry B.
1872	1952	Ward, Fannie
1866	1951	Warfield, David
1876	1958	Warner, H. B.
1878	1964	Warwick, Robert
1924	1963	Washington, Dinah
1867	1945	Watson, Billy
1879	1962	Watson, Lucille
1890	1965	Watson, Minor
1896	1966	Webb, Clifton
1867	1942	Weber, Joe
1905	1973	Webster, Margaret
1876	1926	Welch, Ben
1873	1918	Welch, Joe
1896	1975	Wellman, William
1883	1953	Werrenrath, Reinald
1879	1942	Westley, Helen
1895	1968	Wheeler, Bert
1889	1938	White, Pearl
1890	1967	Whiteman, Paul
1882	1943	Whiting, George
1865	1948	Whitty, Dame May
1906	1966	Whorf, Richard
1895	1948	William, Warren
1877	1922	Williams, Bert
1867	1918	Williams, Evan
1923	1953	Williams, Hank
1917	1972	Wilson, Marie
1884	1969	Winninger, Charles
1904	1959	Withers, Grant
1881	1931	Wolheim, Louis
1907	1961	Wong, Anna May
1888	1963	Woolley, Monty
1889	1938	Woolsey, Robert
1881	1956	Wycherly, Margaret
1886	1966	Wynn, Ed
1906	1964	Wynyard, Diana

Y

Born	Died	Name
1891	1960	Young, Clara Kimball
1887	1953	Young, Roland

Z

Born	Died	Name
1869	1932	Ziegfeld, Florenz
1873	1976	Zukor, Adolph

AWARDS — MEDALS — PRIZES
The Alfred B. Nobel Prize Winners

Alfred B. Nobel, inventor of dynamite, bequeathed $9,000,000, the interest to be distributed yearly to those who had most benefited mankind in physics, chemistry, medicine-physiology, literature, and peace. The first Nobel Prize in Economics was awarded in 1969. No awards given for years omitted. In 1975, each prize was worth $143,000.

Physics

1975 James Rainwater, U.S.
    Ben Mottelson, U.S.-Danish,
    Hage Bohr, Danish
1974 Martin Ryle, British
    Antony Hewish, British
1973 Ivar Giaever, U.S.
    Leo Esaki, U.S.
    Brian D. Josephson, British
1972 John Bardeen, U.S.
    Leon N. Cooper, U.S.
    John R. Schrieffer, U.S.
1971 Dennis Gabor, British
1970 Louis Neel, French
    Hannes Alfven, Swedish
1969 Murray Gell-Mann, U.S.
1968 Luis W. Alvarez, U.S.
1967 Hans A. Bethe, U.S.
1966 Alfred Kastler, French
1965 Richard P. Feynman, U.S.
    Julian S. Schwinger, U.S.
    Shinichiro Tomanaga, Japanese
1964 Nikolai G. Basov, USSR
    Aleksander M. Prochorov, USSR
    Charles H. Townes, U.S.
1963 Maria Goeppert-Mayer, U.S.
    J. Hans D. Jensen, German
    Eugene P. Wigner, U.S.
1962 Lev. D. Landau, USSR
1961 Robert Hofstadter, U.S.
    Rudolf L. Mossbauer, German
1960 Donald A. Glaser, U.S.
1959 Owen Chamberlain, U.S.
    Emilio G. Segre, U.S.
1958 Paval Cerenkov, Ilya Frank,
    Igor J. Tamm, all USSR
1957 Tsung-Dao Lee,

Chen Ning Yang, both U.S.
1956 John Bardeen, U.S.
    Walter H. Brattain, U.S.
    William Shockley, U.S.
1955 Polykarp Kusch, U.S.
    Willis E. Lamb, U.S.
1954 Max Born, British
    Walter Bothe, German
1953 Frits Zernike, Dutch
1952 Felix Bloch, U.S.
    Edward M. Purcell, U.S.
1951 Sir John D. Cockroft, British
    Ernest T. S. Walton, Irish
1950 Cecil F. Powell, British
1949 Hideki Yukawa, Japanese
1948 Patrick M. S. Blackett, British
1947 Sir Edward V. Appleton, British
1946 Percy Williams Bridgman, U.S.
1945 Wolfgang Pauli, U.S.
1944 Isidor Isaac Rabi, U.S.
1943 Otto Sern, U.S.
1939 Ernest O. Lawrence, U.S.
1938 Enrico Fermi, U.S.
1937 Clinton J. Davisson, U.S.
    George P. Thomson, British
1936 Carl D. Anderson, U.S.
    Victor F. Hess, Austrian
1935 James Chadwick, British
1933 Paul A. M. Dirac, British
    Erwin Schrodinger, Austrian
1932 Werner Heisenberg, German
1930 Sir Chandrasekhara V. Raman, Indian
1929 Prince Louis-Victor de Broglie, French

1928 Owen W. Richardson, British
1927 Arthur H. Compton, U.S.
    Charles T. R. Wilson, British
1926 Jean B. Perrin, French
1925 James Franck,
    Gustav Hertz, both German
1924 Karl M. G. Siegbahn, Swedish
1923 Robert A. Millikan, U.S.
1922 Niels Bohr, Danish
1921 Albert Einstein, Ger.-U.S.
1920 Charles E. Guillaume, French
1919 Johannes Stark, German
1918 Max K. E. L. Planck, German
1917 Charles G. Barkla, British
1915 Sir William H. Bragg, British
    William L. Bragg, British
1914 Max von Laue, German
1913 Heike Kamerlingh-Onnes, Dutch
1912 Nils G. Dalen, Swedish
1911 Wilhelm Wien, German
1910 Johannes D. van der Waals, Dutch
1909 Carl F. Braun, German
    Guglielmo Marconi, Italian
1908 Gabriel Lippmann, French
1907 Albert A. Michelson, U.S.
1906 Sir Joseph J. Thomson, British
1905 Philipp E. A. von Lenard, Ger.
1904 Rayleigh, Lord (John W. Strutt), British
1903 Antoine Henri Becquerel, Fr.
    Marie Curie, French
    Pierre Curie, French
1902 Hendrik A. Lorentz,
    Pieter Zeeman, both Dutch
1901 Wilhelm C. Rontgen, German

Chemistry

1975 John Cornforth, Austral.-Brit.,
    Vladimir Prelog, Yugo.-Switz.
1974 Paul J. Flory, U.S.
1973 Ernst Otto Fischer, W. German
    Geoffrey Wilkinson, British
1972 Christian B. Anfinsen, U.S.
    Stanford Moore, U.S.
    William H. Stein, U.S.
1971 Gerhard Herzberg, Canadian
1970 Luis A. Leloir, Arg.
1969 Derek H. R. Barton, British
    Odd Hassel, Norwegian
1968 Lars Onsager, U.S.
1967 Manfred Eigen, German
    Ronald G. W. Norrish, British
    George Porter, British
1966 Robert S. Mulliken, U.S.
1965 Robert B. Woodward, U.S.
1964 Dorothy C. Hodgkin, British
1963 Giulio Natta, Italian
    Karl Ziegler, German
1962 John C. Kendrew, British
    Max F. Perutz, British
1961 Melvin Calvin, U.S.
1960 Willard F. Libby, U.S.
1959 Jaroslav Heyrovsky, Czech
1958 Frederick Sanger, British
1957 Sir. Alexander R. Todd, British
1956 Sir Cyril N. Hinshelwood, British
    Nikolai N. Semenov, USSR

1955 Vincent du Vigneaud, U.S.
1954 Linus C. Pauling, U.S.
1953 Hermann Staudinger, German
1952 Archer J. P. Martin, British
    Richard L. M. Synge, British
1951 Edwin M. McMillan, U.S.
    Glenn T. Seaborg, U.S.
1950 Kurt Adler, German
    Otto P. H. Diels, German
1949 William F. Glauque, U.S.
1948 Arne W. K. Tiselius, Swedish
1947 Sir Robert Robinson, British
1946 James B. Sumner, John H. Northrop, Wendell M. Stanley, all U.S.
1945 Artturi I. Virtanen, Finnish
1944 Otto Hahn, German
1943 Georg de Hevesy, Hungarian
1939 Adolf F. J. Butenandt, German
    Leopold Ruzicka, Swiss
1938 Richard Kuhn, German
1937 Walter N. Haworth, British
    Paul Karrer, Swiss
1936 Peter J. W. Debye, Dutch
1935 Frederic Joliot-Curie, French
    Irene Joliot-Curie, French
1934 Harold C. Urey, U.S.
1932 Irving Langmuir, U.S.
1931 Friedrich Bergius, German
    Carl Bosch, German

1930 Hans Fischer, German
1929 Arthur Harden, British
    Hans von Euler-Chelpin, Swed.
1928 Adolf O. R. Windaus, German
1927 Heinrich O. Wieland, German
1926 Theodor Svedberg, Swedish
1925 Richard A. Zsigmondy, German
1923 Fritz Pergl, Austrian
1922 Francis W. Aston, British
1921 Frederick Soddy, British
1920 Walther H. Nernst, German
1918 Fritz Haber, German
1915 Richard M. Willstatter, German
1914 Theodore W. Richards, U.S.
1913 Alfred Werner, Swiss
1912 Victor Grignard, French
    Paul Sabatier, French
1911 Marie Curie, French
1910 Otto Wallach, German
1909 Wilhelm Ostwald, German
1908 Ernest Rutherford, British
1907 Eduard Buchner, German
1906 Henri Moissan, French
1905 Adolf von Baeyer, German
1904 Sir William Ramsay, British
1903 Svante A. Arrhenius, Swedish
1902 Emil Fischer, German
1901 Jacobus H. van't Hoff, Dutch

Physiology or Medicine

1975 David Baltimore, Howard Temin, both U.S.; Renato Dulbecco, Ital.-U.S.
1974 Albert Claude, Lux.-U.S.; George Emil Palade, Rom.-U S.: Christian Rene de Duve, Belg.
1973 Karl von Frisch, Konrad Lorenz, both Ger.; Nikolaas Tinbergen, Brit.
1972 Gerald M. Edelman, U.S.
    Rodney R. Porter, British

1971 Earl W. Sutherland Jr., U.S.
1970 Julius Axelrod, U.S.
    Sir Bernard Katz, British
    Ulf von Euler, Swedish
1969 Max Delbruck,
    Alfred D. Hershey,
    Salvador Luria, all U.S.
1968 Robert W. Holley,
    H. Gobind Khorana,
    Marshall W. Nirenberg, all U.S.
1967 Ragnar Granit, Swedish

Haldan Keffer Hartline, U.S.
    George Wald, U.S.
1966 Charles B. Huggins,
    Francis Peyton Rous, both U.S.
1965 Francois Jacob, Andre Lwoff, Jacquest Monod, all French
1964 Konrad E. Bloch, American
    Feodor Lynen, German
1963 Sir John C. Eccles, Australian
    Alan L. Hodgkin, British
    Andrew F. Huxley, British

1962 Francis H. C. Crick, British
James D. Watson, U.S.
Maurice H. F. Wilkins, British
1961 Georg von Bekesy, U.S.
1960 Sir F. MacFarlane Burnet, Australian
Peter B. Medawar, British
1959 Arthur Kornberg, U.S.
Severo Ochoa, U.S.
1958 George W. Beadle, U.S.
Edward L. Tatum, U.S.
Joshua Lederberg, U.S.
1957 Daniel Bovet, Italian
1956 Andre F. Cournand, U.S.
Werner Forssmann, German
Dickinson W. Richards, Jr., U.S.
1955 Alex H. T. Theorell, Swedish
1954 John F. Enders,
Frederick C. Robbins,
Thomas H. Weller, all U.S.
1953 Hans A. Krebs, British
Fritz A. Lipmann, U.S.
1952 Selman A. Waksman, U.S.
1951 Max Theiler, U.S.
1950 Philip S. Hench,
Edward C. Kendall, both U.S.
Tadeus Reichstein, Swiss
1949 Walter R. Hess, Swiss

Antonio Moniz, Portuguese
1948 Paul H. Muller, Swiss
1947 Carl F. Cori,
Gerty T. Cori, both U.S.
Bernardo A. Houssay, Arg.
1946 Hermann J. Muller, U.S.
1945 Ernst B. Chain, British
Sir Alexander Fleming, British
Sir Howard W. Florey, British
1944 Joseph Erlanger, U.S.
Herbert S. Gasser, U.S.
1943 Henrik C. P. Dam, Danish
Edward A. Doisy, U.S.
1939 Gerhard Domagk, German
1938 Corneille J. F. Heymans, Belg.
1937 Albert Szent-Gyorgyi, U.S.
1936 Sir Henry H. Dale, British
Otto Loewi, U.S.
1935 Hans Spemann, German
1934 George R. Minot, Wm. P. Murphy,
G. H. Whipple, all U.S.
1933 Thomas H. Morgan, U.S.
1932 Edgard D. Adrian, British
Sir Charles S. Sherrington, Brit.
1931 Otto H. Warburg, German
1930 Karl Landsteiner, U.S.
1929 Christiaan Eijkman, Dutch

Sir Frederick G. Hopkins, British
1928 Charles J. H. Nicolle, French
1927 Julius Wagner-Jauregg, Aus.
1926 Johannes A. G. Fibiger, Danish
1924 Willem Einthoven, Dutch
1923 Frederick G. Banting, Canadian
John J. R. Macleod, Canadian
1922 Archibald V. Hill, British
Otto F. Meyerhof, German
1920 Schack A. S. Krogh, Danish
1919 Jules Bordet, Belgian
1914 Robert Barany, Hungarian
1913 Charles R. Richet, French
1912 Alexis Carrel, U.S.
1911 Allvar Gullstrand, Swedish
1910 Albrecht Kossel, German
1909 Emil T. Kocher, Swiss
1908 Paul Ehrlich, German
Elie Metchnikoff, French
1907 Charles L. A. Laveran, French
1906 Camillo Golgi, Italian
Santiago Roman y Cajal, Sp.
1905 Robert Koch, German
1904 Ivan P. Pavlov, Russian
1903 Niels R. Finsen, Danish
1902 Sir Ronald Ross, British
1901 Emil A. von Behring, German

Literature

1975 Eugenio Montale, Ital.
1974 Eyvind Johnson, Harry Edmund Martinson, both Swedish
1973 Patrick White, Australian
1972 Heinrich Boll, W. German
1971 Pablo Neruda, Chilean
1970 Aleksandr I. Solzhenitsyn, Russ.
1969 Samuel Beckett, Irish
1968 Yasunari Kawabata, Japanese
1967 Miguel Angel Asturias, Guate.
1966 Samuel Joseph Agnon, Israeli
Nelly Sachs, Swedish
1965 Mikhail Sholokhov, Russian
1964 Jean Paul Sartre, French
(Prize declined)
1963 Giorgos Seferis, Greek
1962 John Steinbeck, U.S.
1961 Ivo Andric, Yugoslavian
1960 Saint-John Perse, French
1959 Salvatore Quasimodo, Italian
1958 Boris L. Pasternak, Russian
(Prize declined)
1957 Albert Camus, French
1956 Juan Ramon Jimenez,
Puerto Rican
1955 Halldor K. Laxness, Icelandic

1954 Ernest Hemingway, U.S.
1953 Sir Winston Churchill, British
1952 Francois Mauriac, French
1951 Par F. Lagerkvist, Swedish
1950 Bertrand Russell, British
1949 William Faulkner, U.S.
1948 T. S. Eliot, British
1947 Andre Gide, French
1946 Hermann Hesse, Swiss
1945 Gabriela Mistral, Chilean
1944 Johannes V. Jensen, Danish
1939 Frans. E. Sillanpaa, Finnish
1938 Pearl S. Buck, U.S.
1937 Roger Martin du Gard, French
1936 Eugene O'Neill, U.S.
1934 Luigi Pirandello, Italian
1933 Ivan A. Bunin, French
1932 John Galsworthy, British
1931 Erik A. Karlfeldt, Swedish
1930 Sinclair Lewis, U.S.
1929 Thomas Mann, German
1928 Sigrid Undset, Norwegian
1927 Henri Bergson, French
1926 Grazia Deledda, Italian
1925 George Bernard Shaw, British

1924 Wladyslaw S. Reymont, Polish
1923 William Butler Yeats, Irish
1922 Jacinto Benavente, Spanish
1921 Anatole France, French
1920 Knut Hamsun, Norwegian
1919 Carl F. G. Spitteler, Swiss
1917 Karl A. Gjellerup, Danish
Henrik Pontoppidan, Danish
1916 Verner von Heidenstam, Swed.
1915 Romain Rolland, French
1913 Rabindranath Tagore, Indian
1912 Gerhart Hauptmann, German
1911 Maurice Maeterlinck, Belgian
1910 Paul J. L. Heyse, German
1909 Selma Lagerlof, Swedish
1908 Rudolf C. Eucken, German
1907 Rudyard Kipling, British
1906 Giosue Carducci, Italian
1905 Henryk Sienkiewicz, Polish
1904 Frederic Mistral, French
Jose Echegaray, Spanish
1903 Bjornsterne Bjornson, Norw.
1902 Theodor Mommsen, German
1901 Rene F. A. Sully Prudhomme,
French

Peace

1975 Andrei Sakharov, USSR
1974 Eisaku Sato, Jap., Sean MacBride, Irish
1973 Henry Kissinger, U.S.
Le Duc Tho, N. Vietnamese
1971 Willy Brandt, W. German
1970 Norman E. Borlaug, U.S.
1969 Intl. Labor Organization
1968 Rene Cassin, French
1965 U.N. Children's Fund (UNICEF)
1964 Martin Luther King, Jr., Am.
1963 International Red Cross,
League of Red Cross Societies
1962 Linus C. Pauling, U.S.
1961 Dag Hammarskjold, Swedish
1960 Albert J. Luthuli, South African
1959 Philip J. Noel-Baker, British
1958 Georges Pire, Belgian
1957 Lester B. Pearson, Canadian
1954 Office of the UN High
Commissioner for Refugees
1953 George C. Marshall, U.S.
1952 Albert Schweitzer, French
1951 Leon Jouhaux, French
1950 Ralph J. Bunche, U.S.
1949 Lord John Boyd Orr of Brechin,
British

1947 Friends Service Council, Brit.
Amer. Friends Service Com.
1946 Emily G. Balch,
John R. Mott, both U.S.
1945 Cordell Hull, U.S.
1944 International Red Cross
1938 Nansen International Office
for Refugees
1937 Viscount Cecil of Chelwood
(Lord Edgar A. R. G. Cecil), Brit.
1936 Carlos de Saavedra Lamas, Arg.
1935 Carl von Ossietzky, German
1934 Arthur Henderson, British
1933 Sir Norman Angell, British
1931 Jane Addams, U.S.
Nicholas Murray Butler, U.S.
1930 Nathan Soderblom, Swedish
1929 Frank B. Kellogg, U.S.
1927 Ferdinand E. Buisson, French
Ludwig Quidde, German
1926 Aristide Briand, French
Gustav Stresemann, German
1925 Sir J. Austen Chamberlain, Brit.
Charles G. Dawes, U.S.
1922 Fridtjof Nansen, Norwegian
1921 Karl H. Branting, Swedish

Christian L. Lange, Norwegian
1920 Leon V. A. Bourgeois, French
1919 Woodrow Wilson, U.S.
1917 International Red Cross
1913 Henri La Fontaine, Belgian
1912 Elihu Root, U.S.
1911 Tobias M. C. Asser, Dutch
Alfred H. Fried, Austrian
1910 Permanent International Peace
Bureau
1909 Auguste M. F. Beernaert, Belg.
Paul H. B. B. d'Estournelles de
Constant, French
1908 Klas P. Arnoldson, Swedish
Fredrik Bajer, Danish
1907 Ernesto T. Moneta, Italian
Louis Renault, French
1906 Theodore Roosevelt, U.S.
1905 Baroness Bertha von Suttner,
Austrian
1904 Institute of International Law
1903 Sir William R. Cremer, British
1902 Elie Ducommun,
Charles A. Gobat, both Swiss
1901 Jean H. Dunant, Swiss
Frederic Passy, French

Economics

1975 Tjalling Koopmans, Dutch-U.S.,
Leonid Kantorovich, USSR
1974 Gunnar Myrdal, Swed., Friedrich
A. von Hayek, Austrian

1973 Wassily Leontief, U.S.
1972 Kenneth J. Arrow, U.S.
John R. Hicks, British
1971 Simon Kuznets, U.S.

1970 Paul A. Samuelson, U.S.
1969 Ragnar Frisch, Norwegian
Jan Tinbergen, Netherlandish

Pulitzer Prizes in Journalism, Letters, and Music

The Pulitzer Prizes were endowed by Joseph Pulitzer (1847-1911), publisher of The World, New York, N. Y., in a bequest to Columbia University, New York, N. Y., and are awarded annually by the president of the university on recommendation of the Advisory Board on Pulitzer Prizes for work done during the preceding year. Secretary of the Advisory Board is Prof. Richard T. Baker of Columbia Univ. All prizes are $1,000 (originally $500) in each category, except Meritorious Public Service for which a gold medal is given. No awards given for years omitted.

Pulitzer Prizes in Journalism
Meritorious Public Service

For distinguished and meritorious public service by a United States newspaper.

1918—New York Times. Also special award to Minna Lewinson and Henry Beetle Hough.
1919—Milwaukee Journal.
1921—Boston Post.
1922—New York World.
1923—Memphis (Tenn.) Commercial Appeal.
1924—New York World.
1926—Enquirer-Sun, Columbus, Ga.
1927—Canton (Oh.) Daily News.
1928—Indianapolis Times.
1929—Evening World, New York.
1931—Atlanta (Ga.) Constitution.
1932—Indianapolis (Ind.) News.
1933—New York World-Telegram.
1934—Medford (Ore.) Mail-Tribune.
1935—Sacramento (Cal.) Bee.
1936—Cedar Rapids (Ia.) Gazette.
1937—St. Louis Post-Dispatch.
1938—Bismarck (N. D.) Tribune.
1939—Miami (Fla.) Daily News.
1940—Waterbury (Conn.) Republican and American.
1941—St. Louis Post-Dispatch.
1942—Los Angeles Times.
1943—Omaha World Herald.
1944—New York Times.
1945—Detroit Free Press.
1946—Scranton (Pa.) Times.
1947—Baltimore Sun.
1948—St. Louis Post-Dispatch.
1949—Nebraska State Journal.
1950—Chicago Daily News; St. Louis Post-Dispatch.
1951—Miami (Fla.) Herald and Brooklyn Eagle.
1952—St. Louis Post-Dispatch.
1953—Whiteville (N. C.) News Reporter; Tabor City (N. C.) Tribune.
1954—Newsday (Long Island, N.Y.).
1955—Columbus (Ga.) Ledger and Sunday Ledger-Enquirer.
1956—Watsonville (Cal.) Register-Pajaronian.
1957—Chicago Daily News.
1958—Arkansas Gazette, Little Rock.
1959—Utica (N. Y.) Observer-Dispatch and Utica Daily Press.
1960—Los Angeles Times.
1961—Amarillo (Tex.) Globe-Times.
1962—Panama City (Fla.) News-Herald.
1963—Chicago Daily News.
1964—St. Petersburg (Fla.) Times.
1965—Hutchinson (Kan.) News.
1966—Boston Globe.
1967—The Louisville Courier-Journal and The Milwaukee Journal.
1968—Riverside (Cal.) Press-Enterprise.
1969—Los Angeles Times.
1970—Newsday (Long Island, N.Y.).
1971—Winston Salem (N.C.) Journal & Sentinel.
1972—New York Times.
1973—Washington Post.
1974—Newsday (Long Island, N.Y.).
1975—Boston Globe.
1976—Anchorage Daily News.

Reporting

This category originally embraced all fields, local, national, and international. Later separate categories were created for the different fields of reporting.

1917—Herbert Bayard Swope, New York World.
1918—Harold A. Littledale, New York Evening Post.
1920—John J. Leary, Jr., New York World.
1921—Louis Seibold, New York World.
1922—Kirke L. Simpson, Associated Press.
1923—Alva Johnston, New York Times.
1924—Magner White, San Diego Sun.
1925—James W. Mulroy and Alvin H. Goldstein, Chicago Daily News.
1926—William Burke Miller, Louisville Courier-Journal.

1927—John T. Rogers, St. Louis Post-Dispatch.
1929—Paul Y. Anderson, St. Louis Post-Dispatch.
1930—Russell D. Owens, New York Times. Also $500 to W. O. Dapping, Auburn (N. Y.) Citizen.
1931—A. B. MacDonald, Kansas City (Mo.) Star.
1932—W. C. Richards, D. D. Martin, J. S. Pooler, F. D. Webb, J. N. W. Sloan, Detroit Free Press.
1933—Francis A. Jamieson, Asssociated Press.
1934—Royce Brier, San Francisco Chronicle.
1935—William H. Taylor, New York Herald Tribune.
1936—Lauren D. Lyman, New York Times.
1937—John J. O'Neill, N. Y. Herald Tribune; William L. Laurence, N. Y. Times; Howard W. Blakeslee, A. P.; Gobind Behari Lal, University Service; and David Dietz, Scripps-Howard Newspapers.
1938—Raymond Sprigle, Pittsburgh Post-Gazette.
1939—Thomas L. Stokes, Scripps-Howard Newspaper Alliance.
1940—S. Burton Heath, New York World-Telegram.
1941—Westbrook Pegler, New York World-Telegram.
1942—Stanton Delaplane, San Francisco Chronicle.
1943—George Weller, Chicago Daily News.
1944—Paul Schoenstein, N. Y. Journal-American.
1945—Jack S. McDowell, San Francisco Call-Bulletin.
1946—William L. Laurence, New York Times.
1947—Frederick Woltman, N. Y. World-Telegram.
1948—George E. Goodwin, Atlanta Journal.
1949—Malcolm Johnson, New York Sun.
1950—Meyer Berger, New York Times.
1951—Edward S. Montgomery, San Francisco Examiner.
1952—Geo. de Carvalho, San Francisco Chronicle.

(1) general or spot; (2) special or investigative

1953—(1) Providence (R.I.) Journal and Evening Bulletin; (2) Edward J. Mowery, N.Y. World-Telegram & Sun.
1954—(1) Vicksburg (Miss.) Sunday Post-Herald; (2) Alvin Scott McCoy, Kansas City (Mo.) Star.
1955—(1) Mrs. Caro Brown, Alice (Tex.) Daily Echo; (2) Roland K. Towery, Cuero (Tex.) Record.
1956—(1) Lee Hills, Detroit Free Press; (2) Arthur Daley, New York Times.
1957—(1) Salt Lake Tribune, Salt Lake City, Ut.; (2) Wallace Turner and William Lambert, Portland Oregonian.
1958—(1) Fargo (N. D.) Forum; (2) George Beveridge, Evening Star, Washington, D. C.
1959—(1) Mary Lou Werner, Washington Evening Star; (2) John Harold Brislin, Scranton (Pa.) Tribune, and The Scrantonian.
1960—(1) Jack Nelson, Atlanta Constitution; (2) Miriam Ottenberg, Washington Evening Star.
1961—(1) Sanche de Gramont, N. Y. Herald Tribune; (2) Edgar May, Buffalo Evening News.
1962—(1) Robert D. Mullins, Deseret News, Salt Lake City; (2) George Bliss, Chicago Tribune.
1963—(1) Shared by Sylvan Fox, William Longgood, and Anthony Shannon, N. Y. World-Telegram & Sun; (2) Oscar Griffin, Jr., Pecos (Tex.) Independent and Enterprise.

(1) General Reporting; (2) Special Reporting.

1964—(1) Norman C. Miller, Wall Street Journal; (2) Shared by James V. Magee, Albert V. Gaudiosi, and Frederick A. Meyer, Philadelphia Bulletin.
1965—(1) Melvin H. Ruder, Hungry Horse News (Columbia Falls, Mon.); (2) Gene Goltz, Houston Post.
1966—(1) Los Angeles Times Staff; (2) John A. Frasca, Tampa (Fla.) Tribune.
1967—(1) Robert V. Cox, Chambersburg (Pa.) Public Opinion; (2) Gene Miller, Miami Herald.
1968—Detroit Free Press Staff; (2) J. Anthony Lukas. N. Y. Times.
1969—(1) John Fetterman, Louisville Courier-Journal and Times; (2) Albert L. Delugach, St. Louis Globe Democrat, and Denny Walsh, Life.
1970—(1) Thomas Fitzpatrick, Chicago Sun-Times; (2) Harold Eugene Martin, Montgomery Advertiser & Alabama Journal.
1971—(1) Akron Beacon Journal Staff, (2) William Hugh Jones, Chicago Tribune.
1972—(1) Richard Cooper and John Machacek, Rochester Times-Union; (2) Timothy Leland, Gerard M. O'Neill, Stephen Kurkjian and Anne De Santis, Boston Globe.

1973—(1) Chicago Tribune; (2) Sun Newspapers of Omaha.
1974—(1) Hugh F. Hough, Arthur M. Petacque, Chicago Sun-Times; (2) William Sherman, N.Y. Daily News.
1975—(1) Xenia (Oh.) Daily Gazette; (2) Indianapolis Star.
1976—(1) Gene Miller, Miami Herald; (2) Chicago Tribune.

Criticism or Commentary

(1) Criticism; (2) Commentary

1970—(1) Ada Louise Huxtable, N. Y. Times; (2) Marquis W. Childs, St. Louis Post-Dispatch.
1971—(1) Harold C. Schonberg, N. Y. Times; (2) William A. Caldwell, The Record, Hackensack, N.J.
1972—(1) Frank Peters Jr., St. Louis Post-Dispatch; (2) Mike Royko, Chicago Daily News.
1973—(1) Ronald Powers, Chicago Sun-Times; (2) David S. Broder, Washington Post.
1974—(1) Emily Genauer, Newsday, (N.Y.); (2) Edwin A. Roberts, Jr., National Observer.
1975—(1) Roger Ebert, Chicago Sun Times; (2) Mary McGrory, Washington Star.
1976—(1) Alan M. Kriegsman, Washington Post; (2) Walter W. (Red) Smith, N.Y. Times.

National Reporting

1942—Louis Stark, New York Times.
1944—Dewey L. Fleming, Baltimore Sun.
1945—James B. Reston, New York Times.
1946—Edward A. Harris, St. Louis Post-Dispatch.
1947—Edward T. Folliard, Washington Post.
1948—Bert Andrews, New York Herald Tribune; Nat S. Finney, Minneapolis Tribune.
1949—Charles P. Trussell, New York Times.
1950—Edwin O. Guthman, Seattle Times.
1952—Anthony Leviero, New York Times.
1953—Don Whitehead, Associated Press.
1954—Richard Wilson, Cowles Newspapers.
1955—Anthony Lewis, Washington Daily News.
1956—Charles L. Bartlett, Chattanooga Times.
1957—James Reston, New York Times.
1958—Relman Morin, AP; Clark Mollenhoff, Des Moines Register & Tribune.
1959—Howard Van Smith, Miami (Fla.) News.
1960—Vance Trimble, Scripps-Howard, Washington, D. C.
1961—Edward R. Cony, Wall Street Journal.
1962—Nathan G. Caldwell and Gene S. Graham, Nashville Tennessean.
1963—Anthony Lewis, New York Times.
1964—Merriman Smith, UPI.
1965—Louis M. Kohlmeier, Wall Street Journal.
1966—Haynes Johnson, Washington Evening Star.
1967—Monroe Karmin and Stanley Penn, Wall Street Journal.
1968—Howard James, Christian Science Monitor; Nathan K. Kotz, Des Moines Register.
1969—Robert Cahn, Christian Science Monitor.
1970—William J. Eaton, Chicago Daily News.
1971—Lucinda Franks & Thomas Powers, UPI.
1972—Jack Anderson, United Features.
1973—Robert Boyd and Clark Hoyt, Knight Newspapers.
1974—James R. Polk, Washington Star-News; Jack White, Providence Journal-Bulletin.
1975—Donald L. Barlett and James B. Steele, Philadelphia Inquirer.
1976—James Risser, Des Moines Register.

International Reporting

1942—Laurence Edmund Allen, Associated Press.
1943—Ira Wolfert, No. Am. Newspaper Alliance.
1944—Daniel DeLuce, Associated Press.
1945—Mark S. Watson, Baltimore Sun.
1946—Homer W. Bigart, New York Herald Tribune.
1947—Eddy Gilmore, Associated Press.
1948—Paul W. Ward, Baltimore Sun.
1949—Price Day, Baltimore Sun.
1950—Edmund Stevens, Christian Science Monitor.
1951—Keyes Beech and Fred Sparks, Chicago Daily News; Homer Bigart and Marguerite Higgins, New York Herald Tribune; Relman Morin and Don Whitehead, AP.
1952—John M. Hightower, Associated Press.
1953—Austin C. Wehrwein, Milwaukee Journal.
1954—Jim G. Lucas, Scripps-Howard Newspapers.
1955—Harrison Salisbury, New York Times.
1956—William Randolph Hearst, Jr., Frank Conniff, Hearst Newspapers; Kingsbury Smith, INS.
1957—Russell Jones, United Press.
1958—New York Times.
1959—Joseph Martin and Philip Santora, N. Y. News.

1960—A. M. Rosenthal, New York Times.
1961—Lynn Heinzerling, Associated Press.
1962—Walter Lippmann, N. Y. Herald Tribune Synd.
1963—Hal Hendrix, Miami (Fla.) News.
1964—Malcolm W. Browne, AP; David Halberstam, N. Y. Times.
1965—J. A. Livingston, Philadelphia Bulletin.
1966—Peter Arnett, AP.
1967—R. John Hughes, Christian Science Monitor.
1968—Alfred Friendly, Washington Post.
1969—William Tuohy, L. A. Times.
1970—Seymour M. Hersh, Dispatch News Service.
1971—Jimmie Lee Hoagland, Washington Post.
1972—Peter R. Kann, Wall Street Journal.
1973—Max Frankel, N.Y. Times.
1974—Hedrick Smith, N.Y. Times.
1975—William Mullen and Ovie Carter, Chicago Tribune.
1976—Sydney H. Schanberg, N.Y. Times.

Correspondence

For Washington or foreign correspondence. Category was merged with those in national and international reporting in 1948.

1929—Paul Scott Mowrer, Chicago Daily News.
1930—Leland Stowe, New York Herald Tribune.
1931—H. R. Knickerbocker, Philadelphia Public Ledger and New York Evening Post.
1932—Walter Duranty, New York Times, and Charles G. Ross, St. Louis Post-Dispatch.
1933—Edgar Ansel Mowrer, Chicago Daily News.
1934—Frederick T. Birchall, New York Times.
1935—Arthur Krock, New York Times.
1936—Wilfred C. Barber, Chicago Tribune.
1937—Anne O'Hare McCormick, New York Times.
1938—Arthur Krock, New York Times.
1939—Louis P. Lochner, Associated Press.
1940—Otto D. Tolischus, New York Times.
1941—Bronze plaque to commemorate work of American correspondents on war fronts.
1942—Carlos P. Romulo, Philippines Herald.
1943—Hanson W. Baldwin, New York Times.
1944—Ernest Taylor Pyle, Scripps-Howard Newspaper Alliance.
1945—Harold V. (Hal) Boyle, Associated Press.
1946—Arnaldo Cortesi, New York Times.
1947—Brooks Atkinson, New York Times.

Editorial Writing

1917—New York Tribune.
1918—Louisville (Ky.) Courier-Journal.
1920—Harvey E. Newbranch, Omaha Evening World-Herald.
1922—Frank M. O'Brien, New York Herald.
1923—William Allen White, Emporia Gazette.
1924—Frank Buxton, Boston Herald, Special Prize. Frank I. Cobb, New York World.
1925—Charleston (S. C.) News and Courier.
1926—Edward M. Kingsbury, N. Y. Times.
1927—F. Lauriston Bullard, Boston Herald.
1928—Grover C. Hall, Montgomery Advertiser.
1929—Louis Isaac Jaffe, Norfolk Virginian-Pilot.
1931—Chas. Ryckman, Fremont (Neb.) Tribune.
1933—Kansas City (Mo.) Star.
1934—E. P. Chase, Atlantic (Ia.) News Telegraph.
1936—Felix Morley, Washington Post, George B. Parker, Scripps-Howard Newspapers.
1937—John W. Owens, Baltimore Sun.
1938—W. W. Waymack, Des Moines (Ia.) Register and Tribune.
1939—Ronald G. Callvert, Portland Oregonian.
1940—Bart Howard, St. Louis Post-Dispatch.
1941—Reuben Maury, Daily News, N. Y.
1942—Geoffrey Parsons, New York Herald Tribune.
1943—Forrest W. Seymour, Des Moines (Ia.) Register and Tribune.
1944—Henry J. Haskell, Kansas City (Mo.) Star.
1945—George W. Potter, Providence (R. I.) Journal-Bulletin.
1946—Hodding Carter, Greenville (Miss.) Delta Democrat-Times.
1947—William H. Grimes, Wall Street Journal.
1948—Virginius Dabney, Richmond (Va.) Times-Dispatch.
1949—John H. Crider, Boston (Mass.) Herald, Herbert Elliston, Washington Post.
1950—Carl M. Saunders, Jackson (Mich.) Citizen-Patriot.
1951—William H. Fitzpatrick, New Orleans States.
1952—Louis LaCoss, St. Louis Globe Democrat.
1953—Vermont C. Royster, Wall Street Journal.
1954—Don Murray, Boston Herald.

1955—Royce Howes, Detroit Free Press.
1956—Lauren K. Soth, Des Moines (Ia.) Register and Tribune.
1957—Buford Boone, Tuscaloosa (Ala.) News.
1958—Harry S. Ashmore, Arkansas Gazette.
1959—Ralph McGill, Atlanta Constitution.
1960—Lenoir Chambers, Norfolk Virginian-Pilot.
1961—William J. Dorvillier, San Juan (Puerto Rico) Star.
1962—Thomas M. Storke, Santa Barbara (Cal.) News-Press.
1963—Ira B. Harkey, Jr., Pascagoula (Miss.) Chronicle.
1964—Hazel Brannon Smith, Lexington (Miss.) Advertiser.
1965—John R. Harrison, The Gainesville (Fla.) Sun.
1966—Robert Lasch, St. Louis Post-Dispatch.
1967—Eugene C. Patterson, Atlanta Constitution.
1968—John S. Knight, Knight Newspapers.
1969—Paul Greenberg, Pine Bluff (Ark.) Commercial.
1970—Philip L. Geyelin, Washington Post.
1971—Horance G. Davis, Jr., Gainesville (Fla.) Sun.
1972—John Strohmeyer, Bethlehem (Pa.) Globe-Times.
1973—Roger B. Linscott, Berkshire Eagle, Pittsfield, Mass.
1974—F. Gilman Spencer, Trenton (N.J.) Trentonian.
1975—John D. Maurice, Charleston (W. Va.) Daily Mail.
1976—Philip Kerby, Los Angeles Times.

Editorial Cartooning

1922—Rollin Kirby, New York World.
1924—Jay N. Darling, New York Herald Tribune.
1925—Rollin Kirby, New York World.
1926—D. R. Fitzpatrick, St. Louis Post-Dispatch.
1927—Nelson Harding, Brooklyn Eagle.
1928—Nelson Harding, Brooklyn Eagle.
1929—Rollin Kirby, New York World.
1930—Charles Macauley, Brooklyn Eagle.
1931—Edmund Duffy, Baltimore Sun.
1932—John T. McCutcheon, Chicago Tribune.
1933—H. M. Talburt, Washington Daily News.
1934—Edmund Duffy, Baltimore Sun.
1935—Ross A. Lewis, Milwaukee Journal.
1937—C. D. Batchelor, New York Daily News.
1938—Vaughn Shoemaker, Chicago Daily News.
1939—Charles G. Werner, Daily Oklahoman.
1940—Edmund Duffy, Baltimore Sun.
1941—Jacob Burck, Chicago Times.
1942—Herbert L. Block, Newspaper Enterprise Assn.
1943—Jay N. Darling, New York Herald Tribune.
1944—Clifford K. Berryman, Washington Star.
1945—Bill Mauldin, United Feature Syndicate.
1946—Bruce Alexander Russell, Los Angeles Times.
1947—Vaughn Shoemaker, Chicago Daily News.
1948—Reuben L. (Rube) Goldberg, N. Y. Sun.
1949—Lute Pease, Newark (N. J.) Evening News.
1950—James T. Berryman, Washington Star.
1951—Reginald W. Manning, Arizona Republic.
1952—Fred L. Packer, New York Mirror.
1953—Edward D. Kuekes, Cleveland Plain Dealer.
1954—Herbert L. Block, Washington Post & Times-Herald.
1955—Daniel R. Fitzpatrick, St. Louis Post-Dispatch.
1956—Robert York, Louisville (Ky.) Times.
1957—Tom Little, Nashville Tennessean.
1958—Bruce M. Shanks, Buffalo Evening News.
1959—Bill Mauldin, St. Louis Post-Dispatch.
1961—Carey Orr, Chicago Tribune.
1962—Edmund S. Valtman, Hartford Times.
1963—Frank Miller, Des Moines Register.
1964—Paul Conrad, Denver Post.
1966—Don Wright, Miami News.
1967—Patrick B. Oliphant, Denver Post.
1968—Eugene Gray Payne, Charlotte Observer.
1969—John Fischetti, Chicago Daily News.
1970—Thomas F. Darcy, Newsday.
1971—Paul Conrad, L. A. Times.
1972—Jeffrey K. MacNelly, Richmond News-Leader.
1974—Paul Szep, Boston Globe.
1975—Gary Trudeau, Universal Press Syndicate.
1976—Tony Auth, Philadelphia Inquirer.

Spot News Photography

1942—Milton Brooks, Detroit News.
1943—Frank Noel, Associated Press.
1944—Frank Filan, AP; Earle L. Bunker, Omaha World-Herald.
1945—Joe Rosenthal, Associated Press, for photograph of planting American flag on Iwo Jima.
1947—Arnold Hardy, amateur, Atlanta, Ga.
1948—Frank Cushing, Boston Traveler.
1949—Nathaniel Fein, New York Herald Tribune.
1950—Bill Crouch, Oakland (Cal.) Tribune.

1951—Max Desfor, Associated Press.
1952—John Robinson and Don Ultang, Des Moines Register and Tribune.
1953—William M. Gallagher, Flint (Mich.) Journal.
1954—Mrs. Walter M. Schau, amateur.
1955—John L. Gaunt, Jr., Los Angeles Times.
1956—New York Daily News.
1957—Harry A. Trask, Boston Traveler.
1958—William C. Beall, Washington Daily News.
1959—William Seaman, Minneapolis Star.
1960—Andrew Lopez, UPI.
1961—Yasushi Nagao, Mainichi Newspapers, Tokyo.
1962—Paul Vathis, Associated Press.
1963—Hector Rondon, La Republica, Caracas, Venezuela.
1964—Robert H. Jackson, Dallas Times-Herald.
1965—Horst Faas, Associated Press.
1966—Kyoichi Sawada, UPI.
1967—Jack R. Thornell, Associated Press.
1968—Rocco Morabito, Jacksonville Journal.
1969—Edward Adams, A.P.
1970—Steve Starr, A.P.
1971—John Paul Filo, Valley Daily News & Daily Dispatch of Tarentum & New Kensington, Pa.
1972—Horst Faas and Michel Laurent, AP.
1973—Huynh Cong Ut, AP.
1974—Anthony K. Roberts, AP.
1975—Gerald H. Gay, Seattle Times.
1976—Stanley Forman, Boston Herald American.

Feature Photography

1968—Toshio Sakai, UPI.
1969—Moneta Sleet, Jr., Ebony.
1970—Dallas Kinney, Palm Beach Post.
1971—Jack Dykinga, Chicago Sun-Times.
1972—Dave Kennerly, UPI.
1973—Brian Lanker, Topeka Capitol-Journal.
1974—Slava Veder, AP.
1975—Matthew Lewis, Washington Post.
1976—Louisville Courier-Journal and Louisville Times.

Special Citation

1938—Edmonton (Alberta) Journal, bronze plaque.
1941—New York Times.
1944—Byron Price and Mrs. William Allen White. Also to Richard Rodgers and Oscar Hammerstein 2d, for musical, Oklahoma!
1945—Press cartographers for war maps.
1947—(Pulitzer centennial year.) Columbia Univ. and the Graduate School of Journalism, and St. Louis Post-Dispatch.
1948—Dr. Frank Diehl Fackenthal.
1951—Cyrus L. Sulzberger, New York Times.
1952—Max Kase, New York Journal-American.
1953—The New York Times; Lester Markel.
1957—Kenneth Roberts, for his historical novels.
1958—Walter Lippmann, New York Herald Tribune.
1960—Garrett Mattingly, for The Armada.
1961—American Heritage Picture History of the Civil War.
1964—The Gannett Newspapers.
1973—James T. Flexner, for "George Washington," a four-volume biography.
1976—John Hohenberg, retiring Pulitzer Prize Administrator.

Pulitzer Prizes in Letters
Fiction

For fiction in book form by an American author, preferably dealing with American life.
1918—Ernest Poole, His Family
1919—Booth Tarkington, The Magnificent Ambersons.
1921—Edith Wharton, The Age of Innocence.
1922—Booth Tarkington, Alice Adams.
1923—Willa Cather, One of Ours.
1924—Margaret Wilson, The Able McLaughlins.
1925—Edna Ferber, So Big.
1926—Sinclair Lewis, Arrowsmith. (Refused prize.)
1927—Louis Bromfield, Early Autumn.
1928—Thornton Wilder, Bridge of San Luis Rey.
1929—Julia M. Peterkin, Scarlet Sister Mary.
1930—Oliver LaFarge, Laughing Boy.
1931—Margaret Ayer Barnes, Years of Grace.
1932—Pearl S. Buck, The Good Earth.
1933—T. S. Stribling, The Store.
1934—Caroline Miller, Lamb in His Bosom.
1935—Josephine W. Johnson, Now in November.
1936—Harold L. Davis, Honey in the Horn.
1937—Margaret Mitchell, Gone With the Wind.

1938—John P. Marquand, The Late George Apley.
1939—Marjorie Kinnan Rawlings, The Yearling.
1940—John Steinbeck, The Grapes of Wrath.
1942—Ellen Glasgow, In This Our Life.
1943—Upton Sinclair, Dragon's Teeth.
1944—Martin Flavin, Journey in the Dark.
1945—John Hersey, A Bell for Adano.
1947—Robert Penn Warren, All the King's Men.
1948—James A. Michener, Tales of the South Pacific.
1949—James Gould Cozzens, Guard of Honor.
1950—A. B. Guthrie, Jr., The Way West.
1951—Conrad Richter, The Town.
1952—Herman Wouk, The Caine Mutiny.
1953—Ernest Hemingway, The Old Man and the Sea.
1955—William Faulkner, A Fable.
1956—MacKinlay Kantor, Andersonville.
1958—James Agee, A Death in the Family.
1959—Robert Lewis Taylor, The Travels of Jaimie McPheeters.
1960—Allen Drury, Advise and Consent.
1961—Harper Lee, To Kill a Mockingbird.
1962—Edwin O'Connor, The Edge of Sadness.
1963—William Faulkner, The Reivers.
1965—Shirley Ann Grau, The Keepers of the House.
1966—Katherine Anne Porter, Collected Stories of Katherine Anne Porter.
1967—Bernard Malamud, The Fixer.
1968—William Styron, The Confessions of Nat Turner.
1969—N. Scott Momaday, House Made of Dawn.
1970—Jean Stafford, Collected Stories.
1972—Wallace Stegner, Angle of Repose.
1973—Eudora Welty, The Optimist's Daughter.
1975—Michael Shaara, The Killer Angels.
1976—Saul Bellow, Humboldt's Gift.

Drama

For an American play, preferably original and dealing with American life.

1918—Jesse Lynch Williams, Why Marry?
1920—Eugene O'Neill, Beyond the Horizon.
1921—Zona Gale, Miss Lulu Bett.
1922—Eugene O'Neill, Anna Christie.
1923—Owen Davis, Icebound.
1924—Hatcher Hughes, Hell-Bent for Heaven.
1925—Sidney Howard, They Knew What They Wanted.
1926—George Kelly, Craig's Wife.
1927—Paul Green, In Abraham's Bosom.
1928—Eugene O'Neill, Strange Interlude.
1929—Elmer Rice, Street Scene.
1930—Marc Connelly, The Green Pastures.
1931—Susan Glaspell, Alison's House.
1932—George S. Kaufman, Morrie Ryskind and Ira Gershwin, Of Thee I Sing.
1933—Maxwell Anderson, Both Your Houses.
1934—Sidney Kingsley, Men in White.
1935—Zoe Akins, The Old Maid.
1936—Robert E. Sherwood, Idiot's Delight.
1937—George S. Kaufman and Moss Hart, You Can't Take It With You.
1938—Thornton Wilder, Our Town.
1939—Robert E. Sherwood, Abe Lincoln in Illinois.
1940—William Saroyan, The Time of Your Life.
1941—Robert E. Sherwood, There Shall Be No Night.
1943—Thornton Wilder, The Skin of Our Teeth.
1945—Mary Chase, Harvey.
1946—Russel Crouse and Howard Lindsay, State of the Union.
1948—Tennessee Williams, A Streetcar Named Desire.
1949—Arthur Miller, Death of a Salesman.
1950—Richard Rodgers, Oscar Hammerstein 2d, and Joshua Logan, South Pacific.
1952—Joseph Kramm, The Shrike.
1953—William Inge, Picnic.
1954—John Patrick, Teahouse of the August Moon.
1955—Tennessee Williams, Cat on a Hot Tin Roof.
1956—Frances Goodrich and Albert Hackett, The Diary of Anne Frank.
1957—Eugene O'Neill, Long Day's Journey Into Night.
1958—Ketti Frings, Look Homeward, Angel.
1959—Archibald MacLeish, J. B.
1960—George Abbott, Jerome Weidman, Sheldon Harnick and Jerry Bock, Fiorello.
1961—Tad Mosel, All the Way Home.
1962—Frank Loesser and Abe Burrows, How To Succeed In Business Without Really Trying.
1965—Frank D. Gilroy, The Subject Was Roses.
1967—Edward Albee, A Delicate Balance.
1969—Howard Sackler, The Great White Hope.
1970—Charles Gordone, No Place to Be Somebody.
1971—Paul Zindel, The Effect of Gamma Rays on Man-in-the-Moon Marigolds.
1973—Jason Miller, That Championship Season.
1975—Edward Albee, Seascape.
1976—Michael Bennett, James Kirkwood, Nicholas Dante, Marvin Hamlisch, Edward Kleban, A Chorus Line.

History

For a book on the history of the United States.

1917—J. J. Jusserand, With Americans of Past and Present Days.
1918—James Ford Rhodes, History of the Civil War.
1920—Justin H. Smith, The War with Mexico.
1921—William Sowden Sims, The Victory at Sea.
1922—James Truslow Adams, The Founding of New England.
1923—Charles Warren, The Supreme Court in United States History.
1924—Charles Howard McIlwain, The American Revolution: A Constitutional Interpretation.
1925—Frederick L. Paxton, A History of the American Frontier.
1926—Edward Channing, A History of the U. S.
1927—Samuel Flagg Bemis, Pinckney's Treaty.
1928—Vernon Louis Parrington, Main Currents in American Thought.
1929—Fred A. Shannon, The Organization and Administration of the Union Army, 1861-65.
1930—Claude H. Van Tyne, The War of Independence.
1931—Bernadotte E. Schmitt, The Coming of the War, 1914.
1932—Gen. John J. Pershing, My Experiences in the World War.
1933—Frederick J. Turner, The Significance of Sections in American History.
1934—Herbert Agar, The People's Choice.
1935—Charles McLean Andrews, The Colonial Period of American History.
1936—Andrew C. McLaughlin, The Constitutional History of the United States.
1937—Van Wyck Brooks, The Flowering of New England.
1938—Paul Herman Buck, The Road to Reunion, 1865-1900.
1939—Frank Luther Mott, A History of American Magazines.
1940—Carl Sandburg, Abraham Lincoln: The War Years.
1941—Marcus Lee Hansen, The Atlantic Migration, 1607-1860.
1942—Margaret Leech, Reveille in Washington.
1943—Esther Forbes, Paul Revere and the World He Lived In.
1944—Merle Curti, The Growth of American Thought.
1945—Stephen Bonsal, Unfinished Business.
1946—Arthur M. Schlesinger, Jr., The Age of Jackson.
1947—James Phinney Baxter 3d, Scientists Against Time.
1948—Bernard De Voto, Across the Wide Missouri.
1949—Roy F. Nichols, The Disruption of American Democracy.
1950—O. W. Larkin, Art and Life in America.
1951—R. Carlyle Buley, The Old Northwest: Pioneer Period 1815-1840.
1952—Oscar Handlin, The Uprooted.
1953—George Dangerfield, The Era of Good Feelings.
1954—Bruce Catton, A Stillness at Appomattox.
1955—Paul Horgan, Great River: The Rio Grande in North American History.
1956—Richard Hofstadter, The Age of Reform.
1957—George F. Kennan, Russia Leaves the War.
1958—Bray Hammond, Banks and Politics in America—From the Revolution to the Civil War.
1959—Leonard D. White and Jean Schneider, The Republican Era; 1869-1901.
1960—Margaret Leech, In the Days of McKinley.
1961—Herbert Feis, Between War and Peace: The Potsdam Conference.
1962—Lawrence H. Gibson, The Triumphant Empire: Thunderclouds Gather in the West.
1963—Constance McLaughlin Green, Washington: Village and Capital, 1800-1878.
1964—Sumner Chilton Powell, Puritan Village: The Formation of A New England Town.
1965—Irwin Unger, The Greenback Era.
1966—Perry Miller, Life of the Mind in America.
1967—William H. Goetzmann, Exploration and Empire: the Explorer and Scientist in the Winning of the American West.
1968—Bernard Bailyn, The Ideological Origins of the American Revolution.
1969—Leonard W. Levy, Origin of the Fifth Amendment.
1970—Dean Acheson, Present at the Creation: My Years in the State Department.

1971—James McGregor Burns, Roosevelt: The Soldier of Freedom.
1972—Carl N. Degler, Neither Black Nor White.
1973—Michael Kammen, People of Paradox: An Inquiry Concerning the Origins of American Civilization.
1974—Daniel J. Boorstin, The Americans: The Democratic Experience.
1975—Dumas Malone, Jefferson and His Time.
1976—Paul Horgan, Lamy of Santa Fe.

Biography or Autobiography

For a distinguished biography or autobiography by an American author, preferably on an American subject.

1917—Laura E. Richards and Maude Howe Elliott, assisted by Florence Howe Hall, Julia Ward Howe.
1918—William Cabell Bruce, Benjamin Franklin, Self-Revealed.
1919—Henry Adams, The Education of Henry Adams.
1920—Albert J. Beveridge, The Life of John Marshall.
1921—Edward Bok, The Americanization of Edward Bok.
1922—Hamlin Garland, A Daughter of the Middle Border.
1923—Burton J. Hendrick, The Life and Letters of Walter H. Page.
1924—Michael Pupin, From Immigrant to Inventor.
1925—M. A. DeWolfe Howe, Barrett Wendell and His Letters.
1926—Harvey Cushing, Life of Sir William Osler.
1927—Emory Holloway, Whitman: An Interpretation in Narrative.
1928—Charles Edward Russell, The American Orchestra and Theodore Thomas.
1929—Burton J. Hendrick, The Training of an American: The Earlier Life and Letters of Walter H. Page.
1930—Marquis James, The Raven. (Sam Houston).
1931—Henry James, Charles W. Eliot.
1932—Henry F. Pringle, Theodore Roosevelt.
1933—Allan Nevins, Grover Cleveland.
1934—Tyler Dennett, John Hay.
1935—Douglas Southall Freeman, R. E. Lee.
1936—Ralph Barton Perry, The Thought and Character of William James.
1937—Allan Nevins, Hamilton Fish: The Inner History of the Grant Administration.
1938—Divided between Odell Shepard, Pedlar's Progress; Marquis James, Andrew Jackson.
1939—Carl Van Doren, Benjamin Franklin.
1940—Ray Stannard Baker, Woodrow Wilson, Life and Letters.
1941—Ola Elizabeth Winslow, Jonathan Edwards.
1942—Forrest Wilson, Crusader in Crinoline.
1943—Samuel Eliot Morison, Admiral of the Ocean Sea (Columbus).
1944—Carleton Mabee, The American Leonardo: The Life of Samuel F. B. Morse.
1945—Russell Blaine Nye, George Bancroft: Brahmin Rebel.
1946—Linny Marsh Wolfe, Son of the Wilderness.
1947—William Allen White, The Autobiography of William Allen White.
1948—Margaret Clapp, Forgotten First Citizen: John Bigelow.
1949—Robert E. Sherwood, Roosevelt and Hopkins.
1950—Samuel Flag Bemis, John Quincy Adams and the Foundations of American Foreign Policy.
1951—Margaret Louise Colt, John C. Calhoun: American Portrait.
1952—Merlo J. Pusey, Charles Evans Hughes.
1953—David J. Mays, Edmund Pendleton, 1721-1803.
1954—Charles A. Lindbergh, The Spirit of St. Louis.
1955—William S. White, The Taft Story.
1956—Talbot F. Hamlin, Benjamin Henry Latrobe.
1957—John F. Kennedy, Profiles in Courage.
1958—Douglas Southall Freeman (decd. 1953), George Washington, Vols. I-VI: John Alexander Carroll and Mary Wells Ashworth, vol. VII.
1959—Arthur Walworth, Woodrow Wilson: American Prophet.
1960—Samuel Eliot Morison, John Paul Jones.
1961—David Donald, Charles Sumner and The Coming of the Civil War.
1963—Leon Edel, Henry James: Vol. II. The Conquest of London, 1870-1881; Vol. III, The Middle Years, 1881-1895.
1964—Walter Jackson Bate, John Keats.
1965—Ernest Samuels, Henry Adams.
1966—Arthur M. Schlesinger, Jr., A Thousand Days.
1967—Justin Kaplan, Mr. Clemens and Mark Twain.
1968—George F. Kennan, Memoirs (1925-1950).

1969—B. L. Reid, The Man from New York: John Quinn and his Friends.
1970—T. Harry Williams, Huey Long.
1971—Lawrence Thompson, Robert Frost: The Years of Triumph, 1915-1938.
1972—Joseph P. Lash, Eleanor and Franklin.
1973—W. A. Swanberg, Luce and His Empire.
1974—Louis Sheaffer, O'Neill, Son and Artist.
1975—Robert A. Caro, The Power Broker: Robert Moses and the Fall of New York.
1976—R.W.B. Lewis, Edith Wharton: A Biography.

American Poetry

Before this prize was established in 1922, awards were made from gifts provided by the Poetry Society: 1918—Love Songs, by Sara Teasdale. 1919—Old Road to Paradise, by Margaret Widdemer; Corn Huskers, by Carl Sandburg.

1922—Edwin Arlington Robinson, Collected Poems.
1923—Edna St. Vincent Millay, The Ballad of the Harp-Weaver; A Few Figs from Thistles; Eight Sonnets in American Poetry, 1922; A Miscellany.
1924—Robert Frost, New Hampshire: A Poem with Notes and Grace Notes.
1925—Edwin Arlington Robinson, The Man Who Died Twice.
1926—Amy Lowell, What's O'Clock.
1927—Leonora Speyer, Fiddler's Farewell.
1928—Edwin Arlington Robinson, Tristram.
1929—Stephen Vincent Benet, John Brown's Body.
1930—Conrad Aiken, Selected Poems.
1931—Robert Frost, Collected Poems.
1932—George Dillon, The Flowering Stone.
1933—Archibald MacLeish, Conquistador.
1934—Robert Hillyer, Collected Verse.
1935—Audrey Wurdemann, Bright Ambush.
1936—Robert P. Tristram Coffin, Strange Holiness.
1937—Robert Frost, A Further Range.
1938—Marya Zaturenska, Cold Morning Sky.
1939—John Gould Fletcher, Selected Poems.
1940—Mark Van Doren, Collected Poems.
1941—Leonard Bacon, Sunderland Capture.
1942—William Rose Benet, The Dust Which Is God.
1943—Robert Frost, A Witness Tree.
1944—Stephen Vincent Benet, Western Star.
1945—Karl Shapiro, V-Letter and Other Poems.
1947—Robert Lowell, Lord Weary's Castle.
1948—W. H. Auden, The Age of Anxiety.
1949—Peter Viereck, Terror and Decorum.
1950—Gwendolyn Brooks, Annie Allen.
1951—Carl Sandburg, Complete Poems.
1952—Marianne Moore, Collected Poems.
1953—Archibald MacLeish, Collected Poems.
1954—Theodore Roethke, The Waking.
1955—Wallace Stevens, Collected Poems.
1956—Elizabeth Bishop, Poems, North and South.
1957—Richard Wilbur, Things of This World.
1958—Robert Penn Warren, Promises: Poems 1954-1956.
1959—Stanley Kunitz, Selected Poems 1928-1958.
1960—W. D. Snodgrass, Heart's Needle.
1961—Phyllis McGinley, Times Three: Selected Verse from Three Decades.
1962—Alan Dugan, Poems.
1963—William Carlos Williams, Pictures From Breughel.
1964—Louis Simpson, At the End of the Open Road.
1966—Richard Eberhart, Selected Poems.
1967—Anne Sexton, Live or Die.
1968—Anthony Hecht, The Hard Hours.
1969—George Oppen, Of Being Numerous.
1970—Richard Howard, Untitled Subjects.
1971—William S. Merwin, The Carrier of Ladders.
1972—James Wright, Collected Poems.
1973—Maxine Winokur Kumin, Up Country.
1975—Gary Snyder, Turtle Island.
1976—John Ashbery, Self-Portrait in a Convex Mirror.

General Non-Fiction

For best book by an American, not eligible in any other category.

1962—Theodore H. White, The Making of the President 1960.
1963—Barbara W. Tuchman, The Guns of August.
1964—Richard Hofstadter, Anti-Intellectualism in American Life.
1965—Howard Mumford Jones, O Strange New World.
1966—Edwin Way Teale, Wandering Through Winter.
1967—David Brion Davis, The Problem of Slavery in Western Culture.

1968—Will and Ariel Durant, Rousseau and Revolution.
1969—Norman Mailer, The Armies of the Night; and Rene Jules Dubos, So Human an Animal: How We Are Shaped by Surroundings and Events.
1970—Eric H. Erikson, Gandhi's Truth.
1971—John Toland, The Rising Sun.
1972—Barbara W. Tuchman, Stilwell and the American Experience in China, 1911-1945.
1973—Frances FitzGerald, Fire in the Lake: The Vietnamese and the Americans in Vietnam; and Robert Coles, Children of Crisis, Volumes II and III.
1974—Ernest Becker, The Denial of Death.
1975—Annie Dillard, Pilgrim at Tinker Creek.
1976—Robert N. Butler, Why Survive? Being Old in America.

Pulitzer Prize in Music

For composition in the larger forms of chamber, orchestral or choral music or for an operatic work including ballet, performed or published by a composer resident in the United States. A special posthumous award was granted in 1976 to Scott Joplin.

1943—William Schuman, Secular Cantata No. 2, A Free Song.
1944—Howard Hanson, Symphony No. 4, Op. 34.
1945—Aaron Copland, Appalachian Spring.
1946—Leo Sowerby, The Canticle of the Sun.
1947—Charles E. Ives, Symphony No. 3.

1948—Walter Piston, Symphony No. 3.
1949—Virgil Thomson, Louisiana Story.
1950—Gian-Carlo Menotti, The Consul.
1951—Douglas Moore, Giants in the Earth.
1952—Gail Kubil, Symphony Concertante.
1954—Quincy Porter, Concerto for Two Pianos and Orchestra.
1955—Gian-Carlo Menotti, The Saint of Bleecker Street.
1956—Ernest Toch, Symphony No. 3.
1957—Norman Dello Joio, Meditations on Ecclesiastes.
1958—Samuel Barber, Vanessa.
1959—John La-Montaine, Concerto for Piano and Orchestra.
1960—Elliott Carter, Second String Quartet.
1961—Walter Piston, Symphony No. 7.
1962—Robert Ward, The Crucible.
1963—Samuel Barber, Piano Concerto No. 1.
1966—Leslie Bassett, Variations for Orchestra.
1967—Leon Kirchner, Quartet No. 3.
1968—George Crumb, Echoes of Time and the River.
1969—Karel Husa, String Quartet No. 3.
1970—Charles W. Wuorinen, Time's Encomium.
1971—Mario Davidovsky, Synchronisms No. 6.
1972—Jacob Druckman, Windows.
1973—Elliott Carter, String Quartet No. 3.
1974—Donald Martino, Notturno. (Special citation) Roger Sessions.
1975—Dominick Argento, From the Diary of Virginia Woolf.
1976—Ned Rorem, Air Music.

Special Awards

Awarded in 1976 unless otherwise designated

Books, Allied Arts

Copernicus Award, by Academy of American Poets, for lifetime achievement, $10,000: Robert Penn Warren.

Edgar Allan Poe Award, by Academy of American Poets, for a younger poet, $5,000: Charles Wright for Bloodlines.

Walt Whitman Award, by Academy of American Poets, for an unpublished poet, $1,000: Laura Gilpin.

John Burroughs Medal, by American Museum of Natural History, for natural science writing: Ann Haymond Zwinger for Run, River, Run.

Louis A. Heyn Award, by Society of Southwestern Authors, for book with Southwestern locale: Katherine Gehm for Sarah Winnemucca.

Jane Addams Children's Book Award (1975): Charlotte Pomerantz for The Princess and the Admiral.

American Revolution Round Table Award, for the best book on the Revolution: Thomas Fleming for 1776: Year of Illusions.

R.T. French Co. Tastemaker Award, for the best cookbook overall: Jean Anderson, Elaine Hanna for Doubleday Cookbook.

Harold Morton Landon Translation Award, by the Academy of American Poets: Robert Fitzgerald for Iliad.

National Book Awards, for books by American authors, administered by the National Institute of Arts and Letters; Poetry: John Ashbery for Self-Portrait in a Convex Mirror; Fiction: William Gaddis for JR; Contemporary Affairs: Michael J. Arlen for Passage to Ararat; History and Biography: David Brion Davis for The Problem of Slavery in the Age of Revolution: 1770-1823; Children's Literature: Walter D. Edmonds for Bert Breen's Barn; Arts and Letters: Paul Fussell for The Great War and Modern Memory.

George Freedley Memorial Award, by the Theater Library Assn. for best theater book: Donald Oenslager, posthumously, for Stage Design: Four Centuries of Scenic Invention; best book on films or TV: Robert Sklar for Movie-made America: A Social History of American Movies.

Edgar Awards, by the Mystery Writers of America; Novel: Brian Garfield for Hop-Scotch; Fact Crime Book: Tom Wicker for A Time to Die; Grand Master Award: Graham Greene; Special Edgars: Jorge Luis Borges, Donald J. Sobol; First Novel: Rex Burns for The Alvarez Journal; Paperback: John R. Feegel for Autopsy; Juvenile: Robert C. O'Brien for Z for Zachariah; Special Raven, posthumously: Leo Margulies.

Nebula Awards, by the Science Fiction Writers Assn.: Novel: Joe Haldeman for The Forever War; Novella: Roger Zelazny for Home Is the Hangman; Novelette: Tom Reamy for San Diego Lightfoot Sue; Short Story: Fritz Leiber for "Catch That Zeppelin;" Dramatic Writing: Mel Brooks, Young Frankenstein; Grand Master Award: Jack Williamson.

Bennett Award, by Hudson Review, for an unrecognized major writer, $12,500: Jorge Guillen.

Bancroft Prizes, by Columbia University, for American history and biography, $4,000 each: David Brion Davis for The Problem of Slavery in the Age of Revolution, 1770-1823; R.W.B. Lewis for Edith Wharton: A Biography.

Academy of American Poets Fellowship, for distinguished achievement, $10,000: Robert Hayden.

Golden Kite Award, by the Society of Children's Book Writers: Carol Farley for The Garden is Doing Fine.

Yale Series of Younger Poets Competition: Carolyn Forche for Gathering the Tribes.

Skinner Award, by Women's National Book Assn.: Frances Neal Cheney, Helen Honig Meyer, Barbara Ringer.

Friends of American Writers Award, $1,000: Margot Peters for Unquiet Soul.

Children's Book Award, by Child Study Assn. of Amer.: Carol Farley for The Garden is Doing Fine.

Children's Science Book Awards, by N.Y. Academy of Sciences, $250; Junior: Jean-Claude Deguine for Emperor Penguin; Older: Bruce Buchenholz for Doctor in the Zoo.

Hemingway Prize, by P.E.N. American Center, $6,000: Loyd Little for Parthian Shot.

P.E.N. Translation Prize, $1,000: Richard Howard for A Short History of Decay by E.M. Cioran; Goethe House-P.E.N. Translation Prize, $500: Ralph Manheim for A Sorrow Beyond Dreams by Peter Handke.

Carey-Thomas Award for creative publishing: Pierpont Morgan Library for Early Children's Books and Their Illustration by Gerald Gottlieb.

St. Lawrence Award, by St. Lawrence Univ., for first collection of short fiction: Russell Banks for *Searching for Survivors*.

National Book Critics Circle Awards, for books by American writers; Fiction: E.L. Doctorow for *Ragtime*; Poetry: John Ashbery for *Self Portrait in a Convex Mirror*; Nonfiction: R.W.B. Lewis for *Edith Wharton: A Biography*; Criticism: Paul Fussell for *The Great War and Modern Memory*.

Christian Gauss Award, by Phi Beta Kappa, for literary scholarship, $2,500: Robert Gittings, *Young Thomas Hardy*.

Ralph Waldo Emerson Award, by Phi Beta Kappa, $2,500, posthumously: Marshall G.S. Hodgson for *The Venture of Islam*.

Phi Beta Kappa Award in Science, $2,500: Guido Majno for *The Healing Hand: Man and Wound in the Ancient World*.

National Historical Society Book Award, for U.S. history, $1,000: Ira Berlin for *Slaves Without Masters: The Free Negro in the Antebellum South*.

Alexander Gode Medal, by American Translators Assn.: Frederick Ungar, publisher.

Silver Gavel Award, by American Bar Assn.: John P. MacKenzie for *The Appearance of Justice*.

Lenore Marshall Poetry Prize, by Book-of-the-Month Club, $3,500: Cid Corman for *0/1*.

Prisoners Writing Award, by P.E.N., $100: Fiction: Paul Ferguson; Poetry: Michael F.X. Hogan; Nonfiction: Jonathan Z. Shoher.

Newbery Medal, by Amer. Library Assn., for children's literature: Susan Cooper for *The Grey King*.

Caldecott Medal, by Amer. Library Assn., for children's illustrations: Leo and Diane Dillon for *Why Mosquitoes Buzz in People's Ears: A West African Tale*.

Dexter Prize, by the Society for the History of Technology, $1,000: Bruce Sinclair for *Philadelphia's Philosopher Mechanics: A History of the Franklin Institute, 1824-1865*.

American Medical Writers Assn. Award: *Primary Care: Where Medicine Fails*, ed. by Spyros Andreopolis.

Thomas More Medal, for Catholic literature: John Delaney, editor.

Edward MacDowell Medal for contribution to literature: Lillian Hellman.

Canadian Governor General's Literary Awards, $5,000: Milton Acorn for *The Island Means Minago*; Marion MacRae, Anthony Adamson for *Hallowed Walls*; Brian Moore for *The Great Victorian Collection*; Louis-Edmond Hamelin for *Nordicite canadienne*; Anne Hebert for *Les Enfants du sabbat*; Pierre Perrault for *Chouennes*.

National Institute of Arts and Letters-American Academy of Arts and Letters Awards; Gold Medal for Biography: Leon Edel; National Medal for Literature, $10,000: Allen Tate; E.M. Forster Award, $5,000: Jon Stallworthy; Loines Poetry Award, $2,500: Mona Van Duyn; Zabel Award for criticism, $2,500: Harold Rosenberg; Resenthal Award for fiction, $2,000: Richard Yates for *Disturbing the Peace*; Waite Award for continuing achievement: Rene Wellek; Academy-Institute Awards, $3,000: Robert Coover, Robert Craft, E.L. Doctorow, Eugene D. Genovese, Kenneth Koch, Charles Simic, John Simon, Louis Simpson, Susan Sontag, Louis Zukofsky.

Chicago Friends of Literature Award, $500: Lacey Baldwin Smith for *Elizabeth Tudor*.

Fletcher Pratt Award, by N.Y. Civil War Round Table: David H. Donald, ed., for *Gone for a Soldier: The Civil War Memoirs of Private Alfred Bellard*.

Hadley Cantril Award. for book in social sciences: Alex Inkeles, David Horton Smith for *Becoming Modern*.

National Arts Club Gold Medal for Literature: Norman Mailer.

Lucille Medwick Award, by P.E.N., $500: Harry Smith, poet, editor.

W.A. Dwiggins Award, by Bookbuilders of Boston: Patricia C. Thoma, art director.

American Psychological Foundation National Media Award: Lee Edson for *How We Learn*.

Thomas J. Wilson Prize, by Harvard Univ. press, first book: John Naynard for *Browning's Youth*.

Lamont Poetry Selection, by Academy of American Poets: Lisel Mueller for *The Private Life*.

Laurence L. Winship Award, by Boston Globe, for New England book: Andre Dubus for *Separate Flights*.

Journalism Awards

Drew Pearson Foundation Awards, for investigative reporting: Seymour Hersh, N.Y. Times, $5,000; Maxine Cheshire, Washington Post, $1,000.

Paul Tobenkin Award, by Columbia Univ., for writings against bigotry, $250: Joe H. Stroud, Detroit Free Press.

Meyer Berger Award, by Columbia Univ., $750; Howard Blum, N.Y. Village Voice; Israel Shenker, N.Y. Times.

Sidney Hillman Awards, by Amalgamated Clothing Workers, $750 each: William S. Randall, Stephen D. Solomon, Philadelphia Inquirer.

Handicapped Awareness Award, by Easter Seal Society: Ridgewood (N.J.) News.

Lulu Awards, by Men's Fashion Assn. of Amer.; Large daily: Genevieve Buck, Chicago Tribune; Newspaper magazine: Addis Durning, N.Y. News.

Pictures of the Year Grand Prizes, by National Press Photographers Assn., $1,000; newspaper: Brian Lanker, Eugene (Ore.) Register-Guard; magazine: Steve Raymer, National Geographic; World understanding: Ken Heyman, freelance.

Conservation Communications Award, by National Wildlife Federation: Detroit News.

Sigma Delta Chi Awards, for distinguished service in journalism; Public service: Louisville Courier-Journal; General Reporting: Billy Bowles, Kirk Cheyfitz, James Harper, Tom Hennessey, William J. Mitchell, Julie Morris, Jim Neubacher, Detroit Free Press; Editorial writing: William J. Duncliffe, Boston Herald American; Washington correspondence: James Risser, Des Moines Register; Foreign correspondence: Sydney H. Schanberg, N.Y. Times; News photography: Stanley J. Forman, Boston Herald

American; Editorial cartooning: Tony Auth, Philadelphia Inquirer; Journalism research: Marvin Barrett, Columbia Univ.

Canadian National Newspaper Awards, by Toronto Press Club, $500: Spot news: Jack Cahill, Toronto Star; Feature: Nigel Gibson, Montreal Gazette; Spot photo: Stephen Liard, Toronto Star; Feature photo: Tedd Church, Montreal Gazette; Enterprise reporting: Lysiane Gagnon, Montreal La Presse; Editorial: John W. Grace, Ottawa Journal; Critical writing: Scott Beaven, Calgary Albertan; Sports: Trent Frayne, Toronto Sun; Cartooning: Roy Peterson, Vancouver Sun.

National Headliners Awards, News reporting, under 50,000 circ.: Anchorage Daily News; News reporting, 50,000-150,000 circ.: Fort Myers (Fla.) News-Press; News reporting, over 150,000 circ.: Steven M. Luxenberg, Mark Reutter, Baltimore Sun; Public service: Wall Street Journal; News event, syndicate: Paul Vogle, Alan Dawson, UPI; Spot photo: Stanley J. Forman, Boston Herald American; Local interest: John Keasler, Miami News; Special column: Roy Larson, Chicago Sun-Times; Editorial cartoon: Herbert Block, Washington Post; Feature photo: Greg Schneider, San Bernardino Sun-Telegram; Sports photo: Gerard C. Benene, Philadelphia Inquirer; Sports writing: Phil Elderkin, Christian Science Montior; Newspaper magazine: Chicago Tribune; Investigative reporting: John Fialka, Washington Star.

Charles Stewart Mott Awards, by Education Writers Assn.; Grand prize, $1,000: Jonathan Neumann, Daily Hampshire Gazette (Northampton, Mass.); Other prizes, $500: Breaking news: Diane

Brockett, Washington Star; Larry Nagengast, Wilmington (Del.) Evening Journal Feature: Robert Braun, N. J. Star-Ledger; Donald W. Glickstein, Delaware State News.

Worth Bingham Memorial Award, for investigative reporting, by White House Correspondents Assn., $1,000: James V. Risser, Des Moines Register & Tribune.

Legis 50 Awards, for state government reporting, by Center for Legislative Improvement: Louisville Courier-Journal; Felton West, Houston Post.

Canadian Science Writers Assn. Award, $1,000: Betty Lou Lee, Hamilton Spectator.

World Press Photo Award, by Amsterdam Foundation, First prize, $1,800: Stanley J. Forman, Boston Herald American.

Heywood Broun Award, by the Newspaper Guild, $1,000: Kent Pollock, Philadelphia Inquirer.

Golden Carnation Awards, for nutrition reporting, by Carnation Co.: Eleanor Ostman, St. Paul Pioneer Press-Dispatch; Marge Hanley, Indianapolis News.

Eclipse Awards, by Thoroughbred Racing Assn., $500: Bob Harding, N. J. Star Ledger; John Pineda, Miami Herald Fred Deford, Sports Illustrated.

Front Page Awards, by Newswomen's Club of N.Y.: Deadline News: Deirdre Carmody, N. Y. Times; Feature: Rita Delfiner, N. Y. Post; Series: Joyce Purnick, N. Y. Post; Family: Jane E. Brody, N. Y. Times.

Atomic Industrial Forum Awards, $500: John McPhee, New Yorker; David Perlman, San Francisco Chronicle.

Maria Moors Cabot Awards, for inter-American understanding, by Columbia Univ.: Gold Medals: Sam Summerlin, AP; Enrique Zileri Gibson, Lima (Peru) Caretas.

Suburban Journalist of Year, by Suburban Newspapers of America, $100: Joan Calvano, Pacific Beach (Calif.) Sentinel: Muriel Hardy, Berea (Ohio) News Sun.

John Hancock Co. Awards for Excellence, for consumer understanding of business: Syndicated: Louise Cook, AP; Magazines: Marshall Loeb, Time Business magazine: Gordon Williams, Business Week; Newspapers: Donald Barlett, James Steele, Philadelphia Inquirer; Dick Youngblood, Minneapolis Tribune; Tom Miller, Huntington (W. Va.) Herald-Advertiser.

Univ. of Missouri Award: Cherokee (Ia.) Daily Times.

Minnesota Award, for distinguished service, by Inland Daily Press Assn.: Richard L. Blacklidge, Kokomo (Ind.) Tribune.

Science Writers Award, by American Dental Assn., $1,000 each: Sarah Watke, Green Bay Press-Gazette; Jean Butler, freelance.

Barney Kilgore Award, for college journalism, by Sigma Delta Chi, $2,500; Gregory A. Waskul, Calif. St. Univ.

Golden Quill Award, by Society of Weekly Newspaper Editors: Betty Cox, Madison County (Ky.) Newsweek.

Raymond Clapper Award, by White House Correspondents Assn., $1,000: Brooks Jackson, AP.

Carr Van Anda Award, by Ohio Univ.: Patricia Carbine, Ms.; A. M. Rosenthal, N. Y. Times.

Reuben Awards, by National Cartoonists Society; Outstanding Cartoonist of Year: Bob Dunn, King Features; Editorial: John Pierotti, N.Y. Post; Strip: Russell Myers, Chicago Tribune-N. Y. News; Features: Allan Jaffee, Mad; Sports: Bruce Stark, N. Y. News.

Ernie Pyle Memorial Award, by Scripps-Howard Foundation, for human interest in the tradition of Ernie Pyle, $1,000: Robert Hullihan, Des Moines Register; $500: Carl Hiaasen, Cocoa (Fla.) Today.

Walker Stone Awards, for editorial writing, by Scripps-Howard Foundation, $1,000: David Bowes, Cincinnati Post; $500: Edward C. Domaingue, Hartford Times.

Edward J. Meeman Awards, for conservation reporting, by Scripps-Howard Foundation; Grand Prize, $2,500: Kenneth L. Robison, Idaho Statesman; Other prizes: Gordon Bishop, N.J. Star Ledger ($1,500); John R. Stallard, Madison (Wis.) Capital Times ($1,500); William V. Shannon, N. Y. Times ($1,000); Jim Detjen, Poughkeepsie (N. Y.) Journal ($2,000); Casey Bukro, Chicago Tribune ($750); Whitney Gould, Madison (Wis.) Capital Times ($750); Brian Kelly, Washington Star ($500); Nash Herndon, Winston-Salem Sentinel ($500).

Roy W. Howard Public Service Awards, by Scripps-Howard Foundation; First prize, $2,500: Louisville Courier-Journal; Second prize, $1,000: Charlotte Observer; Third prize, $500: Cincinnati Post.

Broadcasting and Theater Awards

Life Achievement Award, by the American Film Institute: William Wyler.

Roy W. Howard Public Service Award, by Scripps-Howard Foundation; First prize $2,500: KGW-TV, Portland, Ore.; Second prizes, $500: KYTV, Springfield, Mo.; WBBM-TV, Chicago; WCKT, Miami; WMAL, Washington, D.C.

Sidney Hillman Awards, by Amalgamated Clothing Union; $750: CBS television network for Fear on Trial.

National Headliner Club Awards: Daniel Schorr, CBS radio network for stories on Central Intelligence Agency; ABC radio network for Scenes From a War.

George Foster Peabody Awards, by University of Georgia, for public service; Radio: Jim Laurie, NBC, The fall of Vietnam; KMOX, St. Louis, Sleeping Watchdogs; WGMS, Bethesda, Md., Collectors Shelf; Standard School Broadcast, San Francisco; WFMT, Chicago, Stravinsky '75; WSOU-FM, South Orange, N.J., Land of Poetry; Voice of America, Battle of Lexington; WCBS, New York, Life to Share; KDKB, Mesa, Ariz., public service programs; WMAL, Washington, D.C., Suffer the Little Children. Television: WTOP, Washington, D.C., Harambee; WCKT, Miami, investigative reporting; Charles Kuralt, CBS, On the Road to '76; KABC, Los Angeles, Dale Care; CBS, MASH; ABC, Love Among the Ruins; NBC, Weekend; WCBV, Boston, programming; Group W, Call it Macaroni; ABC, Afterschool Specials; Kaiser Broadcasting, Snipets; Alphaventure, Big Blue Marble; CBS, Mr. Rooney Goes to Washington; WWL, New Orleans, Sunday Journal; CBS, American Assassins;

WAPA, San Juan, Las Rosas Blancas; James Killian, public broadcasting.

Antoinette Perry Awards (Tonys), by the League of New York Theaters, 1975-76 season; **Musicals:** best play: A Chorus Line; actress: Donna McKechnie, Chorus Line; actor: George Rose, My Fair Lady; featured actress: Kelly Bishop, Chorus Line; featured actor: Sammy Williams, Chorus Line; director: Michael Bennett, Chorus Line; book: James Kirkwood, Nicholas Dante, Chorus Line; costumes: Florence Klotz, Pacific Overtures; scenic design: Boris Aronson, Pacific Overtures; lighting: Tharon Musser, Chorus Line; choreography: Bob Avian, Michael Bennett, Chorus Line; score: Marvin Hamlisch, Edward Kleban, Chorus Line. Dramas: best play: Travesties; actress: Irene Worth, Sweet Bird of Youth; actor: John Wood, Travesties; featured actress: Shirley Knight, Kennedy's Children; featured actor: Edward Herrman, Mrs. Warren's Profession; director: Ellis Rabb, Royal Family. Special awards: Mathilde Pincus, Arena Stage. Circle in the Square, Thomas H. Fitzgerald.

Emmy Awards, by Academy of Television Arts and Sciences (a selection from among 46 categories): performers, single appearance: Edward Asner, Rich Man, Poor Man, Kathryn Walker, The Adams Chronicles; supporting performers: Fionnuala Flanagan, Rich Man, Poor Man, Gordon Jackson, Upstairs, Downstairs; writer, comedy series: David Lloyd, Mary Tyler Moore Show; director, comedy series: Gene Reynolds, MASH; performers, comedy series: Mary Tyler Moore, Mary Tyler Moore Show; Jack Albertson, Chico and the Man; supporting performers, comedy series; Betty White, Ted Knight, both of Mary Tyler Moore Show; comedy series: Mary Tyler Moore Show; limited series: Upstairs, Downstairs; performers limited series: Rosemary Harris, Notorious Woman, Hal Holbrook, Sandburg's Lincoln; sports: NBC, 1975 World Series, ABC, Monday Night Football.

Miscellaneous Awards

Westinghouse Science Talent Awards, for high school science projects, by Westinghouse Educational Foundation: Edward S. Phinney III, Amherst, Mass., $10,000; Scott T. Cohen, N.Y.C., $8,000; Mark A. Gubrud, Columbia, Md., $8,000; William A. Schwartz, Massapequa, N.Y., Joe Fajans, Teaneck, N.J., Diane H. Wooden, Rockville, Md., $6,000 each.

Miss Black America 1976: Twanna Kilgore, Washington, D. C. **Miss Universe 1976:** Rina Messinger, Israel.

Audubon Medal, for environmental achievement, by National Audubon Society: Maurice F. Strong, UN Environment Program.

Martin Luther King Jr. Woman of the Year Award, by Southern Christian Leadership Conference: Lt. Gov. Thelma Stovall, Ky.

Frederick Douglass Awards, by National Urban League; U. S. District Court Judge Constance Baker Motley; James L. Hicks, N. Y. Amsterdam News; J. Henry Smith, Equitable Life.

National Arts Club Gold Medal: R. Buckminster Fuller.

National Institute of Arts and Letters/American Academy of Arts and Letters Awards: Gold Medal for Music: Samuel Barber; Art awards, $3,000: Gregory Gillespie, William Kienbusch, Julio Fernandez Larraz, Joseph Wolins, Judith Brown, Anthony Padovano, Sidney Simon; Music awards, $3,000: Dominick Argento, Robert Helps, Robert Hall Lewis, Richard Wernick.

Motion Picture Academy Awards
(Oscars)

1927-28
Actor: Emil Jennings, The Way of All Flesh.
Actress: Janet Gaynor, Seventh Heaven.
Picture: Wings, Paramount.
1928-29
Actor: Warner Baxter, In Old Arizona.
Actress: Mary Pickford, Coquette.
Picture: Broadway Melody, MGM.
1929-30
Actor: George Arliss, Disraeli.
Actress: Norma Shearer, The Divorcee.
Picture: All Quiet on the Western Front, Univ.
1930-31
Actor: Lionel Barrymore, Free Soul.
Actress: Marie Dressler, Min and Bill.
Picture: Cimarron, RKO.
1931-32
Actor: Fredric March, Dr. Jekyll and Mr. Hyde; Wallace Beery, The Champ (tie).
Actress: Helen Hayes, Sin of Madelon Claudet.
Picture: Grand Hotel, MGM.
Special: Walt Disney, Mickey Mouse.
1932-33
Actor: Charles Laughton, Private Life of Henry VIII.
Actress: Katharine Hepburn, Morning Glory.
Picture: Cavalcade, Fox.
1934
Actor: Clark Gable, It Happened One Night.
Actress: Claudette Colbert, same.
Picture: It Happened One Night, Columbia.
1935
Actor: Victor McLaglen, The Informer.
Actress: Bette Davis, Dangerous.
Picture: Mutiny on the Bounty, MGM.
1936
Actor: Paul Muni, Story of Louis Pasteur.
Actress: Luise Rainer, The Great Ziegfeld.
Picture: The Great Ziegfeld, MGM.
1937
Actor: Spencer Tracy, Captains Courageous.
Actress: Luise Rainer, The Good Earth.
Picture: Life of Emile Zola, Warner.
1938
Actor: Spencer Tracy, Boys Town.
Actress: Bette Davis, Jezebel.
Picture: You Can't Take It With You, Columbia.
1939
Actor: Robert Donat, Goodbye Mr. Chips.
Actress: Vivien Leigh, Gone With the Wind.
Picture: Gone With the Wind, Selznick International.
1940
Actor: James Stewart, The Philadelphia Story.
Actress: Ginger Rogers, Kitty Foyle.
Picture: Rebecca, Selznick International.
1941
Actor: Gary Cooper, Sergeant York.
Actress: Joan Fontaine, Suspicion.
Picture: How Green Was My Valley, 20th Cent.-Fox.
1942
Actor: James Cagney, Yankee Doodle Dandy.
Actress: Greer Garson, Mrs. Miniver.
Picture: Mrs. Miniver, MGM.

1943
Actor: Paul Lukas, Watch on the Rhine.
Actress: Jennifer Jones, The Song of Bernadette.
Picture: Casablanca, Warner.
1944
Actor: Bing Crosby, Going My Way.
Actress: Ingrid Bergman, Gaslight.
Picture: Going My Way, Paramount.
1945
Actor: Ray Milland, The Lost Weekend.
Actress: Joan Crawford, Mildred Pierce.
Picture: The Lost Weekend, Paramount.
1946
Actor: Fredric March, Best Years of Our Lives.
Actress: Olivia de Havilland, To Each His Own.
Picture: The Best Years of Our Lives, Goldwyn, RKO.
1947
Actor: Ronald Colman, A Double Life.
Actress: Loretta Young, The Farmer's Daughter.
Picture: Gentleman's Agreement, 20th Cent.-Fox.
1948
Actor: Laurence Olivier, Hamlet.
Actress: Jane Wyman, Johnny Belinda.
Picture: Hamlet, Two Cities Film, Universal International.
1949
Actor: Broderick Crawford, All the Kings Men.
Actress: Olivia de Havilland, The Heiress.
Picture: All the King's Men, Columbia.
1950
Actor: Jose Ferrer, Cyrano de Bergerac.
Actress: Judy Holliday, Born Yesterday.
Picture: All About Eve, 20th Century-Fox.
1951
Actor: Humphrey Bogart, The African Queen.
Actress: Vivien Leigh, A Streetcar Named Desire.
Picture: An American in Paris, MGM.
1952
Actor: Gary Cooper, High Noon.
Actress: Shirley Booth, Come Back, Little Sheba.
Picture: Greatest Show on Earth, Cecil B. DeMille, Paramount.
1953
Actor: William Holden, Stalag 17.
Actress: Audrey Hepburn, Roman Holiday.
Picture: From Here to Eternity, Columbia.
1954
Actor: Marlon Brando, On the Waterfront.
Actress: Grace Kelly, The Country Girl.
Picture: On The Waterfront, Horizon-American Corp., Columbia.
1955
Actor: Ernest Borgnine, Marty.
Actress: Anna Magnani, The Rose Tattoo.
Picture: Marty, Hecht and Lancaster's Steven Productions, U.A.
1956
Actor: Yul Brynner, The King and I.
Actress: Ingrid Bergman, Anastasia.
Picture: Around the World in 80 Days, Michael Todd Co., U.A.

1957
Actor: Alec Guinness, The Bridge on the River Kwai.
Actress: Joanne Woodward, The Three Faces of Eve.
Picture: The Bridge on the River Kwai, Columbia.
1958
Actor: David Niven, Separate Tables.
Actress: Susan Hayward, I Want to Live.
Picture: Gigi, Arthur Freed Production, MGM.
1959
Actor: Charlton Heston, Ben-Hur.
Actress: Simone Signoret, Room at the Top.
Picture: Ben-Hur, MGM.
1960
Actor: Burt Lancaster, Elmer Gantry.
Actress: Elizabeth Taylor, Butterfield 8.
Picture: The Apartment, Mirisch Co., U.A.
1961
Actor: Maximilian Schell, Judgment at Nuremberg.
Actress: Sophia Loren, Two Women.
Picture: West Side Story, United Artists.
1962
Actor: Gregory Peck, To Kill a Mockingbird.
Actress: Anne Bancroft, The Miracle Worker.
Picture: Lawrence of Arabia, Columbia.
1963
Actor: Sidney Poitier, Lilies of the Field.
Actress: Patricia Neal, Hud.
Picture: Tom Jones, Woodfall Prod., UA-Lopert Pictures.
1964
Actor: Rex Harrison, My Fair Lady.
Actress: Julie Andrews, Mary Poppins.
Picture: My Fair Lady, Warner Bros.
1965
Actor: Lee Marvin, Cat Ballou.
Actress: Julie Christie, Darling.
Picture: The Sound of Music, 20th Century-Fox.
1966
Actor: Paul Scofield, A Man for All Seasons.
Actress: Elizabeth Taylor, Who's Afraid of Virginia Woolf?
Picture: A Man for All Seasons, Columbia.
1967
Actor: Rod Steiger, In the Heat of the Night.
Actress: Katharine Hepburn, Guess Who's Coming to Dinner.
Picture: In the Heat of the Night.
1968
Actor: Cliff Robertson, Charly.
Actress: Katharine Hepburn, The Lion in Winter, Barbra Streisand, Funny Girl (tie).
Picture: Oliver.
1969
Actor: John Wayne, True Grit.
Actress: Maggie Smith, The Prime of Miss Jean Brodie.

Picture: Midnight Cowboy.
1970
Actor: George C. Scott, Patton (refused).
Actress: Glenda Jackson, Women in Love.
Picture: Patton.
1971
Actor: Gene Hackman, The French Connection.
Actress: Jane Fonda, Klute.
Picture: The French Connection.
1972
Actor: Marlon Brando, The Godfather (refused).
Actress: Liza Minnelli, Cabaret.
Picture: The Godfather.
1973
Actor: Jack Lemmon, Save the Tiger.
Actress: Glenda Jackson, A Touch of Class.
Picture: The Sting.
1974
Actor: Art Carney, Harry and Tonto.
Actress: Ellen Burstyn, Alice Doesn't Live Here Anymore.
Picture: The Godfather, Part II.
1975
Actor: Jack Nicholson, One Flew Over the Cuckoo's Nest.
Actress: Louise Fletcher, One Flew Over the Cuckoo's Nest.
Picture: One Flew Over the Cuckoo's Nest.
Supporting Actor: George Burns, The Sunshine Boys.
Supporting Actress: Lee Grant, Shampoo.
Director: Milos Forman, One Flew Over the Cuckoo's Nest.
Foreign Language Film: Dersu Uzala.
Documentary (feature): F.R. Crawley, James Hager, Dale Hartleben, The Man Who Skied Down Everest; (short): Claire Wilbur, Robin Lehman, The End of the Game.
Short Subject (animated): Bob Godfrey, Great; (live): Bert Salzman, Angel and Big Joe.
Sound: Robert Hoyt, Roger Heman, Earl Madrey, John Carter, Jaws.
Editing: Verna Fields, Jaws.
Costume Design: Ulla-Britt Soderlund, Milena Canonero, Barry Lyndon.
Cinematography: John Alcott, Barry Lyndon.
Art Direction: Ken Adam, Roy Walker, Barry Lyndon.
Set Decoration: Ken Adam, Roy Walker, Barry Lyndon.
Screenplay (original): Frank Pierson, Dog Day Afternoon; (Adapted): Lawrence W. Hauben, Bo Goldman, One Flew Over the Cuckoo's Nest.
Original Score: John Williams, Jaws.
Scoring: Leonard Rosenman, Barry Lyndon; Song: Keith Carradine, I'm Easy (Nashville).
Jean Hersholt Humanitarian Award: Jules S. Stein.
Irving Thalberg Award: Mervyn Leroy.
Special Award: Mary Pickford.

Canadian Film Awards
Source: Canadian Film Institute

1968
Actor: Gerard Parkes, Isabel
Actress: Genevieve Bujold, Isabel
Picture: A Place to Stand
1969
Actor: Chris Wiggins, The Best Damn Fiddler from Calabogie to Kaladar
Actress: Jackie Burroughs, Dulcima
Picture: The Best Damn Fiddler from Calabogie to Kaladar
1970
Actor: Doug McGrath and Paul Bradley (tied), Goin' Down the Road
Actress: Genevieve Bujold, Act of the Heart
Picture: Psychocratie
1971
Actor: Jean Duceppe, Mon oncle Antoine
Actress: Ann Knox, The Only Thing You Know
Picture: Mon oncle Antoine

1972
Actor: Gordon Pinsent, The Rowdyman
Actress: Micheline Lanctot, Vrai nature de Bernadette
Picture: Wedding in White

1973
Actor: Jacques Godin, O.K. Laliberte
Actress: Genevieve Bujold, Kamouraska
Picture: Slipstream

1974
Picture: The Apprenticeship of Duddy Kravitz

1975
Actor: Stuart Gillard, Why Rock the Boat?
Actress: Margot Kidder, Black Christmas and A Quiet Day in Belfast
Picture: Les Ordres

The Spingarn Medal

The Spingarn Medal has been awarded annually since 1914 by the National Association for the Advancement of Colored People for the highest achievement by an American Negro.

1945—Thurgood Marshall
1946—Dr. Percy L. Julian
1947—Channing H. Tobias
1948—Ralph J. Bunche
1949—Charles Hamilton Houston
1950—Mabel Keaton Staupers
1951—Harry T. Moore
1952—Paul R. Williams
1953—Theodore K. Lawless
1954—Carl Murphy
1955—Jack Roosevelt Robinson

1956—Martin Luther King, Jr.
1957—Mrs. Daisy Bates and the Little Rock Nine
1958—Edward Kennedy (Duke) Ellington
1959—Langston Hughes
1960—Kenneth B. Clark
1961—Robert C. Weaver
1962—Medgar Wiley Evers
1963—Roy Wilkins
1964—Leontyne Price

1965—John H. Johnson
1966—Edward W. Brooke
1967—Sammy Davis, Jr.
1968—Clarence M. Mitchell, Jr.
1969—Jacob Lawrence
1970—Leon Howard Sullivan
1971—Gordon Parks
1972—Wilson C. Riles
1973—Damon Keith
1974—Henry (Hank) Aaron
1975—Alvin Ailey

World Almanac Bicentennial Prize

David W. Andersen, Charleston, W. Va., won the top national prize of $1,776.00 in the "Message to America" essay contest sponsored by The World Almanac and Book of Facts and newspaper cosponsors.

Second-place award of $776 went to Mrs. Doris Bogard, Savannah, Ga., and 3d place, $176, to James M. Shaw of Detroit.

Andersen, a program specialist in the Division of Social Service, West Virginia Department of Welfare, won over thousands of entrants from across the country.

All 3 winners were awarded valuable Bicentennial Collections of history books by The World Almanac through their local newspapers, The Charleston Gazette, The Savannah News-Press, and the Detroit News.

Message to America on Her 200th Birthday

By David Andersen

There is a spirit called America. At our two-hundredth birthday the American spirit as personified in the American people represents our greatest heritage and the most unique quality we will pass to future generations. My message to America on its two-hundredth birthday is a reminder and an expression of gratitude to the American people for this spirit.

The boundaries of the American spirit are not limited by national origin, religious conviction, economic standing or educational background. It is the spirit of an unfinished dream, articulated by the philosophers and educators, and moved toward fulfillment by the realization and action of the elected representatives of the American people.

It is the spirit of the American family, and its ability to not only survive but to enhance the lives of its members in an age of rapid change and increasing mobility.

It is the spirit of American young people who still dream of careers, and when necessary feel the freedom to question established priorities and values.

Most of all, the spirit called American is the children. It is the spirit of hope renewed in their birth. It is the spirit of children freely lost in play on our city sidewalks and open fields. It is the spirit of children spontaneously sharing their emotions with the world around them, laughing when happy and crying when hurt.

America is a rich country, but it has not always been so, and may not always be so. The foundation of our country does not exist in a wealthy people. They were a people tied to the earth and possessed of a dream. The limitations of the world's natural resources may not allow us the promise of a continuing expansive materialism. The future may ask of us a more conservative material existence. But if it does America will not have lost its uniqueness or its greatness, for its richness is merely a reflection of its greatness.

America is the most powerful nation in the world, and a leader among nations, but it has not always been so, and may not always be so. America may some day assume the position of its more humble beginnings. The centuries, like the seasons, may color and change the face of the earth. But America's uniqueness and greatness is not tied to its power.

America's greatness, America's uniqueness is its spirit, the American spirit, born in the Revolution, and still a young child at its two hundredth birthday. In the best of times and in the worst of times the American spirit has prevailed.

It was in the heart of the settler, making his way west to a new frontier. It was a part of the technical and scientific skill of those who contributed to man's first step on the moon. It remains an unfinished part of all that we do and will attempt to become.

We have yet to realize the dimensions of our democracy. We are still creating the American dream. We are still realizing and exploring the significance and meaning of justice and equality in our land. Freedom still inspires and gives life to those who seek dignity and self-worth. Peace remains our most precious greeting to the world.

Democracy, justice, equality, freedom, peace, each of these words so vital to who we are as a nation are born and nurtured in the American spirit. Collectively and individually Americans reflect and hold in trust this spirit. We have inherited this spirit from our forefathers. We will pass it to our children. It is our greatness. It is our uniqueness.

It is our soul.

It is our very existence.

There is a spirit called America, and today it is two hundred years old. Happy Birthday America!

National Teacher of the Year Award

Awarded by the Ladies' Home Journal magazine for distinguished service in elementary and secondary schools.

1964—Lawana Trout, English, Charles Page H.S., Sand Springs, Okla.
1965—Richard E. Klinck, sixth grade, Reed Street Elementary, Wheat Ridge, Colo.
1966—Mona Dayton, first grade, Walter Douglas Elementary, Tucson, Ariz.
1967—Roger Tenney, music, Owatonna Junior-Senior H.S., Owatonna, Minn.
1968—David E. Graf, vocational education & industrial arts, Sandwich Comm. H.S., Sandwich, Ill.
1969—Barbara Goleman, language arts, Miami Jackson H.S., Miami, Fla.
1970—Johnnie T. Dennis, physics, math analysis, Walla Walla H.S., Walla Walla, Wash.
1971—Martha Marion Stringfellow, first grade, Lewisville Elementary, Chester Co., S.C.
1972—James Marshall Rogers, American history & Black studies, Durham H.S., Raleigh, N.C.
1973—John A. Ensworth, sixth grade, Kenwood school, Bend, Ore.
1974—Vivian Tom, social studies, Lincoln High, Yonkers, N.Y.
1975—Robert G. Heyer, science, Johanna Junior H.S., St. Paul, Minn.
1976—Ruby S. Murchison, social studies, Washington Drive J.H.S., Fayetteville, N.C.

The Molson Prize

The Molson Prizes have been given annually to recognize and encourage outstanding contributions in the arts, humanities, or social sciences. They are financed from the interest on a gift to the Canada Council by the Molson Foundation. The value of each prize is $20,000.

1963 Donald Creighton; Alain Grandbois
1964 No awards made.
1965 Jean Gascon; Frank Scott
1966 Rev. Georges-Henri Levesque; H. McLennan
1967 Arthur Erickson; Anne Hebert; Marshall McLuhan
1968 Glenn Gould; Jean Le Moyne
1969 Jean-Paul Audet; Morley Callaghan; Arnold Spohr
1970 Northrop Frye; Duncan Macpherson; Yves Pheriault

1971 Maureen Forrester; Rina Lasnier; Norman McLaren
1972 John Deutsch; Alfred Pellan; George Woodcock
1973 W.A.C.H. Dobson; Celia Franca; Jean-Paul Lemieux
1974 Alex Colville, Margaret Laurence; Pierre Dansereau
1975 Jon Vickers; Denise Pelletier; the Orford String Quartet: Andrew Dawes; Terrence Helmer; Kenneth Perkins and Marcel St-Cyr

ARTS AND MEDIA
Notable New York Theater Openings, 1975-76 Season

A Matter of Gravity, comedy by Enid Bagnold; with Katherine Hepburn.

A Musical Jubilee, revue of American theater music; devised by Marilyn Clark and Charles Burr; with Lillian Gish, Tammy Grimes, Larry Kert, John Raitt, Cyril Ritchard, and Dick Shawn.

Bubbling Brown Sugar, a musical history of Harlem; with Josephine Premice and Avon Long.

California Suite, 4 playlets by Neil Simon; directed by Gene Saks; with Tammy Grimes, Barbara Barrie, Jack Weston, and George Grizzard.

Habeas Corpus, farce by Alan Bennett about a doctor and his patients; with Rachel Roberts, Donald Sinden, and Celeste Holm.

Home Sweet Homer, musical by Mitch Leigh; with Yul Brynner and Joan Diener.

Kennedy's Children, drama by Robert Patrick about 5 people in a N.Y. city bar reminiscing about the 60s; with Shirley Knight and Barbara Montgomery.

Knock Knock, comedy by Jules Feiffer; with Neil Flanagan and Daniel Seltzer.

Lamppost Reunion, drama by Louis La Russo about a star singer from Hoboken, N.J.; with Garbiel Dell.

Legend, comedy by Samuel Taylor; with Elizabeth Ashley.

Me and Bessie musical program about Bessie Smith; with Linda Hopkins.

Murder Among Friends, comedy thriller by Bob Berry; with Janet Leigh and Jack Cassidy.

My Fair Lady, revival of the Lerner/Loewe musical; with Ian Richardson, Christine Andreas, George Rose, and Robert Coote.

Pacific Overtures, musical by Stephen Sondheim about Commodore Perry's expedition to Japan in 1853; with Mako.

Pal Joey, revival of the Rodgers/Hart musical; with Christopher Chadman and Joan Copeland.

P.S. Your Cat is Dead, comedy by James Kirkwood; with Keir Dullea and Tony Muscante.

Rex, musical by Richard Rodgers about Henry VIII; with Nicol Williamson and Penny Fuller.

1600 Pennsylvania Avenue, musical by Alan Jay Lerner and Leonard Bernstein; with Ken Howard and Patricia Routledge.

Something's Afoot, musical mystery set in England; with Tessie O'Shea.

Streamers, conclusion of David Rabe's Vietnam trilogy; directed by Mike Nichols.

Summer Brave, rewrite by William Inge of his play "Picnic"; with Alexis Smith, Ernest Thompson, and Jill Eikenberry.

The Belle of Amherst, play by William Luce based on the life of Emily Dickinson; with Julie Harris.

The Heiress, play based on Henry James's novel "Washington Square"; with Jane Alexander and Richard Kiley.

The Lady From the Sea, Ibsen revival with Vanessa Redgrave, Pat Hingle, and John Heffernan.

The Leaf People, drama about a stone age tribe in Brazil encountering modern civilization; with Tom Aldredge and Raymond J. Barry.

The Norman Conquests, trilogy by Alan Ayckbourn; with Richard Benjamin, Paula Prentiss, Estelle Parsons, Ken Howard, Carole Shelley, and Barry Nelson.

The Poison Tree, drama by Ronald Ribman about men in prison; with Cleavon Little, Moses Gunn, and Dick Anthony Williams.

The Royal Family, revival of George S. Kaufman and Edna Ferber play; with Rosemary Harris, Eva LeGallienne, and Sam Levene.

The Runner Stumbles, drama by Milan Stitt about a priest accused of murdering a nun.

The Threepenny Opera, revival of the Brecht/Weill classic.

Travesties, play by Tom Stoppard set in Zurich during the first world war; with John Wood.

Treemonisha, 1915 Scott Joplin opera about freed blacks in Arkansas in 1866; with Carmen Balthrop and Betty Allen.

Vanities, comedy by Jack Heifner; with Susan Merson, Jane Galloway, and Kathy Bates.

Who's Afraid of Virginia Woolf?, revival of the Edward Albee play; with Colleen Dewhurst and Ben Gazzara.

Yentl, drama by Leah Napolin and Isaac Bashevis Singer.

Zalman or the Madness of God, drama by Elie Wiesel; with Joseph Wiseman and Richard Bauer.

Record Long Run Broadway Plays *Still Running June 23, 1976

Fiddler on the Roof	3,242	Voice of the Turtle	1,557	Lightnin'	1,291
Life With Father	3,224	*Barefoot in the Park	1,532	Promises, Promises	1,281
Tobacco Road	3,182	Mame	1,508	The King and I	1,246
Hello Dolly	2,844	*Pippin	1,500	Cactus Flower	1,234
My Fair Lady	2,717	Arsenic and Old Lace	1,444	Sleuth	1,222
Man of La Mancha	2,329	The Sound of Music	1,443	"1776"	1,217
Abie's Irish Rose	2,327	How to Succeed in Business Without Really Trying	1,417	Guys and Dolls	1,200
Oklahoma	2,212			Cabaret	1,166
*Grease	1,780	Hellzapoppin	1,404	Mister Roberts	1,157
Harvey	1,775	The Music Man	1,375	Annie Get Your Gun	1,147
Hair	1,742	Funny Girl	1,348	Butterflies Are Free	1,128
South Pacific	1,694	Oh! Calcutta!	1,316	Pins and Needles	1,108
Born Yesterday	1,643	Angel Street	1,295	Plaza Suite	1,097
Mary, Mary	1,572			Kiss Me Kate	1,070

Plays in London *Still running June 6, 1976

*The Mousetrap	9,778	The Boy Friend	2,084	The Secretary Bird	1,463
Black and White Minstrels	4,354	Canterbury Tales	2,082	The Beggars Opera	1,463
Oliver	2,811	Boeing Boeing	2,036	Simple Spymen	1,404
There's a Girl in my Soup	2,547	Fiddler on the Roof	2,030	Our Boys	1,362
Pyjama Tops	2,498	Blithe Spirit	1,997	Knights of Madness	1,361
*Oh Calcutta	2,407	Worms Eye View	1,745	Maid of the Mountains	1,352
Sound of Music	2,385	Me and My Girl	1,646	Arsenic and Old Lace	1,337
Salad Days	2,283	Reluctant Heroes	1,610	The Farmer's Wife	1,329
My Fair Lady	2,281	*Jesus Christ Superstar	1,605	Annie Get Your Gun	1,304
Sleuth	2,358	Together Again	1,566	The Little Hut	1,261
Hair	2,239	Seagulls over Sorrento	1,551	A Little Bit of Fluff	1,241
Chu Chin Chow	2,238	Oklahoma	1,543	Sailor Beware	1,231
The Man Most Likely To	2,213	Irma La Douce	1,512	One for the Pot	1,221
*No Sex, Please, We're British	2,085	Dry Rot	1,475	Beyond the Fringe	1,184
		Charley's Aunt	1,466		

Symphony Orchestras of the U.S. and Canada
(As of July 26, 1976)
Source: American Symphony Orchestra League, Inc.
Classifications are based on annual budgets of orchestras.

Major Symphony Orchestras

Conductors

Atlanta Symphony	1280 Peachtree St., N.E., Atlanta, GA. 30309	Robert Shaw
Baltimore Symphony	120 West Mount Royal Ave., Baltimore, MD. 21201	Sergiu Comissiona
Boston Symphony	Symphony Hall, Boston, MA. 02115	Seiji Ozawa
Buffalo Philharmonic	26 Richmond Ave., Buffalo, N.Y. 14222	Michael Thomas
Chicago Symphony	220 S. Michigan Ave., Chicago, IL. 60604	Sir Georg Solti
Cincinnati Symphony	1241 Elm St., Cincinnati, OH. 45210	Thomas Schippers
Cleveland Orchestra	11001 Euclid Ave., Cleveland, OH. 44106	Lorin Maazel
Dallas Symphony	P.O. Box 26207, Dallas, TX 75226	Louis Lane
Denver Symphony	1615 California St., Denver, CO. 80202	Brian Priestman
Detroit Symphony	20 Auditorium Dr., Detroit, MI. 48226	Aldo Ceccato
Honolulu Symphony	1000 Bishop St., Honolulu, HA 96813	Robert LaMarchina
Houston Symphony	615 Louisiana, Houston, TX. 77002	Lawrence Foster
Indianapolis Symphony	4600 Sunset Ave., Indianapolis, IN. 46208	John Nelson
Kansas City Philharmonic	210 W. 10th St., Kansas City, MO 64105	Maurice Peress
Los Angeles Philharmonic	135 North Grand, Los Angeles, CA. 90012	Zubin Mehta
Milwaukee Symphony	929 N. Water St., Milwaukee, WI 53202	Kenneth Schermerhorn
Minnesota Orchestra	1111 Nicollet Mall, Minneapolis, MN 55403	S. Skrowaczewski
Montreal Symphony	Place des Arts, Montreal, Que., Can., H2X 1Y9	Rafael Fruhbeck de Burgos
National Symphony	JFK Center for the Performing Arts, Wash., DC 20566	Antal Dorati
New Jersey Symphony	213 Washington St., Newark, NJ 07101	Max Rudolf
New Orleans Philharmonic	203 Carondelet St. New Orleans, LA 70130	W. Torkanowsky
New York Philharmonic	Broadway at 65th St., New York, NY 10023	Pierre Boulez
North Carolina Symphony	PO Box 28026, Raleigh, NC 27611	John Gosling
Philadelphia Orchestra	230 S. 15th St., Philadelphia, PA 19102	Eugene Ormandy
Pittsburgh Symphony	600 Penn Ave., Pittsburgh, PA 15222	William Steinberg
Rochester Philharmonic	20 Grove Pl., Rochester, NY 14605	David Zinman
St. Louis Symphony	718 N. Grand Blvd., St. Louis, MO 63103	George Semkow
San Antonio Symphony	109 Lexington Ave., San Antonio, TX 78205	Victor Alessandro
San Francisco Symphony	War Memorial Veterans' Bldg., San Fran., CA 94102	Seiji Ozawa
Seattle Symphony	305 Harrison St., Seattle, WA 98109	Milton Katims
Syracuse Symphony	411 Montgomery St., Syracuse, NY 13202	Christopher Keene
Toronto Symphony	215 Victoria St., Toronto, Ontario, Can. M5B 1V1	Andrew Davis
Utah Symphony	55 W. 1st So. St., Salt Lake City, UT 84101	Maurice Abravanel
Vancouver Symphony	873 Beatty St., Vancouver, B.C. V6B 2M6	Kazuyoshi Akiyama

Regional Orchestras

Birmingham Symphony	2133 7th Ave. N., Birmingham, AL 35203	Amerigo Marino
Columbus Symphony	101 E. Town St., Columbus, OH 43215	Evan Whallon
Florida Symphony	320 N. Magnolia, Suite 6-A, Orlando, FL 32801	Pavle Despalj
Hartford Symphony	15 Lewis St., Hartford, CT 06103	Arthur Winograd
Louisville Orchestra	333 W. Broadway, Louisville, KY 40202	Jorge Mester
Nashville Symphony	1805 West End Ave., Nashville, TN 37203	Michael Charry
Oakland Symphony	PO Box 1619, Oakland, CA 94612	Harold Farberman
Oklahoma Symphony	512 Civic Center Music Hall, Oklahoma City, OK 73102	Ainslee Cox
Oregon Symphony	1119 SW Park Ave., Portland, OR 97205	Lawrence Smith
Phoenix Symphony	6328 N. 7th St., Phoenix, AZ 85014	Eduardo Mata
Puerto Rico Symphony	GPO Box 2350, San Juan, Puerto Rico 00936	Victor Tevah
Richmond Symphony	15 S. Fifth St., Richmond, VA 23219	Jacques Houtmann
Saint Paul Chamber Orchestra	St. Paul Bldg., 5th and Wabasha, St. Paul, MN 55102	Dennis Russell Davies
San Diego Symphony	PO Box 3175, San Diego, CA 92103	Peter Eros
San Jose Symphony	170 Park Center Plaza, San Jose, CA 95113	George Cleve
Spokane Symphony	W. 245 Spokane Falls Blvd., Spokane, WA 99201	Donald Thulean
Toledo Symphony	1 Stranahan Sq., Toledo, OH 43604	Serge Fournier
Wichita Symphony	225 W. Douglas, Wichita, KS 67202	Francois Huybrechts

Metropolitan Orchestras

Akron Symphony	Thomas Hall, Hill & Center Sts., Akron, OH 44303	Louis Lane
Albany Symphony	19 Clinton Ave., Albany, NY 12207	Julius Hegyi
American Symphony	119 W. 57th St., New York, NY 10019	Kazuyoshi Akiyama
Amarillo Symphony	P.O. Box 2552, Amarillo, TX 79105	Thomas Conlin
Arkansas Orchestra Society	Robinson Aud., Markham & Broadway, Little Rock, AR 72201	Kurt Klippstatter
Austin Symphony	1101 Red River St., Austin, TX 78701	Akiro Endo
Brooklyn Philharmonia	30 Lafayette Ave., Brooklyn, NY 11217	Lukas Foss
Calgary Philharmonic	320 9th Ave. SW, Calgary, Alta., T2P1K6	Franz Paul Decker
Canton Symphony	1001 Market Ave. N., Canton, OH 44702	Robert Marcellus
Cedar Rapids Symphony	605 Dows Bldg., Cedar Rapids, IA 52401	Richard D. Williams
Charlotte Symphony	511 E. Morehead St., Charlotte, NC 28202	Jacques Brourman
Chattanooga Symphony	730 Cherry St., Chattanooga, TN 37402	Richard Cormier
Chautauqua Symphony	Chautauqua Institution, Chautauqua, NY 14722	Sergiu Comissiona
Clarion Music Society	415 Lexington Ave., New York, NY 10017	Newell Jenkins
Colorado Springs Symphony	P.O. Box 1692, Colorado Springs, CO 80901	Charles Ansbacher
Corpus Christi Symphony	P.O. Box 495, Corpus Christi, TX 78403	Cornelius Eberhardt
Dayton Philharmonic	210 N. Main St., Dayton, OH 45402	Charles Wendelken-Wilson
Des Moines Symphony	318 Securities Bldg., Des Moines, IA 50309	Yuri Krasnapolsky
Duluth-Superior Symphony	506 W. Michigan St., Duluth, MN 55802	Joseph Hawthorne
Eastern Music Festival	712 Summit Ave., Greensboro, NC 27405	Sheldon Morgenstern
Edmonton Symphony	P.O. Box 4232, Edmonton, Alberta, Can. T6E 4T2	Pierre Hetu
El Paso Philharmonic	P.O. Box 180, El Paso, TX 79942	Abraham Chavez Jr.
Erie Philharmonic	720 G. Daniel Baldwin Bldg., Erie, PA 16501	Harold Bauer
Evansville Philharmonic	P.O. Box 84, Evansville, IN 47701	Minas Christian
Flint Symphony	1025 E. Kearsley St., Flint, MI 48503	Samuel Jones
Florida Gulf Coast Symphony	P.O. Box 569, St. Petersburg, FL 33731	Irwin Hoffman

Florida West Coast Symphony	P.O. Box 1107, Sarasota, FL 33578	Paul C. Wolfe
Fort Lauderdale Symphony	450 E. Las Olas Blvd., Fort Lauderdale, FL 33301	Emerson Buckley
Fort Wayne Philharmonic	927 S. Harrison, Fort Wayne, IN 4682	Thomas Briccetti
Fort Worth Symphony	4401 Trail Lake Dr., Ft. Worth, TX 76109	John Giordano
Fresno Philharmonic	1362 N. Fresno St., Fresno, CA 93703	Guy Taylor
Glendale Symphony	401 N. Brand Blvd., Glendale, CA 91203	Carmen Dragon
Grand Rapids Symphony	Exhibitors Bldg., Grand Rapids, MI 49502	Theo Alcantara
Hamilton Philharmonic	50 Main St., W. Hamilton, Ont., Can. L8P1H3	Boris Brott
Hartford Symphony	15 Lewis St., Hartford, CT 06103	Arthur Winograd
Hudson Valley Philharmonic	P.O. Box 191, Poughkeepsie, NY 12602	Imre Pallo
Jackson Symphony	P.O. Box 4584 Jackson, MS 39216	Lewis Dalvit
Jacksonville Symphony	333 Laura St., Jacksonville, FL 32202	Willis Page
Kalamazoo Symphony	426 S. Park St., Kalamazoo, MI 49007	Yoshimi Takeda
Knoxville Symphony	618 Gay St., Knoxville, TN 37902	Arpod Joo
Lexington Philharmonic	P.O. Box 838, Lexington, KY 40501	George Zack
London Symphony	520 Wellington St., London, Ont., Can. N6A 3R2	Clifford Evens
Long Beach Symphony	121 Linden Ave., Long Beach, CA 90802	Alberto Bolet
Long Island Symphony	P.O. Box 315, Huntington, NY 11743	Seymour Lipkin
Los Angeles Chamber Orchestra	1777 N. Vine St., Hollywood, CA 90028	Neville Marriner
Madison Symphony	211 N. Carroll St., Madison, WI 53703	Roland Johnson
Memphis Symphony	1503 Monroe, Memphis, TN 38104	Vincent DeFrank
Miami Beach Symphony	420 Lincoln Rd. Mall, Miami Beach, FL 33139	Barnett Breeskin
Miami Philharmonic	1200 Anastasia Ave., Coral Gables, FL 33134	(To be announced)
Midland Odessa Sym. & Chorale	P.O. Box 6266, Midland, TX 79701	Thomas Hohstadt
Monterey County Symphony	P.O. Box 3965, Carmel, CA 93921	Haymo Taeuber
New Haven Symphony	33 Whitney Ave., New Haven, CT 06511	Erich Kunzel
New World, Symphony of the	881 7th Ave., New York NY 10019	Everett Lee
Norfolk Symphony	P.O. Box 26, Norfolk, VA 23501	Russell Stanger
Northeastern Philharmonic	P.O. Box 71, Avoca, PA 18641	Thomas Michalak
Omaha Symphony	478 Aquila Ct., Omaha NE 68102	Thomas Bicetti
Orchestra da Camera	129 East Dr., N. Massapequa, NY 11758	Herbert Grossman
Oregon Symphony	1119 S.W. Park, Portland, OR 97205	Lawrence Smith
Pasadena Symphony	300 E. Green St., Pasadena, CA 91101	Daniel Lewis
Peoria Symphony	416 N.E. Jefferson, Peoria, IL 61603	Robert Kreis
Phoenix Symphony	6328 N. 7th St., Phoenix, AZ 85014	Eduardo Mata
Portland Symphony	30 Myrtle St., Portland, ME 04111	Bruce Hangen
Quebec Symphony	745 Rue St. Cyrille Ouest, Que., Can. G1S 1T3	James de Priest Pierre Dervaux
Queens Symphony	1 Station Sq., Forest Hills, NY 11375	David Katz
Rhode Island Philharmonic	39 The Arcade, Providence, RI 02903	Francis Madeira
Sacramento Symphony	451 Parkfair Dr., Sacramento, CA 95825	Harry Newstone
Saginaw Symphony	P.O. Box 889, Saginaw, MI 48606	Gideon Grau
Santa Barbara Symphony	210 E. Figueroa, Santa Barbara, CA 93101	Ronald Ondrejka
Savannah Symphony	P.O. Box 9505, Savanahh, GA 31402	George Trautwein
Shreveport Symphony	P.O. Box 4057, Shreveport, LA 71104	John Shenaut
South Bend Symphony	215 W. North Shore Drive, South Bend, IN 46617	Herbert Butler
Springfield Symphony	49 Chestnut St., Springfield, MA 01103	Robert Gutter
Thunder Bay Symphony	P.O. Box 2004, Station P, Thunder Bay, Ont. P7B 5E7	Dwight Bennett
Tri-City Symphony	P.O. Box 67, Davenport, IA 52805	James Dixon
Tucson Symphony	443 So. Stone Ave., Tucson, AZ 85701	Gregory Millar
Tulsa Philharmonic	2210 S. Main, Tulsa, OK 74114	Thomas Lewis
Utica Symphony	255 Genesee St., Utica, NY 13501	Fritz Maraffi
Vermont Symphony	P.O. Box 548, Middlebury, VT 05753	Efrain Guigui
Victoria Symphony	748 Johnson St., Victoria, B.C., Can. V8W 1N1	Lazlo Gati
Wheeling Symphony	P.O. Box 368, Wheeling, WV 26003	Jeff Holland Cook
Wichita Symphony	225 W. Douglas, Wichita, KS 67202	Francois Huybrechts
Winnipeg Symphony	555 Main St., Winnipeg, Manitoba, Can. R3B 1C3	Piero Gamba
Winston-Salem Symphony	610 Coliseum Dr., Winston-Salem, NC 27106	John Iuele
Youngstown Symphony	260 Federal Plaza West, Youngstown, OH 44503	Franz Bibo

Recordings

Disc and Tape Sales Up; New Platinum Record Awards Added to Gold

Manufacturers' sales of phonograph records and pre-recorded tapes went up by 7.3% in 1975 to a new high of $2.36 billion, according to the Recording Industry Assn. of America, which also announced that, as of Jan. 1, 1976, it was adding Platinum Record Awards to its well-known Gold Record Awards.

While Gold Awards will still go to single records selling one million copies, Platinum Awards will go to records when they sell 2 million.

Long-play albums and their tape equivalents that sell one million units will get the Platinum Award. Gold Awards will still go to those selling 500,000 units.

In 1975, manufacturers sold 282 million L-P albums for $1.485 billion, and 164 million singles for $183 million.

They sold 100.2 million 8-track tape cartridges for $583 million; 16.4 million pre-recorded tape cassettes for $16.4 million; 1.1 million quadraphonic tapes for $8.2 million, and 400,000 reel-to-reel tapes for $2 million.

The figures represented increases for 8-tracks, L-P albums, and cassettes; the other categories had declines.

Artists and Recording Titles

(A) Album. (S) Single.

Platinum Record Awards in 1976 follow:

The Eagles; Eagles - Their Greatest Hits (A).
Bob Dylan; Desire (A).
Peter Frampton; Frampton Comes Alive (A).
Led Zeppelin; Presence (A).
Johnnie Taylor; Disco Lady (S).
Wings; Wings at the Speed of Sound (A).
The Beatles; Rock 'N' Roll Music (A)
Rolling Stones; Black and Blue (A).

Aerosmith; Rocks (A).

Gold Record Awards during late 1975-76 follow:

August 1975

Captain & Tennille; Love Will Keep Us Together (A).
B.T. Express; Express (S).
Rolling Stones; Made in the Shade (A).
Aerosmith; Toys in the Attic (A).
Pilot; Magic (S).
Marshall Tucker Band; The Marshall Tucker Band (A).

Cat Stevens; Cat Stevens' Greatest Hits (A).
Ohio Players; Honey (A).
Kool & the Gang; Light of Worlds (A).
War; Why Can't We Be Friends? (S).
Bee Gees; Jive Talkin' (S).
Jefferson Starship; Red Octopus (A).
Linda Ronstadt; Don't Cry Now (A).
Freddy Fender; Before the Next Teardrop Falls (A).

September 1975
Paul McCartney & Wings; Listen to What the Man Said (S).
Glen Campbell; Rhinestone Cowboy (S).
Barbra Streisand & James Caan; Funny Lady (Original Soundtrack - A).
Elton John; Someone Saved My Life Tonight (S).
Aerosmith; Aerosmith (A).
Isley Bros.; Fight the Power, Part I (S).
Janis Ian; Between the Lines (A).
James Taylor; Gorilla (A).
Hamilton, Joe Frank & Reynolds; Fallin' in Love (S).
Olivia Newton-John; Please Mister Please (S).
Pink Floyd; Wish You Were Here (A).
Freddy Fender; Wasted Days and Wasted Nights (S).
Spinners; Pick of the Litter (A).
John Denver; Windsong (A).
Dickie Goodman; Mr. Jaws (S).
Tony Orlando & Dawn; Tony Orlando & Dawn's Greatest Hits (A).
Olivia Newton-John; Clearly Love (A).
Seals & Crofts; I'll Play for You (A).
Richard Pryor; Is It Something I Said? (A).

October 1975
Allman Bros. Band; Win, Lose, or Draw (A).
Linda Ronstadt; Prisoner in Disguise (A).
Jackson Browne; For Everyman (A).
Jeff Beck; Blow by Blow (A).
Bruce Springsteen; Born to Run (A).
Graham Central Station; Ain't No 'Bout-a-Doubt It (A).
David Bowie; Fame (S).
Kris Kristofferson & Rita Coolidge; Kris & Rita Full Moon (A).
Rick Wakeman; The Six Wives of Henry VIII (A).
Elton John; Rock of the Westies (A).
John Denver; Rocky Mountain Christmas (A).

November 1975
Black Oak Arkansas; Raunch 'N Roll (A).
Marshall Tucker Band; Where We All Belong (A).
David Crosby & Graham Nash; Wind on the Water (A).
Foghat; Foghat (A).
George Harrison; Extra Texture (A).
Neil Sedaka; Sedaka's Back (A).
Joan Baez; Diamonds and Rust (A).
Billy Joel; Piano Man (A).
Morris Albert; Feelings (S).
Jethro Tull; Minstrel in the Gallery (A).
Spinners; They Just Can't Stop It (S).
Paul Simon; Still Crazy after All These Years (A).
Peoples Choice; Do It Anyway You Wanna (S).
Michael Murphey; Blue Sky - Night Thunder (A).
Chicago; Chicago IX - Chicago's Greatest Hits (A).
John Denver; I'm Sorry (S).
Queen; Sheer Heart Attack (A).
Judy Collins; Judith (A).
The Staple Singers; Let's Do It Again (S).
Neil Sedaka; Bad Blood (S).

December 1975
Silver Convention; Fly, Robin, Fly (S).
Helen Reddy; Helen Reddy's Greatest Hits (A).
Kiss; Alive! (A).
Elton John; Island Girl (S).
Joni Mitchell; The Hissing of Summer Lawns (A).
Seals & Crofts; Seals & Crofts Greatest Hits (A).
Fleetwood Mac; Fleetwood Mac (A).
Art Garfunkel; Breakaway (A).
Earth, Wind, & Fire; Gratitude (A).
O'Jays; Family Reunion (A).
Silver Convention; Save Me (A).
The Who; The Who by Numbers (A).
Bay City Rollers; Saturday Night (S).

Captain & Tennille; The Way I Want to Touch You (S).
Carly Simon; The Best of Carly Simon (A).
Neil Sedaka; The Hungry Years (A).
Rod Stewart; Atlantic Crossing (A).
C.W. McCall; Convoy (S).
Bachman-Turner Overdrive; Head On (A).
Bee Gees; Main Course (A).
Barry Manilow; Trying to Get the Feeling (A).
Glen Campbell; Rhinestone Cowboy (A).
Bay City Rollers; Bay City Rollers (A).

January 1976
Ohio Players; Love Rollercoaster (S).
Black Oak Arkansas; High on the Hog (A).
Barry Manilow; I Write the Songs (S).
The O'Jays; I Love Music (S).
Harold Melvin & The Blue Notes; Wake up Everybody (A).
Hot Chocolate; You Sexy Thing (S).
Rufus - Featuring Chaka Khan; Rufus - Featuring Chaka Khan (A).
Bob Dylan; Desire (A).
Cat Stevens; Numbers (A).
Cat Stevens; Mona Bone Jakon (A).
Donna Summer; Love to Love You Baby (A).
Helen Reddy; No Way to Treat a Lady (A).
Barbra Streisand; A Christmas Album (A).
The Electric Light Orchestra; Face the Music (A).
Creedence Clearwater Revival; Proud Mary (A).
C.W. McCall; Black Bear Road (A).

February 1976
Marshall Tucker Band; Searchin' for a Rainbow (A).
Fleetwood Mac; Bare Trees (A).
Bad Company; Run with the Pack (A).
Natalie Cole; Inseparable (A).
Rhythm Heritage; Theme from S.W.A.T. (S).
Donna Summer; Love to Love You Baby (S).
Sweet; Fox on the Run (S).
The Eagles; Eagles, Their Greatest Hits 1971-75 (A).
Jethro Tull; M.U. - The Best of Jethro Tull (A).
David Bowie; Station to Station (A).
Earth, Wind & Fire; Singasong (S).
Peter Frampton; Frampton Comes Alive (A).

March 1976
Rufus - Featuring Chaka Khan; Sweet Thing (A).
Gary Wright; The Dream Weaver (A).
Barry White; Barry White's Greatest Hits (A).
Leon Russell; Will O' the Wisp (A).
Queen; A Night at the Opera (A).
Captain & Tennille; Song of Joy (A).
Willie Nelson; Red Headed Stranger (A).
Johnny Taylor; Disco Lady (A).
Paul Simon; 50 Ways to Leave Your Lover (S).
Foghat; Fool for the City (A).
Pure Prairie League; Bustin' Out (A).
Carol King; Thoroughbred (A).
Paul McCartney & Wings; Wings at the Speed of Sound (A).
The Four Seasons; December, 1963 (S).
The Outlaws. Waylon Jennings. Willie Nelson. Thompall Glasser; The Outlaws (A).
Brass Construction; Brass Construction (A).

April 1976
Led Zeppelin; Presence (A).
Johnnie Taylos; Eargasm (A).
Frank Zappa; Apostrophe'; (A).
Captain & Tennille; Lonely Night (S).
Nazareth; Love Hurts (S).
Nazareth; Hair of the Dog (A).
Blackbyrds; City Life (A).
Gladys Knight & the Pips; 2nd Anniversary (A).
Barbra Streisand; Lazy Afternoon (A).
The Sylvers; Boogie Fever (S).
Gary Wright; Dream Weaver (S).
Kiss; Destroyer (A).
Rolling Stones; Black and Blue (A).
Parliament; Membership Connection (A).
Olivia Newton-John; Come on Over (A).
Maxine Nightingale; Right Back Where We Started From (S).
Conway Twitty; You've Never Been This Far Before - Baby's Gone (A).

May 1976

Elton John; Here and There (A).
The Doobie Brothers; Takin' It to the Streets (A).
The Brothers Johnson; Look Out for No. 1 (A).
Miles Davis; Bitches Brew (A).
Dr. Hook; Only Sixteen (S).
America; Hideaway (A).
John Sebastian; Welcome Back Kotter (S).
Jimmy Dean; I.O.U. (S).
Aerosmith; Rocks (A).
Dan Fogelberg; Souvenirs (A).
Mac Davis; All the Love in the World (A).
Sweet; Desolation Boulevard (A).

June 1976

Isley Brothers; Harvest for the World (A).
Queen; Bohemian Rhapsody (A).
George Benson; Breezin' (A).
Silver Convention; Get up and Boogie (S).
Ohio Players; Contradiction (A).
Wings; Silly Love Songs (S).

Santana; Amigos (A).
The Beatles; Rock 'N' Roll Music (A).
The Manhattans; Kiss and Say Goodby (S).
Spirit; Twelve Dreams of Dr. Sardonicus (A).
Electric Light Orchestra; Ole' ELO (A).
Henry Gross; Shannon (S).
Chicago; Chicago X (A).
Neil Diamond; Beautiful Noise (A).
Elvin Bishop; Fooled Around and Fell In Love (A).
Donna Summer; Love Trilogy (A).
Daryl Hall & John Oates; Sara Smile (S).
Jefferson Starship; Spitfire (A).

July 1976

Natalie Cole; Natalie (A).
Aretha Franklin; Sparkle (A).
Phoebe Snow; Second Childhood (A).
Johnny Mathis; All-time Greatest Hits (A).
Carpenters; A Kind of Hush (A).
Starland Vocal Band; Afternoon Delight (S).
Boz Scaggs; Silk Degrees (A).

Best-Selling Books of 1975-76

Listed according to frequency of citation on best seller reports for Sept. 1975 through July 1976.
Numbers in parentheses show rank on final list for calendar year 1975, according to Publishers Weekly.

Fiction

1. Curtain; Agatha Christie (3).
2. Ragtime; E. L. Doctorow (1).
3. Trinity; Leon Uris.
4. The Choirboys; Joseph Wambaugh (5).
5. Looking for Mr. Goodbar; Judith Rossner (4).
6. 1876; Gore Vidal.
7. The Greek Treasure; Irving Stone.
8. The Deep; Peter Benchley.
9. Humboldt's Gift; Saul Bellow (10).
10. The Eagle Has Landed; Jack Higgins (6).
11. Shogun; James Clavell (9).
12. In the Beginning; Chaim Potok.
13. Saving the Queen; William F. Buckley Jr.
14. Agent in Place; Helen MacInnes.
15. The Lonely Lady; Harold Robbins.
16. The Gemini Contenders; Robert Ludlum.
17. The Great Train Robbery; Michael Crichton (8).
18. A Stranger in the Mirror; Sidney Sheldon.
19. The Boys from Brazil; Ira Levin.
20. The West End Horror; Nicholas Meyer.
21. Circus; Alistair MacLean.
22. The Moneychangers; Arthur Hailey (2).
23. The R Document; Irving Wallace.
24. The Canfield Decision; Spiro T. Agnew.
25. Dolores; Jacqueline Susann.

General

1. Sylvia Porter's Money Book; Sylvia Porter (5).
2. World of Our Fathers; Irving Howe.
3. Winning through Intimidation (2).
4. Bring on the Empty Horses; David Niven (9).

5. Angels; Billy Graham (1).
6. The Final Day; Bob Woodward and Carl Bernstein.
7. The Relaxation Response; Herbert Benson with Miriam Z. Klipper.
8. The Russians; Hedrick Smith.
9. Doris Day; Her Own Story; A. E. Hotchner.
10. Power; How to Get It, How to Use It; Michael Korda.
11. A Year of Beauty and Health; Beverly and Vidal Sassoon.
12. Scoundrel Time; Lillian Hellman.
13. A Man Called Intrepid; The Secret War; William Stevenson.
14. TM; Discovering Energy and Overcoming Stress; Harold H. Bloomfield (3).
15. Total Fitness in 30 Minutes a Week; Laurence E. Morehouse and Leonard Gross (6).
16. Passages; The Predictable Crises of Adult Life; Gail Sheehy.
17. Spandau; The Secret Diaries; Albert Speer.
18. The Ascent of Man; Jacob Bronowski (4).
19. Breach of Faith; Theodore H. White (10).
20. The Rockefellers; An American Dynasty; Peter Collier and David Horowitz.
21. The Great Railway Bazaar; Paul Theroux.
22. Against Our Will; Susan Brownmiller.
23. The Adams Chronicles; Four Generations of Greatness; Jack Shepherd.
24. The Age of Napoleon; Will and Ariel Durant.
25. Lyndon Johnson and the American Dream; Doris Kearns.

The Bermuda Triangle by Charles Berlitz with J. Manson Valentine, and The Save-Your-Life Diet by David Reuben were (7) and (8) on the final list for 1975, general.

Miss America Winners

For the winners of 1921 through 1958 see the 1972 issue of The World Almanac

		Height	Bust	Waist	Hips	Wgt.	Age	Hair	Eyes
1959	Mary Ann Mobley, Brandon, Miss.	5-5	34-1/2	22	35	114	21	Brown	Brown
1960	Lynda Lee Mead, Natchez, Miss.	5-7	36	24	36	120	20	Brown	Green
1961	Nancy Fleming, Montague, Michigan	5-6	35	22	35	116	18	Brown	Green
1962	Maria Fletcher, Asheville, N.C.	5-5-1/2	35	24	35	118	19	Brown	Hazel
1963	Jacquelyn Mayer, Sandusky, Ohio	5-5	35	24	35	118	19	Brown	Hazel
1964	Donna Axum, El Dorado, Arkansas	5-6-1/2	36	22	36	115	20	Brown	Hazel
1965	Vonda Kay Van Dyke, Phoenix, Ariz.	5-6	35	23	35	124	21	Brown	Brown
1966	Deborah Irene Bryant, Overland Park, Kansas	5-7	36	24	36	124	21	Brown	Brown
1967	Jane Anne Jayroe, Laverne, Oklahoma	5-6	36	23	36	115	19	Brown	Blue
1968	Debra Dene Barnes, Moran, Kansas	5-9	36-1/2	24	36-1/2	135	20	Brown	Blue
1969	Judith Anne Ford, Belvidere, Ill.	5-7	36	24-1/2	36	125	18	Blonde	Blue
1970	Pamela Anne Eldred, Birmingham, Mich.	5-5-1/2	34	21-1/2	34	110	21	Blonde	Green
1971	Phyllis Ann George, Denton, Texas	5-8	36	23	36	121	21	Brown	Brown
1972	Laurie Lea Schaefer, Columbus, Ohio	5-7	36	24	34	118	22	Auburn	Green
1973	Terry Anne Meeuwsen, DePere, Wisconsin	5-8	36	24	36	120	23	Brown	Brown
1974	Rebecca Ann King, Denver, Colorado	5-9	36	25	36	125	23	Brown	Blue
1975	Shirley Cothran, Fort Worth, Texas	5-8	36	24	36	119	21	Brown	Hazel
1976	Tawney Elaine Godin, Yonkers, N.Y.	5-10-1/2	36	24	36	128	18	Brown	Brown

Famous Paintings and Where You Can See Them

These paintings are listed because of their fame, not necessarily their artistic merit, and because they are in public collections. They are listed chronologically.

Giotto: Pieta, 1305; Arena Chapel, Padua.

Fra Filippo Lippi: Adoration of the Child, c. 1435; Staatliches Museum, Berlin.

Piero Della Francesca: Duke of Urbino, 1465; Uffizi Gallery, Florence.

Giovanni Bellini: Pieta, c. 1466; Brera, Milan.

Botticelli: The Birth of Venus, c. 1480; Uffizi.

Hieronymus Bosch: Christ Crowned with Thorns, c. 1500; National Gallery, London.

Leonardo da Vinci: Mona Lisa (La Gioconda), c. 1505; Louvre, Paris.

Michelangelo: Creation of Adam, 1508-12; Sistine Chapel, Vatican, Rome.

Giorgione: Sleeping Venus, c. 1508, Gemaldegalerie, Dresden.

Raphael: The Sistine Madonna, 1515-19; Gemaldegalerie, Dresden.

Titian: The Tribute Money, 1516; Gemaldegalerie.

Durer: The Four Apostles, 1523-26; Alte Pinakothek, Munich.

Holbein: Henry VIII, 1540; National Gallery, Rome.

Pieter Brueghel the Elder: Massacre of the Innocents, 1566; Kunsthistorisches Museum, Vienna.

El Greco: The Burial of Count Orgaz, 1586; Santo Tome, Toledo, Spain.

Rubens: Venus and Adonis, c. 1620; Met., N. Y.

Frans Hals: Laughing Cavalier, 1624; Wallace Collection, London.

Van Dyck: Charles I of England, c. 1635; Louvre.

Ribera: The Martyrdom of St. Bartholomew, 1630-39; Prado, Madrid.

Rembrandt: The Night Watch, 1642; Rijksmuseum, Amsterdam.

Velasquez: Maids of Honor, 1656; Prado, Madrid.

Vermeer: Young Woman with a Water Jug, c. 1658-64; Met., N.Y.

Ruisdael: View of Haarlem, c. 1670; Rijksmuseum.

Murillo: Virgin and Child, c. 1672; Met., N. Y.

Watteau: The Embarkation for Cythera, c. 1712; Louvre.

Hogarth: The Orgy (Rake's Progress), 1734; Soane's Museum, London.

Fragonard: The Love Letter, c. 1769; Met., N. Y.

Gainsborough: The Blue Boy, c. 1770; Huntington Gallery, San Marino, Cal.

John Singleton Copley: Watson and the Shark, 1778; Museum of Fine Arts, Boston.

Joshua Reynolds: Mrs. Siddons as the Tragic Muse, 1784; Huntington Gallery, San Marino, Cal.

John Trumbull: The Declaration of Independence, 1786-94; Capitol, Washington, D. C.

Gilbert Stuart: George Washington, c. 1795; Museum of Fine Arts, Boston. (Others in Met., N. Y., etc.)

David: The Rape of the Sabines, 1799; Louvre.

Goya: The Naked Maja, 1799; Prado, Madrid.

Ingres: Odalisque, 1814; Louvre.

John Constable: The Hay Wain, 1821; National Gallery, London.

Thomas Lawrence: Calmady Children, 1823; Met., N.Y.

John James Audubon: Birds of America (433 of the original 435 paintings), early 19th century; New-York Historical Society.

Joseph M. W. Turner: The Grand Canal, Venice, early 19th century; Met., N. Y.

George Caleb Bingham: Fur Traders Descending the Missouri, 1845; Met., N. Y.

Emanuel Leutze: Washington Crossing the Delaware, 1851; Washington Crossing State Park, Pa.

Rosa Bonheur: The Horse Fair, 1855; Met., N.Y.

Jean-Baptiste Corot: Le Lac de Terni, 1861; Corcoran Gallery, Washington.

Honore Daumier: The Third-Class Carriage, c. 1862; Met., N. Y.

Jean-Francois Millet: Man with the Hoe, 1863; San Francisco Museum.

James McNeil Whistler: Arrangement in Grey and Black—The Artist's Mother, c. 1872; Louvre.

Thomas Eakins: The Gross Clinic, 1875; Jefferson Medical College, Philadelphia.

A. M. Willard: Spirit of '76, 1876; (3 versions): Cleveland City Hall; Western Reserve Historical Society, Cleveland; Abbot Hall, Marblehead, Mass.

Edgar Degas: La Danseuse au Bouquet, 1878; Rhode Island School of Design, Providence.

Edouard Manet: In a Boat, 1879; Met., N. Y.

Pierre Auguste Renoir: Luncheon of the Boating Party, 1881; Phillips Collection, Washington.

Georges Seurat: Sunday Afternoon on the Grande Jatte, 1884-86; Art Institute of Chicago.

Paul Cezanne: Mont Sainte-Victoire, 1885-87; Met., N.Y.

Vincent Van Gogh: Wheat Field and Cypress Trees, 1889; National Gallery, London.

Albert Pinkham Ryder: Toilers of the Sea, c. 1890; Addison Gallery, Andover, Mass.

Paul Gauguin: Ia Orana Maria (Hail Mary), 1891, Met., N. Y.

Henri De Toulouse-Lautrec: At the Moulin Rouge, 1892; Art Institute of Chicago.

Claude Monet: Rouen Cathedral, 1894; Met., N. Y.

Winslow Homer: Gulf Stream, 1899; Art Institute of Chicago.

John Singer Sargent: Wyndham Sisters, 1900; Met., N.Y.

Frederic Remington: Cavalry Charge on the Southern Plains, 1907; Met., N. Y.

Georges Braque: Head of a Woman, 1909; Musee d'Art Moderne, Paris.

Henri Rousseau: The Dream, 1910; Modern Art, N. Y.

Marc Chagall: I and the Village, 1911; Modern Art, N. Y.

Marcel Duchamp: Nude Descending a Staircase, 1912; Philadelphia Museum of Art.

Paul Chabas: September Morn, 1912; Met., N. Y.

Amadeo Modigliani: Portrait of Madame Zboroski, 1917-18; Rhode Island School of Design, Providence.

Piet Mondrian: Composition, 1921; Kunstmuseum, Basel, Switzerland.

Paul Klee: Twittering Machine, 1922; Modern Art, N. Y.

George Bellows: The Dempsey-Firpo Fight, 1924; Whitney Museum of American Art, N. Y.

Vasily Kandinsky: Several Circles, 1926; Guggenheim Museum, N. Y.

Henri Matisse: Odalisque, 1928; Musee d'Art Moderne, Paris.

Grant Wood: American Gothic, 1930; Art Institute of Chicago.

Joan Miro: Man, Woman and Child, 1931; Philadelphia Museum of Art.

Jose Clemente Orozco: Zapatistas, 1931; Modern Art, N. Y.

Maurice Utrillo: Sacred-Heart and Montmartre Square, 1932; Musee d'Art et d'Histoire, Geneva.

William Gropper: The Senate, 1935; Modern Art, N. Y.

Pablo Picasso: Guernica, 1937; Modern Art, N. Y.

Georges Rouault: The Old King, 1937; Carnegie Institute Museum, Pittsburgh.

Thomas Hart Benton: Threshing Wheat, 1939; Swope Gallery, Terre Haute, Ind.

John Steuart Curry: John Brown, 1939; Met., N. Y.

Anna (Grandma) Moses: The Thanksgiving Turkey, 1943; Met., N. Y.

Andrew Wyeth: Christina's World, 1948; Modern Art, N. Y.

Jackson Pollock: Autumn Rhythm, 1950; Met., N. Y.

Salvador Dali: Crucifixion, 1954; Met., N. Y.

Raphael Soyer: Hugo Kastor, 1957; Met., N. Y.

Estimated Advertising Expenditures in the U. S.

Source: Advertising Age; prepared by
Robert J. Coen of McCann-Erickson, Inc.

MEDIUM	1973 Dollars-millions	1973 Per cent of total	1974 Dollars-millions	1974 Per cent of total	1975 Dollars-millions	1975 Per cent of total	% Change '75 vs. '74
Newspapers							
Total...............	7,595	30.2	8,001	29.8	8,442	29.9	+5.5
National............	1,111	4.4	1,194	4.5	1,221	4.3	+2.3
Local..............	6,484	25.8	6,807	25.4	7,221	25.6	+6.1
Magazines							
Total..............	1,448	5.8	1.504	5.6	1,465	5.2	−2.6
Weeklies...........	583	2.3	630	2.3	612	2.2	−2.9
Women's...........	362	1.5	372	1.4	368	1.3	−1.0
Monthlies..........	503	2.0	502	1.9	485	1.7	−3.4
Farm Publications	65	0.3	72	0.3	74	0.3	+3.0
Television							
Total...............	4,493	17.9	4,851	18.1	5,272	18.6	+8.7
Network............	1,968	7.8	2,145	8.0	2,310	8.2	+7.7
Spot...............	1,450	5.8	1,495	5.6	1,630	5.7	+9.0
Local..............	1,075	4.3	1,211	4.5	1,332	4.7	+10.0
Radio							
Total..............	1,690	6.7	1,837	6.9	2,025	7.2	+10.2
Network...........	70	0.3	69	0.3	85	0.3	+22.5
Spot...............	380	1.5	405	1.5	440	1.6	+9.0
Local..............	1,240	4.9	1,363	5.1	1,500	5.3	+10.0
Direct Mail...........	3,698	14.7	3,986	14.9	4,155	14.7	+4.2
Business Papers.......	865	3.4	900	3.4	919	3.2	+2.1
Outdoor							
Total...............	308	1.2	309	1.2	335	1.2	+8.3
National............	200	0.8	203	0.8	220	0.8	+8.3
Local..............	108	0.4	106	0.4	115	0.4	+8.3
Miscellaneous							
Total...............	4,958	19.7	5.270	19.7	5,583	19.7	+5.9
National............	2,590	10.3	2,752	10.3	2,881	10.2	+4.7
Local..............	2,368	9.4	2,518	9.4	2,702	9.5	+7.3
Total							
National............	13,845	55.1	14,725	55.1	15,400	54.5	+4.6
Local...............	11,275	44.9	12,005	44.9	12,870	45.5	+7.2
Grand Total...........	25,120	100.0	26,730	100.0	28,270	100.0	+5.8
Inflation Adjustment. (1967 Dollars)	18,890	—	18,097	—	17,537	—	−9.7

U.S. Television Sets and Stations

Set Ownership
(Nielsen Est. as of Sept. 1975)

Total TV Homes	69,600,000	100%
(Est. 9/1/76)	71,460,000	
Homes with:		
Color TV Sets	51,230,000	74%
B&W only	18,370,000	26
2 or more Sets	30,000,000	43
One Set	39,600,000	57
CATV	9,488,200	14
UHF	63,561,600	91

Station Facilities
(FCC as of June, 1976)

Commercial TV		708
	VHF	513
	UHF	195
Educational TV		253
	VHF	98
	UHF	155
Total TV		961

Network TV Program Ratings

Source: A.C. Nielsen, December, 1975

Program Type	TV Households Rating	TV Households No. (000)	Men 18-34	Men 25-54	Men 55+	Women 18-34	Women 25-54	Women 55+	Working	Teens 12-17	Children 6-11
Today (7:30-8:00)	4.3	2,990	1.1	1.4	3.5	1.3	2.8	5.1	2.6	*	*
CBS News (7:00-8:00)	2.1	1,460	*	*	2.0	*	1.1	2.2	*	*	*
Daytime:											
Drama	7.7	5,340	1.0	*	3.1	6.2	6.4	8.5	2.7	1.4	*
Quiz and Aud. Part.	6.1	4,220	1.5	1.3	4.4	3.5	4.0	6.4	2.0	1.5	1.4
All 10:00-4:30	6.9	4,810	1.3	1.1	3.4	4.9	5.2	7.4	2.3	1.5	1.3
Evening Inform	11.4	7,910	5.4	7.0	14.4	5.1	6.3	14.3	6.1	3.1	3.9
Evening:											
General Drama	16.5	11,480	9.2	10.0	12.5	11.7	12.8	16.0	11.5	10.3	11.2
Susp. & Myst.	18.5	12.890	11.9	13.9	14.7	12.9	14.8	15.0	12.4	10.3	8.4
Situation Comedy	21.2	14,750	12.2	13.0	16.8	15.9	16.6	18.8	16.0	14.1	15.8
Variety	17.6	12,250	9.3	11.4	14.6	11.3	13.5	16.5	12.9	12.0	11.4
Feature Film	16.5	11,500	13.8	13.6	13.1	11.5	13.1	10.9	11.4	10.3	9.0
All 7:30-11:00	18.4	12,800	11.9	13.3	14.7	12.6	14.0	14.8	12.4	11.1	11.8

*Less than 1.0 rating.

50 Leading U.S. Advertisers, 1975

Reprinted by permission of Advertising Age, Sept. 13, 1976
Copyright© Crain Communications Inc. 1976)

Rank	Company	Ad Costs (000)	Sales (000)	Ads as % Sales
	Cars			
2	General Motors Corp.....	$225,000	$35,724,911	0.6
15	Chrysler Corp..........	98,200	7,589,404	1.3
18	Ford Motor Co..........	91,000	24,099,100	0.4
	Food			
4	General Foods Corp.....	203,000	2,987,300	6.8
17	General Mills...........	94,000	2,645,000	3.6
20	Norton Simon Inc.......	86,447	1,308,902	6.6
23	Nabisco Inc............	80,700	1,970,800	4.1
24	Kraftco Corp...........	76,600	4,093,810	1.9
26	McDonald's Corp........	75,000	2,478,000	3.0
30	Standard Brands Inc......	72,000	1,944,979	3.7
36	Pillsbury Co............	65,400	1,421,937	4.6
37	Beatrice Foods Co........	64,000	3,662,432	1.8
39	Kellogg Co.............	60,846	1,213,620	5.0
41	Ralston Purina Co.......	60,000	3,149,100	1.9
	Soaps, cleansers (and allied)			
1	Procter & Gamble Co.....	360,000	4,550,000*	7.9
11	Colgate-Palmolive Co....	108,000	1,100,000	9.8
21	Lever Bros.............	85,000	747,500	11.4
	Tobacco			
9	R. J. Reynolds, Industries Inc...	113,600	4,837,643	2.4
14	Philip Morris Inc.......	99,500	3,642,414	2.7
27	American Brands........	74,000	4,055,300	1.8
43	Brown & Williamson Tobacco Co..	57,000	1,523,100	3.7
48	Liggett Group Inc.......	53,000	812,974	6.5
	Drugs and cosmetics			
5	Bristol-Myers Co........	170,000	1,827,669	9.3
6	Warner-Lambert Co......	169,000	1,218,134	13.9
7	American Home Products..	138,000	2,408,919	5.7
16	Richardson-Merrell......	94,472	658,691	14.3
22	Gillette Co.............	84,000	1,406,906	6.0
33	Sterling Drug Inc.......	69,000	584,949	11.8
44	Schering-Plough Corp....	56,000	423,275	13.2
45	Johnson & Johnson......	$ 55,500	$ 1,267,960	4.4
50	Chesebrough-Pond's Inc...	50,000	475,665	10.5
	Liquor			
12	Heublein Inc...........	103,726	1,682,703	6.2
38	Seagram Co. Ltd........	63,000	1,930,786	3.3
	Oil			
8	Mobil Oil Corp..........	135,900	27,178,955	0.5
	Tires			
35	Goodyear Tire & Rubber Co...	67,807	5,452,473	1.2
	Soft drinks			
25	Coca-Cola Co..........	75,300	2,872,839	2.6
31	PepsiCo Inc............	70,000	1,787,357	3.9
	Appliances, tv, radio			
19	RCA Corp.............	89,000	4,815,800	1.8
31	General Electric Co......	70,000	13,399,000	0.5
	Retail chains			
2	Sears, Roebuck & Co.†....	225,000	11,555,947	1.9
34	J. C. Penney Co........	68,000	7,678,600	0.9
	Chemicals			
27	American Cyanamid Co...	74,000	1,157,066	6.4
	Photographic equipment			
46	Eastman Kodak Co......	55,200	4,958,536	1.1
	Telephone service, equipment			
13	American Telephone & Telegraph...	101,700	29,272,000	0.3
29	International Telephone & Telegraph Corp...	73,085	11,367,747	0.6
	Miscellaneous			
10	U.S. Government.......	113,400		
40	Loews Corp...........	60,467	2,701,836	2.2
42	CBS Inc..............	57,244	1,938,867	3.0
47	Gulf & Western Industries..	55,000	2,529,459	2.2
49	Greyhound Corp.......	53,000	3,748,000	1.4

*Domestic sales estimated by AA. †Percentage shown would be two and a half times more if Sears $285,000,000 in local advertising were added to the $225,000,000 national total. The other retail chain (J. C. Penney) ad total also does not include local advertising.
Note: All add totals are domestic. Whenever possible, AA has reported the company's domestic sales figure in this table, although for some companies only a worldwide sales total was available.

Commercial Broadcast Stations on the Air

Source: Federal Communications Commission (1974)

State	Total	AM	FM	TV
Total.............	7,526	4,357	2,448	721
United States.......	7,426	4,305	2,413	708
Alabama..........	213	136	60	17
Alaska...........	28	18	3	7
Arizona..........	84	54	19	11
Arkansas.........	142	87	47	8
California.........	441	226	162	53
Colorado.........	110	67	32	11
Connecticut.......	64	38	21	5
Delaware.........	16	10	6	—
Dist. of Columbia....	20	7	7	6
Florida..........	317	194	96	27
Georgia..........	268	173	77	18
Hawaii..........	39	25	4	10
Idaho...........	59	43	10	6
Illinois..........	265	123	118	24
Indiana..........	187	86	84	17
Iowa...........	141	74	54	13
Kansas..........	104	60	32	12
Kentucky........	198	110	76	12
Louisiana........	154	92	45	17
Maine...........	61	36	18	7
Maryland........	91	51	33	7
Massachusetts.....	112	64	38	10
Michigan.........	237	124	92	21
Minnesota........	153	89	53	11
Mississippi.......	166	102	53	11
Missouri.........	188	108	57	23
Montana.........	66	41	13	12
Nebraska........	84	48	21	15
Nevada..........	39	21	11	7
New Hampshire.....	46	27	15	4
New Jersey.......	68	37	27	4
New Mexico.......	84	57	19	8
New York........	303	161	113	29
North Carolina......	299	203	78	18
North Dakota......	47	26	9	12
Ohio...........	268	121	120	27
Oklahoma........	115	67	39	9
Oregon..........	117	80	24	13
Pennsylvania......	314	173	118	23
Rhode Island......	24	15	7	2
South Carolina.....	163	104	47	12
South Dakota......	54	30	14	10
Tennessee.......	237	154	66	17
Texas..........	481	284	140	57
Utah...........	47	32	12	3
Vermont.........	26	18	6	2
Virginia.........	207	128	64	15
Washington.......	148	93	40	15
West Virginia......	96	60	27	9
Wisconsin........	200	99	83	18
Wyoming........	35	29	3	3
Other areas.......	100	52	35	13
Puerto Rico.......	89	48	31	10
Guam..........	3	1	1	1
Virgin Islands......	8	3	3	2

Movies of the Year (Sept. 1, 1975 to Sept. 1, 1976)

Listed below, alphabetically, are some of the major films rated by the New York Daily News star system: ★★★★ is for excellent, ★★★1/2 very good, ★★★ good, ★★1/2 fair, ★★ mediocre, ★1/2 poor, ★ very poor, 0★ not worth rating.

Kathleen Carroll, N. Y. Daily News Movie Editor and Critic

Movie	Star Rating	Stars	Director
Sherlock Holmes' Smarter Brother	★★	Gene Wilder, Madeline Kahn	Gene Wilder
All the President's Men	★★★★	Robert Redford, Dustin Hoffman	Alan J. Pakula
All Screwed Up	★★	Luigi Diberti, Lina Polito	Lina Wertmuller
Alpha Beta	★★★	Albert Finney, Rachel Roberts	Anthony Page
Bad News Bears, The	★★1/2	Walter Matthau, Tatum O'Neal	Michael Ritchie
Barry Lyndon	★★1/2	Ryan O'Neal, Marisa Berenson	Stanley Kubrick
Big Bus, The	★★	Joseph Bologna, Stockard Channing	James Frawley
Bingo Long Traveling All-Stars and Motor Kings, The	★★1/2	Billy Dee Williams, James Earl Jones	John Badham
Birch Interval	★★★1/2	Eddie Albert, Rip Torn	Dilbert Mann
Bluebird, The	★★1/2	Elizabeth Taylor, Jane Fonda	George Cukor
Breakheart Pass	★★1/2	Charles Bronson, Ben Johnson	Tom Gries
Buffalo Bill and the Indians	★★★	Paul Newman, Joel Grey	Robert Altman
Clockmaker, The	★★★	Philippe Noiret	Bertrand Tavernier
Conduct Unbecoming	★★★	Richard Attenborough, Trevor Howard	Michael Anderson
Cousin, Cousine	★★★1/2	Marie-Christine Barrault, Victor Lanoux	Jean-Charles Tacchella
Distant Thunder	★★★1/2	Soumitra Chatteril	Sanyajit Ray
Dog Day Afternoon	★★★★	Al Pacino, Charles Durning	Sidney Lumet
Echoes of a Summer	★★★	Richard Harris, Jodie Foster	Don Taylor
Face to Face	★★★1/2	Liv Ullmann, Erland Josephson	Ingmar Bergmann
Family Plot	★★1/2	Bruce Dern, Barbara Harris	Alfred Hitchcock
Gable and Lombard	★★	James Brolin, Jill Clayburgh	Sidney J. Furie
Give 'em Hell, Harry	★★★	James Whitmore	Steve Binder
Grey Gardens	★★★1/2	Edie and Edith Beale	David and Albert Maysles
Hard Times	★★1/2	Charles Bronson, Jack Coburn	Walter Hills
Harry and Walter Go to New York	★★1/2	Elliot Gould, James Caan	Mark Rydell
Hearts of the West	★★★1/2	Jeff Bridges, Alan Arkin	Howard Zieff
Hester Street	★★★	Steven Keats, Carol Kane	John Micklin Silver
Hiding Place, The	★★★1/2	Julie Harris, Eileen Heckart	James F. Collier
Hindenburg, The	★★	George C. Scott, Anne Bancroft	Robert Wise
Hustle	★★★1/2	Burt Reynolds, Catherine Deneuve	Robert Aldrich
Inserts	★1/2	Richard Dreyfuss, Jessica Harper	John Byrum
Killer Elite, The	★★	James Caan, Robert Duval	Sam Peckinpah
Killing of a Chinese Bookie, The	★★	Ben Gazzara, Seymour Cassel	John Cassavetes
Leadbelly	★★★	Roger E. Mosley, Madge Sinclair	Gordon Parks
Let's Do It Again	★★★1/2	Sidney Poitier, Bill Cosby	Sidney Poitier
Lies My Father Told Me	★★★	Yossi Yadin	Jan Kadar
Lipstick	★	Margaux Hemingway, Anne Bancroft	Lamont Johnson
Logan's Run	★★1/2	Michael York, Peter Ustinov	Michael Anderson
Lucky Lady	★★★	Gene Hackman, Liza Minelli	Stanley Doren
Magic Flute, The	★★1/2	Joseph Kostlinger, Irma Urrila	Ingmar Bergmann
Mahogany	★★1/2	Diana Ross, Billy Dee Williams	Berry Gordy
Man Who Fell to Earth, The	★★★1/2	David Bowie	Nicholas Roeg
Man Who Would Be King, The	★★★	Sean Connery, Michael Caine	John Houston
Missouri Breaks, The	★★★1/2	Jack Nicholson, Marlon Brando	Arthur Penn
Mr. Quilp	★★★1/2	Anthony Newley, David Hemmings	Michael Tuchner
Murder By Death	★★★	Peter Falk, Peter Sellers	Robert Moore
Next Stop, Greenwich Village	★★★	Lenny Baker, Shelley Winters	Paul Mazursky
Obsession	★★★	Cliff Robertson, Genevieve Bujold	Brian De Palma
Omen, The	★★★1/2	Lee Remick, Gregory Peck	Richard Donner
One Flew Over the Cuckoo's Nest	★★★★	Jack Nicholson, Louise Fletcher	Milos Forman
Other Side of the Mountain, The	★★★	Marilyn Hassett, Beau Bridges	Larry Peerce
Rancho DeLuxe	★★★1/2	Jeff Bridges, Sam Waterston	Frank Perry
Ritz, The	★★1/2	Jack Weston, Rita Moreno	Richard Lester
Robin and Marion	★★1/2	Sean Connery, Audrey Hepburn	Richard Lester
Romantic Englishwoman, The	★★★	Glenda Jackson, Michael Caine	Joseph Losey
Rooster Cogburn	★★1/2	John Wayne, Katherine Hepburn	Stuart Miller
Sailor Who Fell From Grace With the Sea, The	★★1/2	Sarah Miles, Kris Kristofferson	Lewis John Carlino
Seven Beauties	★★★★	Giancarlo Giannini	Lina Wertmuller
Shootist, The	★★★★	John Wayne, Lauren Bacall	Don Siegel
Silent Movie	★★★	Marty Feldmann, Dom DeLuise	Mel Brooks
"Smile"	★★★1/2	Bruce Dern	Michael Ritchie
Special Section	★★★1/2	Louis Seigner, Michel Lonsdale	Costa-Gavras
Story of Adele H., The	★★★	Isabelle Adjani	Francois Truffaut
Sunshine Boys, The	★★★1/2	Walter Matthau, George Burns	Herbert Ross
Swashbuckler	★★★	Robert Shaw, Peter Boyle	James Goldstone
Swept Away By an Unusual Destiny	★★1/2	Giancarlo Giannini, Mariangela Melato	Lina Wertmuller
Taxi Driver	★★★1/2	Robert De Niro, Cybill Shepard	Martin Scorese
That's Entertainment, Part 2	★★★1/2	Fred Astaire, Gene Kelly	Gene Kelly, et al
Three Days of the Condor	★★★	Robert Redford, Faye Dunnaway	Sydney Pollack
W. C. Fields and Me	★★★	Rod Steiger, Valerie Perrine	Arthur Hiller

State Support of the Arts

Source: Associated Council of the Arts

(Footnotes apply to 1976 figures only.)

State	Appropriations		Per Capita in¢		Rank	Percentage Change
	'75	'76	'75	'76		
Alabama (1)	$125,000	$250,000	3.6	7.2	33	+100%
Alaska	215,600	446,250	71.4	147.7	2	+107%
Arizona (2)	82,500	86,700	4.7	4.8	43	+5%
Arkansas	167,465	283,722	8.7	14.7	14	+69%
California	1,000,000	875,000	5.0	4.3	45	-12%
Colorado (3)	1,251,316	1,900,914	56.7	86.1	4	+52%
Connecticut	394,000	367,532	12.9	12.1	18	-7%
Delaware	43,128	58,353	7.9	10.7	23	+36%
D.C. (4)	30,000	117,500				
Florida (5)	398,994	415,812	5.9	6.1	39	+4%
Georgia	101,640	153,452	2.2	3.4	48	+57%
Hawaii (6)	599,083	998,553	77.8	129.6	3	+67%
Idaho (2)	23,121	43,200	3.2	6.0	39	+87%
Illinois	925,719	1,278,400	8.3	11.5	21	+38%
Indiana	160,964	617,221	3.1	11.8	20	+283%
Iowa	70,767	200,735	2.5	7.1	35	+184%
Kansas	85,780	84,870	3.8	3.7	46	-2%
Kentucky	225,800	290,400	7.0	9.0	28	+29%
Louisiana (2)	59,792	68,614	1.6	1.8	50	+15%
Maine	163,000	156,241	16.4	15.7	12	-4%
Maryland	449,788	463,363	9.2	9.5	25	+3%
Massachusetts	1,600,000	1,000,000	28.1	17.5	11	-38%
Michigan (7)	2,109,000	2,330,000	23.8	26.2	8	+10%
Minnesota (8)	300,000	500,000	7.9	13.1	15	+67%
Mississippi	112,628	160,564	5.1	7.2	34	+43%
Missouri	1,249,209	1,499,600	26.7	32.0	5	+20%
Montana (9)	27,950	48,549	4.0	6.9	36	+74%
Nebraska	129,390	172,517	8.7	11.9	19	+37%
Nevada	15,000	62,695	3.4	12.8	16	+318%
New Hampshire (2)	45,079	59,356	6.2	8.0	31	+32%
New Jersey	792,998	671,464	11.1	9.3	27	-15%
New Mexico	65,000	83,500	6.4	8.2	30	+28%
New York	35,653,000	35,702,900	196.1	196.2	1	+.1%
North Carolina	221,805	248,761	4.4	4.8	42	+12%
North Dakota (2)	5,100	33,850	.8	5.4	41	+564%
Ohio	976,161	1,002,030	9.2	9.4	26	+3%
Oklahoma	95,322	120,000	3.7	4.6	44	+26%
Oregon	53,350	138,695	2.6	6.6	37	+160%
Pennsylvania	1,490,000	1,471,000	12.6	12.4	17	-1%
Rhode Island (10)	267,199	261,006	28.1	27.4	7	-2%
South Carolina	595,696	589,666	23.0	24.7	9	+8%
South Dakota	85,391	100,000	12.8	15.0	13	+17%
Tennessee	411,500	380,400	10.5	9.6	24	-7%
Texas	159,565	410,454	1.4	3.6	47	+157%
Utah	268,400	324,800	25.3	30.6	6	+21%
Vermont	50,000	50,000	11.2	11.2	22	no change
Virginia	265,000	272,055	5.7	5.8	40	+3%
Washington (11)	246,130	263,923	7.2	7.7	32	+7%
West Virginia (12)	276,759	360,000	15.9	20.6	10	+30%
Wisconsin (2)	59,900	102,200	1.4	2.3	49	+7.1%
Wyoming (13)	14,567	27,560	4.4	8.3	29	+89%
TOTAL:	**$54,214,556**	**$57,668,668**				

(1) Earmarked funds totalled $187,000. (2) Money appropriated is for administrative use only. (3) All but $83,000 was earmarked. (4) $87,000 appropriated by D.C. government; $30,000 by Congress. (5) Earmarked funds totalled $300,000. (6) Earmarked funds totalled $252,000. (7) Included in the appropriation is a $680,000 line-item for the Detroit Institute of Art. (8) $75,000 is earmarked for "major institutions" — eligibility and distribution to be determined by the Arts Board, not the legislature. Also, 55% of the funds remaining after "major" monies and administrative funds are subtracted must be granted in the Twin Cities metropolitan area. (9) Earmarked funds totalled $5,000. (10) Earmarked funds totalled $63,250. (11) Earmarked funds totalled $63,585. (12) Earmarked funds totalled $200,-000. (13) $8,900 was earmarked.

Television Network Addresses

ABC
1330 Avenue of Americas
New York, N.Y. 10019

CBC
Canadian Broadcasting Corp.
1500 Bronson Ave.
Ottawa, Ontario, Canada K1G 3J5

CBS
51 W. 52nd St.
New York, N.Y. 10019
Metromedia
277 Park Ave.
New York, N.Y. 10017
NBC
30 Rockefeller Plaza
New York, N.Y. 10020

Westinghouse Broadcasting
(Group W)
90 Park Ave.
New York, N.Y. 10016

PBS
Public Broadcasting Service
15 W. 51st St.
New York, N.Y. 10020

Global Communication
Source: UNESCO; data for 1971-72

Nation	No. of daily newspapers	Copies per 1,000 pop.	No. of radio trans-mitters	Radios per 1,000 pop.	No. of TV trans-mitters[1]	TV sets per 1,000 pop.	No. of film theaters	Theater seats per 1,000 pop.	Avg. visits per year pop.
Algeria	4	18	25	46	13	10	640	14	6
Argentina	180	180	147	424	59	191	1,637	31	2
Australia	58	321	212	220	199	234	1,100	64	3
Austria	31	328	366	287	322	226	835	37	4
Bahrain	3[2]	29	3	341	0	59	9	45	6
Bangladesh	25	N/A	16	N/A	1	N/A	(est 100)	N/A	N/A
Belgium	55	N/A	29	366	17	235	740	41	3
Bolivia	16	33	133	260	1	2	120	13	0.6
Brazil	261	35	994	58	50	66	3,194	19	2
Bulgaria	13	206	26	268	118	150	3,106	82	13
Canada	121	234	729	821	534	334	1,156	30	4
Chile	46	N/A	229	156	25	56	360	27	5
China (P.R.)	N/A	N/A	N/A	19	(est. 20)[4]	0.7	N/A	N/A	N/A
Colombia	36	105	131	130	18	53	378	13	3
Cuba	16	107	110	154	19	66	428	N/A	N/A
Czechoslovakia	27	280	119	266	680	228	3,469	68	7
Denmark	53	364	31	329	25	284	350	28	4
Ecuador	22	43	336	261	14	23	164	18	3
Egypt	14	20	43	144	28	15	246	6	2
Ethiopia	3	2	9	20	6	1	30	1	0.4
Finland	60	425	97	409	70	255	318	21	2
France	106	233	294	312	1,961	244	4,237	39	3
Germany, E.	40	425	106	355	455	283	1,197	21	5
Germany, W.	1,093	330	313	340	958	455	3,171	21	2
Ghana	3	30	23	85	4	2	13	2	0.1
Greece	104	N/A	50	313	17	58	1,034	N/A	15
Guinea	1	1	5	21	—	(no TV)	28	2	N/A
Hungary	27	216	29	244	12	193	3,755	57	7
Iceland	5	439	29	303	59	206	25	44	7
India	821	N/A	137	21	2	0.1	4,716	5	6
Indonesia	120	10	140	114	12	2	490	N/A	N/A
Iran	39	25	38	130	70	33	437	9	0.9
Iraq	7	N/A	21	169	5	25	24	N/A	0.8
Ireland	7	233	12	209	20	168	N/A	N/A	7
Israel	24	183	47	220	21	119	252	59	11
Italy	78	142	1,874	230	1,193	201	10,719	N/A	10
Jamaica	2	69	14	408	11	55	42	21	3
Japan	172	529	889	441	4,991	229	2,673	12	2
Kenya	3	10	18	64	4	2	32	2	0.6
Korea, S.	42	138	123	128	39	28	793	15	4
Kuwait	6	44	14	439	7	165	7	13	4
Lebanon	52	N/A	6	210	8	113	170	30	17
Liberia	1	5	16	255	3	4	8	N/A	0.5
Libya	7	17	12	41	2	0.5	28	9	2
Malaysia	40	77	61	162	18	24	550	31	7
Mexico	200	N/A	590	266	78	57	1,765	28	5
Morocco	6	N/A	35	95	14	14	260	9	1
Netherlands	95	307	34	303	16	245	321	14	2
New Zealand	40	367	58	704	7	249	239	49	N/A
Nigeria	11	N/A	37	23	7	1	183	0.7	1
Norway	79	391	248	313	525	227	450	37	5
Pakistan	98	N/A	22	18	7	2	578	5	0.3
Panama	7	86	114	329	13	82	23	19	3
Paraguay	4	30	37	71	1	20	61+	N/A	N/A
Peru	56	N/A	304	138	19	28	276	N/A	N/A
Philippines	19	17	327	42	15	11	951	N/A	N/A
Poland	44	231	51	177	52	159	2,465	18	3
Portugal	33	N/A	95	146	23	40	485	28	3
Rhodesia	4	15	22	38	3	20	90	9	N/A
Romania	57	173	52	152	111	83	6,244	N/A	9
Saudi Arabia	5	7	11	31	6	19	(no public movies)		
Senegal	1	5	12	67	1	0.4	87	13	1
Singapore	10	193	16	130	2	95	75	29	17
S. Africa	21	47	177	102	N/A	N/A	685	22	N/A
Spain	115	99	463	205	641	169	6,064	129	8
Sri Lanka	17	48	29	66	—	(no TV)	303	10	8
Sweden	108	515	292	367	299	333	1,334	N/A	3
Switzerland	98	390	200	310	446	243	554	32	5
Syria	5	9	11	375	7	22	70	N/A	N/A
Tanzania	7	4	9	11	—	—	36	1	0.4
Thailand	35	24	144	85	30	10	392	12	N/A
Tunisia	4	21	6	49	11	16	104	9	2
Turkey	432	N/A	19	132	7	5	700	N/A	N/A
USSR	639	333	3,034	430	1,466	185	147,200	N/A	19
UK	109	437	396	699	314	299	1,482	25	3
U.S.A.	1,761	314	6,719	1,695	3,695	472	14,300	48	5
Uruguay	29	269	99	507	17	101	180	42	N/A
Venezuela	42	91	235	182	37	89	429	49	3
Vietnam, S.[5]	56	5	22	319	4	26	143	5	1
Yugoslavia	25	89	463	241	348	120	1,393	23	4
Zaire	6	N/A	27	0.9	2	0.3	57	0.8	0.05
Zambia	2	13	20	55	3	4	29	3	N/A

[1]No. of TV transmitters indicates breadth of coverage; mountainous countries require more transmitters. [2]Bahrain, non dailies. [3]Bolivia, data 1963, 64, 68. [4]Originating stations. [5]Vietnam, S., pre-PRG. N/A-not available.

Selected U.S. Daily Newspapers' Circulation

Source: Audit Bureau of Circulations' FAS-FAX Report. Average paid circulation for 6 months to Mar. 31, 1976. †3 months. For the 6 months up to Sept. 30, 1975, 1,630 English language dailies in the U.S. (322 morning, 1,290 evening, 18 all day) had an average audited circulation of 60,230,329. Sunday papers included 602 with audited average circulation of 50,359,875. (m) morning; (e) evening; *Mon.-Fri. average. Brackets indicate joint publication.

Newspaper	Daily	Sunday
Albany, N.Y. Times-Union (m)	76,186	134,006
Albany, N.Y. Knickerbocker News-Union Star (e)	62,069	
Akron Beacon Journal (e)	168,278	216,078
Allentown Call-Chronicle (m&e)	*122,286	151,335
Atlanta Constitution (m)	204,623	
Atlanta Journal (e)	225,948	522,915
Baltimore News-American (e)	*181,525	263,084
Baltimore Sun (m&e)	*350,659	348,812
Birmingham News (e)	*184,776	222,821
Birmingham Post-Herald (m)	*73,899	
Boston Globe (m&e)	449,046	598,637
Boston Herald American (m) & Sunday Advertiser	*313,703	456,009
Buffalo Courier-Express (m)	122,060	270,806
Buffalo News (e)	*279,298	
Charlotte News (e)	57,107	
Charlotte Observer (m)	167,508	226,021
Chicago News (e)	*374,406	
Chicago Sun-Times (m)	*560,124	687,356
Chicago Tribune (m&e)	*747,715	1,110,865
Christian Science Monitor (m)	*172,786	
Cincinnati Enquirer (m)	185,061	284,653
Cincinnati Post (e)	207,596	
Cleveland Plain Dealer (m)	375,100	450,657
Cleveland Press (e)	327,359	
Columbia, S.C. State (m)	101,027	118,409
Columbia, S.C. Record (e)	31,897	
Columbus, Ga. Enquirer (m)	*33,859	65,077
Columbus, Ga. Ledger (e)	*32,202	
Columbus, O. Citizen-Journal (m)	108,771	
Columbus, O. Dispatch (e)	197,704	325,124
Dallas News (m)	257,565	315,987
Dallas Times Herald (e)	*223,524	314,881
Dayton Journal (m)	103,216	
Dayton News (e)	149,199	217,854
Denver Post (e)	*246,146	333,585
Denver: Rocky Mountain News (m)	224,053	246,679
Des Moines Register (m)	229,047	433,865
Des Moines Tribune (e)	93,383	
Detroit Free Press (m)	*622,339	734,738
Detroit News (e)	*627,461	824,776
Ft. Worth Star-Telegram (m&e)	224,652	228,430
Fresno Bee (e)	112,689	133,737
Grand Rapids Press (e)	124,939	136,198
Hackensack Record (e)	*154,063	*198,238
Hartford Courant (m)	183,188	247,957
Hartford Times (e)	*69,133	70,426
Honolulu Advertiser (m)	75,755	
Honolulu Star-Bulletin (e)	116,769	187,342
Houston Chronicle (e)	*303,459	378,272
Houston Post (m)	*292,008	353,537
Indianapolis News (e)	*159,895	
Indianapolis Star (m)	*218,954	†354,965
Jacksonville Journal (e)	54,230	
Jacksonville: Fla. Times Union (m)	147,010	179,971
Kansas City Star (e)	300,619	395,950
Kansas City Times (m)	324,617	
Knoxville News-Sentinel (e)	104,927	161,513
Little Rock: Ark. Democrat (e)	*61,924	111,850
Little Rock: Ark. Gazette (m)	*123,024	147,095
Long Beach Independent (m)	*62,116	137,259
Long Beach Press Telegram (e)	87,355	
Long Island, N.Y.: L. I. Press (e)†	280,702	270,020
Long Island, N.Y.: Newsday (e)	463,376	430,524
Los Angeles Herald-Examiner (e)	*352,459	356,454
Los Angeles Times (m)	1,004,718	1,271,018
Louisville Courier-Journal (m)	210,171	343,668
Louisville Times (e)	161,272	
Memphis Commercial Appeal (m)	204,747	285,457
Memphis Press Scimitar (e)	111,957	
Miami Herald (m)	424,280	521,087
Miami News (e)	78,246	
Milwaukee Journal (e)	343,420	529,089
Milwaukee Sentinel (m)	166,533	
Minneapolis Star (e)	240,594	
Minneapolis Tribune (m)	225,957	604,763
Nashville Banner (e)	86,006	
Nashville Tennessean (m)	128,058	217,416
New Haven Register (e)	*101,595	131,079
New Haven Journal-Courier (m)	*30,555	
New Orleans Times-Picayune (m)	†207,925	†311,696
New Orleans States-Item (e)	†*117,675	
New York News (m)	*1,902,717	2,818,281
New York Post (e)	*505,757	
New York Times (m)	*841,416	1,475,430
Newark Star-Ledger (m)	*†393,095	584,162
Norfolk Ledger-Star (e)	†93,287	
Norfolk Virginian-Pilot (m)	†124,474	†184,320
Oakland Tribune (e)	*173,414	202,936
Oklahoma City Oklahoman (m)	*171,918	287,494
Oklahoma City Times (e)	*87,512	
Omaha World-Herald (m&e)	*235,830	278,826
Orlando Sentinel-Star (m&e)	*184,612	209,763
Philadelphia Bulletin (e)	*554,381	652,024
Philadelphia Inquirer (m)	*412,254	847,442
Philadelphia News (e)	*238,951	
Phoenix Republic (m)	*229,495	†339,874
Phoenix Gazette (e)	†111,553	
Pittsburgh Post Gazette (m)	*188,886	
Pittsburgh Press (e)	*265,114	667,297
Portland, Me. Press-Herald (m)	53,219	
Portland, Me. Express (e) & Maine Sunday Telegram	30,434	108,301
Portland Oregonian (m)	226,235	400,848
Portland: Oregon Journal (e)	*106,528	
Providence Journal (m)	*66,260	209,426
Providence Bulletin (e)	*142,892	
Raleigh News & Observer (m)†	129,438	157,248
Raleigh Times (e)†	32,294	
Richmond News Leader (e)	112,259	
Richmond Times Dispatch (m)	*131,677	199,633
Rochester Democrat-Chronicle (m)	127,619	222,126
Rochester Times-Union (e)	130,416	
Sacramento Bee (e)	*172,603	204,531
Sacramento Union (m)	*92,639	94,917
St. Louis Globe-Democrat (m)	*274,917	275,019
St. Louis Post-Dispatch (e)	*286,031	468,220
St. Paul Dispatch (e)	118,704	
St. Paul Pioneer Press (m)	102,288	240,179
St. Petersburg Independent (e)	35,586	
St. Petersburg Times (m)	203,070	253,935
Salt Lake Tribune (m)	100,788	171,463
Salt Lake City Deseret News (e)	72,088	
San Antonio Express (m)	*80,092	60,080
San Antonio News (e)	*76,243	
San Antonio Light (e)	*126,032	174,394
San Diego Union (m)	*181,907	†297,687
San Diego Tribune (e)	*126,363	
San Francisco Examiner (e)	*150,698	
San Francisco Chronicle (m)	*443,097	637,201
San Jose Mercury (m)*	135,264	230,584
San Jose News (e)*	66,885	
Santa Ana Register (m&e)	*202,037	230,842
Seattle Post-Intelligencer (m)	*185,009	249,010
Seattle Times (e)	*223,478	310,203
South Bend Tribune (e)	111,495	121,326
Spokane Chronicle (e)	641,841	
Spokane Spokesman-Review (m)	74,293	123,480
Springfield, Ill. State Journal-Register (m&e)	72,442	72,092
Springfield, Mass. Union (m)	74,472	
Springfield, Mass. News(e) & Sunday Republican	80,615	140,715
Syracuse Herald-Journal (e) & Sun. Herald-American	123,773	244,840
Syracuse Post-Standard (m)	*83,670	
Tampa Tribune (m)	172,126	203,607
Tampa Times (e)	22,516	
Toledo Blade (e)	173,144	207,503
Tulsa Tribune (e)	†78,488	
Tulsa World (m)	†117,282	†204,431
Wall St. Journal (m) (total)	*1,465,633	
Washington, D.C. Post (m)	*514,849	718,806
Washington, D.C. Star (e)	*390,414	382,025
West Palm Beach Post (m)	*74,660	110,557
West Palm Beach Times (e)	*29,319	
Wichita Eagle (m)	121,102	178,489
Wichita Beacon (e)	47,049	
Winston-Salem Journal (m)	68,002	92,293
Winston-Salem Sentinel (e)	40,289	
Youngstown Vindicator (e)	†99,584	†155,196

Circulation of Leading U.S. Magazines

Source: Audit Bureau of Circulations' FAS-FAX Report

General magazines, exclusive of groups and comics. Based on total average paid circulation during the 6 months prior to Dec. 31, 1975. *Indicates circulation for the 6 months prior to June 30, 1975.

Magazine	Circulation	Magazine	Circulation	Magazine	Circulation
TV Guide	19,168,096	Mechanix Illustrated	1,547,892	Motor Trend	709,886
Reader's Digest	18,142,923	Seventeen	1,521,035	Vogue & Vanity Fair	701,147
Natl. Geographic	9,039,374	Parent's Magazine	1,509,215	Modern Screen	691,137
Family Circle	8,364,442	Sport	1,395,086	Lion Magazine	687,079
Woman's Day	8,167,108	Sunset	1,347,303	TV Radio Mirror	681,608
Better Homes & Gar.	8,126,644	Ebony	1,285,525	Decorating & Craft.	676,765
Ladies' Home		Oui	1,279,625	Scientific American	637,548
Journal	7,067,039	Southern Living	1,225,747	Forbes	629,024
McCall's	6,801,287	Esquire	1,208,390	Modern Romances	626,846
Playboy	5,701,007	Grit	1,202,346	Argosy	625,530
Good Housekeeping	5,250,597	Scouting	1,157,031	Money	622,851
Redbook	4,562,760	Sports Afield	1,123,686	American Girl	618,828
Time	4,325,270	Jr. Scholastic	1,076,105	Jet	615,128
Penthouse	4,209,984	House & Garden	1,070,136	Weight Watchers	614,520
National Enquirer	4,155,762	Psychology Today	1,061,700	Fortune	614,224
Newsweek	2,928,484	Midnight	1,044,837	Simplicity	
Sr. Scholastic	2,906,531	Playgirl	1,042,451	Home Cat.	590,589
American Legion	2,660,002	Photoplay	993,434	Apartment Life	589,762
American Home	2,524,362	Nation's Business	989,352	Golf	573,789
Sports Illustrated	2,267,547	Smithsonian	972,265	Gourmet	556,338
Cosmopolitan	2,095,201	Co-ed	899,439	Lutheran	546,344
U.S. News & World		Mademoiselle	888,597	Catholic Digest	532,168
Report	2,036,140	True	864,409	Modern Photo'y	515,666
Field & Stream	1,992,994	National Lampoon	839,560	Viva	508,088
Boy's Life	1,877,572	House Beautiful	839,467	Flower & Garden	499,877
Outdoor Life	1,797,642	Hustler	826,345	New Yorker	490,876
Workbasket	1,778,379	'Teen	821,114	Harper's Bazaar	487,690
Popular Science	1,776,031	Family Health	805,520	Sat'day Evening Post	483,240
V.F.W. Magazine	1,761,477	Hot Rod	769,257	Saturday Rev/World.	481,487
Glamour	1,740,026	Business Week	761,737	Skiing	467,780
Popular Mechanics	1,736,274	Signature	751,546	National Observer	463,924
True Story	1,702,146	Golf Digest	750,241	Rotarian	462,324
Today's Education	1,647,976	Car & Driver	731,060	Rolling Stone	451,124
People	1,619,822	Popular Photo'y	716,329	Essence	450,402
Elks Magazine	1,600,333	Family Handyman	711,595*	Capper's Weekly	437,360

Sunday Magazines Weekly Circulation

Family Weekly (311 papers) 11,587,985   Parade (113 papers) 19,533,862

Canadian Daily Newspapers of Large Circulation

Source: Audit Bureau of Circulations' FAS-FAX Report of average paid circulation for 6 months ending Mar. 31, 1976. (†) Indicates 3 month circulation average.

For the 6 months up to Sept. 30, 1975, 113 daily newspapers in Canada (23 morning: 89 evening, 1 all day) had an average of 4,764,987; 9 Sunday newspapers had an average circulation of 766,440.

(m) Morning; (e) Evening; *Based on Monday to Friday average. Brackets indicate joint publication.

Newspaper	Daily	Sunday	Newspaper	Daily	Sunday
Calgary Albertan (m)	6,301		Regina Leader Post (e)	65,456	
Calgary Herald (e)	21,550		St. Catharines Standard (e)	†40,775	
Edmonton Journal (e)	167,440		St. John's Telegram (e)	*31,660	
Halifax Chronicle-Herald (m)	(68,670)		Saint John Telegraph-Journal (m)	*(32,612)	
Halifax Mail-Star (m)	(52,275)		Saint John Times Globe (e)	*(29,437)	
Halifax Mail-Star (e)	52,275		Saskatoon Star-Phoenix (e)	48,664	
Hamilton Spectator (e)	†137,909		Sherbrooke: La Tribune (e)	37,752	
Kitchener-Waterloo Record (e)	†65,293		Sudbury Star (e)	36,636	
London Free Press (m & e)	125,931		Toronto Globe and Mail (m)	255,791	
Moncton Times (m)	17,685		Toronto Star (e)	540,491	
Moncton Transcript (e)	23,375		Toronto Sun (m)	*140,493	223,678
Montreal Gazette (m)	116,193		Trois Rivieres Nouvelliste (e)	51,509	
Montreal: La Presse (e)	184,155		Vancouver Province (m)	124,806	
Montreal: Le Devoir (m)	28,922		Vancouver Sun (e)	239,162	
Montreal: Le Journal de Montreal (m)	*165,509	154,943	Victoria Colonist (m)¹	(38,606)	43,916
Montreal-Matin (m)	*125,667	102,378	Victoria Times (e)	(29,518)	
Montreal Star (e)	172,632		Windsor Star (e)	85,142	
Ottawa Citizen (e)	102,571		Winnipeg Free Press (e)	138,645	
Ottawa Journal (e)	82,455		Winnipeg Tribune (e)	86,884	
Ottawa: Le Droit (e)	45,146		(1) Excludes Monday		
Quebec: Le Soleil (e)	140,397				

Circulation of Leading Canadian Magazines

Source: Audit Bureau of Circulations' FAS-FAX Report.

General magazines, exclusive of groups and comics. Statistics based on average paid circulation during the 6 months prior to Dec. 31, 1975.

Magazine	Circulation	Magazine	Circulation	Magazine	Circulation
Reader's Digest (English-French)	1,451,024	Maclean's Magazine (English-French)	891,772	Selection du Reader's Digest	259,869
Chatelaine (English-French)	1,299,844	MacLean's Magazine (English)	741,965	T.V. Hebdo	229,987
Reader's Digest (English)	1,191,155	Time Canada	512,987	Le Maclean	149,807
Chatelaine (English)	1,018,327	Legion Magazine	431,299	Miss Chatelaine	144,212
		Chatelaine (French)	286,868	Actualite	141,036
				Canadian Motorist	131,610

WORLD FACTS
Early Explorers of the Western Hemisphere

The first men to discover the New World or Western Hemisphere are believed to have walked across a "land bridge" from Siberia to Alaska, an isthmus since broken by the Bering Strait. From Alaska, these ancestors of the Indians spread through North, Central, and South America. Anthropologists have placed these crossings at between 18,000 and 14,000 B.C.; but evidence found in 1967 near Puebla, Mex., indicates mankind reached there as early as 35,000-40,000 years ago.

At first, these people were hunters using flint weapons and tools. In Mexico, about 7000-6000 B.C., they founded farming cultures, developing corn, squash, etc. Eventually, they created· complex civilizations — Olmec, Toltec, Aztec, and Maya and, in South America, Inca. Carbon-14 tests show men lived about 8000 B.C. near what are now Front Royal, Va., Kanawha, W. Va., and Dutchess Quarry, N.Y. The Hopewell Culture, based on farming, flourished about 1000 B.C.; remains of it are seen today in large mounds in Ohio and other states.

Norsemen (Norwegian Vikings sailing out of Iceland and Greenland) are credited by most scholars with being the first Europeans to discover America, with at least five voyages around 1000 A.D. to areas they called Helluland, Markland, and Vinland—possibly Labrador, Nova Scotia or Newfoundland, and New England.

The remains of a settlement at L'Anse-aux-Meadows, near the northern tip of Newfoundland, were uncovered by Dr. and Mrs. Helge Ingstad, Norwegian archeologists, 1960-63, with the aid of a grant from the National Geographic Society. They identified the settlement as Norse. Carbon-14 tests from hearths and the remains of a smithy indicated the site was occupied about 900 A.D. and during several hundred years before and after.

Christopher Columbus, most famous of the explorers, was born at Genoa, Italy, but made his discoveries sailing for the Spanish rulers Ferdinand and Isabella. Dates of his voyages, places he discovered, and other information follow:

1492—First voyage. Left Palos, Spain, Aug. 3 with 88 men (est.). Discovered San Salvador (Guanahani or Watling Is., Bahamas) Oct. 12. Also Cuba, Hispaniola (Haiti-Dominican Republic); built Fort La Navidad on latter.

1493—Second voyage, first part, Sept. 25, with 17 ships, 1,500 men. Dominica (Lesser Antilles) Nov. 3; Guadaloupe, Montserrat, Antigua, San Martin, Santa Cruz, Puerto Rico, Virgin Islands. Settled Isabela on Hispaniola. **Second part** (Columbus having remained in Western Hemisphere), Jamaica, Isle of Pines, La Mona Is.

1498—Third voyage. Left Spain May 30, 1498, 6 ships. Discovered Trinidad. Saw South American continent Aug. 1, 1498, but called it Isla Sancta (Holy Island). Entered Gulf of Paria and landed, first time on continental soil. At mouth of Orinoco Aug. 14 he decided this was mainland.

1502—Fourth voyage, 4 caravels, 150 men. St. Lucia, Guanaja off Honduras; Cape Gracias a Dios, Honduras; San Juan River, Costa Rica; Almirante, Portobelo, and Laguna de Chiriqui, Panama.

A.D.	Explorer	Nationality and Employer	Discovery or Exploration
1497	John Cabot	Italian-English	Newfoundland or Nova Scotia
1498	John and Sebastian Cabot	Italian-English	Labrador to Hatteras
1499	Alonso de Ojeda	Spanish	South American coast, Venezuela
1500, Feb.	Vicente y Pinzon	Spanish	South American coast, Amazon River
1500, Apr.	Pedro Alvarez Cabral	Portuguese	Brazil (for Portugal)
1500-02	Gaspar Corte-Real	Portuguese	Labrador
1501	Rodrigo de Bastidas	Spanish	Central America
1513	Vasco Nunez de Balboa	Spanish	Pacific Ocean
1513	Juan Ponce de Leon	Spanish	Florida
1515	Juan de Solis	Spanish	Rio de la Plata
1519	Alonso de Pineda	Spanish	Mouth of Mississippi River
1519	Hernando Cortes	Spanish	Mexico
1520	Ferdinand Magellan	Portuguese-Spanish	Straits of Magellan, Tierra del Fuego
1524	Giovanni da Verrazano	Italian-French	Atlantic Coast-New York harbor
1531	Alfonso de Souza	Portuguese	Rio de Janeiro
1532	Francisco Pizarro	Spanish	Peru
1534	Jacques Cartier	French	Canada, Gulf of St. Lawrence
1536	Pedro de Mendoza	Spanish	Buenos Aires
1536	A. N. Cabeza de Vaca	Spanish	Texas coast and interior
1539	Francisco de Ulloa	Spanish	California coast
1539-41	Hernando de Soto	Spanish	Mississippi River near Memphis
1539	Marcos de Niza	Italian-Spanish	Southwest (now U.S.)
1540	Francisco V. de Coronado	Spanish	Southwest (now U.S.)
1540	Hernando Alarcon	Spanish	Colorado River
1540	Garcia de L. Cardenas	Spanish	Grand Canyon of the Colorado
1541	Francisco de Orellana	Spanish	Amazon River
1542	Juan Rodriquez Cabrillo	Portuguese-Spanish	San Diego harbor
1565	Pedro Menendez	Spanish	St. Augustine
1573	Pedro Marquez	Spanish	Chesapeake Bay
1576	Martin Frobisher	English	Frobisher's Bay, Canada
1577-80	Francis Drake	English	California coast
1582	Antonio de Espejo	Spanish	Southwest (named New Mexico)
1584	Amadas & Barlow (for Raleigh)	English	Virginia
1585-87	Sir Walter Raleigh's men	English	Roanoke Is., N.C.
1595	Sir Walter Raleigh	English	Orinoco River
1602	Bartholomew Gosnold	English	Martha's Vineyard and Massachusetts
1603-09	Samuel de Champlain	French	Canadian interior, Lake Champlain
1604	Samuel de Champlain	French	Mt. Desert Island
1607	Capt. John Smith	English	Atlantic coast
1609-10	Henry Hudson	English-Dutch	Hudson River, Hudson Bay
1634	Jean Nicolet	French	Lake Michigan; Wisconsin
1673	Jacques Marquette, Louis Jolliet	French	Mississippi S to Arkansas

(Continued)

1682........Sieur de la Salle..............French.............Mississippi S to Gulf of Mexico
1789........Alexander Mackenzie...........Canadian...........Canadian Northwest

Arctic Exploration

Early Explorers

1587 — John Davis (England). Davis Strait to Sanderson's Hope, 72° 12′ N.

1596 — Willem Barents and Jacob van Heemskerck (Holland). Discovered Bear Island, touched northwest tip of Spitsbergen, 79° 49′ N, rounded Novaya Zemlya, wintered at Ice Haven.

1607 — Henry Hudson (England). North along Greenland's east coast to Cape Hold-with-Hope, 73° 30′, then north of Spitsbergen to 80° 23′. Returning he discovered Hudson's Touches (Jan Mayen).

1616 — William Baffin and Robert Bylot (England). Baffin Bay to Smith Sound.

1728 — Vitus Bering (Russia). Proved Asia and America were separate by sailing through strait.

1733-40 — Great Northern Expedition (Russia). Surveyed Siberian Arctic coast.

1741 — Vitus Bering (Russia). Sighted Alaska from sea, named Mount St. Elias. His lieutenant, Chirikof, discovered coast.

1771 — Samuel Hearne (Hudson's Bay Co.). Overland from Prince of Wales Fort (Churchill) on Hudson Bay to mouth of Coppermine River.

1778 — James Cook (Britain). Through Bering Strait to Icy Cape, Alaska, and North Cape, Siberia.

1789 — Alexander Mackenzie (North West Co., Britain). Montreal to mouth of Mackenzie River.

1806 — William Scoresby (Britain). North of Spitsbergen to 81° 30′.

1820-3 — Ferdinand von Wrangel (Russia). Completed a survey of Siberian Arctic coast. His exploration joined that of James Cook at North Cape, confirming separation of the continents.

1845 — Sir John Franklin (Britain) was one of many to seek the Northwest Passage — an ocean route connecting the Atlantic and Pacific via the Arctic. His two ships (the Erebus and Terror) were last seen entering Lancaster Sound Jul. 26.

1888 — Fridtjof Nansen (Norway) crossed Greenland's icecap, 1893-96 — Nansen in Fram drifted from New Siberian Is. to Spitsbergen; tried polar dash in 1895, reached Franz Josef Land.

1896 — Salomon A. Andree (Sweden) and companion, in June, made first attempt to reach North Pole by balloon; failed and returned in August. On Jul. 11, 1897, Andree and 2 others started in balloon from Danes Is., Spitsbergen, to drift across pole to America, and disappeared. Over 33 years later, Aug. 6, 1930, Dr. Gunnar Horn (Norway) found their frozen bodies on White Is., 82° 57′ N. 29° 52′ E.

1903-06 — Roald Amundsen (Norway) first sailed Northwest Passage.

Discovery of North Pole

Robert E. Peary began exploring in 1886 on Greenland, when he was 30. With his hq. at McCormick Bay he explored Greenland's coast 1891-92, tried for North Pole 1893, returned with large meteorites. In 1900 he reached northern limit of Greenland and 83° 50′ N; in 1902 he reached 84° 06′ N; in 1906 he went from Ellesmere Is. to 87° 06′ N. He sailed in the Roosevelt, July, 1908, to winter off Cape Sheridan, Grant Land. The dash for the North Pole began Mar. 1 from Cape Columbia, Ellesmere Land. Peary reached the pole, 90° N, Apr. 6, 1909.

Peary had several supporting groups carrying supplies until the last group, under Capt. Robt. A. Bartlett, turned back at 87° 47′N. Peary, Matthew Henson, and 4 Eskimos proceeded with dog teams and sleds. They crossed the pole several times, finally built an igloo at 90°, remained 36 hours. Started south Apr. 7 at 4 p.m. for Cape Columbia. Eskimos were Coqueeh, Ootah, Eginwah, and Seegloo. Adm. Peary died Feb. 20, 1920. Henson, a Negro, born Aug. 8, 1866, died in New York, N.Y., Mar. 9, 1955, aged 88. Ootah, the last survivor, died near Thule, Greenland, May, 1955, aged 80.

1914 — Donald Macmillan (U.S.). Northwest, 200 miles, from Axel Hieberg Island to seek Peary's Crocker Land.

1915-17 — Vihjalmur Stefansson (Canada) discovered Borden, Brock, Meighen, and Lougheed Islands.

1918-20 — Amundsen sailed Northeast Passage.

1926 — Richard E. Byrd and Floyd Bennett (U.S.) reached 87° 44′N. in attempt to fly to North Pole from Spitsbergen.

1926 — Richard E. Byrd and Floyd Bennett (U.S.) first over North Pole by air, May 9.

1926 — Amundsen, Ellsworth, and Umberto Nobile (Italy) flew from Spitsbergen over North Pole May 12, to Teller, Alaska, in dirigible Norge.

1928 — Nobile crossed North Pole in airship Italia May 24, crashed May 25. Amundsen lost while trying to effect rescue by plane.

1928 — Sir Hubert Wilkins and Eielson flew from Point Barrow to Spitsbergen, 84° N.

Submarine Records

On Aug. 3, 1958, the Nautilus, under Comdr. William R. Anderson, became the first ship to cross the North Pole beneath the Arctic ice.

On Aug. 12, 1958, the nuclear submarine Skate, Comdr. James F. Calvert, became the second ship to make an underwater crossing of the North Pole.

In March, 1959, the Skate returned to the Arctic and, on its third attempt, broke through at the North Pole, the first time any ship had been on the surface at 90° N.

The nuclear-powered U. S. submarine Seadragon, Comdr. George P. Steele 2d, made the first east-west underwater transit through the Northwest Passage during August, 1960. It sailed from Portsmouth, N.H., headed between Greenland and Labrador through Baffin Bay, then west through Lancaster Sound and McClure Strait to the Beaufort Sea. Traveling submerged for the most part, the submarine made 850 miles from Baffin Bay to the Beaufort Sea in six days. The vessel made a 300-foot dive to sail under an iceberg in Baffin Bay.

In February, 1960, the nuclear submarine Sargo traveled under the Arctic ice pack to and around the North Pole. The Sargo departed from and returned to Honolulu, and spent 31 days and 4 hours under the ice. The submarine successfully smashed its way through ice three feet thick.

Antarctic Exploration

Early History

Antarctica has been approached since 1773-75, when Capt. Jas. Cook (Britain) reached 71°10′S. Many sea and landmarks bear names of early explorers. Bellingshausen (Russia) discovered Peter I and Alexander I Islands, 1819-21. Nathaniel Palmer (U.S.) discovered Palmer Peninsula, 60°W, 1820, without realizing that this was a continent. Jas. Weddell (Britain) found Weddell Sea, 74°15′S, 1823.

First to announce existence of the continent of Antarctica was Charles Wilkes (U.S.), who followed the coast for 1,500 mi., 1840. Adelie Coast, 140° E, was found by Dumont d'Urville (France), 1840. Ross Ice Shelf was found by Jas. Clark Ross (Britain), 1841-42.

1895 — Leonard Kristensen, Norwegian whaling captain, landed a party on the coast of Victoria Land in Jan. 1895. They were the first ashore on the main continental mass. C. E. Borchgrevink, a member of that party, returned in 1899 with a British expedition, first to winter on Antarctica.

1902-04 — Robert F. Scott (Britain) discovered Edward VII Peninsula. In 1902 he reached 82°17′S, 146°33′E from McMurdo Sound.

1908-09 — Ernest Shackleton, in 1908, introduced the use of Manchurian ponies in Antarctic sledging. In 1909 he reached 88°23′S, discovering a route on to the plateau by way of the Beardmore Glacier and pioneering the way to the Pole.

Discovery of South Pole

1911 — Roald Amundsen (Norway) with four men and dog teams reached the Pole Dec. 14, 1911.

1912 — Capt. Scott reached the Pole from Ross Island Jan. 18, 1912, with four companions (Dr. E. A. Wilson, Lt. Bowers, Capt. Oates, and Petty Officer Edgar Evans), where they found Amundsen's tent. Of Scott's party, Oates and Evans died first; Scott, Wilson, and Boers died in a tent around March 29. They were found Nov. 12, 1912.

1928 — First man to use an airplane over Antarctica was Hubert Wilkins (Britain).

1929 — Richard E. Byrd (U.S.) established Little America on Bay of Whales. On 1600-mi. airplane flight begun Nov. 28 he crossed South Pole Nov. 29 with pilot Bernt Balchen, a radio operator, and a photographer. Dropped U. S. flag over Pole, temp. 16° below zero.

1934-35 — Richard E. Byrd (U.S.) led second expedition to Little America, which explored 450,000 sq. mi. Byrd wintered alone at an advance weather station in 80°08′S.

1934-37 — John Rymill led British Graham Land expedition of 1934-37; discovered that Palmer Peninsula is part of Antarctic mainland.

1935 — Lincoln Ellsworth (U.S.) flew south along Palmer Peninsula's east coast, then crossed continent to Little America, making four landings on unprepared terrain in bad weather, a new feat.

1939-41 — U. S. Antarctic Service built West Base on Ross Ice Shelf under Paul Siple, and East Base on Palmer Peninsula under Richard Black. U. S. Navy plane flights discovered about 150,000 sq. miles of new land.

1940 — Richard E. Byrd (U.S.) charted most of coast between Ross Sea and Palmer Peninsula.

1946-47 — U. S. Navy undertook Operation Highjump under Rear Admiral Byrd. Ships were commanded by Rear Admiral Richard H. Cruzen. Expedition included 13 ships and 4,000 men. Twenty-nine land-based flights from Little America and 35 by seaplanes from tenders photomapped coastline and penetrated beyond Pole.

1946-48 — Ronne Antarctic Research Expedition, Comdr. Finn Ronne, USNR, determined the Antarctic to be one continent with no strait between Weddell Sea and Ross Sea; discovered 250,000 sq. miles of land by flights to 79°S Lat., and made 14,000 aerial photographs over 450,000 sq. miles of land. Mrs. Ronne and Mrs. H. Darlington, who accompanied their husbands, were the first women to winter on Antarctica.

1955-57 — U. S. Navy's Operation Deep Freeze led by Adm. Richard E. Byrd. Supporting U. S. scientific efforts for the International Geophysical Year, the operation was commanded by Rear Adm. George Dufek. It established five coastal stations fronting the Indian, Pacific, and Atlantic Oceans and also three interior stations; explored more than 1,000,000 sq. miles in Wilkes Land. Seven Navy men under Adm. Dufek landed by plane at the Pole Oct. 31, 1956, and landed radar reflectors.

1957-58 — During the International Geophysical year, Jul., 1957, through Dec., 1958, scientists from 12 countries conducted ambitious programs of Antarctic research. A network of some 60 stations on the continent and sub-Arctic islands studied oceanography, glaciology, meteorology, seismology, geomagnetism, the ionosphere, cosmic rays, aurora, and airglow. A party from Ellsworth IGY station (U.S.) south of Weddell Sea under the direction of Captain Finn Ronne explored beyond 1947 flight and delineated Berkner Island imbedded in the Filchner Ice Shelf. Pensacola Mountains, first sighted by Argentines in Oct., 1955, and seen by U. S. Navy in Jan., 1956, were accurately located. New mountain ranges about 11,609 ft. high were discovered in Edith Ronne Land.

Dr. V. E. Fuchs led a 12-man Trans-Antarctic Expedition on the first land crossing of Antarctica. Starting from the Weddell Sea, they reached Scott Station Mar. 2, 1958, after traveling 2,158 miles in 98 days.

1958 — A group of 5 U. S. scientists led by Edward C. Thiel, seismologist, moving by tractor from Ellsworth Station on Weddell Sea, identified a huge mountain range, 5,000 ft. above the ice sheet and 9,000 ft. above sea level. The range, originally seen by a Navy plane, was named the Dufek Massif, for Rear Adm. George Dufek.

1959 — Twelve nations — Argentina, Australia, Belgium, Chile, France, Japan, New Zealand, Norway, South Africa, the Soviet Union, the United Kingdom, and the U. S. — signed a treaty suspending any territorial claims for 30 years and reserving the continent for research.

1960-61 — Scientists at Cape Adare found a wooden building erected in 1899 by the first men (led by C. E. Borchgrevink) to winter on the continent.

1961-62 — Scientists discovered a trough, the Bentley Trench, running from Ross Ice Shelf, Pacific, into Marie Byrd Land, around the end of the Ellsworth Mtns., toward the Weddell Sea, which may be the long-suspected link between the Atlantic and Pacific Oceans.

1962 — First nuclear power plant began operation at McMurdo Sound.

1963 — On Feb. 22 a U. S. plane made the longest nonstop flight ever made in the S. Pole area, covering 3,600 miles in 10 hours. The flight was from McMurdo Station south past the geographical S. Pole to Shackleton Mtns., southeast to the "Area of Inaccessibility" and back to McMurdo Station.

1963 — Three turbine-powered helicopters made the first copter landings on the S. Pole.

1964 — A British survey team was landed by helicopter on Cook Island, the first recorded visit since its discovery in 1775.

1964 — New Zealanders completed one of the last and most important surveys when they mapped the mountain area from Cape Adare west some 400 miles to Pennell Glacier.

1966-67 — Fifteen Antarctic areas set aside as Specially Protected Areas for the conservation of flora and fauna.

Exploring Pre-History

Oldest Fossils of True Man Unearthed

A form of early man, much more like modern man than was previously believed possible, may have lived in East Africa as long as 3.75 million years ago. Fossils recently discovered in Kenya, Ethiopia, and Tanzania have pushed back the date for true man 1,000,000 years earlier than once thought.

The first find, announced by Dr. Mary Leakey in October 1975, included two almost complete lower jaws with most of the teeth still remaining. The fossils came from at least 11 creatures that appear to have belonged to genus Homo. Dated at 3.35 to 3.75 million years old, the fossils are believed to be the oldest reliably dated examples of true man. Dr. Leakey's evidence was supported by fossil finds in Kenya and Ethiopia, reported in March by Dr. Richard Leakey, director of the National Museums of Kenya, and Donald C. Johanson, curator of the Cleveland Museum of Natural History and associate professor of anthropology at Case-Western Reserve University.

Dr. Mary Leakey reported that her new fossils shared many anatomical features with later human fossils discovered previously in Kenya and Ethiopia. The new Kenya and Ethiopia finds included skulls and hand and thigh bones with remarkably advanced features quite similar to those of modern man. They seemed to be from the same type of primitive human creature as the Tanzania fossils. Taken together, these finds indicate that a species of true man, clearly different from Australopithecus, or "near man," evolved contemporaneously with Australopithecus. Until quite recently, Australopithecus was thought to be a transitional stage between ape and man. Dr. Mary Leakey explained, "I think our new discoveries confirm the view that Australopithecus was an off-shoot of the hominid line, an early man who died out." Richard Leakey and Johanson concluded that future discoveries may unearth human remains from a period 4 to 5 million years ago.

These discoveries, together with earlier fossil finds, make it possible to piece together a tentative picture of human evolution. Sketchy evidence suggests that, about 10 to 15 million years ago, a group of slightly manlike creatures developed from apelike creatures. Then, about 5 million years ago, the manlike creatures separated into 2 distinct groups, Homo (true man) and Australopithecus (near man), both essentially human-sized. Homo had a larger brain than Australopithecus. Australopithecus, it is conjectured, then split into a larger and smaller line, both of which lived in Africa virtually unchanged until they died out approximately 1,000,000 years ago. Homo, however, continued to evolve larger brains and, about 1.5 million years ago, Homo erectus appeared and migrated out of Africa.

Dr. Richard Leakey also reported the discovery of the most complete skull found to date of Homo erectus. The skull was dated at 1.5 million years old. Peking man, discovered in China some 50 years ago and believed to be about 500,000 years old, was the best example of Homo erectus prior to the latest find by Leakey's assistant, Bernard Ngeneo. Because Peking man was never reliably dated, it is now considered possible that it, too, is older.

Dr. Johanson's discoveries included more than 15 bones representing 2 young children and 3 to 5 adults who may have been a family. Johanson speculated: "If this is the case, the fossil people may have been living in a group and may have been related to one another. This is evidence for the idea of cooperative behavior which I feel formed the basis for early human survival." He was able to piece together a hand from the fossils. It was essentially the size of modern man's and appeared to be capable of comparable dexterity.

"Living Shrimp" Fossil Found

French marine scientists have reported the discovery of a "living fossil" of a shrimp species which was believed to have become extinct 50 million years ago. According to a spokesman for the University of the Philippines, the fossils — 10 different specimens — were found in May, 1976, off the coast of Lubang Island, in the Philippines, about 75 miles south of Manila. The specimens were found in various stages of development. The find was compared to the 1938 discovery of the living coelecanth, a fish thought to be extinct for 60 million years, off the coast of Madagascar.

Stegosaurus Had Built-in Air-Conditioning

One paleontologist and 2 engineers have suggested that the 2 rows of bony plates protruding from the arched back of the stegosaurus could have functioned as a natural air-conditioning system. The conventional explanation for the bony plates on the back of the 20-foot-long vegetarian dinosaur states that they functioned as armor. Stegosaurus, which lived about 125 to 150 million years ago, weighed about 2 tons

and had a relatively small head and a tail marked by 4 huge spikes.

Using actual fossils of the plates, the scientists discovered that the strange anatomical structure met the sophisticated criteria applied to the design of convective cooling fins in many modern devices, particularly where heat build-up presents a problem or heat transfer is necessary. It is possible that the dinosaur used the fins to dissipate excess body heat.

They noted that the plates, placed in a staggered and interrupted pattern, were arranged in violation of the principle of biological symmetry. The principle states that an animal's left side is the mirror image of the right side. The asymmetrical arrangement of the stegosaurus' fins is one of the most efficient forms that engineers would choose to get the greatest flow of cooling air over the fins.

The hypothesis was proposed by Dr. James O. Farlow, vertebrate paleontologist at Yale University and at the Peabody Museum of Natural History; Carl V. Thomas, formerly at Yale and currently a metallurgical engineering student at Massachusetts Institute of Technology; and Daniel E. Rosner of Yale's Department of Engineering and Applied Sciences.

Neanderthal Man Gains Sophistication

Neanderthal man, who lived as recently as 60,000 years ago, may have been more sophisticated than the hulking, brutish creature he was once thought to be.

Evidence found in an Iraqi cave containing one of the oldest known ritual burials of a human being seems to indicate Neanderthal man knew certain plants possessed medicinal properties.

Columbia University anthropologist Dr. Ralph S. Solecki and Dr. Arlette Leroi-Gourhan, a French expert on identifying pollens, based their conclusion on an examination of a male skeleton and preserved pollen grains found with it. It appeared that the body had been laid out on a bed of branches of a shrub which contains ephedrine, a nerve stimulant. Seven species of wildflowers, six of which are known to have medicinal properties, were strewn around the body.

Although the grave was discovered in 1963, a pollen analysis was not made at that time. Since 1963, the view of Neanderthal man has been changing — he is now considered to be a very close, if not direct, relative of modern man. Most anthropologists have accepted the pollen analyses as evidence that Neanderthal man had a decidedly nonbrutish, esthetic appreciation of flowers as well as a regard for the dead comparable to modern attitudes.

Bronze Age Artifacts Found in Thailand

Evidence that a lively, prosperous Bronze Age culture may have flourished in northeastern Thailand 5,600 years ago is challenging long-held assumptions about the beginnings of technology and civilization. Scholars have long assumed that Southeast Asia played a "minor and derivative role in prehistoric development" and that China and India were the dominant technological cultures in Asia.

In May 1976, Dr. Chester Gorman, an assistant professor of the University Museum at the University of Pennsylvania, and Pifit Charoenwongsa, curator of the National Museum of Thailand, displayed bronze implements and jewelry excavated over the past 2 years at the Thai village of Ban Chiang and other sites. The artifacts were dated, using radiocarbon and thermoluminesence dating techniques, to 3,600 B.C. The date is 600 years earlier than the oldest known Bronze Age artifacts from the Middle East and as much as 2,500 years earlier than Bronze Age materials in India and China. The Tigris-Euphrates Valley in the Middle East was generally considered to be the exclusive birthplace of the Bronze Age.

Some of the artifacts — spearheads, anklets, and bracelets — appear sufficiently sophisticated to indicate evidence of smelting and suggest the Ban Chiang culture had developed an advanced metallurgy long before 3,600 B.C. Gorman and Charoenwongsa evaluated their finds: "If our picture of prehistoric man in Thailand is still far from clear, we do have enough evidence to know we are uncovering remains of a technically innovative society."

New Light on the Saramatians

Excavation for a dam project at Senta, Yugoslavia, has unearthed the remains of an 1,900-year-old city which may add to knowledge of the Sarmatians, Huns, and other predatory neighbors of the Roman Empire. Project head, Laszla Szekeres, director of archeology at the Museum of Subotica, hopes further digging will uncover the grave of Attila the Hun.

The first remains — human bones, pottery shards, and other artifacts — were found in a large sugar-beet field near the Tisza River in the modern Yugoslav province of Vojvodina. The site, near the borders of Hungary and Rumania, is at the approximate intersection of the eastern and western Roman empires in the days of Attila, who died in 453. Further excavation unearthed pit dwellings, walls, granaries, and burial urns, all of which have convinced Szekeres that the settlement was Sarmatian, probably dating from the 2nd and 3rd decades of the first century A.D.

Little is known of the Sarmatians except that they were possibly of Mongolian origin like the Huns. They were thought to have dominated the area northeast of the Black Sea before being pushed further west into the Balkans and other parts of Europe. On the basis of the new evidence, Szekeres believes that, unlike the Huns, the Sarmatians could not have been purely nomadic. Their buildings, though primitive by Roman standards, suggest a higher standard of domestic life than that of the Huns who presumably lived in yurts, Mongolian felt tents. According to Szekeres, "The Sarmatians were clearly a transitional people, and the Hun conquerors living among them presumably adopted some of their ways, although they were never assimilated. . . By the end of the sixth century the Huns had disappeared completely, but these people survived as a group for another two centuries."

Temple of Ikhnaton Unearthed

The Egyptian pharaoh Ikhnaton, who reigned from about 1369 to 1352 B.C., was a monotheist and, consequently, one of the most intriguing pharaohs. In February 1976, a team of University of Pennsylvania archeologists announced the discovery of the foundation of his temple at Thebes. It was the first time one of his temples had been found.

Ikhnaton replaced the many thousands of Egyptian gods with his sun-god, Aton, and built 8 temples to glorify him. The search for these temples began with a systematic study of 40,000 of the pharaoh's distinctive building blocks — called talatats — which have been found over the past 100 years at Karnak and Luxor. The talatats had been used as fill for later temples, especially those built by Ikhnaton's successor, Horemheb, who tried to destroy all memory of the visionary pharaoh. Matching the decorations on the talatats, most of which pictured Ikhnaton and his queen Nefertiti, the team identified 8 temples, but did not know their original locations. Team director Donald B. Redford discovered the site of the foundation, along with 100 new fragments.

The decorated relief shows that Ikhnaton created a peculiarly realistic art style. Instead of the typical rendering of royal figures in a straightlined, impersonal style, Ikhnaton allowed the sculptors to depict him as the misshapen man he was. The reliefs also show that Nefertiti, who is shown twice as many times as Ikhnaton, was the real power behind the throne, but her origins remain unknown.

King Solomon's Mine Found

King Solomon's legendary "lost" gold mine, the Biblical Ophir, may have been found in Saudi Arabia.

The site is in Mahd adh Dhahab (Cradle of Gold) in the mountainous region between Mecca and Medina. Some 3,000 years ago, the mine may have contained half the ancient world's known gold supply and been the source of Israel's great wealth. Dr. Robert W. Luce, a geologist with the U.S. Geological Survey, stated, "Our investigations have now confirmed that the old mine could have been as rich as described in Biblical accounts and, indeed, is a logical candidate to be the lost Ophir."

Based on detailed geologic, geochemical, and geophysical study, researchers believe the long-abandoned mine is the only one near ancient Israel capable of once containing the historically attributed quantities of gold — $125 million at today's prices. Although Ophir was mentioned at least 4 times in the Bible, its exact location was never given.

Mahd adh Dhahab is located within the range of ancient Israel's transport capability. It lies just 400 miles south of the port of Aqaba, on which Solomon's empire relied. Consequently, because Mahd adh Dhahab lies on the north-south trade route that has run to Aqaba for some 4,000 years, it could well have been known to Solomon.

Life-size Clay Soldiers Found in China

Chinese archeologists have discovered a battlefield strewn with realistic 2,200-year-old clay figures of fallen warriors and horses near the tomb of Emperor Chin Shih Huang (221-207 B.C.). Although few Chinese and no outsiders have seen the clay soldiers and horses, reports suggest that the find makes the Chinese relics recently displayed in the U.S. and China look minor in comparison.

The site is the ancient city of Changan which was the capital of China during 5 separate, but not continuous, dynasties between the 11th century B.C. and A.D. 907.

The figures, all different, are mostly in armor and long tunics and wear various types of headdress. The richly decorated figures look very alive and the horses are quite modern in appearance. Some are still semi-buried and upright; others are smashed and scattered. Cheng Hsueh-hua, one of the archeologists working at the site, explained that after the death of Emperor Chin, an uprising against the Chin empire occurred. General Hsiang Yu, the leader of the invading troops, discovered the underground army and smashed some of the figures, stole some of the weapons, and set fire to what remained. The charred wood is still visible in the earth.

Emperor Chin, whose rule marked the shortest dynasty in Chinese history, is credited with having destroyed slave society, replacing it with a feudal society. Under the slave society, human beings were buried with their rulers. Chin is believed to have been the first emperor to take clay figures, not real people, into the next world.

Stockbroker Finds Hadrian Statue

Armed with an electronic mine detector and a Boy Scout knife, Morton Leventhal, a 38-year-old New York City stockbroker and passionate amateur archeologist, stumbled upon a life-size, beautifully carved statue of the Roman emperor Hadrian (ruled A.D. 117-138) while hunting for coins in an agricultural field near Beit Shean, Israel. Beit Shean overlooks the Jordan River about 25 miles south of the sea of Galilee.

The bronze, tentatively dated to between A.D. 117 and 138, is only the second Hadrian known to exist. Although in pieces, the statue was in nearly a perfect state of preservation. It depicts the older Hadrian, bearded and in full battle dress with his right arm raised.

Encouraged by the discovery, the Israeli department of antiquities dug deeper and discovered the head of a second bronze statue, a woman who may have been Hadrian's empress Sabina.

Volcanoes of the World

Source: The Center for Short-Lived Phenomena, Cambridge, Mass.
Last year of eruption in parentheses.

More than 75 per cent of the world's 850 active volcanoes lie within the "Ring of Fire," a zone running along the west coast of the Americas from Chile to Alaska and down the east coast of Asia from Siberia to New Zealand. Twenty per cent of these volcanoes are located in Indonesia. Other prominent groupings are located in Japan, the Aleutian Islands, and Central America. Almost all active volcanic regions are found at the boundaries of the large moving plates which comprise the earth's surface. The "Ring of Fire" marks the boundary between the plates underlying the Pacific Ocean and those underlying the surrounding continents. Other active volcanic regions, such as the Mediterranean Sea and Iceland, are located on plate boundaries.

Major Historical Eruptions

Approximately 7,000 years ago, Mazama, a 3,000-meter-high volcano in southern Oregon, erupted violently, ejecting about 40 cubic kilometers of ash and lava. The ash spread over the entire northwestern United States and as far away as Saskatchewan, Canada. During the eruption, the top of the mountain collapsed, leaving a caldera 10 kilometers across and about one kilometer deep, which filled with rain water to form what is now called Crater Lake.

In 79 A.D., Vesuvio, a 1281-meter-high volcano overlooking Naples Bay, became active after several centuries of quiescence. On October 26 of that year, a heated mud and ash flow swept down the mountain, engulfing the cities of Pompeii, Herculaneum, and Stabiae with debris up to 15 meters deep. Virtually all residents of the 3 towns were killed.

The largest eruptions in recent centuries have been in Indonesia. In 1883, an eruption similar to the Mazama eruption occurred on the island of Krakatau. On August 27, the 800-meter-high peak of the volcano collapsed to 300 meters below sea level, leaving only a small portion of the island standing above the sea. Ash from the eruption covered nearly 1,000,000 square kilometers and colored sunsets around the world for 2 years. A tsunami ("tidal wave") generated by the collapse killed 36,000 people in nearby Java and Sumatra and eventually reached England. A similar, but even more powerful, eruption had taken place 68 years earlier at Tambora volcano on the Indonesian island of Sumbawa.

Major Eruptions 1975-76

Most of the major eruptions of 1975-76 have occurred in the "Ring of Fire." Merapi in Java and Sakura jima in Japan remained active in 1976. Between March 6 and 13, more than 100 lava avalanches occurred at Merapi.

In Siberia, Plotsky Tolbachik erupted violently, emitting lava flows and spreading ash over a 200-square-kilometer area. A new cone, 250 meters in height, was formed during the eruption, and satellite photographs indicated that the ash plume from the eruption drifted nearly 1,000 kilometers eastward over the Pacific Ocean.

After a century of near-quiescence, thermal activity at Mount Baker in Washington increased significantly during 1975-76. Hundreds of new fumaroles were observed, and a small crater lake formed from melted glacier ice. Although no major eruption occurred, the Baker activity was considered the most significant volcanic activity in the contiguous United States since the 1915-16 eruptions at Mount Lassen, California.

Name	Location	Ht. Mt.	Name	Location	Ht. Mt.
Africa			Gede (1949)	Java	2,958
Kilimanjaro	Tanzania	5,895	Zhupanovsky (1959)	USSR	2,958
Cameroon	Cameroons	4,070	Apo	Philippines	2,953
Teide (Tenerife) (1909)	Canary Is.	3,713	Merapi (1976)	Java	2,911
Nyiragongo (1972)	Zaire	3,465	Marapi (1949)	Sumatra	2,891
Nyamuragiga (1971)	Zaire	3,056	Tambora (1913)	Indonesia	2,851
Ol Doinyo Lengai (1960)	Tanzania	2,886	Bezymianny (1969)	USSR	2,800
Fogo (1951)	Cape Verde Is.	2,829	Ruapehu (1975)	New Zealand	2,796
Piton de la Fournaise (1975)	Reunion	2,631	Peuetsagoe (1921)	Sumatra	2,780
Palma (1971)	Canary Is.	2,423	Avachinskaya (1945)	USSR	2,751
Karthala (1972)	Comoro Is.	2,361	Papandajan (1925)	Java	2,665
Erta-Ale (1973)	Ethiopia	615	Balbi	Solomon Is.	2,593
Antarctica			Geureudong	Sumatra	2,590
Erebus (1974)	Ross Island	3,743	Asama (1973)	Japan	2,542
Big Ben (1960)	Heard Island	2,745	Sumbing (1921)	Sumatra	2,508
Melbourne	Victoria Land	2,590	Canlaon (1969)	Philippines	2,465
Darnley (1956)	South Sandwich Islands	1,100	Sinabung	Sumatra	2,460
			Yake Dake (1963)	Japan	2,455
Deception Island (1970)	South Shetland Islands	602	Tandikat (1914)	Sumatra	2,438
			Niigata Yakeyama (1974)	Japan	2,400
Asia-Oceania			Idjen (1936)	Java	2,386
Klyuchevskaya (1974)	USSR	4,850	Alaid (1972)	Kuril Is.	2,339
Kerintji (1968)	Sumatra	3,805	Bromo (1950)	Java	2,329
Fuji	Japan	3,776	Ulawun (1973)	New Britain	2,300
Rindjani (1966)	Indonesia	3,726	Ngauruhoe (1975)	New Zealand	2,291
Semeru (1972)	Java	3,676	Guntur	Java	2,249
Ichinskaya	USSR	3,631	Bamus	New Britain	2,248
Kronotskaya (1923)	USSR	3,528			
Koryakskaya (1957)	USSR	3,456	Chokai (1974)	Japan	2,230
Slamet (1967)	Java	3,432	Butak Petarangan (1939)	Java	2,222
Shiveluch (1964)	USSR	3,395	Sibajak	Sumatra	2,212
Ardjuno-Welirang	Java	3,339	Galunggung (1918)	Java	2,168
Raung (1945)	Java	3,332	Sorikmerapi (1917)	Sumatra	2,145
Dempo (1940)	Sumatra	3,173	Ambulombo (1969)	Indonesia	2,124
Sundoro (1906)	Java	3,150	Tangkuban Perahu (1967)	Java	2,084
Agung (1964)	Bali	3,142	Tokachi (1962)	Japan	2,077
Plosky Tolbachik (1975)	USSR	3,085	Tongariro	New Zealand	1,978
Tjereme (1938)	Java	3,078	Zheltovskaya (1923)	USSR	1,953
Ontake	Japan	3,063	Kaba (1941)	Sumatra	1,952
Mayon (1968)	Philippines	2,990	Sangeang Api (1966)	Indonesia	1,949

Name	Location	Ht. Mt.
Manam (1974)	Papua New Guinea	1,830
Tiatia (1973)	Kuril Islands	1,822
Siau (1974)	Indonesia	1,784
Soputan (1968)	Celebes	1,784
Lamington (1952)	Papua New Guinea	1,780
Kelud (1967)	Java	1,731
Batur (1968)	Bali	1,717
Ternate (1963)	Indonesia	1,715
Lewotobi (1935)	Indonesia	1,703
Bagana (1960)	Solomon Islands	1,702
Kirishima (1956)	Japan	1,700
Ili Boleng (1950)	Indonesia	1,659
Lamongan	Java	1,651
Malinao	Philippines	1,657
Keli Mutu (1968)	Indonesia	1,640
Akita Komaga take (1970)	Japan	1,637
Gamkunoro (1949)	Indonesia	1,635
Aso (1973)	Japan	1,592
Lewotobi Laki-Laki (1968)	Indonesia	1,584
Lokon-Empung (1970)	Celebes	1,579
Bulusan (1933)	Philippines	1,559
Me-akan (1966)	Japan	1,503
Karkar (1975)	Papula New Guinea	1,500
Sarycheva (1965)	Kuril Islands	1,497
Karymskaya (1975)	USSR	1,486
Lopevi (1960)	New Hebrides	1,447
Ibu (1911)	Indonesia	1,340
Ambrim (1953)	New Hebrides	1,334
Catarman (1952)	Philippines	1,332
Mahawu	Celebes	1,331
Awu (1968)	Indonesia	1,320
Ili Lewotolo (1920)	Indonesia	1,319
Langila (1973)	New Britain	1,189
Tongkoko	Celebes	1,149
Komaga take (1942)	Japan	1,140
Sakura jima (1976)	Japan	1,118
Dukono (1971)	Indonesia	1,087
Bangum	New Britain	1,052
Ili Werung (1948)	Indonesia	1,018
Lolobau (1905)	New Britain	932
Paloe (1973)	Indonesia	875
Sirung (1947)	Indonesia	862
Asuncion (1906)	Mariana Is.	857
Miyake jima (1962)	Japan	815
Krakatau (1972)	Indonesia	813
Suwanose jima (1970)	Japan	799
Nila (1968)	Indonesia	781
Mihara (Oshima) (1969)	Japan	758
Batu Tara	Indonesia	748
Ruang (1949)	Indonesia	714
Banda (1901)	Indonesia	685
Teun (1904)	Indonesia	655
Tinakula (1971)	Santa Cruz Is.	650

Central America—Caribbean

Name	Location	Ht. Mt.
Tajumulco	Guatemala	4,220
Tacana	Guatemala	4,092
Acatenango (1972)	Guatemala	3,976
Santiaguito (Santa Maria) (1973)	Guatemala	3,772
Fuego (1975)	Guatemala	3,736
Atitlan	Guatemala	3,537
Irazu (1967)	Costa Rica	3,432
Poas (1972)	Costa Rica	2,704
Pacaya (1976)	Guatemala	2,552
San Miguel (1970)	El Salvador	2,130
Izalco (1966)	El Salvador	1,965
Rincon de la Vieja (1968)	Costa Rica	1,806
El Viejo (San Cristobal) (1976)	Nicaragua	1,745
Ometepe (Concepcion) (1974)	Nicaragua	1,610
Arenal (1975)	Costa Rica	1,552
Pelee (1932)	Martinique	1,397
Conchagua (1947)	El Salvador	1,250
Momotombo (1905)	Nicaragua	1,191
Soutriere (1972)	St. Vincent	1,178
Telica (1971)	Nicaragua	1,010

Name	Location	Ht. Mt.
South America		
Guallatiri (1960)	Chile	6,060
Cotopaxi (1942)	Ecuador	5,897
El Misti (1960)	Peru	5,825
Ubinas (1969)	Peru	5,672
Lascar (1968)	Chile	5,641
Tupungatito (1964)	Chile	5,640
Tolima (1943)	Colombia	5,525
Sangay (1975)	Ecuador	5,230
Tungurahua (1944)	Ecuador	5,016
Pichincha	Ecuador	4,787
Purace (1949)	Colombia	4,600
Reventador (1976)	Ecuador	3,485
Lautaro (1960)	Chile	3,380
Llaima (1957)	Chile	3,124
Villarrica (1971)	Chile	2,840
Hudson (1973)	Chile	2,600
Puyehue (1960)	Chile	2,240
Rinihue	Chile	2,430
Calbuco (1961)	Chile	2,015
Fernandina (1973)	Galapagos Is.	1,546
Alcedo (1954)	Galapagos Is.	1,127
Mid-Pacific		
Mauna Kea	Hawaii	4,206
Mauna Loa (1975)	Hawaii	4,170
Haleakala	Hawaii	3,055
Kilauea (1975)	Hawaii	1,222
Mid-Atlantic Ridge		
Beerenberg (1970)	Jan Mayen Is.	2,277
Tristan da Cunha (1962)	Tristan da Cunha Is.	2,060
Askja (1961)	Iceland	1,510
Hekla (1970)	Iceland	1,491
Faial (1968)	Azores	1,043
Katla (1918)	Iceland	900
Leirhnukur (1975)	Iceland	650
Helgafell (1973)	Iceland	226
Surtsey (1967)	Iceland	174
Europe		
Etna (1975)	Italy	3,290
Vesuvio (1944)	Italy	1,281
Stromboli (1975)	Italy	926
Vulcano	Italy	500
Santorini (1950)	Greece	130
North America		
Citlaltepec	Mexico	5,676
Popocatepetl (1920)	Mexico	5,452
Rainier	Washington	4,395
Wrangell	Alaska	4,320
Colima (1975)	Mexico	3,960
Spurr (1953)	Alaska	3,375
Baker	Washington	3,316
Lassen (1915)	California	3,186
Paricutin (1952)	Mexico	3,170
Redoubt (1966)	Alaska	3,110
Iliamna	Alaska	3,073
Shishaldin (1976)	Aleutian Is.	2,858
Pavlof (1976)	Alaska	2,715
Veniaminof	Alaska	2,560
Chiginagak	Alaska	2,420
Douglas	Alaska	2,328
Pogromni	Alaska	2,286
Katmai (1931)	Alaska	2,285
Mageik (1912)	Alaska	2,210
Tanaga	Aleutian Is.	2,125
Trident (1963)	Alaska	2,070
Kukak	Alaska	2,046
Makushin	Aleutian Is.	2,036
Martin (1912)	Alaska	1,830
Great Sitkin (1974)	Aleutian Is.	1,750
Cleveland (1951)	Aleutian Is.	1,730
Gareloi	Aleutian Is.	1,627
Korovin	Aleutian Is.	1,480
Kanaga	Aleutian Is.	1,348
Aniakchak	Alaska	1,348
Akutan (1974)	Aleutian Is.	1,293
Kiska (1969)	Aleutian Is.	1,220
Augustine (1976)	Alaska	1,210
Little Sitkin	Aleutian Is.	1,195
Okmok (1945)	Aleutian Is.	1,072

Important Islands and Their Areas

Source: National Geographic Society, Washington, D.C.

Figure in parentheses shows rank among the world's 10 largest islands, some islands have not been surveyed accurately; in such cases estimated areas are shown. *See footnotes.

Location-Ownership
Area in Square Miles

Arctic Ocean
Canadian Islands

Axel Heiberg	16,671
Baffin (5)	195,928
Banks	27,038
Bathurst	6,194
Devon	21,331
Ellesmere (10)	75,767
Melville	16,274
Prince of Wales	12,872
Somerset	9,570
Southampton	15,913
Victoria (9)	83,896

USSR Islands

Franz Josef Land	8,000
Novaya Zemlya (two is.)	35,000
Wrangel	2,800

Norwegian Islands

Svalbard	23,940
Nordaustlandet	5,410
Spitsbergen	15,060

Atlantic Ocean

Anticosti, Canada	3,066
Ascension, UK	34
Azores, Portugal	902
Faial	67
Sao Miguel	291
Bahamas	5,380
Bermuda Is., UK	20
Block, Rhode Island	10
Canary Is., Spain	2,808
Fuerteventura	668
Gran Canaria	592
Tenerife	795
Cape Breton, Canada	3,981
Cape Verde Is.	1,557
Faeroe Is., Denmark	540
Falkland Is., UK	4,618
Fernando de Noronha Archipelago, Brazil	7
Macias Nguema Biyogo, Equatorial Guinea	785

British Isles

Great Britain, mainland (8)	84,186
Channel Islands	75
Guernsey	24
Jersey	45
Sark	2
Hebrides	2,744
Ireland	32,598
Irish Republic	27,136
Northern Ireland	5,462
Man	227
Orkney Is.	390
Scilly Is.	6
Shetland Is.	567
Skye	670
Wight	147

Greenland, Denmark (1)	840,000
Iceland	39,768
Long Island, N. Y.	1,396
Madeira Is., Portugal	307
Marajo, Brazil	15,528
Martha's Vineyard, Mass.	91
Mount Desert, Me.	108
Nantucket, Mass.	46
Newfoundland, Canada	42,031
Prince Edward, Canada	2,184
St. Helena, UK	47
South Georgia, UK	1,450
Tierra del Fuego, Chile and Argentina	17,800
Tristan da Cunha, UK	40

Baltic Sea

Aland Is., Finland	581
Bornholm, Denmark	227
Gotland, Sweden	1,164

Caribbean Sea

Antigua, UK	108
Aruba, Netherlands	74
Barbados	166
Cuba	44,218
Isle of Pines	1,182
Curacao, Netherlands	182
Dominica, UK	290
Guadeloupe, France	687
Hispaniola, Haiti and Dominican Republic	29,530
Jamaica	4,232
Martinique, France	425
Puerto Rico, U. S.	3,435
Tobago	116
Trinidad	1,864
Virgin Is., UK	59
Virgin Is., U.S.	133

Indian Ocean

Andaman Is., India	2,500
Madagascar (Malagasy Republic) (4)	226,657
Mauritius	720
Pemba, Tanzania	380
Reunion, France	969
Seychelles	107
Sri Lanka	25,332
Zanzibar, Tanzania	640

Persian Gulf

Bahrain	231

Mediterranean Sea

Balearic Is., Spain	1,936
Corfu, Greece	229
Corsica, France	3,365
Crete, Greece	3,186
Cyprus	3,572
Elba, Italy	86
Euboea, Greece	1,409
Malta	122
Rhodes, Greece	542
Sardinia, Italy	9,262
Sicily, Italy	9,822

Pacific Ocean

Aleutian Is., U. S.	6,821
Adak	289
Amchitka	121
Attu	388
Kanaga	135
Kiska	110
Tanaga	209
Umnak	675
Unalaska	1,064
Unimak	1,600
Canton, U. S., UK*	4
Caroline Is., U. S. trust terr.	463
Christmas, U. S., UK*	94
Diomede, Big, USSR	11
Diomede, Little, U.S.	2
Easter, Chile	68
Fiji	7,055
Vanua Levi	2,242
Viti Levu	4,109
Funafuti, UK, U.S.*	2
Galapagos Is., Ecuador	3,043
Guadalcanal, UK	2,500
Hainan, China	13,000
Hawaiian Is., U.S.	6,450
Hawaii	4,037
Oahu	593
Hong Kong, UK	29
Japan	143,750
Hokkaido	30,100
Honshu (7)	87,804
Iwo Jima	9
Kyushu	14,154
Okinawa	460
Shikoku	7,053
Kodiak, U.S.	3,670
Mariana Is., U.S. trust terr. excluding Guam	182
Guam, U. S.	209
Marquesas Is., France	492
Marshall Is., U.S. trust terr.	69
Bikini*	2
Nauru	8
New Caledonia, France	6,530
New Guinea (2)	305,577
New Hebrides, UK-Fr.	5,700
New Zealand	103,747
Chatham	372
North	44,190
South	58,192
Stewart	674
Philippines	115,830
Leyte	2,787
Luzon	40,880
Mindanao	36,775
Mindoro	3,790
Negros	4,907
Palawan	4,554
Panay	4,446
Samar	5,050
Quemoy, Taiwan	56
Sakhalin, USSR	29,500
Samoa Is.	1,177
American Samoa	76
Tutuila	52
Western Samoa	1,101
Savaii	670
Upolu	429
Santa Catalina, U.S.	72
Tahiti, France	402
Taiwan	13,812
Tasmania, Australia	26,383
Tonga Is.	270
Vancouver, Canada	12,079

East Indies

Bali, Indonesia	2,147
Borneo, Indonesia-Malaysia, UK (3)	280,107
Celebes, Indonesia	69,255
Java, Indonesia	48,763
Madura, Indonesia	2,113
Moluccas, Indonesia	28,766
New Britain, Papua New Guinea	14,050
New Ireland, Papua New Guinea	2,799
Sumatra, Indonesia (6)	182,860
Timor	11,570

Australia, often called an island, is a continent. Its mainland area is 2,941,526 sq. mi.

Islands in minor waters: Manhattan (23 sq. mi.) Staten (58 sq. mi.) and Governors (173 acres), all in New York Harbor, U.S.; Isle Royale (209 sq. mi.), Lake Superior, U.S.; Manitoulin (1,068 sq. mi.), Lake Huron, Canada; Pinang (110 sq. mi.), Strait of Malacca, Malaysia; Singapore (224 sq. mi.), Singapore Strait, Singapore.

Atolls: Bikini (lagoon area, 230 sq. mi., land area 2 sq. mi.), U.S. Trust Territory of the Pacific Islands; Canton (lagoon 20 sq. mi., land 4 sq. mi.), U.S. and UK; Christmas (lagoon 140 sq. mi., land 94 sq. mi.), U.S. and UK; Funafuti (lagoon 84 sq. mi., land 2 sq. mi.), U.S. and UK.

Highest and Lowest Continental Altitudes

Source: National Geographic Society, Washington, D.C.

(In feet)

Continent	Highest Point	Elevation	Lowest Point	Below Sea Level
Asia	Mount Everest, Nepal-Tibet	29,028	Dead Sea, Israel-Jordan	1,302
South America	Mount Aconcagua, Argentina	22,834	Valdes Peninsula, Argentina	131
North America	Mount McKinley, Alaska	20,320	Death Valley, California	282
Africa	Kilimanjaro, Tanzania	19,340	Lake Assal, Afars & Issas Terr.	512
Europe	Mount El'brus USSR Caucasus Mts.	18,510	Caspian Sea, USSR	92
Antarctica	Vinson Massif	16,860	Unknown	...
Australia	Mount Kosciusko, New South Wales	7,310	Lake Eyre, South Australia	52

Height of Mount Everest

Mt. Everest was considered to be 29,002 ft. tall when Edmund Hillary and Tanzing Norgay scaled it in 1953. This triangulation figure had been accepted since 1850. In 1954 the Surveyor General of the Republic of India set the height at 29,028 ft., plus or minus 10 ft. because of snow. The National Geographic Society accepts the new figure, but many mountaineering groups still use 29,002 ft.

High Peaks in United States, Canada, Mexico

Name	Place	Feet	Name	Place	Feet	Name	Place	Feet
McKinley	Alas	20,320	Crestone	Col	14,294	Eolus	Col	14,084
Logan	Can	19,850	Lincoln	Col	14,286	Columbia	Col	14,073
Citlaltepec (Orizaba)	Mexico	18,700	Grays	Col	14,270	Augusta	Alas-Can	14,070
St. Elias	Alas-Can	18,008	Antero	Col	14,269	Missouri	Col	14,067
Popocatepetl	Mexico	17,887	Torreys	Col	14,267	Humboldt	Col	14,064
Foraker	Alas	17,400	Castle	Col	14,265	Bierstadt	Col	14,060
Iztaccihuatl	Mexico	17,343	Quandary	Col	14,265	Sunlight	Col	14,059
Lucania	Can	17,147	Evans	Col	14,264	Split	Cal	14,058
King	Can	16,971	Longs	Col	14,256	Nauhcampatepetl (Cofre de Perote)	Mexico	14,049
Steele	Can	16,644	McArthur	Can	14,253	Handies	Col	14,048
Bona	Alas	16,550	Wilson	Col	14,246	Culebra	Col	14,047
Blackburn	Alas	16,390	White	Cal	14,246	Langley	Cal	14,042
Kennedy	Alas	16,286	North Palisade	Cal	14,242	Lindsey	Col	14,042
Sanford	Alas	16,237	Shavano	Col	14,229	Middle Palisade	Cal	14,040
South Buttress	Alas	15,885	Belford	Col	14,197	Little Bear	Col	14,037
Wood	Can	15,885	Princeton	Col	14,197	Sherman	Col	14,036
Vancouver	Alas-Can	15,700	Crestone Needle	Col	14,197	Redcloud	Col	14,034
Churchill	Alas	15,638	Yale	Col	14,196	Tyndall	Cal	14,018
Fairweather	Alas-Can	15,300	Bross	Col	14,172	Pyramid	Col	14,018
Zinantecatl (Toluca)	Mexico	15,016	Kit Carson	Col	14,165	Wilson Peak	Col	14,017
Hubbard	Alas-Can	15,015	Wrangell	Alaska	14,163	Muir	Cal	14,015
Bear	Alas	14,831	Shasta	Cal	14,162	Wetterhorn	Col	14,015
Walsh	Can	14,780	Sill	Cal	14,162	North Maroon	Col	14,014
East Buttress	Alas	14,730	El Diente	Col	14,159	San Luis	Col	14,014
Matlalcueyetl	Mexico	14,636	Maroon	Col	14,156	Huron	Col	14,005
Hunter	Alas	14,573	Tabeguache	Col	14,155	Holy Cross	Col	14,005
Alverstone	Alas-Can	14,565	Oxford	Col	14,153	Colima	Mexico	14,003
Browne Tower	Alas	14,530	Sneffels	Col	14,150	Sunshine	Col	14,001
Whitney	Cal	14,494	Point Success	Wash	14,150	Grizzly	Col	14,000
Elbert	Col	14,433	Democrat	Col	14,148	Barnard	Cal	13,990
Massive	Col	14,421	Liberty Cap	Wash	14,133	Stewart	Col	13,980
Harvard	Col	14,420	Capitol	Col	14,130	Keith	Cal	13,977
Rainier	Wash	14,410	Pikes Peak	Col	14,110	Ouray	Col	13,971
Williamson	Cal	14,375	Snowmass	Col	14,092	Le Conte	Cal	13,960
Blanca	Col	14,345	Windom	Col	14,087	Meeker	Col	13,911
La Plata	Col	14,336	Russell	Cal	14,086	Kennedy	Can	13,905
Uncompahgre	Col	14,309						

South America

Peak	Country	Feet	Peak	Country	Feet	Peak	Country	Feet
Aconcagua, Argentina		22,834	Laudo, Argentina		20,997	Solo, Argentina		20,492
Ojos del Salado, Arg.-Chile		22,572	Ancohuma, Bolivia		20,958	Polleras, Argentina		20,456
Bonete, Argentina		22,546	Ausangate, Peru		20,945	Pular, Chile		20,423
Tupungato, Argentina-Chile		22,310	Toro, Argentina-Chile		20,932	Chani, Argentina		20,341
Pissis, Argentina		22,241	Illampu, Bolivia		20,873	Aucanquilcha, Chile		20,295
Mercedario, Argentina		22,211	Tres Cruces, Argentina-Chile		20,853	Juncal, Argentina-Chile		20,276
Huascaran, Peru		22,205	Huandoy, Peru		20,852	Negro, Argentina		20,184
Llullaillaco, Argentina-Chile		22,057	Parinacota, Bolivia-Chile		20,768	Quela, Argentina		20,128
El Libertador, Argentina		22,047	Tortolas, Argentina-Chile		20,745	Condoriri, Bolivia		20,095
Cachi, Argentina		22,047	Ampato, Peru		20,702	Palermo, Argentina		20,079
Yerupaja, Peru		21,709	Condor, Argentina		20,669	Solimana, Peru		20,068
Galan, Argentina		21,654	Salcantay, Peru		20,574	San Juan, Argentina-Chile		20,049
El Muerto, Argentina-Chile		21,457	Chimborazo, Ecuador		20,561	Sierra Nevada, Arg.-Chile		20,023
Sajama, Bolivia		21,391	Huancarhuas, Peru		20,531	Antofalla, Argentina		20,013
Nacimiento, Argentina		21,302	Famatina, Arg.		20,505	Marmolejo, Argentina-Chile		20,013
Illimani, Bolivia		21,201	Pumasillo, Peru		20,492	Chachani, Peru		19,931
Coropuna, Peru		21,083				Licancabur, Argentina-Chile		19,425

The highest point in the West Indies is in the Dominican Republic, Pico Duarte (10,417 ft.)

Africa, Australia, and Oceania

Mountain and Country	Feet	Mountain and Country	Feet	Mountain and Country	Feet
Kilimanjaro, Tanzania	19,340	Meru, Tanzania	14,979	Toubkal, Morocco	13,665
Kenya, Kenya	17,058	Wilhelm, New Guinea	14,793	Kinabalu, Malaysia	13,455
Margherita Pk., Uganda-Zaire	16,763	Karisimbi, Zaire-Rwanda	14,787	Kerinci, Sumatra	12,467
Jaja, New Guinea	16,500	Elgon, Kenya-Uganda	14,178	Cook, New Zealand	12,349
Trikora, New Guinea	15,585	Batu, Ethiopia	14,131	Teide, Canary Islands	12,198
Mandala, New Guinea	15,420	Guna, Ethiopia	13,881	Semeru, Java	12,060
Ras Dashan, Ethiopia	15,158	Gughe, Ethiopia	13,780	Kosciusko, Australia	7,310

Europe

Peak	Feet	Peak	Feet	Peak	Feet	Peak	Feet
Alps		Hohberghom	13,842	Fiescherhorn	13,283	**Pyrenees**	
Mont Blanc	15,771	Alphubel	13,799	Grunhorn	13,266	Aneto	11,168
Monte Rosa (highest peak of group)	15,203	Rimpfischhorn	13,776	Lauteraarhorn	13,261	Posets	11,073
Dom	14,911	Aletschorn	13,763	Durrenhorn	13,238	Perdido	11,007
Liskamm	14,852	Strahlhorn	13,747	Allalinhorn	13,213	Vignemale	10,820
Weisshorn	14,780	Dent D'Herens	13,686	Weissmies	13,199	Long	10,479
Taschhorn	14,733	Breithorn	13,665	Lagginhorn	13,156	Estats	10,304
Matterhorn	14,690	Bishom	13,645	Zupo	13,120	Montcalm	10,105
Dent Blanche	14,293	Jungfrau	13,642	Fletschhorn	13,110	**Caucasus (Europe-Asia)**	
Nadelhorn	14,196	Ecrins	13,461	Adlerhorn	13,081	Elbrus	18,510
Grand Combin	14,154	Monch	13,448	Gletscherhorn	13,068	Shkara	17,064
Lenzpitze	14,088	Pollux	13,422	Schalihorn	13,040	Dykh Tau	17,054
Finsteraarhorn	14,022	Schreckhorn	13,379	Scerscen	13,028	Kashtan Tau	16,877
Castor	13,865	Ober Gabelhorn	13,330	Eiger	13,025	Kazbek	16,558
Zinalrothorn	13,849	Gran Paradiso	13,323	Jagerhorn	13,024	Dzhangi Tau	16,565
		Bernina	13,284	Rottalhorn	13,022		

Asia

Peak	Country	Feet	Peak	Country	Feet
Everest	Nepal-Tibet	29,028	Istoro Nal	Pakistan	24,240
K2 (Godwin Austen)	Kashmir	28,250	Tent Peak	India-Nepal	24,165
Kanchenjunga	India-Nepal	28,208	Chomo Lhari	Bhutan-Tibet	24,040
Lhotse I (Everest)	Nepal-Tibet	27,923	Chamlang	Nepal	24,012
Makalu I	Nepal-Tibet	27,824	Kabru	India-Nepal	24,002
Lhotse II (Everest)	Nepal-Tibet	27,560	Alung Gangri	Tibet	24,000
Dhaulagiri	Nepal	26,810	Baltoro Kangri	Kashmir	23,990
Manaslu I	Nepal	26,760	Mussu Shan	Sinkiang	23,890
Cho Oyu	Nepal-Tibet	26,750	Mana	India	23,860
Nanga Parbat	Kashmir	26,660	Baruntse	Nepal	23,688
Annapurna I	Nepal	26,504	Nepal Peak	India-Nepal	23,500
Gasherbrum	Kashmir	26,470	Amne Machin	China	23,490
Broad	Kashmir	26,400	Gauri Sankar	Nepal-Tibet	23,440
Gosainthan	Tibet	26,287	Badrinath	India	23,420
Annapurna II	Nepal	26,041	Nunkun	Kashmir	23,410
Gyachung Kang	Nepal-Tibet	25,910	Lenina Peak	USSR	23,405
Disteghil Sar	Kashmir	25,868	Pyramid	India-Nepal	23,400
Himalchuli	Nepal	25,801	Api	Nepal	23,399
Nuptse (Everest)	Nepal-Tibet	25,726	Pauhunri	India-Tibet	23,385
Masherbrum	Kashmir	25,660	Trisul	India	23,360
Nanda Devi	India	25,645	Kangto	India-Tibet	23,260
Chomo Lonzo	Nepal-Tibet	25,640	Nyenchhen Thanglha	Tibet	23,255
Rakaposhi	Kashmir	25,550	Trisuli	India	23,210
Kamet	India-Tibet	25,447	Pumori	Nepal-Tibet	23,190
Namcha Barwa	Tibet	25,445	Dunagiri	India	23,184
Gurla Mandhata	Tibet	25,355	Lombo Kangra	Tibet	23,165
Ulugh Muz Tagh	Sinkiang-Tibet	25,340	Saipal	Nepal	23,100
Kungur	Sinkiang	25,325	Macha Pucchare	Nepal	22,958
Tirich Mir	Pakistan	25,230	Numbar	Nepal	22,817
Makalu II	Nepal-Tibet	25,120	Kanjiroba	Nepal	22,580
Minya Konka	China	24,900	Ama Dablam	Nepal	22,350
Kula Gangri	Bhutan-Tibet	24,784	Cho Polu	Nepal	22,093
Changtse (Everest)	Nepal-Tibet	24,780	Lingtren	Nepal-Tibet	21,972
Muz Tagh Ata	Sinkiang	24,757	Khumbutse	Nepal-Tibet	21,785
Skyang Kangri	Kashmir	24,750	Hlako Gangri	Tibet	21,266
Communism Peak	USSR	24,590	Mt. Grosvenor	China	21,190
Jongsang Peak	India-Nepal	24,472	Thagchhab Gangri	Tibet	20,970
Pobedy Peak	Sinkiang-USSR	24,406	Damavand	Iran	18,606
Sia Kangri	Kashmir	24,350	Ararat	Turkey	16,946
Haramosh Peak	Pakistan	24,270			

Antarctica

Peak	Feet	Peak	Feet	Peak	Feet
Vinson Massif	16,860	Miller	13,650	Press	12,566
Tyree	16,290	Long Gables	13,620	Falla	12,549
Shinn	15,750	Dickerson	13,517	Rucker	12,520
Gardner	15,375	Giovinetto	13,412	Goldthwait	12,510
Epperly	15,100	Wade	13,400	Morris	12,500
Kirkpatrick	14,855	Fisher	13,386	Erebus	12,450
Elizabeth	14,698	Fridtjof Nansen	13,350	Campbell	12,434
Markham	14,290	Wexler	13,202	Don Pedro Christophersen	12,355
Bell	14,117	Lister	13,200	Lysaght	12,326
Mackellar	14,098	Shear	13,100	Huggins	12,247
Anderson	13,957	Odishaw	13,008	Sabine	12,200
Bentley	13,934	Donaldson	12,894	Astor	12,175
Kaplan	13,878	Ray	12,808	Mohl	12,172
Andrew Jackson	13,750	Sellery	12,779	Frakes	12,064
Sidley	13,720	Waterman	12,730	Jones	12,040
Ostenso	13,710	Anne	12,703	Gjelsvik	12,008
Minto	13,668			Coman	12,000

How Deep Is the Ocean?

Principal Ocean Depths. **Source:** Defense Mapping Agency Hydrographic Center

Name of Area	Location		Depth Meters	Fathoms	Feet	Ship and/or Country	Year

Pacific Ocean

Name of Area	Location		Meters	Fathoms	Feet	Ship and/or Country	Year
Mariana Trench	11°21′N,	142°12′E.	11,034	6,033	36,198	Vityaz (USSR).	1957
	11°19′N,	142°.5′E.	10,863	5,939	35,631	HMS Challenger.	1951
	11°20′N,	142°16′E.	10,815	5,910	35,460	″ (UK)	1951
	11°18.5′N,	142°15.5′E.	10,910	5,967	35,800	Bathyscaph Trieste.	1960
Tonga Trench.	23°15.3′S,	174°44.7′W.	10,882	5,950	35,702	Vityaz (USSR).	1957
	24°00′S,	175°00′W.	10,850	5,933	35,598	Nat'l Geographic.	1965
	23°16′S,	174°46′W.	10,633	5,814	34,884	R/V Horizon (U.S.).	1953
Kuril Trench.	44°15.2′N,	150°34.2′E.	10,542	5,764	34,587	Vityaz (USSR).	1954
	44°18′N,	150°30′E.	10,382	5,677	34,062	Vityaz (USSR).	1953
Philippine Trench	10°24′N,	126°40′E.	10,539	5,763	34,578	Galathea (Danish).	1951
(Mindanao)	10°27′N,	126°39.5′E.	10,497	5,740	34,440	USS Cape Johnson.	1945
Izu Trench.	30°32′N,	142°31′E.	10,374	5,673	34,033	USS Ramapo.	1932
	30°30′N,	142°30′E.	9,985	5,459	32,751	Bathymetric Map (USSR).	1964
	31°54′N,	142°00′E.	9,915	5,420	32,521	Bathymetric Map (USSR).	1964
	30°49′N,	142°18′E.	9,441	5,159	30,954	Mansyu (Japan).	1924
Kermadec Trench	31°52.8′S,	177°20.6′W.	10,047	5,494	32,964	Vityaz (USSR).	1957
	31°51′S,	177°02′W.	9,994	5,465	32,790	Galathea (Danish).	1952
Bonin Trench.	24°30′N,	143°24′E.	9,156	5,005	30,032	Vityaz (USSR).	1964
	24°17′N,	143°23′E.	9,150	5,002	30,012	USS Salt Lake City.	1945
New Britain Trench.	06°34′S,	153°55′E.	9,140	4,998	29,988	Planet (German).	1910
	06°18′S,	153°48′E.	9,103	4,976	29,858	Bathymetric Map (USSR).	1964
	06°18′S,	153°43′E.	8,936	4,886	29,316	SS Blackfin.	1959
Yap Trench.	08°33′N,	138°02′E.	8,527	4,662	27,976	Vityaz (USSR).	1958
	08°08′N,	137°49′E.	8,028	4,390	26,340	USCGG Kukui.	1965
	07°55′N,	137°39′E.	8,028	4,390	26,340	SS Greenfish.	1965
Japan Trench.	36°08′N,	142°43′E.	8,412	4,597	27,591	Bathymetric Map (USSR).	1964
Palau Trench.	07°40′N,	135°04′E.	8,138	4,449	26,693	Stefan (Germany).	1905
	07°31′N,	134°56′E.	7,324	4,005	24,030	USCGG Ironwood.	1966
Aleutian Trench.	50°53′N,	176°23′E.	8,100	4,429	26,574	USCGC Bering Strait.	1953
	51°13′N,	174°48′E.	7,882	4,276	25,656	USCGC Chelan.	1936
	50°51′N,	172°16′E.	7,679	4,199	25,194	Coast & Geodetic.	1936
	50°41′N,	177°11′E.	7,666	4,192	25,152	Coast & Geodetic.	1966
Peru Chile Trench.	23°18′S,	71°41′W.	8,064	4,409	26,454	R/V Spencer F. Baird.	1957
(Atacama Trench)	23°27′S,	71°21′W.	8,064	4,409	26,454	IGY.	
	21°00′S,	71°15′W.	7,920	4,330	25,980	R/V Atlantis.	1955
New Hebrides Trench.	20°36′S,	168°37′E.	7,570	4,138	24,830	Planet (Germany).	1910
Ryukyu Trench.	25°15′N,	128°32′E.	7,507	4,105	24,629	Mansyu (Japan).	1925
	24°00′N,	126°48′E.	7,181	3,926	23,554	Bathymetric Map (USSR).	1964
Mid. America Trench.	14°02′N,	93°39′W.	6,669	3,642	21,852	USS Epce.	1965

Atlantic Ocean

Name of Area	Location		Meters	Fathoms	Feet	Ship and/or Country	Year
Puerto Rico Trench.	19°35′N,	68°17′W.	8,648	4,729	28,374	SS Archerfish.	1961
	19°45′N,	67°49′W.	8,528	4,663	27,978	USS Rehoboth.	1955
	19°44′N,	67°22′W.	8,497	4,646	27,876	USS San Pablo, USS Rehoboth.	1955
	19°53′N,	66°55′W.	8,476	4,635	27,810	USS San Pablo.	1955
	19°41′N,	67°17′W.	8,416	4,602	27,612	USS San Pablo.	1955
	19°45.5′N,	67°09.7′W.	8,604	4,589	27,534	USNS Wyman	1972
	19°42′N,	67°05′W.	8,381	4,583	27,498	R/V Vema (U.S.).	1954
Cayman Trench.	19°12′N,	80°00′W.	7,535	4,120	24,720	R/V Vema (U.S.).	1960
	18°59′N,	80°12′W.	7,211	3,943	23,658	(British Admiralty).	1955
	18°59′N,	80°23′W.	7,191	3,932	23,592	″ ″	1955
	19°03′N,	80°22′W.	7,491	4,096	24,576	(Germany).	1937
So. Sandwich Trench.	55°14′S,	26°29′W.	8,252	4,512	27,072	USS Eltanin.	1963
	55°08′S,	26°04′W.	8,246	4,509	27,054	USS Eltanin.	1963
	55°08′S,	26°05′W.	8,219	4,494	26,964	USS Eltanin.	1963
	55°07′S,	26°46′W.	8,264	4,518	27,113	Meteor (Germany).	1926
Romanche Gap.	00°16′S,	18°35′W.	7,864	4,300	25,800	R/V Vema (U.S.).	1957
	00°13′S,	18°26′W.	7,729	4,226	25,356	USS Albatross.	1948
Brazil Basin.	09°10′S,	23°02′W.	6,119	3,346	20,076	R/V Vema (U.S.).	1956

Indian Ocean

Name of Area	Location		Meters	Fathoms	Feet	Ship and/or Country	Year
Java Trench.	10°15′S,	109°E′(approx.).	7,725	4,224	25,344	Natl Geographic.	1967
	10°20′S,	110°10′E.	7,450	4,073	24,442	(British Admiralty).	1928
	10°19′S,	108°50′E.	7,457	3,977	23,862	Australian Navy Hydrographer.	1962
Ob Trench.	(no position).		6,874	3,759	22,553	Nat'l Geographic.	1967
Vema Trench.	(no position).		6,402	3,501	21,004	Nat'l Geographic.	1967
Agulhas Basin.	(no position).		6,195	3,388	20,325	Nat'l Geographic.	1967
Diamantina Trench.	35°00′S,	105°35′E.	6,062	3,315	19,800	Nat'l Geographic.	1967

Arctic Ocean

Name of Area	Location		Meters	Fathoms	Feet	Ship and/or Country	Year
Eurasia Basin.	82°23′N,	19°31′E.	5,450	2,980	17,880	Fidor Lithke (USSR).	1955

Mediterranean Sea

Name of Area	Location		Meters	Fathoms	Feet	Ship and/or Country	Year
Ionian Basin.	36°32′N,	21°06′E.	5,150	2,816	16,896	USS Tanner.	1955
	35°51′N,	22°18′E.	5,005	2,737	16,420	Calypso (French).	1955
	36°34′N,	21°08′E.	5,093	2,717	16,302	R/V Chain.	1959

Continental Statistics

Source: National Geographic Society, Washington, D.C.

Continents	Area (sq. mi.)	% of Earth	Population (est.)	% World Total	Highest Point (in feet)	Lowest Point
Asia	16,988,000	29.5	2,352,700,000	58.5	Everest, 29,028	Dead Sea, −1,302
Africa	11,506,000	20.0	413,000,000	10.3	Kilimanjaro, 19,340	Lake Assal, −512
North America	9,390,000	16.3	347,000,000	8.6	McKinley, 20,320	Death Valley, −282
South America	6,795,000	11.8	217,000,000	5.4	Aconcagua, 22,834	Valdes Penin., −131
Europe	3,745,000	6.5	667,300,000	16.6	El'brus, 18,510	Caspian Sea−92
Australia	2,968,000	5.2	13,800,000	0.3	Kosciusko, 7,310	Lake Eyre, −52
Antarctica	5,500,000	9.6	—	—	Vinson Massif, 16,860	Not Known

Est. World Population 4,019,000,000

Ocean Area and Average Depth

Four major bodies of water are recognized by geographers and mapmakers. They are: the Pacific, Atlantic, Indian and Arctic Oceans. The Atlantic and Pacific Oceans are considered divided at the equator into the No. and So. Atlantic; the No. and So. Pacific. The Arctic Ocean is the name for waters north of the continental land masses in the region of the Arctic Circle.

	Sq. Miles	Avg. Depth in Feet		Sq. Miles	Avg. Depth in Feet
Pacific Ocean	64,186,300	13,739	Hudson Bay	281,900	305
Atlantic Ocean	33,420,000	12,257	East China Sea	256,600	620
Indian Ocean	28,350,500	12,704	Andaman Sea	218,100	3,667
Arctic Ocean	5,105,700	4,362	Black Sea	196,100	3,906
South China Sea	1,148,500	4,802	Red Sea	174,900	1,764
Caribbean Sea	971,400	8,448	North Sea	164,900	308
Mediterranean Sea	969,100	4,926	Baltic Sea	147,500	180
Bering Sea	873,000	4,893	Yellow Sea	113,500	121
Gulf of Mexico	582,100	5,297	Gulf of California	59,100	2,375
Sea of Okhotsk	537,500	3,192	Persian Gulf	88,800	328
Sea of Japan	391,100	5,468			

The Malayan Sea is not considered a geographical entity but a term used for convenience for waters between the South Pacific and the Indian Ocean.

Principal World Rivers

Source: National Geographic Society, Washington, D.C. (Length in miles)

River	Outflow	Lgth	River	Outflow	Lgth	River	Outflow	Lgth
Albany	James Bay	610	Japura	Amazon River	1,750	Rhone	Gulf of Lions	505
Amazon	Atlantic Ocean	4,000	Jordan	Dead Sea	200	Rio de la Plata	Atlantic Ocean	150
Amu	Aral Sea	1,578	Kootenay	Columbia River	485	Rio Grande	Gulf of Mexico	1,885
Amur	Tatar Strait	2,700	Lena	Laptev Sea	2,680	Rio Roosevelt	Aripuana	400
Angara	Yenisey River	1,151	Loire	Bay of Biscay	634	Saguenay	St. Lawrence R.	434
Arkansas	Mississippi	1,459	Mackenzie	Arctic Ocean	2,635	St. John	Bay of Fundy	418
Back	Arctic Ocean	605	Madeira	Amazon River	2,013	St. Lawrence	Gulf of St. Law.	800
Brahmaputra	Bay of Bengal	1,800	Magdalena	Caribbean Sea	956	St. Maurice	St. Lawrence R.	350
Bug, Southern	Dnieper River	532	Marne	Seine River	326	Salween	Andaman Sea	1,500
Bug, Western	Wisla River	481	Mekong	S. China Sea	2,600	Sao Francisco	Atlantic Ocean	1,988
Canadian	Arkansas River	906	Meuse	North Sea	580	Saskatchewan	Lake Winnipeg	1,205
Churchill, Man.	Hudson Bay	1,000	Mississippi	Gulf of Mexico	2,348	Seine	English Chan.	482
Churchill, Que.	Atlantic Ocean	532	Missouri	Mississippi	2,533	Shannon	Atlantic Ocean	230
Colorado	Gulf of Calif.	1,450	Murray-Darling	Indian Ocean	2,310	Snake	Columbia River	1,038
Columbia	Pacific Ocean	1,243	Negro	Amazon	1,400	Sungari	Amur River	1,150
Congo	Atlantic Ocean	2,718	Nelson	Hudson Bay	1,600	Syr	Aral Sea	1,370
Danube	Black Sea	1,776	Niger	Gulf of Guinea	2,600	Tajo, Tagus	Atlantic Ocean	626
Dnieper	Black Sea	1,420	Nile	Mediterranean	4,145	Tennessee	Ohio River	652
Dniester	Black Sea	877	Ob-Irtysh	Gulf of Ob	3,460	Thames	North Sea	215
Don	Sea of Azov	1,224	Oder	Baltic Sea	567	Tiber	Tyrrhenian Sea.	252
Drava	Danube River	447	Ohio	Mississippi	1,306	Tigris	Euphrates	1,180
Dvina, North	White Sea	824	Orange	Atlantic Ocean	1,300	Tisza	Danube River	600
Dvina, West.	Gulf of Riga	634	Orinoco	Atlantic Ocean	1,600	Tocantins	Para River	1,677
Ebro	Mediterranean	565	Ottawa	St. Lawrence R.	790	Ural	Caspian Sea	1,575
Elbe	North Sea	724	Paraguay	Parana River	1,584	Uruguay	Rio de la Plata	1,000
Euphrates	Persian Gulf	2,235	Parana	Rio de la Plata	2,500	Usumacinta	Gulf of Mexico	270
Fraser	Str. of Georgia	850	Peace	Slave River	1,195	Volga	Caspian Sea	2,290
Gambia	Atlantic Ocean	700	Pilcomayo	Paraguay River	1,000	Weser	North Sea	454
Ganges	Bay of Bengal	1,560	Po	Adriatic Sea	405	Wisla	Bay of Danzig	675
Garonne	Bay of Biscay	357	Purus	Amazon River	2,100	Yangtze	E. China Sea	3,400
Hsi	S. China Sea	1,200	Red	Mississippi	1,270	Yellow (See Huang)		
Huang	Yellow Sea	3,000	Red River of N.	Lake Winnipeg	545	Yenisey	Kara Sea	2,566
Indus	Arabian Sea	1,800	Rhine	North Sea	820	Yukon	Bering Sea	1,979
Irrawaddy	Bay of Bengal	1,300				Zambezi	Indian Ocean	1,700

Major Rivers in North America
Source: U.S. Geological Survey

River	Source or Upper Limit of Length	Outflow	Miles
Alabama	Gilmer County, Ga.	Mobile River	735
Albany	Lake St. Joseph, Ont., Can.	James Bay	320
Allegheny	Potter County, Pa.	Ohio River	325
Altamaha-Ocmulgee	Junction of Yellow and South Rivers, Newton County, Ga.	Atlantic Ocean	392
Apalachicola-Chattahoochee	Towns County, Ga.	Gulf of Mexico, Fla.	524
Assiniboine	Eastern Saskatchewan	Red River	450
Arkansas	Lake County, Col.	Mississippi River, Ark.	1,459
Atchafalaya	Red River, La.	Grand Lake, La.	135
Attawapiskat	Attawapiskat, Ont., Can.	James Bay	465
Black (N.W.T)	Contwoyto Lake	Chantrey Inlet	600
Big Black (Miss.)	Webster County, Miss.	Mississippi River	330
Big Horn	Junction of Wind and Popo Agie Rivers, Fremont County, Wy.	Yellowstone River, Mon.	336
Black (Mo.-Ark.)	Junction Middle and West Forks, Reynolds County, Mo.	White River	280
Bow	Rocky Mountains	South Saskatchewan River	315
Brazos	Junction of Salt and Double Mountain Forks, Stonewall County, Tex.	Gulf of Mexico	870
Canadian	Las Animas County, Col.	Arkansas River, Okla.	906
Cape Fear	Junction of Haw and Deep Rivers, Chatham County, N.C.	Atlantic Ocean	202
Cedar (Iowa)	Dodge County, Minn.	Iowa River, Ia.	329
Cheyenne	Junction of Antelope Creek and Dry Fork, Converse County, Wy.	Missouri River	290
Churchill	Methy Lake	Hudson Bay	1,000
Cimarron	Colfax County, N. M.	Arkansas River, Okla.	600
Clark Fork-Pend Oreille	Silver Bow County, Mon.	Columbia River, B.C.	505
Colorado (Ariz.)	Rocky Mountain National Park, Col. (90 miles in Mexico)	Gulf of Cal., Mexico	1,450
Colorado (Texas)	West Texas	Matagorda Bay	840
Columbia	Columbia Lake, British Columbia	Pacific Ocean, bet. Ore. and Wash.	1,243
Columbia, Upper	Columbia Lake, British Columbia	To mouth of Snake River	890
Colville	Brooks Range	Beaufort Sea	350
Connecticut	Third Connecticut Lake, N.H.	L.I. Sound, Conn.	407
Coosa	Junction of Etowah and Oostanaula River, Floyd County, Ga.	Alabama River	286
Copper	Alaska Range	Gulf of Alaska	280
Coppermine (N.W.T.)	Lac de Gras	Coronation Gulf (Atlantic Ocean)	525
Cumberland	Letcher County, Ky.	Ohio River	720
Delaware	Schoharie County, N.Y.	Liston Point, Delaware Bay	390
Deschutes	Lava Lake, Deschutes County, Ore.	Columbia River	250
Des Moines	Junction of East and West Forks, Humboldt County, Ia.	Mississippi River	327
Dolores	Dolores County, Col.	Colorado River	230
Flint	Hapeville, Fulton County, Ga.	Apalachicola River	265
Fraser	Near Mount Robson (on Continental Divide)	Strait of Georgia	850
French Broad	Junction of North and West Forks, Transylvania County, N.C.	Tennessee River	210
Gila	Catron County, N.M.	Colorado River, Ariz.	630
Grand (Mich.)	Jackson County, Mich.	Lake Michigan	260
Great Whale (Que.)	Lake Bienville	Hudson Bay	230
Green (Ky.)	Lincoln County, Ky.	Ohio River, Ky.	360
Green (Ut.-Wy.)	Junction of Wells and Trail Creeks, Sublette County, Wy.	Colorado River, Ut.	730
Hamilton (Lab.)	Lake Ashuanipi	Atlantic Ocean	600
Hudson	Henderson Lake, Essex County, N.Y.	Upper N.Y. Bay, N.Y.,-N.J.	306
Humboldt	Wells, Nev.	Humboldt Lake	390
Illinois	St. Joseph County, Ind.	Mississippi River	420
Iowa	Hancock County, Ia.	Mississippi River	291
James (N.D.-S.D.)	Wells County, N.D.	Missouri River, S.D.	710
James (Va.)	Junction of Jackson and Cowpasture Rivers, Botetourt County, Va.	Hampton Roads	340
Jefferson-Beaverhead-Red Rock	Source of Red Rock River in Beaverhead County, Mon.	Missouri River	217
John Day	Blue Mountains, Grant County, Ore.	Columbia River	281
Kanawha-New	Junction of North and South Forks of New River, N.C.	Ohio River	352
Kentucky	Junction of North and Middle Forks, Lee County, Ky.	Ohio River	259
Klamath	Lake Ewauna, Klamath Falls, Ore.	Pacific Ocean	250
Koyukuk	Endicott Mountains, Alaska	Yukon River	470
Kuskokwim	Alaska Range	Kuskokwim Bay	680
Liard	Southern Yukon, Alaska	Mackenzie River	570
Licking	Magoffin County, Ky.	Ohio River	350
Little Colorado	Latitude 34°, Apache County, Ariz.	Colorado River	300
Little Missouri	Crook County, Wy.	Missouri River	560
Mackenzie	Great Slave Lake	Arctic Ocean	900
Milk	Junction of North and South Forks, Alberta Province	Missouri River, Mon.	625
Minnesota	Big Stone Lake, Minn.	Mississippi River, St. Paul, Minn.	332
Mississippi	Lake Itasca, Minn.	Mouth of Southwest Pass	2,348

River	Source or Upper Limit of Length	Outflow	Miles
Mississippi, Upper	Lake Itasca, Minn.	To mouth of Missouri R.	1,171
Mississippi-Missouri-Red Rock	Source of Red Rock River, Mon.	Mouth of Southwest Pass	3,710
Missouri	Junction of Jefferson, Madison, and Gallatin Rivers, Madison County, Mon.	Mississippi River	2,315
Missouri-Red Rock	Source of Red Rock River, Mon.	Mississippi River	2,533
Mobile-Alabama-Coosa	Gilmer County, Ga.	Mobile Bay	780
Neches	Van Zandt County, Tex.	Sabine Lake	280
Nelson (Manitoba)	Lake Winnipeg	Hudson Bay	410
Neosho	Morris County, Kan.	Arkansas River, Okla.	460
Neuse	Junction of Eno, Little, and Flat Rivers, Durham County, N.C.	Pamlico Sound	260
New	Junction of North and South Forks, Ashe County, N.C.	Kanawha River	255
Niobrara	Niobrara County, Wy.	Missouri River, Neb.	431
Noatak	Brooks Range, Alas.	Kotzebue Sound	350
North Canadian	Union County, N.M.	Canadian River, Okla.	760
North Platte	Junction of Grizzly and Little Grizzly Creeks, Jackson County, Col.	Platte River, Neb.	618
Nueces	Edwards County, Tex.	Nueces Bay	338
Ohio	Junction of Allegheny and Monogahela Rivers, Pittsburgh, Pa.	Mississippi River, Ill.-Ky.	981
Ohio-Allegheny	Potter County, Pa.	Mississippi River	1,306
Osage	East-central Kansas	Missouri River, Mo.	500
Ottawa	Lake Capimitchigama	St. Lawrence	696
Ouachita	Polk County, Ark.	Red River, La.	605
Owyhee	Elko County, Nev.	Snake River	250
Pearl	Neshoba County, Miss.	Gulf of Mexico, Miss.-La.	411
Peace	Stikine Mountains, B.C.	Slave River	1,054
Pecos	Mora County, N.M.	Rio Grande, Tex.	735
Pee Dee	Junction of Yadkin and Uwharrie Rivers, Montgomery County, N.C.	Winyah Bay	233
Pee Dee-Yadkin	Watauga County, N.C.	Winyah Bay, S.C.	435
Pend Oreille	Near Butte, Mon.	Columbia River	490
Platte	Junction of North and South Platte Rivers, Neb.	Missouri River, Neb.	310
Porcupine	Ogilvie Mountains, Alaska	Yukon River, Alaska	460
Potomac	Garrett County, Md.	Chesapeake Bay	383
Powder	Junction of South and Middle Forks, Wy.	Yellowstone River, Mon.	375
Red (Okla.-Tex.-La.)	Curry County, N.M.	Mississippi River	1,270
Red River of the North	Junction of Otter Tail and Boise de Sioux Rivers, Wilkin County, Minn.	Lake Winnipeg, Manitoba	545
Republican	Junction of North Fork and Arikaree River, Neb.	Kansas River, Kan.	445
Rio Grande	San Juan County, Col.	Gulf of Mexico	1,885
Roanoke	Junction of North and South Forks, Montgomery County, Va.	Albemarle Sound, N.C.	380
Rock (Ill.-Wis.)	Dodge County, Wis.	Mississippi River, Ill.	300
Sabine	Junction of South and Caddo Forks, Hunt County, Tex.	Sabine Lake, Tex.-La.	380
Sacramento	Siskiyou County, Cal.	Suisun Bay	377
St. Francis	Iron County, Mo.	Mississippi River, Ark.	425
St. Johns (Fla.)	Lake Washington, Brevard County, Fla.	Atlantic Ocean	276
St. Joseph	Hillsdale County, Mich.	Lake Michigan	210
St. Lawrence	Lake Ontario	Gulf of St. Lawrence (Atlantic Ocean)	800
Salmon (Idaho)	Custer County, Ida.	Snake River, Ida.	420
San Joaquin	Junction of South and Middle Forks, Madera County, Cal.	Suisun Bay	350
San Juan	Silver Lake, Archuleta County, Col.	Colorado River, Ut.	360
Santee-Wateree-Catawba	McDowell County, N.C.	Atlantic Ocean, S.C.	538
Saskatchewan, North	Rocky Mountains	Lake Winnipeg	1,100
Saskatchewan, South	Rocky Mountains	Lake Winnipeg	1,205
Savannah	Junction of Seneca and Tugaloo Rivers, Anderson County, S.C.	Atlantic Ocean, Ga.-S.C.	314
Scioto	Auglaize County, O.	Ohio River	237
Severn (Ontario)	Sandy Lake	Hudson Bay	610
Skeena (B.C.)	Skeena Mountains	Pacific Ocean	360
Smoky Hill	Cheyenne County, Col.	Kansas River, Kan.	540
Snake	Teton County, Wy.	Columbia River, Wash.	1,038
South Platte	Junction of South and Middle Forks, Park County, Col.	Platte River, Neb.	424
Stikine	Stikine Range, B.C.	Pacific Ocean	310
Susitna	Alaska Range	Cook Inlet	300
Susquehanna	Otsego Lake, Otsego County, N.Y.	Chesapeake Bay, Md.	444
Tallahatchie	Tippah County, Miss.	Yazoo River, Miss.	301
Tallapoosa	Near Embry in Paulding County, Ga.	Alabama River	268
Tanana	Wrangell Mountains	Yukon River, Alaska	620
Tar-Pamlico	Person County, N.C.	Pamlico Bay	215
Tennessee	Junction of French Broad and Holston Rivers	Ohio River, Ky.	652
Tennessee-French Broad	Bland County, Va.	Ohio River	900
Tombigbee	Prentiss County, Miss.	Mobile River, Ala.	525
Tongue	Junction of North and South Forks, Sheridan County, Wy.	Yellowstone River	246
Trinity	North of Dallas, Tex.	Galveston Bay, Tex.	360
Wabash	Darke County, O.	Ohio River, Ill.-Ind.	529
Washita	Hemphill County, Tex.	Red River, Okla.	500
White (Ark.-Mo.)	Madison County, Ark.	Mississippi River	720
Willamette	Douglas County, Ore.	Columbia River	270
Wisconsin	LeVieux Desert, Vilas County, Wis.	Mississippi River	430
Yellowstone	Park County, Wy.	Missouri River, N.D.	671
Yukon	Junction of Lewes and Pelly Rivers, Yukon	Bering Sea, Alaska	1,770

Flows of Largest Rivers in the United States

(Ranked according to average discharge in cubic feet per second (cfs) at mouth)
Source: U.S. Geological Survey (Average discharges for the period 1941-70)

Rank	River	Average Discharge	Length[a] (miles)	Drainage Area	Most Distant Source	Maximum Discharge at Gauging Station Farthest Downstream	(date)
1	Mississippi	°640,000	°3,710	d1,247,300	Beaverhead Co., Mont.	2,080,000	2-17-37
2	Columbia	262,000	1,243	258,000	Columbia Lake, B.C.	1,240,000	Jun. 1894
3	Ohio	258,000	1,306	203,900	Potter Co., Pa.	1,850,000	2-1-37
4	St. Lawrence	°243,000	—	°302,000		ʲ314,000	May 1870
5	Yukon	°240,000	1,770	327,600	Coast Mountain, B.C.	1,030,000	6-22-64
6	ʰAtchafalaya	183,000	135	95,105	Curry Co., N. Mex.	—	
7	Missouri	76,300	2,533	529,400	Beaverhead Co., Mont.	892,000	Jun. 1844
8	Tennessee	64,000	900	40,910	Bland Co., Va.	500,000	2-17-48
9	Red	ʲ62,300	1,270	93,244	Curry Co., N. Mex.	233,000	4-17-45
10	Kuskokwim	62,000	680	49,000	Alaska Range, Alaska	392,000	6-5-64
11	Mobile	61,400	780	43,800	Gilmer, Co., Ga.	—	
12	Snake	50,000	1,038	109,000	Teton Co., Wyo.	409,000	Jun. 1894
13	Arkansas	45,100	1,459	160,600	Lake Co., Col.	536,000	5-27-43
14	Copper	ʲ43,000	280	24,000	Alaska Range, Alaska	ᵏ280,000	7-15-71
15	Tanana	ʲ41,000	620	44,000	Wrangell Mtn., Alaska	186,000	8-18-67
16	Susitna	ᵐ40,000	300	20,000	Alaska Range, Alaska	90,700	6-7-64
17	Susquehanna	37,190	444	27,570	Otsego Co., N.Y.	1,080,000	6-23-72
18	Willamette	35,660	270	11,200	Douglas Co., Ore.	500,000	12-4-1861
19	Alabama	32,400	735	22,600	Gilmer Co., Ga.	267,000	3-7-61
20	White	32,100	720	28,000	Madison Co., Ark.	343,000	4-17-45
21	Wabash	30,400	529	33,150	Darke Co., Oh.	428,000	3-30-13
22	Pend Oreille	29,900	490	25,820	Near Butte, Mont.	171,300	6-13-48
23	Tombigbee	27,300	525	20,100	Prentiss Co., Miss.	280,000	1874 and 1900
24	Cumberland	°26,900	720	18,080	Letcher Co., Ky.	201,000	2-18-50
25	Stikine	°26,000	310	20,000	Stikine Range, B.C.	120,000	6-26-55
26	Sacramento		377	27,100	Siskiyou Co., Cal.	ᵖ332,000	12-25-64
27	Apalachicola	24,700	524	19,600	Towns Co., Ga.	293,000	3-20-29
28	Illinois	22,800	420	27,900	St. Joseph Co., Ind.	123,000	May 1943
29	Koyukuk	°22,000	470	32,400	Endicott Mtns., Alaska	266,000	6-6-64
30	Porcupine	ʲ20,000	460	45,000	Ogilvie Mtns., Alaska	289,000	5-25-71
31	Hudson	19,500	306	13,370	Essex Co., N.Y.	215,000	3-19-36
32	Allegheny	19,290	325	11,700	Potter Co., Pa.	365,000	3-18-36
33	Delaware	ˢ17,200	390	11,440	Schoharie Co. N.Y.	329,000	8-20-55

(a)-Because river lengths and methods of measurement may change from time to time, the length figures given are subject to revision; (b)-about 25 percent of flow occurs in the Atchafalaya River; (c)-the length from mouth to source of the Mississippi River in Minnesota is 2,348 miles; (d)-at Baptiste Collete Bayou, Louisiana; (e)-at international boundary lat. 45° (f)-maximum monthly discharge; (g)-period 1957-70; (h)-continuation of Red River; (i)-flow of Quachita River added; (j)-period 1956-69; (k)-provisional; (l)-period 1962-69; (m)-based on records of Chilitna, Talkeetna, and Yetna Rivers; (n)-period 1931-60; (o)-period 1954-63; summer records only; (p)-discharge of American river not included; (q)-period 1960-69; (r)-period 1964-69; (s)-at Liston Point on Delaware Bay.

Large Rivers in Canada

Source: "Facts from Canadian Maps" Published by Canada Department of Energy Mines and Resources
(Ranked according to mean discharge in cubic feet per second (cfs))

Rank	River	Mean Discharge	Length (miles)	Drainage Area (sq. mi.)
1	St. Lawrence River.................................	348,000	1,900	396,000¹
2	Mackenzie (to head of Finlay)......................	343,000	2,635	697,000
3	Fraser...	125,000	850	84,800
4	Columbia (International Boundary to head of Columbia Lake).........	98,700	498	59,700²
5	Nelson (to head of Bow)............................	83,600	1,600	414,000³
6	Yukon (International Boundary to head of Nisutlin)..........	82,000	714	114,800⁴
7	Ottawa..	69,000	790	56,500
8	Churchill (to head of Ashuanipi)...................	55,700	532	30,800
9	Churchill (to head of Churchill Lake)..............	42,400	1,000	108,600
10	Saskatchewan (to head of Bow).....................	24,800	1,205	130,000

(1) Including 195,000 sq. mi. in U.S.A. (2) Including 20,000 sq. mi. in U.S.A. (3) Including 69,500 sq. mi. in U.S.A. (4) Including 9,000 sq. mi. in U.S.A.

The Largest Lake in Each Province of Canada

Source: Standard Encyclopedia of the World's Rivers and Lakes, 1965 & The Canada Yearbook, 1970-1971.

Province	Largest within:	Largest partly in:	Shared with	Origin	Area sq. miles	Ft. above sea level
Alta.	Claire.			Natural	545	699
		Athabasca	Sask.	Natural	940	699
B.C.	Kootenay.			Natural	168	1,745
Man.	Winnipeg.			Natural	9,465	713
Nfld.	Melville.			Natural	1,133	S.L.
N.B.	Grand.			Natural	65	Tidal
N.W.T.	Great Bear.			Natural	12,275	511
N.S.	Bras d'Or.			Natural	360	Tidal
Ont.	Nipigon.			Natural	1,870	855
		Huron	U.S.A.	Natural	15,353	580
P.E.I.						
Que.	Mistassini.			Natural	840	1,220
Sask.	Wollaston.			Natural	796	1,300
		Athabasca	Alta.	Natural	2,180	699

The Largest Lake in Each State of the U.S.

Source: National Geographic Society, Washington, D.C.

*indicates reservoir

State	Largest entirely within state	Largest partly in another state	Shared with	Origin	Total Area in square miles	Feet above sea level	Maximum depth feet	Shoreline length miles
Ala.	Guntersville			Man-made	108.8	595	94	962
		Walter F. George	Ga.	Man-made	71	190	90	640
Alaska.	Iliamna			Natural	1,150	150	1,289	230
Ariz.	Theodore Roosevelt			Man-made	27	2,136	280	88
		Powell	Ut.	Man-made	252	3,700	580	1,800
Ark.	Ouachita			Man-made	63	578	179	690
		Bull Shoals	Mo.	Man-made	71	654	175	740
Cal.	Salton Sea			Natural	360	-235	48	—
		Tahoe	Nev.	Natural	192	6,229	1,644	71
Col.	Blue Mesa*			Man-made	14	7,519	325	95
		Navajo*	N.M.	Man-made	24	6,085	382	150
Conn.	Candlewood			Man-made	8	429	85	75
Del.	Lum's Pond			Man-made	.34	44	22	5
Fla.	Okeechobee			Natural	700	14	15	96
Ga.	Sidney Lanier			Man-made	59	1,070	156	540
		Clark Hill	S.C.	Man-made	109	330	150	1,200
Ha.	Waita*			Man-made	.66	242	—	4
Ida.	Pend Oreille			Natural	136	2,063	1,200	127
Ill.	Carlyle*			Man-made	41	445	40	83
		Michigan	Wis., Ind., Mich.	Natural	22,300	579	923	1,660
Ind.	Monroe*			Man-made	29	556	75	100
		Michigan	Wis., Ill., Mich.	Natural	22,300	579	923	1,660
Ia.	Rathbun*			Man-made	18	904	55	180
Kan.	Tuttle Creek*			Man-made	25	1,079	90	112
Ky.	Cumberland			Man-made	79	760	183	1,255
		Kentucky	Tenn.	Man-made	250	359	90	2,380
La.	Pontchartrain			Natural	621	sea lev.	18	112
Me.	Moosehead			Natural	117	1,042	246	190
Md.	Deep Creek			Man-made	6	2,462	72	62
		Conowingo*	Pa.	Man-made	13	109	110	38
Mass.	Quabbin*			Man-made	39	524	150	104
Mich.	Houghton			Natural	31	1,138	20	30
		Superior	Wis., Mich., Ont.	Natural	31,700	600	1,333	2,980
Minn.	Red			Natural	452	1,172		
		Superior	Wis., Mich., Ont.	Natural	31,700	600	1,333	2,980
Miss.	Grenada			Man-made	100	231	102	282
Mo.	Lake of the Ozarks			Man-made	93	659	148	1,300
Mon.	Fort Peck*			Man-made	375	2,246	220	1,540
Neb.	McConaughty			Man-made	50	3,260	130	105
Nev.	Pyramid			Natural	169	3,789	330	66
		Mead	Ariz.	Man-made	247	1,221	432	550
N.H.	Winnipesaukee			Natural	70	504	169	240
N.J.	Hopatcong			Man-made	4	924	58	32
N.M.	Elephant Butte*			Man-made	57	4,450	176	201
N.Y.	Oneida			Natural	80	369	55	63
		Erie	Mich., Pa., Ont., Oh.	Natural	9,910	570	210	856
N.C.	Mattamuskeet			Natural	67	3	5	—
		John H. Kerr*	Va.	Man-made	76	300	99	800
N.D.	Sakakawea			Man-made	575	1,850	180	1,600
		Oahe*	S.D.	Man-made	556	1,617	200	2,250
Oh.	Lake St. Mary's			Man-made	17	869	10	60
•		Erie	Mich., Pa., N.Y., Ont.	Natural	9,910	570	210	856
Okla.	Eufaula			Man-made	160	585	87	600
Ore.	Klamath			Natural	145	4,143	45	165
		Goose Lake	Cal.	Natural	194	4,716	24	90
Pa.	Wallenpaupack			Man-made	9	1,185	60	52
		Erie	Mich., N.Y., Oh., Ont.	Natural	9,910	570	210	856
R.I.	Scituate			Man-made	5	284	94	38
S.C.	Marion			Man-made	173	75	55	300
S.D.	Francis Case			Man-made	159	1,375	140	540
		Oahe*	N.D.	Man-made	556	1,617	200	2,250
Tenn.	Watts Bar			Man-made	61	741	75	783
		Kentucky	Ky.	Man-made	250	359	90	2,380
Tex.	Sam Rayburn*			Man-made	179	164	74	—
		Toledo Bend*	La.	Man-made	284	172	92	—
Ut.	Great Salt Lake			Natural	1,438	4,200	36	334
Vt.	Bomoseen			Natural	4	413	—	—
		Champlain	N.Y., Que.	Natural	437	95	400	379
Va.	Smith Mountain			Man-made	31	795	200	500
		John H. Kerr*	N.C.	Man-made	76	300	99	800
Wash.	F.D. Roosevelt			Man-made	123	1,288	375	325
W. Va.	Summersville			Man-made	4	1,652	267	65
Wis.	Winnebago			Natural	215	747	21	78
		Superior	Minn., Mich., Ont.	Natural	31,700	600	1,333	2,980
Wyo.	Yellowstone			Natural	137	7,733	309	110
		Flaming Gorge*	Utah	Man-made	—	6,040	437	—

Famous Waterfalls

Source: National Geographic Society, Washington, D. C.

Height = total drop in one or more leaps. † = falls of more than one leap; * = falls that diminish greatly seasonally; ** = falls that reduce to a trickle or are dry for part of each year. If river names not shown, they are same as the falls. R. = river; L. = lake; (C) = cascade type. See notes following list.

Name and Location	Ft.
Africa	
Angola	
Duque de Braganca,	
Lucala R.	344
Ruacana, Cunene R.	406
Ethiopia	
Dal Verme,	
Dorya R.	98
Fincha	508
Tesissat, Blue Nile R.	140
Lesotho	
*Maletsunyane	630
Rhodesia-Zambia	
*Victoria, Zambezi R.	355
South Africa	
*Augrabies, Orange R.	480
Howick, Umgeni R.	364
† Tugela	2,014
Highest fall	597
Tanzania-Zambia	
*Kalambo	726
Uganda	
Kabalega (Murchison) Victoria	
Nile R.	130
Asia	
India—*Cauvery	330
*Gokak, Ghataprabha R.	170
*Jog (Gersoppa), Sharavathi R.	830
Japan	
*Kegon, Daiya R.	330
Laos	
Khon Cataracts,	
Mekong R. (C)	70
Australasia	
Australia	
New South Wales	
† Wentworth	614
Highest fall	360
Wollomombi	1,100
Queensland	
Coomera	210
Tully	885
† Wallaman, Stony Cr.	1,137
Highest fall	937
New Zealand	
Bowen	540
Helena	890
Stirling	505
† Sutherland, Arthur R.	1,904
Highest fall	815
Europe	
Austria—†Gastein	492
Highest fall	280
‡ *Golling, Schwarzbach R.	250
† Krimml	1,312
France—*Gavarnie	1,385

Name and Location	Ft.
Great Britain—Scotland	
Glomach	370
Wales	
Cain	150
Rhaiadr	240
Iceland—Detti	144
† Gull, Hvita R.	105
Italy—Frua, Toce R. (C)	470
Norway	
Mardalsfossen (Northern)	1,535
† Mardalsfossen (Southern)	2,150
† **Skjeggedal, Nybuai R.	1,378
**Skykkje	984
Vetti, Morka - Koldedola R.	900
Voring, Bjoreio R.	597
Sweden	
† Handol	427
† Tannforsen, Are R.	120
Switzerland	
† Diesbach	394
Giessbach (C)	1,982
Handegg, Aare R.	150
Iffigen	120
Pissevache, Salanfe R.	213
† Reichenbach	656
Rhine	79
† Simmen	459
Staubbach	984
† Trummelbach	1,312
North America	
Canada	
Alberta	
Panther, Nigel Cr.	600
British Columbia	
† Della	1,443
Takakkaw, Daly Glacier	1,200
Northwest Territories	
Virginia, S. Nahanni R.	294
Quebec	
Montmorency	274
Canada—United States	
Niagara: American	193
Horseshoe	186
United States	
California	
*Feather, Fall R.	640
Yosemite National Park	
Bridalveil	620
*Illilouette	370
*Nevada, Merced R.	594
**Ribbon	1,612
**Silver Strand, Meadow Br.	1,170
*Vernal, Merced R.	317
† **Yosemite	2,425
Yosemite (upper)	1,430
Yosemite (lower)	320
Yosemite (middle) (C)	675
Colorado	
† Seven, South Cheyenne Cr.	300

Name and Location	Ft.
Hawaii	
Akaka, Kolekole Str.	442
Idaho	
**Shoshone, Snake R	212
Twin, Snake R	120
Kentucky	
Cumberland	68
Maryland	
*Great, Potomac R. (C)	71
Minnesota	
**Minnehaha	53
New Jersey	
Passaic	70
New York	
*Taughannock	215
Oregon	
† Multnomah	620
Highest fall	542
Tennessee	
Fall Creek	256
Washington	
Mt. Rainier Natl. Park	
Narada, Paradise R	168
Sluiskin, Paradise R	300
Palouse	197
**Snoqualmie	268
Wisconsin	
*Big Manitou, Black R. (C)	165
Wyoming	
Yellowstone Pk. Tower	132
*Yellowstone (upper)	109
*Yellowstone (lower)	308
Mexico	
El Salto	218
**Juanacatlan, Santiago R.	72
South America	
Argentina—Brazil	
Iguazu	230
Brazil	
Glass	1,325
Patos-Maribondo, Grande R.	115
Paulo Afonso, Sao Francisco R.	275
Uruqupunga, Parana R.	40
Brazil-Paraguay	
Sete Quedas, or Guaira	
Parana R.	130
Colombia	
Catarata de Candelas,	
Cusiana R	984
*Tequendama, Bogota R.	427
Ecuador	
*Agoyan, Pastaza R.	200
Guyana	
Kaieteur, Potaro R	741
King George VI, Kamarang R.	1,600
† Marina, Ipobe R.	500
Highest fall	300
Venezuela—† *Angel	3,212
Highest fall	2,648
Cuquenan	2,000

The earth has thousands of waterfalls, some of considerable magnitude. Their importance is determined not only by height but volume of flow, steadiness of flow, crest width, whether the water drops sheerly or over a sloping surface, and in one leap or a succession of leaps. A series of low falls flowing over a considerable distance is known as a cascade.

Sete Quedas or Guaira is the world's greatest waterfall when its mean annual flow (estimated at 470,000 cusecs, cubic feet per second) is combined with height. A greater volume of water passes over Boyoma Falls (Stanley Falls), though not one of its seven cataracts, spread over nearly 60 miles of the Congo River, exceeds 10 feet.

Estimated mean annual flow, in cusecs, of other major waterfalls are: Niagara, 212,200; Paulo Afonso, 100,000; Urubupunga, 97,000; Iguazu, 61,600; Patos-Maribondo, 53,000; Victoria, 38,400; and Kaieteur, 23,400.

Notable Bridges in North America

Source: State Highway Engineers; Canadian Civil Engineering — ASCE

Asterisk (*) designates Railroad Bridge. Span of a bridge is distance (in feet) between its supports.

Suspension

Year	Bridge	Location	Longest Span
1964	Verrazano-Narrows	New York, N.Y.	4,260
1937	Golden Gate	San Fran. Bay, Cal.	4,200
1957	Mackinac	Sts. of Mackinac	3,800
1931	Geo. Washington	Hudson River	3,500
1952	Tacoma	Washington	2,800
1936	¹Transbay	San Fran. Bay, Cal.	2,310
1939	Bronx-Whitestone	East R., N.Y.C.	2,300
1970	Quebec Road	Quebec	2,190
1951	Del. Memorial	Wilmington, Del.	2,150
1968	Del. Mem. (new)	Wilmington, Del.	2,150
1957	Walt Whitman	Phila., Pa.	2,000
1929	Ambassador	Detroit-Canada	1,850
1961	Throgs Neck	Long Is. Sound	1,800
1926	Benjamin Franklin	Philadelphia	1,750
1924	Bear Mt., N.Y.	Hudson River	1,632
1952	²Wm. Preston Lane Mem.	Sandy Point, Md.	1,600
1903	Williamsburg	East R., N.Y.C.	1,600
1969	Newport	Narragansett Bay, R.I.	1,600
1883	Brooklyn	East R., N.Y.C.	1,595
1930	Mid-Hudson, N.Y.	Poughkeepsie	1,500
1964	Vincent Thomas	Los Angeles Harbor	1,500
1909	Manhattan	East R., N.Y.C.	1,470
1936	Triborough	East R., N.Y.C.	1,380
1931	St. Johns	Portland, Ore.	1,207
1929	Mount Hope	Rhode Island	1,200
1939	Deer Isle	Maine	1,080
1931	Maysville (Ky.)	Ohio River	1,060
1867	Cincinnati	Ohio River	1,057
1971	Dent	Clearwater Co., Ida.	1,050
1900	Miampimi	Mexico	1,030
1849	Wheeling, W. Va.	Ohio River	1,010
1929	Royal Gorge	Colorado	880
1938	Thousand Islands	St. Lawrence R.	800
1933	Anthony Wayne	Ohio	782
1915	Belpre, O.-W. Va.	Ohio River	775
1904	E. Liv'p'l, O.-W. Va.	Ohio River	750
1933	South 10th St.	Pittsburgh, Pa.	750
1932	Waldo-Hancock	Maine	750
1935/59	Memorial Twin (Ill.)	Mississippi R.	740

Cantilever

Year	Bridge	Location	Longest Span
1917	*Quebec (Railway)	Quebec	1,800
1970	Chester, Pa.	Delaware River	1,644
1958	New Orleans, La.	Mississippi R.	1,575
1936	Transbay	San Fran. Bay	1,400
1968	Baton Rouge, La.	Mississippi R.	1,235
1955	Nyack-Tarrytown	Hudson River	1,212
1930	Longview, Wash.	Columbia River	1,200
1909	Queensboro	East R., N.Y.C.	1,182
1927	Carquinez Strait	California	1,100
1958	Parallel Span		1,100
1968	Isaiah D. Hart	Jacksonville, Fla.	1,088
1957	²Richmond	San Fran. Bay, Cal.	1,070
1929	Grace Memorial	Charleston, S.C.	1,050
1963	Newburgh-Beacon	Hudson R., N.Y.	1,000
1975	Caruthersville, Mo.	Mississippi R.	920
1969	Ohio River	Pt. Pleasant, W.Va.	900
1940	Natchez	Mississippi R.	875
1938	Blue Water	Pt. Huron, Mich.	871
1972	Vicksburg	Mississippi River	870
1954	Sunshine Skyway	St. Petersburg, Fla.	864
1940	*Baton Rouge	Mississippi R.	848
1899	*Cornwall	St. Lawrence R.	843
1940	Greenville	Mississippi R.	840
1961	Helena, Ark.	Mississippi R.	840
1963	Brent Spence	Covington, Ky.	831
1963	Cincinnati, Oh.	Ohio River	830
1956	Earl C. Clements	Ohio R., Ill.-Ky.	825ᵃ
1930	*Vicksburg	Mississippi R.	825
1929	Louisville	Ohio River	820
1943	Jeff'rson Barr'ks., Mo.	Mississippi R.	804
1950	Maurice J. Tobin	Boston, Mass.	800
1935	Rip Van Winkle	Catskill, N.Y.	800
1938	Cairo	Ohio River, Ill.-Ky.	800
1940	Ludlow Ferry	Potomac R.	800
1932	Washington Mem.	Seattle, Wash.	800
1936	North Bend, Ore.	Coos Bay	793
1936	McCullough	Coos Bay, Ore.	793
1935	²Huey P. Long	New Orleans	790
1916	*Memphis (Harahan)	Mississippi R.	790
1892	*Memphis	Mississippi R.	790
1949	Memphis-Arkansas	Mississippi R.	790
1904	*Mingo Jct., W. Va.	Ohio River	769
1910	*Beaver, Pa.	Ohio River	767
1966	⁵S.N. Pearman	Charleston, S.C.	760
1940	Owensboro	Ohio River	750
1911	Sewickley, Pa.	Ohio River	750
1928	Outerbridge, N.Y.-N.J.	Arthur Kill	750
1964	Sunshine, Don'ville	Mississippi, La.	750
1931	Coal Grove	Ohio R., Ky.-Oh.	722
1964	Ohio River	Henderson, Ky.	720
1929	US-421	Ohio R., Ind.-Ky.	720
1973	I-275	Ohio R., Boone Co., Ky.	720
1956	Talmadge Memorial	Savannah, Ga.	710
1940	Bridge of the Gods	Oregon	705
1927	Bellaire, Oh.	Ohio River	700
1955	Belpre, Oh.-W. Va.	Ohio River	700
1930	Cairo, Ill.	Mississippi R.	700
1964	John F. Kennedy	Louisville, Ky.	700
1974	Clay Wade Bailey	Ohio R., Ky.-Oh.	675
1928	Goethals, N.Y.-N.J.	Arthur Kill	672
1905	*Thebes, Ill.	Mississippi R.	671
1957	Rappahannock	White Stone, Va.	648
1959	Corpus Christi	Nueces Co., Tex.	620
1968	Reedy Point	Ches. & Del. Can.	600
1960	Summit	Ches. & Del. Can.	600
1959	Castleton	Hudson R., N.Y.	600
1943	Gold Star	New London, Conn.	540
1934	Gastineau Channel	Juneau, Alaska	516
1918	MacArthur, Ill.-Ia.	Mississippi R.	480
1960	West River	Brattleboro, Vt.	440
1953	Luck Peak Reservoir	nr. Boise, Ida.	432
1965	Jeremiah Morrow	Warren Co., Oh.	427
1952	I-680 Eastbound (Mormon)	Missouri R. (Nebr.-Ia.)	420
1975	I-680 Westbound	Missouri R. (Nebr.-Ia.)	420

Simple Truss

Year	Bridge	Location	Longest Span
1917	*Metropolis	Ohio River	720
1929	Irvin S. Cobb	Ohio River-Ill.-Ky.	716
1922	*Tanana River	Nenana, Alaska	700
1933	*Henderson	Ohio River-Ind.-Ky.	665
1967	I-77, Ohio River	Marietta, Oh.	650
1917	MacArthur, Ill.-Mo.	St. Louis	647
1919	Louisville	Ohio River	644
1933	Atchafalaya	Morgan City, La.	608
1924	*Castleton	Hudson River	598
1906	Elizabethtown	Great Miami R., Oh.	586
1889	*Cincinnati	Ohio River	542
1951	Allegheny River	Allegheny Co., Pa.	533
1914	Pittsburgh	Allegheny R.	531
1930	*Martinez	California	528
1967	Tanana River	Alaska	500
1963	216 Nenana River	Rex, Alaska	406

Steel Truss

Year	Bridge	Location	Longest Span
1940	Gov. Nice Mem.	Potomac River, Md.	800
1975	I-24	Tenn R., Ky.	720
1938	US-62, Ky.	Green River	700
1952	US-62, Ky.	Cumberland River	700
1940	Jamestown	Jamestown, R.I.	640
1940	Greenville	Mississippi R., Ark.	640
1949	Memphis	Mississippi R., Ark.	621
1938	US-22	Delaware River, N.J.	540
1972	Mississippi River	Muscatine, Ia.	512
1896	Newport	Ohio River, Ky.	511
1931	US-60	Cumberland River, Ky.	500
1958	Lake Oahe	Mobridge, S.D.	500
1958	Lake Oahe	Gettysburg, S.D.	500
1910	McKinley, St. Louis	Mississippi River	500
1963	Millard E. Tydings	Susquehanna R., Md.	490
1955	Four Bears	Missouri R., N.D.	475
1930	Lake Champlain	Lake Champlain, N.Y.	434
1947	Mayo	Suwanee R., Fla.	420
1929	Clarendon	White River, Ark.	400
1931	US-60	Tennessee R., Ky.	400
1965	Moyie Springs	Moyie River, Ida.	378
1944	US-68	Tennessee R., Ky.	368
1931	Tennessee R.	Benton Co.-Humphrey Co.	366
1929	Augusta	White River, Ark.	360
1932	US-62	Kentucky River	360

1951	SR-80	Fishing Creek, Ky.	360
1953	Lake Francis Case	Chamberlain, S.D.	336
1876	*High Bridge, Ky.	Kentucky River	332
1963	US-68	Cumberland R., Ky.	321
1939	US-431	Green & Rough R., Ky.	320
1940	Deep Creek Lake	Deep Creek Lake, Md.	300
1953	Montague Twp.	Delaware River, N.J.	300
1958	Little Colorado	Cameron, Ariz.	296
1950	Somerset	Cumberland R., Ky.	280
1951	Comm. Isaac Hull.	Housatonic R., Conn.	254

Continuous Truss

1966	Astoria, Ore.	Columbia R.	1,232
1966	Marquam	Willamette R., Ore.	1,044
1969	Miss. R.	Dyersburg, Tenn.	900
1969	Irondequoit Bay.	Rochester, N.Y.	891
1943	Dubuque, Ia.	Mississippi R.	845
1953	John E. Mathews	Jacksonville, Fla.	810
1957	Kingston-Rhinecliff	Hudson R., N.Y.	800
1918	*Sciotoville.	Ohio River	775
1929	Madison-Milton	Ohio River	727
1966	Matthew E. Welsh	Mauckport, Ind.	707*
1975	Girard Point.	Philadelphia, Pa.	700
1929	Chain of Rocks.	Mississippi R.	699
1966	Braga	Taunton R., Mass	682
1938	Port Arthur-Orange.	Texas	680
1929	*Cincinnati.	Ohio River	675
1928	Cape Girardeau, Mo.	Mississippi R.	672
1946	Chester, Ill.	Mississippi R.	670
1930	Quincy, Ill.	Mississippi R.	628
1934	Bourne.	Cape Cod Canal	616
1935	Sagamore.	Cape Cod Canal	616
1965	Clarion River.	Clarion Co., Pa.	612
1965	Rio Grande Gorge.	Taos, N.M.	600
1941	Columbia River.	Kettle Falls, Wash.	600
1954	Columbia River.	Umatilla, Ore.	600
1954	Columbia River.	The Dalles, Ore.	576
1962	W. Br. Feather River	Oroville, Cal.	576
1936	Meredosia.	Illinois River	567
1936	Mark Twain Mem.	Hannibal, Mo.	562
1957	Mackinac.	Mackinac Straits, Mich.	560
1937	Homestead	Pittsburgh.	553
1961	Ship Canal	Seattle, Wash.	552
1932	Pulaski Skyway	Passaic R., N.J.	550
1973	I-95, Thames River	New London, Conn.	540
1927	Ross Island.	Portland, Ore.	535
1936	South Omaha.	Missouri R., Neb.-Ia.	525
1932	Savanna, Ill.-Sabula.	Mississippi R.	520
1962	Columbia River.	Beebe, Wash.	520
1970	Snake River.	Central Ferry, Wash.	520
1954	Columbia River.	Pasco, Wash.	520
1962	Columbia River.	Vantage, Wash.	520
1974	New Lyons Fulton.	Mississippi R. (Ia.-Ill.)	500
1958	Stevenson, Ala.	Tennessee River	500
1958	Pecos River	Val Verde Co., Tex.	480
1922	Memorial.	Missouri River, N.D.	475
1962	Martinez, Cal.	Carquinex Strait.	475
1967	Mississippi River.	Minneapolis, Minn.	456
1963	I-75 Ky. (Twin)	Kentucky R.	448
1960	Mississippi River	Red Wing, Minn.	432
1963	International.	Sault Ste. Marie, Mich.	430
1956	Decatur, Nebr.	Missouri R. (Nebr.-Ia.)	420
1939	Florence, Ala.	Tennessee River	420
1975	I-680.	Missouri R. (Ia.-Neb.)	420
1952	Bellevue, Nebr.	Missouri R. (Nebr.-Ia.)	420
1939	Brownville, Nebr.	Missouri R. (Nebr.-Ia.)	420
1930	Plattsmouth, Nebr.	Missouri R. (Nebr.-Ia.)	403

Continuous Box and Plate Girder

1953	Neches River	Orange County, Tex.	850
1967	San Mateo-Hayward Twp. No. 2	San Fran. Bay, Cal.	750
1963	Gunnison River	Gunnison, Col.	720
1969	San Diego-Coronado.	San Diego Bay, Cal.	660*
1972	Ship Channel	Houston, Tex.	630
1967	Poplar St.	St. Louis, Mo.	600
1971	Lake Koocanusa	Lincoln Co., Mon.	500
1967	Mississippi R.	LaCrescent, Minn.	450
1972	Sitka Harbor.	Sitka, Alaska.	450
1974	I-430	Arkansas R.	430
1972	Kansas City.	Missouri R., Kan.-Mo.	425
1967	Chattanooga.	Tennessee R., Tenn.	420
1975	Yukon River.	Taylor Highway, Alaska	410
1972	I-75, Tennessee River	Loudon Co., Tenn.	400
1941	Susquehanna.	Susquehanna R., Md.	400
1963	Lake Charles B'Pass.	Louisiana.	399
1971	St. Croix River.	Hudson, Minn.	390
1957	Conn. Turnpike	Quinnipiac R.	387
1960	Route 34	New Haven, Conn.	379
1971	S.H. No. 1	Pendleton, Ark.	377
1960	Tennessee River.	Chattanooga, Tenn.	375

1966	I-80, LeClaire, Ia.	Mississippi R.	370
1971	Sacramento R.	Bryte, Cal.	370
1963	I-40, Tennessee River	Benton Co., Tenn.	365
1967	San Mateo Creek	Hillsborough, Cal.	360
1950	US-62, Kentucky Dam.	Tennessee R., Ky.	350
1961	Whiskey Creek.	Trinity Co., Cal.	350
1972	Franklin Falls	Snoq'lmie Pass, Wash.	350
1971	Don Pedro Reserv.	Tuolumne Co., Cal.	350
1970	Columbia River.	Brewster, Wash.	343
1968	Dartmouth.	Minneapolis.	340
1967	Lexington Ave.	St. Paul.	340
1971	Cumberland River.	Nashville, Tenn.	330
1969	Buffalo Creek.	Armstrong Co., Pa.	325
1970	Arkansas R.	Dardanelle, Ark.	325
1969	Arkansas R.	Morrilton, Ark.	322
1963	Western Ky. Pkwy.	Green River, Ky.	320
1965	Blue Grass Pkwy.	Kentucky River, Ky.	320
1962	I-65, Cumberland R.	Nashville, Tenn.	320
1956	SR-6, Cumberland R.	Nashville, Tenn.	320
1967	I-71 (twin)	Kentucky R., Ky.	320
1936	Kentucky River.	Frankfort, Ky.	315
1929	Washington Ave.	Minneapolis.	315
1959	William H. Putnam	Conn. River, Conn.	311
1971	Copper River.	Chitina, Alaska	310
1973	Main Street	Little Rock, Ark.	303
1967	Rouge River.	Detroit, Mich.	300
1972	Mission Valley.	San Diego, Cal.	300
1953	US-42	Kentucky River, Ky.	300
1950	Guthrie	Guthrie, Ariz.	300
1942	Charter Oak	Hartford, Conn.	300
1970	Sacramento River.	Elkhorn, Cal.	285
1964	West Camas Slough	Camas, Wash.	284
1950	US-231	Green River, Ky.	276
1964	Duwamish R. (Twins)	Seattle.	275
1940	Lakefront.	Cleveland, Oh.	271
1951	SR-61.	Green River, Ky.	260
1954	Wenatchee River.	Wenatchee, Wash.	260
1971	Lake Bornoseen.	Castleton, Vt.	260
1975	I-80N, Snake River.	King Hill, Ida.	260
1973	East 148 St.	Seattle, Wash.	258
1975	S-39, Snake River.	American Falls, Ida.	256
1962	Snohomish River.	Monroe, Wash.	255
1965	Susitna River	Alaska	250
1940	Thomas A. Edison.	Raritan River	250
1965	Barren River.	165, Kentucky.	250
1954	Garden State Pkwy.	Raritan River, N.J.	250
1958	P't Wash'gt'n Narr.	Bremerton, Wash.	250
1966	Lake Francis Case	Platte, S.D.	250
1973	Swinomish Slough	Mt. Vernon, Wash.	246
1972	Arkansas River	Pine Bluff, Ark.	243
1948	Baldwin.	Connecticut R.	240
1968	Sharon.	Sharon, Vt.	239
1962	Lake Sharpe	Pierre, S.D.	235
1959	Mulholland Dr.	Los Angeles, Cal.	235
1968	11th (Twins)	Anacostia R., Wash., D.C.	234
1967	White River	Hartford, Vt.	233
1968	Royalton	Royalton, Vt.	225
1975	U.S.1, Raritan R.	New Brunswick, N.J.	222
1964	Theodore Roosevelt	Potomac R., Wash., D.C.	222
1961	W'r'w Wilson Mem.	Potomac River.	222
1969	Snohomish	Monroe, Wash.	222
1973	Chattahoochee R.	Ft. Gaines, Ga.	220
1940	Tallulah River.	Tallulah Gorge, Ga.	220
1970	Chulitna River	Alaska	220

Continuous Plate

1965	New Chain of Rocks.	Mississippi R., Ill.	5,411*
1973	Great Congress Gty.	Schenectady, N.Y.	1,870
1971	Congress St.	Troy, N.Y.	1,420
1966	I-480.	Missouri R., Ia.-Neb.	425
1970	I-435.	Missouri R., Mo.	425
1972	I-80.	Missouri R., Ia.-Neb.	425
1970	Green River	Hendersonville, N.C.	350
1969	Fort Smith	Arkansas River	340
1971	Audubon Pkwy.	Green R., Ky.	330
1974	Green River Pkwy.	Green R., Ky.	330
1974	Camp Nelson	Kentucky, R.	330
1974	Queen Isabella Cswy.	Port Isabel, Tex.	310
1957	Snake River	Alpine Jct., Wy.	264
1974	I-90.	Chamberlain, S.D.	250
1973	Lewis & Clark	Williston, N.D.	235
1971	Washburn.	Missouri R., Mo.	235
1965	Grant-Marsh	Missouri R., N.D.	235
1964	Galveston Bay	Galveston Co., Tex.	215
1957	Freeway.	Arkansas River	210

I-Beam Girder

1941	US-31E.	Rolling Fork R., Ky.	340

1948	US-27	Licking River, Ky.	316
1947	US-31E	Green River, Ky.	316
1941	US-62	Rolling Fork, Ky.	240
1942	Licking River	Owingsville, Ky.	240
1954	Fuller Warren	Jacksonville, Fla.	224

Steel Arch

1931	Bayonne, N.J.	Kill Van Kull	1,652
1972	Fremont	Portland, Ore.	1,255
1964	Port Mann	British Columbia	1,200
1959	Glen Canyon	Colorado River	1,028
1967	Trois-Rivieres	St. Lawrence R., P.Q.	1,100
1962	Lewiston-Queenston	Niagara River, Ont.	1,000
1976	Perrine	Twin Falls, Ida.	993
1917	*Hell Gate	East R., N.Y.C.	977
1941	Rainbow	Niagara Falls	950
1972	I-40, Mississippi R.	Memphis, Tenn.	900"
1970	Lake Quinsigamond	Worcester, Mass.	849
1966	Charles Braga	Somerset, Mass.	840
1967	Lincoln Trail	Ohio R., Ind.-Ky.	825
1961	Sherman Minton	Louisville, Ky.	800
1936	Henry Hudson	Harlem River	800
1936	French King	Conn. R. (Rt. 2, Mass.)	782
1931	West End	Pittsburgh	778
1972	Piscataqua R.	I-95, N.H.-Me.	756
1963	Cold Spring Canyon	Santa Barbara, Cal.	700
1973	I-24, Paducah, Ky.	Ohio River	700
1955	Pa.-N.J. Turnpike	Delaware River	682
1964	Burro Creek	(Wikieup) Ariz.	680
1954	Newark-Bayonne	Newark Bay, N.J.	670
1924	*Michigan Central	Niagara Falls	640
1955	Missouri River	Jefferson City, Mo.	640
1929	Navajo	Colorado River, Ariz.	616
1961	Duluth Harbor	Lake Superior	600
1961	St. Louis Bay	Superior, Wis.	600
1938	Middletown	Connecticut	600
1936	Yaquina Bay	Oregon	600
1954	Gt. S. Bay.	West Islip, N.Y.	600
1963	Fire Is. Inlet	Fire Is., N.Y.	600
1916	Colorado River	Ariz.-Cal.	592
1917	Cuyahoga River	Cleveland, Oh.	591
1973	I-280	Mississippi R. (Ia.-Ill.)	570
1929	Palmyra Boro	Delaware R., N.J.	550
1949	Chesapeake City	Ches. & Del. Can.	540
1941	St. Georges	Ches. & Del. Can.	540
1940	Centennial	Miss. R., Ill.-Ia.	539
1967	Gerald Desmond	Long Bea. H'b'r, Cal.	527
1874	Eads, St. Louis	Mississippi R.	520
1951	Hastings, Minn.	Mississippi R.	514
1888	Washington, N.Y.C.	Harlem River	509
1962	Alex'der Hamilton	Harlem R., N.Y.	505
1848	High Bridge, N.Y.C.	Harlem River	496
1967	Arkansas River	Ozark, Ark.	474
1974	Prairie DuChien	Mississippi R. (Ia.-Wisc.)	462
1956	Wabash Memorial	Wabash River, Ind.	441

Concrete Arch

1934	New River	Ripplemead, Va.	1,321[9]
1932	Clark Memorial	Wabash River	1,033[9]
1971	Selah Creek (twin)	Selah, Wash.	549
1968	Cowlitz River	Mossyrock, Wash.	520
1931	Westinghouse	Pittsburgh	425
1923	Cappelen	Minneapolis	400
1930	Jack's Run	Pittsburgh	400
1973	Elwha River	Port Angeles, Wash.	380
1931	Bixby Creek	Monterey Coast, Cal.	330
1953	Arroyo Seco	Pasadena, Cal.	320
1927	Mendota	Ft. Snelling, Minn.	304
1915	Rocky River	Cleveland, Oh.	280
1929	10th Ave.	Minneapolis	266
1929	U.S. 1, Raritan River	New Brunswick, N.J.	222
1963	I-95, Edgewood Ave.	Ft. Lee, N.J.	216
1918	Third Ave.	Minneapolis	211
1929	Chisholm Pk.	Rumford, Me.	210
1934	Waldport	Alsea Bay, Ore.	210
1925	Key	Potomac R.,Wash.D.C.	208
1930	Cornwall, Conn.	Housatonic R.	184

Twin Concrete Trestle

1963	Slidell, La.	L. Pontchartrain.	28,547[9]

Concrete Slab Dam

1927	Conowingo Dam	Maryland	4,611
1952	John H. Kerr Dam	Roanoke River, Va.	2,785
1936	Hoover Dam	Boulder City, Nev.	1,324

Drawbridges
Vertical Lift

1959	*Arthur Kill	N.Y.-N.J.	558
1935	*Cape Cod Canal	Massachusetts	544
1960	*Delair, N.J.	Delaware River.	542
1937	Marine Parkway	New York City	540
1931	Burlington, N.J.	Delaware R.	534
1912	*A-S-B Fratt.	Kansas City	428
1945	*Harry S. Truman	Kansas City	427
1932	*M-K-T R.R.	Missouri R.	414
1969	Wilm'gtn Mem.	Wilmington, N.C.	408
1930	Duluth	Minnesota.	386
1941	Main St.	Jack'ville, Fla.	386
1922	*Cincinnati	Ohio River	365
1967	Benj. Harrison Mem.	James River, Va.	363
1961	Corpus Christi Harbor	Corpus Christi, Tex.	344[4]
1933	Troy-Menands	Hudson River.	341
1962	Sand Island Access	Oahu, Hawaii.	340
1941	U.S. 1&9, Passaic R.	Newark, N.J.	332
1929	Carlton	Bath-Woolwich, Me.	328
1930	*Martinez	California	328
1960	St. Andrews Bay	Panama City, Fla.	327
1929	*Penn-Lehigh	Newark Bay	322
1920	*Chattanooga	Tennessee R.	310
1936	Triboro, N.Y.C.	Harlem River	310
1936	Hardin	Illinois River.	309
1960	Sacramento River.	Rio Vista, Cal.	306
1957	Claiborne Ave.	New Orleans.	305
1927	Cochrane	Mobile, Ala.	300
1928	James River	Newport News	300
1929	San Mateo	California	300
1926	*Missouri Pacific	Kragen, Ark.	300
1956	Sidney Lanier	Brunswick, Ga.	295
1928	Jordan	Chesapeake, Va.	284
1960	Interstate	Columbia River, Ore.-Wash.	279
1959	Houghton-Hancock	Michigan	268
1924	Yankton, S.D.	Missouri R. (Nebr.-SD)	250
1952	U.S. 1&9, Hackensack R.	Jersey City, N.J.	222
1948	Stickle	Passaic R., Newark, N.J.	222

Bascule

1926	Fort Madison	Mississippi R.	525[4]
1969	Pearl River	Slidell, La.	482
1916	Keokui Municipal.	Mississippi R., Ia.	377
1917	SR-8, Tennessee River	Chattanooga, Tenn.	306
1940	Lorain, Ohio	Black River	295
1958	Morrison	Portland, Ore.	285
1969	Elizabeth River.	Chesapeake, Va.	281
1957	Craig Memorial	I-280, Toledo, Oh.	271
1952	Downtown	Norfolk, Va.	230

Swing Bridges

1950	Douglass Memorial	Anac'tia R., Wash. D.C.	386
1945	Lord Delaware	Mattaponi River, Va.	252
1957	Eltham	Pamunkey River, Va.	237
1939	Chickahominy River.	Route 5, Va.	222
1930	Nansemond River.	Route 125, Va.	200

Swing Span

1908	*Willamette R.	Portland, Ore.	521
1903	*East Omaha.	Missouri R.	519
1952	Yorktown	York River, Va.	500
1897	*Duluth, Minn.	St. Louis Bay	486
1899	*C.M.&N.R.R.	Chicago	474
1897	Sioux City, Ia.	Missouri R. (Nebr.-Ia.).	470
1914	*Coos Bay	Oregon	458

Floating Pontoon

1963	Evergreen Pt.	Seattle, Wash.	7,518
1969	Lacey V. Murrow	Seattle.	6,561
1961	Hood Canal.	Pt. Gamble, Wash.	6,471

(1) The Transbay Bridge has 2 spans of 2,310 ft. each. (2) A second bridge in parallel will be completed. (3) The Richmond Bridge has twin spans 1,070 ft. each. (4) Railroad and vehicular bridge. (5) Two spans each 760 ft. (6) Two spans each 707 ft. (7) Two spans each 660 ft. (8) Two spans each 825 ft. (9) Total length of bridge. (10) Dumbarton has 7 spans each 225 ft. long. (11) Two spans each 900 ft.

Construction Details of Large and Unusual Bridges

Verrazano-Narrows Bridge, between Staten Island and Brooklyn, N.Y., has a suspension span of 4,260 ft., longest in the world and exceeding the Golden Gate Bridge, San Francisco, by 60 ft. One level in use Nov., 1964, second opened Jun. 28, 1969. The name is a compromise; it spans the Narrows and commemorates a visit to New York Harbor in Apr., 1524, de-duced from certain notes left by Giovanni da Verrazano, Italian navigator sailing for Francis I of France.

Allegheny River Bridge (Interstate 80) near Emlenton, Pa., 270 ft. above the water, tallest in eastern U.S., a continuous truss, 688 ft. long, 1968.

Angostura, suspension type, span 2,336 feet, 1967 at Ciudad Bolivar, Venezuela. Total length, 5,507.

Charles Braga Bridge over Taunton River between Fall River and Somerset, Mass. It is 5,780 feet long.

Bendorf Bridge on the Rhine River, 5 mi. n. of Coblenz, completed 1965, is a 3-span cement girder bridge, 3,378 ft. overall length, 101 ft. wide, with the main span 682 ft.

Burro Creek Bridge with 4 spans over Burro Creek on highway 93 near Kingman, Ariz. Main span steel truss 680 ft. Others plate girder, 110 and 2 of 85 ft. 1966.

Champlain Bridge at Montreal crossing the St. Lawrence River was opened 1962. It is 4 miles long. Three others connect Montreal with the South Bank, the Jacques Cartier, Victoria, and Mercier bridges.

Chesapeake Bay Bridge-Tunnel, opened Apr. 15, 1964 on US-13, connects Virginia Beach-Norfolk with the Eastern Shore of Virginia. Shore to shore, 17.6 miles. Twelve miles of trestles, 4 man-made islands, 2 mile-long tunnels, and 2 bridges.

Corpus Christi, Tex., has a high level port entrance bridge. It is a cantilever truss with anchor spans 310 ft. and main span 620 ft., total length approx. 5,862 ft.

Cross Bay Parkway Bridge (N.Y.), 3,000 feet long with 6 traffic lanes, 11 eight foot wide precast, prestressed concrete T girders to support spans 130 feet long each with main span 275 feet.

Delaware Memorial Bridge over Delaware River near Wilmington. A twin suspension bridge paralleling the original 250 ft. upstream has a 2,150-ft. main span suspended from 440-ft. towers.

Eads Bridge across the Mississippi R. between St. Louis and E. St. Louis, built in 1874 has 4 main spans 1,520 ft., 2,502 ft., and 1,118 ft. crossing Miss. R., a railroad and a road.

Evergreen Point Bridge in Wash. consists of 33 floating concrete pontoons weighing 4,700 tons each, held in place by 77 ton crete anchors. Pontoon structure is 6,561 ft. long; with approaches bridge is 12,596 ft. long.

Fremont Bridge, Part of Stadium Freeway, Portland, Ore., crossing Willamette R. 1,255 ft. steel arch span with two 452 ft. flanking steel arch spans. 1971.

Frontenac Bridge, Quebec, suspension, span 2,190 ft., open 1970.

Gladesville Bridge at Sydney, Australia, has the longest concrete arch in the world (1,000 ft. span).

George Washington Bridge, New York City, 4th longest suspension bridge in the world, spans the Hudson River between W. 178th St., Manhattan, and Ft. Lee, N.J.; 4,760 ft. between anchorages, two levels, 14 traffic lanes. Triborough Bridge connects Manhattan, the Bronx, and Queens; project comprises a suspension bridge, a vertical lift bridge, and a fixed bridge, all connected by long viaducts. The famous Brooklyn Bridge over the East River, connecting Manhattan, and Brooklyn, was completed in 1883, breaking all previous records by spanning 1,595 ft.

Golden Gate Bridge, crossing San Francisco Bay, has the second longest single span, 4,200 ft.

Hampton Roads Bridge-Tunnel, Va. A crossing completed in 1957 consisting of 2 man-made islands, 2 concrete trestle bridges, and one tunnel, under Hampton Roads with a length of 7,479 ft. A parallel facility with a 7,315 ft. tunnel is now open to traffic.

Hood Canal Floating Bridge, Wash., 23 floating concrete pontoons 4,980 tons each. Roadway is supported on crete T-beam sections mounted on pontoons 20 feet above canal. Floating section is 6,471 ft. long, overall 7,866 ft.

International Bridge, a series of 8 arch and truss bridges crossing St. Mary's and the Soo Locks between Mich. and Ontario. Two-mile toll completed 1962.

Lacy V. Murrow Floating Bridge, Wash., 25 floating pontoons of 4,558 tons each. Bridge with approaches is 8,583 ft.

Lake Pontchartrain Twin Causeway, a twin-span crete trestle bridge and 24-mile link within metropolitan New Orleans that connects the north and south shore. First span opened 1956, second 1969.

Lavaca Bay Causeway, Tex., 2.2 miles long, consisting of one 260 ft. continuous plate girder unit and 194 precast, prestressed concrete spans of 60 ft. length. 1961.

Newport Bridge between Newport and Jamestown, R. I. Total length 11,248 ft., a main suspension span of 1,600 feet, 2 side spans each 688 feet long. It has U.S.A.'s first prefabricated wire strands.

New York City bridges, see Verrazano-Narrows Bridge and George Washington Bridge above.

Ogdensburg-Prescott Internat'l Bridge across the St. Lawrence River from Ogdensburg, N.Y., to Johnston, Ont., opened 1970, is 13,510 ft. long with approaches and 7,260 ft. between abutments.

Oland Island Bridge in Sweden was completed in 1972. It is 19,882 feet long, Europe's longest.

Oosterscheldebrug, opened Dec. 15, 1965, is a 3.125-mile causeway for automobiles over a sea arm in Zeeland, the Netherlands. It completes a direct connection between Flushing and Rotterdam.

Poplar St. Bridge over the Mississippi at St. Louis, a 5-span continuous orthotropic deck plate girder bridge, longest span 600 ft. Eight lanes, 2,165 ft. long.

Quebec Road, suspension, span 2,190 feet, 1969, Quebec, Canada.

Rio-Niteroi, Guanabara Bay, Brazil, under construction, will be world's longest continuous box and plate girder bridge, 8 miles, 3,363 feet long, with a center span of 984 feet and a span on each side of 656 feet.

Robert Opie Norris Bridge, Rappahannock R. between Greys Pt. and White Stone, Va. 9,989 ft. long. Main spans are two 144 foot cantilever truss spans with a 360 foot truss span suspended between them.

Rockville Bridge, world's longest 4-track stone arch bridge, 3,810 ft., with 48 arches. Part of the Penn-Central RR system west of Harrisburg, Pa. It contains 440 million lbs. of stone, 100,000 cubic yds. of masonry and crosses the Susquehanna Riv. to Rockville, Pa.

Royal Gorge Bridge, 1,053 ft. above the Arkansas River in Colorado, is the highest bridge above water. Opened Dec. 8, 1929, it is 1,260 ft. long with a main span of 880 ft., width 18 ft.

San Mateo-Hayward Bridge across San Francisco Bay is first major orthotropic bridge in U.S. It is 6.7 miles long, 4.9 mile low-level concrete trestle and 1.8 miles high-level steel bridge.

Seven Mile Bridge is the longest of an expanse of bridges connecting the Florida Keys. It was built by the Florida East Coast Railway between 1904 and 1916, now a state highway.

Shenandoah River Bridges, one spans the south fork, 1,924 ft. long, the other the north fork, 1,090 ft. long, Warren County, Va.

Straits of Mackinac Bridge, completed in 1957, is the longest suspension bridge between anchorages and with approaches extends nearly 5 mi. between Mackinaw City and St. Ignace, Mich.

Sunshine Skyway, a 15-mile-long bridge-causeway with twin roadbeds that crosses Tampa Bay at St. Petersburg, Fla., a system of twin bridges 864 feet long and 4 smaller bridges with 6 causeways.

Tagus River Bridge near Lisbon, Portugal, longest suspension bridge outside the United States, has a 3,323-ft. main span. Opened Aug. 6, 1966, it was named Salazar Bridge for the former premier.

Thomas A. Edison Memorial Bridge (causeway) across Sandusky Bay between Martin Point and Danbury, Oh., is 2.67 miles long. The main bridge is 2,044 feet long.

Thousand Island Bridge, St. Lawrence River. American span 800 ft.; Canadian 750 ft.

Union St. Bridge in Woodstock, Vt., a timber lattice truss with a span of 122 feet built in 1969 using old time procedure of hand drilled holes and wooden pegs.

Vancouver Bridge, Canada's longest railway lift span connecting Vancouver and North Vancouver over Burrard Inlet. It is in 3 sections, the longest 493 ft. Spans are part of a project that includes a 2-mile tunnel under Vancouver Hts.

Woodrow Wilson Memorial Bridge across the Potomac River at Alexandria, Va., is over a mile long.

Zoo Bridge across the Rhine at Cologne, with steel box girders, has a main span of 850 ft.

The Interstate Highway 610 crossing of the Houston Ship Channel in Texas is 6,300 feet in length and consists of various lengths of prestressed concrete beam and slab approach spans and a 1,233 foot main unit of two 471'6" plate girder units and one 290 ft. simple span.

Underwater Vehicular Tunnels in North America
Over 3,000 feet in length

Name	Location	Waterway	Lgth. Ft.
Bart Trans-Bay Tube (Rapid Transit)	San Francisco, Cal.	S.F. Bay	3.6 miles
Brooklyn-Battery	New York, N.Y.	East River	9,117
Holland Tunnel	New York, N.Y.	Hudson River	8,557
Lincoln Tunnel	New York, N.Y.	Hudson River	8,216
Baltimore Harbor Tunnel	Baltimore, Md.	Patapsco River	7,650
Hampton Roads	Norfolk, Va.	Hampton Roads	7,479
Queens Midtown	New York, N.Y.	East River	6,414
Thimble Shoal Channel	Cape Henry, Va.	Chesapeake Bay	5,738
Sumner Tunnel	Boston, Mass.	Boston Harbor	5,650
Chesapeake Channel	Cape Charles, Va.	Chesapeake Bay	5,450
Louis-Hippolyte Lafontaine Tunnel	Montreal, Que.	St. Lawrence River	5,280
Detroit-Windsor	Detroit, Mich.	Detroit River	5,135
Callahan Tunnel	Boston, Mass.	Boston Harbor	5,046
Midtown Tunnel	Norfolk, Va.	Elizabeth River	4,194
Baytown Tunnel	Baytown, Tex.	Houston Ship Channel	4,111
Posey Tube	Oakland, Cal.	Oakland Estuary	3,500
Downtown Tunnel	Norfolk, Va.	Elizabeth River	3,350
Webster St.	Alameda, Cal.	Oakland Estuary	3,350
Bankhead Tunnel	Mobile, Ala.	Mobile River	3,109
I-10 Twin Tunnel	Mobile, Ala.	Mobile River	3,000

Land Vehicular Tunnels in U.S. Over 1,000 feet in length.

Name	Location	Lgth. Ft.	Name	Location	Lgth. Ft.
Eisenhower Memorial	Route 70, Col.	8,941	Battery Park	New York City	2,300
Copperfield	Copperfield, Ut.	6,989	Battery St.	Seattle, Wash.	2,140
Allegheny (Twin)	Penna. Turnpike	6,070	Big Oak Flat	Yosemite Natl. Park	2,083
Liberty Tubes	Pittsburgh, Pa.	5,920	Prudential	Boston, Mass.	1,980
Zion Natl. Park	Rte. 1, Utah	5,766	Internatl. Underpass	Los Angeles, Cal.	1,910
East River Mt. (Twin)	Interstate 77, W.Va.-Va.	5,661	Street-Car	Providence, R.I.	1,793
Tuscarora (Twin)	Penna. Turnpike	5,326	Broadway	San Francisco, Cal.	1,616
Kittatinny (Twin)	Penna. Turnpike	4,727	9th Street Expy.	Washington, D.C.	1,610
Lehigh	Penna. Turnpike	4,379	F.D. Roosevelt Dr.	42-48 Sts. NYC	1,600
Blue Mountain (Twin)	Penna. Turnpike	4,339	Lowry Hill	Minneapolis	1,496
Wawona	Yosemite Natl. Park	4,233	Wheeling	Interstate 70, W. Va.	1,490
Squirrel Hill	Pittsburgh, Pa.	4,225	Mt. Baker Ridge (3)	Seattle, Wash.	1,466
Big Walker Mt.	Route I-77, Va.	4,200	Knowls Creek	Lane County, Ore.	1,430
Fort Pitt	Pittsburgh, Pa.	3,560	Mule Pass	Near Bisbee, Ariz.	1,400
Mall Tunnel	Dist. of Columbia	3,400	Arch Cape	Oregon Coast Hwy. 9.	1,228
Caldecott	Oakland, Cal.	3,371	Queen Creek	Superior, Ariz.	1,200
Kalihi	Honolulu, Ha.	2,780	West Rock	New Haven, Conn.	1,200
Memorial	W. Va. Tpke. (I-77)	2,669	Green River	Route I-80, Wyo.	1,135
Cross-Town	178 St. N.Y.C.	2,414	Nouanu Pali	Koolau Mt. Oahu, Ha.	1,080
F.D. Roosevelt Dr.	81-89 Sts. NYC	2,400	Elk Creek	Umpqua Hwy 45, Ore.	1,080
Dewey Sq.	Boston, Mass.	2,400	Golden	Clear Cr'k Canyon, Col.	1,068

World's Longest Railway Tunnels
Source: Railway Directory & Year Book. Tunnels over 4 miles in length.

Tunnel	Date	Miles	Yds	Operating Railway	Country
Simplon No. I and II	1922	12	559	Swiss Fed. & Italian St.	Switz.-Italy
Apennine	1934	11	892	Italian State	Italy
Cotthard	1882	9	562	Swiss Federal	Switzerland
Lotschberg	1913	9	140	Bern-Lotschberg-Simplon	Switzerland
Hokuriku	1962	8	1,089	Japanese National	Japan
Mont Cenis (Frejus)	1871	8	855	Italian State	France-Italy
Cascade	1929	7	1,397	Great Northern	United States
Flathead Tunnel, Mont.	1970	6	1,758	Great Northern	United States
Arlberg	1884	6	650	Austrian Federal	Austria
Moffat	1928	6	373	Denver & Rio Grande	United States
Shimizu	1931	6	50	Japanese National	Japan
Kvineshei	1943	5	1,112	Norwegian State	Norway
Rimutaka	1955	5	821	New Zealand Gov.	New Zealand
Ricken	1910	5	608	Swiss Federal	Switzerland
Grenchenberg	1915	5	581	Swiss Federal	Switzerland
Otira	1923	5	564	New Zealand Gov.	New Zealand
Tauern	1909	5	551	Austrian Federal	Austria
Haegebostad	1943	5	467	Norwegian State	Norway
Ronco	1889	5	277	Italian State	Italy
Hauenstein (Lower)	1916	5	95	Swiss Federal	Switzerland
Connaught	1916	5	39	Canadian Pacific	Canada
Karawanken	1906	4	1,683	Austrian Federal	Austria-Yugo.
New Tanna	1964	4	1,663	Japanese National	Japan
Somport	1928	4	1,572	French National	France-Spain
Tanna	1934	4	1,493	Japanese National	Japan
Ulrikken	1964	4	1,338	Norwegian State	Norway
Hoosac	1875	4	1,230	Boston & Maine	United States
Monte Orso	1927	4	1,230	Italian State	Italy
Lupacino	1958	4	1,178	Italian State	Italy
Vivola	1927	4	1,004	Italian State	Italy
Monte Adone	1934	4	760	Italian State	Italy
Jungfrau	1912	4	750	Jungfrau	Switzerland
Borgallo	1884	4	700	Italian State	Italy
Severn	1886	4	628	Western Region	Great Britain
Lusse (Vosges)	1937	4	474	French National	France

Major World Dams

Source: Bureau of Reclamation. Dept. of the Interior. Revised September 1975. *Replaces existing dam.
Volume in cubic yards. Capacity (Gross) in acre feet. Year of completion. U.C. under construction.
Type: A—Arch. B—Buttress. E—Earthfill. G—Gravity. R—Rockfill. MA—Multi-arch.

Name of Dam	Type	Year	River and Basin	Country	Height Feet	Crest Length Feet	Volume (1,000 C.Y.)	Res. Cap. (1,000 A.F.)
Afsluitdijk	E	1932	ZuiderZee	Netherlands	62	10,500	82,927	4,864
Akosombo-Main	R	1965	Volta	Ghana	463	2,100	10,400	120,000
Almendra	A	1970	Turmes-Douro	Spain	662	1,860	2,188	2,148
Alpe Gera	G	1965	Cornor-Adda-Po	Italy	584	1,710	2,252	53
Bagdad Tailings	E	1973	Maroney Gulch	U.S.A.	121	2,601	37,304	40
Beas	E	1975	Beas-Indus	India	435	6,400	45,800	6,600
W.A.C. Bennett*	E	1967	Peace-Mackenzie	Canada	600	6,700	57,203	57,006
Bhakra	G	1963	Sutlend-Indus	India	742	1,700	5,400	8,000
Bratsk	GE	1964	Angara	USSR	410	16,864	18,283	137,220
Brouwershavense Gat		1972		Netherlands	118	20,341	35,316	466
Castaic	E	1973	Castaic Cr.	U.S.A.	340	5,200	44,000	432
Charvak	E	1970	Chirchik-Sir Darya	USSR	551	2,483	24,983	1,620
Chirkey	A	1975	Sulak-Caspian Sea	USSR	764	1,109	1,602	2,252
Chivor	R	1975	Bata	Colombia	778	919	14,126	661
Cochiti	E	1975	Rio Grande	U.S.A.	253	26,891	64,631	513
Copper Cities Tailing 2	E	1973	Tinhorn Wash.	U.S.A.	325	7,598	30,003	4
Cougar	R	1964	S.F. McKenzie	U.S.A.	519	1,600	13,000	219
Dartmouth	R		Mitta-Mitta	Australia	591	2,264	20,012	5,232
Dneprodzerzhinsk	GE	1964	Dnieper	USSR	112	118,090	28,503	1,994
Don Pedro*	ER	1971	Tuolume-San Joaquin	U.S.A.	585	1,900	16,760	2,030
Dworshak	G	1974	N. Fork Clearwater	U.S.A.	717	3,287	6,500	3,453
El Chocon	E	1974	Limay	Argentina	282	7,546	17,004	17,025
Emosson	A	1974	Barberine	Switz.	590	1,818	1,400	182
Esperanza Tailings	E	1973	Santa Cruz	U.S.A.	121	10,600	39,704	5
Fort Peck	E	1940	Missouri	U.S.A.	250	21,026	125,612	19,133
Fort Randall	E	1956	Missouri	U.S.A.	165	10,700	50,205	5,701
Gardiner*	E	1968	South Saskatchewan	Canada	223	16,700	85,743	8,000
Garrison	E	1956	Missouri	U.S.A.	203	11,300	66,506	24,321
Gepatsch	R	1965	Faggenbach-Inn	Austria	500	1,908	9,810	113
Glen Canyon	A	1964	Colorado	U.S.A.	710	1,560	4,901	27,000
Goscheneralp	E	1960	Goschener	Switz.	508	1,771	12,230	61
Grand Coulee	G	1942	Columbia	U.S.A.	550	4,173	10,585	9,724
Grande Dixence	G	1962	Dixence-Rhone	Switz.	935	2,280	7,792	324
Guri	GER	1968	Caroni-Orinoco	Venezuela	348	2,264	4,917	14,349
Haringvliet	E		Haringvliet	Netherlands	79	18,044	26,160	527
High Aswan (Saad-El-Aali)	ER	1970	Nile	Egypt	364	12,565	57,203	137,000
Hirakud	GE	1956	Mahandi	India	202	15,748	25,100	6,600
Hoover	A	1936	Colorado	U.S.A.	726	1,244	4,400	29,755
Hungry Horse	AG	1953	S.Fork Flathead	U.S.A.	564	2,115	3,086	3,468
Ilha Solteira	EG	1973	Parana Rio de la Plata	Brazil	295	20,308	29,454	27,730
Irkutsk	GE	1956	Angara	USSR	144	8,989	16,219	37,290
Ivankova	EG	1937	Volga-Caspian S.	USSR	98	31,398	20,207	908
Jari	E	1967	Jari	Pakistan	234	5,700	42,400	400
Daniel Johnson*	MA	1968	Manicougan-St. Lawrence	Canada	703	4,311	2,950	115,000
Kakhovka	EG	1955	Dnieper	USSR	121	5,380	46,617	14,755
Kanev	E	1974	Dnieper	USSR	82	52,950	49,520	2,125
Kapchagay	E	1970	Ili	USSR	164	1,542	5,078	22,813
Kariba	A	1959	Zambesi	Rhodesia-Zambia	420	2,025	1,350	130,000
Keban	RG	1974	First (Euphrates)	Turkey	679	3,881	20,900	25,110
Kiev	E	1964	Dnieper	USSR	72	177,448	57,552	3,021
King Paul (Kremasta)	ER	1965	Acheloos	Greece	541	1,510	10,686	3,850
Kremenchug	EG	1961	Dnieper	USSR	108	39,844	41,192	10,945
Kurobegawa No. 4	A	1964	Kurobe	Japan	610	1,603	1,782	162
Lauwerszee	E	1969	Lauwerszee	Netherlands	75	42,650	46,532	40
Ludington	E	1973	Lake Michigan	U.S.A.	170	29,301	37,703	83
Luzzone	A	1963	Brenno di Luzzone	Switz.	682	1,738	1,739	70
Mangla	E	1967	Jhelum	Pakistan	380	11,000	85,872	5,150
Marimbondo	E	1975	Grande	Brazil	295	12,297	24,328	5,184
Mauvoisin	A	1957	Drance de Bagnes	Switz.	777	1,706	2,655	146
Mica	R	1974	Columbia	Canada	794	2,600	42,000	20,000
Mingechaur	E	1953	Kura	USSR	262	5,085	20,400	12,970
Navajo	E	1963	San Juan	U.S.A.	407	3,648	26,841	1,709
New Bullards Bar	A	1970	North Yuba-Sacramento	U.S.A.	637	2,200	2,700	960
New Cornelia Tailings	E	1973	Ten Mile Wash, Ariz.	U.S.A.	98	35,600	274,026	20
New Melones	R	1975	Stanislaus-San Joaquin	U.S.A.	625	1,600	15,970	2,400
Oahe	E	1963	Missouri	U.S.A.*	245	9,300	92,008	23,591
Okutadami	G	1961	Tadami	Japan	515	1,575	2,145	487
Oroville	E	1968	Feather-Sacramento	U.S.A.	770	6,920	78,008	3,538
Owen Falls	G	1954	Lake Victoria-Nile	Uganda	100	2,725	n	166,000
Place Moulin	AG	1965	Buthier-Dora Baltea	Italy	502	2,181	1,962	81
Reza Shah Kabir	A	1975	Karoun	Iran	656	1,247	1,570	2,351
Rybinsk	GE	1941	Volga-Caspian S.	USSR	98	2,060	3,329	20,590
Sakuma	G	1956	Tenryu	Japan	510	963	1,465	265
San Luis	E	1967	San Luis-San Joaquin	U.S.A.	382	18,600	77,666	2,039
Saratov	E	1967	Volga-Caspian S.	USSR	131	37,204	52,843	10,458
Shasta	G	1945	Sacramento	U.S.A.	602	3,460	8,711	4,552
Swift	E	1958	Lewis-Columbia	U.S.A.	610	2,100	15,800	756
Tabka	E	1975	Euphrates	Syria	197	14,764	60,168	11,350
Talbingo	R	1971	Tamut	Australia	530	2,300	18,950	747
Tarbella	ER	1975	Indus	Pakistan	486	9,000	186,000	11,100
Trinity	E	1962	Trinity-Klamath	U.S.A.	537	2,600	29,252	2,448
Tsimlyansk	EG	1952	Don	USSR	128	43,411	44,323	17,715
Tuttle Creek	E	1962	Big Blue-Missouri	U.S.A.	154	7,500	22,937	413
Twin Buttes	E	1963	Concho-Colorado, Texas	U.S.A.	134	42,463	21,442	641
Twin Buttes Tailings	E	1973	Santa Cruz	U.S.A.	239	11,299	38,604	209
Vilyui	ER	1967	Vilyui	USSR	246	2,297	3,793	29,104
Volga-22d congress USSR	ERG	1958	Volga-Caspian S.	USSR	144	13,108	33,020	27,160
Volga-V. I. Lenin	EG	1955	Volga-Caspian S.	USSR	148	12,405	44,298	47,020
Yellowtail	A	1966	Bighorn-Missouri	U.S.A.	525	1,480	1,456	1,375
Zeya	G	1975	Zeya	USSR	369	2,343	3,139	55,452

Major Public and Private Dams and Reservoirs in U.S.

Source: Corps of Engineers, U.S. Army

Heights over 330 feet.

Height—Difference in elevation in feet, between lowest point in foundation and top of dam, exclusive of parapet or other projections.
Length—Overall length of barrier in feet; main dam and its integral features as located between natural abutments.
Volume—Total volume in cubic yards of all material in main dam and its appurtenant works.
Year—Date structure was originally completed for use. (UC) Under construction subject to revision.
River——Mainstream.
Purpose—I-Irrigation; C-Flood Control; H-Hydroelectric; N-Navigation; S-Water Supply; R-Recreation; D-Debris Control; O-Other.
Parentheses after name indicate type of dam as follows: (RE)-Earth; (PG)-Gravity; (ER)-Rockfill; (CB)-Buttress; (VA)-Arch; (MV)-Multi-arch; (OT)-Other.
*Replacing existing dam.

Name of dam	State	River	Ht.	Lgth.	Vol. (1,000)	Purpose	Yr.
Oroville (RE)	Cal.	Feather River	742	6800	78000	IR	1968
Hoover (VA)	Nev.	Colorado River	726	1242	4400	IHCO	1936
Dworshak (PG)	Ida.	North Fork of Clearwater	717	3287	6500	HCR	1972
Glen Canyon (VA)	Ariz.	Colorado River	710	1560	4901	HCSR	1964
Auburn (PG)	Cal.	N.F. American	680	3500	6000	ISCH	UC
New Bullards Bar (VA)	Cal.	North Yuba River	635	2200	2600	S D	1970
New Melones (ER)	Cal.	Stanislaus River	625	1600	15970	IH	UC
Swift Dam (RE)	Wash.	North Fork Lewis River	610	2100	15800	HR	1958
Mossyrock Dam (VA)	Wash.	Cowlitz River	605	1300	1231	HCR	1968
Shasta (PG)	Cal.	Sacramento River	602	3460	8711	ISHN	1945
Kopperston No. 3 Refuse Bank (DT)	W.Va.	Jones Br of Toney Cr	580	1100		O	1963
Don Pedro (RE)	Cal.	Tuolumne River	568	1800	16000	H I	1971
Hungry Horse (VA)	Mon.	South Fork of Flathead River	564	2115	3086	IHCN	1953
Grand Coulee (PG)	Wash.	Columbia River	550	4173	10585	IHCN	1942
Ross Dam (VA)	Wash.	Skagit River	540	1235	905	HR	1949
Trinity (RE)	Cal.	Trinity River	537	2600	29410	IHCR	1962
Yellowtail (VA)	Mon.	Bighorn River	525	1480	1546	ICHR	1966
Cougar (ER)	Ore.	South Fork McKenzie River	519	1600	13000	HCIR	1964
Flaming Gorge (VA)	Ut.	Green River	502	1285	987	HCSR	1964
Fontana Dam (PG)	N.C.	Little Tennessee River	480	2365	3576	H	1944
New Exchequer (ER)	Cal.	Merced River	479	1240	5169	H I	1926
Morrow Point (VA)	Col.	Gunnison River	468	741	365	HCRO	1968
Carters Main Dam (ER,RE)	Ga.	Coosawattee River	464	1950	15000	CHR	1974
Detroit (PG)	Ore.	North Santiam River	463	1580	1500	HCRI	1953
Anderson Ranch (RE)	Ida.	South Fork Boise River	456	1350	9653	IHCR	1950
Union Valley (RE)	Cal.	Silver Cr	453	1800	10000	S H	1963
Elmore Mine Refuse Dump (OT)	W.Va.	Tr-Guyandotte River	447	1975		O	1973
Round Butte Dam (RE,ER)	Ore.	Deschutes River	440	1450	9600	HR	1964
Pine Flat Lake (PG)	Cal.	Kings River	440	1840	2400	CIRH	1954
Kopperston No. 4 Dam (OT)	W.Va.	Crane Fk of Clear Fk	435	1100		O	1963
Jocassee (ER)	S.C.	Keowee River	435	1800	11600	H	1973
Mud Mountain Dam (ER)	Wash.	White River	425	700	2300	C	1948
Libby Dam (PG)	Mon.	Kootenai River	420	3055	13760	HC	1973
Owyhee Dam (VA)	Ore.	Owyhee River	417	833	538	ICR	1932
Lower Hell Hole (ER)	Cal.	Rubicon River	410	1550	8315	S D	1966
Mammoth Pool (RE)	Cal.	San Joaquin River	406	820	5535	H S	1960
Navajo (RE)	N.M.	San Juan River	402	3648	26840	IR	1963
Stirrat No. 15 Embankment (OT)	W.Va.	Rockhouse Br. of Island Cr.	400	1200		O	1973
Toxaway Lake (RE)	S.C.	Jocassee River	400	1000		H	1972
Diablo Dam (VA)	Wash.	Skagit River	400	1142	350	HR	1930
Trout Lake Dam (RE)	Col.	Lake Fork San Miguel River	395	870		H	1906
Brownlee Dam (ER)	Ida.	Snake River	395	1380	6700	H	1959
Summersville Dam (ER)	W.Va.	Cauley River	393	2280	13565	CRSO	1965
Blue Mesa (RE)	Col.	Gunnison River	390	785	3093	HCRO	1966
Pyramid (ER)	Cal.	Piru Creek	386	1080	6952	I R	1973
Boundary Dam (VA)	Wash.	Pend Oreille River	385	740	240	HR	1967
San Luis (RE)	Cal.	San Luis Creek	382	18000	77664	ISHR	1967
Green Peter (PG)	Ore.	Middle Santiam River	378	1517	1142	CHRI	1967
Pacoima (VA)	Cal.	Pacoima Creek	365	640	226	C	1929
Yale Dam (RE)	Wash.	Lewis River	357	1600	4200	HR	1952
Abiquiu Dam (RE)	N.M.	Rio Chama	354	1540	11793	CDD	1963
Arrowrock (VA)	Ida.	Boise River	350	1150	636	IC	1915
Pardee (PG)	Cal.	Mokelumne River	345	1337	615	S	1929
Hills Creek (RE)	Ore.	Middle Fork Willamette River	341	2306	10800	CHIS	1962
Folsom (PG)	Cal.	American River	340	10200	8980	ISHC	1956
Whitman Cr. Embankment (OT)	W.Va.	Whitman Cr. of Coopers Fk.	340	625		O	1952
Reservoir No. 22 (VA)	Col.	Boulder Creek	340	1090		S	1953
Gross Dam (PG)	Col.	South Boulder Creek	340	1050	592	S	1955
Castaic (RE)	Cal.	Castaic Cr.	340	5200	44000	I R	1973
Casitas (RE)	Cal.	Coyote Creek	334	2000	9112	ISC	1959
Smith Dam (RE)	Ore.	Smith River	333	1150	2500	H	1962
Upper Baker Dam (PG)	Wash.	Baker River	332	1220	628	HR	1961

World's Largest Dams

Source: Bureau of Reclamation, Dept. of the Interior

Based on total volume of structure. All dams listed are predominantly earthfill or rockfill and may contain concrete sections. UC—Under Construction.

Name of Dam	Cubic Yards	Completed	Name of Dam	Cubic Yards	Completed
New Cornelia Tailings, U.S.A.	274,026,000	1973	Kiev, USSR	57,552,000	1964
Tarbella, Pakistan	186,000,000	1975	W.A.C. Bennett, Canada	57,203,000	1967
Fort Peck, U.S.A.	125,612,000	1940	High Aswan Saad-El-Aili, Egypt	57,203,000	1970
Oahe, U.S.A.	92,008,000	1963	Saratov, U.S.S.R.	52,843,000	1967
Mangla, Pakistan	85,872,000	1967	Mission Tailings, No. 2, U.S.A.	52,435,000	1973
Gardiner, Canada	85,743,000	1968	Fort Randall, U.S.A.	50,205,000	1956
Afsluitdijk, Netherlands	82,927,000	1932	Kanev, USSR	49,520,000	1974
Oroville, U.S.A.	78,008,000	1968	Kakhovka, USSR	46,617,000	1955
San Luis, U.S.A.	77,666,000	1967	Volga, V.I. Lenin, USSR.	44,298,000	1955
Garrison, U.S.A.	66,506,000	1956	Castaic, U.S.A.	44,000,000	1971
Cochiti, U.S.A.	64,631,000	1975	Jari, Pakistan	42,400,000	1967
Tabka, Syria	60,168,000	1975	Kremenchug, USSR	41,192,000	1961

Superlative U. S. Statistics

Source: National Geographic Society, Washington, D.C.

Area for fifty states	Total	3,615,122 sq. mi.
	Land 3,536,855 sq. mi. — Water 78,267 sq. mi.	
Largest state	Alaska	586,412 sq. mi.
Smallest state	Rhode Island	1,214 sq. mi.
Largest county	San Bernardino County, California	20,119 sq. mi.
Smallest county	New York, New York	23 sq. mi.
Northernmost city	Barrow, Alaska	71° 17′N.
Northernmost point	Point Barrow, Alaska	71° 23′N.
Southernmost city	Hilo, Island of Hawaii	19° 43′N.
Southernmost town	Naalehu, Island of Hawaii	19° 03′N.
Southernmost point	Ka Lae (South Cape), Island of Hawaii	18° 56′N. (155° 41′W.)
Easternmost city	Eastport, Maine	66° 59.5′W.
Easternmost town	Lubec, Maine	66° 59′W.
Easternmost point	West Quoddy Head, Maine	66° 57′W.
Westernmost city	Lihue, Island of Kauai, Hawaii	159° 22′W.
Westernmost town	Adak, Aleutians, Alaska	176° 45′W.
Westernmost point	Cape Wrangell, Attu Island, Aleutians, Alaska	172° 27′E.
Highest city	Leadville, Colorado	10,200 ft.
Lowest town	Calipatria, California	—183 ft.
Highest point on Atlantic coast	Cadillac Mountain, Mount Desert Is., Maine	1,530 ft.
Largest and oldest national park	Yellowstone National Park (1872), Wyoming	3,468 sq. mi.
	Montana, Idaho	
Largest national monument	Glacier Bay, Alaska	4,383 sq. mi.
Highest waterfall	Yosemite Falls—Total in three sections	2,425 ft.
	Upper Yosemite Fall	1,430 ft.
	Cascades in middle section	675 ft.
	Lower Yosemite Fall	320 ft.
Longest river	Mississippi-Missouri	3,710 mi.
Highest mountain	Mount McKinley, Alaska	20,320 ft.
Lowest point	Death Valley, California	—282 ft.
Deepest lake	Crater Lake, Oregon	1,932 ft.
Rainiest spot	Mt. Waialeale, Hawaii	Annual Aver. rainfall 460 inches
Largest gorge	Grand Canyon, Colorado River, Arizona; 217 miles	
	long, 4 to 18 miles wide, 1 mile deep	
Deepest gorge	Hells Canyon, Snake River, Idaho	7,900 ft.
Strongest surface wind	Mount Washington, New Hampshire recorded 1934	231 mph
Biggest dam	Ft. Peck, Missouri River, Montana	125,628,000 cu. yds. material used
Tallest building	Sears Tower, Chicago, Illinois	1,454 ft.
Largest building	Boeing 747 Manufacturing Plant, Everett, Washington, 205,600,000	
	cu. ft.; covers 47 acres.	
Tallest structure	TV tower, Blanchard, North Dakota	2,063 ft.
Longest bridge span	Verrazano-Narrows, New York	4,260 ft.
Highest bridge	Royal Gorge, Colorado	1,053 ft. above water
Deepest well	Gas well, Washita County, Oklahoma	31,441 ft.

The Forty-Nine States, Including Alaska

Area for forty-nine states	Total	3,608,672 sq. mi.
	Land 3,530,430 sq. mi. — Water 78,242 sq. mi.	

The Forty-Eight States

Area for forty-eight states	Total	3,022,260 sq. mi.
	Land 2,963,998 sq. mi. — Water 58,262 sq. mi.	
Largest state	Texas	267,338 sq. mi.
Northernmost town	Angle Inlet, Minnesota	49° 22′N.
Northernmost point	Northwest Angle, Minnesota	49° 23′N.
Southernmost city	Key West, Florida	24° 33′N.
Southernmost mainland city	Florida City, Florida	25° 27′N.
Southernmost point	Key West, Florida	24° 33′N.
Westernmost town	La Push, Washington	124° 38′W.
Westernmost point	Cape Alava, Washington	124° 44′W.
Highest mountain	Mount Whitney, California	14,494 ft.

Note to users: The distinction between cities and towns varies from state to state. In this table the U.S. Bureau of the Census usage was followed.

U. S. Coastline by States*

Source: NOAA, Department of Commerce

State	Coastline[1]	Shoreline[2]	State	Coastline[1]	Shoreline[2]
Atlantic coast	**2,069**	**28,673**	**Gulf coast**	**1,631**	**17,141**
Connecticut	(-)	618	Alabama	53	607
Delaware	28	381	Florida	770	5,095
Florida	580	3,331	Louisiana	397	7,721
Georgia	100	2,344	Mississippi	44	359
Maine	228	3,478	Texas	367	3,359
Maryland	31	3,190			
Massachusetts	192	1,519	**Pacific coast**	**7,623**	**40,298**
New Hampshire	13	131	Alaska	5,580	31,383
New Jersey	130	1,792	California	840	3,427
New York	127	1,850	Hawaii	750	1,052
North Carolina	301	3,375	Oregon	296	1,410
Pennsylvania	(-)	89	Washington	157	3,026
Rhode Island	40	384			
South Carolina	187	2,876	**Arctic coast, Alaska**	**1,060**	**2,521**
Virginia	112	3,315			
			United States	**12,383**	**88,633**

*In statute miles (Apr. 1, 1961). (-) Represents zero.

(1) Figures are lengths of general outline of seacoast. Measurements were made with a unit measure of 30 minutes of latitude on charts as near the scale of 1:1,200,000 as possible. Coastline of sounds and bays is included to a point where they narrow to width of unit measure, and includes the distance across at such point.

(2) Figures obtained in 1939-40 with a recording instrument on the largest-scale charts and maps then available. Shoreline of outer coast, offshore islands, sounds, bays, rivers and creeks is included to the head of tidewater or to a point where tidal waters narrow to a width of 100 feet.

Highest and Lowest Altitudes in the U.S.

Source: U. S. Geological Survey. (Minus sign means below sea level; elevations are in feet.)

State	Highest Point Name	County	Elev.	Lowest Point Name	County	Elev.
Alabama	Cheaha Mountain	Cleburne	2,407	Gulf of Mexico		Sea level
Alaska	Mount McKinley		20,320	Pacific Ocean		Sea level
Arizona	Humphreys Peak	Coconino	12,633	Colorado R.	Yuma	70
Arkansas	Magazine Mountain	Logan	2,753	Ouachita R.	Ashley Union	55
California	Mount Whitney	Inyo-Tulare	14,494	Death Valley	Inyo	—282
Canal Zone	Cerro Galera	Balboa District	1,205	Atlantic Ocean		Sea level
Colorado	Mount Elbert	Lake	14,433	Arkansas R	Prowers	3,350
Connecticut	Mount Frissell	Litchfield	2,380	L. I. Sound		Sea level
Delaware	On Ebright Road	New Castle	442	Atlantic Ocean		Sea level
Dist. of Col.	Tenleytown	N. W. part	410	Potomac R.		1
Florida	West boundary	Walton	345	Atlantic Ocean		Sea level
Georgia	Brasstown Bald	Towns-Union	4,784	Atlantic Ocean		Sea level
Guam	Mount Lamlam	Agat District	1,329	Pacific Ocean		Sea level
Hawaii	Mauna Kea	Hawaii	13,796	Pacific Ocean		Sea level
Idaho	Borah Peak	Custer	12,662	Snake R.	Nez Perce	710
Illinois	Charles Mound	Jo Daviess	1,235	Mississippi R.	Alexander	279
Indiana	Franklin Township	Wayne	1,257	Ohio R.	Posey	320
Iowa	NE of Sibley	Osceola	1,670	Mississippi R.	Lee	480
Kansas	Mount Sunflower	Wallace	4,039	Verdigris R.	Montgomery	680
Kentucky	Black Mountain	Harlan	4,145	Mississippi R.	Fulton	257
Louisiana	Driskill Mountain	Bienville	535	New Orleans	Orleans	—5
Maine	Mount Katahdin	Piscataquis	5,268	Atlantic Ocean		Sea level
Maryland	Backbone Mountain	Garrett	3,360	Atlantic Ocean		Sea level
Massachusetts	Mount Greylock	Berkshire	3,491	Atlantic Ocean		Sea level
Michigan	Mount Curwood	Baraga	1,980	Lake Erie		572
Minnesota	Eagle Mountain	Cook	2,301	Lake Superior		602
Mississippi	Woodall Mountain	Tishomingo	806	Gulf of Mexico		Sea level
Missouri	Taum Sauk Mt.	Iron	1,772	St. Francis R.	Dunklin	230
Montana	Granite Peak	Park	12,799	Kootenai R.	Lincoln	1,800
Nebraska	Johnson Township	Kimball	5,426	S.E. cor. State	Richardson	840
Nevada	Boundary Peak	Esmeralda	13,143	Colorado R.	Clark	470
New Hampshire	Mt. Washington	Coos	6,288	Atlantic Ocean		Sea level
New Jersey	High Point	Sussex	1,803	Atlantic Ocean		Sea level
New Mexico	Wheeler Peak	Taos	13,161	Red Bluff Res.	Eddy	2,817
New York	Mount Marcy	Essex	5,344	Atlantic Ocean		Sea level
North Carolina	Mount Mitchell	Yancey	6,684	Atlantic Ocean		Sea level
North Dakota	White Butte	Slope	3,506	Red River	Pembina	750
Ohio	Campbell Hill	Logan	1,550	Ohio R.	Hamilton	433
Oklahoma	Black Mesa	Cimarron	4,973	Little River	McCurtain	287
Oregon	Mount Hood	Clackamas-Hood R.	11,235	Pacific Ocean		Sea level
Pennsylvania	Mt. Davis	Somerset	3,213	Delaware R.	Delaware	Sea level
Puerto Rico	Cerro de Punta	Ponce	4,389	Atlantic Ocean		Sea level
Rhode Island	Jerimoth Hill	Providence	812	Atlantic Ocean		Sea level
Samoa	Lata Mtn.	Tau Island	3,160	Pacific Ocean		Sea level
South Carolina	Sassafras Mountain	Pickens	3,560	Atlantic Ocean		Sea level
South Dakota	Harney Peak	Pennington	7,242	Big Stone Lake	Roberts	962
Tennessee	Clingmans Dome	Sevier	6,643	Mississippi R.	Shelby	182
Texas	Guadalupe Peak	Culberson	8,751	Gulf of Mexico		Sea level
Utah	Kings Peak	Duchesne	13,528	Beaverdam Cr.	Washington	2,000
Vermont	Mount Mansfield	Lamoille	4,393	Lake Champlain	Franklin	95
Virginia	Mount Rogers	Grayson-Smyth	5,729	Atlantic Ocean		Sea level
Virgin Islands	Crown Mt.	Is. St. Thomas	1,556	Atlantic Ocean		Sea level
Washington	Mount Rainier	Pierce	14,410	Pacific Ocean		Sea level
West Virginia	Spruce Knob	Pendleton	4,863	Potomac R.	Jefferson	240
Wisconsin	Timms Hill	Price	1,952	Lake Michigan		581
Wyoming	Gannett Peak	Fremont	13,804	B. Fourche R.	Crook	3,100

International Boundary Lines of the U.S.

The length of the northern boundary of the conterminous U.S. — the U.S.-Canadian border, excluding Alaska — is 3,987 miles according to the U.S. Geological Survey, Dept. of the Interior. The length of the Alaskan-Canadian border is 1,538 miles. The length of the U.S.-Mexican border, from the Gulf of Mexico to the Pacific Ocean, is approximately 1,933 miles (1963 boundary agreement).

Geodetic Datum Point of North America

The geodetic datum point of the U.S. is the National Ocean Survey's triangulation station Meades Ranch in Osborne County, Kansas, at latitude 39° 13'26''. 686 N and longitude 98° 32'30''. 506 W. (Frequently this is referred to as the geodetic center of the U.S., which has no meaning.) This geodetic datum point is a fundamental point from which all latitude and longitude computations originate for North America and Central America.

Statistical Information About the U.S.

In the *Statistical Abstract of the United States* the Bureau of the Census, U.S. Dept. of Commerce, annually publishes a summary of social, political, and economic information. A book of more than 1,000 pages, it presents in 34 sections comprehensive data on population, housing, health, education, employment, income, prices, business, banking, science, defense, trade, government finance, foreign country comparison, and other subjects. Special features include comprehensive data for states and metropolitan areas and a summary of recent trends. The book is prepared under the direction of William Lerner, Data User Services Division, Bureau of the Census. Supplements to the *Statistical Abstract* are *Pocket Data Book USA, 1976; County and City Data Book, 1972; Congressional District Data Book, 93rd Congress* with supplements for the 3 states that redistricted for the 94th Congress; *Historical Statistics of the United States, Colonial Times to 1970.* Information concerning these and other publications may be obtained from the Supt. of Documents, Government Printing Office, Wash., D.C. 20402, or from the U.S. Bureau of the Census, Data User Services Division, Wash., D.C. 20233.

States: Settled, Capitals, Entry into Union, Area, Rank

The Original Thirteen States — The 13 colonies that seceded from Great Britain and fought the War of Independence (American Revolution) became the 13 original states. They were Massachusetts, Rhode Island, Connecticut, New Hampshire, New York, New Jersey, Pennsylvania, Delaware, Maryland, Virginia, North Carolina, South Carolina, and Georgia.

State	Set-tled*	Capital	Entered Union Date	Order**	Extent in Miles Long	Extent in Miles Wide	Area in square miles Land	Area in square miles Inland Water	Area in square miles Total	Rank in Area
Ala.	1702.	Montgomery	Dec. 14, 1819	22	330	200	50,708	901	51,609	29
Alaska.	1784.	Juneau	Jan. 3, 1959	49	(a)900	800	566,432	19,980	586,412	1
Ariz.	1848.	Phoenix	Feb. 14, 1912	48	390	335	113,417	492	113,909	6
Ark.	1785.	Little Rock	June 15, 1836	25	275	240	51,945	1,159	53,104	27
Cal.	1769.	Sacramento	Sept. 9, 1850	31	770	375	156,361	2,332	158,693	3
Col.	1858.	Denver	Aug. 1, 1876	38	390	270	103,766	481	104,247	8
Conn.	1635.	Hartford	Jan. 9, 1788	5	90	75	4,862	139	5,009	48
Del.	1683.	Dover	Dec. 7, 1787	1	110	35	1,982	75	2,057	49
D.C.		Washington			...	...	61	6	67	51
Fla.	1565.	Tallahassee	Mar. 3, 1845	27	460	400	54,090	4,470	58,560	22
Ga.	1733.	Atlanta	Jan. 2, 1788	4	315	250	58,073	803	58,876	21
Hawaii		Honolulu	Aug. 21, 1959	50	...	...	6,425	25	6,450	47
Ida.	1842.	Boise	July 3, 1890	43	490	305	82,677	880	83,557	13
Ill.	1720.	Springfield	Dec. 3, 1818	21	380	205	55,748	652	56,400	24
Ind.	1733.	Indianapolis	Dec. 11, 1816	19	265	160	36,097	102	36,291	38
Ia.	1788.	Des Moines	Dec. 28, 1846	29	300	210	55,941	349	56,290	25
Kan.	1727.	Topeka	Jan. 29, 1861	34	400	200	81,787	477	82,264	14
Ky.	1774.	Frankfort	June 1, 1792	15	350	175	39,650	745	40,395	37
La.	1699.	Baton Rouge	Apr. 30, 1812	18	280	275	44,930	3,593	48,523	31
Me.	1624.	Augusta	Mar. 15, 1820	23	235	205	30,920	2,295	33,215	39
Md.	1634.	Annapolis	Apr. 28, 1788	7	200	120	9,891	686	10,577	42
Mass.	1620.	Boston	Feb. 6, 1788	6	190	110	7,826	431	8,257	45
Mich.	1668.	Lansing	Jan. 26, 1837	26	400	310	56,817	1,399	58,216	23
Minn.	1805.	St. Paul	May 11, 1858	32	400	350	79,289	4,779	84,068	12
Miss.	1699.	Jackson	Dec. 10, 1817	20	340	180	47,296	420	47,716	32
Mo.	1735.	Jefferson City	Aug. 10, 1821	24	300	280	68,995	691	69,686	19
Mon.	1809.	Helena	Nov. 8, 1889	41	580	315	145,587	1,551	147,138	4
Neb.	1847.	Lincoln	Mar. 1, 1867	37	415	205	76,483	744	77,227	15
Nev.	1850.	Carson City	Oct. 31, 1864	36	485	315	109,889	651	110,540	7
N.H.	1623.	Concord	June 21, 1788	9	185	90	9,027	277	9,304	44
N.J.	1664.	Trenton	Dec. 18, 1787	3	160	70	7,521	315	7,836	46
N.M.	1605.	Santa Fe	Jan. 6, 1912	47	390	350	121,412	254	121,666	5
N.Y.	1614.	Albany	July 26, 1788	11	320	310	47,831	1,745	49,576	30
N.C.	1650.	Raleigh	Nov. 21, 1789	12	520	200	48,798	3,788	52,586	28
N.D.	1766.	Bismarck	Nov. 2, 1889	39	360	210	69,273	1,392	70,665	17
Oh.	1788.	Columbus	Mar. 1, 1803	17	230	205	40,975	247	41,222	35
Okla.	1889.	Oklahoma City	Nov. 16, 1907	46	585	210	68,782	1,137	69,919	18
Ore.	1811.	Salem	Feb. 14, 1859	33	375	290	96,184	797	96,981	10
Pa.	1682.	Harrisburg	Dec. 12, 1787	2	300	180	44,966	367	45,333	33
R.I.	1636.	Providence	May 29, 1790	13	50	35	1,049	165	1,214	50
S.C.	1670.	Columbia	May 23, 1788	8	285	215	30,225	830	31,055	40
S.D.	1856.	Pierre	Nov. 2, 1889	40	380	245	75,955	1,092	77,047	16
Tenn.	1757.	Nashville	June 1, 1796	16	430	120	41,328	916	42,244	34
Tex.	1691.	Austin	Dec. 29, 1845	28	760	620	262,134	5,204	267,338(b)	2
Ut.	1847.	Salt Lake City	Jan. 4, 1896	45	345	275	82,096	2,820	84,916	11
Vt.	1724.	Montpelier	Mar. 4, 1791	14	155	90	9,267	342	9,609	43
Va.	1607.	Richmond	June 25, 1788	10	425	205	39,780	1,037	40,817	36
Wash.	1811.	Olympia	Nov. 11, 1889	42	340	230	66,570	1,622	68,192	20
W. Va.	1727.	Charleston	June 20, 1863	35	225	200	24,070	111	24,181	41
Wis.	1766.	Madison	May 29, 1848	30	300	290	54,464	1,690	56,154	26
Wy.	1834.	Cheyenne	July 10, 1890	44	365	275	97,203	711	97,914	9

*First permanent settlement. **The order for the original 13 states is the order in which they ratified the constitution. (a) Aleutian Islands and Alexander Archipelago are not considered in these lengths. (b) Total area of Texas reduced one sq. mile by Chamizal boundary solution between U.S. and Mexico, 1963.

The Continental Divide

Source: U.S. Geological Survey, Department of the Interior

Continental Divide: watershed, created by mountain ranges or table-lands of the Rocky Mountains, from which the drainage is easterly or westerly; the easterly flowing waters reaching the Atlantic Ocean chiefly through the Gulf of Mexico, and the westerly flowing waters reaching the Pacific Ocean through the Columbia River, or through the Colorado River, which flows into the Gulf of California.

The location and route of the Continental Divide across the United States may briefly be described as follows:

Beginning at point of crossing the United States-Mexican boundary, near long. 108°45'W., the Divide, in a northerly direction, crosses New Mexico along the western edge of the Rio Grande drainage basin, entering Colorado near long. 106°41'W.

Thence by a very irregular route northerly across Colorado along the western summits of the Rio Grande and of the Arkansas, the South Platte, and the North Platte River basins, and across Rocky Mountain National Park, entering Wyoming near long. 106°52'W.

Then in a northwesterly direction, forming the western rims of the North Platte, Big Horn, and Yellowstone River basins, crossing the southwestern portion of Yellowstone National Park.

Thence in a westerly and then a northerly direction forming the common boundary of Idaho and Montana, to a point on said boundary near long. 114°00' W.

Thence northeasterly and northwesterly through Montana and the Glacier National Park, entering Canada near long. 114°04'W.

Chronological List of Territories

Name of Territory	Date of Organic Act			Organic Act Effective			Admission as State			Yrs. Terr.
Northwest Territory (a)	Jul.	13,	1787	No fixed date						
Territory south of Ohio River	May	26,	1790	No fixed date	Jun.	1,	1796(b)			6
Mississippi	Apr.	7,	1798	When President acted	Dec.	10,	1817			19
Indiana	May	7,	1800	Jul. 4, 1800	Dec.	11,	1816			16
Territory northwest of Ohio River	May	7,	1800	Jul. 4, 1800	Mar.	1,	1803(c)			2
Orleans	Mar.	26,	1804	Oct. 1, 1804	Apr.	30,	1812(d)			7
Michigan	Jan.	11,	1805	Jun. 30, 1805	Jan.	26,	1837			31
Louisiana-Missouri (e)	Mar.	3,	1805	Jul. 4, 1805	Aug.	10,	1821			16
Illinois	Feb.	3,	1809	Mar. 1, 1809	Dec.	3,	1813			9
Alabama	Mar.	3,	1817	When Miss. became a State	Dec.	14,	1819			2
Arkansas	Mar.	2,	1819	Jul. 4, 1819	Jun.	15,	1836			17
Florida	Mar.	30,	1822	No fixed date	Mar.	3,	1845			23
Indian (organized 1834)*										
Wisconsin	Apr.	20,	1836	Jul. 3, 1836	May	29,	1848			12
Iowa	Jun.	12,	1838	Jul. 3, 1838	Dec.	28,	1846			7
Oregon	Aug.	14,	1848	Date of act	Feb.	14,	1859			10
Minnesota	Mar.	3,	1849	Date of act	May	11,	1858			9
New Mexico	Sept.	9,	1850	On President's proclamation	Jan.	6,	1912			61
Utah	Sept.	9,	1850	Date of act	Jan.	4,	1896			44
Washington	Mar.	2,	1853	Date of act	Nov.	11,	1889			36
Nebraska	May	30,	1854	Date of act	Mar.	1,	1867			12
Kansas	May	30,	1854	Date of act	Jan.	29,	1861			6
Colorado	Feb.	28,	1861	Date of act	Aug.	1,	1876			15
Nevada	Mar.	2,	1861	Date of act	Oct.	31,	1864			3
Dakota	Mar.	2,	1861	Date of act	Nov.	2,	1889			28
Arizona	Feb.	24,	1863	Date of act	Feb.	14,	1912			49
Idaho	Mar.	3,	1863	Date of act	Jul.	3,	1890			27
Montana	May	26,	1864	Date of act	Nov.	8,	1889			25
Wyoming	Jul.	25,	1868	When officers were qualified	Jul.	10,	1890			22
Oklahoma	May	2,	1890	Date of act	Nov.	16,	1907			17
Hawaii	Apr.	30,	1900	Jun. 14, 1900	Aug.	21,	1959			59
Alaska	Aug.	24,	1912	Nov. 5, 1912	Jan.	3,	1959			47

(a) Included present Ohio, Indiana, Illinois, Michigan, Wisconsin, Eastern Minnesota; (b) as the State of Tennessee; (c) as the State of Ohio; (d) as the State of Louisiana; (e) organic act for Missouri Territory of June 4, 1812, became effective Dec. 7, 1812.

*Indian Territory was set aside in 1834 for the "5 civilized Indian tribes"—Cherokee, Choctaw, Chickasaw, Creek, and Seminole. In 1889, part of it was included in the Territory of Oklahoma. In 1906, Indian Territory and the Territory of Oklahoma were merged to form the state of Oklahoma.

Geographic Centers, U.S. and Each State

Source: U. S. Geological Survey, Department of the Interior

United States, including Alaska and Hawaii — South Dakota; Butte County, 17 miles W of Castle Rock, 14 miles E of junction of borders of South Dakota, Montana, and Wyoming. approx. lat. 44°58′N. long. 103°46′W.

Conterminous U. S. (48 States)—Near Lebanon, Smith Co., Kansas. lat. 39°50′N. long. 98°35′W.

North American Continent—The geographic center is in Pierce County, North Dakota, 6 miles W of Balta, latitude 48°10′, longitude 100°10′W.

STATES

State	County	Locality
Alabama—Chilton, 12 miles SW of Clanton.		
Alaska—lat. 63°50′N, long. 152°W. Approx. 60 mi. NW of Mt. McKinley.		
Arizona—Yavapai, 55 miles ESE of Prescott.		
Arkansas—Pulaski, 12 miles NW of Little Rock.		
California—Madera, 38 miles E of Madera.		
Colorado—Park, 30 miles NW of Pikes Peak.		
Connecticut—Hartford, at East Berlin.		
Delaware—Kent, 11 miles S of Dover.		
District of Columbia—Near Fourth and "L" Streets, NW.		
Florida—Hernando, 12 miles NNW of Brooksville.		
Georgia—Twiggs, 18 miles SE of Macon.		
Hawaii—Hawaii, 20°15′N,156°20′W, off Maui Island.		
Idaho—Custer, at Custer, SW of Challis.		
Illinois—Logan, 28 miles NE of Springfield.		
Indiana—Boone, 14 miles NW of Indianapolis.		
Iowa—Story, 5 miles NE of Ames.		
Kansas—Barton, 15 miles NE of Great Bend.		
Kentucky—Marion, 3 miles NNW of Lebanon.		
Louisiana—Avoyelles, 3 miles SE of Marksville.		
Maine—Piscataquis, 18 miles north of Dover.		

State	County	Locality
Maryland—Prince Georges, 4⅗ miles NW of Davidsonville.		
Massachusetts—Worcester, north part of city.		
Michigan—Wexford, 5 miles NW of Cadillac.		
Minnesota—Crow Wing, 10 miles SW of Brainerd.		
Mississippi—Leake, 9 miles WNW of Carthage.		
Missouri—Miller, 20 miles SW of Jefferson City.		
Montana—Fergus, 12 miles west of Lewistown.		
Nebraska—Custer, 10 miles NW of Broken Bow.		
Nevada—Lander, 26 miles SE of Austin.		
New Hampshire—Belknap, 3 miles E of Ashland.		
New Jersey—Mercer, 5 miles SE of Trenton.		
New Mexico—Torrance, 12 miles SSW of Willard.		
New York—Madison, 12 miles S of Oneida and 26 miles SW of Utica.		
North Carolina—Chatham, 10 miles NW of Sanford.		
North Dakota—Sheridan, 5 miles SW of McClusky.		
Ohio—Delaware, 25 miles NNE of Columbus.		
Oklahoma—Oklahoma, 8 miles N of Oklahoma City.		
Oregon—Crook, 25 miles SSE of Prineville.		
Pennsylvania—Centre, 2⅗ miles SW of Bellefonte.		
Rhode Island—Kent, 1 mile SSW of Crompton.		
South Carolina—Richland, 13 miles SE of Columbia.		
South Dakota—Hughes, 8 miles NE of Pierre.		
Tennessee—Rutherford, 5 mi. NE of Murfreesboro.		
Texas—McCulloch, 15 miles NE of Brady.		
Utah—Sanpete, 3 miles N of Manti.		
Vermont—Washington, 3 miles E of Roxbury.		
Virginia—Buckingham, 5 miles SW of Buckingham.		
Washington—Chelan, 10 mi. WSW of Wenatchee.		
West Virginia—Braxton, 4 miles E of Sutton.		
Wisconsin—Wood, 9 miles SE of Marshfield.		
Wyoming—Fremont, 58 miles ENE of Lander.		

There is no generally accepted definition of geographic center, and no satisfactory method for determining it. The geographic center of an area may be defined as the center of gravity of the surface, or that point on which the surface of the area would balance if it were a plane of uniform thickness.

No marked or monumented point has been established by any government agency as the geographic center of either the 50 states, the conterminous United States, or the North American continent. A monument was erected in Lebanon, Kan., conterminous U.S. center, by a group of citizens.

Origin of the Names of U.S. States

Source: State officials, the Smithsonian Institution, and the Topographic Division, U.S. Geological Survey.

Alabama—Indian for tribal town, later a tribe (Alabamas or Alibamons), of the Creek confederacy.

Alaska—Russian version of Aleutian (Eskimo) word, alakshak, for "peninsula" or "great lands."

Arizona—Spanish version of Pima Indian word for "little spring place," or Aztec arizuma, meaning "silver-bearing."

Arkansas—French variant of Kansas, a Sioux Indian name for "south wind people."

California—Bestowed by the Spanish conquistadors (possibly by Cortez). It was the name of an imaginary island, an earthly paradise, in "Las Serges de Esplandian," a Spanish romance written by Montalvo in 1510. Baja California (Lower California, in Mexico) was first visited by Spanish in 1533. The present U.S. state was called Alta (Upper) California.

Colorado—Spanish, red, first applied to Colorado River.

Connecticut—From Mohican and other Algonquin words meaning "long river place."

Delaware—Named for Lord De La Warr, early governor of Virginia; first applied to river, then to Indian tribe (Lenni-Lenape), and the state.

District of Columbia—For Columbus, 1791.

Florida—Named by Ponce de Leon on Pascua Florida, "Flowery Easter," on Easter Sunday, 1513.

Georgia—For King George II of England by James Oglethorpe, colonial administrator, 1732.

Hawaii—Possibly derived from native word for homeland, Hawaiki or Owyhee.

Idaho—Shoshone derivation. State calls it "light on the mountains."

Illinois—French for Illini or land of Illini, Algonquin word meaning men or warriors.

Indiana—Means "land of the Indians."

Iowa—Indian word variously translated as "one who puts to sleep" or "beautiful land."

Kansas—Sioux word for "south wind people."

Kentucky—Indian word variously translated as "dark and bloody ground," "meadow land" and "land of tomorrow."

Louisiana—Part of territory called Louisiana by LaSalle for French King Louis XIV.

Maine—From Maine, ancient French province.

Maryland—For Queen Henrietta Maria, wife of Charles I of England.

Massachusetts—From Indian tribe named after "large hill place" identified by Capt. John Smith as near Milton, Mass.

Michigan—From Chippewa words mici gama meaning "great water," after the lake of the same name.

Minnesota—From Dakota Sioux word meaning "cloudy water" or "sky-tinted water" of the Minnesota River.

Mississippi—Probably Chippewa: mici zibi, "great river" or "gathering-in of all the waters."

Missouri—Indian tribe named after Missouri River, meaning "muddy water."

Montana—Latin or Spanish for "mountainous."

Nebraska—From Omaha or Otos Indian word meaning "broad water" or "flat river," describing the Platte River.

Nevada—Spanish, meaning snow-clad.

New Hampshire—Named 1629 by Capt. John Mason of Plymouth Council for county in England.

New Jersey—The Duke of York, 1664, gave a patent to John Berkeley and Sir George Carteret to be called Nova

Caesaria, or New Jersey, after England's Isle of Jersey.

New Mexico—Spaniards in Mexico applied term to land north and west of Rio Grande in the 16th Century.

New York—For Duke of York and Albany who received patent to New Netherland from his brother Charles II and sent an expedition to capture it, 1664.

North Carolina—In 1619 Charles I gave a large patent to Sir Robert Heath to be called Province of Carolana, from Carolus, Latin name for Charles. A new patent was granted by Charles II to Earl of Clarendon and others. Divided into North and South Carolina, 1710.

North Dakota—Dakota is Sioux for friend or ally.

Ohio—Iroquois word for "beautiful river."

Oklahoma—Choctaw coined word meaning red man, proposed by Rev. Allen Wright, Choctaw-speaking Indian.

Oregon—Origin unknown.

Pennsylvania—William Penn, the Quaker, who was made full proprietor by King Charles II in 1681, suggested Sylvania, or woodland, for his tract. The king's government owed Penn's father, Admiral William Penn, £16,000, and the land being granted in part settlement, the king added the Penn to Sylvania, against the desires of the modest proprietor, in honor of the admiral.

Puerto Rico—Spanish for Rich Port.

Rhode Island—Named Roode Eylandt by Adriaen Block, Dutch explorer, because of its red clay. Name of Roger Williams' settlement was added to give the small state its long, official title: State of Rhode Island and Providence Plantations.

South Carolina—See North Carolina.

South Dakota—See North Dakota.

Tennessee—From 1784 to 1788 this was the State of Franklin, or Frankland. Tanasi was the name of Cherokee villages on the Little Tennessee River.

Texas—Variant of word used by Caddo and other Indians meaning friends or allies, and applied to them by the Spanish in eastern Texas. Also written texias, tejas, teysas.

Utah—From a Navajo word meaning upper, or higher up, as applied to a Shoshone tribe called Ute. Spanish form is Yutta, English Uta or Utah. Proposed name Deseret, "land of honeybees," from Book of Mormon, was rejected by Congress.

Vermont—From French words Vert, green, and Mont, mountain. The Green Mountains were said to have been named by Samuel de Champlain. The Green Mountain Boys were Gen. Stark's men in the Revolution. When the state was formed, 1777, Dr. Thomas Young suggested combining vert and mont into Vermont.

Virginia—Named by Sir Walter Raleigh, who fitted out the expedition of 1584, in honor of Queen Elizabeth, the Virgin Queen of England.

Washington—Named after George Washington. When the bill creating the Territory of Columbia was introduced in the 32d Congress, the name was changed to Washington because of the existence of the District of Columbia.

West Virginia—So named when western counties of Virginia refused to secede from the United States, 1863.

Wisconsin—An Indian name, spelled Ouisconsin and Misconsing by early chroniclers. Believed to mean "grassy place" in Chippewa. Congress made it Wisconsin.

Wyoming—The word was taken from Wyoming Valley, Pa., which was the site of an Indian massacre and became widely known by Campbell's poem, Gertrude of Wyoming. In Algonquin it means "large prairie place."

Accession of Territory by the U.S.

Source: Statistical Abstract of the United States

Division	Yr.	Sq. mi.[1]	Division	Yr.	Sq. mi.[1]	Division	Yr.	Sq. mi.[1]
Total (1970).....		3,628,062	Texas............	1845	390,143	American Samoa...	1900	76
			Oregon...........	1846	285,580	Canal Zone[4]......	1904	553
United States.....		3,615,122	Mexican cession....	1848	529,017	Corn Islands[5]......	1914	4
Territory in 1790[2]		888,685	Gadsden Purchase...	1853	29,640	Virgin Islands, U.S...	1917	133
Louisiana Purchase.	1803	827,192	Alaska...........	1867	586,412	Trust Territory of		
By Treaty with Spain			Hawaii...........	1898	6,450	the Pacific Is......	1947	8,489
Florida..........	1819	58,560	The Philippines[3]...	1898	115,600	All other[6]..........	....	42
Other areas......	1819	13,443	Puerto Rico........	1899	3,435			
			Guam............	1899	212			

(1) Gross area (land and water), (2) Includes drainage basin of Red River on the north, south of 49th parallel sometimes considered a part of the Louisiana Purchase, (3) Area not included in total; became Republic of the Philippines July 4, 1946. (4) Under U.S. jurisdiction by treaty with Panama. (5) Leased from Nicaragua for 99 years but returned Apr. 25, 1971; Area not included in total. (6) See index for Outlying Areas; U.S.

Confederate States and Secession

The American Civil War, 1861-1865, grew out of sectional disputes over the employment of slavery in the South and the contention of Southern legislators that the states retained many sovereign rights, including the right to secede from the Union.

The principal product of the South was cotton, harvested by slave labor. For 50 years Northern leaders had been trying to curtail slavery, but were checkmated in Congress by Southern legislators. Extreme partisans in the North, called Abolitionists, demanded the immediate end of slavery for moral reasons.

The Southern states argued that the U.S.Constitution was a contract between sovereign states, which could withdraw (secede) when state rights were violated. This has led Southern historians to call the Civil War the War Between the States. Actually the war was not fought by state against state but by one federal regime against another, the Confederate government in Richmond assuming control over the economic, political, and military life of the South, under protest from Georgia and South Carolina.

Early Slavery Laws

Milestone U.S. laws on the slavery issue included the Missouri Compromise of 1820 which admitted Missouri as a slave state but prohibited slavery in the Louisiana Territory north of Arkansas; the Compromise of 1850, which admitted California as a free state, omitted action on slavery in organizing Utah and New Mexico as territories, ended slave trade in the District of Columbia, amended the Fugitive Slave Act to punish any who aided a fugitive, and abolished trial by jury for fugitives; Kansas-Nebraska Act, 1854, which left choice of slavery in Kansas and Nebraska to residents there (squatter sovereignty).

Harriet Beecher Stowe's *Uncle Tom's Cabin*, 1851-1852, intensified feeling against slavery.

Tension increased when the Supreme Court ruled Mar. 6, 1857, that Dred Scott, a Negro, did not become free when taken to a free state and did not have rights as a citizen; also that the Missouri Compromise on slavery was unconstitutional.

John Brown's attempt to arm slaves at Harpers Ferry, Oct. 16-18, 1859, inflamed partisans.

Abraham Lincoln's stand for free soil (no slavery) in new states and territories, and his general condemnation of slavery, caused Southern fanatics to threaten secession if he were elected. When Sen. Stephen A. Douglas split the Democratic party by his stand against secession, Republican Lincoln's election was assured. Even before inauguration Lincoln had Sen. William H. Seward (N.Y.) offer a resolution that the Constitution never be altered to interfere with slavery where established, that the Fugitive Slave Law be amended to include trial by jury, that all states repeal laws contrary to the Constitution.

Secession of States

South Carolina voted an ordinance of secession from the Union repealing its 1788 ratification of the U.S. Constitution on Dec. 20, 1860, to take effect Dec. 24. Other states seceded in 1861 and their votes in convention were:

Mississippi, Jan. 1861, by 84 to 15.
Florida, Jan. 10, 1861, by 62 to 7.

Alabama, Jan. 11, 1861, by 61 to 39.
Georgia, Jan. 19, 1861, by 208 to 89.
Louisiana, Jan. 26, 1861, by 113 to 17.
Texas, Feb. 1, 1861, by 166 to 7, ratified by popular vote Feb. 23, 1861 (for 34,794; against 11,325).
Virginia had delayed action, but when President Lincoln called for troops after Fort Sumter fell (Apr. 14, 1861), it voted for secession Apr. 17, 1861, by 88 to 55, ratified by popular vote May 23, 1861 (for secession, 128,884; against, 32,134).
Arkansas, May 6, 1861, by 69 to 1.
North Carolina, May 21, 1861, voted secession but refused by two-thirds vote to submit it to people for ratification.
Tennessee, May 7, 1861, entered a military league with the Confederacy (popular vote, June 8, for secession, 104,019; against 47,238).
Missouri Unionists stopped secession in the convention at Jefferson City Feb. 28 and at the second session in St. Louis Mar. 9. The legislature condemned secession Mar. 7. Under the protection of Confederate troops, secessionist members of the legislature adopted a resolution of secession at Neosho, Oct. 31, 1861. The Confederate Congress seated the secessionists' representatives.
Kentucky did not secede and its government remained Unionist. In a part occupied by Confederate troops,Kentuckians approved secession and the Confederate Congress admitted their representatives.
The Maryland legislature voted against secession Apr. 27, 53 to 13. Delaware did not secede. Western Virginia held conventions at Wheeling, named a pro-Union governor June 11, 1861; admitted to Union as West Virginia June 30, 1863; its constitution provided for gradual abolition of slavery.

Confederate Government

Forty-two delegates from South Carolina, Georgia, Alabama, Mississippi, Louisiana and Florida met in convention at Montgomery, Ala., Feb. 4, 1861. The Congress adopted a provisional constitution of the Confederate States of America Feb. 8, 1861, and on the next day elected Jefferson Davis (Miss.), provisional president, and Alexander H. Stephens (Ga.), provisional vice president. Davis was inducted into office at Montgomery, Feb. 18, 1861.

A permanent constitution was adopted Mar. 11, 1861. It provided that the president should be elected for a single term of 6 years; it also abolished the African slave trade. The Congress moved to Richmond, Va., July 20, 1861. Jefferson Davis was elected president, October, 1861; inaugurated Feb. 22, 1862.

Jefferson Davis (1808-1889) was a West Point graduate, 1828; served in Black Hawk and Mexican Wars; senator from Mississippi, 1847-1851; secretary of war, 1853-1857; senator, 1857-1861.

The Congress adopted a flag, consisting of a red field with a white stripe in the middle third, and a blue jack with a circle of white stars, going two-thirds of the way down the flag. This flag was unfurled in Montgomery, Mar. 4, 1861. Later the more popular flag was the red field with blue diagonal cross bars that held 13 white stars, designed by Gen. P. G. T. Beauregard.

(See also Civil War, U. S., in Index)

Dixie

The name Dixie is popularly associated with the southern states of the U.S. Several possible origins have been suggested.

One is said to be the French word dix (ten) which was printed on $10 bills used in early Louisiana which were called "dixies" by Americans. Louisiana became known as "Dix's Land" or "Land of the Dixies."

Some sources suggest that the name originated from a kind-hearted Dutch farmer, Dixie (Dixye), who unsuccessfully tried to cultivate tobacco in Harlem, N.Y. City, in the late 1700s. When he sold his slaves to a farmer in Piedmont County, S.C., they are said to have longed to return to Dixie's farm and sang of its joys.

In the South many consider Dixie a derivation from the "Mason-Dixon Line" which divided the free and slave states.

Public Lands of the U. S.

Source: Bureau of Land Management, U.S. Dept. of the Interior

Acquisition of the Public Domain 1781-1867

Acquisition	Area* (in Acres)	Land	Water	Total	Cost¹
State Cessions (1781-1802)		233,415,680	3,409,920	236,825,600	²$6,200,000
Louisiana Purchase (1803)³		523,446,400	6,465,280	529,911,680	23,213,568
Red River Basin⁴		29,066,880	535,040	29,601,920	
Cession from Spain (1819)		43,342,720	2,801,920	46,144,640	6,674,057
Oregon Compromise (1846)		180,644,480	2,741,760	183,386,240	
Mexican Cession (1848)		334,479,360	4,201,600	338,680,960	16,295,149
Purchase from Texas (1850)		78,842,880	83,840	78,926,720	15,496,448
Gadsden Purchase (1853)		18,961,920	26,880	18,988,800	10,000,000
Alaska Purchase (1867)		362,516,480	12,787,200	375,303,680	7,200,000
Total		**1,804,716,800**	**33,053,440**	**1,837,770,240**	**$85,079,222**

*All areas except Alaska were computed in 1912, and have not been adjusted for the recomputation of the area of the United States which was made for the 1950 Decennial Census.
(1.) Cost data for all except "State Cessions" obtained from U.S. Geological Survey.
(2.) Paid by Federal Government for Georgia Cession, 1802 (56,689,920 acres).
(3.) Excludes areas eliminated by Treaty of 1819 with Spain.
(4.) Basin of the Red River of the North, south of the 49th parallel.

Disposition of Public Lands 1781 to 1970 (In acres)

Disposition by methods not elsewhere Classified¹		Granted to States for:	
Granted or sold to homesteaders	303,500,000	Support of common schools	77,600,000
Granted to railroad corporations	287,500,000	Reclamation of swampland	64,900,000
Granted to veterans as military bounties	94,300,000	Construction of railroads	37,100,000
Confirmed as private land claims²	61,100,000	Support of misc. institutions⁶	21,700,000
Sold under timber and stone law³	34,000,000	Purposes not elsewhere classified⁷	117,500,000
Granted or sold under timber culture law⁴	13,900,000	Canals and rivers	6,100,000
Sold under desert land law⁵	10,900,000	Construction of wagon roads	3,400,000
	10,700,000	**Total granted to States**	**328,300,000**
		Grand Total	**1,144,200,000**

(1.) Chiefly public, private, and preemption sales, but includes mineral entries, script locations, sales of townsites and townlots.
(2.) The Government has confirmed title to lands claimed under valid grants made by foreign governments prior to the acquisition of the public domain by the United States.
(3.) The law provided for the sale of lands valuable for timber or stone and unfit for cultivation.
(4.) The law provided for the granting of public lands to settlers on condition that they plant and cultivate trees on the lands granted.
(5.) The law provided for the sale of arid agricultural public lands to settlers who irrigate them and bring them under cultivation.
(6.) Universities, hospitals, asylums, etc.
(7.) For construction of various public improvements (individual items not specified in the granting act) reclamation of desert lands, construction of water reservoirs, etc.

Land Owned by the Federal Government (in acres)

Agency (June 30, 1973)	Public Domain	Acquired	Total
Bureau of Land Management	471,420,276.0	2,363,288.4	473,783,564.4
U.S. Forest Service	160,243,743.0	26,980,669.5	187,224,412.5
U.S. Fish and Wildlife Service	24,412,086.2	3,670,695.4	28,082,781.6
U.S. Park Service	19,744,722.0	4,937,649.7	24,682,371.7
U.S. Army	7,069,415.0	3,955,552.0	11,024,967.0
Bureau of Reclamation	5,734,706.5	1,866,933.1	7,601,639.6
U.S. Air Force	6,945,640.0	1,441,700.0	8,387,340.0
Corps of Engineers	734,304.3	6,907,389.2	7,641,693.5
Bureau of Indian Affairs	4,204,417.4	765,386.0	4,969,803.4
U.S. Navy	2,284,072.1	1,278,067.7	3,562,139.8
Atomic Energy Commission	1,435,910.1	666,593.8	2,102,503.9
Other	522,188.7	1,413,767.2	1,935,955.9
Total	**704,751,481.3**	**56,247,692.0**	**760,999,173.3**

The Homestead Act; Sale of Public Land

The Homestead Act became effective Jan. 1, 1863, the same day President Lincoln's Emancipation Proclamation became effective. Its purpose was to open the vacant lands of America's vast public domain to agricultural settlement.

To qualify for a homestead a person had to be a citizen of the United States or express his intention of becoming one, be over 21 years of age or the head of a household, and own less than 160 acres of land.

To acquire title to 160 acres of public land the homesteader had to establish residence on the land and bring a portion under cultivation. After 6 months residence he could purchase the land for $1.25 per acre, or after 5 years residence he could acquire title for a $15 filing fee.

Originally passed by Congress on May 20, 1862, the Homestead Act was later amended to increase acreage limitations under certain conditions. Under the Homestead Act and its several amendments, more than a million families received title to over 248,000,000 acres of public land across the plains, prairies and mountains of western United States. But as subsequent waves of settlers moved onto vacant land the supply of arable land dwindled; by the late 1930s some homesteaders had settled on submarginal lands that would not support a farm family. In 1937 Congress passed the Bankhead-Jones Act authorizing the Government to repurchase bankrupt farms to relieve the plight of such families. Under this program about 2,000,000 acres of homestead land was returned to Federal ownership.

By the time of its 100th anniversary the Homestead Act had accomplished its purpose—the transformation of a wilderness into productive farmland. Now outdated, the Homestead Act will always be a part of the American heritage.

Public Land Sale

From time to time the Bureau of Land Management sells public land to private individuals. Public land is always sold for its fair market value as determined by public auction. The Federal Govt. offers no free land. Persons wishing to purchase public land should contact the Bureau of Land Management, Wash., D. C. 20240, or one of the Bureau's Land Offices in the public land states.

The Bureau stresses that it is the only authoritative source of information on the sale of land under its jurisdiction.

National Parks, Other Areas Administered by Nat'l Park Service

Figures given are date area was set aside by Congress or proclaimed by president, and area in acres.

National Parks

Acadia, Me. (1916) 37,722. Includes Mount Desert Island, half of Isle au Haut, Schoodic Point on mainland. Highest elevation on Eastern seaboard.

Arches, Utah (1929) 73,379. Contains giant red sandstone arches and other products of erosion.

Big Bend, Texas (1935) 708,118. On Rio Grande River.

Bryce Canyon, Utah (1923) 37,277. Spectacularly colorful and unusual display of erosion effects in Southwestern Utah.

Canyonlands, Utah (1964). 337,570. At junction of Colorado and Green Rivers, extensive evidence of prehistoric Indians.

Capitol Reef, Utah (1937) 241,866. A 70-mile uplift of sandstone cliffs dissected by high-walled gorges.

Carlsbad Caverns, N.M. (1923) 46,756. Largest known underground caverns, not yet fully explored.

Crater Lake, Ore. (1902) 160,290. Extraordinary blue lake in crater of extinct volcano encircled by lava walls 500 to 2,000 feet high.

Everglades, Fla. (1934) 1,400,533. Largest remaining subtropical wilderness in Continental U.S.; abundant wildlife includes rare birds.

Glacier, Mont. (1910) 1,013,599. Superb Rocky Mountain scenery, numerous glaciers and glacial lakes. Part of Waterton-Glacier International Peace Park established by U.S. and Canada in 1932.

Grand Canyon, Ariz. (1908) 1,218,375. Most spectacular part of Colorado River's greatest canyon.

Grand Teton, Wyo. (1929) 310,418. Most impressive part of the Teton Mountains, winter feeding ground of largest American elk herd.

Great Smoky Mountains, N.C.-Tenn. (1926) 517,014. Largest eastern mountain range, magnificent forests.

Guadalupe Mountains, Texas (1966) 76,398. Extensive and significant Permian limestone fossil reef; tremendous earth fault.

Haleakala, Hawaii (1960) 27,824. 10,023 foot dormant volcano on Maui.

Hawaii Volcanoes, Hawaii (1916) 229,177. Contains Kilauea and Mauna Loa, active volcanoes on the island of Hawaii.

Hot Springs, Ark. (1832) 5,801. Government supervised bath houses use waters of 45 of the 47 natural hot springs.

Isle Royale, Mich. (1931) 539,280. Largest island in Lake Superior, noted for its wilderness area and wildlife.

Kings Canyon, Calif. (1890) 460,136. Mountains wilderness, dominated by Kings River Canyons and High Sierra, contains giant sequoias.

Lassen Volcanic, Calif. (1907) 106,372. Contains Lassen Peak, most recently active volcano in continental U.S., and other volcanic phenomena.

Mammoth Cave, Ky. (1926) 52,129. 144 miles of surveyed underground passages, beautiful natural formations, river 360 feet below surface.

Mesa Verde, Colo. (1906) 52,036. Most notable and best preserved prehistoric cliff dwellings in the United States.

Mount McKinley, Alaska (1917) 1,939,493. Highest Mountain in North America, large glaciers, and unusual wildlife.

Mount Rainier, Wash. (1899) 285,404. Greatest single-peak glacial system in the U.S. radiates from this dormant volcano.

North Cascades, Wash. (1968) 504,785. Spectacular mountainous region with many glaciers, lakes, and rugged peaks.

Olympic, Wash. (1909) 897,909. Mountain wilderness containing finest remnant of Pacific Northwest rain forest, active glaciers, Pacific shoreline, rare elk.

Petrified Forest, Ariz. (1906) 94,189. Extensive petrified wood and Indian artifacts. Contains part of Painted Desert.

Redwood, Calif. (1968) 62,147. Forty miles of Pacific coastline, virgin groves of ancient redwoods.

Rocky Mountain, Colo. (1915) 263,793. Beautiful scenery on the continental divide includes 107 named peaks over 11,000 feet.

Sequoia, Calif. (1890) 386,823. Groves of giant sequoias, highest mountain in conterminous United States — Mount Whitney (14,494 feet).

Shenandoah, Va. (1926) 190,532. Portion of the Blue Ridge Mountains; this park overlooks much of the famous Shenandoah Valley.

Virgin Islands, Virgin Islands (1956) 14,470. Covers 3/4ths of St. John Island, lush growth, lovely beaches, Indian relics, evidence of colonial Danes.

Voyageurs, Minn. (1971) 219,128. Abundant lakes, forests, wildlife, unusual recreation.

Wind Cave, S.D. (1903) 28,060. Limestone Caverns in Black Hills. Extensive wildlife includes a herd of bison.

Yellowstone, Ida., Mont., Wyo., (1872) 2,219,823. Oldest and largest National Park. World's greatest geyser area has about 3,000 geysers and hot springs; the spectacular falls and impressive canyons of the Yellowstone River are major attractions.

Yosemite, Calif. (1890) 760,916. Yosemite Valley, the nation's highest waterfall, 3 groves of giant sequoias, and mountainous terrain.

Zion, Utah (1909) 146,553. Unusual shapes and landscapes have resulted from the effects of erosion and faulting activity, Zion Canyon, with sheer walls ranging up to 2,500 feet, is readily accessible.

National Historical Parks

Appomattox Court House, Va. (1930) 995. Where Lee surrendered to Grant.

Boston, Mass. (1974) 35. Includes Faneuil Hall, Old North Church, Bunker Hill, Paul Revere House.

Chalmette, La. (1907) 142. Scene of part of the Battle of New Orleans.

Chesapeake and Ohio Canal, Md.-W. Va.-D.C. (1961) 20,239. 185 mile historic canal; D.C. to Cumberland, Md.

City of Refuge, Hawaii (1955) 181. Until 1819, a sanctuary for Hawaiians vanquished in battle, and those guilty of crimes or breaking taboos.

Colonial, Va. (1930) 9,834. Includes most of Jamestown Island, site of first successful English colony; Yorktown site of Cornwallis' surrender to George Washington; Cape Henry Memorial, approximate site of the first landing of the Jamestown colonists; and the Colonial Parkway.

Cumberland Gap, Ky.-Tenn.-Va. (1940) 20,273. Mountain pass of the Wilderness Road which carried the first great migration of pioneers into America's interior.

George Rogers Clark, Vincennes, Ind. (1966) 24. Commemorates American defeat of British in West during Revolution.

Harpers Ferry, Md., W. Va. (1944) 1,909. At the confluence of the Shenandoah and Potomac Rivers the site of John Brown's 1859 raid on the Army arsenal. Scene of several Civil War battles.

Independence, Pa., (1948) 22. Contains several properties in Philadelphia associated with the Revolutionary War and the founding of the U.S.

Minute Man, Mass. (1959) 746. Where the colonial Minute Men battled the British, April 19, 1775. Also contains Nathaniel Hawthorne's home.

Morristown, N.J. (1933) 1,544. Sites of important military encampments during the Revolutionary War; Washington's headquarters 1777, 1779-80.

Nez Perce, Ida. (1965) 2,113. Illustrates the history and culture of the Nez Perce Indian country. 22 separate sites.

San Juan Island, Wash. (1966) 1,752. Commemorates the peaceful relations of the U.S., Canada and Great Britain since the 1872 boundary disputes at this site.

Saratoga, N.Y. (1938) 2,432. Scene of a major battle which became a turning point in the War of Independence.

Sitka, Alaska (1910) 108. Scene of last major resistance of the Tlingit Indians to the Russians, 1804.

National Memorial Park

Theodore Roosevelt, N.D. (1947) 70,409. Part of T.R.'s Elkhorn Ranch along the Little Missouri River. Has bison and some original prairie.

National Battlefields

Big Hole, Mont. (1910) 656. Site of major battle with Nez Perce Indians.

Cowpens, S.C. (1929) 826. Revolutionary War Battlefield.

Fort Necessity, Pa. (1931) 911. First battle of French and Indian War.

Petersburg, Va. (1926) 1,515. Scene of 10-month Union campaign 1864-65.

Stones River, Tenn. (1927) 331. Civil War battle leading to Sherman's "March to the Sea."

Tupelo, Miss. (1929) 1.0. Crucial battle over Sherman's supply line.

Wilson's Creek, Mo. (1960) 1,750. Civil War battle for control of Missouri.

National Battlefield Parks

Kennesaw Mountain, Ga. (1917) 2,884. Two major battles of Atlanta campaign.

Manassas, Va. (1940) 3,032. Two early Civil War battles.

Richmond, Va. (1936) 746. Site of battles defending Confederate capital.

National Battlefield Sites

Antietam, Md. (1890) 1,800. End of first Confederate invasion of North.

Brices Cross Roads, Miss. (1929) 1. Civil War Battlefield.

National Military Parks

Chickamauga and Chattanooga, Ga.-Tenn. (1890) 8,093. Four Civil War Battlefields.

Fort Donelson, Tenn. (1928) 545. Site of first major Union victory.

Fredericksburg and Spotsylvania County, Va. (1927) 6,019. Sites of several major Civil War battles and campaigns.

Gettysburg, Pa. (1895) 3,864. Major Confederate defeat in North.

Guilford Courthouse, N.C. (1917) 220. Revolutionary War battle site.

Horseshoe Bend, Ala. (1956) 2,040. On Tallapoosa River, place where Gen. Andrew Jackson broke the power of the Creek Indian Confederacy.

Kings Mountain, S.C. (1931) 3,945.Revolutionary War battle.

Moores Creek, N.C. (1926) 77. Pre-Revolutionary War battle.

Pea Ridge, Ark. (1956) 4,300. Civil War battle.

Shiloh, Tenn. (1894) 3,753. Major Civil War battle; site includes some well-preserved Indian burial mounds.

Vicksburg, Miss. (1899) 1,741. Union victory gave North control of the Mississippi and split the Confederacy in two.

National Memorials

Arkansas Post, Ark. (1960) 385. First permanent French settlement in the lower Mississippi River Valley.

Chamizal, El Paso Texas (1966) 55. Commemorates 1963 settlement of 99-year border dispute with Mexico.

Coronado, Ariz. (1952) 2,834. Commemorates first European exploration of the Southwest under Francisco Vasquez Coronado.

DeSoto, Fla. (1948) 30. Commemorates 16th-century Spanish explorations.

Federal Hall, N.Y. (1939) 0.45. First seat of U.S. government under the Constitution.

Fort Caroline, Fla. (1950) 129. On St. Johns River, overlooks site of second attempt by French Huguenots to colonize. N.A.

Fort Clatsop, Ore. (1958) 125. Lewis and Clark encampment 1805-06.

General Grant, N.Y. (1958) 0.76. Tombs of Gen. and wife.

Hamilton Grange, N.Y. (1962) 0.71. Home of Alexander Hamilton.

John F. Kennedy Center for the Performing Arts, D.C. (1972) 18. Memorial to late president.

Johnstown Flood, Pa. (1964) 110. Commemorates tragic flood.

Lincoln Boyhood, Ind. (1962) 200. Farm Lincoln grew up on.

Lincoln Memorial, D.C. (1911) 164.

Lyndon B. Johnson Grove on the Potomac, D.C. (1973) 15. Memorial to late president.

Mount Rushmore, S.D. (1925) 1,278. World famous sculpture of 4 presidents.

Perry's Victory and International Peace Memorial, Ohio (1936) 26. American naval victory, War of 1812.

Roger Williams, R.I. (1965) 5. Memorial to founder of Rhode Island.

Thaddeus Kosciuszko, Pa. (1972) 0.02. Memorial to Polish hero of American Revolution.

Theodore Roosevelt Island, D.C. (1947) 88.5. Woods and statuary honor 25th president.

Thomas Jefferson Memorial, D.C. (1943) 18.

Washington Monument, D.C. (1848) 106.

Wright Brothers, N.C. (1927) 431. Site of first powered flight.

National Historic Sites

Abraham Lincoln Birthplace, Hodgenville, Ky. (1916) 117.

Adams, Quincy, Mass. (1946) 8. Home of Presidents John Adams, John Quincy Adams, and celebrated descendants.

Allegheny Portage Railroad, Pa. (1964) 760. Part of the Pennsylvania Canal system.

Andersonville, Andersonville, Ga. (1970) 488. Noted Civil War prison.

Andrew Johnson, Greeneville, Tenn. (1935) 17. Home of the President.

Bent's Old Fort, Colo. (1960) 178. Old West fur-trading post.

Carl Sandburg Home, N.C. (1968) 247. Poet's farm home for 22 years.

Christiansted, St. Croix; Virgin Islands (1952) 27. Commemorates Danish colony.

Clara Barton, Md. (1974) 1. Home of founder of American Red Cross.

Edison, West Orange, N.J. (1955) 20. Home and laboratory.

Eisenhower, Gettysburg, Pa. (1967) 493. Home of 34th president. Not open to public.

Ford's Theatre, Washington, D.C. (1866) 0.25. Includes theater, now restored, where Lincoln was assassinated, house where he died, and Lincoln Museum.

Fort Bowie, Ariz. (1964) 1,000. Focal point of operations against Geronimo and the Apaches.

Fort Davis, Texas (1961) 460. Frontier outpost battled Comanches and Apaches.

Fort Laramie, Wyo. (1938) 571. Military post on Oregon Trail.

Fort Larned, Kan. (1964) 718. Military post on Sante Fe Trail.

Fort Point, San Francisco, Calif. (1970) 29. Largest West Coast fortification.

Fort Raleigh, N.C. (1941) 159. First English settlement.

Fort Smith, Ark. (1961) 19. Active post from 1817 to 1890.

Fort Union Trading Post, Mont., N.D. (1966) 398. Principal fur-trading post on upper Missouri, 1828-1867.

Fort Vancouver, Wash. (1948) 212. Hdqts. for Hudson's Bay Company in 1825. Early military and political seat of Pacific N.W.

Golden Spike, Utah (1957) 2,203. Commemorates completion of first transcontinental railroad in 1869.

Grant-Kohrs Ranch, Mont. (1972) 1,564. Ranch house and part of 19th century ranch.

Hampton, Md. (1948) 45. 18th-century Georgian mansion.

Herbert Hoover, West Branch, Iowa (1965) 187. Birthplace and boyhood home of 31st president.

Home of Franklin D. Roosevelt, Hyde Park, N.Y. (1944) 188. Birthplace, home and "Summer White House"

Hopewell Village, Pa. (1938) 848. 19th-century iron making village.

Hubbell Trading Post, Ariz. (1965) 160. Indian trading post.

Jefferson National Expansion Memorial, St. Louis, Mo. (1935) 91. Commemorates westward expansion with park and memorial arch.

John Fitzgerald Kennedy, Brookline, Mass. (1967) .09. Birthplace and childhood home of the President.

John Muir, Martinez, Calif. (1964) 9. Home of early conservationist and writer.

Knife River Indian Villages, N.C. (1974) 1,304. Remnants of 5 Hidatsa villages.

Lincoln Home, Springfield, Ill. (1971) 12. Lincoln's residence when he was elected President, 1860.

Longfellow, Cambridge, Mass. (1972) 2. Longfellow's home, 1837-82, and Washington's hq. during Boston Siege, 1775-76. No federal facilities.

Lyndon B. Johnson, Johnson City, Texas (1969) 241. Birthplace and boyhood home of the 36th president.

Mar-A-Largo, Florida (1969) 17. Mansion expresses the affluent Palm Beach life of the 1920s.

Martin Van Buren, N.Y. (1974) 42. Lindenwald, Home of 8th president, near Kingston.

Puukohola Heiau, Hawaii (1972) 77. Ruins of temple built by King Kamehameha.

Sagamore Hill, Oyster Bay, N.Y. (1962) 85. Home of President Theodore Roosevelt from 1885 until his death in 1919.

Saint-Gaudens, Cornish, N.H. (1964) 86. Home, studio and gardens of American sculptor Augustus Saint-Gaudens.

Salem Maritime, Mass. (1938) 9. Only port never seized from the Patriots by the British. Major fishing and whaling port.

San Juan, Puerto Rico (1949) 53. 16th-century Spanish fortifications.

Saugus Iron Works, Mass. (1968) 9. Reconstructed 17th-century colonial ironworks.

Sewall-Belmont House, D.C. (1974) 0.35. National Women's Party headquarters 1929-74.

Springfield Armory, Mass. (1974) 55. Small arms center of world for nearly 200 years.

Theodore Roosevelt Birthplace, N.Y., N.Y. (1962) 0.11.

Theodore Roosevelt Inaugural, Buffalo, N.Y. (1966) 1. Wilcox House where he took oath of office, 1901.

Tuskegee Institute, Ala. (1974) 70. College founded by Booker T. Washington in 1881 for blacks, includes student-made brick buildings.

Vanderbilt Mansion, Hyde Park, N.Y. (1940) 212. Mansion of 19th-century financier.

Whitman Mission, Wash. (1936) 98. Site where Dr. and Mrs. Marcus Whitman ministered to the Indians until slain, 1847.

William Howard Taft, Cincinnati, Ohio (1969) 0.78. Birthplace and early home of the 27th president, 1909-13; Chief Justice, 1921-30.

National Capital Parks

District of Columbia — Maryland — Virginia (1790) 7,052. Includes 367 reservations.

White House

Washington, D.C. (1792) 18. Presidential residence since November 1800.

National Seashores

	State	Year	Acreage
Assateague Island	Md.-Va.	1965	39,631
Canaveral	Fla.	1975	67,500
Cape Cod	Mass.	1961	44,600
Cape Hatteras	N.C.	1937	30,326
Cape Lookout**	N.C.	1966	24,732
Cumberland Island	Ga.	1972	36,876
Fire Island	N.Y.	1964	19,357

Gulf Island, Fla.-Miss. (1971) 142,009. White Sand beaches, primitive off-shore islands, historic forts.

	State	Year	Acreage
Padre Island	Tex.	1962	133,918
Point Reyes	Calif.	1962	65,291

National Lakeshores

Apostle Islands, Wis. (1970) 42,012. Picturesque islands and coastal portion of Bayfield Peninsula on south shore of Lake Superior.

	State	Year	Acreage
Indiana Dunes	Ind.	1966	8,330
Pictured Rocks	Mich.	1966	70,822

Sleeping Bear Dunes, Mich. (1970) 71,105. Notable for its beaches, massive sand dunes, forests, lakes. **Benzie and D. H. Day State Parks open to public.**

National River

	State	Year	Acreage
Buffalo	Ark.	1972	94,146

National Scenic Rivers and Riverways

	State	Year	Acreage
Lower Saint Croix**	Minn.-Wis.	1972	7,845
Ozark	Mo.	1964	79,587
Saint Croix**	Minn.-Wis.	1968	62,728

National Recreation Areas

	State	Year	Acreage
Amistad	Tex.	1965	62,452
Bighorn Canyon	Mont.-Wy.	1964	140,434
Chickasaw	Okla.	1976	9,294
Coulee Dam	Wash.	1946	10,001
Curecanti	Colo.	1965	41,572
Cuyahoga	Oh.	1974	29,112
Delaware Water Gap	N.J.-Pa.	1965	47,676
Gateway	N.Y.-N.J.	1972	26,172
Glen Canyon	Ariz.-Utah	1958	1,235,080
Golden Gate	Calif.	1972	34,938
Lake Chelan	Wash.	1968	61,890
Lake Mead	Ariz.-Nev.	1936	1,492,795
Lake Meredith	Tex.	1965	45,964
Ross Lake	Wash.	1968	117,574
Shadow Mountain	Colo.	1952	19,004
Whiskeytown-Shasta-Trinity	Calif.	1962	42,497

National Scenic Trail

	State	Year	Acreage
Appalachian	Me. to Ga.	1968	52,034

*Not open to the public **No federal facilities

National Monuments

Name	State	Year	Acreage
Agate Fossil Beds	Nebr.	1965	3,054
Alibates Flint Quarries and Texas Panhandle Pueblo Culture	Tex.	1965	93
Aztec Ruins	N.M.	1923	27
Badlands	S.D.	1929	243,302
Bandelier	N.M.	1916	29,661
Biscayne	Fla.	1968	103,701
Black Canyon of the Gunnison	Colo.	1933	13,672
Booker T. Washington	Va.	1956	224
Buck Island Reef	Virgin Isls.	1961	880
Cabrillo	Calif.	1913	144
Canyon de Chelly	Ariz.	1931	83,840
Capulin Mountain	N.M.	1916	775
Casa Grande Ruins	Ariz.	1892	473
Castillo de San Marcos	Fla.	1924	20
Castle Clinton	N.Y.	1946	1
Cedar Breaks	Utah	1933	6,155
Chaco Canyon	N.M.	1907	21,510
Channel Islands	Calif.	1938	18,388
Chiricahua	Ariz.	1924	10,648
Colorado	Colo.	1911	17,669
Craters of the Moon	Idaho	1924	53,545
Custer Battlefield	Mont.	1879	765
Death Valley	Calif.-Nev.	1933	2,067,832
Devils Postpile	Calif.	1911	798
Devils Tower	Wyo.	1906	1,347
Dinosaur	Colo.-Utah	1915	211,051
Effigy Mounds	Iowa	1949	1,475
El Morro	N.M.	1906	1,279
Florissant Fossil Beds**	Colo.	1969	5,992
Fort Frederica	Ga.	1936	215
Fort Jefferson	Fla.	1935	47,125
Fort McHenry National Monument & Historic Shrine.	Md.	1925	43
Fort Matanzas	Fla.	1924	299
Fort Pulaski	Ga.	1924	5,616
Fort Stanwix	N.Y.	1935	16
Fort Sumter	S.C.	1948	64
Fort Union	N.M.	1954	721
Fossil Butte	Wyo.	1972	8,178
G. Washington Birthplace	Va.	1930	456
George Washington Carver	Mo.	1943	210
Gila Cliff Dwellings	N.M.	1907	533
Glacier Bay	Alas.	1925	2,805,269
Grand Portage	Minn.	1951	710
Gran Quivira	N.M.	1909	611
Great Sand Dunes	Colo.	1932	36,827
Hohokam Pima**	Ariz.	1972	1,555
Homestead Nat'l. Monument of America	Nebr.	1936	195
Hovenweep	Colo-Utah.	1923	785
Jewel Cave	S.D.	1908	1,275
John Day Fossil Beds	Ore.	1974	14,402
Joshua Tree	Calif.	1936	559,960
Katmai	Alaska	1918	2,792,137
Lava Beds	Calif.	1925	46,821
Lehman Caves	Nev.	1922	640
Montezuma Castle	Ariz.	1906	842
Mound City Group	Ohio	1923	68
Muir Woods	Calif.	1908	554
Natural Bridges	Utah	1908	7,779
Navajo	Ariz.	1909	360
Ocmulgee	Ga.	1934	683
Oregon Caves	Ore.	1909	466
Organ Pipe Cactus	Ariz.	1937	330,690
Pecos	N.M.	1965	341
Pinnacles	Calif.	1908	14,498
Pipe Spring	Ariz.	1923	40
Pipestone	Minn.	1937	282
Rainbow Bridge	Utah	1910	160
Russell Cave	Ala.	1961	310
Saguaro	Ariz.	1933	78,978
Saint Croix Island**	Me.	1949	35
Scotts Bluff	Nebr.	1919	2,988
Statue of Liberty	N.J.-N.Y.	1924	58
Sunset Crater	Ariz.	1930	3,040
Timpanogos Cave	Utah	1922	250
Tonto	Ariz.	1907	1,120
Tumacacori	Ariz.	1908	10
Tuzigoot	Ariz.	1939	58
Walnut Canyon	Ariz.	1915	2,249
White Sands	N.M.	1933	145,335
Wupatki	Ariz.	1924	35,253
Yucca House*	Colo.	1919	10

Declaration of Independence

The Declaration of Independence as adopted by the Continental Congress in Philadelphia, on July 4, 1776. John Hancock was president of the Congress and Charles Thomson was secretary. A copy of the Declaration, engrossed on parchment, was signed by members of Congress on and after Aug. 2, 1776. On Jan. 18, 1777, Congress ordered that "authenticated copies, with the names of the members of Congress subscribed the same, be sent to each of the United States, and that they be desired to have same put upon record." Authenticated copies were printed in broadside form in Baltimore, where the Continental Congress was then in session. The following text is that of the original printed by John Dunlap at Philadelphia for the Continental Congress.

IN CONGRESS, July 4, 1776.

A DECLARATION

By the REPRESENTATIVES of the

UNITED STATES OF AMERICA,

In GENERAL CONGRESS assembled

When in the Course of human Events, it becomes necessary for one People to dissolve the Political Bands which have connected them with another, and to assume among the Powers of the Earth, the separate and equal Station to which the Laws of Nature and of Nature's God entitle them, a decent Respect to the Opinions of Mankind requires that they should declare the causes which impel them to the Separation.

We hold these Truths to be self-evident, that all Men are created equal, that they are endowed by their Creator with certain unalienable Rights, that among these are Life, Liberty, and the Pursuit of Happiness—That to secure these Rights, Governments are instituted among Men, deriving their just Powers from the Consent of the Governed, that whenever any Form of Government becomes destructive of these Ends, it is the Right of the People to alter or to abolish it, and to institute new Government, laying its Foundation on such Principles, and organizing its Powers in such Form, as to them shall seem most likely to effect their Safety and Happiness. Prudence, indeed, will dictate that Governments long established should not be changed for light and transient Causes; and accordingly all Experience hath shewn, that Mankind are more disposed to suffer, while Evils are sufferable, than to right themselves by abolishing the Forms to which they are accustomed. But when a long Train of Abuses and Usurpations, pursuing invariably the same Object, evinces a Design to reduce them under absolute Despotism, it is their Right, it is their Duty, to throw off such Government, and to provide new Guards for their future Security. Such has been the patient Sufferance of these Colonies; and such is now the Necessity which constrains them to alter their former Systems of Government. The History of the present King of Great-Britain is a History of repeated Injuries and Usurpations, all having in direct Object the Establishment of an absolute Tyranny over these States. To prove this, let Facts be submitted to a candid World.

He has refused his Assent to Laws, the most wholesome and necessary for the public Good.

He has forbidden his Governors to pass Laws of immediate and pressing Importance, unless suspended in their Operation till his Assent should be obtained; and when so suspended, he has utterly neglected to attend to them.

He has refused to pass other Laws for the Accommodation of large Districts of People, unless those People would relinquish the Right of Representation in the Legislature, a Right inestimable to them, and formidable to Tyrants only.

He has called together Legislative Bodies at Places unusual, uncomfortable, and distant from the Depository of their public Records, for the sole Purpose of fatiguing them into Compliance with his Measures.

He has dissolved Representative Houses repeatedly, for opposing with manly Firmness his Invasions on the Rights of the People.

He has refused for a long Time, after such Dissolutions, to cause others to be elected; whereby the Legislative Powers, incapable of Annihilation, have returned to the People at large for their exercise; the State remaining in the mean time exposed to all the Dangers of Invasion from without, and Convulsions within.

He has endeavoured to prevent the Population of these States; for that Purpose obstructing the Laws for Naturalization of Foreigners; refusing to pass others to encourage their Migrations hither, and raising the Conditions of new Appropriations of Lands.

He has obstructed the Administration of Justice, by refusing his Assent to Laws for establising Judiciary Powers.

He has made Judges dependent on his Will alone, for the Tenure of their Offices, and the Amount and payment of their Salaries.

He has erected a Multitude of new Offices, and sent hither Swarms of Officers to harrass our People, and eat out their Substance.

He has kept among us, in Times of Peace, Standing Armies, without the consent of our Legislatures.

He has affected to render the Military independent of and superior to the Civil Power.

He has combined with others to subject us to a Jurisdiction foreign to our Constitution, and unacknowledged by our Laws; giving his Assent to their Acts of pretended Legislation:

For quartering large Bodies of Armed Troops among us:

For protecting them, by a mock Trial, from Punishment for any Murders which they should commit on the Inhabitants of these States:

For cutting off our Trade with all Parts of the World:

For imposing Taxes on us without our Consent:

For depriving us, in many Cases, of the Benefits of Trial by Jury:

For transporting us beyond Seas to be tried for pretended Offences:

For abolishing the free System of English Laws in a neighbouring Province, establishing therein an arbitrary Government, and enlarging its Boundaries, so as to render it at once an Example and fit Instrument for introducing the same absolute Rule into these Colonies:

For taking away our Charters, abolishing our most valuable Laws, and altering fundamentally the Forms of our Governments:

For suspending our own Legislatures, and declaring themselves invested with Power to legislate for us in all Cases whatsoever.

He has abdicated Government here, by declaring us out of his Protection and waging War against us.

He has plundered our Seas, ravaged our Coasts, burnt our towns, and destroyed the Lives of our People.

He is, at this Time, transporting large Armies of foreign Mercenaries to compleat the works of Death, Desolation, and Tyranny, already begun with circumstances of Cruelty and Perfidy, scarcely paralleled in the most barbarous Ages, and totally unworthy the Head of a civilized Nation.

He has constrained our fellow Citizens taken Captive on the high Seas to bear Arms against their Country, to become the Executioners of their Friends and Brethren, or to fall themselves by their Hands.

He has excited domestic Insurrections amongst us, and has endeavoured to bring on the Inhabitants of our Frontiers, the merciless Indian Savages, whose known Rule of Warfare, is an undistinguished Destruction, of all Ages, Sexes and Conditions.

In every stage of these Oppressions we have Petitioned for Redress in the most humble Terms: Our repeated Petitions have been answered only by repeated Injury. A Prince, whose Character is thus marked by every act which may define a Tyrant, is unfit to be the Ruler of a free People.

Nor have we been wanting in Attentions to our British Brethren. We have warned them from Time to Time of Attempts by their Legislature to extend an unwarrantable Jurisdiction over us. We have reminded them of the Circumstances of our Emigration and Settlement here. We have appealed to their native Justice and Magnanimity, and we have conjured them by the Ties of our common Kindred to disavow these Usurpations, which, would inevitably interrupt our Connections and Correspondence. They too have been deaf to the Voice of Justice and of Consanguinity. We must, therefore, acquiesce in the Necessity, which denounces our Separation, and hold them, as we hold the rest of Mankind, Enemies in War, in Peace. Friends.

We, therefore, the Representatives of the UNITED STATES OF AMERICA, in General Congress, Assembled, appealing to the Supreme Judge of the World in the Rectitude of our Intentions, do, in the Name, and by Authority of the good People of these Colonies, solemnly Publish and Declare, That these United Colonies are, and of Right ought to be, Free and Independent States; that they are absolved from all Allegiance to the British Crown, and that all political Connection between them and the State of Great-Britain, is and ought to be totally dissolved; and that as Free and Independent States, they have full Power to levy War, conclude Peace, contract Alliances, establish Commerce, and to do all other Acts and Things which Independent States may of right do. And for the support of this declaration, with a firm Reliance on the Protection of divine Providence, we mutually pledge to each other our lives, our Fortunes, and our sacred Honor.

JOHN HANCOCK, President.

Attest.
CHARLES THOMSON, Secretary.

Signers of the Declaration of Independence

Delegate and State	Vocation	Birthplace	Born		Died	
Adams, John (Mass.)	Lawyer	Braintree (Quincy), Mass.	1735, Oct.	30	1826, July	4
Adams, Samuel (Mass.)	Political Leader	Boston, Mass.	1722, Sept.	27	1803, Oct.	2
Bartlett, Josiah (N. H.)	Physician, Judge	Amesbury, Mass.	1729, Nov.	21	1795, May	19
Braxton, Carter (Va.)	Farmer	Newington, Va.	1736, Sept.	10	1797, Oct.	10
Carroll, Chas. of Carrollton (Md.)	Lawyer	Annapolis, Md.	1737, Sept.	19	1832, Nov.	14
Chase, Samuel (Md.)	Judge	Princess Anne, Md.	1741, Apr.	17	1811, June	19
Clark, Abraham (N. J.)	Surveyor	Elizabeth, N. J.	1726, Feb.	15	1794, Sept.	15
Clymer, George (Pa.)	Merchant	Philadelphia, Pa.	1739, Mar.	16	1813, Jan.	23
Ellery, William (R. I.)	Judge	Newport, R. I.	1727, Dec.	22	1820, Feb.	15
Floyd, William (N. Y.)	Soldier	Brookhaven, N. Y.	1734, Dec.	17	1821, Aug.	4
Franklin, Benjamin (Pa.)	Printer, Publisher	Boston, Mass.	1706, Jan.	17	1790, Apr.	17
Gerry, Elbridge (Mass.)	Merchant	Marblehead, Mass.	1744, July	17	1814, Nov.	23
Gwinnett, Button (Ga.)	Merchant	Down Hatherly, England	1732		1777, May	19
Hall, Lyman (Ga.)	Physician	Wallingford, Conn.	1724, Apr.	12	1790, Oct.	19
Hancock, John (Mass.)	Merchant	Braintree (Quincy), Mass.	1737, Jan.	12	1793, Oct.	8
Harrison, Benjamin (Va.)	Farmer	Berkeley, Va.	1726, Apr.	5	1791, Apr.	24
Hart, John (N. J.)	Farmer	Stonington, Conn.	(1707-1711?)		1779, May	11
Hewes, Joseph (N. C.)	Merchant	Kingston, N. J.	1730, Jan.	23	1779, Nov.	10
Heyward, Thos. Jr. (S. C.)	Lawyer, Farmer	St. Luke's Parish, S. C.	1746, July	28	1809, Mar.	6
Hooper, William (N. C.)	Lawyer	Boston, Mass.	1742, June	28	1790, Oct.	14
Hopkins, Stephen (R. I.)	Judge, Educator	Providence, R. I.	1707, Mar.	7	1785, July	13
Hopkinson, Francis (N. J.)	Judge, Author	Philadelphia, Pa.	1737, Sept.	21	1791, May	9
Huntington, Samuel (Conn.)	Judge	Windham County, Conn.	1731, July	3	1796, Jan.	5
Jefferson, Thomas (Va.)	Lawyer	Old Shadwell, Va.	1743, Apr.	13	1826, July	4
Lee, Francis Lightfoot (Va.)	Farmer	Stratford, Va.	1734, Oct.	14	1797, Jan.	11
Lee, Richard Henry (Va.)	Farmer	Stratford, Va.	1732, Jan.	20	1794, June	19
Lewis, Francis (N. Y.)	Merchant	Landaff, Wales	1713, Mar.		1803, Dec.	30
Livingston, Philip (N. Y.)	Merchant	Albany, N. Y.	1716, Jan.	15	1778, June	12
Lynch, Thomas Jr. (S. C.)	Farmer	Winyah, S. C.	1749, Aug.	5	1779, (at sea)	
McKean, Thomas (Del.)	Lawyer	New London, Pa.	1734, Mar.	19	1817, June	24
Middleton, Arthur (S. C.)	Farmer	Charleston, S. C.	1742, June	26	1787, Jan.	1
Morris, Lewis (N.Y.)	Farmer	Morisania, N. Y. (N.Y.C.)	1726, Apr.	8	1798, Jan.	22
Morris, Robert (Pa.)	Merchant	Liverpool, England	1734, Jan.	20	1806, May	9
Morton, John (Pa.)	Judge	Ridley, Pa.	1724		1777, Apr.	
Nelson, Thos. Jr. (Va.)	Farmer	Yorktown, Va.	1738, Dec.	26	1789, Jan.	4
Paca, William (Md.)	Judge	Abingdon, Md.	1740, Oct.	31	1799, Oct.	23
Paine, Robert Treat (Mass.)	Judge	Boston, Mass.	1731, Mar.	11	1814, May	12
Penn, John (N. C.)	Lawyer	Near Port Royal, Va.	1741, May	17	1788, Sept.	14
Read, George (Del.)	Judge	Near North East, Md.	1733, Sept.	18	1798, Sept.	21
Rodney, Caesar (Del.)	Judge	Dover, Del.	1728, Oct.	7	1784, June	29
Ross, George (Pa.)	Judge	New Castle, Del.	1730, May	10	1779, July	14
Rush, Benjamin (Pa.)	Physician	Byberry, Pa. (Philadelphia)	1745, Dec.	24	1813, April	19
Rutedge, Edward (S. C.)	Lawyer	Charleston, S. C.	1749, Nov.	23	1800, Jan.	23
Sherman, Roger (Conn.)	Lawyer	Newton, Mass.	1721, Apr.	19	1793, July	23
Smith, James (Pa.)	Lawyer	Dublin, Ireland	1713		1806, July	11
Stockton, Richard (N. J.)	Lawyer	Near Princeton, N. J.	1730, Oct.	1	1781, Feb.	28
Stone, Thomas (Md.)	Lawyer	Charles County, Md.	1743		1787, Oct.	5
Taylor, George (Pa.)	Ironmaster	Ireland	1716		1781, Feb.	23
Thornton, Matthew (N. H.)	Physician	Ireland	1714		1803, June	24
Walton, George (Ga.)	Judge	Prince Edward County, Va.	1741		1804, Feb.	2
Whipple, William (N. H.)	Merchant, Judge	Kittery, Me.	1730, Jan.	14	1785, Nov.	28
Williams, William (Conn.)	Merchant	Lebanon, Conn.	1731, Apr.	23	1811, Aug.	2
Wilson, James (Pa.)	Judge	Carskerdo, Scotland	1742, Sept.	14	1798, Aug.	28
Witherspoon, John (N. J.)	Educator	Gifford, Scotland	1723, Feb.	5	1794, Nov.	15
Wolcott, Oliver (Conn.)	Judge	Windsor, Conn.	1726, Dec.	1	1797, Dec.	1
Wythe, George (Va.)	Lawyer	Elizabeth City, Va.	1726		1806, June	8

How the Declaration of Independence Was Adopted

On June 7, 1776, Richard Henry Lee, who had issued the first call for a congress of the colonies, introduced in the Continental Congress at Philadelphia a resolution declaring "that these United Colonies are, and of right ought to be, free and independent states, that they are absolved from allegiance to the British Crown, and that all political connection between them and the state of Great Britain is, and ought to be, totally dissolved."

The resolution, seconded by John Adams on behalf of the Massachusetts delegation, came up again June 10 when a committee of 5, headed by Thomas Jefferson, was appointed to express the purpose of the resolution in a declaration of independence. The others on the committee were John Adams, Benjamin Franklin, Robert R. Livingston, and Roger Sherman.

Drafting the Declaration was assigned to Jefferson, who worked on a portable desk of his own construction in a room at Market and 7th Sts. The committee reported the result June 28, 1776. The members of the Congress suggested a number of changes, which Jefferson called "deplorable." They didn't approve Jefferson's arraignment of the British people and King George III for encouraging and fostering the slave trade, which Jefferson called "an execrable commerce." They made 86 changes, eliminating 480 words and leaving 1,337. In the final form capitalization was erratic. Jefferson had written that men were endowed with "inalienable" rights; in the final copy it came out as "unalienable" and has been thus ever since.

The Lee-Adams resolution of independence was adopted by 12 yeas July 2 — the actual date of the act of independence. The Declaration, which explains the act, was adopted July 4, in the evening.

After the Declaration was adopted, July 4, 1776, it was turned over to John Dunlap, printer, to be printed on broadsides. The original copy was lost and one of his broadsides was attached to a page in the journal of the Congress. It was read aloud July 8 in Philadelphia, Easton, Pa., and Trenton, N. J. On July 9 at 6 p.m. it was read by order of Gen. George Washington to the troops assembled on the Common in New York City (City Hall Park).

The Continental Congress on July 19, 1776, adopted the following resolution:

"Resolved, That the Declaration passed on the 4th, be fairly engrossed on parchment with the title and stile of "The Unanimous Declaration of the thirteen United States of America' and that the same, when engrossed, be signed by every member of Congress."

Not all delegates who signed the engrossed Declaration were present on July 4. Robert Morris (Pa.), William Williams (Conn.) and Samuel Chase (Md.) signed on Aug. 2, Oliver Wolcott (Conn.), George Wythe (Va.), Richard Henry Lee (Va.) and Elbridge Gerry (Mass.) signed in August and September. Matthew Thronton (N. H.) joined the Congress Nov. 4 and signed later. Thomas McKean (Del.) rejoined Washington's Army before signing and said later that he signed in 1781.

Charles Carroll of Carrollton was appointed a delegate by Maryland on July 4, 1776, presented his credentials July 18, and signed the engrossed Declaration Aug. 2. Born Sept. 19, 1737, he was 95 years old and the last surviving signer when he died Nov. 14, 1832.

Two Pennsylvania delegates who did not support the Declaration on July 4 were replaced.

The 4 New York delegates did not have authority from their state to vote on July 4. On July 9 the New York state convention authorized its delegates to approve the Declaration and the Congress was so notified on July 15, 1776. The 4 signed the Declaration on Aug. 2.

The original engrossed Declaration is preserved in the National Archives Building in Washington.

Independence Hall, American Patriotic Shrine

Independence Hall is the central and main building of a group in Philadelphia, located in Independence Square and facing Chestnut St. It is connected with arcades with 2 buildings, the East and West Wings, and 2 separate corner buildings. Of the latter, Congress Hall is at 6th St., and Old City Hall at 5th St.

Independence Hall originally was the State House. It was begun in 1732, and completed in 1759. The East and West Wings were intended to house offices. Tower and spire were completed by June 1753.

The Pennsylvania Assembly occupied Assembly Hall in 1735, before the whole structure was completed. In 1775 it gave the use of the room to the Second Continental Congress. Here, on June 16, 1775, George Washington accepted command of the Continental Army. Here the Declaration of Independence was adopted on July 4, 1776; the Articles of Confederation and Perpetual Union were signed beginning on July 9, 1778, and the Constitution of the United States was framed by the Constitutional Convention in 1787.

Congress Hall, at the west end of the group, was erected in 1787 and was the seat of the United States Congress from 1790 to 1800, when the Congress moved to Washington, D.C. The Court House, or Old City Hall, at the east end, was built in 1790 for the municipal courts, and was the first seat of the United States Supreme Court.

Independence Hall and the other buildings in Independence Square form the nucleus around which has been developed the Independence National Historical Park, established in 1956. Much restoration work has been done.

The Liberty Bell; Its History and Significance

The Liberty Bell, in Independence Hall, Philadelphia, is an object of great reverence to Americans because of its association with the historic events of the War of Independence.

The original Province bell, ordered to commemorate the 50th anniversary of the Commonwealth of Pennsylvania, was cast by Thomas Lister, Whitechapel, London, and reached Philadelphia in Aug. 1752. It bore an inscription from Leviticus XXV, 10: "Proclaim liberty throughout all the land unto all the inhabitants thereof."

The bell was cracked by a stroke of its clapper in Sept. 1752 while it hung on a truss in the State House yard for testing. Pass & Stow, Philadelphia founders, recast the bell, adding 1 1/2 ounces of copper to a pound of the original metal to reduce brittleness. It was found that the bell contained too much copper, injuring its tone, so Pass & Stow recast it again, this time successfully.

In June 1753 the bell was hung in the wooden steeple of the State House, erected on top of the brick tower. In use while the Continental Congress was in session in the State House, it rang out in defiance of British tax and trade restrictions, and proclaimed the Boston Tea Party and the first public reading of the Declaration of Independence.

On Sept. 18, 1777, when the British Army was about to occupy Philadelphia, the bell was moved in a baggage train of the American Army to Allentown, Pa., where it was hidden in the Zion Reformed Church until June 27, 1778. It was moved back to Philadelphia after the British left.

In July 1781 the wooden steeple became insecure and had to be taken down. The bell was lowered into the brick section of the tower. Here it was hanging in July, 1835, when it cracked while tolling for the funeral of John Marshall, chief justice of the United States. Because of its association with the War of Independence it was not recast but remained mute in this location until 1846, the year of the Mexican War, when it was placed on exhibition in the Declaration Chamber of Independence Hall.

In 1876, when many thousands of Americans visited Philadelphia for the Centennial Exposition, it was placed in its old walnut frame in the tower hallway. In 1877 it was hung from the ceiling of the tower by a chain of 13 links. It was returned again to the Declaration Chamber and in 1896 taken back to the tower hall, where it occupied a glass case. In 1915 the case was removed so that the public might

continued on page 475

Constitution of the United States

The Original Seven Articles

PREAMBLE

We, the people of the United States, in order to form a more perfect Union, establish justice, insure domestic tranquility, provide for the common defense, promote the general welfare, and secure the blessings of liberty to ourselves and our posterity, do ordain and establish this Constitution for the United States of America.

ARTICLE 1.
Section 1 —Legislative powers; in whom vested:

All legislative powers herein granted shall be vested in a Congress of the United States, which shall consist of a Senate and House of Representatives.

Section 2 —House of Representatives, how and by whom chosen. Qualifications of a Representative. Representatives and direct taxes, how apportioned. Enumeration. Vacancies to be filled. Power of choosing officers, and of impeachment.

1. The House of Representatives shall be composed of members chosen every second year by the people of the several States, and the electors in each State shall have the qualifications requisite for electors of the most numerous branch of the State Legislature.

2. No person shall be a Representative who shall not have attained to the age of twenty-five years, and been seven years a citizen of the United States, and who shall not, when elected, be an inhabitant of that State in which he shall be chosen.

3. *(Representatives and direct taxes shall be apportioned among the several States which may be included within this Union, according to their respective numbers, which shall be determined by adding to the whole number of free persons, including those bound to service for a term of years, and excluding Indians not taxed, three-fifths of all other persons.) (The previous sentence was superseded by Amendment XIV, section 2.)* The actual enumeration shall be made within three years after the first meeting of the Congress of the United States, and within every subsequent term of ten years, in such manner as they shall by law direct. The number of Representatives shall not exceed one for every thirty thousand, but each State shall have at least one Representative; and until such enumeration shall be made, the State of New Hampshire shall be entitled to choose three, Massachusetts eight, Rhode Island and Providence Plantations one, Connecticut five, New York six, New Jersey four, Pennsylvania eight, Delaware one, Maryland six; Virginia ten, North Carolina five, South Carolina five, and Georgia three.

4. When vacancies happen in the representation from any State, the Executive Authority thereof shall issue writs of election to fill such vacancies.

5. The House of Representatives shall choose their Speaker and other officers; and shall have the sole power of impeachment.

Section 3—Senators, how and by whom chosen. How classified. Qualifications of a Senator, President of the Senate, his right to vote. President pro tem., and other officers of the Senate, how chosen. Power to try impeachments. When President is tried, Chief Justice to preside. Sentence.

1. The Senate of the United States shall be composed of two Senators from each State. *(chosen by the Legislature thereof,) (The preceding five words were superseded by Amendment XVII, section 1.)* for six years; and each Senator shall have one vote.

2. Immediately after they shall be assembled in consequence of the first election, they shall be divided as equally as may be into three classes. The seats of the Senators of the first class shall be vacated at the expiration of the second year, of the second class at the expiration of the fourth year, and of the third class at the expiration of the sixth year, so that one-third may be chosen every second year; *(and if vacancies happen by resignation, or otherwise, dur-*

Origin of the Constitution

The War of Independence was conducted by delegates from the original 13 states, called the Congress of the United States of America and generally known as the Continental Congress. In 1777 the Congress submitted to the legislatures of the states the Articles of Confederation and Perpetual Union, which were ratified by New Hampshire, Massachusetts, Rhode Island, Connecticut, New York, New Jersey, Pennsylvania, Delaware, Virginia, North Carolina, South Carolina, and Georgia, and finally, in 1781, by Maryland.

The first article of the instrument read: "The stile of this confederacy shall be the United States of America." This did not signify a sovereign nation, because the states delegated only those powers they could not handle individually, such as power to wage war, establish a uniform currency, make treaties with foreign nations and contract debts for general expenses (such as paying the army). Taxes for the payment of such debts were levied by the individual states. The president under the Articles signed himself "President of the United States in Congress assembled," but here the United States were considered in the plural, a cooperating group. Canada was invited to join the union on equal terms but did not act.

When the war was won it became evident that a stronger federal union was needed to protect the mutual interests of the states. The Congress left the initiative to the legislatures. Virginia in Jan. 1786 appointed commissioners to meet with representatives of other states, with the result that delegates from Virginia, Delaware, New York, New Jersey, and Pennsylvania met at Annapolis. Alexander Hamilton prepared for their call by asking delegates from all states to meet in Philadelphia in May 1787 "to render the Constitution of the Federal government adequate to the exigencies of the union." Congress endorsed the plan Feb. 21, 1787. Delegates were appointed by all states except Rhode Island.

The convention met May 14, 1787. George Washington was chosen president (presiding officer). The states certified 65 delegates, but 10 did not attend. The work was done by 55, not all of whom were present at all sessions. Of the 55 attending delegates, 16 failed to sign, and 39 actually signed Sept. 17, 1787, some with reservations. Some historians have said 74 delegates (9 more than the 65 actually certified) were named and 19 failed to attend. These 9 additional persons refused the appointment, were never delegates and never counted as absentees. Washington sent the Constitution to Congress with a covering letter and that body, Sept. 28, 1787, ordered it sent to the legislatures, "in order to be submitted to a convention of delegates chosen in each state by the people thereof."

The Constitution was ratified by votes of state conventions as follows: Delaware, Dec. 7, 1787, unanimous; Pennsylvania, Dec. 12, 1787, 43 to 23; New Jersey, Dec. 18, 1787, unanimous; Georgia, Jan. 2, 1788, unanimous; Connecticut, Jan. 9, 1788, 128 to 40; Massachusetts, Feb. 6, 1788, 187 to 168; Maryland, Apr. 28, 1788, 63 to 11; South Carolina, May 23, 1788, 149 to 73; New Hampshire, June 21, 1788, 57 to 46; Virginia, June 25, 1788, 89 to 79; New York, July 26, 1788, 30 to 27. Nine states were needed to establish the operation of the Constitution "between the states so ratifying the same" and New Hampshire was the 9th state. The government did not declare the Constitution in effect until the first Wednesday in Mar. 1789 which was Mar. 4. After that North Carolina ratified it Nov. 21, 1789, 197 to 77; and Rhode Island May 29, 1790, 34 to 32. Vermont in convention ratified it Jan. 10, 1791, and by act of Congress approved Feb. 19, 1791, was admitted into the Union as the 14th state, Mar. 4, 1791.

ing the recess of the Legislature of any State, the Executive thereof may make temporary appointments until the next meeting of the Legislature, which shall then fill such vacancies.) (The words in parenthesis were superseded by Amendment XVII, section 1.)

3. No person shall be a Senator who shall not have attained to the age of thirty years, and been nine years a citizen of the United States, and who shall not, when elected, be an inhabitant of that State for which he shall be chosen.

4. The Vice President of the United States shall be President of the Senate, but shall have no vote, unless they be equally divided.

5. The Senate shall choose their other officers, and also a President pro tempore, in the absence of the Vice President, or when he shall exercise the office of President of the United States.

6. The Senate shall have the sole power to try all impeachments. When sitting for that purpose, they shall be on oath or affirmation. When the President of the United States is tried, the Chief Justice shall preside: and no person shall be convicted without the concurrence of two-thirds of the members present.

7. Judgment in cases of impeachment shall not extend further than to removal from office, and disqualification to hold and enjoy any office of honor, trust or profit under the United States: but the party convicted shall nevertheless be liable and subject to indictment, trial, judgment and punishment, according to law.

Section 4—Times, etc., of holding elections, how prescribed. One session in each year.

1. The times, places and manner of holding elections for Senators and Representatives, shall be prescribed in each State by the Legislature thereof; but the Congress may at any time by law make or alter such regulations, except as to the places of choosing Senators.

2. The Congress shall assemble at least once in every year, and such meeting shall (be on the first Monday in December.) (The words in parenthesis were superseded by Amendment XX, section 2). unless they shall by law appoint a different day.

Section 5—Membership, quorum, adjournments, rules. Power to punish or expel, Journal. Time of adjournments, how limited, etc.

1. Each House shall be the judge of the elections, returns and qualifications of its own members, and a majority of each shall constitute a quorum to do business; but a smaller number may adjourn from day to day, and may be authorized to compel the attendance of absent members, in such manner, and under such penalties as each House may provide.

2. Each House may determine the rules of its proceedings, punish its members for disorderly behavior, and, with the concurrence of two-thirds, expel a member.

3. Each House shall keep a journal of its proceedings, and from time to time publish the same, excepting such parts as may in their judgment require secrecy; and the yeas and nays of the members of either House on any question shall, at the desire of one-fifth of those present, be entered on the journal.

4. Neither House, during the session of Congress, shall, without the consent of the other, adjourn for more than three days, nor to any other place than that in which the two Houses shall be sitting.

Section 6—Compensation, privileges, disqualifications in certain cases.

1. The Senators and Representatives shall receive a compensation for their services, to be ascertained by law, and paid out of the Treasury of the United States. They shall in all cases, except treason, felony and breach of the peace, be privileged from arrest during their attendance at the session of their respective Houses, and in going to and returning from the same; and for any speech or debate in either House, they shall not be questioned in any other place.

2. No Senator or Representative shall, during the time for which he was elected, be appointed to any civil office under the authority of the United States, which shall have been created, or the emoluments whereof shall have been increased during such time; and no person holding any office under the United States, shall be a member of either House during his continuance in office.

Section 7—House to originate all revenue bills. Veto. Bill may be passed by two-thirds of each House, notwithstanding, etc. Bill, not returned in ten days, to become a law. Provisions as to orders, concurrent resolutions, etc.

1. All bills for raising revenue shall originate in the House of Representatives; but the Senate may propose or concur with amendments as on other bills.

2. Every bill which shall have passed the House of Representatives and the Senate, shall, before it becomes a law, be presented to the President of the United States; if he approves he shall sign it, but if not he shall return it, with his objections to that House in which it shall have originated, who shall enter the objections at large on their journal, and proceed to reconsider it. If after such reconsideration two-thirds of that House shall agree to pass the bill, it shall be sent, together with the objections, to the other House, by which it shall likewise be reconsidered, and if approved by two-thirds of that House, it shall become a law. But in all such cases the votes of both Houses shall be determined by yeas and nays, and the names of the persons voting for and against the bill shall be entered on the journal of each House respectively. If any bill shall not be returned by the President within ten days (Sundays excepted) after it shall have been presented to him, the same shall be a law, in like manner as if he had signed it, unless the Congress by their adjournment prevent its return, in which case it shall not be a law.

3. Every order, resolution, or vote to which the concurrence of the Senate and House of Representatives may be necessary (except on a question of adjournment) shall be presented to the President of the United States; and before the same shall take effect, shall be approved by him, or being disapproved by him, shall be repassed by two-thirds of the Senate and House of Representatives, according to the rules and limitations prescribed in the case of a bill.

Section 8—Powers of Congress.

The Congress shall have power

1. To lay and collect taxes, duties, imposts and excises, to pay the debts and provide for the common defense and general welfare of the United States; but all duties, imposts and excises shall be uniform throughout the United States;

2. To borrow money on the credit of the United States;

3. To regulate commerce with foreign nations, and among the several States, and with the Indian tribes;

4. To establish a uniform rule of naturalization, and uniform laws on the subject of bankruptcies throughout the United States;

5. To coin money, regulate the value thereof, and of foreign coin, and fix the standard of weights and measures;

6. To provide for the punishment of counterfeiting the securities and current coin of the United States;

7. To establish post-offices and post-roads;

8. To promote the progress of science and useful arts, by securing for limited times to authors and inventors the exclusive right to their respective writings and discoveries;

9. To constitute tribunals inferior to the Supreme Court;

10. To define and punish piracies and felonies committed on the high seas, and offenses against the law of nations;

11. To declare war, grant letters of marque and reprisal, and make rules concerning captures on land and water;

12. To raise and support armies, but no appropriation of money to that use shall be for a longer term than two years;

13. To provide and maintain a navy;

14. To make rules for the government and regulation of the land and naval forces;

15. To provide for calling forth the militia to execute the laws of the Union, suppress insurrections and repel invasions;

16. To provide for organizing, arming, and disciplining the militia, and for governing such part of them as may be employed in the service of the United States, reserving to the States respectively, the appointment of the officers and the authority of training and militia according to the discipline prescribed by Congress;

17. To exercise exclusive legislation in all cases whatsoever, over such district (not exceeding ten miles square

as may, by cession of particular States, and the acceptance of Congress, become the seat of the Government of the United States, and to exercise like authority over all places purchased by the consent of the Legislature of the State in which the same shall be, for the erection of forts, magazines, arsenals, dockyards, and other needful buildings; — And

18. To make all laws which shall be necessary and proper for carrying into execution the foregoing powers, and all other powers vested by this Constitution in the Government of the United States, or in any department or officer thereof.

Section 9—Provision as to migration or importation of certain persons. Habeas corpus, bills of attainder, etc. Taxes, how apportioned. No export duty. No commercial preference. Money, how drawn from Treasury, etc. No titular nobility. Officers not to receive presents, etc.

1. The migration or importation of such persons as any of the States now existing shall think proper to admit, shall not be prohibited by the Congress prior to the year one thousand eight hundred and eight, but a tax or duty may be imposed on such importation, not exceeding ten dollars for each person.

2. The privilege of the writ of habeas corpus shall not be suspended, unless then in cases of rebellion or invasion the public safety may require it.

3. No bill of attainder or ex post facto law shall be passed.

4. No capitation, or other direct, tax shall be laid, unless in proportion to the census or enumeration herein before directed to be taken. (Modified by Amendment XVI.)

5. No tax or duty shall be laid on articles exported from any State.

6. No preference shall be given by any regulation of commerce or revenue to the ports of one State over those of another: nor shall vessels bound to, or from, one State, be obliged to enter, clear, or pay duties in another.

7. No money shall be drawn from the Treasury, but in consequence of appropriations made by law; and a regular statement and account of the receipts and expenditures of all public money shall be published from time to time.

8. No title of nobility shall be granted by the United States: and no person holding any office of profit or trust under them, shall, without the consent of the Congress, accept of any present, emolument, office, or title, of any kind whatever, from any king, prince, or foreign state.

Section 10—States prohibited from the exercise of certain powers.

1. No State shall enter into any treaty, alliance, or confederation; grant letters of marque and reprisal; coin money; emit bills of credit; make anything but gold and silver coin a tender in payment of debts; pass any bill of attainder, ex post facto law, or law impairing the obligation of contracts, or grant any title of nobility.

2. No State shall, without the consent of the Congress, lay any imposts or duties on imports or exports, except what may be absolutely necessary for executing its inspection laws: and the net produce of all duties and imposts, laid by any State on imports or exports, shall be for the use of the Treasury of the United States; and all such laws shall be subject to the revision and control of the Congress.

3. No State shall, without the consent of Congress, lay any duty of tonnage, keep troops, or ships of war in time of peace, enter into any agreement or compact with another State, or with a foreign power, or engage in war, unless actually invaded, or in such imminent danger as will not admit of delay.

ARTICLE II.

Section 1—President: his term of office. Electors of President; number and how appointed. Electors to vote on same day. Qualification of President. On whom his duties devolve in case of his removal, death, etc. President's compensation. His oath of office.

1. The Executive power shall be vested in a President of the United States of America. He shall hold his office during the term of four years, and together with the Vice President, chosen for the same term, be elected as follows

2. Each State shall appoint, in such manner as the Legislature thereof may direct, a number of electors, equal to the whole number of Senators and Representatives to which the State may be entitled in the Congress: but no Senator or Representative, or person holding an office of trust or profit under the United States, shall be appointed an elector.

(The electors shall meet in their respective States, and vote by ballot for two persons, of whom one at least shall not be an inhabitant of the same State with themselves. And they shall make a list of all the persons voted for, and of the number of votes for each; which list they shall sign and certify, and transmit sealed to the seat of the Government of the United States, directed to the President of the Senate. The President of the Senate shall, in the presence of the Senate and House of Representatives, open all the certificates, and the votes shall then be counted. The person having the greatest number of votes shall be the President, if such number be a majority of the whole number of electors appointed; and if there be more than one who have such majority, and have an equal number of votes, then the House of Representatives shall immediately choose by ballot one of them for President; and if no person have a majority, then from the five highest on the list the said House shall in like manner choose the President. But in choosing the President, the votes shall be taken by States, the representation from each State having one vote; a quorum for this purpose shall consist of a member or members from two-thirds of the States, and a majority of all the States shall be necessary to a choice. In every case, after the choice of the President, the person having the greatest number of votes of the electors shall be the Vice President. But if there should remain two or more who have equal votes, the Senate shall choose from them by ballot the Vice President.)

(This clause was superseded by Amendment XII.)

3. The Congress may determine the time of choosing the electors, and the day on which they shall give their votes; which day shall be the same throughout the United States.

4. No person except a natural born citizen, or a citizen of the United States, at the time of the adoption of this Constitution, shall be eligible to the office of President; neither shall any person be eligible to that office who shall not have attained to the age of thirty-five years, and been fourteen years a resident within the United States.

(For qualification of the Vice President, see Amendment XII.)

5. In case of the removal of the President from office, or of his death, resignation, or inability to discharge the powers and duties of the said office, the same shall devolve on the Vice President, and the Congress may by law provide for the case of removal, death, resignation or inability, both of the President and Vice President, declaring what officer shall then act as President, and such officer shall act accordingly, until the disability be removed, or a President shall be elected.

(This clause has been modified by Amendment XX, sections 3 and 4).

6. The President shall, at stated times, receive for his services, a compensation, which shall neither be increased nor diminished during the period for which he shall have been elected, and he shall not receive within that period any other emolument from the United States, or any of them.

7. Before he enter on the execution of his office, he shall take the following oath or affirmation:

"I do solemnly swear (or affirm) that I will faithfully execute the office of President of the United States, and will to the best of my ability, preserve, protect and defend the Constitution of the United States."

Section 2—President to be Commander-in-Chief. He may require opinions of cabinet officers, etc., may pardon. Treaty-making power. Nomination of certain officers. When President may fill vacancies.

1. The President shall be Commander-in-Chief of the Army and Navy of the United States, and of the militia of the several States, when called into the actual service of the United States; he may require the opinion, in writing, of the principal officer in each of the executive departments, upon any subject relating to the duties of their respective offices, and he shall have power to grant reprieves and pardons for offenses against the United States, except in cases of impeachment.

2. He shall have power, by and with the advice and consent of the Senate, to make treaties, provided two-thirds of the Senators present concur; and he shall nominate, and by and with the advice and consent of the Senate, shall appoint ambassadors, other public ministers and consuls, judges of the Supreme Court, and all other officers of the United States, whose appointments are not herein otherwise provided for, and which shall be established by law: but the Congress may by law vest the appointment of such inferior officers, as they think proper, in the President alone, in the courts of law, or in the heads of departments.

3. The President shall have power to fill up all vacancies that may happen during the recess of the Senate, by granting commissions, which shall expire at the end of their next session.

Section 3—President shall communicate to Congress. He may convene and adjourn Congress, in case of disagreement, etc. Shall receive ambassadors, execute laws, and commission officers.

He shall from time to time give to the Congress information of the state of the Union, and recommend to their consideration such measures as he shall judge necessary and expedient; he may, on extraordinary occasions, convene both Houses, or either of them, and in case of disagreement between them, with respect to the time of adjournment, he may adjourn them to such time as he shall think proper; he shall receive ambassadors and other public ministers; he shall take care that the laws be faithfully executed, and shall commission all the officers of the United States.

Section 4—All civil offices forfeited for certain crimes.

The President, Vice President, and all civil officers of the United States, shall be removed from office on impeachment for, and conviction of, treason, bribery, or other high crimes and misdemeanors.

ARTICLE III.

Section 1—Judicial powers, Tenure. Compensation.

The judicial power of the United States, shall be vested in one Supreme Court, and in such inferior courts as the Congress may from time to time ordain and establish. The judges, both of the Supreme and inferior courts, shall hold their offices during good behavior, and shall at stated times, receive for their services, a compensation, which shall not be diminished during their continuance in office.

Section 2—Judicial power; to what cases it extends. Original jurisdiction of Supreme Court; appellate jurisdiction. Trial by jury, etc. Trial, where.

1. The judicial power shall extend to all cases, in law and equity, arising under this Constitution, the laws of the United States, and treaties made, or which shall be made, under their authority; to all cases affecting ambassadors, other public ministers and consuls; to all cases of admiralty and maritime jurisdiction; to controversies to which the United States shall be a party; to controversies between two or more States; between a State and citizens of another State; between citizens of different States, between citizens of the same State claiming lands under grants of different States, and between a State, or the citizens thereof, and foreign states, citizens or subjects.

(This section is modified by Amendment XI.)

2. In all cases affecting ambassadors, other public ministers and consuls, and those in which a State shall be party, the Supreme Court shall have original jurisdiction. In all the other cases before mentioned, the Supreme Court shall have appellate jurisdiction, both as to law and fact, with such exceptions, and under such regulations as the Congress shall make.

3. The trial of all crimes, except in cases of impeachment, shall be by jury; and such trial shall be held in the State where the said crimes shall have been committed; but when not committed within any State, the trial shall be at such place or places as the Congress may by law have directed.

Section 3— Treason Defined — Proof of, Punishment of.

1. Treason against the United States, shall consist only in levying war against them, or in adhering to their enemies, giving them aid and comfort. No persons shall be convicted of treason unless on the testimony of two witnesses to the same overt act, or on confession in open court.

2. The Congress shall have power to declare the punishment of treason, but no attainder of treason shall work corruption of blood, or forfeiture except during the life of the person attainted.

ARTICLE IV.

Section 1—Each State to give credit to the public acts, etc., of every other State.

Full faith and credit shall be given in each State to the public acts, records, and judicial proceedings of every other State. And the Congress may by general laws prescribe the manner in which such acts, records and proceedings shall be proved, and the effect thereof.

Section 2—Privileges of citizens of each State. Fugitives from justice to be delivered up. Persons held to service having escaped, to be delivered up.

1. The citizens of each State shall be entitled to all privileges and immunities of citizens in the several States.

2. A person charged in any State with treason, felony, or other crime, who shall flee from justice, and be found in another State, shall on demand of the Executive authority of the State from which he fled, be delivered up, to be removed to the State having jurisdiction of the crime.

(3. No person held to service or labor in one State, under the laws thereof, escaping into another, shall in consequence of any law or regulation therein, be discharged from such service or labor, but shall be delivered up on claim of the party to whom such service or labor may be due.) (This clause was superseded by Amendment XIII.)

Section 3—Admission of new States. Power of Congress over territory and other property.

1. New States may be admitted by the Congress into this Union; but no new State shall be formed or erected within the jurisdiction of any other State; nor any State be formed by the junction of two or more States, or parts of States, without the consent of the Legislatures of the States concerned as well as of the Congress.

2. The Congress shall have power to dispose of and make all needful rules and regulations respecting the territory or other property belonging to the United States; and nothing in this Constitution shall be so construed as to prejudice any claims of the United States, or of any particular State.

Section 4—Republican form of government guaranteed. Each state to be protected.

The United States shall guarantee to every State in this Union a Republican form of government, and shall protect each of them against invasion; and on application of the Legislature, or of the Executive (when the Legislature cannot be convened) against domestic violence.

ARTICLE V.

Constitution: how amended; proviso.

The Congress, whenever two-thirds of both Houses shall deem it necessary, shall propose amendments to this Constitution, or, on the application of the Legislatures of two-thirds of the several States, shall call a convention for proposing amendments, which, in either case, shall be valid to all intents and purposes, as part of this Constitution, when ratified by the Legislatures of three-fourths of the several states, or by conventions in three-fourths thereof, as the one or the other mode of ratification may be proposed by the Congress; provided that no amendment which may be made prior to the year one thousand eight hundred and eight shall in any manner affect the first and fourth clauses in the Ninth Section of the First Article; and that no State, without its consent, shall be deprived of its equal suffrage in the Senate.

ARTICLE VI.

Certain debts, etc., declared valid. Supremacy of Constitution, treaties, and laws of the United States. Oath to support Constitution, by whom taken. No reli-

gious test.

1. All debts contracted and engagements entered into, before the adoption of this Constitution, shall be as valid against the United States under this Constitution, as under the Confederation.

2. This Constitution, and the laws of the United States which shall be made in pursuance thereof; and all treaties made, or which shall be made, under the authority of the United States, shall be the supreme law of the land; and the judges in every State shall be bound thereby, any thing in the Constitution or laws of any State to the contrary notwithstanding.

3. The Senators and Representatives before mentioned, and the members of the several State Legislatures, and all executive and judicial officers, both of the United States and of the several States, shall be bound by oath or affirmation, to support this Constitution; but no religious test shall ever be required as a qualification to any office or public trust under the United States.

ARTICLE VII.

What ratification shall establish Constitution.

The ratification of the Conventions of nine States, shall be sufficient for the establishment of this Constitution between the States so ratifying the same.

Done in convention by the unanimous consent of the States present the Seventeenth day of September in the year of our Lord one thousand seven hundred and eighty seven, and of the independence of the United States of America the Twelfth. In witness whereof we have hereunto subscribed our names.

George Washington, President and deputy from Virginia.
New Hampshire—John Langdon, Nicholas Gilman.
Massachusetts—Nathaniel Gorham, Rufus King.
Connecticut—Wm. Saml. Johnson, Roger Sherman.
New York—Alexander Hamilton.
New Jersey—Wil: Livingston, David Brearley, Wm. Paterson, Jona: Dayton.
Pennsylvania—B. Franklin, Thomas Mifflin, Robt. Morris, Geo. Clymer, Thos. FitzSimons, Jared Ingersoll, James Wilson, Gouv. Morris.
Delaware—Geo: Read, Gunning Bedford Jun., John Dickinson, Richard Bassett, Jaco: Broom.
Maryland—James McHenry, Daniel of Saint Thomas Jenifer, Danl. Carroll.
Virginia—John Blair, James Madison Jr.
North Carolina—Wm. Blount, Rich'd. Dobbs Spaight, Hugh Williamson.
South Carolina—J. Rutledge, Charles Cotesworth Pinckney, Charles Pinckney, Pierce Butler.
Georgia—William Few, Abr. Baldwin.
Attest: William Jackson, Secretary.

Ten Original Amendments—The Bill of Rights

In Force Dec. 15, 1791

(The First Congress, at its first session in the City of New York, Sept. 25, 1789, submitted to the states 12 amendments to clarify certain individual and state rights not named in the Constitution. They are generally called the Bill of Rights.

(Influential in framing these amendments was the Declaration of Rights of Virginia, written by George Mason (1725-1792) in 1776. Mason, a Virginia delegate to the Constitutional Convention, did not sign the Constitution and opposed its ratification on the ground that it did not sufficiently oppose slavery or safeguard individual rights.

(In the preamble to the resolution offering the proposed amendments, Congress said: "The conventions of a number of the States having at the time of their adopting the Constitution, expressed a desire, in order to prevent misconstruction or abuse of its powers, that further declaratory and restrictive clauses should be added, and as extending the ground of public confidence in the government will best insure the beneficent ends of its institution, be it resolved," etc.

(Ten of these amendments now commonly known as one to 10 inclusive, but originally 3 to 12 inclusive, were ratified by the states as follows: New Jersey, Nov. 20, 1789; Maryland, Dec. 19, 1789; North Carolina, Dec. 22, 1789; South Carolina, Jan. 19, 1790; New Hampshire, Jan. 25, 1790; Delaware, Jan. 28, 1790; New York, Feb. 24, 1790; Pennsylvania, Mar. 10, 1790; Rhode Island, June 7, 1790; Vermont, Nov. 3, 1791; Virginia, Dec. 15, 1791; Massachusetts, Mar. 2, 1939; Georgia, Mar. 8, 1939; Connecticut, Apr. 19, 1939. These original 10 ratified amendments follow as Amendments I to X inclusive.

(Of the two original proposed amendments which were not ratified by the necessary number of states, the first related to apportionment of Representatives; the second, to compensation of members.)

AMENDMENT I.

Religious establishment prohibited. Freedom of speech, of the press, and right to petition.

Congress shall make no law respecting an establishment of religion, or prohibiting the free exercise thereof; or abridging the freedom of speech, or of the press; or the right of the people peaceably to assemble, and to petition the Government for a redress of grievances.

AMENDMENT II.

Right to keep and bear arms.

A well-regulated militia, being necessary to the security of a free State, the right of the people to keep and bear arms, shall not be infringed.

AMENDMENT III.

Conditions for quarters for soldiers.

No soldier shall, in time of peace be quartered in any house, without the consent of the owner, nor in time of war, but in a manner to be prescribed by law.

AMENDMENT IV.

Right of search and seizure regulated.

The right of the people to be secure in their persons, houses, papers, and effects, against unreasonable searches and seizures, shall not be violated, and no warrants shall issue, but upon probable cause, supported by oath or affirmation, and particularly describing the place to be searched, and the persons or things to be seized.

AMENDMENT V.

Provisions concerning prosecution. Trial and punishment—private property not to be taken for public use without compensation.

No person shall be held to answer for a capital, or otherwise infamous crime, unless on a presentment or indictment of a Grand Jury, except in cases arising in the land or naval forces, or in the militia, when in actual service in time of war or public danger; nor shall any person be subject for the same offense to be twice put in jeopardy of life or limb; nor shall be compelled in any criminal case to be a witness against himself, nor be deprived of life, liberty, or property, without due process of law; nor shall private property be taken for public use without just compensation.

AMENDMENT VI.

Right to speedy trial, witnesses, etc.

In all criminal prosecutions, the accused shall enjoy the right to a speedy and public trial, by an impartial jury of the State and district wherein the crime shall have been committed, which district shall have been previously ascertained by law, and to be informed of the nature and cause of the accusation; to be confronted with the witnesses against him; to have compulsory process for obtaining witnesses in his favor, and to have the assistance of counsel for his defense.

AMENDMENT VII.

Right of trial by jury.

In suits at common law, where the value in controversy shall exceed twenty dollars, the right of trial by jury shall be preserved, and no fact tried by a jury shall be otherwise reexamined in any court of the United States, than according to the rules of the common law.

AMENDMENT VIII.

Excessive bail or fines and cruel punishment prohibited.

Excessive bail shall not be required, nor excessive fines imposed, nor cruel and unusual punishments inflicted.

AMENDMENT IX.

Rule of construction of Constitution.

The enumeration in the Constitution, of certain rights, shall not be construed to deny or disparage others retained by the people.

AMENDMENT X.

Rights of States under Constitution.

The powers not delegated to the United States by the Constitution, nor prohibited by it to the States, are reserved to the States respectively, or to the people.

Amendments Since the Bill of Rights

AMENDMENT XI.

Judicial powers construed.

The judicial power of the United States shall not be construed to extend to any suit in law or equity, commenced or prosecuted against one of the United States by citizens of another State, or by citizens or subjects of any foreign state.

(This amendment was proposed to the Legislatures of the several States by the Third Congress on March 4, 1794, and was declared to have been ratified in a message from the President to Congress, dated Jan. 8, 1798.

(It was on Jan. 5, 1798, that Secretary of State Pickering received from 12 of the States authenticated ratifications, and informed President John Adams of that fact.

(As a result of later research in the Department of State, it is now established that Amendment XI became part of the Constitution on Feb. 7, 1795, for on that date it had been ratified by 12 States as follows:

(1. New York, Mar. 27, 1794. 2. Rhode Island, Mar. 31, 1794. 3. Connecticut, May 8, 1794. 4. New Hampshire, June 16, 1794. 5. Massachusetts, June 26, 1794. 6. Vermont, between Oct. 9, 1794, and Nov. 9, 1794. 7. Virginia, Nov. 18, 1794. 8. Georgia, Nov. 29, 1794. 9. Kentucky, Dec. 7, 1794. 10. Maryland, Dec. 26, 1794. 11. Delaware, Jan. 23, 1795. 12. North Carolina, Feb. 7, 1795.

(On June 1, 1796, more than a year after Amendment XI had become a part of the Constitution (but before anyone was officially aware of this), Tennessee had been admitted as a State; but not until Oct. 16, 1797, was a certified copy of the resolution of Congress proposing the amendment sent to the Governor of Tennessee (John Sevier) by Secretary of State Pickering, whose office was then at Trenton, New Jersey, because of the epidemic of yellow fever at Philadelphia; it seems, however, that the Legislature of Tennessee took no action on Amendment XI, owing doubtless to the fact that public announcement of its adoption was made soon thereafter.

(Besides the necessary 12 States, one other, South Carolina, ratified Amendment XI, but this action was not taken until Dec. 4, 1797; the two remaining States, New Jersey and Pennsylvania, failed to ratify.)

AMENDMENT XII.

Manner of choosing President and Vice-President.

(Proposed by Congress Dec. 9, 1803; ratification completed June 15, 1804.)

The Electors shall meet in their respective States and vote by ballot for President and Vice-President, one of whom, at least, shall not be an inhabitant of the same State with themselves; they shall name in their ballots the person voted for as President, and in distinct ballots the person voted for as Vice-President, and they shall make distinct lists of all persons voted for as President, and of all persons voted for as Vice-President, and of the number of votes for each, which lists they shall sign and certify, and transmit sealed to the seat of the Government of the United States, directed to the President of the Senate; the President of the Senate shall, in the presence of the Senate and House of Representatives, open all the certificates and the votes shall then be counted;—The person having the greatest number of votes for President, shall be the President, if such number be a majority of the whole number of Electors appointed; and if no person have such majority, then from the persons having the highest numbers not exceeding three on the list of those voted for as President, the House of Representatives shall choose immediately, by ballot, the President. But in choosing the President, the votes shall be taken by States, the representation from each State having one vote; a quorum for this purpose shall consist of a member or members from two-thirds of the States, and a majority of all the States shall be necessary to a choice. *(And if the House of Representatives shall not choose a President whenever the right of choice shall devolve upon them, before the fourth day of March next following, then the Vice-President shall act as President, as in case of the death of other constitutional disability of the President.)* *(The words in parentheses were superseded by Amendment XX, section 3.)* The person having the greatest number of votes as Vice-President, shall be the Vice-President, if such number be a majority of the whole number of Electors appointed, and if no person have a majority, then from the two highest numbers on the list, the Senate shall choose the Vice-President; a quorum for the purpose shall consist of two-thirds of the whole number of Senators, and a majority of the whole number shall be necessary to a choice. But no person constitutionally ineligible to the office of President shall be eligible to that of Vice-President of the United States.

THE RECONSTRUCTION AMENDMENTS

(Amendments XIII, XIV, and XV are commonly known as the Reconstruction Amendments, inasmuch as they followed the Civil War, and were drafted by Republicans who were bent on imposing their own policy of reconstruction on the South. Post-bellum legislatures there—Mississippi, South Carolina, Georgia, for example—had set up laws which, it was charged, were contrived to perpetuate Negro slavery under other names.)

AMENDMENT XIII.

Slavery abolished.

(Proposed by Congress Jan. 31, 1865; ratification completed Dec. 6, 1865. The amendment, when first proposed by a resolution in Congress, was passed by the Senate, 38 to 6, on Apr. 8, 1864, but was defeated in the House, 95 to 66 on June 15, 1864. On reconsideration by the House, on Jan. 31, 1865, the resolution passed, 119 to 56. It was approved by President Lincoln on Feb. 1, 1865, although the Supreme Court had decided in 1798 that the President has nothing to do with the proposing of amendments to the Constitution, or their adoption.)

1. Neither slavery nor involuntary servitude, except as a punishment for crime whereof the party shall have been duly convicted, shall exist within the United States or any place subject to their jurisdiction.

2. Congress shall have power to enforce this article by appropriate legislation.

AMENDMENT XIV

Citizenship rights not to be abridged.

(The following amendment was proposed to the Legisla-

tures of the several states by the 39th Congress, June 13, 1866, and was declared to have been ratified in a proclamation by the Secretary of State, July 28, 1868.

(The 14th amendment was adopted only by virtue of ratification subsequent to earlier rejections. Newly constituted legislatures in both North Carolina and South Carolina (respectively July 4 and 9, 1868), ratified the proposed amendment, although earlier legislatures had rejected the proposal. The Secretary of State issued a proclamation, which, though doubtful as to the effect of attempted withdrawals by Ohio and New Jersey, entertained no doubt as to the validity of the ratification by North and South Carolina. The following day (July 21, 1868), Congress passed a resolution which declared the 14th Amendment to be a part of the Constitution and directed the Secretary of State so to promulgate it. The Secretary waited, however, until the newly constituted Legislature of Georgia had ratified the amendment, subsequent to an earlier rejection, before the promulgation of the ratification of the new amendment.)

1. All persons born or naturalized in the United States, and subject to the jurisdiction thereof, are citizens of the United States and of the State wherein they reside. No State shall make or enforce any law which shall abridge the privileges or immunities of citizens of the United States; nor shall any State deprive any person of life, liberty, or property, without due process of law; nor deny to any person within its jurisdiction the equal protection of the laws.

2. Representatives shall be apportioned among the several States according to their respective numbers, counting the whole number of persons in each State, excluding Indians not taxed. But when the right to vote at any election for the choice of Electors for President and Vice-President of the United States, Representatives in Congress, the executive and judicial officers of a State, or the members of the Legislature thereof, is denied to any of the male inhabitants of such State, being twenty-one years of age, and citizens of the United States, or in any way abridged, except for participation in rebellion, or other crime, the basis of representation therein shall be reduced in the proportion which the number of such male citizens shall bear to the whole number of male citizens twenty-one years of age in such State.

3. No person shall be a Senator or Representative in Congress, or Elector of President and Vice-President, or hold any office, civil or military, under the United States, or under any State, who, having previously taken an oath, as a member of Congress, or as an officer of the United States, or as a member of any State Legislature, or as an executive or judicial officer of any State, to support the Constitution of the United States, shall have engaged in insurrection or rebellion against the same, or given aid or comfort to the enemies thereof. But Congress may by a vote of two-thirds of each House, remove such disability.

4. The validity of the public debt of the United States, authorized by law, including debts incurred for payment of pensions and bounties for services in suppressing insurrection or rebellion, shall not be questioned. But neither the United States nor any State shall assume or pay any debt or obligation incurred in aid of insurrection or rebellion against the United States, or any claim for the loss or emancipation of any slave; but all such debts, obligations and claims, shall be held illegal and void.

5. The Congress shall have power to enforce, by appropriate legislation, the provisions of this article.

AMENDMENT XV.
Race no bar to voting rights.

(The following amendment was proposed to the legislatures of the several States by the 40th Congress, Feb. 26, 1869, and was declared to have been ratified in a proclamation by the Secretary of State, Mar. 30, 1870.)

1. The right of citizens of the United States to vote shall not be denied or abridged by the United States or by any State on account of race, color, or previous condition of servitude.

2. The Congress shall have power to enforce this article by appropriate legislation.

AMENDMENT XVI.
Income taxes authorized.

(Proposed by Congress July 12, 1909; ratification completed Feb. 3, 1913.)

The Congress shall have power to lay and collect taxes on incomes, from whatever sources derived, without apportionment among the several States, and without regard to any census or enumeration.

AMENDMENT XVII.
United States Senators to be elected by direct popular vote.

(Proposed by Congress May 13, 1912; ratification completed Apr. 8, 1913.)

1. The Senate of the United States shall be composed of two Senators from each State, elected by the people thereof, for six years; and each Senator shall have one vote. The electors in each State shall have the qualifications requisite for electors of the most numerous branch of the State Legislatures.

2. When vacancies happen in the representation of any State in the Senate, the executive authority of such State shall issue writs of election to fill such vacancies: Provided, That the Legislature of any State may empower the Executive thereof to make temporary appointments until the people fill the vacancies by election as the Legislature may direct.

3. This amendment shall not be so construed as to affect the election or term of any Senator chosen before it becomes valid as part of the Constitution.

AMENDMENT XVIII.
Liquor prohibition amendment.

(Proposed by Congress Dec. 18, 1917; ratification completed Jan. 16, 1919. Repealed by Amendment XXI, effective Dec. 5, 1933.)

(1. After one year from the ratification of this article the manufacture, sale, or transportation of intoxicating liquors, within, the importation thereof into, or the exportation thereof from the United States and all territory subject to the jurisdiction thereof, for beverage purposes is hereby prohibited.

(2. The Congress and the several States shall have concurrent power to enforce this article by appropriate legislation.

(3. This article shall be inoperative unless it shall have been ratified as an amendment to the Constitution by the Legislatures of the several States, as provided in the Constitution, within seven years from the date of the submission hereof to the States by the Congress.)

(The total vote in the Senates of the various States was 1,310 for, 237 against — 84.6% dry. In the lower houses of the States the vote was 3,782 for, 1,035 against — 78.5% dry.

(The amendment ultimately was adopted by all the States except Connecticut and Rhode Island.)

AMENDMENT XIX.
Giving nationwide suffrage to women.

(Proposed by Congress June 4, 1919; ratification certified by Secretary of State Aug. 26, 1920.)

1. The right of citizens of the United States to vote shall not be denied or abridged by the United States or by any State on account of sex.

2. Congress shall have power to enforce this Article by appropriate legislation.

AMENDMENT XX.
Terms of President and Vice President to begin on Jan. 20; those of Senators, Representatives, Jan. 3.

(Proposed by Congress Mar. 2, 1932; ratification completed Jan. 23, 1933.)

1. The terms of the President and Vice President shall end at noon on the 20th day of January, and the terms of Senators and Representatives at noon on the 3rd day of January, of the years in which such terms would have ended if this article had not been ratified; and the terms of their successors shall then begin.

2. The Congress shall assemble at least once in every year, and such meeting shall begin at noon on the 3rd day of January, unless they shall by law appoint a different day.

3. If, at the time fixed for the beginning of the term of the President, the President elect shall have died, the Vice President elect shall become President. If a President shall not have been chosen before the time fixed for the begin-

ning of his term, or if the President elect shall have failed to qualify, then the Vice President elect shall act as President until a President shall have qualified; and the Congress may by law provide for the case wherein neither a President elect nor a Vice President shall have qualified, declaring who shall then act as President, or the manner in which one who is to act shall be selected, and such person shall act accordingly until a President or Vice President shall have qualified.

4. The Congress may by law provide for the case of the death of any of the persons from whom the House of Representatives may choose a President whenever the right of choice shall have devolved upon them, and for the case of the death of any of the persons from whom the Senate may choose a Vice President whenever the right of choice shall have devolved upon them.

5. Sections 1 and 2 shall take effect on the 15th day of October following the ratification of this article (Oct., 1933).

6. This article shall be inoperative unless it shall have been ratified as an amendment to the Constitution by the Legislatures of three-fourths of the several States within seven years from the date of its submission.

AMENDMENT XXI.
Repeal of Amendment XVIII.
(Proposed by Congress Feb. 20, 1933; ratification completed Dec. 5, 1933.)

1. The eighteenth article of amendment to the Constitution of the United States is hereby repealed.

2. The transportation or importation into any State, Territory, or Possession of the United States for delivery or use therein of intoxicating liquors, in violation of the laws thereof, is hereby prohibited.

3. This article shall be inoperative unless it shall have been ratified as an amendment to the Constitution by conventions in the several States, as provided in the Constitution, within seven years from the date of the submission hereof to the States by the Congress.

AMENDMENT XXII.
Limiting Presidential terms of office.
(Proposed by Congress Mar. 21, 1947; ratification completed Feb. 27, 1951.)

1. No person shall be elected to the office of the President more than twice, and no person who has held the office of President, or acted as President, for more than two years of a term to which some other person was elected President shall be elected to the office of the President more than once. But this Article shall not apply to any person holding the office of President when this Article was proposed by the Congress, and shall not prevent any person who may be holding the office of President, or acting as President, during the term within which this Article becomes operative from holding the office of President or acting as President during the remainder of such term.

2. This article shall be inoperative unless it shall have been ratified as an amendment to the Constitution by the Legislatures of three-fourths of the several States within seven years from the date of its submission to the States by the Congress.

AMENDMENT XXIII.
Presidential vote for District of Columbia.
(Proposed by Congress June 17, 1960; ratification completed Mar. 29, 1961.)

1. The District constituting the seat of Government of the United States shall appoint in such manner as the Congress may direct:

A number of electors of President and Vice President equal to the whole number of Senators and Representatives in Congress to which the District would be entitled if it were a State, but in no event more than the least populous State; they shall be in addition to those appointed by the States, but they shall be considered, for the purposes of the election of President and Vice President, to be electors appointed by a State; and they shall meet in the District and perform such duties as provided by the twelfth article of amendment.

2. The Congress shall have power to enforce this article by appropriate legislation.

AMENDMENT XXIV.
Barring poll tax in federal elections.
(Proposed by Congress Aug. 27, 1962; ratification completed Jan. 23, 1964.)

1. The right of citizens of the United States to vote in any primary or other election for President or Vice President, for electors for President or Vice President, or for Senator or Representative in Congress, shall not be denied or abridged by the United States or any State by reason of failure to pay any poll tax or other tax.

2. The Congress shall have power to enforce this article by appropriate legislation.

AMENDMENT XXV.
Presidential disability and succession.
(Proposed by Congress July 6, 1965; ratification completed Feb. 10, 1967.)

1. In case of the removal of the President from office or of his death or resignation, the Vice President shall become President.

2. Whenever there is a vacancy in the office of the Vice President, the President shall nominate a Vice President who shall take office upon confirmation by a majority vote of both houses of Congress.

3. Whenever the President transmits to the President pro tempore of the Senate and the Speaker of the House of Representatives his written declaration that he is unable to discharge the powers and duties of his office, and until he transmits to them a written declaration to the contrary, such powers and duties shall be discharged by the Vice President as Acting President.

4. Whenever the Vice President and a majority of either the principal officers of the executive departments or of such other body as Congress may by law provide, transmit to the President pro tempore of the Senate and the Speaker of the House of Representatives their written declaration that the President is unable to discharge the powers and duties of his office, the Vice President shall immediately assume the powers and duties of the office as Acting President.

Thereafter, when the President transmits to the President pro tempore of the Senate and the Speaker of the House of Representatives his written declaration that no inability exists, he shall resume the powers and duties of his office unless the Vice President and a majority of either the principal officers of the executive department or of such other body as Congress may by law provide, transmit within four days to the President pro tempore of the Senate and the Speaker of the House of Representatives their written declaration that the President is unable to discharge the powers and duties of his office. Thereupon Congress shall decide the issue, assembling within forty-eight hours for that purpose if not in session. If the Congress, within twenty-one days after receipt of the latter written declaration, or, if Congress is not in session, within twenty-one days after Congress is required to assemble, determines by two-thirds vote of both houses that the President is unable to discharge the powers and duties of his office, the Vice President shall continue to discharge the same as Acting President; otherwise, the President shall resume the powers and duties of his office.

AMENDMENT XXVI.
Lowering voting age to 18 years.
(Proposed by Congress Mar. 23, 1971; ratification completed June 30, 1971.)

1. The right of citizens of the United States, who are 18 years of age or older, to vote shall not be denied or abridged by the United States or any state on account of age.

2. The Congress shall have the power to enforce this article by appropriate legislation.

PROPOSED EQUAL RIGHTS AMENDMENT
(Proposed by Congress Mar. 22, 1972; ratification completed, as of mid-1976, by 34 states, rejected by 1 state; needed total of 38 for adoption before deadline, Mar. 22, 1979.)

1. Equality of rights under the law shall not be denied or abridged by the United States or by any State on account of sex.

2. The Congress shall have the power to enforce, by appropriate legislation, the provisions of this article.

3. This amendment shall take effect two years after the date of ratification.

Statue of Liberty National Monument

Since 1886, the Statue of Liberty Enlightening the World has stood as a symbol of freedom in New York harbor. It also commemorates French-American friendship for it was given by the people of France, designed by Frederic Auguste Bartholdi (1834-1904). A $2.5 million building housing the American Museum of Immigration was opened by Pres. Nixon Sept. 26, 1972, at the base of the statue. It houses a permanent exhibition of photos, posters, and artifacts tracing the history of American immigration. In addition, there is a small immigration library. The Monument is administered by the National Park Service.

Nearby Ellis Island, gateway to America for more than 12 million immigrants between 1892 and 1954, was proclaimed part of the National Monument in 1965 by Pres. Johnson. It can be visited between May and October.

Edouard de Laboulaye, French historian and admirer of American political institutions, suggested that the French present a monument to the United States, the latter to provide pedestal and site. Bartholdi visualized a colossal statue at the entrance of New York harbor, welcoming the peoples of the world with the torch of liberty.

The French approved the idea and formed the Franco-American Union to raise funds, which eventually reached $250,000. Bartholdi began work about 1874 in Paris. He made several models and one, 36 ft. tall, enabled him to compute the statue in sections. Wooden battens were made and sheets of copper 3/32 of an inch thick were hammered into shape by hand. A framework of 4 steel supports was designed by Gustave Eiffel, creator of the Eiffel Tower.

On Washington's birthday, Feb. 22, 1877, Congress approved the use of a site on Bedloe's Island suggested by Bartholdi. This island of 12 acres had been owned in the 17th century by a Walloon named Isaac Bedloe, who came to New Amsterdam in 1639. He died in 1673 and his wife sold the island for £80. In later years it was owned by the City of New York and the U.S. Government. It was called Bedloe's until Aug. 3, 1956, when Pres. Eisenhower approved a resolution of Congress changing the name to Liberty Island.

The statue was finished May 21, 1884, and formally presented to U.S. Minister Morton July 4, 1884, by Ferdinand de Lesseps, head of the Franco-American Union, promoter of the Panama Canal, and builder of the Suez Canal.

On Aug. 5, 1884, the Americans laid the cornerstone for the pedestal. This was to be built on the foundations of Fort Wood, which had been erected by the Government in 1811. The American committee had raised $125,000, but when the pedestal was 15 ft. high, this was found to be inadequate. Joseph Pulitzer, owner of the New York World, appealed on Mar. 16, 1885, for general donations. By Aug. 11, 1885, he had raised $100,000. The pedestal was made of concrete with granite facing and steel girders were built into it to connect with framework of the statue.

The statue arrived dismantled, in 214 packing cases, in the steamship Isere, which reached New York from Rouen, France, in June, 1885. The last rivet of the statue was driven Oct. 28, 1886, when Pres. Grover Cleveland dedicated the monument.

The total cost of statue and pedestal was estimated at $500,000.

Funds for permanently lighting the statue were raised by the World in 1916 and President Wilson turned on the lights Dec. 2, 1916.

At the celebration of the statue's 50th anniversary, in 1936, Pres. Franklin D. Roosevelt said: "The realization that we are all bound together by hope of a common future rather than by reverence for a common past has helped us to build upon this continent a unity unapproached in any similar area or similar size population in the whole world. For all our millions of people, there is a unity in language and speech, in law and economics, in education and in general purpose which nowhere finds its match.

"It was the hope of those who gave us this statue and the hope of the American people in receiving it that the Goddess of Liberty and the Goddess of Peace were the same."

The statue weighs 450,000 lbs. or 225 tons. The copper sheeting weighs 200,000 lbs. There are 167 steps from the land level to the top of the pedestal, 168 steps inside the statue to the head, and 54 rungs on the ladder leading to the arm that holds the torch. Visitors may enter the head, which holds from 30 to 40 persons, but not the torch. The statue is open daily.

Dimensions of the Statue

	Ft.	In.
Height from base to torch (45.3 meters)	151	1
Foundation of pedestal to torch (91.5 meters)	305	1
Heel to top of head	111	1
Length of hand	16	5
Index finger	8	0
Circumference at second joint	3	6
Size of finger nail . . . . 13x10 in.		
Head from chin to cranium	17	3
Head, thickness from ear to ear	10	0
Distance across the eye	2	6
Length of nose	4	6
Right arm, length	42	0
Right arm, greatest thickness	12	0
Thickness of waist	35	0
Width of mouth	3	0
Tablet, length	23	7
Tablet, width	13	7
Tablet, thickness	2	0

Emma Lazarus' Famous Poem

A poem by Emma Lazarus is graven on a tablet within the pedestal on which the statue stands:

The New Colossus

Not like the brazen giant of Greek fame,
With conquering limbs astride from land to land;
Here at our sea-washed, sunset gates shall stand
A mighty woman with a torch, whose flame
Is the imprisoned lightning, and her name
Mother of Exiles. From her beacon-hand
Glows world-wide welcome; her mild eyes command
The air-bridged harbor that twin cities frame.
"Keep ancient lands, your storied pomp!" cries she
With silent lips. "Give me your tired, your poor,
Your huddled masses yearning to breathe free,
The wretched refuse of your teeming shore.
Send these, the homeless, tempest-tost to me,
I lift my lamp beside the golden door!"

continued from page 466

touch it. On Jan. 1, 1976, just after midnight to mark the opening of the Bicentennial Year, the bell was moved to a new glass and steel pavilion behind Independence Hall for easier viewing by the larger number of visitors expected during the year.

The measurements of the bell follow: circumference around the lip, 12 ft.; circumference around the crown, 7 ft. 6 in.; lip to the crown, 3 ft.; height over the crown, 2 ft. 3 in.; thickness at lip, 3 in.; thickness at crown, 1⅛ in.; weight, 2080 lbs., length of clapper, 3 ft. 2 in.; cost, £60 14s 5d.

Lincoln's Address at Gettysburg, 1863

Fourscore and seven years ago our fathers brought forth on this continent a new nation, conceived in liberty and dedicated to the proposition that all men are created equal.

Now we are engaged in a great civil war, testing whether that nation or any nation so conceived and so dedicated can long endure. We are met on a great battle field of that war. We have come to dedicate a portion of that field, as a final resting-place for those who here gave their lives that that nation might live. It is altogether fitting and proper that we should do this.

But, in a larger sense, we can not dedicate — we can not consecrate — we can not hallow — this ground. The brave men, living and dead, who struggled here, have consecrated it, far above our poor power to add or detract. The world will little note, nor long remember, what we say here, but it can never forget what they did here. It is for us the living, rather, to be dedicated here to the unfinished work which they who fought here have thus far so nobly advanced. It is rather for us to be here dedicated to the great task remaining before us — that from these honored dead we take increased devotion to that cause for which they gave the last full measure of devotion — that we here highly resolve that these dead shall not have died in vain — that this nation, under God, shall have a new birth of freedom — and that government of the people, by the people, for the people, shall not perish from the earth.

History of the Address

President Lincoln delivered his address at the dedication of the military cemetery at Gettysburg, Pa., Nov. 19, 1863. The battle had been fought July 1-3, 1863. He was preceded by Edward Everett, former president of Harvard, secretary of state and senator from Massachusetts, then 69 and one of the nation's great orators. Everett gave a full resume of the battle, Lincoln's speech was so short that the photographer did not get his camera adjusted in time. The report that newspapers ignored Lincoln's address is not entirely accurate; Everett's address swamped their columns, but the greatness of Lincoln's speech was immediately recognized. Everett wrote him: "I should be glad if I could flatter myself that I came as near the central idea of the occasion in 2 hours as you did in 2 minutes."

Five copies of the Gettysburg address in Lincoln's hand are extant. The first and 2d drafts, prepared in Washington and Gettysburg just before delivery, are in the Library of Congress. The 3d draft, written at the request of Everett to be sold at a fair in New York for the benefit of soldiers, was given the Illinois State Historical Library by popular subscription.

The 4th copy was written out by Lincoln for George Bancroft, the historian, and remained in custody of the Bancroft family until 1929, when it was acquired by Mrs. Nicholas H. Noyes, of Indianapolis, Ind. In 1949 Mrs. Noyes

presented this copy to the Cornell University Library, Ithaca, N.Y. The 5th copy, usually described as the clearest and best, was also written by Lincoln for George Bancroft, for facsimile reproduction in a volume to be sold for the benefit of soldiers and sailors in Baltimore, where Bancroft lived. It is called the 2d Bancroft copy. It passed to Bancroft's stepchildren, named Bliss, and was sold for $54,000 by the estate of Dr. William J. A. Bliss in New York Apr. 27, 1949, to Oscar B. Cintas, former Cuban ambassador to the United States. He died in May 1957 and willed it to the Lincoln Room of the White House, where it was placed in Mar. 1959. Lincoln's spelling of battle field and can not as separated words in that version is reproduced above.

Sen. John Sherman Cooper (R. Ky.), president of the Lincoln Sesquicentennial Commission, on June 17, 1959, presented a Latin translation of Lincoln's Gettysburg Address to the Apostolic Delegation of the Roman Catholic Church, in Washington, D. C. It was engrossed on vellum and was to be sent to Pope John XXIII for deposit in the Vatican Library. The presentation took place in the presence of government officials and members of the diplomatic corps. The translation was made by the Rt. Rev. Edwin Ryan of White Plains, N. Y. The Latin version was ordered printed in the Congressional Record.

Washington's Letter on Bigotry and Persecution

During a tour of various New England states in 1790, then Pres. George Washington was greeted by various leaders in Newport, R. I. Among the clergy was Moses Seixas, the warden of the Hebrew congregation, who greeted Washington and praised the new government for its opposition to bigotry. Washington acknowledged the greeting in a letter to the congregation:

Gentlemen:

While I received with much satisfaction, your address replete with expressions of affection and esteem; I rejoice in the opportunity of assuring you, that I shall always retain a grateful remembrance of the cordial welcome I experienced in my visit to Newport from all classes of Citizens.

The reflection on the days of difficulty and danger which are past is rendered the more sweet, from a consciousness that they are succeeded by days of uncommon prosperity and security. If we have wisdom to make the best use of the advantages with which we are now favored, we cannot fail, under the just administration of a good Government, to become a great and happy people.

The Citizens of the United States of America have a right to applaud themselves for having given to mankind examples of an enlarged and liberal policy; a policy worthy of imitation. All possess alike liberty of conscience and immunities of citizenship. It is now no more that toleration is spoken of, as if it was by the

indulgence of one class of people, that another enjoyed the exercise of their inherent natural rights. For happily the Government of the United States, which gives to bigotry no sanction, to persecution no assistance, requires only that they who live under its protection, should demean themselves as good citizens, in giving it on all occasions their effectual support.

It would be inconsistent with the frankness of my character not to avow that I am pleased with your favorable opinion of my administration, and fervent wishes for my felicity. May the Children of the Stock of Abraham, who dwell in this land, continue to merit and enjoy the good will of the other Inhabitants; while everyone shall sit in safety under his own vine and fig tree, and there shall be none to make him afraid. May the father of all mercies scatter light and not darkness in our paths, and make us all in our several vocations useful here, and in his own due time and way everlastingly happy.

Go. Washington

Famous Fairs and Expositions

1851	Great Exhibition opened, Crystal Palace, Hyde Park, London.
1853 July 14	New York World's Fair opened, Crystal Palace, N. Y. C.
1867 Apr. 1	International Exhibition, Paris.
1873 May 1	International Exhibition, Vienna.
1876 May-Nov.	Centennial Expos., Philadelphia.
1889 May 6-Nov. 6.	Universal Exposition, Paris.
1893 May 1-Oct. 30.	World's Columbian Exposition, Chicago.
1898 June 1-Oct. 31	Trans-Mississippi International Exposition, Omaha.
1900 Apr. 15.	International Exposition, Paris.
1901 May 1-Nov. 2.	Pan-American Expo: Buffalo.
1904 Apr. 20-Dec. 1	Louisiana Purchase Exposition, St. Louis.
1905 June 1	Lewis and Clark Centennial Exposition opened, Portland, Ore.
1907 Apr. 26	Jamestown, Va., Tercentenary Exposition, opened.
1909 June 1-Oct. 16	Alaska-Yukon-Pacific Exposition, Seattle.
1909 Sept. 25-Oct. 2.	Hudson-Fulton Celebration, N.Y.
1910 Apr. 23	International Exhibition, Brussels.
1913 Apr. 26	International Exposition opened, Ghent, Belgium.
1915 Feb. 20-Dec. 4.	Panama-Pacific International Exposition, San Francisco.
1915	Panama-California Exposition, San Diego.
1922-23	Brazilian Expos., Rio de Janeiro.
1924-25	British Empire Expos., Wembley.
1926 May 31-Nov. 30.	Sesquicentennial Expos. Phila.
1931	International Colonial and Overseas Exposition, Paris.
1933 May 27-Nov. 12.	Century of Progress, Chicago.
1934 May 26-Oct. 31.	Century of Progress, Chicago.
1936	Texas Centennial Expos., Dallas.
1936-1937	Great Lakes Expos., Cleveland.
1937 May 1-Oct. 31.	International Exposition, Paris.
1939 Feb. 18-Oct. 29	Golden Gate International Exposition, San Francisco.
1940	Golden Gate, San Francisco.
1939 Apr. 20-Oct. 31.	New York World's Fair, N.Y.C.
1940 May 11-Oct. 21.	New York World's Fair, N.Y.C.
1957 Apr. 26-Oct. 30.	Jamestown, Va., 350th Anniv.
1958 Apr. 17-Oct. 19.	World's Fair, Brussels.
1962 Apr. 21-Oct. 21.	Century 21 Exposition, Seattle.
1964 Apr. 22-Oct. 18.	New York World's Fair, N.Y.C.
1965 Apr. 21-Oct. 17.	New York World's Fair, N.Y.C.
1967 Apr. 28-Oct. 27.	Universal Exhibition (Expo 67), Montreal.
1968 Apr. 6-Oct. 6.	HemisFair 1968, San Antonio.
1970 Mar. 15-Sept. 13.	Expo '70 (Japan World Exposition), Osaka, Japan.
1974 May 4-Nov. 3.	Expo 74, Spokane, Wash.
1981	Expo '81, Universal Exposition, Los Angeles.

U. S. Bicentennial—1976

The 200th anniversary of the independence of the United States was celebrated in 1976. Observances were held in each of the 50 states and many communities, including reenactments of historic events and varied cultural and scientific projects.

Forms of Address for Persons of Rank and Public Office

In these examples John Smith is used as a representative American name. The salutation Dear Sir is always permissible when addressing a person not known to the writer.

President of the United States

Address: The President, The White House, Washington, D.C. 20500. Also, The President and Mrs. ——.
Salutation: Dear Sir or Mr. President or Dear Mr. President. More intimately: My dear Mr. President. Also: Dear Mr. President and Mrs. ——
The vice president takes the same forms.

Cabinet Officers

Address: Mr. John Smith, Secretary of State, Washington, D.C. or The Hon. John Smith. Similar addresses for other members of the cabinet. Also: Secretary and Mrs. John Smith.
Salutation: Dear Sir, or Dear Mr. Secretary. Also: Dear Mr. and Mrs. Smith.

The Bench

Address: The Hon. John Smith, Chief Justice of the United States. The Hon. John Smith, Associate Justice of the Supreme Court of the United States. The Hon. John Smith, Associate Judge, U. S. District Court.
Salutations: Dear Sir or Dear Mr. Chief Justice. Dear Mr. Justice. Dear Judge Smith.

Members of Congress

Address: The Hon. John Smith, United States Senate, Washington, D.C. 20510, or Sen. John Smith, etc. Also The Hon. John Smith, House of Representatives, Washington, D.C. 20515, or Rep. John Smith, etc.
Salutation: Dear Mr. Senator or Dear Mr. Smith; for Representative, Dear Mr. Smith.

Officers of Armed Forces

Address: Careful attention should be given to the precise rank, thus: General of the Army John Smith, Fleet Admiral John Smith. The rules for Air Force are same as Army.
Salutation: Dear Sir, or Dear General. All general officers, whatever rank, are entitled to be addressed as generals. Likewise a lieutenant colonel is addressed as colonel and first and second lieutenants are addressed as lieutenant.
Warrant officers and flight officers are addressed as Mister. Chaplains are addressed as Chaplain. A Catholic chaplain may be addressed as Father. Cadets of the United States Military Academy and Air Force Academy are addressed as Cadet. Noncommissioned officers are addressed by their titles. In the U. S. Navy all men from midshipman at Annapolis up to and including lieutenant commander are addressed as Mister.

Ambassador, Governor, Mayor

Address: The Hon. John Smith, followed by his title. He can be addressed either at his embassy, or at the Department of State, Washington, D.C. A foreign ambassador is His Excellency.
Salutation: Dear Mr. Ambassador. A foreign ambassador is Your Excellency.
Governors and mayors are often addressed as The Hon. John Smith, Governor of ——, or The Hon. John Smith, Mayor of ——; also Governor John Smith, State House, Albany, N.Y., or Mayor John Smith, City Hall, Erie, Pa.

The Clergy

Address: His Holiness, the Pope, or His Holiness Pope (name), State of Vatican City, Italy.
Salutation: Your Holiness or Most Holy Father.
Also: His Eminence, John, Cardinal Smith; salutation: Your Eminence. An archbishop or a bishop is addressed The Most Reverend, and the salutation is Your Excellency. A monsignor who is a papal chamberlain is The Very Reverend Monsignor and the

salutation is Dear Sir or Very Reverend Monsignor; a monsignor who is a domestic prelate is The Right Reverend Monsignor and salutation is Right Reverend Monsignor. A priest is addressed Reverend John Smith. A brother of an order is addressed Brother — ———. A sister takes the same form.

A bishop of the Protestant Episcopal Church is The Right Reverend John Smith; salutation is Right Reverend Sir, or Dear Bishop Smith. If a clergyman is a doctor of divinity, he is addressed: The Reverend John Smith, D.D., and the salutation is Reverend Sir, or Dear Dr. Smith. When a clergyman does not have the degree the salutation is Dear Mr. Smith.

A bishop of the Methodist Church is addressed Bishop John Smith with titles following.

Royalty and Nobility

An emperor is to be addressed in a letter as Sir, or Your Imperial Majesty.

A king or queen is addressed as His Majesty (Name), King of (Name), or Her Majesty (Name), Queen of (Name). Salutation: Sir, or Madam, or May it please Your Majesty.

Princes and princesses and other persons of royal blood are addressed as His (or Her) Royal Highness, and saluted with May it please Your Royal Highness.

A duke or marquis is My Lord Duke (or Marquis), a duke is His (or Your) Grace.

The National Anthem — The Star-Spangled Banner

The Star-Spangled Banner was ordered played by the military and naval services by President Woodrow Wilson in 1916. It was designated the National Anthem by Act of Congress, Mar. 3, 1931. It was written by Francis Scott Key, of Georgetown, D. C., during the bombardment of Fort McHenry, Baltimore, Md., Sept. 13-14, 1814. Key was a lawyer, a graduate of St. John's College, Annapolis, and a volunteer in a light artillery company. When a friend, Dr. Beanes, a physician of Upper Marlborough, Md., was taken aboard Admiral Cockburn's British squadron for interfering with ground troops, Key and J. S. Skinner, carrying a note from President Madison, went to the fleet under a flag of truce on a cartel ship to ask Beanes' release. Admiral Cockburn consented, but as the fleet was about to sail up the Patapsco to bombard Fort McHenry he detained them, first on H. M. S. Surprise, and then on a supply ship.

Key witnessed the bombardment from his own vessel. It began at 7 a.m., Sept. 13, 1814, and lasted, with intermissions, for 25 hours. The British fired over 1,500 shells, each weighing as much as 220 lbs. They were unable to approach closely because the Americans had sunk 22 vessels in the channel. Only four Americans were killed and 24 wounded. A British bomb-ship was disabled.

During the bombardment Key wrote a stanza on the back of an envelope. Next day at Indian Queen Inn, Baltimore, he wrote out the poem and gave it to his brother-in-law, Judge J. H. Nicholson. Nicholson suggested the tune, Anacreon in Heaven, and had the poem printed on broadsides, of which two survive. On Sept. 20 it appeared in the Baltimore American. Later Key made 3 copies; one is in the Library of Congress and one in the Pennsylvania Historical Society.

The copy that Key wrote in his hotel Sept. 14, 1814, remained in the Nicholson family for 93 years. In 1907 it was sold to Henry Walters of Baltimore. In 1934 it was bought at auction in New York from the Walters estate by the Walters Art Gallery, Baltimore, for $26,400. The Walters Gallery in 1953 sold the manuscript to the Maryland Historical Society for the same price.

The flag that Key saw during the bombardment is preserved in the Smithsonian Institution, Washington. It is 30 by 42 ft., and has 15 alternate red and white stripes and 15 stars, for the original 13 states plus Kentucky and Vermont. It was made by Mary Young Pickersgill. The Baltimore Flag House, a museum, occupies her premises, which were restored in 1953.

The Star-Spangled Banner

I

Oh, say can you see by the dawn's early light
    What so proudly we hailed at the twilight's last gleaming?
Whose broad stripes and bright stars thru the perilous fight.
    O'er the ramparts we watched were so gallantly streaming?
And the rocket's red glare, the bombs bursting in air.
    Gave proof through the night that our flag was still there.
Oh, say does that star-spangled banner yet wave
    O'er the land of the free and the home of the brave?

II

On the shore, dimly seen through the mists of the deep,
    Where the foe's haughty host in dread silence reposes,
What is that which the breeze, o'er the towering steep,
    As it fitfully blows, half conceals, half discloses?
Now it catches the gleam of the morning's first beam.
    In full glory reflected now shines on the stream:
'Tis the star-spangled banner! O long may it wave
    O'er the land of the free and the home of the brave!

III

And where is that band who so vauntingly swore
    That the havoc of war and the battle's confusion,
A home and a country should leave us no more!
    Their blood has washed out their foul footsteps' pollution.
No refuge could save the hireling and slave
    From the terror of flight, or the gloom of the grave:
And the star-spangled banner in triumph doth wave
    O'er the land of the free and the home of the brave!

IV

Oh! thus be it ever, when freemen shall stand
    Between their loved homes and the war's desolation!
Blest with victory and peace, may the heav'n rescued land
    Praise the Power that hath made and preserved us a nation.
Then conquer we must, when our cause it is just,
    And this be our motto: "In God is our trust."
And the star-spangled banner in triumph shall wave
    O'er the land of the free and the home of the brave!

Code of Etiquette for Display and Use of the U.S. Flag

Although the Stars and Stripes originated in 1777, it was not until 146 years later that there was a serious attempt to establish a uniform code of etiquette for the U.S. flag. The War Department issued Feb. 15, 1923, a circular on the rules of flag usage. These were adopted almost in their entirety June 14, 1923, by a conference of 68 patriotic organizations in Washington. Finally, on June 22, 1942, a joint resolution of Congress codified "existing rules and customs pertaining to the flag for civilians."

When to Display the Flag—The flag should be displayed on all days when the weather permits, especially on legal holidays and other special occasions, on official buildings when in use, in or near polling places on election days, and in or near schools when in session. A citizen may fly the flag at any time he wishes. It is customary to display the flag only from sunrise to sunset on buildings and on stationary flagstaffs in the open. However, it may be displayed at night on special occasions, preferably lighted. In Washington, the flag now flies over the White House both day and night. It flies over the Senate wing of the Capitol when the Senate is in session and over the House wing when that body is in session. It flies day and night over the east and west fronts of the Capitol, without floodlights at night but receiving light from the illuminated Capitol Dome. It flies 24 hours a day at several other places, including the Fort McHenry Nat'l. Monument in Baltimore, where it inspired Francis Scott Key to write The Star Spangled Banner.

How to Fly the Flag—The flag should be hoisted briskly and lowered ceremoniously, and should never be allowed to touch the ground or the floor. When hung over a sidewalk from a rope extending from a building to a pole, the union should be away from the building. When hung over the center of a street it should have the union to the north in an east-west street and to the east in a north-south street. No other flag may be flown above or, if on the same level, to the right of the U.S. flag, except that at the United Nations Headquarters the UN flag may be placed above flags of all member nations and other national flags may be flown with equal prominence or honor with the flag of the U.S. At services by Navy chaplains at sea, the church pennant may be flown above the flag.

When two flags are placed against a wall with crossed staffs, the U.S. flag should be at right—its own right, and its staff should be in front of the staff of the other flag; when a number of flags are grouped and displayed from staffs, it should be at the center and highest point of the group.

Church and Platform Use—In an auditorium, the flag may be displayed flat, above and behind the speaker. If on a staff in a church chancel or on a speaker's platform, it should be in the position of honor at the clergyman's or speaker's right as he faces the congregation or audience. Any other flag in the chancel or on the platform should be displayed at the clergyman's or speaker's left. If elsewhere than in chancel or on platform, the flag should be displayed at the right of the congregation or audience as they face the speaker.

When the flag is displayed horizontally or vertically against a wall, the stars should be at the observer's left.

When to Salute the Flag—All persons present should face the flag, stand at attention and salute on the following occasions: (1) When the flag is passing in a parade or in a review, (2) During the ceremony of hoisting or lowering, (3) When the National Anthem is played and the flag is displayed, and (4) During the Pledge of Allegiance. Those present in uniform should render the military salute. When not in uniform, men should remove the hat with the right hand holding it at the left shoulder, the hand being over the heart. Men without hats should salute in the same manner. Aliens should stand at attention. Women should salute by placing the right hand over the heart.

On Memorial Day, the flag should fly at half-staff until noon, then be raised to the peak.

As provided by Presidential proclamation the flag should fly at half-staff for 30 days from the day of a death of a president or former president; for 10 days from the day of death of a vice president, chief justice or retired chief justice of the U.S., or speaker of the House of Representatives; from day of death until burial of an associate justice of the Supreme Court, cabinet member, former vice president, or Senate president pro tempore, majority or minority Senate leader, or majority or minority House leader; for a U.S. senator, representative, territorial delegate, or the resident commissioner of Puerto Rico, on day of death and the following day within the metropolitan area of the District of Columbia and from day of death until burial within the decedent's state, congressional district, territory or commonwealth; and for the death of the governor of a state, territory, or possession of the U.S., from day of death until burial within that state, territory, or possession.

When used to cover a casket, the flag should be placed so that the union is at the head and over the left shoulder. It should not be lowered into the grave nor touch the ground.

Prohibited Uses of the Flag—The flag should not be dipped to any person or thing. It should never be displayed with the union down save as a distress signal. It should never be carried flat or horizontally, but always aloft and free.

It should not be displayed on a float, motor car or boat except from a staff.

It should never be used as a covering for a ceiling, nor have placed upon it any word, design, or drawing. It should never be used as a receptacle for carrying anything. It should not be used to cover a statue or a monument.

The flag should never be used for advertising purposes, nor be embroidered on such articles as cushions or handkerchiefs, printed or otherwise impressed on boxes or used as a costume or athletic uniform. Advertising signs should not be fastened to its staff or halyard.

The flag should never be used as drapery of any sort, never festooned, drawn back, nor up, in folds, but always allowed to fall free. Bunting of blue, white and red always arranged with the blue above and the white in the middle, should be used for covering a speaker's desk, draping the front of a platform, and for decoration in general.

An Act of Congress approved Feb. 8, 1917, provided certain penalties for the desecration, mutilation or improper use of the flag within the District of Columbia. A 1968 federal law provided penalties of up to a year's imprisonment or a $1,000 fine or both, for publicly burning or otherwise desecrating any flag of the United States. In addition, many states have laws against flag desecration.

How to Dispose of Worn Flags—The flag, when it is in such condition that it is no longer a fitting emblem for display, should be destroyed in a dignified way, preferably by burning in private.

Pledge of Allegiance to the Flag

I pledge allegiance to the flag of the United States of America and to the republic for which it stands, one nation under God, indivisible, with liberty and justice for all.

This, the current official version of the Pledge of Allegiance, has developed from the original pledge, which was first published in the Sept. 8, 1892, issue of the Youth's Companion, a weekly magazine then published in Boston. The original pledge contained the phrase "my flag," which was changed more than 30 years later to "flag of the United States of America." An act of Congress in 1954 added the words "under God."

The authorship of the pledge has been in dispute for many years. The Youth's Companion stated in 1917 that the original draft was written by James B. Upham, an executive of the magazine who died in 1910. A leaflet circulated by the magazine later named Upham as the originator of the draft "afterwards condensed and perfected by him and his associates of the Companion force."

Francis Bellamy, a former member of the Youth's Companion editorial staff, publicly claimed authorship of the pledge in 1923. The United States Flag Assn., acting on the advice of a committee named to study the controversy, upheld in 1939 the claim of Bellamy, who had died 8 years earlier. The Library of Congress issued in 1957 a report attributing the authorship to Bellamy.

The Flag of the U.S.—The Stars and Stripes

The 50-star flag of the United States was raised for the first time officially at 12:01 a.m. on July 4, 1960, at Fort McHenry National Monument in Baltimore, Md. The 50th star had been added for Hawaii; a year earlier the 49th, for Alaska. Before that, no star had been added since 1912, when N. M. and Ariz. were admitted to the Union.

History of the Flag

The true history of the Stars and Stripes has become so cluttered by a volume of myth and tradition that the facts are difficult, and in some cases impossible, to establish. For example, it is not certain who designed the Stars and Stripes, who made the first such flag, or even whether it ever flew in any sea fight or land battle of the American Revolution. Historians disagree on many details of the history of the Stars and Stripes and the flags that preceded it.

One thing all agree on is that the Stars and Stripes originated as the result of a resolution offered by the Marine Committee of the Second Continental Congress at Philadelphia and adopted Jun. 14, 1777. It read:

Resolved: that the flag of the United States be thirteen stripes, alternate red and white; that the union be thirteen stars, white in a blue field, representing a new constellation.

Congress gave no hint as to the designer of the flag, no instructions as to the arrangement of the stars, and no information on its appropriate uses. Historians have been unable to find the original flag law.

The resolution establishing the flag was not even published until Sept. 2, 1777, more than 11 weeks after its passage. Despite repeated requests by the American commander, Gen. George Washington, for the "Standard of the United States" for his army, he did not get the flags until 1783, after the Revolutionary War was over. And there is no certainty that they were the Stars and Stripes.

Early Flags

Although it was never officially adopted by the Continental Congress, many historians consider the first flag of the United States to have been the Grand Union (sometimes called Great Union) flag. This was a modification of the British Meteor flag, which had the red cross of St. George and the white cross of St. Andrew combined in the blue canton. For the Grand Union flag, 6 horizontal stripes were imposed on the red field, dividing it into 13 alternate red and white stripes. On Jan. 1, 1776, when the Continental Army came into formal existence, this flag was unfurled on Prospect Hill, Somerville, Mass. Washington wrote that "we hoisted the Union Flag in compliment to the United Colonies."

One of several flags about which controversy has raged for years is at Easton, Pa. Containing the devices of the national flag in reversed order, this has been in the public library at Easton for over 150 years. Supporters of the movement contend that this flag was actually the first Stars and Stripes, and that it was first displayed on July 8, 1776, on the occasion of the public reading of the Declaration of Independence at the court house in Easton. This flag has 13 red and white stripes in the canton, 13 white stars centered in a blue field.

A flag was hastily improvised from garments by the defenders of Fort Schuyler at Rome, N.Y., Aug. 3-22, 1777, and this has led to the assumption that it was the Stars and Stripes. Historians believe it was the Grand Union Flag.

The Sons of Liberty had a flag of 9 red and white stripes, to signify 9 colonies, when they met in New York in 1765 to oppose the Stamp Tax. By 1775, the flag had grown to 13 red and white stripes, with a rattlesnake on it.

At Concord, Apr. 19, 1775, the minute men from Bedford, Mass., are said to have carried a flag having a silver arm with sword on a red field.

At Cambridge, Mass., the Sons of Liberty used a plain red flag with a green pine tree on it.

In June 1775, Washington went from Philadelphia to Boston to take command of the army, escorted to New York by the Philadelphia Light Horse Troop. It carried a yellow flag which had an elaborate coat of arms — the shield charged with 13 knots, the motto "For These We Strive" — and a canton of 13 blue and silver stripes.

In Feb., 1776, Col. Christopher Gadsden, member of the Continental Congress, gave the South Carolina Provincial Congress a flag "such as is to be used by the commander-in-chief of the American Navy." It had a yellow field, with a rattlesnake about to strike and the words "Don't Tread on Me." Benjamin Franklin's paper, the Pennsylvania Gazette, had suggested sending a cargo of rattlesnakes to London parks to retaliate for British injustice.

At the battle of Bennington, Aug. 16, 1777, patriots used a flag of 7 white and 6 red stripes with a blue canton extending down 9 stripes and showing an arch of 11 white stars over the figure 76 and a star in each of the upper corners. The stars are seven-pointed. This flag is preserved in the Historical Museum at Bennington, Vt.

At the Battle of Cowpens, Jan. 17, 1781, the 3d Maryland Regt. is said to have carried a flag of 13 red and white stripes, with a blue canton containing 12 stars in a circle around one star.

Legends about the Flag

Who Designed the Flag? No one knows for a certainty. Francis Hopkinson, a signer of the Declaration of Independence and designer of seals for the State Department, the Treasury Board, and of a naval flag, declared he also had designed the flag and in 1781 asked Congress to reimburse him for his services. Congress did not do so. Dumas Malone of Columbia Univ. wrote: "This talented man . . . designed the American flag."

Who Called the Flag Old Glory? — The flag is said to have been named Old Glory by William Driver, a sea captain of Salem, Mass. One legend has it that when he raised the flag on his brig, the Charles Doggett, in 1824, he said: "I name thee Old Glory." But his daughter, who presented the flag to the Smithsonian Institution, said he named it at his 21st birthday celebration Mar. 17, 1824, when his mother presented the homemade flag to him.

Washington Coat-of-Arms Legend — The idea that the flag was suggested by Washington's coat of arms was publicized by Martin F. Tupper, an English writer, in a play in the 1870s. It rests on a coincidence and has no validity.

Washington's Invocation Legend — Circulation has been given to this speech attributed to General Washington: "We take the stars from heaven, the red from our mother country, separating it by white stripes, thus showing that we have separated from her, and the white stripes shall go down to posterity representing liberty." There is no proof that Washington ever said this.

The Betsy Ross Legend — The widely publicized legend that Mrs. Betsy Ross made the first Stars and Stripes in June 1776, at the request of a committee composed of George Washington, Robert Morris, and George Ross, an uncle, was first made public in 1870, by a grandson of Mrs. Ross. Historians have been unable to find a historical record of such a meeting or committee. Dr. Milo Milton Quaife wrote: "No record has ever been found of the creation by Mrs. Ross of the first Stars and Stripes." The New Century Cyclopedia of Names (1954) says: "There is documentary evidence that she was paid in May, 1777, for 'making ships' colours, etc.' but no direct documentary evidence has been found to link her with the flag adopted by the Continental Congress on June 14, 1777, as the national emblem, and most historians now doubt if she made it."

Adding New Stars

The flag of 1777 was used until 1795. Then, on the admission of Vermont and Kentucky to the Union, Congress passed an act that after May 1, 1795, the flag should have 15 stripes, alternate red and white, and 15 white stars on a blue field in the union.

When new states were admitted it became evident that the flag would become burdened with stripes. Congress thereupon ordered that after July 4, 1818, the flag should have 13 stripes, symbolizing the 13 original states; that the union have 20 stars, and that whenever a new state was admitted a new star should be added on the July 4 following admission. No law designates the permanent arrangement of the stars. However, since 1912 when a new state has been admitted, the new design has been announced by executive order. No star is specifically identified with any state.

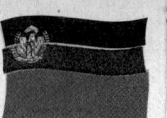
AFGHANISTAN

ALBANIA

ALGERIA

ANDORRA

ANGOLA

ARGENTINA

AUSTRALIA

AUSTRIA

BAHAMAS

BAHRAIN

BANGLADESH

BARBADOS

BELGIUM

BENIN

BHUTAN

BOLIVIA

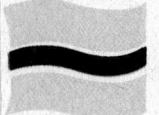
BOTSWANA

BRAZIL

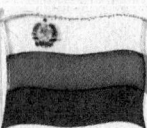
BULGARIA

BURMA

BURUNDI

CAMBODIA

CAMEROON

CANADA

CAPE VERDE

CENTRAL AFRICAN
REPUBLIC

CHAD

CHILE

CHINA (MAINLAND)

CHINA (TAIWAN)

COLOMBIA

COMORO ISLANDS

CONGO

COSTA RICA

CUBA

CYPRUS

CZECHOSLOVAKIA

DENMARK

DOMINICAN REPUBLIC

Flags shown are *national* flags in common use and vary slightly from official *state* flags, most particularly by omitting coats of arms in some cases.

ECUADOR

EGYPT

EL SALVADOR

EQUATORIAL GUINEA

ETHIOPIA

FIJI

FINLAND

FRANCE

GABON

GAMBIA

GERMAN DEM. REP.

GERMANY, FED. REP. OF

GHANA

GREECE

GRENADA

GUATEMALA

GUINEA

GUINEA-BISSAU

GUYANA

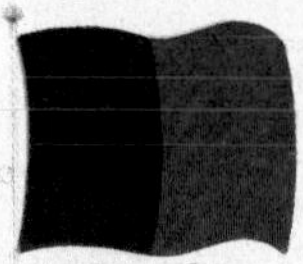

HAITI

HONDURAS

HUNGARY

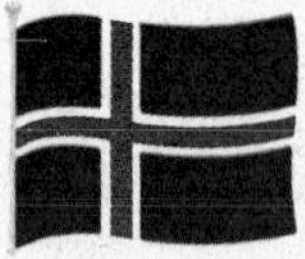

ICELAND

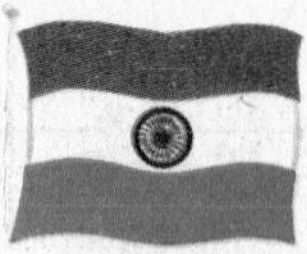

INDIA

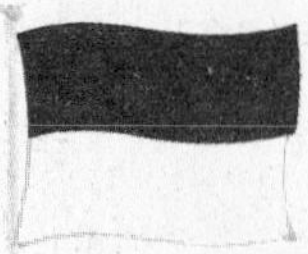

INDONESIA

IRAN

IRAQ

IRELAND

ISRAEL

ITALY

IVORY COAST

JAMAICA

JAPAN

JORDAN

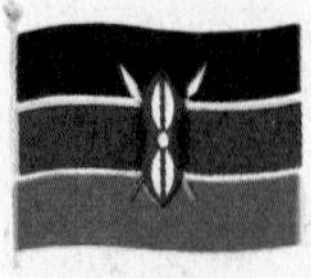

KENYA

KOREA, NORTH

KOREA, SOUTH

KUWAIT

LAOS

LEBANON

LESOTHO

LIBERIA

LIBYA

LIECHTENSTEIN

LUXEMBOURG

MADAGASCAR

MALAWI

MALAYSIA

MALDIVES

MALI

MALTA

MAURITANIA

MAURITIUS

MEXICO

MONACO

MONGOLIA

MOROCCO

MOZAMBIQUE

NAURU

NEPAL

NETHERLANDS

NEW ZEALAND

NICARAGUA

NIGER

NIGERIA

NORWAY

OMAN

PAKISTAN

PANAMA

PAPUA NEW GUINEA

PARAGUAY

PERU

PHILIPPINES

POLAND

PORTUGAL

QATAR

RHODESIA

ROMANIA

RWANDA

SAN MARINO

484

SAO TOME & PRINCIPE	SAUDI ARABIA	SENEGAL	SEYCHELLES	SIERRA LEONE
SINGAPORE	SOMALIA	SOUTH AFRICA	SPAIN	SRI LANKA
SUDAN	SURINAM	SWAZILAND	SWEDEN	SWITZERLAND
SYRIA	TANZANIA	THAILAND	TOGO	TONGA
TRINIDAD & TOBAGO	TUNISIA	TURKEY	UGANDA	U.S.S.R.
UNITED ARAB EMIRATES	UNITED KINGDOM	UNITED STATES	UPPER VOLTA	URUGUAY
VATICAN CITY	VENEZUELA	VIETNAM	WESTERN SAMOA	YEMEN
YEMEN, P.D.R. OF	YUGOSLAVIA	ZAIRE	ZAMBIA

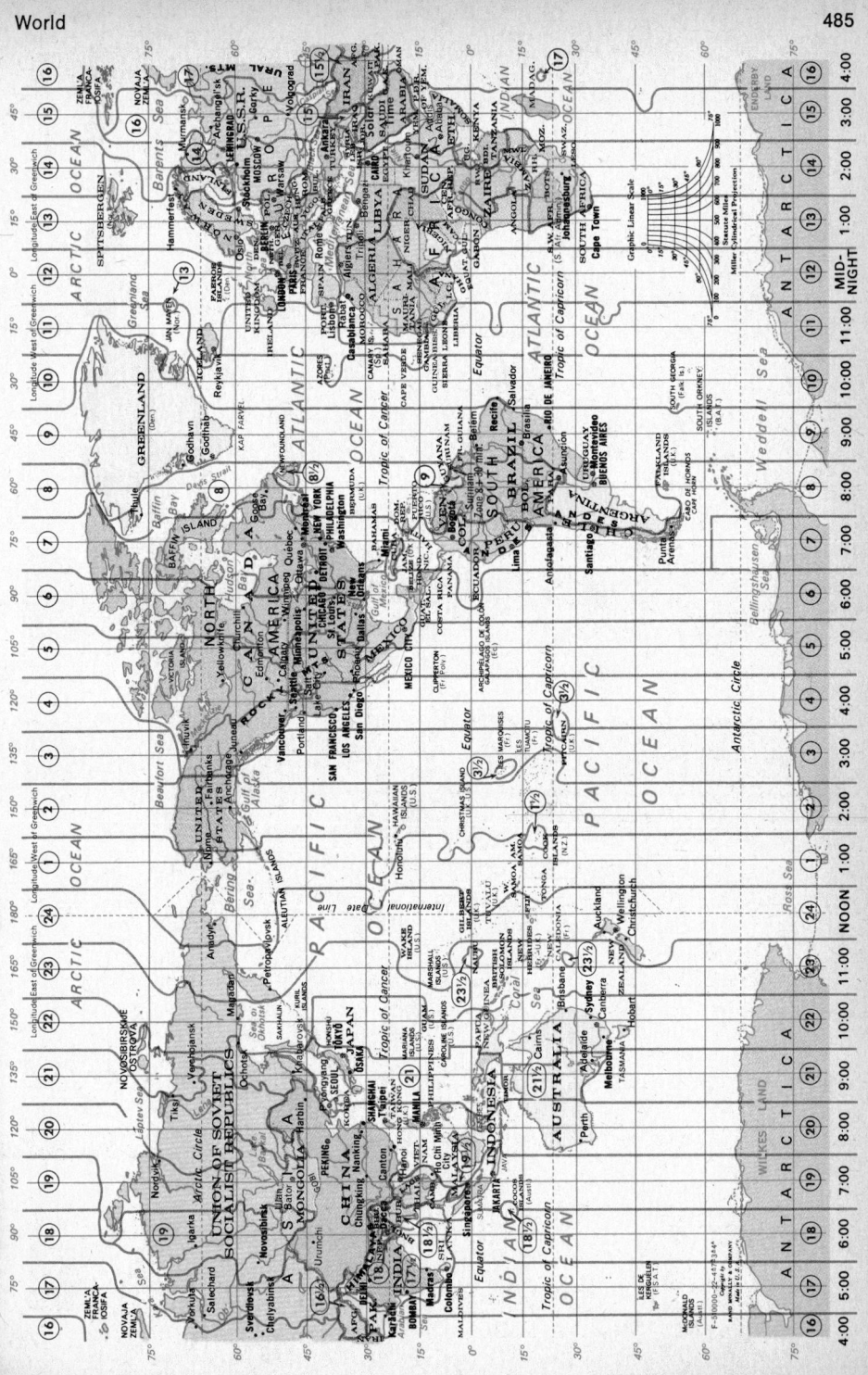

ARCTIC OCEAN
North Pole
ASIA
U.S.S.R.
Anadyr
BERING SEA
GREENLAND (Den.)
Greenland Sea
JAN MAYEN (Nor.)
FAEROE ISLANDS (Den.)
ICELAND
Reykjavík
Angmagssalik
ELLESMERE ISLAND
BAFFIN ISLAND
Baffin Bay
Davis Strait
Labrador Sea
NEWFOUNDLAND
St. John's
Goose Bay
Schefferville
Fort George
BELCHER ISLANDS
York Factory
Churchill
Hudson Bay
Repulse Bay
Yellowknife
Port Radium
Uranium City
Inuvik
Cambridge Bay
VICTORIA ISLAND
BANKS ISLAND
MELVILLE ISLAND
PRINCE OF WALES ISLAND
Beaufort Sea
POINT BARROW
BROOKS RA.
UNITED STATES
Nome
Bethel
Anchorage
Valdez
Seward
KODIAK ISLAND
ALASKA PENINSULA
Bristol Bay
Gulf of Alaska
Juneau
Skagway
Whitehorse
Ketchikan
Prince Rupert
QUEEN CHARLOTTE ISLANDS
Dawson Creek
Prince George
VANCOUVER ISLAND
Victoria
Vancouver
Seattle
Portland
Spokane
CANADA
Edmonton
Calgary
Saskatoon
Regina
Winnipeg
Flin Flon
Sudbury
Timmins
Moosonee
Québec
MONTREAL
Ottawa
TORONTO
Halifax
Portland
BOSTON
Providence
Albany
Buffalo
DETROIT
CLEVELAND
NEW YORK
PHILADELPHIA
WASHINGTON
Norfolk
Richmond
Raleigh
Charlotte
Columbia
Charleston
Savannah
Jacksonville
PITTSBURGH
Cincinnati
Louisville
Nashville
Atlanta
Montgomery
Mobile
Birmingham
Memphis
Little Rock
ST. LOUIS
CHICAGO
Milwaukee
Madison
Indianapolis
Baltimore
Kansas City
Omaha
Saint Paul
Minneapolis
Duluth
Fargo
Bismarck
Pierre
Cheyenne
Denver
Wichita
Oklahoma City
Fort Worth
Dallas
Houston
New Orleans
Tampa
Miami
San Antonio
Laredo
Brownsville
Great Falls
Boise
Salt Lake City
GREAT BASIN
Reno
SACRAMENTO
SAN FRANCISCO
LOS ANGELES
San Diego
Las Vegas
Phoenix
Albuquerque
Santa Fe
El Paso
UNITED STATES
Mount Shasta
Mount Whitney
Mount Rainier
CAPE MENDOCINO
PACIFIC OCEAN
ATLANTIC OCEAN
BERMUDA (UK)
BAHAMAS
Nassau
Havana
CUBA
HAITI
DOM. REP.
San Juan
PUERTO RICO (U.S.)
JAMAICA
Kingston
Guantánamo
Port-au-Prince
WEST INDIES
CARIBBEAN SEA
GUAT.
HONDURAS
NICARAGUA
COSTA RICA
PANAMA
CANAL ZONE
Colón
Barranquilla
Maracaibo
VENEZUELA
Medellín
BOGOTÁ
COLOMBIA
SOUTH AMERICA
Tropic of Cancer
GULF OF MEXICO
MEXICO
MEXICO CITY
Guadalajara
Mazatlán
La Paz
CABO SAN LUCAS
BAJA CALIFORNIA
Hermosillo
Chihuahua
Torreón
Monterrey
Tampico
Veracruz
Mérida
YUCATAN PENINSULA
BELIZE
Belmopan
Guatemala
San Salvador
EL SALVADOR
Tegucigalpa
Managua
Bluefields
San José
Panamá
Acapulco
Oaxaca
Villahermosa
CABO CORRIENTES
SIERRA MADRE OCCIDENTAL
SIERRA MADRE ORIENTAL
YUKON R.
MACKENZIE MTS.
Arctic Circle
ROCKY MOUNTAINS
GREAT SLAVE LAKE
Great Bear Lake
Lake Athabasca
Tropic of Cancer

F-520000-21-3853-343ᴬ
Copyright by
RAND MᶜNALLY & COMPANY
Made in U.S.A.

(Inset map, lower left)
U.S.S.R.
Kavača
KOMANDORSKIE OSTROVA
UNITED STATES
BERING SEA
PRIBILOF ISLANDS
Bethel
ALEUTIAN ISLANDS
ATTU ISLAND
UNIMAK ISLAND
Unalaska
PACIFIC OCEAN

Statute Miles　0　200　400　600　800
Kilometers　0　200　400　600　800　1000　1200
Longitude West of Greenwich

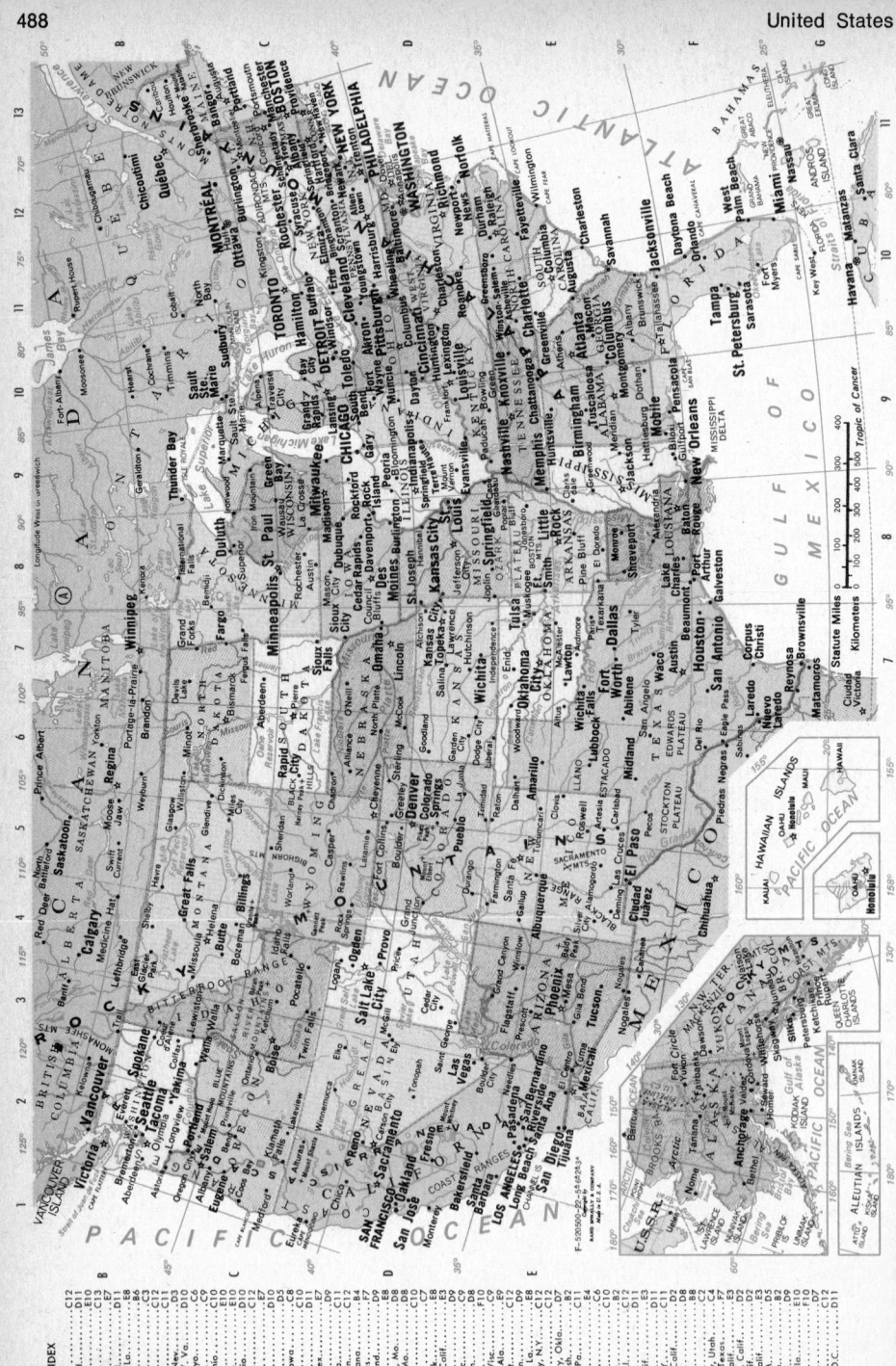

U.S.A. Miami
BAHAMAS
Nassau
SAN SALVADOR
Havana
CUBA
Mérida
ISLA DE PINOS
Santiago de Cuba
CAYMAN IS.
(U.K.)
HAITI
JAMAICA
Port-au-Prince
Kingston
DOM.
REP.
Santo
Domingo
PUERTO
RICO
VIRGIN (U.K. and U.S.)
San Juan IS.
ANTIGUA (U.K.)
BARBUDA
GUADELOUPE (Fr.)
DOMINICA (U.K.)
MARTINIQUE (Fr.)
Fort-de-France
Bridgetown
BARBADOS
GRENADA
Port of Spain
TRINIDAD
AND
TOBAGO
Tropic of Cancer

WEST INDIES
CARIBBEAN SEA
NETHERLANDS
ANTILLES
LESSER ANTILLES

Guatemala
BELIZE
Belmopan
HONDURAS
Tegucigalpa
EL San Salvador
SALV.
NICARAGUA
Managua
Bluefields
COSTA
San José RICA
David
PANAMA
C.Z.
Colón
Panamá
Bucaramanga
Cúcuta
San Cristóbal
Ciudad Bolívar
Ciudad Guayana
Barquisimeto
Barcelona
CARACAS
Maracaibo
Santa
Marta
Barranquilla
Cartagena

ISLA DEL
COCO (C.R.)
ISLA DE
MALPELO
(Col.)
ARCHIPIÉLAGO
DE COLÓN
GALAPAGOS ISLANDS
(EC.)
ISLA ISABELA

Medellín
Manizales
Nevado del Tolima
BOGOTÁ
Cali
Buenaventura
COLOMBIA
Tumaco
CABO DE
SAN FRANCISCO
Esmeraldas
Quito
Mitú
ECUADOR
Guayaquil
Cuenca
Golfo de Guayaquil
Piura
Chiclayo
Cajamarca
Trujillo
Chimbote
Callao
LIMA
Huancayo
Ica
Cuzco

VENEZUELA
Puerto Ayacucho
Mt. Roraima
San Fernando
de Atabapo
GUYANA
Georgetown
Paramaribo
SURI-
NAM
FR. GUIANA
Cayenne
Boa Vista
Amapá
Macapá
ILHA DE
MARAJÓ

Leticia
Fonte Boa
Óbidos
Manaus
Santarém
Pôrto de
Moz
Belém
São Luís
Parnaíba
Fortaleza
Natal
João
Pessoa
Recife
Maceió
Aracaju
Salvador

SELVAS
BRAZIL
Pôrto
Velho
Rio
Branco
Cobija
Riberalta
SERRA DOS PARECIS
PLANALTO DO
MATO
GROSSO
Teresina
Marabá
Carolina
Pôrto Nacional
Barra
Juàzeiro
Caruaru
Penedo

PERU
Nevado
Huascarán
Cerro de Pasco
Huaraz
Pucallpa
Iquitos
Lago Titicaca
Puno
Volcán Misti
Arequipa
Mollendo
Arica
Iquique
Antofagasta

Guajará Mirim
Trinidad
Nevado
Illampu
LA PAZ
Oruro
Sucre
Potosí
BOLIVIA
Santa Cruz
Corumbá
Tarija
San Salvador
de Jujuy

Mato Grosso
Cuiabá
GROSSO
Goiânia
Brasília
Goiás
Montes
Claros
Belo Horizonte
Governador
Valadares
Vitória
CABO DE SÃO TOMÉ
Campos
Ilhéus
Itabuna
Belmonte

Tropic of Capricorn

Campo
Grande
Campinas
Londrina
Ponta Grossa
SÃO PAULO
RIO DE JANEIRO
Santos
Curitiba
Florianópolis

PARAGUAY
ASunción
Pilar
Concepción
Pedro Juan Caballero

Salta
San Miguel
de Tucumán
Cerro Ojos
del Salado
Santiago del
Estero
Córdoba
Santa
Fe
Rosario
BUENOS AIRES
La Plata
Mar del
Plata

ARGENTINA
San Juan
Cerro
Aconcagua
Mendoza
Viña del Mar
Valparaíso
SANTIAGO
Talca
Concepción
Talcahuano
Temuco
Valdivia
Osorno
Puerto Montt

URUGUAY
Montevideo
Paysandú
Salto
Pelotas
Pôrto Alegre
Rio Grande
Rocha
Santa
Maria
Río de la Plata
CABO
SAN ANTONIO
Bahía Blanca
Viedma

PACIFIC OCEAN
ATLANTIC OCEAN

ISLA SAN FÉLIX
(Chile)
ISLA SAN AMBROSIO
(Chile)
PUNTA MORRO
Coquimbo
ISLAS JUAN FERNÁNDEZ
(Chile)
ISLA
ALEJANDRO
SELKIRK
ISLA
ROBINSON
CRUSOE

Neuquén
PATAGONIA
ISLA DE
CHILOÉ
Monte
San Valentín
CABO DOS BAHÍAS
Comodoro Rivadavia
Golfo San Jorge
Rawson
Golfo San Matías
ISLA
WELLINGTON
Puerto Natales
Río Gallegos
Punta Arenas
TIERRA DEL FUEGO
Ushuaia
CABO DE HORNOS
CAPE HORN
FALKLAND
ISLANDS
(U.K.)
Stanley
SOUTH GEORGIA
(Falk. Is.)

Statute Miles 0 200 400 600 800
Kilometers 0 200 400 600 800 1000 1200

Longitude West of Greenwich

F-540000-21-4548264*
Copyright by
RAND MᶜNALLY & COMPANY
Made in U.S.A.

CARIBBEAN SEA
CANAL
ZONE
(U.S.)
Colón (Pan.)
Chepo
PANAMA
Gatún
Panamá
Balboa Heights
La Chorrera
Penonomé
Bay of Panama

Map of Europe

Statute Miles
Kilometers

Longitude West of Greenwich Longitude East of Greenwich

F-580000-21-9588485⁴
Copyright by
RAND M⁹NALLY & COMPANY
Made in U.S.A.

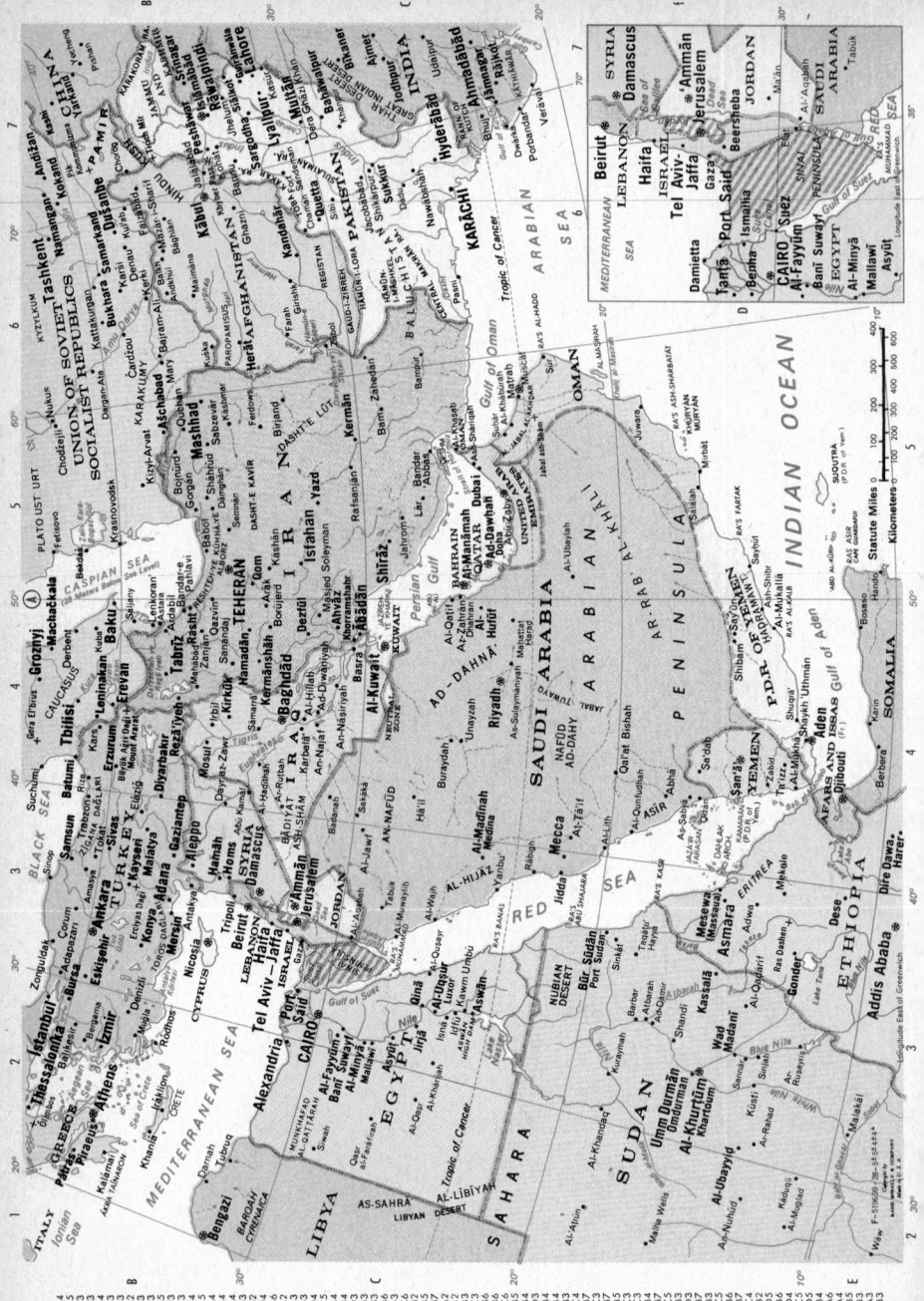

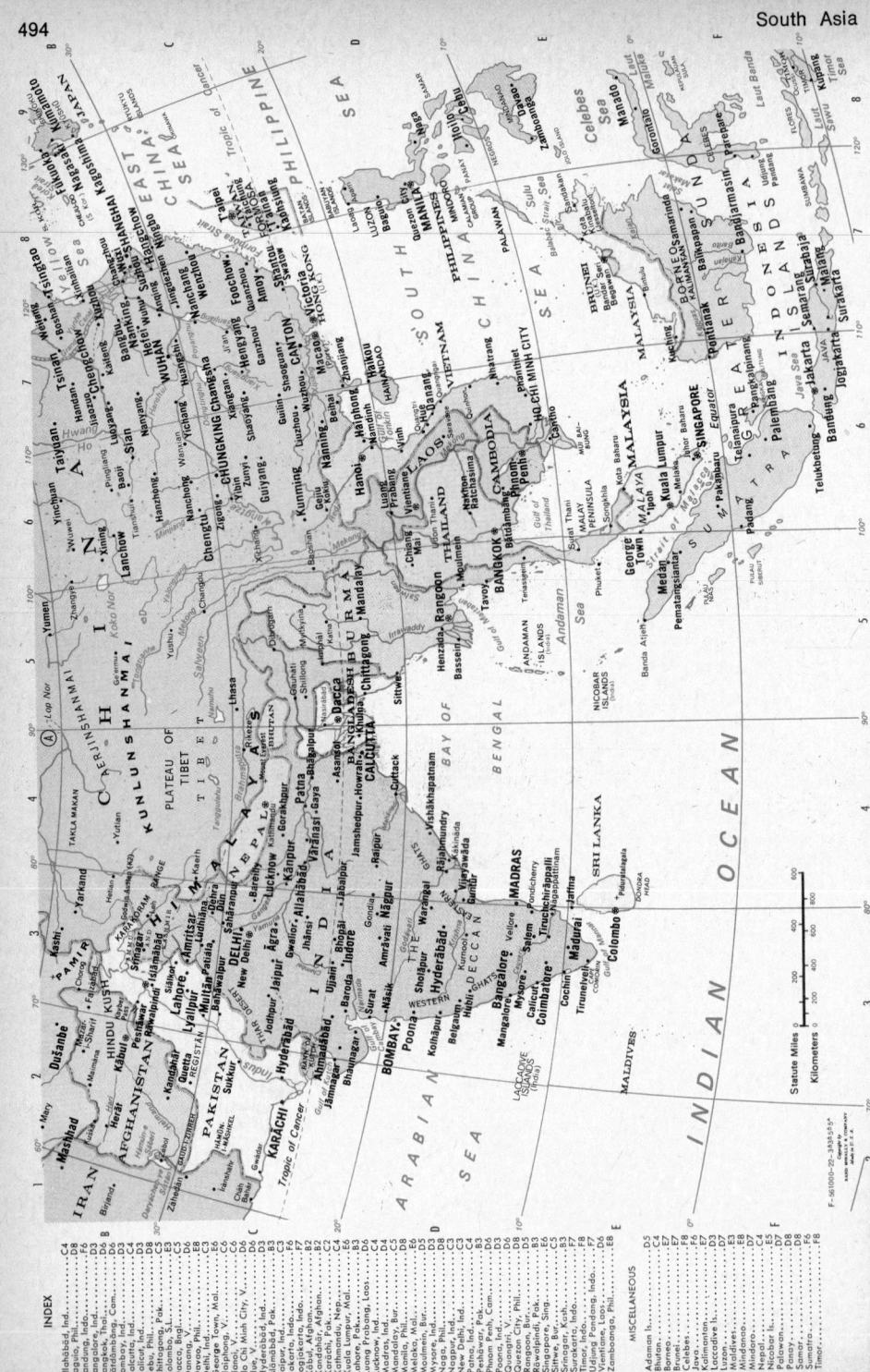

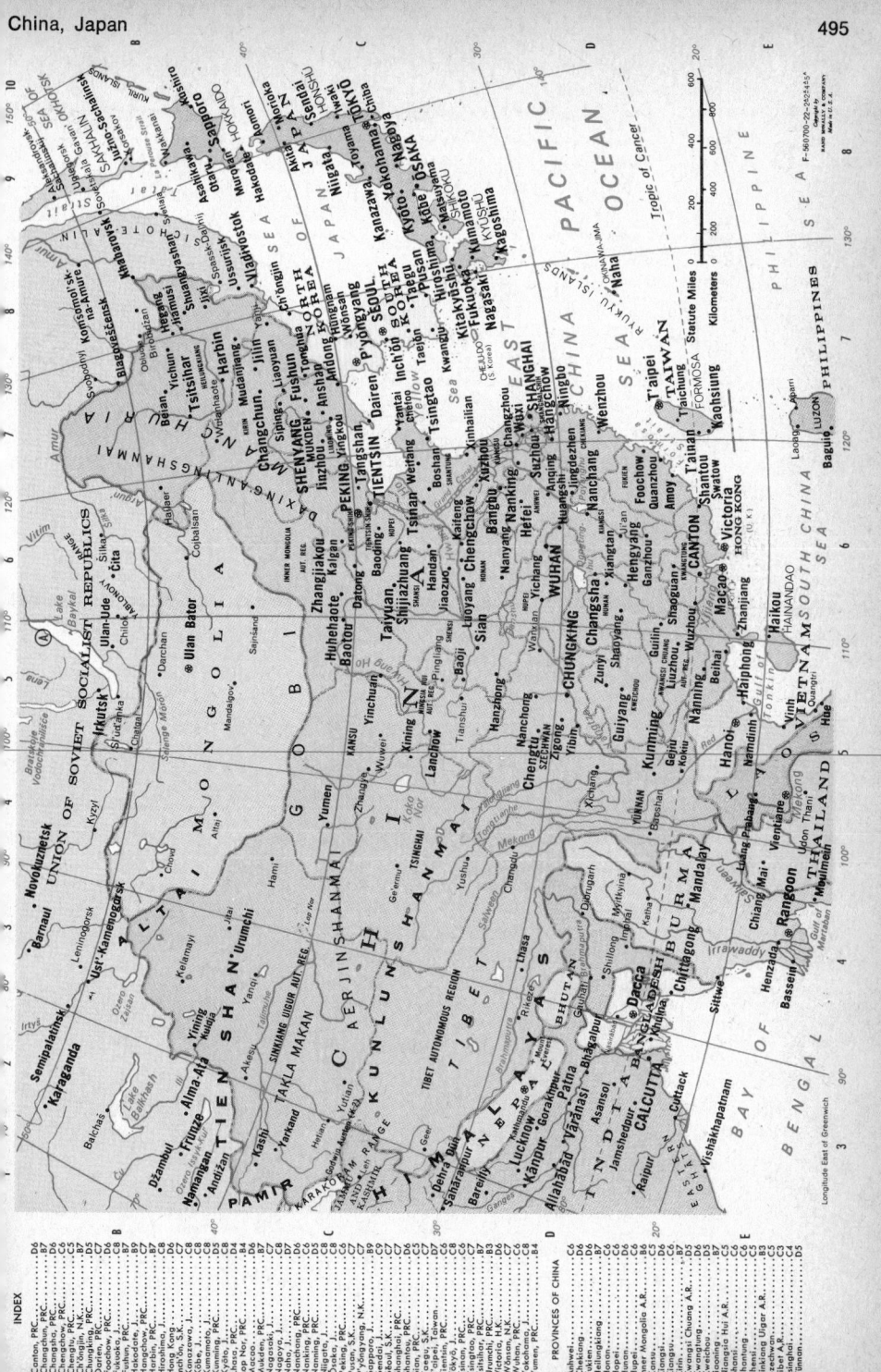

CANADA

Capital: Ottawa. Area: 3,851,809 sq. mi. Population (Govt. est., Jan. 1976): 22,998,000. Monetary unit: Canadian dollar.

Government and Politics

Prime Minister Pierre Trudeau's Liberal government, re-elected in 1974 with a slight majority of 18 seats, has been plagued by scandals and controversy.

Many of the major policies of the Trudeau government have generated intense criticism from large segments of the Canadian public. Trudeau's attempt to implement bilingualism by making French as well as English an official operative language provoked renewed controversy. The Government's bilingual training program for federal civil servants — a top priority with the P.M. — was dealt a severe blow when the Commissioner of Official Languages said that 89% of the program's graduates were unable to use their second official language on the job.

Another highly controversial policy was the government's wages and prices restraint policy. On October 13, 1975, Prime Minister Trudeau announced mandatory guidelines on incomes and prices for federal employees, large companies, and professionals. Parliament subsequently passed an Anti-Inflation Act to control wages and prices by setting up a tough Anti-Inflation Review Board (AIB). Attributing spiralling double-digit inflation to excessive wage demands, which reached unprecedented levels of 30 to 40 per cent for some groups in 1975, the government claimed Canadians had been demanding too much from the economy. Calling for restraint, Trudeau also tried to reduce unemployment, which rose from 5.4% in 1974 to 8.1% in April 1975.

The new guidelines allowed individual wage earners a maximum 12% increase in wages in the first year, 8% in the 2nd year, and 6% in the 3rd year. All professionals, such as doctors, lawyers, accountants, and engineers, were subjected to increased fee limits of the lesser of 12% or $2,400. Certain professional categories like teachers and executives were allowed overall average group increases of $2,400 a year.

The directives applied to the 1,500 largest companies in Canada, defined as firms having more than 500 employees, although construction companies were affected if they had 20 employees or more. By June 1976, all companies including trust and loan companies as well as chartered banks were brought under the controls. Under the existing regulations (July 1976) companies can choose between using as a base year for profit margin calculations either the latest fiscal year completed previous to May 1, 1976, or the average of the five fiscal years completed before October 14, 1975. The allowable net margin of profit has been reduced from 95% of the base to 85%.

With the exception of two provinces — Saskatchewan and Quebec — which administer their own wage and price controls under separate anti-inflation boards, the provincial governments apply the federal guidelines to salaries, prices, and rents under their jurisdiction.

Appeals from AIB decisions are heard by an administrator who is empowered to order a reduction in price or salary increases. If the administrator's order is disobeyed, stiff penalties ranging from a fine of up to $5,000, or one year in jail can be levied. In February 1976, the administrator handed down a $125,000 penalty against the Irving Pulp and Paper Ltd. for contravening the anti-inflation guidelines by paying employees more than the 14% granted by the AIB.

The new restraint program incurred the wrath of business and organized labor. Union leaders accused the government of trying to make "labor" the scapegoat in the inflation crisis. Invoking the overwhelming support of its members, the Canadian Labour Congress staged a massive demonstration against the anti-inflation program and withdrew from the Economic Council of Canada and the tripartite Canadian Labour Relations Council.

Still more controversial was the Federal government's bill to abolish the death penalty, which won Parliamentary approval for abolition in June 1976. It was a personal victory for the prime minister, who has been a vehement critic of the death penalty. Parliamentary rules were relaxed, individual MPs were allowed a "free vote" according to their conscience, but abolition passed in the House of Commons by only 133 votes to 125 with 38 of the 139 Liberals voting against the bill; 18 of the 95 Conservatives (including the party's new leader Joseph Clark) supported the bill; all 16 New Democratic Party MPs voted for the bill while all 11 Social Credit MPs were against it.

Under the new bill there are two degrees of murder. First-degree murder includes premediated murder, or murder of a policeman or prison guard, or murder occurring while commiting or attempting rape, indecent assault, kidnapping and forcible confinement or hijacking. Those convicted of 1st degree murder will face a minimum 25-year sentence before becoming eligible for parole. Second-degree murder, which includes all other types of killings, such as crimes of passion, carries a minimum 10-year jail term before parole eligibility. The bill also introduced stricter gun controls.

A major political highlight of 1976 was the election of Joseph (Joe) Clark as leader of the Progressive Conservative Party, replacing Robert Stanfield. Narrowly defeating the front-runner Claude Wagner on the fourth ballot by 1,187 votes to 1,122, Mr. Clark, a 36-year-old Albertan, has had only four years experience in parliament. If he wins the next Federal election, expected in 1978, the new PC leader would be the youngest Prime Minister in Canadian history.

Foreign Relations

Since 1972 Canada has been pursuing a "Third Option" of "enlightened self-interest" in foreign policy, seeking diversification in political and economic relations. Based on the view that foreign policy is an extension of domestic policy and must be relevant to Canadian needs and interests, the new thrust is towards strengthening Canadian independence and tional sovereignty by reducing Canadian vulnerability to the United States. To achieve these goals, Canada gave very high priority in 1975-76 to her relations with countries like Japan and those in the European Community which could serve as counterweights to the United States.

In addition to strengthening bilateral relations with individual European countries, Canada has recently cooperated more closely with the European Community (EC), signing a "Framework Agreement for Commercial and Economic Co-operation between Canada and the European Communities." The document serves as the basis for a "new contractual link" between Canada and the EC. The concrete benefits to be derived from the agreement for either party are not immediately obvious. The EC could potentially benefit from a secure supply of many raw materials, especially uranium, and greater investment opportunities. At best, Canada could hope for more favorable tariffs on manufactured products.

The new "Japanese connection" is not intended to foster the development of trade by increasing exports of Canada's diminishing natural resources. Instead, the Canadian design is to "export" space by attracting the establishment in Canada of Japanese heavy industries to process raw materials, especially the refining of metals, the processing of agricultural products, and the manufacture of pulp and paper.

Despite these new ventures Canada cannot neglect relations with the United States. Canadian efforts to diversify foreign relations are not an attempt to supplant U.S. influence but merely to supplement it by finding a balance to the country's growing dependence on a single country.

Canadian-American bilateral trade amounts to about $40 billion per annum. The United States takes 67% of Canadian exports and supplies 69% of the country's imports. Canada takes 21% of United States exports and supplies 25% of United States imports. The United States market absorbs up to 35% of all the goods produced in Canada. By contrast Canada buys less than 2% of all goods produced in the U.S. By the end of 1971 American investors controlled 27% of the assets of all non-financial Canadian corporations. In some key industries U.S. control exceeds 75%. Canadian direct investors in the United States own less than one half of one percent of U.S. corporate assets. Given the extent of U.S. investment and trade with Canada a large measure of cooperation is inevitable and essential to promote and sustain the economy.

The two countries cooperate in several areas. Notable is the ratification of the Canada-United States Extradition Treaty in Ottawa, March 1976. Replacing arrangements which date back to 1842, the new treaty will help the law enforcement authorities of the two countries to deal more effectively with some of the most dramatic and intractable problems faced by contemporary society on this continent, such as hijacking of aircraft, political kidnapping, and drug offenses.

Several contentious issues marred Canada-U.S. relations during 1975-76. A Parliamentary Statute eliminated the Canadian editions of Time and Readers Digest; Saskatchewan nationalized the province's potash industry, which included large U.S. holdings; the Canadian Radio-Television Commission deleted from local cable transmissions commercial messages originating in the U.S.; and the American and Canadian governments exacerbated their disputes surrounding two major hydroelectric projects.

Most contentious was Canada's energy policy. The Canadian government decided to increase the price of oil and gas exported, principally to the United States, and to gradually phase out oil exports over the next ten years. The increase in oil and gas prices was felt necessary to bring them in line with world prices.

Canada's most significant departure in foreign policy was its unilateral declaration extending Canadian fisheries jurisdiction to 200 miles off-shore effective January 1, 1977. Within the designated area of jurisdiction Canada will set limits and impose quotas on allowable catches for foreign fishing fleets. Such action is necessary to conserve stock and protect Canada's coastal fishing communities.

Canada has reinforced her sovereignty by making bilateral fishing agreements with Norway, Poland, the Soviet Union, Spain, and Portugal, adding them to an agreement with France entered into in 1972. Canada now will permit foreign vessels to fish in the area concerned under Canadian authority and control.

Also making news was the Canadian nuclear sales policy. Canada is one of the strongest supporters of the Treaty on the Non-Proliferation of Nuclear Weapons. Objecting to India's detonation of a nuclear explosive device in 1974, the Canadian government has tightened its nuclear safeguards by insisting in all nuclear sales agreements that the recipients cannot use the material supplied for any non-peaceful or explosive purpose. The agreements also call for inspection. Under these conditions Canada in 1976 entered into negotiations for nuclear cooperation and sales with the Republic of Korea, Argentina, Spain, and Finland.

An interesting aspect of Canadian foreign policy in 1976 was the prime minister's self-styled "Gateway to Latin American" visit to Cuba, Mexico, and Venezuela. However, Canada-Latin American relations are not a matter of high priority; Canada still rejects membership in the Organization of American States.

The Economy

Measured by constant-dollar gross national product (GNP), real output increased marginally by 0.2% in 1975, which was considerably below the real GNP increase of 2.8% in 1974. Growth in 1975 was uneven: real GNP declined 0.8% in the first quarter and then rose 0.8% in the second quarter, 1% in the third quarter, and 0.4% in the final quarter. In the first quarter of 1976, the GNP, seasonally adjusted at annual rates, increased 4.4% to a level of $176.5 billion. However, after adjustment for price changes, real GNP for the first quarter grew by only 2.7%. This increase left real GNP over 5% higher than at the trough of the recession one year ago.

Agricultural output, as measured by the index of real domestic product, fell 1.6% in 1975 compared with declines of 5.2% in 1974 and 3% in 1973. In the agricultural sector, wheat and feed grain production in Canada rose significantly in 1975, with the total wheat harvest up 28.5% to 627 million bushels and the combined oats, barley, and rye feed grain crop 10.3% above levels of a year earlier. Growth was slower in the animal production sector. Estimated shipment of cattle from farms rose 15.6% from 1974, but because of the greatly reduced inventory of cattle on farms, total production was down 1%. Calf production dropped 25.7% below the 1974 level, hog slaughter also declined while poultry production fell 10.6% in volume from 1974 and egg production showed a slight 0.02% decrease.

Industrial production, which began to decline in the second quarter of 1974, did not recover until the final quarter of 1975. Total industrial output in 1975 was 4.5% below the level of 1974. The largest decline was in mining, especially non-metals.

All non-durable manufacturing industries suffered output declines in 1975, except the food and beverage and the printing and publishing industries. The largest decline was 19% in the paper and allied industries, which were plagued by declining world demand and long work stoppages.

The output of durable goods was 5.5% below in 1974, but output began rising in the second quarter.

Among service industries, output in community, business, and personal services increased 4%, while that of retail trade rose 1.3%.

The volume of residential construction declined by 10.7% in 1975. Despite a severe decline during the first half of 1975, housing starts accelerated as the year went on, totalling 231,456, compared with 222,-123 in 1974 giving an increase of 4.2%. Single detached starts in 1975 declined slightly below the 1974 level; semi-detached and row housing units achieved new levels of popularity; apartment starts declined and rural starts fell 5.8% to the lowest level since 1972. Housing completions declined 15.7% in 1975, reaching only 216,964, compared with 257,243 in 1974.

The average selling price of all types of housing in Canada was 11.8% higher in 1975. This increase is considerably below the 27.1% gain between 1973 and 1974.

Current-dollar expenditure on residential construction in 1975 on a national accounts basis rose 3.8% to $7.9 billion. This compares with 16.8% and 24.1% year-over-year increases in 1974 and 1973 respectively. In 1971 dollars, residential construction expenditure acutally declined 10.7% to $4.8 billlion from $5.3 billion in 1974.

The Canadian labor force increased by 354,000 or 3.6%, a growth rate just below the average growth of 3.7% for the previous four years. In 1974, the growth rate was 4.1%. The 1975 percentage growth rate hides important changes in certain sectors of the labor force. The number of adult women in the work force increased by 159,000, or 6.9%, up from 108,000, or 4.9% in 1974. The number of young people in the labor force grew by 92,000, or 3.5%, compared with 158,000, or 6.3% in 1974. The adult male labor force rose by 104,000, or 2.2%, as compared with 117,000, or 2.5% in the previous year.

Employment declined in the first quarter of 1975 but recovered sufficiently to register moderate gains in the remaining three quarters. In 1975, employment increased by 178,000, or 1.9% compared with an increase of 383,000, or 4.4% the previous year.

The average number unemployed in 1975 was 697,-000, an increase of 176,000 since 1974. As a percentage of the labor force, the 1975 unemployment rate increased to 6.9% from 5.4% in the previous year.

Industrial disputes resulted in a record 11.5 million man-days being lost in 1975 through work stoppages, surpassing the 1974 record of 9.3 million. A breakdown shows that manufacturing lost 5.8 million man-days; construction, 1.5 million; transportation and communication, 1.4 million; and mining, 1.2 million man-days. The major work stoppages included 2.8 million man-days lost in the pulp and paper industry, 690,000 man-days lost among the inside postal workers, 500,000 man-days lost at five Quebec asbestos mines and 246,000 man-days lost due to the Toronto teachers' strike.

On the average, prices increases in 1975 were below the 1974 level. The GNP implicit price deflator rose 9.7% in 1975, compared with 13.8% in 1974, while the consumer price index (CPI) increased 10.8% in 1975, compared with 10.9% in 1974. The difference between these two indicators reflects primarily the changes in export and import trade. The implicit deflator for imports rose 13.9% in 1975 compared with 20.7% in 1974, whereas export prices advanced only 10.4% or about one-third of the 1974 rate. The imbalance between value of total imports and exports of goods in 1975 produced a record current account deficit on a balance of payments basis of $5.1 billion in 1975, compared with $1.6 billion in 1974. In terms of total volume of trade, exports declined by 6.7% in 1975, while total imports decreased by 2.6%.

The implicit price index for gross national expenditures (GNE) increased 9.7% in 1975, a drop in percentage increase from 13.8% in 1974. The implicit deflator for total domestic demand, which is the sum of the final demands by Canadians for both domestically produced and imported goods and services, rose 11% in 1975 compared to 11.9% in 1974.

The volume of business investment in plant and equipment increased by 4.7% in 1975, compared with an increase of 7.9% in 1974. The increase was based primarily on activity in the first quarter of 1975. Nonresidential construction increased in volume by 7.4% during 1975, while machinery and equipment investment rose by only 2.5%. Investment in energy accounted for one-fifth of private investment, or about 4% of GNE, in 1975, and half of this was put into the generation of electricity.

The Land
Canada is the world's 2d largest country in land size, extending south from the North Pole to the U.S. border and including all the islands of the Arctic from near Greenland to near the Alaskan border. Its seacoast, one of the longest in the world, includes 17,-860 miles of mainland and 41,810 miles of islands.

A great sweep of the nation, stretching across the northern territories and prairies through northern Ontario and Quebec down to the Atlantic provinces, is known as the Canadian Shield, where past ice ages scraped most soil and vegetation off the land. This is the world's oldest surface rock, and it is here that most Canadian mineral discoveries have been made.

Canada's continental climate, while generally temperate, can run to freezing cold and blistering heat. The range is well beyond 100 degrees Fahrenheit.

History
French explorer Jacques Cartier is generally regarded as the founder of Canada. But his 1534 exploration of the Gulf of St. Lawrence followed by 37 years the sighting of Newfoundland in 1497 by English seaman John Cabot. Centuries prior to that, increasing evidence shows, Vikings had reached Newfoundland and Canada's Atlantic coast.

France pioneered Canadian settlement and the French have multiplied to become about 27% of the Canadian population today. Quebec was settled as early as 1608, Montreal in 1642; New France was declared a colony in 1663.

Britain and France clashed in Canada as a result of European rivalries and British expansion in America. Britain acquired Acadia (later Nova Scotia) in 1713, and captured Quebec in 1759, obtaining control of the rest of New France in 1763. The Quebec Act in 1774 gave the French rights to their own language, religion, and civil law. This was one reason why the French-Canadian settlers did not join American colonists in the War of Independence.

During the American Revolution, many former colonials moved north to settle in Canada, proudly calling themselves United Empire Loyalists.

The fur trade and exploration opened up the western plains and led Canadians across the continent to the Pacific. Alexander Mackenzie scrawled on a rock by the Pacific "From Canada, by land, 1793."

In Upper and Lower Canada (later called Ontario and Quebec) and in the Maritimes, legislative assemblies appeared in the 18th century and reformers called for responsible government. But the War of 1812 with the U.S. intervened. The war ended in a stalemate that was symbolic of the end to armed conflict between Canada and the U.S.

In 1837 political agitation for more democratic government culminated in rebellions in Upper and Lower Canada. The British sent Lord Durham to investigate and, in a famous report, he recommended union of the two parts into one colony called Canada. The union lasted until Confederation brought 2 additional colonies, Nova Scotia and New Brunswick, to join the new country in 1867. During the period 1840 to 1867, the Canadian colonies won the right to internal self-government.

The Dominion of Canada was launched on July 1, 1867, by the proclamation of the British North America Act, which became the country's written constitution, establishing a federal system of government on the model of a British parliament and cabinet structure under the crown. Canada was proclaimed a self-governing Dominion within the British Empire in 1931. Empire has now given way to Commonwealth, and Canada remains an independent member.

World War I had much to do with the development of Canadian nationhood. The pride it engendered and the industrial base it created in Canada led to the demand for full sovereignty.

But the achievement of nationhood was dulled by the blight of the Great Depression in the 1930s. It took World War II and Canada's accomplishments in it to revive the country's pride and sense of direction. It also fired the furnaces of industry, converting the country into an urban, industrial state.

Industrial Boom

On the Pacific coast a chain of rivers and lakes was reversed to flow backwards through the mountains to power electric generators for the huge aluminum smelters at Kitimat. The Columbia and Kootenay Rivers and Arrow Lakes were dammed to provide electricity. Oil wells and mineral strikes led to an El Dorado. Immense iron ore resources were discovered and developed in the wilds of Labrador. Uranium was unearthed in northern Ontario and turned into nuclear power.

Canada joined with the U.S. to build the St. Lawrence River Seaway, and Ottawa shared costs with the provinces to complete the Trans-Canada Highway, the longest in the world. Two million immigrants arrived in Canada in the 2 decades after World War II and the country imported a billion dollars a year of foreign capital to finance a new industrial boom.

Economic System

Canada has a "mixed economy" — a mixture of private and public ownership. Despite a long historical tradition of state aid which has been necessary because of Canada's harsh climate and sparse population, private enterprise has flourished. But like Sweden, with which it vies for the 2d highest standard of living in the world, Canada accepts the idea of state capitalism and collectivism.

Most hydroelectric and many transportation and communication facilities are owned by either federal, provincial, or municipal governments. Air Canada, one of the largest airlines in the world, is a federal crown corporation, while the competing Canadian Pacific airline is privately owned. Canadian National Railways is another crown corporation. Its chief rival is the Canadian Pacific company. The Canadian Broadcasting Corp. is publicly owned, although independently managed. There are also private radio chains and private television networks.

Social Security

Under the British North America Act (1867), the provinces are responsible for welfare programs to benefit their citizens. The federal government helps the provinces bear the cost of welfare programs. Federal payments reimburse up to 50% of the cost of welfare assistance provided by the provinces. Ottawa has also used its fiscal strength to launch the social security system and help bring about a certain uniformity in the existing programs, ensuring a high level of equity in programs among the provinces.

In the mid-1960s the federal government conceived of a universal and compulsory medicare and hospitalization system. Strenuous provincial opposition to the federal government's proposals delayed implementation of a revised plan until 1968.

Following a three-year review of the social security system, the federal government in 1976 proposed a new program for supplementing incomes of the "working poor" by about $1,200 a year for a family of four when the program begins, perhaps in 1978 or 1979. Ottawa's proposal involves a cost-sharing arrangement whereby the federal government will pay two-thirds of the cost of the supplementary program with the rest being paid by the provinces. While Ontario opposed the plan and New Brunswick and Prince Edward Island took no position, even the 7 provinces which agreed in principle were reluctant to give a firm commitment to undertake their share of the cost. Since the provincial governments are trying to cut their spending, they are afraid that if the program is implemented, the cost of supplementary income could escalate and lead to further increases in public expenditure. To overcome provincial opposition, the federal government has threatened to introduce the program unilaterally by assuming the full cost of payments, administering the plan through the tax system rather than through the provincial welfare offices.

The Social Security system in Canada covers several schemes: Family Allowances, Shared Cost Welfare Programs of the Federal and Provincial Governments; Old Age Security; Guaranteed Income Supplement; The Canada Pension Plan; and Veterans Benefits. Payments under almost all of these schemes are adjusted to the cost of living index.

Provinces of Canada

Alberta

CAPITAL: Edmonton. AREA: 255,285 sq. mi., rank 4th. POPULATION: 1,804,000 (est. Jan. 1976). FLOWER: The Wild Rose. ENTERED CONFEDERATION: 1905.

The vast area of Alberta was controlled by the Hudson's Bay Co. until 1870, at which time it was transferred to the Northwest Territories.

Along with Saskatchewan, Alberta is nicknamed the "sunshine" province because of its good weather. The weather is strongly affected by the "Chinook," a warm wind blowing eastward over the Rockies. The Rocky Mountains provide such famous tourist attractions as Banff and Jasper parks, Lake Louise and the Columbian ice fields.

Wheat and cattle gave Alberta its start but the economy was transformed by the discovery of huge petroleum and natural gas supplies at Leduc near Edmonton in 1947.

Alberta's economy gave a spectacular performance in 1975 and the bonanza growth rate of the economy shows no sign of declining in 1976. Economic growth is expected to continue at a "heady pace" with expansion in production of oil, gas, petroleum and petrochemicals products. Estimates for 1975 show total capital and repair expenditures in the province grew by 25%, from $4.5 billion in 1974 to $5.7 billion in 1975. The forecasts for the sustained economic activity in Alberta are supported by the vast amount of capital investment in the economy. In 1975, the growth rate of capital investment was more than 10 percentage points greater than the national level. In addition, Alberta's contribution to the total Canadian capital and repair expenditure amounted to 12% despite the fact that the province provides between 8.5 and 9% of the Canadian output.

Government spending in the 1976-77 fiscal year is expected to reach $2.93 billion, an increase of 7.7% over the previous year's expenditures. However, if the previous year expenditures estimate is used as the base, expenditure for the current fiscal year increased close to 16%, far above the 11% ceiling imposed on annual increase in governmental expenditure. Despite record levels of government spending, and the province's high cash deficit of $162.1 million at the end of December 1975, compared with a healthy cash surplus of $329.4 million at the end of 1974, no new personal or corporate tax increases have been levied. The previous deficit and increase in expenditure are to be defrayed from high incomes derived from oil and gas royalties in the province. In the first quarter of 1976, the Alberta government received $539.8 million for royalties, land rentals and the sale of Crown reserves. This compares with revenue of $376.8 million for the corresponding period of 1975. As a result of the enormous revenues from oil and gas royalties, the provincial government has kept individual income tax at low levels. Albertans enjoy the lowest tax rate in Canada. The personal income tax rate is 26% compared with 30.5% in Ontario and British Columbia and 42.5% in Manitoba.

Premier of Alberta is Peter Lougheed, leader of the Progressive Conservative party in the province. The Conservatives, who gained office in 1971 bringing an end to 36 years of Social Credit rule, were reelected in 1975 with a healthy 69 to 6 majority.

British Columbia

CAPITAL: Victoria. AREA: 366,255 sq. mi., rank 3d. POPULATION: 2,481,000 (est. Jan. 1976). FLOWER: The Dogwood. ENTERED CONFEDERATION: 1871.

Canada's most westerly province, British Columbia, on the Pacific coast, has mild winters and moderate summer temperatures which give the province the warmest climate in Canada and make it a haven for tourists and retired people. The interior is a series of rugged mountain ranges.

In 1849 the territory of the province became a British colony. The first significant settlement of the area took place in 1858 with the Fraser River gold rush. The full emergence of British Columbia as a distinct province came about by the union of the two former British colonies of Victoria and British Columbia.

The new Social Credit government's budget, introduced in March 1976, called for expenditures totaling $3.6 billion, an increase of 5.4% over the budget of the previous New Democratic government which was defeated in the December 11, 1975 provincial election. The newly elected Socreds budget imposed an additional $500 in taxes on the average B.C. household; car insurance rates were doubled and tripled; the provincial sales tax increased from 5% to 7%, taxes on cigarettes rose to 12 cents on a pack of 25; corporate income tax for large companies rose to 15%, and the provincial individual income tax rate went up 2% to 32.5%. Through these increases in taxes and fees the government expects to raise an additional $267.5 million in revenues to finance current spending.

The size of the labor force grew to 1,107,000 in April 1975. The average number unemployed in April 1975 was reported as 93,000, up from 62,000 in the corresponding period the year before. The unemployment rate for the same period was 8.4%. The unemployment rate is expected to climb to new record levels in 1976.

In the field of manufacturing, value of shipments amounted to $7.4 billion in 1974, an increase of 16.1% over the 1973 total of $6.3 billion.

British Columbia is the third largest mineral-producing province in Canada. The value of mineral production totalled $1.2 billion in 1975, compared with $1.1 billion in 1974, and $978.0 million in 1973. B.C. is the second leading producer of copper; in 1975 copper production amounted to 531.9 million lbs., the total value of which was $333.8 million.

Farm cash receipts from farming operations were $399.1 million in 1975, an increase over the figure of $372.5 million in 1974. The income from field crops accounted for $135.4 million of the 1975 total, and livestock and products made up $251.2 million. The largest income producer was dairy products, which yielded $11.6 million in cash receipts.

The new Premier of British Columbia is William Bennett, leader of the provincial Social Credit Party (or Socreds).

Manitoba

CAPITAL: Winnipeg. AREA: 251,000 sq. mi., rank 6th. POPULATION: 1,023,000 (est. Jan. 1976). FLOWER: The Prairie Crocus. ENTERED CONFEDERATION: 1870.

Most easterly of the Prairie provinces, Manitoba is called the "keystone" province because it links the eastern and western halves of the country.

Previously called the Red River Colony, and controlled by the Hudson's Bay Co., the area was purchased by the Dominion of Canada in 1870. The Red River Colony is of great historical importance because it was the site of the Riel rebellion that occurred in 1869. The execution of Riel in 1885 had a dramatic impact on the course of Canadian history.

Manitoba's economy remained almost at a standstill in 1975. The province's economic growth, which underwent expansion in the early 1970's, seems to have levelled off. The estimated gross provincial product for 1975 was $6.5 billion, up from the $6 billion reached in 1974, but when inflation is taken into account, the real growth rate is almost nil.

The provincial labor force was 418,000 in April 1975, an increase of 2,000 over the corresponding period in 1974. The number of unemployed was 19,-000 in April 1975, compared with 13,000 a year earlier, while unemployment reached a rate of 4.5%.

The outlook for the manufacturing sector is dim as farm machinery, the strongest area of activity in this sector, is expected to decline with the anticipated drop in farm income. In the first three quarters of 1975, total shipments of manufactured goods were $1.84 billion, 10% greater than in the same period in 1974. The value of shipments of goods manufactured in the province increased 23.9% in 1974 to $2.2 billion from $1.8 billion in 1973.

Estimated value of construction totalled $1 billion in 1975, above the figure of $984.9 million for 1974. Residential construction declined to $307.5 million from $321.8 million in 1974. In 1975 a total of 6,947 building permits were issued for which the estimated value of construction is placed at $291.1 million.

Agriculture is one of the principal sectors of the provincial economy. Total farmers' cash receipts amounted to $906.1 million in 1975, surpassing the 1974 figure of $842.4 million. Income from field crops was $554.4 million in 1975, up from $503.1 in 1974. More modest gains occurred in the livestock and products sector which grew to $338.2 million from $329 million.

The New Democratic Party under the leadership of Premier Edward Schreyer has established a firm foothold on the government of Manitoba, winning two consecutive elections in 1969 and 1973.

New Brunswick

CAPITAL: Fredericton. AREA: 27,835 sq. mi., rank 8th. POPULATION: 684,000 (est. Jan. 1976). FLOWER: The Purple Violet. ENTERED CONFEDERATION: 1867.

The rectangular Atlantic province has an extensive

seacoast and the world's highest tides on the Bay of Fundy.

New Brunswick's economy performed outstandingly in 1975. Capital spending in the province reached a record $1.14 billion in 1975, or 20.7% above the previous year. The increase in capital spending was well above the national increase in capital spending of 14.6%. Real gross provincial product (GPP) increased by an estimated 3.4% in 1975, a decline from the 4.5% growth rate in 1974. Total output in current dollars reached $3.3 billion in 1975, or 13.8% above the 1974 total, but inflation accounted for over 10 of the advance.

The average number employed in 1975 was 231,-000, compared with 227,000 in the previous year. Unemployment levels in 1975 averaged 25,000, up from 19,000 in 1974. The unemployment rate of 9.9% was one of the highest in recent years.

Total value of mineral production was $218.7 million in 1974, compared with $163.5 million in 1973. The year 1975 was a very active one for mineral exploration in New Brunswick and total value should surpass previous records. Mining accounts for about 10% of the gross provincial product.

The total value of construction rose to $835.5 million in 1975 compared with $758.5 million in 1974. The total number of building permits issued in New Brunswick was 4,990, while the estimated value of construction was placed at $231.7 million.

Net public debt per capita as of March 31, 1975 was $658, compared with $589 at the corresponding period in 1974.

The province is governed by the Progressive Conservative Party under Premier Richard Hatfield.

Newfoundland

CAPITAL: St. John's. AREA: 156,185 sq. mi., rank 7th. POPULATION: 554,000 (est. Jan. 1976). FLOWER: The Pitcher-Plant. ENTERED CONFEDERATION: 1949.

Newfoundland consists of 2 parts: an Atlantic island of 43,359 sq. mi. and the 112,826 sq. mi. of Labrador. Both sections are hilly, rugged, and generally barren.

The economy of Newfoundland remained in a recession during 1975, but the economic outlook for 1976 was optimistic. Estimated gross provincial product for 1975 was given as $2.28 billion, which was above the 1974 projected figure of $2.03 billion. GPP during 1976 was expected to grow in real terms by 2% to $2.57 billion. The budget introduced for the fiscal year 1976-1977 provided for public spending totaling $1.25 billion.

To meet the province's budgetary requirements the Government increased the gasoline and diesel fuel tax by 2 cents a gallon to 27 cents, while the provincial corporation tax was raised to 14% from 13 , retroactive to Jan. 1. The province's single and most important source of revenue is the federal government. Newfoundland is expected to receive close to $225 million in tax equalization payments from the federal government to offset its expenditures.

The total registered labor force grew to an average of 193,000 in 1975, 8,000 higher than the previous year; the average number employed increased by a net 3,000 but the average number unemployed increased by 35,000 or 18% for the year.

The value of manufacturing output was adversely affected by the international recession and two major industrial disputes which caused manufacturing activity in Newfoundland to decline significantly during 1975, with the gross value of manufacturing shipments falling by 8% in current value terms.

The Tories were re-elected to office in Newfoundland in September 1975. The Progressive Conservative Party was returned with a comfortable majority, receiving 30 of the 51 seats — 2 less than it had at dissolution of the legislature August 25. The provincial Liberals won 16 seats, the Liberal Reform secured 4, and there was one independent. Newfoundland's Premier is Frank Moores.

Nova Scotia

CAPITAL: Halifax. AREA: 21,425 sq. mi., rank 9th. POPULATION: 830,000 (est. Jan. 1976). FLOWER: The Trailing Arbutus. ENTERED CONFEDERATION: 1867.

Nova Scotia is called "The Wharf of North America" because of its many excellent harbors, of which Halifax, the capital, is the most extensive and famous.

Of the Canadian provinces, Nova Scotia has the longest history, beginning with John Cabot's visit to Cape Breton in 1497. The province gained its name in 1621 with the establishment of New Scotland.

Once considered the wealthiest of the British North American colonies, the province has long been looked upon as a "have not" province, because its economy has not kept pace with rapid industrialization.

Nova Scotia showed real growth of more than 5% in 1975, far ahead of the nation as a whole, while the gross provincial product increased to $4.36 billion or 15.2% over the previous year. The provincial government's 1976-77 budget was the first to exceed $1 billion in Nova Scotia, representing an increase of about 10 over the last year. To meet this record government expenditure, taxes were increased in several areas including corporations, liquor and beer sales, cigarettes, car registrations, and telephones, as well as an increase in provincial sales tax to 8%. The federal government was expected to contribute close to $537 million or almost 50% of the province's total revenues in the form of federal transfer payments or cost-shared programs.

The labor force underwent some expansion in 1975. The annual average size of the labor force in 1974 grew to 299,000 over 281,000 in 1973. For April 1975, the number unemployed was 27,000, the actual unemployment rate being 9.2%, which was above the annual average unemployment rate in 1974 of 6.7%.

Despite a decline in the manufacturing sector, mineral production, value of construction, farm cash income, and fisheries registered some gains. The record growth was in tourism. Visitors from the United States increased 13% over 1974. Total number of visitors rose by 7%. The average U.S. tourist spends twice as much as the typical Canadian guest. Tourist expenditure in Nova Scotia amounted to a record $88.1 million in 1975.

The Liberal Party, headed by Premier Gerald Regan, was re-elected in 1974.

Ontario

CAPITAL: Toronto. AREA: 412,582 sq. mi., rank 2d. POPULATION: 8,290,000 (est. Jan. 1976). FLOWER: The White Trillium. ENTERED CONFEDERATION: 1867.

The first big wave of settlers in Ontario consisted of Loyalists forced to flee from the rebelling American colonies. At the time, the area was part of Quebec. Conflict between the English-speaking settlers and the French-speaking inhabitants led to the division of the province. Upper Canada later became Ontario. The vast industrialization of the region following World War II led to the arrival of millions of immigrants. Between 1946 and 1972, Ontario alone received over 60% of all immigrants into Canada, a fact which has drastically altered the ethnic and racial composition of the province.

Ontario occupies the heartland of Canada, stretching from the Great Lakes to Hudson and James Bays in the north.

Ontario's economy was expected to recover in 1976 from the 1975 slump. The economic growth rate was expected to surpass the predicted 5% real gain in gross national product. Estimated GPP for Ontario in 1975 was placed at $62.1 billion, surpassing the $57.1 billion in 1974. However, the real gross provincial product declined by a larger percentage than the national level.

Massive cutbacks in provincial spending and tax increases to reduce government deficits have had a major impact on the population. Tax increases on cigarettes and beer and fee increases for health premiums and uninsured motor vehicle drivers are expected to yield up to 19.4% more in government revenues. At the same time, severe government restraints should keep the growth in spending down to 10.4%.

The actual size of the labor force for the month of April 1975 was 3,736,000, while the number employed was 3,487,000; the unemployment rate was 6.6%, an increase over the annual average unemployment rate of 4.1% in 1974.

Manufacturing, the primary sector in Ontario's economy, declined in total output for many areas of industrial activity, accounting for the weak performance of the economy in 1975. The estimated value of shipments of all of Ontario's manufacturing industries in September 1975 was $3.77 billion, only slightly above the June total of $3.76 billion.

Ontario's mineral production declined in total value to $2.3 billion in 1975 from $2.4 billion in 1974. The metal group makes up $1.9 billion of 1975 total value. The province is the leading Canadian producer of zinc, nickel, and copper.

Total value of construction increased to $9.3 billion in 1975 from $8.4 billion in 1974; residential construction declined by $16 million in 1975 from the previous year. The value of building permits in 1975 reached $4.3 billion for a total of 91,298 permits issued.

The agricultural sector registered slight gains in 1975 over the previous year. Total farm cash receipts reached $2.5 billion in 1975, compared with $2.4 billion in 1974. Of the 1975 total, income from crops accounted for $763 million and income from livestock and products made up $1.6 billion. Cattle, hogs, and dairy products yielded incomes in 1975 of $528 million, $303.2 million, and $490.9 million respectively.

The Conservative Party was re-elected in September 1975. It must, however, govern with a minority which limits its effectiveness. The Conservative Party has captured political office in every election during the last 33 years. The incumbent Conservative Premier is William Davis who was first elected as Premier in 1971.

Prince Edward Island

CAPITAL: Charlottetown. AREA: 2,184 sq. mi., rank 10th. POPULATION: 120,000 (est. Jan. 1976). FLOWER: Lady's Slipper. ENTERED CONFEDERATION: 1873.

Prince Edward Island in the Gulf of St. Lawrence is the smallest province of Canada both in area and population. It is often called "The Garden of the Gulf."

The projected gross provincial product for Prince Edward Island for 1975 was set at $457.5 million. This exceeds the previous year's total by $25 million or 5.9%. However, when the 11% increase in the consumer price index is taken into account, in real terms the GPP growth declined by 4.7%.

The labor force for the peak employment month, August 1975, reached 51,000, of which 49,000 were employed, resulting in an unemployment rate of 3.9%. By comparison, the labor force declined by 41,-000 in January 1976, and the number employed decreased to 38,000, giving rise to a 7.3% unemployment rate.

The province's manufacturing output is the smallest in Canada. In an effort to expand this sector, the provincial government has encouraged development of two industrial parks now nearing completion. The PEI development promoters are aiming to attract light industrial firms that employ from 35 to 50 workers. Other new manufacturing ventures include a garment industry creating 250 to 275 new jobs.

Tourism, potatoes, and fisheries account for the major share of the island's economy. The tourist industry experienced a slight setback in 1975 despite a marginal increase in the total number of tourists over the record 600,000 who visited the island in 1974. Tourist spending is expected to reach about $29 million in 1975, compared with more than $30 million in 1974.

The Liberals are in office in P.E.I. under Premier Alexander Campbell.

Quebec

CAPITAL: Quebec City. AREA: 594,860 sq. mi., rank 1st. POPULATION: 6,224,000 (est. Jan. 1976). FLOWER: The White Garden Lily. ENTERED CONFEDERATION: 1867.

Quebec was founded by Champlain in 1608 as a French colony and continues to struggle today to maintain its French heritage and culture. Quebec City, the provincial capital, dates to about 1625. The commercial and industrial center of the province is located in Montreal, Canada's largest city. Scene of Expo '67, Montreal was the site of the 1976 Olympic Games.

The rocky and barren Canadian shield spreads over the largest part of the province north of the St. Lawrence River. South of the river, the Appalachian Mountains run east and south to the U.S.A. A fertile agricultural band called the St. Lawrence Lowlands surrounds the western end of the river. Quebec experiences the most severe climatic conditions in Canada. In the north and northwest the winters are long and harsh, the summers short and hot. The upper St. Lawrence Valley has a more moderate climate, but in the lower reaches of the river from Quebec to Gaspe winter arrives early and is followed by a late spring and hot summer.

Quebec, along with Ontario, forms the industrial backbone of Canada.

Quebec's economy remained buoyant throughout 1975 and is expected to expand greatly in 1976 because of tourism and retail sales resulting from the Olympic Games in the summer. For 1975, gross provincial product was estimated at $37.3 billion, up from $33.7 billion calculated from the previous year. The government is confronted with the major problem of off-setting a huge billion dollar deficit for the 1976 Olympics.

The Quebec government imposed a 33.3% duty on the transfer of immovable property to non-resident Canadians to discourage undue foreign speculation in Quebec land. The government continues to support high investment outlays to promote growth in the industrial segment of the economy. Government investment for 1976-77 will grow to $3.5 billion, compared with $3 billion in 1975-76, an increase of 15%.

The actual number of persons in the labor force for April 1975 was 2,631,000, and the actual number employed was 2,358,000. Unemployment in April 1975 reached 273,000, resulting in an unemployment rate as high as 10.4%.

Labor unrest remains a problem. During 1975, 95,-000 teachers, 5,200 provincial government employees, 80,000 hospital workers, 5,500 nurses, 9,200 Hydro-Quebec workers among others answered various strike calls by their leaders. To curb the disruption caused by striking employees the government has passed legislation which empowers it to order strikers back to work.

The value of shipments of goods locally manufactured increased by 28.1% in 1974. The food and beverage industries accounted for $3.9 billion; paper and allied industries $2.4 billion; and primary metal industry $1.8 billion of the 1974 total.

Quebec ranks fourth in mineral production, the 1975 value of which was $1.1 billion, a decrease of $49.9 million over the previous year.

Value of construction increased by almost $820 million to reach $6.3 billion in 1975. During 1975, 50,-116 building permits were issued; the estimated value of construction is set at $2.0 billion.

Total farm cash receipts from farming operations rose to $1.3 billion in 1975 — up by $175.4 million. Income from field crops was $137 million, and income from livestock and products was $1 billion. The largest producer of income was dairy products which alone made up $512 million of the total.

As the prime site for the majority of the 1976 Olympic events, Quebec's largest city, Montreal, was the center of international attention in 1976. Amidst controversy arising from accusations of mismanagement, bribery, corruption, and rapidly escalating costs of construction of the Olympic site, the Quebec government took control of the Olympic Village Project in April, 1976. Given the blunt refusal of the federal government to finance any part of the Olympics venture, the government established Quebec's Olympics Installation Board and undertook action to negotiate a $700-million loan with a consortium of Canadian and U.S. banks to defray part of the $950-million Olympics deficit.

The Liberal Party, headed by Premier Robert Bourassa, controls the government of the province.

Saskatchewan

CAPITAL: Regina. AREA: 251,700 sq. mi., rank 5th. POPULATION: 929,000 (est. Jan. 1976). FLOWER: The Prairie Lily. ENTERED CONFEDERATION: 1905.

Formerly part of the Northwest Territories, Saskatchewan became a province in 1905. The southern portion is an arable plain devoted to the production of wheat.

Saskatchewan's economy, which is very closely tied to the performance of the agricultural sector, remained buoyant in 1975 as demand for major grain crops was sustained. The outlook for 1976 calls for a similar pattern of growth with a real growth rate of 5% to 6%.

The actual size of the labor force in April 1975 was 371,000, compared with 354,000 in the same month in 1974. The unemployment rate stood at 3.8% in April

1975, one of the lowest in the nation.

Industrial production declined in 1975. In the first nine months factory shipments of $769.6 million were only $10.5 million ahead of 1974 levels.

The provincial mining industry performed better than the manufacturing sector. In 1975, the estimated value of mineral production was set at $826.5 million, which was up from the previous year's amount of $790.3 million. The 1975 total value of mineral production is largely attributed to potash production, which was $346.8 million, and petroleum crude, which accounted for $389.7 million. Saskatchewan is the sole producer of potash in Canada, and its petroleum crude output is the second highest in the country.

The value of construction work performed moved upwards to $1.07 billion from $918.4 million in 1974. In 1975, residential construction increased to $290.6 million over $273.5 million in 1974. The number of building permits issued amounted to 9,513 and the estimated value of construction for permits issued was placed at $430.1 million.

The dominant sector of the economy is agriculture. Saskatchewan's economy is highly sensitive and vulnerable to fluctuations in production, demand, or price levels in the agricultural sector. In 1975, gross farm cash receipts were estimated at $1.9 billion, compared to $1.7 billion in 1974. Net income to farmers reached a record $1.3 billion in 1975, which was 12.5% above the 1974 level. High farm operating costs and soaring land prices coupled with the effects of inflation erode the real growth rate in farming operations.

Saskatchewan elected the first democratic socialist government in North America in 1944. Defeated by the Liberals in 1964, the socialists regained office under the New Democratic Party label in 1971. Premier of the province is Allan Blakeney.

Approximate Land and Freshwater Areas
Source: Canada Year Book

Province or Territory	Land sq. miles	Freshwater sq. miles	Total sq. miles	Percentage of Total Area
Newfoundland	143,045	13,140	156,185	4.1
Island of Newfoundland	41,164	2,195	43,359	1.1
Labrador	101,881	10,945	112,826	3.0
Prince Edward Island	2,184	—	2,184	0.1
Nova Scotia	20,402	1,023	21,425	0.6
New Brunswick	27,835	519	28,354	0.7
Quebec	523,860	71,000	594,860	15.4
Ontario	344,092	68,490	412,582	10.7
Manitoba	211,775	39,225	251,000	6.5
Saskatchewan	220,182	31,518	251,700	6.5
Alberta	248,800	6,485	255,285	6.6
British Columbia	359,279	6,976	366,255	9.5
Yukon Territory	205,346	1,730	207,076	5.4
Northwest Territories	1,253,438	51,465	1,304,903	33.9
Franklin	541,753	7,500	549,253	14.3
Keewatin	218,460	9,700	228,160	5.9
Mackenzie	493,225	34,265	527,490	13.7
Canada	**3,560,238**	**291,571**	**3,851,809**	**100.0**

The Government of Canada

Canada is a constitutional monarchy with a parliamentary system of government. It is also a federal state. The head of state is Queen Elizabeth, represented in Canada, a self-governing member of the Commonwealth of Nations, by a resident Governor-General, appointed by Her Majesty on the advice of the federal cabinet.

The cabinet is drawn from members of the party holding the largest number of seats in the House of Commons. Its members are appointed by the

Governor-General on the advice of the prime minister, the leader of the party. The prime minister is the head of the executive branch of government which is composed of the cabinet and the Governor-General, the formal title of the body being "the governor-in-council," also known constitutionally as the Privy Council.

Canada has a bicameral Parliament. The House of Commons, the more important chamber, is composed of 264 members elected at least every 5 years. The prime minister chooses the date within this period.

The upper house is the senate, comprised of 102 Senators who now are appointed to serve until 75. Prime ministers are free to choose appointees, the tradition being that they are party patronage nominations. The British North America Act requires that 30 members come from the Atlantic provinces, 24 from Quebec, 24 from Ontario, and 24 from the 4 western provinces.

Legislation becomes law by receiving 3 "readings" in the Commons, passing in the Senate and obtaining assent from the Governor-General. Financial bills can be introduced only in the Commons.

Each province has a modified version of the Ottawa pattern. Each province has a unicameral legislature. The executive head in the province is referred to usually as the Premier.

Head of State and Cabinet

Queen Elizabeth, succeeded to the throne in 1952, is represented by Governor-General Rt. Hon. Jules Leger, appointed 1974.

(listed according to precedence) (Sept. 15, 1976)

Prime Minister — Pierre Elliott Trudeau
President of the Queen's Privy Council for Canada — Allan J. MacEachen
Industry, Trade and Commerce — Jean Chretien
Finance — Donald S. Macdonald
Labor — John Carr Munro
Justice and Attorney General — Stanley R. Basford
Secretary of State for External Affairs — Donald Jamieson
President of Treasury Board — Robert K. Andras
National Defence — James Richardson
Transport — Otto E. Lang
Supply and Services — Jean-Pierre Goyer
Energy, Mines and Resources— Alastair W. Gillespie
Agriculture — Eugene F. Whelan
Indian Affairs and Northern Development — W. Warren Allmand
*Science and Technology — James H. Faulkner
Veterans Affairs — Daniel J. MacDonald

National Health and Welfare — Marc Lalonde
Communications — Jeanne Sauve
Leader of the Government in the Senate — Raymond J. Perrault
*Urban Affairs — Barnett J. Danson
Public Works — J. Judd Buchanan
Fisheries and Environment — Romeo LeBlanc
Regional Economic Expansion — Marcel Lessard
Manpower and Immigration — Jack (Bud) Cullen
*Small Businesses — Leonard S. Marchand
Secretary of State — John Roberts
National Revenue — Monique Begin
Postmaster General — Jean-Jacques Blais
Solicitor General — Francis Fox
Consumer and Corporate Affairs — Anthony C. Abbott
*Fitness and Amateur Sport — Iona Campagnolo
Titled Minister unless otherwise stated or *Minister of State.

Governors-General of Canada Since Confederation, 1867

Name	Term	Name	Term
The Viscount Monck of Ballytrammon . . .	1867-1868	General The Baron Byng of Vimy	1921-1926
The Baron Lisgar of Lisgar and Bailieborough	1869-1872	The Viscount Willingdon of Ratton	1926-1931
The Earl of Dufferin	1872-1878	The Earl of Bessborough	1931-1935
The Marquis of Lorne	1878-1883	The Baron Tweedsmuir of Elsfield	1935-1940
The Marquis of Lansdowne	1883-1888	Major General The Earl of Athlone	1940-1946
The Baron Stanley of Preston	1888-1893	Field Marshal The Viscount Alexander of Tunis	1946-1952
The Earl of Aberdeen	1893-1898	The Right Hon. Vincent Massey	1952-1959
The Earl of Minto . . . . ·.	1898-1904	General The Right Hon. Georges P. Vanier	1959-1967
The Earl Grey	1904-1911	The Right Hon. Roland Michener	1967-1974
Field Marshal H.R.H. The Duke of Connaught	1911-1916	The Right Hon. Jules Leger	1974
The Duke of Devonshire	1916-1921		

Prime Ministers of Canada

Name	Party	Term	Name	Party	Term
Sir John A. Macdonald . . .	Conservative	1867-1873 1878-1891	Arthur Meighen	Conservative Unionist	1920-1921 1926
Alexander Mackenzie . . .	Liberal	1873-1878	W. L. M. King	Liberal	1921-1926 1926-1930 1935-1948
Sir John J. C. Abbott	Conservative	1891-1892			
Sir John S. D. Thompson . .	Conservative	1892-1894			
Sir Mackenzie Bowell . . .	Conservative	1894-1896	R. B. Bennett	Conservative	1930-1935
Sir Charles Tupper	Conservative	1896	Louis St. Laurent	Liberal	1948-1957
Sir Wilfrid Laurier	Liberal	1896-1911	John G. Diefenbaker	Prog. Cons.	1957-1963
Sir Robert L. Borden	Conservative Unionist	1911-1920	Lester B. Pearson	Liberal	1963-1968
			Pierre Elliott Trudeau . . .	Liberal	1968

The Political Parties

Canadian parties, from whatever point in the political spectrum they begin, tend to move to the middle of the road where most of the votes lie. They all take much the same kind of moderate line.

The Canadian political spectrum has embraced a plethora of political parties. Since the year of Confederation, 1867, there have been over 45 different party labels in official existence and contesting elections. Most of these parties have never attained any national prominence; indeed, the majority disappeared into oblivion without electing a single candidate.

The four political parties that have dominated Canadian political life are:

Conservatives—The oldest party, they have adopted the prefix "Progressive" and moved to the left, advocating farm support programs and endorsing an extension of social welfare. Their support comes from older voters, Protestants, and English-speaking rural residents.

Liberals—Originally the Canadian equivalent of the American Jacksonian Democrats, favoring strict representation by population and the rural pioneer against the urban elite, they now get most of their electoral support from the middle and upper classes in cities, from ethnic voters, and among French-speaking Canadians. Liberals are cautious about extending the welfare state.

New Democratic Party—Successor to the Cooperative Commonwealth Federation, which combined the agrarian protest movement in western Canada with a democratic socialism of the British Labor Party variety, the N.D.P. was founded in 1961. It now attempts to attract the vote of middle-class Canadians and fuse it with the party's labor support.

Social Credit — Adopting the unorthodox monetary theories of its English founder, Major C. H. Douglas, Social Credit has appealed to the have-nots, especially now in rural Quebec.

Political power in Canada has been completely dominated by the 2 major parties — the Progressive Conservatives and the Liberals. Since 1867 these 2 parties have alternated in forming the government and in monopolizing political power. In the 30 federal elections conducted in Canada, the Conservatives have won 12, holding power for 47 years; the Liberals have gained office in 18 elections, governing the country for 61 years. A noteworthy feature of these 2 parties' political rule has been the tendency for one or the other to remain entrenched in office for a considerable length of time.

Although the Conservatives and the Liberals have been the only 2 parties to form the government of Canada and have clearly dominated Canadian political life, the role of 3d parties in Canadian politics has been significant. Since 1961, 2 minority parties, the New Democratic Party and Social Credit, have exerted some measure of influence on political outcomes. The NDP, Canada's most persistent 3d party, has been the more important of the 2. Pressure from the NDP on the left has pushed the 2 major parties to a position close to the center stream of the political spectrum. Minority party success at the polls has not been particularly spectacular. At best the NDP has succeeded in obtaining 31 seats or 12% with 18% of the popular vote.

In contrast to the NDP, the Social Credit Party is to the extreme right. The SC came into national prominence in the 1962 election following a sudden sweep in the Province of Quebec when the party succeeded in winning 26 of the 75 seats in that province. This victory increased the party's federal strength to 30 seats (12%), the highest it has ever been. In the 1974 election the party received only 11 seats of the total 264 and captured a mere 5% of the popular vote.

Canada: Party Representation by Regions, 1949-1974

Canada[1]	1949	1953	1957	1958	1962	1963	1965	1968	1972	1974
Liberal	193	171	105	40	100	129	131	155	109	141
Conservative	41	51	112	208	116	95	97	72	107	95
New Dem.	13	23	25	8	19	17	21	22	31	16
Soc. Cred.	10	15	19	—	30	24	14	14	15	11
Other	5	5	4	—	—	—	2	1	2	1
Ontario										
Liberal	56	51	21	15	44	52	51	64	36	55
Conservative	25	33	61	67	35	27	25	17	40	25
New Dem.	1	1	3	3	6	6	9	6	11	8
Quebec										
Liberal	68	66	62	25	35	47	56	56	56	60
Conservative	2	4	9	50	14	8	8	4	2	3
Soc. Cred.	—	—	—	—	26	20	9	14	15	11
Atlantic										
Liberal	26	27	12	8	14	20	15	7	10	13
Conservative	7	5	21	25	18	13	18	25	22	17
New Dem.	1	1	—	—	1	—	—	—	—	1
Western										
Liberal	43	27	10	1	7	10	9	27	7	13
Conservative	7	9	21	66	49	47	46	25	42	49
New Dem.	11	21	22	5	12	11	12	16	19	6
Soc. Cred.	10	15	19	—	4	4	5	—	—	—

[1]Total seats in 1968, 1972 and 1974 elections include one each for Yukon and Northwest Territories.

Canadian Armed Forces

In Feb., 1968, Canada carried out the unification of its traditionally separate services: the Royal Canadian Navy, the Canadian Army, and the Royal Canadian Air Force. The first step towards a unified force was taken in 1964 when the 3 services were brought together under one control with common logistics and supply and training systems, but retaining their separate legal entities. The positions of Chairman of the Chiefs of Staff and Chiefs of the Navy, Army, and Air Force were abolished and replaced by the Chief of the Defense Staff. On Feb. 1, 1968, the 3 services ceased to exist. They were unified into the Canadian Armed Forces in which all officers, men, and women are managed within a single body, with a common uniform.

Chief of the Defense Staff: General J. A. Dextraze
Vice Chief of the Defense Staff: Vice Admiral R. H. Falls

Air Defense Command	— Lieut. Gen. W. K. Carr	**Canadian Forces Europe**	— Maj. Gen. J. W. Quinn
Air Transport Command	— Maj. Gen. K. E. Lewis	**Maritime Command**	— Vice Admiral D. S. Boyle
Communications Command	— Brig. Gen. L. H. Wylie	**Mobile Command**	— Lieut. Gen. J. Chouinard
Training Command	— Rear Admiral R. S. Stephens		

Regular Forces Strength

March 31	Navy	Army	Air Force	Total	March 31	Navy	Army	Air Force	Total
1945	92,529	494,258	174,254	761,041	1973	......	......	......	82,402
1955	19,207	49,409	49,461	118,077	1974	......	......	......	81,243
1965	19,756	46,264	48,144	114,164	1975	......	......	......	78,114

Canadian Military Participation in Major Conflicts

Northwest Rebellion (1885)[1]
Participants—3,323
Killed—38
Last veteran died at the age of 104 in 1971.
South African War (1899-1902)
Participants—7,368[2]
Killed—89
Living Veterans—less than 50
First World War (1914-1918)
Participants—626,636[3]

Killed—61,332[4]
Living Veterans—96,900
Second World War (1939-1945)
Participants—1,086,343 (inc. 45,423 women)
Killed—37,714 (inc. 8 women)
Living Veterans—801,000
Korean War (1950-1953)
Participants—25,583
Killed—314
Living Veterans—25,000

[1]First battle in history to be fought entirely by Canadian troops. [2]Includes Canadians in the South African constabulary and 8 nursing sisters. [3]Includes 2,854 nursing sisters. [4]Includes 21 nursing sisters and 1,563 airmen serving with the British air forces.

Canadian Peacekeeping Operations

Since World War II Canada has played a vital role in cooperating with the United Nations in its capacity as a peacekeeping agency for the preservation of peace and the promotion of international security. Canadians have participated in almost all UN peacekeeping operations to date — in Egypt, Israel, Syria, Lebanon, Cyprus, Korea, India, Pakistan, West New Guinea, the Congo, Yemen, and Nigeria.

Nearly 900 Canadian soldiers served in the Gaza Strip following the Israeli-Egyptian crisis of 1956 until the force was disbanded in 1967.

In the Congo, a 300-man signals unit provided communications for the UN Force from 1960 to 1964.

Canadian participation in the International Commission for Control and Supervision in Vietnam and Laos began in 1954 and at the high point of participation in 1973, following the U.S. military withdrawal from Vietnam, there were 245 Canadian Forces personnel involved in the supervision of the ceasefire. The Canadian Vietnam supervisory contingent was withdrawn in July 1973 and the Laos mission was withdrawn in the spring of 1974.

Canada's largest peacekeeping commitment at the present time (mid-1976) is in the Middle East where Canadians participate in the United Nations Emergency Force (UNEF), and in the United Nations Disengagement Observer Force (UNDOF). Canada shares with Poland the logistics support role for UNEF in the Sinai and UNDOF in the Golan Heights. Canada's current overall participation in UNEF/UNDOF is approximately 1,000 personnel — about 850 Canadians are serving with UNEF and about 150 with UNDOF.

Th UN Force in Cyprus is another of Canada's large military commitments. Since 1964 Canadian participation included provision of a reduced infantry battalion and a Canadian element in the UN Headquarters—a total of approximately 580 officers and men. However, in July 1974, following the troubles in Cyprus, Canada, at the request of the UN, augmented the Cyprus contingent by an additional force of approximately 480 officers and men and some additional military equipment. About 515 Canadians presently serve in the Peacekeeping Force in Canada.

Other Canadian peacekeeping operations in 1975 are as follows:
— 11 Canadian Forces personnel with UN Military Observer Group, India-Pakistan.
— 20 Canadian officers with the UN Truce Supervisory Organization, Israel.
— 2 Canadian Forces personnel in Korea with the UN Military Armistice Commission.

Canadian Winners of the Victoria Cross

The Victoria Cross is Britain's highest military honor. It has been accorded to 94 Canadians since its inception in 1856. The cross was originally cast from metal of a Russian cannon captured during the Crimean War. Canadian winners in World War II:

Name	Unit	Theater of War & Date
Sgt. Mjr. J. R. Osborn	Winnipeg Grenadiers	Hong Kong, Dec. 19, 1941
Lt. Col. C. E. Merritt	S. Sask. Regiment	Dieppe, Aug. 19, 1942
Capt. J. W. Foote	Royal Hamilton Light Infantry	Dieppe, Aug. 19, 1942
Capt. F. T. Peters	Royal Navy	Oran, North Africa, Nov. 8, 1942
Capt. Paul Triquet	Royal 22d Regiment	Casa Berardi, Dec. 14, 1943
Maj. C. F. Hoey	Lincolnshire Regiment	Burma, Feb. 16, 1944
Maj. John K. Mahoney	Westminster Regiment	Melfa River, May 24, 1944
P.O.A.C. Mynarksi	RCAF	Camria, France, June 12, 1944
Flt. Lieut. D. E. Hornell	RCAF	"Northern waters", June 25, 1944
Sqd. Ldr. Ian Bazalgette	RCAF	Trossy St. Maximin, Aug. 4, 1944
Maj. D. V. Currie	South Alberta Regiment	Normandy, Aug. 20, 1944
Pvt. E. A. Smith	Seaforth Highlanders	Savio River, Italy, Oct. 22, 1944
Sgt. Aubrey Cosens	Queen's Own Rifles	Holland, Feb. 26, 1945
Maj. F. A. Tilston	Essex Scottish	Hochwald Forest, Mar. 1, 1945
Cpl. F. G. Topham	1st Canadian Parachute Battalion	Germany, Mar. 24, 1945
Lt. R. H. Gray	Royal Canadian Navy	Pacific, Aug. 9, 1945

Superlative Canadian Statistics

Area	Total: Land 3,560,238 sq. mi.; Water 291,571 sq. mi.	3,851,809 sq. mi.
Largest city in area	Whitehorse	162 sq. mi.
Smallest city in area (east)	Thetford Mines, Que.	7 sq. mi.

Smallest city in area (west).. Prince George, B.C. . . . . 17 sq. mi.
Northernmost point . . . . Cape Columbia, N.W.T. . . . . 83°07′N.
Northernmost town . . . . Inuvik, N.W.T. . . . . 68°21′N.
Southernmost point . . . . . . Middle Island (Lake Erie), Ont. . . . . 42°41′N.
Southernmost town . . . . Kingsville, Ont. . . . . 42°02′N.
Westernmost point . . . . Mount St. Elias, Yukon. . . . . 141°W.
Westernmost town . . . . Dawson, Yukon. . . . . 139°25′W.
Easternmost point . . . . Cape Spear, Nfld. . . . . 52°37′W.
Easternmost town . . . . St. John's, Nfld. . . . . 52°43′W.
Highest City . . . . Rossland, B.C. at R.R. Stn. (49°05′N117°47′W). . . . . 3,465 ft.
Highest town . . . . Lake Louise, Alta. . . . . 5,051 ft.
Highest waterfall . . . . Takakkaw Falls, B.C. (51°30′N116°29′W) . . . . 1,248 ft.
Longest river . . . . Mackenzie (from head of Finlay R.). . . . . 2,635 mi.
Highest mountain . . . . Mt. Logan. . . . . 19,850 ft.
Rainiest spot . . . . Henderson Lake, Vancouver Is. yrly avg. rainfall . . . . 262.0 inches
Highest lake . . . . Chilco Lake (51°20′N124°05′W) 75.1 sq. mi. . . . . 3,842 ft.

Canadian Government Budget

(in millions of dollars)
Source: Canadian Statistical Review, Apr. 1976

Expenditures

Fiscal Year or Month	National Defense	Health and Welfare	Agriculture	Post Office	Public Works	Transport	Veterans Affairs	Payments to Provinces	Total Expenditures
1971-72...	1,895.2	2,706.1	286.1	413.3	336.8	512.4	423.3	1,425.5	14,840.9
1972-73...	1,932.2	2,916.0	322.3	496.5	374.1	598.9	452.3	1,501.4	16,120.7
1973-74...	2,232.0	3,775.0	426.0	591.0	470.0	827.0	538.0	1,874.0	20,056.0
1974-75...	2,509.0	5,199.0	664.0	732.0	524.0	1,303.0	619.0	2,639.0	26,055.0
Apr.	203.0	328.0	17.0	62.0	20.0	54.0	50.0	182.0	2,648.0
Jul.	232.0	760.0	27.0	71.0	48.0	76.0	55.0	201.0	2,730.0
Oct.	242.0	821.0	175.0	71.0	56.0	88.0	58.0	175.0	2,786.0

Revenues[1]

Fiscal Year or Month	Personal Income Tax	Corporation Income Tax	Sales Tax	Other Excise Tax[2]	Excise Duties	Customs Duties	Estate Taxes	Post Office	Total Budgetary Revenues
1971-72...	5,582.0	2,183.1	1,984.7	388.4	606.6	988.6	132.4	403.8	14,226.6
1972-73...	7,172.8	2,653.5	2,288.7	400.4	638.0	1,181.8	61.4	470.1	16,601.6
1973-74...	7,925.0	3,411.0	2,693.0	695.0	686.0	1,385.0	15.0	480.0	19,383.0
1974-75...	10,069.0	4,285.0	2,900.0	2,083.0	748.0	1,809.0	7.0	485.0	24,909.0
Apr.	556.0	793.0	48.0	19.0	57.0	136.0	—	35.0	1,829.0
Jul.	1,080.0	392.0	251.0	134.0	92.0	186.0	—	39.0	2,371.0
Oct.	1,096.0	308.0	335.0	175.0	71.0	155.0	2.0	42.0	2,340.0

(1) This statement includes only receipts relating to budgetary revenue. Excluded are non-budgetary revenues such as Old Age Security Fund taxes, Prairie Farm Assistance Act levies, employer and employee contributions to government-held funds.
(2) Beginning in Dec. 1973, this category includes oil export tax.

Canadian Foreign Trade

Source: Canadian Statistical Review (April, 1976)
(in millions of dollars)

Year and Month	Exports including re-exports				Imports			
	All Countries	U.S.	U.K.	All other countries	All countries	U.S.	U.K.	All other countries
1969.	14,931	10,614	1,113	3,204	14,130	10,243	791	3,096
1970.	16,820	10,917	1,485	4,404	13,951	9,917	738	3,296
1971.	17,744	12,006	1,361	4,377	15,607	10,941	837	3,827
1972.	20,140	13,932	1,358	4,780	18,678	12,878	950	4,844
1973.	25,419.5	17,129.0	1,604.3	6,686.3	23,323.6	16,502.0	1,005.3	5,816.0
1974.	32,176.7	21,325.1	1,902.9	8,948.7	31,639.3	21,305.9	1,126.5	9,207.0
1975 Apr.	2,620.7	1,781.2	134.6	704.9	2,875.6	2,039.1	90.2	746.4
Oct.	2,979.6	2,047.8	102.3	829.5	3,100.1	2,208.5	106.2	785.5

Assets and Deposits of Chartered Banks in Canada

(in thousands of dollars)
Source: Supplement to the Canada Gazette (July 10, 1976)

Bank	Assets	Deposits
Royal Bank of Canada.	27,452,761	24,960,324
Canadian Imperial Bank of Commerce.	24,975,011	22,820,245
Bank of Montreal	19,806,995	17,981,920
Bank of Nova Scotia	17,224,115	15,368,510
Toronto-Dominion Bank	15,666,910	14,019,856
Banque Canadienne Nationale	5,315,833	4,935,411
Banque Provinciale du Canada	3,364,988	3,181,672
Mercantile Bank of Canada	1,505,909	1,367,008
Bank of British Columbia	727,229	660,546
Unity Bank of Canada.	166,789	142,705

Canadian Consumer Price Index

Source: Canadian Statistical Review, April 1976 (1971:100)

Year and Month	All Items	Food	Shelter	Clothing	Trans-portation	Health, Personal	Recreation, Education	Tobacco, Alcohol	Total Services
1973.....	150.4	162.0	168.7	138.6	136.8	156.4	145.2	136.3	167.6
1974.....	125.0	143.4	120.7	118.0	115.8	119.4	116.4	111.8	120.5
1975.....	138.5	161.9	130.9	125.1	129.4	133.0	128.5	125.3	133.4
1976 Jan..	145.1	166.8	139.5	128.0	138.4	139.1	132.6	128.3	142.4
Feb...	145.6	166.3	140.6	128.9	139.0	140.7	133.0	128.5	143.0

Personal Expenditure on Consumer Goods and Services in Current Dollars

(millions of dollars)
Source: Statistics Canada

	1967	1968	1969	1970	1971	1972	1973	1974
Food, Beverage, and Tobacco...............	9,240	9,739	10,471	11,217	12,026	13,474	15,765	18,415
Clothing and Footwear.....................	3,354	3,364	3,908	4,034	4,382	4,868	5,678	6,703
Gross Rent, Fuel and Power................	7,247	7,960	8,742	9,861	10,592	11,402	12,592	14,253
Furniture, Furnishings,...................								
Household Equipment and Operation.......	4,024	4,322	4,658	4,785	5,211	5,936	6,943	8,163
Medical Care and Health Services.........	1,789	1,902	1,912	1,758	1,679	1,866	2,112	2,413
Transportation and Communication.........	5,940	6,458	6,863	6,946	7,775	8,741	10,080	11,496
Recreation, Entertainment,...............								
Education and Cultural Services.........	3,334	3,682	4,104	4,467	5,041	5,960	6,466	7,449
Personal Goods and Services..............	5,497	6,034	6,683	7,135	7,667	8,468	9,568	10,917
Net Expenditure Abroad...................	-463	-10	151	126	95	129	.163	128
Total...................................	39,972	43,704	47,492	50,327	54,468	60,580	69,367	79,910
Durable Goods...........................	5,915	6,494	6,975	6,799	7,762	8,984	10,588	12,103
Semi-Durable Goods......................	5,539	5,953	6,426	6,645	7,224	8,108	9,497	11,267
Non-Durable Goods.......................	13,219	14,019	15,073	16,186	17,357	19,354	22,521	26,629
Services................................	15,299	17,238	19,018	20,697	22,125	24,134	26,761	29,911

Number of Canadian Households with Television Sets[1]

Source: Statistics Canada (April 1974)

Province	Number Households	Black & White			Color		
		One Set	Two Sets or More	No Sets	One Set	Two Sets or More	No Sets
Newfoundland........................	125	86	13	27	39	*	85
Prince Edward Island................	30	21	*	8	11	*	19
Nova Scotia.........................	222	136	19	68	97	*	122
New Brunswick.......................	169	105	17	46	78	*	88
Quebec..............................	1,764	1,093	236	435	832	44	888
Ontario.............................	2,540	1,474	242	825	1,315	79	1,147
Manitoba............................	311	172	24	114	158	8	145
Saskatchewan........................	273	147	17	109	158	9	106
Alberta.............................	519	274	34	211	307	15	198
British Columbia....................	749	390	42	317	404	20	325
Total...........................	6,703	3,896	647	2,159	3,398	183	3,122

(1) Estimates in thousands. *Less than 4,000.

Canadian Sea Fish Catch and Exports[1]

(in millions of pounds)
Source: Canadian Statistical Review-April, 1975

Year and month	Total[2] Value ($1,000)	Landings of Sea Fish							Exports to[3]		Exports By Type	
		Total Quantity	Nfld	P.E.I.	N.S.	N.B.	Que.	B.C.	Total United States	Other	Salmon	Lobster
1971..........	192,993	2,466.1	871.6	97.5	658.1	370.1	240.2	228.7	607.6	438.3	169.3	58.5	22.5
1972..........	219,820	2,215.1	649.3	59.9	654.0	394.5	182.1	336.7	642.0	443.6	169.3	77.6	19.8
1973..........	296,288	2,190.4	675.9	62.9	615.4	286.1	161.3	388.8	752.6	491.6	211.1	93.1	20.1
1974..........	259,108	1,839	517	36	624	353	118	293	551.4	394.6	155.0	78.5	18.2
1975..........	225,423	1,518	191	30	582	268	108	252	598.6	397.2	201.3	50.3	19.1
1976 Jan......	4,870	59.4	22.4	0.2	31.2	0.6	1.6	3.4	42.9	26.1	16.8	2.8	1.8

[1] Monthly totals for current years are not equivalent to annual data due to receipt of additional statistics which cannot be allocated months.
[2] Includes also seaweeds and other species such as whales, worms, etc.
[3] Exports include sea and freshwater fish and shellfish products but exclude bait, meal, oils, offal, livers, fish roe, n.e.s. and fishery foods and feeds n.e.s.

Population and Area of Canada by Provinces

Source: Statistics Canada

Province, territory	Capital	Area in square miles			1966 Census	1971 Census	July 1975 Estimate
		Land	Fresh Water	Total			
Newfoundland...........	St. John's.......	143,045	13,140	156,185	493,396	522,105	550,000
Prince Edward Island.....	Charlottetown...	2,184		2,184	108,645	111,645	119,000
Nova Scotia...........	Halifax..........	20,402	1,023	21,425	756,039	788,960	823,000
New Brunswick.........	Fredericton......	27,385	519	28,354	616,788	634,555	676,000
Quebec...............	Quebec..........	523,860	71,000	594,860	5,780,845	6,027,765	6,193,000
Ontario..............	Toronto..........	344,092	68,490	412,582	6,960,870	7,703,110	8,237,000
Manitoba.............	Winnipeg........	211,775	39,225	251,000	963,066	988,245	1,020,000
Saskatchewan.........	Regina..........	220,182	31,518	251,700	955,344	926,245	920,000
Alberta..............	Edmonton........	248,800	6,485	255,285	1,463,203	1,627,870	1,772,000
British Columbia......	Victoria.........	359,279	6,976	366,255	1,873,674	2,184,620	2,462,000
Northwest Territories.....	Yellowknife......	1,253,438	51,465	1,304,903	28,738	34,805	38,000
Yukon Territory.......	Whitehorse......	205,345	1,730	207,076	1,382	18,390	21,000
Total...............	....	3,560,238	291,571	3,851,809	20,014,880	21,568,315	22,831,000

Canadian Shipping Traffic*

Source: Canadian Statistical Review, Apr. 1976 (thousand short tons)

Year and Month	Halifax	Saint John	Quebec	Montreal	Toronto	Vancouver	All Ports	Coastwise
1971	10,999	7,438	10,811	21,690	4,710	30,813	286,606	122,536
1972	11,355	10,263	14,901	20,431	4,534	29,894	298,076	122,403
1973	13,703	12,181	15,946	21,177	4,170	39,126	320,498	122,436
1974	13,256	9,997	12,957	19,626	4,497	36,684	303,341	118,475
1975 Jan.	961	896	502	579	143	2,994	15,387	5,118
May	1,235	1,216	1,282	1,993	588	3,646	36,060	14,850
Sept.	820	839	781	2,197	334	2,368	25,566	10,375

*Total cargo handled includes cargo loaded and unloaded in foreign and coastwise shipping.

Canadian Cities with Metropolitan Populations Over 100,000

Source: Statistics Canada

	Metro Area* (thousands)	City**		Metro Area* (thousands)	City**
Montreal, Que.	2,798	1,214,352	Windsor, Ont.	266	203,300
Toronto, Ont.	2,741	712,786	Kitchener, Ont.	238	111,804
Vancouver, B.C.	1,137	426,256	Halifax, N.S.	224	122,035
Ottawa-Hull, Ont.	626	365,921	Victoria, B.C.	208	61,761
Winnipeg, Man.	570	246,246	Sudbury, Ont.	154	90,535
Edmonton, Alta.	529	438,152	Regina, Sask.	151	139,469
Hamilton, Ont.	520	309,173	Chicoutimi-Jonquiere, Que.	137	62,323
Quebec, Que.	499	186,088	St. John's Nfld.	132	88,102
Calgary, Alta.	444	403,319	Saskatoon, Sask.	130	126,449
St. Catharines-Niagara, Ont.	311	176,885	Saint John, N.B.	112	89,039
London, Ont.	296	223,222	Thunder Bay, Ont.	112	108,411

*1974 Estimates. **1974 Census.

Population by Mother Tongue, for Canada and Provinces, 1971

Source: Statistics Canada

Province	English	French	German	Indian, Eskimo	Italian	Dutch	Polish	Ukrainian	Other
Newfoundland	514,520	3,635	515	1,620	175	120	45	50	1,430
Prince Edward Island	103,105	7,360	140	145	35	280	40	30	510
Nova Scotia	733,560	39,330	2,000	2,710	1,495	1,850	555	435	7,020
New Brunswick	410,400	215,730	1,110	2,725	755	665	155	110	2,905
Quebec	789,185	4,867,250	31,025	21,050	135,455	4,660	15,480	11,385	152,265
Ontario	5,971,570	482,045	184,880	28,590	344,285	77,475	73,985	80,230	460,050
Manitoba	662,720	60,550	82,720	31,665	7,265	10,385	15,900	72,925	44,130
Saskatchewan	685,920	31,605	75,885	26,020	2,045	4,695	7,675	53,385	39,025
Alberta	1,263,935	46,500	92,800	29,920	15,570	20,670	13,730	70,895	73,855
British Columbia	1,807,250	38,035	89,020	18,550	31,030	23,955	7,100	20,055	149,620
Yukon	15,345	450	565	1,030	75	100	55	150	620
Northwest Territories	16,305	1,160	425	15,800	175	80	60	205	595
Total	12,973,810	5,793,650	561,085	179,825	538,360	144,920	134,780	309,855	932,020

Immigration to Canada, by Country of Last Permanent Residence

Source: Canadian Statistical Review, April 1976

Year	Total	U.K. and Ireland	France	Germany	Netherlands	Greece	Italy
1972	122,006	18,317	2,742	2,025	1,471	4,016	4,608
1973	184,102	28,100	3,586	2,564	1,898	5,833	5,468
1974	218,465	39,748	4,232	3,621	2,103	5,632	5,226

Year	Portugal	Other Europe	Asia	Australasia	United States	West Indies	All Other
1972	8,737	8,871	23,831	2,148	22,618	8,214	14,408
1973	13,483	10,949	43,193	2,671	25,242	19,180	22,031
1974	16,333	11,799	50,566	2,594	26,541	23,670	26,400

Births and Deaths in Canada by Province

Source: Statistics Canada

Province	Births 1974	Births 1973	Deaths 1974	Deaths 1973	Province	Births 1974	Births 1973	Deaths 1974	Deaths 1973
Nfld.	11,267	11,895	2,972	3,163	Manitoba	17,609	17,268	8,562	8,491
P.E.I.	1,937	1,875	993	911	Sask.	15,213	14,713	7,765	7,574
N.S.	12,955	13,448	6,919	7,042	Alberta	29,645	29,416	11,687	10,784
N.B.	11,699	11,697	5,359	5,138	B.C.	35,321	34,142	19,775	17,962
Quebec	84,564	87,627	41,957	42,816					
Ontario	125,958	125,180	61,642	60,426	Total	346,168	347,261	167,631	164,307

Marriages, Divorces, and Rates in Canada

(Rates per 1,000 population)

Year	Marriages No.	Marriages Rate	Divorces No.	Divorces Rate	Year	Marriages No.	Marriages Rate	Divorces No.	Divorces Rate
1940	125,799	10.8	2,416	0.21	1970	188,428	8.8	29,775	1.37
1950	125,083	9.1	5,386	0.39	1972	200,470	9.2	32,364	1.48
1960	130,338	7.3	6,980	0.39	1973	199,064	9.0	36,704	1.66
1965	145,519	7.4	8,974	0.45	1974	198,824	8.9	45,019	2.00

NATIONS OF THE WORLD

The nations of the world are listed in alphabetical order, except for Canada and the United States (see Index for listings). Initials in the following articles include UN (United Nations), OAS (Organization of American States), NATO (North Atlantic Treaty Org.), EC (European Communities or Common Market), OAU (Org. of African Unity), CENTO (Central Treaty Org. of the Middle East). Areas based primarily upon U.S. State Department figures.

See special color section for maps and flags of all nations.

Afghanistan

Area: 253,861 sq. mi. Population (UN est. 1975): 19,280,000. Capital: Kabul. Monetary unit: Afghani.

Afghanistan is a landlocked republic occupying a mountainous area much of which is 4,000 ft. and more above sea level. It is slightly smaller than Texas. Its neighbors are Iran, Pakistan, and the USSR. The northeast tip of the country just touches China's Sinkiang Province.

The Hindu Kush mountains tower 16,000 ft. above the capital of Kabul and reach a height of more than 25,000 ft. some 200 miles to the E. Trade with Pakistan flows through the 35-mile long Khyber Pass from Kabul to Peshawar. The climate is dry, with extreme temperatures.

Resources and Industries. Much of the country's exports (which totalled $210 million in 1974) are agricultural products, but natural gas exports to the USSR is the leading trade item. Other items: cotton, wool, karakul pelts, hides, oilseeds, and fruit. Hand-woven carpets, cotton, wool, fruits and nuts, and sheepskin coats are exported. Some 4 million head of broadtail karakul sheep are raised, as well as goats and camels. The sheep provide the principal meat, and the tightly curled, glossy black coats of the new-born lambs are a valuable fur. Minerals include copper, lead, gas, coal, zinc, iron, silver, asbestos, and oil. The country has received considerable economic aid from the U.S., USSR and China. The USSR is Afghanistan's largest trading partner.

Textile mills, cement factories, highways and irrigation projects are among recent developments.

History and Government. Afghanistan was so named in about the middle of the 18th Century. In ancient times it was known as Aryana, in the Middle Ages as Khorasan. Pushtuns (Pathans) comprise 53.5% of the population; Tajiks (who speak a Persian dialect) 36.7%; Uzbeks 6%; Hazaras 3%.

In 1964 a Grand Assembly approved a new constitution providing for an elected Lower House, partly-elected Upper House, an independent judiciary, a prime minister chosen by the king. The last king was Mohammed Zahir Shah, who ascended the throne Nov. 8, 1933, on the assassination of his father, Mohammad Nadir Shah. Leading a July 17, 1973, coup, Gen. Mohammad Daud, the king's brother-in-law, proclaimed Afghanistan a republic with himself as president and premier.

Bordering on both Russia and China, Afghanistan has been traditionally neutral. Armed forces: over 88,000.

Education and Religion. Education is free and, where facilities are available, compulsory. The University of Kabul was established in 1932. Principal languages are Pushtu and Persian. English is taught. Islam is the predominant religion.

Albania

Area: 11,100 sq. mi. Population (UN est. 1975): 2,480,000. Capital: Tirana. Monetary unit: Lek.

Albania, a Balkan communist republic, is a narrow mountainous land, slightly larger than Maryland, extending for 225 mi. along the E coast of the Adriatic. Yugoslavia and Greece are its neighbors. Mt. Korab, 9,066 ft., is the tallest peak.

Resources and Industries. Still a preponderantly agricultural nation, Albania in the 1960s pressed programs of industrialization and agricultural modernization with the aid of China.

New industrial installations included chemical fertilizer, textile, electric cable, and electric power plants. A slowdown was reported in the 1970s.

Principal exports include petroleum, bitumen, chrome, iron, and copper; cotton textiles, wood products, and tobacco. More than half of Albania's foreign trade is with communist China.

History and Government. Albania has been overrun by warring armies for over 2,000 years. It declared its independence from the Turks in 1912; this was backed by a conference of European powers which placed Prince William of Wied on the throne in 1914. He fled within months because of uprisings. During World War I armies of several nations occupied the land by turns. In 1920, a republic was set up. In 1925, Ahmed Zogu seized the presidency; in 1928 he proclaimed himself king, assuming the title Zog I.

King Zog fled in 1939 when Italy invaded and annexed Albania. When Italy surrendered to the Allies in 1943, German troops took over; they left in 1944 and communist partisans seized power. Gen. Enver Hoxha was named provisional president; a communist front won a 1945 election; in 1946 a new constitution, modeled on that of the USSR, was adopted under Hoxha's leadership.

The U.S. and Britain voted against Albanian admission to the UN in 1946; it finally won admission in 1955 with Britain voting "yes" and the U. S. abstaining. In 1955 it was admitted to the Warsaw Pact. Its policies have been strongly pro-Stalinist, anti-Khrushchev, pro-China and hostile to Tito's Yugoslav regime. The USSR broke relations with Albania in Dec. 1961 and in 1962 barred it from Warsaw Pact meetings. Albania withdrew from the pact in 1968.

In 1970 China and Albania signed a new treaty providing for expanded trade and additional Chinese financial credits for Albania. In 1971, after years of mistrust, Albania resumed diplomatic relations with Yugoslavia and Greece.

Education and Religion. Historically, the largest segment of the population was Moslem, followed by Orthodox Christians and Roman Catholics. All religious institutions and public worship were made illegal in 1967. Primary education nominally is compulsory and free under the constitution.

Ethnically the Albanians are divided into 2 groups: Ghegs in the north and Tosks in the south.

Defense. Military strength totals 38,000.

Algeria

Area: 919,951 sq. mi. Population (Govt. est. 1975): 16,780,000. Capital: Algiers. Monetary unit: Dinar.

Algeria, an independent "Islamic Socialist" republic more than 3 times the size of Texas, is located in northern Africa extending for 640 mi. along the Mediterranean Sea between Tunisia and Morocco. The southern Saharan Departments extend into the Sahara Desert and border on Niger, Mali, and Mauritania. The Tell, located on the coast, comprises fertile plains from 50 to 100 mi. wide. Several chains of the Atlas Mtns., running roughly E-W and reaching altitudes of 7,000 ft., separate the coast regions from inland plateaus and the Sahara, and its vast mineral deposits. Algiers, the capital, is the largest city.

Resources and Industries. Agricultural products include wheat, barley, oats, corn, potatoes, artichokes, flax, tobacco, wine, and olive oil. Dates, pomegranates and figs grow abundantly. Cattle raising is important. There are large deposits of oil, iron, zinc, lead, mercury, coal, copper.

Exports consist of wines, fruits, iron and zinc ores, phosphate rock, cork, tobacco products, vegetables, liquefied natural gas and petroleum. Algeria is the world's 14th largest oil-producing nation. Oil is exported to pay for necessary food imports. Imports in 1973 totalled $2,125 million, exports $1,775 million.

In 1967-71 most foreign oil distribution and producing companies were nationalized. Industrialization has progressed with an oil refinery, natural gas liquefication, iron, steel, fertilizer, plastics, and textile factories, financed with oil revenues, and wage and import curbs.

History and Government. The fertile Tell plains have attracted a succession of conquerors to Algeria from before the time of Christ. Once ruled by Carthage, the country after 146 B.C. came under control of the Romans. But it was the Arabs, who arrived in the 7th Century, who were to have the most lasting influence on the country. In 1518 Algiers and the coastal area came under Turkish domination. France took control in 1830, annexed Algeria in 1842 and began to develop the land.

From 1954-62 growing Arab nationalism led to warfare between the French and the Algerians. The political impasse was not broken until French president Charles de Gaulle negotiated with the Front de Liberation Nationale (FLN). Algeria in a referendum July, 1962, voted overwhelmingly for independence; de Gaulle proclaimed it independent July 3.

Internal strife continued, however, between opposing Algerian factions, and Ahmed Ben Bella, with Army support, assumed control in Aug. 1962.

A constitution was approved Sept. 8, 1963, and Premier Ben Bella, sole candidate, was elected president for a 5-year term Sept. 15. Nationalization of lands and industries proceeded rapidly. Algeria received a $100 million long-term industrial loan from the USSR in 1963; French aid continued.

Ben Bella was arrested and deposed June 19, 1965, in a bloodless, army-backed coup d'etat led by Col. Houari Boumediene (born Mohammed Boukharouba), defense minister. Col. Boumediene, on July 11, announced a new cabinet with himself as president. Algeria is a member of the UN, OAU, and Arab League.

Education and Religion. The population before independence included approx. 1 million Europeans. 80 of them Algerian-born, since reduced to about 80,000. Most Algerians are Arabs and Berbers, of Moslem faith. French is still widely used. There are 3 universities and 21 technical institutes.

Defense. Armed forces, modernized with USSR aid, total 63,000.

Andorra

Area: 180 sq. mi. Population (1976 Census): 26,500. Capital: Andorra la Vella. Monetary units: Franc, Peseta.

Andorra is a tiny principality of valleys and mountains set high in the Pyrenees on the border of France and Spain. It has two co-princes, the president of France and the Spanish Catholic bishop of Urgel, whose representatives are charged with the administration of justice, but the country has enjoyed practical sovereignty since 1278. It pays an annual tribute of 960 francs to France and 460 pesetas to the bishop of Urgel.

Actual government is in the hands of a Council-General of 24 members elected by universal suffrage, who enact laws and elect a syndic general, the top administrator. Women won voting rights in 1970.

The main industry is tourism (247 hotels), followed by sheep-raising. Andorra has considerable iron, lead, alum, stone, and timber. Skiing, trout fishing, and chamois hunting are among tourist attractions.

The official language is Catalan; Spanish and

French are spoken; principal religion is Roman Catholicism.

Angola

Area: 481,351. Population (Govt. est. 1972): 5,800,-000. Capital: Luanda.

Angola stretches 1,000 mi. along the Atlantic in SW Africa, bordering Namibia (South-West Africa), Zambia, and Zaire. **Cabinda,** an enclave separated from the rest of the country by the short Atlantic coast of Zaire, borders on the Congo Republic.

Most of Angola, which is twice the size of Texas, consists of a plateau elevated 3,000 to 5,000 feet above sea level, rising sharply from a narrow coastal strip. There is also a temperate highland area in the west-central region, a desert in the south, and a tropical rain forest covering Cabinda.

Resources and Industries. Angola produces 5% of world's coffee. Other products are corn, sugar, palm oil, cotton, wheat, tobacco, cacao, sisal, wax, fish, and fishmeal. Livestock totaled 4.4 million head in 1971. Angola is an important exporter of iron and diamonds. Copper, manganese, sulphur, and phosphates are also found. Exploitation of large oil fields in Cabinda is growing. Manufactures include alcohol, cotton goods, paper, footwear, soap, and sugar.

History and Government. Portuguese settlers arrived in the Congo region in 1491, and founded Luanda, 1575. Angola became a major slaving center, with about 3 million slaves sent to the New World until the middle of the nineteenth century. Portugal increased its colonization efforts in the 20th Century. The white population rose to about 400,000, with the rest divided among four major and many minor Bantu tribal groups.

A 1961 insurrection against Portuguese rule continued until 1974, when the new regime in Portugal offered independence. By then, the independence movement was divided into three groups, the National Front, based in Zaire, the Soviet-backed Popular Movement, and the moderate National Union. Each group's power was in part tribally based. Fighting broke out in 1975 between followers of the National Front and Popular Movement; over 3,000 were killed in Luanda. After independence on Nov. 11, 1975, the Popular Front won control of most of the country, led by 15,000 Cuban troops. Some resistance continued in 1976. The fighting had halved economic output, and helped drive most of the whites from the country. The USSR promised military and economic assistance.

Education and Religion. About 550,000 students attended school under the Portuguese, and literacy had increased to 30%. Portuguese was the only nationwide language. About 2.2 million Angolans are Roman Catholic. The rest adhere to local cults, excepting some Protestants.

Argentina

Area: 1,072,067 sq. mi. Population (Govt. est. 1975): 25,380,000. Capital: Buenos Aires. Monetary unit: Peso.

Argentina, 4 times the size of Texas, extends from Bolivia 2,300 miles to Tierra del Fuego and from the Andes to the South Atlantic, and is the 2d largest and 2d most populous country in South America.

The mountains are grouped into 4 isolated systems: the Andean, Central, Misiones, and Southern. Aconcagua is the highest peak in the Western Hemisphere, altitude 22,834 ft.

East of the Andes are great plains, heavily wooded and called the Gran Chaco in the north, and the fertile, treeless Pampas, given over to wheat and cattle raising, in the central region. Patagonia, in the south, is bleak and arid; petroleum and sheep are its main products.

Rio de la Plata is the estuary of one of the world's

great drainage systems. It is a wide gulf of mostly fresh water, 170 mi. long, 140 mi. wide at its mouth. On its banks are 3 important cities, Buenos Aires and La Plata in Argentina, and Montevideo in Uruguay. Emptying into it are the Parana River, 2,500 mi. long, and the Uruguay, 1,000, both starting far to the north in Brazil. Further south, other large rivers flow from the Andes, in the west, to the Atlantic, including the Colorado and Negro.

Resources and Industries. The mountains of Argentina contain deposits of coal, lead, zinc, iron, sulphur, silver, copper, and gold. Petroleum is important.

Cotton, wheat, barley, rye, linseed, oats, alfalfa are important. Sugar, wine, cotton, fruit, corn, sorghum, tobacco, and peanuts are produced. Sheep, cattle, horses, goats, and pigs form the chief wealth of the ranches. In 1975 there were 58 million cattle and 39 million sheep, both high in world rankings. Meat processing is the chief industry. Flour milling is 2d. Argentina is one of the world's largest meat exporters.

Railroads are state-owned.

Also important in the country's growing industrialization are chemicals, textiles, sugar-refining, and machinery. But successive governments were unable to control inflation, which reached a 500% annual rate in 1976, and balance of payment problems.

Foreign trade, in thousands of U. S. dollars:

	Imports	Exports
1973	$2,235,000	$3,266,000
1974	$3,656,000	$3,931,000

History and Government. Discovered 1515-16 by Spanish explorers headed by Juan Diaz de Solis, Argentina remained under Spanish domination until the provinces, in a revolt, established an independent republic, May 25, 1810. In 1863 a liberal constitution was adopted. The present constitution, proclaimed May 1, 1956, is essentially that of 1863.

There are 22 provinces which elect their own governors and legislatures, and a Federal District, Buenos Aires (area 72 sq. mi.), whose mayor is appointed by the president, and a national territory (Tierra del Fuego).

The president and vice president must be Roman Catholic and Argentine by birth. They are elected for 4-year terms by direct popular vote. Congress consists of a Senate of 69 and a House of Deputies. Voting is compulsory for both men and women.

After the election of Juan D. Peron, an army officer, as president in 1946, Argentine democracy was replaced by dictatorship. By concessions to labor Peron built a following; he then suppressed freedom of speech and press and religious schools and ran the country deeply into debt. Civilians, clericals and part of the armed forces unseated Peron Sept. 19, 1955, and he went into exile. A provisional government was replaced November, 1955, by a military junta, which restored civil liberties, dissolved the Peronist party and returned expropriated property.

In the first free elections in 12 years, Feb. 22, 1958, Dr. Arturo Frondizi was elected president. Dissension among military leaders, democratic parties and the Peronist unions which had supported Dr. Frondizi resulted in a bloodless military coup Mar. 29, 1962. Another election and another military coup followed. In March 1971, Lt. Gen. Alejandro A. Lanusse took over as president; he ordered a return to civilian government.

In March 1973 elections, Hector J. Campora, a follower of Peron, was elected president. On July 13, 1973, Campora resigned and Peron, 77, returned and was elected president Sept. 23, taking office Oct. 12. His 3d wife, Maria Estela, was elected vice president.

Peron died July 1, 1974, and Mrs. Peron, 43, succeeded, becoming the first woman president in the Western Hemisphere. Her influence was curbed by violent struggle between left and right Peronists, and she was removed by the military, March 24, 1976.

Terrorist violence increased in the 1970's with hundreds of political slayings by left and right, and lucrative kidnapings netting tens of millions of dollars.

Argentina is a member of the UN and OAS.

Education and Religion. The population is about 92% Roman Catholic, the constitutional religion since 1810. There are 600,000 Jews. Primary education is free, secular, and compulsory. There are 400,000 students attending national universities in Cordoba (founded in 1613), Buenos Aires and 9 other cities, and numerous private universities. The language is Spanish. The people are of Spanish and Italian descent, with many European & Mediterranean ethnic minorities.

Defense. The 3 services total over 133,500 plus several hundred thousand reserves.

Australia

Area: 2,965,368 sq. mi. (7,682,300 sq. km.). Population (Govt. est. 1975): 13,500,000. Capital: Canberra. Monetary unit: Australian dollar.

The continent of Australia, an island almost the size of the 48 conterminous U.S. states, is SE of Asia and below Indonesia. The Indian O. is W and S, the Pacific E; they meet N of Australia in the Timor and Arafura Seas. The Great Barrier Reef is along the NE coast. About 150 mi. S of the state of Victoria lies the island state, Tasmania. Branches of the Pacific are the Coral Sea, NE, and the Tasman Sea, SE.

The Tropic of Capricorn bisects Australia. The Great Dividing Range along the E coast has Mt. Kosciusko, 7,316 ft., in New South Wales. The W plateau rises to 2,000 ft., with arid areas in the Great Sandy and Great Victoria Deserts. The NW part of Western Australia and Northern Territory are arid and torrid. There are several areas reserved for aborigines in the Northern Territory. The NE has heavy rainfall and Cape York Peninsula has jungles. The Murray River rises in New South Wales, flows 1,600 mi. to the Indian Ocean and fuels power plants.

States and territories of Australia with their areas in sq. mi. and 1974 est. populations were:

	Area	Population
New South Wales	309,418	4,743,400
Victoria	87,854	3,631,900
Queensland	666,699	1,967,900
South Australia	379,824	1,218,200
Western Australia	974,843	1,094,700
Tasmania	26,171	400,700
Northern Territory	519,633	101,200
Australian Capital Terr.	926	180,500
Totals	2,965,368	13,338,300

The capitals are: NSW, Sydney; Vic., Melbourne; Qld., Brisbane; S.A., Adelaide; W.A., Perth; Tas., Hobart; N. T., Darwin; Capital Terr., Canberra.

Home of the kangaroo, Australia also is the habitat of other strange flora and fauna: the koala, or living teddy bear; the platypus, wombat, dingo, Tasmanian devil, a blind mole, and barking and frilled lizards.

By 1973, Australia had added almost 3 million people through immigration since World War II. About one-half was British. In 1975, emigration exceeded immigration for the first time in 28 years. Australia's 80,000 aborigines are mostly detribalized.

The Melbourne Cup horse race is the biggest annual sports event; cricket, tennis, and football are played extensively. Excellent beaches are numerous.

Resources and Industries. Almost from earliest days of settlement a primary producing country, Australia has become highly industrialized. More than 25% of the total labor force of approx. 5,550,000 work in factories; about 15% are engaged in rural occupations.

Wool and meat are important primary products. With an annual clip of more than 1.9 billion lbs., Australia produces 30% of the world's wool, 50% of its merino wool; it is the largest exporter of beef and second in lamb. It is also one of the largest wheat producers, with 10.5 million tons in 1974, much of it exported. Other important products are sugar, wine, fruit, vegetables, meat, grains, minerals, including uranium, gold, coal, copper, iron, silver, lead, nickel, tin, bauxite, rutile and petroleum products.

Discovery of vast iron ore deposits in Western Australia brought a mining boom to desolate areas in 1965. New oil and gas was discovered 1965-1968, nickel in 1969, uranium in 1972 and 1974.

Principal manufactures include iron and steel, textiles, electrical and radio equipment, drugs, chemicals, paints, machinery, metal work, clothing, motor cars and engines, aircraft, and ships. Unemployment rose to 5.3% of the work force in 1975. Gross domestic product in 1973-74 was $A58,558 million ($US72.7 billion).

In recent years exports of mineral and industrial products have increased considerably. Foreign aid takes 0.52% of gross national product, one of the highest rates in the world.

Australia changed its currency from pounds-shillings-pence to dollars and cents Feb. 14, 1966, with its dollar worth half the old Australian pound. It will complete adoption of metric weights and measures by 1980.

Foreign trade, in thousands of U.S. dollars:

	Imports	Exports
1974	$11,078,000	$10,785,000
1975	$9,811,000	$11,575,000

Tourism is rapidly expanding. In 1974 Australia had 532,683 overseas visitors.

History and Government. Australia has been settled by Europeans since 1788. The Commonwealth, proclaimed Jan. 1, 1901, is a self-governing federation of 6 states and 2 territories. Parliament consists of the Crown (represented by the governor-general), the Senate and House of Representatives.

Gough Whitlam, chosen in 1972 as the first Labor prime minister in 23 years, ended restrictions on non-white immigrants, ended the draft and military aid to South Vietnam, and recognized China and North Vietnam.

The Liberal-National coalition won a major victory in 1975 elections, winning a record parliamentary majority. Malcolm Fraser was chosen Prime Minister.

Pension acts provide for payments of war, old age and invalid pensions; also cover the blind, the ill, and the unemployed. The National Health Scheme provides free drugs and subsidizes hospital and medical expenses.

A maternity act provides for the payment of a maternity allowance for every child born in Australia. Social security for children includes child endowment payments for children under 16.

Education and Religion. Education is free and compulsory. There are 17 universities and 3 university colleges. The Church of England claims 37.7% of the population, the remainder being Roman Catholic, 23.3%; Presbyterian, 9.7%; Methodist, 10.8%.

Defense. Armed forces total 69,100.

Australian External Territories

Norfolk Island was taken over by Australia, 1914. It has an area of 13.5 sq. mi. and a population (est. 1973) of 1,500. The soil is very fertile and is suitable for citrus fruits, bananas, and coffee. Many of the inhabitants are descendants of the Bounty mutineers; some moved to Norfolk in 1856 from Pitcairn Is.

Coral Sea Islands Territory, 1 sq. mi., is administered from Norfolk Is.

Territory of Ashmore and Cartier Islands, area 2 sq. mi., in the Indian Ocean came under the authority of Australia May 1934 and are administered as part of Northern Territory. **Heard** and **McDonald Islands** are administered by the Department of Science.

Cocos (Keeling) Islands, 27 small coral islands in the Indian Ocean 1,300 miles NW of Australia. Pop. (est. 1973): 654; area: 5 sq. mi.

Christmas Island, 52 sq. mi., pop. 2,884 (census 1973), 230 mi. S. of Java, was transferred by Britain in 1958. It has phosphate deposits.

Australian Antarctic Territory was claimed by Australia in 1933, including 2,472,000 sq. mi. of territory S of 60th parallel S. Lat. and between 160th-45th meridians E. Long.

Austria

Area: 32,374 sq. mi. Population (Govt. est. 1975): 7,520,000. Capital: Vienna. Monetary unit: Schilling.

Austria is a republic in the mountainous region of central Europe, 360 mi. long, 160 mi. wide — slightly smaller than Maine. Mountain passes cross frontiers; the Brenner, below the Stubai Alps, has been a major route to Italy since ancient times.

Principal river, the Danube, flows from Bavaria in NW to Czechoslovakia, E. Others are the Enns, Inn, Drau, Ill, Mur, and Salzach, some furnishing hydroelectric power. There are numerous lakes and popular spas, such as Bad Gastein and Bad Ischl.

Resources and Industries. Austria produces iron ore, oil, timber, magnesite, aluminum, coal, lignite, cement, and copper. It is an important source of high-grade graphite. Hydroelectric power has been widely developed. Manufactures include steel, machinery, vehicles, electrical and optical instruments, glassware, sporting goods, paper, yarns, textiles, fertilizers, chemicals, and artistic leather goods.

Although farmland is limited, Austria produces about 85% of its foodstuffs. It grows wheat, rye, barley, oats, corn, potatoes, sugar beets. Vineyards flourish in Lower Austria and in Burgenland.

Over 11 million tourists visit annually. The Salzburg Festival, the Vienna State Opera, skiing and spas are among attractions.

Principal exports are iron, steel, paper, textiles, machinery, chemicals, metal products, vehicles, aluminum, electric power. Trade is heavy with West Germany, Italy, and the U.S.

Foreign trade in thousands of U.S. dollars:

	Imports	Exports
1974	$9,020,000	$7,161,000
1975	$9,391,000	$7,518,000

History and Government. Austria, the East Mark (Ost Mark) of Charlemagne (788 A.D.) came under the Hapsburgs in 1278. Tyrol was added 1363, Bohemia (Czech.) and Hungary, 1526. The Turks were twice turned back at Vienna, 1529 and 1683. Austrian dominance of German lands was challenged in the 18th century and Empress Maria Theresa (ruled 1740-1780) lost Silesia to Frederick II (the Great) of Prussia. Austria took slices of Poland in the partitions of 1772, 1793 and 1795. Austria was the scene of several of Napoleon's battles, and helped defeat him. The Congress of Vienna, 1815, awarded it Istria, Illyria, and the Italian provinces of Lombardy and Venetia. Austria lost Lombardy to Italy 1859 and Venetia 1866, after Prussia defeated Austria.

Under the Dual Monarchy of Austria-Hungary, established 1867 to recognize the aspirations of the Magyars, Francis Joseph was Emperor of Austria and King of Hungary. The nation had an area of 261,259 sq. mi., population c. 51 million. It contained Austria, Hungary, Bohemia, Transylvania, Polish Galicia, Trentino, Slavonia, Croatia, Bosnia, Herzegovina, Banat. After Archduke Francis Ferdinand, heir to the Austrian throne, and his consort were assassinated in Sarajevo, Bosnia, June 28, 1914, Austria declared war on Serbia, which helped precipitate World War I. It was dismembered after that war; became a republic composed of 9 small states in 1918.

Between the 2 world wars Austria had a turbulent political history. Socialists introduced some socio-economic changes. These were checked by Chancellor Engelbert Dollfuss, 1934. Dollfuss was murdered by Nazi conspirators July 25, 1934. Germany, under Hitler, occupied Austria Mar. 13, 1938, and proclaimed its union with Germany. It was reestablished as a republic in 1945.

Dr. Karl Renner was president of the provisional government after liberation by the Allies, 1945. After 17 years of occupation, delayed by tactics of the Soviet Union, a 1955 treaty restored the frontiers of Jan. 1, 1938, prohibited union with Germany, required support of democratic institutions. Austria formally regained sovereignty July 27, 1955. It declared perpetual neutrality.

The president is elected by secret ballot for a 6-year term. He appoints the chancellor; Parliamentary elections Oct. 10, 1971, gave the Socialist party a majority of seats; Socialist candidates were elected president in each postwar election.

Austria belongs to the UN and the EFTA. In 1972 Austria and 5 other EFTA members joined with Common Market members in pacts for abolition of industrial tariffs.

Education and Religion. The predominant religion is Roman Catholicism. Elementary education is compulsory between the ages of 6 and 15. There are universities in Vienna, Graz, Innsbruck, Linz, Klagenfurt, and Salzburg. The language is German.

Defense. Armed forces total 52,000.

The Bahamas

Area: 4,404 sq. mi. Population (Govt. est. 1975): 205,000. Capital: Nassau. Monetary unit: Bahamian dollar.

The Commonwealth of the Bahamas achieved full independence from Great Britain on July 10, 1973. The Bahamas comprise nearly 700 islands (30 inhabited) and over 2,000 islets in the western Atlantic. They extend 760 mi. NW to SE from a point 50 mi. off Florida to about 70 mi. from Haiti.

Christopher Columbus first set foot in the New World on the island of San Salvador (also called Watling Is.) on the eastern fringe of the Bahamas in 1492. British settlement started in 1647; the islands became a British colony in 1783. Internal self-government was granted in 1964. General elections in 1967 led to the selection of the first black prime minister, Lynden O. Pindling.

The prime minister leads the majority party of the 38-member, elected Assembly. The 16-member Senate is appointed by the governor-general (nominally representing the British queen) on the advice of the prime minister and the opposition leader. The Bahamas belong to the UN and the Commonwealth.

Tourism is the main industry; second is international banking and investment management. Rum is exported. Fruit and vegetables are grown mostly for local use. There are cement and pharmaceutical plants. Other exports are salt, lobster, tomatoes, cucumbers, handicrafts.

English is the only spoken language; protestantism is the predominant religion. All government elementary and high schools are free; elementary education is compulsory. About 85% of the population is of African descent.

Bahrain

Area: 231 sq. mi. Population: (Govt. est. 1974): 260,000. Capital: Manama. Monetary unit: Dinar.

Bahrain, long a British Protected State, declared its complete independence Aug. 14, 1971. It includes the main island, Bahrain, and several smaller islands ·midway along the Persian (also called Arabian) Gulf, about 20 mi. off the Arabian Peninsula's NE coast.

Pearls, shrimp, fruit, and vegetables were the mainstays of the economy until oil was discovered in 1932. By the 1970s, oil reserves showed signs of depletion. Contributions were made to the economy by a large refinery handling oil pumped undersea from Saudi Arabia as well as local oil, by a large aluminum smelter using local natural gas, and by increased use of Bahrain as a trans-shipment center. Bahrain took part in the 1973-74 Arab oil embargo against the U. S. and other nations. The government bought controlling interest in the oil industry in 1975.

Long ruled by the Khalifa family, Bahrain in 1861 gave Great Britain responsibility for defense and foreign relations. When Britain announced it would withdraw by the end of 1971, Bahrain sought to form a federation with the 7 Trucial Sheikdoms and Qatar.

The attempt failed and Bahrain declared itself independent. It is ruled by an Emir, a Prime Minister, and a Council of Ministers (cabinet). A 1973 constitution created a parliament, the National Assembly; 30 members are elected by male citizens 18 or over; 14 Cabinet members also sit in the Assembly. The first Assembly, elected in 1973 and dominated by leftists, was dissolved by the emir in 1975.

Most Bahrainis are of north Arabian descent, half of them Sunni Moslems, half of the Shi'ites. Arabic is the official language; Persian and English are also spoken. Education and health care are free.

The future of a small U. S. Navy base remained in doubt.

Bangladesh

Area: 55,126 sq. mi. Population (UN est. 1975): 76,820,000. Capital: Dacca. Monetary unit: Taka.

East Pakistan, the smaller but more populous of the 2 sections of Pakistan, achieved independence as Bangladesh (Bengal Nation) during the Dec. 3-16, 1971, India-Pakistan war. It is mostly a low plain cut by the Ganges and Brahmaputra Rivers and is bounded by India, Burma, and the Bay of Bengal. It is subject to heavy monsoon rains. A Nov. 13, 1970, cyclone killed at least 300,000 persons in coastal areas.

Resources and Industries. Bangladesh is primarily agricultural, with small, fertile farms. The area normally produces most of the world's jute, used in twine and sacks, and has large rice crops. Resources include rivers for irrigation and hydroelectric power, and natural gas. Small industries include cement, textile, jute, and fertilizer plants. Food shipments and other aid were provided by India, the U.S., USSR, and others. In Mar., 1972, Bangladesh announced nationalization of banks and some industries. Offshore oil deposits have been found, some in areas disputed by India, but 1974 floods and high world oil prices caused famine deaths to soar.

History and Government. British rule in the Indian sub-continent, dating from the 18th Century, ended in Aug. 1947 when India and Pakistan became independent. Pakistan's government power was centered in W. Pakistan, while E. Pakistan, with about 56% of the population, demanded greater economic benefits and political reforms. There were riots in 1968-69.

In Dec. 1970 elections, the Awami League, which demanded greater autonomy for E. Pakistan, won a majority in the National Assembly. But Pakistan Pres. A. M. Yahya Khan postponed the Assembly sessions. A general strike and riots swept E. Pakistan and on Mar. 25, 1971, W. Pakistani troops launched attacks on rebellious Bengalis. Awami League leaders declared independence the next day. Months of fighting followed in which it was estimated a million or more died as, it was charged, W. Pakistani troops conducted repressive attacks on the populace and guerrilla forces. Some 10 million fled to India, which supported their cause.

India and Pakistan each declared on Dec. 3, 1971, that the other had launched war. Pakistani troops surrendered Dec. 15 in the East; the Pakistan government accepted India's offer of a cease-fire on both east and west fronts Dec. 16. India had recognized Bangladesh as independent Dec. 6.

Sheik Mujibur Rahman, Awami League leader arrested in Mar. 1971, was freed by Pakistan and became Bangladesh prime minister Jan. 12, 1972.

Bangladesh joined the Commonwealth in 1972 and the UN in 1974.

A constitution took effect Dec. 16, 1972. In 1973 elections, Sheik Mujib's Awami League party won 305 of 313 seats. The government assumed emergency powers in 1974 to curb widespread violence. In 1975 a presidential form of government went into effect. Mujib was assassinated in 1975.

In Aug. 1973 India and Pakistan agreed to exchange war prisoners, leading to release of Bangladesh and Pakistani nationals stranded in each other's country.

By 1974 most prisoners were returned to Pakistan which then accepted more than 100,000 Biharis out of 500,000 who sought to leave Bangladesh.

Most of the Bangladesh people are Moslem Bengalis. The official language is Bengali.

Barbados

Area: 166 sq. mi. Population (UN est. 1975): 250,000. Capital: Bridgetown. Monetary unit: Barbados dollar.

Barbados achieved full independence from Great Britain Nov. 30, 1966. Furthest east of the West Indies, the island is about 2 1-2 times the size of the District of Columbia; it lies alone in the Atlantic almost completely surrounded by coral reefs. Its highest point is Mt. Hillaby, 1,115 ft. The name Barbados (bearded) was believed given it by Portuguese or Spanish sailors, referring to bearded fig trees.

An English ship visited in 1605; English settlers arrived in 1627. Slaves were imported, but freed in 1834. Most of the islanders are Negroes; the language is English and the religion of most is Anglican.

A charter of 1652 provided for a governor-general, council, and assembly. Self-rule was achieved gradually; universal suffrage was granted in 1950, cabinet government in 1958, full internal self-government in 1961. It has a parliament and prime minister and, as a member of the Commonwealth, a governor-general.

Sugar, molasses, rum, cotton, and building lime are the main products; there is a lively flying fish industry and, thanks mainly to the attractions of excellent beaches, the tourist business has boomed. But unemployment is high. In 1973 Barbados joined other West Indies states in the Caribbean Common Market.

With over 1,400 persons per sq. mi., the population density is one of the world's highest. Barbados has a high literacy rate.

Belgium

Area: 11,779 sq. mi. Population (Govt. est. 1975): 9,790,000. Capital: Brussels. Monetary unit: Franc.

Belgium's seacoast of 40 mi. borders on the North Sea at the Strait of Dover. Slightly larger than Maryland, the country shares borders with the Netherlands, Germany, Luxembourg, and France. The Meuse (Maas) River crosses the country from France to the Netherlands. The Scheldt (Escaut, Schelde) makes Antwerp an ocean port via the Netherlands.

Brussels, Bruges, Ghent, and Antwerp are noted for art and architecture; Liege and Charleroi are important industrially. Antwerp is the world's 3d largest port.

Resources and Industries. Coal is the nation's only important mineral. Although Belgium is essentially a manufacturing country, agriculture and forestry are profitable industries. The principal crops are oats, rye, wheat, potatoes, barley, and sugar beets.

Important industries are mining, steel manufacture, glassware, diamond cutting, food and beverages, fishing, textiles, and chemicals. Beurs voor Diamant in Antwerp is the world's largest diamond trading center.

Belgium lives by its foreign trade; about 40% of its entire production is sold abroad (75% of steel and glass). The Belgium-Luxembourg Economic Union is one of the world's foremost exporters of steel.

Foreign trade of Belgium-Luxembourg, in thousands of U. S. dollars:

	Imports	Exports
1974	$29,918,000	$28,328,000
1975	$30,688,000	$28,807,000

History and Government. Belgium, land of the Belgae conquered by Julius Caesar, was for 1800 years ruled by conquerors, including Rome, the Franks, Burgundy, Spain, Austria, and France. After the fall of Napoleon, 1815, Belgium was made a part of the Netherlands. Belgium became an independent constitutional monarchy in 1830 and chose Prince Leopold of Saxe-Coburg king, as Leopold I.

By the treaty of London, Apr. 19, 1839, Austria, France, Great Britain, Netherlands, Prussia, and Russia guaranteed the inviolability of Belgium; this was the "scrap of paper" repudiated by Germany when its troops entered Belgium, Aug. 2, 1914. After World War I Belgium was awarded 382 sq. mi. of territory formerly held by Germany, including Malmedy.

During World War II, Leopold III surrendered to Germany, May 28, 1940, to avoid bloodshed. His cabinet maintained a government-in-exile in London. Nevertheless, Belgium suffered heavily. Ancient churches, houses, and records were ruined at Nivelles, Mons, Tournai, Liege, Louvain; the University Library at Louvain, burned in both World Wars, was each time restored with U. S. aid. About 50,000 Belgians died, some in Nazi prison camps.

In 1950 Belgians voted 57% in favor of recalling Leopold III (who had been in Switzerland since being freed from German internment), but Socialists forced the king to abdicate and his son became King Baudouin I July 17, 1951. Born Sept. 7, 1930, he was the son of Leopold's first wife, Princess Astrid of Sweden. Baudouin married (Dec. 15, 1960) Dona Fabiola de Mora y Aragon of Spain.

Universal suffrage is in force and those who fail to vote are fined. Women have voted since 1949.

Parliament consists of a Senate with members elected for 4 years, partly directly and partly indirectly; the number elected directly is equal to half the number of members of the House of Representatives. The representatives are directly elected, for 4 years, by proportional representation (one for every 40,000 population).

The Flemings of northern Belgium speak Dutch while French is the language of the Walloons in the south. The language difference has been a perennial source of controversy, particularly as it affects education, with Flemish parents unwilling to have their children taught in French.

Disagreement between the 2 groups became embittered in 1968 elections in which minority extremist parties increased their strength. In 1971 and 1974 Belgium sought to solve the problem through creation of decentralized administrative and cultural communities.

Belgium is a member of the UN, NATO, EC, and the Benelux economic union.

Education and Religion. Roman Catholicism is the religion of the great majority. Part of the income of the ministers of the Catholic, Jewish, Church of England, and Protestant Evangelical religions is paid by the government. There are universities in Ghent, Liege, Brussels, Mons, Antwerp, and Louvain and agricultural, technical, art, and music schools.

Defense: Armed forces total 87,000.

Benin

Area: 43,483 sq. mi. Population (Govt. est. 1975): 3,110,000. Capitals: Porto-Novo, Cotonou. Monetary unit: CFA franc.

The Republic of Benin, former Overseas Territory in French West Africa, is a narrow strip 415 mi. long and 77 mi. wide, bounded by the Republics of the Niger and Upper Volta, Nigeria, the Gulf of Guinea and the Republic of Togo. It is about as large as Tennessee.

In accordance with the 1958 French constitution, Benin became fully independent Aug. 1, 1960, and became a member of the UN Sept. 20. Benin signed agreements Apr. 24, 1961, providing for close ties with France.

Under the constitution the president and National Assembly are elected for 5-year terms. Pres. Hubert Maga, elected Dec. 11, 1960, was deposed Oct. 28, 1963, and replaced by a provisional government headed by Gen. Christophe Soglo. The constitution of the second republic was adopted Dec. 19, 1963; several coups followed. In Oct. 1972 Maj. Mathieu Kerekou became president in a military coup.

Principal products: palm oil, kernels and nuts; peanuts, cotton, kapok, coffee, tobacco.

Small industries were constructed in the late 1960s, including a bicycle plant, cotton mill and peanut-oil plant. Oil was discovered offshore in 1969. The 1972-73 drought slowed economic development. France gives the nation an annual subsidy.

French is the official language. About 65% of the people are animists; 15%, in the S, are Christians; 13%, in the N, are Moslems.

Bhutan

Area: 19,305 sq. mi. Population (Govt. est. 1974): 1,034,774. Capital: Thimphu. Monetary unit: Ngultrum. (Indian Rupee is used.)

The tiny kingdom of Bhutan or Druk-Yul (Dragon-Nation) is a constitutional monarchy in the eastern Himalayas, adjoining Tibet and India. It is 190 mi. long from east to west and 90 mi. across, with both mountains and jungles. Over half the people are Bhotias of Tibetan origin and are Buddhists; a minority are Hindus of Nepalese descent, with indigenous Buddhist groups in the east.

Agriculture is the chief industry. The principal products are rice, corn, wheat, oranges, cardamom, yak butter, lac, wax, cloth, elephants, ponies, and timber.

The ruler of the kingdom is the "Dragon King," Jigme Singye Wangchuk (born 1955), who inherited the throne July 24, 1972, and was crowned June 2, 1974. Bhutan joined the UN in 1971.

Modernization has begun, including the country's first road network usable by automobiles, linking central Bhutan and India. There is also airline service from India. Dzongs (castle-monasteries) and game sanctuaries are among attractions.

Bolivia

Area: 424,162 sq. mi. Population (Govt. est. 1975): 5,630,000. Capital: Sucre. Seat of govt.: La Paz. Monetary unit: Peso.

Bolivia is a landlocked nation, over 8 times the size of N.Y. State. It lies across the Andes. The great central plateau, at an altitude of 12,000 ft., over 500 mi. long, lies between two great cordilleras having 3 of the highest peaks in South America. About 65% of the population are Indians; 10% are white, and 25% are mixed (cholo).

Lake Titicaca, on the Peruvian-Bolivian border, is the highest lake in the world on which steamboats ply (12,506 ft.), and is the 2d largest lake in South America (est. 3,200 sq. mi.).

The legal capital is Sucre, but La Paz, a city more accessible, is the actual seat of government. La Paz lies in the heart of a gigantic canyon about 3 mi. wide, 10 mi. long and 1,500 ft. deep, at an altitude of about 11,800 ft., and framed with high Andean peaks. Its huge cathedral seats 12,000 was dedicated 1933.

Resources and Industries. Agriculture claims 65% of the work force. Products include potatoes, sugar, coffee, barley, cocoa, highland rice, corn, bananas, citrus, rubber, and cinchona bark.

The most important industry is mining. There are large deposits of tin, silver, copper, lead, zinc, petroleum, antimony, bismuth, wolfram, gold, iron, cadmium, borate of lime, and natural gas. More than 12% of the world's output of tin is produced in Bolivia, running to 28,000 tons or more annually. The 3 largest tin producers were nationalized in 1952. The oilfields and plants of a U.S. company were nationalized in Oct. 1969. High world tin and oil prices yielded a $140 million 1974 trade surplus.

Bolivian miners' attempts to negotiate better working conditions with the government-owned mining corp. were led in 1967-68 by a group of priests. An agreement was reached in 1968; the corporation agreed to permit union activities and provide better conditions. Troops occupied the mines in 1976 after further strikes.

Bolivia receives aid from the U. S., the Inter-American Development Bank, the World Bank and the International Monetary Fund. It is a member of the UN and OAS. In May 1969 Bolivia joined Chile, Colombia, Ecuador and Peru in an Andean Common Market.

History and Government. Once part of the ancient Inca empire, Bolivia was under Spanish domination for centuries before it gained independence Aug. 6, 1825, naming itself after Simon Bolivar, famed liberator.

Bolivia's 16th constitution, adopted in 1967, provides for strong executive power, nationalization of mines, and agrarian reform. The Congress it provided for was dissolved in Sept. 1969.

Dr. Victor Paz Estenssoro, elected to a 3d term as President May 31, 1964, was ousted Nov. 4 and the government was taken over in one of a series of military coups. Military and civilian anti-Communist forces under Col. Hugo Banzer Suarez took over the government in a brief conflict, Aug. 19-22, 1971. In 1973 the government pressed school-building and oil-exploration programs. In 1974 Brazil contracted to build steel, cement and petrochemical plants in Bolivia and a pipeline to carry Bolivian natural gas 1,000 mi. to Sao Paulo, Brazil.

Unrest continued as peasants and miners staged protests. In 1974 Banzer dismissed civilian members of his cabinet, banned political parties and labor unions, and postponed elections until 1980.

Education and Religion. Primary education is free and compulsory. Adult illiteracy at 58% is being lowered. There are 8 universities. Roman Catholicism is predominant; Spanish is the official language.

Defense. Bolivia's armed forces total 27,000.

Botswana

Area: 219,815 sq. mi. Population (Govt. est. 1975): 690,000. Capital: Gaborone. Monetary unit: South African rand.

The former British Protectorate of Bechuanaland received full independence Sept. 30, 1966, and joined the UN Oct. 17, 1966.

In the center of Southern Africa and populated predominantly by blacks, Botswana shares borders with the Republic of South Africa, South-West Africa (Namibia), and Rhodesia. It also claims to border on Zambia, its nearest black-ruled neighbor. It is slightly smaller than Texas.

The Kalahari Desert, supporting nomadic Bushmen and many wild animals, spreads over the southwestern areas of Botswana; there are swamplands and farming areas in the north, and rolling plains in the east where livestock are grazed.

Cattle is the largest industry. Large copper, coal, and nickel deposits were discovered in 1967 and diamonds in 1969. Corn, sorghum, beans, and peanuts are raised in the north. Tourism is flourishing; black-maned lions and swamp antelopes are hunted.

Many workers have become migrant laborers in South Africa and much of the country's chief export, meat, goes to that country, as well as to the EC, Zambia, and Hong Kong.

In 1885, Bechuanaland was made a British protectorate after local chiefs appealed to Great Britain for aid to halt encroachment on their territories by Boers of South Africa's Transvaal and Germans of S.W. Africa.

It is a republic with a president, a House of Chiefs (which handles questions of tradition) and a National Assembly.

Brazil

Area: 3,286,470 sq. mi. Population (Govt. est. 1975): 107,661,000. Capital: Brasilia. Monetary unit: Cruzeiro.

Brazil is the largest nation in South America in area and population. Larger in area than the 48 states in conterminous U.S., it is smaller than the 50 states. It has a coastline on the Atlantic Ocean of 4,603 mi., and extends 2,689 from N to S and 2,684 from E to W. The northern part is the great, heavily-wooded basin of the Amazon (1,465,637 sq. mi. in Brazil) which rises in the Peruvian Andes and empties into the Atlantic.

The Amazon basin has a network of rivers which are navigable for 15,814 mi. The Amazon River by itself flows 2,093 mi. through Brazil, and is navigable for 2,300 mi., to the Peruvian riverport of Iquitos.

The majestic falls of the Iguazu, 230 ft. high but extremely wide, are on the Brazil-Argentina border; Glass Falls, in Bahia west of Salvador, are 1,325 ft. high. Tallest mountain is Pico da Neblina, 10,046 ft., on the Venezuela border.

The south central region, favored by climate, resources, and communications, has 45% of the population and produces 75% of agricultural goods and 80% of industrial output.

Brasilia, the capital city, was inaugurated Apr. 21, 1960, superseding Rio de Janeiro. Fast-growing Sao Paulo is the largest city in South America.

Resources and Industries: Brazil has vast mineral wealth and exploitation is being spurred. It is among world leaders in output of quartz crystal and beryl, sheet mica, manganese, columbium and tantalum, and iron ore. It has large deposits of iron (one-third of the world's reserves) and monazite, a source of thorium, alternate to uranium as a supplier of fissionable material. Gold output is about 142,000 troy oz. annually. Also important are nickel, chrome, diamonds, coal, tungsten, tin, bauxite, various gem stones. New oil finds have raised hopes for self-sufficiency.

Cotton weaving is among important manufacturing industries, occupying 14% of workers. Brazil produces 7.5 million tons of steel annually, 30% in the Volta Redonda national mills. About 1 million autos are produced a year. Aluminum, petrochemical, cement, pharmaceutical, plastics, food and beverage, electrical appliances, shipbuilding, ceramics, shoe, tire, paper, glass, and heavy machinery industries are growing.

Brazil, world's greatest coffee grower, supplies about 30% of the coffee consumed in the U.S. Cotton, soybeans, sugar, cocoa, iron ore, and industrial products are also important exports. There are large crops of bananas, manioc, oranges, pineapples, rice, and corn.

Brahman (zebu) cattle of India thrive in Brazil, which is 3rd among world leaders with 98 million cattle. It also has 47 million hogs and 25 million sheep.

Brazil's economy boomed in the 1970s, with heavy government investment and planning; the gross national product was up 10% in 1974, though income maldistribution remained a problem. Exports also showed strong gains. But inflation, though slowed, remained a problem. A 3,150-mi. Trans-Amazon Highway, stretching from the Atlantic coast to Peru, is nearing completion.

West Germany agreed in 1975 to supply Brazil with the technology for a complete nuclear energy industry, in exchange for uranium.

Foreign trade in thousands of U.S. dollars:

	Imports	Exports
1974	$14,168,000	$7,952,000
1975	$13,558,000	$8,658,000

History and Government. Pedro Alvares Cabral, a Portuguese navigator, is generally credited as the first European to reach Brazil, 1500.

Brazil was developed as a colony of Portugal until the royal house of Braganca, fleeing from Lisbon before Napoleon's army in 1807, transferred the seat of government to Rio de Janeiro, March, 1808. Brazil thereupon became a kingdom under Dom Joao VI. After his return to Portugal, his son Pedro I, proclaimed the independence of the country, Sept. 7, 1822, and was acclaimed emperor. The second emperor, Dom Pedro II, was driven from the throne Nov. 15, 1889, by a revolution which established a republic, the United States of Brazil. In Jan. 1967 a new constitution changed the name to Federative Republic of Brazil.

There are 21 states, with limited autonomy, a federal district and 4 territories: Roraima, Rondonia, Amapa and Fernando de Noronha Is.

Brazil is a member of both the UN and OAS.

A military junta took control in 1930. Getulio Vargas became provisional president until 1933, when he was elected president under a new constitution. Out in 1945, he was reelected in 1950, but in 1954 the army forced him to retire.

In 1964, after a succession of presidents, economic and social problems brought the ouster of Pres. Joao Goulart, in a part-military, part-civilian coup. A new constitution, adopted in 1967, strengthened the powers of the presidency, reducing those of congress. The next 4 presidents were all military leaders. On Jan. 15, 1974, an electoral college consisting of representatives of congress and of the state legislatures, elected Gen. Ernesto Geisel president. In 1974 elections, the democratic opposition took control of the chamber of deputies; but cases of torture by police elements were still being reported.

Education and Religion. Roman Catholicism is the predominant religion.

There are 65 universities in Brazil as well as other institutions of higher education, with a total of 700,000 students in 1972. Primary, 5-year schools number more than 167,000 and there are more than 24,000 median level schools. Primary and secondary schools are free. A national program has reduced adult illiteracy to 18%. The language is Portuguese.

Armed forces total over 200,000.

Bulgaria

Area: 42,829 sq. mi. Population (Govt. est. 1974): 8,720,000. Capital: Sofia. Monetary unit: Lev.

The People's Republic of Bulgaria, fronting on the Black Sea, is about the size of Ohio. It is bounded by Romania, Turkey, Greece, and Yugoslavia. The Balkan Mtns. stretch across the center of the country with the Danubian Plain in the north and the Rhodope Mtns. and Thracian Plain in the south.

Resources and Industries. Under communism after World War II, farms were collectivized, resources nationalized, and foreign trade made a government monopoly. The principal crops are wheat, fruit, rye, barley, oats, corn, potatoes, and tobacco. The country has been industrialized under a nationalized planned economy which emphasizes electric power, chemicals, coal, machinery, metals, textiles, building materials, fur, leather goods, and oil. About 70% of the work force is non-agricultural.

In 1971 productive enterprises were centralized into some 60 state economic amalgamations. The index of industrial production (1970 = 100) reached 142 in 1974. Tourism is promoted and nearly 4 million tourists visit Bulgaria annually.

About 73% of trade is with nations of the communist bloc. Exports include machinery, industrial and agricultural vehicles, chemicals, vegetables, tobacco, rose attar, lead, zinc, cement, and wine.

Foreign trade, in thousands of U. S. dollars:

	Imports	Exports
1974	$4,326,000	$3,836,000
1975	$5,324,000	$4,614,000

History and Government. The Bulgars settled Bulgaria in the 7th cent., became Christians in the 9th, and set up a powerful empire in the 10th-12th. The Turks conquered in 1396. A revolt in 1876 led to autonomy in 1878 and an independent kingdom in 1908. Bulgaria expanded after the first Balkan war but lost its Aegean coastline in World War I, when it sided with Germany.

Under the influence of King Boris III, Bulgaria joined the Axis in World War II, occupying considerable Balkan territory. In 1944 Bulgaria withdrew from the war, but the USSR refused to recognize its neutrality and declared war Sept. 5. Four days later, an anti-fascist government seized power and declared war on Germany. In a plebiscite Sept. 8, 1946, the monarchy was abolished and a republic voted. Georgi Dimitrov, Communist party leader, became the first premier.

The 1971 constitution provides that the National Assembly, elected for 5 years, is the supreme organ of government. The Assembly chooses a premier and a State Council whose president is the head of state. Only one slate is permitted, dominated by the Communist party.

Bulgaria belongs to the UN and the Warsaw Pact.

Education and Religion. Bulgarian is a Slavic language, the earliest to be written. Elementary education is obligatory from 7 to 14 years of age. There are 27 higher educational establishments, with over 100,-000 students. The main religion is Eastern Orthodox. There are several hundred thousand Moslems. Religious observance is discouraged.

Defense. Armed forces total 152,000.

Burma

Area: 261,789 sq. mi. Population (UN est. 1975): 31,240,000. Capital: Rangoon. Monetary unit: Kyat.

The Union of Burma, slightly smaller than Texas, is a republic in the western part of the former Indochinese peninsula. It is bounded by China, Laos, Thailand, India, Bangladesh, and the Bay of Bengal. Rivers flowing from the rugged mountains in the north provide habitable valleys down the peninsula. The largest is the Irrawaddy which is navigable for 900 mi.

The Burma Road, from Lashio to Kunming in Yunnan Province, China, was the principal military supply line from Burma into China 1938-1942.

Rangoon, on the Gulf of Martaban, is the chief port. Mingaladon airport, near Rangoon, handles international traffic.

Resources and Industries. Mineral wealth is great; included are petroleum, lead, silver, tin, tungsten, zinc, rubies, sapphires, and jade. Principal products are rice, cotton, maize, teakwood, tobacco, tin, silver, rubber, and petroleum. In value of exports, rice accounted for 40% until recent declines. Production in some industries also declined in the 1960s.

History and Government. Burma was a Buddhist monarchy in the Middle Ages. Britain, through 3 wars, gained Lower Burma in 1824 and Upper Burma in 1884 and administered them as part of India until 1937, when Burma became a self-governing unit of the British Commonwealth. It was overrun by Japan in World War II. Burma became independent outside the Commonwealth by treaty effective Jan. 4, 1948, and a member of the UN in 1948.

The constitution which went into effect in 1948 created a parliamentary democracy and provided for nationalization of certain industries. In a 1958 political crisis, Gen. Ne Win took over the government from Premier U Nu. Elections were held in 1960 and the Union party, headed by U Nu, won a large majority; he again became premier in April, 1960.

Political and economic problems continued and the government was again taken over by Gen. Ne Win, Mar. 2, 1962; he set up a Revolutionary Council with himself as chief of state, setting aside the constitution. In 1972 he became premier.

The Ne Win government pursued a socialistic program and nationalized nearly all of industry and trade, which had been controlled by Indian and Chinese minorities. It continued a neutralist foreign policy, and isolated the nation from most foreign contacts. On Jan. 4, 1974, a new constitution, aimed at making Burma a "socialist republic" under one-party rule, was adopted. Ne Win continued as premier.

Recurrent problems facing the government have been the need to stimulate production, rebellions staged by Chinese-backed Communist forces, and pressures from groups seeking greater autonomy for local ethnic groups. Communist guerrillas became more active after the communist victories in Indochina in 1975.

Education and Religion. The Burmans are the main ethnic group; others are Karens, Shans, Kachins, Chins, etc. Burmese or one of its variants is spoken by nearly three-fourths of the population. Higher education is provided at the Universities of Rangoon, Mandalay and 5 smaller cities. A state-controlled system of schools was introduced after 1948.

The chief religion is Buddhism (about 90%).

Defense. Armed forces total about 150,000.

Burundi

Area: 10,739 sq. mi. Population (UN est. 1975): 3,760,000. Capital: Bujumbura. Monetary unit: Burundi franc.

Burundi, a country the size of Maryland in east central Africa, became independent July 1, 1962. Formerly part of the Belgian UN Trusteeship of Ruanda-Urundi, it is bordered by Rwanda, Tanzania, Lake Tanganyika and Zaire. Much of the country is grasslands and mountains.

For 3 centuries in the present Burundi and Rwanda area, the Tutsi, a minority tribe, were overlords and political masters of the Hutu. (The Tutsi tend to be extremely tall; the Hutu, the vast majority of the population, are of average height; a 3d tribe, the Twa, are pygmies.) Under German control in the late 19th century, the area was taken over by Belgium in World War I; the League of Nations in 1923 gave the king of Belgium a mandate over the combined Ruanda-Urundi territory; Belgium received a UN Trusteeship in 1946.

Burundi became an independent constitutional monarchy in 1962 with Mwami Mwambutsa IV as king; there were a premier and cabinet, an Assembly elected by universal suffrage and a Senate. The government was mainly supported by the Uprena party, a coalition of moderate Tutsi and Hutu. Two premiers were slain by extremists and in Oct. 1965 a 3d, Leopold Biha, was severely wounded. Hutu extremists opposed the power of the minority Tutsi in the government; Tutsi extremists, accused of receiving Chinese aid, opposed the government as too moderate.

In July 1966 the king's son, Prince Charles, 19, deposed him, appointing Michael Micombero premier. Extremist Tutsi returned to power; on Sept. 1 Prince Charles was proclaimed King Mwami Ntare V. But in a coup d'etat Nov. 28, he was overthrown by Micombero, who declared himself president and Burundi a republic. Ntare was killed in April 1972, supposedly during an attempt to seize power.

A Hutu revolt, starting Apr. 29, 1972, was put down; it was estimated 10,000 Tutsi were slain by rebels and 100,000 Hutu by government troops. In 1973 renewed fighting was reported and thousands of Hutu fled to Tanzania and Zaire.

The economy is agricultural, with 90% of the people farmers or livestock raisers. Coffee is the main crop and export. Much of the land is over-grazed and eroded. The nation receives aid from Belgium and the UN. It is a member of the UN and OAU.

Cotton production has become increasingly important. With outside technical aid, tea plantations have been established.

Over half the population is Christian, mostly Roman Catholic. Many others believe in a supreme deity, Imana, called the Principle of Good. Kirundi, a Bantu tongue, and French are the official languages; Swahili is also widely used. (See also Rwanda.)

Cambodia

Area: 69,898 sq. mi. Population (UN est. 1974): 7,890,000. Capital: Phnom Penh. Monetary unit: Riel.

Cambodia, or Khmer, is in southeast Asia and, with Vietnam and Laos, comprised the former associated states of French Indochina. It is slightly larger than N.D. It is bordered by Laos, Thailand, the Gulf of Siam and South Vietnam. Three-fourths is forested; the central part is level, forming a basin for the Mekong River. The climate is tropical.

Resources and Industries. The country is largely undeveloped; 50% of the land is virgin forest. Main industries are forestry, fishing, and agriculture, rice occupying about 80% of the land usage. Other products are rubber, maize, pepper, kapok, palm-sugar, tobacco, cotton, silk, oil seeds, beans. Cattle flourish; the forests have valuable hardwoods. Some iron, copper, manganese and gold exist. Industry includes textiles, paper, plywood. An oil refinery opened in 1968.

Continuing warfare created a rice shortage; until 1970 Cambodia exported rice, but it now imports.

History and Government. Early kingdoms dating from that of Founan in the 1st century A.D. culminated in the great Khmer civilization which flourished from the 9th century to the 13th. The Khmer "God Kings" built a series of monumental cities, distinguished for their temple tower architecture and striking wall sculptures. Most famous temple is that of Angkor Wat.

Cambodia came under French protection in 1863. A national constitution promulgated May 6, 1947, replaced the former absolutism. Cambodia became an associated state within the French Union by a treaty of Nov. 8, 1949, but declared its independence from France Nov. 9, 1953. It is a UN member.

Prince Norodom Sihanouk was king, 1941-55; he abdicated in favor of his father, Norodom Suramarit, who died Apr. 3, 1960. On June 13, 1960, Sihanouk, refusing to become king again, was named chief of state. Sihanouk broke off relations with the U.S. in 1965 after an attack by S. Vietnamese planes on Vietcong forces fleeing into Cambodia. In 1968 Sihanouk said Viet communists were arming Cambodian insurgents. In July 1969 relations with the U.S. were restored. In 1969-70 the U.S. bombed N. Viet forces in Cambodia but did not announce that until 1973.

In Mar. 1970, while Sihanouk was in Europe, the Cambodian government demanded, without result, that N. Vietnam and the Vietcong withdraw their troops, estimated at 40,000, from Cambodia. On Mar. 18, 1970, Sihanouk's premier, Lt. Gen. Lon Nol, took power. Sihanouk later announced in Peking the formation of a government-in-exile.

In Oct. 1970 the monarchy was abolished and Cambodia's name was changed to the Khmer Republic. Lon Nol was voted president in June 1972.

The Lon Nol government charged increasing attacks on its troops by the communist forces and appealed for arms from other nations. The U.S. provided heavy military and economic aid.

On Apr. 30, 1970, U.S. President Nixon announced that U.S. troops were moving into Cambodia to drive communist forces from S. Vietnam border area sanctuaries. More than 30,000 U.S. troops and over 40,000 S. Vietnamese took part in the operations. On June 30 Nixon announced the end of the U.S. incursion.

Khmer Rouge forces completed their takeover April 17, 1975, after 5 years of war in which over 100,000 died. Sihanouk was named chief of state for life April 25, but Red commander Khieu Samphan emerged as the leading figure and Sihanouk resigned in 1976.

The new government immediately evacuated all cities and towns, sending virtually the entire population to clear jungle, forest and scrub for rice cultivation, reportedly with no tools. Refugees in Thailand reported arbitrary killings and massive hardship deaths, totalling 500,000 by some reports.

The government claimed international neutrality, though Chinese advisors were reported present. Border clashes with Thailand occurred, but ties were later restored. At least 15 U.S. troops were killed in the May 14, 1975, recovery of the merchant ship Mayaguez, seized by Cambodia two days earlier.

Education and Religion. The national language is Cambodian, or Khmer; French is widely spoken and English is taught. In 1965 there were over 4,000 schools and 37 faculties of higher learning. Buddhism is the majority religion.

Cameroon

Area: 183,568 sq. mi. Population (UN est. 1975): 6,400,000. Capital: Yaounde. Monetary unit: CFA franc.

Cameroon, which became a republic in 1960, lies on the western coast of Africa, bounded N and NW by Nigeria, NE by Chad, E by Central African Republic, S by People's Republic of Congo, Gabon and Equatorial Guinea, W by Gulf of Guinea. It is larger than California.

Cameroon was composed of 2 states: East Cameroon, formerly the Republic of Cameroon, previously a French mandate and trusteeship; and West Cameroon, formerly British Southern Cameroons. A united republic was declared May 20, 1972. Douala has the principal seaport and one of 9 airports.

The population comprises some 200 tribes, including Bantu, Semitic and Sudanese peoples, Kirdis, Foulbes and Bamilekes. There are about 600,000 Christians and 600,000 Moslems; others are animists.

Resources and Industries. Mainly agricultural, Cameroon exports cocoa, coffee, palm products, leather, timber, rubber, peanut oil, tea, bananas, cotton, and tobacco.

Aluminum processing is the most important manufacturing industry. Trade is heavy with France and United Kingdom. Import and export totals are each over $350 million annually. New railroad and power dam construction and agricultural modernization were pressed in the 1970s.

History and Government. Cameroon embraces the larger part of the former German protectorate of Kamerun which was occupied by France and Britain in 1916, and placed under trusteeship, 1919. France passed a statute Dec. 31, 1958, conferring internal autonomy on the French trusteeship as a step toward complete independence which took effect Jan. 1, 1960.

Following a referendum by the UN in former British Cameroons, the southern section joined the republic to form the Federal Republic of Cameroon Oct. 1, 1961. (The northern section of British Cameroons voted to become part of Nigeria.) Cameroon belongs to the UN and OAU.

The president and the 120-member national assembly are elected for 5-year terms by direct universal suffrage.

Canada

See Index

Cape Verde Islands

Area: 1,557 sq. mi. Population (UN est. 1975): 290,000. Capital: Praia.

The Cape Verde Islands, 15 in number, lie in the North Atlantic Ocean, 280 miles west of Dakar, Africa. Principal products are coffee, which is exported, fruits, salt, tuna, hides, and grain. An 8-year drought continued in 1975, with Portugal and the UN supplying nearly all the country's food.

The uninhabited Cape Verde Islands were discovered by the Portuguese in 1460. The first Portuguese colonists landed in 1462; African slaves were brought soon after. Most Cape Verdeans descend from both groups. Many Cape Verdeans, who have a relatively high educational level, served as officials in Portuguese African colonies, and also led the independence movement in Guinea-Bissau.

After over 500 years of Portuguese rule, the Cape Verdes became independent July 5, 1975. All 56 members of the new national assembly belonged to the Party for the Independence of Guinea-Bissau and the Cape Verde Islands, though the party's resistance activities had been confined to Guinea-Bissau. The party favored unification of the 2 former colonies, and several agreements were signed in 1976 unifying their policies.

Most of the population speaks only Portuguese. Roman Catholicism is practiced by 98%.

Central African Republic

Area: 241,313 sq. mi. Population (UN est. 1974): 2,610,000. Capital: Bangui. Monetary unit: CFA franc.

The Central African Republic in equatorial Africa is 350 mi. NE of the Gulf of Guinea and is bounded by Chad, Sudan, Congo, Zaire, and Cameroon. Slightly N of the equator, it is mostly rolling plateau, average alt. about 2,000 ft., with rivers draining S to the Congo and N to Lake Chad. Landlocked, it is slightly smaller than Texas.

As the French territory of Ubangi-Shari, it achieved partial self-government in 1958. Complete independence was proclaimed Aug. 13, 1960. The republic is a UN member.

A few months after his election in 1960, Pres. David Dacko dissolved all political parties. He was re-elected Jan. 1965, running as the sole candidate. The country became a center for Chinese political activities.

On Jan. 1, 1966, Col. Jean Bedel Bokassa deposed Dacko; a few days later Pres. Bokassa broke off diplomatic relations with Peking. He was named president-for-life Mar. 8, 1972. Elizabeth Domitien became premier in 1975, the first woman to assume such a post in Africa.

French is the official language; Sangho is a lingua franca of the 4 ethnic groups: Banda, M'Baka, Zande, Mandjia-Baya.

Diamonds are the main export. Export earnings amount to about $70 million annually. Uranium, iron, and copper have been found. Cotton, coffee, and peanuts are the chief cash crops; production was increased in the late 1960s. There are large herds of cattle and sheep; lumber exports have increased. About 87% of the population is agricultural.

Small factories for textiles, processed food, soap, beer and for motorbike assembly and radios have been set up.

Republic of Chad

Area: 495,752 sq. mi. Population (Govt. est. 1975): 4,030,000. Capital: N'Djamena. Monetary unit: CFA franc.

A former French Overseas Territory in Equatorial Africa, 500 mi. NE of the Gulf of Guinea, 550 mi. S of the Mediterranean, Chad is bounded N by Libya, E by Sudan, S by Central African Republic, W by Cameroon, Nigeria, Niger. It is four-fifths the size of Alaska.

Sudanic Moslem groups predominate in the north, and Bantu animists and Christians in the south. Chad has a southern wooded savanna, a steppe, and a desert, part of the Sahara, in the N. On the W is Lake Chad.

Chad proclaimed complete independence Aug. 11, 1960, and joined the UN Sept. 20. There is a president and a National Assembly elected by universal adult suffrage. Chad is a member of the OAU and UN. French is the official language; but in 1974 the nation began replacing French names with African ones. The capital, Fort-Lamy, became N'Djamena.

Cotton is the main export; others are refrigerated meat, leather, dried fish, and sodium carbonate. Uranium has been found.

In 1969-71, with the aid of French troops, government forces fought many skirmishes with rebellious Arab nomads in the northeast. French troops began leaving in 1972, and completed withdrawal in 1975. Chad had accused Libya of aiding the rebels. In 1973 Chad broke off diplomatic relations with Israel, and Libya reportedly responded by halting aid to the rebels. Some fighting continued.

Years of drought which began in 1969 afflicted Chad and other nations in the Sahel, the sub-Sahara region of West Africa. U.S. gifts of food were increased in 1972 and other Western nations aided in 1973; the U.S. provided over 40% of food shipments, over twice as much as any other nation.

President Ngarta Tombalbaye, who had ruled since independence, was killed in a military coup in April, 1975.

Chile

Area: 286,396 sq. mi. Population (Govt. est. 1975): 10,250,000. Capital: Santiago. Monetary unit: Peso.

The Republic of Chile lies along the southern half of the west coast of South America, a narrow strip of land 2,620 mi. long between the towering Andes and the South Pacific. It is slightly larger than Texas.

Most of Chile lies in the temperate zone, but the Atacama Desert in the north is one of the world's driest regions, with little or no rainfall. The Christ of the Andes, a heroic-size statue in Uspallata Pass, symbolizes peace between Chile and Argentina.

Tierra del Fuego is the largest (18,800 sq. mi.) island in the archipelago of the same name at the southern tip of South America, an area of majestic mountains, tortuous channels, and high winds. It was discovered 1520 by Magellan; he named the island Land of Fire because of its many Indian bonfires. Part of the island is in Chile, part in Argentina. Punta Arenas, on a mainland peninsula in Chile, is a center of sheep-raising and the world's southernmost city (pop. over 64,000); Puerto Williams, pop. 949, at a Chilean naval base on Navarino Is., is the southernmost settlement. Beagle Channel, between Navarino and the main island, and Mt. Darwin were named for Charles Darwin's visit to the area aboard the ship Beagle.

Possessions in Pacific: Sala y Gomez and **Easter Is. (Rapa Nui),** with huge stone statues, both over 2,000 mi. to the W, **San Ambrosio** and **San Felix,** 600 mi. W, and **Juan Fernandez Islands** 450 mi. W., the place where Alexander Selkirk, who reputedly was the inspiration for Defoe's Robinson Crusoe, lived for 4 years.

Resources and Industries. The arid deserts of northern Chile contain incalculable mineral wealth. Mining industries account for more than 70% of Chile's exports. Nitrate production is about 100,000 metric tons a month. About 47% of the world's supply of iodine is a by-product of Chilean nitrate works. Chile produces about 10% of world copper output.

The provinces of Atacama and Coquimbo have enormous iron deposits estimated at a billion tons. Coal reserves are estimated at 2 billion tons. Oil wells, mostly in Tierra del Fuego, partly supply Chile's needs and natural gas offers an export potential. Other minerals are gold, silver, molybdenum, cobalt, zinc, manganese, borate, mica, mercury, iodine, salt, sulphur, marble, onyx. Chile has abundant waterpower. Patagonia, the sparsely populated southern third of the nation, is undergoing extensive industrial development.

There are many large dairy farms. Wheat, rice, barley, oats, beans, lentils, apples, melons, peaches, plums, nectarines, peas, and potatoes are grown in abundance. Sugar beet, automotive, and textile industries are being developed. Vineyards cover 250,000 acres and much wine is exported. Forests have large reserves of hard and soft woods. Coastal waters have shellfish, lobster, tuna, swordfish, sardines. Chile ranks 15th in weight of its fish catch.

Besides minerals the exports are mainly fishmeal, barley, oats, wine, onions, garlic, leather, lentils, fruits, fish, sea-food, cellulose, newsprint, wood.

Chile is served by 15 international airlines. The Pan American Highway runs 2,000 mi. from Arica in the N to Puerto Montt.

In the late 1960s the government pressed a wide program of social and economic reforms.

In 1970 Dr. Salvador Allende Gossens, a Marxist, was elected president and in July 1971 a constitutional amendment provided for full nationalization of copper mines owned by 3 U.S. companies, with compensation to be negotiated. A policy of nationalizing large industries and banks and expropriating large farms was launched. In 1972 middle class groups staged street demonstrations protesting food shortages and socialist policies. Strikes and riots increased in 1973. Food shortages and inflation continued.

A U.S. Senate Foreign Relations subcommittee in 1973 accused the International Telephone & Telegraph Corp. and the U.S. Central Intelligence Agency (CIA) of conspiring to prevent Allende's election in 1970. The Allende government nationalized ITT phone systems in Chile, without compensation. The CIA was also accused of aiding anti-Allende groups after the election.

In an attack on the Presidential Palace, Sept. 11, 1973, a military junta seized power and said Allende killed himself. A few thousand were killed in street fighting and junta reprisals. The junta named Gen. Augusto Pinochet Ugarte president, swore in a mostly military cabinet and broke off diplomatic relations with Cuba, which Allende had resumed. Pinochet announced the junta would "exterminate Marxism."

A year after the coup, some 5,000 Allende sympathizers were reported still in prison camps, some reportedly subjected to torture; at least 80 had been executed, and about 15,000 people, mostly foreigners, had been allowed to leave the country. Inflation, which had raged under the Allende administration, reached 400% in 1974. The Pinochet government agreed to pay U.S. companies for property expropriated under Allende.

History and Government. Diego de Almagro entered Chile for Pizarro 1536 and Valdivia completed Spanish conquest 1540.

Independence was gained 1810-18, under Jose de San Martin and Bernardo O'Higgins; the latter as supreme director, 1817-1823, sought social and economic reforms until deposed. Chile defeated Peru and Bolivia in 1836-39 and 1879-84, taking Tacna and Arica provinces from Peru, returned Tacna, 1929. Arica (town) and Antofagasta are now free ports for landlocked Bolivia.

Under the suspended constitution the president is elected for 6 years, the 50 senators for 8 and 150 deputies for 4. Voting age was lowered from 21 to 18 in 1970. Chile is a member of the UN and OAS.

About two-thirds of the Chileans are of mixed Spanish and Indian descent; about one-fourth of Spanish only; a small percentage are Indian only; there are some of German and other European descent.

Education and Religion. Education is free and compulsory between 7 and 15. Literacy is 88%. There are 9 universities. The Roman Catholic religion is dominant. The language is Spanish.

People's Republic of China

Area: 3,691,502 sq. mi. Population (Chinese Govt. est. 1974): "Almost 800 million." Capital: Peking. Monetary unit: Jen MinPi.

China, with about one-fifth of the world's population, occupies a territory in the eastern part of Asia slightly larger than the United States.

The mainland is of rolling topography, rising to high elevations in the N in the Khinghan Mtns., separating Manchuria and Mongolia; the Tarabagata Mtns. in Sinkiang; the Himalayan and Kunlun Mtns., in the SW in Tibet. Its length from N to S is 1,860 mi. and its breadth from E to W more than 2,000 mi.

The eastern half of China is one of the best-watered lands in the world. Three great river systems, the Yangtze, the Hwang (Yellow) and the Si (Si Kiang) provide water for vast farmlands.

China comprises 22 provinces, including Taiwan, which it claims; 5 autonomous regions (Inner Mongolia, Sinkiang-Uighur, Kwangsi-Chuang, Ningsia-Hui, Tibet-Chamdo) and 3 municipalities — Peking, Tientsin, and Shanghai. The government has pressed birth control programs.

History. One of the oldest of monarchies, with a history reaching back to 2205 B.C., China became a republic Jan. 1, 1912, following the Wuchang Uprising inspired by Dr. Sun Yat-sen, begun Oct. 10, 1911.

For a period of 50 years after the Sino-Japanese War, 1894-95, China was involved in conflicts with Japan. On Sept. 18, 1931, Japan seized the Northeastern Provinces (Manchuria) and set up a puppet state called Manchukuo. The border province of Jehol was cut off as a buffer state in 1933. Japan invaded China in the vicinity of Peking July 7, 1937, precipitating war. After its defeat in World War II Japan returned all seized land.

After the war with Japan ended, Aug. 15, 1945, internal disturbances arose involving the Kuomintang, communists, and other factions. Manchuria was lost by the Kuomintang regime in 1948, and China proper came under domination of Chinese Communist armies during 1949-1950. The Kuomintang government moved to Taipei, Taiwan (Formosa), 90 mi. off the mainland, Dec. 8, 1949.

The People's Republic of China was proclaimed in Peking (Peiping) Sept. 21, 1949, by the Chinese People's Political Consultative Conference under Mao Tse-tung, communist leader. Chou En-lai was named premier and foreign minister Oct. 1, 1949.

The communist regime and the USSR signed a 30-year treaty of "friendship, alliance and mutual assistance," Feb. 15, 1950, repudiating the 1945 treaty between the Soviet Union and nationalist China authorized by the Yalta Agreement. Great Britain recognized the People's Republic in 1950 and France did so in 1964. By 1975, over 100 nations had recognized the regime.

The U.S. refused recognition, and after its consular officers met with abuse, withdrew them. On Nov. 26, 1950, the People's Republic sent armies into Korea against U.S. troops and forced a stalemate.

By the 1960s, relations with the USSR deteriorated, with disagreements on borders, ideology and leadership of world communism. The USSR cancelled aid accords, and China, with Albania, launched anti-Soviet propaganda drives.

On Mar. 2, 1969, Chinese and Russian soldiers fought one of a series of clashes on an island in the Ussuri River on the border between the two nations in the Far East. The island, called Chenpao by Chinese and Damansky by Russians, was claimed by both nations. Both sides reported dead and wounded. There were later clashes and reports of skirmishes to the west on the Sinkiang-USSR border. In 1970, ambassadors were exchanged for the first time since 1966. In 1974 China seized (but later returned) a Soviet helicopter on spy charges. Border talks through 1975 were unsuccessful, and minor skirmishes took place on both fronts in 1976.

China has sought to promote revolutionary movements in Africa, Asia and South America. The program suffered serious setbacks, 1965-66. By the 1970s, China was reported sending military and economic aid to several established governments.

In April 1971, after the U.S. relaxed restrictions on visits by its citizens, a U.S. table tennis team was invited to the People's Republic.

On Oct. 25, 1971, the UN General Assembly ousted the Taiwan government from the UN and seated Communist China in its place. The U.S. had supported the mainland's admission but opposed Taiwan's expulsion.

U.S. Pres. Nixon visited China Feb. 21-28, 1972, on invitation from Premier Chou En-lai, ending years of antipathy between the 2 nations. They agreed to continue progress toward normalization of relations. In April, U.S. businessmen made purchases at the Canton export fair. China and the U.S. moved close to formal diplomatic relations by opening liaison offices in each other's capitals, May-June 1973.

In 1973, because of food shortages, China ordered 6 million tons of grain from the U.S., Australia and other countries. Two-way trade with the U.S. neared $1 billion in 1974, but declined in 1975.

Government. On Feb. 27, 1957, Mao Tse-tung, then chief of state, condemned the Stalinist terror but admitted an est. 800,000 anti-communist Chinese were executed 1949-54. Leniency for political criticism, proposed by Mao Tse-tung, led to anti-communist disturbances among students and a quick return to repressive measures. In 1958, the regime announced all "rights" in government service had been removed.

Early in 1966, a long, widespread purge of "antiparty intellectuals" was launched; it was viewed as a possible symptom of a struggle for power and the succession to the aging Mao. Premier Chou En-lai called the purge a "cultural revolution." Ousted from office and denounced were the chief of the Army's General Staff, minister of culture, the party propaganda chief, 3 university presidents, newspaper editors and writers, opera producers, youth officials, economists, Peking's mayor, etc. Education, industrial production and foreign relations were disrupted.

In August 1966, Defense Minister Lin Piao emerged as top deputy and heir apparent to Mao. But in 1972 China said Lin died in a 1971 plane crash trying to flee to the USSR after attempting a coup.

By late 1968-69 the long disruption had tapered off; much power was taken from the students and given to Revolutionary Committees and the military, and some purge victims were restored to office. In 1974 a new ideological campaign was launched; it was aimed at the teachings of the ancient sage, Confucius, but its purpose was obscure. Once again, production suffered. In 1976, aging leaders Mao Tse-tung, Chou En-lai, and Chuh Teh died.

Resources and Industry. China began limited industrialization around 1910, but agriculture is still dominant. Wheat, barley, corn, koaliang, and millet and other cereals, peas and soy beans are produced in the north; rice, sugar and indigo in the south. Rice is the staple food of the Chinese and mainland China is the world's largest producer. Fiber crops include abutilon, hemp, jute, ramie, and flax. Cotton is produced mostly in the Yangtze and Yellow River valleys. Tea is cultivated principally in the west and south. Silk production has flourished for 4,000 years. Livestock is raised in large numbers. Food shortages remain but improved distribution has reduced the incidence of famine. Most of the work force is agricultural.

China is the world's 3d largest coal producer. Other minerals are iron ore, tin, antimony, tungsten, molybdenum, salt. Petroleum production reached 1.5 million barrels per day in 1975, much of it sold to Japan.

Application of radical theories to industry and agriculture resulted in erratic economic development. Serious food shortages existed beginning in 1959 after floods, drought, and failure of the "Great Leap Forward" 5-year plan. The regime was forced to obtain grain from Argentina, Mexico, Canada and Australia. Light industries dependent on agriculture for their raw materials also were affected — cotton textiles, knitted goods, vegetable oils, sugar, and cigarets. The "people's commune" system of agriculture in effect since 1958 was drastically modified in 1960-61 to increase individual incentives to stimulate production, but collectivization was renewed in 1963-64. Thousands fled to overcrowded Hong Kong.

Education has been radically revised since the cultural revolution; university enrollment has fallen. Millions of urban dwellers and non-manual workers were moved to rural areas.

In 1969-1972, after the "cultural revolution" eased off, industry and agriculture showed production gains.

China leads all nations in number of hogs, is 3d in sheep, 4th in cattle. Its fish catch is 2d in value to Japan's.

Defense. Regular forces total 3,250,000. There is a growing stockpile of nuclear weapons and intermediate range missiles. Military spending declined 25% 1971-75.

On Oct. 16, 1964, China exploded a low-yield atomic bomb in Sinkiang Province, becoming the 5th nation to possess such power. An explosion of a hydrogen bomb was announced June 17, 1967. The nation's first orbiting space satellite was launched Apr. 24, 1970.

Religion. Buddhism had the largest following. Confucianism, which reveres God but stresses ethical and philosophical principles rather than divine revelation, had wide acceptance. Taoism (after Lao Tze, b. 604 B.C.) is more metaphysical and looks to immortality. Islam, at one time, had 50 million followers; there were 3,280,000 Roman Catholics and 700,000 Protestants. On the mainland foreign missionaries and church schools are no longer tolerated.

Manchuria, 404,428 sq. mi., is divided into 3 provinces. Seized by Japan in 1931, it was renamed Manchukuo, a puppet "independent" nation, Mar. 1, 1932. In 1945 it was returned to China.

Kwantung is the southern part of the Liaotung peninsula, the southernmost portion of Manchuria. Russia in 1898 forced China to lease it Kwantung and constructed the fortified city of Port Arthur (Lushun) and the nearby ice-free port of Dairen (Luta).

Japan seized Port Arthur in 1905, and at the close of the Russo-Japanese War took over the lease in the Treaty of Portsmouth. It was turned over to the USSR by the Yalta Agreement, Feb. 11, 1945, which also internationalized Dairen. Following the 1950 Soviet-Chinese treaty the USSR gave the Changchun railroad, Port Arthur, and Dairen to Communist China.

Inner Mongolia was organized by the People's Republic as an Autonomous Region on May 12, 1947. Its boundaries have undergone frequent changes. In 1950 it comprised northern Chahar and parts of former Manchuria. Suiyan province was incorporated June 1954, and parts of Jehol in Aug. 1955. Population is about 6,200,000 of which less than 20% are Mongol. Capital: Huhehot (Kweisui).

Outer Mongolia: *For People's Republic of Mongolia, see Mongolia in Index.*

Sinkiang Uigur Autonomous Region, in Central Asia, comprising Chinese Turkestan, Kulia and Kashgaria, is 633,802 sq. mi.; pop. (est. 1958), 6 million, of whom 75% are Uigurs, a Turkic Moslem group, with a heavy Chinese increase in recent years. Urumchi is the capital. It is China's richest region in strategic materials, including tungsten, wolfram, molybdenum, copper, zinc, coal, uranium and oil.

Tibet, 470,000 sq. mi., is a thinly populated region of high plateaus and massive mountains. The Himalayas ring it on the S, the Kunluns on the N. Lofty passes link it with India and Nepal to the S; roads lead into China proper. The capital is Lhasa. The average altitude is 15,000 ft. Jiachan, 15,870 ft., is believed to be the highest inhabited town on earth. Agricultural methods are primitive. Cereals are the main crops. The religion was Lamaism, a form of Buddhism. Pop. (1964 est.) 1,300,000.

With only token resistance, Tibet accepted suzerainty of Communist China under a pact signed May 23, 1951. A communist Tibetan Autonomous Government was announced Dec. 20, 1953, revising the quasi-religious administration of the Dalai and Panchen Lamas.

A revolt against the communists occurred in 1959, when the latter attempted to arrest the Dalai Lama.

The Tibetan cabinet denounced the 1951 treaty. The communists crushed the revolt and placed the Panchen Lama on the Tibetan throne. The Dalai Lama fled to India. The Panchen Lama was demoted Dec. 1964. A new ruler was sponsored by Peking Sept. 9, 1965, when it announced election of Ngapo Ngawang Jigme as chairman of the newly-established Tibet Autonomous Region. Revolts continued in 1965 and 1966.

A reform program, including land redistribution and abolition of serfdom (practiced in some monasteries), was announced July 3, 1959.

The International Commission of Jurists at Geneva in 1961 charged the Communist regime with genocide in Tibet. About 20,000 Tibetans have fled to India since the Chinese takeover.

Republic of China

Area: 13,592. Population (Govt. rpt. 1975): 16,171, 569. Capital: Taipei. Monetary unit: Taiwan dollar.

The Kuomintang government of China, after its defeat in 1949, moved to the island of Taiwan, where it still governs. Both the Taipei and Peking governments assert that Taiwan is an integral part of China.

Taiwan lies 110 mi. E of the mainland, but the term Taiwan is used by the Nationalist government to include 14 other islands nearby and 64 others comprising the Penghu group.

Taiwan was ceded by China to Japan in 1895, after the Sino-Japanese War and was returned to China as a province, 1945, after World War II.

A range of mountains forms the backbone of the island. The eastern half is exceedingly steep and craggy but the western slope is flat, fertile and well cultivated, yielding 2 rice crops a year. The principal crops, besides rice, are tea, sugar, sweet potatoes, ramie, jute, turmeric, and camphor. Minerals include gold, silver, copper, and coal.

The **Penghus** (Pescadores), 50 sq. mi., pop. (1974) 115,613, lie between Taiwan and the coast of China.

The islands of **Quemoy** and **Matsu** are within a few miles of the mainland.

The 1947 constitution is still formally in effect. The National Assembly is the supreme organ. Members are elected on the basis of territorial and professional representation. The Assembly elects the president and vice president, who serve 6-year terms. An elected Legislative Yuan (Council), serves as the legislature. The cabinet, appointed by the president, is responsible to the Yuan. Most Yuan members have remained in office since 1948, representing areas of mainland China. A Provincial Assembly is elected every four years.

Generalissimo Chiang Kai-shek, except for a period of semi-retirement, was virtual ruler since 1927. Upon his death in 1975, his son, Premier Chiang Ching-Kuo, became the effective ruler. The government was a founding member of the UN. On Oct. 25, 1971, the UN General Assembly expelled the Taiwan government from the UN and admitted the Peking government in its place. By July 1975 only 26 nations, including the U.S., still recognized the Taipei regime, but informal commercial relations continued with many others.

Although agriculture remains a vital and growing part of the economy, industrial production has grown much more rapidly. Important industries include textiles, clothing, electrical and electronic equipment, TV sets, processed foods, chemicals, glass, metals, and machinery. Living standards have improved dramatically, and 93% of adults are literate. College enrollment is 300,000.

Foreign trade, with 1975 imports at $US 5.3 billion and exports at $US 5.9 billion, has also shown strong and steady growth. Gross national product was $US 14.4 billion in 1975.

U.S. economic aid, begun in 1951 and totaling $1.5 billion, essentially terminated June 30, 1965. Military aid, which totaled $2.5 billion, continued, but at a re-

duced scale. U.S. private investment was about $500 million. The republic has extended technical assistance to some 30 countries in Asia, Africa, and Latin America.

Defense. Armed forces total 494,000. The government signed a mutual defense treaty with the U.S., in force Mar. 3, 1955. It provides for consultation on threats of attack and promises that if Taiwan is subject to unprovoked attack the U.S. will act according to its constitutional procedures. About 2,300 U.S. troops are stationed on Taiwan.

Colombia

Area: 455,355 sq. mi. Population (Gov't. est. 1975): 4,720,000. Capital: Bogota, Monetary unit: Peso.

The Republic of Colombia, in the extreme northwest of South America, extends up the Isthmus of Panama to the Republic of Panama. It has a coastline of 913 mi. on the Pacific, and 1,094 mi. on the Caribbean Sea. It borders Venezuela and Brazil on the E, and Ecuador and Peru on the S. Its area is greater than those of Texas and California combined.

Three great ranges of the Andes, the Western, Central and Eastern Cordilleras, run through the country from N to S. The eastern range consists mostly of high table lands, cool and healthful, and densely populated. The Magdalena River, in the NE, rises in the high Andes and flows N into the Caribbean Sea near Barranquilla. It is navigable for over 800 mi. The Magdalena Valley is a plain of rich alluvial land.

Snow-crested mountains standing almost directly over the Equator are one of many examples of scenic splendor. Tourists are also attracted by Tequendama Falls near Bogota, 427 ft. high.

Bogota, the capital, founded in 1538, is in the Andes, 8,660 ft. above sea level.

Resources and Industries. Colombia is second to Brazil in exports of coffee, which accounts for about half of its export trade. Rice, tobacco and cotton are cultivated, besides cocoa, maize, potatoes, sugar and bananas. Dye-woods, rubber, balsam and copaiba trees are important.

The country is rich in minerals. It has become a producer of petroleum, and gas resources are plentiful. Seventy-five miles from Bogota are the Muzo emerald mines which have been in operation for 4 centuries. Colombia produces 95% of the world's gem emeralds. Other minerals are gold, silver, copper, lead, mercury, cinnabar, manganese, platinum, coal, iron, nickel, salt. Colombia is accelerating expansion of its hydro-electric power which has est. potential of 85 million kw. Food processing is the leading manufacturing industry; other products are textiles, hides, rubber goods, steel, paper, cement, and chemicals. Textiles have become a major export.

Loans from international agencies have helped expand industry and modernize agriculture. An oil pipeline from the Orito field in the SE, crosses the Andes to the Pacific; it was finished in 1969.

The government has sought to reduce vast land holdings, increase the size of small farms, and put idle land into production. From 1961 to 1970 the Institute for Land Reform acquired or developed 9,800,-000 acres; more than 95,000 families were given title to farm plots.

History and Government. The country, conquered and ruled for 300 years by Spain, won its freedom in the revolt of the Spanish-American colonies 1810-1824. The liberator, Simon Bolivar, established the Republic of Greater Colombia in 1819; Venezuela and Ecuador withdrew in 1829-1830. From the remainder of the confederation evolved the Republic of Colombia under a constitution dated Aug. 5, 1886. Panama withdrew Nov. 3, 1903, becoming a separate republic. Colombia is a member of the UN and OAS.

The Congress consists of a Senate of 118 members and a House of Representatives with 210 members, elected directly by the people for 4-year terms. The president is elected by direct vote for 4 years and is ineligible for immediate re-election. Political violence and banditry have resulted in repeated states of emergency since the 1950s. Nevertheless, political and civil freedoms are respected.

Education and Religion. Most of the people are of mixed Indian and white descent; the next largest group is white; the smallest groups are Indians and Negroes. Education is free but not compulsory. National Univ., founded 1572, is in Bogota. Roman Catholicism prevails. Spanish is the language.

Defense. Armed forces total 64,300.

Comoro Islands

Area: 693 sq. mi. Population: (UN est. 1974): 262,000. Capital: Moroni. Monetary unit: CFA franc.

The Comoro Islands are a volcanic archipelago in the Mozambique Channel between NW Madagascar and SE Africa. An active volcano is on Grand Comoro. Leading crops are vanilla, copra, perfume plants, and tropical fruits. Perfume is distilled and exported.

The islands were controlled by Moslem sultans until the French acquired them 1841-1909. They were ruled as part of Madagascar 1912-1947, and became an autonomous French Overseas Territory in 1961. A 1974 referendum overwhelmingly favored independence, with only the Christian island of Mayotte preferring association with France. The French National Assembly decided in June, 1975 to allow each of the islands to decide its own fate. The Comoro Chamber of Deputies unilaterally declared the country's independence July 6, 1975. In a referendum in 1976, Mayotte voted overwhelmingly to remain French.

The inhabitants are predominantly Moslem, deriving from Arab, African, and East Indian ancestors.

People's Republic of Congo

Area: 132,046 sq. mi. Population (est. 1976): 1,070,-000. Capital: Brazzaville. Monetary unit: CFA franc.

Formerly the French Middle Congo Overseas Territory, the People's Republic of the Congo straddles the Equator. It is bounded on the E and S by Zaire; on the W by Cabinda (an Angolan enclave), the Atlantic and Gabon; on the N by Cameroon and Central African Republic. It is twice the size of Missouri.

Complete independence was proclaimed Aug. 15, 1960, and the republic joined the UN Sept. 20. Fulbert Youlou was elected president Nov. 21, 1959, and resigned in Aug. 1963 in a coup sparked by trade unions. Under his successor, President Alphonse Massamba-Debat, the country came under Communist China's influence and announced a "scientific Socialist state" with one-party control.

In Aug. 1965 the U. S. withdrew its embassy staff, a step short of breaking off relations, charging harassment of American officials. Massamba-Debat was ousted in a military coup, Sept. 4, 1968. Maj. Marien Ngouabi became president Jan. 1, 1969.

In Jan. 1970, the earlier name, Republic of the Congo-Brazzaville, was changed to People's Republic of the Congo. The government advocates socialism.

The nation has received aid from both France and Communist China. Agriculture declined in the 1970s.

Forests are a prime resource, covering 54 million acres, and wood products form a major export. Chief commercial agricultural products are palm oil and kernels, cocoa, coffee, bananas, and peanuts. Industrialization has progressed and its output now accounts for 11% of the total national product. Potash reserves are extensive. Two-thirds of government revenues comes from offshore oil.

Costa Rica

Area: 19,653 sq. mi. Population (Govt. est. 1975): 1,970,000. Capital: San Jose. Monetary Unit: Colon.

Costa Rica, in Central America, borders Nicaragua on the N and Panama on the S. The lowlands by the Caribbean are tropical. The interior plateau, with an altitude of about 4,000 ft., is temperate.

San Jose, the capital, situated inland (103 mi. by rail from Puerto Limon on the Atlantic, 93 by rail from Puntarenas on the Pacific) is the country's industrial and cultural center. Limon and Puntarenas are the principal ports. Puerto Limon occupies one of the sites where Columbus landed on his fourth and last visit to America.

Resources and industries. A 1962 law giving new industries a tax holiday of up to 10 years brought in a wide variety of factories. The Irazu volcano near San Jose erupted from Mar. 1963 to Dec. 1964, dropping millions of tons of ash which severely damaged coffee, vegetable, and dairy crops. Coffee of a high quality is the chief cash crop and export, followed by bananas, sugar, cocoa, beef, cotton, fish, and hemp.

Despite growing, small-scale industrialization, agriculture remains the mainstay of the economy, employing half the work force. New industries include fiberglass products, aluminum processing, textiles, fertilizer, roofing, and cement.

The forests are extensive, and the lumber industry is important. Gold and silver are mined on the Pacific slope. Other minerals are quartz, alabaster, granite, oil, alum, slate, onyx, mercury, sulphur, copper.

Chief imports are flour, industrial machinery, gasoline, leather, hardware and tools. Nearly half of the foreign trade is with the U. S.

The nation has a comparatively high standard of living and of social services.

History and Government. Once a part of the Confederation of Central America, 1824-1829, Costa Rica has been independent since 1821.

An unusual constitution was adopted Nov. 8, 1949. It abolishes the army as a permanent institution. The legislative power is vested in a chamber of deputies, 57 in number, with 4-year terms, under universal suffrage. The president, elected for 4 years, appoints a cabinet of 12. Deputies may not serve successive terms but may be reelected after an intervening 4 years. A president may not be reelected. There is a fine for not voting.

In Feb. 1974 a liberal, Daniel Oduber Quiros, was elected president.

Religion and Education. Primary education is compulsory, and literary is 87%. Higher education is free. There are universities in Cartago, Heredia, San Jose and Turrialba. The language is Spanish; English is taught in the public schools. Roman Catholicism is predominant.

Defense. Order within the country is kept by a civil guard and police forces. Costa Rica is a member of the UN and OAS.

Cuba

Area: 44,218 sq. mi. Population (Est. 1976): 9,470,-000. Capital: Havana. Monetary unit: Peso.

Cuba, "Pearl of the Antilles," is an island, the largest in the West Indies, and a nation about the size of Pennsylvania. The Straits of Florida lie to the N, the Gulf of Mexico to the W, the Caribbean to the S.

Key West, Fla., is about 90 mi. N. The Windward Passage, 50 mi. wide, separates Cuba from Haiti to the E, and Jamaica lies 90 mi. to the S. Cuba's length is 730 mi.; its breadth averages 50 mi. The coastline, including the larger keys, is about 2,500 mi. It has numerous harbors, notably that of Havana, one of the finest in the world.

The Isle of Pines, off the SW coast, is 1,180 sq. mi. in area. Mountains rise in Pinar del Rio Province in the W, and in Oriente in the E, with Pico Turquino, 6,467 ft., the highest.

Havana, pop. over 1,770,000, is the busiest port. Santiago de Cuba, in the SE, is the next largest port.

Resources and Industries. Chief barometer of the

nation's economy is the sugar industry which represents about 80% of exports. American-owned sugar mills, seized by the revolutionary regime in 1960, represented an investment of about $275 million, producing about 40% of Cuba's output.

Tobacco, cigars, and cigarettes rank 2d. Other products are molasses, coffee, pineapples, bananas, citrus fruit, and coconuts. Textiles, cabinet woods (mahogany and cedar), dye-woods, fibers, gums, resins, and oils are important. Iron, copper, manganese, nickel, and salt are some of the minerals. Industries include rayon, cement, chemicals.

Poor sugar crops and food shortages resulted in collectivization of farms and stringent labor controls under the revolutionary government. Rationing of food, shoes, clothing, gasoline, was ordered. Some rationing and economic difficulties continued in the 1970s, despite massive aid from the USSR and assistance from other Communist countries. Health and education services were improved.

History. Cuba was discovered by Christopher Columbus in Oct. 1492. Its name derives from the Indian Cubanacan. Except for British occupation of Havana, 1762-63, Cuba remained Spanish until 1898.

Under Spanish governors Cubans were denied citizenship, slavery was retained until 1886, and patriots who revolted were executed. On Oct. 10, 1868, Carlos Manuel de Cespedes led Cubans in a proclamation of independence. Their 10-years' war ended in 1878 with guarantees of rights by Spain, which Spain failed to carry out. A full-scale movement began Feb. 24, 1895, under Jose Marti, with the military under the command of Maximo Gomez, Antonio Maceo, and Calixto Garcia. The Spanish governor, Valeriano Weyler, destroyed sugar plantations, banned export of tobacco and held patriots in "reconcentration camps." A U. S. offer to mediate was rejected by Spain.

The movement to help Cuba gain its independence was speeded by the sinking of the U.S.S. Maine in Havana harbor. The U. S. declared war on Spain Apr. 25, 1898, and defeated it in the short Spanish-American War. In the Treaty of Paris, Dec. 10, 1898, Spain gave up all claims to Cuba. The U. S. formally withdrew May 20, 1902, when Tomas Estrada Palma was inaugurated first president of the republic.

Under 1903 and 1934 agreements, the U. S. leases a site for its naval base at Guantanamo Bay, in the SE.

In 1952 Fulgencio Batista seized control of the government and imposed a dictatorship. Opposition to the corrupt Batista regime became vigorous in 1956 under leadership of Fidel Castro, born 1927, lawyer and former leader of student opposition. The rebels in 1958 carried on intensified guerrilla warfare. Batista quit Jan. 1, 1959. He died in Spain Aug. 6, 1973.

Castro proclaimed Dr. Manuel Urrutia Lleo provisional president. Urrutia dissolved the Cuban Congress, Jan. 6, 1959. Castro became premier Feb. 16.

Pres. Urrutia resigned after accusing communists of plotting treason. The government, quickly dominated by left-wing extremists, began a program of sweeping economic and social changes, led by an agrarian reform law in May 1959. It executed hundreds of dissidents, and ousted moderates.

The National Institute of Agrarian Reform nationalized cattle and tobacco lands and instituted a system of cooperatives. All private enterprise was brought under control by a Central Planning Board created Feb. 20, 1960. By the end of 1960 all Cuban banks and industrial companies had been nationalized, including an est. $1 billion worth of U. S.-owned properties.

Soviet, Communist Chinese, and Czechoslovakian economic penetration was extended by trade and credit agreements, including sugar purchases and USSR credits for construction of factories, etc.

Citing the open hostility of the regime, the U. S. cut back Cuba's remaining 1960 sugar quota by 700,000 tons. On Oct. 19 the U. S. imposed an extensive embargo on exports to Cuba and, Feb. 4, 1962, President Kennedy ordered a total embargo.

On Apr. 17, 1961 about 1,400 Cuban exiles, who had trained in the U.S. and Guatemala, landed at the Bahia de Cochinos (Bay of Pigs) on Cuba's southern coast. They were overwhelmed and killed or imprisoned. The attempt created severe criticism in Congress of activities of the U.S Central Intelligence Agency. It was revealed in 1975 that CIA agents had plotted to kill Castro in 1959 or 1960. President Kennedy previously had declared there would be no intervention by the U. S. On Dec. 21, 1962, Castro agreed to release 1,113 prisoners in exchange for medical supplies worth a reputed $53 million. American drug concerns and religious groups raised the supply.

In the fall, 1962, the U.S. ascertained that the Soviet Union was delivering nuclear missiles and other weapons to Cuba and building bases. On Oct 22 President Kennedy warned that any missile launched from Cuba would be regarded as an attack by the Soviet Union and would call for full retaliation. He asked Premier Khrushchev to halt this "clandestine, reckless and provocative threat to world peace." Khrushchev removed the missiles.

The OAS nations voted July 26, 1964, 15-4, a resolution for mandatory sanctions against Cuba and for strengthening defenses against Cuban subversion efforts. The sanctions were lifted in 1975, with the tacit support of the U.S.

Cuba complained of numerous raids by infiltrators, 1964-70.

In Feb. 1973, Cuba and the U.S. signed an agreement providing for extradition or punishment of hijackers of planes or vessels, and for each nation to bar activity from its territory against the other.

In 1974, U.S. President Ford said relations with Cuba could be improved, adding that the U. S. would act in concert with the other OAS nations.

In 1975, France expelled three Cuban diplomats in connection with a probe of a world-wide terrorist network.

More than 650,000 Cubans have gone into exile since the Castro takeover, most of them to the U.S.

In 1975 and 1976, Cuba sent 15,000 troops to aid one faction in the Angola civil war.

Cuba is a member of the UN and Comecon.

Education and Religion. Education is compulsory between the ages of 6 and 14. Among the institutions of higher learning is the University of Havana, founded in 1721. The Roman Catholic religion is dominant. The language is Spanish with English widely understood. Education was nationalized June 7, 1961, and many Catholic schools were seized. Many Catholic priests of Spanish origin were deported.

Defense. Armed forces total 108,000.

Cyprus

Area: 3,572 sq. mi. Population (UN. est. 1975): 640,-000. Capital: Nicosia. Monetary unit: Pound.

Cyprus, former British Crown Colony, became a republic Aug. 16, 1960, and joined the Commonwealth, UN, and Council of Europe. It is the third largest island in the Mediterranean Sea, 40 mi. S of Turkey, 60 mi. W of Syria, and 350 mi. E of Crete. Two mountain ranges run E-W, separated by a wide, fertile plain. It is smaller than Connecticut.

Four-fifths of the inhabitants were Greek Orthodox Christians until 1974, nearly all the rest were Turkish Moslems. Greek and Turkish are official languages; English is widely spoken.

Resources and Industries. Cyprus is mainly agricultural, with cereals, grapes, wine, carobs, citrus fruits, potatoes, and olives as principal crops. Agricultural products account for about 60% of the island's exports. Minerals are important but declining — copper, iron pyrites, asbestos, gypsum, chrome, and umber. Manufacturing is limited mainly to light industries. Exports include shoes and clothing. Cement and oil refining industries are under development. The economy was disrupted by the 1974-76 political crisis.

The nation suffers an unfavorable balance of trade, offset by tourism.

History and Government. Cyprus was inhabited as early as the New Stone Age in the 4th millennium B.C. Achaeans from Greece traded with the early Cypriots from 1600 B.C., set up colonies after the end of the Trojan War (c. 1184 B.C.). From the middle of the 8th century B.C., Cyprus was dominated successively by Phoenicians, Assyrians, Egyptians, Persians, Alexander and the Ptolemies, Romans, Byzantines, Moslems, Crusaders, Venetians, and Turks. Great Britain took over administration in 1878 under an agreement with Turkey, annexed the island in 1914, made it a Crown Colony in 1925.

Agitation for enosis (union) with Greece resulted in the British abolishing the legislative council in 1931. Demands for enosis were renewed after World War II; the Turkish minority was opposed. Widespread violence in 1955-56, led by EOKA, an underground Greek organization, brought harsh disciplinary measures, including the temporary exiling of Archbishop Makarios III, head of the Independent Orthodox Church in Cyprus and leader of the enosis movement.

In 1959, conflict was brought to a temporary halt by an agreement signed by British, Greek, Turkish, and Cypriot leaders. Cyprus would become a republic, with a president elected from and by the ethnic Greek community, and a vice president from and by the Turkish community. A 70-30% proportion of the Greek and Turkish communities was to be represented in the House of Representatives. Greek and Turkish Communal Chambers dealt with religious, educational, and other communal affairs. Britain retained 2 military enclaves, Akrotiri and Dhekelia.

Archbishop Makarios was elected president for a 5-year term and Dr. Fazil Kutchuk, a Turkish Cypriot, vice president, Dec. 14, 1959. The constitution was approved April 6, 1960; independence became final Aug. 16, 1960, and Pres. Makarios took office.

Communal strife again broke out in December, 1963, following proposals by Makarios to make changes in the constitution which the Turkish minority felt would reduce their rights.

The UN Security Council approved Mar. 4, 1964, a resolution providing for an international peace-keeping force and UN troops took stations Mar. 27.

Tension worsened after Turkey charged that Turkish Cypriots had been massacred. Turkey bombed and strafed Greek areas Aug. 7-10, 1964. Both sides accepted a cease-fire.

War between Greece and Turkey over Cyprus appeared imminent in Nov. 1967 but was averted mainly because of mediation work by Cyrus R. Vance, special envoy of U.S. President Johnson.

Archbishop Makarios, whose term as president had been twice extended by Parliament, was re-elected Feb. 25, 1968, by an overwhelming popular vote, and again on Feb. 8, 1973.

The Cypriot National Guard, led by officers from the Army of Greece, seized the government July 15, 1974, and named Nikos Sampson, an advocate of union with Greece, president. Makarios fled the country. On July 20, Turkey invaded the island; Greece mobilized its forces but did not intervene. A cease-fire was arranged July 22. On the 23d, Sampson turned over the presidency to Glafkos Clerides (on the same day, Greece's military junta resigned). A peace conference collapsed Aug. 14; fighting resumed. Greek Cypriots and Turks charged each other with massacres and atrocities. By Aug. 16 Turkish forces had occupied the NE 40% of the island, despite the presence of UN peace forces. On Aug. 19 the U.S. ambassador to Cyprus was slain by a bullet during a riot in Nicosia. Makarios resumed the presidency in December.

Turkish Cypriots voted overwhelmingly June 8, 1975 to form a separate Turkish Cypriot federated state. A president and assembly were elected in 1976.

Some 200,000 refugees had left the Turkish-controlled area, replaced by thousands of Turks from the mainland.

Czechoslovakia

Area: 49,371 sq. mi. Population (Govt. est. 1975): 14,800,000. Capital: Prague. Monetary unit: Koruna.

Czechoslovakia is a central European socialist republic about 600 mi. long and 50 to 100 mi. wide — about the area of New York State. It is bounded by West Germany (Bavaria), East Germany (Saxony), Poland, the Soviet Union, Austria and Hungary.

The Vltava (Moldau) and Labe (Elbe) flow from Bohemia to Germany; the Danube separates Slovakia from Hungary. The Carpathian Mtns. are in the E and NE; tallest are the Tatras, with Gerlachovka peak 8,737 ft.

Resources and Industries. Czechoslovakia has considerable natural resources, developed by farming, mining and industry. The nation is highly industrialized but agriculture is important; chief crops are wheat, sugar beets, potatoes, rye, hops.

Coal and iron are mined; oil, imported mainly from the USSR, is refined at Bratislava. Jachymov has Europe's richest deposits of pitchblende (for uranium and radium). Czechoslovakia is a major exporter of arms and machinery. Ostrava and Kosice are important steel centers. There is a large glass and china industry; other products include chemicals, beer, aircraft, wood pulp, textiles, shoes.

Imports for 1974 were valued at $9 billion, exports at $8.7 billion.

History and Government. In Feb. 1948 Czechoslovakia became a unitary socialist republic composed of 2 Slav nations—the Czechs and the Slovaks—with a socialist constitution, nationalized industry and one-slate elections. The Czechs make up 65% of the population and Slovaks about 30%. In addition, there are some 450,000 Hungarians, 200,000 Germans, 200,000 gypsies, 100,000 Ruthenian-Ukrainians and 100,000 Poles. Large numbers of Hungarians were moved out of Slovakia and many Slovaks were moved from Hungary to Slovakia in 1945-46. An estimated 3 million Sudeten Germans were transferred to Germany under the Potsdam Agreement.

Bohemia, Moravia and Slovakia were part of the Great Moravian Empire when overrun by the Magyars 906 A.D. Bohemia and Moravia later became part of the Holy Roman Empire. Under the kings of Bohemia, Prague in the 14th century was the cultural center of Central Europe. In 1526 Ferdinand, brother of Holy Roman Emperor Charles V, became king of Bohemia and Hungary. Later the lands became part of Austria-Hungary.

In 1914-1918 Thomas G. Masaryk and Eduard Benes formed a provisional government with the support of Slovak leaders, of whom Milan Stefanik organized freedom fighters in foreign countries. When Austria fell, Oct. 28, 1918, they proclaimed the Republic of Czechoslovakia Oct. 30. Masaryk became president, Benes foreign minister and Stefanik minister of war. Benes succeeded Masaryk in 1935.

By 1938 Adolf Hitler of Nazi Germany had worked up disaffection among German-speaking citizens in Sudetenland and demanded its cession. To avoid war, Prime Minister Neville Chamberlain of Great Britain, with the acquiescence of France, signed an agreement with Hitler at Munich, Sept. 30, 1938, agreeing to the cession, with a guarantee of peace by Hitler and Mussolini. Nazi Germany occupied Sudetenland Oct. 1-2. President Benes resigned Oct. 5.

Hitler on Mar. 15, 1939, dissolved Czechoslovakia, made protectorates of Bohemia and Moravia, and supported the autonomy of Slovakia, which was proclaimed independent Mar. 14, 1939, with Jozef Tiso president.

Soviet troops with some Czechoslovak contingents entered eastern Czechoslovakia in 1944 and reached

Prague in May 1945; Benes returned as president. In May 1946 elections, the Communist Party won 38% of the votes, largest for a single party, and Benes accepted Klement Gottwald, a communist, as prime minister. Tiso was executed in 1947.

In Feb. 1948 a crisis resulted in the resignation of 12 anti-Communist ministers and Benes accepted a new Gottwald Cabinet Feb. 25. Jan Masaryk, son of Thomas Masaryk, had not resigned as foreign minister. He was found dead March 10, apparently a suicide, but there was widespread speculation he was murdered.

In May 1948 a new constitution was approved; Benes refused to sign it. On May 30 the voters were offered a one-slate ballot and the communists won full control. Benes resigned June 7, Gottwald became president and Benes died Sept. 3.

In Jan. 1968 a liberalization movement spread explosively through Czechoslovakia. Antonin Novotny, long the Stalinist boss of the nation, was deposed as party leader and succeeded by Alexander Dubcek, a Slovak, who declared he intended to make communism democratic. On Mar. 22 Novotny resigned as president and was succeeded by Gen. Ludvik Svoboda. On Apr. 6, Premier Joseph Lenart resigned and was succeeded by Oldrich Cernik, whose new cabinet was pledged to carry out democratization and economic reforms.

In July 1968 the USSR and 4 hard-core Warsaw Pact nations demanded an end to liberalization. On Aug. 20, Russian, Polish, East German, Hungarian and Bulgarian military forces invaded Czechoslovakia.

Some Soviet troops remained and Soviet pressure brought agreements from officials that the liberal policies would be "normalized." Despite demonstrations and riots by students and workers, press censorship was imposed, many liberal leaders were ousted from office and promises of loyalty to Soviet policies were made by some old-line Communist party leaders.

On Apr. 17, 1969, Dubcek resigned as leader of the Communist party and was succeeded by Gustav Husak. In Jan. 1970, Premier Cernik was ousted. Censorship was tightened and the Communist Party expelled a third of its members. In 1972, more than 40 liberals were jailed on subversion charges. In 1973, amnesty was offered to some of the 40,000 who fled the country after the 1968 invasion, but repressive policies remained in force through 1976.

On Jan. 2, 1969, Czechoslovakia became a federal state. In addition to a federal president, premier and Assembly for the Czechoslovak Socialist Republic, there were separate governments, a Czech Socialist Republic and a Slovak Socialist Republic, each with a National Council, a premier and Cabinet. The central government retained control over foreign affairs, defense and finance. In the Federal Assembly, a House of People was chosen by electoral districts; a House of Nations had 75 Czech and 75 Slovak members.

West Germany and Czechoslovakia resumed diplomatic relations in 1973 and declared the 1938 Munich pact void.

Education and Religion. An estimated 75% of the population is Roman Catholic, the rest are Protestant (Hussite), Greek Orthodox, etc.

Institutions of higher learning are Charles University in Prague, founded in 1348; the Universities of Brno, Bratislava, Kosice, Hradec Kralove, Plzen; also technical universities. Czech and Slovak are official languages.

Defense. Military forces total 200,000.

Denmark

Area: 17,028 sq. mi. **Population including Faeroe Islands and Greenland (Govt. est. 1975):** 5,150,000. **Capital:** Copenhagen. **Monetary unit:** Kroner.

Denmark occupies the peninsula of Jutland, thrusting out to the N from Germany, which is its only land neighbor, between the North Sea and the Baltic Sea, and adjacent islands. The Skagerrak separates it from Norway; the Kattegat and Oresund from Sweden. The country consists of low undulating plains. It is about the size of New Hampshire and Massachusetts combined.

The **Faeroe Islands** in the North Atlantic, about 300 mi. NE of the Shetlands, and 850 mi. from Denmark proper, 18 inhabited, have an area of 540 sq. mi. and pop. (est. 1975) of 40,000. They are self-governing in most matters.

Resources and Industries. About 7.5% of the population lives by agriculture on more than 70% of the usable land. Denmark exports much butter, cheese, poultry, eggs, bacon, and beef. Its fishing industry ranks 9th in the world. Tourist trade accounts for 10% of foreign exchange. Denmark exports machinery, ships, textiles, furniture, iron and steel goods. Most raw materials and fuels have to be imported, but manufactures have increased; industrial exports surpass agricultural.

Denmark is the world's largest exporter of pork and 3rd largest of meat in general.

The first cooperative consumers' society was established 1866; the system currently has about 1,548 affiliated societies and includes 917,000 households, about 51%.

More than a million tourists visit Denmark annually. Many leave their children in Danish camps while visiting other countries.

Foreign trade in thousands of U.S. dollars:

	Imports	Exports
1974	$10,076,000	$7,819,000
1975	$10,346,000	$8,705,000

History and Government. The origin of Copenhagen dates back to ancient times, when the fishing and trading place named Havn (port) grew up on a cluster of islets, but Bishop Absalon (1128-1201) is regarded as the actual founder of the city. On one of the islets he built a stronghold against the pirating Wends and the remnants of this still exist underground in front of Christiansborg. Elsinore (Helsingor) contains the reputed grave of Hamlet, the Danish prince immortalized by Shakespeare.

Denmark is a constitutional monarchy with a Queen. A new constitution, signed June 5, 1953, substituted a unicameral parliament, the Folketing, of 179 members (including 2 each from Greenland and the Faeroes) for the former two-chamber Rigsdag. A cabinet of ministers, which must have the support of a majority in the Folketing, conducts the government. A system of proportional representation has led to a variety of parties, with 10 parties holding seats after 1975 elections.

The Queen of Denmark is Margrethe II (born Apr. 16, 1940) who succeeded to the throne Jan. 14, 1972, after the death of her father, King Frederik IX. She was married June 10, 1967, to Count Henri Marie Andre Laborde de Monpezat of France who became Prince Henrik of Denmark. They had 2 sons: Prince Frederik (born May 26, 1968), heir to the throne, and Prince Joachim (born June 7, 1969).

Denmark has public assistance, health insurance, disability and old-age pensions, workmen's compensation and unemployment insurance. Pensions are paid to anyone aged 67.

Denmark is a member of the UN and NATO, and joined the EC Jan. 1, 1973.

Education and Religion. Evangelical Lutheranism is the established religion, but there is complete religious freedom. Education is compulsory and includes vocational courses. The University of Copenhagen was founded in 1479; there are 3 other universities and a variety of technical & professional colleges.

Defense. Military forces total 34,400.

Greenland

Greenland, a huge island between the North Atlantic and the Polar Sea, is separated from the North

American continent by Davis Strait and Baffin Bay. Its total area is 840,000 sq. mi., 705,234 of which are ice-capped. Most of the island is a lofty plateau 9,000 to 10,000 ft. in altitude. The average thickness of the ice cap is 1,000 ft. The population (est. 1975) is 50,000. The capital is Godthaab. Under the 1953 Danish constitution the colony became an integral part of the realm with representatives in the Folketing. Fish and fur are exported.

Dominican Republic

Area: 18,704 sq. mi. Population (Govt. est. 1975): 4,700,000. Capital: Santo Domingo. Monetary unit: Peso.

The Dominican Republic occupies the eastern two-thirds of the Island of Hispaniola (discovered by Columbus in 1492), second largest of the Greater Antilles, lying between Cuba on the W and Puerto Rico on the E. The boundary between it and the Republic of Haiti, which occupies the western part of the island, is 241 mi. long. It has a coastline of 979 mi. It is twice the size of New Hampshire. Climate is generally sub-tropical.

The city of Santo Domingo, founded 1496, is the oldest settlement by Europeans in the hemisphere and has the supposed ashes of Columbus in an elaborate tomb in its ancient cathedral.

Resources and Industries. The land is fertile. Chief products are sugar, cocoa, coffee, tobacco, corn, peanuts, bananas, and livestock products.

The country has nickel, gold, copper, iron, salt, chalk, bauxite, marble, amber, kaolin.

Chief manufactures are sugar, molasses, rum, alcohol, cement, peanut oil, chocolate, tobacco products, cordage, textiles, apparel, lumber, furniture. The U. S. buys more than 50% of its exports, mostly sugar, cocoa, and coffee, and supplies about 60% of imports.

Agricultural products, including sugar, showed strong gains in the early 1970s. A large nickel refining plant opened in 1972.

History and Government. Spain ceded Santo Domingo to France, 1795. Toussaint L'Ouverture, Haitian leader, seized it, 1801. Spain returned intermittently 1803-1821, and several native republics came and went. From 1822 to 1844 Haiti governed it. The republic was formed 1844. Spain occupied it 1861-63.

The country was occupied by U.S. Marines from 1916 until 1924, when a constitutionally elected government was installed.

In 1930, Gen. Rafael Leonidas Trujillo Molina was elected president. Trujillo remained in power, ruling the nation with an iron hand (though turning the presidency over to his brother, Hector, in 1952 and to Joaquin Balaguer in 1960) until his assassination May 30, 1961.

Balaguer resigned under pressure Jan. 17, 1962. Pending general elections, the country was governed by a 7-member Council of State headed by Rafael F. Bonnelly who was named president Jan. 18, 1962. He was succeeded by Juan Bosch, elected president Dec. 20, 1962, in the first free elections in 38 years. Bosch was overthrown Sept. 25, 1963, and his regime replaced by an army-backed civilian triumvirate led by Donald Reid Cabral.

On April 24, 1965, a revolt was launched by followers of Bosch and others, including some communists, and led by Col. Francisco Caamano Deno. The Reid Cabral government was ousted, but the rebel regime was replaced Apr. 28 by a 3-man counter-revolutionary junta led by Gen. Elias Wessin y Wessin; on May 7 it was succeeded by a 5-man regime headed by Gen. Antonio Imbert Barreras, another anti-Bosch leader; fighting continued in Santo Domingo.

A force of 405 U. S. Marines landed by helicopter April 28. U.S. forces were expanded to a high of 24,-000.

At U. S. urging, the Organization of American States sent an Inter-American Peace Force to Santo Domingo May 23, under a Brazilian commander with the head of U. S. forces as deputy commander. Some U. S. forces were withdrawn and the Inter-American Force consisted of 11,200 men, including 9,400 U.S. troops, 1,100 Brazilians, and units from Honduras, Nicaragua, Paraguay, and Costa Rica.

On Sept. 3, Hector Garcia-Godoy became provisional president under sponsorship of the OAS with agreement by all major local groups.

An election was held June 1, 1966; Balaguer defeated Bosch, 754,409 votes to 517,783. The Balaguer Reformist party won control of Congress. The new president was inaugurated July 1. The Inter-American Peace Force completed their departure Sept. 20. Balaguer was reelected, 1970 and 1974, the latter time without real opposition.

In 1971, scores of leftists were reported killed by rightist terrorists.

Education and Religion. The population is mostly mixed white and Negro, plus about 15% whites and a slightly larger percentage of blacks. Roman Catholicism is the state religion. Education is free and compulsory by law, but illiteracy is still widespread. The language is Spanish. The University of Santo Domingo was established 1538.

Defense. Armed forces total 15,800. The nation is a member of the UN and OAS.

Ecuador

Area: 105,685 sq. mi. Population (Govt. est. 1975): 6,730,000. Capital: Quito. Monetary unit: Sucre.

On the NW coast of South America, Ecuador (Sp. for Equator) extends 100 mi. into the Northern Hemisphere, 400 into the Southern. It is bounded by Colombia, Peru, and the Pacific. Two ranges of the Andes run N and S, splitting the country into 3 zones: hot, humid lowlands on the coast; temperate highlands between the ranges, and rainy, tropical lowlands to the E. There are 22 peaks over 14,000 ft.; highest is Chimborazo, 20,561 ft.; many are snowcapped; some volcanoes have erupted in recent years. Ecuador is larger than Arizona.

The **Galapagos Islands**, 600 mi. to the W, are the home of huge tortoises and other unusual animals. Charles Darwin visited the islands aboard the Beagle in 1835; his studies of wildlife there provided most of the facts for his theory of evolution.

Ecuador and Peru have long disputed their Amazon Valley boundary. Ecuador claims jurisdiction over Pacific waters 200 mi. out from its coast. It has seized and fined U.S. fishing boats within that limit. The U.S. adopted its own 200 mile limit in 1976.

Guayaquil, Ecuador's largest city, is the chief seaport and, together with Quito, is served by major airlines. Rail lines link Quito with Guayaquil and San Lorenzo on the coast. Quito is famed for its 17th century churches.

Resources and Industries. The country is rich in minerals with large deposits of copper, iron, lead, coal, and sulphur. In 1972 Ecuador became an important exporter of oil, brought by pipeline from eastern Ecuador to the Pacific. Modern farm methods have helped make Ecuador the world's largest exporter of bananas. Other products are rice, cereals, potatoes, fruits, cocoa, coffee, kapok, rubber, mangrove bark, fish.

Industry now contributes 20% to national income, with production increases in cement, edible oils, textiles, sugar, chemicals, petroleum products, paper. Ecuador is the chief source of light but strong balsa wood, and was the original home of the Cinchona tree, source of quinine.

History and Government. Spain conquered the region, which was the northern Inca empire, in the 16th century. Liberation forces defeated the Spanish May 24, 1822, near Quito. Ecuador became part of the Great Colombia Republic but seceded, May 13, 1830.

In June 1968 elections, Dr. Jose Maria Velasco Ibarra, who had been elected president 4 times but had been ousted 3 times by coups, was again chosen by the voters. In June 1970, he assumed dictatorial powers. On Feb. 15, 1972, he was ousted by a military junta. A new junta took over in 1976, after strikes, inflation, and other economic problems arose.

Education and Religion. Roman Catholicism is the chief religion. Primary education is compulsory. The language is Spanish. The population is over one-third Indian and one-third mixed; whites, mostly of Spanish descent, and Negroes are minority groups.

Defense. Armed forces total about 22,000.

Egypt

Area (1966): 386,872 sq. mi. Population (Govt. est. 1975): 37,230,000. Capital: Cairo. Monetary unit: Egyptian pound.

The Arab Republic of Egypt occupies the NE corner of Africa on the Mediterranean. On the E lie Israel and the Red Sea which separates Egypt from Saudi Arabia. Libya is to the W and Sudan to the S. The Gulf of Suez and the Suez Canal (linking the gulf to the Mediterranean) separate Egypt's main area in Africa from the Sinai Peninsula in Asia.

Alexandria, founded 332 B.C., is the chief port. Cairo, largest city, is rich in archeological treasures, cafes, bazaars. Tourist attractions include the pyramids, Sphinx, temple ruins at Karnak and Luxor, and other ancient monuments.

Resources and Industries. Productive acreage lies in the Valley of the Nile and in its delta, or Lower Egypt, north of Cairo. The Nile flows through 960 mi. in Egypt, and covers 2,850 sq. mi. with waters and marshes. Irrigated lands produce cotton, cereals, vegetables, and sugar cane. Fruit is plentiful and includes grapes, dates, figs, pomegranates, peaches, apricots, oranges, lemons, bananas, and olives. Egypt is one of the world's largest producers of cotton.

The billion-dollar Aswan High Dam project, begun 1960, completed 1971, provided irrigation for more than a million acres of land and a potential of 10 billion kwh of electricity per year. Artesian wells, drilled in the Western Desert, reclaimed 43,000 acres, 1960-66.

A variety of minerals is found in Egypt; petroleum is most important, with fields in the Red Sea, Sinai, and the Western Desert. Other minerals are phosphate rock, salt, iron, manganese, cement, gold, gypsum, kaolin, titanium.

A series of decrees in July, 1961, nationalized about 90% of industry and reduced land holdings to 52 acres per family. In 1974 an economic liberalization was begun, with more emphasis on private domestic and foreign investment.

Egypt has textile plants, chemical, steel, cement and fertilizer factories, and a film industry supplying the Middle East, Africa, and Asia. Principal exports are cotton, rice, petroleum, textiles, refrigerators, tires, cement, electrical instruments.

History and Government. Archeological records of ancient empires in Egypt go back to 4000 B.C. A high civilization of rulers and priests dominated the lowly serfs. Hyksos, Assyrians, Persians, Greeks (Alexander of Macedon), Romans, Saracens, Turks, French (Napoleon) and British invaded Egypt. Under Turkish sultans the khedive as hereditary viceroy had wide authority but repeated insolvency led to regulation by European powers. Britain, which supervised the administration after 1882, made Egypt a protectorate 1914-1922. Britain then recognized Egypt as a sovereign state but reserved defense, security of British communications, and the Sudan.

The sultan became King Fouad I in 1922 and a constitution was adopted in 1923. King Fouad I died in 1936 and was succeeded by his son, Farouk, who abdicated in 1952 and left the country. His son was named nominal ruler under a regency council, Aug. 5, 1952,

but the crown was abolished when Egypt was declared a republic, June 18, 1953.

In 1936 an Anglo-Egyptian treaty of alliance revised the conditions of association. Britain agreed to a condominium over the Sudan, with British and Egyptian troops cooperating, obtained the right to retain 10,000 soldiers and 400 airmen to defend the Suez Canal for 20 years until Egypt would take over, and also held naval bases in Alexandria and Port Said.

Egypt became a charter member of the UN and in 1944 led in organizing the Arab League. In 1947 Egypt brought before the UN Security Council a demand for unification of Egypt and Sudan and evacuation of all British troops from the Suez. In Oct. 1951 Egypt abrogated its 1936 treaty with Britain. The Sudan, with UN support, became independent in 1956.

Delays in reforms, corruption in public office and royal extravagance led to an uprising July 23, 1952, led by the Society of Free Officers which named Maj. Gen. Mohammed Naguib commander in chief and forced Farouk to abdicate. Naguib became premier Sept. 7, 1952. When the republic was proclaimed June 18, 1953, Naguib became its first president and premier. Lt. Col. Gamal Abdel Nasser, the principal influence behind the revolt, removed Naguib and succeeded him as premier on Apr. 18, 1954. On June 23, 1956, voters elected Nasser president. Nasser died in 1970 and was replaced as president by Vice President Anwar Sadat.

A new constitution, guaranteeing individual rights, was approved Sept. 11, 1971. At the same time, Egypt adopted the name Arab Republic of Egypt, dropping the name United Arab Republic, which it had used since its brief union with Syria, 1958-1961. Egypt has a president, premier, and National Assembly all of whose 350 members must be members of the only legal party, the Arab Socialist Union. Three factions within the party, left, right and center, are allowed to run candidates.

In July, 1956, the United States and Great Britain withdrew support for loans to start the Aswan High Dam. President Nasser nationalized the Suez Canal and seized control of the assets of the canal company. Later he obtained credits and technicians from the USSR to build the dam.

When the state of Israel was proclaimed in 1948, Egypt joined other Arab nations invading Israel and was defeated. No peace treaties were made and Egypt later denied Israeli shipping the use of the Suez Canal.

After terrorist raids across its border, Israel invaded Egypt's Sinai Peninsula, Oct. 29, 1956. Egypt rejected a cease-fire demand by Britain and France; on Oct. 31 the 2 nations dropped bombs and on Nov. 5-6 landed forces. Egypt and Israel accepted a UN cease-fire, followed by Britain and France; fighting ended Nov. 7.

A UN Emergency Force guarded the 117-mile long border between Egypt and Israel until May 19, 1967, when it was withdrawn at Nasser's demand. Egyptian troops entered the Gaza Strip and the heights at Sharm el Sheikh and 3 days later closed the Strait of Tiran leading into the Gulf of Aqaba to all Israeli shipping. Full-scale war broke out June 5 and before it ended under a UN cease-fire June 10, Israel had captured Gaza and the Sinai Peninsula, controlled the east bank of the Suez Canal and reopened the gulf.

Sporadic fighting with Israel broke out late in 1968. In 1969-70 there were almost daily artillery duels across the Suez Canal, ground forays and air raids in which Israeli planes penetrated deep into Egypt. Military and economic aid was received from the USSR and it was est. in 1971 there were 19,000 or more Soviet military personnel in Egypt. Israel and Egypt agreed, Aug. 7, 1970, to a cease-fire and peace negotiations proposed by the U.S. Negotiations, pressed by the UN and U.S., failed to achieve results, but the cease-fire continued into 1973.

In July 1972 Sadat ordered most of the 20,000 Soviet military advisers and personnel to leave Egypt. They complied, leaving behind bases and equipment they had installed for the Egyptians.

In a surprise attack Oct. 6, 1973 (Yom Kippur, most sacred day on the Jewish calendar), Egyptian forces crossed the Suez Canal into the Sinai. (At the same time, Syrian forces attacked Israelis on the Golan Heights.) Egypt was supplied by a USSR military airlift; the U.S. responded with an airlift to Israel. Israel counter-attacked, crossed the canal, surrounded Suez City and trapped the Egyptian 3d Army in its Sinai bridgehead. A UN cease-fire took effect Oct. 24; a UN peace-keeping force went to the area.

A disengagement agreement was signed Jan. 18, 1974, mainly through the efforts of U.S. Secretary of State Henry Kissinger. Under it, Israeli forces withdrew from the canal's W bank; limited numbers of Egyptian forces occupied a strip along the E bank from the Mediterranean to the Gulf of Suez; UN forces took over a buffer zone, E of the Egyptians; Israelis, further E, could have only limited forces adjoining the UN zone. Withdrawals to the new lines were completed Mar. 4. A second accord was signed in 1975, with Israel yielding Sinai oil fields.

The U.S. and Egypt resumed, in Feb. 1974, diplomatic relations, severed by Egypt after the 1967 war. In June, U. S. President Nixon announced during an Egyptian visit that he would provide Egypt nuclear technology for peaceful purposes. Major arms deals with Britain and France were set in 1975.

Iran, Saudi Arabia, and Kuwait provided aid and low interest loans in 1975 and 1976.

Education and Religion. There are 3 ethnic elements: the Fellahin, basic Egyptian group; the Bedouin, nomadic Arabs; Nubians, a mixed group. Moslems form 92% of the population and Coptic Christians, whose liturgical language is the only surviving remnant of ancient Egyptian culture, about 7%.

Education is compulsory for all children beginning at age 7 and free through high school. There is a famous seat of Moslem learning in the University of Al-Azhar in Cairo, founded about 968 A.D. Seven modern universities are in Cairo, Alexandria, and other cities. Arabic is the official language.

Defense. Military forces total 323,500 with reserves of about 530,000.

The Suez Canal

The Suez Canal, 103 mi. long, links the Mediterranean and the Red Sea. It was begun April 25, 1859, by a French corporation under Ferdinand de Lesseps and opened Nov. 17, 1869. Benjamin Disraeli, British prime minister, obtained control for Britain Nov. 24, 1875, by buying 176,752 shares from the Khedive Ismail of Egypt for about $20 million.

The British ended a 74-year military occupation of the canal area June 13, 1956. On July 26, Egypt nationalized the canal, seizing it from French and British stockholders. It had barred Israeli ships and cargoes destined for Israel since 1948.

A final agreement between Egypt and the Universal Suez Canal Co., signed July 13, 1958, called for payments to stockholders of $64,400,000. Final payments were made Jan. 1, 1963.

After nationalization, Egypt widened and deepened the canal, improving its capacity. The canal was closed to all shipping by Cairo during the Israeli-Arab War in June 1967. Subsidies to replace lost canal revenues were paid the UAR by Saudi Arabia, Kuwait, and Libya. In 1974, operations to clear the canal of war debris began, with aid from the U.S. and others. The canal was reopened June 5, 1975, with Israeli cargoes in 3rd party ships allowed passage.

El Salvador

Area: 8,260 sq. mi. Population (Govt. est. 1975): 4,010,000. **Capital: San Salvador. Monetary unit: Colon.**

El Salvador, Smallest of the 6 Central American republics and the only one without an Atlantic seacoast, is bounded by Guatemala, Honduras and a Pacific coastline of about 160 mi. A country of mountains, including many volcanoes, and upland plains, it is entirely within the tropics, but tropic heat is modified by the elevation. It is about the size of Massachusetts.

The 3 racial types are white, 5%; mixed white and Indian descent, 85%; Indian, 10%.

Resources and Industries. Mountain slope plantations make El Salvador the world's 8th largest producer and a large exporter of coffee. Cotton production has made large strides; coffee represents about one-half of the value of exports, cotton 8%. Primarily agricultural, the country is becoming industrialized; it produces cement, refined sugar, and textiles.

Economic development has been helped by U.S. aid.

History and Government. El Salvador became independent of Spain in 1821; member of the Central American Federation until 1839. The constitution provides for a unicameral legislative system, the National Assembly of Deputies, elected by popular vote. Voting is compulsory for all over 18 years of age. Executive power is vested in the president who is elected for a 5-year term by direct, popular vote and is ineligible for immediate reelection.

In July 1969, a dispute over the presence of 300,000 Salvadorean workers and settlers in Honduras broke into open warfare between the two nations, 2,000 people were killed. After 5 days, the OAS arranged a truce. In 1970, after new clashes, a demilitarized zone was agreed on. Clashes continued in 1974.

Education and Religion. Education is free but illiteracy rate is high. The language is Spanish. The dominant religion is Roman Catholicism.

Defense. Military forces number about 5,100. El Salvador is a member of the UN and OAS.

Equatorial Guinea

Area: 10,832 sq. mi. Population (UN est. 1975): 310,-000. Capital: Malabo. Monetary unit: Ekuele.

The Republic of Equatorial Guinea, which received its independence from Spain on Oct. 12, 1968, consists of the Province of Masie Nguema Biyogo, including Masie Nguema Biyogo Is., in the Gulf of Guinea off the W coast of Africa and Pagalu Is., 370 mi. SW, and the Province of Rio Muni, on the mainland facing the gulf. Malabo, the capital, is on Masie Nguema Biyogo Is., which has an area of 780 sq. mi. and population (est. 1972) of 90,000.

Self-government and independence were achieved in steps, with local elections in 1960 and increased autonomy in 1964. Masie Nguema Biyogo was elected the first president. In 1971 he assumed complete control of the government and in 1972 was named president for life.

Important exports are cocoa and timber for plywood. Other exports are coffee, bananas, and palm oil.

Most of the population is nominally Roman Catholic. Spanish is the official language; numerous African languages are also spoken. By the late 1960s Nigerian workers and settlers numbered almost half the Masie Nguema Biyogo island population, but most have emigrated charging mistreatment and cruelty. Before a 1969 confrontation, there were about 7,000 Europeans, mostly Spanish, but many left during the dispute.

Relations with Cameroon and Gabon have cooled due to boundary disputes. The U.S. suspended relations in 1976. The USSR, China, and N. Korea maintain relations.

The nation is a member of the UN and OAU.

Ethiopia

Area: 457,142 sq. mi. Population (Govt. est. 1975): 27,950,000. Capital: Addis Ababa. Monetary unit: Ethiopian dollar.

Ethiopia is a ruggedly mountainous state in NE Africa. It faces on the Red Sea, but its main rivers are important tributaries of the Nile: the Abbai or Blue Nile, one of the 2 main branches of that mighty river, has its source in Ethiopia's Lake Tana. The country is as large as Texas, Oklahoma, and New Mexico combined.

Resources and Industries. Economy is some 70% agricultural but industrial resources are potentially great, including vast hydroelectric power. Industries include food processing, cement, shoes, textiles.

Fertile soil and abundant rainfall produce 2 crops annually. Coffee, wheat, barley, millet, tobacco, and sugar are principal crops. Coffee of extremely high quality from Kaffa, in SW Ethiopia, reputed birthplace of the coffee plant, accounts for half of the country's foreign exchange. Over 185,000 tons are exported annually. Value of exports in 1974 rose to $268 million; imports totaled $277 million.

Cattle, sheep, mules, and goats are raised. Hides and skins, oilseeds, and vegetables also are exported. Mineral resources include platinum, gold, silver, manganese, tin, copper, asbestos, potash, sulphur, mica, cement, and salt. There are known deposits of coal and iron.

Ethiopia has used large credits from the World Bank and other agencies for road building (there are over 4,000 mi. of all-weather roads). Aid and investment funds are received from the U. S. and other western nations and from communist countries. Ethiopia is a member of the UN and Addis Ababa is hq. for the Organization of African Unity.

History and Government. The Ethiopian monarchy derived from a number of earlier kingdoms, descendants of ancient Hamite and Semite tribes. Italy invaded the country in 1880 and acquired a sphere of influence and later organized its colony of Eritrea. In 1936 Italy invaded Ethiopia without declaring war. The League of Nations applied sanctions against Italy, which proved ineffective. Mussolini added Ethiopia to Italy. British forces freed Ethiopia in 1941.

The last emperor, Haile Selassie I, 225th consecutive Solomonic ruler, was born July 23, 1892, crowned Nov. 2, 1930. He established a parliament and judiciary system, 1931, and promulgated a new constitution 1955, but barred all political parties.

A 1973 famine killed over 100,000 people, causing unrest. An army mutiny, strikes and student demonstrations led to the dethronement of Selassie Sept. 12, 1974, and the execution of 60 former officials in November. The ruling junta pledged to form a one-party socialist state. The influence of the Coptic Church was curbed. The monarchy was abolished March 21, 1975. A famine in the east killed thousands in 1975.

Education and Religion. Ethiopian culture has been influenced by Greece and Egypt. Christianity was for centuries the predominant religion, embraced in 330 A.D.; the Coptic, Monophysite branch is practiced. Until 1952 the Egyptian Coptic patriarch was the head of the church, but the archbishop has since been an Ethiopian. The population is largely composed of a mixture of Hamites, Semites, and Negroes. The largest religious groups are Coptic Christians and Moslems; others practice tribal religions.

There are 2 universities and a number of colleges. The official language is Amharic; English is widely taught.

Eritrea, which had been an Italian colony since 1890, was administered after World War II by Great Britain; the UN General Assembly voted to return it to Ethiopia and the action became effective Sept. 11, 1952. In 1970-76 secessionist guerrillas were active in Eritrea, receiving military and political support from Arab and Moslem states.

Fiji

Area: 7,055 sq. mi. Population (UN est. 1975): 580,000. Capital: Suva. Monetary unit: Fiji dollar.

The Fiji Islands lie in the South Pacific, E of Australia and N of New Zealand. There are about 840 islands (106 inhabited), many of them mountainous, with tropical forests and large fertile areas. The capital, Suva, is on Viti Levu, the largest island (4,011 sq. mi.).

Descendants of the native Fijians (Melanesians and Polynesians) form about 43% of the population but have been protected by law in ownership of 83% of the land. Descendants of Indian contract laborers, brought to the islands in the late 19th Century, make up slightly over 51%. Most of the others are of Chinese or European descent. English is the official language. Most of the Fijians are Christians; the Indians are about 80% Hindu, 15% Moslem. Literacy is about 85%.

A British colony since 1874, Fiji received gradual measures of self-government in the 1960s. On Oct. 10, 1970, Fiji became a fully independent parliamentary democracy, with a Senate, a House of Representatives, a prime minister, and, as a member of the Commonwealth, a governor-general representing the British Queen. It is a member of the UN.

Sugar is the main export, along with molasses, coconut products, timber, ginger and gold. Tourism is important. A cement factory, shipyards and small manufacturing plants have been built.

Finland

Area: 130,119 sq. mi. Population (Govt. est. 1975): 4,710,000. Capital: Helsinki. Monetary unit: Markka.

Finland is a republic in northern Europe, with Sweden, Norway, and the USSR for neighbors. South and central Finland are mostly flat areas with low hills; there are mountainous areas, 3,000-4,000 ft., in the N. It is half the size of Texas.

About 70% of the land is forested. Lakes and canal waterways are navigable for 3,000 mi. Rail and air transport is well developed.

Aland, constituting an autonomous department, is a group of small islands, 572 sq. mi., in the Gulf of Bothnia, 25 mi. from Sweden, 15 mi. from Finland. It is demilitarized. Mariehamn is the principal port.

Resources and Industries. Rapid industrialization has taken place with 25% of output exported. Forest products (paper, etc.) are 55% of exports, metals 25%, foods 5%. Principal crops are oats, barley, wheat, rye, potatoes, hay. There are machinery, metal, shipbuilding, textiles, leather, and chemicals industries. In 1972, 2 million tourists visited Finland.

Foreign trade, in thousands of U. S. dollars:

	Imports	Exports
1974	$6,864,000	$5,527,000
1975	$7,602,000	$5,487,000

History and Government. The early Finns probably migrated from the Ural area at about the beginning of the Christian era. Swedish settlers brought the country into the kingdom of Sweden, 1154 to 1809, when Finland became an autonomous grand duchy of the Russian Empire. Russian exactions created a strong national spirit; on Dec. 6, 1917, Finland declared its independence and on July 17, 1919, became a republic. On Nov. 30, 1939, the Soviet Union invaded Finland, and although the Finns took heavy toll, in March, 1940, they were forced to cede 16,173 sq. mi., including the Karelian Isthmus, Viipuri, and an area on Lake Ladoga. When Germany attacked the USSR June 22. 1941. Finland again was involved. An armistice was signed Sept. 19, 1944. and the USSR took the former cessions, plus Petsamo in the N, and a lease for 50 years on Porkkala, near Helsinki, for a military base. The treaty of Feb. 10, 1947, also exacted $300 million in goods in term payments. In April. 1948. Finland signed a treaty of mutual assistance and friendship with the USSR; in Jan. 1956 Russia returned Porkkala.

The president is chosen for a term of six years by an electoral college of 300 named by direct vote; he appoints the cabinet. There is a single legislative chamber. the Eduskunta. numbering 200, elected to 4-year terms. Voting is by proportional representation. The prime minister and cabinet normally represent a coalition of parties in the Eduskunta. including the Communists.

Education and Religion. The Evangelical Lutheran Church is the leading religion. and both Finnish and Swedish are official languages. There is no illiteracy. There are 8 universities (the oldest founded 1640) and several institutes on the university level.

Defense. Military strength for 1972-73 was 36,300.

Finland is a member of the UN. Nordic Council and EFTA. and has a trade agreement with the EC and a cooperation accord with the Council for Mutual Economic Assistance. Only 20% of trade is with the USSR. but the latter supplies 80% of oil imports.

France

Area: 211,000 sq. mi. Population (Census 1975): 52,658,253. Capital: Paris. Monetary unit: Franc.

France has coastlines on the Atlantic and Mediterranean and is about four-fifths the size of Texas. It shares borders with Belgium, Luxembourg, Germany. Switzerland. Italy. Andorra. and Spain. It is separated from England by the English Channel and the Strait of Dover. The Rhine River is on the German boundary. the Jura Mts. form the Swiss boundary and the Pyrenees Mtns. rise along the borders of Andorra and Spain.

Mont Blanc, on the Franco-Italian border, is the tallest in Europe W of the Caucasus, 15,771 ft. A highway tunnel. 7.25 mi.. under Mont Blanc, was opened in 1965. linking France and Italy.

There are 4 important rivers. the Seine, the Loire. the Garonne, and the Rhone. There are some 5,005 mi. of navigable rivers and canals.

The island of Corsica, in the Mediterranean W of Italy and N of Sardinia. is an official region of France comprising 2 departments. It has an area of 3,369 sq. mi. and a population of 220,000. The capital is Ajaccio, birthplace of Napoleon.

Resources and Industries. Agriculturally. France is a country of small diversified farms involving 45,800,000 acres and 12% of the employed. making France the biggest food producer in Western Europe. Agricultural exports were valued at more than $7 billion in 1975. Leading crops are wheat, barley, corn, oats. rice. and a wide variety of fruits and vegetables. Cattle. poultry. forestry. and fishing are large-scale. France is the world's 4th ranking producer of beef. and of pork. Approx. half of the farm population belongs to cooperative unions.

The country is rich in minerals. and the basins of Pas de Calais and Lorraine are noted for their huge coal deposits. iron ore. bauxite, pyrites, mineral oils, auriferous ore, asphalt. rock salt. and potash salts. The iron ore deposits in eastern France and the bauxite deposits in central France are among the richest in the world. Power stations produced about 174 million kwh in 1973. one-third hydro and 8% nuclear.

France tested atomic bombs in the Sahara beginning in 1960 and. beginning in 1966 exploded nuclear devices at Mururoa, an atoll 750 mi. SE of Tahiti. continuing the tests through 1974. (France was not a signer of the 1963 treaty banning such tests.) Australia and New Zealand protested the tests and in

1973 the International Court of Justice asked France to suspend the tests.

Manufacturing includes chemicals, silk and cotton textiles, perfumes. automobiles. aircraft. ships. instruments. plastics. electronic equipment. Index of industrial production (1970   100) was 116 in Dec. 1975.

France leads the world in wine-making. producing over 1.5 billion gallons a year.

Foreign trade in thousands of U-S. dollars

	Imports	Exports
1974	$49,723,000	$46,388,000
1975	$51,667,000	$52,991,000

History and Government. The monarchial system was overthrown by the French Revolution (1789-1793) and succeeded by the First Republic: thereafter successively followed by the First Empire under Napoleon (1804-1814). a monarchy (1814-1848). the Second Republic (1848-1852). the Second Empire (1852-1870). the Third Republic (1871-1946). the Fourth Republic (1946-1958). Fifth Republic (1958).

France suffered severe losses in manpower and wealth in the first World War. 1914-1918. when it was invaded by Germany. By the Treaty of Versailles. France exacted return of Alsace and Lorraine. French provinces seized by Germany in 1871. Germany invaded France again in May. 1940. occupied Paris June 14. 1940. and signed an armistice with a government that made its hq. in Vichy. Marshal Philippe Petain became chief of state. After France was liberated by the Allies Sept. 1944. Gen. Charles de Gaulle became premier of the provisional government. serving from Nov. 1944 to Jan. 1946.

De Gaulle again became premier June 1. 1958. His proposed constitution for the Fifth Republic and new French Community was approved by the voters by an overwhelming margin. De Gaulle was elected first president of the Fifth Republic Dec. 21. 1958; inaugurated Jan. 8. 1959. De Gaulle ran for reelection Dec. 5. 1965; he failed to win a majority of the votes. In a runoff. Dec. 19. de Gaulle won with about 55%.

The constitution provides for a strong executive branch headed by the president. and a legislature composed of a National Assembly and a Senate.

A constitutional amendment adopted by referendum Oct. 28. 1962. provided that future presidents be elected by popular vote rather than by an electoral college. The president. elected for 7 years. appoints the premier (formerly invested by the Assembly). and may dissolve the Assembly and call for new elections: he may call for referendums on specific issues and may assume full powers in a national emergency.

Women. who had less than equal rights under provisions of the 1804 Code Napoleon. won the right to take jobs. open checking accounts and own their own businesses by a 1966 law.

In May 1968 rebellious students at the Sorbonne and elsewhere rioted. battled police and were joined by some 10 million workers who launched nationwide strikes and took over many factories. The government awarded pay increases to the strikers May 26; on May 30 de Gaulle dissolved the Assembly. A threat of civil war was eased as Army tank units. loyal to the government. maneuvered in Paris outskirts. By early June. normalcy was returned. In elections to the Assembly in late June 1968. de Gaulle's backers won a landslide victory.

In Nov. 1968 de Gaulle weathered an economic storm. refusing to devalue the franc. But on Apr. 28. 1969. he resigned from office after losing a nationwide referendum on his proposals for constitutional reform.

A nationwide election for a successor. June 1. resulted in a runoff election June 15 in which the winner was Georges Pompidou. who had been de Gaulle's premier from 1962 until July 1968. Pompidou died Apr. 2. 1974. Valery Giscard d'Estaing. a conservative. was elected president. May 19. 1974. with 50.81   of the vote. defeating Socialist Francois

Mitterrand.

Education and Religion. Primary, secondary and higher education are free and instruction is compulsory between the ages of 6 and 16.

The country is 90% Roman Catholic, 2% Jewish and 2% Protestant, with some Moslems.

Both employers and employes contribute to the old-age pension fund. There is provision for family allowances and compulsory social insurance for illness, maternity, disability and death. A profit-sharing and participation plan begun in 1959 was expanded in 1967. By 1974, over 4 million employes were covered.

Defense. Military forces total 502,000; reserves number over 45,000.

France is a member of the UN and EC.

In 1966, France withdrew all its troops from the integrated military command of NATO, though 60,-000 remain stationed in Germany. NATO headquarters and bases were removed from France. France continued to attend political meetings of NATO.

Afars and Issas Territory

The French Territory of the Afars and the Issas, formerly French Somaliland, borders Ethiopia and Somalia and is separated by the Straits of Bab-el-Mandeb from Yemen.

The area is 8,800 sq. mi. and population (est. 1974), 150,000; the capital is Djibouti. France took control of the area in gradual steps, beginning in 1862.

The territory has few industries, except fishing and livestock. Salt is its most valuable product. Half of Ethiopia's foreign commerce passes along the rail line from Addis Ababa and through the port of Djibouti.

In a referendum Mar. 19, 1967, the territory elected to remain French. There were clashes between Afar and Issa tribes in 1975, the Afars being ethnically similar to Ethiopians and the Issas to Somalis.

Mayotte

Formerly part of Comoros, Mayotte voted in 1976 to become an overseas department of France. An island NW of Madagascar, area is 144 sq. mi., pop. 36,-000.

Reunion

Reunion, Overseas Department, is an island in the Indian Ocean, about 420 miles east of Madagascar, and has belonged to France since 1665. The area is 969 sq. mi.; the population (1975) 476,675, is 30% of French extraction. Capital: Saint-Denis. The chief products are sugar, rum, corn, perfume essences, vanilla, and spices. It elects 3 deputies, 2 senators to the French Parliament.

Guadeloupe

Guadeloupe, Overseas Department in the West Indies' Leeward Islands, consists of 2 large islands, Basse-Terre and Grande-Terre, separated by the Salt River, plus Marie Galante and the Saintes group to the S and, to the N, Desirade, St. Barthelemy, and over half of St. Martin (the Netherlands portion is St. Maarten). A French possession since 1635, the department is represented in the French Parliament by 2 senators and 3 deputies; administration consists of a prefect (governor) and an elected General Council.

Area of the islands is 687 sq. mi.; population (1975) 24,530, mainly descendants of slaves; capital is Basse-Terre on Basse-Terre Is. The land is fertile; sugar, rum, and bananas are exported; tourism is an important industry.

Martinique

Martinique, one of the Windward Islands, in the West Indies, has been a possession since 1635, and a Department since March, 1946. It is represented in the French Parliament by 2 senators and 3 deputies. Mt. Pelee, a volcano, erupted May 8, 1902, destroying

the city of St. Pierre and 30,000 inhabitants. The island was the birthplace of Napoleon's Empress Josephine.

It has an area of 426 sq. mi. and population (1975) 324,832, mostly descendants of slaves. The capital is Fort-de-France. It is a popular tourist stop. The chief exports are sugar, rum, bananas, pineapples, and cocoa.

St. Pierre and Miquelon

St. Pierre and Miquelon, an Overseas Territory, are 2 groups of rocky islands near the SW coast of Newfoundland, inhabited by fishermen. A governor, assisted by a Council, rules the islands. The exports are chiefly fish products. The St. Pierre group has an area of 10 sq. mi.; Miquelon, 83 sq. mi. Total population (est. 1974), 5,450. The capital is St. Pierre. A deputy and a senator are elected to the French Parliament.

French Guiana

French Guiana, an Overseas Department, is on the NE coast of South America with Surinam on the W and Brazil on the E and S. Its area is 37,740 sq. mi.; population (1975), 55,125. Guiana sends one senator and one deputy to the French Parliament. Guiana has a prefect and a Council General of 15 elected members; capital is Cayenne.

In 1944 France closed the famous penal colony, Devil's Island, and repatriated 2,800 inmates.

Immense forests of rich timber cover 90% of the land. The principal crops are rice, corn, manioc, cacao, bananas, and sugar cane. Placer gold mining is the most important industry. Exports are cocoa, bananas, wood, gold, fish glue, rum, rosewood essence, shrimp, and hides.

Pacific Islands

French Polynesia, Overseas Territory, comprises 130 islands widely scattered among 5 archipelagos in the South Pacific; administered by a governor, Territorial Assembly and a Council with headquarters at Papeete, Tahiti, one of the **Society Islands.** A deputy and a senator are elected to the French Parliament.

Other groups are the **Marquesas Islands,** the **Tuamotu Archipelago,** the **Gambier Islands** and the **Austral Islands.**

Total area of the islands administered from Tahiti is 1,544 sq. mi.; pop. (est. 1974), 130,000, more than half on Tahiti. Tahiti is picturesque and mountainous with a productive coastline bearing coconut, banana and orange trees, sugar cane and vanilla.

Tahiti was visited by Capt. James Cook in 1769 and by Capt. Bligh in the Bounty, 1788-89. Its beauty impressed Herman Melville, Paul Gauguin, Charles Darwin and Robert Louis Stevenson who called Tahitians "God's sweetest works."

New Caledonia and its dependencies, an Overseas Territory, are a group of islands in the Pacific Ocean about 1,115 mi. E of Australia and approx. the same distance NW of New Zealand. Dependencies are the **Loyalty Islands,** the **Isle of Pines, Huon Islands** and the **Chesterfield Islands.**

New Caledonia, the largest, has 6,530 sq. mi. Total area of the territory is 8,548 sq. mi.; population (est. 1974) 130,000. The group was acquired by France in 1853.

The territory is administered by a governor and government council. There is a popularly elected Territorial Assembly. A deputy and a senator are elected to the French parliament. Capital: Noumea.

Mining is the chief industry. New Caledonia is the world's third largest nickel producer. Other minerals found are chrome, cobalt, manganese, antimony, mercury, cinnebar, silver, gold, lead, and copper. Agricultural products include coffee, copra, cotton, manioc (cassava), corn, tobacco, bananas, and pineapples.

Wallis and Futuna Islands, 2 archipelagos raised to status.of Overseas Territory July 29, 1961, are in the SW Pacific S of the Equator between Fiji and Samoa. The islands have a total area of 106 sq. mi. and population (est. 1972) of 7,500. **Alofi,** attached to Futuna, is uninhabited. Capital: Mata-Utu. Chief products are copra, yams, taro roots, bananas. A senator and a deputy are elected to the French parliament.

French Antarctica

French Southern and Antarctic Lands, Overseas Territory, comprises **Adelie Land,** on Antarctica, and 4 island groups in the Indian Ocean. Adelie, discov. 1840, has 2 research bases, a coastline of 185 mi. and tapers 1,240 mi. inland to the South Pole. The US does not recognize national claims in Antarctica. There are 2 huge glaciers, Ninnis, 22 mi. wide, 99 mi. long, and Mertz, 11 mi. wide, 140 mi. long. The Indian Ocean groups are:

Kerguelen Archipelago, discovered 1772, has 300 islands. The chief is 87 mi. long, 74 mi. wide, and has Mt. Ross, 6,429 ft. tall. Principal research station is Port-aux-Francais. Seals often weigh 2 tons; there are blue whales, coal, peat, semi-precious stones. **Crozet Archipelago** (discov. 1772), covers 195 sq. mi. Eastern Island rises to 6,560 ft. **Saint Paul,** in southern Indian Ocean, has warm springs and tropical climate, with earth at places heating to 120° to 390° F. **New Amsterdam,** nearby, has temperate climate, produces cod and rock lobster.

New Hebrides

New Hebrides, a condominium administered since 1906 by France and Great Britain, is a group of 11 main islands and about 69 islets 250 mi. NE of New Caledonia and 500 mi. W of Fiji. It has 5,790 sq. mi. and population (est. 1974) of 90,000, mostly Melanesian. It has 2 administrations—French and British. Chief products are copra, frozen fish, cocoa, and coffee.

Gabon Republic

Area: 102,317 sq. mi. Population (UN est. 1975): 530,000. Capital: Libreville. Monetary unit: CFA franc.

A former French Overseas Territory, Gabon is on the west coast of Equatorial Africa, straddling the Equator and bounded by Cameroon, Equatorial Guinea, People's Republic of Congo, and the Atlantic. Heavily forested, the country consists of coastal lowlands, plateaus in N, E and S, mountains in N, SE, and center. It is about the size of Colorado.

Gabon's economy is thriving; exports far exceed imports in value. Valuable timber, plywood, and veneers were the main exports until the late 1960s when manganese, crude oil and uranium topped them in value. There are also huge iron ore deposits. New rail lines will aid resource exploitation. Foreign private investment has been welcomed.

Agriculture, roads, port facilities, and hydroelectric power are being developed. Main crops are cocoa, coffee, rice, peanuts, palm products, cassava, bananas, but some food is imported.

Gabon proclaimed independence Aug. 17, 1960; it became a UN member Sept. 20. It is a republic, with an elected president and unicameral National Assembly. The first president, Leon M'ba, died in 1967; he was succeeded Dec. 1 by vice president Omar Bongo, who declared a one-party state.

Dr. Albert Schweitzer, Nobel Peace Prize winner, founded a hospital for lepers and others in 1913 at Lambarene. He died Sept. 4, 1965.

The Gambia

Area: 4,003 sq. mi. Population (Govt. est. 1975):

520,000. Capital: Banjul. Monetary unit: Dalasi.

Gambia is a former British colony and protectorate in western Africa. It includes the island of Banjul at the mouth of the Gambia River and a 10-mile wide strip of territory on each side of the river. Except for its Atlantic coastline, Gambia is surrounded by Senegal.

Gambia attained internal self-government Oct. 4, 1963. Its legislature comprises a speaker and 32 elected members. Britain granted complete independence to the colony Feb. 18, 1965.

In April 1970, after a referendum, Gambia became a republic within the Commonwealth. Former Prime Minister Dawda K. Jawara became the first president.

Peanuts are the main export. Rice and other foods are also grown. Tourism has become important. Britain provides development aid.

English is the official language. Islam is the main religion.

Germany

Now comprises 2 nations: Federal Republic of Germany (West Germany), German Democratic Republic (East Germany).

Germany, prior to World War II, was a central European nation composed of numerous states which had a common language and traditions and which had been united in one country since 1871; since World War II it has been split in 2 parts (see below).

History and Government. Germanic tribes were defeated by Julius Caesar, 55 and 53 B. C. but Roman expansion N of the Rhine was stopped with the wiping out of 3 legions under Varus in 9 A.D. Charlemagne, ruler of the Franks, consolidated Saxon, Bavarian, Rhenish, Frankish and other lands; after him the eastern part became the German Empire. The Thirty Years' War, 1618-1648, split Germany into small principalities and kingdoms. After Napoleon, Austria contended with Prussia for dominance, but lost the Seven Weeks' War to Prussia, 1866. Otto von Bismarck, Prussian chancellor, formed the North German Confederation, 1867.

In 1870 Bismarck maneuvered Napoleon III into declaring war. After the quick defeat of France Bismarck formed the **German Empire** and on Jan. 18, 1871, in Versailles, proclaimed King Wilhelm I of Prussia German emperor (Deutscher kaiser).

The German Empire reached its peak before World War I in 1914, with 208,780 sq. mi., plus a colonial empire. After that war Germany ceded Alsace-Lorraine to France; Eupen and Malmedy to Belgium; parts of Silesia to Poland and Czechoslovakia; part of Schleswig to Denmark; lost all of its colonies as well as the ports of Memel and Danzig.

Republic of Germany, 1919-1933, adopted the Weimar constitution; met reparation payments and elected Friedrich Ebert and Gen. Paul von Hindenburg presidents.

Third Reich, 1933-1945. Adolf Hitler, born in Austria, 1889, led the National Socialist German Workers' (Nazi) party after World War I. In 1923 he attempted to unseat the Bavarian government in the "Beer Hall putsch," and was imprisoned. He wrote Mein Kampf while in prison. President von Hindenburg named Hitler chancellor Jan. 30, 1933; on Aug. 3, 1934, the day after Hindenburg's death, the cabinet joined the offices of president and chancellor and made Hitler fuehrer (leader). Hitler abolished freedom of speech and assembly, and began a long series of persecutions climaxed by the murder of millions of Jews and opponents.

Hitler repudiated the Versailles treaty and reparations agreements. He remilitarized the Rhineland 1936 and annexed Austria (Anschluss, 1938). At Munich he made an agreement with Neville Chamberlain, British prime minister, enabling him to annex Czechoslovakia. He signed a non-aggression treaty with the Soviet Union, 1939. He declared war on Poland Sept. 1, 1939, precipitating World War II.

With total defeat near, Hitler committed suicide in Berlin Apr. 1945. The victorious Allies voided all acts and annexations of Hitler's Reich.

Postwar changes. The zones of occupation administered by the Allied Powers and later relinquished gave the Soviet Union Saxony, Saxony-Anhalt, Thuringia, and Mecklenburg, and the former Prussian provinces of Saxony and Brandenburg.

The territory E of the Oder-Neisse line within 1937 boundaries comprising the provinces of Silesia, Pomerania, West Prussia and the southern part of East Prussia, totaling about 41,220 sq. mi., population (1939) 9,600,000, was taken by Poland. Northern East Prussia was taken by the Soviet Union. Several million Germans emigrated from these territories to W. Germany.

The Western Allies ended the state of war with Germany in 1951. The USSR did so in 1955.

There was also created the area of Greater Berlin, within but not part of the Soviet zone, administered by the 4 occupying powers under the Allied Command. In 1948 the Soviet Union withdrew and established its single command in East Berlin. The Communists cut off supplies, whereupon the Allies utilized a gigantic airlift to bring food to West Berlin during 1948-1949. In Aug. 1961 the East Germans built a wall dividing Berlin, after over 3 million E. Germans had emigrated.

East Germany

Area: 40,646 sq. mi. Population (UN est. 1975); 16,850,000. Capital: East Berlin. Monetary unit: DDR Mark.

The German Democratic Republic was proclaimed in the Soviet sector of Berlin Oct. 7, 1949. Wilhelm Pieck was named president, reelected 1953, and 1957 (died Sept. 7, 1960); Willi Stoph, prime minister; Walter Ulbricht, Communist party secretary. The unicameral legislature is called the Volkskammer or People's Chamber. A ministry of state security, the SSD, and a militarized People's Police were organized.

The Soviet Union proclaimed East Germany a sovereign republic Mar. 25, 1954, but kept Soviet troops there on grounds of security and the 4-power Potsdam agreement.

The Volkskammer approved a constitutional amendment Sept. 12, 1960, that abolished the presidency, replacing it with a new Council of State designated as East Germany's highest governing body, with Walter Ulbricht as chairman.

Ulbricht negotiated a treaty with Poland placing Poland's boundary at the line formed by the Oder and Neisse Rivers. The U.S. registered its disapproval, declaring that it violated the Potsdam agreement and that no boundaries could be settled "unilaterally or bilaterally" outside a peace treaty. The Republic also ratified an agreement with Czechoslovakia, accepting the expulsion of over 2 million Germans from Sudetenland as "permanent and just." Its industry was integrated with other communist nations.

The Volkskammer abolished, 1952, the 5 traditional provinces of East Germany as administrative units in favor of 14 districts of 217 counties. Brandenburg, Mecklenburg, Saxony, and Thuringia were divided into 3 districts each, Saxony-Anhalt into 2.

Coincident with the entrance of West Germany into the European Defense Community, May 27, 1952, the East German government decreed a prohibited zone 3 mi. deep along its 600-mile border with West Germany and cut Berlin's telephone system into 2 sections. Berlin was further divided by erection of a fortified wall, 1961, but the exodus of refugees from East Germany into Western sectors continued though on a much smaller scale. By 1974, 37,000 had crossed

to the west since 1961, plus thousands of retired people.

The regime signed a 20-year treaty of friendship and co-operation with the USSR June 12, 1964.

East Germany suffered severe economic problems until the mid-1960s. A "new economic system" was introduced, easing the former central planning controls and allowing factories to make "profits" provided they were reinvested in operations or distributed to workers as bonuses. By the early 1970s, the economy was highly industrialized, and was the world's ninth greatest industrial power. In May 1972 the few remaining private firms were ordered sold to the government. The nation was credited with the highest standard of living among communist countries. Exports in 1975 totaled $10,088 million, with imports of $11,290,000.

On Apr. 8, 1968, a new constitution, announced as approved by 94.49% of voters, went into effect. It reaffirmed Communist party control and close ties with the USSR. A 1974 amendment removed all mention of reunification.

In May 1971 Ulbricht resigned as leader of the Communist party and was replaced by Erich Honecker, but retained his post as chairman of the Council of State. Ulbricht died Aug. 1, 1973.

Travel restrictions between the 2 Germanies were eased in the first formal treaty signed by the 2, in May 1972, and millions of W. Germans have since visited the GDR. The GDR gained admission to the UN in Sept. 1973.

The U.S. and East Germany established diplomatic relations Sept. 4, 1974. East Germany agreed to negotiate claims of U.S. citizens for properties seized under the Nazis.

Regular armed forces total 143,000. An est. 370,000 Soviet troops are stationed in East Germany.

West Germany

Area (including West Berlin): 95,815 sq. mi. Population (Govt. est. 1975): 61,830,000. Capital: Bonn. Monetary unit: Deutsche Mark.

The climate and terrain are varied, with fertile lowlands in the N, rolling farmlands and forests in the center, and mountainous areas in the S.

The Federal Republic of Germany was proclaimed May 23, 1949, in Bonn, after a constitution had been drawn up by a consultative assembly formed by representatives of the 11 laender (states) in the French, British and American zones. Later reorganized into 9 units, the laender numbered 10 with the addition of the Saar Jan. 1, 1957: Schleswig-Holstein, Hamburg, Lower Saxony, Bremen, North Rhine-Westphalia, Hesse, Rhineland-Palatinate, Baden-Wuerttemberg, Bavaria, Saarland. Berlin also was granted land (state) status, but the 1945 occupation agreements placed restrictions on it.

The occupying powers, the U.S., Britain, and France, restored the civil status, Sept. 21, 1949. The U. S. resumed diplomatic relations July 2, 1951. The powers lifted controls and the republic became fully independent May 5, 1955.

Parliament has 2 chambers, serving 4-year terms. The Bundestag, lower house, is elected. It has 496 voting members from the republic and 22 nonvoting observers from West Berlin. The Bundesrat, upper house, represents the states; it has 41 delegates from the laender and 4 non-voting members from West Berlin. The Bundesrat president serves one year and acts as deputy to the federal president.

The federal president is elected for a 5-yr. term by the Federal Assembly, convened for this purpose only and made up of deputies of the Bundestag and an equal number of delegates from the land parliaments. Re-election is possible only once. The president concludes treaties with foreign states, and signs laws, which must be countersigned by the chancellor and the minister in charge. The chancellor is elected for a four-year term by the Bundestag.

Dr. Konrad Adenauer, Christian Democrat, was made chancellor Sept. 15, 1949, re-elected 1953, 1957, 1961. Dr. Ludwig Erhard, Christian Democrat, was elected 1963. Kurt Georg Kiesinger was elected chancellor Dec. 1, 1966, heading a coalition government of Christian Democrats and Social Democrats. Willy Brandt, heading a coalition of Social Democrats and Free Democrats, became chancellor Oct. 21, 1969.

In 1970 Brandt signed friendship treaties with the USSR and Poland. In 1971, the U.S., Britain, France and the USSR signed an agreement on Western access to West Berlin. In 1972 the Bundestag approved the USSR and Polish treaties and East and West Germany signed their first formal treaty, implementing the agreement easing access to West Berlin. In 1973 a West Germany-Czechoslovakia pact normalized relations and nullified the 1938 "Munich Agreement." In 1974 Bonn agreed to extend $350 million yearly in long-term credits to East Germany until 1981.

In May 1974 Brandt resigned, saying he took full responsibility for "negligence" for allowing an East German spy to become a member of his staff. Helmut Schmidt, Brandt's finance minister, succeeded him.

West Germany is a member of NATO, EC, European Coal and Steel Community and Council of Europe. Both West and East Germany gained full membership in the UN in Sept. 1973.

Resources and Industries. West Germany has experienced tremendous economic growth since 1950. It is one of the world's top industrial nations, though a recession slowed growth in the mid-1970's.

West Germany leads Western Europe as a steel producer. Shipyards annually produce more than 1 million gross registered tons of shipping, more than half of it for export. The oil industry has a refining capacity of more than 133 million tons annually. Some of the 2.6 million foreigners working in West Germany left during a 1974-75 economic slowdown. The FRG leads European countries in provisions for worker participation in industry.

The merchant fleet on Jan. 1, 1974, had 702 vessels over 1,000 gross tons each.

Some of more important crops are wheat, rye, barley, oats, potatoes, sugar beets and hay. Other commercial products are fruit, tobacco, hops, nuts.

Principal minerals are coal, lignite, iron, zinc, lead, copper, salt, potash, and petroleum. Bulk of mining is in North Rhine-Westphalia, Central Germany, the Harz, and Westerwald. Oil comes chiefly from Emsland near the Netherlands border, and Lower Saxony. Iron and steel production is greatest in the Ruhr and Saar.

Frankfurt Rhine-Main airport, 3d largest in Europe, handles annually about 5 million passengers and is 2d largest in freight shipments.

Foreign trade, in thousands of U.S. dollars:

	Imports	Exports
1974	$70,240,000	$90,590,000
1975	$75,619,000	$91,620,000

Education and Religion. The Federal Republic and West Berlin have 46 universities, several technical universities and over 100 musical, theological, and other institutions of higher education. School attendance is compulsory, ages 6 to 15.

Complete religious freedom is guaranteed by the constitution. The country (1970) is 49% Protestant, 44.6% Roman Catholic. The Evangelical Church in Germany (EKD) was formed by the Lutheran, United and Reformed churches after World War II, supplanting an earlier group.

Defense. Armed Forces, 1975, total 495,000. About 214,000 U.S., 55,000 British, and 60,000 French troops are stationed in West Germany.

Helgoland, an island of 130 acres in the North Sea, was taken from Denmark by a British Naval force in 1807 and later ceded to Germany to become a part of Schleswig-Holstein province in return for rights in East Africa. The heavily fortified island was surrendered to Great Britain, May 23, 1945, demilitarized in 1947 and returned to West Germany, Mar. 1, 1952. It is a free port.

The Saar (Fr. Sarre), 10th land (state) of the Federal Republic, is an industrial and mining area N of Lorraine, originally 738 sq. mi., now extended to about 991 and population (1973) of 1.1 million. Capital: Saarbrucken. After World War II it had semi-autonomy and economic links to France until it became a German state again Jan. 1, 1957.

Ghana

Area: 92,100 sq. mi. Population (Govt. est. 1975): 9,870,000. Capital: Accra. Monetary unit: Cedi.

The Republic of Ghana, a member of the UN and the Commonwealth, is composed of the former British Gold Coast colony including Ashanti and Northern Territories, and British Togoland, former UN trusteeship. Slightly smaller than Oregon, it faces the Gulf of Guinea in Western Africa, bounded N by Upper Volta, E by Togo and W by the Ivory Coast.

Resources and Industries. Ghana is rich in mineral wealth. It ranks among world leaders in production of diamonds (mostly industrial type), manganese, gold, and bauxite.

Ghana is the world's leading cocoa producer; it exports up to 470,000 tons annually, about 30% of world output. Timber is 2d in value, including mahogany and rare woods.

The huge Akosombo hydroelectric project on the Volta River, partly financed by U.S., was completed in 1965 and began serving Ghana's 1st giant industry, an aluminum reduction plant near the port of Tema, built by U.S. companies. In 1972-73 the government pressed a program of both small and large farms, "Operation Feed-Yourself," to cut costly food imports.

History and Government. Named after an earlier African state along the Niger River, 800-1076 A.D., Ghana has long been settled by the Adansi, Akwamu, Ga and other tribes, and was ruled by Great Britain for 113 years. Its independence was gained by rapid steps after 1951 when Britain granted the colony a new constitution and its chief spokesman, Kwame Nkrumah, was elected prime minister. The UN General Assembly on Dec. 13, 1956, approved termination of the British Togoland trusteeship and merger of the territory with the new state following a 1956 plebiscite.

Full independence within the Commonwealth, with a British governor-general, was effective Mar. 6, 1957. Ghana became a republic July 1, 1960, but remained within the Commonwealth. Kwame Nkrumah became president.

In 1964 a referendum gave Nkrumah dictatorial powers and made Ghana a one-party Socialist state.

Nkrumah built hospitals and schools, raised the literacy rate, created a state-owned airline and ship line, but ran the country into debt, jailed hundreds of political dissenters and was accused of corruption.

On Feb. 24, 1966, a National Liberation Council of Army and police officers took over the government. The Council expelled Communist Chinese and East German teachers and technicians. It promised a "balanced neutrality" and slashed expenditures.

Elections were held in Aug. 1969 and Ghana returned to civilian rule, with an elected National Assembly, a prime minister and a president.

On Jan. 13, 1972, a National Redemption Council, headed by Army Col. Ignatius K. Acheampong, took over the government in a bloodless coup. His government has sought national self-reliance.

Greece

Area: 50,547 sq. mi. Population (Govt. est. 1975):

9,050,000. Capital: Athens. Monetary unit: Drachma.

Greece occupies the southern part of the Balkan peninsula, reaching into the Mediterranean Sea with the Ionian Sea on the W and the Aegean Sea on the E. Its neighbors are Albania, Yugoslavia, Bulgaria and Turkey. The Pindus Mtns. run through the country N to S. Total length of the heavily indented coastline is 9,385 mi. Hundreds of islands account for 8,918 sq. mi. of the total land area, which is approx. that of Alabama; 166 islands are inhabited, among them Crete, Rhodes, Milos, Kerkira (Corfu), Chios, Lesbos, Samos. Principal seaport is Piraeus, near Athens.

Resources and Industries. One-fourth of the total area is arable: 13,350,000 of the total of 16,074,000 acres are covered by mountains, lakes and rivers. Four-fifths of the forests are state-owned. Chief agricultural products are wheat, rye, barley, oats, corn, rice, cotton, tobacco, olives, citrus fruits, raisins, and figs. Sheep are the most important livestock.

Heavily damaged in World War II, Greece's industrial and agricultural output has far surpassed prewar levels thanks to economic development programs helped in part by U.S. aid. Hydroelectric development is remedying the lack of coal. Principal industries are textiles, food-processing, wine, cement, chemicals, aluminum.

Greek-owned merchant marine tonnage is the largest in the world, but much of it is registered under other flags.

Over 50% of exports are industrial goods; agricultural exports include tobacco, cotton, citrus fruits, raisins, vegetables. Ores, esp. bauxite, are also important. Aiding the economy is the tourist industry, which produced $436 million in 1974.

Foreign trade, in thousands of U.S. dollars:

	Imports	Exports
1974	$4,385,000	$2,030,000
1975	$5,457,000	$2,288,000

History and Government. The achievements of Ancient Greece in art, architecture, science, mathematics, philosophy, drama, literature and democracy became legacies for succeeding ages. Greece reached the height of its glory and power, particularly in the Athenian city-state, in the 5th century B.C.

Greece fell under Roman rule in the 2d and 1st centuries B.C. In the 4th century A.D. it became part of the Byzantine Empire and, after the fall of Constantinople to the Turks in 1453, part of the Ottoman Empire.

Greece won its war of independence from Turkey 1821-1829, and became a kingdom under guarantee of Britain, France and Russia, 1830. A republic was established 1925; the monarchy was restored, 1935, and George II, King of the Hellenes, resumed the throne. In Oct., 1940, Greece rejected an ultimatum from Italy. Nazi support resulted in the defeat and occupation of Greece by Germans, Italians and Bulgarians. By the end of 1944 the invaders withdrew. Communist resistance forces were defeated by Royalist and British troops.

A plebiscite recalled King George II. He died Apr. 1, 1947, and was succeeded by his brother, Paul I.

Communists waged guerrilla war 1947-49 against the government but were defeated with the aid of the U.S. (acting under the Truman Doctrine).

A period of reconstruction and rapid development followed, mainly with conservative governments under Premier Constantine Karamanlis. The Center Union led by George Papandreou won elections in 1963 and 1964. King Constantine, who succeeded his father March 6, 1964, forced Papandreou to resign. A period of political maneuvers ended in the military takeover of April 21, 1967, by Col. George Papadopoulos. King Constantine tried to reverse the consolidation of the harsh dictatorship Dec. 13, 1967, but failed and fled to Italy. Papadopoulos was ousted Nov. 25, 1973, in a coup led by rightist Brig. Demetrius Ioannides.

Greek army officers serving in the National Guard of Cyprus staged a coup on the island July 15, 1974. Turkey invaded Cyprus a week later, precipitating the collapse of the Greek junta, which was implicated in the Cyprus coup.

The military turned the government over to former Premier Karamanlis, called back from exile. Karamanlis named a civilian cabinet, including anti-junta elements, freed political prisoners, and sought to settle the Cyprus crisis. Karamanlis held elections Nov. 17, 1974, which gave his party a large parliamentary majority, though local elections in 1975 showed leftist gains. A referendum held Dec. 8, 1974, resulted in the proclamation of a parliamentary republic.

Education and Religion. Greek Orthodox Church is the official church. Nine years of education is compulsory. There are 6 schools of university rank in Athens, and others in Thessaloniki, Patras and Ioannina.

Defense. Military strength totaled 161,000.

Greece is a member of the UN and an associate member of EC. It withdrew its forces from NATO during the 1974 crisis with Turkey over Cyprus.

Dodecanese and Crete

The **Dodecanese** are a group of 13 islands in the southeastern Aegean Sea. They were occupied by Italy during the Balkan War of 1912 against Turkey and though claimed by Greece were retained by Italy. Rhodes is the capital.

After World War II the islands were ceded to Greece at the Paris Conference of Foreign Ministers, June 27, 1946, and annexed Mar. 7, 1948.

Crete, largest Greek island and 5th largest in Mediterranean, original site of Minoan civilization, lies SE of the Peloponnesus peninsula and is 160 mi. long, 35 mi. wide, with area of 3,207 sq. mi. Principal towns: Heraklion (Candia) and Khania (Canea).

Grenada

Area: 133 sq. mi. Population: (est. 1976) 119,000. Capital: St. George's. Monetary unit: Grenadian dollar.

Southernmost in the long arc of the Windward Islands, Grenada (pronounced gren-ay-dah) lies in the SE Caribbean, 90 mi. N of the Venezuelan coast. The main island is mountainous and roughly 21 mi. by 12; the nation's territory includes Carriacou and Petit Martinique, 13 sq. mi. together.

Formerly a British Associated State with limited self-government, Grenada became fully independent Feb. 7, 1974 during a general strike. It is the smallest independent nation in the Western Hemisphere. It is a member of the Commonwealth group of nations and the UN.

First European visitor was Christopher Columbus, 1498. First European settlers were French, 1650. The island was held alternately by France and England until final British occupation, 1784. Beginning in 1925, self-government was gradually increased.

Over 50% of the population is of African descent; over 40% of mixed descent, including descendants of indentured laborers from India; there are a few Carib Indians, descendants of the original inhabitants, and a few whites. About 60% are Roman Catholics; others include Anglicans and Methodists. The language is English; a French-African patois is also spoken.

The economy is agricultural; main products are nutmegs, bananas, cocoa, sugar, rum, and mace.

Guatemala

Area: 42,042 sq. mi. Population (est. 1976): 6,064,-000. Capital: Guatemala City. Monetary unit: Quetzal.

Guatemala lies between Mexico on the N and El Salvador and Honduras on the S. To the east is Belize (British Honduras) which Guatemala claims. It is about the size of Ohio. It faces on both the Caribbean and the Pacific. There are numerous volcanoes in the south, more than a half dozen over 11,000 ft. About 41% of the population is pure Indian and most of the remainder is of mixed Spanish and Indian descent.

There are famous Mayan ruins in Uaxatcun, Tikal and other sites in the north, at Zaculeu in the west and at Quirigua, about 140 mi. from Guatemala City.

Santo Tomas and Puerto Barrios, main ports on the Atlantic, are connected by rail and road with Guatemala City in the highlands and ports on the Pacific.

Resources and Industries. Agriculture is the most important industry, the Guatemalan soil being exceedingly fertile. Coffee accounts for a third of the exports. Other important export crops are sugar, meat, bananas, cotton, chicle gum. Rare woods and cattle are important. Silver, gold, copper, iron, lead, zinc, and nickel are found. A search for oil is being pressed in the north, where natural gas has been found. Shoes and textiles are manufactured.

History and Government. The old Mayan Indian empire flourished in what is today Guatemala for over 1,000 years before the Spanish conquest.

Guatemala was a Spanish colony 1524-1821; briefly a part of Mexico and then of the U.S. of Central America; the republic was established in 1839.

Since 1945 when a liberal government was elected to replace the long-term dictatorship of Jorge Ubico, the country has seen a swing toward socialism, an armed revolt, renewed attempts at social reform and a military coup. Assassinations and political violence from left and right plagued the country. Leftist guerrillas killed a U. S. ambassador in 1968 and a West German ambassador in 1970.

A 1976 earthquake killed 20,000 Guatemalans and left over 1 million homeless.

In Mar. 1974 Gen. Kjell Laugerud Garcia was elected president, amidst charges of voting fraud.

Education and Religion. Roman Catholicism is the dominant religion. Education is compulsory. There are 5 universities in Guatemala City, with divisions in Quezaltenango. The language is Spanish.

Guatemala is a member of the UN and OAS.

Guinea

Area: 94,925 sq. mi. Population (UN est. 1975): 4,420,000. Capital: Conakry. Monetary unit: Syli.

Guinea, a former French Overseas Territory, is in western Africa with the Atlantic on the W, Guinea-Bissau, Senegal and Mali on the N, Ivory Coast on the E and Liberia and Sierra Leone on the S. Chief tribes are the Fullah, Malinke, and Soussou. Guinea is about the size of Oregon.

Guinea has a variety of climates, from the humid coastal tropics (Conakry, the capital has an average annual rainfall of 169") to cooler plateaus and uplands. Wildlife is varied and abundant, including elephant, hippopotamus, buffalo, antelope, lion, leopard, chimpanzee.

Resources and Industries. Although Guinea is still primarily an agricultural country, the importance of minerals to its economy is growing. Bauxite, iron and diamonds (both gem and industrial) are the principal minerals. Bauxite mines have been developed by both private Western and Soviet programs.

Economic progress has been aided by large grants from both communist and non-communist countries. Acceleration of agricultural output is a government goal. Chief agricultural exports are bananas and pineapples. Production of rice, the staple food of the population, has been expanded. Other crops include corn, palm nuts, coffee, and honey.)

History and Government. With France's acquiescence, Guinea proclaimed itself an independent republic Oct. 2, 1958. Premier Sekou Toure became first president. The nation's first constitution was adopted Nov. 12, 1958. It provided for rule by a president with a term of 7 years and a National Assembly elected by universal suffrage. The Political Bureau of the single legal party, the Parti Democratique de Guinee, exercises great power in making governmental decisions. Guinea is a member of the UN and OAU. French is the official language.

Guinea has agreements with Czechoslovakia, East Germany, Poland, USSR and Communist China, and has criticized U.S. policies in Africa, but continues to avow a neutral course. France and Guinea restored diplomatic relations in 1975, after a 10-year suspension.

Guinea-Bissau

Area: 13,948 sq. mi. Population (UN est. 1975): 530,-000. Capital: Bissau.

Portuguese Guinea, a colonial possession of Portugal, achieved independence as Guinea-Bissau, a republic, Sept. 10, 1974. Almost twice the size of New Jersey, it is in West Africa, facing the Atlantic to the W with Senegal to the N and Guinea to the E and S. The land is mostly level and low, with forests, swamps and numerous offshore islands.

Portuguese mariners explored the area in the mid-15th century; the slave trade flourished in the 17th and 18th centuries, but in the 19th colonization began. In the early 20th century, Portuguese troops put down uprisings in the interior.

Beginning in the 1960s, the African Party for the Independence of Guinea-Bissau and the Cape Verde Islands conducted guerrilla warfare against Portuguese troops and formed a government in the interior with an elected National Assembly. The party's founder, Dr. Amilcar Cabral was slain in nearby Guinea in 1973 and his brother Luiz became Guinea-Bissau's first president. The Soviet Union, which had supplied arms to the rebels, handed over several MIG jets after independence.

The Cape Verde Islands, once linked with Portuguese Guinea, lie in the Atlantic some 300 mi. NW of Bissau. The islands, independent in 1975, were expected to merge with Guinea-Bissau.

Most of the Guinea-Bissau population is black with about 2,200 white and 10,000 of mixed descent. Most follow tribal religions; a large minority are Moslems.

There is little industry. Chief products are peanuts, palm oil, and hides. In 1972 a large deposit of bauxite and traces of oil were discovered. The country belongs to the UN and OAU.

Guyana

Area: 83,000 sq. mi. Population (Govt. est. 1975): 794,348. Capital: Georgetown. Monetary unit: Guyana dollar.

British Guiana, a British colony for 152 years, became the independent nation of Guyana on May 26, 1966, and a republic in 1970. It was the first South American nation to become independent since Venezuela in 1830.

Fronting on the Atlantic in northern South America, Guyana borders on Venezuela, Brazil and Surinam. It is about the size of Kansas. The population is about 55% of East Indian (from India) descent, 35.5% of African descent, 10% others (American Indians, Chinese, and European's). Ethnic tensions have influenced political life.

Dense tropical forests cover much of the land, although a flat coastal area up to 40 mi. wide, where 90% of the population lives, provides rich alluvial soil for agriculture.

Sugar and rice are the main cash crops and account

for almost half the total exports. Other products are coconuts, coffee, cocoa, citrus and other fruits, shrimp, timber, and livestock.

The main industry is the mining of bauxite ore; Guyana is the 5th largest producer of the mineral, supplying 4.5% of the world's needs; the industry has been nationalized. Also exported are gold and diamonds. Deposits of a wide range of other minerals have been found but not yet exploited.

Manufacturing has shown an average 5% annual growth; products include cigarettes, rum, clothing, furniture, drugs, soap, food products, and insecticides.

Guyana was visited in 1499 by Spanish sailors. Originally a Dutch possession, the country became a British possession in 1814. African slaves and indentured servants from India were brought in to work on plantations. The Indians soon outnumbered the Negro population and still do. Venezuela has claimed ownership of the western half of Guyana. In 1970 an agreement suspended the claim for 12 years. The Surinam border is also disputed.

Guyana has an elected Assembly, which chooses the president. A prime minister heads the government. It is a UN and Commonwealth member.

Most of the economy has been nationalized and reorganized along communist lines, though political freedoms continue in force.

Haiti

Area: 10,714 sq. mi. Population (Govt. est. 1975): 4,580,000. Capital: Port-Au-Prince. Monetary unit: Gourde.

Haiti occupies the western third of the island known as Hispaniola, the second largest of the Greater Antilles, lying between Cuba on the W and Puerto Rico on the E. The boundary which separates Haiti from the Dominican Republic to the E is 241 mi. long. Haiti is a little larger in area than Maryland.

Blacks comprise over 90% of the population, the remainder being mixed descendants of both slaves and French settlers.

Resources and Industries. Major mineral exports are bauxite and copper. Other minerals are gold, silver and cement.

Coffee is the chief product, along with sisal, cotton, sugar, bananas, cocoa, tobacco, and rice, molasses and rum are produced; valuable woods are exported.

Haiti encourages tourism and is served by several major airlines, with an international jet airport at Port-au-Prince. However, tourist spending and private foreign investment in Haiti dwindled under the regime of President Francois Duvalier. They revived in 1971 after his death. Economic improvement was reported, 1972-74, but drought and famine struck in 1975.

History and Government. Haiti, visited by Columbus, 1492, and a French colony from 1677, attained its independence, 1804, following the rebellion begun by Toussaint L'Ouverture. There were Republican constitutions in 1806 and 1816. In 1811 Henri Christophe proclaimed himself king in the north; the south continued to be a republic, with a president. Henri died in 1820 and President Jean Pierre Boyer reunited the nation. Following a period of political violence, 1910-1915, the U. S. occupied the country. The occupation terminated Aug. 14, 1934.

Five regimes failed between 1950-1957. In Sept., 1957, Dr. Duvalier was elected president for a 6-year term. In June 1964 a new constitution made Dr. Duvalier president-for-life. There were unsuccessful outbreaks against his rule in 1963 and 1970. He died Apr. 21, 1971, and was succeeded by his son, Jean-Claude Duvalier, 19, as president-for-life.

Haiti is a member of the UN and OAS.

Education and Religion. Roman Catholicism and Voodoo are the main religions. Education is officially compulsory, but illiteracy rate is est. at 85%. French is the official language of the country, but French Creole, a dialect, is spoken by the majority.

Honduras

Area: (Govt. est.): 43,277 sq. mi. Population (UN est. 1975): 3,040,000. Capital: Tegucigalpa. Monetary unit: Lempira.

Honduras is a republic in Central or Middle America, bounded on the N by the Caribbean; E and S by Nicaragua; S by Pacific Ocean and El Salvador; W by Guatemala. It is about the size of Pennsylvania.

The Caribbean coast is 500 mi. long. On the Pacific side the coast, on the Gulf of Fonseca, is 40 mi. long. There are ports on both coasts. The country is mountainous, very fertile, with rich forests. The inhabitants are mostly of mixed Spanish and Indian descent.

At Copan, near the western border, are the imposing remains of a large Mayan city which flourished around the 4th century A.D.; it had disappeared by the time Spaniards arrived in 1576.

Resources and Industries. Minerals are abundant but undeveloped and include gold, silver, copper, lead, zinc, iron, antimony and coal. The chief export is bananas, coffee, timber, cotton, sugar, tobacco, and cattle raising are important. A peasant movement to spur land reform gained force in the 1970.

Manufacturing industries are small but growing; they include clothing, textiles, cement, chemicals, food products. In 1974 the government said it would nationalize the lumber industry; lumber export is controlled by the government.

History and Government. Honduras became independent after freeing itself from Spain, Sept. 15, 1821, and from the Fed. of Central America, 1838.

Pres. Ramon Villeda Morales, elected Nov. 15, 1957, was overthrown in a military coup Oct. 3, 1963, and replaced by a military regime headed by Oswaldo Lopez Arellano. The country returned to constitional government and Lopez was inaugurated president June 6, 1965.

The 1965 constitution provided for a president and Congress, both elected for 6 years. In free elections, Mar. 28, 1971, Ramon Ernesto Cruz was chosen president. In Dec. 1972 Lopez seized the presidency again; he was ousted by the army in 1975 over charges of pervasive bribery by United Brands Co. of the U.S.

Honduras and El Salvador fought a 5-day war in July 1969 over the presence in Honduras of 300,000 Salvadorean workers and settlers. After new clashes in 1970, a demilitarized zone was agreed on. But minor clashes took place in 1976.

Honduras is a member of the UN and OAS.

Education and Religion. Education is secular and free. The literacy rate is about 50%. Roman Catholicism is the prevailing religion. The language is Spanish.

Hungary

Area: 35,919 sq. mi. Population (Govt. est. 1975): 10,540,000. Capital: Budapest. Monetary unit: Forint.

The Hungarian People's Republic, in central Europe, is bounded by Czechoslovakia, the USSR, Romania, Yugoslavia and Austria. It is about the size of Indiana.

The Danube forms the Czech border in the NW, then swings S to bisect the country. The eastern half of Hungary is mainly a great fertile plain, the Alfold; the west and north are hilly.

Resources and Industries. Before World War II, Hungary was primarily agricultural, but industry has surpassed it in value. The index of industrial production (1970 100) was 136 for 1975. Most means of production have been nationalized.

Major economic reforms were launched early in 1968, switching from a central planning system to one where market forces and a profit principle control much of production. Productivity was reportedly increased.

About 70% of foreign trade is with Eastern bloc countries. Foreign trade in thousands of US dollars.

	Imports	Exports
1974	$5,576,000	$5,130,000
1975	$7,176,000	$6,090,000

In addition to a wide range of grains and vegetable crops, fruit production has expanded. Near Tokay, in the northeast, the best-known Hungarian wines are vinted.

Industries include iron and steel, machines, machine tools, chemicals, vehicles, railways and communications equipment, milling, and distilling. Hungary has become an important supplier of industrial products to communist bloc countries. Hungary produces large amounts of bauxite. Also important is natural gas.

Tourism from both E and W Europe has increased.

History and Government. Earliest settlers, chiefly Slav and Germanic, were overrun by Huns and Magyars from the east. Stephen I (997-1038) was made king by Pope Silvester II in 1001 A.D. The country suffered repeated Turkish invasions in the 15th-17th centuries. After the defeats of the Turks, 1686-1697, Austria dominated, but Hungary obtained concessions until it regained internal independence in 1867, with the emperor of Austria as king of Hungary in a dual monarchy with a single diplomatic service. Defeated with the Central Powers in 1918, Hungary lost Transylavania to Romania, Croatia and Bacska to Yugoslavia, Slovakia and Carpatho-Ruthenia to Czechoslovakia. A republic under Michael Karoly and a bolshevist revolt under Bela Kun were followed by a vote for a monarchy in 1920 with Admiral Nicholas Horthy as regent.

Hungary joined Germany in World War II; he was removed and Nazi supporters put in power, 1944. Russian troops captured most of the country, 1945. By terms of an armistice with the Allied powers Hungary agreed to give up territory acquired by the 1938 dismemberment of Czechoslovakia and to return to its borders of 1937.

Hungary declared for a republic Feb. 1, 1946, and elected Zoltan Tildy president. In 1947 the communists forced Tildy out. A Soviet-type constitution was adopted Aug. 18, 1949, which vests formal power in a Presidential Council and a National Assembly of 349 members elected for 4-year-terms. Hungary is a member of the UN and Warsaw Pact.

Premier Imre Nagy, in office since mid-1953, was ousted for his moderate policy of favoring agriculture and consumer production, April 18, 1955.

In 1956, popular demands for the ousting of Erno Gero, Communist party secretary, and for formation of a government by Nagy, resulted in the latter's appointment Oct. 23; demonstrations against communist rule developed into open revolt when police fired on demonstrators. Gero called in Soviet forces. On Nov. 4 Soviet forces launched a massive attack against Budapest with 200,000 troops, 2,500 tanks and armored cars.

Estimates varied from 6,500 to 32,000 dead. Many rebels were reported executed and thousands deported. Between 170,000 and 196,000 persons fled the country (though some have since returned). The U.S. received 38,248 under a refugee emergency program. In the spring of 1963 the regime freed many anti-communists and captives from the revolution in a sweeping amnesty.

Nagy was executed by the Russians. Janos Kadar, sponsored by the USSR, became first secretary of the Hungarian Workers (Communist) party. By the 1970's, Hungary led the communist nations in tolerance for cultural freedoms and small private enter-

prise.

In 1973 Hungary agreed to pay the U.S. $18,900,000 for nationalized U.S. properties in Hungary, but minor disputes have prevented full trade relations.

Education and Religion. There is no state religion, and all are tolerated. About two-thirds of the population were Roman Catholics; most of the remainder, Calvinists.

Public school education is compulsory and free from 6 to 16. Most church schools were nationalized in 1948. There are 91 insititutes of higher learning. The language is Hungarian (Magyar).

Jozsef Cardinal Mindszenty, Roman Catholic primate, was jailed in 1949. He was freed by the 1956 insurgents and granted refuge in the U. S. Embassy. In 1971 he went into exile in Vienna. In 1975 he was removed as primate by Pope Paul VI.

Defense. Military forces totaled 105,000. About 40,000 USSR troops are stationed in Hungary. Hungary is a member of the UN and the Warsaw Pact.

Iceland

Area: 39,702 sq. mi. Population (Govt. est. 1976): 220,000. Capital: Reykjavik. Monetary unit: Krona.

The Republic of Iceland is an island of volcanic origin, close to the Arctic Circle in the North Atlantic. There are geysers and hot springs and the climate is modified by the Gulf Stream. Iceland is about the size of Virginia.

Natural hot water from volcanic springs is piped into towns and provides heat for office buildings, homes and hot houses. In Jan. 1973 a volcanic eruption on Heimaey forced evacuation of 5,500 residents of the small island off the SE coast of Iceland.

Resources and Industries. Agriculture engages about 11% of the population; industry and services 70%; fisheries 14%. About six-sevenths of the land is unproductive and only about 65,000 acres are under cultivation, producing potatoes, turnips, and hay. The fishing industry is most important. It includes herring, cod and haddock. Fish products, in salted, smoked, canned or frozen form, account for two-thirds of exports.

Iceland's largest industrial plants include an ammonium nitrate factory, an aluminum smelter, a cement factory, and a diatomite plant. Hydroelectric power is being developed.

History and Government. Iceland was an independent republic, 930-1262; then it joined with Norway. The two came under Danish rule in 1380. Denmark acknowledged Iceland as a sovereign state, 1918, united with Denmark only in that the Danish King Christian X, was also king of Iceland. In 1941 the Althing (Parliament) voted to dissolve all ties with Denmark, and adopted the constitution of a republic. The republic, with a president and prime minister, was proclaimed June 17, 1944.

Iceland celebrated the 1,000th anniversary of the Althing, the oldest parliamentary assembly in the world, in 1930. The prime minister and his cabinet are responsible to the Althing. There is universal suffrage for men and women at age 20.

In 1972 Iceland barred foreign ships from fishing within 50 mi. of its coast, and expanded its fishing limit to 200 miles in 1974. British trawlers defied the ban and in 1973 were fired on by Icelandic gunboats. A 1976 accord reduced British fishing activities with the 200-mile limit. Iceland claimed that fish stocks had been threatened.

A conservative coalition won power in June 1974 and stopped plans to oust U. S. NATO Air Force and Navy personnel, which totalled 2,900 in 1975.

Education and Religion. The Icelandic language has maintained its purity, as in Eddas and Sagas, for 1,000 years. Danish and English also are taught. Eight years of elementary education is compulsory. There is no illiteracy. The national church is Evangelical Lutheran, but there is complete religious freedom.

Defense: Iceland has no Army, Navy, Air Force or forts. It is a charter member of NATO. It is also a member of the UN, Council of Europe and Nordic Council.

India

Area: 1,229,737 sq. mi. Population (Govt. est. 1974): 598,170,000. Capital: New Delhi. Monetary unit: Rupee.

An independent republic since 1950 and a member of the Commonwealth, India occupies most of the subcontinent of India. It is a third the size of the U.S.

India's climate varies from tropical heat in the south to the nearly Arctic cold of the Himalayas. Approximately 22.3% of the area is forested.

The population is 80% rural, 20% urban. The annual increase rate, 2-1/2%, causes food and housing shortages. In 1967 the government supplemented its birth control programs with monetary inducements to men to volunteer for sterilization. Strong birth control measures were introduced in 1976 at the federal and state levels.

Sikkim, bordered by Tibet, Bhutan, Nepal and India, formerly British protected, became a protectorate of India in 1950. Area, 2,818 sq. mi.; population 1974, 210,000; capital, Gangtok. In Apr. 1973 the chogyal, the hereditary ruler asked Indian troops to help suppress demonstrations against his rule. In May he and India signed an agreement providing for a legislative assembly. In Sept. 1974 India's Parliament voted to make Sikkim an associate Indian state, absorbing it into India. The monarchy was abolished in an April, 1975 referendum.

Kashmir, a predominantly Moslem region in the northwest, has been in dispute between India and Pakistan since 1947 when British rule was ending and Indian and Pakistani troops entered the area. A cease-fire was negotiated by the UN, Jan. 1, 1949; it gave Pakistan control of one-third of the area, in the west and northwest, and India the remaining two-thirds, the Indian state of Jammu and Kashmir. In late Aug. 1965, clashes broke out along the line and soon involved the armed forces of the 2 nations in a spreading war.

On Sept. 20, 1965, the UN Security Council demanded a cease-fire; both sides agreed. The USSR invited India and Pakistan to a conference at Tashkent, USSR, and on Jan. 10, 1966, the 2 signed the "Tashkent Declaration," pledging to withdraw their forces to behind the old cease-fire line. A new truce line, slightly altering the old cease-fire line, was agreed on in Dec. 1972, accommodating changes made during Dec. 1971 fighting.

There were also clashes in April 1965 along the Assam-East Pakistan border and in the **Rann** (swamp) **of Cutch** area along the West Pakistan-Gujarat border near the Arabian Sea. An international arbitration commission on Feb. 19, 1968, awarded 90% of the Rann to India, 10% to Pakistan.

France, 1952-54, peacefully yielded to India its 5 colonies on the Bay of Bengal, former French India, comprising Pondicherry, Kirkal, Mahe, Yanaon, and Chandernagor, totalling 196 sq. mi. and 346,000 pop.

Goa, 1,426 sq. mi., pop., 1962, 626,978, which had been ruled by Portugal since 1505 A.D., was taken by India by military action Dec. 18, 1961, together with 2 other Portuguese enclaves, Daman and Diu, located about 250 mi. S. of Bombay.

India is a union of 22 states and 9 centrally administered union territories.

Resources and Industries. Agriculture occupies 70% of the workers. Principal food products are rice, corn, millet, wheat, barley, coffee, sugar cane, spices, tea, cashew nuts. Other important products include cotton, copra, coir, jute, linseed, rubber, lumber.

Severe droughts in northern areas have repeatedly

threatened mass starvation and brought large shipments of grain from the U.S. In July 1967 plentiful rains broke the drought; there were bumper crops, 1968-72; the drought and food shortages returned in 1972-75, but a bumper crop in 1976 assured self-sufficiency.

Indian agriculture has made progress with high-yield seeds, fertilizers, irrigation and limited mechanization.

For many years India has had large textile industries with a wide variety of cotton, woolen, and silk products. In the 1960s, other industries, including steel, processed foods, cement, machinery, chemicals, and fertilizers came into prominence, along with many finished products such as sewing machines, typewriters, bicycles, telephones, and transportation equipment.

India's 1st nuclear power plant, built with U.S. help, was dedicated in 1970 near Bombay; Canada helped India build 2 reactors. In May 1974 India exploded a nuclear device underground, assertedly for peaceful development. Canada halted shipments of nuclear equipment and material to India. Restricted shipments from both the U.S. & Canada resumed in 1976. An Indian space satellite was launched by the USSR April 19, 1975.

The 1975 index of industrial production (1970 100) was 119. Much industrial production, distribution and prices are regulated by law. Railroads, airlines, banks, insurance, and coal industries are state-owned, as are some steel plants.

India is a leading producer of coal, mica, and manganese; also important are salt, iron ore, bauxite, and gypsum. Exports include tea, sugar, raw and processed jute, cotton fabrics, and other textiles, tanned hides and skins, manganese ore, pepper, tobacco. Largest trade is with the U.S. There are indications of offshore oil in the Bay of Bengal.

Foreign trade, in thousands of U.S. dollars:

	Imports	Exports
1974	$4,932,000	$3,876,000
1975	$6,094,000	$2,203,000
		(6 mo.)

History and Government. India has one of the oldest civilizations in the world. Excavations trace the Indus Valley civilization back for at least 5,000 years. Paintings in the mountain caves of Ajanta in South India, richly carved temples, the Taj Mahal in Agra and the Kutab Minar in Delhi are among relics of the past.

Vasco da Gama established Portuguese trading posts 1498-1503. The Dutch followed. The British East India Co. sent Capt. William Hawkins, 1609, to get concessions from the Mogul emperor for spices and textiles. Operating as the East India Co. the British gained control of most of India. The British parliament assumed political direction; under Lord Bentinck, 1828-35, rule by rajahs was curbed, infanticide stopped, suttee (suicide of a widow on her husband's funeral pyre) made illegal. After the Sepoy troops mutinied, 1857-58, the British supported the native rulers.

Nationalism grew rapidly after World War I. The National Congress and the Moslem League demanded constitutional reform. A leader emerged in Mohandas K. Gandhi (called Mahatma, or Great Soul), born Oct. 2, 1869, assassinated Jan. 30, 1948. A Hindu, trained in law in England, he began advocating self-rule, non-violence, pursuit of native handicrafts, removal of untouchability (which forced millions of poor to remain menials by heredity) in 1919. In 1930 he launched "civil disobedience," including boycott of British goods and rejection of taxes without representation.

In 1935 Britain gave India a constitution providing a bicameral federal congress. Suffrage was granted about 30 million. Mohammed Ali Jinnah, head of the Moslem League, sought creation of a Moslem nation, Pakistan.

Following more than 40 years' active struggle for freedom by both Hindus and Moslems, the British government announced Feb. 20, 1947, its intention to partition India into 2 dominions and set June, 1948, for British withdrawal from India. Aug. 15, 1947, was designated Indian Independence Day. India became a self-governing member of the Commonwealth and a member of the UN. The dominion became a democratic republic, Jan. 26, 1950.

It was estimated that more than 11 million refugees (Hindus and Moslems) crossed the India-Pakistan borders in a mass transferral of some of the two peoples during 1947; about 200,000 were killed in communal fighting.

The constitution provides for a president, elected for a 5-year term by an electoral college consisting of members of both houses of Parliament (Council of States and House of the People), and elected members of the lower houses of the federating states. A Council of Ministers (cabinet) is headed by a prime minister who is the practical head of the government. The federating states have governors, appointed by the president, at the head of state organizations similar to the federal system.

Prime Minister Mrs. Indira Gandhi, named Jan. 19, 1966, succeeded Lal Bahadur Shastri, who on June 2, 1964, succeeded India's first prime minister, Jawaharlal Nehru. Mrs. Gandhi, Nehru's daughter, was no relation to Mahatma Gandhi. Nehru, prime minister from the beginning of India's independence in 1947, died May 27, 1964.

Long the dominant power in India's politics, the Congress party lost some of its near monopoly by 1967. The party split into New and Old Congress parties in 1969. Mrs. Gandhi's New Congress party won control of the House.

Threatened with adverse court rulings in a voting law case, an opposition protest campaign and strikes, Gandhi invoked emergency provisions of the constitution June, 1975. As many as 175,000 opponents were arrested and press censorship imposed. Measures to control prices, protect small farmers and improve productivity were adopted, with some success.

After Pakistan troops began attacks on Bengali separatists in East Pakistan, Mar. 25, 1971, some 10 million refugees fled into India. On Aug. 9, India and the USSR signed a 20-year friendship pact while U.S.-India relations soured. India and Pakistan went to war Dec. 3, 1971, on both the East and West fronts. Pakistan troops in the East surrendered Dec. 16; Pakistan agreed to a cease-fire in the West Dec. 17.

India and Pakistan signed a pact agreeing to withdraw troops from their borders and seek peaceful solutions, July 3, 1972. In Aug. 1973 India agreed to release 93,000 Pakistanis held prisoner since 1971; the return was completed in Apr. 1974. The two countries resumed full relations in 1976.

Education and Religion. The constitution provides for free, compulsory education through age 14, though this is not yet universally enforced. There are now 96 universities, some 2,000 colleges, and 27 research institutes.

There are 14 language groups, 12 originating from Sanskrit, and over 1,600 "mother tongues." Hindi is spoken by 30%, with Urdu, the principal Moslem language, spoken by 5%. Hindi became the official language in Jan. 1965 with English the associate official language. Much government work and instruction at universities is done in English. English-language dailies outsell those of any other language.

The religion of 83% of the people is Hinduism. The constitution guarantees freedom of worship. Moslems are the largest minority, 61,417,934 in the 1971 census; there were 14,223,382 Christians, 10,378,797 Sikhs, 3,812,325 Buddhists, 2,604,646 Jains. Hindus totaled 453,292,086.

Defense. Military forces total 56,000.

Indonesia

Area: 735,268 sq. mi. Population (Govt. est. 1974): 127,590, **Capital: Jakarta. Monetary unit: Rupiah.**

Indonesia, world's largest archipelago, lies along the Equator SE of Asia, N and NW of Australia. Indonesia comprises about 13,000 islands, including Java (one of the most densely populated areas in the world with 1,500 persons to the sq. mi.), Sumatra, Kalimantan (most of Borneo), Sulawesi (Celebes) and West Irian (Irian Jaya, the west half of New Guinea). Among others are Bangka, Billiton, Madura, Bali, Timor. The land area is 6 times that of New Mexico.

Many races are included, the principal ones being Achinese, Bataks, Menangkabaus, Javanese, Sundanese, Madurese, Balinese, Sasaks, Menadonese, Buginese, Dayaks and Papuans.

The capital, called Batavia by the Dutch, is Jakarta, on the island of Java.

Resources and Industries. Indonesia is one of the richest countries in natural resources. There are vast supplies of tin, oil and coal, and sizable deposits of bauxite, manganese, copper, nickel, gold, and silver.

Agriculture occupies 80% of the population. Products include rice, maize, casava, peanuts, soybeans, tobacco, coffee, rubber, cinchona, pepper, kapok, coconuts, palm oil, tea, sugar, and indigo.

Inflation spiraled during the 1960's, but by 1969 comparative stability was achieved and a 5-year development plan was undertaken. Oil accounts for more than half of export income, followed by rubber and timber. Indonesia is the world's 13th largest oil producer. There are food processing, textile and other small factories.

History and Government. Until March, 1942, Indonesia was a Netherlands overseas territory. Following Japanese military occupation, 1942-1945, nationalists, led by Dr. Sukarno and Dr. Hatta, proclaimed a republic Aug. 17, 1945. Four years of intermittent warfare between Netherlands and Indonesian forces ended with agreements signed Nov. 2, 1949, transferring sovereignty over all Indonesia, except Netherlands New Guinea (West Irian) to a new interim government effective Dec. 27, 1949. Dr. Sukarno was elected president, Dec. 16, 1949. On July 20, 1950, the member states agreed to form a strongly centralized government; a unitarian state with an amended constitution was proclaimed Aug. 15 and its name formally changed to Republic of Indonesia. It joined the UN 1950.

After the Dutch in Nov. 1957 rejected proposals for new negotiations over West Irian, Indonesia's government stepped up the seizure of Dutch property. A U.S. mediator's plan was adopted in 1962, providing that West Irian be turned over temporarily to the UN, then to Indonesia. Under the agreement Indonesia pledged to hold a plebiscite allowing the people of West Irian the choice of staying with Indonesia or separating from it. The UN turned the area over to Indonesia May 1, 1963. In 1969, voting by tribal chiefs and other representatives favored staying with Indonesia.

President Sukarno suspended the original elected 257-member Parliament Mar. 5, 1960, announced a new 261-member appointed group, Mar. 27, and swept aside anti-leftist criticism. He was named president-for-life May 18, 1963.

The USSR announced in 1964 plans to step up its contributions of modern arms to Indonesia to aid in attempting to "crush" the new nation. Malaysia, formation of which Indonesia opposed. In 1964 and 1965 Indonesia staged numerous guerrilla raids into Malaysia.

Indonesia withdrew from the UN in Jan. 1965. Many anti-American demonstrations were staged at U.S. consulates, including stonings, during the year.

Indonesia's large, pro-Peking Communist party tried to seize complete control Sept. 30, 1965, taking strategic points and murdering 6 high generals. The army smashed the coup and later intimated that Sukarno had played a role in it. In Central and East Java, Reds seized control of several districts and fighting continued. It was later reported that at least

100,000 communists were executed.

Gen. Suharto was named head of the Army. He was named president for a 5-year term by the Consultative Assembly Mar. 27, 1968. He was reelected in Mar. 1973.

On Aug. 11, 1966, Indonesia and Malaysia signed an agreement ending the Sukarno policy of hostility to Malaysia. On Sept. 28 Indonesia resumed membership in the UN. The U. S. resumed economic aid.

In July 1971, in the first popular vote in 16 years, a coalition party backing the Suharto government won a strong majority in the House of Representatives.

The former territory of Portuguese Timor became Indonesia's 27th province, July 17, 1976. The area had been occupied by Indonesian troops during a local civil war.

Education and Religion. 90% of the inhabitants are Moslems, the remainder Christians, Hindus and Buddhists. There is compulsory primary education for children 6 to 12. There are 26 state universities, more than 10 vocational or religious institutions, and a number of private universities. Literacy is about 60%. Many languages are spoken; the official one is Bahasa Indonesia, derived from Malay.

Armed Forces total 266,000.

Iran

Area: 636,363 sq. mi. Population (Govt. est. 1975): 33,020,000. Capital: Tehran. Monetary unit: Rial.

A constitutional monarchy, Iran is a mountainous land, much of it a high plateau region, in SW Asia. Slightly larger than Alaska, it has coastlines on the Caspian Sea, Persian Gulf and Gulf of Oman. For neighbors it has the USSR, Afghanistan, Pakistan, Iraq and Turkey. Large salt deserts comprise 25% of the land but there are many oases and forest areas.

Tehran, Isfahan, Shiraz and Abadan have jet airports. Shiraz is noted for ancient ruins of Persepolis.

Resources and Industries. Iran is the world's 4th largest oil producer and 2d largest exporter; petroleum provides most of its foreign exchange and government income. Iran refused to join the 1973-74 Arab oil embargo, but did join in raising oil prices.

In 1974 Iran invested some of its oil wealth in a multi-billion dollar trade pact with France including nuclear energy facilities; a 25% interest in West Germany's Krupp enterprises, and a $1.2 billion loan to Britain. In 1975, Iran signed an 8-year agreement to facilitate $25 billion in purchases in the U.S., to further Iran's five-year development plan, including 8 large nuclear power plants.

Other mineral wealth includes chromite, copper, iron, lead, manganese, zinc, barite, sulphur and coal. Also mined are emeralds and turquoise.

Foreign trade, in thousands of U. S. dollars:

	Imports	Exports
1974	$5,672,000	$21,554,000
1975	$10,963,000	$19,978,000

The first Iranian steel mill, near Isfahan, was built by the Soviet Union and paid for by natural gas piped to the USSR. Iran has contracted with the French for development of a petrochemical industry. There are cement, vehicle assembly and sugar refining plants.

Agriculture is a prime industry; wheat, barley, corn, rice, fruits, gums, wool, tobacco, raw silk, sugar beets, and cotton are the chief products. Some wines are famous, as are Persian carpets. Sturgeon fishing in Caspian Sea is important, especially for caviar. Major dams built in the 1960s provide hydroelectric power and aid irrigation.

Under Shah Mohammed Reza Pahlavi's rule, Iran has undergone economic and social change. Improvements included land reform, the spread of literacy and wide gains in women's rights.

History and Government. Iran is the official name to the country long referred to as Persia. The Iranians, who came from the E during the 2d millenium B.C., were an Indo-European people related to the Aryans of India, and included Medes, Persians, and other groups. Use of the name Iran became widespread in the 1920s and 1930s.

In 549 B.C. Cyrus the Great united the Medes and Persians in the Persian Empire, conquered Babylonia, 538 B.C., restored Jerusalem to the Jews. Darius I began the invasion of Greece, was defeated at Salamis, 480 BC. and Plataea, 479 B.C. Alexander the Great of Macedon defeated Darius III 333 B.C.

Subsequently Persia was ruled by the Seleucids; the Parthians, beginning c. 250 B.C.; the Sassanians, c. 226 A.D. Arabs brought Islam to Persia in the 7th century and for many years the religious-political Caliphate ruled the land. Omar Khayyam (c. 1050-c. 1123) wrote his famous Rubaiyat and created a calendar renowned for its accuracy.

Mongols invaded the country in 1250 and again under Tamerlane c. 1370. After the downfall of the Mongols in 1502 Persia became a monarchy under a shah.

In 1906 a constitution was enacted. It provided for an executive with power vested in a cabinet and government officials who act in the name of the shah. The legislature has a national assembly (Majlis) elected for 4 years and a senate of 60, 30 elected and 30 nominated by the shah. Women voted and were elected to the legislature for the first time in 1963. Only one party is tolerated. The government killed about 100 purported terrorists in 1976 street battles.

The shah is Mohammed Reza Pahlavi (born Oct. 26, 1919), ascended in 1941. After divorcing his first two wives for failing to bear a male heir, the shah married Farah Diba Dec. 21, 1959; Crown Prince Reza Pahlavi was born Oct. 31, 1960.

British and Russian forces entered Iran Aug. 25, 1941, withdrawing later. Britain and the USSR signed an agreement Jan. 29, 1942, to respect Iranian integrity and give economic aid. In 1946 a Soviet attempt to take over the Azerbijan region in the NW was defeated when a puppet regime was ousted by force.

In 1951 the Majlis nationalized the oil industry, the Anglo-Iranian Oil Co. closed its refinery.

The shah in 1954 signed an agreement with a consortium of British, U.S., Dutch and French companies. In 1973 a new agreement gave the National Iranian Oil Co. control over all operations.

In 1969-74 Iran and Iraq were involved in a dispute over Iran's right to use the Shatt al Arab, a border river estuary, for shipping. Border clashes, reflecting rivalry for power in the Persian Gulf area, continued in 1974. Iraq acceeded to Iran's border claims in a June 13, 1975 pact. In late 1971, Iran occupied 3 islands at the mouth of the gulf, claimed by states of the United Arab Emirates. Iran in the 1970's modernized its military forces, aided by multi-billion dollar purchases from the U.S. Economic aid to Egypt, and military aid against leftist Oman rebels advanced Iran's regional status in the 1970s.

Education and Religion. The Shiah branch of Islam predominates. Education is free and nominally compulsory. There are 7 universities. A Literacy Corps of high school and college graduates teaches in rural areas in lieu of military service. A Health Corps is patterned after the Literacy Corps. The language is Farsi (Persian), written in Arabic script.

Defense. Military strength totals 250,000.

Iran is a member of the UN and CENTO.

Iraq

Area: 172,000 sq. mi. Population (Govt. est. 1975): 1,120,000. Capital: Baghdad. Monetary unit: Dinar.

Iraq, constitutionally an "Arab, Islamic republic," occupies Mesopotamia, the area around the Euphrates and Tigris Rivers, about twice the size of Utah. It is bounded by Turkey, Iran, the Persian (also called Arabian) Gulf, Kuwait, Saudi Arabia, Jordan, and Syria.

The country is mostly alluvial plain. The temperature varies widely: 120°F in the shade is common, contrasted with severe frosts in the winter.

Resources and Industries. Wheat, barley, rice, dates, millet, and cotton are the chief crops, with tobacco grown in the Kurdish hills. Sheep are raised in the north and wool and skins are exported; textiles are produced.

Iraq is the world's 6th largest oil producer. Most of its national income is from oil. New fields were developed with USSR aid, 1970-72. In June 1972 Iraq nationalized the Western-controlled Iraq Petroleum Co., and nationalized other U.S. oil interests in Oct. 1973. Exports, 1974, were $7.551 billion.

History and Government. The Tigris-Euphrates valley was the site of the ancient cities of Eridu, Ur, Nineveh and Babylon. The Sumerian culture of 3000 B.C. influenced Crete, Egypt, and Greece.

Iraq, then known as Mesopotamia, was taken from Turkey in World War I. The League of Nations gave a mandate to Britain, which ended 1932 when Iraq was recognized as a sovereign state.

Emir Faisal, then king of the Hejaz, was chosen ruler by a referendum in 1921; a constitutional monarchy was created in 1924. On his death, 1933, he was succeeded by his son Ghazi, who died, 1939; succeeded by his son, Faisal II.

King Faisal was assassinated July 14, 1958, when the Free Officers, led by Brig. Gen. Abdul Karim Kassem revolted and proclaimed Iraq "part of the Arab nation." Gen. Kassem became premier of a republic. Iraq received Soviet arms aid. It withdrew from the Baghdad pact and 3 U.S. arms agreements.

After several coups, the government was taken over by a group headed by Gen. Ahmed Hassan al-Bakr, a member of the international Baath Socialist party, July 17, 1968.

On June 7, 1967, Iraq broke diplomatic relations with the U. S. following Egyptian charges that America was aiding Israel in the 6-day, 1967 war, but U.S. exports and diplomatic contacts grew in the 1970s.

In 1969, in a series of trials, Iraq condemned and executed more than a score of citizens as spies for Israel, Iran and the U.S. It had border clashes for several years with Iran in a dispute over navigation rights on the Shatt al Arab, a border river estuary, till a 1975 pact conceded Iranian claims. Iraq reportedly maintained 12,000 troops in Jordan as part of the Arab confrontation with Israel. It withdrew them in 1971. In April 1972 Iraq and the USSR signed a friendship pact. Soviet military aid was increased; several thousand Soviet advisers were sent. In Mar. 1973 Kuwait charged Iraqi troops entered its territory in a border dispute. In the 1973 "Yom Kippur" war, Iraq sent forces to aid Syria, but disputes with Syria persisted over sharing of river waters.

Years of battling with the Kurds, a minority in the northeast area, led to a 1970 recognition by the government of partial Kurdish autonomy. Renewed fighting resulted in total defeat for the Kurds in 1975, when Iran withdrew support. Egyptian Arab immigrants have reportedly been settled in Kurdish areas.

Education and Religion. Elementary and secondary education is free and compulsory. Arabic is spoken by 75%, Kurelish by 20%. The people are preponderantly Moslems, divided between the Sunni and Shiah sects, Christians number 250,000.

Defense. Military strength is 135,000.

Ireland

Area 26,600 sq. mi. Population (Govt. est. 1975): 3,130,000. Capital: Dublin. Monetary unit: Irish pound.

Ireland, or Eire, an island in the Atlantic near the European mainland, is a republic about the size of W. Va. It is separated from Great Britain on the E by the Irish Sea and the North Channel and on the SE by St. George's Channel. The northern one-sixth of the island is part of the United Kingdom.

Ireland consists mainly of a central plateau surrounded by isolated groups of hills and mountains. Ireland's coastline is much indented by the sea, affording many inlets and coves. The mean annual temperature ranges from 48°F, in the N to 52°F, in the S. There are numerous lakes (called loughs); the best known are those of Killarney. The most important river is the Shannon, about 250 mi. long. Tallest mountains are in SW; Carrantuohill, 3,414 ft. in Kerry; Brandon Hill on the coast, 3,127 ft.

Tourist attractions include the scenery, historic houses, cultural and folk festivals and medieval banquets. The famous Blarney stone is in an old castle in the village of Blarney, 4 mi. NW of Cork.

Emigration had been high and for years the population remained static. Since 1961, however, emigration has decreased and steady population growth has resumed.

Resources and Industries. About 28% of the work force is employed in agriculture, forestry and fishing. The nearness of the Gulf Stream causes considerable rainfall; lush pastures of the "Emerald Isle" support an extensive cattle and dairy industry. Important crops are potatoes, wheat, oats, barley, sugar beets, fruits and vegetables. Food and animals comprise 43% of the exports.

Industrialization increased, 1962-74, with over 750 new factories, many with foreign participation. Major industries are tobacco, food processing, vehicle assembly, metals, textiles, chemicals and brewing. Gains have been recorded in electrical and nonelectrical machinery, fertilizers and computers.

A mining boom, following discovery of zinc, lead and silver deposits, brought new strength to the economy. The index for general industrial production rose (1970=100) to 124 in 1974. Natural gas was discovered off the SE coast in May 1974.

Tourism normally provides Ireland with earnings of up to $250 million annually.

Foreign trade, in thousands of U. S. dollars:

	Imports	Exports
1974	$3,812,000	$2,630,000
1975	$3,768,000	$3,177,000

A switch to decimal currency was made in 1971.

History and Government. Celtic tribes invaded the islands about the 4th century B. C.; their Gaelic culture and literature flourished and spread to Scotland and elsewhere in the 5th century A. D., the same century in which St. Patrick converted the Irish to Christianity. Invasions by Norsemen began in the 8th century, but were ended with defeat of the Danes by the Irish King Brian Boru in 1014. English invasions started in the 12th century; for over 700 years the Anglo-Irish struggle continued with bitter rebellions and savage repressions.

The Easter Monday Rebellion (1916) failed but was followed by guerrilla warfare and harsh reprisals by British troops, the "Black and Tans." The Dail Eireann, or Irish parliament, reaffirmed independence in Jan. 1919. The British offered dominion status to Ulster (6 counties) and southern Ireland (26 counties) Dec. 1921. The constitution of the Irish Free State, a British dominion, was adopted Dec. 11, 1922. By treaty with Britain Northern Ireland could vote itself out, which it did, Dec. 12, 1922.

A new constitution adopted by plebiscite came into operation Dec. 29, 1937. It declared the name of the state Eire in the Irish language and Ireland in the English and declared it a sovereign democratic state.

On Dec. 21, 1948, an Irish law declared the country a republic rather than a dominion and withdrew it from the Commonwealth. In 1949 the British Parliament recognized both actions, but re-asserted its claim to incorporate the 6 northeastern counties in the United Kingdom. This claim has not been recognized by Ireland. *See United Kingdom — Northern Ireland.*

First president was William T. Cosgrave, 1922-32. Eamon de Valera, hero of the rebellion, was president 1932-38, 1959-66, 1966-73. He was prime minister 1937-48, 1951-54, 1957-59.

Following Feb. 28, 1973, elections the Fianna Fail party was ousted from power after 16 years, although it won 69 seats, by a coalition of Fine Gael, 54 seats, and Labor, 19. Independents won 2. Liam Cosgrave became prime minister.

The parliament is composed of a house, Dail Eireann, of 144 elected members, and a senate, Seanad Eireann, of 60, 11 of them nominated by the prime minister, 6 by the universities and the rest elected from 5 panels of candidates representing public interests.

Irish governments have favored peaceful unification of all Ireland. Ireland cooperated with England against terrorist groups. In 1974 Ireland and Britain agreed to create a Council of Ireland, a body with limited functions of which both the Republic and Northern Ireland would be represented.

Education and Religion. Roman Catholicism is the prevailing religion, claiming more than 90% of the population. About 4% belong to Protestant churches. In a 1972 referendum voters repealed a Constitutional provision giving the Roman Catholic Church a "special position."

Elementary education is free and compulsory. The Irish language is a required study, though English is the native tongue of most. All daily newspapers are in English.

Defense. Armed forces total 13,200.

Ireland is a member of the UN, Council of Europe and the EC.

Israel

Area: (pre-1967) 8,017 sq. mi.; (post 1967) over 30,000 sq. mi. Population (Govt. est. 1975, pre-1967 territory): 3,410,000. Capital: Jerusalem. Monetary unit: Israeli pound.

The state of Israel was re-established, as a republic, in 1948. It occupies part of the ancient land first called Canaan, then Israel, then Palestine. About the size of New Jersey, it faces the Mediterranean to the W, Lebanon to the N, Syria and Jordan to the E, and Egypt to the SW.

The coastal plain on the W is 120 mi. long, 15 wide, fertile and well watered. In the center is the plateau of Judea. A triangular-shaped semi-desert region, the Negev, extends from south of Beersheba to an apex at the head of the Gulf of Aqaba. The eastern border drops sharply into the depressed valley of the River Jordan and the Dead Sea, which is 46 mi. long, with an average width of 8 mi., 1,296 ft. below sea level, lowest point on the earth's surface.

Israel's area, as defined by armistices with the Arab nations, includes all the land assigned to it under the 1947 partition resolution of the UN General Assembly, as well as Western Galilee and a corridor to Jerusalem. By the terms of the armistice with Syria, July 20, 1949, last of the Arab states to end military action after the creation of modern Israel, demilitarized zones were set up on the eastern edge of Lake Huleh and the southeastern shore of the Sea of Galilee, site of Israel's Ein Gev settlement.

In the Israel-Arab war of June 1967 Israel occupied the Sinai Peninsula, the west bank of the Jordan and a small area of Syria. Parts of Sinai were surrendered in 1974 and 1975 accords.

Non-Jewish population (1974): Moslem, 392,500; Christian, 84,500; Druse and others, 41,600. Martial law for the Arab minority was ended in 1966.

The chief ports are Haifa, Ashdod, and Eilat.

Resources and Industries. Citrus fruit is the most valuable agricultural product. Other principal crops include wheat, barley, durra, olives, melons, grapes, figs, tomatoes, bananas, cotton. Since 1955 total cultivated area has been increased from 412,500 to well over 1 million acres, of which 454,000 acres are under irrigation. Wine making is extensive.

Israel has deposits of limestone, sandstone, gypsum, copper, iron, phosphates, magnesium, manganese, ceramic clays. The valley of Jordan and the Dead Sea yield rock salt, sulphur, and potash.

Israel's over-all economy and industrialization have both grown rapidly. The economy has been aided by German reparations payments, U. S. aid, international loans and contributions. West Germany completed payment of $860 million in reparations (cash and goods) in 1965. The 2 countries also set up full diplomatic relations.

The index of industrial production (1970=100) was 138 in 1975.

The Negev region in the south is Israel's primary development area, receiving nearly half of the immigrants. It has large phosphate deposits, copper, oil, natural gas, and potash.

A 150-mi. pipeline, major link in Israel's national water plan, was completed in June 1964 and began carrying water from Lake Kinneret (Sea of Galilee) to the Negev. Desalinization plants have been built.

In 1970 Israel completed construction of a 160-mi., 42-inch, oil pipeline from Elath on the Gulf of Aqaba to Ashkelon on the Mediterranean.

Israel's first atomic reactor at Nahal Rubin began operations in July, 1960. The nation launched its first successful solid-fuel rocket 50 mi. into the atmosphere July 5, 1961, for meteorological study. Israel has denied reports that it had assembled 10-20 atom bombs.

Israel's main exports are citrus fruits, polished diamonds, chemicals, textiles and fashion goods, machinery, plastics, tires, and pharmaceutical products. In 1975, Israel signed agreements with the U.S. to facilitate investments in Israel, and with the Common Market allowing free trade.

Tourism is second only to citrus products in earnings, over $150 million annually.

Foreign trade in thousands of U. S. dollars:

	Imports	Exports
1974	$4,179,000	$1,734,000
1975	$4,140,000	$1,835,000

History and Government. The Jewish people lived in Israel from before 1200 B.C.; many were driven from the land by various conquerors. The Judaic moral and ethical code and the Bible originated here. The modern Zionist movement for a homeland in Palestine, led by Dr. Chaim Weizmann, caused the cabinet of Great Britain to give its support in the Balfour Declaration, Nov. 2, 1917. Under the Palestine Mandate, about four-fifths of historic Palestine was detached in 1922 to form Trans-Jordan, now the Kingdom of Jordan. When the Nazi persecutions began in Germany great numbers of Jews set out for Palestine. The UN General Assembly voted Nov. 29, 1947, to partition Palestine into two independent states by Oct. 1, 1948. A separate enclave of Jerusalem, area 289 sq. mi., was to be administered by a UN official. Britain gave up its mandate May 15, 1948.

A new state, the Republic of Israel, was proclaimed May 14, 1948. A few hours later, the armies of Egypt, Jordan, Syria, Lebanon and Iraq, with Saudi Arabian contingents, crossed the frontiers at several points. They were defeated.

Separate armistices with the Arab nations were signed in 1949, but no general peace settlement was obtained. The Arab nations continued policies of economic boycott, blockade in the Suez Canal, political warfare and local incitement.

After persistent terrorist provocations, Israel invaded Egypt's Sinai, Oct. 29, 1956, aided briefly by British and French forces. A UN ceasefire was arranged Nov. 6.

An uneasy truce between Israel and the Arab countries, supervised by a UN Emergency Force, prevailed until May 19, 1967, when the UN force withdrew at the demand of Egypt's President Gamal Abdel Nasser. Egyptian forces rapidly reoccupied the Gaza Strip and closed the Gulf of Aqaba to Israeli shipping. In a full-scale 6-day war that started June 5, the Israelis took the Gaza strip, occupied the Sinai Peninsula to the Suez Canal, and captured Old Jerusalem, Syria's Golan Heights and Jordan's West Bank. The fighting was halted June 10 by UN-arranged cease-fire agreements.

By 1969-70 there were almost daily Egyptian-Israeli artillery duels across the Suez Canal as well as ground forays and air raids with Israeli planes penetrating deep into Egypt. Palestinian guerrilla raids and Israeli reprisals continued across the Jordanian, Syrian, and Lebanese frontiers; there were also encounters with Syrian and Jordanian forces.

It was est. in 1970 there were 10,000 or more Soviet military men in Egypt, and increasing supplies of Soviet planes and anti-aircraft missiles, some of which Israel charged were manned by Russians. In July 1972 most of the Russians, then est. at 20,000, were sent home by Egypt.

In June 1970 the U.S. proposed a 3-month, standstill cease-fire and peace negotiations. Israel, Egypt and Jordan agreed. Palestinian guerrilla groups said they would continue attacks.

The cease-fire was formally ended by Egypt Mar. 7, 1971, but continued unofficially. Terrorist attacks continued in 1972-73 and Israel made reprisal raids in Lebanon and Syria.

Egypt and Syria launched a surprise war on Israel, Oct. 6, 1973 (Yom Kippur, most solemn day on the Jewish calendar). Egypt and Syria were supplied by massive USSR military airlifts; the U.S. responded with an airlift to Israel. Israel counter-attacked, driving the Syrians back, and crossing the Suez Canal to surround Suez City and trap the Egyptian 3d Army in its Sinai salient.

Israel and Egypt agreed to a UN cease-fire which took effect Oct. 24; a UN peace-keeping force went to the area. A disengagement agreement was signed Jan. 18, 1974, following negotiations by U.S. Secretary of State Henry Kissinger. Israel withdrew from the canal's W bank. A second withdrawal was completed in 1976; Israel yielded additional Sinai territory including an oil field. Some 200 unarmed American technicians were stationed to monitor the cease-fire. The U.S. agreed to provide substantial arms aid to Israel.

Israel and Syria agreed to disengage June 1; Israel completed withdrawing from its salient (and a small part of the land taken in the 1967 war) June 25.

In the wake of the war, Golda Meir, long Israel's premier resigned; severe inflation gripped the nation. Palestinian guerillas staged massacres, killing scores of civilians 1974-75. Israel conducted preventive attacks in Lebanon through 1975. By mid-1974 the USSR had replenished arms and equipment lost by Syria in 1973.

Israeli forces raided Entebbe, Uganda, July 3, 1976, and rescued 103 hostages seized by Arab and German terrorists.

Israel is a parliamentary democracy. The first constituent assembly (Knesset), was formed Feb. 14, 1949, with 120 members, including 8 Arabs. The assembly elected Dr. Chaim Weizmann first president of Israel Feb. 17, 1949. He died Nov. 9, 1952. Israel's first premier was David Ben-Gurion.

The Knesset (Parliament) members are elected by universal suffrage for 4-year terms by all citizens over 18, under proportional representation.

Israel had diplomatic relations with 70 nations. Specialists in many fields shared their knowledge with those in less developed nations in Africa and elsewhere. But nearly all European Communist and black African nations broke off relations with Israel in 1972-74, the latter reportedly at the urging of Libya.

Education. Israel has compulsory education from 5 years of age to 16. Total enrollment in 6,620 schools in 1974 was 1,014,414. Of these, 146,377 were enrolled in Arab schools.

Over 60,000 students attend 7 universities and other specialized institutes.

Defense. Military service is compulsory for men and, between ages 18-26, unmarried women. Military forces total 146,000 which can be raised to 400,000 in 3 days by mobilization of reservists.

Israel became a member of the UN in 1949.

Italy

Area: 116,303 sq. mi. Population (Govt. est. 1975): 55,810,000. Capital: Rome. Monetary unit: Lira.

The Republic of Italy occupies a long peninsula shaped like a boot, extending SE from the Alps into the Mediterranean, with the island of Sicily separated from the mainland by the 2-mi. Strait of Messina at the toe of the boot. The country is about 700 mi. long and not over 220 mi. wide. Its area is about the same as Arizona's. Lying directly W of mid-Italy is the major island of Sardinia, slightly smaller than Sicily.

Sicily, 9,927 sq. mi., pop. (1971) 4,680,715, is an island 180 by 120 mi., seat of a region that embraces the island of **Pantelleria**, 32 sq. mi., and the **Lipari** group, 44 sq. mi., pop. 14,000, including 2 active volcanoes: **Vulcano**, 1,637 ft. and **Stromboli**, 3,038 ft. From prehistoric times Sicily has been settled by various peoples; a Greek state had its capital at Syracuse. Rome took Sicily from Carthage 215 B.C. **Mt. Etna**, 10,705 ft. active volcano, is tallest peak. Sicily leads in citrus fruits, also produces wheat, grapes, wine, sulphur, salt, olives. Cattle and sheep are raised.

Sardinia, 9,283 sq. mi., pop. (1971) 1,473,800, lies in the Mediterranean, 115 mi. W. of Italy and 7-1/2 mi. S of Corsica. Like Sicily, it is under a regional administration. It is 160 mi. long, 68 mi. wide, mountainous, with mining of coal, zinc, lead, copper; it raises grapes, olives, tobacco, also cattle and sheep. In 1720 Sardinia was added to the possessions of the Dukes of Savoy in Piedmont and Savoy to form the Kingdom of Sardinia. Giuseppe Garibaldi is buried on the nearby isle of Caprera. Capital: Cagliari.

Elba, 87 sq. mi., pop. 30,000, lies 6 mi. west of Tuscany. Industries include fishing, iron mining, wine making. Napoleon I lived in exile on Elba 1814-1815.

Capri, 4 sq. mi., pop. c. 9,000, 20 mi. SW of Naples, is famous for its beauty and equable climate.

The allure of historical monuments, great museums of painting and sculpture, imposing churches, as well as good living attracted 35.5 million tourists in 1973.

The 3.4-mi. Great St. Bernard tunnel, between Italy and Switzerland, first auto tunnel in the Alps, was opened Mar. 19, 1964. The Mont Blanc tunnel, 7.25-mi. linking Italy and France, was opened July 16, 1965.

Resources and Industries. Italy has enjoyed an extraordinary industrial growth since World War II. But in 1973-74, a fourfold increase in international oil prices helped disrupt the economy. Taxes were boosted in July 1974. Western aid helped ease the crisis in 1975. but inflation and decline in confidence continued in 1976.

Grapes, olives, citrus fruits, vegetables, wheat, rice, and cattle are the major agricultural products, but rural declines have necessitated increasing food imports. The wines of Italy have great variety. Chianti from Tuscany is popular, as are Asti Spumante, Orvieto, Capri.

White marble is quarried at Carrara, Volterra and Pisa; colored marble at Verona, Siena and Vicenza. Alabaster comes chiefly from Volterra.

Natural gas is found in the valley of the Po, the Marches, Abruzzi, Apulia, Basilicata, and Sicily.

In 1973 electric plants produced about 145.5 billion kwh. There were nuclear power plants. The electrical industry was nationalized in 1962.

Steel production was 23.8 million metric tons in 1974. Italy is a heavy producer of industrial and electrical machinery, automobiles (1.6 million passenger cars in 1974), steel products, typewriters, shoes, textiles, synthetic fabrics, machine tools. Its chemical industry has expanded rapidly.

The index of industrial production (1970=100) was 119.5 for 1974.

Italy's merchant marine ranks high. It has over 635 ships of more than 1.000 gross tons.

Tourism brings in $2.5 billion a year.

Foreign trade, in thousands of U.S. dollars:

	Imports	Exports
1974	$40,927,000	$30,253,000
1975	$38,366,000	$34,821,000

History and Government. Divided and dismembered since the fall of the Roman Empire, Italy began to reunite after the war of 1859 when Lombardy came under the crown of King Victor Emmanuel II of Sardinia. By plebiscite in 1860, Parma, Modena, Romagna and Tuscany joined, followed by Sicily and Naples, and by the Marches and Umbria. The first Italian parliament declared Victor Emmanuel king of Italy Mar. 17, 1861. Mantua and Venetia were added in 1866 as an outcome of the Austro-Prussian war. The Papal States were taken by Italian troops Sept. 20, 1870, on the withdrawal of the French garrison. The states were annexed to the kingdom by plebiscite. Italy recognized the State of Vatican City as independent Feb. 11, 1929.

Fascism appeared in Italy Mar. 23, 1919, led by Benito Mussolini, who took over the government at the invitation of the king Oct. 28, 1922. Mussolini acquired dictatorial powers and was called duce (leader). He made war on Ethiopia and proclaimed Victor Emmanuel III emperor, defied the sanctions of the League of Nations, joined the Berlin-Tokyo axis, sent troops to fight for Franco against the Republic of Spain and joined Germany in World War II.

After Fascism was overthrown in 1943, Italy declared war on Germany and Japan and contributed to the Allied victory. It surrendered conquered lands and lost its colonies. Mussolini was killed by partisans Apr. 28, 1945.

Victor Emmanuel III abdicated May 9, 1946; his son Humbert II was king until June 10, when Italy became a republic after a referendum, June 2-3.

The senate has 322 members elected for 5-year terms, plus 5 whom the president may appoint for life. Ex-presidents are eligible for life membership. The chamber of deputies has 630 members elected for 5 years. Titles of nobility are no longer recognized. Reorganization of the Fascist party is forbidden. The cabinet normally represents a coalition of the Christian Democrats, largest of Italy's many parties, and one or 2 other parties. After June 1976 elections, the Communists were given several important parliamentary posts. Voting age was lowered to 18 in 1975.

Twenty regional governments now perform functions previously belonging to central and local governments. Six were governed by the Communist Party or Communist-led coalitions in 1975.

Trieste. Following prolonged negotiations an agreement was signed Oct. 5, 1954, by Italy and Yugoslavia which gave Italy provisional administration over the northern section and the seaport of Trieste, with 90 sq. mi. and about 300,000 pop., and Yugoslavia the part of Istrian peninsula it had occupied, 200 sq. mi. and 73,500 pop., and provision for emergency access to the port. A formal agreement signed Nov. 10, 1975, confirmed this division as permanent.

Italy is a member of NATO, EC, and Council of Europe; admitted to the UN Dec. 14, 1955.

Education and Religion. Roman Catholicism is the state religion. In 1974 Italians voted by a 3-to-2 margin to retain a 3-year-old law permitting divorce which was opposed by the church.

Italy has 36 state universities, including Bologna (founded 1088), and 24 other institutes of higher education. Education is compulsory between the ages of 6 and 14.

Defense. Military forces total 421,000. A large proportion are committed to NATO.

Ivory Coast

Area: 124,503 sq. mi. Population (Govt. est. 1975): 6,500,000. Capital: Abidjan. Monetary unit: CFA franc.

The Republic of Ivory Coast, a former French Overseas Territory in West Africa, is on the coast of the Gulf of Guinea. Roughly oblong in shape and about the area of New Mexico, it is bounded by Liberia, Guinea, Mali, Upper Volta and Ghana and has 340 mi. of coastline on the Atlantic. Abidjan, the capital, is the chief port. A new port, San Pedro, opened in 1971.

Under the 1958 constitution of France, Ivory Coast became fully independent Aug. 7, 1960. Its present constitution was adopted Oct. 31, 1960. It signed an agreement, 1961, retaining close ties with France. Ivory Coast is a member of the West African Monetary Union with Benin, Niger, Senegal, Togo, and Upper Volta.

Agriculture, forestry, stock raising and fishing occupy 90% of the population. Chief export crops are coffee, cocoa, tropical woods and bananas; cotton, pineapples, rubber, rice, oil palms also are raised. Electric power, lumbering, and industrialization are being expanded.

The Ivory Coast has been the most prosperous of tropical African nations, with per 1975 capita income of $558. It has a favorable balance of trade. Exports grew and continued to exceed imports in 1975. The number of small factories also increased.

About 12% of the people are Catholics or Protestants; 23% are Moslems and the rest animists. French is the official language. Literacy is 65%, among the highest in Africa.

Jamaica

Area: 4,411 sq. mi. Population (UN est. 1975): 2,030,000. Capital: Kingston. Monetary unit: Jamican dollar.

Jamaica is a mountainous island in the Caribbean Sea, 90 mi. S of Cuba. Its area is 12% less than that of Connecticut.

Temperatures range from 80 to 86 on the coast and down to 40 in the Blue Mtns. Montego Bay and Ocho Rios are among popular resort areas; most of about 500,000 annual tourists are American.

Jamaica was visited by Columbus, 1494, and ruled by Spanish (under whom native Arawak Indians died out) until seized by the English, 1655. The island figures largely in the history of the buccaneers of the West Indies around the time of Sir Henry Morgan, once its governor. Port Royal, old haunt of the pirate, was largely destroyed by earthquake, 1692.

Jamaica won independence from Britain Aug. 6, 1962. There is a governor-general representing the British crown, an elected house of representatives and an appointed senate; executive power lies with a prime minister and cabinet.

Principal exports are bauxite (world's largest production) and alumina. Other products include sugar cane, coffee, bananas, rum, coconuts, ginger, molasses, cocoa, pimento, fruits, cigars, and petroleum products. About 50% of sugar cane is worked by worker-coops. Value of imports exceeds that of exports but earnings from tourism help offset this. Manufacturing plants have grown in number, aided by government-sponsored incentives. In 1974 Jamaica sought a large increase in taxes paid by U.S. and Canadian companies which mine bauxite on the island. The socialist government acquired 50% ownership of the companies in 1956. Political violence flared in 1975-76.

Japan

The World Almanac is sponsored in Japan by the Mainichi Newspapers, 1-1 Hitotsubashi, Chiyoda-ku, Tokyo 100; phone 03-212-0321. Mainichi founded 1876, Osaka, Japan; circulation 5,124,682 (m), 2,627,161 (e). (Mainichi Daily News, English Language 53,154); president Toshio Hiraoka; vice president, executive editor Jibei Inano.

Area: 143,574 sq. mi. Population (Govt. est. 1975): 110,950,000. Capital: Tokyo. Monetary unit: Yen.

Japan consists of 4 main islands: Honshu ("mainland"), 88,952 sq. mi.; Hokkaido, 30,304; Kyushu, 16,-191; and Shikoku, 7,240. Total area is about twice that of Missouri. The islands lie in the North Pacific separated from the Soviet Union and Korea by the Sea of Japan and from China by the East China Sea.

The Japanese coast is deeply indented, measuring 16,654 mi. The northern islands are a continuation of the Sakhalin mountain chain running through Hokkaido and the main island. The continuation of the Kunlun mountain range of China appears in the southern islands, the ranges meeting in the Japanese Alps. In the vast transverse fissure crossing the main island from the Sea of Japan to the Pacific rises a group of volcanoes, mostly extinct or dormant, with Fuji-San (Fujiyama), 60 mi. SW of Tokyo, lifting its white cone 12,388 ft.

Most important ports are Kobe, the world's 3d busiest, Nagoya, Yokohama, and Osaka. **Tokyo**, the capital, is the second most populous city of the world. It has a modern business section centering about the Ginza, a major avenue. The Imperial Palace, surrounded by a moat on a 250-acre site, and the white-marble Diet building, erected in 1936, are also in Tokyo. Its International Airport is Asia's busiest. Tokyo Tower is a 1,089-ft. steel structure built for radio-TV broadcasting and sightseeing.

At Kamakura, 30 mi. SW of Tokyo, is the Great Buddha or Daibutsu, a bronze figure 42 ft. 6 in. tall with base, cast in 1252. The Hakone hot spring area is noted for the reflection in Lake Ashino of Fuji-San. Also famous is the Toshogu Shrine at Nikko, where a national park of 347,000 acres preserves the natural beauty of Japanese flora. Kyoto, for 1,000 years a capital city, with massive temples and colorful shrines, is a cultural center.

The 2.34-mi. Kanmon undersea highway tunnel connecting Honshu and Kyushu is the world's first double-deck tunnel, with one level for vehicles and one for pedestrians.

Resources and Industries. More than half the arable land is used for growing rice, the chief food. Wheat, barley, potatoes, tobacco, tea, beans, peaches, pears, apples, grapes, persimmons, and mandarins are also produced. Minerals include some amounts of gold, silver, copper, lead, zinc, chromite, white arsenic, coal, sulphur, salt, and petroleum, but most minerals have to be imported.

The principal industries are iron and steel products, transportation equipment, machinery, electronics, shipbuilding, precision instruments, chemicals, fertilizers, textiles (cotton, wool, silks, synthetics), ceramics, wood products, fisheries. The 1974 fish catch of 10.8 million metric tons, led all nations.

Japan is 2d to the U.S. in motor vehicle production; about 7 million autos, trucks and buses are produced annually. It is also 2d to the U.S. in number of telephones in use (35 million in 1973). The index of industrial production (1970=100) was 126 in 1974.

Japan's shipyards lead the world, especially in construction of super tankers and bulk carriers of over 300,000 tons. Japan's own merchant fleet included 2,145 ships of 1,000 or more gross tons in 1974, 3d among nations.

Electric power production was about 460 billion kwh in 1974, close to half from hydroelectric plants. An atomic power station at Tokai, near Tokyo, began commercial distribution of electricity in 1967.

Major exports are steel and related products, clothing, chemicals, motor vehicles, optical goods, ships, radio and TV sets, toys.

Tourism is an increasingly important source of foreign exchange; in 1972, 723,744 visitors spent over $210 million.

The U.S. is Japan's biggest customer, taking about one-fourth of all its exports. In 1973, value of imports topped that of exports for the first time in many years; the deficit continued through 1975.

Foreign trade in thousands of U.S. dollars:

	Imports	Exports
1974	$62,110,000	$55,536,000
1975	$57,881,000	$55,844,000

History and Government. According to Japanese legend, the empire was founded by Emperor Jimmu, 660 B.C. Political power was held by successive families of shoguns (military dictators), 1192-1867, until recovered by the Emperor Meiji in 1868. The Portuguese and Dutch had minor trade with Japan in the 16th and 17th centuries, U.S. Commodore Matthew C. Perry opened it to U.S. trade in a treaty ratified 1854. Japan fought China, 1894-95, gaining Taiwan. In war with Russia, 1904-05, Russia's fleet was wiped out at Tsushima; Russia ceded S half of Sakhalin and gave concessions in China. Japan annexed Korea 1910. In World War I Japan ousted Germany from Shantung, took over German Pacific islands as mandates from the League of Nations. Japan took Manchuria 1931, started war with China 1932. Japan launched war against the U.S. by attack on Pearl Harbor Dec. 7, 1941. Japan surrendered Aug. 14, 1945.

In a new constitution adopted May 3, 1947, Japan renounced the right to wage war; the emperor was acknowledged as hereditary symbol of the nation, but gave up claims to divinity; the Diet became the sole law-making authority. The House of Councilors has 252 members elected for 6 yr. terms and the House of Representatives 491 members, elected for 4 yrs., both by popular vote. The constitution separates church and state. Japan has granted suffrage to women and lowered the voting age to 20.

The emperor is Hirohito, the 124th of his line, born April 29, 1901, succeeded to the throne Dec. 25, 1926. The crown prince is Akihito Tsugu No Miya, born Dec. 23, 1933.

The U.S. and 48 other non-communist nations signed a peace treaty and the U.S. a bilateral defense agreement with Japan, in San Francisco Sept. 8, 1951, restoring Japan's sovereignty as of April 28, 1952. Under the treaty, Japan was reduced territorially to the 4 main islands, but it was to have an opportunity eventually to regain the Ryukyu and Bonin Islands. Japan signed separate treaties with Nationalist China, 1952; India, 1952; a declaration with USSR ending a technical state of war, 1956. In Dec. 1965 Japan and South Korea agreed to resume diplomatic relations.

On June 26, 1968, the U.S. returned to Japanese control the Bonin Islands, the Volcano Islands (including Iwo Jima) and Marcus Island. On May 15, 1972, Okinawa, the other Ryukyu Islands and the Daito Islands were returned to Japan by the U.S., but it was agreed the U.S. would continue to maintain large military bases on Okinawa. Japan and the USSR have failed to resolve disputed claims of sovereignty over four of the Kurile Is.

On Sept. 29, 1972, Japan and mainland China agreed to resume diplomatic relations; Japan and Taiwan severed relations.

Education and Religion. The principal forms of religion are Buddhism, with 12 sects, and Shintoism with 13. There are over 100,000 Shinto shrines, 106,-634 Buddhist temples and several thousand Christian churches.

Nine years of education is compulsory, consisting of 6 years of elementary and 3 years of lower secondary education. There were 405 colleges and universities and 500 junior colleges in 1973. English is required study in lower secondary schools.

Defense. Legislation effective July 1, 1954, established new Self-Defense Forces. Military strength is 236,000.

During 1969 the U.S. began turning over 50 military installation sites, a third of its facilities in Japan, to the Japanese. The U.S. reduced its forces in Japan in 1971.

Jordan

Area: 37,297 sq. mi. (including West Bank). Population (Govt. est. 1975): 2,700,000. Capital: Amman. Monetary unit: Dinar.

Jordan is a constitutional monarchy in SW Asia. The country's former name, Transjordan, was dropped Apr. 26, 1949, after it occupied the West Bank lands, W of the Jordan River, in favor of the constitutional name, Hashemite Kingdom of Jordan.

About 12% of the land is fertile; the rest is arid. In the extreme south is its only port, Aqaba, on the Gulf of Aqaba. It shares the Dead Sea (1,296 ft. below sea level) with Israel. Jordan is slightly larger than Indiana.

Resources and Industries. The fertile western portions have a high agricultural potential. Principal crops are tomatoes, vegetables, wheat, barley, olives, grapes, citrus fruits, and bananas.

Industries include tobacco, flour milling, distilling, building materials, olive oil, soap, mother-of-pearl, textiles, plastics, cement, steel, batteries, leather.

Potash from the Dead Sea and phosphate rock are the main minerals. Phosphate is 30% of value of exports.

As a result of the Lebanese civil war dozens of foreign corporations have shifted their Middle East headquarters from Beirut to Amman.

History and Government. The area was part of the Ottoman Empire from the 16th century until World War I. It was set up within the Palestine Mandate Sept. 1, 1922, and gained independence as Transjordan in 1946. Abdullah Ibn Al Husein, born 1882, was proclaimed king May 25, 1946; he was assassinated by an Arab extremist, 1951. His eldest son became King Talal I. Parliament removed Talal on medical advice, installing his son King Hussein I (born 1935) May 11, 1952. His marriage to Sherifa Deena (a daughter was born 1956) was dissolved 1958.

Legislature has a senate of 30 named by the king and a lower house of 60 elected by manhood suffrage. Jordan is a member of the UN and Arab League.

After creation of Israel May 14, 1948, Jordan joined in the Arab attack on Israel and seized areas of central Palestine including the West Bank and the old city of Jerusalem. Several hundred thousand Palestinian refugees fled into Jordan. But Jordan lost all the territories to Israel in the June 1967 war.

In 1968-70 Palestinian guerrillas based in Jordan continued raids on Israel, including artillery attacks. Israel staged reprisal raids against commando bases inside Jordan.

Fighting between Jordanian troops and Palestinian commandos in 1970 included a 10-day civil war in Sept. in which 3,500 commandos were killed. In renewed fighting in July 1971 Jordanian troops dispersed thousands of commandos from their bases. Syria, Algeria and Libya suspended relations with Jordan, and Iraq closed its border. Syria reopened its border in 1972.

In the Oct. 1973 Arab war on Israel, Jordan sent troops to aid Syria, but the Israel-Jordan border remained peaceful.

In Oct. 1974 an Arab summit meeting designated the Palestine Liberation Organization as sole representative of Arabs on the West Bank. Jordan accepted the move. Arab oil states agreed to pay Jordan a $350 million annual subsidy. Jordan and Syria entered a military cooperation pact in 1975, and conducted joint military maneuvers.

Education and Religion. The population is chiefly Arab, of whom the majority are Moslems; there are 250,000 Christians and 10,000 Moslem Circassians. The language is Arabic. Public school education is growing. The Jordanian Univ. was established in 1962.

Defense. Military forces total 78,000. The U.S. has provided military aid, but a dispute erupted in 1975 over the number and deployment of Hawls antiaircraft missiles that Jordan sought to purchase.

Kenya

Area: 224,960 sq. mi. Population (Govt. est. 1975): 13,400,000. Capital: Nairobi. Monetary unit: Kenya shilling.

Kenya, former British Colony and Protectorate which became independent in 1963, extends from its Indian Ocean coast NE to Somalia, N to Ethiopia, W to Uganda, and S to Tanzania. It has twice the area of New Mexico.

The northern three-fifths is arid. Most economic production is centered in the south, a low coastal area and a plateau varying from 3,000 to 10,000 ft. The main products are coffee, tea, cereals, cotton, sisal, dairy products, hides, bark extract, timber, and minerals. Kenya is the largest producer of tea in Africa.

In 1953 Kenya became the scene of terroristic activities of the Mau Mau, an oath-bound unit of some of the Kikuyu, Meru, Embu and other tribes which killed Africans and whites during an 8-year rebellion.

Kenya won independence Dec. 12, 1963. Jomo Kenyatta, once imprisoned as a Mau Mau leader, became its first prime minister. It became a republic within the Commonwealth Dec. 12, 1964, and Kenyatta became its first president. The National Assembly is a unicameral legislature.

Since independence, Kenya's economy has continued to grow, including both agriculture and manufacturing. Tourism has boomed, with hundreds of thousands of overseas visitors each year. Schools and health centers have increased. Drought caused setbacks in 1971 and 1973.

In Jan. 1968 Kenya and Somalia resumed diplomatic relations as efforts were made to end 4 years of skirmishes caused by "invasions" of nomadic Somali herders seeking grass and water.

From 1968 through 1973 thousands of Asians holding old British passports were ordered evicted from Kenya. In 1973 it was announced Swahili would become the national language, with English still used for international communications.

The majority of the people are Christians, with some ethnic Moslem minorities. Swahili is the official language, and English is also widely spoken.

Years of political stability ended in 1974-75, with opposition charges of corruption and repression.

In 1976, relations with Uganda deteriorated over the latter's territorial claims, and its alleged mistreatment of Kenyan citizens, and over alleged Kenyan cooperation with an Israeli rescue mission in Uganda.

The U.S. agreed in 1976 to sell several jet fighters to Kenya, in order to bolster its military forces, among the smallest in Africa.

North Korea

Area: 46,768 sq. mi. Population (UN est. 1975): 15,850,000. Capital: Pyongyang. Monetary unit: Won.

The Democratic People's Republic of Korea was formed May 1, 1948. The U.S. did not recognize it.

North Korea has good mineral resources that are fairly well developed. The country ranks among the first 5 in the world in the output of tungsten, graphite and magnesite. Other products of significance include lead, zinc, pyrite, cement, iron ore, copper, gold, phosphate, salt and fluorspar. A well-developed hydroelectric system and sizeable reserves of coal provide power needs for industry, which had been developed during the period of Japanese rule, 1910-45. Agriculture is collectivized and industry nationalized.

North Korea is slightly larger than N. Y. State.

The import and export trade is largely with Communist countries, particularly China and Russia.

The USSR signed a military aid treaty with North Korea July 6, 1961, pledging defense protection and financial help. A similar treaty was signed with Communist China. (See Index for Korean War.)

Soviet prestige declined in the early 1960s as North Korea sided with the Chinese in the Sino-Soviet dispute. By 1974 North Korea apparently had good relations with both Communist super-powers.

North Korean patrol boats seized the U.S. Navy intelligence ship Pueblo on Jan. 23, 1968, charged it had entered North Korean territorial waters and held its crew captive. The 82 surviving crew members were freed Dec. 23 (Korean time).

North Korean planes shot down a U S. Navy intelligence plane over the Sea of Japan Apr. 15, 1969 (Korean time). No survivors were found.

In July 1972 North and South Korea agreed they would seek reunification of the two nations by peaceful means, but little progress was made by 1975.

North Korea's armed forces totaled 467,000, including a large air force.

South Korea

Area: 38,031 sq. mi. Population (UN est. 1975): 33,095,000. Capital: Seoul. Monetary unit: Won.

Korea, Land of the Morning Calm, is a mountainous peninsula in NE Asia between the Yellow Sea and the Sea of Japan. South Korea is about the size of Indiana.

Resources and Industries. Once chiefly an agricultural country, South Korea has a cultivated area of about 5,095,655 acres. Main crops are rice, barley, wheat, tobacco, and beans, but the mountainous terrain, poor soil, and cold winters limit yields. Population growth has been sharply curbed.

Division of Korea in 1945 left the South with only light industry and about 10% of power generating capacity. Large infusions of foreign aid helped build an industrial base especially in mining of tungsten (supplies 6% of world's needs), coal, iron ore, bismuth, fluorspar, graphite, and cement. The fishing, timber, rubber, glass, shipbuilding, electronics, and silk industries have expanded rapidly; chemical and fertilizer plants and oil refineries have been built. Growth was at record highs, 1971-73, but oil price increases caused soaring inflation in 1974-75.

U.S. support in South Korea has been military, financial, technical and educational. Since 1954 it has totaled more than $2.5 billion. Index of industrial production (1970 = 100) was 230 for 1974.

Foreign trade in thousands of U.S. dollars:

	Imports	Exports
1973	$4,218,000	$3,221,000
1974	$6,844,000	$4,713,000

History and Government. Korea, once called the Hermit Kingdom, has a recorded history since the 1st century B.C. It was united in a kingdom under the Silla Dynasty, 668 A.D. It was at times associated with the Chinese empire; the treaty that concluded the Sino-Japanese war of 1894-95 recognized Korea's complete independence. In 1910 Japan forcibly annexed Korea as Chosun.

At the Potsdam conference, July, 1945, the 38th parallel was designated as the line dividing the Soviet and the American occupation. Russian troops entered Korea Aug. 10, 1945, U.S. troops entered Sept. 8, 1945. The Soviet military organized socialists and communists and blocked efforts to let the Koreans unite their country. A UN commission to supervise elections in Korea in 1948 was denied admission to North Korea. (See Index for Korean War.)

The South Koreans formed the Republic of Korea in May 1948 with Seoul as the capital. Dr. Syngman Rhee was chosen president July 20 and the republic was formally proclaimed Aug. 15, 1948. President Rhee was reelected to a 4th term Mar. 15, 1960, when 85 years old. A movement spearheaded by college students forced his resignation Apr. 26, amid charges of corruption and election fraud.

A constitutional amendment passed June 15, 1960, replaced an autocratic presidential system with a cabinet system. But in an army coup May 16, 1961, Gen. Park Chung Hee became chairman of the ruling junta. He was formally elected president Oct. 15, 1963; a referendum Nov. 22, 1972, provided more presidential powers and allowed him to be reelected for 6 year terms unlimited times. In 1974 scores of political dissidents were jailed in a long series of trials. Eight accused of subversion were executed in 1975. An assassin, firing at Park, fatally wounded Mrs. Park.

North Korean raids across the border tapered off in 1971, but 2 South Korean soldiers were killed in 1973; in 1974, 2 South Korean boats were sunk and North Koreans fired on a U.S. helicopter south of the neutral zone. In July 1972 South and North Korea agreed on a common goal of reunifying the 2 nations by peaceful means. Red Cross delegates from both nations met to find ways to aid divided families.

Education and Religion. Christianity, Confucianism, Buddhism, and Chondogyo are principal religions.

Ten years of education are free and compulsory, and literacy surpasses 90%. Well over 200,000 students attend universities and institutions of higher education.

Defense. Military strength is over 625,000. By Mar. 1973 South Korea withdrew the last of 50,000 troops that had been aiding the South Vietnam government.

During 1970-71 U.S. forces authorized in South Korea were reduced; in 1976 there were 38,000. South Korean troops replaced most U.S. forces on the armistice border.

Kuwait

Area: 7,780 sq. mi. Population (Govt. est. 1975): 1,000,000. Capital: Kuwait City. Monetary unit: Kuwaiti dinar.

Kuwait, a small Arab state formerly under British protection, became fully independent June 19, 1961. It extends along the NW coast of the Persian (also called Arabian) Gulf, bordered by Iraq and Saudi Arabia. Kuwait City is a principal Gulf port. In area, Kuwait is slightly larger than Connecticut.

Resources and Industries. Oil, first exported in 1946, is Kuwait's economic mainstay; the tiny nation was the world's 7th largest producer in 1975. Reserves are about 10 billion tons, 15% of the world's total.

Crude oil production in 1975 was 670 million barrels. Annual payments to the Kuwait government in royalties and taxes are about $8 billion. Per capita income was estimated at more than $10,000 in 1974. The country had some $18 billion in foreign assets in 1976.

Revenues from oil from a former Kuwait-Saudi neutral zone are split 50-50 with Saudi Arabia.

History and Government. Kuwait is governed by members of the Al-Sabah dynasty founded in 1756. Under a treaty of 1899 Great Britain administered foreign relations and guaranteed territorial integrity until Kuwait became fully independent, 1961, by mutual agreement. Kuwait joined the Arab League 1961, the UN 1963. The nation's first constitution was proclaimed in Jan. 1963, when the first elections for a 50-member national assembly were held. The majority of the population are non-Kuwaiti (including many Palestinians) and do not have voting rights.

The Emir Sabah Al-Salim Al-Sabah became ruler Nov. 27, 1965, after the death of his older brother.

Iraqi troops crossed the Kuwait border in Mar. 1973 but soon withdrew; Iraq demanded possession of 2 islands claimed by Kuwait. Kuwait has ordered 20 Mirage F1 fighters from France (reportedly for transfer to Egypt), and other advanced weapons from the U.S.

Education and Religion. The government has utilized its enormous national income to create a welfare state with free medical care, education and social security. A $2 billion fund has been set aside to aid other Arab nations. There are no taxes except customs duties. Educational facilities are being rapidly expanded. There were, in 1973, 225 schools of all types, with 150,000 students and over 9,000 teachers. The University of Kuwait was opened in Oct. 1966. Islam is the official religion, and Arabic the official language.

Laos

Area: 91,428 sq. mi. Population (UN est. 1975): 2,300,000. Capital: Vientiane. Monetary unit: Kip.

Laos is a republic in SE Asia, one of the 3 former French Indo-Chinese states. It is bounded by China, Vietnam, Cambodia, Thailand and Burma. It is landlocked, smaller than Oregon, largely jungle and mountains.

Laos became a French protectorate in 1893 and a member of the Indo-Chinese Union in 1899. Nationalist aims grew in the 1940s, and the king promulgated a constitution May 11, 1947, providing for a constitutional monarchy under the Luang Prabang dynasty, and a parliamentary government. Laos became independent by a treaty with France July 19, 1949.

Conflicts among neutralist, communist and conservative factions created a chaotic political situation despite 1954 agreements. Although Laos was intended to be neutral, rivalry between the communist Pathet Lao movement in the northern third of the country, led by Prince Souphanouvong, and rightwing and neutralist factions prevented integration of the Pathet Lao into the royalist army. Armed conflict increased after 1960 with the arrival of Russian arms and North Vietnamese troops.

The 3 factions formed a coalition government in June 1962, with neutralist Prince Souvanna Phouma as premier. A 14-nation conference in Geneva signed agreements July 23, 1962, guaranteeing neutrality and independence of Laos.

By 1964 the Pathet Lao had withdrawn from the coalition, and, with aid from N. Vietnamese troops, renewed sporadic attacks on government positions. Both Laos and U. S. planes bombed the Ho Chi Minh trail, supply line from N. Vietnam to communist forces in northern Laos and S. Vietnam. An estimated 2.75 million tons of bombs were dropped on Laos during the fighting.

In 1970 communist forces seized more territory in central and southeast Laos. On March 6 U.S. President Nixon confirmed that the U.S. had stepped up air support and military aid to Laos government forces. There were an est. 67,000 North Vietnamese troops in Laos, and some 15,000 Thai "irregulars" financed by the U.S. Laotian and North Vietnamese forces continued fighting in 1972.

Following a Feb. 21, 1973, ceasefire, the neutralists and Pathet Lao signed an agreement Sept. 14 for a coalition government and withdrawal of foreign troops. The coalition, with Souvenna Phouma as premier and Souphanouvong as president of a National Political Council, took office in Apr. 1974.

After Pathet Lao military gains, Souvanna Phouma

in May 1975 ordered government troops to cease fighting, and Pathet Lao troops took effective control of the country. The formal coalition remained in effect. The U. S. withdrew its huge aid mission, but retained a reduced diplomatic presence. A Lao People's Democratic Republic was proclaimed Dec. 3, 1975.

Chief products are tin, rice, maize, tobacco, cotton, opium, citrus fruits, benzoin, shellac, teakwood, and coffee. The population comprises peoples of Thai, Indonesian, and Chinese origin. Lao and French are the most important languages. Buddhism was the state religion under the monarchy.

Lebanon

Area: 4,015 sq. mi. Population (UN est. 1974): 2,780,000. Capital: Beirut. Monetary unit: Lebanese pound.

The Republic of Lebanon, in SW Asia, occupies a strip along the Mediterranean coast about 120 mi. long and 30 to 35 mi. wide, extending from the Israeli frontier on the S to Syria on the E and N. It is smaller than Connecticut. There is a narrow coastal strip and 2 main mountain ranges running N and S with fertile land between. Beirut, with one-third of the country's population, is the chief sea and airport.

Resources and Industries. Trade provides two-thirds of national income. Agriculture employs half the workers; chief crops are apples, citrus fruit, olives, tobacco, grapes, vegetables, cereals. Manufacturing is growing rapidly; important are food products, textiles, leather goods, cement, oil refining. Tripoli and Sidon are terminals of oil pipelines from Iraq and Saudi Arabia. Large hydroelectric and irrigation projects are being developed.

Lebanon has a free enterprise economy and banking secrecy. Private capital from other Arab states has poured into the country. Literacy and life expectancy are higher than in most Arab countries.

History and Government. Lebanon was formed from 5 former Turkish Empire districts and became, along with Syria, an independent state Sept. 1, 1920, administered under French Mandate 1920-1941. In 1944 France yielded its powers. French troops withdrew in 1946.

Attempts to undermine the pro-western administration led to a revolt in May 1958. The U.S. sent Marines in reply to a government call for help. The revolt dwindled, American forces withdrew, in Oct. 1958.

On Dec. 28, 1968, an Israeli helicopter raid on Beirut Airport destroyed 13 Lebanese airliners; Israel had accused Lebanon of aiding Arab terrorists. Lebanon's efforts to restrict Palestinian commandos caused armed clashes in 1969. Continued commando raids against Israeli civilians, 1970-75, brought Israeli reprisal and preventive raids against guerrilla camps and Lebanese villages.

An estimated 35,000 people were killed and billions of dollars of damage inflicted in 1975-76 communal fighting. Palestinian units and leftist Lebanese Moslems fought against the Maronite militia, the Phalange, and other Christian groups. Several Arab countries provided political and arms support to the various factions.

Up to 15,000 Syrian troops intervened in 1976, and fought Palestinian groups. Arab League troops from several nations attempted to impose a cease-fire.

The republic's constitution instituted a democratic parliamentary regime. There is a unicameral legislature (Chamber of Deputies) of 99, elected every 4 years. The president is elected for a 6-year term. Traditionally he is a Christian, the premier a Moslem. All public positions are divided among the various religious communities according to the provisions of the 1943 National Covenant. Lebanon is a member of the UN and Arab League.

Education and Religion. Christians (mostly Maronites) number nearly half the population, Moslems most of the remainder, divided into Sunni and Shilite sects. There are 8 universities and institutions of higher learning in Beirut. Arabic is the official language; French and English are widely spoken.

Lesotho

Area: 11,716 sq. mi. Population (Govt. est. 1975): 1,040,000. Capital: Maseru. Monetary unit: S. Afr. Rand.

The former British dependency, Basutoland, became independent as the Kingdom of Lesotho Oct. 4, 1966. An African state without white settlers, it is about the size of Maryland and completely surrounded by the Republic of South Africa.

The land is mountainous, altitudes ranging from 5,000 to 11,000 ft. There are air, rail and road links with South Africa. Agriculture has been advanced with U.S. and UN technical aid. Maize, sorghum, barley, beans, and peas are grown. The main industry is livestock raising which produces wool and mohair, the chief exports. There are small industries including diamond polishing. About 110,000 men work in South African mines. Up to 70% of males work abroad. Tourism is being promoted.

In 1868, Lesotho became a British protectorate upon the request of Moshesh, the paramount chieftain, who sought protection against the Boers of South Africa. The government consists of a king, an elected National Assembly of 60, a Senate, Cabinet and prime minister. In 1970, elections were suspended by Prime Minister Leabua Jonathan.

Liberia

Area: 43,000 sq. mi. Population (UN est. 1975): 1,710,000. Capital: Monrovia. Monetary unit: U. S. dollar, also Liberian silver and copper coinage.

The Republic of Liberia is in West Africa adjacent to Sierra Leone, Guinea and Ivory Coast, and has an Atlantic coast of about 350 mi. Much of the country is forest. It is slightly larger than Ohio.

Liberia has no natural harbors. The Free Port of Monrovia, built 1945-48 with U.S. funds, was turned over to the Liberian government in 1964, with payments to be concluded by 1999. The country is served by several international airlines.

Resources and Industries. Iron ore and rubber are the main products; loans from the U.S. and other Western nations helped increase production in the 1960s. In 1970 a U.S. company began developing nation's timber resources. Diamonds and gold are mined; other products are fibers, palm kernels, rice, cassava, coffee, cocoa, and sugar. U.S. aid is promoting schools, hospitals, and food production.

History and Government. Liberia was founded in 1822 when a settlement was made at Monrovia by black freedmen from the U.S. with the assistance of American colonization societies. It was declared a republic July 26, 1847. Its constitution is modeled on that of the U.S. Only persons of African descent may acquire citizenship and only citizens may own real estate.

There is a president elected for one 8-year term only, a Senate of 18 elected for 6 years and a House of Representatives of 52, elected for 4 years. William V. S. Tubman, president since 1943, died July 23, 1971. Descendants of freedmen dominate politics.

Education and Religion. About 10% are Christian, 10-20% Moslem, the rest nativists. There are nearly 1,200 schools, one university and two colleges. English is the official language, but African languages are spoken by the majority.

Libya

Area: 679,536 sq. mi. Population (Govt. est. 1975): 2,440,000. Capital: Tripoli. Monetary unit: Libyan Dinar.

Libya is an Arab republic comprising 10 provinces in the former states of Tripolitania, Cyrenaica and Fezzan. Larger than Alaska, it is on the North African coast, bounded by the Mediterranean, Egypt, Sudan, Chad, Niger, Algeria and Tunisia.

Resources and Industries. Discovery of major oil fields in the northern part of the country beginning in 1957 brought prosperity and an improved standard of living to the country.

In 1973 Libya expropriated 51% of several U.S. oil firms' assets. In 1974 it took over complete owner-SHIP. It joined the 1973-74 Arab oil embargo.

In the 1960s-70s, several hundred schools were built. Homes, hospitals, roads and power stations were constructed. Per capita gross national product rose from $145 in 1959 to $2,984 in 1973. Education and health services are provided free.

Libya had been basically agricultural, producing dates, olives, lemons, almonds, figs, grapes, and tobacco. Carpets, leather goods and embroidered fabrics are also produced.

In 1973 "people's committees" took over many factories, firms, radio and TV stations, hospitals, and farms, with government approval.

History and Government. Libya has come under the domination successively of Carthage, Rome, the Vandals, the Ottoman Empire and Italy. After World War II Tripoli and Cyrenaica were placed under British administration, the Fezzan under French.

Emir Mohammed Idris El Senussi, ruler of the Senussi tribesmen, was recognized by Great Britain as emir of Cyrenaica, June, 1949. Libya, as a sovereign state, was approved by the UN, 1949, effective Jan. 2, 1952. A constituent assembly approved a constitutional monarchy and named the emir as king of Libya, Dec. 3, 1950. A hereditary monarchy was proclaimed by King Idris I, Dec. 24, 1951.

On Sept. 1, 1969, a Revolutionary Command Council headed by Col. Muammar el-Qaddafi overthrew the government and announced formation of the Arab Republic of Libya.

In Aug. 1972 Libya and Egypt agreed to prepare unification by Sept. 1, 1973. But Egypt put off the union and in Aug. 1974 charged that Qaddafi conspired in the bombing of an Egyptian presidential palace. Qaddafi and Tunisia's president, Habib Bourguiba, announced in Jan. 1974 their nations would unite, but Bourguiba soon dropped the plan.

In the mid-1970s, it was widely reported that Libya had financed and armed violent revolutionary groups throughout the Arab world, and had aided terrorist groups of various nationalities.

Education and Religion. Libya's population is mostly Arab Moslems and Islam is the state religion. Schools were taken over by the "people's committees" in 1973. There are 2 universities.

Defense. In 1970, Libya arranged to buy jet planes from France and received tanks and other arms from the USSR; the U.S. turned over its Wheelus Air Force Base to Libya. The USSR sold over $1 billion in advanced arms in 1975; 1,000 Soviet advisers were present. Armed forces total 32,000.

Liechtenstein

Area: 61 sq. mi. Population (Govt. est. 1974): 23,700. Capital: Vaduz. Monetary unit: Swiss franc.

Liechtenstein is a principality on the Upper Rhine between Austria and Switzerland. It is slightly smaller than the District of Columbia. It received independence in 1866 when the German Confederation dissolved and was in an economic union with Austria from 1852 to 1918. By treaty with Switzerland (1920-23) that country administers its posts and telegraphs, customs and foreign interests.

The country is highly industrialized. Industries are machines and tools, cotton spinning and weaving, precision instruments, false teeth, pharmaceuticals, ceramics and canned food. Finely engraved postage stamps are sold around the world. Exports from 1974 were valued at $206 million. Foeign workers constitute about 34% of the resident population.

Under the constitution, granted in 1921, legislative powers rest in a Landtag of 15 members, elected for four years by direct vote, on a basis of male suffrage and proportional representation. The reigning prince is Franz Joseph II. Taxes are low and consequently many international corporations have made their headquarters there.

The country is predominantly Catholic. German is the language.

Luxembourg

Area: 999 sq. mi. Population (Govt. est. 1975): 360,0 00. Capital: Luxembourg. Monetary unit: Luxembourg franc.

Luxembourg is a European Grand Duchy, bounded by Germany, Belgium and France. It measures only 55 mi. long by 34 mi. wide, smaller than Rhode Island.

Resources and Industries. About 9,500 farmers cultivate 336,000 acres. The principal crops are oats, wheat, rye, barley, and potatoes.

Luxembourg's iron ore deposits, in the south, are the basis for an important steel industry. It employs 17% of the labor force, and accounts for 45% of total industrial production, and 65% of the value of exports. The country also produces chemicals, beer, tires, tobacco, and metal products, cement, roses, and dairy products.

History and Government. Luxembourg, founded about 963, passed under the domination of Burgundy, Spain, Austria and France from 1443 to 1815, when it regained autonomy. It left the Germanic Confederation in 1866, its neutrality guaranteed by the Treaty of London, 1867. Overrun by Germany in 2 World Wars, Luxembourg abolished its unarmed neutrality in 1948. Customs union with Netherlands and Belgium was adopted 1948. Luxembourg is a member of the UN, NATO, OECD, Council of Europe, Western European Union and the EC.

As a Grand Duchy, Luxembourg is governed under the constitution of 1868, with modifications. Legislative power rests with a Council of State of 21, chosen for life, and a 59-member elected Chamber of Deputies with executive power delegated to a minister of state and a Cabinet. Grand Duke Jean became chief of state Nov. 12, 1964.

The population is almost entirely Roman Catholic. Official languages are French and German; national language is Luxembourgeois.

Madagascar

Area: 203,035 sq. mi. Population (Est. 1974): 7,655,- 134. Capital: Tananarive. Monetary unit: Malagasy franc.

Madagascar is a large island off the SE coast of Africa, from which it is separated by the 240-mi. wide Mozambique Channel. It is about 980 mi. long and 360 mi. wide at its greatest breadth. It is a little smaller than Texas. There is a humid coastal strip on the E, fertile valleys in the mountainous center plateau region, and a wider coastal strip on the W.

The name of the nation and the island is Madagascar; the nation was officially the Malagasy Republic from 1958 to 1975, when the name was changed to Democratic Republic of Madagascar.

The people consist of many ethnic groups, including those of SE Asian, Arab and African descent. They speak Malagasy, a language of Malayan origin; but coastal tribes have distinct dialects, and have charged dominance by the highland Merinas. Over 3 million are animists; 3 million are Christians, about equally divided between Catholics and Protestants; about 9% are Moslems.

Madagascar became a French protectorate, 1885, and a French colony 1896. It proclaimed itself autonomous 1958. Independence came June 26, 1960.

Discontent with inflation and French domination of the university led to student demonstrations, followed by a coup in May 1972. President Philibert Tsiranana was ousted. The new regime has nationalized most French-owned industrial, trade, & agricultural interests, closed French air and naval bases and a U.S. space tracking station, and obtained Chinese assistance.

Most of the population is engaged in agriculture. Chief crops are coffee, cloves, vanilla (producing 80% of the world's supply), rice, livestock, sugar, sisal, tobacco, peanuts, etc. Small factories have been established. Chromium and graphite are exploited.

Malawi

Area: 45,747 sq. mi. Population (Govt. est. 1975): 5,040,000. Capital: Lilongwe. Monetary unit: Kwacha.

Malawi, in SE Africa, stretches 560 mi. north and south along Lake Malawi (Lake Nyasa), most of which belongs to Malawi. High mountains, dense forests and broad plains make it a scenic country. It is about the size of Pennsylvania.

The area became a British protectorate, Nyasaland, in 1891. From 1953 to 1963 it was a member of the Federation of Rhodesia and Nyasaland. On Feb. 1, 1963, it became internally self-governing and, on July 6, 1964, achieved independence, taking the name Malawi. It became a republic July 6, 1966.

About 85% of the workforce is agricultural, with only a few light industries. Four crops—tea, tobacco, peanuts, and cotton — account for 90% of the exports. Other important products are sugar, rubber, soybeans, and coffee.

Since 1967, factories have been built for textiles, shoes, sugar, farm implements, and other products formerly imported. Main trading partners are the United Kingdom, South Africa and the U.S. Malawi is dependent on Mozambique for her rail trade routes to the sea. The country maintains a pro-Western foreign policy. Construction continued in 1974 on a new capital at Lilongwe.

The Univ. of Malawi was built partly with U.S. aid; the first class graduated in July 1969. Population is mostly African; there are about 11,000 Indians and 7,000 of European descent.

Malaysia

Area: 128,328 sq. mi. Population (Govt. east. 1975): 11,930,000. Capital: Kuala Lumpur. Monetary unit: Ringgit.

Occupying the southern part of the Malay Peninsula in SE Asia and the northern part of the island of Borneo, Malaysia produces about 35% of the world's output of both rubber and tin. Total area is larger than Arizona.

Malaysia was created Sept. 16, 1963. It included the old Federation of Malaya (11 Malayan states which had become an independent constitutional monarchy Aug. 31, 1957), plus the formerly-British Singapore, Sabah (former British North Borneo) and Sarawak (former British Colony in NW Borneo).

Indonesia harassed the new nation with guerrilla action 1963-65. After Indonesian President Sukarno lost power, Malaysia and Indonesia agreed Aug. 11, 1966, to restore normal relations.

On Aug. 9, 1965, the separation of Singapore from Malaysia was announced under an agreement by Malaysia and Singapore officials that this was the best way to end tensions between the ethnic Chinese, largest group in Singapore, and the Malays, who were in control of the Malaysia government.

With Singapore's departure, the Malays numbered 44% of Malaysian's population and ethnic Chinese 36%; 10% are Indians.

Forming East Malaysia are Sabah (capital, Kota Kinabalu) and Sarawak (capital, Kuching). They lie on the N Coast of the island of Borneo and have a total pop. of 1,900,000 (1975), area of 77,638 mi.

A monarch is elected by a council of hereditary rulers of the Malayan states every 5 years. There is a Senate, House of Representatives, prime minister and Cabinet. The ruling National Front dominates political life.

In May 1969 at least 180 persons died in riots between ethnic Chinese and Malays in Kuala Lumpur. Communist guerrillas renewed activities in 1971 and intermittently thereafter.

Resources and industries. Rubber, tin, timber, iron ore, palm oil and copra are the main products. Rubber, much of it produced by new high-yield trees, accounts for 30% of exports. A million tourists visited in 1974.

Other agricultural products are rice, coconuts, tapioca, sugar, pepper, camphor. Small-scale industry includes rubber goods, pottery, cement, pewterware, furniture, bricks, tiles, soap, fertilizers, processing plants. Oil output is increasing.

Religion and Language. The Malays and some others are Moslems; other religions are Buddhism, Christianity, and Hinduism. Malay is the official language in W. Malaysia; Malay and English are official in E. Malaysia.

Defense. After 1971 Malaysia increased its armed forces to 61,100 to compensate for reduction of British Southeast Asia forces. Britain, Australia, and New Zealand maintain small forces in Malaysia.

Republic of Maldives

Area: 115 sq. mi. Population (Govt. census 1974): 128,697. Capital: Male. Monetary unit: Rupee.

The Maldive Islands are a group of 19 atolls containing 1,087 islands, 203 of which are inhabited. Totaling about twice the area of the District of Columbia, they are in the Indian Ocean 300 mi. SW of the southern tip of India. The country obtained independence from Great Britain on July 26,1965; Britain retained its RAF base until March 1976. The Maldives became a member of the UN, 1965.

The islands had been a British-protected state since 1887, with Britain responsible for their defense and foreign relations until the 1965 agreement. Long a sultanate, the islands became briefly a republic in 1953 and a sultanate again in 1954. After a referendum, the country became a republic once more, Nov. 11, 1968, with a president and legislature (Majlis).

The people are Moslems and seafarers. Coconuts, fruit, and millet are grown; chief occupation is fishing; production of processed fish, marketed in Ceylon, is the main industry. Also exported are coir, copra, and shells. Tourism is increasing.

revenues to the government.

Mali

Area: 464,873 sq. mi. Population (UN est. 1975): 5,700,000. Capital: Bamako. Monetary unit: Mali franc.

The Republic of Mali, a one-time French Overseas Territory in West Africa, is a landlocked nation larger than Texas but smaller than Alaska. It is a vast plain in the upper basins of the Senegal and Niger Rivers, extending N into the Sahara.

From the 11th to 15th centuries the area was part of the great Mali Empire which stretched from the western Sudan to the Atlantic; Timbuktu was a renowned center of Islamic learning.

Under provisions of the 1958 French constitution French Sudan became the Sudanese Republic, an autonomous republic, and formed with neighboring Senegal Jan. 17, 1959, the Mali Federation. Complete independence was proclaimed June 20, 1960. Senegal withdrew from the federation Aug. 20, 1960, and Sudan took the name Republic of Mali Sept. 22. Mali signed economic and cultural agreements with France. On June 8, 1963, Mali and Senegal reached customs, trade and railway traffic agreements, with use of Senegalese harbors by Mali.

On Nov. 19, 1968, a coup ended the socialist regime of President Modibo Keita; Lt. Moussa Traore became president Dec. 6, 1968.

The country is mainly agricultural and pastoral. Millet, rice and peanuts are the chief crops. Cotton, rubber and river fishing are also important. Livestock raising is a major prop of the economy. Famine, following a long drought, struck Mali in 1973-74. Aid was sent by many nations, 40% of it from the U. S., but loss of livestock and dislocation of 700,000 Tuareg nomads remained problems.

The people are mostly Moslem, with a minority of Christians. French is the official language.

Malta

Area: 122 sq. mi. Population (Govt. est. 1975): 27,-704. Capital: Valetta. Monetary unit: Pound.

Malta lies in the Mediterranean 58 mi. S of Sicily and 180 mi. from Africa. The island of Malta itself is 95 sq. mi.; the other islands in the group are Gozo, 26 sq. mi., and Comino, one sq. mi.

For 35 centuries Malta was under successive rule by Phoenicians, Carthaginians, Romans, Arabs, Normans, the Knights of Malta, France and Britain (which annexed Malta in 1814). It achieved limited self-government in 1887; home rule, 1961. On Sept. 21, 1964, it became independent, with the British monarch as head of state, and agreed to permit British forces to maintain a base for 10 years. Malta became a republic Dec. 13, 1974. It is a member of the Commonwealth, Council of Europe and UN. A House of Representatives with 65 members is elected by universal suffrage; the prime minister and Cabinet derive authority from the House.

Population density is high; there is continuous emigration, much of it to Australia, the United Kingdom and Canada. Recently, the number of returning migrants has exceeded emigration.

A Labor party victory in June 1971 elections led to the ouster of NATO naval hq. In 1972 Malta agreed to Britain's use of its military bases for 7 years in return for greatly increased payments; USSR forces would be barred. Malta is non-aligned.

Leading industries are ship repairing, food and beverages, textiles and tourism. Tourists rose to 334,-000 in 1975. Historic sites, a casino and village fetes are among attractions. Maltese is a Semitic language with Italian influences, written in Latin characters. Nearly all inhabitants are Roman Catholic.

Mauritania

Area: 419,229 sq. mi. Population (Govt. est. 1975): 1,320,000. Capital: Nouakchott. Monetary unit: Ouguiya.

The Islamic Republic of Mauritania, former French Overseas Territory in West Africa, is bounded by the Atlantic Ocean, Spanish Sahara, Algeria, Mali and Senegal. Population is 80% Moorish. Mauritania is about four-fifths the size of Alaska.

The economy has been agricultural and pastoral. Products include dates, grain, meat, fish. There are large herds of cattle, camels, sheep and goats, and large deposits of iron and copper.

A large new iron mine was opened in 1963 to add to the nation's large annual production. Fishing was being expanded; a copper mine opened in 1971, with annual yield of 30,000 metric tons; a new cattle slaughterhouse and freezing plant was opened. Mauritania has received aid from France and China. Drought and famine struck in 1973-74; aid was sent by Western nations, 40% of it from the U. S.

Mauritania became fully independent Nov. 28, 1960. Prime Minister Mokhtar Ould Daddah, appointed June 26, 1959, became president by popular vote in Aug. 1962. In 1976, Mauitania annexed the southern part of former Spanish Sahara, rich in phosphates.

Mauritius

**Area: 787 sq. mi. Population (Govt. est. 1975): 860,0
00. Capital: Port Louis. Monetary unit: Rupee.**

Mauritius, an island in the Indian Ocean 550 mi. E
of Madagascar, became an independent nation within
the Commonwealth on Mar. 12, 1968, after 158 years
of British rule. It has a parliamentary government.

Mauritius has one of the world's most complex racial, religious and political mixtures as well as one of
the world's highest population densities. There are
over 408,000 Hindus; 224,000 of mixed European and
African descent and whites; 130,000 Moslems and 25,-
000 Chinese. Although the official language is English, French is spoken by many persons, and Creole, a
French patois, is the lingua franca. Chinese and Indian languages are also spoken. The country had a
nearly one-crop economy, sugar. However, a tea
industry has been developed, foreign investment has
been welcomed, and tourism is growing. Commonwealth subsidies support sugar prices and aid the
economy. The literacy rate and life expectancy are
very high.

Mauritius was uninhabited until 1638 when the
Dutch settled there, introduced sugar cane and gave
the island its present name in honor of Prince Maurice of Nassau. The French took over in 1721 and imported African slaves. The British, who seized the
island in 1810, brought Hindus and Moslems from
India to work the sugar plantations.

Mexico

**Area: 761,601 sq. mi. Population (Govt. est. 1975):
60,150,000. Capital: Mexico City. Monetary unit:
Peso.**

Mexico is the second most populous nation in Latin
America and 3d largest in area.

With progress in housing, health, farm, and industrial programs, Mexico has attempted to join the
ranks of the developed nations; life expectancy, for
example, from 39 years in 1940 to 61 years in 1972.

Streams of foreign visitors (3.36 million in 1974)
find spectacular scenery, striking art and architecture, remains of Indian civilizations, cosmopolitan
and colonial cities, and luxurious resorts.

The Sierra Madre Occidental Mtns. run NW-SE
near the west coast. The Sierra Madre Oriental Mtns.,
a continuation of the Rockies, run near the Gulf of
Mexico coast nearly as far S as Veracruz.

Between the 2 ranges lies the central plateau of
Mexico, altitude frgm 5,000 to 8,000 ft. and with the
vegetation of the temperate zone. The lowlands along
the coast are tropical, rising to subtropical in the
foothills, with a heavy rainfall on the Gulf side. Along
the Pacific slope and in the interior irrigation is needed. Mexico is nearly 3 times the size of Texas.

Tampico and Veracruz, on the Gulf, are the busiest
of Mexico's 49 ocean ports.

Mexico's population is composed of descendants of
the Toltecs, Aztecs, Mayas, and the Spaniards who
conquered and colonized the country.

Resources and Industries. Mexico is rich in minerals and timber. It is one of the top 5 producers of silver; also important are gold, copper, lead, zinc,
antimony, mercury, arsenic, amorphous graphite,
molybdenum, sulphur, coal, and opal. Mexico is the
world's 15th largest petroleum producer and is self-
sufficient in oil; vast new reserves have been uncovered in Yucatan. The industry is nationalized. Natural gas is sold to the U. S. Electric power generated in
1973 rose to 37 billion kwh.

Farming, stock raising, and fishing are important.
The land is rich, but the rugged topography and lack
of sufficient rainfall are major obstacles. Crops and
farm prices are controlled, as are export and import.
Large estates have been expropriated; since 1915 the
government has distributed about 160 million acres
to small farmers through landholding communities
(ejidos). Four million peasants are still without land,
and five million others hold minimal plots. Major ir-

rigation projects in Sonora and Sinaloa have increased production of cotton and wheat.

Principal export crops are cotton, coffee, cane
sugar, tomatoes, cattle, fruit fresh and frozen meats.

Mexico is the 5th largest coffee producer; other
major crops are corn, rice, tobacco, garbanzos, cocoa,
sisal, bananas. About 50% of the world supply of sisal
comes from Yucatan, in southern Mexico.

Mexican industry is producing products formerly
imported, especially in iron and steel, chemicals,
electric goods. Other products are cotton, wool and
synthetic textiles, flour, beverages, soap, cigarettes
and cigars, rubber, paper, rubber products, cement,
shoes, glass, furniture, and tiles. Mexico is famous for
industrial and native handicraft in silver, pottery,
leather, wood, fibers and textiles. The U.S. buys a
large portion of Mexico's exports.

Index of industrial production (1970 = 100) was 130
in 1974.

Foreign trade, in thousands of U.S. dollars:

	Imports	Exports
1974	$6,519,000	$3,545,000
1975	$6,631,000	$2,909,000

History and Government. Mexico was the site of
advanced Indian civilizations before the Spanish con-
guest. The Mayas, an agricultural people, moved up
from Yucatan and built immense stone pyramids and
invented a calendar. The Toltecs were overcome by
the Aztecs, who founded Tenochtitlan 1325 A.D., now
Mexico City. Hernando Cortes, Spanish conquistador,
destroyed the Aztec empire, 1519-1521.

After 3 centuries of Spanish rule the people rose,
under Fr. Miguel Hidalgo y Costilla (a priest), 1810,
Fr. Morelos y Payon (another priest), 1812, and Gen.
Agustin Iturbide, who made independence effectual
Sept. 27, 1821, but made himself emperor as Agustin
I. A republic was declared in 1823.

Mexican territory extended into the present
American Southwest and California until Texas revolted and established a republic in 1836; the Mexican legislature refused recognition but was unable to
enforce its authority there. After numerous clashes,
the U.S.-Mexican War, 1846-48, resulted in the loss by
Mexico of the lands north of the Rio Grande.

French arms supported an Austrian archduke on
the throne of Mexico as Maximilian I, 1864-67, but
pressure from the U.S. forced France to withdraw. A
dictatorial rule by Porfirio Diaz, president 1877-80,
1884-1911, led to fighting by rival forces until the new
constitution of Feb. 5, 1917 provided social reform.
Since then Mexico has developed large-scale programs of social security, labor protection and school
improvement. A constitutional provision requires
management to share profits with labor.

Mexico is a federal democratic republic of 31
states, with president, legislature and judiciary elected by the universal suffrage; and a federal district
containing Mexico City. The president is elected for 6
years and thereafter ineligible; senators serve for 6
years and deputies for 3 years; they are ineligible for
reelection until one term has intervened.

The Institutional Revolutionary party has been
dominant in politics since 1929. Radical opposition,
including some guerrilla activity, has been contained
by strong measures. In 1970 the legal voting age was
lowered from 21 to 18.

Education and Religion. Education is secular, with
primary education compulsory up to 15 years of age.
Vocational instruction particularly in agriculture is
promoted. The National University of Mexico continues an educational foundation of 1551 A.D. Spanish is
the official language though 1 million speak only Indian languages, and 4 million others are bilingual.
Literacy has reached 65% of the population.

Most of the people are Roman Catholics. All church
real estate is vested in the nation, but care of church
buildings is the responsibility of the clergy.

Defense. The armed forces total 82,500 regulars,
250,000 part-time conscripts. Mexico is a member of
the UN and OAS.

(See also Index for Mexico City.)

Monaco

**Area: 600 acres. Population (est. 1974): 25,000.
Capital: Monaco. Monetary unit: French franc.**

Monaco is a small principality on the Mediterranean surrounded on all but the sea side by France. It is noted for its mild climate and magnificent scenery. There is a local police force of 200.

Resources and Industries. Monaco's fame as a tourist resort and international conference city is widespread. Its revenues derive from indirect taxation, a tobacco monopoly, postage and the gambling tables of the Monte Carlo Casino.

History and Government. An independent principality for over 300 years, Monaco has belonged to the House of Grimaldi except during the French Revolution. It was placed under the protectorate of Sardinia in 1815, and under that of France, 1861. The Prince of Monaco was an absolute ruler until a constitution was promulgated in 1911.

A new constitution, proclaimed Dec. 17, 1962, provided for female suffrage and abolition of capital punishment, and established a court to guarantee liberties. The legislature (National Council) consists of 18 members elected for 5 years.

The ruler of Monaco is Prince Rainier III who succeeded his grandfather, Prince Louis II, who died May 9, 1949. He married Grace Kelly, American motion picture actress, Apr. 18, 1956. A daughter, Princess Caroline Louise Marguerite, was born Jan. 23, 1957. The heir apparent, Prince Albert Alexandre Louis Pierre, was born Mar. 14, 1958. Princess Stephanie Marie Elisabeth was born Feb. 1, 1965.

In 1967 the government purchased for $8 million the holdings of Aristotle Onassis in the Societe des Bains de Mer, owner of the Casino and other interests. The prince launched a program of reclaiming land from the sea and developing new tourist facilities.

Mongolia

Area: 604,247 sq. mi. Population (Govt. est. 1975): 1,450,000. Capital: Ulan Bator. Monetary unit: Tughrik.

The Mongolian People's Republic comprises Outer Mongolia in northeastern Asia. It is bounded on the N by the Siberian provinces of USSR, and on 3 other sides by Mainland China. It is larger than Alaska. Much of Mongolia is a high plateau with vast grasslands; arid lands in the south are part of the Gobi Desert.

Resources and Industries. In the early 1970s Mongolia was changing from a nomadic culture to one of settled agriculture and growing industries with aid from the USSR and East European nations. Irrigation and scientific farming methods were pressed to increase grain crops and fodder for the large livestock herds, which have been collectivized since 1958. Food processing, textile, chemical, brick and cement factories were established in growing cities in the north. Electric power plants were built, running on coal; Mongolia has large coal deposits as well as tungsten, copper, molybdenum, gold, tin.

History and Government. One of the world's oldest countries, Mongolia reached the zenith of its power in the 13th Century when Genghis Khan and his successors conquered all of China and extended their influence as far W as Hungary and Poland. In later centuries, the empire dissolved and Mongolia came under the suzerainty of China.

With the advent of the 1911 Chinese revolution, Mongolia, with Russian backing, declared its independence. A Mongolian Communist regime was established July 11, 1921.

The constitution vests power in the elected Great People's Khural from which is drawn a Council of Ministers. Actual power is in the hands of the

Communist party and its 9-man Politburo.

Mongolia has sided with the Russians in the Sino-Soviet dispute. A Mongolian-Soviet mutual assistance pact was signed Jan. 15, 1966, and thousands of Soviet troops are based in the country. Mongolia is a UN member.

Education and Religion. There are primary, secondary and technical schools, and 7 higher educational institutes. Buddhist Lamaism is the leading religion, though only one monastery has survived government repression. Khalkha Mongol is the main language, written since 1941 mostly in the Cyrillic alphabet.

Morocco

Area: 171,953 sq. mi. Population (UN est. 1975): 17,500,000. Capital: Rabat. Monetary unit: Dirham.

The Kingdom of Morocco lies on the NW tip of Africa separated from Europe by the 8-mile-wide Strait of Gibraltar. It is bounded by Algeria, Mauritania, the Mediterranean and the Atlantic.

It consists of 5 natural regions: A series of mountain ranges (Riff, facing Gibraltar; Middle Atlas, extending NW of Marrakesh; Upper Atlas, and Anti-Atlas); a series of rich plains in the W; the alluvial plains of Haouz in the SW; the "mesata," a well-cultivated series of plateaus in the center; a pre-Saharan zone extending from S to E.

The inhabitants largely are a mixture of Arabs and the original Berbers.

Resources and Industries. Morocco is primarily agricultural and pastoral. Cereals rank first among agricultural products, including barley, wheat and corn. Fruit and vineyards are abundant and dates a staple crop. Carpets, leather goods, clothing and textiles are among the manufactures.

Morocco ranks 3d in world production of phosphate rock and is first in phosphate exports. It produces 5% of the world's cobalt. Other minerals are antimony, manganese, zinc, lead, oil and coal.

In the late 1960s, a number of dams were constructed for irrigation, including a large project built with U.S. aid. Foreign-owned agricultural lands were nationalized in 1973.

Tourism attracts 1,500,000 visitors annually.

History and Government. Morocco is a remnant of an early empire founded by the Arabs at the close of the 7th Century which encompassed all NW Africa and most of the Iberian Peninsula.

Part of Morocco came under Spanish rule in the 19th Century; in the early 20th France took control of the rest. A general uprising of tribes in 1910 led to the dispatch of a French expeditionary force that occupied Fez in 1911. Uprisings continued for 2 decades until the exile of Abdelkarim el Khattabi in 1926 and the surrender of Sidi Ali Hociene in 1933.

Morocco became independent Mar. 2, 1956, after agreement by France to end its protectorate. Spain signed similar agreements.

Tangier, a seaport which had been internationalized, was turned over to Moroccan control in 1956. Ifni, a small Spanish enclave on the Atlantic coast, was turned over to Morocco June 30, 1969.

Morocco annexed over 70,000 sq. mi. of phosphate-rich land Apr. 14, 1976, two-thirds of former Spanish Sahara, with the remainder annexed by Mauritania. Spain had withdrawn in February. Polisario, a guerrilla movement, proclaimed the region independent Feb. 27, and launched attacks with Algerian support.

Mohammed V, Sultan since 1927 (with the title of king since 1957), died Feb. 26, 1961. His eldest son became King Hassan II.

Under a constitution approved by referendum Dec. 7, 1962, Morocco became a constitutional monarchy. The first Parliament was elected May 17, 1963.

A new constitution was approved by voters in July 1970, providing for a unicameral, elected Chamber of Deputies. An attempted army revolt failed in July 1971. Air force pilots tried unsuccessfully to assassinate the king in Aug. 1972.

Morocco accepted U.S. military and economic aid. It has agreements with France on economic, technical and cultural cooperation. It is a member of the UN, OAU and Arab League.

Education and Religion. Trade schools and agricultural training centers have been developed, in addition to regular schools. The main university is in Rabat. Arabic is the official language; French is also widely used. The population is Sunni Moslem.

Defense. Armed forces total 61,000.

Mozambique

Area: 303,373 sq. mi. Population (UN est. 1975): 9,240,000. Capital: Maputo. Monetary unit: Mozambique escudo.

The Peoples' Republic of Mozambique faces the Indian Ocean and Mozambique Channel in SW Africa, and borders on Tanzania, Malawi, Zambia, Rhodesia, South Africa, and Swaziland. It is somewhat larger than Texas.

Coastal lowlands comprise 44% of the country, with plateaus rising in steps to the mountains along the western border.

Resources and Industries. Agriculture dominates the economy, and cashews, cotton, sugar, copra, sisal, and tea are exported. Fishing is important. Coal is the leading mineral currently produced, but tantalite, copper, iron, bauxite, and gold have been found. Manufactures include cement, alcohol, food products, and textiles. A vast hydro-power complex is being built with South African help at Cabora Bassa on the Zambezi River, which bisects the country.

History and Government. The first Portuguese post on the Mozambique coast was established in 1505, on the trade route to the East. Mozambique became independent June 25, 1975, after a ten-year war against Portuguese colonial domination. The 1974 revolution in Portugal paved the way for the orderly transfer of power to Frelimo (Front for the Liberation of Mozambique), which had earlier gained complete control of the independence movement. Frelimo took over local administration Sept. 20, 1974, over the opposition, in part violent, of some blacks and whites. The new government, led by Maoist Pres. Samora Machel, promised a gradual transition to a communist system, beginning with indoctrination to combat "individualism" and capitalist or traditionalist values. All private schools were closed. Rural collective farms were called for in a July 27, 1975, directive. All private homes were nationalized in 1976. Economic problems included the emigration of most of the country's 160,000 whites, a politically untenable economic dependence on white-ruled South Africa, and a large external debt.

Mozambique closed its border with Rhodesia Mar. 3, 1976, and some border clashes were reported.

The population is divided into various Bantu tribes, with those in the south more influenced by Portuguese culture and language. Catholicism and Islam have made many converts, and Protestant missions are present. The majority of the population is illiterate, though schools in 1970 enrolled over one-half million students.

Nauru

Area: 8 sq. mi. Population (census 1972): 6,817. Capital: Yaren. Monetary unit: Australian dollar.

Nauru, one of the world's smallest nations, became an independent republic Jan. 31, 1968, after 80 years of foreign rule. In the western Pacific 26 mi. S of the Equator and 1,300 mi. NE of Australia, Nauru is comfortably affluent because of its high-grade phosphate deposits.

Phosphate exports provide one of the world's highest per capita revenues for the 3,500 native Nauruans (883 Chinese, 627 Europeans and 1,787 Pacific Islanders also live in Nauru, many working in the phosphate industry). The deposits are expected to be nearly exhausted by 1990.

The island was discovered in 1798 by the British but was formally annexed to the German Empire in 1886. After World War I, Nauru became a League of Nations mandate administered by Australia. During World War II the Japanese occupied the island and shipped 1,200 Nauruans to the fortress island of Truk as slave laborers.

In 1947 Nauru was made a UN trust territory, administered by Australia on behalf of the 3 trust powers: Australia, Great Britain and New Zealand. Because of its small size, Nauru has not sought UN membership.

An elected Parliament has 18 members.

Nepal

Area: 54,362 sq. mi. Population (Govt. est. 1975): 12,570,000. Capital: Katmandu. Monetary unit: Nepalese rupee.

Nepal is a monarchy in the Himalayas, bounded on the N by China (Tibet) and E, S and W by India. It is about the size of Arkansas.

There are many fertile valleys lying in the slopes of the lofty mountains, including Mt. Everest, on the Tibet border. The capital is in the valley of Katmandu, 15 mi. long and 20 wide, which is noted for its many, lavishly decorated shrines.

Virtually closed to the outside world for centuries, Nepal is now linked to India and Pakistan by modern roads and air service and to Tibet by road.

Nepal has established a 500 sq. mi. game preserve for elephants, tigers, rhinoceroses, leopards, boars, crocodiles and over 500 species of birds.

Resources and Industries. Nepal has rich forests and quartz deposits. The country exports jute, rice, grain, cattle, hides, wheat and drugs. Nepal is a net exporter of food. Trade is 90% with India. Tourism provides vital funds.

Two-thirds of a 3,000 mile road network has been completed with aid from the U.S., India, China, and other nations. Hydroelectric power is also being developed.

History and Government. Nepal was originally a group of petty principalities, the inhabitants of one of which, the Gurkhas, became dominant about 1769. In 1951 King Tribhubana Bir Bikram, member of the Shah family, ended the system of rule by hereditary premiers of the Ranas family, who had kept the kings virtual prisoners, and established a cabinet system of government.

Tribhubana was succeeded by his son, Mahendra Bir Bikram Shah Dev, who died Jan. 31, 1972, and was succeeded by his son, Birendra Bir Bikram Shah Dev. A new constitution was promulgated Dec. 16, 1962, providing for a three-tier system of indirectly elected councils topped by a National Assembly or National Panchayat.

Education and Religion. There are more than 2,400 English schools in addition to thousands of Sanskrit and Nepali schools and other institutions of learning. Over a dozen languages are spoken, including Nepali, the official language. Buddha was born at Lumbini in South-Central Nepal. Hinduism and Buddhism are the main religions. Polygamy, child marriage and the caste system were officially abolished in 1963.

The Netherlands

Area (land): 14,192 sq. mi. Population (Govt. est. 1976): 13,733,578. Capital: Amsterdam. Monetary unit: Guilder.

The Kingdom of the Netherlands, a constitutional monarchy in NW Europe, is bounded by Germany, Belgium, and the North Sea. Its surface is flat, with an average height above sea level of 37 ft., with much land below sea level, reclaimed and protected by dikes, of which there are 1,500 mi. The country is about twice the area of New Jersey.

Since 1927 the government has been draining the IJsselmeer, formerly the Zuider Zee, and converting the reclaimed land into farms. The total will add over 550,000 acres. By 1972, 410,000 acres had been reclaimed. Work is also progressing on damming the southwest estuaries.

The Hague is the seat of government, but Amsterdam is the sole capital of the kingdom and the inaugurations of sovereigns are held there.

Rotterdam, located along the principal mouth of the Rhine, handles the most cargo of any ocean port in the world.

Resources and Industries. About 43% of total land area is given to pasture, farming takes 22%, heath, dunes and forest 8%, horticulture 3.4%. Of the arable land 80% is in holdings of fewer than 50 acres and about 20% of fewer than 10 acres. Cereals, potatoes, sugar beets, vegetables and fruits are raised. Agriculture and fishing engage about 6% of the workers. Dairy products are a major export. In pork exports the nation ranks 2d to Denmark. Flowers, bulbs, seeds and trees are grown commercially.

The most important industries are metals and machinery, food, chemicals, textiles, oil refining. Amsterdam is famous for diamond cutting; Delft for pottery. Eindhoven has electrical and radio factories. Natural gas reserves are large. Index of industrial production (1970 = 100) was 115 for 1975.

Canals, of which there are 3,478 mi., are important in transportation. The Rhine, Meuse and Schelde reach the sea through the Netherlands and carry enormous traffic.

The 1973-74 Arab oil embargo against Western nations was not lifted from the Netherlands until July 1974; the Dutch had refused Arab demands to condemn Israel.

Foreign trade in thousands of U.S. dollars:

	Imports	Exports
1974	33,816,000	33,568,000
1975	34,375,000	34,853,000

History and Government. After the empire of Charlemagne (d. 814) fell apart, the Netherlands (Holland, Belgium, Flanders) split among counts, dukes and bishops, passed to Burgundy and thence to Charles V of Spain. His son, Philip II, tried to check the Dutch drive toward political freedom and Protestantism (1568-1573). William the Silent, prince of Orange, led a confederation of the northern provinces, called Estates, in the Union of Utrecht, 1579. The Estates retained individual sovereignty, but were represented jointly in the States-General, a body that had control of foreign affairs and defense. In 1581 they repudiated allegiance to Spain. The rise of the Dutch republic to naval, economic and artistic eminence came in the 17th Century.

The United Dutch Republic ended 1795 when the French formed the Batavian Republic. Napoleon made his brother Louis king of Holland, 1806; Louis abdicated 1810 when Napoleon annexed Holland. In 1813 the French were expelled. In 1815 the Congress of Vienna formed a kingdom of the Netherlands, including Belgium, under William I. In 1830, the Belgians seceded and formed a separate kingdom.

The constitution, promulgated 1814, and subsequently revised, assures a hereditary constitutional monarchy. Executive power rests in the crown (the queen and ministers). Legislative powers are exercised jointly by the crown and Parliament (States-General) of 2 chambers: First Chamber, 75 members, elected for 6 years (one half every 3d year) by the provincial legislatures, and the Second Chamber, 150 deputies, elected for 4 years directly. Universal suffrage for all citizens over 18 and proportional representation are in force. The sovereign exercises the executive authority through a Council of Ministers, the president thereof corresponding to a prime minister. There is a State Council named by the sovereign, of which she is president, to be consulted on all legislative and some executive matters.

The reigning sovereign since Sept. 6, 1948, is Queen Juliana Louise Emma Marie Wilhelmina, born April 30, 1909. Queen Juliana on Jan. 7, 1937, married Prince Bernhard of Lippe-Biesterfeld, the Prince of the Netherlands. They have 4 daughters. Princess Beatrix Wilhelmina Armgard, born Jan. 31, 1938, heir presumptive, married Claus von Ambsberg, West German diplomat, Mar. 10, 1966. On Apr. 27, 1967, Princess Beatrix gave birth to the first of three sons, Willem-Alexander, Prince of Orange, first male heir to the throne in 3 generations.

Surinam, a Dutch associated state on the northern coast of South America, became independent in 1975. About 160,000 Surinamers, one third of the population, emigrated to the Netherlands, adding to problems of unemployment.

Education and Religion. There is complete liberty of worship. The royal family belongs to the Netherlands Reformed Church. The population is 40.4% Roman Catholic; 33.7% Protestant; others 2.3%; nonchurch members 23.6%. Education is obligatory from ages 6 through 15. Instruction is free in both public and denominational schools and teachers are paid by the state. There are 13 universities.

Defense. Military forces total 112,500.

The Netherlands is a member of the UN, NATO, EEC, Council of Europe and Benelux.

Netherlands Antilles

The **Netherlands Antilles**, constitutionally on a level of equality with the Netherlands homeland within the Kingdom, consist of 2 groups of islands in the West Indies. **Curacao, Aruba** and **Bonaire** are near the South American coast; **St. Eustatius, Saba** and the southern part of **St. Maarten** are SE of Puerto Rico. Northern two-thirds of St. Maarten belong to French Guadeloupe; the French call the island St. Martin. Total area of the 2 groups is 395 sq. mi., including: Aruba 70, Bonaire 112, Curacao 180, St. Eustatius 12, Saba 5, St. Maarten (Dutch part) 16.

The Netherlands Antilles population (est. 1975) was 240,000. Willemstad is the capital. Chief products are corn, pulse, salt and phosphate; principal industry is the refining of crude oil from Venezuela. Tourism is an important industry, as are electronics and shipbuilding.

New Zealand

Area: 103,736 sq. mi. (268,676 sq. km.). Population (Govt. est. 1976): 3,148,000. Capital: Wellington. Monetary unit: New Zealand dollar.

The main islands of New Zealand lie in the South Pacific about 1,300 mi. E of Australia; total area is about that of Colorado. Including remote islands to the N and the Ross Dependency to the S, the reach of New Zealand is from the tropics to Antarctica.

Snow-topped mountains, smoking volcanoes, deep fjords, boiling geysers, golden beaches and the glowworm caves of Waitomo are among attractions.

New Zealand comprises **North Island,** 44,281 sq. mi.; **South Island,** 58,093 sq. mi.; **Stewart Island,** 670 sq. mi.; **Chatham Islands,** 372 sq. mi. Both the North and South Islands slightly exceed 500 mi. in length. Cook Strait, separating the two, is only 16 mi. wide at its narrowest.

In 1965, the **Cook Islands** (pop. 1974, 19,522; area 93 sq. mi.) became self-governing although New Zealand retains responsibility for defense and foreign affairs. Niue (pop. 1974, 3,992; area 100 sq. mi.) lies 400 mi. to W (pop. 1974, 3,992; area 100 sq. mi.). **Tokelau Is.,** (pop. 1974, 1,574; area 4 sq. mi.) are 300 mi. N of Samoa.

Wellington and Auckland, on North Is., are the chief ports. South Is. has the picturesque Southern Alps and Tasman, Fox and Franz Josef Glaciers. There are 15 named peaks over 10,000 ft., the highest being Mt. Cook, 12,349 ft. Christchurch and Dunedin are the main cities of South Is.

Resources and Industries. New Zealand is largely dependent on agricultural products for export income; wool, meat and dairy products account for over 70% of the total value. Next to Australia, New Zealand is the world's largest exporter of meat (mostly lamb).

Imports totaled $3.65 billion (in U.S. dollars) in 1974; exports were $2.44 billion.

Agriculture engages 12% of the population, manufacturing industries 25%. Private enterprise is basic in the economy, but state ownership or regulation affects many industries. Transportation, broadcasting, mining, and forestry are largely state-owned.

Food processing is the largest industry.

The pulp and paper industry on North Is. is partly powered by natural steam from volcanic areas. The first iron and steel plant commenced production in 1968. Natural gas was discovered at Kapuni, North Is., 1967, and is piped to several towns. A large hydroelectric plant at Lake Manapouri, South Is., began providing power for an aluminum smelter in 1971.

About 300,000 tourists visit New Zealand annually, over 55,000 of them from the U.S.

History and Government. New Zealand was discovered in 1642 by Abel Janszoon Tasman, a Dutch navigator, and its coasts were explored by British Capt. James Cook, 1769-1770. British sovereignty was proclaimed in 1840, with organized settlement commencing in the same year. Representative institutions were granted in 1853. The Colony became a Dominion in 1907 and is an independent member of the Commonwealth.

The native Maoris are Polynesians. Early in the 19th Century they numbered an est. 200,000; violence and European diseases cut them to 40,000 by the end of the century. Recently they have increased at 3% annually and totaled 249,800 in 1975.

Government consists of a governor-general, representing the British Crown; a House of Representatives whose members are elected by universal suffrage for 3-year terms (4 of 87 members are elected directly by the Maori people); a prime minister and Cabinet who are members of the House and accountable to it. In Nov. 1975 elections the National (conservative) party returned to power after 3 years of Labour party rule.

In July 1973, to protest France's testing of nuclear devices above Mururoa Atoll, a New Zealand Navy frigate cruised just outside the French South Pacific island's 12-mi. limit but within the test area.

New Zealand is a member of the UN, Commonwealth, and ANZUS.

New Zealand's tax rates reach a maximum of 50 cents per dollar at the $12,240 income level. "Cradle-to-grave" social security includes maternity, school, medical, hospital, medicine, pension and other benefits.

Education and Religion. Education is free and compulsory between the ages of 6 and 14. There are 7 universities. The Anglican and Presbyterian Churches have the largest followings.

Defense. Military forces total 12,685.

Ross Dependency, administered by New Zealand since 1923, comprises 160,000 sq. mi. of Antarctic territory.

Nicaragua

Area: 57,143 sq. mi. Population (Govt. est. 1975): 2,160,000. Capital: Managua. Monetary unit: Cordoba.

Nicaragua, largest of the Central or Middle American States, lies between the Caribbean and the Pacific with more than 200 mi. of coastline on each. The country is bordered by Honduras on the N and Costa Rica on the S. The Cordillera range of mountains, including many volcanic peaks, runs NW-SE through the middle of the country. Between this range and a range of volcanic peaks to the W lie Lake Managua, 38 Mi. by 15, and Lake Nicaragua, 100 mi. by 45, of great importance to the transport system. The government-owned Pacific Railroad, Corinto to Leon and Managua to Granada, 171 mi., is the principal rail line.

Resources and Industries. The nation has valuable forests and some gold and silver is mined. It is essentially an agricultural country, but industrialization, including oil refining, is growing. On the broad tropical plains of the east coast, bananas, cotton, fruit and yucca are cultivated. Products of the western half include coffee, sugar, corn, beans, cocoa, rice, sesame, tobacco and wheat.

Cotton, coffee, meat, and sugar account for most of the value of exports.

A severe earthquake, Dec. 23, 1972, destroyed much of Managua; about 6,000 died and 200,000 were left homeless. The nation was also hit by severe drought, lasting into 1973.

History and Government. After gaining independence from Spain, 1821, Nicaragua was united for a short period with Mexico then with the United Provinces of Central America, finally becoming an independent republic, 1838.

The constitution, revised in 1960, provided for a Congress of 2 chambers: a House of Deputies of 45 members and a Senate of 18 members, all elected by popular vote. Ex-presidents also serve in the Senate and are appointed for life. The president is elected for 5 years and may not succeed himself.

Gen. Anastasio Somoza Debayle was elected president 1967. He resigned 1972 and was succeeded by a 3-man National Junta. He was elected president again Sept. 1, 1974. The Somozas, richest Nicaraguan family, have dominated politics for four decades.

Education and Religion. Roman Catholicism is the prevailing religion. There are 3 universities. Spanish is the official language, but English is spoken by Jamaican blacks on the Caribbean coast and some Indian dialects survive. Nicaragua is a UN and OAS member.

Niger

Area: 489,206 sq. mi. Population (Govt. est. 1975): 4,600,000. Capital: Niamey. Monetary unit: CFA franc.

The Republic of the Niger, a former French Overseas Territory in the heart of West Africa, is bounded by Libya, Algeria, Chad, Upper Volta, Dahomey, Nigeria and Mali. Chief access to the country, a vast plateau almost twice the size of Texas, is by air. The Niger River flows through the western corner.

Niger became fully independent Aug. 3, 1960. It signed a bilateral agreement Apr. 24, 1961, retaining close ties with France. Hamani Diori, president since independence, was overthrown in a military coup, Apr. 15, 1974.

Niger is an agricultural and pastoral land. Peanuts are the principal cash crop; livestock (cattle, sheep, camels, donkeys, goats) are second in importance. Cotton is being promoted. Drought and famine struck in 1973-74; aid was sent by several nations, half of it by the U.S. Half the country's livestock died during the drought. A new drought struck in 1975-76.

Uranium mines began production in 1971; known reserves of uranium are fifth greatest in the world.

The people are predominantly Moslems. French is the official language.

Nigeria

The World Almanac is sponsored in Nigeria by the Daily and Sunday Times, 3 Kakawa St., Lagos, Nigeria; founded 1925; circulation 190,000 daily, 244,500 Sunday; published by The Daily Times of Nigeria, Ltd.

Area: 356,669 sq. mi. Population (UN est. 1975): 62,930,000. Capital: Lagos. Monetary unit: Naira.

The Federal Republic of Nigeria, Africa's most

populous country, became independent of Britain in 1960. Larger than Texas and Oklahoma combined, it lies on the southern side of the West African bulge, between Dahomey and Cameroon, with Niger to the N and Chad NE. It comprises nearly 250 tribal and linguistic groups, including the Hausas in the N, Ibos in the E. Yorubas in the W.

The northern desert region gives way to savannah and open woodland; tropical rain forests are in the south, with mangrove swamps along the coast.

Nigeria's rich natural resources include oil, coal, iron, limestone and natural gas. It produces much of the world's columbium ore (for steel alloys).

By 1975, Nigeria became the world's 8th largest petroleum producer; oil accounted for 90% of export value with cocoa 2d. Other exports are tobacco, tin, palm products, peanuts, cotton lint, hides and skins, lumber, rubber and peanuts. Under an "indigenization" program, 55 categories of businesses were to be run by blacks only by 1974. Oil revenues have made possible a massive economic development program, largely using private enterprise.

Foreign trade in thousands of U.S. dollars:

	Imports	Exports
1974	2,734,000	9,559,000
1975—6 mo.	2,487,000	3,688,000

Nigeria became a sovereign country Oct. 1, 1960, and a republic Oct. 1, 1963. It is a member of the UN and Commonwealth. Its first constitution provided for 4 regions with local autonomy, and a federal Parliament and prime minister.

In 1966 there were 2 military coups and periods of political assassination and inter-tribal strife, ending a long period of coalition governments of the majority Northern Region and other regions.

On May 30, 1967, the Eastern Region seceded, proclaiming itself the Republic of Biafra. The move plunged the country into civil war. Casualties in the war were estimated at over 1 million, including many "Biafrans" (mostly Ibos) who died of starvation despite international efforts to provide relief. The secessionists, after steadily losing ground, capitulated Jan. 12, 1970; Gen Odumegwu Ojukwu, rebel leader, fled to the Ivory Coast. Gen. Gowon announced a general amnesty. In July 1975 Gowon himself was ousted in a military coup.

Nigeria led in the formation of the West African Economic Community, linking 15 French, English, and Portuguese-speaking countries.

The northern parts of the nation are predominantly Moslem; there are many animists, Christians and Moslems in the south.

Several universities cap a school system with over four million students. English is the official language; 250 African tongues are also spoken.

Nigeria's armed forces, largest in black Africa with 208,000 men, has received Soviet assistance.

Norway

Area: 125,181 sq. mi. Population (Govt. est. 1976) 4,017,000. Capital: Oslo. Monetary unit: Krone.

Norway occupies the W part of the Scandinavian Peninsula in NW Europe. It shares borders with Sweden, Finland and the USSR. The rocky W coast is deeply cut by fjords of scenic grandeur. Norway's area is about that of New Mexico.

The country's greatest length is 1,100 mi.; its width varies from 270 to only 4 mi. at the narrowest point. The coastline, including the fjords and largest of the 150,000 islands, is 17,000 mi. long. The climate is mild and moist on the W coast, but fairly cold and dry in the E.

The midnight sun is a phenomenon of the northern area where the sun does not set from the middle of May until the end of July, and does not rise above the horizon from approximately Nov. 20 to Jan. 24.

Resources and Industries. Only 3% of the land, 4,300 sq. mi., is cultivated; rivers and lakes occupy 5,000; forests 29,455. The rest is mostly barren.

Forests supply a sizable wood and paper industry. Large quantities of cod, herring, mackerel and salmon are caught. Norway has the world's 6th largest fish catch. Mines yield copper, pyrites, nickel, iron, zinc, lead. North Sea oil production began in 1971. Norway became a net oil exporter by 1976, with pipes to Germany and the UK. Norway has harnessed its waterfalls to provide power. Important industries by rank, are engineering (including shipbuilding), metallurgical, food, beverages, chemical, paper and pulp, mining. Farm products include oats, rye, potatoes, dairy products and fruits. Industry and mining employ 33.6% of workers, agriculture and fisheries 9.5%.

Norway's merchant marine fleet is the world's 4th largest. Its earnings helped offset the unfavorable balance of trade. Foreign trade in thousands of U.S. dollars:

	Imports	Exports
1974	8,414,000	6,274,000
1975	9,718,000	7,207,000

History and Government. The first supreme ruler of Norway was Harald the Fairhaired who came to power in 872 A.D. Between 800 and 1000, Norway's Vikings raided and occupied parts of Europe. Christianity was introduced 1030.

The country was united with Denmark 1381-1814, with Sweden 1814-1905. Germany attacked Norway Apr. 9, 1940, and held it until liberation May 8, 1945.

Norway is a constitutional monarchy. The king is Olav V (born July 2, 1903); he became king Sept. 21, 1957. The heir to the throne, Crown Prince Harald, was born Feb. 21, 1937.

Legislative power is vested in the Storting, whose 155 members are elected for 4 years. Executive power is held by a prime minister and his cabinet.

Social security includes health and unemployment insurance and pensions.

Education and Religion. The Evangelical Lutheran religion is endowed by the state. All religions enjoy complete freedom of worship. Education is free at all levels and compulsory from ages 7 to 16. Universities are subsidized by the state.

Defense. Armed forces total 35,000, plus a Home Guard of 80,000.

Norway is a member of UN, NATO, EFTA, Nordic Council and Council of Europe. A trade agreement was reached with the EC in 1973. Norwegians rejected EC membership in a 1972 referendum.

Svalbard

Svalbard is a group of mountainous islands in the Arctic Ocean, c. 23,957 sq. mi., pop. varying seasonally from 1,500 to 3,000. The largest, West Spitsbergen, c. 15,000 sq. mi., seat of governor, is about 370 mi. N of Norway. By a treaty signed in Paris, 1920, major European powers recognized the sovereignty of Norway, which incorporated it 1925. Both Norway and the U.S.S.R. mine rich coal deposits. Mt. Newton (West Spitsbergen) is 5,633 ft. tall.

Oman

Area: 82,000 sq. mi. Population (UN est. 1975): 770,-000. Capital: Muscat. Monetary unit: Omani riyal.

The Sultanate of Oman (formerly Muscat and Oman) is an independent monarchy occupying the SE corner of the Arabian Peninsula and including the tip of a nearby peninsula, Ruus-al-Jebal, to the N. The Sultanate has a coastline of 1,000 mi. along the Gulf of Oman to the NE and the Arabian Sea to the SE. Climate is generally hot and dry.

There is a narrow coastal plain up to 10 mi. wide, a range of barren mountains with Jebal Akhdar, the highest, reaching c. 9,900 ft., and a wide, stony, mostly waterless plateau averaging 1,000 ft. in altitude. The Sultanate is the size of Utah.

Exports are mainly oil, dates and some dried fish, limes and pomegranates. Cultivated areas also produce bananas, grapes, wheat, vegetables, coconuts and frankincense. Goats and sheep are raised.

Oil was discovered in 1964 and production began in 1967. By 1975 Oman was the world's 17th largest producer.

The people are predominantly Arab, but there are also Indians, Baluchi, Negroes and others. The language is Arabic, but Hindi, Urdu, Baluchi and others are also spoken. The religion is mainly Islam of the Ibadhi sect.

A long history of rule by other lands ended with ouster of the Persians in 1744. On July 23, 1970, Sultan Said bin Taimur was overthrown by his son, who became Sultan Qabus bin Said. The new sultan changed the nation's name to Sultanate of Oman. He launched a domestic development program and battled leftist rebels in the southern Dhofar area. The government received arms aid and over 3,500 advisors from Iran; the guerrillas reportedly got arms from the U.S.S.R., Iraq, and Southern Yemen.

Pakistan

Area: 310,403 sq. mi. Population (Gov. est. 1975): 70,260,000. Capital: Islamabad. Monetary unit: Rupee.

Pakistan became a sovereign nation Aug. 14, 1947, when what had been the British Empire of India achieved independence and was partitioned into 2 countries, Pakistan and India. At first a dominion, Pakistan declared itself a republic on Mar. 23, 1956.

Pakistan was divided in 2 sections, West Pakistan and East Pakistan. The 2 areas were nearly 1,000 mi. apart on opposite sides of India.

East Pakistan became the separate, independent nation of Bangladesh as a result of its 1971 rebellion and the Dec. 3-17, 1971, Pakistan-India war.

Pakistan (the former West Pakistan) adjoins Iran, Afghanistan, China, India and the Arabian Sea. In the NE is Kashmir, ownership long disputed with India.

Pakistan is a land of rugged mountains and river valleys, where irrigation aids agriculture, the occupation of 60% of the people. The Indus flows for over 1,000 mi. in Pakistan from the base of the Himalayas to the Arabian Sea and with its tributaries supplies reservoirs, canals and hydroelectric plants. In the W, in the Hindu Kush Mts., the highest is Tirich Mir. In the N are Rakaposhi, Nanja Parbat, and Mt. K2 (Godwin Austen), 28,250 ft., 2d highest in the world. The climate is mostly dry with little rainfall and summer temperatures up to 120°F.

Resources and Industries. Rice, wheat, cotton, oilseeds, tobacco, sugar, flour, wool and fish are important products. Minerals include sulphur, gypsum, salt, chromite, cement, petroleum, extensive natural gas, coal, asbestos, antimony, magnesite and silica.

Pakistan manufactures cotton textiles (its largest industry), wool, silk, leather, rayon, cement, card and paper board, sugar, chemicals, dyes, synthetic fertilizers, surgical implements.

Foreign trade in thousands of U.S. dollars:

	Imports	Exports
1974	1,738,000	1,105,000
1975	2,125,000	1,005,000

History and Government. The land now called Pakistan shares the 5,000-year history of the India-Pakistan sub-continent. At the present day sites of Harappa and Mohenjo Daro, the Indus Valley Civilization, with large cities and elaborate irrigation systems, flourished c. 4000-2500 B.C.

A lasting influence on Pakistan was the arrival of Islam with the first Arab invasion of 712 A.D.

After World War I the Moslems of British India began agitation for minority rights in elections.

Mohammad Ali Jinnah (1876-1948) was the principal architect of Pakistan. A lawyer who studied in England, he was a leader of the Moslem League from 1916, and worked for dominion status for India. From 1940 he advocated a separate Moslem state.

When the British withdrew Aug. 14, 1947, the Islamic majority areas of India acquired self-government as Pakistan, with dominion status in the Commonwealth.

Pakistan became a republic in 1956. In Oct. 1958, Gen. Mohammad Ayub Khan took power in a coup. He was elected president in 1960 and reelected in 1965. Pakistan had a National Assembly (legislature) with equal membership from East and West Pakistan, and 2 Provincial Assemblies.

Ayub resigned Mar. 25, 1969, after several months of violent rioting and unrest, most of it in East Pakistan. There were demands for a parliamentary form of government, for direct elections and economic reforms. In East Pakistan, which had about 56% of the population, there were demands for autonomy.

The government was turned over to Gen. Agha Mohammad Yahya Khan and martial law was declared; Yahya assumed the presidency.

The Awami League, which sought regional autonomy for East Pakistan, won a majority in Dec. 1970 elections to a National Assembly which was to write a new constitution. In March 1971 Yahya postponed the Assembly. Rioting and strikes broke out in the East.

On Mar. 25, 1971, government troops launched attacks in the East. The Easterners, aided by India, proclaimed the independent nation of Bangladesh. In months of widespread fighting, countless thousands were killed. Some 10 million Easterners fled into India.

Full scale war between India and Pakistan had spread to both the East and West fronts by December 3. Pakistan troops in the East surrendered Dec. 16; Pakistan agreed to a cease-fire in the West Dec. 17.

Zulfikar Ali Bhutto, leader of the Pakistan People's party, which had won the most West Pakistan votes in the Dec. 1970 elections, became president Dec. 20. In 1972 he announced new land reforms and said the government would control management of major industries.

On July 3, 1972, Pakistan and India signed a pact agreeing to withdraw troops from their borders and seek peaceful solutions to all problems.

In Aug. 1973 India agreed to release 93,000 Pakistani prisoners held since 1971. The return was completed in April 1974. Pakistan agreed to repatriate 200,000 Bengali nationals stranded in Pakistan, and agreed to accept some Biharis (non-Bengalis) unwanted in Bangladesh. India and Pakistan agreed in 1976 to resume full diplomatic relations.

A new constitution adopted Apr. 10, 1973, made Pakistan a federal Islamic republic, with a 2-chamber Parliament and a president, but with executive power given to the prime minister. Bhutto became prime minister Aug. 14.

Education and Religion. Most of the population is Moslem. Education is free through the tenth grade. Urdu is the national language, English, Punjabi, Sindhi, Pushtu, Baluchi, and others are widely spoken.

Defense. Armed forces total 392,000.

Pakistan is a member of the UN and CENTO. Following clashes between India and China in 1962, Pakistan made commercial and aid agreements with Communist China. U.S. aid to both Pakistan and India was suspended during the 1966 war over Kashmir but both economic aid and "nonlethal" military aid were resumed in 1966. The embargo was modified in 1973 and lifted in 1975.

Panama

Area: 28,753 sq. mi. Population (Govt. est. 1975): 1,670,000. Capital: Panama. Monetary unit: Balboa.

The Republic of Panama occupies the isthmus of Panama, connecting Central and South America. Smaller than South Carolina, it has a shoreline of 477 mi. on the Caribbean and 767 mi. on the Pacific. Its width varies from about 37 to 110 mi. It is bounded by Colombia and Costa Rica, and is bisected by the 10-mi. wide U.S. Canal Zone.

Resources and Industries. Panama has extensive forests, and exports mahogany. Only half the rich arable land is cultivated. Sufficient cement, clay and salt are produced for domestic needs. Bananas are the largest export, rivaled by products of a large petroleum refinery (which imports crude oil). Also exported are pineapples, cocoa, coconuts, sugar, shrimp. A vast copper mining plan has been approved.

Due to easy Panama ship regulations and strictures in the U.S., merchant tonnage registered in Panama since World War II ranks high in size. Registered number of ships more than 1,000 gross tons each is over 1,300.

History and Government. The coast of Panama was sighted by Rodrigo de Bastidas, sailing with Columbus for Spain in 1501, and was visited by Columbus in 1502. Vasco Nunez de Balboa crossed the isthmus and "discovered" the Pacific Ocean Sept. 13, 1513. Spanish colonies were ravaged by Francis Drake, 1572-95, and Henry Morgan, 1668-71. Morgan destroyed the old city of Panama which had been founded in 1519. Freed from Spain, Panama joined Colombia in 1821. Separatist forces in Panama sought to gain independence from Colombia several times.

Panama declared its independence from Colombia Nov. 3, 1903, with U.S. recognition. U.S. Naval forces deterred action by Colombia. On Nov. 18, 1903, Panama granted use, occupation and control of the Canal Zone to the U.S. by treaty, ratified Feb. 26, 1904. *(See also Canal Zone and Panama Canal.)*

Rioting began Jan. 9, 1964, in a dispute over the flying of the U.S. and Panamanian flags and terms of the 1903 treaty. At least 21 Panamanians and 3 U.S. soldiers died in the rioting.

In 1967 new treaties were proposed, but Panama rejected them in 1970. In Feb. 1974 the U.S. and Panama agreed to negotiate a new treaty which would give the U.S. the right to operate and protect the canal for a certain period, with Panama sharing in the revenues, and would also set a date for final transfer of jurisdiction to Panama. Opposition by U.S. Senators stalled the talks.

Panama adopted its 4th constitution in 1972, providing for a president, Legislative Council and an elected Assembly. The Assembly gave Gen. Omar Torrijos powers as head of government.

Education and Religion. Most Panamanians are Roman Catholics. Education is compulsory, ages 7-15. Two universities are in Panama City. Spanish is the official language; English is widely spoken.

Papua New Guinea

Area: 178,260 sq. mi. Population (Govt. est. 1975): 2,760,000. Capital: Port Moresby. Monetary unit: Kina.

Papua New Guinea occupies the eastern half of the island of New Guinea, second largest in the world. It lies N of Australia and just S of the Equator, and borders on Irian Jaya, controlled by Indonesia. Thickly forested mountains cover much of the center of the country, with lowlands along the coasts. Included in the country are the nearby islands of the Bismarck and Solomon groups, including the **Admiralty Is.**, **New Ireland, New Britain** and **Bougainville;** the latter two enjoy some autonomy. A secession movement in copper-rich Bougainville led to violence in 1973. Papua New Guinea is somewhat larger than California.

Leading exports are copper, gold, silver, timber, coffee, coconut products, fish, and cocoa. Exports amount to $200 million annually. Livestock raising is being developed. Natural gas has been found.

The southern half of the country was first claimed by Britain in 1884, and transferred to Australia in 1905. The northern half was claimed by Germany in 1884, but captured in the first World War by Australia, which was granted a League of Nations mandate and then a UN trusteeship over the area. The two territories were administered jointly after 1949, were given self-government Dec. 1, 1973, and became independent Sept. 16, 1975. Australia promised $1 billion in aid for the 5 years starting 1976-77, and pledged assistance in defense and foreign affairs.

Apart from 40,000 Australians, Europeans, and Chinese, the population descends from a huge number of indigenous Melanesian tribes, many living in almost complete isolation. More than 700 languages are spoken, many of them mutually unintelligible, with pidgin English the medium of communication. Over 250,000 students attend school. The University of Papua New Guinea opened in 1966.

Paraguay

Area: 157,047 sq. mi. Population (UN est. 1975): 2,650,000. Capital: Asuncion. Monetary unit: Guarani.

The Republic of Paraguay, one of the 2 landlocked countries of South America, is bounded by Bolivia (also landlocked), Brazil and Argentina. Extensive plains are excellent for pastures and farms, and the mountain slopes are covered with luxuriant forests. Paraguay is about the size of California. The Paraguay River, the most important waterway, is 1,800 mi. long.

Resources and Industries. Timber resources are large. Most of the population is agricultural and pastoral, with cattle breeding the principal industry. Most important agricultural crops are corn, wheat, cotton, beans, peanuts, tobacco, and citrus fruits.

Chief exports are beef and other food products: cotton, wood products, hides, tobacco, yerba mate (tea), vegetable oils.

The first stages of a large hydroelectric project were completed in 1968-70; a highway to Brazil to aid trade shipments for the landlocked nation was completed.

In 1974 Paraguay and Brazil announced partnership plans to build a 10-million-kilowatt hydroelectric plant, largest in the world, at Itaipu on the Parana River, the border between the 2 nations.

History and Government. Visited by Sebastian Cabot in 1527 and settled as a Spanish possession in 1535. Paraguay gained its independence from Spain in 1811, and fought Brazil, Argentina and Uruguay (War of the Triple Alliance). 1865-1870.

A new constitution, adopted in 1967, provided for a president, a Senate, and a House of Representatives.

In elections held Feb. 11, 1973, Gen. Alfredo Stroessner, who had ruled Paraguay since 1954, was reelected president for a 5-year term. Suppression of the opposition and of Indians has been charged by international civil rights groups.

Education and Religion. Roman Catholicism is the established religion but others are guaranteed freedom. Primary education is compulsory, ages 7-14. Spanish is the official language; but Spanish and Guarani, an Indian tongue spoken exclusively by half the population, are designated national languages.

Peru

Area: 496,222 sq. mi. Population (Govt. est. 1975): 15,870,000. Capital: Lima. Monetary unit: Sol.

Peru, on the Pacific coast of South America, is bounded by Ecuador, Colombia, Brazil, Bolivia, Chile and the Pacific. It has a Pacific coastline of 1,410 mi. and an extreme width, from western coast to eastern jungle, of about 800 mi. It is about the size of Arizona, New Mexico and Texas combined.

The Andes reach 22,205 ft. (Mt. Huascaran); 7 peaks tower above 19,000 ft. The uplands of western slopes of the Andes are well watered as are the eastern slopes and lowlands reaching the Amazon basin, where the port of Iquitos loads ocean-going vessels for a 2,300-mi. trip down the Amazon through Brazil.

The coastal area on the west is almost rainless, but the soil is fertile, and irrigation, using rivers pouring down from the Andes, has made the area highly productive.

Lima, the capital, is in the coastal region and is also the nation's commercial center. Callao, the chief seaport, is 7 mi. west of Lima.

Inca and earlier Chimu ruins make Peru a mecca for archeologists, notably at Cuzco, Chan Chan, and the Andean city of Machu Picchu.

A severe earthquake hit northern Peru May 31, 1970, destroying many towns and killing 66,794.

Resources and Industries. Agriculture and stock raising occupy half the population.

The leading agricultural product is cotton. Wool, hides, skins, sugar, coffee, rice, potatoes, beans, barley and tobacco also are produced. Corn, native to Peru, is a staple food.

Peru is normally the world's·top fishing nation; it takes about a sixth of total world tonnage, mostly anchovies from the plankton-rich waters of the coastal Peru current. Most of the take is ground into fish meal for poultry and livestock feed. But in 1972 the industry was crippled by a disappearance of anchovies from offshore waters. In 1973 the government nationalized the crippled industry. In 1974 a shift in the ocean currents brought at least some of the anchovies back.

The mountains are rich in minerals. The Toquepala copper mine in the southern Andes is one of the world's largest. Lead, zinc, and iron are also mined. The steel industry has expanded. The first petroleum shipments from eastern fields went down the Amazon in 1974, but total reserves remain unknown.

Fishmeal is the leading export, with copper 2d. Other exports are cotton, sugar, iron ore, lead, zinc, coffee, and wool.

In 1968-74, the military government converted large farmlands into cooperatives, expropriated several large U.S. companies with compensation, forced foreign mining companies to expand investments, and ordered local industries to turn over 50% of ownership to their workers.

History and Government. The powerful Inca empire had its seat at Cuzco in the Andes (alt. 11,000 ft.) when Francisco Pizarro, Spanish conquistador, began raiding Peru for its wealth, 1532. In 1533 he had the ruling Inca, Atahualpa, fill a room with gold, then executed him and enslaved the natives.

Lima was the seat of Spanish viceroys until the Argentine liberator, Jose de San Martin, captured it in 1821; Spain was defeated by Simon Bolivar and Antonio J. de Sucre and recognized Peruvian independence, 1824. Chile defeated Peru and Bolivia, 1879-84, and took Tarapaca, Tacna, and Arica; returned Tacna, 1929.

The constitution provided for a president and a bicameral legislature, all elected for 6-year terms. On Oct. 3, 1968, a military coup ousted Pres. Fernando Belaunde Terry. Food shortages, escalating debt, and strikes helped lead to another coup, Aug. 29, 1976.

Education and Religion. Roman Catholicism is the state religion.

About 46% of the population is Indian; 43% is mestizo (mixed); 11% is of Spanish descent, with small percentages of Negroes, Chinese, and Japanese.

Education is free and compulsory, ages 7-16. There are 33 universities. Spanish and Quechua are the official languages; Aymara is also spoken. About 5 million Indians do not speak Spanish. The government has tried to preserve the Indian heritages. Peru is a member of the UN and OAS.

Philippines

Area: 115,707 sq. mi. Population (Govt. est. 1975): 42,760,000. Capital: Quezon City. Monetary unit: Peso.

The Republic of the Philippines occupies an archipelago in the western Pacific, 500 mi. from the SE coast of Asia. Over 7,100 islands extend 1,150 mi. N to S, 682 E to W.

Eleven of the islands comprise the bulk of the area. The country is about the size of Arizona.

The archipelago has a coastline of 10,850 mi. Manila Bay, with an area of 770 sq. mi., and a circumference of 120 mi., is the finest harbor in the Far East.

Resources and Industries. Forests, which cover 42% of the area, provide a variety of products from lumber and resins to medicinal plants. The fishing industry is being modernized.

The islands are rich in mineral resources. Gold, silver, gypsum, sulfur, mercury, phosphates, zinc, nickel, copper, iron, coal, chromite, and manganese are mined.

Chief agricultural products are manila hemp, copra, sugar, rice, corn, pineapple, and tobacco.

In the late 1960s self-sufficiency in rice production was achieved after introduction of "miracle" high-yield varieties.

In 1972 and 1974 severe floods destroyed crops in central Luzon. In 1974 the first in a series of flood-control dams, built with U.S. aid, was dedicated.

Manufacturing has shown steady gains, mostly in processing or assembly of food, clothing, pharmaceuticals, paper products, appliances. Tourists number over 200,000 annually, providing further income.

History and Government. The archipelago was visited by Magellan, 1521. The Spanish founded Manila, 1571. The islands, named for King Philip II of Spain, were ceded by Spain to the U.S. in the Treaty of Paris, Dec. 10, 1898, following the Spanish-American War. The U.S. paid Spain $20 million for the territory.

Japan attacked the Philippines Dec. 8, 1941 (Far Eastern time). Gen. Douglas MacArthur was put in command of the U.S.-Filipino forces (15,000 Americans, 40,000 in Filipino Army, 100,000 Filipino reservists). Japan conquered the islands in May. 1942. It was ousted by Sept. 1945.

On July 4, 1946, independence was proclaimed in accordance with an act passed by the U.S. Congress in 1934, providing for Philippine independence in 1946. A republic, with a president, Senate and House, was established.

All natural resources of the Philippines belong to the state and their exploitation is limited to citizens of the Philippines or corporations and associations of which 60% of the capital is owned by citizens. In 1946 the right to develop natural resources and to own and operate public utilities until 1974 was extended to U.S. citizens.

President Ferdinand E. Marcos in 1966 concluded a pact reducing U.S. base leases from 99 to 25 years. There were riots by radical youth groups and terrorism by leftist guerrillas and outlaws, increasing from 1970. On Sept. 21, 1972, Marcos declared martial law. Ruling by decree, he ordered land reform, cut crime and stabilized prices. On Jan. 17, 1973, he proclaimed a new constitution, established a parliamentary government with himself as president. Diplomatic and trade ties were set with China in 1975 and with the USSR in 1976.

Government troops battled Moslem (Moro) secessionists in 1973-76 in southern Mindanao.

Education and Religion. Primary and secondary education is free, instruction is largely in English. The literacy rate, at 83%, is one of the highest in Asia. There are several universities, with a total of 500,000 students.

The official national language is Filipino, based on Tagalog. English and Spanish, also official, are commonly used in government and commerce. Some 87 native languages are spoken, belonging to the Malayo-Polynesian family.

About 83% of the inhabitants are Roman Catholics and about 10% belong to the Philippine Independent Church, organized by a Filipino priest, Fr. Gregorio Aglipay. Other Christians, Moslems, Buddhists are among minorities.

Defense. The Philippines and U.S. have treaties for U.S. military and naval bases and a 1951 Mutual Defense Treaty. President Marcos sought renegotiation of U.S. defense arrangements in 1975. Military forces total 67,000. The republic is a member of the UN.

Poland

Area: 120,359 sq. mi. Population (Govt. est. 1975): 34,020,000. Capital: Warsaw. Monetary unit: Zloty.

The Polish People's Republic, in Central Europe, is bounded by the Baltic Sea, USSR, Czechoslovakia, and East Germany. It is about the size of New Mexico.

Its terrain consists largely of lowlands, often forested; there are mountains in the south. Gdynia, Gdansk (once Danzig), Szczecin, Swinoujscie, and Kolobrzeg are the principal ports.

Resources and Industries. About 30% of the population was still engaged in agriculture in 1973. Chief crops are rye, wheat, barley, oats, potatoes, sugar beets, tobacco, flax. Hogs are important. Coal mining, shipbuilding, textiles, chemicals, woodworking, and metal industries are important. Products include automobiles, tractors, heavy machinery, aircraft. Key industries are nationalized and operate under a planned economy. About 85% of the farms and some businesses are privately operated. The index of industrial production (1970 = 100) was 171 in 1975; Poland has become the world's 10th largest industrial power.

Poland produces 7% of world bituminous and lignite coal output and much zinc. Other minerals are sulphur, cement, salt, cadmium, iron, and copper. Imported raw materials supply aluminum plants and oil refineries. Foreign trade in thousands of U.S. dollars:

	Imports	Exports
1974	$10,860,000	$8,320,000
1975	12,536,000	10,282,000

History and Government. Poland was a great power from the 14th to the 17th centuries. In 3 partitions (1772, 1793, 1795) it was apportioned among Prussia, Russia, and Austria. Overrun by the Austro-German armies in World War I, its independence, self-declared on Nov. 11, 1918, was recognized by the Treaty of Versailles, June 28, 1919.

Nazi Germany and the Soviet Union invaded Poland Sept. 1-27, 1939, and divided the country. During the war, some 6 million Polish citizens were killed by the Nazis, half of them Jews. With Germany's defeat, a Polish government-in-exile in London was recognized by the U.S., but the Soviet Union pressed the claims of a rival group. The election of 1947 was completely dominated by the communists.

In compensation for 69,860 sq. mi. ceded to the USSR, 1945, Poland received approx. 40,000 sq. mi. of German territory east of the Oder-Neisse line comprising Silesia, Pomerania, West Prussia, and part of East Prussia.

The 1952 constitution describes Poland as a people's republic with a Sejm (parliament) elected for 4-year terms by direct ballot. The Sejm elects a Council of State and a Council of Ministers (cabinet). Policy is decreed by the Communist party Politburo. Two other parties exist: the United Peasant and Democratic parties.

During 12 years of rule by Stalinists, large estates were abolished, industries nationalized, schools secularized, and some Roman Catholic prelates jailed. Farm production fell off. Harsh working conditions caused a riot by workmen in Poznan June 28-29, 1956.

A new Politburo, committed to development of a more independent Polish Communism, was named Oct. 1956, with Wladyslaw Gomulka as first secretary of the Communist party. Collectivization of farms was ended and many collectives were abolished.

In 1970 Poland and West Germany signed a treaty to normalize relations.

In Dec. 1970 workers in port cities rioted because of price rises and new incentive wage rules. On Dec. 20 Gomulka resigned as party leader; he was succeeded by Edward Gierek; the incentive rules were dropped, price rises were revoked. In June 1971 a new 5-year plan was announced, placing more stress on housing and consumer goods production.

Poland was the first Communist state to get most-favored nation trade terms from the U.S. A 10-year

W. Germany cooperation pact was signed in 1974.

Education and Religion. Education is free and compulsory. There are 87 institutions of higher learning.

Roman Catholicism is the predominant religion. A law promulgated Feb. 13, 1953, required government consent to high church appointments. In 1956 Gomulka agreed to permit religious liberty and religious publications, provided the church kept out of politics. In 1961 religious studies in public schools were halted. Government relations with the Church improved in the 1970s. The number of priests and churches was greater in 1971 than in 1939, and 24 seminaries continued to function.

Defense. Military forces total 293,000. Poland is a UN and Warsaw Pact member.

Portugal

Area: 35,340 sq. mi. Population (UN est. 1974): 8,740,000. Capital: Lisbon. Monetary unit: Escudo.

Portugal occupies the SW part of the Iberian Peninsula and is bordered by Spain and the Atlantic. It is about the size of Indiana. The Azores Islands, in the Atlantic, 740 mi. W. of Portugal, have an area of 904 sq. mi. and a population (1970) of 291,028. The Madeira Islands, 360 mi. off the NW coast of Africa, have an area of 307 sq. mi. and a population (1970) of 253,220. Both groups were offered partial autonomy in 1976.

Portugal is mountainous, but about two-thirds of the land is cultivated.

Resources and Industries. Wheat, corn, oats, barley, rye and rice are important crops. Wines, olive oil, sardines, anchovies, resins, and fruits are major industries. Forests of pine, oak, and chestnut cover 19% of the country, and the nation leads the world in cork production. Among main industries are textiles, pottery, shipbuilding, petrochemical products, paper, and glassware. Tourism is important, as well as remittances from Portuguese workers abroad. A trade agreement was signed with the EC in 1973.

History and Government. Portugal, an independent state since the 12th century, was a kingdom until a revolution in 1910 drove out King Manoel II and a republic was proclaimed.

From 1932 a strong, repressive government was headed by Premier Antonio de Oliveira Salazar. Illness forced his retirement in Sept. 1968; he was succeeded by Marcello Caetano. Portugal was the last European nation to hold an extensive empire in Africa, maintaining over 140,000 troops there to battle various independence movements.

On Apr. 25, 1974, the government was seized by a military junta led by Gen. Antonio de Spinola, who was named president.

The new government reached agreements providing independence for Guinea-Bissau, Mozambique, Cape Verde Islands, Angola, and Sao Tome and Principe. Up to 1 million colonists fled to Portugal. Spinola resigned Sept. 30, 1974, in face of increasing pressure from leftist officers. Despite a 64% victory for democratic parties in April 1975, the Soviet-supported Communist party increased its influence. Banks, insurance companies, transport, and other industries were nationalized. A counter-coup in November halted this trend. Free elections under the new constitution were held in 1976, with the Socialist party gaining a parliamentary plurality.

Education and Religion. The dominant religion is Roman Catholicism. Primary education is compulsory. There are 9 universities.

Defense. Military forces, which totaled over 200,000, have been rapidly demobilized. A 1951 agreement gave the U.S. rights to use defense facilities in the Azores. Portugal is a member of NATO and the U.N.

Portuguese Timor was annexed by Indonesia May 3, 1976, after 9 months of fighting between local factions. Portuguese troops had withdrawn in 1975.

Macao

Macao, with an area of 6 sq. mi., is an enclave, a

peninsula and 2 small islands, at the mouth of the Canton River in China. Portugal granted broad autonomy in 1976. Population (UN est. 1974): 270,000.

Qatar

Area: 4,000 sq. mi. Population (UN est. 1975): 90,-000. Capital: Doha. Monetary unit: Riyal.

Qatar, formerly a British Protected State, declared its complete independence Sept. 1, 1971. It occupies a peninsula extending into the Persian (also called Arabian) Gulf from the coast of Arabia.

A mainly arid land, slightly larger than Connecticut, Qatar was the world's 17th largest petroleum producer in 1975. Production started in 1949 and provides an income of several hundred million dollars a year. Doha has become a modern town with seawater desalting plants. Commercial fishing, government-aided agriculture, and herds of camels, sheep, and goats are also important.

Qatar was under Turkish control from 1872 to 1915. In a treaty signed in 1916 Qatar gave Great Britain responsibility for its defense and foreign relations. After Britain announced it would remove its military forces from the Persian Gulf area by the end of 1971, Qatar sought a federation with other British Protected States in the area; this failed and Qatar declared itself independent. It is a monarchy, ruled by an emir aided by a prime minister, Council of Ministers, and Advisory Council. Its first ruler under independence, Emir Ahmed bin Ali al-Thani, was replaced by his cousin, Khalifa bin Hamad al-Thani, Feb. 22, 1972, in a bloodless coup. Qatar is a member of the UN and Arab League.

Most Qataris are Arabs of the Sunni branch of Islam. Arabic is the official language. Education is free and compulsory, ages 6-16.

Rhodesia

Area: 150,333 sq. mi. Population (Govt. est. 1975): 6,420,000. Capital: Salisbury. Monetary unit: Rhodesian dollar.

Rhodesia is mostly high plateau country, bordered by the Zambezi River and Zambia to the N, Mozambique to the E, the Republic of South Africa to the S, and Botswana to the W. It is almost the size of California.

Victoria Falls on the Zambezi, partly in Zambia, are 355 ft. high, 5,580 ft. wide.

The vast majority of the people are Africans (mostly Bantus); there are about 270,000 whites and small minorities of Asians and people of mixed descent. English is the official language but the majority speak Bantu languages.

Rich farmlands and mineral deposits are the mainstays of the economy. Leading exports are tobacco, asbestos, meat, sugar, copper, clothing, iron, chemical products, cotton, coal, and chrome.

Britain took over the area as Southern Rhodesia in 1923 from the British South Africa Co. and granted internal self-government. Under a 1961 constitution, there was a governor representing the British Crown, a prime minister and Legislative Assembly with voting restricted to maintain whites in power. On Nov. 11, 1965, Prime Minister Ian D. Smith announced his country's unilateral declaration of independence. Britain termed the act illegal, and demanded Rhodesia broaden voting rights to provide for eventual rule by the majority Africans.

Urged by Britain, the UN imposed sanctions, including embargoes on oil shipments to Rhodesia, which were backed by most nations including the U.S. Some oil and gasoline reached Rhodesia, however, from South Africa and Mozambique, before the latter became independent in 1975. Some African nations denounced Britain for refusing to use force against the Rhodesian government. In May 1968, the UN Security Council ordered a trade embargo.

Rhodesia claimed the sanctions were ineffective. A new constitution came into effect Mar. 2, 1970, providing for a republic with a president and prime minister. The election law effectively prevented full black representation through income tax requirements.

A proposed British-Rhodesian settlement was dropped in May 1972 when a British commission reported most Rhodesian blacks opposed it. In 1972-74 there were small clashes between black nationalist guerrillas and Rhodesian security forces. Intermittent negotiations between the government and various black groups failed to prevent increasing skirmishes. By mid-1976, over 1,000 soldiers and civilians had been killed.

In 1974, and again in 1976, U.S. Pres. Ford sought repeal of a U.S. law allowing U.S. import of Rhodesian chrome.

Romania

Area: 91,699 sq. mi. Population (UN est. 1975): 21,180,000. Capital: Bucharest. Monetary unit: Leu.

The Socialist Republic of Romania, a Balkan state in SE Europe, is almost the size of Oregon. It is bounded by the USSR, the Black Sea, Bulgaria, Yugoslavia, and Hungary. The Danube flows along the southern border and through eastern Romania into the Black Sea. The Carpathian Mtns. enclose the north-central Transylvanian plateau. There are wide plains S and E of the mountains.

Resources and Industries. Romania has become industrialized, industry accounting for 64% of the total national product by 1974. Industrial growth rate for 1974 was 15%. But 40% of labor was still agricultural in 1973.

Main industries are iron-steel, other metallurgy, machinery, oil and chemicals, building materials, timber, textiles, footwear, food processing. All industry is nationalized.

There is considerable mineral wealth: oil, natural gas, coal, salt, bauxite, manganese, lead, zinc, gold, silver. In 1975, Romania produced 108 million barrels of crude oil, more than any other European country except the USSR, while 8.8 million tons of steel were produced.

State farms and cooperatives own over 90% of arable land. Romania is the world's 6th largest corn producer; also important are wheat, sugar beets, grapes and fruits. In 1974, 3.9 million foreigners visited Black Sea and other Romanian resorts.

In 1975 Romania had 14 million sheep, 9 million hogs, 6 million cattle.

Imports in 1974 were valued at $5.14 billion, exports at $4.87 billion.

History and Government. Romania's earliest known people were merged with invading Proto-Thracians, preceding by centuries the Dacians. The Dacian kingdom was occupied by Rome, 106 A.D.-271 A.D.; the people and language were Romanized. The principalities of Wallachia and Moldavia, dominated by Turkey, were united in 1859, became Romania in 1861. In 1877 Romania proclaimed independence from Turkey, became an independent state by the Treaty of Berlin, 1878, and kingdom, 1881, under Carol I. In 1886 Romania became a constitutional monarchy with a bicameral legislature.

Romania helped Russia in its war with Turkey, 1877-78. After World War I it acquired Bessarabia, Bukovina, Transylvania and Banat. In 1940 it ceded Bessarabia and Northern Bukovina to the USSR and part of Southern Dobrudja to Bulgaria.

Marshal Ion Antonescu, leader of a militarist movement, came to power and forced Romania to join Germany against the USSR in World War II in 1941. In 1944 Antonescu was overthrown by King Michael with Soviet help and Romania joined the Allies.

With occupation by Soviet troops the National Democratic Front, headed by the Communist party, displaced the National Peasant party. A People's Republic was proclaimed, Dec. 30, 1947, and Michael was forced to abdicate. Land owners were dispossessed and most banks, factories and transportation units were nationalized. A new constitution on the Soviet model was voted Sept. 24, 1952. A modification, March 1961, replaced the Presidium with the State Council, elected by the Grand National Assembly from its own membership. A Council of Ministers is the administrative body. The Assembly has 349 deputies, elected for 4-year terms.

On Aug. 22, 1965, a new constitution proclaimed Romania a Socialist, rather than a People's Republic. Since 1966, Romania has adopted an independent attitude toward the USSR, a stand pointed up by the visit of U.S. President Nixon in Aug. 1969. Romanian President Nicolae Ceausescu visited the U.S. in 1970 and 1973. The U.S. granted most-favored-nation tariff treatment in 1975. Since 1959, USSR troops have not been permitted to enter Romania. In 1974, Ceausescu declared Russia was Romania's top ally.

Education and Religion. Education is compulsory for 10 years, all education is free. There are 7 universities, and 35 other higher education institutes. The language has a Latin base, with traces of French, Greek, Slav and Turkish influences.

Romanian Orthodox clergy and those of 14 other denominations are paid by the state, but church and state are called separated. Roman Catholic orders have been abolished and the Greek Catholic Church has been absorbed by the Romanian Orthodox.

Defense. Military forces total 171,000. Romania is a member of the UN and Warsaw Pact.

Rwanda

Area: 10,169 sq. mi. Population (Govt. est. 1975): 4,200,000. Capital: Kigali. Monetary unit: Rwanda franc.

The Republic of Rwanda, which became independent July 1, 1962, had been part of the former Belgian UN Trusteeship of Ruanda-Urundi. Rwanda lies in East Central Africa, bounded N by Uganda, E by Tanzania, W by Zaire and S by Burundi.

The source of the Nile River, long sought by explorers and geographers, has been located in the headwaters of the Kagera (Akagera) River, SW of Kigali.

About the size of Maryland, Rwanda is one of the most densely populated nations in Africa. The population includes the Hutu (90% of population), the Tutsi (Watusi, 8%) and the Twa (2%). For centuries the Tutsi (an extremely tall race) subjugated the Hutu (average height) and the Twa (pygmies). A civil war broke out in 1960 and Tutsi power was ended. (See Index for Burundi.)

The majority of Rwandans are Christians. French and Kinyarwanda are the official languages.

A Legislative Council, organized in Oct. 1960, declared Rwanda a republic Jan. 28, 1961, and a referendum, Sept. 25, abolished the monarchic system. The new government was dominated by the Hutu. A president and National Assembly are elected for 4-year terms. The government was overthrown in a 1973 military coup. Rwanda is a member of the UN and OAU.

Coffee is the principal cash crop; cotton, tea, pyrethrum, tobacco, cattle and hides also are produced. Minerals include tin, gold, wolframite.

Kagera (Akagera) National Park, in the northeast, covers a tenth of the country; here the ecology of East Central Africa is preserved. Lake Kivu, on the nation's western border with Zaire, is 4,788 ft. above sea level and is considered one of Africa's most beautiful lakes.

San Marino

Capital: San Marino. Area: 23.5 sq. mi. Population (Govt. est. 1975): 19,621. Monetary unit: Italian and San Marino lira.

San Marino, one of the world's smallest nations, lies on the slopes of Mt. Titano in the Apennines near the Adriatic, in north central Italy. It is one-third the size of the District of Columbia.

Principal industries are printing postage stamps, tourism, woolen goods, paper, cement, industrial ceramics. Cradle-to-grave social security is provided. A ceremonial army of 180 men is maintained.

History and Government. The republic claims to be the oldest state in Europe and to have been founded in the 4th century. It has had a treaty of friendship with Italy since 1862. It is a member of the International Court of Justice.

San Marino is governed by a Grand Council of 60 members elected by popular vote, 2 of whom are chosen to exercise executive power for a term of 6 months. Women were allowed to vote for the first time Sept. 13, 1964. A Sept. 1973 law gave them the right to hold public office and make legal contracts. Three women were elected to the Council in 1974.

Sao Tome and Principe

Area: 372 sq. mi. Population (UN est. 1975): 80,000. Capital: Sao Tome.

The Democratic Republic of Sao Tome and Principe became independent July 12, 1975. The nation is comprised of the islands of Sao Tome and Principe, which lie in the Gulf of Guinea about 125 miles off West Central Africa. Each of the two islands is made up of northeast and southwest lowlands with volcanic hills in the center.

Cocoa is the principal product, followed by coffee and coconut palm products. Low cocoa prices, the emigration of most of the 1,000 whites, and the repatriation of Cape Verdean plantation foremen stymied the economy at independence.

The islands were uninhabited when discovered in 1471 by the Portuguese, who brought the first settlers — convicts and exiled Jews. Sugar planting was replaced by the slave trade as the chief economic activity until coffee and cocoa were introduced in the nineteenth century.

Portugal agreed in 1974 to turn the colony over to the Gabon-based Movement for the Liberation of Sao Tome and Principe, which proclaimed as the first president its East-German-trained leader Manuel Pinto da Costa.

Nearly all the population is black, with many laborers imported in recent years from Angola and Mozambique.

Saudi Arabia

Area: 873,000 sq. mi. Population (est. 1973): 8,100,-000. Capital: Riyadh. Monetary unit: Riyal.

Saudi Arabia occupies four-fifths of the Arabian Peninsula, with the Red Sea on most of its W coast and the Persian Gulf (also called Arabian Gulf) on the E. The highlands of the W, up to 9,000 ft., slope as an arid, barren desert to the Persian Gulf. Its neighbors are Jordan, Iraq, Kuwait, Bahrain, Qatar, United Arab Emirates, Oman and the 2 Yemens. It is more than 3 times the size of Texas.

Saudi Arabia comprises 4 provinces: the former sultanate of **Nejd**, the old kingdom of **Hejaz, Asir** and **El Hasa** (now known as the Eastern Province).

The Hejaz contains the holy cities of Islam — Medina where the Mosque of the Prophet enshrines the tomb of Mohammed, who died in the city June 7, 632, and Mecca, his birthplace, containing a great mosque sheltering the sacred shrine, the Kaaba. More than 600,000 Moslems from 60 nations pilgrimage to Mecca annually.

Two major airports, Dhahran and Jidda, handle the bulk of international traffic. Jidda, on the Red Sea, is the main seaport.

Resources and Industries. Saudi Arabia possesses

the world's largest oil reserves and is the 3d largest producer, accounting for 13% of 1975 world total. Production centers along the Persian gulf. Refineries and piers for tankers are at Ras Tanura, and a pipeline runs to the Lebanese coast. Operations are mostly in the hands of the Arabian American Oil Co. (Aramco), formerly owned by several American companies. Most of the oil is shipped to Western Europe. Government income from oil was $30 billion annually in recent years. Gold, currency reserves, and investments in Western countries reached $45 billion by 1976. In 1973, the Saudi government acquired 25% ownership of Aramco's operations, and in 1974 increased that to 60%. A 100% takeover was agreed upon in 1976.

A five year $140 billion development plan was approved in 1975, calling for the importation of 500,000 workers.

An agricultural country except for oil and recently discovered gold, silver, and rich iron ore, Saudi Arabia's products are dates, wheat, barley, fruit, hides, wool. Camels, horses, donkeys, and sheep are raised. It receives UN technical assistance. Industries are being developed with private Western technical assistance.

History and Government: Nejd, long an independent state and center of the Wahhabi sect, fell under Turkish rule in the 18th century, but in 1913 Ibn Saud, founder of the Saudi dynasty, overthrew the Turks and captured the Turkish province of Hasa; took the Hejaz in 1925 and by 1926, most of Asir. The discovery of oil by an American oil company in the 1930s tranformed the new country.

The form of government is a hereditary monarchy. Crown Prince Khalid was proclaimed king on Mar. 25, 1975, after the assassination of King Faisal. There is no constitution and no parliament. The king exercises authority together with a Council of Ministers.

Education and Religion. Elementary, secondary and higher education are free, but not compulsory.

Development of education is extensive, but illiteracy was still high in 1974. Population is almost entirely Moslem.

Defense. Regular military forces total 47,000, about 12,000 of which are deployed in Syria and Jordan. Saudi Arabia is a member of the UN and Arab League. Billions of dollars in arms have been purchased from Britain, France, and the U.S., including advanced jet fighters and missiles.

Beginning with the 1967 Arab-Israeli war, Saudi Arabia provided large annual financial gifts to Egypt; aid was later extended to Syria, Jordan, and Palestinian guerrilla groups, as well as to other Moslem countries.

Faisal played a leading role in the 1973-74 Arab oil embargo against the U.S. and other nations in an attempt to force them to adopt an anti-Israel policy.

Senegal

Area: 76,124 sq. mi. Population (Govt. est. 1975): 4,140,000. Capital: Dakar. Monetary unit: CFA franc.

A former French Overseas Territory on the Atlantic coast of western Africa, Senegal borders Mauritania, Mali, Guinea, and Guinea-Bissau and surrounds Gambia on 3 sides. It is the size of South Dakota.

Senegal became an autonomous state in 1958 and with the Sudanese Republic formed the Mali Federation, Jan. 17, 1959. The federation became completely independent June 20, 1960, but after political conflict arose Senegal withdrew from the federation Aug. 20, 1960. The Sudanese Republic assumed the name Mali. The president and National Assembly are elected by universal suffrage.

About 70% of the population is engaged in agriculture and stock raising; peanuts are the mainstay of the economy. Dakar is an important seaport, handling 6,000 ships annually. Phosphates are an important export, along with peanut oil and canned fish. Developing industries include food processing, chemicals, cement. A long drought brought famine in 1972-73. Food supplies were sent to Senegal and its neighbors; 40% was from the U.S.

French is the official language, but the majority speak various tribal languages. Over 80% of the population is Moslem.

Seychelles

Area: 107 sq. mi. Population (UN est. 1974): 60,000. Capital: Victoria. Monetary unit: Seychelles rupee.

The Seychelles are a group of 86 islands and islets in the Indian Ocean 700 miles N of Madagascar. Largest island is Mahe, 57 sq. mi., on which lies Victoria, the capital, which has a port and coaling station.

Most of the working population is engaged in agriculture or fishing. Coconut products are the chief exports, followed by cinnamon, guano, shark fins, and tortoise shell. Vanilla, tea, and patchouli are also grown. An international airport was opened in 1972 to serve the growing tourist industry.

The islands were occupied by France in 1768, and seized by Britain in 1794. Ruled as part of Mauritius from 1814, the Seychelles became a separate colony in 1903. Several island groups were detached in 1965. The ruling party had opposed independence as impractical, but pressure from the OAU and the UN Committee on Colonialism became irresistible, and independence was declared June 29, 1976.

The population descends almost entirely from early French settlers and African slaves. Most of the people speak Creole, a French patois; 5% speak French. English is also used. Literacy is fairly high, with over 11,000 students in school. Over 98% of the population profess Christianity.

Sierra Leone

Area: 27,925 sq. mi. Population (Govt. est. 1974): 2,710,000. Capital: Freetown. Monetary unit: Leone.

Sierra Leone, former British Colony and Protectorate, became an independent state within the Commonwealth Apr. 27, 1961. It is in the SW corner of the West African bulge. The coastline on the Atlantic is about 210 mi.; the country extends inland about 180 mi., between Guinea and Liberia. It is a bit smaller than South Carolina. Its name, meaning Mountain of the Lion, was applied by an early Portuguese mariner because of thunderstorms around its coastal peaks.

Freetown, the capital, was founded in 1787 by the British government as a home for destitute freed slaves. Their descendants, known as Creoles, number more than 80,000.

Principal exports are industrial diamonds, iron ore, bauxite, cocoa, coffee, palm kernels, kola nuts, ginger, piassava (palm fiber). More than 80% are employed in agriculture.

Successive steps toward independence followed introduction of the first constitution in 1951. The Sierra Leone People's Party was dominant until a military junta took over in March 1967.

Col. A. T. Juxon-Smith, who headed the coup, was himself ousted in another coup, Apr. 8, 1968, led by non-commissioned officers. The nation was returned to civilian rule with swearing-in of Siaka Stevens as prime minister, Apr. 26. Sierra Leone became a republic Apr. 19, 1971, and Stevens was named president.

English is the official language but the majority speak Krio (pidgin English) or tribal languages. Most of the people are animists; there are over 700,000 Moslems and over 100,000 Christians.

Singapore

Area: 226 sq. mi. Population (Govt. est. 1975): 2,250,000. Capital: Singapore. Monetary unit: Singapore dollar.

Singapore is an island republic 25 mi. long and 14

mi. wide at the southern tip of the Malay Peninsula in SE Asia. About 3 times the size of the District of Columbia, the main island is linked to the mainland by a three-quarter mile long causeway. The narrow Straits of Singapore separate it from its isles to the south.

Singapore, the capital, is the world's 4th largest port and the largest in SE Asia.

Founded in 1819 by Sir Thomas Stamford Raffles, Singapore was a British colony until 1959 when it became autonomous within the Commonwealth. On Sept. 16, 1963, it joined with Malaya, Sarawak and Sabah to form the Federation of Malaysia.

Tensions between Malayans, dominant in the federation, and ethnic Chinese, dominant in Singapore, led to an agreement under which Singapore became a separate nation, Aug. 9, 1965. It has a one-house Parliament, elected by compulsory suffrage; a president elected by Parliament, and a prime minister. Most British and Australian troops were removed in 1975.

Singapore's population is 74% Chinese, 14% Malay and 11% Indians, Pakistanis, Ceylonese, Eurasians, etc. Administration is in English. Industries include shipbuilding, oil refining, electronics, banking, textiles, and food, rubber, and lumber processing. Manufacturing has replaced shipping as the basis of the economy, pushing per capita income to second place in Asia, following Japan. Standards of health, education, and housing are high.

Tourism is an important source of income; there were over a million visitors in 1973.

Primary education for 6 years is free but not compulsory. There are 2 universities, 2 technical colleges, and an institute of education. Literacy exceeds 75%.

Armed forces total 30,000. Singapore is a member of the Commonwealth and UN.

Somalia

Area: 246,155 sq. mi. Population (UN est. 1975): 3,170,000. Capital: Mogadishu. Monetary unit: Somali shilling.

The Somali Democratic Republic is composed of the former protectorate of British Somaliland and the former Italian UN trusteeship of Somalia in eastern Africa. It is bordered by the Gulf of Aden, Indian Ocean, Kenya, Ethiopia, and the French Territory of Afars and Issas. It is about the size of Texas. The population is 99% Moslem.

Resources and Industries. Somalia has a weak economy and long depended on outside aid, part of it from the U.S., Italy, Great Britain, and the USSR. Principal occupations are livestock-raising and agriculture. Products include incense, sugar, bananas, sorghum, corn, gum, hides, kapok.

Its mineral resources, largely undeveloped, include iron, tin, gypsum, sandstone, bauxite, meerschaum, titanium, and others. In 1968 the government announced discovery of large uranium deposits.

History and Government. Many of the Somali peoples are nomadic and include large numbers in Kenya and Ethiopia. The Italian Protectorate of Somalia, acquired from 1885 to 1927, extended along the Indian Ocean from the Gulf of Aden to the Juba River. The UN in 1949 approved eventual creation of Somalia as a sovereign state and in 1950 Italy took over the trusteeship held by Great Britain since World War II.

British Somaililand was formed in the 19th century in the northwest. Britain gave it independence June 26, 1960, and on July 1 it joined with the former Italian part to create the independent Somali Republic.

On Oct. 21, 1969, a Supreme Revolutionary Council seized power in a bloodless army and police coup, named a mainly civilian cabinet to aid it, and abolished the Assembly. It made Somali, a Hamitic language spoken by most of the population, the official language, and decreed a standardized spelling using Latin letters. In May, 1970, several foreign companies were nationalized.

A severe drought in 1975 killed tens of thousands, and spurred efforts to resettle nomads on collective farms. The U.S. charged in 1975 that Soviet naval facilities at Berbera included a missile storage site.

Republic of South Africa

Area: 471,819 sq. mi. Population (Govt. est. 1975): 25,470,000. Capitals: Pretoria and Cape Town. Monetary unit: Rand.

The Republic of South Africa occupies the southern portion of the continent and includes the former colonies of the **Cape of Good Hope, Natal,** the **Transvaal** and the **Orange Free State,** which became provinces. It is close to twice the size of Texas.

Cape Town, seat of Parliament, is the legislative capital and Pretoria the administrative capital. Largest cities are Johannesburg, Cape Town and Durban.

Estimated population of government-designated racial groups in 1974 was: Bantu, 17.7 million; white, 4.1 million; Colored (mixed) 2.4 million; Asians, 709 thousand. Among Bantu, the 1970 census reported the largest groups to be: Zulu, 4,026,058; Xhosa 3,930,087; Tswana, 1,719,367; Sotho, 3,471,000.

Kruger National Park, an 8,000-sq.-mi. wild game preserve; Cape Peninsula, and the Drakensberg Mtns. are among numerous tourist attractions.

Resources and Industries. Corn, wool, wheat, tobacco, sugar, fruit, peanuts, wine, karakul, butter and cheese are major agricultural products. Industry products include steel, tires, electric motors, textiles, furniture, plastics.

South Africa leads the world in production of gold, gem diamonds and antimony; it is among top producers of platinum, chrome, copper, uranium, vanadium, vermiculite, manganese and asbestos. Coal, iron, lead and zinc resources are large. Annual production of more than 50 minerals is est. at over $6 billion.

South Africa has enjoyed an industrial boom. Index numbers of industrial production (1970=100) was 124 in 1975 for manufacturing. An advanced nuclear energy industry has developed.

Foreign trade (in thousands of U.S. dollars), excluding gold:

	Imports	Exports
1974	$7,222,000	$4,988,000
1975	$7,589,000	$5,315,000

History and Government. The Cape of Good Hope area was settled by Dutch, beginning in the 17th century. Britain seized the Cape in 1806. Many Dutch trekked north and founded 2 republics, the Transvaal and the Orange Free State. Diamonds were discovered, 1867, and gold, 1886. The Dutch (Boers) resented encroachments by the British and others; the Anglo-Boer War followed, 1899-1902. Britain won and, effective May 31, 1910, created the Union of South Africa, incorporating the British colonies of the Cape and Natal, the Transvaal and the Orange Free State.

After a referendum, the Union became the Republic of South Africa, May 31, 1961, and withdrew from the Commonwealth.

With the election victory of Daniel Malan's National party in 1948, the policy of separate development of the races, or apartheid, already existing unofficially, became official. This called for separate development, separate residential areas and ultimate political independence for the whites, Bantus, Asians and Coloreds. In 1959 the government passed acts providing the eventual creation of several Bantu nations or Bantustans on 13% of the country's land area, though most Bantu leaders have opposed the plan. In 1963, the Transkei, an area in the SE, became the first of these partially self-governing territories or "Homelands." By 1974 there were 10. Transkei independence was scheduled for 1976.

The white-operated government includes a president chosen for a 7-year term by the Senate and Assembly, and a prime minister. Members of the partly appointed, partly indirectly-elected Senate, and of the elected Assembly, are chosen for 5-year terms; all members must be white. There is a separate, advisory Indian Council, partly elected, partly appointed. In 1969, a Colored People's Representative Council was created. There is an elected Provincial Council in each of the 4 provinces. At least 140 persons, mostly Bantus, were killed in June 1976 riots protesting apartheid and discrimination.

Education and Religion. There are 16 universities, 11 of them for white students; enrollment exceeds 90,000 (93% whites). Primary education is free to all citizens, and literacy among Bantus is high.

Dutch Protestant churches predominate, with Anglicans and Methodists next. The majority of Bantus are Christian. Hindus, Moslems, and Jews are present. English and Afrikaans are official languages.

Defense. Military forces total 50,500.

South-West Africa or Namibia

South-West Africa, a sparsely populated land twice the size of California, became the object of international dispute in 1966. Made a German protectorate in 1884, it was surrendered to South Africa in 1915 and was administered by that country under an old League of Nations mandate. South Africa refused to accept UN authority under the trusteeship system.

Other African nations charged South Africa imposed apartheid, built military bases and exploited S-W Africa; 36 African states called on the UN to take over the mandate. The UN General Assembly in May 1968 created an 11-nation council to take over administration of S-W Africa and lead it to independence. In April 1968 the council charged that South Africa had blocked its effort to visit S-W Africa.

In 1968 the UN General Assembly gave the area the name Namibia. In Jan. 1970 the UN Security Council condemned South Africa for "illegal" control of the area. In an advisory opinion in June 1971 the International Court of Justice declared South Africa was occupying the area illegally. In 1973, a South African-style "homeland," Ovamboland in the northern area, was given limited self-government.

Most of S-W Africa is a plateau, 3,600 ft. high, with plains in the N. Kalahari Desert to the E. Orange River on the S. the Atlantic on the W. Area is 318,261 sq. mi.; population (Govt. est. 1975) 852,000 including about 100,000 whites; capital, Windhoek. There is a South African administrator; voters choose 18 members of a Legislative Assembly and send 6 members to the South African Assembly; 4 are appointed to the South African Senate.

Products include cattle, sheep, diamonds, copper, lead, zinc, fish. People include Namas (Hottentots), Ovambos (Bantus), Bushmen, and others.

Spain

Area: 194,883 sq. mi. Population (Govt. est. 1975): 35,470,000. Capital: Madrid. Monetary unit: Peseta.

Spain, a constitutional monarchy, occupies the entire Iberian peninsula in Western Europe, except for Portugal. It is separated from France by the Pyrenees.

The interior is a high arid plateau traversed E and W by mountain ranges. Spain is twice the size of Wyoming.

The **Balearic Islands** in the western Mediterranean, 1,935 sq. mi., are a province of Spain; they include **Majorca** (Mallorca), with the capital, Palma; **Minorca, Cabrera, Ibiza,** and **Formentera.** The **Canary Islands**, 2,807 sq. mi., in the Atlantic W of Morocco, form 2 provinces, including the islands of **Tenerife, Palma, Gomera, Hierro, Grand Canary, Fuerteventura,** and **Lanzarote** with Las Palmas and Santa Cruz thriving ports. **Ceuta** and **Melilla,** small enclaves on Morocco's Mediterranean coast, are part of Metropolitan Spain.

Spanish Sahara, a former overseas province on the NW coast of Africa, was relinquished to Morocco and Mauritania when the last Spanish troops withdrew in February, 1976.

Spain has sought return of Gibraltar, in British control since 1704. (See Index.)

Resources and Industries. Only about 40% of the land is cultivable, the remainder is arid or mountainous. Farm mechanization and irrigation are increasing.

Principal agricultural products are wheat, barley, oats, rye, olives, grapes, lemons, oranges and other fruit, onions, almonds, esparto, flax, hemp, pulse and cork. Tobacco, cotton, and rice are also grown. Wine making is a large industry. Spain has abundant minerals, including lead, iron, copper, zinc, coal, cobalt, mercury, silver, sulphur and phosphates.

Between 1960 and 1975 Spain changed from an agricultural nation into one of the world's top industrial powers. Manufacturing includes machinery, cotton and woolen goods, shoes, paper, automobiles, ships, cork and cement. Spain's fish catch is one of the world's largest, by value. Coal production is more than 13 million metric tons annually. Foreign trade in thousands of U.S. dollars:

	Imports	Exports
1974	$15,298,000	$7,036,000
1975	$16,097,000	$7,691,000

The index of general industrial production (1970=100) was 143 in 1975. A trade pact with the USSR was signed in 1972. Spain recognized Communist China in 1973. More than 35 million tourists spend over $3 billion a year in Spain.

History and Government. Spain was settled by Iberians, Basques and Celts, partly overrun by Carthaginians, conquered by Rome c. 200 B.C. The Visigoths, in power by the 5th Century A.D., adopted Christianity but by 711 A.D. lost to the Islamic invasion from Africa. Christian reconquest from the N led to a Spanish nationalism. In 1469 the kingdoms of Aragon and Castile were united by the marriage of Ferdinand II and Isabella I, and the last Moorish power broken by the fall of the kingdom of Granada, 1492. Spain became a bulwark of Roman Catholicism.

Spain obtained a colonial empire with the discovery of America by Columbus, 1492, the conquest of Mexico by Cortes and Peru by Pizarro. It also controlled the Netherlands and parts of Italy and Germany. Spain lost its American colonies in the early 19th century. It lost Cuba, the Philippines and Puerto during the Spanish-American War, 1898.

Primo de Rivera became dictator in 1923. King Alfonso XIII revoked the dictatorship, 1930, but was forced to leave the country 1931. A republic was proclaimed which disestablished the church, curtailed its privileges and secularized education. A conservative reaction occurred 1933 but was followed by a Popular Front (1936-1939) composed of socialists, communists, republicans, and anarchists.

Army officers headed a revolt against the government, 1936, under Francisco Franco. In a destructive 3-yr. war, in which one million were said to have died, Franco received help from Italy and Germany, while the Soviet Union, France and Mexico were active on behalf of the republic. War ended Mar. 28, 1939. Franco was named caudillo, or leader of the nation.

Spain was neutral in World War II but its relations with fascist countries caused its exclusion from the UN in 1946. It was admitted in 1955.

Dec. 14, 1966, a new constitution, was approved by the people in a plebiscite. The new law implied a liberalization of government policy, but enforcement was limited.

In July 1969, Franco and the Cortes designated Prince Juan Carlos, then 31, as the future king and chief of state. After Franco's death, Nov. 20, 1975, Juan Carlos was sworn in as king. A transitional government planned political and social reforms in 1976.

Education and Religion. Franco reestablished Catholicism as the state religion. Primary education is compulsory and free. There are 17 universities, enrolling 27% of college-age youth. More than two-thirds speak Castilian; Basque is spoken in the N; Galician in the NW, and Catalan in the NE. Non-Castilians have protested cultural and political repression, and some concessions have been granted.

Defense. Military forces total 302,300. Under a 1953 agreement with the U.S., renewed in 1970 and in 1976, Spain received military aid and the U.S. was granted use of bases.

Sri Lanka

Area: 25,332 sq. mi. Population (UN est. 1975): 13,990,000. Capital: Colombo. Monetary unit: Rupee.

Sri Lanka, formerly Ceylon, is an island republic in the Indian Ocean 20 mi. off the southern tip of India. Its greatest length from N to S is 270 mi., and its greatest width, 140 mi. The coastal area is flat, but the central part is mountainous with the highest peak, Pidurutalagala, 8,281 ft. The climate is hot, with high relative humidity. There are many mountain streams, navigable only by small river craft. Colombo is served by world airlines.

Resources and Industries. Minerals and metals include graphite, limestone, iron, precious and semiprecious stones, ilmenite, monazite, zircon, quartz. Manufactures include plywood, paper, glassware, ceramics, cement, chemicals, textiles, fertilizers, and vegetable oil products.

Principal agricultural products are tea, rubber, coconuts, rice, cacao, cinnamon, citronella, tobacco. Accounting for 90% of exports are tea, rubber, and coconuts. Food imports are necessary.

A major source of precious stones, the island produces about 20 varieties including sapphires, rubies, alexandrites, topaz, tourmalines, and cat's-eyes. Most are mined at pits in Ratnapura.

History and Government. The island was known to the ancient world as Taprobane (Greek for coppercolored) and later as Serendip (from Arabic). Colonists from northern India subdued the indigenous Veddahs about 543 B.C.; their descendants, the Sinhalese, still form most of the population. Descendants of Tamil immigrants from southern India account for one-fifth of the population, though many are being repatriated. Parts of the maritime areas were occupied in turn by the Portuguese in 1505 and by the Dutch in 1658. The British seized the island in 1796 and it became a Crown colony in 1802.

As Ceylon it became an independent member of the Commonwealth in 1948. It is a member of the UN.

Prime Minister W. R. D. Bandaranaike, appointed Apr. 12, 1956, was assassinated Sept. 25, 1959. In new elections, the Freedom party was victorious. Its leader, Mrs. Sirimavo Bandaranaike, widow of the former prime minister, was sworn in to the office.

In April, 1962, the government expropriated service and terminal facilities of one British and 2 U.S. oil companies. In March 1965 elections, the conservative, pro-Western United National party won the largest number of seats and its leader, Dudley Senanayake, became prime minister.

In Dec. 1965, the new government agreed to pay compensation for the seized oil companies. The U.S. in Feb. 1966, agreed to resume economic aid, which had been cut off when the oil companies were expropriated.

After May 1970 elections, Mrs. Bandaranaike became prime minister again. In 1971 the nation suffered economic problems and terrorist activities by ultra-leftists, thousands of whom were executed. Unemployment among graduates and food shortages plagued the nation from 1973 to 1976. Massive land reform and nationalization of foreign-owned plantations was undertaken in the mid-1970s.

On May 22, 1972, Ceylon became the Republic of Sri Lanka with a president, prime minister, and a unicameral National Assembly.

Education and Religion. All education is free in government schools from kindergarten to university. The majority of the population, Sinhalese, belongs to the Buddhist faith. The Tamils are mostly Hindu. Sinhalese became the official language in 1961, but laws must also be written in Tamil. Literacy is 81%.

Defense. Armed forces total 13,600.

Sudan

Area: 967,491 sq. mi. Population (Govt. est. 1975): 17,760,000. Capital: Khartoum. Monetary unit: Pound.

Sudan proclaimed itself a republic Jan. 1, 1956. It is bounded by Egypt, the Red Sea, Ethiopia, Uganda, Kenya, Zaire, the Central African Republic, Chad and Libya. It is about the size of Texas, Alaska and New Mexico combined and is the largest country in Africa.

The northern zone consists of the Libyan Desert, in the W, and the mountainous Nubian Desert, extending to the Red Sea on the E, separated by the narrow valley of the Nile; the central zone contains large fertile areas, including the rainlands of Kassala and Tokar, the Gezira Plain and the pastures and gum forests of Kordofan; in the southern equatorial belt the soil is richest and watered by tropical rains.

The White Nile flows N through the center of the country; the Blue Nile, flowing from the mountains of Ethiopia, joins the White at Khartoum; the combined river flows N in a huge S curve to enter Egypt N of Wadi Halfa.

Resources and Industries. The Sudan is the world's principal source of gum arabic. Chief grain crop is durra (sorghum), the country's staple food. Cotton is the principal export; American and extra-long staple cottons are grown in the fertile Gezira, between the White and Blue Niles. Other important products are sesame, peanuts, rice, coffee, sugarcane, tobacco, wheat, dates, hides, mahogany, chrome. Live camels and sheep are exported to Egypt. A livestock industry for export to Arab states is being developed. There are textile and food-processing factories.

History and Government. In the 1820s Egypt took over the Sudan, defeating the last of earlier empires, including the Fung. In the 1880s a revolution was led by Mohammed Ahmed who called himself the Mahdi (leader of the faithful) and his followers, the dervishes. British Gen. Charles Gordon (Chinese Gordon), who had earlier put down the slave trade in the Sudan, was sent by Egypt to evacuate its troops; he was besieged and slain at Khartoum, 1885.

In 1898 Horatio Kitchener led an Anglo-Egyptian force which crushed the Mahdi's successors.

In Oct. 1951 the Egyptian Parliament abrogated its 1899 and 1936 treaties with Great Britain, and amended the constitution, Oct. 16, to provide for a separate Sudanese constitution.

Sudan voted for complete independence effective Jan. 1, 1956. A 5-member Supreme Commission (Council of State) and a Cabinet were sworn in.

A parliamentary government was set up but in 1958 Gen. Ibrahim Abboud took power; he resigned under pressure in 1964; a Constituent Assembly was elected in 1965 which approved a coalition government.

In May 1969, in a second military coup, a Revolutionary Council took power, but a civilian premier and cabinet were appointed and the new government announced it would create a socialist state. It also announced plans to negotiate an end to guerrilla warfare, which had beset the southern third of the nation for years. The northern 12 provinces are predominantly Arab-Moslem and have been dominant in the central government. The 3 southern provinces, in which there was a strong separatist movement, are Negro and predominantly pagan, with small Christian and Moslem minorities. A peace agreement, giving the South regional autonomy, was reached in 1972. Renewed flare-ups occurred in 1975.

The government nationalized a number of businesses in May 1970. An attempted communist coup in July 1971 failed, leading to a temporary diplomatic break with the USSR. Soviet arms shipments were announced in 1975.

Diplomatic relations with the U.S., broken by Sudan during the 1967 Arab-Israeli war, were restored in 1972; locally-owned firms were denationalized and foreign firms compensated.

On Mar. 2, 1973, the U. S. ambassador and the charge d'affaires and a Belgian diplomat were slain in Khartoum by 8 Palestinian terrorists. The 8 were freed and turned over to a Palestinian liberation group in Egypt.

Education and Religion. Sudanese inhabitants are Arabs, Negroes, and Nubians (of mixed Arab and Negro blood); the Arabs and Nubians are Mohammedans. Higher education is available at Khartoum Univ. Arabic is the national language; many tribal languages are spoken in the South.

Surinam

Area: 63,251 sq. mi. Population: (UN est. 1975): 420,000. Capital: Paramaribo. Monetary unit: Surinam florin.

Surinam is on the N coast of South America, between the Atlantic Ocean and Brazil; to the E is French Guiana, to the W is Guyana, both of which have disputed parts of their Surinam borders. Surinam is about the size of Washington State.

Most of the population is concentrated along the coast, where dikes permit agriculture. Farther inland is a forest belt; to the south, largely unexplored hills cover three-fourths of the country.

Minerals abound, especially bauxite, which is the major export, in raw or refined form. Hydroelectric power and lumbering are being developed. Rice is the major crop; sugar, fruits, and shrimp are also important, but food must be imported.

The Netherlands acquired Surinam in 1667 from Britain, in exchange for New Netherlands (New York). The 1954 Dutch constitution raised the colony to a level of equality with the Netherlands and the Netherlands Antilles. In the 1970s the Dutch government pressured for Surinam independence, which came Nov. 25, 1976, despite objections from East Indians and some Bush Negroes. Some 40% of the population emigrated to the Netherlands in the months before independence. A Legislative Council (Staten) is elected by universal suffrage for four-year terms; a Council of Ministers is responsible to the Staten. The Netherlands promised $1.5 billion in aid for the first decade of independence.

The population is extremely diverse; East Indians make up over 35%, Creoles (racially mixed descendants of freed African slaves) 30%, Javanese 15%, Bush Negroes (forest-dwelling descendants of runaway slaves) 10%; the remainder is composed of European, Chinese, and Amerindian groups. Dutch is the official language, but the Creole tongue Sranan Tongo is universally understood. Nearly all major world religions are represented.

Swaziland

Area: 6,705 sq. mi. Population (Govt. est. 1975): 490,000. Capital: Mbabane. Monetary unit: Lilangeni.

The Kingdom of Swaziland is in SE Africa, almost completely surrounded by the Republic of South Africa except for part of the E border which adjoins Mozambique. The Swazis came under British protection in 1903.

The example of neighboring former British territories Bechuanaland and Basutoland, which became the independent nations of Botswana and Lesotho in 1966, encouraged the drive for Swazi independence; Swaziland was economically the most healthy of the 3. In 1967, it achieved full self-government under a constitution and on Sept. 6, 1968, it became independent and a member of the Commonwealth.

The constitution provided for a partly-elected, partly-appointed Assembly and Senate, and a prime minister; the former paramount chief, Sobhuza II,

became King Sobhuza, a constitutional head of state. The royal house of Swaziland traces back 400 years, and remains one of Africa's last ruling dynasties. In April 1973 the king repealed the constitution and assumed full powers.

Polygamy has been the common marital status, but women have the right to vote.

About 97% of the residents are Swazi, a Bantu group. South African whites constitute a small minority; English and Siswati are the official languages.

The country is rich in mineral resources, including one of the world's largest asbestos mines, the Havelock Mine, and iron ore resources estimated at some 47 million tons. In addition, coal is exported. Tourism has grown with 250,000 visitors a year.

In recent years Swaziland developed a timber and pulp industry, a railway link to ports in Mozambique, hydro-electric power, and roads. The major export items are asbestos, iron ore, wood pulp, citrus fruits, and sugar. The land is fertile and has abundant water, producing such other crops as corn, cotton, rice, pineapples, and cattle. About 8,000 Swazis hold jobs in South Africa, which has a customs union with Swaziland.

Sweden

Area: 173,665 sq. mi. Population (Census 1975): 8,208,600. Capital: Stockholm. Monetary unit: Krona.

Sweden occupies the eastern and larger part of the Scandinavian peninsula in NW Europe. Its greatest N-S length is 977 mi.; greatest width 311 mi. The country is 10% larger than California. Sweden is separated from Norway on the W by the Kjolen Mtns., and from Finland on the E by the Baltic Sea except in the N where the 2 meet along the Tornea River.

Stockholm and Goteborg are the largest ports.

Resources and Industries. Although half of the country is forested, Sweden contains much productive land on which the Swedes have attained high efficiency in agriculture. Of the total land area, 9.9% is cultivated, 2.5% pasture. Chief agricultural products are dairy products, beef, pork, grains, potatoes, sugar beets, and vegetable oils.

Main natural resources are forests, iron ore, and water power. Coal and oil have to be imported. Industry employs 35% of the work-population, agriculture 7%. Swedish steel is of especial value for toolmaking. Other metals produced are lead, copper, zinc, gold, and silver. In 1975, 79.2 billion kwh were produced; the Stornorrforsen hydroelectric plant on the Ume River is the largest in Western Europe.

Although over 95% of the economy is in private hands, the government holds a large interest in water power production and the railroads are operated by a public agency. Worker participation in management is expanding.

Consumer cooperatives are in extensive operation, with 1,700,000 member households. Cooperatives also are important in agriculture and housing.

Shipping is privately operated. The merchant fleet included (1975) about 480 units totaling about 8 million tons d.w.

Sweden is one of the leading exporters of iron ore and cellulose. About one-fourth of the exports come from pulp, lumber, paper, and other forestry products. Other important products are machinery, instruments, autos, iron and steel, ships.

Foreign trade in thousands of U. S. dollars:

	Imports	Exports
1974	$16,455,000	$15,937,000
1975	17,874,000	17,439,000

History and Government. Sweden is a parliamentary democracy with a king as head of state and a prime minister as chief executive. The Riksdag (Parliament) has 349 members; all citizens 18 and over may vote.

King Gustaf VI Adolf died at the age of 90, Sept. 15, 1973. He was succeeded by his grandson, Carl XVI Gustaf, born 1946. Only symbolic powers are left to the king.

In elections Sept. 16, 1973, the Social Democrats, in power 41 years, and the non-Socialist parties each won 175 of the seats, then numbering 350.

About 20% of the national income is redistributed through the social welfare system which includes compulsory health insurance, pensions, unemployment and industrial injuries insurance, family and educational allowances. Unemployment during 1975 averaged 1.6%. Per capita GNP, 1975, was the highest in the world.

The U. S. and Sweden in 1974 ended a 15-month diplomatic "freeze" and exchanged ambassadors.

Sweden is a member of the Nordic Council, UN, EFTA, and Council of Europe and has a trade agreement with EC. Sweden distributes 1% of its GNP in foreign aid.

Education and Religion. The population is homogeneous, except for 650,000 foreign workers, mostly Northern Europeans. About 95% of the people are Lutheran, which is the state religion. Education is compulsory and illiteracy is non-existent. There are 6 state universities with several branches.

Defense. Full mobilizable strength exceeds 750,-000. Military service is compulsory for men. The air force is among the largest in Europe.

Switzerland

Area: 15,941 sq. mi. Population (Govt. est. 1975): 6,400,000. Capital: Bern. Monetary unit: Franc.

Switzerland, a federal republic in Central Europe, is bounded by France, Germany, Austria, Liechtenstein, and Italy. It is twice the size of New Jersey.

Switzerland is the most mountainous of all European countries. The Alps cover 60% of land area, the Jura 10%; running between them NE to SW are the midlands, about 30%. Swiss lakes are famous for their beauty. The Rhine, Rhone, and feeders of the Danube and Po originate in Switzerland.

Resources and Industries. Switzerland's abundant streams power 431 major hydroelectric plants, providing most of electricity output. Most important industries, in descending order: machinery, instruments, watches, textiles, foodstuffs (cheese, chocolate, etc.). Steel, chemicals, and pharmaceuticals are also important. Machine-making employs 26% of all factory workers and accounts for 34% of exports. Included are textile machinery, machine tools, dynamo-electric plants, transformers, and diesels . . . 20% of workers are foreign residents.

Foreign trade in thousands of U.S. dollars:

	Imports	Exports
1974	$14,441,000	$11,929,000
1975	$13,305,000	$12,957,000

Switzerland is one of the world's great banking centers. Stability of its currency brings funds from many quarters. Nearly 7 million tourists visit annually.

History and Government. Switzerland, the Helvetia of ancient times, is a federation of 22 cantons (19 full cantons and 6 half cantons), 3 of which in 1291 created a defensive league and later were joined by other districts. (Voters in the French-speaking Jura approved a breakaway canton in 1974.) In 1648 the Swiss Confederation obtained its independence from the Holy Roman Empire. The cantons were joined under a federal constitution in 1848, with large powers of local control retained by each canton. Legislative authority vests in a parliament of 2 chambers, a Standerat or State Council to which each canton sends 2 members; and a lower house, Nationalrat or National Council.

Executive power is vested in the 7-member Bundesrat (Federal Council). The president is selected from members of the Federal Council, serves for a year, and customarily is succeeded by the vice president. Women won the right to vote in federal elections in 1971; some were elected to parliament.

Switzerland enters into no military alliance and is not a member of UN or NATO. It is, however, a member of UN agencies such as the ILO, WHO, UNESCO, FAO. In 1972 it signed an agreement with the EC for gradual abolition of industrial tariffs.

Geneva is the seat of a number of UN agencies, International Committee of the Red Cross, League of Red Cross Societies, Int'l. Union for Telecommunications. The Universal Postal Union is in Bern.

Education and Religion. Primary education has been free and compulsory since 1874. There are 9 universities. Swiss German dialects are spoken by a majority of the people in 16 of the cantons; other languages are French, Italian, and Romansch.

There is complete freedom of worship; 47.8% of the people are Protestants, 49.4% Roman Catholics.

Defense. Service in the national militia is compulsory. Its easily mobilized divisions comprise more than 625,000 men. The air force has about 300 combat craft.

Syria

Area: 71,498 sq. mi. Population (Govt. est. 1975): 7,350,000. Capital: Damascus. Monetary unit: Syrian pound.

The Syrian Arab Republic has a short coastline on the eastern shore of the Mediterranean, then stretches E and S with fertile valleys and plains alternating with mountains and desert. Main rivers are Euphrates and Orontes. Chief seaport is Latakia. Syria is about the size of South Dakota.

Resources and Industries. Syria is primarily an agricultural and stock-raising nation. Cotton, barley, wheat, olives, fruits, vegetables, meat, textiles, and wool are the main exports. Growing industries include flour milling, oil refining, textiles, cement, tobacco, glassware, sugar, and brassware. In 1965 the Socialist regime nationalized most industries. Oil production is growing. Royalties, collected from Iraqi and Saudi Arabian pipelines crossing to Mediterranean ports, fluctuate due to political conditions. In 1973 a $300 million power and irrigation dam was completed on the upper Euphrates, leading to a dispute with Iraq over water use.

History and Government. One of the world's ancient inhabited lands, the state of Syria was formed from former Turkish Empire Sanjaks (districts). Syria was made a separate entity by the Treaty of Sevres 1920 and divided into the states of Syria and Greater Lebanon. Both were administered under a French League of Nations mandate 1920-1941.

Syria was proclaimed a republic by the occupying French Sept. 16, 1941, and exercised full independence effective Jan. 1, 1944. French troops left in 1946.

Syria joined with Egypt in Feb. 1958 in the United Arab Republic but seceded Sept. 30, 1961. The Socialist Baath party and military leaders seized power in Mar. 1963. The Baath, a pan-Arab organization, became the only legal party. A 1973 constitution provides for a 186-member People's Council but gives most powers to the president.

In the Israeli-Arab war of June 1967, Israel seized and occupied the Golan Heights area inside Syria, from which Israeli settlements had for years been shelled by Syria.

Syria aided Palestinian guerrillas fighting Jordanian forces in Sept. 1970, and, after a renewal of that fighting in July 1971, broke off relations with Jordan. But by 1975 the 2 countries had entered a military coordination pact.

Syria received large shipments of arms from the USSR in 1972-73 and on Oct. 6, 1973, joined Egypt in an attack on Israel. (For details, see article on Israel.) Arab oil states agreed in 1974 to give Syria $1 billion a year to aid anti-Israel moves. Military supplies used or lost in the 1973 war were replaced by the USSR in 1974. At least 16,000 Syrian troops entered Lebanon in 1976 to mediate in a civil war. Armed forces total 177,500.

Education and Religion. The population is composed mainly of Sunni Moslems but there are many Christians. Arabic is the official language but about

12% of the population are Kurds, Armenians, Turks, etc. Syria has universities in Damascus, Aleppo, and Latakia.

Tanzania

Area: 363,708 sq. mi. Population (Govt. est. 1975): 15,160,000. Capital: Dar es Salaam. Monetary unit: Tanzanian shilling.

The Republic of Tanganyika and the Republic of Zanzibar, an island in the Indian Ocean off the coast of Tanganyika, joined into a single nation, the United Republic of Tanzania, Apr. 26, 1964. The new central government at Dar es Salaam (Haven of Peace), an important port and capital of Tanganyika, was given jurisdiction over defense, foreign affairs, and public services. In 1973 Dodoma, in the country's center, was named the future capital.

Julius K. Nyerere, Tanganyika's president, became president of the new nation; Zanzibar's president became first vice president.

In 1967 the government set on a socialist course; it nationalized all banks and many industries; some of the latter were taken over completely, in others the government took a part interest. The government also ordered that Swahili, not English, be used in all official business.

Tanzania is a member of the UN and Commonwealth. In 1974 a road to Zambia was completed with U.S. aid and in 1975 a railroad to Zambia was finished with aid from the People's Republic of China.

Tanganyika

Tanganyika stretches from the Indian Ocean on the E to 3 of Africa's Great Lakes: Victoria, Tanganyika and Nyasa. Its area is 362,688 sq. mi., larger than Texas and Oklahoma combined; pop. is over 14 million. Most of the people are Bantus and speak Swahili.

Snow-capped Mt. Kilimanjaro, tallest in Africa, rises 19,340 ft. in the N. Nearby are the famed Serengeti Plains, teeming with vast herds of wild animals.

Principal products are sisal, cotton, coffee, tea, tobacco, and hides. Nine million people have been moved into cooperative villages. Both gem and industrial diamonds are mined, as are gold, salt, tin, and mica. Diamonds accounted for 91% of the mineral income in 1973.

Factories include food processing, clothing.

Arab colonization began in the 8th century A.D.; Portuguese sailors explored the coast by about 1500. Other Europeans followed.

In 1885 Germany established German East Africa of which Tanganyika formed the bulk. It became a League of Nations mandate and, after 1946, a UN trust territory, both under Britain.

Constitutional changes gave it autonomy in Sept. 1960. It became independent Dec. 9, 1961, and a republic within the Commonwealth a year later.

Moslems & Christians each claim 30% of the population. The state has taken control of church schools.

Zanzibar

Zanzibar, the Isle of Cloves, lies 23 mi. off the coast of Tanganyika; its area is 640 sq. mi. The island of Pemba, 25 mi. to the NE, area 380 sq. mi., is included in the administration. The population is mainly African and Arab. The total area of the 2 islands is about that of Rhode Island; population (Govt. est. 1967): 354,360.

Chief industry is the production of cloves and clove oil, of which Zanzibar and Pemba produce the bulk of the world's supply.

Zanzibar was for centuries the center for Arab slave-traders. Portugal ruled for 2 centuries until ousted by Arabs around 1700. Zanzibar became a British Protectorate in 1890. Independence came Dec. 10, 1963. Revolutionary forces overthrew the Sultan Jan. 12, 1964. The new government ousted American and British diplomats and newsmen, slaughtered thousands of Arabs, and nationalized farms. Union with Tanganyika followed, 1964.

Thailand

Area: 198,455 sq. mi. Population (Govt. est. 1975): 41,280,000. Capital: Bangkok. Monetary unit: Baht.

Thailand is a constitutional monarchy in SE Asia bordered by Burma, Laos, Cambodia, the Gulf of Thailand (or Siam), and Malaysia. It is about twice the size of Colorado with large areas under irrigation.

Bangkok, the capital, is a modern city. Its Don Muang airfield is one of the largest and most modern in SE Asia, served by 38 international airlines. It is also an important port. There is an extensive inland waterway system and network of roads.

Resources and Industries. There are large forests, teakwood being an important article of export. Agriculture occupies 78% of the population.

Thailand is the world's 5th largest producer of tin ore; other minerals are iron, manganese, tungsten, antimony. Offshore natural gas was discovered, 1974.

The chief crop is rice, the staple food and a major export, with 850,000 metric tons shipped in 1973. Other important exports are tin, rubber, corn, teak, tapioca, jute, and sugar. Coconuts, tobacco, pepper, peanuts, beans, and cotton are produced.

Foreign investment in industry is encouraged — auto assembly plants, pharmaceuticals, textiles, electrical goods. Over 1 million tourists visited in 1974.

History and Government. Thailand, an ancient monarchy, noted for picturesque architecture and pageantry, is the only country in SE Asia never taken over by a colonial power, thanks to King Mongkut and his son King Chulalongkorn who ruled from 1851 to 1910, modernized the country, and signed trade treaties with both Britain and France.

Thailand underwent a bloodless revolution in 1932. King Prajadhipok, a liberal, signed a new constitution, establishing a limited monarchy, but he refused to sign a measure abdicating the royal power of life and death and resigned. He was succeeded by his nephew, Prince Ananda, who was found dead of a bullet wound, June 9, 1946, and the legislature named his brother, Prince Phumiphol Aduldet (Bhumibol Adulyadej) (born 1927), to succeed him. The new king formally took the throne May 5, 1950, as Rama IX.

A military-civilian junta, headed by Gen. Thanom Kittikachorn, took over the government in Nov. 1971. Civilians, led by students, overwhelmed police, Oct. 1973, and forced Thanom to resign as premier. A civilian cabinet was named. After free elections in January 1975, a coalition government was sworn in.

There was sporadic terrorism in the NE and far S, 1965-76, by communists and ethnic minorities.

Education and Religion. Education is compulsory between 7 and 14. There are 12 universities, 31 training colleges and many vocational schools. The language is Thai, derived from Pali and Sanskrit. Literacy has been high for several decades. About 15% of the population is ethnic Chinese. English is widely used.

About 94% of the people are Buddhists; others are: 1.5 million Moslems, some Christians, etc.

Defense. Military strength is 204,000. Thailand is a member of the UN.

U.S. forces in Thailand, mostly airmen, totaled 45,-000 in 1973. The U.S. withdrew most of its forces during 1973 and 1974. The new Thai government obtained U.S. agreement to withdraw all troops by 1976, except for some 270 advisers.

The last of 11,000 Thai troops were withdrawn from South Vietnam in 1972. About 15,000 Thai "irregular" forces, financed by the U.S., returned from Laos in 1974.

Togo

Area: 21,853 sq. mi. Population (Govt. est. 1975): 2,220,000. Capital: Lome. Monetary unit: CFA franc.

The republic of Togo is composed of part of the one-time German colony of Togoland, surrendered in 1914, and administered by France as a UN trusteeship, 1946-1960.

Togo is a thin sliver of land on the southern edge of the West African bulge. It is bounded by Upper Volta, Dahomey, the Atlantic and Ghana.

In 1958 France got UN approval to end its trusteeship; the republic was proclaimed Apr. 27, 1960.

A draft constitution on the U.S. model was published Mar. 20, 1961. It provided for a president and a 46-member unicameral parliament. First president, Sylvanus Olympio, elected Apr. 9, 1961, was assassinated by a military junta, Jan. 13, 1963. His elected successor, Nicolas Grunitzky, was replaced by Gnassingbe Eyadema, head of the armed forces.

Togo has received aid from France, the U.S. and West Germany. Tourism is a growing industry.

Principal commercial products: phosphates, coffee, cocoa, palm kernels, copra, cotton, kapok and peanuts. There are textile and shoe factories. Togo has led efforts toward West African economic unity.

French, Ewe and Cabrai are official languages. The population is divided between Bantus in the South and Hamitic tribes in the North.

Tonga

Area: 269 sq. mi. Population (Govt. est. 1974): 100,-000. Capital: Nukualofa. Monetary unit: Pa'anga.

The Kingdom of Tonga, a constitutional monarchy, comprises 150 volcanic and coral islands (45 inhabited) in the South Pacific, NE of New Zealand and S of Samoa. The capital, Nukualofa, is on the main island, Tongatapu.

The islands were first visited by the Dutch in the early 17th Century. A series of civil wars ended in 1845 with establishment of the Tupou dynasty. In 1900 Tonga became a British protectorate. On June 4, 1970, Tonga became completely independent and a member of the Commonwealth.

Government consists of a king, a prime minister and an elected Legislative Assembly.

Agriculture and fishing are the mainstays of the economy. Chief exports are coconut products and bananas. Tourism is being encouraged.

Tongans are Polynesians; languages: Tongan, English. Education is free and compulsory, ages 6-14; medical care is free; religion is Christianity.

Trinidad and Tobago

Area: 1,979 sq. mi. Population (Govt. est. 1974): 1,070,000. Capital: Port of Spain. Monetary unit: Trinidad and Tobago Dollar.

Trinidad, area 1,864 sq. mi., is the most southerly of the West Indies, lying off the NE coast of South America approx. 7 mi. from Venezuela. It was discovered by Columbus in 1498. Tobago, 116 sq. mi. lies 20 mi. to the NE of Trinidad.

Second largest of the old British West Indies and a British possession since 1802, Trinidad and Tobago won independence Aug. 31, 1962. A governor-general represents the British crown. A prime minister is the actual executive. Parliament consists of a 24-member Senate, appointed by the prime minister and the opposition, and a 36-member House of Representatives, elected by universal suffrage. The country is a member of the UN, Commonwealth and OAS.

Middle Eastern oil is refined and exported, mostly to the U. S. Other exports are sugar, asphalt, rum, cocoa, coffee, citrus, bananas, cement, bitters. Oil production has increased with offshore finds.

The nation is one of the most prosperous in the West Indies, but unemployment averages 13%.

Trinidad claims to have originated the steel band, calypso songs and the limbo dance. Tourism is an important source of revenue.

The population is mixed: Black 43%, East Indian (descended from immigrants from India) 36%; mixed races, Europeans and Chinese comprise the rest.

Religions include Roman Catholic 36%, Protestant 34%, Hindu 23%, Moslem 6%.

Public primary and secondary education is free to age 18. Some units of the Univ. of West Indies are in Trinidad, some in Jamaica. There are 4 technical institutes.

Tunisia

Area: 63,378 sq. mi. Population (Govt. est. 1975): 5,770,000. Capital: Tunis. Monetary unit: Dinar.

Tunisia is a former French protectorate which became independent Mar. 20, 1956. It is on the Mediterranean coast of Africa wedged between Algeria and Libya. It is about the size of Florida. The people are mostly Arabs, with some Berbers and Europeans.

Resources and Industries. The chief pursuit is agriculture; an abundance of grains, dates, olives, citrus fruits, figs, vegetables, and wine grapes, is produced. Livestock is extensively raised. Phosphates, iron, oil, lead and zinc are leading minerals.

Industries include food processing, textiles, clothing, leather, oil refining, construction materials. Principal exports are olive oil, wine, iron ore, lead, phosphate, fruits, oil and grains. A farm collectivization program was dropped in 1970. Private local and foreign investment is encouraged, and the economy has prospered.

Tourism is growing (over 700,000 in 1974) and attractions include numerous well-preserved Roman ruins, excellent beaches, and resorts on Djerba Is., reputed home of the Lotus Eaters of the Odyssey.

The tourist industry earns over $100 million a year. New industries include steel and auto-assembly plants, a paper mill and sugar refinery.

History and Government. Site of ancient Carthage, and a former Barbary state under the suzerainty of Turkey, Tunisia became a protectorate of France under a treaty signed May 12, 1881. After receiving increasing measures of self-government since 1947, a constituent assembly, elected Mar. 25, 1956, chose a government headed by Habib Bourguiba, named premier Apr. 10. The basic law, adopted by the assembly, Apr. 13, vested sovereignty in the people, ignoring the titular ruler, Mohammed el Amim, bey of Tunis. The assembly unanimously voted, July 25, 1957, to end the monarchy. It proclaimed a republic; Bourguiba became president; he was re-elected three times. Bourguiba was named president for life of the single legal party in 1974; a new constitutional provision assured the party chief of the national presidency.

Although Tunisia is a member of the Arab League, Bourguiba in the 1960s urged negotiations to end Arab-Israeli disputes and was denounced by other members. In 1966 he broke relations with Egypt but resumed them after the 1967 Israeli-Arab war. He again urged negotiations with Israel in June 1973.

Tunisia and Libya announced in Jan. 1974 that the 2 nations would merge, but Bourguiba soon dropped the plan.

Education and Religion. The majority of the population is Moslem. Europeans number fewer than 100,-000. Arabic is the national and official language. From 1956-1974 Tunisia raised the number of primary school students from 200,000 to 943,000, secondary from 15,500 to 178,000, and higher education from 1,350 to 15,000.

Defense. The armed forces total over 24,000.

Turkey

Area: 301,380 sq. mi. Population (Govt. est. 1975): 39,180,000. Capital: Ankara. Monetary unit: Lira.

About 90% of Turkey's population lives in the Asian portion of the country on the Anatolian Peninsula — an area of 292,184 sq. mi. The remainder live in the European part which is bordered by Bulgaria and Greece. A republic since 1923, Turkey is a little larger than Texas and has extensive coastlines on the

Black Sea, the Mediterranean and the Aegean. Its Asian neighbors are the USSR, Iran, Iraq and Syria.

Central Turkey has wide plateaus, with hot dry summers and cold winters with snow remaining until May. High mountains ring the interior on all but the W side. More than 20 peaks top 10,000 ft.

The world's 4th longest suspension bridge, linking Europe and Asia across the Bosporus, opened in 1973.

Resources and Industries. About 64% of the labor force is engaged in agriculture, the products including tobacco (it is the world's 6th largest producer), cereals, cotton, olive oil, wool, mohair, silk, figs, nuts, fruits, sugar, opium, and gums. About 45 million acres are in forests, nearly one-fourth of land area.

In June 1971 Turkey agreed to stop all opium poppy production, in return for $37.5 million in economic aid from the U.S. In 1974 it announced it would resume opium production, with U.S. and U.N. controls, for medical use only.

There are large deposits of antimony, borate, copper and chrome (of which Turkey is one of the world's largest producers). Other minerals include manganese, lead, zinc, coal, iron, oil, silver, mercury, sulphur, molybdenum, magnesite and asbestos.

Turkey manufactures silk, cotton and woolen yarn and cloth, steel, foundry products, sugar, footwear, office furniture, cement, paper, glassware and appliances. About one million tourists visit each year.

Foreign trade, in thousands of U.S. dollars:

	Imports	Exports
1974	$3,720,000	$1,532,000
1975	$4,640,000	$1,401,000

History and Government. Just before World War I, Turkey, or the Ottoman Empire, ruled what is now Syria, Lebanon, Iraq, Jordan, Israel, Arabia, Yemen and islands in the Aegean Sea.

Turkey joined Germany and Austria in World War I and its defeat resulted in loss of much territory and fall of the sultanate. A republic was declared Oct. 29, 1923, with Mustafa Kemal Ataturk first president. The Caliphate (spiritual leadership of Islam) was renounced 1924. Turkey was permitted (1936) to refortify the Dardanelles and Bosporus, to close them if threatened, but to permit free passage of merchant vessels in peace or war.

The present constitution, adopted July 9, 1961, provides for a bicameral legislature composed of a Senate of 150 and a National Assembly of 450 deputies. The president is elected by Parliament to a 7-year term and is ineligible for reelection. A premier is chosen from a leading party.

Turkey is a member of the UN, CENTO, NATO, Council of Europe and an associate in EC. Communism is outlawed, and many leftist terrorists have been jailed. Martial law, imposed in 1971, was ended in 1973.

Long embroiled with Greece over Cyprus, off Turkey's south coast, Turkey invaded the island July 20, 1974, after Greek officers seized the Cypriot government as a step toward unification with Greece. Turkey sought a new government for Cyprus, with Greek Cypriot and Turkish Cypriot zones. In reaction to Turkey's moves, the U. S. Congress cut off military aid in 1975. Turkey, in turn, suspended the use of most U. S. bases. A new base accord was tentatively reached in March, 1976.

Education and Religion. About 99% of the population is Moslem. There are about three million Kurds and one million in other ethnic minorities. Public elementary education is free and compulsory; higher public education is free.

Defense. Armed forces total 453,000.

Uganda

Area: 91,134 sq. mi. Population (Govt. est. 1975): 11,550,000. Capital: Kampala. Monetary unit: Uganda shilling.

The Republic of Uganda, a former British protectorate, is in east-central Africa with Kenya to the E, Lake Victoria and Tanzania to the S, Lakes Albert and Edward (also called Lakes Sese Seko and Idi Amin) and Zaire to the W, Sudan to the N. It is about the size of Oregon. On the border with Zaire, the Rewenzori Range rises 16,000 ft. In the SW there are several volcanoes over 11,000 ft. high.

Uganda is the world's 5th largest coffee exporter; coffee provided 68% of 1973 export earnings. Cotton, tea, maize, peanuts, sisal, oil seeds, tobacco, sugar, are also produced. Copper and tin are important exports. The expulsion of Asians and Europeans threw the economy into chaos in the 1970's.

Uganda became independent Oct. 9, 1962; a republic Oct. 9, 1963. It is a member of the UN, OAU and Commonwealth.

Milton Obote, then prime minister, seized full power Feb. 23, 1966. Gen. Idi Amin seized control Jan. 25, 1971, and was named president; over 90,000 of his opponents were reported killed in subsequent years. Amin was named president for life in 1976.

In 1972 Amin expelled nearly all of Uganda's 45,-000 Asians (Indians and Pakistanis), many of them business and professional men. Britain, the U.S. and some other nations accepted the deportees. In 1973 the U.S., Canada and Norway ended economic aid programs; and the U.S. withdrew all diplomatic personnel. Amin seized all British firms.

Nearly half the population is Christian (mostly Roman Catholics). English, Luganda, and Luo are the main languages. Idi Amin and others are Moslems.

At Owen Falls on the Victoria Nile, outlet of Lake Victoria, a major dam and hydroelectric project has been constructed.

Union of Soviet Socialist Republics

Area: 8,647,250 sq. mi. Population (Govt. est. 1975): 254,380,000. Capital: Moscow. Monetary unit: Ruble.

The Union of Soviet Socialist Republics—in area the largest country in the world—stretches across 2 continents from the North Pacific to the Baltic Sea. It occupies the northern part of Asia and the eastern half of Europe. Its western borders brush against Norway, Finland, the Baltic, Poland, Czechoslovakia, Hungary and Romania. To the S are the Black Sea, Turkey, Iran, Afghanistan, China, Mongolian Peoples Republic and North Korea. In the far NE, Bering Strait separates it from Alaska.

The vast territory of the USSR, one-sixth of the earth's land surface, contains every phase of climate, except the distinctly tropical, and a varied topography. The European portion is a vast low plain with the Ural Mtns. on its eastern edge, the Caucasus Mtns. and others on the S. The Urals, separating the European from the Asiatic portions of the country, stretch N-S for 2,500 mi. The Asiatic portion also consists largely of an immense plain, with mountain ranges on the S and in the E.

There are some 150,000 rivers and 250,000 lakes. The larger European rivers include the Dnieper, flowing into the Black Sea, the Volga and the Ural into the Caspian Sea, the Don into the Sea of Azov, the Western Dvina into the Baltic and the Northern Dvina into the White Sea. The Asiatic section is drained by the Ob, the Yenisei and the Lena, each over 2,000 mi. long, flowing into the Arctic Ocean, and the Amur, flowing into the Pacific.

The Caspian Sea, with its S end in Iran, is the world's largest lake in surface area (143,550 sq. mi.). Other lakes are the Aral Sea (25,300 sq. mi.), Lake Baykal (11,780 sq. mi.), Lake Balkhash (6,720 sq. mi.), Lake Ladoga (6,835 sq. mi.).

In Moscow, the Kremlin, ancient citadel of the Czars, forms the nerve center of the federated republics. Leningrad (formerly St. Petersburg and Petrograd), in the delta of the Neva River, is the 2d largest city. Kiev, the 1,000-year-old capital of the Ukrainian SSR, is the industrial center of the south. The Crimea and the eastern shore of the Black Sea, beneath the towering Caucasus Mtns., are resort areas.

Beginning in 1939 the USSR by means of military action and negotiation overran contiguous territory and independent republics, including all or part of Lithuania, Latvia, Estonia, Poland, Czechoslovakia, Romania, Germany, Tannu Tuva, and Japan.

Political Organization

The USSR is a federation consisting of 15 union republics, within certain of which are further subdivisions. Four of the union republics contain 20 autonomous soviet socialist republics and 8 autonomous regions; the largest union republic, the Russian Soviet Federal Socialist Republic, has also 10 national districts. Nationalist agitation has occasionally been reported in several of the republics. The Union Republics are:

Republic	Area, sq. miles	Pop. (Est. 1974)
Russian SFSR	6,593,391	132,900,000
Ukrainian SSR	232,046	48,600,000
Kazakh SSR	1,064,092	13,900,000
Uzbek SSR	158,069	13,300,000
Byelorussian SSR	80,154	9,300,000
Azerbaijan SSR	33,436	5,500,000
Georgian SSR	26,911	4,900,000
Moldavian SSR	13,012	3,800,000
Lithuanian SSR	26,173	3,300,000
Tadzhik SSR	54,019	3,300,000
Kirghiz SSR	76,642	3,200,000
Armenian SSR	11,306	2,700,000
Latvian SSR	24,695	2,500,000
Turkmen SSR	188,417	2,400,000
Estonian SSR	17,413	1,400,000

The Russian Soviet Federal Socialist Republic, contains over 50% of the population of the Soviet Union and includes 76% of its territory. Its territories stretch from the old Estonian, Latvian and Finnish borders and the Byelorussian and Ukrainian lines on the W, to the shores of the Pacific, and from the Arctic on the N to the Black and Caspian Seas and the borders of Kazakh SSR, Mongolia and Manchuria on the S. Siberia, divided into a number of administrative units, encompasses a large part of the RSFSR area. Capital: Moscow.

Parts of Eastern and Western Siberia have been transformed by steel mills, huge dams, oil and gas industries, electric railroads and highways.

Ukrainian SSR is the most densely populated of the major constituent republics. It borders on the Black Sea, with Poland, Czechoslovakia, Hungary and Romania on the W and SW. The population is 75% Ukrainian. Capital: Kiev.

The Ukraine contains the arable black soil belt, the chief wheat-producing section of the Soviet Union. Sugar beets, potatoes and livestock are important.

The Donets Basin has large deposits of coal, iron and other metals. There are chemical and machine industries and salt mines.

Byelorussian SSR (White Russia), bordering on Poland, suffered greatly under the Czars from periodical pogroms and from inter-ethnic struggles. In the World Wars it was a field for military operations. Capital: Minsk. Chief industries include machinery, tools, appliances, tractors, clocks, cameras, steel, cement, textiles, paper, leather, glass. Main crops are grain, flax, potatoes, sugar beets.

Azerbaijan SSR boasts near Baku, the capital, important oil fields. Its natural wealth includes deposits of iron ore, cobalt, etc. Irrigation has boosted cotton production. A high-yield winter wheat also is grown, as are fruits. It produces iron, steel, cement, fertilizers, synthetic rubber, electrical and chemical equipment. It borders on Iran and Turkey.

Georgian SSR, which lies in the western part of Transcaucasia, contains the largest manganese mines in the world. There are rich timber resources and coal mines. Basic industries are food, textiles, iron, steel. Grain, tea, tobacco, fruits, grapes are grown. Capital: Tbilisi (Tiflis). Despite massive party and government purges since 1972, illegal private enterprise and Georgian nationalist feelings persist; at-

tempts to repress them have led to violence.

Armenian SSR is mountainous, sub-tropical, extensively irrigated. Copper, zinc, aluminum, molybdenum, and marble are mined. Instrument making is important. Capital: Erevan.

Uzbek SSR, most important economically of the Central Asia republics, produces 67% of USSR cotton, 50% of rice, 33% of silk, 34% of astrakhan, 85% of hemp. Industries include iron, steel, cars, tractors, TV and radio sets, textiles, food. Mineral wealth includes coal, sulphur, copper and oil. Capital: Tashkent.

Turkmen SSR in Central Asia, produces cotton, maize, carpets, chemicals. Minerals: oil, coal, sulphur, barite, lime, salt, gypsum. The Kara Kum desert occupies four-fifths of the area. Capital: Ashkhabad.

Tadzhik SSR borders on China and Afghanistan. Over half the population are Tadzhiks, mostly Moslems, speaking an Iranian dialect. Chief occupations are farming and cattle breeding. Cotton, grain, rice and a variety of fruits are grown. Heavy industry, based on rich mineral deposits, coal and hydroelectric power, has replaced handicrafts. Capital: Dushanbe.

Kazakh SSR extends from the lower reaches of the Volga in Europe to the Altai Mtns. on the Chinese border. It has vast deposits of coal, oil, iron, tin, copper, lead, zinc, etc. Fish for its canning industry are caught in Lake Balkhash and the Caspian and Aral Seas. The capital is Alma-Ata. About 50% of the population is Russian or Ukrainian, working in the virgin-grain lands opened up after 1954, and in the growing industries. Kazakhstan is third among industrial republics in the USSR.

Kirghiz SSR is in the eastern part of Soviet Central Asia, on the frontier of Sinkiang (western China). The people, once nomadic, breed cattle and horses and grow tobacco, cotton, rice, sugar beets. New industries include machine and instrument making, chemicals. Capital: Frunze.

Moldavian SSR in the SW part of the USSR, is a fertile black earth plain bordering Romania, and includes Bessarabia. It is an agricultural region that grows grains, fruits, vegetables and tobacco. Textiles, wine, food and electrical equipment industries have been developed. Capital: Kishinev.

Lithuanian SSR, on the Baltic, produces cattle, hogs, electric motors and appliances. The capital is Vilnius (Vilna). **The Latvian SSR** on the Baltic and the Gulf of Riga, has timber and peat resources estimated at 3 billion tons. In addition to agricultural products it produces rubber goods, dyes, fertilizers, glassware, telephone apparatus, TV and radio sets, railroad cars. The capital is Riga. **The Estonian SSR** also on the Baltic, has textiles, shipbuilding, timber, roadmaking and mining equipment industries and a shale oil refining industry. Tallinn is the capital. The 3 Baltic states were provinces of imperial Russia before World War I, were independent nations between World Wars I and II, and became SSRs, within the USSR, in 1940. They were occupied by Germany 1941-44. The U.S. has never formally recognized the incorporation of Lithuania, Latvia and Estonia into the USSR.

Economics and Production

The economic foundation of the USSR is the socialist ownership of the instruments and means of production. Socialist property exists in 2 forms: (1) State property; (2) Cooperative and collective farm property. State property includes the land, minerals, waters, forests, mills, factories, mines, rail, water and air transport, banks, communications, large agricultural enterprises and the bulk of dwellings.

The common enterprises of collective farms and cooperative organizations, their output and common buildings constitute their socialized property. Members may use small plots of land attached to their dwellings.

"Backyard" farms, from which farmers may sell

produce and keep the profit, produced 61% of potatoes, a third of vegetables, meat and milk, 43% of eggs, and 21% of wool in 1973.

Cultivated land in 1972 was about 518.7 million acres. About 25% of the work force engaged in agriculture in 1973, and 40% of the population lived in rural areas. There were 31,500 collective farms and 17,300 state farms. In 1975 there were 111 million cattle (topped by India and the U.S.), 58 million hogs (2d to China) and 141 million sheep (2d to Australia). The fish catch is 2d only to Japan's.

In poor crop years, the USSR has been forced to make huge purchases of grain from Canada and other countries. About $1.1 billion worth was ordered from the U. S. in 1972, with additional amounts for 1973 and 1974. Further huge orders and a 5-year trade commitment were made in 1975 and 1976 from the U. S. and Canada, to compensate for drought shortfalls. Nevertheless, food shortages and rationing were intermittently reported.

The USSR is incalculably rich in natural resources. It claims to possess 58% of the world's coal deposits, 59% of its oil, 41% of iron ore, 88% of manganese, 54% of potassium salts, 30% of phosphates, and 25% of all timber land.

In 1973, the USSR produced 26% of world iron ore output, 19.5% of steel, 22% of coal, 16% of gold. Oil production and steel production in 1975 led the world. The index of industrial production (1970 = 100) was 133 for 1974.

In 1966 many major factories were put on an incentive profit-sharing system, while bonuses to farms and farm workers (called "Socialist competition") were introduced to spur food production. In 1973 steps were taken to group factories into "production associations" partly resembling large U.S. corporations.

In 1971 a proposed new 5-year plan stressed growth in consumer goods, but subsequent adjustments restored priority to heavy industry, and reduced overall goals. The 1976-80 plan called for slower growth, emphasizing modernization of plants and higher farm investment.

Foreign Trade

Exports include petroleum and its products, iron and steel, rolled non-ferrous metals, industrial plant equipment, arms, lumber, cotton, asbestos, gold, manganese and others. 60% of its trade is with Socialist nations, 25% with the West, which supplies advanced technology. The USSR had a $5 billion trade deficit with the West in 1975, financed by gold sales and loans.

Foreign trade, in thousands of U.S. dollars:

	Imports	Exports
1973	$21,108,000	$21,463,000
1974	$24,877,000	$27,381,000

Early History

The first Russian state centered on Kiev in the 9th century. In the 13th century the Mongols overran the country. It recovered under the grand dukes and princes of Muscovy, or Moscow, and by 1480 freed itself from the Mongols. Ivan the Terrible was the first to be formally proclaimed Czar (1547). Peter the Great (1682-1725), extended the domain and in 1721 founded the Russian Empire.

Revolution of 1917

The abortive Revolution of 1905 demonstrated the insecurity of the czarist regime and led to mild concessions. The 1917 Revolution began in March with a series of sporadic strikes for higher wages by factory workers. A provisional democratic government under Prince Georgi Lvov was established but was quickly followed in May by the second provisional government, led by Alexander Kerensky. The Kerensky government and the freely-elected Constituent Assembly were overthrown in a communist coup led by Vladimir Ilyich Lenin Nov. 7.

Lenin's death Jan. 21, 1924, resulted in an internal power struggle from which Joseph Stalin eventually emerged the absolute ruler of Russia. Stalin secured his position at first by exiling opponents such as Leon Trotsky. But from the 1930s to 1953 he resorted to a series of "purge" trials, mass executions and mass exiles in work camps. These measures, along with forced collectivization of agriculture, resulted in millions of deaths, according to most estimates. In 1975 it was estimated there still were 10,000 political prisoners, mostly in labor camps.

Khrushchev, Brezhnev

After Stalin died, Mar. 5, 1953, Nikita Khrushchev was elected first secretary of the Central Committee. In 1956 he condemned Stalin and his tyrannical methods before the Soviet Communist Party Congress in Moscow, said Stalin cultivated a "cult of personality" and subverted communist aims. Khrushchev lifted some restrictions, extended barter and trade policies. The names of Stalin, Molotov, Malenkov and other supporters of Stalin were eliminated from regions, cities and other sites in 1961-62 after Stalin's body was removed from the Lenin-Stalin tomb in Moscow.

Khrushchev was elected premier by the Supreme Soviet, Mar. 27, 1958, succeeding Marshal Bulganin.

Under Khrushchev the open antagonism of Poles and Hungarians toward domination by Moscow was brutally suppressed in 1956. He advocated peaceful co-existence with the capitalist countries, but continued arming the USSR with nuclear weapons. He aided the Cuban revolution under Fidel Castro but withdrew Soviet missiles from Cuba during confrontation by U.S. President Kennedy, Sept.-Oct. 1962.

The USSR, the U. S. and Great Britain initialed a joint treaty July 25, 1963, banning above-ground nuclear tests.

The co-existence and economic reform policies, as well as border disputes, alienated the leaders of Albania and Communist China.

Khrushchev was suddenly deposed, Oct. 14-15, 1964, and replaced as party first secretary by Leonid I. Brezhnev, 57, and as premier by Aleksei N. Kosygin, 60. Brezhnev's title was changed in 1966 to general secretary. Internal controls were tightened.

Communist China's Premier Chou En-lai visited the new USSR chiefs in Nov. 1964 but the visit failed to heal the growing rift between the 2 communist powers.

In 1968, the U. S. and USSR joined 59 other nations in signing a treaty to bar spread of nuclear weapons.

In Aug. 1968 Russian, Polish, East German, Hungarian and Bulgarian military forces invaded Czechoslovakia to put a curb on liberalization policies of the Czech government. The USSR declared it had a duty to intervene in nations where socialism was "imperiled," according to the "Brezhnev Doctrine."

In March 1969 troops of the USSR and Communist China fought the first of a series of clashes on a disputed island in the Ussuri River on the border between the 2 nations in the Far East, north of Vladivostok. In 1970 ambassadors were exchanged, after a lapse; but both nations increased their border forces. In the 1970s the USSR forged close ties with India and Bangladesh.

The USSR in 1971 continued heavy arms shipments to Egypt. In July 1972 Egypt ordered most of the 20,-000 Soviet military personnel in that country to leave. The USSR then increased arms shipments to Syria. When Egypt and Syria attacked Israel in Oct. 1973, the USSR launched huge arms airlifts to the 2 Arab nations. In 1974, the Soviet replenished the arms used or lost by the Syrians in the 1973 war, and continued some shipments to Egypt.

Massive Soviet military aid to North Vietnam in the late 1960s and early 1970s helped assure Communist victories throughout Indo-China in 1975. Similar aid helped leftist factions gain control of Angola in 1976.

'Detente'

During the May 1972 visit of U.S. President Nixon,

the U. S. and USSR reached temporary agreements to freeze intercontinental missiles at their current levels, to limit defensive missiles to 200 each, to cooperate on health and environment problems, to stage a joint space flight and to set up commissions for trade and scientific cooperation.

In the June 1973 visit of Brezhnev to the U.S., agreements were signed to seek ways to promote trade, peace and cultural and scientific exchanges. Meanwhile, under Brezhnev, dissident intellectuals were repressed and purge-type trials resumed. Andrei Sakharov, creator of the USSR hydrogen bomb, and other Soviet dissidents warned Western nations that aid given Russia would be used against them.

On Aug. 1, 1975, 35 countries of Europe and North America signed a European security declaration tacitly approving current boundaries and urging freer movement of people and ideas.

Government

The first Soviet constitution was adopted in 1918 for the RSFSR. The USSR was formed in Dec. 1922 and the first Union constitution adopted 1923. The current constitution was adopted 1936. Each Union republic is organized similarly to the central government.

The mainly nominal legislative authority is the Supreme Soviet consisting of 2 chambers, the Soviet of the Union and the Soviet of Nationalities. The first house is elected on the basis of population, the second has deputies from each major national homeland. The Supreme Soviet normally meets briefly twice a year, serves for a 4-year term. It elects a 36-member Presidium which serves between sessions.

Titular chief of state, chairman of the Presidium of the Supreme Soviet, Nikolai V. Podgorny, was chosen Dec.9, 1965.

Elections for the Supreme Soviet are by universal suffrage but from single slates of candidates approved by the party; voters are offered a choice only to strike out names.

The highest judicial organ is the Supreme Court, whose members are elected by the Supreme Soviet for 5-year terms. Other courts are elected within the constituent republics. All cases are decided by judges; there are no citizens' juries.

The highest executive and administrative organ of state power is the Council of Ministers (premier and deputies), with over 100 members appointed by and theoretically responsible to the Supreme Soviet.

The Communist party of the USSR is the only legal party. Its highest organ is the Party Congress of about 1,500 representatives meeting once every 4 years, though delays have been frequent. It elects a Central Committee, the party's directive body, and other committees. The Central Committee elects from its number a Politburo which makes party policy between Central Committee meetings; and a Secretariat, the party's chief executive body. The Politburo consists of 16 full members and several candidate members.

Membership in the Communist party in 1973 was reported at about 14,800,000.

Education

Education is free. It is compulsory from ages 7 to 15/16. In 1973-74 there were 49.2 million students in primary, secondary, and technical schools, and 9.1 million in universities, institutes, and other places of higher education, half of them in correspondence or evening courses. There were 7.5 million children 3-7 years old in kindergartens.

Social Benefits

All workers are entitled to free public health services, paid vacations, sickness insurance, pensions for men at 60 and women at 55. State payments are made to mothers on the birth of the 3d and successive children. In 1974 there were 44 million receiving pensions.

Religion

Separation of church and state was effected in 1918. Nine branches of Christianity are represented, led by the Orthodox Church, which in 1967 had 20,-000 congregations. Islam has the second largest following. Jewish and Buddhist faiths are also present. It is illegal to teach religion in classes to persons under 18.

Since 1970 many Jews have sought to leave the USSR. About 100,000 left in 1970-74. Emigration was sharply curtailed in 1975, after the U. S. Congress limited export credits and linked tariff cuts to freedom of emigration.

Defense

Armed forces on active duty are est. (1975) to total 3,575,000 (including support troops). The Army had about 1.8 million men. There were 31 divisions stationed in satellite nations (20 of them in East Germany); 63 divisions in European Russia; 6 in Central USSR, 23 in the Caucasus, 43 facing China. Several thousand military aid personnel were stationed in Syria, Iraq, Cuba, Somalia, and other countries.

Navy personnel totals 500,000. The main power of the Soviet fleets is its 265 submarines, some 75 of which are nuclear-powered. Some are equipped with ballistic nuclear missiles.

Air Force personnel totals 400,000; there is a total of about 8,000 combat aircraft including intercontinental bombers. Air Defense service has 500,000 men, border and security troops number 430,000. Strategic rocket forces number 350,000.

In 1975 the USSR reportedly had 1,618 land-based intercontinental nuclear missiles, and 784 submarine-borne missiles. The USSR was advancing development of multiple warhead (MIRV) missiles, and of more accurate and more powerful missiles.

The USSR is a member of the UN and Warsaw Pact.

United Arab Emirates

Area: 32,278 sq. mi. Population (UN est. 1975): 656,-000. Capital: Abu Dhabi. Monetary unit: Dirham.

The United Arab Emirates, formerly known as the Trucial States or Trucial Sheikdoms, were British Protected States until they merged to become an independent nation Dec. 2, 1971. The UAE stretches 400 mi. along the Persian (also called Arabian) Gulf and the Gulf of Oman. It borders on Saudi Arabia, Qatar and Oman.

The 7 sheikdoms signed treaties with Britain in the 19th century giving Britain control of defense and foreign relations. When Britain withdrew in 1971, the 7 sought to federate with Bahrain and Qatar. The attempt failed. The UAE was formed by 6 of the 7, Abu Dhabi, Dubai, Sharja, Ajman, Fujaira and Umm al Quaiwan. The 7th, Ras al Khaima, joined shortly after. Abu Dhabi city became the capital; the Abu Dhabi ruler became president. There is a prime minister, a Supreme Council of Rulers and a National Council or legislature.

Abu Dhabi, Dubai and Sharja have large and increasing oil production, the 9th largest in the world. In Sept. 1974 Abu Dhabi acquired a 60% interest in the Abu Dhabi Petroleum Co.; full nationalization came in 1975. Revenues total $5-6 billion a year.

Abu Dhabi has the greatest population of the seven, followed closely by Dubai. The population is 72% Arab; the rest are Iranians, Indians and Pakistanis.

Armed forces total 31,000.

United Kingdom

Area: 94,209 sq. mi. Population (Govt. est. 1975): 55,962,000. Capital: London. Monetary Unit: Pound.

The United Kingdom of Great Britain and Northern Ireland comprises England, Wales, Scotland and

Northern Ireland.

The British Isles lie off the W. coast of Europe, with the North Atlantic on the N and W. Separating Britain from the mainland are the North Sea on the E, the Strait of Dover on the SE and the English Channel on the S. The Thames, 210 mi. from its source to the North Sea, is England's longest river.

England has an area of 50,331 sq. mi. and Wales has 8,016 sq. mi.; combined population (est. 1972), 49,029,000; Scotland, 30,411 sq. mi., 5,210,000; Northern Ireland, 5,451 sq. mi., 1,549,000.

The climate of the British Isles is mild and somewhat warmer than that of the continent because of the Gulf Stream modifying the temperature, which has a mean of 48°. Rainfall averages 41 inches a year.

Queen and Royal Family. The ruling sovereign is Elizabeth II of the House of Windsor, born Apr. 21, 1926, eldest daughter of King George VI. She succeeded to the throne Feb. 6, 1952, and was crowned June 2, 1953. As Princess Elizabeth, she was married Nov. 20, 1947 to Lt. Philip Mountbatten, born June 10, 1921, former Prince of Greece. He was created Duke of Edinburgh Nov. 19, 1947, H.R.H. Prince Philip Nov. 20, 1947, and given the title Prince of the United Kingdom Feb. 22, 1957. They have 4 children. Prince Charles Philip Arthur George, born Nov. 14, 1948, is the Prince of Wales and heir apparent.

Parliament is the legislative governing body for the United Kingdom, with certain powers over dependent units. It consists of 2 Houses. The **House of Lords** includes hereditary and life peers and peeresses, certain judges, 2 archbishops and 21 bishops of the Church of England. Total membership is over 1,000 but daily attendance averages 270. Women became eligible to sit in the House of Lords for the first time in 1958. **The House of Commons** has 635 members, who are elected by direct ballot and divided as follows: England 516; Wales 36; Scotland 71; Northern Ireland 12.

Clergymen of the Church of England, ministers of the Church in Scotland and Roman Catholic clergymen are disqualified from sitting as members, as are certain government officers and sheriffs. Women have had the right to vote since 1918.

A two-tier system of local government controls a large variety of social and economic activity. Reforms occurred in 1974-75.

Resources and Industries. Great Britain's major occupations are manufacturing and trade. Metals and metal-using industries contribute more than 50% of the exports. Agriculture provides wheat, barley, oats, sugar beets, rye, livestock products and garden truck. Of about 60 million acres of land in England, Wales and Scotland, 47 million are farmed, of which 17.4 million are arable, the rest pastures.

Large oil and gas fields have been found in the North Sea. Commercial oil production began in 1975; self-sufficiency is expected by 1980, with projected output of two million barrels a day. There are large deposits of coal; 1975 output was 127 million tons. Limestone, igneous rock and iron ore are valuable products. Other important minerals are salt, clay, chalk, gypsum, lead ore, tin ore and silica.

There are 150 civil and 50 service airports in Great Britain. The railroads, nationalized since 1948, have been reduced in total length, with a basic network of 11,326 mi. designated for modernization and development.

There are about 19 million telephones. Broadcast receiving licenses in 1974 totaled 9,381,000 for black-and-white TV, 8,294,000 for color.

The government in 1967 took ownership of 14 steel companies which comprised 90% of the nation's steel-making industry, paying shareholders over $1.4 billion. Further industry takeovers and intervention were foreseen in 1974 government proposals.

The Labor government raised taxes, 1966-69; devalued the pound to $2.40 in 1967 and took various measures to improve exports and cut imports. The Conservative government put a freeze on prices, wages and rents in 1972 to combat inflation. In 1973 it substituted "restraints." A Labor government, elected in 1974, obtained trade union approval of wage curbs; yet inflation continued, and the pound dropped to record lows in 1976.

Britons backed continued EC membership by a 67% vote in a referendum June 5, 1975.

On Feb. 15, 1971, Britain completed a changeover to decimal currency. By 1975 it had in part converted to the metric system as well.

Tourism ranks high in earnings. Visitors from abroad totaled nearly 9 million in 1975, of whom 1.3 million were from the U. S. Index of industrial production (1970 = 100) was 102.3 in 1975. The merchant marine totaled 31,415,000 gross registered tons in Sept. 1975, comprising over 10% of active world shipping. About 2 million tons of shipping were under construction in 1975.

The world's first power station using atomic energy to create electricity for civilian use began operation Oct. 17, 1956, at Calder Hall in Cumbria.

Britain's aid to less developed countries totalled $723 million in 1974.

The United Kingdom is a member of the UN, Commonwealth, NATO, CENTO, Council of Europe and, since Jan. 1, 1973, EC.

Britain imports all of its cotton, rubber, sulphur, four-fifths of its wool, half of its food and iron ore, also certain amounts of paper, tobacco, chemicals. Manufactured goods made from these basic materials have been exported since the industrial age began.

Main exports are machinery, chemicals, woolen and synthetic textiles, clothing, autos and trucks, iron and steel, locomotives, ships, jet aircraft, farm machinery, drugs, radio, TV, radar and navigation equipment, scientific instruments, arms, whisky.

Foreign trade in thousands of U.S. dollars:

	Imports	Exports
1974	$54,142,000	$38,639,000
1975	53,262,000	43,760,000

Religion and Churches. The Church of England is Protestant Episcopal. The queen is its temporal head, with rights of appointment to archbishoprics, bishoprics and other offices. There are 2 provinces, Canterbury and York, each headed by an archbishop. About 55% of the population is baptized into the Church, less than 20% is confirmed. Most famous church is Westminster Abbey (1050-1760), site of coronations, tombs of Elizabeth I, Mary of Scots, kings, poets and of the Unknown Warrior.

Roman Catholic Church membership in the United Kingdom was about 5,500,000 in 1974. There were about 14,000 Methodist churches and 601,000 full members in 1974.

Others: There are an est. 410,000 Jews in Great Britain; 80% of them are Orthodox; more than half live in the London area. There are 191,000 Baptists and 192,410 members of the United Reformed Church (Congregational and Presbyterian). The Calvinistic Methodist (Presbyterian) Church of Wales has 102,000 communicants. The Unitarians have 330 chapels. The Society of Friends has 21,000 members. There are 72,000 Mormons. The Church of Christ Scientist has 302 branches in Great Britain and Ireland. The Presbyterian Church in Ireland has a membership in Northern Ireland of about 140,000. The number of Hindus and Moslems has been growing steadily with immigration.

The Church of Scotland is Presbyterian. It is presided over by a moderator, chosen annually. Members numbered 1,100,000 in 1974.

Education. Education is free and compulsory from 5 to 16. The most celebrated British universities are Oxford and Cambridge, each dating to the 13th century. There are 40 other universities.

Social Welfare. National Insurance provides for virtually universal compulsory insurance covering sickness, maternity, unemployment and industrial accidents, and death benefits and pensions for widows, orphans and the aged. The National Health Service provides free medical and nursing care, small dental fees and minimum charges for certain appliances and prescriptions. Under the Family Allowance Act the government pays 90 pence a week for each child of compulsory school age, after the first, and one pound each for the third or more. Supplementary benefits provide for those not fully protected by National Insurance. Contributions vary according to sex and classification (employed, self-employed, non-employed). In the case of employed, the employer pays slightly over half.

Defense: Armed forces total 345,100 (1975). Britain exploded its 1st atomic bomb in 1952 and has a stockpile of these weapons. A 10-year program to cut forces 10% and almost eliminate Britain's non-European presence was announced in 1974.

Wales

The Principality of Wales in western Britain has an area of 8,017 sq. mi. and a population (est. 1974) of 2,759,000.

England and Wales are administered as a unit. More than one-fourth the population of Wales speak both English and Welsh; under 50,000 speak Welsh solely. Welsh nationalism is advocated by a segment. The UK government favors creation of an elected Welsh Assembly.

Early Anglo-Saxon invaders drove Celtic peoples into the mountains of Wales, terming them Waelise (Welsh, or foreign). There they developed a distinct nationality. Members of the ruling house of Gwynedd in the 13th century fought England but were crushed, 1283. Edward of Caernarvon, son of Edward I of England, was created Prince of Wales, 1301.

Cardiff is the capital, pop. (1974) 284,700.

Scotland

Scotland, a kingdom now united with England and Wales in Great Britain, occupies the northern 37% of the main British island, and the Hebrides, Orkney, Shetland and smaller islands. Length, 275 mi., breadth approx. 150 mi., area, 30,411 sq. mi., population (est. 1974) 5,226,000.

The Lowlands, a belt of land approximately 60 miles wide from the Firth of Clyde to the Firth of Forth, divide the farming region of the Southern Uplands from the granite Highlands of the north. Only one-tenth of the land area, the Lowlands contain three-quarters of the population and most of the industry. The Highlands, famous for hunting and fishing, have been opened to industry by many hydroelectric power stations.

Edinburgh, pop. (est. 1974) 475,042, is the capital. It lies on the Firth of Forth in the County of Lothian and has notable memorials of its royal and cultural history. Glasgow, pop. (est. 1974) 905,032, is the largest city, 3d largest in Britain, and Britain's greatest industrial center. It is a shipbuilding complex on the Clyde and an ocean port. Aberdeen, pop. (est. 1972) 212,237, NE of Edinburgh, is a major port, center of granite industry, fish processing, and North Sea oil exploitation. Dundee, pop. (1972) 182,842, NE of Edinburgh, is an industrial and fish processing center.

History. Scotland was called Caledonia by the Romans who battled early Picts and Celtic tribes and occupied southern areas from the 1st to the 4th centuries. The Scots were an Irish tribe from Scotia (an early name for Ireland). Missionaries from Britain introduced Christianity in the 4th century; St. Columba, an Irish monk, converted most of Scotland in the 6th century.

The Kingdom of Scotland was founded in 1018. William Wallace, patriot leader, defeated an English army, 1297, and Robert Bruce defeated another, 1314. John Knox led the Scottish Reformation in the 16th century.

In 1603 James VI of Scotland, son of Mary, Queen of Scots, succeeded to the throne of England as James I, and effected the Union of the Crowns. In 1707 Scotland received representation in the British Parliament, resulting from the union of former separate Parliaments. Its executive in the British cabinet is the Secretary of State for Scotland. The growing Scottish National Party urges independence. The UK government has proposed creation of an elected Scotland Assembly.

There are 8 universities. Memorials of Robert Burns, Sir Walter Scott, John Knox, Mary, Queen of Scots draw many tourists, as do the beauties of the Trossachs, Loch Katrine, Loch Lomond and abbey ruins.

Industries. Engineering products are the most important industry, with growing emphasis on lighter products such as office machinery, autos, electronics and other consumer goods and less dependence on locomotives, ships, boilers, pumps, valves and other industrial machinery. Oil has been discovered offshore in the North Sea, stimulating on-shore support industries.

Scotland produces fine woolens, worsteds, tweeds; silks, fine linens and jute. It is known for its special breeds of cattle and sheep. Fisheries have large hauls of herring, cod, whiting. Whisky is the biggest export.

Atomic projects produce plutonium and electrical energy at Dounreay, Chapelcross, Hunterston.

The Hebrides are a group of c. 500 islands, 100 inhabited, off the W coast. The Inner Hebrides include **Skye, Mull** and **Iona**, the last famous for the arrival of St. Columba, 563 AD. The Outer Hebrides include **Lewis** and **Harris**. Industries include sheep raising and weaving. **The Orkney Islands,** c. 90, are to the NE. The capital is Kirkwall, on Pomona Is. Fish curing, sheep raising and weaving are occupations. NE of the Orkneys are the 200 **Shetland Islands,** 24 inhabited, home of Shetland pony. The Orkneys and Shetlands have become centers for the North Sea oil industry.

Northern Ireland

Six of the 9 counties of Ulster, the NE corner of Ireland, constitute Northern Ireland, with the parliamentary boroughs of Belfast and Londonderry. The country has an area of 5,451 sq. mi. and a population (1975 est.) 1,537,000. Belfast is the capital and chief industrial center.

Industries. Shipbuilding, including large tankers, has long been an important industry, centered in Belfast, the largest port. Linen manufacture is also important, along with apparel, rope, and twine. Growing diversification has added engineering products, synthetic fibers, and electronics. There are large numbers of cattle, hogs, and sheep; potatoes, poultry, and dairy foods are also produced. There is an agricultural surplus, mostly shipped to England.

Government. An act of the British Parliament, 1920, divided Northern from Southern Ireland, each with a parliament and government. When Ireland became a dominion, 1921, and later a republic, Northern Ireland chose to remain a part of the United Kingdom. It elects 12 members to the British House of Commons.

During 1968-69, large demonstrations were conducted by Roman Catholics who charged they were discriminated against in voting rights, housing, and employment. The Catholics, a minority comprising about a third of the population, demanded abolition of property qualifications for voting in local elections. Violence and terrorism intensified, involving branches of the Irish Republican Army (outlawed in the Irish Republic), Protestant groups, police, and up to 15,000 British troops.

A succession of Northern Ireland prime ministers pressed reform programs but failed to satisfy extremists on both sides. About 1,400 were killed in 7 years of bombings and shootings, some in England itself. Britain suspended the Northern Ireland parliament Mar. 30, 1972, and imposed direct British rule. A coalition government was formed in 1973 when moderates won election to a new one-house Assembly. But a Protestant general strike overthrew the government in 1974. Direct rule continued in 1976, after the failure of a constitutional convention to achieve a settlement.

Education and Religion. Northern Ireland is 2/3 Protestant, 1/3 Roman Catholic. Elementary education is compulsory through age 15. There are 2 universities and 24 technical colleges.

Channel Islands

The Channel Islands, area 75 sq. mi., est. pop. 1974 130,000, off the NW coast of France, the only parts of the one-time Dukedom of Normandy belonging to England, are **Jersey, Guernsey** and the dependencies of Guernsey — **Alderney, Brechou, Great Sark, Little Sark, Herm, Jethou and Lihou.** Jersey and Guernsey have separate legal existences and lieutenant governors named by the Crown. The islands were the only British soil occupied by German troops in World War II.

Isle of Man

The Isle of Man, area 227 sq. mi., est. 1974 pop. 60,000, is in the Irish Sea, 20 mi. from Scotland, 30 mi. from Cumberland. It is rich in lead and iron. The island has its own laws and a lt. gov. appointed by the Crown. The Tynwald (legislature) consists of the Legislative Council, partly elected, and House of Keys, elected. Capital: Douglas. Farming, tourism, fishing (kippers, scallops) are chief occupations. Man is famous for the Manx tailless cat.

Gibraltar

Gibraltar, a dependency on the southern coast of Spain, guards the entrance to the Mediterranean. The width of the strait dividing Europe from Africa varies from 7.75 mi. at the narrowest part to 23.75 at the widest. The Rock has been in British possession since 1704. There is a large harbor and a naval base. The Rock is 2.75 mi. long, 3/4 of a mi. wide and 1,396 ft. in height; a narrow isthmus connects it with the mainland. Est. pop. 1974: 30,000.

In 1966 Spain called on Britain to give "substantial sovereignty" of Gibraltar to Spain and imposed a partial blockade. In 1967, residents voted 12,138 for remaining under Britain, 44 for returning to Spain. A new constitution, May 30, 1969, gave an elected House of Assembly more control in domestic affairs. A UN General Assembly resolution requested Britain to end Gibraltar's colonial status by Oct. 1, 1969. No settlement has been reached.

British West Indies

Swinging in a vast arc from the coast of Venezuela NE, then N and NW toward Puerto Rico are the Windward and Leeward Islands, forming a coral and volcanic barrier sheltering the Caribbean from the open Atlantic. Many of the islands are self-governing British possessions. Universal suffrage was instituted 1951-54; ministerial systems were set up 1956-1960.

Moving northward from the southern end of the arc lie the British **Windward Islands: St. Vincent,** (1973 pop. 100,000, area 150 sq. mi., capital Kingstown), **St. Lucia** (1974 pop. 110,000, area 238 sq. mi., capital Castries) and **Dominica** (1974 pop. 70,000, area 290 sq. mi., capital Roseau).

Further north, in the **Leeward Islands,** are **Montserrat** (1970 pop. 12,300, area 33 sq. mi., capital Plymouth), **Antigua** (1974 pop. 70,000, area 171 sq. mi., capital St. John's), and **St. Kitts (St. Christopher)-Nevis-Anguilla,** three islands (1974 pop. 70,000, area 138 sq. mi., capital Basseterre on St. Kitts). Nearby are the small **British Virgin Islands.**

Britain granted self-government to 5 of these islands and island groups in 1967-1969; each became an Associated State, with Britain controlling foreign affairs and defense. These were Antigua, Dominica, St. Lucia, the St. Kitts-Nevis-Anguilla Federation, and St. Vincent.

Anguilla declared its independence from St. Kitts June 16, 1967. A 1976 constitution provides for an autonomous elected government. Area is 35 sq. mi., pop. 5,000.

Sugar is the major crop of Antigua and St. Kitts; bananas are the main product of the Windwards; Dominica produces cocoa; Antigua, Montserrat, St. Kitts, and St. Vincent have Sea Island cotton; St. Vincent has arrowroot; Dominica grows citrus fruits. Imports include foods, clothing, machinery. Tourism is growing. Dominica tried in 1975 to suppress leftist terrorists.

The three **Cayman Islands,** a dependency, lie S of Cuba, NW of Jamaica. Population is 10,423 (1970), most of it on Grand Cayman. It is a free port; in the 1970s Grand Cayman became a tax-free refuge for foreign funds and branches of many Western banks were opened there in the 1970s. Total area: 93 sq. mi. Capital: Georgetown.

The **Turks and Caicos Islands,** at the SE end of the Bahama Islands, are a separate British possession. There are about 30 islands, only 6 inhabited, pop. est. 6,000, area 166 sq. mi., capital Grand Turk. Salt, crayfish and conch shells are the main exports.

Bermuda

Bermuda is a British dependency governed by a royal governor and an Assembly, the oldest legislative body among British dependencies. Capital is Hamilton.

It is a group of 360 small islands of coral formation, 20 inhabited, comprising 21 sq. mi. in the western Atlantic, 580 mi. E of North Carolina. Population, 1974, was 60,000 (about 63% of African descent). Density is high.

The Assembly dates from 1620. In elections May 22, 1968, the first on the basis of universal adult suffrage, the predominantly white United Bermuda party won 30 of the 40 Assembly seats (26 of 40 in 1976 elections); 16 of the 40 elected were blacks. A black, Sir Edward Richards, became prime minister in 1971. The Assembly runs local affairs. Bermuda adopted a dollar-decimal currency in 1970.

Gov. Richard Sharples and an aide were slain by gunmen in 1973. The police commissioner was shot to death in 1972.

The U.S. has air and naval bases under long-term lease, and a NASA tracking station.

Bermuda boasts many resort hotels, serving over 280,000 visitors a year. The government raises most revenue from import duties. Exports: lilies, drugs, cosmetics.

Belize

Belize (formerly called British Honduras) is in Central America facing the Caribbean to the E, with Mexico on the N and Guatemala on the W. Population (UN est. 1974) 140,000, area 8,866 sq. mi., capital Belmopan.

Internal self-government was granted by Britain in 1964.

The area has long been claimed by Guatemala, but also was promised independence by Britain. In Apr. 1968, a mediator proposed that British Honduras be made independent but have close association with Guatemala. The proposal was rejected by Belize.

Main export is sugar, along with citrus fruits, mahogany and other hardwoods, chicle, seafood.

South Atlantic Dependencies

Falkland Islands and Dependencies, a British dependency, lies 300 mi. E of the Strait of Magellan at the southern end of South America.

The Falklands or Islas Malvinas include about 200 islands with an area of 4,618 sq. mi. and pop. (1970) of 2,045. Sheep-grazing is the main industry; wool is the principal export. There are indications of large oil and gas deposits. The islands are also claimed by Argentina. **South Georgia,** area 1,450 sq. mi., and pop. 439, and the uninhabited **South Sandwich Islands** are dependencies of the Falklands.

British Antarctic Territory, south of 60° S lat., was made a separate colony in 1962 and comprises mainly the **South Shetland Islands,** the **South Orkneys and Graham's Land.** A chain of meteorological stations is maintained.

St. Helena, an island 1,200 mi. off the W. coast of Africa and 1,800 E of South America, has 47 sq. mi. and est. pop., 1970 of 4,952. Flax, lace and rope making are the chief industries. After Napoleon Bonaparte was defeated at Waterloo the Allies exiled him to St. Helena, where he lived from Oct. 16, 1815, to his death, May 5, 1821. His remains were transferred to Paris in 1840. Capital is Jamestown.

Tristan da Cunha is the principal of a group of islands of volcanic origin, total area 40 sq. mi., half way between the Cape of Good Hope and South America. The other islands are inaccessible, Gough (or Diego Alvarez) and the 3 Nightingale Is. A volcanic peak 6,760 ft. high erupted in 1961. The 262 inhabitants were removed to England, but most returned in 1963. The islands are dependencies of St. Helena.

Ascension is an island of volcanic origin, 34 sq. mi. in area, 700 mi. NW of St. Helena, through which it is administered. It is a communications relay center for Britain, and has a U. S. satellite tracking center. Est. pop., 1971, was 1,232, half of them communications workers. The island is noted for sea turtles.

Asian and Indian Ocean Dependencies

Brunei has been since 1888 a protected sultanate on the N side of the Island of Borneo, between the Malaysian states of Sarawak and Sabah. Its area is 2,226 sq. mi., the size of Delaware, with population (1974 UN est.), 140,000, two-thirds Malay and indigenous races, one-third of Chinese descent.

A 1959 constitution was amended, 1965, to provide for general elections to the Legislative Council, some members of which are appointed. There is a sultan and a British high commissioner. A 1971 agreement gave Brunei full internal self-government.

Brunei's rich Seria oilfield provides tax revenues well in excess of expenditures. Rubber is also exported. Some of the surplus has been spent on a growing program of schools and social services.

Hong Kong is a Crown Colony at the mouth of the Canton River in China, 90 mi. south of Canton. Its nucleus is Hong Kong Island, 35 1/2 sq. mi., acquired from China 1841, on which is located Victoria, the capital. Opposite is Kowloon Peninsula, 3 sq. mi. and Stonecutters Island, 1/4 sq. mi., added, 1860. An additional 355 sq. mi. known as the New Territories, comprised of a mainland area and islands, were leased from China, 1898, for 99 years. Total area of the colony is 391 sq. mi., with a population, 1974 UN est., of 4,250,000 including fewer than 20,000 British. From 1949 to 1962 Hong Kong absorbed more than a million refugees from the mainland. The flow of refugees continued, on a lesser scale, into the 1970's.

Hong Kong harbor was long an important British naval station and one of the world's great trans-shipment ports. Britain announced in 1975 a reduction of its garrison to 6,400 men.

Principal industries are shipbuilding and textiles; also iron and steel, apparel, fishing, cement, and small manufactures. American tourists spend an est. $29 million yearly.

Spinning mills, among the best in the world, and low wages compete with textiles elsewhere and have resulted in protective measures in some countries. Hong Kong also has a booming electronics industry. The U. S. is the largest market for Hong Kong products.

During 1967 Communist China launched a campaign against British authority in Hong Kong, including demonstrations, strikes, riots, bombings, border incidents and slowdowns in supplying food. The campaign later subsided.

British Indian Ocean Territory was formed Nov. 1965, embracing islands formerly dependencies of Mauritius or Seychelles: the Chagos Archipelago (including Diego Garcia), Aldabra, Farquhar and Des Roches. (The latter three are to be transferred to Seychelles, which became independent in 1976.) Population, 558. In 1973 the U. S. Navy established a communications station on Diego Garcia and in 1975 began constructing a naval base. The USSR and Asian nations opposed the step.

Pacific Ocean Dependencies

Pitcairn Island is in the Pacific, halfway between South America and Australia. The island was discovered in 1767 by Carteret but was not inhabited until 23 years later when the mutineers of the Bounty landed there. The area is 18 sq. mi. and population, 1974, was 78. It is a British colony and is administered by a British Representative in New Zealand and a local Council. The uninhabited islands of Henderson, Ducie and Oeno are in the Pitcairn group.

The British Solomon Islands, a protectorate, number 10 large islands and 4 groups of small islands with a total area of 11,500 sq. mi. and population, est. 1974, of 180,000, mostly Melanesians. The Solomons lie E of New Guinea. The chief islands in the group are Guadalcanal, Malaita, San Cristobal, New Georgia, Santa Isabel, Choiseul, Shortland, Mono or Treasury, Vella Lavella, Ganongga, Gizo, Rendova, Russell, Florida and Rennel. Among the groups of islands are the Lord Howe, Santa Cruz, Tucopia, Mitre, Duff or Wilson and Reef. Self-government was set for 1975 and independence for 1977. Exports: copra, timber, nuts, and trochus shell.

The Gilbert Islands were proclaimed a protectorate in 1892. Self-government was granted in 1971. The dependency includes the Gilbert Islands (16), Phoenix Islands, Ocean Island, Line Islands, composed of Fanning, Washington and Christmas Islands, the last the largest atoll in the Pacific (also claimed by the U. S.). The total area is 264 sq. mi. and the population, 1973 census, 52,000. Exports: chiefly copra and phosphates. Tuvalu, formerly called the Ellice Islands, was separated from Gilbert Islands administration, 1976; its 9 islands have an area of 10 sq. mi., pop. (1973 census) 6,000.

New Hebrides, a condominium jointly administered since 1906 by Great Britain and France, is a group of 11 main islands and about 69 islets lying 500 mi. W of Fiji, with an aggregate area of 5,790 sq. mi. Population, 1974 UN est. 90,000, mostly Melanesian. Chief products are copra, cotton, cocoa, fish and coffee. British and French resident commissioners are joint heads of the administration; representative bodies were elected in 1975. Banks (309 sq. mi.) and Torres (40 sq. mi.) Islands, with pop. of 2,640, are attached to the New Hebrides for administration.

United States
(See Index for listings)

Upper Volta

Area: 105,869 sq. mi. Population (UN est. 1975): 6,030,000. Capital: Ouagadougou. Monetary unit: CFA franc.

The Republic of Upper Volta, one-time French Overseas Territory, is an inland plateau region in west Africa, bounded by Mali, Niger, the Ivory Coast, Ghana, Togo and Dahomey. It is the size of Colorado.

Most of the population lives in the southern part of the country, where population density reaches one of the highest levels in Africa — 125 people per sq. mi.

More than 80% of the people are subsistence farmers. Greatest wealth is in livestock, mostly cattle and sheep, accounting for 50% of exports. Principal market crops are cotton, rice, peanuts and karite. Climate is extremely dry but irrigation efforts, using water from the Black Volta, White Volta and pumped from underground, have been started with aid from the UN Special Fund. Several hundred thousand seasonal farm workers migrate each year. There are rich manganese deposits, which have not yet been exploited. A long drought brought famine in 1973-74 to Ivory Coast and Ghana; the U. S. provided 40% of the aid sent to the area.

Upper Volta became an autonomous state in 1958. It became fully independent Aug. 5, 1960 and a member of the UN. It signed a bilateral agreement, 1961, maintaining close ties with France.

A constitution, adopted 1960, provided for a presidential form of government and a unicameral National Assembly. In 1966 the army chief of staff, Gen. Sangoule Lamizana, took over the presidency during demonstrations against austerity measures. A new constitution, providing for a premier, was adopted 1970. In Feb. 1974 Lamizana dissolved the Assembly, suspended the constitution, and named a mostly military cabinet. A border dispute with Mali was resolved, July 1975.

Uruguay

Area: 68,548 sq. mi. Population (Govt. est. 1975): 3,060,000. Capital: Montevideo. Monetary unit: Peso.

Uruguay is one of the smallest republics in South America. Slightly larger than Missouri, it is a country of rich, rolling, grassy plains on the South Atlantic coast. Brazil and Argentina are its neighbors, with the Uruguay River forming the boundary line with Argentina.

Resources and Industries. Some 70% of Uruguay's area is devoted to stock raising which provides more than 2/3 of agricultural production. Meat and wool accounted for most export earnings, until the European Common Market cut off beef imports in 1973. The chief products are meat, wool, hides, corn, wheat, citrus fruits, rice, oats and linseed. Meat-packing, metallurgical, textile and wine-making industries are large.

More than half of the population lives in one city, Montevideo. More than a third of the workers are employed by the government. The state owns the power, telephone, railroad, cement, oil-refining and other industries, and employs a large social welfare bureaucracy.

Uruguay's standard of living was one of the highest in South America. Economic stagnation, inflation, plus floods, drought and a cold wave in 1967 and a general strike in 1968 brought attempts by the government to strengthen the economy through a series of devaluations of the peso and wage and price controls. But inflation continued. The cost of living rose 1,200% between 1968 and 1976.

History and Government. Once a part of the Spanish Viceroyalty of Rio de la Plata and later a province of Brazil, Uruguay declared its independence, Aug. 25, 1825. The constitution provides for a president, a Chamber of Deputies and a Senate elected for 5-year terms. Suffrage is universal.

Uruguay has one of the world's most extensive social welfare programs with old age pensions, child welfare.

Leftist guerrillas, drawn from the upper classes and called Tupamaros, increased terrorist actions in 1970; a U. S. police adviser was slain in Aug. In 1971 the guerrillas kidnaped and, after 8 months, freed the British ambassador. Violence continued and in Feb. 1973 President Juan Maria Bordaberry agreed to military control of his administration. In June he abolished Congress and set up a Council of State in its place. By 1974 the military had apparently defeated the Tupamaros, using severe repressive measures, including mass arrests and torture, according to many reports. The economic decline continued. Bordaberry was removed by the military in a 1976 coup.

Education and Religion. Church and state are separate and there is complete religious tolerance. Preponderant religion is Roman Catholic. Education, including college, is free; primary education is compulsory. The language is Spanish.

Defense. Armed forces total 21,000, all paid volunteers. Uruguay is a member of the UN and OAS.

State of Vatican City

Area: 108.7 acres. Population: about 700.

The popes for many centuries, with brief interruptions, held temporal sovereignty over mid-Italy (the so-called Papal States), comprising an area of some 16,000 sq. mi., with a population in the 19th century of more than 3 million. This territory was incorporated in the new Kingdom of Italy, the sovereignty of the pope being confined to the palaces of the Vatican and the Lateran in Rome and the villa of Castel Gandolfo, by an Italian law, May 13, 1871. This law also guaranteed to the pope and his successors a yearly indemnity of over $620,000. This allowance, however, remained unclaimed.

A Treaty of Conciliation, a Concordat and a financial convention were signed Feb. 11, 1929, by Cardinal Gasparri and Premier Mussolini. The documents established the independent state of Vatican City, and gave the Catholic religion special status in Italy. The treaty (Lateran Agreement) was made part of the Constitution of Italy (Article 7) in 1947.

Vatican City includes St. Peter's, the Vatican Palace and Museum covering over 13 acres, the Vatican gardens, and neighboring buildings between Viale Vaticano and the Church. Thirteen buildings in Rome, outside the boundaries, enjoy extra-territorial rights; these buildings house congregations or officers necessary for the administration of the Holy See.

The legal system is based on the code of canon law, the apostolic constitutions and the laws especially promulgated for the Vatican City by the pope. In cases not covered the Italian law of Rome applies. The Secretariat of State represents the Holy See in its diplomatic relations. By the Treaty of Conciliation the pope is pledged to a perpetual neutrality unless his mediation is specifically requested. This, however, does not prevent the defense of the Church whenever it is persecuted. A total of 84 nations maintain diplomatic representatives in Vatican City. The U.S. does not have an official ambassador, but in June 1970 President Nixon named Henry Cabot Lodge to be his personal envoy.

The present sovereign of the State of Vatican City is the Supreme Pontiff Paul VI, Giovanni Battista Montini, born in Concesio, Italy, Sept. 26, 1897, elected June 21, 1963, in succession to Angelo Giuseppe Roncalli, John XXIII, who died June 3, 1963.

Venezuela

Area: 352,143 sq. mi. Population (Gov. est. 1975): 11,990,000. Capital: Caracas. Monetary unit: Bolivar.

Venezuela, a land of wide plains and lofty mountains, lies within the torrid zone in northern South America, with a 1,750-mi. coast on the Caribbean and Atlantic. Its neighbors are Guyana, Brazil and Colombia. It includes 72 islands totaling 14,650 sq. mi., the largest being Margarita, 40 mi. by 20, which is one of Venezuela's 20 states and an important pearl center. Venezuela is more than twice the size of California.

The Orinoco River with its tributaries drains about four-fifths of the country. About 1,700 mi. in length and 13.5 mi. across at its widest point, it is the 2d largest river system in South America, and is navigable for about 700 mi.

Caracas, the capital, is 12 mi. inland from its port, La Guaira. It is noted for its modern architecture. In its Pantheon are enshrined the ashes of Simon Bolivar, South American liberator (1783-1830.).

Resources and Industries. Mining, agriculture, fishing and manufacturing are the chief industries. Venezuela in 1975 was the world's 5th largest oil producer. Lake Maracaibo is the largest oil field in South America. Venezuela helped found the Organization of Petroleum Exporting States (OPEC). On Jan. 1, 1976, the government nationalized the oil industry with compensation. Development has begun of the Orinoco tar belt, believed to contain the world's largest oil reserves. Iron ore production was nationalized Jan. 1, 1975.

Other minerals are iron, gold, copper, coal, salt, nickel, manganese, asbestos, diamonds and mica. Iron ore production was 26 million tons in 1974 and is the 2d most important export, next to oil.

Coffee is the major agricultural market product. Exports also include cocoa, canned fish, fruit, sugar, steel products. Industries include steel, petrochemicals, textiles, containers, tobacco products, paper, tires, shoes. Tourists increased from 95,000 in 1965 to 453,331 in 1973.

Construction is booming, including a new $3.8 billion city, Ciudad Guyana, 300 mi. SE of Caracas; and a 4,175-ft. bridge across the Orinoco opened in 1967.

Oil profits help finance the extensive industrial development. The gross national product rose from $8.9 billion in 1966 to over $25.2 billion in 1974. Government efforts at income redistribution were thwarted by inflation in 1974-5.

History and Government. Columbus first set foot on the South American continent on the peninsula of Paria, Aug. 1498. Alonso de Ojeda, 1499, found Lake Maracaibo, called the land Venezuela, or Little Venice, because natives had houses on stilts. Venezuela was under Spanish domination until 1821. The republic was formed after secession from the Colombian Federation in 1830.

The 1961 constitution provided for a strong central government; a president, Senate and Chamber of Deputies elected for 5 years by direct universal vote, and a Supreme Court appointed by the Congress for 5 years. Member: UN, OAS.

Education and Religion. The language is Spanish, with Amerindian languages spoken by about 200,000 people and Roman Catholic is the religion of the majority. All education, including college, is free. Primary education is compulsory. Illiteracy has been reduced to about 13%.

Defense. Armed forces total 44,000.

Vietnam

Area: 126,436 sq. mi. Population (UN est. 1973): 42,650,000. Capital: Hanoi. Monetary unit: Dong.

Vietnam occupies the eastern half of the Indo-Chinese peninsula, bounded on the N by China, on the E and S by the South China Sea, and on the W by Cambodia and Laos. It consists of the historic regions Tonkin, Annam, and Cochin China. Principal cities are Saigon, Hanoi, Haiphong, Hue and Danang.

Vietnam is long and narrow, with a coastline of 1,400 miles. About 24% of the country is readily arable, including the densely settled Red River valley in the North, narrow coastal plains in the center; and the wide, often marshy Mekong River Delta in the South. The rest consists of semi-arid plateaus and barren mountains, with some stretches of tropical rain forest.

Resources and Industries. The chief occupation is agriculture, with rice the staple food. Other crops are corn, sugar cane, sweet potatoes, coffee, tea, cotton, manioc, tobacco. Timber, fishing, and rubber are important. In the North, the land is worked in collective units of about 40,000 people; in the South, small private owners still prevail.

There are rich coal deposits in the North, with 1971 output of 2 million metric tons of hard coal. There are deposits of iron ore, manganese, bauxite, apatite, chromite, and phosphates. Exploratory oil drilling was begun in 1973 off the southern coast. Development of industry and transport in all parts of the country were hampered by years of warfare. Food processing and textiles were the leading industries.

History and Government. Vietnam's recorded history began in Tonkin before the Christian era. Settled by Viets from central China, Vietnam was held by China, 111 B.C.-939 A.D., and was a vassal state during subsequent periods. Vietnam defeated the armies of Kublai Khan, 1288. Conquest by France began in 1858 and ended in 1884 with protectorate status.

In 1940 Vietnam was occupied by Japan; during the occupation nationalist aims gathered force. A number of groups formed the Vietminh (Independence) League, headed by Ho Chi Minh, communist guerrilla leader. In Aug. 1945 the Vietminh forced out Bao Dai, former emperor of Annam, head of a regime sponsored by Japan. France, seeking to reestablish colonial control, battled communist and nationalist forces, 1946-1954, and was finally defeated at Dienbienphu, May 8, 1954. Meanwhile, on July 1, 1949, Bao Dai had formed a State of Vietnam, with himself as chief of state, with French approval. Communist China backed Ho Chi Minh.

A cease-fire accord signed in Geneva July 21, 1954, divided Vietnam along the Ben Hai River. It provided for a buffer zone, withdrawal of French troops from the North and elections to determine the country's future. Under the agreement the communists gained control of territory north of the 17th parallel, 22 provinces with area of 62,000 sq. mi. and 13 million pop., with its capital at Hanoi and Ho Chi Minh as president. South Vietnam came to comprise the 39 southern provinces with approx. area of 65,000 sq. mi. and pop. of 12 million. Some 900,000 North Vietnamese fled to South Vietnam. Neither South Vietnam nor the U.S. signed the agreement.

On Oct. 26, 1955, Ngo Dinh Diem, premier of the interim government of South Vietnam, proclaimed the Republic of Vietnam and became its first president, following a referendum on Oct. 23.

The Democratic Republic of Vietnam, established in the North, adopted a constitution Dec. 31, 1959, based on communist principles and calling for reunification of all Vietnam. President Ho Chi Minh, reelected July 15, 1960, by unanimous vote of the National Assembly, had held office since 1945. He died Sept. 3, 1969, and was succeeded as president by Ton Duc Thang.

North Vietnam sought to take over South Vietnam beginning in 1954. Fighting persisted from 1956, with the communist Vietcong, aided by North Vietnam, pressing war in the South and South Vietnam receiving U.S. aid. Northern aid to Vietcong guerrillas was intensified in 1959, and large-scale troop infiltration began in 1964, with Russian and Chinese arms assistance. Large Northern forces were stationed in border areas of Laos and Cambodia.

A serious political conflict arose in the South in 1963 when Buddhists denounced authoritarianism and brutality. This paved the way for a military coup Nov. 1-2, 1963, which overthrew Diem.

Several military coups followed. In elections Sept. 3, 1967, Chief of State Nguyen Van Thieu was chosen president. A 60-member Senate was also elected Sept. 3 and a 137-member House on Oct. 22. Thieu was reelected in a one-candidate election, Oct. 3, 1971.

In 1964, the U.S. began air strikes against North Vietnam. Beginning in 1965, the raids were stepped up and U.S. troops became combatants. U.S. troop strength in Vietnam, which reached a high of 543,400 in Apr. 1969, was ordered reduced by U.S. President Nixon in a series of withdrawals, beginning in June 1969. U.S. bombings were resumed in 1972-73.

A ceasefire agreement which President Nixon said would bring "peace with honor" was signed in Paris Jan. 27, 1973 (EST), by the U.S., North and South Vietnam, and the Vietcong, to take effect the same day (Jan. 28 in Vietnam). It provided for withdrawal of U.S. troops (about 23,000 were still in Vietnam) and return of U.S. prisoners (590), both within 90 days, an International Commission to supervise the ceasefire, and for the U.S. and North Vietnam to respect the South Vietnamese people's right to self-determination. U.S. aid was curbed in 1974 by the U.S. Congress. Despite the agreement heavy fighting continued for two years throughout Indochina.

Massive numbers of North Vietnamese troops, aided by tanks, launched attacks against remaining government outposts in the Central Highlands in the first months of 1975. Government retreats turned into a rout, and the Saigon regime surrendered April 30. Conquest of the country was effectively completed within days.

A Provisional Revolutionary Government assumed control, aided by officials and technicians from Hanoi, and first steps were taken to transform society along communist lines. Ultimate reunification of the two Vietnams was called for, though both countries applied for UN membership.

The U.S. accepted over 130,000 Vietnamese fleeing the new regime, while some thousands more sought refuge in other countries.

The war's toll included — Combat deaths: U.S. 46,-079; South Vietnam over 200,000; other allied forces 5,225. Civilian casualties were over a million. Displaced war refugees in South Vietnam totaled over 6,500,000.

After the fighting ended, eight Northern divisions remained stationed in the South, while Southern forces of over 900,000 were demobilized, adding to severe economic problems. Some urban residents were resettled in the countryside; an unknown number were sent to long-term re-education camps. Some military resistance against the new regime was periodically reported.

The first National Assembly representing both parts of the country met June 24, 1976, with 249 representatives from the North and 243 from the South.

The country was officially reunited July 2, 1976, as the Socialist Republic of Vietnam. The former North Vietnamese capital, flag, anthem, emblem, and currency were applied to the new state.

Nearly all major government posts went to officials of the former Northern government; Ton Duc Thang continued as President and Pham Van Dong as prime minister.

Education and Religion. Taoism and Buddhism are the prevalent religions, with many people combining practices of both. Roman Catholics number 1.5 million. The Caodai sect claims 2 million followers, Hoa Hao has 1 million; both are indigenous groups. Hoa Hao leaders and tens of thousands of followers were reportedly arrested in 1976.

Schools enroll about 10 million.

Vietnamese is the language of 88% of pop.; Chinese, Khmer, Montagnan tribal languages are spoken. English and French are also used in education.

Defense. Armed forces totalled some 700,000.

(See also Vietnam in Index.)

Western Samoa

Area: 1,133 sq. mi. Population (Govt. est. 1975): 160,000. Capital: Apia. Monetary unit: Tala.

Western Samoa, which became an independent nation Jan. 1, 1962, comprises 4 inhabited islands, and several uninhabited islets, of a group in the South Pacific lying about 2,613 mi. SW of Hawaii. Largest of the islands are **Savaii** and **Upolu.** Eastern Samoa, the smaller part of the group with its capital at Pago Pago, is a dependency of the U.S.

Western Samoa was a German colony, 1899 to 1914, when New Zealand landed troops and took over. It became a New Zealand mandate under the League of Nations and, in 1945, a New Zealand UN Trusteeship.

An elected local government took office in Oct. 1959 and the country became fully independent in 1962. New Zealand has continued economic aid and educational assistance. Western Samoa changed from pounds to decimal currency July 10, 1967.

The population is composed almost solely of Polynesians. The islands are fertile. Chief products are tropical hardwoods, fish, cocoa, coconuts, bananas, taro, coffee, bark cloth (tapa), mats.

Robert Louis Stevenson's grave is on a hill near Apia.

Arab Republic of Yemen

Area: 75,289 sq. mi. Population (UN est. 1975): 6,670,000. Capital: Sana. Monetary unit: Riyal.

Yemen is an ancient, mountainous country, near the southern tip of the Arabian Peninsula on the Red Sea. Its neighbors are the People's Democratic Republic of Yemen (formerly Southern Yemen) and Saudi Arabia. Parts of the northern and eastern borders are undefined. It is about the size of Nebraska.

Hodeida, Mocha and Loheiya are major ports. Marib and Sana are archeological sites.

Resources and Industries. On the plateau of El Jebel, the most fertile section of Arabia, coffee, cotton, qat (a narcotic shrub), barley and grain (millet is the staple), are grown. Hides, dates, cotton, sesame, herbs, fruits and precious stones are exported. There are periodic droughts. Per capita GNP is among the lowest in the world. A prolonged drought has forced imports of food.

The remittances from 400,000 Yemens living in Arab oil countries provide most of foreign earnings.

History and Government. Yemen's territory once was part of the ancient kingdom of Sheba, or Saba, a prosperous link in trade between Africa and India. A Biblical reference speaks of its gold, spices and precious stones as gifts borne by the Queen of Sheba to King Solomon.

Yemen became independent in 1918, after years of Ottoman Turkish rule. Imam Ahmed ruled 1948-1962. The king was reported assassinated Sept. 26, 1962, and a revolutionary group headed by Brig. Gen. Abdullah al-Salal declared the country to be the Yemen Arab Republic. He became president.

The Imam Ahmed's heir, the Imam Mohamad al-Badr, fled to the mountains where tribesmen joined royalist forces; internal warfare between them and the republican forces continued. Egyptian president Nasser sent 70,000 troops to aid the republicans; Saudi Arabia supported the royalists with military aid.

After Egypt's defeat in the June 1967 Israeli-Arab war, Egypt announced it would withdraw its troops from Yemen; the last of them left Nov. 29, 1967, and Saudi Arabia said it would stop aiding the royalists.

This was accompanied by a bloodless coup Nov. 5, 1967. Leadership was taken over by a Presidential Council headed by Abdul Rahman al-Iryani, who later became president.

Fighting continued between the republican and royalist forces. Saudi Arabia announced in Feb. 1968 it was renewing its aid to the royalists, charging that both Russia and Syria, as well as Southern Yemen, were aiding the republicans.

In April 1970 hostilities ended with an agreement between Yemen and Saudi Arabia and appointment of several royalists to the Yemen government.

There were border skirmishes with forces of the People's Democratic Republic of Yemen in 1972-73. The U.S. and Yemen in 1972 resumed diplomatic relations, broken by Yemen after the 1967 Arab-Israeli war.

On June 13, 1974, an Army group, led by Col. Ibrahim al-Hamidi, seized the government. The country is ruled by a 7-man Command Council, which appoints the prime minister.

About 10% of the population is urban. The rest live in small villages on the coast and in the highlands. Literacy is about 15-20%.

Yemen is a member of the UN and Arab League.

People's Democratic Republic of Yemen

Area: 112,000 sq. mi. Population (Census 1974): 1,630,000. Capitals: Aden and Medina as-Shaab. Monetary unit: Dinar.

This nation became independent as the People's Republic of Southern Yemen Nov. 30, 1967, after 129 years of British rule. It changed its name to People's Democratic Republic of Yemen on Nov. 30, 1970. It consists of the port city of Aden, 17 states of the former South Arabian Federation, 3 small sheikdoms, 3 larger sultanates, Quaiti, Kathiri and Mahri, which made up the Eastern Aden Protectorate, Socotra, the largest island in the Arabian Sea, Kamaran, an island in the Red Sea near the coast of North Yemen, and Perim, an island in the strait between the Gulf of Aden and the Red Sea.

Aden, mentioned in the Bible, has been a port for trade in incense, spices and silk between the East and West for 2,000 years. British rule began in 1839. Aden provided Britain with a controlling position at the southern entrance to the Red Sea.

With only 1% of the land fertile and few mineral deposits, the Port of Aden has been the area's most valuable natural resource. The port is 10 mi. across, well-sheltered and deep. In 1966 more than 6,000 ships put in at Aden for refueling, servicing and transshipment of goods, bringing over 227,000 visitors. Cotton and grains are grown.

But, with the closing of the Suez Canal after the Israeli-Arab War in June 1967, the port lost much of its business. Local products exported are cotton, fish, coffee, hides. The canal was reopened in 1975.

A war for independence began in 1963. The National Liberation Front (NLF) and the Egypt-supported Front for the Liberation of Occupied South Yemen, waged a guerrilla war against the British and local dynastic rulers. The 2 groups vied with each other for control. The NLF won out. In 1969, the left wing of the NLF seized power and inaugurated a thorough nationalization of the economy.

The new government broke off relations with the U.S. and nationalized some foreign firms. Aid has been furnished by the USSR and China, with the USSR supplying most military aid.

In 1972-73 there were border skirmishes with forces of the Yemen Arab Republic. South Yemen aided leftist guerrillas in neighboring Oman, organized in the Popular Front for the Liberation of Oman.

Yugoslavia

Area: 98,766 sq. mi. Population (Govt. est. 1975): 21,330,000. Capital: Belgrade. Monetary unit: Dinar.

The Socialist Federal Republic of Yugoslavia is a rugged mountainous land, densely forested, which rises from the eastern shore of the Adriatic Sea. Fertile plains and lowlands comprise 29%. Its neighbors are Italy, Austria, Hungary, Romania, Bulgaria, Greece, and Albania. It is about the size of Wyoming.

The federation comprises 6 republics: Serbia, Croatia, Slovenia, Montenegro, Bosnia-Herzegovina and Macedonia, and 2 autonomous provinces: Kosovo and Voyvodina.

Resources and Industries. Agriculture occupies 48% of the population. Chief crops are maize, wheat, barley, rye, tobacco, hops and fruits, sugar beets, sunflower. Principal minerals are coal, iron, copper, chrome, antimony, manganese, lead, zinc, mercury, salt and bauxite. Timber cutting and processing is a major industry. Iron, steel, chemicals, are also important. The majority of industrial enterprises are concentrated in the northwestern areas.

Most industry is socialized and private enterprise is restricted to small-scale production. Since 1952 workers are guaranteed a basic wage and a share in cooperative profits.

Management of industrial enterprises is handled by workers' councils. Farmland is 85% privately owned but farms are restricted to 25 acres.

Yugoslavia has conducted several large-scale programs to improve its economy. Beginning in the late 1950s, successful efforts were made to strengthen agriculture by improving fertilizers, grain varieties and livestock.

Tourism was promoted, particularly along the country's colorful Adriatic coast. Large numbers of visitors from nations of the West provided an important source of foreign income.

Beginning in 1965, reforms designed to decentralize the administration of economic development and to force industries to produce more efficiently in competition with foreign producers were introduced.

Yugoslavia has developed considerable trade with Western Europe as well as with the USSR and Eastern European countries and elsewhere. While its import-export balance has continued to show deficits, money earned by Yugoslavs working temporarily in Western Europe, and money brought in by tourists come close to making these up. In 1970 a trade treaty was signed with the EC. Unemployment and inflation became serious in 1975.

The index for industrial production (1970=100) was 147 for 1975.

Foreign trade in thousands of U.S. dollars:

	Imports	Exports
1974	$8,071,000	$4,071,000
1975	$7,697,000	$4,072,000

History and Government. Serbia, which had since 1389 been a vassal principality of Turkey, was established as an independent kingdom by the Treaty of Berlin, 1878. Montenegro, independent since 1389, also obtained international recognition in 1878. After the Balkan wars its boundaries were enlarged by the annexation of Old Serbia and Macedonia, 1913. When the Austrian Archduke Francis Ferdinand and wife were assassinated at Sarajevo June 28, 1914, the Austrian government forced war on Serbia, the onset of World War I, 1914-1918.

When the Austro-Hungarian empire collapsed, the Kingdom of the Serbs, Croats, and Slovenes was formed from the former provinces of Croatia, Dalmatia, Bosnia, Herzegovina, Slovenia, Voyvodina and the independent state of Montenegro, with Peter I of Serbia as king. The name was later changed to Yugoslavia. Peter (d. 1921) was succeeded by his son Alexander I, assassinated in 1934. Prince Paul, regent, was overthrown in Mar. 1941 and Crown Prince Peter became king. Germany invaded April, 1941, and King Peter II fled to London.

Many Yugoslav partisan troops continued to operate. Among these were the Chetniks led by Draja Mikhailovich, who fought other partisans led by Josip Broz, known as Marshal Tito. Tito, backed by the USSR and Britain from 1943, was in control by the time the Germans had been driven from Yugoslavia in 1944. The Chetnicks were charged with collaboration with the Nazis, and Mikhailovich was executed July 17, 1946, by the Tito regime.

A constituent assembly proclaimed Yugoslavia a republic Nov. 29, 1945. It became a federated republic Jan. 31, 1946, and Marshal Tito, a communist, became head of the government. By terms of a treaty with Italy, the greater part of Venezia-Giulia, Zara, Pelagosa, and adjacent islands were ceded to Yugoslavia.

The Stalin policy of dictating to all communist nations was rejected by Tito. He accepted economic aid and military equipment from the U. S. and received aid in foreign trade also from France and Great Britain.

Yugoslavia is governed by the president, as chairman of a 9-man collective presidency (created in 1971), a premier, and a parliament (Federal Assembly), from which cabinet members are drawn.

A new constitution, approved by the Assembly in Feb. 1974, provided that representatives in the Assembly be chosen by subordinate assemblies consisting of delegates from labor organizations, local communities, and units of the Socialist Alliance of Working People, largely dominated by the League of Communists. The constitution provided that Tito remain president indefinitely.

Tito supported the liberalization government of Czechoslovakia in 1968 before the Russian invasion, but he paid a friendship visit to Moscow in 1972.

A separatist movement among Croatians, 2d to the Serbs in numbers, brought arrests and a change of leaders in the Crotian Republic in Jan. 1972. Violence by extreme Croatian nationalists, and fears of Soviet political intervention, have led to restrictions on political and intellectual dissent, which had previously been freer than in other East European countries.

Education and Religion. Education is free, and compulsory to age 14. There are 9 universities. Main languages are Slovene, Macedonian, Serbo-Croat. All religions are recognized. Serbo-Orthodox compromise 42%, Roman Catholic 32%. Moslem 12%. Serbians, Montenegrins, and Macedonians use Cyrillic, Croatians and Slovenians use Latin letters.

Complete social security is in force, including unemployment, medical, maternity benefits.

Defense. Military forces total 230,000, plus 500,000 reservists and 1 million in the Territorial Defense Force.

Zaire

Area: 905,063 sq. mi. Population (Govt. est. 1975): 24,900,000. Capital: Kinshasa. Monetary unit: Zaire.

The Democratic Republic of Congo changed its name to Republic of Zaire on Oct. 27, 1971; the Congo River was changed to Zaire (its traditional name) and in 1972 Zairians with Christian names were ordered to change them to African names.

Zaire lies in Equatorial Africa, entirely inland except for 25 mi. on the Atlantic Ocean, N of the mouth of the Zaire River. It is larger than Texas and Alaska combined.

Along the eastern border lie several of Africa's Great Lakes. North of the Equator, on the Uganda border, stand the Ruwenzori Mtns., believed to be the "Mountains of the Moon" of ancient legend. Mt. Margherita is 16,763 ft.

The Zaire River, one of the world's longest, rises near the Zambian border in the SE and flows 2,718 mi. N, then W and finally SW, emptying into the South Atlantic.

Wildlife is abundant and includes most of the species Africa is famous for: elephant, lion, gorilla, hippopotamus, crocodile, python, etc.

Resources and Industry. There are extensive mineral deposits in the Katanga, Ituri and Kivu highlands. Zaire in 1973 produced 7% of the world's copper, 67% of its cobalt, and a third of its industrial diamonds. Also produced are cadmium, gold, silver, tin, germanium, zinc, iron, tungsten, manganese, uranium, zinc, and radium.

Tropical rain forests cover much of the land; trees often are 150 to 200 ft. tall. They include mahogany, ebony, teak, copal, palms, cedars, gum, and resin trees. Bananas, coffee, rubber, mangoes, plantain, manioc, rice, sugar cane, and coconuts are grown. Chief agricultural exports are fats and oil, timber, coffee, cotton, rubber, tea, cocoa, and bananas. With only 1% of arable land under cultivation, Zaire imports much of its food, leading to foreign payments problems. Oil from offshore Atlantic wells supplies national needs.

History and Government. Leopold II, king of the Belgians, formed an international group to exploit the Congo in 1876. In 1877 Henry M. Stanley explored the Congo and in 1878 the king's group sent him back to organize the region and win over the native chiefs. The Conference of Berlin, 1884-85, organized the Congo Free State with Leopold as king and chief owner. Exploitation of native laborers on the rubber plantations caused international criticism and led to granting of a colonial charter, 1908.

Belgian and Congolese leaders agreed Jan. 27, 1960, that the Congo would become independent June 30. In the first general elections, May 31, the National Congolese movement of Patrice Lumumba won 35 of 137 seats in the National Assembly, lower House of Parliament. He was appointed premier June 21, and formed a coalition cabinet.

Widespread violence caused Europeans and others to flee. Pres. Moise Tshombe of Katanga seceded from the republic July 11, but ended the secession in 1963. Katanga was the seat of the Union Miniere copper mines. The UN Security Council Aug. 9, 1960, called on Belgium to withdraw its troops and sent a UN contingent to guard against civil war. President Kasavubu removed Lumumba as premier. Lumumba fought for control backed by Ghana, Guinea and India. On Feb. 12, 1961, Lumumba was murdered.

The last UN troops left the Congo June 30, 1964, and Tshombe became president.

On Sept. 7, 1964, leftist rebels set up a "People's Republic" in Stanleyville. Tshombe hired foreign mercenaries and sought to rebuild the Congolese Army. In Nov. and Dec. 1964 rebels slew scores of white hostages and thousands of Congolese; Belgian paratroops, dropped from U. S. transport planes, rescued hundreds. By July 1965 the rebels had lost their effectiveness.

In 1965 Gen. Joseph D. Mobutu was named president. He later changed his name to Mobutu Sese Seko. In March 1966 Mobutu took over from Parliament all of its legislative powers. On July 1 he renamed Leopoldville, Kinshasa; Stanleyville, Kisangani; and Elisabethville, Lubumbashi.

In 1969-74, political stability under Mobutu was reflected in improved economic conditions. In 1970, he was elected to a 7-year term as president. In 1974 most foreign-owned businesses were ordered sold to Zaire citizens.

Education and Religion. The population is principally Bantu. More than 200 tribes are represented. Swahili, Lingala, Tshiluba and Kikongo are widely spoken; French is the official language. There are an estimated 9 million African Christians, predominantly Roman Catholic. There are 3 universities.

Zambia

Area: 290,724 sq. mi. Population (Govt. est. 1975): 4,900,000. Capital: Lusaka. Monetary unit: Kwacha.

The Republic of Zambia is a land-locked country in South Central Africa, bordering Zaire, Tanzania, Malawi, Mozambique, Rhodesia, Botswana, Southwest Africa (Namibia) and Angola. It is slightly larger than Texas.

The terrain is mostly high plateau covered with thick forest and suitable for both farming and grazing. The country is rich in minerals, including copper (10% of world production), zinc, cobalt, gold, lead, vanadium, manganese, and coal. Copper provides most of export revenue.

Victoria Falls on the Zambezi River, the border with Rhodesia, is 3 times the width and more than twice the height of Niagara.

As Northern Rhodesia, the country was under the administration of the South Africa Company, 1889 until 1924, when the office of governor was established, and, subsequently, a legislature.

A new constitution, announced in 1963, granted self-government effective Jan. 22, 1964. The United National Independence Party (UNIP) won the first elections Jan. 21 and its leader, Kenneth D. Kaunda, became prime minister. He was elected president and, on Oct. 24, 1964, Zambia became an independent republic within the Commonwealth. It has a National Assembly of 125 elected members and 10 nominated by the president. In 1973 a new constitution provided for a one-party system, with a government role for the UNIP Central Committee.

After the white government of Rhodesia declared its independence from Britain Nov. 11, 1965, relations between Zambia and Rhodesia became strained and use of their jointly owned railroad was disputed.

Britain gave Zambia an extra $12 million aid in 1966 after imposing an oil embargo on Rhodesia, and Zambia set up a temporary airlift to carry copper out from its mines and gasoline in. In Aug. 1968 a 1,058-mi. pipeline was completed, bringing oil from Tanzania. In 1973 a truck road to carry copper to Tanzania's port of Dar es Salaam was completed with U. S. aid. A railroad, built with Chinese aid across Tanzania, reached the Zambian border in 1974.

As part of a program of government participation in major industries, a government corporation in 1970 took over 51% of the ownership of 2 foreign-owned copper mining companies, paying with bonds. Privately-held land and other enterprises were nationalized in 1975, as were all newspapers.

United Nations

History, Membership, Organization and Purpose

The 1st regular session of the United Nations General Assembly was scheduled to open in September, 1976. *See Chronology for developments at UN sessions during 1976.*

Foundations of the United Nations were laid at the Dumbarton Oaks Conference in Washington between the United States, the United Kingdom, and the Soviet Union, Aug. 21-Sept. 28, 1944, and between the United States, the United Kingdom, and the Republic of China, Sept. 29-Oct. 7, 1944. Proposals to establish an organization of nations for maintenance of world peace led to the United Nations Conference on International Organization at San Francisco, Apr. 25-June 26, 1945, where the charter of the United Nations was drawn up. It was signed June 26 by 50 nations, and by Poland, one of the original 51, on Oct. 15, 1945. The charter came into effect Oct. 24, 1945, when the requisite ratification by the 5 permanent members of the Security Council, China, France, Soviet Union, United Kingdom and United States, and a majority of other signatories had been completed.

United Nations headquarters are located in New York, N.Y., between First Ave. and Roosevelt Drive and E. 42nd St. and E. 48th St. The General Assembly Bldg. (opened 1952), Secretariat, Conference and Library bldgs. are interconnected. A new UN office building-hotel was opened in New York in 1976. The Dag Hammarskjold Library, built by a $6,200,000 grant from the Ford Foundation, was dedicated Nov. 16, 1961. It has room for 400,000 vols. To build the headquarters the U.S. Government advanced an interest-free loan of $65,000,000, payable in annual installments until 1982. John D. Rockefeller, Jr., contributed $8,000,000 for land and the City of New York contributed an est. $26,500,000 for adapting the site. United Nations has a post office originating its own stamps. *See Postal Information.*

A European office at Geneva includes Secretariat and agency staff members. Other offices of UN bodies and related organizations are scattered throughout the world.

Roster of the United Nations

(As of mid-1976)

The 144 members of the United Nations, with the dates on which they became members.

Member	Date	Member	Date	Member	Date
Afghanistan	Nov. 19, 1946	Gambia	Sept. 21, 1965	Netherlands	Dec. 10, 1945
Albania	Dec. 14, 1955	Germany, East	Sept. 18, 1973	New Zealand	Oct. 24, 1945
Algeria	Oct. 8, 1962	Germany, West	Sept. 18, 1973	Nicaragua	Oct. 24, 1945
Argentina	Oct. 24, 1945	Ghana	Mar. 8, 1957	Niger	Sept. 20, 1960
Australia	Nov. 1, 1945	Greece	Oct. 25, 1945	Nigeria	Oct. 7, 1960
Austria	Dec. 14, 1955	Grenada	Sept. 17, 1974	Norway	Nov. 27, 1945
		Guatemala	Nov. 21, 1945		
Bahamas	Sept. 18, 1973	Guinea	Dec. 12, 1958	Oman	Oct. 7, 1971
Bahrain	Sept. 21, 1971	Guinea-Bissau	Sept. 17, 1974		
Bangladesh	Sept. 17, 1974	Guyana	Sept. 20, 1966	Pakistan	Sept. 30, 1947
Barbados	Dec. 9, 1966			Panama	Nov. 13, 1945
Belgium	Dec. 27, 1945	Haiti	Oct. 24, 1945	Papua	
Benin	Sept. 20, 1960	Honduras	Dec. 17, 1945	New Guinea	Oct. 10, 1975
Bhutan	Sept. 21, 1971	Hungary	Dec. 14, 1955	Paraguay	Oct. 24, 1945
Bolivia	Nov. 14, 1945			Peru	Oct. 31, 1945
Botswana	Oct. 17, 1966	Iceland	Nov. 19, 1946	Philippines	Oct. 24, 1945
Brazil	Oct. 24, 1945	India	Oct. 30, 1945	Poland	Oct. 24, 1945
Bulgaria	Dec. 14, 1955	Indonesia	Sept. 28, 1950	Portugal	Dec. 14, 1955
Burma	Apr. 19, 1948	Iran	Oct. 24, 1945		
Burundi	Sept. 18, 1962	Iraq	Dec. 21, 1945	Qatar	Sept. 21, 1971
Byelorussian SSR.	Oct. 24, 1945	Ireland	Dec. 14, 1955		
		Israel	May 11, 1949	Romania	Dec. 14, 1955
Cambodia	Dec. 14, 1955	Italy	Dec. 14, 1955	Rwanda	Sept. 18, 1962
Cameroon	Sept. 20, 1960	Ivory Coast	Sept. 20, 1960		
Canada	Nov. 9, 1945			Saudi Arabia	Oct. 24, 1945
Central African R.	Sept. 20, 1960	Jamaica	Sept. 18, 1962	Senegal	Sept. 28, 1960
Chad	Sept. 20, 1960	Japan	Dec. 18, 1956	Sierra Leone	Sept. 27, 1961
Chile	Oct. 24, 1945	Jordan	Dec. 14, 1955	Singapore	Sept. 21, 1965
China[4]	Oct. 24, 1945			Somalia	Sept. 20, 1960
Colombia	Nov. 5, 1945	Kenya	Dec. 16, 1963	South Africa[5]	Nov. 7, 1945
Comoros	Oct. 17, 1975	Kuwait	May 14, 1963	Spain	Dec. 14, 1955
Congo	Sept. 20, 1960			Sri Lanka	Dec. 14, 1955
Costa Rica	Nov. 2, 1945	Laos	Dec. 14, 1955	Sudan	Nov. 24, 1956
Cuba	Oct. 24, 1945	Lebanon	Oct. 24, 1945	Surinam	Dec. 4, 1975
Cyprus	Sept. 20, 1960	Lesotho	Oct. 17, 1966	Swaziland	Sept. 24, 1968
Czechoslovakia	Oct. 24, 1945	Liberia	Nov. 2, 1945	Sweden	Nov. 19, 1946
		Libya	Dec. 14, 1955	Syria[2]	Oct. 24, 1945
Denmark	Oct. 24, 1945	Luxembourg	Oct. 24, 1945		
Dominican Rep.	Oct. 24, 1945			Thailand	Dec. 16, 1946
		Malagasy Rep.	Sept. 20, 1960	Togo	Sept. 20, 1960
Ecuador	Dec. 21, 1945	Malawi	Dec. 1, 1964	Trinidad & Tob.	Sept. 18, 1962
Egypt[22]	Oct. 24, 1945	Malaysia[11]	Sept. 17, 1957	Tunisia	Nov. 12, 1956
El Salvador	Oct. 24, 1945	Maldives	Sept. 21, 1965	Turkey	Oct. 24, 1945
Equatorial Guinea	Nov. 12, 1968	Mali	Sept. 28, 1960		
Ethiopia	Nov. 13, 1945	Malta	Dec. 1, 1964	Uganda	Oct. 25, 1962
		Mauritania	Oct. 27, 1961	Ukrainian SSR	Oct. 24, 1945
Fiji	Oct. 13, 1970	Mauritius	Apr. 24, 1968	Union of Soviet	
Finland	Dec. 14, 1955	Mexico	Nov. 7, 1945	Soc. Repub's.	Oct. 24, 1945
France	Oct. 24, 1945	Mongolia	Oct. 27, 1961	United Arab	
		Morocco	Nov. 12, 1956	Emirates	Dec. 9, 1971
Gabon	Sept. 20, 1960	Nepal	Dec. 14, 1955	United Kingdom	Oct. 24, 1945
				United States	Oct. 24, 1945

United Rep. of ...		Venezuela	Nov. 15, 1945	Yugoslavia	Oct. 24, 1945
Tanzania[3]	Dec. 14, 1961				
Upper Volta	Sept. 20, 1960	Yemen	Sept. 30, 1947	Zaire	Sept. 20, 1960
Uruguay	Dec. 18, 1945	Yemen, South	Dec. 14, 1967	Zambia	Dec. 1, 1964

(1.) The Federation of Malaya joined the UN on Sept. 17, 1957. On Sept. 16, 1963, its name to Malaysia following the admission to the new federation of Singapore, Sabah (North Borneo) and Sarawak. Singapore became an independent State Aug. 9, 1965 and a member of th UN Sept. 21.

(2.) Egypt and Syria were original members of the United Nations from Oct. 24, 1945. Following a plebiscite held on Feb. 21, 1958, the United Arab Republic was established by a union of Egypt and Syria and continued as a single Member of the United Nations. On Oct13, 1961, Syria resumed its separate membership.

(3.) Tanganyika was a member of the United Nations from Dec. 14, 1961 and Zanzibar was a member from Dec. 16, 1963. Following the ratification, on Apr. 26, 1964, of Articles of Union between Tanganyika and Zanzibar, the United Republic of Tanganyika and Zanzibar continued as a single Member of the United Nations, later changing its name to United Republic of Tanzania.

(4.) The General Assembly voted Oct. 25, 1971 to expel the Chinese government on Taiwan and admit the Peking government in its place.

(5.) The General Assembly rejected the credentials of the South African government delegates Sept. 30, 1974, and suspended the country from the Assembly Nov. 12.

Operations of the United Nations under Its Charter

The following article describes both the powers of the United Nations and its present organization. It is based on the provisions of the charter of the United Nations, and on an official report furnished by the Secretariat. The text of the Charter may be obtained from the Office of Public Information, United Nations, N. Y.

General Assembly

Pres. of 30th Session — Gaston Thorn, Luxembourg.

The General Assembly is composed of representatives of all the member nations. Each nation may send not more than five delegates and five alternate delegates to each session. Each nation is entitled to one vote.

The General Assembly meets in regular annual sessions and in special session when necessary. Special sessions are convoked by the Secretary General at the request of the Security Council or of a majority of the members of the UN. A president and seventeen vice presidents are chosen at each regular session.

Any matter within the scope of the charter may be brought before the General Assembly, which may make recommendations on all except issues on the agenda of the Security Council. However, the General Assembly in November, 1950, decided that if the Security Council, because of lack of unanimity of its permanent members, fails to exercise its primary responsibility for the maintenance of international peace and security, in any case where there appears to be a threat to the peace, breach of the peace or act of aggression, the Assembly may consider it and recommend collective measures including, in the case of a breach of peace or act of aggression, the use of armed forces to maintain or restore peace. In such cases, the General Assembly may be convened within 24 hours in an emergency special session.

On important questions a two-thirds majority of members present and voting is required; on other questions a simple majority is sufficient. Questions that require a two-thirds majority include: recommendations on maintenance of international peace and security, election of non-permanent members of the Security Council, election of members of the Economic and Social Council, election of members of the UN that are to designate the members of the Trusteeship Council, admission of members to the UN (who must first be recommended by the Security Council), suspension and expulsion of members, trusteeship questions and budgetary matters.

The General Assembly must approve the budget and apportion expenses among members. A member in arrears will have no vote if the amount of arrears equals or exceeds the amount of the contributions due for the preceding two full years. The General Assembly may permit such a member to vote if it is satisfied that the failure is due to conditions beyond control.

A general or steering committee co-ordinates the proceedings of the Assembly and is composed of 25 members — the president of the Assembly, the 17 vice-presidents, and the chairmen of the seven main committees. A nine-member Credentials Committee, appointed at the start of each session examines and reports on delegates' credentials. Two standing committees, one on administration and budget and one on

contributions, operate throughout the year, with 13 members each, chosen to assure wide geographic representation.

The General Assembly may establish ad hoc and subsidiary organizations. Among these are 15 ongoing Special Bodies, which are semi-autonomous, and which may include governments which are not members of the UN. These bodies are:

UN Capital Development Fund (UNCDF), New York, 24 member nations; UN Children's Fund (UNICEF), New York, 30; UN Conference on Trade and Development (UNCTAD), Geneva, Switz., 12; UN Development Program (UNDP), New York, 48; UN Disaster Relief Office (UNDRO), Geneva; UN Environment Program (UNEP), Nairobi, Kenya, 58; UN Fund for Population Activities (UNFPA), New York; UN Habitat and Human Settlements Foundation (UNHHSF), New York; UN Industrial Development Organization (UNIDO), Vienna, Austria, 45; UN Institute for Training and Research (UNITAR), New York; UN Office of High Commissioner for Refugees (UNHCR), Geneva, 31; UN Relief and Works Agency for Palestine Refugees in the Near East (UNRWA), Beirut, Lebanon; UN Research Institute for Social Development (UNRISD), Geneva; UN University (UNU), Tokyo, Japan; World Food Council, Rome, Italy, 36.

Security Council

The Security Council consists of 15 members, 5 with permanent seats. The remaining 10 are elected for 2-year terms by the General Assembly; they are not eligible for immediate re-election.

Permanent members of the Council: China, France, USSR, United Kingdom, United States.

Non-permanent members were Guyana, Italy, Japan, Sweden, Tanzania (until Dec. 31, 1976), and Benin, Libya, Pakistan, Panama, Romania (until Dec. 31, 1977).

The presidency of the Council is held monthly in turn by the member states in English alphabetical order.

The Security Council has the primary responsibility within the UN for maintaining international peace and security. The Council may investigate any dispute that threatens international peace and security. When the Security Council is handling a dispute or situation the General Assembly makes no recommendation unless the Council requests it.

The Security Council functions continuously, each member being represented at all times. It may change its place of meeting. Any member of UN at UN headquarters may participate in its discussions and a nation not a member of UN may appear if it is a party to a dispute.

Decisions on procedural questions are made by an affirmative vote of 9 members. On all other matters the affirmative vote of 9 members must include the concurring votes of all permanent members; it is this clause which gives rise to the so-called "veto." A party to a dispute must refrain from voting.

The Security Council may decide to enforce its decisions without the use of arms. Such measures include interruption of economic relations, break in transportation and communications, and severance of diplomatic relations. If such measures fail the Council may call on UN members to furnish armed forces, assistance and facilities, based on agreements made by the Council with the states and subject to ratification by the members of the UN "in accordance with their constitutional processes."

The right of individual or collective self-defense is not prohibited by membership in the UN, and if a member nation is attacked it may do what is necessary, reporting this to the Security Council, which may take independent action. However, the Council encourages regional arrangements or agencies by means of which local disputes can be settled without getting as far as the Council, after the Council has approved this method.

The Security Council directs the various truce supervisory forces deployed in the Middle East, India-Pakistan, and Cyprus.

Economic and Social Council

The Economic and Social Council consists of 54 members elected by the General Assembly for 3-year terms of office. The council is responsible under the General Assembly for carrying out the functions of the United Nations with regard to international economic, social, cultural, educational, health and related matters. The council meets usually twice a year.

The Economic and Social Council had the following commissions in 1974:

Functional Commissions: Statistical; Population; Social Development; Narcotic Drugs; Human Rights (and its Sub-Commission on the Prevention of Discrimination and the Protection of Minorities); Status of Women; Transnational Corporations.

Regional Economic Commissions: Africa (Addis Ababa, Ethiopia, 44 member nations); Asia and the Pacific (Bangkok, Thailand, 31); Europe (Geneva, Switz., 34); Latin America (Santiago, Chile, 31); Western Asia (Beirut, Lebanon, 12).

Trusteeship Council

The administration of Trust territories is subject to the supervision of the United Nations. Administering authorities are required to render an account of their stewardship to the Trusteeship Council. The Council may entertain petitions from private persons or organizations regarding conditions in the Trust territories and may dispatch missions to study conditions there.

The membership of the Council is made up of (1) countries which administer trust territories (United States); (2) countries which are permanent members of the Security Council but which do not administer trust territories (China, France, the United Kingdom, USSR); and (3) as many other countries as may be necessary to ensure equal representation in the Council between administering and non-administering members. There are currently no members in the third category.

Since Papua New Guinea, part of which had been an Australian trust territory, became independent in 1975, the only remaining trust territory is the Pacific Islands, administered by the U.S.

Non-Self-Governing Territories

Members of the United Nations responsible for the administration of non-self-governing territories not under trusteeships recognize the principle that the interests of the inhabitants are paramount and promote their welfare. They are bound by the charter to transmit to the Secretary-General technical information concerning economic, social, and educational conditions in the territories. This information is summarized, analyzed, and classified by the Secretariat.

Since 1961 a Special Committee on Colonial Countries has been studying the implementation of the 1960 General Assembly declaration on the granting of independence to colonial countries and peoples. This committee also receives the reports on non self-governing territories.

International Court of Justice

The International Court of Justice is the principal judicial organ of the United Nations. All members are ipso facto parties to the statute of the Court, as are three nonmembers — Liechtenstein, San Marino, and Switzerland. Other states may become parties to the Court's statute on conditions determined in each case by the General Assembly on the recommendation of the Security Council.

The jurisdiction of the Court comprises cases which the parties submit to it and matters especially provided for in the charter or in treaties. The Court gives advisory opinions and renders judgments. Its decisions, which are final, are binding between the parties concerned and in respect to a particular dispute. If any party to a case fails to heed a judgment of the Court, the other party may have recourse to the Security Council, which may decide what is to be done.

The Court consists of 15 judges elected for 9-year terms by a majority in both the General Assembly and the Security Council. No two of the judges may be nationals of the same state. Retiring judges are eligible for re-election. The Court remains permanently in session, except during the judicial vacations. A quorum of 9 judges suffices to constitute the Court. All questions are decided by majority. In the event of a tie, the President of the Court or the judge who acts in his place casts the deciding vote.

Judges
Nine year term in office ending 1985:
Taslim Olawala Elias, Nigeria.
Hermann Mosler, W. Germany.
Shigeru Oda, Japan.
Salah El Dine Tarazi, Syria.
Manfred Lachs, Poland.
Nine year term in office ending 1982:
Isaac Forster, Senegal.
Andre Gros, France.
Jose Maria Ruda, Argentina.
Nagendra Singh, India.
Sir Humphrey Waldock, Britain.
Nine year term in office ending 1979:
Hardy C. Dillard, U.S.
Louis Ignacio-Pinto, Benin.
Federico de Castro, Spain.
Platon D. Morozov, USSR.
Eduardo Jimenez de Arechaga, Uruguay.

The president until 1976 is Jimenez de Arechaga, Uruguay, and the vice president is Nagendra Singh, India.

Specialized Agencies

These agencies are autonomous entities with their own memberships and organs which have a functional relationship with the UN.

International Labor Org. (ILO) aims to promote social justice; improve labor conditions and living standards; and promote economic stability. (Geneva, 126 member nations)

Food & Agriculture Org. (FAO) aims to increase production from farms, forests, and fisheries; improve distribution, marketing, and nutrition. (Rome, 135)

United Nations Educational, Scientific, & Cultural Org. (UNESCO) aims to promote collaboration among nations in the fields of education, science, and culture. (Paris, 135 and 2 associate members)

World Health Org. (WHO) aims to aid the attainment of the highest possible level of health. (Geneva, 145, 3 assoc.)

International Bank for Reconstruction & Develop-

ment **(World Bank)** aims to help in the economic development of members by facilitating investment of capital; promote foreign investment and supplement private investment by providing loans for productive purposes out of its capital funds raised by it and its other resources; and to promote growth of international trade and equilibrium in balance of payments. (Washington, D. C., 127)

International Development Assn. (IDA) aims to further economic development of less developed members by financing on terms bearing less heavily on balance of payments than those of conventional loans. (Washington, D.C., 114)

International Finance Corp. (IFC) aims to further economic development in member countries by encouraging private enterprise, particularly in less developed areas. It is empowered to invest in private enterprises in association with private investors, and without government guarantee of repayment in cases where sufficient private capital is not available on reasonable terms; and to bring together private capital and management. (Washington, D. C., 100)

International Monetary Fund (IMF) aims to promote international monetary co-operation and currency stabilization. Sells currency to help members meet temporary foreign payments difficulties. (Washington, D. C., 128)

International Civil Aviation Org. (ICAO) promotes international civil aviation standards and regulations. (Montreal, 129)

Universal Postal Union (UPU) aims to perfect postal services and promote international collaboration. To this end, members agree to handle other members mail by the best means used for their own mail. (Berne, 154)

International Telecommunication Union (ITU) sets up international regulations of radio, telegraph, telephone and space radio-communications. Allocates radio frequencies. (Geneva, 147)

World Meteorological Org. (WMO) aims to co-ordinate, standardize and improve world meteorological work and weather data exchange. (Geneva, 143)

Intergovernmental Maritime Consultative Org. (IMCO) aims to promote co-operation on technical matters affecting international shipping. (London, 88, 1 assoc.)

World Intellectual Property Organization (WIPO) seeks to protect, through international cooperation,

literary, industrial, scientific, and artistic "intellectual property." (Geneva, 61)

Related Organizations

These autonomous bodies have working agreements with the UN.

International Atomic Energy Agency (IAEA) aims to promote the safe, peaceful uses of atomic energy. (Vienna, 106)

General Agreement on Tariffs and Trade (GATT) was drafted in 1946. It establishes and administers code for orderly conduct of international trade. Aids export promotion in developing countries. (Geneva, 85)

Secretariat

The Secretariat is composed of a Secretary General appointed by the General Assembly upon the recommendation of the Security Council and such staff as the organization may require.

The Secretary General is the chief administrative officer of the UN. He may bring to the attention of the Security Council any matter that threatens international peace. He reports to the General Assembly.

Kurt Waldheim (Austria), Secretary General, was chosen to succeed U Thant by the UN Security Council and General Assembly for a 5-year term beginning Jan. 1, 1972.

United Nations Budget

Secretary General Waldheim proposed a 1976-77 program budget of $737,005,000, exclusive of trust funds and special contributions. This does not include expenses for the Specialized or the Related Organizations.

The US contributes 25% of the regular budget, the Soviet Union 12.97%, with Japan, W. Germany, France, China, and Britain all contributing over 5%.

Sources of Information

Public Inquiries Unit, Office of Public Information, United Nations, N. Y. Provides pamphlets, study guides, speakers, films; arranges group visits, provides information on UN activities: (212) 754-1234.

UN Publications: UN Bookshop, United Nations, N.Y.

United Nations Assn. of the United States of America Inc., 345 E. 46th St., New York, N.Y.

Major International Organizations
(See also United Nations)

THE COMMONWEALTH, originally called the British Commonwealth of Nations, is an association of nations and dependencies loosely joined by a common interest based on having been parts of the old British Empire. The British monarch is the symbolic head of the Commonwealth.

There are 33 self-governing independent nations which are full members of the Commonwealth, plus various colonies and protectorates. As of August, 1975, the members were the United Kingdom of Great Britain and Northern Ireland and eleven other nations recognizing the British monarch, represented by a governor-general, as their head of state: Australia, Bahamas, Barbados, Canada, Fiji, Grenada, Jamaica, Mauritius, New Zealand, Papua New Guinea Trinidad and Tobago; and 23 countries with their own heads of state: Bangladesh, Botswana, Cyprus, Gambia, Ghana, Guyana, India, Kenya, Lesotho, Malawi, Malaysia, Malta, Nigeria, Seychelles, Sierra Leone, Singapore, Sri Lanka (Ceylon), Swaziland, Tanzania, Tonga, Uganda, Western Samoa, Zambia. In addition, Nauru and various Caribbean islands take part in certain Commonwealth activities.

The Commonwealth facilitates consultation among member states through meetings of prime ministers and finance ministers, and through a permanent Secretariat established in 1949. Members consult on economic, scientific, educational, financial, legal, and military matters, and try to coordinate policies.

Population (est. 1975) was about 900 million in the member nations; total area, over ten million sq. mi.

EUROPEAN COMMUNITIES (EC) is the collective designation of three organizations with common membership: the European Economic Community (Common Market), the European Coal and Steel Community, and the European Atomic Energy Community. The nine full members are: Belgium, Denmark, France, West Germany, Ireland, Italy, Luxembourg, Netherlands, United Kingdom. The Common Market also includes as associate members Greece, Turkey, Cyprus, Malta, 46 other nations in Africa, The Caribbean, and the Pacific are affiliated under the Lome Convention. The Common Market also has trade agreements with other nations, including EFTA members, Israel, and several Arab nations have trade agreements with other countries.

A coordinated structure for the communities went into effect July 1, 1967, though the component organizations date back to 1951 and 1957. A Council of Ministers, an expert Commission, a European Parliament and a Court of Justice comprise the permanent structure. The communities aim to integrate their economies, coordinate social developments, and ultimately, bring about political union of the democratic states of Europe.

A 1975 agreement provides that direct elections for the European Parliament would be held in member countries in 1978, and that a uniform Western Europe passport would be issued in that year.

EUROPEAN FREE TRADE ASSOCIATION (EFTA), consisting in 1975 of Austria, Iceland, Norway, Portugal, Sweden, Switzerland and associate member Finland, was created by treaty Jan. 4, 1960, effective May 3, to gradually reduce customs duties and quantitative restrictions between members on industrial products. By Dec. 31, 1966, tariffs and restrictions had been eliminated. The United Kingdom and Denmark withdrew to become members of EEC Jan. 1, 1973. Other EFTA members joined in an industrial tariff elimination pact with EEC in 1972.

NORTH ATLANTIC TREATY ORG. (NATO) was created April 4, 1949, in a treaty signed in Washington, effective Aug. 24, by Belgium, Canada, Denmark, France, Iceland, Italy, Luxembourg, the Netherlands, Norway, Portugal, the United Kingdom, and the U.S. Greece, Turkey, and West Germany have joined since. The members agreed to settle disputes by peaceful means; to develop their individual and collective capacity to resist armed attack; to regard an attack on one as an attack on all, and to take necessary action to repel an attack under Article 51 of the United Nations Charter.

Parallel military and civilian institutions comprise NATO's permanent structure. The civilian side includes the North Atlantic Council, a Defense Planning Committee, an international Secretariat, and specialized committees. A Military Committee includes professional military representatives from all member nations except France, which maintains liaison. North Atlantic Council meetings may consist of heads of government, cabinet ministers, or permanent NATO representatives, who hold ambassadorial rank. The Military Committee may include Chiefs of Staff of the member nations.

Armed forces of NATO members include forces assigned to NATO commands, forces earmarked for NATO commands, and forces under national command. The NATO military command has five branches: Allied Command Europe, Allied Command Atlantic, Allied Command Channel, Canada-U.S. Regional Planning Group, and Allied Air Force, Central Europe.

Following announcement in 1966 of nearly total French withdrawal from the military affairs of NATO, the organization moved its headquarters in 1967 from Paris to Brussels. In August, 1974, Greece announced a total withdrawal of armed forces from NATO, in response to Turkish intervention in Cyprus. Nevertheless, Greece has continued to participate in NATO political and military planning activities.

ORGANIZATION OF AFRICAN UNITY (OAU), formed May 25, 1963 by 30 African countries (46 by 1976) to coordinate cultural, political, scientific and economic policies; to end colonialism in Africa; to promote a common defense of members' independence. It holds annual conferences of heads of state, has a council of foreign ministers meeting at least twice a year, a secretary-general and a mediation-arbitration commission. Hq. is in Addis Ababa, Ethiopia. The OAU has helped formulate common policies on problems of trade, sea law, etc.

ORGANIZATION OF AMERICAN STATES (OAS) was formed in Bogota, Colombia, in 1948. Hq. are in Washington, D.C. It has a Permanent Council, Inter-American Economic and Social Council, and Inter-American Council for Education, Science and Culture, a Juridical Committee, and a Commission on Human Rights. The Permanent Council can call meetings of foreign ministers to deal with urgent security matters. A General Assembly meets annually. A Secretary General and Assistant are elected for 5-year terms. There are 25 members, each with one vote in the various organizations: Argentina, Barbados, Bolivia, Brazil, Chile, Colombia, Costa Rica, Cuba, Dominican Republic, Ecuador, El Salvador, Grenada, Guatemala, Haiti, Honduras, Jamaica, Mexico, Nicaragua, Panama, Paraguay, Peru, Trinidad-Tobago, U.S., Uruguay, Venezuela. In 1962, the OAS excluded Cuba from OAS activities but not from membership.

ORGANIZATION FOR ECONOMIC COOPERATION AND DEVELOPMENT (OECD) was established in 1960 to promote stable economic growth in member countries and the world at large, and to help expand free trade. Nearly all the industrialized "free market" countries belong, with Yugoslavia as an associate member. OECD is active in collecting and disseminating economic and environmental information, and in channeling resources to developing countries. Members in 1976 were: Australia, Austria, Belgium, Canada, Denmark, Finland, France, West Germany, Greece, Iceland, Ireland, Italy, Japan, Luxembourg, Netherlands, New Zealand, Norway, Portugal, Spain, Sweden, Switzerland, Turkey, United Kingdom, United States.

ORGANIZATION OF PETROLEUM EXPORTING COUNTRIES (OPEC) was created in 1960 at Venezuelan initiative. The group has successfully maintained high oil prices, and has tried to advance members' interests in trade and development dealings with industrialized oil-consuming nations. Members in 1976 were Algeria, Ecuador, Gabon, Indonesia, Iran, Iraq, Kuwait, Libya, Nigeria, Qatar, Saudi Arabia, United Arab Emirates, Venezuela.

LEAGUE OF ARAB STATES (THE ARAB LEAGUE) was created March 22, 1945, by Egypt, Iraq, Jordan, Lebanon, Saudi Arabia, Syria and Yemen. Joining later were Algeria, Bahrain, Kuwait, Libya, Mauritania, Morocco, Oman, Qatar, Somalia, Southern Yemen, Sudan, Tunisia and United Arab Emirates. Cairo is headquarters for the Secretary-General. The League mediates disputes between Arab states, represents Arab states in certain international negotiations, and coordinates a military, economic, and diplomatic offensive against Israel. The League fosters cultural, economic, and communications ties among the Arab states.

WARSAW TREATY ORGANIZATION (WARSAW PACT) was created May 14, 1955, as a mutual defense alliance by Albania, Bulgaria, Czechoslovakia, East Germany, Hungary, Poland, Romania and the USSR. It provides for a unified military command with headquarters in Moscow; if one member is attacked, the others will aid it with all necessary steps including armed force; joint maneuvers are held; there is a Political Consultative Committee and economic cooperation is advanced. Albania was barred from meetings in 1962, withdrew in 1968.

Heads of States and Prime Ministers
Data to Mid-1976

Country	Head of State, Title	Born	Acceded or Elected	Premier or Prime Minister
Afghanistan	Mohammad Daoud, pres.		July 19, 1973	Mohammad Daoud
Albania	Maj.-Gen. Haxhi Lleshi, pres.	1913	July, 1953	Maj. Gen. Mehmet Shehu
Algeria	Houari Boumediene, pres.	1925	June 19, 1965	
Andorra	Pres. of France & Spanish bishop of Urgel			
Angola				L. Nascimento
Argentina	Lt. Gen. Jorge Rafael Videla, pres.	Aug. 2, 1925	Mar. 29, 1976	
Australia (C).	Sir John R. Kerr, gov-gen.(*).	Sept. 24, 1914	July 11, 1974	Malcolm Fraser
Austria	Rudolf Kirchschlaeger, pres.	Mar. 20, 1915	June 23, 1974	Dr. Bruno Kreisky
Bahamas (C)	Milo B. Butler, gov.-gen.(*).	Aug. 11, 1906	Aug. 1, 1973	Lynden O. Pindling

Country	Head of State, Title	Born	Acceded or Elected	Premier or Prime Minister
Bahrain	Isa bin Sulman al-Khalifa, sheik	July 3, 1933	Dec. 16, 1961	Khalifa bin Sulman al-Khalifa
Bangladesh (C)	Abu Sadat Mohammad Sayem		Nov. 6, 1976	
Barbados (C)	Sir Arleigh W. Scott, gov.-gen.(*)	May 18, 1967		Errol W. Barrow
Belgium	Baudouin I, king	Sept. 7, 1930	July 17, 1951	Leo Tindemans
Benin	Maj. Mathieu Kerekou, pres	1933	Oct. 28, 1972	Maj. Mathieu Kerekou
Bhutan	Jigme Singye Wangchuk, king	Nov. 11, 1955	July 24, 1972	
Bolivia	Gen. Hugo Banzer Suarez, pres	May 10, 1926	Aug. 21, 1971	
Botswana (C)	Sir Seretse Khama, pres	July 1, 1921	Sept. 10, 1966	
Brazil	Gen. Ernesto Geisel, pres	Aug. 3, 1907	Jan. 15, 1974	
Bulgaria	Todor Zhivkov, pres	Sept. 7, 1911	July 7, 1971	Stanko Todorov
Burma	Ne Win	1911	Mar. 2, 1962	Sein Win
Burundi	Michel Micombero, pres	1939	Nov. 28, 1966	
Cambodia	Khieu Samphan, chief of state		Apr. 14, 1976	Tol Saut
Cameroon	Ahmadou Ahidjo, pres	Aug. 24, 1924	Jan. 1, 1960	
Canada (C)	Jules Leger, gov.-gen.(*)	Apr. 4, 1913	Jan. 14, 1974	Pierre E. Trudeau
Cape Verde	Aristedes Pereira, pres		July 5, 1975	Pedro Pires
Central African Rep.	Gen. Jean-Bedel Bokassa, pres	Feb. 22, 1920	Jan. 1, 1966	Elisabeth Donitien
Chad	Gen. Felix Malloum	Sept. 10, 1932	April 16, 1975	
Chile	Augusto Pinochet Ugarte, pres	Nov. 25, 1915	June 27, 1974	
China, People's Republic	Wu Teh, chmn., People's Cong.		July, 1976	Hua Kuo-Feng
China (Taiwan)	Yen Chia-kan		Apr. 6, 1975	Chiang Ching-kuo
Colombia	Alfonso Lopez Michelsen, pres	June 30, 1913	Aug. 7, 1974	
Comoro Is.	Ali Soilih		Jan. 2, 1976	Abdallah Mohammed
Congo, People's Rep.	Maj. Marien Ngouabi, pres	1937	Jan. 1, 1969	Henri Lopes
Costa Rica	Daniel Oduber Quiros, pres	Aug. 25, 1921	May 8, 1974	
Cuba	Osvaldo Dorticos Torrado, pres	1919	July 17, 1959	Fidel Castro
Cyprus (C)	Archbishop Makarios	Aug. 13, 1913	Dec. 14, 1959	
Czechoslovakia	Gustav Husak	1913	May 29, 1975	Lubomir Strougal
Denmark	Margrethe II, queen	Apr. 16, 1940	Jan. 14, 1972	Anker Joergensen
Dominican Rep.	Dr. Joaquin Balaguer, pres	1908	July 1, 1966	
Ecuador	V. Adm. Alfredo Poveda Burbano, junta head		Jan. 11, 1976	
Egypt	Anwar Sadat, pres	Dec. 25, 1918	Oct. 17, 1970	Mamdouh Salem
El Salvador	Arturo Armando Molina, pres	Aug. 6, 1927	July 1, 1972	
Equatorial Guinea	Masie Nguema Biyogo, pres	Jan. 1, 1924	Oct. 12, 1968	
Ethiopia	Tafari Banti, chmn., mil. cncl.	1921	Nov. 28, 1974	
Fiji (C)	Sir George Cakobau, gov.-gen.(*)	Nov. 6, 1912	Jan. 13, 1973	Sir Kamisese K. T. Mara
Finland	Dr. Urho Kekkonen, pres	Sept. 3, 1900	Feb. 15, 1956	Martti Miettunen
France	Valery Giscard D'Estaing, pres	Feb. 2, 1926	May 19, 1974	Raymond Barre
Gabon	Omar Bongo, pres	Dec. 30, 1935	Dec. 2, 1967	Leon Mebiame
Gambia (C)	Sir Dawda Kairaba Jawara, pres	May 16, 1924	Apr. 24, 1970	
Germany, West	Walter Scheel, pres	July 8, 1919	May 15, 1974	Helmut Schmidt
Germany, East	Willi Stoph, chmn. council of state	July 9, 1914	Aug. 1973	Horst Sindermann
Ghana (C)	Col. Ignatius K. Acheampong	Sept. 23, 1931	Jan. 13, 1972	
Greece	Constantine Tsatsos	1899	June 19, 1975	Constantine Caramanlis
Grenada (C)	Leo V. de Gale, gov.-gen.(*)		Feb. 7, 1975	Eric Matthew Gairy
Guatemala	Gen. Kjell Laugerud-Garcia, pres	Jan. 24, 1930	July 1, 1974	
Guinea	Ahmed Sekou Toure, pres	Jan. 19, 1922	Oct. 2, 1958	Lansana Beavogui
Guinea-Bissau	Luis Cabral, pres	1931	Sept. 24, 1973	Francisco Mendes
Guyana (C)	Arthur Chung, pres	Jan. 10, 1918	Feb. 23, 1970	Linden Forbes Burnham
Haiti	Jean-Claude Duvalier, pres	July 3, 1951	Apr. 21, 1971	
Honduras	Col. Juan Alberto Melgar Castro		Apr. 22, 1975	
Hungary	Pal Losonczi, pres	1919	Apr. 14, 1967	Gyorgy Lazar
Iceland	Kristjan Eldjarn, pres	Dec. 16, 1916	Aug. 1, 1968	Geir Hallgrimsson
India (C)	Fakhruddin Ali Ahmed, pres	May 13, 1905	Aug. 24, 1974	Indira Nehru Gandhi
Indonesia	Gen. Suharto, pres	June 8, 1921	Mar. 11, 1967	
Iran	Mohammed Reza Pahlavi, shah	Oct. 26, 1919	Sept. 18, 1941	Amir Abbas Hoveyda
Iraq	Ahmed Hassan al-Bakr, pres	1912	July 17, 1968	
Ireland	Cearbhall O Dalaigh	Feb. 12, 1911	Dec. 19, 1974	Liam Cosgrave
Israel	Prof. Ephraim Katzir, pres	May 16, 1916	Apr. 10, 1973	Yitzhak Rabin
Italy	Giovanni Leone, pres	Nov. 3, 1908	Dec. 24, 1971	Giulio Andreotti
Ivory Coast	Felix Houphouet-Boigny, pres	Oct. 18, 1905	Nov. 27, 1960	
Jamaica (C)	Florizel A. Glasspole, gov.-gen.(*)	Sept. 25, 1909	June 27, 1973	Michael Manley
Japan	Hirohito, emperor	Apr. 29, 1901	Dec. 25, 1926	Takeo Miki
Jordan	Hussein I, king	Nov. 14, 1935	May 2, 1952	Zaid al-Rifai
Kenya (C)	Jomo Kenyatta, pres	1890	Dec. 12, 1964	
Korea, Republic	Park Chung Hee, pres	Sept. 30, 1917	Nov. 26, 1963	Choi Kyu-hah
Korea, People's Dem. Rep.	Kim Il-sung, pres	1912		Kim Il
Kuwait	Sabah al-Salim al-Sabah, emir	1915	Nov. 24, 1965	Jaber al-Ahmed al-Jaber
Laos	Prince Souphanouvong, chief of st.	1912	Dec. 3, 1975	Kaysone Phomvihan
Lebanon	Suleiman Franjieh, pres	June 14, 1910	Sept. 23, 1970	Rashid Karami
Lesotho (C)	Motlotlehi Moshoeshoe II, king	1898	Oct. 4, 1969	Chief Leabua Jonathan
Liberia	William R. Tolbert, Jr., pres	May 13, 1913	July 23, 1971	
Libya	Muammar el-Qaddafi, chmn., revolutionary cncl.	1942	Sept. 1, 1969	Abdul Salam Jalloud
Liechtenstein	Franz Joseph II, prince	Aug. 16, 1906	July 26, 1938	Dr. Walter Kieber
Luxembourg	Jean, grand duke	Jan. 5, 1921	Nov. 12, 1964	Gaston Thorn
Madagascar	Didier Ratsiraka, pres	November, 1936	Feb. 12, 1975	
Malawi (C)	Dr. H. Kamuzu Banda, pres	1906	July 6, 1966	
Malaysia (C)	Sultan Yahaya Putra, king		June 19, 1975	Abdul Razak
Maldives, Rep. of	Amir Ibrahim Nasir, pres	Sept. 2, 1926	Nov. 11, 1968	
Mali	Moussa Traore, pres	Sept. 25, 1936	Nov. 19, 1968	
Malta (C)	Sir Anthony Mamo, pres	Jan. 9, 1909	Dec. 13, 1974	Dom Mintoff

Country	Head of State, Title	Born	Acceded or Elected	Premier or Prime Minister
Mauritania	Moktar Ould Daddah, pres.	Apr. 25, 1925	Nov., 1958	
Mauritius (C)	Sir Raman Osman gov.-gen.(*).	Aug., 1902	Dec. 27, 1972	Sir Seewoosagur Ramgoolam
Mexico	Jose Lopez Portillo.	1920	July 4, 1976	
Monaco	Rainier III, prince	May 31, 1923	May 9, 1949	
Mongolia	Yumjaagiyn Tsendenbal, presidium chmn.	Sept. 17, 1916	June 11, 1974	Jambyn Batmunkh
Morocco	Hassan II, king.	July 11, 1929	Mar. 3, 1961	Ahmed Osman
Mozambique	Samora Machel, pres.	1934	June 25, 1975	Joachim Chissano
Nauru (C)	Hammer DeRoburt, pres.	Sept. 25, 1922	Jan. 31, 1968	
Nepal	Birendra Bir Bikram, king.	Dec. 28, 1945	Jan. 31, 1972	Tulsi Giri
Netherlands	Juliana, queen	Apr. 30, 1909	Sept. 6, 1948	Joop M. den Uyl
New Zealand (C)	Sir Denis Blundell, gov.-gen.(*).	May 29, 1907	Sept. 27, 1972	Robert D. Muldoon
Nicaragua	Gen. Anastasio Somoza Debalye, pres.		Dec. 1, 1974	
Niger	Seyni Kountche, chief of state		Apr. 17, 1974	
Nigeria (C)	Lt. Gen. Olusegun Obasanjo.		Aug. 5, 1975	
Norway	Olav V, king.	July 2, 1903	Sept. 21, 1957	Odvar Nordli
Oman	Qabus bin Said, sultan.	Nov. 18, 1940	July 23, 1970	
Pakistan	Fazal Elahi Chaudhri, pres.	1904	Aug. 14, 1973	Zulfikar Ali Bhutto
Panama	Demetrio B. Lakas, pres.	Aug. 29, 1925	Mar., 1972	Gen. Omar Torrijos Herrera
Papua New Guinea (C)	John Guise, gov.-gen.(*).		Sept. 16, 1975	Michael Somare
Paraguay	Gen. Alfredo Stroessner, pres.	Nov. 3, 1912	Aug. 15, 1954	
Peru	Gen. Francisco Morales Bermudez, pres.	1922	Aug. 29, 1975	Guillermo Arbulu Galliani
Philippines	Ferdinand Marcos, pres.	Sept. 11, 1917	Dec. 30, 1965	
Poland	Henryk Jablonski, chmn. council of state		Mar. 28, 1972	Piotr Jaroszewicz
Portugal	Antonio Ramalho Eanes, pres.	Jan. 25, 1935	June 28, 1976	Mario Soares
Qatar	Khalifa bin Hamad Al-Thani.	Feb., 1929	Feb. 22, 1972	Khalifa bin Hamad Al-thani
Rhodesia	Clifford W. Dupont, pres.	Dec. 6, 1905	Mar. 2, 1970	Ian Smith
Romania	Nicolae Ceausescu, state council pres.	Jan. 26, 1918	Dec. 7, 1967	Manea Manescu
Rwanda	Maj. Gen. Juvenal Habyalimana, pres.		July 5, 1973	
San Marino	Co-regents			
Sao Tome & Principe.	Manuel Pinto da Costa, pres.		July 12, 1975	Miguel Trovoda
Saudi Arabia	Khalid Bin Abdul Aziz, king.	1913	Mar. 25, 1975	Khalid Bin Abdul Aziz
Senegal Rep.	Leopold S. Senghor, pres.	Oct. 9, 1906	Sept., 1960	Abdou Diouf
Seychelles (C).	James Mancham.	1940	June 29, 1976	Albert Rene
Sierra Leone (C)	Siaka P. Stevens, pres.	1906	Apr. 28, 1971	S. S. Ibrahim Koroma
Singapore (C)	Benjamin H. Sheares, pres.	Aug. 12, 1907	Jan. 2, 1971	Lee Kuan Yew
Somali, Dem. Rep.	Maj. Gen. Mohamed Siad Barre, pres.	1912	Oct. 15, 1969	
South Africa	Nicolaas Diederichs.	Nov. 11, 1903	Apr. 19, 1975	B. John Vorster
Spain	Juan Carlos I, king.	Jan. 5, 1938	Nov. 22, 1975	Adolfo Suarez Gonzalez
Sri Lanka (Ceylon) (C)	William Gopallawa, pres.	Sept. 16, 1897	May 22, 1972	Mrs. Sirimavo Bandaranaike
Sudan	Gaafar al-Nimeiry, pres.	1929	May 25, 1969	
Surinam	Johan H. E. Ferrier.		Nov. 25, 1976	Henk Arron
Swaziland (C)	Sobhuza II, king.	July 22, 1899	Apr. 25, 1967	Prince Makhosini Damini
Sweden	Carl XVI Gustaf, king.	Apr. 30, 1946	Sept. 15, 1973	Olof Palme
Switzerland (1).	Rudolf Gnaegi, pres.	1917	Jan. 1, 1976	
Syria	Hafez al-Assad, chief of state.	Mar., 1930	Mar. 14, 1971	Abdel Rahman Khleifawi
Tanzania (C)	Julius K. Nyerere, pres.	1922	Apr. 26, 1964	Rashid M. Kawawa
Thailand	Bhumibol Adulyadej, king.	Dec. 5, 1927	June 9, 1946	Seni Pramoj
Togo (C)	Gen. Gnassingbe Eyadema, pres.	1932	Jan. 13, 1967	
Tonga (C)	Taufa'ahau Tupou IV, king.	July 4, 1918	July 5, 1967	Prince Fatafehi Tu'pelehake
Trinidad-Tobago (C).	Sir Ellis E. I. Clarke, pres.	Dec. 28, 1917	July 31, 1976	Eric E. Williams
Tunisia	Habib Bourguiba, pres.	Aug. 3, 1903	July 25, 1957	Hedi Nouira
Turkey	Fahri Koruturk, pres.	1903	Apr. 6, 1973	Suleyman Demirel
Uganda (C)	Field Marshall Idi Amin, pres.	1925	Jan. 25, 1971	
USSR	Nikolai V. Podgorny, presidium pres.	Feb. 18, 1903	Dec. 9, 1965	Aleksei N. Kosygin
United Arab Emirates.	Zayed bin Sultan al-Nahayan, pres.	1923	Dec. 2, 1972	
United Kingdom (C).	Elizabeth II, queen.	Apr. 21, 1926	Feb. 6, 1952	James Callaghan
United States	Gerald R. Ford, pres.	July 14, 1913	Aug. 9, 1974	
Upper Volta	Gen. Sangoule Lamizana, pres.	1921	Jan. 3, 1966	
Uruguay	Aparicio Mendez, pres.	1904	Sept. 1, 1976	
Vatican City	Giovanni Battista Montini, Pope Paul VI.	Sept. 26, 1897	June 21, 1963	
Venezuela	Carlos Andres Perez, pres.	Oct. 27, 1922	Mar. 12, 1974	
Vietnam	Ton Duc Thang.	1888	Sept. 23, 1969	Pham Van Dong
Western Samoa (C)	Malietoa Tanumafili II, king.	Jan. 4, 1913	Jan. 1, 1962	Tupua Tamasese Lealof IV
Yemen, People's Dem. Rep. of.	Salem Robaye Ali, council pres.	1934	June 23, 1969	Ali Nasser Mohammed
Yemen Arab Rep.	Lt. Col. Ibrahim Al-Hamadi, pres.	1944	June 13, 1974	Abdulaziz Abdul Ghani
Yugoslavia	Josip Broz Tito, pres.	May 25, 1892	Jan. 31, 1946	Dzemal Bijedic
Zaire	Mobutu Sese Seko, pres.	Oct. 14, 1930	Nov. 24, 1965	
Zambia (C).	Kenneth Kaunda, pres.	Apr. 28, 1924	Oct. 24, 1964	M. Elijah Mudenda

(1) President serves one-year term, the vice president customarily succeeds him.
(C) Member of the Commonwealth of Nations.
(*) gov.-gen. acts as representative of the British monarch, who is recognized as head of state.

Ambassadors and Envoys
As of May 1976
The address of foreign embassies to the United States is Washington, D.C.

Countries	Envoys from United States	Envoys to United States
Afghanistan	Theodore L. Eliot Jr., Amb.	Abdullah Malikyar, Amb.
Algeria	Richard B. Parker, Amb.	Abdelkader Maadini, Charge
Argentina	Robert C. Hill, Amb.	Rafael Maximiano Vazquez, Amb.
Australia	James W. Hargrove, Amb.	Nicholas F. Parkinson, Amb.
Austria	Wiley T. Buchanan, Amb.	Arno Halusa, Amb.
Bahamas	Seymour Weiss, Amb.	Livingston B. Johnson, Amb.
Bahrain	Joseph W. Twinam, Amb.	
Bangladesh	Davis E. Boster, Amb.	Mustafizur Rahman Siddiqi, Amb.
Barbados	Theodore R. Britton Jr., Amb.	Maurice A. King, Amb.
Belgium	Leonard K. Firestone, Amb.	Willy Van Cauwenbrg, Amb.
Benin	James E. Engle, Amb.	Thomas S. Boya, Amb.
Bolivia	William P. Stedman Jr., Amb.	Alberto Crespo, Amb.
Botswana	David B. Bolen, Amb.	Amos M. Dambe, Amb.
Brazil	John Hugh Crimmins, Amb.	Joao Baptista Pinheiro, Amb.
Bulgaria	Martin F. Herz, Amb.	Lubomir D. Popov, Amb.
Burma	David L. Osborn, Amb.	Tin Lat, Amb.
Burundi	David E. Mark, Amb.	Clement Sambira, Charge
Cambodia[1]		
Cameroon	Herbert J. Spiro, Amb.	Eric Dikoko Quan, Charge
Canada	Thomas O. Enders, Amb.	Jack Warren, Amb.
Centr. African Rep.	Anthony C. E. Quainton, Amb.	Christophe Maidou, Amb.
Chad	Vacant.	Bawoyeu Alingue, Amb.
Chile	David H. Popper, Amb.	Manuel Trucco, Amb.
China (Taiwan)	Leonard Unger, Amb.	James C. H. Shen, Amb.
China, People's Rep.[2]	Thomas S. Gates, Jr., Amb.	Huang Chen[1]
Colombia	Phillip V. Sunchez, Amb.	Julio Cesar Turbay-Ayala, Amb.
Congo (Brazzaville)[3]		
Costa Rica	Terence A. Todman, Amb.	Rodolfo Silva Vargas, Amb.
Cuba[4]		
Cyprus	William R. Crawford Jr., Amb.	Nicos G. Dimitriou, Amb.
Czechoslovakia	Thomas X. Byrne, Amb.	Jaromir Johanes, Amb.
Denmark	John Gunther Dean, Amb.	Otto Borch, Amb.
Dominican Republic	Robert A. Hurwitch, Amb.	Horacio Vicioso-Soto, Amb.
Ecuador	Richard J. Bloomfield, Amb.	Jose C. Cardenas, Amb.
Egypt	Hermann F. Eilts, Amb.	Ashraf A. Ghorbal, Amb.
El Salvador	James F. Campbell, Amb.	Francisco Bertrand Galindo, Amb.
Equatorial Guinea[5]		
Estonia[5]		Ernst Jackson, Consul General
Ethiopia	Arthur W. Hummel Jr., Amb.	Ghebeyehou Mekbib, Charge
Fiji	Armistead I. Selden Jr., Amb.	S. K. Sikivou, Amb.
Finland	Mark E. Austad, Amb.	Leo Tuominen, Amb.
France	Kenneth Rush, Amb.	Jacques Kosciusko-Morizet, Amb.
Gabon	Andrew L. Steigman, Amb.	Vincent Mavoungou, Amb.
Gambia	O. Rudolph Aggrey, Amb.	Vacant
Germany, East	John Sherman Cooper, Amb.	Rolf Sieber, Amb.
Germany, West	Martin J. Hillenbrand, Amb.	Berndt von Staden, Amb.
Ghana	Vacant.	Samuel Ernest Quarm, Amb.
Greece	Jack B. Kubisch, Amb.	Menelas D. Alexandrakis, Amb.
Grenada	Theodore R. Britton Jr., Amb.	Marie McIntyre, Amb.
Guatemala	Francis E. Meloy Jr., Amb.	Federico A. Maldonado Gularte, Amb.
Guinea	William C. Harrop, Amb.	Habib Bah, Amb.
Guinea-Bissau	Vacant.	Gil Vicente Vaz Fernandez, Amb.
Guyana	Max V. Krebs, Amb.	Laurence E. Mann, Amb.
Haiti	Heyward Isham, Amb.	Georges Salomon, Amb.
Honduras	Vacant.	Roberto Lazarus, Amb.
Hungary	Eugene V. McAuliffe, Amb.	Ferenc Esztergalyos, Amb.
Iceland	James J. Blake	Haraldur Kroyer, Amb.
India	William B. Saxbe, Amb.	Triloki Nath Kaul, Amb.
Indonesia	David D. Newsom, Amb.	Roesmin Nurjadin, Amb.
Iran	Richard Helms, Amb.	Ardeshir Zahedi, Amb.
Iraq[6]		
Ireland	Walter J. P. Curley Jr., Amb.	John G. Molloy, Amb.
Israel	Malcolm Toon, Amb.	Simcha Dinitz, Amb.
Italy	John A. Volpe, Amb.	Roberto Gaja, Amb.
Ivory Coast	Robert S. Smith, Amb.	Timothee N'Guetta Ahoua, Amb.
Jamaica	Sumner Gerard, Amb.	Alfred A. Rattray, Charge
Japan	James D. Hodgson, Amb.	Fumihiko Togo, Amb.
Jordan	Thomas R. Pickering, Amb.	Abdullah Salah, Amb.
Kenya	Anthony D. Marshall, Amb.	Ernest M. Mungai, Charge
Korea, South	Richard L. Sneider, Amb.	Pyong-choon Hahm, Amb.
Kuwait	Frank E. Maestrone, Amb.	Khalid M. Jaffar, Amb.
Laos	Vacant.	Somphong Vanitsaveth, Charge
Latvia[5]		Dr. Antole Dinbergs, Charge
Lebanon	Vacant.	Najati Kabbani, Amb.
Lesotho	David B. Bolen, Amb.	Teboho J. Mashologu, Amb.
Liberia	W. Beverly Carter Jr., Amb.	S. Edward Peal, Amb.
Libya	Vacant.	Shaban F. Gashut, Charge
Lithuania[5]		Joseph Kajeckas, Charge
Luxembourg	Rosemary L. Ginn, Amb.	Adrien Meisch, Amb.

Countries	Envoys from United States	Envoys to United States
Madagascar	Vacant	Charles Randrianasolo, Charge
Malawi	Robert A. Stevenson, Amb.	Jacob T. X. Muwamba, Amb.
Malaysia	Francis T. Underhill Jr., Amb.	Zain Azraai, Amb.
Maldives, Rep.	John H. Reed, Amb.	Vacant
Mali	Ralph J. McGuire, Amb.	Mamadou Boubacar Kante
Malta	Robert P. Smith, Amb.	Joseph Attard-Kingswell, Amb.
Mauritania	Holsey G. Handyside, Amb.	Mohamed Said Hamody, Amb.
Mauritius	Robert V. Keeley, Amb.	Pierre Guy Girald Balancy, Amb.
Mexico	Joseph J. Jova, Amb.	Dr. Jose Juan de Olloqui, Amb.
Morocco	Robert Anderson, Amb.	Abdelhadi Boutaleb, Amb.
Mozambique	William A. De Pree, Amb.	
Nauru	James W. Hargrove, Amb.	Vacant
Nepal	Marquita M. Maytag, Amb.	Padma Bahadur Khatri, Amb.
Netherlands	Kingdon Gould Jr., Amb.	Age R. Tammenoms Bakker, Amb.
New Zealand	Armistead I. Selden Jr., Amb.	Lloyd White, Amb.
Nicaragua	James D. Theberge, Amb.	Dr. Guillermo Sevilla-Sacasa, Amb.
Niger	L. Douglas Heck, Amb.	Illa Salifou, Amb.
Nigeria	Donald B. Easum, Amb.	Edward Olusola Sanu, Amb.
Norway	William A. Anders, Amb.	Soren Christian Sommerfelt, Amb.
Oman	William D. Wolle, Amb.	Ahmed Macki, Amb.
Pakistan	Henry A. Byroade, Amb.	Sahabzada Yaqub-Khan, Amb.
Panama	William J. Jorden, Amb.	Nicolas Gonzalez-Revilla, Amb.
Papua, New Guinea	Mary S. Olmsted, Amb.	Paulias Nguna Matane, Amb.
Paraguay	George W. Landau, Amb.	Miguel Solano-Lopez, Amb.
Peru	Robert W. Dean, Amb.	Carlos Garcia-Bedoya, Amb.
Philippines	William H. Sullivan, Amb.	Eduardo Z. Romualdez, Amb.
Poland	Richard T. Davies, Amb.	Witold Trampczynski, Amb.
Portugal	Frank C. Carlucci, Amb.	Joao Hall Themido, Amb.
Qatar	Robert P. Paganelli, Amb.	Abdullah Saleh Al-Mana, Amb.
Romania	Harry G. Barnes Jr., Amb.	Nicolae M. Nicolae, Amb.
Rwanda	Robert E. Fritts, Amb.	Joseph Nizeyimana, Amb.
Sao Tome and Principe	Andrew L. Steigman, Amb.	
Saudi Arabia	William J. Porter, Amb.	Ali Abdallah Alireza, Amb.
Senegal	O. Rudolph Aggrey, Amb.	Andre Coulbary, Amb.
Seychelles	Anthony D. Marshall, Amb.	
Sierra Leone	Michael A. Samuels, Amb.	Philip J. Palmer, Amb.
Singapore	John H. Holdridge, Amb.	Dr. Ernest Steven Monteiro, Amb.
Somali, Democratic Rep.	James L. Loughran, Amb.	Dr. Adbullaha Ahmed Addou, Amb.
South Africa	William G. Bowdler, Amb.	R. F. Botha, Amb.
Spain	Wells Stabler, Amb.	Jaime Alba, Amb.
Sri Lanka (Ceylon)	John H. Reed, Amb.	Neville Kanakaratne, Amb.
Sudan	William D. Brewer, Amb.	Francis M. Deng, Amb.
Surinam	J. Owen Zurhellen Jr., Amb.	
Swaziland	David B. Bolen, Amb.	J.L.F. Simelane, Amb.
Sweden	David S. Smith, Amb.	Wilhelm Wachtmeister, Amb.
Switzerland	Nathaniel Davis, Amb.	Raymond Probst, Amb.
Syrian Arab Rep.	Richard W. Murphy, Amb.	Sabah Kabbani, Amb.
Tanzania	James W. Spain, Amb.	Paul Bomani, Amb.
Thailand	Charles S. Whitehouse, Amb.	Upadit Pachariyangkun, Amb.
Togo	Nancy V. Rawls, Amb.	Messanvi Kokou Kekeh, Amb.
Tonga	Armistead I. Selden Jr., Amb.	Vacant
Trinidad and Tobago	Albert B. Fay, Amb.	Victor C. McIntyre, Amb.
Tunisia	Edward W. Mulcahy, Amb.	Ali Hedda, Amb.
Turkey	William B. Macomber Jr., Amb.	Melih Esenbel, Amb.
Uganda[7]		S. M. Nsubuga, Charge
USSR	Walter J. Stoessel Jr., Amb.	Anatoliy F. Dobrynin, Amb.
United Arab Emirates	Michael Sterner, Amb.	Saeed Ahmad Ghobash, Amb.
United Kingdom	Anne L. Armstrong, Amb.	Sir Peter Ramsbotham, Amb.
Upper Volta	Pierre R. Graham, Amb.	Telesphore Yaguibou, Amb.
Uruguay	Ernest V. Siracusa, Amb.	Jose Perez Caldas, Amb.
Venezuela	Viron P. Vaky, Amb.	Miguel Angel Burelli, Amb.
Vietnam[1]		
Western Samoa	Armistead I. Selden Jr., Amb.	Vacant
Yemen, South[8]		
Yemen Arab Rep.	Thomas J. Scotes, Amb.	Yahya M. Al-Mutawakel, Amb.
Yugoslavia	Laurence H. Silberman, Amb.	Dimce Belovski, Amb.
Zaire	Walter L. Cutler, Amb.	Ndagano Bulumba, Amb.
Zambia	Jean M. Wilkowski, Amb.	Siteke Gibson Mwale, Amb.

Ambassadors at Large: U. Alexis Johnson, Ellsworth Bunker, Robert J. McCloskey, T. Vincent Learson

(1) U.S. embassy closed in 1975 during Communist takeover; (2) no formal relations; liaison offices; (3) U.S. embassy closed in 1965; West Germany acts as protective power; (4) relations severed in 1961; Switzerland protects U.S. interests; (5) U.S. does not officially recognize 1940 annexation by USSR; (6) relations severed in 1967, limited staff returned in 1972; Belgium protects U.S. interests; (7) U.S. embassy closed in 1973; West Germany protects U.S. interests; (8) U.S. embassy closed in 1969; UK serves as protective power; (9) U.S. severed relations in 1976.

Special Missions
U.S. Mission to North Atlantic Treaty Organization, Brussels—Robert Strausz-Hupe
U.S. Mission to the European Communities, Brussels—Deane R. Hinton
U.S. Mission to the International Atomic Energy Agency, Vienna—Gerald F. Tape
U.S. Mission to the United Nations, New York—William W. Scranton
U.S. Mission to the European Office of the UN & Other Internatl. Organizations, Geneva—Henry Catto, Jr.
U.S. Mission to the Organization for Economic Cooperation and Development, Paris—William C. Turner
U.S. Mission to the Organization of American States—William S. Mailliard

U.S. Aid to Foreign Nations

Source: Bureau of Economic Analysis, U.S. Department of Commerce

Data shown by country includes the military supplies and services furnished under the Foreign Assistance Act and direct Defense Department appropriations. This aid is principally to the Southeast Asia countries. Data shown includes credits which have been extended to private entities in the country specified.

Grants are largely outright gifts for which no payment is expected or which at most involve an obligation on the part of the receiver to extend aid to the U.S. or other countries to achieve a common objective.

Net grants and credits take into account all known returns to the U.S. government, including reverse grants, returns of grants, and payments of principal. A minus sign indicates that the total of these returns to the U.S. is greater than the total of grants or credits.

Other assistance represents the transfer of U.S. farm products in exchange for foreign currencies, less the government's disbursements of the currencies as grants, credits, or for purchases. The net acquisitions of currencies represents net transfers of resources to foreign currencies in addition to those classified as grants or credits.

Amounts do not include investments in international financial institutions in 1975 as follows: Asian Development Bank, $29.76 million; Inter-American Development Bank, $267.68 million; International Development Assn., $356.65 million.

In millions of dollars or equivalent (*Less than $500,000)

Calendar Year 1975	Total	Net grants	Net credits	Net other
TOTAL..............	$8,039	$5,162	$2,848	$29
Military grants...........	2,916	2,916	—	—
Other grants, credits, ass't.	5,122	2,246	2,848	29
Western Europe..........	270	17	249	4
Austria.................	-2	—	-2	—
Belgium-Luxembourg....	18	—	18	—
Denmark...............	15	—	15	—
Finland................	7	—	7	—
France.................	-15	—	-15	—
Germany, West.........	33	—	33	*
Iceland................	3	—	3	*
Ireland................	-18	—	-18	—
Italy..................	-13	—	-13	—
Malta.................	15	14	1	—
Netherlands...........	56	—	56	—
Norway................	92	—	92	—
Portugal..............	15	*	15	—
Spain.................	94	3	91	*
Sweden...............	4	—	4	—
Switzerland...........	28	—	28	*
United Kingdom.......	-89	—	-89	—
Yugoslavia............	38	—	34	4
Atomic EC............	-6	—	-6	—
Coal-Steel EC........	-6	—	-6	—
Other & unspecified.....	1	—	1	—
Eastern Europe..........	-58	*	-30	-28
Hungary..............	-1	—	-1	—
Poland...............	9	*	37	-28
Romania..............	20	—	20	—
Soviet Union..........	-86	—	-86	—
Near East & South Asia....	1,932	847	1,034	50
Afghanistan...........	1,932	847	1,034	50
Bangladesh...........	380	47	333	*
Cyprus...............	14	14	*	—
Egypt................	87	27	13	47
Greece...............	112	*	112	*
India.................	243	170	79	-5
Iran..................	-103	1	-104	*
Israel................	803	423	379	*
Jordan................	63	67	-5	*
Kuwait...............	-5	—	-5	—
Lebanon..............	37	1	36	—
Nepal................	8	8	*	1
Pakistan..............	134	24	103	7
Saudi Arabia..........	-11	—	-11	—
Sri Lanka (Ceylon).......	20	6	14	*
Syria.................	18	*	18	—
Turkey...............	72	4	68	*
Yemen (Sana).........	6	6	—	—
Other & unspecified.....	37	38	—	—
East Asia & Pacific.......	1,152	355	796	1
Australia..............	-23	—	-23	—
Cambodia.............	78	44	34	*
China-Taiwan.........	191	*	191	*
Hong Kong............	19	*	19	*
Indonesia.............	164	15	149	*
Japan................	10	-2	12	*
Korea (So.)...........	313	4	309	*
Laos.................	14	14	*	—
Malaysia..............	3	2	1	—
New Zealand..........	30	—	30	*
Papua New Guinea......	*	*	—	—
Philippines............	76	39	37	*
Thailand..............	10	12	-2	—
Singapore.............	15	*	15	—
Trust Terr. Pacific.......	79	79	—	—
Vietnam (So.)..........	159	134	26	*
Other & unspecified......	14	14	—	—
Africa.................	401	212	186	3
Algeria................	41	8	33	—
Botswana..............	8	3	4	—
Cameroon.............	5	5	*	—
Chad.................	4	4	—	—
Ethiopia...............	30	10	19	*
Gabon................	4	*	3	—
Ghana................	6	7	-1	*
Guinea...............	9	1	9	*
Ivory Coast............	1	2	-1	*
Kenya................	8	5	3	*
Lesotho...............	4	4	—	—
Gabon................	4	*	3	—
Liberia................	-1	6	-7	—
Madagascar............	2	1	1	—
Malawi................	5	1	4	—
Mali..................	11	11	*	*
Mauritania............	3	3	*	—
Morocco...............	8	16	-9	1
Niger.................	10	10	*	—
Nigeria...............	7	7	*	—
Senegal...............	8	6	2	*
Sierra Leone...........	4	4	*	—
Somalia...............	6	6	*	—
Sudan................	13	10	4	-1
Tanzania..............	37	20	17	*
Togo.................	3	3	*	—
Tunisia...............	12	12	-4	4
Upper Volta...........	6	6	—	—
Zaire.................	96	3	93	*
Zambia...............	5	*	5	—
Other & unspecified......	46	38	11	—
Western Hemisphere......	818	201	617	*
Argentina.............	-4	*	-4	—
Bahamas..............	21	—	21	—
Bermuda..............	-5	—	-5	—
Bolivia................	11	7	3	*
Brazil................	193	13	179	*
Canada...............	75	—	45	—
Cayman Islands........	2	—	2	—
Chile.................	128	11	117	*
Colombia..............	36	18	18	*
Costa Rica............	10	3	6	*
Dominican Republic......	36	10	25	*
Ecuador..............	6	7	-1	—
El Salvador............	7	3	3	—
Guatemala............	20	7	13	—
Guyana...............	16	1	15	—
Haiti.................	11	9	2	—
Honduras.............	24	11	12	*
Jamaica..............	25	2	23	—
Mexico...............	70	2	68	—
Nicaragua.............	13	4	9	—
Panama...............	23	12	11	—
Paraguay.............	7	3	3	—
Peru.................	49	11	38	*
Uruguay..............	*	1	-1	*
Venezuela.............	-18	1	-20	*
Other & unspecified......	92	65	35	—
International organizations & unspecified areas.....	607	613	-6	—

National Population Density, Natural Increase, Life Expectancy

Source: United Nations Demographic Yearbooks, 1964, 1974

Country	Density[1]	Natural Increase[2] 1964[3]	1974[3]	Life Expectancy[4]
Afghanistan	29	N.A.	24.0	37.5*
Algeria	7	N.A.	32.2	50.7*
Argentina	9	13.5	13.5	64.14
Australia	2	12.9	10.5	67.63
Austria	90	6.2	0.3	67.4
Bangladesh	521	N.A.	N.A.	N.A.
Belgium	321	4.5	0.7	67.79
Bolivia	5	16-25[5]	24.9	49.71
Brazil	12	27-36[6]	28.3	57.61
Bulgaria	78	8.2	7.4	68.58
Burma	45	15	22.9	47.5*
Cambodia	44	21.7	29.0	44.2
Cameroon	13	N.A.	20.3	41.0*
Canada	2	16.2	8.1	69.34
Chad	3	20	22.7	29.0
Chile	14	21.7	19.1	60.48
China	86	23	17.8	50.0*
Colombia	21	26-32[5]	34.0	44.18
Costa Rica	38	38.2	23.2	61.87
Cuba	79	17-25[5]	19.6	66.8*
Czechoslovakia	115	7.4	8.1	66.80
Denmark	117	7.7	4.0	70.7
Ecuador	25	25-35[5]	33.5	51.04
Egypt	36	N.A.	22.5	51.6
Ethiopia	22	N.A.	20.6	38.5*
Finland	14	8.3	3.7	65.89
France	96	7.4	4.8	68.6
Germany, E.	159	4.0	-2.9	68.85
Germany, W.	250	7.2	-1.6	67.41
Ghana	40	N.A.	28.8	46.0*
Greece	68	N.A.	7.6	70.09
Guatemala	51	30.5	28.0	48.29
Guinea	18	22	22.1	26.0
Haiti	163	22.8	24.2	44.5*
Honduras	26	25-35[5]	31.9	49.0*
Hong Kong	4,066	24.5	14.1	67.36
Hungary	112	3.1	5.8	66.87
Iceland	2	18.7	13.4	70.7
India	179	18.9	26.1	41.89
Indonesia	86	21.6	28.9	47.5
Iran	19	25-28[5]	28.8	50.0*
Ireland	44	11.1	11.5	68.58
Israel	159	16.0	20.4	70.23
Italy	184	10.4	6.1	67.97
Ivory Coast	15	22.8	23.3	41.0*
Jamaica	182	32.4	23.3	62.65
Japan	295	10.8	12.8	70.49
Kenya	22	N.A.	30.3	46.9
Korea, N.	128	N.A.	27.6	57.7*
Korea, S.	340	N.A.	24.6	63.00
Kuwait	52	N.A.	35.9	66.14
Lebanon	268	N.A.	20.2	N.A.
Liberia	15	N.A.	28.9	45.8
Libya	1	N.A.	30.1	52.1*
Malawi	41	N.A.	24.0	38.5*
Mali	44	33	23.2	37.2*
Mexico	29	35.4	34.3	61.03
Morocco	38	27.4	33.0	50.5*
Mozambique	12	N.A.	20.4	41.0*
Netherlands	332	13.0	5.8	71.2
Niger	4	25	28.9	41.0*
Nigeria	66	N.A.	24.7	37.2
Norway	12	7.9	5.0	71.24
Pakistan	85	26-30[5]	24	53.72
Panama	22	N.A.	32.3	64.26
Papua N.G.	6	N.A.	25	46.8*
Paraguay	6	29-38[5]	30.7	52.59
Peru	12	24-35[5]	33.7	62.5
Philippines	138	N.A.	32.7	48.81
Poland	108	10.5	10.2	66.83
Portugal	95	13.5	8.2	67.99*
Puerto Rico	341	23.2	16.8	68.92
Rhodesia	16	34	34.0	51.4*
Romania	89	7.2	11.8	66.27
Rwanda	157	38.3	28.5	41.0*
Saudi Arabia	4	N.A.	27.3	42.3*
Senegal	22	26.6	23.5	41.0*
Singapore	3,819	26.4	14.6	65.1
Somalia	5	N.A.	21.9	38.5*
Spain	70	13.5	10.9	69.69
Sudan	7	33.2	30.5	47.6*
Sri Lanka	208	N.A.	21.8	64.8
Sweden	18	6.0	2.8	72.12
Switzerland	157	9.6	4.4	70.15
Syria	38	N.A.	32.2	54.49
Tanzania	16	21.22[5]	25	40-41*
Thailand	80	22	32.4	53.6
Togo	39	26	25.4	31.6
Tunisia	34	21	30.3	51.7*
Turkey	49	N.A.	25.0	53.7*
Uganda	47	22	25.6	47.5*
USSR	11	14.0	9.5	64.0
United Kingdom	229	7.4	1.1	67.81
United States	23	11.8	5.9	67.4
Upper Volta	22	18.6	20.3	32.1
Uruguay	17	N.A.	11.3	65.51
Venezuela	13	30-40[5]	33.1	66.41*
Vietnam, N.	146	N.A.	21.4	50.0*
Vietnam, S.	111	17	21.4	50.0*
Yugoslavia	83	11.4	9.4	65.59
Zaire	10	N.A.	21.7	37.64
Zambia	6	32	29.1	43.5*

(1) Persons per sq. kilometer, 1974. (2) Excess of births over deaths per 1,000 people. (3) Or latest available prior data. (4) For males at birth, except (*)both sexes; life expectancy figures are for a variety of years, and may not reflect recent changes. (N.A.) Not available. (5) Estimate.

Gross National Product Estimates

For Calendar Year 1973 in Current Market Prices—U.S..$
Compiled by Agency for International Development

Nation	GNP Total $ Millions	GNP Per Capita
Afghanistan	1,466	81
Algeria	7,730	504
Angola	2,980	492
Argentina	31,385	1,246
Australia	52,160	3,998
Austria	27,900	3,710
Bahrain	216	935
Bangladesh	7,730	100
Belgium	45,740	4,686
Bolivia	1,014	202
Brazil	77,220	750
Burma	2,416	82
Burundi	284	74
Cambodia	627	81
Cameroon	1,418	232
Canada	118,900	5,372
Central African Rep.	302	176
Chad	350	88
Chile	7,640	777
China (Taiwan)	10,226	663
Colombia	9,968	413
Congo	425	423
Costa Rica	1,461	775
Cyprus	963	1,459
Dahomey	348	122
Denmark	27,350	5,342
Dominican Republic	2,378	509
Ecuador	2,496	371
Egypt	9,100	259
El Salvador	1,335	344
Ethiopia	2,240	83
Fiji		640
Finland	17,060	3,661
France	255,060	4,851
Gabon	634	1,248
Germany, West	348,170	5,618
Ghana	2,857	287
Greece	16,290	1,780
Guatemala	2,545	454
Guinea	575	137
Guinea-Bissau	158	275
Guyana	294	380
Haiti	694	143
Honduras	869	291
Hong Kong	5,998	1,435
Iceland	1,025	4,835
India	71,000	117
Indonesia	15,370	115
Iran	25,598	762
Iraq	6,680	645
Ireland	6,560	2,165
Israel	8,950	2,732
Italy	138,270	2,520
Ivory Coast	2,393	511
Jamaica	1,714	868
Japan	413,070	3,812
Jordan	575	286
Kenya	2,249	172
Korea, South	12,380	376
Kuwait	7,165	8,449
Laos	320	100
Lebanon	2,841	874
Lesotho	97	99
Liberia	417	248
Libya	6,230	2,984
Luxembourg	1,829	5,226
Madagascar	1,258	174
Malawi	535	112
Malaysia	6,565	554
Mali	397	73
Malta	353	1,096
Mauritania	245	196
Mexico	48,650	870

Morocco	5,012	286	Portugal	11,200	1,308	Tanzania	1,834	127
Mozambique	2,905	334	Rhodesia	2,493	406	Thailand	9,180	232
Nepal	1,078	90	Qatar	511	5,938	Togo	393	185
Netherlands	59,670	4,440	Rwanda	280	71	Tunisia	2,515	459
New Zealand	11,710	3,930	Saudi Arabia	7,520	1,299	Turkey	22,036	576
Nicaragua	1,065	503	Senegal	1,014	252	Uganda	1,715	161
Niger	525	125	Sierra Leone	455	162	United Arab -		
Nigeria	14,802	250	Singapore	4,283	1,929	Emirates	1,425	6,736
Norway	18,750	4,735	Somalia	236	79	United Kingdom	174,800	3,120
Oman	355	492	South Africa	26,125	1,077	United States	1,294,900	6,155
Pakistan	8,340	126	Spain	60,230	1,728	Upper Volta	450	79
Panama	1,418	904	Sri Lanka	2,612	198	Uruguay	2,585	865
Papua New -			Sudan	2,300	135	Venezuela	16,120	1,357
Guinea	945	365	Swaziland	140	310	Yemen, South	175	110
Paraguay	979	402	Sweden	50,100	6,155	Yemen, North	500	80
Peru	9,080	617	Switzerland	40,870	6,346	Zaire	3,129	147
Philippines	10,330	246	Syria	2,379	345	Zambia	2,425	503

Cost of Living in Various Cities of the World

This comparison of the cost of living in various cities was drawn up in 1976 by the UN Statistical Office, based on prices for goods, services and housing for international officials stationed in these cities. Figures show relative costs, based on about 120 items. New York City was assigned the index figure 100. Thus, while expenditure for certain items might be $1,000 in New York, it would be $1,240 for them in Paris and $900 in Rio de Janeiro. Figures with an asterisk (*) omit cost of housing (rent, utilities, and domestic service) in cities where they are furnished at nominal cost by governments.

Index	City	Index	City	Index	City
*134	Abidjan, Ivory Coast	120	The Hague, Netherlands	118	Ouagadougou, Upper Volta
*127	Accra, Ghana	84	Havana, Cuba	88	Panama City, Panama
86	Addis Ababa, Ethiopia	76	Islamabad, Pakistan	124	Paris, France
*83	Aden, Yemen (Dem.)	107	Jakarta, Indonesia	92	Port-au-Prince, Haiti
*114	Algiers, Algeria	82	Kabul, Afghanistan	71	Port Louis, Mauritius
92	Amman, Jordan	*105	Kampala, Uganda	79	Port-of-Spain, Trinidad
75	Ankara, Turkey	76	Katmandu, Nepal	77	Prague, Czechoslovakia
*99	Apia, Western Samoa	*125	Kigali, Rwanda	80	Quito, Ecuador
80	Asuncion, Paraguay	95	Kingston, Jamaica	96	Rabat, Morocco
93	Athens, Greece	132	Kinshasa, Zaire	85	Rangoon, Burma
86	Baghdad, Iraq	88	Kuala Lumpur, Malaysia	90	Rio de Janeiro, Brazil
133	Bamako, Mali	96	Kuwait, Kuwait	94	Rome, Italy
83	Bangkok, Thailand	*122	Lagos, Nigeria	99	Sana, Yemen (Rep.)
*149	Banqui, Cen. African Rep.	*82	LaPaz, Bolivia	95	San Jose, Costa Rica
102	Beirut, Lebanon	*127	Libreville, Gabon	87	San Salvador, El Salvador
87	Belgrade, Yugoslavia	90	Lima, Peru	75	Santiago, Chile
67	Bogota, Colombia	91	London, United Kingdom	103	Seoul, South Korea
116	Bonn, West Germany	*104	Lusaka, Zambia	95	Singapore, Singapore
*137	Brazzaville, Congo	91	Managua, Nicaragua	79	Suva, Fiji
102	Bridgetown, Barbados	79	Manila, Philippines	97	Sydney, Australia
97	Budapest, Hungary	73	Mbabane, Swaziland	103	Tananarive, Malagasy
46	Buenos Aires, Argentina	92	Mexico City, Mexico	90	Tegucigalpa, Honduras
77	Cairo, Egypt	92	Mogadishu, Somalia	87	Tehran, Iran
87	Caracas, Venezuela	*102	Monrovia, Liberia	*110	Tokyo, Japan
69	Colombo, Sri Lanka	72	Montevideo, Uruguay	*131	Tripoli, Libya
139	Conakry, Guinea	86	Montreal, Canada	91	Tunis, Tunisia
116	Copenhagen, Denmark	80	Nairobi, Kenya	*109	Ulan Bator, Mongolia
95	Damascus, Syria	71	New Delhi, India	62	Valetta, Malta
115	N'Djamena, Chad	100	New York, U.S.	108	Vienna, Austria
*102	Freetown, Sierra Leone	*123	Niamey, Niger	78	Warsaw, Poland
126	Geneva, Switzerland	79	Nicosia, Cyprus	92	Washington, D.C., U.S.
68	Georgetown, Guyana	*133	Nouakchott, Mauretania	103	Yaounde, Cameroon

Population of World's Largest Urban Areas

City populations often cannot be used to compare urban areas because city limits may fall short of or exceed the built-up or urban area. The problem of comparison is compounded by the difficulty in obtaining reliable population data for a common year. The ranking of urban areas below represents one attempt at comparing the world's largest urban areas, taking into account, where necessary and within the limits of available data, urban development extending outward from the principal city named in the table. Thus, the Tokyo area included Tokyo plus neighboring smaller cities, towns and villages. (Some computations include Yokohama as part of Tokyo's urban population.) New York's urban area in 1970 included part or all the population of 10 New Jersey and 5 New York counties in addition to the 5 boroughs of New York City.

New York, N.Y. (census 1970)	16,206,841	Bombay, India (census 1971)	5,970,575
Tokyo, Japan (est. 1973)	11,612,311	Seoul, S. Korea (census, 1970)	5,433,198
Shanghai, China (est. 1970)	10,820,000	Essen (Ruhr-Gebiet), W. Germany (est. 1971)	5,425,000
Mexico City, Mexico (est. 1974)	10,766,791	Cairo, Egypt (est. 1970)	4,961,000
Paris, France (est. 1970)	9,250,647	Philadelphia, Pa. (census 1970)	4,817,914
Buenos Aires, Argentina (est. 1974)	8,925,000	Rio de Janeiro, Brazil (est. 1973)	4,658,000
Osaka, Japan (census, 1973)	7,838,722	Jakarta, Indonesia (census 1971)	4,576,009
Sao Paulo, Brazil (est. 1973)	7,693,000	Victoria-Hong Kong (est. 1975)	4,370,000
Peking, China (est. 1970)	7,570,000	Tientsin, China (est. 1970)	4,280,000
Moscow, USSR (est. 1974)	7,528,000	Leningrad, USSR (1974)	4,243,000
London, England (est. 1973)	7,281,000	Detroit, Mich. (census, 1970)	4,199,931
Los Angeles-Long Beach, Calif. (census, 1970)	7,032,075	Bangkok, Thailand (est. 1973)	3,967,081
Calcutta, India (census 1971)	7,031,382	Teheran, Iran (est. 1973)	3,774,048
Chicago, Ill. (census 1970)	6,978,947	Karachi, Pakistan (est. 1972)	3,650,000

Delhi-New Delhi, India (census, 1971)......... 3,647,023	Yokahama, Japan (est. 1973)................ 2,494,975
Madras, India (census 1971)................. 3,169,930	Pittsburgh, Pennsylvania (census, 1970)........ 2,401,245
Lima, Peru (census, 1972)................... 3,158,417	Manchester, England (est. 1973)............. 2,389,260
Madrid, Spain (census 1970)................. 3,146 071	Dallas-Ft. Worth, Texas (census, 1970)........ 2,377,979
Berlin, E. and W. Germany (est. 1973, 1974)..... 3,136,774	St. Louis, Missouri (census 1970)............. 2,363,017
Istanbul, Turkey (est. 1973)................. 3,135,354	Birmingham, England (est. 1973)............. 2,358,980
San Francisco-Oakland, Calif. (census 1970)... 3,109,519	Chungking, China (est. 1970)................ 2,300,000
Santiago, Chile (est. 1971)................. 3,068,652	Singapore (est. 1975)..................... 2,250,000
Manila, Philippines (est. 1973).............. 3,000,000	Canton, China (est. 1970)................. 2,200,000
Sydney, Australia (est. 1973)............... 2,874,380	Caracas, Venezuela (est. 1970)............. 2,175,400
Washington, D.C.-Md.-Va. (census, 1970)....... 2,861,123	Lahore, Pakistan (census, 1972)............. 2,148,000
Bogota, Colombia (census, 1973)............. 2,850,000	Nagoya, Japan (est. 1973)................. 2,075,249
Shenyang (Mukden), China (est. 1970)......... 2,800,000	Baltimore, Maryland (census 1970)........... 2,070,670
Rome, Italy (census, 1971)................. 2,799,836	Cleveland, Ohio (census 1970)............... 2,064,194
Montreal, Quebec (est. 1973)............... 2,775,000	Rangoon, Burma (est. 1973)................ 2,056,118
Boston, Mass. (census, 1970)............... 2,753,700	Newark, New Jersey (census 1970).......... 2,054,928
Toronto, Ontario (est. 1973)............... 2,692,000	Alexandria, Egypt (est. 1970)............... 2,032,000
Melbourne, Australia (est. 1973)............ 2,583,900	Budapest, Hungary (est. 1971)............. 2,027,300
Wuhan, China (est. 1970).................. 2,560,000	Kinshasa, Zaire (est. 1974)................ 2,008,352
Athens, Greece (census, 1971)............. 2,540,000	Taipei, China (est. 1974)................. 2,000,409

Population of Important World Cities

Source: Latest census reports and latest official estimates; *(asterisk) denotes capital;
Gr. denotes Greater, or metropolitan area   See index for U.S. and Canadian cities

Afghanistan
*Kabul, Gr...... 534,350
Kandahar...... 133,799
Albania
*Tirana......... 171,300
Algeria
*Algiers, Gr.... 1,116,493
Constantine... 243,558
Oran........... 327,493
Angola
*Luanda, Gr..... 475,328
Argentina
*Buenos Aires, Gr.
.... 8,925,000
Cordoba, Gr..... 825,000
La Plata, Gr..... 510,000
Mendoza, Gr..... 470,806
Rosario, Gr..... 875,000
San Miguel, Gr.. 365,757
Australia
Adelaide, Gr.... 842,693
Brisbane, Gr.... 867,784
*Canberra, Gr.... 198,700
Melbourne, Gr.. 2,503,450
Newcastle, Gr... 351,010
Perth, Gr....... 703,199
Sydney, Gr.... 2,807,828
Austria
Graz........... 249,211
Linz........... 204,627
*Vienna, Gr...... 1,940,000
Bahamas
*Nassau, Gr..... 101,503
Bahrain
*Manama, Gr..... 145,000
Bangladesh
Chittagong..... 492,153
*Dacca, Gr...... 1,629,402
Khulna........ 467,881
Narayanganj... 442,673
Barbados
*Bridgetown, Gr... 115,000
Belgium
Antwerp, Gr.... 1,155,000
*Brussels, Gr.... 2,000,000
Ghent, Gr...... 320,000
Liege, Gr...... 880,000
Belize (Br. Honduras)
*Belize, Gr...... 48,421
Benin
Cotonou........ 111,100
*Porto-Novo...... 74,500
Bermuda
*Hamilton, Gr..... 18,000
Bolivia
*La Paz......... 700,000
Santa Cruz..... 200,000
*Sucre......... 53,000
Botswana
*Gaborone........ 17,718
Brazil
Belem.......... 762,000
Belo Horizonte.. 1,542,000
*Brasilia, Gr..... 800,000

Curitiba........ 760,000
Fortaleza..... 1,059,000
Niteroi......... 324,367
Porto Alegre... 1,105,000
Recife........ 1,352,000
Rio de Janeiro.. 4,658,000
Salvador...... 1,311,000
Santos........ 262,048
Sao Paulo, Gr.. 7,693,000
Bulgaria
Plovdiv....... 305,091
*Sofia........ 1,055,100
Burma
Mandalay....... 393,000
*Rangoon..... 2,056,118
Burundi
*Bujumbura, Gr.... 78,810
Cambodia (Khmer Rep.)
*Phnom-Penh..... 393,995
Cameroon
Douala, Gr..... 350,000
*Yaounde....... 200,000
Central African Rep.
*Bangui, Gr..... 187,000
Chad
*N'Djamena, Gr... 179,000
Chile
*Santiago, Gr.... 3,068,652
Valparaiso...... 292,847
China
Anshan........ 1,050,000
Canton........ 2,200,000
Changchun..... 1,200,000
Chungking..... 2,300,000
Fushun........ 1,080,000
Harbin........ 1,670,000
Kunming...... 1,100,000
Lanchow...... 1,450,000
Nanking....... 1,750,000
*Peking....... 7,570,000
Port Arthur,
  Dairen...... 1,650,000
Shanghai..... 10,820,000
Shenyang..... 2,800,000
Sian.......... 1,500,000
Taiyuan...... 1,350,000
Tangshan...... 950,000
Tientsin...... 4,280,000
Tsinan....... 1,100,000
Tsingtao...... 1,300,000
Wuhan........ 2,560,000
China (Taiwan)
*Taipei........ 2,000,149
Colombia
Barranquilla.... 816,706
*Bogota, Gr.... 2,818,300
Bucaramanga... 347,400
Cali.......... 1,100,000
Cartagena..... 347,600
Medellin...... 1,207,800
Congo, People's Rep.
*Brazzaville, Gr... 175,000
Costa Rica
*San Jose, Gr.... 418,000

Cuba
Camaguey..... 196,900
*Havana, Gr.... 1,755,000
Santiago de Cuba. 277,600
Cyprus
*Nicosia, Gr.... 116,125
Czechoslovakia
Bratislava..... 328,765
Brno.......... 343,860
Ostrava....... 292,404
*Prague...... 1,095,615
Denmark
Arhus........ 245,212
*Copenhagen, Gr. 1,383,073
Dominican Republic
*Santo Domingo... 671,402
Ecuador
Guayaquil...... 860,600
*Quito........ 597,133
Egypt
Alexandria.... 2,032,000
*Cairo........ 4,961,000
Giza.......... 711,900
Port Said...... 313,000
Suez.......... 315,000
El Salvador
*San Salvador, Gr.. 600,000
Ethiopia
*Addis Ababa... 1,083,420
Asmara........ 296,044
Fiji
*Suva.......... 60,000
Finland
*Helsinki, Gr.... 837,553
France
Bordeaux, Gr.... 555,152
Grenoble, Gr.... 332,423
Lille, Gr...... 881,439
Lyon, Gr...... 1,074,823
Marseille, Gr.... 964,412
Nantes, Gr..... 393,731
Nice, Gr...... 392,635
*Paris, Gr..... 9,250,647
Strasbourg..... 334,668
Toulouse, Gr.... 439,764
Gabon
*Libreville, Gr..... 73,000
Gambia
*Banjul, Gr..... 52,640
Germany (West)
Berlin (West).. 2,047,948
Bochum....... 338,022
*Bonn........ 283,260
Bremen....... 584,265
Cologne...... 832,396
Dortmund..... 632,317
Duesseldorf.... 628,498
Duisburg...... 435,281
Essen........ 674,000
Frankfurt...... 663,422
Gelsenkirchen... 333,202
Hamburg..... 1,751,621
Hannover...... 505,106
Mannheim..... 325,386

Muelheim (Ruhr).. 191,100
Munich....... 1,336,576
Nuremberg..... 514,657
Stuttgart...... 624,835
Wuppertal...... 409,715
Germany (East)
*Berlin (East).. 1,088,827
Dresden..... 505,408
Karl Marx Stadt
  (Chemnitz).... 301,826
Leipzig...... 575,913
Ghana
*Accra, Gr...... 738,498
Kumasi, Gr..... 345,117
Greece
*Athens-Piraeus. 2,540,000
Thessaloniki
  (Salonika), Gr... 557,360
Guatemala
*Guatemala City... 730,991
Guinea
*Conakry, Gr..... 197,267
Guyana
*Georgetown, Gr... 167,078
Haiti
*Port-au-Prince,
  Gr.......... 493,932
Honduras
*Tegucigalpa, Gr.. 302,483
Hong Kong
Victoria, Gr.... 4,370,000
Hungary
*Budapest...... 2,043,959
Iceland
*Reykjavik, Gr.... 110,000

India
Agra, Gr...... 634,622
Ahmedabad, Gr. 1,741,522
Allahabad, Gr.... 513,036
Bangalore, Gr.. 1,653,779
Bombay...... 5,970,575
Calcutta, Gr... 7,031,382
*Delhi........ 4,065,698
Howrah....... 737,877
Hyderabad, Gr.. 1,796,339
Indore, Gr..... 560,936
Jaipore, Gr..... 636,768
Kanpur, Gr.... 1,275,242
Lucknow, Gr.... 813,982
Madras, Gr.... 3,169,930
Madurai, Gr.... 711,501
Nagpur, Gr..... 930,459
Poona, Gr..... 1,135,034
Surat, Gr...... 493,001
Varanasi, Gr.
  (Benares)..... 606,721

Indonesia
Bandung..... 1,201,730
*Jakarta...... 4,576,009
Jogjakarta..... 342,267
Makassar...... 434,766
Malang....... 422,428
Medan........ 635,562

Palembang...... 532,961
Semarang...... 646,590
Surabaja...... 1,556,255
Iran
Abadan......... 306,000
Isfahan........ 575,000
Mashhad....... 562,000
Shiraz......... 356,000
Tabriz......... 493,000
*Teheran...... 4,200,000
Iraq
*Baghdad, Gr.... 2,183,800
Basra......... 370,900
Mosul......... 293,100
Ireland
Cork.......... 128,235
*Dublin, Gr...... 650,153
Israel
Haifa, Gr....... 351,900
*Jerusalem..... 326,400
Tel Aviv-Jaffa,
Gr.......... 1,150,000
Italy
Bari.......... 356,733
Bologna....... 491,873
Catania........ 413,670
Florence....... 461,602
Genoa........ 841,978
Milan......... 1,724,173
Naples....... 1,277,438
Palermo....... 661,477
*Rome....... 2,799,836
Trieste....... 277,752
Turin......... 1,183,864
Venice........ 363,062
Ivory Coast
*Abidjan, Gr...... 510,000
Jamaica
*Kingston, Gr.... 475,548
Japan
Amagasaki..... 538,411
Fukuoka....... 914,877
Hiroshima..... 740,792
Kawasaki..... 1,001,368
Kitakyushu.... 1,051,076
Kobe......... 1,338,705
Kyoto........ 1,435,254
Nagoya...... 2,075,249
Osaka........ 2,841,937
Sakai......... 681,805
Sapporo...... 1,130,828
Sendai........ 564,404
*Tokyo, Gr..... 11,612,311
Yokohama..... 2,494,975
Jordan
*Amman....... 580,000
Kenya
Mombasa, Gr.... 301,000
*Nairobi, Gr..... 630,000
Korea, Dem. People's Rep. of
*Pyong Yang..... 840,000
Korea, Republic of
Inchon........ 646,013
Pusan........ 1,880,710
*Seoul........ 5,536,377
Taegu........ 1,082,750
Kuwait
*Kuwait, Gr..... 560,000
Laos
*Vientiane..... 145,000
Lebanon
*Beirut, Gr....... 938,940
Lesotho
*Maseru, Gr..... 29,049
Liberia
*Monrovia........ 96,226
Libya
Bengazi........ 170,000
*Tripoli....... 264,000
Luxembourg
*Luxembourg...... 78,032
Macao
*Macao......... 241,413
Madagascar
*Tananarive, Gr... 377,600
Malawi
*Blantyre-Limbe, Gr......... 169,000

*Zomba, Gr....... 19,666
Malaysia
*Kuala Lumpur... 500,000
Pinang......... 280,000
Maldives, Rep. of
*Male.......... 15,740
Mali
*Bamako, Gr..... 196,800
Malta
*Valletta....... 15,401
Mauritania
*Nouakchott..... 120,000
Mauritius
*Port Louis, Gr... 370,000
Mexico
Chihuahua, Gr... 363,850
Guadalajara, Gr. 1,856,878
Juarez, Gr....... 497,267
Leon......... 468,887
*Mexico Gr.... 10,766,791
Monterrey, Gr... 1,543,399
Puebla, Gr...... 521,885
Tijuana, Gr...... 458,514
Torreon........ 356,240
Mongolian Rep.
*Ulan Bator...... 310,000
Morocco
Casablanca, Gr. 1,561,280
Fez, Gr......... 379,790
Marrakech, Gr... 390,480
Meknes, Gr..... 362,840
*Rabat—Sale..... 534,270
Tangier........ 187,994
Mozambique
Maputo, Gr..... 383,775
Namibia
*Windhoek....... 61,260
Nepal
*Katmandu, Gr.... 210,000
Netherlands
*Amsterdam, Gr.. 1,023,695
Eindhoven, Gr... 346,543
The Hague, Gr... 697,869
Rotterdam, Gr.. 1,059,626
Utrecht, Gr..... 463,471
New Zealand
Auckland, Gr.... 747,339
Christchurch, Gr. 313,210
*Wellington, Gr... 337,680
Nicaragua
*Managua....... 398,514
Niger
*Niamey....... 102,000
Nigeria
Ibadan........ 758,332
Kano......... 357,098
*Lagos, Gr..... 1,476,837
Ogbomosho..... 386,650
Norway
Bergen, Gr..... 182,265
*Oslo, Gr....... 645,413
Oman
*Muscat........ 6,000
Pakistan
Hyderabad, Gr... 834,000
*Islamabad....... 77,000
Karachi, Gr.... 3,650,000
Lahore, Gr..... 2,148,000
Lyalpur, Gr.... 1,109,000
Rawalpindi, Gr... 615,000
Panama
*Panama....... 418,013
Papua New Guinea
*Port Moresby.... 80,000
Paraguay
Asuncion, Gr.... 550,000
Peru
Arequipa...... 304,653
Callao........ 296,220
*Lima, Gr..... 3,158,417
Philippines
Cebu........ 384,000
Davao....... 591,500
Manila, Gr.... 3,000,000
*Quezon City..... 896,200
Poland
Gdansk (Danzig).. 394,000
Krakow....... 651,300
Lodz......... 777,800

Poznan......... 495,200
Szczecin........ 355,600
*Warsaw, Gr..... 1,775,000
Wroclaw (Breslau) 557,200
Portugal
*Lisbon, Gr..... 1,640,000
Porto, Gr...... 1,314,794
Qatar
*Doha.......... 95,000
Rhodesia
*Salisbury, Gr..... 502,000
Romania
*Bucharest...... 1,681,603
Saudi Arabia
Jidda........ 500,000
Mecca........ 185,000
*Riyadh....... 225,000
Senegal
*Dakar, Gr....... 581,000
Seychelles
*Victoria....... 14,500
Sierra Leone
*Freetown....... 214,443
Singapore
*Singapore..... 2,250,000
Somalia
*Mogadishu..... 230,000
South Africa
*Cape Town, Gr.. 1,125,000
Durban, Gr.... 1,040,000
Johannesburg, Gr......... 2,550,000
*Pretoria, Gr..... 575,000
Spain
Barcelona, Gr... 3,165,000
Bilbao....... 410,490
*Madrid....... 3,580,000
Malaga....... 374,452
*Seville....... 548,072
Valencia...... 653,690
Zaragoza...... 479,845
Sri Lanka (Ceylon)
*Colombo, Gr.... 2,700,000
Sudan
*Khartoum, Gr.... 675,000
Omdurman..... 258,532
Surinam
*Paramaribo..... 110,867
Sweden
Goteborg, Gr.... 685,699
Malmo, Gr.... 450,619
*Stockholm, Gr.. 1,352,359
Switzerland
Basel, Gr....... 381,453
*Berne, Gr...... 284,737
Geneva, Gr..... 321,083
Zurich, Gr...... 719,324
Syria
Aleppo........ 639,361
*Damascus, Gr.... 923,253
Tanzania
*Dar es Salaam.... 343,911
Thailand
*Bangkok, Gr.... 3,967,081
*Thonburi....... 627,989
Togo Rep.
*Lome......... 192,745
Trinidad and Tobago
*Port of Spain, Gr.. 310,000
Tunisia
*Tunis, Gr....... 685,000
Turkey
*Ankara, Gr..... 1,553,897
Istanbul, Gr.... 3,135,354
Izmir, Gr...... 819,276
Uganda
*Kampala....... 331,889
USSR
Alma-Ata...... 776,000
Baku......... 884,000
Barnaul...... 459,000
Chelyabinsk.... 910,000
Dniepropetrovsk.. 903,000
Donetsk....... 905,000
Erevan....... 818,000
Frunze....... 452,000
Gorky....... 1,213,000
Irkutsk....... 473,000
Ivanovo...... 434,000
Karaganda..... 541,000

Kazan........ 904,000
Khabarovsk..... 462,000
Kharkov..... 1,280,000
Kiev........ 1,764,000
Krasnodar..... 491,000
Krasnoyarsk... 698,000
Krivoy Rog.... 600,000
Kuibyshev.... 1,094,000
Leningrad, Gr.. 4,066,000
Lvov........ 579,000
Makeyevka..... 396,000
Minsk........ 996,000
*Moscow, Gr.... 7,300,000
Novokuznetsk... 508,000
Novosibirsk.... 1,199,000
Odessa....... 941,000
Omsk........ 876,000
Perm........ 881,000
Riga........ 755,000
Rostov....... 823,000
Saratov....... 790,000
Sverdlovsk.... 1,073,000
Tashkent...... 1,461,000
Tbilisi....... 927,000
Ufa........ 821,000
Vladivostok.... 472,000
Volgograd..... 852,000
Voronezh..... 693,000
Yaroslavl..... 538,000
Zaporozh'ye... 697,000
United Arab Emirates
*Abu Dhabi..... 55,000
Dubai....... 66,000
United Kingdom
England
Birmingham... 1,013,366
Bristol....... 426,170
Coventry..... 334,839
Leeds........ 501,080
Leicester..... 283,549
Liverpool...... 606,834
*London, Gr.... 7,418,020
Manchester..... 542,430
Newcastle..... 222,153
Nottingham..... 299,758
Sheffield..... 519,703
Wales
*Cardiff....... 278,221
Swansea...... 172,566
Scotland
Aberdeen..... 186,006
Dundee...... 182,084
*Edinburgh..... 453,422
Glasgow...... 896,958
Northern Ireland
*Belfast....... 360,150
Londonderry.... 53,744
Upper Volta
*Ouagadougou.... 110,000
Uruguay
*Montevideo.... 1,202,757
Venezuela
Barquisimeto.... 330,815
*Caracas, Gr.... 2,500,000
Maracaibo..... 650,002
Valencia...... 366,154
Vietnam
Danang....... 492,194
Haiphong..... 182,490
*Hanoi....... 414,620
Hue........ 209,043
Saigon....... 1,825,297
Western Samoa
*Apia, Gr....... 30,593
Yemen
*Sana....... 120,000
Yemen, Southern
Aden, Gr....... 285,373
Yugoslavia
Belgrade...... 800,000
Sarajevo..... 244,000
Skopje....... 313,000
Zagreb....... 566,000
Zaire
*Kinshasa..... 2,008,352
Kananga..... 601,239
Lubumbashi.... 403,623
Luluabourg.... 506,033
Zambia
*Lusaka, Gr..... 415,000

NORTH AMERICAN CITIES

Their History, Business and Industry, Educational Facilities, Cultural Advantages, Tourist Attractions and Transportation

Akron, Ohio

The World Almanac is sponsored in the Akron area by the Akron Beacon Journal, 44 E. Exchange St., Akron, OH. 44328, (216) 375-8111, a Knight-Ridder newspaper; founded 1809; circulation 169,433 daily, 217,814 Sunday; John S. Knight, editor emeritus; William Ott, president and publisher; Mark Ethridge, editor and vice president.

Population: 267,600 (city); 696,010 (metro) 5th in state; total employed, 272,500; 1975 average metro household buying income, $15,500.

Area: 56 sq. mi. (city), 413 sq. mi. (metro) on Ohio Canal 30 mi. south of Lake Erie; founded 1825; Summit County seat.

Industry: approx. $2 billion value added by Akron area mfg. industry in 1975; home plants of Firestone, Goodyear, Goodrich, General and many smaller rubber firms employ 33,100, use 40% of entire world rubber supply; other products mfd. in area include auto bodies, salt, clay, matches, rubber toys, road building equipment, missile components.

Transportation: Akron-Canton Airport served by 3 major carriers; Akron Muni Airport; Conrail covers 9 former private rail and trunk lines; birthplace of trucking industry, served by 70 common and 50 contract carriers; metro transit system; Greyhound and Continental Trailways; city bisected east-west and north-south by interstate highway systems.

Communications: 5 TV, one cablevision, and 5 radio stations; 2 public broadcast TV outlets.

New construction: $13 million Northeastern Ohio Universities College of Medicine; $16 million Ohio Edison Co. headquarters; total of $127.2 million in new construction started in 1975.

Federal facilities: new $17 million downtown federal office bldg.; Army Reserve Center; Navy-Marine Reserve Center.

Medical facilities: major hospitals including specialized children's treatment center; State of Ohio Fallsview Mental Health Center.

Education: University of Akron and School of Law; Kent State University; Firestone Conservatory of Music.

Sports: NBA Cleveland Cavaliers and WTT Nets play in nearby Richmond Township Coliseum; Firestone Country Club, home of the World Series of Golf, American Golf Classic, and site of the 1975 PGA championship; 35,000-seat Akron Rubber Bowl; Derby Downs, home of the All-American Soap Box Derby.

Cultural attractions: E. J. Thomas Performing Arts Center; Blossom Music Center; Stan Hywet mansion; Akron Art Institute; Akron Symphony Orchestra. **Other attractions:** Children's Zoo; John Brown Home; Simon Perkins Mansion; Railway Museum.

Accommodations: Nearly 2,500 Class A hotel and motel rooms in the metro area.

Further information: Akron Regional Development Board, Delaware Bldg., or Akron Convention Bureau, 1 Cascade Plaza, both Akron, Ohio 44308.

Albany, New York

The World Almanac is sponsored in the Albany-Schenectady-Troy area by The Times-Union and Knickerbocker News-Union Star, 645 Albany-Shaker Road, Albany, N.Y. 12201; (518) 453-5454; Times-Union founded 1856; Knickerbocker News 1843; Union-Star 1855; circulation Times-Union (morn) 77,289, Sunday Times-Union 135,-946, Knickerbocker News-Union Star (aft) 63,811, publisher Robert J. Danzig.

Population: 115,781 (city), 286,742 (county); total employed 99,047.

Area: 19.6 sq. mi. on west bank of Hudson River, 150 miles north of New York City; state capital and Albany County seat.

Industry: chief products are felts, woolen goods, meat products, paper products, iron and brass castings, drugs and medicines; 295 manufacturing firms.

Commerce: 5 savings banks, 9 commercial banks.

Transportation: 2 major freight lines; 4 airlines at Albany County Airport; New York State Thruway, Adirondack Northway; Port of Albany.

Communications: 4 TV and 11 radio stations.

Medical facilities: 5 major hospital complexes including a Veteran's Administration installation.

Cultural facilities: Albany Symphony Orchestra, art museum, 90 church buildings, city libraries.

Educational facilities: Albany Law School, Albany College of Pharmacy, Albany Medical College, the State University of New York at Albany, Siena College, Saint Rose College, Albany Junior College, and Maria College; 24 elementary schools, 1 senior high school, 25 private and parochial schools.

New construction: Albany is completing a major revamping of its downtown area. The $1-billion South Mall includes a 44-story state office tower, 4 large state agency buildings, as well as cultural buildings.

Recreational facilities: municipal golf course, private clubs, 2 large city parks with tennis, baseball, swimming facilities.

Other attractions: Dudley Observatory, Fort Crailo in Rensselaer, Joseph Henry Memorial Building, Ten Broeck Mansion, First Church in Albany (Reformed), Schuyler Mansion, State Capitol.

Government: 2d only to Washington, Albany is the most important governmental city in the U.S.; home city of the governor, state officials and 30,000 state employees.

History: founded 1609 when Henry Hudson terminated his voyage in the Half Moon at the location where Albany was later settled by the Dutch.

Further information: Albany Chamber of Commerce, 508 Broadway, Albany, N.Y. 12207.

Albuquerque, New Mexico

The World Almanac is sponsored in the Albuquerque area by the Albuquerque Tribune, 701 Silver Ave. SW, Albuquerque, N.M. 87103; (505) 842-2300; founded June 22, 1922, by Carl Magee; a Scripps-Howard Newspaper since Sept. 24, 1923; circulation 41,450; editor Ralph Looney; sponsors Tribune Annual Spelling Bee.

Population: 286,300 (city), 361,400 (metro area); first in state, 58th in nation; total employed, 159,200.

Area: 81 sq. mi. on Rio Grande and U.S. 66. Bernalillo County seat.

Industry: electronics with GTE-Lenkurt, Gulton, Sparton Sandia Laboratories, General Electric; clothing with Levi Strauss, Pioneer Wear; movie production center.

Commerce: retail sales $1.35 billion; per capita income $4,374; bank resources $1.39 billion in 10 banks.

Transportation: Santa Fe Railway, Amtrak; Continental Trailways, and Greyhound bus lines; Albuquerque Intl. Airport, hub for 7 airlines, average 594 air movements daily.

Communications: 4 TV and 18 radio stations.

Federal facilities: Kirtland AFB, Air Force Special Weapons Center, Air Force Weapons Laboratory; Bureau of Indian Affairs, Forest Service, Social Security.

Medical facilities: 9 major hospitals.

Cultural facilities: symphony orchestra, 26 art galleries, 5 museums, 8 library branches.

Educational facilities: Univ. of N.M., Univ. of Albuquerque, 117 public schools.

Recreational facilities: Sandia Peak ski area with longest tramway in North America; 80 city parks, 16 swimming pools, 9 golf courses, 83 tennis courts; Cibola National Forest; Rio Grande Zoo.

Convention facilities: $9.2 million convention center with underground parking facility and 300-room hotel; 118 motels and hotels.

Sports: Dukes AAA baseball, Chaparrals hockey.

History: founded Feb. 7, 1706; named for Duke of Albuquerque, viceroy of New Spain.

Further information: Chamber of Commerce, 401 Second NW, Albuquerque, NM.

Allentown, Pennsylvania

The World Almanac is sponsored in the Allentown-Bethlehem-Easton area by Call-Chronicle Newspapers, 101 N. 6th St., Allentown, 18105; (215) 433-4241; Call founded 1883, daily circulation 101,000, Sunday 151,000; Chronicle founded 1870, circulation 21,000; publisher Donald P. Miller, executive editor Edward D. Miller; sponsors Park & Shop, housing development, newspaper-in-the-classroom, newsprint recycling.

Population: Allentown 109,871; Bethlehem 72,686; Easton 30,256; metro area 543,620, 3d in state; total employed 229,934.

Area: 5,000 sq. mi. (metro) in eastern Pa. at Lehigh and Delaware rivers; Lehigh County seat.

Industry: Bethlehem Steel Corp., 2d largest in U.S.; home offices for Mack Truck Inc., Air Products & Chemicals, New Jersey Zinc Co., Allen Products (ALPO); area leads in textile production; transistor developed in Western Electric here.

Commerce: retail center for east-central Pa.; retail sales (1975) $1.6 billion; average family buying power $14,090.

Transportation: 4 major rail lines, 5 bus lines; 9 federal and state highways intersect area; jet airport averages 335 movements per day on 6 airlines.

Communications: 3 TV and 12 radio stations.

Medical facilities: 6 major hospitals.

Cultural facilities: Allentown Art Museum (including Kress Renaissance and Baroque collection), Bethlehem Bach Choir, Allentown Symphony, 7 theater

groups (plus 4 summer); Allentown Band is oldest continuing concert band in U.S.; 10 colleges including Lehigh Univ., Muhlenberg, Cedar Crest, and Lafayette serve 12,000 students.

Other attractions: center of "Pennsylvania Dutch" area, covered bridges; 1,400-acre park system; 1,170-acre game preserve, pre-Cambrian mountain range, access to Appalachian Trail, many historic houses, Allentown Fair, folk festivals, Liberty Bell Shrine.

Sports: fishing, small game hunting, auto racing at Pocono Raceway, Allentown Jets basketball, Olympic bicycle racing.

History: settled in 1600s by Germans seeking religious freedom; Allentown founded 1762; hiding place for Liberty Bell during Revolutionary War; GAR founded Flag Day here 1906; Allentown one of 5 First Defender Companies in Civil War.

Further information: Chambers of Commerce in Allentown: 462 Walnut St. 18105; Bethlehem: 11 W. Market St. 18018; Easton: 157 S. 4th St. 18042.

Amarillo, Texas

The World Almanac is sponsored in the Amarillo area by the Amarillo Globe-News, 900 S. Harrison, Amarillo, Tex., 79166, (806) 376-4488; a division of Southwestern Newspapers Corp., and publisher of Daily News, Globe-Times and Sunday News-Globe; daily circulation, 75,249; Sunday 69,585; James L. Whyte, vice president and general manager; Jerry Huff, executive editor.

Population: 145,790 city; 165,425 metro area; 11th in state; total employed 78,440.

Area: 68.98 sq. mi. in central panhandle of Texas at junction of Interstates 40 and 27 in Potter and Randall counties. Potter County seat.

Industry: 3-state hub of $8 billion agribusiness market including wheat, beef and produce, value $25 million; ASARCO, Inc., copper refinery; Santa Fe rail welding plant; Bell Helicopter, Levi Strauss, Iowa Beef Processors, oil and gas, and coal-burning elec-

tricity plants.

Commerce: wholesale-retail center for 5-state area; retail sales $550 million 1975; bank resources $751.3 million, 5 banks, 5 savings and loan associations; 104th in wholesale sales ($800 million) among 230 metro areas.

Transportation: served by 5 airlines; 3 railroads, 4 bus lines, 23 truck lines; 2 interstate, 4 federal and one state highway intersect Amarillo.

Communications: 4 TV, 9 radio stations.
Medical: 5 hospitals including VA facilities in metro area; mental health centers.
Culture, recreation: Amarillo Symphony; Fine Arts complex; Civic Center complex; summer musical, "Texas"; regional history museum; Discovery Center; 46 parks, 3 colleges.

Sports: drag racing, college and high school football, basketball, hockey, Gold Sox baseball.
History: settled 1887 as railroad crew camp, incorporated 1892; named for yellow lake clay.
Further information: Amarillo Chamber of Commerce, Amarillo Bldg., 301 Polk, Amarillo, Tex. 79101.

Anchorage, Alaska

The World Almanac is sponsored in the Anchorage area by the Anchorage Daily Times, 820 W. 4th Avenue, Anchorage, AK 99510; (907) 279-5622; founded 1915; circulation 47,000; editor-publisher Robert B. Atwood; sponsors Spelling Bee, Kodak Photo Contest.

Population: city, borough unified in 1975. Total population of new municipality is 200,000 (1976), half of state's population.
Area: 927 sq. mi. (census district), at head of Cook Inlet on south central coast.

Industry and commerce: business center for most of Alaska; aviation, oil companies, railroading, shipping, and national defense activities are largest elements in area's economy; headquarters for construction of $7 billion trans-Alaska oil pipeline.

Transportation: Anchorage International Airport is major refueling stop on transpolar flights; thousands of small planes make city one of country's busiest air traffic centers with 5 airports and 25% of world's seaplanes in area; headquarters of Alaska Railroad; $10 million port.
Communications: 4 TV and 8 radio stations; 2 daily newspapers.
Medical facilities: 5 hospitals.

Cultural facilities: annual Festival of Music; 4 theater groups; fine arts museum; community concert organization, opera company, civic symphony.
Educational facilities: 57 elementary and secondary schools enroll 36,000; Univ. of Alaska, Alaska Methodist Univ.
Recreation: 2 major ski areas; cross-country skiing and bicycling; annual Fur Rendezvous with dogsled races; Iditarod dogsled race to Nome; Chugach National Forest.
Convention facilities: 5 major hotels and motels offer facilities for over 1,000 persons.
History: founded 1915 as headquarters for Alaska Railroad; twice winner of All America city award, for coping with rapid growth, and for swift recovery from catastrophic 1964 earthquake.
Further information: Chamber of Commerce, 612 F St., Anchorage, AK. 99501.

Atlanta, Georgia

Population: 477,100 (city), 1,791,400 (metro), first in state, 18th in nation; total employed, 734,800 (metro).
Area: 136 sq. mi. in north central Georgia, on Piedmont plateau of Blue Ridge foothills, 1,050 ft. above sea level; 4,326 sq. mi. in 15-county metro area.
Industry: 2,200 manufacturers produce more than 3,500 commodities; 432 of Fortune 500 firms operate in Atlanta; Ford assembly plant, 2 GM assembly plants, Lockheed-Ga. Co.; home base for Coca-Cola, Fuqua Ind., Delta Air Lines, Equifax, Scripto, Genuine Parts.
Commerce: financial, retail, wholesale center of Southeast; massive Merchandise Mart; 6th Federal Reserve District hdqtrs.; 78 banks, 294 branches with resources of $6.2 billion (metro); 22 savings and loan associations with assets of $3.5 billion (1975).
Transportation: founded as railroad center, now served by 6 lines of 2 systems; Greyhound and Trailways bus terminals used by 3 companies with 250 buses in and out daily; 9 passenger airlines, 2 commuter carriers, one freight-only carrier; more than 1,100 scheduled flights daily; non-stop passenger service to 99 cities from Hartsfield International Airport, 25 million passengers (1975); rapid transit system under construction for 52.9 mi. rapid rail, 8 mi. of rapid busways coordinated with street bus operations; 6 legs of 3 interstate highways intersect 100-acre downtown interchange; 63 mi. highway encircles city.
Communications: 7 TV stations; 33 radio stations;

Protestant Radio and TV Center; largest Bell system toll-free dialing area; one of nation's 5 TV and radio network control centers; 10 daily newspapers.
New construction: luxury hotels, indoor downtown amusement center, office towers, and parks; condominiums; total value 1975 city building permits $134.3 million.
Medical facilities: 55 hospitals (metro), VA hospital; National Center for Disease Control, National Cancer Center at Emory Univ. Medical School.
Federal facilities: 29,500 federal, non-military employees; Ft. McPherson, hdqtrs. U.S. Army Forces Command; Ft. Gillem; Dobbins AFB; NAS Atlanta.
Cultural facilities: Memorial Arts Center with museum, symphony orchestra, ballet, School of Art; Civic Center with auditorium-theater-exhibition hall; 24 degree-granting schools including Ga. Tech., Ga. State Univ., Emory Univ., Atlanta Univ.
Sports: NBA Hawks; NFL Falcons; NL Braves; NHL Flames; stadium seats 52,000, Omni arena, 16,500.
Convention facilities: 545,000 delegates attended 700 conventions in 1975; Ga. World Congress Center with largest single display room in U.S., equal to 8 football fields; 20,000 hotel rooms with 10,000 to be added within next 5 years.
History: named 1845, chartered 1847; burned by Gen. Wm. Sherman 1864.
Further information: Chamber of Commerce, 1300 Commerce Building, Atlanta, Ga. 30303.

Augusta, Georgia

The World Almanac is sponsored in the Augusta area by The Chronicle-Herald, 725 Broad St., 30903; (404) 724-0851; Chronicle established in 1785, circulation 50,000; Herald 20,000; Sunday, 72,000; William S. Morris III publisher, E.B. Skinner general manager, L.C. Harris editor, David L. Playford managing editor, Herald; W.H. Eanes managing editor, Chronicle.

Population: 55,600 (city), 277,200 (metro area); total employed, 101,300 (metro).
Area: 1,713 sq. mi. (metro: Richmond, Columbia

counties, Ga.; Aiken County, S.C.) straddling Savannah River; Augusta County seat.
Industry: diversified; Continental Can, Du Pont,

Procter & Gamble, Lily-Tulip, Olin, Dymo, Monsanto.

Commerce: wholesale, retail center of 17 counties in 2 states; 1975 retail sales, $697.9 million; per capita income, $3,638; per family income, $12,178; effective buying income, $1.008 billion; 4 banks, 3 savings-loan assns.; distribution center.

Transportation: 5 railroads, 26 truck lines, 3 airlines at modern airport and in-city field for executive planes; Interstate 20, other federal highways; river shipping.

Communications: 3 TV and 10 radio stations.

Medical facilities: 5 major hospitals, including Eisen-hower Memorial at Ft. Gordon, Medical College of Georgia.

Federal facilities: Ft. Gordon and Savannah River (AEC) Plant.

Cultural facilities: Augusta College, Paine College; museum, art gallery, arts council with 25 affiliates.

Recreational facilities: hunting, fishing, boating, camping; 7 golf courses; home of Masters Golf Tournament.

History: founded as fort 1717; named for wife of Prince of Wales 1735; capital of Georgia, 1778.

Further information: Chamber of Commerce of Greater Augusta, 624 Greene St., Augusta, Ga. 30902.

Austin, Texas

The World Almanac is sponsored in the Austin area by The Austin American-Statesman, 308 Guadalupe St., Austin, Texas, 78701; (512) 476-2661; Statesman founded 1871; American 1914; combined 1924; published by Newspapers, Inc.; circulation, American-Statesman (morn.) 73,630. American-Statesman (aft.) 39,770. American-Statesman (Sunday) 116,360. The Austin American-Statesman, a division of Texas Newspapers Inc. Jim Fain publisher, Bill Meroney general manager, Ray Mariotti editor.

Population: 283,700 (city), 334,000 (metro area), 6th in state, 56th in nation; total employed 158,500.

Area: 91 sq. mi. in mid-Texas on Colorado River.

Industry: electronics — Texas Instruments, IBM, Motorola, Tracor; Glastron (Conroy) boats, Westinghouse Electric; county has 360 manufacturing firms.

Commerce: wholesale, retail center for 10 counties (750,000 pop.) in triangle of Dallas-Fort Worth, San Antonio, Houston; retail sales (1972) $616 million; bank assets $1.4 billion in 14 banks; 7 savings associations with assets $442 million; 33 insurance home offices.

Transportation: 3 airlines; 3 railroads, Amtrak; 4 bus lines; 13 motor freight carriers; U.S. Interstate 35, State 71, 79, 183, 290.

Communications: 4 TV and cable, 12 radio stations.

Medical facilities: 7 hospitals, 1,032 beds; 389 physicians; 174 dentists.

Federal facilities: Bergstrom AFB; Internal Revenue Service center with 3,300 employees.

Cultural facilities: University of Texas System & UT at Austin; Lyndon Baines Johnson Library dedicated 1971; other libraries; Texas Memorial & Art Museums; 85,000-seat stadium; law and other graduate schools; 4 small colleges. O. Henry Home, Laguna Gloria, Elizabet Ney & French Legation museums; 4 local theater companies, Austin Symphony, 2 ballet companies. City library, branches and mobile service. Austin public school district, 76 schools, 55,000 students.

State facilities: Capitol and office building complex; 5 special schools for handicapped; psychiatric hospital, 36,578 employes.

Convention facilities: city center seats 5,000.

Recreational facilities: 2 lakes; 7,000 acres of parks, pools, 6 golf courses, tennis courts; 3 annual fiestas: Aqua (motor boat racing), Laguna Gloria, and Highland Lakes arts and crafts.

Further information: Chamber of Commerce, 901 W. Riverside Dr., Austin, Texas 78701.

Bakersfield, California

The World Almanac is sponsored in the Bakersfield and Kern County area by The Bakersfield Californian (eves. and Sunday), 1707 Eye Street, Bakersfield, Cal. 93302, phone 805-323-7631; founded 1866 as Havilah Courier, christened The Bakersfield Californian 1897; circulation 57,941 daily, 64,423 Sunday; president Berenice Fritts Koerber, publisher Donald H. Fritts, executive director Alfred T. Fritts, managing editor James E. Griffith.

Population: 76,400 city, 193,200 metro, 348,700 Kern County.

Area: approximately 8,060 square miles in Kern County of which Bakersfield is county seat, in California's San Joaquin Valley.

Industry: oil, gas, agriculture, military; oil valuation $535 million; total agriculture production $744.3 million; Edwards AFB and China Lake Naval Test Station in eastern Kern County.

Commerce: retail sales in Kern $1.217 billion; total bank deposits $860 million.

Transportation: 2 railroads, 3 airlines, 2 bus lines, Interstate 5, Highway 99.

Communications: 3 TV and 8 radio stations.

Cultural facilities: symphony orchestra, Cunningham Art Gallery; 4-year state college, city college; community theater.

History: Kern County organized April 2, 1866, from portions of Los Angeles and Tulare counties; discovery of gold on Kern River in 1851 brought influx of settlers; oil discovered in 1865, with major boom in 1909; gold mining town of Havilah first county seat, moved to Bakersfield in 1875.

Baltimore, Maryland

The World Almanac is sponsored in the Baltimore area by the Baltimore News American, 301 E. Lombard St., Baltimore, Md. 21203; (301) 752-1212; founded in 1773 as the Maryland Journal and Baltimore Advertiser; Baltimore American founded 1799; Baltimore Evening News founded 1872; adopted present name 1964; daily circulation, 199,247; Sunday 272,182; publisher Mark F. Collins; general manager Roy W. Anderson; executive editor Thomas J. White; American Medical Association Award, Howard W. Blakeslee and Albert Lasker Award; sponsors I am An American Day Parade.

Population: __45,050 (city), 2,120,540 (metro), first in state, 7th in U.S; total employment 305,150 (city), 854,765 (metro).

Area: 91 sq. mi. (city), 2,225 sq. mi. (metro); on Patapsco River, a tributary of Chesapeake Bay.

Industry: highly diversified, none dominating; most important are steel fabricating, shipbuilding, and repairing; manufacture of electrical equipment and food containers; food processing, sugar, petroleum, chemicals, copper; added value of manufacturing in 1975 was $3.8 billion.

Commerce: metro area consists of city and 5 adjacent counties; estimated buying income $4,182 per capita; retail sales about $5 billion in 1975, ranked 16th in metro areas nationally; area has 209 shopping centers with 3,591 stores; home ownership 57%.

Transportation: 3 railroads including Amtrak; Baltimore-Washington International Airport, used by 12 lines, served 2,773,400 passengers in 1975; 150 certified truck lines; tunnel carries motor traffic through city under the harbor; buses operated by state authority carry 410,000 passengers daily.

Port facilities: 120 steamship lines serve port, the nation's 4th largest and the farthest inland on the Atlantic Coast; in 1975, 4,193 ships moved 41 million short tons of international cargo; port was 2d largest container cargo port on the Atlantic and Gulf Coasts; leading cargos are petroleum products, ores, grain, coal, bananas, automobiles.

Communications: 3 daily newspapers in city, 2 more in metro area; 3 VHF TV stations, 2 UHF public broadcast stations; 25 radio stations.

Cultural facilities: Enoch Pratt Free Library with 31 agencies and 2.2 million volumes; metro county libraries have 28 branches; Baltimore Symphony Orchestra; Maryland Ballet Co.; Baltimore Opera Co.; Baltimore Museum Of Arts, Walters Art Gallery, Peale Museum, Carroll Mansion, Md. Academy of Sciences, Morris A. Mechanic Theater, and Center Stage.

Educational facilities: 30 colleges and 9 junior colleges, including Johns Hopkins Univ. and medical institutions, Univ. of Md. (downtown and county campuses), Loyola, Goucher, and Towson State colleges, Morgan State Univ.; Peabody Conservatory of Music;

Md. Inst. College of Art; St. Mary's Seminary and Univ.; Ner Israel Rabbinical College.

Medical facilities: 26 general hospitals, with 8,664 beds in metro area, including the renowned Johns Hopkins and the Univ. of Md. and its Institute for Emergency Medicine.

Sports: Memorial Stadium, home of football Colts and baseball Orioles; horse racing, including Preakness at Pimlico, and the International Race at Laurel; Bowie and Timonium tracks nearby. Chesapeake Bay's 1,700 sq. mi. of open water are noted for fishing, boating, and waterfowl hunting; ocean and ski resorts within 3-hour drive.

Convention facilities: Civic Center, 45 meeting rooms, 87,160 sq. ft. of exhibition space; 7 hotels downtown and over 100 motels in or near the city.

Other attractions: Fort McHenry Historic Shrine where Francis Scott Key wrote "The Star Spangled Banner;" U.S. frigate Constellation; the Flag House; Baltimore and Ohio Transportation Museum; Edgar Allan Poe's home and grave; Babe Ruth's home; annual Preakness Festival Week in May; Mother Seton House. Most of the central business district rebuilt in last 15 years; Inner Harbor project will provide World Trade Center, Academy of Science Building, restoration of early 19th century rowhouses, a floating restaurant, a marina, an aquarium, and new hotels. Many old neighborhoods are experiencing a revival with early townhouses being preserved.

History: founded 1729 by act of the Provincial Assembly of the Maryland Colony which was established by members of the Calvert family, the Lords of Baltimore; early economy based on shipment of tobacco, grain, flour, and on shipbuilding; privateering in the War of 1812 tempted British to try to capture the American "nest of pirates." When economic growth was threatened by completion of the Erie Canal, the city's business leaders countered by building the nation's first railroad, the Baltimore and Ohio.

Further information: Chamber of Commerce Metro Baltimore, 22 Light St., Baltimore Promotion Council, 102 St. Paul St., 21202.

Baton Rouge, Louisiana

The World Almanac is sponsored in the Baton Rouge area by the Morning Advocate and State-Times, 525 Lafayette St., B.R., La. 70821; (504) 383-1111; founded 1842; combined daily circ., 112,000; Sunday, 104,000; pres., Charles P. Manship Jr.; Publisher, Douglas L. Manship; Director of news and production, Richard Palmer; bus. mgr., Charles Garvey; executive editor, all newspapers, Jim Hughes; managing editors, Edwin Price Jr. (Morning Advocate), Jack Lord (State-Times).

Population: 165,963 (city), 392,400 (metro); total 1974 city-parish employment, 168,475.

Area: city, 42.83 sq. mi.; parish, 407.01 sq. mi.; on east bank of Mississippi River, 80 mi. northeast of New Orleans; state capitol, East Baton Rouge Parish seat.

Industry: northern anchor of 100-mi. long petrochemical complex along Mississippi River.

Commerce: marketing center for major trade area of 400,000; bank resources, $1.6 billion; 6 banks, 7 savings and loan associations.

Transportation: major transfer point on southern federal interstate system; 2 airports with 4 airlines; 2 bus lines; 4 railroad trunk lines; Port of Baton Rouge handled over 55 million tons in 1974.

Communications: 4 TV and 9 radio stations.

Cultural facilities: 6 museums, 4 theaters, symphony, planetarium, 5 art galleries.

Educational facilities: Louisiana State Univ., founded

1860, center of 8-campus system; Southern Univ., largest Negro land-grant college in U.S., center of 3-college system.

Sports: LSU Tigers and Southern Jaguars home stadia, football, basketball, track.

Other attractions: state capitol; city-parish zoo and arboretum; 67 parks; major recreational lakes.

History: first noted by French explorer Iberville in 1699, Baton Rouge (French: red stick) was already occupied by the Istrouma (also translates red stick) Indians; Louisiana's capital since 1836; government structure is a city-parish combination with a mayor-president and city-parish council.

Further information: Chamber of Commerce, P.O. Box 1868, Baton Rouge, 70821; Louisiana Tourist Commission, P.O. Box 44291, Capitol Station, Baton Rouge, 70804.

Billings, Montana

The World Almanac is sponsored in the Billings area by the Billings Gazette, 401 N. Broadway, Billings, Mont., 59101; telephone (406) 245-3071; founded 1885; member of Lee Enterprises, Inc., since 1960; circulation, daily 56,575; Sunday, 59,231; publisher George Remington, editor William N. Roesgen.

Population: 70,666 (city), 85,889 (metro area), first in state; total employed 41,800 (non-agri.).

Area: south central Montana on Yellowstone River, 125 mi. from Yellowstone Park, Yellowstone County seat.

Industry: 3 oil refineries, beet sugar refinery, 2 packing plants, 3d largest livestock auction yards in U.S., center for Northern Great Plains coal industry.

Commerce: wholesale-retail center for eastern Montana, northern Wyoming; retail sales (1974) $323 million; bank debits (1975) $4.9 billion; 6 banks, 2 savings and loan associations, 274 wholesale firms, 804 retail firms; per capita income $3,545.

Transportation: 3 airlines, one railroad, 2 bus lines, 98 motor carriers, Interstates 90 and 94.

Communications: 2 TV and 5 radio stations, one weekly, one daily newspaper.

Medical facilities: 2 hospitals, 400 beds, 11 clinics, 128 doctors, 40 dentists.

Cultural facilities: 3 art galleries, symphony orchestra, 2 western museums, studio theater, liberal arts college, business college, private (church-related) college, 2 nursing schools, voc.-tech. program; 30 public, 8 parochial schools.

New construction: $24 million shopping center, $10 million auditorium, $11 million hospital expansion, $6 million bank building.

Other attractions: big game hunting, fishing, boating, skiing, within hour's drive; 21 city parks, 3,200 hotel-motel rooms, convention facilities for 5,000.

History: founded 1882 with arrival of Northern Pacific Railroad; named after Frederic Billings, then NP president; now largest city in 500-mile radius.

Further information: Tourist Information Bureau, Billings Chamber of Commerce, P.O. Box 2519, Billings, 59103.

Binghamton, New York

The World Almanac is sponsored in the Binghamton area by The Evening Press and The Sunday Press, Vestal Parkway East, Binghamton, N.Y. 13902; (607) 798-1234; founded 1904; circulation daily 72,649, Sunday 75,280; president and publisher Robert R. Eckert, editor Laurence S. Hale, managing editor George R. Venizelos.

Population: 60,500 (city), 302,800 (metro area), 12th in state; total employed 114,200.

Area: 10.98 sq. mi. at junction of Chenango and Susquehanna rivers. Broome County seat.

Industry: GAF, second largest producer of film in country; computers, IBM; electronics & simulators, Singer Co.; shoes, Endicott Johnson Corp.; a major railroad center.

Commerce: wholesale-retail center of area producing $490 million a year; 5 banks; national headquarters of Security Mutual Life Insurance Co.

Transportation: 3 airlines, major being Allegheny, out of Broome County Airport; intersection Interstates 81 & 88 and Route 17; Erie-Lackawanna and Delaware and Hudson freight rail carriers.

Communications: 3 TV and 4 radio stations.

Medical facilities: 2 major hospitals.

Cultural facilities: Roberson Center Arts & Sciences; State Univ. at Binghamton; Broome County College; Tri-Cities Opera Co.; symphony orchestra; public library; civic theater.

Other attractions: municipal parks zoo; major state park on outskirts; new Veterans Memorial Arena.

Sports: Dusters pro-hockey team.

History: Settled 1800; became rail center by 1848, with roads replacing old Chenango Canal that fed Erie Canal; named for Philadelphia patriot and multi-millionaire William Bingham.

Birmingham, Alabama

The World Almanac is sponsored in the Birmingham area by The Birmingham Post-Herald, 2200 Fourth Ave., N. Birmingham, Ala. 35202; telephone (205) 325-2222; Post founded 1921 by Scripps-Howard Newspapers; Herald founded 1887; circulation, 75,630; editor Duard LeGrand, vice president W. H. Metz, managing editor George Cook; major public service projects include Goodfellow Christmas Fund, Alabama Favorite Teacher selection.

Population: 292,994 (city, 1974 est.), 641,900 (county, 1974 est.), employment 347,800 (1976, metro).

Area: 82 sq. mi. in north central Alabama; state's largest city; Jefferson County seat.

Industry: heavy manufacturing in metals; U.S. Steel is area's largest employer; U.S. Pipe and Foundry and American Cast Iron Pipe Co. are in top 10 employers; South Central Bell's 5-state headquarters located in city.

Commerce: wholesale-retail center for Alabama; retail sales, (1975) $3.319 billion; bank debits (1975) $61.1 billion; 13 banks (county); 6 bank holding companies; 7 savings and loan assns.

Transportation: 5 major rail freight lines, Amtrak; Greyhound and Continental Trailways bus lines; Eastern, Delta, United, and Southern air lines with modern airport terminal completed in 1973; 75 truck line terminals; 3 interstate highways, I-65, I-59 and I-20 all under construction.

Communications: 3 commercial TV stations, one PBS TV outlet, and 15 radio stations.

Medical facilities: Univ. of Alabama in Birmingham Medical Center covers 60 sq. blocks; heart surgery team brings patients from all over the world; Veterans Administration hospital, in same complex, is the base of organ transplant program; Baptist Medical

Centers have 2 major hospitals; 13 other hospitals.
Cultural facilities: symphony orchestra, Oscar Wells Museum of Art with more than $4 million in assets; Civic Opera; 4 resident civic theaters; 2 resident ballet companies.
Education: Samford Univ., Birmingham-Southern, Miles, and Daniel Payne colleges; Jefferson State and Lawson State Junior colleges.
Convention facilities: civic center with exhibition hall, theater, music hall, and coliseum; several new convention hotels and motels in civic center area.
Sports: Birmingham Bulls (WHA) moved from Toronto in '76; nicknamed "Football Capital of the South" for Univ. of Alabama and Auburn Univ. games played at municipal stadium, Legion Field.
Other attractions: world's 2d largest cast iron statue,

Vulcan, mythical god of the forge, overlooks Birmingham from Red Mountain as a symbol of the steel industry; Arlington Shrine, antebellum home that housed federal troops during Civil War; Botanical Gardens complex with Japanese Garden; Jimmie Morgan Zoo; extensive city park system.
History: chartered 1871; soon became known as the "Magic City" because of its rapid growth brought on by the presence of the 3 ingredients in steelmaking — coal, iron ore, and lime; mining died out in recent years and most iron ore is now imported by ship and barge to Birmingport on Warrior River from South America; coal mining, in decline since the 1940s, is on the upswing.
Further information: Chamber of Commerce, 1914 Sixth Ave. N., Birmingham, AL 35203.

Bismarck, North Dakota

The World Almanac is sponsored in western North Dakota by the Bismarck Tribune, 222 Fourth St., Bismarck, N.D., 58501; (701) 223-2500; founded 1873 as weekly, became daily 1881; circ. 27,600; publisher A. G. Sorlie, editor John O. Hjelle, advertising director J. Joe Miller; major awards include Pulitzer Prize Gold Medal, 1937.

Population: 38,123 (1975 census), 3d in state; total employed 19,280.
Area: 14 sq. mi. on Missouri River. State capital and Burleigh County seat.
Industry: agriculture, printing, trucking, farm machinery, state government, electric power, manufacturing, concrete products, railroad, insurance, livestock sales rings, lignite coal.
Commerce: retail trade area radius 100 miles, serving 150,000 people; retail sales (1975) $432 million; bank deposits (1975) $486 million; 5 banks, 5 building and loan associations.
Transportation: 2 rail lines, Amtrak; airport, hub for 3 airlines; 13 truck lines; 4 bus lines; U.S. Highways 18 and 83, I-94.
Communication: one daily newspaper; 3 AM, 2 FM radio stations; 2 TV stations.
New construction: 1975 building permits, $40 million (1,190 housing units).
Medical facilities: 2 hospitals, 450 bed capacity, served by 70 M.D.s.

Federal facilities: federal buildings house 20 offices; 14th Radar Bomb Scoring Detachment.
Cultural facilities: Bismarck Junior College; Mary College; 72,000-volume public library; state library; state museum; Elan Gallery; 45 churches.
Recreation: 20 parks with over 1,250 acres; indoor artificial ice arena; 3 golf courses; 5 swimming pools; playgrounds; tennis courts; YMCA; duck and goose hunting; fishing; nearby Fort Lincoln State Park.
Convention facilities: 8,000 seat Civic Center; 1,300 rooms; 5 banquet and meeting facilities for groups of 200-700.
Other attractions: Dakota Zoo; Garrison Dam; United Tribes of North Dakota Educational Technical Center; state capitol.
History: founded 1872 as Edwinton, a rail town; name changed to Bismarck in 1873 to encourage German investment capital.
Further information: Chamber of Commerce, 412 Sixth St., Bismarck, N.D., 58501.

Bloomington, Illinois

The World Almanac is sponsored in Bloomington-Normal and central Illinois by The Daily Pantagraph, 301 W. Washington St., Bloomington, Ill. 61701; (309) 829-9411; founded 1837 by Jesse W. Fell; circulation 51,747; president and publisher Davis U. Merwin; editor Harold Liston; general manager William Diesel; managing editor Gene Smedley.

Population: 77,367 Bloomington-Normal, 114,192 (metro area) McLean County; mid-way between Chicago and St. Louis in central Illinois.
Industry: over 50 industries in county, ranks 9th in insurance cities in U.S., home offices of State Farm, Country Companies, Union Auto; uniform diversity of non-agricultural employment in all major work force areas; leads nation in corn and soybean production with 2,316 farms in county.
Commerce: 1975 metro retail sales $312.9 million; per household income $15,535; per household retail sales, $8,192.
Transportation: new terminal at B-N Airport, 3 bus lines, 6 federal and state highways, 4 railroads, Am-

trak, 35 interstate and 23 intrastate motor carriers, Ozark Airlines.
Communications: 6 radio stations.
Medical facilities: 3 hospitals; Watson-Gailey Foundation Eye Bank.
Cultural facilities: Illinois Wesleyan Univ., 1,650, in Bloomington; Illinois State Univ., 20,500, in Normal; 49 churches; home of American Passion Play; B-N Symphony, community players, amateur musical.
History: incorporated 1850; site of A. Lincoln's "Lost Speech" and David Davis mansion, state historical shrine; city's Stevenson family has produced 3 generations of leadership; vice president Adlai E.; governor, presidential candidate and UN Ambassador,

Adlai E. II; and U.S. Senator Adlai E. III.
Further information: Association of Commerce and

Industry of McLean County, 210 S. East St., Bloomington, Ill. 61701.

Boise, Idaho

The World Almanac is sponsored in the Boise area by the Idaho Statesman, 1200 N. Curtis Road, Boise, Idaho 83704; (208) 376-2121; founded 1864 as Tri-Weekly; daily circulation 60,282; Sunday 68,764; publisher Robert B. Miller Jr., general manager C. Ralph Guilieri, managing editor Gary L. Watson; a Gannett newspaper.

Population: 86,800 (city), 120,200 (metro area), first in state, 224th in nation; total employed 76,848.
Area: 1,054 sq. mi. on Boise River at foot of Salmon River Mountains. State capital and Ada County seat.
Industry: mobile home and recreational trailers produced $225 million in 1975; world headquarters Boise Cascade Corp., Morrison-Knudsen Co., and Albertson Food Stores.
Commerce: wholesale and retail center for southwest Idaho; retail sales $353.6 million (1975); bank resources $6,980 million in 5 banks with 24 branches; 4 savings and loan associations, and 7 insurance company offices.
Transportation: 2 major airlines, 2 feeder airlines, one rail freight line, 4 bus lines, 17 common carrier truck lines.

Communications: 4 TV and 9 radio stations.
Medical facilities: 3 major hospital complexes including a Veteran's Administration facility.
Cultural facilities: Boise Philharmonic Orchestra, art gallery, state museum, Boise Little Theatre, new $1.4 million public library, Boise State University.
Other attractions: 33 parks, Southwestern Idaho Fairgrounds, 2 major recreational lakes, scenic mountain areas; Bogus Basin ski resort offers one of the world's longest illuminated ski runs.
History: founded 1863; name derived from "les bois" (the trees), a description for area used by French fur trappers in 1811.
Further information: Boise Chamber of Commerce, P. O. Box 2368, or Department of Commerce & Development, Idaho Statehouse, both Boise, Idaho 83701.

Boston, Massachusetts

The World Almanac is sponsored in the Boston area by The Boston Herald American, 300 Harrison Avenue, Boston, Mass. 02106; (617) 426-3000. Herald American established 1972; daily circulation 13,076; Sunday (Herald Advertiser) 456,007. Publisher Robert C. Bergenheim, executive editor Sam Bornstein, general manager Dennis Mulligan. Pulitzer prize, Sigma Delta Chi distinguished service awards, Heywood Broun award, AP first place, 3 UPI first places, World Press Photo award.

Population: 641,071 (city); 2,899,401 (metro area of 92 cities and towns around Boston); 5th largest metro area in nation; total employed, 266,505.
Area: 50 sq. mi. on Massachusetts Bay; state capital and Suffolk County seat.
Commerce: northeast center for finance and insurance; home for 50 insurance companies and regional hqs. for most U.S. and foreign companies; banking center for New England with total deposits of $12.264 billion (1972); birthplace of mutual fund, accounts for 35% of the nation's mutual fund holdings; retail center for northern New England; median family income $8,133 (city), $11,449 (metro); major electronics industry and publishing center.
Transportation: terminating point for 2 railroads, Penn Central and Boston & Maine; Logan International Airport, operated by Mass. Port Authority, terminal for 38 scheduled airlines, including 10 commuter lines, 8th busiest in world, served 10 million passengers in 1974; Volpe International terminal; 5 interstate highways.
Communications: 2 newspapers, 7 TV and 31 radio stations.
New construction: John Hancock Tower; Blue Cross-Blue Shield, Mass. Hqs.; Stone & Webster Engineering Hqs.; Federal Reserve Tower; Faneuil Hall Market Area; National Shawmut Bank; West End residential-office complex, Atlantic Ave. waterfront.
Medical facilities: health care is Boston's largest industry in terms of dollars invested; major institutions: Mass. General, Children's & New England medical centers; Boston City, Beth Israel, Deaconess hospitals; Harvard, Boston Univ., and Tufts medical schools; Lahey Clinic.
Federal facilities: 50 federal agencies employ 45,700 (military-facilities not included.)
Cultural facilities: the "Athens of America"; Boston Public Library includes capacity for 500,000 books on

open shelf, plus large lecture hall; Boston Symphony Orchestra; Boston Pops; opera company; Boston Ballet; Museum of Fine Art; Museum of Science and Hayden Planetarium; New England Aquarium; Isabella Stewart Gardner Museum; Museum of Transportation; Children's Museum.
Educational facilities: 16 degree-granting institutions in the city and 47 in the metro area, including Harvard, Boston College, Boston Univ., Tufts, M.I.T., Brandeis, Univ. of Mass., Suffolk, Emmanuel, Simmons, and Wentworth Inst.
Recreation: 2,327 acres of city recreation area, includes historic Boston Common and Public Garden; Metropolitan District Commission provides extensive facilities, including beaches and harbor islands.
Convention facilities: 49 hotels equipped to handle conventions; exhibition halls include Commonwealth Pier Exhibition Hall with 168,000 sq. ft. and John B. Hynes Veterans Auditorium in Prudential Center with 154,000 sq. ft. and auditorium seating 5,800.
Sports: pro teams include Red Sox (baseball), Celtics (basketball), New England Patriots (football), Bruins (hockey), Astros and Minutemen (soccer), and Lobsters (tennis).
Other attractions: "The Freedom Trail," a 1 1/2-mile walk through historic Boston; Beacon Hill and Back Bay historical districts; U.S.S. Constitution, "Old Ironsides," oldest commissioned ship in U.S. Navy; reconstruction of Boston Tea Party ship, the "Beaver."
Nicknames: The Hub (of the Universe), Bean Town.
History: capital city of commonwealth, founded 1630; from 1770, Boston was scene of many events leading to American Revolution, including Boston Tea Party on Dec. 16, 1773; incorporated Feb. 23, 1822.
Further information: Boston Chamber of Commerce, 125 High St., Boston, Mass.

Bridgeport, Connecticut

The World Almanac is sponsored in the Bridgeport area by The Bridgeport Post (evening), The Bridgeport Telegram (morning), and The Bridgeport Sunday Post, published by The Post Publishing Co., 410 State Street, Bridgeport, Conn. 06602; (203) 333-0161; circulation Post, 77,264, Telegram, 12,131, Sunday Post, 90,907; John E. Pfriem president and general manager, Leonard E. Gilbert managing editor.

Population: 152,000 (State Health Dept. estimate 1975), 2d in state; planning region, 326,800; 8-town district labor force, 183,500.

Area: 17.5 sq. mi. on north shore of Long Island Sound at mouth of the Pequonnock River.

Industry: "Industrial Capital of Connecticut"; products include tools, metallic cartridges, wiring devices, brass goods, valves, corsets, electrical apparatus and appliances; nearby are Sikorsky Aircraft and Avco Lycoming; General Electric has new corporate headquarters in Fairfield, one mile from city line.

Commerce: retail sales, $404.7 million (1975); downtown renewal includes completed complex with Gimbels and Sears stores, mall, 2,000-car parking garage, U.S. courthouse; also 2 new bank buildings, major addition to another; new state courthouse; construction started on downtown residential project.

Transportation: $3 million railroad station opened in 1975, to be connected with planned $7 million multi-transportation center with bus terminal, 1,500-car

parking garage. City served by Conn. Turnpike (Interstate 95); historic U.S. 1 (Boston Post Road); 2 airlines at municipal Sikorsky Memorial Airport; Conrail; 2 national bus lines; summer ferry to Port Jefferson, L.I.

Medical facilities: 3 general hospitals, state mental health center; new $5.5 million municipal convalescent hospital, only one of kind in state.

Cultural facilities: Univ. of Bridgeport, Fairfield Univ., Sacred Heart Univ., Housatonic Community College; Museum of Art, Science, Industry; P. T. Barnum museum; symphony orchestra; American Shakespeare theater in adjoining town of Stratford.

Recreational facilities: "The Park City" has 1,200 acres of parks, including Seaside with 2-mile shoreline; zoo; municipal indoor ice-skating rink; new $16 million jai alai fronton, largest in world.

Further information: Bridgeport Area Chamber of Commerce, 180 Fairfield Ave., Bridgeport, Conn. 06604.

Buffalo, New York

The World Almanac is sponsored in the Buffalo area by The Courier-Express, 785 Main St., Buffalo, NY 14240; (716) 847-5353; founded 1926, as merger of Courier and Express by William J. Conners Sr.; circulation mornings 132,232, Sunday 269,217; publisher William J. Conners III, asst. to publisher William J. Conners IV; treasurer R. C. Lyons, gen. mgr. Donald J. Maul; sponsors hole-in-one tournament, learn to swim program, ski school, Goodfellows.

Population: 1,349,211 (metro area), 462,768 (city); 2d in state; metro area 24th in U.S.; employment about 500,000 (metro); hub of broad 8 county area with population of 1,758,000.

Area: 49.6 sq. mi. city, 1,567 sq. mi. metro; at western end of N.Y. State on Lake Erie, Niagara River, and U.S.-Can. boundary. Metro area includes cities of Niagara Falls, Lockport, Tonawanda, N. Tonawanda, Lackawanna.

Industry: 1,602 manufacturing establishments with $6.3 billion in shipments, highly diversified; headquarters for Carborundum, Buffalo Forge, Trico Products, Fisher-Price Toys; large plants for National Gypsum, Bethlehem Steel, Chevrolet, Ford, Westinghouse, Union Carbide.

Commerce: wholesale and financial center for western N.Y. area; retail sales $3.2 billion (metro); average income per household after taxes (metro) $13,721; distribution center for northeastern U.S. and Canada; $6.5 billion in trade between U.S. and Canada handled each year; 13 commercial banks, 4 savings banks, 11 savings and loans.

Transportation: Greater Buffalo Int. Airport served by 4 scheduled airlines with 2.7 million passengers, 141,544 scheduled and non-scheduled flights in 1974; 6 major railroads, 10 freight terminals; about 150 motor carriers; highway system includes New York State Thruway. Direct highway and rail service to all parts of Canada; direct water service to entire Great Lakes-St. Lawrence Seaways system, overseas, and Atlantic seaboard.

Communications: 2 Buffalo newspapers, 3 additional dailies and one Sunday in surrounding cities; 5 TV and 20 AM and FM radio stations; 5 cable systems.

Cultural facilities: Buffalo Philharmonic in Kleinhans Music Hall; Albright-Knox Art Gallery; Studio Arena theater; Museum of Science; Historical Museum; Zoological Gardens (23 acres); Shaw Festival at Niagara-on-the-Lake, Ontario; Performing Arts Center (Artpark) in Lewiston.

Educational facilities: State Univ. at Buffalo (now building $650 million new campus), State College at Buffalo, Niagara University, Canisius College; 5 other colleges; several 2-year institutions.

Convention facilities: newly rebuilt Memorial Auditorium seats up to 17,000; new Buffalo convention center now being built; new Niagara Falls Convention Center seats up to 12,000; additional facilities available at several hotels and motels.

Sports attractions: Bills football (NFL), Sabres hockey (NHL), Braves basketball (NBA); Rich Stadium.

Recreation: abundant facilities for water and winter sports and activities; near both U.S. and Canada vacationlands.

Other attractions: Niagara Falls and river areas from Buffalo to Lake Ontario; Robert Moses and Adam Beck hydro stations, St. Lawrence Seaway, Welland Canal Locks, Aquarium (Niag. Falls), Our Lady of Victory Basilica (Lackawanna); Old Fort Niagara; Letchworth and Allegany state parks.

Further information: Chamber of Commerce, 238 Main, Buffalo, N.Y. 14202.

Calgary, Alberta, Canada

The World Almanac is sponsored in the Calgary and southern Alberta area by the Calgary Albertan, 830 Tenth Ave., S.W., Calgary, Alberta, T2R Ob1; (403) 263-7730; founded 1902; circulation 36,301; publisher Bruce L. Rudd; managing editor Les Buhasz; business manager Al Vogt.

Population: 470,043.

Area: 162 sq. mi., one of Canada's highest cities (elevation 3,440 feet); in foothills of Rocky Mountains, 150 miles north of the Montana-Alberta border.

Industry: over 400 firms directly connected with the oil industry have headquarters in Calgary; also chemical, fertilizer, and supply industries, and older agricultural industries; assistance in locating industrial information is provided by L.A. Harris, Director, Industrial Development, City Hall, Calgary, Alberta.

Transportation: 2 railways; Greyhound bus lines; International Airport served by 6 airlines.

Communications: 3 TV and 6 radio stations; 2 cable TV channels.

Medical facilities: 6 major hospital complexes.

New construction: building permits in 1975 totaled $3.9 million.

Cultural facilities: 2,700-seat auditorium, Glenbow Museum; Allied Arts Centre; centennial planetarium; symphony orchestra, live theatre; University of Calgary enrolls over 12,000.

Other attractions: Calgary Exhibition and Stampede in July; Heritage Park reconstructs life in early days; Calgary Zoo and Natural History Park show lifesize dinosaurs; 626 ft. rotating Calgary Tower gives panoramic view of city, seats 200 for dining and 300 in observation area.

Sports: every active sport; facilities for hockey, football, and curling; Stampeders of Canadian Football League; Cowboys (WHA).

Convention facilities: Calgary Convention Centre accommodates 2,400 in one large room, 10 smaller rooms accommodate from 18 to 220.

History: began as Mounted Police outpost; as early as 1885, when the railway arrived, had a population of 1,800; discovery of oil in 1914 at Turner Valley contributed to Calgary's present prominence.

Further information: Chamber of Commerce, 300 Canada Permanent Building, 315 Eighth Ave., S.W.; Tourist and Convention Bureau, Mewata Park, 1300 Sixth Ave., S.W., both Calgary, Alberta.

Charleston, West Virginia

The World Almanac is sponsored in the Charleston area by The Charleston Gazette, 1001 Virginia St., E., Charleston, W. Va. 25330; (304) 348-5140; Circulation (morn) 55,641, (Sun.) 102,348; founded 1873 as the Kanawha Chronicle, became The Charleston Gazette 1898; W. E. Chilton III publisher; Harry G. Hoffmann editor; Dallas C. Higbee executive editor.

Population: 71,505 (city), 229,500 (Kanawha County), most populous county in state; county labor force, 85,800.

Area: 29.3 sq. mi. at meeting place of Elk and Kanawha rivers; state capital.

Industry: diversified industrial complex, with coal and chemicals dominating; center for production of limestone, lumber, salt brines, vitreous clays and natural gas; also glass, petroleum products, alloys.

Commerce: wholesale, retail center for central and southern West Virginia; city retail sales, $426.3 million; average family income, $13,497.

Transportation: 2 rail freight lines, Amtrak, bus lines, state's busiest airport; barge lines, 3 interstate highways.

Communications: 3 TV and 7 radio stations.

New construction: One Valley Square; Physicians office bldg. at Charleston Area Medical Center Memorial Division.

Medical facilities: 6 hospitals, 2 of them major complexes.

Cultural facilities: modern civic center and auditorium, Sunrise Cultural and Art Center, symphony orchestra, Community Music Assn., Light Opera Guild, Kanawha Players, State Museum, Morris Harvey College, W. Va. Univ. Graduate Center.

Other attractions: Coonskin Park, Kanawha State Forest, 6 golf courses, public tennis, International League baseball.

History: first settlement, Fort Lee, 1788; Virginia Assembly established Charles Town 1794; named Charleston 1818.

Further information: Chamber of Commerce, 818 Virginia St., East, Charleston, W. Va. 25301.

Charlotte, North Carolina

The World Almanac is sponsored in the Charlotte area by The Charlotte Observer, 600 S. Tryon St., Charlotte, N.C. 28233; (704) 374-7070; founded 1886 as Charlotte Chronicle; changed to Charlotte Daily Observer, March 1892; sold to Knight Newspapers Inc. 1955; circulation 167,508 daily, 226,021 Sunday; president and publisher Rolfe Neill; editor C.A. McKnight; executive editor David Lawrence.

Population: 306,000 (city), 397,850 (Mecklenburg County), 615,000 (Charlotte-Gastonia metro area), 65th in nation; labor force 299,000.

Area: 105 sq. mi. in Piedmont section of N.C., a plateau extending from the Appalachians to the Coastal Plains.

Industry: over 600 manufacturing companies, industrial chemicals, textiles, food products, machinery, printing and publishing.

Commerce: major trucking center, photographic and data processing center, 1,400 wholesale firms with $6.7 billion sales; retail sales (SMSA 1976) $1.8 billion; EBI per household $14,982; 16 banks, 11 mortgage banks, 6 building and loan associations.

Transportation: 115 trucking firms, 2 major railway lines; 4 bus lines; 5 airlines with 198 air movements

per day.
Communications: 5 TV and 12 radio stations.
Medical facilities: an outstanding center in Southeast, 7 hospitals including 3 large general.
Cultural facilities: Opera Assn.; symphony orchestra; Oratorio Society; Mint Museum (art); Coliseum Auditorium, Civic Center; Johnson C. Smith Univ.; Univ. of N.C. — Charlotte; Davidson College; Queens College; Central Piedmont Community College; Kings College; Biscayne-Southern College.
Sports: Charlotte Checkers (Southern Hockey League); Charlotte Motor Speedway (NASCAR) with

World 600 and National 500 races; Kemper Open golf tournament; NCNB Tennis Classic; Charlotte Orioles (professional baseball).
Other attractions: 2 major recreational lakes; nature museum; Carowinds, a family entertainment park.
History: incorporated 1768; named for Queen Charlotte of England; played major part in American Revolution; county was the gold mining capital of the country before 1849; U.S. Mint was built in Charlotte in 1836 to serve the gold mining industry.
Further information: Chamber of Commerce, P.O. Box 1867, Charlotte, N.C. 28233.

Chattanooga, Tennessee

The World Almanac is sponsored in the Chattanooga area by the Chattanooga News-Free Press, 400 E. 11th St., Chattanooga, Tenn., 37401; (615)756-6900, circulation 63,000 daily and 66,000 Sunday; Publisher Roy McDonald, president Frank McDonald, senior vice president Everett Allen, vice president and editor Lee Anderson, secretary J.W. Hoback, treasurer Clifford Welch.

Population: 169,952 (city), 370,857 (metro area); 4th in state, 89th in nation; 168,400 employed.
Area: 2,109.8 sq. mi. Metropolitan shopping area at juncture of Tennessee River and north Georgia boundary line.
Industry: over 600 manufacturers employ 55,000; receipts added by manufacture in 1973, $754 million; agriculture grossed $19 million in 1973.
Commerce: wholesale and retail center; wholesale sales (1973), $721 million; bank assets, $1.29 billion; 9 banks, 2 mortgage banks, 4 savings and loan assns., 3 major life insurance companies.
Transportation: 2 major freight lines, 2 bus lines, 13 federal and state highways; modern municipal airport serves 4 airlines.
New construction: development of $5 million Bicentennial library.
Communications: 5 TV, 20 radio stations, and 2 newspapers.

Medical facilities: speech and hearing rehabilitation center; children and adults rehabilitation and education center; 12 major hospital complexes including psychiatric hospital.
Cultural facilities: Univ. of Tenn. at Chattanooga; 3 liberal arts colleges; state tech community college; state area vocational-tech school; symphony orchestra, opera assn., civic chorus.
Other attractions: multi-million dollar vacation complex; Chattanooga Choo-Choo, in one of the world's largest restaurants, in restored railroad terminal; recreational lakes, mountains, museums.
History: explored by DeSoto in 1540, settled 1828 at Ross's Landing, incorporated 1839, scene of decisive battles of Chickamauga, Lookout Mountain, Chattanooga, and Missionary Ridge during Civil War.
Further information: Chattanooga Convention and Visitors Bureau, Memorial Auditorium, Chattanooga, Tenn.

Chicago, Illinois

The World Almanac is sponsored in the Chicago area by the Chicago Tribune, 435 N. Michigan Ave., Chicago, Ill., 60611; (312) 222-3232; founded 1847 by Joseph Medill; circulation daily 747,715, Sunday 1,110,865; publisher Stanton R. Cook; editor Clayton Kirkpatrick; major awards include 8 Pulitzer prizes won by staff members; sponsors college-pro All Star football game, Nutcracker Ballet, Golden Gloves, and Chicago Tribune swimming meet. Co-sponsors Coho Fishing Derby; Golden Helmet Awards; Golden Basketball Awards.

Population: est. 3,108,700 (city), 2d largest in nation; est. 7,610,000 (8-county metro area in Illinois and Indiana); est. 1,116,300 households in city and est. 2,511,200 in metro area; total employed 3,401,100.
Area: 227 sq. mi. on SW shore of Lake Michigan.
Industry: metro area is leading producer of steel, telephone equipment, radios, TV sets, confectionery products, household products, diesel engines, and frozen and canned foods. Largest industry is primary metals worth $8.4 billion; food and related products follow at $8.3 billion; then come non-electrical machinery, metal products, electrical machinery equipment, chemicals & allied products, petroleum & coal products, printing & publishing, and transportation equipment. Chicago accounts for 5% of the gross national product.
Commerce: 14,460 manufacturers have sales of $41 billion in metro area; 57,000 retailers do a $22 billion business; wholesale sales are estimated at $44 billion. Average spendable family income $17,017. Midwest Stock Exchange markets stocks and bonds; 7th Federal Reserve District Bank; world's leading grain futures market; Chicago Board of Trade; Mercantile Exchange.
Transportation: 3 major airports with 31 commercial airlines handled over 38 million passengers in 1975;

O'Hare is world's largest and busiest commercial airport. Lake, ocean and river shipping makes city link between Mississippi River and St. Lawrence Seaway; 1975 overseas cargo tonnage totaled nearly 2 million tons. Amtrak rail system headquarters. Over 12 major highways, expressways, tollways.
New construction: total industrial construction, development, and investment for 1975, $454 million; total commercial construction for 1975, $950 million, of which total shopping center construction accounted for $554 million.
Convention facilities: 1,067 trade shows and conventions in 1975 attended by over 2 million people.
Educational facilities: 95 institutions of higher learning, include University of Chicago, Illinois Institute of Technology, Northwestern University; Univ. of Ill. — Circle Campus; 6 medical schools; 3 dental colleges and one college of pharmacy and osteopathy.
Medical facilities: over 150 hospitals.
Recreation: 568 parks with an area of 6,700 acres; 73 swimming pools; baseball diamonds, golf courses, bicycle paths, handball courts, etc.
Cultural facilities: Art Institute; Museum of Contemporary Art; Museum of Science and Industry; Field Museum of Natural History; Shedd Aquarium is largest in world; Adler Planetarium; Lincoln Park and

Brookfield Zoos; museums of Academy of Science and Historical Society.

Sports: NFL Bears, American (baseball) League White Sox, National (baseball) League Cubs, NHL Black Hawks, NBA Bulls, N.A. Soccer League Sting, American Soccer League Cats.

History: Indians named area Checagou after area's strong-smelling wild onions; incorporated 1837 with population of 4,170.

Further information: Visitors Bureau and Information Center, Association of Commerce and Industry, 130 South Michigan Avenue, Chicago, Ill. 60603.

Cincinnati, Ohio

The World Almanac is sponsored in the Cincinnati area by The Post, a Scripps-Howard Newspaper, 800 Broadway, Cincinnati, Ohio 45202; (513) 721-1111; founded 1881 by Alfred and Walter Wellman; evening circulation 207,596; editor Walter Friedenberg; business manager Earl Brown.

Population: 425,300 (city), 1,377,000 (metro area), 3d in state, 21st in nation; total employed 553,600 (Apr. '76).

Area: 2,150 sq. mi. (metro) in SW Ohio; SE Indiana and 3 north central counties in Ky.

Industry: home of Proctor and Gamble, Federated Department Stores, Kroger Foods, Armco Steel, U.S. Shoe, Western-Southern Life Insurance, Baldwin Piano and Organ, Cincinnati Milacron; also the home of GM, Ford, and GE plants; production of jet engines, playing cards, cosmetics, chemicals, machine tools, printing and publishing.

Commerce: retail sales ('76 E&P est.) $3.9 billion; bank assets $4.2 billion, deposits $3.2 billion (1974); (metro area) with 41 banks with 180 branches; 71 savings and loan associations in metro area.

Transportation: 7 truck lines and Amtrak; 101 common motor carriers; Greater Cincinnati Airport with 300 incoming-outgoing flights daily serving 7 airlines; Lunken Airport with 4 hard surface runways and FAA control tower; Port of Cincinnati with 100 barge lines, making up 6.1% of total Ohio River traffic of 136 million tons; 2 major transcontinental bus lines; city-owned local bus lines; metro freeway.

Communications: 5 TV, 12 AM, 22 FM radio stations; 2 daily newspapers.

New construction: development of Yeatman's Cove (Riverfront Park) scheduled for Fall '76 completion; Ft. Square South development being approved for downtown; addition to downtown Stouffer's Inn

underway; Formica $28 million expansion-renovation; library expansion for downtown in planning; Town Center-WCET-TV partially completed; I-275 construction underway at various points.

Medical facilities: 27 hospitals with over 9,078 beds; 88.3 physicians per 100,000 population; UC Medical Center where Sabin oral vaccine was discovered; Burn Institute and VA Hospital.

Cultural facilities: Art Museum, Historical Society, symphony orchestra, Krohn Conservatory, Lloyd Library, May Festival, Taft Museum, Summer Opera, Museum of Natural History, Shubert Theater, Contemporary Arts Center, UC Observatory, Playhouse in the Park.

Educational facilities: Cincinnati, Xavier Univs.; Edgecliff, Mt. St. Joseph, Hebrew Union, Thomas More, Bible Seminary colleges; 8 technical and 2-year colleges; 47 vocational schools.

Convention facilities: numerous hotels and restaurants, Convention and Exposition Center, Cincinnati Gardens, Emery Auditorium, Taft Auditorium, Riverfront Coliseum, and Music Hall.

Other attractions: zoo, Reds, baseball world champions, Bengals, football, Swords and Stingers, ice hockey, Fountain Square Plaza, River Downs Race Track, Kings Island Amusement Park, Delta Queen and New Mississippi Queen travel riverboats.

Further information: Chamber of Commerce, 120 W. Fifth St., Cincinnati, Ohio 45202.

Cleveland, Ohio

The World Almanac is sponsored in the Cleveland area by The Cleveland Press, 901 Lakeside Ave., Cleveland, Ohio 44114; (216) 623-1111; founded 1878 by E. W. Scripps; circulation 327,359; editor Thomas L. Boardman; managing editor Richard R. Campbell; business manager William Holcombe; major awards include Pulitzer Prize, Lasker Award.

Population: 655,100 (city), 1,984,000 (metro area), first in state, total employed 855,000 (non-agricultural).

Area: 1,519 sq. mi., SMSA 4 county area; along southern shore of Lake Erie, east and west of Cuyahoga River.

Industry: city has been described as "an industrial powerhouse;" bills itself "The Best Location in the Nation." Within 500 miles are: more than 50% of populations of the U.S. and Canada, more than 55% of U.S. manufacturing plants, more than 50% of retail sales in the U.S. and more than 60% of U.S. product value. No single industry dominates economy — steel and metal products are mainstays; manufacturing complex occupied essentially with primary metals, fabricated metal products, machinery, tools, automotive products. Important industries include making of electric motors, products of petroleum, rubber, plastic, stone, clay and glass, chemicals, paints, wearing apparel, measuring instruments, electronic components, food products, and publishing-printing. Value of products is $15 billion a year. Retail sales are almost $5 billion with average family spending about $6,000 on retail merchandise. More than 50% of

families earn more than $10,000 a year.

Transportation: Hopkins Airport with more than 5 million passengers each year; Burke Lakefront Airport, 5 minutes from Public Square and capable of handling intermediate jets; Port of Cleveland visited by more than 50 overseas steamship lines and Great Lakes fleet; largest city on Lake Erie and 3d largest on Great Lakes. Cleveland is only U.S. city with airport-to-downtown rail service. Ride takes 20 minutes and costs about $10 less than a cab ride. Amtrak train service.

Communications: Cleveland Press, evening daily; Cleveland Plain Dealer, morning daily plus Sunday; numerous foreign language newspapers; 5 TV stations; 12 AM and 14 FM radio stations.

New construction: projects on the drawing boards include a 32-acre complex of offices, stores and apartments, and a gateway and jetport on Lake Erie. A $61 million Justice Center is about to open.

Cultural facilities: Cleveland Orchestra; Play House, nation's oldest and largest resident professional theater; Museum of Art; Karamu House for interracial arts; Western Reserve Historical Society; Health Museum; Natural Science Museum; Cultural Gardens;

zoo; Blossom Music Center; Salvador Dali Museum; Garden Center; Sea World; aquarium.

Educational facilities: Case Western Reserve Univ., Baldwin-Wallace College, Cleveland State Univ., Cuyahoga Community College, John Carroll Univ.; Notre Dame and Ursuline colleges.

Sports attractions: NFL Browns, American League Indians, NBA Cavaliers, NHL Barons, and World Team Tennis Nets; also golfing, horse and car racing, boating.

Other attractions: downtown Convention Center is largest city-owned convention facility in U.S.; public library is 2d in size of book collection to New York. Public Square, hub of city, marked by 52-story Terminal Tower. "The Forest City" is encircled by "Emerald Necklace," 18,000 acres of metropolitan parks. Cleveland Clinic, known for medical research, attracts patients from throughout the world.

History: settlement established in summer, 1796 by Gen. Moses Cleaveland, was capital of the Western Reserve, became a city in 1836.

Further information: Greater Cleveland Growth Assn., 690 Union Commerce Bldg., Cleveland 44115.

Columbia, South Carolina

The World Almanac is sponsored in the Columbia area by Columbia Newspapers, Inc., P.O. box 1333, Columbia, S. C. 29202; phone (803) 771-6161; circulation, The State (am) 100,965; The Columbia Record (pm) 32,543; The State (Sun.) 117,751 (ABC 3/31/76); Ambrose G. Hampton, publisher; Ben R. Morris, co-publisher; Arthur D. Cooper, associate publisher, president and general manager; James W. Holton Jr., assistant general manager and advertising director; William E. Rone, editorial page editor (The State); Thomas N. McLean, editor, The Columbia Record.

Population: 113,542 (1970 census), city corporate limits; 2-county metro area (Richland and Lexington) estimated 370,000 (Fed-State Co-op '75).

Area: 105 sq. mi. (Richland County); 1,525 sq. mi. (metro); center of South Carolina, at confluence of Broad and Saluda Rivers (at Columbia).

Government: state capital with about 100 agencies (state); 19 (federal) agencies: government employees total more than 25,000; Fort Jackson Military Post numbers over 25,000 personnel.

Industry: more than 50 national firms such as General Electric, Allied Chemical, Continental Can, Burlington, Litton, Bendix, M. Lowenstein, Rockwell Int., Square D, Westinghouse, Colite Ind., Tamper, Shakespeare, Allis-Chalmers; fibres, heavy equipment, electronics, textiles, fertilizer, and cement products.

Commerce: retail sales (metro) $880 million ('75); consumer spendable income $1.4 billion; median household income (metro) $15,500; 11 commercial (main) banking institutions.

Transportation: Metropolitan Airport with 4 major airlines and freight service; 3 rail freight lines, Amtrak; 44 motor freight companies; 3 interstate, 6 federal, and 5 state highways.

Communications: 4 TV and 8 radio stations.

Medical facilities: 6 general hospitals, including modern Richland Memorial; William S. Hall Psychiatric Institute; 2 state mental hospitals.

Cultural facilities: Town Theatre, the oldest continuous community theater in nation; 3 other theaters; Museum of Art and Sciences; Gibbes Planetarium; Township Auditorium, home of Artist Series; Dreher Auditorium with Philharmonic Orchestra, City Ballet, Lyric Theatre and Choral Society; Fraser Hall.

Recreation facilities: 13 golf courses; city park system; 2 municipal pools; wide range of hunting activities; Riverbanks Zoological Park, part of 135-acre complex; Lake Murray, water sports.

Sports: Williams-Brice Stadium, home of Univ. of South Carolina Fighting Gamecock football team; Carolina Coliseum for basketball, conventions.

Educational facilities: 22,000-student Univ. of South Carolina; 4 private colleges; Technical Education Center; Lutheran Seminary.

History: established 1786 as state capital; burned in 1865 by Union General Sherman.

Further information: Chamber of Commerce, 1308 Laurel St., Columbia, S.C. 29202.

Columbus, Georgia — Phenix City, Alabama

The World Almanac is sponsored in the Columbus, Ga. - Phenix City, Ala., area by the Columbus Enquirer and the Columbus Ledger, 17 W. 12th Street, Columbus, GA 31902; phone (404) 322-8831; combined daily circulation 64,638; Sunday 63,819. Enquirer founded 1828, awarded Pulitzer Prize 1926; Ledger founded 1886, awarded Pulitzer Prize 1955. Published by the R. W. Page Corporation; M. R. Ashworth, president-emeritus; Glenn Vaughn, vice-president and general manager; J. Carrol Dadisman, vice-president and executive editor. Owned by Knight-Ridder Newspapers, Inc.

Population: 163,600 (Columbus); 29,900 (Phenix City); 223,500 (metro); 78,000 employed (metro).

Area: 1,100 sq. miles (metro: Muscogee and Chattahoochee counties, Ga.; Russell County, Ala.) straddling the Chattahoochee River.

Industry: major textile production center: Swift, Fieldcrest, Cartersville, Columbus Mills, Bibb Mfg., Reeves Bros., West Point Pepperell. International hqs. Tom's Foods Ltd. and Burnham Van Lines; lumber products, beverages, concrete, bakery goods, and paper.

Commerce: center of west Georgia—east Alabama finance, agriculture, textiles, hydroelectric power; metro retail sales $626.2 million; avg. household buying income $12,042; 9 banks, 6 savings and loan associations.

Federal facilities: Ft. Benning, world's largest infantry school, $244 million annual disbursements.

Transportation: 2 rail lines, 2 bus lines; Delta, Eastern, Southern airlines; 33 truck lines; Chattahoochee is navigable river.

Communications: 3 TV and 10 radio stations.

New construction: Peachtree Mall, Columbus East Industrial Park, Fieldcrest Mills, Chattahoochee Promenade, I-185.

Medical facilities: 5 hospitals.

Cultural facilities: Museum of Arts and Crafts, Springer Theater (state theater of Georgia), Three Arts Theater, Bradley Memorial Library; Columbus College, Chattahoochee Valley Community College.

Sports: Astros, Southern baseball league.

History: Columbus founded 1828; gained early prominence as shipping center for cotton, fish; birthplace of Coca-Cola formula. Phenix City founded 1883, growing from a Creek Indian trading post.

Further information: Columbus Chamber of Commerce, P.O. Box 1200, Columbus, GA 31902, or Phenix City-Russell County Chamber of Commerce, P.O. Box 1326, Phenix City, AL 36867.

Columbus, Ohio

The World Almanac is sponsored in the Columbus area by the Columbus Citizen-Journal, 34 S. Third St., Columbus, Oh. 43216; (614) 461-5000; Citizen founded 1899, Journal 1811; circ. 113,752 a.m. daily except Sun.; owned by E. W. Scripps Co.; editor Charles Egger, business manager Gregory A. Dembski, managing editor Jack Keller.

Population: 595,500 (city), 19th in nation, 1,126,000 (metro area), 1976 ests.; 2d in state, total employed 457,200.

Area: 173.2 sq. mi., central Ohio; state capital, Franklin County seat.

Industry: diversified; 1,019 manufacturers including General Motors, Rockwell International, Western Electric, White-Westinghouse, Borden (natl. hqs.); planes, missiles, refrigerators, mining machinery, telephones, glass products, auto parts; est. 1975 production-workers payroll $989 million; home office of Battelle Memorial Institute with world-wide research laboratories.

Commerce: wholesale, retail center for central, southern Ohio, parts of W. Va., Ky. Retail sales, $2,961 billion; bank assets, $8.6 billion; 7 banks, 20 savings & loan assns.; 41 insurance co. home offices, assets $3.9 billion. Per capita income, $4,911. Defense Construction Supply Center, world's largest; 21% of employment is government.

Transportation: 92 truck lines, 3 intercity bus lines, 4 railroads, 8 airlines using Port Columbus International with 750 air movements daily; 12 major highways.

Communications: 4 TV stations, 12 radio stations.

Medical facilities: 18 hospitals, medical centers; Children's Hospital leads nation in children admitted; Ohio State Univ. School of Medicine.

Cultural facilities: Ohio Theatre; symphony orchestra, public library with 22 branches; art museums, Center of Science and Industry, Ohio Historical Center with recreated early 19th Century village.

Other attractions: 104 parks, Park of Roses, world's largest; Ohio Railway Museum; zoo, boating.

Educational facilities: Ohio State, Capital, Franklin univs., Ohio Dominican College, Columbus College of Art & Design, Columbus Technical Institute.

Sports: Ohio Stadium; Owls (hockey), Beulah Park (thoroughbreds), Scioto Downs (harness); Muirfield Memorial golf tournament initiated in 1976.

History: founded 1812 as state capital, named for Christopher Columbus.

Further information: Chamber of Commerce, P. O. Box 1527, Columbus, Oh. 43216.

Corpus Christi, Texas

The World Almanac is sponsored in the Corpus Christi area by The Caller and The Times, P.O. Box 9136, Corpus Christi, Texas, 78408; Caller (a.m.) founded 1883; Times (p.m.) founded 1911; merged 1929; Caller circ. 60,510, Times 28,544, Sunday 85,009; publisher Edward H. Harte; president Allan P. Johnson III; editor Gregory E. Fayre; associate editor editorial page John L. Stallings.

Population: 216,000 (est.); labor force 95,400.

Area: 328 sq. mi. (226 water), 210 miles SW of Houston on Corpus Christi Bay; Nueces County seat.

Industry: oil refineries, offshore oil rig fabrication; chemical, petrochemical, synthetics, aluminum, and zinc plants.

Commerce: Port of Corpus Christi handled 44.6 million tons in 1975; 72-foot-deep superport proposed for 1977; economic hub of south Texas; farming, ranching, oil, and gas production, commercial fishing, tourist trade; 13 banks have deposits in excess of $710 million.

Transportation: 3 airlines, 2 bus lines, 3 railroads but no passenger service.

Medical facilities: 9 hospitals, including a children's center, with 1,497 beds.

Federal facilities: Corpus Christi Naval Air Station is headquarters for Naval Air Training Command; Corpus Christi Army Depot is Army's only complete helicopter overhaul plant; combined payroll more than $100 million.

Cultural facilities: Corpus Christi Museum, Art Museum of South Texas, Japanese art museum, symphony, little theatre, Del Mar College, Texas A&I Univ. at Corpus Christi.

Recreation: public beaches and fishing piers on the bay and along Gulf of Mexico on Mustang Island and in 88-mile-long Padre Island National Seashore; surf and charter boat fishing, sailing, city marina with public launching ramps, large public tennis center, 3 private tennis clubs, 5 golf courses, Gulf States League baseball.

History: Spanish explorer Alonzo de Pineda discovered Corpus Christi Bay in 1519. Blas Maria de la Garza Falcon established San Petronilla Ranch on Petronilla Creek about 1765; city grew from a frontier trading post est. in 1839; city incorporated Feb. 16, 1852.

Further information: Corpus Christi Chamber of Commerce, P.O. Box 640, Corpus Christi, Tex. 78403.

Dallas, Texas

The World Almanac is sponsored in Dallas by The Dallas Morning News, Communications Center, Dallas, Tex. 75222; telephone (214) 745-8222; published by the oldest business in Texas, the News was founded in 1842 by Samuel Bangs; circulation, 315,987 Sunday, 257,565 daily; president Joe M. Dealey, executive editor Tom J. Simmons. Winner of numerous national awards including Freedoms Foundation and National Headliner. Sponsors Teen-age Citizenship Tribute, Fly-the-Flag program, Spelling Bee, Sports Show, Involved Citizen Award, etc.

Population: city, 830,900 (8th in nation); county, 1,407,500; Dallas-Fort Worth metro area, 2,559,800 (10th in nation); total employed, 1,125,100 with 4.2% unemployment.

Area: 900 sq. mi. astride Trinity River in north Texas, about 75 miles south of Oklahoma border; elevation from 450 to 750 feet.

Industry: banking and insurance capital of the Southwest, Dallas ranks 3d among U.S. cities in the number of million-dollar-net-worth companies with 656 such firms. Manufacturing accounts for one-fourth of employment, about evenly divided between durable (including electronics, aviation, aerospace, and machinery) and non-durable (including food products, apparel, and printing-publishing).

Commerce: a $4 billion wholesale market ($8 billion retail), Dallas ranks first nationally in giftware, home furnishing and floor covering wholesaling, 2d in apparel and toys. Metro retail sales totaled $8.3 billion in 1975, while estimated buying income reached $14 billion and bank deposits $14.7 billion.

Transportation: Dallas-Fort Worth Airport is the nation's largest. In 1975, it was the nation's 4th busiest with 341,418 total operations; 7.3 million passengers enplaned there. City is served by 12 major commercial and 4 commuter air lines, 8 railroads, 2 transcontinental bus lines, 87 motor freight lines, 3 taxicab companies with 464 cabs. Dallas Transit System serves 100,000 people daily on 73 lines, 481 route miles.

Communications: 2 metropolitan daily newspapers, numerous suburban dailies, 4 commercial VHF TV stations, public television, 1 UHF station, 17 AM and 20 FM radio stations, 2 city magazines.

New construction: $383 million in building permits in 1975 ($227 million nonresidential); projects include 300-acre, $300 million office park and $210 million Union Terminal area redevelopment.

Medical facilities: 59 hospitals with 9,597 beds, 500 bassinets. Baylor University Medical Center was recently chosen No. 4 among the country's top 13 "super hospitals."

Culture: symphony orchestra, civic opera, summer musicals, civic ballet, Sunday Concert series — among others — offer varied programs; drama at Dallas Theater Center, Theater Three, National Children's Theater, Repertory Theater and 4 dinner theaters; 7 museums; SMU's Owens Fine Arts Center with a collection of paintings and sculpture; numerous art galleries.

Education: 125,000 students attend 28 colleges and universities within 50 miles of Dallas; Southern Methodist Univ., the Univ. of Texas at Dallas, Univ. of

Dallas, North Texas State, Univ. of Texas at Arlington, Baylor Univ. College of Dentistry, Southwestern Medical School; the Dallas Community College System with 37,000 students on 4 campuses and 3 more under construction.

Convention facilities: 3 major convention centers, including expanded Dallas Convention Center with more combined meeting-exhibit space (611,000 sq. ft.) than any other in U.S.; 26,000 air-conditioned hotel rooms. Dallas consistently ranks in top 5 convention cities. In 1975, 1,152,000 people attended 818 conventions.

Sports: professional sports include football, baseball, tennis, golf, hockey, soccer, and rodeo. Cotton Bowl is site of annual New Year's Day football game and SMU home games.

Other attractions: Six Flags Over Texas, Dallas Zoo, Hawaii Kai, Lion Country Safari. Fair Park is home of State Fair of Texas 16 days each October; museums of fine arts, health and science, natural history; Hall of State; Garden Center and Music Hall; excellent lakes, golf courses, parks, luxury hotels, and restaurants.

History: first settler was Tennessee frontiersman John Neely Bryan who established a trading post and plotted the townsite in 1844; incorporated 1856; named for Vice-President George Millifin Dallas. Since 1931, the city has had council-manager form of government. Spectacular population growth began after World War II, when aircraft manufacturing augmented an economy that had been built first on cotton, then on oil, banking, and insurance. Diversified economic expansion fed the growth of the 1960s.

Further information: Dallas Chamber of Commerce, Fidelity Union Tower, Dallas, Texas 75201.

Dayton, Ohio

The World Almanac is sponsored in the Dayton area by The Journal Herald, 37 So. Ludlow St., Dayton, Ohio, 45401;(513) 225-2421; founded as Dayton Repertory; circulation 103,993; editor Dennis Shere, managing editor William Worth, editorial page editor Alvin P. Sanoff, Modern Living department editor Virginia Hunt.

Population: 239,700 (city), 862,700 (metro), 4th in state, 43d in nation; total employed 345,000 (1974).
Area: 46.64 sq. mi. (1975) at junction Mad, Miami, and Stillwater rivers; Montgomery County seat.
Industry: NCR Corp., McCall Printing Co., General Motors Corp. (Delco Moraine, Delco Products, Delco-Air, Inland Mfg. and Frigidaire); more than 800 other manufacturing facilities.
Commerce: retail sales (1973), $2,107 billion; average effective buying household income, $14,331.
Transportation: 2 airports, 6 airlines, 4 trunk rail systems, 6 bus lines, Dayton Regional Transit Auth.
Communications: 4 TV and 10 radio stations.
Medical facilities: 10 hospitals, including a VA facility.
Federal facilities: Wright Patterson AFB, headquarters for Air Force Logistics Command and Aeronautical Systems Div.; Defense Electronics Supply Center, Federal Bldg.
Convention facilities: new downtown convention and exhibition center.

New construction: Stouffer's hotel, Courthouse Sq. Plaza, which includes new dept. store, bank building, utilities bldg., and the Mead Corp. Tower; Univ. of Dayton Law School, Wright State Med. School.
Educational facilities: Univ. of Dayton (new law school), Wright State Univ. (new med. school); 2 jr. colleges; Sinclair (downtown campus), Miami-Jacobs (business); United Theological Seminary.
Cultural facilities: Dayton Art Institute, Philharmonic Orchestra, opera, ballet, 4 amateur theatrical groups, 2 professional companies, Diehl band shell, Deed's carillon, 2 new dinner theaters.
Sports: Dayton Gems (IHL); Amateur Trapshoot Hdqtrs., college sports, Bogie Busters Tourn., DABC (1975).
Other attractions: Air Force Museum, Carillon Park, Paul Lawrence Dunbar home, Wright Bros. Memorial, Aviation Hall of Fame, Old Courthouse Museum.
History: "Birthplace of Aviation."
Further information: Dayton Area Chamber of Commerce, 111 W. First St., Dayton, Ohio 45402.

Denver, Colorado

The World Almanac is sponsored in the Denver area by the Rocky Mountain News, 400 W. Colfax Ave., Denver, Col. 80201; (303) 892-5000; founded 1859 by William N. Byers; circulation daily 224,053, Sunday 246,679; editor Michael Balfe Howard, business manager William W. Fletcher; sponsors Colorado-Wyoming spelling bee, Golden Wedding party, Huck Finn Day, Showagon.

Population: 553,435 (city), 1,511,722 (metro area), first in state, 26th in nation; total employed 700,000.
Area: 116.4 sq. mi. on S. Platte River at edge of Great Plains near Rocky Mountains. State capital.

Industry: Gates Rubber Co. is world's largest maker of v-belts and hose, 6th largest U.S. rubber company; Samsonite Corp. is world's largest luggage manufacturer, also makes furniture; Adolph Coors Co. is na-

tion's 4th largest brewer of beer; center for smokeless industry with 1,500 manufacturing firms.
Commerce: largest distribution center in region embracing one-third of U.S. geographical area; retail sales, $8 billion (1975); bank deposits $4.55 billion, 92 banks, 16 savings and loan associations and 45 insurance company home offices; per capita income, $4,800.
Transportation: 6 major rail freight lines, Amtrak; Continental and Greyhound bus lines; 3 interstate highways intersect city; Stapleton International Airport is nation's 10th largest, with 620 daily flights, hub for 6 trunk airlines; Frontier Air Lines; United Air Lines Flight Training Center.
Communications: 5 TV and 32 radio stations.
Medical facilities: largest medical center between Kansas City and San Francisco; one of 17 regional comprehensive cancer centers with operations to begin in 1976; Univ. of Colorado Medical Center, National Jewish Hospital, Children's Asthma Research Institute and Hospital (CARIH); 22 major hospitals.
Federal facilities: largest complex of federal offices outside Washington, D.C., with 37,700 federal employes; site of Energy Research and Development Administration's Rocky Flats plant, U.S. Mint, Lowry

AFB, Air Force Accounting and Finance Center, Fitzsimons Army Medical Center, Army's Rocky Mountain Arsenal.
Cultural facilities: symphony orchestra, 3 nonprofessional orchestras, 3 choral groups, Denver Art Museum, 6 theater companies; 3-sq.-block convention center; 12,000-seat Red Rocks outdoor theater.
Educational facilities: Univ. of Denver, Colorado School of Mines; Colorado Women's, Metropolitan State, Loretto Heights, and Regis colleges; Univ. of Colorado School of Medicine, Iliff School of Theology.
Recreational facilities: 150 parks, 8,030 acres of mountain parks, 36 golf courses in metro area, City Park Zoo, 2 amusement parks; many ski areas.
Sports: pro teams include Broncos, NFL; Bears, baseball, American Assn.; Nuggets, NBA; NHL hockey team scheduled for 1976-77 season.
Other attractions: Museum of Natural History, Botanic Gardens, State Historical Museum.
History: founded 1858 with discovery of gold, fast became supply center for mountain mining camps; named for territorial governor.
Further information: Denver Chamber of Commerce, 1301 Welton St., Denver 80204; Hospitality Center, 280 14th St., Denver 80202.

Des Moines, Iowa

The World Almanac is sponsored in Iowa by the Des Moines Register and Tribune, 715 Locust St., Des Moines, Ia. 50304; (515) 284-8000; founded 1849; circulation evening Tribune 98,169, morning Register 236,846, Sunday Register 447,233; president and publisher David Kruidenier, editorial chairman Kenneth MacDonald, editor Michael Gartner, business manager Louis Norris; sales director J. Robert Hudson.

Population: 201,404 (city, 1970), 328,900 (1975 SMSA)
Area: 66 sq. mi., at juncture of Raccoon and Des Moines rivers, south central Iowa. State capital and Polk County seat.
Industry: considered to be 2d largest insurance center in nation (56 home companies) and 2d largest tire center with Firestone, Armstrong plants; publishing center — Meredith Co., Better Homes and Gardens, Wallace-Homestead, others; farm implements — North American headquarters and plant of Massey-Ferguson, John Deere; lawn and garden equipment, sporting goods, food products, cosmetics, dental equipment, automotive accessories, concrete forms, nozzles, tools; 700 wholesale and jobbing firms; Standard Oil credit card center, bulk mail center.
Commerce: retail sales in metro area, $955 million (1975); per capita income, $5,611 (1974); average household income, $15,542.
Transportation: newly enlarged in-city airport, 4 major airlines; 4 bus lines; 6 railroads; 69 truck lines, Interstate Highways 80 and 35.
New Construction: civic theater, major hospital additions, 2 state office bldgs., $75 million dam and 5,400-

acre reservoir.
Communications: 13 radio, 4 TV, cablevision.
Medical facilities: 11 hospitals with 2,700 beds.
Cultural facilities: art center, Center of Science and Industry, community playhouse, drama workship, Drake University, symphony orchestra; Grand View Junior, Area Community, and 2 bible colleges; College of Osteopathic Medicine and Surgery, ballet.
Recreation: 1,400 acres of parks, 9 public golf courses, 11 public pools, tennis, YMCA; 2 huge reservoirs.
Other attractions: AAA baseball, Drake Relays, Missouri Valley and Big Eight (Iowa State U.) conferences; 15,000-seat auditorium; boys and girls state basketball tournaments, State Fair, Living History Farm, Children's Zoo, 36-story Ruan Center, tallest in Iowa, Terrace Hill (Governor's Mansion), state capitol and state historical bldg.
History: founded 1843 as a fort to protect rights of Indians; incorporated 1853, became Iowa capital 1857.
Further Information: Chamber of Commerce, 8th and High Sts., Des Moines, Iowa 50309.

Detroit, Michigan

The World Almanac is sponsored in the Detroit area by The Detroit News, 615 Lafayette, Detroit, Mich. 48231 (313) 222-2000; founded 1873 by James E. Scripps; circulation (D) 627,461 (S) 824,776; president and publisher Peter B. Clark Sr., v.p. R.M. Spitzley, exec. v.p. J. T. Dorris, v.p. and editor Martin S. Hayden; major awards won include Pulitzer Prize, Nat'l Headliners; 66 community projects include NCAA Indoor Track Championships, Policeman and Fire Fighter of the Month, Science Fair, Scholastic Writing and Art Awards, Spelling Bee.

Population: 1,500,000 (city), 4,250,000 (metro area), (1972); first in state, 5th in U.S.
Area: 139.6 sq. mi. on the Detroit River, a Great Lakes connecting link and the world's busiest inland waterway.
Industry: "The Motor City"; area plants produce 25% of the nation's cars and trucks, employing more than 200,000. Nonautomotive manufacturing and nonmanufacturing firms employ more than 1.4 million. Other

products are machine tools, iron products, metal stampings, hardware, industrial chemicals, drugs, paint, wire products.
Commerce: total metro personal income per household was $14,111 (1971); area retail sales were $8.6 billion.
Transportation: served by 5 railroads, over 200 inter-city truck lines, 19 airlines, and 31 scheduled steamship lines serving more than 40 countries.

Communications: 9 TV and 18 radio stations.

New construction: $500 million riverfront development, Renaissance Center, will be built on east side waterfront area, incorporating living units, business offices and hotels; other projects include 660-acre, $284 million downtown residential developments, and a 235-acre, $500 million mid-town medical center.

Cultural facilities: symphony orchestra, International Institute, Meadow Brook music and drama programs, Institute of Arts, concert band, and the annual Freedom Festival, celebrating Canada's Dominion Day, July 1, and U.S. Independence Day, July 4.

Educational facilities: 11 colleges and universities are located in the metro area, including Wayne State Univ., Univ. of Detroit, and branches of the Univ. of Michigan and Michigan State Univ.

Convention facilities: 75-acre, $100 million Civic Center, including Cobo Hall and Convention Arena with 400,000 sq. ft. of exhibit space, more than 24,000 rooms in 250 hotels and motels.

Sports: Tigers baseball (American League), NFL Lions, NHL Red Wings, NBA Pistons; 6 winter skiing areas within short driving distance.

Other attractions: Chrysler, Ford, and General Motors auto plants; Henry Ford Museum and Greenfield Village historical displays, Cranbrook Institute (science museum and arts), Belle Isle (1,000-acre park), zoo, public library, historical museum, and Fort Wayne Military Museum.

History: founded 1701 by the Frenchman Cadillac as a strategic frontier fort and trading post, ceded to the British in 1763 and turned over to the U.S. in 1796 as a village of 2,500; reoccupied by the British for a year in the War of 1812. Completion of the Erie Canal in 1825 opened a cheap water transport route from New York to the Northwest and made Detroit an important commercial center. R. E. Olds built Detroit's first auto factory in 1899; and Henry Ford, who hand-built his first car in 1896, formed his first company in 1899, and the present Ford Motor Co. in 1903. The area's industries made it the "Arsenal of Democracy" in World War II.

Further information: Greater Detroit Chamber of Commerce, 150 Michigan Ave.; Cities Reporting and Information Dept., City-County Bldg.; Detroit Convention Bureau, 1400 Book Bldg., all Detroit, Mich. 48226.

Edmonton, Alberta, Canada

The World Almanac is sponsored in central and northern Alberta by the Edmonton Journal, 10006-101 St., Edmonton, Alberta, T5J 2S6; telephone (403) 425-9120; founded November 11, 1903. A division of Southam Press Limited; circulation 175,000. Publisher J. Patrick O'Callaghan; editor Andrew Snaddon. Sponsor Learn to Ski, curl, play golf, tennis, and Shape Up Fitness programs; literary awards, Newspaper in the Classroom.

Population: (est.) 461,559 (city), 555,000 (metro), capital of Alberta, largest Alberta city, 5th in Canada; total metro employed 371,850; Mar. 31, 1976.

Area: 123.34 sq. mi. on North Saskatchewan River.

Industry: 2d largest refining center in Canada, 7,000 producing wells; petrochemical industries include plastics, fertilizers, man-made fibers, steel tube mills; 2d largest meat processing center in Canada; prosperous mixed farming.

Commerce: major supply center for Northwest Territories, Yukon, northeastern B.C., and Canadian Arctic; originating terminus of 5 oil and natural gas pipelines east and west from Alberta, Alaska, and the Canadian north; retail sales (est. '75) $1,900 billion; mfg. shipments (est. '75) $1.6 billion; trading area population (est.) 1,100,000.

Transportation: Alaska and Mackenzie highways; Canadian National, Canadian Pacific, Pacific Northern, Great Slave, and Alberta Resources railroads; 4 airports, 6 airlines, 169,907 itinerant movements in '75, 5th busiest in Canada.

Communications: 3 TV, 3 cable TV, and 8 radio stations.

Medical facilities: 5 general and 5 auxiliary hospitals, 2 rehabilitation centers, 9 nursing homes.

Cultural facilities: Edmonton Symphony Orchestra, Edmonton Art Gallery, Centennial Library, Provincial Museum and Archives, Univ. of Alberta, Northern Alberta Institute of Technology, Grant McEwan Community College, Alberta and Edmonton ballet companies, Canada's most active professional theatre, Edmonton Opera, Northern Alberta Jubilee Auditorium, Queen Elizabeth Planetarium.

Other attractions: Klondike Days, annual celebration of the 1898 Yukon gold rush is held in mid-July; Valley Zoo, Fort Edmonton, Mayfair Park; Alberta Game Farm, Elk Island Park and many lakes nearby.

Sports: CFL Edmonton Eskimos, WHA Edmonton Oilers, Western Major Fastball League Monarchs; 16,000 seat Coliseum opened in 1974; 45,000 seat sport complex is being built for the 1978 Commonwealth Games; Kinsmen Field House indoor track seats 4,000.

History: Fort Edmonton built in 1795, named after town now a borough of London, England. Oil discovered at Leduc (20 miles south) in 1947 rocketed the city into prominence as one of the world's leading petrochemical centers.

El Paso, Texas

The World Almanac is sponsored in the El Paso area by the El Paso Herald-Post, 401 Mills Ave., El Paso, Tex. 79999; (915) 747-6700; Herald founded 1881, Post 1922, merged (under Scripps-Howard) 1931; circulation 38,-730. Robert W. Lee, editor; Robert McBrinn, managing editor.

Population: 377,000 (city); with twin city, Juarez, Mexico, 1,180,000; 5th in state, 45th in nation; total employed, 137,250.

Area: 160,742 sq. mi. western tip of Texas where Rio Grande cuts boundaries of Texas, New Mexico, and Mexico at foot of the Rockies (including Franklin Mtns.); El Paso County seat.

Industry: manufacturing payroll, $193.9 million in 1975, manufacturing employment, 28,900; clothing largest employer, including Farah, Levi Straus, Mann, Hicks-Ponder, Billy the Kid. Juarez-El Paso border in-bond industries at 80 and 21,000 employed, including electronic and other, such as RCA, GTE

Sylvania, General Instruments, American Hospital Supply, and Allen Bradley; home of El Paso Natural Gas, ASARCO, Inc., Peyton Packing, Tony Lama Boots, Phelps-Dodge, Standard and Texaco refineries, Old El Paso (Pet Foods) and Ashley's of Texas canned Mexican foods; nut processing, cattle, pecans, cotton, and other agriculture.

Commerce: wholesale-retail center for west Texas, New Mexico, northern Mexico; retail sales in 1975, $1.25 billion; 1975 bank deposits $1.1 billion; bank clearings, $7.1 billion; 19 banks, 6 savings and loan associations. Value added in 1975, $375.1 million including $193.9 million in labor. Exports in 1974, $448 million, with $510 million in imports.

Transportation: 4 major rail lines, Amtrak; 8 bus lines, 26 truck lines, 5 major highways; Gateway to Mexico busiest crossing point on U.S. border with 57 million crossings in 1975; International Airport, 4 airlines with 130,667 flights in 1975 and 1,107,968 passengers, 12,356 tons of freight.

Communications: 5 TV and 14 radio stations.

New construction: 1975 buildings permits totaled $112.6 million.

Medical facilities: 17 hospitals with 3,139 beds; area cancer treatment center; Univ. of Texas System School of Nursing.

Federal facilities: Ft. Bliss (U.S. Army Air Defense Center, Allied Students Missile Center, Sgts. Major Academy). William Beaumont Army Medical Center, and nearby McGregor Range, White Sands Missile Range, and Holloman AFB in New Mexico.

Cultural facilities: Univ. of Texas at El Paso, El Paso Community College, El Paso Symphony, Museum of Art with Kress Collection, University ballet, opera companies, theater groups, and Chamizal National Memorial theater; $20 million civic-convention center; public libraries.

Other attractions: annual Dec. Sun Carnival and Sun Bowl football game; Tigua Indian community arts and crafts center, missions that pre-date those of the Californias, horse racing in nearby·New Mexico, horse and dog racing in Juarez; zoo, Cavalry Museum, Wilderness Park Museum, Guadalupe Mountains and Big Bend National Parks within 300 miles; exotic Juarez, Mexico.

Further information: Convention and Visitors Bureau, Five Civic Center Plaza, El Paso, Texas 79901.

Erie, Pennsylvania

The World Almanac is sponsored in the Erie area by The Erie Daily Times, 205 W. 12th St., Erie, Pa. 16501; (814) 456-8531; founded in 1888; circulation 74,000 daily, 92,000 Sunday; Edward M. Mead, Michael Mead, co-publishers; executive editor Joseph Meagher, managing editor Len Kholos.

Population: 129,231 (city), 186,652 (metro area), 3d in state; total employed, 53,946.

Area: 19.53 sq. mi. at tip of northwestern Pa.

Commerce: Erie County, pop. 220,000, produces $133 million in exports, highest per capita export in U.S.; tourism — 5 miles of beaches, good fishing, boating, winter sports; seaport — 60 or more oceangoing vessels each year; over 506 industrial plants producing machinery and parts; iron and steel forgings, hardware, meters, plastics, paper (Hammermill), furniture, and toys; General Electric producing Amtrak passenger trains.

New construction: main street transformed into pedestrian walkway; 200-room Hilton Hotel; "Mid City Towers," a 14-story apt. bldg.; $36 million Hamot Medical Center building project; Millcreek shopping mall, $80 million, largest single-design shopping center under one roof in U.S.

Special awards: All America City through 1974.

Transportation: 4 railroads, Boston-Chicago Amtrak line; airport; 35 trucking companies, 4 bus lines.

Cultural facilities: Penn State Univ. extension, Gannon, Mercyhurst, and Villa Maria colleges; Philharmonic Society, Council of the Arts, theater groups; new field house for plays, entertainment, sports.

History: Named after Eriez Indians; site of building of ship Niagara with which Oliver Hazard Perry defeated British in 1813 in Lake Erie battle.

Further information: Chamber of Commerce, 1006 State, Erie, Pa. 16501.

Evansville, Indiana

The World Almanac is sponsored in southwestern Indiana, western Kentucky and southeastern Illinois by the Evansvile Press, 201 N.W. Second Street, Evansville, Ind. 47701; (812) 424-7711; founded July 2, 1906, by E. W. Scripps and J. C. Harper; circulation, 47,000; editor, William R. Burleigh; managing editor, Paul Knue.

Population: 138,764 (city), 287,600 (metro area), 4th in state.

Area: 47 sq. mi. at bend of Ohio River in southwest corner of state; Vanderburgh County seat.

Industry: Whirlpool Corp. plants (refrigeration and air conditioning); Mead Johnson & Co. (pharmaceutical division of Bristol-Myers Co.); Alcoa Warrick Operations (aluminum) just east of city; 277 manufacturing firms.

Commerce: retail sales, $813 million (1975); effective buying income per household, $12,906 (1975); home offices of CrediThrift of America, Inc.; 5 banks, 7 savings and loan associations.

Transportation: world headquarters of Atlas Van Lines; 4 railroads; 5 commercial barge lines; 4 interstate bus lines; Allegheny, Delta, Eastern air lines.

Communications: 2 daily newspapers; 4 TV and 6 radio stations.

Medical facilities: 4 general and mental hospitals; branch of Indiana University Medical School.

Cultural facilities: Philharmonic Orchestra, Museum of Arts and Science, Mesker Zoo, Univ. of Evansville, Indiana State Univ., Evansville; national headquarters of Phi Mu Alpha music fraternity. Abraham Lincoln boyhood home nearby.

Sports: Evansville Triplets baseball of American Assn. (AAA), farm team of Detroit Tigers.

Further information: Chamber of Commerce, Southern Securities Building, Evansville, Ind. 47708.

Fort Wayne, Indiana

The World Almanac is sponsored in the Fort Wayne area by The Journal-Gazette, 600 W. Main St., Fort Wayne, Ind., 46802; (219) 423-3311; established June 14, 1899 by consolidation of The Journal and The Daily Gazette; circulation daily 62,870, Sundays 103,784; president-publisher Richard G. Inskeep; secretary-treasurer Naomi Erb; editor Larry W. Allen; managing editor James P. Lovette.

Population: 188,600 (city); 374,550 (metro area); total employed 159,700.

Area: 50.4 sq. mi. at confluence of St. Joseph, St. Mary's, and Maumee rivers. Allen County seat.

Industry: General Electric and International Harvester largest employers; Magnavox, Essex International, and Central Soya home offices; several firms manufacture about 85% of world's diamond wire dies.

Commerce: wholesale and retail center for northeastern Indiana, southeastern Michigan, northwestern Ohio; retail sales (metro) over $1 billion; bank deposits $1,527 billion; 5 banks, 4 savings-and-loan assns.; 6 life insurance companies, including Lincoln National Life, based here.

Transportation: 2 major rail freight lines; Amtrak; 56 motor freight lines including home-based North American Van, Elway Express, Scott, and Transport Motor; I-69 connects city with Indianapolis and Indiana Toll Road; U.S. 30 dual lane to Chicago; municipal airport; hq. for 122d Tactical Fighter Wing, Indiana Air National Guard.

Communications: 7 radio, 3 TV stations.

Medical facilities: 4 hospitals including VA.

Cultural facilities: Philharmonic Orchestra; Fine Arts and Performing Arts complex; 9 universities and colleges; 3 museums; Foellinger outdoor theater.

Sports: Komet hockey team (IHL) plays at Allen Co. War Memorial Coliseum.

Other attractions: replica of 3d Fort Wayne (1815); children's zoo; 70 parks and playgrounds; 11 golf courses; 36 shopping centers.

History: first white settlement in Indiana (circa 1692).

Further information: Chamber of Commerce, 826 Ewing St., Ft. Wayne, Ind.

Fort Worth, Texas

The World Almanac is sponsored in the Fort Worth area by the Fort Worth Star-Telegram, 400 West Seventh, Fort Worth, Texas 76101 (817) 336-9271; circulation (morn.) 84,682, (eve.) 136,600, (Sun.) 219,485. Established in 1906. Publisher Amon G. Carter Jr.; executive editor Jack Tinsley; vice-president and general manager James H. Hale.

Population: 407,000 (city, 1976 est.); metro area 851,800 (1976 est.); 4th largest Texas city; work force of 367,330 (1976 avg.), unemployment average 4.9%.

Area: 233 sq. mi. on the Trinity River in north central Texas; Tarrant County seat.

Commerce: all types of manufacturing; wholesale and retail center for large area including west Texas; retail sales $2.3 billion (1976 est.); effective buying income $3.8 billion (1976 est.); bank deposits $2.9 billion (47 Tarrant County banks); over 60 mortgage institutions, insurance companies and savings and loans associations.

Transportation: Dallas-Fort Worth Regional Airport, 17 miles from downtown; Meacham Field, general aviation airport, many smaller airports; 9 railroads; Amtrak, 38 motor carriers, and 5 bus companies.

Communications: 2 TV and 18 area radio stations; 1 daily newspaper, several weekly and monthly publications.

Medical facilities: over 20 hospitals.

Federal facilities: 14 federal agencies and Carswell AFB; reserve training centers.

Cultural facilities: Casa Manana, America's first permanent musical arena theater; symphony, opera; Van Cliburn Piano Competition; museums include Kimball Art Museum, Amon Carter Museum of Western Art, Fort Worth Museum of Science & History, and Fort Worth Art Center.

Educational facilities: 3 campuses of Tarrant County Junior College; Texas Christian Univ., Univ. of Texas at Arlington, Texas Wesleyan College, Southwestern Baptist Seminary, Texas Woman's Univ., and other technical and vocational schools.

Recreation: 6 Flags over Texas, Forest Park and Fort Worth Zoological Park; several other parks.

Convention facilities: Tarrant County Convention Center, Will Rogers Memorial Center.

Sports attractions: Texas Rangers baseball; Fort Worth Texans in hockey; Colonial National Golf Tournament; TCU football, other college and semipro teams.

Other attractions: Fat Stock Show and Rodeo; Miss Texas Pageant.

History: founded 1849 as a frontier Army post on the Chisholm Trail; became major railhead.

Further Information: Chamber of Commerce, 700 Throckmorton St., Fort Worth, Tex. 76102.

Fresno, California

The World Almanac is sponsored in the Fresno area by The Fresno Bee, 1626 E Street, Fresno, Cal. 93721; phone (209) 268-5221; founded 1922; circulation daily 112,689, Sunday 133,737; president Eleanor McClatchy, editor C. K. McClatchy, managing editor George Gruner.

Population: 177,900 (city), 448,600 (county); total employed 193,500.

Area: one of largest counties in the state, 3,819,456 acres; located in geographical center of the state midway between San Francisco and Los Angeles.

Agriculture: leading county in U. S. in annual value of agricultural production; state's leading county in production of raisin grapes, processing tomatoes, barley, figs, turkeys, nectarines, cantaloupes, alfalfa seed, peaches; 2d leading county in plums, naval/misc. oranges, pomegranates, sweet potatoes, safflower, sheep, lambs, onions, wool, cotton lint, boysenberries, garlic, fall lettuce, wine grapes.

Industry: 475 diversified manufacturing establishments; food processing is major industry; 2d in importance is production of beverages, primarily wine, brandy and spirits; metro retail sales (1975) $1.3 billion.

Transportation: airports, daily service by 5 airlines; freeways connect to all major metropolitan areas in California; served by 23 common truck carriers, 2 interstate bus lines and 2 mainline railroads with freight handling facilities.

Communications: 5 TV and 16 radio stations.

Medical facilities: 6 general hospitals, including a Veteran's Administration installation.

Cultural facilities: Community and Convention Center; community philharmonic, opera, ballet, and theater; California State Univ.-Fresno, Pacific College, 3 community colleges.

Recreation: golf courses; tennis courts; swimming pools; 3 national parks; Yosemite, Sequoia, and Kings Canyon with groves of giant Sequoia trees plus facilities for boating, sailing, hunting, fishing, skiing, hiking, pack trips and camping.

Other attractions: city zoo, nationally famous rodeo, county fair, underground gardens, Kearney Museum; downtown malls with one of the best outdoor art displays in the West.

History: area explored by the Spaniards in the early 1800s and visited by fur trappers before 1840; settlement began when gold miners came in the 1850s; county created Apr. 19, 1856, from parts of Mariposa, Merced, and Tulare counties.

Halifax, Nova Scotia, Canada

The World Almanac is sponsored in Nova Scotia by The Chronicle-Herald and The Mail-Star, 1650 Argyle St., Halifax; phone (902) 426-2811; circulation Chronicle (morning) 68,165, Mail-Star (aft.) 49,805; publisher and president Graham W. Dennis, chairman of the board Ira B. MacCallum, general-manager Fred G. Mounce, managing editor Jack E. Regan, secretary-treasurer W. D. Coleman.

Population: 122,035 (1971); labor force 57,305; employed 53,170.
Area: 24.19 sq. mi. of land, on the southeast coast of the province; capital city.
Industry: leading industrial area in Atlantic provinces; establishments include oil refineries, electronic equipment manufacturers, ship yards, car assembly plant, plastic fabricators, metal works, breweries, and fish processing; 3d largest and one of Canada's most diversified scientific research centers.
Commerce: financial center of region, regional head offices for all major banks and investment houses; retail sales over $320 million annually in Halifax County; average family income $13,720 (1973); all 3 levels of government constitute employment for 12,000; armed forces have over 14,000 stationed in city.
Transportation: 2 major passenger-freight rail lines, 8 container lines call regularly at eastern-most commercial port on mainland North America; only Canadian container port with 3 sea-shore cranes; handled 143,000, 20-foot equivalent containers (1975), over 620,000 tons break bulk general cargo; international airport.
Communication: 5 radio and 2 TV stations.
New construction: building permits issued for $80.1 million worth of construction last year.
Education: 6 degree-granting universities, 48 common and 3 private schools, one technical institute.
Medical facilities: 9 hospitals (3 teaching).
Cultural facilities: Atlantic Symphony Orchestra, 1 professional live theatre and 2 amateur, 2 public libraries.
Parks: 3 major parks (403 acres).
Sports: home of Halifax Voyageurs of the AHL.
History: founded in 1749; meeting place of first legislative assembly in Canada (1758).

Hamilton, Ontario, Canada

The World Almanac is sponsored in Hamilton and the Niagara Peninsula by The Spectator (a division of Southam Press Ltd.), 44 Frid St., Hamilton, Ontario; phone (416) 526-3333; founded in 1846; circulation 140,000; publisher John D. Muir, business manager Gordon Bullock, managing editor Alex Beer.

Population: 311,886 (city), 408,466 (Hamilton-Wentworth region); 3d in province, 6th in Canada; total work force 260,000 (1974 region).
Area: 54.4 sq. mi. (city), 426 sq. mi. (region), at the west end of Lake Ontario.
Industry: 56.5% of Canada's steel is produced at the Steel Company of Canada and Dominion Foundaries and Steel Limited; city ranks 3d in Canada in industrial production; about 2,000 plants in the region, manufacturing iron and steel products, electrical apparatus, agricultural equipment, tires, food products, wire, heavy machinery, chemicals, and textiles.
Commerce: retail sales (1973) $952 million; average weekly wage (1974) $192.42; 7th in Canada in total retail sales, 6th in annual wage.
Transportation: Hamilton Street Railway, Canadian National and Canadian Pacific railways, as well as the Toronto, Hamilton, and Buffalo line; western terminus for GO Transit (provincial rapid transit system); provincial highways through Toronto to Windsor and Buffalo pass through region; city airport 9 miles south at Mount Hope.
Communications: one TV, one community programming cable station, 4 radio stations.
New construction: Plans call for a 15,000-seat hockey arena; convention center slated for 1978; $5.2 million art gallery under construction.
Medical facilities: 5 major hospitals including medical center at McMaster Univ.; Hamilton Psychiatric Hospital; St. Peter's Centre for chronically ill and geriatric patients.
Educational facilities: McMaster Univ., Mohawk College of Applied Arts and Technology.
Cultural facilities: Hamilton Place, theater-auditorium; Hamilton Art Gallery; Hamilton Philharmonic Orchestra; Hamilton Players Guild; Multicultural Centre.
Convention facilities: convention center slated for 1978, will have 17 meeting rooms, banquet space for up to 2,300 people in one room, 15-story office tower; 590 hotel rooms between 3 hotels in downtown core; banquet facilities for up to 700.
Other attractions: Dundurn Castle, restored prime minister's residence circa 1850; Whitehearn, restored Victorian home; Royal Botanical Gardens; Canadian Football League Hall of Fame; one of the largest park systems per capita in Canada; Hess Village, boutiques and restaurants in old restored homes; Bruce Trail winds through region along the Niagara Escarpment.
Sports: Hamilton Tiger-Cats, football; 2 municipal golf courses; Hamilton Fincups, hockey; Royal Hamilton Yacht Club.
History: explorer Sieur de La Salle discovered Hamilton area in 1669; city takes name from George Hamilton, who laid out streets on part of the farm he bought in 1813.
Further information: Hamilton and District Visitors and Convention Bureau, 58 Jackson Street West; Hamilton; District Chamber of Commerce, 155 James St. South.

Hartford, Connecticut

The World Almanac is sponsored in the Hartford area by The Hartford Times, 10 Prospect St., Hartford, Conn. 06103; phone (203) 249-8211; founded 1817 by Frederick D. Bolles and John M. Niles; circulation 82,289 afternoons and 80,200 Sunday; publisher Lionel S. Jackson, assistant publisher Charles A. Betts, editor William P. Pike, Pulitzer citation as a newspaper; sponsor of Times Farm Camp for less privileged children.

Population: 156,500 (city), 823,200 (county); total employed greater Hartford, 335,500.
Area: 17.2 sq. miles.
Industry: "Insurance City", headquarters for 33 insurance firms employing 39,950; East Hartford is home office of United Technologies, one of the world's largest aircraft firms, manufacturers of Pratt & Whitney jet engines, employer of 52,000.

Commerce: total retail sales (county, 1973) $2.12 billion; per household consumer spendable income (1973) $14,628.
Transportation: intersection of highways 84 and 91; Amtrak, Penn Central Railroad; Bradley International Airport with 8 scheduled airlines, several providing cargo service.
New construction: Hartford Civic Center complex, including $18 million Aetna Life & Casualty shopping arcade, 20-story Sheraton Hotel, 10,000 seat coliseum, 70,000 sq. ft. exhibition hall, and 17,000 sq. ft. assembly hall.
Communications: 6 radio and 4 TV stations.
Educational facilities: Trinity College, Univ. of Hartford, Graduate Center of Rensselaer Polytechnic Institute, St. Joseph College, Hartford Seminary Foundation, Univ. of Connecticut Law School, Greater Hartford Community College.
Cultural facilities: Wadsworth Atheneum, the oldest public art museum in America; Mark Twain House; symphony orchestra; Conn. Opera Association; stage company; Mark Twain Masques; ballet company.
Sports: Greater Hartford Open (golf), Aetna World Cup (tennis); Bicentennials, Yankees (soccer); New England Whalers (hockey).
History: founded 1636 by Thomas Hooker and company of settlers from Newtown (Cambridge), Mass.; became Connecticut's capital city 1665.
Further information: Chamber of Commerce, 250 Constitution Plaza, Hartford, Conn. 06103.

Honolulu, Hawaii

The World Almanac is sponsored in Hawaii by The Honolulu Advertiser, P.O. Box 3110, Honolulu, Ha., 96802; (808) 537-2977; founded July 2, 1856, as Pacific Commercial Advertiser by Henry M. Whitney; circulation 76,196 mornings, 184,528 Sunday; president and publisher Thurston Twigg-Smith, editor-in-chief George Chaplin, executive editor Buck Buchwach, managing editor Mike Middlesworth; awards from American Political Science Assn., American Assn. for the Advancement of Science, others.

Population: 704,500 (metro); 82% of state population; total employed, 266,900.
Area: 595 sq. mi., encompassing Oahu Island. State capital.
Commerce: major destination for U.S., Japanese tourists; persons staying a night or more, 2.8 million in 1975, up from 687,000 a decade earlier; average daily visitor census, 69,000 in 1975; tourist spending, $1.3 billion in 1975, up from $225 million in 1965; visitor dollars top military spending, $982.8 million in 1975; sugarcane and pineapple major agriculture export crops; retail sales (statewide), $3.4 billion; total income, $5.5 billion; per capita income, $6,426; per capita disposable personal income, $5,341; Pacific Basin business and financial center.
Transportation: dependent on ships, planes for most goods; passengers arrive mostly by air; 19 airlines serve airport; 8 domestic carriers, 9 foreign, 2 inter-island; inter-island hydrofoil.
Communications: 5 TV, 32 radio stations; 2 daily newspapers.
Medical facilities: 16 hospitals, including Tripler Army Medical Center; Univ. of Hawaii School of Medicine.
Federal facilities: 7 major military bases, including Pearl Harbor Naval Base.
Cultural facilities: 10-campus, University of Hawaii with 60,000 students; main campus at Manoa in Honolulu, 21,260 students in 1975; university stresses oceanography, tropical environment problems and resources, tsunami research, volcanology, interrace relations; East-West Center, Inc., at Manoa, public education corp. funded by federal government, attracts international students and researchers; Bernice Pauahi Bishop Museum is center for studies of Pacific cultures, houses artifacts, maintains floating square-rigger Falls of Clyde, plus branch museum in Waikiki; Polynesian Cultural Center showcases native dances, music, arts; Honolulu Academy of Art.
Recreation: surfing, swimming, sailing, fishing, football, basketball, baseball.
Other attractions: Waikiki Beach, extinct volcano Diamond Head, Arizona Memorial, balmy weather, tradewinds, multi-racial population, cultural diversity, Polynesian heritage.
History: Honolulu ("sheltered bay" in Hawaiian) was a small village when first westerners called aboard 2 British ships in 1786, 8 years after Capt. James Cook became first known European to discover Hawaiian Islands.
Further information: Hawaii Visitors Bureau, 2270 Kalakaua Avenue, Honolulu, Hawaii 96815.

Houston, Texas

The World Almanac is sponsored in the Southwest by The Houston Post, 4747 Southwest Freeway, Houston, Tex. 77001, phone: (713) 621-7000; founded in 1836; Oveta Culp Hobby, chairman of the board and editor; William P. Hobby, president. Circulation: daily 292,008; Saturday, 329,188; Sunday 353,537. Awards include Pulitzer Prize, Grand Prix, Editor & Publisher. Community events sponsored: Educational Services, Science Engineering Fair, Spring Art Festival, travel shows, Houston Post Family Night at the Shrine Circus, the Rodeo, the Ice Capades.

Population: (city) 1,468,000; 5th in nation; (SMSA) 2,510,000; total employed, (SMSA) 1,101,300; total wages & salaries, (SMSA) $13.2 billion.
Area: 507 sq. mi. (city) on upper center Gulf Coast prairies, 41 ft. above sea level; Harris County seat; connected to Gulf of Mexico by 50-mile inland waterway, the Ship Channel.
Industry: nation's 9th largest mfg. area; supplies nation with 66% petrochemicals, 80% synthetic rubber, 25% natural gas; 9 refineries, 200 chemical plants, 3,500 mfg. plants; produces $2 billion annually in steel, 10 million board feet of lumber monthly, 33% nation's rice; 250 firms in underwater, offshore & oceanographic markets; exports chemicals, oilfield equip., machinery, food supplies.
Commerce: metro retail sales, $7.2 billion; average spendable family income, $13,227 (1974); per capita income, $5,954 (1974); 179 metro banks with resources of $13.5 billion & deposits of $11.4 billion; 8 foreign banks.
Transportation: Port of Houston (nation's 3d in tonnage) connects with 250 world ports by 120 steamship lines, hosts 4,000 ships yearly; 12 major airlines, 2 airports; 6 major rail systems; 34 common carrier truck lines; 200-mile freeway system; bus transit system.
Communications: 2 daily newspapers; 29 radio stations; 5 commercial, one educational TV station.
New construction: non-residential contract awards (1974) $1.1 billion; residential units completed value

$713.3 million (1974).

Medical facilities: Texas Medical Center (city's largest employer) includes 29 institutions on 200 acres, 11 hospitals plus medical, dental, nursing schools, employs 17,000 with annual budget of $300 million; total 55 hospitals including VA.

Federal facilities: Lyndon B. Johnson Space Center, $202 million manned-spacecraft center; Ellington AFB.

Cultural facilities: 11 theatrical organizations perform at $3 million Alley Theatre & Miller Outdoor Theatre; Houston Symphony Orchestra, Grand Opera Assn., Houston Ballet Foundation perform in $7.5 million Jones Hall for Performing Arts; 30 major art galleries including Museum of Fine Arts (permanent collection valued at $14 million) and Contemporary Arts Museum; 28-branch library.

Education: 24 major universities including Rice Univ., Univ. of Houston, Texas Southern Univ.; 2 major medical schools including Baylor College of Medicine and Univ. of Texas Health Science Center (8 Houston branches); 7th largest school district in nation; total enrollment, 211,408; 22 school districts in Harris County, total enrollment, 454,194; private and parochial school enrollment, 30,000.

Recreational facilities: 258 parks and playgrounds; 5 municipal golf courses; 34 municipal swimming pools; Astroworld 60-acre amusement park; botanical garden, arboretum, Hermann Park & Zoo; 50 community centers; 28 Harris County parks; 70 miles of Gulf beaches in one hour's driving distance.

Convention facilities: world's largest single facility Astrohall and Abercrombie Arena, 991,000 sq. ft., next to Astrodome with its 60,000-seat capacity for conventions; downtown locations include Albert Thomas Convention Center (300,000 sq. ft.); Coliseum (50,000 sq. ft.) 11,500 seats; adjoining Music Hall seats 3,036; Exposition Hall, 83,000 sq. ft. exhibit area.

Sports: pro teams Astros baseball, Oilers football, Aeros hockey, Rockets basketball; sports events centers are Astrodome and Summit.

Climate: temperatures moderated by winds from Gulf of Mexico, abundant rainfall; average daily temp. 68.1° (1975); total yearly precip. 50.97 inches (1975).

Scientific facilities: 9th among nation's science centers; research in petroleum, chemicals, medicine, earth sciences, aerospace, oceanography; $214 million spent on science and research (1972).

History: founded 1836 by J. K. and A. C. Allen; city eventually encompassed Old Harrisburgh which was an 1826 townsite laid out by John Harris; named for Gen. Sam Houston, commander of the Texas Army, which won independence from Mexico for the Republic of Texas Apr. 21, 1836; Houston was first president of the Republic, later governor of the state of Texas; both Houston and Harrisburg were for brief periods capitals of the Republic.

Further information: Houston Convention & Visitors Council, 10006 Main, Houston 77002; Houston Chamber of Commerce, 1100 Milam, Houston 77052.

Huntington, West Virginia

The World Almanac is sponsored in the Huntington-Ashland-Ironton area by The Herald-Dispatch (morn.), and The Huntington Advertiser (aft.), Huntington Publishing Company, 946 Fifth Avenue, Huntington, West Virginia 25720, member of the Gannett Group; circulation 62,934, Sunday 54,918. Publisher and president Harold E. Burdick, business manager James D. Hoffman, managing editors, C. Donald Hatfield (Advertiser), and Donald G. Mayne (Herald-Dispatch).

Population: 74,315 (city), 297,200 (5-county metro area); largest city in the state.

Area: 15.86 sq. mi., on Ohio River near where West Virginia, Ohio, and Kentucky meet.

Industry: center for coal transport and for handcrafted glass; leading industries are Ashland Oil, Armco Steel Co., Huntington Alloys, Inc., Division of International Nickel Co.

Commerce: largest port for inland vessels in U.S. handles nearly 20 million tons of materials per year, moved by 7 freight companies; 1975 total retail sales in metro area, $750.1 million.

Transportation: Tri-State Airport, with the longest runway in the state, is served by 2 airlines, 500 air movements a month; 18 truck lines; urban bus transport system; 2 interstate bus lines.

Communications: 4 TV and 11 radio stations.

Cultural facilities: Marshall University; Ashland Community College (University of Kentucky); The Huntington Galleries of Art.

Medical facilities: 5 general hospitals with 1,076 total beds; 3 specialty hospitals including a VA hospital.

New construction: $32 million renewal program calls for large shopping mall, riverfront marina, civic center (to be finished in 1977), and additional convention facilities.

Further information: Chamber of Commerce, 522 Ninth Street, Huntington, W. Va. 25701.

Indianapolis, Indiana

The World Almanac is sponsored in the Indianapolis area by The Indianapolis Star, The Indianapolis News, 307 N. Pennsylvania St., Indianapolis, IN 46206; phone (317) 633-1240. News founded 1869; Star 1903; cir. Star 218,954; News 159,895; Sunday Star 354,965; publisher-Eugene S. Pulliam; president-William A. Dyer Jr.; Star editor Frank Crane, News editor Dr. Harvey Jacobs; Pulitzer Prizes-News, Star; Nat'l. Headliners first prize-Star.

Population: 745,739 (consolidated city 1970), nation's 11th largest; 1,111,173 (metro 1970); total employed 496,000.

Area: 379.4 sq. mi.; geographic center of state; state capital and Marion County seat.

Industry: over 1,400 diversified manufacturers including plane and auto engines and parts, electronics, pharmaceuticals, machinery; 1975 manufacturing payroll over $1.4 billion.

Commerce: commercial center for Indiana; retail sales $3.4 billion; per capita personal income $5,600; 6 banks with resources over $5.5 billion; home offices of over 60 insurance companies.

Transportation: 9 airlines; 5 rail freight lines; Amtrak; 3 interstate bus lines; 67 truck lines; 7 interstate freeway routes.

New construction: projects totaling over $314.4 million under construction in 1976.

Communications: 6 TV stations and 18 radio stations.

Medical facilities: 16 hospitals, over 7,700 beds.

Federal facilities: Fort Harrison incl. Army Finance and Acctng. Center, U.S.A. Admin. Center.

Cultural facilities: Museum of Art and Oldfields Museum of Decorative Arts; Indiana State Museum; Indianapolis Zoo; Children's Museum; Conner Prairie Pioneer Settlement and Museum of Indiana Heritage; Clowes Hall, home of symphony orch.; Civic Theatre, oldest U.S. amateur theatrical group;

repertory theatre.

Education facilities: Butler Univ., Indiana Central Univ., Marian College, Christian Theological and St. Mauer's seminaries, Indiana Univ., Purdue Univ. at Indianapolis, with nation's largest medical center.

Convention facilities: Indiana Convention-Exposition Center, Indiana State Fairgrounds.

Recreational facilities: 13,000 park acres, 16 municipal swimming pools, 12 golf courses; pro basketball and hockey in 18,000-seat domed sports arena, home of the Pacers NBA; Racers WHA; Loves WTA; minor league baseball.

Other attractions: Indianapolis 500; Yankee 300; annual National Drag Racing championships.

History: sesquicentennial in 1971; important before Civil War, with nation's first union railway station (1853); home of James Whitcomb Riley, Booth Tarkington and President Benjamin Harrison.

Additional information: Indianapolis Chamber of Commerce, 320 N. Meridian St., Indianapolis, IN 46204, (317) 635-4747.

Jacksonville, Florida

The World Almanac is sponsored in the Jacksonville area by The Florida Times-Union and The Jacksonville Journal, One Riverside Ave. 32202; phone (904) 791-4111; circulation, Times-Union 146,600, Journal 57,600, combined Sunday 178,200, publisher J. J. Daniel, president Robert R. Feagin, vice president John A. Tucker, executive editor John S. Walters; Journal won Pulitzer Prize for photography in 1967.

Population: 578,300 (1975); total employment, 236,-900 (1975).

Area: 840 sq. mi., includes nearly all of Duval Co. in northeast Fla.; largest incorporated developed area in Western Hemisphere.

Industry: 590 industries, added value total of $505 million annually; Offshore Power Systems investing $250 million in floating nuclear power plant production facility to employ 10,000 when completed.

Commerce: emphasis on finance, distribution; home or regional headquarters for 34 insurance companies; 1974 retail sales, $1.8 billion; effective buying income per household in 1974, $12,104.

Transportation: 3 major railroads and Amtrak; 16 major truck lines; 6 airlines averaging 118 air movements daily; 2 interstate bus lines; port handled 15 million tons in 1974.

Communications: 4 TV and 18 radio stations.

New construction: $146 million in building permits issued in 1975; 37-story Independent Life building, tallest in Florida.

Medical facilities: 10 general hospitals and one naval hospital with total of 3,158 beds.

Federal facilities: 2 naval air stations, one naval station add $400 million yearly to economy.

Cultural facilities: Cummer Art Gallery, Jacksonville Art Museum, Children's Museum; Jacksonville Symphony, Ballet Guild, 4 community theaters.

Education: Univ. of North Florida, Jacksonville Univ., Edward Waters College, Florida Jr. College.

Sports: Gator Bowl; Greater Jacksonville Open, $165,000 PGA tournament.

Other attractions: Civic Auditorium, Coliseum, Jacksonville Zoo, Fort Caroline, Kingsley Plantation; 8 miles of public beaches.

History: founded in 1822 by Isaiah Hart, named for Andrew Jackson; fire in 1901 destroyed 2,368 buildings, left 10,000 homeless; city and county governments merged in 1968 after referendum.

Further information: Chamber of Commerce, 604 Hogan St., or Convention & Visitors Bureau, Hemming Park, Jacksonville, 32202.

Kalamazoo, Michigan

The World Almanac is sponsored in the Kalamazoo area by The Kalamazoo Gazette, 401 S. Burdick, Kalamazoo, Mich. 49003; telephone (616)345-3511, founded 1833; circulation daily 57,555, Sunday 63,282, owned and operated by Boothe Newspapers Inc.; president James E. Sauter, editor Daniel M. Ryan, manager Ralph H. Bastien Jr.

Population: 84,100 (city), 202,800 (county); total employed (Kalamazoo-Portage SMSA) 115,100.

Area: located equidistant to the 3d and 5th largest metro areas in nation — Chicago and Detroit, 140 miles away.

Industry: paper-making is the traditional industry, with 5 large plants. Checker Motors Corp. manufactures cars; large Fisher Body Division body stamping plant; Upjohn Company, pharmaceuticals.

Commerce: shopping center for large part of southwestern Michigan. In 1959, city became first in country to close downtown streets and create a pedestrian mall; now known as "Mall City." Retail sales (1975) 663 million; 4 banks had combined assets in 1975 of $754 million, 2 savings and loan associations have assets of over $200 million.

Transportation: 2 railroads provide freight service, Amtrak passenger service; 34 general carriers provide trucking services; airport with freight and passenger service; 3 bus lines.

Cultural facilities: 5 auditoriums offering music and theatrical performances, 6 live arts theaters, an art center, symphony orchestra, Kalamazoo Civic Players.

Educational facilities: 3 colleges and one university with combined student enrollment over 27,000.

Other attractions: Kalamazoo Nature Center, 83 lakes (county), National Junior Tennis Championships, 2 major hospitals, Kalamazoo Hotel-Business-Convention Center, IHL Kalamazoo Wings (hockey).

Further information: Kalamazoo County Chamber of Commerce, 500 W. Crosstown, Kalamazoo, Mich. 49008, telephone (616)381-4000.

Kansas City, Missouri

The World Almanac is sponsored in the Kansas City area by The Kansas City Star, 1729 Grand Ave., Kansas City, Mo. 64108; telephone (816) 421-1200; founded by William Rockhill Nelson; circulation morning 317,238, evening 295,494, Sunday 388,576; president and editor W. W. Baker, executive assistant to the president George

Burg, general manager Frank S. McKinney, executive editor Cruise Palmer, advertising director W. W. Meyer.

Population: 511,600 (city); 1,307,800 (metro area), 27th in nation; total employed, 565,600

Area: 316.3 sq. mi., at confluence of Missouri and Kansas rivers.

Industry: 2d in nation in automotive assembly; first in production of vending machines, greeting cards, underground freezer space, and winter wheat trading. Top employers: U.S. government, General Motors, TWA, Bendix, Western Electric, Ford. Presently Kansas City is a leading hard wheat center, stocker and feeder market, and is among the top 5 cities in flour production and grain elevator capacity.

Commerce: total retail sales in 1974, $3.874 billion; the center of a 7-county metro area: Jackson, Clay, Platte, Cass, and Ray counties in Missouri; Johnson and Wyandotte counties in Kansas.

Transportation: 9 airlines with 400 scheduled arrivals and departures daily at Kansas City International Airport; 169 truck lines and 4 barge companies; city is one of the nation's major rail centers.

New construction: $250 million Crown Center business and apartment complex covers 25 square blocks; new medical center of University of Missouri and Univ. of Kansas; American Royal Arena; Mercantile Bank Building; United Missouri Bank headquarters; 30-story office and retail building downtown; 27 story IBM bldg.; H. Roe Bartle exposition hall; Worlds of Fun recreation center. More than 6 large hotels and several hospital additions.

Cultural facilities: Starlight Theater, nation's 2d largest outdoor theater; William Rockhill Nelson Gallery of Art, among the 10 top American museums with the 3d largest Oriental collection outside China; Performing Arts Foundation formed in 1965 to present festival events; University of Missouri at Kansas City; Rockhurst College; Kansas City Art Institute; University of Kansas Medical Center. Within commuting distance are University of Kansas, Park College, William Jewell College, Truman Library in Independence. Linda Hall Library of Science and Technology is one of the largest privately endowed technical reference libraries in the nation.

Recreational facilities: more than 100 parks cover 5,345 acres, including Swope Park, 2d largest in nation, with fine zoo.

Sports: The American Royal Livestock and Horse Show each fall attracts entries from throughout the country; home of the Chiefs of the NFL, Royals, American League baseball, Kings, NBA.

History: Kansas City's beginnings can be traced to a trading post of French fur trappers about 1826. It became an important trade and transportation center as the overland routes of the Oregon and Santa Fe Trails spread westward. As agricultural production boomed, it became an important market and distribution center for crops from throughout the middle west.

Further information: Chamber of Commerce of Greater Kansas City, 920 Main, Kansas City, Missouri.

Kitchener-Waterloo, Ontario, Canada

The World Almanac is sponsored in the Kitchener-Waterloo area by the Kitchener-Waterloo Record, 225 Fairway Road, Kitchener, Ont.; phone (519) 579-2231: founded 1878; circulation 65,293, president and publisher K. A. Baird.

Population: 130,228 (Kitchener) and 48,468 (Waterloo), 286,281 (metro area); total employed 93,100.

Area: 51.74 sq. mi. (Kitchener) and 25.47 sq. mi. (Waterloo), 65 miles west of Toronto.

Industry: highly diversified industry (359 companies), rubber, plastics, electronics, metal fabrication, brewing, distilling, meat packing, footwear, furniture, food processing, automotive components; Budd Automotive Co., largest autoframe manufacturer in Canada; Deilcraft furniture plant is the largest under one roof in North America.

Agricultural: hog and dairy area; Waterloo County's 1,976 farms accounted for $90 million production in 1975.

Commerce: wholesale and retail center for area; metro retail sales (1975) $526.3 million; 7 banks, 61 branches; 8 trust companies, 20 branches; 36 life insurance offices, 21 other insurance offices; Waterloo, "The Hartford of Canada," head office for 6 insurance companies.

Transportation: 2 major rail lines, 34 truck lines, on Ontario's key highway 401; Waterloo-Wellington Airport; 45 mi. from Toronto International.

Communications: one TV and 4 radio stations.

Medical facilities: 2 major hospitals.

Cultural facilities: symphony orchestra, Kitchener-Waterloo Art Gallery, Doon Pioneer Village; 28 mi. from famed Stratford Festival Theatre.

Educational facilities: Univ. of Waterloo, Wilfrid Laurier Univ., Conestoga College.

Other attractions: nationally-known farmers market; Canada's largest annual Oktoberfest celebration; Woodside, national historic park, boyhood of W. L. Mackenzie King, Canadian prime minister 22 years.

History: founded 1807 by German settlers; retains strong Germanic flavor.

Further information: Kitchener Chamber of Commerce, 68 King East; Waterloo Chamber of Commerce, Waterloo Square.

Knoxville, Tennessee

The World Almanac is sponsored in the Knoxville area by The Knoxville News-Sentinel, 204 West Church Ave., Knoxville, TN 37901. Sentinel founded in 1886; News in 1921 by Scripps-Howard Newspapers; Sentinel purchased by Scripps-Howard in 1926 and combined with News. Circulation 103,311 daily; 161,434 Sunday; editor Ralph L. Millett Jr., managing editor Harold E. Harlow.

Population: 181,527 (city), 309,763 (county), 454,330 (metro area), 3d in state; total employed metro area, 180,500.

Area: city 77.6 sq. mi., county 528 sq. mi., located almost in exact center of that portion of United States lying east of the Mississippi River and south of Great Lakes.

Industry: major manufacturing industries are primary metals and chemicals; nearly 500 plants representing 51 diversified major industries (coal and zinc mining, marble quarrying, meat packing, steel fabrication, industrial controls eqpt., furniture, auto safety eqpt., refuse eqpt., apparel) with Aluminum Co. of America, Union Carbide Corp. Nuclear Div. at Oak Ridge, included in Knoxville market.

Commerce: wholesale and retail trade center of a

multi-county area in east Tennessee, Virginia, Kentucky, N. Carolina; county retail sales (1975) $972 million.

Transportation: 2 rail lines, 5 airlines, 2 inter-state bus lines, 25 motor freight carriers; interstate Highways I-40 and I-75 intersect in heart of city.

New construction: continuance of downtown redevelopment program, over $112 million expended since 1972; in progress, 30 story bank bldg., Univ. of Tenn. Neyland Stadium enlarged to seat 80,290.

Cultural facilities: Univ. of Tennessee, Knoxville College, Knoxville Symphony Orchestra, 10 museums, art gallery, auditorium-coliseum, city-county library (612,684 book volume), Zoological Park; university-community theater, choral society, opera workshop.

Sports: Univ. of Tennessee football and other major sports; Knoxville Sox, Chicago White Sox farm club.

Other attractions: Great Smoky Mountains National Park, 39 miles from Knoxville, offers year-round scenic beauty, skiing in season; within 30 miles of Knoxville, 6 TVA lakes offer 2,320 miles of shoreline providing fishing, boating, swimming. Oak Ridge, known for its nuclear developments, 22 miles from Knoxville; American Museum of Atomic Energy and Oak Ridge National Lab.

Further information: Chamber of Commerce, 301 E. Church Ave., or Tourist Bureau, 811 Henley St., both Knoxville, Tenn. 37902.

Las Vegas, Nevada

The World Almanac is sponsored in the Las Vegas area by the Las Vegas Review-Journal, 1111 W. Bonanza, Las Vegas, 89101; phone (702) 385-4241; founded as a weekly 1909; purchased 1956 by Donald W. Reynolds, present publisher; member Donrey Media Group; circulation 68,230 weekdays, 73,399 Sundays; general manager Wm. Wright; editor Don Digilio.

Population: 357,010 greater Las Vegas (1975); 1975 total employment 143,300.

Area: southern Nevada, 7,927 sq. miles, 283 miles NW of Phoenix, 289 miles NE of Los Angeles.

Industry: 24-hour tourism; hotel/gaming/recreation payroll $437 million, approx.; 1975 tourist volume 9.2 million; convention and tourist revenue $2.2 billion, gaming revenue $770 million.

Commerce: 6 banks total resources over $1.5 billion, 5 savings & loans, total savings $349 million; retail sales $1.7 billion, average spendable family income $13,865.

Transportation: McCarran Int'l Airport, total 6.5 million yearly passengers, 7 major airlines, plus foreign carriers, U.S. Customs Port of Entry, 3 bus lines, daily auto traffic entering area 16,000.

Communications: 5 TV stations, 12 radio stations, 3 newspapers.

Medical facilities: 8 hospitals, 15 convalescent homes, acupuncture clinics.

Federal facilities: Nellis AFB, 8,200 military, 1400 civilian personnel, $96 million annual federal payroll.

Cultural facilities: cultural arts; arts & crafts; centers for cultural & athletic programs; drama theater; music; dance; beautification; museum; educational displays, historical societies, collectors organizations, libraries.

Education: total enrollment Clark County school district, Univ. of Nevada Las Vegas, community college, 94,105.

Recreation: Lake Mead recreation area, Hoover Dam; Mt. Charleston, Lee & Kyle canyons, skiing; Valley of Fire, Lost City Museum, one-day drive to ghost towns; Death Valley.

Convention facilities: Las Vegas Convention Center 45 acres, 50,000 sq. ft. under roof, 500,000 sq. ft. exhibit area; 7,500 seat rotunda, 11 hotels with convention facilities; over 393 conventions in city each year.

Sports: 12 golf courses, 125 tennis courts, 16,000 seat Las Vegas stadium, UNLV basketball, baseball, football, track, and swimming.

History: first recorded group to enter the Las Vegas Valley was Antonio Armijo's party in early 1839. Las Vegas, Spanish for "The Meadows," first settled by Europeans in June of 1855, by a 30 man Mormon group under William Bringhurst; city of Las Vegas founded May 15, 1905, as a result of public land auction by the railroad.

Further information: Las Vegas Chamber of Commerce, 2301 East Sahara, Las Vegas, Nev. 89105.

Lethbridge, Alberta, Canada

The World Almanac is sponsored in the Lethbridge area by The Lethbridge Herald, 504 7th St., S., Lethbridge, Alberta; phone (403) 328-4411; founded as weekly in 1907; circulation, weekdays, 24,913, Saturdays, 26,861; editor and publisher Cleo W. Mowers, general manager Donald Doram, managing editor Donald H. Pilling.

Population: 46,818, 3d in province.

Area: 23 square miles; located on Oldman River, 60 miles north of Montana border, 125 miles south of Calgary.

Industry: heavily dependent on agriculture; federally inspected packing plants slaughtered 25% of cattle slaughtered in Alberta in 1975; large dryland grain growing, ranching area and extensive irrigation district; brewery, distillery, flour mill, foundry, oilseed processing, mobile home construction.

Commerce: 1975 retail sales of $270 million, 17% more than 1974; 5 banks, 4 trust companies, 11 finance companies.

Transportation: CP Rail; 2 bus lines; depots for 50 trucking firms; regional airline flies out of Lethbridge Airport.

New construction: building permits valued at $43.6 million in 1975, compared with $42.5 million in 1974.

Communications: 2 radio, 2 TV stations.

Medical facilities: 2 general hospitals, one long-term care hospital, 4 nursing homes for the aged.

Cultural facilities: Canada agriculture research station, Univ. of Lethbridge, Lethbridge Community College, Alexander Galt Museum, Nikka Yuko Centennial Japanese Garden, symphony orchestra and chorus, local theater groups, Bowman Arts Centre, Yates Memorial Centre.

Other attractions: 4 major parks, 4 artificial ice arenas, 2 golf courses, Stewart Game Farm.

Sports: Expos, Montreal Expos farm team; Broncos, Western Canada Hockey League.

History: early coal-mining town, named Lethbridge Oct. 16, 1885, after a coal executive. A whisky traders' depot, Fort Whoop-Up, was booming, 5 miles southwest of what is now Lethbridge, in the 1860's. First settlers in area came 15 years later, many from the United States.

Little Rock, Arkansas

The World Almanac is sponsored in Arkansas by the Arkansas Gazette, 112 West Third Street, Little Rock 72203, phone (501) 376-6161; founded 1819 at Arkansas Post, A. T., by Wm. E. Woodruff, moved to Little Rock 1821; circulation 121,135 daily, 143,635 Sunday; Hugh B. Patterson Jr., publisher and president; J. O. Powell, editorial director; Robert R. Douglas, managing editor; J. R. Williamson, executive vice president-general manager.

Population: 142,000 (city), 367,700 (metro); 152,500 employed.

Area: 110 sq. mi. at point where Ozarks-Ouachita highlands meet central coastal plain at geographical center of state.

Industry: 378 manufacturing plants, employing 31,-500 persons, and including Allis-Chalmers, Armstrong Rubber Co., Timex, AMF Cycle Division, Remington Arms, Jacuzzi Bros., Teletype, Westinghouse, CPC, International, and General Electric.

Commerce: Retail sales (estimated 1975) $1.158 billion; bank resources (Jan., 1976) $1.5 billion; building permits (1975) $74 million; 11 banks, 6 building & loan associations, 4 old line insurance companies.

Transportation: 3 trunkline railroads, 5 federally certified airlines, 8 bus lines, 14 common carrier barge lines.

Communications: 3 commercial TV, one ETV, 13 radio stations.

Medical facilities: 10 hospitals including UA Medical Center, 2 VA hospitals, and Ark. State Hospital for Nervous Diseases.

Federal facilities: Little Rock AFB, Military Airlift (MAC) Command; Camp Joseph T. Robinson, Arkansas National Guard headquarters and training center; U.S. National Guard Bureau's Non-Commissioned Officers Institute.

Cultural facilities: Univ. of Arkansas at Little Rock with Schools of Law, Medicine, Nursing, and Pharmacy; UA School of Graduate Technology; Philander Smith, Shorter, and Arkansas Baptist colleges; Arkansas State Symphony, Arkansas Arts Center, 3 major public libraries, convention center-auditorium-hotel.

History: French explorer Bernard de la Harpe noted "le petit roche" on his map of the Arkansas River Valley in 1722.

Further information: Chamber of Commerce, Continental Bldg., Markham & Main Streets; Arkansas Parks & Tourist Dept., State Capitol — both Little Rock, Ark. 72201.

Los Angeles, California

Population: 2.7 million (city), 6.9 million (county), 10.2 million, 5-county urban area (July '75); first in state, 2d county in nation, 3d urban area; total civilian employed 2.9 million (county, March '76); labor force 3.2 million (county, March '76).

Area: 463.7 sq. mi. on Pacific, 418 mi. south of San Francisco, 145 mi. north of Mexico. Los Angeles County seat, one of 78 cities in county.

Industry: leading aerospace industry with 17 of the top 100 and 7 of top 10 defense contractors in nation located in Southern California; center of entertainment industry with more than 600 firms in movie work; women's clothing, sportswear, electronics, rubber tires, printing, furniture, paper, autos, auto parts, chemicals; manufacturing work force (county, March '76) 779,000; agriculture 9,200; mining and oil 11,200; construction 94,300; transportation, utilities, and communication 175,900; trade 698,600; finance, insurance, and real estate 186,500; services and misc. 643,600; government 487,400; among nation's leaders in agriculture; farm income $152.5 million, cattle slaughter 1.3 million, sea fish harvested 599.6 million pounds (county '75).

Commerce: total taxable retail sales $16.1 billion; median family income $14,562; average per capita income $5,475, (county '75); personal income $37.9 billion (county '74). Approx. 80 banks, 1,077 branches; more than 65 savings and loans; bank deposits $26.1 billion (county '75); S&L savings $20.6 billion (county '75). International trade through Los Angeles Customs District: imports $8.4 billion, exports $4.9 billion.

Transportation: Santa Fe, Union Pacific, Southern Pacific railroads; Amtrack; Continental and Greyhound bus lines; Southern California Rapid Transit District plus other local and inter-city bus lines; Airport Transit Bus and Gray Line tours; 4.9 million vehicles in county, one of largest concentrations in nation; 3.7 million cars, 644,575 trucks, 330,635 trailers, 194,355 motorcycles (county '75); 148.4 mi. freeway (city), 477.9 mi. (county, Jan. '76); 40 domestic and international airlines serving Los Angeles International Airport, 453,596 landings and take-offs, 23.7 billion passengers, 1.42 billion pounds cargo ('75); 9 other airports; more than 46 miles of commercial waterfront in Los Angeles-Long Beach Harbor which served 4,804 commercial ships, 50 million tons of cargo ('75).

Communications: 13 TV stations (7 UHF, 6 VHF), approx. 75 radio stations, 60 commercial; more than 45 newspapers in English and foreign languages, more than 25 publishing daily (county).

New construction: building permits, $1.7 billion (county '75), including $733.9 million residential, 17,-730 new housing units.

Medical facilities: 186 medical hospitals with 34,683 beds, 24 psychiatric hospitals with 2,431 beds, 424 nursing homes with 39,795 beds (county, June '76).

Educational facilities: 1,280 elementary schools, 146 jr. high, 160 sr. high, approx. 880 private (county '76); 450 elementary, 75 jr. high, 49 sr. high (city '76); 62 city, 95 county, 82 municipally-operated libraries. UCLA, Univ. Southern Cal., Cal. Institute Technology (Cal Tech), Loyola, Marymount, Pepperdine (Los Angeles and Malibu campuses) Univ.; Claremont Colleges; Woodbury, Occidental, Whittier, Mt. St. Marys colleges; four campuses of Cal. State Univ. and colleges at Long Beach, Los Angeles, Northridge, Dominguez Hills.

Cultural facilities: 1,838 churches (county '71); Huntington Art Gallery and Library; Hollywood Bowl; Greek Theater; Griffith Park Planetarium; Mt. Wilson and Mt. Palomar observatories; Los Angeles Museum; Music Center, County Art Museum, UCLA Botanical Gardens, Southwest Museum.

Recreational facilities: 273 city parks and playgrounds plus 122 county parks; 5 public golf courses; 15 public beaches within 35 miles of downtown; oceans, mountains, lakes, deserts, Disneyland, Marineland, Knott's Berry Farm, Magic Mountain, Lion Country Safari within 2 hour's drive.

Convention facilities: 15,000 hotel rooms (city), 25,-000 rooms (county); large convention center.

Sports: collegiate sports including Rose Bowl; pro teams in football (Rams), basketball (Lakers), volleyball (Stars), tennis (Strings), hockey (Kings), soccer (Aztecs, Skyhawks).

History: discovered 1542 by Portuguese navigator Juan Rodriguez Cabrillo; Mission San Gabriel founded Sept. 1771; city formally founded Sept. 4, 1781, by Spanish colonial governor as El Pueblo de Nuestra Senora la Reina de los Angeles de porciuncula; inc.-Apr. 4, 1850.

Further information: Chamber of Commerce, P.O. Box 3696, Terminal Annex, Los Angeles, Cal. 90051.

Louisville, Kentucky

The World Almanac is sponsored in Kentucky and southern Indiana by The Courier-Journal and The Louisville Times, 525 West Broadway, Louisville, Kentucky 40202, (502), 582-4011; Courier-Journal founded 1868; Times 1884; Courier circulation 210,171, Times 161,272, Sunday 343,668; chairman of the board Barry Bingham Sr., editor and publisher Barry Bingham Jr.; major awards include 6 Pulitzer prizes.

Population: 327,500 (city), 929,600 (metro area); first in state; total employed 348,700.
Area: 65.2 sq. mi. (city), 1,392 sq. mi. (metro); on southern bank of Ohio River.
Industry and Commerce: 10th in total industrial shipments; famous for baseball bats, cigarettes, railroad repair shops, electrical appliances, farm machinery, motor vehicles, plumbing fixtures, and whiskey; 900 manufacturing firms in area; estimated retail sales (Jefferson County, 1975) $2.235 billion.
Transportation: 5 trunk-line railroads, 2 terminal railroads, 87 inter-city truck lines; 5 barge lines; 5 bus lines; 7 airlines, and 2 municipal airports.
Communications: 14 radio and 4 TV stations, one educational.
Medical facilities: 18 hospitals, 5,835 total beds.
Cultural facilities: Louisville Orchestra, Kentucky Opera Association, Art Center Association, J.B. Speed Art Museum. 20 private art galleries, Macauley Theatre, Actors Theatre, The Children's Theatre, Louisville Civic Ballet, Louisville-Jefferson County Youth Orchestra, The Louisville Free Public Library (23 branches); 678 churches, 46 denominations.

Education: 11 colleges and universities, 4 business colleges and technical schools in area.
Recreation: 147 public parks, covering more than 7,000 acres.
Convention facilities: Kentucky Fair & Exposition Center, largest ground-level exhibit hall and auditorium complex in North America with 650,000 sq. ft., 20,000-plus seating, parking for 27,000 cars; new 100,000 sq. ft. Commonwealth Convention Center in downtown Louisville; Louisville Gardens, downtown, handles up to 7,000.
Sports: Kentucky Derby, held annually at Churchill Downs since 1875, attended annually by over 125,000; Louisville Downs harness racing.
Other: Belle of Louisville excursion steamboat; Churchill Downs Museum; Louisville Zoo, American Printing House for the Blind; Kentucky Railway Museum.
History: founded by explorer George Rogers Clark, in 1778; named after King Louis XVI of France.
Further information: Louisville Area Chamber of Commerce, 300 West Liberty, Louisville, Ky. 40202.

Lubbock, Texas

The World Almanac is sponsored in the Lubbock area by the Lubbock Avalanche-Journal, 8th St. and Ave. J., Lubbock, Texas, 79408; (806) 762-8844; founded 1900 as Leader, became Avalanche 1908, daily 1921; Plains Journal weekly founded 1923; consolidated 1926; circulation (morn) 58,285, (eve) 15,779, (Sat) 69,014, (Sun) 76,-453; member Southwestern Newspaper Corp.; general manager Robert R. Norris; editor Jay Harris.

Population: 177,920 (city), 201,200 (metro area), 8th in state; total employed 79,770.
Area: 82.2 sq. mi.; center of South Plains territory of northwest Texas.
Industry: vegetable oils, cotton seed flour, grain sorghum, livestock, petroleum, sand and gravel; 228 manufacturing companies.
Commerce: wholesale and retail center for west Texas and eastern New Mexico; retail sales $499 million; bank resources: $679 million; 8 banks and 6 savings and loan associations.
Transportation: 12 motor freight carriers; 2 major railroads, and 3 bus lines; Lubbock Regional Airport, 3 major airlines averaging 60 air movements per day; 6 major federal and state highways.
Communications: 4 TV and 9 radio stations.
Medical facilities: 8 hospitals, Lubbock State School for Mentally Retarded; medical school being constructed on Texas Tech campus, county teaching hospital under construction.

Federal facilities: Reese AFB, federal building, Federal Aviation Admin., and National Weather Service, U.S. Customs port of entry.
Cultural facilities: symphony orchestra, Theatre Centre; Museum of Texas Tech Univ., Moody Planetarium; Ranching Heritage Center (authentic ranch houses dating to 1835), Lubbock Christian College; Memorial Convention Center under construction; Texas Tech Univ., Lubbock Cultural Affairs Council, and Lubbock Garden & Arts Center.
Recreational facilities: 39 city parks, 1,750 acres; Mackenzie State Park, state's largest, with Prairie Dog Town, Buffalo Lakes; Municipal Auditorium, 3,200 seats; Municipal Coliseum, 10,000 capacity; annual Panhandle South Plains Fair.
Sports: Texas Tech, and Christian College sports; Tech Jones Stadium, site of annual Coaches All-American football game; indoor rodeos.
Further information: Chamber of Commerce, P.O. Box 561, Lubbock, Texas 79408.

Macon, Georgia

The World Almanac is sponsored in the Macon area by The Macon Telegraph & News, 120 Broadway, Macon, GA 31208; phone (912) 743-2621; acquired by Knight-Ridder Newspapers Inc., 1969; circulation, Telegraph (morn) 50,294, News (eve) 20,941, Sat. 64,911, Sun. 77,811; general manager Bert Struby, executive editor Frank Caperton, News editor Joseph Parham.

Population: 122,432 (city), 226,782 (metro), 3d in state; labor force, 93,470.
Area: 52 sq. mi., 6 miles northwest of geographic center of Georgia; Bibb County seat.
Industry: textiles; Bibb Company, longtime industry leader, headquartered in area; 2 textile-related plants — YKK Zipper Co. of Japan, and Texprint, Inc.; forestry; Armstrong Cork Co. acoustical tile plant is area's largest; pulpwood also is used to manufacture cardboard packaging; tobacco, Brown & Williamson Tobacco Corp. opened $200 million cigarette

plant in 1976; Levi Strauss apparel manufacturing plant; Kaolin (clay) deposits are mined in area and processed in numerous ways; Government Employees Insurance Co. regional office.

Federal facilities: Warner Robins Air Logistics Center and Robins AFB. 16 miles from Macon are area's largest employers.

Educational facilities: Wesleyan College, nation's oldest college for women, and Mercer Univ. with law school; Macon Jr. College.

Other attractions: Ocmulgee National Monument displays archeological remains of 3 prehistoric Indian civilizations; $4.5 million coliseum seats 10,000.
History: settled when U.S. established Fort Hawkins

in 1806; chartered in 1823, named for Nathaniel Macon of North Carolina.
Further information: Chamber of Commerce, 305 Coliseum Drive, Macon, Ga. 31201.

Madison, Wisconsin

The World Almanac is sponsored in Madison by Madison Newspapers, Inc., publisher of The Capital Times and the Wisconsin State Journal, 1901 Fish Hatchery Road, Madison, Wis., 53713; (608) 252-6100; circulation, Wisconsin State Journal (m) 74,082, The Capital Times (eve) 40,903, combined daily 114,985, Sunday Wisconsin State Journal 118,492.

Population: 168,671 (city), 290,272 (county), 2d in state; metro work force 150,200.
Area: 52 sq. mi. (city), 1,194 sq. mi. (county), in south central Wisconsin, state capital and Dane County seat.
Commerce: home office of 29 insurance firms; 375 industrial firms, 26 banks, 7 savings and loans, retail sales $632 million; average effective buying income $16,577.
Transportation: Dane County regional airport, 3 airlines, 3 railroads, Amtrak (within county), major Interstate highway system; 3 bus lines, 30 common carriers, city owned bus system.
Communications: 4 TV, 2 cable, 6 AM and 9 FM radio stations.
Medical facilities: 9 hospitals, including U.W. and VA; 20 major clinics, approx. 600 physicians.
Federal facilities: Forest Products Laboratory.
Cultural facilities: Dane County Coliseum; Madison Civic Center, 2 art centers, ballet company, dinner

playhouse, 11 drama groups, 8 music organizations, 15 Catholic, 150 Protestant, and one Greek Orthodox Church, 2 synagogues.
Education: University of Wisconsin, (38,545 enrolled), 35 elementary, 10 middle, 5 high schools; 15 parochial, one vocational-technical; Madison Area Technical College, Madison Business College, and Edgewood College, and 7 city and 32 university libraries.
Recreation: 5 lakes with total of 18,000 acres of water surface, and 4,676 acres of parks.
Sports: Blues, hockey; University of Wisconsin in Big Ten.
Other attractions: U. of W. Arboretum, Vilas Zoo, numerous political organizations, weekly Farmer's Market (May-Sept.), World Dairy Exposition headquarters.
Further information: Greater Madison Chamber of Commerce, 615 E. Washington Ave., Madison, Wis. 53701.

Memphis, Tennessee

The World Almanac is sponsored in the Memphis area by The Memphis Press-Scimitar, 495 Union Ave., Memphis, Tenn. 38101; phone (901) 526-2141; Scimitar founded 1880 by G. P. M. Turner; Press 1906 by Scripps-McRae League, predecessor of Scripps-Howard Newspapers; circulation 114,500; editor Milton R. Britten, associate editor Ed Ray, managing editor Van Pritchartt Jr.

Population: 667,150 (city), 853,100 (metro area); first in state, 16th in nation; 332,500 employed.
Area: 280 sq. mi., Shelby County seat, on east bank of the Mississippi River.
Industry: extensive cotton marketing-warehousing and processing of cotton seed into vegetable oil products; headquarters of Holiday Inns Inc., Cook Industries (cotton and grain) and Conwood Corp. (tobacco and food products). Other large industries include Schering-Plough (drugs), International Harvester (cotton pickers, hay balers), and Firestone (tires).
Commerce: wholesale-retail center for large parts of Tennessee, Arkansas, and Mississippi; retail sales (1975) $2.7 billion; bank deposits $2.2 billion; 7 banks, 6 savings-loan assns. Per capita personal income $4,610 (1973).
Transportation: 11 airlines, 150 arrivals a day; 8 trunk line railroads, 82 motor freight lines, 7 barge lines; river port handled 10.4 million tons of freight in 1973.
Communications: 4 TV and 19 radio stations.
Medical facilities: Univ. of Tennessee Center for Health Sciences and a VA hospital in complex with public hospital; 3 private hospitals and St. Jude Hospital, research center for childhood illnesses, particularly leukemia.
Federal facilities: Naval Air Station, Naval Air Technical Training Center, Defense Depot Memphis, and Air Force's 164th Air Transport Group.
Cultural facilities: Memphis Symphony Orchestra,

opera theater, Theatre Memphis, Brooks Art Gallery, Chucalissa Indian Village & Museum, Memphis Museum; annual performances of Metropolitan Opera.
Educational facilities: Memphis State Univ., Southwestern College, LeMoyne-Owen College, Christian Brothers College, U-T Center for Health Sciences, Shelby State Community College, State Technical Institute, Southern College of Optometry, Mid-South Bible College.
Recreational facilities: Meeman-Shelby Forest state park, 12,500 acres; 137 other parks.
Convention facilities: $27 million Cook Convention Center, 1.3 million sq. ft., seating 16,500.
Sports: Liberty Bowl, home of Memphis State University football team and site of Liberty Bowl game; Mid-South Coliseum, home of MSU basketball team; Memphis Blues, International Baseball League (AAA); Danny Thomas Memphis Classic golf tournament.
Other attractions: Cotton Carnival each May; Mid-South Fair each September; Beale Street, home of the blues, where composer W. C. Handy lived; Mid-America Mall; Libertyland.
History: DeSoto, exploring Mississippi River, stopped here in 1541; Ft. Adams established in 1797; Memphis incorporated in 1826; Yellow fever in 1878 nearly depopulated city, but its population grew back to 64,589 in 1890.
Further information: Memphis Area Chamber of Commerce 42 S. 2d St., Memphis, Tenn. 38103.

Mexico City (Ciudad de Mexico), Mexico

Population: 8,299,209 (UN est. 1974).
Area: about 53 sq. mi. within the 573 sq. mi. Federal District (Distrito Federal; population, 1976 est. 11 million); in central Mexico at an altitude of 7,349 ft.
Industry and commerce: capital of Mexico; the politi-

cal and economic hub of the nation; manufactures include steel, automobiles, appliances, textiles, rubber goods, furniture, and electrical equipment; marketing center of Mexico.
Transportation: center of modern highway and rail

system; 25-mi. subway system; served by most international air lines, Mexico City is 4 hrs. by jet from New York and 3 hrs. from Los Angeles.

Communications: major media center for Mexico and parts of Latin America; major film center.

Cultural facilities: Palace of Fine Arts and Ballet Folklorico; National Palace (Diego Rivera murals); National University with over 90,000 students; National Museum of Anthropology; city itself is an architectural exhibit of Aztec ruins, baroque cathedrals, and ultra-modern buildings.

Other attractions: Xochimilco with the "floating gardens" and gondolas; Chapultepec Castle, palace of the French-supported Emperor and Empress of Mexico, Maximilian and Carlota; 22-ton Aztec Calendar Stone; 2 volcanoes, Popocatepetl (17,887 ft.) and Iztaccihuatl (17,343 ft.); sports centers.

History: traditionally founded 1321 by Aztecs, city was called Tenochtitlan; captured by Spanish under Cortez in 1519 and again in 1521; occupied by the U. S. in 1847 and by the French from 1863 to 1867.

Further information: Mexican National Tourist Council, Mariano Escobedo 726, Mexico, D.F., or 405 Park Ave., New York 10022; or 9701 Wilshire Blvd., Beverly Hills, Cal. 90212.

Miami, Florida

The World Almanac is sponsored in the Miami area by The Miami Herald, 1 Herald Plaza, Miami, Fla. 33101; phone (305) 350-2111; founded Dec. 1, 1910, by Frank B. Shutts; circulation 477,556 daily, 502,778 Sunday; chairman James L. Knight, editor Don Shoemaker, executive editor Larry Jinks, managing editor Ron Martin; newspaper or staff writers have won or shared in 5 Pulitzer prizes, the latest in 1976, and numerous other honors.

Population: 354,000 (city), 1,369,917 (metro); first in state, 24th in nation; total employed in metro area, 650,500.

Area: 53.8 sq. mi., land and water, on Biscayne Bay at mouth of Miami River in southeast Florida; largest of 27 municipalities in Dade County; Dade County seat.

Industry: 4,900 light manufacturing plants; tourism and aviation are mainstays of economy; 1,000 hotels and motels employ 50,000 and handle 13 million visitors a year; aviation accounts for 70,000 jobs; Eastern (largest industrial employer), National, and Pan American operate bases; winter agriculture center.

Commerce: center of Pan-American finance and commerce, with 97 banks, 16 savings and loan associations, Federal Reserve Bank branch; retail sales (1975) $5.5 billion; Port of Miami busy in waterborne commerce as well as Caribbean cruise center, with 20 cruise sailings weekly.

Transportation: Miami International, served by 109 air carriers, handled more than 12 million travelers in 1975; Seaboard Coast Line, Amtrak, and all-freight Fla. East Coast Railroads operate in Miami, as do Greyhound and Trailways buses; 65 truck lines.

Communications: 5 commercial and 5 educational or closed-circuit TV stations, 38 radio stations.

New construction: major new office buildings downtown, topped by 40-story One Biscayne Tower, in a $500 million building surge; work underway on $75 million Omni International, Miami "megastructure" with shops, a hotel, restaurants, and entertainment.

Medical facilities: 38 hospitals, 11,171 beds; over 13,-000 beds at 54 nursing and convalescent homes in metro area; 2,904 members of Dade County Medical Association; Jackson Memorial Hospital one of area's leading research facilities.

Federal facilities: Homestead Air Force Base south of Miami with 8,900 men and women; Federal Aviation Administration; Coast Guard bases; 2 federal hospitals; oceanographic center; 12,400 U.S. employees.

Cultural facilities: Philharmonic, Opera Guild, and other musical groups perform regularly; 18 auditoriums, including new downtown Gusman Hall; resident and touring theatrical productions; 6 major art museums; 12 playhouses, and 55 night clubs and theater restaurants, some in major hotels.

Educational facilities: 8 colleges and universities, plus 3 campuses of Miami-Dade Community College, total enrollment of 62,000; Univ. of Miami is largest independent institution of higher learning in southeast; Florida International Univ.; public school system with 244,439 students.

Recreational facilities: 14 miles of public beach on ocean and bay; 362 parks and playgrounds, 11 stadiums and grandstands; resort-oriented, Miami offers 45 golf courses and 57 marinas for boaters, with 43,-000 pleasure crafts registered; 95 movie houses.

Convention facilities: newly expanded Miami Beach Convention Hall can handle largest conventions; 655 conventions brought 345,000 delegates to Miami Beach in 1975; 248 brought 84,985 delegates to Miami proper during the year.

Sports: pro football Miami Dolphins and U. of Miami play in Orange Bowl, which seats 80,050; stadium also hosts Orange Bowl game, Orange Blossom classic, North-South All-Star Shrine Game; Miami Stadium is spring home for Baltimore Orioles; Miami Toros, professional soccer; parimutuel wagering at 5 horse and greyhound tracks, jai-alai fronton.

Other attractions: balmy subtropical climate, with mean annual temperature of 75.3 degrees; 532 Protestant, 49 Catholic churches, and 41 Jewish synagogues; city is bilingual with 400,000 Latin American residents; one of nation's largest Jewish communities; marine stadium features powerboat and regatta racing, twilight concerts; Everglades National Park, 40 miles south of Miami, is virgin wilderness.

History: America's newest big city, Miami had only 3 houses in 1895 in a community called Fort Dallas. Julia Tuttle persuaded Henry M. Flagler to extend his railroad south from West Palm Beach to stimulate Miami development. City was incorporated in 1896, when railroad arrived.

Further information: Miami-Metro Department of Publicity and Tourism, 499 Biscayne Blvd., Miami, Fla. 33132.

Milwaukee, Wisconsin

The World Almanac is sponsored in the Milwaukee area by The Milwaukee Journal, Journal Square, Milwaukee, Wis. 53201; telephone (414) 224-2000; founded 1882 by Lucius W. Nieman; circulation 343,420 daily, 529,089 Sunday; chairman of the board Irwin Maier; publisher Donald B. Abert; president of The Journal Co. Donald B. Abert; editor Richard H. Leonard; major awards include 2 Pulitzer Prizes to the newspaper and 2 to staff members.

Population: 680,390 (city); 1,415,900 (SMSA); city 12th and metro area 20th in U.S.; total employment 615,-900 (metro area).

Area: 95.8 sq. mi. on shore of Lake Michigan, Milwaukee County seat.

Industry: largest U.S. producer of diesel and gasoline engines, outboard motors, motorcycles, tractors, padlocks, beer; 4th largest U.S. automaking center; graphic arts and food processing are largest nondurable goods employers; location for 11 "Fortune 500" industries.

Commerce: wholesale and retail trade center for Wisconsin, upper Michigan; total retail sales $3.9 billion (SMSA); wholesale trade $5.5 billion (SMSA).

Average household spendable income $14,565 (SMSA); 79 banks with $4.8 billion deposits; 49 savings and loan associations home offices in the (SMSA), with deposits of $3.3 billion.

Transportation: 4 major rail lines; Amtrak. 5 major airlines provide direct service to East and West coasts, south, southeast, southwest, and Florida for 2 million users of Gen. Mitchell field; 30 U.S. and foreign-flag ship lines use Milwaukee's St. Lawrence Seaway port, handling nearly 4.3 million tons annually including 596,400 tons overseas cargo; port of Milwaukee gateway for 350 cities in 31 states and overseas ports. Wisconsin ranks 11th in foreign trade-exports and imports; 4 inter-city bus lines, 68 motor freight carriers; I-94, 5 federal and 14 state highways intersect Milwaukee.

Communications: morning, evening, and Sunday metropolitan newspaper; 4 commercial, 2 educational TV stations; 28 AM and FM radio stations.

Medical facilities: 21 major hospitals and medical centers, including 600 bed VA hospital.

Cultural facilities: Milwaukee Symphony, Repertory Theater, 2 opera and one operetta companies; Mid-America Ballet; Milwaukee Art Center; Milwaukee museum; University of Wisconsin-Milwaukee, Marquette University, Medical College of Wisconsin, 8 other colleges and vocational schools enroll over 45,-000 annually; $13 million Performing Arts Center; $15.9 million exhibition addition to convention-arena-auditorium complex; Mitchell Park Conservatory; Milwaukee County Stadium, and Milwaukee County Zoo are parts of 13,000 acre county park system.

Sports: baseball, Brewers (American League); basketball, Bucks (NBA), Marquette Univ., Univ. Wisconsin-Milwaukee; football, Green Bay Packers (NFL) play 5 of 11 home games in Milwaukee.

History: founded by Solomon Juneau, (1818), one of many French trappers in area in early 1800s; incorporated as town 1837; as city 1846.

Further information: Metropolitan Milwaukee Association of Commerce, 828 N. Broadway, Milwaukee, Wis. 53202.

Minneapolis, Minnesota

Population: 413,800 (city), 1,222,100 (metro); first in state, 29th in nation; total employed (city, non-agricultural, 1974) 303,914.

Area: 59 sq. mi. (city), 4,000 sq. mi. (10-county metro area) around St. Anthony Falls near junction of Minnesota and Mississippi rivers.

Industry: diverse; major electronics-computer manufacturing center, including Honeywell, Control Data, Medtronics; headquarters for nation's 4 largest grain millers, including General Mills, Pillsbury, and International Multifoods.

Commerce: $13,038 median household income; $3.6 billion total retail sales metro area (1975); 24 commercial banks, 6 savings and loan associations; headquarters for Ninth Federal Reserve District; world trade center, 12th among U.S. metro areas in exports.

Transportation: Amtrak regional terminal, 5 trunk railroads; 150 trucking firms; 5 major barge lines headquartered in city; Mpls.-St. Paul International Airport, 650 flights daily.

Communications: 4 commercial, 2 educational TV stations; 39 radio stations.

Medical facilities: 21 hospitals, including a leading heart hospital at Univ. of Minn.

Federal facilities: Farm Credit Administration regional office; FBI regional office, Environmental Protection Agency district office.

Cultural facilities: Minnesota Orchestra, 7 art galleries-museums, Tyrone Guthrie Theatre, Walker Art Center, Univ. of Minnesota.

Sports: Minnesota Twins (American League), Minnesota Vikings (NFL), Minnesota North Stars (NHL), Minnesota Kicks (NASL).

Other attractions: 153 parks, 22 lakes; 57-story IDS Tower; Mpls. Aquatennial celebration in July; average yearly snowfall, 41 inches.

History: first visited in 1680s by Fr. Louis Hennepin who discovered and named St. Anthony Falls on the Mississippi River; French fur traders used the area in 18th century; incorporated 1871. Falls became power source for lumber and milling operations in 19th century.

Further information: Greater Minneapolis Chamber of Commerce Information, 15 S. 5th St., Minneapolis, Minn. 55402.

Mobile, Alabama

The World Almanac is sponsored in the Mobile area by The Mobile Press Register, 304 Government St., 36630; phone (205) 433-1441; circulation, Register (morn.) 47,500, Press (eve.) 56,600, combined (Sat., Sun.) 99,000; Register founded 1813, Press 1928; William J. Hearin publisher and president, Fallon Trotter executive editor, John Fay associate executive editor.

Population: 196,600 (city), 400,600 (metro), 2d city in state, 68th in nation; total employed (metro), 125,000.

Area: 142 sq. mi., at head of Mobile Bay.

Industry: home of Alabama State Docks, a $300 million complex where 33 ocean-going ships can be docked at one time; over $1.9 billion is invested in diversified industry, including paper and paper products, forest products, shipbuilding, chemicals, roofing, paints, alumina, oil, aircraft engines, and metals.

Commerce: wholesale-retail center for large portion of southwest Alabama and southeast Mississippi; Mobile County retail sales (1975), $737 million.

Transportation: served by 4 major railroads, one of the great river systems, 3 major airlines, 55 truck lines and about 100 steamship lines.

Communications: 2 TV and 12 radio stations.

Medical facilities: Univ. of South Alabama Medical College and 5 modern hospitals.

Cultural facilities: Municipal Auditorium-Theater complex seats 16,000; art gallery, museum, amateur dramatic theater, public library and branches; Univ. of South Alabama, Spring Hill, Mobile Colleges, and Bishop State Junior College.

Annual attractions: America's Junior Miss Pageant, Senior Bowl football game, and Mardi Gras.

History: founded in 1702 by Jean Baptiste Le Moyne; 6 flags have flown over the city since then.

Further information: Chamber of Commerce, Commercial Guaranty Bank Bldg., Mobile, Ala.

Montgomery, Alabama

The World Almanac is sponsored in the Montgomery area by the Advertiser-Journal, 200 Washington Street, Montgomery AL 36102; phone: (205) 262-1611; Advertiser founded 1828, Journal 1881; circulation Advertiser (morn) 51,184; Journal (eve) 25,959; combined Sunday 75,446; publisher Harold Martin, managing editor Ben R. Davis.

Population: 146,000 (city), 244,000 (metro); 147th in nation; total employed, 102,300.
Area: 50.34 sq. mi. (city), 442 sq. mi. (county).
Industry: machinery manufacture, glass products, textiles, refrigeration equipment, axles, furniture, food products, paper, and fertilizers; over 250 industries.
Commerce: wholesale-retail center for 13 counties in central Alabama; retail trade area sales (1974), $1 billion; 7 banks, 3 savings & loans associations, 6 insurance company home offices; state capital.
Transportation: 5 railroads, 3 airlines, 2 national bus lines; Interstates 65 and 85 intersect in the city; Alabama River navigable to the Gulf of Mexico.
Medical facilities: 4 general hospitals and a VA hospi-

tal; over 1,700 beds.
Military: home of Maxwell Air Force Base, The Air University, and Gunther Field.
Cultural facilities: Art Guild, Civic Ballet, Little Theater, and a Community Concert Series; Museum of Fine Arts; 5 major colleges and universities.
Sports: Rebels, farm team of Detroit; Blue-Gray Football Classic; Southeastern Championship Rodeo.
History: incorporated 1819; Jefferson Davis inaugurated president of the Confederate States of America, Feb. 18, 1861, in Montgomery.
Other attractions: a riverboat, accommodating 300 passengers, makes regular-scheduled excursions on the now navigable Alabama River.

Montreal, Quebec, Canada

The World Almanac is sponsored in the Montreal area by The Gazette, a Southam newspaper, 1000 St. Antoine Street, Montreal H3C 3R7, Quebec, Canada; phone (514) 861-1111; founded 1778 by Fleury Mesplet; circulation 122,651 daily; publisher Ross Munro; exec. assistant to the publisher Robert McConnell; editorial page editor Tim Creery; executive editor R. Lindsay Crysler; managing editor Brodie Snyder; sponsors Christmas fund; 8 National Newspaper Awards in last 4 years.

Population: 1,214,300 (city), 2,761,000 (metro); after Paris, the 2d largest French-speaking city in the world, 67% French origin, 12% Anglo-Saxon, 21% other origins; Canada's largest urban center.
Area: 68 sq. mi. on an island 30 sq. mi. in the St. Lawrence River where the Ottawa and Richelieu rivers flow into it at the head of the St. Lawrence Seaway; metro area extends over 1,000 sq. mi.; the 769 ft. Mount Royal dominates the Island which averages 100 ft. above sea level.
Industry: Canada's industrial hub ($7 billion, value of shipments of goods of own manufacture).
Commerce: retail sales of $5 billion, headquarters of many of Canada's largest financial institutions, home of the Montreal and Canadian Stock Exchanges, about 75% of countries have consulates or representatives in Montreal.
Transportation: $1 billion St. Lawrence Seaway, Port of Montreal; 14 miles long, 42 miles of harbour with 140 berths; $500 million Mirabel jetport opened in 1975 with multi-million electric train link to downtown planned for early 1980's; existing 14 mile Metro to expand to 46 miles by 1981; world headquarters of International Civil Aviation Organization and International Air Transport Association serving 2 major airports; headquarters of Canadian National and Canadian Pacific railways.
Communications: 5 TV stations, 16 radio stations, 7 daily newspapers; headquarters for Bell Canada, CN-CP Telecommunications.
Educational facilities: Concordia University, McGill University, Universite de Montreal, Universite de Quebec; enrollment 78,000; faculty 5,500.
Cultural facilities: Place des Arts with 3,000 seat hall

and 2 theaters, attracting the finest forms of artistic, cultural, and musical entertainment; the Montreal Museum of Fine Arts, the Musee de l'Art Contemporain; some of the world's most beautiful churches, including the Mary Queen of The World Basilica, a half-size replica of St. Peter's in Rome.
Sports: $1 billion Olympic complex; including a 56,000 permanent seat stadium, home of the National Baseball League Expos and the Canadian Football League Alouettes; 7,200 seat Velodrome, 2 50-meter pools, 25-meter diving pool, and a scuba diving pool — 15-meter depth; the Montreal Forum, home of the National Hockey League Canadiens.
Recreational facilities: within an hour of the Laurentien and Eastern townships skiing, hunting, and fishing resort areas; over 5,000 restaurants of all lands; over 100 cinemas, 19 museums, 13 city libraries, the Montreal Botanical Gardens, St. Helen's Island Park, Dow Planetarium, Montreal Municipal Golf Course.
Convention facilities: over 15,000 hotel and motel rooms with 5,000 plus under construction; full facilities for conventions.
Medical facilities: over 80 hospitals with 26,000 beds, including the renowned Montreal Neurological Institute, and the Montreal Children's Hospital.
History: Montreal was first visited by Jacques Cartier in 1535; founded under the name of Ville Marie in 1642; Old Montreal, some 1,000 acres in all, is the largest such restoration in North America and retains the general atmosphere of the 18th century.
Further information: Convention and Visitor's Bureau of Greater Montreal, 1270 Sherbrooke St. W., H3G 1H7; The Montreal Tourist Bureau, 85 Notre Dame Street East, Montreal, Quebec.

Nashville, Tennessee

The World Almanac is sponsored in Nashville by The Tennessean, 1100 Broadway, 37202; phone (615) 255-1221; founded as The Tennessean in 1907 but incorporated publications date to 1812; circulation daily 134,700, Sunday 236,400; president Amon Carter Evans, publisher John Seigenthaler; 3 Pulitizer prizes, 8 Headliner awards, 3 Sigma Delta Chi awards.

Population: 480,000 ('76 est.) in unified metro government. 2d in state; labor force 268,000.
Area: 533 sq. mi., straddling Cumberland River, in north central part of state.
Industry: music, 52% of U.S. singles are recorded in 40 studio complexes; clothing, headquarters of Genesco, world's largest and most diversified clothing and footwear manufacturer; insurance, 2 of largest U.S. companies located here; world's largest auto glass plant; chemicals, printing (especially religious materials), aerostructures, tires, air conditioning,

heating equipment.
Commerce: retail center for middle Tennessee, south Kentucky; retail sales (1975) $1,773 million; bank resources, over $3.5 billion in 8 banks, 108 branches.
Transportation: 9 U.S. highways and 6 branches of the interstate system radiate from Nashville; 9 commercial airlines with 192 daily flights; 2 railroads, Amtrak; bus service, 73 motor freight lines.
Communications: 5 TV stations (one public), and 22 AM and FM radio stations.
Medical facilities: 18 hospitals (6,019 beds), 2 medical

schools, VA hospital, speech-hearing center.

Cultural: symphony orchestra; replica of Parthenon with art gallery; public and state libraries; botanic garden and art center, 3 community theaters.

Educational facilities: 15 colleges and universities; 137 public schools, 39 private schools.

Convention facilities: 10,000-seat auditorium; Opryland convention center under construction.

Other attractions: Grand Ole Opry, Opryland U.S.A. ($32 million theme park featuring music); Country Music Hall of Fame; Hermitage (home of Andrew Jackson); Belle Meade antebellum mansion.

Recreation facilities: water sports, outdoor activity on Old Hickory and Percy Priest lakes.

History: settled in 1780 as a fort in then western North Carolina; incorporated, 1784, with first written charter west of Alleghenies.

Further information: Chamber of Commerce, 161 4th Ave. N., Nashville, Tenn. 37219.

New Haven, Connecticut

The World Almanac is sponsored in the greater New Haven area by the New Haven Register (founded 1812) and the New Haven Journal-Courier (founded 1755); circulation Register (eve.) 103,222, Sunday 128,095; Journal-Courier (morn.) 31,327; president and publisher Lionel S. Jackson, vp and general manager Donald A. Spargo, vp and treasurer Lionel S. Jackson Jr., vp and editor Robert J. Leeney.

Population: 135,500 (city), 360,400 (metro); 3d in state.

Area: 21.1 sq. mi. southern coast of Conn. on north shore of Long Island Sound; county seat.

Industry: 1,000 firms in immediate area; principal products are guns, hardware, rubber goods, paper products, machinery, and tools.

Commerce: wholesale-retail center for southern Conn.; retail city sales (1974), 336.5 million, highest in Conn.; serves 850,000 people within a radius of 25 miles; busy harbor, particularly with cargo ships delivering oil.

Transportation: Conrail, Amtrak Cosmopolitan turbotrain; 25 major truck lines: 14 federal and state highways; Tweed-New Haven Airport served by 3 airlines; limo service to N. Y. airports, 2 bus lines.

Communications: VHF, 2 UHF TV stations, and 6 radio stations.

Medical facilities: Yale Medical Center; Yale-New Haven Hospital; Hospital of St. Raphael.

Cultural facilities: Yale Univ. Library with over 6 million books one of the world's largest collections; Yale's Peabody Museum of Natural History, Art Gallery and Beinecke Rare Book Library; New Haven Historical Society; Cultural Center; 2 legitimate theaters, and The New Haven Symphony.

Educational facilities: Yale Univ. and graduate schools; Albertus Magnus, Southern Conn. State, South Central Community, Quinnipiac Colleges; Univ. of New Haven.

Recreational facilities: Yale Bowl, Woolsey Hall, Ingalls Rink, the Coliseum, 15 parks, including Frederick Brewster's estate, East and West Rock scenic drives, 50 playgrounds, West Rock Nature Center; 7 golf courses, 30 tennis courts, 6 skating rinks.

Convention facilities: Coliseum-convention center with a 19-story hotel nearby.

Sports: AHL nighthawks; West Haven Yankees (baseball).

History: founded 1638 by Puritans; named after Newhaven in England; incorporated 1638, became a part of Conn. 1662; first mayor was Roger Sherman, signer of Declaration of Independence.

Further information: New Haven Chamber of Commerce, 152 Temple St., New Haven, Conn. 06510.

New Orleans, Louisiana

The World Almanac is sponsored in the New Orleans area by The States-Item, 3800 Howard Ave., New Orleansa. 70140; phone (504) 586-3560; founded Jan. 3, 1880, by Maj. Henry J. Hearsey, circulation 130,188 daily, 117,130 Saturday; editor Walter G. Cowan, associate editor Charles A. Ferguson, city editor William U. Madden; sponsors Women Against Crime Crusade and Football Fund for Underprivileged.

Population: 593,471 (city), 1,034,316 (metro area); first in state; total employed, 399,000 in Mar., 1976.

Area: 363.5 sq. mi. of which 199.4 are land.

Industry: Port of New Orleans, 2d largest in nation, handled 32 million tons of cargo valued at $8.3 billion in 1975.

Commerce: trade center for lower Mississippi valley. Bank resources $5.1 billion in 1975.

Transportation: rail hub for north, east and west-bound commerce. Amtrak passenger service to Chicago, New York, Los Angeles. New Orleans International Airport serves major airlines; Lakefront Airport private aviation.

New construction: $50 million, 27-story Hyatt-Regency Hotel opening beside Superdome; tallest building, 51-story One Shell Square.

Communications: 4 commercial TV stations and educational channel.

Medical facilities: major medical center with Charity Hospital, 2 schools of medicine and one of dentistry; Oschner Clinic, Touro Infirmary.

Cultural facilities: Center for the Performing Arts seats 2,317 for operas, concerts; museums include Louisiana State Museum, Isaac Delgado Museum of Art, the Middle American Research Institute of Tulane University and many small galleries.

Educational facilities: Tulane Univ., Louisiana State Univ. in New Orleans, Loyola, Dillard, Southern Univ. in New Orleans, Xavier, St. Mary's Dominican.

Other attractions: Louisiana Superdome seats 80,000 for major events; French Quarter remains major historic tourist attraction.

Sports: New Orleans Saints (NFL), New Orleans Jazz (NBA). Sugar Bowl is major college attraction.

History: named after the Duke of Orleans, founded on the edge of a swamp within crescent of the Mississippi River 100 miles upstream from the Gulf of Mexico by Jean Baptiste Le Moyne, Sieur de Bienville; became capital of Louisiana Territory in 1722, when Adrien de Pauger laid out what is now the French Quarter; became part of U. S. with signing of Louisiana Purchase in 1803.

Further information: Chamber of Commerce of Greater New Orleans, 301 Camp St., New Orleans, La. 70130.

New York City, New York

The World Almanac is sponsored in the greater New York City metropolitan area by the Daily News and Sunday News, 220 E. 42d St., New York, N. Y. 10017, phone (212) 949-1234; New York News Inc. founded June 26, 1919, by Joseph Medill Patterson; circulation daily 1,902,717; Sunday 2,818,281; president and publisher W. H. James, vice president and editor Michael J. O'Neill, managing editor William J. Brink, treasurer Robert J. Rohrbach, secretary Valfrid E. Palmer; Pulitzer Prizes for news photography, cartoon, editorial writing and international and local investigative reporting; sponsors Golden Gloves, National Spelling Bee championships for New York City, Long Island, Westchester, and other major school events as community service programs.

Population: 7,567,000 (city), 10,927,827 (consolidated area), N.Y. City, Westchester, Nassau, Suffolk counties); first in state and nation; total employed 3,199,-900; per capita personal income $6,306.

Area: 300 sq. mi. at mouth of Hudson River; embraces 5 boroughs — Manhattan, Bronx, Brooklyn, Queens, and Staten Island.

Industry: nation's leader in manufacturing and service industries; produces 25.2% of America's apparel, 15.7% of printing and publishing; 22,300 manufacturing establishments (Oct. 1974).

Commerce: nation's richest port, handling annual 195 million tons of maritime cargo; Wall Street, world's largest financial center, with New York and American Stock exchanges; wholesale-retail center for New York, New Jersey and southwestern Connecticut, retail sales $15.9 billion (1975); 33 commercial banks, resources $143.7 billion; 43 savings banks, resources $51.1 billion; World Trade Center, twin 110-story towers, cost $850 million.

Transportation: Kennedy International Airport handles 42% of nation's overseas air travel and 52% of export-import air tonnage, served by 57 scheduled air carriers; LaGuardia Airport served by 15 domestic airlines; 4 heliports. Penn Central Railroad, Amtrak; 2 major rail terminals, Pennsylvania and Grand Central stations; 40 interstate bus lines; subway network covers every borough except Staten Island; ferry and the 4,260-ft. Verrazano-Narrows Bridge (world's longest suspension span) link Staten Island to Manhattan and Brooklyn; 18 bridges connect Manhattan with other boroughs, George Washington Bridge over the Hudson connects New Jersey; 5 tunnels under the Hudson and East rivers.

Communications: 13 TV stations (6 commercial, 2 educational, 1 municipal, 2 Spanish, 2 CATV); 39 AM and FM radio stations; WPIX-TV and WPIX-FM are broadcast affiliates of The News.

Medical facilities: 106 hospitals, (17 municipal, 28 private, 61 voluntary non-profit); 5 major medical research centers specialize in cancer, heart diseases, sickle cell anemia, and other research; Sloan-Kettering Institute for Cancer Research; 4 VA hospitals.

Federal facilities: Fort Wadsworth, Staten Island; Governors Island, many federal agencies represented in buildings at Federal Plaza and 90 Church St.

Educational facilities: 6 universities, 23 colleges, including 5 medical colleges, 4 law schools, 3 colleges of pharmacy, 2 colleges of dentistry, 2 institutes of art and architecture; 954 schools in the public school system; more than 1,000 private schools; public libraries total 201.

Cultural facilities: Lincoln Center for the Performing Arts (Philharmonic, Ballet Company, Metropolitan Opera, and other theatrical arts), Carnegie Hall, Brooklyn Academy of Music. Broadway and Off-Broadway alliance for varied theatrical productions; Shakespeare Festival at Delacorte Theatre; 42 museums including American Museum of Natural History, Metropolitan Museum of Art, Museum of the Performing Arts, Museum of Modern Art, Whitney Museum, and South Street Seaport Museum.

Other attractions: United Nations; botanic gardens in the Bronx and Brooklyn; Central Park and Prospect Park; Bronx Zoo and 4 other zoos; 13 municipal golf courses, 527 tennis courts, 37 outdoor swimming pools.

Sports: NBA Knicks, Nets; NHL Rangers, Islanders; NL Mets and NFL Jets play in Shea Stadium; AL Yankees play in Yankee Stadium; NFL Giants scheduled to play in new Giant Stadium, E. Rutherford, N.J.; tennis WTT Sets; soccer NASL Cosmos.

History: discovered by Giovanni da Verrazano in 1524; in 1626 Peter Minuit bought the island from the Manhattan Indians for about $24 in goods and trinkets; settlement named New Amsterdam. In 1664, British troops occupied city without resistance and named it New York in honor of the Duke of York, brother of the King. On Jan. 1, 1898, Manhattan and large areas to the NE, E, and S were consolidated into one city of New York.

Further information: Department of Commerce and Industry, 225 Broadway; Convention and Visitors Bureau, 90 East 42d St. both New York, N.Y.

Newark, New Jersey

Population: 390,300; first in state, swells on weekdays with non-residents working and attending school; 1,876,500 (metro area) including Essex, Morris, and Union counties; 134,282 employed (city).

Area: 25.4 sq. mi. (city), 15 miles SW of New York City; Essex County seat.

Industry: wide diversity of manufacturers, fine craftsmanship; more than 10,000 businesses, major banking and insurance center. Headquarters for several national firms.

Transportation: international airport; major port; 5 railroads; world's largest privately owned bus system; one of world's largest truck terminals; world's largest containerized shipping center.

Communication: 5 radio stations, one VHF public TV station and 2 UHF TV stations.

Medical facilities: 6 major hospitals with new home of the College of Medicine and Dentistry completed in 1975; Beth Israel Medical Center.

Federal facilities: new federal building; old federal courthouse.

Cultural facilities: museum, library, New Jersey Historical Society, New Jersey Symphony Orchestra, Opera Theater of N.J., Garden State Ballet, Newark Community Center of the Arts, and Symphony Hall.

Educational facilities: New Jersey College of Medicine and Dentistry; Rutgers Univ.; Seton Hall Univ. Law School; New Jersey Institute of Technology; Essex County College.

Recreational facilities: parks cover 783.97 acres; 7 pools, 74 playgrounds, one ice rink, 2 lakes.

Convention facilities: large hotel and 2 motor inns.

Other attractions: 7 famous works of sculpture, including "John F. Kennedy" by Jacques Lipchitz and a seated Abraham Lincoln by Gutzon Borglum; Sacred Heart, one of the largest Gothic cathedrals in the world, and the historic Plume House, built in 1710.

History: founded in 1666, incorporated 1836; British troops ravaged the town during the Revolution.

Further information: Greater Newark Chamber of Commerce, 1180 Raymond Blvd., Newark, N.J. 07102.

Norfolk, Virginia

The World Almanac is sponsored in the Norfolk metro. area by The Virginian-Pilot and Ledger-Star, 150 W. Brambleton Ave., Norfolk, Va. 23501; phone (804) 446-2000; Va. founded 1865, Ledger, 1876; circulation: LS (eve.) 94,851; VP (morn.) 125,248; VP (Sun.) 183,832; Frank Batten publisher, Derek Dunn-Rankin president & general manager, Perry Morgan exec. editor, Robert H. Mason VP editor, George J. Hebert LS editor.

Population: 283,700 (city), 754,600 (metro); first in state; civilian employed, 268,800; military pop., 84,-600.
Area: 915 sq. mi. in SE Virginia.
Industry: General Electric, Ford Motor Co., Norfolk Shipbuilding & Drydock Corp.
Commerce: retail sales (1975) $2.2 billion; average household income, $13,217.
Transportation: Port of Hampton Roads, world's finest naural harbor, ranks first in export tonnage (43,851,670 tons handled 1974) among Atlantic ports; biggest coal port in world; International Airport, 4 major airlines; Chesapeake Bay Bridge-Tunnel supplies direct north highway route; 6 trunk line railroads, 50 common carrier trucking companies, 2 bus companies.
Communications: 5 TV, 13 AM, 12 FM radio stations.
Medical facilities: 12 hospitals including oldest and 2d largest naval hospital in U.S.
Federal facilities: greatest concentration of naval installations in world; approx. 36 major commands include Atlantic Fleet, Second Fleet, NATO Supreme Allied Command Atlantic (SACLANT), Armed Forces Staff College, and Commandant 5th Naval Dist.
Cultural facilities: symphony orchestra, Feldman Chamber Quartet, repertory theater, dinner and little theaters, civic and univ. ballet; Chrysler Museum collection; winter home Barter Theater; Va. Opera Assoc.; yearly Festival of the Arts.
Educational facilities: Old Dominion Univ., Norfolk State, Virginia Wesleyan, Tidewater Community Colleges; Eastern Va. Medical School.
Recreational facilities: General Douglas MacArthur Memorial, Adam Thoroughgood House (1636), Gardens-by-the-sea; Dismal Swamp located in Chesapeake; resort city of Virginia Beach offers 38 mi. of swimming, fishing and surfing; camping facilities at Seashore State Park. Hermitage Foundation Museum.
Convention facilities: Scope, $30 million cultural and convention center.
Sports: Tidewater Tides, International League baseball; Tidewater Sharks, SHL.
Climate: Average temp. 70° to 52°.
Further information: Chamber of Commerce, 475 St. Paul Blvd., Norfolk, Va. 23501.

Oakland, California

Population: 336,600; employed living in Oakland, 143,300.
Area: 53.4 sq. mi.; seat of Alameda County.
Industry: food processing, fabricated metal products, transportation equipment, chemicals and paint; Port of Oakland is 2d in containerized cargo; home base for Kaiser Industries.
Commerce: 8,133 retail outlets with taxable sales (Jan. 1976) of $1.1 billion; effective buying income for family, $8,959 per annum.
Transportation: western terminus for Southern Pacific, Santa Fe, and Western Pacific railroads; International Airport is major airfreight terminal and center for supplemental air carriers; headquarters for Bay Area Rapid Transit, underground, underwater 75-mile subway connecting 15 communities.
Medical facilities: 9 hospitals include Children's Hospital Medical Center, Kaiser Foundation, and the Veterans Administration.
New construction: Pacific Telephone Bldg., Wells Fargo Bldg., Clorox Bldg.; 16 square block city center project, and major downtown garage under construction.
Cultural facilities: museum, half garden, half gallery design, has divisions of Natural Science, History, and Art; symphony, Chinese Community Cultural Center.
Educational facilities: Univ. of California at Berkeley, Mills College, College of Holy Names, Cal. State, Hayward, Chabot, California College of Arts and Crafts, Peralta Community College.
Recreational facilities: 26,000 acre Regional Park System serving the East Bay; zoo in 100-acre Knowland State Park has large collection of gibbons and aerial tram; Lake Merritt Park includes botanical garden, wildfowl refuge, natural science center, and Children's Fairyland.
Sports: Raiders (football), Athletics (baseball), Golden State Warriors (basketball).
Other attractions: Oakland Coliseum, over 50,000 capacity, for theatrical entertainment, exhibits, conventions and circus; Jack London Square.
History: area explored in 1772, settled in 1850; incorporated as town in 1852, as city in 1854.
Further information: Chamber of Commerce, 1320 Webster St., Oakland, Cal. 94612.

Oklahoma City, Oklahoma

The World Almanac is sponsored in the Oklahoma City area by The Daily Oklahoman and Oklahoma City Times, Oklahoma City, Okla. 73125; phone (405) 232-3311; The Oklahoman founded in 1894; Times in 1888; Oklahoma Publishing Co. acquired The Oklahoman 1903 and the Times 1916; circulation Oklahoman 181,000; Times 92,000; Sunday, 304,000; editor and publisher E. L. Gaylord, executive editor Charles L. Bennett.

Population: (1976 est.) 391,000 (city), 788,000 (metro); largest in state; labor force 355,600.
Area: city area, among nation's largest, is 647.5 sq. mi.; metro area, 3,491 sq. mi.; located in state's center on Canadian River.
Industry: oil, with about 1,500 producing wells in metro area, employs about 13,000; Tinker AFB, one of world's largest air depots, employs 17,200 civilians and 3,500 military on $100 million installation; FAA and other aviation employ some 30,000, with annual payroll of $300 million; agricultural and ranching area; manufactured goods include aircraft, telecommunications equipment, computers, oil field machinery, oil and greases, building materials, feed, flour, meat, and tires.
Commerce: regional, national, and international marketing center; effective buying income, $13,228 per household (metro), consumer sales near $2.6 billion (metro).
Transportation; 5 passenger airlines; 4 primary federal and 3 major state highways, with I-40 and I-35 intersecting the city; fully planned urban expressway system, major bus, truck, and rail lines.
Medical facilities: Oklahoma Univ. Health Sciences Center and 25 hospitals and clinics.
Cultural facilities: symphony and junior symphony; Oklahoma Art Ctr.; Lyric Theater at Oklahoma City Univ.; Warehouse Theater; Oklahoma Theater Ctr.; Southwest Repertory Theater, Univ. of Oklahoma.
Education: Univ. of Oklahoma, Oklahoma City Univ., Central State Univ.
Convention facilities: $23 million Myriad Convention Center, seating 15,000 in the center of a downtown redevelopment project, hosts 350 conventions yearly with more than 150,000 delegates.
Other attractions: National Cowboy Hall of Fame; 130 municipal parks; major college sports; pro sports: Oklahoma City 89ers, American Assn. base-

ball; International Softball headquarters.
History: founded by land run, Apr. 22, 1889.

Further information: Chamber of Commerce, 1 Santa Fe Plaza, Oklahoma City, Okla. 73102.

Omaha, Nebraska

The World Almanac is sponsored in Nebraska by The Omaha World-Herald, World-Herald Square, Omaha, Neb. 68102; phone (402) 444-1000; Evening World, founded 1885 by G. M. Hitchcock, acquired Daily Herald, founded 1865; adopted present name 1889; circulation 240,778 daily, 276,854 Sunday; president Harold W. Andersen, executive editor Louis G. Gerdes; 3 Pulitzer Prizes; sponsors Midwest Spelling Bee, Newspapers in the Classroom, Music in the Parks, Show Wagon, Good Fellows charities, college scholarships.

Population: 383,800 (city), 587,000 (metro) (1976 est.) first in state, 68th in U.S.; 261,750 work force.

Area: eastern Nebraska, 83 sq. mi. of rolling hills on Missouri River; Douglas County seat.

Industry: manufacturing shipments valued at $2.1 billion annually; 600 plants employ 40,000; food processing center; 2d in frozen food production; 3d largest livestock market in salable receipts.

Commerce: major trade center; 1,000 wholesale firms, $1.6 billion retail sales, 50th in buying income per household ($16,238); 28 banks, $2 billion deposits; 11 savings and loans, $2 billion assets; 4th largest insurance center in U.S. (36 home offices, including Mutual of Omaha). Also headquarters Union Pacific, Northern Natural Gas, Northwestern Bell, ConAgra.

Transportation: 7 major airlines; 4th largest rail center, served by 8 major railroads, Amtrak, 122 truck lines, Interstates 80 and 29, bus, 3 barge lines; 2.6 million tons carried on Missouri River annually; port of entry, foreign trade zone.

Communications: Nebraska's largest daily newspaper, 6 TV, 17 radio stations.

Medical facilities: 16 hospitals 4,680 beds; 2 medical schools (Nebraska U., Creighton U.), 8 nursing schools, Eppley Institute for Cancer Research.

Federal facilities: Strategic Air Command's global headquarters at Offutt Air Base; Missouri River Division of the U.S. Army Corps of Engineers.

Cultural facilities: Orpheum performing arts center, symphony orchestra, opera company, ballet society; 10 live theatre groups, 15 art galleries, 7 museums, Joslyn Art Museum's $20 million collection.

Educational facilities: 3 universities, 4 colleges educate 27,000 students; 30 adult education schools.

Recreation: 5,000 acres of public parks include 100 tennis courts, 25 pools, 10 golf courses, ice rinks.

Other attractions: 1,200-acre Fontenelle Forest, Henry Doorly Zoo, Boys Town; Omaha Royals baseball, Ak-Sar-Ben horse racing, NCAA College World Series; (10th among 50 largest U.S. cities in quality of life, (January 1975 Harper's magazine).

History: Lewis and Clark, 1804; Indian trading post, 1825; Mormon settlement, 1846; Omaha (named after Indian tribe) laid out when Nebraska Territory opened, 1854; chartered as city, 1867.

Further information: Chamber of Commerce, 1620 Dodge St., Omaha, 68102.

Orange County, California

The World Almanac is sponsored in Orange County by The Register, 625 N. Grand, Santa Ana, Cal. 92711; telephone (714) 835-1234; circulation combined daily 206,849, Sunday 234,857; founded in 1905, purchased in 1935 by the late R. C. Hoiles, founder of Freedom Newspapers Inc., 24-paper chain. Son Clarence H. Hoiles, chairman of the board and publisher The Register; son Harry Hoiles, co-publisher and president of Freedom Newspapers Inc.; general manager, Richard Wallace; executive editor, Jim Dean; managing editor, Mike Maloney; research and promotion director, Jim Lyons Sr.

Population: 1,722,094 as of special census Jan. 1976, 2d most populous county in state, fastest growing U.S. metropolitan area, up 22% since 1970, compares to 212,364 in 1950, 2.5 million projected for 1990. County encompasses 26 cities: largest, Anaheim, 196,382 population; county seat Santa Ana, 179,499; unincorporated areas, 217,299.

Area: 511,040 acres in S. Cal. from Pacific Ocean inland 25 miles to Cleveland National Forest; 42-mile coastline stretches from Long Beach past Huntington Beach surfing, Newport Beach yacht harbor, Laguna Beach art colony, Dana Point small-craft harbor to San Clemente and Camp Pendleton. County lies at center of developing San Diego-to-Santa Barbara megalopolis.

Industry and Commerce: median family income (1975) $16,560, 1976 est. $18,350; total personal income, 1976 est. $13.2 billion; $5.7 billion, 1975 retail sales, with eating and drinking estab. comprising the largest segment at $1 billion; employment, 800,600 (1975), with 151,900 in manufacturing, 143,100 in trades, 111,000 in services, 92,100 in government, 31,-300 in insurance, real estate, and finance; 8,000 in agriculture, a $145.3 million industry in 1975. Biggest manufacturing employer, Rockwell International's Autonetics, Minuteman missiles and electronic calculators, sewing and reading machines firm; Hughes Aircraft Co., 2d; McDonald-Douglas Astronautics, 3d. Other major employers include corporate or major unit headquarters for international firms such as Philco-Ford Aeronutronics, Beckman Instruments, Fluor Corp., AMF-Voit, Hunt-Wesson Foods. County is center for such industries as tourism, sailboat construction, fiberglass products, glass containers, food processing, computers, and agriculture, with nursery stock 1975 top crop at $55 million, followed by strawberries, $22 million; oranges, $15 million.

Transportation: 8 major freeways, including main Los Angeles-San Diego artery; nation's 2d busiest airport with 618,889 tower operations in 1975; transit district with countywide bus network including freeway commuter buses and Dial-A-Ride in some areas.

New construction: 15,399 new housing units built in 1975, with total $887.3 million in new construction valuation; first 4 months 1976 total $489.9 million building valuation, up 157.7% over same period 1975; average price new home (1975) $57,640.

Communications: Local UHF, 12 other TV stations, over 40 radio stations.

Federal facilities: Marine Corps Air Station at El Toro, Los Alamitos Naval Air Station, Seal Beach Naval Weapons Station, Santa Ana Marine Corps Lighter-Than-Air (helicopter) Station, federal building in Santa Ana, General Services Admin. Building in Laguna Niguel; Cleveland National Forest; Marine Corps Camp Pendleton nearby.

Medical facilities: Univ. of Cal. medical school at Irvine, 65 hospitals and convalescent hospitals.

Recreation: 781 acres of beaches, over 13,000 acres regional parks, 141 scenic sea cliffs, 3 yacht basins, 2 fishing lakes, wilderness campgrounds, 35 golf courses.

Other attractions: Disneyland, 10 million visitors in 1975; Knott's Berry Farm, 5 million visitors in 1975; Lion Country Safari, Movieland Wax Museum, and Cars of Stars, air and car museums; Los Alamitos racetrack, auto races, motorcycle park, mid-summer Laguna Beach Arts Festival-Pageant of the Masters, Santa Ana zoo. Mediterranean climate attracts new residents, development, visitors.

Convention facilities: Anaheim Convention Center, hotels in Anaheim, Buena Park, Irvine, Newport Beach.

Sports: AL Angels, school sports.

Cultural, Educational facilities: 2 major tax-supported universities, 4 private liberal arts colleges, 6 community colleges, multiple trade and special interest schools; 76 tax-supported high schools; 35 city and county libraries; symphony orchestra society; 2 master chorales, 6 ballet companies, 32 community theater groups, 6 performing arts support groups, 4 major art museums, art associations.

History: first Spanish expedition 1769 by Capt. Gaspar de Portola, recorded first reported earthquake in the state; county formed March 11, 1889, from Los Angeles Co.; Glenn Martin tested his first plane near Santa Ana; Madame Modjeska resided in local forest hideaway; Toastmasters International founded in Santa Ana 1924; Howard Hughes set new world's speed record in Santa Ana 1935 with 351 mph flight. Swallows traditionally return each year to Mission San Juan Capistrano on March 19.

Further information: Anaheim Visitor and Convention Bureau, 800 W. Katella Ave., Anaheim; Orange County Chamber of Commerce, One City Blvd. W., Orange.

Orlando, Florida

The World Almanac is sponsored in the Orlando area by the Sentinel Star, 633 N. Orange Ave., Orlando, Fla. 32802; phone (305) 420-5000; Sentinel and Evening Star founded as dailies in 1913; merged 1931; acquired by Tribune Co. of Chicago in 1965; combined to create "all day" newspaper in 1973; circulation, 177,494 weekdays, 170,939 Saturday, 203,186 Sunday.

Population: 122,405 (city), 602,632 (metro); 236,800 employed (metro) as of April, 1976; 1976 estimated buying income per household, $13,586.

Area: 30.1 sq. mi. (city), 2,528 sq. mi. (metro) in east central Florida; 52 lakes inside city limits; av. temperature 72.5; Orange County seat.

Industry: center of citrus belt; 6 regional home and 10 national home insurance company offices; Martin Marietta Co., aerospace division; General Electric plant; Westinghouse Electric Co., minicomputer division; 16 industrial parks; naval training center training approximately one-third of men in Navy and all women recruits, 25 commands, new nuclear power school.

Commerce: 53 commercial banks in metro area; total deposits, nearly $1.5 billion; 6 savings and loan assns. based in metro area; 30 major shopping centers with 4 regional malls; retail sales, $2.2 billion in 1975.

Transportation: 4 major commercial airlines serving jetport at McCoy, 1975 passenger total, 3,208,348; Seaboard Coastline Railroad, Amtrak, 9 intercity bus lines, 195 common carrier truck lines and 7 freight forwarding services; every major Florida market less than 4 hours by highway.

Communications: 16 radio and 6 TV stations.

Medical facilities: 15 hospitals in metro area.

Cultural facilities: Florida Symphony Orchestra, Loch Haven Art Center, John Young Museum and Planetarium, Central Florida Civic Theater, Orlando Public Library with 12 community libraries and approximately 620,000 volumes; Rollins College, Florida Tech Univ., Valencia and Seminole community colleges.

Other attractions: Walt Disney World, destination resort 18 miles from downtown Orlando visited annually by 12.5 million people; Sea World; Barnum & Bailey Circus World; Church Street Station, renovated area in downtown Orlando; Stars Hall of Fame, wax museum.

Convention facilities: metro area ranks 6th in world in number of hotel rooms; 30,006 rooms; approximately 750 conventions attended by some 300,000 in 1975.

Sports: Minnesota Twins spring training site; Tangerine Bowl Sports Week; 2 PGA tournaments, $200,000 Walt Disney World Tournament, $200,000 Florida Citrus Open; Ben White Raceways, training ground for trotters; Seminole Harness Raceway; Sanford-Orlando Kennel Club; Jai-Alai fronton.

Additional information: Orlando Area Chamber of Commerce. P.O. Box 1913, Orlando, Fla. 32802.

Ottawa, Ontario, Canada

Population: 303,000 (city), 626,000 (metro region including greater Ottawa and Hull, Que.); Canada's 5th largest city, linked with neighboring city of Hull (pop. 130,000) by 5 bridges.

Area: 30,481 acres (city), 1,100 sq. mi. (region) on Ontario-Quebec border at the Chaudiere Falls on the Ottawa River.

National Capital Region: Ottawa and Hull, occupying 1800 square miles of eastern Ontario and western Quebec, form the National Capital Region of Canada; it includes 24 municipalities and 2 regional governments.

Industry: major employer is the federal government; E.B. Eddy Co. largest private employer.

Commerce: capital city of Canada with a large tourist business and developing convention capacity; some 57 hotels and motels, 5,180 rooms.

Transportation: 45 miles of parkways and bicycle paths in and around the city; Canadian Pacific and Canadian National railways; International Airport, nation's 5th busiest, more than 85 scheduled flights daily by 5 airlines.

Cultural facilities: $45 million National Arts Centre with 2,300-seat opera house-concert hall, a theatre and an experimental studio; Ottawa Little Theatre.

National museums: National Gallery of Canada, Museum of Man, Museum of Natural Sciences, Museum of Science and Technology, Canadian War Museum, National Aeronautical Collection.

Other attractions: Gothic-style Parliament buildings, housing Canada's House of Commons and Senate; Peace Tower, memorial to Canada's war dead; Central Canada Exhibition; Ottawa's oldest building, the Bytown Museum; Royal Mint; Rideau Canal provides boating facilities in summer, skating in winter; the Experimental Farm, 1,300 working acres in the heart of Ottawa; Winter Fair; 80 camping and trailer parks, 7 city beaches; mountain lake recreation facilities.

Sports: Ottawa Rough Riders, CFL; Ottawa 67's, hockey.

History: founded 1827 as Bytown, incorporated as Ottawa 1855; named after Outaouac (or Outaouais Indian tribe); became capital of Canada 1857.

Further information: Canada's Capital Visitors and Convention Bureau, 251 Laurier Ave. West, Ottawa, Ont., K1P-5J6.

Pensacola, Florida

The World Almanac is sponsored in the Pensacola area by the Pensacola News-Journal, 101 E. Romana St., Pensacola, Fla. 32501; (904) 433-0041; predecessor The Floridian founded 1821, first daily News 1899, Journal 1898; merged 1924; combined circulation daily 86,204, Sunday 71,612; member Gannett Group; publisher James H. Jesse, editor J. Earle Bowden.

Population: 60,705 (city), 295,159 (county), 450,000 (primary trade area).

Area: southern end of 759 sq. mi: Escambia County at westernmost edge of Florida Panhandle.

Industry: U.S. Navy employs 15,200 military, 5,000 civilian personnel; major manufacturers are Monsanto, St. Regis Paper, Armstrong Cork, Tenneco, Westinghouse, Air Products and Chemical, American Cyanamid, Vanity Fair; major industries are food and kindred products, lumber, printing, stone, clay, glass, and concrete.

Commerce: wholesale, retail center for 4 counties in west Florida, one in Alabama; effective buying income $1.400 billion; retail sales 1974 $1.085 million; 17 banks, 4 savings and loan banks, 26 mortgage firms; tourist industry $60 million, and farm and forest income $18.33 million annually.

Transportation: 2 railways, 2 airlines, 2 bus lines, 16 truck lines; 3 U.S. highways, Interstate 10.

Communications: one TV, 9 radio stations.

Medical facilities: 5 hospitals in addition to the U.S. Naval Aviation Medical Center.

Cultural facilities: public library; 5 museums: Historical Museum, T. T. Wentworth Museum, Hispanic Museum, Transportation Museum, Museum of Naval Aviation; little theater; symphony orchestra; Art Association; Arts Council, Inc.; Oratorio Society.

Other attractions: historic forts, Pensacola Beach, Gulf Islands National Seashore, Seville Quarter.

Sports: PGA tournament, Falstaff Classic Amateur Golf Classic, intercollegiate basketball, greyhound racing.

History: colonized in 1559, failed; city founded in 1698, existing under 5 flags until ceded by Spain to U.S. in 1813.

Philadelphia, Pennsylvania

The World Almanac is sponsored in the Philadelphia area by The Philadelphia Inquirer, 400 N. Broad St., Philadelphia, Pa. 19101; phone (215) 854-2000; established 1829, lineage traced to Pennsylvania Packet, founded 1771; circulation 410,254 daily, 847,442 Sunday; Pulitzer Prizes 1975, 1976; published by Philadelphia Newspapers, Inc.; president Sam S. McKeel; vice president and general manager David Gelsanliter; executive editor Eugene L. Roberts Jr.; editor Creed C. Black; managing editor Gene Foreman; sponsors Delaware Valley Science Fair, Book & Author Luncheons, Old Newsboys Day. PNI also publishes the Philadelphia Daily News, an afternoon tabloid, at same address; founded 1925; circulation 238,951; editor Gilman Spencer; managing editor Mort Persky; sponsors Secret Witness rewards, sports clinics.

Population: 1,804,100 (4th in U.S.); 4,778,900 (metro area: 5 counties in Pa., 3 in N.J.): employment (metro area): 1,838,800.

Area: 130 sq. mi. (city); 3,575 sq. mi. (metro area); city located in southeastern Pa. on Delaware and Schuylkill rivers; 90 mi. from N.Y.C., 136 mi. from Wash., D.C., 60 mi. from Atlantic City.

Industry: diversified, with over 90% of all U.S. basic industries represented; major center for textiles and apparel, food processing, petroleum (largest oil refining region on East Coast), printing and publishing, instruments, chemicals and pharmaceuticals; companies headquartered in metro area include Sun Oil, Campbell Soup, American Stores, Scott Paper, Leeds & Northrup, Smithkline, Rohm & Haas, Food Fair, Crown Cork & Seal, Pennwalt.

Commerce: 17 commercial banks, over $20 billion in deposits; 4 mutual savings banks, over $7.7 billion; retail sales (1975 metro), $13.4 billion; average household income (1975 metro), $16,751.

Transportation: biggest fresh-water port in world (50 mi. of waterfront); largest international port in N. Atlantic; foreign trade (1975), 76.6 million tons; 2 new marine terminals for containerized cargo; rail service provided by Conrail (Penn Central, Reading), Chessie System (B&O), and Amtrak; over 250 truck lines, vast highway network, 6 bridges in metro area for motor traffic between Pa. and N.J.; International Airport completed $174 million terminal expansion, now capable of doubling number of passengers handled in 1975 (7.5 million); Cargo City, $50 million air freight facility; area transit (SEPTA) conveyed 278.7 million passengers on subway, el, rail commuter, bus and streetcar lines in 1975.

Communications: 3 major daily newspapers: Inquirer, Bulletin, and News; 23 AM, 23 FM, 6 commercial TV stations; cable TV.

New construction: Market St. East, $300 million reconstruction of major retail area; Franklin Town, privately financed $400 million redevelopment of 50-acre midcity site (will provide 4,000 residential units, employment for 20,000); Penn's Landing, $120 million waterfront development.

Medical facilities: 97 hospitals with 23,000 beds.

Federal facilities: Phila. Naval Base; Defense Industrial Supply Center; Defense Personnel Support Center; U.S. Navy Aviation Supply Office Compound; U.S. Mint; Frankford Arsenal; Ft. Dix and McGuire AFB (metro area).

Cultural facilities: Phila. Orchestra; Pa. Ballet; Opera Co. of Phila.; Acad. of Music; Museum of Art; Franklin Inst.; Pa. Acad. of the Fine Arts; Rodin Museum; University Museum; Acad. of Natural Sciences; Barnes Fdtn.; Robin Hood Dells (East and new West); Walnut St. Theater (oldest in America); Shubert, Forrest, and New Locust theaters; community and summer theaters.

Educational facilities: 54 colleges and universities within 25 mi. of City Hall; 6 medical schools in city; University City Science Center.

Convention facilities: Civic Center, 321,000 sq. ft. of exhibit space, 57 meeting rooms incl. 12,500-seat Convention Hall; 522 hotels/motels in metro area with 18,000 first-class rooms.

Recreational facilities: over 8,000 acres of parks incl. 4,079-acre Fairmount Park; hundreds of playgrounds, swimming pools, golf courses, tennis courts, ice-skating rinks; close to seashore, mountains.

Sports: NL Phillies and NFL Eagles (Veterans Stadium); NBA 76ers and NHL Flyers (Spectrum); NAHL Firebirds (Civic Center); NASL Atoms and Penn Relays (Franklin Field); Army-Navy football (J. F. Kennedy Stadium); horse racing at Liberty Bell, Keystone, and Garden State in metro area.

Other attractions: city was focal point of nation's Bicentennial with famed historic district and Benjamin Franklin Parkway centers of interest; many preserved, restored or reconstructed historic bldgs.; Liberty Bell housed in new pavilion; history comes to life on giant IMAX screen (70'x100') and other multimedia exhibits in $11.6 million Living History Museum; Afro-American Historical and Cultural Museum; Mummers Museums; city hall; Elfreth's

Alley; Franklin Court; Society Hill; Fairmount Park mansions; Zoo (America's first); Mummers Parade (Jan. 1); Freedom Week (June 27-July 4); nearby attractions incl. Valley Forge, Longwood Gardens.

History: Wm. Penn founded his "Greene Countrie Towne" as Quaker colony in 1682; gave it name that means "City of Brotherly Love"; national capital 1790-1800; historical shrines incl. Independence Hall,

Liberty Bell, Carpenters' Hall, Franklin's grave, Betsy Ross House, Gloria Dei Church, Christ Church, USS Olympia, Fort Mifflin.

Further information: City Representative, 1660 Municipal Services Bldg., Phila., Pa. 19107; Phila. Tourist Bureau, 1525 J. F. Kennedy Blvd., Phila., Pa. 19102.

Phoenix, Arizona

The World Almanac is sponsored in the Phoenix area by The Phoenix Gazette, 120 East Van Buren Street, Phoenix, Arizona 85004; phone (602) 271-8000; founded Oct. 28, 1880, as Arizona Gazette by Charles H. McNeil; circulation 102,338; publisher Mrs. Eugene C. Pulliam, assistant publisher Mason Walsh, managing editor Alan D. Moyer; sponsors Christmas Fund Drive, Music Memory Programs, Science Fair, Phoenix Suns Christmas Day Basketball Game, Family Symphony Concerts, and other events.

Population: 683,000 (city), 1,313,000 (metro); capital and largest city in state, 15th (city) in nation; total employed 515,600.

Area: 273.4 sq. mi. (city), 9,226 sq. mi. (metro), in south central Arizona.

Industry: electronic equipment manufacturers, Honeywell Information Systems, and Motorola, Inc. each employ more than 2,500; aircraft and parts manufacturers, AiResearch, a division of The Garrett Corp., and Sperry Flight Systems each employ more than 2,500; other major employers are E. L. Gruber (apparel), Goodyear Aerospace, General Electric, Western Electric Cable, Reynolds Metals, Marathon Steel, Arizona Public Service, Salt River Project, Mountain Bell, Amerco, Greyhound, American Express, and Phoenix Newspapers.

Commerce: wholesale-retail center for state; retail sales (1975) $4.1 billion; effective household buying income, $14,371; bank and S&L assets $10.6 billion; 12 banks with 217 area offices, 7 S&Ls with 88 offices in metro area.

Transportation: transportation center of the Southwest; Sky Harbor International Airport served by 10 airlines, 3,964,942 passengers (1975); 2 railroads; 2 transcontinental bus lines; 10 transcontinental truck lines; 25 transcontinental heavy equipment haulers; 34 interstate and 39 intrastate truck lines.

Communications: 6 TV and 32 radio stations.

New construction: In 1975, 9,959 new residential building units were permitted; total value all types of building permits, $484 million.

Medical facilities: Barrow Neurological Institute; 21 general care hospitals, Veterans' Hospital; other special service facilities.

Cultural facilities: art museum, public library, symphony orchestra, Indian museums, zoo, botanical gardens, community and professional theaters; Civic Plaza convention center; Gammage Auditorium.

Educational facilities: Arizona State Univ., American Graduate School of International Management; 4 community colleges; Maricopa Technical College (vocational); 56 public and parochial high schools.

Sports: 50 golf courses and $200,000 Phoenix Open; inland surfing beach; ice skating rinks; amusement park; pro hockey, basketball, baseball teams; auto, greyhound, and horse racing; annual Fiesta Bowl (holiday football game).

Other attractions: Frank Lloyd Wright's Taliesin West; Paolo Soleri's Arcosanti; Firebird Festival of the Arts; Dons' Club guided tours of Arizona; full calendar of events including state and county fairs and rodeos, horse shows, regattas, polo tournaments.

History: founded 1870, on site of ancient Indian settlement; the Hohokam tribe, which flourished ca. 500-1200 A.D., developed an intricate system of irrigation canals which form the base of the canal system in use today.

Pittsburgh, Pennsyvania

The World Almanac is sponsored in the Pittsburgh area by The Pittsburgh Press, 34 Blvd. of the Allies, Pittsburgh, Pa. 15222; phone (412) 263-1100; founded June 23, 1884, as Evening Penny Press by Thomas J. Keehan; circulation 265,114 daily, 667,297 Sunday; editor John Troan, business manager Robert Hartmann, executive editor Leo Koeberlein, managing editor Ralph Brem; sponsors Press Old Newsboys Fund for Children's Hospital which raised $363,300 in 1975.

Population: 520,117 (city), 2,401,245 (4-county metro area), 2d in state and 24th in nation; metro area labor force of 997,300 is 6th in nation.

Area: 55.5 sq. mi. at juncture of Allegheny and Monongahela rivers which form Ohio River; Allegheny County seat; altitude, 702 feet.

Industry: one-fifth of nation's steelmaking capacity concentrated in metro area; western Pennsylvania mines produce 44 million tons of bituminous coal annually; 6,000 different products made in area; home of world's first full-scale nuclear power plant, world's largest manufacturers of aluminum, steel rolls, rolling mill machinery, air brakes, plate and window glass, and safety equipment; 3d largest headquarters city in nation.

Commerce: retail sales (1974) $6.1 billion; exports abroad of products manufactured here totaled $650 million (1975); average household effective buying income (Allegheny County) $16,023.

Transportation: 7 scheduled airlines handled 7,359,-581 passengers on 101,621 flights at International Airport (1975); 19 railroads; Continental Trailways and Greyhound bus lines; over 400 common carriers;

Port Authority Transit vehicles carried 109.6 million passengers (1975) over 165 routes, 5 trolley lines; 9 major highways serve the city; rapid and mass transit plan under development.

Communications: 2 daily newspapers; 5 TV (including country's first educational station) and 27 radio stations.

New construction: $32 million, 140,000 sq. ft. convention center underway for completion in 1978.

Medical facilities: 21 hospitals include Univ. of Pittsburgh Health and Medical complex where Dr. Jonas Salk developed polio vaccine; VA installation.

Federal facilities: Federal Building contains scores of U.S. government offices (information center: 412/644-3456) Army base at Oakdale; Air Force base.

Cultural facilities: Heinz Hall is home of the opera co., ballet, civic light opera, youth symphony and symphony orchestra; 3 community and 2 legitimate theaters; Frick Art Museum; Carnegie Museum and Art Gallery, home of the new Pittsburgh International series, a biennial one-man art show starting in 1977 and offering a $55,000 prize; American Wind Symphony.

Educational facilities: Univ. of Pittsburgh, Duquesne Univ.; Point Park, Chatham, Carlow, Robert Morris, and La Roche colleges, Carnegie-Mellon Univ., Community College of Allegheny Co.; 18 Carnegie public libraries, 3 bookmobiles, community libraries.

Sports: NL Pirates, NFL Steelers, NHL Penguins; World Team Tennis Triangles.

Other attractions: Highland Park Zoo, children's zoo, Twilight Zoo, aquarium, aviary, Buhl Planetarium, Allegheny Observatory, Phipps Conservatory, Fort Pitt Museum; 4 amusement parks; 2 operating passenger inclines; folk festival; Three Rivers Arts Festival every June; harness racing; river cruises; Civic Arena; Three Rivers Stadium.

History: first hunters and trappers came through in 1714; city dates from Nov. 25, 1758, when English forces under Brig. Gen. John Forbes occupied the ruins of Fort Duquesne, which French soldiers had burned and abandoned, and built a new and bigger fortress called Fort Pitt. When incorporated in 1816, it already had a reputation as a "Smoky City" from factories and coal-burning homes. Massive "Renaissance Plan" has cleared the skies and rebuilt the heart of the city during the past 25 years.

Further information: Chamber of Commerce, 411 Seventh Ave.; Convention and Visitors Bureau, 3001 Jenkins Arcade; both Pittsburgh, Pa. 15222.

Portland, Maine

The World Almanac is sponsored in the Portland area by the Maine Sunday Telegram, 390 Congress, Portland, Me, 04104; phone (207) 775-5811; published by Guy Gannett Publishing Co., founded 1921; circulation 108,684 president Jean Gannett Hawley; editor Ernest Chard; also publishes morning Press Herald, circulation 54,955, and Evening Express, 29,852.

Population: 66,500 (city), 230,000 (metro area), first in state; total employed, 27,500 (1975).

Area: 21.6 sq. mi.; peninsula on Casco Bay; Cumberland County seat.

Industry: Atlantic Coast's 2d busiest oil shipping center, east terminus Montreal pipeline; fishing fleet base, seafood shipping center; landbased products: printed materials, clothing, metal, processed food, electronic parts, wooden goods.

Commerce: tourist center, regional retail-wholesale hub, large shopping complex, 1,000 retail, 350 wholesale, 600 service enterprises; retail sales (1975), $225 million; median family income (1975), $11,600.

Transportation: municipal jetport, Delta airline; 3 rail freight lines, integrated bus system, Greyhound, Continental bus terminals, 25 truck lines; Maine Turnpike, Interstate 95 and 295 highways connect to all New England; deep water anchorage, auto cruise ferries year round to Yarmouth, Nova Scotia.

Communications: 3 TV, 5 AM, 4 FM stations.

New construction: Cumberland County Civic Center, vocational school, elementary school.

Medical facilities: medical center, 2 hospitals.

Cultural facilities: symphony orch., Kotzschmar organ, one of world's largest; public, historical libraries; Victorian, art museums; Henry Longfellow home (1785); branch Univ. of Maine, Westbrook College, art, vocational, and business schools; Portland Headlight, oldest lighthouse in country.

Recreation: 18-hole municipal golf course, 9 others in area; scenic cruises; swimming, tennis, fishing within easy travel; scenic parks.

Convention facilities: 2 large assembly halls, meeting rooms in modern hotels and motels.

Further information: Tourist Bureau, 142 Free St., Portland, Maine.

Portland, Oregon

The World Almanac is sponsored in the Portland area by The Oregon Journal, 1320 SW Broadway, Portland, Ore. 97201; phone (503) 221-8275; founded Mar. 1902; circulation 106,279; editor Donald J. Sterling Jr.; managing editor Edward F. O'Meara.

Population: 371,800 (city), 1,094,300 (metro) in 1975; 1st in state; 34th in nation; total employed, 456,200.

Area: 80 sq. mi., at juncture of Columbia and Willamette rivers.

Industry: electrical and electronic industries along with lumber and wood products, food, and paper; ranks first in manufacture of logging, lumbering equipment; home of Georgia-Pacific, Louisiana-Pacific (forest products), Tektronix (oscilloscopes), Omark (saw cutting chain), Hyster (lifts, hoists, lumber handling), White Stag, Pendleton, Jantzen (clothing).

Commerce: wholesale-retail center for large part of Oregon, SW Washington; retail sales metro area (1975), $3.34 billion. There are 16 banks, 11 savings and loan associations.

Transportation: 4 major rail freight lines, Amtrak, Greyhound, Trailways buses; 10th largest freshwater port in U.S., with 27-mile frontage, 29 marine berths; 11 million tons of cargo pass over docks annually; more than 1,000 ships visit annually, most active harbor in U.S.; hub for 9 airlines, flights to all parts of world.

Communications: 5 TV and 19 radio stations.

Medical facilities: 17 major hospitals, Univ. of Oregon Medical School, VA hospital.

Cultural facilities: art museum, Oregon Symphony Orchestra, Opera Association, Oregon Historical Society, Portland State Univ., Univ. of Portland, and Lewis & Clark, Reed, and Concordia Colleges.

Other attractions: annual Rose Festival, Rose Show; park system includes Washington Park, Hoyt Arboretum International Rose Test Garden, Portland Zoo, Oregon Museum of Science and Industry; Forest Park is largest forest area in a U.S. city's limits.

Sports: Trail Blazers of the NBA play at the Memorial Coliseum.

History: chartered 1851 with population of 821; named after Portland, Me., rather than Boston, Mass., on flip of coin by 2 early citizens.

Further information: Chamber of Commerce, 824 SW 5th, Portland, Oregon 97204.

Providence, Rhode Island

The World Almanac is sponsored in the Providence area by The Providence Journal-Bulletin, 75 Fountain St., Providence. R.I. 02902; phone (401) 277-7000; Journal founded 1829, Bulletin 1863, Sunday Journal 1883; circulation, Journal (morn) 67,106, Bulletin (eve) 144,924, Sunday Journal 207,767; publisher John C. A. Watkins, president Michael P. Metcalf, v.p. and asst. publ. Edwin P. Young, v.p.-admin. Charles P. O'Donnell, v.p. and exec. editor Charles McC. Hauser.

Population: 175,100 (city), 952,000 (metro); total employed 115,084.

Area: 18.91 sq. mi., at the head of Narragansett Bay; state capital.

Industry: jewelry, silverware, plated ware, costume jewelry are largest industries; Textron is based in Providence; 1,235 manufacturing companies in the city.

Commerce: wholesale-retail center for entire state; retail sales $2.5 billion (metro); consumer spendable income per household $13,037 (metro); Allendale Insurance, world's largest mutual insurer of industrial firms, is based outside of city in Johnston; home of Narragansett Capital, largest small business investment company in nation; 2 savings and loan assns., 2 mutual savings banks, one cooperative bank, 6 commercial banks.

Transportation: Penn Central Railroad, fast "Turbo-Liner" passenger service between Boston, Providence, and N.Y.; 5 bus lines; 45 locally-based common carriers and contract truckers; 9 major highways link Providence to every corner of R.I.; 6 major airlines out of T. F. Green Airport in Warwick (15 min. away); port is 3d largest in New England with 25 wharves and docks, 10.5 miles of commercial waterfront on the bay.

Communications: 3 TV and 8 radio stations.

Medical facilities: 7 hospitals; one VA hospital.

Cultural facilities: Trinity Square Repertory Co., R. I. Philharmonic, R. I. School of Design Museum.

Education: Brown University, founded 1764, is 7th oldest college in nation; 7-year M.D. program inaugurated 1973; Providence and R. I. colleges, and R.I. School of Design.

Recreation: one of America's most attractive recreational areas centers around Providence: 69 salt water beaches, 25 fresh water beaches, 50 golf and country clubs, 4 ski areas, 29 yacht clubs, 27 parks, all within 45 minutes of city.

Convention facilities: R.I. Civic Center (seats 12,000).

Sports: America's Cup races since 1930; Newport-Bermuda race starts at Newport every other year; Reds (hockey), Oceaneers (soccer).

Other attractions: largest collection of original early American homes of any city; located along Benefit St., they have been preserved by the Providence Preservation Society.

History: founded 1636 by Roger Williams; incorporated 1832; official state name is "Rhode Island and Providence Plantations."

Further information: Chamber of Commerce, 10 Dorrance St., Providence, R. I. 02903.

Quebec City, Quebec, Canada

Population: 186,088 (city), 480,500 (metro); oldest city in Canada (1608) and the capital city of the province of Quebec.

Area: 30 sq. mi.; natural citadel on north shore of St. Lawrence River at confluence with St. Charles River; 400 miles from Gulf of St. Lawrence; 167 miles east of Montreal; older part is built on a cliff 360 ft. above the St. Lawrence.

Industry: some 300 industrial firms, ranging from primary industry products to a variety of consumer products, employ over 16,000 people; food and beverage, leather footwear and leather products, textiles, apparel, wood products, pulp and paper, printing and publishing, iron and steel products, non-ferrous metal and chemical products.

Commerce: Quebec harbor, one of the busiest seaports of Canada, accommodates the largest ocean-going vessels with year-round facilities, an important container terminal on the North Atlantic coast; Provincial Government, with more than 15,000 employees, is the largest single employer and consumer in the city.

Transportation: Canadian Pacific and Canadian National railroads; Air Canada, Quebecair, Nordair; major bus center.

Communications: 3 TV stations (2 French, 1 bilingual); 7 radio stations (6 French, 1 English), 2 newspapers (French).

Medical facilities: 5 large general hospitals, many smaller ones.

Cultural facilities: historic character, cultural appeal and natural beauty make tourism important area of economic activity; annual "Carnaval" in Feb. is internationally known; annual summer festival (July) changes the city into an open theater for numerous artistic events; Expo-Quebec, an annual provincial exhibition (industrial, commercial, and agricultural), draws over 500,000 people a year.

Educational facilities: Laval University, the first in North America; Quebec University; 3 colleges for general and vocational training, numerous private schools.

Sports: home of WHA Nordiques.

Other attractions: only walled city in North America with fortifications standing today as they were 125 years ago; the Citadel, built from 1823-1832, contains within its walls 25 buildings, including the summer residence of Governor-General of Canada, Parliament buildings (1886), Quebec Museum, Battlefield Park, Ursulines Museum, Seminary (1663), Talon cellars, Notre Dame des Victoires Church, and Tresor Street.

History: founded 1608 by French explorer Samuel de Champlain; cradle of French civilization in America; once the key to the interior of the North American continent.

Raleigh, North Carolina

The World Almanac is sponsored in eastern North Carolina by The News & Observer and The Raleigh Times, 215 S. McDowell St., Raleigh, NC 27602, (919) 821-1234; circulation N&O (morn) 126,839, Times (eve) 32,031, N&O Sunday 155,266; publisher Frank Daniels Jr., editorial director Claude Sitton, editor Times A. C. Snow, managing editor N&O Bob Brooks, Times Mike Yopp.

Population: 150,000 (city), 275,000 (county), 500,000 (metro area); 4th in state; 200,000 employed (metro area).

Area: 45 sq. mi. in geographical center of state where piedmont joins coastal plain; alt. 363 ft.; state capital

and Wake Co. seat.

Industry: major industry is government, employing 25% of work force; also electrical machinery, foods, and textiles.

Commerce: financial, retail center of eastern N.C.;

retail sales (1975) $1.3 billion; 13 banks with $50 billion debits; income average per household $16,000.

Education: 6 colleges; N.C. State Univ. largest, with Univ. of N.C. (Chapel Hill), and Duke Univ. (Durham) within 30 mi. form Research Triangle; 5,000 acre Triangle Park employs 10,000 in drug, fiber, biomedical, and engineering research.

Transportation: 3 rail and 5 bus lines; airport has 4 airlines and 46 flights daily.

Communications: 4 TV and 13 radio stations.

New construction: $98 million (1975).

Medical facilities: 3 hospitals, 818 beds; major mental hospital, 2,765 beds; 350 doctors.

Convention facilities: 30 motels, 4,000 rooms.

Cultural facilities: 3 museums, state fairgrounds; Dorton Arena seats 9,111, Memorial Auditorium 3,000, and Reynolds Coliseum 12,000.

Recreation: 4,200-acre Umstead Park; Carter Stadium; 100 city parks.

Sports: one pro golf meet; college sports.

History: founded 1792; Andrew Johnson birthplace.

Further information: Chamber of Commerce, 411 S. Salisbury St., Raleigh, NC 27602.

Regina, Saskatchewan, Canada

The World Almanac is sponsored in southern Saskatchewan by The Leader-Post, 1964 Park St., Regina, Sask., S4P 3GA, phone (306) 527-8511; founded 1883 by Nicholas Flood Davin; circulation 66,650; president Michael Sifton, Toronto; executive vice-president Max Macdonald; editor W. Ivor Williams; managing editor C.E.W. Bell; business manager William Duffus; advertising manager George Crawford; MacLaren Trophy for editorial page reproduction excellence.

Population: 150,610, first in province, 17th in nation; labor force, 65,000.

Area: 34.5 sq. mi., 100 miles north of Canada-U.S. border; provincial capital.

Industry: over 260 manufacturing industries; gross production value (1975) $290 million, 37.6% of Saskatchewan total.

Commerce: service center for oil, potash; grain production area; retail sales (1975) $447.6 million, 24.7% of province.

Transportation: 2 rail lines, 2 airlines, 3 bus lines, and 80 trucking companies; main Trans-Canada highway bisects; city-run transit system, including Telebus, hybrid system with demand/response taxi service and mass transit, provides to-and-from service to user's home.

Communications: 2 TV and 6 radio stations.

Medical facilities: 4 major hospitals, 1,735 beds.

Cultural facilities: Saskatchewan Centre of Arts, multi-purpose theater-convention center with: Jubilee theater (seats 450) stage, ballroom, reception hall and dining room; Centennial theater (seats 2,029); Hanbidge Hall convention area, 12,200 square feet, 9 meeting rooms, seats 1,600, serves 1,200. Regina Symphony; Globe Repertory; Museum Natural History; Norman Mackenzie Art Gallery; RCMP Museum.

Educational facilities: Regina University; 13 collegiates; 92 elementary; Wascana Institute of Applied Arts and Sciences.

Recreation facilities: Saskatchewan Roughriders (Canadian pro football); 137 parks and playgrounds; 9 golf courses; 6 swimming pools; 6 indoor ice rinks.

Other attractions: Wascana Centre, 2,000-acre development, with man-made lake, public buildings, parks, recreation in heart of city.

History: founded 1882, and since that time headquarters for RCMP training depot. Will mark 75th anniversary of incorporation as a city in 1978.

Further information: Regina Chamber of Commerce, 2145 Albert Street, Regina, Saskatchewan.

Reno, Nevada

The World Almanac is sponsored in the northern Nevada area by the Nevada State Journal and Reno Evening Gazette, 401 West 2d St., Reno, Nev. 89504; phone (702) 786-8989; Journal founded 1870; Gazette 1876; combined daily circulation 48,396, Sunday 39,389; publisher Ronald H. Einstoss, executive editor Warren L. Lerude.

Population: est. 1975 pop. of 88,800 (city), 153,900 county (including Sparks with 34,500); 2d largest in the state; 1975 labor force, 77,800.

Area: 36.8 sq. mi. (including Stead annexation), in northwestern part of state at the eastern foot of the Sierra Nevada; Washoe County seat.

Industry: gross gaming revenue for county, $193.2 million (1975) netted state taxes of $9.7 million; 80,-283 delegates attended 196 conventions, staying in 13,603 rooms, paying $2.5 million in room taxes; warehousing continues to grow because of Nevada's liberal free port law with est. 10-12 million sq. ft. in the county; marriages (33,032) outnumbered divorces (3,371).

Commerce: taxable sales in metro area (including Sparks) for 1975, $785 million; assessed valuation (city) $524.4 million; median household income $13,-746; bank resources, $1.8 billion.

Transportation: 12 motor freight lines, 3 freight railroads, Amtrak, 3 commercial bus lines and 3 commercial airlines; airport handled 1,044,716 passengers (1975) as international port of entry; U.S. 395 and Interstate 80.

Communications: 3 TV, 10 radio stations; one CTV.

New construction: 116 commercial, 1,326 residential units totaling $109.2 million new assessed valuation (1975, includes county).

Medical facilities: 3 hospitals, including VA.

Educational facilities: Univ. of Nevada-Reno, 8,225 enrollment (1976); community college, 6,000 enrollment; public school enrollment, 31,830; parochial, 1,269.

Cultural facilities: 1,428 seat Pioneer Theater Auditorium and 8,000 seat Centennial Coliseum; Fleischman Atmospherium Planetarium, and 280,000-volume library; national air races; rodeo; little theater; Nevada Historical Society; Nevada Opera Guild, Reno Philharmonic Orchestra, Nevada Art Gallery.

Recreation: 21 ski resorts within a 2-hour drive; Lake Tahoe and Pyramid Lake offer fishing, boating, swimming, and sun-bathing; medium game hunting; camping; historic Virginia City mining town and tourist attraction within 1/2-hour drive.

Sports: semi-pro Aces hockey, Silver Sox minor league baseball.

History: est. 1868 with public auction of land by Central Pacific RR; named after Civil War hero Gen. Jesse L. Reno.

Further information: Chamber of Commerce, P.O. Box 3499, Reno, Nev. 89505.

Richmond, Virginia

The World Almanac is sponsored in the Richmond area by the Richmond Times-Dispatch and News Leader, 333 E. Grace St., Richmond, Va. 23213; (804) 649-6000; Times-Dispatch founded 1950 by James A. Cowardin, circulation 131,237 daily, 199,884 Sunday; News Leader founded 1896 by Joseph Bryan, circulation 112,305; publisher D. Tennant Bryan; president Alan S. Donnahoe, executive editor John E. Leard, Times-Dispatch managing editor Alf Goodykoontz, News Leader managing editor J. A. Finch.

Population: 233,100 (city), 569,500 (metro area), total employed (non-agricultural) 278,000.

Area: 62.5 sq. mi. (city), located at fall line of James River, 90 miles from Atlantic Ocean.

Industry: tobacco, with 10,000 workers, and chemicals, with 8,200 are leaders in employment; Philip Morris cigarette plant which began production in 1974 is world's largest and most modern; printing, publishing, manufacture of paper and allied products, and food.

Commerce: wholesale-retail center for central Virginia; retail sales $1.6 billion in 1975, per capita income $5,691, family $13,403, total income $2.88 billion.

Transportation: 4 major railroads, 5 intercity bus lines, 3 commercial air lines, one commuter air line, 50 motor truck lines; 3 interstate, 6 U. S., and 9 state highways; deepwater terminal accessible to ocean-going ships.

Communications: 4 TV, 16 radio stations.

Medical facilities: Medical College of Virginia known worldwide for heart and kidney transplants, medical research; 21 other hospitals, including McGuire VA Hospital.

Federal facilities: Defense General Supply Center, Fifth Federal Reserve Bank, U. S. Fourth Circuit Court, Ft. Lee (Quartermaster Corps).

Cultural facilities: Va. Museum and Theater with

professional artists make city a center for dramatic, other performing arts; variety of other drama groups; symphony orchestra.

Educational facilities: Virginia Commonwealth Univ. has state's largest enrollment; Univ. of Richmond, Virginia Union Univ., Union Theological Seminary (Presbyterian), Randolph-Macon College.

Recreational facilities: Coliseum for athletic, entertainment events; city-owned Mosque auditorium, Parker Field, City Stadium, numerous parks.

Convention facilities: large downtown hotels near Mosque and Coliseum.

Sports: Braves (IL baseball), Robins (hockey), national ranked track and tennis events.

Other attractions: St. John's Church, scene of Patrick Henry's "Liberty or Death" speech; Virginia Capitol, designed by Thomas Jefferson; White House of the Confederacy; Civil War battlefields.

History: exploration here in 1607 by Capt. John Smith, first settlement 1609, incorporated as town 1742, made Va. capital 1780, Confederate Capital 1861-65; burned 1781 by Benedict Arnold, and 1865 when cotton, tobacco stockpiles fire set by fleeing Confederates spread to city; damaged by floods 1771, 1969, 1972.

Further information: Chamber of Commerce, 201 E. Franklin St., Richmond, Va. 23219.

Roanoke, Virginia

The World Almanac is sponsored in the Roanoke area by The Roanoke Times and The World-News, 201-203 Campbell Avenue, Roanoke, Va. 24010, telephone (703) 981-3000; Times founded 1886, World-News founded 1889; Robert Benson, president; Barton W. Morris Jr., publisher; circulation combined daily, 114,129; Sunday 113,189.

Population: 109,500 (City, Jan. 1, 1976), 214,300 (metro area); labor force 106,980.

Area: 43.25 sq. mi.; Metro SMSA includes Roanoke City, Salem City, Roanoke, Craig, Botetourt counties; located at southern extremity of Shenandoah Valley midway between Maryland and Tennessee.

Industry: 22% of work force in manufacturing. Leading firms are General Electric, Eaton Corp., ITT, Singer, Burlington Industries, Mohawk Rubber, Ingersoll Rand.

Commerce: headquarters Shenandoah Life Ins. Co., Estate Life Ins. Co., Appalachian Power Co., Advance Stores, Mick or Mack Groceries; Regional Allstate Ins. Co. offices; Kroger (central warehouse); retail sales metro area (1975) $689.1 million; average spendable family income, $13,647 (metro area); retail center for 20 counties and parts of West Virginia and North Carolina.

Transportation: Norfolk & Western Railway Co. headquarters. 2 airlines; Trailways and Greyhound buses; Amtrak east-west route Norfolk to Cincinnati. 30 interstate trucking firms with terminals; Highways Interstate 81, Spur 581, US 11, US 460, US 220, US 221, Blue Ridge Parkway.

Communications: 3 TV and 12 radio stations.

Medical facilities: 4 general, 4 specialty hospitals, VA facility; state hospital.

Cultural facilities: 2 civic centers with auditorium, coliseums and exhibit halls, symphony orchestra, art center, theaters, Roanoke College, Hollins College, Virginia Western Community College, National Business College; commuting distance from Va. Polytechnic Inst. and State Univ.; concert and lecture series.

Other attractions: Mill Mt. Park rising 1,000 ft. in center of city; children's zoo; Transportation and Historical Museum; Smith Mt.; Fairy Stone and Claytor Lakes state parks; Natural Bridge, Dixie Caverns, Peaks of Otter.

Sports: professional ice hockey, baseball; school sports, winter skiing nearby, public recreation and parks programs.

History: formerly named Big Lick, Roanoke, an Indian word for shell money, became a city in 1884 with the linking of the Shenandoah Valley Railroad with Norfolk and Western Railroad.

Further information: Roanoke Valley Chamber of Commerce, 14 West Kirk Avenue, P.O. Box 20, Roanoke, Va. 24001.

Rochester, New York

The World Almanac is sponsored in the Rochester area by Gannett Rochester Newspapers, 55 Exchange St., Rochester, N. Y. 14614; phone (716) 232-7100; circulation, Democrat and Chronicle (morn) 127,619; Times-Union (eve), 130,416; Democrat and Chronicle, (Sun.) 222,126; publisher Eugene C. Dorsey; executive editor Stuart Dunham; director of advertising James E. McKearney, Jr.; Times-Union reporters awarded a 1972 Pulitzer Prize.

Population: 295,011 (1970 adj.); 5-county metro area 974,000 (1975 est.); 412,700 employed; unemployment 6.3%.

Area: 675 sq. mi. (Monroe County) straddling Genesee River, on Lake Ontario; 2,966 sq. mi. (metro); Monroe County seat.

Industry: world leader in production of photographic optical, and scientific instruments, with Eastman Kodak (48,775 employees), Xerox (14,000), and Bausch & Lomb (5,000), all founded in Rochester, the most prominent; other fields include machinery, food products, apparel, printing and publishing; industrial wage increase, 41% since 1969.

Commerce: retail sales (1975 est.) over $2 billion; 20 commercial and savings banks, with assets of $5.8 billion; 1974 median household income (Monroe County) $14,759, (metro area) $13,716, 49th in nation.

Transportation: Monroe County Airport, with 3 major airlines and several freight companies; rail freight service by 4 lines, Amtrak; port of Rochester; over 75 motor freight firms.

Communications: 4 TV and 15 radio stations.

New construction: First Federal Bldg., 22 story office tower.

Medical facilities: one of the nation's most advanced health care centers: 8 general hospitals, including Strong Memorial Hospital.

Cultural facilities: Eastman Theater, part of Univ. of Eastman School of Music, and home of the Philharmonic Orchestra; Memorial Art Gallery; Museum and Science Center, including Strasenburgh Planetarium; George Eastman House of Photography; 3 resident theatre companies.

Educational facilities: 8 private and 2 public 4-year colleges; 3 community colleges.

Recreational facilities: Finger Lakes area, with 13 parks, summer and winter sports, golf, tennis, bowling; 16-park Monroe County system, including Seneca Park Zoo, Highland Park, with Lilac Festival (May).

Convention facilities: 2d largest used site in N.Y.; War Memorial, 7,500 cap., Dome Arena, 5,000 cap.; 4,600 rms. available.

Sports: International League Red Wings, top Baltimore Orioles farm team; AHL Amerks, North American Soccer League Lancers, National Lacrosse League Griffins; thoroughbred racing and Finger Lakes Race Track, (Canandaigua).

Further information: Chamber of Commerce, 55 St. Paul St., 14604 or Convention and Publicity Bureau, 100 Exchange St., 14614.

Rockford, Illinois

The World Almanac is sponsored in the Rockford area by the Rockford Newspapers, Inc., 97 East State Street, Rockford, Ill., 61105, phone (815) 962-4433, publisher of the Morning Star, Register-Republic, and Sunday Register-Star; combined daily circulation 80,100; Sunday 77,000. Publisher Brian Donnelly, managing editor Gene Cryer. Member of the Gannett Group.

Population: 150,000 (city), 241,000 (county), 126,200 work force (metro).

Area: 36.8 sq. mi. (city) on Rock River in extreme north central Illinois; Winnebago County seat; 519 sq. mi. (county).

Industry: 575 manufacturing establishments; products include machine tools (Sundstrand, Ingersoll Milling Machine, Barber-Colman, Greenlee Bros.), screws and bolts (Rockford Products, Elco, Camcar, National Lock), pharmaceuticals (Warner-Lambert American Chicle) and paints (Valspar). Chrysler Corp. assembly plant is in nearby Belvidere.

Commerce: retail "magnet" for northern Illinois and southern Wisconsin; 12 shopping centers and new central district mall; retail sales (1975) $697.5 million; 20 commercial banks, resources (1975) $806.5 million; 4 savings and loan associations, resources (1975) $343.9 million.

Transportation: Amtrak; 4 rail freight lines; 3 bus lines; 50 truck lines; Ozark Air Lines; U.S. 51, U.S. 20 and Interstate 90.

Communications: 3 TV and radio stations; 2 cable TV operations; 7 weekly newspapers; 2 daily newspapers.

Medical facilities: 3 hospitals; 2 public supported extended care facilities.

Cultural facilities: symphony orchestra; concert band; civic theater; 2 male and one mixed choral organizations; Rock Valley College, Rockford College.

Education: 101 public schools (K-12); 18 parochial and private schools (K-12); Rockford College (4 years, liberal arts); Rock Valley College (2 years, liberal arts); UI-Rockford School of Medicine.

Recreation: 18 forest preserves; 102 parks; 1 state park; 6 public golf courses; 4 country club courses; 56 public tennis courts; 3 indoor tennis facilities.

Agriculture: 240,000 acres tilled farmland (1975 estimated value $220 million); 5,000 people on 1,180 farms in county.

Attractions: Children's Farm; Time Museum; Tinker Swiss Cottage; Rockford Museum.

History: founded in 1834 by Germanicus Kent and Thatcher Blake beside fording place across Rock River; incorporated in 1852.

Further information: Rockford Area Chamber of Commerce, 815 E. State St., Rockford, Ill. 61101.

Sacramento, California

The World Almanac is sponsored in the Sacramento area by The Sacramento Bee, 21st & Q, Sacramento, Cal. 95816; telephone (916) 442-5011; founded 1857; circulation daily 172,603, Sunday 204,531; president Eleanor McClatchy, editor C. K. McClatchy, managing editor Frank McCulloch.

Population: 262,100 (city), 693,000 (county), 889,000 (metro); total employed (county) 266,700.

Area: 94 sq. mi. (city), 997 sq. mi. (county) in Sacramento Valley, 85 mi. northeast of San Francisco.

Industry: 475 manufacturing plants including Campbell Soup, Procter and Gamble, Libby McNeil and Libby, California Almond Growers Exchange, Del Monte, Teichert Construction, and Aerojet-General.

Commerce: state capital; wholesale-retail center for large area of Sacramento Valley; retail sales (1975), $2.1 billion; bank debits, $8.1 billion (city).

Transportation: 3 county operated airports, including metropolitan airport, plus numerous private airports; $55-million Port of Sacramento gives access to the Pacific; 2 mainline transcontinental rail carriers; junction 4 major highways.

Communications: 6 TV and 21 radio stations.

New construction: downtown Mall; Old Sacramento being restored as state and federal historical project; Rancho Seco Atomic Power Plant; regional sewage treatment plant; 2 major hotels.

Medical facilities: 10 major hospitals, Univ. of California Medical School in nearby Davis.

Federal facilities: 2 large Air Force bases, Army

depot, many regional federal offices.

Cultural facilities: Sacramento Earl Warren Community Center complex; Eagle Theater; symphony orchestra; ballet; Civic Theater; Crocker Art Gallery; California State Univ., Sacramento; McGeorge College of Law; Lincoln Univ. Law School, and 3 community colleges.

Other attractions: zoo, 95 public parks; 74 playgrounds; 12 public and 4 private golf courses, Sutter's Fort, State Capitol, Stanford Home, Pony Express Terminal, Fairytale Town, and Governor's Mansion; fishing, hunting, boating, camping, hiking, and skiing in nearby high Sierras; annual State Fair at Cal Expo.

History: founded by John Augustus Sutter Jr. in 1839; James Marshall discovered gold at Sutter's Mill, in 1848, 35 miles northeast, gateway to Mother Lode Country; Pony Express and Central Pacific Railroad which crossed the Sierra Nevada were part of early history.

St. Louis, Missouri

The World Almanac is sponsored in the St. Louis area by the Post-Dispatch, 900 N. 12th Blvd. 63101; telephone (314) 621-1111; founded Dec. 12, 1878 by Joseph Pulitzer; circulation 275,121 daily, 455,121 Sunday; editor and publisher Joseph Pulitzer Jr., managing editor Evarts A. Graham Jr., general manager Alex T. Primm, director of promotion and public affairs William J. Isam; major awards include 5 Pulitzer Prizes to the newspaper and 11 to staff members.

Population: 556,000 (city), 991,000 (county), 2,481,000 (metro), 10th in nation in payroll employment (902,-700 in April 1976).

Area: 4,935 sq. mi. (metro) just south of confluence of Missouri and Mississippi rivers.

Industry: 2d to Detroit in auto and truck assembly with Ford, GM, and Chrysler plants; McDonnell Douglas headquarters, aerospace manufacturer; other headquarters include nation's largest shoe company, Interco; Anheuser-Busch, world's largest brewer; Monsanto, General Dynamics, Ralston-Purina, Pet, Inc., Chromalloy American, Consolidated Aluminum, Emerson Electric, Brown Group; grain market with 74.7 million bushel annual yield; 3,200 manufacturing concerns employing 245,600 persons.

Commerce: $6.3 billion retail sales (est. 1976 metro); $13,492 median family income; 177 banking institutions, total deposits $8.7 billion (1975).

Transportation: 10 major airlines with 6.4 million passenger movements (1975); 2d largest rail center in nation, 14 trunk line railroads; largest inland river port in nation; 9 major highways; 14 motor-bus lines; 350 motor freight lines.

Communications: 6 TV and 28 radio stations.

New construction: industrial and commercial contracts totaled $324 million (1975); residential $285 million; Mercantile Center, $150 million office, store and hotel complex; Gateway Convention Center, $34 million; General American, $9 million; Boatmen's Bank Tower, $28 million.

Medical facilities: 67 hospitals with 16,170 beds; Washington Univ. and St. Louis Univ. medical schools and affiliated hospitals provide specialized treatment in many areas.

Federal facilities: Military Personnel Records Center, Defense Mapping Agency Aerospace Center, Army Mobility Equipment Command, Scott AFB.

Cultural facilities: Art Museum; Museum of Science and Natural History; restored historic homes; symphony orchestra; Mississippi River Festival near Edwardsville in summer; Municipal Theatre (Muny Opera) offers Broadway shows in big outdoor theater in Forest Park.

Educational facilities: 4 major universities: Washington, St. Louis, Univ. of Missouri at St. Louis, and Southern Illinois Univ. at Edwardsville; private colleges; 3-branch junior college system.

Recreational facilities: Jefferson National Expansion Memorial with 630-foot Gateway Arch on riverfront; 1,326-acre Forest Park with 3 golf courses, ball fields, floral displays, zoo, McDonnell Planetarium and Jefferson Memorial displaying Lindbergh trophies; National Museum of Transport; Six Flags Over Mid-America with world's tallest roller coaster; Grant's Farm with President Grant's cabin and animal displays; Missouri Botanical Garden with floral displays and advanced research display greenhouse, the Climatron.

Convention facilities: 12,000 hotel rooms; 90,000 sq. ft. exhibit space in Kiel Auditorium; 240,000 sq. ft. exhibit space in Gateway Convention Center to be completed May 1977.

Sports: Busch Stadium home of the Cardinals baseball and football teams; St. Louis Blues (NHL); soccer Stars.

Other attractions: climate has 4 distinct seasons; spring and autumn warm, winters mild, summers hot with 90-degree temperatures; average temperature 54.1 degrees; average precipitation 35.3 inches; downtown area contains significant architecture including Eads Bridge, Old Post Office, Old Courthouse, Old Cathedral, Spanish International Pavilion which now contains a hotel tower; Louis Sullivan's Wainwright Building that is being refurbished, and restoration of Laclede's Landing area on riverfront adjoining Gateway Arch.

History: named for French King Louis IX by fur trapper Pierre Laclede whose trading post became major fur market and gateway to the West; starting point of Lewis and Clark expedition and other explorations.

Further information: Convention and Visitors Bureau, 500 N. Broadway, or Regional Commerce and Growth Assn., 10 S. Broadway, both St. Louis, Mo.

St. Paul, Minnesota

The World Almanac is sponsored in the St. Paul area by the St. Paul Dispatch and Pioneer Press, 55 E. 4th St., St. Paul, Minn. 55101; phone (612) 222-5011; founded 1849 as Minnesota Pioneer by James Goodhue; circulation, Pioneer Press (morn) 105,482, Dispatch (eve) 123,569, Sunday Pioneer Press 238,332. Bernard H. Ridder Jr., president, Ridder Pub., Inc. and vice-chairman Knight-Ridder Newspapers, Inc.; publisher Thomas L. Carlin, executive editor John R. Finnegan, editor William G. Sumner. First newspaper published in Minnesota.

Population: 292,000 (city); 782,300 (metro), 2d in state, 46th in nation; total employed (3-county metro area, 1975), 301,775.

Area: 55 sq. mi. in eastern Minnesota on banks of Mississippi River close to Minnesota and Wisconsin vacationlands; state capital and Ramsey County seat.

Industry: West Publishing, world's largest law book publisher; international center for electronics and computer technology; Union Stockyards is largest livestock center in nation (3,561,626 head in 1974). Headquarters 3M Co., Am. Hoist & Derrick Co., Burlington Northern RR, Univac, Brown & Bigelow, Whirlpool, Economics Laboratory, Hoerner-Waldorf Corp., St. Paul Companies (insurance).

Commerce: retail sales (1975) $1.9 billion (metro); median household income, $14,285; 25 banks and 6 savings and loan associations.

Transportation: 5 major and 2 regional rail lines, Amtrak; 21 intercity truck firms, 37 terminals; 3 interstate bus lines; 730-mile public transit system; metropolitan airport, hub of 8 commercial airlines, headquarters for Northwest and North Central airlines, averages 824 air movements per day; Downtown Airport; 60 firms operate barges on Mississippi River, using a 9-foot channel downtown.

Communications: 4 commercial and 2 educational TV stations; 29 radio stations.

Medical facilities: 12 private hospitals; a 611 bed community hospital and research center: St. Paul-Ramsey Hospital.

Federal facilities: Ft. Snelling; area headquarters for HUD, HEW; district headquarters for IRS, FCC, Immigration and Naturalization Service; U.S. District Court.

Cultural facilities: Minnesota Symphony Orchestra; Univ. of Minnesota Institute of Agriculture, Hamline Univ., St. Thomas, St. Catherine, Bethel, Concordia, and Macalester colleges, and William Mitchell College of Law; $66 million city school system with 80 public schools and 61 private schools.

Recreational facilities: more than 900 lakes in metro area, 438 tennis courts, 148 swimming beaches, 513 parks, 50 golf courses, 27 ski centers; 52 neighborhood recreation centers, 35 miles of parkways, 100 miles of hiking and biking trails.

Convention facilities: Civic Center complex with 101,000 sq. ft. exhibit space, seating for 35,000 in 4 main buildings, 15 meeting halls; 50 hotels and motels.

Other attractions: Winter Carnival in Jan., Minnesota State Fair, Como Park Zoo and Conservatory; onyx statue of Indian God of Peace in City Hall, Minnesota Historical Society Museums, Arts & Science Center, Fort Snelling State Park.

History: once called "Pig's Eye" for first settler, Pierre "Pig's Eye" Parrant; changed to St. Paul when Father Lucien Galtier built St. Paul's Chapel 1841; became town 1847, city 1854.

Further information: St. Paul Area Chamber of Commerce, Osborn Bldg., St. Paul, Minn. 55102.

St. Petersburg, Florida

The World Almanac is sponsored in Florida's Suncoast area by The St. Petersburg Times and Evening Independent, 490 1st Ave. S., St. Petersburg, Fla. 33701; phone (813) 893-8111. Times founded 1884, Independent 1906; circulation, Times (morn) 188,922; Independent (evening) 33,888; Sunday Times 235,181. Nelson Poynter, chairman of the board, The Times Publishing Co.; Eugene C. Patterson, editor of The Times and president of The Times Publishing Co.; Robert Stiff, editor, The Independent; John B. Lake, executive vice president and publisher, The Times Publishing Co.

Population: 236,362 (city), 685,400 (Pinellas County), 1,423,200 (metro); Pinellas County March 1976 employment 225,600; unemployment 9.1%.

Industry and Commerce: tourism, over 3.8 million visited county in 1974, spending about $1.4 billion; industries include General Electric, Honeywell, Sperry, Milton Roy Co., Eckerd Drugs, Jim Walter Research, All-State Insurance regional office, U.S. Homes headquarters, Morgan Yacht. County 1975 retail sales over $2.1 billion.

Transportation: U.S. 19, 41 and 98 link city to rest of Gulf Coast Florida; Interstates 275, 75 and 4 link St. Petersburg with Tampa, Orlando, and east coast; Tampa International Airport 25 minutes from downtown St. Petersburg; other airports are St. Petersburg-Clearwater International and Albert Whitted. Amtrak, Seaboard Coast Line railroads; Greyhound and Trailways bus lines.

Communications: 6 TV and 46 radio stations.

Convention and Tourist facilities: Over 52,000 units can house 160,000 visitors. Bayfront Center seats 9,400 in arena, 2,200 in auditorium. Pinellas restaurants can serve 90,000 people at one time. Disney World 2 hours away.

Medical facilities: 7 major hospitals; Bay Pines veterans complex to be greatly expanded adding 1,150 new beds at cost of $110 million; All Children's Hospital.

Cultural facilities: Museum of Fine Arts, Gulf Coast Symphony, Historical Museum, community theatres, Eckerd College Free Institutions Forums, varied musical, theatrical, and dance events at Bayfront Center Complex.

Educational facilities: Univ. of South Florida's downtown Bayboro Campus to expand enrollment from 1,700 to 7,500. First building phase of $5 million to start 1977. Stetson College of Law, Eckerd College, St. Petersburg Junior College.

Recreational facilities: 76 parks on 1,800 acres, many with recreational buildings, pools, tennis courts, boat ramps, and picnic areas; municipal and private marinas; deep sea fishing, golf courses, baseball fields.

Sports: St. Louis Cardinals and New York Mets spring training; spectator sports include greyhound racing, baseball, jai alai, horse racing, NFL football, basketball, pro tennis, boat racing, soccer.

Additional information: St. Petersburg Chamber of Commerce, 225 4th St. S., St. Petersburg, Fla. 33701.

Salt Lake City, Utah

The World Almanac is sponsored in the Salt Lake City area by the Salt Lake Tribune, 143 S. Main St., Salt Lake City, Utah 84110; phone (801) 524-4545; founded Apr. 15, 1871; circulation, 99,608 daily, 169,317 Sunday; publisher John W. Gallivan; executive editor, Arthur C. Deck; 1957 Pulitzer Prize; civic projects; statewide civic beautification awards, Sub for Santa program, Community Christmas Tree, Arbor Day tree plantings; Spring Garden Festival; Ski Race; No Champs Tennis Tourn.

Population: (1975 est.) 192,400 (city); 502,700 (county); 775,200 (metro); 1st in state; 49th in nation; 52% of state pop. lives within 30 miles; state capital and Salt Lake County seat.

Area: nestled in a vast valley (elev. 4,327 ft.) surrounded by Wasatch and Oquirrh mountains.

Industry: labor force, 236,900; effective buying income, $3.1 billion (1975), per family income, $13,-201; 46% of state construction in county; total construction value, $245 million (1975 record high); employers are Hill Air Force Base (30 miles north), local defense industries, and Kennecott Copper; metro area becoming major center for electronics, apparel manufacturing; mining, smelting, refining; distribution, warehousing center of West.

Commerce: trade center of Mountain West.

Transportation: 6 air lines, customs office, International Airport; geographic center of 11 western states; hub of central transcontinental highway system; 3 railroads, all major western truck, bus lines.
Communications: 2 daily newspapers; 3 commercial and 2 public TV, 18 radio stations.
New construction: downtown ZCMI Mall, 70 shops, 27-story office bldg.
Medical facilities: 10 hospitals, including Univ. of Utah Medical Center, major research in transplant surgery.
Cultural facilities: Utah Symphony Orchestra among 12 best in U.S.; Mormon Tabernacle Choir, Ballet West, Repertory Dance Theatre.
Other attractions: Temple Square, home of 3.5 million member Church of Jesus Christ of Latter Day Saints; Salt Palace Civic Auditorium; 700 acres in 22 parks, 25 playgrounds, 10 golf courses, 85 tennis courts; near Great Salt Lake (7 times more salty than ocean); Hogle Zoological Gardens, Kennecott Copper's Bingham Mine.
Sports: 9 major ski resorts; Golden Eagles (Central Hockey League), Salt Lake Gulls, baseball; Bonneville Salt Flats.
Education: Univ. of Utah, Westminster College.
Other: 4 well-defined seasons, mean annual temperature is 50.9°F.
History: founded July 24, 1847, By Brigham Young and contingent of pioneers.
Further information: Chamber of Commerce, 19 E. 2d So.; Utah Travel Council, Council Hall, Salt Lake City, Utah.

San Antonio, Texas

The World Almanac is sponsored in the San Antonio area by the S. A. Express (morning) and S. A. News (evening), P.O. Box 2171, San Antonio, Tex. 78297; tel. (512) 225-7411; circulation daily, Express 80,092, News 76,243, Sunday Express-News 160,080; chairman K. Rupert Murdoch, publisher and editor Charles O. Kilpatrick; Express-News Corp. is a division of News America, Inc.

Population: 786,181 city; 908,756 Bexar County; total employed, 349,450.
Area: Bexar County, 1,247 sq. mi., 2 1/2 hours from Gulf Coast and Mexican border.
Industry: 5 military bases include Kelly AFB, largest employer; fast-growing medical industry; diverse manufacturing, tourism, construction, trade, and service industries.
Commerce: center for 100 mile radius retail trade area, truck crops, livestock production; retail sales (1975), $4.2 billion.
Federal facilities: Kelly AFB, hq. AF Air Security Service; Randolph AFB, hq. AF Air Training Command & AF Personnel Center; Brooks AFB, hq. AF Aerospace Medical Division; Lackland AFB with Wilford Hall USAF Medical Center; Fort Sam Houston, hq. Fifth Army, & Army Health Services Command, Brooke Army Medical Center.
Medical facilities: University of Texas Medical, Dental, Nursing schools; Audie Murphy VA Hospital; Southwest Research Institute; Southwest Foundation of Research and Education.
Transportation: International Airport, 6 major airlines; 3 rail freight, 2 Amtrak lines.
Education facilities: Univ. of Texas at San Antonio; Trinity, St. Mary's universities; Our Lady of the Lake, Incarnate Word colleges; 2 jr. colleges, San Antonio College, St. Philip's College; permanent extension of National University of Mexico.
Convention facilities: Convention Center with large arena, theater, exhibit, meeting space.
Cultural facilities: symphony orchestra; Institute of Texan Cultures, Mexican Cultural Institute, Witte Museum, McNay Art Institute.
Other attractions: historic Alamo, old Spanish missions of San Jose, Concepcion, Capistrano, Espada; Hemis Fair Plaza with 622-foot observation tower-restaurant; downtown River Walk; zoo; annual events: Fiesta San Antonio, Livestock Show & Rodeo, Folklife Festival; pro sports: Spurs (NBA); Thunder (NASL); minor league baseball, Brewers.
Further information: Greater San Antonio Chamber of Commerce, 602 E. Commerce, P. O. Box 1628, San Antonio, Tex. 78296.

San Bernardino, California

The World Almanac is sponsored in the San Bernardino area by the Sun-Telegram, 399 North D St., San Bernardino, Cal. 92401, phone (714) 889-9666; Telegram founded 1873, Sun 1894; daily circulation 76,696, Sunday 82,-103; member Gannett chain; editor-publisher James Geehan, advertising director, Carl B. Shaver, managing editor Kent Freeland.

Population: 102,303 (city), 1,220,000 (2-county metro area); 43d in state, 148th in nation; total employed 41,221.
Area: 47.22 sq. mi. at base of Cajon Pass, 58 miles east of Los Angeles; county seat.
Industry: 165 business and industrial firms including Culligan, Edginton Oil, Fleetwood Enterprises, Hanford Foundry, Knudsen Dairy, Mode O'Day, Pepsi Cola and Seven-Up bottling plants, Santa Fe Railway, TRW Systems.
Commerce: trading center for 20,189 sq. mi. San Bernardino county, largest in the nation; retail sales (1975) $546 million; 7 banks, 22 branches, 11 savings and loan associations; 2 major shopping center complexes, each parking over 5,000 cars.
Transportation: Santa Fe, Southern Pacific, and Union Pacific rail lines, Amtrak; Greyhound and Continental bus lines; major interstate highways leading from Mexico to Canada and West to East Coast; municipal airport and nearby Ontario International Airport, over 1.2 million passengers (1975).
Communications: 15 radio and one VHF educational TV station access to 5 Los Angeles channels.
Medical facilities: 3 major hospitals with 995 beds; major research and training center for heart surgery and hip and knee replacement surgery.
Federal facilities: Norton Air Force Base.
cultural facilities: symphony orchestra, Civic Light Opera, nearby Redlands Bowl (summer concerts); National Orange Show with orange festival every spring; Convention Center-Exhibit Hall complex.
Educational facilities: California State College, junior college, 3 major universities nearby.
History: founded 1852 by Mormons who purchased land from Spanish grant holders.
Further information: Chamber of Commerce, 546 West 6th St., San Bernardino, Cal. 92401.

San Diego, California

The World Almanac is sponsored in San Diego by The San Diego Union and Evening Tribune (Copley Newspapers), P.O. Box 191, San Diego 92112; (714) 299-3131; Union founded 1868 (pioneer daily of Southwest); circulation, Union (morn) 181,907, Tribune (eve) 126,363, Sunday Union 297,687; publisher Helen K. Copley, general manager Al De Bakcsy, Union exec. editor Gerald L. Warren, Tribune editor Fred Kinne.

Population: 770,344 (1976, city); 1,559,505 (county); 11th in U.S. (official state estimate); total civilian employment, 553,200.
Area: (county) 4,255 sq. mi.; 70 mi. Pacific Coast, San Clemente to Mexican border.
Industry: tourism, manufacturing, military, and agriculture; manufactured products earn $2.9 billion a year; non-military payroll $4.1 billion, military $875.2 million; tourist spending over $500 million; corporations with bases or divisions include Bendix, Burroughs, Control Data, Cubic, General Dynamics, Gulf, Honeywell, International Harvester's Solar division, NCR Corp., Pacific Southwest Airlines, Rohr, Sea World, Teledyne Ryan, TraveLodge, Wickes Van Camp sea food, Foodmaker (Jack-in-the-Box); aerospace, rapid transit design and manufacture, oceanography, nuclear energy, medicine important; also shipbuilding, tuna fishing, clothing, ocean shipping; among top 20 counties in farm products (avocados, cut flowers, eggs); Marine Corps Recruit Depot, Naval Training Center, North Island and Miramar Naval Air Stations, Naval Electronics Lab and Undersea Center, Marine Corps base at Camp Pendleton.
Transportation: freeway system state's 2d largest; urban transit service, 35-cent fare, Mexican border to 35 miles north; Amtrak, 9 airlines, bus lines; primary airport Lindbergh Field.
Communications: Some 30 TV and radio stations.

Medical facilities: Salk Institute for Biological Studies, Scripps Clinic & Research Foundation; Naval Hospital; many hospitals.
Educational and Cultural facilities: San Diego State Univ., U.S. International Univ., Univ. of San Diego, Univ. of California, San Diego (3 colleges and Scripps Institution of Oceanography), Point Loma College; symphony; Old Globe Theatre (functioning reproduction of Shakespeare's Globe Theatre); opera; ballet; Fine Arts and Timken Galleries; La Jolla Museum of Contemporary Art.
Other attractions: world famous zoo and wild animal park; Balboa Park, central 1,400 acres containing museums, zoo, Fleet Space Theatre (computerized planetarium), many other attractions; Mission Bay Park includes Sea World; "Old San Diego" State Historical Park; "Star of India" ship-museum; visits to neighboring Mexico (Tijuana); 70 miles of beaches.
Sports: NFL Chargers, NL Padres, WHA Mariners; tennis, soccer, volleyball teams; racing at Del Mar, Caliente.
History: area discovered 1542 by Cabrillo, founded in 1769 by Father Serra.
Other attractions: climate sunny; summer and winter resort; average temp. 68° in summer, 57° in winter, rainfall mainly December to March; famous "place names" include La Jolla (part of city of San Diego); 70 golf courses, including Torrey Pines; large convention facilities; off-shore "whale watching."

San Francisco, California

The World Almanac is sponsored in the San Francisco-Oakland area by the San Francisco Examiner, P.O. B. 3100, Rincon Annex, S.F., Cal. 94119 (415) 781-2424; founded June 12, 1865; circulation daily Examiner, 176,286; Sunday Examiner & Chronicle, 667,121; president and editor, R.A. Hearst; executive editor Thomas Eastham; general manager, Wells Smith; major awards: Pulitzer Prize, Freedoms Foundation; Examiner sponsors Examiner Games, Golden Gloves, Distinguished Ten, Bay to Breakers Race.

Population: 671,100, 3d in state, 13th in nation; total employed: 250,000.
Area: 44.6 sq. mi. on the northern tip of a peninsula. San Francisco County seat.
Industry: food products, printing, publishing, fabricated metal products; west's financial capital and administrative center for many of the nation's leading corporations; West Coast operations' headquarters for a majority of the federal agencies; finance, insurance, and real estate; chief port of the Pacific Coast.
Commerce: wholesale-retail trade employment, 92,-100; services 110,200; manufacturing 47,800; total retail outlets 21,978, taxable sales $3 billion; 40 banks with 157 branches; 25 savings and loans with 39 branches; total deposits in banks $19.2 billion.
Transportation: 27 major airlines serve the Bay Area; International Airport processed 17,503,778 passengers, 649 million lbs. of freight (1975); Municipal Railway (intra-city); AC-Transit and Bay Area Rapid Transit System (BART) to East Bay cities; Greyhound bus and Southern Pacific Railroad to Peninsula areas; Golden Gate Bridge District Bus and Ferry service to Marin County; Port of San Francisco services available: LASH, BULK, general cargo, containerization and barge service.
Communications: 2 major newspapers; 118 others serving the Bay Area; 45 radio stations, 7 TV channels received directly, one TV cable system.
Medical facilities: 21 general hospitals with over

6,516 total beds and 5 specialty hospitals with over 1,935 beds; 3,033 physicians/surgeons and 772 dentists; Univ. of Cal. Medical Center, with 42 buildings, is a general teaching and research institute and is the largest kidney transplant center in the world.
Cultural facilities: San Francisco Opera, Spring Opera, Western Opera Theater, symphony, ballet, Civic Light Opera, American Conservatory Theater, Japanese Cultural Center, Chinese Cultural Center, International Film Festival, 3 museums, 29 libraries, and 540 churches.
Educational facilities: 103 public elementary schools with a total enrollment of 35,439 and 11 junior high and 18 high schools with a combined enrollment of 38,859 students; Univ. of California, San Francisco; California State Univ., Univ. of San Francisco, Lone Mountain College, and City College of San Francisco.
Recreational facilities: 120 parks and many mini-parks, 78 playgrounds, 6 golf courses, numerous tennis courts, 10 swimming pools, 5 1/2 miles of ocean beach, 1 lake, 1 fishing pier, Marina small craft harbor and 3 yacht clubs.
Convention facilities: 124 hotels and motels with over 20,000 rooms.
Sports: Candlestick Park, home of the NL Giants and the NFL 49ers.
Other attractions: zoo and 1,013-acre Golden Gate Park containing the California Academy of Sciences, De Young Museum, Japanese Tea Garden, and Arboretum; cable cars, Fisherman's Wharf, Chinatown,

the Ferry Building, Coit Tower, the Palace of Fine Arts, and Grace Cathedral.
History: San Francisco Bay discovered 1769 by Sgt. Jose Ortega; pueblo of Yerba Buena established 1834, renamed San Francisco on January 3, 1847; incorporated April 15, 1850.
Further information: Chamber of Commerce, 465 California St., San Francisco, Cal. 94104.

San Jose, California

The World Almanac is sponsored in the San Jose area by The Mercury and News, 750 Ridder Pk. Dr., San Jose, Cal. 95190; (408) 289-5000; Mercury founded June 20, 1851; News July 23, 1883; combined daily circulation 200,-376; Sunday Mercury News; 224,393; publisher Joseph B. Ridder; general manager P. A. Ridder; business manager W. H. Lindsay; executive editor Paul Conroy.

Population: 557,700 (city), 1,178,000 (metro area coextensive with Santa Clara County); total employed 533,200 (metro).
Area: broad alluvial 832,256-acre valley at south end of San Francisco Bay.
Industry: largest county in northern California for manufacturing employment and total wages; called "Silicone Valley" due to high technology semi-conductor and other electronics firms; IBM, Fairchild Semi-conductor, Hewlett-Packard, Varian Associates, Intel Corp., National Semi-conductor; diversity shown by Ford Motor Co., Lockheed Missiles & Space, FMC Corp., Syntex Laboratories; county a major producer of cut flowers.
Commerce: leading retail trade center of northern California, $3.30 billion in sales; 135 shopping centers; 3d nationally in median household income among U.S. metro areas with 2 million and over population, 74% of households earn $10,000 and over annually, 54% earn $15,000 & over annually (metro).
Transportation: Municipal Airport served by 13 airlines; highway system interconnected with interstate in north-south, east-west directions; Southern Pacific and Western Pacific railroads.

Education: San Jose State, Santa Clara, and Stanford universities, plus community colleges have total enrollments of 118,399; 37% of adult pop. is college educated (metro).
Cultural facilities: symphony, First State Capital Museum, Rosicrucian Egyptian Temple, Science Museum and Planetarium, De Saisset Gallery & Museum, Villa Montalvo estate and arboretum, City Gallery, Triton Museum of Art, New Almaden Museum.
Sports: Earthquakes (soccer); Bees, farm club for KC Royals; Sunbirds, women professional baseball; 8 reservoirs with boat ramps, 2 with camping; outlet to S.F. Bay for ocean sports.
Other attractions: Japanese Tea Gardens, Lick Observatory, Winchester Mystery House (St. Monument).
History: founded 1777, first civil settlement in Cal.; county is one of the original 27 in Cal.; first public school in Cal., San Jose Granary, 1795; first Cal. state capitol, Dec. 15, 1849.
Further information: Chamber of Commerce Metro-San Jose, One Paseo de San Antonio, San Jose, Cal. 95113, (408) 998-7000.

San Juan, Puerto Rico

The World Almanac is sponsored in Puerto Rico by the San Juan Star, GPO Box 4187, San Juan, Puerto Rico 00936; telephone (809) 782-4200; founded Nov. 2, 1959; circulation 42,000 daily, 43,000 Sunday; president and general manager John A. Zerbe Jr.; vice president and editor Andrew T. Viglucci; major awards include 1961 Pulitzer Prize for editorial writing; APME citations 1960, 1965; staff awards include 1970 LAPA Mergenthaler Award, 1972 Overseas Press Club Award; National Spelling Bee 1975 champion.

Population: 463,244 (city), 936,700 (metro area) first in commonwealth.
Area: 47 sq. mi. in Caribbean, capital city.
Industry: seat of Puerto Rico's tourism industry with 19 luxury hotels and several dozen high rise condominiums. City is also the commercial and shipping hub of the island and is a major stop for cruise ships plying the Caribbean. Major industries are electronics, pharmaceuticals, and an expanding petrochemical industry serviced by 3 major refineries. Petrochemical industry represents $1.5 billion in investments. Center of island's rum industry with the Bacardi distillery on San Juan Bay, the largest in the world. More than 75 per cent of all rum sold in U.S. is Puerto Rican rum.
Transportation: San Juan International Airport handles more than 500,000 passengers monthly with 3 major U.S. airlines and 10 foreign lines. Isla Grande Airport handles small aircraft traffic.
Education: seat of the Rio Piedras campus of the University of Puerto Rico, the public university system, InterAmerican University, College of the Sacred Heart, UPR Medical Sciences campus and UPR Law School, World University, and several junior and regional colleges.
Federal facilities: Ft. Buchanan army base with 9-hole golf course on grounds.
Cultural facilities and events: The Casals Festival, guided for 15 years by the late Maestro Casals, is an annual June event bringing together some of the world's finest musicians; The Puerto Rico Institute of Culture is housed in a restored Dominican convent; El Morro, the Spanish-built fortress that guards the entrance to San Juan Harbor; numerous art museums in Old San Juan; the Puerto Rico Symphony Orchestra in concerts spread over the year; the capitol building and governor's mansion.
Convention facilities: new Condado Convention Center built by state government seats 5,000 for meetings, 3,000 for meals.
New construction: Old City restoration program, Riomar Hotel, Ramada Inn; new banking district located in Hato Rey, Melia Puerto Rico Hotel in Isla Verde.
Sports: Hiram Bithorn Stadium, winter baseball, track, and outdoor events; Roberto Clemente Coliseum, basketball, boxing, and indoor events; soccer, cockfighting arenas (legal); preparations for 1979 PanAm Games.
History: discovered by Columbus on his 2d voyage to the New World in 1493, colonized by Juan Ponce de Leon, Puerto Rico's first Spanish governor; since 1952 a commonwealth freely associated with the United States. Free market with U.S. and same currency, common citizenship.
Further information: Chamber of Commerce, 100 Tetuan St., Old San Juan; Dept. of Tourism, Banco de Ponce Bldg., Hato Rey, P.R.

Santa Ana, California
See Orange County, California

Saskatoon, Saskatchewan, Canada

The World Almanac is sponsored in northern Saskatchewan by the Saskatoon Star-Phoenix, 204 Fifth Ave. North, Saskatoon, Sask., S7K 2P1; (306) 652-9200; Daily Star and Phoenix, founded in 1906 and 1902 respectively, merged in 1928 into the Star-Phoenix; circulation daily, 50,491; publisher Michael C. Sifton, executive vice president James K. Struthers.

Population: 136,000, 2d in prov., 17th in nation.
Area: 38.5 sq. mi. land, 1.5 sq. mi. water, on S. Sask. River, center of agricultural province.
Commerce: retail, wholesale, service, distribution hub for 400,000 in 100-mi. radius trading area; world's richest, largest potash reserves; meat packing, grain milling dominant; garment and electronics newest; base for northern mineral explorations; retail sales (1974) $328 million.
Transportation: 2 railways, 2 airlines, 2 bus lines, air and bus terminals on Yellowhead Highway, easiest access through Rockies from prairies to West Coast ports.
Communications: One daily, 2 TV, 5 radio stations, one farm weekly, one community weekly.
Medical facilities: 3 major hospitals, 6 nursing homes; Univ. hospital known for kidney transplants, open-heart surgery; $26 million expansion planned.

Cultural facilities: $7 million, 2,000-seat Centennial Auditorium, convention facilities for over 1,800; Mendel Art Gallery/Civic Conservatory; Western Development Museum houses N. America's largest display of antique cars, farm implements and 1910 Pioneer Village; theme pavilion for summer fair.
Education: Univ. of Sask. (17,500 students), famed for agriculture, space, Arctic, physics, medicine, veterinary college; Kelsey Institute for Applied Arts and Science (4,700 students); School for Deaf.
Recreation: 1,456 acres parkland; wild animal farm; man-made ski mountain; camping, fishing.
History: founded 1883 as temperance colony; incorporated 1906; battle sites of 1885 Riel Rebellion nearby.
Further information: Board of Trade, Bessborough Hotel, Saskatoon, Sask. S7K 3GB.

Savannah, Georgia

The World Almanac is sponsored in the Savannah area by the Savannah News-Press, 111 W. Bay St., Savannah, Ga. 31401, phone (912) 236-9511, publisher of the Savannah Morning News and Savannah Evening Press; combined daily circulation 75,900; Sunday 67,274. Donald E. Harwood, general manager; Wallace M. Davis Jr., executive editor.

Population: 116,000 (city), 195,000 (metro).
Area: 37 sq. mi. on Savannah River, 18 miles from Atlantic Ocean.
Industry: world's largest pulpwood-to-paper container plant owned by Union Camp Corp; Savannah Sugar Refining Corp., nation's 3d largest seller; jet aircraft manufacture (Grumman American Aviation), tea packaging (Tetley), fertilizer materials, ship repair, titanium dioxide production (American Cyanamid).
Commerce: hub of "Coastal Empire," economic center of 8 Georgia and 3 South Carolina counties; Southeast's leading foreign trade port, 80 steamship lines, 41 deep water terminals; retail sales (1975) $817 million; 7 commercial banks, resources (1974) $8.6 billion; 4 savings and loan associations.

Transportation: 2 rail freight lines, Amtrak; Greyhound, Trailways bus lines; 74 truck lines; Delta, National airlines.
Communications: 4 TV and 14 radio stations.
Medical facilities: 6 hospitals.
Cultural facilities: symphony orchestra, ballet guild, dance theater, little theater, Telfair Academy of Arts and Sciences; maritime museum, science museum, military museum; $10.4 million Civic Center; Savannah State, Armstrong State colleges.
Sports: Savannah Braves, Southern League.
History: founded 1733 by Gen. James Oglethorpe, first planned U.S. city; much of old city is national historic landmark, largest in country.
Further information: Chamber of Commerce, P.O. Box 530, Savannah, Georgia 31402.

Schenectady, New York

Population: 77,958; total employed, 38,000.
Area: 11.3 sq. mi., 13 miles northwest of Albany.
Industry: General Electric, employing about 27,000, is largest employer. Other firms manufacture industrial chemicals, pollution control and measuring devices, and military vehicles.
Commerce: there are 2,100 retail establishments with net sales of over $200 million; 9 banks with total deposits over $500 million.

Cultural facilities: Union College, Schnectady Community College, 66 homes and buildings built between 1700-1850; the Schenectady Museum and County Historical Society.
Other attractions: 5 hospitals, 87-acre Industrial Park; 65 schools; 175 churches; 25 parks, 5 golf courses, 30 tennis courts, 18 playgrounds.
Further information: Schenectady County Chamber of Commerce, 101 State St., Schnectady, NY. 12305.

Seattle, Washington

The World Almanac is sponsored in the Seattle area by The Seattle Times, Fairview Ave. N. & John St., P.O. Box 70, Seattle, Wash. 98111; phone (206) MA 2-0300; founded 1896 by Alden J. Blethen; circulation 223,478 daily,

310,203 Sunday; publisher John A. Blethen; president W. J. Pennington; vice president and general manager Harold G. Fuhrman.

Population: 503,000 (city), 1,416,700 (metro); first in state, 23d in nation; total employed (metro) 608,000.
Area: 91.6 sq. mi. between Puget Sound and Lake Washington; King County seat.
Industry: headquarters for Boeing, 45,000 employes, world's largest manufacturer of commercial jet aircraft; Port of Seattle has $800 million current value of properties and facilities including Seattle-Tacoma airport; nation's 4th largest containerized-shipping seaport; area has 2,313 employer units; major industries are transportation products, retail trade, shipbuilding, wood products, and food products.
Commerce: business center for western Wash. and Alaska; major import-export center for Far East; principal supply point for construction of Trans-Alaska oil pipeline; total retail sales (1975) $4.55 billion; per capita income (1975) $6,074; 29 commercial banks.
Transportation: 3 transcontinental railroads, Amtrak; International Airport served by 12 scheduled airlines, 6 commuter airlines, handled 6.11 million passengers (1975); ferries serve Puget Sound, Canada, and Alaska.
Communications: 3 daily newspapers in metro area; 5 TV, 26 AM and 20 FM stations.
Medical facilities: 26 hospitals, including Univ. of Wash. Health Sciences Center and Fred Hutchinson Cancer Research Center.

Educational facilities: Three 4-year colleges: Univ. of Wash., Seattle Univ., and Seattle Pacific College; 7 community colleges.
Cultural facilities: symphony orchestra, opera association, art museum and 10 other museums, 2 professional theater companies.
Recreation: major boating center; several nearby ski areas; Mt. Rainier, North Cascades, and Olympic National Parks within 2-hour drive.
Sports: NBA SuperSonics; Sounders, North American Soccer League; Kingdome, new domed stadium seating 65,000 (football) and 60,000 (baseball), home of NFL Seahawks, a new American League baseball team.
Other attractions: $50 million Seattle Center, site of 1962 world's fair, has 14,000-seat coliseum, opera house, playhouse, arena, Space Needle, and Pacific Science Center.
History: settled 1851, named for an Indian chief who befriended the settlers; virtually destroyed by fire in 1889, quickly rebuilt; Alaska Gold Rush of 1897 spurred economic and population growth and propelled Seattle toward its status as the Northwest's principal city.
Further information: Chamber of Commerce, 215 Columbia St., or Convention and Visitors Bureau, 1815 7th Ave., Seattle, Wash.

Shreveport, Louisiana

The World Almanac is sponsored in the Shreveport area by the Shreveport Journal (eves. except Sunday), 222 Lake St., Shreveport, La. 71130; phone (318) 424-0373; founded 1895 as The Judge, given present name in 1897; circulation 50,000; president Douglas F. Attaway, vice-president D. Wesley Attaway, editor Stanley R. Tiner.

Population: 195,783 (1975); total employed approximately 130,000.
Area: 85 sq. mi., on Red River in Caddo Parish, northwest Louisiana.
Industry: oil, gas, timber, agriculture, largest manufacturer of telephones in the world, steel products, glassware, car batteries; Barksdale Air Force Base across Red River in Bossier Parish.
Commerce: wholesale-retail center for Ark-La-Tex area; retail sales (1975) over one billion dollars; total bank deposits $1.4 billion; 11 banks, 2 savings and loan companies.
Transportation: 6 railroads, 4 airlines, one bus line, 16 motor-freight lines; Interstate Hwy. 20; north-south toll road and Red River barge traffic proposed for 1980s.
Communications: 3 TV and 9 radio stations.
Cultural facilities: State Exhibit Museum and Planetarium, 2 art galleries; Norton Arts Gallery and Barnwells Memorial Garden and Arts Center, symphony orchestra, civic opera, 5 colleges, 5 community theaters, headquarters for the American Rose Society, garden center and conservatory, Men's Camellia Club.
Other attractions: Shreve Square, restoration project downtown on riverfront; Louisiana State Fair; Holiday-in-Dixie spring festival; 12 hospitals, LSU Medical School, speech and hearing center.
Sports: college basketball (Centenary College); Louisiana Downs race track across Red River in Bossier Parish, 7 golf courses, Cross Lake 8,960 acres, boating-fishing waters, skiing, and yacht club.
History: founded 1836 as Shreve Town, named for riverboat Capt. Henry M. Shreve who cleared massive logjam on river; starting point for the Texas Trail during westward expansion; Louisiana capital for 2 years during Civil War; 3d largest city in Louisiana.

Sioux Falls, South Dakota

The World Almanac is sponsored in the Sioux Falls area by the Sioux Falls Argus-Leader, 200 S. Minnesota Ave., Sioux Falls, S.D. 57102, tel. (605) 336-1130; a Speidel newspaper; founded 1885; circulation 47,038 daily, 54,679 Sunday; publisher William H. Leopard, executive editor Anson Yeager.

Population: 72,444 (city), 95,209 (metro area) according to 1970 census; largest in state.
Area: 33.81 square miles in southeastern South Dakota at junction of interstates 29 and 90; Minnehaha County seat.
Federal facilities: Earth Resources Observation Systems Data Center of the U.S. Dept. of Interior is nearby.
Industry & commerce: located in the nation's breadbasket, Sioux Falls Stockyards is the 4th largest public market in the U.S. John Morrell & Co. is the largest of 170 manufacturers. There are 24 banks with clearings in excess of $1.5 billion and 3 savings and loan associations. Wholesale and retail center for South Dakota, parts of Minnesota and Iowa; yearly retail sales over $390 million, wholesale over $750 million; average spendable family income is $17,000.
Transportation: served by 3 major rail lines, 4 bus lines, 5 major highways. Joe Foss Field with modern terminal is within 2 miles of business district, has 3

major airlines offering 35 daily flights.
Medical facilities: 4 hospitals including Royal C. Johnson Veterans Hospital and Crippled Children's Hospital and School.
Communications: 2 TV and 9 radio stations.
Culture & Education: public library, convention center, Civic Fine Arts Center, Sioux Falls Symphony, Community Playhouse. Augustana College, Sioux

Falls College, North American Baptist Seminary, the South Dakota School For the Deaf, a vocational school, business college, 2 nurses training schools, 3 high schools, 29 public, 8 parochial schools, 91 churches.

Further information: Chamber of Commerce, 101 W. 9th, Sioux Falls, S.D. 57102.

Springfield, Illinois

The World Almanac is sponsored in the Springfield area by The State Journal-Register (morn. and eve.), oldest newspaper in Illinois, 313 S. 6th St., Springfield, Ill. 62701; (217) 544-5711; Circulation, 72,442; John P. Clarke, publisher; Edward H. Armstrong, editor; Patrick Coburn, managing editor.

Population: 96,200 (city), 175,700 (metro), 6th in state; total employed, 85,567.
Area: 50 sq. mi. on Sangamon River in center of state; state capital and Sangamon County seat.

Commerce: state and federal offices; 11 banks, 6 savings and loan assns.; 7 insurance company home offices; 125 national, regional, and state assns.; 27 civic clubs; 36 social service orgs.; 167 women's orgs.; annual retail sales of $563.47 million.
Transportation: 4 railroads; 38 truck carriers; one airport; nearby barge facilities.
Communications: one TV station and 7 radio stations.
Medical facilities: 3 hospitals with 1,434 beds, 296 doctors, 13 clinics, 10 nursing homes.
Cultural facilities: municipal band; opera; symphony; chorus; Theatre Guild; State Museum; Lincoln

Historical Sites; New Salem State Park; Old State Capitol; art assns.; summer theater; Illinois Country Opry; Clayville renovated stagecoach stop; arts & crafts festivals; Oliver Parks Telephone Museum; Saddle Tramp Gap western ranch; new Lincoln Library; Lincoln Memorial Garden; Nelson Recreation Center; Henson Robinson Children's Zoo; convention center under construction.
Education: Sangamon State Univ.; Lincoln Land Community College; Springfield College, Southern Illinois School of Medicine.
Recreation: 26 district parks; swimming, boating, skiing at 5 parks on Lake Springfield; public golf, tennis.
Special events: Ill. State Fair; Old Capitol Art Fair; NCAA college division world series; International Carillon Festival; Midwest Charity Horse Show.

Springfield, Massachusetts

The World Almanac is sponsored in the Springfield area by The Springfield Union, Sunday Republican, and Daily News, 1860 Main St., Springfield, Ma. 01101; phone (413) 787-2411. Union founded 1864; Republican 1824; Daily News 1880; circulation, Union, 74,993; Republican 137,460; Daily News, 81,274; publisher, Sidney R. Cook; Union-Republican editor Arnold S. Friedman; Daily News editor Richard C. Garvey.

Population: 168,460 (city); 523,677 (metro); 3d in state (city), 4th in New England, 84th in U.S.; 66,613 employed in city.
Area: 33.1 sq. mi. in SW part of state; I-91 skirts city; Hampden County seat.
Industry: 227 manufacturing plants produce boxes, childrens' games, wallets, auto tires, handguns, plastics, envelopes, hair shampoo, chemicals, paper; major employers Monsanto, Milton Bradley, Smith & Wesson, Breck.
Commerce: metro retail sales, $1.5 billion; avg. household spendable income $13,530; Mass Mutual Life Ins. Co., number 10 in U.S.; Baystate West, a combined. highrise shopping mall, office-hotel complex.
Transportation: Amtrak, 2 rail lines, 5 bus lines, Bradley International Airport (Hartford-Springfield) 18 miles south, major truck depot.
Communications: 3 TV, 9 radio stations.
Medical facilities: 6 major hospital complexes.
Educational facilities: College belt of N.E.; North

Adams State, Williams, Smith, Hampshire, Amherst, Univ. of Massachusetts at Amherst, Mount Holyoke, Our Lady of the Elms, American International, Springfield, Western New England and Law School, Westfield State, Greenfield and Holyoke Community colleges, Springfield Technical Community College.
Cultural facilities: State West Theater; quadrangle complex, 2 museums of art; library, natural history museum including planetarium; 146 churches and 7 synagogues; Tanglewood festival, 155 parks; civic center.
Sports: Indians (AHL) hockey; Basketball Hall of Fame.
History: founded 1636 by William Pynchon; first U.S. musket developed at city's armory (now a U.S. landmark) 1795; Springfield rifle developed in 1903 and produced here as was the Garand M-1 rifle.
Further information: Chamber of Commerce, 1500 Main St.; Convention and Visitors Bureau, Springfield, Mass.

Syracuse, New York

The World Almanac is sponsored in the Syracuse area by the Herald-Journal, Clinton Square, Syracuse, N.Y., 13201; telephone (315) 473-7700; founded Jan. 15, 1877, by Arthur Jenkins; circulation 123,773 daily, 244,840 Sunday Herald-American Post-Standard; publisher, Stephen Rogers; editor, William D. Cotter; sponsors college scholarship fund for police.

Population: 197,297 (city), 636,507 (metro), 5th in state, 66th in nation; 254,900 employed.

Area: 25.82 sq. mi. near center of state; interstate routes 90 and 81 intersect at Syracuse.

Industry: some 500 manufacturing plants produce electrical and non-electrical machinery, primary metals, food, transportation equipment, chemicals, pharmaceuticals, paper, candles, china; new $100 million Schlitz brewery, world's largest ever built at one time, opened in 1975 in suburban Lysander as did major Miller brewery north of city; major employers: General Electric, Carrier Corp., Crucible Steel, Crouse-Hinds, Allied Chemical.
Commerce: retail sales (1975 est.) $1.9 billion; average household spendable income (1975 est.) $12,800.
Transportation: 2 rail freight lines, Amtrak; 3 bus lines, 169 truck lines; 3 airlines.

Communications: 4 TV, 14 radio stations.
Medical facilities: 4 major hospital complexes.
Cultural facilities: Syracuse Univ., State Univ. College of Environmental Science and Forestry, and Le Moyne, Maria Regina, and Onondaga community colleges; Everson Museum of Art; symphony; $22 million county office-cultural center.
Sports: Syracuse Univ. football; Chiefs (baseball).
History: first explored 1615 by French; salt deposits led to area development, known as "Salt City;" "crossroads" since Indian days; became city 1847.
Further information: Chamber of Commerce, One MONY Plaza, Syracuse, N.Y. 13202.

Tallahassee, Florida

The World Almanac is sponsored in the north Florida-south Georgia Panhandle area by The Tallahassee Democrat, 227 N. Magnolia Drive, Tallahassee, Florida 32302; (904) 599-2100; founded 1905; circulation 40,753 (eve), 44,376 Sunday; member Knight-Ridder Newspapers, Inc., W. H. Harwell Jr. president and general manager; Malcolm B. Johnson, vice president and editor.

Population: 63,300 (city) 141,100 (metro); total employment 63,300.
Area: 26.14 sq. mi. between Gulf of Mexico and Georgia line; state capital and Leon County seat.
Commerce: 44% of economic base is state government; small manufacturers; agriculture only 1.1% of economic base; retail-wholesale center serving 17 county area; 2 shopping malls and 10 shopping centers containing 232 outlets; retail sales (1975) $587 million; effective buying income per household is $14,046, 3d highest in state; 15 commercial banks (resources, $320 million) and 3 savings & loan (resources $215 million).
Transportation: 3 major airlines, 2 commuter flight services, one railroad, 5 motor carriers.
Communications: 8 radio, 9 TV stations by cable.
Medical facilities: major hospital, retardation hospital, university hospital.
Recreational facilities: 5 recreation centers, 10 play-

grounds, 45 ball fields, 21 tennis courts; salt water fishing in Gulf of Mexico, bass fishing in Lake Jackson; deer, dove, quail, duck, geese hunting; 4 golf courses, PGA Tallahassee Open Invitational.
Other attractions: college athletic events at Florida State Univ., and Florida A&M; symphony, ballet, repertory theater, opera, touring plays, and art exhibits; 1845 historic capitol and other historic sites; Apalachicola National Forest; Junior Museum; Wakulla Springs, Maclay Gardens State Park, LeMoyne Art Gallery, Natural Bridge State Historic Memorial, Florida State Univ. "Flying High" Circus.

History: established as state capital 1823; Tallahassee means "old town" or "deserted fields" in Creek; area prospered with large plantations and antebellum mansions, many still standing.

Further information: Chamber of Commerce, P.O. Box 1639, Tallahassee, Florida 32302. (904) 224-8116.

Tampa, Florida

The World Almanac is sponsored in the Tampa Bay area by The Tampa Tribune and The Tampa Times, 202 S. Parker St., Tampa, Fla. 33606, (813) 272-7711; Times founded 1893, Tribune 1894; combined circulation 192,302; D. T. Bryan, chairman of board, A. S. Donnahoe, president; J. S. Bryan III, executive vice president; R. F. Pittman Jr., vice president/general manager; J. Clendinen, chairman of editorial board; J. Urbanski, business manager; P. Hogan, Tribune managing editor; B. Witwer, Times managing editor.

Population: 293,300 (city), 602,500 (county); total employed in county, 200,400.
Area: 84.45 sq. mi., halfway between the northern edge of Florida and southern tip; Hillsborough County seat.
Industry: Tampa port activity ranking 8th in nation for imports and ranking 4th in nation for exports; principal export cargo, phosphate; Ybor City section well known for cigar manufacturing; beer breweries, Anheuser-Busch and Joseph Schlitz.
Commerce: retail sales (1975) $1.788 billion; 42 banks, resources $2.051 billion, 8 savings & loan assns.
Transportation: 21 freight lines, Amtrak, 5 bus lines; city-owned bus system expanding into county, 48 truck lines, junction of I-75 & I-4, Int'l Airport, 9 major airlines.
Communications: 6 TV and 21 radio stations.
New construction: Univ. of So. Fla. continuing expansion; Tampa Medical Center; expansion of Busch Gardens, Westinghouse Electric, Tampa municipal beach; Ybor City Square, Tampa Wholesale Co., waste water treatment plant, Florida State fairgrounds; port expansion, county expressway system

expansion.
Medical facilities: 6 major hospitals.
Federal facilities: MacDill AFB, Federal Bldg.
Cultural facilities: Florida Gulf Coast Symphony; 2 museums; $2.4 million library; 5 local community theaters, Gasparilla Art Fair.
Education: Univ. of South Florida, Univ. of Tampa, Florida College, and Hillsborough Community College with 2 campuses.
Other attractions: Lowry Park Zoo; Busch Gardens; Ybor City (Latin Quarter); 26 parks, 11 picnic areas; annual Gasparilla Pirate Invasion; site for Florida State Fair.
Sports: pro-football Tampa Bay Buccaneers with 71,-500 capacity seat stadium; NASL (Soccer) Tampa Bay Rowdies, Tampa Tarpons (baseball farm team for the Cincinnati Reds); Cincinnati Reds spring training headquarters; greyhound racing, jai-alai.
History: Fort Brooke est. 1824 on site of present Tampa; incorporated 1885.
Further information: Greater Tampa Chamber of Commerce, 801 E. Kennedy Blvd., Tampa, Fla. 33602, (813) 228-7777.

Toledo, Ohio

The World Almanac is sponsored in the Toledo area by The Blade, 541 Superior St., Toledo, Ohio 43660; phone (419) 259-6000; founded 1835; circulation, 170,784 daily, 206,688 Sunday; publishers Paul Block Jr. and William Block; associate publisher John D. Willey; editor Bernard Judy; executive editor Joseph O'Conor; managing editor William Rosenberg.

Population: 389,100 (city), 783,300 (metro), 5th in state, 45th in nation; total employed, 298,000.

Area: 85.3 sq. mi. at juncture of Maumee River and Lake Erie, in northwestern Ohio.

Industry: glass, headquarters for Owens-Illinois, Owens Corning & Libbey-Owens-Ford; automotive parts, largest producer in nation, home of American Motors Jeep, Toledo Scale, and Haughton Elevator; largest petroleum refining center between Chicago and the East Coast.

Commerce: growing port on Great Lakes, annual overseas cargo runs to 500,000 tons; 2d in international tonnage, 3d in total tonnage, 11th among all ports, only inland foreign trade zone in the nation; total retail sales $2.31 billion; spendable income per household: $15,865.

Transportation: 9 railroads, 4 major airlines, 120 motor freight lines, 2 interstate bus lines; 13 major highways converge here, permitting the rapid flow of goods to almost 60% of the nation's consumers.

Communications: 4 TV, 15 radio stations and one cablevision company.

Medical facilities: 12 major hospital complexes, including the Medical College of Ohio Hospital.

Cultural facilities: Museum of Art with largest display of antique glass in the world; Peristyle used for the performing arts; symphony, opera society.

Education: Univ. of Toledo and its Community and Technical College; Michael J. Owens Technical College; Bowling Green State Univ.

Other attractions: Municipal Zoo among top 10 in the nation; modern 2,500 seat Masonic Auditorium with a Great Hall annex.

Sports: Mud Hens, farm club of the Cleveland Indians, at the Lucas County Recreation Center.

History: founded in 1836; took its name from sister city, Toledo, Spain.

Further information: Convention and Visitors Bureau, 218 Huron, Toledo, Ohio 43604.

Toronto, Ontario, Canada

The World Almanac is sponsored in the metropolitan Toronto area by The Toronto Star, One Yonge St., Toronto, Ontario, M5E 1E6. (416) 367-2000; established 1892, Joseph E. Atkinson, publisher, 1899-1948; circulation daily 493,049; Saturday, 778,562; Chairman, Beland H. Honderich; president, William A. Dimma; vice-president, Burnett M. Thall; editor-in-chief, Martin Goodman. Canada's largest newspaper in circulation, display and classified advertising linage; winner of 33 national newspaper awards and sponsor of the Santa Claus Fund and Fresh Air Fund.

Population: 685,333 (city), 2,152,269 (metro); 2d largest city in Canada, 13th in North America; labor force: 850,000.

Area: 241 sq. mi., on northwest shore of Lake Ontario; provincial capital.

Industry: Canada's leading commercial and industrial center; 6300 manufacturing establishments; value of 1975 factory shipments: $13.5 billion; principal industries: slaughtering and meat packing, clothing, printing and publishing, machinery, electrical goods, furniture, food products, rubber goods, sheet metal products.

Commerce: retail sales (1976 est.) $7.9 billion; headquarters for Eaton's and Simpson's, Canada's largest department stores; head offices of 12 trust companies and 4 of 10 federally chartered banks; value of cheques cashed (1975), $938.6 billion; Toronto Stock Exchange, 4th in North America, traded shares worth $4.1 billion in 1975; per capita disposable income: $5,380.

Transportation: 10 railway lines carry 325 freight and passenger trains daily; 9500 trucks use 12 major highways; Transit Commission carries 358 million passengers annually on 710 miles of routes; 6.17 miles of line now under construction will extend subways to 33 miles in 1977; 3 million tons of cargo unloaded (1975) at this major Great Lakes port; 25 airlines handle 11 million passengers annually at International Airport.

Communications: 6 TV stations including educational and French-language channels; 10 AM and 4 FM radio stations; 3 daily newspapers; 42 foreign language newspapers.

New construction: value of building permits (1975) $1.2 billion; $200-million Eaton Centre with 300 shops and $7-million convention and exhibition building on 100,000 sq. ft. of waterfront.

Medical facilities: 26 active-treatment hospitals including renowned Hospital for Sick Children; special treatment centers: Clarke Institute for Psychiatry, Addiction Research Centre, Ontario Crippled Chil-

dren's Centre.

Cultural facilities: 30 local groups offer alternate theatre; National Ballet of Canada and Canadian Opera Company perform in 3,200-seat O'Keefe Centre; symphony orchestra and Mendelssohn Choir at Massey Hall; touring shows at Royal Alexandra Theatre; 77 public libraries; Royal Ontario Museum; $40-million collection of Henry Moore sculptures housed in Art Gallery of Ontario.

Educational facilities: 2 universities, York and Toronto, Canada's largest (1975-76 enrollment: 46,-643); Ryerson Polytechnical Institute, 4 colleges of applied arts and technology, 2 teachers' colleges, Royal Conservatory of Music, Ontario College of Art, Osgoode Hall Law School.

Recreational facilities: Canadian National Exhibition, world's biggest annual fair; Ontario Place, 100 acres of offshore islands with restaurants, marina, and 1,000-seat Cinesphere for film showings; Toronto Islands have 3 yacht clubs, 560 acres of beaches and picnic grounds; Harborfront, 86-acre sports, arts, and entertainment park.

Convention facilities: Canada's top convention center; 266,000 visitors attended 501 conventions in 1975 and spent $62.5 million; total rooms, 18,631.

Sports: 9 public golf courses; thoroughbred and harness racing; NHL Maple Leafs play in 16,435-seat Gardens; new Toronto team plays AL baseball and Argonauts play Canadian Football League games in 54,000-seat Exhibition Stadium.

Other attractions: Ontario Science Centre, designed for participation and involvement; Black Creek Pioneer Village, living displays of upper Canada; McMichael Conservation collection of works by Canada's famed Group of Seven painters; Metro Zoo has 500 species roaming 5 continental areas covering 700 acres; CN Tower, world's tallest free-standing structure, opened for dining and sight-seeing in June 1976.

History: town of York founded 1793 on site of French fort as capital of British colony of upper Canada; incorporated as city 1834 and named Toronto from

Indian word for meeting place.
Further information: Convention and Tourist Bureau, 85 Richmond St. West, Suite 300, Toronto, Ontario. M5H 1H9.

Troy, New York

Population: 62,918.
Area: 9.8 sq. mi., 8 miles northeast of Albany.
Industry: known for manufacture of collars and shirts; military equipment, precision machines, automobile parts, abrasive materials, metals.
Commerce: 7 banks.
Cultural facilities: Rensselaer Polytechnic Institute Fieldhouse (seating 7,500); Troy Music Hall, Junior Museum, Historical Society.

Other attractions: 21 playgrounds, 3 hospitals, Russell Sage College, Hudson Valley Community College, Emma Willard School for Girls, 31 public and parochial schools.

Further information: Greater Troy Chamber of Commerce, 28 Second St., Troy, N.Y. 12180.

Tucson, Arizona

The World Almanac is sponsored in the Tucson area by The Arizona Daily Star, 4850 S. Park Ave., Tucson 85726: (602)294-4433; founded 1877 as a weekly, Michael E. Pulitzer, editor and publisher; William J. Woesterdiek, executive editor; Frank E. Johnson, managing editor; Stephen E. Auslander, editorial section director; Frank Delehanty, business manager; William Waters, Public affairs editor; sponsors Sportsmen's Fund for less-chance youngsters.

Population:330,700 within city limits, 360,000 in Pima County (Special Census 1975) 157,600 employed in county, out of total civilian labor force of 168,700.
Area: Sonoran Desert of southern Arizona, elev. 2,500 ft.; Santa Catalina Mts. immediately N and E reach 9,000 ft.; Pima County seat.
Industry: Hughes Aircraft, various aircraft-reclamation plants handling surplus craft from Davis-Monthan AFB; electronics, light manufacturing, and tourism; center of the "copper circle" — hundreds of millions of development dollars have been invested in the area by Anaconda, Duval, American Smelting and Refining, Kennecott, Magma, Pima and other mining operations.
Transportation: International Airport served by AeroMexico and Hughes AirWest (to and from Mexico), most major airlines nationally and Cochise Airlines within Arizona; 3 smaller airports; 2 national, one local bus line; Southern Pacific Railroad; trucks.
Communications:2 newspapers; 5 TV and 18 radio stations.
Medical facilities:10 hospitals, including Arizona

winter; summer brings some rain, mostly after July 1, and temperatures of about 100° F.
Culture: Univ. of Arizona; Tucson Museum of Art; Tucson Symphony; Arizona Civic Theater; Tucson Civic Ballet; many musical, drama, and dance groups; Tucson Boys Chorus, Los Changuitos Feos mariachi group provide local flavor.

Convention facilities: convention center accommodates 10,000 theater-style in arena; sit-down functions 5,000; meeting-rooms 1,000 theater-style; music hall, 2,300; contiguous exhibit space 64,000 sq. ft.

Sports: Toros, farm club of Oakland Athletics; Cleveland Indians spring training site; Tucson Open golf tournament; collegiate athletics.

History: Presidio of Tucson est. 1775; Mission San Xavier del Bac founded nearby by Rev. Eusebio Francisco Kino, S. J., who first visited area in 1692.

Bicentennial plans: fiestas, parades, commemorative publications with "Colonial heritage" theme.

Further information: Tucson Chamber of Commerce, P.O. Box 991, Tucson, 85702.

Tulsa, Oklahoma

The World Almanac is sponsored in the Tulsa area by The Tulsa Tribune, 315 So. Boulder, Tulsa, Oklahoma, 74102; phone (918) 582-1101; founded 1904 as The Tulsa Democrat, renamed the Tulsa Tribune in 1920; circulation, 88,210; editor Jenkin Lloyd Jones; managing editor Gordon Fallis; executive editor Jenkin Lloyd Jones Jr.

Population: 350,200 (city), 492,200 (metro); 254,700 employed.
Area: 175 sq. mi., on Arkansas River at 96th meridian.
Industry: petroleum, 30,000 employed by 825 oil and oil-related firms with $185 million annual payroll, Sun Oil and Texaco refineries; aviation, 15,000 in aviation and aerospace industries, including Rockwell International, McDonnell Douglas, and American Airlines; world's largest manufacturer of industrial heaters and winches; 1,200 diversified manufacturing plants.
Commerce: retail sales (1975) $1.285 billion; 17 banks (resources $1,914 billion), 10 savings and loan assns.; per capita income, $4,565.
Transportation: Tulsa Port of Catoosa, nation's most inland port, head of Arkansas-Verdigris navigation channel, total 1975 barge tonnage, 364,564; 4 rail freight lines; 3 bus lines; 32 truck lines; 6 airlines with 1,373,352 passenger movements (1975).

Communications: 2 daily newspapers, 3 TV and 15 radio stations.
New construction: building permits valued at $259.5 million (1975).
Medical facilities: 5 hospitals, 2,250 beds; Osteopathic College, Univ. of Oklahoma medical school branch.
Federal facilities: District Corps of Engineers, 1,200 employees; hq. Southwestern Power Administration.
Cultural facilities: Univ. of Tulsa, Oral Roberts Univ., American Christian and Tulsa junior colleges, Philharmonic, opera, civic ballet, 2 art museums, including Thomas Gilcrease Institute of American History and Art.
Convention facilities: Assembly Center seats 10,000; 355 conventions with 140,440 attendance (1975).
Sports: Tulsa Oilers, St. Louis Cardinals farm team; pro hockey in Central Hockey League; intercollegiate athletics; 4 public and 7 country club golf courses.
Further information: Metropolitan Tulsa Chamber of Commerce, 616 S. Boston Ave., Tulsa, Okla. 74127.

Vancouver, British Columbia, Canada

The World Almanac is sponsored in the Vancouver area by The Vancouver Sun, 2250 Granville Street, Vancouver, B. C., V6H 3G2; phone (604) 732-2111; founded 1886: circulation 241,388; publisher Stu Keate; editorial director Bruce Hutchison; managing editor Bruce Larsen; sponsors world's largest free Salmon Derby; Sun Family Pops Concerts; Sun Tournament of Soccer Champions and many other community services.

Population: 435,000 (city), 1,180,900 (metro area), first in province, 3d in Canada.
Area: 44 sq. mi. on the Pacific coast at the mouth of the north arm of the Fraser River; scenic beauty of the city accented by the towering, snowcapped Coast Mountains to the north and rich greenery of agricultural land to the east and south.
Industry: 98 miles of waterfront, stretching up Burrard Inlet, the largest cargo port on the Pacific and Canada's 2d busiest, with 38.5 million tons handled in 1975; major cargos: grain, lumber, coal, mineral ore, chemicals, and manufactured goods; tourism a major industry with an estimated 7.5 million visitors bringing in $540 million in 1975.
Commerce: retail sales: $2.9 billion in 1975; value of shares traded on the Vancouver stock exchange $314.5 million in 1975.
Transportation: western terminus of Canada's 2 national railways: Canadian National Railway and Canadian Pacific; headquarters of provincially operated British Columbia Railway, which is linked to the U.S. by Amtrak along the Burlington Northern Railway right-of-way; 3 major long-distance bus carriers; Provincial Stage Lines, Trailways, and Greyhound; International Airport served by 7 major airlines handled more than 4.7 million passengers in 1975.

Communications: 11 AM-5 FM radio, and 2 local TV stations; also 5 U.S. network TV outlets.
Medical facilities: General and St. Paul's are largest hospitals; Royal Columbian in New Westminster, Burnaby General, Lion's Gate in North Vancouver, and Riverview Psychiatric Hospital are also major facilities.
Cultural facilities: symphony orchestra, opera association, several professional theatre groups, Centennial and Maritime Museums, and Art Gallery. Queen Elizabeth Theatre is the major arts facility.
Other attractions: Pacific National Exhibition, Gastown, Chinatown, the H. R. MacMillan Planetarium, Bloedel Conservatory, public aquarium, 1,000 acre Stanley Park, zoo, 18 golf courses, Grouse Mountain and Mount Seymour ski areas, Univ. of British Columbia, Simon Fraser Univ., and 18 public beaches.
Sports: professional teams; B. C. Lions (CFL football); Canucks (NHL hockey); Whitecaps (NASL soccer); Exhibition Park racetrack (thoroughbreds); and several amateur teams and sports activities.
History: discovered by Spaniards; first mapped 1791; taken possession by Capt. George Vancouver for British 1792; Hudson's Bay Company post established early 1800s; city incorporated 1886.

Washington, District of Columbia

The World Almanac is sponsored in the Washington, D.C., area by the Washington Star, 225 Virginia Ave. SE, Washington, D.C. 20061; phone (202) 484-5000; founded Dec. 16, 1852; publisher Joe L. Allbritton; editor James Bellows; managing editor Sidney Epstein; awards received by newspaper and staff include 8 Pulitzer Prizes.

Population: 726,700 (city), 3,015,300 (metro area including D.C. and parts of Maryland and Virginia).
Industry: U.S. Capital, federal government employs 410,000 civilian and military personnel, about 30% of the labor force, with annual payroll over $6.21 billion; government related activity, law, journalism, professional and trade associations, unions, lobbying groups, and scientists provide another large portion of employment base; tourism a major industry.
Commerce: metro area first in per capita income of 10 largest markets, $6,189; bank clearings for D.C. approx. $12.2 billion a year.
Transportation: circumferential highway; 100-mile rapid rail-transit system to be completed 1982, with downtown subway opened in March, 1976; Metroliner to New York, long distance rail and bus service; National Dulles, and Baltimore-Washington International airports. National Visitors Center built at Union Station; Concorde service inaugurated.
Communications: several national magazines; news bureaus of major newspapers, wire services, and TV networks; 21 FM, 23 AM radio stations; 6 TV stations; 2 daily metropolitan newspapers, over 30 weekly newspapers.
Educational facilities: American, Catholic, George-

town, George Washington, and Howard universities, and Gaulladet College; nearby Univ. of Maryland and George Mason Univ.
Medical facilities: major medical research center; National Institutes of Health, Walter Reed Hospital, Bethesda Naval Medical Center; about 40 general hospitals and 3 teaching hospitals.
Cultural facilities: Kennedy Center with 3 performance halls and Wolf Trap Farm Park in nearby Vienna, Va., present major concerts, ballet, opera; Arena Stage, Ford's Theatre, National Theater, many community theater groups; Smithsonian Institution, including major art collections; Corcoran Gallery of Art, Library of Congress; D.C. Public Library with 19 branches.
Sports: pro sports include football (Redskins), basketball (Bullets), hockey (Capitals), soccer (Diplomats).
History: named for George Washington and Christopher Columbus; Georgetown in the District of Columbia first settled 1665, then annexed by the city when D.C. created as seat of federal government by Act of Congress 1790; governed by elected mayor and city council with budget controlled by Congress.
Further information: Convention and Visitors Bureau, 1129 20th St. NW, Washington, D.C. 20036.

West Palm Beach, Florida

The World Almanac is sponsored in Palm Beach County, Florida, by Palm Beach Newspapers, Inc., 2751 S. Dixie Highway, West Palm Beach, Fla. 33405, phone (305)833-7411; publisher of The Palm Beach Post and The Palm Beach Times; combined daily circulation 103,979; Sunday, The Palm Beach Post-Times 110,557.

Population: (1975) 65,248 (city), 516,914 (metro); total labor force: 187,300 (April 1976).
Area: 41.75 sq. mi. (city), 2,023 sq. mi. (metro); south-

east Fla., 8th largest county east of the Mississippi; 2d largest county in Fla., Palm Beach County seat.
Industry: on top of Fla.'s "Gold Coast;" Pratt & Whit-

ney Aircraft, IBM, ITT, RCA, U.S. Sugar Corp., Atlantic Sugar Assn.; Osceola Farms Co., Sugar Cane Growers Cooperative of Fla., Gulf & Western Food Products Co., Rinker Materials, Solitron Devices, Inc.; construction and tourism.

Commerce: 47 general service banks, 14 savings and loans, total assets $3.8 billion (1975); retail sales $1.6 billion (1974); per capita income $6,622 (1974).

Transportation: 2 rail freight lines, Amtrak; Greyhound, Trailways bus lines; 15 truck lines; Delta, Eastern, National, United, Mackey, Shawnee airlines, Commutaire commuter service; Palm Beach County Transportation Authority (bus).

Communications: 2 TV, 12 radio stations, cable TV; 2 daily newspapers, winter-season daily newspaper, society journal magazine.

Medical facilities: 10 hospitals, 1,853 beds.

Cultural facilities: Society of Four Arts, Flagler Museum, Norton Gallery of Art, Science Museum, 6 community theaters, 3 legitimate theaters, Florida Atlantic Univ., Palm Beach Junior College, Palm Beach Atlantic College, West Palm Beach Audit., Lion Country Safari.

Sports: Expos, baseball; Atlanta Braves spring training; greyhound racing, jai-alai fronton, 70 golf courses, 2 polo fields, county fairgrounds, Palm Beach International Speedway, tennis facilities, water sports.

History: founded late 1800s by workers and business people associated with the construction of the famed Royal Poinciana Hotel in Palm Beach by Henry Morrison Flagler who set aside 48 homesites on the western shore of Lake Worth; inc. 1894.

Further information: Chamber of Commerce, 501 N. Flagler Dr.; Area Planning Board of Palm Beach County, 2300 Palm Beach Lakes Blvd.

Wichita, Kansas

The World Almanac is sponsored in the Wichita area by the Wichita Eagle and Beacon Publishing Co., Inc., 825 East Douglas, Wichita, Kansas, 67202; phone (316) 268-6000; founded 1872 as weeklies; became dailies 1884; consolidated 1961; circulation: Eagle (morn) 121,102, Beacon (eve) 47,049, Sunday Eagle and Beacon 178,489. Britt Brown, chairman; Eugene Lambert, president and publisher; W. Davis Merritt, Jr., executive editor; Keith Ashley and Lynne Holt, managing editors.

Population: Jan., 1975, (city) 264,669, first in state; (SMSA) 378,745, first in state; SMSA employment (Dec. 1975) 191,300.

Area: (city) 95.98 sq. mi. in Sedgwick County at juncture of Big and Little Arkansas rivers; Sedgwick County seat. Elevation 1,280 feet, average rainfall 30.06; Mean temp.; Jan.—31.5, July—80.3.

Industry: 60% of all U.S. general aviation aircraft is manufactured in Wichita. Aircraft employment: Beech (city) 6,127 (total) 7,525; Cessna 10,500; Gates Learjet 2,030; Boeing 8,000. Other fields: meat processing, flour milling, grain storage, petroleum refining, natural gas, chemicals; largest non-aero manufacturer Coleman Co.

Commerce: wholesale-retail center for large part of Kansas and northern Oklahoma. Metro (SMSA) retail sales (1975) $1.6 billion; bank resources (16 city banks) $1.43 billion; median household income $12,-250.

Transportation: 4 major rail freight lines, Amtrak; Continental bus lines; 54 truck lines; 8 major highways; Mid-Continent Airport, 5 airlines, averages 622 air movements per day; National Flying Farmers headquarters.

Communications: 4 TV, 7 AM and 6 FM radio stations.

Medical facilities: world's largest speech and hearing rehabilitation center (Institute of Logopedics); 5 hospital complexes including VA installation.

Federal facility: McConnell Air Force Base.

Educational facilities: Wichita State University and WSU Medical Branch; Friends University; Kansas Newman College.

Cultural facilities: Wichita Symphony Orchestra; Wichita Art Museum; Wichita Art Association (museum) and Children's Theater; Century II auditorium and convention complex; community theater; city library; 443 churches. Mid-America All Indian Center.

Other attractions: city-county zoo; 52 parks; recreation lakes; Cow Town (restoration of 1872 Wichita); Historical Museum; National Junior Livestock Show.

Sports: Aeros, Chicago Cubs farm team. National Baseball Congress (semi-pro) headquarters and tournaments.

History: founded 1870, became railhead (shipping point) for cattle herds driven up Chisholm Trail; named after Wichita Indians.

Further information: Chamber of Commerce, 350 West Douglas, Wichita, Kansas, 67202.

Wilmington, Delaware

The World Almanac is sponsored in Delaware by The News-Journal Co., 831 Orange St., Wilmington, DE 19899, (302) 654-5351, publisher of The Morning News, Evening Journal, and Saturday News Journal, circulation: 134,-247 and The Sunday News Journal, circulation: 68,371 (subject to audit). President and publisher, Andrew Fisher; executive vice president and general manager, Frederick Walter; executive editor, Frederick W. Hartmann; editor of the editorial page, James E. O'Brien.

Population: 75,800 (Wilmington) largest in state; 410,-000 (New Castle County); 535,000 (metro).

Area: 15.1 sq. mi. at the confluence of the Brandywine, Christina, and Delaware rivers.

Industry: one of the largest chemical and petrochemical centers in the U.S.; autos, utilities, steel; about 400 manufacturing firms; offices for many insurance firms and holding companies.

Commerce: port is major auto importing center; retail sales (SMSA 1975) $1.9 billion; est. 1976 personal income in SMSA $4.4 billion; est. personal income per household $25,085. State has 12 state-chartered commercial banks, 19 state-chartered savings and loans, 5 national banks, 2 mutual savings banks, 2 federally chartered savings and loans, 1 non-deposit trust company.

Transportation: 2 major railway lines, 3 bus lines, more than 60 trucking firms, airport.

Communications: 1 public TV station; 6 radio stations.

Medical facilities: Wilmington Medical Center (4 divisions); 2 private hospitals; Alfred I. du Pont Institute.

Cultural attractions: Grand Opera House, Winterthur Museum, Hagley Museum, Old Brandywine Village, Fort Christina Park, Wilmington Symphony Orchestra, Wilmington Opera Society, Wilmington Drama League, Museum of Natural History; University of Delaware (Neward), Delaware State College (Dover), Delaware Technical and Community College.

Sports: Delaware Park, Brandywine Raceway, Dover Downs (Dover), Harrington Raceway (Harrington); Univ. of Delaware football.
Other attractions: Rehoboth Beach (100 mi.); Longwood Gardens and Brandywine River Museum (both in nearby Pa.); several state parks and recreation areas, historic old New Castle, Hillendale Museum.

History: founded as Fort Christina in 1638; named for Queen of Sweden; name changed to Willington in 1731 and then to Wilmington in 1739 in honor of the Earl of Wilmington; it is the first city in the first state of the union.
Further information: Delaware State Chamber of Commerce, 1102 West St., Wilmington, Del. 19801.

Windsor, Ontario, Canada

The World Almanac is sponsored in Windsor and a large part of southwestern Ontario including Essex, Kent, and Lambton counties by The Windsor Star (Cir. 82,726), 167 Ferry St., Windsor 12, Ontario; a division of Southam Press Ltd.; published daily since 1890 (present name since 1957); publisher E. H. Wheatley; general manager A. H. Fast; editor R. M. Pearson.

Population: 203,000 (city), 258,655 (metro), 539,700 (tri-county); 10th in nation; total employed 106,000.
Area: 50 sq. mi., one-half mile across Detroit River from Detroit, Mich.; largest Canadian city on U.S.-Canada border.
Industry: autos and feeder plants, more than 25% national production (Chrysler, Ford, GM); tool and die shops; alcoholic beverages (home office Hiram Walker and Sons); food processing (H. J. Heinz, Green Giant); pharmaceutical supplies (Wyeth Ltd., C. E. Jamieson Ltd.); salt mining; zinc and plastic die-casting; agriculture (rich producer early vegetables) tomatoes, corn, soybeans, peaches, tobacco; tourism (largest port of entry in nation for U.S. visitors).
Commerce: retail sales $588.2 million (2% above national average); personal disposable income $1.338 billion (10% above national average); average weekly income $201.17; 6 banks, 7 loan companies, 68 branches.
Transportation: 7 rail lines; 2 airlines; linked to Detroit by suspension bridge and underwater tunnel; western terminus Highway 401; major harbor terminal (deep water port); private marinas; yacht club; municipal bus line.
Communications: 6 radio, 1 TV outlet; access to Detroit's 50 radio and 6 TV outlets; 1 monthly magazine; 1 daily newspaper.
Medical facilities: 4 major hospitals including burn unit.
Cultural facilities: Univ. of Windsor; St. Clair Community College; Light Opera Association; Art Gallery of Windsor; symphony orchestra; Hiram Walker Museum; public libraries; Cleary Auditorium and Convention Centre.
Other attractions: 60 parks and playgrounds, sunken gardens; close access to Great Lakes resort areas; site of International Freedom Festival; access to Detroit Ethnic Festival.
Further information: Chamber of Commerce, 500 Riverside Drive West; Tourist Information, 135 Ouellette Avenue, both Windsor, Ont.

Winnipeg, Manitoba, Canada

The World Almanac is sponsored in the Winnipeg area by the Winnipeg Free Press, 300 Carlton St., Winnipeg, Man., Canada; phone (204) 943-9331; founded 1872; daily circulation 138,645; publisher Richard C. Malone; president R. H. Shelford; editor Peter McLintock; managing editor Don Nicol; the newspaper and its staff have received numerous awards for outstanding journalism.

Population: 585,000, first in province.
Area: 220 sq. mi., junction Red and Assiniboine rivers, near center of North America; capital of province of Manitoba.
Industry: manufacturing is single largest source of jobs; 1,291 establishments, 54,284 employees; value of factory shipments, $2.5 billion.
Commerce: retail sales over 2.1 billion; Winnipeg Commodity Exchange is only gold futures market in Canada; headquarters Canada Grains Council, Canadian Grain Commission, Canadian International Grains Institute, Canadian Wheat Board.
Transportation: International Airport, Canada's 6th busiest, served by 7 airlines; 2 national rail lines and one railroad to U.S.; 5 national and regional bus lines; major trucking hub.
Communications: 6 TV and 12 radio stations.
New construction: valued at $224 million (1975) compared with $225 million (1974).
Medical facilities: one of Canada's largest medical teaching centers; research in immunology, transplant-tissue rejection, cancer, blood diseases, endrocrinology, respiratory diseases, neo-natal, pre-natal medicine; of Manitoba's 85 active treatment hospitals, 13 are in Winnipeg, including 2 major teaching centers, plus Univ. of Manitoba Rh Inst.
Cultural facilities: Art Gallery, Royal Winnipeg Ballet, Contemporary Dancers, Winnipeg Symphony Orchestra, Manitoba Chamber Orchestra, Manitoba Theatre Centre, Manitoba Opera Assn., Cercle Moliere, Museum of Man and Nature, Rainbow Stage, Manitoba Theatre Workshop, plus over 20 amateur theater groups.
Educational facilities: Univ. of Manitoba with 4 affiliated colleges, Univ. of Winnipeg, and Red River Community College.
Sports attractions: Blue Bombers (Canadian Football League); Jets (WHA champions); Assiniboia Downs horse racing.
Other attractions: major zoo; Red River Exhibition and multi-cultural Folklorama festival in summer; French Canadian festival in winter; museums and planetarium.
History: first colony, Lord Selkirk Settlers, 1812; incorporated Nov. 8, 1873; on Jan. 1, 1972, amalgamated city government replaced 7 cities, 4 urban municipalities, one town, and a metropolitan government.
Additional information: Chamber of Commerce, 177 Lombard Ave.; Tourist Information: 101 Legislative Bldg.; and Tourist and Convention Assn. of Manitoba, 400-365 Hargrave St.

Winston-Salem, North Carolina

The World Almanac is sponsored in the Piedmont Triad area by the Winston-Salem Journal and The Sentinel, 416-20 Marshall St., Winston-Salem, N. C. 27102; phone (919) 725-2311; Sentinel founded 1856, Journal 1897; brought under one ownership in 1927; now an affiliate of Media General; Charles W. Crowder, publisher-general manager.

Population: 137,000 (city), 229,000 (Forsyth County); 1976 est.

Area: 61.34 square miles (city), 419 square miles (county) in north central North Carolina.

Industry: R. J. Reynolds Industries with diversified interests in tobacco, food, shipping, oil, packaging; Western Electric; Jos. Schlitz Brewery; Westinghouse; Hanes Corp.; Hanes Dye and Finishing; Brenner Industries; Bahnson; Graveley Corp.; Dennis Inc.; Wachovia Corp.

Commerce: total retail sales (city 1975) nearly $900 million; part of the Piedmont Triad which, with Greensboro and High Point, comprise a rapidly growing industrial and business area.

Transportation: headquarters for Piedmont Airlines at Smith Reynolds Airport; city also served by regional airport with 4 airlines; 2 bus lines; 54 motor-freight carriers.

Communications: 4 TV, 10 radio stations.

Medical facilities: Bowman Gray School of Medicine of Wake Forest Univ.; Baptist, Forsyth Memorial,

Medical Park, Reynolds hospitals.

Cultural facilities: one of the nation's first arts councils, formed in 1949; N.C. School of the Arts; Wake Forest Univ., Salem College, Winston-Salem State Univ.; Old Salem, restoration of colonial town.

Convention facilities: Hyatt House hotel complex sits across from the Benton Convention Center; hotels and motels offer 2,700 rooms.

Recreation: more than 50 public parks, 10 community centers, 10 swimming centers, fishing and boating on Winston and Salem lakes; 17 golf courses, including Tanglewood.

Sports: Polar Twins, Southern Hockey League; Red Sox, Carolina League farm club of Boston Red Sox; stock car racing; Wake Forest football at Groves Stadium, basketball at Memorial Coliseum.

History: Salem founded 1766 by members of the Moravian Church; Winston founded 1849; merged in 1913.

Further information: Chamber of Commerce, 2640 N. Marshall St., Winston-Salem, N.C. 27101.

Yakima, Washington

The World Almanac is sponsored in the Yakima area by the Yakima Herald-Republic (morning and evening Mon.-Fri.) (mornings Sat. and Sun.), 114 North Fourth St., Yakima, Wash. 98907; phone (518) 248-1251; founded 1903 as The Yakima Republic, given present name in 1970; circulation 38,958 daily and 43,056 Sunday; publisher James E. Tonkin, editorial page editor J.M. (Tom) Thomas, managing editor Stephen M. Kent.

Population: 48,290 (1975 est.); average monthly work force 36,146.

Area: 11.78 square miles east of Cascade Mountains in southcentral Washington, 142 miles SE of Seattle, Yakima County seat.

Industry: agriculture, timber, first in the nation in production of apples, hops, and mint; first in the number of fruit trees.

Commerce: retail sales $264 million; EBI per capita $3,803; bank deposits $1.7 billion.

Transportation: Hughes Airwest and Cascade Airways; Burlington Northern, Union Pacific railroads; Greyhound; on Interstate 82, U.S. Routes 12 and 97.

Communications: one daily, one weekly newspaper, 4 TV, 8 radio stations.

New construction: 824 building permits totalling $15 million, 1974.

Medical facilities: 3 hospitals with 440 beds; 140 physicians, 60 dentists.

Federal facilities: U.S. Army Yakima Firing Center, 409 permanent personnel, trains active and reserve units on 263,131 acres.

Cultural facilities: Yakima Valley Museum, Yakima Valley Regional Library, Allied Arts Council, 95 churches.

Education: Yakima Valley College, 7 public school districts in and around city.

Recreation: 5 theaters, 6 drive-in theaters, hunting, fishing, skiing.

Convention facilities: Bicentennial Pavilion; over 1,400 hotel and motel units.

Sports: 1975 American Legion baseball champions; fishing, hunting, skiing in the Cascades, 45 minutes from city.

History: founded Jan. 27, 1886 as North Yakima on route of Northern Pacific Railroad.

Further information: Greater Yakima Chamber of Commerce, P.O. Box 1498, Yakima, Wash. 98907.

Youngstown, Ohio

The World Almanac is sponsored in the Youngstown area by The Vindicator, Vindicator Sq., Youngstown, Oh. 44501; phone (216) 747-1471; founded 1863 by J. H. Odell; Wm. F. Maag began daily Sept. 25, 1889; daily circulation 103,094, Sunday 160,004; president, publisher, general manager William J. Brown; advertising manager William Mittler; managing editor Irving L. Mansell.

Population: 140,909 (city) Ohio's 7th largest; 536,836 (metro) 63d largest in U.S.; Mahoning County seat.

Area: 35 sq. mi. in northeastern Ohio at juncture of Ohio Turnpike, I-80, Ohio Rt. 11.

Industry: historically a strong iron and steel center, still important producer with Youngstown Sheet & Tube, Republic Steel, and U.S. Steel; local steel supplied to big nearby plants of General Motors-Packard Electric Div. in Warren and GMAD plant in Lordstown, where Chevrolet Vegas and trucks are made; GF Business Equipment sells office furnishings worldwide; Commercial Shearing does worldwide tunnel frame and hydraulics business; other fabricators use local steel, rubber.

Commerce: wholesale-retail center for large area of northeast Ohio and western Penn.; retail sales for metro area (est.) over $1 billion; estimated value

added by mfg. $1.7 billion.

Transportation: rail and truck transport center with 7 railroads and 92 motor freight terminals; airport served by 2 major airlines, headquarters for Beckett Aviation, largest fleet of executive aircraft in U. S.

Communications: 3 TV, 5 radio stations.

Medical facilities: 6 large hospitals in area.

Cultural facilities: symphony orchestra with downtown bldg.; ballet guild; Youngstown Playhouse in own modern bldg.; Butler Institute of American Art.

Educational facilities: Youngstown State Univ. with over 15,500 students and graduate program; medical college being established; 55 public and parochial schools; branches of Kent State Univ. in nearby Warren and Salem.

Recreational facilities: 10 parks, 44 playgrounds, golf course, 6 swim pools; Mill Creek Park, 2,383 acres.

Washington, Capital of the U. S.

The Capitol

The Capitol (building) since 1961 has presented an entirely new east central front, the central portion having been reconstructed and extended. It was moved forward 32 1/2 ft. The former facade of Virginia sandstone was reproduced in Georgia marble, the original wall becoming an interior wall. The new section added 78 offices and other important facilities. The cost of the extension project was $11.4 million; improved illumination and other work brought the total to $24 million.

The original plan for the Capitol was drawn by Dr. William Thornton, of Tortola, West Indies, and accepted April 5, 1793. It had a central section, nearly square, a low dome and rectangular buildings north and south. The southeast cornerstone of the north section was laid by President Washington with Masonic ceremonies Sept. 18, 1793. Sandstone from Aquia Creek, Va., was used. The northern wing was completed first. The Congress occupied it in Nov. 1800. The Supreme Court met there in Feb. 1801, and other local courts also used the Capitol. In charge of early construction were architects Stephen H. Hallet, Geo. Hadfield, and James Hoban, who was architect of the White House. Benjamin H. Latrobe was architect of the South or House wing which was occupied in 1807, but not completed until 1811. All the interiors were burned by the British in 1814. Latrobe had charge of the rebuilding until 1818 when Charles Bulfinch became the architect for 11 years. Congress reoccupied the Capitol in 1819 and the central rotunda area was finished in 1829.

The present Senate and House wings were designed and constructed under the architect Thomas U. Walter from 1851 to 1863. The wing extensions are white marble from Lee, Mass., and the columns are from Maryland. Daniel Webster spoke at the laying of the cornerstone.

The House moved in Dec. 16, 1857; the Senate Jan. 4, 1859. In 1860 the Supreme Court moved into the former Senate Chamber, and in 1864 the old Hall of the House was designated Statuary Hall. The court moved into its own building in 1935.

The original dome of the Capitol, wood covered with copper, was replaced, 1856, by the present dome of cast iron, completed 1865. Its greatest exterior diameter is 135 ft. 5 in. The rotunda is 96 ft. in diameter; height from floor to base of lantern is 180 ft. 3 in. In the "eye" of the dome is a fresco by Constantino Brumidi, the "Apotheosis of Washington." Below the dome runs a 300-ft. frieze in fresco, portraying American history from Columbus, 1492, to Kitty Hawk, 1903. Brumidi painted part of it by 1880. Costaggini added panels by 1888. Allyn Cox completed the frieze in 1953 and it was dedicated in 1954.

The Statue of Freedom on the dome, 19 1/2 ft. tall, is of bronze and weighs 14,985 pounds. At its base are the words "E Pluribus Unum" (Out of Many One). It was modeled in plaster by Thomas Crawford in Rome and cast in bronze. It cost $23,796, exclusive of erection.

Inaugurations of presidents and vice presidents are usually held on a platform erected over the great steps on the east front. The oath of office of the president is usually given by the chief justice of the United States.

Prayer Room

A nondenominational room for meditation and prayer is located off the rotunda. Decorated in blue, it has a white oak altar with an open Bible and candelabra, 10 seats, and 2 kneeling benches.

National Statuary Hall

Statuary Hall was created in 1864 to occupy the former Hall of the House of Representatives. States were invited to contribute not more than two statues of distinguished persons judged worthy of national commemoration by the States. In 1933 the number of statues in Statuary Hall was limited to one statue from each state, others to be placed in other parts of the Capitol. Early in 1976 it became necessary to rearrange the statues again. To date 91 statues have been contributed by 50 states. The statues in Statuary Hall:

Alabama—Gen. Jos. Wheeler, U.S.A., C.S.A.
Arizona—John C. Greenway, U.S.A.
Arkansas—Uriah M. Rose, jurist.
California—Junipero Serra, mission founder.
Colorado—Dr. Florence Rena Sabin, scientist.
Florida—Dr. John Gorrie, inventor.
Georgia—Alex H. Stephens, statesman.
Hawaii—King Kamehameha I, uniter of islands.
Idaho—Geo. L. Shoup, first governor.
Illinois—Frances E. Willard, WCTU head.
Indiana—Lew Wallace, U.S.A., author.
Iowa—Saml. J. Kirkwood, governor.
Kansas—John J. Ingalls, senator.
Kentucky—Henry Clay, statesman.
Louisiana—Huey P. Long, senator.
Maine—Hannibal Hamlin, vice president.
Michigan—Lewis Cass, statesman.
Minnesota—Henry M. Rice, senator.
Mississippi—Jefferson Davis, statesman.
Missouri—Thos. H. Benton, senator.
Montana—Charles Marion Russell, artist.
Nebraska—Wm. Jennings Bryan, statesman.
Nevada—Patrick A. McCarran, senator.
New Hampshire—Daniel Webster, statesman.
North Carolina—Zebulon B. Vance, governor.
North Dakota—John Burke, U.S. treasurer.
Ohio—William Allen, senator, governor.
Oklahoma—Sequoyah, Cherokee leader.
Oregon—Rev. Jason Lee, pioneer.
Pennsylvania—Robert Fulton, inventor.
South Dakota—Gen. W.H.H. Beadle, educator.
Tennessee—John Sevier, first governor.
Texas—Sam Houston, pioneer leader.
Utah—Brigham Young, Mormon leader.
Vermont—Ethan Allen, revolutionary leader.
Virginia—Robt. E. Lee, U.S.A., C.S.A.
Washington—Dr. Marcus Whitman, pioneer.
West Virginia—Francis H. Pierpont, statesman.
Wisconsin—Robt. M. La Follette Sr., statesman.
Wyoming—Esther Hobart Morris, suffragette.

Located Elsewhere
Alaska—E. L. "Bob" Bartlett, senator.
New Mexico—Dennis Chavez, senator.

Under the dome in the **Great Rotunda** are statues and busts of Washington (Va.), Andrew Jackson (Tenn.), James A. Garfield (Ohio).

Adjoining it, the **South Small Rotunda** has statues of George Clinton (N.Y.), Stephen F. Austin (Tex.), and John Peter Muhlenberg (Pa.). The corridor leading from Statuary Hall to the House has statues of Jonathan Trumbull (Conn.), Wm. King (Me.), Father Jacques Marquette (Wis.), Wade Hampton (S.C.), Will Rogers (Okla.), E. L. "Bob" Bartlett (Alaska), and Dr. John McLoughlin (Ore.).

In the foyer of the former Senate and Supreme Court Chamber are statues of John Stark (N.H.), Dennis Chavez (N.M.). In the corridor leading to the Senate wing are statues of Dr. Ephraim McDowell (Ky.), first to use ether as anaesthetic, John Hanson (Md.), 9th president of the Continental Congress, and John M. Clayton (Del.), secretary of state, Wm. E. Borah (Ida.), Edward D. White (La.), and Maria L. Sanford (Minn.).

In the **Hall of Columns** on the first floor, House wing, are statues of E. Kirby Smith (Fla.), Zachariah Chandler (Mich.), Jas. Harlan (Ia.), Francis P. Bair Jr. (Mo.), Gen. Philip Kearny (N.J.), Gen. Jas. Shields (Ill.), John Winthrop (Mass.), Oliver P. Morton (Ind.), J. Sterling Morton (Neb.), Rev. Thos. Starr King (Cal.), J. L. McCurry (Ala.), J. P. Clarke (Ark.), Geo. W. Glick (Kan.), Jas. Z. George (Miss.), Roger Williams (R.I.), Jacob Collamer (Vt.), John E. Kenna (W. Va.), Joseph Ward (S.D.), Eusebio F. Kino, S. J. (Ariz.), and Father Damien (Ha.).

In a new area on the first floor, the Main Hall, are statues of Roger Sherman (Conn.), Caesar Rodney (Del.), Dr. Crawford W. Long (Ga.), Samuel Adams (Mass.), Charles Carroll of Carrollton (Md.), Richard Stockton (N.J.), Robert R. Livingston (N.Y.), Charles B. Aycock (N.C.), Nathanael Greene, and John C. Calhoun (S.C.).

Office Buildings for Members

Members of Congress meet constituents and transact other business in five office buildings on Capitol Hill, two for the Senate and three for the House.

The original Senate building, now named the Richard Brevard Russell Office Building, was completed in 1909, enlarged in 1933; the second Senate building, now named the Everett McKinley Dirksen Office Building, was constructed in 1958. A subway connects both with the Capitol.

The original House building (1908) was named for former Speaker Joseph G. Cannon (R. Ill.), the second (1933) for former Speaker Nicholas Longworth (R. Oh.), and the third (1964) for former Speaker Sam Rayburn (D. Tex.). The Rayburn Building has underground transportation to the Capitol.

Also on Capitol Hill is the bell tower and statue memorial to Sen. Robert A. Taft of Ohio (1889-1953). It was erected by popular subscription and dedicated Apr. 14, 1959, by President Eisenhower.

Hours for Visiting

The Capitol is normally open from 9 a.m. to 4:30 p.m. daily. The Capitol is closed Christmas, New Year's Day, and Thanksgiving Day. Should either the House or the Senate remain in session beyond closing time, the wing of the Capitol in use stays open until the session closes.

Tours through the Capitol, including the House and Senate Galleries, are conducted from 9 a.m. to 4 p.m. without charge. It is not necessary to take a tour to see the Capitol. Visitors desiring to hear debate in either chamber for a longer period than the tour allows must obtain a visitor's card from their Senator or Representative.

The White House

The White House, the president's residence, stands on 18 acres on the south side of Pennsylvania Avenue, between the Treasury and the Executive Office Building. The main building, 170 by 85 ft., has 6 floors, with the East Terrace, 135 by 35 ft., leading to the East Wing, a 3-story building, 139 by 82 ft., used for offices and as an entrance for official functions. The West Terrace, 174 by 35 ft., contains offices and new press facilities above the boarded over swimming pool, and leads to the Executive Office, 3 stories high, 148 by 98 ft., erected in 1902 and enlarged several times since.

The White House was designed by James Hoban, an Irish-born architect, in a competition that paid $500. The main facade resembles the Duke of Leinster's house in Dublin. President Washington chose the site, which was included on the plan of the Federal City prepared by the French engineer, Major Pierre L'Enfant. The cornerstone was laid Oct. 13, 1792. President Washington never lived in the house. President John Adams entered in Nov. 1800, and Mrs. Adams hung her washing in the uncompleted East Room.

The walls are of sandstone, quarried at Aquia Creek, Va. The exterior walls were painted during the course of construction, causing the building to be termed the "White House." For many years, however, it was generally referred to as the "President's House" or the "President's Palace." Thos. Jefferson developed the east and west terraces and built one-story offices, woodsheds, and a wine cellar. On Aug. 24, 1814, during Madison's administration, the house was burned by the British. James Hoban completed rebuilding by Dec. 1817, and President Monroe moved in.

The south portico was added in 1824 and the north colonnade and porch in 1829 by Benjamin Latrobe, surveyor of public buildings, based on sketches by Hoban, approved by Jefferson. In 1948 President Truman had a second-floor balcony built into the south portico. In 1948 he had Congress authorize complete rebuilding because the White House was unsafe. During its reconstruction he lived in Blair House, 1651 Pennsylvania Ave.

Reconstruction cost $5,761,000. The interior was completely removed, new underpinning 24 ft. deep was placed under the outside walls and a steel frame was built to support the interior.

The Green Room, used for informal receptions, is in American Sheraton style, with green silk moire on the walls, a white marble fireplace, and white enamel wainscoting and door trim. On the west wall hangs a portrait of Benjamin Franklin, painted in 1767. Most of the furniture now in the room was made in New York City about 1815-1825 by Duncan Phyfe or his contemporaries.

The Blue Room, an oval drawing room, is the main reception room. The parquet floor is exposed; the walls are covered with wallpaper reproduced from a French docu-

ment of 1800. Portraits of Washington, Adams, Jefferson, Jackson, Monroe, and Tyler, as well as two seascapes by Fitz Hugh Lane of Boston harbor and Baltimore harbor decorate the walls. Seven chairs and a French clock from Monroe's original 1817 furnishings remain in the room.

The Red Room, used as a parlor, is furnished in the Empire period, hung in red twill satin with gold scroll borders. There are a Savonnerie carpet of the period and a marble-topped gueridon labeled by Charles Honore Lannuer. There are portraits of Pierce, Polk, T. Roosevelt, Abigail Adams, Dolley Madison, Angelica Van Buren, Audubon, and Alexander Hamilton in the room. Also there is a marble bust of Martin Van Buren by Hiram Powers.

The State Dining Room has a large chief table. Other tables are brought in for large dinners but do not remain there. Centerpiece of the main table is a French bronze-dore plateau purchased by Monroe in 1817. China in use was ordered during the Lyndon B. Johnson Administration. Chairs are in Queen Anne style. The room is paneled in oak with Corinthian pilasters, painted white.

The Family Dining Room, used for breakfasts and luncheons, has a portrait of Mrs. Theodore Roosevelt by Theobold Chartran.

The President's Dining Room is on the second floor. It is furnished with American Federal furniture, an 18th Century chandelier, and blue silk window hangings. There is a mahogany sideboard once owned by Daniel Webster.

The Diplomatic Reception Room, an oval room on the ground floor, is used as the entrance to the mansion at state functions. It has scenic wallpaper based on 1820 engravings, and a new Aubusson style rug with seals of the 50 states, installed in June 1971.

The Library, on the ground floor, has the painted decor of an early American room. In Aug. 1963, 2,780 titles were selected to be placed in the library. All but a few are by American authors. They were chosen by a committee headed by the late James T. Babb, librarian emeritus of Yale University.

The Lincoln Bedroom which contains an ornately carved bed and furniture of his period, is at the east end of the second floor. It served as Lincoln's cabinet room and in it he signed the Emancipation Proclamation of Jan. 1, 1863. A portrait of Jackson, admired by Lincoln, hangs there today. Seven pieces of furniture have Lincoln associations. The bed was used in the State Bedroom during the Lincoln administration. In the room is a copy of the Gettysburg Address, written out by Lincoln and donated to the White House by the will of Oscar B. Cintas, one-time Cuban ambassador, who died in 1957.

The Treaty Room, one door removed from Lincoln's cabinet room was used by Andrew Johnson as his cabinet room, and was so used until 1902, when it became a sitting room. Here in 1899 was signed the peace protocol, a forerunner to the final treaty of peace with Spain. It is now a waiting or meeting room for the President and contains some of the original Victorian furniture. There are portraits of Presidents A. Johnson, Grant, and Taylor and paintings of McKinley observing the signing of the treaty, and of Lincoln and Grant in conference.

The Queen's Bedroom is assigned to distinguished women guests, and has sheltered five queens — Queen Mother Elizabeth and Queen Elizabeth II of Britain, Wilhelmina and Juliana of the Netherlands, Queen Mother Frederika of Greece. The English overmantel mirror was presented by Princess Elizabeth in 1951.

The Yellow Oval Room, directly above the Blue Room is used as a private sitting room by the president and first lady.

The Map Room, on the ground floor, a top-secret war room during World War II, was redecorated in 1970 at the request of President and Mrs. Nixon. Furnished in American Chippendale style, it contains 4 American landscape paintings and a portrait of Benjamin Franklin which was taken from Franklin's Philadelphia home by a British officer quartered there during the American Revolution.

The President's Office, oval in form, is in the West Wing and looks out on the rose garden. The office was added in 1909 to the West Wing, which had been built 7 years earlier by Theodore Roosevelt. The West Wing also contains the Roosevelt Room and the Cabinet Room.

Visiting Hours

The White House is open from 10 a.m. to 12 noon, Tuesday through Friday, except on holidays. Also Saturdays, 10 a.m. to 2 p.m. Jun. 1 through Labor Day, and 10 a.m. to noon Labor Day through May 31. Only the public rooms in the basement and the first floor rooms may be visited. No permit is required.

President's Guest House

Blair House, the President's Guest House, fronts on Pennsylvania Ave., northwest of the White House grounds. It is supervised by the Dept. of State and is the official residence of heads of state who visit Washington. Built 1824, it was the home of Francis Preston Blair (1791-1876), political leader and Lincoln advisor. President Truman lived there 1948-1952 during rebuilding of the White House, and 2 Puerto Rican fanatics tried to shoot their way in Nov. 1, 1950, killing one guard and wounding 2 others.

Restoration and refurnishing began in 1963 and the house was reopened Jan. 14, 1964, on the occasion of the visit of President Antonio Segni of the Italian Republic. The Blair House Fine Arts Committee continues to provide for the house.

Other Centers of Interest

Arlington National Cemetery

Arlington National Cemetery, on the former Custis-Lee estate in Virginia, is the site of the **Tomb of the Unknown Soldier** and the final resting place of John Fitzgerald Kennedy, president of the United States, who was buried there Nov. 25, 1963. A torch burns day and night over his grave. The remains of his brother Sen. Robert F. Kennedy (N.Y.) were interred on June 8, 1968, in an area adjacent. Many other famous Americans also are buried at Arlington, as well as American soldiers from every major war.

Arlington National Cemetery, administered by the Department of the Army, was established June 15, 1864, on land originally the estate of George Washington Parke Custis. The land was part of the District of Columbia from 1791 until 1847, when Arlington County was returned to Virginia.

The Unknown Soldier of World War I was entombed on the east front of the Arlington Memorial Amphitheater Nov. 11, 1921, in the presence of President Warren G. Harding. The tomb is inscribed: *Here, rests in honored glory an American soldier known but to God.* The body had been chosen at Chalons-sur-Marne from unidentified dead in Europe. On Memorial Day, May 30, 1958, two unidentified servicemen, one of whom died in World War II and one in the Korean War, were placed in crypts beside the first, in ceremonies led by President Eisenhower and Vice President Nixon. The president placed the Medal of Honor on each of the two coffins.

As of Mar. 31, 1976, a total of 167,612 interments had been made in Arlington National Cemetery. Among the unknown dead are 2,111 who died on the battlefields of Virginia in the Civil War and 167 who lost their lives when the battleship Maine was blown up in Havana Harbor Feb. 15, 1898. The total of unknown dead interred in Arlington National Cemetery is 4,724.

Arlington House, The Robert E. Lee Memorial

On a hilltop above the cemetery, stands Arlington House, the Robert E. Lee Memorial, which from 1955 to 1972 was officially called the Custis-Lee Mansion. The house has a portico 60 ft. wide, with 8 Doric columns, and faces the Potomac. With its two wings the house extends 140 ft. It was built by George Washington Parke Custis, grandson of Martha Washington and father of Mary Ann Randolph Custis, who married Lee in this house in 1831. Here Lee wrote his resignation from the U.S. Army, Apr. 20, 1861. The house became a military hq. and was confiscated by the government. The U.S. Supreme Court restored it to the legal heir, George Washington Custis Lee, grandson of the builder, who sold the entire estate (including the mansion) to the Government in 1883 for $150,000.

The mansion and grounds are administered by the National Park Service of the Dept. of the Interior.

U.S. Marine Corps War Memorial

North of the National Cemetery, approximately 350 yards, stands the bronze statue of the raising of the United States flag on Iwo Jima, executed by Felix de Weldon from the photograph by Joe Rosenthal, and presented to the nation by members and friends of the U.S. Marine Corps, at a cost of $850,000. It was dedicated Nov. 10, 1954, and is under the administration of the Dept. of the Interior, National Park Service.

Folger Shakespeare Library

The Folger Shakespeare Library on Capitol Hill, Washington, D. C., is a research institution devoted to the advancement of learning in the background of Anglo-American civilization in the 16th and 17th centuries and in most aspects of the continental Renaissance. It has the largest collection of Shakespeareana in the world with 79 copies of the First Folio. Its collection of English books printed before 1640 is the largest in the Western Hemisphere. It also has extensive source materials for the history of theater and drama from the Middle Ages to the end of the 19th century, both English and American. The library owns approximately 250,000 books and manuscripts, about half of them rare.

The library was founded and endowed by Henry Clay Folger, a former president of the Standard Oil Co. of New York, and his wife, Emily Jordan Folger. He left its administration to the trustees of his alma mater, Amherst College. The exhibition gallery and replica Elizabethan Theatre are open free 10 a.m. to 4:30 p.m. daily; closed federal holidays and on Sundays after Labor Day to April 15.

Library of Congress

Established by and for Congress in 1800, the Library of Congress has extended its services over the years to other Government agencies and other libraries, to scholars, and to the general public, and it now serves as the national library. Two buildings, an ornate Italian Renaissance structure (1897) and a modern annex (1939), cover 6 acres of the 15²/₃-acre library site and contain 35 acres of floor space. In addition the library occupies 10 other buildings dispersed throughout the Metropolitan area. In Oct. 1965 Congress passed a law authorizing construction of a third library building, the James Madison Memorial Building; completion is expected in 1980.

Dr. Daniel J. Boorstin became the 12th Librarian of Congress on November 12, 1975.

The library had over 3,000 volumes when it was destroyed in the burning of the Capitol, Aug. 24-25, 1814. In Jan. 1815 Congress bought Thomas Jefferson's library of some 6,000 volumes. In 1851 fire destroyed about half the collections. In 1866 the science library of the Smithsonian Institution was transferred to the library, and in 1870 the library became the repository for materials deposited for copyright. Today the library's collections contain more than 70 million items, including more than 17 million volumes and pamphlets.

In addition to providing a variety of reference and bibliographic services to other government agencies, the Library of Congress serves as a cataloging and bibliographic center for libraries throughout the country. Its cataloging data is available on printed cards (a service offered since 1901), on magnetic tapes for libraries using computers, and in book catalogs. A recent program called Cataloging in Publication makes cataloging information available in books themselves so that they can be processed and put into circulation almost immediately after their delivery to libraries.

The library's exhibit halls are open to the public. Guided tours are given every 20 minutes from 9 a.m. through 4:20 p.m. and every 30 minutes 4:30 p.m. through 8:30 p.m., Monday through Friday; every 30 minutes, Saturday, Sunday and holidays from 9 a.m. through 4:30 p.m.; arrangements for groups should be made in advance with the Tour Coordinator. Many of the library's treasures are on permanent exhibit and changing exhibits feature interesting selections from the library's collection of photographs.

rare books, music, maps, and manuscripts. These are sometimes seen outside Washington as well, as traveling exhibits circulated by the Library of Congress to libraries and museums elsewhere in the country. The library's resources are also made available to the public through publication of guides, bibliographies, catalogs, and facsimiles. An annual list of **Publications in Print** is available free of charge from Central Services Division, Library of Congress, Washington, DC 20540. A monthly **Calendar of Events** listing exhibits currently on view, literary programs, chamber music, and concerts scheduled is also available from the same address. Information about the Library of Congress, publications, posters, color slides, and greeting and postal cards are available at the Information Counter, in the west entrance ground floor lobby of the Library of Congress Building.

Thomas Jefferson Memorial

The Thomas Jefferson Memorial stands on the south shore of the Tidal Basin in West Potomac park. It is a circular stone structure, with Vermont marble on the exterior and Georgia white marble inside and combines architectural elements of the dome of the Pantheon in Rome and the rotunda designed by Jefferson for the University of Virginia. The central circular chamber, 86 1/4 ft. in diameter, is dominated by a 19-ft. tall full-length figure of Thomas Jefferson by the American sculptor Rudulph Evans. The architects were John Russell Pope and his associates Otto R. Eggers and Daniel P. Higgins. The Memorial was dedicated by President F. D. Roosevelt Apr. 13, 1943, the 200th anniversary of Jefferson's birth.

On the pediment over the portico is a sculptured group by Adolph A. Weinman showing Jefferson standing before the committee appointed by the Continental Congress to draft the Declaration of Independence. On the interior walls are four panels with inscriptions from Jefferson's writings. On the frieze of the main entablature are Jefferson's lines: "I have sworn upon the altar of God eternal hostility against every form of tyranny over the mind of man."

The memorial is open daily from 8 a.m. to midnight, except Christmas Day.

John F. Kennedy Center

John F. Kennedy Center for the Performing Arts, designated by Congress as the National Cultural Center and the official memorial in Washington to President Kennedy, was opened September 8, 1971. The white marble building, designed by Edward Durell Stone, houses a 2,300-seat Opera House, a 2,750-seat Concert Hall, the 1,150-seat Eisenhower Theater, the 224-seat American Film Institute Theater, an unfinished 500-seat studio theater, and 3 restaurants. All facilities are in full operation throughout the year. Tours are available daily, free of charge, between 10:00 a.m. and 1:15 p.m.

Lincoln Memorial

The Lincoln Memorial in West Potomac Park, on the axis of the Capitol and the Washington Monument, consists of a large marble hall enclosing a heroic statue of Abraham Lincoln in meditation sitting on a large armchair. It was dedicated on Memorial Day, May 30, 1922. The Memorial was designed by Henry Bacon. The statue was made by Daniel Chester French. Murals and ornamentation on the bronze ceiling beams are by Jules Guerin.

The memorial, built on bedrock, is of white Colorado-Yule marble. There are 2 Doric columns at the entrance and 36 others in the colonnade. The frieze above the 36 columns bears the names of the 36 states existing at the time of Lincoln's death. On the attic parapet are recorded names of the 48 states existing in 1922.

Inside are 3 memorials to Lincoln. The seated figure of Lincoln is 19 ft. from head to foot and the classic armchair is 12 1/2 ft. tall. Over the back of the chair a flag is draped in marble. The statue was fashioned out of 28 blocks of Georgia white marble. On the north wall is inscribed the Second Inaugural Address. On the south wall is the Gettysburg Address.

The walls of the interior are Indiana limestone. The panels between the overhead girders are of Alabama marble saturated with melted beeswax to produce translucency. The interior floor and the wall base are of pink Tennessee marble. The cost of the Memorial was $2,957,000 and of the statue $88,400.

The memorial is open daily from 8 a.m. to midnight, except Christmas Day.

Mount Vernon

Mount Vernon on the south bank of the Potomac, 16 miles below Washington, D. C., is part of a large tract of land in northern Virginia which was originally included in a royal grant made to Lord Culpepper, who in 1674 granted 5,000 acres to Nicholas Spencer and John Washington. The division between Spencer and Washington put John Washington's son Lawrence in possession of the Washington half in 1690. Later it became the property of Lawrence Washington's son Augustine, the father of George Washington.

The present house is an enlargement of one apparently built on the site of an earlier one by Augustine Washington, who lived there 1735-1738. His son Lawrence came there in 1743, when he renamed the plantation Mount Vernon in honor of Admiral Vernon under whom he had served in the West Indies. Lawrence Washington died in 1752 and was succeeded as proprietor of Mount Vernon by his half-brother, George Washington.

To Mount Vernon in 1759 Washington brought his wife, Martha Dandridge Custis, having previously enlarged the house from 1-1/2 to 2-1/2 stories. Just before the Revolution he planned additions, and when he was called away to war his kinsman Lund Washington supervised the work, which was completed after Washington returned in 1783. During the Revolution Washington visited Mount Vernon only twice, on the way to and from Yorktown in 1781. In 1789 he left to become president and lived in New York and Philadelphia, with brief visits to the plantation. He came back in 1797 and died in Mount Vernon Dec. 14, 1799. He was buried in the old family vault. He had made plans for a new burial vault and this was built in 1831. Both his remains and those of Martha, who died in 1802, were transferred there.

Mount Vernon was left to Washington's nephew, U.S. Supreme Court Justice Bushrod Washington, and by him to his nephew, John Augustine Washington, whose son, John A. Washington Jr., was the last private owner. In 1853 Miss Ann Pamela Cunningham of South Carolina organized the Mount Vernon Ladies' Assn., which bought the mansion and 200 acres, since extended to just under 500 acres. The Association reassembled original Washington furniture and repaired the buildings. It restored the kitchen garden, flower garden, and experimental botanical garden, reconstructed the greenhouse, and built a museum. Several trees planted by Washington still exist, and the boxwood dates from 1798.

The Association preserves house and tomb with the visitor's fee. The regent of the Mount Vernon Ladies' Association is Mrs. Thomas Turner Cooke. About 31 states are represented by vice regents. The Resident Director is Chas. C. Wall.

National Arboretum

The National Arboretum, established in 1927 for the study of trees and plants, has become one of Washington's great show places. Occupying 415 acres of rolling land along the Anacostia River in the northeastern section of the city, it is administered by the secretary of agriculture through the Northeast Region of the Agricultural Research Service.

The Arboretum is open every day of the year except Christmas. The visiting hours are as follows: April through October—8 a.m. to 7 p.m. Monday through Friday; 10 a.m. to 7 p.m. Saturdays and Sundays. November through March —8 a.m. to 5 p.m. Monday through Friday; 10 a.m. to 5 p.m. Saturdays and Sundays.

National Archives

The Declaration of Independence, the Constitution of the United States, and the Bill of Rights are on permanent display in the National Archives Exhibition Hall. They are sealed in glass-and-bronze cases filled with inert helium gas. They can be lowered at a moment's notice into a large shockproof and fireproof safe.

The National Archives holds the permanently valuable federal records of the United States government, 1774 to the present. As a research institution, it is designed to preserve these records and make them available to government agencies, scholars, students, writers, and the general public.

The National Archives and Records Service is a part of the General Services Administration. Through the Presidential Libraries Office it administers the Franklin D. Roosevelt Library at Hyde Park, N. Y., the Harry S. Truman Library at Independence, Mo., the Dwight D. Eisenhower Library at Abilene, Kan., the Herbert Hoover Library at West Branch, Iowa, the Lyndon Baines Johnson Library at Austin, Tex., and the John Fitzgerald Kennedy Library, temporarily at Waltham, Mass.

The National Archives and Records Service is headed by Dr. James B. Rhoads, archivist of the United States, Pennsylvania Ave. and 8th St. N.W. For research information, call 202-523-3220. For visitor information, call 202-523-3216.

National Gallery of Art

The National Gallery of Art, situated in an area bounded by Constitution Avenue and the Mall, between Third and Seventh Streets, was established by Joint Resolution of Congress Mar. 24, 1937, and opened Mar. 17, 1941. Although technically a bureau of the Smithsonian Institution, the gallery is an autonomous organization governed by its own board of trustees. The chairman of the board is the chief justice of the United States. Other members are the secretaries of state and of the treasury, the secretary of the Smithsonian Institution, and five distinguished private citizens.

The collections comprise gifts of over 300 donors (none of the works were acquired with Government funds) and cover the various European schools of art from the 13th century to the present.

· The building was erected with funds given by Andrew W. Mellon, who also gave his collection of 126 paintings and 26 pieces of sculpture, which included such masterpieces as Raphael's Alba Madonna, the Niccolini-Cowper Madonna, and St. George and the Dragon, van Eyck's Annunciation, Botticelli's Adoration of the Magi, and 9 Rembrandts. Twenty-one paintings came from the Hermitage in Leningrad. Also in this collection are the Vaughan Portrait of George Washington, by Gilbert Stuart, and The Washington Family, by Edward Savage.

The Samuel H. Kress Collection includes the great tondo of the Adoration of the Magi by Fra Angelico and Fra Filippo Lippi, the Laocoon by El Greco, and fine examples by Giorgione, Titian, Grunewald, Durer, Memling, Bosch, Juan de Flandes, Francois Clouet, Poussin, Watteau, Chardin, Boucher, Fragonard, David, and Ingres. Also included are a number of masterpieces of sculpture, especially of the Italian and French schools.

The Widener Collection of over 100 paintings includes 14 Rembrandts, 8 Van Dycks, 2 Vermeers, and examples of Italian, Spanish, English, and French painting, and Italian and French sculpture and decorative arts.

The Chester Dale Collection includes masterpieces by Manet, Cezanne, Renoir, Toulouse-Lautrec, Monet, Modigliani, Pissarro, Degas, van Gogh, Gauguin, Matisse, Picasso, Braque, and such American artists as Gilbert Stuart, Childe Hassam, and George Bellows.

Several major works of art by some of the most important artists of the last hundred years, including Picasso, Cezanne, Gauguin, and the American painter Walt Kuhn, have been given to the gallery by the W. Averell Harriman Foundation in memory of Marie N. Harriman.

The Collection of Edgar William and Bernice Chrysler Garbisch includes more than 300 American naive paintings and watercolors covering the eighteenth and nineteenth centuries. Among them are Edward Hicks' Cornell Farm, Winthrop Chandler's portraits of Captain Samuel Chandler

and Mrs. Samuel Chandler, and Linton Park's Flax Scutching Bee.

Pictures to round out the collection have been bought with funds provided by the late Ailsa Mellon Bruce, daughter of Andrew W. Mellon. Preeminent among them is the portrait of Ginevra de' Benci, the only generally acknowledged painting by Leonardo da Vinci outside Europe; Georges de la Tour's Repentant Magdalen, one of the rarest paintings of the 17th Century; and Pablo Picasso's Nude Woman, the key work of the artist's analytical cubist period. Among others are: Rubens' Daniel in the Lions' Den; Claude Lorrain's Judgment of Paris; Saint George and the Dragon, attributed to van der Weyden; and a number of American paintings, including Cole's second set of The Voyage of Life.

Cezanne's great early portrait of his father and 351 paintings by George Catlin, mostly of North and South American Indians, are among recent acquisitions given by Paul Mellon, president of the gallery and son of Andrew Mellon. A fine collection of French impressionist pictures are on loan to the gallery from Mr. and Mrs. Mellon.

Among other works donated to the gallery's collection are Vermeer's A Lady Writing, given by Harry Waldron Havemeyer and Horace Havemeyer Jr., in memory of their father, Horace Havemeyer; Copley's Watson and the Shark, given by Ferdinand Lammot Belin; Goya's Victor Guye, given by William Nelson Cromwell; and Mondrian's Lozenge in Red, Yellow and Blue, given by Herbert and Nannette Rothschild.

The National Gallery's rapidly expanding graphic arts holdings number about 62,000 items and date from the twelfth century to the present. Almost half of these works were the gift of Lessing J. Rosenwald, who had gathered one of the world's great collections of prints and drawings.

The Index of American Design contains over 17,000 watercolor renderings and 500 photographs of American crafts and folk arts from before 1700 until 1900.

The gallery's Education Department gives daily talks on the gallery's collection. The Extension Service lends films, slide programs, and slide sets to schools, colleges, and civic groups in more than 4000 communities in the United States and Canada. Nearly all of the gallery's services are available to the public free of charge.

Construction is in progress for the expansion of the National Gallery in the block immediately east of the present building. Funds for this project have come from the Mellon family. The architect is I. M. Pei. Expected to open in stages, the East Building will provide space for temporary exhibitions, for the National Gallery's growing collection of 20th century paintings and sculpture, for a Center for Advanced Study in the Visual Arts, and for a greatly expanded library and photographic archive. The first stage, a concourse housing major new restaurant facilities called the Café/Buffet, opened in 1976 and will eventually link the present and the new buildings.

Open daily except Christmas and New Year's, from 10 a.m. to 5 p.m. Monday through Saturday and noon to 9 p.m. Sunday. During the summer open Monday through Saturday 10 a.m. to 9 p.m., noon to 9 p.m. Sunday.

National Geographic Society

The National Geographic Society, founded in 1888 "for the increase and diffusion of geographic knowledge," is the world's largest nonprofit scientific and educational institution. The Society produces the illustrated monthly National Geographic, books, maps, globes, atlases, other educational materials, and television programs. Its activities are supported by the dues of 9,000,000 members.

The society's 10-story headquarters building in Washington, D. C., was dedicated by President Lyndon B. Johnson in 1964. It attracts many thousands of visitors, including members of the society from all over the world. Explorers Hall offers exhibits, artifacts, and mementos depicting the organization's research and exploration activities.

In 1968 the society occupied its new Membership Center Building on a 100-acre tract near Gaithersburg, Md. The building accommodates 1,200 employees charged with handling membership files, correspondence, changes of address, and other clerical operations.

Executive officers are: Robert E. Doyle, president; Owen R. Anderson, vice president and secretary; Gilbert M. Grosvenor, vice president and editor; Melvin M. Payne, chairman of the board; Melville Bell Grosvenor, chairman emeritus and editor-in-chief; Thomas W. McKnew, advisory chairman of the board; Robert E. Doyle, vice president and secretary; Thomas M. Beers, vice president and associate secretary; Hilleary F. Hoskinson, treasurer.

The Pentagon

The Pentagon, headquarters of the Department of Defense, is the world's largest office building, twice as large as the Merchandise Mart in Chicago and with 3 times the floor space of the Empire State Building in New York. Situated on the Virginia side of the Potomac River, it houses 26,000 employees in offices that occupy 3,707,745 square feet.

The Pentagon was completed Jan. 15, 1943, at a cost of about $83,000,000. It covers 34 acres and has 204 acres of lawns and terraces. It is 5 stories high and consists of 5 rings of buildings connected by 10 corridors, with a 5-acre pentagonal court in the center. Each of the outer-most sides of the building is 921 ft. long and the perimeter is seven-eighths of a mile. Total length of corridors is 17 1/2 miles. There is a partial mezzanine below the first floor and a partial basement below that.

Smithsonian Institution

The Smithsonian Institution is one of the world's great historical, scientific, educational, and cultural establishments. It comprises numerous facilities, mostly in the metropolitan Wash., D.C., area. It was founded by an Act of Congress in 1846, pursuant to a bequest of James Smithson, a British scholar-scientist, to the United States to found at Washington "an establishment for the increase and diffusion of knowledge among men." The Smithsonian, ever since its founding, has been a center for basic scientific research; it engages in programs of education and it is also the largest museum-gallery complex in the world. About 20 million persons visit its halls annually. S. Dillon Ripley became the 8th secretary of the Smithsonian Feb. 1, 1964.

The Anacostia Neighborhood Museum, the first of its kind in the nation, opened in 1967 in a low-income urban community. The museum develops and presents exhibits on topics of interest to the residents of the community as well as the greater Washington area. The staff also conducts independent research in the areas of Afro-American history, minority and ethnic studies, and the history of the Anacostia community and Washington, D.C. Independent programs and activities, such as teacher workshops, seminars, and a circulating library of children's books on African and Afro-American history serve the local school community.

The Arts and Industries Building reopened in May 1976 with an exhibit entitled "1876: A Centennial Exhibition" which displays actual items from the Centennial exhibition in Philadelphia as well as others of the same era. The four halls are devoted to various subjects including machinery, with a large number of the machines in operation; items from the military, U.S. Treasury and the Patent Office; manufactured articles; and displays from many of the 37 states in existence in 1876 and from the foreign countries represented in the Philadelphia exhibition.

The Freer Gallery of Art, the gift of Detroit industrialist Charles Lang Freer, is an outstanding museum and research center in art of the Far and Near East. The gallery also houses the Whistler Peacock Room and his etchings and paintings.

The Hirshhorn Museum and Sculpture Garden, opened in 1974, houses works in the Joseph H. Hirshhorn collection which were donated in 1966 to the people of the United States. Primary emphasis is on art of the 20th century although the sculpture section ranges from antiquity to works of the most significant European and American contemporaries.

The National Museum of History and Technology has exhibits illustrating American culture, civil and military history, and the history of science and technology. The mu-

seum consists of 3 floors of exhibitions, and food facilities for its visitors. In the rotunda the visitor will find the original Star-Spangled Banner and a Foucault pendulum demonstrating the earth's rotation. "A Nation of Nations" is a museum within a museum tracing the peopling of America through 6,000 objects. Other major exhibits feature gowns of the first ladies, the Petroleum Hall, the history of transportation, American political and military history, numismatics, philately, ceramics and glass, musical instruments, timekeeping, physical and medical sciences, graphic arts, electricity, photography, and news reporting. National treasures on display include the desk on which Thomas Jefferson drafted the Declaration of Independence and Samuel Morse's first telegraph. A popular attraction is an authentic 19th century country storepost office where mail is hand-stamped with a "Smithsonian Station" postmark.

The National Museum of Natural History serves as a national and international center for the natural sciences. It maintains the largest reference collection in the nation and conducts a broad program of basic research on man, plants, animals, fossil organisms, rocks, minerals, and materials from outer space. Exhibits show aspects of life and cultures in Asia, Africa, the Pacific, and North and South America. Other exhibits include fossil plants and invertebrate animals, mammals, fishes, amphibians, dinosaurs, and primitive reptiles. There are halls of North American archeology, osteology, and physical anthropology. Also on view are geology exhibits on the earth, the moon, and meteorites as well as a Hall of Minerals and Gems which includes the 45 1/2-carat blue Hope diamond and the largest gem emerald on public exhibit, the 858-carat Gachala emerald. The World of Mammals, the Hall of Birds, the Fenykovi Elephant, and the Insect Zoo are additional major exhibits.

The National Air and Space Museum, which opened in a newly constructed building July 1, 1976, houses exhibits on space exploration, air travel and related scientific and technical topics. Its Milestones of Flight Gallery exhibits 'famous firsts' of air and space development such as the Wright Flyer, Lindbergh's "Spirit of St. Louis", John Glenn's Mercury capsule, the Friendship 7 craft, the Apollo 11 command module Columbia, and a moon rock. Aspects of space exploration and air travel are displayed in galleries titled the Space Hall, Hall of Air Transportation, Satellites and Sounding Rockets, Vertical Flight, and Life in the Universe. Other exhibit galleries focus on balloons and airships, flight technology, sea-air operations, and various kinds of military aviation. There is a giant screen theater with presentations related to air and space travel and the Albert Einstein Spacearium presents programs of sky and space simulation.

The National Collection of Fine Arts presents a panorama of American painting, sculpture, and graphic art from the 18th century to today with 17,000 works in its collections and approximately 20 special exhibitions each year. It is housed in the historic Old Patent Office Building; its Lincoln Gallery was the site of Abraham Lincoln's second inaugural reception. **The Renwick Gallery,** a curatorial department of the National Collection of Fine Arts, is a national showcase for American creativity in design, crafts, and the decorative arts. In addition to special temporary exhibitions, two rooms refurnished in the late 19th century period can be seen.

The National Portrait Gallery, also located in the Old Patent Office Bldg., exhibits the likenesses of persons who have made significant contributions to the history, development, and culture of the people of the United States. The gallery's temporary exhibitions are based on a variety of historical themes.

The National Zoological Park is noted for its outstanding collections including two giant pandas from China. Its research includes investigation in animal behavior, ecology, nutrition and reproduction physiology, pathology, and clinical medicine. Conservation-oriented studies cover maintenance of wild population and long-term captive breeding and care of endangered species.

The Smithsonian Associates was founded to stimulate interest and active participation in the Smithsonian's work. Its membership programs for adults and young people include seminars, lectures, workshops, demonstrations, concerts, theater, exhibition previews, dramas, films, tours, and field and camping trips. *Smithsonian*, a monthly magazine of the arts, sciences, and history, is available to members of the Associates.

The **Smithsonian Institution Traveling Exhibition Service** (SITES) organizes and circulates exhibitions for art and science museums, colleges, and other educational institutions around the United States and Canada. More than 200 exhibitions are on continuous tour with 75 or 80 openings of these shows occurring monthly across the country.

Washington Monument

The **Washington Monument** is a tapering shaft or obelisk of white marble, 555 ft., 5-1/8 inches in height and 55 ft., 1-1/2 inches square at base. Eight small windows, 2 on each side, are located at the 500-ft. level, where Washington points of interest are indicated.

The capstone weighs 3,300 lbs. and was placed Dec. 6, 1884. The monument was dedicated Feb. 21, 1885, and opened Oct. 9, 1888. It weighs 81,120 tons. It is dressed with white Maryland marble in 2-ft. courses. The first 150 ft. are backed by rubble masonry. From that point to 452 ft. Maine granite was used as backing, and above 452 ft. marble was used. The face of the monument is primarily marble from Maryland. Set into the interior wall are 190 memorial stones from states, foreign countries, and organizations. An iron stairway has 50 landings and 898 steps. A modern elevator takes sightseers to the 500-ft. level in one minute, compared with 12 "precarious minutes" in 1888.

The erection of the monument by the Washington National Monument society with funds obtained by popular subscription was authorized by Congress in 1848. The cornerstone was laid July 4 of the same year. Work progressed slowly until 1854 when $300,000 had been subscribed and 152 ft. of the shaft erected. In that year the enterprise became controversial and contributions ceased. Work was resumed in 1880 at government expense by the Corps of Engineers.

The Monument is open 7 days a week, 9 a.m. to 5 p.m. Extended summer hours are 8 a.m. to 12 midnight. It is closed Christmas Day.

Famous Churches

The **National Shrine of the Immaculate Conception**, at Fourth St. and Michigan Ave., NE, Washington, D.C. is the largest Catholic church in the United States and one of the largest in the world. Built by all the bishops and Catholics of the U.S., it honors the Blessed Virgin Mary as Patroness of the United States. The Shrine is impressive not only in size but also in beauty, its blue and gold dome and soaring bell-tower having become Washington landmarks. Open daily from 7 a.m. to 8 p.m., Sunday masses, 7:30, 9:00, 10:30 a.m., 12 noon, 1:30 and 4 p.m. (5:15 p.m. Sat. eve.). Free guided tours 9 a.m. to 5 p.m. daily; Sunday tours 2 p.m. to 4 p.m. Carillon concerts on Sundays and preceding organ and choral concerts. Organ recitals every Sun. at 7:00 p.m. (June through August) and 4th Friday organ recitals (Sept. through May).

Washington Cathedral, Massachusetts and Wisconsin Aves., NW, is atop Mt. Saint Alban, the highest point in Washington, D.C. It is the seat of the Presiding Bishop of the Episcopal Church and of the Bishop of Washington. Started in 1907, the cathedral is nearly complete. The nave will be finished and opened in 1976, with a festival dedicatory ceremony to take place July 8, marking the visit of Queen Elizabeth to the nation's capital. The west facade will be completed by 1980. When complete it will be the 6th largest cathedral in the world. Notables buried in the cathedral include Woodrow Wilson, Adm. George Dewey, Cordell Hull, and Frank B. Kellogg. The cathedral is considered one of the finest examples of Gothic architecture in the country.

Several Protestant churches commemorate the association of presidents with their congregations. **St. John's Episcopal Church**, across Lafayette Sq. from the White House, designed by Benj. Latrobe in 1815, was regularly attended by Madison and F. D. Roosevelt and at times by other presidents. **New York Ave. Presbyterian Church**, 1313 New York Ave., NW, preserves the pew in which Lincoln sat, also an original manuscript of the first draft of his first proposal to abolish slavery. The church was rebuilt on same site in 1950-51.

The **National Presbyterian Church**, on a 13-acre tract, at Nebraska Ave. and Van Ness St., NW, was dedicated on May 10, 1970. The Church traces its origin to a group of stonemasons who met in a carpenter's shop in the grounds of the White House in 1795, later becoming the First Presbyterian Church in the District of Columbia. The Church of the Covenant, founded in 1883, united with the original Presbyterian body in 1930 to become the congregation of the National Presbyterian Church. President Eisenhower was baptized by the pastor, Dr. Edward L. R. Elson, and became a member of the Church on Feb. 1, 1953. He laid the cornerstone of the new Church on his 77th birthday, Oct. 14, 1967, and the Chapel of the Presidents is dedicated to him. The Chapel of the Presidents contains the Eisenhower pew, and pews representing 16 additional presidents who worshipped with the congregation. The oldest president's pew, occupied by Jackson, Polk, Pierce, Buchanan, and Cleveland, is on view together with much historic memorabilia.

The **Islamic Center**, 2551 Massachusetts Ave. NW, a magnificent monument of Islamic culture and outstanding landmark for visitors, a mosque for worship, and an institute for study of Islamic culture.

Cherry Blossom Time

Cherry blossom time in Washington is looked upon as the opening of spring. The famous cherry trees encircle the Tidal Basin in West Potomac Park and for 2 miles line the roadside in East Potomac Park. A gift by the Mayor of Tokyo to the city of Washington, the original 3,000 trees were propagated from the trees on the Arawaka River in a suburb of Tokyo. The first trees were planted by Mrs. William Howard Taft, wife of the president, and by Viscountess Chinda, wife of the Japanese Ambassador, Mar. 27, 1912. Today many of the 650 trees around the Tidal Basin have white blossoms, while some have pink; deep pink blossoms are in East Potomac Park. The trees usually are in full blossom the first week in April, but no precise date can be given earlier than 10 days prior to full blossom, which lasts about one week.

Other Points of Interest

Pan American Union Building, 17th St. and Constitution Ave., NW, houses the General Secretariat of the Organization of American States, the oldest major international organization in the world, representing 25 countries of the western hemisphere. Of traditional Spanish architecture with a tropical garden courtyard, the building is one of the more gracious sights in Washington. It contains the Hall of the Americas assembly room, permanent and temporary exhibits of Latin American art, the Columbus Memorial Library, and behind the building, the Aztec Gardens.

National Society, Daughters of the American Revolution on a block bounded by 17th and 18th Sts., and C and D Sts. NW.

American National Red Cross, 17th and D Sts. NW, occupies 3 white marble buildings of neoclassic design, embellished with a Corinthian portico, colonnades, and bronze doors. The Red Cross Museum is in the east building.

Federal Reserve Building, Constitution Ave., between 20th and 21st Sts. NW, is a 4-story white marble building of Georgian design, with formal gardens and fountains, and tasteful but relatively simple interiors, built 1937. An annex, the William McChesney Martin Building, was occupied in 1974.

The **Corcoran Gallery of Art**, 17th St. between New York Ave., and E St. NW, Washington, was donated by William Wilson Corcoran in 1859. Other donors, including Sen. W. A. Clark, have augmented its collection. The gallery is open 11 a.m. to 5 p.m., Tuesday through Sunday; closed Mondays, and on Jan. 1, July 4, Thanksgiving, and Dec. 24, 25, and 31. Admission is $1.00; free on Tues. and Weds. and at all times to senior citizens, children under 12 accompanied by an adult, and members.

N.Y. City Museums, Libraries, Centers of Interest

See Index for Statue of Liberty

The New York Aquarium, in Coney Island, exhibits marine life from all climes, with over 3,000 live specimens including whales, sharks, seals, sea lions, fish, penguins; whale and dolphin training sessions.

The New York Botanical Garden covers 250 acres in the Bronx. It offers seasonal botanical and educational exhibits and concerts. There are specialized gardens, a museum of plant evolution and uses, a botanical library, and a plant and book shop.

The Frick Collection, 1 E. 70th St., was founded by Henry Clay Frick (1849-1919). The principal part of the collection consists of 14th-19th Century paintings as well as sculpture and Chinese and French enamels.

The Solomon R. Guggenheim Museum, 5th Ave. and 89th St.; permanent collection contains over 3,000 paintings, drawings, sculptures, and graphic works by paintings, drawings, sculptures, and graphic works by 19th and 20th Century artists. The museum's unique spiral building was designed by Frank Lloyd Wright.

The Hayden Planetarium, facing 81st St. near Central Park W., presents changing sky shows with a Zeiss projector in the world's largest planetarium dome; "Astronomia," an exhibit of astronomy fact and fantasy throughout history; Guggenheim Space Theater shows, and a new (1976) "Hall of the Sun."

The Hispanic Society of America is a free public museum and reference library devoted to the art and literature of Spain and Portugal. It is on Audubon Terrace, between 155th and 156th Sts., west of Broadway. Collections run from ancient to modern.

The Jewish Museum, 5th Ave. at 92d St., offers exhibitions of Jewish art and ceremonial objects and exhibits of Jewish interest. The permanent collection of Judaica is considered the most comprehensive in the world. There are lectures, guided tours, and a book and print shop.

The Metropolitan Museum of Art, 5th Ave. at 82d St. With over 1 million works of art, the museum's collection is the largest of its kind in the Western Hemisphere. Great masters of all the ages of art are included in the collections; Egyptian, Greek, Roman, Ancient Near Eastern, Islamic, Far Eastern, Medieval, Arms and Armor, European, Pre-Columbian, American, Contemporary Arts, Musical Instruments, Costume Institute, and Junior Museum. A new American Bicentennial Wing is to be completed in 1978.

The Cloisters, in Manhattan's Fort Tryon Park, is a branch of the Metropolitan devoted to Medieval art and architecture in 5 cloisters and other early European structures.

The Museum of the American Indian, Heye Foundation, Broadway at 155th St., maintains the world's largest collection of American Indian materials, extensive archeological and ethnological displays from North, Central, and South America, as well as study and photographic facilities.

The Museum of Modern Art, 11 W. 53d St., presents 20th Century painting, sculpture, drawings, prints, architectural and industrial design, photography, and film. A library contains about 30,000 vols. and a reference collection of more than 100,000 photographs. The film department has more than 12 million ft. of film. Bookstore, restaurant, and gift shop.

The American Museum of Natural History occupies a group of buildings at Central Park West between 77th and 81st Sts. There are large exhibits of man and beast from the most primitive times to the present, with extensive reconstruction of fossilized remains, dioramas of men and animals in their natural settings, dinosaurs, birds, Indians, Eskimos, and glass models of protozoa, rotifers, and coelenterates. The collections of gems, mollusks, meteorites, and ocean life are famous. Live shows include dance, drama, sand-painting, and crafts.

The Museum of the City of New York on 5th Ave. at 103d St., illustrates the history and life of the city. Its collections include dioramas, paintings, prints, maps, photographs, portraits, miniatures, vehicles, ship models, costumes, silver, furniture, theatrical and musical memorabilia, toys, and rare books.

The New-York Historical Society, founded 1804, is at 170 Central Park W. between 76th and 77th Sts. The society maintains a museum devoted to Americana; a large gallery of American portrait, landscape, and genre paintings; a reference library of American, and especially New York, history; manuscripts from all periods of the nation's past; maps, prints, broadsides, and photographs. Of special interest are the original watercolor drawings by John James Audubon for his *Birds of America.* Also, fire engine, carriage, toy collections.

The American Numismatic Society, founded 1858, maintains a museum of coins and other currency, ancient and modern medals, and decorations at Broadway and 156th St.

The New York Public Library: In 1975, its resources were placed at more than 34.5 million items of which over 9 million were books, over 10 million manuscripts, over 6 million pictures, 3.5 million posters, photographs, and broadsides, 6 million pamphlets, scrapbooks, and clippings. Of this total, 4 million books and the pictures are in the collections of the Branch Libraries which are maintained by N.Y. City and which operate 82 branch libraries in Manhattan, the Bronx and Staten Island and 3 bookmobiles. The Research Libraries, based at 5th Ave. and 42d St., include the Performing Arts Research Center, in Lincoln Center, and the Schomburg Center for Research in Black Culture, 103 W. 135th St.

Seamen's Church Institute, 15 State St., facing Manhattan's Battery Park, has dining room, cafeteria, collections of ships' bells and models, marine paintings, gym, sauna, and showers, all open to public.

South Street Seaport Museum, on the East River waterfront in lower Manhattan, is a growing restoration of earlier eras of New York's port. At piers off South St. at Fulton, the museum has 8 ships, including an iron-hulled windjammer, the world's longest square-rigger, and the original Ambrose Lightship. Ashore on Fulton St. are museum galleries, a 19th Century printshop, and a bookshop. Special features include puppet and craft shows, songfests, plays for children and adults, and seminars on nautical subjects. Restorations will include 100 early buildings with art shops, apartments, offices, restaurants.

The Staten Island Institute of Arts and Sciences, founded 1881, has a museum of art, natural science, conservation, and Indian life at 75 Stuyvesant Pl., St. George, S.I., and library at 51 Stuyvesant Pl. It offers lectures and classes for children and adults.

Whitney Museum of American Art, Madison Ave. at 75th St., holds exhibitions of group and individual artists, historical and contemporary. Comprehensive permanent collection of American art. Has downtown branches at 55 Water St.

Zoos. One of the world's largest zoos is the N.Y. Zoological Society Park (the Bronx Zoo), Pelham Parkway and Southern Blvd., the Bronx. About 3,000 mammals, birds, reptiles are displayed in its 252 acres, including African Plains exhibit, World of Birds, Children's Zoo, and nocturnal animals in World of Darkness. The city's Parks Administration runs the Central Park Zoo and the adjoining Children's Zoo at 5th Ave. and 64th St. in Manhattan, the Prospect Park Zoo and Children's Farmyard in Brooklyn, and the Queens Zoo and Children's Farm in Flushing Meadows-Corona Park, Queens. The Staten Island Zoological Society operates the Staten Island Zoo and Children's Zoo in Barrett Park, West New Brighton.

Brooklyn Centers

Brooklyn Academy of Music, 30 Lafayette Ave., presents a Sept.-through-May program of music, dance, theater, and film.

Brooklyn Botanic Garden, Eastern Parkway, Washington and Flatbush Aves., has 50 acres of gardens, including rose, herb, wild flower, and Japanese, and a fragrance garden for the blind.

The Brooklyn Museum, Eastern Parkway and Washington Ave., estab. 1897, has comprehensive exhibitions in all major fields of art. An Outdoor Sculpture Garden contains ornaments from razed N.Y. area buildings.

The Brooklyn Public Library occupies the Ingersoll Building, Grand Army Plaza, and 58 branches. The Ingersoll Building has 7 major-subject divisions and a children's room, and telephone reference service.

Houses of Worship

Central Synagogue (Reform), Lexington Ave. at 55th St., is the oldest Jewish house of worship in N.Y. City (1872), and combines 2 earlier congregations founded in 1839 and 1846. Its modern community house, 123 E. 55th St., includes a religious school, chapel, meeting rooms. Since 1934, the synagogue has presented the weekly Message of Israel program on a nationwide radio network.

John Street United Methodist Church, 44 John St., erected 1841, on site of Wesley Chapel of 1768, "first Methodist preaching-house in America," houses oldest Methodist Society, formed 1766. Has noontime services for office workers, and a museum.

Marble Collegiate Church (Collegiate Reformed Protestant Dutch), 5th Ave. and W. 29th St., erected 1854, is notable for the preaching by Dr. Norman Vincent Peale.

Mormon Visitors Center, 2 Lincoln Sq. (B'way at 65th St.), opened 1976. Has meeting house, sports and drama facilities, genealogy research library, displays of Mormon history, open to public.

Plymouth Church of the Pilgrims (Congregational), Orange and Hicks Sts., Brooklyn, is a Nat'l. Historic Site, built 1847, present structure 1849. Has windows illustrating Puritan influence on America and pew where Lincoln sat to hear Henry Ward Beecher, the first minister. In 1860 Beecher raised funds at an auction here to purchase the freedom of a slave girl, Pinky.

Riverside Church (Interdenominational), Riverside Drive and W. 122d St. The chief donor was John D. Rockefeller Jr. The tower, reminiscent of Chartres, is 100 ft. square, rises 392 ft.; it has the world's largest carillon, with 74 bells, and is open to public.

Russian Orthodox Cathedral of the Transfiguration (Orthodox Church in America), 228 N. 12th St., Brooklyn, is of a design similar to Moscow's Cathedral of the Assumption, with 5 onion-shaped domes. A screen of icons includes one from the 13th century.

Cathedral of St. John the Divine on Morningside Heights, Amsterdam Ave. and W. 112th St. (Episcopal), is one of the world's largest cathedrals. It was begun 1892 as a Romanesque building; the design was changed to Gothic. The church is 601 ft. long, 146 ft. wide at nave, and will be 330 ft. wide at transept. Two front towers will rise to over 250 ft.

St. Mark's-in-the-Bowery (Episcopal), 2d Ave. and E. 10th St., originally a chapel built on the farm of Director General Peter Stuyvesant in 1660, rebuilt in 1799. A statue of Stuyvesant in the churchyard was presented by Queen Wilhelmina of the Netherlands in 1915. The church has a theater and poetry center.

St. Patrick's Cathedral (Roman Catholic) occupies a block facing 5th Ave., between E. 50th and E. 51st Sts., opposite Rockefeller Center. It was begun in 1858 in granite and marble in a Gothic revival style designed by James Renwick. It was opened in part in 1877 and dedicated May 25, 1879. It has 2 spires, 330 ft. tall, and a 26-ft. rose window. St. Patrick's is the cathedral church of the Archdiocese of N.Y.

St. Paul's Chapel of Trinity Parish (Episcopal), Broadway and Vesey St., is the oldest colonial church edifice in Manhattan. It was opened Oct. 30, 1766.

Much of the interior decoration was by L'Enfant, who laid the plans for Washington, D.C. There is a unique collection of 14 Waterford Irish cut glass chandeliers.

St. Peter's Church (Roman Catholic), Barclay and Church Sts., has the form of a Greek temple with large porch, wide steps, granite pillars, erected 1836-38 to replace the original church of 1785 of the first Catholic parish of New York.

St. Thomas Church (Episcopal), 5th Ave. at 53d St., is the 4th church building, consecrated 1916, of a parish founded in 1823. The limestone Gothic edifice was designed by architects Bertram G. Goodhue and Ralph Adams Cram. It has 2 organs; recitals are given Thursdays at noon. It also has the only church-affiliated boarding choir school in the U.S.; choir recitals are given Wednesdays at noon.

St. Vartan Armenian Cathedral (Armenian Church of America), 2d Ave. and 35th St. In 5th-7th century style, it is the cathedral church of the Eastern North America Diocese.

Temple Emanu-El, 5th Ave. and 65th St., was erected 1929 by Congregation Emanu-El (Reform), which dates from 1845. It was built of limestone in early Romanesque style, its auditorium 77 ft. wide by 150 ft. long and 103 ft. high, one of the largest temples in the world. Noteworthy are the high arch at the entrance, the rose window, mosaics, and 6 bronze doors.

Trinity Church (Episcopal) faces Broadway at the head of Wall St. It was built 1841-46 of brown sandstone in perpendicular Gothic, designed by Richard Upjohn, is 78 ft. wide by 202 ft. long. The first church was completed in 1697. In the churchyard are buried Alexander Hamilton, Robert Fulton, Capt. James Lawrence, and Revolutionary soldiers who died in British prisons.

Historic Sites

Castle Clinton, Battery Park, lower Manhattan, is an 1811 fort, restored 1975; historical exhibits.

Edgar Allan Poe Cottage, Grand Concourse and Kingsbridge Rd., Bronx, is a restored cottage, built 1812, in which Poe lived 1846-49, and in which his wife, Virginia Clem, died, 1847.

Federal Hall National Memorial, Wall and Fassau Sts., is a Greek Revival structure of 1842, originally the Custom House, later the U.S. Sub-Treasury. The site was first occupied by the Colonial City Hall and next by Federal Hall, where the Stamp Act Congress, Continental and U.S. Congresses met, and George Washington took the oath of office as president.

Fraunces Tavern, Broad and Pearl Sts., was erected 1719 as the DeLancey mansion, acquired 1762 by Samuel Fraunces and operated as the Queen's Head Tavern. The Long Room was the scene of Washington's farewell to his officers, Dec. 4, 1783. It was restored by the Sons of the Revolution in the State of New York and is their headquarters. It contains a Revolutionary War museum and art gallery, free to the public.

General Grant National Memorial (Grant's Tomb), Riverside Dr. and W. 122d St., is a formal Roman-style mausoleum, 165 ft. tall, where Gen U.S. Grant, 18th president, and Mrs. Grant are buried.

The Morris-Jumel Mansion and Museum, W. 160th St. and Edgecombe Ave., is a 3-story Georgian mansion with 4-pillared portico built in 1765 by retired British Lt. Col. Roger Morris. From Sept. 14-Oct. 18, 1776, it was the headquarters of Gen. George Washington. In 1810 Stephen Jumel bought 36 of the original 100 acres of the property. In 1833, the widowed Eliza Jumel married Aaron Burr in the mansion's front parlor.

Washington Square, at the foot of 5th Ave., is the best known landmark of **Greenwich Village,** a colorful community and tourist attraction. Facing the lower end of 5th Ave. is the marble **Washington Arch,** designed by Stanford White to mark the centennial of the first inauguration and completed in 1895.

Important Buildings

Battery Park City. On a mile-long, 100-acre site reclaimed from the Hudson River, running north from

Battery Park in lower Manhattan, buildings will provide 16,000 housing units, 6 million sq. ft. of office space, a hotel, and entertainment, cultural, shopping, and recreational facilities. Occupancy to begin in 1978.

City Hall, headquarters of the mayor, the City Council, and the Board of Estimate of the City of New York, is in City Hall Park (the original Common), bounded by Broadway, Park Row, and Chambers St. Erected 1803-1812, it is an adaptation of French Renaissance with clock cupola surmounted by a figure of Justice.

The Coliseum, facing Columbus Circle between W. 58th and W. 60th Sts., is New York's principal center for national and international exhibitions. Opened in 1956, it cost about $35 million. The Coliseum has over 320,000 sq. ft. of exhibition space.

Empire State Building, 5th Ave., between W. 33d and 34th Sts., is one of the world's tallest buildings (see also World Trade Center, below), 1,250 ft. high plus a 222-ft. television and FM radio transmitting tower. The building was completed May 1, 1931. More than 1.5 million persons annually visit the 86th and 102d floor observatories. On a clear day viewers can see a distance of 80 mi. It also has the Guinness World Records Exhibit Hall.

Lincoln Center for the Performing Arts was opened Sept. 23, 1962, with a concert in Philharmonic (later renamed Avery Fisher) Hall. The center is located between W. 62d and 66th Sts., Amsterdam and Columbus Aves. It is a private, nonprofit, tax-exempt corporation of 8 constituent organizations. The New York State Theater opened in 1964; the Vivian Beaumont Theater, which includes the Mitzi E. Newhouse Theater, and the Library-museum of the Performing Arts, 1965; the Metropolitan Opera House, 1966; the Juilliard School of Music, including Alice Tully Hall, 1969.

Madison Square Garden Center, Pennsylvania Plaza (7th-8th Aves., 31st-33d Sts.). The huge development, above the modernized underground Pennsylvania RR station, includes a 29-story office building and the Sports and Entertainment Center which has the Garden Arena seating over 20,000, the 5,000-seat Felt Forum, 48 bowling lanes, the National Art Museum of Sport, and an Exposition Rotunda for trade and walk-around shows.

Pan Am Building, north of Grand Central Station, is one of the world's largest commercial office buildings. It has 59 floors rising 808 ft., with provision for a rooftop heliport, and was erected over the tracks of Grand Centra Terminal. It covers an area of 3 1/2 acres. Estimated office population is 17,000.

Rockefeller Center, the largest privately-owned business and entertainment center in America was started Sept., 1931. Its area includes the 3 blocks from 48th to 51st Sts. between 5th Ave. and the Ave. of the Americas, a large portion of the 51st-52d St. block and 4 blockfronts on the west side of the Ave. of the Americas between 47th and 51st Sts. There are 21 buildings. It has 175,000 daily visitors; over 66,000 work there.

The surface area of Rockefeller Center covers 24 acres; almost one half are leased for a long period from Columbia University. Rockefeller Center pays Columbia an annual rental of nearly $4 million. The lease with options for renewal runs until 2069.

The part of Rockefeller Center comprising theaters and radio and television studios is often referred to as Radio City. Studios of the National Broadcasting Co. are located in the 70-story RCA building (850 ft. tall). There is an observation roof on the 70th Floor.

Radio City Music Hall, Ave. of the Americas and W. 50th St., largest indoor theater in the world, seats 6,000 people. Its stage, 144 ft. wide by 67 ft. deep, has a proscenium arch 60 ft. high and 100 ft. wide. Has first-run films and stage spectacles with the Rockettes, Symphony Orchestra, and guest artists, plus concerts and other special events.

New York Stock Exchange, visitors' entrance 20 Broad St., has visitors' gallery, films, guided tours, Mon. through Fri., 10 a.m. to market closing.

American Stock Exchange, visitors' entrance 78 Trinity Pl., has visitors' gallery, guides, multi-media shows, and other exhibits, Mon. through Fri. during trading hours.

United Nations Headquarters occupies over 16 acres between 1st Ave. and F.D.R. (East River) Drive, E. 42d and E. 48th Sts. Most unusual is the Secretariat Bldg., 505 ft. high at front entrance, 286 ft. long and only 72 ft. wide. The 2 sides have 5,400 windows; the end walls are of 2,000 tons of Vermont marble. General Assembly Bldg. has a hall 165 ft. long, 115 ft. wide. Conference Bldg. houses 3 Council chambers, etc. There are guided tours daily.

World Trade Center, dedicated Apr. 4, 1973, on Manhattan's lower west side, has twin towers of 110 stories, 1,350 ft. each (2d in height to Chicago's Sears Tower) and 4 other buildings, with total of 9 million sq. ft. of office space. In 1976, over 35,000 of an eventual 50,000 persons worked in the North and South Towers. Atop the South Tower is the world's highest observation deck. Construction of this office complex for international trade, a Port Authority of N.Y. and N.J. facility, is to be completed in 1977.

A Guide to Avenue and Street Addresses in N.Y. City

To find the location of a number on the following avenues of Manhattan, cancel the last figure of the number, divide the remainder by 2 and add the given key number. Thus: Where is 596 7th Ave.? Divide 59 by 2 equals 30, plus 12 equals 42d St.

Ave. A	add	4	Up to 600	add	18	8th Ave.	add	9
Ave. B	add	3	Up to 775	add	20	9th Ave.	add	13
Ave. C	add	3	From 775 to 1286			10th Ave.	add	13
Ave.D.	add	3	see exception below:			11th ave.	add	15
1st Ave.	add	4	Up to 1500	add	45	Amsterdam Ave.	add	59
2d Ave.	add	3	Above 2,000	add	24	Audubon Ave.	add	165
3d Ave.	add	10	Ave. of Americas (6th Ave.)			Columbus Ave.	add	60
4th Ave.	add	8	subtract 12 or 13			Convent Ave.	add	127
5th ave. to 200	add	13	7th Ave.	add	12	Edgecomb Ave.	add	134
Up to 400	add	16	Above 1800	add	20	Ft. Wash. Ave.	add	158

Lenox Ave.	add	110
Lexington Ave.	add	22
Madison Ave.	add	27
Manhattan Ave.	add	100
Park Ave.	add	34
Pleasant Ave.	add	101
St. Nicholas Ave.	add	110
Wadsworth Ave.	add	175
West End Ave.	add	59

Exceptions

Broadway: Up to 754 below East 8th St.
     Above 754, apply above rule but deduct following key numbers:
     From 754 to 858 deduct 29.
     From 857 to 958 deduct 25.
     Above 1000 deduct 31.

Riverside Drive: Below 567, drop last figure, add 75, do not divide by 2.
     Above 577, drop last figure, add 78.
Central Park West: Drop last figure, add 60.
5th Ave.: From 775 to 1286, drop last figure and deduct 18 from remainder.

Street Addresses

North of the Washington Square area, most Manhattan streets are numbered. Each street has about 100 building numbers on each block. These building numbers rise east and west from Fifth Ave.

Notable Tall Buildings in North American Cities

Height from sidewalk to roof, including penthouse and tower if enclosed as integral part of structure; actual number of stories beginning at street level. Asterisks (*) denote buildings still under construction Jan. 1977.

City	Hgt. ft.	Stories
New York City		
World Trade Center (2 towers)	1,350	110
Empire State, 34th St. & 5th Ave.	1,250	102
TV tower, 222 ft., makes total	1,472	
Chrysler, Lexington Ave. & 43d St.	1,046	77
60 Wall Tower, 70 Pine St.	950	67
40 Wall Tower	927	71
RCA, Rockefeller Center	850	70
1 Chase Manhattan Plaza	813	60
Pan Am Bldg., 200 Park Ave.	808	59
Woolworth, 233 Broadway	792	60
1 Penn Plaza	764	57
Exxon, 1251 Ave. of Americas	750	54
1 Liberty Plaza	743	50
Citibank	741	57
One Astor Plaza	730	54
Union Carbide Bldg., 270 Park Ave.	707	52
General Motors Bldg.	705	50
Metropolitan Life, 1 Madison Ave.	700	50
500 5th Ave.	697	60
9 W. 57th St.	688	50
Chem. Bank, N.Y. Trust Bldg.	687	50
55 Water St.	687	53
Chanin, Lexington Ave. & 42d St.	680	56
Gulf & Western Bldg., 15 Columbus Circle	679	44
Marine Midland Bldg., 140 Bway	677	52
McGraw Hill, 1221 Ave. of Am.	674	51
Lincoln, 60 E. 52d Street	673	53
1633 Broadway	670	48
American Brands, 245 Park Ave.	648	45
Irving Trust, 1 Wall St.	640	50
345 Park Ave.	634	44
Grace Plaza, 1114 Ave. of Am.	630	50
1 New York Plaza	630	50
Home Insurance Co. Bldg.	630	44
1 Dag Hammarskjold Plaza	628	50
Waldorf-Astoria, 301 Park Ave.	625	47
Burlington House, 1345 Ave. of Am.	625	50
Olympic Tower, 643 5th Ave.	620	50
10 E. 40th St.	620	48
General Electric, Lexington Ave.	616	50
New York Life, 51 Madison Ave.	615	40
Penney Bldg., 1301 Ave. of Am.	609	46
Celanese Bldg., 1211 Ave. of Am.	592	45
U.S. Court House, 505 Pearl St.	590	37
Federal Bldg., Foley Square	587	41
Time & Life, 1271 Ave. of Am.	587	47
Cooper Bregstein Bldg., 1250 Bway	580	40
1185 Ave. of Americas	580	42
Municipal, Park Row & Centre St.	580	34
1 Madison Square Plaza	576	42
Westvaco Bldg., 299 Park Ave.	574	42
Socony Mobil Bldg., East 42d St.	572	45
Sperry Rand Bldg., 1290 Ave. of Am.	570	43
600 3d Ave.	570	42
N.Y. General, 230 Park Ave.	565	35
1 Bankers Trust Plaza	565	40
30 Broad St.	562	48
Sherry-Netherland, 5th Ave. & 59th St.	560	40
Continental Can, 633 3d Ave.	557	39
Sperry & Hutchinson, 330 Madison	555	39
Galleria, 117 E. 57th St.	552	57
Interchem Bldg., 1133 Ave. of Am.	552	45
919 3d Ave.	550	47
Burroughs Bldg., 605 3d Ave.	550	44
Bankers Trust, 33 E. 48 St.	547	41
Transportation Bldg., 225 Bway	546	45
Equitable Life, 1285 Ave. of Am.	540	42
Ritz Tower, Park Ave. & 57th St.	540	41
Bankers Trust, 6 Wall St.	540	39
1166 Ave. of Americas	540	44
Equitable, 120 Broadway	538	42
1700 Broadway	533	41
Downtown Athletic Club, 19 West St.	530	45
Nelson Towers, 7th Ave. & 34th St.	525	45
Hotel Pierre, 5th Ave. & 61st St.	525	44
House of Seagram, 375 Park Ave.	525	38
Random House, 825 3d Ave.	522	40
3 Park Ave.	522	42
Du Mont Bldg., 515 Madison Ave.	520	42
26 Broadway	520	31
Newsweek Bldg., 444 Madison Ave.	518	43
Sterling Drug. Bldg., 90 Park Ave.	515	41
First National City Bank	515	41
Bank of New York, 48 Wall St.	513	32
Navarre, 512 7th Ave.	513	43
Williamsburg Savings Bank, Bklyn.	512	42
ITT—American, 437 Madison Ave.	512	40
International, Rockefeller Center	512	41
1407 Broadway Realty Corp.	512	44
United Nations, 405 E. 42 St.	505	39
2 New York Plaza	504	40
22 E. 40th St.	503	43
60 Broad St.	503	39
Americana Hotel	501	51
World Apparel Center, 1411 Bway	501	42
Akron, Ohio		
First National Tower Bldg.	330	28
Cascade, 10 W. Bowery	316	24
Edison Tower, 76 S. Main St.	280	19
Albany, N.Y.		
Office Tower, So. Mall	589	44
State Office Building	388	34
Agency (four bldgs.), So. Mall	310	23
University Towers	286	22
Atlanta, Ga.		
Peachtree Center Plaza Hotel	723	71
First National Bank, 2 Peachtree	556	44
Equitable Building, 100 Peachtree	453	34
101 Marietta Tower, 101 Marietta St.	446	36
National Bank of Georgia, 34 Peachtree	439	32
Peachtree Summit No. 1	406	31
Tower Place, 3361 Piedmont Road	461	29
Atlanta Hilton Hotel	383	32
Peachtree Center Harris Bldg.	382	31
Southern Bell Telephone	380	
Trust Company Bank	377	28
Coastal States Insurance, 260 Peachtree	377	27
Peachtree Center Cain Building	376	30
Peachtree Center Building, 230 Peachtree	374	31
Life of Georgia Tower	371	29
Peachtree Center South, 225 Peachtree	332	27
Gas Light Tower, 235 Peachtree	331	27
Hyatt Regency Hotel, 265 Peachtree	330	23
100 Colony Square, 1175 Peachtree	328	25
Georgia Power Building, 270 Peachtree	318	22
Fairmont Hotel, 180 14th St.	310	28
400 Colony Square, 1201 Peachtree	308	23
Atlanta Center Building, 260 Piedmont Ave.	301	23
Merchandise Mart, 240 Peachtree	300	22
Austin, Tex.		
Austin National Bank	328	26
American Bank	313	21
State Capitol	309	
Univ. of Texas Admin. Bldg.	307	29
J. Frank Dobie Univ. Center	299	29
Westgate Bldg.	261	24
Baltimore, Md.		
U.S. Fidelity & Guaranty Co.	529	40
Maryland National Bank Bldg.	509	34
World Trade Center Bldg.	405	32
Saint-Paul Apartments Bldg.	385	37
Arlington Federal Savings and Loan Assn. Bldg.	370	28
Blaustein Bldg.	370	30
Charles Plaza Apts. So.	350	31
Charles Center South	330	26
Tower Bldg.	330	16
Baltimore Arts Tower	319	15
First National Bank of Maryland	315	22
Lord Baltimore Hotel	315	24
Mercantile-Safe Deposit and Trust Co.	315	21
Charles Plaza Apts. No.	315	28

City	Hgt. ft.	Stories
Baltimore Hilton Hotel	302	29
One Charles Center Bldg	301	24
Baltimore Gas and Electric Co. Bldg	300	22
Chesapeake & Potomac Telephone Co.	300	16

Baton Rouge, La.

City	Hgt. ft.	Stories
State Capitol	460	34
American Bank Bldg	310	25
Hilton Hotel	290	28
La. Natl. Bank Bldg	277	21

Birmingham, Ala.

City	Hgt. ft.	Stories
First Natl. Southern Natural Bldg	390	30
South Central Bell Hdqts. Bldg	390	30
City Federal Bldg	325	27
Cabana Motel	287	21
Daniel Bldg	283	20

Boston, Mass.

City	Hgt. ft.	Stories
John Hancock Tower	790	60
Prudential Tower	750	52
Boston Co. Bldg., Court St.	601	41
First National Bank of Boston	591	37
Employers Commercial Union Co's	507	40
New England Merch. Bank Bldg	500	40
U.S. Custom House	496	32
John Hancock Bldg	495	26
State St. Bank Bldg	477	34
Keystone Custodian Funds	400	32
State Office Bldg	350	22
Federal Bldg. & Post Office	345	22
Suffolk County Courthouse	330	19
Sheraton-Boston Hotel	310	29
State Service Center	300	23

Buffalo, N.Y.

City	Hgt. ft.	Stories
Marine Midland, Main St.	529	40
City Hall	378	32
Rand Bldg., not incl. 40-ft. beacon	351	29
Erie County Savings Bank, Main St.	350	26
Manuf. & Trades Trust Co.	317	21
Liberty Bank	305	23
Electric Tower	294	18

Calgary, Alta.

City	Hgt. ft.	Stories
Calgary Tower	626	
Norcen Tower	508	33
Scotia Tower	504	38
Oxford Square North	463	34
Shell Tower	460	34
Oxford Square South	449	33
Three Bow Valley Square	432	35
Sun Oil Bldg	397	34
Western Centre	385	40
Two Bow Valley Square	378	39
Mobil Tower	369	29
One Palliser Square	350	28
Mount Royal House	330	34
Standard Life Bldg	327	25
Place Concorde (Twin Towers)	321	34
Penthouse Towers	312	34
International Hotel	301	34
Two Calgary Place	300	24

Charlotte, N.C.

City	Hgt. ft.	Stories
NCNB Plaza, 101 S. Tryon	503	40
Jefferson First Union Tower	433	32
Wachovia Center, 400 S. Tryon	420	32
Southern National Center, 1200 S. College	300	22
NCNB Bldg., 200 S. Tryon	299	18
Bank of NC Bldg., 112 S. Tryon	280	20

Chicago, Ill.

City	Hgt. ft.	Stories
Sears Tower (World's Tallest)	1,454	110
Standard Oil (Indiana)	1,136	80
John Hancock Center	1,127	100
Water Tower Plaza (a)	859	74
First Natl. Bank	850	60
IBM Bldg	695	52
Civic Center (City Hall)	662	31
Lake Point Towers	645	70
Board of Trade, add 81 ft. statue	605	44
Prudential Bldg., 130 E. Randolph	601	41
Antenna tower, 311 ft., makes total	912	
1000 Lake Shore Plaza Apts	590	55
Marina City Apts., 2 buildings	588	61

City	Hgt. ft.	Stories
Mid Continental Plaza	580	50
Pittsfield, 55 E. Washington St.	557	38
Kemper Insurance Bldg	555	45
Newberry Plaza, State & Oak	553	56
Harbor Point	550	54
LaSalle Natl. Bank, 135 S. LaSalle St.	535	44
One LaSalle Street	530	49
111 E. Chestnut St.	529	56
*River Plaza, Rush & Hubbard	524	56
Pure Oil, 35 E. Wacker Drive	523	40
United Ins. Bldg., 1 E. Wacker Dr.	522	41
Lincoln Tower, 75 E. Wacker Dr.	519	42
Carbide & Carbon, 230 N. Mich.	503	37
Walton Colonnade	500	44
Edgewater Beach Apts., 5445 Sheridan	449	39
LaSalle-Wacker, 221 N. LaSalle St.	491	41
Amer. Nat'l. Bank, 33 N. LaSalle St.	479	40
Bankers, 105 W. Adams St.	476	41
Brunswick Bldg	475	37
Continental Companies	475	45
American Furniture Mart	474	24
Sheraton Hotel, 505 N. Mich. Ave.	471	42
Playboy Bldg., 919 N. Mich. Ave.	468	37
188 Randolph Tower	465	45
Tribune Tower, 435 N. Mich. Ave.	462	36
Equitable Life, 401 N. Michigan	457	35
Roanoke, 11 S. LaSalle St.	452	37
(a) World's tallest reinforced concrete bldg.		

Cincinnati, Ohio

City	Hgt. ft.	Stories
Carew Tower	574	48
Central Trust Tower	495	34
Dubois Tower, 5th & Walnut	423	32
Kroger Bldg	345	25
U. of Cinn., Sander Hall	297	27
Terrace Hilton Hotel	273	19

Cleveland, Ohio

City	Hgt. ft.	Stories
Terminal Tower	708	52
Erieview Plaza Tower	529	40
Justice Center, 1250 Ontario	420	26
Federal Bldg	419	32
Cleveland Trust Tower No. 1	383	29
Ohio-Bell Telephone	365	22
Park Centre	320	26
Central Natl. Bank Bldg	305	23
Diamond Shamrock Bldg	300	23
CEI Bldg	300	22
Union Commerce Bldg	289	21
Standard Bldg	282	21
East Ohio Bldg	275	21
Bond Court, 1300 E. 9th	270	20

Columbus, Ohio

City	Hgt. ft.	Stories
State Office Tower, 30 E. Broad	624	41
LeVeque-Lincoln Tower, 50 W. Broad	555	47
Nationwide Plaza	485	40
Borden Building, 180 E. Broad	438	34
Columbus Center, 100 E. Broad	357	20
Ohio Bell Building, 150 E. Gay St.	348	26
88 E. Broad St.	324	20
Ohio National Plaza, E. Broad	317	25
Motorists Building, 471 E. Broad	297	21
Midland Building, 250 E. Broad	278	21

Dallas, Tex.

City	Hgt. ft.	Stories
First International Bldg	710	56
First National Bank	625	52
Republic Bank Tower	598	50
Southland Life Tower	550	42
2001 Bryan St.	512	40
Republic Bank Bldg., not incl. 150-ft. ornamental tower	452	36
One Main Place	445	34
Ling-Tempco-Vought Tower	434	31
Mercantile Natl. Bank Bldg., not incl. 115-ft. weather beacon	430	31
Mobil Bldg	430	31
Fidelity Union Tower	400	33
Southwestern Bell Toll Bldg	372	22
Court House & Fedl. Office Bldg	362	16
Mercantile Dallas Bldg	360	22
Sheraton Hotel	352	38
*Hyatt Hotel, 303 Reunion Blvd.	343	30
Elm Place, 1005-09 Elm St.	341	22
Main Tower	336	26

City	Hgt. ft.	Stories
Park Central No. 3	327	20
Adolphus Tower	327	27
Bell Telephone Bldg.	326	23
Davis Bldg.	323	21
Manor House, Bank of Service & Trust.	319	26
Preston Tower	316	29
Tower Petroleum Bldg.	315	23
Adolphus Hotel.	312	25
Fairmont Hotel.	308	24
Baptist Annuity Center	303	17
Life Bldg.	302	22
Santa Fe Bldg. (1st unit).	300	20

Dayton, Ohio

City	Hgt. ft.	Stories
Winters Bank Bldg.	404	30
*Mead Tower, 10 W. 2d St.	365	28
Centre City Office Bldg.	297	21
Hulman Bldg.	295	23
Grant-Deneau Bldg.	290	22

Denver, Colo,

City	Hgt. ft.	Stories
Brooks Towers, 1020 15th St.	504	42
First of Denver Plaza	415	32
Colorado Nat'l. Bank, 17th & Curtis.	389	26
First National Bank	385	28
Security Life Bldg.	384	33
Lincoln Center.	367	30
Western Fed. Savings.	354	27
Colorado State Bank.	352	27
Brooks Tower Annex.	350	30
Mountain Bell, 17th & Curtis	330	21
D&F Tower.	330	20
Prudential Tower Plaza.	322	26
Denver Club Building.	277	23

Des Moines, Iowa

City	Hgt. ft.	Stories
Ruan Center.	457	36
Financial Center, 7th & Walnut.	345	25
Equitable Bldg.	318	19
State Capitol.	275	4

Detroit, Mich.

City	Hgt. ft.	Stories
Detroit Plaza Hotel	748	70
City Natl. Bank Bldg., 637 Griswold.	557	47
Guardian, 500 Griswold.	485	40
*Renaissance Center (4 bldgs.)	479	39
Book Tower, 1227 Wash. Blvd.	472	35
Cadillac Tower, 51 Cadillac Sq.	437	40
David Stott, 1150 Griswold.	436	38
Mich. Cons. Gas Co. Bldg.	430	32
Fisher, W. Grand Blvd. & 2d St.	420	28
J. L. Hudson Bldg.	397	28
McNamara Federal Office Bldg.	393	27
Detroit Bank & Trust Bldg.	370	28
Walker Cisler	365	25
David Broderick Tower.	358	34
Buhl, 535 Griswold.	350	26
Michigan Bell Telephone.	340	19
1st Federal Savings & Loan Assn.	338	23
Pontchartrain Motor Hotel.	336	23
Michigan Bell Telephone.	327	17
Commonwealth Bldg.	325	25
1300 Lafayette East.	325	30
First National Bldg.	319	25
City-County Bldg.	317	20
The Executive Plaza, 1200 6th Ave.	313	21
Sheraton Cadillac Hotel	310	28
Mich. Blue Cross/Blue Shield.	307	22
The Jeffersonian	305	29

Edmonton, Alta.

City	Hgt. ft.	Stories
AGT Tower, 10020-100 St.	441	34
T-D Bank Tower.	390	30
CN Tower, 1004-104 Ave.	365	26
Royal Trust Tower	325	25
Edmonton House.	315	34

Fort Wayne, Ind.

City	Hgt. ft.	Stories
Ft. Wayne Natl. Bank.	339	26
Lincoln Natl. Bank.	312	23

Fort Worth, Tex.

City	Hgt. ft.	Stories
Ft. Worth Natl. Bank.	454	37
Continental Natl. Bank Bldg.	380	30
First National Bank, 500 W. 7th.	300	21
Continental Life Ins. Bldg.	282	23
Electric Service Bldg., 800 Main St.	275	20

City	Hgt. ft.	Stories
W. T. Waggoner Bldg.	270	22
Service Life Center.	270	19

Halifax, N.S.

City	Hgt. ft.	Stories
Fenwick Towers.	300	31

Harrisburg, Pa.

City	Hgt. ft.	Stories
State Capitol.	272	6
Presbyterian Apts., 322 N. 2nd Ave.	260	23

Hartford, Conn.

City	Hgt. ft.	Stories
Travelers Ins. Co. Bldg.	527	34
Hartford Plaza.	420	22
Hartford Natl. Bank & Trust.	360	26
One Financial Plaza, 755 Main.	335	26

Honolulu, Hawaii

City	Hgt. ft.	Stories
Ala Moana Hotel.	390	38
Pacific Trade Center.	360	30
Discovery Bay.	350	42
Hyatt Regency Waikiki.	350	39
*Mehelani Waikiki Lodge.	350	43
Hemmeter Center.	350	39
Regency Tower, 2525 Date St.	350	42
Yacht Harbor Towers.	350	40
Chateau Waikiki.	349	39
Rainbow Plaza.	348	37
*2121 Ala Wai Blvd.	347	41
Royal Kuhio.	346	39
Waipuna.	343	38
The Villa on Eaton Square.	335	37
Kukui Plaza.	333	33
The Skyrise.	333	38
Diamond Head Vista.	322	35
*Ke Aloha at Waikiki.	330	35
Reed & Martin Apt. Bldg.	321	36
1350 Ala Moana	309	33
Mott-Smith Laniloa.	303	34
Ala Moana Bldg.	300	23

Houston, Tex.

City	Hgt. ft.	Stories
One Shell Plaza (not incl. 285 ft. TV tower).	714	50
1100 Milam Bldg.	651	47
Exxon Bldg.	606	44
2 Houston Center.	570	40
Dresser Tower.	550	40
Pennzoil, 700 Milam.	523	36
Entex Bldg.	518	35
Tenneco Bldg.	502	33
Conoco Bldg.	465	32
One Allen Center.	452	34
Gulf Bldg.	428	37
First City Natl. Bank.	410	32
Houston Lighting & Power.	410	27
Neils Esperson Bldg.	409	31
Hyatt Regency Houston.	401	34
Houston Natural Gas Bldg.	386	28
Bank of the Southwest.	369	24
Sheraton-Lincoln Hotel.	352	28
Two Shell Plaza.	341	26
American General Life.	337	25
Transco.	333	25
609 Fannin Bldg.	325	22
Holiday Inn.	325	30
Capital Natl. Bank.	320	21
Post Oak Central.	318	25
St. Luke's Hospital.	316	26
500 Jefferson Bldg.	316	21
Marathon Manufacturing Co. Bldg.	313	21
Sterling Bldg.	312	22
Melrose Bldg.	308	21
Chamber of Commerce Bldg.	306	22
Control Data Center.	303	22
First National Life Bldg.	302	22
Prudential Bldg.	300	21
Kellogg Bldg.	300	22

Indianapolis, Ind.

City	Hgt. ft.	Stories
Indiana Natl. Bank Tower.	504	37
City-County Bldg.	377	26
Indiana Bell Telephone.	320	20
Blue Cross-Blue Shield Bldg.	302	18
Riley Towers (2 bldgs.).	294	30
Indiana Bell "220" Bldg.	284	20
Monument Circle.	284	. . .
Market Square Office Bldg.	283	20

City	Hgt. ft.	Stories
*Merchants Plaza Office Bldg./		
Regency Hyatt Hotel	271	17

Jacksonville, Fla.

City	Hgt. ft.	Stories
Independent Life & Accident Ins. Co...	535	37
Gulf Life Ins. Co. Bldg.	432	28
Prudential Ins. Co. of America	295	22
Blue Cross-Blue Shield	287	20
Atlantic National Bank	278	19

Jersey City, N.J.

Medical Center (5 bldgs.; 332 ft., 294 ft., 274 ft., (2) 273 ft.)

Kansas City, Mo.

City	Hgt. ft.	Stories
Kansas City Power and Light Bldg.	476	32
City Hall	443	29
Federal Office Bldg.	413	35
Commerce Tower	402	32
Southwest Bell Telephone Bldg.	394	27
*Pershing Road Associates,		
2333 Grand	352	28
A. T. & T. Long Line Bldg.	331	20
Bryant Bldg.	319	26
Federal Reserve Bldg.	311	21
City Center Square, 1100 Main	302	30
Holiday Inn	300	28

Las Vegas, Nev.

City	Hgt. ft.	Stories
Las Vegas Hilton	346	30
Landmark Hotel	308	27
Sahara Hotel	294	24
Dunes Hotel	277	24
Mint Hotel	275	26
Union Plaza Hotel	272	22

Little Rock, Ark.

City	Hgt. ft.	Stories
First National Bank	454	33
Worthen Bank & Trust	375	28
Union National Bank	331	24
Tower Bldg.	300	18

Los Angeles, Calif.

City	Hgt. ft.	Stories
United Cal.Bank.	858	62
Security Pacific Natl. Bank	738	55
Atlantic Richfield Plaza (2 bldgs.)	699	52
Crocker-Citizen Plaza	620	42
Theme Towers (2 Bldgs.)	571	44
Union Bank Square	516	41
City Hall	454	28
Equitable Life Bldg.	454	34
Occidental Life Bldg.	452	32
Mutual Benefit Life Ins. Bldg.	435	31
Broadway Plaza	414	33
1900 Ave. of Stars	398	27
1 Wilshire Bldg.	395	28
Calif. Fed. Savings & Loan Bldg.	363	28
Century City Office Bldg.	363	24
Bunker Hill Towers	349	32
International Industries Plaza	347	24
City Natl. Bank Bldg.	344	24
Wilshire West Plaza	327	24

Louisville, Ky.

City	Hgt. ft.	Stories
First Natl. Bank	512	40
Citizen's Plaza	420	30
Galt House	325	25
Louisville Trust Bldg.	312	24
800 Apartments Bldg.	290	29

Memphis, Tenn.

City	Hgt. ft.	Stories
100 N. Main Bldg.	430	37
Commerce Square	396	31
Sterick Bldg.	365	31
Clark, 5100 Poplar	365	32
First Natl. Bank Bldg.	332	25
Hyatt Regency	329	28
Lowenstein's Towers	296	25
Lincoln American Life Tower	290	22
White Station Tower	280	24

Miami, Fla.

City	Hgt. ft.	Stories
One Biscayne Corp.	456	40
First Federal Savings & Loan	375	32
Dade County Court House	357	28
Ferre Bldg.	340	30
Flagler Center Bldg.	318	25
Brickell Bay Club	286	29

City	Hgt. ft.	Stories
Palm Bay Club	279	24

Milwaukee, Wis.

City	Hgt. ft.	Stories
First Wisc. Center & Office Tower	625	42
City Hall	350	9
Wisconsin Telephone Co.	313	19
Marine Plaza Bldg.	288	22
Allen-Bradley Co.	280	17
Marshall & Ilsley Bank	277	21
Regency House Apts.	274	27
Prospect Towers Apts.	268	23
Juneau Village Apts.	265	28
Marc Plaza Hotel	265	24
Carl Sandburg Dorm. (U. of Wis.)	264	26
Locust Court Apts.	262	24

Minneapolis, Minn.

City	Hgt. ft.	Stories
IDS Center	772	57
Foshay Tower, not including 163-ft.		
antenna tower	447	32
Hennepin County Government Center.	403	24
First Natl. Bank Bldg.	366	28
Municipal Building	355	14
North Western Bell Telephone	350	26
Cedar-Riverside	337	39
Dane Tower	311	26
Northwest Financial Center	300	24
Midwest Federal Savings & Loan	276	20

Montreal, Que.

City	Hgt. ft.	Stories
Place Victoria	624	47
Place Ville Marie	616	49
Canadian Imperial Bank		
of Commerce	580	45
Le Complexe Desjardins		
La Tour du Sud	498	40
La Tour du L'Est	428	32
La Tour du Nord	355	27
Chateau Champlain Hotel	480	38
CIL House	429	32
Royal Bank	397	22
Sun Life	390	26
Banque Canadienne National	390	32
Place du Canada	372	33
Alexis Nihon Plaza	331	33
Bell Telephone	324	22
Le Cartier Apts.	320	32

Nashville, Tenn.

City	Hgt. ft.	Stories
Natl. Life & Acc. Ins. Co.	452	31
Nashville Life & Casualty Tower	409	30
First American Natl. Bank	354	28
Hyatt Regency	300	28
Third Natl. Bank Bldg.	292	20
Andrew Jackson State Office Bldg.	286	17

Newark, N.J.

City	Hgt. ft.	Stories
National Newark & Essex Bank	465	36
Raymond-Commerce	448	36
Prudential Corporate Bldg.	369	27
Western Electric Bldg.	359	31
Gateway 1, tower	355	30
Prudential Insurance Company	353	21
American Insurance Company	326	21
N. J. Bell Telephone Co.	275	21
Gateway 2, Western Electric	272	20
Mutual Benefit Life Ins. Co.	271	18

New Haven, Conn.

City	Hgt. ft.	Stories
Knights of Columbus Hqs.	319	23

New Orleans, La.

City	Hgt. ft.	Stories
One Shell Square	697	51
Plaza Tower	531	45
Marriott Hotel	450	42
Bank of New Orleans	438	31
Int'l. Trade Mart Bldg.	407	33
225 Baronne St.	362	28
Hibernia Bank Bldg.	355	23
American Bank Bldg.	330	23
Canal LaSalle Bldg.	288	24
Charity Hospital of Louisiana	279	19
Lykes Center, 300 Poydras	276	22

Oakland, Cal.

City	Hgt. ft.	Stories
Ordway Bldg., 2150 Valdez St.	404	28
Kaiser Bldg.	390	28
Clorox Bldg.	330	24

City	Hgt. ft.	Stories
City Hall	319	15
Tribune Tower	305	21
United Cal. Bank Bldg.	297	18
Blue Cross Bldg.	296	21
Telephone Bldg.	289	15
565 Bellevue Apts.	270	25

Oklahoma City, Okla.

City	Hgt. ft.	Stories
Liberty Tower	500	36
First National Bank	493	33
City National Bank Tower	440	32
Kerr-McGee Center	393	30
Fidelity Plaza	310	15
Southwestern Bell Telephone	303	15
Hotel Oklahoma	298	24
The Regency Tower	288	25

Omaha, Neb.

City	Hgt. ft.	Stories
Woodmen Tower	469	30
Northwestern Bell Telephone Hdqrs.	334	16
Masonic Manor	320	22
First Natl. Bank	295	22
Mutual of Omaha	269	13

Ottawa, Ont.

City	Hgt. ft.	Stories
Place de Ville, Tower C	368	29
Place Bell Canada	318	26
DBS Tower	308	26
Holiday Inn	308	28
Parliament Bldgs., Peace Tower	291	
Skyline Hotel	286	25
L'Esplanade Laurier (2 towers)	285	22

Philadelphia, Pa.

City	Hgt. ft.	Stories
City Hall Tower, incl. 37-ft. statue of Wm. Penn	548	7
1818 Market St.	500	40
Fidelity Mutual Life Ins. Bldg.	490	38
Phila. Saving Fund Society	490	39
Central Penn Natl. Bank	490	36
Centre Square	490	38, 40
Industrial Valley Bank Bldg.	482	32
Philadelphia National Bank	475	25
2000 Market St. Bldg.	435	29
Fidelity Bank Bldg.	410	30
Two Girard Plaza	404	30
Lewis Tower, 15th & Locust	397	33
Fifteen Hundred Locust	390	44
Philadelphia Electric Co.	384	27
Penn Mutual Life	375	20
The Drake, 15th & Spruce	375	33
Medical Tower, 255 So. 17th	364	33
State Bldg., 1400 Spring Garden	351	18
United Engineers, 17th & Ludlow	344	20
Packard, 15th & Chestnut	340	25
Inquirer Building	340	18
Dorchester	339	32
Transportation Centre	336	18
Land Title, Broad & Chestnut	331	22
Suburban Station Bldg.	330	21

Phoenix, Ariz.

City	Hgt. ft.	Stories
Valley National Bank	483	40
Arizona Bank Downtown	407	31
First National Bank	372	27
First Federal Savings Bldg.	341	26
Regency Apts.	297	21
Hyatt-Regency Hotel	281	21
Del Webb TowneHouse	280	23
United Bank Square	272	20
Del Webb Bldg.	271	17

Pittsburgh, Pa.

City	Hgt. ft.	Stories
U.S. Steel Bldg.	841	64
Gulf, 7th Ave. and Grant St.	582	44
University of Pittsburgh	535	42
Mellon Bank Bldg.	520	41
1 Oliver Plaza	511	39
Grant, Grant St. at 3rd Ave.	485	40
Koppers, 7th Ave. and Grant	475	34
Equibank Bldg.	445	34
Pittsburgh National Bldg.	424	30
Alcoa Bldg., 425 Sixth Ave.	410	30
Westinghouse Bldg.	355	23
Oliver, 535 Smithfield St.	347	25
Gateway Bldg. No. 3	344	24
Smithfield Plaza	341	26
Federal Bldg., 1000 Liberty Ave.	340	23

City	Hgt. ft.	Stories
Bell Telephone, 416 7th Ave.	339	21
Hilton Hotel	333	22
Frick, 437 Grant St.	330	20
301 Fifth Ave.	322	24
Washington Plaza Apts.	300	23
Commonwealth, 316 Fourth Ave.	300	21

Portland, Ore.

City	Hgt. ft.	Stories
First Natl. Bank of Oregon	538	41
Georgia Pacific Bldg.	367	27

Providence, R.I.

City	Hgt. ft.	Stories
Industrial National Bank	420	26
Rhode Island Hospital Trust Tower	408	30
First Hartford Realty Corp.	301	23

Richmond, Va.

City	Hgt. ft.	Stories
First & Merchants Natl. Bank	313	26
City Hall	310	18
Central National Bank Bldg.	282	24
First National Bank Bldg.	262	19
Fidelity Bankers Life	261	23

Rochester, N.Y.

City	Hgt. ft.	Stories
Xerox Tower	443	30
Lincoln First Tower	390	26
Eastman Kodak Bldg.	360	19
First Federal Bank Plaza	305	22
Marine Midland Bank Bldg.	280	22

St. Louis, Mo.

City	Hgt. ft.	Stories
Gateway Arch	630	
Mercantile Trust Bldg.	485	35
Laclede Gas. Bldg., 8th & Olive	400	34
S. W. Bell Telephone Bldg.	398	31
Civil Courts	387	13
Queeny Tower	321	19
Counsil House Plaza	320	27
Park Plaza Hotel	310	30
Pierre Laclede Tower	309	24
Stauffer's Riverfront Inn, 3rd St.	301	30
Pet, Inc. Bldg.	300	22
Riverfront Holiday Inn	290	28
Mansion House	285	28
500 Broadway	282	22
Inn of the Spanish Pavilion	280	23
Continental Bldg.	277	23
Railroad Exchange Bldg.	277	21
University Club Bldg.	276	23
77 Bonhomme Bldg.	275	25
Boatman's Bank Tower	275	22
Equitable Bldg.	275	21
Lennox Hotel	275	25
Boatmen's Tower	275	22
Park Tower Apts.	270	24

St. Paul, Minn.

City	Hgt. ft.	Stories
First Natl. Bank Bldg., incl. 100-ft. sign	517	32
Osborn Bldg.	368	20
Kellogg Square Apts.	366	32
Northwestern Bell Telephone Bldg.	340	15
American National Bank Bldg.	335	25
St. Paul Cathedral	307	
U.S. Post Office Bldg.	274	12
St. Paul Hilton Hotel	273	24
City Hall & Court House	261	18

Salt Lake City, Utah

City	Hgt. ft.	Stories
L.D.S. Church Office Bldg.	420	30
Beneficial Life Tower	351	27
City & County Bldg.	290	
State Capitol	285	
Univ. Club Bldg.	277	24
Kennecott Bldg.	267	18

San Antonio, Tex.

City	Hgt. ft.	Stories
Tower of the Americas	622	
Tower Life	404	30
Nix Professional Bldg.	375	23
Natl. Bank of Commerce	310	24
First Natl. Bank Tower	302	20
Frost Bank Tower	300	21
Alamo National Bldg.	288	23
Milam Bldg.	280	20

San Diego, Cal.

City	Hgt. ft.	Stories
So. Cal. First Natl. Bank Bldg.	388	27
Crocker Natl. Bank Bldg.	340	25
Financial Square	339	24
*Central Federal	320	22
Union Bank	320	22

City	Hgt. ft.	Stories
Little America Westgate Hotel	303	19
San Diego Gas & Electric Bldg.	293	21
Charter Oil Bldg.	281	23
Security Pacific Natl. Bank Bldg.	278	18
Home Tower	278	18

San Francisco, Cal.

City	Hgt. ft.	Stories
Transamerica Pyramid	853	48
Bank of America	778	52
Security Pacific Bank	569	45
One Market Plaza, Spear St.	565	43
Wells Fargo Bldg.	561	43
Standard Oil, 575 Market St.	551	39
Aetna Life	529	38
First & Market Bldg.	529	38
Metropolitan Life	524	38
Hilton Hotel	493	46
Pacific Gas & Electric	492	34
Union Bank	487	37
Pacific Insurance	476	34
*Bechtel Bldg., Fremont St.	475	33
Hartford Bldg.	465	33
Mutual Benefit Life	438	32
Russ Bldg.	435	31
Telephone Bldg.	435	26
*Embarcadero Center, No. 3	412	31
Levi Strauss	412	31
Calif. State Automobile Assn.	399	29
Alcoa Bldg.	398	27
St. Francis Hotel	395	32
Shell Bldg.	386	29
Del Monte	378	28
Great Western Savings	359	26
Union Square Hyatt House Hotel	355	35
Equitable Life Bldg.	355	25
Grosvenor Plaza	354	29
International Bldg.	350	22
450 Sutter Street	343	26
Cathedral Apartments	340	21
Royal Towers	330	24
Fairmont Hotel	330	29
Bechtel Bldg., Beale St.	327	23
Standard Oil Bldg.	327	22
*Bank of Tokyo	324	23

Seattle, Wash.

City	Hgt. ft.	Stories
Seattle-1st Natl. Bank Bldg.	609	50
Space Needle	605	
Bank of Calif., 900 4th Ave.	536	42
Rainer Bank Tower, 4th & Univ.	536	40
L. C. Smith Bldg.	500	42
Federal Office Bldg.	487	37
1600 Bell Plaza	480	33
Washington Plaza Hotel	397	40
Financial Center	389	30
Safeco Ins. Co. of America	325	22
Northern Life Tower	314	27
Norton Bldg.	310	21
Pacific Bldg.	298	22
Washington Bldg.	289	21
Exchange Bldg.	275	23
IBM Bldg.	272	20
Park Place	270	21
Plaza 600	270	20

Springfield, Mass.

City	Hgt. ft.	Stories
Valley Bank Tower	370	29
Chestnut Towers	290	34

Syracuse, N.Y.

City	Hgt. ft.	Stories
State Tower	315	22
Mony Office Bldg.	268	19
Carrier Tower	268	19

Tampa, Fla.

City	Hgt. ft.	Stories
First Financial Tower	458	36

City	Hgt. ft.	Stories
Exchange Natl. Bldg.	280	22

Toledo, Ohio

City	Hgt. ft.	Stories
Owens-Corning Fiberglas Tower	400	30
Owens Illinois Bldg.	368	27
Toledo Trust Bldg.	288	21

Toronto, Ont.

City	Hgt. ft.	Stories
CN Tower, world's tallest self-supporting structure	1815	...
First Canadian Place	935	72
Commerce Court	784	57
Toronto-Dominion Bank Tower (TD Centre)	740	56
Royal Trust Tower (TD Centre)	600	46
Manufacturers Life Centre	545	51
Royal Bank Plaza—South Tower	480	41
Bank of Commerce	476	34
Four Seasons-Sheraton Hotel	470	43
Simpson Tower	470	33
Two Bloor St. West	463	34
390 Bay St.	452	33
Two Bloor St. East	442	35
Harbour Castle Hotel	438	38
Commercial Union Tower (TD Centre)	420	32
Royal York Hotel	407	28
Harbour Square Apts.	403	34
Leaside Towers Apts.	387	43
100 Bloor St. West	370	29
Hyatt Regency Hotel	365	31
York Centre	360	27
Carltoncourt	355	29
Summerhill Square Apts.	354	37
Hotel Toronto	350	32
MacDonald Block	349	24
Sutton Place Hotel	340	32
Richmond-Adelaide Centre	340	26

Tulsa, Okla.

City	Hgt. ft.	Stories
Bank of Oklahoma Tower	667	50
1st National Tower	516	41
4th Natl. Bank of Tulsa	412	32
National Bank of Tulsa	400	24
Cities Service Bldg.	388	28
Univ. Club Tower	377	32
Philtower	343	23

Vancouver, B.C.

City	Hgt. ft.	Stories
Harbour Centre	481	31
Royal Bank Tower	468	37
Scotiabank Tower	451	36
T-D Bank Tower	410	31
200 Granville Square	403	30
Sheraton-Landmark Hotel	394	41
First Bank Tower	386	30
Hyatt Regency Hotel	357	36
Hotel Vancouver	352	22
Oceanic Plaza	342	26
Board of Trade Tower	342	26
MacMillan Bloedel Bldg.	340	28
Guinness Tower	328	23
Marine Bldg.	321	21
Four Seasons Hotel	311	30
Martello Tower	300	31

Wilmington, Del.

City	Hgt. ft.	Stories
Hercules Tower	287	23
American Life Ins. Co. Bldg.	282	21

Winnipeg, Man.

City	Hgt. ft.	Stories
Richardson Bldg., 1 Lombard Place	439	34
55 Nassau St.	354	39
North Star Inn	300	30
1 Evergreen Place	294	32

Winston-Salem, N.C.

City	Hgt. ft.	Stories
Wachovia Bldg.	410	30
Reynolds Bldg.	315	21

Tall Buildings in Other Cities

Figures denote number of stories. Height in feet is in parentheses.

Cape Canaveral, Fla., Vehicle Assembly Bldg., 40 (552); Albuquerque, N.M., National Bldg., 18 (272); Allentown, Pa., Power & Light Bldg., 23 (320); Amarillo, Texas, American Natl. Bank, 33 (374); Bethlehem, Pa., Martin Tower, 21 (332); Charleston, W. Va., Kanawha Valley Bldg., 20 (384); Cuyahoga Falls, Ohio, Cathedral Tower Restaurant, 60 (554); Frankfort, Ky., Capital Plaza Office Tower, 28 (338); Galveston, Tex., American National Ins., 20 (358); Greenville, S.C., Daniel Bldg., 22 (305); Knoxville, Tenn., *United American Bank, 30 (400); Lansing, Mich., Michigan Natl. Tower, 25 (300, not including antenna tower); Lincoln, Neb., State Capitol (432); Long Beach, Cal., International Tower, 27 (277); Mobile, Ala., First Natl. Bank, 33 (420); Niagara Falls, Ont., Skylon, (520); Norfolk, Va., Va. Natl. Bank, 23 (304); Reading, Pa., Berks County Courthouse (280); So. Bend, Ind., American National Bank Bldg., 25 (312); Tacoma, Wash., Washington Plaza, 23 (290); Tallahassee, Fla., State Capitol Tower, 22 (345).

STATES AND OTHER AREAS OF THE U.S.

Their Resources, Histories, Industries, Agriculture, Mineral Products, Tourist Attractions, Nicknames, State Symbols

Areas of the states are total land and water areas reported by the Geography Division, Bureau of the Census; populations are July 1, 1975, estimates by the Bureau of the Census, including armed forces personnel in each state but excluding such personnel stationed overseas; agricultural figures are based on reports of the Dept. of Agriculture and state agencies; mineral statistics are those reported by the Bureau of Mines; manufacturing statistics are from the Bureau of the Census. Per capita income figures are preliminary from the Dept. of Commerce, Bureau of Economic Analysis. Travel expenditure figures are from the U.S. Travel Data Center.

For maps and for descriptive articles on cities, see Index.

Alabama

Heart of Dixie, Cotton State

AREA: 51,609 sq. mi.; rank, 29th. POPULATION (U.S. est. 1975): 3,614,000; rank, 21st. CAPITAL: Montgomery. MOTTO: We Dare Defend Our Rights. FLOWER: Camellia. BIRD: Yellowhammer. TREE: Southern pine. SONG: Alabama. ENTERED UNION: Dec. 14, 1819; rank, 22d.

Alabama lies in the cotton belt of the Old South but introduction of new and diversified industries has given the state a more balanced economy. Natural wealth includes coal, which underlies about 7,000 sq. mi. in the northern region; iron, bauxite and timber.

Alabama ranks 2d behind Arkansas in production of bauxite and is a large producer of asphalt and mica. But bituminous coal accounts for over 50% of the value of its total mineral production, which in 1975 rose 22% to an estimated $933 million. Also important are cement, stone and petroleum.

Abundant water for hydroelectric power and river shipping has contributed to the growth of Alabama's economy. Three Tennessee Valley Authority dams and a large nuclear power plant are in the northern part of the state. Historic sites, fishing and hunting are among Alabama's attractions.

With two-thirds of the state's land area in timber, Alabama is a leading producer of pulp, paper, plywood, and paperboard.

Iron and steel production is the most important of Alabama's manufacturing industries; there is also a large segment of manufacturing devoted to primary metal products of wide diversity, particularly structural steel. Other important industry groupings include chemicals and fertilizers, textile mill products and apparel, processing of foods, stone-clay-glass products, transportation equipment, electrical and other machinery. Value added by manufacture is over $5 billion a year.

Industrial growth in 1975 saw $1.5 billion invested in 906 new or expanded plants, providing 12,864 new jobs. Per capita personal income was $4,557 in 1975 (U. S. average was $5,834).

Birmingham, center of the steel industry, has long been known as "the Pittsburgh of the South."

At Huntsville is the George C. Marshall Space Flight Center of NASA and a space and rocket museum.

Agriculture remains a vital part of the economy. Cotton has been dethroned by soybeans as king among Alabama's crops and is rivaled by corn, pecans, and peanuts. Among the states, Alabama ranked 4th in production of pecans in 1975, 2d in peanuts. Also important are potatoes, watermelons, tobacco, and peaches.

Livestock, especially poultry, has grown in importance. Alabama was 4th among the states in number of chickens in 1975. Farm receipts for livestock and livestock products in 1975 totaled $770 million; for crops, the total was $546 million. Forest product sales totaled $122 million.

There are 56 institutions of higher education. Per pupil expenditure in public schools in 1974-75 was $933, ranking 49th among the states.

Earliest traces of mankind in the area date to 10,-000 years ago. First Europeans were Spanish explorers in the early 1500's. The French made the first permanent settlement, on Mobile Bay, 1701-02; later, English settled in the northern areas. France ceded the entire region to England at the end of the French and Indian War, 1763, but Spanish Florida claimed the Mobile Bay area until U. S. troops took it, 1813. Gen. Andrew Jackson broke the power of the Creek Indians, 1814, and they were removed to Oklahoma.

The Confederate States were organized at Montgomery, Feb. 4, 1861, and Jefferson Davis took the oath as president at State Capitol there, Feb. 18. Davis' "first White House" now is a state shrine; also notable are the house in Tuscumbia where Helen Keller was born June 27, 1880, and the Statue of Vulcan near Birmingham.

Tourists spent an estimated $718 million in Alabama in 1974.

At Russell Cave National Monument, near Bridgeport, may be seen a detailed record of occupancy by humans from about 7000 B.C. to 1650 A.D., including tools, weapons and pottery. The exhibit is free.

The George Washington Carver Museum at Tuskegee Institute, Tuskegee, contains records of the famous black scientist's contributions to agronomy, and dioramas of achievements by blacks.

The University of Alabama Museum of Natural History, in Tuscaloosa, displays Alabama fossils, shells and aboriginal materials and collections. Mound State Monument, Moundville, an adjunct of the museum, shows aboriginal burials.

Famous Alabamians include Gov. George Wallace, Hank Aaron, Tallulah Bankhead, Nat King Cole, Hank Williams, Jesse Owens, Helen Keller, Harper Lee, Joe Louis, George Washington Carver, Hugo L. Black, William C. Handy, Booker T. Washington, William C. Gorgas.

(See also Index for Birmingham, Mobile, Montgomery, Phenix City.)

Alaska

No official nickname

AREA: 585,412 sq. mi.; rank, 1st. POPULATION: 352,000; (U. S. est. 1975); rank, 50th. CAPITAL: Juneau. FLOWER: Forget-me-not. BIRD: Willow ptarmigan. TREE: Sitka spruce. SONG: Alaska's Flag. FISH: King salmon. MOTTO: North to the Future. ENTERED UNION: Jan. 3, 1959; rank, 49th.

Alaska became the 49th state Jan. 3, 1959. Largest political division of the U.S., it is two and one-fifth times the size of Texas. Alaska occupies the NW part of North America, separated from the rest of the continental U.S. by Canada's British Columbia. Alaska's general coastline runs 6,640 mi.; including all its islands, 33,904 mi. It has mountain ranges, volcanoes, fjords and glaciers.

About one-sixth of the population are Eskimos and Indians.

Pt. Barrow in Arctic Alaska is the northernmost spot in the state. The Yukon River flows E to W 1,200 mi. through central Alaska, from the Canadian border to the Bering Sea. In south central Alaska stands Mt. McKinley, 20,320 ft., highest point in North America.

In west central Alaska, off the tip of the Seward Peninsula, lies Little Diomede Is., only 2.4 mi. from the Big Diomede Is., owned by the USSR. The Alaska

Peninsula and the Aleutian Islands into which it tapers, extends SW and W for 1,200 mi., with numerous volcanoes; at the base of the peninsula is Katmai National Monument, containing the Valley of 10,000 Smokes, scene of a 1912 volcanic eruption.

Alaska's Panhandle stretches SE; it is a narrow strip of mainland and islands, with fjords and Glacier Bay National Monument (containing the Muir Glacier, 2 mi. wide and 250 ft. high), facing the Pacific, W of British Columbia.

Vitus Bering, a Danish explorer working for Russia, was the first European to land in Alaska, 1741. Alexander Baranov, first governor of Russian America, set up headquarters at Archangel, near present Sitka, in 1799. Secretary of State William H. Seward in 1867 bought Alaska from Russia for $7.2 million, a bargain which some called "Seward's Folly." In 1896, gold was discovered and the famed Gold Rush was on. Many of the fortune hunters settled in Alaska as farmers or traders.

Resources and Industries. Principal income is from fisheries, minerals (esp. oil), wood products, tourism and furs. Salmon, halibut, herring, cod, and shellfish are frozen or canned; Alaska is a leader in value of its commercial catch, about $144 million in 1975.

Processing of fish and other foods is the largest manufacturing industry, followed by forest products.

Spruce, yellow cedar, and hemlock are plentiful; there also are red cedar, and birch. Commercial timberland of Alaska's vast forest totals 28 million acres. The forest products industry in SE is expanding as pulp mills increase. Timber products value is over $134 million yearly.

Furs produced are those of the seal, sable, ermine, wolverine, land otter, muskrat, beaver, mink, red fox, blue fox, lynx, marten. Wildlife includes the gray wolf, moose, caribou, and 5 kinds of bear: black, grizzly, polar, Kodiak, and glacier. There are plenty of sea fowl, but whales, walrus, sea lion, and sea otter have diminished.

The seal herd on the Pribilof Islands is owned by the federal government and seal harvesting is managed by the U.S. Commerce Dept. Reindeer herds are multiplying and their meat is marketed.

Oil production, mainly from offshore fields in Cook Inlet, had an est. value of $360 million in 1975. Total mineral production value was est. at $524 million.

Sale of leases for the vast North Slope oil discovery area at Prudhoe Bay brought the state $900 million in 1969. After long delay caused by ecological controversy, Congress in Nov. 1973 authorized construction of a $6-billion, 796-mi., trans-Alaska pipeline to carry oil from Prudhoe Bay to the south Alaska port of Valdez. Oil was to start flowing by mid-1977.

The value of gold production in 1975 was $2.6 million. Alaska also has natural gas, tin, bituminous coal and mercury.

Principal ports are in the Panhandle where Juneau, the capital, is on the mainland shore; N of it is Skagway, historic entry to Klondike gold fields via Chilkoot Pass and White Pass. Sitka, Wrangell, and Ketchikan (center of salmon industry), are on islands of the Alexander group.

At the head of Cook Inlet, in S Central Alaska, is the state's largest city, Anchorage. Seward, S of Anchorage, is government-terminus for the government-owned Alaska Railroad, which runs N to Fairbanks. Nine domestic airlines serve Alaska. International lines flying via Arctic routes make stops; Fairbanks has the northern most international airport on the continent. Nearby is Eielson AFB. Ships transport 90% of the goods and foods to and from Alaska, linking some 50 Alaskan ports with Seattle, etc.

More than 235,000 tourists visit Alaska annually, spending some $299 million.

There are 2 motor routes to Alaska. The newer is by way of Marine Highway, a 450-mile ferry route from Prince Rupert, B.C., to Skagway. Motorists leaving the ferry at Haines may drive to Fairbanks, Anchorage, etc., with part of the route passing through

Canada. The older route is the Alaska Highway, from British Columbia.

There are 9 institutions of higher education.

Pay of public school teachers, $16,906 in 1975, is the highest in the 50 states. Average per capita income was $8,815 in 1975, highest in the U. S. The Alaskan cost of living was also the highest in the U.S.

The Alaska State Museum in Juneau features Eskimo and Indian exhibits, mounted wildlife specimens, rocks and minerals and historical exhibits.

The University of Alaska Museum, in College, near Fairbanks, maintains cultural and natural history collections for research and for the public.

Famous Alaskans include pioneer pilot Carl Eielson, prospector Joe Juneau, painter Sydney Laurence, former Gov. Ernest Gruening, Congressman James Wickersham.

(See also Index for Anchorage.)

Arizona
Grand Canyon State

AREA: 113,909 sq. mi.; rank, 6th. POPULATION (U.S. est. 1975): 2,224,000; rank, 32d. CAPITAL: Phoenix. MOTTO: Ditat Deus, God Enriches. FLOWER: Giant cactus or saguaro. BIRD: Cactus wren. TREE: Paloverde. SONG: Arizona. ENTERED UNION: Feb. 14, 1912, rank, 48th.

Arizona leads the nation in copper production with half of the total U.S. output, but its rapidly-growing manufacturing industries, such as machinery, aerospace, and electronics, form the largest source of income. Agriculture and tourism are also important.

Sunshine and a wealth of scenic attractions give Arizona a mounting tourist business; out-of-state visitors spent an est. $807 million in 1974.

The climate is dry in southern regions and the northern plateau, but high mountains and forests in central areas have heavy snows in winter. Highest point is Humphreys Peak, 12,633 ft. Over 44% of the land is owned by the U.S. government.

The only point in the U.S. at which 4 states meet is the juncture of Arizona, Utah, Colorado and New Mexico.

Arizona is noted for the Grand Canyon of the Colorado, an immense, vari-colored fissure 217 mi. long, 4 to 13 mi. wide at the brim, 4,000 to 5,500 ft. deep. Nature has given Arizona the Painted Desert, extending for 30 mi. along U.S. 66; the Petrified Forest; Canyon Diablo, 225 ft. deep and 500 ft. wide, and Meteor Crater, 4,150 ft. across, 570 ft. deep, made by a prehistoric meteor. The state has 17 national monuments, 2 national parks. Rodeos and historic sites of Indian and Spanish eras are other attractions.

The 1975 est. value of the state's copper production was $1 million. Arizona also ranks high among the states in pumice, silver, molybdenum and gold. Total value of mineral production in 1975 was est. at $1.2 billion.

Cotton is a major crop; Arizona's harvest ranked 5th among the states in 1975. Cash receipts for all crops in 1975 were $607 million; receipts from livestock and livestock products, $618 million. The state ranks 10th in number of sheep. Fruit production is important; Arizona ranks high in lemons, oranges, grapefruit, and grapes. Lettuce, melons, and alfalfa are valuable crops.

Manufacturing has expanded in recent years. Value added by manufacture is over $2.6 billion a year. Electrical machinery, including electronic components, accounts for $340 million of this total.

Federal spending on defense contracts, construction projects, air bases, etc., is an important factor in Arizona's economy. Per capita personal income was $5,329 in 1975.

Schools include the Univ. of Arizona at Tucson, Arizona State Univ. at Tempe, and Northern Arizona Univ. at Flagstaff. The new observatory of the National Science Foundation is located on Kitt Peak near Tucson. Taliesin West is the Frank Lloyd Wright architectural school near Phoenix.

Marcos de Niza, a Franciscan, and Estevan, a black slave, explored the Arizona area in 1539. Eusebio Francisco Kino, Jesuit missionary, taught Indians Christianity and farming, 1690-1711, and left a chain of missions. Spain ceded Arizona to Mexico, 1821. The U. S. took over at the end of the Mexican War, 1848. The area below the Gila River was obtained from Mexico in the Gadsden Purchase, 1854. Long Apache wars did not end until 1886, with Geronimo's surrender.

Museums include Arizona State Museum, Tucson, which stresses the archeology and ethnology of the Southwest. The Museum of Northern Arizona, 3 mi. N of Flagstaff, has exhibits illustrating the geology and paleontology of the area.

The Southwestern Arboretum, on U.S. 60 and 70 near Superior, has over 6,000 plants and trees from arid regions of the world, from lowly cactus to lofty boojum tree. The Phoenix Zoo is one of the nation's largest. The Arizona-Sonora Desert Museum, near Tucson, displays animals and plants of the desert.

Famous Arizonans include Cochise, Geronimo, Helen Jacobs, Zane Grey, Barry Goldwater, Percival Lowell, Stewart Udall, Frank Lloyd Wright, William H. Pickering, George W. P. Hunt, Morris Udall.

(See also Index for Phoenix and Tucson.)

Arkansas
Land of Opportunity

AREA: 53,104 sq. mi.; rank, 27th. POPULATION (U.S. est. 1975): 2,116,000; rank, 33d. CAPITAL: Little Rock. MOTTO: Regnat Populus, Let the People Rule. FLOWER: Apple blossom. BIRD: Mockingbird. TREE: Pine. SONG: Arkansas. ENTERED UNION: June 15, 1836; rank, 25th.

Arkansas is an important agricultural state with growing industries and has valuable mineral production. It has thermal springs and is popular with sportsmen.

First European explorers were Hernando de Soto, 1541; Louis Jolliet, 1673; La Salle, 1682. First settlement was by the French under Henri de Tonty, 1686, at Arkansas Post. In 1762 the area was ceded by France to Spain, then back again in 1800 and was part of the Louisiana Purchase by the U. S. in 1803. Arkansas seceded from the Union in 1861, only after the Civil War began, and many Arkansans (over 10,000) fought on the Union side. The state rejoined the Union in 1868.

Manufacturing is growing in importance with a 64% increase in employees in a 10-year period. New and expanded factories provided 13,000 new jobs in 1974. Per capita income was $4,383 in 1975. Lumber, petroleum, bauxite, and cotton are major products.

The $1.2 billion Arkansas River program, involving navigation, flood control, and power developments and construction of 17 dams and locks in Arkansas and Oklahoma, was completed to Catoosa, near Tulsa, Okla., in 1971 and provided an important boost to the area's economy.

The state has 18.5 million acres of oak, hickory, gum, cypress, and pine, and forest industries have a $500 million annual payroll. Cotton accounts for 48% of farm income and Arkansas ranked first among the states in rice production in 1975, and 4th in cotton production in 1975. It was 3d in number of chickens, 6th in turkeys. Farm receipts for 1975 totaled $2.2 billion.

Arkansas produces by far the greatest amount of bauxite (aluminum ore) produced in the U.S. It has the only diamond field in the U.S. and ranks 1st in bromine and vanadium.

But petroleum is the state's main mineral product; 1975 output was valued at $130 million; that of bauxite was $22 million. Natural gas and stone were also important. Total value of mineral production was est. at $414 million, up slightly from the record 1974 figure.

Arkansas has 29 institutions of higher learning.

Fresh-water fishing, duck-hunting in southeast lowlands, and recreation areas in 21 state parks and 3 national forests attract visitors. There are several reservoir-recreation areas, as at Norfork, Bull Shoals, Nimrod and Dardanelle, and others are being created. There are 47 hot springs in government-operated Hot Springs National Park, which entirely surrounds the city of Hot Springs, about 50 mi. SW of Little Rock. Spring water ranges from 95° to 147°F. and is piped in insulated conduits for baths and drinking. Blanchard Caverns, near Mountain View, are among the nation's largest.

Out-of-state visitors spent more than $535 million in Arkansas in 1974. There are 93 airports.

Historic attractions in Little Rock include the Territorial Capital Restoration, a block of 13 original frame and brick buildings, including the governor's home, furnished as in 1820-36, and an early print shop of the Arkansas Gazette, oldest newspaper west of the Mississippi. The Old State House in Little Rock was the state capitol 1836-1912; it houses many historical exhibits.

The Little Rock Museum of Science and Natural History occupies the building where Gen. Douglas MacArthur was born; also in MacArthur Park is the Arkansas Museum of Fine Arts.

Famous Arkansans include Hattie Caraway, "Dizzy" Dean, Orval Faubus, James W. Fulbright, Douglas MacArthur, John L. McClellan, Winthrop Rockefeller, Edward Durell Stone, Thyra Samter Winslow, Opie Read, Archibald Yell.

(See also Index for Little Rock.)

California
Golden State

AREA: 158,693 sq. mi.; rank, 3d. POPULATION (U. S. est. 1975): 21,185,000; rank, 1st. CAPITAL: Sacramento. MOTTO: Eureka, I Have Found It. FLOWER: California poppy. BIRD: Valley quail. TREE: Redwood. SONG: I Love You, California. ENTERED UNION: Sept. 9, 1850; rank 31st.

California is the leading state in agriculture, manufacturing, and population.

Third largest in area, California also has, within only 85 mi. of each other, the highest and lowest points in the conterminous 48 states; Mt. Whitney, 14,494 ft., and Death Valley, 282 ft. below sea level.

The U.S. Bureau of the Census estimated California's population as of July 1, 1964, at 18,084,000 and New York's at 17,915,000, giving California 1st place; New York had been in 1st place from 1820 through the census of 1960. In the 1970 census, New York had 18,241,266; California, 19,953,134. California also has the most dogs and cats — an est. 50 million.

Among scenic regions are the Yosemite Valley, Lassen and Sequoia-Kings Canyon national parks, Lake Tahoe, the Mojave and Colorado deserts, San Francisco Bay, and Monterey Peninsula. National forests cover one-fifth of the state.

Oldest living things on earth are believed to be a stand of Bristlecone pines in the Inyo National Forest, est. to be 4,600 years old.

The world's tallest tree, the Howard Libbey redwood, 362 ft. with a girth of 44 ft., stands on Redwood Creek, Humboldt County.

California's huge fruit and vegetable production is fed by large irrigation systems. Receipts from crops in 1975 totaled $8.6 billion (tops in U.S.); from livestock, $2.9 billion (2d in U.S.); total receipts were $8.2 billion (most in U.S.).

The state ranked 1st in numbers of chickens, 2d in turkeys, 3d in sheep, 7th in cattle, as of Jan. 1, 1976.

California produces the most apricots, avocados, grapes and raisins, peaches, persimmons, pomegranates, plums, prunes, lemons, nectarines, olives, dates, almonds, walnuts, and sugar beets. Its total vegetable crop is the largest; it ranks 2d to Florida in oranges and was also 2d in grapefruit, cotton, and barley, 3d in rice.

It was 2d to Alaska in commercial fishing in 1975 with a catch valued at $130 million.

The state's giant aerospace industries employ a third of all its manufacturing employees. Value added by manufacture is over $36.7 billion (1973); transportation equipment, especially aircraft and missiles, led; food products, particularly frozen and canned foods, were 2d; electrical machinery, including electronic components, was 3d followed by ordnance, other machinery, metal products. Per capita income was $6,555 in 1975, 7th highest in the U.S.

Gold, discovered at Sutter's sawmill Jan. 24, 1848, set off the historic Gold Rush and gave initial impetus to California's development, but petroleum is the leading mineral product today.

Oil output in 1975 was valued at an est. $1.9 billion, over half the state's total mineral production value, $2.9 billion, up 9% and 3d highest in the U.S. after Texas and Louisiana. California is a leader in output of asbestos, cement, boron, gypsum, and tungsten.

The Oroville Dam, main unit in the world's largest water project — the $2.8 billion Feather River Project — was dedicated May 4, 1968.

Tourists spend about $7.3 billion a year in California.

There are some 200 institutions of higher learning. Three of the world's largest observatories are located on Palomar Mtn., Mt. Hamilton, and Mt. Wilson.

The Tournament of Roses and the Rose Bowl football game at Pasadena are held annually on Jan. 1. Winter sports are featured in many mountain areas.

Vandenberg AFB, 170 mi. NW of Los Angeles, is center of an interservice missile range.

First European visitors were Juan Rodriguez Cabrillo, 1542, and Francis Drake, 1579. First settlement was the Spanish Alta California mission at San Diego, 1769, first in a string founded by Franciscan Father Junipero Serra. U. S. traders and settlers arrived in the 19th century and staged the abortive Bear Flag Revolt, 1846; the Mexican War began later in 1846 and U.S. forces occupied California; Mexico ceded the province to the U.S. in 1848, the same year the Gold Rush began.

Among museums the Pasadena Art Museum has collections of modern German painting, American painting, Oriental art and prints. The Santa Barbara Museum of Art has exhibits of Greek and Roman sculpture, Oriental art, old master and modern paintings, primitive arts, American paintings, and old and modern European drawings. The Santa Barbara Historical Society Museum displays and interprets objects of state and local history and operates the Gledhill Library for historical research. In Sacramento, the Crocker Art Gallery has collections of paintings, drawings, prints, sculpture, and crafts representing all European schools, American glass, and pottery from 5th century B.C. to contemporary American.

The J. Paul Getty Museum in Malibu opened in 1974 with collections of Greek and Roman antiquities, 18th Century French furniture and Western European paintings.

Famous Californians include Luther Burbank, W. R. Hearst, Joe DiMaggio, Jack London, Richard Nixon, Herbert Hoover, William Saroyan, Earl Warren, John Steinbeck, Gertrude Atherton, Bret Harte.

(See also Index for Bakersfield, Fresno, Los Angeles, Oakland, Orange County, Sacramento, San Bernardino, San Diego, San Francisco, San Jose, Santa Ana.)

Colorado
Centennial State

AREA: 104,247 sq. mi.; rank, 8th. **POPULATION** (U.S. est. 1975): 2,534,000; rank, 28th. **CAPITAL:** Denver. **MOTTO:** Nil Sine Numine, Nothing Without Deity. **FLOWER:** Columbine. **BIRD:** Lark bunting. **TREE:** Colorado blue spruce. **ANIMAL:** Big horn sheep. **SONG:** Where the Columbines Grow. **ENTERED UNION:** Aug. 1, 1876; rank, 38th.

Once primarily a mining and grazing state, Colorado now draws the largest segment of its income from manufacturing, followed by agriculture, tourism, and mining. Its snow-capped peaks, ski centers, ghost towns and health spas make it a popular vacation-recreation area.

Early civilization centered around Mesa Verde 2,000 years ago. The U. S. acquired eastern Colorado in the Louisiana Purchase, 1803; Lt. Zebulon M. Pike explored the area, 1806, discovering the peak that bears his name. After the Mexican War, 1846-48, U.S. immigrants settled in the east, former Mexicans in the south.

The total of value added by Colorado's varied manufacturing industries is over $2.7 billion yearly. Important industry groups are processing of meat, dairy and other food products, as well as machinery, electronics, metals, and stone-clay-glass products. Research and aerospace industries are growing. Per capita income was $5,839 in 1975.

Farm receipts in 1975 totaled $2 billion, about 70% from livestock and livestock products. Colorado ranked 4th among the states in the number of sheep in 1976, 11th in cattle. Its sugar beet crop is the 2d largest in the U.S. Other important crops are wheat, corn, barley, alfalfa, potatoes, apples, peaches, pears.

Gold was discovered on the Platte in 1858 and at Leadville in 1860.

Climax, near Leadville, now produces most of the world's molybdenum. Colorado produces a rich variety of minerals and is a leader among the states in output of tin, vanadium, tungsten, carbon dioxide, uranium, lead, zinc, and pyrites. Total 1975 mineral production was valued at $901 million, up 20% from 1974; petroleum accounted for $324 million of the total, up 14%.

With Utah and Wyoming, Colorado shares the world's richest oil shale deposits, still to be developed.

Colorado is the highest state in the Union, with an average altitude of 6,800 ft. It has 54 of the nation's highest mountains and 1,500 peaks over 10,000 ft. Highest is Mt. Elbert, 14,433 ft. Frozen Lake, altitude 12,940 ft., is the highest lake in the 48 conterminous states.

Six major rivers—the Colorado, Rio Grande, Arkansas, North Platte, South Platte, and Republican — rise in Colorado, supply water to 19 states. The western rivers have cut great canyons; the Black Canyon of the Gunnison and the Royal Gorge of the Arkansas, 1,000 to 1,500 ft. deep. One of the world's highest bridges crosses the Arkansas 1,053 ft. above the river at Royal Gorge.

The Federal Government owns 36.4% of the land, including 2 National Parks, 6 monuments, 2 Recreation Areas, 12 forests, 2 Indian reservations, 7 major military reservations.

Colorado has 39 institutions of higher education.

Attractions for an annual 8 million tourists include Rocky Mountain National Park, Garden of the Gods, Great Sand Dunes and Dinosaur National Monuments, Pikes Peak and Mt. Evans Highways, Mesa Verde National Park (pre-historic cliff dwellings). The Grand Mesa tableland comprises Grand Mesa Forest, 659,584 acres, with 200 lakes stocked with trout. Other attractions include the U.S. Air Force Academy near Colorado Springs, Denver Western Stock Show, Colorado State Fair, horse, dog, and auto races, rodeos, and pioneer celebrations. Thirty-one major ski areas operate from November to May. Tourists spend some $1.5 billion a year.

Big game include deer, bear, elk, mountain lion, gray wolf, coyote. There are thousands of miles of trout streams and 2,000 fishing lakes.

The old mining towns of Aspen and Central City have become cultural centers.

Museums include the Colorado Springs Fine Arts Center which has paintings, prints and drawings by contemporary artists, exhibits of the cultural history of the SW and Latin America, and the John F. Huckel collection of 112 Navajo sand painting reproductions.

The University of Colorado Museum, in Boulder, has more than a million objects in its exhibits of rocks, plants and early peoples as well as an art gallery.

Famous Coloradans include Lowell Thomas, Paul Whiteman, William N. Byers, Frederick Bonfils, Harry Tammen, Jack Dempsey, Douglas Fairbanks, Ralph Edwards, Byron R. White, M. Scott Carpenter.

(See also Index for Denver.)

Connecticut

Constitution State

AREA: 5,009 sq. mi.; rank 48th. **POPULATION** (U.S. est. 1975): 3,095,000; rank, 24th. **CAPITAL:** Hartford. **MOTTO:** Qui Transtulit, Sustinet; He Who Transplanted, Still Sustains. **FLOWER:** Mountain laurel. **BIRD:** American robin. **TREE:** White oak. Fifth of the 13 original states to ratify the Constitution, Jan. 9, 1788.

Connecticut's heavily industrialized cities are in sharp contrast to its picturesque New England villages and scenic countryside. Despite its small size, the state has large and diverse manufacturing industries, mainly of high-value specialty products. Per capita income was $6,854 in 1975, 2d only to Alaska.

It is a leading maker of jet engines, helicopters, nuclear subs, pins and needles, silverware, hardware, cutlery, and ball bearings. Ranking 48th in area, it is 16th in value added by manufacturing, a total of over $7.9 billion annually. Its factories employ over 30% of the non-farm work force. Hartford is headquarters for many of the nation's largest insurance companies. The Greenwich-Stamford area has one of the world's highest concentrations of multinational corporation headquarters.

Poultry and dairy products account for the largest part of farm receipts, which totaled $220 million in 1975. Much of the soil is stony, but tobacco, potatoes, fruits, and vegetables are grown. Greenhouse, nursery, and forest products are valued at over $21 million annually.

The vacation-recreation industry is important. Attractions include historic sites, charming villages, the American Shakespeare Theatre in Stratford, famed museums, boating on Long Island Sound, and winter sports.

There are 85 state parks, 29 state forests, recreation areas, and historic sites, covering 163,000 acres.

Tourism brings Connecticut about $491 million a year from out-of-state vacationers.

Mineral production is mostly of sand, stone, and gravel for construction of roads and buildings. Total value for 1975 was $33 million.

Adriaen Block, Dutch explorer, was the first European visitor, 1614. By 1633, settlers from Plymouth Bay started colonies along the Connecticut River and in 1637 defeated the Pequot Indians, opening the area to more settlements. In the Revolution, Connecticut men fought in most major campaigns and beat off British raids on Danbury and other towns. Connecticut privateers captured British merchant ships; the state was nicknamed "The Provision State" for the large amount of food it furnished the Continental Army.

Free public schools were established in New Haven, 1642; Hartford, 1643. Compulsory education in elementary and Latin grammar schools was established in 1650.

There are 46 institutions of higher education.

Museums include the P. T. Barnum Museum, Bridgeport; American Clock and Watch Museum, Bristol; trolley museums, East Haven and Warehouse Point; Hill-Stead Museum, a country house with paintings by famous impressionists, Farmington; Museum of American Art, New Britain; Lyman Allyn Museum, New London; Bruce Museum, Greenwich; Wadsworth Atheneum and State Library Museum, Hartford.

In New Haven, museums include the Winchester Gun Museum, with 5,000 items from the 15th century to present. The Yale University Art Gallery's collections range from ancient to modern. The Peabody Museum at Yale has collections in paleontology, mineralogy, zoology and, archeology.

Mystic Seaport, Mystic, is a recreated 19th century village, including smithy, chapel, and schoolhouse. At the docks lie the wooden whaleship, Charles W. Morgan, the squarerigger, Joseph Conrad, and the Gloucester fishing schooner, L. A. Dunton.

Famous "Nutmeggers" include Phineas T. Barnum, Ethan Allen, Walter Camp, Samuel Colt, Nathan Hale, Isaac Hull, J. Pierpont Morgan, Abraham Ribicoff, Harriet Beecher Stowe, Mark Twain, Noah Webster, Emma Hart Willard, Katharine Hepburn, Jonathan Edwards.

(See also Index for Bridgeport, Hartford, New Haven.)

Delaware

First State, Diamond State

AREA: 2,057 sq. mi.; rank, 49th. **POPULATION:** (U.S. est. 1975); 575,000; rank, 47th. **CAPITAL:** Dover. **MOTTO:** Liberty and Independence. **FLOWER:** Peach blossom. **BIRD:** Blue hen chicken. **TREE:** American holly. **SONG:** Our Delaware. First of original 13 states to ratify the Constitution, Dec. 7, 1787.

Delaware occupies part of the Delmarva Peninsula, so-called because Delaware and parts of Maryland and Virginia share the peninsula separating Delaware and Chesapeake Bays. Delaware is 96 mi. long and from 9 to 35 mi. wide. The land slopes from rolling hills (442 ft. highest elevation) in the N to a near sea-level plain.

Second smallest of the states in area, Delaware has the 3d highest per capita income in the U.S., $6,799 in 1975. It has large chemical and other industries, the hqs. of many large corporations, prosperous farms, and important shellfish production.

Important in Delaware's total of value added by manufacture are canned and frozen foods, leather and metal products, textiles and machinery. Total value added by manufacture is over $1.5 billion.

Broiler chickens are the largest item of farm income. Farm receipts for 1975 were $279 million.

Mineral production is mainly sand, gravel, and stone used for construction. Total value in 1975 was est. at $4.8 million. There is also a sizable commercial fishing catch, valued at $1.6 million in 1975.

Delaware's major tourist attractions include several famed beaches, racetracks, and historic sites and museums. Annual value of tourism is about $158 million.

The Dutch first settled in Delaware near present Lewes, 1631, but were wiped out by Indians. Swedes settled at present Wilmington, 1638; Dutch settled anew, 1651, near New Castle and seized the Swedish settlement, 1655, only to lose all Delaware and New Netherland to the British, 1664. Delaware troops served in Washington's New Jersey campaigns and at the Brandywine, near home, where Washington suffered defeat. Delaware troops also fought in the southern campaigns and, finally, at Yorktown. In the Civil War, over 10% of Delaware's total population served in the Union Army.

Fort Christina Monument marks the site of founding of New Sweden. Holy Trinity (Old Swedes) Church erected 1698 is the oldest Protestant church in the U.S. still in use. Center New Castle comprises a unique survival of a colonial capital nearly in its late 18th century form. The home of John Dickinson, "Penman of the Revolution," and drafter of the Articles of Confederation, has been restored near Dover.

Museums include the Delaware Art Center in Wilmington which has collections of Pre-Raphaelite English paintings and American paintings. The Henry Francis du Pont Winterthur Museum, at Winterthur near Wilmington, has 100 American period rooms from 17th to early 19th centuries (reservations are required to visit some of them). The Hagley Museum at Wilmington includes many of the old du Pont powder mills and other exhibits illustrating the development of American industry. The Delaware Museum of Natural History is in Greenville.

The Delaware State Museum, Dover, has varied exhibits on Delaware history and life and a collection on the development of the Victor Talking Machine and related sound recording.

Delaware has 10 institutions of higher education.

Famous Delawareans include E. I. du Pont, Caesar Rodney, Howard Pyle, Henry Seidel Canby, John P. Marquand.

(See also Index for Wilmington.)

Florida
Sunshine State

AREA: 58,560 sq. mi.; rank, 22d. POPULATION (U.S. est. 1975): 8,357,000; rank, 8th. CAPITAL: Tallahassee. MOTTO: In God We Trust. FLOWER: Orange blossom. BIRD: Mockingbird. TREE: Sabal palm. SONG: Old Folks at Home. ENTERED UNION: Mar. 3, 1845; rank 27th.

Florida's many miles of beaches and other resort areas offer fun in the sun to millions of vacationers. The state also has a tremendous agricultural output, producing 80% of the nation's citrus fruits and ranking 2d only to California in production of vegetables. Its growing and diversified manufacturing industries provide even more income than its agriculture. Per capita income was $5,517 in 1975 (U.S. average: $5,834).

The Florida peninsula juts southward 500 mi. between the Atlantic and the Gulf of Mexico; Cuba is only 90 mi. from its southern tip. It has some 30,000 lakes; Okeechobee, covering 700 sq. mi., is the 4th largest natural lake inside the U.S. The land is flat or rolling; highest point is 345 ft. in the NW.

First European to see Florida was Ponce de Leon, 1513. France established a colony, Fort Caroline, on the St. Johns River, 1564; Spain settled St. Augustine, 1565, and Spanish troops massacred most of the French. Britain's Francis Drake burned St. Augustine, 1586. Britain held the area briefly, 1763-83, returning it to Spain. After Andrew Jackson led a U.S. invasion, 1818, Spain ceded Florida to the U.S., 1819. The Seminole War, 1835-42, resulted in removal of most Indians to Oklahoma. Florida seceded from the Union, 1861, was readmitted, 1868.

Tourism is a major industry; about 27.3 million visitors spend some $5.5 billion annually in Florida. It offers a wide variety of tourist attractions in addition to climate, resorts, and water sports. Many tourists have become permanent residents.

Major tourist objectives are metropolitan Miami, with the nation's greatest concentration of luxury hotels at Miami Beach; Palm Beach; St. Augustine, oldest city in U.S.; Daytona Beach, Fort Lauderdale, all on the E coast; Sarasota, Tampa, Key West, St. Petersburg on the W; Walt Disney World, an entertainment and vacation development near Orlando, visited by 12.5 million persons in 1975.

Everglades National Park, 3d largest of U.S. national parks, preserves the beauty of the vast Everglades swamp. Castillo de San Marcos (St. Augustine), Fort Matanzas, Fort Jefferson (Dry Tortugas), De Soto National Memorial (Bradenton), and Fort Caroline (Jacksonville) are national monuments.

The John F. Kennedy Space Center is another big tourist attraction. From it the nation's first earth satellite was launched Jan. 31, 1958; first U.S. manned space flight, May 5, 1961; first manned orbital flight, Feb. 20, 1962 (Col. John H. Glenn), as well as the first man-on-the-moon launch, July 16, 1969.

Key West became the 1st U.S. city to get its fresh water from the sea when a desalting plant, capable of producing 3.5 million gallons a day, opened 1967.

Florida produces most of the nation's oranges and grapefruit; 1975 output was an est. 7.8 million tons of oranges and 1.9 million tons of grapefruit, both several times the amount produced by California and with a total value of $563 million. It also produces vegetables, avocados, watermelons, limes, tangerines, sugarcane, peanuts, cotton, tobacco, strawberries.

Florida also ranks high in chickens. The cattle industry has grown in importance. Crop and livestock receipts for 1975 totaled $2.3 billion.

Manufacturing has made great gains and provides payrolls totaling $3 billion. Leading industries, in terms of value added by manufacturing, are food processing, chemicals, electrical equipment, transportation equipment, metal products, paper. Total added in 1973 was $6.5 billion.

Florida leads the U.S. in production of phosphate rock and is 2d to New York in titanium. Total mineral production value in 1974 was est. at $1.5 billion, up 39% from 1974 with most of the increase due to raised petroleum and phosphate prices.

The commercial catch of fish and shellfish is worth over $70 million a year, high among the states.

Florida has 17 airports with scheduled service, 62 scheduled airlines, and 5 major railroads. There are 14 deepwater ports which handle domestic and foreign trade valued at $1.8 billion a year.

Florida has 74 institutions of higher learning.

Museums include the Florida State Museum in Gainesville, with exhibits in archeology, ethnology, paleontology, ornithology, history, and industry. Castillo de San Marcos in St. Augustine is a Spanish fort built 1672-1696 which is now a national monument. Marineland of Florida, 18 mi. S of St. Augustine, has some 2,500 marine specimens ranging from sharks and porpoises to tiny tropical fish; trained porpoises and pilot whales perform in shows. Miami's Seaquarium and Orlando's Sea World have similar shows.

At Pensacola is the Naval Aviation Museum, with exhibits tracing flight development into the space age; Fort Pickens, built 1829, where Geronimo was imprisoned; the T. T. Wentworth Museum, with exhibits of local historical interest; the Pensacola Historical Museum.

At Lake Wales are the 205-ft. Singing Tower with a carillon of 53 bells (the largest weighs 11 tons) and Mountain Lake Sanctuary, with trails and picnic area, given "to the American people" by publisher Edward Bok in thanks for "the successful life they gave" him.

In Sarasota, the John and Mable Ringling Museum of Art, willed to the state, contains works by Rembrandt, Rubens, Hals, Tiepolo, Velasquez, Murillo, Gainsborough, Reynolds, and other masters. The Ringling Museum of the Circus includes elaborately decorated wagons, costumes, and printed bills showing performers at fairs and circuses from the 16th to 20th centuries; the Asolo Theater presents operas.

Also in Sarasota, the Circus Hall of Fame gives circus acts and puppet shows, displays mementos such as a coach given Tom Thumb by Queen Victoria, a sleigh P. T. Barnum gave Jenny Lind.

Famous Floridians include Henry M. Flagler, Rex Beach, Irving Bacheller, James Weldon Johnson, Marjorie Kinnan Rawlings, MacKinlay Kantor, Gen. Joseph W. Stilwell, Henry B. Plant.

(See also Index for Jacksonville, Miami, Orlando, Pensacola, St. Petersburg, Tallahassee, Tampa, West Palm Beach.)

Georgia
Empire State of the South, Peach State

AREA: 58,876 sq. mi.; rank, 21st. POPULATION (U.S. est. 1975): 4,926,000; rank, 14th. CAPITAL: Atlanta. MOTTO: Wisdom, Justice, Moderation. FLOWER: Cherokee rose. BIRD: Brown thrasher. TREE: Live oak. SONG: Georgia. Fourth of the 13 original states to ratify The Constitution, Jan. 2, 1788.

Largest in area of the states east of the Mississippi, Georgia is rich in a number of natural resources and in its growing, diversified industries.

There are large deposits of marble in the mountainous N, along with fertile plains and industry centers in the NW. The central Georgia Piedmont plateau boasts rich farmlands and a flourishing textile industry. The SE coastal plain produces pecans and peanuts and its forests yield a wealth of pulpwood and turpentine. Islands off its 100-mi. Atlantic coast provide resort havens. The state also has large deposits of clay, limestone, and talc.

Okefenokee in the SE is one of the largest swamps in the U.S., a wetland wilderness and peat bog covering 660 sq. mi. A large part of it is a National Wildlife Refuge, a home for wild birds, alligators, bear, deer.

Highest point in the state is Brasstown Bald in the NE, 4,784 ft.; Stone Mtn., near Atlanta, is 1,686 ft.

Manufacturing has grown many times over since World War II, but the textile industry remains the largest, both in terms of number of workers and value added by manufacture. Also of great importance are paper products, transportation equipment, apparel, food products, and chemicals.

Value added by manufacture totals over $8.6 billion a year. Per capita income was $4,969 in 1975.

Georgia ranks high among the states in forest products, particularly in pulpwood and turpentine.

Georgia is by far the nation's largest producer of peanuts, harvesting 863,000 tons in 1975, three times that of any other state. It is among the leading growers of pecans, peaches, and rye.

It ranked 2d among the states in numbers of chickens, about 35 million in 1975, and also had a large hog production. Farm receipts totaled over $2.2 billion in 1975, more than half from livestock.

Georgia is also a leader in production of marble, zirconium, bauxite, and kyanite. Total value of mineral production in 1975 was an est. $320 million.

Savannah and Brunswick are the main ports. The state is served by 6 major railroads and 10 airlines.

Notable among attractions are the Little White House in Warm Springs where Pres. Franklin D. Roosevelt died Apr. 12, 1945, the 2,500-acre Callaway Gardens, Jekyll Island State Park, the restored 1850s farming community of Westville; Dahlonega, site of America's first gold rush; Helen, a mountain village with Alpine motif, Stone Mountain and Six Flags over Georgia.

Georgia has also become a sports center, with professional baseball, basketball, football, hockey.

Andersonville Prison Park and National Cemetery are on the site of the Confederate prison camp in which a total of 50,000 Union soldiers were confined, Feb. 1864 to Apr. 1865.

There are 66 institutions of higher learning.

Gen. James Oglethorpe established the first settlements, 1733, for poor and religiously-persecuted Englishmen. Oglethorpe defeated a Spanish army from Florida at Bloody Marsh, 1742. In the Revolution, Georgians seized the Savannah armory, 1775, and sent the munitions to the Continental Army. Led by Light-Horse Harry Lee, Elijah Clarke, Andrew Pickens and Anthony Wayne, Georgians fought see-saw campaigns with Cornwallis' British troops, twice liberating Augusta and forcing final evacuation by the British from Savannah, 1782.

Famous Georgians include Jimmy Carter, Ty Cobb, Margaret Mitchell, Erskine Caldwell, Joel Chandler Harris, Laurence Stallings, John C. Fremont, James Bowie, Joseph Wheeler, Lucius D. Clay.

(See also Index for Atlanta, Augusta, Columbus, Macon, Savannah.)

Hawaii
Aloha State

AREA: 6,450 sq. mi.; rank, 47th. POPULATION (U.S. est. 1975): 865,000; rank, 40th. CAPITAL: Honolulu. MOTTO: The Life of the Land Is Perpetuated in Righteousness. FLOWER: Hibiscus. BIRD: Nene (Hawaiian goose). TREE: Kukui (candlenut). SONG: Hawaii Ponoi. ENTERED UNION: Aug. 21, 1959, rank, 50th.

Hawaii, prosperous paradise of the Pacific, became the 50th state Aug. 21, 1959, and the 50-star U. S. flag

became official the following July 4.

The Hawaiian Islands lie in the North Pacific, 2,397 mi. from San Francisco (5 hrs. by commercial jet). They consist of 8 major islands (7 inhabited) and 124 minor islands.

The principal islands are Hawaii, the largest; Oahu, on which are Honolulu and Pearl Harbor; Lanai, Maui, Molokai, Kauai, Niihau and Kahoolawe.

The islands are volcanic. Highest point is Mauna Kea, on Hawaii, an extinct volcano 13,796 ft. above sea level. Its twin is Mauna Loa, about 100 ft. lower but an active volcano. Average annual rainfall is 22.9 inches at Honolulu Airport, 133.57 inches in Hilo, and 486 inches atop Waialeale, a mountain on Kauai. Honolulu is subtropical (all-time range, 57° to 88°) but Mauna Kea is often snowcapped.

Lake Waiau, at 13,020 ft. near the summit of Mauna Kea, is one of the highest lakes in the U.S.

Ka Lae, or South Cape, on the island of Hawaii, is the southernmost point in the 50 states.

Polynesians from islands 2,000 mi. to the south settled the Hawaiian Islands, probably about 700 A.D. First European visitor was British Capt. James Cook, 1778. Missionaries arrived, 1820, taught religion, reading and writing. King Kamehameha III and his chiefs created the first Constitution and a Legislature which set up a public school system. Sugar production began in 1835; it became the dominant industry. In 1893, Queen Liliuokalani was deposed, followed, 1894, by a republic headed by Sanford B. Dole. Annexation by the U.S. came in 1898.

Hawaii has a very heterogeneous population with Americans of Polynesian, Asian, European, and African extraction.

Many of the Polynesians intermarried with the other racial groups, which arrived mainly in the 19th Century.

The 1970 Census gave as racial origins: Japanese, 28.3%; Caucasian, 39.2%; the remainder, Hawaiian, Chinese, Filipino, Korean, etc., with many of mixed racial descent.

Major sources of income are tourism, defense expenditures, sugar and pineapple production, in that order. Visitors totaled 2.8 million in 1975, with an average 68,600 present daily. Tourists spend about $891 million each year.

Value added by manufacturing, led by food processing, was $410 million in 1973. There were 4,100 farms, with a total of 2.3 million acres; farm receipts for 1975 were $375 million. The commercial fishing catch was valued at $6 million in 1975.

Mineral production, mostly cement and stone for construction, was valued at $42 million in 1975.

Per capita income was $6,426 in 1975, 9th highest in the U.S.

More than 5,800 ships put into Honolulu in 1974. Honolulu International Airport has an average of over 319,000 arrivals and departures annually.

A marine exposition is scheduled for 1978, bicentennial of Capt. Cook's arrival in the islands.

There are 13 institutions of higher education.

Famous Hawaiians include Duke Kahanamoku, Don Ho, Patsy Mink, Daniel K. Inouye, Father Joseph Damien, Bette Midler.

(See also Index for Honolulu.)

Idaho
Gem State

AREA: 83,557 sq. mi.; rank, 13th. POPULATION (U.S. est. 1975): 820,000; rank, 41st. CAPITAL: Boise. MOTTO: Esto Perpetua, Let It Be Forever. FLOWER: Lewis mock orange (syringa). BIRD: Mountain bluebird. TREE: Western white pine. SONG: Here We Have Idaho. ENTERED UNION: July 3, 1890; rank, 43d.

A land of rugged grandeur, Idaho nevertheless ranks high in agricultural production.

Exploration of the Idaho area began with Lewis and Clark, 1805; they returned through Idaho, 1806. Next came fur traders, setting up posts, 1809-34, and missionaries, establishing missions, 1830s-1850s. Mormons made their first permanent settlement at Franklin, 1860. Idaho's Gold Rush began that same year, and brought thousands of permanent settlers. Strangest of the Indian Wars was the 1,300-mi. trek in 1877 of Chief Joseph and the Nez Perce tribe, pursued by troops that caught them a few miles short of the Canadian border. By 1890, Idaho adopted a progressive Constitution and became a state that year.

The Snake River runs through Hells Canyon, which averages 5,510 ft. in depth for 40 mi., at one point 7,900 ft., exceeding Grand Canyon, and is 10 mi. from rim to rim at widest point. The Snake has several noted waterfalls: Shoshone, Twin, American.

Idaho is the nation's leading potato producer, growing about 75 million cwt. annually. It ranks high in sugar beets, barley, wheat, hops, and apples.

It is an important wool producer and was 8th among the states in number of sheep in 1975 with 536,000. Farm marketing receipts in 1975 totaled $1.3 billion, two-thirds from crops, the rest from livestock.

Manufacturing gains have been mainly in processing of potatoes and other foods, phosphates, paper, etc. Total value added by manufacturing was est. at over $976 million. Per capita income was $4,980 in 1975.

Discovery of silver in 1884 at Coeur d'Alene caused a stampede; Idaho still leads the nation in production of that metal. It also ranks high among the states in antimony, lead, cobalt, garnet, phosphate rock, vanadium, zinc, and mercury. Total mineral production in 1974 was estimated at $260 million, up 25%.

With 39% of its area in forests, Idaho produces much lumber, with the world's largest white pine lumber mill at Lewiston. Yellow pine, Douglas fir, white spruce, larch, hemlock abound; the DeVoto Grove has cedars 1,000 years old. Total value of forest products is more than $153 million a year.

Hells Canyon, Brownlee, and Oxbow Dams are 3 recent hydro-electric projects on the Snake River. The National Reactor Testing Station of the AEC on Upper Snake River Plains has more than a score of reactors in operation.

Tourism brings in an est. $337 million annually, making it an important industry.

The state offers excellent hunting and fishing and Lake Pend Oreille, which has a 111-mile shoreline, is home of the world's largest trout, Kamloop rainbow.

Craters of the Moon National Monument, 18 mi. W of Arco, is a jagged landscape; lava covers the area.

The Nez Perce National Historic Park, in northern Idaho, includes many sites visited by the Lewis and Clark Expedition. The State Historical Museum in Boise has displays of early Idaho Indian life, the fur trade, mining, farm and pioneer mementos.

There are 9 institutions of higher education.

Famous Idahoans include William E. Borah, Fred T. Dubois, Chief Joseph and Sacajawea, woman guide for Lewis and Clark.

(See also Index for Boise.)

Illinois
The Inland Empire

AREA: 56,400 sq. mi.; rank, 24th. POPULATION: (U.S. est. 1975): 11,145,000; rank, 5th. CAPITAL: Springfield. MOTTO: State Sovereignty, National Union. FLOWER: Native violet. BIRD: Cardinal. TREE: White oak. Song: Illinois. SLOGAN: Land of Lincoln. ENTERED UNION: Dec. 3, 1818; rank, 21st.

Illinois ranks high among the states as both an agricultural and industrial empire. It has large coal and oil reserves and boasts highly developed rail, water, and air transportation facilities. The soil is rich and level.

Fur traders were the first Europeans in Illinois, followed shortly, 1673, by Louis Jolliet and Father Jacques Marquette, and, 1680, La Salle, who built a fort near present Peoria. First settlements were French, at Fort St. Louis on the Illinois River, 1692.

and Kaskaskia, 1700. France ceded the area to Britain, 1763, and in 1778 American Gen. George Rogers Clark took it from the British without a shot. Defeat of Indian tribes in Black Hawk War, 1832, inspired new immigration, as did railroads in 1850s.

Illinois ranks 4th highest among the states in terms of value added by manufacture with a total of close to $30 billion. Manufacturing payrolls total $14.3 billion.

Major manufacturing lines are machinery (particularly construction and farm), processing of food products (especially grain, beverages and bakery), electrical machinery (communications, electronic components and appliances), primary metals (mainly iron and steel), transportation equipment (for railroads, aircraft, and cars) and chemicals. Rockford is one of the nation's machine-tool centers; Peoria is a distilling center. Per capita income was $6,750 in 1975 (U.S. average: $5,834).

In 1975 Illinois ranked 2d to California in receipts from farm crops, $3.6 billion. It stood 7th in receipts for livestock and livestock products and was 4th in total cash farm receipts, $5.6 billion.

Illinois and Iowa vie closely with each other for the largest corn crop. Illinois produces the most soybeans; in 1976 it ranked 2d to Iowa in number of hogs and stood high in cattle and milk cows.

The state has large coal and oil reserves. It ranks high among the states in annual bituminous coal production, est. at $679 million in 1975. Petroleum production, 2d in value to coal, was est. to be worth $258 million. The state is a leader in output of fluorspar, tripoli, stone, and peat. Total 1975 minerals were valued at $1.3 billion.

A major research and development installation of the Atomic Energy Commission is the Argonne National Laboratory, Lemont, Ill., directed by the Univ. of Chicago, which also operates the Argonne Cancer Research Hospital in Chicago. At Batavia, W of Chicago, the AEC completed the nation's largest atom-smasher in 1971.

Illinois has 147 institutions of higher education.

The Illinois State Fair is held annually in August in Springfield. Attendance is over 700,000.

State forests, parks, and conservation areas cover 283,430 acres. Some are associated with the history of the Middle West, including Lincoln's home and tomb in Springfield; the restored Fort de Chartres, seat of French 18th century authority; old settlements such as Kaskaskia.

The Illinois State Museum in Springfield has large collections of local art and archeology, art of the ancient Near East, and antique furnishings.

Located in Springfield is a state memorial including Abraham Lincoln's tomb and the Lincoln home which the family occupied 1844-1860. The Old State Capitol Building has been restored.

New Salem State Park, 20 mi. NW of Springfield, contains the restored pioneer village of New Salem where Lincoln lived as storekeeper, surveyor, and postmaster, 1831-37. Annual performances are staged of Robert Sherwood's Abe Lincoln in Illinois.

Famous Illinoisans include Abraham Lincoln, William Jennings Bryan, Jane Addams, Adlai Stevenson, Carl Sandburg, Mary Garden, Ernest Hemingway, James T. Farrell, Frank Lloyd Wright.

(See also Index for Bloomington, Chicago, Rockford, Springfield.)

Indiana
Hoosier State

AREA: 36,291 sq. mi.; rank, 38th. POPULATION (U.S. est. 1975): 5,311,000; rank, 12th. CAPITAL: Indianapolis. MOTTO: Cross-roads of America. FLOWER: Peony. BIRD: Cardinal. TREE: Tulip (yellow poplar). SONG: On the Banks of the Wabash. ENTERED UNION: Dec. 11, 1816; rank, 19th.

Indiana is heavily industrialized, yet is also important among the states for its agricultural output. It ranks among the top states in production of both steel and corn; it quarries much of the building limestone used in the U.S. and is a large producer of coal.

Pre-historic Indian Mound Builders of 1,000 years ago were the earliest known inhabitants. French explorer La Salle visited the present South Bend area, 1679 and 1681. A French trading post was built, 1731-32, at Vincennes. France ceded the area to Britain, 1763. During the Revolution, American Gen. George Rogers Clark captured Vincennes, 1778, and defeated British forces 1779; at war's end Britain ceded the area to the U.S. Miami Indians defeated U.S. troops twice, 1790, but were beaten, 1794, at Fallen Timbers by Gen. Anthony Wayne. At Tippecanoe, 1811, Gen. William H. Harrison defeated Tecumseh's Indian confederation.

There are sand dunes and lakes in the N, a level plain through most of the central area, and hills in the S.

The Calumet region in the state's NW corner, including Gary, Hammond, East Chicago, and Whiting, has one of the world's greatest concentrations of heavy industry, especially steel, cement, and oil-refining plants. Gary was a sand dune in 1906 when U.S. Steel began constructing mills there; in 1970 it had a pop. of 175,415.

Per capita income was $5,587 in 1975.

Another vast steel complex has been developed further E along Lake Michigan, including a deep-water port at Burns Harbor in the famed Dunes area, a large plant of the Midwest Steel Div. of the National Steel Corp., plus Bethlehem Steel Corp. works.

While steel and other metal industries are responsible for $1.8 billion of the $14 billion in value added annually by manufacture, electrical machinery, including television sets and household appliances, is a close 2d with $1.9 billion. Auto parts, aircraft and other transportation equipment is next, with $1.6 billion; farm and other machinery, 4th; chemicals, 5th; processing of food products, 6th.

Indiana is a leader in production of pre-fabricated wood products, mobile homes, and band instruments. Furniture is manufactured in over 40 cities.

Corn is the principal crop and much of it goes to fatten the hogs. Among the states, Indiana ranks 3d in hogs and corn, 8th in chickens. Farm marketing receipts for 1975 totaled $2.9 billion, 8th highest among the states.

Coal accounts for about half of the value of mineral production which in 1975 totaled $475 million. Portland cement, petroleum, limestone, clay, and gypsum are also important.

Indiana limestone, from vast quarries in the southern part of the state, sheathes tens of thousands of buildings, including the Empire State, Rockefeller Center, the United Nations, the Pentagon, the National Cathedral and many federal and state buildings.

Spending by out-of-state tourists is est. at $910 million a year.

Indiana has 27 state parks and recreation areas, including Dunes State Park on Lake Michigan; prehistoric Indian mounds; over 1,000 lakes; French Lick and other mineral spas; Wyandotte Cave, 3d largest in the U.S.; the Indianapolis 500-mile auto race, and the famous post office, Santa Claus.

Lincoln's boyhood home in Spencer County and the grave of his mother, Nancy Hanks Lincoln, are part of the Lincoln Boyhood National Memorial. State memorials commemorate the capture of Vincennes by George Rogers Clark in the Revolution, the defeat of Indian forces at Tippecanoe, and the Rappite and Robert Owen communities at New Harmony.

Spring Mill, Conner Prairie, and Billie Creek are restored pioneer settlements. The restored Whitewater Canal is at Brookville.

There are 64 institutions of higher education.

Famous "Hoosiers" include Wendell L. Willkie, Wilbur Wright, Lew Wallace, Cole Porter, Hoagy Carmichael, James Whitcomb Riley, Ernie Pyle, Booth Tarkington, Gene Stratton Porter, George Jean Nathan.

(See also Index for Evansville, Fort Wayne, Indianapolis.)

Iowa
Hawkeye State

AREA: 56,290 sq. mi.; rank, 25th. POPULATION (U.S. est. 1975): 2,870,000; rank, 25th. CAPITAL: Des Moines. MOTTO: Our Liberties We Prize and Our Rights We Will Maintain. FLOWER: Wild rose. BIRD: Eastern goldfinch. TREE: Oak. SONG: Iowa. ENTERED UNION: Dec. 28, 1846; rank, 29th.

Iowa, the heart of the rich Midwest farm belt, is one of the nation's wealthiest agricultural states, but its industrial growth has been so great that the value of its manufacturing output has become more than twice that of its farms.

Many industries process farm products or produce farm implements. However, the fast-growing industrial economy includes a wide variety of manufacturing plants, with electronic items, home appliances, tires, railway equipment, furnaces, automobile accessories, chemicals and fertilizers, vending machines, office furniture, and gypsum wallboard among the diversified products. Value added by manufacture is over $4.8 billion a year. Per capita income was $5,899 in 1975 ($65 above U.S. average).

Iowa's broad plains contain some of the finest soil in the world. Its huge harvests support the nation's richest livestock industry. Iowa had by far the most hogs, 12.6 million in 1976, twice as many as Illinois, the next largest raiser. In cattle, with 7.5 million, Iowa was 2d only to Texas. It also had large numbers of chickens, turkeys, and sheep.

In field crops, Iowa ranked 2d in corn, and soybeans, and 3d in oats.

Receipts for livestock and livestock products totaled $4 billion in 1975, tops in the nation. In receipts for crops, Iowa stood 4th. Its total farm receipts were $6.9 billion, 2d only to California.

Iowa's forests produce hardwood lumber.

Mineral production was valued at $171 million in 1975. Products, in order of value, were cement, limestone, sand and gravel, gypsum, and coal.

Visitors from other states add more than $520 million to Iowa's economy annually.

Tourist attractions include the Herbert Hoover birthplace and library near West Branch, tulip festivals at Pella and Orange City in May, Iowa State Fair at Des Moines in August, several rodeos, the National Hot Air Balloon Races. The Little Brown Church in the Vale, near Nashua, inspired a well-known hymn. There are 95 state parks and other recreation areas. Effigy Mounds National Monument at Marquette is a prehistoric Indian burial site.

The Davenport Municipal Art Gallery has a collection of paintings and memorabilia of the Iowa painter Grant Wood, as well as other American, Mexican, Haitian, and European paintings. The State Historical Building, Des Moines, has Indian artifacts.

In Decorah, the Norwegian-American Museum preserves homes of pioneers from Norway.

Waterloo's Museum of History and Science has exhibits on Iowa history, pioneer life, Indian lore, and earth sciences, and a planetarium.

Iowa has 63 institutions of higher education.

A thousand years ago several groups of pre-historic Indian Mound Builders dwelt on Iowa's fertile plains. Father Jacques Marquette and Louis Jolliet gave France its claim to the area, 1673. It became U.S. territory through the 1803 Louisiana Purchase. Indian tribes were moved into the area from states further east, but by mid-19th century were forced to move on to Kansas. Before and during the Civil War, Iowans strongly supported Abraham Lincoln and became traditional Republicans.

Famous Iowans include Herbert Hoover, Buffalo Bill Cody, Billy Sunday, Susan Glaspell, Harry Hansen, Marquis Childs, James Norman Hall, Carl Van Vechten, Grant Wood, Henry Wallace, James A. Van Allen, Meredith Willson.

(See also Index for Des Moines.)

Kansas

Sunflower State

AREA: 82,264 sq. mi.; rank, 14th. POPULATION (U.S. est. 1975): 2,267,000; rank, 31st. CAPITAL: Topeka. MOTTO: Ad Astra per Aspera, To the Stars through Difficulties. FLOWER: Sunflower. BIRD: Western meadowlark. TREE: Cottonwood. SONG: Home on the Range. ENTERED UNION: Jan. 29, 1861; rank, 34th.

Rolling fields of wheat, clusters of oil well derricks, great herds of cattle, and towering grain storage elevators feature the landscape of Kansas, the geographical center of the 48 conterminous states. The land rises from broad plains in the east, 680 ft. above sea level, to slightly over 4,000 ft. in the west.

Manufacturing, farming, and mining (especially petroleum and natural gas) are major factors in the Kansas economy. Large industry fields include transportation equipment, food processing, machinery, and chemicals. Value added by manufacture is $3.3 billion a year. Per capita income was $5,968 in 1975.

Most of the land of Kansas is devoted to agriculture, and much of that to growing wheat. Kansas ranked first among the states in its wheat crop in 1975, 2d in sorghum, 5th in cattle. Total farm receipts for 1975 were $3.7 billion, 7th highest in the U.S. Forest products, particularly walnut lumber are valued at about $14 million a year.

Wichita ranks first in the nation in production of general aircraft.

Kansas stands high in petroleum production and has large reserves of natural gas. It ranks first among the states in helium production.

Petroleum production in 1975 was valued at an est. $518 million, over half the total mineral production value, $998 million, up $109 million. Also important are natural gas and salt.

Coronado marched through the Kansas area, 1541; French explorers came next. The U.S. took over in the Louisiana Purchase, 1803. In the pre-war North-South struggle over slavery, so much violence swept the area it was called Bleeding Kansas; it was deeply involved in the Civil War. Railroad construction after the war made Abilene and Dodge City terminals of large cattle drives from Texas. Sale of alcoholic beverages was prohibited from 1880 to 1948.

In Abilene, the boyhood home of the late Pres. Dwight D. Eisenhower, is the Eisenhower Center, with the Eisenhower Home, Museum, and Library. Near them, in a chapel named "Place of Meditation," the 34th president was buried Apr. 2, 1969.

The Agricultural Hall of Fame and National Center, 14 mi. W of Kansas City, Kan., displays farm equipment of the past such as a wooden-wheeled corn planter, anvils, wheat drills, etc. In Dodge City are extensive reproductions of the original Front Street, saloons, and Boot Hill cemetery.

The Wichita Art Museum has works by many modern artists. The Kansas State Historical Society in Topeka has displays and period rooms of Midwest history.

In Lawrence, the Univ. of Kansas has a Museum of Natural History which presents a panorama of North American mammals from the Arctic to the tropics; a Museum of Art, with European and American painting and sculpture and European and Oriental decorative arts; and the Snow Entomological Museum, with over 2 million insects.

It is estimated that tourists spend over $520 million a year in the state.

Kansas has 52 institutions of higher learning.

Kansas has developed an extensive recreation system around its reservoirs, lakes, and roadside parks.

Famous Kansans include John Brown, Dwight D. Eisenhower, Gen. Hugh Johnson, Walter P. Chrysler, Amelia Earhart, Osa Johnson, Brock Pemberton, Walter Johnson, Alf M. Landon.

(See also Index for Wichita.)

Kentucky

Blue Grass State

AREA: 40,395 sq. mi.; rank, 37th. POPULATION (U.S. est. 1975): 3,396,000; rank, 23d. CAPITAL: Frankfort. MOTTO: United We Stand, Divided We Fall. FLOWER: Goldenrod. BIRD: Cardinal. SONG: My Old Kentucky Home. TREE: Kentucky coffee tree. ENTERED UNION: June 1, 1792; rank, 15th.

Kentucky was the first area west of the Alleghenies settled by American pioneers. First permanent settlers, led by James Harrod, founded Harrodsburg, 1774. Daniel Boone blazed the Wilderness Trail through the Cumberland Gap and founded Boonesboro, 1775. Indian attacks, spurred by the British, were unceasing until, during the Revolution, Gen. George Rogers Clark, leading Kentucky volunteers, captured British forts in Indiana and Illinois, 1778; Boone, captured by Indians, escaped and warned Boonesboro of a coming Indian attack, which was repulsed. In 1792, after Virginia dropped its claims to the region, Kentucky became the 15th state.

Kentucky rises from an elevation of less than 260 ft., at the Mississippi, to over 4,000 ft. in the Cumberland and Pine mountains. Over 42% of the state is forested, and lumbering, particularly of hardwoods, is an important industry. Forest products are valued at over $50 million a year.

Tobacco is the principal crop, 2d only to that of North Carolina. Corn, soybeans, wheat, fruit, hogs, and cattle, especially milk cows, are also important. Farm receipts in 1975 totaled $585 million from livestock; $761 million from crops.

In 1975 Kentucky produced more coal than West Virginia. It also produced important amounts of petroleum, natural gas, fluorspar, clay, and stone. But coal accounts for over 90% of the total mineral value, est. at $3.4 billion for 1975, up 25% from 1974.

In 1966 Kentucky enacted a law requiring surface and strip miners of coal to restore and regrade earth removed by their operations, but problems have remained.

Manufacturing has shown needed growth and diversity. Leading fields are food processing and beverages (including liquor), tobacco products, machinery, chemicals, transportation equipment and apparel. Value added by manufacture is over $6.5 billion a year. Per capita income was $4,668 in 1975 (U.S. average: $5,834).

Tourists bring in an est. $798 million a year. There are 48 state and national parks and shrines.

Two of the largest man-made lakes in the world, Kentucky Lake and Lake Barkley, parallel each other in Western Kentucky, creating a 170,000-acre isthmus called the Land Between the Lakes National Recreation Area.

Lexington, heart of the Bluegrass country, has the University of Kentucky and Transylvania, oldest college west of the Alleghenies (1780), and a large tobacco market, and holds annual trotting and running races and a horse show. The Kentucky Derby is run annually at Churchill Downs, Louisville.

Fort Knox, repository for the nation's gold reserve, also contains the George S. Patton Jr. Military Museum of World War II equipment.

Mammoth Cave, 40 mi. from Bowling Green, is in a national park. Discovered 1799, it has 150 mi. of passageways, rooms with 200-ft. ceilings, blind fish, and an Echo River 360 ft. below ground.

Old Fort Harrod State Park, Harrodsburg, contains the reconstructed fort with stockade, blockhouses, the log cabin in which Thomas Lincoln and Nancy Hanks, Abraham Lincoln's parents, were married, and a museum with relics of Shakertown, Ky.

Abraham Lincoln Birthplace National Historic Site, 3 mi. from Hodgenville, contains the original Thomas Lincoln farm and cabin.

My Old Kentucky Home, one mi. E of Bardstown, was the home of John Rowan, senator and state chief justice. Stephen Foster, a relative, visited the Rowan family in 1852 and is said to have written My Old Kentucky Home on a desk preserved in the house.

Kentucky has 38 institutions of higher learning.

Famous Kentuckians include Abraham Lincoln, Vice Presidents Adlai Stevenson and Alben Barkley, Henry Clay, Jefferson Davis, Louis D. Brandeis, Kit Carson, Irvin S. Cobb, Elizabeth Madox Roberts, John Fox Jr., Robert Penn Warren, Mary Anderson.

(See also Index for Louisville.)

Louisiana
Pelican State

AREA: 48,523 sq. mi.; rank 31st. **POPULATION** (U.S. est. 1975): 3,791,000; rank, 20th. **CAPITAL:** Baton Rouge. **MOTTO:** Union, Justice, Confidence. **FLOWER:** Southern magnolia. **BIRD:** Eastern brown pelican. **SONG:** Give Me Louisiana. **TREE:** Bald cypress. **ENTERED UNION:** Apr. 30, 1812; rank, 18th.

Louisiana blends a wealth of historic charm, rich natural resources, and giant modern industries. Fertile soil, huge mineral deposits and over 7,500 mi. of navigable waterways linking the nation's heart with deepsea ports are factors basic to the state's wealth.

Mardi Gras and other festivals, the beat of Dixieland jazz in its birthplace, and nostalgic relics of the days of French and Spanish rule and the prosperous pre-Civil War era are among the attractions which bring Louisiana an est. $850 million a year in tourist revenues.

In total value of its 1975 mineral output, $8.8 billion (up 8%), Louisiana was 2d only to Texas among the 50 states. It was first in value of its salt production, 2d in petroleum, natural gas, and sulphur. Much of the oil and sulphur comes from offshore deposits.

The lush Louisiana land produces one of the nation's largest crops of sweet potatoes. It is 2d to Texas in rice, 3d in sugarcane. Also important are pecans, soybeans, cotton, and corn.

Farm receipts in 1975 included $890 million from crops, $371 million from livestock.

Total value added by manufacture is over $4.8 billion annually. Per capita income was $4,729 in 1975.

Leading manufacturing industries include chemicals, food processing, petroleum and coal products (especially oil refining), paper (particularly paperboard), lumber and wood products, transportation equipment, stone clay-glass products, apparel.

Louisiana supplies most of the nation's muskrat fur; there are also opossum, raccoon, mink, otter and large numbers of game birds. The annual catch of fresh and salt water fish, shrimp, and oyster is valued at about $88 million. Lake Pontchartrain covers 630 sq. mi.

Much of the land is a rich alluvial plain; there are also rolling hills, bluffs on the Mississippi, and coastal marshes. The elevation ranges from 5 ft. below sea level, protected by vast levees, to 535 above.

Louisiana is rich in historical relics and traditions. The area was first visited, 1530, by Cabeza de Vaca and Panfilo de Narvaez. The region was claimed for France by LaSalle, 1682. First permanent settlement was by French at Fort St. Jean Baptiste (now Natchitoches), 1717. France ceded the region to Spain, 1762, took it back, 1800, and sold it to the U.S., 1803, in the Louisiana Purchase. During the Revolution, Spanish Louisiana aided the Americans. Admitted to statehood, 1812, Louisiana was the scene of the Battle of New Orleans, 1815. The state seceded from the Union, 1861, was readmitted, 1868.

Louisiana Creoles are descendants of early French and/or Spanish settlers. About 4,000 Acadians, French settlers in Nova Scotia, Canada, were forcibly transported by the British to Louisiana in 1755 (an event commemorated in Longfellow's Evangeline) and settled near Bayou Teche; their descendants became known as Cajuns. Another group, the Islenos, were descendants of Canary Islanders brought to Louisiana by a Spanish governor in 1770. Traces of Spanish and French survive in local dialects.

Louisiana has 30 institutions of higher education.

Famous Louisianians include Zachary Taylor, Leonidas K. Polk, Braxton Bragg, Judah P. Benjamin, Pierre Beauregard, Huey Long, Grace King.

(See also Index for Baton Rouge, New Orleans, Shreveport.)

Maine
Pine Tree State

AREA: 33,215 sq. mi.; rank, 39th. **POPULATION** (U.S. est. 1975): 1,059,000; rank, 38th. **CAPITAL:** Augusta. **MOTTO:** Dirigo, I Direct. **FLOWER:** Pine cone and tassel. **BIRD:** Chickadee. **TREE:** Eastern white pine. **SONG:** State of Maine Song. **ENTERED UNION:** Mar. 15, 1820; rank, 23d.

Maine is noted for its scenic and vacation attractions, lobsters, potatoes, poultry, forest products, fishing and hunting.

Largest of the 6 New England states, it is the farthest east and borders on only one other state, New Hampshire. Its rugged coast, because of deep indentations, measures 3,478 mi. Tides are often high; in Passamaquoddy Bay they average 20 ft.

Mt. Cadillac, on Mt. Desert Is., 1,532 ft., is the highest Atlantic seacoast point N of Brazil; West Quoddy Head, Long 66° 57' W, is the farthest east point on the U.S. Atlantic coast. Lubec is the most easterly town on the U.S. mainland.

Maine's rocky coast was explored by John and Sebastian Cabot, 1498-99. French settlers arrived, 1604, at the St. Croix River; English, 1607, on the Kennebec. In 1691, Maine was made part of Massachusetts. Joining that colony's protests against Britain, Maine staged its own Tea Party at York. In the Revolution, a Maine regiment fought at Bunker Hill; a British fleet destroyed Falmouth (now Portland), 1775, but the British ship Margaretta was captured near Machiasport. In 1820, Maine broke off from Massachusetts, became a separate state.

Maine's coastal waters produce an annual 20 million lbs. of lobsters, 75% of the nation's total, and 50% of its soft-shelled clams. The state packs over 150 million cans of sardines a year, tops among the states. The fish and shellfish catch is valued at $48 million annually.

Maine grows about 12% of the nation's potatoes, trailing Idaho and Washington, and is the leading supplier of seed potatoes. It produces 90% of the nation's low bush blueberries. Also grown are apples, sweet corn, peas, beans. Farm income totaled $355 million in 1975, with poultry and eggs the largest item.

With more than 80% of its area forested, Maine turns out wood products ranging from boats to toothpicks, paper, lumber, and Christmas trees. Over 98% of the forest land is privately owned. Forest products are valued at over $700 million a year. Spruce, white pine, and birch are the most important woods. Also vital to Maine's economy are processed foods, shoes, and textiles. Boatyards build fishing and sailing craft.

Per capita income was $4,785 in 1975 (U.S. average: $5,834).

Granite, cement, and feldspar account for much of the 1975 value of mineral products, $38 million.

Maine's scenic seacoast, beaches, lakes, mountains, and resorts make it a popular vacationland; tourism produces $542 million a year. There are 26 state parks, including Baxter, where Mt. Katahdin, tallest of the state's 10 mountains over 4,000 ft., rises 5,268 ft. Maine has over 2,500 lakes, 1,300 wooded islands and 5,000 streams. Moosehead Lake is 40 mi. long and 2 to 10 mi. wide. Deer, grouse, black bear abound; game fish include salmon, tuna, trout, bass. There are over 45 public skiing facilities. Acadia National Park and Bar Harbor are on Mt. Desert Island.

Museums include the Bowdoin College Museum, Brunswick, which has portraits by American masters; also Assyrian, Greek, and Roman sculpture.

The Colby College Art Museum, Waterville, has paintings by classic and contemporary Europeans and Americans.

The Farnsworth Library and Museum, Rockland,

has 19th and 20th century American fine art.

The Portland Museum of Art comprises the Sweat Museum of American Art and the Sweat Mansion, a Federal-style house built in 1800. Other historic homes in Portland are the Tate House, 1755, and the Victoria Mansion, 1859.

There are 25 institutions of higher learning.

Famous "Down Easters" include Longfellow, Kenneth Roberts, Edna St. Vincent Millay, Kate Douglas Wiggin, Ben Ames Williams, James G. Blaine, Hiram and Hudson Maxim, Cyrus H. K. Curtis.

(See also Index for Portland.)

Maryland

Old Line State, Free State

AREA: 10,577 sq. mi.; rank, 42d. POPULATION (U.S. est. 1975): 4,098,000; rank, 18th. CAPITAL: Annapolis. MOTTO: Fatti Maschi, Parole Femine; Manly Deeds, Womanly Words. FLOWER: Black-eyed Susan. BIRD: Baltimore oriole. TREE: White oak. SONG: Maryland, My Maryland. Seventh of the original 13 states to ratify Constitution; Apr. 28, 1788.

Maryland stretches from the Atlantic Ocean to the Allegheny Mountains with 2 major interruptions, Chesapeake Bay, and the District of Columbia. Both contribute importantly to the state's economy.

The bay cuts off the low coastal plain of the Eastern Shore from the rest of the state, provides both commercial and sports fishing and leads to the port of Baltimore, which handles some $3 billion in imports and exports a year. The 7.11-mi. Chesapeake Bay Highway Bridge spans the bay near Annapolis.

The national capital area provides a market for much of Maryland's produce, and large-scale employment in federal offices, as well as adding to the crowds which enjoy its recreational facilities.

Virginia's Capt. John Smith first explored Maryland, 1608. William Claiborne set up a trading post on Kent Is. in Chesapeake Bay, 1631. Britain granted land to Lord Baltimore (Cecilius Calvert), 1632; his brother Leonard Calvert led 200 settlers to St. Marys River, 1634. An informal Maryland Convention, 1774, headed pre-Revolutionary agitation. The bravery of Maryland troops in the Revolution, as at the Battle of Long Island, won the state its nickname, The Old Line State. In the War of 1812, when a British fleet tried to take Fort McHenry, Marylander Francis Scott Key wrote The Star-Spangled Banner.

Maryland has a diversified economy. Leading industries in number of workers are wholesale and retail trade, government, services, manufacturing. Value added by manufacture totals over $4.7 billion annually. Important manufacturing industries are food products, primary metals, electrical equipment, printing and publishing, apparel, machinery. Per capita income was $6,437 in 1975, 9th highest in the U.S.

Almost half of the land area is covered with forests. About 40% of timber cut is softwood. Stone and cement are leading mineral products; mineral output was valued at $152 million in 1975.

Seafood is an important industry. In a typical year, the fish and shellfish catch has a value of about $22 million. Striped bass is the principal contributor to the fin fish revenues, while oysters account for about 60% of the shellfish, followed by soft-shelled clams.

Most of Maryland's farms are fertile though not extensive. The state's largest cash crops are tobacco, corn, soybeans, apples, and tomatoes. Commercial broilers and dairy products are important. Farm receipts in 1975 totaled $646 million.

The first U.S. steam locomotive, Peter Cooper's Tom Thumb, was built in Baltimore and made its first run on the tracks of the Baltimore & Ohio R.R., 1830.

There are 52 institutions of higher education.

Famous racing events include the Preakness, at Pimlico track, Baltimore; the International at Laurel Race Course, and John B. Campbell Handicap at Bowie. Annapolis is a center for yacht races. Ocean City is a popular summer resort.

Famous historic sites include restored Fort McHenry, Baltimore, near which Francis Scott Key wrote the Star-Spangled Banner in 1814; Antietam Battlefield near Hagerstown (1862); South Mountain Battlefield (1862); Edgar Allan Poe house, Baltimore. The State House, Annapolis (1772), is the oldest still in use in the U.S.

The U.S. Frigate Constellation, which was launched at Baltimore in 1797, has been made a National Historic Landmark in Baltimore.

The Chesapeake Bay Maritime Museum in St. Michael's exhibits the last surviving oyster sloop, a cottage-type lighthouse and models of Baltimore clippers, log canoes, bugeyes, and skipjacks.

Tourism is valued at $902 million a year.

Famous Marylanders include Upton Sinclair, H. L. Mencken, James M. Cain, Benjamin Banneker.

(See also Index for Baltimore.)

Massachusetts

Bay State, Old Colony

AREA: 8,257 sq. mi.; rank, 45th. POPULATION (U.S. est. 1975): 5,828,000; rank, 10th. CAPITAL: Boston. MOTTO: Ense Petit Placidam sub Libertate Quietem: By the Sword We Seek Peace, but Peace Only under Liberty. FLOWER: Mayflower. BIRD: Chickadee. TREE: American elm. SONG: All Hail to Massachusetts. Sixth of the original 13 states to ratify Constitution, Feb. 6, 1788.

Massachusetts has played important roles in the political, intellectual, and economic development of the U.S.

The Pilgrims, seeking religious freedom, made their first settlement at Plymouth, 1620; the following year they gave thanks for their survival with the first Thanksgiving Day. Indian opposition reached a high point in King Philip's War, 1675-76, won by the colonists. Demonstrations against British restrictions set off the "Boston Massacre," 1770, and Boston "tea party," 1773. First bloodshed of the Revolution was at Lexington, 1775.

In Massachusetts ports, a great shipping industry, including the famed China trade, developed, along with large whaling and fishing interests. Abundant waterpower helped create a variety of industries.

Religious freedom, at first restricted by the Puritans, was eventually achieved. In 1867, Mary Baker Eddy founded Christian Science in Lynn. Heavy immigration of Irish, Italians, Poles, Czechs, and French Canadians increased the number of Catholics.

The first free American public school, the Mather, was founded in Dorchester (Boston) in 1639. The state has 119 institutions of higher learning including Harvard and Mass. Institute of Technology.

Commercial fishing, in the rich waters off Massachusetts and the Grand Banks off Newfoundland, was one of the area's earliest industries. Whalers sailed the oceans around the world. Modern trawlers with huge nets help bring in a catch valued at about $78 million in 1975, ranking high among the states.

Massachusetts was a pioneer in the manufacture of textiles and shoes and in creation of specialized machinery for them. The Bay State remains one of the top producers of shoes. A power loom, perfected by Francis Cabot Lowell in 1822, launched cotton manufacturing in Lowell.

Production of electrical machinery, including electronics and communications equipment, has become the leading manufacturing division, in terms of numbers of employees and value added by manufacture. Also important are apparel, metal and food products, and plastics. The state is a leader in production of medical instruments and mini-computers.

Total value added by manufacture is over $11.7 billion a year, placing Massachusetts, despite its relatively small size, 11th among the states. A third of the state's workers are employed in manufacturing. Per capita income was $6,159 in 1975 (U.S. average: $5,834).

Massachusetts' cranberry crop is the nation's 2d largest. Also important are dairy and poultry products, apples, peaches, maple syrup. Farm receipts totaled $201 million in 1975. Mineral production for that year was valued at an est. $52.3 million, mostly of stone, sand, and gravel.

Because of the state's numerous recreational areas and historic landmarks, tourism has become an important factor in the economy of the state. Tourists generate an est. $1.5 billion annually.

Cape Cod has summer theaters, sports, and an artists' colony at Provincetown. Tanglewood, in the Berkshires, has the summer concerts of the Boston Symphony Orchestra.

In New Bedford, the Old Dartmouth Historical Society and Whaling Museum has a large and unique collection of whaling implements, scrimshaw, and logbooks as well as furniture, costumes, and firearms. In Old Deerfield are Memorial Hall (1799), Hall Tavern (1765), Parson Ashley House (1732).

In Pittsfield, the Berkshire Athenaeum has memorabilia of Herman Melville, who lived there while writing Moby Dick; a scrimshaw and whaling collection, and a large library. The Berkshire Museum, Pittsfield, has paintings by Rubens, Van Dyck, Reynolds, Murillo, the Hudson River artists, etc.; mineral and animal rooms; one of the sledges with which Robert E. Peary reached the North Pole.

In Plymouth, Pilgrim Hall contains relics of the Mayflower Pilgrims, including swords of Myles Standish, Bibles of Gov. William Bradford and John Alden, and the cradle of Peregrine White, first child born in the colony.

Old Sturbridge Village, in Sturbridge, is a recreated early New England village of 35 authentic homes and shops, shown functioning.

The Sterling and Francine Clark Art Institute, Williamstown, displays 14th-17th century European paintings, a large collection of Impressionists, sculpture, silver, and drawings.

The Worcester Art Museum presents a survey of art through 50 centuries, stressing early American painting, pre-Columbian, and contemporary arts. Also in Worcester, the John W. Higgins Armory displays medieval armor, and the American Antiquarian Society has a collection of early printing.

Famous "Bay Staters" include Samuel, John, and John Quincy Adams, Hancock, Revere, Bryant, Emerson, Hawthorne, Holmes, Whittier, Poe, Thoreau, Alger, James, Emily Dickinson, Louisa May Alcott, Lucy Stone, Clara Barton, Whistler, Sargent, Homer, Morse, Elias Howe.

(See also Index for Boston, Springfield.)

Michigan
Great Lake State, Wolverine State

AREA: 58,216 sq. mi.; rank, 23d. **POPULATION** (U.S. est. 1975): 9,157,000; rank, 7th. **CAPITAL:** Lansing. **MOTTO:** Si Quaeris Peninsulam Amoenam Circumspice, If You Seek a Pleasant Peninsula, Look about You. **FLOWER:** Apple blossom. **BIRD:** Robin. **TREE:** White pine. **SONG** (unofficial): Michigan, My Michigan. **ENTERED UNION:** Jan. 26, 1837; rank, 26th.

Bordering on 4 of the 5 Great Lakes, Michigan is divided into an Upper and Lower Peninsula by the Straits of Mackinac, which link Lakes Michigan and Huron. The 2 parts of the state are connected by the Mackinac Bridge, which has the 3d longest suspension span in the U. S. To the N, separating Michigan from Canada, is the Sault Ste. Marie (Soo) Ship Canal, one of the world's most heavily used waterways.

Rich orchards near the shores of Lake Michigan grow large fruit crops; the Upper Peninsula produces important amounts of iron, copper, and other minerals, and the state's lakes and forests make it a highly popular vacationland.

While Michigan has the world's greatest concentration of motor vehicle manufacturers, it is also a leader in many other lines including prepared cereals, pickles, machine tools, hardware, steel springs, furniture, padding and upholstering, industrial patterns, nonferrous castings, industrial leather belts, paperboard mills, and gray iron foundries.

The state ranked 6th in the U. S. in terms of value added by manufacture, $27.1 billion. Motor vehicles and equipment accounted for $8.3 billion of that and also provided the most jobs, almost 400,000. Other major industry groups were primary metals and metal products, machinery, food, and chemicals. Per capita income was $6,240 in 1975, 10th highest in the U.S.

Tourist attractions are many and visitors spend $2.3 billion annually, 6th highest among the states. The state has 36,000 mi. of streams, over 11,000 lakes and the longest freshwater shoreline (facing 4 of the Great Lakes). Water sports, music festivals, skiing, winter carnivals, fishing, and hunting are among attractions.

There are 4 national forests, 80 state parks and recreational areas, and numerous canoe trails.

Farm receipts in 1975 totaled $1.7 billion, more than half from crops. The state ranked 6th in the U.S. in number of milk cows. It grew the most tart and sweet cherries and ranked high in apples, pears, grapes, and sugar beets. Truck farm vegetables were valued at $160 million; forest products at $1.75 billion.

Iron ore is the largest source of Michigan's income from minerals. With continued depletion of high-grade iron ore deposits, production of high-grade pellets from low-grade taconite iron ore has increased, amounting to over 85% of the total output.

Michigan was 2d only to Minnesota among the states in value of iron ore output, $340 million in 1975, up 60%. It was also a leading producer of gypsum, peat, iodine, bromine, salt, magnesium compounds, lime, gravel, cement. Total output was est. at $1.2 billion.

There are 93 institutions of higher education.

French fur traders and missionaries visited the region, 1616, set up a mission at Sault Ste. Marie, 1641, and a settlement there, 1668. The whole region went to Britain, 1763. During the Revolution, the British led attacks from the area on American settlements to the south until Anthony Wayne defeated their Indian allies at Fallen Timbers, Ohio, 1794. The British returned, 1812, seized Fort Mackinac and Detroit. Oliver H. Perry's Lake Erie victory and William H. Harrison's troops, who carried the war to the Thames River in Canada, 1813, freed Michigan once more.

Famous Michiganders include Gerald Ford, Henry Ford, Robert Ingersoll, Thomas Dewey, Milton A. McRae, James Oliver Curwood, Stewart Edward White, Paul de Kruif, Gen. George Custer, Edgar Guest, Ellen Burstyn, Betty Hutton, Diana Ross, Mike Marshall, Danny Thomas.

(See also Index for Detroit and Kalamazoo.)

Minnesota
North Star State, Gopher State

AREA: 84,068 sq. mi.; rank, 12th. **POPULATION** (U.S. est. 1975): 3,926,000; rank, 19th. **CAPITAL:** St. Paul. **MOTTO:** L'Etoile du Nord, Star of the North. **FLOWER:** Showy lady's-slipper. **BIRD:** Loon. **TREE:** Red (Norway) pine. **SONG:** Hail! Minnesota. **ENTERED UNION:** May 11, 1858; rank, 32d.

Minnesota is a land rich in natural resources. Its fertile prairies support large crops and an important dairy industry, its mines yield most of the iron ore produced in the U.S., its forests produce mountains of pulpwood, its manufacturing is varied and vigorous, its thousands of lakes and other attractions lure millions of sportsmen and vacationers.

Known as the "land of 10,000 lakes," Minnesota actually has 12,034 over 10 acres in size. Lake Itaska is the source of the Mississippi River. Two-thirds of the state is rolling prairie. Highest point is Eagle Mt. in the NE, 2,301 ft.

Fishing, hunting, water sports, and winter sports

are among attractions for more than 5.5 million vacationers who spend some $1.7 billion yearly. There are numerous state parks and recreation areas.

Minnesota produces about 63% of the iron ore mined in the U.S., despite depletion of the high-grade ore in the famed Mesabi and other ranges in the NE part of the state. Lost production from the huge open pit and underground mines is being replaced by high-grade pellets refined from low-grade taconite iron ore. By 1975, shipments of taconite pellets comprised about 77% of the total iron ore value.

One taconite company, Reserve Mining, was enjoined in 1974 from polluting Lake Superior drinking waters but won a stay of the court order.

Iron ore production in 1975 was valued at $1.01 billion, the major part of the total mineral production.

Manufacturing has grown and diversified. Largest industries are food processing and machinery. Also important are electrical machinery, chemicals, paper, stone-clay-glass products, apparel, lumber, fabricated metal products. Value added by manufacture is $6.7 billion.

Per capita income was $5.754 in 1975.

Much of the land is richly fertile. With $3.9 billion in farm receipts for 1975, Minnesota ranked 6th among the states. About 55% of that income was from livestock products, the rest from crops. Ranking 3d in number of milk cows in 1975, the state was the leader in butter, turkeys, and non-fat dry milk.

Minnesota's farms grew the most oats and it ranked among the top states in spring wheat, corn, rye, alfalfa, and sugar beets.

Forest products have a yearly estimated value of $576 million, most of it in pulpwood.

Nationally known is the Mayo Clinic at Rochester, founded by Drs. William J. and Charles H. Mayo.

Minnesota has 66 institutions of higher learning.

The Minnesota Orchestra, the Tyrone Guthrie Theater in Minneapolis, and the St. Olaf College Choir in Northfield are widely known.

Other attractions are the St. Paul Winter Carnival, Minneapolis Aquatennial, and State Fair. Minnehaha Falls in Minneapolis became famous in Longfellow's "Song of Hiawatha." A new Minnesota zoo is to open in Apple Valley in 1977.

Fur traders and missionaries from French Canada opened the region in the 17th century. Britain took the area east of the Mississippi, 1763. The U.S. took over that portion after the Revolution and in 1803 bought the western area as part of the Louisiana Purchase. The U.S. built present Fort Snelling, 1820, bought lands from the Indians, 1837. In the Civil War, Minnesota was first to offer troops to the Union. Sioux Indians staged a bloody uprising, 1862, and were driven from the state.

Famous Minnesotans include Hubert Humphrey, Walter F. Mondale, Charles Lindbergh, Sinclair Lewis, F. Scott Fitzgerald, Thorstein Veblen, Cass Gilbert, Paul Manship, E. G. Marshall, Blanche Yurka.

(See also Index for Minneapolis and St. Paul.)

Mississippi
Magnolia State

AREA: 47,716 sq. mi.; rank, 32d. **POPULATION** (U.S. est. 1975): 2,346,000; rank, 29th. **CAPITAL:** Jackson. **MOTTO:** Virtute et Armis, By Valor and Arms. **FLOWER:** Magnolia. **TREE:** Magnolia. **BIRD:** Mockingbird. **SONG:** Go, Mississippi! **ENTERED UNION:** Dec. 10, 1817; rank, 20th.

Mississippi's economy, long based on one crop, "King Cotton," has become balanced and diversified, thanks to promotion of industry, other crops, tourism, and federal agency installations.

The land slopes from the NE hills, where the high point is Woodall Mt. (806 ft.), to the Delta, a cotton-producing alluvial plain in the W and NW lying between the Yazoo River and the Mississippi, which flows along the state's western border. The land also slopes to the S where the sandy beaches on the Gulf of Mexico have created a popular vacationland.

Hernando de Soto explored the area, 1540, discovered the Mississippi River, 1541. La Salle traced the river from Illinois to its mouth and claimed the entire valley for France, 1682. First settlement was the French Fort Maurepas, near Ocean Springs, 1699. The area was ceded to Britain, 1763; American settlers followed. During the Revolution, Spain seized part of the area and refused to leave even after the U.S. acquired title at the end of the Revolution, finally moving out, 1798. Mississippi seceded 1861. Union forces captured Corinth and Vicksburg and destroyed Jackson and much of Meridian.

Soybeans have taken over as Mississippi's largest crop; the state ranks 3d in cotton production. Other important farm products include pecans, sweet potatoes, rice, and sugarcane. Poultry and eggs are also important. Farm receipts totaled $1.3 billion in 1975.

Biloxi has a large seafood industry, operating deep-sea trawlers for shrimp and oysters. Value of the catch is over $15 million a year. Home-pond catfish production was valued at $28 million in 1974.

With more than 50% of the land classified as forest, timber products yielded over $1 billion in 1974. The state produces the most hardwood pulpwood, much hardwood lumber, and slashpine products, including fiberboard, kraft paper, newsprint.

Petroleum production was valued at $305 million for 1975. Natural gas output was valued at $25 million; total value of mineral production was est. at $388 million.

Mississippi has achieved considerable industrial expansion. The main fields have been lumber, along with furniture and paper, food processing, apparel, chemicals, electronics, machinery.

Per capita income was $4,041 in 1975, lowest in the nation. Annual pay for public school teachers was $8,338 in 1974, also the nation's lowest. But the legislature provided 25% increases in 1975.

A $250 million NASA space installation is used as a center for International Earth Sciences by NOAA and NASA.

There are 45 institutions of higher learning.

Mississippi became the last state to abandon prohibition, adopting a local-option law May 21, 1966.

Tourism is of growing economic importance. It is estimated that out-of-state tourists spend over $398 million a year in the state.

Gulfport holds an annual yacht regatta and a fishing rodeo in July, Biloxi has a Mardi Gras, Pass Christian has a tarpon rodeo. A dozen cities sponsor pilgrimages each spring featuring visits to ante-bellum mansions.

In Vicksburg National Military Park, visitors may see remains of forts, trenches, and other works of the 1863 siege of the city.

The Old Court House Museum in Vicksburg, built in 1858 by slave labor, has a museum with relics of the siege of Vicksburg, including flags, weapons, newspapers printed on the back of wallpaper, etc.

The Lauren Rogers Library and Museum of Art in Laurel contains works of 19th and early 20th century Americans and Europeans, local artifacts, and an unusual basket collection (about half of them Indian). Pre-historic Indian mounds include one covering 8 acres 12 mi. NE of Natchez.

Famous Mississippians include Jefferson Davis, James Street, William Faulkner, Eudora Welty, Dana Andrews, B. B. King, Bobby Gentry, Elvis Presley, and Leontyne Price.

Missouri
Show Me State

AREA: 69,686 sq. mi.; rank, 19th. **POPULATION** (US. est. 1975): 4,763,000; rank, 15th. **CAPITAL:** Jefferson City. **MOTTO:** Salus Populi Suprema Lex Esto, The Welfare of the People Shall Be the Supreme Law. **FLOWER:** Hawthorn. **BIRD:** Eastern bluebird. **TREE:** Dogwood. **SONG:** Missouri Waltz. **ENTERED UNION:** Aug. 10, 1821; rank, 24th.

The gateway through which the pioneers passed on

their way West, Missouri today is a leading manufacturing state, with aerospace and a wide variety of other industries; it is the nation's largest producer of lead; it ranks high among the states in agricultural products; its areas of scenic and historic interest attract over 28 million vacationers each year.

Gently rolling hills in the N and W produce large crops, and support cattle, sheep, and hogs. The Ozark highlands in the S are famed for fishing, hunting, and rugged scenery, including numerous caves and springs. The "delta" area in the SE produces soybeans, cotton, and melons.

The Mississippi forms the state's boundary on the E; the Missouri forms part of the boundary in the W, then flows across the state to join the Mississippi above St. Louis.

Manufacturing, paced by the state's large aerospace industries, is the top income producer and employs more persons than any other segment of the economy. Value added by manufacture is over $9.1 billion yearly. Transportation equipment, including space capsules, rocket engines, aircraft, and auto assemblies, ranks first, followed by food processing, esp. meat packing, grain milling, beer, and other beverages. Also important are chemicals, printing, metal products, machinery, shoes. Corncob pipes and charcoal are well-known products.

Agriculture is also an important income producer. Farm receipts in 1975 totaled $2.5 billion, 60% from livestock products. Missouri ranked 4th among the states in hogs, cattle, and turkeys. It has large soybean, corn, and clover crops. Also important are winter wheat, tobacco, apples, peaches, alfalfa, popcorn.

Missouri is rich in minerals. Its output of lead, valued at $221 million for 1975, was the largest in the U.S. Total mineral production value was worth $672 million. It was also a leader in barite and lime. Other products include cement, coal, iron ore, copper, zinc, asphalt.

Per capita income was $5,387 in 1975.

Tourism, described as the 3d largest industry, produces $1.3 billion annually. There is a wide variety of vacation facilities; large resort areas include Lake of the Ozarks, Lake Taneycomo and Table Rock Lake.

Missouri has endeared itself to generations of Americans with its river lore, folk tales, and especially the writings of Mark Twain (Samuel L. Clemens). Statues of 2 of his creations, Tom Sawyer and Huckleberry Finn, stand in Hannibal, his boyhood home. His birthplace near Florida, Mo., has been enshrined in Mark Twain State Park.

The farm birthplace of notorious bandit Jesse James (1847-1882) is near Excelsior Springs. A log cabin built by U.S. Grant is near St. Louis. Near Diamond, the farm where George Washington Carver, agricultural scientist, was born is now a National Monument. The Harry S. Truman Library, near Independence, contains presidential papers and memorabilia. Mr. Truman is buried in the library courtyard.

The St. Joseph Museum in St. Joseph stresses the natural history and wildlife of the region and has exhibits on Indian tribes from Alaska to Florida. Also in St. Joseph is the Pony Express Museum.

There are 81 institutions of higher learning. The nation's first Journalism School, founded 1908, is at the University of Missouri in Columbia.

DeSoto visited the area, 1541. French hunters and lead miners made the first settlement, c. 1735, at Ste. Genevieve. The U.S. acquired Missouri as part of the Louisiana Purchase, 1803. The fur trade and the Santa Fe Trail provided prosperity and adventure; St. Louis became the "jump-off" point for pioneers on their way West. Pro- and anti-slavery forces battled each other there during the Civil War.

Famous Missourians include Harry Truman, John J. Pershing, Omar Bradley, Mark Twain, Zoe Akins, Sara Teasdale, T. S. Eliot, Luman H. Long, George Washington Carver, Shelley Winters, Gladys Swarthout, Helen Traubel, Thomas Hart Benton, Ken Holtzman, Mel Stottlemyre, Bernarr Macfadden.

(See also Index for Kansas City and St. Louis.)

Montana
Treasure State

AREA: 147,138 sq. mi.; rank, 4th. **POPULATION** (U.S. est. 1975): 748,000; rank, 43d. **CAPITAL:** Helena. **MOTTO:** Oro y Plata, Gold and Silver. **FLOWER:** Bitterroot. **TREE:** Ponderosa pine. **BIRD:** Western meadowlark. **SONG:** Montana. **ENTERED UNION:** Nov. 8, 1889; rank, 41st.

The Rocky Mountains, with snow-capped peaks, forested slopes, broad valleys, and many lakes, cover the western 40% of Montana; the rest is High Plains country devoted to grazing and farming. Montana is rich in minerals, hydroelectric power, and impressive scenery. Highest mountain is Granite Peak, 12,799 ft.

Agriculture plays a vital role in Montana's economy, along with manufacturing, mining, tourism, recreation. Per capita income was $5,434 in 1975.

Oceans of grain cover much of Montana's plains; it ranks high among the states in wheat and barley output. Also grown are rye, oats, flaxseed, sugar beets, and potatoes. Montana ranks 6th in sheep and high in cattle. Farm receipts totaled over $1.1 billion in 1975, more than half from crops.

Manufacturing industries have grown, with value added by manufacture over $515 million a year. Processing of forest products and primary metal industries are most important and have the most employees, followed by food processing. Wood products include: pulp, plywood, and lumber. The state ships more than 3 million Christmas trees annually.

Total mineral production for 1975 was est. at $560 million, with petroleum accounting for $237 million and copper $128 million. Other products include silver, gold, natural gas. Increasing amounts of coal are strip-mined: 14 million tons in 1974, 21 million in 1975.

Out-of-state tourists spend an est. $398 million annually. Tourist attractions include hunting, fishing, skiing, dude ranching.

Hunters annually take about 100,000 deer, 17,000 antelope, 10,000 elk, 1,100 black bear, 500 moose, 600 mountain goats.

Glacier National Park, on the Continental Divide, is a scenic and recreational wonderland, with 60 glaciers, 200 lakes and many trout streams.

Flathead Lake, in the NW, covers 189 sq. mi. Fort Peck Reservoir, in the NE, covers 382.8 sq. mi.

French explorers, the Verendrye brothers, visited the region, 1742. The U.S. acquired the area partly through the Louisiana Purchase, 1803, and partly through the explorations of Lewis and Clark, 1805-06. Fur traders and missionaries established posts in the early 19th century. Indian uprisings hit their highwater mark in the Battle of the Little Big Horn, in which Col. George Custer and his 264 men were wiped out, 1876. The coming of the Northern Pacific Railway, 1883, spurred farming, cattle raising, and mining and brought population growth.

Important historical site is Custer Battlefield National Cemetery, in Big Horn County (near Hardin).

There are 7 Indian reservations, covering over 5 million acres; tribes are Blackfeet, Crow, Confederated Salish & Kootenai, Assiniboine, Gros Ventre, Sioux, Northern Cheyenne, Chippewa, Cree. Population of the reservations is approximately 25,500.

The Museum of the Plains Indian, on the Blackfeet Reservation near Browning, features exhibits of historic and contemporary arts and crafts of the Northern Plains Indians and an Indian craft shop.

There are 12 colleges and universities.

The Historical Society of Montana, in Helena, has paintings, dioramas, and other exhibits of Montana's Indian and buffalo days, mining camps, frontier settlements, cattle roundups. Outstanding is the collection of nearly 100 Charles M. Russell paintings.

Famous Montanans include Gary Cooper, Myrna Loy, Mike Mansfield, Chet Huntley, Charles M. Rus-

sell, Will James, Jeannette Rankin.
(See also Index for Billings.)

Nebraska
Cornhusker State

AREA: 77,227 sq. mi.; rank, 15th. POPULATION (U.S. est. 1975): 1,546,000; rank, 35th. CAPITAL: Lincoln. MOTTO: Equality Before the Law. FLOWER: Goldenrod. TREE: Cottonwood. BIRD: Western meadowlark. SONG: Beautiful Nebraska. ENTERED UNION: Mar. 1, 1867; rank, 37th.

Fields of corn, wheat, and sorghum cover the Nebraska plain, which slopes gently toward the Missouri River, the eastern border of the state; vast herds of cattle roam the grassy sandhills which rise to the W and end in the broken tablelands marking the foothills of the Rockies.

With more than 23 million acres under cultivation, Nebraska is an agricultural stronghold, an important grain and livestock producer. Many of its manufacturing industries are agriculture-related.

But manufacturing has expanded and diversified, broadening the state's economic base. Firms making electronic components, auto accessories, pharmaceuticals, and other sophisticated products have joined the older industries.

Processing of meat, grain, and dairy products is by far the largest manufacturing field and employs the largest number of workers, accounting for more than a third of the total value added by manufacture, which is estimated at almost $2 billion.

Other important manufacturing fields are electrical machinery and other machinery, especially farm equipment; chemicals, metal products, transportation equipment, instruments, and related products. Per capita income was $6,175 in 1975 ($341 above the U.S. average).

Nebraska ranked 5th among the states in total farm receipts for 1975; $4 billion, with the larger part coming from livestock products. Its cattle herds ranked 4th among the states; it had 6.5 million cattle in 1976. It ranked 6th in hogs. Nebraska was also a leader in sorghum, winter wheat, corn, and rye. Also important are soybeans, sugar beets, and oats.

Mineral production in Nebraska was valued at $103 million for 1975. Oil continued to be the most important product, valued at $45 million. Other products included cement, lime, pumice, sand, and gravel.

Nebraska has a unicameral or one-house legislature with 49 members elected on a non-partisan ballot. All electric power facilities are state or municipally owned.

Nebraska has 30 institutions of higher education.

Arbor Lodge State Park at Nebraska City is a memorial to J. Sterling Morton, founder of Arbor Day, which is observed as a legal holiday on his birthday, Apr. 22. Boys Town is just west of Omaha.

The Sheldon Memorial Art Gallery at the Univ. of Nebraska, Lincoln, in a building designed by Philip Johnson, has works by many leading modern artists.

The Joslyn Art Museum, Omaha, has works by Titian, El Greco, Rembrandt, Goya, Renoir, etc.; exhibits of furniture, the early West, fur trade, Indian art.

Pioneer Village, Minden, has some 30,000 items of Americana displayed in a rural schoolhouse, depot, general store, fort, fire house, sod house, Pony Express station, etc. The Stuhr Museum of the Prairie Pioneer has 57 original 19th century buildings near Grand Island.

The House of Yesterday, Hastings, has exhibits of pioneer days and natural science and the J. M. McDonald Planetarium. The Strategic Aerospace Museum is in Bellevue.

Spanish and French explorers and fur traders visited the area prior to the 1803 Louisiana Purchase. Lewis and Clark passed through, 1804-06. First permanent settlement was Bellevue, near Omaha, 1823. Many Civil War veterans settled under free land terms of the 1862 Homestead Act; struggles followed between homesteaders and ranchers. Under

Gov. Charles W. Bryan, farm mortgage moratoriums were declared, 1933, during the Depression.

Famous Nebraskans include William Jennings and Charles W. Bryan, the Rev. Edward J. Flanagan, Willa Cather, Mignon Eberhart, Rollin Kirby, Clare Briggs, Gen. Alfred Gruenther, Roscoe Pound, Darryl Zanuck, Susette (Bright Eyes) La Flesche.
(See also Index for Omaha)

Nevada
Sagebrush State, Battle Born State

AREA: 110,540 sq. mi.; rank, 7th. POPULATION (U.S. est. 1975): 592,000; rank, 46th. CAPITAL: Carson City. MOTTO: All for Our Country. FLOWER: Sagebrush. BIRD: Mountain bluebird. TREE: Single-leaf pinon. SONG: Home Means Nevada. ENTERED UNION: Oct. 31, 1864; rank, 36th.

Nevada lies mostly in the Great Basin, a rugged plateau region broken by mountain chains running N-S. It is enclosed on the E by the Rockies and the Wasatch Range in Utah, and on the W by California's Sierra Nevada and Cascade Ranges which rob the clouds of moisture, making Nevada's climate extremely dry.

One of the smallest states in population, Nevada has attracted large numbers of outsiders, starting with the famed rush to the Comstock Lode (1859) and other gold and silver mines. Today, the attractions are legalized gambling, highly-developed entertainment and recreation facilities, and lenient divorce laws requiring only 6-weeks residence. New floods of visitors were attracted in the 1970s by lenient marriage laws.

Spending by visitors, $950 million a year, is the biggest factor in Nevada's economy. More than 12 million from out of state, about 50 times the state population, visit annually.

Tourist-connected industries—hotels, casinos, amusement and recreation facilities—make up the largest employment category. Per capita income was $6,524 in 1975, 8th highest in the U.S.

State collections from gaming were $72,455,288 in 1974-75, up $7,775,297 from 1973-74. This income provides about 45% of the state's revenue. Gross gambling receipts for 1975 were $1.2 billion. Nevada officials state that Florida, California, and New York have higher gambling revenues from pari-mutuel race betting.

There are big resort areas, with skiing as well as sunbathing, near Lake Tahoe, Reno, Las Vegas. Ghost towns, rodeos, trout fishing, water skiing, and deer hunting are other attractions.

Large recreation areas include those at Pyramid Lake, wholly within the state; Lake Tahoe, partly in California; Lake Mead, formed by Hoover Dam, and Lake Mohave, formed by Davis Dam, both in Lake Mead National Recreation Area, shared with Arizona.

Mineral production value for 1975 was est. at $229 million with copper accounting for $97 million. Nevada is also a leader in gold, mercury, lithium, barite, and silver. With rising prices, old gold mines have been reopened.

Nevada is the largest manufacturer of gaming devices. Also important are electronic devices, chemicals, forest products, suntan lotion, stone-clay-glass products. About $161 million is the est. value added annually by growing manufacturing industries. Warehousing has become a major industry; the state has no inventory tax on goods not sold in Nevada.

Farm receipts totaled $142 million for 1975, more than 80% from livestock products. The dry climate makes much of the state more suitable for grazing than for crops, although large-scale irrigation has expanded the growing areas.

The Nevada Test Site, NW of Las Vegas, is a proving ground for various atomic devices.

There are 6 state institutions of higher learning.

The Nevada State Museum, Carson City, occupies a former U.S. Mint, and exhibits coins, habitat groups of mammals and birds of the Great Basin area, Indian baskets, full-scale replicas of underground mining operations, and thousands of arrowheads.

Nevada was first explored by Spaniards in 1776. Fur trader Peter Skene Ogden trapped the region, 1825 and 1828; Jedediah Smith, another trader, crossed the state, 1826 and 1827. The area was acquired by the U.S., 1848, at the end of the Mexican War. First settlement, Mormon Station, now Genoa, was established 1849. In the early 20th century, Nevada adopted progressive measures such as the initiative, referendum, recall and woman suffrage.

Famous Nevadans include Dr. Robert C. Lynch, Sarah Winnemucca Hopkins, Pat McCarran, Walter Van Tilburg Clark.

(See also Index for Las Vegas, Reno.)

New Hampshire

Granite State

AREA: 9,304 sq. mi.; rank, 44th. **POPULATION** (U.S. est. 1975): 818,000; rank, 42d. **CAPITAL:** Concord. **MOTTO:** Live Free or Die. **FLOWER:** Purple lilac. **BIRD:** Purple finch. **TREE:** Paper (white) birch. **SONG:** Old New Hampshire. Ninth of the original 13 states to ratify the Constitution, June 21, 1788.

One of the 6 New England states, New Hampshire is a land of impressive mountains, picturesque lakes, swift rivers, and, in the north, thick forests. Mountain slopes provide excellent ski trails. Numerous lakes and streams afford fishing for trout, bass, pickerel, perch, whitefish.

Abundant water power early turned New Hampshire into an industrial state, and manufacturing is still the principal source of income. Soil and climate have curtailed agricultural growth, but scenic and recreation resources have been developed and the tourist-vacation business, over $400 million a year, ranks 2d in its contribution to the state's economy. Per capita income was $5,210 in 1975.

In 1964, to raise funds to support education, the state ran the first legal sweepstakes lottery in the U.S. since 1894 (in that year, a lottery in Louisiana was outlawed). Profits from the state lottery are turned over to local school districts.

Most important industrial products are shoes and boots, electrical and other machinery, wool and other textiles, and paper. Most factories are concentrated along the Merrimack and Connecticut Rivers, and in the seacoast area. Manufacturing employs about 100,-000 workers. Value added by manufacture is $1.5 billion a year.

Farm receipts for 1975 totaled $72 million, about 55% from dairy and poultry products. Crops include apples, peaches, hay, corn, and maple syrup.

Mineral products, mainly sand, gravel, and stone for construction, were valued at $13 million for 1975.

Recreation and vacation attractions include Lake Winnipesaukee, largest of 1,300 lakes and ponds; the White Mountains, with skiing and scenic beauty; beaches on the Atlantic Coast, and historic sites.

One-third of the state is over 2,000 ft. above sea level. Highest land in northeast U.S. is the Presidential Range of the White Mountains, with Mt. Washington, 6,288 ft. (first cog railway in world opened 1869). National forests cover 677,559 acres; 142 state forests and parks, 63,805 acres.

State-owned parks include areas in Crawford and Franconia Notches; the latter includes the Old Man of the Mountains, described by Nathaniel Hawthorne as the Great Stone Face.

Portsmouth is the state's only port. Manchester is the largest city.

First explorers to visit the New Hampshire area were England's Martin Pring, 1603, and Samuel Champlain, 1605. First settlement was Little Harbor, near Rye, 1623. Indian raids were halted, 1759, by Robert Rogers' Rangers. Before the Revolution, New Hampshire men seized a British fort at Portsmouth, 1774, and drove the royal governor out, 1775. Three regiments served in the Continental Army and scores

of privateers raided British shipping.

New Hampshire shared the educational pioneering of Massachusetts Bay from 1642; it established its first free public library at Dublin, 1822.

There are 24 institutions of higher education.

The MacDowell colony at Peterborough, established in 1908 in honor of Edward MacDowell, is a summer haven for writers, composers, artists.

The Currier Gallery of Art, Manchester, exhibits silver by Paul Revere, textiles, hooked rugs, pewter, and glass, and works by old and modern masters.

The New Hampshire Historical Society, Concord, has a museum displaying New Hampshire furniture, silver, pewter, glass, china, quilts, costumes, etc.

Famous men and women included Daniel Webster, Salmon P. Chase, Franklin Pierce, Robert Frost, Charles A. Dana, Horace Greeley, Sarah Buell Hale, Mary Baker Eddy, Ralph Adams Cram, Daniel Chester French, Augustus Saint-Gaudens.

New Jersey

Garden State

AREA: 7,836 sq. mi.; rank, 46th. **POPULATION** (U.S. est. 1975): 7,316,000; rank, 9th. **CAPITAL:** Trenton. **MOTTO:** Liberty and Prosperity. **FLOWER:** Purple violet. **BIRD:** Eastern goldfinch. **TREE:** Red oak. **SONG:** New Jersey Loyalty Song. Third of the original 13 states to ratify the Constitution, Dec. 18, 1787.

Smallest of the Middle Atlantic states, New Jersey has the most people (953.1) per sq. mi. of the 50 states, ranks near the top in manufacturing, is rich in poultry and vegetable production, and has a flourishing resort industry. About 63% of the state's land area is in farms and forests.

There are vast shipping facilities, and New Jersey divides authority over important airports, harbors, tunnels, and bridges with the Port Authority of N.Y. and N. J. and the states of Delaware and Pennsylvania.

New Jersey has a heavy concentration of factories, highways, railroads, and farms, and is a leader in many fields.

Highly industrialized, New Jersey ranks 7th among the states in value added by manufacture, over $17.7 billion annually. It ranks 1st among the states in chemical products, having large pharmaceutical, synthetics, basic chemical, and paint industries.

Per capita income was $6,629 in 1975, 5th highest in the U.S.

It is also a leader in other manufacturing lines: apparel, food processing, electrical and other machinery, stone-clay-glass products, printing, rubber and plastics, petroleum products, leather products. It has a large concentration of research installations.

New Jersey also ranks high in the U. S. in gross income per farm acre. Chief crops are tomatoes, corn, asparagus, apples, cranberries, peaches, spinach. Poultry and dairy products are also important.

Total farm receipts in 1975 were $331 million, two-thirds from crops.

Mineral production is mostly stone, sand, and gravel, mainly for construction work. Zinc, peat, and clays are among other products. Total value was $122 million in 1975.

Large refineries, which process oil from out of state, have a total crude capacity of more than 500,-000 barrels a day.

The commercial fishing catch is valued at over $19 million a year.

There are 64 institutions of higher learning.

Atlantic City, Ocean City, Cape May, Asbury Park, Point Pleasant, Wildwood, are among more than 100 resorts. The tourist industry generates over $1.2 billion in business annually. There are 40 state parks with 55,717 acres. The 10 state forests comprise 176,-652 acres. There are several historic sites relating to the Revolutionary War period.

In Camden, the Walt Whitman House, home of the poet from 1884 until his death, Mar. 26, 1892, contains books, mementos, and furnishings used by Whitman. The U. S. Army Signal Corps Museum, Fort Monmouth, contains communications equipment from the earliest visual methods to modern satellites.

The Montclair Art Museum exhibits art of many periods and lands, emphasizing the American. The Newark Museum is a museum of art, science and industry, including American paintings and sculpture; Chinese, Japanese and Tibetan art; collections of birds, insects, minerals, shells, glass, ceramics, and jewelry. The New Jersey Historical Society Museum, Newark, has old New Jersey rooms and collections of New Jersey furniture, paintings, china, costumes, etc.

The Garden State Arts Center is an amphitheater for concerts and stage shows at Telegraph Hill Park.

The Johnston Historical Museum, adjacent to the national hq. of the Boy Scouts of America, New Brunswick, depicts Scouting history, has a weather station, ham radio station, and 22-acre Outdoor Museum of Nature and Conservation.

The Edison National Historic Site, West Orange, displays Thomas Alva Edison's chemical laboratory, machine shop, and library; a reproduction of the "Black Maria," Edison's first movie studio; originals or replicas of his phonograph, incandescent lamp, and movie camera. In South Orange, the New Jersey Fire Museum displays 19th Century hand-pumpers, hose carts, helmets, etc.

In Trenton, the New Jersey State Museum displays the state's achievements in the arts, sciences, history, technology, and industry, and has a planetarium.

The New Jersey Meadowlands, lying close to the state's northeastern metropolitan centers, are the target of new development plans, including a New Jersey Sports Complex with a football stadium and race track. The Football Giants (formerly N.Y. Giants) planned to play their 1976 football season in the stadium.

The state's network of modern highways gives New Jersey more miles of roads per sq. mi. of area than any other state. There are 16 airlines and 17 railroads. New Jersey has the most rail trackage per sq. mi. in the U.S.

The Lenni Lenape (Delaware) Indians had mostly peaceful relations with European colonists who arrived after the explorers Verrazano, 1524, and Henry Hudson, 1609. The Dutch were first. When the British took New Netherland, 1664, the area between the Delaware and Hudson Rivers was given to Lord John Berkeley and Sir George Carteret. New Jersey was the scene of nearly 100 battles, large and small, during the Revolution, including Trenton, 1776, Princeton 1777, Monmouth, 1778. The state abolished slavery, 1846.

Famous New Jerseyites include Cleveland, Wilson, Hamilton, Paine, Burr, Molly Pitcher, Gen. George McClellan, Edison, Whitman, James Fenimore Cooper, George Inness, Paul Robeson, Alexander Woolcott, Joyce Kilmer, Stephen Crane.

(See also Index for Newark.)

New Mexico
Land of Enchantment

AREA: 121,666 sq. mi.; rank, 5th. POPULATION (U.S. est. 1975): 1,147,000; rank, 37th. CAPITAL: Santa Fe. MOTTO: Crescit Eundo, It Grows as it Goes. FLOWER: Yucca. BIRD: Roadrunner. TREE: Piñon (nut pine). SONGS: O, Fair New Mexico, Asi Es Nuevo Mejico. ENTERED UNION: Jan. 6, 1912; rank, 47th.

New Mexico is a land of contrasts, presenting remnants of old Indian and Spanish cultures along with nuclear and space research centers; mountains over 13,000 ft., and a cavern 829 ft. below ground; ski slopes, and desert vistas.

Vast areas are made fertile by irrigation through dams and reservoirs on the Rio Grande, San Juan, Pecos, Canadian, Cimarron, Gila, and San Francisco Rivers.

The climate is dry and invigorating; annual rainfall is 7" to 16"; mean temperature is 50°, reaching 100° on the plains in summer.

National forests cover 13,281 sq. mi. Douglas fir, Ponderosa pine, and spruce are cut for timber. Almost 34% of the land is federally owned.

Minerals are New Mexico's richest natural resource, and the state leads the U.S. in output of uranium and potassium salts.

Mineral production reached a total value of $2.16 billion in 1975, up 11%. Petroleum accounted for the largest single part of this, $770 million, followed by natural gas, $452 million, and copper, $179 million. New Mexico ranks high among the states in perlite, and carbon dioxide (dry ice) production. Its rich variety of minerals also includes gold, silver, zinc, lead, molybdenum.

Farm receipts accounted for $636 million for 1975, more than two-thirds from livestock products. New Mexico ranked 7th among the states in number of sheep. Cotton, pecans, and sorghum are the most important field crops. Also grown are corn, peanuts, beans, onions, and lettuce.

Manufacturing industries have grown and diversified. Principal lines are food products, chemicals, ordnance, transportation equipment, lumber, electrical machinery, stone-clay-glass products. Value added by manufacture is over $416 million annually.

Federal government activities, especially nuclear and space research and testing, have played a large role in New Mexico's economic growth. Nuclear and space centers are at Los Alamos, White Sands, Holloman, Kirtland, and Sandia.

Per capita income was $4,482 in 1975.

New Mexico's most awe-inspiring natural wonder, Carlsbad Caverns, had 790,000 visitors in 1975. A national park, the caverns are on 3 levels and have the largest natural cave "room" in the world, 1,500 by 300 ft., 300 ft. high.

There are 4 large Indian reservations and 19 inhabited pueblos, including Acoma, the "sky city," built atop a 357-ft. mesa. There are pueblo ruins from 1000 A.D. in Chaco Canyon.

Skiing, hunting, fishing, ghost towns, and dude ranches help tourism show steady gains. Visitors spend more than $472 million in the state annually.

Franciscan Marcos de Niza and his black slave Estevan explored the area, 1539, seeking gold. First settlements were at San Juan Pueblo, 1598, and Santa Fe, 1610. Settlers alternately traded and fought with the Apaches, Comanches and Navahos. Trade on the Santa Fe Trail to Missouri started 1821. In the Mexican War, Gen. Stephen Kearney took Santa Fe, 1846. In the 1870s, cattlemen staged the famed Lincoln County War in which Billy (the Kid) Bonney played a leading role. Pancho Villa raided Columbus, 1916.

Santa Fe is the 2d oldest city in the U.S. It and Taos have large artist colonies. Albuquerque (1706) is the state's largest city.

There are 17 institutions of higher education.

The Museum of Navaho Ceremonial Art, Santa Fe, housed in a modernized version of a ceremonial hogan, has over 600 sandpaintings, recordings of 2,000 Navaho chants; books, manuscripts, baskets, blankets.

The Museum of New Mexico, Santa Fe, maintains the oldest public building in the U.S., the Palace of the Governors (built 1610), a hall of modern Indian culture, collected works of artists of the SW, folk art exhibits.

The Roswell Museum and Art Center, Roswell, has 19th and 20th century art collections, archeology and geology exhibits, the Robert H. Goddard rocket collection.

Famous New Mexicans include Kit Carson, Archbishop John Lamy, Billy (the Kid) Bonney, Pat Garrett, Lew Wallace, Peter Hurd, Bill Mauldin, Kim Stanley.

(See also Index for Albuquerque.)

New York
Empire State

AREA: 49,576 sq. mi.; rank, 30th. POPULATION (U.S. est. 1975): 18,120,000; rank, 2d. CAPITAL: Albany. MOTTO: Excelsior, Ever Upward. FLOWER: Rose. BIRD: Bluebird. TREE: Sugar maple. Eleventh of the original 13 states to ratify the Constitution, July 26, 1788.

New York is the nation's leading manufacturing state and within its borders are the financial capital of the nation, the largest city and port, the headquarters of the United Nations, the head offices of many of the greatest national corporations and insurance companies, and a great variety of industries.

New York's manufacturing industries outrank those of all other states in number, employees, and payrolls, but are 2d to California in value added by manufacture ($33.6 billion, 1973).

Value added by manufacture in New York exceeded that of every other state in apparel ($3.2 billion), printing and publishing ($4.2 billion), instruments ($3.5 billion), and in the miscellaneous group, which includes jewelry, silverware, toys and sporting goods, pens and pencils, etc. ($1.2 billion).

The state produces more than 33% of the nation's instruments, 24% of apparel, 21% of printing and publishing, 17% of the miscellaneous category. It is one of the largest producers of both leather and paper products.

Average non-farm employment for 1975 was 7 million. Wages and salaries totaled nearly $60 billion.

The bi-state Port Authority of New York and New Jersey handled 19% of the nation's foreign trade (by value) in 1974 by U.S. Commerce Dept. figures. The 3 Customs Districts (New York, Buffalo, and Ogdensburg) handled 25% of U.S. exports and imports by value in 1974.

Kennedy International Airport in N.Y. City handled about 50% of the nation's overseas air travel and is the nation's largest air cargo center, handling half of export-import air tonnage (by value).

The state Barge Canal System is 800 mi. long. There are 34 railroads and 535 landing facilities, including 27 seaplane bases and 79 heliports. The Verrazano-Narrows Bridge has the world's longest suspension span.

Rich, rolling farmlands support a large agricultural output. New York usually ranks 1st among the states in production of timothy, maple syrup, cottage cheese; it is 2d to Washington in apples and 2d to California in grapes (it has large wine and grape juice industries).

It is also a leader in milk production, with the 2d largest number of milk cows in the U.S., and is high in vegetables, melons, cherries, and other fruit; it is 7th among the states in potatoes, 8th in hay. Also important are corn, oats, wheat, peaches. Poultry and egg production is also high. Farm production supports large canning and freezing industries in the state.

Farm receipts for 1975 were est. at $1.5 billion, with more than two-thirds of the total from livestock and dairy products. Commercial fishing produced $28 million in 1975.

The state has a rich and varied mineral industry, normally ranking 1st in the U.S. in zinc, talc, titanium, emery, abrasive garnet, and wollastonite, and among the leaders in salt. Other products include lead, gypsum, petroleum, clay, stone, iron. Total value for 1975 was $392 million.

Per capita income was $6,603 in 1975, 6th highest among the states.

There are 285 institutions of higher education, most in any state. Expenditure per pupil in public schools is highest of any state, $2,241 in 1975; average pay of teachers, $15,000, is only topped in Alaska.

New York was the nation's most populous state from 1820 through 1964. As of July 1, 1964, the U.S. Census Bureau estimated California's pop. reached 18,084,000, New York's 17,915,000 (including Armed Forces stationed in the 2 states; without them, New York still led 17,870,000 to 17,749,000). By July 1, 1965, the Bureau estimated California led in both categories. In the 1970 Census, California had 19,953,134; New York had 18,241,266.

In 1609 Henry Hudson discovered the river that bears his name and Samuel de Champlain explored the lake, far upstate, which was named for him. In 1614 and 1624, the Dutch built posts near Albany; in 1626 they settled Manhattan. A British fleet seized New Netherland, 1664. In New York, 92 of the 300 or more engagements of the Revolution were fought, including the Battle of Bemis Heights-Saratoga, a turning point of the war.

Tourism and business travel provide $3.4 billion a year to businesses in the state. Major vacation areas include the Adirondack and Catskill Mtns., Finger Lakes, Great Lakes, Thousand Islands, Long Island, N.Y. City, and Niagara Falls. The 128 state parks are visited annually by over 45 million persons.

Sunnyside, the home of Washington Irving, "as full of angles and corners as an old cocked hat," is in Tarrytown. The Dutch Church of Sleepy Hollow (1697), North Tarrytown, overlooks a bridge commemorating Irving's story of the "headless horseman;" Irving is buried close by in Sleepy Hollow Cemetery. Also in Tarrytown is Lyndhurst, 19th century mansion of Jay Gould, maintained by the National Trust for Historic Preservation.

The Franklin D. Roosevelt National Historic Site, in Hyde Park, includes the graves of President and Mrs. Roosevelt, the home occupied by the Roosevelt family from 1867, greenhouse, etc. The Roosevelt Library has historic papers, trophies, and ship models.

In Cooperstown are the National Baseball Hall of Fame and Museum with a wide collection of mementos of the national game; nearby is Abner Doubleday Field, said to be where baseball originated in 1839. Near Cooperstown are Fenimore House, hq. of the State Historical Society, with collections including James Fenimore Cooper memorabilia and an art gallery; the Farmers' Museum; the Village Crossroads, with blacksmith shop, etc; the Carriage and Harness Museum.

The restored Fort Ticonderoga, overlooking the waters connecting Lakes George and Champlain, has relics of the French and Indian War and the Revolution in which the fort played important roles.

A new N.Y. State Museum, "Man and Nature in N.Y.," was opened in Albany in 1976.

The Corning Glass Center, Corning, has a museum and the Steuben factory, where visitors may see crystal glass formed and engraved. Also in the Finger Lakes area are the Curtiss Museum of aviation and the Wine Museum at Hammondsport and several wineries which offer tours to visitors. In Binghamton, the Roberson Center for the Arts and Sciences has art and historical collections.

Philipsburg Manor, in North Tarrytown, a trading center of the early 1700s, includes the restored Frederick Philipse home, a dam, and grist mill. Van Cortlandt Manor, Croton-on-Hudson, has the restored Van Cortlandt home and ferry house.

In Kingston, the Senate House, seat of the first Senate of the state, exhibits early historical objects; its museum has works by John Vanderlyn, local historical painter. In Newburgh, Washington's Hq., the Jonathan Hasbrouck House has Revolutionary relics.

The Suffolk Museum and Carriage House, Stony Brook, L.I., has early American paintings and furniture, apothecary shop, tavern, Wells Fargo, Conestoga, and gypsy wagons, etc.

The Remington Art Memorial Museum, Ogdensburg, has paintings and bronzes by Frederic Remington (1861-1909), born in nearby Canton.

Famous New Yorkers include Van Buren, Fillmore, Theodore and Franklin Roosevelt, Alfred E. Smith, Charles Evans Hughes, Julia Ward Howe, Elizabeth Cady Stanton, Melville, Whitman, Henry and William James, Peter Cooper, George Eastman.

(See also index for Albany, Binghamton, Buffalo, N.Y. City, Rochester, Schenectady, Syracuse, Troy.)

North Carolina

Tar Heel State, Old North State

AREA: 52,586 sq. mi.; rank, 28th. POPULATION (U.S. est. 1975): 5,451,000; rank, 11th. CAPITAL: Raleigh. MOTTO: Esse Quam Videri; To Be, Rather Than to Seem. FLOWER: Dogwood. BIRD: Cardinal. TREE: Pine. SONG: The Old North State. Twelfth of the original 13 states to ratify the Constitution, Nov. 21, 1789.

From a low coastal plain, with Capes Hatteras, Lookout, and Fear jutting into the Atlantic, North Carolina rises to a central Piedmont plateau region and, in the W, to the scenic Blue Ridge and Great Smoky Mountains. Mt. Mitchell, 6,684 ft., is the highest peak E of the Mississippi.

Modernization of production methods has brought North Carolina increasing prosperity from its factories. Per capita personal income was $4,801 in 1975, $1,033 below U.S. average.

The state leads the U.S. in production of textiles, bricks, household furniture, and cigarettes.

In 1975, 116 new industrial plants opened and 219 expanded their facilities, creating an est. 18,590 new jobs through an investment of $701 million.

About 757,700 workers are employed in factories. The textile industry is the state's largest, with shipments valued at about $23.8 billion annually.

North Carolina ranks 1st among the states in tobacco production; in 1975 it was valued at $950 million. It was also first in sweet potatoes, 4th in peanuts. Other large crops are cotton, corn, and soybeans. Also grown are wheat, oats, barley, peaches, apples. In crop receipts, the state ranked 9th in 1975 with $1.7 million; it was also 9th in total crop and livestock receipts, $2.7 billion. The state ranked 3d in turkeys, 5th in chickens in 1975.

Mineral production value was est. at $162 million for 1975. North Carolina ranked 1st in mica, feldspar, and lithium; it was also a leader in talc and asbestos.

Tourism is important; in 1975 travelers spent an est. $1.14 billion in the state. Sports include golfing, skiing at mountain resorts, fishing, hunting.

Among attractions are the Great Smoky Mtns. (half in Tennessee), the Blue Ridge Parkway and the Cape Hatteras and Cape Lookout National Seashores.

Other attractions include the restored Fort Raleigh National Historic Site, Roanoke Is., where Virginia Dare, first child of English parents in the New World, was born Aug. 18, 1587; Wright Brothers National Memorial near Kitty Hawk with aviation exhibits and a reproduction of the plane in which Wilbur and Orville Wright made their first flights, 1903; Guilford Court House and Moore's Creek battles, sites of Revolutionary battles. The battleship North Carolina, a war memorial, is berthed at Wilmington.

In Asheville is one of the world's largest rayon plants as well as Biltmore Industries, native craft plants set up by Mrs. George W. Vanderbilt in 1901 to continue handweaving traditions of the area. Just S of Asheville is the 19th century Biltmore mansion of the Vanderbilts, which has a large collection of paintings, antiques, and Ming china. Also in Asheville, the Thomas Wolfe Memorial was the home of the author.

Bennett Place, 6 mi. NW of Durham, is the site where Gen. Joseph E. Johnston surrendered the last Confederate army to Gen. William Sherman.

The Mint Museum of Art, Charlotte, has collections of paintings, sculpture, and ceramics. The North Carolina Museum of Art, Raleigh, exhibits American and European paintings, sculpture and decorative art. Tryon Palace, New Bern, is the reconstructed colonial capitol of 1770-1794.

Old Salem, in Winston-Salem, includes buildings erected by the Moravians from 1766 on.

There are 114 institutions of higher education.

The first English colony in America was the first of 2 established by Sir Walter Raleigh on Roanoke Is., 1585 and 1587. The first group returned to England; the second, the "Lost Colony," disappeared without trace. Permanent settlers came from Virginia, c.

1660. Roused by British repressions, the colonists drove out the royal governor, 1775; the province's Congress was the first to vote for independence. Ten regiments were furnished to the Continental Army. Cornwallis' forces were defeated at Kings Mountain, 1780, and forced out after Guilford Courthouse, 1781.

Famous men and women included James K. Polk, Dolley Madison, Gaylord and Jim Perry, Jim (Catfish) Hunter, and Enos Slaughter.

(See also Index for Charlotte, Raleigh, and Winston-Salem.)

North Dakota

Sioux State, Flickertail State

AREA: 70,665 sq. mi.; rank, 17th. POPULATION (U.S. est. 1975): 635,000; rank, 45th. CAPITAL: Bismarck. MOTTO: Liberty and Union, Now and Forever, One and Inseparable. FLOWER: Wild prairie rose. BIRD: Western meadowlark. TREE: American elm. SONG: North Dakota Hymn. ENTERED UNION: Nov. 2, 1889; rank, 39th or 40th, with South Dakota.

The eastern plains of North Dakota are rich in grain and support large numbers of livestock, in sharp contrast to the rough, colorful Badlands in the west which have elements of scenic beauty and include Theodore Roosevelt National Memorial Park.

North Dakota's economy is based on agriculture and mining; but manufacturing industries, especially processing of food, have grown in number and size. Most of the usable land is in farms and ranches.

North Dakota led the other states in production of spring and durum wheat, barley, and flaxseed in 1975 and was 2d to Kansas in total wheat. It was also a leader in rye, oats, sugar beets, and potatoes. Farm receipts for 1975 totaled $2 billion. In 1975 there were 2.3 million cattle in the state.

Mineral production in 1975 was valued at $177 million, up 11% from 1973. The larger part of this was from petroleum. Other products include natural gas, natural gas liquids, coal (lignite), salt, peat.

Per capita income was $5,855 in 1975, $21 above U.S. average.

Tourism brings in over $269 million a year.

There are 65 state parks and historic sites. The International Peace Garden, on a 2,200-acre tract extending across the border into Manitoba, commemorates the friendly relations between the U.S. and Canada. The state is known for its waterfowl, grouse, and deer hunting, bass, trout, and northern pike fishing. Lake Sakakawea, formed by the Garrison Dam across the Missouri River, is 609 sq. mi. in area.

A museum with exhibits of pioneer life, the Northern Plains Indians and natural history of the area, is maintained by the State Historical Society on the State Capitol grounds, Bismarck.

Pierre La Verendrye was the first (1738) French fur trader in the area, followed later by English traders. The U.S. acquired half the territory in the Louisiana Purchase, 1803. Lewis and Clark built Fort Mandan, spent the winter of 1804-05 there. In 1818, American ownership of the other half was confirmed by agreement with Britain. First permanent settlement was at Pembina, 1812. Missouri River steamboats reached the area, 1832; the first railroad, 1873, bringing many homesteaders. The state was first to hold a presidential primary, 1912; other progressive measures were the referendum and recall.

There are 15 institutions of higher learning.

Famous North Dakotans include Vilhjalmur Stefansson, Maxwell Anderson, Eric Sevareid, Lawrence Welk, Peggy Lee, Dorothy Stickney.

(See also Index for Bismarck.)

Ohio

Buckeye State

AREA: 41,222 sq. mi.; rank, 35th. POPULATION (U.S. est. 1975): 10,759,000; rank, 6th. CAPITAL: Columbus. MOTTO: With God, All Things Are Possible. FLOWER: Scarlet carnation. BIRD: Cardinal.

TREE: **Ohio buckeye. SONG: Beautiful Ohio. ENTERED UNION: Mar. 1, 1803; rank, 17th.**

Ohio is the nation's 3d greatest industrial state; it ranks among the wealthiest states in livestock and crop receipts, and is a leader in output of lime, coal, and coke.

Ohio leads the U.S. in a wide variety of products: tires, machine tools, playing cards, business machines, glassware, cutlery, dishwashers, clay.

Per capita income was $5,883 in 1975, $49 above national average.

Total value added by manufacture was $31.1 billion. Of this, autos, aircraft, boats, and parts accounted for $2.9 billion; iron, steel, and other metals, $2.9 billion; machinery, especially industrial, $3.4 billion; electrical machinery, especially household appliances, $2.4 billion. Also important are metal products, chemicals, rubber and plastic products, food processing.

Farm receipts for 1975 totaled over $2.7 billion, 10th among the states, with three-fourths of it from livestock products. Ohio has large numbers of milk cows, hogs, and sheep; it ranks high in milk production. It is also a large producer of corn, grapes, clover, popcorn, oats, soybeans, and other crops.

Mineral production was valued at a total $1.1 billion for 1975, with the largest item being bituminous coal. Ohio was the top state in lime production and one of the leaders in clays, salt, gypsum sand, and gravel. Other important products include petroleum, cement, gypsum, and natural gas.

It was estimated that the value of the tourist industry was more than $1.9 billion for 1975.

There are 64 state parks, over 300 roadside parks, and many historic memorials, including Fallen Timbers Battlefield, prehistoric Indian mounds, and the restored first settlement, Schoenbrunn (1772).

The National Rifle and Pistol Matches are held at Camp Perry and the Grand American Trapshoot at Vandalia.

Unusual museums include the Air Force Museum and Paul Lawrence Dunbar House, Dayton; Dental Museum, Bainbridge; Auto-Aviation Museum, Cleveland; Ohio Historical Museum, Columbus.

In Canton, the Pro Football Hall of Fame has a museum and daily movies; the Stark County Historical Society has industry and historical museums.

The state is served by 27 railroads and 21 scheduled airlines. It has busy ports on Lake Erie.

There are 129 institutions of higher education.

LaSalle visited the Ohio area, 1669; American furtraders arrived, beginning 1685; the French and Indians sought to drive them out. During the Revolution, Virginians defeated the Indians, 1774, but hostilities were renewed, 1777. The region became U.S. territory after the Revolution. First organized settlement was at Marietta, 1788. Indian warfare ended with Anthony Wayne's victory at Fallen Timbers, 1794. In the War of 1812, Oliver H. Perry's victory on Lake Erie and William H. Harrison's invasion of Canada, 1813, ended British incursions.

Famous Ohioans include Grant, Hayes, Garfield, William H. and Benjamin Harrison, McKinley, Taft, Harding, Sherman, Rickenbacker, Edison, Orville Wright, George Bellows, Ambrose Bierce, Paul Laurence Dunbar, Sherwood Anderson, John D. Rockefeller Sr. and Jr., Bob Hope, John Glenn.

(See also index for Akron, Cincinnati, Cleveland, Columbus, Dayton, Toledo, Youngstown.)

Oklahoma
Sooner State

AREA: **69,919 sq. mi.; rank, 18th. POPULATION (U.S. est. 1975): 2,712,000; rank, 27th. CAPITAL: Oklahoma City. MOTTO: Labor Omnia Vincit, Labor Conquers All Things. FLOWER: Mistletoe. BIRD: Scissortailed flycatcher. TREE: Redbud. SONG: Oklahoma! ENTERED UNION: Nov. 16, 1907; rank, 46th.**

Most of Oklahoma is a great, rolling plain sloping S and E with a mean altitude of 1,300 ft. There are 4 mountainous areas; the Ozark Plateau in the NE, the Ouachitas in the SE, the Arbuckles in the S central and the Wichitas in the SW. In the western Panhandle, the land rises toward the Rockies with Black Mesa, 4,973 ft., the highest point.

Oil, wheat, and cattle are the basic ingredients of Oklahoma's economy, but manufacturing industries have gained increasing importance. Per capita income was $4,996 in 1975.

The $1.2 billion Arkansas River Navigation System, involving shipping, flood control, and power dams, was completed to Catoosa, near Tulsa, in 1971. It made Catoosa a "seaport," with barge shipping to the Mississippi and beyond.

The state's output of petroleum was valued at $1.4 billion for 1975, accounting for much of the total value of mineral production, $2.3 billion. The state is one of the leaders in the U.S. in petroleum production, and in total mineral production.

Natural gas was the 2d most important mineral with production valued at $531 million. Other minerals include helium, in which the state is a leader, gypsum, zinc, cement, coal, copper, silver.

Oklahoma's rich plains produced the nation's 2d largest winter wheat crop in 1975 as well as large crops of sorghum, broomcorn, other grains, and peanuts. Its cattle herd was the 6th largest in the U.S. Total farm receipts were $1.8 billion, more than half from livestock products.

While much of Oklahoma's manufacturing industry is based on processing of the state's own meat, wheat, and oil, other lines have become important rivals. Value added by manufacture exceeds $2.6 billion annually. Important lines include food processing, machinery (especially construction and oil equipment), transportation equipment, metal products, petroleum, and coal products.

There are 44 institutions of higher education.

Total tourist revenues are estimated at more than $711 million annually. Attractions include 30 state parks, large lakes and reservoirs such as Eufaula (102,500 acres) and Lake Texoma (93,080 acres); Ouachita National Forest (176,000 acres), rodeos, Indian powwows, the National Cowboy Hall of Fame in Oklahoma City, bass fishing, and quail hunting.

The Will Rogers Memorial, Claremore, has collections of the great humorist's saddles and ropes, as well as trophies; his tomb is also there. In Anadarko, the Southern Plains Indian Museum and Crafts Center exhibits Indian arts and has a crafts sales shop. The Woolaroc Museum near Bartlesville has 55,000 exhibits in a panorama of New World history, and a collection of paintings of the West.

The Fort Gibson Stockade, restored with many of the original buildings, near Muskogee, was established 1824 and was the army's largest outpost in the Indian lands.

Near Tahlequah is the Cherokee Cultural Center with a restored 1700 Cherokee village.

The first permanent white settlement in the area was made in 1796 by Maj. Jean Pierre Chouteau on the site of present-day Salina, Okla.

Part of the Louisiana Purchase, 1803, Oklahoma was known as Indian Territory (but was not given territorial government) after it became the home of the "Five Civilized Tribes"—Cherokee, Choctaw, Chickasaw, Creek, and Seminole—1828-1846. The land was also used by Comanche, Osage, and other Plains Indians. As white settlers pressed west, land was opened for homesteading by runs and lottery, a run being a race for a claim at a specific time. The first run took place Apr. 22, 1889; the most famous was the run to the Cherokee Outlet, 1893. The portion thus opened was organized as a Territory; this and Indian Territory were joined by Congress in the State of Oklahoma, admitted to the Union Nov. 16, 1907.

Famous Oklahomans include Will Rogers, Gen. Patrick J. Hurley, Jim Thorpe, Maria Tallchief, Kay Starr, Mickey Mantle, Allie Reynolds, Johnny Bench, Wiley Post, Roger Miller, Woodie Guthrie.

(See also Index for Oklahoma City and Tulsa.)

Oregon
Beaver State

AREA: 96,981 sq. mi.; rank, 10th. **POPULATION** (U.S. est. 1975): 2,288,000; rank, 30th. **CAPITAL:** Salem. **MOTTO:** The Union. **FLOWER:** Oregon grape. **BIRD:** Western meadowlark. **ANIMAL:** Beaver. **TREE:** Douglas fir. **SONG:** Oregon, My Oregon. **ENTERED UNION:** Feb. 14, 1859; rank, 33d.

Oregon is rich in timber, fish and wildlife, water power, and scenic beauty, with lofty mountain ranges, deep river gorges, and broad, fertile valleys.

Half of Oregon, or about 30 million acres, is thickly forested and the state leads the nation in value of forest products, over $3 billion a year. Production of lumber, furniture, paper, and other forest products provides jobs for about 75,000 workers and is a major factor in the state's economy.

Also important are food processing, transportation equipment, machinery, fabricated metal. Total value added by manufacture is over $4.3 billion a year.

Per capita income was $5,610 in 1975.

Oregon's agriculture is rich and varied. While farmers grow fair-sized crops of wheat, oats, potatoes, and other staples, the state is a leader in production of berries, pears, cherries, filberts, walnuts, vegetables. It also ranks high in number of turkeys and of sheep. Farm receipts for 1975 were over $1 billion, two-thirds from crops, the rest livestock.

Stone, nickel, cement, lime are important in mineral production, valued at $88 million for 1975.

Hydroelectric power, from both privately-owned and publicly-owned utilities, is abundant. A federal agency, the Bonneville Power Administration, sells electric power, much of it from a series of great dams across the Columbia River, to many of the utilities and to large industrial plants. Among users are plants for the refining and processing of metals from out of state, including aluminum.

The Columbia River brings ocean shipping to Portland, 100 mi. inland but one of the Pacific Coast's principal ports, and to other river ports.

The commercial fish catch, including salmon, tuna, halibut, sole, cod, and shellfish, was worth over $28 million in 1975.

Tourism is an important industry, est. at over $891 million annually. There are 237 state parks, and both state and national forests. Crater Lake, a national park, is a body of sapphire blue water in a former volcano, 6 mi. in diameter and 1,932 ft. deep—deepest lake in the U.S. Oregon Dunes National Recreation Area was created in 1972.

Snow-capped Mt. Hood, which rises 11,235 ft., is the highest point in the state; nearby are scenic recreation areas.

Fort Clatsop National Memorial includes a replica of the fort in which the Lewis and Clark expedition spent the winter of 1805-06. Oregon Caves National Monument contains stone waterfalls. Skiing and the annual Pendleton Round-Up are other attractions.

A summer Shakespearean Festival is staged annually in Ashland.

Oregon has 43 institutions of higher education.

The Univ. of Oregon in Eugene has a Museum of Art with oriental, Pacific Northwest and other art collections. It also has a Museum of Natural History.

American Capt. Robert Gray discovered and sailed into the Columbia River, 1792; Lewis and Clark, traveling overland, wintered at the mouth of the river, 1805-06. Fur traders followed. Settlers arrived in the Willamette Valley, 1834. In 1843 the first large wave of settlers arrived via the Oregon Trail. Early in the 20th Century, the "Oregon System," reforms which included the initiative, referendum, recall, direct primary, and woman suffrage, was adopted.

Famous Oregonians include Dr. John McLoughlin, Ernest Haycox, Stewart Holbrook, John Reed, Childe Hassam, Ernest Bloch, Mrs. Ruth Tooze, Chief Joseph, Joaquin Miller, Jane Powell, Maurine Neuberger, Sally Struthers, Mickey Lolich.

(See also Index for Portland.)

Pennsylvania
Keystone State

AREA: 45,333 sq. mi.; rank, 33d. **POPULATION** (U.S. est. 1975): 11,827,000; rank, 4th. **CAPITAL:** Harrisburg. **MOTTO:** Virtue, Liberty and Independence. **FLOWER:** Mountain laurel. **BIRD:** Ruffed grouse. **TREE:** Eastern hemlock. Second of the original 13 states to ratify the Constitution, Dec. 12, 1787.

Pennsylvania has extensive mineral resources and fertile farmlands, is a leader in manufacturing, and boasts a wealth of historic landmarks and scenic attractions.

Roughly rectangular in shape, Pennsylvania has prosperous farmlands in the SE and the W. Through the center, running NE-SW, are parallel mountain ridges with valleys between. Highest point is Mt. Davis in the SW, 3,213 ft.

Many of the nation's largest steel plants are in Pennsylvania, with the greatest concentration in the Pittsburgh area. Pennsylvania ranks 1st among the states in steel wire and structural metal.

Mill and factory products are many and varied; value added by manufacture is over $26.8 billion. Primary metals (mainly steel) are the most important, over $4.7 billion. Other large lines are machinery and electrical machinery, food processing, chemicals, metal products, women's dresses, and men's suits.

Per capita income was $5,874 in 1975, $40 above the national average.

Pennsylvania produces almost all of the nation's anthracite coal; it ranked 3d in 1975 in output of bituminous coal. Also important are cement, stone, petroleum, lime, clays, zinc, iron. Mineral production value, 1975, was $2.7 billion, up 16%.

Prosperous farms, such as those in the Pennsylvania Dutch country in the SE, brought in total livestock and crop receipts for the state of $1.6 billion in 1975, much of it from dairy and poultry products. The state ranked high in number of cows, chickens, turkeys.

The state ranks high in its output of grapes, peaches, apples, and cherries. It claims 1st place in scrapple, pretzels, mushrooms, and plantation-grown Christmas trees. It also ranks high in ice cream. Forest products are valued at over $7 billion annually.

Pennsylvania is among the leading states in hunting, fishing, golf, and winter sports. Tourism reportedly produces sales of $2.29 billion a year, 7th highest in the U.S.

There are more than 100 state and federal parks, recreation areas, and historic sites. Scenic attractions include the Delaware Water Gap in the east and the 1,000-ft. deep Pine Creek Gorge in the north. Folk festivals, country fairs, and fall foliage in the Poconos draw many visitors.

Washington Crossing State Park, where Continental troops crossed the Delaware to attack Hessian-British forces in Trenton, Christmas Night 1776, has restored buildings and picnic areas.

Longwood Gardens, near Kennett Square, include conservatories and rock, heather, flower, and water gardens; arboretum, illuminated fountains, open-air theater; open every day of the year.

Lancaster County and nearby areas in the southeast are known as Pennsylvania Dutch Country. Descendants of early German, Swiss, and Dutch settlers, many of them Amish or Mennonites, still maintain many of the early customs and "old world" culture which make their farms, festivals, and market places attractive to tourists.

The William Penn Memorial Museum, Harrisburg, has collections of folk art, ironwork, glass, pewter, china, textiles, stage coaches, sleighs; replicas of artisans' shops, period rooms; fine arts, planetarium.

There are 175 institutions of higher learning.

First settlers were Swedish, 1643, on Tinicum Is. In 1655 the Dutch seized the settlement but lost it to the British, 1664. The region was given by Charles II to William Penn, 1681. Philadelphia (brotherly love) was the capital of the colonies during most of the Revolution, and of the U.S., 1790-1800. Pennsylvanians aided in the siege of Boston; Philadelphia was taken by the British, 1777; Washington's troops encamped at Valley Forge in the bitter winter of 1777-78. The Declaration of Independence, 1776, and the Constitution, 1787, were signed in Philadelphia.

Famous Pennsylvanians include Betsy Ross, Benjamin Franklin, Robert E. Peary, Andrew Carnegie, George C. Marshall, Stephen Foster, Marion Anderson, Mary Roberts Rinehart, Maxwell Anderson.

(See also Index for Allentown, Erie, Philadelphia, Pittsburgh.)

Rhode Island
Little Rhody, Ocean State

AREA: 1,214 sq. mi.; rank, 50th, **POPULATION** (U. S. est. 1975): 927,000; rank, 39th, **CAPITAL:** Providence. **MOTTO:** Hope. **FLOWER:** Violet. **BIRD:** Rhode Island red (hen). **TREE:** Red maple. **SONG:** Rhode Island. Thirteenth of original 13 states to ratify the Constitution, May 29, 1790.

Rhode Island is the smallest of the 50 states but has the longest official name: State of Rhode Island and Providence Plantations. It is not an island, although its Narragansett Bay, extending from the Atlantic 37 mi. inland, contains many islands, the largest of which is named Rhode Is.

Tiny Rhode Island is densely populated and highly industrialized. It is 2d to New Jersey in population density. The 1970 Census showed New Jersey averaging 953.1 persons per sq. mi.; Rhode Island 905.5.

Industries show more than $1.9 billion in value added annually by manufacturing. Until 1940, textile mills, dating back to a 1793 cotton mill, employed more workers than all other Rhode Island industries put together. Employment in the mills fell off sharply but jobs in other fields increased.

The state also pioneered in the manufacture of jewelry and silverware and remains tops in the U. S. Other leading industry groups are primary metal processing, metal products, machinery, rubber, and plastics, food processing, chemicals, apparel. The tourist industry produces over $143 million annually.

Per capita income was $5,917 in 1975; U.S. average was $5,834.

Only 1% of the labor force is engaged in farming, and farm receipts in 1975 totaled $26 million. Dairy and poultry (notably Rhode Island reds) are the most important lines; potatoes and apples are principal crops. The fish and shellfish catch is valued at over $18 million annually.

There are 13 institutions of higher education.

Rhode Island is distinguished historically for its battle for freedom of conscience and action, begun by Roger Williams, founder of Providence, who was exiled from Massachusetts Bay Colony in 1636, and Anne Hutchinson, exiled in 1638. The first Baptist church in the U.S. was founded in Providence in 1638. Rhode Island gave protection to Quakers in 1657 and to Jews from Holland in 1658.

The colonists broke the power of the Narragansett Indians in the Great Swamp Fight, 1675, the decisive battle in King Philip's War. British trade restrictions angered the colonists and they burned the British revenue cutter Gaspee, 1772. The colony declared its independence May 4, 1776. Gen. John Sullivan and Lafayette won a partial victory, 1778, but failed to oust the British.

The Rhode Island Historical Society in Providence occupies the historic John Brown House, with rooms containing furniture by 18th century cabinet makers. Also in Providence, the Rhode Island School of Design has collections of classic art, 18th century American furniture, 19th century paintings, etc.

Providence is a major manufacturing and educational center, and a port handling over 9 million tons of cargo per year.

Newport became famous as the summer capital of society in the mid-19th century. Touro Synagogue (1763) is the oldest in the U.S., a national historic site.

The Newport Historical Society has a marine museum; extensive exhibits of silver, furniture, china, etc.; a grist mill, several forts, a Seventh Day Baptist meeting house built 1729.

In Pawtucket, the Old Slater Mill Museum is a restored 1793 cotton mill, considered the first to spin yarn successfully in this country; it has demonstrations of hand spinning and weaving.

Famous Rhode Islanders include Nathanael Greene, Gilbert Stuart, Oliver and Matthew C. Perry, Jabez Gorham, George M. Cohan, Nelson Eddy, Ambrose Burnside, Oliver and Christopher La Farge.

(See also Index for Providence.)

South Carolina
Palmetto State

AREA: 31,055 sq. mi.; rank, 40th. **POPULATION** (U. S. est. 1975): 2,818,000; rank, 26th. **CAPITAL:** Columbia. **MOTTO:** Dum Spiro, Spero, While I Breathe, I Hope; and Animis Opibusque Parati, Prepared in Mind and Resources. **FLOWER:** Carolina (yellow) jessamine. **BIRD:** Carolina wren. **SONG:** Carolina. **TREE:** Palmetto. Eighth of the original 13 states to ratify the Constitution, May 23, 1788.

In South Carolina, the land slopes from the Blue Ridge Mountains in the NW, through thick pine forests and fertile farmlands with great fields of tobacco and cotton, to semi-tropic beaches and busy ports on the Atlantic. Deep-sea and inland fishing, hunting, antebellum houses, public gardens, and famed shore resorts are among the state's attractions.

Efforts to diversify industry and expand foreign trade and tourism have been highly successful. Per capita income was $4,521 in 1975.

Manufacturing is by far the major source of income; value added by manufacture is over $5.8 billion annually. The textile industry is still the most important, comprising about 40% of the value of all manufactured products, and employing the most workers. The mills rank high in cotton goods, and are a major producer of synthetic and woolen goods.

Other important manufacturing lines are chemicals, apparel, paper, lumber, food processing, machinery, and stone-clay-glass products.

In 1975, new industrial investment was valued at $511 million; it was estimated this would provide 6,020 new jobs. Major areas of expansion were in chemical, textile, and metal-working fields.

Farms have become fewer but larger. South Carolina grows more peaches than any other state except California; it ranks 3d in tobacco. Also grown are cotton, peanuts, sweet potatoes, pecans, etc. Poultry and eggs are important revenue producers; the state has large sales of chickens and turkeys.

Total farm receipts for 1975 were $812 million.

The state's mineral production value for 1975 was est. at $105 million. It is a leader in production of vermiculite, used in insulation, and of kyanite and kaolin used in ceramics. Also produced are mica, cement, and stone, including Winnsboro blue granite. Lumber for pulp and saw-timber is a major resource, especially the loblolly pine.

Income from tourism has risen; 33 million out-of-state visitors spent an est. $911 million in 1975.

Attractions include state parks, famed gardens, historic sites, coastal islands, shore resorts such as Myrtle Beach, fishing, and quail hunting.

There are many historic churches and white-pillared houses in Charleston, Columbia, and Beaufort. Gardens near Charleston include Middleton Place, Magnolia, and Cypress; Brookgreen, south of Myrtle Beach, has 340 outdoor statues; other gardens are Edisto, at Orangeburg; Glencairn, at Rock Hill.

Fort Sumter National Monument is in Charleston Harbor. Charleston Museum, estab. 1773, has exhibits of interior paneling, furniture, arts, crafts, and utensils from early South Carolina days.

The first English colonists settled, 1670, on the Ashley River, moved to the site of Charleston, 1680. The colonists seized the government, 1775, and the royal governor fled. In 1780 the British took Charleston, but British troops were defeated at Kings Mountain that year, and at Cowpens and Eutaw Springs, 1781. In the 1830s, South Carolinians, angered by Federal protective tariffs, adopted the Nullification Doctrine, holding a state can void an act of Congress. The state was the first to secede and, in 1861, Confederate troops fired on and forced the surrender of U. S. troops at Fort Sumter, in Charleston Harbor, launching the Civil War.

There are 55 institutions of higher education.

Famous South Carolinians include Andrew Jackson, John C. Calhoun, Francis Marion, James F. Byrnes, Julia Peterkin, DuBose Heyward.

(See also Index for Columbia.)

South Dakota
Coyote State, Sunshine State

AREA: 77,047 sq. mi.; rank, 16th. **POPULATION** (U.S. est. 1975): 683,000; rank, 44th. **CAPITAL:** Pierre. **MOTTO:** Under God, the People Rule. **FLOWER:** American pasque. **BIRD:** Ringnecked pheasant. **SONG:** Hail, South Dakota. **TREE:** Black Hills spruce. **ENTERED UNION:** Nov. 2, 1889; rank, 39th or 40th (entered at same time as North Dakota).

South Dakota is a rectangle split down the middle by the Missouri R. and a chain of huge lakes formed behind dams on the river. In the E are rich farmlands which produce large crops of rye, oats, and other grains. In the W are rolling grasslands which support millions of cattle and sheep, as well as vast acreages of wheat. In the far W are the Black Hills with Harney Peak, 7,242 ft., the highest point E of the Rockies.

With more than 43,000 farms and ranches, occupying most of the land area, agriculture is South Dakota's basic industry. Its livestock and livestock products account for three-quarters of farm income. Mining and lumbering are large natural resource industries. Per capita income was $4,980 in 1975, $854 below U. S. average.

The state normally ranks first in the U.S. in size of its rye crop and high in spring wheat, flaxseed, oats, and barley. In 1976 South Dakota ranked 5th in sheep, 9th in cattle, and 10th in hogs. Total farm receipts for 1975 were $1.8 billion.

Large areas are reclaimed by irrigation and plans were under way for additional hundreds of thousands of acres to be fed from the Oahe Reservoir.

South Dakota leads the nation in gold production; the Homestake Mine in Lawrence County is the largest in the U. S. Gold accounted for $49 million of the state's total mineral production value which was $100 million for 1975. The state was also a leader in production of beryllium. Other products include silver, petroleum, uranium, cement.

Processing of foods produced by farms and ranches is the largest of South Dakota's manufacturing industries. Also important are lumber and wood products, and machinery, including farm equipment. Total value added by manufacture is over $330 million.

South Dakota has 8,400 sq. mi. of Indian reservations. The Indians, mostly Sioux, are est. at 32,365.

There are 17 institutions of higher education and 12 state parks, 35 recreation areas, and 49 roadside parks. Pheasant, duck, and geese are abundant. There are large herds of deer and elk and about 5,000 bison in state and private herds.

Mount Rushmore, in the Black Hills, has an altitude of 6,200 ft. Sculptured on its granite face are the heads of Washington, Jefferson, Lincoln, and Theodore Roosevelt. These busts by Gutzon Borglum are proportionate to men 465 ft. tall. Rushmore is visited by about 2 million persons annually.

Other tourist attractions include Custer State Park, with the world's largest herd of bison; the Black Hills Passion Play at Spearfish; Badlands National Monument, 170 sq. mi. of barren, eroded "moonscape."

The "Great Lakes of South Dakota" are 4 reservoirs created behind Oahe, Big Bend, Fort Randall, and Gavins Point Dams on the Missouri River with total water surface area of 571,000 acres.

Nine million out-of-state tourists, it is estimated, spend $258 million a year in South Dakota.

Fort Sisseton State Park, 18 mi. SE of Britton, is a restored army frontier post of 1864. The Sioux Indian Museum in Rapid City features historic and contemporary arts of the Sioux, and an Indian craft shop.

The French Verendrye brothers explored the region, 1742-43. Lewis and Clark passed through the area, 1804, and recrossed it on their return from the Pacific, 1806. First American settlement was at Sioux Falls, 1857, but there were few other settlements until after gold was discovered, 1874, on the Sioux Reservation. Miners rushed in; the U.S. first tried to stop them, then relaxed its opposition. Custer's defeat by the Sioux followed, and in 1877 the Sioux relinquished the land and the "great Dakota Boom" began. Miners and settlers poured in. A new Indian uprising came in 1890, climaxed by the massacre of Indian families at Wounded Knee.

Famous South Dakotans include Sakajawea, Sitting Bull, Crazy Horse, Dr. Ernest O. Lawrence.

(See also Index for Sioux Falls.)

Tennessee
Volunteer State

AREA: 42,244 sq. mi.; rank, 34th. **POPULATION** (U.S. est. 1975): 4,188,000; rank, 17th. **CAPITAL:** Nashville. **MOTTO:** Agriculture, Commerce. **FLOWER:** Iris. **BIRD:** Mockingbird. **TREE:** Tulip poplar. **SONG:** Tennessee Waltz. **ENTERED UNION:** June 1, 1796; rank, 16th.

Eastern Tennessee is rugged country with the Great Valley separating the Great Smoky Mtns., on the state's E border, from the Cumberland Mtns.; the Central Basin is a rolling area containing the famed Bluegrass country; from there the state slopes W to the bottom lands of the Mississippi.

Manufacturing has taken top place in Tennessee's economy: Among important products are chemicals (especially plastic fibers), textiles, apparel, electrical machinery. Other lines are food processing, furniture, lumber, paper, metal products, leather.

Value added by manufacture is over $8.8 billion annually. Per capita income was $4,766 in 1975 (U.S. average: $5,834).

There are 24 research centers including Oak Ridge, TVA, and Arnold Engineering Development Center for rocket research.

Tennessee ranks 6th among the states in tobacco production. Farm receipts for 1975 totaled $967 million, more than half of it from crops, the rest from livestock. It has large numbers of hogs and cattle.

Forest products are also important, providing full-time jobs to 40,000 persons and contributing over $500 million annually to the economy. The state is known as the U.S. hardwood flooring center.

Tennessee produces a wide range of minerals and is a leader in production of zinc and pyrites. Other products include silver, copper, coal. Total mineral production was valued at $444 million for 1975.

Tourism is of increasing importance; tourists spend about $986 million annually in Tennessee. "Country and Western" music and the "Nashville sound" have made that city a leading recording center.

With 6 other states, Tennessee shares in federal reservoir developments on the Tennessee and Cumberland River systems. The Tennessee Valley Authority built Norris Dam on the Clinch River and operates a number of other dams in the state. Their reservoirs cover 756,321 acres.

Tennessee has a number of natural wonders—Reelfoot Lake, the reservoir basin of the Mississippi River formed by an earthquake (1811); Lookout Mountain, a rock-faced promontory carved by the currents of the Tennessee River and overlooking Moccasin Bend, at Chattanooga; Fall Creek Falls, 256 ft. high; and the west half of Great Smoky Mountains National Park.

The American Museum of Atomic Energy in Oak Ridge has displays, models, lectures. The Hermitage, 13 mi. E of Nashville, home of Andrew Jackson, contains personal effects of the 7th president. The Ancestral Home of James K. Polk, in Columbia, has various articles used by Pres. Polk in the White House. The home, tailor shop, and grave of Pres. Andrew Johnson are a national monument at Greeneville. The

Parthenon, in Centennial Park, Nashville, is a replica of the Parthenon of Athens. There are 26 state parks.

There are 67 institutions of higher education.

Spanish explorers first visited the area, 1541. English traders crossed the Great Smokies from the east while France's Marquette and Jolliet sailed down the Mississippi on the west, 1673. First permanent settlement was by Virginians on the Watauga River, 1769. During the Revolution, these colonists helped win the Battle of Kings Mountain, N.C., 1780, and joined other eastern campaigns. In the Civil War, hundreds of engagements were fought in the state. It seceded from the Union 1861, but of a total of 145,000 Tennessean soldiers, 30,000 fought for the Union.

Famous Tennesseans include Jackson, Johnson, Polk, Crockett, Houston, Farragut, Cordell Hull, Grace Moore, Pat Boone, Dinah Shore.

(See also Index for Chattanooga, Knoxville, Memphis, Nashville.)

Texas
Lone Star State

AREA: 267,338 sq. mi.; rank, 2d. **POPULATION** (U.S. est. 1975): 12,237,000; rank, 3d. **CAPITAL:** Austin. **MOTTO:** Friendship (from Indian word, Tejas—Friends). **FLOWER:** Bluebonnet. **TREE:** Pecan. **BIRD:** Mockingbird. **SONG:** Texas, Our Texas. **ENTERED UNION:** Dec. 29, 1845; rank, 28th.

Texas leads all other states in many categories, among them oil, cattle, sheep, and cotton. While these are basic to the Texas economy, manufacturing, as measured in terms of value added, makes a greater contribution than either mineral output or farm receipts. It is 2d only to Alaska in area.

Texas normally produces a third of the nation's total petroleum output. The state's 1975 petroleum production was valued at $9.6 billion, more than twice that of Louisiana, its nearest rival. Texas is also the top producer of asphalt, sulphur, graphite, natural gas, natural gas liquids, and magnesium chloride; Louisiana and Texas are the leading producers of natural gas. Texas ranks 2d among the states in output of salt, helium, and bromine, and 3d in cement.

The total value of the state's annual mineral pruduction is by far the greatest of any state, $16 billion in 1975, a 16.8% increase over 1974.

Texas ranked 3d in 1975 in cash receipts for crops, $2.9 billion; 3d for livestock products, $2.9 billion; 3d in total farm receipts, $5.8 billion.

It led all states in 1976 in number of cattle, 16.6 million (giving the state more cattle than people), and in sheep, 2.7 million; it ranked 4th in turkeys and 10th in chickens. It grew the largest crops of pecans, sorghum, and cotton, and the 3d largest of rice, peanuts and sweet potatoes. It also grows large amounts of vegetables and melons; its varied output includes oranges, grapefruit, peaches, winter wheat, and roses. Irrigation has reclaimed large arid areas.

The largest of its many livestock expositions are held annually in Fort Worth, San Antonio, Houston, and El Paso; its largest cattle auction in Amarillo.

Manufacturing industries have shown tremendous growth. Value added by manufacture was over $17.7 billion a year. About 20% of the total value is in chemicals, the largest manufacturing industry. Other important lines are petroleum refining, processing of foods, transportation equipment, machinery, primary metals. Per capita income was $5,387 in 1975, $447 below U.S. average.

Texas ranks high among the states in commercial fishing with the 1975 catch valued at $93 million.

About 22 million tourists spend over $3.2 billion dollars annually in Texas. There are 70 state parks, recreation areas, and historic sites; Big Bend and Guadalupe Mtns. National Parks, Padre Is. National Seashore, and Fort Davis National Historic Site. Named for Pres. Lyndon B. Johnson are a National Historic Site, a National Park and a State Park, marking his birthplace, boyhood home, and ranch, all near Johnson City, and a library in Austin.

Texas lists 376 museums; included were renowned art and historical collections.

Texas has 145 institutions of higher education.

It is the only state that was an independent republic, recognized by the U.S., before annexation. Over it have flown the flags of Spain, France, Mexico, the Lone Star Flag of the Republic, the Confederate States, and the U.S.

Alonso de Pineda sailed along the Texas coast, 1519; Cabeza de Vaca and Coronado visited the interior, 1541. Spaniards made the first settlement at Ysleta, near El Paso, 1682. Americans moved into the vast, empty land early in the 19th century. Mexico, of which Texas was a part, won independence from Spain, 1821; Santa Anna became dictator, 1835; Texans rebelled, Santa Anna wiped out defenders of the Alamo, 1836; Sam Houston's Texans defeated Santa Anna at San Jacinto and independence was proclaimed the same year. In 1845, Texas was admitted to the Union; it seceded, 1861.

Famous Texans include Stephen Austin, Sam Houston, James Bowie, J. Frank Dobie, Katharine Ann Porter, Lyndon Johnson, Chester Nimitz, Frank Robinson, Howard Hughes, Mary Martin.

(See also Index for Amarillo, Austin, Corpus Christi, Dallas, El Paso, Fort Worth, Houston, Lubbock, San Antonio.)

Utah
Beehive State

AREA: 84,916 sq. mi.; rank, 11th. **POPULATION** (U.S. est. 1975): 1,206,000; rank, 36th. **CAPITAL:** Salt Lake City. **MOTTO:** Industry. **FLOWER:** Sego lily. **BIRD:** California gull. **TREE:** Blue spruce. **EMBLEM:** Beehive. **SONG:** Utah, We Love Thee. **ENTERED UNION:** Jan. 4, 1896; rank, 45th.

Wrested from the wilderness by Mormon settlers in the mid-19th Century, Utah is for the most part a mountainous area, broken by fertile irrigated valleys, several deserts and 2 large lakes, Great Salt Lake in the N and Lake Powell in the S.

Great Salt Lake is 4,200 ft. above sea level, but has no known outlet. Its salt density varies from 20% to 25%, 2d only to that of the Dead Sea; it covers more than 1,500 sq. mi.; it is crossed by a 13-mi., rock-fill railroad causeway.

Manufacturing has become the state's major industry, well ahead of mining, agriculture, and tourism. Value added by manufacture in 1975 was an est. $1.2 billion. Transportation equipment was the most important line, followed by food products, machinery, metal products, printing-publishing, and electrical equipment. Per capita income was $4,819 in 1975.

Utah is an important center for research on, and production of, intercontinental missiles, rocket engines, solid fuel propellants, supersonic engines, aircraft navigational systems, and military computer components.

Utah is a rich storehouse of a wide variety of minerals. Among the states, it is a leading producer of copper, gold, silver, ashphalt, molybdenum, lead, vanadium, beryllium, sodium sulphate, and potassium salts.

Copper and petroleum have by far the greatest value among Utah's mineral products. In 1975, copper production was valued at $231 million, 2d only to Arizona's, and petroleum was worth $310 million; total mineral production value was $938 million.

The nation's largest open-pit copper mine at Bingham Canyon, normally employs about 7,000 persons and produces about 20% of the newly-mined copper in the U.S. There are large smelters and refineries.

With Colorado and Wyoming, Utah shares what may be the world's richest oil shale deposits.

Utah ranked 7th among the states in number of sheep in 1976 with 590,000. It also raises large flocks of turkeys. It is a leader in apricots and cherries. Other crops include barley, sugar beets, alfalfa, winter wheat, potatoes. Farm receipts for 1975 included $226 million from livestock, $93 million from crops.

Over 66% of the land is owned by the U.S.

Tourists spend about $630 million a year in Utah.

Utah is a great recreational area, with 11,000 mi. of fishing streams and 147,000 acres of lakes and reservoirs, numerous winter sports areas, and camp grounds. Natural wonders may be seen at Zion, Canyonlands, Bryce Canyon, Arches, and Capitol Reef National Parks, and Dinosaur, Rainbow Bridge, Timpanogos Cave and Natural Bridges National Monuments. The Lake Powell Recreation Area and Flaming Gorge Dam are other attractions.

Works by Utah artists, and archeological, botanical, mineral, and fossil collections may be seen at the Brigham Young University Collections in Provo.

In 1776, when the American colonies were declaring independence, 2 Spanish Franciscans visited the Utah area, the first white men to do so. American fur traders followed. Permanent settlement began with the arrival of the Mormons, 1847. They made the arid land bloom and created a prosperous economy; in 1849 they organized the State of Deseret and asked admission to the Union. This was not achieved until 1896, after a long period of controversy over the Mormon Church's doctrine of polygamy, which it discontinued in 1890.

Mormons comprise 72% of the population.

Famous Utahans include Brigham Young, George Romney, Ivy Baker Priest, Philo Farnsworth, Maude Adams, Laraine Day, Loretta Young.

(See also Index for Salt Lake City.)

Vermont
Green Mountain State

AREA: 9,609 sq. mi.; rank, 43d. POPULATION (U.S. est. 1975): 471,000; rank, 48th. CAPITAL: Montpelier. MOTTO: Freedom and Unity. FLOWER: Red clover. TREE: Sugar maple. BIRD: Hermit thrush. SONG: Hail, Vermont. ENTERED UNION: Mar. 4, 1791; rank, 14th.

Vermont, first state to join the Union after the original 13, was the home of the Green Mountain Boys of the American Revolution. They took their name from the Green Mountains which form the N-S backbone of the state. There are rich marble quarries in the western part of the state and large granite beds in the E. The Connecticut River runs along the E boundary, Lake Champlain forms much of the W line; among the many lakes is Memphremagog which lies partly in Canada to the N. Seven peaks rise over 4,000 ft. with Mt. Mansfield, 4,393 ft., the highest.

Vermont has long been known for its stoneworking, forest, and dairy industries. Per capita income was $4,925 in 1975.

Principal manufactured goods are machine tools, computer components, stone and clay products, lumber, furniture, and paper. Value added by manufacture is over $688 million a year.

Large milk and butter production accounts for most of the total value of farm receipts which was $217 million for 1974. For its small size, Vermont has a large number of milk cows.

The state ranks high in output of marble, granite, limestone; it is a leader in asbestos and talc.

Tourism is important; the accent is on recreation. Visitors spend more than $307 million a year. Skiing has experienced a tremendous growth. There are more than 95 miles of ski lifts in the state.

Vermont has 74 state parks and forests covering 141,000 acres. The Long Trail is popular for hiking and camping. There is fishing for trout, salmon, bass, muskellunge; hunting for deer and game birds.

The Shelburne Museum, 7 mi. S of Burlington, preserves 35 early American buildings; stagecoach inn; covered bridge, side-wheeler, old trains, folk art, etc.; Webb gallery of paintings by Rembrandt, Goya, Corot, Manet, Cassatt.

The Bennington Museum displays early American glass, furniture, pottery, and what is said to be the oldest Stars and Stripes flag in existence.

Champlain explored the lake that bears his name and separates Vermont from New York, 1609. First American settlement was Fort Dummer, 1724, near Brattleboro. With the Revolution, Ethan Allen and

Benedict Arnold captured Fort Ticonderoga and Seth Warner took Crown Point, both in N.Y., 1775. Britain's Burgoyne recaptured them, 1777, but John Stark defeated part of Burgoyne's forces near Bennington. In the War of 1812, Thomas MacDonough defeated a British fleet on Champlain off Plattsburgh, 1814. In the Civil War, Confederate soldiers, operating from Canada, robbed St. Albans banks.

Vermont has 23 institutions of higher learning.

Famous Vermonters include Chester Arthur, Calvin Coolidge, Stephen A. Douglas, Adm. George Dewey, Dorothy Canfield Fisher, John Dewey.

Virginia
Old Dominion

AREA: 40,817 sq. mi.; rank, 36th. POPULATION (U.S. est. 1975): 4,967,000; rank, 13th. CAPITAL: Richmond. MOTTO: Sic Semper Tyrannis, Thus Ever to Tyrants. FLOWER: American dogwood. BIRD: Cardinal. TREE: American dogwood. SONG: Carry Me Back to Old Virginia. Tenth of the original 13 states to ratify the Constitution, June 25, 1788.

The Commonwealth of Virginia is famed for its colonial heritage, for the statesmen it produced, its historic homes and estates, and great battlefields on which the fate of the nation was decided in both the 18th and 19th centuries.

Virginia's coastal plain, the Tidewater, consists mostly of 4 peninsulas formed by Chesapeake Bay and the Potomac, Rappahannock, York, and James Rivers. The central Piedmont plateau rises westward to the Blue Ridge Mtns. Beyond the Blue Ridge and between them and the Alleghenies on the W border lies the Shenandoah Valley, a rich farming region.

Virginia's manufacturing industries have grown and diversified. They provide jobs for 386,000, over 5 times the number employed in agriculture. Total value added by manufacture is $6.9 billion, with payrolls totaling $3 billion; value of shipments was estimated at $14.7 billion.

Largest lines were chemicals, textiles, food products, and clothing. Other important lines were lumber, furniture, paper, electrical machinery, transportation equipment, cigarettes, metal products, stone-clay-glass products, shipbuilding.

The federal government is a major employer with large military installations at Hampton Roads and many U.S. agencies near Washington, D.C.

Per capita income was $5,671 in 1975.

Hampton Roads, a large natural harbor at the mouth of the James, is the major port, a leader in bulk export tonnage.

Agriculture remains a vital factor in the economy. Virginia ranks among the leaders in the U.S. in its crops of tobacco, peanuts, apples, and sweet potatoes. Other important crops are corn, vegetables, barley, peaches. It has large numbers of turkeys; its Smithfield hams are famous. Farm receipts for 1975 totaled $977 million, more than half from crops.

Coal is Virginia's leading mineral commodity, in terms of both tonnage and value, and usually accounts for about 70% of the value of total mineral production, which was $1.1 billion in 1975. Also important are lime, zinc, stone.

The fish catch was worth $33 million in 1975.

With its wealth of historical attractions and recreational facilities, such as Shenandoah National Park in the Blue Ridge Mts. and Virginia Beach, on the Atlantic, the state drew 25 million out-of-state travelers who spent about $1.2 billion in 1974.

Virginia was the birthplace of 8 presidents. It has many historic shrines, including Washington's birthplace, Wakefield; his home and grave at Mount Vernon; Jefferson's Monticello, near Charlottesville, and the Univ. of Virginia he designed; Robert E. Lee's birthplace, Stratford Hall, and grave at Lexington.

Colonial Williamsburg is a restoration of the 18th century buildings and living conditions in what was the capital of Virginia when Washington, Jefferson, Patrick Henry, and George Mason were young men.

There are over 800 buildings.

At Jamestown, first permanent English settlement, are foundations and ruins of early buildings, relics, statues and monuments.

At Yorktown, where the surrender of British Gen. Cornwallis to American and French forces virtually ended the American Revolution, may be seen colonial buildings, earthworks and cannons.

In Fredricksburg, the James Monroe Law Office and Museum is the original building in which Pres. Monroe practiced law in the 1780s, containing the desk at which he signed the Monroe Doctrine.

Appomattox Court House National Monument includes the rebuilt Wilmer McLean house in which Gen. Lee surrendered to Gen. Grant, Apr. 9, 1865.

Fort Monroe Casement Museum has relics of the imprisonment in the fort of Jefferson Davis and Chief Black Hawk, and of the battle between the Monitor and Merrimac. The Quartermaster Museum, Fort Lee, exhibits clothing, saddles, etc., of American soldiers from the Revolution on. The War Memorial Museum of Virginia, in Newport News, displays World War I and II weapons and equipment.

In Lexington are Washington and Lee University and Virginia Military Institute, both closely linked with leaders and action in the Civil War. Also in Lexington is the George C. Marshall Research Library and Museum with displays of the life of the famed World War II general and statesman.

At Staunton is the Woodrow Wilson birthplace, with memorabilia of his family. The Gen. Douglas MacArthur Memorial in Norfolk contains the general's sarcophagus, flags of 30 units he commanded, documents, and murals of events in his life.

English settlers founded Jamestown, 1607. Virginians took over much of the government from royal Gov. Dunmore in 1775, forcing him to flee. Virginians under George Rogers Clark freed the Ohio-Indiana-Illinois area of British forces. Benedict Arnold burned Richmond and Petersburg, for the British, 1781. That same year, Britain's Cornwallis was trapped at Yorktown and surrendered.

Though a slave state, Virginia was one of the last to secede, 1861. It was the scene of major Civil War battles, ending with Robert E. Lee's surrender at Appomattox.

There are 73 institutions of higher education.

Famous Virginians include Washington, Jefferson, Madison, Monroe, William Harrison, Tyler, Taylor, Wilson, Patrick Henry, John Marshall, Joseph E. Johnston, Poe, Cabell, Cather, Ellen Glasgow, Booker T. Washington, Lewis and Clark, Richard E. Byrd.

(See also Index for Norfolk, Richmond, Roanoke.)

Washington
Evergreen State

AREA: 68,192 sq. mi.; rank, 20th. **POPULATION** (U.S. est. 1975): 3,544,000; rank, 22d. **CAPITAL:** Olympia. **MOTTO:** Al-Ki, By and By, **FLOWER:** Coast **rhododendron. TREE:** Western hemlock. **BIRD:** Willow goldfinch. **SONG: Washington, My Home.** **ENTERED UNION:** Nov. 11, 1889; rank, 42d.

The state of Washington in the Pacific Northwest is a leader in many ways — in lumber, in fruit and other crops, and in aircraft production; its ports on Puget Sound are gateways to Alaska and the Far East; the great dams on the Columbia River provide power for production of aluminum and irrigation for the rich Columbia Basin.

The lofty Cascade Range splits the state, running N-S. To the W, the Puget Sound lowlands support dairy, poultry, and truck-farming. On the E slopes of the Cascades are great fruit orchards; further E, plateau country provides sheep and cattle lands and a rich wheat belt.

The Columbia River cuts a zig-zag course across Washington from the NE, then flows W along the Oregon border to the Pacific.

Puget Sound has many deep harbors beside which Seattle, Tacoma, Everett, and other great cities have grown. Foreign trade, mainly with Japan and Canada, has increased greatly in the last 20 years.

Manufacturing industries employ 244,000 workers with payrolls of $2.6 billion and value added by manufacture over $5.7 billion a year. Transportation equipment, mostly aircraft, but including ships and trucks, accounts for $1.5 billion.

Other important manufacturing lines are lumber, food processing, paper, metal products, chemicals, machinery. The Atomic Energy Commission plant at Hanford produces nuclear fuels and electricity. Per capita income was $6,226 in 1975 (U.S. average: $5,834).

Washington's large production of fruits, berries, and other crops places it first among the states in apples, blueberries, hops, and red raspberries; it is among the top producers of potatoes, winter wheat, pears, grapes, apricots, filberts, cranberries, cherries, asparagus, strawberries. It ranks 3d in winter wheat. Farm receipts for 1975 totaled $2.02 billion, three-fourths from crops, the rest from livestock.

The commercial fishing catch is valued at $56 million a year. Salmon accounts for half the total, followed by halibut, and bottomfish.

Mineral production in 1975 was valued at an est. $143 million. Sand and gravel, silver, cement, zinc, and lead were the most important products.

Large aluminum reduction plants, using refined ore from out-of-state and hydro-electric power, have expanded. Aluminum output is 25% of U.S. total.

A series of great dams on the Columbia, including the massive Grand Coulee in the NE, and Bonneville on the Oregon border, provide power and irrigation.

More than half the state is in forests; one-sixth of the nation's standing sawtimber is in Washington. Towering Douglas firs and Ponderosa pines, western hemlocks, and red cedars are among commercially important trees; income, $1.4 billion a year.

There are 43 institutions of higher education.

Spain's Bruno Hezeta sailed the coast, 1775. American Capt. Robert Gray sailed up the Columbia River, 1792. Canadian fur traders set up Spokane House, 1810; Americans under John Jacob Astor established a post at Fort Okanogan, 1811. Missionary Marcus Whitman settled near Walla Walla, 1836. Final agreement on the border of Washington and Canada was made with Britain, 1846, and gold was discovered in the state's northeast, 1855, bringing new settlers. The 2 World Wars brought great industrial expansion.

The state has 3 national parks, Mt. Rainier, North Cascades, and Olympic National Park. Its state parks and national forests of nearly 10 million acres have large hunting, fishing, and recreation areas.

The Washington State Historical Society, Tacoma, has exhibits of the fur trade, Indian, and Eskimo arts, and pioneer cabins, schoolhouse, and covered wagon.

Tourists, it has been estimated, spend about $1 billion annually in the state.

Famous Washingtonians include Bing Crosby, Patrice Munsel, Eric Johnston, Guthrie McClintic, Upton Close, Dr. Marcus Whitman.

(See also Index for Seattle, Yakima.)

West Virginia
Mountain State

AREA: 24,181 sq. mi.; rank, 41st. **POPULATION** (U.S. est. 1975): 1,803,000; rank, 34th. **CAPITAL:** Charleston. **MOTTO:** Montani Semper Liberi, **Mountaineers Always Free. FLOWER: Rhododendron maximum. BIRD: Cardinal. TREE: Sugar maple. SONGS: The West Virginia Hills, This Is My West Virginia, and West Virginia, My Home, Sweet Home. ENTERED UNION:** June 20, 1863; rank, 35th.

West Virginia's fortunes have long been based on those of the bituminous coal industry; the state produces 17% of the U.S. total, 2d only to Kentucky. Increased output of coal and natural gas, plus growth in the chemical, steel, glass, and tourist industries, have aided the economy.

The terrain is mountainous, with the Alleghenies

running NE-SW in the eastern half of the state; the western half is a plateau sloping down to the Ohio River which forms most of the boundary on the W.

Early explorers included George Washington, 1753, and Daniel Boone. The area became part of Virginia and often objected to rule by the eastern part of the state. When Virginia seceded, 1861, the Wheeling Conventions repudiated the act and created a new state, Kanawha, subsequently changed to West Virginia. It was admitted to the Union as such, 1863. In the late 19th and early 20th centuries, the state was torn by industrial warfare. In recent years, it has had serious economic troubles.

Coal accounts for 94% of the total value of mineral production. In 1975 total production was valued at an est. $2.9 billion.

West Virginia produces and markets more natural gas than any other state east of the Mississippi. Also important are petroleum, salt, stone, cement, lime.

Production of a wide variety of chemicals, based on the state's resources of salt brine, gas, oil, and coal, and including synthetic fibers and plastics, dominates the manufacturing field, accounting for about 36% of the $2.9 billion in value added annually by manufacture. Large plants are in the Ohio and Kanawha valleys, where electric power is abundant. The state is also a major producer of steel, glass, pottery.

Farm receipts totaled $147 million for 1975; the hilly terrain is not conducive to large-scale agriculture. Poultry, dairy products, cattle, and sheep accounted for most receipts. Apples and peaches are profitable. About 79% of the state is forested.

Per capita income was $4,815 in 1975; national average was $5,834.

Tourism is being promoted and an est. 10 million visitors spend over $480 million annually. More than a million acres have been set aside for recreation in 34 state parks, 9 state forests, and Monongahela, George Washington, and part of Jefferson National Forests.

Attractions include Harpers Ferry National Historical Park, mineral water resorts at White Sulphur, and Berkeley Springs, trout fishing, turkey, deer, and bear hunting.

Part of the town of Harpers Ferry has been restored to its condition in 1859, when John Brown seized the U.S. Armory. Still standing is the fire-engine house in which Brown and a score of followers were besieged and captured by a force of U.S. Marines under Robert E. Lee, then a U.S. colonel.

The State Museum in Charleston displays local relics and artifacts from prehistoric cultures (as early as 8,000 B.C.), Indians, and pioneers.

The Huntington Galleries, Huntington, has collections of 19th and 20th century European and American paintings, furniture, and decorative arts. The Oglebay Mansion-Museum displays colonial furniture and 19th century glassware.

There are 28 institutions of higher education.

Famous West Virginians include Stonewall Jackson, Dwight Morrow, Michael Owens, John W. Davis, Newton D. Baker, Pearl Buck, Eleanor Steber.

(See also Index for Charleston, Huntington.)

Wisconsin
Badger State

AREA: 56,154 sq. mi.; rank, 26th. **POPULATION** (U.S. est. 1975): 4,607,000; rank, 16th. **CAPITAL:** Madison. **MOTTO:** Forward. **FLOWER:** Butterfly violet. **BIRD:** Robin. **TREE:** Sugar maple. **ANIMAL:** Badger. **FISH:** Muskellunge. **SONG:** On, Wisconsin! **ENTERED UNION:** May 29, 1848; rank, 30th.

Known as America's Dairyland, Wisconsin produces more milk and cheese than any other state and agriculture is a vital part of the state's economy. However, manufacturing, including processing of foods, has become the state's largest employer and biggest income producer.

Reforestation has kept the paper and wood product industries important. There are 14 ports on Lakes Michigan and Superior. Per capita income was $5,627 in 1975.

The state has an abundance of recreation resources; water and winter sports, hunting and fishing are among its attractions. Vacationers, it is estimated, spend $1.4 billion a year.

Wisconsin's rolling pasturelands and large crops support the nation's largest herd of milk cows, about 1.8 million; 80% of its farms are dairy farms.

The state produces the most milk, cheese, hay, and alfalfa in the U.S. It ranks 4th in oats, 7th in corn. It is also a leading producer of butter, corn, cranberries, and maple syrup. In addition to cattle, it also has large numbers of hogs and turkeys.

Farm receipts for 1975 totaled $2.5 billion, 11th highest among the states, four-fifths of it from livestock.

About 40% of income produced in Wisconsin comes from manufacturing and, with over 532,000 factory employees, the state ranks among the top 12. Value added by manufacturing is over $10.8 billion a year.

Most important products, in terms of value added, are: machinery, especially engines, turbines, industrial, and construction; food products, including dairy, meat and beer; transportation equipment, especially motor vehicle parts and equipment, and mobile homes; iron and steel, metal products, paper. Wisconsin is the top producer of motorcycles, beer, and canned vegetables.

Mineral production for 1975 was valued at $113 million. Zinc, lime, cement, and stone are important. Iron mining ceased in 1965 except for an open-pit taconite operation which by 1975 had increased production to nearly a million tons of pellets.

Most of Wisconsin's timber production goes into pulp and paper, but the state is also a leading producer of hardwood plywood and veneer.

Wisconsin borders Lake Superior to the north and Lake Michigan to the east. It has over 8,500 lakes, of which Winnebago is the largest. Water sports, iceboating and fishing for trout, bass, and muskellunge are popular, as are skiing and hunting for deer, bear, and wildfowl. Public parks and forests take up one-seventh of the land area; there are 49 state parks, 9 state forests, 2 national forests. Wisconsin produces 900,000 mink pelts per year, one-third the U.S. total.

Other attractions include small towns which preserve Swiss, Scandinavian, German, and other European cultures, visits to breweries and cheese factories, Indian festivals, and the Dells (scenic gorges) of the Wisconsin River.

The Circus World Museum in Baraboo has over 100 circus wagons and other displays, and presents circus shows daily, early May-early Sept.

There are 58 institutions of higher learning and the State University system has the 4th largest enrollment in the U.S.

Jean Nicolet was the first European to see the Wisconsin area, arriving in Green Bay, 1634. French missionaries and fur traders followed; the British took over, 1763. Thanks to the Revolution, the U.S. won the land but the British were not ousted until after the War of 1812. Lead miners came next and then farmers. Railroads were started in 1851, serving growing wheat harvests and iron mines. In the 20th Century, Wisconsin became an industrial state and also took the lead in dairy products.

Famous Wisconsinites include Robert and Philip LaFollette, Joseph R. McCarthy, Marc Mitscher, Thorstein Veblen, Thornton Wilder, Edna Ferber, Alfred Lunt, Frank Lloyd Wright, Harry Houdini.

(See also Index for Madison, Milwaukee.)

Wyoming
Equality State

AREA: 97,914 sq. mi.; rank, 9th. **POPULATION** (U.S. est. 1975): 374,000; rank, 49th. **CAPITAL:** Cheyenne. **MOTTO:** Equal Rights. **FLOWER:** Indian paintbrush. **BIRD:** Western meadowlark. **TREE:** Plains cottonwood. **SONG:** Wyoming State Song.

ENTERED UNION: July 10, 1890; rank, 44th.

Wyoming's towering mountains and rolling plains provide spectacular scenery, grazing ranges for sheep and cattle, and a wealth of mineral resources. Ranges of the Rockies cover the western two-thirds of the state; the eastern third is Great Plains country.

The most important industry is mining, particularly of oil and natural gas. Agriculture, especially livestock, runs 2d. Tourism and manufacturing are growing. Per capita income was $5,942 in 1975, $108 above U.S. average.

Wyoming has large reserves of coal, oil, gas, oil shale, iron ore, and gypsum.

Production of petroleum in 1975 was valued at $925 million. Total mineral production value for the year was est. at $1.6 billion. The state ranked first in the U.S. in sodium carbonate and bicarbonate production, 2d in uranium. Also important are coal, natural gas, clays, and iron ore.

Wyoming is 2d among the states in wool production, and in 1975 its sheep numbered 1.3 million, exceeded only by Texas; it also had 1.6 million cattle. Principal crops include wheat, oats, sugar beets, corn, potatoes, barley, and alfalfa. Livestock receipts for 1975 totaled $262 million; crops, $358 million.

Much of Wyoming's manufacturing is based on its mining and agricultural products. Leading lines include petroleum and coal products, including coke; processed foods, timber and wood, construction materials, food service equipment, pocket transits, iron and steel, electronic components. Value added by manufacture is about $171 million annually.

Wyoming is a source of 3 important river systems; the Missouri, Colorado, and Columbia. Both power and irrigation are provided by a growing number of dams and reservoirs. Tourism produces an est. annual $311 million.

The French explorers, Francois and Louis Verendrye, were the first European visitors, 1743. John Colter, American, was first to traverse Yellowstone Park, 1807-08. Trappers and fur traders followed in the 1820s. Forts Laramie and Bridger became important stops on the pioneer trail to the West Coast. Indian wars followed massacres of army detachments in 1854 and 1866. Population grew after the Union Pacific crossed the state, 1869. Women won the vote, for the first time in the U.S., from the Territorial Legislature, 1869.

Yellowstone National Park, 3,472 sq. mi. carved from the NW corner of Wyoming and the adjoining edges of Montana and Idaho, is the oldest of U.S. national parks, established 1872. It has some 10,000 geysers, plus hot springs, mud volcanoes, fossil forests, a volcanic glass (obsidian) mountain, the 1,000-ft.-deep canyon and 308-ft.-high waterfall of the Yellowstone River, and a wide variety of animals living free in their natural habitat.

Grand Teton National Park, with mountains 13,000 ft. high, comprises 299,326 acres; the National Elk Refuge covers 25,000 acres. Devils Tower, a cluster of rock columns 865 ft. high, became the first National Monument in the U.S. in 1906. Fort Laramie, partly preserved, partly restored, is a National Historic Site. The annual Cheyenne Frontier Days Celebration, last full week in July, is the state's largest rodeo. Hunting, fishing, and skiing are other attractions.

The Buffalo Bill Historical Center in Cody has a museum with personal effects of William F. Cody (Buffalo Bill), as well as the Whitney Gallery of Modern Art with Indian art and paintings by Frederic Remington, Charles M. Russell, George Catlin, etc.

The Bradford Brinton Memorial Ranch, near Big Horn, has collections of western painting and sculpture, antiques, Indian arts, hunting trophies.

There are 8 institutions of higher education.

Famous Wyomingites include Jim Bridger, Nellie Tayloe Ross, Buffalo Bill Cody.

District of Columbia

AREA: 67 sq. mi. POPULATION (U.S. est. 1975): 716,000; MOTTO: Justitia omnibus, Justice for all.

FLOWER: American beauty rose. TREE: Scarlet oak. BIRD: Wood thrush. The city of Washington is coextensive with the District of Columbia.

The District of Columbia is the seat of the federal government of the United States. It lies on the west central edge of Maryland on the Potomac River, opposite Virginia. Its area was originally 100 sq. mi. taken from the sovereignty of Maryland and Virginia. Virginia's portion south of the Potomac was given back to that state in 1846.

The 23d Amendment, ratified in 1961, granted residents of the District the right to vote for president and vice president for the first time and gave them 3 members in the Electoral College. Residents cast the first such votes in Nov. 1964.

Congress, which has legislative authority over the District under the Constitution, experimented with various forms of municipal government until 1878 when it established a government of 3 commissioners appointed by the president. The Reorganization Plan of 1967 substituted a single commissioner (also called mayor) and assistant, and a 9-member City Council; funds were still appropriated by Congress; residents had no vote in local government (except to elect school board members).

In Sept. 1970, Congress approved legislation giving the District one delegate to the House of Representatives. The delegate could vote in committee but not on the House floor. The first was elected 1971.

In May 1974 voters approved a charter giving them the right to elect their own mayor and a 13-member city council in Nov. 1974. The first mayor and council took office Jan. 2, 1975. The district won the right to levy its own taxes but Congress retained power to kill council actions.

Proposals for a "federal town" for the deliberations of the Continental Congress were made in 1783, 4 years before the adoption of the Constitution that gave the Confederation a national government. Rivalry between northern and southern delegates over the site appeared in the First Congress, meeting in New York in 1789. John Adams, presiding officer of the Senate, cast the deciding vote of that body for Germantown, Pa. In 1790 Congress compromised by making Philadelphia the temporary capital for 10 years. The Virginia members of the House wanted a capital on the eastern bank of the Potomac; they were defeated by the Northerners, while the Southerners defeated the Northern attempt to have the nation assume the war debts of the 13 original states, the Assumption Bill fathered by Alexander Hamilton. Hamilton and Jefferson arranged a compromise: the Virginia men voted for the Assumption Bill, and the Northerners conceded the capital to the Potomac. President Washington chose the site in Oct. 1790 and persuaded landowners to sell their holdings to the government at £25, then about $66, an acre. The capital was named Washington.

Washington appointed Pierre Charles L'Enfant, a French engineer who had come over with Lafayette, to plan the capital on an area not over 10 mi. square. The L'Enfant plan was considered grandiose, for streets 100 to 110 feet wide and one avenue 400 feet wide and a mile long on the Potomac pastures seemed foolhardy. But Washington endorsed his plans. When L'Enfant ordered a wealthy landowner to remove his new manor house because it obstructed a vista, and demolished it when the owner refused, Washington stepped in and dismissed L'Enfant. The official map was completed by Andrew Ellicott and Benjamin Banneker.

On Sept. 18, 1793, Pres. Washington laid the cornerstone of the north wing of the Capitol. The occasion was expected to drum up sales of city lots, but there were few purchasers. Washington bought several lots. In the next few years Robert Morris and others invested. By 1799 the Senate wing of the Capitol had been roofed, the walls of the president's house were up and the Treasury building was ordered. On June 3, 1800, Pres. John Adams moved to Washington and on June 10, Philadelphia ceased to be the temporary capital. The City of Washington was incorporated in 1802; the District of Columbia was created as a municipal corporation in 1871, embracing Washington, Georgetown, and Washington County.

(See also Index for Washington, D. C.)

Outlying U. S. Areas

Commonwealth of Puerto Rico

Estado Libre Asociado de Puerto Rico

AREA: 3,435 sq. mi. POPULATION (1976 est.): 3,112,000. CAPITAL: San Juan. SONG: La Borinquena. TREE: Ceiba. BIRD: Reinita. FLOWER: Maga.

Puerto Rico is a hilly, tropical island lying between the Atlantic to the N and the Caribbean to the S; it is the easternmost of the West Indies group called the Greater Antilles, of which Cuba, Hispaniola and Jamaica are the larger units. It lies about 1,600 mi. SE of New York, 500 mi. N of Venezuela. It is roughly rectangular, 105 mi. long by 35 wide. Numerous small islands include Vieques, Culebra, and Mona.

The soil of the coast plain is fertile and there are many lush valleys, but there are dry areas in the S which need irrigation and an extensive system has been constructed by the government. The climate is mild, with a mean temperature of 76°; the mean maximum is 82°, and the mean minimum 73°. Highest point is Cerro de Punta, 4,389 ft.

Pres. Truman, on Aug. 5, 1947, signed an act giving Puerto Rico the right to choose its chief executive by popular vote. An act of 1950, affirmed by special election, June 4, 1951, permitted Puerto Rico to draft its own constitution. One similar to that of the U. S. was approved in a convention Feb. 4, 1952, and ratified by a popular vote March 3, 1952. Pres. Truman signed, July 3, 1952, a Congressional resolution approving the new constitution, elevating Puerto Rico to the status of a free commonwealth associated with the U. S., effective July 25, 1952.

In a July 23, 1967, referendum, Puerto Ricans strongly favored continuation of commonwealth status. The vote was: commonwealth, 425,081; statehood, 273,315; independence, 4,205.

The Legislative Assembly consists of a Senate and House of Representatives, elected by direct vote every 4 years. Eight senatorial districts elect 2 senators each; 40 representative districts one member each; also 11 senators and 11 representatives at large. Puerto Rico's directly elected resident commissioner in the U.S. Congress has only committee voting privileges. Puerto Ricans were granted American citizenship under the Organic Act of 1917. They do not vote for president unless they move to the U.S., where they come under local laws.

Executive power is vested in a governor elected by direct vote. There are 12 executive departments each headed by a secretary. The judiciary consists of a Supreme Court and lower courts.

The Commonwealth's "Operation Bootstrap" program for economic development has radically raised the standard of living; per capita income for 1975 was $1,980, up $1,069 from 1965.

Puerto Rico derives its largest income from manufacturing, $1.80 billion in 1975. Products include textiles and apparel, electrical and electronic equipment, plastics, chemicals, petrochemicals, petroleum products, processed foods, metal, leather.

Gross capital investment in 1975 reached $1.86 billion; gross product was $7.11 billion.

Mineral production is mainly of construction materials, with cement accounting for a large part of the value; total value for 1975 was $47 million.

Agriculture, a large source of income, rose in 1975 to $333 million. Income from dairy and livestock products has surpassed that from sugar. Also important are tobacco, coffee, pineapples, coconuts, fruits, garden truck, rum, molasses.

Off-island trade is chiefly with the United States.

	Imports	Exports
1974	$4,262,000,000	$3,339,000,000
1975	$4,950,700,000	$2,138,400,000

The flow of migrants to mainland U.S. after 1945 was reversed in 1963. In 1975 39,574 more persons moved to Puerto Rico than departed. These changes are caused mainly by employment conditions, mainland and Puerto Rican. Unemployment on the island is usually over 12%; it reached 20% in 1976.

San Juan, with its international airport and resort hotels, is the center of the tourism industry. Visitors totaled 1,339,000 in 1975, down from 1,441,002 in 1974, but their spending rose to $375 million, up from $360.3 million.

Spanish is the official language but most persons also speak English. Public school education is free and compulsory at the elementary school level; English is taught as a secondary language and is compulsory in all 8 grades. Chief religion is Roman Catholicism.

Puerto Rico (or Borinquen, after the original Arawak Indian name Boriquen) was discovered by Columbus, Nov. 19, 1493. Ponce de Leon conquered it for Spain, 1509, and established the first settlement at Caparra, across the bay from San Juan.

Sugarcane was introduced, 1515, and slaves were imported 3 years later. Gold mining petered out, 1570. Spaniards fought off a series of British and Dutch attacks; slavery was abolished, 1873. The U.S. took the island during the Spanish-American War, 1898, without any major battle.

Famous Puerto Ricans include Luis Munoz Marin, Dona Felisa Rincon de Gautier, Pablo Casals, Roberto Clemente, Orlando Cepeda, Jose Ferrer, Rita Moreno, Jose Feliciano.

(See also Index for San Juan.)

Canal Zone and Panama Canal

For Panama Canal cargo traffic see Index.

The Canal Zone has been, in effect, a U. S. Government reservation. It is a strip of land extending 5 mi. on each side of the axis of the Canal, under jurisdiction of the U.S. by treaty with the Republic of Panama.

Efforts to change the zone's status have been made by both nations for several years.

The canal connects the Caribbean with the Bay of Panama on the Pacific. Because of the geographic loop made by the Isthmus of Panama, the Caribbean end of the canal, which could be called the eastern end, is actually further west than the Pacific end.

The zone has an area of 553 sq. mi. of which 371 are land. Population (1973 est.) was 46,000. About 11,000 U.S. army, air force, and navy personnel are normally stationed in the zone. The capital is Balboa Heights.

The Canal Zone government and the Panama Canal Co. are the 2 operating agencies, both headed by an individual who acts as governor of the Canal Zone and president of the company. The governor is appointed by the president of the U.S. As governor he reports directly to the secretary of the army; as president of the company he reports to its board of directors, appointed by the secretary of the army. The Canal Zone government maintains civil government. The company operates the canal, the Panama Railroad, and a ship between New Orleans and the Canal Zone.

A French syndicate under Ferdinand de Lesseps failed to complete a canal, 1880-89, and a second French company failed in 1899. The U. S. bought their rights and offered Colombia compensation for a canal zone, but Colombia failed to ratify the treaty, Oct. 1903. Panama declared itself independent of Colombia Nov. 3, 1903, and was recognized by Pres. Theodore Roosevelt Nov. 6. American naval forces discouraged action by Colombia. On Nov. 18 Panama granted the canal strip to the U.S. by treaty, ratified Feb. 26, 1904, compensation $10 million, with annual payments of $250,000 after 9 years, and a guarantee of Panama's independence.

Under terms of the 1903 treaty, Panama granted the U.S. perpetual sovereignty over the Canal Zone.

The canal was opened to traffic Aug. 15, 1914. In 1922, Colombia accepted $25 million from the U. S. plus special land transportation privileges, and agreed to recognize Panama. The U. S. increased its annual payment to Panama to $430,000 and withdrew its guarantee of independence.

A further treaty regulating relations between the U. S. and Panama was signed Jan. 25, 1955, increasing the annuity paid Panama to $1.9 million, (actually increasing it to $2.3 million because of devaluation of the U.S. dollar.) In addition, the U. S. gave Panama $28 million worth of real estate and buildings no longer needed by the Canal Zone administration. U. S. citizen and non-citizen employees were guaranteed equality of pay and opportunity. In addition, the U. S. agreed to build the high level bridge over the Pacific entrance to the canal. The bridge was opened Oct. 12, 1962, as a link in the Inter-American Highway.

Negotiations for a new treaty began after Panamanian riots protesting the 1903 and 1955 treaties caused the death of 21 Panamanians and 3 U. S. soldiers, Jan. 9, 1964. Preliminary agreement was reached in 1967, but in 1970, after a change of government, Panama declared the proposal unacceptable.

In Mar. 1973, the U. S. vetoed a Panama-backed resolution in the UN Security Council which called on the U. S. and Panama to negotiate a new treaty to "guarantee full respect for Panama's effective sovereignty over all its territory." The U. S. said it wished to negotiate with Panama "without outside pressure."

In Feb. 1974, U. S. and Panama representatives agreed on principles for negotiating a new treaty which would set a date for giving Panama jurisdiction over the canal area but give the U. S. the right to operate and protect the canal for a certain period, with Panama sharing in the revenues, until a date set for final transfer to Panama.

Virgin Islands

CAPITAL: Charlotte Amalie, on St. Thomas Is. AREA: 133 sq. mi. POPULATION: (1975 est.) 100,000. FLOWER: Yellow cedar.

The Virgin Islands of the United States, an unincorporated territory administered by the Interior Dept., lie to the E of Puerto Rico at the western end of the Lesser Antilles, 1,629 mi. SE of New York. There are about 100 islands in the Virgins, of which more than 50 islands and islets in the western area belong to the U.S.; the remainder are the British Virgin Islands.

The 3 largest and most populous of the U.S. islands are St. Croix, St. Thomas, and St. John. Formerly the Danish West Indies, the islands were purchased by the U.S. from Denmark for $25 million (effective Mar. 31, 1917) for defense purposes. The islands were discovered by Columbus in 1493. About 80% of the population is of Negro descent.

Mean winter temperature is 78°; summer, 82°. Virgin Islands National Park occupies about three-fourths of St. John, smallest of the 3 principal islands.

The inhabitants have been citizens of the U.S. since 1927. Legislation originates in a unicameral house of 15 senators, elected for 2 years.

The governor, formerly appointed by the president of the U.S., was popularly elected for the first.time in Nov. 1970 and took office Jan. 4, 1971, for a 4-year term. In 1972 a U.S. law gave the Virgin Islands one delegate to the U.S. House of Representatives; the delegate may vote in committee but not on the House floor.

Tourism is the largest industry, but it was hurt by a series of murders in 1973 and early 1974. Principal exports are watch movements, jewelry, rum, wool textile products, thermometers, bay rum.

Minor Caribbean Islands

Quita Sueno Bank, Roncador Cay, Serrana Bank and Seranilla Bank lie in the Caribbean between Nicaragua and Jamaica. They are uninhabited. They were to be turned over to Colombia under a 1972 agreement, but this still awaited U.S. Senate action.

Navassa lies between Jamaica and Haiti, covers about 2 sq. mi., is reserved by the U.S. for a lighthouse and is uninhabited.

American Samoa

CAPITAL: Pago Pago, Island of Tutuila. AREA: 76 sq. mi. POPULATION: (1975 est.) 31,000. MOTTO: Samoa Muamua Le Atua - In Samoa, God Is First. SONG: Amerika Samoa. FLOWER: Padgo. PLANT: Ava.

Blessed with spectacular scenery and delightful South Seas climate, American Samoa is the most southerly of all lands under U. S. ownership. It is an unincorporated territory consisting of 6 small islands of the Samoan group: **Tutuila** (where Pago Pago, the capital, lies by a crescent bay beneath tall mountains), **Aunuu**, the **Manua Islands (Tau, Olosega and Ofu)**, and **Rose**. Also administered as part of American Samoa is **Swain's Is.**, 210 mi. to the NW, acquired by the U.S. in 1925. The islands are 2,300 mi. SW of Hawaii.

American Samoa became U. S. territory by a treaty with the United Kingdom and Germany in 1899, confirmed by local chiefs in 1900 and 1904. Pago Pago had been a U.S. navy coaling station under an 1872 commercial treaty.

Western Samoa, comprising the larger islands of the Samoan group, was a New Zealand mandate and UN Trusteeship until it became an independent nation Jan. 1, 1962. *(See Index.)*

Tutuila has an area of 52 sq. mi. Tau has an area of 17 sq. mi., and the islets of Ofu and Olosega, 5 sq. mi. with a population of a few thousand. Swain's Island has nearly 2 sq. mi. and a population of about 100. Highest peak is Lata, on Tau Is., 3,056 ft.

About 70% of the land is forest. Chief products and exports are fish products, copra, and handicrafts. Taro, bread-fruit, yams, coconuts, pineapples, oranges, and bananas are also produced.

Formerly under jurisdiction of the navy, since July 1, 1951, it has been administered by the Interior Dept., which appoints a governor and a lieutenant governor. It has a bicameral legislature and an elected delegate to represent the territory before U.S. agencies in Washington.

The American Samoans are of Polynesian origin. They are nationals of the U. S.

Wake, Midway, Other Islands

Wake Island, and its sister islands, **Wilkes** and **Peale,** lie in the Pacific Ocean on the direct route from Hawaii to Hong Kong, about 2,000 mi. W of Hawaii and 1,290 mi. E of Guam. The group is 4.5 mi. long, 1.5 mi. wide, and totals less than 3 sq. mi. Population (1970 census) was 1,647.

The U.S. flag was hoisted over Wake Island, July 4, 1898, by Gen. F. V. Greene, commanding 2d Detachment, Philippine Expedition. Formal possession was taken Jan. 17, 1899; Wake has been administered by the U.S. Air Force since 1972.

The **Midway Islands,** acquired in 1867, consist of 2, **Sand** and **Eastern,** in the North Pacific 1,150 mi. NW of Hawaii, with area of about 2 sq. mi., administered by the Navy Dept: Population (1975 est.) was 2,256.

Johnston Atoll, SW of Hawaii, area 1 sq. mi., pop. 1,007 (1970 census), is under Air Force control, and **Kingman Reef,** S of Hawaii, is under Navy control.

Howland, Jarvis, and **Baker Islands** south of the Hawaiian group, uninhabited since World War II, are under the Interior Dept.

Palmyra is an atoll SW of Hawaii, 4 sq. mi. Privately owned, it has been under the Interior Dept. since 1961.

Guam

The World Almanac is sponsored on Guam by the Pacific Daily News, 90 O'Hara St., Agana, GU 96910; phone 777-9711; successor in 1970 to Guam Daily

News; circulation throughout Micronesia, 20,350; a Gannett newspaper; president and publisher Robert E. Udick, editor Joe Murphy, managing editor George Blake.

CAPITAL: Agana. AREA: 209 sq. mi. POPULATION: (1974 est.) 100,000.

Guam, the largest of the Mariana Islands, is an unincorporated U.S. territory. It was ceded to the U.S. by Spain in the treaty of Paris, Dec. 10, 1898. It is 30 mi. long and 4 to 8.5 mi. wide. Distance from Manila, 1,499 mi.; from San Francisco, 5,053 mi. Mean annual temp. is 81°, average annual rainfall, July to Sept., 70 in. The island is volcanic and mountains rise 700 to 1,329 ft. Highest peak is Mt. Lamlam.

Magellan arrived in the Marianas Mar. 6, 1521, and called them the Ladrones (thieves). They were colonized in 1668 by Spanish missionaries who renamed them the Mariana Islands in honor of Maria Anna, queen of Spain.

When Spain ceded Guam to the U. S., it sold the other Marianas to Germany. Japan obtained a League of Nations mandate over the German islands in 1919; in Dec. 1941 it seized Guam; the island was retaken by the U.S. in July 1944. Guam has U.S. Navy and Air Force bases.

Guam is under the jurisdiction of the Dept. of the Interior. It is administered under the Organic Act of 1950, which provides for a governor, a 21-member unicameral legislature, elected biennially by the residents, who are American čitizens but do not vote for president.

Beginning in Nov. 1970, Guamanians elected their own governor, previously appointed by the U.S. president. He took office in Jan. 1971. In 1972 a U.S. law gave Guam one delegate to the U.S. House of Representatives; the delegate may vote in committee but not on the House floor.

School attendance is compulsory. The University of Guam provides higher education. English is the official language. Chief religion is Roman Catholicism.

The Guamanians are of primarily Chamorro (Micronesian) stock, with some of mixed Spanish or Filipino descent.

Copra, fish, and handicraft products are exported. Tourism has become a major aspect of Guam's economy. Over 125,000 tourists, most from Japan, visit annually.

Islands Under Trusteeship

The U. S. Trust Territory of the Pacific Islands, also called Micronesia, includes 3 major archipelagoes: the Caroline Islands, Marshall Islands, and Mariana Islands (except Guam: see above). There are 2,141 islands, 98 of them inhabited; land area total 687 sq. mi. but the islands are scattered over 3 million sq. mi. of Micronesia in the western Pacific N of the Equator and E of the Philippines. Total pop. est. (1974) at 115,000.

The Marianas

In process of becoming a U.S. commonwealth in 1976 were the Northern Mariana Islands, which since 1947 had been part of the Trust Territory of the Pacific Islands, assigned to U.S. administration by the United Nations. The Northern Marianas comprise all the Marianas except Guam, stretching N-S in a 500-mi. arc of tropical islands east of the Philippines and southeast of Japan.

Residents of the islands on June 17, 1975, voted 78% in favor of becoming a commonwealth of the U.S. rather than continuing with the Carolines and Marshalls in the U.S.-UN Trusteeship. On March 24, 1976, U.S. Pres. Ford signed a Congressionally-approved commonwealth covenant giving the Marianas control of domestic affairs and giving the U.S. control of foreign relations and defense, and the right to maintain military bases on the islands.

Establishment of the commonwealth awaited adoption of a constitution and acceptance of the change in status by the UN Security Council.

Ferdinand Magellan was the first European to visit the Marianas, 1521. Spain, Germany, and Japan held the islands in turn until World War II when the U.S. seized them in bitter battles on 2 of the main islands, Saipan and Tinian.

Population in 1976 was 14,335, mostly on Saipan. English is the official language; Roman Catholicism is the major religion. The people are descendants of the early Chamorros, Spanish, Japanese, Filipinos, and Mexicans. Land area is 181.9 sq. mi.

Tourism is an important industry; visitors are mostly from Japan. Crops include sugar, cotton, coco-nuts, maize, rice, tobacco, coffee, and breadfruit.

The Carolines and Marshalls.

In 1885, many of the Carolines, Marshalls and Marianas were claimed by Germany. Others, held by Spain, were sold to Germany at the time of the Spanish-American War, 1898. After the outbreak of World War I, Japan took over the 3 archipelagoes and, following that war, League of Nations mandates over them were awarded to Japan.

After World War II, the United Nations assigned them (1947) as a Trust Territory to be administered by the U.S. They were placed under administration of the U.S. Interior Dept. in 1951.

There is a high commissioner, appointed by the U.S. president. Saipan is the headquarters of the administration. The Congress of Micronesia, an elected legislature with limited powers, held its first meeting in 1965. It has a Senate of 12 members and a House of Representatives of 21.

In 1969, a commission of the Congress of Micronesia recommended that Micronesia be given internal self-government in free association with the U.S.

A U.S. offer of commonwealth status, similar to Puerto Rico's, was rejected by Micronesian leaders in 1970.

In 1974 talks, tentative agreement was reached on parts of a U. S. plan for self-government for the Marshalls and Carolines in free association with the U. S. (which would be responsible for foreign affairs and defense).

Among the noted islands are the former Japanese strongholds of Palau, Peleliu, Truk, and Yap in the Carolines; Bikini and Eniwetok, where U.S. nuclear tests were staged, and Kwajalein, another World War II battle scene, all in the Marshalls.

Many of the islands are volcanic with luxuriant vegetation; others are of coral formation. Only a few are self-sustaining. Principal exports are copra, trochus shells, fish products, handicrafts, and vegetables.

Disputed Pacific Islands

In the central Pacific, S and SW of Hawaii, lie 25 islands claimed by the U.S.; 18 of them are also claimed by the United Kingdom, and 7 by New Zealand. All are S of the Equator except Christmas Island.

Those claimed by the UK are:

The Line Islands, S of Hawaii, including Christmas, Flint, Malden, Starbuck, Vostok, and Caroline; only Christmas is inhabited. All are administered by the UK.

Also, the Phoenix Islands, SW of Hawaii, including Canton and Enderbury; and Birnie, Gardner, Hull, McKean, Sydney, and Phoenix. All are inhabited and administered by the UK except for Canton and Enderbury which are under joint U.S. and UK administration.

Also, the Tuvalu (Ellice) Islands, further to the SW, including Funafuti, Nukufetau, Nukulailai, and Nurakita; all inhabited and all administered by the UK.

Those claimed by New Zealand are:

The Tokelau (Union) Islands, S of the Phoenix group, including Nukunono, Atafu, and Fakaofu. All are inhabited and administered by New Zealand.

Also, the Northern Cook Islands, E of the Tokelaus, including Danger, Manahiki, Rakahanga, and Penrhyn (Tongareva). All are inhabited and administered by New Zealand.

MEMORABLE DATES

Consult also Chronology, Aviation Records, Polar Explorations, Fast Ocean Passages, Train Records, Marine Disasters, Political Assassinations, Earthquakes, Fires, Tornadoes, Amendments to the Constitution, Noted Personalities, Astronomical Data, Space Exploration, Sports and other classifications.

B.C. or B.C.E.
Before Christ or Before Common Era

3000
Indus Valley civilization sites at Mohenjo-Daro and Harappa in West Pakistan. Civilization had complex form of government, elaborate irrigation and drainage system, writing, well planned streets, houses of several stories. Ended about **1500 B. C.**
Pyramids begun by kings of Egypt at Sakkara. Cheops built great pyramid at Giza. Sphinx built about **2900 B.C.**

c. 1792-1750
Hammurabi ruled Semitic kingdom of Babylon; wrote extensive code of laws. Ruled Canaan in days of Abraham.

c. 1450 or c. 1275
Moses led the Israelites out of Egypt.

1360
Ikhnaton introduced monotheistic worship of Aton, or sun, in Egypt. A successor, Tutankhamen, revived polytheistic orthodoxy **1350 B. C.** Tutankhamen buried at Thebes **1344 B. C.**, tomb opened by Howard Carter and Lord Carnarvon **1923-24 A. D.**

1184
Troy (Ilium) fell to Greeks after 10-year siege, according to Homer's Iliad. Excavations show numerous battles were waged on site, NW corner of Asia Minor, 3 mi. from Hellespont (Dardanelles).
In 1871 A. D. Heinrich Schliemann, German archeologist, excavated site of Troy on hill of Hissarlik and found layered remains of 7 cities. Dorpfeld found 2 more. Schliemann identified 2d city with Homer's Troy, but objects found in 6th city correspond better with Greek remains of **1200 to 1100 B. C.** found at Agamemnon's Mycenae in Greece.

1000
On death of **King Saul c. 1000 B. C.** David became king of Israel, but for 7 1/2 years ruled only the southern kingdom of Judah. Thereafter he ruled all Israel, made Jerusalem capital. Solomon, son of David and Bathsheba, ruled **c. 973-933 B. C.**

753
Romulus founded Rome, according to legend.

612
Babylonians destroyed Nineveh, Assyrian capital. Nebuchadnezzar's Babylonians defeated Egyptians at Carchemish **605 B.C.** Built famed hanging gardens. Destroyed Solomon's temple **589 B. C.**

563
Gautama (Sakyamuni) Buddha, "the Enlightened," born near Himalayas; died **483 B. C.**, aged 80. Taught that pain in life is caused by desire; if desire is overcome, pain ends.

551
Confucius (Latinized form of K'ung-fu-tze) Chinese social philosopher, born; died **478 B. C.**

490
King Darius' Persian army landed at Marathon to march on Athens. Athenian infantry (10,000) routed 30,000 Persians.

484-480
Persian King Xerxes assembled a large army at Sardis to invade Greece. His Phoenicians and Egyptians built 2 ship bridges across Hellespont from Abydos (Nagara) to Sestos, 2,000 yds. long. One bridge of planks and dirt rested on 360 ships; the other on 314. Herodotus reported army crossing took 7 days and 7 nights.
At Thermopylae Pass, 480 B.C., Leonidas and 300 Spartans, supported by 700 Thespians and 400 Thebans, held off Persians until overcome. Persians took Athens and Attica. Athenians under Themistocles destroyed Persian fleet at Salamis under eyes of Xerxes, won land battle. Rallying about 70,000 from Greek states, they routed Persians at Plataea **479 B. C.**

438
Parthenon completed at Athens; Ictinus and Callicrates, designers; Phidias, chief sculptor.

431
Peloponnesian Wars began between Athens and Sparta. Wars ended **404 B.C.** with Sparta victorious.

399
Socrates, Greek philosopher, condemned by Athenian state, drank poison hemlock. Plato, his student, recorded 35 dialogues, famed philosophical work. Xenophon, another student, recorded memorabilia.

356
Alexander "The Great" of Macedon born. Ruthless and energetic military leader, defeated Persians at Granicus, Issus, Arbela; conquered Asia Minor and Egypt, burned Persian capital, Persepolis, carried war to the Punjab in India. Founded Alexandria in Egypt. Died of fever at Babylon **323 B. C.**

300
Invention of Mayan calendar in Yucatan (approximate date) giving solar year 365.24 days and lunar month 29.52 days. Now considered more exact than older calendars of Babylon, Assyria, Egypt, Greece.

264
Rome began first Punic War against Carthage, rich commercial seaport on Bay of Tunis. In 241 B. C. Carthage ceded Sicily and Lipari Islands; in 239 B. C. Rome annexed Sardinia and Corsica.

218-146
Hannibal, Carthaginian general, in a campaign against Rome during 2d Punic War, crossed from Spain to Italy via the Alps with 20,000 infantry, 6,000 cavalry, and about 40 elephants. Defeated Romans at Lake Trasimene **217 B. C.** and Cannae **216 B. C.** Victories nullified by Fabius, "the delayer," hence "Fabian tactics." War closed with defeat of Carthage in Africa by Publius Scipio **202 B. C.** Hannibal, after career in Asia Minor, committed suicide in Bithynia upon betrayal to Romans, c. **183 B.C.**
Third Punic War 149-146 B. C., ended with total destruction of Carthage. Later, Roman colony built there; eventually destroyed by Saracens **698 A. D.**

60-27
Julius Caesar formed political triumvirate with Pompey and Crassus 60 B.C.; defeated Helvetia, Belgae, 58-57 B. C.; entered Britain 55 and 54 B. C. Crossed Rubicon River into Italy, despite Senate orders, defeated Pompey at Pharsalus 48 B. C. Defeated Pharnaces at Zela, Asia Minor, 47 B. C. Lived with Cleopatra, queen of Egypt, in Rome 46-44 B. C. Was dictator but refused crown.
Caesar assassinated in Roman Senate by group led by Cassius and Brutus 44 B. C. Caesar's will made his grand-nephew, Gaius Octavius, successor; he formed new triumvirate, Octavius ruling West, Mark Antony East and Lepidus Africa. At Philippi 42 B. C. Antony defeated Cassius and Brutus, both committed suicide. Antony joined Cleopatra in Alexandria; they had 3 sons. Octavius defeated their fleet at Actium 31 B. C.; they committed suicide. Octavius received title of Augustus (venerated) 27 B. C., called first Roman emperor. Roman advance into northern Europe ended 9 A. D. when Germans under Arminius defeated Varus. Augustus died 14 A. D.

4
Birth of Jesus Christ in Bethlehem.

1 B. C. and 1 A. D.
The year 1 B. C. is the first year before the beginning of the Christian era. The year 1 A. D. is the first year of the Christian era. Jan. 1, 1 B. C. is just one year before Jan. 1, 1 A. D. The elapsed number of

years between a date B. C. and the same date A. D. is one less than the sum of the years. The Christian era was calculated by the monk Dionysius Exiguus in the 6th century after Christ. He placed Jesus' birth on Dec. 25 in the year 753 of Rome and decided 754 should be the first year of the Christian era. Biblical scholars find his calculations in error and place the birth of Jesus in the Roman year 750 (4 B. C.) or earlier.

A.D.
The Christian or Common Era

29
Crucifixion of Jesus in reign of Roman emperor Tiberius; Pontius Pilate procurator in Judea. The Roman Catholic church gives the date of the crucifixion as **April 7, 30 A. D.**

43
Roman Emperor Claudius subdued Britons; occupation of 300 years begun.

64
Persecution of Christians by Nero; burning of Rome. Apostles Paul and Peter martyred c. 67.

70
Jerusalem destroyed by Titus. Christians persecuted, worship in catacombs of Rome.

79
Pompeii, Herculaneum and Stabii destroyed by eruption of Mt. Vesuvius.

180
Death of Marcus Aurelius; onset of Roman decline.

311
Emperor Galerius, on deathbed, agreed to tolerance of Christians. Emperor Constantine 313 promulgated Edict of Milan, made Christianity legal.

325
Council of Nicaea called by Constantine in Bithynia, Asia Minor, to get churchmen to define orthodox Christian belief. Divinity of Christ and Holy Trinity endorsed; minority view of Arius rejected.

330
Constantine dedicated Byzantium capital of Eastern Empire, henceforth called Constantinople, now Istanbul. Baptized a Christian on his deathbed by Eusebius 337.

380
Theodosius, Roman emperor, made Christianity based on Nicene creed official religion, banned worship of old pagan gods.

410
Rome sacked by Alaric, the Goth; by Genseric, the Vandal, 455.

432
Bishop (later Saint) Patrick, was missionary to Ireland; labored 30 years, converting inhabitants to Christianity. In 563 Irish Missionary (later Saint) Columba founded church on Iona, Scottish island. In 597 St. Augustine founded church at Canterbury in England.

449
Anglo-Saxon migrations from continent to Britain.

483
Justinian I, Byzantine emperor, born; died 565. During reign had Tribonian prepare Justinian Code (Corpus Juris Civilis) which became basic Roman law used later as a model by many modern European states.

570
Mohammed born in Mecca; Hegira, flight from Mecca to Medina, July 16, 622 is beginning of Moslem calendar. Saracens crossed to Spain 711, established Moorish kingdom, lasted until 1492.

731
Great period of **Mayan empire** began; ended 987.

732
Charles Martel, Frankish ruler, defeated 90,000 Moors at Tours, France; height of Moslem invasion of Western Europe.

800
Charlemagne, king of Franks, proclaimed Holy Roman Emperor by Pope Leo III on Christmas Day in St. Peter's. Charlemagne fought Saxons, Lombards, Saracens 30 years to Christianize them; extended empire from Atlantic to eastern boundaries of Hungary. Died 814, aged 72, was buried in his cathedral at Aix.

1000
Leif Ericsson's Norsemen reach Vinland (land of grape vines). Variously identified as Labrador, New England coast and Martha's Vineyard.

1014
Brian Boru, Irish king, defeated Danes at Clontarf.

1027
Second Maya empire in Yucatan. Disintegrated 1480. Destruction of Tayasal, Guatemala, Itza capital, by Spanish governor of Yucatan in 1697 ended Mayan millennium.

1054
Final break between Eastern (Orthodox) and Western (Roman) church came when Pope Leo IX excommunicated Michael Cerularius and his followers. Eastern Orthodox Church became established religion of Russia under the Czars. Russian patriarchate formed 1589.

1066
William of Normandy conquered England at Hastings Oct. 14; Harold, last Saxon king of England, slain.

1096
First crusade, preached by Peter of Amiens, supported by Pope Urban II, raised 100,000 men. Captured Jerusalem 1099, Acre, 1104. Second, 1146, lost Jerusalem to Saladin, a Kurd. Third, 1189, Richard I of England took Jaffa. Fourth, 1200, besieged Constantinople 1204. Fifth, 1216, achieved 10-year truce. Sixth, 1238, lost ground. Seventh, 1245, led by Louis IX (St. Louis) of France who was captured 1250. Eighth, 1270, led by Louis, who died near Tunis 1270. Children's crusade, 1212, 50,000 children (est.); most died of disease and hunger or were sold as slaves in North Africa.

1162
Genghis Khan, Mongol chief, born; died 1227. Captured Peking 1215, defeated Russians 1223, conquered most of Central Asia and massacred population of Herat, Afghanistan. By 1241 Mongols under Batu had burned Moscow and Kiev and invaded Poland, Hungary and the Danube Valley.

1215
Magna Carta, the great charter of England, signed by King John at Runnymede at insistence of 2,000 English barons who refused to fight on foreign soil and demanded end of illegal levies by king. Charter guaranteed privileges of nobility, church free from secular interference, right of freemen to legal protection. Freemen were privileged class; common people were villein farmers, practically serfs. But 400 years later Edward Coke and Puritans demanded protection for the common people under these rights by jury developed. It reads: *No freeman shall be taken or imprisoned, or dispossessed, or outlawed, or banished, or in any way destroyed, nor will we go upon him, nor send upon him, except by the legal judgment of his peers or by the law of the land.*

1271
Marco Polo started with father and uncle for Cathay (China), Mongol kingdom of Kublai Khan. Served under Khan, returned to Venice 1295. Wrote Travels.

1274
Thomas Aquinas, scholastic philosopher, died.

1300
Dante and Giotto flourished; dawn of Renaissance.

1309
Clement V, French pope, made Avignon seat of church; Urban V returned to Rome 1367, warfare caused him to return to Avignon, 1370. Gregory XI finally reentered St. Peter's 1377. During the Great Schism, 1378-1417, French and Italian factions chose popes for Avignon and Rome; breach healed by Martin V 1417.

1346
Battle of Crecy, France, Aug. 26. Edward III of England defeated larger French force of Philip VI; first use of English longbow in continental warfare.

1348
Black Death (bubonic plague) reached Venice, rapidly spreading to rest of Europe by 1349. An estimated one-fourth of European population killed.

1382
John Wycliffe, English forerunner of Reformation, directed translation of Vulgate Bible into English vernacular. Supported bill in Parliament declaring it sinful for clergy to hold property. By elevating Scriptures above church authority he anticipated Lutheran doctrine by 150 years.

1415
John Huss, Bohemian preacher, follower of Wycliffe, agitator of ecclesiastic reforms, burned at stake in Konstanz, Germany, **July 6** for heresy after German Emperor Sigismund revoked his safe-conduct.

1429
Joan of Arc, Maid of Orleans, obeying "voices" of saints, rallied French against English, raised siege of Orleans, effected coronation of Charles VII at Rheims. Through carelessness or treachery she was captured by Burgundians **May 24, 1430,** and sold to English for 10,000 livres. Placed on trial before bishop of Beauvais at Rouen for magic, disobeying parents, wearing male attire, and heresy, she made a retraction (which she later revoked), but was given life imprisonment. Tricked to resume male attire, she was condemned to death by a French court and burned at Rouen by the English **May 30, 1431.** Sentence revoked 25 years later.

1453
Constantinople captured by Ottoman Turks.
End of 100-years' war between England and France, begun 1338. England lost all French land except Calais which the French captured 1558.

1456
Johann Gutenberg completed first Bible printed from movable type; 2 vols., 42 lines 2 columns to page. Printing took 5 years.

1457
Johann Fust and Peter Schoeffler produced a psalter, the first book printed in colors, and having printers' name, date and place.

1475
William Caxton printed first book in English, translation of a French history of Troy, at Bruges. He moved to Westminster, London, where he printed the first dated book in England 1477.

1492
Christopher Columbus, Genoese navigator, gained support of Spain's Queen Isabella for westward voyage. Left Palos de la Frontera **Aug. 3** with Santa Maria, 100 tons, 52 men; Pinta 50 tons, 18 men; Nina, 40 tons, 18 men. On **Oct. 12** at 2 a.m., Rodrigo de Triana on Pinta discovered land. Columbus landed on Guanahani (Watling Is.), Bahamas, called it San Salvador. Discovered Cuba and Hispaniola (Haiti or San Domingo); built first fort, La Navidad, there. *For later voyages see Index.*

1497
John Cabot, Venetian employed by English, reached Canada. His son Sebastian joined 2d voyage **1498.** English claim to Canada was based on their discoveries.
Amerigo Vespucci, Italian-born Spanish navigator, asserted he reached American mainland (New World) a year before Columbus.

1498
Savonarola, who preached against luxury and power of clergy, burned as heretic in Florence **May 23.**
Vasco da Gama, Portuguese navigator, reached India, discovering all-sea, around-Africa route from W. Europe.

1506
Pope Julius II (della Rovere) started new St.
Peter's; employed Michelangelo, Bramante, Raphael.

1509
Henry VIII became king of England. Defeated Scots at **Flodden Field** 1513. Named Defender of the Faith by Pope Leo X for attacking Luther 1521. When pope refused to annul his marriage to **Catherine of Aragon** for lack of male issue, Henry divorced Catherine, married **Anne Boleyn 1533.** Act of Supremacy abrogated pope's authority, made king head of church in England **1534.** He ordered monasteries closed **1536.**

1517
Martin Luther, Augustinian monk, preached faith over works, attacked abuse of selling papal indulgences, posted 95 theses (propositions) on Wittenberg church door Oct. 31. Diet of Worms, under Charles V **Jan. 1521** ordered recantation. Luther, backed by German princes, refused; put Scriptures above papal authority. Translated Greek New Testament into German 1522. Became head of German evangelical movement, broke with Rome, married a former nun. Augsburg Confession, basic Lutheran creed, presented to Diet there by Melanchthon 1530.

1519
Hernando Cortes began conquest of Mexico.

1520
Fernando Magellan discovered Strait of Magellan; killed in Philippines 1521. His crew completed first circumnavigation of the world arriving in Spain **Sept. 6, 1522.** Voyage proved the world round, showed large proportion of water to land, and revealed the Americas to be a "New World."

1524
Giovanni da Verrazano, Italian, explored New England coast for French, probably New York Bay.

1526
William Tyndale produced in Cologne first printed version of New Testament in English, suppressed in England. Tyndale executed for heresy **Oct. 6, 1536,** at Vilvarde, near Brussels.

1529
Turks failed in siege of Vienna; 2d siege, **1683,** was broken by Polish King John Sobieski's landmark victory.

1531-35
Francisco Pizarro conquered Peru for Spain.

1534
John Calvin, French-born religious reformer, published his Institutes of the Christian Religion, influential Protestant doctrine. Rejected Lutheran doctrine of consubstantiation; believed in religious base of citizenship, original sin, infant damnation. Influence extended to Scottish Presbyterians, English and New England Puritans.
Jacques Cartier, sent by Francis I of France, in 2 voyages 1534-36 discovered St. Lawrence River, reached site of Montreal. Basis of French claims to Canada.

1535
Miles Coverdale published first complete Bible in English. Also worked on first authorized Bible, "The Great Bible," completed **1539.** Other editions: Whittingham's New Testament, with Calvin's introduction **1557;** Geneva Bible **1560;** Bishop's Bible **1568.**

1540
Francisco Coronado, searching for gold and "Seven Cities of Cibola," explored Southwest north of Rio Grande with 70 horse and 30 foot soldiers. Hernando de Alarcon discovered Colorado River. Don Garcia Lopez de Cardenas discovered Grand Canyon.

1541
Hernando de Soto discovered Mississippi River.

1545
Council of Trent, in Austrian Tyrol, urged on Pope Paul III by Emperor Charles V, to define Catholic dogma and remedy ecclesiastical abuses, opened **Dec. 13;** continued intermittently until 1563; reiterated supreme papal authority, outlined Roman Catholic faith.

1555
Bishops Ridley and Latimer burned at Oxford Oct.

16; Archbishop Cranmer of Canterbury burned **Mar. 21, 1556; 2̄77** other religious leaders burned in attempt of Queen Mary Tudor (Bloody Mary) to restore Catholic authority. Elizabeth I became queen **1558,** made Anglican communion official church.

1560

Some 1,200 Huguenots hanged at Amboise. Catherine de Medici, regent of France for son, Charles IX, by **Edict of Jan. 1562,** granted Huguenots right to worship outside walled towns. Infraction of edict led to massacre of Huguenots at Vassy **Mar. 1, 1562,** beginning of 8 religious wars. Massacre of St. Bartholomew **Aug. 24, 1572,** encouraged by Charles IX on marriage of sister, Marguerite de Valois to Henry of Navarre (non-Catholic). Henry III, who caused assassination of Catholic leaders Duc de Guise and Cardinal of Lorraine, was himself murdered **Aug. 1, 1589.** Henry IV (of Navarre) first Bourbon king, promulgated **Edict of Nantes Apr. 13, 1598,** giving Huguenots and Catholics equality before law. Henry converted to Catholicism; assassinated **May 14, 1610.** Revocation of edict by Louis XIV **Oct. 23, 1685,** led to large Huguenot emigration to England and America.

1564

William Shakespeare born; traditional date **Apr. 23;** Baptismal record **Apr. 26.**

1565

St. Augustine, Fla. founded by Pedro Menendez, Spaniard. Razed by Francis Drake **1586.**

1579

Francis Drake claimed California for Britain. Left metal plate found in Marin Co. **1936.**

1582

First Catholic New Testament in English issued at Rheims; Old Testament translated at Douai **1609.**

1587

Mary, Queen of Scots, executed on charge of treason against Elizabeth I.

Virginia Dare, first child born of English parents in the New World, on Roanoke Is., N.C., **Aug. 18,** 7 days after **Sir Walter Raleigh's** 2d expedition with 117 persons landed. (First, **1585,** returned to England **1586.**) By **1590** all trace of settlement had vanished except for a tree inscribed enigmatically "Croatoan."

1588

Spanish Armada, 132 ships, 33,000 soldiers, sent by Philip II of Spain against England, destroyed by Drake's attacks and storms **July 21-29.** Only 50 ships returned to Spain. Fading of Spanish power; flourishing of Elizabethan England.

1590

Edmund Spenser began The Faerie Queen. First Shakespeare poem, Venus and Adonis, registered **1593.** First play to appear in quarto, Titus Andronicus registered **1594.** Romeo and Juliet performed **1597.**

1600

Shakespeare's most productive decade opened. He retired to Stratford-on-Avon **1610;** died **Apr. 23, 1616,** the same date **Cervantes** died. First folio of 36 plays published **1623:** 2d; **1632:** 3d; **1663:** 4th, **1675.**

1605

Gunpowder Plot of Guy Fawkes to blow up King James I and Parliament foiled when 36 barrels of gunpowder were found in Parliament's cellar **Nov. 4.**

1607

Capt. John Smith and 105 cavaliers in 3 ships landed on Virginia coast and started first permanent English settlement in New World at Jamestown **May 13.**

1609

Henry Hudson, English explorer of Northwest Passage, employed by Dutch East India Co.; sailed sloop Half Moon into New York harbor **Sept.** and up river to Albany. In **1610,** in English ship Discovery, 55 tons, explored Hudson Bay.

Spaniards settled Santa Fe, N.M., erected presidio.

1611

King James version of English Bible published; ordered by James I in **1604** it reconciled earlier versions and became basic Protestant Bible.

1618

Thirty Years' War began in Bohemia between Catholic and Protestant armies; ended **1648** with Peace of Westphalia, Alsace given to France. Holland and Switzerland received independence.

1619

House of Burgesses, first representative assembly in New World, elected by popular vote **July 30** at Jamestown, Va., establishing principle of self-government for royal colony.

First Negro laborers—indentured servants—in English N. American colonies, landed by Dutch at Jamestown, **Aug.**

1620

Plymouth Pilgrims, Puritan separatists from Church of England, some living in Leyden, Holland, since **1609,** left Plymouth, England, **Sept. 16** on Mayflower, 101 passengers, 48 crew. Original destination Virginia, they reached Cape Cod **Nov. 9-19,** explored coast, landed **Dec. 21** (Dec. 11, Old Style) at Plymouth, so named for Plymouth, England. Mayflower Compact, signed on shipboard, was agreement to form a local government and abide by its laws; elected own first Governor, John Carver. Started first house **Dec. 25.** Half of colony perished during hard winter.

1624

Dutch left 8 men from ship, New Netherland, on Manhattan **May.** Rest proceeded to Albany.

1626

Peter Minuit bought Manhattan from Man-a-hat-a Indians **May 6** for trinkets valued at $24.

1636

Harvard College founded **Oct. 28.**

1642

Great Rebellion of the Puritan Parliament against the civil and religious policies of Charles I of England began **July** after Charles rejected Parliament's demands for control of militia and church affairs and for right to appoint and dismiss the king's ministers.

Oliver Cromwell led army of Roundheads for Parliament, defeated Charles' Cavaliers at **Marston Moor 1644** and **Naseby 1645.** Charles was delivered to Parliament by the Scots **1648.** Beheaded **1649.**

Galileo died, **Newton** was born (100 years after **Copernicus** published heliocentric theory.) Galileo defended theory: "Holy Spirit intended to teach us in the Bible how to go to Heaven, not how the heavens go." But in **1616** the Inquisition at Rome declared the assertion of earth's motion to be heretical and placed works of Copernicus, Kepler, and Galileo on the Index of Forbidden Books.

1648

Taj Mahal outside Agra, India, completed by Mogul Emperor Shah Jehan in memory of his favorite wife Mumtaz Mahal. Begun in **1630.**

1649

Charles I condemned by House of Commons sitting as high court; beheaded, **Jan. 30.**

Commonwealth ruled by Commons and Council of State (John Milton, Latin secretary) with Cromwell at head. Cromwell made protector for life (actually dictator), **1653.**

Cromwell died 1658. His son Richard resigned rule. Puritan government collpased and Parliament called Charles II to rule the nation.

1660

Restoration under Charles II, "Merry Monarch." Charles' Cavalier Parliament restored Anglican church and refused freedom of worship to "dissenters."

1664

King Charles II ordered Col. Nicolls and 300 men to seize New Netherland (Manhattan and environs) from Dutch, granted territory to his brother James, Duke of York. Peter Stuyvesant, Dutch director-general, yielded peacefully; province of New Netherland and city of New Amsterdam became New York. The Dutch recaptured both **Aug. 9, 1673,** but ceded all by treaty to Britain **Nov. 10, 1674.**

1665

Great Plague in London killed 68,000. In **1666** great fire destroyed 13,200 houses, 89 churches.

1676

Nathaniel Bacon led planters, oppressed by taxes, against Gov. Berkeley at Jamestown, burned town, Bacon died suddenly; 23 followers executed.

Bloody Indian war in New England ended Aug. 12. King Philip, Wampanog chief, and many Narragansett Indians killed.

1682

Robert Cavelier, Sieur de la Salle, claimed lower Mississippi River country for Louis XIV, called it Louisiana Apr. 9. Had built French outposts in Illinois, established fort at Lavaca, Tex. 1684 with 400 men, killed by his own men in a mutiny on Trinity River, Tex., Mar. 19, 1687.

1683

William Penn signed treaty with Indians.

1689

King William's War, British in America vs. French and Indians, began; ended 1697.

1692

Witchcraft delusion at Salem (now Danvers, Mass.), inspired by preaching; 19 persons hanged, 1 man crushed to death. Executions in Europe of women for witchcraft between 1484 and 1782 believed to have reached 300,000. Last in England 1716, in Scotland 1722.

1696

Capt. William Kidd, American, hired by British king and nobles to fight pirates and take booty, became pirate. Returned to New York with treasure 1698, buried it on Gardiner's Island. Arrested and sent to England for trial. He was hanged 1701.

1704

Indians attacked Deerfield, Mass., Feb. 28-29, killed 40, carried off 100.

Gibraltar taken by Britain from Spain July 24; formally ceded by Spain in Treaty of Utrecht 1713.

Boston News Letter, first regular newspaper, started by John Campbell, postmaster. (Publick Occurences was suppressed after one issue 1690.)

1709

British-Colonial troops captured French fort, Port Royal, Nova Scotia, in Queen Anne's War 1701-13. France yielded Nova Scotia by treaty 1713.

1712

Slaves revolted in New York Apr. 6. Six committed suicide, 21 were executed. Second rising, 1741; 13 slaves hanged, 13 burned, 71 deported.

1720

"Mississippi Bubble." John Law, a Scot, comptroller of finance in France, issued paper currency without security to back trading scheme. On basis of wild stories of gold in Louisiana, shares reached $4,000 value before collapse; provoked large immigration to Louisiana.

1728

Pennsylvania Gazette founded by Samuel Keimer in Philadelphia. Benjamin Franklin bought interest 1729.

1735

Freedom of the press recognized in New York by acquittal of John Peter Zenger, editor Weekly Journal, on charge of libeling British Gov. Cosby by criticizing his conduct in office.

1740-1741

Capt. Vitus Bering, Dane employed by Russians, discovered Alaska.

1743

King George's War. British and colonials vs. French. Siege of Louisbourg, Cape Breton Is. was led by Gov. William Shirley of Massachusetts. Surrendered June 17, 1745. Returned to France by Treaty of Aix la Chapelle 1748.

1746

English defeated Scots at Culloden Moor, near Inverness, Apr. 16, routing Stuart pretender, Prince Charles. The last battle fought on British soil, it terminated attempts of Stuarts to recover the English throne.

1751

Publication of the Encyclopedie, great popularizer of the Enlightenment, began in France.

1752

Benjamin Franklin, flying kite in thunderstorm, proved lightning is electricity June 15.

Gregorian calendar adopted by Great Britain and American colonies, dropping 11 days after Sept. 2; next day Sept. 14.

1754

French and Indian War (in Europe called 7 Years War, started 1756) started after French occupied uncompleted British post, called it Ft. Duquesne (site of Pittsburgh). Col. George Washington with Virginia troops clashed with French at Great Meadows, dug in at Ft. Necessity; capitulated and withdrew July 3, 1754. Boston's 3,000 provincial troops took French forts in Nova Scotia June 16, 1755. French and Indians ambushed Gen. Edward Braddock's expedition 10 mi. from Ft. Duquesne (now Braddock, Pa.) July 9; Braddock fatally wounded, 714 killed. Gen. Sir William Johnson defeated French and Indians under Baron Dieskau at Lake George Sept. 8. British moved Acadian French from Nova Scotia to Louisiana Nov. Britain formally declared war May 18, 1756. Surrendered Ft. William Henry (Lake George) to Montcalm. Montcalm at Ft. Ticonderoga, N.Y., repulsed 17,000 British July 8, 1758. French gave up Louisburg, Ft. Frontenac, Ft. Duquesne in 1758; Niagara, Ticonderoga, Crown Point in 1759. British captured Quebec Sept. 18, 1759 in battles in which Montcalm and Gen. James Wolfe (Br.) died. Peace signed Feb. 10, 1763. French lost Canada and American Midwest.

Samuel Johnson published his English Dictionary.

1756

Black Hole of Calcutta. Nawab of Bengal, attacking British East India Co., threw 146 British prisoners into room less than 20 ft. square June 20; only 23 survived overnight. Lord Robert Clive with 3,000 troops routed the nawab's force of 50,000 June 23, 1757.

First Partition of Poland by Austria, Prussia, and Russia. Second and third partitions of 1793 and 1795 erased Poland from map of Europe, not to re-emerge until after World War I.

1776-1783; American Revolution; See Pp 714-715

1781

Bank of North America incorporated in Philadelphia May 26. First chartered bank, Bank of Pennsylvania Mar. 1, 1780 operated 1782-1784.

1783

Massachusetts Supreme Court outlawed slavery, noting the words in the state Bill of Rights "all men are born free and equal."

1784

First successful daily newspaper, Pennsylvania Packet & General Advertiser, published Sept. 21.

1785

First steamboat experiment by John Fitch. Fitch demonstrated 3 mph steamboat with 12 mechanical oars on Delaware River Aug. 22, 1787. He operated steamboat between Trenton and Philadelphia 1790.

1786

Delegates from 5 states at Annapolis asked Congress to call convention in Philadelphia to write practical constitution for the 13 states.

1787

Shays' rebellion in Massachusetts, led by Capt. Daniel Shays; attempt to seize U. S. Arsenal in Springfield failed Jan. 25.

Northwest Ordinance adopted July 13 by Continental Congress made effective Ordinance of 1784 drafted by Jefferson. Determined government of Northwest Territory north of Ohio River, west of New York; 5,000 male voters could establish Legislature; 60,000 inhabitants could get statehood. Guaranteed freedom of religion, support for schools, no slavery.

James Rumsey, encouraged by George Washington, ran steamboat with power pump on Potomac Dec. 3 and 11. Patented 1791.

Constitutional convention opened at Philadelphia May 14 with George Washington presiding. Constitution adopted by delegates Sept. 17; ratification by 9th state, New Hampshire, **June 21, 1788,** meant adoption; declared in effect **Mar. 4, 1789.**

1788

First British settlement in Australia, a penal colony at Port Jackson, now Sydney.

1789

George Washington chosen president by all electors voting (73 eligible, 69 voting, 4 absent); John Adams, vice president, 34 votes, **Feb.** First U. S. Congress called **Mar. 4,** at Federal Hall, N. Y. City; regular sessions began **Apr. 6.** Washington inaugurated there **Apr. 30.** Supreme Court created by Federal Judiciary Act **Sept. 24.**

The French Revolution began **June 20** when the delegates to the Third Estate (Commons) met on a tennis court and took an oath not to disband until the king had granted France a constitution; Paris mob stormed the Bastille **July 14** to capture ammunition; released 7 non-political prisoners. France was declared a limited monarchy under Louis XVI; the king and family were arrested **June 21, 1791;** Revolutionary Tribunal set up on **Aug. 19, 1792;** National Convention opened **Sept. 17, 1792,** a republic was established on **Sept. 22.** Louis was beheaded **Jan. 21, 1793;** the Reign of Terror began **May 31, 1793;** Charlotte Corday killed Marat **July 13, 1793;** Queen Marie

Antoinette was beheaded **Oct. 16, 1793;** Danton **Apr. 5, 1794;** Robespierre **July 28, 1794.** Revolutionary Tribunal abolished **Dec. 15, 1794.** Moderate Directory of 5 men established to rule France 1795.

1791

Continued attacks on settlements north of Ohio River by Indians armed by British, led Washington to send Gen. Arthur St. Clair and Gen. Wilkinson to area with 1,400 men. St. Clair was surprised near Wabash River in Ohio **Nov. 4,** lost 630 killed.

1792-94

Gen. Anthony Wayne made commander, took 2 years to train American Legion; established string of forts. Routed Indians (Ottawas, Shawnees, Miamis, Iroquois) at Fallen Timbers on Maumee River **Aug. 20, 1794,** checked British at Ft. Miami.

Whiskey Rebellion, west Pennsylvania farmers protesting "discriminatory" liquor tax of **1791,** was suppressed by 15,000 militiamen **Sept. 1794.** Alexander Hamilton used incident to establish authority of the new federal government in enforcing its laws.

1795

Gen. Wayne built Ft. Wayne; signed peace with Indians at Fort Greeneville.

U. S. bought peace from Algiers and Tunis by paying $800,000, supplying a frigate and annual trib-

---

American Revolution and War of Independence;

Great Britain, after acquiring Canada from France in 1763, tightened up colonial administration in North America. The 13 colonies, used to self-government, resented duties on commerce and objected to paying for troops now quartered among them. **The Sugar Act of 1764** placed duties on lumber, foodstuffs, molasses and rum. **The Stamp Act of 1765** required revenue stamps to help defray cost of royal troops. The colonists formed Sons of Liberty groups and rejected British goods. Nine colonies, led by New York and Massachusetts at **Stamp Act Congress** in New York **Oct. 7-25, 1765,** adopted Declaration of Rights opposing taxation without representation in Parliament and trial without jury by admiralty courts. In the Virginia House of Burgesses, Patrick Henry warned King George III of consequences declaring, "If this be treason make the most of it." Parliament repealed Stamp Act on **Mar. 17, 1766.**

Townshend Acts of 1767 levied taxes on glass, painter's lead, paper and tea imports. In 1770 all duties except tax on tea were repealed, but principle of right to tax was maintained. British troops fired into a mob **Mar. 5, 1770,** killed 5 including Crispus Attucks, a Negro, reportedly leader of the group; later called the **Boston Massacre.** Tea ships of East India Co., turned back at Boston, New York, Philadelphia in May 1773. Cargo ship burned at Annapolis **Oct. 14.** Cargo thrown overboard at **Boston Tea Party Dec. 16.** Parliament ordered port closed until tea was paid for, sent 4 regiments to Boston, suppressed town meetings and elective representation in Massachusetts.

Samuel Adams, in Boston, began uniting patriot leaders by Committees of Correspondence. Virginia called for first **Continental Congress** in Philadelphia **Sept. 5-Oct. 26,** 1774. On **Mar. 23,** 1775, Patrick Henry addressed revolutionary convention, Richmond, Va., with famous exclamation: "Give me liberty or give me death!"

Battles of 1775

Paul Revere and William Dawes on night of **Apr. 18,** rode to alert Samuel Adams and John Hancock at Lexington and others that 700 British were on way to **Concord** to destroy arms. At **Lexington, Mass., Apr. 19** Minutemen lost 8 killed, 10 wounded. On return from Concord the harassed British lost 273.

Col. Ethan Allen (joined by Col. Benedict Arnold)

captured **Ft. Ticonderoga,** N. Y., **May 10;** also Crown Point. Colonials headed for Bunker Hill, fortified Breed's Hill, Charlestown, Mass., repulsed British under Gen. William Howe twice before retreating **June 17;** British casualties 1,000; called **Battle of Bunker Hill.** Continental Congress **June 15** named George Washington commander-in-chief; he took command in Cambridge **July 3.** Maj. Gen. Richard Mongomery led troops against Canada via New York, captured **Montreal** Nov. 13, Col. Arnold marched via Maine wilderness attacked Quebec Dec. 30-31; Montgomery killed. Colonials returned to New York State June 1776.

Declaration of Independence

Virginia voted for independence **May 15.** In Continental Congress **June 7,** 1776, Richard Henry Lee (Va.) moved "that these united colonies are and of right ought to be free and independent states." Resolutions adopted **July 2. Declaration of Independence** **July 4.** See Index for article.

Col. Moultrie's batteries at Charleston, S.C., repulsed British sea attack **June 28.** Washington, with 10,000 men lost **Battle of Long Island** to Gen. William (Lord) Howe and Gen. Sir Henry Clinton with 15,000 **Aug. 27,** evacuated New York.

Nathan Hale, 21, executed as spy, without trial, by British **Sept. 22.**

Washington repulsed Howe at Harlem Heights Sept. 16, retreated to White Plains, N.Y. Brig. Gen. Arnold's Lake Champlain fleet was defeated at **Valcour Oct. 11,** but British returned to Canada. Howe failed to destroy Washington's army at **White Plains Oct. 28.** Hessians captured **Ft. Washington,** Manhattan, and 3,000 men Nov. 16; **Ft. Lee,** N.J., Nov. 18.

Washington in Pennsylvania, recrossed Delaware River Dec. 25-26, defeated 1,400 Hessians at **Trenton,** N.J., **Dec. 26.**

Brandywine and Saratoga, 1777

Washington defeated Lord Cornwallis at **Princeton Jan. 3.** Continental Congress adopted Stars and Stripes **June 14.** See Flag article. Maj. Gen. John Burgoyne with 8,000 from Canada captured **Ft. Ticonderoga July 6.** Brig. Gen. Nicholas Herkimer, to raise St. Leger's siege of **Ft. Stanwix,** routed Indians at **Oriskany,** N. Y. Aug. 6. Burgoyne's Hessians defeated by Brig. Gen. John Stark and the Green Mountain

ute of $25,000 Nov. 28. (See 1801.)

1796

Washington's Farewell Address as president delivered **Sept. 19.** Gave strong warnings against permanent alliances with foreign powers, partiality toward favorite nations, big public debt, large military establishment and devices of "small artful, enterprising minority" to control or change government; praised reciprocal checks of Constitution; stressed need for enlightened public opinion; declared "religion and morality lead to political prosperity."

Vaccination discovered by Edward Jenner **May 14;** laid foundation for modern immunology.

1797

U. S. frigate United States launched at Philadelphia **July 10;** Constellation at Baltimore **Sept. 7;** Constitution (Old Ironsides) at Boston **Sept. 20.**

France ordered capture of all neutral ships carrying British cargoes.

1798

War with France threatened over French raids on U. S. shipping and rejection of U. S. diplomats. Congress voided all treaties with France, ordered Navy to capture French armed ships. Navy (45 ships) and 365 privateers captured 84 French ships. U. S. Constellation took French warship Insurgente **1799.**

Napoleon stopped French raids after becoming First Consul.

Napoleon invaded Egypt and won Battle of the Pyramids **July 1798;** British Adm. Nelson destroyed French fleet **Aug. 1-2** in Aboukir Bay. Rosetta stone, found in Egypt by one of Napoleon's officers **1799,** contained 3 identical inscriptions in ancient Egyptian hieroglyphics, demotic (common) Greek, and classical Greek. Jean Champollion, a young French scholar, compared these writings and deciphered ancient Egypt's hieroglyphics. Napoleon fled secretly to France **1799,** became First Consul **Nov. 9-10, 1799,** after coup d'etat.

1801

Tripoli declared war June 10 against U. S., which refused added tribute to commerce-raiding Arab corsairs. U. S. frigate Philadelphia captured in Tripoli harbor **Oct. 1803** burned by Stephen Decatur **Feb. 16, 1804,** to block harbor. Expedition under William Eaton forced Tripoli to conclude peace **June 4, 1805.**

1803

Robert Emmet convicted of treason by British in Ireland; executed in Dublin **Sept. 19.**

Louisiana Purchase. Pres. Jefferson sent James Monroe to Paris to join Robert R. Livingston, U. S. minister, in offering up to $10 million for the Isle of

---

Origins, Battles, Results, 1763-1783

Boys near **Bennington,** Vt. **Aug. 16.** Arnold raised siege of Ft. Stanwix.

Howe defeated Washington near **Brandywine Creek,** Pa., **Sept. 11** and occupied Philadelphia. Congress moved to Lancaster, Pa. Inconclusive battle of Germantown, Pa., **Oct. 4.** Washington's army wintered at Valley Forge.

Americans massed at Bemis Heights, near Saratoga, under Maj. Gen. Horatio Gates, attacked by Burgoyne **Sept. 19.** At nearby **Freeman's Farm,** Gen. Arnold and Col. Daniel Morgan's riflemen repulsed British, inflicted great losses. Gen Clinton took **Fts. Clinton and Montgomery** below West Point Oct. 6, but did not support Burgoyne. Americans beat back Burgoyne at Bemis Heights **Oct. 7** and cut off British escape route. Burgoyne surrendered 5,000 men at **Saratoga,** N. Y., **Oct. 17.**

Marquis de la Fayette (Lafayette), aged 20, made major general.

Articles of Confederation and Perpetual Union adopted by Continental Congress Nov. 15.

Help from France

France recognized independence of 13 Colonies, signed treaty of aid with Benjamin Franklin, Silas Deane, Arthur Lee on **Feb. 6, 1778.** Sent fleet under Adm. d'Estaing. British evacuated Philadelphia in consequence **June 18.** Washington harassed British at Monmouth Court House, N. J., **June 28.** Wyoming Massacre **July 3** in Pa. by British and Indian force. British overran Georgia in December.

George Rogers Clark who took Cahokia and Kaskaskia (Ill.) 1778, took **Vincennes** Feb. 1779. Maj. Gen. Anthony Wayne **July 15** stormed **Stony Point,** on Hudson, but withdrew after victory.

John Paul Jones on the Bonhomme Richard defeated Serapis in British North Sea waters **Sept. 23, 1779.** French fleet and Maj. Gen. Benjamin Lincoln's men were repulsed at Savannah Oct. 9.

Benedict Arnold's Treason

Three Continental soldiers, Paulding, Williams and Van Wart, captured Major John Andre, adjutant general of the British army, in disguise at Tarrytown, N. Y., **Sept. 23, 1780,** finding papers betraying West Point, signed by Gen. Arnold, in his socks. He had lost his way after rendezvous with Arnold at Haverstraw, N.Y. Arnold, informed of Andre's capture, escaped from headquarters in Highlands, near present Garri-

son, N. Y., by barge to British sloop Vulture off Verplanck's Point.

Andre was found guilty by board of American officers at Tappan, N. Y., hanged as spy **Oct. 2.** Washington refused to intercede. Arnold made brigadier general in British army; burned New London, Conn., 1781. His wife, Peggy Shippen of Philadelphia, adjudged innocent by Washington, since proved implicated. Arnold died in London. Andre's body removed to Westminster Abbey 1821.

Road to Yorktown

Charleston, S. C., fell to the British **May 12, 1780,** but a segment of Lord Cornwallis' forces led by Maj. Patrick Ferguson was defeated near **Kings Mountain,** N. C., **Oct. 7** by militiamen commanded by Cols. John Sevier, Isaac Shelby, William Campbell and Benjamin Cleveland. Operations in South under Cornwallis and Col. Banastre Tarleton in 1781 were checked by Maj. Gen. Nathanael Greene and Brig. Gen. Daniel Morgan. **Cowpens,** S. C., **Jan. 17** was a victory, but **Guilford Court House,** N. C., **Mar. 15** was a British gain. Greene's harassments caused Cornwallis to retire to Wilmington, N. C., and thence to Yorktown, Va.

While Lafayette waited near Yorktown, Adm. De Grasse landed 3,000 French and stopped Adm. Thomas Graves' British fleet in Hampton Roads. Adm. Barras joined De Grasse. Washington and Rochambeau joined forces and left 2,000 men to mislead Sir Henry Clinton in New York, marched to Annapolis, and took boats to James River near Williamsburg, arriving **Sept. 26.** When siege of Cornwallis began **Oct. 6,** British had 6,000, Americans 8,846, French 7,800. Clinton decided too late to relieve Cornwallis. Graves sailed from New York with 7,000 **Oct. 17** too late to reach Cornwallis who surrendered **Oct. 19, 1781.**

Independence, 1782

A new British cabinet agreed to recognize independence **March 1782.** Preliminary agreement signed in Paris **Nov. 30;** treaty **Sept. 3, 1783.** Congress ratified it **Jan. 14, 1784.** Washington ordered army disbanded **Nov. 3, 1783.** British evacuated N.Y. City **Nov. 25.** Washington bade farewell to his officers at Fraunces Tavern, N.Y. City, **Dec. 4;** resigned **Dec. 23,** retired to Mount Vernon, Va. *For casualties of war see Index.*

Orleans (New Orleans) and West Florida. Napoleon, who had recovered Louisiana from Spain by secret treaty, offered all of Louisiana, stretching to Canadian border, for $11,250,000 in bonds, plus $3,750,000 indemnities to American citizens with claims against France. U. S. took title **Dec. 20.**

1804
Lewis and Clark expedition ordered by Pres. Jefferson to explore what is now northwest U. S. Started from St. Louis **May 14**; ended **Sept. 23, 1806.** An Indian woman named Sacajawea served as guide and interpreter.

Alexander Hamilton (ex-Sec. of the Treasury) and Vice Pres. Aaron Burr, after years of bitter political rivalry, fought a duel **July 11** on the Hudson Palisades, Weehawken, N.J. Hamilton was mortally wounded, died **July 12.**

Code Napoleon systematized French law under the auspices of Napoleon Bonaparte. It became a model for many countries.

John Stevens, of Hoboken, N.J., operated experimental steamboat with twin-screw propellers for 9 mi.

1805
Napoleon, emperor since **May 18, 1804,** defeated Austrians at Ulm **Oct. 17;** Russo-Austrians at Austerlitz, "masterpiece of battles," **Dec. 2.** Dissolved Holy Roman Empire. Made brothers Joseph, king of Naples, Louis, king of Holland.

Lord Nelson defeated French-Spanish fleet at Cape Trafalgar **Oct. 21;** lost his own life.

1806
Napoleon defeated Prussians at Jena **Oct. 14.** In 1807 he defeated Russians at Eylau; signed peace of Tilsit with Czar Alexander I. Made brother Jerome king of Westphalia; allotted Finland to Russia.

1807
Robert Fulton made first practical steamboat trip on Clermont (open boat, 140 by 13 ft., 7 ft. draft, side paddle wheels). Left **New York Aug. 17,** reached Albany, 150 mi., in 32 hrs.

Aaron Burr was tried for treason in Richmond, Va., **May 22.** Charged with "assembling an armed force . . . to seize the city of New Orleans . . . and to separate the western from the Atlantic states," he was acquitted **Sept. 1.** Chief Justice John Marshall sitting as U.S. Circuit Court judge ruled that treason must be attested to by 2 witnesses. After trial Burr went to Europe to avoid prosecution on Hamilton murder charge.

1808-09
French occupied Madrid in March; Rome in April; Napoleon made brother Joseph king of Spain in Peninsular War begun by British 1808, Continued until 1814. Napoleon defeated Austrians at Wagram **July 6, 1809;** annexed Papal States.

Phoenix, world's first ocean-going steamboat, built by John Stevens, left New York for Philadelphia **June 8, 1809.**

1811
William Henry Harrison, governor of Indiana Territory, defeated Indians under the Prophet, brother of Tecumseh, in battle of Tippecanoe **Nov. 7.**

1812
Napoleon invaded Russia June 22 with first modern conscript army of 500,000 men; Russian army, outnumbered 3 to 1, retreated and used "scorched earth" policy. Napoleon's army defeated Russians at Borodino **Sept. 7;** took Moscow **Sept. 14.** Moscow destroyed by fire; lacking shelter and supplies, Napoleon ordered retreat **Oct. 19.** Army suffered from cold, starvation and Cossack attacks; only 30,000 survived.

1813
Napoleon with 180,000 French decisively defeated at Leipzig by 200,000 allied Prussians, Austrians, Russians, under Austrian Gen. Schwartzenberg in Battle of the Nations **Oct. 16-19.**

1814
Allies entered Paris Mar. 21; Napoleon abdicated **Apr. 11;** Louis XVIII restored to throne, **May 3;** Congress of Vienna opened **Nov. 3.** Napoleon exiled to Elba.

1815
Napoleon re-entered France Mar. 1, assumed command for the famed "Hundred Days," **Mar. 20-June 22.** Defeated at Waterloo, Belgium, **June 18,** by Duke of Wellington (British), Count von Blucher (Prussian) and allies. Deported to St. Helena; died there **May 5, 1821.**

Holy Alliance, formed by Russia, Austria and Prussia; signed in Paris **Sept. 26;** promulgated in Frankfort **Feb. 2, 1816** and acceded to, **1818,** by the rulers of Great Britain and France.

1817
Rush-Bagot treaty signed **Apr. 28-29** limited U. S., Canadian naval armaments on the Great Lakes.

1820
Henry Clay's Missouri Compromise bill passed by Congress **Mar. 3.** Slavery was allowed in Missouri, but not elsewhere west of the Mississippi River north of 36° 30′ latitude (the southern line of Missouri). Repealed **1854.**

1822
Brazil proclaimed independence from Portugal **Sept. 7.** Dom Pedro, son of Portugal's King John VI, was crowned emperor **Dec. 1;** abdicated **1831;** succeeded by his son. A republic proclaimed **1888.**

Mexico separated from Spain, made Iturbide emperor May; formed republic **Oct. 1823.**

1823
Monroe Doctrine declared **Dec. 2.**

Mississippi River first ascended by steamboat, the Virginia, as far as Fort Snelling, Minn., **Apr. 21-May 10,** 729 mi.

Gas vacuum (internal combustion) engine operated successfully by Samuel Brown in London.

1824
Simon Bolivar liberator of Venezuela, Colombia, Ecuador, Peru broke Spanish power in South America.

1825
Great Britain repeals laws against trade unions.

First railroad to use steam locomotive (on level grade only) Stockton & Darlington RR opened in England **Sept. 27** with Stephenson's engine "Locomotion." First public railroad to use steam exclusively for passenger and freight traffic, Liverpool & Manchester, opened **Sept. 15, 1830.**

Erie Canal opened, first boat left Buffalo **Oct. 26,** reached N.Y. City **Nov. 4.** Canal cost $7 million but cut travel time by one-third, shipping costs one-tenth; opened Great Lakes area, made N. Y. City chief Atlantic port.

First iron steamboat built in America, the Codorus, at York, Pa., by John Elgar.

John Stevens, of Hoboken, N.J., built and operated first steam locomotive in U.S.

1827
Slavery in New York State abolished July 4.

Steamship Curacao, first European-built oceanic vessel to use steam power only, crossed the Atlantic **April** from Antwerp to Paramaribo, Dutch Guiana. The Royal William launched in Montreal **Apr. 29, 1831** left there **Aug. 18, 1833,** crossed to Europe in 25 days using only steam.

1828
First passenger railroad in U. S., Baltimore & Ohio, was begun **July 4,** first 14 mi. opened to horsedrawn railcar traffic **May 24, 1830.**

1830
Mormon church organized by Joseph Smith in Fayette, N. Y., **Apr. 6.**

Revolution in France. Charles X abdicated **Aug. 2** and was succeeded by the duke of Orleans as Louis Philippe I. There were revolts in Brunswick, Saxony and Belgium. Belgium became independent kingdom.

First regularly scheduled passenger train service in United States using steam power opened at Charleston on South Carolina Railroad **Dec. 25** with 3

1/2-ton U. S.-built locomotive, Best Friend of Charleston.

1831

Nat Turner, a Negro slave from Virginia, led a band of men in a slave rebellion, killed 57 whites, in August. Army called in, Turner captured, tried and hanged.

1832

Black Hawk War (Ill.-Wis.) **Apr. - Sept.** pushed Sac & Fox Indians west across Mississippi.

South Carolina convention passed **Ordinance of Nullification** Nov. 1832 against permanent tariff protection policy, declaring that if the federal government attempted to enforce the tariff the state would consider itself no longer a member of the Union. Congress Feb. 1833 passed a compromise tariff act, whereupon South Carolina repealed its act.

British Reform Bill: middle class enfranchised; step toward political democracy **Mar. 23.**

1833

Slavery in British Empire outlawed **Aug. 28** as of Aug. 1, 1834. About 700,000 were liberated at cost of £20 million. (Slavery was abolished in Britain **June**

22, 1772. Slave trade was suppressed 1807.)

Oberlin College, first in U. S. to adopt coeducation. Oberlin refused to bar students on account of race 1835.

1835

Texas proclaimed independence from Mexico in convention **Nov. 1,** provisional government formed. Stephen Austin and Sam Houston leaders.

Gold discovered on Cherokee land in Georgia. Indians forced to cede lands **Dec. 20** and to cross Mississippi.

1836

Texans besieged in Alamo (San Antonio) by Mexicans under Santa Anna **Feb. 23-Mar. 6;** garrison including William Travis, Jim Bowie and David Crockett died defending the fort. At San Jacinto **Apr.** 21 Sam Houston and 800 Texans defeated 3,000 Mexicans. Santa Anna signed treaties ending hostilities, promised to recognize Texan independence but Mexican Congress repudiated treaties.

Marcus Whitman, H. H. Spaulding and wives reached Fort Walla Walla on Columbia River, Oregon. First white women to cross plains.

War of 1812 Between U.S. and Great Britain

The War of 1812, coming only 30 years after the end of the Revolution, had 3 major causes: (1) Britain, blockading France, seized American ships trading with France; (2) Britain, refusing to recognize naturalized American sailors, seized 4,000 by 1810 and impressed two-thirds into British service; (3) Britain armed Indians who raided western border. Under Pres. Jefferson U.S., 1807 and 1809, stopped trade with Europe which ruined American shippers. Under Pres. Madison 1810 trade with Britain only was stopped.

War might have been averted. The British raised the blockade for American ships **June 16, 1812,** but the news did not reach U. S. by **June 18** when Congress by a small majority voted a declaration of war. Congress voted to raise army from 11,744 to 44,500 and to use militia. The navy had 20 major ships of 500 guns. The West favored war; New England opposed it. The British were handicapped by war with France.

War on Land

Americans made many blunders due to poor leadership and refusal of regulars to work with militia. Brig. Gen. William Hull surrendered Detroit **Aug. 16, 1812,** Maj. Gen. Stephen Van Rensselaer with 2,300 took Queenston Heights, Canada, **Oct. 13,** but retired when regulars did not support. Brig. Gen. William H. Harrison had 1,000 casualties near Ft. Malden. Brig. Gen. Zebulon M. Pike took York (Toronto) **Apr. 27, 1813,** died in explosion. Gen. Henry Dearborn **May 27** took Ft. George and Queenston Heights aided by amphibious assault led by Col. Winfield Scott and Master Commandant Oliver Hazard Perry. British defeated 2,000 Americans a few days later.

Battle of the Thames, Ontario, Can., **Oct. 5, 1813.** Harrison with 3,500 men took Ft. Malden, pursued British 85 mi. Cavalry charge by Kentucky riflemen routed British and Indians, killing Shawnee chief, Tecumseh. Detroit frontier was safe for U. S. Both Brig. Gen. Wade Hampton with 4,000 and Maj. Gen. James Wilkinson with 6,000 mismanaged attempts to invade Canada. British recaptured Fts. George and Niagara, burned Buffalo; Americans burned Newark and Queenston.

Battle of Lundy's Lane. Brig. Gen. Winfield Scott led fighting of Brown's army at Lundy's Lane, on road to Burlington **July 25, 1814;** result a draw with heavy losses, Scott was wounded.

Burning of Washington. in **August** British landed 4,000 men under Adm. Sir George Cockburn and Maj. Gen. Robert Ross. At Bladensburg, Md., **Aug. 24, 1814,**

Ross routed 5,000 hastily assembled U. S. troops, then burned Capitol and White House; Maryland militia stopped British **Sept. 12** from reaching Baltimore; Ross was killed.

Battle of New Orleans. Maj. Gen. Andrew Jackson, who had defeated the Creek Indians at Horseshoe Bend on the Tallapoosa **Mar. 27, 1814,** and captured British base at Pensacola, Fla., in Nov.; on **Dec. 23** engaged 2,000 British east of New Orleans. **Jan. 8, 1815,** 5,300 British under Maj. Gen. Sir Edward Pakenham attacked American entrenchments at Chalmette. Jackson had 3,500, a reserve of 1,000, 20 guns and an armed schooner. British had over 2,000 casualties. Pakenham was killed; Americans lost 71. British withdrew and left by sea **Jan. 18.** On **Feb. 8** they took Mobile. News came **Feb. 14** that a treaty of peace had been signed at Ghent **Dec. 24, 1814.** U.S. ratified it **Feb. 17, 1815.**

War at Sea

Brilliant American gunnery brought naval victories. USS Essex captured Alert **Aug. 13, 1812.** USS Constitution, 44 guns, Capt. Isaac Hull, destroyed Guerriere **Aug. 19;** thereafter, Constititution was called **Old Ironsides.** USS Wasp took Frolic **Oct. 18.** USS United States, Capt. Stephen Decatur, defeated Macedonian off Azores **Oct. 25.** Constitution beat Java **Dec. 29, 1812.** USS Chesapeake captured by Shannon **June 1, 1813;** Capt. James Lawrence, dying, called out: "Don't give up the ship!" USS Enterprise took Boxer **Sept. 5.**

Battle of Lake Erie. Commodore Oliver H. Perry defeated British fleet near Put-in-Bay **Sept. 10, 1813.** Perry sent message to Harrison: "We have met the enemy and they are ours: 2 ships, 2 brigs, 1 schooner, 1 sloop."

USS Essex, Capt. David Porter, first U. S. warship to sail around South America, was defeated off Valparaiso, Chile, **Mar. 28, 1814.**

Bombardment of Ft. McHenry, Baltimore, for 25 hours. **Sept. 13-14, 1814,** by British fleet failed. Francis Scott Key wrote words to Star Spangled Banner.

Battle of Lake Champlain. Commodore Thomas Macdonough defeated fleet of Sir George Prevost near Plattsburg **Sept. 11, 1814** while Brig. Gen. Thomas Macomb held 4,500 ready to oppose 11,000. British withdrew to Canada.

U. S. frigate President was captured **Jan. 1815.** Constitution captured Cyane and Levant **Feb. 20, 1815.** U.S. sloop Hornet captured Penguin **Mar. 23.**

The War of 1812 gave recognition to westerners, made Andrew Jackson a political power.

Seminole Indians in Florida under Osceola began attacks Nov. 1, 1836, protesting forced removal. The unpopular 8-year war ended Aug. 14, 1842; Indians sent to Oklahoma. War was the most costly Indian war; 1,500 soldiers died, $30 million spent.

1838

The Great Western, a steamship 236 ft. long, 450 horsepower, 1,340 gross tons, left Bristol, England, **Apr. 8**, arrived in N. Y. City **Apr. 23**. The Sirius, 178 ft. long, 703 tons, left Queenstown **Apr. 4**, reached N.Y. City **Apr. 22**, using only steam power.

1839

Belgium and the Kingdom of the Netherlands were separated by treaties signed by those 2 countries and by Great Britain, France, Austria, Prussia and Russia at London **Apr. 19**. To the treaties was annexed a document declaring Belgium independent and perpetually neutral (called "scrap of paper" by Germany in World War I when it invaded Belgium.)

Opium War broke out between China and Britain. China tried to prohibit opium trade in Canton. British resisted and took Canton. War ended **Aug. 1842.**

1840

Antarctic was found to be a continent by Comdr. Charles Wilkes of first U. S. exploring expedition; named Wilkes Land **Jan.-Feb.**

1841

First emigrant wagon train for California, 47 persons, left Independence, Mo., **May 1**, reached Stanislaus River, **Nov. 4.**

First passenger train on Erie R.R. **June 30.**

1842

First use of anesthetic (sulphuric ether gas) by Dr. Crawford W. Long in Jefferson, Ga. Dr. William T. G. Morton, dentist, used ether for painless extraction of tooth **Sept. 30, 1846**; administered ether in tumor operation **Oct. 16, 1846** at Massachusetts General Hospital, Boston.

1844

First message over first telegraph line sent from U.S. Supreme Court room **May 24** to Baltimore by inventor **Samuel F. B. Morse**: "What hath God wrought!"

Joseph Smith, founder of Mormons, and brother Hyrum killed in Carthage, Ill., jail by mob **June 27.**

1845

Texas voted for annexation to U. S. **July 4**. Congress admitted Texas as 28th state **Dec. 29.**

1846

Mexican War. Pres. James K. Polk ordered **Gen. Zachary Taylor** to seize disputed Texan land settled by Mexicans. After border clash, U. S. declared war **May 13**; Mexico **May 23.**

Bear flag of Republic of California raised by American settlers at Sonoma **June 14**. Gen. John C. Fremont took charge **July 5**. Commodore J. S. Sloat took Monterey **July 7**, declared California annexed to U. S. Commodore Robert Stockton succeded Sloat, was ordered to recognize Gen. Kearny as governor and commander-in-chief in California. Kearny was defeated by Mexicans **Dec. 6**, retreated to San Diego.

Gen. Taylor defeated Mexicans at Buena Vista **Feb. 23, 1847**. Gen. Winfield Scott with 12,000 troops (est.) took Vera Cruz **Mar. 27**; Mexico City **Sept. 14**, captured dictator Santa Anna. By treaty, **Feb. 1848** Mexico ceded claims to Texas, California, Arizona, New Mexico, Nevada, Utah, part of Colorado. U. S. assumed $3 million American claims and paid Mexico $15 million.

Treaty with Great Britain June 15, set boundary in Oregon Territory at 49th parallel (extension of existing line). Water boundary settled 1873. Expansionists in U. S. seeking boundary farther North used slogan "54° 40' or fight!"

Mormons, after violent clashes with settlers over polygamy, left Nauvoo, Ill., for West under Brigham Young, settled **July 1847** at Salt Lake City, Utah.

1847

First adhesive U. S. postage stamps on sale July 1;

Benjamin Franklin 5c, Washington 10c.

1848

Gold discovered Jan. 24 by James W. Marshall, who was erecting sawmill in partnership with Capt. John A. Sutter on American River, branch of the Sacramento, near Coloma, Cal. Small finds of gold were reported 45 mi. northwest of Los Angeles 1841-44.

Louis Philippe dethroned in France; Second Republic set up **Feb. 26.**

In Austria **Ferdinand I** abdicated **Dec. 2** in favor of his nephew Franz Josef. In Hungary, freedom was briefly declared under Louis Kossuth; revolts in Ireland, Lombardy, Venice, Denmark and Schleswig-Holstein.

Communist Manifesto written by Karl Marx (1818-1883) and Friedrich Engels (1820-1895); still the basic doctrine of communism.

1850

Sen. Henry Clay's Compromise of 1850 passed; admitted California as 31st state **Sept. 9**, slavery forbidden; made Utah and New Mexico territories without decision on slavery; amended Fugitive Slave Law punishing those who aided fugitives and abolished jury trial for fugitives, ended slave trade in Dist. of Columbia.

Jenny Lind's first American concert at Castle Garden, New York City, **Sept. 11**; P. T. Barnum was manager.

Taiping Rebellion, led by Hung Hsiu-ch'uan, began in Kwangsi province, China. One of the largest civil wars in history, it resulted in the death of an estimated 20 to 40 million, devastated entire provinces and nearly toppled the Manchu dynasty. The Taiping movement, aimed at foreign exploitation, was finally suppressed 1864 by Tseng Kuo-fan with the help of the "Ever Victorious Army" of Gen. Charles G. (Chinese) Gordon.

1851

New York & Hudson River R.R., New York to Albany, opened **Oct.**

1852

Louis Napoleon crowned emperor of the French.

Uncle Tom's Cabin, by Harriet Beecher Stowe, published.

1853

Commodore Matthew C. Perry, U.S.N., received by Lord of Toda, Japan, **July 14**; negotiated treaty to open Japan to U.S. ships. Ratified **Mar. 8, 1854.**

Crimean War. A dispute between Greek Orthodox and Roman monks over holy places held by Turkey in Palestine led Russian Czar Nicholas I to extend protection to Greeks. Russia occupied Turkish-held Moldavia and Wallachia. Turkey declared war **Oct. 4, 1853**. Britain and France, fearing Russian expansion declared war on Russia **May 28, 1854**. Fighting concentrated in the Crimea and included famous **Charge of the Light Brigade** at Balaklava **Oct. 25, 1854**; 400 of 607 killed; Russian defeat at Inkerman **Nov. 5, 1854**; fall of Sebastopol **Sept. 11, 1855. Florence Nightingale** established first dressing stations. By Treaty of Paris **Mar. 30, 1856**, Russia ceded part of Bessarabia to Moldavia, freed Danube for navigation. Black Sea closed to warships (later repudiated).

1854

Republican party started at Ripon, Wis., **Feb. 28**; first state organization, Jackson, Mich., **July 6**. Opposed Kansas-Nebraska Act (became law **May 30**) which left issue of slavery in Kansas and Nebraska to vote of settlers.

Henry D. Thoreau wrote Walden.

1855

Walt Whitman published Leaves of Grass; **Henry W. Longfellow** wrote Song of Hiawatha.

1856

First railroad train crossed Mississippi River on the river's first bridge at **Rock Island, Ill.-Davenport, Ia., Apr. 21.**

Republican party's first nominee for president, John C. Fremont **June-Nov.**, defeated by James Buchanan. Abraham Lincoln made 50 speeches for Fremont.

Lawrence, Kan., sacked May 21 by slavery party; abolitionist John Brown led anti-slavery men against Missourians at Osawatomie, Kan., **Aug. 30.**

1857

Dred Scott decision of U. S. Supreme Court, 6-3, that a Negro slave did not become free when taken into a free state and had no rights as a citizen. Abraham Lincoln denounced decision. Minnesota outlawed slavery.

Great Mutiny in India (Sepoy Rebellion) began in Merrut **May 10** when Indian soldiers revolted against British officers; crushed **1858.** British East India Co. abolished and India placed under crown rule as a result of mutiny.

John D. Lee, a Mormon, led raid against wagon train at Mountain Meadows **Sept. 11,** killed 120, spared only 17 children under 7. U. S. Army supplies burned. Government sent 6,000 troops to suppress "rebellion." Mormon Church unjustly accused.

1858

First Atlantic cable completed by Cyrus W. Field **Aug. 5.** Queen Victoria and President Buchanan exchanged greetings, but cable failed **Sept. 1.** Field tried again in 1865, succeeded in 1866.

Lincoln-Douglas debates in Illinois **Aug. 21-Oct. 15.**

1859

Dixie, composed by Daniel D. Emmett, was first performed by him with Bryant's Minstrels at Mechanics Hall, N.Y. City **Apr. 4.**

First commercially productive oil well, drilled near Titusville, Pa., by Edwin L. Drake **Aug. 27,** started boom.

Abolitionist John Brown with 21 men seized U.S. Armory at Harpers Ferry (then Va.) **Oct. 16.** U.S. Marines under Lt. Col. Robert E. Lee captured raiders, killing 11. One Marine and 5 civilians also killed. Brown was hanged for treason by Virginia **Dec. 2** as were 5 of his band, at Charleston (now Charles Town, W. Va.).

Darwin's Origin of Species published.

1860

Abraham Lincoln, Republican, elected president by 1,866,352 popular and 180 electoral votes; Stephen A. Douglas had 1,375,157 and 12; John C. Breckinridge, 845,763 and 72; John Bell 589,581 and 39. Lincoln took office **Mar. 4, 1861.**

First Pony Express between Sacramento, Cal., and St. Joseph, Mo., 1,980 mi. apart, started from each place at 5 p.m., **Apr. 3;** 80 men used 429 horses, changed every 10 mi. There were 190 relay stations. The service ended **Oct. 24, 1861,** when first transcontinental telegraph line was completed.

Giuseppe Garibaldi led 1,000 volunteers to Sicily in **May** to unify Italy by force; deposed Francis II of Naples; named Victor Emmanuel king of Italy.

1861-65—Civil War.
See Article, Pages 720-721

1861

Emancipation of Russian serfs by Alexander II.

1863

Draft riots in N.Y. City killed an estimated 1,000, including Negroes who were hung by mobs **July 13-16;** protested provision allowing money payment in place of military service. Property loss about $1.5 million. Payment in place of service ended **1864.**

1864

Sand Creek massacre of Cheyenne and Arapaho Indians by Col. John M. Chivington **Nov. 29** in a raid by 900 cavalrymen who killed between 150-500 men, women and children; 9 soldiers died. The tribes were awaiting surrender terms when attacked.

1866

Ku Klux Klan formed secretly in South to terrorize Negroes who voted. Disbanded **1869-1871.** A 2d Ku Klux Klan was organized 1915.

First post of the Grand Army of the Republic formed at Decatur, Ill., **Apr. 6.** First national encampment met. **Nov. 2** in Indianapolis. For years this Union veterans organization was a political force in the nation. Last encampment held **Aug. 31, 1949,** in Indianapolis; 6 of the 16 surviving veterans attended.

1867

Alaska sold to U.S. by Russia for $7.2 million (2 cents an acre) **Mar. 30** through efforts of Secretary of State William H. Seward and Sen. Charles Sumner.

Emperor Maximilian of Mexico executed by Juarez supporters **June 19.** He was an Austrian archduke placed on throne **Apr. 10, 1864,** by French.

Dominion of Canada established **July 1.**

Abolition of the Shogunate and restoration of the Mikado marked beginning of Meiji reforms that industrialized and modernized Japan; feudalism abolished 1871; Constitution promulgated 1889.

1868

The World Almanac, a publication of the New York World newspaper, appeared for the first time.

Thomas D'Arcy McGee, a "Father of Confederation," shot in first Canadian political assassination.

Pres. Andrew Johnson, blocked by Senate in attempt to remove Edwin M. Stanton, secretary of war, for opposing his policies, was impeached for violation of Tenure of Office Act by House; tried by Senate and acquitted **March-May.** Stanton resigned.

1869

Financial "Black Friday" in New York **Sept. 24;** caused by gold corner attempt.

Transcontinental railroad completed; golden spike driven at Promontory, Utah **May 10** marking the junction of Central Pacific and Union Pacific.

Woman suffrage law passed in Territory of Wyoming **Dec. 10.**

1870

Franco-Prussian War. Napoleon III, French emperor, tricked into declaring war on Prussia by Bismarck, Prussian chancellor, over Spanish succession issue; surrendered with large army at Sedan **Sept. 4.** Nationalists declared republic **Sept. 4.**

The troops of Victor Emmanuel II, under Gen. Cadorna, took possession of Rome **Sept. 20** in the name of the kingdom of Italy. Rome and the rest of the Papal States then were annexed after a plebiscite taken **Oct. 2.**

1871

William I of Hohenzollern proclaimed German emperor (kaiser) at Versailles **Jan. 18.** Paris "Red Republicans" organized commune **Mar. 18-May 29;** burned Hotel de Ville, Tuileries palace, executed 67 hostages. Communards overcome by French army; deaths est. 20,000.

Treaty of Frankfort ended Franco-Prussian War **May 23.** France ceded Alsace, most of Lorraine, paid 5 billion francs indemnity.

The Law of Guarantees, passed by the Italian Parliament **May 13,** granted the pope and his successors possession of the Vatican, the Lateran and the villa of Castel Gandolfo and a yearly 3,225,000 lire, or about $645,000. The money was not claimed.

Great fire destroyed Chicago Oct. 8-11; loss est. at $196 million. Supposedly started in Mrs. O'Leary's barn, 558 DeKoven St., by cow upsetting lantern.

Henry M. Stanley sent by James Gordon Bennett, owner of New York Herald, to find David Livingstone, missionary; greeted him **Nov. 10** at Ujiji in Central Africa, now Tanzania, with "Dr. Livingstone, I presume?"

1872

Amnesty Act restored civil rights to citizens of the South **May 22** except 500 Confederate leaders.

1873

Panic began in N.Y. City with bank failures **Sept. 20.**

First U. S. postal card issued **May 1.**

1874

"Boss" William Tweed of N. Y. City convicted of fraud **Nov. 19** and sentenced to 12 years in prison; the court released him from Blackwells Island prison **June 1875** on a technicality; he was committed to Ludlow St. jail in a civil suit, escaped **Dec. 4, 1875,** and went to Cuba, then to Spain; brought back to N.Y.

City **Nov. 1876;** died in jail **Apr. 12, 1878.**
1875
Congress passed first Civil Rights Act. Mar. 1 which guaranteed equal rights to Negroes in public accommodations and jury duty. Act invalidated in **1883** by Supreme Court ruling that the federal government can protect only political, not social, rights.
First Kentucky Derby held **May 17,** at Churchill Downs, Louisville, Ky.
Mary Baker Eddy published "Science and Health".
1876
Samuel J. Tilden, Democrat, received majority of 250,807 popular votes for president over Rutherford B. Hayes, Republican, and had 184 electoral votes against 163, with returns from South Carolina, Florida, Louisiana and Oregon, 22 electoral votes, in dispute. Bitter contest for delegates with charges of corruption; issue left to Congress, which appointed electoral commission, 8 Republicans, 7 Democrats; Hayes given presidency by strict party vote.
Col. George A. Custer and 264 soldiers of the 7th Cavalry killed **June 25** in "last stand," Battle of the Little Big Horn, Mont., in Sioux Indian War, by Indian tribes united by Sitting Bull; fighting led by Chiefs Gall and Crazy Horse.
James Butler (Wild Bill) Hickok, shot dead from behind by Jack McCall, a desperado, in Deadwood, S.D., **Aug. 2.** A vigilance committee acquitted McCall

---

For origins of the Civil War see Index for Confederate States and Secession.
South Carolina, Georgia, Alabama, Mississippi, Louisiana, and Florida formed the Confederate States of America **Feb. 8, 1861,** chose Jefferson Davis provisional president; were joined later by Texas, North Carolina, Arkansas, Virginia, and Tennessee.

First Year of War — 1861

Gen. Pierre Beauregard, on Confederate Government orders, demanded surrender of Ft. Sumter in Charleston, S.C., harbor **Apr. 11,** Maj. Robert Anderson, USA, refused. Bombardment started at 4:30 a.m. **April 12.** Anderson surrendered **Apr. 14.**
Pres. Lincoln called for 75,000 militia from states by quotas **April 15.**
Battle of Bull Run or Manassas. Brig. Gen. Irvin McDowell attacked Beauregard's forces on the Warrenton Road **July 21,** pushed them back to Henry House hill. Gen. Joseph E. Johnston's army from Winchester, including forces commanded by Brig. Gen. Thomas J. Jackson and Gen. E. Kirby Smith reinforced Confederates, and with help of Gen. Jubal Early's brigade routed Federals. Brig. Gen. B. E. Bee, CSA, said: "Look, there is Jackson standing like a stone wall!" McDowell had 28,455 troops, 18,500 engaged, 2,708 casualties; Confederates had 32,072 available, 18,000 engaged, 1,967 casualties. Congress **July 22** authorized an army of 500,000.

Events of 1862

Forts Henry and Donelson — Brig. Gen. U.S. Grant with 17,000 attacked **Ft. Henry** on Tennessee River; it fell **Feb. 6.** Grant rushed troops across 10 mi. of bogs to **Ft. Donelson** on the Cumberland, sent his "unconditional surrender" message to Brig. Gen. Simon B. Buckner, CSA, who gave up with 11,500 **Feb. 16.**
Shiloh — Gen. Albert S. Johnston, CSA, with 40,000 men surprised Grant at **Shiloh Church** near **Pittsburg Landing,** Tenn. **Apr. 6;** Johnston was killed. Gen. Beauregard retreated **Apr. 7** after Brig. Gen. Don Carlos Buell reinforced Grant with about 20,000 men. U.S. had 44,895 engaged, with 1,734 killed of 13,047 total casualties; CSA, 1,728 killed of 10,699 casualties.
New Orleans — Fighting ships and gunboats under Flag Officer David G. Farragut took New Orleans Apr. 25. Farragut made rear admiral.
Monitor and Merrimack — Confederates rebuilt scuttled US frigate Merrimack into ironclad Virginia. Sank Cumberland, USN, destroyed Congress, USN, at Hampton Roads, Va., **Mar. 8.** Three other U.S. ships ran aground including Minnesota. Monitor, flat-decked ironclad, 900 tons, 172 ft. long with revolving turret and 2 11-in. guns, built by John Ericsson at $275,000 cost; Lt. John L. Worden commander, crew of 58, badly damaged Virginia **Mar. 9.** After Union took Virginia's base, Confederates scuttled ship **May 11.**
Peninsular Campaign — McClellan moved Army of the Potomac by sea to Fort Monroe, Va., 70 mi. from Richmond. Confederates sent Stonewall Jackson up Shenandoah Valley to divert U.S. troops; Jackson lost

Major Events of Civil War, 1861-1865;

at **Kernstown,** Va., but routed U.S. troops at **McDowell, Front Royal, Winchester, Cross Keys, Port Republic, Mar. 23-June 9.** McClellan's advance troops clashed with Maj. Gen. James Longstreet at **Williamsburg May 5.** On **May 25,** 2 U.S. corps crossed to south side of Chickahominy leaving 3 on north side. Gen. Joseph E. Johnston attacked south side **May 30. Battle of Fair Oaks** or **Seven Pines,** was repulsed. Johnston was wounded and Lee took over Army of Northern Virginia.
Gen. Lee started **Seven Days' Battles** at Mechanicsville, Va. **June 26.** McClellan withdrew to **Gaines Mill** (1st Cold Harbor) where Lee with 57,000 assaulted Brig. Gen. Fitz-John Porter's 34,000 **June 29, Frayser's Farm** or Glendale **June 30;** stopped Stonewall Jackson at **White Oak Swamp June 30.** At Malvern Hill July 1 Confederates had 5,500 casualties, mostly from U.S. artillery; Union casualties were 2,000. Despite this success McClellan withdrew army to Harrison's Landing. With over 115,000 men available against Confederates' 95,000, McClellan from **June 25-July 1** had 1,734 killed, 8,062 wounded, 6,053 missing; CSA had 3,478 killed, 16,261 wounded, 875 missing. McClellan's army was sent to join Gen. John Pope's in northern Virginia.
Second Bull Run (Manassas). Stonewall Jackson and Maj. Gen. A. P. Hill, CSA, attacked Maj. Gen. Nathaniel P. Banks (part of Pope's Army of Virginia) at Cedar Mountain, Va. **Aug. 9.** Jackson destroyed Pope's supplies at **Manassas Aug. 26.** Major battle was fought **Aug. 30.** Pope was checked by Jackson and Longstreet, withdrew; was relieved.
Antietam (Sharpsburg). Lee with 50,000 crossed Potomac **Sept. 4** to Frederick, Md., moved across South Mountain to Hagerstown, Md. McClellan, fought Longstreet and D. H. Hill at **South Mountain Sept. 14,** Lee dropped back to Antietam Creek near Sharpsburg, Md., **Sept. 15;** Jackson took **Harpers Ferry** where only 1,300 cavalry of 12,000 USA escaped. McClellan attacked **Sept. 17;** stopped Lee, but failed to use reserve and let Lee withdraw across Potomac. U.S. had 70,000 engaged, 13,000 casualties; CSA had 50,000 engaged, 13,000 casualties.
Fredericksburg, Va. Lincoln relieved McClellan, gave Army of the Potomac to Maj. Gen. Ambrose E. Burnside. Burnside crossed Rappahannock, made frontal attacks on Marye's Heights above Fredericksburg **Dec. 13.** Lee, Longstreet and Jackson with 75,000 repulsed him. USA lost 12,653; CSA 5,377.
Preliminary proclamation, **Sept. 22,** by President Lincoln announced that **Jan. 1, 1863,** slaves would be declared free in territory then in rebellion.

Events of 1863

Lincoln's Emancipation Proclamation Jan. 1 declared free forever the slaves in Arkansas, Texas, Louisiana (certain parishes already occupied excepted); Mississippi, Alabama, Florida, Georgia, South Carolina, North Carolina, Tennessee, and Virginia (West Virginia and other portions excepted). About 3 million slaves were thus declared free.
Chancellorsville, Va. — Maj. Gen. Joseph E. Hook-

but the U.S. Court in Yankton, S.D., found him guilty and he was hanged.

1877

Molly Maguires, Irish terrorist society in Scranton, Pa., mining areas, broken up by hanging of 11 leaders for murders of mine officials and police.

1878

First commercial telephone exchange opened, New Haven, Conn., **Jan. 28, 1878.** First private exchange, used by physicians, reported in use **July 1877** at Hartford, Conn.

1879

F. W. Woolworth opened his first five-and-ten store in Utica, N.Y., **Feb. 22.**

Henry George published Progress & Poverty, advocating single tax on land.

1881

Pres. James A. Garfield shot in Washington, D.C., **July 2;** died in Elberon, N.J., **Sept. 19.**

Federation of Organized Trades and Labor Unions formed **Aug. 2** at Terre Haute, Ind.; later joined with 25 independent unions to form the American Federation of Labor at Columbus, Oh., **Dec. 1886.**

1882

Prof. Robert Koch announced, in Berlin, discovery of the tuberculosis bacillus **Mar. 24.**

1883

Brooklyn Bridge opened May 24; panic on it **May**

Emancipation and Lincoln's Assassination

er succeeded Burnside and with 90,000 available, attempted to envelop Lee May 2. Jackson led 32,000 around US Army, drove in right of Maj. Gen. O. O. Howard. Jackson wounded by own troops **May 2** died **May 10;** succeeded by Maj. Gen. J. E. B. Stuart. Maj. Gen. John Sedgwick forced Confederates out of Marye's Heights; was pushed back May 4. Hooker overruled his advisers and withdrew across Rappahannock. U.S. casualties 17,197; CSA 13,000. Lincoln called for 100,000 men for 6 months June 15.

Gettysburg — Lee with 76,224 and 272 guns, invaded Penn. Army of the Potomac had 115,256, about 90,000 effective, 362 guns. Lincoln gave Maj. Gen. George G. Meade top command June 28. 1st U.S. Cavalry under Gen. John Buford pushed back at Gettysburg by Lt. Gen. A. P. Hill, CSA, **July 1.** Lt. Gen. Richard S. Ewell, CSA, forced U.S. back to Cemetery Hill; U.S. took Culp's Hill, extended line to Round Top. Lee's attacks checked **July 2.** On **July 3** Maj. Gen. George E. Pickett, Maj. Gen. Isaac Trimble, and Brig. Gen. James J. Pettigrew with 15,000 made assault on foot from Seminary Ridge vs. U.S. center held by Gen. W. S. Hancock; were repulsed with 4,500 casualties. Lee retreated into Virginia; Meade did not pursue. Losses: U.S. 3,155 killed, 14,529 wounded, 5,365 missing; CSA, 3,903 killed, 12,709 wounded, 5,425 missing. Many of the missing were prisoners. Total casualties estimated at 23,049 USA, 20,451 CSA.

Vicksburg — Gen. William T. Sherman took **Jackson, Miss., May 14.** Lt. Gen. John C. Pemberton, CSA, commanding 30,000 men, was defeated at **Champion's Hill** and **Black River Bridge,** and besieged in Vicksburg by Grant. He surrendered **July 4;** Grant paroled prisoners. Gen. Nathaniel Banks with 15,000 captured **Port Hudson July 8,** giving U.S. control of Mississippi River.

Tennessee — Maj. Gen. William S. Rosecrans, USA took **Chattanooga Sept. 9.** Braxton Bragg CSA, drove him back to **Chickamauga** but Maj. Gen. George H. Thomas checked Bragg **Sept. 18-20;** was called "Rock of Chickamauga." Hooker took **Lookout Mt.,** fought "Battle Above the Clouds" **Nov. 24.** Sherman and Thomas dislodged Bragg at **Missionary Ridge Nov. 25.** Bragg retreated to Georgia.

Events of 1864

Grant made general in chief Mar. 12. Sherman succeeded him in West. Draft for 500,000 men to serve 3 yrs. or duration begun **Mar. 10; 20,000 more Mar. 14.**

Rear Adm. David G. Farragut won naval battle of **Mobile Bay Aug. 5.**

Wilderness, Spotsylvania — Bloody battles followed when Grant crossed the Rapidan and was attacked by Lee in the "Wilderness," tangled woods west of Fredericksburg, **May 5.** Grant attacked Lee at **Spotsylvania Court House May 10** (2d Wilderness). Maj. Gen. Francis C. Barlow USA took Spotsylvania salient, including **Bloody Angle May 12** (3d Wilderness). U.S. killed and wounded May 5-12 est. 26,813, missing 4,183. Maj. Gen. Philip H. Sheridan's cavalry defeated Maj. Gen. J.E.B. Stuart at **Yellow Tavern,**

Va., **May 11;** Stuart was fatally wounded, died **May 12** in Richmond.

Cold Harbor — Lee took strong position near the Chickahominy. Grant made frontal attacks **June 3,** lost 7,000 casualties in 30 minutes, 11,000 June 1-3.

USS Kearsarge — Capt. John A. Winslow defeated CSS Alabama, Capt. Raphael Semmes, off Cherbourg, France, **June 19;** Alabama surrendered and sank.

Early vs. Sheridan — Lee sent Maj. Gen. Jubal A. Early to hold Shenandoah Valley. Sheridan defeated Early at **Winchester Sept. 19, Fisher's Hill Sept. 22.** Early surprised Gen. Horatio Wright at **Cedar Creek Oct. 19;** Sheridan's famous ride from Winchester rallied troops, brought victory.

Sherman's Campaign for Atlanta — Sherman defeated J. E. Jonston at **Resaca, Ga., May 14-15.** Johnston repulsed Sherman at **Kenesaw Mtn. June 27** (U.S. casualties 3,000, CSA 600), but told Jefferson Davis he could not annihilate Sherman's large forces, was superseded by Gen. J. B. Hood, CSA, **July 17.** Lt. Gen. William J. Hardee, CSA, defeated at **Peach Tree Creek July 20.** Hardee defeated in battle of **Atlanta July 22** by Gen. J. B. McPherson who was killed. Sherman occupied Atlanta **Sept. 2,** burned it **Nov. 15,** started **March to the Sea,** reached Savannah **Dec. 21.** Thomas defeated Hood at **Nashville,** Tenn.

Events of 1865

Confederates evacuated Columbia, S.C., and **Charleston, S.C., Feb. 17,** lost Cape Fear River forts **Feb. 20-21.** Brig. Gen George A. Custer defeated Early at **Waynesboro, Va., Mar. 2.** Confederates evacuated **Petersburgh** and **Richmond Apr. 2-3.** Lee surrendered 27,805 to Grant at **Appomattox Court House, Va., Apr. 9.** J. E. Johnston surrendered 31,243 to Sherman at **Durham Station,** N.C., **Apr. 18.**

Murder of Lincoln

Lincoln was shot by John Wilkes Booth, an actor, in Ford's Theatre, in Washington, D.C., **April 14,** died **April 15.** Booth died of a bullet wound **April 26,** in burning barn, on a farm near Bowling Green, Va. Hanged for complicity in Lincoln's assassination were Mrs. Mary E. Surratt, David E. Herold, George A. Atzerodt, and Lewis Payne (Powell) **July 7.** Also convicted of conspiracy were Dr. Samuel A. Mudd, who set Booth's broken ankle, Samuel Arnold, Michael O'Laughlin, and Edward Spangler. All were sentenced to life imprisonment except Spangler, who received a 6-year sentence. They were sent to Dry Tortugas prison, off Key West, where O'Laughlin died during an 1867 outbreak of yellow fever. Dr. Mudd's unselfish services as a physician during the outbreak won him a pardon; Arnold and Spangler were freed with Dr. Mudd in 1869. John H. Surratt, son of Mary E., fled to Europe, was brought back, tried and freed. Booth's body was buried under the stone floor of a naval prison in Washington, D. C., later reburied in the Booth family plot in Baltimore.

Slavery was abolished by adoption of the 13th amendment to the U.S. Constitution **Dec. 18.**

30, 12 trampled to death.

1884
Financial panic in N.Y. City **May 5-7**.

1885
Gen. Charles G. (Chinese) Gordon, British governor of the Sudan, sent there to aid Egyptian troops, was slain **Jan. 26** by a Moslem soldier, at Khartoum. Several thousand whites were massacred by troops of the Mahdi, Sudanese leader. Gen. Kitchener defeated the Mahdi's army **Sept. 2, 1898**.

First electric street railway in U.S. opened in Baltimore by Leo Daft **Aug. 10**.

Canadian rebel Louis Riel hanged for treason at Regina, following crushing of Northwest Rebellion.

Last spike driven Nov. 7 in Canadian Pacific Railway at Craigellachie, British Columbia, completed Canadian transcontinental railway.

1886
Haymarket riot, evening of **May 4**, followed bitter labor battles for 8-hour day in Chicago, attacks on strike-breakers, police violence and attempts of anarchists to incite workers. A bomb killed 7 police and wounded 66. Eight anarchists found guilty. Gov. John P. Altgeld denounced trial as unfair.

Geronimo, Apache Indian, surrendered **Mar. 27** to U.S. Gen. George Crook in Sonora, Mex., but fled the next day and finally surrendered **Sept. 4** to U. S. Gen. Nelson A. Miles in Arizona.

Dr. Arthur Conan Doyle created famous detective Sherlock Holmes, in story, A Study in Scarlet.

1887
Flood in Hwang-ho River, China; 900,000 persons perished.

1888
Great blizzard in eastern U. S. **Mar. 11-14; 400** deaths.

1889
Crown Prince Rudolf of Austria and Baroness Maria Vetsera found slain in his hunting lodge, Mayerling, near Vienna **Jan. 29**.

Johnstown, Pa., flood May 31; 2,200 lives lost.

Universal Exhibition in Paris **May 6-Nov. 6**. Eiffel Tower (984.25 ft.) opened. First automobile exhibited, a Benz.

Dom Pedro II, emperor of Brazil, forced off throne by planters after he freed slaves. Died in Paris **1891**; last emperor on American soil.

1890
First execution by electrocution; William Kemmler **Aug. 6** at Auburn Prison, Auburn, N. Y., for murder.

Battle of Wounded Knee, S. D., **Dec. 29**, the last major conflict between Indians and U. S. troops, occurred when a band of Sioux were captured and brought to Wounded Knee Creek where Col. J. W. Forsyth ordered them disarmed. Some Indians resisted, sparking the battle which killed about 200 Indian men, women, and children; 29 soldiers died, 33 wounded. (See 1973, 1974.)

Castle Garden closed as immigration depot and Ellis Island opened Dec. 31; closed 1954.

1892
Homestead, Pa., strike at Carnegie steel mills, near Pittsburgh; conflict between 300 Pinkerton guards and strikers; 7 guards and 11 strikers and spectators shot to death, many wounded **July 6**.

1893
Ford's Theatre building, Washington, D.C., where Lincoln was shot, used by Pension Bureau, collapsed **June 9** killing 22.

1894
Chinese-Japanese War began **July 25**; Battle of Yalu **Sept. 17**; Treaty of Shimonoseki **April 17, 1895** gave Japan the Liaotung Peninsula, Formosa (Taiwan) and the Pescadores.

Jacob S. Coxey led 500 unemployed from the Midwest into Washington, D. C., **Apr. 29**. Coxey was arrested for trespassing on the Capitol grounds. Strike of employees of Pullman Co., South Chicago, Ill., June, led Eugene V. Debs to call sympathetic strike of American Railway Union. Pres. Cleveland

called out Federal troops over protest of Gov. Altgeld (Ill.). Debs and 3 others were imprisoned 6 months for contempt of court. Strike ended **Aug. 7**.

Thomas A. Edison's kinetoscope (invented 1887) given first public showing at 1155 Broadway, N.Y. City **Apr. 14**, was patented **1891** for U. S. only.

Capt. Alfred Dreyfus found guilty of betraying French army secrets **Dec. 22** in sensational frame-up; real culprit, Major Esterhazy, acquitted; Dreyfus condemned to Devil's Island, off French Guiana. Recalled for second trial by efforts of Emile Zola and Georges Clemenceau; again condemned **Sept. 9, 1899**. Public clamor led to pardon **Sept. 19**. Further proofs of innocence led to complete exoneration **1906**. He served as a lieutenant colonel in World War I.

1895
Cuban Revolution resumed **Feb. 20**; Gen. Antonio Maceo, leader of the insurrection, was killed in action **Dec. 7, 1896**.

X-rays discovered by Wilhelm Konrad Roentgen, a German physicist; Nobel prize winner **1901**.

1896
Guglielmo Marconi received first wireless (radio) patent from Britain **June 2**.

William Jennings Bryan delivered "Cross of Gold" speech at Democratic National Convention in Chicago **July 8**. Bryan nominated for president but defeated by Republican William McKinley.

1897
Eugene V. Debs formed Social Democratic party.

1898
Radium discovered by Pierre Curie, his wife, Marie, and G. Bemont in Paris.

1898—Spanish-American War
See Article Page 723

1899
South African (Boer) War began **Oct. 11**; Ladysmith relieved **Feb. 28, 1900**; Pretoria fell **June 5, 1900**; war ended **May 31, 1902** with loss of independence of Boer republics, Transvaal and Orange Free State, now in Republic of South Africa. British losses: 5,773 killed; 16,171 dead of wounds or disease; 22,829 wounded. Boers engaged est. 65,000; losses unknown.

Filipino insurgents (est. 12,000 under arms) unable to get recognition of independence from U. S. started guerrilla war **Feb. 4**. Crushed with capture **Mar. 23, 1901** of leader, Emilio Aguinaldo, by Brig. Gen. Frederick Funston.

Open Door Policy of U. S. Secy. of State John Hay supported by 6 nations. Policy was to make China an open market for international commerce and to preserve its integrity as a nation.

Boxer anti-foreign uprising started in China; Westerners and Westernized Chinese murdered.

1900
Carry Nation, Kansas anti-saloon agitator, began raiding with hatchet.

Boxers in China killed German minister **June 20**. Foreigners besieged in Peking legations. Relief expedition of 18,000 American, British, French, Japanese, and Russian troops took Tientsin **July 13**; Peking **Aug. 14**. U. S. had 2,500 men under Maj. Gen. A. R. Chaffee. Germans arrived and Field Marshal Count Alfred von Waldersee led army of occupation. Russia refused to yield parts of Manchuria. Dowager empress of China accepted allied terms **Sept. 1901**. All except U. S. exacted large concessions and indemnity of $333 million payable in 39 years. U.S. used half its $25 million share to provide Chinese students scholarships.

Campaign to wipe out yellow fever in Cuba begun **June 26** by Drs. Walter Reed, Aristides Agramonte, Jesse Lazear, and James Carroll.

1901
Pres. William McKinley was shot at the Pan-American Exposition in Buffalo, N. Y., **Sept. 6** by Leon Czolgosz, anarchist; died **Sept. 14**. Theodore Roosevelt, 42, became youngest U. S. president.

Marconi signalled letter "S" by wireless telegraph across Atlantic from Cornwall, England, to Newfoundland **Dec. 12**.

1902

Anglo-Japanese alliance formed **Jan. 30** to protect Japan against encroaching Russians.

Cuban Republic inaugurated. American occupation under Gen. Leonard Wood ended **May 20.**

First International Arbitration Court opened in The Hague, Holland, **October.**

1903

First automobile trip across U. S. from San Francisco to New York **May 23-Aug. 1.**

Treaty between U. S. and Colombia to have U. S. dig Panama Canal signed **Jan. 22, 1903,** rejected by Colombia. Panama declared independence **Nov. 3;** recognized by Pres. Theodore Roosevelt **Nov. 6.**

First successful flight in heavier-than-air mechanically propelled airplane by **Orville Wright** (1871-1948) **Dec. 17, 1903,** rising from base of Kill Devil Hill, 4 miles south of Kitty Hawk, N. C., 120 ft. in 12 sec. Fourth flight same day by **Wilbur Wright** (1867-1912), 852 ft., in 59 sec. Plane patented **May 22, 1906.**

1904

Russo-Japanese War began **Feb. 6.** Port Arthur surrendered to Japanese **Jan. 2, 1905.** Peace treaty signed in Portsmouth, N. H., **Sept. 5, 1905.**

New York subway opened **Oct. 27.**

1905

Russian revolution crushed by Czar Nicholas II. Resulted in creation of Duma (parliament) to placate liberals. First meeting **May 10;** dissolved **July.**

Norway dissolved union with Sweden.

1906

San Francisco earthquake and fire **Apr. 18-19.** Dead: 452. Loss: $350 million.

Harry K. Thaw, Pittsburgh millionaire, shot and killed architect Stanford White on roof of Madison Square Garden, N.Y. (26th and Madison) **June 25** on ground of avenging honor of wife Evelyn Nesbit.

1907

Financial panic in the U.S.

Standard Oil of Indiana fined $29,240,000 by Judge K. M. Landis in U. S. Court, Chicago, for accepting freight rebates **Apr. 3.** Set aside **July 22, 1908.** Railroads found guilty of giving rebates.

First round-world cruise of U.S. "Great White Fleet"; 16 battleships, 12,000 men; exhibited U.S. naval strength.

1909

Admiral Robert E. Peary reached North Pole **Apr. 6** on 6th attempt, accompanied by Matthew Henson, a black, and 4 Eskimos.

Louis Bleriot flew across the English Channel from Calais to Dover, 31 mi. in 37 min., **July 25.**

1910

Boy Scouts of America founded **Feb. 8.**

Glenn H. Curtiss won $10,000 offered by the New York World for first continuous flight, Albany to N.Y. City, 137 mi., 152 min., **May 29.**

Dynamite explosion at Los Angeles Times **Oct. 1** caused fire killing 21 in labor dispute.

1911

Italian-Turkish war began **Sept. 29.** Italians made first combat use of aircraft in warfare; Libya acquired by Italy.

First transcontinental airplane flight (with numerous stops) by C. P. Rodgers, New York to Pasadena, **Sept. 17-Nov. 5;** time in air 82 hr., 4 min.

Capt. Roald Amundsen, Norwegian explorer, reached South Pole **Dec. 14.**

Mexican Revolution. Porfirio Diaz, president of Mexico since 1877 (except 1880-84),resigned **May 25** after successful revolt by Francisco L. Madero who succeeded him. People living in poverty wanted restoration of communal lands (ejidos), better conditions. In 1912 Madero, supported by Gen. Huerta, put down revolts. In **Feb. 1913** Huerta helped depose Madero; Madero, his brother, and Vice Pres. Suarez were murdered. Pres. Wilson refused recognition to Huerta and "government by assassination." Venustiano Carranza, rallying Maderos, was opposed by Gen. Francisco (Pancho) Villa in north. When American sailors were arrested at Tampico **Apr. 9, 1914,** the U.S. sent Atlantic fleet to Veracruz. Huerta re-

---

Spanish-American War of 1898; U.S. Becomes Naval Power

Spanish misrule in Cuba led to repeated attempts by Cuban patriots to gain rights of citizenship, abolition of slavery, and finally independence. When South America broke from Europe in the 1820s proslavery influence in the U.S. blocked movements to free Cuba and Puerto Rico. But in 1852, President Fillmore refused to join Great Britain and France in guaranteeing Spanish authority in Cuba. In 1854, the Ostend Manifesto, written largely by James Buchanan, urged the U.S. to buy Cuba or seize it to abolish oppression. Grant's administration offered to buy Cuba, but Spain rejected the offer.

In Cuba revolts led by Narciso Lopez and Joaquin de Aguero, 1848-1851, were suppressed and the leaders executed. In 1868, a major revolt was led by Carlos de Cespedes and Manuel de Quesada; it lasted 10 years. In 1873, the Virginius expedition, flying the American flag, was seized by the Spaniards, and Americans and Cubans aboard were shot. This did not stop supplying of arms from the U.S. In 1895, the insurrection had spread so widely under Generals Calixto Garcia, Maximo Gomez, and Antonio Macea that Spain landed 150,000 troops, but by 1896 over half of the island was in the hands of the patriots. The U.S. offered to mediate but was repulsed. The country was laid waste by Spanish troops and the accounts of suffering increased sentiment in the U.S. in favor of a free Cuba.

The U.S. battleship Maine, under Capt. Charles D. Sigsbee, sent to Havana in January on goodwill tour, was blown up **Feb. 15, 1898;** 264 men, 2 officers killed. U.S. inquiry, Capt. William T. Sampson, board president, blamed external explosion **Mar. 2.** Spanish inquiry **Mar. 28** blamed internal explosion. Congress **Mar. 9** voted $50 million for defense. President McKinley **Mar. 27** demanded Spain grant armistice for negotiation with Cuba via U.S., end relocation of noncombatants in special military enclaves. Spain **Mar. 31** offered to arbitrate Maine charges, end relocation, but wanted Cubans to ask for armistice. After appeal by foreign ministers Spain granted armistice **Apr. 9.** McKinley **Apr. 11** asked Congress for authority to intervene in Cuba. Congress **Apr. 20-25** debated joint resolution recognizing independence of Cuba, asked Spain to withdraw and empowered president to enforce it; adopted it with statement war existed since **Apr. 21.** Spain declared war **Apr. 24.**

Commodore George Dewey, with 6 warships, destroyed the Spanish fleet (10 ships) in Manila Bay **May 1,** occupied Cavite. Spain, 167 dead; U.S., 7 wounded. Marines landed at Guantanamo **May 11.** Maj. Gen. William R. Shafter landed 10,000 men at Daiquiri and Siboney, including 1st U.S. Volunteer Cavalry (Rough Riders) recruited by Lt. Col. Theodore Roosevelt. El Caney and San Juan Hill were captured **July 1.**

Admiral Cervera's fleet left Santiago harbor **July 3,** was destroyed by ships of acting Rear Adm. Sampson and Commodore Winfield S. Schley; 353 Spaniards killed, 151 wounded; 1 American killed. Santiago surrendered **July 17.** Maj. Gen. Nelson A. Miles took Puerto Rico **July 25-28.** Armistice signed **Aug. 12.** Peace treaty signed in Paris **Dec. 10** eliminated Spain from lands discovered by Columbus. U. S. acquired Puerto Rico, Guam and Philippines, paying $20 million for all Spanish claims in latter; guaranteed Cuban independence (ratified **Feb. 6, 1899.**) U.S. had treaty rights in Cuba until 1934; granted Philippines independence **July 4, 1946.**

signed **July 14, 1914**, Carranza occupied Mexico City **Aug. 20**. Villa, supported by Zapata, warred on Carranza. U.S. recognized Carranza **Oct. 19, 1915**, placed embargo on arms to other generals. Villa raided Santa Isabel, Mexico, **Jan. 10, 1916**, killed several Americans; raided Columbus, N. M., **Mar. 9, 1916**, killed 17. Gen. John J. Pershing with 12,000 sent into Mexico **Mar. 15**. Fight at Parral and Chihuahua **Apr. 12**. Carranza's troops attacked **June 21**. U. S. troops withdrawn **Feb. 4, 1917**. Carranza called constitutional convention, **Feb. 15, 1917**, became legal president **May 1, 1917**. He restored some of the land, nationalized coal and oil, expropriated some foreign holdings. Discontent caused new uprising and he was ambushed and killed. Obregon became president **Dec. 1, 1920**. Villa was killed in ambush at Parral **July 20, 1923**.

Chinese Revolution led by Sun Yat-sen overthrew Manchu dynasty. Republic formed **Feb. 12, 1912**; Yuan shih-K'ai elected president **Feb. 15**.

Parliament Act of 1911 reduced the power of British House of Lords to a suspensory veto which could delay but not kill bills.

1912

Capt. Robert F. Scott and 4 companions reached South Pole **Jan. 17**; all 5 died on return journey.

White Star liner Titanic wrecked on maiden trip, from Southampton to N.Y. City; hit iceberg off Newfoundland **Apr. 14-15**; U. S. reported 1,517 lost; British Board of Trade reported 1,503 lost. There were 2,307 persons aboard. The ship was 882 1/2 ft. long, cost $7.5 million.

War in Balkans against Turkéy by Montenegro, Bulgaria, Serbia, and Greece **Oct. 8-Dec. 3**. Turks driven from Europe except for Constantinople (Istanbul) area.

1913

Sixteenth Amendment effective **Feb. 25** empowered Congress to levy and collect income taxes.

1914

Ford Motor Co. raised basic wage rates from $2.40 for 9-hr. day to $5 for 8-hr. day, **Jan. 5**.

First ship passed through Panama Canal **Aug. 15**.

Second International: Brussels meeting of Interna-

Principal Events of World War I,

Origins. Since the defeat of France by Prussia in 1870-71 major powers of Europe had kept peace by diplomatic negotiations and a balance of power. Triple Alliance, of Germany, Austria and Italy was defensive, with reservations; Triple Entente was an understanding between Britain, France and Russia. Nationalist aspirations in the Balkans had resulted in several wars and Italy had fought with Turkey and Ethiopia, Austria annexed Bosnia, Herzegovina, former Turkish Balkan provinces, in 1908. Russia backed Serbia's efforts to get a port on the Adriatic. Germany's industrial expansion led to building of powerful navy, which Britain matched 2 for one. Germany's universal military service led France to adopt 3-year training.

On **June 28, 1914**, Archduke Francis Ferdinand, heir to Austrian throne, was assassinated, with his wife, by Gavrillo Princip, Bosnian Serb terrorist, in Sarajevo, Bosnia. Austria-Hungary, through Count Berchthold, foreign minister, made 10 demands on Serbia for suppression of anti-Austrian agitation. Serbia conceded all but 2, which called for Austrian enforcement police inside Serbia. It asked reference to The Hague peace tribunal. Austria demanded all or nothing.

Russia, fearing Austrian action was aimed at Russia, supported Serbia. Germany backed Austria. Britain, France, Italy proposed mediation, Sir Edward Grey, British foreign minister, **July 26** proposed conference of 4 major powers; Germany refused to join.

Austria declared war on Serbia July 28. Germany, citing Russian mobilization, declared war on Russia **Aug. 1**; on France **Aug. 3**. Germans entered Belgium in violation of treaty, of which Britian was cosigner. Britain asked Germany to guarantee neutrality of Belgium by midnight **Aug. 4**; Germany refused; British declared war **Aug. 4**. Italy, declaring German aggression made Triple Alliance inoperative, proclaimed neutrality. Japan declared war on Germany **Aug. 23** because of Anglo-Japanese treaty on Far East. Turkey joined Central Powers **Nov. 23**.

Lord Kitchener became British sec. for war. Belgian forts at Liege stopped Germans until **Aug. 7**, delayed German schedule. Germans entered Brussels **Aug. 20**; pushed back British Expeditionary Force (Sir John French) at Mons **Aug. 23-24**; burned most of Louvain **Aug. 25**. Von Hindenburg and Ludendorff defeated Russians at **Tannenberg**, East Prussia, **Aug. 26-31**; at Masurian Lakes **Sept. 5-10**.

In first **Battle of the Marne, Sept. 5-10**, French under Joseph Joffre, Ferdinand Foch and Joseph Gallieni, stopped German advance of Von Kluck and Von Bulow toward Paris; forced them back to Aisne where trench warfare began. British repulsed Germans at Ypres **Oct. 16-Nov. 24**. Belgians lost Antwerp **Oct. 9**. Russians forced Austrians back in Galicia. Austrians took and lost Belgrade **Dec. 2-15**.

British bombarded Dardanelles forts Nov. 3; declared war on Turkey, annexed Cyprus **Nov. 5**. Japan took German-leased Tsingtao **Nov. 6**.

1915—Submarine War Begins

In 1915 the war became a desperate battle of attrition on land and sea. British sank German cruiser Bluecher **Jan. 24**. Germany ordered submarine blockade of Britain to start **Feb. 18**. U. S. held Germany to "strict accountability" for American losses. Germans used liquid fire in Vosges **Mar. 3**. Roving German cruiser Dresden sunk in Pacific **Mar. 15**. Three British, French battleships sunk at Dardanelles **Mar. 18**. Turks sank British battleship Lord Nelson **Apr. 6**. Germans introduced poison gas at Ypres **Apr. 22**, Canadians saved the line. Allies landed at Gallipoli **Apr. 25**. Germans torpedoed Gulflight, U.S. tanker, **Apr. 30**, 2 Americans lost.

German sub sank Cunard liner **Lusitania** off Old Head of Kinsale, Ireland, **May 7**; of 1,959 aboard, including 702 crew, 1,198, including 124 Americans, died. This started a series of protests by U.S. to Germany. Secy. of State William J. Bryan resigned **June 8**; considered Wilson's Lusitania note too severe. After sinking Arabic **Aug. 19** Germans agreed not to sink liners without warning, but U.S. considered promises inadequate. U.S. dismissed Austrian Ambassador Dumba and Germans Boy-Ed and Von Papen for illegal activities.

South Africans under Gen. Botha captured German S. W. Africa. Italy declared war on Austria-Hungary **May 23**, on Turkey **Aug. 20**, on Germany **Aug. 27**. Bulgaria declared war on Serbia **Oct. 14**; Allies against Bulgaria **Oct. 15-19**. Germans occupied Russian Baltic ports, took Vilna; Austrians occupied Serbia. Allies landed at Salonika **Oct. 5**. Sir John French replaced by Sir Douglas Haig on British front **Dec. 15**. Allies began evacuation of Gallipoli (Dardanelles) **Dec. 19**.

1916—Vast Battles

Germany announced Feb.10 that armed merchant ships would be considered warships and sunk without warning. U.S. retorted **Feb. 15** international law permitted self-defense of commercial ships. Germans made huge effort vs. Verdun **Feb. 21**, took Ft. Douau-

tional Socialist Bureau **July**. Members included 5 men later heads of governments: Lenin (Russia); Ebert (German Republic); Stauning (Denmark); Branting (Sweden); MacDonald (Britain).

1915

First telephone talk, New York to San Francisco, **Jan. 25** by Alexander Graham Bell and Thomas A. Watson.

First successful wireless from moving Lackawanna train to station, **Feb. 7.**

Twenty-one Demands presented by Japan to China; called for almost complete control of China.

1916

Gregory Rasputin, confessor to czarina, killed in Petrograd (Leningrad) **Dec.**

Bomb exploded during San Francisco Preparedness Day Parade **July 22**, killed 10, wounded 40. Thomas J. Mooney, 33, labor organizer; Warren K. Billings, shoe worker, were convicted of murder. Mooney was sentenced to death, Billings to life imprisonment. Pres. Wilson interceded for Mooney, who got life imprisonment 1918. Mooney was par-

doned by Gov. C. L. Olson **Jan. 7, 1939**; Billings freed **Oct. 16, 1939.**

1917

The 18th (Prohibition) Amendment to the Constitution was submitted to the states by Congress **Dec. 18**. On **Jan. 16, 1919**, the 36th state (Nebraska) ratified it, whereupon, by proclamation of the sec. of state, it became effective **Jan. 16, 1920**. The **Volstead (Prohibition Enforcement) Act** was passed by Congress **Oct. 1919**, was vetoed by Pres. Wilson, passed over his veto **Jan. 17, 1920**. New York, Montana and Wisconsin canceled their enforcement acts by 1929; Franklin D. Roosevelt, as 1932 presidential candidate, endorsed repeal; 21st Amendment repealed 18th; ratification completed **Dec. 5, 1933.**

Balfour Declaration Nov. 2 favored establishment of a national homeland in Palestine for Jewish people.

1918

Romanovs killed. Czar Nicholas II of Russia, the Empress Alexandra; their daughters, Olga, Tatiana, Marie, Anastasia; their son, Alexis, and aides were

1914-1918; Why U.S. Intervened

mont **Feb. 25**. Germany declared war on Portugal **Mar. 8**. Russians invaded Persia **Mar. 10**. Wilson threatened **Apr. 18-19** to break relations unless Germany revised sub warfare; Germany met most of U.S. demands.

Uprising in Ireland Apr. 24-May 1. Patrick Pearse et al, executed; Sir Roger Casement hanged **Aug. 3**. Britain adopted conscription **May 24**. **Jutland** naval battle **May 31-June 1**: British Admirals Jellicoe and Beatty lost 5 major cruisers, 8 destroyers, 6,091 men; German Admirals Scheer and von Hipper lost 2 major ships, also cruisers, destroyers, 2,545 men. **Battle of Ypres June 2.** Lord Kitchener drowned when Hampshire sunk off Orkneys June 5. **Battle of the Somme July 1-10**; second battle July 11-Aug. 3. Romania joined Allies Aug. 16 was defeated by January, 1917. U.S., Nov. 29, protested deportation of Belgian workers into Germany.

Germany and its allies called for peace negotiations **Dec. 12, 1916** to halt bloodshed. Germany told the Vatican it was fighting for the integrity of its frontiers and development in peaceful competition. On **Dec. 18, 1916**, President Wilson asked the belligerents to state their aims and terms; in order to end rival alliances he asked formation of a League of Nations and protection of "weak peoples." The Allies called the German offer "empty and insincere." They also told President Wilson they wanted "restorations, reparations, indemnities."

1917—U. S. Enters War

When **Germany began unrestricted submarine war**, the U.S. **Feb. 3** broke relations, refused negotiations until order was rescinded. Wilson **Feb. 26** asked Congress to order arming of merchant ships; when Senate refused Wilson armed them by executive order **Mar. 12**. Intercepted note of German Foreign Sec. **Zimmerman** to German minister in Mexico suggested Mexico be asked to enter war to recover U.S. Southwest **Feb. 28**. U.S. declared war on Germany **Apr. 6**, adopted selective conscription **May 18**, registered men aged 21-30 **June 5**. First of American Expeditionary Force (AEF) landed in France **June 26**; Gen. John J. Pershing, commander-in-chief, Adm. William S. Sims, chief Naval Operations, Europe. U.S. declared war on Austria-Hungary **Dec. 7.**

Collapse of Russian Empire. When navy and army revolted **Mar. 11-15** Czar Nicholas II abdicated. Provisional govt. made **Kerensky** premier July 20. Offensive in Galicia failed. In **April** Germans moved **Lenin** and associates from Switzerland to Russia via

Sweden to disrupt war. Bolshevists overthrew **Kerensky** Nov. 7, formed socialist republic of workers and peasants with Lenin president of Council of Commissars; made peace with Germany, Austria-Hungary, Bulgaria and Turkey at **Brest-Litovsk Mar. 3, 1918**. Russians withdrew from Lithuania, Estonia, Latvia, Ukraine, Poland, Finland, Aland Is., Erivan, Kars, Batum.

Other Fronts. Huge losses by Allies at Vimy, Arras, Cambrai, Passchendaele, Verdun. Petain succeeded Nivelle as French commander-in-chief. British took Jaffa, Baghdad, Jerusalem. Germans forced Italians back to Piave River.

1918—Victory for U. S. and Allies

German submarine war, **Feb. 1, 1917-Feb. 1, 1918**, cost U. S. 69 ships (171,061 tons); U. S. seized 686,494 German-Austrian tonnage. British lost 1,169 ships. Allies & neutrals lost 6,617,000 tons.

President Wilson presented his 14 points for peace to Congress **Jan. 8**. Asked open diplomacy; freedom of seas; restoration of Alsace-Lorraine to France; independence for Poland and Austrian minorities; "a general association of nations" to guarantee political and economic independence.

Collapse of Russian front released German troops for powerful thrusts on West front. **Battle of the Somme, Mar. 21-Apr. 6**. Gen. Foch made supreme commander **Mar. 26**. Battle of the Aisne May 27-June 5; AEF took Cantigny **May 28**. Germans reached Marne, AEF fought at **Chateau Thierry, Belleau Woods**. German retreat began July 19. AEF took St. Mihiel salient Sept. 12-20, fought at Meuse-Argonne Sept. 20-Nov. 11. British broke Hindenburg line Sept. 27.

Bulgaria gave up **Sept. 30**; Czar Ferdinand abdicated. Turkish armistice **Oct. 30**. Italians defeated Austrians at **Vittorio Veneto**, Austria and Hungary formed separate republics **Nov. 1**, Austria surrendered **Nov. 4.**

Germans accepted President Wilson's terms and recalled submarines **Oct. 20**; U. S. troops reached Sedan **Nov. 7**; revolution in Kiel and Hamburg **Nov. 7**; Bavaria proclaimed a republic **Nov. 8**; Kaiser abdicated **Nov. 9**, fled to Holland. Armistice signed in Marshal Foch's railway coach, near Compiegne, France, took effect **Nov. 11**; bugles sounded "cease firing" at 11 a.m. German fleet surrendered to British **Nov. 21**; AEF entered Mainz **Dec. 6**; crossed Rhine **Dec. 13.**

shot by Bolshevist orders in Ekaterinburg **July 16**; in Perm **July 12** the Bolshevists assassinated the Czar's brother, Grand Duke Michael.

Influenza epidemic killed estimated 20 million throughout world, 548,000 in U.S.

1919

Rosa Luxemburg and Karl Liebknecht, leading German socialists and founders of the Spartacan party, shot and killed **Jan.** by soldiers who were taking them to prison.

Peace conference opened in Paris **Jan. 18**; treaty, including Pres. Wilson's proposed League of Nations, signed in palace at Versailles **June 28** between German representatives, Allied powers and U.S. Pres. Wilson submitted treaty to Senate **July 10**. ratified by Germany **July 10**, Britain **July 26**, Italy **Oct. 7**, France **Oct. 13**, Japan **Oct. 27**. Not signed by China. Rejected by U.S. Senate **Nov. 19** which considered American sovereignty not properly safeguarded in League of Nations.

First Transatlantic Flight U.S. Navy seaplane NC-4, commanded by Lt. Com. Albert Cushing Read, left Rockaway, N.Y., **May 8**; stopped at Trepassey, Newfoundland; left **May 16**, reached Azores **May 17**; Lisbon **May 27**; Plymouth, England, **May 31**; covered 4,500 mi. John Alcock and A. W. Brown made **June 14-15**, a non-stop air flight from Newfoundland to Ireland. A British dirigible, R-34, left Scotland **July 2** and descended in Mineola, N. Y., **July 6**. It left for England **July 10** and arrived there **July 13**. A round-trip transcontinental air race, New York to San Francisco, was won by **Lt. W.B. Maynard** and **Lt. Alex Pearson Oct. 8-18**

1920

League of Nations held first meeting at Geneva, Switzerland, **Jan. 10**; was dissolved **Jan. 10, 1946**.

The 19th (Woman Suffrage) Amendment, having been adopted by Congress, 1918-1919, and ratified by Tennessee (36th state to do so) Aug. 18, 1920, was proclaimed adopted **Aug. 26** by the sec. of state. It had been first introduced in Congress in 1878; by 1918, women had won the vote under laws of 15 states, mostly in the West and Midwest, but including New York. The amendment gave women full, nationwide voting rights.

Nicola Sacco, 29, shoe factory employee and radical agitator, and **Bartolomeo Vanzetti**, 32, fish peddler and anarchist, accused of killing 2 men in payroll holdup at South Braintree, Mass., **Apr. 15**. Found guilty **1921** they became objects of 6-year campaign for release on grounds of want of conclusive evidence and prejudice of court. Appeals failing, they were executed at Charlestown, Mass., prison **Aug. 22, 1927**. Trial sharply criticized by Wickersham Commission on law procedure.

Wall St., N.Y. City, bomb explosion killed 30, injured 100; did $2 million damage **Sept. 16**.

1921

Joint Congressional resolution declaring peace with Germany, Austria, and Hungary signed **July 2** by Pres. Harding. Treaties with the 3 were signed in **Aug.**

Limitation of Armaments Conference met in Washington **Nov. 12, 1921—Feb. 6, 1922**. U.S., Britain, France, Italy, Japan agreed to curtail naval construction. Nine powers outlawed poison gas and restricted submarine attack on merchantmen. U.S., Britain, France, Japan agreed on integrity of China. Ratified **Aug. 5, 1925**.

1922

Roof of Knickerbocker (movie) Theatre collapsed in Washington, D. C., **Jan. 28**; 98 dead.

Violence during coal-mine strike at Herrin, Ill., **June 22-23** cost 36 lives, 21 of them non-union miners.

Fascist march on Rome Oct 30; Mussolini's power in Italy began.

1923

Occupation of Ruhr by French and Belgian troops to enforce reparations began **Jan. 11**.

First sound-on-film moving picture "Phonofilm" was shown by Lee de Forest at Rivoli Theatre, N.Y. City, beginning **Apr.**

Beer Hall Putsch in Munich led by Gen. Ludendorff and Adolf Hitler **Nov. 8-9**. Several supporters killed in street clashes. Ludendorff was arrested and paroled; Hitler was wounded. He was arrested **Nov. 12** and imprisoned at Landsberg where he wrote Mein Kampf (served 9 months of 5-year sentence).

1924

Dawes Reparation Plan accepted by Allies and Germany in London **Aug. 16**: Owen D. Young put in charge. French troops began evacuation of the Ruhr **Aug. 18**.

Nellie Tayloe Ross elected governor of Wyoming **Nov. 9** after death of her husband **Oct. 2**; installed **Jan. 5, 1925**, first woman governor. Miriam (Ma) Ferguson was elected governor of Texas **Nov. 9**; installed **Jan. 20, 1925**.

1925

John T. Scopes was found guilty of having taught evolution in Dayton, Tenn., high school and was fined $100 and costs **July 24**. William Jennings Bryan, chief counsel for prosecution, died in Dayton **July 26**. Clarence Darrow, chief defense counsel, died **Mar. 13, 1938**. Scopes died **Oct. 21, 1970**. The last state law prohibiting teaching evolution in public schools was ruled unconstitutional by the Mississippi Supreme Court **Dec. 2, 1970**.

By Treaty of Locarno Oct. 16 Germany agreed to demilitarization of Rhineland and security of Franco-German and Belgo-German frontiers.

1926

Dr. Robert H. Goddard demonstrated practicality of rockets **Mar. 16** at Auburn, Mass., with first liquid, fuel rocket flight; rocket traveled 184 ft. in 2.5 secs.

General strike paralyzed Britain **May 3-12**. Parliament passed act making general strike criminal conspiracy against nation.

Germany admitted to the League of Nations Sept. 8. Locarno treaties with Germany (1925) went into effect **Sept. 14**.

1927

About 1,000 U.S. Marines landed in China **Mar. 5** to protect property in civil war. U.S. and British consulates looted by nationalists **Mar. 24**.

Capt. Charles A. Lindbergh, U.S. air mail pilot, left Roosevelt Field, N. Y., at 7:52 a.m., **May 20** alone in monoplane, Spirit of St. Louis, competing for Raymond Orteig's offer of $25,000 for first New York-Paris non-stop flight. Reached Le Bourget airfield, Paris. 5:21 p.m. (10:21 p.m. Paris time) **May 21**, 3,610 mi. in 33 hrs. 29 min., 30 sec. Returned on U.S. cruiser Memphis with plane; welcomed by Pres. Coolidge in Washington **June 11**, given rank of colonel. Tremendous ticker tape parade, N. Y. City **June 13**.

The Jazz Singer, with Al Jolson, demonstrated part-talking pictures in N.Y. City **Oct. 6**.

1928

First all-talking picture, Lights of New York, presented at Strand, N.Y. City, **July 6**.

Kellogg-Briand Peace Pact signed **Aug. 27** by 62 nations; condemned the use of war as an instrument of national policy.

Dirigible Graf Zeppelin, Capt. Hugo Eckener, with 20 passengers and 38 crew, flew from Friedrichshafen, Germany to Lakehurst, N.J., **Oct. 11-15**; returned **Oct. 29-31**. Made round-the-world trip from Friedrichshafen with 20 passengers **Aug. 14-Sept. 4, 1929**, via Tokyo, Los Angeles, Lakehurst.

Stalin issued **first 5-year plan**: rapid, ruthless industrialization of Russian economy.

1929

"St. Valentine's Day massacre" in Chicago **Feb. 14**; gangsters killed 7 rivals.

The Papal State, extinct since **1870**, revived as State of Vatican City, at Rome **June 7**.

Albert B. Fall, former sec. of the interior, was convicted of accepting a bribe of $100,000 from Edward L. Doheny in the leasing of the Elk Hills **(Teapot Dome)** naval oil reserve. He was sentenced **Nov. 1** to $100,000 fine and a year in prison.

Stock Market crash Oct. 29 marked end of postwar prosperity as stock prices plummeted. Decline in value estimated at $15 billion by end of 1929; stock losses for 1929-1931 estimated at $50 billion; worst American depression began.

1930

London Naval Reduction Treaty signed by U.S., Britain, Italy, France and Japan **Apr. 22**; in effect **Jan. 1, 1931.** Set proportional reductions of the navies of each country. Its terms expired **Dec. 31, 1936.**

Joseph F. Crater, a justice of the state Supreme Court in N.Y. City, vanished **Aug. 6.**

1931

British Parliament gave legal status to declaration of Imperial Conference of 1926 proclaiming Britain and the dominions, including Canada, completely equal and "in no way subordinate one to another."

Mukden Incident occurred **Sept. 18** when Japanese troops attacked Mukden garrison and then overran Manchuria. China protested to League of Nations.

1932

Japan sends troops into China Jan. 27 following murder of Japanese Buddhist priest in Shanghai.

Manchuria became Manchukuo (Japanese puppet state) **Feb. 18;** Henry Pu Yi, Manchu emperor who abdicated in 1912, installed as ruler **Mar. 9.**

Charles Lindbergh Jr. kidnaped **Mar. 1,** found dead, **May 12.**

Bonus March on Washington **May 29** by World War I veterans demanding Congress pay their bonus in full. Army, under Gen. Douglas MacArthur, disbanded the marchers on Pres. Hoover's orders.

1933

Adolf Hitler became German chancellor **Jan. 30.**

German Reichstag building in Berlin was destroyed **Feb. 27** by fire believed set by Nazis, although Marinus van der Lubbe, Dutch communist, was found guilty; beheaded **Jan. 10, 1934.**

All banks in the U.S. were ordered closed by Pres. Roosevelt **Mar. 6.**

Gold standard dropped by U.S.; announced by Pres. Roosevelt on **Apr. 19** and ratified by Congress **June 5.**

Spain, by parliamentary edict, May 17 disestablished the Roman Catholic church.

Germany quit the League of Nations **Oct. 14.**

Pres. Roosevelt accorded diplomatic recognition to the Soviet Union **Nov. 16.**

Prohibition ended in the U.S. as Utah, 36th state, ratified 21st Amendment to Constitution **Dec. 5,** repealing 18th (Prohibition) Amendment.

1934

The Dionne sisters, first quintuplets to survive beyond infancy, were born **May 28** in Callender, Ont., Canada; to Mr. and Mrs. Oliva Dionne.

Pres. von Hindenburg of Germany died **Aug. 2. Adolf Hitler** consolidated offices of president and chancellor, became "fuehrer."

Long March by Chinese Communists started **Oct.** Mao Tse-tung led 100,000 in 6,000-mi. trek from south to north China; only 20,000 completed journey and reached Yenan **Oct. 1935.**

1935

Hitler renounced Versailles Treaty, ordered conscription in Germany **Mar. 10.**

Will Rogers, 56, comedian, and Wiley Post, 36, aviator, were killed **Aug. 15** when Post's plane crashed in a fog near Point Barrow, Alaska.

Social Security Act passed by Congress **Aug. 14.**

Ethiopia appealed to League of Nations against Italy. Italy invaded Ethiopia **Oct. 2-4.**

Economic sanctions against Italy went into effect **Nov. 18** supported by 52 nation-members of the League of Nations, and by one non-member, Egypt. The sanctions ended **July 15, 1936.**

1936

British King George V, 70, died **Jan. 20** and was succeeded by his eldest son, Prince of Wales, 42, who took the title of King Edward VIII. He abdicated **Dec. 11, 1936,** and was succeeded by his brother, the Duke of York, who became King George VI. The ex-ruler was created Duke of Windsor with the title of "His Royal Highness." He gave up the throne, he said, because he could not marry "the woman I love," Mrs. Wallis Warfield of Baltimore, Md., who obtained a divorce **Oct. 27** in Ipswich, England, from Ernest A. Simpson, an insurance agent. Edward and "Wally" were married **June 3, 1937** in Monts, France.

Reoccupation of demilitarized Rhineland zone, in violation of the Locarno pact, begun by German troops **May. 7.**

Emperor Haile Selassie of Ethiopia escaped Italian advance by boarding British cruiser **May 1.** Premier Mussolini of Italy announced end of war **May 5,** proclaimed annexation of Ethiopia with King Victor Emmanuel emperor. Haile Selassie restored 1941; deposed Sept. 12, 1974.

Revolt against Spain's republican government began **July 17** in Morocco and spread to Spain, included much of the army and air force and half of the navy; Gen. Francisco Franco proclaimed head of the nationalist (insurgent) government **Oct. 1;** seige of Madrid begun by insurgents **Oct. 21;** Loyalist government moved to Valencia, **Nov. 6.**

Japan and Germany signed an anti-Comintern pact **Nov. 25.** Italy joined **Nov. 6, 1937.**

1937

Spanish insurgents took Malaga **Feb. 8.** Warships of Great Britain, France, Italy and Germany **March 13** began to police the coasts of Spain under a 27-nation neutrality agreement, effectively blockading the Loyalists, but not the insurgents (Nationalists), from receiving supplies. An est. 70,000 Italian troops and several thousand Germans were aiding Nationalists. Loyalists shifted government to Barcelona **Oct. 28.**

Fighting in China, west of Peking, was renewed by Japanese; **July 29** they bombed Tientsin destroying Nankai Univ.; **Aug. 9** they took formal possession of Peking; **Aug. 11** they landed marines at Shanghai and shelled Nankow; other eastern cities were hit by Japanese planes **Oct. 23.** Chinese forces abandoned Shanghai and Japanese took control **Nov. 8.** Premier Chiang Kai-shek moved to Hankow **Dec. 12.**

Japanese bombs sank the U. S. gunboat Panay **Dec. 12** with loss of 2 lives; and several American oil carriers (the captain of one died) on the Yangtze River above Nanking. The Japanese apologized and paid indemnity.

Hitler repudiated war guilt clause of Versailles Treaty **Jan. 30.** (Treaty blamed Germany for World War I.) Hitler stated that Germany was free from obligations imposed upon her by the treaty.

Amelia Earhart Putnam, aviator, and co-pilot Fred Noonan lost **July 2** near Howland Is. in the Pacific.

Italy gave notice Dec. 11 of withdrawal from the League of Nations.

1938

Insurgent air raids killed 1,000 in Barcelona **Mar. 7;** Insurgents took Lerida, cutting Loyalist Spain in half **Apr. 15.**

Hitler invaded Austria Mar. 11. After resignation of Chancellor Kurt von Schuschnigg and Pres. Wilhelm Miklas **Mar. 13** the new chancellor, Arthur Seyss-Inquart, proclaimed the union of Germany and Austria. This was ratified by a popular vote, excluding Jews, in Austria **Apr. 10.**

Douglas G. Corrigan of Los Angeles flew from Brooklyn to Dublin **July 17-18.** Having no permit or passport, he jokingly said he flew the "wrong way."

At a conference in Munich, Britain and France yielded **Sept. 30** to Nazi demands for the cession of the Sudetenland to Germany by Czechoslovakia, thus ending a 15-day international crisis during which British Prime Minister Neville Chamberlain made 2 flying visits to Hitler. Mussolini backed Hitler's territorial demands. Hitler signed a "peace declaration" with Britain **Sept. 30,** occupied Sudetenland **Oct. 1-10.** Eduard Benes, president of Czechoslovakia, resigned **Oct. 5.**

1939

Uranium atom was first measured in U. S. at Columbia Univ. **Jan. 25. In 1940, uranium 235, a rare isotope, proved to be prime fissionable form.

The **Loyalist Spanish government** surrendered Barcelona to the insurgents **Jan. 26.** Madrid surrendered **Mar. 24;** war ended **Mar. 29** with Franco victor.

The **Republic of Czechoslovakia** was dissolved **Mar. 14;** Hungarian troops seized Carpatho-Ukraine **Mar. 14;** Nazis occupied Bohemia and Moravia which became German protectorates **Mar. 16.**

Japanese troops in Manchukuo and Soviet and Mongol troops near Lake Bor began 6-month border fight **May 11; 20,000** killed.

Germany and Italy signed military pact **May 22.**

Germany and Soviet Union signed a non-aggression treaty **Aug. 24;** Germany invaded Poland **Sept. 1;** USSR invaded Poland **Sept. 17;** Britain and France declared war on Germany **Sept. 3.**

N. Y. World's Fair opened **Apr. 30,** closed **Oct. 31;** reopened **May 11, 1940** and finally closed **Oct. 21.**

Pres. Roosevelt proclaimed a limited national emergency **Sept. 8,** an unlimited emergency **May 27, 1941.** Both ended by Pres. Truman **Apr. 28, 1952.**

Russia invaded Finland Nov. 30.

Principal Events of World War II, 1939-1945

Major Belligerents — German army invaded Poland **Sept. 1, 1939;** Norway and Denmark **April 9, 1940;** the Netherlands, Belgium, and Luxemburg **May 10, 1940;** invaded France, reaching Paris **June 14.** Occupied France (Vichy) signed an armistice with Germany **June 22, 1940.** Germany invaded Russia **June 22, 1941,** unoccupied France and Italy **Nov. 11, 1942.** Surrendered unconditionally **May 7, 1945 (May 6 EST).** War with Germany formally declared ended by Britain, France, Australia, New Zealand on **July 9, 1951;** by U.S. **Oct. 19, 1951.**

Great Britain declared war on Germany **Sept. 3, 1939,** as did Australia and New Zealand. Union of South Africa declared war **Sept. 6; Canada Sept. 10.** Britain declared war on Italy **June 11, 1940;** on Finland, Hungary, and Romania, **Dec. 7, 1941;** on Japan **Dec. 8, 1941;** on Bulgaria **Dec. 13, 1941;** on Thailand **Jan. 25, 1942.**

France declared war on Germany **Sept. 3, 1939;** on Italy **June 11, 1940.** Free French (de Gaulle) declared war on Japan **Dec. 8, 1941.**

Italy (under Benito Mussolini) declared war on Great Britain and France **June 10, 1940;** on the U.S. **Dec. 11, 1941.** Surrendered unconditionally **Sept. 8, 1943.** Declared war against Germany **Oct. 13, 1943,** against Japan **July 14, 1945.** Signed treaty of peace **Feb. 10, 1947,** in Paris, with Britain, France, U.S. and USSR.

Japan invaded French Indochina **Sept. 22, 1940;** attacked Pearl Harbor naval station and the Philippines by air **Dec. 7, 1941** and declared war on the U.S., Great Britain, Australia, Canada, New Zealand and the Union of South Africa **Dec. 7, 1941;** on the Netherlands **Jan. 11, 1942.** Japan accepted the Allied terms unconditionally **Aug. 14, 1945;** signed surrender terms **Sept. 1, 1945 (Sept. 2,** Tokyo time) on board USS Missouri; signed treaty of peace with all big powers (except USSR) and a total of 49 nations at San Francisco **Sept. 8, 1951.**

Union of Soviet Socialist Republics (Russia) signed non-aggression pact with Germany **Aug., 1939;** invaded Poland, **Sept. 17, 1939,** and Finland, **Nov. 30, 1939.** Signed peace with Finland **Mar. 12, 1940.** Russia was invaded by Germany and Romania **June 22, 1941.** Finland declared war on Russia **June 25, 1941.** Armistice with Finland **Sept. 19, 1944,** peace treaty **Feb. 10, 1947.** Declared war on Japan **Aug. 8, 1945,** effective **Aug. 9.** Signed treaties of peace with Italy, Hungary, Romania, Bulgaria and Finland **Feb. 10, 1947.**

U.S. declared war on Japan Dec. 8, 1941. Germany and Italy declared war on U.S. **Dec. 11, 1941.** A few hours later U.S. declared war on Germany and Italy; also Bulgaria, Hungary and Romania **June 5, 1942;** signed peace treaties with Italy, Bulgaria, Hungary and Romania **Feb. 10, 1947;** with Japan **Sept. 8, 1951.**

German Blitzkrieg forces outflanked the Maginot Line **May 13, 1940,** and quickly occupied northern France.

Retreat from Dunkirk by British Expeditionary Force took place **May 26-June 4, 1940,** when 900 vessels took 338,226 troops across the English Channel, 26,175 of them French.

Nazi bombing of Britain began **July 10, 1940,** and reached its height **Sept. 7, Oct. 15,** and **Dec. 29.**

Coventry was destroyed **Nov. 14;** Birmingham was hit **Nov. 19-22.** Many London churches were burned **Dec. 29.** Desperate attacks on German aircraft by RAF stopped threat of invasion. Of this defense Prime Minister Churchill said: "Never in the field of human conflict was so much owed by so many to so few."

Pearl Harbor. Some 360 Japanese planes attacked Hickam and Wheeler Fields and U. S. Pacific fleet (86 ships) anchored at Pearl Harbor, Hawaii on **Dec. 7, 1941.** (7:55 a.m. Hawaiian time; 1:25 p.m. EST.) Totally destroyed: battleship Arizona. Severely damaged: battleships Oklahoma, Nevada, California, West Virginia, 3 destroyers, 1 target ship, 1 minelayer. Damaged and repaired: battleships Pennsylvania, Maryland, Tennessee; cruisers Helena, Honolulu, Raleigh. Casualties: navy and marines, 2,086 officers and men killed, 749 wounded; army, 194 officers and men killed, 360 wounded.

Planes over Tokyo. Lt. Col. James H. Doolittle, with 16 B-25s and 79 pilots and crewmen, took off **Apr. 18, 1942,** from carrier Hornet, 688 mi. from Tokyo; 13 dropped 500-lb. bombs on Tokyo, 2 on Nagoya, Kobe. Eight airmen were captured off China coast; 3 were shot, others imprisoned. Total dead, 9. One plane landed near Vladivostok and was interned by Russians; the crew escaped to Iran.

Loss and recapture of Philippines. Manila and Cavite taken by Japan **Jan. 2, 1942.** U.S. forces in Bataan were attacked by 200,000 Japanese **Jan. 10.** Gen. Douglas MacArthur ordered to leave Philippines, reached Australia **Mar. 17,** vowed, "I shall return." Maj. Gen. Jonathan M. Wainwright defended Bataan until **Apr. 8, 1942.** Japan took 35,000 U.S. and Filipino troops prisoner, including 5,000 Marines, forced them into prison via the "Death March" of Bataan. Wainwright surrendered **Corregidor May 6** with 11,-574 troops. Gen. MacArthur returned to the Philippines near Palo on Leyte, **Oct. 20, 1944.** U.S. returned to Luzon **Jan. 9, 1945.** Manila was taken **Feb. 3:** Corregidor reoccupied **Feb. 16-Mar. 1.**

Germany attacked the Soviet Union **June 22, 1941;** took Minsk, Smolensk, Kiev, Kharkov, Orel; besieged Leningrad, fought a long battle in the ruins of Stalingrad **Aug. 1942** and extended the German lines to the Caucasus Mts.; tide turned in **Nov. 1942;** the Russians encircled Stalingrad and the Nazi army there surrendered **Jan. 31, 1943.** Russian army reached the Oder River **Feb. 1945.**

North African Campaign began **Aug. 6, 1941,** when Marshal Graziani led Italian forces against the British with some success. The first counteroffensive in **Dec.** relieved Tobruk, where British had held out 8 months. The British pushed the Germans under Rommel back to El Agheila but Rommel regained the lost ground. He captured Tobruk with its garrison of 25,-000 British **June 21, 1942,** and pushed the British back to within 70 mi. of Alexandria. On **Oct. 23,** the British, heavily reinforced and under Lt. Gen. Bernard L. Montgomery, attacked Rommel at El Alamein, Egypt, and inflicted heavy losses on the Germans and Italians, driving them back over 1,000 mi. to Tunisia.

1940

Finnish-Russian peace signed in Moscow **Mar. 12.**

Estonia, Latvia, and Lithuania annexed by Soviet Russia **July 14.**

1941

The Four Freedoms termed essential by Pres. Roosevelt in a speech to Congress **Jan. 6:** freedom of speech and expression, freedom of worship, freedom from want, and freedom from fear.

U.S. Marines occupied Iceland **July 7** on invitation from that country.

The Atlantic Charter, an 8-point joint U.S.-British declaration of principles, issued by Pres. Roosevelt and Prime Minister Churchill **Aug. 14** after conference aboard battleship off Newfoundland.

Pres. Roosevelt and Secretary of State Hull Nov. 17 received special Japanese envoys, Saburo Kurusu and Admiral Nomura, for conference on the Far East.

Japan attacked U.S. fleet at Pearl Harbor **Dec. 7** as first act of war. (*See World War II.*)

Hitler ordered policy of genocide as the "final solu-

Summary of Aerial Naval and Military Actions

North African Invasion by U.S. and Britain landed 150,000 American and 140,000 British troops in French Algeria **Nov. 8, 1942** (Nov. 7 EST), with Lt. Gen. Dwight D. Eisenhower in command; Axis forces were driven from Africa by **May 12, 1943.** U.S. 7th Army under Maj. Gen. George S. Patton Jr. and British-Canadian 8th Army landed on Sicily **July 10.** Mussolini was forced to resign **July 25** and escaped to German lines **Sept. 12.** The Italian mainland was invaded and Italy surrendered **Sept. 8, 1943,** but heavy fighting with Germans followed and they were not dislodged until spring of **1945.**

Battle of the Coral Sea on **May 7-8, 1942,** took heavy toll of ships and planes on both sides, was first battle fought by naval planes from ships that had neither sight nor range of enemy. U.S. lost carrier (Lexington), 66 planes, 543 men; Japan lost 80 planes, 900 men. **Battle of Midway June 3-6, 1942,** U. S. lost 1 carrier (Yorktown), 1 destroyer, 150 planes, 307 men; Japan lost 4 carriers, 253 planes, 3,500 men. The Japanese navy halted its advance toward Australia and withdrew northward.

Guadalcanal, in the southern Solomon Islands, assaulted by U. S. Marines **Aug. 7, 1942,** in one of the most costly Allied Pacific campaigns, finally won by the Allies in **Jan. 1943.**

U.S. Return to Philippines: battle for Leyte Gulf, biggest naval action ever fought, **Oct. 22-27, 1944,** in 3 engagements destroying Japanese naval power. Battles were fought in Surigao Strait, off Samar and off Cape Engano. Ships engaged: U.S. 166, Japanese 65. Airplanes, U.S. 1,280; Japanese 716. Losses for Philippine campaign — Japan: 3 large carriers, 3 light carriers, one escort carrier, 4 battleships, 14 cruisers, 32 destroyers, 11 submarines, total 68. U. S.: one light carrier, 3 escort carriers, 6 destroyers, 3 destroyer escorts, one high-speed transport, 7 submarines, total 21. U.S. lost one ship to a kamikaze (suicide) plane at Leyte and 5 in subsequent actions. Total plane losses for Philippine campaign from **Oct., 1944-Jan. 1945:** Japan (est.) 7,000, including 722 kamikaze; U. S. 967.

D-Day: Invasion of France — Invasion of France by Allies **June 6, 1944.** About 1,000 planes and gliders dropped paratroopers on Cotentin Peninsula near Normandy, 5 a.m. London time. About 1,000 RAF, 1,400 U.S. bombers attacked installations. First assault troops landed 6:30 a.m. on beaches along line Carentan-Bayeux-Caen; U.S. on west, British-Canadians on east. Total Allied strength available 2,876,439, including 17 British divisions of which 3 Canadian; 20 U. S. divisions, one French, one Polish. Gen. Dwight D. Eisenhower was Supreme Commander of Allied Expeditionary Forces.

British took Bayeux June 7; Carentan fell **June 13,** U.S. took Cherbourg **June 27;** British-Canadians took Caen **July 9** after desperate fighting Lt. Gen. George S. Patton Jr. with 3d U.S. Army attacked south and west of St. Lo **Aug. 1.** Canadians took Falaise **Aug 16.** German army routed **Aug. 23** in the Argentan-Falaise gap by U.S.-Canadian armies and Allied aircraft.

Allies were then free to overrun northern France and liberate Paris **Aug. 25.**

Allies invaded Southern France **Aug. 14-15, 1944,** east of the Rhone River, with 1,000 ships(641 U.S., 316 British).

The Ardennes Bulge was a violent counterattack by 15 German divisions (Gen. von Rundstedt commander-in-chief) launched **Dec. 16, 1944.** By **Dec. 19,** the 1st U. S. Army was pushed out of Germany and the Germans penetrated 60 mi. west of Celles, Belgium. Patton's 3d U.S. Army rescued besieged Americans at Bastogne, Belgium, **Dec. 26** and Nazi drive was stopped by **Dec. 28.** Near Malmedy, Belgium, Germans shot captured American soldiers with machine guns and left them dead on the field. U. S. casualties estimated at 80,000; Germans lost 220,000 dead and prisoners.

Rhine Crossing — On **Mar. 7, 1945,** the 9th Armored Div., 3d Corps, First Army, found Ludendorff Bridge at Remagen on the Rhine intact; Gen. Eisenhower ordered Gen. Omar N. Bradley to put 5 divisions across.

Iwo Jima assaulted by U. S. joint expeditionary force **Feb. 19, 1945,** with land action by U. S. Marines; invasion used 495 ships, including 17 aircraft carriers and 1,170 planes. U. S. troops engaged, 111,308 of which 75,144 were assault troops. Island was conquered by **Mar. 16.** U. S. lost 4,590 killed; Japanese deaths est. over 20,000.

Okinawa, principal Japanese base in the Ryukyu group, was invaded **Apr. 1, 1945,** in the final land campaign in the Far East. U.S. used 1,300 vessels, including airplane carriers. After 83 days of fighting the end was marked by the formal suicide of the 2 Japanese generals. U. S. men engaged up to **June 30, 1945,** reached 176,491 army, 88,500 marines, 18,000 navy. Japanese strength at start was 77,199. U. S. losses were 49,151 of which 12,520 were killed or missing, 36,631 wounded. The Japanese lost 110,071 killed, wounded and 7,400 prisoners.

U. S. lost 763 aircraft; Japan lost 7,830 of which 1,020 were destroyed on the ground. U. S. lost 36 ships sunk, 369 damaged; Japan lost 16 sunk. The Yamato, world's largest battleship, full load displacement 72,809 tons, 861 ft. long, 3,333 personnel, was sunk by 10 aerial torpedoes; 300 survived.

V-E Day — German armies began surrendering **May 4, 1945.** Unconditional surrender signed **May 7** at 2:41 a.m., French time, in Rheims Hq., designating cessation of operations **May 9** at 12:01 a.m., London time (**May 8,** 6:01 p.m., Eastern U.S. War Time). Surrender also signed in Berlin. **May 8** celebrated as V-E Day.

Atomic bombs — First atomic bomb ever used in war was dropped by U.S. plane **Aug. 6, 1945,** on Hiroshima, Japan (pop. 343,969). Second U.S. bomb dropped on Nagasaki (pop. 252,630) **Aug. 9, 1945.** Estimates of dead from bombs and radiation exposure vary: Hiroshima, 80,000 to over 200,000; Nagasaki, 39,000 to 74,000. Japan surrendered **Aug. 14.** Formal surrender aboard USS Missouri **Sept. 2, 1945,** Far Eastern Time, celebrated as V-J Day.

Consult Index for additional listings under World War II.

tion" to the Jewish "problem." By end of war an estimated 6 million Jews had been killed in Nazi concentration camps. Other religious, ethnic, and political groups were also persecuted and some 4 to 6 million members were murdered by Nazis.

1942

Fire swept through Cocoanut Grove, a Boston night club, Nov. 28, killing 491 and injuring scores.

First nuclear chain reaction (fission of uranium isotope, U-235) at Univ. of Chicago, under physicists Arthur Compton, Enrico Fermi, et al., **Dec. 2.**

1943

Pres. Roosevelt signed **June 10** the pay-as-you-go income tax bill. Starting **July 1** wage and salary earners were subject to a paycheck withholding tax.

Race riot in Detroit June 21; 34 dead, 700 injured. Riot in Harlem section of N.Y. City; 6 Negroes killed.

1945

Yalta Conference met in the Crimea, USSR, **Feb. 3-11.** Roosevelt, Churchill and Stalin agreed Russia would enter war against Japan.

Pres. Roosevelt, 63, died of cerebral hemorrhage in Warm Springs, Ga. **Apr. 12.**

Mussolini caught by partisans near Dongo while trying to flee to Switzerland; executed **Apr. 28.**

Hitler committed suicide in ruined chancellery, Berlin, **Apr. 30,** with wife Eva Braun. Goebbels and wife poisoned children, committed suicide.

United Nations Conference on International Organization of 46 nations, San Francisco, opened **Apr. 25;** closed **June 26** with address by Pres. Truman and adoption of UN charter.

Potsdam, Germany, conference of Truman, Stalin, and Churchill **July 17-Aug. 2.** After July 25 Clement Atlee, new prime minister, replaced Churchill.

First atomic bomb, produced at Los Alamos, N. M., exploded at Alamogordo, N. M., **July 16.** Bomb dropped on Hiroshima **Aug. 6,** on Nagasaki **Aug. 9.**

U.S. forces entered Korea south of 38th parallel to displace Japanese **Sept. 8.**

Gen. Douglas MacArthur took over supervision of Japan **Sept. 9.**

Vidkun Quisling, pro-Nazi premier of Norway, executed by a firing squad in Oslo **Oct. 23.**

1946

William Joyce, "Lord Haw Haw," broadcaster for Nazis, hanged in London for treason **Jan. 3.**

The first General Assembly of the United Nations opened in London **Jan. 10.**

League of Nations in Geneva, Switzerland, transfered physical assets to the United Nations **Apr. 18.**

Philippines given independence by U.S. **July 4;** Manuel Roxas elected first president of new republic.

Twenty-two Nazi leaders convicted of war crimes **Sept. 30** by International Tribunal in Nuremberg. Eleven Nazis were sentenced to death by hanging **Oct. 1.** Hermann Goering committed suicide by poison in Nuremberg Prison, 2 hours before he was scheduled to be hanged **Oct. 15.** The 10 other top Nazis were hanged individually. They were: Hans Frank, Wilhelm Frick, Col. Gen. Alfred Jodl, Gestapo Chief Ernst Kaltenbrunner, Field Marshal Wilhelm Keitel, Alfred Rosenberg, Fritz Sauckel, Arthur Seyss-Inquart, Julius Streicher, Foreign Minister Joachim von Ribbentrop.

Others executed for war crimes: Gen. Anton Dostler, Nazi, hanged in Rome Dec. 1, 1945, for shooting 15 U.S. soldiers without trial; Joseph Kramer, "Beast of Belsen" and 10 others hanged Dec. 14, by British for atrocities at Belsen and Auschwitz concentration camps; Gen. Yamashita, Japanese commander in Philippines, hanged Feb. 23, 1946; Lt. Gen. Homma, who ordered Bataan death march, shot near Manila Apr. 3, 1946; Marshal Ion Antonescu, dictator of Romania, hanged June 1, 1946; Karl Hermann Frank, Nazi ruler in Czechoslovakia, hanged in Prague May 22 for ordering massacre at Lidice; 48 Nazi officers and guards hanged by the U.S. Army at Landsberg,

Germany, May, 1947, for mass murders at Mauthausen camp.

Pres. Truman proclaimed the cessation of hostilities of World War II **Dec. 31.**

1947

British Labor government took ownership of coal mines, cables and wireless communications **Jan. 1.**

Peace treaties for Hitler's European satellites, imposing $1.33 billion in reparations, signed **Feb. 10.**

Truman doctrine. Pres. Truman asked Congress to appropriate $400 million for aid to Greece and Turkey to combat Communist terrorism **Mar. 12.** Approved **May 15.**

The United Nations Security Council voted unanimously **Apr. 2** to place under U. S. trusteeship the Pacific islands formerly mandated to Japan.

Taft-Hartley Labor Act approved by U.S. Senate **May 13.** The House concurred **June 4.** The measure was vetoed by Pres. Truman **June 20,** but Congress overrode the veto.

Proposals known later as the Marshall Plan, under which the U.S. would extend financial aid to all European countries "willing to assist in the task of recovery," were made by Sec. of State George C. Marshall **June 5.** Congress authorized the spending in the next 3 1/2 years of some $12 billion on Marshall Plan aid, which was credited with restoring economic health to free Europe and halting the march of communism in those countries cooperating.

Hindu India and Moslem Pakistan, formerly parts of British India, gained independence Aug. 15.

1948

British Labor Government nationalized railways Jan. 1.

Mohandas K. Gandhi, Hindu spiritual leader and champion of freedom for India, was shot and killed by a Hindu fanatic in New Delhi **Jan. 30.**

Czechoslovakia joined the communist block in Eastern Europe after Pres. Benes yielded **Feb. 25** to an ultimatum to install a pro-Soviet cabinet. He resigned **June 7;** succeeded by Klement Gottwald, communist. Benes died **Sept. 3.** Communists reported Jan Masaryk, foreign minister, committed suicide **Mar. 10.**

A land blockade of Berlin's Allied sectors was started **Apr. 1** by the Soviet military, which refused to permit U.S. and British supply trains to pass through the Soviet zone of Germany. This blockade and a Western counter-blockade were lifted **Sept. 30, 1949,** after British and U.S. planes had airlifted 2,343,315 tons of food and coal into West Berlin.

Charter of the Organization of American States signed **Apr. 30** at 9th International Conference of American States at Bogota, Colombia.

The Free State of Israel was proclaimed in Tel Aviv **May 14** as the British evacuated Palestine. First de facto recognition came from the U.S. **May 14.** Soviet Russia granted recognition **May 17.** Chaim Weizmann elected president by the Constituent Assembly **Feb. 14, 1949.**

The Cominform (Communist Information Bureau) at a Prague meeting **June 28,** denounced Marshal Tito and other leaders of the Yugoslav Communist party as deserters from the Marxist-Leninist doctrine.

Alger Hiss, former State Department official, was indicted **Dec. 15** on 2 perjury charges after he had denied passing secret documents to Whittaker Chambers, a former magazine editor, for transmission to a communist spy ring. A jury failed to reach an agreement **July 8, 1949.** His second trial Nov. 17, 1949-Jan. 21, 1950 ended with conviction on 2 counts and a sentence of 5 years in federal prison. Appeals to higher courts were rejected and Hiss began his sentence **Mar. 22, 1951.** He was released **Nov. 27, 1954,** his term shortened for good conduct.

Former Premier Hideki Tojo and 6 other Japanese war leaders were hanged **Dec. 23** as war criminals.

Joseph Cardinal Mindszenty, Roman Catholic primate of Hungary, arrested by Communist government in Budapest on charges of treason **Dec. 27.**

Convicted, given life imprisonment **Feb. 8, 1949.** All persons taking part in the cardinal's prosecution were excommunicated by Pope Pius XII. Mindszenty freed **Oct. 31, 1956.** After 15 years in U.S. Embassy in Budapest the cardinal left Hungary **Sept. 28, 1971,** for West Europe. He died **May 6, 1975,** in Vienna.

1949
Mildred E. (Axis Sally) Gillars was convicted by a federal jury in N.Y. City **Mar. 10** of treason in broadcasting Nazi propaganda during war. She received 10 to 30 years in prison. Freed **1961.**

North Atlantic Treaty Organization (NATO) established **Mar. 18** by U.S., Canada and 10 Western European nations, agreeing that "an armed attack against one or more of them in Europe and North America shall be considered an attack against all."

Ireland severed last ties with Britain by leaving Commonwealth **Apr. 18.**

End of American A-bomb monopoly revealed by Pres. Truman's announcement **Sept. 23** that an atomic explosion had been set off in the USSR.

Mrs. I. Toguri D'Aquino, (Tokyo Rose) of Japanese wartime broadcasts, was sentenced in San Francisco **Oct. 7** to 10 years in prison for treason. Paroled **1956.**

Eleven leaders of U.S. Communist party convicted **Oct. 14,** after 9-month trial in N.Y. City, of advocating violent overthrow of U.S. Government. Federal Judge Harold R. Medina **Oct. 21** sentenced 10 defendants to 5 years in prison each and the 11th, a war veteran, to 3 years. Supreme Court upheld the convictions **June 4, 1951.** Seven surrendered **July 2, 1951;** of the other 4, hunted as fugitives, one, Gus Hall, was captured **Oct. 8, 1951,** and given 3 additional years. Robert G. Thompson was captured **Aug. 27, 1953.** Five defense lawyers, cited for contempt during the trial, received sentences ranging from one to 6 months **Apr. 24, 1952.**

Nationalist China's government fled to Formosa (Taiwan) **Dec. 7.** Chinese Communists took Yunnan and Kunming as Nationalists deserted.

1950
Great Britain recognized Communist China Jan. 6 one day after breaking diplomatic relations with Chiang Kai-shek's nationalist Chinese regime.

U.S. Jan. 14 recalled all consular officials from Communist China after the latter seized the American consulate general in Peking.

Masked bandits robbed Brink's Inc., Boston express office, **Jan. 17** of $2,775,395.12, of which $1,218,211.29 was in cash. Case solved 1956 by FBI; 8 men sentenced to life.

Pres. Truman authorized AEC to produce the hydrogen bomb (H-bomb), **Jan. 31.**

Dr. Klaus J. E. Fuchs, German-born atomic research physicist at Harwell, England, pleaded guilty **Mar. 1** to violating the Official Secrets Act and received 14 years in prison. He had communicated atomic information to Russian agents since 1942. Released **June 23, 1959,** went to E. Germany.

The Army seized all railroads Aug. 27, on orders of Pres. Truman to prevent a general strike after unions had rejected terms of an 18-cents-an-hour raise for yardmen but none for trainmen. Roads returned to owners **May 23, 1952** after new contract.

In an attempt to kill Pres. Truman, 2 members of a Puerto Rican nationalist movement attacked Blair

Korean War and U.S. Intervention

Republic of Korea was invaded June 25, 1950 (June 24 EST) by over 60,000 North Korean troops spearheaded by over 100 Russian-built tanks. UN Security Council demanded cessation of hostilities and withdrawal to 38th parallel (Russia not present, having staged "walkout" from Council). On **June 27,** Council asked UN members to help carry out its demand. Pres. Truman **June 27,** ordered Gen. of the Army Douglas MacArthur to aid South Korea, and the U.S. 7th Fleet to protect Taiwan against possible aggression and keep the Chinese Nationalist forces from attacking the mainland. Requested by the UN to name a commander, the president designated Gen. MacArthur **July 8, 1950.**

North Korean forces took Seoul, South Korean capital **June 29.** U.S. ground forces entered the conflict **June 30.** Truman termed the intervention a "police action."

The war had 3 phases:

(1) The North Korean drive as checked by U.S. and allied troops, with help of a brilliant landing by U.S. Marines at **Inchon Sept. 15.** Pyongyang, North Korean capital, was taken **Oct. 20.** U.S. 7th Div. reached Manchurian border **Nov. 20.**

(2) Counter-attack by 200,000 Chinese Communist "volunteers," who crossed Yalu River **Nov. 26,** forced evacuation of 105,000 UN troops and 91,000 Korean civilians at Hungnam **Dec. 24.** The Chinese pushed across 38th parallel, drove 70 mi. into South Korea. The UN General Assembly **Feb. 1, 1951,** named Communist China the aggressor in Korea. UN troops pushed Chinese back across parallel **Apr. 3,** stopped offensive by 600,000 Chinese **Apr. 22-30.**

(3) Removal of Gen. MacArthur from command **Apr. 11, 1951,** and start of negotiations for truce along 38th parallel **July 10, 1951.**

Pres. Truman removed Gen. MacArthur from all Far East commands and replaced him with Gen. Matthew B. Ridgway, commander of 8th Army. MacArthur had wished to pursue Chinese across Yalu River to their air depots in Manchuria and on **Mar. 25** had threatened Communist China with air and naval attack. He had been warned to clear all announcements of policy through Washington. The president opposed his views. Senate inquiry **May 3-June 27, 1951,** found that MacArthur was not charged with insubordination, but had disregarded the president's order to clear policy statements through the Defense Department.

Cease-fire and armistice talks began **July 1951** and dragged on with numerous breakdowns until **July 27, 1953** (July 26, EST) when armistice was signed; fighting ended 12 hrs. later. A military armistice commission supervised truce; 10 joint UN-Communist teams policed demilitarized zone; Neutral Nations Supervisory Commission watched military movements in ports; voluntary repatriation of prisoners was provided and Communists won privilege of interviewing prisoners refusing repatriation.

Prisoner repatriation began Aug. 6, 1953, at Panmunjom, ended **Sept. 6, 1953.** UN turned over 75,790 prisoners (70,150 North Koreans and 5,640 Chinese). Communists released 12,760, including 7,850 South Koreans, 3,597 Americans, 945 Britons; 228 Turks.

The Supervisory Commission, made up of members from Czechoslovakia, Poland, Sweden, and Switzerland, was reduced one-half in **Sept. 1955** on repeated complaints that the communist members were spying in South Korea. Repeated reports indicated that the North Koreans had violated many terms of the armistice, built numerous airfields and received naval vessels. The UN Command expelled the commission from South Korea in **June 1956,** on grounds that its Czech and Polish members and the North Korean government had frustrated the operation of the armistice agreement. The UN Command announced in **June 1957,** that it could no longer be bound by armistice provisions controlling importation of military equipment into Korea, but would modernize UN forces "to restore the relative balance of military strength that the armistice was intended to preserve."

House in Washington, **Nov. 1.** *(See Assassinations).*

U. S. Dec. 8 banned shipments to Communist China and to Asiatic ports trading with it.

1951

Ilse Koch was sentenced to life imprisonment by a German court in Frankfurt **Jan. 15** for inciting the murder of a Buchenwald prisoner.

With Sen. Estes Kefauver (D. Tenn.) as chairman, the Senate Committee to Investigate Organized Crime in Interstate Commerce exposed nationwide criminal organizations that reaped huge illegal profits, used these funds to enter legitimate businesses, influenced politicians, and bought protection. Preliminary report **Feb. 28** said gambling take was over $20 billion a year.

Julius Rosenberg, his wife, Ethel, and Morton Sobell, all U.S. citizens, were found guilty **Mar. 29** of conspiracy to commit wartime espionage. Rosenbergs sentenced to death, Sobell to 30 years; appeals denied. David Greenglass, brother of Mrs. Rosenberg and a state witness, received 15 years in prison. Rosenbergs executed at Sing Sing prison, Ossining, N.Y., **June 19, 1953.** Sobell released **Jan. 14, 1969.**

Pres. Truman relieved Gen. Douglas MacArthur of his command in the Far East **Apr. 11.** *(See Korean War).*

European Coal and Steel Plan proposed by French Foreign Minister Robert Schuman **May 9.** France, West Germany, Italy, Belgium, Netherlands, and Luxembourg agreed to conference. Ratified **June 16, 1952.**

UN General Assembly voted arms embargo against Communist China **May 18.**

Tariff concessions by the U.S. to the Soviet Union, Communist China, and all communist-dominated lands were suspended **Aug. 1.**

Transcontinental television inaugurated **Sept. 4** with Pres. Truman's address at the Japanese Peace Treaty Conference in San Francisco.

Japanese Peace Treaty signed in San Francisco **Sept. 8** by U.S. and 48 other nations.

War between Germany and the U.S. formally ended **Oct. 19.** Great Britain and France ended war with Germany **July 9.**

1952

Queen Elizabeth II proclaimed queen of United Kingdom and Canada **Feb. 6,** marking first time monarch was specifically enthroned in name of Canada.

U.S. seizure of nation's steel mills was ordered by Pres. Truman **Apr. 8** to avert a strike by 600,000 CIO United Steelworkers. Seizure was ruled illegal by the Supreme Court **June 2.** Strike followed **June 3,** was settled **July 24.**

First jetliner passenger service opened **May 2,** British DeHavilland Comet, London to Johannesburg.

Peace contract between West Germany, U.S., Great Britain, and France was signed in Bonn **May 26.** Allied high commissions abolished.

Puerto Rico became an "associated free state" or commonwealth of the U.S. **July 25** after Pres. Truman gave approval to a new constitution.

West Germany agreed Sept. 10 to pay Israel and Jews $822 million over 12 to 14 years as indemnity for damages inflicted by Nazis.

Britain successfully completed its first atomic test off northwest Australia **Oct. 3** detonating a bomb aboard a naval vessel.

First hydrogen device explosion Nov. 1 at AEC Eniwetok proving grounds in Pacific reported by witnesses but not officially confirmed for more than a year. Pres. Eisenhower told Congress **Feb. 2, 1954,** that the 1952 test was "the first full-scale thermonuclear explosion in history."

Alan Nunn May, British scientist who gave atom secrets to the USSR, was released from prison **Dec. 29,** after serving 6 yr. 8 mo. of his 10-yr. term.

1953

Joseph Stalin died Mar. 5. By 1955, Nikita Khrushchev emerged as dominant political leader of USSR.

Mau Mau or "Hidden Ones" of Kenya's Kikuyu tribe, formed to force whites from Kenya and to regain ancestral lands from government, climaxed sporadic violence **Mar. 26,** by murdering 71 and wounding 100 fellow Kikuyus who remained loyal to colonial government. Jomo Kenyatta, tribal leader, found guilty **Apr. 8** of organizing Mau Mau, sentenced to 7 years on **Dec. 12, 1963.** Kenya became independent and Jomo Kenyatta became prime minister and president **Dec. 12, 1964.**

Mount Everest was conquered May 29 by Edmund P. Hillary of New Zealand and Tensing Norkay, a Nepalese living in India.

Demonstration by workers in East Berlin against increased work quotas **June 16** erupted into an anti-communist riot by 20,000 to 50,000 persons **June 17.** Soviet troops quelled disturbances, killed 16.

Lavrenti P. Beria, chief of Soviet secret police, was dismissed **July 10** as an enemy of the people. He was executed **Dec. 23** along with 6 of his aides.

First USSR announcement of H-bomb explosion **Aug. 20;** AEC reported explosion occurred **Aug. 12.**

1954

Nautilus, first atomic-powered submarine, was launched at Groton, Conn., **Jan. 21.**

Five members of Congress were wounded in the House **Mar. 1** by 4 Puerto Ricans, one a woman, who fired pistols at random from a spectators' gallery, shouting for Puerto Rican independence. The wounded recovered; the attackers were imprisoned.

Dien Bien Phu, French military outpost in NW Vietnam, fell to the Vietminh army of Ho Chi Minh **May 7.**

Geneva Conference on Far Eastern Affairs was held **Apr. 26-July 21** by 19 nations, including Communist China. Free elections in Korea foundered on communist objections to UN supervision. Armistice, effective **Aug. 11,** ended 7 1/2 years of war in Indochina with French withdrawal; Vietminh received 62,000 sq. mi. and 13 million people in North Vietnam, Cambodia and Laos became independent.

Racial segregation in public schools was unanimously ruled unconstitutional by the Supreme Court **May 17.**

Southeast Asia Treaty Organization (SEATO) formed by collective defense pact signed in Manila **Sept. 8** by the U. S., Britain, France, Australia, New Zealand, Philippines, Pakistan, and Thailand.

Agreement signed in Paris Oct. 23 provided for West German sovereignty, rearmament and entrance into NATO and the Western European Union.

Condemnation of Sen. Joseph R. McCarthy (R. Wis.) voted by Senate, 67-22, **Dec. 2** for contempt of a Senate elections subcommittee, for abuse of its members and for insults to the Senate during investigation **Apr. 22-June 17** of charges brought by the Dept. of the Army against him growing out of his investigation of alleged subversive activities.

1955

Afro-Asian conference of 29 nations met in Bandung, Indonesia, **Apr.** Conference gave expression to the new nationalism of developing nations.

Federal Republic of West Germany became a sovereign state **May 5.** Pres. Eisenhower signed an order ending U. S. occupation but troops remained on a contractual basis.

The Warsaw Pact, a 20-yr. mutual defense treaty, was signed at Warsaw **May 14** by USSR, Albania, Bulgaria, Czechoslovakia, Hungary, Poland, Romania, and East Germany. Albania was barred from meetings **1963;** withdrew from pact **1968.**

A meeting of heads of state "at the summit" proposed by U. S., Great Britain, and France to the USSR, took place **July 18-23** in Geneva, Switzerland, with Pres. Eisenhower representing the U.S.

Juan D. Peron, president and dictator of Argentina, was deposed **Sept. 19** after a revolt begun **June 16** by naval and marine corps units.

Rosa Parks refused **Dec. 1** to give her seat to a white man on a bus in Montgomery, Ala. Bus segregation ordinance declared unconstitutional by a federal court following boycott and NAACP protest.

Merger of America's 2 largest labor organizations was effected **Dec. 5** under the name American

Federation of Labor and Congress of Industrial Organizations. George Meany became president, Walter Reuther became vice president in charge of the industrial department. The merged AFL-CIO had a membership estimated at 15 million.

Vietnam War and U.S. Intervention

American combat involvement in Vietnam for about 12 years made the Vietnam War the longest in U.S. history. U.S. interest in the area began when Pres. Harry S. Truman June 27, 1950, sent a 35-man military advisory team to aid the French in their fight against communist forces in North Vietnam.

After the French stronghold of Dien Bien Phu fell to communist forces May 8, 1954, France and North Vietnam agreed at the Geneva Conference on Indochina, May 8 to July 21, to partition Vietnam pending reunification elections. Pres. Eisenhower offered South Vietnam economic aid Oct. 24, 1954, and agreed to help train the South Vietnamese army Feb. 12, 1955. In July, the South Vietnamese government refused a North Vietnamese request to prepare for reunification elections on grounds that free elections would be impossible in North Vietnam.

North Vietnam announced Dec. 1960 the formation of the National Liberation Front (Vietcong) of South Vietnam; terrorism in the South increased. The number of U.S. military advisers in South Vietnam rose from about 2,000 in Dec. 1961 to over 15,000 by the end of 1963.

Ngo Dinh Diem, South Vietnam president since 1955, was assassinated during a military coup Nov. 1, 1963. Stable government did not return to South Vietnam until June, 1965, when Gen. Nguyen Van Thieu assumed command of a military government.

The major American commitment in Vietnam began after the U.S. destroyers Maddox and C. Turner Joy were reportedly attacked Aug. 2, 1964, by North Vietnamese torpedo boats in the Gulf of Tonkin. The U.S. Congress Aug. 7 passed the Gulf of Tonkin Resolution giving the president power to "take all necessary measures to repel any armed attack against the forces of the U.S. and to prevent further aggression." In Feb. 1965, Pres. Johnson ordered continuous bombing raids over North Vietnam below the 20th parallel.

U.S. commanders were authorized to commit 23,-000 advisers to combat June 8, 1965. U.S. army, navy, air and marine forces committed in Vietnam reached 184,300 men by year's end. The U.S. began bombing strikes in the Hanoi-Haiphong area June 29, 1966. By Dec. 31, 1966, U.S. forces in Vietnam reached 385,300 men, not including some 60,000 men in the U.S. fleet and some 33,000 men stationed in Thailand.

The unconventional conflict in South Vietnam required the use of new ground warfare tactics. "Search and destroy" missions and "free-fire zones" for artillery were the most publicized of these new tactics because of their potential hazard to non-combatants. Armed helicopters were used extensively because of their mobility.

As the fighting and American casualties escalated, large-scale protests against the war erupted in the U.S. Thousands of war protesters marched Oct. 21-22, 1967, in Washington, D.C., and hundreds were arrested when they stormed the Pentagon. Nevertheless, American troop strength climbed to 474,300 men in Dec., 1,500 more than peak U.S. strength in Korea during the Korean War.

In the "Tet offensive" Jan. 30, 1968, the Vietcong and North Vietnamese attacked 30 provincial capitals in South Vietnam. The city of Hue was held by the Vietcong for 25 days, with bitter street fighting ending Feb. 24. Saigon was heavily attacked and the U.S. Embassy was occupied for 6 hrs. Record casualties were suffered on both sides. President Johnson Mar. 31 announced a bombing halt over 90% of North Vietnam and asked Hanoi for a peaceful response.

While the fighting continued, preliminary peace talks between the U.S. and North Vietnam opened in Paris May 10. In Chicago, police and troops clashed with 10,000-15,000 anti-war demonstrators during the Democratic National Convention Aug. 26-29.

Expanded peace talks, including representatives from South Vietnam and the Vietcong, opened in Paris Jan. 18, 1969. American forces in South Vietnam reached a final peak of 543,400 men in Apr. 1969. U.S. battle deaths Apr. 3 totaled 33,641 men, surpassing by 12 those killed in the Korean War. Withdrawal of U.S. combat troops began July 8, 1969, and on Nov. 3 Pres. Nixon announced a Vietnamization policy which would transfer the fighting to South Vietnamese forces.

Protests in the U.S. continued, however, as hundreds of thousands of Americans demonstrated opposition to the Vietnam War Oct. 15 in a nationwide "moratorium." Some 250,000 demonstrators gathered in Washington, D.C., Nov. 15 in the largest anti-war protest in U.S. history.

As the Paris talks continued, U.S. and South Vietnamese forces invaded neutral Cambodia Apr. 30, 1970, to destroy communist supply bases in border area sanctuaries. On May 4 at Kent State Univ. in Ohio, 4 students were slain and 9 wounded when National Guardsmen opened fire during a demonstration against the Cambodian incursion; 100 U.S. colleges were closed down to protest the Cambodian invasion and Kent State killings. A year later, during massive anti-war protests in Washington, D.C., between May 3-5, police arrested some 12,614 people, at least 7,000 of them on the first day — a record high for arrests in a civil disturbance in U.S. history.

Pres. Nixon revealed Jan. 25, 1972, that secret peace negotiations had been conducted since the previous June by presidential adviser Henry A. Kissinger. In the biggest communist attack since 1968, North Vietnamese forces Mar. 30 launched an offensive in force against South Vietnam through the demilitarized zone (DMZ) between the 2 Vietnams. Bombing of North Vietnam resumed Apr. 15, the first intensive bombing of North since 1968. Quang Tri, capital city of South Vietnam's northernmost province, fell to Hanoi troops May 1. The mining of Haiphong and other North Vietnamese ports was ordered by Pres. Nixon May 8. After initial setbacks, South Vietnamese troops brought the invasion to a halt.

The last U.S. combat troops left Vietnam Aug. 11. Hanoi announced Oct. 26 that secret talks had achieved a tentative agreement. But the peace talks broke down and, on Dec. 18 Pres. Nixon ordered the heaviest bombing of the war against North Vietnam. B-52 bombers were used for the first time against targets in Hanoi; some 15 were shot down by Hanoi's surface-to-air missiles.

Peace talks resumed Jan. 8, 1973, and Pres. Nixon ordered a halt to all offensive military operations against North Vietnam Jan. 15. Peace pacts were formally signed in Paris Jan. 27 by the U.S., and North and South Vietnam, and the Vietcong. A cease-fire began in Vietnam on Jan. 28. Between Feb. 12 and Apr. 1, 590 American POWs were released by North Vietnam. Some 1,359 Americans were reported missing in Indochina. The last American troops left Vietnam Mar. 29, officially ending any direct U.S. military role. U.S. combat deaths were counted at 46,079 as of Aug. 25, 1973. Total dead were estimated at some 2 million.

1956

At 20th Congress of Soviet Communist party in Moscow Feb. 14-25 party chief Nikita S. Khrushchev and other leaders denounced Joseph Stalin, repudiated cruelties of Stalinism, and proclaimed a policy of peaceful coexistence with the West. New party line helped to alienate Chinese communists and hasten Sino-Soviet split.

Workers in Poznan, Poland, revolted June 28; uprising crushed with 44 killed, many wounded.

Principles of Organization of American States outlined in Panama Declaration signed in Panama City July 22 by Pres. Eisenhower and heads of 18 other Western Hemisphere states.

Egypt seized Suez Canal July 26 under nationalization decree after Pres. Gamal Abdel Nasser denounced Western withdrawal of proposed Aswan dam financing.

Polish Communist leaders Oct. 19-21 defied Kremlin leadership and elected Wladyslaw Gomulka to head more independent government.

Hungarian revolt against Soviet-dominated regime began Oct. 23, was crushed Nov. 4 by Soviet Army.

Israel invaded Egypt's Sinai Peninsula Oct. 29, saying an Arab attack was imminent. France and Britain landed forces Nov. 5-6. U.S. condemned attack, supported cease-fire demand by UN. Egypt and Israel accepted cease-fire. Britain and France followed, fighting stopped Nov. 7.

UN established first international police force Nov. 5 to supervise truce in Middle East.

1957

Britain set off its first hydrogen bomb in Pacific test May 15.

Soviet Union announced Aug. 26 that it had successfully tested an intercontinental ballistic missile.

Sen. Strom Thurmond (D. S.C.) held Senate floor for 24 hrs., 18 min., Aug. 28-29, eclipsing filibuster record of Sen. Wayne Morse (D. Ore.) in 1953.

First underground nuclear explosion set off by Atomic Energy Commission in Nevada Sept. 19.

A federal-state controversy over admission of Negroes to the previously all-white Central High School in Little Rock, Ark., reached a showdown Sept. 4 when National Guardsmen ordered out by Gov. Orval Faubus (D.) barred 9 Negro students from entering the school. A conference between Faubus and Pres. Eisenhower brought no result but Faubus complied Sept. 21 with a federal court order to remove the National Guardsmen. The Negroes entered school Sept. 23 but were ordered to withdraw by local authorities because of fear of mob violence. Pres. Eisenhower sent federal troops to Little Rock Sept. 24 to enforce the court's order and the school began operation on an integrated basis.

First man-made satellite, Sputnik I, was launched by Soviet scientists Oct. 4. The 184-lb. sphere circled the earth about every 1-1/2 hours in an elliptical orbit at altitudes ranging from some 140 to 560 mi. above earth. The Russians Nov. 3 launched Sputnik II, weighing 1,120 lbs., carrying a live dog, Laika, as the world's first space passenger and orbiting the earth about every 103.7 minutes at altitudes ranging from some 160 mi. to about 1,062 mi. Soviet authorities announced the dog's death Nov. 10.

1958

First U. S. earth satellite to go into orbit, Explorer I, launched by Army Jan. 31 at Cape Canaveral, Fla.

Gen. Charles de Gaulle became French premier June 1 averting threatened civil war; De Gaulle constitution, increasing power of executive, overwhelmingly adopted Sept. 28. De Gaulle elected Dec. 21 as first president of 5th Republic.

Arab nationalist rebels seized Iraqi government July 14, killed King Faisal II, proclaimed republic. Pres. Eisenhower sent U.S. marines to Lebanon July 15 to forestall alleged effort by Soviet Union and United Arab Republic (Egypt and Syria) to engineer overthrow of Lebanon regime. Withdrawal of U. S.

troops began Aug. 12.

Jet airliner passenger service across Atlantic was opened Oct. 4 by British Overseas Airways Corp.

First domestic jet airline passenger service in U.S. opened by National Airlines Dec. 10 between New York and Miami.

1959

Fidel Castro seized power in Cuba following collapse of Fulgencio Batista's government Jan. 1.

St. Lawrence Seaway opened Apr. 25.

The George Washington, first U.S. ballistic-missile submarine, launched at Groton, Conn., June 9.

N.S. Savannah, world's first atomic-powered merchant ship, launched July 21 at Camden, N.J.

Soviet Premier Khrushchev paid unprecedented visit to U.S. Sept. 15-27, made transcontinental tour.

1960

A wave of sit-ins began Feb. 1 when 4 Negro college students in Greensboro, N.C., refused to move from a Woolworth lunch counter when they were denied service. By Sept. 1961 more than 70,000 students, whites and blacks, had participated in sit-ins.

First French nuclear test explosion set off Feb. 13 in Sahara Desert.

A U-2 reconnaissance plane of the U.S., piloted by Francis Gary Powers, was shot down in the Soviet Union May 1. Soviet Premier Khrushchev refused to participate in the Paris summit conference scheduled for May 16 unless Pres. Eisenhower apologized for U-2 flights over the USSR; the Big Four leaders went to Paris but the conference did not take place. Powers was freed Feb. 10, 1962, in exchange for convicted Soviet spy Rudolf Abel, who was serving a 30-year term imposed by U. S. in 1957.

Adolf Eichmann's capture in Argentina by Israeli agents announced May 22; former Nazi SS general accused of playing a major role in killing of millions of Jews. After 4-month trial in Jerusalem, sentenced by Israeli court Dec. 15, 1961, hanged for crimes against humanity May 31, 1962.

1961

The U. S. severed diplomatic and consular relations with Cuba Jan. 3.

Maj. Yuri Gagarin of the Soviet Union became Apr. 12 the first human orbital traveler; he was launched into orbit from Siberia in a spacecraft called Vostok I and returned to earth after one circuit of the globe.

Invasion of Cuba "Bay of Pigs" Apr. 17 by Cuban exiles attempting to overthrow the regime of Premier Fidel Castro was repulsed.

Commander Alan B. Shepard Jr. was rocketed from Cape Canaveral, Fla., 116.5 mi. above the earth in a Mercury capsule May 5 in the first U. S. manned sub-orbital space flight; he landed safely in the Atlantic 302 mi. away.

East Germany closed the border between East and West Berlin Aug. 12-13 to stop the exodus of East Germans to the West; the East Germans built a wall dividing the city.

Dag Hammarskjold, sec. general of the UN, was killed in a plane crash near Ndola, Northern Rhodesia, Sept. 18.

Nuclear blasts of 25 megatons and over 50 megatons, largest man-made explosions to date, were set off by the Soviet Union Oct. 23 and Oct. 30, respectively, despite world protests.

1962

Lt. Col. John H. Glenn Jr. became the first American in orbit Feb. 20 when he circled the earth 3 times in the Mercury capsule Friendship 7.

A truce agreement Mar. 18 ended the 7-yr. Moslem revolt against French rule in Algeria. Algerians cast an overwhelming vote for independence in a referendum July 1 and French President Charles de Gaulle declared the country independent July 3.

The 3d Soviet astronaut was sent into orbit Aug. 11 and the 4th followed him into a nearly identical orbit Aug. 12, both descended Aug. 15. They were Maj. Andrian G. Nikolayev, who made a record 64 orbits of the earth, and **Lt. Col. Pavel R. Popovich**, who made 48 orbits.

The largest cash robbery to date in U. S. history occurred **Aug. 14** when a gang held up a U. S. mail truck near Plymouth, Mass., and stole $1,551,277.

A Soviet offensive buildup in Cuba was revealed to the American people **Oct. 22** by Pres. Kennedy, who ordered a naval and air quarantine on shipment of offensive military equipment to the island. Pres. Kennedy and Soviet Premier Khrushchev reached agreement **Oct. 28** on a formula to end the crisis. Kennedy announced **Nov. 2** that Soviet missile bases in Cuba were being dismantled.

1963

The first woman space traveler, Soviet **Jr. Lt. Valentina V. Tereshkova,** was launched into orbit in Vostok VI **June 16;** landed **June 19** after 48 orbits.

U.S. Supreme Court ruled, 8-1, **June 17** that state and local laws requiring recitation of the Lord's Prayer or Bible verses in public schools were unconstitutional.

A limited nuclear test-ban treaty was agreed upon **July 25** by the U. S., the Soviet Union, and Britain, barring all nuclear tests except those conducted underground. It became effective **Oct. 10.**

The biggest robbery to date occurred **Aug. 8** when an armed holdup gang stole more than $7 million (£2.5 million) in currency from a mail train near Cheddington, England. Some of the money was recovered and a dozen men were sentenced to prison.

Washington demonstration by 200,000 persons **Aug. 28** in support of Negro demands for equal rights. Highlight was speech in which Dr. Martin Luther King said: "I have a dream that this nation will rise up and live out the true meaning of its creed, 'We hold these truths to be self evident: that all men are created equal'."

Pres. John F. Kennedy was shot and fatally wounded by an assassin **Nov. 22** as he rode in a motorcade through downtown Dallas, Tex. **Gov. John B. Connally Jr. of Texas,** riding in the same car, was also shot but not fatally injured. Vice Pres. Lyndon B. Johnson was inaugurated president shortly afterward in Dallas. **Lee Harvey Oswald** was arrested and charged with the murder of the president. Oswald was shot and fatally wounded **Nov. 24** by **Jack Ruby,** 52, a Dallas nightclub owner, who was convicted of murder **Mar. 14, 1964,** and was sentenced to death. The murder conviction was reversed by the Texas Court of Criminal Appeals. Ruby died of natural causes **Jan. 3, 1967** while awaiting re-trial.

1964

Pope Paul VI toured the Holy Land **Jan. 4-6,** the first pope to visit there since Christianity began, the first to travel by air, and, the first to leave Italy in over 150 years.

Three civil rights workers were reported missing in Mississippi **June 22.** The bodies of Michael Schwerner, Andrew Goodman and James E. Chaney were found buried near Philadelphia, Miss., **Aug. 4.** Twenty-one white men were arrested. On **Oct. 20, 1967,** an all-white federal jury convicted 7 of conspiracy in the slayings.

The Warren Commission released **Sept. 27** a report concluding that Lee Harvey Oswald was solely responsible for the Kennedy assassination.

Soviet Premier Khrushchev was ousted as premier and Soviet Communist party chief **Oct. 14-15.** Aleksei N. Kosygin replaced him as premier and Leonid I. Brezhnev took over the party leadership.

Communist China conducted a successful test explosion of its first atomic bomb **Oct. 16.**

1965

A Selma to Montgomery, Ala., civil rights march was led by Dr. Martin Luther King Jr., **Mar. 21-25.** The march started with 3,200 and swelled to 25,000. They were guarded along the way by 4,000 troops dispatched by Pres. Johnson.

U.S. armed forces sent to Dominican Republic to protect U.S. citizens and prevent a revolution **Apr. 28.** The Organization of American States **May 23** set up a peace-keeping force to maintain order.

Los Angeles riot by discontented blacks living in Watts area resulted in death of 35 persons and property damage est. at $200 million **Aug. 11-16.**

Pope Paul VI visited N.Y. City **Oct. 4** and delivered a personal appeal for peace to the UN. It was the first time a pope had come to America.

Massive electric power failure blacked out most of northeastern U.S., parts of 2 Canadian provinces the night of **Nov. 9-10.** Approximately 80,000 sq. mi. with a population of 30 million were affected. In N.Y. City over 800,000 were trapped in the subways for hours.

Independence from Britain proclaimed in Rhodesia by minority white regime **Nov. 11.**

1966

Kwame Nkrumah, president of Ghana since independence in 1957, was overthrown **Feb. 24.**

France withdrew all its armed forces from the integrated NATO military alliance **July 1.**

Medicare, government program to pay part of the medical expenses of citizens over 65, began **July 1.**

Edward Brooke (R. Mass.) elected **Nov. 8** as first Negro U.S. senator in 85 years.

1967

Rep. Adam Clayton Powell (D. N.Y.) was denied **Mar. 1** his seat in 90th Congress because House of Representatives charged him with misuse of government funds and nepotism. Reelected in 1968, he was seated by the 91st Congress but was fined $25,000 and stripped of his 22 years' congressional seniority.

In 6-day Israeli-Arab war June 5-10, Israel smashed armed forces of United Arab Republic (Egypt), Syria and Jordan; Israel captured territory 4 times its own area. **A U.S. communications ship, the U.S.S. Liberty,** was attacked by Israeli planes and torpedo boats **June 8** in international waters off the Sinai Peninsula. Thirty-four U.S. crewmen were killed and 75 wounded. Israel apologized for the attack, which it called accidental.

Pres. Johnson and Soviet Premier Aleksei Kosygin met **June 23 and 25** at Glassboro State College in N.J.; agreed not to let any crisis push them into nuclear war.

Black riots in Newark, N.J., July 12-17 killed some 26, injured 1,500; over 1,000 arrested. In Detroit, Mich., **July 23-30** at least 40 died, 2,000 injured, and 5,000 left homeless by rioting, looting, burning in city's black ghetto. Quelled by 4,700 federal paratroopers and 8,000 National Guardsmen.

Thurgood Marshall sworn in **Oct. 2** as first black U.S. Supreme Court Justice. **Carl B. Stokes** (D. Cleveland) and **Richard G. Hatcher** (D. Gary, Ind.), elected first black mayors of major U.S. cities **Nov. 7.**

Dr. Christiaan Barnard, Capetown, South Africa, performed first successful human heart transplant **Dec. 3** on Louis Washkansky, who lived for 18 days.

1968

U.S.S. Pueblo and 83-man crew seized in Sea of Japan **Jan. 23** by North Koreans; 82 men released **Dec. 22.**

White racism cited as chief cause of black violence in Kerner Commission report on civil disorders **Feb. 29.**

Pres. Johnson said Mar. 31 he would not seek or accept the Democratic nomination for president.

The Rev. Dr. Martin Luther King Jr., 39, assassinated **Apr. 4** in Memphis, Tenn. Riots in Washington, D.C., caused Pres. Johnson to call out troops. By **Apr. 14** racial violence erupted in 125 cities in 29 states. James Earl Ray, an escaped convict, pleaded guilty to the slaying, was sentenced to 99 years.

Six New Left students' protest at Univ. of Nanterre, France, **May 2** grew into nearly a month of civil violence and by **May 24** 10 million strikers paralyzed country. De Gaulle saved regime with broad reforms. **Sen. Robert F. Kennedy,** 42 (D. N.Y.), shot **June 5** in Hotel Ambassador, Los Angeles, after celebrating Cal. and S.D. presidential primary victories. Died

June 6. Sirhan Bishara Sirhan, a Jordanian Arab living in Los Angeles, convicted of murder.

Soviet Union and other Warsaw Pact nations invaded Czechoslovakia **Aug. 20-21** to crush Alexander Dubcek's liberal regime.

1969

Unarmed U.S. reconnaissance plane, with 31 aboard, shot down by North Korean jets **Apr. 15** in the Sea of Japan about 100 mi. from the mainland. No survivors found.

Charles de Gaulle resigned as president of France **Apr. 28** after narrowly losing a referendum.

A car driven by Sen. Edward M. Kennedy (D. Mass.) plunged off a bridge into a tidal pool on Chappaquiddick Is., Martha's Vineyard, Mass., **July 18.** The body of Mary Jo Kopechne, a 28-year-old secretary, was found drowned, in the car.

U.S. astronaut Neil A. Armstrong, 38, commander of the Apollo 11 mission, became the first man to set foot on the moon **July 20.** After stepping onto the moon Armstrong said: "That's one small step for a man, one giant leap for mankind." Air Force **Col. Edwin E. Aldrin Jr.** accompanied Armstrong.

1970

The 31-month Nigerian civil war ended with the surrender **Jan. 12** of secessionist Biafra after a loss of about 2 million lives.

A federal jury Feb. 18 found the defendants in the turbulent 21-week trial of the "Chicago 7" innocent of conspiring to incite riots during the 1968 Democratic National Convention. However, 5 were convicted of crossing state lines with intent to incite riots.

The U.S. cast its first veto in the UN Security Council **Mar. 17** when it joined Britain in rejecting a resolution calling on UN members to cut all communications with Rhodesia.

Millions of Americans participated in anti-pollution demonstrations **Apr. 22** to mark the first Earth Day.

The first women generals in American history were named by Pres. Nixon **May 15** when he promoted Col. Elizabeth P. Hoisington, director of the Women's Army Corps, and Col. Anna Mae Hays, chief of the Army Nurse Corps, to the rank of brigadier general.

The Norwegian explorer Thor Heyerdahl and a multi-national crew of 7 set sail from Morocco **May 17** in a frail papyrus boat, the Ra II, in an attempt to prove that ancient Egyptians could have reached the new world. The craft sailed into Bridgetown Harbor, Barbados, **July 12.**

A postal reform measure was signed by Pres. Nixon **Aug. 12,** creating an independent U.S. Postal Service, thus relinquishing governmental control of the U.S. mails after almost 2 centuries.

Egypt's Pres. Gamal Abdel Nasser, 52, most powerful leader in Arab world, died **Sept. 28.**

Salvador Allende Gossens, 62, first democratically elected Marxist head of government in the world, was sworn in as Chile's president **Nov. 3.**

Charles de Gaulle, 79, died of a heart attack in Colombey-les-Deux Eglises **Nov. 9.**

1971

Charles Manson, 36, and 3 of his followers were found guilty **Jan. 26** of first-degree murder in the brutal slaying in 1969 of actress Sharon Tate and 6 others.

A treaty prohibiting installation of nuclear weapons on the seabed beyond any nation's 12-mi. coastal zone was signed by 63 nations **Feb. 11.**

A Constitutional Amendment lowering the voting age to 18 in all elections was approved in the Senate by a vote of 94-0 **Mar. 10.** The proposed 26th Amendment received House approval by a 400-19 vote **Mar. 23;** Ohio ratified it on **June 30** making it law.

Civil war between East and West Pakistan beginning **Mar. 25** brought death from war and starvation to hundreds of thousands and caused 9 million refugees to pour into India.

A court-martial jury of 6 officers **Mar. 29** after 13 days deliberation, convicted Lt. William L. Calley Jr., of premeditated murder of 22 South Vietnamese men, women and children at Mylai on **Mar. 16, 1968.** he was sentenced to life imprisonment **Mar. 31.** Sentence reduced to 20 years **Aug. 20, 1971,** by Lt. Gen. Albert O. Conner.

Haiti's Francois (Papa Doc) Duvalier, 64, died **Apr. 21.** His son Claude, 19, succeeded him **Apr. 22.**

Amtrak, the nation's new rail passenger system, went into operation **May 1** with the goal to "get people back on trains."

Publication of classified Pentagon papers on the U.S. involvement in Vietnam was begun **June 13** by the New York Times. In a 6-3 vote, the U.S. Supreme Court **June 30** upheld the right of the Times and the Washington Post to publish the documents under the protection of the First Amendment. Daniel Ellsberg, admitted leaker of the 47-volume Pentagon analysis, was arraigned **June 28** on charges of unauthorized possession of secret documents.

Pres. Nixon began a sweeping new economic program **Aug. 15** calling for a 90-day wage, price and rent freeze, to be effective immediately. He also freed the dollar for devaluation against other currencies by cutting its tie with gold.

More than 1,000 N.Y. State troopers and police stormed the Attica State Correctional Facility where 1,200 inmates held 38 guards hostage **Sept. 13,** ending a 4-day rebellion in the maximum-security prison. Nine hostages and 28 convicts were shot to death in the assault.

Chile virtually expropriated the Anaconda and Kennecott copper mines **Sept. 28** when Pres. Allende subtracted $774 million from proposed compensation for the U.S. owners. He claimed the deduction was for "excess profits" harvested by the U.S. firms over 16 years.

Communist China was granted UN membership when the General Assembly by a vote of 76 to 35, with 17 abstentions, adopted an Albanian resolution **Oct. 25** to seat Mao Tse-tung's communists and oust Chiang Kai-shek's nationalists.

India invaded Pakistan Dec. 3 in defense of splinter nation of Bangladesh, formerly East Pakistan. Following India's victory in the 14-day war, Shiek Mujibur Rahman, the father of the secessionist rebellion, became the prime minister of Bangladesh **Jan. 12.**

Pres. Nixon announced Dec. 18 an 8.57% devaluation of the U.S. dollar to allow American goods to be more competitive in the world market, while raising the price of certain imports; the devaluation was accomplished by a $3 increase in the price of gold, from $35 an ounce to $38.

1972

Pres. Nixon arrived in Peking Feb. 21 for an 8-day visit to China, which he called a "journey for peace." The unprecedented visit ended with a joint communique pledging that both powers would work for "a normalization of relations".

By a vote of 84 to 8, the Senate approved **Mar. 22** a Constitutional Amendment banning legal discrimination against women because of their sex and sent the measure to the states for ratification.

Britain imposed direct rule over North Ireland **Mar. 30,** ending 51 years of semi-autonomous rule by the North Ireland government.

Alabama Gov. George C. Wallace, campaigning at a Laurel, Md., shopping center **May 15,** was shot and seriously wounded as he greeted a large, enthusiastic crowd. Arthur H. Bremer, 21, was sentenced **Aug. 4** to 63 years in prison for the shooting of Wallace and 3 bystanders.

In the first visit of a U.S. president to Moscow, Pres. Nixon arrived **May 22** for a week of summit talks with Kremlin leaders which culminated in a landmark arms pact aimed at a standoff between the missile forces of the 2 nuclear giants.

The Environmental Protection Agency announced **June 14** a near-total ban on agricultural and other uses of the pesticide DDT, to be effective Dec. 31.

Five men were arrested June 17 for breaking into the offices of the Democratic National Committee in the Watergate office complex in Washington, D.C.

Hurricane Agnes hit Florida June 19 and went on a 10-day rampage up 250-mi. of eastern seaboard with winds and rains which unleashed "the most extensive" floods in the country's history, causing 118 deaths and more than $3 billion in property damage.

The White House announced July 8 that the U.S. would sell the Soviet Union at least $750 million of American wheat, corn and other grains over a period of 3 years. Soviet bought most of it in 1st year.

Less than 2 weeks after Sen. Thomas F. Eagleton received the Democrats' nomination for vice-president, he confirmed July 25 reports that he had under gone electroshock treatment on 2 occasions in the 1960s. Eagleton withdrew as nominee July 31. R. Sargent Shriver was named as vice presidential candidate Aug. 8.

By a vote of 88 to 2, the Senate Aug. 3 ratified the strategic arms treaty limiting the U.S. and Russia to 2 antiballistic missile sites each. In White House ceremonies Oct. 3 Pres. Nixon and Soviet Foreign Min. Andrei Gromyko signed and exchanged the final documents implementing the accords, which also limited the 2 powers' land-based and submarine-borne nuclear missile forces.

Eight Arab guerrillas, members of the Black September terrorist group, invaded the Israeli dormitory in the Olympics village in Munich early Sept. 5 killing 2 members of the Israeli squad. Twenty-three hours later, after tense negotiations, 5 of the terrorists and 9 hostages were killed.

Life ended publication with its Dec. 29 issue after 36 years as the leading weekly pictorial magazine.

1973

All mandatory wage and price controls were ended by Pres. Nixon Jan. 11.

All state laws that limited a woman's right to an abortion during the first 3 months of pregnancy were overturned Jan. 22 by the U.S. Supreme Court, 7-2.

The end of the military draft was announced Jan. 27 by Defense Sec. Melvin R. Laird.

U. S. Sec. of the Treasury George P. Shultz announced Feb. 12 a 10% devaluation of the U.S. dollar against nearly all major world currencies.

Some 200-300 members of the militant American Indian Movement Feb. 27 seized the trading post and church at historic Wounded Knee on the Oglala Sioux Reservation in South Dakota. The insurgents demanded that the U.S. Senate Foreign Relations Committee hold hearings on treaties made with Indians, and that the Senate start a "full-scale investigation" of government treatment of Indians. After numerous negotiation failures both sides signed an agreement May 5 stipulating removal of government armored personnel carriers and concurrent surrender of weapons by the insurgent Indians. The hamlet was evacuated May 8.

Palestinian terrorists invaded a reception Mar. 1 at the Saudi Arabian embassy in Khartoum, Sudan, and held 6 diplomats hostage. After a breakdown of negotiations between the gunmen and Sudanese government officials, the 8 Palestinians Mar. 2 tortured and executed 2 U.S. envoys and a Belgian charge d'affaires. Terrorists arrested; later freed.

James W. McCord, a key figure in the Watergate conspiracy, said Mar. 23 in a letter to the court that he and others had been under "political pressure" to plead guilty and remain silent. He said there were others involved who had escaped indictment.

Pres. Nixon responded to the Watergate crisis in an address over radio and television Apr. 30. Although he himself had not played a role in the Watergate case, he said, he accepted, as "top man in the organization," full responsibility for those "people whose zeal exceeded their judgment." Earlier the same day 3 of his top aides resigned: chief of staff H. R. Halde-

man, domestic affairs assistant John D. Ehrlichman and presidential counsel John W. Dean 3d. Atty. Gen. Richard G. Kleindienst also resigned.

The West German Bundestag ratified a treaty May 11 establishing formal relations with the German Democratic Republic in East Germany.

Presiding Judge William M. Byrne dismissed May 11 all government charges of espionage, theft, and conspiracy against Daniel Ellsberg and Anthony J. Russo Jr., the defendants in the 89-day Pentagon Papers trial. The decision precluded a retrial, but did not vindicate the defendants nor resolve the major constitutional issues in the controversial case. The crucial revelation leading to dismissal of the case came Apr. 27 when Judge Byrne released a Justice Dept. memorandum stating that 2 of the convicted Watergate defendants, E. Howard Hunt and G. Gordon Liddy, had broken into the office of Ellsberg's psychiatrist with the intention of stealing Ellsberg's medical records. Byrne released E. Howard Hunt's grand jury testimony May 14 in which Hunt stated that the White House had conceived the plot and supervised and paid for the break-in.

Hearings by the Senate Select Committee on Presidential Campaign Activities into the Watergate scandal opened in Washington, D.C., May 17 chaired by Sam J. Ervin (D.,N.C.).

Pres. Nixon released a statement May 22 in which he asserted that he made legitimate efforts to restrict investigation into some matters related to the Watergate affair because they impinged on national security. The president further stated that his concern over foreign policy leaks and the publication of the Pentagon Papers led to the establishment in 1971 of a small White House investigative unit, the "plumbers," supervised by John D. Ehrlichman.

Pres. Nixon set a freeze June 13 on retail prices. The freeze included prepared-food prices but excluded rents, interest, dividends, and raw food.

The U.S. and USSR signed 9 agreements during Soviet Communist party Gen. Sec. Leonid I. Brezhnev's June 16-25 visit to the U. S. One agreement obliged the 2 nations to enter into immediate consultations if relations between them or between one of them and some other country "appear to involve risk of nuclear conflict."

John Dean, former presidential counsel, June 25 testified to a widespread cover-up of the Watergate conspiracy. He said the cover-up had spread from the White House staff and the Committee to Re-elect the President to the Justice Dept. and to the "Oval Office" of the president.

Former Pres. Juan D. Peron returned June 20 to Argentina after almost 20 years of exile. He was re-elected president of Argentina Sept. 23, but died 9 months later, July 1, 1974.

The Federal Trade Commission July 9 charged 8 of the largest U.S. oil companies with conspiracy to monopolize the refining of petroleum products. The commission said the 23-year conspiracy had led to shortages of gasoline, forcing "substantially higher prices" on American consumers, and caused some independent petroleum marketers to close down.

The Senate Armed Services Committee July 16 began a probe into allegations that the U.S. Air Force had made secret B-52 bombing raids into Cambodia in 1969 and 1970. Defense Sec. James R. Schlesinger verified the secret raids July 16 describing them as "fully authorized" and necessary for the protection of U.S. servicemen. The Defense Dept. disclosed July 17 that some 3,500 secret bombing raids had been made over Cambodia in the 14-month period beginning Mar. 1969, while Cambodia was officially recognized as a neutral country.

Herbert Kalmbach, formerly attorney and fund raiser for Pres. Nixon, told the Senate Watergate Committee July 16 that he had raised $220,000 for the 7 defendants in the Watergate trial, believing the money was intended for legal fees and support of the defendant's families.

White House tape recording of all conversation in

the president's offices since Mar. 1971 was revealed by Alexander P. Butterfield, former presidential deputy assistant, in a surprise appearance before the Senate Watergate Committee **July 16**. On **July 23** citing separation of powers and executive privilege, Pres. Nixon refused to release any tapes to Senate investigators.

The U. S. officially ceased bombing in Cambodia at midnight **Aug. 14** in accord with a June Congressional action. The bombing halt was preceded by several days of intensive bombing around Phnom Penh.

Forty-six years of civilian rule in Chile ended **Sept. 11** when a 4-man military Junta overthrew Pres. Salvador Allende Gossens in a violent military coup. Allende's Popular Unity Coalition was the world's first freely-elected Marxist government.

Henry A. Kissinger's nomination as Sec. of State was confirmed **Sept. 21**.

Pres. Nixon's 1972 campaign finance aides revealed **Sept. 28** that campaign fund raisers had collected a record $60.2 million.

The 4th and biggest Arab-Israeli War in 25 years erupted **Oct. 6** along the 103-mile-long Suez Canal and on the Golan Heights. The war began on the afternoon of Yom Kippur, the Jewish Holy Day of Atonement, and was marked by heavy troop and materiel losses on both sides. UN observers in the Middle East reported that Egyptian forces had crossed the Suez Canal at 5 points and that Syrian forces had attacked at 2 points on the Golan Heights. By **Oct. 11** the Egyptian army had established a bridgehead of about 60,000 men in the Sinai. The Egyptian army's advance was greatly aided by use of new Russian SAM-6 missiles which stymied the Israeli air offensive against the bridgehead.

After losing ground on both fronts, Israel counterattacked. Israel claimed **Oct. 12** that its forces had pushed to within 18 mi. of Damascus, despite the arrival of Iraqi and Jordanian forces on the Syrian front. Israel **Oct. 16** said it had sent a task force across the Suez Canal to attack Egyptian tanks, artillery and missile sites on the west bank. By **Oct. 24**, this Israeli force had isolated the city of Suez and the Egyptian 3d Army in Sinai.

The UN Security Council **Oct. 22** passed, 14-0, a U.S.-USSR sponsored resolution calling for a cease-fire in place. Fighting continued until a 2d cease-fire went into effect **Oct. 24** with UN supervision.

A total ban on oil exports to the U.S. was imposed by Arab oil-producing nations **Oct. 19-21**. The ban was lifted **Mar. 18, 1974**.

The U.S. **Oct. 25** suddenly placed its military forces on a world-wide "precautionary alert." The crisis ended when the USSR and U.S. joined in a Security Council vote barring the superpowers from participation in a Middle East peace-keeping force. A 7,000-man UN peace-keeping force was approved **Oct. 27** for an initial period of 6 months.

Vice President Spiro T. Agnew Oct. 10 resigned and pleaded "nolo contendere" (no contest) to charges of tax evasion on payments made to him by Maryland contractors. Agnew was sentenced to 3-years probation and fined $10,000.

Atty. Gen Elliot Richardson resigned, and his deputy William D. Ruckelshaus and Watergate Special Prosecutor Archibald Cox were fired by Pres. Nixon **Oct. 20** when Cox threatened to secure a judicial ruling that Pres. Nixon was violating a court order to turn tapes over to Judge John Sirica.

A massive expression of public outrage was followed **Oct. 23** by an agreement among Congressional leaders that the House Judiciary Committee should inquire into the possible impeachment of Pres. Nixon.

Leon Jaworski, conservative Texas Democrat, was named **Nov. 1** by the Nixon administration to be special prosecutor to succeed Archibald Cox, with the understanding Jaworski would have "complete freedom" to investigate administrative wrongdoing.

Congress overrode Nov. 7 Pres. Nixon's veto of the war powers bill which curbed the president's power to commit armed forces to hostilities abroad without Congressional approval.

The U.S. and Egypt announced **Nov. 7** they would renew diplomatic relations.

Sentencing 6 Watergate break-in defendants **Nov. 9**, Federal Judge John J. Sirica dealt E. Howard Hunt 2 1/2-8 years and a $10,000 fine; James W. McCord Jr. 1-5 years; Frank A. Sturgis, Eugenio R. Martinez, and Virgilio R. Gonzalez 1-4 years; Bernard L. Barker 18 months to 6 years. The 7th defendant, G. Gordon Liddy, had already been sentenced to 20 years, reflecting his refusal to cooperate with the prosecution.

Watergate Special Prosecutor Archibald Cox's firing, **Oct. 20**, was ruled illegal by Washington, D.C., Federal Court **Nov. 14**.

Alaska pipeline bill, permitting construction of 789-mi. pipe from Alaska's North Shore oilfield to port of Valdez, signed by Pres. Nixon **Nov. 16**.

Greek Pres. George Papadopoulos was deposed **Nov. 25** in bloodless military coup after student-worker riots.

Egil Krogh Jr., former head of the "plumbers," White House investigative unit, pleaded guilty **Nov. 30** to violating civil rights of Daniel Ellsberg's psychiatrist, Dr. Lewis J. Fielding, in burglary of Fielding's office. Krogh was sentenced **Jan. 24, 1974**, to 6 months.

Gerald Rudolph Ford was sworn in **Dec. 6** as 40th vice president under XXVth Amendment procedures.

Pres. Nixon disclosed his financial records **Dec. 8**, showing large income tax deductions based on gift of his vice presidential papers to the National Archives. He said he would let a joint Congressional committee decide if he owed more taxes.

Allocations for fuel oil and gasoline were announced by energy chief William Simon **Dec.12**, giving priorities to essential services.

A 3-day work week was ordered by British government **Dec. 13** because of Arab oil embargo and coal miners' slowdown.

Spanish Premier Louis Carrero Blanco was assassinated **Dec. 20** in Madrid. Basque terrorists claimed credit.

Arab nations doubled oil prices and said they would increase oil flow to some nations by 10%, but would continue embargo against U.S., the Netherlands and Denmark, after meetings **Dec. 23-25**.

1974

U.S. oil companies reported huge profits for the 4th quarter of 1973, during the Arab oil embargo, in their **Jan. 1974** reports. Exxon profits were up 59% over the same period of 1972; Mobil, 68%; Texaco, 70%; Ashland, 52%.

A disengagement agreement was reached by Israel and Egypt **Jan. 17** with U.S. aid. Egyptian forces occupied a narrow strip on the east side of the Suez Canal; a UN-patrolled buffer zone separated them from Israeli forces further east; Israelis withdrew from west of the canal.

Impeachment proceedings against Pres. Nixon began as the House voted its Judiciary Committee full inquiry powers **Feb. 6**.

Alexander Solzhenitsyn, Nobel Prize-winning author, was deported by Soviet Russia to West Germany **Feb. 13**. He had exposed the Soviet prison camp system in Gulag Archipelago, book published in Paris. His family was also allowed to leave Russia.

Herbert W. Kalmbach, Pres. Nixon's personal lawyer and fundraiser, pleaded guilty **Feb. 25** to promising a contributor an ambassadorship for a $100,000 contribution. Sentenced **June 17**, he got 6 to 8 months and a $10,000 fine.

Seven former White House and campaign aides of Pres. Nixon were indicted **Mar. 1** for taking part in the cover-up of the Watergate scandals. The 7 were former chief of staff H. R. Haldeman, former Atty. Gen. and campaign director John N. Mitchell, Presidential Domestic Assistant John D. Ehrlichman, former Special Counsel Charles W. Colson, former campaign aide Robert C. Mardian, former campaign committee attorney Kenneth W. Parkinson, former Haldeman aide Gordon C. Strachan.

Arab nations ended their oil embargo against the U.S. **Mar. 18** but continued it against Denmark and the Netherlands, designating them "unfriendly."

Pres. Nixon said Apr. 3 he would pay $432,787.13 in back taxes plus interest for 1969 through 1972, after Joint Congressional Committee, acting on request from Nixon, found him liable.

Lt. Gov. Ed Reinecke of California was indicted **Apr. 3** for lying to the Senate Judiciary Committee. Convicted **July 27,** he resigned and received an 18-month suspended sentence.

W. A. Boyle, deposed United Mine Workers president, was convicted **Apr. 11** of murder for ordering the slayings of union rival Joseph A. Yablonski and Yablonski's wife and daughter. The conviction carried a mandatory life sentence.

Arab guerrillas killed 18, mostly women and children, in attack on Qiryat Shemona, Israel, **Apr. 11.**

Charging Soviet Russia was trying to influence Egyptian actions by putting off requests for more arms, Pres. Anwar Sadat said **Apr. 18** Egypt would end its reliance on Soviet arms aid.

Portugal's Premier Marcello Caetano was ousted **Apr. 25** by a military group pledging democracy and peace for Portugal's African territories.

Former Atty. Gen. John N. Mitchell and former Commerce Sec. Maurice H. Stans were acquitted **Apr. 28** in N.Y. City Federal Court of attempting to impede an official probe of financier Robert L. Vesco in return for a $200,000 cash donation to the 1972 Nixon re-election campaign.

Impeachment hearings were opened **May 9** against Pres. Nixon by the House Judiciary Committee.

Arab terrorists seized 90 students in the Israeli town of Maalot **May 15** after murdering a family of 3. Israeli troops freed the hostages, but 21 students, one Israeli soldier, and the 3 terrorists died.

Ex-Atty. Gen. Richard G. Kleindienst pleaded guilty **May 16** to a misdemeanor charge that he did not testify accurately and fully before a Congressional committee probing handling of an ITT anti-trust settlement. He received 30 days and a $100 fine, both suspended, **June 7.**

India exploded a nuclear device May 18, becoming the 6th nation with nuclear bomb capability.

Jeb Stuart Magruder, former deputy director of the Committee to Re-elect the President, was sentenced **May 21** to 10 months to 4 years for his role in the Watergate break-in and cover-up.

Northern Ireland's Protestant-Catholic coalition government collapsed after a strike; the British government took over direct rule of Ulster **May 29.**

Israel and Syria signed a disengagement agreement **May 31.** Israel gave up some of the Golan Heights territory she had taken in 1967 and 1973; forces on both sides were limited in strips separated by a UN-patrolled buffer zone.

Charles W. Colson, ex-counsel to the president, pleaded guilty **June 3** to attempting to obstruct justice; he was sentenced **June 21** to 1 to 3 years and fined $5,000.

Mrs. Alberta Williams King, 69, mother of slain civil rights leader Dr. Martin Luther King Jr., was shot and killed **June 30,** along with a church deacon, in Atlanta's Ebenezer Baptist Church. Marcus Wayne Chenault, 23, of Dayton, Oh., was convicted **Sept. 12.**

Pres. Juan Domingo Peron of Argentina, 78, died **July 1;** he was succeeded by his vice president and wife, Maria Estela (Isabel) Martinez de Peron.

Turkey announced July 1 it would again allow the growth and sale of opium, but under strict control; in 1971 Turkey had promised the U.S. to outlaw the trade; the U.S. had agreed to give Turkey $35.7 million over 4 years.

John D. Ehrlichman and 3 White House "plumbers" were found guilty **July 12** of conspiring to violate the civil rights of Dr. Lewis Fielding, formerly psychiatrist to Daniel Ellsberg, by breaking into his

Beverly Hills, Cal., office. **On July 31,** Ehrlichman, Nixon domestic aide, drew 20 mos. to 5 yrs.; G. Gordon Liddy got 1 to 3 years.; Bernard L. Barker and Eugenio Martinez won suspended sentences.

Turkey invaded Cyprus July 20. Earlier, 650 Greek officers, **July 15,** led the Cypriot National Guard in a violent coup, overthrowing Pres. Makarios, who fled to London. Negotiations brought a promise from Greece to replace gradually the 650 Greek officers but she refused to recall them immediately. The Turkish invasion followed, ostensibly to protect the Turkish minority, 18% of the Cyprus population.

Greece's military government resigned July 23: former Premier Constantine Karamanlis returned from exile to become chief of state. On Cyprus, fighting continued until Turkey, in possession of the NE third of the island, declared a cease-fire **Aug. 16.**

The U.S. Supreme Court ruled, 8-0, **July 24** that Pres. Nixon had to turn over 64 tapes of White House conversations sought by Watergate Special Prosecutor Leon Jaworski.

The House Judiciary Committee, in televised hearings **July 24-30,** recommended 3 articles of impeachment against Pres. Nixon. The first, voted 27-11, **July 27,** charged Nixon with taking part in a criminal conspiracy to obstruct justice in the Watergate cover-up. The second, voted 28-10, **July 29,** charged he "repeatedly" failed to carry out his constitutional oath in a series of alleged abuses of power. The third, voted 27-17, **July 30,** accused him of unconstitutional defiance of committee subpoenas. The House of Representatives **Aug. 20,** without debate, voted 412-3 to accept the committee report, which included the recommended impeachment articles.

Ex-presidential counsel John W. Dean 3d was sentenced **Aug. 2** to 1 to 3 years, on his plea of guilty to conspiracy to obstruct justice.

Pres. Richard M. Nixon resigned and Vice Pres. Gerald R. Ford was sworn in as president **Aug. 9.** Nixon's support in the Watergate struggle began eroding **Aug. 5** when Nixon released 3 tapes, admitting he originated plans to have the FBI stop its probe of the Watergate break-in for political as well as national security reasons. Supporters in both House and Senate said, **Aug. 6-7,** they would vote for his impeachment.

Former N.Y. Gov. Nelson A. Rockefeller was nominated to be vice president by Pres. Ford **Aug. 20.**

Portugal began dissolving its African empire **Aug. 26,** signing an agreement to free Portuguese Guinea **Sept. 10;** the new nation became Guinea-Bissau.

The U.S. and East Germany established diplomatic relations **Sept. 4.**

An unconditional pardon to ex-Pres. Nixon for all federal crimes that he "committed or may have committed" while president was issued by Pres. Gerald Ford **Sept. 8,** one month after Nixon resigned. Ford's press secretary, J. F. terHorst resigned in protest. The administration also announced a **Sept. 6** agreement under which the ex-president's papers and tapes would be held for 3 years; after that Nixon could destroy the tapes.

Ethiopian Emperor Haile Selassie, 82, was peacefully deposed **Sept. 12** by armed forces leaders who had been strengthening their power since Feb.

Conditional amnesty to Vietnam era draft evaders and deserters who would be willing to work up to 2 years in public service jobs was proposed by Pres. Ford **Sept. 16.** Organized exiles condemned the program and few took advantage of it.

Charges against Wounded Knee defendants Dennis J. Banks and Russell C. Means, Indian leaders, were dismissed **Sept. 16** by Federal Judge Fred J. Nichol in the 1973 takeover of the South Dakota village. Nichol said that during the trial the FBI had been shown to lie and suborn perjury.

The court martial conviction of Lt. William L. Calley Jr. in the 1968 massacre of civilians in Mylai South Vietnam, was overturned **Sept. 25** by Federal Court Judge J. Robert Elliott in Columbus, Ga.

The provisional president of Portugal, Gen. Antonio de Spinola, resigned **Sept. 30** with several associates, accused of a right-wing plot; the government was left chiefly in the hands of leftist officers and civilians.

A temporary restraining order, barring the Ford administration from carrying out its Sept. 6 agreement on returning Nixon's tapes, was issued **Oct. 21** by Federal Judge Charles Richey.

Leaders of 20 Arab nations declared Palestine Liberation Organization leader Yasir Arafat the "sole legitimate representative" of Palestinian Arabs **Oct. 28.** The UN General Assembly had voted **Oct. 14** to give the PLO a voice at its meetings.

Ex-Pres. Nixon underwent surgery for a blood clot **Oct. 29,** suffered internal bleeding and shock, but recovered; in Long Beach, Cal. hospital.

Nixon's ex-attorney, Edward L. Morgan, pleaded guilty **Nov. 8** to backdating documents falsely to give former Pres. Richard M. Nixon a $576,000 tax deduction.

South Africa was suspended from taking part in the UN General Assembly session **Nov. 12.**

Ex-Pres. Nixon underwent surgery for phlebitis and suffered vascular shock in a Long Beach, Cal. hospital in **Nov.**

Dominated by Arab and Communist nations, the UN General Assembly welcomed Palestine Liberation Organization leader Yasir Arafat **Nov. 13** and backed his demands for a sovereign Palestine state.

A limit of 2,400 ICBMs each for the U.S. and USSR was tentatively agreed on by Pres. Ford and Soviet leader Leonid Brezhnev **Nov. 24** at Vladivostok.

A second heart was placed in the chest of a 58-year-old man to help his own heart **Nov. 18** by Dr. Christiaan Barnard in Capetown, South Africa.

The Irish Republican Army was outlawed by the British House of Commons **Nov. 19;** police powers were strengthened.

Democracy returned to Greece as a newly-elected Parliament met after 7-year hiatus. **Dec. 9.**

Court-ordered busing for desegregation was rejected, 3-2, by the Boston School Committee **Dec. 16;** 3 members were fined for contempt of court.

Nelson A. Rockefeller was sworn in as the 2d unelected vice president of the U.S. **Dec. 19.**

Charges that the CIA abused its powers by conducting massive domestic operations were published **Dec. 21.**

1975

Found guilty of Watergate cover-up charges Jan. 1 were ex-Attorney General John N. Mitchell, ex-presidential advisers H.R. Haldeman and John D. Ehrlichman, all for perjury, conspiracy and obstruction of justice, and attorney Robert C. Mardian, for conspiracy to obstruct justice. Mardian got 10 mos. to 8 years in prison, the others 2 1/2 to 8 years.

A budget deficit of $51.9 billion, largest in the nation's peacetime history, was projected in the $349.4 billion budget Pres. Ford presented to Congress **Feb. 3.**

A separate nation, in the part of Cyprus occupied by Turkish troops, was proclaimed **Feb. 13** by Turkish Cypriots.

Boston Dr. Kenneth C. Edelin was found guilty **Feb. 15** of manslaughter after performing a legal abortion.

Senate filibuster rules were reformed **Mar. 7;** vote of 3/5 of Senate, rather than previous 2/3, made sufficient to invoke cloture and end a filibuster.

Saudi Arabian King Faisal, 70, was shot dead **Mar. 25** in Riyadh by a nephew, who was beheaded **June 18.**

Tax cuts, individual rebates, and bonuses for some retirees, along with an end to oil depletion allowances for large oil companies and extended unemployment insurance were approved by Congress **Mar. 26.**

Warfare between Lebanese Moslems and Christians, which would last more than a year, broke out **Apr. 1.**

Cambodian government surrendered to the Communist Khmer Rouge **Apr. 16,** ending 5 years of warfare.

South Vietnam government surrendered to the Communist Vietcong and North Vietnamese **Apr. 30,** shortly after evacuation of last Americans and many South Vietnamese refugees.

Maurice H. Stans, chief fund-raiser for the Nixon reelection campaign, was fined $5,000 **May 14** after pleading guilty to 5 violations of federal campaign laws.

U.S. merchant ship Mayaguez and crew of 39 seized by Cambodian forces in Gulf of Siam **May 12.** In rescue operation, U.S. Marines attacked Tang Is., planes bombed air base; Cambodia surrendered ship and crew; U.S. losses were 15 killed in battle and 23 dead in a helicopter crash.

Congress voted $405 million for South Vietnam refugees **May 16;** 140,000 were flown to U.S., 130,000 were resettled in U.S.

Gulf Oil Corp. admitted May 16 it had paid $5 million in illegal gifts to foreign politicians; many other large U.S. corporations admitted making gifts and bribes to do business in foreign countries.

The Suez Canal was reopened June 5 to all but Israeli ships, 8 years after Egypt closed it during the 1967 Arab-Israeli war. It was cleared of debris mainly by the U.S.

U.S. unemployment reached 9.2%, high point of the year, the Labor Dept. reported **June 6.**

Illegal CIA operations, including records on 300,-000 persons and groups, infiltration of agents into black, anti-war and political movements, monitoring of overseas phone calls, mail surveillance, and drug-testing, were described by a "blue-ribbon" commission headed by Vice Pres. Rockefeller **June 10.** Information on assassination plots against foreign leaders was ordered withheld by Pres. Ford. The commission recommended a Congressional oversight committee.

N.Y. City default on notes was avoided **June 10** by creation of a state Municipal Assistance Corp. (Big MAC) to refinance $3 billion in short-term indebtedness.

A U.S. Apollo and a USSR Soyuz linked together 140 mi. above the Atlantic **July 17.** The crews exchanged visits and shared meals in the 2 crafts.

Large U.S. grain companies were indicted July 21 and Aug. 7 for conspiring to steal grain from foreign shipments.

James R. Hoffa, Teamsters ex-president, disappeared **July 30.** The FBI entered the search **Aug. 3.**

A non-binding Security and Cooperation document was signed by 33 European nations, Canada and the U.S. **Aug. 1** at Helsinki. It froze postwar European borders; the nations agreed to broaden detente, renounce force and aid to terrorists, respect human freedoms, aid families to unite across borders, reduce forces and tension in the Mediterranean.

Communist Pathet Lao completed takeover of Laos **Aug. 23.**

Second-stage Sinai agreement was signed by Israel and Egypt **Sept. 4,** providing for new Israeli withdrawals from oil wells and strategic passes in the Sinai, Egypt to permit nonmilitary shipments to and from Israel through the Suez Canal, and a team of 200 U.S. civilians to operate an early-warning system at the passes.

Two assassination attempts against Pres. Ford, by women in California, failed. Lynette Alice (Squeaky) Fromme, a Charles Manson follower, pointed a pistol at him **Sept. 5** in Sacramento, but a Secret Service agent grabbed the gun. Sara Jane Moore, a political activist, fired a revolver at the president **Sept. 22** in San Francisco, but bystander Oliver Sipple deflected the gun.

William L. Calley's court-martial conviction for the murder of 22 Vietnamese, overturned in lower courts, was reinstated by the U.S. Court of Appeals in New Orleans, **Sept. 10.**

Mother Elizabeth Bayley Seton was canonized the Catholic Church's first U.S.-born saint, by Pope Paul VI **Sept. 14.**

FBI agents captured Patricia (Patty) Hearst, kidnaped Feb. 4, 1974, in San Francisco Sept. 18 with others. She was indicted for bank robbery; a San Francisco Jury convicted her Mar. 20, 1976.

Oil prices were raised 10% by the Organization of Petroleum Exporting Countries Oct. 1.

Price controls on domestic oil were temporarily restored in a compromise between Pres. Ford and Congress Sept. 25. Controls extension had been vetoed by Ford earlier.

A 5-year grain agreement under which the U.S. would sell and the USSR would purchase 6 to 8 million tons of grain per year was announced Oct. 20.

Pres. Ford refused federal loan guarantees to N. Y. City Oct. 29 to save it from threatened bankruptcy, claiming such guarantees would be "a bailout."

For events of 1976 and late 1975,
see Chronology.

100 Years Ago

In 1876, the United States celebrated its Centennial with a $10-million World Exhibition in Philadelphia, Pa. Ten million people visited the 236-acre fairgrounds which featured some 100 exhibits dedicated to American social, industrial, and cultural progress. On display were the self-binding reaper, the web printing press, the typewriter, the Corliss engine, and Alexander Graham Bell's first telephone, patented that year. Fifty foreign nations also sent exhibits in honor of the 100th birthday of the United States.

The opening ceremonies of the exhibition which were attended by Pres. U. S. Grant and Brazil's Emperor Don Pedro, the first major foreign potentate to visit the U. S., were disrupted by 5 women, including Susan B. Anthony, who presented a declaration of women's rights.

Custer's Last Stand

On June 25, during the Second Sioux War, 36-year-old Col. George A. Custer and more than 260 soldiers of the 7th Cavalry were massacred at the Battle of Little Big Horn, Mont., by 3,500 Sioux and Cheynne braves led by Sitting Bull and Crazy Horse. President Grant had sent Custer to search out and destroy the local Sioux. The Sioux were finally defeated and forced to surrender on Oct. 31.

The House of Representatives, July 2, impeached Grant's secretary of war, William W. Belknap, on 5 charges, including taking a $1,500-bribe in return for allowing a trading establishment at Ft. Sill, a U. S. military post, to continue in operation. Belknap resigned immediately. The Senate, Aug. 1, acquitted the war secretary because many senators believed they could not try an official who had resigned.

On Aug. 2, James McCall, a desperado, shot and killed James Butler "Wild Bill" Hickock in Deadwood, S. Dak. The local vigilante committee acquitted McCall, but the U. S. Court in Yankton, S. Dak., convicted him and McCall was hanged.

Colorado joined the union as the 38th state in August.

In the election of 1876, the Democrat, Samuel J. Tilden, who had destroyed New York City's Tweed Ring, won a popular majority of 250,000 votes over the Republican candidate, Rutherford B. Hayes. Hayes, a relative unknown from Ohio, had been nominated on the convention's 7th ballot. The Republican favorite, James G. Blaine, had come into disfavor just before the convention when he had been accused of taking railroad graft. In the electoral college, Tilden won 184 votes against Hayes' 163, but 22 votes — from South Carolina, Florida, Louisiana, and Oregon — were disputed. A bitter contest for votes, marked by charges of corruption and buying of votes, followed. The final decision was left to Congress which appointed an electoral commission composed of 8 Republicans and 7 Democrats. In early 1877, the commission gave the election to Hayes with a strict party-line vote.

Discontent Boils in Balkans

The Balkans remained a hotbed of anti-Turkish discontent. Turkish efforts to suppress an April uprising in Bulgaria led to war with Serbia and Montenegro in

July and pressure from the European powers for Turkish reforms. In order to placate the Europeans, in December, Turkey proclaimed a constitution and parliamentary government. However, because the Turks refused to make any actual concessions or cede further authority to Europe in its dominions, the situation in the Balkans remained volatile.

On the other side of the world, Korea ended several centuries of stringent isolationism as a "hermit kingdom," by opening its ports to Japan. China completed its first railroad in the same year.

In England, Benjamin Disraeli was named the Earl of Beaconsfield. In Germany, the Bayreuth Festspielhaus opened with the first complete performance of Richard Wagner's "Ring of Nibelungen." Johannes Brahms composed his Symphony No. 1. Stephane Mallarme, a leader of the French symbolist poets, published his dramatic poem, "L'Apres-midi d'un faune." Pierre-Auguste Renoir, one of the most famous of the French Impressionists, painted "Le Moulin de la galette," one of his masterpieces. Henry James published his first novel, *Roderick Hudson*. Mark Twain's *The Adventures of Tom Sawyer* was published and sold by subscription. The book became a best-seller, but was, nevertheless, banned by the Denver Public Library.

First Telephone Conversation

On Mar. 10, in his Boston, Mass., home, Alexander Graham Bell spoke the words, "Come here Watson, I want you," the first distinguishable telephone message, to Thomas Watson who was listening on a receiver on another floor in the same house. On Oct. 9, the first telephone conversation over outside wires took place between Cambridge and Boston.

Using the "broom-action" principle, Melville Reuben Bissell of Grand Rapids, Mich., invented the first practical carpet sweeper. The patent was obtained Sept. 19.

Johns Hopkins University opened in 1876 in Baltimore, Md., as the first U. S. establishment primarily for graduate study. Yale University awarded the first Doctor of Philosophy degree to a black, Edward Alexander Bouchet. He had graduated from Yale in 1874 where he had become the first black elected to Phi Beta Kappa.

Eight professional baseball teams were incorporated into the U. S. National Baseball League, administered by one set of enforceable rules. Previously, amateur games had been riddled with bribery and betting. Yale University won the first intercollegiate football championship and the first U. S. tennis tournament was held at Nahant, Mass.

Dr. Felix Adler founded the New York Society for Ethical Culture in New York City. The movement which became international emphasized moral excellence as the goal of mankind. The first free kindergarten opened in Florence, Mass., and Juliet Corison opened the New York Cooking School, the first such school in the U. S.

George Sand, the French writer, and Michael Bakunin, the Russian socialist, politician and writer, died in 1876. Konrad Adenauer, Jack London, Pablo Casals, Bruno Walter, and Eugenio Pacelli, who would become Pope Pius XII, were born in the same year.

Some Notable Marine Disasters Since 1865

(Figures Indicate Estimated Lives Lost)

1865, Apr. 27—Sultana; a Mississippi River steamer blew up; 1,400.

1868, Mar. 18—Magnolia; steamboat blew up on Ohio River; 80.

1868, Apr. 9—Sea Bird; steamer burned on Lake Michigan; 100.

1868, Dec. 4—United States and America; steamboats collided, burned, on Ohio River near Warsaw, Ky.; 72.

1869, Oct. 27—Stonewall; steamer burned on Mississippi River below Cairo, Ill.; 200.

1870, Jan. 24—Oneida; American ship sank in collision off Yokohama; 115.

1870, Jan. 28—City of Boston; American steamer of Inman Line vanished between New York and Liverpool; 191.

1871, July 30—Westfield; Staten Island ferryboat exploded in New York Harbor; 100.

1872, Nov. 7—Mary Celeste; American half-brig sailed from New York for Genoa; found abandoned in Atlantic 4 weeks later in mystery of sea; crew never heard from; loss of life unknown.

1873, Jan. 22—Northfleet; British steamer foundered off Dungeness, England; 300.

1873, Apr. 1—Atlantic; British (White Star) steamer wrecked off Nova Scotia; 547.

1873, Nov. 23—Ville de Havre; French steamer, New York to Havre, sank after collision with Loch Earn; 230.

1875, Nov. 7—Schiller; German mail steamer wrecked off Scilly Islands; 200.

1875, Nov. 4—Pacific; American steamer sank after collision off Cape Flattery; 236.

1875, Dec. 6—Deutschland; German steamer, Bremen to New York, wrecked at mouth of Thames; 157.

1877, Nov. 24—Huron; U. S. warship wrecked off North Carolina; 100.

1878, Jan. 31—Metropolis; American steamer wrecked off North Carolina; 100.

1878, Sept. 3—Princess Alice; British steamer sank after collision in Thames; 700.

1878, Dec. 18—Byzantin; French steamer sank after Dardanelles collision; 210.

1880, Nov. 24—Uncle Joseph; French steamer sank in collision off Spezzia, Greece; 250.

1881, May 24—Victoria; steamer capsized in Thames River, Canada; 200.

1883, Jan. 19—Cambria; German steamer hit iceberg in North Sea; 389.

1884, Jan. 18—City of Columbus; American steamer wrecked off Gay Head Light, Mass.; 103.

1887, Nov. 15—Wah Yeung; British steamer burned at sea; 400.

1890, Feb. 17—Duburg; British steamer wrecked, China Sea; 400.

1890, Sept. 19—Ertogrul; Turkish frigate foundered off Japan; 540.

1891, Mar. 17—Utopia; British steamer sank in collision off Gibraltar; 574.

1895, Jan. 30—Elbe; German steamer sank in collision with British steamer Crathie in North Sea; 335.

1895, Mar. 11—Reina Regenta; Spanish cruiser foundered near Gibraltar; 400.

1898, Feb. 15—Maine; U.S. battleship blown up in Havana Harbor; 266.

1898, July 4—La Bourgogne, Cromartyshire; French steamer and British sailing ship collided off Nova Scotia; 560.

1898, Nov. 26—Portland; American steamer wrecked off Cape Cod; 157.

1900, June 30—Main, Bremen and Saale; German steamers destroyed in $10 million dock fire at Hoboken, N.J.; 145.

1901, Feb. 22—Rio de Janeiro; American mail steamer wrecked in San Francisco Harbor; 128.

1903, June 7—Libau; French steamer sank in collision near Marseilles; 150.

1904, June 15—General Slocum; excursion steamer burned in East River, New York City; 1,030.

1904, June 28—Norge; steamer wrecked on Rockall Reef off Scotland; 590.

1906, Jan. 22—Valencia; American steamer lost off Vancouver Island; 129.

1906, Aug. 4—Sirio; Italian steamer wrecked off Cape Palos, Spain; 350.

1907, Feb. 12—Larchmont; American steamer sank in Long Island Sound; 131.

1908, Mar. 23—Matsu Maru; Japanese steamer sank in collision near Hakodate, Japan; 300.

1909, Aug. 1—Waratah; British steamer, Sydney to London, vanished; 300.

1910, Feb. 9—General Chanzy; French steamer wrecked off Minorca, Spain; 200.

1911, Sept. 25—Liberte; French battleship exploded at Toulon; 285.

1912, Mar. 5—Principe de Asturias; Spanish steamer wrecked off Spanish coast; 500.

1912, Apr. 14-15—Titanic; British (White Star) liner hit iceberg in North Atlantic; 1,517.

1912, Sept. 28—Kichemaru; Japanese steamer sank off Japanese coast; 1,000.

1913, Mar. 1—Calvados; British steamer lost in Sea of Marmora, Turkey; 200.

1914, May 29—Empress of Ireland; Canadian steamer sank after collision with collier in St. Lawrence River; 1,024.

1915, May 7—Lusitania; British (Cunard Line) steamer torpedoed by German submarine, sank off Ireland; 1,198.

1915, July 24—Eastland; excursion steamer capsized in Chicago River; 812.

1916, Feb. 26—Provence; French cruiser sank in Mediterranean; 3,100.

1916, Aug. 29—Hsin Yu; Chinese steamer sank off Chinese coast; 1,000.

1917, Dec. 6—Mont Blanc, Imo; French ammunition ship and Belgian steamer collided in Halifax Harbor; 1,600.

1918, Apr. 25—Kiang-Kwan Chinese steamer sank in collision off Hankow; 500.

1918, July 12—Kawachi; Japanese battleship blew up in Tokayama Bay; 500.

1918, Oct. 25—Princess Sophia; Canadian steamer sank off Alaskan coast; 398.

1919, Jan. 17—Chaonia; French steamer lost in Straits of Messina, Italy; 460.

1919, Sept. 9—Valbanera; Spanish steamer lost off Florida coast; 500.

1921, Mar. 18—Hong Kong; steamer wrecked in South China Sea; 1,000.

1922, Aug. 26—Niitaka; Japanese cruiser sank in storm off Kamchatka, USSR; 300.

1923, Apr. 23—Mossamedes; Portuguese mail steamer went aground at Cape Frio, Africa; 220.

1924, Jan. 10—L-24; British submarine in collision off Portland, England; 48.

1924, Mar. 19—No. 43; Japanese submarine in collision off Sasebo, Japan; 49.

1925, Sept. 25—S-51; American submarine in collision with steamer City of Rome off Block Island, R. I.; 34.

1925, Nov. 11—M-1; British submarine in English Channel collision; 69.

1927, Oct. 25—Principessa Mafalda; Italian steamer blew up, sank off Porto Seguro, Brazil; 314.

1927, Dec. 17—S-4; American submarine in collision off Provincetown, Mass.; 40.

1928, Nov. 12—Vestris; British steamer sank in gale off Virginia coast; 113.

1934, Sept. 8—Morro Castle; American steamer, Havana to New York, burned off Asbury Park, N. J.; 125.

1939, May 23—Squalus; American submarine sank off Portsmouth, N. H.; 26.

1941, June 16—O-9; American submarine lost in test dive off Maine; 33.

1942, Feb. 18—Truxton and Pollux; American destroyer and cargo ship ran aground, sank off Newfoundland; 204.

1942, Oct. 2—Curacao; British cruiser sank after collision with liner Queen Mary; 335.

1947, Jan. 19—Himera; Greek steamer hit a mine off Athens; 392.

1947, Apr. 16—Grandcamp; French freighter exploded in Texas City, Tex., Harbor, starting fires; 510.

1949, Sept. 17—Noronic; Canadian Great Lakes steamer burned at Toronto; 119.

1950, Jan. 12—Truculent; British submarine in Thames collision; 65.

1951, Apr. 16—Affray; British submarine lost in English Channel; 75.

1952, Apr. 26—Hobson and Wasp; American destroyer and aircraft carrier collided in Atlantic; 176.

1952, Sept. 24—La Sibylle; French submarine lost off Toulon; 48.

1953, Oct. 16—Leyte; U.S. aircraft carrier damaged by explosion below decks in Boston; 37.

1954, May 26—Bennington; U.S. aircraft carrier damaged by explosions, fire, off Quonset Point, R. I.; 103.
1954, Sept. 26—Toya Maru; Japanese ferry sank in Tsugaru Strait, Japan; 1,172.
1956, July 26—Andrea Doria and Stockholm; Italian liner and Swedish liner collided off Nantucket; 51.
1957, July 14—Eshghabad; Soviet ship ran aground in Caspian Sea; 270.
1959, Jan. 30—Hans Hedtoft; Danish passenger-freighter hit iceberg, Greenland; 95.
1960, Dec. 19—Constellation; U.S. aircraft carrier burned in Brooklyn Navy Yard; 50.
1961, Apr. 8—Dara; British liner burned in Persian Gulf; 212.
1961, July 8—Save; Portuguese ship ran aground off Mozambique; 259.
1963, Feb. 3—Marine Sulphur Queen; American tanker vanished in Gulf of Mexico; 39.
1963, Apr. 10—Thresher; U.S. Navy atomic submarine sank in North Atlantic; 129.
1964, Feb. 10—Voyager, Melbourne; Australian destroyer sank after collision with Australian aircraft carrier Melbourne off New South Wales; 82.
1965, Nov. 13—Yarmouth Castle; Panamanian registered cruise ship burned, sank off Nassau; 89.
1966, Oct. 26—Oriskany; U.S. aircraft carrier caught fire, Gulf of Tonkin; 43.
1967, July 29—Forrestal; U.S. aircraft carrier caught fire off North Vietnam; 134.

1968, Jan. 25—Dakar; Israeli submarine vanished in Mediterranean; 69.
1968, Jan. 27—Minerve; French submarine vanished in Mediterranean; 52.
1968, May 21—Scorpion; U.S. nuclear submarine sank in Atlantic near Azores; 99.
1969, Jan. 14—Enterprise; U.S. aircraft carrier suffered fires and explosions off Hawaii; 27.
1969, June 2—Evans; U.S. destroyer cut in half by Australian carrier Melbourne, S. China Sea; 74.
1970, Mar. 4—Eurydice; French submarine sank in Mediterranean near Toulon; 57.
1970, Dec. 15—Namyong-Ho; South Korean ferry sank in Korea Strait; 308.
1973, May 5— Three river boats collided near Dacca, Bangladesh; c. 250.
1973, Dec. 24— Ferry capsized off coast of Ecuador; nearly 200.
1974, Feb. 22— Ferry capsized off Chungmu, So. Korea; 157.
1974, May 1— Motor launch capsized off Bangladesh coast; 250.
1974, Sept. 26— Soviet destroyer burned and sank in Black Sea; est. 200.
1974, Oct. 25— Ferry capsized off Bangladesh coast; over 200.
1975, Aug. 9— Two Chinese riverboats collided and sank near Canton; c. 500.

(See also Chronology)

Floods, Tidal Waves

Date, Location, Number of Deaths—See also Chronology

1887	. . . .	Hwang-ho Riv., China.	900,000	1962	Sept. 27	Barcelona, Spain.	445
1889	May 31	Johnstown, Pa.	2,200	1963	Oct. 9	Dam collapse, Vaiont, Italy.	1,800
1900	Sept. 8	Galveston, Tex.	5,000	1965	June 11	Sanderson, Tex.	10
1903	June 15	Heppner, Ore.	325	1966	Nov. 4-6	Florence, Venice, Italy. . . .	113
1911	. . . .	Yangtze River, China.	100,000	1967	Jan. 18-24	Eastern Brazil.	894
1913	Mar. 25-27	Ohio, Indiana.	732	1967	Mar. 19	Rio de Janeiro, Brazil.	436
1915	Aug. 17	Galveston, Tex.	275	1968	Aug. 7-14	Gujarat state, India.	1,000
1927	. . . .	Mississippi River Valley. . .	214	1968	Oct. 7	Northeastern India.	780
1928	Mar. 13	Collapse of St. Francis		1969	Jan. 18-26	Southern California.	91
		Dam, Santa Paula, Cal. . . .	450	1969	Mar. 17	Mundau Valley, Alagoas,	
1928	Sept. 13	Lake Okeechobee, Fla. . . .	2,000			Brazil.	218
1937	Jan. 22	Ohio, Miss. Valleys.	250	1969	July 4	Northern Ohio.	41
1939	. . . .	Northern China.	200,000	1969	Oct. 1-8	Tunisia.	500
1947	. . . .	Honshu Island, Japan. . . .	1,900	1969	Aug. 25	Western Virginia.	189
1951	Aug.	Manchuria	1,800	1969	Sept. 15	South Korea.	250
1953	Jan. 31	Western Europe.	2,000	1970	May 20	Central Romania.	160
1954	Aug. 17	Farahzad, Iran.	2,000	1970	July 22	Himalayas, India.	500
1955	Oct. 7-12	India, Pakistan.	1,700	1971	Feb. 26	Rio de Janeiro, Brazil.	130
1959	Nov. 1	Western Mexico.	2,000	1972	June 9	Rapid City, S.D.	236
1959	Dec. 2	Frejus, France.	412	1972	Aug. 7	Luzon Is., Philippines.	454
1960	Oct. 10	East Pakistan.	6,000	1974	Mar. 29	Tubaro, Brazil	1,000
1960	Oct. 31	East Pakistan.	4,000	1974	Aug. 12	Monty-Long, Bangladesh. . .	2,500
1962	Feb. 17	German North Sea coast. . .	343	1975	Jan. 11	Southern Thailand.	131

Major Earthquakes

Source: U.S. Geological Survey, National Earthquake Information Service, and historical records.

Magnitude of earthquakes (Mag.), distinct from deaths or damage caused, is measured on the Richter scale, on which each higher number represents a tenfold increase. Adopted in 1935, the scale has been applied in the following table to earthquakes as far back as reliable seismograms are available.

Date		Place	Deaths	Mag.		Date	Place	Deaths	Mag.
526	May 20	Syria, Antioch	250,000	N.A.		1908	Dec. 28	Italy, Messina	83,000	7.5
856	. . . .	Greece, Corinth	45,000	"		1915	Jan. 13	Italy, Avezzano	29,980	7.5
1057	. . . .	China, Chihli	25,000	"		1920	Dec. 16	China, Kansu	100,000	8.6
1268	. . . .	Asia Minor, Cilicia . .	60,000	"		1923	Sept. 1	Japan, Tokyo	99,330	8.3
1290	Sept. 27	China, Chihli	100,000	"		1927	May 22	China, Nan-Shan	200,000	8.3
1293	May 20	Japan, Kamakura	30,000	"		1932	Dec. 26	China, Kansu	70,000	7.6
1531	Jan. 26	Portugal, Lisbon	30,000	"		1933	Mar. 2	Japan	2,990	8.9
1556	Jan. 24	China, Shensi	830,000	"		1933	Mar. 10	Cal., Long Beach	115.	6.3
1667	Nov.	Caucasia, Shemaka . .	80,000	"		1934	Jan. 15	India, Bihar-Nepal. . .	10,700	8.4
1693	Jan. 11	Italy, Catania	60,000	"		1935	May 31	India, Quetta	30,000	7.5
1730	Dec. 30	Japan, Hokkaido. . . .	137,000	"		1939	Jan. 24	Chile, Chillan	28,000	8.3
1737	Oct. 11	India, Calcutta.	300,000	"		1939	Dec. 26	Turkey, Erzincan	30,000	7.9
1755	June 7	Northern Persia. . . .	40,000	"		1946	May 31	Eastern Turkey	1,300	6.0
1755	Nov. 1	Portugal, Lisbon	60,000	8.75*		1946	Dec. 21	Japan, Honshu.	2,000	8.4
1783	Feb. 4	Italy, Calabria	30,000	N.A.		1948	June 28	Japan, Fukui	5,131	7.3
1797	Feb. 4	Ecuador, Quito	41,000	N.A.		1949	Aug. 5	Ecuador, Pelileo. . . .	6,000	6.8
1811	Dec. 16	Missouri, New Madrid		7.2*		1950	Aug. 15	India, Assam	1,530	8.7
1822	Sept. 5	Asia Minor, Aleppo . .	22,000	N.A.		1953	Mar. 18	NW Turkey	1,200	7.2
1828	Dec. 28	Japan, Echigo	30,000	"		1954	Sept. 9-12	Northern Algeria. . . .	1,250	6.8
1868	Aug. 13-15	Peru and Ecuador . . .	40,000	"		1956	June 10-17	" Afghanistan	2,000	7.7
1875	May 16	Venezuela, Colombia	16,000	"		1957	July 2	Northern Iran	2,500	7.4
1896	June 15	Japan, sea wave	27,120	"		1957	Dec. 13	Western Iran	2,000	7.1
1906	Apr. 18-19	Cal., San Francisco . .	452	8.3		1960	Feb. 29	Morocco, Agadir. . . .	12,000	5.8
1906	Aug. 16	Chile, Valparaiso . . .	20,000	8.6		1960	May 21-30	Southern Chile	5,000	8.3

1962	Sept. 1	Northwestern Iran..	12,230	7.1
1963	July 26	Yugoslavia, Skopje..	1,100	6.0
1964	Mar. 27	Alaska.............	114	8.5
1966	Aug. 19	Eastern Turkey....	2,520	6.9
1968	Aug. 31	Northeastern Iran..	12,000	7.4
1970	Mar. 28	Western Turkey....	1,086	7.4
1970	May 31	Northern Peru.....	66,794	7.7
1971	Feb. 9	Southern California.	65	6.5
1972	Apr. 10	Southern Iran......	5,057	6.9
1972	Dec. 23	Nicaragua.........	5,000	6.2
1974	Dec. 28	Pakistan (9 towns)...	5,200	6.3
1975	Sept. 6	Turkey (Lice, etc.)....	2,312	6.8
1976	Feb. 4	Guatemala.........	22,778	7.5
1976	May 6	Northeast Italy.....	946	6.5

(*) estimated from earthquake intensity.
(N.A.) not available.

Fires

Date, Location and Number of Deaths. *See also Chronology*

1871	Oct. 8	Chicago, $196 million loss......	250
1871	Oct. 9	Peshtigo, Wis., forest fire......	1,182
1876	Dec. 5	Brooklyn (N.Y.), theater........	295
1877	June 20	St. John, N. B., Canada.........	100
1881	Dec. 8	Ring Theater, Vienna...........	850
1887	May 25	Opera Comique, Paris..........	200
1887	Sept. 4	Exeter, England, theater........	200
1894	Sept. 1	Hinckley, Minn., forest fire......	413
1897	May 4	Charity bazaar, Paris..........	150
1900	June 30	Hoboken, N. J., docks..........	326
1902	Sept. 20	Church, Birmingham, Ala.......	115
1903	Dec. 30	Iroquois Theater, Chicago.......	602
1904	Feb. 7	Baltimore, Md................	0
1908	Jan. 13	Rhoads Thea., Boyertown, Pa....	170
1908	Mar. 4	School, Collinwood, Oh........	176
1911	Mar. 25	Triangle factory, N. Y. City......	145
1914	June 26	1,000 bldgs., Salem, Mass.......	0
1918	Apr. 13	Norman, Okla., state hospital....	38
1918	Oct. 12	Cloquet, Minn., forest fire......	400
1919	June 20	Mayaguez Theater, San Juan....	150
1923	May 17	School, Camden, S. C..........	76
1924	Dec. 24	School, Hobart, Okla..........	35
1929	May 15	Clinic, Cleveland, Oh..........	125
1930	Apr. 21	Penitentiary, Columbus, Oh......	320
1931	July 24	Pittsburgh, Pa., home for aged...	48
1938	May 16	Atlanta, Ga., Terminal Hotel.....	35
1940	Apr. 23	Dance hall, Natchez, Miss.......	198
1942	Nov. 28	Cocoanut Grove, Boston........	491
1943	Sept. 7	Gulf Hotel, Houston...........	55
1944	July 6	Ringling Circus, Hartford.......	168
1946	June 5	LaSalle Hotel, Chicago.........	61
1946	Dec. 7	Winecoff Hotel, Atlanta........	119
1946	Dec. 12	New York, ice plant, tenement...	37
1949	Apr. 5	Hospital, Effingham, Ill........	77
1950	Jan. 7	Davenport, Ia., Mercy Hospital...	41
1953	Mar. 29	Largo, Fla., nursing home.......	35
1953	Apr. 16	Chicago, metalworking plant.....	35
1957	Feb. 17	Home for aged, Warrenton, Mo...	72
1957	Nov. 16	Niagara Falls, N. Y., tenement....	18
1958	Mar. 19	New York City loft building.....	24
1958	Nov. 8	Tenement, Montreal, Canada....	21
1958	Dec. 1	Parochial school, Chicago.......	95
1958	Dec. 16	Store, Bogota, Colombia........	83
1959	Mar. 5	School near Little Rock, Ark.....	24
1959	June 23	Resort hotel, Stalheim, Norway..	34
1960	Mar. 12	Pusan, Korea, chemical plant....	68
1960	June 11	Liverpool, England, store.......	22
1960	July 14	Mental hospital, Guatemala City.	225
1960	Nov. 13	Movie theater, Amude, Syria....	152
1961	Jan. 6	Thomas Hotel, San Francisco....	20
1961	May 15	Tenement, Hong Kong.........	25
1961	Dec. 8	Hospital, Hartford, Conn........	16
1961	Dec. 17	Circus, Niteroi, Brazil.........	323
1963	May 4	Theater, Diourbel, Senegal......	64
1963	Nov. 18	Surfside Hotel, Atlantic City, N.J.	25
1963	Nov. 23	Rest home, Fitchville, Oh.......	63
1963	Dec. 29	Roosevelt Hotel, Jacksonville, Fla.	22
1964	May 8	Apartment building, Manila.....	30
1964	Dec. 18	Nursing home, Fountaintown, Ind.	20
1965	Mar. 1	Apartment, LaSalle, Canada.....	28
1965	Dec. 20	Jewish center, Yonkers, N. Y.....	12
1966	Mar. 11	Numata, Japan, 2 ski resorts....	31
1966	Aug. 13	Melbourne, Australia, hotel.....	29
1966	Sept. 12	Anchorage, Alaska, hotel........	14
1966	Oct. 17	N. Y. City bldg. (firemen).......	12
1966	Dec. 7	Erzurum, Turkey, barracks......	68
1967	Feb. 7	Restaurant, Montgomery, Ala....	25
1967	May 22	Store, Brussels, Belgium........	322
1967	July 16	State prison, Jay, Fla..........	37
1968	Jan. 9	Brooklyn, N. Y., tenement......	13
1968	Feb. 16	Moberly, Mo., tavern.........	12
1968	Feb. 26	Shrewsbury, England, hospital...	22
1968	May 11	Vijayawada, India, wedding hall	58
1968	Nov. 18	Glasgow, Scotland, factory.....	24
1969	Jan. 26	Victoria Hotel, Dunnville, Ont....	13
1969	Dec. 2	Nursing home, Notre Dame, Can.	54
1970	Jan. 9	Nursing home, Marietta, Oh.....	27
1970	Mar. 20	Hotel, Seattle, Wash..........	19
1970	Nov. 1	Dance hall, Grenoble, France....	145
1970	Nov. 5	Nursing home, Pointe-aux-Trembles, Que.	17
1970	Dec. 20	Hotel, Tucson, Arizona........	28
1971	Mar. 6	Psychiatric clinic, Burghoezli, Switzerland...........	28
1971	Apr. 20	Hotel, Bangkok, Thailand......	24
1971	Oct. 19	Nursing home, Honesdale, Pa....	15
1972	July 5	Sherborne, England, hospital....	30
1973	Feb. 6	Paris, France, school..........	21
1973	Nov. 6	Fukui, Japan, train...........	28
1973	Nov. 29	Kumamoto, Japan, department store...	107
1973	Dec. 2	Seoul, Korea, theater.........	50
1974	Feb. 1	Sao Paulo, Brazil, bank building...	189
1974	June 30	Port Chester, N.Y., discotheque..	24
1974	Nov. 3	Seoul, So. Korea, hotel discotheque........	88
1975	Dec. 12	Mina, Saudi Arabia, Tent City....	138

Major Railroad Wrecks in the U.S.

Source: Federal Railroad Admin., Office of Safety
Date, Location and Number of Deaths. *See also Chronology*

1876	Dec. 29	Ashtabula, Oh................	92
1880	Aug. 11	Mays Landing, N. J...........	40
1887	Aug. 10	Chatsworth, Ill..............	81
1888	Oct. 10	Mud Run, Pa................	55
1896	July 30	Atlantic City, N. J...........	60
1903	Dec. 23	Laurel Run, Pa..............	53
1904	Aug. 7	Eden, Col..................	96
1904	Sept. 24	New Market, Tenn...........	56
1906	Mar. 16	Florence, Col...............	35
1906	Oct. 28	Atlantic City, N.J...........	40
1906	Dec. 30	Washington, D. C............	53
1907	Jan. 2	Volland, Kan...............	33
1907	Jan. 19	Fowler, Ind................	29
1907	Feb. 16	New York City..............	22
1907	Feb. 23	Colton, Cal................	26
1907	July 20	Salem, Mich................	33
1907	Sept. 15	Canaan, N. H...............	24
1910	Mar. 1	Wellington, Wash............	96
1910	Mar. 21	Green Mountain, Ia..........	55
1911	Aug. 25	Manchester, N.Y............	29
1912	July 4	East Corning, N. Y..........	39
1912	July 5	Ligonier, Pa................	23
1913	Sept. 2	North Haven, Conn..........	21
1914	Aug. 5	Tipton Ford, Mo.............	43
1914	Sept. 15	Lebanon, Mo...............	28
1916	Mar. 29	Amherst, Oh................	27
1917	Feb. 27	Mount Union, Pa............	20
1917	Sept. 28	Kellyville, Okla.............	23
1917	Dec. 20	Shepherdsville, Ky..........	46
1918	June 22	Ivanhoe, Ind...............	68
1918	July 9	Nashville, Tenn.............	101
1918	Nov. 2	Brooklyn, N.Y., Malbone St. Tunnel..	97
1919	Jan. 12	South Byron, N. Y...........	22
1919	July 1	Dunkirk, N. Y...............	12
1919	Dec. 20	Onawa, Maine..............	23
1921	Feb. 27	Porter, Ind.................	37
1921	Dec. 5	Woodmont, Pa..............	27
1922	Aug. 5	Sulphur Spring, Mo..........	34
1922	Dec. 13	Humble, Tex................	22
1923	Sept. 27	Lockett, Wy................	31
1925	June 16	Hackettstown, N. J..........	50
1925	Oct. 27	Victoria, Miss..............	21
1926	Sept. 5	Waco, Col..................	30
1928	Aug. 24	I.R.T subway, N.Y., Times Sq....	18
1938	June 19	Saugus, Mont...............	47
1939	Aug. 12	Harney, Nev................	24

1940	Apr. 19	Little Falls, N. Y.	31	1951	Feb. 6	Woodbridge, N. J.	84
1940	July 31	Cuyahoga Falls, Ohio.	43	1951	Nov. 12	Wyuta, Wyo.	17
1943	Aug. 29	Wayland, N. Y.	27	1951	Nov. 25	Woodstock, Ala.	17
1943	Sept. 6	Frankford Junction, Philadelphia	79	1953	Mar. 27	Conneaut, Ohio.	21
1943	Dec. 16	Between Rennert and Buie, N.C.	72	1956	Jan. 22	Los Angeles, Cal.	30
1944	July 6	High Bluff, Tenn.	35	1956	Feb. 28	Swampscott, Mass.	13
1944	Aug. 4	Near Stockton, Ga.	47	1956	Sept. 5	Springer, N. M.	20
1944	Sept. 14	Dewey, Ind.	29	1957	June 11	Vroman, Col.	12
1944	Dec. 31	Bagley, Utah.	50	1958	Sept. 15	Elizabethport, N. J.	48
1945	Aug. 9	Michigan, N. D.	34	1960	Mar. 14	Bakersfield, Cal.	14
1946	Apr. 25	Naperville, Ill.	45	1962	July 28	Steelton, Pa.	19
1947	Feb. 18	Gallitzin, Pa.	24	1966	Dec. 28	Everett, Mass.	13
1950	Feb. 17	Rockville Centre, N. Y.	31	1971	June 10	Salem, Ill.	11
1950	Sept. 11	Coshocton, Ohio.	33	1972	Oct. 30	Chicago, Ill.	45
1950	Nov. 22	Richmond Hill, N. Y.	79				

World's worst train wreck occurred Dec. 12, 1917, Modane, France, passenger train derailed, 543 killed.

Historic Assassinations Since 1865

1865—Apr. 14. U. S. President Abraham Lincoln, shot in Washington, D. C.; died Apr. 15.

1881—Mar. 13. Alexander II, of Russia—July 2. James A. Garfield, president of the United States, in Washington; died Sept. 19.

1900—July 29. Umberto I, king of Italy.

1901—Sept. 6. U. S. President William McKinley in Buffalo, N.Y., died Sept. 14. Leon Czolgosz executed for the crime Oct. 29.

1913—Feb. 23. Francisco. I. Madero, president of Mexico and Jose Pino Suarez, the vice-president.— Mar. 18. George, king of Greece.

1914—June 28. Archduke Francis Ferdinand of Austria-Hungary and his wife in Sarajevo, Bosnia (later part of Yugoslavia), by Gavrillo Princip.

1916—Dec. 30. Grigori Rasputin, politically powerful Russian monk.

1918—July 12. Grand Duke Michael of Russia, at Perm.—July 16. Nicholas II, abdicated as czar of Russia; his wife, the Czarina Alexandra, their son, Czarevitch Alexis, and their daughters, Grand Duchesses Olga, Tatiana, Marie, Anastasia, and 4 members of their household were murdered by Bolsheviks at Ekaterinburg.

1920—May 20. Gen. Venustiano Carranza, president of Mexico, in Tiaxcaltenago.

1922—Aug. 22. Michael Collins, Irish revolutionary.

1923—July 20. Gen. Francisco "Pancho" Villa, ex-rebel leader, in Parral, Mexico.

1928—July 17. Gen. Alvaro Obregon, president-elect of Mexico, in San Angel, Mexico.

1933—Feb. 15. In Miami, Fla., Joseph Zangara, anarchist, shot at President-elect Franklin D. Roosevelt, but a woman seized his arm, and the bullet fatally wounded Mayor Anton J. Cermak, of Chicago, who died Mar. 6. Zangara was electrocuted on Mar. 20, 1933.

1934—July 25. In Vienna, Engelbert Dollfuss, Chancellor of Austria, by Nazi, in the chancellery. Otto Planetta convicted and hanged.

1935—Sept. 8. U. S. Senator Huey P. Long, shot in Baton Rouge, La., by Dr. Carl Austin Weiss, who was slain by Long's bodyguards.

1940—Aug. 20. Leon Trotsky (Lev Bronstein), 63, exiled Russian war minister, near Mexico City. Killer identified as Ramon Mercador del Rio, a Spaniard, served 20 years in Mexican prison.

1948—Jan. 30. Mohandas K. Gandhi, 78, shot in New Delhi, India, by Nathuran Vinayak Godse, 36— Sept. 17. Count Folke Bernadotte, UN mediator for Palestine, ambushed in Jerusalem.

1951—July 20. King Abdul ibn Hussein of Jordan.

1956—Sept. 21. Anastasio Somoza, president of Nicaragua, in Leon; died Sept. 29.

1957—July 26. President Carlos Castillo Armas of Guatemala, in Guatemala City by one of his own guards, who then committed suicide.

1958—July 14. King Faisal of Iraq; his uncle, Crown Prince Abdul Illah, and July 15, Premier Nuri as-Said, by rebels in Baghdad.

1959—Sept. 25. Prime Minister S.W.R.D. Bandaranaike of Ceylon, by Buddhist monk in Colombo.

1961—Jan. 17. Ex-Premier Patrice Lumumba of the Congo, in Katanga Province—May 30. Dominican dictator Rafael Leonidas Trujillo-Molina shot to death by assassins near Ciudad Trujillo.

1963—Jan. 13. President Sylvanus Olympio of Togo, by ex-soldiers at Lome.—June 12. Medgar W. Evers, NAACP's Mississippi field secretary, in Jackson, Miss.—Nov. 12. President Ngo Dinh Diem of the Republic of Vietnam and his brother, Ngo Dinh Nhu, in a military coup.—Nov. 22. U. S. President John F. Kennedy fatally shot in Dallas, Tex.; accused Lee Harvey Oswald murdered while awaiting trial.

1965—Jan. 21. Irani Premier Hassan Ali Mansour fatally wounded by assassin in Teheran; 4 executed. —Feb. 21. Malcolm X, Negro nationalist, fatally shot in N. Y. City; 3 sentenced to life.

1966—Sept. 6. Prime Minister Hendrik F. Verword of South Africa stabbed to death in parliament at Capetown by drifter later ruled insane.

1968—Apr. 4. Rev. Dr. Martin Luther King Jr. fatally shot in Memphis, Tenn.; James Earl Ray sentenced to 99 years.—June 5. Sen. Robert F. Kennedy (D-N.Y.) fatally shot in Los Angeles; Sirhan Sirhan, resident alien, convicted of murder.

1969—July 5. Tom Mboya, Kenya's minister of economic planning and development, in Nairobi.—Oct. 17. A. A. Shermarke, president of Somalia, at Las Anos, Somalia.

1971—Nov. 28. Jordan Prime Minister Wasfi Tal, in Cairo, by Palestinian guerrillas.

1973—Mar. 2. U. S. Ambassador Cleo A. Noel Jr., U. S. Charge d'Affaires George C. Moore and Belgian Charge d'Affaires Guy Eid tortured and killed by Palestinian guerrillas in Khartoum.

1974—Aug. 15. Mrs. Park Chung Hee, wife of president of South Korea, hit by bullet meant for her husband. Police said plot was organized in No. Korea.— Aug. 19. U. S. Ambassador to Cyprus, Rodger P. Davies, killed by sniper's bullet in Nicosia.

1975—Feb. 11. President Richard Ratsimandrava, 43, of Madagascar, machine-gunned in Tananarive.— Mar. 25. King Faisal of Saudi Arabia shot by nephew Prince Musad Abdel Aziz, 31, in royal palace, Riyadh.

1975—May 21. U.S. Col. Paul R. Shaffer Jr. and U.S. Lt. Col. John H. Turner slain by 3 Iranian terrorists in Tehran.

1975—Aug. 15. Bangladesh President Sheik Mujibur Rahman and wife and son killed in army coup.

1976—Feb. 13. Nigerian head of state, Gen. Murtala Ramat Mohammed, slain by self-styled "young revolutionaries." Several arrests were made.

Assassination Attempts

1910—Aug. 6. N. Y. City Mayor Wm. J. Gaynor shot and seriously wounded by discharged city employee.

1912—Oct. 14. Former U. S. President Theodore Roosevelt shot and seriously wounded by demented man in Milwaukee.

1950—Nov. 1. In an attempt to assassinate President Truman, 2 men identified as members of a Puerto Rican nationalist movement — Griselio Torresola and Oscar Collazo — tried to shoot their way into Blair House. Torresola was killed, and a guard, Pvt. Leslie Coffelt was fatally shot. Collazo, wounded, recovered and was tried and convicted Mar. 7, 1951 for the murder of Coffelt. His death sentence was commuted to life imprisonment by President Truman.

1970—Nov. 27. Pope Paul VI unharmed by knife-wielding assailant dressed as priest who attempted to attack him in Manila airport. Benjamin Mendoza,

Bolivian, charged with attempted murder.

1972—May 15. Alabama Gov. George Wallace shot in Laurel, Md.; seriously crippled.

1972—Dec. 7. Mrs. Ferdinand E. Marcos, wife of the Philippine president, was stabbed and seriously injured in Pasay City, Philippines.

See also Chronology and Memorable Dates.

Major Kidnapings

Edward A. Cudahy Jr., 16, in Omaha, Neb., **Dec. 18, 1900.** Returned Dec. 20 after $25,000 paid. Pat Crowe confessed.

Robert Franks, 13, in Chicago, **May 22, 1924**, by two youths, Loeb and Leopold, who killed boy. Demand for $10,000 ignored. Loeb died in prison, Leopold paroled 1958, freed 1963.

Charles A. Lindbergh Jr., 20 mos. old, in Hopewell, N.J., **Mar. 1, 1932;** found dead May 12. Ransom of $50,000 was paid to man identified as Bruno Richard Hauptmann, 35, paroled German convict who entered U.S. illegally. Hauptmann passed ransom bill and $14,000 marked money was found in his garage. He was convicted after spectacular trial at Flemington, and electrocuted in Trenton, N.J., prison, Apr. 3, 1936.

William A. Hamm Jr., 39, in St. Paul, **June 15, 1933.** $100,000 paid. Alvin Karpis given life, paroled in 1969.

Charles F. Urschel, in Oklahoma City, **July 22, 1933.** Released July 31 after $200,000 paid. George (Machine Gun) Kelly and 5 others given life.

George Weyerhaeuser, 9, in Tacoma, Wash., **May 24, 1935.** Returned home June 1 after $200,000 paid. Kidnapers given 20 to 60 years.

Charles Mattson, 10, in Tacoma, Wash., **Dec. 27, 1936.** Found dead Jan. 11, 1937. Kidnaper asked $28,000, failed to contact.

Arthur Fried, in White Plains, N. Y., **Dec. 4, 1937.** Body not found. Two kidnapers executed.

Peter Levine, 12, in New Rochelle, N. Y., **Feb. 24, 1938.** Dismembered body found May 29.

Robert C. Greenlease, 6, son of a Kansas City, Mo., motor car dealer, taken from school **Sept. 28, 1953**, and held for $600,000. Body found Oct. 7, when Mrs. Bonnie Brown Heady and Carl A. Hall were arrested. They pleaded guilty and were executed Dec. 18.

Peter Weinberger, 32 days old, Westbury, N.Y., **July 4, 1956**, for $2,000 ransom, not paid. Child found dead. Angelo John LaMarca, 31, convicted, executed.

Cynthia Ruotolo, 6 wks. old, taken from carriage in front of Hamden, Conn. store **Sept. 1, 1956.** Body found in lake.

Lee Crary, 8, in Everett, Wash., **Sept. 22, 1957**, for $10,-000 ransom, not paid. Escaped after 3 days, led police to George E. Collins, convicted.

Eric Peugeot, 4, taken from playground at St. Cloud golf course, Paris, **Apr. 12, 1960.** Released unharmed 3 days later after payment of undisclosed sum to kidnaper who had demanded $100,000. Two sentenced to prison.

Frank Sinatra Jr., 19, from hotel room in Lake Tahoe, Cal., **Dec. 8, 1963.** Released Dec. 11 after his father paid $240,000 ransom. John W. Irwin, Barry W. Keenan and Joseph C. Amsler sentenced to prison; most of ransom recovered.

Barbara Jane Mackle, 20, abducted **Dec. 17, 1968**, from Atlanta, Ga., motel, was found unharmed 3 days later, buried in a coffin-like wooden box 18 inches underground, after her father had paid $500,000 ransom; Gary Steven Krist sentenced to life, Ruth Eisenmann-Schier to 7 years; most of ransom recovered.

Anne Katherine Jenkins, 22, abducted **May 10, 1969**, from her Baltimore apartment, freed 3 days later after her father paid $10,000 ransom; Edward Lee Dull and Marie Calvert charged with crime.

Mrs. Roy Fuchs, 35, and 3 children held hostage 2 hours **May 14, 1969**, in Long Island, N.Y., released after her husband, a bank manager, paid kidnapers $129,000 in bank funds; 4 men arrested, ransom recovered.

C. Burke Elbrick, U.S. ambassador to Brazil, kidnaped by Brazilian revolutionaries in Rio de Janeiro **Sept. 4, 1969;** released 3 days later after Brazil yielded to kidnapers' demands by publishing manifesto and releasing 15 political prisoners.

Patrick Dolan, 18, found shot to death near Sao Paulo, Brazil, **Nov. 5, 1969**, after he was kidnaped and $12,500 paid.

Sean M. Holly, U.S. diplomat, in Guatemala **Mar. 6, 1970;** freed 2 days later upon release of 3 terrorists from prison.

Lt. Col. Donald J. Crowley, U.S. air attache, in Dominican Republic **Mar. 24, 1970;** released after government allowed 20 prisoners to leave the country.

Count Karl von Spreti, W. German ambassador to Guatemala, **Mar. 31, 1970;** slain after Guatemala refused demands for $700,000 and release of 22 prisoners.

Rudy W. Martinez, Guatemalan coffee exporter, by terrorists **Apr. 23, 1970;** released on payment of large ransom.

Pedro Eugenio Aramburu, former Argentine president, by terrorists **May 29, 1970;** body found July 17.

Ehrenfried von Holleben, W. German ambassador to Brazil, by terrorists **June 11, 1970;** freed after release of 40 prisoners.

Daniel A. Mitrione, U.S. diplomat, **July 31, 1970**, by terrorists in Montevideo, Uruguay; body found Aug. 10 after government rejected demands for release of all political prisoners.

Aloysio Dias Gomide, Brazilian vice consul, in Montevideo, **July 31, 1970;** released Feb. 21, 1971, after wife paid ransom estimated at over $250,000.

James R. Cross, British trade commissioner, **Oct. 5, 1970**, by French Canadian separatists in Quebec; freed Dec. 3 after 3 kidnapers and relatives flown to Cuba by government.

Pierre Laporte, Quebec Labor Minister, by separatists Oct. 10, 1970; body found Oct. 18.

Eugen Beihl, W. German businessman, by Basque separatists, in San Sebastian, Spain, **Dec. 1, 1970;** released Dec. 25 unharmed.

Giovanni E. Bucher, Swiss ambassador **Dec. 7, 1970**, by revolutionaries in Rio de Janeiro; freed Jan. 16, 1971, after Brazil released 70 political prisoners.

Geoffrey Jackson, British ambassador, in Montevideo, **Jan. 8, 1971**, by Tupamaro terrorists. Held as ransom for release of imprisoned terrorists, he was released Sept. 9, after the prisoners escaped.

Four U.S. airmen, in Ankara, by Turkish leftist terrorists on **Mar. 4, 1971.** $400,000 ransom was not paid, but the 4 were released unharmed Mar. 8.

Ephraim Elrom, Israel consul general in Istanbul, **May 17, 1971.** Held as ransom for imprisoned terrorists, was found dead May 23.

Mrs. Virginia Piper, 49, abducted **July 27, 1972**, from her home in suburban Minneapolis; found unharmed near Duluth 2 days later after her husband paid $1 million ransom to the kidnapers.

Victor E. Samuelson, Exxon executive, **Dec. 6, 1973**, in Campana, Argentina, by Marxist guerrillas, freed Apr. 29, 1974, after payment of record $14.2 million ransom.

J. Paul Getty 3d, 17, grandson of the U.S. oil mogul, released by kidnapers **Dec. 15, 1973**, in southern Italy after family paid $2.8 million ransom. Kidnapers had severed his right ear, sent it with ransom demand.

Patricia (Patty) Hearst, 19, taken from her Berkeley, Cal., apartment **Feb. 4, 1974.** Symbionese Liberation Army demanded her father, Randolph A. Hearst, publisher, give millions to poor. Hearst offered $2 million in food; the Hearst Corp. offered $4 million worth. Kidnapers objected to way food was distributed. Patricia, in message, said she had joined SLA; she was identified by FBI as taking part in a San Francisco bank holdup, **Apr. 15;** she claimed, in message, she had been coerced. Again identified by FBI in a store holdup, **May 16**, she was classified by FBI as "an armed, dangerous fugitive." FBI, **Sept. 18, 1975**, captured Patricia and others in San Francisco; they were indicted on various charges, Patricia for bank robbery. A San Francisco jury convicted her, **Mar. 20, 1976.**

J. Reginald Murphy, 40, an editor of Atlanta (Ga.) Constitution, kidnaped **Feb. 20, 1974**, freed **Feb. 22** after payment of $700,000 ransom by the newspaper. Police arrested William A. H. Williams, a contractor; most of the money was recovered.

J. Guadalupe Zuno Hernandez, 83, father-in-law of Mexican President Luis Echeverria Alvarez, seized by 4 terrorists **Aug. 28, 1974;** government refused to negotiate; he was released **Sept. 8.**

E. B. Reville, Hepzibah, Ga., banker and wife Jean kidnaped **Sept. 30, 1974.** Ransom of $30,000 paid. He was found alive; Mrs. Reville was found dead of carbon monoxide fumes in car trunk **Oct. 2.**

Jack Teich, Kings Point, N.Y., steel executive, seized

Nov. 12, 1974; released Nov. 19 after payment of $750,000.

Samuel Bronfman, 21, heir to Seagram liquor fortune, abducted Aug. 9, 1975, in Purchase, N.Y.; $2.3 million ransom paid by father, Edgar. FBI and N.Y.C. police rescued

Samuel Aug. 17 in Brooklyn, N.Y., apartment, recovered ransom, and arrested Mel Patrick Lynch, a city fireman, and Dominic Byrne, a limousine operator.

See also Chronology.

Some Major Tornadoes Since 1925

Source: National Climatic Center, NOAA, Dept. of Commerce

Date		Place	Dead	Date		Place	Dead
1925	Mar. 18	Mo., Ill., Ind.	689	1953	May 11	Waco, Tex.	114
1926	Nov. 25	Belleville to Portland, Ark.	53	1953	June 8	Flint to Lakeport, Mich.	116
1927	Apr. 12	Rock Springs, Tex.	74	1953	June 9	Worcester and vicinity, Mass.	90
1927	May 9	Arkansas, Poplar Bluff, Mo.	92	1953	Dec. 5	Vicksburg, Miss.	38
1927	Sept. 29	St. Louis, Mo.	72	1955	May 25	Udall, Kan.	80
1929	Apr. 25	SE-Central Ga.	40	1957	May 20	Williamsburg, Kan. to Ruskin	
1930	May 6	Hill & Ellis Co., Tex.	41			Heights, Mo.	48
1932	Mar. 21	Ala. (series of tornadoes)	268	1958	June 4	Northwestern Wisconsin	30
1936	Apr. 5	Tupelo, Miss.	216	1959	Feb. 10	St. Louis, Mo.	21
1936	Apr. 6	Gainesville, Ga.	203	1960	May 5, 6	SE Oklahoma, Arkansas	30
1938	Sept. 29	Charleston, S. C.	32	1965	Apr. 11	Ind., Ill., Mich., Wis.	271
1942	Mar. 16	Central to NE Miss.	75	1966	Mar. 3	Jackson, Miss.	57
1942	Apr. 27	Rogers & Mayes Co., Okla.	52	1966	Mar. 3	Mississippi, Alabama	61
1944	June 23	Ohio, Pa., W. Va., Md.	150	1967	April 21	Illinois.	33
1945	Apr. 12	Okla.-Ark.	102	1968	May 15	Arkansas	34
1947	Apr. 9	Texas, Okla. & Kan.	169	1969	Jan. 23	Mississippi	32
1948	Mar. 19	Bunker Hill & Gillespie, Ill.	33	1971	Feb. 21	Mississippi delta	110
1949	Jan. 3	La. & Ark.	58	1973	May 26-7	South, Midwest (series)	47
1952	Mar. 21	Ark., Mo., Tenn. (series)	208	1974	Apr. 3-4	Ala., Ga., Tenn., Ky., Oh.	350

Number of Tornadoes in U.S. Since 1924, Deaths

Year	No.	Deaths	Year	No.	Deaths	Year	No.	Deaths	Year	No.	Deaths
1924	130	376	1937	147	29	1950	199	70	1964	703	73
1925	119	794	1938	213	183	1951	264	34	1965	901	296
1926	111	144	1939	152	87	1952	240	230	1966	585	99
1927	163	540	1940	124	65	1953	422	515	1967	929	114
1928	203	92	1941	118	53	1954	550	36	1968	660	131
1929	197	274	1942	167	384	1955	595	126	1969	608	66
1930	192	179	1943	152	58	1956	503	83	1970	652	72
1931	94	36	1944	169	275	1957	856	191	1971	889	156
1932	151	394	1945	121	210	1958	563	66	1972	741	27*
1933	258	362	1946	106	78	1959	604	58	1973	1109†	87
1934	147	47	1947	165	313	1960	616	47	1974	945	361
1935	180	70	1948	183	140	1961	698	51	1975	917	59
1936	151	552	1949	249	212	1962	658	28	**Total**	**21,033**	**9,054**
						1963	464		**Average**	**404**	**174**

*Record low; †Record high.

Hurricanes, Typhoons, Blizzards, Other Storms

Date, Locations, Number of Deaths—*See also Chronology*—Names of hurricanes and typhoons in italics

1888 Mar. 11-14	Blizzard, Eastern U.S.	400
1900 Sept. 8	Hurricane, Galveston, Tex.	6,000
1926 Sept. 16-22	Hurricane, Fla., Ala.	372
1926 Oct. 20	Hurricane, Cuba.	600
1928 Sept. 12-17	Hurricane, W. Indies, Fla.	4,000
1930 Sept. 3	Hurricane, San. Domingo.	2,000
1938 Sept. 21	Hurricane, New England.	600
1942 Oct. 15-16	Hurricane, Bengal, India.	11,000
1944 Sept. 12-16	Hurricane, N.C. to New Eng.	389
1953 Sept. 25-27	Typhoon, Vietnam, Japan.	1,300
1954 Aug. 30	*H. Carol,* Northeast U.S.	68
1954 Oct. 12-16	*H. Hazel,* Eastern U.S., Haiti.	347
1955 Aug. 12-13	*H. Connie,* Carolinas, Va., Md.	43
1955 Aug. 18-19	*H. Diane,* Eastern U.S.	400
1955 Sept. 19	*H. Hilda,* Mexico.	200
1955 Sept. 22-28	*H. Janet,* Caribbean	500
1956 Feb. 1-29	Blizzard, Western Europe.	1,000
1957 June 27-30	*H. Audrey,* La., Tex.	430
1958 Feb. 15-16	Blizzard, NE U.S.	171
1959 Sept. 17-19	*T. Sarah,* Far East.	2,000
1959 Sept. 26-27	*T. Vera,* Honshu, Japan.	4,466
1960 Sept. 4-12	*H. Donna,* Caribbean, E. U. S.	148
1961 Oct. 31	*H. Hattie,* Br. Honduras.	400
1962 Feb. 17	Flooding, German Coast.	343
1962 Sept. 27	Flooding, Barcelona, Spain.	445
1963 May 28-29	Windstorm, E. Pakistan.	22,000
1963 Oct. 4-8	*H. Flora,* Cuba, Haiti.	6,000
1964 Oct. 4-7	*H. Hilda,* La., Miss., Ga.	38
1964 June 30	*T. Winnie,* N. Philippines	107
1964 Sept. 5	*T. Ruby,* Hong Kong and China	735
1964 Sept. 14	Flooding, Central S. Korea	563
1964 Nov. 12	Flooding, S. Vietnam.	7,000
1965 May 11-12	Windstorm, E. Pakistan	17,000
1965 June 1-2	Windstorm, E. Pakistan.	30,000
1965 Sept. 7-10	*H. Betsy,* Fla., Miss., La.	74
1965 Dec. 15	Windstorm, E. Pakistan.	10,000
1966 June 4-10	*H. Alma,* Honduras, SE U. S.	51
1966 Sept. 24-30	*H. Inez,* Carib., Fla., Mex.	293
1967 July 9	*T. Billie,* Japan.	347
1967 Sept. 5-23	*H. Beulah,* Carib., Mex., Tex.	54
1967 Dec. 12-20	Blizzard, Southwest, U.S.	51
1968 Nov. 18-28	*T. Nina,* Philippines.	63
1969 Aug. 17-18	*H. Camille,* Miss., La.	258
1970 July 30-Aug 5	*H. Celia,* Cuba, Fla., Tex.	31
1970 Aug. 20-21	*H. Dorothy,* Martinique.	42
1970 Sept. 15	*T. Georgia,* Philippines	300
1970 Oct. 14	*T. Sening,* Philippines.	583
1970 Oct. 15	*T. Titang,* Philippines.	526
1970 Nov. 13	Cyclone, East Pakistan, est.	300,000
1971 Aug. 1	*T. Rose,* Hong Kong.	130
1972 June 19-29	*H. Agnes,* Fla. to N. Y.	118
1972 Dec. 3	*T. Theresa,* Philippines.	169
1973 June-Aug.	Monsoon rains in India.	1,217
1974 June 11	Storm *Dinah,* Luzon Is., Philip.	71
1974 July 11	*T. Gilda,* Japan, S. Korea.	108
1974 Sept. 19-20	*H. Fifi,* Honduras.	2,000
1974 Dec. 25	Cyclone leveled Darwin, Aus.	50
1975 Sept. 13-27	*H. Eloise,* Caribbean—NE U.S.	71
1976 May 22	*T. Olga,* floods, Philippines.	60

Explosions

Date, Location, Number of Deaths—*See also Marine Disasters, Fires and Chronology*

1910 Oct. 1	Los Angeles Times Bldg.	21	
1913 Mar. 7	Dynamite, Baltimore harbor.	55	
1915 Sept. 27	Gasoline tank car, Ardmore, Okla.	47	
1917 Apr. 10	Munitions plant, Eddystone, Pa.	133	
1917 Dec. 6	Halifax Harbor, Canada.	1,654	
1918 July 2	Explosives, Split Rock, N.Y.	50	
1918 Oct. 4	Shell plant, Morgan Station, N.J.	64	
1919 May 22	Food plant, Cedar Rapids, Ia.	44	

1920 Sept. 16	Wall Street, New York, bomb	30	
1924 Jan. 3	Food plant, Pekin, Ill.	42	
1937 Mar. 18	New London, Tex., school	294	
1940 Sept. 11	Hercules Powder, Kenvil, N. J.	51	
1942 June 5	Ordnance plant, Elwood, Ill.	49	
1944 Apr. 14	Bombay, India, harbor	700	
1944 July 17	Port Chicago, Calif., pier	322	
1944 Oct. 21	Liquid gas tank, Cleveland	135	
1947 Apr. 16	Texas City, Tex., pier	561	
1948 July 28	Farben works, Ludwigshafen, Ger.	184	
1950 May 19	Munition barges, S. Amboy, N. J.	30	
1956 Aug. 7	Dynamite trucks, Cali, Colombia	1,100	
1958 Apr. 18	Sunken munitions ship, Okinawa	40	
1958 May 22	Nike missiles, Leonardo, N. J.	10	
1959 Apr. 10	World War II bomb, Philippines	38	
1959 June 2	Gas truck, Penn. Turnpike	10	
1959 June 28	Rail tank cars, Meldrin, Ga.	25	
1959 Aug. 7	Dynamite truck, Roseburg, Ore.	13	
1959 Nov. 2	Jamuri Bazar, India, explosives	46	
1959 Dec. 13	Dortmund, Ger., 2 apt. bldgs.	26	
1960 Mar. 4	Belgian munition ship, Havana	100	
1960 Oct. 25	Gas, Windsor, Ont., store	11	
1962 Jan. 16	Gas pipeline, Alberta, Canada	19	
1962 Mar. 3	Gasoline truck, Syria	31	

1962 Oct. 3	Telephone Co. office, N. Y. City	23	
1963 Jan. 2	Packing plant, Terre Haute, Ind.	16	
1963 Mar. 9	Dynamite plant, S. Africa	45	
1963 Mar. 9	Steel plant, Belecke, W. Germany	19	
1963 Aug. 13	Explosives dump, Gauhiti, India	32	
1963 Oct. 31	State Fair Coliseum, Indianapolis	73	
1964 July 23	Bone, Algeria, harbor munitions	100	
1965 Mar. 4	Gas pipeline, Natchitoches, La.	17	
1965 Aug. 9	Missile silo, Searcy, Ark.	53	
1965 Oct. 21	Bridge, Tila Bund, Pakistan	80	
1965 Oct. 30	Cartagena, Colombia	48	
1965 Nov. 24	Armory, Keokuk, Iowa	20	
1966 Oct. 13	Chemical plant, La Salle, Que.	11	
1967 Feb. 17	Chemical plant, Hawthorne, N.J.	11	
1967 Dec. 25	Apartment bldg., Moscow	20	
1968 Apr. 6	Sports store, Richmond, Ind.	43	
1970 Apr. 8	Subway construction, Osaka, Japan	73	
1971 June 24	Tunnel, Sylmar, Cal.	17	
1971 June 28	School, fireworks, Pueblo, Mex.	13	
1971 Oct. 21	Shopping center, Glasgow, Scot.	20	
1973 Feb. 10	Liquified gas tank, Staten Is., N.Y.	40	
1975 Dec. 27	Chasnala, India, mine	431	
1976 Apr. 13	Lapua, Finland, munitions works	45	

Principal Mine Disasters in the U. S.

Source: Bureau of Mines

Note: Prior to 1968, only disasters with losses of 50 or more lives are listed; for 1968-72, all disasters in which 5 or more men are killed are listed. Only fatalities to mining company employees are included. All Bituminous-coal mines unless otherwise noted.

Date	Location	Killed	Date	Location	Killed
1855 Mar.	Coalfield, Va.	55	1915 Mar. 2	Layland, W. Va.	112
1867 Apr. 3	Winterpock, Va.	69	1917 Apr. 27	Hastings, Col.	121
1869[1] Sept. 6	Plymouth, Pa.	110	1917[2] Jun. 8	Butte, Mon.	163
1883 Feb. 16	Braidwood, Ill.	69	1917 Aug. 4	Clay, Ky.	62
1884 Jan. 24	Crested Butte, Col.	59	1919[1] Jun. 5	Wilkes-Barre, Pa.	92
1884 Mar. 13	Pocahontas, Va.	112	1922 Nov. 6	Spangler, Pa.	77
1891 Jan. 27	Mount Pleasant, Pa.	109	1922 Nov. 22	Dolomite, Ala.	90
1892 Jan. 7	Krebs, Okla.	100	1923 Feb. 8	Dawson, N.M.	120
1895 Mar. 20	Red Canyon, Wy.	60	1923 Aug. 14	Kemmerer, Wy.	99
1896[1] June 28	Pittston, Pa.	58	1924 Mar. 8	Castle Gate, Ut.	171
1900 Jan. 1	Scofield, Ut.	200	1924 Apr. 28	Benwood, W. Va	119
1902 May 19	Coal Creek, Tenn.	184	1925 Feb. 20	Sullivan, Ind.	52
1902 July 10	Johnstown, Pa.	112	1925 May 27	Coal Glen, N.C.	53
1903 June 30	Hanna, Wy.	169	1925 Dec. 10	Acmar, Ala.	53
1904 Jan. 25	Cheswick, Pa.	179	1926 Jan. 13	Wilburton, Okla.	91
1905 Feb. 20	Virginia City, Ala.	112	1926[2] Nov. 3	Ishpeming, Mich.	51
1907 Jan. 29	Stuart W. Va.	84	1927 Apr. 30	Everettville, W. Va.	97
1907 Dec. 6	Monongah, W. Va	361	1928 May 19	Mather, Pa.	195
1907 Dec. 16	Yolande, Ala.	57	1929 Dec. 17	McAlester, Okla	61
1907 Dec. 19	Jacobs Creek, Pa.	239	1930 Nov. 5	Millfield, Oh.	79
1908 Mar. 28	Hanna, Wy.	59	1932 Dec. 23	Moweaqua, Ill.	54
1908 Nov. 28	Marianna, Pa.	154	1940 Jan. 10	Bartley, W. Va.	91
1908 Dec. 29	Switchback, W. Va.	50	1940 Mar. 16	St. Clairsville, Oh.	72
1909 Jan. 12	Switchback, W. Va.	67	1940 Jul. 15	Portage, Pa.	63
1909 Nov. 13	Cherry, Ill.	259	1942 May 12	Osage, W. Va.	56
1910 Jan. 31	Primero, Col.	75	1943 Feb. 27	Washoe, Mon.	74
1910 May 5	Palos, Ala.	90	1944 Jul. 5	Belmont, Oh.	66
1910 Oct. 8	Starkville, Col.	56	1947 Mar. 25	Centralia, Ill.	111
1910 Nov. 8	Delagua, Col.	79	1951 Dec. 21	West Frankfort, Ill.	119
1911 Apr. 7	Throop, Pa.	72	1968[3] Mar. 6	Calumet, La.	21
1911 Apr. 8	Littleton, Ala.	128	1968 Aug. 7	Greenville, Ky.	9
1911 Dec. 9	Briceville, Tenn.	84	1968 Nov. 20	Farmington, W. Va.	78
1912 Mar. 20	McCurtain, Okla.	73	1970 Dec. 30	Hyden, Ky.	38
1912 Mar. 26	Jed, W. Va.	83	1971[3] Apr. 12	Rosiclare, Ill.	7
1913 Apr. 23	Finleyville, Pa.	96	1972[2] May 2	Kellogg, Ida.	91
1913 Oct. 22	Dawson, N.M.	263	1972 Jul. 22	Blacksville, W. Va.	9
1914 Apr. 28	Eccles, W. Va.	181	1972 Dec. 16	Itmann, W. Va.	5
1914 Oct. 27	Royalton, Ill.	52	1976 Apr. 11	Partridge, Ky.	26

World's worst mine disaster killed 1,549 workers in Honkeiko Colliery in Manchuria Apr. 25, 1942.

(1) Anthracite mine. (2) Metal mine. (3) Nonmetal mine.

Record Oil Spills, 1967-1971

Source: U. S. Geological Survey, Conservation Division

Name and Place	Date	Cause of Spill	Barrels
Tanker, Torrey Canyon, England	Mar. 18, 1967	Grounding	700,000
Tanker, World Glory, South Africa	June 13, 1968	Hull failure	322,000
Tanker, Atlantic Ocean	Mar. 27, 1971	Sinking	220,000
Tanker, Keo, Massachusetts	Nov. 5, 1969	Hull failure	210,000

Storage tank, Sewaren, N. J.	Nov. 1969	Tank failure	200,000
Pipeline, West Delta area, La.	Oct. 15, 1967	Anchor dragging	160,000
Tanker, Japan.	Nov. 30, 1971	Tanker broke in half	149,080
Tanker, R. C. Stoner, Wake Island.	Sept. 6, 1967	Grounding	143,300
Tanker, Andron, West African coast.	May 5, 1968	Sinking	117,000

Some Notable Aircraft Disasters Since 1937

Date	Aircraft	Site of Accident	Deaths
1937 May 6	German zeppelin Hindenburg	Burned at mooring, Lakehurst, N. J.	36
1944 Aug. 23	U.S. Air Force B-24	Hit school, Freckelton, England.	76[1]
1945 July 28	U.S. Army B-25	Hit Empire State bldg., N.Y.C.	14[1]
1949 Nov. 1	Eastern Air Lines DC-4	Rammed by Bolivian P-38, Wash., D.C.	55
1952 Dec. 20	U. S. Air Force C-124	Fell, burned, Moses Lake, Wash.	87
1953 Mar. 3	Canadian Pacific Comet Jet.	Karachi, Pakistan	11[2]
1953 June 18	U. S. Air Force C-124	Crashed, burned near Tokyo.	129
1955 Nov. 1	United Air Lines DC-6B	Exploded, crashed near Longmont, Col.	44[3]
1956 June 20	Venezuelan Super-Constellation	Crashed in Atlantic off Asbury Park, N. J.	74
1956 June 30	TWA Super-Const., United DC-7.	Collided over Grand Canyon, Arizona.	128
1957 Aug. 11	Maritime, Central Airways DC-4	Crashed in swamp near Quebec.	79
1960 Dec. 16	United DC-8 jet, TWA Super-Constellation	Collided over New York City	134[5]
1961 Sept. 10	President Airlines DC-6	Crashed at Shannon, Ireland.	83
1962 Mar. 4	Br. Caledonian Airlines DC-7C	Crashed near Douala, Cameroun.	111
1962 Mar. 16	Flying Tiger Super-Const.	Vanished in Western Pacific	107
1962 June 3	Air France Boeing 707 jet	Crashed on takeoff from Paris.	130
1962 June 22	Air France Boeing 707 jet	Crashed in storm, Guadeloupe, W. I.	113
1963 June 3	Chartered Northw. Airlines DC-7.	Crashed in Pacific off British Columbia.	101
1963 Nov. 29	Trans-Canada Airlines DC-8F	Crashed after takeoff from Montreal.	118
1963 Dec. 8	Pan American Boeing 707.	Crashed near Elkton, Md.	82
1965 Feb. 8	Eastern Air Lines DC-7B.	Plunged into Atlantic after takeoff, New York	84
1965 May 20	Pakistani Boeing 720-B.	Crashed at Cairo, Egypt, airport.	121
1966 Jan. 24	Air India Boeing 707 jetliner.	Crashed on Mont Blanc, France-Italy.	117
1966 Feb. 4	All-Nippon Boeing 727.	Plunged into Tokyo Bay.	133
1966 Mar. 5	BOAC Boeing 707 jetliner.	Crashed on Japan's Mount Fuji.	124
1966 Dec. 24	U. S. military-chartered, CL-44.	Crashed into village in South Vietnam.	129[1]
1967 Mar. 9	TWA DC-9, Beechcraft.	Collided in air at Urbana, Oh.	26
1967 Apr. 20	Swiss Britannia turboprop	Crashed at Nicosia, Cyprus	126
1967 July 19	Piedmont Boeing 727, Cessna 310.	Collided in air, Hendersonville, N. C.	82
1968 Apr. 20	S. African Airways Boeing 707.	Crashed on takeoff, Windhoek, SW Africa	122
1968 May 3	Braniff International Electra.	Crashed in storm near Dawson, Tex.	85
1969 Mar. 16	Venezuelan DC-9.	Crashed after takeoff from Maracaibo, Venezuela.	155[7]
1969 Mar. 20	United Arab Ilyushin-18.	Crashed at Aswan airport.	87
1969 June 4	Mexican Boeing 727.	Rammed into mountain near Monterrey, Mexico.	79
1969 Nov. 20	Nigerian VC-10.	Crashed near Iju, Nigeria.	87
1969 Dec. 8	Olympia Airways DC-6B.	Crashed near Athens in storm.	93
1970 Feb. 15	Dominican DC-9.	Crashed into sea on takeoff from Santo Domingo.	102
1970 July 3	British chartered jetliner.	Crashed near Barcelona, Spain.	112
1970 July 5	Air Canada DC-8.	Crashed near Toronto International Airport.	108
1970 Aug. 9	Peruvian turbojet.	Crashed after takeoff from Cuzco, Peru.	101[1]
1970 Oct. 2	Chartered Martin 404.	Crashed in Rocky Mts. near Silver Plume, Col.	30[8]
1970 Nov. 14	Southern Airways DC-9.	Crashed in mountains near Huntington, W. Va.	75[9]
1970 Dec. 31	Soviet Aeroflot Ilyushin 18.	Crashed on takeoff, Leningrad.	90
1971 July 30	All-Nippon Boeing 727, Japanese Air Force F-86.	Collided over Morioka, Japan.	162[7]
1971 Aug. 11	Soviet Aeroflot Tupolev-104.	Crashed at Irkutsk airport, USSR.	97
1971 Sept. 4	Alaska Airlines Boeing 727.	Crashed into mountain near Juneau, Alaska.	111
1972 Mar. 14	Danish Airliner.	Crashed near Dubai, United Arab Emirates.	112
1972 Aug. 14	E. German Ilyushin-62.	Crashed on take-off East Berlin.	156
1972 Oct. 13	Aeroflot Ilyushin-62.	E. German airline crashed near Moscow.	176
1972 Dec. 4	Chartered Spanish airliner.	Crashed on take-off, Canary Islands.	155
1972 Dec. 29	Eastern Airlines Lockheed Tristar.	Crashed on approach to Miami Int'l. Airport.	100
1973 Jan. 22	Chartered Boeing 707.	Burst into flames during landing, Kano Airport, Nigeria.	176
1973 Apr. 10	British Vanguard turboprop.	Crashed during snowstorm at Basel, Switzerland.	104
1973 June 3	Soviet Supersonic TU-144.	Exploded in air near Goussainville, France.	14[11]
1973 July 11	Brazilian Boeing 707.	Crashed on approach to Orly airport Paris.	122
1973 July 31	Delta Airlines jetliner.	Crashed, landing in fog at Logan Airport, Boston.	89
1973 Aug. 13	Spanish Caravelle jet.	Exploded and crashed near La Coruna, Spain.	85
1973 Dec. 23	French Caravelle jet.	Crashed in Morocco.	106
1974 Jan. 31	Pan American Boeing 707 jet.	Crashed in Pago Pago, American Samoa.	96
1974 Mar. 3	Turkish DC-10 jet.	Crashed at Ermenoville near Paris.	346
1974 Apr. 22	Pan American 707 jet.	Crashed in Bali, Indonesia.	107
1974 Sept. 8	TWA 707 jet.	Crashed in Ionian Sea off Greece, after bomb explosion; Arab guerrilla group claimed responsibility.	80
1974 Dec. 1	TWA-727.	Crashed in storm, Upperville, Va.	92
1974 Dec. 4	Dutch-chartered DC-8.	Crashed in storm near Colombo, Sri Lanka.	191
1975 Apr. 4	Air Force Galaxy C-58.	Crashed near Saigon, So. Vietnam, after takeoff with load of orphans.	172
1975 June 24	Eastern Airlines 727 jet.	Crashed short of landing strip in storm, JFK Airport, N.Y.	113
1975 Aug. 3	Chartered 707.	Hit mountainside, Agadir, Morocco.	188
1975 Aug. 20	Czech Ilyushin.	Crashed in landing at Damascus, Syria.	26

(1) Including those on the ground and in buildings. (2) First fatal crash of commercial jet plane. (3) Caused by bomb planted by John G. Graham in insurance plot to kill his mother, a passenger. (4) First crash of commercial helicopter. (5) Including all 128 aboard the plane and 6 on ground. (6) Including 74 Army recruits. (7) Killed 84 on plane and 71 on ground. (8) Including 13 members of Wichita State U. football team. (9) Including 43 Marshall U. football players and coaches. (10) Airline-fighter crash, pilot of fighter parachuted to safety, was arrested for negligence. (11) First supersonic plane crash killed 6 crewmen and 8 on the ground; there were no passengers.

ASTRONOMY AND CALENDAR

Edited by Dr. Kenneth L. Franklin, Astronomer
American Museum-Hayden Planetarium

Celestial Events Highlights, 1977

(All times are Greenwich Mean Time)

Most of the planet action this year occurs in the morning sky. Early in 1977, the planets in the evening are Venus and Saturn. By April, Venus becomes unobservable, passing into the morning sky to be seen at dawn for nearly all of the remainder of the year. Venus and Mars have a double conjunction (May 13 and June 3), and Venus passes Jupiter on July 30 and Saturn on Sept. 18. Take pictures of Venus and the moon on the morning of July 12. In August, reading from east to west, we find Venus, Jupiter and Mars in the morning sky. These are joined by Saturn in September.

The moon occults no bright stars this year — only planets, but few occultations are visible in the North American continent. Notice of an occultation should be considered an invitation to see the moon and a planet close in the sky. There are eight occultations of Uranus alone. Binocular or telescope observation is necessary, but these are good opportunities to find Uranus.

The moon is eclipsed twice, the first a minor penumbral eclipse, the second a penumbral one. The two solar eclipses are an annular eclipse moving across Africa and a total eclipse almost totally over the eastern Pacific Ocean.

1977 is the centennial of Mars, or at least of its "canals" and satellites. A hundred years ago when Mars made a close approach to the earth, G. Schiaparelli first detected "canali" and A. Hall found Phobos and Deimos.

January

Mercury is at inferior conjunction on the 6th, 62.5 million miles from earth. On the 18th, it looks like a bright star south of the crescent moon in the dawn sky. Greatest western elongation occurs on the 22d, 25° from the sun.

Venus is south of the crescent moon in the evenings of the 22d and 23rd, and is farthest from the sun (47°) on the 24th. Venus is in the faint region south of the Great Square of Pegasus, so there is no competition from the stars.

Mars, for most of this month is too faint and near the sun to be seen in the morning sky.

Jupiter, on New Year's Eve, 1976, may be found slightly to the north of the gibbous moon. About 2 a.m., Jan. 1 in Greenwich (EST: Dec. 31, 9 p.m.), the moon will occult Jupiter in Aries for observers in South America and Antarctica. The moon and Jupiter approach close again on the 28th. Watch also on the 27th.

Saturn is north of the moon on the evening of the 7th for Western Hemisphere observers. It is in retrograde motion in Cancer.

Moon occults Jupiter on the 1st (GMT), passes Saturn on the 8th, occults Uranus on the 14th, passes Mercury and Mars on the 18th, Venus on the 23rd and Jupiter on the 28th. Perigee (227,700 miles) is on the 16th; apogee (251,200 miles) on the 28th.

Jan. 3 — Earth at perihelion, 91.44 million miles away from the sun.

Jan. 4 — Quadrantid meteors spoiled by the full moon.

Jan. 6 — Mercury at inferior conjunction.

Jan. 15 — Jupiter is stationary in Taurus.

Jan. 19 — Sun enters Capricornus.

Jan. 24 — Venus is at greatest eastern elongation, 47° from the sun.

Jan. 29 — Mercury is at greatest western elongation, 25° from the sun.

February

Mercury is at zero magnitude when it passes 0°.1 south of Mars on the 12th, hard to see in the dawn twilight.

Venus, in the faint watery constellations, continues to brighten, and makes a great scene with the crescent moon, 3° to the south, the evening of the 21st.

Mars passes close to Mercury on the 12th; binoculars may be needed to find it in the bright dawn sky.

Jupiter is 2° north of the quarter moon on the 24th.

Saturn is in opposition on the 2d in Cancer, and passes 6° north of the full moon on the 4th.

Moon passes Saturn on the 4th, occults Uranus on the 10th, at perigee (230,100 miles) on the 11th, passes Mars and Mercury on the 16th, Venus on the 21st, Jupiter on the 24th and at apogee (251,200 miles) on the 25th.

Feb. 2 — Saturn in opposition.

Feb. 16 —Sun enters Aquarius.

March

Mercury is in superior conjunction on the 16th and is 8° south of Venus on the 27th when it appears as a star of magnitude minus 1.2.

Venus attains greatest brilliancy (-4.3 magnitude) on the 1st, is 8° north of the crescent moon on the 21st, and 8° north of Mercury on the 27th. Look at Venus through a good telescope or binoculars. What shape is it?

Mars is 6° south of the morning crescent moon on the 17th.

Jupiter is 2° north of the moon on the 24th.

Saturn is passed by the moon twice this month, 6° north of the moon on the 3rd and on the 30th.

Moon passes Saturn on the 3rd, at perigee (227,700 miles) on the 8th, occults Uranus on the 9th, passes Mars on the 17th, Venus on the 21st, Jupiter on the 24th, at apogee (251,700 miles) on the 24th, and passes Saturn again on the 30th.

Mar. 1 — Venus at greatest brilliancy.

Mar. 9 — Occultation of Uranus.

Mar. 11 — Sun enters Pisces.

Mar. 16—Mercury in superior conjunction.

Mar. 20 — Vernal equinox at 17:43 GMT (12:43 EST). Spring begins in the northern hemisphere, Autumn in the southern.

Mar. 24 — Ceres in opposition.

April

Mercury is at greatest eastern elongation, 19° from the sun, on the 10th, 5° north of the moon on the 16th and at inferior conjunction on the 30th.

Venus is lost this month, being in inferior conjunction on the 6th.

Mars is slowly emerging from the sun into the

morning sky, 4° south of the moon on the 15th.

Jupiter, becoming lost in the evening twilight, is 3° north of the moon on the 21st.

Saturn resumes its eastward motion on the 11th, and is passed by the moon on the 27th.

Moon is partially eclipsed on the 4th, at perigee (224,400 miles) and occults Uranus again on the 5th, passes Mars on the 15th, Venus on the 16th, gives the sun an annular eclipse on the 18th, passes Mercury on the 19th, Jupiter on the 21st while at apogee (252,300 miles), and passes Saturn on the 27th.

April 2 — Pluto at opposition, 2,747.7 million miles away, in Virgo, about 4° east of Epsilon Virginis.

April 4 — Partial eclipse of the moon.

April 5 — Occultation of Uranus.

April 6 — Venus at inferior conjunction.

April 10 — Mercury at greatest eastern elongation, 19°.

April 11 — Saturn stationary in Cancer.

April 18 — Annular eclipse of the sun; sun enters Aries.

April 22 — The Lyrids, a weak meteor shower.

April 24 — Venus stationary.

April 30 — Uranus in opposition in Libra; Mercury in inferior conjunction.

May

Mercury is 2° south of the moon on the 16th and at greatest western elongation (25°) on the 27th.

Venus is at greatest brilliancy in the morning sky on the 11th, passes 1°.3 north of Mars on the 13th, and is occulted by the crescent moon on the 14th, visible in North America. Binoculars are not necessary but are a help, because, at about 7 a.m. (EDT), the event occurs in daylight for eastern observers. Look for Mars to the southeast about a degree away.

Mars, passing 1°.3 south of Venus on the 13th, is passed 2° to the north by the moon after the occultation of Venus on the 14th.

Jupiter is lost in the evening twilight.

Saturn is 6° north of the moon on the 24th.

Moon occults Uranus on the 3rd, at perigee (222,300 miles) on the 4th, occults Venus on the 14th, just before it passes Mars; it passes Mercury on the 16th, at apogee (252,600 miles) on the 18th, passes Saturn on the 24th, and occults Uranus (again) on the 30th.

May 3 — Occultation of Uranus.

May 4 — Eta Aquarids, a weak meteor shower, washed out by full moon.

May 11 — Venus at greatest brilliancy.

May 13 — Juno at opposition, Venus passes 1°.3 north of Mars, Sun enters Taurus.

May 14 — Occultation of Venus.

May 27 — Mercury at greatest western elongation (25°).

May 30 — Occultation of Uranus.

June

Mercury overtakes the sun this month, being in superior conjunction on the 30th.

Venus is 1°.2 south of Mars overtaking it in Pisces on the 3rd, is 2° south of the moon on the 12th, and is at greatest elongation 46° west of the sun on the 15th in Aries.

Mars is passed by Venus, 1°.2 to the south, on the 3rd, and is occulted by the moon on the 12th.

Jupiter is in conjunction with the sun on the 4th.

Saturn, still in Cancer, is 6° north of the moon on the 20th.

Moon at perigee (221,900 miles) on the 1st, occults Mars on the 12th and passes 2° north of Venus some four hours later, at apogee (252,500 miles) on the 14th, passes Saturn on the 20th, occults Uranus on the 27th, and at perigee (223,200 miles) again on the 30th.

June 3 — Venus and Mars in conjunction, 1°.2

apart.

June 4 — Jupiter in conjunction with the sun.

June 5 — Neptune at opposition.

June 12 — Occultation of Mars.

June 15 — Venus at greatest elongation west, 46°.

June 20 — Sun enters Gemini.

June 21 — Summer solstice at 12:14 GMT (7:14 a.m. EST); Summer begins.

June 27 — Occultation of Uranus.

June 30 — Mercury in superior conjunction.

July

Mercury, coming out of conjunction, is difficult to locate in the bright evening sky, but it is 0°.4 north of Saturn on the 20th (GMT). Use a telescope on this on the evening of the 19th; and again on the evening of the 27th when Mercury passes 0°.1 south of Regulus. Mercury then is about 25° east of the sun.

Venus is occulted by the moon on the morning of the 12th. This is a good opportunity to photograph bright Venus and the crescent moon. Venus, in the hyades this month, passes close to Epsilon Tauri on the 14th, is 3° north of Aldebaran on the 15th and 1°.6 south of Jupiter on the 30th.

Mars is 2° north of the moon on the 11th, in western Taurus.

Jupiter is becoming apparent in the dawn sky, 4° north of the moon on the 13th, and 1°.6 north of Venus on the 30th.

Saturn is nearly lost in the evening twilight, 6° north of the thin crescent moon on the 18th and 0°.4 south of Mercury on the 20th.

Moon is full twice this month, on the 1st and the 30th, at apogee (252,000 miles) on the 12th, occults Venus on the 12th, passes 4° south of Jupiter on the 13th, 6° south of Mercury and Saturn on the 18th, occults Uranus on the 24th, and at perigee (225,800 miles) on the 28th.

July 5 — Earth at aphelion, 94.55 million miles.

July 12 — Occultation of Venus.

July 20 — Mercury in conjunction with Saturn; Sun enters Cancer.

July 24 — Occultation of Uranus.

July 28 — Mercury 0°.1 south of Regulus; Delta Aquarids, but the moon is nearly full.

July 30 — Venus and Jupiter in conjunction.

August

Mercury is at greatest eastern elongation, 27° from the sun, on the 8th. Watch for Mercury's occultation on the 16th.

Venus is 4° north of the moon on the 11th and 7° south of Pollux on the 23rd.

Mars is 5° north of Aldebaran on the 1st, and 4° north of the moon on the 10th.

Jupiter is 4° north of the moon on the 10th.

Saturn is in conjunction on the 13th.

Moon at apogee (251,400 miles) and passes Mars on the 9th, passes Jupiter on the 10th, Venus on the 11th, occults Mercury on the 16th, does not occult Uranus as it passes it on the 20th, and at perigee (228,900 miles) on the 24th.

Aug. 8 — Mercury at greatest eastern elongation, 27°.

Aug. 10 — Sun enters Leo.

Aug. 12 — Perseid meteor shower peaks. Watch a night or two on either side of this date. This is the Old Faithful of meteor showers and there is no moon this month.

Aug. 13 — Saturn in conjunction.

Aug. 16 — Occultation of Mercury.

September

Mercury is in inferior conjunction on the 5th, and greatest western elongation (18°) on the 21st.

Venus is 5° north of the moon on the 10th, 0°.4 south of Saturn on the 18th and 0°.4 north of Regulus on the 22nd.

.**Mars** is 0°.5 north of Jupiter in Gemini on the 4th, and 5° north of the moon on the 7th.

Jupiter is 0°.5 south of Mars on the 4th, and 5° north of the moon on the 7th.

Saturn is slowly emerging into the dawn sky, 5° north of the moon on the 11th.

Moon at apogee (251,100 miles) on the 5th, passes Jupiter and Mars within two hours on the 7th, passes Venus on the 10th, and Saturn on the 11th, at perigee (229,300 miles) on the 18th, and experiences a penumbral eclipse on the 27th.

Sept. 4 — Mars and Jupiter in conjunction.

Sept. 5 — Mercury in inferior conjunction.

Sept. 16 — Sun enters Virgo.

Sept. 21 — Mercury at greatest western elongation, 18°.

Sept. 22 — Venus 0°.4 north of Regulus.

Sept. 23 — ,Autumnal equinox at 3:30 a.m. GMT (Sept. 22, 10:30 p.m. EST); Autumn begins.

Sept. 27 — Penumbral eclipse of the moon.

October

Mercury is in superior conjunction on the 18th.

Venus is 4° north of the waning crescent moon on the 11th, too close to the sun for observation.

Mars is 6° north of the moon on the 6th, and 6° south of Pollux on the 13th.

Jupiter is 5° north of the moon on the 4th, and begins its retrograde motion on the 24th in Gemini.

Saturn is 5° north of the moon on the 9th.

Moon at apogee (251,400 miles) on the 3rd, passes Jupiter on the 4th, Mars on the 6th, Saturn on the 9th, Venus on the 11th, totally eclipses the sun on the 12th, at perigee (226,300 miles) on the 15th and at apogee (252,000 miles) again on the 31st.

Oct. 7 — Pluto is in conjunction.

Oct. 12 — Total solar eclipse.

Oct. 18 — Mercury in superior conjunction.

Oct. 21 — Orionid meteors disturbed by the nearly full moon.

Oct. 24 — Jupiter is stationary.

Oct. 30 — Sun enters Libra.

November

Mercury is too close to the sun to be interesting for most of this month.

Venus is also very close but being brighter it may

be found by diligent searching. On the 3rd, it is 4° north of Spica, is occulted by the moon on the 10th, and is 0°.9 from Uranus on the 20th.

Mars is becoming as bright as a zero magnitude star this month. It is 7° north of the moon on the 3rd.

Jupiter is 5° north of the moon on the 1st and the 28th.

Saturn is 0°.8 north of Regulus on the 3rd, and 5° north of the moon on the 5th.

Moon passes Jupiter on the 1st, Mars on the 3rd, Saturn on the 5th, occults Venus on the 10th, at perigee (223,200 miles) on the 12th, at apogee (252,500 miles) on the 27th, and passes Jupiter on the 28th.

Nov. 3 — Saturn 0°.8 north of Regulus.

Nov. 4 — Uranus in conjunction; weak Taurid meteor shower with last quarter moon.

Nov. 10 — Occultation of Venus.

Nov. 20 — Venus and Uranus are in conjunction.

Nov. 22 — Sun enters Scorpius.

Nov. 29 — Sun enters Ophiuchus.

December

Mercury is at greatest eastern elongation (21°) on the 3rd, 6° south of the moon on the 12th, and at inferior conjunction on the 21st.

Venus is too close to the sun for observation.

Mars is 7° north of the moon on the 1st, begins its retrograde motion in Cancer on the 13th and is 8° north of the moon on the 28th.

Jupiter is at opposition in Gemini on the 23rd, and 5° north of the moon on the 25th.

Saturn is 5° north of the moon on the 3rd, begins its retrograde motion in Leo on the 12th, and is 5° north of the moon again on the 30th.

Moon passes Mars on the 1st, Saturn on the 3rd, at perigee (221,600 miles) on the 10th, passes Mercury on the 12th, at apogee (252,600 miles) on the 24th, passes Jupiter on the 25th, Mars on the 28th, and Saturn on the 30th.

Dec. 3 — Mercury at greatest eastern elongation, 21°.

Dec. 8 — Neptune in conjunction.

Dec. 12 — Saturn stationary.

Dec. 13 — Mars stationary; the Geminid meteor shower may well be good.

Dec. 16 — Sun enters Sagittarius.

Dec. 21 — Mercury at inferior conjunction; winter solstice at 11:24 p.m. GMT (6:24 p.m. EST).

Dec. 22 — The weak Ursid meteor shower is not hurt too much by the moon this year.

Astronomical Signs and Symbols

☉ The Sun	⊕ The Earth	⛢ Uranus	☐ Quadrature
☾ The Moon	♂ Mars	♆ Neptune	☍ Opposition
☿ Mercury	♃ Jupiter	♇ Pluto	☊ Ascending Node
♀ Venus	♄ Saturn	☌ Conjunction	☋ Descending Node

Two heavenly bodies are in "conjunction" (☌) when they are due north and south of each other, either in Right Ascension (with respect to the north celestial pole) or in Celestial Longitude (with respect to the north ecliptic pole). If the bodies are seen near each other, they will rise and set at nearly the same time. They are in "opposition" (☍) when their Right Ascensions differ by exactly 12 hours, or their Celestial Longitudes differ by 180°. One of the two objects in opposition will rise while the other is setting. "Quadrature" (☐) refers to the arrangement when the coordinates of two bodies differ by exactly 90°. These terms may refer to the relative positions of any two bodies as seen from the earth, but one of the bodies is so frequently the sun that mention of the sun is omit-

ted; otherwise both bodies are named. The geocentric angular separation between sun and object is termed "elongation." Elongation is limited only for Mercury and Venus; the "greatest elongation" for each of these bodies is noted in the appropriate tables and is approximately the time for longest observation. When a planet is in its "ascending" (☊) or "descending" (☋) node, it is passing northward or southward, respectively, through the plane of the earth's orbit, across the celestial circle called the ecliptic. The term "perihelion" means nearest to the sun, and "aphelion," farthest from the sun. An "occultation" of a planet or star is an eclipse of it by some other body, usually the moon.

Planets and the Sun

The planets of the solar system, in order of their distance from the sun, are Mercury, Venus, Earth, Mars, Jupiter, Saturn, Uranus, Neptune and Pluto. Uranus, Neptune and Pluto are not included in the celestial list because they are too faint to be seen without optical aid. Both Uranus and Neptune are visible through good field glasses, but Pluto is so distant and so small that only large telescopes or long exposure photographs can make it visible.

Since Mercury and Venus are nearer to the sun than is the earth, their motions about the sun are seen from the earth as wide swings first to one side of the sun and then to the other, although they are both passing continuously around the sun in orbits that are almost circular. When their passage takes them either between the earth and the sun, or beyond the sun as seen from the earth, they are invisible to us. Because of the laws which govern the motions of planets about the sun, both Mercury and Venus require much less time to pass between the earth and the sun than around the far side of the sun, so their periods of visibility and invisibility are unequal.

The planets that lie farther from the sun than does the earth may be seen for longer periods of time and are invisible only when they are so located in our sky that they rise and set about the same time as the sun when, of course, they are overwhelmed by the sun's great brilliance. None of the planets has any light or exterior heat of its own but each shines only by reflecting sunlight from its surface. Mercury and Venus, because they are between the earth and the sun, show phases very much as the moon does. The planets farther from the sun are always seen as full, although Mars does occasionally present a slightly gibbous phase — like the moon when not quite full.

The planets move rapidly among the stars because they are very much nearer to us than the stars are. The stars are also in motion, some of them at tremendous speeds, but they are so far away that their motion does not change their apparent positions in the heavens sufficiently for anyone to perceive that change in a single lifetime. The very nearest star is about 7,000 times as far away as the most distant planet.

Visible Planets of the Solar System

Mercury, Venus, Mars, Jupiter and Saturn

Mercury

Mercury, nearest planet to the sun, is also the smallest of the nine planets known to be orbiting the sun. Its diameter is 3,100 miles and its mean distance from the sun is 36,000,000 miles.

Mercury moves with great speed in its journey about the sun, averaging about 30 miles a second to complete its circuit in 88 of our days. Mercury rotates upon its axis over a period of nearly 59 days, thus exposing all of its surface periodically to the sun. It is believed that the surface passing before the sun may have a temperature of about 800° F., while the temperature on the side turned temporarily away from the sun does not fall as low as might be expected. This night temperature has been described by Russian astronomers as "room temperature" — possibly about 70°. This would contradict the former belief that Mercury did not possess an atmosphere, for some sort of atmosphere would be needed to retain some of the fierce solar radiation that must strike Mercury at its small distance from the sun. A shallow but dense layer of carbon dioxide would produce the "greenhouse" effect, in which heat accumulated during exposure to the sun would not completely escape at night. The actual presence of a carbon dioxide atmosphere is in dispute.

This uncertainty about conditions upon Mercury and its motion arise from its short angular distance from the sun as seen from the earth, for Mercury is always too much in line with the sun to be observed against a dark sky, but is always seen during either morning or evening twilight.

Mariner 10 made three passes by Mercury in 1974 and 1975. A large fraction of the surface was photographed from varying distances, revealing a degree of cratering similar to that of the moon. An atmosphere of hydrogen and helium may be made up of gases of the solar wind temporarily concentrated by the disturbing presence of Mercury. The discovery of a weak but permanent magnetic field was a surprise. It has been held that both a fluid core and rapid rotation (such as that of earth) were necessary for the generation of a planetary magnetic field. Mercury may demonstrate these conditions to be unnecessary, or the field may reveal something about the history of Mercury.

Venus

Venus is slightly smaller than the earth. Its diameter is about 200 miles less than the earth's diameter. Venus moves about the sun at a mean distance of 67,000,000 miles in 225 of our days. Its synodical revolution — its return to the same relationship with the earth and the sun, which is a result of the combination of its own motion and that of the earth — is 584 days. Venus will, then, be nearer to the earth every 19 months than any of the other planets of the solar system. We have never been able to see the surface of Venus because the planet is covered with a dense, white, cloudy atmosphere that conceals whatever is below it. This same cloud reflects sunlight efficiently so that when Venus is favorably situated, it is the third brightest object in the sky, exceeded only by the sun and the moon.

Ordinary telescopic observation has been unable to reveal much about the nature of the surface of Venus, not even its period of axial rotation. Spectral analysis of sunlight reflected from Venus' cloud tops has shown features that can best be explained by identifying the material of the clouds as sulphuric acid (oil of vitriol). Infrared spectroscopy from a balloon-borne telescope nearly 20 miles above the earth's surface gave indications of a small amount of water vapor present in the same region of the atmosphere of Venus. In 1956, a breakthrough in our knowledge came from radio astronomers at the Naval Research Laboratories in Washington, D. C. Their observations indicated a temperature for Venus of about 600° F., in marked contrast to minus 125° F., previously found at the cloud tops. Subsequent radio work confirmed a high temperature and produced evidence for this temperature to be associated with the solid body of Venus. With this peculiarity in mind, space scientists devised experiments for the U.S. space probe Mariner 2 to perform when it flew by in 1962. Mariner 2 confirmed the high temperature and the fact that it pertained to the ground rather than to some special activity of the atmosphere. In addition, Mariner 2 was unable to detect any radiation belts similar to the earth's so-called Van Allen belts. Nor was it able to detect the existence of a magnetic field even as weak as 1/100,000 of that of the earth.

An international scientific drama occurred in 1966 when a Russian space probe, Venus 4, and the American Mariner 5 arrived at Benus within a few hours of each other. Venus 4 was unique in that it was designed to allow an instrument package to land gently on the planet's surface via parachute. It ceased transmission of information after 75 minutes when the temperature it read went above 500° F. After considerable controversy, it was agreed that it still had 20 miles to go to reach the surface. The U.S. probe, Mariner 5, went around the dark side of Venus at a distance of about 6,000 miles. Again, it detected no significant magnetic field, but its radio signals passed to earth through Venus' atmosphere twice — once on the night side and once on the day side. The results are startling. Venus' atmosphere is nearly all carbon dioxide and must exert a pressure at the planet's surface of up to 100 times the earth's normal sea-level pressure of one atmosphere. Since the earth and Venus are about the same size, and were presumably formed at the same time by the same general process from the same mixture of chemical elements, one is faced with the question: which is the planet with the unusual history — earth or Venus?

In the last several years, astronomers using radar techniques involving powerful transmitters as well as sensitive receivers and computers have succeeded in determining the rotation period of Venus. It turns out to be 243 days clockwise — in other words, contrary to the spin of most of the other planets and to its own motion around the sun. If it were exactly 243.16 days, Venus would always present the same face toward the earth at every inferior conjunction. This rate and sense of rotation allows a "day" on Venus of 117.4 earth days. Any part of Venus will receive sunlight on its clouds for over 58 days and will be in darkness for 58 days.

Mariner 10 passed Venus before traveling on to Mercury. The carbon dioxide molecule found in such abundance in the atmosphere is rather opaque to certain ultraviolet wavelengths, enabling sensitive television cameras to take pictures of the Venusian cloud cover. Photos radioed to earth show a spiral pattern in the clouds from equator to the poles. Long-lived features in the clouds have been detected moving at speeds of the order of a hundred miles per hour or more. If this is typical of the wind speed over the ground of Venus, it can account for the transfer of heat to the night side in spite of the low rotation rate of the planet.

Recent radar observations have shown surface features below the clouds. Large craters have been identified. Before the end of 1977, we should have radar-derived pictures of Venus that are as revealing as ordinary telescopic views of our moon taken by earth-based telescopes.

Mars

Mars is the first planet beyond the earth, away from the sun. Mars' diameter is about 4,200 miles, although a determination of the radius and mass of Mars by the space-probe, Mariner 4, which flew by Mars on July 14, 1965 at a distance of less than 6,000 miles, indicated that these dimensions were slightly larger than had been previously estimated. While Mars orbit is also nearly circular, it is somewhat more eccentric than the orbits of many of the other planets, and Mars is more than 30 million miles farther from the sun in some parts of its year than it is at others. Mars takes 687 of our days to make one circuit of the sun, traveling at about 15 miles a second. Mars rotates upon its axis in almost the same period of time that the earth does — 24 hours and 37 minutes. Mars' mean distance from the sun is 141 million miles, so that the temperature on Mars would be lower than that on the earth even if Mars' atmosphere were about the same as ours. The atmosphere is not, however, for Mariner 4 reported that atmospheric pressure on Mars is between 1% and 2% of the earth's atmospheric pressure. This thin atmosphere appears to be largely carbon dioxide. No evidence of free water was found.

There appears to be no magnetic field about Mars. This would eliminate the previous conception of a dangerous radiation belt around Mars similar to the Van Allen Belt around the earth. The same lack of a magnetic field would expose the surface of Mars to an influx of cosmic radiation about 100 times as intense as that on earth.

Deductions from years of telescopic observation indicate that 5/8ths of the surface of Mars is a desert of reddish rock, sand and soil. The rest of Mars is covered by irregular patches that appear generally green in hues that change through the Martian year. These were formerly held to be some sort of primitive vegetation, but with the findings of Mariner 4 of a complete lack of water and oxygen, such growth does not appear possible. The nature of the green areas is now unknown. They may be regions covered with volcanic salts whose color changes with changing temperatures and atmospheric conditions, or they may be gray, rather than green. Optical experiments show that when large gray areas are placed beside large red areas, the gray areas will appear green to the eye.

Mars' axis of rotation is inclined from a vertical to the plane of its orbit about the sun by about 25° and therefore has seasons as does the earth, except that the Martian seasons are longer because Mars' year is longer. White caps form about the winter pole of Mars, growing through the winter and shrinking in summer. These polar caps were thought to be frozen water which, when it melted, nourished the green areas. In view of the negative findings of Mariner 4, however, the caps are thought to be carbon dioxide.

The canals of Mars have become more of a mystery than they were before the voyage of Mariner 4. Markings forming a network of fine lines crossing much of the surface of Mars have been seen there by men who have devoted much of their professional time to the study of the planet, but no canals have shown clearly enough upon previous photographs to be universally accepted. A few of the 21 photographs sent back to earth by Mariner 4 covered areas crossed by canals. The pictures show faint, ill-defined, broad, dark markings, but no positive identification of the nature of the markings.

Mariners 6 & 7 in 1969 sent back many more photographs of higher quality than those of the pioneering Mariner 4. These pictures showed cratering similar to the earlier views, but in addition showed two other types of terrain. Some regions seemed featureless for many square miles, but others were chaotic, showing high relief without apparent organization into mountain chains or craters.

Mariner 9, the first artificial body to be placed in an orbit about Mars, has transmitted over 10,000 photographs covering 100% of the planet's surface. Preliminary study of these photos and other data shows that Mars resembles no other planet we know. Using terrestrial terms, however, scientists describe features that seem to be clearly of volcanic origin. One of these features is Nix Olympica, apparently a caldera whose outer slopes are over 300 miles in diameter. Some features may have been produced by cracking (faulting) of the surface and the sliding of one region over or past another. Many craters seem to have been produced by impacting bodies such as may have come from the nearby asteroid belt. Features near the south pole may have been produced by glaciers that are no longer present. Flowing water, non-existent on Mars at the present time, probably carved canyons, one 10 times longer and 3 times deeper than the Grand Canyon.

Although the Russians landed a probe on the Martian surface, it transmitted for only 20 seconds. The U.S., in its Viking program, expects to land two very sophisticated craft on Mars in mid-1976 in an attempt to detect, among other things, if life exists or has ever existed on the planet.

Mars' position in its orbit and its speed around that

orbit in relation to the earth's position and speed bring Mars fairly close to the earth on occasions about two years apart and then move Mars and the earth too far apart for accurate observation and photography. Every 15-17 years, the close approaches are especially favorable for an all-out astronomical attack on Mars.

Mars has two satellites. They are small, estimated to be about 5 and 10 miles in diameter if their surfaces have properties similar to that of our moon. They were discovered in 1877 by Asaph Hall. The outer satellite is named Deimos and it revolves around Mars in about 31 hours. The inner satellite, Phobos, whips around Mars in a little more than 7 hours, making three trips around the planet each Martian day.

The Mariner flights of 1969 produced a photograph accidentally taken showing Phobos, silhouetted against the planet. An analysis of the image gives dimensions of Phobos as about 14 miles by 8 miles, proportions resembling those of a potato. The ability of Phobos to reflect light appears to be even less than that of the earth's moon. Mariner 9 has confirmed those results and added information that Phobos and Deimos are pitted with large craters and are of irregular shape, suggesting a history of fragmentation.

Jupiter

Jupiter is the largest of the planets. Its equatorial diameter is 88,000 miles, 11 times the diameter of the Earth. Its polar diameter is about 6,000 miles shorter. This is caused by the almost fluid condition of its atmosphere and its extremely rapid rate of rotation. Jupiter's day is just under 10 hours long. For a planet of this size, this rotational speed is amazing, and it moves a point on Jupiter's equator at a speed of 22,-000 miles an hour, as compared with 1,000 miles an hour for a point on the Earth's equator. Jupiter is at an average distance of 480 million miles from the sun and takes almost 12 of our years to make one complete circuit of the sun.

The only directly observable chemical constituents of Jupiter's atmosphere are methane (CH_4) and ammonia (NH_3), but it is reasonable to assume the same mixture of elements available to make Jupiter as to make the sun. This would mean a large fraction of hydrogen and helium must be present also, as well as water (H_2O). The temperature at the tops of the clouds may be about minus 260° F. The clouds are probably ammonia ice crystals, becoming ammonia droplets lower down. There may be a space before water ice crystals show up as clouds; in turn, these become water droplets near the bottom of the entire cloud layer. The total atmosphere may be only a few hundred miles in depth, pulled down by the surface gravity (= 2.64 times Earth's) to a relatively thin layer. Of course, the gases become denser with depth until they may turn into a slush or a slurry. Perhaps there is no solid surface—no real interface between solid and gas. Its temperature may approach 1,000° F. Long before the center is reached, hydrogen and helium become a fluid metal and perhaps a solid metal near the center. Jupiter's cloudy atmosphere is a fairly good reflector of sunlight and makes it far brighter than any of the stars among which it wanders.

Jupiter has 14 satellites. Four of these are large and bright, rivaling our own moon and the planet Mercury in diameter, and may be seen through a field glass. They move rapidly around Jupiter and their change of position from night to night is extremely interesting to watch. The other satellites are much smaller and in all but one instance much farther from Jupiter and cannot be seen except through powerful telescopes. The 4 outermost satellites are revolving around Jupiter clockwise as seen from the north, contrary to the motions of the great majority of the satellites in the solar system and to the direction of revolution of the planets around the sun. The reason for this retrograde motion is not known, but one theory is that Jupiter's tremendous gravitational power may have captured 4 of the minor planets or asteroids that move about the sun between Mars and Jupiter, and that these 4 would be running backwards. Jupiter's mass is more than twice the mass of all the other planets put together, and accounts for Jupiter's tremendous gravitational field and so, probably, for its numerous satellites and its dense atmosphere.

In December, 1973, Pioneer 10 passed about 80,000 miles from the equator of Jupiter and was whipped into a path taking it out of our solar system in about 50 years. In December, 1974, Pioneer 11 passed within 30,000 miles of Jupiter, moving roughly from south to north, over the poles. Photographs from both encounters reveal much detail in the clouds, including what appear to be cyclonic storms. The Great Red Spot shows a spiral nature suggesting it is a long lived hurricane-like feature. The magnetic field is eccentric and tilted. It is stronger than was thought and of the opposite sign to that of the earth. The action of the trapped particles — the Jovian Van Allen Belts — is too violent to let man pass through in present spacecraft without serious radiation injury. Analysis of the paths of the Pioneers and of other facts about Jupiter indicate the planet may be almost entirely fluid, with a gaseous atmosphere and liquid ball, except for, perhaps, an earth-size core that is solid.

Both Pioneers contain a pictorial message that has been included for the benefit of extra-solar system finders of the derelicts. Before Pioneer 11 leaves the solar system, it will make a visit to Saturn in September, 1979.

Saturn

Saturn, last of the planets visible to the unaided eye, is almost twice as far from the sun as Jupiter, almost 900 million miles. It is second in size to Jupiter but its mass is much smaller. Saturn's specific gravity is less than that of water. Its diameter is about 71,000 miles at the equator; its rotational speed spins it completely around in a little more than 10 hours, and its atmosphere is much like that of Jupiter, except that its temperature at the top of its cloud layer is at least 100° colder. At about 300° F. below zero, the ammonia would be frozen out of Saturn's clouds. The theoretical construction of Saturn resembles that of Jupiter; it is either all gas, or it has a small dense center surrounded by a layer of liquid and a deep atmosphere.

Saturn has 10 satellites. The 10th having been discovered by the French astronomer Audouin Dollfus in December, 1966. The newly found satellite is a few thousand miles outside of the edge of Saturn's ring system. Its discovery was made possible by an edge-on presentation of the rings.

Saturn's ring system begins about 7,000 miles above the visible disk of Saturn, lying above its equator and extending about 35,000 miles into space. The diameter of the ring system, including Saturn itself, is about 170,000 miles; the rings are estimated to be no thicker than 10 miles. In 1973, radar observation showed the ring particles to be large chunks of material averaging a meter on a side.

The rings cannot be seen except in a telescope of at least 3-inch aperture. Because of Saturn's inclination, as stated above, there are two periods during Saturn's journey around the sun when the rings are presented to us edge-on. At these times, the rings disappear. Nothing that is only 10 miles wide can be seen from a distance of nearly 900 million miles. The rings are receding from a favorable position to be seen. They were edge-on in 1966 and reached maximum visibility again in 1973.

Pioneer 11 was guided to pass Jupiter in such a way that Jupiter will swing Pioneer 11 into an orbit that will bring it near Saturn in 1979. If the space craft is functioning adequately at that time, it will send us the photos and physical data possible only from a close fly-by. This will complete man's initial on-site inspection of the classical planets.

Planetary Configurations, 1977

Greenwich Mean Time (0 designates midnight; 12 designates noon)

Mo.	d.	h.	m.	
Jan.	1	2	—☌♃☽	♃ 0°.8 N occultation
	3	10	—	⊕ at perihelion
	6	8	—☌☿☉	inferior
	8	0	—☌♄☽	♄ 6° N
	12	12	—☌☿♂	☿ 4° N
	18	1	—☌☿☽	☿ 2° S
	18	12	—☌♂☽	♂ 6° S
	23	11	—☌♀☽	♀ 3° S
	24	12	—	♀ gr. elong. E (47°)
	28	10	—☌♃☽	♃ 1° N
	29	0	—	☿ gr. elong. W (25°)
Feb.	2	10	—☍♄☉	
	4	04	—☌♄☽	♄ 6° N
	12	19	—☌☿♂	☿ 0°.1 S
	16	12	—☌♂☽	♂ 6° S
	16	17	—☌☿☽	☿ 7° S
	21	17	—☌♀☽	♀ 3° N
	24	22	—☌♃☽	♃ 2° N
Mar.	1	2	—	♀ gr. brilliancy
	3	9	—☌♄☽	♄ 6° N
	16	5	—☌☿☉	superior
	17	12	—☌♂☽	♂ 6° S
	20	17	43	Vernal Equinox; Spring begins
	21	13	—☌♀☽	♀ 8° N
	24	15	—☌♃☽	♃ 2° N
	27	19	—☌☿♀	☿ 8° S
	30	17	—☌♃☽	♃ 6° N
Apr.	4	04	—☍☽☉	☽ partial eclipse
	6	6	—☌♀☉	inferior
	10	16	—	☿ gr. elong. E (19°)
	15	12	—☌♂☽	♂ 4° S
Apr.	16	20	—☌♀☽	♀ 5° N
	18	11	—☌☽☉	☉ annular eclipse
	19	16	—☌♀☽	♀ 5° N
	21	09	—☌♃☽	♃ 3° N
	27	01	—☌♄☽	♄ 6° N
	30	17	—☌☿☉	inferior
May	11	23	—	♀ gr. brilliancy
	13	18	—☌♀♂	♀ 1°.3
	14	11	—☌♀☽	♀ 1° S occultation
	14	12	—☌♂☽	♂ 2° S
	16	07	—☌☿☽	☿ 2° S
	20	13	—☌♃*	♃ 5° N of Aldebaran
	24	11	—☌♄☽	♄ 6° N
	27	23	—	☿ gr. elong. W (25°)
June	3	13	—☌♀♂	♀ 1°.2 S
	4	10	—☌♃☉	
	12	11	—☌♂☽	♂ 0°.1 N occultation
	12	15	—☌♀☽	♀ 2° S
	15	05	—☌☿☽	☿ 2° N
	15	07	—	♀ gr. elong. W (46°)
	16	15	—☌☿*	☿ 5° N of Aldebaran
	20	07	—☌☿♃	☿ 0°.1 N
	20	21	—☌♄☽	♄ 6° N
	21	12	14	Summer Solstice; Summer begins

Mo.	d.	h.	m.	
[June]	30	00	—☌☿☉	superior
July	5	20	—	⊕ aphelion
	11	11	—☌♂☽	♂ 2° N
	12	09	—☌♀☽	♀ 1° N occultation
	13	19	—☌♃☽	♃ 4° N
	15	19	—☌♀*	♀ 3° N of Aldebaran
	18	03	—☌☿☽	☿ 6° N
July	18	09	—☌♄☽	♄ 6° N
	20	01	—☌☿♄	☿ 0°.4 N
	28	03	—☌☿*	☿ 0°.1 S of Regulus
	30	06	—☌♀♃	♀ 1°.6 S
Aug.	1	12	—☌♂*	♂ 5° N of Aldebaran
	8	20	—	☿ gr. elong. E (27°)
	9	11	—☌♂☽	♂ 4° N
	11	14	—☌♀☽	♀ 4° N
	13	06	—☌♄☉	
	16	23	—☌☿☽	☿ 0°.9 S occultation
	23	17	—☌♀*	♀ 7° S of Pollux
Sept.	4	22	—☌♂♃	♂ 0°.5 N
	5	06	—☌☿☉	☿ inferior
	7	07	—☌♃☽	♃ 5° N
	7	09	—☌♂☽	♂ 5° N
	10	21	—☌♀☽	♀ 5° N
	11	13	—☌♄☽	♄ 5° N
	18	13	—☌♀♄	♀ 0°.4 S
	21	08	—	☿ gr. elong. W (18°)
	22	03	—☌♀*	♀ 0°.4
	23	03	30	Autumnal Equinox; Autumn begins
	27	08	—☍☽☉	☽ penumbral eclipse
Oct.	4	21	—☌♃☽	♃ 5° N
	6	03	—☌♂☽	♂ 6° N
	9	04	—☌♄☽	♄ 5° N
	11	01	—☌♀☽	♀ 4° N
	11	21	—☌☽☉	☉ total eclipse
	13	14	—☌♂*	♂ 6° S of Pollux
	18	23	—☌☿☉	superior
Nov.	1	05	—☌♃☽	♃ 5° N
	3	12	—☌♄*	♄ 0°.8 N of Regulus
Nov.	3	14	—☌♂☽	♂ 7° N
	3	20	—☌♀*	♀ 4° N
	5	18	—☌♄☽	♄ 5° N
	10	00	—☌♀☽	♀ 0°.1 N occultation
	15	19	—☌☿*	☿ 3° N of Antares
	28	08	—☌♃☽	♃ 5° N
Dec.	1	13	—☌♂☽	♂ 7° N
	3	3	—☌♄☽	♄ 5° N
	3	8	—☌☿☽	☿ gr. elong. E (21°)
	10	23	—☌♀*	♀ 5° N of Antares
	12	00	—☌☿☽	☿ 6° S
	21	14	—☌☿☉	inferior
	21	23	24	Winter Solstice; Winter begins
	23	01	—☍♃☉	
	25	07	—☌♃☽	♃ 5° N
	28	18	—☌♂☽	♂ 8° N
	30	09	—☌♄☽	♄ 5° N

Planetary Configurations, 1978

As a service to those who wish to consult the planetary configurations for early 1978 in the preceding fall, THE WORLD ALMANAC publishes the configurations for January, February, March, and April, 1978.

Jan.	1	23	—	⊕ perihelion
	11	9	—	☿ gr. elong. W (23°)
	22	00	—☍♂☉	
	22	05	—☌♀☉	superior
Feb.	16	04	—☍♄☉	
	27	03	—☌☿☉	superior
Mar.	12	22	—☌☿♀	☿ 1°.3 N
	20	23	34	vernal equinox; spring begins
	24	17	—	☿ gr. elong. E (19°)
	28	19	—☌☿♀	☿ 4° N
Apr.	11	17	—☌☿☉	inferior

Right Ascension of Mean Sun, 1977

0^h Greenwich Mean Time

Date	h	m	Date	h	m	Date	h	m	Date	h	m	Date	h	m	Date	h	m
Jan. 1	18	41.9	Mar. 1	22	34.8	May 10	03	10.7	July 9	07	07.2	Sept. 7	11	04.0	Nov. 6	15	00.4
11	19	21.2	11	23	14.3	20	03	50.1	19	07	46.7	17	11	43.4	16	15	39.7
21	20	00.8	21	23	53.7	30	04	29.5	29	08	26.1	27	12	22.8	26	16	19.1
31	20	40.3	31	00	33.2	June 9	05	08.9	Aug. 8	09	05.4	Oct. 7	13	02.2	Dec. 6	16	58.4
Feb. 10	21	19.8	Apr. 10	01	12.6	19	05	48.3	18	09	45.2	17	13	41.6	16	17	37.8
20	21	59.3	20	01	52.0	29	06	27.8	28	10	24.6	27	14	21.0	26	18	07.2
			30	02	31.3												

Rising and Setting of Planets, 1977

Greenwich Mean Time(0 designates midnight)

Venus, 1977

Date	20° N. Latitude Rise	Set	30°N. Latitude Rise	Set	40° N. Latitude Rise	Set	50° N. Latitude Rise	Set	60° N. Latitude Rise	Set
Jan. 1	9:31	20:54	9:43	20:42	9:58	20:27	10:18	20:07	10:50	19:35
15	9:23	21:06	9:29	20:59	9:37	20:52	9:47	20:42	10:03	20:26
Feb. 1	9:05	21:12	9:04	21:13	9:03	21:14	9:01	21:16	8:58	21:18
15	8:42	21:08	8:36	21:15	8:28	21:23	8:17	21:34	7:59	21:51
Mar. 1	8:10	20:52	7:58	21:04	7:44	21:18	7:25	21:37	6:54	22:08
15	7:21	20:14	7:06	20:28	6:48	20:46	6:23	21:11	5:42	21:52
Apr. 1	5:44	18:34	5:31	18:47	5:14	19:04	4:51	19:27	4:14	20:04
15	4:40	17:14	4:31	17:22	4:20	17:33	4:05	17:48	3:42	18:11
May 1	3:40	16:01	3:35	16:06	3:29	16:12	3:20	16:20	3:07	16:33
15	3:08	15:28	3:03	15:33	2:58	15:39	2:50	15:47	2:37	15:59
June 1	2:45	15:13	2:38	15:20	2:29	15:29	2:16	15:42	1:57	16:01
15	2:33	15:13	2:23	15:23	2:10	15:36	1:52	15:54	1:24	16:22
July 1	2:27	15:20	2:12	15:34	1:54	15:52	1:29	16:18	0:48	16:59
15	2:28	15:31	2:10	15:49	1:48	16:11	1:17	16:42	0:24	17:35
Aug. 1	2:37	15:48	2:17	16:08	1:52	16:34	1:16	17:10	0:13	18:12
15	2:51	16:03	2:31	16:22	2:06	16:48	1:30	17:24	0:27	18:26
Sept. 1	3:13	16:16	2:56	16:33	2:34	16:55	2:03	17:26	1:12	18:17
15	3:33	16:22	3:19	16:36	3:03	16:52	2:39	17:16	2:02	17:53
Oct. 1	3:55	16:25	3:47	16:33	3:37	16:42	3:24	16:55	3:04	17:16
15	4:13	16:24	4:11	16:26	4:09	16:29	4:05	16:33	3:59	16:38
Nov. 1	4:36	16:23	4:41	16:18	4:47	16:12	4:55	16:04	5:07	15:52
15	4:56	16:25	5:07	16:14	5:20	16:01	5:38	15:43	6:05	15:16
Dec. 1	5:22	16:31	5:39	16:15	5:59	15:55	6:27	15:27	7:13	14:41
15	5:47	16:44	6:07	16:24	6:32	15:59	7:07	15:24	8:08	14:23

Mars, 1977

Date	20° N. Latitude Rise	Set	30°N. Latitude Rise	Set	40° N. Latitude Rise	Set	50° N. Latitude Rise	Set	60° N. Latitude Rise	Set
Jan 1	5:51	16:42	6:13	16:20	6:41	15:52	7:20	15:13	8:32	14:02
15	5:42	16:33	6:03	16:12	6:31	15:44	7:10	15:06	8:19	13:57
Feb. 1	5:28	16:25	5:48	16:05	6:13	15:40	6:49	15:04	7:50	14:03
15	5:15	16:19	5:33	16:01	5:55	15:38	6:26	15:08	7:18	14:16
Mar. 1	4:59	16:12	5:14	15:57	5:33	15:39	5:59	15:13	6:40	14:31
15	4:42	16:06	4:53	15:54	5:08	15:39	5:28	15:19	5:59	14:48
Apr. 1	4:18	15:56	4:26	15:49	4:35	15:39	4:47	15:27	5:07	15:08
15	3:57	15:48	4:01	15:44	4:06	15:39	4:12	15:33	4:22	15:23
May 1	3:32	15:37	3:32	15:38	3:32	15:38	3:31	15:39	3:30	15:40
15	3:10	15:28	3:07	15:32	3:02	15:37	2:55	15:43	2:45	15:54
June 1	2:44	15:16	2:36	15:24	2:26	15:34	2:12	15:48	1:50	16:10
15	2:23	15:06	2:11	15:18	1:57	15:32	1:37	15:51	1:06	16:23
July 1	2:00	14:54	1:45	15:09	1:26	15:28	1:00	15:54	0:18	16:36
15	1:41	14:44	1:23	15:01	1:01	15:23	0:30	15:54	23:39	16:46
Aug. 1	1:18	14:30	0:59	14:50	0:33	15:15	23:59	15:50	22:56	16:53
15	1:01	14:16	0:40	14:38	0:13	15:05	23:35	15:43	22:26	16:53
Sept. 1	0:40	13:58	0:18	14:20	23:51	14:48	23:10	15:28	21:57	16:41
15	0:21	13:39	23:59	14:01	23:31	14:29	22:51	15:09	21:38	16:23
Oct. 1	23:58	13:14	23:37	13:36	23:10	14:03	22:31	14:42	21:21	15:52
15	23:35	12:49	23:15	13:09	22:49	13:35	22:12	14:12	21:06	15:18
Nov. 1	23:02	12:12	22:43	12:31	22:18	12:56	21:43	13:31	20:43	14:31
15	22:29	11:36	22:10	11:55	21:47	12:18	21:14	12:52	20:17	13:49
Dec. 1	21:42	10:48	21:24	11:06	21:01	11:29	20:28	12:02	19:33	12:58
15	20:51	9:58	20:32	10:16	20:08	10:40	19:35	11:13	18:38	12:10

Jupiter, 1977

Date	20° N. Latitude Rise	Set	30°N. Latitude Rise	Set	40° N. Latitude Rise	Set	50° N. Latitude Rise	Set	60° N. Latitude Rise	Set
Jan. 1	14:03	2:59	13:47	3:15	13:28	3:34	13:00	4:02	12:16	4:46
15	13:06	2:03	12:51	2:19	12:31	2:38	12:04	3:05	11:20	3:50
Feb. 1	12:01	0:58	11:45	1:14	11:26	1:34	10:58	2:01	10:13	2:47
15	11:10	0:08	10:54	0:24	10:34	0:45	10:06	1:13	9:19	1:59
Mar. 1	10:20	23:20	10:03	23:36	9:43	23:57	9:14	0:26	8:25	1:14
15	9:33	22:35	9:16	22:52	8:55	23:14	8:25	23:44	7:34	0:34
Apr. 1	8:38	21:42	8:20	22:00	7:58	22:22	7:26	22:54	6:33	23:47
15	7:53	21:00	7:35	21:18	7:12	21:41	6:39	22:14	5:43	23:10
May 1	7:04	20:12	6:45	20:32	6:21	20:56	5:46	21:30	4:48	22:29
15	6:21	19:32	6:01	19:51	5:37	20:16	5:01	20:51	4:00	21:53
June 1	5:30	18:42	5:10	19:03	4:44	19:28	4:08	20:05	3:03	21:09
15	4:48	18:02	4:27	18:23	4:01	18:49	3:24	19:26	2:17	20:33
July 1	4:00	17:15	3:39	17:36	3:13	18:03	2:34	18:41	1:26	19:50
15	3:18	16:34	2:57	16:55	2:30	17:22	1:51	18:01	0:42	19:10
Aug. 1	2:26	15:43	2:05	16:04	1:38	16:31	0:59	17:10	23:48	18:21
15	1:42	14:59	1:21	15:20	0:54	15:48	0:15	16:27	23:04	17:38
Sept. 1	0:48	14:04	0:26	14:26	23:59	14:53	23:20	15:32	22:09	16:43
15	0:01	13:17	23:39	13:40	23:12	14:06	22:33	14:45	21:22	15:56
Oct. 1	23:05	12:21	22:43	12:42	22:16	13:09	21:37	13:48	20:27	14:59
15	22:13	11:29	21:51	11:50	21:24	12:17	20:45	12:56	19:35	14:07
Nov. 1	21:06	10:22	20:45	10:44	20:17	11:11	19:38	11:50	18:28	13:00
15	20:08	9:24	19:46	9:46	19:19	10:13	18:40	10:52	17:29	12:03
Dec. 1	18:59	8:15	18:37	8:37	18:10	9:04	17:30	9:43	16:19	10:55
15	17:56	7:13	17:34	7:34	17:07	8:02	16:27	8:41	15:16	9:53

Saturn, 1977

Date	20° N. Latitude Rise	Set	30° N. Latitude Rise	Set	40° N. Latitude Rise	Set	50° N. Latitude Rise	Set	60° N. Latitude Rise	Set
Jan. 1	20:03	8:59	19:48	9:14	19:28	9:33	19:02	10:00	18:18	10:44
15	19:04	8:01	18:48	8:16	18:29	8:36	18:01	9:03	17:16	9:48
Feb. 1	17:51	6:49	17:35	7:05	17:15	7:25	16:47	7:53	16:00	8:40
15	16:46	5:46	16:30	6:02	16:10	6:23	15:41	6:52	14:53	7:39
Mar. 1	15:47	4:47	15:30	5:04	15:09	5:25	14:40	5:54	13:51	6:43
15	14:48	3:50	14:31	4:06	14:10	4:28	13:41	4:57	12:51	5:47
Apr. 1	13:39	2:41	13:22	2:58	13:01	3:19	12:31	3:49	11:41	4:39
15	12:44	1:46	12:27	2:03	12:05	2:24	11:35	2:54	10:45	3:44
May 1	11:42	0:44	11:26	1:01	11:04	1:22	10:35	1:52	9:45	2:42
15	10:50	23:51	17:50	23:51	10:13	0:29	9:43	0:58	8:54	1:48
June 1	9:49	22:49	9:33	23:05	9:12	23:26	8:43	23:54	7:55	0:42
15	9:00	21:58	8:43	22:14	8:23	22:34	7:55	23:03	7:08	23:49
July 1	8:04	21:01	7:49	21:17	7:29	21:36	7:02	22:03	6:17	22:48
15	7:17	20:12	7:01	20:27	6:43	20:46	6:16	21:12	5:33	21:55
Aug. 1	6:19	19:12	6:05	19:27	5:46	19:45	5:21	20:10	4:40	20:51
15	5:32	18:24	5:18	18:38	5:00	18:55	4:36	19:19	3:57	19:58
Sept. 1	4:35	17:24	4:21	17:37	4:05	17:54	3:42	18:17	3:04	18:54
15	3:47	16:35	3:34	16:48	3:18	17:04	2:56	17:26	2:20	18:01
Oct. 1	2:52	15:38	2:40	15:50	2:24	16:06	2:03	16:27	1:29	17:01
15	2:03	14:48	1:51	15:00	1:36	15:14	1:16	15:35	0:43	16:08
Nov. 1	1:02	13:46	0:51	13:57	0:36	14:11	0:17	14:31	23:45	15:03
15	0:11	12:53	0:00	13:05	23:46	13:19	23:26	13:38	22:55	14:09
Dec. 1	23:10	11:52	22:59	12:04	22:45	12:17	22:26	12:36	21:56	13:07
15	22:16	10:58	22:04	11:09	21:50	11:23	21:31	11:42	21:01	12:12

The Planets and the Solar System

Name of Planet	Mean Daily Motion ″	Orbital Velocity Miles Per Sec.	Sidereal Revolution Days	Synodical Revolution Days	Dist. from Sun in Millions of Miles Max.	Min.	Approx. miles from Earth in Millions Max.	Min.	Light at Perihelion	Aphelion
Mercury....	14732.420	29.75	87.9693	115.9	43.403	28.597	136	50	10.58	4.59
Venus.....	5767.668	21.76	224.7009	583.9	67.726	66.813	161	25	1.94	1.89
Earth......	3548.329	18.51	365.2564	—	94.555	91.445	—		1.03	0.97
Mars.......	1886.519	14.99	686.9796	779.9	154.936	128.471	248	35	0.524	0.360
Jupiter.....	299.183	8.12	4332.0466	398.9	507.046	460.595	600	368	0.0408	0.0336
Saturn.....	119.884	5.99	10775.056	378.1	937.541	838.425	1031	745	0.01230	0.00984
Uranus.....	42.355	4.23	30572.21	369.7	1859.748	1699.331	1953	1606	0.00300	0.00250
Neptune....	21.650	3.38	60050.04	367.5	2821.686	2760.386	2915	2667	0.00114	0.00109
Pluto......	14.351	2.95	89952.8	366.7	4551.386	2756.427	4644	2663	0.00114	0.00042

Light at Perihelion and Aphelion is solar illumination in units of mean illumination at Earth.

Name of Planet	Mean Longitude of:* Ascending Node ° ′ ″	Perihelion ° ′ ″	Inclination* of Orbit to Ecliptic ° ′ ″	Mean Distance*	Eccentricity* Nof Orbit	Mean Longitude at the Epoch* ° ′ ″
Mercury....	48 03 38	77 06 00	7 00 15	0.387099	0.205630	288 54 57
Venus.....	78 28 27	131 14 58	3 23 40	0.723332	0.006784	132 39 22
Earth......	- -	102 32 51	- -	1.000000	0.016719	- -
Mars......	49 22 53	335 38 18	1 50 59	1.523691	0.093384	295 50 34
Jupiter.....	100 12 23	14 01 10	1 18 20	5.202168	0.0479528	64 59 27
Saturn.....	113 29 00	93 15 04	2 29 14	9.569096	0.0574163	134 17 37
Uranus.....	73 58 29	167 51 28	0 46 18	19.14567	0.0465173	218 58 06
Neptune....	131 34 22	54 07 15	1 46 18	29.94882	0.0121468	254 10 44
Pluto......	109 54 01	223 31 14	17 08 17	39.39304	0.2468242	192 34 25

*Consistent for the standard Epoch: 1977 Feb. 26.0 Ephemeris Time

Sun and Planets	Semi-Diameter At Unit Distance ′ ″	At Mean Least Dist. ″	In Miles Mean S.D.)	Volume ⊕=1.	Mass. ⊕=1.	Density ⊕=1.	Axial Rotation d.	h.	m.	s.	Gravity at Surface ⊕=1.	Reflecting Power Pct.	Probable Temperature °F.
Sun..........	15 59.63	—	432000	1300000.	332000.	0.26	24	16	48		27.9		+10,000
Mercury.......	3.34	5.45	1505	0.056	0.0543	0.68	59				0.38	0.07	+ 600
Venus........	8.41	30.40	3805	0.910	0.8136	0.94	243 (R)				0.88	0.76	+ 100
Earth........			3959	1.000	1.000	1.00		23	56	4	1.00	0.39	+ 50
Moon.........	2.44	932.58	1080	0.020	0.0120	0.60	27	7	43	12	0.16	0.07	+ 215
Mars.........	4.68	8.94	2070	0.150	0.1069	0.71		24	37	23	0.39	0.15	+ 0
Jupiter........	1 35.19	22.60	43450	1312.	318.35	0.24		9	50		2.65	0.51	- 150
Saturn........	1 18.95	9.24	35750	763.	95.3	0.12		10	14		1.17	0.50	- 250
Uranus........	34.28	1.88	14750	53.	14.54	0.28		10	45 (R)		1.05	0.66	- 350
Neptune.......	36.56	1.26	15750	65.	17.2	0.26		15	48		1.23	0.62	- 400

The planet Pluto was located by C. W. Tombaugh of Lowell Observatory Mar. 13, 1930. Its mass is about 0.18 of the mass of the Earth. It rotates on its axis in 6 days 9 hours. Its average distance from the sun is 3,664,000,-000 miles. On Apr. 2 at 16 hours, GMT, it is in opposition in Virgo at right ascension 13 hrs. 8 mins. 43 secs. and declination, North 10 degrees 53 minutes 51 seconds, west of Epsilon Virginis. Pluto will then have a magnitude of about 14. (R) Venus and Uranus are in retrograde motion, rotating in opposite direction from other planets.

Four Eclipses in 1977

Greenwich Mean Time

First Eclipse

A **partial eclipse of the moon, April 4.** Less than 20% of the diameter of the moon enters umbra of the earth's shadow in this eclipse. The beginning of the umbral phase is visible in western Africa, western Europe, the Atlantic Ocean, South America, part of Antarctica, North America except the northwestern part, and the eastern part of the Pacific Ocean.

The end will be visible in western Africa, the extreme western part of Europe, the Atlantic Ocean, Part of Antarctica, South America, North America except the extreme northwestern part, and the eastern half of the Pacific Ocean.

Circumstances of the Eclipse

Moon enters penumbra.	April 4, 2:05.0
Moon enters umbra....	4,3:30.2
Middle of eclipse.......	4, 4:18.2
Moon leaves umbra....	4, 5:06.4
Moon leaves penumbra.	4, 6:31.5

Second Eclipse

An **annular eclipse of the sun, April 18.** Partial phases of this eclipse will be visible throughout southern and eastern Africa south of Egypt, and the southern Arabian Peninsula. The path of central eclipse begins in the south Atlantic Ocean, makes landfall in South West Africa, leaves land in Tanzania and ends in the Indian Ocean south of Sri Lanka. The maximum duration of the annular phase is 6 minutes, 59.5 seconds.

Circumstances of the Eclipse

Eclipse begins.........	April 18, 7:32.7
Central eclipse begins..	18, 8:43.1
Central eclipse at local noon...............	18, 10:18.0
Central eclipse ends....	18, 12.:18.5
Eclipse ends..........	18, 13:28.8

Third Eclipse

A **penumbral eclipse of the moon, September 27.** In a penumbral eclipse, no part of the moon enters the umbra, so no part shows the distinct outline of the earth's shadow. The part of the moon closest to the umbra may exhibit a sensible darkening, but it may not catch the eye. The beginning of the penumbral phase is calculated as being visible from the extreme western part of Africa, North America, South America, the Atlantic Ocean, part of the arctic regions, most of the Pacific Ocean, and part of Antarctica. The end is visible in the extreme northwestern part of South America, North America except the northeastern part, the Pacific Ocean, part of the arctic regions, Australia, part of Antarctica, and the eastern part of Asia.

Circumstances of the Eclipse

Moon enters penumbra.	Sept. 27, 06:18.3
Middle of eclipse.......	27, 08:29.3
Moon leaves penumbra.	27, 10:40.2

Fourth Eclipse

A **total eclipse of the sun, October 12.** Partial phases of this eclipse will be visible from all 50 of the United States, western and southeastern Canada, Mexico and Central America. The path of totality begins in the Pacific Ocean, runs north of and parallel to the Hawaiian Island chain, enters South America in the Darien region of Columbia and ends in Venezuela. Maximum duration is 2 minutes 37.4 seconds.

Circumstances of the Eclipse

Eclipse begins.........	Oct. 12, 17:47.6
Central eclipse begins..	12, 18:48.5
Central eclipse at local noon...............	12, 20:14.4
Central eclipse ends....	12, 22:04.9
Eclipse ends..........	12, 23:05.7

Morning and Evening Stars, 1977

(Greenwich Mean Time)

	Morning	Evening		Morning	Evening
Jan.	Mercury (from Jan. 6)	Mercury (to Jan. 6)	Aug.	Venus	Mercury
	Mars	Venus		Mars	Saturn (to Aug. 13)
	Saturn	Jupiter		Jupiter	
Feb.	Mercury	Venus		Saturn (from Aug. 13)	
	Mars	Jupiter	Sept.	Mercury (from Sept. 5)	Mercury (to Sept. 5)
	Saturn (to Feb. 2)	Saturn (from Feb. 2)		Venus	
Mar.	Mercury (to Mar. 16)	Mercury (from Mar. 16)		Mars	
				Jupiter	
	Mars	Venus		Saturn	
		Jupiter	Oct.	Mercury (to Oct. 18)	Mercury (from Oct. 18)
		Saturn		Venus	
Apr.	Mercury (from Apr. 30)	Mercury (to Apr. 30)		Mars	
	Venus (from Apr. 6)	Venus (to Apr. 6)		Jupiter	
	Mars	Jupiter		Saturn	
		Saturn	Nov.	Venus	Mercury
May	Mercury	Jupiter		Mars	
	Venus	Saturn		Jupiter	
	Mars			Saturn	
June	Mercury (to June 30)	Mercury (from June 30)	Dec.	Mercury (from Dec. 21)	Mercury (to Dec. 21)
	Venus	Jupiter (to June 4)		Venus	Jupiter (to Dec. 23)
	Mars	Saturn		Mars	
	Jupiter (from June 4)			Jupiter (to Dec. 23)	
July	Venus	Mercury		Saturn	
	Mars	Saturn			
	Jupiter				

Astronomical Constants; Speed of Light

The following astronomical constants were adopted in 1968, in accordance with the resolutions and recommendations of the International Astronomical Union (Hamburg 1964): Velocity of light, 299,792.5 kilometers per second, or about 186,282 statute miles per second; solar parallax, 8'.794; constant of nutation, 9'.210; and constant of aberration, 20'.496.

Star Tables, 1977

These tables include stars of visual magnitude 2.5 and brighter. Co-ordinates are for the epoch Jan. 0.463, 1977. Where no parallax figures are given, the trigonometric parallax figure is smaller than the margin for error and the distance given is obtained by indirect methods. Stars of variable magnitude designated by V.

To find the time when star is on meridian, subtract R.A.M.S. of the sun table on page 756 from the star's right ascension, first adding 24h to the latter, if necessary. Mark this result P.M., if less than 12h; but if greater than 12, subtract 12h and mark the remainder A.M.

Star	Magnitude	Parallax "	Light Yrs.	Right Ascen. h. m.	Decli- nation ° '
α Andromedae (Alpheratz)	2.06	0.02	90	0 07.2	+28 57
β Cassiopeiae	2.26	0.07	45	0 07.9	+59 01
α Phoenicis	2.39	0.04	93	0 25.1	-42 25.8
α Cassiopeiae (Schedir)	2.16	0.01	150	0 39.2	+56 25
β Ceti	1.02	0.06	57	0 42.3	-18 07
γ Cassiopeiae	2.13v	0.03	96	0 55.3	+60 36
β Andromedae	2.02	0.04	76	1 08.3	+35 30
α Eridani (Achernar)	0.51	0.02	118	1 36.9	-57 21
γ Andromedae	2.14		260	2 02.5	+42 13
α Arietis	2.00	0.04	76	2 05.9	+23 21
α Ursae Min. (Pole Star)	1.99v		680	2 09.2	+89 10
o Ceti	2.00v	0.01	103	2 18.2	-3 05
β Persei (Algol)	2.06v	0.03	105	3 06.7	+40 52
α Persei	1.80	0.03	570	3 22.7	+49 47
α Tauri (Aldebaran)	0.86v	0.05	68	4 34.6	+16 28
β Orionis (Rigel)	0.14v		900	5 13.3	-8 14
α Aurigae (Capella)	0.05	0.07	45	5 15.0	+45 59
γ Orionis (Bellatrix)	1.64	0.03	470	5 23.9	+6 20
β Tauri (El Nath)	1.65	0.02	300	5 24.8	+28 35
δ Orionis	2.20v		1500	5 30.8	-0 19
ε Orionis	1.70		1600	5 35.0	-1 13
ζ Orionis	1.79	0.02	1600	5 39.6	-1 57
κ Orionis	2.06		2100	5 46.7	-9 41
α Orionis (Betelgeuse)	0.41v		520	5 53.9	+7 24
β Aurigae	1.86	0.04	88	5 57.8	+44 57
β Canis Majoris	1.96	0.01	750	6 21.7	-17 57
α Carinae (Canopus)	-0.72		98	6 23.4	-52 41
γ Geminorum	1.93	0.03	105	6 36.4	+16 25
α Canis Majoris (Sirius)	-1.42	0.38	8.7	6 44.1	-16 41
ε Canis Majoris	1.48		680	6 57.7	-28 56
δ Canis Majoris	1.85		2100	7 07.5	-26 21
η Canis Majoris	2.46		2700	7 23.2	-29 15
β Geminorum (Castor)	1.97	0.07	45	7 33.1	+31 56
α Canis Minoris (Procyon)	0.37	0.29	11.3	7 38.1	+5 17
β Geminorum (Pollux)	1.16	0.09	35	7 43.9	+28 05
ζ Puppis	2.23		2400	8 02.8	-39 56
γ Velorum	1.88		520	8 08.8	-47 16
ε Carinae	1.97		340	8 22.0	-59 26
δ Velorum	1.95	0.04	76	8 44.1	-54 37
γ Velorum	2.24	0.02	750	9 07.1	+32 30
β Carinae	1.67	0.04	86	9 13.0	-69 37
? Carinae	2.25		750	9 16.5	-59 11
κ Velorum	2.45	0.01	470	9 21.3	-54 55
α Hydrae	1.98	0.02	94	9 26.5	-8 34
α Leonis(Regulus)	1.36	0.04	84	10 07.1	+12 05
γ Leonis	1.99	0.02	90	10 18.7	+19 58
β Ursae Majoris (Merak)	2.37	0.04	78	11 00.5	+56 30
α Ursae Majoris (Dubhe)	1.81	0.03	105	11 02.3	+61 53
β Leonis (Denebola)	2.14	0.08	43	11 47.9	+14 42
γ Ursae Majoris (Phecda)	2.44	0.02	90	11 52.6	+53 49
α Crucis	1.39		370	12 25.3	-62 58
γ Crucis	1.69		220	12 29.9	-56 59
γ Centauri	2.17		160	12 40.2	-48 50
β Crucis	1.28		490	12 46.4	-59 34
ε Ursae Majoris (Alioth)	1.79	0.01	68	12 53.0	+56 05
ζ Ursae Majoris (Mizar)	2.26	0.04	88	13 23.0	+55 03
α Virginis (Spica)	0.91v	0.02	220	13 24.0	-11 02
ε Centauri	2.33		570	13 38.4	-53 21
η Ursae Majoris (Alkaid)	1.87		210	13 46.6	+49 26
β Centauri	0.63	0.02	490	14 02.2	-60 16
θ Centauri	2.04	0.06	55	14 05.3	-36 15
α Bootis (Arcturus)	0.06	0.09	36	14 14.6	+19 18
η Centauri	2.39v		390	14 34.0	-42 03
α Centauri	0.01	0.75	4.4	14 38.0	-60 44
α Lupi	2.32		430	14 40.0	-47 17
ε Bootis	2.37	0.01	103	14 44.0	+27 10
β Ursae Minoris	2.04	0.03	105	14 50.8	+74 15
α Coronae Borealis	2.23v	0.04	76	15 33.7	+26 47
δ Scorpii	2.34		590	15 59.0	-22 33
α Scorpii (Antares)	0.92v	0.02	520	16 28.0	-26 23
α Trianguli Australis	1.93	0.02	82	16 46.2	-68 59
γ Scorpii	2.28	0.05	66	16 48.7	-34 15
η Ophiuchi	2.46	0.05	69	17 09.1	-15 42
? Scorpii	1.60		310	17 32.0	-37 05
α Ophiuchi	2.09	0.06	58	17 33.9	+12 35
θ Scorpii	1.86	0.02	650	17 35.7	-42 59
η Scorpii	2.39		470	17 40.9	-39 01
γ Draconis	2.21	0.02	108	17 56.1	+51 29
ε Sagittarii	1.81	0.02	124	18 22.6	-34 24
α Lyrae (Vega)	0.04	0.12	26.5	18 36.2	+38 46
σ Sagittarii	2.12		300	18 53.8	-26 20
α Aquilae (Altair)	0.77	0.20	16.5	19 49.7	+8 48
γ Cygni	2.22		750	20 21.4	+40 11
α Pavonis	1.95		310	20 23.8	-56 49
α Cygni (Deneb)	1.26		1600	20 40.6	+45 12
ε Cygni	2.46	0.04	75	20 45.3	+33 53
α Cephei	2.44	0.06	52	21 18.0	+62 29
ε Pegasi	2.31		780	21 43.1	+9 46
α Gruis	1.76	0.05	64	22 06.8	-47 04
β Gruis	2.17v		280	22 41.3	-47 00
α Piscis Austrinis (Fomalhaut)	1.19	0.14	22.6	22 56.4	-29 45
β Pegasi	2.50v	0.02	210	23 02.7	+27 57
α Pegasi	2.50	0.03	109	23 03.6	+15 05

Aurora Borealis and Aurora Australis

The Aurora Borealis, also called the Northern Lights, is a broad display of rather faint light in the northern skies at night. The Aurora Australis, a similar phenomenon, appears at the same time in southern skies. The aurora appears in a wide variety of forms. Sometimes it is seen as a quiet glow, almost foglike in character; sometimes as vertical streamers in which there may be considerable motion; sometimes as a series of luminous expanding arcs. There are many colors, with white, yellow, and red predominating.

The auroras are most vivid and most frequently seen at about 20 degrees from the magnetic poles, along the northern coast of the North American continent and the eastern part of the northern coast of Europe. They have been seen as far south as Key West and as far north as Australia and New Zealand, but such occasions are rare.

While the cause of the auroras is not known beyond question, there does seem to be a definite correlation between auroral displays and sun-spot activity. It is thought that atomic particles expelled from the sun by the forces that cause solar flares speed through space at velocities of 400 to 600 miles per second. These particles are entrapped by the earth's magnetic field, forming what are termed the Van Allen belts. The encounter of these clouds of the solar wind with the earth's magnetic field weakens the field so that previously trapped particles are allowed to impact the upper atmosphere. The collisions between solar and terrestrial atoms result in the glow in the upper atmosphere called the aurora. The glow may be vivid where the lines of magnetic force converge near the magnetic poles.

The auroral displays appear at heights ranging from 50 to about 600 miles and have given us a means of estimating the extent of the earth's atmosphere.

The auroras are often accompanied by magnetic storms whose forces, also guided by the lines of force of the earth's magnetic field, disrupt electrical communication.

Comet Table 1977-1986

Name	Year of First Perihelion	Due to Return	Period in Years	Perihelion Dist.	Aphelion Dist.	Inclination to Ecliptic Degree	Long. of Ascend. Node Degree	From Asc. Node to Perihelion Degree
Johnson	1949	Jan. 1977	6.77	2.20	4.95	14	118	206
Dutoit-Neujmin-Delporte	1941	Jan. 1977	6.31	1.68	5.15	3	188	116
Van Houten*	1961	Jan. 1977	15.75	3.94	8.63	7	23	15
Kopff	1906	Mar. 1977	16.41	1.57	5.34	5	120	163
Faye	1843	Mar. 1977	7.41	1.62	5.98	9	199	204
Grigg-Skjellerup	1902	Mar. 1977	5.12	1.00	4.94	21	213	359
Encke	1786	July 1977	3.30	0.34	4.08	12	334	186
Temple I	1867	Jan. 1978	5.50	1.50	4.74	10	68	179
Arend-Rigaux	1950	Jan. 1978	6.84	1.44	5.76	18	122	329
Temple II	1873	Jan. 1978	5.26	1.36	4.68	12	119	191
Wolf-Harrington	1924	Feb. 1978	6.55	1.62	5.38	18	254	187
Whipple	1933	Mar. 1978	7.47	2.48	5.16	10	188	190
DeVico-Swift	1844	Mar. 1978	6.31	1.62	5.20	4	24	325
Tuschinshan I	1965	Apr. 1978	6.64	1.49	5.57	10	96	23
Comas-Sola	1927	Apr. 1978	8.55	1.77	6.60	13	63	40
Daniel	1909	May 1978	7.09	1.66	5.72	20	68	11
Ashbrook-Jackson	1948	July 1978	7.43	2.28	5.33	12	2	349
Tuschinshan II	1965	Aug. 1978	6.80	1.78	5.40	7	288	203
Clark*	1969	Dec. 1978	5.52	1.56	4.68	10	59	209
Van Biesbroeck	1954	Dec. 1978	12.41	2.41	8.30	7	149	134
Tuttle-Giacobini-Kresak	1858	Dec. 1978	5.56	1.15	5.13	14	105	39
Jackson-Neujmin	1936	Dec. 1978	8.39	1.42	6.83	14	163	196
Shajn-Schaldach	1949	Jan. 1979	7.27	2.23	5.27	6	167	215
Giacobini-Zinner	1900	Jan. 1979	6.52	0.99	5.98	32	195	172
Holmes	1892	Jan. 1979	7.05	2.16	5.20	19	328	23
Honda-Mrkos-Pajdusakova	1969	Mar. 1980	5.28	0.58	5.48	13	233	185
Wirtanen	1947	Apr. 1980	5.84	1.26	5.25	12	84	35
Kohoutek*	1975	Aug. 1980	5.67	1.56	4.80	5	274	169
Halley	240BC	May 1986	76.1	0.59	35.3	162	58	112

*One appearance only.

Most of the comets in the table will not be seen except by professional astronomers or by well-equipped amateurs. At any given time, these observers may be able to follow about a half dozen comets of which the public is unaware. An easily seen comet is rare, one or two every ten to fifteen years.

Comets are named for their discoverers, up to three independent observers being so honored. If a comet becomes unusual, it may be well-known by these names. Usually, however, a preliminary designation is used. This is the year followed by a letter of the alphabet assigned in the order of discovery during that year. About two years later, after any likely late discoveries, comets are given their permanent designation which states the year of their perihelion passage and a Roman numeral giving the order of passage during that year. Well-known periodic comets will receive these designations at each appearance, but the literature and the Comet Table will continue to identify them, by their discoverers' names.

Largest Telescopes Are in Northern Hemisphere

Most of the world's major astronomical installations are in the northern hemisphere, while many of astronomy's major problems are found in the southern sky. This imbalance has long been recognized and is being remedied at this time. For several years, large telescopes have been under construction in South America and Australia. Many of these will soon be in use.

In the northern hemisphere the largest reflector is the 236-inch mirror at the Special Astrophysical Observatory in the Caucasus in the Soviet Union. The largest reflectors in the U.S. include 3 in California: at Palomar Mtn., 200 inches; at Lick Observatory, Mt. Hamilton, 120 inches; and at Mt. Wilson Observatory, 100 inches. Also in the U.S. are a 158 inch reflector at Kitt Peak, Arizona, dedicated in June 1973, and a 107-inch telescope at the McDonald Observatory on Mt. Locke in Texas. A telescope at the Crimean Astrophysical observatory in the Soviet Union has a 104-inch mirror.

Placed in service in 1975 were three large reflectors for the southern hemisphere. Associated Universities for Research in Astronomy (AURA), the operating organization of Kitt Peak National Observatory, dedicated the 158-inch reflector (twin of the telescope on Kitt Peak) at Cerro Tololo International Observatory, Chile; the European Southern Observatory began using its 150-inch reflector at La Silla, Chile; and the Anglo-Australian telescope, 140 inches in diameter, opened at Siding Spring Observatory in Australia.

Optical Telescopes

Optical astronomical telescopes are of two kinds, refracting and reflecting. In the first, light passes through a lens which brings the light rays into focus, where the image may be examined after being magnified by a second lens, the eye-piece, or directly photographed.

The reflector consists of a concave parabolic mirror, generally of Pyrex or now of a relatively heat insensitive material, cervit, coated with silver or aluminum, which reflects the light rays back toward the upper end of the telescope, where they are either magnified and observed by the eye-piece or, as in the case of the refractors, photographed. In most reflecting telescopes, the light is reflected again by a secondary mirror and comes to a focus after passing through a hole in the side of the telescope, where the eye-piece or camera is located, or after passing through a hole in the center of the primary mirror.

World's Largest Refractors
Location and diameter in inches

Yerkes Obs., Williams Bay, Wis.	40
Lick Obs., Mt. Hamilton, Cal.	36
Astrophys. Obs., Potsdam, E. Germany	32
Paris Observatory, Meudon, France	32
Allegheny Obs., Pittsburgh, Pa.	30
Univ. of Paris, Nice, France	30
Royal Greenwich Obs., Herstmonceux, England	28
Union Obs., Johannesburg, South Africa	26.5
Universitats-Sternwarte, Vienna, Austria	26.5
University of Virginia	26
Obs., Academy of Sciences, Pulkova, USSR	26
Astronomical Obs., Belgrade, Yugoslavia	26
Leander McCormick Obs., Charlottesville, Va.	26
Obs. Mitaka, Tokyo-to, Japan	26
US Naval Obs., Washington, D.C.	26
Mt. Stromlo Obs., Canberra, Australia	26

World's Largest Reflectors

Major Planetariums in the United States

Academy Planetarium, U.S..Air Force Academy.
Adler Planetarium, Chicago, Ill.
American Museum-Hayden Planetarium, N. Y.C.
Buhl Planetarium, Pittsburgh, Pa.
Charles Hayden Planetarium, Boston, Mass.
Einstein Spacearium, Washington, D.C.
Fels Planetarium, Philadelphia, Pa.
Fernbank Science Center Planetarium, Atlanta, Ga.

Griffith Planetarium, Los Angeles, Cal.
La. Arts and Science Planetarium, Baton Rouge, La.
McDonnell Planetarium, St. Louis, Mo.
Morehead Planetarium, Chapel Hill, N.C.
Morrison Planetarium, San Francisco, Cal.
Robert T. Longway Planetarium, Flint, Mich.
Strassenburgh Planetarium, Rochester, N.Y.

The Sun

The sun, the controlling body of our solar system, is a star whose dimensions cause it to be classified among stars as average in size, temperature, and brightness. Its proximity to the earth makes it appear to us as tremendously large and bright. A series of thermo-nuclear reactions involving the atoms of the elements of which it is composed produces the heat and light that make life possible on the earth.

The sun has a diameter of 864,000 miles and is distant, on the average, 92,900,000 miles from the earth. It is 1.41 times as dense as water. The light of the sun reaches the earth in 499.012 seconds or slightly more than 8 minutes. The average solar surface temperature has been measured by several indirect methods which agree closely on a value of 6,000° Kelvin or about 10,000° F. The interior temperature of the sun is about 35,000,000 F.°.

When sunlight is analyzed with a spectroscope, it is found to consist of a continuous spectrum composed of all the colors of the rainbow in order, crossed by many dark lines. The "absorption lines" are produced by gaseous materials in the atmosphere of the sun. More than 60 of the natural terrestrial elements have been identified in the sun, all in gaseous form because of the intense heat of the sun.

Spheres and Corona

The radiating surface of the sun is called the photosphere, and just above it is the chromosphere. The chromosphere is visible to the naked eye only at times of total solar eclipses, appearing then to be a pinkish-violet layer with occasional great prominences projecting above its general level. With proper instruments the chromosphere can be seen or photographed whenever the sun is visible without

waiting for a total eclipse. Above the chromosphere is the corona, also visible to the naked eye only at times of total eclipse. Instruments also permit the brighter portions of the corona to be studied whenever conditions are favorable. The pearly light of the corona surges millions of miles from the sun. Iron, nickel, and calcium are believed to be principal contributors to the composition of the corona, all in a state of extreme attenuation and high ionization that indicates temperatures on the order of a million degrees Fahrenheit.

Sunspots

There is an intimate connection between sunspots and the corona. At times of low sunspot activity, the fine streamers of the corona will be much longer above the sun's equator than over the polar regions of the sun, while during high sunspot activity, the corona extends fairly evenly outward from all regions of the sun, but to a much greater distance in space. Sunspots are dark, irregularly-shaped regions whose diameters may reach tens of thousands of miles. The average life of a sunspot group is from two to three weeks, but there have been groups that have lasted for more than a year, being carried repeatedly around as the sun rotated upon its axis. The record for the duration of a sunspot is 18 months. Sunspots reach a low point every 11.3 years, with a peak of activity occurring irregularly between two successive minima.

The sun is 400,000 times as bright as the full moon and gives the earth 6 million times as much light as do all the other stars put together. Actually, most of the stars that can be easily seen on any clear night are brighter than the sun.

The Moon

The moon completes a circuit around the earth in a period whose mean or average duration is 27 days 7 hours 43.2 minutes. This is the moon's sidereal period. Because of the motion of the moon in common with the earth around the sun, the mean duration of the lunar month — the period from one new moon to the next new moon — is 29 days 12 hours 44.05 minutes. This is the moon's synodical period.

The mean distance of the moon from the earth according to the American Ephemeris is 238,857 miles. Because the orbit of the moon about the earth is not circular but elliptical, however, the maximum distance from the earth that the moon may reach is 252,710 miles and the least distance is 221,463 miles. All distances are from the center of one object to the

center of the other.

The moon's diameter is 2,160 miles. If we deduct the radius of the moon, 1,080 miles, and the radius of the earth, 3,963 miles from the minimum distance or perigee, given above, we shall have for the nearest approach of the bodies' surfaces 216,420 miles.

The moon rotates on its axis in a period of time exactly equal to its sidereal revolution about the earth — 27.321666 days. The moon's revolution about the earth is irregular because of its elliptical orbit. The moon's rotation, however, is regular and this, together with the irregular revolution, produces what is called "libration in longitude" which permits us to see first farther around the east side and then farther around the west side of the moon. The moon's variation north or south of the ecliptic permits us to see farther over first one pole and then the other of the moon and this is "libration in latitude." These two libration effects permit us to see a total of about 60% of the moon's surface over a period of time. The hidden side of the moon was photographed in 1959 by the Soviet space vehicle Lunik III. Since then many excellent pictures of nearly all of the moon's surface have been transmitted to earth by Lunar Orbiters launched by the U.S.

The tides are caused mainly by the moon, because of its proximity to the earth. The ratio of the tide-raising power of the moon to that of the sun is 11 to 5.

Harvest Moon and Hunter's Moon

The Harvest Moon, the full moon nearest the Autumnal Equinox, ushers in a period of several successive days when the moon rises soon after sunset. This phenomenon gives farmers in temperate latitudes extra hours of light in which to harvest their crops before frost and winter come. The 1977 Harvest Moon falls on Sept. 27. Harvest moon in the south temperate latitudes falls on Apr. 4.

The next full moon after Harvest Moon is called the Hunter's Moon, accompanied by a similar phenomenon but less marked; — Oct. 26, northern hemisphere, May 3, southern hemisphere.

Moon's Perigee and Apogee, 1977

		Perigee								Apogee			
		Hour				**Hour**				**Hour**			**Hour**
Day	GMT	EST		Day	GMT	EST		Day	GMT	EST	Day	GMT	EST
Jan.	16	10	05	July	28	02	21*	Jan.	28	06	01	July	12	08	03
Feb.	11	04	23*	Aug.	24	09	04	Feb.	25	03	22*	Aug.	9	00	19*
Mar.	8	23	18	Sept.	18	09	04	Mar.	24	22	17	Sept.	5	8	13
Apr.	5	21	16	Oct.	15	09	04	Apr.	21	12	07	Oct.	3	14	09
May	4	05	00	Nov.	12	12	07	May	18	18	13	Oct.	31	08	03
June	1	15	10	Dec.	10	23	18	June	14	21	16	Nov.	27	21	16
June	30	00	19*		*Previous date.							Dec.	24	21	16

The Zodiac

The sun's apparent yearly path among the stars is known as the **ecliptic**. The zone 16° wide, 8° on each side of the ecliptic, is known as the **zodiac**. Inside of this zone are the apparent paths of the sun, moon, earth, and major planets. Beginning at the point on the ecliptic which marks the position of the sun at the vernal equinox, and thence proceeding eastward, the zodiac is divided into twelve signs of 30° each, as shown herewith.

These signs are named from the twelve constellations of the zodiac with which the signs coincided in the time of the astronomer Hipparchus, about 2,000 years ago. Owing to the precession of the equinoxes, that is to say, to the retrograde motion of the equinoxes along the ecliptic, each sign in the zodiac has, in the course of 2,000 years, moved backward 30° into the constellation west of it; so that the sign Aries is now in the constellation Pisces, and so on. The vernal equinox will move from Pisces into Aquarius about the middle of the 26th Century. The signs of the zodiac with their Latin and English names are as follows:

Spring	1. ♈ Aries.	The Ram.	Autumn	7. ♎ Libra.	The Balance.
	2. ♉ Taurus.	The Bull.		8. ♏ Scorpio.	The Scorpion.
	3. ♊ Gemini.	The Twins.		9. ♐ Sagittarius.	The Archer.
Summer	4. ♋ Cancer.	The Crab.	Winter	10. ♑ Capricorn.	The Goat.
	5. ♌ Leo.	The Lion.		11. ♒ Aquarius.	The Water Bearer.
	6. ♍ Virgo.	The Virgin.		12. ♓ Pisces.	The Fishes.

The Earth: Size, Computation of Time, Seasons

Size and Dimensions

The earth is the fifth largest planet and the third from the sun. Its mass is 6 sextillion, 588 quintillion short tons. Using the parameters of an ellipsoid adopted by the International Astronomical Union in 1964 and recognized by the International Union of Geodesy and Geophysics in 1967, the length of the equator is 24,901.55 miles, the length of a meridian is 24,859.82 miles, the equatorial diameter is 7,926.41 miles, and the area of this reference ellipsoid is approximately 196,938,800 square miles.

The earth is considered a solid, rigid mass with a dense core of magnetic, probably metallic material. The outer part of the core is probably liquid. Around the core is a thick shell or mantle of heavy crystalline rock which in turn is covered by a thin crust forming the solid granite and basalt base of the continents and ocean basins. Over broad areas of the earth's surface the crust has a thin cover of sedimentary rock such as sandstone, shale, and limestone formed by weathering of the earth's surface and deposition of sands, clays, and plant and animal remains.

The temperature in the earth increases about 1°F. with every 100 to 200 feet in depth, in the upper 100 kilometers of the earth, and the temperature near the core is believed to be near the melting point of the core materials under the conditions at that depth. The heat of the earth is believed to be derived from radioactivity in the rocks, pressures developed within the earth, and original heat (if the earth in fact was formed at high temperatures).

Atmosphere of the Earth

The earth's atmosphere is a blanket composed of nitrogen, oxygen and argon, in amounts of about 78.21, and 1% by volume. Also present in minute quantities are carbon dioxide, hydrogen, neon, helium, krypton and xenon.

Water vapor displaces other gases and varies from nearly zero to about 4% by volume. The height of the ozone layer varies from approximately 12 to 21 miles above the earth. Traces exist as low as 6 miles and as high as 35 miles. Traces of methane have been found.

The atmosphere rests on the earth's surface with the weight equivalent to a layer of water 34 ft. deep. For about 300,000 ft. upward the gases remain in the proportions stated. Gravity holds the gases to the earth. The weight of the air compresses it at the bottom, so that the greatest density is at the earth's surface. Pressure, as well as density, decreases as height increases because the weight pressing upon any layer is always less than that pressing upon the layers below.

The temperature of the air drops with increased height, until the **tropopause** is reached. This may vary from 25,000 to 60,000 ft. The atmosphere below the tropopause is the **troposphere**; the atmosphere for about twenty miles above the tropopause is the stratosphere, where the temperature generally increases with height except at high latitudes in winter. A temperature maximum near the 30-mile level is called the stratopause. Above this boundary is the mesosphere where the temperature decreases with height to a minimum, the mesopause, at a height of 50 miles. Extending above the mesosphere to the outer fringes of the atmosphere is the thermosphere, a region where temperature increases with height to a value measured in thousands of degrees Fahrenheit. The lower portion of this region, extending from 50 to about 400 miles in altitude, is characterized by a high ion density, and is thus called the ionosphere. The outer region is called exosphere; this is the region where gas molecules traveling at high speed may escape into outer space, above 600 miles.

Latitude, Longitude

Position on the globe is measured by means of meridians and parallels. Meridians, which are imaginary lines drawn around the earth through the poles, determine longitude. The meridian running through Greenwich, England, is the prime meridian of longitude, and all others are either east or west. Parallels, which are imaginary circles parallel with the equator, determine latitude. The length of a degree of longitude varies as the cosine of the latitude. At the equator a degree is 69.171 statute miles; this is gradually reduced toward the poles. Value of a longitude degree at the poles is zero.

Latitude is reckoned by the number of degrees north or south of the equator, an imaginary circle on the earth's surface everywhere equidistant between the two poles. According to the IAU Ellipsoid of 1964, the length of a degree of latitude is 68.708 statute miles at the equator and varies slightly north and south because of the oblate form of the globe; at the poles it is 69.403 statute miles.

Computation of Time

The earth rotates on its axis and follows an elliptical orbit around the sun. The rotation makes the sun appear to move across the sky from East to West. It determines day and night and the complete rotation, in relation to the sun, is called the apparent or true solar day. This varies but an average determines the mean solar day of 24 hours.

The mean solar day is in universal use for civil purposes. It may be obtained from apparent solar time by correcting observations of the sun for the equation of time, but when high precision is required, the mean solar time is calculated from its relation to sidereal time. These relations are extremely complicated, but for most practical uses, they may be considered as follows:

Sidereal time is the measure of time defined by the diurnal motion of the vernal equinox, and is determined from observation of the meridian transits of stars. One complete rotation of the earth relative to the equinox is called the sidereal day. The mean sidereal day is 23 hours, 56 minutes, 4.091 seconds of mean solar time.

The Calendar Year begins at 12 o'clock precisely local clock time, on the night of Dec. 31-Jan. 1. The day and the calendar month also begin at midnight by the clock. The interval required for the earth to make one absolute revolution around the sun is a sidereal year; it consisted of 365 days, 6 hours, 9 minutes, and 9.5 seconds of mean solar time (approximately 24 hours per day) in 1900, and is increasing at the rate of 0.0001-second annually.

The Tropical Year, on which the return of the seasons depends, is the interval between two consecutive returns of the sun to the vernal equinox. The tropical year consisted of 365 days, 5 hours, 48 minutes, and 46 seconds in 1900. It is decreasing at the rate of 0.530 seconds per century.

In 1956 the unit of time interval was defined to be identical with the second of Ephemeris Time, 1/31,556,925.9747 of the tropical year for 1900 January 0d 12th hour E.T. A physical definition of the second based on a quantum transition of cesium (atomic second) was adopted in 1964. The atomic second is equal to 9,192,631,770 cycles of the emitted radiation. In 1967 this atomic second was adopted as the unit of time interval for the Intern'l System of Units.

The Zones and Seasons

The five zones of the earth's surface are torrid, lying between the Tropics of Cancer and Capricorn; North Temperate, between Cancer and the Arctic Circle; South Temperate, between Capricorn and the Antarctic Circle; the Frigid Zones, between the polar Circles and the Poles.

The inclination or tilt of the earth's axis with respect to the sun determines the seasons. These are commonly marked in the North Temperate Zone, where spring begins at the vernal equinox, summer at the summer solstice, autumn at the autumnal equinox and winter at the winter solstice.

In the South Temperate Zone, the seasons are reversed. Spring begins at the autumnal equinox, summer at the winter solstice, etc.

If the earth's axis were perpendicular to the plane of the earth's orbit around the sun there would be no change of seasons. Day and night would be of nearly constant length and there would be equable conditions of temperature. But the axis is tilted 23° 27' away from a perpendicular to the orbit and only in March and September is the axis at right angles to the sun.

The points at which the sun crosses the equator are the equinoxes, when day and night are most nearly equal. The points at which the sun is at a maximum distance from the equator are the solstices. Days and nights are then most unequal.

In June the North Pole is tilted 23° 27' toward the sun and the days in the northern hemisphere are longer than the nights, while the days in the southern hemisphere are shorter than the nights. In December the North Pole is tilted 23° 27' away from the sun and the situation is reversed.

The Seasons in 1977

In 1977 the 4 seasons will begin as follows: add one hour to EST for Atlantic Time; subtract one hour for Central, two hours for Mountain, 3 hours for Pacific, 4 hours for Yukon, 5 hours for Alaska-Hawaii and six hours for Bering Time. Also shown in Greenwich Mean Time.

		Date	GMT	EST
Vernal Equinox	Spring	Mar. 20	17:43	12:43 pm
Summer Solstice	Summer	June 21	12:14	7:14 am
Autumnal Equinox	Autumn	Sept. 23	03:30	10:30 pm (22d)
Winter Solstice	Winter	Dec. 21	23:24	6:24 pm

Poles of The Earth

Source: National Oceanic and Atmospheric Admn.

The geographic (rotation) poles, or points where the earth's axis of rotation cuts the surface, are not absolutely fixed in the body of the earth. The pole of rotation describes an irregular curve about its mean position.

Two periods have been detected in this motion: (1) an annual period due to seasonal changes in barometric pressure, load of ice and snow on the surface and to other phenomena of seasonal character; (2) a period of about 14 months due to the shape and constitution of the Earth.

In addition there are small but as yet unpredictable irregularities. The whole motion is so small that the actual pole at any time remains within a circle of 30 or 40 feet in radius centered at the mean position of the pole.

The pole of rotation for the time being is of course the pole having a latitude of 90° and an indeterminate longitude.

Magnetic Poles

The **north magnetic Pole** of the earth is that region where the magnetic force is vertically downward and the **south magnetic pole** that region where the magnetic force is vertically upward. A compass placed at the magnetic poles experiences no directive force.

There are slow changes in the distribution of the earth's magnetic field. These changes were at one time attributed in part to a periodic movement of the magnetic poles around the geographical poles, but later evidence refutes this theory and points, rather, to a slow migration of "disturbance" foci over the earth.

There appear shifts in position of the magnetic poles due to the changes in the earth's magnetic field. The center of the area designated as the north magnetic pole was estimated to be in about latitude 70.5° N and longitude 96° W in 1905; from recent nearby measurements and studies of the secular changes, the position in 1970 is estimated as latitude 76.2° N and longitude 101° W. Improved data rather than actual motion account for at least part of the change.

The position of the south magnetic pole in 1912 was near 71° S and longitude 150° E; the position in 1970 is estimated at latitude 66° S and longitude 139.1° E.

The direction of the horizontal components of the magnetic field at any point is known as magnetic north at that point, and the angle by which it deviates east or west of true north is known as the magnetic declination, or in the mariner's terminology, the **variation of the compass.**

A compass without error points in the direction of magnetic north. (In general this is *not* the direction of the magnetic north pole.) If one follows the direction indicated by the north end of the compass, he will travel along a rather irregular curve which eventually reaches the north magnetic pole (though not usually by a great-circle route). However, the action of the compass should not be thought of as due to any influence of the distant pole, but simply as an indication of the distribution of the earth's magnetism at the place of observation.

Rotation of The Earth

The speed of rotation of the earth about its axis has been found to be slightly variable. The variations may be classified as:

(A) **Secular.** Tidal friction acts as a brake on the rotation and causes a slow secular increase in the length of the day, about 1 millisecond per century.

(B) **Irregular.** The speed of rotation may increase for a number of years, about 5 to 10, and then start decreasing. The maximum difference from the mean in the length of the day during a century is about 5 milliseconds. The accumulated difference in time has amounted to approximately 44 seconds since 1900. The cause is probably motion in the interior of the earth.

(C) **Periodic.** Seasonal variations exist with periods of one year and six months. The cumulative effect is such that each year the earth is late about 30 milliseconds near June 1 and is ahead about 30 milliseconds near Oct. 1. The maximum seasonal variation in the length of the day is about 0.5 millisecond. It is believed that the principal cause of the annual variation is the seasonal change in the wind patterns of the Northern and Southern Hemispheres. The semi-annual variation is due chiefly to tidal action of the sun, which distorts the shape of the earth slightly.

The secular and irregular variations were discovered by comparing time based on the rotation of the earth with time based on the orbital motion of the moon about the earth and of the planets about the sun. The periodic variation was determined largely with the aid of quartz-crystal clocks. The introduction of the cesium-beam atomic clock in 1955 made it possible to determine in greater detail than before the nature of the irregular and periodic variations.

Astronomical Twilight—Meridian of Greenwich

Date 1977		20° Begin h m	20° End h m	30° Begin h m	30° End h m	40° Begin h m	40° End h m	50° Begin h m	50° End h m	60° Begin h m	60° End h m
Jan.	1	5 16	6 50	5 30	6 35	5 45	6 21	6 00	6 07	6 18	5 49
	11	5 19	6 56	5 33	6 43	5 46	6 30	6 00	6 17	6 15	6 01
	21	5 21	7 01	5 32	6 51	5 43	6 40	5 55	6 30	6 06	6 18
Feb.	1	5 21	7 07	5 29	6 58	5 38	6 51	5 45	6 44	5 51	6 38
	11	5 18	7 11	5 24	7 05	5 29	7 01	5 32	6 59	5 32	7 01
	21	5 13	7 15	5 17	7 12	5 17	7 12	5 16	7 14	5 09	7 23
Mar.	1	5 08	7 18	5 08	7 19	5 06	7 21	4 59	7 29	4 44	7 45
	11	5 00	7 21	4 58	7 24	4 50	7 32	4 38	7 46	4 12	8 12
	21	4 52	7 24	4 45	7 32	4 33	7 44	4 14	8 04	3 37	8 43
Apr.	1	4 42	7 28	4 31	7 39	4 14	7 57	3 47	8 25	2 53	9 21
	11	4 32	7 32	4 18	7 47	3 56	8 09	3 20	8 47	2 03	10 10
	21	4 23	7 36	4 04	7 54	3 37	8 23	2 52	9 11	0 37	11 47
May	1	4 14	7 41	3 52	8 04	3 19	8 37	2 22	9 39		
	11	4 08	7 46	3 41	8 13	3 03	8 53	1 49	10 09		
	21	4 02	7 52	3 32	8 22	2 48	9 07	1 13	10 46		
June	1	3 58	7 58	3 26	8 30	2 36	9 20	0 21	11 52		
	11	3 56	8 03	3 22	8 36	2 29	9 30				
	21	3 57	8 06	3 22	8 40	2 28	9 35				
July	1	3 59	8 07	3 25	8 41	2 30	9 35				
	11	4 03	8 06	3 30	8 39	2 40	9 30				
	21	4 08	8 03	3 39	8 33	2 52	9 18	1 12	11 23		
Aug.	1	4 15	7 56	3 48	8 23	3 09	9 01	1 49	10 20		
	11	4 20	7 50	3 56	8 13	3 22	8 46	2 21	9 46		
	21	4 24	7 41	4 05	8 01	3 34	8 27	2 47	9 15		
Sept.	1	4 29	7 31	4 14	7 46	3 51	8 08	3 13	8 43	1 40	10 02
	11	4 32	7 20	4 20	7 33	4 02	7 50	3 33	8 16	2 36	9 12
	21	4 35	7 11	4 26	7 19	4 14	7 31	3 52	7 52	3 11	8 31
Oct.	1	4 38	7 02	4 33	7 05	4 25	7 13	4 10	7 28	3 41	7 54
	11	4 40	6 53	4 40	6 53	4 35	6 58	4 26	7 05	4 07	7 23
	21	4 43	6 47	4 45	6 44	4 45	6 43	4 41	6 46	4 32	6 55
Nov.	1	4 46	6 41	4 52	6 34	4 56	6 30	4 58	6 27	4 56	6 27
	11	4 50	6 38	4 59	6 28	5 06	6 21	5 13	6 14	5 17	6 08
	21	4 55	6 36	5 06	6 25	5 16	6 15	5 26	6 04	5 37	5 52
Dec.	1	5 00	6 37	5 13	6 24	5 25	6 11	5 38	5 58	5 53	5 42
	11	5 06	6 40	5 20	6 26	5 34	6 12	5 48	5 57	6 06	5 38
	21	5 11	6 45	5 25	6 30	5 39	6 16	5 55	6 00	6 15	5 40
	31	5 15	6 50	5 30	6 35	5 44	6 21	6 00	6 06	6 18	5 48

Latitude, Longitude and Altitude of North American Cities

Source: National Ocean Survey (NOAA) for geographic position.
Source for Canadian Cities: Geodetic Survey of Canada, Dept. of Energy, Mines and Resources.
Altitudes U.S. Geological Survey and various sources. °Approx. altitude at downtown business area U.S.; in Canada at tower of major airport.

City	Lat. N ° ' "	Long. W ° ' "	Alt.* Feet
Abilene, Texas.	32 27 54	99 42 48	1710
Akron, Ohio	41 05 00	81 30 44	874
Albany, N.Y.	42 39 01	73 45 01	20
Albuquerque, N.M.	35 05 01	106 39 05	4,945
Allentown, Pa.	40 36 11	75 28 06	255
Alert, N.W.T.	82 29 50	62 21 15	95
Altoona, Pa.	40 30 55	78 24 03	1,180
Amarillo, Tex.	35 12 27	101 50 04	3,685
Anchorage, Alaska	61 10 00	149 59 00	118
Ann Arbor, Mich.	42 16 59	83 44 52	880
Asheville, N.C.	35 35 42	82 33 26	1,985
Ashland, Ky.	38 28 36	82 38 23	536
Atlanta, Ga.	33 45 10	84 23 37	1,050
Atlantic City, N.J.	39 21 32	74 25 53	10
Augusta, Ga.	33 28 20	81 58 00	143
Augusta, Me.	44 18 53	69 46 29	45
Austin, Tex.	30 16 09	97 44 37	505
Bakersfield, Cal.	35 22 30	119 01 18	400
Baltimore, Md.	39 17 26	76 36 45	20
Bangor, Me.	44 48 13	68 46 18	20
Baton Rouge, La.	30 26 58	91 11 00	57
Battle Creek, Mich.	42 18 58	85 10 48	820
Bay City, Mich.	43 36 04	83 53 15	595
Beaumont, Tex.	30 05 20	94 06 09	20
Belleville, Ont.	44 09 30	77 22 30	280
Bellingham, Wash.	48 45 02	122 28 36	60
Berkeley, Cal.	37 52 10	122 16 17	40
Bethlehem, Pa.	40 37 16	75 22 34	235
Billings, Mont.	45 47 00	108 30 04	3,120
Biloxi, Miss.	30 23 48	88 53 00	20
Binghamton, N.Y.	42 06 03	75 54 47	865
Birmingham, Ala.	33 31 01	86 48 36	600
Bismarck, N.D.	46 48 23	100 47 17	1,674
Bloomington, Ill.	40 28 35	88 59 36	800
Boise, Idaho	43 37 07	116 11 58	2,704
Boston, Mass.	42 21 24	71 03 25	21
Bowling Green, Ky.	36 59 18	86 27 03	510
Brattleboro, Vt.	42 51 06	72 33 48	300
Brandon, Man.	49 51 00	99 57 00	1,265
Brantford, Ont.	43 07 30	80 15 30	705
Bridgeport, Conn.	41 10 49	73 11 22	10
Brockton, Mass.	42 05 02	71 01 25	130
Brownsville, Tex.	25 54 07	97 29 58	35
Buffalo, N.Y.	42 52 52	78 52 21	585
Burlington, Ont.	43 18 30	79 46 30	875
Burlington, Vt.	44 28 34	73 12 46	110
Butte, Mont.	46 01 06	112 32 11	5,765
Calgary, Alta.	51 02 46	114 03 24	3,557
Cambridge, Mass.	42 22 01	71 06 22	20
Camden, N.J.	39 56 41	75 07 14	30
Canton, Ohio	40 47 50	81 22 37	1,030
Carson City, Nev.	39 10 00	119 46 00	4,680
Cedar Rapids, Iowa	41 58 01	91 39 53	730
Central Islip, N.Y.	40 47 24	73 12 00	80
Champaign, Ill.	40 07 05	88 14 48	740
Charleston, S.C.	32 46 35	79 55 53	9
Charleston, W.Va.	38 21 01	81 37 52	601
Charlotte, N.C.	35 13 44	80 50 45	720
Charlottetown, P.E.I.	46 14 00	63 07 45	181
Chattanooga, Tenn.	35 02 41	85 18 32	675
Cheyenne, Wyo.	41 08 09	104 49 07	6,100
Chicago, Ill.	41 52 28	87 38 22	595
Churchill, Man.	58 45 15	94 10 00	94
Cincinnati, Ohio	39 06 07	84 30 35	550
Cleveland, Ohio	41 29 51	81 41 50	660
Colorado Springs	38 50 07	104 49 16	5,980
Columbia, Mo.	38 57 03	92 19 46	730
Columbia, S.C.	34 00 02	81 02 00	190
Columbus, Ga.	32 28 07	84 59 24	265
Columbus, Ohio	39 57 47	83 00 17	780
Concord, N.H.	43 12 22	71 32 25	290
Corpus Christi, Tex.	27 47 51	97 23 45	35
Dallas, Tex.	32 47 09	96 47 37	435
Dartmouth, N.S.	44 38 39	63 34 34	476
Davenport, Iowa	41 31 19	90 34 33	590
Dawson, Yukon	64 03 30	139 26 00	1,211
Dayton, Ohio	39 45 32	84 11 43	574
Daytona Beach, Fla.	29 12 44	81 01 10	7
Decatur, Ill.	39 50 42	88 56 47	682
Denver, Colo.	39 44 58	104 59 22	5,280
Des Moines, Iowa	41 35 14	93 37 00	805
Detroit, Mich.	42 19 48	83 02 57	585
Dodge City, Kans.	37 45 17	100 01 09	2,480
Dubuque, Iowa	42 30 12	90 40 30	620
Duluth, Minn.	46 46 56	92 06 24	610
Durham, N.C.	36 00 00	78 54 45	405
Eau Claire, Wis.	44 48 48	91 29 42	790
Edmonton, Alta.	53 32 45	113 29 15	2,373
El Paso, Tex.	31 45 36	106 29 11	3,695
Elizabeth, N.J.	40 39 43	74 12 59	21
Enid, Okla.	36 23 42	97 52 30	1,240
Erie, Pa.	42 07 15	80 04 57	685
Eugene, Ore.	44 03 16	123 05 30	422
Eureka, Cal.	40 46 54	124 09 24	45
Evansville, Ind.	37 58 20	87 34 21	385
Fairbanks, Alaska	64 48 00	147 51 00	448
Fall River, Mass.	41 42 06	71 09 18	40
Fargo, N.D.	46 52 30	96 47 18	900
Flagstaff, Ariz.	35 11 36	111 39 06	6,900
Flint, Mich.	43 01 18	83 41 00	750
Ft. Smith, Ariz.	35 23 06	94 25 06	440
Fort Wayne, Ind.	41 04 21	85 08 26	790
Fort Worth, Tex.	32 44 55	97 19 44	670
Fredericton, N.B.	45 57 40	66 38 30	67
Fresno, Cal.	36 44 12	119 47 11	285
Gadsden, Ala.	34 00 57	86 00 41	555
Gainesville, Fla.	29 39 36	82 19 48	175
Gallup, N.M.	35 31 30	108 44 30	6,540
Galveston, Tex.	29 18 10	94 47 43	5
Gary, Ind.	41 36 12	87 20 19	590
Grand Junction, Col.	39 04 06	108 33 06	4,590
Grand Rapids, Mich.	42 58 03	85 40 13	610
Great Falls, Mont.	47 30 06	111 17 06	3,340
Green Bay, Wis.	44 30 48	88 00 50	590
Greensboro, N.C.	36 04 17	79 47 25	839
Greenville, S.C.	34 50 50	82 24 01	966
Guelph, Ont.	43 32 30	80 15 30	1,075
Gulfport, Miss.	30 22 04	89 05 36	20
Halifax, N.S.	44 38 39	63 34 34	476
Hamilton, Ont.	43 15 17	79 52 28	776
Hamilton, Ohio	39 23 59	84 33 47	600
Harrisburg, Pa.	40 15 43	76 52 59	365
Hartford, Conn.	41 46 12	72 40 49	40
Helena, Mont.	46 35 33	112 02 24	4,155
Hilo, Hawaii	19 43 30	155 05 24	40
Holyoke, Mass.	42 12 29	72 36 36	115
Honolulu, Hawaii	21 18 22	157 51 35	21
Houston, Tex.	29 45 26	95 21 37	40
Hull, Que.	45 26 00	75 44 00	225
Huntington, W.Va.	38 25 12	82 26 33	565
Huntsville, Ala.	34 43 54	86 35 12	640
Indianapolis, Ind.	39 46 07	86 09 46	710
Iowa City, Iowa	41 39 37	91 31 53	685
Jackson, Mich.	42 14 43	84 24 22	940
Jackson, Miss.	32 17 56	90 11 06	298
Jacksonville, Fla.	30 19 44	81 39 42	20
Jersey City, N.J.	40 43 50	74 03 56	20
Johnstown, Pa.	40 19 35	78 55 03	1,185
Joplin, Mo.	37 05 36	94 30 42	990
Juneau, Alaska	58 18 12	134 24 30	50
Kalamazoo, Mich.	42 17 29	85 35 14	755
Kansas City, Kan.	39 07 04	94 38 24	750
Kansas City, Mo.	39 04 56	94 35 20	750
Kenosha, Wis.	42 35 43	87 50 11	610
Key West, Fla.	24 33 30	81 48 12	5
Kingston, Ont.	44 13 30	76 30 00	310
Kitchener, Ont.	43 26 59	80 29 17	1,031
Knoxville, Tenn.	35 57 39	83 55 07	890
Lafayette, Ind.	40 25 11	86 53 39	550
Lancaster, Pa.	40 02 25	76 18 29	355
Lansing, Mich.	42 44 01	84 33 15	830
Laredo, Tex.	27 30 22	99 30 30	440
La Salle, Que.	45 25 30	73 38 30	100
Las Vegas, Nev.	36 10 20	115 08 37	2,030
Laval, Que.	45 35 30	73 45 30	100
Lawrence, Mass.	42 42 16	71 10 08	65
Lethbridge, Alta.	49 41 30	112 49 00	2,990
Lexington, Ky.	38 02 50	84 29 46	955
Lihue, Hawaii	21 58 48	159 22 30	210
Lima, Ohio	40 44 35	84 06 20	865
Lincoln, Nebr.	40 48 59	96 42 15	1,150
Little Rock, Ark.	34 44 42	92 16 37	286
London, Ont.	42 59 00	81 15 00	912
Long Beach, Cal.	33 46 14	118 11 18	35
Lorain, Ohio	41 28 05	82 10 49	610
Los Angeles, Cal.	34 03 15	118 14 28	340
Louisville, Ky.	38 14 47	85 45 49	450
Lowell, Mass.	42 38 25	71 19 14	100
Lubbock, Tex.	33 35 05	101 50 33	3,195
Macon, Ga.	32 50 12	83 37 36	335
Madison, Wis.	43 04 23	89 22 55	860

City	Lat. N (° ′ ″)	Long. W (° ′ ″)	Alt.* Feet
Manchester, N.H.	42 59 28	71 27 41	175
Marshall, Texas	32 33 00	94 23 00	410
Memphis, Tenn.	35 08 46	90 03 13	275
Meriden, Conn.	41 32 06	72 47 30	190
Mexico City, Mexico	19 25 45	99 07 00	7,347
Miami, Fla.	25 46 37	80 11 32	10
Milwaukee, Wis.	43 02 19	87 54 15	635
Minneapolis, Minn.	44 58 57	93 15 43	815
Minot, N.D.	48 14 18	101 17 48	1,550
Mississauga, Ont.	43 33 00	79 35 00	260
Mobile, Ala.	30 41 36	88 02 33	5
Moline, Ill.	41 30 31	90 30 49	585
Moncton, N.B.	46 05 30	64 47 30	75
Montgomery, Ala.	32 22 33	86 18 31	160
Montpelier, Vt.	44 15 36	72 34 41	485
Montreal, Que.	45 30 30	73 33 20	117
Moose Jaw, Sask.	50 23 30	105 32 30	1,810
Muncie, Ind.	40 11 28	85 23 16	950
Nashville, Tenn.	36 09 33	86 46 55	450
Natchez, Miss.	31 33 48	91 23 30	210
Newark, N.J.	40 44 14	74 10 19	55
New Bedford, Mass.	41 38 13	70 55 41	15
New Britain, Conn.	41 40 08	72 46 59	200
New Haven, Conn.	41 18 25	72 55 30	40
New Orleans, La.	29 56 53	90 04 10	5
New York, N.Y.	40 45 06	73 59 39	55
Niagara Falls, N.Y.	43 05 34	79 03 26	570
Niagara Falls, Ont.	43 05 30	79 03 30	585
Nome, Alaska	64 30 00	165 25 00	25
Norfolk, Va.	36 51 10	76 17 21	10
North Bay, Ont.	46 18 30	79 27 30	925
Oakland, Cal.	37 48 03	122 15 54	25
Ogden, Utah	41 13 31	111 58 21	4,295
Oklahoma City	35 28 26	97 31 04	1,195
Omaha, Nebr.	41 15 42	95 56 14	1,040
Orlando, Fla.	28 32 42	81 22 38	70
Oshawa, Ont.	43 54 00	78 52 00	350
Ottawa, Ont.	45 25 40	75 42 45	374
Paducah, Ky.	37 05 13	88 35 56	345
Pasadena, Cal.	34 08 44	118 08 41	830
Paterson, N.J.	40 55 01	74 10 21	100
Pensacola, Fla.	30 24 51	87 12 56	15
Peoria, Ill.	40 41 42	89 35 33	470
Peterborough, Ont.	44 18 00	78 19 30	685
Philadelphia, Pa.	39 56 58	75 09 21	100
Phoenix, Ariz.	33 27 12	112 04 28	1,090
Pierre, S.D.	44 22 18	100 20 54	1,480
Pittsburgh, Pa.	40 26 19	80 00 00	745
Pittsfield, Mass.	42 26 53	73 15 14	1,015
Pocatello, Idaho	42 52 24	112 27 00	4,460
Port Arthur, Texas	29 52 30	93 56 15	10
Portland, Me.	43 39 33	70 15 19	25
Portland, Ore.	45 31 06	122 40 35	77
Portsmouth, N.H.	43 04 30	70 45 24	20
Portsmouth, Va.	36 50 07	76 18 14	10
Prince Rupert, B.C.	54 19 00	130 19 00	125
Providence, R.I.	41 49 32	71 24 41	80
Provo, Utah	40 14 06	111 39 24	4,550
Pueblo, Col.	38 16 17	104 36 33	4,690
Quebec City, Que.	46 48 46	71 12 20	239
Racine, Wis.	42 43 49	87 47 12	630
Rapid City, S.D.	44 04 48	103 13 42	3,230
Raleigh, N.C.	35 46 38	78 38 21	365
Reading, Pa.	40 20 09	75 55 40	265
Regina, Sask.	50 27 02	104 36 30	1,894
Reno, Nev.	39 31 27	119 48 40	4,490
Richmond, Va.	37 32 15	77 26 09	160
Roanoke, Va.	37 16 13	79 56 44	905
Rochester, Minn.	44 01 21	92 28 03	990
Rochester, N.Y.	43 09 41	77 36 21	515
Rockford, Ill.	42 16 07	89 05 48	715
Sacramento, Cal.	38 34 57	121 29 41	30
Saginaw, Mich.	43 25 52	83 56 05	595
St. Catharines, Ont.	43 09 30	79 14 30	362
Saint John, N.B.	45 16 00	66 04 30	80
St. Cloud, Minn.	45 34 00	94 10 24	1,040
St. John's, Nfld.	47 34 00	52 43 30	200
St. Joseph, Mo.	39 45 57	94 51 02	850
St. Louis, Mo.	38 37 45	90 12 22	455
St. Paul, Minn.	44 57 19	93 06 07	780
St. Petersburg, Fla.	27 46 18	82 38 19	20
Salem, Ore.	44 56 24	123 02 00	155

City	Lat. N (° ′ ″)	Long. W (° ′ ″)	Alt.* Feet
Salina, Kan.	38 50 06	97 36 30	1,229
Salt Lake City, Utah	40 45 23	111 53 26	4,390
San Angelo, Tex.	31 27 39	100 26 03	1,845
San Antonio, Tex.	29 25 37	98 29 06	650
San Bernardino, Cal.	34 06 30	117 17 28	1,080
San Diego, Cal.	32 42 53	117 09 21	20
San Francisco, Cal.	37 46 39	122 24 40	65
San Jose, Cal.	37 20 16	121 53 24	90
San Juan, P.R.	18 27 00	66 04 15	35
Santa Barbara, Cal.	34 25 18	119 41 55	100
Santa Cruz, Cal.	36 58 18	122 01 18	20
Santa Fe, N.M.	35 41 11	105 56 10	6,950
Sarasota, Fla.	27 20 12	82 31 54	20
Saskatoon, Sask.	52 07 50	106 39 41	1,653
Sault Ste. Marie, Ont.	46 31 30	84 20 00	650
Savannah, Ga.	32 04 42	81 05 37	20
Schenectady, N.Y.	42 48 42	73 55 42	245
Scranton, Pa.	41 24 32	75 39 44	725
Seattle, Wash.	47 36 32	122 20 12	10
Sheboygan, Wis.	43 45 36	87 44 54	630
Sherbrooke, Que.	45 24 00	71 53 30	625
Sheridan, Wyo.	44 47 48	106 57 42	3,740
Shreveport, La.	32 30 46	93 44 58	204
Sioux City, Iowa	42 29 46	96 24 30	1,110
Sioux Falls, S.D.	43 32 35	96 43 35	1,395
Somerville, Mass.	42 23 15	71 06 07	13
South Bend, Ind.	41 40 33	86 15 01	710
Spartanburg, S.C.	34 57 03	81 56 06	875
Spokane, Wash.	47 39 32	117 25 33	1,890
Springfield, Ill.	39 47 58	89 38 51	610
Springfield, Mass.	42 06 21	72 35 32	85
Springfield, Mo.	37 13 03	93 17 32	1,300
Springfield, Ohio	39 55 38	83 48 29	980
Stamford, Conn.	41 03 09	73 32 24	35
Steubenville, Ohio	40 21 42	80 36 53	660
Stockton, Cal.	37 57 30	121 17 16	20
Sudbury, Ont.	46 28 30	80 58 30	917
Superior, Wis.	46 43 14	92 06 07	630
Sydney, N.S.	46 08 30	60 11 00	50
Syracuse, N.Y.	43 03 04	76 09 14	400
Tacoma, Wash.	47 14 59	122 26 15	110
Tallahassee, Fla.	30 26 42	84 16 54	150
Tampa, Fla.	27 56 58	82 27 25	15
Terre Haute, Ind.	39 28 03	87 24 26	496
Texarkana, Texas	33 25 48	94 02 30	324
Thunder Bay, Ont.	48 25 00	89 14 00	650
Toledo, Ohio	41 39 14	83 32 39	585
Topeka, Kan.	39 03 16	95 40 23	930
Toronto, Ont.	43 39 12	79 23 00	532
Trenton, N.J.	40 13 14	74 46 13	35
Trois-Rivieres, Que.	46 21 00	72 33 00	115
Troy, N.Y.	42 43 45	73 40 58	35
Tucson, Ariz.	32 13 15	110 58 08	2,390
Tulsa, Okla.	36 09 12	95 59 34	804
Urbana, Ill.	40 06 42	88 12 06	. . .
Utica, N.Y.	43 06 12	75 13 33	415
Vancouver, B.C.	49 16 30	123 07 30	388
Victoria, B.C.	48 25 40	123 21 45	. . .
Waco, Tex.	31 33 12	97 08 00	405
Walla Walla, Wash.	46 04 08	118 20 24	936
Washington, D.C.	38 53 51	77 00 33	25
Waterbury, Conn.	41 33 13	73 02 31	260
Waterloo, Iowa	42 29 40	92 20 20	850
West Palm Beach, Fla.	26 43 00	80 03 12	15
Wheeling, W.Va.	40 04 03	80 43 20	650
Whitehorse, Yukon	60 43 15	135 03 15	2,305
White Plains, N.Y.	41 02 00	73 45 48	220
Wichita, Kan.	37 41 30	97 20 16	1,290
Wichita Falls, Tex.	33 54 34	98 29 28	945
Wilkes-Barre, Pa.	41 14 32	75 53 17	640
Wilmington, Del.	39 44 46	75 32 51	135
Wilmington, N.C.	34 14 12	77 55 24	35
Windsor, Ont.	42 19 50	83 03 00	590
Winnipeg, Man.	49 53 06	97 08 20	765
Winston-Salem, N.C.	36 05 52	80 14 42	860
Worcester, Mass.	42 15 37	71 48 17	475
Yakima, Wash.	46 35 42	120 30 48	1,060
Yellowknife, N.W.T.	62 28 15	114 22 00	674
Yonkers, N.Y.	40 55 55	73 53 54	10
York, Pa.	39 57 35	76 43 36	370
Youngstown, Ohio	41 05 57	80 39 02	840
Yuma, Ariz.	32 42 54	114 37 24	160
Zanesville, Ohio	39 56 18	82 00 30	720

World Cities

City	Lat. N (° ′ ″)	Long. W (° ′ ″)	Alt.* Feet
London, UK (Greenwich)	51 30 00N	0 0 0	245
Paris, France	48 50 14N	2 20 14E	300
Berlin, Germany	52 32 00N	13 25 00E	110
Rome, Italy	41 53 00N	12 30 00E	95
Warsaw, Poland	52 15 00N	21 00 00E	360
Moscow, U.S.S.R.	55 45 00N	37 42 00E	394
Athens, Greece	37 58 00N	23 44 00E	300
Jerusalem, Israel	31 47 00N	35 13 00E	2,500
Johannesburg, So. Afr.	26 10 00S	28 02 00E	5,740
New Delhi, India	28 38 00N	77 12 00E	770
Peking, China	39 54 00N	116 28 00E	600
Rio de Janeiro, Brazil	22 53 43S	43 13 22W	30
Tokyo, Japan	35 45 00N	139 45 00E	30
Sydney, Australia	33 52 00S	151 12 00E	25

Calendar Adjustment Tables

The tables below will allow you to determine the approximate time of the rise or set of the sun and moon at your specific location. Rise and set times of the moon for your location can be more than one-half hour later than the times given on the following pages.

First find your latitude and longitude or that of a nearby city in the tables on pages 766-767. On the calendar tables look for the time given for the nearest latitude to your south. Compare that time with the time given for the next latitude to your north.

On Table A below, find the difference between the two latitudes in the top row. Run your finger down the column until you reach the row that indicates how far north you are of the southern latitude. Adjust the time given for the southern latitude by the number of minutes shown in Table A.

Now compare the time given for the southern latitude on the day you're seeking and for the next day. Using Table B, find the time difference between the two days. Run your finger down the column until you reach the row that belongs to the longitude nearest you. Add the minutes given there to your previous figure.

Finally, to adjust for local time, you must determine how many degrees of longitude you are from your time zone meridian: Atlantic — 60°, Eastern — 75°, Central — 90°, Mountain — 105°, Pacific — 120° and Alaska-Hawaii — 150°. For every degree of longitude west of the meridian you must add 4 minutes of time; for every degree of longitude east, subtract 4 minutes.

Example: Find the moonrise time for Superior, Wisconsin for March 7, 1977. Superior is at 92° 06' longitude and 46° 43' latitude.

Calendar time given for 40° — 20:18
Calendar time given for 50° — 20:28
Difference — 10 minutes
Table A at 30 min. and 6° 40' — 7 minutes
First adjusted time — 20:15
Time for 40° on March 8 — 21:27
Difference between Mar. 7 and Mar. 8 — 9 minutes
Table B at 10 min. and 90° 00' — 2 minutes
Second adjusted time — 20:17
Local time adjustment 2° x 4 min. — 8 minutes
Moonrise on March 7 — about 20:25 p.m.

Table A: Latitude Adjustment

Diff. in Min. / Lat.	10	20	30	40	50	60	70	80	90	100	110	120
0°20	0	1	1	1	2	2	2	3	3	3	4	4
40	1	1	2	3	3	4	5	5	6	7	7	8
1 00	1	2	3	4	5	6	7	8	9	10	11	12
20	1	3	4	5	7	8	9	11	12	13	15	16
40	2	3	5	7	8	10	12	13	15	17	18	20
2 00	2	4	6	8	10	12	14	16	18	20	22	24
20	2	5	7	9	12	14	16	19	21	23	26	28
40	3	5	8	11	13	16	19	21	24	27	29	32
3 00	3	6	9	12	15	18	21	24	27	30	33	36
20	3	7	10	13	17	20	23	27	30	33	37	40
40	4	7	11	15	18	22	26	29	33	37	40	44
4 00	4	8	12	16	20	24	28	32	36	40	44	48
20	4	9	13	17	22	26	30	35	39	43	48	52
40	5	9	14	19	23	28	33	37	42	47	51	56
5 00	5	10	15	20	25	30	35	40	45	50	55	60
20	5	11	16	21	27	32	37	43	48	53	59	64
40	6	11	17	23	28	34	40	45	51	57	62	68
6 00	6	12	18	24	30	36	42	48	54	60	66	72
20	6	13	19	25	32	38	44	51	57	63	70	76
40	7	13	20	27	33	40	47	53	60	67	73	80
7 00	7	14	21	28	35	42	49	56	63	70	77	84
20	7	15	22	29	37	44	51	59	66	73	81	88
40	8	15	23	31	38	46	54	61	69	77	84	92
8 00	8	16	24	32	40	48	56	64	72	80	88	96
20	8	17	25	33	42	50	58	67	75	83	92	100
40	9	17	26	35	43	52	61	69	78	87	95	104
9 00	9	18	27	36	45	54	63	72	81	90	99	108
20	9	19	28	37	47	56	65	75	84	93	103	112
40	10	19	29	39	48	58	68	77	87	97	106	116

Table B: Longitude Adjustment

Diff. in Min. / Long.	10	20	30	40	50	60	70	80	90	100	110	120
50°	1	3	4	6	7	8	10	11	12	14	15	17
55	2	3	5	6	8	9	11	12	14	15	17	18
60	2	3	5	7	8	10	12	13	15	17	18	20
65	2	4	5	7	9	11	13	14	16	18	20	22
70	2	4	6	8	10	12	14	16	18	19	21	23
75	2	4	6	8	10	12	15	17	19	21	23	25
80	2	4	7	9	11	13	16	18	20	22	24	27
85	2	5	7	9	12	14	16	19	21	24	26	28
90	2	5	8	10	12	15	18	20	22	25	28	30
95	3	5	8	11	13	16	18	21	24	26	29	32
100	3	6	8	11	14	17	19	22	25	28	31	33
105	3	6	9	12	15	18	20	23	26	29	32	35
110	3	6	9	12	15	18	21	24	28	31	34	37
115	3	6	10	13	16	19	22	26	29	32	35	38
120	3	7	10	13	17	20	23	27	30	33	37	40
125	4	7	10	14	17	21	24	28	31	35	38	42
130	4	7	11	14	18	22	25	29	32	36	40	43
135	4	8	11	15	19	22	26	30	34	38	41	45
140	4	8	12	16	19	23	27	31	35	39	43	47
145	4	8	12	16	20	24	28	32	36	40	44	48
150	4	8	12	17	21	25	29	33	38	42	46	50
155	4	9	13	17	22	26	30	34	39	43	47	52
160	4	9	13	18	22	27	31	36	40	44	49	53
165	5	9	14	18	23	28	32	37	41	46	50	55
170	5	9	14	19	24	28	33	38	42	47	52	57

1st Month   January, 1977   31 Days

Greenwich Mean Time

NOTE: Light figures indicate Sun. **Dark** figures indicate **Moon.** *Degrees are North Latitude.*
CAUTION: Must be converted to local time. For instruction see page 768.

Day of month / week / year	Sun on meridian / Moon phase (h m s)	20° Rise Sun/Moon	20° Set Sun/Moon	30° Rise Sun/Moon	30° Set Sun/Moon	40° Rise Sun/Moon	40° Set Sun/Moon	50° Rise Sun/Moon	50° Set Sun/Moon	60° Rise Sun/Moon	60° Set Sun/Moon
1 Sa	12 02 50	6 34	17 31	6 55	17 10	7 21	16 44	7 58	16 08	9 02	15 04
1		14 32	3 01	14 17	3 16	13 57	3 35	13 30	4 01	12 46	4 44
2 Su	12 03 18	6 35	17 32	6 55	17 11	7 21	16 45	7 58	16 09	9 01	15 06
2		15 18	3 51	15 00	4 08	14 39	4 29	14 09	4 58	13 19	5 47
3 Mo	12 03 45	6 35	17 32	6 56	17 12	7 21	16 46	7 58	16 10	9 00	15 07
3		16 06	4 41	15 48	4 58	15 26	5 21	14 54	5 52	14 02	6 43
4 Tu	12 04 13	6 35	17 33	6 56	17 13	7 21	16 47	7 57	16 11	9 00	15 09
4		16 56	5 30	16 39	5 48	16 17	6 10	15 47	6 41	14 56	7 32
5 We	12 04 40	6 36	17 34	6 56	17 13	7 21	16 48	7 57	16 12	9 01	15 10
5	12 10 ○	17 49	6 18	17 33	6 35	17 13	6 56	16 45	7 24	16 00	8 11
6 Th	12 05 06	6 36	17 35	6 56	17 14	7 21	16 49	7 57	16 14	8 57	15 13
6		18 43	7 05	18 29	7 20	18 12	7 38	17 49	8 03	17 11	8 43
7 Fr	12 05 32	6 36	17 35	6 56	17 15	7 21	16 50	7 56	16 15	8 56	15 15
7		19 37	7 50	19 27	8 02	19 13	8 17	18 53	8 37	18 27	9 08
8 Sa	12 05 57	6 36	17 36	6 56	17 16	7 21	16 51	7 56	16 16	8 55	15 17
8		20 32	8 33	20 25	8 42	20 16	8 53	20 05	9 07	19 46	9 29
9 Su	12 06 22	6 36	17 37	6 56	17 17	7 21	16 52	7 55	16 18	8 54	15 19
9		21 27	9 16	21 24	9 21	21 20	9 27	21 15	9 35	21 07	9 47
10 Mo	12 06 47	6 36	17 37	6 56	17 18	7 20	16 53	7 55	16 19	8 53	15 21
10		22 23	9 58	22 24	9 59	22 25	10 00	22 27	10 01	22 30	10 07
11 Tu	12 07 11	6 36	17 38	6 56	17 18	7 20	16 54	7 54	16 20	8 52	15 23
11		23 20	10 40	23 25	10 37	23 32	10 33	23 40	10 28	23 54	10 21
12 We	12 07 34	6 37	17 39	6 56	17 19	7 20	16 55	7 53	16 22	8 50	15 25
12	19 55 ☾		11 24		11 17		11 28		10 52		10 39
13 Th	12 07 57	6 37	17 39	6 56	17 20	7 20	16 56	7 53	16 23	8 49	15 27
13		0 18	12 10	0 27	11 59	0 39	11 46	0 54	11 28	1 19	11 00
14 Fr	12 08 19	6 37	17 40	6 56	17 21	7 19	16 57	7 52	16 24	8 48	15 29
14		1 18	12 59	1 31	12 45	1 47	12 28	2 09	12 04	2 45	11 26
15 Sa	12 08 40	6 37	17 41	6 56	17 22	7 19	16 58	7 51	16 26	8 46	15 31
15		2 20	13 53	2 35	13 36	2 55	13 16	3 22	12 47	4 07	12 00
16 Su	12 09 01	6 37	17 41	6 55	17 23	7 18	17 00	7 51	16 27	8 45	15 34
16		3 21	14 50	3 39	14 32	4 01	14 10	4 32	13 38	5 23	12 46
17 Mo	12 09 21	6 37	17 42	6 55	17 23	7 18	17 01	7 50	16 29	8 43	15 36
17		4 22	15 50	4 40	15 32	5 02	15 10	5 34	14 38	6 27	13 46
18 Tu	12 09 40	6 37	17 43	6 55	17 24	7 18	17 02	7 49	16 30	8 41	15 38
18		5 20	16 51	5 37	16 35	5 58	16 14	6 28	15 45	7 17	14 58
19 We	12 09 59	6 37	17 43	6 55	17 25	7 17	17 03	7 48	16 32	8 39	15 41
19	14 11 ●	6 14	17 52	6 29	17 38	6 47	17 21	7 13	16 57	7 54	16 18
20 Th	12 10 17	6 37	17 44	6 54	17 26	7 16	17 04	7 47	16 34	8 38	15 43
20		7 03	18 51	7 15	18 40	7 30	18 27	7 50	18 09	8 22	17 41
21 Fr	12 10 34	6 37	17 44	6 54	17 27	7 16	17 05	7 46	16 35	8 36	15 45
21		7 49	19 47	7 58	19 41	8 08	19 32	8 22	19 21	8 43	19 03
22 Sa	12 10 51	6 37	17 45	6 54	17 28	7 15	17 06	7 45	16 37	8 34	15 48
22		8 32	20 41	8 36	20 39	8 42	20 35	8 50	20 30	9 01	20 23
23 Su	12 11 06	6 36	17 46	6 54	17 29	7 15	17 08	7 44	16 38	8 32	15 50
23		9 12	21 34	9 13	21 35	9 14	21 36	9 15	21 38	9 17	21 40
24 Mo	12 11 21	6 36	17 46	6 53	17 30	7 14	17 09	7 43	16 40	8 30	15 53
24		9 50	22 24	9 47	22 29	9 44	22 35	9 39	22 43	9 32	22 55
25 Tu	12 11 35	6 36	17 47	6 53	17 30	7 13	17 10	7 42	16 42	8 28	15 55
25		10 28	23 14	10 22	23 22	10 14	23 33	10 04	23 46	9 48	
26 We	12 11 48	6 36	17 48	6 52	17 31	7 12	17 11	7 40	16 43	8 26	15 58
26		11 07		10 57		10 45		10 30		10 05	0 08
27 Th	12 12 01	6 36	17 48	6 51	17 32	7 12	17 12	7 39	16 45	8 24	16 00
27	05 11 ☽	11 46	0 04	11 34	0 15	11 19	0 29	10 58	0 48	10 25	1 19
28 Fr	12 12 12	6 36	17 49	6 51	17 33	7 11	17 14	7 38	16 47	8 21	16 03
28		12 28	0 53	12 13	1 07	11 55	1 24	11 29	1 48	10 49	2 27
29 Sa	12 12 23	6 35	17 49	6 51	17 34	7 10	17 15	7 36	16 48	8 19	16 06
29		13 12	1 43	12 55	1 59	12 35	2 19	12 06	2 46	11 19	3 32
30 Su	12 12 33	6 35	17 50	6 50	17 35	7 09	17 16	7 35	16 50	8 17	16 08
30		13 58	2 32	13 41	2 50	13 19	3 11	12 48	3 41	11 58	4 32
31 Mo	12 12 42	6 35	17 51	6 50	17 36	7 08	17 17	7 34	16 52	8 15	16 11
31		14 48	3 22	14 30	3 39	14 08	4 02	13 37	4 32	12 46	5 24

2d Month   February, 1977   28 Days

Greenwich Mean Time

NOTE: Light figures indicate Sun. **Dark** figures indicate **Moon**. *Degrees are North Latitude.*
CAUTION: Must be converted to local time. For instruction see page 768.

Day of month / week / year	Sun on meridian / Moon phase (h m s)	20° Rise Sun/Moon	20° Set Sun/Moon	30° Rise Sun/Moon	30° Set Sun/Moon	40° Rise Sun/Moon	40° Set Sun/Moon	50° Rise Sun/Moon	50° Set Sun/Moon	60° Rise Sun/Moon	60° Set Sun/Moon
1 Tu 32	12 12 50	6 35	17 51	6 50	17 36	7 08	17 18	7 33	16 53	8 13	16 13
		15 39	4 11	15 23	4 28	15 02	4 49	14 33	5 19	13 45	6 07
2 We 33	12 12 58	6 34	17 52	6 49	17 37	7 07	17 19	7 31	16 55	8 11	16 15
		16 33	4 58	16 18	5 14	16 00	5 33	15 35	6 00	14 53	6 43
3 Th 34	12 13 04	6 34	17 52	6 48	17 38	7 06	17 20	7 30	16 56	8 08	16 18
		17 28	5 45	17 16	5 58	17 01	6 14	16 41	6 36	16 09	7 11
4 Fr 35	12 13 10 03 56 ☉	6 34	17 53	6 48	17 39	7 05	17 22	7 28	16 58	8 06	16 21
		18 24	6 30	18 15	6 40	18 05	6 52	17 51	7 09	17 28	7 34
5 Sa 36	12 13 15	6 33	17 53	6 47	17 40	7 04	17 23	7 27	17 00	8 03	16 23
		19 20	7 13	19 16	7 20	19 10	7 28	19 02	7 38	18 50	7 54
6 Su 37	12 13 19	6 33	17 54	6 46	17 40	7 03	17 24	7 25	17 01	8 01	16 26
		20 17	7 56	20 17	7 59	20 16	8 02	20 15	8 06	20 14	8 12
7 Mo 38	12 13 23	6 32	17 54	6 46	17 41	7 02	17 25	7 24	17 03	7 58	16 28
		21 15	8 40	21 19	8 38	21 23	8 36	21 30	8 33	21 39	8 30
8 Tu 39	12 13 25	6 32	17 55	6 45	17 42	7 01	17 26	7 22	17 05	7 56	16 31
		22 13	9 24	22 21	9 18	22 31	9 11	22 44	9 02	23 05	8 48
9 We 40	12 13 27	6 32	17 55	6 44	17 43	6 59	17 28	7 20	17 07	7 53	16 34
		23 13	10 09	23 24	10 00	23 39	9 48	23 59	9 32		9 08
10 Th 41	12 13 28	6 31	17 56	6 43	17 44	6 58	17 29	7 19	17 08	7 51	16 36
			10 58		10 45		10 29		10 07	0 30	9 32
11 Fr 42	12 13 28 04 07 ☾	6 31	17 56	6 42	17 44	6 57	17 30	7 17	17 10	7 48	16 39
		0 13	11 49	0 28	11 33	0 46	11 14	1 11	10 47	1 53	10 03
12 Sa 43	12 13 28	6 30	17 57	6 42	17 45	6 56	17 31	7 15	17 12	7 45	16 42
		1 13	12 43	1 30	12 26	1 51	12 04	2 21	11 34	3 10	10 44
13 Su 44	12 13 27	6 30	17 57	6 41	17 46	6 55	17 32	7 13	17 14	7 43	16 44
		2 13	13 40	2 31	13 23	2 53	13 00	3 24	12 29	4 16	11 37
14 Mo 45	12 13 25	6 29	17 58	6 40	17 47	6 53	17 33	7 12	17 15	7 40	16 47
		3 10	14 39	3 21	14 22	3 49	14 01	4 20	13 31	5 10	12 42
15 Tu 46	12 13 22	6 28	17 58	6 39	17 48	6 52	17 35	7 10	17 17	7 37	16 50
		4 04	15 38	4 20	15 24	4 40	15 05	5 07	14 39	5 51	13 57
16 We 47	12 13 19	6 28	17 59	6 38	17 48	6 51	17 36	7 08	17 19	7 34	16 52
		4 54	16 37	5 08	16 25	5 24	16 10	5 46	15 49	6 22	15 17
17 Th 48	12 13 15	6 27	17 59	6 37	17 49	6 50	17 37	7 06	17 20	7 32	16 55
		5 41	17 34	5 51	17 25	6 03	17 15	6 20	17 00	6 46	16 30
18 Fr 49	12 13 10 03 37 ●	6 27	18 00	6 36	17 50	6 48	17 38	7 04	17 22	7 29	16 57
		6 25	18 29	6 31	18 24	6 39	18 18	6 50	18 10	7 06	17 58
19 Sa 50	12 13 04	6 26	18 00	6 35	17 51	6 47	17 39	7 02	17 24	7 26	17 00
		7 06	19 22	7 09	19 21	7 12	19 20	7 16	19 19	7 23	19 16
20 Su 51	12 12 58	6 25	18 01	6 34	17 51	6 46	17 40	7 00	17 26	7 23	17 03
		7 45	20 14	7 44	20 17	7 43	20 20	7 41	20 25	7 39	20 33
21 Mo 52	12 12 52	6 25	18 01	6 33	17 52	6 44	17 42	6 58	17 27	7 21	17 05
		8 24	21 05	8 20	21 11	8 14	21 19	8 06	21 30	7 55	21 47
22 Tu 53	12 12 44	6 24	18 01	6 32	17 53	6 43	17 43	6 57	17 29	7 18	17 08
		9 03	21 55	8 55	22 05	8 45	22 17	8 32	22 33	8 12	23 00
23 We 54	12 12 36	6 23	18 02	6 31	17 54	6 41	17 44	6 55	17 31	7 15	17 10
		9 42	22 45	9 31	22 57	9 18	23 13	8 59	23 35	8 30	
24 Th 55	12 12 27	6 23	18 02	6 30	17 54	6 40	17 45	6 53	17 32	7 12	17 13
		10 23	23 34	10 10	23 49	9 53		9 30		8 53	0 09
25 Fr 56	12 12 18	6 22	18 03	6 29	17 55	6 38	17 46	6 51	17 34	7 09	17 15
		11 06		10 50		10 31	0 08	10 04	0 34	9 20	1 16
26 Sa 57	12 12 08 02 50 ☽	6 21	18 03	6 28	17 56	6 37	17 47	6 49	17 36	7 06	17 18
		11 51	0 24	11 34	0 40	11 13	1 01	10 43	1 30	9 55	2 17
27 Su 58	12 11 58	6 21	18 03	6 27	17 57	6 36	17 48	6 47	17 37	7 03	17 21
		12 39	1 13	12 21	1 30	11 59	1 52	11 29	2 22	10 38	3 12
28 Mo 59	12 11 47	6 20	18 04	6 26	17 57	6 34	17 49	6 45	17 39	7 00	17 23
		13 29	2 01	13 12	2 18	12 50	2 40	12 21	3 10	11 32	3 59

3d Month   March, 1977   31 Days

Greenwich Mean Time

NOTE: Light figures indicate Sun. **Dark** figures indicate **Moon**. *Degrees are North Latitude.*
CAUTION: Must be converted to local time. For instruction see page 768.

Day of month week year	Sun on meridian Moon phase		20° Rise Sun Moon	20° Set Sun Moon	30° Rise Sun Moon	30° Set Sun Moon	40° Rise Sun Moon	40° Set Sun Moon	50° Rise Sun Moon	50° Set Sun Moon	60° Rise Sun Moon	60° Set Sun Moon
	h m s		h m	h m	h m	h m	h m	h m	h m	h m	h m	h m
1 Tu 60	12 11 35		6 19 14 21	18 04 2 49	6 25 14 05	17 58 3 05	6 33 13 46	17 51 3 25	6 42 13 19	17 41 3 53	6 58 12 35	17 26 4 38
2 We 61	12 11 23		6 18 15 15	18 05 3 35	6 24 15 02	17 59 3 50	6 31 14 45	17 52 4 07	6 40 14 23	17 42 4 31	6 55 13 46	17 28 5 10
3 Th 62	12 11 11		6 17 16 10	18 05 4 21	6 23 16 00	17 59 4 32	6 30 15 48	17 53 4 46	6 38 15 31	17 44 5 06	6 52 15 04	17 31 5 36
4 Fr 63	12 10 58		6 17 17 07	18 05 5 05	6 22 17 01	18 00 5 14	6 28 16 53	17 54 5 23	6 36 16 42	17 46 5 37	6 49 16 25	17 33 5 57
5 Sa 64	12 10 44 17 13 ☉		6 16 18 05	18 06 5 50	6 21 18 03	18 01 5 54	6 27 18 00	17 55 5 59	6 34 17 56	17 47 6 06	6 46 17 50	17 36 6 17
6 Su 65	12 10 30		6 15 19 04	18 06 6 34	6 20 19 06	18 01 6 34	6 25 19 08	17 56 6 34	6 32 19 11	17 49 6 35	6 43 19 17	17 38 6 35
7 Mo 66	12 10 16		6 14 20 04	18 06 7 19	6 18 20 10	18 02 7 15	6 23 20 18	17 57 7 10	6 30 20 28	17 51 7 03	6 40 20 44	17 41 6 53
8 Tu 67	12 10 01		6 13 21 05	18 07 8 05	6 17 21 15	18 03 7 57	6 22 21 27	17 58 7 48	6 28 21 45	17 52 7 34	6 37 22 12	17 43 7 14
9 We 68	12 09 46		6 13 22 06	18 07 8 54	6 16 22 20	18 03 8 42	6 20 22 37	17 59 8 28	6 26 23 00	17 54 8 08	6 34 23 38	17 46 7 38
10 Th 69	12 09 31		6 12 23 08	18 07 9 46	6 15 23 24	18 04 9 31	6 19 23 44	18 00 9 13	6 24 8 48	17 55	6 31 8 07	17 48
11 Fr 70	12 09 15		6 11 10 40	18 08	6 14 10 23	18 05	6 17 10 02	18 01	6 21 0 12	17 57 9 33	6 28 0 58	17 51 8 45
12 Sa 71	12 08 59 11 35 ☾		6 10 0 08	18 08 11 36	6 13 0 25	18 05 11 19	6 16 0 47	18 02 10 57	6 19 1 17	17 59 10 26	6 25 2 08	17 53 9 35
13 Su 72	12 08 43		6 09 1 05	18 08 12 34	6 11 1 23	18 06 12 17	6 14 1 45	18 03 11 55	6 17 2 15	18 00 11 25	6 22 3 06	17 56 10 35
14 Mo 73	12 08 26		6 08 2 00	18 08 13 32	6 10 2 16	18 07 13 17	6 12 2 36	18 05 12 57	6 15 3 04	18 02 12 30	6 19 3 50	17 58 11 46
15 Tu 74	12 08 09		6 08 2 50	18 09 14 30	6 09 3 04	18 07 14 17	6 11 3 22	18 06 14 01	6 13 3 46	18 03 13 38	6 16 4 24	18 00 13 02
16 We 75	12 07 52		6 07 3 37	18 09 15 26	6 08 3 48	18 08 15 16	6 09 4 02	18 07 15 04	6 11 4 21	18 05 14 47	6 13 4 50	18 03 14 21
17 Th 76	12 07 35		6 06 4 21	18 09 16 20	6 07 4 29	18 08 16 14	6 08 4 38	18 08 16 07	6 08 4 51	18 07 15 56	6 10 5 11	18 05 15 40
18 Fr 77	12 07 18		6 05 5 02	18 10 17 13	6 05 5 06	18 09 17 11	6 06 5 11	18 09 17 08	6 06 5 18	18 08 17 04	6 07 5 29	18 08 16 58
19 Sa 78	12 07 00 18 33 ●		6 04 5 42	18 10 18 05	6 04 5 42	18 10 18 07	6 04 5 43	18 10 18 08	6 04 5 44	18 10 18 11	6 04 5 45	18 10 18 14
20 Su 79	12 06 43		6 03 6 21	18 10 18 56	6 03 6 18	18 10 19 01	6 03 6 14	18 11 19 07	6 02 6 09	18 11 19 16	6 01 6 01	18 13 19 29
21 Mo 80	12 06 25		6 02 6 59	18 10 19 47	6 02 6 53	18 11 19 55	6 01 6 45	18 12 20 05	6 00 6 34	18 13 20 20	5 58 6 17	18 15 20 42
22 Tu 81	12 06 07		6 02 7 39	18 11 20 37	6 01 7 29	18 12 20 48	5 59 7 17	18 13 21 02	5 58 7 01	18 15 21 22	5 55 6 36	18 18 21 53
23 We 82	12 05 49		6 01 8 19	18 11 21 26	5 59 8 07	18 12 21 40	5 58 7 51	18 14 21 58	5 55 7 30	18 16 22 22	5 52 6 57	18 20 23 01
24 Th 83	12 05 31		6 00 9 01	18 11 22 16	5 58 8 46	18 13 22 32	5 56 8 28	18 15 22 52	5 53 8 03	18 18 23 19	5 49 7 22	18 22
25 Fr 84	12 05 13		5 59 9 45	18 12 23 05	5 57 9 29	18 13 23 22	5 55 9 08	18 16 23 43	5 51 8 40	18 19	5 46 7 54	18 25 0 05
26 Sa 85	12 04 54		5 58 10 31	18 12 23 53	5 56 10 14	18 14	5 53 9 53	18 17	5 49 9 23	18 21 0 13	5 42 8 33	18 27 1 02
27 Su 86	12 04 36 22 27 ☽		5 57 11 20	18 12	5 55 11 02	18 15 0 10	5 51 10 41	18 18 0 32	5 47 10 11	18 23 1 02	5 39 9 22	18 30 1 52
28 Mo 87	12 04 18		5 56 12 10	18 12 0 40	5 53 11 54	18 15 0 57	5 50 11 34	18 19 1 18	5 45 11 06	18 24 1 46	5 36 10 20	18 32 2 33
29 Tu 88	12 04 00		5 55 13 02	18 13 1 26	5 52 12 48	18 16 1 42	5 48 12 30	18 20 2 00	5 42 12 06	18 26 2 26	5 33 11 26	18 35 3 07
30 We 89	12 03 42		5 55 13 56	18 13 2 11	5 51 13 44	18 16 2 24	5 46 13 30	18 21 2 40	5 40 13 10	18 27 3 01	5 30 12 39	18 37 3 35
31 Th 90	12 03 23		5 54 14 51	18 13 2 56	5 50 14 43	18 17 3 05	5 45 14 33	18 22 3 17	5 38 14 19	18 29 3 33	5 27 13 57	18 40 3 58

4th Month   April, 1977   30 Days

Greenwich Mean Time

NOTE: Light figures indicate Sun **Dark** figures indicate **Moon**. *Degrees are North Latitude.*

CAUTION: Must be converted to local time. For instruction see page 768.

Day/week, year	Sun on meridian / Moon phase	Body	20° Rise	20° Set	30° Rise	30° Set	40° Rise	40° Set	50° Rise	50° Set	60° Rise	60° Set
1 Fr / 91	12 03 05	Sun	5 53	18 13	5 49	18 18	5 43	18 23	5 36	18 30	5 24	18 42
		Moon	15 48	3 39	15 43	3 46	15 38	3 53	15 31	4 03	15 19	4 19
2 Sa / 92	12 02 48	Sun	5 52	18 14	5 47	18 18	5 42	18 24	5 34	18 32	5 21	18 44
		Moon	16 46	4 23	16 46	4 26	16 46	4 28	16 45	4 32	16 45	4 37
3 Su / 93	12 02 30	Sun	5 51	18 14	5 46	18 19	5 40	18 25	5 32	18 33	5 18	18 47
		Moon	17 46	5 08	17 50	5 06	17 56	5 04	18 03	5 01	18 13	4 56
4 Mo / 94	12 02 12 4 09 ☽	Sun	5 50	18 14	5 45	18 19	5 38	18 26	5 29	18 35	5 15	18 49
		Moon	18 48	5 55	18 57	5 49	18 07	5 41	19 21	5 31	19 44	5 16
5 Tu / 95	12 01 55	Sun	5 49	18 14	5 44	18 20	5 37	18 27	5 27	18 37	5 12	18 52
		Moon	19 52	6 44	20 04	6 34	20 19	6 22	20 40	6 05	21 13	5 39
6 We / 96	12 01 37	Sun	5 49	18 15	5 43	18 21	5 35	18 28	5 25	18 38	5 09	18 54
		Moon	20 56	7 36	21 11	7 23	21 30	7 06	21 56	6 43	22 39	6 07
7 Th / 97	12 01 20	Sun	5 48	18 15	5 41	18 21	5 34	18 29	5 23	18 40	5 06	18 57
		Moon	21 58	8 31	22 16	8 15	27 37	7 55	23 07	7 28	23 56	6 43
8 Fr / 98	12 01 03	Sun	5 47	18 15	5 40	18 22	5 33	18 30	5 21	18 41	5 03	18 59
		Moon	22 59	9 29	23 16	9 12	23 38	8 50		8 20		7 29
9 Sa / 99	12 00 47	Sun	5 46	18 16	5 39	18 22	5 31	18 31	5 19	18 43	5 00	19 01
		Moon	23 56	10 28		10 11		9 49	0 09	9 19	1 00	8 28
10 Su / 100	12 00 30 19 15 ☾	Sun	5 45	18 16	5 38	18 23	5 29	18 32	5 17	18 44	4 57	19 04
		Moon		11 27	0 12	11 11	0 33	10 51	1 02	10 23	1 49	9 37
11 Mo / 101	12 00 14	Sun	5 44	18 16	5 37	18 24	5 27	18 33	5 14	18 46	4 54	19 06
		Moon	0 48	12 25	1 03	12 12	1 21	11 54	1 46	11 31	2 27	10 52
12 Tu / 102	11 59 59	Sun	5 44	18 16	5 36	18 24	5 26	18 34	5 12	18 48	4 51	19 09
		Moon	1 36	13 22	1 48	13 11	2 03	12 58	2 23	12 39	2 55	12 10
13 We / 103	11 59 43	Sun	5 43	18 17	5 35	18 25	5 24	18 35	5 10	18 49	4 48	19 11
		Moon	2 20	14 16	2 29	14 09	2 40	14 00	2 54	13 48	3 17	13 28
14 Th / 104	11 59 28	Sun	5 42	18 17	5 33	18 25	5 23	18 36	5 08	18 51	4 45	19 14
		Moon	3 02	15 09	3 07	15 05	3 13	15 01	3 22	14 55	3 35	14 45
15 Fr / 105	11 59 14	Sun	5 41	18 17	5 32	18 26	5 21	18 37	5 06	18 52	4 42	19 16
		Moon	3 41	16 00	3 43	16 00	3 45	16 01	3 48	16 01	3 52	16 01
16 Sa / 106	11 58 59	Sun	5 40	18 18	5 31	18 27	5 20	18 38	5 04	18 54	4 39	19 19
		Moon	4 20	16 51	4 18	16 55	4 15	16 59	4 12	17 06	4 08	17 15
17 Su / 107	11 58 45	Sun	5 40	18 18	5 30	18 27	5 18	18 39	5 02	18 55	4 36	19 21
		Moon	4 58	17 41	4 53	17 48	4 46	17 57	4 37	18 09	4 24	18 28
18 Mo / 108	11 58 32 10 35 ●	Sun	5 39	18 18	5 29	18 28	5 18	18 40	5 00	18 57	4 34	19 24
		Moon	5 37	18 31	5 28	18 41	5 18	18 54	5 03	19 12	4 41	19 40
19 Tu / 109	11 58 19	Sun	5 38	18 19	5 28	18 29	5 15	18 41	4 58	18 59	4 31	19 26
		Moon	6 17	19 21	6 05	19 34	5 51	19 50	5 31	20 13	5 01	20 49
20 We / 110	11 58 06	Sun	5 37	18 19	5 27	18 29	5 13	18 42	4 56	19 00	4 28	19 29
		Moon	6 58	20 10	6 44	20 26	6 27	20 45	6 03	21 11	5 25	21 54
21 Th / 111	11 57 54	Sun	5 37	18 19	5 26	18 30	5 11	18 43	4 54	19 02	4 25	19 31
		Moon	7 41	20 59	7 25	21 16	7 06	21 37	6 38	22 06	5 54	22 54
22 Fr / 112	11 57 42	Sun	5 36	18 19	5 25	18 30	5 11	18 44	4 52	19 03	4 22	19 33
		Moon	8 27	21 48	8 10	22 05	7 48	22 27	7 19	22 57	6 30	23 47
23 Sa / 113	11 57 30	Sun	5 35	18 20	5 24	18 31	5 10	18 45	4 50	19 05	4 19	19 36
		Moon	9 14	22 35	8 57	22 52	8 35	23 13	8 03	23 43	7 15	
24 Su / 114	11 57 19	Sun	5 35	18 20	5 23	18 32	5 08	18 46	4 48	19 06	4 16	19 38
		Moon	10 03	23 21	9 46	23 37	9 26	23 56	8 57		8 09	0 31
25 Mo / 115	11 57 09	Sun	5 34	18 20	5 22	18 32	5 07	18 47	4 46	19 08	4 13	19 41
		Moon	10 53		10 38		10 20		9 54	0 23	9 11	1 07
26 Tu / 116	11 56 58 14 42 ☽	Sun	5 33	18 21	5 21	18 33	5 06	18 48	4 45	19 09	4 11	19 43
		Moon	11 45	0 05	11 32	0 19	11 17	0 36	10 55	1 00	10 20	1 37
27 We / 117	11 56 49	Sun	5 33	18 21	5 20	18 34	5 04	18 49	4 43	19 11	4 08	19 46
		Moon	12 38	0 49	12 28	1 00	12 16	1 14	12 00	1 32	11 34	2 01
28 Th / 118	11 56 40	Sun	5 32	18 21	5 19	18 34	5 03	18 50	4 41	19 12	4 05	19 48
		Moon	13 33	1 31	13 26	1 39	13 19	1 49	13 08	2 02	12 52	2 22
29 Fr / 119	11 56 31	Sun	5 31	18 22	5 18	18 35	5 02	18 51	4 39	19 14	4 02	19 51
		Moon	14 29	2 14	14 26	2 18	14 24	2 23	14 20	2 30	14 14	2 40
30 Sa / 120	11 56 23	Sun	5 31	18 22	5 17	18 36	5 00	18 52	4 37	19 16	3 59	19 53
		Moon	15 27	2 57	15 29	2 57	15 31	2 58	15 34	2 58	15 39	2 58

5th Month   May, 1977   31 Days

Greenwich Mean Time

NOTE: Light figures indicate Sun. **Dark** figures indicate **Moon**. *Degrees are North Latitude.*

CAUTION: Must be converted to local time. For instruction see page 768.

Day of month week year	Sun on meridian Moon phase			20° Rise Sun Moon	20° Set Sun Moon	30° Rise Sun Moon	30° Set Sun Moon	40° Rise Sun Moon	40° Set Sun Moon	50° Rise Sun Moon	50° Set Sun Moon	60° Rise Sun Moon	60° Set Sun Moon
	h	m	s	h m	h m	h m	h m	h m	h m	h m	h m	h m	h m
1 Su	11	56	15	5 30	18 23	5 16	18 36	4 59	18 53	4 35	19 17	3 57	19 56
121				16 27	3 42	16 34	3 38	16 41	3 33	16 52	3 27	17 08	3 17
2 Mo	11	56	08	5 29	18 23	5 15	18 37	4 58	18 54	4 34	19 19	3 54	19 58
122				17 30	4 30	17 41	4 22	17 53	4 12	18 11	3 58	18 39	3 38
3 Tu	11	56	02	5 29	18 23	5 15	18 38	4 57	18 55	4 32	19 20	3 51	20 01
123	13	03		18 35	5 21	18 49	5 09	19 06	4 54	19 30	4 34	20 09	4 03
4 We	11	55	56	5 28	18 24	5 14	18 38	4 56	18 56	4 30	19 22	3 49	20 03
124				19 40	6 15	19 57	6 00	20 17	5 42	20 46	5 16	21 33	4 35
5 Th	11	55	50	5 28	18 24	5 13	18 39	4 54	18 57	4 28	19 23	3 46	22 06
125				20 45	7 14	21 02	6 57	21 24	6 36	21 55	6 06	22 46	5 18
6 Fr	11	55	45	5 27	18 24	5 12	18 39	4 53	18 58	4 27	19 25	3 43	20 08
126				21 45	8 15	22 03	7 57	22 24	7 35	22 54	7 04	23 44	6 13
7 Sa	11	55	41	5 27	18 25	5 11	18 40	4 52	18 59	4 25	19 26	3 41	20 11
127				22 41	9 16	22 57	8 59	23 17	8 38	23 43	8 09		7 20
8 Su	11	55	37	5 26	18 25	5 11	18 41	4 51	19 00	4 24	19 28	3 38	20 13
128				23 32	10 17	23 46	10 02		9 44		9 18	0 27	8 37
9 Mo	11	55	34	5 26	18 26	5 10	18 41	4 50	19 01	4 22	19 29	3 36	20 15
129					11 16		11 04	0 02	10 49	0 24	10 29	0 59	9 56
10 Tu	11	55	32	5 25	18 26	5 09	18 42	4 49	19 02	4 20	19 31	3 33	20 18
130	04	08	☾	0 19	12 12	0 29	12 03	0 41	11 53	0 58	11 39	1 23	11 16
11 We	11	55	30	5 25	18 26	5 08	18 43	4 48	19 03	4 19	19 32	3 31	20 20
131				1 02	13 05	1 08	13 01	1 16	12 55	1 27	12 47	1 43	12 34
12 Th	11	55	29	5 24	18 27	5 08	18 43	4 47	19 04	4 17	19 34	3 28	20 23
132				1 42	13 57	1 45	13 56	1 48	13 55	1 53	13 53	2 00	13 50
13 Fr	11	55	28	5 24	18 27	5 07	18 44	4 46	19 05	4 15	19 35	3 25	20 25
133				2 21	14 48	2 20	14 50	2 19	14 54	2 18	14 58	2 16	15 05
14 Sa	11	55	28	5 23	18 27	5 06	18 45	4 45	19 06	4 14	19 36	3 23	20 27
134				2 59	15 38	2 54	15 44	2 49	15 51	2 42	16 02	2 31	16 18
15 Su	11	55	28	5 23	18 28	5 06	18 45	4 44	19 07	4 13	19 38	3 21	20 30
135				3 37	16 27	3 29	16 37	3 20	16 48	3 07	17 04	2 48	17 29
16 Mo	11	55	29	5 23	12 28	5 05	18 46	4 43	19 08	4 12	19 39	3 19	20 32
136				4 16	17 17	4 05	17 29	3 52	17 44	3 34	18 04	3 07	18 39
17 Tu	11	55	31	5 22	18 29	5 05	18 47	4 42	19 09	4 10	19 41	3 16	20 35
137				4 57	18 06	4 43	18 21	4 27	18 39	4 04	19 05	3 29	19 46
18 We	11	55	33	5 22	18 29	5 04	18 47	4 41	19 10	4 09	19 42	3 14	20 37
138	02	51	●	5 39	18 56	5 24	19 12	5 05	19 33	4 38	20 01	3 56	20 48
19 Th	11	55	36	5 22	18 30	5 03	18 48	4 40	19 11	4 08	19 43	3 12	20 39
139				6 24	19 44	6 07	20 02	5 46	20 23	5 17	20 53	4 29	21 43
20 Fr	11	55	39	5 21	18 30	5 03	18 48	4 40	19 12	4 07	19 45	3 10	20 41
140				7 10	20 32	6 53	20 49	6 31	21 11	6 01	21 41	5 11	22 31
21 Sa	11	55	43	5 21	18 30	5 02	18 49	4 39	19 13	4 05	19 46	3 08	20 44
141				7 59	21 19	7 42	21 35	7 21	21 55	6 51	22 23	6 02	23 09
22 Su	11	55	47	5 21	18 31	5 02	18 50	4 38	19 13	4 04	19 47	3 06	20 46
142				8 49	22 03	8 33	22 18	8 13	22 36	7 46	23 01	7 01	23 41
23 Mo	11	55	52	5 21	18 31	5 02	18 50	4 37	19 14	4 03	19 49	3 04	20 48
143				9 40	22 46	9 22	22 59	9 09	23 14	8 45	23 34	8 07	
24 Tu	11	55	57	5 20	18 32	5 01	18 51	4 37	19 15	4 02	19 50	3 02	20 50
144				10 31	23 28	10 20	23 38	10 07	23 49	9 48		9 18	0 06
25 We	11	56	03	5 20	18 32	5 01	18 51	4 36	19 16	4 01	19 51	3 00	20 52
145				11 24		11 16		11 06		10 53	0 04	10 33	0 28
26 Th	11	56	09	5 20	18 32	5 00	18 52	4 35	19 17	4 00	19 52	2 58	20 54
146	03	20	☽	12 17	0 10	12 13	0 15	12 08	0 22	12 02	0 32	11 51	0 46
27 Fr	11	56	16	5 20	18 33	5 00	18 53	4 35	19 18	3 59	19 53	2 56	20 56
147				13 13	0 51	13 13	0 53	13 13	0 52	13 12	0 59	13 12	1 04
28 Sa	11	56	23	5 20	18 33	5 00	18 53	4 34	19 18	3 58	19 55	2 54	20 58
148				14 10	1 33	14 14	1 32	14 19	1 29	14 26	1 26	14 37	1 21
29 Su	11	56	31	5 19	18 34	4 59	18 54	4 34	19 19	3 57	19 56	2 53	21 00
149				15 10	2 18	15 18	2 12	15 28	2 05	15 42	1 55	16 04	1 40
30 Mo	11	56	39	5 19	18 34	4 59	18 54	4 33	19 20	3 56	19 57	2 51	21 02
150				16 13	3 06	16 25	2 56	16 40	2 44	17 00	2 27	17 33	2 02
31 Tu	11	56	47	5 19	18 34	4 59	18 55	4 33	19 21	3 56	19 58	2 50	21 04
151				17 18	3 58	17 33	3 44	17 52	3 28	18 18	3 05	19 01	2 29

6th Month   June, 1977   30 Days

Greenwich Mean Time

NOTE: Light figures indicate Sun. **Dark** figures indicate **Moon**. *Degrees are North Latitude.*

CAUTION: Must be converted to local time. For instruction see page 768.

Day of month week year	Sun on meridian Moon phase h m s	20° Rise Sun Moon	20° Set Sun Moon	30° Rise Sun Moon	30° Set Sun Moon	40° Rise Sun Moon	40° Set Sun Moon	50° Rise Sun Moon	50° Set Sun Moon	60° Rise Sun Moon	60° Set Sun Moon
1 We	11 56 56	5 19	18 35	4 58	18 55	4 32	19 22	3 55	19 59	2 48	21 06
152	20 31 ☉	18 23	4 54	18 40	4 38	19 02	4 18	19 32	3 50	20 22	3 05
2 Th	11 57 05	5 19	18 35	4 58	18 56	4 32	19 22	3 54	20 00	2 47	21 07
153		19 27	5 55	19 45	5 37	20 07	5 15	20 38	4 44	21 59	3 54
3 Fr	11 57 15	5 19	18 36	4 58	18 56	4 32	19 23	3 54	20 01	2 45	21 09
154		20 27	6 57	20 44	6 40	21 05	6 18	21 34	5 47	22 21	4 56
4 Sa	11 57 25	5 19	18 36	4 58	18 57	4 31	19 24	3 53	20 02	2 44	21 11
155		21 23	8 01	2 37	7 45	21 55	7 15	22 20	6 57	22 59	6 11
5 Su	11 57 35	5 19	18 36	4 58	18 57	4 31	19 24	3 52	20 03	2 43	21 12
156		22 13	9 03	22 24	8 49	22 39	8 33	27 58	8 10	23 28	7 33
6 Mo	11 57 46	5 19	18 37	4 58	18 58	4 31	19 25	3 52	20 04	2 42	21 14
157		22 59	10 02	23 07	9 52	23 16	9 40	23 30	9 23	23 50	8 56
7 Tu	11 57 57	5 19	18 37	4 58	18 58	4 30	19 25	3 51	20 05	2 41	21 15
158		23 41	10 58	23 45	10 52	23 50	10 44	23 57	10 34		10 17
8 We	11 58 08	5 19	18 37	4 57	18 59	4 30	19 26	3 51	20 05	2 40	21 17
159	15 07 ☾		11 52		11 50		11 47		11 43	0 08	11 36
9 Th	11 58 20	5 19	18 38	4 57	18 59	4 30	19 27	3 51	20 06	2 39	21 18
160		0 21	12 44	0 21	12 45	0 22	12 47	0 23	12 49	0 24	12 52
10 Fr	11 58 32	5 19	18 38	4 57	19 00	4 30	19 27	3 50	20 07	2 38	21 19
161		0 59	13 34	0 56	13 39	0 53	13 45	0 48	13 53	0 40	14 06
11 Sa	11 58 44	5 19	18 38	4 57	19 00	4 30	19 28	3 50	20 08	2 37	21 20
162		1 38	14 24	1 31	14 32	1 23	14 43	1 13	14 56	0 56	15 18
12 Su	11 50 56	5 19	18 39	4 57	19 00	4 30	19 28	3 50	20 08	2 37	21 21
163		2 16	15 13	2 07	15 75	1 55	15 39	1 39	15 58	1 14	16 29
13 Mo	11 59 09	5 19	18 39	4 57	19 01	4 30	19 29	3 50	20 09	2 36	21 22
164		2 56	16 03	2 44	16 17	2 28	16 34	2 07	16 58	1 34	17 37
14 Tu	11 59 21	5 19	18 39	4 58	19 01	4 30	19 29	3 50	20 09	2 36	21 23
165		3 38	16 52	3 23	17 08	3 05	17 28	2 40	17 55	1 59	18 41
15 We	11 59 34	5 20	18 39	4 58	19 01	4 30	19 29	3 50	20 09	2 35	21 24
166		4 22	17 41	4 05	17 58	3 45	18 20	3 16	18 50	2 30	19 39
16 Th	11 59 47	5 20	18 40	4 58	19 02	4 30	19 30	3 49	20 10	2 35	21 25
167	18 23 ●	5 08	18 30	4 50	18 47	4 29	19 09	3 59	19 39	3 09	20 29
17 Fr	12 00 00	5 20	18 40	4 58	19 02	4 30	19 30	3 49	20 11	2 35	21 25
168		5 56	19 17	5 38	19 34	5 17	19 55	4 47	20 24	3 57	21 11
18 Sa	12 00 13	5 20	18 40	4 58	19 02	4 30	19 31	3 49	20 11	2 35	21 26
169		6 45	20 02	6 29	29 18	6 09	20 37	5 40	21 03	4 53	21 46
19 Su	12 00 26	5 20	18 41	4 58	19 03	4 30	19 31	3 49	20 11	2 35	21 26
170		7 36	20 46	7 21	20 59	7 03	21 16	6 38	21 38	5 57	22 13
20 Mo	12 00 40	5 20	18 41	4 58	19 03	4 30	19 31	3 50	20 12	2 35	21 27
171		8 28	21 28	8 15	21 39	8 01	21 52	7 40	22 09	7 07	22 36
21 Tu	12 00 53	5 21	18 41	4 59	19 03	4 30	19 31	3 50	20 12	2 35	21 27
172		9 20	22 09	9 11	22 17	8 59	22 25	8 44	22 37	8 20	22 55
22 We	12 01 05	5 21	18 41	4 59	19 03	4 31	19 32	3 50	20 12	2 35	21 27
173		10 12	22 50	10 07	22 54	10 00	22 58	9 51	23 04	9 36	23 12
23 Th	12 01 19	5 21	18 42	4 59	19 04	4 31	19 32	3 50	20 12	2 36	21 22
174		11 06	23 31	11 04	23 31	11 02	23 30	10 59	23 30	10 55	23 29
24 Fr	12 01 32	5 21	18 42	4 59	19 04	4 31	19 32	3 51	20 12	2 36	21 27
175	12 44 ☽	12 01		12 03		12 06		12 10	23 57	12 16	23 47
25 Sa	12 01 45	5 22	18 42	5 00	19 04	4 32	19 32	3 51	20 12	2 36	21 27
176		12 57	0 13	13 04	0 09	13 12	0 04	13 22		13 39	
26 Su	12 01 57	5 22	18 42	5 00	19 04	4 32	19 32	3 51	20 12	2 37	21 27
177		13 57	0 58	14 07	0 50	14 20	0 40	14 37	0 27	15 04	0 06
27 Mo	12 02 10	5 22	18 42	5 00	19 04	4 32	19 32	3 52	20 12	2 38	21 27
178		14 59	1 46	15 12	1 34	15 29	1 20	15 53	1 00	16 31	0 29
28 Tu	12 02 22	5 22	18 42	5 01	19 04	4 33	19 32	3 52	20 12	2 39	21 26
179		16 02	2 38	16 18	2 24	16 39	2 05	17 07	1 40	17 54	1 00
29 We	12 02 34	5 23	18 42	5 01	19 04	4 33	19 32	3 53	20 12	2 39	21 26
180		17 06	3 35	17 24	3 18	17 46	2 57	18 16	2 28	19 08	1 40
30 Th	12 02 46	5 23	18 42	5 01	19 04	4 34	19 32	3 54	20 12	2 40	21 25
181		18 08	4 36	18 26	4 19	18 48	3 57	19 18	3 26	20 08	2 34

7th Month   July, 1977   31 Days

Greenwich Mean Time

NOTE: Light figures indicate Sun. **Dark** figures indicate **Moon.** *Degrees are North Latitude.*

CAUTION: Must be converted to local time. For instruction see page 768.

Day of month / week / year	Sun on meridian / Moon phase (h m s)	20° Rise Sun/Moon	20° Set Sun/Moon	30° Rise Sun/Moon	30° Set Sun/Moon	40° Rise Sun/Moon	40° Set Sun/Moon	50° Rise Sun/Moon	50° Set Sun/Moon	60° Rise Sun/Moon	60° Set Sun/Moon
1 Fr / 182	12 02 57 ☺	5 23	18 43	5 02	19 04	4 34	19 32	3 54	20 12	2 41	21 24
		19 07	5 40	19 23	5 23	19 43	5 02	20 10	4 32	20 54	3 42
2 Sa / 183	12 03 09	5 24	18 43	5 02	19 04	4 35	19 32	3 55	20 11	2 43	21 23
		20 01	6 43	20 14	6 29	20 31	6 10	20 53	5 44	21 28	5 02
3 Su / 184	12 03 20	5 24	18 43	5 02	19 04	4 35	19 32	3 56	20 11	2 44	21 23
		20 50	7 46	21 00	7 34	21 12	7 19	21 28	6 59	21 54	6 26
4 Mo / 185	12 03 31	5 24	18 43	5 03	19 04	4 36	19 31	3 56	20 11	2 45	21 22
		21 36	8 45	21 42	8 37	21 49	8 27	21 59	8 13	22 14	7 41
5 Tu / 186	12 03 41	5 25	18 43	5 03	19 04	4 36	19 31	3 57	20 10	2 46	21 21
		22 18	9 42	22 20	9 37	22 23	9 32	22 26	9 25	22 32	9 14
6 We / 187	12 03 51	5 25	18 43	5 04	19 04	4 37	19 31	3 58	20 10	2 48	21 20
		22 58	10 36	22 56	10 35	22 54	10 35	22 52	10 34	22 48	10 33
7 Th / 188	12 04 01	5 25	18 43	5 04	19 04	4 37	19 31	3 59	20 09	2 49	21 20
		23 37	11 28	23 32	11 31	23 25	11 35	23 17	11 41	23 05	11 50
8 Fr / 189	12 04 11 / 04 39 ☾	5 26	18 43	5 05	19 04	4 38	19 30	4 00	20 09	2 51	21 18
			12 19		12 26	23 57	12 34	23 43	12 46	23 22	13 04
9 Sa / 190	12 04 20	5 26	18 43	5 05	19 04	4 39	19 30	4 01	20 08	2 52	21 16
		0 16	13 09	0 07	13 19		13 31		13 49	23 41	14 16
10 Su / 191	12 04 28	5 26	18 43	5 06	19 03	4 39	19 30	4 02	20 07	2 54	21 15
		0 55	13 58	0 44	14 11	0 30	14 23	0 11	14 49		15 25
11 Mo / 192	12 04 37	5 27	18 42	5 06	19 03	4 40	19 29	4 03	20 07	2 56	21 14
		1 36	14 48	1 22	15 08	1 05	15 22	0 42	15 48	0 04	16 31
12 Tu / 193	12 04 44	5 27	18 42	5 07	19 03	4 41	19 29	4 04	20 06	2 57	21 12
		2 19	15 37	2 03	15 54	1 44	16 14	1 17	16 43	0 33	17 31
13 We / 194	12 04 52	5 28	18 42	5 07	19 03	4 41	19 28	4 05	20 05	2 59	21 10
		3 04	16 20	2 47	16 43	2 20	17 05	1 57	17 35	1 08	18 25
14 Th / 195	12 04 59	5 28	18 42	5 08	19 02	4 42	19 28	4 06	20 04	3 01	21 09
		3 52	17 13	3 34	17 31	3 13	17 52	2 43	18 22	1 52	19 11
15 Fr / 196	12 05 05	5 28	18 42	5 08	19 02	4 43	19 27	4 07	20 03	3 03	21 07
		4 41	18 00	4 24	18 16	4 03	18 36	3 34	19 03	2 46	19 48
16 Sa / 197	12 05 11 / 08 37 ●	5 29	18 42	5 09	19 01	4 44	19 27	4 08	20 02	3 05	21 05
		5 32	18 45	5 16	18 59	4 57	19 16	4 31	19 40	3 48	20 18
17 Su / 198	12 05 17	5 29	18 42	5 10	19 01	4 44	19 26	4 09	20 01	3 07	21 04
		6 24	19 28	6 11	19 40	5 54	19 54	5 32	20 13	4 56	20 43
18 Mo / 199	12 05 21	5 29	18 41	5 11	19 01	4 45	19 25	4 10	20 00	3 09	21 02
		7 16	20 10	7 06	20 18	6 53	20 29	6 36	20 42	6 09	21 03
19 Tu / 200	12 05 26	5 30	18 41	5 10	19 00	4 46	19 25	4 11	19 59	3 11	21 00
		8 09	20 51	8 02	20 56	7 54	21 02	7 42	21 10	7 25	21 22
20 We / 201	12 05 30	5 30	18 41	5 11	19 00	4 47	19 24	4 13	19 58	3 13	20 58
		9 02	21 32	8 59	21 33	8 55	21 34	8 50	21 36	8 43	21 39
21 Th / 202	12 05 33	5 31	18 41	5 12	18 59	4 48	19 23	4 14	19 57	3 15	20 56
		9 56	22 13	9 57	22 11	9 58	22 07	10 00	22 03	10 02	21 56
22 Fr / 203	12 05 35	5 31	18 40	5 12	18 59	4 49	19 23	4 15	19 56	3 17	20 54
		10 52	22 56	10 57	22 50	11 02	22 42	11 11	22 31	11 23	22 14
23 Sa / 204	12 05 37 / 19 38 ☽	5 32	18 40	5 13	18 58	4 49	19 22	4 16	19 55	3 20	20 52
		11 49	23 42	11 57	23 32	12 08	23 19	12 23	23 02	12 46	22 35
24 Su / 205	12 05 39	5 32	18 40	5 13	18 58	4 50	19 21	4 18	19 54	3 22	20 50
		12 48		13 00		13 15		13 36	23 38	14 10	23 02
25 Mo / 206	12 05 40	5 32	18 39	5 14	18 57	4 51	19 20	4 19	19 52	3 24	20 47
		13 49	0 31	14 04	0 17	14 22	0 01	14 49		15 31	23 36
26 Tu / 207	12 05 40	5 32	18 39	5 15	18 57	4 52	19 19	4 20	19 51	3 26	20 45
		14 50	1 24	15 07	1 08	15 29	0 48	15 58	0 21	16 48	
27 We / 208	12 05 39	5 33	18 39	5 15	18 56	4 53	19 18	4 22	19 50	3 29	20 43
		15 52	2 21	16 09	2 04	16 31	1 42	17 02	1 12	17 53	0 22
28 Th / 209	12 05 38	5 33	18 38	5 16	18 56	4 54	19 17	4 23	19 48	3 31	20 40
		16 51	3 22	17 08	3 04	17 29	2 43	17 57	2 12	18 45	1 21
29 Fr / 210	12 05 37	5 34	18 38	5 16	18 55	4 55	19 16	4 24	19 47	3 33	20 38
		17 47	4 24	18 01	4 08	18 20	3 48	18 44	3 20	19 24	2 34
30 Sa / 211	12 05 34 / 10 52 ☺	5 34	18 37	5 17	18 54	4 56	19 15	4 26	19 45	3 35	20 36
		18 38	5 27	18 50	5 13	19 04	4 56	19 24	4 33	19 54	3 56
31 Su / 212	12 05 32	5 34	18 37	5 18	18 54	4 57	19 14	4 27	19 44	3 38	20 33
		19 26	6 28	19 34	6 18	19 44	6 05	19 57	5 48	20 18	5 21

8th Month   August, 1977   31 Days

Greenwich Mean Time

NOTE: Light figures indicate Sun. **Dark** figures indicate **Moon**. *Degrees are North Latitude.*
CAUTION: Must be converted to local time. For instruction see page 768.

Day of month / week / year	Sun on meridian / Moon phase h m s	20° Rise Sun/Moon	20° Set Sun/Moon	30° Rise Sun/Moon	30° Set Sun/Moon	40° Rise Sun/Moon	40° Set Sun/Moon	50° Rise Sun/Moon	50° Set Sun/Moon	60° Rise Sun/Moon	60° Set Sun/Moon
1 Mo 213	12 05 28	5 35	18 36	5 18	18 53	4 58	19 13	4 29	19 42	3 40	20 31
		20 11	7 27	20 15	7 20	20 20	7 13	20 27	7 02	20 39	6 45
2 Tu 214	12 05 24	5 35	18 36	5 19	18 52	4 58	19 12	4 30	19 41	3 42	20 28
		20 53	8 23	20 53	8 21	20 53	8 18	20 54	8 14	20 55	8 08
3 We 215	12 05 19	5 35	18 35	5 19	18 51	4 59	19 11	4 31	19 39	3 45	20 26
		21 33	9 17	21 30	9 19	21 25	9 21	21 20	9 23	21 12	9 27
4 Th 216	12 05 14	5 36	18 35	5 20	18 50	5 00	19 10	4 33	19 38	3 47	20 23
		22 13	10 10	22 06	10 15	21 57	10 21	21 46	10 30	21 29	10 44
5 Fr 217	12 05 08	5 36	18 34	5 21	18 50	5 01	19 09	4 34	19 36	3 50	20 20
		22 53	11 01	22 43	11 10	22 30	11 20	22 14	11 35	22 48	11 58
6 Sa 218	12 05 02	5 36	18 34	5 21	18 49	5 02	19 08	4 36	19 34	3 52	20 18
	20 40 ☾	23 33	11 51	23 21	12 03	23 05	12 18	22 43	12 37	22 10	13 09
7 Su 219	12 04 55	5 37	18 33	5 22	18 48	5 03	19 07	4 37	19 33	3 54	20 15
			12 41		12 55	23 42	13 13	23 17	13 37	22 36	14 17
8 Mo 220	12 04 47	5 37	18 33	5 22	18 47	5 04	19 06	4 39	19 31	3 57	20 13
		0 16	13 31	0 01	13 47		14 07	23 55	14 34	23 08	15 20
9 Tu 221	12 04 39	5 37	18 32	5 23	18 46	5 05	19 04	4 40	19 29	3 59	20 10
		1 00	14 20	0 44	14 37	0 23	14 58		15 27	23 49	16 16
10 We 222	17 04 30	5 38	18 31	5 24	18 45	5 06	19 03	4 41	19 28	4 02	20 07
		1 46	15 08	1 29	15 25	1 08	15 46	0 38	16 16		17 05
11 Th 223	12 04 21	5 38	18 31	5 24	18 45	5 07	19 02	4 43	19 26	4 04	20 05
		2 35	15 55	2 18	16 11	1 57	16 32	1 27	17 00	0 38	17 46
12 Fr 224	12 04 11	5 38	18 30	5 25	18 43	5 08	19 00	4 44	19 24	4 06	20 02
		3 25	16 41	3 09	16 55	2 49	17 14	2 22	17 39	1 37	18 19
13 Sa 225	12 04 01	5 39	18 29	5 25	18 43	5 09	18 59	4 46	19 22	4 09	19 59
		4 17	17 25	4 03	17 37	3 45	17 53	3 22	18 14	2 43	18 47
14 Su 226	12 03 50	5 39	18 29	5 26	18 42	5 10	18 58	4 47	19 20	4 12	19 56
	21 31 ●	5 09	18 08	4 58	18 17	4 44	18 29	4 25	18 45	3 55	19 09
15 Mo 227	12 03 39	5 39	18 28	5 27	18 41	5 11	18 57	4 49	19 18	4 14	19 54
		6 03	18 50	5 55	18 52	5 45	19 00	5 31	19 14	5 10	19 29
16 Tu 228	12 03 27	5 39	18 27	5 27	18 40	5 12	18 55	4 50	19 17	4 16	19 51
		6 57	19 32	6 53	19 34	6 47	19 37	6 40	19 41	6 29	19 47
17 We 229	12 03 14	5 40	18 27	5 28	18 39	5 13	18 54	4 52	19 15	4 18	19 48
		7 52	20 14	7 51	20 12	7 51	20 10	7 50	20 08	7 49	20 04
18 Th 230	12 03 01	5 40	18 26	5 28	18 38	5 14	18 52	4 53	19 13	4 21	19 45
		8 47	20 57	8 51	20 51	8 55	20 45	9 01	20 36	9 10	20 23
19 Fr 231	12 02 48	5 40	18 25	5 29	18 37	5 15	18 51	4 55	19 11	4 23	19 42
		9 44	21 41	9 52	21 32	10 01	21 21	10 13	21 06	10 33	20 43
20 Sa 232	12 02 34	5 41	18 25	5 29	18 36	5 16	18 50	4 56	19 09	4 26	19 39
		10 43	22 29	10 53	22 16	11 07	22 01	11 26	21 40	11 56	21 08
21 Su 233	12 02 19	5 41	18 24	5 30	18 35	5 16	18 48	4 58	19 07	4 28	19 37
		11 42	23 20	11 56	23 05	12 13	22 46	12 38	22 20	13 17	21 39
22 Mo 234	12 02 04	5 41	18 23	5 31	18 34	5 17	18 47	4 59	19 05	4 30	19 34
	01 04 ☽	12 42		12 58	23 57	13 19	23 36	13 47	23 07	14 34	22 19
23 Tu 235	12 01 49	5 41	18 22	5 31	18 32	5 18	18 45	5 01	19 03	4 33	19 31
		13 42	0 14	13 59		14 21		14 51		15 41	23 12
24 We 236	12 01 33	5 42	18 21	5 32	18 31	5 19	18 44	5 02	19 01	4 35	19 28
		14 40	1 12	14 57	0 54	15 19	0 33	15 48	0 02	16 37	
25 Th 237	12 01 16	5 42	18 21	5 32	18 30	5 20	18 42	5 04	18 59	4 38	19 25
		15 36	2 11	15 51	1 58	16 11	1 34	16 37	1 05	17 20	0 17
26 Fr 238	12 01 00	5 42	18 20	5 33	18 29	5 21	18 41	5 05	18 57	4 40	19 22
		16 28	3 12	16 41	2 58	16 57	2 39	17 19	2 14	17 54	1 33
27 Sa 239	12 00 43	5 42	18 19	5 33	18 28	5 22	18 39	5 07	18 55	4 42	19 19
		17 17	4 13	17 27	4 01	17 38	3 46	17 55	3 27	18 20	2 55
28 Su 240	12 00 25	5 43	18 18	5 34	18 27	5 23	18 38	5 08	18 53	4 45	19 16
	20 10 ○	18 02	5 12	18 08	5 04	18 16	4 54	18 20	4 40	18 41	4 18
29 Mo 241	12 00 07	5 43	18 17	5 34	18 26	5 24	18 36	5 10	18 50	4 47	19 13
		18 45	6 09	18 48	6 05	18 50	5 59	18 54	5 52	19 00	5 41
30 Tu 242	11 59 49	5 43	18 17	5 35	18 25	5 25	18 35	5 11	18 48	4 50	19 10
		19 27	7 04	19 25	7 04	19 23	7 04	19 21	7 03	19 17	7 02
31 We 243	11 59 30	5 43	18 16	5 36	18 23	5 26	18 33	5 13	18 46	4 52	19 07
		20 07	7 58	20 02	8 02	19 56	8 06	19 47	8 12	19 34	8 21

9th Month

September, 1977

30 Days

Greenwich Mean Time

NOTE: Light figures indicate Sun. **Dark** figures indicate **Moon.** *Degrees are North Latitude.*
CAUTION: Must be converted to local time. For instruction see page 768.

Day of month / week	year	Sun on meridian / Moon phase (h m s)	20° Rise Sun/Moon	20° Set Sun/Moon	30° Rise Sun/Moon	30° Set Sun/Moon	40° Rise Sun/Moon	40° Set Sun/Moon	50° Rise Sun/Moon	50° Set Sun/Moon	60° Rise Sun/Moon	60° Set Sun/Moon
1 Th	244	11 59 11	5 44	18 15	5 36	18 22	5 27	18 31	5 14	18 44	4 54	19 04
			20 48	8 51	20 39	8 58	20 29	9 06	20 15	9 18	19 53	9 37
2 Fr	245	11 58 52	5 44	18 14	5 37	18 21	5 28	18 30	5 16	18 42	4 57	19 01
			21 29	9 42	21 17	9 52	21 03	10 05	20 44	10 23	20 14	10 50
3 Sa	246	11 58 33	5 44	18 13	5 37	18 20	5 29	18 28	5 17	18 40	4 59	18 58
			22 11	10 33	21 57	10 46	21 40	11 02	21 16	11 24	20 38	12 00
4 Su	247	11 58 13	5 44	18 12	5 38	18 19	5 30	18 27	5 19	18 38	5 01	18 55
			22 55	11 23	22 39	11 38	22 19	11 57	21 52	12 23	21 08	13 05
5 Mo	248	11 57 53 / 14 33 ☾	5 44	18 11	5 38	18 17	5 31	18 25	5 20	18 36	5 04	18 52
			23 40	12 12	23 23	12 29	23 02	12 49	22 33	13 18	21 46	14 05
6 Tu	249	11 57 33	5 45	18 10	5 39	18 16	5 32	18 23	5 22	18 33	5 06	18 49
				13 00		13 17	23 49	13 39	23 20	14 08	22 31	14 57
7 We	250	11 57 13	5 45	18 10	5 39	18 15	5 33	18 22	5 23	18 31	5 08	18 46
			0 27	13 48	0 10	14 04		14 25		14 54	23 25	15 41
8 Th	251	11 56 52	5 45	18 09	5 40	18 14	5 33	18 20	5 25	18 29	5 11	18 43
			1 17	14 34	1 00	14 49	0 40	15 08	0 12	15 35		16 17
9 Fr	252	11 56 32	5 46	18 08	5 41	18 12	5 35	18 18	5 27	18 27	5 14	18 40
			2 07	15 18	1 53	15 32	1 34	15 48	1 09	16 11	0 28	16 47
10 Sa	253	11 56 11	5 46	18 07	5 41	18 11	5 35	18 17	5 28	18 25	5 16	18 37
			2 59	16 02	2 47	16 13	2 32	16 26	2 10	16 44	1 37	17 12
11 Su	254	11 55 50	5 46	18 06	5 42	18 10	5 36	18 15	5 29	18 23	5 18	18 34
			3 53	16 45	3 43	16 52	3 32	17 01	3 16	17 14	2 51	17 33
12 Mo	255	11 55 29	5 46	18 05	5 42	18 09	5 37	18 14	5 31	18 20	5 20	18 31
			4 47	17 27	4 41	17 31	4 34	17 36	4 24	17 42	4 08	17 52
13 Tu	256	11 55 08 / 09 23 ●	5 46	18 04	5 43	18 08	5 38	18 12	5 32	18 18	5 22	18 28
			5 42	18 10	5 40	18 10	5 38	18 10	5 34	18 10	5 29	18 10
14 We	257	11 54 47	5 46	18 03	5 43	18 06	5 39	18 10	5 34	18 16	5 25	18 25
			6 39	18 53	6 41	18 45	6 43	18 45	6 46	18 38	6 51	18 29
15 Th	258	11 54 75	5 47	18 02	5 44	18 05	5 40	18 09	5 35	18 14	5 27	18 22
			7 37	19 38	7 43	19 31	7 50	19 21	8 00	19 09	8 16	18 49
16 Fr	259	11 54 04	5 47	18 01	5 44	18 04	5 41	18 07	5 37	18 12	5 29	18 19
			8 36	20 26	8 45	20 15	8 58	20 01	9 14	19 42	9 40	19 13
17 Sa	260	11 53 43	5 47	18 00	5 45	18 02	5 42	18 05	5 39	18 09	5 32	18 16
			9 36	21 17	9 49	21 03	10 05	20 45	17 28	20 21	11 04	19 42
18 Su	261	11 53 22	5 47	18 00	5 45	18 01	5 43	18 04	5 40	18 07	5 34	18 13
			10 37	22 10	10 52	21 54	11 12	21 34	11 39	21 06	12 23	20 20
19 Mo	262	11 53 00	5 47	17 59	5 46	18 00	5 44	18 02	5 41	18 05	5 36	18 10
			11 37	23 07	11 54	22 50	12 15	22 28	12 44	21 58	13 34	21 09
20 Tu	263	11 52 39 / 06 18 ☽	5 48	17 58	5 46	17 59	5 45	18 00	5 43	18 00	5 39	18 09
			12 35		12 52	23 48	13 14	23 27	13 43	22 58	14 33	22 09
21 We	264	11 52 18	5 48	17 57	5 47	17 58	5 46	17 59	5 44	18 01	5 41	18 03
			13 31	0 05	13 47		14 06		14 34		15 19	23 20
22 Th	265	11 51 57	5 48	17 56	5 48	17 56	5 47	17 57	5 46	17 58	5 44	18 00
			14 23	1 05	14 36	0 49	14 54	0 30	15 17	0 04	15 55	
23 Fr	266	11 51 36	5 48	17 55	5 48	17 55	5 48	17 55	5 47	17 56	5 46	17 57
			15 11	2 04	15 72	1 51	15 36	1 35	15 54	1 13	16 22	0 38
24 Sa	267	11 51 15	5 48	17 54	5 49	17 54	5 49	17 54	5 50	17 54	5 48	17 54
			15 57	3 02	16 04	2 52	16 13	2 40	16 26	2 24	16 45	1 59
25 Su	268	11 50 54	5 49	17 53	5 49	17 53	5 50	17 52	5 50	17 52	5 51	17 51
			16 40	3 58	16 44	3 52	16 48	3 45	16 55	3 36	17 04	3 20
26 Mo	269	11 50 33	5 49	17 52	5 50	17 51	5 51	17 51	5 52	17 50	5 53	17 48
			17 22	4 53	17 22	4 51	17 22	4 49	17 22	4 46	17 22	4 41
27 Tu	270	11 50 13 / 08 17 ☉	5 49	17 51	5 50	17 50	5 52	17 49	5 53	17 47	5 55	17 45
			18 02	5 47	17 59	5 49	17 54	5 51	17 48	5 55	17 39	5 59
28 We	271	11 49 52	5 49	17 50	5 51	17 49	5 52	17 47	5 55	17 45	5 58	17 42
			18 43	6 40	18 36	6 46	18 27	6 53	18 15	7 02	17 57	7 16
29 Th	272	11 49 32	5 50	17 49	5 51	17 48	5 53	17 46	5 56	17 43	6 00	17 39
			19 24	7 32	19 13	7 41	19 01	7 52	18 44	8 07	18 17	8 31
30 Fr	273	11 49 13	5 50	17 49	5 52	17 46	5 53	17 44	5 58	17 41	6 02	17 36
			20 06	8 24	19 53	8 35	19 37	8 50	19 15	9 10	18 40	9 43

10th Month　　　　　October, 1977　　　　　31 Days

Greenwich Mean Time

NOTE: Light figures indicate Sun **Dark** figures indicate **Moon**. *Degrees are North Latitude.*
CAUTION: Must be converted to local time. For instruction see page 768.

Day of month / week / year	Sun on meridian Moon phase (h m s)		20° Rise Sun/Moon	20° Set Sun/Moon	30° Rise Sun/Moon	30° Set Sun/Moon	40° Rise Sun/Moon	40° Set Sun/Moon	50° Rise Sun/Moon	50° Set Sun/Moon	60° Rise Sun/Moon	60° Set Sun/Moon
1 Sa	11 48 53		5 50	17 48	5 53	17 45	5 55	17 42	5 59	17 39	6 05	17 33
274			20 49	9 14	20 34	9 29	20 15	9 46	19 50	10 11	19 08	10 50
2 Su	11 48 34		5 50	17 47	5 53	17 44	5 56	17 41	6 01	17 36	6 07	17 30
275			21 34	10 04	21 17	10 20	20 57	10 40	20 29	11 07	19 42	11 53
3 Mo	11 48 15		5 51	17 46	5 54	17 43	5 57	17 39	6 02	17 34	6 10	17 27
276			22 20	10 53	22 03	11 10	21 42	11 31	21 13	12 00	20 24	12 48
4 Tu	11 47 57		5 51	17 45	5 54	17 42	5 58	17 37	6 04	17 32	6 12	17 24
277			23 08	11 40	22 52	11 57	22 31	12 18	22 02	12 47	21 14	13 35
5 We	11 47 38	09 21 ☾	5 51	17 44	5 55	17 40	5 59	17 36	6 05	17 30	6 14	17 21
278			23 58	12 26	23 42	12 42	23 23	13 02	22 56	13 30	22 13	14 14
6 Th	11 47 21		5 51		5 55		6 00					
279				13 11		13 25		13 43	23 55	14 07	23 18	14 46
7 Fr	11 47 03		5 52	17 42	5 56	17 38	6 01	17 33	6 08	17 26	6 19	17 15
280			0 48	13 54	0 35	14 06	0 18	14 21		14 41		15 13
8 Sa	11 46 46		5 52	17 42	5 57	17 37	6 02	17 31	6 10	17 24	6 22	17 12
281			1 40	14 37	1 30	14 46	1 16	14 57	0 58	15 12	0 29	15 35
9 Su	11 46 30		5 52	17 41	5 57	17 36	6 03	17 30	6 12	17 21	6 24	17 09
282			2 34	15 19	2 26	15 25	2 17	15 32	2 07	15 41	1 44	15 55
10 Mo	11 46 14		5 52	17 40	5 58	17 35	6 04	17 28	6 13	17 19	6 26	17 06
283			3 28	16 01	3 27	16 03	3 19	16 06	3 13	16 09	3 03	16 13
11 Tu	11 45 58		5 53	17 39	5 59	17 33	6 05	17 26	6 15	17 17	6 29	17 03
284			4 27	16 45	4 24	16 43	4 24	16 40	4 27	16 37	4 25	16 32
12 We	11 45 43	20 31 ●	5 53	17 38	5 59	17 32	6 07	17 25	6 16	17 15	6 31	17 00
285			5 22	17 30	5 26	17 24	5 31	17 17	5 38	17 07	5 49	16 52
13 Th	11 45 29		5 53	17 38	6 00	17 31	6 08	17 23	6 18	17 13	6 34	16 57
286			6 22	18 18	6 30	18 08	6 40	17 56	6 54	17 40	7 16	7 14
14 Fr	11 45 15		5 54	17 37	6 00	17 30	6 09	17 22	6 20	17 11	6 36	16 54
287			7 24	19 09	7 36	18 56	7 50	18 40	8 10	18 17	8 43	17 42
15 Sa	11 45 01		5 54	17 36	6 01	17 29	6 10	17 20	6 21	17 09	6 39	16 51
288			8 26	20 03	8 41	19 48	8 59	19 28	9 25	19 01	10 07	18 18
16 Su	11 44 49		5 54	17 35	6 02	17 28	6 11	17 19	6 23	17 07	6 41	16 49
289			9 29	21 00	9 45	20 43	10 06	20 22	10 35	19 53	11 23	19 04
17 Mo	11 44 36		5 55	17 35	6 02	17 27	6 12	17 17	6 24	17 05	6 44	16 46
290			10 29	22 00	10 46	21 42	11 08	21 21	11 38	20 51	12 28	20 02
18 Tu	11 44 24		5 55	17 34	6 03	17 26	6 13	17 16	6 26	17 03	6 46	16 43
291			11 27	22 59	11 43	22 44	12 04	22 24	12 32	21 56	13 19	21 11
19 We	11 44 13	12 46 ☽	5 55	17 33	6 04	17 25	6 14	17 15	6 28	17 01	6 49	16 40
292			12 20	23 59	12 35	23 45	12 53	23 28	13 18	23 05	13 57	22 27
20 Th	11 44 02		5 56	17 32	6 04	17 24	6 15	17 13	6 29	16 59	6 51	16 37
293			13 09		13 21		13 36		13 56		14 27	23 47
21 Fr	11 43 53		5 56	17 32	6 05	17 23	6 16	17 12	6 31	16 57	6 54	16 34
294			13 55	0 57	14 04	0 46	14 14	0 33	14 29	0 15	14 51	
22 Sa	11 43 43		5 56	17 31	6 06	17 22	6 17	17 10	6 32	16 55	6 56	16 31
295			14 38	1 53	14 43	1 46	14 50	1 37	14 58	1 25	15 10	1 07
23 Su	11 43 35		5 57	17 30	6 06	17 21	6 18	17 09	6 34	16 53	6 59	16 29
296			15 20	2 47	15 21	2 44	15 23	2 40	15 25	2 34	15 28	2 26
24 Mo	11 43 27		5 57	17 30	6 07	17 20	6 19	17 08	6 36	16 51	7 01	16 26
297			16 00	3 41	15 57	3 41	15 55	3 42	15 51	3 42	15 45	3 44
25 Tu	11 43 19		5 58	17 29	6 08	17 19	6 20	17 06	6 37	16 49	7 04	16 23
298			16 40	4 33	16 34	4 37	16 27	4 42	16 17	4 49	16 03	5 00
26 We	11 43 13	23 35 ●	5 58	17 28	6 09	17 18	6 22	17 05	6 39	16 47	7 06	16 20
299			17 20	5 25	17 11	5 32	17 00	5 42	16 45	5 55	16 21	6 15
27 Th	11 43 07		5 58	17 28	6 09	17 17	6 23	17 04	6 41	16 46	7 09	16 18
300			18 01	6 16	17 49	6 27	17 35	6 40	17 15	6 58	16 43	7 27
28 Fr	11 43 02		5 59	17 27	6 10	17 16	6 24	17 02	6 42	16 44	7 11	16 14
301			18 44	7 07	18 30	7 20	18 12	7 37	17 48	8 00	17 09	8 37
29 Sa	11 42 58		5 59	17 27	6 11	17 15	6 25	17 01	6 44	16 42	7 14	16 12
302			19 28	7 57	19 12	8 13	18 52	8 32	18 25	8 58	17 40	9 42
30 Su	11 42 54		6 00	17 26	6 12	17 14	6 26	17 00	6 46	16 40	7 16	16 09
303			20 14	8 46	19 57	9 03	19 36	9 24	19 07	9 53	18 19	10 40
31 Mo	11 42 51		6 00	17 25	6 12	17 13	6 27	16 59	6 47	16 38	7 19	16 07
304			21 02	9 34	20 45	9 51	20 24	10 13	19 54	10 42	19 06	11 31

11th Month   November, 1977   30 Days

Greenwich Mean Time

NOTE: Light figures indicate Sun. **Dark** figures indicate **Moon.** *Degrees are North Latitude.*

CAUTION: Must be converted to local time. For instruction see page 768.

Day of month / week / year	Sun on meridian / Moon phase (h m s)	20° Rise Sun/Moon (h m)	20° Set Sun/Moon (h m)	30° Rise Sun/Moon (h m)	30° Set Sun/Moon (h m)	40° Rise Sun/Moon (h m)	40° Set Sun/Moon (h m)	50° Rise Sun/Moon (h m)	50° Set Sun/Moon (h m)	60° Rise Sun/Moon (h m)	60° Set Sun/Moon (h m)
1 Tu 305	11 42 49	6 01	17 25	6 13	17 13	6 28	16 57	6 49	16 37	7 21	16 04
		21 50	10 21	2 34	10 37	21 14	10 58	20 46	11 26	20 01	12 13
2 We 306	11 42 48	6 01	17 24	6 14	17 12	6 29	16 56	6 51	16 35	7 24	16 02
		22 40	11 06	22 25	11 21	22 07	11 40	21 43	12 05	21 02	12 47
3 Th 307	11 42 48	6 01	17 24	6 14	17 11	6 30	16 56	6 52	16 33	7 27	15 59
		23 30	11 49	23 18	12 02	23 03	12 18	22 43	12 40	22 10	13 15
4 Fr 308	11 42 48 / 3 58 ☾	6 02	17 23	6 15	17 10	6 32	16 54	6 54	16 32	7 29	15 56
			12 31		12 41		12 54		13 11	23 22	13 38
5 Sa 309	11 42 50	6 03	17 23	6 16	17 09	6 33	16 53	6 56	16 30	7 32	15 54
		0 22	13 12	0 12	13 19	0 01	13 28		13 40		13 59
6 Su 310	11 42 52	6 03	17 23	6 17	17 09	6 34	16 52	6 57	16 29	7 34	15 51
		1 14	13 53	1 08	13 57	1 01	14 01	0 52	14 08	0 37	14 17
7 Mo 311	11 42 55	6 04	17 22	6 18	17 08	6 35	16 51	6 59	16 27	7 37	15 49
		2 08	14 35	2 06	14 35	2 04	14 35	2 01	14 35	1 56	14 35
8 Tu 312	11 42 59	6 04	17 22	6 19	17 07	6 36	16 50	7 01	16 25	7 39	15 47
		3 04	15 18	3 06	15 15	3 09	15 10	3 12	15 03	3 18	14 53
9 We 313	11 43 04	6 05	17 21	6 19	17 07	6 37	16 49	7 02	16 24	7 42	15 44
		4 03	16 05	4 09	15 57	4 16	15 47	4 27	15 34	4 43	15 14
10 Th 314	11 43 09	6 05	17 21	6 20	17 06	6 39	16 48	7 04	16 22	7 45	15 42
		5 04	16 54	5 14	16 43	5 26	16 29	5 43	16 09	6 10	15 39
11 Fr 315	11 43 16 / 07 09 ●	6 06	17 21	6 21	17 06	6 40	16 47	7 06	16 21	7 47	15 39
		6 07	17 48	6 21	17 34	6 37	17 16	7 01	16 51	7 38	16 11
12 Sa 316	11 43 23	6 06	17 20	6 22	17 05	6 41	16 46	7 07	16 20	7 50	15 37
		7 12	18 46	7 28	18 29	7 48	18 09	8 15	17 40	9 01	16 53
13 Su 317	11 43 31	6 07	17 20	6 23	17 04	6 42	16 46	7 09	16 18	7 52	15 35
		8 16	19 47	8 33	19 29	8 54	19 08	9 24	18 38	10 14	17 47
14 Mo 318	11 43 40	6 08	17 20	6 23	17 04	6 43	16 44	7 10	16 17	7 55	15 33
		9 17	20 49	9 34	20 32	9 55	20 12	10 25	19 43	11 13	18 55
15 Tu 319	11 43 50	6 08	17 20	6 24	17 03	6 44	16 43	7 12	16 16	7 57	15 30
		10 14	21 51	10 29	21 36	10 49	21 18	11 15	20 53	11 58	20 12
16 We 320	11 44 01	6 09	17 19	6 25	17 03	6 46	16 42	7 14	16 14	8 00	15 28
		11 06	22 51	11 19	22 39	11 35	22 24	11 57	22 05	12 32	21 33
17 Th 321	11 44 12 / 4 52 ☽	6 09	17 19	6 26	17 02	6 47	16 42	7 15	16 13	8 02	15 26
		11 54	23 48	12 04	23 40	12 16	23 30	12 32	23 16	12 58	22 54
18 Fr 322	11 44 25	6 10	17 19	6 27	17 02	6 48	16 41	7 17	16 12	8 05	15 24
		12 39		12 45		12 52		13 03		13 18	
19 Sa 323	11 44 38	6 10	17 19	6 28	17 02	6 49	16 40	7 18	16 11	8 07	15 22
		13 20	0 44	13 23	0 39	13 26	0 34	13 30	0 26	13 36	0 14
20 Su 324	11 44 52	6 11	17 19	6 28	17 01	6 50	16 40	7 20	16 10	8 10	15 20
		14 00	1 37	13 59	1 36	13 58	1 35	13 56	1 34	13 53	1 32
21 Mo 325	11 45 06	6 12	17 19	6 29	17 01	6 51	16 39	7 22	16 09	8 12	15 18
		14 40	2 29	14 35	2 32	14 29	2 36	14 22	2 41	14 10	2 48
22 Tu 326	11 45 22	6 12	17 18	6 30	17 01	6 52	16 38	7 23	16 08	8 14	15 16
		15 19	3 20	15 11	3 27	15 01	3 35	14 48	3 46	14 28	4 03
23 We 327	11 45 38	6 13	17 18	6 31	17 00	6 53	16 38	7 25	16 07	8 17	15 15
		15 59	4 11	15 48	4 21	15 35	4 33	15 17	4 49	14 48	5 15
24 Th 328	11 45 55	6 14	17 18	6 32	17 00	6 54	16 37	7 26	16 06	8 19	15 13
		16 41	5 02	16 28	5 14	16 11	5 30	15 48	5 51	15 12	6 26
25 Fr 329	11 46 13 / 17 31 ☉	6 14	17 18	6 33	17 00	6 56	16 37	7 28	16 05	8 21	15 11
		17 25	5 52	17 09	6 07	16 50	6 25	16 23	6 51	15 40	7 32
26 Sa 330	11 46 32	6 15	17 18	6 33	17 00	6 57	16 36	7 29	16 04	8 24	15 10
		18 10	6 42	17 53	6 58	17 32	7 18	17 04	7 47	16 16	8 33
27 Su 331	11 46 51	6 15	17 18	6 34	16 59	6 58	16 36	7 30	16 03	8 26	15 08
		18 57	7 30	18 40	7 47	18 19	8 09	17 49	8 38	17 00	9 27
28 Mo 332	11 47 11	6 16	17 18	6 35	16 59	6 59	16 36	7 32	16 02	8 28	15 06
		19 45	8 17	19 29	8 34	19 08	8 55	18 39	9 25	17 52	10 13
29 Tu 333	11 47 32	6 17	17 18	6 36	16 59	7 00	16 35	7 33	16 02	8 30	15 05
		20 34	9 03	20 19	9 19	20 00	9 38	19 34	10 06	18 51	10 50
30 We 334	11 47 53	6 17	17 18	6 37	16 59	7 01	16 35	7 35	16 01	8 32	15 04
		21 24	9 46	21 11	10 01	20 55	10 18	20 32	10 42	19 56	11 20

12th Month   December, 1977   31 Days

Greenwich Mean Time

NOTE: Light figures indicate Sun. **Dark** figures indicate **Moon**. *Degrees are North Latitude.*
CAUTION: Must be converted to local time. For instruction see page 768.

Day of month / week / year	Sun on meridian / Moon phase	20° Rise Sun/Moon	20° Set Sun/Moon	30° Rise Sun/Moon	30° Set Sun/Moon	40° Rise Sun/Moon	40° Set Sun/Moon	50° Rise Sun/Moon	50° Set Sun/Moon	60° Rise Sun/Moon	60° Set Sun/Moon
1 Th	11 48 15	6 18	17 19	6 37	16 59	7 02	16 35	7 36	16 01	8 34	15 02
335		22 14	10 28	22 04	10 40	21 51	10 54	21 33	11 14	21 05	11 44
2 Fr	11 48 38	6 18	17 19	6 38	16 59	7 03	16 35	7 37	16 00	8 36	15 01
336		23 05	11 09	22 58	11 18	22 49	11 28	22 37	11 43	22 18	12 05
3 Sa	11 49 01	6 19	17 19	6 39	16 59	7 04	16 34	7 39	15 59	8 38	15 00
337	21 16 ☾	23 57	11 49	23 53	11 54	23 49	12 01	23 42	12 10	23 33	12 23
4 Su	11 49 25	6 20	17 19	6 40	16 59	7 05	16 34	7 40	15 59	8 40	14 59
338			12 29		12 31		12 33		12 36		12 41
5 Mo	11 49 50	6 20	17 19	6 41	16 59	7 06	16 34	7 41	15 59	8 42	14 58
339		0 50	13 10	0 50	13 08	0 50	13 06	0 50	13 03	0 50	12 58
6 Tu	11 50 15	6 21	17 19	6 41	16 59	7 07	16 34	7 42	15 58	8 44	14 57
340		1 46	13 53	1 50	13 47	1 54	13 40	2 01	13 31	2 11	13 16
7 We	11 50 41	6 22	17 20	6 42	16 59	7 08	16 34	7 43	15 58	8 45	14 56
341		2 44	14 40	2 51	14 30	3 01	14 18	3 15	14 03	3 36	13 38
8 Th	11 51 07	6 22	17 20	6 43	16 59	7 08	16 34	7 44	15 58	8 47	14 55
342		3 45	15 30	3 56	15 17	4 10	15 01	4 30	14 40	5 02	14 05
9 Fr	11 51 34	6 23	17 20	6 44	17 00	7 09	16 34	7 46	15 58	8 49	14 55
343		4 48	16 26	5 03	16 10	5 21	15 51	5 47	15 24	6 28	14 40
10 Sa	11 52 01	6 24	17 20	6 44	17 00	7 10	16 34	7 47	15 57	8 50	14 54
344	17 33 ●	5 53	17 26	6 10	17 09	6 31	16 47	7 00	16 17	7 49	15 28
11 Su	11 52 29	6 24	17 21	6 45	17 00	7 11	16 34	7 48	15 57	8 51	14 54
345		6 57	18 29	7 15	18 12	7 37	17 50	8 07	17 20	8 57	16 30
12 Mo	11 52 57	6 25	17 21	6 46	17 00	7 12	16 34	7 49	15 57	8 53	14 53
346		7 59	19 33	8 15	19 17	8 36	18 58	9 05	18 30	9 51	17 45
13 Tu	11 53 25	6 25	17 21	6 46	17 01	7 12	16 34	7 50	15 57	8 54	14 53
347		8 56	20 37	9 10	20 24	9 28	20 07	9 53	19 44	10 32	18 08
14 We	11 53 53	6 26	17 22	6 47	17 01	7 13	16 35	7 50	15 57	8 55	14 52
348		9 48	21 38	9 59	21 28	10 13	21 16	10 32	20 59	11 02	20 33
15 Th	11 54 22	6 26	17 22	6 48	17 01	7 14	16 35	7 51	15 58	8 56	14 52
349		10 35	22 36	10 43	22 30	10 53	22 23	11 05	22 12	11 25	21 56
16 Fr	11 54 51	6 27	17 23	6 48	17 02	7 15	16 35	7 52	15 58	8 57	14 52
350		11 19	23 32	11 23	23 30	11 28	23 27	11 35	23 23	11 45	23 17
17 Sa	11 55 21	6 28	17 23	6 49	17 02	7 15	16 35	7 53	15 58	8 58	14 52
351	10 37 ☽	12 00		12 01		12 01		12 02		12 02	
18 Su	11 55 50	6 28	17 24	6 49	17 02	7 16	16 36	7 53	15 58	8 59	14 52
352		12 40	0 25	12 37	0 27	12 33	0 29	12 27	0 31	12 19	0 35
19 Mo	11 56 20	6 29	17 24	6 50	17 03	7 16	16 36	7 54	15 59	9 00	14 53
353		13 20	1 17	13 13	1 22	13 05	1 29	12 53	1 37	12 36	1 51
20 Tu	11 56 49	6 29	17 24	6 50	17 03	7 17	16 37	7 55	15 59	9 01	14 53
354		14 00	2 08	13 50	2 16	13 37	2 27	13 21	2 42	12 55	3 04
21 We	11 57 19	6 30	17 25	6 51	17 04	7 18	16 37	7 55	15 59	9 01	14 53
355		14 41	2 58	14 28	3 10	14 12	3 24	13 51	3 44	13 17	4 15
22 Th	11 57 49	6 30	17 25	6 51	17 04	7 18	16 38	7 56	16 00	9 02	14 54
356		15 23	3 48	15 08	4 02	14 50	4 20	14 24	4 44	13 44	5 23
23 Fr	11 58 19	6 31	17 26	6 52	17 05	7 19	16 38	7 56	16 00	9 02	14 54
357		16 08	4 38	15 51	4 54	15 31	5 14	15 02	5 41	14 16	6 26
24 Sa	11 58 49	6 31	17 26	6 52	17 05	7 19	16 39	7 57	16 01	9 02	14 55
358		16 54	5 27	16 37	5 44	16 15	6 05	15 46	6 34	14 57	7 23
25 Su	11 59 18	6 32	17 27	6 53	17 06	7 19	16 39	7 57	16 02	9 03	14 56
359	12 49 ○	17 42	6 15	17 25	6 32	17 04	6 53	16 34	7 23	15 45	8 12
26 Mo	11 59 52	6 32	17 28	6 53	17 06	7 20	16 40	7 57	16 02	9 03	14 57
360		18 31	7 01	18 15	7 17	17 55	7 38	17 27	8 06	16 42	8 52
27 Tu	12 00 17	6 32	17 28	6 54	17 07	7 20	16 41	7 57	16 03	9 03	14 58
361		19 20	7 45	19 06	8 00	18 49	8 19	18 25	8 44	17 46	9 25
28 We	12 00 47	6 33	17 29	6 54	17 08	7 20	16 41	7 58	16 04	9 03	14 59
362		20 11	8 28	19 59	8 41	19 45	8 56	19 25	9 18	18 54	9 57
29 Th	12 01 16	6 33	17 29	6 54	17 08	7 21	16 42	7 58	16 05	9 03	15 00
363		21 01	9 09	20 52	9 19	20 42	9 31	20 27	9 48	20 05	10 13
30 Fr	12 01 45	6 34	17 30	6 55	17 09	7 21	16 43	7 58	16 06	9 02	15 01
364		21 52	9 49	21 47	9 56	21 40	10 04	21 31	10 15	21 18	10 32
31 Sa	12 02 14	6 34	17 30	6 55	17 10	7 21	16 43	7 58	16 07	9 02	15 02
365		22 43	10 28	22 42	10 32	22 40	10 36	22 37	10 41	22 33	10 49

The Julian Period

How many days have you lived? To determine this, you must multiply your age by 365, add the number of days since your last birthday until today, and account for all the leap years. Chances are your answer would be wrong. Astronomers, however, find it convenient to express dates and long time intervals in days rather than in years, months and days. This is done by placing events within the Julian period.

The Julian period was devised in 1582 by Joseph Scaliger and named after his father Julius (not after the Julian calendar). Scaliger had Julian Day (JD) # 1 begin at noon, Jan. 1, 4713 B. C., the most recent time that three major chronological cycles began on the same day — 1) the 28-year solar cycle, after which

dates in the Julian calendar (e.g., Feb. 11) return to the same days of the week (e.g., Monday); 2) the 19-year lunar cycle, after which the phases of the moon return to the same dates of the year; and 3) the 15-year indiction cycle, used in ancient Rome to regulate taxes. It will take 7980 years to complete the period, the product of 28, 19 and 15.

Noon of Dec. 31, 1976, marks the beginning of JD 2,443,144; that many days will have passed since the start of the Julian period. The JD at noon of any date in 1977 may be found by adding to this figure the day of the year for that date, which is given in the left hand column in the chart below. Simple JD conversion tables are used by astronomers.

Lunar Calendar, Chinese New Years, Vietnamese Tet

The ancient Chinese lunar calendar is divided into 12 months of either 29 or 30 days (compensating for the fact that the mean duration of the lunar month is 29 days, 12 hours, 44.05 minutes). The calendar is synchronized with the solar year by the addition of extra months at fixed intervals.

The Chinese calendar runs on a sexagenary cycle, i.e., 60 years. The cycles 1861-1923 and 1924-1983, with the years grouped under their twelve animal designations, are printed below. The year 1977 is found in the sixth column, under Snake, and is known as a "Year of the Snake." Readers can find the animal name for the year of their birth, marriage, etc., in the same chart. (Note: the first 3-7 weeks of each of the western years belong to the previous Chinese year and animal designation.)

Both the western (Gregorian) and traditional lunar calendars are used publicly in China, and two New Year's celebrations are held. On Taiwan, in overseas Chinese communities, and in Vietnam, the lunar calendar has been used only to set the dates for traditional festivals, with the Gregorian system in general use.

The four-day Chinese New Year, Hsin Nien, and the three-day Vietnamese New Year festival, Tet, begin at the first new moon after the sun enters Aquarius. The day may fall, therefore, between Jan. 21 and Feb. 19 of the Gregorian calendar. Feb. 18, 1977 marks the start of the new Chinese year. The date is fixed according to the date of the new moon in the Far East. Since this is west of the International Date Line the date may be one day later than that of the new moon in the United States.

Rat	Ox	Tiger	Hare (Rabbit)	Dragon	Snake	Horse	Sheep (Goat)	Monkey	Rooster	Dog	Pig
1864	1865	1866	1867	1868	1869	1870	1871	1872	1873	1874	1875
1876	1877	1878	1879	1880	1881	1882	1883	1884	1885	1886	1887
1888	1889	1890	1891	1892	1893	1894	1895	1896	1897	1898	1899
1900	1901	1902	1903	1904	1905	1906	1907	1908	1909	1910	1911
1912	1913	1914	1915	1916	1917	1918	1919	1920	1921	1922	1923
1924	1925	1926	1927	1928	1929	1930	1931	1932	1933	1934	1935
1936	1937	1938	1939	1940	1941	1942	1943	1944	1945	1946	1947
1948	1949	1950	1951	1952	1953	1954	1955	1956	1957	1958	1959
1960	1961	1962	1963	1964	1965	1966	1967	1968	1969	1970	1971
1972	1973	1974	1975	1976	1977	1978	1979	1980	1981	1982	1983

Days Between Two Dates

Table covers period of two ordinary years. Example—Days between Feb. 10, 1973 and Dec. 15, 1974; subtract 41 from 714; answer is 673 days. For leap year, such as 1976, one day must be added after Feb. 28.

Date	Jan.	Feb.	Mar.	April	May	June	July	Aug.	Sept.	Oct.	Nov.	Dec.	Date	Jan.	Feb.	Mar.	April	May	June	July	Aug.	Sept.	Oct.	Nov.	Dec.
1	1	32	60	91	121	152	182	213	244	274	305	335	1	366	397	425	456	486	517	547	578	609	639	670	700
2	2	33	61	92	122	153	183	214	245	275	306	336	2	367	398	426	457	487	518	548	579	610	640	671	701
3	3	34	62	93	123	154	184	215	246	276	307	337	3	368	399	427	458	488	519	549	580	611	641	672	702
4	4	35	63	94	124	155	185	216	247	277	308	338	4	369	400	428	459	489	520	550	581	612	642	673	703
5	5	36	64	95	125	156	186	217	248	278	309	339	5	370	401	429	460	490	521	551	582	613	643	674	704
6	6	37	65	96	126	157	187	218	249	279	310	340	6	371	402	430	461	491	522	552	583	614	644	675	705
7	7	38	66	97	127	158	188	219	250	280	311	341	7	372	403	431	462	492	523	553	584	615	645	676	706
8	8	39	67	98	128	159	189	220	251	281	312	342	8	373	404	432	463	493	524	554	585	616	646	677	707
9	9	40	68	99	129	160	190	221	252	282	313	343	9	374	405	433	464	494	525	555	586	617	647	678	708
10	10	41	69	100	130	161	191	222	253	283	314	344	10	375	406	434	465	495	526	556	587	618	648	679	709
11	11	42	70	101	131	162	192	223	254	284	315	345	11	376	407	435	466	496	527	557	588	619	649	680	710
12	12	43	71	102	132	163	193	224	255	285	316	346	12	377	408	436	467	497	528	558	589	620	650	681	711
13	13	44	72	103	133	164	194	225	256	286	317	347	13	378	409	437	468	498	529	559	590	621	651	682	712
14	14	45	73	104	134	165	195	226	257	287	318	348	14	379	410	438	469	499	530	560	591	622	652	683	713
15	15	46	74	105	135	166	196	227	258	288	319	349	15	380	411	439	470	500	531	561	592	623	653	684	714
16	16	47	75	106	136	167	197	228	259	289	320	350	16	381	412	440	471	501	532	562	593	624	654	685	715
17	17	48	76	107	137	168	198	229	260	290	321	351	17	382	413	441	472	502	533	563	594	625	655	686	716
18	18	49	77	108	138	169	199	230	261	291	322	352	18	383	414	442	473	503	534	564	595	626	656	687	717
19	19	50	78	109	139	170	200	231	262	292	323	353	19	384	415	443	474	504	535	565	596	627	657	688	718
20	20	51	79	110	140	171	201	232	263	293	324	354	20	385	416	444	475	505	536	566	597	628	658	689	719
21	21	52	80	111	141	172	202	233	264	294	325	355	21	386	417	445	476	506	537	567	598	629	659	690	720
22	22	53	81	112	142	173	203	234	265	295	326	356	22	387	418	446	477	507	538	568	599	630	660	691	721
23	23	54	82	113	143	174	204	235	266	296	327	357	23	388	419	447	478	508	539	569	600	631	661	692	722
24	24	55	83	114	144	175	205	236	267	297	328	358	24	389	420	448	479	509	540	570	601	632	662	693	723
25	25	56	84	115	145	176	206	237	268	298	329	359	25	390	421	449	480	510	541	571	602	633	663	694	724
26	26	57	85	116	146	177	207	238	269	299	330	360	26	391	422	450	481	511	542	572	603	634	664	695	725
27	27	58	86	117	147	178	208	239	270	300	331	361	27	392	423	451	482	512	543	573	604	635	665	696	726
28	28	59	87	118	148	179	209	240	271	301	332	362	28	393	424	452	483	513	544	574	605	636	666	697	727
29	29	—	88	119	149	180	210	241	272	302	333	363	29	394	—	453	484	514	545	575	606	637	667	698	728
30	30	—	89	120	150	181	211	242	273	303	334	364	30	395	—	454	485	515	546	576	607	638	668	699	729
31	31	—	90	—	151	—	212	243	—	304	—	365	31	396	—	455	—	516	—	577	608	—	669	—	730

PERPETUAL CALENDAR

The number shown for each year indicates which calendar to use for that year. For earlier years, or for Julian calendar, see page 784.

7

1977

JANUARY

S	M	T	W	T	F	S
						1
2	3	4	5	6	7	8
9	10	11	12	13	14	15
16	17	18	19	20	21	22
23	24	25	26	27	28	29
30	31					

FEBRUARY

S	M	T	W	T	F	S
		1	2	3	4	5
6	7	8	9	10	11	12
13	14	15	16	17	18	19
20	21	22	23	24	25	26
27	28					

MARCH

S	M	T	W	T	F	S
		1	2	3	4	5
6	7	8	9	10	11	12
13	14	15	16	17	18	19
20	21	22	23	24	25	26
27	28	29	30	31		

APRIL

S	M	T	W	T	F	S
					1	2
3	4	5	6	7	8	9
10	11	12	13	14	15	16
17	18	19	20	21	22	23
24	25	26	27	28	29	30

MAY

S	M	T	W	T	F	S
1	2	3	4	5	6	7
8	9	10	11	12	13	14
15	16	17	18	19	20	21
22	23	24	25	26	27	28
29	30	31				

JUNE

S	M	T	W	T	F	S
			1	2	3	4
5	6	7	8	9	10	11
12	13	14	15	16	17	18
19	20	21	22	23	24	25
26	27	28	29	30		

JULY

S	M	T	W	T	F	S
					1	2
3	4	5	6	7	8	9
10	11	12	13	14	15	16
17	18	19	20	21	22	23
24	25	26	27	28	29	30
31						

AUGUST

S	M	T	W	T	F	S
	1	2	3	4	5	6
7	8	9	10	11	12	13
14	15	16	17	18	19	20
21	22	23	24	25	26	27
28	29	30	31			

SEPTEMBER

S	M	T	W	T	F	S
				1	2	3
4	5	6	7	8	9	10
11	12	13	14	15	16	17
18	19	20	21	22	23	24
25	26	27	28	29	30	

OCTOBER

S	M	T	W	T	F	S
						1
2	3	4	5	6	7	8
9	10	11	12	13	14	15
16	17	18	19	20	21	22
23	24	25	26	27	28	29
30	31					

NOVEMBER

S	M	T	W	T	F	S
		1	2	3	4	5
6	7	8	9	10	11	12
13	14	15	16	17	18	19
20	21	22	23	24	25	26
27	28	29	30			

DECEMBER

S	M	T	W	T	F	S
				1	2	3
4	5	6	7	8	9	10
11	12	13	14	15	16	17
18	19	20	21	22	23	24
25	26	27	28	29	30	31

8

JANUARY

S	M	T	W	T	F	S
1	2	3	4	5	6	7
8	9	10	11	12	13	14
15	16	17	18	19	20	21
22	23	24	25	26	27	28
29	30	31				

FEBRUARY

S	M	T	W	T	F	S
			1	2	3	4
5	6	7	8	9	10	11
12	13	14	15	16	17	18
19	20	21	22	23	24	25
26	27	28	29			

MARCH

S	M	T	W	T	F	S
				1	2	3
4	5	6	7	8	9	10
11	12	13	14	15	16	17
18	19	20	21	22	23	24
25	26	27	28	29	30	31

APRIL

S	M	T	W	T	F	S
1	2	3	4	5	6	7
8	9	10	11	12	13	14
15	16	17	18	19	20	21
22	23	24	25	26	27	28
29	30					

MAY

S	M	T	W	T	F	S
		1	2	3	4	5
6	7	8	9	10	11	12
13	14	15	16	17	18	19
20	21	22	23	24	25	26
27	28	29	30	31		

JUNE

S	M	T	W	T	F	S
					1	2
3	4	5	6	7	8	9
10	11	12	13	14	15	16
17	18	19	20	21	22	23
24	25	26	27	28	29	30

JULY

S	M	T	W	T	F	S
1	2	3	4	5	6	7
8	9	10	11	12	13	14
15	16	17	18	19	20	21
22	23	24	25	26	27	28
29	30	31				

AUGUST

S	M	T	W	T	F	S
			1	2	3	4
5	6	7	8	9	10	11
12	13	14	15	16	17	18
19	20	21	22	23	24	25
26	27	28	29	30	31	

SEPTEMBER

S	M	T	W	T	F	S
						1
2	3	4	5	6	7	8
9	10	11	12	13	14	15
16	17	18	19	20	21	22
23	24	25	26	27	28	29
30						

OCTOBER

S	M	T	W	T	F	S
	1	2	3	4	5	6
7	8	9	10	11	12	13
14	15	16	17	18	19	20
21	22	23	24	25	26	27
28	29	30	31			

NOVEMBER

S	M	T	W	T	F	S
				1	2	3
4	5	6	7	8	9	10
11	12	13	14	15	16	17
18	19	20	21	22	23	24
25	26	27	28	29	30	

DECEMBER

S	M	T	W	T	F	S
						1
2	3	4	5	6	7	8
9	10	11	12	13	14	15
16	17	18	19	20	21	22
23	24	25	26	27	28	29
30	31					

9

JANUARY

S	M	T	W	T	F	S
	1	2	3	4	5	6
7	8	9	10	11	12	13
14	15	16	17	18	19	20
21	22	23	24	25	26	27
28	29	30	31			

FEBRUARY

S	M	T	W	T	F	S
				1	2	3
4	5	6	7	8	9	10
11	12	13	14	15	16	17
18	19	20	21	22	23	24
25	26	27	28	29		

MARCH

S	M	T	W	T	F	S
					1	2
3	4	5	6	7	8	9
10	11	12	13	14	15	16
17	18	19	20	21	22	23
24	25	26	27	28	29	30
31						

APRIL

S	M	T	W	T	F	S
	1	2	3	4	5	6
7	8	9	10	11	12	13
14	15	16	17	18	19	20
21	22	23	24	25	26	27
28	29	30				

MAY

S	M	T	W	T	F	S
			1	2	3	4
5	6	7	8	9	10	11
12	13	14	15	16	17	18
19	20	21	22	23	24	25
26	27	28	29	30	31	

JUNE

S	M	T	W	T	F	S
						1
2	3	4	5	6	7	8
9	10	11	12	13	14	15
16	17	18	19	20	21	22
23	24	25	26	27	28	29
30						

JULY

S	M	T	W	T	F	S
	1	2	3	4	5	6
7	8	9	10	11	12	13
14	15	16	17	18	19	20
21	22	23	24	25	26	27
28	29	30	31			

AUGUST

S	M	T	W	T	F	S
				1	2	3
4	5	6	7	8	9	10
11	12	13	14	15	16	17
18	19	20	21	22	23	24
25	26	27	28	29	30	31

SEPTEMBER

S	M	T	W	T	F	S
1	2	3	4	5	6	7
8	9	10	11	12	13	14
15	16	17	18	19	20	21
22	23	24	25	26	27	28
29	30					

OCTOBER

S	M	T	W	T	F	S
		1	2	3	4	5
6	7	8	9	10	11	12
13	14	15	16	17	18	19
20	21	22	23	24	25	26
27	28	29	30	31		

NOVEMBER

S	M	T	W	T	F	S
					1	2
3	4	5	6	7	8	9
10	11	12	13	14	15	16
17	18	19	20	21	22	23
24	25	26	27	28	29	30

DECEMBER

S	M	T	W	T	F	S
1	2	3	4	5	6	7
8	9	10	11	12	13	14
15	16	17	18	19	20	21
22	23	24	25	26	27	28
29	30	31				

10

JANUARY

S	M	T	W	T	F	S
		1	2	3	4	5
6	7	8	9	10	11	12
13	14	15	16	17	18	19
20	21	22	23	24	25	26
27	28	29	30	31		

FEBRUARY

S	M	T	W	T	F	S
					1	2
3	4	5	6	7	8	9
10	11	12	13	14	15	16
17	18	19	20	21	22	23
24	25	26	27	28	29	

MARCH

S	M	T	W	T	F	S
						1
2	3	4	5	6	7	8
9	10	11	12	13	14	15
16	17	18	19	20	21	22
23	24	25	26	27	28	29
30	31					

APRIL

S	M	T	W	T	F	S
		1	2	3	4	5
6	7	8	9	10	11	12
13	14	15	16	17	18	19
20	21	22	23	24	25	26
27	28	29	30			

MAY

S	M	T	W	T	F	S
				1	2	3
4	5	6	7	8	9	10
11	12	13	14	15	16	17
18	19	20	21	22	23	24
25	26	27	28	29	30	31

JUNE

S	M	T	W	T	F	S
1	2	3	4	5	6	7
8	9	10	11	12	13	14
15	16	17	18	19	20	21
22	23	24	25	26	27	28
29	30					

JULY

S	M	T	W	T	F	S
		1	2	3	4	5
6	7	8	9	10	11	12
13	14	15	16	17	18	19
20	21	22	23	24	25	26
27	28	29	30	31		

AUGUST

S	M	T	W	T	F	S
					1	2
3	4	5	6	7	8	9
10	11	12	13	14	15	16
17	18	19	20	21	22	23
24	25	26	27	28	29	30
31						

SEPTEMBER

S	M	T	W	T	F	S
	1	2	3	4	5	6
7	8	9	10	11	12	13
14	15	16	17	18	19	20
21	22	23	24	25	26	27
28	29	30				

OCTOBER

S	M	T	W	T	F	S
			1	2	3	4
5	6	7	8	9	10	11
12	13	14	15	16	17	18
19	20	21	22	23	24	25
26	27	28	29	30	31	

NOVEMBER

S	M	T	W	T	F	S
						1
2	3	4	5	6	7	8
9	10	11	12	13	14	15
16	17	18	19	20	21	22
23	24	25	26	27	28	29
30						

DECEMBER

S	M	T	W	T	F	S
	1	2	3	4	5	6
7	8	9	10	11	12	13
14	15	16	17	18	19	20
21	22	23	24	25	26	27
28	29	30	31			

11

JANUARY

S	M	T	W	T	F	S
			1	2	3	4
5	6	7	8	9	10	11
12	13	14	15	16	17	18
19	20	21	22	23	24	25
26	27	28	29	30	31	

FEBRUARY

S	M	T	W	T	F	S
						1
2	3	4	5	6	7	8
9	10	11	12	13	14	15
16	17	18	19	20	21	22
23	24	25	26	27	28	29

MARCH

S	M	T	W	T	F	S
1	2	3	4	5	6	7
8	9	10	11	12	13	14
15	16	17	18	19	20	21
22	23	24	25	26	27	28
29	30	31				

APRIL

S	M	T	W	T	F	S
			1	2	3	4
5	6	7	8	9	10	11
12	13	14	15	16	17	18
19	20	21	22	23	24	25
26	27	28	29	30		

MAY

S	M	T	W	T	F	S
					1	2
3	4	5	6	7	8	9
10	11	12	13	14	15	16
17	18	19	20	21	22	23
24	25	26	27	28	29	30
31						

JUNE

S	M	T	W	T	F	S
	1	2	3	4	5	6
7	8	9	10	11	12	13
14	15	16	17	18	19	20
21	22	23	24	25	26	27
28	29	30				

JULY

S	M	T	W	T	F	S
			1	2	3	4
5	6	7	8	9	10	11
12	13	14	15	16	17	18
19	20	21	22	23	24	25
26	27	28	29	30	31	

AUGUST

S	M	T	W	T	F	S
						1
2	3	4	5	6	7	8
9	10	11	12	13	14	15
16	17	18	19	20	21	22
23	24	25	26	27	28	29
30	31					

SEPTEMBER

S	M	T	W	T	F	S
		1	2	3	4	5
6	7	8	9	10	11	12
13	14	15	16	17	18	19
20	21	22	23	24	25	26
27	28	29	30			

OCTOBER

S	M	T	W	T	F	S
				1	2	3
4	5	6	7	8	9	10
11	12	13	14	15	16	17
18	19	20	21	22	23	24
25	26	27	28	29	30	31

NOVEMBER

S	M	T	W	T	F	S
1	2	3	4	5	6	7
8	9	10	11	12	13	14
15	16	17	18	19	20	21
22	23	24	25	26	27	28
29	30					

DECEMBER

S	M	T	W	T	F	S
		1	2	3	4	5
6	7	8	9	10	11	12
13	14	15	16	17	18	19
20	21	22	23	24	25	26
27	28	29	30	31		

12

1976

JANUARY

S	M	T	W	T	F	S
				1	2	3
4	5	6	7	8	9	10
11	12	13	14	15	16	17
18	19	20	21	22	23	24
25	26	27	28	29	30	31

FEBRUARY

S	M	T	W	T	F	S
1	2	3	4	5	6	7
8	9	10	11	12	13	14
15	16	17	18	19	20	21
22	23	24	25	26	27	28
29						

MARCH

S	M	T	W	T	F	S
	1	2	3	4	5	6
7	8	9	10	11	12	13
14	15	16	17	18	19	20
21	22	23	24	25	26	27
28	29	30	31			

APRIL

S	M	T	W	T	F	S
				1	2	3
4	5	6	7	8	9	10
11	12	13	14	15	16	17
18	19	20	21	22	23	24
25	26	27	28	29	30	

MAY

S	M	T	W	T	F	S
						1
2	3	4	5	6	7	8
9	10	11	12	13	14	15
16	17	18	19	20	21	22
23	24	25	26	27	28	29
30	31					

JUNE

S	M	T	W	T	F	S
		1	2	3	4	5
6	7	8	9	10	11	12
13	14	15	16	17	18	19
20	21	22	23	24	25	26
27	28	29	30			

JULY

S	M	T	W	T	F	S
				1	2	3
4	5	6	7	8	9	10
11	12	13	14	15	16	17
18	19	20	21	22	23	24
25	26	27	28	29	30	31

AUGUST

S	M	T	W	T	F	S
1	2	3	4	5	6	7
8	9	10	11	12	13	14
15	16	17	18	19	20	21
22	23	24	25	26	27	28
29	30	31				

SEPTEMBER

S	M	T	W	T	F	S
			1	2	3	4
5	6	7	8	9	10	11
12	13	14	15	16	17	18
19	20	21	22	23	24	25
26	27	28	29	30		

OCTOBER

S	M	T	W	T	F	S
					1	2
3	4	5	6	7	8	9
10	11	12	13	14	15	16
17	18	19	20	21	22	23
24	25	26	27	28	29	30
31						

NOVEMBER

S	M	T	W	T	F	S
	1	2	3	4	5	6
7	8	9	10	11	12	13
14	15	16	17	18	19	20
21	22	23	24	25	26	27
28	29	30				

DECEMBER

S	M	T	W	T	F	S
			1	2	3	4
5	6	7	8	9	10	11
12	13	14	15	16	17	18
19	20	21	22	23	24	25
26	27	28	29	30	31	

13

JANUARY

S	M	T	W	T	F	S
					1	2
3	4	5	6	7	8	9
10	11	12	13	14	15	16
17	18	19	20	21	22	23
24	25	26	27	28	29	30
31						

FEBRUARY

S	M	T	W	T	F	S
	1	2	3	4	5	6
7	8	9	10	11	12	13
14	15	16	17	18	19	20
21	22	23	24	25	26	27
28	29					

MARCH

S	M	T	W	T	F	S
		1	2	3	4	5
6	7	8	9	10	11	12
13	14	15	16	17	18	19
20	21	22	23	24	25	26
27	28	29	30	31		

APRIL

S	M	T	W	T	F	S
					1	2
3	4	5	6	7	8	9
10	11	12	13	14	15	16
17	18	19	20	21	22	23
24	25	26	27	28	29	30

MAY

S	M	T	W	T	F	S
1	2	3	4	5	6	7
8	9	10	11	12	13	14
15	16	17	18	19	20	21
22	23	24	25	26	27	28
29	30	31				

JUNE

S	M	T	W	T	F	S
			1	2	3	4
5	6	7	8	9	10	11
12	13	14	15	16	17	18
19	20	21	22	23	24	25
26	27	28	29	30		

JULY

S	M	T	W	T	F	S
					1	2
3	4	5	6	7	8	9
10	11	12	13	14	15	16
17	18	19	20	21	22	23
24	25	26	27	28	29	30
31						

AUGUST

S	M	T	W	T	F	S
	1	2	3	4	5	6
7	8	9	10	11	12	13
14	15	16	17	18	19	20
21	22	23	24	25	26	27
28	29	30	31			

SEPTEMBER

S	M	T	W	T	F	S
				1	2	3
4	5	6	7	8	9	10
11	12	13	14	15	16	17
18	19	20	21	22	23	24
25	26	27	28	29	30	

OCTOBER

S	M	T	W	T	F	S
						1
2	3	4	5	6	7	8
9	10	11	12	13	14	15
16	17	18	19	20	21	22
23	24	25	26	27	28	29
30	31					

NOVEMBER

S	M	T	W	T	F	S
		1	2	3	4	5
6	7	8	9	10	11	12
13	14	15	16	17	18	19
20	21	22	23	24	25	26
27	28	29	30			

DECEMBER

S	M	T	W	T	F	S
				1	2	3
4	5	6	7	8	9	10
11	12	13	14	15	16	17
18	19	20	21	22	23	24
25	26	27	28	29	30	31

14

JANUARY

S	M	T	W	T	F	S
						1
2	3	4	5	6	7	8
9	10	11	12	13	14	15
16	17	18	19	20	21	22
23	24	25	26	27	28	29
30	31					

FEBRUARY

S	M	T	W	T	F	S
		1	2	3	4	5
6	7	8	9	10	11	12
13	14	15	16	17	18	19
20	21	22	23	24	25	26
27	28	29				

MARCH

S	M	T	W	T	F	S
			1	2	3	4
5	6	7	8	9	10	11
12	13	14	15	16	17	18
19	20	21	22	23	24	25
26	27	28	29	30	31	

APRIL

S	M	T	W	T	F	S
						1
2	3	4	5	6	7	8
9	10	11	12	13	14	15
16	17	18	19	20	21	22
23	24	25	26	27	28	29
30						

MAY

S	M	T	W	T	F	S
	1	2	3	4	5	6
7	8	9	10	11	12	13
14	15	16	17	18	19	20
21	22	23	24	25	26	27
28	29	30	31			

JUNE

S	M	T	W	T	F	S
				1	2	3
4	5	6	7	8	9	10
11	12	13	14	15	16	17
18	19	20	21	22	23	24
25	26	27	28	29	30	

JULY

S	M	T	W	T	F	S
						1
2	3	4	5	6	7	8
9	10	11	12	13	14	15
16	17	18	19	20	21	22
23	24	25	26	27	28	29
30	31					

AUGUST

S	M	T	W	T	F	S
		1	2	3	4	5
6	7	8	9	10	11	12
13	14	15	16	17	18	19
20	21	22	23	24	25	26
27	28	29	30	31		

SEPTEMBER

S	M	T	W	T	F	S
					1	2
3	4	5	6	7	8	9
10	11	12	13	14	15	16
17	18	19	20	21	22	23
24	25	26	27	28	29	30

OCTOBER

S	M	T	W	T	F	S
1	2	3	4	5	6	7
8	9	10	11	12	13	14
15	16	17	18	19	20	21
22	23	24	25	26	27	28
29	30	31				

NOVEMBER

S	M	T	W	T	F	S
			1	2	3	4
5	6	7	8	9	10	11
12	13	14	15	16	17	18
19	20	21	22	23	24	25
26	27	28	29	30		

DECEMBER

S	M	T	W	T	F	S
					1	2
3	4	5	6	7	8	9
10	11	12	13	14	15	16
17	18	19	20	21	22	23
24	25	26	27	28	29	30
31						

Julian and Gregorian Calendars; Leap Year

Calendars based on the movements of sun and moon have been used since ancient times, but none has been perfect. The Julian calendar, under which western nations measured time until 1582 A. D., was authorized by Julius Caesar in 46 B.C., the year 709 of Rome. His expert was a Greek, Sosigenes. The Julian calendar, on the assumption that the true year was 365 1/4 days long, gave every fourth year 366 days. The Venerable Bede, an Anglo-Saxon monk, announced in 730 A.D. that the 365-day Julian year was 11 min., 14 sec. too long, making a cumulative error of about a day every 128 years, but nothing was done about it for over 800 years.

By 1582 the accumulated error was estimated to have amounted to 10 days. In that year Pope Gregory XIII decreed that the day following Oct. 4, 1582, should be called Oct. 15, thus dropping 10 days.

However, with common years 365 days and a 366-day leap year every fourth year, the error in the length of the year would have recurred at the rate of a little more than 3 days every 400 years. So 3 of every 4 centesimal years (ending in 00) were made common years, not leap years. Thus 1600 was a leap year, 1700, 1800 and 1900 were not, but 2000 will be. Leap years are those divisible by 4 except centesimal years, which are common unless divisible by 400.

The Gregorian calendar was adopted at once by France, Italy, Spain, Portugal and Luxembourg. Within 2 years most German Catholic states, Belgium and parts of Switzerland and the Netherlands were brought under the new calendar, and Hungary followed in 1587. The rest of the Netherlands, along with Denmark and the German Protestant states made the change in 1699-1700 (though the German Protestants retained the old reckoning of Easter until 1776).

The British Government imposed the Gregorian calendar on all its possessions, including the American colonies, in 1752. The British decreed that the day following Sept. 2, 1752, should be called Sept. 14, a loss of 11 days. All dates preceding were marked O.S., for Old Style. In addition New Year's Day was moved to Jan. 1 from Mar. 25. (e.g., under the old reckoning, Mar. 24, 1700 had been followed by Mar. 25, 1701.) George Washington's birth date, which was Feb. 11, 1731, O.S., became Feb. 22, 1732, N.S. In 1753 Sweden too went Gregorian, retaining the old Easter rules until 1844.

In 1793 the French Revolutionary Government adopted a calendar of 12 months of 30 days each with 5 extra days in September of each common year and a 6th extra day every 4th year. Napoleon reinstated the Gregorian calendar in 1806.

The Gregorian system later spread to non-European regions, first in the European colonies, then in the independent countries, replacing traditional calendars at least for official purposes. Japan in 1873, Egypt in 1875, China in 1912 and Turkey in 1917 made the change, usually in conjunction with political upheavals. In China, the republican government began reckoning years from its 1911 founding — e.g., 1948 was designated the year 37. After 1949, the Communists adopted the Common, or Christian Era year count, even for the traditional lunar calendar.

In 1918 the revolutionary government in Russia decreed that the day after Jan. 31, 1918, Old Style, would become Feb. 13, 1918, New Style. Greece followed in 1923. (In Russia the Orthodox Church has retained the Julian calendar, as have various Middle Eastern Christian sects.) For the first time in history, all major cultures have been brought under one calendar.

To change from the Julian to the Gregorian calendar, add 10 days to dates Oct. 5, 1582, through Feb. 28, 1700; after that date add 11 days through Feb. 28, 1800, 12 days through Feb. 28, 1900, and 13 days through Feb. 28, 2100.

Julian Calendar

To find which of the 14 calendars printed on pages 782-783 applies to any year under the Julian system, find the century for the desired year in the three left-hand columns below; read across. Then find the year in the four top rows; read down. The number in the intersection is the calendar designation for that year.

Century			00	Year (last two figures of desired year)																							
				01	02	03	04	05	06	07	08	09	10	11	12	13	14	15	16	17	18	19	20	21	22	23	24	25	26	27	28
				29	30	31	32	33	34	35	36	37	38	39	40	41	42	43	44	45	46	47	48	49	50	51	52	53	54	55	56
				57	58	59	60	61	62	63	64	65	66	67	68	69	70	71	72	73	74	75	76	77	78	79	80	81	82	83	84
				85	86	87	88	89	90	91	92	93	94	95	96	97	98	99													
0	700	1400	12	7	1	2	10	5	6	7	8	3	4	5	13	1	2	3	11	6	7	1	9	4	5	6	14	2	3	4	12
100	800	1500	11	6	7	1	9	4	5	6	14	2	3	4	12	7	1	2	10	5	6	7	8	3	4	5	13	1	2	3	11
200	900	1600	10	5	6	7	8	3	4	5	13	1	2	3	11	6	7	1	9	4	5	6	14	2	3	4	12	7	1	2	10
300	1000	1700	9	4	5	6	14	2	3	4	12	7	1	2	10	5	6	7	8	3	4	5	13	1	2	3	11	6	7	1	9
400	1100	1800	8	3	4	5	13	1	2	3	11	6	7	1	9	4	5	6	14	2	3	4	12	7	1	2	10	5	6	7	8
500	1200	1900	14	2	3	4	12	7	1	2	10	5	6	7	8	3	4	5	13	1	2	3	11	6	7	1	9	4	5	6	14
600	1300	2000	13	1	2	3	11	6	7	1	9	4	5	6	14	2	3	4	12	7	1	2	10	5	6	7	8	3	4	5	13

Gregorian Calendar

Pick desired year from table below or on page 782. The number shown with each year shows which calendar to use for that year, as shown on pages 782-783. (The Gregorian calendar was inaugurated Oct. 15, 1582. From that date to Dec. 31, 1582, use calendar 6.)

1583-1799

1583...7	1603...4	1623...1	1643...5	1663...2	1683...6	1703...2	1723...6	1743...3	1763...7	1783...4
1584...8	1604...12	1624...9	1644...13	1664...10	1684...14	1704...10	1724...14	1744...11	1764...8	1784...12
1585...3	1605...7	1625...4	1645...1	1665...5	1685...2	1705...5	1725...2	1745...6	1765...3	1785...7
1586...4	1606...1	1626...5	1646...2	1666...6	1686...3	1706...6	1726...3	1746...7	1766...4	1786...1
1587...5	1607...2	1627...6	1647...3	1667...7	1687...4	1707...7	1727...4	1747...1	1767...5	1787...2
1588...13	1608...10	1628...14	1648...11	1668...8	1688...12	1708...8	1728...12	1748...9	1768...13	1788...10
1589...1	1609...5	1629...2	1649...6	1669...3	1689...7	1709...3	1729...7	1749...4	1769...1	1789...5
1590...2	1610...6	1630...3	1650...7	1670...4	1690...1	1710...4	1730...1	1750...5	1770...2	1790...6
1591...3	1611...7	1631...4	1651...1	1671...5	1691...2	1711...5	1731...2	1751...6	1771...3	1791...7
1592...11	1612...8	1632...12	1652...9	1672...13	1692...10	1712...13	1732...10	1752...14	1772...11	1792...8
1593...6	1613...3	1633...7	1653...4	1673...1	1693...5	1713...1	1733...5	1753...2	1773...6	1793...3
1594...7	1614...4	1634...1	1654...5	1674...2	1694...6	1714...2	1734...6	1754...3	1774...7	1794...4
1959...1	1615...5	1635...2	1655...6	1675...3	1695...7	1715...3	1735...7	1755...4	1775...1	1795...5
1596...9	1616...13	1636...10	1656...14	1676...11	1696...8	1716...11	1736...8	1756...12	1776...9	1796...13
1597...4	1617...1	1637...5	1657...2	1677...6	1697...3	1717...6	1737...3	1757...7	1777...4	1797...1
1598...5	1618...2	1638...6	1658...3	1678...7	1698...4	1718...7	1738...4	1758...1	1778...5	1798...2
1599...6	1619...3	1639...7	1659...4	1679...1	1699...5	1719...1	1739...5	1759...2	1779...6	1799...3
1600...14	1620...11	1640...8	1660...12	1680...9	1700...6	1720...9	1740...13	1760...10	1780...14	....
1601...2	1621...6	1641...3	1661...7	1681...4	1701...7	1721...4	1741...1	1761...5	1781...2	....
1602...3	1622...7	1642...4	1662...1	1682...5	1702...1	1722...5	1742...2	1762...6	1782...3	....

Standard Time Differences — North American Cities

At 12 o'clock noon, Eastern Standard Time, the standard time in N.A. cities is as follows:

Akron, Ohio	12.00 NOON	Fort Worth, Texas	11.00 A.M.	Philadelphia, Pa.	12.00 NOON
Albuquerque, N.M.	10.00 A.M.	Frankfort, Ky.	12.00 NOON	*Phoenix, Ariz.	10.00 A.M.
Atlanta, Ga.	12.00 NOON	Galveston, Tex.	11.00 A.M.	Pierre, S. Dak.	11.00 A.M.
Austin, Tex.	11.00 A.M.	Grand Rapids, Mich.	12.00 NOON	Pittsburgh, Pa.	12.00 NOON
Baltimore, Md.	12.00 NOON	Halifax, N.S.	1.00 P.M.	Portland, Me.	12.00 NOON
Birmingham, Ala.	11.00 A.M.	Hartford, Conn.	12.00 NOON	Portland, Oreg.	9.00 A.M.
Bismarck, N. Dak.	11.00 A.M.	Helena, Mont.	10.00 A.M.	Providence, R.I.	12.00 NOON
Boise, Idaho	10.00 A.M.	*Honolulu, Hawaii	7.00 A.M.	*Regina, Sask.	11.00 A.M.
Boston, Mass.	12.00 NOON	Houston, Tex.	11.00 A.M.	Reno, Nev.	9.00 A.M.
Buffalo, N.Y.	12.00 NOON	*Indianapolis, Ind.	12.00 NOON	Richmond, Va.	12.00 NOON
Butte, Mont.	10.00 A.M.	Jacksonville, Fla.	12.00 NOON	Rochester, N.Y.	12.00 NOON
Calgary, Alta.	10.00 A.M.	Juneau, Alaska	9.00 A.M.	Sacramento, Calif.	9.00 A.M.
Charleston, S.C.	12.00 NOON	Kansas City, Mo.	11.00 A.M.	St. John's, Nfld	1.30 P.M.
Charleston, W. Va.	12.00 NOON	Knoxville, Tenn.	12.00 NOON	St. Louis, Mo.	11.00 A.M.
Charlotte, N.C.	12.00 NOON	Lexington, Ky.	12.00 NOON	St. Paul, Minn.	11.00 A.M.
Charlottetown, P.E.I.	1.00 P.M.	Lincoln, Nebr.	11.00 A.M.	Salt Lake City, Utah.	10.00 A.M.
Chattanooga, Tenn.	12.00 NOON	Little Rock, Ark.	11.00 A.M.	San Antonio, Tex.	11.00 A.M.
Cheyenne, Wyo.	10.00 A.M.	Los Angeles, Calif.	9.00 A.M.	San Diego, Calif.	9.00 A.M.
Chicago, Ill.	11.00 A.M.	Louisville, Ky.	12.00 NOON	San Francisco, Calif.	9.00 A.M.
Cleveland, Ohio.	12.00 NOON	*Mexico City.	11.00 A.M.	Santa Fe, N.M.	10.00 A.M.
Colorado Spr., Colo.	10.00 A.M.	Memphis, Tenn.	11.00 A.M.	Savannah, Ga.	12.00 NOON
Columbus, Ohio.	12.00 NOON	Miami, Fla.	12.00 NOON	Seattle, Wash.	9.00 A.M.
Dallas, Tex.	11.00 A.M.	Milwaukee, Wis.	11.00 A.M.	Shreveport, La.	11.00 A.M.
*Dawson, Yuk.	8.00 A.M.	Minneapolis, Minn.	11.00 A.M.	Sioux Falls, S. Dak.	11.00 A.M.
Dayton, Ohio.	12.00 NOON	Mobile, Ala.	11.00 A.M.	Spokane, Wash.	9.00 A.M.
Denver, Colo.	10.00 A.M.	Montreal, Que.	12.00 NOON	Tampa, Fla.	12.00 NOON
Des Moines, Iowa.	11.00 A.M.	Nashville, Tenn.	11.00 A.M.	Toledo, Ohio	12.00 NOON
Detroit, Mich.	12.00 NOON	New Haven, Conn.	12.00 NOON	Topeka, Kan.	11.00 A.M.
Duluth, Minn.	11.00 A.M.	New Orleans, La.	11.00 A.M.	*Tucson, Ariz.	10.00 A.M.
El Paso, Tex.	10.00 A.M.	New York, N.Y.	12.00 NOON	Tulsa, Okla.	11.00 A.M.
Erie, Pa.	12.00 NOON	Nome, Alaska	6.00 A.M.	Vancouver, B.C.	9.00 A.M.
Evansville, Ind.	11.00 A.M.	Norfolk, Va.	12.00 NOON	Washington, D.C.	12.00 NOON
Fairbanks, Alaska.	7.00 A.M.	Okla. City, Okla.	11.00 A.M.	Wichita, Kan.	11.00 A.M.
Flint, Mich.	12.00 NOON	Omaha, Nebr.	11.00 A.M.	Wilmington, Del.	12.00 NOON
*Fort Wayne, Ind.	12.00 NOON	Peoria, Ill.	11.00 A.M.	Winnipeg, Man.	11.00 A.M.

*Cities with an asterisk do not observe daylight savings time. During much of the year, it is necessary to add one hour to the cities which do observe daylight savings time to get the proper time relation.

Standard Time Differences — World Cities

The time indicated in the table is fixed by law and is called the legal time, or, more generally, Standard Time. *Indicates morning of the following day. At 12 o'clock noon, Eastern Standard Time, the standard time in foreign cities is as follows:

Alexandria.	7:00 P.M.	Copenhagen.	6:00 P.M.	Liverpool	5:00 P.M.	Seoul.	2:00 A.M.*
Amsterdam.	6:00 P.M.	Dacca.	11:00 P.M.	London.	5:00 P.M.	Shanghai.	1:00 A.M.*
Athens.	7:00 P.M.	Delhi.	10:30 P.M.	Madrid.	6:00 P.M.	Singapore.	12:30 A.M.*
Auckland.	5:00 A.M.*	Djakarta.	12:00 MID.	Manila.	1:00 A.M.*	Stockholm.	6:00 P.M.
Baghdad.	8:00 P.M.	Dublin.	5:00 P.M.	Melbourne.	3:00 A.M.*	Sydney.	
Bangkok.	12:00 MID.	Gdansk.	6:00 P.M.	Montevideo.	2:00 P.M.	(Australia)	3:00 A.M.*
Belfast.	5:00 P.M.	Geneva.	6:00 P.M.	Moscow.	8:00 P.M.	Tashkent.	11:00 P.M.
Berlin.	6:00 P.M.	Havana.	12:00 NOON	Nagasaki.	2:00 A.M.*	Teheran.	8:30 P.M.
Bogota.	12:00 NOON	Helsinki.	7:00 P.M.	Oslo.	6:00 P.M.	Tel Aviv.	7:00 P.M.
Bombay.	10:30 P.M.	Hong Kong.	1:00 A.M.*	Paris.	6:00 P.M.	Tokyo.	2:00 A.M.*
Bremen.	6:00 P.M.	Istanbul.	7:00 P.M.	Peking.	1:00 A.M.*	Valparaiso.	1:00 P.M.
Brussels.	6:00 P.M.	Jerusalem.	7:00 P.M.	Prague.	6:00 P.M.	Vladivostok.	3:00 A.M.*
Bucharest.	7:00 P.M.	Johannes-		Rangoon.	11:30 P.M.	Vienna.	6:00 P.M.
Budapest.	6:00 P.M.	burg.	7:00 P.M.	Rio de Janeiro	2:00 P.M.	Warsaw.	6:00 P.M.
Buenos Aires	2:00 P.M.	Karachi.	10:00 P.M.	Rome.	6:00 P.M.	Wellington.	
Calcutta.	10:30 P.M.	Le Havre.	6:00 P.M.	Saigon.	1:00 A.M.*	(N.Z.)	5:00 A.M.*
Cape Town.	7:00 P.M.	Leningrad.	8:00 P.M.	Santiago.		Yokohama.	2:00 A.M.*
Caracas.	1:00 P.M.	Lima.	12:00 NOON	(Chile).	1:00 P.M.	Zurich.	6:00 P.M.
		Lisbon.	6:00 P.M.				

Chronological Eras, 1977

The year 1977 of the Christian Era comprises the latter part of the 201st and the beginning of the 202d year of the independence of the United States of America.

Era	Year	Begins in 1977	Era	Year	Begins in 1977
Byzantine	7486	Sept. 14	Japanese	2637	Jan. 1
Jewish	5738	Sept. 13 (sunset)	Grecian (Seleucidae)	2289	Sept. 14 or Oct. 14
Olympiads.	2753	July 1	Diocletian	1694	Sept. 11
(First year of Olympiad 689)			Indian (Saka)	1899	Mar. 22
Roman (Ab Urbe Condita).	2730	Jan. 14	Mohammedan (Hegira)	1398	Dec. 12
Nabonassar (Babylonian).	2726	Apr. 29			(sunset)

Chronological Cycles, 1977

Dominical Letter	B	Golden Number (Lunar Cycle)	II	Roman Indiction	15
Epact	10	Solar Cycle	26	Julian Period (year of)	6690

Standard Time, Daylight Saving Time, and Others

Source: Defense Mapping Agency Hydrographic Center; Department of Transportation; National Bureau of Standards; U.S. Naval Observatory

Standard Time

Standard time is reckoned from Greenwich, England, recognized as the Prime Meridian of Longitude. The world is divided into 24 zones, each 15° of arc, or one hour in time apart. The Greenwich meridian (0°) extends through the center of the initial zone, and the zones to the east are numbered from 1 to 12 with the prefix "minus" indicating the number of hours to be subtracted to obtain Greenwich Time.

Westward zones are similarly numbered, but prefixed "plus" showing the number of hours that must be added to get Greenwich Time. While these zones apply generally to sea areas, it should be noted that the Standard Time maintained in many countries does not coincide with zone time. A graphical representation of the zones is shown on the Standard Time Zone Chart of the World published by the Defense Mapping Agency Hydrographic Center, Washington, D.C. 20390.

The United States and possessions are divided into eight Standard Time zones, as set forth by the Uniform Time Act of 1966, which also provides for the use of Daylight Saving Time therein. Each zone is approximately 15° of longitude in width. All places in each zone use, instead of their own local time, the time counted from the transit of the "mean sun" across the Standard Time meridian which passes near the middle of that zone.

These time zones are designated as Atlantic, Eastern, Central, Mountain, Pacific, Yukon, Alaska-Hawaii, and Bering, and the time in these zones is basically reckoned from the 60th, 75th, 90th, 105th, 120th, 135th, 150th, 165th meridians west of Greenwich. The line wanders to conform to local geographical regions. The time in the various zones is earlier than Greenwich Time by 4, 5, 6, 7, 8, 9, 10, and 11 hours respectively.

High Precision Time and Frequency are broadcast by U.S. Navy Stations which are maintained on frequency with the aid of Atomic Clocks (cesium beam and atomic hydrogen masers). The stations are as follows: NBA: NSS: NLK: NAA: NPM: NWC: NPN: NPG: NDT: Omega.

Loran-C Navigational Transmissions at 100 KHz of the East Coast, Central Pacific, Mediterranean, Northwest Pacific and the Norwegian sea chains may be used for time and frequency comparisons.

Standard Frequency Stations

The National Bureau of Standards (NBS) radio stations WWV at Fort Collins, Colorado, and WWVH on the island of Kauai, Hawaii, broadcast a number of technical services continuously night and day. These services are: 1. standard radio frequencies, 2.5, 5, 10, 15, 20, and 25 MHz (WWV) and 2.5, 5, 10, 15, and 20 MHz (WWVH); 2. standard time voice announcements (WWV—male, 7.5 seconds before the minute; WWVH — female, 15 seconds before the minute); 3. standard time intervals of one second and one minute; 4. corrections to adjust atomic time to astronomical time; 5. standard audio frequencies of 500 and 600 Hz on alternate minutes and a 440 Hz tone (the musical pitch A above middle C) once each hour; 6. a slow time code at 100 Hz giving the day, hour, and minute in binary coded decimal form; 7. hourly radio propagation forecasts (WWV only); 8. geophysical alerts on events in process and summaries of solar and geophysical events of the last 24 hours; and 9. storm warnings; 10. Omega Polar Cap Disturbance warnings. The NBS also broadcasts time and frequency signals from its low frequency station (60kHz) WWVB, also located at Fort Collins, Colorado.

Each hour there are periods with no tone modulation during which the carrier, seconds ticks, minute time announcements, and 100 Hz time code continue. They occur from 45 to 51 minutes after each hour on WWV and from 8 to 11 and 15 to 20 minutes after each hour on WWVH and the 46th through the 50th minute on WWV

The National Research council of Canada continually transmits precision time signals from Ottawa over station CHU on 3 frequencies, 3330, 7335, and 14670 kHz.

Storm warnings cover the waters of the Atlantic and eastern Pacific from WWV and the Pacific from WWVH and are given at the 8th, 9th, and 10th minute of each hour from WWV and at the 48th, 49th, and 50th minute of each hour from WWVH. Times of issue are 0500, 1100, 1700, and 2300 UTC from WWV, and 0000, 0600, 1200, and 1800 UTC from WWVH.

The time and frequency broadcasts are controlled by the NBS atomic frequency standards, which realize the internationally defined cesium resonance frequency with an accurancy of 1 part in 10^{13}. (The Cesium atom invariably resonates at a little over 9 billion oscillations per second.)

The atomic time scale is uniform and does not reflect the variable rotational speed of the earth. The time signals are adjusted by introducing a leap second about once a year (at the end of June or December) so that the broadcast time never departs more than nine-tenths of a second from mean solar time, determined by the rotational position of the earth.

Special Publication 432 describes in detail the standard frequency and time service of the National Bureau of Standards. Single copies may be obtained upon request from the National Bureau of Standards, Boulder, Colorado, 80302. Quantities may be obtained from the Superintendent of Documents, U.S. Gov. Printing Office, Wash., D.C. 20402, at 60c per copy.

24-Hour Time

24-hour time is widely used in scientific work throughout the world. In the United States it is used also in operations of the Armed Forces. In Europe it is used in preference to the 12-hour a.m. and p.m. system. With the 24-hour system the day begins at midnight and hours are numbered 0 through 23.

International Date Line

The Date Line is a zig-zag line that approximately coincides with the 180th meridian, and it is where each calendar day begins. The date must be advanced one day when crossing in a westerly direction and set back one day when crossing in an easterly direction.

The line is deflected between north latitude 48° and 75°, so that all Asia lies to the west of it.

Daylight Saving Time

Daylight Saving Time is achieved by advancing the clock one hour. Under the Uniform Time Act, which became effective in 1967, all states, the District of Columbia and U. S. possessions were to observe Daylight Saving Time beginning at 2 a.m. on the last Sunday in April and ending at 2 a.m. on the last Sunday in October. Any state could, by law, exempt itself; a 1972 amendment to the act authorized states split by time zones to take that into consideration in exempting themselves. Arizona, Hawaii, Puerto Rico, the Virgin Islands, American Samoa, and part of Indiana are now exempt. Some local zone boundaries in Kansas, Texas, Florida, and Michigan have been modified in the last several years by the Dept. of Transportation, which oversees the act. To conserve energy Congress put most of the nation on year-round Daylight Saving Time for two years effective Jan. 6, 1974 through Oct. 26, 1975; but a further bill, signed in October, 1974, restored Standard Time from the last Sunday in that month to the last Sunday in February, 1975.

Legal or Public Holidays

Technically there are no national holidays in the United States; each state has jurisdiction over its holidays, which are designated by legislative enactment or executive proclamation. In practice, however, most states observe the Federal legal public holidays, even though the President and Congress can legally designate holidays only for the District of Columbia and for Federal employees.

Federal legal public holidays are: New Year's, Washington's Birthday, Memorial Day, Independence Day, Labor Day, Columbus Day, Veterans Day, Thanksgiving, and Christmas.

1977

Chief Legal or Public Holidays

When a holiday falls on a Sunday it is usually observed on the following Monday. For some holidays, government and business closing practices vary. In most states, the office of the Secretary of State can provide details of holiday closings.

Jan. 1 (Saturday) — New Year's Day. All the states (several states will celebrate on Dec. 31, 1976.)

Feb. 12 (Saturday) — Lincoln's Birthday. Alas., Ariz., Cal., Col., Conn., Ill., Ind., Ky., Me., Md., Mo., Mon., Neb., N.J., N.M., N.Y., Pa., Ut., Vt., Wash., W.Va In Del. and Ore., celebrated Feb. 7.

Feb. 21 (Third Monday in Feb.) — Washington's Birthday. All the states except Kan., N.C., R.I. (celebrated Feb. 22 in La.) In several states, the holiday is called Presidents' Day or Washington-Lincoln Day.

Apr. 8 — Good Friday. Observed in all the states. A legal holiday in Conn., Del., Fla., Ha., Ind., Ia., La., Md., N.J., N.D., Pa., Tenn. Partial holiday in N.M. and Wis.

May 30 (Monday) — Memorial Day. All the states except Ala., Miss., S.C., (Confederate Memorial Day in Virginia.)

July 4 (Monday) — Independence Day. All the states.

Sept. 5 (First Monday in Sept.) — Labor Day. All the states.

Oct. 10 (Second Monday in Oct.) — Columbus Day. All the states except Alas., Ark., Ia., Kan., Mich., Miss., Nev., N.C., N.D., Okla., Ore., S.C., S.D., Wash. (Discoverer's Day in Hawaii; Landing Day in Wis.).

Oct. 24 (Fourth Monday in October) — Armistice Day (Veterans Day). In 1978, the U.S. government will resume celebrating this holiday on Nov. 11, the traditional date. Nearly all the states will observe Nov. 11 in 1977.

Nov. 8 (First Tuesday after first Monday in Nov.) — General Election Day. All the states except Ala., Alas., Ark., Conn., Ga., Ha., Id., Ky., Me., Mass., Mich., Miss., Mont., Neb., Nev., N.M., N.C., N.D., Oh., Okla., Ore., R.I., S.C., S.D., Ut., Vt., Wash. Observed Nov. 2 in Mo. (Observed usually only when presidential or general elections are held. Primary election days are observed as holidays or part holidays in some states.)

Nov. 11 (Friday) — Armistice Day (Veterans Day.) Nearly all the states.

Nov. 24 (Fourth Thursday in Nov.) — Thanksgiving Day. All the states. Okla. and Wash. also observe the day after Thanksgiving.

Dec. 25 (Sunday) — Christmas. All the states. (Most states will observe Christmas on Dec. 26 in 1977.)

Other Legal or Public Holidays

Dates are for 1977 observance, when known.

Jan. 8 — Battle of New Orleans. In Louisiana.

Jan. 15 — Martin Luther King Birthday. Ky., Md., Mass. Observed on Jan. 16 in N.Y. Many schools and black groups in other states also observe the day.

Jan. 17 (Third Mon. in Jan.) — Robert E. Lee's Birthday. Ala., Miss., S.C. Lee-Jackson Day in Va.

Jan. 19 — Robert E. Lee's Birthday. Ark., Fla., Ga., Ky., La.; Confederate Heroes' Day in Tex.

Jan. 20 — Inauguration Day. In the District of Columbia; observed every fourth year.

Jan. 30 — Franklin D. Roosevelt's Birthday. In Ky.

Feb. 14 — Admission Day. In Arizona.

Feb. 22 — Mardi Gras (Shrove Tuesday). Ala., La., and some Fla. counties.

March 1 — Town Meeting Day (First Tuesday in March.) In Vermont.

March 2 — Texas Independence Day. In that state.

March 17 — Evacuation Day. In Boston and Suffolk County, Mass.

March 25 — Maryland Day. In that state.

March 25 — Kuhio Day. In Hawaii.

March 28 — Seward's Day. In Alaska.

April 11 — Easter Monday. In North Carolina.

April 13 — Thomas Jefferson's Birthday. In Alabama.

April 18 — Patriot's Day (Third Monday in April.) Me. and Mass.

April 21 — San Jacinto Day. In Texas.

April 22 — Arbor Day. In Nebraska.

April 25 — Fast Day (Fourth Mon. in Apr.) In New Hampshire.

April 25 — Confederate Memorial Day (Fourth Monday in April.) Alabama and Miss.

April 26 — Confederate Memorial Day. In Fla., Ga.

April 29 — Arbor Day (Last Friday in April.) In Utah.

May 8 — Harry Truman's Birthday. In Missouri.

May 10 — Confederate Memorial Day. In South Carolina.

June 3 — Birthday of Jefferson Davis. Fla., Ga., Ky., S.C.; in Ala., Miss., observed on first Monday in June.

June 3 — Confederate Memorial Day. In Ky., La.

June 10 — Kamehameha Day. In Hawaii.

June 14 — Flag Day. In Pa. Observed June 12 in N.Y.

July 24 — Pioneer Day. In Utah.

Aug. 1 — Colorado Day (First Monday in August.) In that state.

Aug. 8 — VJ Day (Second Monday in August.) In Rhode Island.

Aug. 16 — Bennington Battle Day. In Vermont.

Aug. 19 — Admission Day (Third Friday in August.) In Hawaii.

Aug. 27 — Lyndon Johnson's Birthday. In Texas.

Aug. 30 — Huey Long's Birthday. In Louisiana.

Sept. 9 — Admission Day. In California.

Sept. 12 — Defenders' Day. In Maryland.

Oct. 10 — Pioneers' Day (Second Monday in Oct.) In So. Dakota.

Oct. 10 — Discoverer's Day. In Hawaii.

Oct. 18 — Alaska Day. In that state.

Oct. 31 — Nevada Day. In that state.

Dec. 10 — Wyoming Day. In that state.

Days Usually Observed

Not legal or public holidays:

All Saints' Day, Nov. 1. A public holiday in Ha.

American Indian Day (Sept. 23 in 1977.) Always fourth Friday in September.

Arbor Day. Tree-planting day. First observed April 10, 1872, in Nebraska. Now observed in every state in the Union except Alaska (often on the last Friday in April.) A legal holiday in Utah (always last Friday in April), and in Nebraska (April 22.)

Armed Forces Day (May 21 in 1977.) Always third

Saturday in that month, by presidential proclamation. Replaced Army, Navy, and Air Force Days.

Bill of Rights Day, Dec. 15. By Act of Congress. Bill of Rights took effect Dec. 15, 1791.

Bird Day. Often observed with Arbor Day.

Child Health Day (Oct. 3 in 1977.) Always first Monday in October, by presidential proclamation.

Citizenship Day, Sept. 17. President Truman, Feb. 29, 1952, signed bill designating Sept. 17 as annual Citizenship Day. It replaced I Am An American Day, formerly 3rd Sunday in May and Constitution Day, formerly Sept. 17.

Easter Sunday (April 10 in 1977.)

Elizabeth Cady Stanton Day, Nov. 12. Birthday of pioneer leader for equal rights for women.

Farmers' Day (Oct. 10 in 1977.) In Fla.

Father's Day (June 19, in 1977.) Always third Sunday in that month.

Flag Day, June 14. By presidential proclamation. It is a legal holiday in Pennsylvania.

Forefathers' Day, Dec. 21. Landing on Plymouth Rock, in 1620. Is celebrated with dinners by New England societies, especially "Down East."

Frances Willard Day, Sept. 28. Observed in Minnesota to honor the educator and temperance leader.

Nathan Bedford Forrest's Birthday, July 13. Observed in Tennessee to honor the Civil War general.

Four Chaplains Memorial Day, February 3.

Gen. Douglas MacArthur Day, Jan. 26. A memorial day in Arkansas.

Gen. Pulaski Memorial Day, Oct. 11. Native of Poland and Revolutionary War hero; died (Oct. 11, 1779) from wounds received at the siege of Savannah, 'Ga. Observed officially in Indiana.

Gen. von Steuben Memorial Day, Sept. 17. By presidential proclamation.

Georgia Day, Feb. 12. Observed in that state.

Groundhog Day, Feb. 2. A popular belief is that if the groundhog sees his shadow this day, he returns to his burrow and winter continues 6 weeks longer.

Halloween, Oct. 31. The evening before All Saints or All-Hallows Day. Informally observed in the United States with masquerading and pumpkin-decorations. Traditionally an occasion for children to play pranks.

Andrew Jackson's Birthday, Mar. 15. Observed in Tennessee.

Leif Ericsson Day, Oct. 9. Observed in Minnesota.

Loyalty Day, May 1. By act of Congress.

May Day. Name popularly given to May 1st. Celebrated as Labor Day in most of the world, and by some groups in the U.S. Observed in many schools as a Spring Festival.

Minnesota Day, May 11. In that state.

Mother's Day (May 8 in 1977.) Always second Sunday in that month:

National Aviation Day, Aug. 19. By presidential proclamation.

National Day of Prayer. By presidential proclamation each year on a day other than a Sunday.

National Freedom Day, February 1. To commemorate the signing of a document abolishing slavery, Feb. 1, 1865. By presidential proclamation.

National Maritime Day, May 22. First proclaimed 1935 in commemoration of the departure of the SS Savannah, from Savannah, Ga., on May 22, 1819, on the first successful transatlantic voyage under steam propulsion. By presidential proclamation.

Pan American Day, April 14. In 1890 the First International Conference of American States, meeting in Washington, was held on that date. A resolution was adopted which resulted in the creation of the organization known today as the Pan American Union. By presidential proclamation.

Poetry Day, Oct. 15.

Primary Election Day. Observed usually only when presidential or general elections are held.

Reformation Day, Oct. 31. Observed by Protestant groups.

Sadie Hawkins Day, first Saturday after November 11.

St. Patrick's Day, March 17. Observed by Irish Societies, especially with parades.

St. Valentine's Day, Feb. 14. Festival of a martyr beheaded at Rome under Emperor Claudius. Association of this day with lovers has no connection with the saint and probably had its origin in an old belief that on this day birds begin to choose their mates.

Senior Citizens' Day (Fourth Sun. in Sept.) In Ind.

Susan B. Anthony Day, Feb. 15. Birthday of a pioneer crusader for equal rights for women.

United Nations Day, Oct. 24. By presidential proclamation, to commemorate founding of United Nations.

Verrazano Day, April 17. Observed by New York State, to commemorate the probable discovery of New York harbor by Giovanni da Verrazano in April, 1524.

Will Rogers Day, Nov. 4. In Oklahoma.

Wright Brothers Day, Dec. 17. By presidential designation, to commemorate first successful flight by Orville and Wilbur Wright, Dec. 17, 1903.

Youth Honor Day, Oct. 31. Iowa day of observance.

Other Holidays, Anniversaries, Events — 1977

(See also Calendars in Index)

Jan. 7, 1927	— First transatlantic phone service.
Jan. 9 (Sun.)	— Superbowl game.
Feb. 1, 1902	— Langston Hughes born.
Feb. 14 (Mon.)	— St. Valentine's Day.
Mar. 20 (Sun.)	— Spring begins, 12:43 PM, EST.
Mar. 26, 1827	— Ludwig van Beethoven dies.
Apr. 1 (Fri.)	— April Fool's Day.
Apr. 12, 1777	— Henry Clay born.
Apr. 22 (Fri.)	— Earth Day.
Apr. 24, 1877	— Reconstruction ends, US troops quit La.
May 1 (Sun.)	— Law Day.
May 3, 1802	— Washington, D.C. incorporated.
May 7 (Sat.)	— Kentucky Derby.
May 14, 1727	— Thomas Gainsborough baptized.
May 20, 1902	— Cuban independence in effect.
May 21, 1927	— Lindberg lands in Paris.
May 30 (Mon.)	— Indianapolis 500.
June 14, 1777	— Continental Congress adopts Stars & Stripes.
June 21 (Tues.)	— Summer begins, 7:14 AM, EST.
June 28, 1902	— US authorizes Panama Canal.
July 1, (Fri.)	— Dominion Day, or Canada Day.
July 14 (Thurs.)	
	— Bastille Day.
July 17, 1577	— Frobisher lands at Baffin Land, Canada.
July 31, 1877	— Thomas A. Edison gets phonograph patent.
Aug. 7, 1927	— Canada-US Peace Bridge dedicated.
Aug. 11, 1877	— First discovery of a Mars moon.
Aug. 23, 1927	— Sacco and Vanzetti executed.
Setp. 14, 1927	— Isadora Duncan dies.
Sept. 16 (Fri.)	— Mexico Independence Day.
Sept. 22 (Thurs.)	
	— Autumn begins, 10:30 PM, EST.
Sept. 28, 1902	— Emile Zola dies.
Oct. 15, 1777	— Burgoyne surrenders at Saratoga.
Nov. 1, 1952	— First hydrogen bomb exploded.
Nov. 15, 1777	— Articles of Confederation adopted.
Dec. 7, 1902	— Thomas Nast dies.
Dec. 21 (Wed.)	— Winter begins, 6:24 PM, EST.

Tides and Their Causes
Source: National Ocean Survey (NOAA)

The tides are a natural phenomenon involving the alternating rise and fall in the large fluid bodies of the earth caused by the combined gravitational attraction of the sun and moon. The combination of these two variable force influences, as modified by certain factors such as depth of the water, configuration of the shoreline, and geographic location produce the complex recurrent cycle of the tides. Tides may occur in both oceans and seas, to a limited extent in large lakes, the atmosphere, and, to a very minute degree, in the earth itself. The period between succeeding tides varies as the result of many factors and force influences.

The tide-generating force represents the difference between (1) the centrifugal force produced by the revolution of the earth around the common center-of-gravity of the earth-moon system and (2) the gravitational attraction of the moon acting upon the earth's overlying waters. Similar tide-producing forces exist in the earth-sun system. Since, on the average, the moon is only 238,857 miles from the earth compared with the sun's much greater distance of 93,000,000 miles, this closer distance outranks the much smaller mass of the moon compared with that of the sun, and the moon's tide-raising force is, accordingly, 2¹/₅ times that of the sun.

The effect of the tide-generating forces of the moon and sun acting tangentially to the earth's surface (the so-called "tractive force") tends to cause a maximum accumulation of the waters of the oceans at two diametrically opposite positions on the surface of the earth and to withdraw compensating amounts of water from all points 90° removed from the positions of these tidal bulges. The presence of the continents, as well as other factors, prevents the total free movement of water. However, as the earth rotates beneath the maxima and minima of these tide-generating forces, a sequence of two high tides, separated by two low tides, ideally is produced each day.

Twice in each lunar month, when the sun, moon, and earth are directly aligned, with the moon between the earth and the sun (at new moon) or on the opposite side of the earth from the sun (at full moon), the sun and the moon exert their gravitational force in a mutual or additive fashion. Higher high tides and lower low tides are produced. These are called spring tides. At two positions 90° in between, the gravitational forces of the moon and sun — imposed at right angles—tend to counteract each other to the greatest extent, and the range between high and low tides is reduced. These are called neap tides. This semi-monthly variation between the spring and neap tides is called the phase inequality.

The inclination of the moon's orbit to the equator also produces a difference in the height of succeeding high tides and in the extent of depression of succeeding low tides which is known as the diurnal inequality. In extreme cases, this phenomenon can result in only one high tide and one low tide each day. The changing distance of the moon from the earth in each lunar month due to the elliptical orbit of the moon produces a difference in the height of the tides known as the lunar parallactic inequality. The changing distance of the earth from the sun during the earth's annual revolution around the sun similarly introduces the solar parallactic inequality.

The actual amount of the uplift of the waters in the deep ocean may amount to only one or two feet. However, as this tide approaches shoal waters and its effects are augmented the tidal range may be greatly increased. In Nova Scotia along the narrow channel of the Bay of Fundy, the range of tides or difference between high and low waters, may reach 43 1/2 feet or more (under spring tide conditions) due to resonant amplification.

At New Orleans, the periodic rise and fall of the tide varies with the state of the Mississippi, being about 10 inches at low stage and zero at high. The Canadian Tide Tables for 1972 gave a maximum range of nearly 50 feet at Leaf Basin, Ungava Bay.

In every case, actual high or low tide can vary considerably from the average due to weather conditions such as strong winds, abrupt barometric pressure changes, or prolonged periods of extreme high or low pressure. •

The Average Rise and Fall of Tides
Source: National Ocean Survey (NOAA)

Places	Ft.	In.	Places	Ft.	In.	Places	Ft.	In.
Baltimore	1	1	Mobile, Ala.	1	6	San Diego, Calif.	4	1
Boston, Mass.	9	6	New London, Conn.	2	7	Sandy Hook, N.J.	4	7
Charleston, S.C.	5	2	Newport, R.I.	3	6	San Francisco, Calif.	4	0
Colon, Panama	1	1	New York, N.Y.	4	6	Savannah, Ga.	7	5
Eastport, Me.	18	2	Old Pt. Comfort, Va.	2	6	Seattle, Wash.	7	7
Galveston, Tex.	1	5	Philadelphia, Pa.	5	11	Tampa, Fla.	2	10
Halifax, N.S.	4	5	Portland, Me.	9	0	Vancouver, B.C.	10	6
Key West, Fla.	1	4	St. John's, Nfld.	2	7	Washington, D.C.	2	11

Wind Chill Table
Source: National Oceanic and Atmospheric Administration

Both temperature and wind cause heat loss from body surfaces. A combination of cold and wind makes a body feel colder than the actual temperature. The table shows, for example, that a temperature of 20 degrees Fahrenheit, plus a wind of 20 miles per hour, causes a body heat loss equal to that in minus 9 degrees with no wind. In other words, the wind makes 20 degrees feel like minus 9.

Top line of figures shows actual temperatures. Column at left shows wind speeds.

MPH	35	30	25	20	15	10	5	0	−5	−10	−15	−20	−25	−30	−35	−40	−45
5	33	27	21	16	12	7	1	−6	−11	−15	−20	−26	−31	−35	−41	−47	−52
10	21	16	8	2	−2	−9	−15	−22	−27	−34	−40	−45	−52	−58	−64	−70	−77
15	16	9	1	−6	−11	−18	−25	−31	−38	−45	−51	−58	−65	−72	−78	−85	−92
20	12	3	−4	−9	−17	−24	−32	−40	−46	−52	−60	−68	−74	−81	−88	−96	−103
25	7	0	−7	−15	−22	−29	−37	−45	−52	−58	−67	−75	−81	−89	−96	−104	−110
30	5	−2	−11	−18	−26	−33	−41	−49	−56	−63	−70	−78	−87	−94	−101	−109	−117
35	4	−4	−12	−20	−27	−35	−43	−52	−58	−67	−74	−83	−90	−98	−105	−113	−121
40	3	−4	−13	−21	−29	−36	−45	−54	−60	−69	−76	−84	−92	−101	−107	−116	−124
45	2	−6	−15	−23	−31	−38	−46	−54	−63	−70	−78	−85	−94	−101	−108	−118	−126
50	1	−7	−15	−23	−31	−38	−47	−56	−63	−70	−79	−87	−96	−103	−112	−120	−128

(Wind speeds greater than 50 mph have little additional chilling effect.)

National Weather Service Watches and Warnings

Source: National Weather Service, NOAA, Dept. of Commerce

National Weather Service forecasters issue a Tornado Watch for a specific area where it is reasonably possible that tornadoes may occur during the valid time of the watch. A Watch is to alert people to watch for tornado activity and listen for a Tornado Warning. A Tornado Warning means that a tornado has been sighted or indicated by radar, and that safety precautions should be taken at once. A Hurricane Watch means that an existing hurricane poses a threat to coastal and inland communities in the area specified by the Watch. A Hurricane Warning means hurricane force winds and/or dangerously high water and exceptionally high waves are expected in a specified coastal area within 24 hours.

Definitions

Tornado—A violent rotating column of air pendant from a thundercloud, usually recognized as a funnel-shaped vortex accompanied by a loud roar. With rotating winds est. up to 300 mph., it is the most destructive storm. Tornado paths have varied in length from a few feet to nearly 300 miles (avg. 5 mi.); diameter from a few feet to over a mile (average 220 yards); average forward speed, 25-40 mph.

Cyclone—An atmospheric circulation of winds rotating counterclockwise in the northern hemisphere and clockwise in the southern hemisphere. Tornadoes, hurricanes, and the Lows shown on weather maps are all examples of cyclones having various sizes and intensities. Cyclones are usually accompanied by precipitation or stormy weather.

Hurricane—A severe cyclone originating over tropical ocean waters and having winds 74 miles an hour or higher. (In the western Pacific, such storms are known as typhoons.) The area of strong winds takes the form of a circle or an oval, sometimes as much as 500 miles in diameter. In the lower latitudes hurricanes usually move toward the west or northwest at 10 to 15 mph. When the center approaches 25° to 30° North Latitude, direction of motion often changes to northeast, with increased forward speed.

Blizzard—A severe weather condition characterized by low temperatures and by strong winds bearing a great amount of snow (mostly fine, dry snow, picked up from the ground). The National Weather Service specifies, for blizzard, a wind of 35 miles an hour or higher, temperatures 20°F. or lower, and sufficient falling and/or blowing snow to reduce visibility to less than 1/4 of a mile. For "severe blizzard" wind speeds of 45 mph or more, temperature near or below 10°F., and visibility reduced by snow to near zero.

Monsoon—A name for seasonal winds (derived from Arabic "mausim," a season). It was first applied to the winds over the Arabian Sea, which blow for six months from northeast and six months from southwest, but it has been extended to similar winds in other parts of the world. The monsoons are strongest on the southern and eastern sides of Asia.

Flood—The condition that occurs when water overflows the natural or artificial confines of a stream or other body of water, or accumulates by drainage over low-lying areas.

National Weather Service Marine Warnings and Advisories

Source: National Weather Service, NOAA, Dept. of Commerce

Small Craft Advisory: A Small Craft Advisory alerts mariners to sustained (exceeding two hours) weather and/or sea conditions either present or forecast, potentially hazardous to small boats. Hazardous conditions may include winds of 18 to 33 knots and/or dangerous wave or inlet conditions. It is the responsibility of the mariner, based on his experience and size or type of boat, to determine if the conditions are hazardous. When a mariner becomes aware of a Small Craft Advisory, he should immediately obtain the latest marine forecast to determine the reason for the Advisory. The visual signal is a red pennant by day, a red over white light at night.

Gale Warning: Two red pennants displayed by day and a white light above a red light at night to indicate that winds within the range 34 to 47 knots are forecast for the area.

Storm Warning: A single square red flag with a black center displayed during daytime and two red lights at night to indicate that winds 48 knots and above, no matter how high the speed, are forecast for the area. However, if the winds are associated with a tropical cyclone (hurricane), the storm warning display indicates that winds within the range 48 to 63 knots are forecast.

Hurricane Warning: Displayed only in connection with a hurricane or typhoon. Two square red flags with black centers displayed by day and a white light between two red lights at night to indicate that winds 64 knots and above are forecast for the area.

Primary sources of dissemination are commercial radio, TV, U.S. Coast Guard Radio stations, and NOAA VHF-FM broadcasts. These broadcasts on 162.40 and 162.55 MHz can usually be received 20-40 miles from the transmitting antenna site, depending on terrain and quality of the receiver used. Where transmitting antennas are on high ground, the range is somewhat greater, reaching 60 miles or more.

The frequencies 162.55 and 162.40 MHz require narrow band FM receivers of +5 kilohertz deviation. In selecting a suitable receiver, special attention should be paid to the manufacturer's rating of the receiver's sensitivity. Generally speaking, a receiver with a sensitivity of one microvolt or less should pick up a broadcast at a distance of about 40-50 miles depending upon antenna height and terrain.

Dissemination is also made by means of visual displays (flags, pennants, and lights). These are indicated under each warning and advisory category.

Hurricane Names in 1977

The National Weather Service has used girls' names to identify hurricanes in the Atlantic, Caribbean, and Gulf of Mexico since 1953. A semi-permanent list of 10 sets of names in alphabetical order was established in 1971. Hurricane season begins June 1 and ends Nov. 30.

Names assigned to hurricanes: 1977 — Anita, Babe, Clara, Dorothy, Evelyn, Frieda, Grace, Hannah, Ida, Jodie, Kristina, Lois, Mary, Nora, Odel, Penny, Raquel, Sophia, Trudy, Virginia, and Willene.

Hurricanes and typhoons in the Eastern North Pacific are also identified by girls' names: 1977 — Ava, Bernice, Claudia, Doreen, Emily, Florence, Glenda, Heather, Irah, Jennifer, Katherine, Lillian, Mona, Natalie, Odessa, Prudence, Roslyn, Sylvia, Tillie, Victoria, and Wallie.

Monthly Normal Temperature and Precipitation

Source: National Climatic Center, NOAA, Dept. of Commerce

These normals are based on records for the 30-year period 1941 to 1970 inclusive. See explanation on page 796. For stations that did not have continuous records from the same instrument site for the entire 30 years, the means have been adjusted to the record at the present site.

AP indicates airport station; those not so marked are city office stations.

T, Temperature in Fahrenheit; P, precipitation in inches; L, less than .05 inch.

	Jan.		Feb.		Mar.		Apr.		May		June		July		Aug.		Sept.		Oct.		Nov.		Dec.	
Stations	T.	P.	T.	P.	T.	P.	T.	P.	T.	P.	T.	P.	T.	P.	T.	P.	T.	P.	T.	P.	T.	P.	T.	P.
Albany, N. Y. (AP)	22	2.2	24	2.1	33	2.6	47	2.7	58	3.3	68	3.0	72	3.1	70	2.9	62	3.1	51	2.6	40	2.8	26	2.9
Albuquerque, N. M. (AP)	35	0.3	40	0.4	46	0.5	56	0.5	65	0.5	75	0.5	79	1.4	77	1.3	70	0.8	58	0.8	45	0.3	36	0.5
Anchorage, Alaska (AP)	12	0.8	18	0.8	24	0.6	35	0.6	46	0.6	55	1.1	58	2.1	56	2.3	48	2.4	35	1.4	21	1.0	13	1.1
Asheville, N. C. (AP)	38	3.4	39	3.6	46	4.7	56	3.5	64	3.3	71	4.0	74	4.9	73	4.5	67	3.6	57	3.3	46	2.9	39	3.6
Atlanta, Ga. (AP)	42	4.3	45	4.4	51	5.8	61	4.6	69	3.7	76	3.7	78	4.9	78	3.5	72	3.2	62	2.5	51	3.4	44	4.2
Baltimore, Md. (AP)	42	2.9	44	2.8	53	3.7	65	3.1	75	3.6	83	3.8	87	4.1	85	4.2	79	3.1	68	2.8	56	3.1	44	3.3
Barrow, Alaska (AP)	-15	0.2	-19	0.2	-15	0.2	-1	0.2	19	0.2	33	0.4	39	0.9	38	1.0	30	0.6	15	0.6	-1	0.3	-12	0.2
Birmingham, Ala. (AP)	44	4.8	47	5.3	53	6.2	63	4.6	71	3.6	77	4.0	80	5.2	79	4.3	74	3.6	63	2.6	52	3.7	45	5.2
Bismarck, N. D. (AP)	8	0.5	14	0.4	25	0.7	43	1.4	54	2.2	64	3.6	71	2.2	69	2.0	58	1.3	47	0.8	29	0.6	16	0.5
Boise, Ida. (AP)	29	1.5	36	1.2	41	1.0	49	1.1	57	1.3	65	1.1	75	0.2	72	0.3	63	0.4	52	0.8	40	1.3	32	1.4
Boston, Mass. (AP)	29	3.7	30	3.5	38	4.0	49	3.5	59	3.5	68	3.2	73	2.7	71	3.5	65	3.2	55	3.0	45	4.5	33	4.2
Buffalo, N. Y. (AP)	24	2.9	24	2.6	32	2.9	45	3.2	55	3.0	66	2.2	70	2.9	68	3.5	62	3.3	52	3.0	40	3.7	28	3.0
Burlington, Vt. (AP)	17	1.7	19	1.7	29	1.9	43	2.6	55	3.0	65	3.5	70	3.5	67	3.7	59	3.1	49	2.7	37	2.9	23	2.2
Caribou, Me. (AP)	11	2.0	13	2.1	24	2.2	37	2.4	50	3.0	60	3.4	65	4.0	62	3.8	54	3.5	44	3.3	31	3.5	16	2.6
Charleston, S. C. (AP)	49	2.9	51	3.3	57	4.8	65	3.0	72	3.8	78	6.3	80	8.2	80	6.4	75	5.2	66	3.1	56	2.1	49	3.1
Chicago, Ill. (AP)	24	1.9	27	1.6	37	2.7	50	3.8	60	3.4	71	4.0	75	4.1	74	3.1	66	3.0	55	2.6	40	2.2	29	2.1
Cincinnati, Oh.	32	3.4	34	3.0	43	4.1	55	3.9	64	4.0	73	3.9	76	4.0	75	3.0	68	2.7	58	2.2	45	3.1	34	2.9
Cleveland, Oh. (AP)	27	2.6	28	2.2	36	3.1	48	3.5	58	3.5	68	3.3	71	3.5	70	3.0	64	2.8	54	2.6	42	2.8	30	2.4
Columbus, Oh. (AP)	28	2.9	30	2.3	39	3.4	51	3.7	61	4.1	70	4.1	74	4.2	72	2.9	65	2.4	54	1.9	42	2.7	31	2.4
Dallas, Tex. (AP)	45	2.0	49	2.6	56	3.0	66	4.7	74	4.9	82	3.3	86	1.8	86	2.4	78	3.3	68	3.2	56	2.6	48	2.3
Denver, Col. (AP)	30	0.6	33	0.7	37	1.2	48	1.9	57	2.6	66	1.9	73	1.8	72	1.3	63	1.1	52	1.1	39	0.8	33	0.4
Des Moines, Iowa (AP)	19	1.1	24	1.1	34	2.3	50	2.9	61	4.2	71	4.9	75	3.3	73	3.3	64	3.1	54	2.1	38	1.4	25	1.1
Detroit, Mich. (AP)	26	1.9	27	1.8	35	2.3	48	3.1	58	3.4	69	3.0	73	3.0	72	3.0	65	2.3	54	2.5	41	2.3	30	2.2
Dodge City, Kan. (AP)	31	0.5	35	0.6	41	1.1	54	1.7	64	3.1	74	3.3	79	3.1	78	2.6	69	1.7	58	1.7	43	0.6	33	8.5
Duluth, Minn. (AP)	9	1.2	12	0.9	24	1.8	39	2.6	49	3.4	59	4.4	66	3.7	64	3.8	54	3.1	45	2.3	28	1.7	14	1.4
Eureka, Cal.	47	7.4	48	5.2	48	4.8	50	3.0	53	2.1	55	0.7	56	0.1	57	0.3	57	0.7	54	3.2	52	5.8	49	6.6
Fairbanks, Alaska (AP)	-12	0.6	-3	0.5	10	0.5	29	0.3	47	0.7	59	1.4	61	1.9	55	2.2	44	1.1	25	0.7	3	0.7	-10	0.7
Ft. Worth, Tex. (AP)	45	1.8	49	2.4	55	2.5	65	4.3	73	4.5	81	3.1	85	1.8	85	2.3	78	3.2	68	2.7	56	2.0	48	1.8
Fresno, Cal. (AP)	45	1.8	50	1.7	54	1.6	60	1.2	67	0.3	74	0.1	81	L	78	L	74	0.1	64	0.4	54	1.2	46	1.7
Galveston, Tex.	54	3.0	56	2.7	61	2.6	69	2.6	76	3.2	81	4.1	83	4.4	83	4.4	80	5.6	73	2.8	64	3.2	57	3.7
Grand Junction, Col. (AP)	27	0.6	34	0.6	41	0.8	52	0.8	62	0.6	71	0.6	79	0.5	75	1.1	67	0.8	55	0.9	40	0.6	30	0.6
Gr. Rapids, Mich. (AP)	23	1.9	25	1.5	33	2.5	47	3.4	57	3.2	67	3.4	72	3.1	70	2.5	62	3.3	52	2.6	39	2.8	27	2.2
Helena, Mon. (AP)	18	0.6	25	0.4	31	0.7	43	0.9	52	1.8	59	2.4	68	1.0	66	1.0	56	1.0	45	0.6	32	0.6	23	0.6
Honolulu, Ha. (AP)	72	4.4	72	2.5	73	3.2	75	1.4	77	1.0	79	0.3	80	0.6	81	0.8	80	0.7	79	1.5	77	3.0	74	3.7
Houston, Tex. (AP)	52	3.6	55	3.5	61	2.7	69	3.5	76	5.1	81	4.5	83	4.1	83	4.4	79	4.7	71	4.1	61	4.0	55	4.0
Huron, S. D. (AP)	13	0.4	18	0.8	29	1.1	46	2.0	57	2.8	67	3.8	74	2.2	72	2.0	61	1.8	50	1.5	32	0.7	19	0.5
Indianapolis, Ind. (AP)	28	2.9	31	2.4	40	3.8	52	3.9	62	4.1	72	4.2	75	3.7	73	2.8	66	2.9	56	2.5	42	3.1	31	2.7
Jacksonville, Fla. (AP)	55	2.8	56	3.6	61	3.6	68	3.1	74	3.2	79	6.3	81	7.4	81	7.9	78	7.8	71	4.5	61	1.8	55	2.6
Juneau, Alaska (AP)	24	3.9	28	3.4	32	3.6	39	3.8	47	3.3	53	2.9	56	4.7	54	5.0	49	6.9	42	7.9	33	5.5	27	4.5
Kansas City, Mo. (AP)	28	1.3	33	1.3	41	2.6	55	3.5	65	4.3	74	5.6	79	4.4	77	3.8	69	4.2	59	3.2	44	1.5	32	1.5
Knoxville, Tenn. (AP)	41	4.7	43	4.7	50	4.9	60	3.6	68	3.3	76	3.6	78	4.7	77	3.2	72	2.8	61	2.7	49	3.6	42	4.5
Lander, Wy. (AP)	20	0.5	26	0.7	31	1.2	43	2.4	53	2.6	61	1.9	71	0.6	69	0.4	58	1.1	47	1.2	32	0.9	23	0.5
Little Rock, Ark. (AP)	40	4.2	43	4.4	50	4.9	62	5.3	70	5.3	78	3.5	81	3.4	81	3.0	73	3.6	62	3.0	50	3.9	42	4.1
Los Angeles, Cal.	57	3.0	48	2.8	59	2.2	62	1.3	65	0.1	68	L	73	L	74	L	73	0.2	68	0.3	63	2.0	58	2.2
Louisville, Ky. (AP)	33	3.5	36	3.5	44	5.1	56	4.1	65	4.2	73	4.1	77	3.8	76	3.0	69	2.9	58	2.4	45	3.3	36	3.3
Marquette, Mich.	18	1.5	20	1.5	27	1.9	40	2.6	50	2.9	60	3.4	66	3.1	66	3.0	57	3.5	49	2.4	34	3.0	24	2.0
Memphis, Tenn. (AP)	41	4.9	44	4.7	51	5.1	63	5.4	71	4.4	79	3.5	82	3.5	80	3.3	74	3.0	63	2.6	51	3.9	43	4.7
Miami, Fla. (AP)	67	2.2	68	2.0	71	2.1	75	3.6	78	6.1	81	9.0	82	6.9	83	6.7	82	8.7	78	8.2	72	2.7	68	1.6
Milwaukee, Wis. (AP)	19	1.6	23	1.1	31	2.2	45	2.8	54	2.9	65	3.6	70	3.4	69	2.7	61	3.0	51	2.0	37	2.0	24	1.8
Minneapolis, Minn. (AP)	12	0.7	17	0.8	28	1.7	45	2.0	57	3.4	67	3.9	72	3.7	70	3.1	60	2.7	50	1.8	32	1.2	19	0.9
Mobile, Ala. (AP)	51	4.7	54	4.8	59	7.1	68	5.6	75	4.5	80	6.1	82	8.9	82	6.9	78	6.6	69	2.6	59	3.4	53	5.9
Moline, Ill. (AP)	22	1.7	26	1.3	36	2.6	51	3.8	61	3.9	71	4.4	75	4.6	73	3.4	65	3.8	54	2.7	39	1.9	27	1.8
Nashville, Tenn. (AP)	38	4.8	41	4.4	49	5.0	60	4.1	69	4.1	77	3.4	80	3.8	79	3.2	72	3.1	61	2.2	48	3.5	40	4.5
Newark, N. J. (AP)	31	2.9	33	3.0	41	3.9	52	3.4	62	3.6	71	3.0	76	4.0	75	4.3	68	3.4	58	2.8	46	3.6	35	3.5
New Haven, Conn. (AP)	29	3.2	30	3.1	37	4.0	48	3.7	57	3.7	67	2.7	72	3.1	71	3.8	65	3.1	55	3.1	44	4.3	32	4.1
New Orleans, La. (AP)	53	4.5	56	4.8	61	5.5	69	4.2	75	4.2	80	4.7	82	6.7	82	5.3	78	5.6	70	2.3	60	3.9	55	5.1
New York City, N. Y.	32	2.9	33	3.1	41	4.0	52	3.6	62	3.4	72	2.9	77	3.9	75	4.5	68	3.2	58	3.0	47	3.8	35	3.6
Nome, Alaska (AP)	6	0.9	5	0.8	7	0.8	19	0.7	35	0.7	46	1.0	50	2.4	49	3.6	42	2.4	29	1.4	16	1.0	4	0.7
Norfolk, Va. (AP)	41	3.4	41	3.3	48	3.4	58	2.7	67	3.3	75	3.6	78	5.7	77	5.9	72	4.2	62	3.1	52	2.9	42	3.1
Okla. City, Okla. (AP)	37	1.1	41	1.3	48	2.1	60	3.5	68	5.2	77	4.2	82	2.7	81	2.6	73	3.6	62	2.6	49	1.4	40	1.3
Omaha, Neb. (AP)	23	0.8	28	1.0	37	1.6	52	3.0	63	4.1	72	4.9	77	3.7	76	4.0	66	3.3	56	1.9	40	1.1	28	0.8
Parkersburg, W. Va.	33	3.1	35	2.8	43	3.8	55	3.5	64	3.6	72	4.0	75	4.3	74	3.3	67	2.8	57	2.1	45	2.5	35	2.8
Philadelphia, Pa. (AP)	34	3.9	34	3.0	47	3.5	53	6.7	60	4.1	75	7.9	78	2.4	79	2.0	71	3.4	59	2.2	48	0.6	39	6.3
Phoenix, Ariz. (AP)	51	0.1	58	1.4	57	1.7	67	0.1	81	0.1	88	L	94	1.3	93	L	85	L	74	L	61	1.4	55	L
Pittsburgh, Pa. (AP)	30	2.0	29	1.8	48	3.9	49	4.7	56	5.9	71	3.1	73	2.2	73	3.4	67	3.6	56	4.5	44	2.7	33	2.2
Portland, Me. (AP)	23	2.6	23	2.6	38	2.6	46	9.9	51	6.3	64	4.9	71	1.7	71	3.5	58	2.2	49	3.4	38	2.4	34	9.6
Portland, Ore. (AP)	39	3.7	45	1.9	48	2.5	52	1.3	59	1.4	64	1.5	70	0.1	66	1.4	64	3.3	54	3.1	44	11.6	45	10.0
Providence, R. I. (AP)	28	3.5	29	3.5	37	4.0	47	3.7	57	3.5	66	2.7	72	2.9	70	3.9	63	3.3	54	3.3	43	4.5	32	4.1
Raleigh, N. C. (AP)	41	3.2	42	3.3	49	3.4	60	3.1	67	3.3	74	3.7	78	5.1	77	4.9	71	3.8	60	2.8	50	2.8	41	3.1
Rapid City, S. D. (AP)	22	0.5	26	0.6	31	1.0	45	2.1	55	2.8	64	3.7	73	2.1	72	1.5	61	1.2	50	0.9	35	0.5	27	0.4
Reno, Nev. (AP)	32	1.2	37	0.9	40	0.7	47	0.5	55	0.7	62	0.4	69	0.3	67	0.2	60	0.2	50	0.4	40	0.7	33	1.1
Richmond, Va. (AP)	38	2.9	39	3.0	47	3.4	58	2.8	67	3.4	74	3.5	78	5.6	76	5.1	70	3.6	59	2.9	49	3.2	39	3.2
St. Louis, Mo. (AP)	31	1.9	35	2.1	43	3.0	57	3.9	66	3.9	75	4.4	79	3.7	77	2.9	70	2.9	59	2.8	45	2.5	35	2.0
Salt Lake City, Ut. (AP)	20	1.5	32	0.9	42	2.7	48	1.6	62	1.7	70	0.2	77	1.1	77	1.2	62	4.1	54	0.7	41	2.5	33	2.3
San Antonio, Tex. (AP)	51	1.7	55	2.1	61	1.5	70	2.5	76	3.1	82	2.8	84	1.7	85	2.4	79	3.7	71	2.8	60	1.8	53	1.5
San Diego, Cal. (AP)	56	1.7	60	1.6	58	2.3	62	0.1	63	L	68	L	69	L	71	L	69	L	67	L	61	1.6	58	0.2
San Francisco, Cal. (AP)	48	4.4	51	3.0	53	2.5	55	1.6	58	0.4	62	0.1	63	L	63	0.0	64	0.2	61	1.0	55	2.3	50	4.0
San Juan, P. R. (AP)	75	3.7	75	2.5	76	2.0	78	3.4	79	6.5	81	5.6	81	6.4	81	7.0	81	6.1	81	5.6	79	5.5	77	4.7
Sault Ste. Marie, Mich.	14	1.9	15	1.5	24	1.7	38	2.2	49	3.0	59	3.3	64	2.6	63	3.1	55	3.9	46	2.9	33	3.3	20	2.4
Savannah, Ga. (AP)	50	2.9	52	2.9	58	4.4	66	2.9	73	4.2	79	5.9	81	7.9	81	6.5	76	5.6	67	2.8	57	1.9	50	3.3
Sea.-Tac. Wash. (AP)	38	5.8	42	4.2	44	3.6	49	2.5	55	1.7	60	1.5	65	0.7	64	1.1	60	2.0	52	3.9	45	5.9	41	5.9
Spokane, Wash. (AP)	25	2.5	32	1.7	38	1.5	46	1.1	55	1.5	62	1.4	70	0.4	68	0.6	60	0.8	48	1.4	36	2.2	29	2.4
Springfield, Mo. (AP)	33	1.7	37	2.2	44	3.0	57	4.3	65	4.9	74	4.7	78	3.6	77	2.9	69	4.1	59	3.4	46	2.3	36	2.5
Syracuse, N. Y. (AP)	24	2.7	25	2.8	33	3.0	47	3.1	57	3.0	67	3.1	72	3.1	70	3.5	63	2.7	53	3.1	41	3.3	28	3.1
Tampa, Fla. (AP)	60	2.3	62	2.9	66	3.9	72	2.1	77	2.4	81	6.5	82	8.4	82	8.0	81	6.4	75	2.5	67	1.8	62	2.2
Trenton, N.J.	32	2.8	33	2.7	41	3.8	52	3.2	62	3.4	71	3.2	76	4.7	74	4.2	67	3.2	57	2.5	46	3.3	35	3.3
Vicksburg, Miss.	48	4.9	51	5.3	57	0.5	66	5.4	73	4.2	79	3.3	82	3.6	81	3.0	76	2.8	67	2.3	56	4.1	50	5.5
Washington, D. C. (AP)	36	2.6	37	2.5	45	3.3	56	2.9	66	3.7	75	3.5	79	4.1	77	4.7	71	3.1	60	2.7	48	2.9	37	3.0
Wilmington, Del. (AP)	32	2.9	34	2.8	42	3.7	52	3.2	62	3.4	71	3.2	76	4.3	74	4.0	68	3.4	57	2.6	46	3.5	35	3.3

Annual Climatological Data

Source: National Oceanic & Atmospheric Administration, National Climatic Center

Station 1975	Elev. ft.	Highest	Date	Lowest	Date	Total (in.)	Greatest in 24 hrs.	Date	Total (in.)	Greatest in 24 hrs.	Date	Fastest MPH	Date	Clear*	Cloudy*	Prec .01 in. or more	Snow, sleet 1 in. or more
Albany, N.Y.	275	97	8/3	-17	2/10	47.05	2.29	10/17-18	59.9	8.8	12/20-21	45	1/30	61	192	152	19
Albuquerque, N.M.	5311	97	8/8	1	1/4	8.01	0.74	9/3-4	14.7	4.1	2/21-22	56	2/22	184	83	54	5
Anchorage, Alaska	114	78	7/9	-34	1/5	13.04	1.76	9/10-11	59.4	5.5	4/26	35	12/16	69	239	121	22
Asheville, N.C.	2140	92	9/4	8	12/19	56.92	3.41	9/23	13.8	5.0	11/23	40	1/1	93	152	126	4
Atlanta, Ga.	1010	96	9/4	13	12/19	66.00	2.25	4/2-3	0.6	0.6	11/23	49	12/31	98	181	145	0
Baltimore, Md.	148	99	8/26	13	1/15	51.82	3.45	7/13	12.5	4.4	2/4	50	4/3	81	172	126	5
Barrow, Alaska	31	64	7/7	-53	1/3	4.83	0.51	7/10	21.8	1.9	4/13-14	32	2/7	58	193	106	7
Birmingham, Ala.	620	96	9/4	14	12/19	55.27	3.15	1/24-25	T	T	12/18	49	1/10	66	191	135	0
Bismarck, N.D.	1647	106	7/28	-27	12/17	21.50	1.89	7/31	59.0	9.5	3/26	54	1/11	81	175	115	13
Boise, Ida.	2838	108	7/27	-5	1/2	13.69	0.64	2/12-13	25.5	3.2	1/9-10	42	7/29	109	170	102	11
Boston, Mass.	15	102	8/2	4	12/24	45.79	2.58	11/12-13	41.4	11.6	12/20-21	40	1/29	109	167	125	8
Buffalo, N.Y.	705	92	8/2	-4	12/24	38.53	3.57	8/29-30	82.7	6.8	4/4-5	47	2/26	46	225	168	23
Burlington, Vt.	332	99	8/2	-16	12/20	32.51	1.39	7/14-15	83.8	8.9	12/25-26	42	4/19	61	215	159	27
Charleston, S.C.	40	96	5/25	21	12/19	56.19	3.43	8/7-8	0.0	0.0	. . .	44	4/3	102	185	134	0
Charleston, W. Va.	939	96	8/1	2	2/10	50.99	1.91	8/14	32.7	12.6	1/12-13	35	6/5	62	198	160	10
Chicago, Ill.	607	94	8/11	-6	2/9	42.05	3.83	4/18	53.3	9.6	4/2-3	43	11/30	80	190	145	14
Cincinnati, Oh.	869	94	8/13	6	1/13	44.23	2.25	10/17-18	16.6	3.9	3/10	35	3/24	78	190	142	3
Cleveland, Oh.	777	95	8/2	-8	2/10	40.81	2.13	8/24-25	54.7	8.1	3/14	45	4/19	63	212	170	17
Columbus, Oh.	812	96	8/2	0	2/10	39.04	2.15	2/23	18.4	2.5	1/19	37	6/15	67	186	151	7
Concord, N.H.	342	101	8/2	-25	2/10	42.28	2.44	9/26-27	74.1	9.3	2/5-6	40	1/30	88	166	128	20
Dallas, Tex.	551	100	9/18	17	1/13	29.10	3.76	7/24-25	4.1	3.7	2/23	39	2/4	132	113	75	1
Denver, Col.	5283	95	8/7	-11	2/6	15.51	1.56	8/12-13	64.1	8.3	3/31-41	45	12/27	134	116	91	21
Des Moines, Ia.	938	99	8/23	-14	2/9	31.61	6.18	8/27	48.8	5.9	1/2-3	42	1/11	104	168	104	15
Detroit, Mich.	633	95	8/1	-6	2/10	34.59	3.06	8/29-30	46.8	6.3	12/25-26	52	3/24	82	181	149	14
Dodge City, Kan.	2582	103	8/31	-2	1/12	18.83	1.57	7/6	16.4	3.4	2/16	56	11/20	155	111	71	8
Duluth, Minn.	1428	93	7/29	-24	1/12	29.41	1.82	11/19-20	109.3	14.0	11/19-20	54	3/23	78	179	142	27
Fairbanks, Alaska	436	94	7/11	-57	1/6	8.46	0.99	7/20-21	57.6	8.2	1/27	30	9/18	66	210	104	19
Fresno, Cal.	328	106	7/26	23	12/31	6.33	0.73	10/30	0.0	0.0	. . .	31	10/22	209	74	46	0
Galveston, Tex.	7	93	7/28	29	1/13	48.54	7.71	5/29-30	0.0	0.0	. . .	45	2/23	N/A	N/A	94	7
Grand Rapids, Mich.	784	93	8/1	-3	2/10	41.25	2.25	6/14-15	73.0	9.8	4/2-3	66	11/10	64	218	154	27
Helena, Mont.	3828	96	7/27	-24	2/6	20.94	1.63	7/30-31	68.9	11.1	1/25-26	65	7/3	73	209	125	21
Honolulu, Ha.	7	90	9/2	56	12/9	24.39	5.49	11/24-25	0.0	0.0	. . .	36	1/31	70	91	82	0
Houston, Tex.	96	96	9/3	21	1/13	50.97	3.75	10/25-26	T	T	1/12	30	5/9	95	168	112	0
Huron, S.D.	1281	109	7/28	-19	2/9	18.38	1.60	6/8-9	72.7	17.6	3/23-24	54	7/31	117	153	93	15
Indianapolis, Ind.	792	91	8/23	-4	2/10	46.72	3.73	6/25	34.8	5.3	3/14	49	5/26	83	189	140	11
Jackson, Miss.	310	95	7/21	17	12/19	70.23	6.90	10/15-16	T	T	12/24	36	5/29	100	150	134	0
Jacksonville, Fla.	26	95	8/24	23	12/19	50.15	5.40	5/27	T	T	3/4	62	5/27	88	155	139	0
Juneau, Alaska	12	90	7/7	-10	2/13	46.32	1.55	7/2-3	170.2	20.1	1/12-13	41	2/23	35	299	223	40
Kansas City, Mo.	1014	103	8/11	-2	2/9	34.07	4.69	4/23-24	28.1	6.1	11/25-26	41	12/14	133	144	97	8
Lander, Wy.	5563	94	8/5	-18	1/12	14.01	1.61	5/20-21	160.7	20.8	5/20-21	47	9/1	109	129	82	31
Little Rock, Ark.	257	98	9/2	14	12/18	45.08	2.37	5/27-28	5.4	2.4	3/13	46	5/20	122	153	119	3
Los Angeles, Cal.	97	104	9/23	37	1/29	7.32	1.77	2/2-3	0.0	0.0	. . .	46	5/25	151	93	29	0
Louisville, Ky.	477	94	9/3	12	12/19	56.31	3.54	4/24-25	15.1	6.4	3/9-10	42	1/25	69	185	141	5
Marquette, Mich.	677	96	8/1	-10	2/9	30.79	1.95	5/19	124.9	15.3	2/24-25	45	1/11	71	203	151	30
Memphis, Tenn.	258	98	9/3	17	1/13	58.68	5.95	3/11-12	5.9	3.9	1/12	35	1/8	111	161	121	1
Miami, Fla.	7	93	4/4	42	12/22	39.10	2.84	10/18-19	0.0	0.0	. . .	35	7/4	70	100	134	0
Milford, Ut.	5028	98	7/8	-13	1/3	9.12	1.00	5/19-20	60.9	8.6	5/19-20	52	5/4	158	107	76	22
Milwaukee, Wis.	672	92	8/19	-9	2/9	29.15	1.95	4/27-28	61.8	10.2	4/2	54	1/11	75	195	137	15
Minneapolis, Minn.	834	98	7/29	-22	2/9	35.15	2.65	6/11-12	78.7	8.4	11/20-21	50	7/23	80	193	125	27
Mobile, Ala.	211	95	7/5	22	12/19	86.58	7.02	11/6-7	0.1	0.0	. . .	35	4/30	80	168	155	0
Moline, Ill.	582	98	8/12	-8	1/20	28.95	1.65	7/23	57.7	10.1	2/23-24	43	12/14	104	176	130	13
Nashville, Tenn.	590	94	9/3	11	12/19	60.58	4.66	3/12	4.2	3.9	1/12	42	1/10	86	169	119	1
New Orleans, La.	4	94	5/27	25	1/14	80.50	8.72	11/5-6	0.0	0.0	. . .	46	1/10	85	165	132	0
New York, N.Y.	132	98	8/2	15	1/21	61.21	87	9/24-25	15.2	7.8	2/12	30	4/3	N/A	N/A	132	4
Nome, Alaska	13	76	7/14	-44	3/22	13.24	1.67	7/9-10	73.1	9.0	2/3-4	40	12/30	103	198	113	26
Norfolk, Va.	24	96	8/26	19	12/20	50.53	3.63	7/16	1.1	0.8	3/2	43	3/24	102	163	124	0
Oklahoma City, Okla.	1285	96	8/31	7	12/18	35.25	2.92	7/24	6.2	2.8	12/24-25	49	1/19	151	116	87	1
Omaha, Neb.	977	103	9/1	-19	2/9	23.98	1.59	9/4-5	51.2	12.1	1/10	44	11/20	124	134	107	14
Philadelphia, Pa.	5	99	8/2	13	2/10	52.13	2.78	7/13-14	13.9	4.6	2/4-5	47	4/3	81	173	120	6
Phoenix, Ariz.	1112	116	8/4	27	1/5	4.51	0.79	9/7	0.0	0.0	. . .	55	11/28	248	49	24	0
Pittsburgh, Pa.	1137	96	8/2	-3	2/10	46.42	2.40	7/8-9	40.6	5.4	3/14	47	1/25	69	199	168	12
Portland, Me.	43	103	8/2	-20	12/20	48.72	2.79	12/25-26	63.9	9.0	12/17-18	41	4/20	93	177	138	18
Portland, Ore.	21	95	7/26	26	12/18	39.06	2.01	1/12-13	0.1	0.1	2/1	37	1/31	70	233	164	0
Providence, R.I.	51	104	8/2	-4	12/24	50.83	3.13	11/12-13	31.3	7.9	2/12-13	39	2/25	79	171	132	9
Raleigh, N.C.	434	97	8/25	10	12/19	46.83	3.73	11/12-13	3.2	2.6	11/23	35	3/24	96	159	114	1
Rapid City, S.D.	3162	105	8/7	-20	2/9	17.46	1.69	6/18	79.4	9.8	12/31	57	6/9	117	142	99	22
Reno, Nev.	4404	103	7/26	-8	1/2	6.95	0.91	9/9-10	42.5	6.8	2/4	66	2/12	160	116	54	13
Richmond, Va.	164	99	8/26	13	12/19	61.31	3.16	7/11-12	6.0	2.7	1/20	40	1/1	82	176	132	2
Rochester, N.Y.	547	95	8/1	-4	12/20	30.60	1.39	9/25-26	89.9	6.7	12/9-10	56	4/19	55	222	165	26
St. Louis, Mo.	535	101	8/12	0	2/9	40.21	2.43	1/9-10	34.0	7.8	2/23-24	41	8/25	105	151	119	9
Salt Lake City, Ut.	4220	100	6/6	1	12/31	17.92	1.12	4/25-26	93.7	8.8	4/25-26	39	6/2	113	153	105	26
San Antonio, Tex.	788	96	7/29	15	1/13	25.67	2.27	5/23-24	T	T	1/12	46	5/8	110	135	74	0
San Diego, Cal.	13	103	9/23	40	1/3	8.37	1.73	3/5-6	0.0	0.0	. . .	30	11/28	156	103	37	0
San Francisco, Cal.	8	94	5/29	30	1/30	17.25	1.86	3/21	T	T	1/31	41	1/31	183	103	65	0
San Juan, P.R.	13	96	6/8	66	1/8	51.26	3.44	9/15-16	0.0	0.0	. . .	44	7/19	64	73	206	0
Sault Ste. Marie, Mich.	721	97	7/31	-22	1/12	33.88	1.62	6/16-17	115.9	8.5	3/24	40	11/10	66	206	163	37
Savannah, Ga.	46	95	8/24	19	12/19	51.18	3.50	9/7-8	0.0	0.0	. . .	36	1/25	99	183	125	9
Seattle, Wash.	400	90	7/5	22	11/29	44.48	1.81	12/1-2	5.7	2.6	12/12	41	1/8	61	236	164	1
Sioux City, Ia.	1095	98	7/5	-24	2/9	26.31	1.78	6/18	37.9	7.5	1/10-11	47	11/12	108	157	101	11
Spokane, Wash.	2356	102	7/10	-10	1/11	21.27	0.86	7/12-13	94.3	8.9	2/6-7	48	12/2	81	197	132	32
Springfield, Mo.	1268	98	7/6	3	2/9	53.94	4.83	6/9-10	35.2	11.9	2/23	45	5/20	130	135	115	6
Syracuse, N.Y.	410	92	8/2	-8	12/24	51.90	4.14	9/25-26	101.5	7.1	4/4	44	4/19	52	211	164	32
Tampa, Fla.	19	98	8/22	30	12/19	43.44	3.13	6/18	0.0	0.0	. . .	29	10/31	99	137	112	0
Trenton, N.J.	56	98	8/3	11	1/21	59.41	6.11	7/20-21	16.7	4.1	2/12	47	4/4	90	171	131	6
Washington, D.C.	10	98	8/3	17	12/19	50.50	5.31	9/25-26	13.1	4.2	2/4-5	43	4/4	80	175	125	4
Williston, N.D.	1899	104	7/28	-27	12/17	18.86	1.91	6/8-9	78.8	9.3	3/27-28	43	10/4	85	186	111	20
Wilmington, Del.	74	97	8/2	10	2/10	49.61	2.71	7/12-13	11.3	3.9	2/4-5	43	4/3	78	180	131	4

*To get partly cloudy days deduct the total of clear and cloudy days from 365 (1 yr.). T—trace. (1) Date shown is the starting date of the storm (in some cases it lasted more than one day).

Normal Temperatures, Highs, Lows, Precipitation

Source: National Climatic Center, NOAA, Dept. of Commerce

These normals are based on records for the thirty-year period 1941-1970. (See explanation on page 796.) The extreme temperatures (thru 1975) are listed for the stations shown and may not agree with the state's records shown on page 794.

AP indicates airport station; those not so marked are city office stations. The minus (—) sign indicates temperatures below zero. Fahrenheit thermometer registration.

State	Station	Normal temperature January Max.	January Min.	July Max.	July Min.	Extreme temperature Highest	Lowest	Normal annual precipitation (inches)
Alabama	Mobile (AP)	61	41	91	73	102	8	66.98
Alabama	Montgomery (AP)	59	38	92	72	102	5	50.69
Alaska	Juneau (AP)	29	18	64	48	86	—22	54.67
Arizona	Phoenix (AP)	65	38	105	78	116	19	7.05
Arkansas	Little Rock (AP)	50	29	93	70	108	—4	48.52
California	Los Angeles	67	47	83	64	110	28	14.05
California	San Francisco (AP)	55	41	71	54	106	24	19.53
Colorado	Denver (AP)	44	16	87	59	103	—25	15.51
Connecticut	*New Haven (AP)	37	22	81	63	100	—8	46.02
Delaware	Wilmington (AP)	40	24	86	66	102	—4	40.25
Dist. of Col.	Washington (AP)	44	28	88	69	101	3	38.89
Florida	Jacksonville (AP)	65	45	90	72	105	12	54.47
Florida	Key West (AP)	74	65	87	79	95	46	39.99
Florida	Miami (AP)	76	59	89	76	96	34	59.80
Georgia	Atlanta (AP)	51	33	87	69	98	—3	48.34
Hawaii	Honolulu (AP)	79	65	87	73	92	53	22.90
Idaho	Boise (AP)	36	21	91	59	111	—23	11.50
Illinois	Chicago (AP) Midway	32	17	84	65	101	—16	34.44
Indiana	Indianapolis (AP)	36	20	85	65	99	—20	38.74
Iowa	Des Moines (AP)	28	11	85	65	104	—24	30.85
Iowa	Dubuque (AP)	27	11	84	62	97	—28	35.71
Kansas	*Wichita (AP)	42	22	92	69	113	—12	28.41
Kentucky	Louisville (AP)	42	25	87	66	101	—20	43.11
Louisiana	New Orleans (AP)	62	44	90	73	100	14	56.77
Maine	Portland (AP)	31	12	79	57	100	—39	40.80
Maryland	Baltimore (AP)	42	25	87	66	102	—7	40.46
Massachusetts	Boston (AP)	36	23	81	65	99	—4	42.52
Michigan	Detroit (AP) City	32	19	83	63	105	—16	30.96
Michigan	Sault Ste. Marie	22	6	75	53	98	—28	31.70
Minnesota	Minn.-St. Paul (AP)	21	3	82	61	101	—34	25.94
Mississippi	**Vicksburg	57	41	90	73	101	2	49.50
Missouri	St. Louis (AP)	40	23	88	69	106	—11	35.89
Montana	Helena (AP)	28	8	84	52	105	—38	11.38
Nebraska	Omaha (AP)	33	12	89	66	110	—22	30.18
Nevada	Winnemucca (AP)	40	15	92	50	106	—34	8.63
New Hampshire	Concord (AP)	31	10	83	57	102	—29	36.17
New Jersey	Atlantic City (AP)	43	27	84	66	106	—8	42.36
New Mexico	Albuquerque (AP)	47	24	92	65	105	—17	7.77
New Mexico	Roswell (AP)	55	21	95	62	110	—8	11.62
New York	Albany (AP)	30	13	84	60	98	—28	33.36
New York	New York (AP) La Guardia	38	26	84	69	107	—2	41.61
No. Carolina	Charlotte (AP)	51	34	89	70	100	2	43.38
No. Carolina	Raleigh (AP)	51	30	88	67	98	0	42.54
No. Dakota	Bismarck (AP)	19	—3	84	57	109	—43	16.16
Ohio	Cincinnati (AP) Abbe.	40	24	87	66	109	—17	40.03
Ohio	Cleveland (AP)	33	20	82	61	98	—19	34.99
Oklahoma	Oklahoma City (AP)	48	26	93	70	108	—1	31.37
Oregon	Portland	44	33	79	55	107	—3	37.61
Pennsylvania	Harrisburg (AP)	39	24	87	65	107	—8	37.65
Pennsylvania	Philadelphia (AP)	40	24	87	67	104	—5	39.93
Rhode Island	Block Island (AP)	38	26	76	63	91	—4	40.45
So. Carolina	Charleston (AP)	60	37	89	71	103	8	52.12
So. Dakota	Huron (AP)	23	2	87	61	112	—39	19.44
So. Dakota	Rapid City (AP)	34	10	86	59	110	—27	17.12
Tennessee	Nashville (AP)	48	29	90	69	103	—6	46.00
Texas	Amarillo (AP)	50	24	94	67	104	—9	19.67
Texas	Galveston	59	48	87	79	101	8	42.20
Texas	Houston (AP)	63	42	94	73	101	19	48.19
Utah	Salt Lake City (AP)	37	18	93	61	107	—18	15.17
Vermont	Burlington (AP)	26	8	81	59	98	—27	32.54
Virginia	Norfolk (AP)	49	32	87	70	103	8	44.68
Washington	Seattle-Tacoma (AP)	43	33	75	54	99	6	38.79
Washington	Spokane (AP)	31	20	84	55	108	—25	17.42
West Virginia	Parkersburg	41	24	86	65	106	—27	38.44
Wisconsin	Madison (AP)	26	9	82	60	98	—30	30.16
Wisconsin	Milwaukee (AP)	27	11	80	59	99	—24	29.07
Wyoming	Cheyenne (AP)	37	14	85	55	98	—27	15.06
Puerto Rico	San Juan (AP)	81	67	87	74	96	60	64.21

*Closed June 14,1969.   **Closed December 1966.

Mean Annual Snowfall (inches) based on record thru 1972: Boston, Mass. 42.8, Sault Ste. Marie, Mich., 108.2, Albany, N.Y., 67.3, Rochester, N.Y., 86.3, Burlington, Vt., 79, Cheyenne, Who., 51.7, Juneau, Alaska, 106.3.

Wettest Spot: Mount Waialeale, Hawaii, on the island of Kauai, is the rainiest place in the world, according to the National Geographic Society, with an average annual rainfall of 460 inches.

Highest Temperature: A temperature of 136° F. observed at Azizia, Tripolitania in Northern Africa on Sept. 13, 1922, is generally accepted as the world's highest temperature recorded under standard conditions.

The record high in the United States was 134° in Death Valley, Calif., July 10, 1913.

Lowest Temperature: A record low temperature of —126.9° F. (—88.3° C.) was recorded at the Soviet Antarctic staton Vostok on Aug. 24, 1960.

The record low in the United States was —80° at Prospect Creek, Alaska, Jan. 23, 1971.

The lowest official temperature on the North American continent was recorded at 81 degrees below zero in February, 1947, at a lonely airport in the Yukon called Snag.

These are the meteorological champions—the official temperature extremes—but there are plenty of other claimants to thermometer fame. However, sun readings are unofficial records, since meteorological data to qualify officially must be taken on instruments in a sheltered and ventilated location.

Record Temperatures by States Through 1975

State	Lowest °F	Highest	Latest Date	Location	Approximate Elevation in Feet
Alabama	-27		Jan. 30, 1966	New Market	725
		112	Sept. 5, 1925	Centerville	345
Alaska	-79.8		Jan. 23, 1971	Prospect Creek Camp	1,100
		100	Jun. 27, 1915	Fort Yukon	*419
Arizona	-40		Jan. 7, 1971	Hawley Lake	8,180
		127	Jul. 7, 1905	Parker	345
Arkansas	-29		Feb. 13, 1905	Pond	1,250
		120	Aug. 10, 1936	Ozark	396
California	-45		Jan. 20, 1937	Boca	5,532
		134	Jul. 10, 1913	Greenland Ranch	-178
Colorado	-60		Feb. 1, 1951	Taylor Park	9,206
		118	Jul. 11, 1888	Bennett	5,484
Connecticut	-32		Jan. 22, 1961	Coventry	480
		105	Jul. 22, 1926	Waterbury	409
Delaware	-17		Jan. 17, 1893	Millsboro	535
		110	Jul. 21, 1930	Millsboro	20
Dist. of Col.	-15		Feb. 11, 1899	Washington	112
		106	Jul. 20, 1930	Washington	112
Florida	-2		Feb. 13, 1899	Tallahassee	193
		109	Jun. 29, 1931	Monticello	207
Georgia	-17		Jan. 27, 1940	CCC Camp F-16	1,000
		112	Jul. 24, 1952	Louisville	337
Hawaii	18		Feb. 20, 1962	Mauna Loa Slope Obs.	11,146
		100	Apr. 27, 1931	Pahala	850
Idaho	-60		Jan. 18, 1943	Island Park Dam	6,285
		118	Jul. 28, 1934	Orofino	1,027
Illinois	-35		Jan. 22, 1930	Mount Carroll	817
		117	Jul. 14, 1954	E. St. Louis	410
Indiana	-35		Feb. 2, 1951	Greensburg	954
		116	Jul. 14, 1936	Collegeville	672
Iowa	-47		Jan. 12, 1912	Washta	1,157
		118	Jul. 20, 1934	Keokuk	614
Kansas	-40		Feb. 13, 1905	Lebanon	1,812
		121	Jul. 24, 1936	Alton (near)	1,651
Kentucky	-34		Jan. 24, 1963	Bonnieville (closed Oct. 1966)	730
	-34		Jan. 28, 1963	Cynthiana	719
		114	Jul. 28, 1930	Greensburg	581
Louisiana	-16		Feb. 13, 1899	Minden	194
		114	Aug. 10, 1936	Plain Dealing	268
Maine	-48		Jan. 19, 1925	Van Buren	510
		105	Jul. 10, 1911	North Bridgton	450
Maryland	-40		Jan. 13, 1912	Oakland	2,461
		109	Jul. 10, 1936	Cumberland and Frederick	623-325
Massachusetts	-34		Jan. 18, 1957	Birch Hill Dam	840
		106	Jul. 4, 1911	Lawrence	51
Michigan	-51		Feb. 9, 1934	Vanderbilt	785
		112	Jul. 13, 1936	Mio	963
Minnesota	-59		Feb. 16, 1903	Pokegama Dam	1,280
		114	Jul. 6, 1936	Moorhead	940
Mississippi	-19		Jan. 30, 1966	Corinth	420
		115	Jul. 29, 1930	Holly Springs	600
Missouri	-40		Feb. 13, 1905	Warsaw	700
		118	Jul. 14, 1954	Warsaw	687
Montana	-70		Jan. 20, 1954	Rogers Pass	5,470
		117	Jul. 5, 1937	Medicine Lake	1,950
Nebraska	-47		Feb. 12, 1899	Camp Clarke	3,700
		118	Jul. 24, 1936	Minden	2,169
Nevada	-50		Jan. 8, 1937	San Jacinto	5,200
		122	Jun. 23, 1954	Overton	1,240
New Hampshire	-46		Jan. 8, 1968	Mt. Washington	6,262
		106	Jul. 4, 1911	Nashua	125
New Jersey	-34		Jan. 5, 1904	River Vale	70
		110	Jul. 10, 1936	Runyon	18
New Mexico	-50		Feb. 1, 1951	Gavilan	7,350
		116	Jul. 14, 1934	Orogrande	4,171
New York	-52		Feb. 9, 1934	Stillwater Reservoir	1,670
		108	Jul. 22, 1926	Troy	35
North Carolina	-29		Jan. 30, 1966	Mt. Mitchell	6,525
		109	Sept. 7, 1954	Weldon	81
North Dakota	-60		Feb. 15, 1936	Parshall	1,929
		121	Jul. 6, 1936	Steele	1,857
Ohio	-39		Feb. 10, 1899	Milligan	800
		113	Jul. 21, 1934	Gallipolis (near)	673
Oklahoma	-27		Jan. 18, 1930	Watts	958
		120	Jul. 26, 1943	Tishomingo	670
Oregon	-54		Feb. 10, 1933	Seneca	4,700
		119	Aug. 10, 1898	Pendleton	1,074
Pennsylvania	-42		Jan. 5, 1904	Smethport	1,469
		111	Jul. 10, 1936	Phoenixville	100
Rhode Island	-23		Jan. 11, 1942	Kingston	100
		102	Jul. 30, 1949	Greenville	420
South Carolina	-13		Jan. 26, 1940	Longcreek (near)	1,631
		111	Jun. 28, 1954	Camden	170
South Dakota	-58		Feb. 17, 1936	McIntosh	2,277
		120	Jul. 5, 1936	Gannvalley	1,750
Tennessee	-32		Dec. 30, 1917	Mountain City	2,471
		113	Aug. 9, 1930	Perryville	377

State	Lowest °F	Highest	Latest Date	Station	Approximate Elevation
Texas	-23		Feb. 8, 1933	Seminole	3,275
		120	Aug. 12, 1936	Seymour	1,291
Utah	-50		Jan. 5, 1913	Strawberry Tunnel	7,650
		116	June 28, 1892	Saint George	2,880
Vermont	-50		Dec. 30, 1933	Bloomfield	915
		105	July 4, 1911	Vernon	310
Virginia	-29		Feb. 10, 1899	Monterey	3,008
		110	July 15, 1954	Balcony Falls	725
Washington	-48		Dec. 30, 1968	Mazama	2,120
	-48		Dec. 30, 1968	Winthrop	1,755
		118	Aug. 5, 1961	Ice Harbor Dam	475
West Virginia	-37		Dec. 30, 1917	Lewisburg	2,200
		112	July 10, 1936	Martinsburg	435
Wisconsin	-54		Jan. 24, 1922	Danbury	908
		114	July 13, 1936	Wisconsin Dells	900
Wyoming	-63		Feb. 9, 1933	Moran	6,770
		114	July 12, 1900	Basin	3,500

Canadian Normal Temperatures, Highs, Lows, Precipitation

Source: Atmospheric Environment Service, Dept. of Environment

These normals are based on varying periods of record over the thirty-year period 1941 to 1970 inclusive. Extreme temperatures are based on varying periods of record for each station thru 1970. AP indicates airport station; those not so marked are city office stations. The minus (—) sign indicates temperatures below zero. Fahrenheit thermometer registration.

Province	Station	Normal January Max.	Normal January Min.	Normal July Max.	Normal July Min.	Extreme Highest	Extreme Lowest	Precipitation Normal Annual (inches)
Alberta	Calgary (AP)	23	2	74	49	97	-49	17.21
Alberta	Edmonton (Industrial AP)	14	3	74	53	94	-55	17.58
British Columbia	Prince George (AP)	19	2	72	46	94	-58	24.43
British Columbia	Victoria (AP)	43	32	71	52	97	4	33.72
British Columbia	Vancouver (AP)	41	31	72	55	92	0	42.05
Manitoba	Churchill (AP)	-11	-25	63	45	91	-49	15.61
Manitoba	Winnipeg (AP)	8	-10	79	56	105	-49	21.06
Newfoundland	Gander (AP)	28	14	71	52	96	-17	42.45
Newfoundland	St. John's (AP)	31	19	68	51	87	-10	59.50
New Brunswick	Fredericton (AP)	25	7	78	55	98	-35	41.74
New Brunswick	Moncton (AP)	26	9	76	55	99	-26	43.27
New Brunswick	Saint John (AP)	28	9	72	53	91	-34	55.13
Nova Scotia	Halifax (AP)	29	14	74	55	93	-14	54.94
Nova Scotia	Sidney (AP)	31	17	74	55	95	-13	52.78
Ontario	Ottawa (AP)	21	4	80	59	100	-33	33.50
Ontario	Sudbury (AP)	17	-1	77	55	97	-36	32.87
Ontario	Toronto (AP)	28	13	81	58	101	-24	29.61
Ontario	Windsor (AP)	31	18	82	62	101	-15	32.91
Prince Edward Island	Charlottetown (AP)	27	13	75	58	98	-23	41.69
Quebec	Montreal (AP)	22	6	79	61	96	-36	37.05
Quebec	Quebec City (AP)	19	3	77	56	96	-33	42.85
Quebec	Val-d'Or (AP)	12	-9	74	52	94	-47	35.52
Saskatchewan	Prince Albert (AP)	5	-17	77	51	100	-58	15.31
Saskatchewan	Regina (AP)	10	-9	79	53	110	-58	15.66
North West Territories	Alert	-19	-33	44	34	68	-57	6.15
North West Territories	Yellowknife (AP)	-12	-27	69	53	90	-60	9.84
Yukon Territory	Dawson	-13	-26	72	48	95	-73	12.81
Yukon Territory	Whitehorse	6	-9	68	47	94	-62	10.24

Low and High Temp. Records Through 1967

Source: Atmospheric Environment Service, Dept. of Environment

Province	Lowest °F	Highest	Latest Dates	Station	Approximate Elevation
Alberta	—78		Jan. 11, 1911	Fort Vermilion	915
		108	Jul. 12, 1886	Medicine Hat	2,365
British Columbia	—74		Jan. 31, 1947	Smith River	2,208
		112	Jul. 17, 1941	Chinook Cove	1324
		112	Jul. 17, 1941	Lillooet	950
		112	Jul. 17, 1941	Lytton	600
Manitoba	—63		Jan. 9, 1899	Norway House	720
		112	Jul. 12, 1936	Emerson	792
		112	Jul. 11, 1936	St. Albans	1,180
Newfoundland	—56		Mar. 7, 1968	Twin Falls	1,499
		107	Aug. 11, 1914	Northwest River	200
New Brunswick	—53		Feb. 1, 1955	Sisson Dam	915
		103	Aug. 18, 1935	Nespisquit Falls	350
		103	Aug. 18, 1935	Woodstock	150
		103	Aug. 19, 1935	Rexton	20
Nova Scotia	—42		Jan. 31, 1920	Upper Stewiacke	75
		101	Aug. 19, 1935	Collegeville	250
Ontario	—73		Jan. 23, 1935	Iroquois Falls	800
		108	Jul. 20, 1919	Biscotasing	1,300
		108	Jul. 11, 1936	Atikokan	1,289
		108	Jul. 13, 1936	Fort Frances	1,160
Prince Edward Island	—35		Jan. 26, 1884	Kilmahumaig	20
		98	Aug. 19, 1935	Charlottetown	74
Quebec	—66		Feb. 5, 1923	Doucet	1,236
		104	Jul. 6, 1921	Barrage Temiscaminigue	595
		104	Aug. 15, 1928	Bark Lake	1,195
Saskatchewan	—70		Feb. 1, 1893	Prince Albert	1,432
		113	Jul. 5, 1937	Midale	1,908
		113	Jul. 5, 1937	Yellow Grass	1,899
North West Territories	—71		Dec. 26, 1917	Fort Smith	665
		103	Jul. 18, 1941	Fort Smith	680
Yukon Territory	—81		Feb. 3, 1947	Snag	1,925
		95	Jun. 18, 1950	Mayo	1,625

Canadian Monthly Normal Temperature and Precipitation

Source: Atmospheric Environment Service, Dept. of Environment
Normal refers to the mean daily temperature and total monthly precipitation based on varying periods of record over the thirty-year period 1941 to 1970 inclusive. In most cases no adjustment factor was used.
AP indicates airport station; Those not so marked are city office stations.
T, Temperature in Fahrenheit; P, Precipitation in inches; L, less than .05 inch.

Stations	Jan. T	P	Feb. T	P	Mar. T	P	Apr. T	P	May T	P	Jun. T	P	Jul. T	P	Aug. T	P	Sept. T	P	Oct. T	P	Nov. T	P	Dec. T	P
Calgary, Alta. (AP)	12	0.7	19	0.8	24	0.8	38	1.2	49	2.0	56	3.6	62	2.7	59	2.2	51	1.4	42	0.7	27	0.6	18	0.6
Charlottetown, P.E.I. (AP)	20	3.8	20	3.2	27	3.0	37	2.9	49	3.1	58	3.1	66	2.9	65	3.5	58	3.6	48	3.9	39	4.5	26	3.9
Churchill, Man. (AP)	-17	0.6	-16	0.5	-5	0.7	12	0.9	28	1.1	43	1.6	54	1.9	53	2.3	42	2.0	30	1.6	10	1.6	-7	0.8
Dawson, Yukon	-20	0.8	-9	0.6	7	0.5	29	0.4	46	0.9	57	1.5	60	2.1	55	2.0	44	1.1	26	1.1	2	1.0	-14	1.0
Edmonton, Alta. (Indus. AP)	6	1.0	13	0.8	22	0.7	39	0.9	52	1.4	58	2.9	63	3.2	61	2.8	52	1.4	42	0.7	24	0.7	13	0.8
Fredericton, N.B.(AP)	16	3.7	17	3.6	28	2.7	39	2.9	51	3.2	61	3.1	67	3.4	64	3.4	56	3.2	46	3.4	35	4.3	21	4.4
Frobisher Bay, N.W.T. (AP)	-15	0.9	-13	1.1	-8	0.8	7	0.8	26	0.9	38	1.4	46	2.0	44	2.2	36	1.7	23	1.6	9	1.4	-5	1.0
Halifax, N.S. (AP)	21	5.3	20	5.0	28	4.0	37	4.2	48	3.8	58	3.1	64	3.1	64	4.2	57	3.7	48	4.6	39	6.4	27	7.0
Hamilton, Ont.	25	2.2	26	2.3	33	2.7	45	2.7	56	3.0	67	2.3	72	2.9	71	2.9	62	2.4	52	2.5	40	2.3	29	2.3
Kitchener, Ont.	20	2.3	21	2.1	30	2.8	44	2.7	54	3.2	65	3.2	69	3.5	68	3.0	60	2.8	49	2.8	37	3.0	25	2.9
London, Ont. (AP)	21	3.0	22	2.5	31	2.8	44	3.0	54	2.9	65	3.1	69	3.2	67	2.8	60	3.1	50	2.9	38	3.2	26	3.4
Moncton, N.B. (AP)	18	4.2	18	3.9	27	3.6	38	3.3	49	3.1	59	3.5	65	3.1	64	3.1	56	2.8	46	3.5	36	4.4	22	4.2
Montreal, Que. (AP)	14	2.9	16	2.7	28	2.7	43	2.9	55	2.6	65	3.2	70	3.3	68	3.4	59	3.1	49	2.9	36	3.4	20	3.4
Ottawa, Ont. (AP)	12	2.3	15	2.2	26	2.4	42	2.6	54	2.7	65	2.8	69	3.2	67	3.2	58	3.1	48	2.6	34	3.0	18	3.0
Quebec City, Que. (AP)	11	3.3	13	3.0	24	2.7	38	2.9	51	3.1	61	4.0	67	4.2	64	4.0	56	4.1	45	3.2	32	3.9	17	3.9
Regina, Sask. (AP)	1	0.7	6	0.6	17	0.7	38	0.9	51	1.6	59	3.2	66	2.2	64	1.9	53	1.4	41	0.7	23	0.7	9	0.6
Saint John, N.B. (AP)	19	5.7	18	5.1	27	4.1	37	4.4	48	4.0	56	3.7	62	3.5	61	3.8	54	4.0	46	4.3	37	6.0	24	6.1
St. John's, Nfld. (AP)	25	5.7	24	6.1	28	5.2	34	4.4	42	3.9	51	3.4	59	3.2	60	4.5	54	4.4	45	5.4	38	6.3	30	6.6
Saskatoon, Sask. (AP)	-2	0.7	5	0.7	16	0.6	38	0.8	51	1.3	60	2.2	66	2.0	63	1.7	52	1.3	41	0.7	22	0.7	7	0.7
Sault Ste. Marie, Ont. (AP)	13	3.2	11	2.1	23	2.2	38	2.2	48	3.3	58	3.4	64	2.8	62	2.6	56	3.7	47	3.1	34	4.1	20	3.7
Toronto, Ont. (AP)	21	2.1	22	1.9	30	2.3	43	2.5	54	2.8	65	2.4	69	2.9	68	2.8	60	2.4	50	2.3	38	2.4	26	2.2
Vancouver, B.C. (AP)	36	5.8	40	4.5	42	3.6	48	2.4	54	1.8	59	1.7	63	1.1	63	1.4	58	2.4	50	4.8	43	5.5	39	6.5
Victoria, B.C. (AP)	37	5.7	40	3.8	42	2.7	47	1.7	53	1.2	58	1.1	61	0.7	61	0.9	57	1.4	50	3.4	43	5.0	40	5.7
Whitehorse, Yukon (AP)	-2	0.7	8	0.5	18	0.5	32	0.4	45	0.5	54	1.1	57	1.3	54	1.4	46	1.1	33	0.7	16	0.8	4	0.7
Windsor, Ont. (AP)	24	2.1	26	2.0	34	2.6	47	3.2	57	3.2	68	3.2	72	3.2	70	3.2	63	2.3	53	2.4	40	2.4	28	2.5
Winnipeg, Man. (AP)	-1	0.9	4	0.7	17	1.0	38	1.4	51	2.2	62	3.1	67	3.1	66	2.9	55	2.0	44	1.3	24	1.0	7	0.9
Yellowknife, N.W.T. (AP)	-19	0.5	-14	0.4	-1	0.4	18	0.4	39	0.5	54	0.6	61	1.3	57	1.4	44	1.1	30	1.2	6	0.9	-11	0.7

Canadian Annual Climatological Data

Source: Atmospheric Environment Service, Dept. of Environment

Station 1975	Elev. ft.	Temperature Highest	Date D./Mo.	Lowest	Date D./Mo.	Precipitation Total (in.)	Greatest in 24 hrs.	Date D./Mo.	Snow or Sleet Total (in.)	Greatest in 24 hrs.	Date D./Mo.	Wind Fastest MPH	Date D./Mo.	No. of Days Prec. .01 in. or more	Snow, sleet 1 in. or more
Calgary	3540	93	27/7	-31	10/1	14.50	0.64	4/5	72.2	6.7	9/12	44	30/12	118	71
Charlottetown	186	93	19/7	-12	4/2	41.32	2.25	22/12	166.0	8.5	6/2	40	2/1	182	90
Churchill	115	93	4/7	-44	12/1	11.82	0.66	14/6	49.2	4.4	12.1	46	12/1	140	82
Dawson	1062	89	29/6	-63	5/1	9.83	0.38	30/9	41.2	5.8	26/9	27	21/2	113	49
Edmonton	2358	89	12/7	-31	10/1	17.52	1.57	27/6	45.6	4.5	4/2	37	6/10	140	61
Frederickton	74	99	2/8	-25	1/2	44.41	2.22	13/11	149.3	12.1	12/1	33	4/4	170	64
Frobisher Bay	68	71	29/6	-44	31/1	16.83	1.24	27/8	84.6	6.0	31/3	51	25/9	133	96
Halifax	461	90	23/6	-10	4/2	50.30	2.78	2/10	89.0	9.3	6/2	54	28/6	166	65
Hamilton	808	97	31/7	-7	22/12	37.19	1.67	23/8	54.5	6.4	7/3	34	10/11	147	43
London	912	94	31/7	-7	22/12	37.45	1.34	24/8	94.9	8.6	3/4	44	10/11	171	69
Moncton	248	93	2/8	-24	11/2	45.50	1.79	13/11	167.9	15.4	7/1	35	8/1	160	69
Montreal	98	100	1/8	-18	19/12	46.87	2.89	26/9	98.0	10.1	3/4	50	2/6	165	60
Ottawa	413	96	1/8	-21	20/1	34.87	1.51	20/7	78.6	10.5	3/4	37	3/4	150	54
Quebec City	245	94	1/8	-24	10/2	48.38	2.50	20/3	129.0	13.0	3/4	45	3/4	166	47
Regina	1884	99	29/7	-31	12/2	18.78	5.24	25/6	54.7	6.5	26/3	41	18/10	114	67
Saint John	352	92	2/8	-17	18/1	56.40	6.08	3/11	158.2	16.7	7/1	46	14/4	162	67
Saint John's	463	85	20/7	-10	3/2	51.50	3.17	23/8	145.9	12.8	10/2	63	2/5	218	103
Saskatoon	1645	95	27/7	-37	12/2	14.10	1.43	19/5	46.1	3.7	2/2	36	20.1	131	67
Sault Ste. Marie	620	96	31/7	-26	22/1	33.83	1.42	5/9	111.3	7.9	8/2	51	10/11	160	75
Thunder Bay	644	99	30/7	-31	22/1	23.46	1.16	10/1	71.7	8.3	19/11	33	25/10	128	54
Toronto	578	92	23/6	-29	20/1	27.32	2.24	23/8	62.3	8.3	20/12	48	29/1	138	41
Vancouver	16	82	23/7	19	10/1	51.95	2.39	29/10	46.8	8.7	30/11	48	30/3	163	25
Victoria	67	84	4/7	22	10/1	42.56	1.77	2/12	36.1	6.9	11/1	29	15/11	159	23
Waterloo-Wellington	1125	93	1/8	-12	20/1	39.31	2.90	24/8	76.6	5.5	2.4	41	10/11	167	70
Whitehorse	2289	83	11/7	-57	19/1	12.17	0.64	13/9	54.5	3.5	17/10	32	19/12	133	77
Windsor	637	96	1/8	-3	10/2	37.91	1.41	29/8	59.2	6.4	26.12	39	10/11	155	53
Winnipeg	786	96	28/7	-29	12/12	23.37	2.14	22/6	52.4	7.2	24/1	41	11/1	131	54
Yellowknife	682	88	11/7	-50	16/1	9.58	1.27	29/8	58.3	6.3	29/10	30	11/8	124	79

Explanation of Normal Temperatures

Normal temperatures listed in the tables on pages 791 and 793 are based on records of the National Weather Service for the 30-year period from 1941-1970 inclusive.

To obtain the average maximum temperature for any month, the daily maximum temperatures are added; the total is then divided by the number of days in that month. The average minimum temperature for the month is obtained by adding the daily minimum temperatures during that month and dividing by the number of days in that month.

The normal maximum temperature for January, for example, is obtained by adding the average maximums for January, 1941, January, 1942, etc., through January, 1970. The total is then divided by 30. The normal minimum temperature is obtained in a similar manner by adding the average minimums for each January in the 30-year period and dividing by 30. The normal temperature for January is one-half of the sum for the normal maximum and minimum temperatures for that month.

The mean temperature for any one day is one-half the total of the maximum and minimum temperatures for that day.

Speed of Winds in the U.S.

Miles per hour — average thru 1973. High thru 1974. Wind velocities in true values.
Source: National Climatic Center, NOAA, Dept. of Commerce

Stations	Avg.	High	Stations	Avg.	High	Stations	Avg.	High
Albany, N. Y.	8.8	71	Helena, Mont.	7.9	73	Pensacola, Fla.	8.2	(b)59
Albuquerque, N. M.	8.9	90	Jacksonville, Fla.	8.7	82	Philadelphia, Pa.	9.6	73
Atlanta, Ga.	9.1	70	Key West, Fla.	11.3	122	Pittsburgh, Pa.	9.4	58
Bismarck, N.D.	10.7	72	Knoxville, Tenn.	7.3	73	Portland, Ore.	7.7	88
Boston, Mass.	12.7	61	Little Rock, Ark.	8.2	65	Rochester, N.Y.	9.6	73
Buffalo, N. Y.	12.3	91	Louisville, Ky.	8.4	61	St. Louis, Mo.	9.5	(b)91
Cape Hatteras, N. C.	11.8	(b)110	Memphis, Tenn.	9.2	57	Salt Lake City, Utah.	8.7	71
Chattanooga, Tenn.	6.3	82	Miami, Fla.	9.0	(a)74	San Diego, Calif.	6.7	51
Chicago, Ill.	10.4	60	Minneapolis, Minn.	10.6	92	San Francisco, Calif.	10.5	58
Cincinnati, Ohio	7.1	49	Mobile, Ala.	9.4	(b)63	Savannah, Ga.	8.3	66
Cleveland, Ohio	10.8	74	Montgomery, Ala.	6.8	60	Spokane, Wash.	8.6	59
Denver, Colo.	9.0	56	Nashville, Tenn.	7.9	73	Toledo, Ohio	9.5	72
Detroit, Mich.	10.2	46	New Orleans, La.	8.4	(b)98	Washington, D. C.	9.3	78
Fort Smith, Ark.	7.7	58	New York, N. Y.(c)	9.5	70	Mt. Wash'ton, N. H.	35.2	231
Galveston, Texas	11.0	(d)100	Omaha, Nebr.	10.9	109			

(a) Highest velocity ever recorded in Miami area was 132 mph, at former station in Miami Beach in September, 1926.
(b) previous location. (c) Data for Central Park. Battery Place data through 1960, avg. 14.5, high 113. (d) Recorded before anemometer blew away. Estimated high 120.

Speed of Winds in Canada

Source: Atmospheric Environment Service. Dept. of Environment

Miles-per-hour average in most cases is for the period of record 1955 to 1972. High is based on varying periods of record dependent on the origin of the station thru 1972.

Stations	Avg.	High	Stations	Avg.	High	Stations	Avg.	High
Calgary	13.3	65	London	10.2	63	Sault Ste. Marie	9.5	55
Charlottetown	12.0	64	Moncton	11.6	62	Thunder Bay	8.8	50
Churchill	14.7	78	Montreal	9.8	51	Toronto	10.7	56
Dawson	4.2	32	Ottawa	9.4	54	Vancouver	7.5	55
Edmonton	9.2	44	Quebec City	10.4	68	Victoria	11.0	68
Fredericton	8.8	50	Regina	13.4	60	Whitehorse	9.4	50
Frobisher Bay	10.3	80	Saint John	11.8	60	Windsor	10.6	57
Halifax	11.4	60	Saint John's	15.1	85	Winnipeg	12.0	56
Hamilton	7.9	41	Saskatoon	11.2	65	Yellowknife	10.0	45

Wind Guide

The National Weather Service classifies winds according to their strength, measured in miles per hour, with official descriptive names or designations, shown in the table below. A similar classification is the Beaufort Scale, in which winds are designated as Force 1, Force 2, etc.

Name	MPH	Beau	Name	MPH	Beau	Name	MPH	Beau	Name	MPH	Beau
Calm	less than 1	0	Moderate breeze	13-18	4	Near gale	32-38	7	Storm	55-63	10
Light air	1-3	1	Fresh breeze	19-24	5	Gale	39-46	8	Violent storm	64-73	11
Light breeze	4-7	2	Strong breeze	25-31	6	Strong gale	47-54	9	Hurricane	74 and up	12
Gentle breeze	8-12	3									

The Beaufort Scale further classifies 74-82 mph as Force 12; 83-92, Force 13; 93-103, Force 14; 104-114, Force 15; 115-124, Force 16; 125-136, Force 17.

Temperature-Humidity (Discomfort) Index

The temperature-humidity index, THI, is a measure of summertime human discomfort resulting from the combined effects of temperature and humidity. (The THI may be calculated by adding wet-bulb and dry-bulb temperatures, multiplying the sum by 0.4 and adding 15.)

The following chart shows the combinations of temperature degrees and humidity percentages which produce discomfort for most persons (the equivalent of a THI value of 75) and those which produce acute discomfort for almost everyone (equivalent to a THI of 80).

Discomfort Temp.-Humid.	Acute Discomfort Temp.-Humid.	Discomfort Temp.-Humid.	Acute Discomfort Temp.-Humid.	Discomfort Temp.-Humid.	Acute Discomfort Temp.-Humid.
75°—100%	81°—100%	82°—49%	88°—54%	90°—14%	96°—20%
76°— 91%	82°— 93%	83°—43%	89°—49%	91°—10%	97°—16%
77°— 82%	83°— 86%	84°—38%	90°—43%	92°— 7%	98°—13%
78°— 75%	84°— 78%	85°—33%	91°—38%	93°— 5%	99°—11%
79°— 68%	85°— 71%	86°—29%	92°—34%	94°— 3%	100°— 8%
80°— 61%	86°— 65%	87°—25%	93°—30%	95°— 1%	101°— 6%
81°— 55%	87°— 59%	88°—20%	94°—26%	96°— 1%	102°— 3%
		89°—17%	95°—23%	97°— 1%	103°— 1%

From 95 degrees up there is discomfort at any humidity. When the temperature is over 102 degrees there is acute discomfort at any humidity.

The Meaning of "One Inch of Rain"

An acre of ground contains 43,560 square feet. Consequently, a rainfall of 1 inch over 1 acre of ground would mean a total of 6,272,640 cubic inches of water. This is equivalent of 3,630 cubic feet.

As a cubic foot of pure water weighs about 62.4 pounds, the exact amount varying with the density, it follows that the weight of a uniform coating of 1 inch of rain over 1 acre of surface would be 226,512 pounds, or 1/4 short tons. The weight of 1 U.S. gallon of pure water is about 8.345 pounds. Consequently a rainfall of 1 inch over 1 acre of ground would mean 27,154 gallons of water.

Weights and Measures

Source: National Bureau of Standards, Department of Commerce

U.S. Moving, Inch by 24.5 Mm, to Metric System

The U.S. is the only industrial country in the world which is not on the metric system and is not yet involved in an official changeover program.

On Jul. 2, 1971, following the report of a metric conversion study committee, Commerce Secy. Maurice H. Stans recommended a gradual U.S. changeover during a 10-year period at the end of which the U.S. would be predominantly, but not exclusively, on the metric system. Proposals to that effect are now pending in Congress.

The International System (Metric)

Two systems of weights and measures exist side by side in the United States today, with roughly equal but separate legislative sanction: the U.S. Customary System and the International (Metric) System. Throughout U.S. history, the Customary System (inherited from, but now different from, the British Imperial System) has been, as its name implies, customarily used; a plethora of federal and state legislation has given it, through implication, standing as our primary weights and measures system. However, the Metric System (incorporated in the scientists' new SI or Systeme International d'Unites) is the only system that has ever received specific legislative sanction by Congress. The "Law of 1866" reads:

It shall be lawful throughout the United States of America to employ the weights and measures of the metric system; and no contract or dealing, or pleading in any court, shall be deemed invalid or liable to objection because the weights or measures expressed or referred to therein are weights or measures of the metric system.

Over the last 100 years, the Metric System has seen slow, steadily increasing use in the United States and, today, is of importance nearly equal to the Customary System.

On Feb. 10, 1964, the National Bureau of Standards issued the following bulletin:

Henceforth it shall be the policy of the National Bureau of Standards to use the units of the International System (SI), as adopted by the 11th General Conference on Weights and Measures (October 1960), except when the use of these units would obviously impair communication or reduce the usefulness of a report.

What had been the Metric System became the International System (SI), a more complete scientific system.

Seven units have been adopted to serve as the base for the International System as follows: **Length**—meter; **Mass**—kilogram; **Time**—second; **Electric Current**—ampere; **Thermodynamic Temperature**—kelvin; **Amount of Substance**—Mole; and **Light Intensity**—Candela.

Prefixes

The following prefixes, in combination with the basic unit names, provide the multiples and submultiples in the International System. For example, the unit name "meter," with the prefix "kilo" added, produces "kilometer," meaning "'1,000 meters.'"

Prefix	Symbol	Multiples and Submultiples	Equivalent	Prefix	Symbol	Multiples and Submultiples	Equivalent
tera	T	10^{12}	trillionfold	centi	c	10^{-2}	hundredth part
giga	G	10^9	billionfold	milli	m	10^{-3}	thousandth part
mega	M	10^6	millionfold	micro	cu	10^{-6}	millionth part
kilo	k	10^3	thousandfold	nano	n	10^{-9}	billionth part
hecto	h	10^2	hundredfold	pico	p	10^{-12}	trillionth part
deka	da	10	tenfold	femto	f	10^{-15}	quadrillionth part
deci	d	10^{-1}	tenth part	atto	a	10^{-18}	quintillionth part

Tables of Metric Weights and Measures

Linear Measure

10 millimeters (mm)	= 1 centimeter (cm)
10 centimeters	= 1 decimeter (dm) = 100 millimeters
10 decimeters	= 1 meter (m) = 1,000 millimeters
10 meters	= 1 dekameter (dam)
10 dekameters	= 1 hectometer (hm) = 100 meters
10 hectometers	= 1 kilometer (km) = 1,000 meters

Area Measure

100 square millimeters (mm²)	= 1 square centimeter (cm²)
10,000 square centimeters	= 1 square meter (m²) = 1,000,000 square millimeters
100 square meters	= 1 are (a)
100 ares	= 1 hectare (ha) = 10,000 square meters
100 hectares	= 1 square kilometer (km²) = 1,000,000 square meters

Volume Measure

10 milliliters (mL)	= 1 centiliter (cL)
10 centiliters	= 1 deciliter (dL) = 100 milliliters
10 deciliters	= 1 liter (L) = 1,000 milliliters
10 liters	= 1 dekaliter (daL)
10 dekaliters	= 1 hectoliter (hL) = 100 liters
10 hectoliters	= 1 kiloliter (kL) = 1,000 liters

Cubic Measure

1,000 cubic millimeters (mm³)	= 1 cubic centimeter (cm³)
1,000 cubic centimeters	= 1 cubic decimeter (dm³) = 1,000,000 cubic millimeters
1,000 cubic decimeters	= 1 cubic meter (m³) = 1 stere = 1,000,000 cubic centimeters = 1,000,000,000 cubic millimeters

Weight

10 milligrams (mg)	= 1 centigram (cg)
10 centigrams	= 1 decigram (dg) = 100 milligrams
10 decigrams	= 1 gram (g) = 1,000 milligrams
10 grams	= 1 dekagram (dag)
10 dekagrams	= 1 hectogram (hg) = 100 grams
10 hectograms	1 kilogram (kg) = 1,000 grams
1,000 kilograms	= 1 metric ton (t)

Table of U.S. Customary Weights and Measures

Linear Measure

12 inches (in)	= 1 foot (ft)
3 feet	= 1 yard (yd)
5 1/2 yards	= 1 rod (rd), pole, or perch (16 1/2 feet)
40 rods	= 1 furlong (fur) = 220 yards = 660 feet
8 furlongs	= 1 statute mile (mi) = 1,760 yards = 5,280 feet
3 miles	= 1 league = 5,280 yards = 15,840 feet
6076.11549 feet	= 1 International Nautical Mile

Liquid Measure

When necessary to distinguish the liquid pint or quart from the dry pint or quart, the word "liquid" or the abbreviation "liq" should be used in combination with the name or abbreviation of the liquid unit.

4 gills	= 1 pint (pt) = 28.875 cubic inches
2 pints	= 1 quart (qt) = 57.75 cubic inches
4 quarts	= 1 gallon (gal) = 231 cubic inches = 8 pints = 32 gills

Area Measure

Squares and cubes of units are sometimes abbreviated by using "superior" figures. For example. ft² means square foot, and ft³ means cubic foot.

144 square inches	= 1 square foot (ft²)
9 square feet	= 1 square yard (yd²)=1,296 square inches
30 1/4 square yards	= 1 square rod (rd²)=272 1/4 =square feet
160 square rods	= 1 acre=4,840 square yards =43,560 square feet
640 acres	= 1 square mile (mi²)
1 mile square	= 1 section (of land)
6 miles square	= 1 township=36 sections=36 square miles

Cubic Measure

30 1/4 square yards	= 1 square rod (rd²)=262 1/4(in²)
1 cubic foot (ft³)	
27 cubic feet	= 1 cubic yard (yd³)

Gunter's or Surveyors' Chain Measure

7.92 inches (in)	= 1 link
100 links	= 1 chain (ch)=4 rods=66 feet
80 chains	= 1 statute mile (mi)=320 rods =5,280 feet

Troy Weight

24 grains	= 1 pennyweight (dwt)
20 pennyweights	= 1 ounce troy (oz t)=480 grains
12 ounces troy	= 1 pound troy (lb t)=240 pennyweights=5,760 grains

Dry Measure

When necessary to distinguish the dry pint or quart from the liquid pint or quart, the word "dry" should be used in combination with the name or abbreviation of the dry unit.

2 pints (pt)	= 1 quart (qt)=(67,2006 cubic inches)
8 quarts	= 1 peck (pk)=(537.605 cubic inches) =16 pints
4 pecks	= 1 bushel (bu)=(2,150.42 cubic inches)=32 quarts

Avoirdupois Weight

When necessary to distinguish the avoirdupois ounce or pound from the troy ounce or pound, the word "avoirdupois" or the abbreviation "avdp" should be used in combination with the name or abbreviation of the avoirdupois unit.

(The "grain" is the same in avoirdupois and troy weight.)

27 11/32 grains	= 1 dram (dr)
16 drams	= 1 ounce (oz)=437 1/2 grains
16 ounces	= 1 pound (lb)=256 drams =7,000 grains
100 pounds	= 1 hundredweight (cwt)°
20 hundredweights	= 1 ton=2,000 pounds°

In "gross" or "long" measure, the following values are recognized:

112 pounds	= 1 gross or long hundredweight°
20 gross or long hundredweights	= 1 gross or long ton=2,240 pounds°

°When the terms "hundredweight" and "ton" are used unmodified, they are commonly understood to mean the 100-pound hundredweight and the 2,000-pound ton, respectively: these units may be designated "net" or "short" when necessary to distinguish them from the corresponding units in gross or long measure.

Tables of Equivalents

When the name of a unit is enclosed in brackets thus, [71 hand], this indicates (1) that the unit is not in general current use in the United States, or (2) that the unit is believed to be based on "custom and usage" rather than on formal definition. See above about superior figures in Area Measure.

Equivalents involving decimals are, in most instances, rounded off to the third decimal place except where they are exact, in which cases these exact equivalents are so designated.

Lengths

Angstrom (A)	0.1 nanometer (exactly) 0.000 1 micron (exactly) 0.000 000 1 millimeter (exactly) 0.000 000 004 inch
1 cable's length	120 fathoms 720 feet 219.456 meters (exactly)
1 centimeter (cm)	0.3937 inch
1 chain (ch) (Gunter's or surveyors)	66 feet 20.1168 meters (exactly)
1 chain (engineers)	100 feet 30.48 meters (exactly)
1 decimeter (dm)	3.937 inches
1 dekameter (dam)	32.808 feet
1 fathom	6 feet 1.8288 meters (exactly)
1 foot (ft)	0.3048 meter (exactly)
1 furlong (fur)	10 chains (surveyors) 660 feet 220 yards 1/8 statute mile 201.168 meters
[1 hand]	4 inches
1 inch (in)	2.54 centimeters (exactly)
1 kilometer (km)	0.621 mile 3,280.8 feet 3 statute miles
1 league (land)	4.828 kilometers
1 link (Gunter's or surveyors)	7.92 inches 0.201 meter
1 link (engineers)	1 foot 0.305 meter
1 meter (m)	39.37 inches 1.094 yards
1 micron (μ) [the Greek letter mu]	0.001 millimeter (exactly) 0.000 039 37 inch
1 mil	0.001 inch (exactly) 0.025 4 millimeter (exactly)

1 mile (mi) (statute or land)	5,280 feet 1.609 kilometers
1 International Nautical Mile (INM)	1,852 kilometers (exactly) 1.150779 statute miles 6,076.11549 feet
1 millimeter (mm)	0.039 37 inch
1 nanometer (nm)	0.001 micron (exactly) 0.000 000 039 37 inch (exactly)
1 point (typography)	0.013 837 inch (exactly) 0.351 millimeter
1 rod (rd), pole, or perch	16 1/2 feet 5 1/2 yards 5.029 meters
1 yard (yd)	0.9144 meter (exactly)

Areas or Surfaces

1 acre	43,560 square feet 4,840 square yards 0.405 hectare
1 are (a)	119.599 square yards 0.025 acre
1 hectare (ha)	2.171 acres
[1 square (building)]	100 square feet
1 square centimeter (cm²)	0.155 square inch
1 square decimeter (dm²)	15.500 square inches
1 square foot (ft²)	929.030 square centimeters
1 square inch (in²)	6.452 square centimeters
1 square kilometer (km²)	247.105 acres 0.386 square mile
1 square meter (m²)	1,196 square yards 10.764 square feet
1 square mile (mi²)	258.999 hectares
1 square millimeter (mm²)	0.002 square inch
1 square rod (rd²) sq. pole, or sq. perch	25.293 square meters
1 square yard (yd²)	0.836 square meter

Capacities or Volumes

1 barrel (bbl) liquid. . . . . 31 to 42 gallons°

°There are a variety of "barrels," established by law or usage. For example: federal taxes on fermented liquors are based on a barrel of 31 gallons: many state laws fix the "barrel for liquids" as 31 1/2 gallons; one state fixes a 36-

gallon barrel for cistern measurement; federal law recognizes a 40-gallon barrel for "proof spirits"; by custom, 42 gallons comprise a barrel of crude oil or petroleum products for statistical purposes, and this equivalent is recognized "for liquids" by four states.

1 barrel (bbl), standard, for fruits, vegetables, and other dry commodities except dry cranberries.........	7,056 cubic inches 105 dry quarts 3.281 bushels, struck measure
1 barrel (bbl), standard, cranberry	5,826 cubic inches 86⁴⁵/₆₄ dry quarts 2,709 bushels, struck measure
1 bushel (bu) (U.S.) (struck measure)	2,150.42 cubic inches (exactly) 35.238 liters
[1 bushel, heaped (U.S.)]	2,747.715 cubic inches 1,278 bushels, struck measure°

°Frequently recognized as 1 1/4 bushels, struck measure.

[1 bushel (bu) (British Imperial) (struck measure)]	1.032 U.S. bushels, struck measure 2,219.36 cubic inches
1 cord (cd) firewood.................	128 cubic feet
1 cubic centimeter (cm³)...............	0.061 cubic inch
1 cubic decimeter (dm³)............	61.024 cubic inches
1 cubic inch (in³).........	0.554 fluid ounce 4.433 fluid drams 16.387 cubic centimeters
1 cubic foot (ft³)........	7,481 gallons 28,317 cubic decimeters
1 cubic meter (m³).................	1.308 cubic yards
1 cubic yard (yd³)...............	0.765 cubic meter
1 cup, measuring.................	8 fluid ounces ½ liquid pint
[1 dram, fluid (fl dr) (British)].	0.961 U.S. fluid dram 0.217 cubic inch 3.552 milliliters
1 dekaliter (dal).................	2.642 gallons 1.135 pecks
1 gallon (gal) (U.S.)........	231 cubic inches 3.785 liters 0.833 British gallon 128 U.S. fluid ounces
[1 gallon (gal) British Imperial].......	277.42 cubic inches 1.201 U.S. gallons 4.546 liters 160 British fluid ounces
1 gill.................	7.219 cubic inches 4 fluid ounces 0.118 liter
1 hectoliter (hl).................	26.417 gallons 2.838 bushels
1 liter (l)...........	1.057 liquid quarts 0.908 dry quart 61.024 cubic inches
1 milliliter (ml)................	0.271 fluid dram 16.231 minims 0.061 cubic inch
1 ounce, liquid (U.S.).................	1.805 cubic inches 29.573 milliliters 1.041 British fluid ounces
[1 ounce, fluid (fl oz) (British)].....	0.961 U. S. fluid ounce 1.734 cubic inches 28.412 milliliters

1 peck (pk)........................	8.810 liters
1 pint (pt), dry............	33.600 cubic inches 0.551 liter
1 pint (pt) liquid............	28.875 cubic inches (exactly) 0.473 liter
1 quart (qt) dry (U.S.)......	67.201 cubic inches 1.101 liters 0.969 British quart
1 quart (qt) liquid (U.S.)....	57.75 cubic in (exactly) 0.946 liter 0.833 British quart
[1 quart (qt) (British)]......	69.354 cubic inches 1.032 U.S. dry quarts 1.201 U.S. liquid quarts
1 tablespoon........................	3 teaspoons° 4 fluid drams ½ fluid ounce
1 teaspoon...................·.....	¹/₃ tablespoon° 1¹/₃ fluid drams°

°The equivalent "1 teaspoon — 1¹/₃ fluid drams" has been found by the bureau to correspond more closely with the actual capacities of "measuring" and silver teaspoons than the equivalent "1 teaspoon — 1 fluid dram" which is given by many dictionaries.

Weights or Masses

1 assay ton∞ (AT)........................	29.167 grams

∞Used in assaying. The assay ton bears the same relation to the milligram that a ton of 2,000 pounds avoirdupois bears to the ounce troy; hence the weight in milligrams of precious metal obtained from one assay ton of ore gives directly the number of troy ounces to the net ton.

1 carat (c).................	200 milligrams 3.086 grains
1 dram avoirdupois (dr avdp)... gamma, see microgram	27¹¹/₃₂ (=27.344) grains 1,722 grains
1 grain.......................	64.799 milligrams
1 gram.......................	15.432 grains 0.035 ounce, avoirdupois
1 hundredweight, gross or long∞ (gross cwt)...	112 pounds 50.802 kilograms
1 hundredweight, net or short (cwt. or net cwt.)........	100 pounds 45,359 kilograms
1 kilogram (kg).................	2,205 pounds
1 microgram (γ [the Greek letter gamma]................	0.000001 gram (exactly)
1 milligram (mg).....................	0.015 grain
1 ounce, avoirdupois (oz avdp).......	437.5 grains (exactly) 0.911 troy ounce 28.350 grams
1 ounce, troy (oz t)........	480 grains 1.097 avoirdupois ounces 31.103 grams
1 pennyweight (dwt).......	1.555 grams
1 pound, avoirdupois (lb avdp)........	7,000 grains 1.215 troy pounds 453.592 37 grams (exactly)
1 pound, troy (lb t).......	5,760 grains 0.823 avoirdupois pound 373.242 grams
1 ton, gross or long ∞ (gross ton).............	2,240 pounds 1.12 net tons (exactly) 1.016 metric tons

∞∞The gross or long ton and hundredweight are used commercially in the United States to only a limited extent, usually in restricted industrial fields. These units are the same as British "ton" and "hundredweight."

1 ton, metric (t)...........	2,204.623 pounds 0.984 gross ton 1.102 net tons
1 ton, net or short (sh ton)..	2,000 pounds 0.893 gross ton 0.907 metric ton

Density of Gases and Vapors

Source: National Bureau of Standards (kilograms per cubic meter)

Gas	Wt.	Gas	Wt.	Gas	Wt.
Acetylene.............	1.171	Ethylene...............	1.260	Methyl fluoride..........	1.545
Air...................	1.293	Fluorine...............	1.696	Mono methylamine.....	1.38
Ammonia.............	.759	Helium................	.178	Neon..................	.900
Argon................	1.784	Hydrogen..............	.090	Nitric oxide............	1.341
Arsene...............	3.48	Hydrogen bromide......	3.50	Nitrogen...............	1.250
Butane-iso............	2.60	Hydrogen chloride......	1.639	Nitrosyl chloride........	2.99
Butane-n.............	2.519	Hydrogen iodide.......	5.724	Nitrous oxide..........	1.997
Carbon dioxide........	1.977	Hydrogen selenide......	3.66	Oxygen................	1.429
Carbon monoxide......	1.250	Hydrogen sulfide.......	1.539	Phosphine.............	1.48
Carbon oxysulfide.....	2.72	Krypton...............	3.745	Propane...............	2.020
Chlorine..............	3.214	Methane...............	.717	Silicon tetrafluoride.....	4.67
Chlorine monoxide.....	3.89	Methyl chloride........	2.25	Sulfur dioxide..........	2.927
Ethane...............	1.356	Methyl ether..........	2.091	Xenon.................	5.897

Tables of Interrelation of Units of Measurement

Bold face type indicates exact values

Units of Length

Units	Inches	Links	Feet	Yards	Rods	Chains	Miles	Cm	Meters
1 inch=	**1**	0.126 263	0.083 333	0.027 778	0.005 051	0.001 263	0.000 016	**2.54**	0.025 4
1 link=	7.92	**1**	**0.66**	0.22	0.04	0.01	0.000 125	20.117	0.201 168
1 foot=	**12**	1.515 152	**1**	0.333 333	0.060 606	0.015 152	0.000 189	**30.48**	0.304 8
1 yard=	**36**	4.545 45	**3**	**1**	0.181 818	0.045 455	0.000 568	**91.44**	0.914 4
1 rod=	**198**	**25**	**16.5**	**5.5**	**1**	0.25	0.003 125	502.92	5.029 2
1 chain=	**792**	**100**	**66**	**22**	**4**	**1**	0.012 5	2011.68	20.116 8
1 mile=	**63 360**	**8000**	**5280**	**1760**	**320**	**80**	**1**	160 934.4	1609.344
1 cm=	0.3937	0.049 710	0.032 808	0.010 936	0.001 988	0.000 497	0.000 006	**1**	**0.01**
1 meter=	39.37	4.970 970	3.280 840	1.093 613	0.198 839	0.049 710	0.000 621	**100**	**1**

Units of Area

Units	Sq. inches	Sq. links	Sq. feet	Sq. yards	Sq. rods	Sq. chains
1 sq. inch=	**1**	.015 942 3	0.006 944	0.00 771 605	0.000 025 5	0.000 001 594
1 sq. link=	62.726 4	**1**	0.435 6	0.0484	0.0016	0.000 1
1 sq. foot=	**144**	2.295 684	**1**	0.111 111 1	0.003 673 09	0.000 220 568
1 sq. yard=	**1296**	20.661 16	**9**	**1**	0.033 057 85	0.002 066 12
1 sq. rod=	39 204	**625**	272.25	30.25	**1**	0.062 5
1 sq. chain=	627 264	**10 000**	**4 356**	**484**	**16**	**1**
1 acre=	6 272 640	**100 000**	**43 560**	**4 840**	**160**	**10**
1 sq. mile=	4 014 489 600	**64 000 000**	**27 878 400**	**3 097 600**	**102 400**	**6400**
1 sq. cm=	0.155 000 3	0.002 471 05	0.001 076	0.000 119 599	0.000 003 954	0.000 000 247
1 sq. meter=	1550.003	24.710 54	10.763 91	1.195 990	0.039 536 86	0.002 471 054
1 hectare=	15 500 031	247.105	107 639.1	11 959.90	395.368 6	24.710 54

Units	Acres	Sq. miles	Sq. cm	Sq. meters	Hectares
1 sq. inch=	0.000 000 159 423	0.000 000 000 249 10	**6.451 6**	**0.000 645 16**	0.000 000 065
1 sq. link=	**0.000 01**	0.000 000 015 625	404.685 642 24	0.040 468 56	0.000 004 047
1 sq. foot=	0.000 022 956 84	0.000 000 035 870 06	**929.030 4**	**0.092 903 04**	0.000 009 290
1 sq. yard=	0.000 206 611 6	0.000 000 322 830 6	8 361.273 6	**0.836 127 36**	0.000 083 613
1 sq. rod=	0.006 25	0.000 003 765 625	252 928.526 4	25.292 852 64	0.002 529 285
1 sq. chain=	**0.1**	0.000 156 25	**4 046 856**	404.685 642 24	0.040 468 564
1 acre=	**1**	0.001 562 5	40 468 564	4046.856 422 4	0.404 685 642
1 sq. mile=	**640**	**1**	25 899 881 103	2 589 988.11	258.998 811 034
1 sq. cm=	0.000 000 024 711	0.000 000 000 038 610	**0.000 1**	**0.000 1**	**0.000 000 01**
1 sq. meter=	0.000 247 105 4	0.000 000 386 102 2	**10 000**	**1**	**0.0001**
1 hectare=	2.471 054	0.003 861 022	**100 000 000**	**10 000**	**1**

Units of Mass Not Greater Than Pounds and Kilograms

	Grains	Pennyweights	Avdp drams	Avdp ounces
1 grain=	**1**	0.041 666 67	0.036 571 43	0.002 285 71
1 pennyweight=	**24**	**1**	0.877 714 3	0.054 857 14
1 dram avdp=	27.343 75	1,139 323	**1**	0.062 5
1 ounce avdp=	437.5	18.229 17	**16**	**1**
1 ounce troy=	**480**	**20**	17.554 29	1.097 143
1 pound troy=	**5760**	**240**	210.651 4	13.165 71
1 pound avdp=	**7000**	291.666 7	**256**	**16**
1 milligram=	0.015 432	0.000 643 015	0.000 564 383	0.000 035 274
1 gram=	15.432 36	0.643 014 9	0.564 383 4	0.035 273 96
1 kilogram=	15 432.36	643.014 9	564.383 4	35.273 96

Units	Troy ounces	Troy pounds	Avdp pounds	Milligrams	Grams	Kilograms
1 grain=	0.002 083 33	0.000 173 611	0.000 142 857	64.798 91	0.064 798 91	0.000 064 799
1 pennyw't.=	0.05	0.004 166 667	0.003 428 571	1555.173 84	1.555 173 84	0.001 555 174
1 dram avdp=	0.056 966 15	0.004 747 179	0.003 906 25	1771.845 195	1.771 845 195	0.001 771 845
1 oz avdp=	0.911 458 3	0.075 954 86	0.062 5	28 349.523 125	28.349 523 125	0.028 349 52
1 oz troy=	**1**	0.083 333 333	0.068 571 43	31 103.476 8	31.103 476 8	0.031 103 48
1 lb troy=	**12**	**1**	0.822 857 1	373 241.721 6	373.241 721 6	0.373 241 722
1 lb avdp=	14.583 33	1.215 278	**1**	453 592.37	453.592 37	0.453 592 37
1 milligram=	0.000 032 151	0.000 002 679	0.000 002 205	**1**	**0.001**	0.000 000 001
1 gram=	0.032 150 75	0.002 679 229	0.002 204 623	**1000**	**1**	**0.001**
1 kilogram=	32.150 75	2.679 229	2.204 623	**1000 000**	**1000**	**1**

Units of Mass Not Less Than Avoirdupois Ounces

Units	Avdp oz	Avdp lb	Short cwt	Short tons	Long tons	Kilograms	Metric tons
1 oz av=	**1**	**0.0625**	0.000 625	0.000 031 25	0.000 027 902	0.028 349 523	0.000 028 350
1 lb av=	**16**	**1**	**0.01**	0.000 5	0.000 446 429	0.453 592 37	0.000 453 592
1 sh cwt=	**1 600**	**100**	**1**	0.05	0.044 642 86	45.359 237	0.045 359 237
1 sh ton=	32 000	**2000**	**20**	**1**	0.892 857 1	907.184 74	0.907 184 74
1 long ton=	35 840	**2240**	22.4	**1.12**	**1**	1016.046 908 8	1.016 046 909
1 kg=	35.273 96	2.204 623	0.022 046 23	0.001 102 311	0.000 984 207	**1**	**0.001**
1 metric ton=	35 273.96	2204.623	22.046 23	1.102 311	0.984 206 5	**1000**	**1**

Continued on next page

Continued from previous page

Units of Volume

Units	Cubic inches	Cubic feet	Cubic yards	Cubic cm	Cubic dm	Cubic meters
1 cubic inch=	1	0.000 578 704	0.000 021 433	16.387 064	0.016 387	0.000 016 387
1 cubic foot=	1728	1	0.037 037 04	28 316.846 592	28.316 847	0.028 316 847.
1 cubic yard=	46 656	27	1	764 554.857 984	764.554 858	0.764 554 858
1 cubic cm=	0.061 023 74	0.000 035 315	0.000 001 308	1	0.001	0.000 000 001
1 cubic dm=	61.023 74	0.035 314 67	0.001 307 951	1 000	1	0.001
1 cubic meter	61 023.74	35.314 67	1.307 951	1 000 000	1000	1

Units of Capacity (Liquid Measure)

Units	Minims	Fluid drams	Fluid ounces	Gills	Liquid pt
1 minim=	1	0.016 666 7	0.002 083 33	0.000 520 833	0.000 130 208
1 liquid dram=	60	1	0.125	0.031 25	0.007 812 5
1 liquid ounce=	480	8	1	0.25	0.062 5
1 gill=	1920	32	4	1	0.25
1 liquid pint=	7680	128	16	4	1
1 liquid quart=	15 360	256	32	8	2
1 gallon=	61 440	1024	128	32	8
1 cubic inch=	265.974	4.432 900	0.554 112 6	0.138 528 1	0.034 632 03
1 cubic foot=	459 603.1	7660.052	957.506 5	239.376 6	59.844 16
1 milliliter=	16.230 73	0.270 512 18	0.033 814 02	0.008 453 506	.002 113 376
1 liter=	16 230.73	270.512 18	33.814 02	8.453 506	2.113 376

Units	Liquid quarts	Gallons	Cubic inches	Cubic feet	Liters
1 minim=	0.000 065 104 17	0.000 016 276 04	0.003 759 766	0.000 002 175 790	0.000 061 611 52
1 liq. dram=	0.003 906 25	0.000 976 562 5	0.225 585 9	0.000 130 547 4	0.03 696 691
1 liquid oz=	0.031 25	0.007 812 5	1.804 687 5	0.001 044 379	0.029 573 53
1 gill=	0.125	0.031 25	7.218 75	0.004 177 517	0.118 294 118 25
1 liquid pt=	0.5	0.125	28.875	0.016 710 07	0.473 176 473
1 liquid qt=	1	0.25	57.75	0.033 420 14	0.946 352 946
1 gallon=	4	1	231	0.133 680 6	3.785 411 784
1 cubic in.=	0.017 316 02	0.004 329 004	1	0.000 578 703 7	0.016 387 064
1 cubic foot=	29.922 08	7.480 519	1728	1	28.316 846 592
1 liter=	1.056 688	0.264 172 05	61.023 74	0.035 314 67	1

Units of Capacity (Dry Measure)

Units	Dry pints	Dry quarts	Pecks	Bushels	Cubic in.	Liters
1 dry pint=	1	0.5	0.062 5	0.015 625	33.600 312 5	.550 610 47
1 dry quart=	2	1	0.125	0.031 25	67.200 625	1.101 220 9
1 peck=	16	8	1	0.25	537.605	8.809 767 5
1 bushel=	64	32	4	1	2150.42	35.239 07
1 cubic inch=	0.029 761 6	0.014 880 9	0.001 860 10	0.000 465 025	1	0.016 387 064
1 liter=	1.816 166	0.908 083	0.113 510 37	0.028 377 59	61.023 74	1

Weight of Water

1	cubic inch	.0360	pound	1	imperial gallon	10.0	pounds
12	cubic inches	.433	pound	11.2	imperial gallons	112.0	pounds
1	cubic foot	62.4	pounds	224	imperial gallons	2240.0	pounds
1	cubic foot	7.48052	U.S. gal	1	U. S. gallon	8.33	pounds
1.8	cubic feet	112.0	pounds	13.45	U.S. gallons	112.0	pounds
35.96	cubic feet	2240.0	pounds	269.0	U. S. gallons	2240.0	pounds

Temperature Conversion Table

The numbers in **bold face type** refer to the temperature either in degrees Celsius or Fahrenheit which are to be converted. If converting from degrees Fahrenheit to Celsius, the equivalent will be found in the column on the left, while if converting from degrees Celsius to Fahrenheit the answer will be found in the column on the right.
For temperatures not shown. To convert Fahrenheit to Celsius subtract 32 degrees and multiply by 5, divide by 9; to convert Celsius to Fahrenheit, multiply by 9, divide by 5 and add 32 degrees.

Celsius		Fahrenheit	Celsius		Fahrenheit	Celsius		Fahrenheit
—273.2	—459.7	....	— 17.8	**0**	32	35.0	**95**	203
—184	—300	....	— 12.2	**10**	50	36.7	**98**	208.4
—169	—273	—459.4	— 6.67	**20**	68	37.8	**100**	212
—157	—250	—418	— 1.11	**30**	86	43	**110**	230
—129	—200	—328	4.44	**40**	104	49	**120**	248
—101	—150	—238	10.0	**50**	122	54	**130**	266
— 73.3	—100	—148	15.6	**60**	140	60	**140**	284
— 45.6	— 50	— 58	21.1	**70**	158	66	**150**	302
— 40.0	— 40	— 40	23.9	**75**	167	93	**200**	392
— 34.4	— 30	— 22	26.7	**80**	176	121	**250**	482
— 28.9	— 20	— 4	29.4	**85**	185	149	**300**	572
— 23.3	— 10	. 14	32.2	**90**	194			

Water boils at 212° Fahrenheit at sea level. For every 550 feet above sea level, boiling point of water is lower by about 1° Fahrenheit. Methyl alcohol boils at 148° Fahrenheit. Average human oral temperature, 98.6° Fahrenheit. Water freezes at 32° Fahrenheit. Although "Centigrade" is still frequently used, the International Committee on Weights and Measures and the National Bureau of Standards have recommended since 1948 that this scale be called "Celsius."

Squares, Square Roots (approx), Cubes and Cube Roots (approx) of Nos. 1 to 100

No.	Sq.	Cube	Sq. Root	Cube Root	No.	Sq.	Cube	Sq. Root	Cube Root	No.	Sq.	Cube	Sq. Root	Cube Root
1	1.000	1.000	1.000	1.000	35	1225	42875	5.916	3.271	68	4624	314432	8.246	4.081
2	4	8	1.414	1.259	36	1296	46656	6.000	3.301	69	4761	328509	8.306	4.101
3	9	27	1.732	1.442	37	1369	50653	6.082	3.332	70	4900	343000	8.366	4.121
4	16	64	2.000	1.587	38	1444	54872	6.164	3.362	71	5041	357911	8.426	4.140
5	25	125	2.236	1.710	39	1521	59319	6.245	3.391	72	5184	373248	8.485	4.160
6	36	216	2.449	1.817	40	1600	64000	6.324	3.420	73	5329	389017	8.544	4.179
7	49	343	2.645	1.913	41	1681	68921	6.403	3.448	74	5476	405224	8.602	4.198
8	64	512	2.828	2.000	42	1764	74088	6.480	3.476	75	5625	421875	8.660	4.217
9	81	729	3.000	2.080	43	1849	79507	6.557	3.503	76	5776	438976	8.717	4.235
10	100	1000	3.162	2.154	44	1936	85184	6.633	3.530	77	5929	456533	8.775	4.254
11	121	1331	3.316	2.224	45	2025	91125	6.708	3.556	78	6084	474552	8.831	4.272
12	144	1728	3.464	2.289	46	2116	97336	6.782	3.583	79	6241	493039	8.888	4.290
13	169	2197	3.605	2.351	47	2209	103823	6.855	3.608	80	6400	512000	8.944	4.308
14	196	2744	3.741	2.410	48	2304	110592	6.928	3.634	81	6561	531441	9.000	4.326
15	225	3375	3.873	2.466	49	2401	117649	7.000	3.659	82	6724	551368	9.055	4.344
16	256	4096	4.000	2.519	50	2500	125000	7.071	3.684	83	6889	571787	9.110	4.362
17	289	4913	4.123	2.571	51	2601	132651	7.141	3.708	84	7056	592704	9.165	4.379
18	324	5832	4.242	2.620	52	2704	140608	7.211	3.732	85	7225	614125	9.219	4.396
19	361	6859	4.358	2.668	53	2809	148877	7.280	3.756	86	7396	636056	9.273	4.414
20	400	8000	4.472	2.714	54	2916	157464	7.348	3.779	87	7569	658503	9.327	4.431
21	441	9261	4.582	2.758	55	3025	166375	7.416	3.803	88	7744	681472	9.380	4.448
22	484	10648	4.690	2.802	56	3136	175616	7.483	3.825	89	7921	704969	9.434	4.464
23	529	12167	4.795	2.843	57	3249	185193	7.549	3.848	90	8100	729000	9.486	4.481
24	576	13824	4.899	2.884	58	3364	195112	7.615	3.870	91	8281	753571	9.539	4.497
25	625	15625	5.000	2.924	59	3481	205379	7.681	3.893	92	8464	778688	9.591	4.514
26	676	17576	5.099	2.962	60	3600	216000	7.746	3.914	93	8649	804357	9.643	4.530
27	729	19683	5.196	3.000	61	3721	226981	7.810	3.936	94	8836	830584	9.695	4.546
28	784	21952	5.291	3.036	62	3844	238328	7.874	3.957	95	9025	857375	9.746	4.562
29	841	24389	5.385	3.072	63	3969	250047	7.937	3.979	96	9216	884736	9.798	4.578
30	900	27000	5.477	3.107	64	4096	262144	8.000	4.000	97	9409	912673	9.848	4.594
31	961	29791	5.567	3.141	65	4225	274625	8.062	4.020	98	9604	941192	9.899	4.610
32	1024	32768	5.656	3.174	66	4356	287496	8.124	4.041	99	9801	970299	9.949	4.626
33	1089	25937	5.744	3.207	67	4489	300763	8.185	4.061	100	10000	1000000	10.000	4.641
34	1156	39304	5.831	3.239										

Square Roots and Cube Roots, (approx) 1000 to 2000

No.	Square Root	Cube Root	No.	Square Root	Cube Root	No.	Square Root	Cube Root	No.	Square Root	Cube Root
1000	31.62	10.00	1255	35.43	10.79	1765	42.01	12.09	1510	38.86	11.47
1005	31.70	10.02	1260	35.50	10.80	1770	42.07	12.10	1515	38.92	11.49
1010	31.78	10.03	1265	35.57	10.82	1775	42.13	12.11	1520	38.99	11.50
1020	31.94	10.07	1275	35.71	10.84	1785	42.25	12.13	1530	39.12	11.52
1025	32.02	10.08	1280	35.78	10.86	1790	42.31	12.14	1535	39.18	11.54
1030	32.09	10.10	1285	35.85	10.87	1795	42.37	12.15	1540	39.24	11.55
1035	32.17	10.12	1290	35.92	10.89	1800	42.43	12.16	1545	39.31	11.56
1045	32.33	10.15	1300	36.06	10.91	1810	42.54	12.19	1555	39.43	11.59
1050	32.40	10.16	1305	36.12	10.93	1815	42.60	12.20	1560	39.50	11.60
1060	32.56	10.20	1315	36.26	10.96	1825	42.72	12.22	1570	39.62	11.62
1065	32.63	10.21	1320	36.33	10.97	1830	42.78	12.23	1575	39.69	11.63
1075	32.79	10.24	1330	36.47	11.00	1840	42.90	12.25	1585	39.81	11.66
1080	32.86	10.26	1335	36.54	11.01	1845	42.95	12.26	1590	39.87	11.67
1085	32.94	10.28	1340	36.61	11.02	1850	43.01	12.28	1595	39.94	11.68
1090	33.02	10.29	1345	36.67	11.04	1855	43.07	12.29	1600	40.00	11.70
1095	33.09	10.31	1350	36.74	11.05	1860	43.13	12.30	1605	40.06	11.71
1100	33.17	10.32	1355	36.81	11.07	1865	43.19	12.31	1610	40.12	11.72
1105	33.24	10.34	1360	36.88	11.08	1870	43.24	12.32	1615	40.19	11.73
1110	33.32	10.35	1365	36.95	11.09	1875	43.30	12.33	1620	40.25	11.74
1115	33.39	10.37	1370	37.01	11.11	1880	43.36	12.34	1625	40.31	11.76
1120	33.47	10.38	1375	37.08	11.12	1885	43.42	12.35	1630	40.37	11.77
1125	33.54	10.40	1380	37.15	11.13	1890	43.47	12.36	1635	40.44	11.78
1130	33.62	10.42	1385	37.22	11.15	1895	43.53	12.37	1640	40.50	11.79
1135	33.69	10.43	1390	37.28	11.16	1900	43.59	12.39	1645	40.56	11.80
1140	33.76	10.45	1395	37.35	11.17	1905	43.65	12.40	1650	40.62	11.82
1145	33.84	10.46	1400	37.42	11.19	1910	43.70	12.41	1655	40.68	11.83
1150	33.91	10.48	1405	37.48	11.20	1915	43.76	12.42	1660	40.74	11.84
1155	33.99	10.49	1410	37.55	11.21	1920	43.82	12.43	1665	40.80	11.85
1160	34.06	10.51	1415	37.62	11.23	1925	43.87	12.44	1670	40.87	11.86
1165	34.13	10.52	1420	37.68	11.24	1930	43.93	12.45	1675	40.93	11.88
1170	34.21	10.54	1425	37.75	11.25	1935	43.99	12.46	1680	40.99	11.89
1175	34.28	10.55	1430	37.82	11.27	1940	44.05	12.47	1685	41.05	11.90
1180	34.35	10.57	1435	37.88	11.28	1945	44.10	12.48	1690	41.11	11.91
1185	34.42	10.58	1440	37.95	11.29	1950	44.16	12.49	1695	41.17	11.92
1190	34.50	10.60	1445	38.01	11.31	1955	44.22	12.50	1700	41.23	11.93
1195	34.57	10.61	1450	38.08	11.32	1960	44.27	12.51	1705	41.29	11.95
1200	34.64	10.63	1455	38.14	11.33	1965	44.33	12.53	1710	41.35	11.96
1205	34.71	10.64	1460	38.21	11.34	1970	44.38	12.54	1715	41.41	11.97
1210	34.79	10.66	1465	32.28	11.36	1975	44.44	12.55	1720	41.47	11.98
1215	34.86	10.67	1470	38.34	11.37	1980	44.50	12.56	1725	41.53	11.99
1220	34.93	10.69	1475	38.41	11.38	1985	44.55	12.57	1730	41.59	12.00
1225	35.00	10.70	1480	38.47	11.40	1990	44.61	12.58	1735	41.65	12.02
1235	35.14	10.73	1490	38.60	11.42	1995	44.67	12.59	1745	41.77	12.04
1245	35.28	10.76	1500	38.73	11.45	2000	44.72	12.60	1755	41.89	12.06

Electrical Units

The **watt** is the unit of power (electrical, mechanical, thermal, etc.). Electrical power is given by the product of the voltage and the current.

Energy is sold by the **joule**, but in common practice the billing of electrical energy is expressed in terms of the **kilowatt-hour**, which is 3,600,000 joules or 3.6 megajoules.

The **horsepower** is a non-metric unit sometimes used in mechanics. It is equal to 746 watts.

The **ohm** is the unit of electrical resistance and represents the physical property of a conductor which offers a resistance to the flow of electricity, permitting just 1 ampere to flow at 1 volt of pressure.

Mathematical Formulas

To find the CIRCUMFERENCE of a:

Circle — Multiply the diameter by 3.14159265 (usually 3.1416).—

To find the AREA of a:

Circle—Multiply the square of the diameter by .785398 (usually .7854).

Rectangle—Multiply the length of the base by the height.

Sphere (surface)—Multiply the square of the radius by 3.1416 and multiply by 4.

Square—Square the length of one side.

Trapezoid—add the two parallel sides, multiply by the height and divide by 2.

Triangle—Multiply the base by the height and divide by 2.

To find the VOLUME of a:

Cone—Multiply the square of the radius of the base by 3.1416, multiply by the height, and divide by 3.

Cube—Cube the length of one edge.

Cylinder—Multiply the square of the radius of the base by 3.1416 and multiply by the height.

Pyramid—Multiply the area of the base by the height and divide by 3.

Rectangular Prism—Multiply the length by the width by the height.

Sphere—Multiply the cube of the radius by 3.1416, multiply by 4 and divide by 3.

Multiplication and Division Table

A number in the top line (19) multiplied by a number in the last column on the left (18) produces the number where the top line and the side line meet (342), and so on throughout the table.

A number in the table (342) divided by the number at the top of that column (19) results in the number (18) at the extreme left; also, a number in the table (342) divided by the number (18) at the extreme left gives the number (19) at the top of the column, and so on throughout the table.

1	2	3	4	5	6	7	8	9	10	11	12	13	14	15	16	17	18	19	20	21	22	23	24	25	1
2	4	6	8	10	12	14	16	18	20	22	24	26	28	30	32	34	36	38	40	42	44	46	48	50	2
3	6	9	12	15	18	21	24	27	30	33	36	39	42	45	48	51	54	57	60	63	66	69	72	75	3
4	8	12	16	20	24	28	32	36	40	44	48	52	56	60	64	68	72	76	80	84	88	92	96	100	4
5	10	15	20	25	30	35	40	45	50	55	60	65	70	75	80	85	90	95	100	105	110	115	120	125	5
6	12	18	24	30	36	42	48	54	60	66	72	78	84	90	96	102	108	114	120	126	132	138	144	150	6
7	14	21	28	35	42	49	56	63	70	77	84	91	98	105	112	119	126	133	140	147	154	161	168	175	7
8	16	24	32	40	48	56	64	72	80	88	96	104	112	120	128	136	144	152	160	168	176	184	192	200	8
9	18	27	36	45	54	63	72	81	90	99	108	117	126	135	144	153	162	171	180	189	198	207	216	225	9
10	20	30	40	50	60	70	80	90	100	110	120	130	140	150	160	170	180	190	200	210	220	230	240	250	10
11	22	33	44	55	66	77	88	99	110	121	132	143	154	165	176	187	198	209	220	231	242	253	264	275	11
12	24	36	48	60	72	84	96	108	120	132	144	156	168	180	192	204	216	228	240	252	264	276	288	300	12
13	26	39	52	65	78	91	104	117	130	143	156	169	182	195	208	221	234	247	260	273	286	299	312	325	13
14	28	42	56	70	84	98	112	126	140	154	168	182	196	210	224	238	252	266	280	294	308	322	336	350	14
15	30	45	60	75	90	105	120	135	150	165	180	195	210	225	240	255	270	285	300	315	330	345	360	375	15
16	32	48	64	80	96	112	128	144	160	176	192	208	224	240	256	272	288	304	320	336	352	368	384	400	16
17	34	51	68	85	102	119	136	153	170	187	204	221	238	255	272	289	306	323	340	357	374	391	408	425	17
18	36	54	72	90	108	126	144	162	180	198	216	234	252	270	288	306	324	342	360	378	396	414	432	450	18
19	38	57	76	95	114	133	152	171	190	209	228	247	266	285	304	323	342	361	380	399	418	437	456	475	19
20	40	60	80	100	120	140	160	180	200	220	240	260	280	300	320	340	360	380	400	420	440	460	480	500	20
21	42	63	84	105	126	147	168	189	210	231	252	273	294	315	336	357	378	399	420	441	462	483	504	525	21
22	44	66	88	110	132	154	176	198	220	242	264	286	308	330	352	374	396	418	440	462	484	506	528	550	22
23	46	69	92	115	138	161	184	207	230	253	276	299	322	345	368	391	414	437	460	483	506	529	552	575	23
24	48	72	96	120	144	168	192	216	240	264	288	312	336	360	384	408	432	456	480	504	528	552	576	600	24
25	50	75	100	125	150	175	200	225	250	275	300	325	350	375	400	425	450	475	500	525	550	575	600	625	25
	2	3	4	5	6	7	8	9	10	11	12	13	14	15	16	17	18	19	20	21	22	23	24	25	

Common Fractions Reduced to Decimals

8ths	16ths	32ds	64ths		8ths	16ths	32ds	64ths		8ths	16ths	32ds	64ths	
			1	.015625				23	.359375				45	.703125
		1	2	.03125	3	6	12	24	.375			23	46	.71875
			3	.046875				25	.390625				47	.734375
	1	2	4	.0625				26	.40625	6	12	24	48	.75
			5	.078125				27	.421875				49	.765625
		3	6	.09375		7	14	28	.4375			25	50	.78125
			7	.109375				29	.453125				51	.796875
1	2	4	8	.125				30	.46875		13	26	52	.8125
			9	.140625				31	.484375				53	.828125
		5	10	.15625	4	8	16	32	.5			27	54	.84375
			11	.171875				33	.515625				55	.859375
	3	6	12	.1875				34	.53125	7	14	28	56	.875
			13	.203125				35	.546875				57	.890625
		7	14	.21875		9	18	36	.5625			29	58	.90625
			15	.234375				37	.578125				59	.921875
2	4	8	16	.25				38	.59375		15	30	60	.9375
			17	.265625				39	.609375				61	.953125
		9	18	.28125	5	10	20	40	.625			31	62	.96875
			19	.296875				41	.640625				63	.984375
	5	10	20	.3125				42	.65625	8	16	32	64	1.
			21	.328125				43	.671875					
		11	22	.34375		11	22	44	.6875					

World Weights and Measures

Source: National Bureau of Standards, Department of Commerce

Denominations	Where Used	Amer. Equiv.
Almude.	Portugal.	4.423 gal
Ardeb.	Egypt.	5.6189 bu
Arratel (Libra).	Portugal.	1.012 lb
Arroba.	Argentina.	25.32 lb
"	Brazil.	32.38 lb
"	Cuba.	25.36 lb
"	Paraguay.	25.32 lb
"	Venezuela.	25.40 lb
" (liquid)	Cuba, Spain, and Venezuela.	4.263 gal
Arshine.	USSR.	28 in
" (sq)	"	5.44 sq ft
Artel.	Morocco.	1.12 lb
Baril.	Argentina and Mexico.	20.077 gal / 20.0787 gal
Barile (wine).	Malta.	11.2 gal
Berkovets.	USSR.	361.128 lb
Bongkal.	Malaysia.	832 grains
Bouw.	Sumatra.	7,096.5 sq meter
Bu.	Japan.	0.12 inch
Bushel.	British.	1.03205 U.S. bu
Caballeria.	Cuba.	33.162 acres
Caban (cavan).	Philippines.	2.13 bu / 19.8 gal
Caffiso.	Malta.	5.40 gal
Candy.	Bombay.	560 lb
"	India (Madras).	500 lb
Cantaro.	Malta.	175 lb
Carat (metric).	World.	3.086 grains
Catty.	China.	1.333$^1/_3$ lb
" (see Kin)	Japan.	
"	Java, Malacca.	1.36 lb
"	Thailand.	2$^2/_3$ lb
" (stand)	Thailand.	1.32 lb
"	Sumatra.	2.12 lb
Centaro.	Central America.	4.2631 gal
Centner.	Brunswick.	117.5 lb
"	Bremen.	127.5 lb
"	Denmark, Norway.	110.23 lb
"	Germany.	113.44 lb
"	Sweden.	93.7 lb
Chetvert.	USSR.	5.957 bu
Ch'ih.	China.	12.60 in
" (metric)	China.	39.37 in=1 meter
Cho.	Japan.	2.451 acres
Coomb.	England.	4.1282 bu
Coyan.	Thailand.	2,645.5 lb
Cuadra.	Argentina.	4.2 acres
"	Paraguay.	94.71 yd
" (sq)	Paraguay.	1.85 acres
"	Uruguay.	1.82 acres
Cwt. (hund. weight).	British.	112 lb
Dessiatine.	USSR.	2.6997 acres
Drachma.	Greece.	49.38 grains
Dunam.	Israel.	0.22239 acre
Fanega (dry).	Ecuador, Salvador.	1.5745 bu
"	Chile.	2.75268 bu
" (dry)	Guatemala, Spain.	1.57744 bu
"	Mexico.	2.57716 bu
" (dry)	Spain.	1.57501 bu
" (liquid)	Spain.	16 gal
" (dry)	Trinidad & Tobago.	110 lb
" (double)	Uruguay.	7.776 bu
" (single)	Uruguay.	3.888 bu
"	Venezuela.	3.334 bu
Feddan.	Egypt.	1.04 acres
Frail (raisins).	Spain.	50 lb
Frasco.	Argentina.	2.51 liq qt
Frasila.	Zanzibar.	35 lb
Fuder.	Luxembourg.	264.18 gal
Funt.	USSR.	0.9028 lb
Gallon.	British.	1.20094 U.S. gal
Garniec.	Poland.	1.0567 gal
Jerib.	Iran.	2.471 acres
Joch.	Austria.	1.422 acres
"	Hungary.	1.067 acres
Kantar.	Egypt.	99.05 lb
"	Morocco.	112 lb
"	Turkey.	124.45 lb
Ken.	Japan.	5.97 feet
Kin.	Japan.	1.32 lb
Klafter.	Austria.	2.074 yd
Klafter.	Germany.	1.90 yd
Koku.	Japan.	5.119 bu
Kwan.	Japan.	8.2673 lb
Last.	Belgium, Holland.	85.134 bu
"	England.	82.56 bu
"	Germany.	2 metric tons
"	Prussia.	112.29 bu
League (land).	Paraguay.	4.633 acres
Li.	China.	1890 ft
"	China.	0.01260 in =1/1000 ch'ih)
Libra (lb).	Argentina.	1.0128 lb
"	C. America, Chile.	1.014 lb
"	Cuba.	1.0143 lb
"	Mexico.	1.01467 lb
"	Peru, Venezuela.	1.0143 lb
"	Uruguay.	1.0127 lb
Load, timber.	England.	50 cu ft
Manzana.	Nicaragua.	1.742 acres
"	Costa Rica.	1.727 acres
"	Salvador.	1.727 acres
Marco.	Bolivia.	0.507 lb
Maund.	Bengal.	82$^2/_7$ lb
Mil.	Denmark.	4.68 miles
Milla.	Nicaragua.	1.1594 miles
"	Honduras.	1.1493 miles
Mina.	Greece.	0.95 lb
Morgen.	Germany.	0.63 acre
Oka (Oke).	Greece.	2.82 lb
Oke.	(Egypt).	2.7514 lb
"	Turkey.	2.826 lb
Pic.	Egypt.	22.83 inches
Picul.	Borneo—Celebes.	135.64 lb
"	China.	133$^1/_3$ lb
"	Java.	136.16 lb
"	Philippines.	139.44 lb
Pie.	Argentina.	0.9471 ft
"	Spain.	0.91416 ft
Pik.	Turkey.	27.9 inches
Pood.	USSR.	36,113 lb
Pund (lb).	Denmark.	1.102 lb
Quart.	British.	1.20094 liq qt
"	"	1.03205 dry qt
Quarter.	"	8.256 bu
Quintal.	Argentina.	101.3 lb
"	Brazil.	129.54 lb
"	Castile, Peru, Chile.	101.43 lb
"	Mexico.	101.47 lb
Rotl.	Israel.	6.35 lb
Sagene.	USSR.	7 feet
Salm.	Malta.	8.26 bu
Se.	Japan.	0.02451 acre
Seer.	India.	2 2/35 lb
Shaku.	Japan.	11.9303 in
Sho.	Japan.	1.91 liq qt
Skalpund.	Sweden.	0.937 lb
Stone.	British.	14 lb
Sun.	Japan.	1.193 inches
Tael (Kuping).	China.	575.64 grs (troy)
Tan.	Japan.	0.25 acre
To.	Japan.	2.05 pecks
Tonde (cereal).	Denmark.	3.9480 bu
Tonde (land).	Denmark.	1.36 acres
Tonne.	France.	2204.62 lb
Tsubo.	Japan.	35.58 sq ft
Ts'un.	China.	1.26 inches
Tunna (wheat).	Sweden.	4.16 bu
Tunnland.	"	1.22 acres
Vara.	Argentina.	34.0944 inches
"	Costa Rica, Salva.	32.913 inches
"	Guatemala.	32.909 inches
"	Honduras.	32.874 inches
"	Nicaragua.	33.057 inches
"	Chile and Peru.	32.913 inches
"	Cuba.	33.386 inches
"	Mexico.	32.992 inches
Vedro.	USSR.	3.249 gal
Verst.	"	0.663 mile
Vloka.	Poland.	41.50 acres
Wey.	Scotland, Ireland.	40 bu

The metric carat of 200 milligrams is now very generally in use. The word carat also is used to denote the proportion of aloy in a metal. Thus, pure gold is 24 carats fine.

Chemical Elements, Discoverers, Atomic Weights

Atomic weights, based on the exact number 12 as the assigned atomic mass of the principal isotope of carbon, carbon 12, are provided through the courtesy of the International Union of Pure and Applied Chemistry and Butterworth Scientific Publications.

For the radioactive elements, with the exception of uranium and thorium, the mass number of either the isotope of longest half-life (marked with a star) or the better known isotope (marked with two stars) is given.

Chemical element	Symbol	Atomic number	Atomic weight	Year discov.	Discoverer
Actinium	Ac	89	227*	1899	Debierne
Aluminum	Al	13	26.9815	1825	Oersted
Americium	Am	95	243*	1944	Seaborg, et al.
Antimony	Sb	51	121.75	1450	Valentine
Argon	Ar	18	39.948	1894	Rayleigh, Ramsay
Arsenic	As	33	74.9216	13th c.	Magnus
Astatine	At.	85	210*	1940	Corson, et al.
Barium	Ba	56	137.34	1808	Davy
Berkelium	Bk	97	249**	1949	Thompson, Ghiorso, Seaborg
Beryllium	Be	4	9.0122	1798	Vanquelin
Bismuth	Bi	83	208.980	15th c.	Valentine
Boron	B	5	10.811a	1808	Davy
Bromine	Br	35	79.904b	1826	Balard
Cadmium	Cd	48	112.40	1817	Stromeyer
Calcium	Ca	20	40.08	1808	Davy
Californium	Cf	98	249**	1950	Thompson, et al.
Carbon	C	6	12.01115a	B.C.	
Cerium	Ce	58	140.12	1803	Klaproth
Cesium	Cs	55	132.905	1861	Bunsen, Kirchoff
Chlorine	Cl	17	35.453b	1774	Scheele
Chromium	Cr	24	51.996b	1797	Vanquelin
Cobalt	Co	27	58.9332	1735	Brandt
Copper	Cu	29	63.546b	B.C.	
Curium	Cm	96	247*	1944	Seaborg, et al.
Dysprosium	Dy	66	162.50	1886	Boisbaudran
Einsteinium	Es	99	254*	1952	Ghiorso, et al.
Erbium	Er	68	167.26	1843	Mosander
Europium	Eu	63	151.96	1901	Demarcay
Fermium	Fm	100	257*	1953	Ghiorso, et al.
Fluorine	F	9	18.9984	1771	Scheele
Francium	Fr	87	223*	1939	Perey
Gadolinium	Gd	64	157.25	1886	Marignac
Gallium	Ga	31	69.72	1875	Boisbaudran
Germanium	Ge	32	72.59	1886	Winkler
Gold	Au	79	196.967	B.C.	
Hafnium	Hf	72	178.49	1923	Coster, Hevesy
Hahnium	Ha	105	262*	1970	Ghiorso, et al.
Helium	He	2	4.0026	1895	Ramsay
Holmium	Ho	67	164.930	1879	Cleve
Hydrogen	H	1	1.00797a	1766	Cavendish
Indium	In	49	114.82	1863	Reich, Richter
Iodine	I	53	126.9044	1811	Courtois
Iridium	Ir	77	192.2	1804	Tennant
Iron	Fe	26	55.847b	B.C.	
Krypton	Kr	36	83.80	1898	Ramsay, Travers
Lanthanum	La	57	138.91	1839	Mosander
Lawrencium	Lr	103	260*	1961	Ghiorso, T. Sikkeland, A.E. Larsh, and R. M. Latimer
Lead	Pb	82	207.19	B.C.	
Lithium	Li	3	6.939	1817	Arfvedson
Lutetium	Lu	71	174.97	1907	Welsbach, Urbain
Magnesium	Mg	12	24.312	1830	Liebig, Bussy
Manganese	Mn	25	54.9380	1774	Gahn
Mendelevium	Md	101	258*	1955	Ghiorso, et al.
Mercury	Hg	80	200.59	B.C.	
Molybdenum	Mo	42	95.94	1782	Hjelm
Neodymium	Nd	60	144.24	1885	Welsbach
Neon	Ne	10	20.183	1898	Ramsay, Travers
Neptunium	Np	93	237*	1940	McMillan, Abelson
Nickel	Ni	28	58.71	1751	Cronstedt
Niobium(Form. Columbium)	Nb	41	92.906	1801	Hatchett
Nitrogen	N	7	14.0067	1772	Rutherford
Nobelium	No	102	259*	1958	Ghiorso, et al.
Osmium	Os	76	190.2	1804	Tennant
Oxygen	O	8	15.9994a	1774	Priestly, Scheele
Palladium	Pd	46	106.4	1803	Wollaston
Phosphorus	P	15	30.9738	1669	Brandt
Platinum	Pt	78	195.09	1735	Ulloa
Plutonium	Pu	94	242**	1940	Seaborg, et al.
Polonium	Po	84	210**	1898	P. and M. Curie
Potassium	K	19	39.102	1807	Davy
Praseodymium	Pr	59	140.907	1885	Welsbach
Promethium	Pm	61	147**	1945	Glendenin, Marinsky
Protactinium	Pa	91	231*	1917	Hahn, Meltner
Radium	Ra	88	226*	1898	P. & M. Curie, Bemont
Radon	Rn	86	222*	1900	Dorn
Rhenium	Re	75	186.2	1925	Noddack, Tacke
Rhodium	Rh	45	102.905	1803	Wollaston
Rubidium	Rb	37	85.47	1861	Bunsen, Kirchoff
Ruthenium	Ru	44	101.07	1845	Claus

Chemical element	Symbol	Atomic number	Atomic weight	Year discov.	Discoverer
Rutherfordium	Rf	104	261*	1969	Ghiorso, et al.
Samarium	Sm	62	150.35	1879	Boisbaudran
Scandium	Sc	21	44.956	1879	Nilson
Selenium	Se	34	78.96	1817	Berzelius
Silicon	Si	14	28.086a	1823	Berzelius
Silver	Ag	47	107.868b	B.C.	
Sodium	Na	11	22.9898	1807	Davy
Strontium	Sr	38	87.62	1790	Crawford
Sulfur	S	16	32.064a	B.C.	
Tantalum	Ta	73	180.948	1802	Eckeberg
Technetium	Tc	43	99**	1937	Perrier and Segre
Tellurium	Te	52	127.60	1782	Von Reichenstein
Terbium	Tb	65	158.924	1843	Mosander
Thallium	Tl	81	204.37	1861	Crookes
Thorium	Th	90	232.038	1828	Berzelius
Thulium	Tm	69	168.934	1879	Cleve
Tin	Sn	50	118.69	B.C.	
Titanium	Ti	22	47.90	1789	Gregor
Tungsten (Alternate Wolfram)	W	74	183.85	1783	d'Elhujar
Uranium	U	92	238.03	1789	Klaproth
Vanadium	V	23	50.942	1830	Sefstrom
Xenon	Xe	54	131.30	1898	Ramsay, Travers
Ytterbium	Yb	70	173.04	1878	Marignac
Yttrium	Y	39	88.905	1794	Gadolin
Zinc	Zn	30	65.37	B.C.	
Zirconium	Zr	40	91.22	1789	Klaproth

a. Atomic weights so designated are known to be variable because of natural variations in isotopic composition. The observed ranges are: hydrogen±0.0001; boron±0.003; carbon±0.0005; oxygen±0.0001; silicon±0.001; sulfur±0.003.

b. Atomic weights so designated are believed to have the following experimental uncertainties: chlorine±0.001; chromium±0.001; iron±0.003; bromine±0.001; silver±0.001; copper±0.001.

Medical Signs and Abbreviations

Source: American Medical Association

℞ (Lat. Recipe)	take	a.c.	before meals	gr	grain	pulvis	powder
℈	drachm	ad	to, up to	gtt	drops	q. 3 h	every three hours
f ℈	fluid drachm	ad libitum	at pleasure	h.s.	at bedtime	q.i.d.	four times daily
℥	ounce	agit	shake	inject	injection	q.s.	as much as is sufficient
f ℥	fluid ounce	aqua	water	lb	pound	sig	sign, write
℥ ss	half an ounce	b.i.d.	twice daily	m	mix	solutio	a solution
℥ i	one ounce	cap	capsule	mg	milligram	ss	one-half
℥ iss	one ounce and a half	cum, or c	with	ml	milliliter	stat	at once
℥ii	two ounces	e.m.p.	as directed	non. rep. or n.r.		tab	tablet
m	minim, or drop	fiant (ft)	make		do not repeat	t.i.d.	three times daily
o	pint	gargarisma	a gargle	p.c.	after meals	ung	ointment
aa	of each	Gm	gram	p.r.n.	as circumstances may require	ut dict	as directed

Bell Time on Shipboard

Source: Maritime Administration

Time, A.M.		Time, A.M.		Time, A.M.		Time, P.M.		Time, P.M.		Time, P.M.	
1 Bell	12:30	1 Bell	4:30	1 Bell	8:30	1 Bell	12:30	1 Bell	4:30	1 Bell	8:30
2 Bells	1:00	2 Bells	5:00	2 Bells	9:00	2 Bells	1:00	2 Bells	5:00	2 Bells	9:00
3 "	1:30	3 "	5:30	3 "	9:30	3 "	1:30	3 "	5:30	3 "	9:30
4 "	2:00	4 "	6:00	4 "	10:00	4 "	2:00	4 "	6:00	4 "	10:00
5 "	2:30	5 "	6:30	5 "	10:30	5 "	2:30	5 "	6:30	5 "	10:30
6 "	3:00	6 "	7:00	6 "	11:00	6 "	3:00	6 "	7:00	6 "	11:00
7 "	3:30	7 "	7:30	7 "	11:30	7 "	3:30	7 "	7:30	7 "	11:30
8 "	4:00	8 "	8:00	8 "	Noon	8 "	4:00	8 "	8:00	8 "	Midnight

Breaking the Sound Barrier; Speed of Sound

The prefix Mach is used to describe supersonic speed. It derives from Ernst Mach, a Czech-born German physicist, who contributed to the study of sound. When a plane moves at the speed of sound it is Mach 1. When twice the speed of sound it is Mach 2. When it is near but below the speed of sound its speed can be designated at less than Mach 1, for example, Mach .0. Mach is defined as "in jet propulsion, the ratio of the velocity of a rocket or a jet to the velocity of sound in the medium being considered."

When a plane passes the sound barrier—flying faster than sound travels—listeners in the area hear thunderclaps, but pilots do not hear them.

Sound is produced by vibrations of an object and is transmitted by alternate increase and decrease in pressures that radiate outward through a material media of molecules—somewhat like waves spreading out on a pond after a rock has been tossed.

The frequency of sound is determined by the number of times the vibrating waves undulate per second, and is measured in cycles per second. The slower the cycle of waves, the lower the sound. As frequencies increase, the sound is higher.

Sound is audible to human beings only if the frequency falls within a certain range. The human ear is usually not sensitive to frequencies of less than 20 vibrations per second, or more than about 20,000 vibrations per second-although this range varies among individuals. Anything at a pitch higher than the human ear can hear is termed ultrasonic.

Intensity or loudness is the strength of the pressure of these radiating waves, and is measured in decibels. The human ear responds to intensity in a range from zero to 120 decibels. Any sound with pressure over 120 decibels is painful.

The speed of sound is generally placed at 1088 ft. per second at sea level at 32°F. It varies in other temperatures and in different media. Sound travels faster in water than in air, and even faster in iron and steel. While in air it travels a mile in 5 seconds, it does a mile under water in 1 second, and through iron in ¹/₃ of a second. It travels through ice cold vapor at approximately 4,708 ft. per sec., ice-cold water, 4,938; granite, 12,960; hardwood, 12,620; brick, 11,-960; glass, 16,410 to 19,690; silver, 8,658; gold, 5,717.

Great Inventions and Scientific Discoveries

Invention	Date	Inventor	Nation
Adding machine	1642	Pascal	French
Adding machine	1885	Burroughs	U.S.
Addressograph	1892	Duncan	U.S.
Aerosol spray	1941	Goodhue	U.S.
Air brake	1868	Westinghouse	U.S.
Air conditioning	1911	Carrier	U.S.
Air pump	1650	Guericke	German
Airplane, automatic pilot	1929	Green	U.S.
Airplane, experimental	1896	Langley	U.S.
Airplane jet engine	1939	Ohain	German
Airplane with motor	1903	Orville and Wilbur Wright	U.S.
Airplane, hydro	1911	Curtiss	U.S.
Airship	1852	Giffard	French
Airship, rigid dirigible	1900	Zeppelin	German
Arc tube	1923	Alexanderson	U.S.
Autogyro	1920	de la Cierva	Spanish
Automobile, differential gear	1885	Benz	German
Automobile, electric	1892	Morrison	U.S.
Automobile, exp'mtl.	1875	Marcus	Austrian
Automobile, gasoline	1887	Daimler	German
Automobile, gasoline	1892	Duryea, C. E.	U.S.
Automobile, magneto	1897	Bosch, R.	German
Automobile muffler	....	Maxim, H.P.	U.S.
Automobile self-starter	1911	Kettering	U.S.
Automobile, steam	1889	Roper	U.S.
Babbitt metal	1839	Babbitt	U.S.
Bakelite	1907	Baekeland	Belg., U.S.
Balloon	1783	Montgolfier	French
Barometer	1643	Torricelli	Italian
Bicycle, modern	1884	Starley	English
Bifocal lens	1780	Franklin	U.S.
Block signals, railway	1867	Hall	U.S.
Bomb, depth	1916	Tait	U.S.
Bottle machine	1903	Owens	U.S.
Braille printing	1829	Braille	French
Burner, gas	1855	Bunsen	German
Calculating machine	1823	Babbage	English
Camera, Polaroid Land	1948	Land	U.S.
Car coupler	1873	Janney	U.S.
Carburetor, gasoline	1876	Daimler	German
Card time recorder	1894	Cooper	U.S.
Carding machine	1797	Whittemore	U.S.
Carpet sweeper	1876	Bissell	U.S.
Cash register	1879	Ritty	U.S.
Cathode ray tube	1878	Crookes	English
Cellophane	1911	Brandenberger	Swiss
Celluloid	1870	Hyatt	U.S.
Cement, Portland	1845	Aspdin	English
Chronometer	1735	Harrison	English
Circuit breaker	1925	Hilliard	U.S.
Clock, pendulum	1657	Huygens	Dutch
Coaxial cable system	1929	Affel, Es. pensched	U.S.
Coke oven	1893	Hoffman	Austrian
Compressed air rock drill	1871	Ingersoll	U.S.
Comptometer	1887	Felt	U.S.
Computer, automatic sequence	1939	Aiken et al.	U.S.
Condenser microphone (telephone)	1920	Wente	U.S.
Cotton gin	1793	Whitney	U.S.
Cream separator	1880	DeLaval	Swedish
Cultivator, disc	1878	Mallon	U.S.
Cystoscope	1877	Nitze	German
Dental plate, rubber	1855	Goodyear	U.S.
Diesel engine	1895	Diesel	German
Dynamite	1866	Nobel	Swedish
Dynamo, continuous current	1860	Picinotti	Italian
Dynamo, hydrogen cooled	1915	Schuler	U.S.
Electric battery	1800	Volta	Italian
Electric fan	1882	Wheeler	U.S.
Electrocardiograph	1903	Einthoven	Dutch
Electroencephalograph	1929	Berger	German
Electromagnet	1824	Sturgeon	English
Electron spectrometer	1944	Deutsch, Elliott, Evans	U.S.
Electron tube multigrid	1913	Langmuir	U.S.
Electroplating	1805	Brugnatelli	Italian
Electrostatic generator	1929	Van de Graaff	U.S.
Elevator brake	1852	Otis	U.S.
Elevator, push button	1922	Larson	U.S.
Engine, automobile	1879	Benz	German
Engine, coal-gas 4-cycle	1877	Otto	German
Engine, compression ignition	1883	Daimler	German
Engine, electric ignition	1880	Benz	German
Engine, gas, compound	1926	Eickemeyer	U.S.
Engine, gasoline	1872	Brayton, Geo.	U.S.
Engine, gasoline	1886	Daimler	German
Engine, steam, piston	1705	Newcomen	English
Engine, steam, piston	1769	Watt	Scottish
Engraving, half-tone	1893	Ives	U.S.
Filament, tungsten	1915	Langmuir	U.S.
Flanged rail	1831	Stevens	U.S.
Flatiron, electric	1882	Seeley	U.S.
Furnace (for steel)	1861	Siemens	German
Galvanometer	1820	Sweigger	German
Gas discharge tube	1922	Hull	U.S.
Gas lighting	1792	Murdoch	Scottish
Gas mantle	1885	Welsbach	Austrian
Gasoline (lead ethyl)	1922	Midgely	U.S.
Gasoline, cracked	1913	Burton, W.M.	U.S.
Gasoline, high octane	1930	Ipatieff	Russian
Geiger counter	1913	Geiger	German
Glass, laminated safety	1909	Benedictus	French
Glider	1853	Cayley	English
Gun, breechloader	1811	Thornton	U.S.
Gun, Browning	1916	Browning	U.S.
Gun, magazine	1875	Hotchkiss	U.S.
Gun, silencer	1909	Maxim, H. P.	U.S.
Guncotton	1846	Schoenbein	German
Gyrocompass	1911	Sperry	U.S.
Gyroscope	1852	Foucault	French
Harvester	1836	Moore	U.S.
Harvester-thresher	1888	Matteson	U.S.
Helicopter	1939	Sikorsky	U.S.
Hydrometer	1768	Baume	French
Ice-making machine	1851	Gorrie	U.S.
Iron lung	1928	Drinker, Slaw.	U.S.
Kaleidoscope	1817	Brewster	English
Kinetoscope	1887	Edison	U.S.
Kodak	1888	Eastman, Walker	U.S.
Lacquer, nitrocellulose	1921	Flaherty	U.S.
Lamp, arc	1879	Brush	U.S.
Lamp, incandescent	1879	Edison	U.S.
Lamp, incand., frosted	1924	Pipkin	U.S.
Lamp, incand., gas	1916	Langmuir	U.S.
Lamp, Klieg	1911	Kliegl, A.&J.	U.S.
Lamp, mercury vapor	1912	Hewitt	U.S.
Lamp, miner's safety	1816	Davy	English
Lamp, neon	1915	Claude	French
Lathe, turret	1845	Fitch	U.S.
Launderette	1934	Cantrell	U.S.
Lens, achromatic	1758	Dollond	English
Lens, fused bifocal	1908	Borsch	U.S.
Leydenjar (condenser)	1745	von Kleist	German
Lightning rod	1752	Franklin	U.S.
Linoleum	1860	Walton	English
Linotype	1885	Mergenthaler	U.S.
Lock, cylinder	1865	Yale	U.S.
Locomotive, electric	1851	Vail	U.S.
Locomotive, exp'mtl.	1801	Trevithick	English
Locomotive, exp'mtl.	1812	Fenton et al	English
Locomotive, exp'mtl.	1813	Hedley	English
Locomotive, exp'mtl.	1814	Stephenson	English
Locomotive practical	1829	Stephenson	English
Locomotive, 1st U.S.	1830	Cooper, P.	U.S.
Loom, power	1785	Cartwright	English
Loudspeaker, dynamic	1924	Rice, Kellogg	U.S.
Machine gun	1861	Gatling	U.S.
Machine gun, improved	1872	Hotchkiss	U.S.
Machine gun (Maxim)	1883	Maxim, H.S.	U.S., Eng.
Magnet, electro	1828	Henry	U.S.
Mantle, gas	1885	Welsbach	Austrian
Mason jar	1858	Mason, J.	U.S.
Match, friction	1827	John Walker	English
Mercerized textiles	1843	Mercer, J.	English
Meter, induction	1888	Shallenberger	U.S.

Invention	Date	Inventor	Nation
Metronome	1816	Malzel	Austrian
Micrometer	1636	Gascoigne	English
Microphone	1877	Berliner	U.S.
Microscope, compound	1590	Janssen	Dutch
Microscope, electronic	1931	Knoll, Ruska	German
Monitor, warship	1861	Ericsson	U.S.
Monotype	1887	Lanston	U.S.
Motor, AC	1892	Tesla	U.S.
Motor, induction	1887	Tesla	U.S.
Motorcycle	1885	Daimler	German
Movie machine	1894	Jenkins	U.S.
Movie, panoramic	1952	Waller	U.S.
Movie, talking	1927	Warner Bros.	U.S.
Mower, lawn	1868	Hills	U.S.
Mowing machine	1831	Manning	U.S.
Neoprene	1930	Carothers	U.S.
Nylon synthetic	1930	Carothers	U.S.
Nylon	1937	Du Pont lab.	U.S.
Oil cracking furnace	1891	Gavrilov	Russian
Oil filled power cable	1921	Emanueli	Italian
Oleomargarine	1868	Mege-Mouries	French
Ophthalmoscope	1851	Helmholtz	German
Paper machine	1809	Dickinson	U.S.
Parachute	1785	Blanchard	French
Pen, ballpoint	1888	Loud	U.S.
Pen, fountain	1884	Waterman	U.S.
Pen, steel	1780	Harrison	English
Pendulum	1581	Galileo	Italian
Percussion cap	1814	Shaw	U.S.
Phonograph	1877	Edison	U.S.
Photo, color	1892	Ives	U.S.
Photo film, celluloid	1887	Goodwin	U.S.
Photo film transparent	1878	Eastman, Goodwin	U.S.
Photoelectric cell	1895	Elster	German
Photographic paper	1898	Baekeland	U.S.
Photography	1835	Fox-Talbot	English
Photography	1837	Daguerre	French
Photography	1839	Niepce	French
Photophone	1880	Bell	U.S.
Phototelegraphy	1925	Bell lab	U.S.
Piano	1709	Cristofori	Italian
Piano, player	1863	Foumeaux	French
Pin, safety	1849	Hunt	U.S.
Pistol (revolver)	1835	Colt	U.S.
Plow, cast iron	1797	Newbold	U.S.
Plow, disc	1896	Hardy	U.S.
Pneumatic hammer	1890	King	U.S.
Powder, smokeless	1863	Schultze	German
Printing press, rotary	1846	Hoe	U.S.
Printing press, web	1865	Bullock	U.S.
Propeller, screw	1804	Stevens	U.S.
Propeller, screw	1837	Ericsson	Swedish
Punch card accounting	1884	Hollerith	U.S.
Radar	1922	Taylor, Young	U.S.
Radio amplifier	1907	De Forest	U.S.
Radio beacon	1928	Donovan	U.S.
Radio crystal oscillator	1918	Nicolson	U.S.
Radio receiver, cascade tuning	1913	Alexanderson	U.S.
Radio receiver, heterodyne	1913	Fessenden	U.S.
Radio transmitter triode modulation	1914	Alexanderson	U.S.
Radio tube-diode	1905	Fleming	English
Radio tube oscillator	1915	De Forest	U.S.
Radio tube triode	1907	De Forest	U.S.
Radio, signals	1895	Marconi	Italian
Radio, magnetic detector	1902	Marconi	Italian
Radio FM 2-path	1929	Armstrong	U.S.
Rayon	1883	Swan	English
Razor, electric	1931	Schick	U.S.
Razor, safety	1895	Gillette	U.S.
Reaper	1834	McCormick	U.S.
Record, cylinder	1887	Bell, Tainter	U.S.
Record, disc	1887	Berliner	U.S.
Record, long playing	1948	Goldmark	U.S.
Record, wax cylinder	1888	Edison	U.S.
Refrigerants, low-boiling, fluorine compound	1930	Midgely and co-workers	U.S.
Refrigerator car	1868	David	U.S.
Resin, synthetic	1931	Hill	English

Invention	Date	Inventor	Nation
Rifle, repeating	1860	Spencer	U.S.
Rocket engine	1929	Goddard, R.H.	U.S.
Rubber, vulcanized	1839	Goodyear	U.S.
Saw, band	1808	Newberry	English
Saw, circular	1777	Miller	English
Searchlight, arc	1915	Sperry	U.S.
Sewing machine	1846	Howe	U.S.
Shoe-sewing machine	1860	McKay	U.S.
Shrapnel shell	1784	Shrapnel	English
Shuttle, flying	1733	Kay	English
Sleeping-car	1858	Pullman	U.S.
Slide rule	1620	Oughtred	English
Soap, hardwater	1928	Bertsch	German
Spectroscope	1859	Kirchoff, Bunsen	German
Spectroscope (mass)	1918	Dempster	U.S.
Spinning jenny	1767	Hargreaves	English
Spinning mule	1779	Crompton	English
Steamboat, exp'mtl.	1783	Jouffroy	French
Steamboat, exp'mtl.	1785	Fitch	U.S.
Steamboat, exp'mtl.	1787	Rumsey	U.S.
Steamboat, exp'mtl.	1788	Miller	Scottish
Steamboat, exp'mtl.	1803	Fulton	U.S.
Steamboat, exp'mtl.	1804	Stevens	U.S.
Steamboat, practical	1802	Symington	Scottish
Steamboat, practical	1807	Fulton	U.S.
Steam car	1770	Cugnot	French
Steam turbine	1884	Parsons	English
Steel	1856	Bessemer	English
Steel alloy	1891	Harvey	U.S.
Steel alloy, high-speed	1901	Taylor, White	U.S.
Steel, electric	1900	Heroult	French
Steel, manganese	1884	Hadfield	English
Steel, stainless	1916	Brearley	English
Stereoscope	1838	Wheatstone	English
Stethoscope	1819	Laennec	French
Stethoscope, binaural	1840	Cammann	U.S.
Stock ticker	1870	Edison	U.S.
Storage battery, electric	1812	Ritter	German
Stove, electric	1896	Hadaway	U.S.
Submarine	1891	Holland	U.S.
Submarine, even keel	1894	Lake	U.S.
Submarine, torpedo	1776	Bushnell	U.S.
Tank, military	1914	Swinton	English
Tape recorder, magnetic	1899	Poulsen	Danish
Telegraph, magnetic	1837	Morse	U.S.
Telegraph, quadruplex	1874	Edison	U.S.
Telegraph, railroad	—	Woods	U.S.
Telegraph, wireless, high frequency	1896	Marconi	Italian
Telephone	1876	Bell	U.S.-Can.
Telephone amplifier	1912	De Forest	U.S.
Telephone, automatic	1891	Stowger	U.S.
Telephone, radio	1902	Poulsen, Fessenden	U.S.
Telephone, radio	1906	De Forest	U.S.
Telephone, radio, l. d.	1915	AT&T	U.S.
Telephone, recording	1898	Poulson	Danish
Telephone, wireless	1899	Collins	U.S.
Telescope	1608	Lippershey	Neth.
Telescope	1609	Galileo	Italian
Telescope, astronomical	1611	Kepler	German
Teletype	1928	Morkrum, Kleinschmidt	U.S.
Television, iconoscope	1923	Zworykin, V.	U.S.
Television, electronic	1927	Farnsworth, P.	U.S.
Television, (mech. scanner)	1926	Baird	Scottish
Thermometer	1593	Galileo	Italian
Thermometer	1710	Reaumur	French
Thermometer, mercury	1714	Fahrenheit	German
Time recorder	1890	Bundy	U.S.
Time, self-regulator	1918	Bryce	U.S.
Tire, double-tube	1845	Thompson	English
Tire, pneumatic	1888	Dunlop	Irish
Toaster, automatic	1918	Strite	U.S.
Tool, pneumatic	1865	Law	English
Torpedo, marine	1804	Fulton	U.S.
Tractor, crawler	1900	Holt	U.S.
Transformer A.C.	1885	Stanley	U.S.
Transistor	1947	Shockley, Brattain, Bardeen	U.S.
Trolley car, electric	1884	Van Depoel	U.S.
	-87	Sprague	U.S.
Tungsten, ductile	1912	Coolidge	U.S.

Invention	Date	Inventor	Nation
Turbine, gas	1899	Curtis, C.G.	U.S.
Turbine, hydraulic	1849	Francis	U.S.
Turbine, steam	1896	Curtis, C.G.	U.S.
Type, movable	1450	Gutenberg	German
Typewriter	1868	Soule, Glidden	U.S.
Vacuum cleaner, electric	1907	Spangler	U.S.
Washer, electric	1907	Hurley Co.	U.S.
Welding, atomic hydrogen	1924	Langmuir, Palmer	U.S.
Welding, electric	1877	Thomson	U.S.
Wind tunnel	1923	Munk	U.S.
Wire, barbed	1874	Glidden	U.S.
Wire, barbed	1875	Haisn	U.S.
X-ray tube	1913	Coolidge	U.S.
Zipper	1891	Judson	U.S.

Discoveries and Innovations: Chemistry, Physics, Biology, Medicine

Product	Date	Discoverer	Nation
Acetylene gas	1892	Wilson	U.S.
ACTH	1949	Armour & Co.	U.S.
Adrenalin	1901	Takamine	Japan
Aluminum, electrolytic process	1886	Hall	U.S.
Aluminum, isolated	1825	Oersted	Danish
Analine dye	1856	Perkin	English
Anesthesia, ether	1842	Long	U.S.
Anesthesia, local	1885	Koller	Austria
Anesthesia, spinal	1898	Bier	German
Anti-rabies	1885	Pasteur	French
Antitoxin, diphtheria	1891	Von Behring	German
Antiseptic surgery	1867	Lister	English
Argyrol	...	Barnes	U.S.
Arsphenamine	1910	Ehrlich	German
Aspirin	1889	Dresser	German
Atomic numbers	1913	Moseley	English
Atomic theory	1803	Dalton	English
Atomic time clock	1947	Libby	U.S.
Atom-smashing theory	1919	Rutherford	English
Atabrine	...	Mietzsch, et al	German
Aureomycin	1948	Duggar	U.S.
Bacitracin	1945	Johnson et al	U.S.
Bacteria (described)	1676	Leeuwenhoek	Dutch
Barbital	1903	Fischer	German
Bleaching powder	1798	Tennant	English
Blood, circulation	1628	Harvey	English
Bordeaux mixture	1885	Millardet	French
Bromine from sea	1924	Edgar-Kramer	U.S.
Calcium carbide	1888	Wilson	U.S.
Calculus	1670	Newton	English
Carbon oxides	1925	Fisher	German
Carbomycin	1952	Tanner	U.S.
Camphor synthetic	1896	Haller	French
Canning (food)	1804	Appert	French
Chlorine	1810	Davy	English
Chloroform	1831	Guthrie, S.	U.S.
Chloromycetin	1947	Burkholder	U.S.
Classification of plants and animals	1735	Linnaeus	Swedish
Cocaine	1860	Niermann	German
Combustion explained	1777	Lavoisier	French
Conditioned reflex	1914	Pavlov	Russian
Conteben	1950	Belmisch, Mietzsch, Domagh	German
Cortisone	1936	Kendall	U.S.
Cortisone, synthesis	1946	Sarett	U.S.
Cosmic rays	1910	Gockel	Swiss
Cyanimide	1905	Frank-Caro	German
Cyclotron	1930	Lawrence	U.S.
DDT	1874	Zeidler	German
(Not applied as insecticide until 1939)			
Deuterium (heavy hydrogen)	1932	Urey, Brick-Wedde Murphy	U.S.
DNA (structure)	1951	Crick	English
		Watson	U.S.
		Wilkins	English
Electric resistance (law)	1827	Ohm	German
Electric waves	1888	Hertz	German
Electrolysis	1852	Faraday	English
Electromagnetism	1819	Oersted	Danish
Electron	1897	Thomson, J.	English
Electron diffraction	1936	Thomson, G.	English
		Davisson	U.S.
Electroshock treatment	1938	Cerletti, Bini	Italy
Erythromycin	1952	McGuire	U.S.
Evolution, natural selection	1858	Darwin	English
Falling bodies, law	1590	Galileo	Italian
Gases, law of combining volumes	1808	Gay-Lussac	French
Geometry, analytic	1619	Descartes	French
Gold (cyanide process for extraction)	1887	MacArthur-Forest	British
Gravitation, law	1687	Newton	English
Holograph	1948	Gabor	British
Human heart transplant	1967	Barnard	S. Africa
Indigo, synthesis of	1880	Baeyer	German
Induction, electric	1830	Henry	U.S.
Insulin	1922	Banting, Best, MacLeod	Canada
Intelligence testing	1905	Binet and Simon	French
Isniazid	1952	Hoffman-La-Roche	U.S.
		Domagh	German
Isotopes, theory	1912	Soddy	English
Laser (light amplification by stimulated emission of radiation)	1958	Townes, Schawlow	U.S.
Light, velocity	1675	Roemer	Danish
Light, wave theory	1690	Huygens	Dutch
Lithography	1796	Senefelder	Bohemia
Lobotomy	1935	Egas Oniz	Portugal
LSD-25	1943	Hoffman	Swiss
Mendelian laws	1866	Mendel	Austrian
Mercator's projection (map)	1568	Mercator	(Kremer) Flemish
Methanol	1925	Patard	French
Milk condensation	1853	Borden	U.S.
Molecular hypothesis	1811	Avogadro	Italian
Motion, laws of	1687	Newton	English
Neomycin	1949	Waksman & Lechevalier	U.S.
Neutron	1932	Chadwick	English
Nitric acid	1648	Glauber	German
Nitric oxide	1772	Priestley	English
Nitroglycerin	1846	Sobrero	Italian
Ohm's law	1827	Ohm, Georg	German
Oil cracking process	1891	Dewar	U.S.
Oxygen	1774	Priestley	English
Ozone	1840	Schonbein	German
Paper, from wood pulp, sulfate process	1884	Dahl	German
Paper, sulfite process	1867	Tilghman	U.S.
Penicillin	1929	Alex. Fleming	English
Practical use	1941	Florey-Chain	English
Periodic law and table of elements	1869	Mendelejeff	Russian
Planetary motion, laws	1609	Kepler	German
Plutonium fission	1940	Kennedy, J.W.	U.S.
		Wahl, A. C.	U.S.
		Seaborg, G. T.	U.S.
		Segre, Emilio	U.S.
Polymixin	1947	Ainsworth	English
Positron	1932	Anderson	U.S.
Proton	1919	Rutherford	English
Psychoanalysis	1900	Freud	Austrian
Quantum theory	1900	Planck	German
Quasars	1963	Matthews & Sandage	U.S.
Quinine-synthetic	1918	Rabe	German
Radioactivity	1896	Becquerel	French
Radium	1898	Curie, Pierre	French
		Curie, Marie	Polish
Relativity theory	1905	Einstein	German

Product	Date	Discoverer	Nation
Reserpine	1949	Jal Vaikl	India
Salvarsan (606)	1910	Ehrlich	German
Schick test, diphtheria	1913	Schick	U.S.
Silicon	1823	Berzelius	Swedish
Streptomycin	1945	Waksman	U.S.
Sulfanilamide theory	1908	Gelmo	German
Sulfanilamide	1934	Domag	German
Sulfadiazine	1940	Roblin	U.S.
Sulfapyridine	1938	Ewins Phelps	English
Sulfathiazole	. . .	Fosbinder, Walter	U.S.
Sulfuric acid	1831	Phillips	English
Sulfuric acid, lead	1746	Roebuck	English
Terramycin	1950	Finlay, et al	U.S.
Tuberculin	1890	Koch	German
Uranium fission (theory)	1939	Hahn, Strassmann	German
		Borr	Danish
		Einstein	U.S.
		Fermi	Italian
		Pegram	U.S.
		Wheeler	U.S.

Product	Date	Discoverer	Nation
Uranium fission, atomic reactor	1942	Enrico Fermi, Leo Seilard	U.S.
Vaccine, measles	1954	Enders, John	U.S.
		Peebles, T.	U.S.
Vaccine, polio	1955	Sabin, Alb. E.	U.S.
Vaccine, polio	1953	Salk, Jonas E.	U.S.
Vaccine, rabies	1885	Pasteur	French
Vaccine, smallpox	1796	Jenner, Edw.	English
Vaccine, typhus	1909	Nicolle, J.	French
Van Allen belts, radiation	1958	Van Allen	U.S.
Vitamin A	1913	McCollum, Davis	U.S.
Vitamin B	1916	McCollum	U.S.
Vitamin C	1912	Holst, Froelich	Norway
Vitamin D	1922	McCollum	U.S.
Wassermann test, syphilis	1906	Wassermann	German
Xerography	1938	Carlson	U.S.
X-ray	1895	Roentgen	German

Playing Cards and Dice Chances

Poker Hands (Four-Suit)

Hand	Number Possible	Odds Against
Royal Flush	4	649,739 to 1
Other Straight Flush	36	72,192 to 1
Four of a kind	624	4,164 to 1
Full House	3,744	693 to 1
Flush	5,108	508 to 1
Straight	10,200	254 to 1
Three of a kind	54,912	46 to 1
Two Pairs	123,552	20 to 1
One Pair	1,098,240	4 to 3 (1.37 to 1)
Nothing	1,302,540	1 to 1
Total	2,598,960	

Dice
Totals Probabilities on Two Dice

Total	Odds Against (Single toss)	Total	Odds Against (Single toss)
2	35 to 1	8	31 to 5
3	17 to 1	9	8 to 1
4	11 to 1	10	11 to 1
5	8 to 1	11	17 to 1
6	31 to 5	12	35 to 1
7	5 to 1		

Dice
Probabilities of Consecutive Winning Plays

No. Consecutive Wins	By 7, 11, or Point.	No. Consecutive Wins	By 7, 11, or Point
1	244 in 495	6	1 in 70
2	24 in 100	7	1 in 141
3	3 in 25	8	1 in 287
4	1 in 17	9	1 in 582
5	1 in 34		

Pinochle Auction
Odds Against Finding in "Widow" of Three Cards

Open Places	Odds Against	Open Places	Odds Against
1	5 to 1	4	3 to 2 for
2	2 to 1	5	2 to 1 for
3	Even		

Bridge
The odds—Against suit distribution in a hand of 4-4-3-2 are about 4 to 1, against 5-4-2-2 about 8 to 1, against 6-4-2-1 about 20 to 1, against 7-4-1-1 about 254 to 1, against 8-4-1-0 about 2,211 to 1, and against 13-0-0-0 about 158,753,389,899 to 1.

Simple Interest Table

	Time	4%	5%	6%	7%	8%
$1.00	1 month	$.003	$.004	$.005	$.005	$.006
..	2 months	.007	.008	.010	.011	.013
..	3	.010	.013	.015	.017	.020
..	6	.020	.025	.030	.035	.040
..	12	.040	.050	.060	.070	.080
$100.00	1 day	.011	.013	.016	.019	.022
..	2 days	.022	.027	.032	.038	.044
..	3	.033	.041	.050	.058	.067

	Time	4%	5%	6%	7%	8%
$100.00	4 days	$.045	$.053	$.066	$.077	$.889
..	5	.056	.069	.082	.097	.111
..	6	.067	.083	.100	.116	.133
..	1 month	.334	.416	.500	.583	.667
..	2 months	.667	.832	1.000	1.166	1.333
..	3	1.000	1.250	1.500	1.750	2.000
..	6	2.000	2.500	3.000	3.500	4.000
..	12	4.000	5.000	6.000	7.000	8.000

Colors of the Spectrum

Color, an electromagnetic wave phenomenon, is a sensation produced through the excitation of the retina of the eye by rays of light. The colors of the spectrum may be produced by viewing a light beam refracted by passage through a prism, which breaks the light into its wave lengths.

Customarily, the primary colors of the spectrum are thought of as those 6 monochromatic colors which occupy relatively large areas of the spectrum: red, orange, yellow, green, blue and violet. However, Sir Isaac Newton named a 7th, indigo, situated between blue and violet on the spectrum. Aubert estimated (1865) the solar spectrum to contain approximately 1,000 distinguishable hues of which according to Rood (1881) 2 million tints and shades can be distinguished; Luckiesh stated (1915) that 55 distinctly different hues have been seen in a single spectrum.

By many physicists only 3 primary colors are recognized: red, yellow and blue (Mayer, 1775); red, green and violet (Thomas Young, 1801); red, green and blue (Clerk Maxwell, 1860).

The color sensation of black is due to complete lack of stimulation of the retina, that of white to complete stimulation. The infra-red and ultra-violet rays, below the red (long) end of the spectrum and the violet end (short end) respectively, are invisible. Heat is the principal effect of the infra-red rays and chemical action that of the ultra-violet rays.

Copyright Law of the U.S.

Source: Copyright Office, Library of Congress

An author, or other owner who derives his rights from the author, may obtain protection for a literary, musical, or artistic work by complying with the provisions of the copyright law (Title 17 of the United States Code). The law gives the copyright owner the exclusive right to print, reprint, publish, copy and sell the copyrighted work; to revise or adapt it; and, with certain limitations, to perform and record it. Applications for registration of claims to copyright are filed with the Copyright Office, Library of Congress, Washington, D.C. 20559. Application forms and information circulars covering various subjects are furnished by the Copyright Office free upon request.

Categories of Works

The copyright law provides that the application for registration of any work shall specify to which of the following classes the work in which copyright is claimed belongs:

(A) Books, including composite and cyclopedic works, directories, gazetteers and other compilations; (B) periodicals, including newspapers; (C) lectures, sermons and addresses prepared for oral delivery; (D) dramatic or dramatico-musical compositions; (E) musical compositions; (F) maps; (G) works of art, models or designs for works of art; (H) reproductions of a work of art; (I) drawings or sculptural works of a scientific or technical character; (J) photographs; (K) prints and pictorial illustrations including prints or labels used for articles of merchandise; (L) motion-picture photoplays; (M) motion pictures other than photoplays; and (N) sound recordings.

How Copyright Is Secured

Between the time a work is created and the time statutory copyright is secured, it is protected, while unpublished, by the common law against unauthorized copying or other use, without any action being required by the Copyright Office.

Copyright in a published work is secured by publishing the work with the required notice of copyright, and it is important that all copies published bear the notice. The law provides that the notice shall consist of either the word "Copyright," or the abbreviation "Copr.," or the symbol © , accompanied by the name of the copyright owner. If the work is a printed literary, musical or dramatic work, the notice shall include also the year in which the copyright was secured by publication. For example: © John Doe 1976. In the case, however, of copies of works specified in classes F through K above, the notice may consist of the symbol © accompanied by the initials, monogram, mark, or symbol of the owner, provided that his name appears on some accessible part of the copies. The notice required to secure copyright for sound recordings fixed and first published on or after Feb. 15, 1972 is the symbol ℗ , the year date of first publication of the sound recording, and the name of the copyright owner. For example: ℗ 1976 Doe Records, Inc. NOTE: Copyright for a sound recording protects against unauthorized reproduction of the same series of sounds; it is not a substitute for registration of the musical or literary work recorded.

Promptly after publication, there should be sent to the Copyright Office, Library of Congress, Washington, D.C. 20559, two copies of the best edition of the work, together with an application for registration and a $6 fee.

Manufacturing Requirements

For books and periodicals to be copyrightable, if they are by American authors, or by foreign authors who are domiciled in the U.S. at the time of first publication, the typesetting, printing, and binding of the copies used for first publication must have been done in the U.S. The only general exception to this rule is that a book or periodical in the English language manufactured and first published abroad may secure a 5-year ad interim copyright, provided that registra-

tion is made within 6 months of the date of first publication abroad. If ad interim copyright is secured, the importation of 1,500 copies is permitted. Books by American authors manufactured abroad may generally not be imported while they are under U.S. copyright protection, unless an Import Statement issued by the Copyright Office at the time of the ad interim registration is presented to U.S. Customs at the port of entry. Further information may be obtained from the Copyright Office.

Copyright for Unpublished Works

Statutory copyright may be had for certain classes of unpublished works by depositing in the Copyright Office one copy of the work, together with an application for registration and the $6 fee. Works for which registration may be made in unpublished form include those in classes C, D, E, G, I, J, L and M, above. There are special provisions concerning what should be deposited in the case of 3-dimensional works of art and motion pictures; information about them is obtainable from the Copyright Office. NOTE: Certain kinds of material are not registrable in unpublished form. These include "book material" such as fiction, nonfiction, poetry, directories and catalogs, as well as manuscripts of articles, stories and other works that are to be first published as contributions to periodicals. Such works are, as mentioned above, protected by the common law against unauthorized use while unpublished.

Duration of Copyright

The original term of copyright endures for 28 years, measured from the exact date of first publication of the work; or in the case of works registered in unpublished form, from the date of registration. During the last (the 28th) year of the first term, the copyright may be renewed by filing in the Copyright Office an application for renewal and a fee of $4. If they are not received by the Copyright Office before the original term has expired the work falls into the public domain and the copyright cannot be restored.

Fees

All copyright fees are established by law. Remittances should be in the form of checks or money orders made payable to the Register of Copyrights. The schedule of fees follows:

Registration of copyright claims (including a certificate bearing the Copyright Office seal) for all classes of works, $6.

For registration of a claim to renewal, $4.

Each additional certificate, $2.

Other certifications, including certifications of photocopies of Copyright Office records, $3.

For recording each assignment, agreement or other document of 6 pages or fewer, listing no more than one title, $5. For each page over 6 and each title over one, 50c.

Searches: for each hour spent by the Copyright Office staff in searching the official records, $5.

International Protection

The U.S. has copyright relations with some 60 countries, under which works of American authors are protected in those countries, and the works of their authors are protected in the U.S. The basic feature of this protection is "national treatment," under which the alien author is treated by a country in the same manner that it treats its own authors. Relations exist by virtue of bilateral agreements or through the Buenos Aires Convention or the Universal Copyright Convention. Legislation implementing the latter convention, which became effective Sept. 16, 1955, gives the works of foreign authors the benefit of exemptions from the manufacturing requirements of the U.S. copyright law, provided the works are first published abroad with a copyright notice including the symbol © , the name of the copyright owner and the year date of first publication, and that the work either is by an "author" who is a citizen of a foreign country which belongs to the Convention or is first published in a foreign member country. Conversely, works of U.S.. authors are exempt from certain burdensome requirements in particular foreign member countries.

Trademarks: How to Obtain and Protect Them

A trademark, as defined by Act of Congress, "includes any word, name, symbol, or device, or any combination thereof, adopted and used by a manufacturer or merchant to identify his goods and distinguish them from those manufactured or sold by others." Rights in trademarks are acquired by use, which must continue if those rights are to be preserved. In order to be eligible for registration a mark must be in use in commerce which may be lawfully regulated by Congress.

Trademarks are registered on the Principal Register and the Supplemental Register of the U.S. Patent and Trademark Office. "Coined, arbitrary, fanciful or suggestive marks, usually called technical marks, if otherwise qualified." may be registered on the Principal Register. A trademark that is merely descriptive of goods, or their regional origin, or is primarily a surname, is placed on the Supplemental Register.

The Trademark Act of 1946 provides that "For the purposes of registration on the supplemental register, a mark may consist of any trademark, symbol, label package, configuration of goods, name, word, slogan, phrase, surname. geographical name, numeral, or device, or any combination of any of the foregoing, but such mark must be capable of distinguishing the applicant's goods or services."

A trademark cannot be registered if it comprises immoral, deceptive or scandalous matter, or matter that may disparage or falsely suggest a connection with persons living or dead, institutions, beliefs, or national symbols. It cannot use the flag or coat of arms or other insignia of the United States, any state, municipality or foreign nation. It cannot use a portrait, signature or name of a living individual without his consent, or those of a deceased President of the United States without consent of his widow.

An application for registration must be filed in the name of the owner of the mark, who may submit his case or be represented by an attorney at law, or other person authorized to practice in trademark matters. A complete application comprises a written application, a drawing of the mark, five specimens or facsimiles and the filing fee.

The Patent and Trademark Office publishes a pamphlet, General Information Concerning Trademarks, which describes the way applications. and drawings are to be prepared and gives sample forms for applications. The Patent and Trademark Office, upon request, will supply forms for the registration of a trademark in the name of (1) an individual, (2) a firm, and (3) a corporation. If facilities permit, the Office will make drawings from the applicant's direction and at his expense. If the application is allowed, the trademark will be published in the Trademark Official Gazette so that anyone who considers that he will be damaged by the new mark may file his opposition in 30 days.

The Trademark Act of 1946 also provides for the registration of service marks, certification marks and collective marks. A service mark is a title, symbol or name used in sale or advertising of services to identify them. A certification mark is used by others than the owner to certify origin or quality, such as work by a union. A collective mark is used by members of a cooperative, an association or other group and indicates membership in a union or other organization. A digest of registered trademarks may be inspected at the Patent and Trademark Office.

A trademark is registered for 20 years and may be renewed for periods of 20 years if still in use in commerce regulated by Congress, or if nonuse is due to special circumstances which excuse nonuse and is not due to any intention to abandon the mark. The fee for the original application is $35, and for the renewal is $25, with lesser fees for corrections. amendments, abstracts of title and other services.

The pamphlet, General Information Concerning Trademarks, is a general guide. The Trademark Rules of Practice of the Patent Office with Forms and Statutes is also published. The Trademark Official Gazette, issued weekly, contains information concerning trademarks published for opposition, registered, and renewed. For these and other trademark publications inquiries may be addressed to the Supt. of Documents, Government Printing Office, Washington, D.C. 20402.

Patents and How to Apply for Them

A patent for an invention is granted by the United States Patent and Trademark Office to the inventor of any new and useful process, machine, manufacture, or composition of matter, or any new and useful improvements in these categories. The grant to the patentee is of "the right to exclude others from making, using or selling the invention throughout the United States" for the term of 17 years. A patent is also granted for certain distinct and new varieties of plants, also for 17 years.

Patents for new, original and ornamental designs for articles of manufacture may be obtained for 3 1/2, 7, and 14 years, as requested by the inventor. The filing fee on each design application is $20; the issue fee is $10 for a 3 1/2-yr. term, $20 for 7 years and $30 for 14 years.

Except in special circumstances, an application must be made by the inventor; if 2 are associated in the invention both must apply; if the inventor is mentally ill or dead, application may be made by the guardian or administrator of the estate. The specification must include a written description of the invention and of the manner and process of making and using it, and is required to be in such full, clear, concise, and exact terms as to enable any person skilled in the art to which the invention pertains, or with which it is most nearly connected, to make and use the same. The claims are full descriptions of the subject matter of the invention. A drawing is required by the statute in all cases which admit of drawings. The filing fee is $65, with $2 additional for each claim in excess of 10, and $10 additional for each claim in independent form in excess of one.

The Patent and Trademark Office examines the application to determine whether the invention is new and useful and whether the application otherwise complies with the law. If the application is allowed, a notice is sent the applicant and the final fee of $100, plus $10 for each page or portion thereof of specification as printed and $2 for each sheet of drawing, is due within 3 months. The terms "patent applied for" and "patent pending" have no legal significance but falsely using this marking is punishable by a fine.

If the Patent and Trademark Office rejects an application, the applicant may ask for reconsideration, giving reason; if rejected again he may appeal to the Board of Appeals of the Patent and Trademark Office, and if rejected there, may go to the Court of Customs and Patent Appeals or file a civil action in the U.S. District Court for the District of Columbia.

Under certain conditions a license must be obtained before an application for a patent can be filed in a foreign country. The Commissioner of Patents and Trademarks may order an invention kept secret if publication would hurt the national safety or defense. Copies of the Patent Laws, (37 Code of Federal Regulations) and General Information Concerning Patents, can be obtained from the Superintendent of Documents, Government Printing Office, Washington, D.C. 20402.

Delegates from over 40 nations took part in Washington May 25-June 19, 1970, in a diplomatic conference on a Patent Cooperation Treaty. It was unanimously approved and was signed by representatives of 20 governments, including the United States, Great Britain, Germany, Canada, and Japan, with many others expected to sign later. The treaty will simplify the filing of patent applications on the same invention in different countries by means of centralized filing procedures and standardized formalities.

U. S. Passport, Visa, and Health Requirements

Source: Passport Office, U.S. Dept. of State and U.S. Public Health Service

Passports are issued by the United States Department of State to citizens and nationals of the United States for the purpose of documenting them for their foreign travel and identifying them as Americans. Some countries require a visa, or stamp of approval, to be affixed to the passport by the consulate of the country to be visited, while others waive this formality. Also some countries, which do not require visas, require tourist cards from visitors making a short stay.

Unless specifically endorsed, passports may not be used for travel into or through Cambodia, Cuba, North Korea or Vietnam, or for travel into or through other countries or areas as determined to be in the national interest by the Secretary of State.

How to Obtain a Passport

An applicant for a passport who has never been previously issued a passport in his own name, must execute an application in person before (1) a Passport Agent; (2) a clerk of any Federal court; (3) a clerk of any State court of record or a judge or clerk of any probate court; (4) a postal employee designated by the Postmaster at a Post Office which has been selected to accept passport applications; or (5) a diplomatic or consular officer of the U.S. abroad. A wife/husband who is to be included in the passport must appear with the applicant and execute the application. Passport Agencies are located at Boston (John F. Kennedy Bldg., Government Center), Chicago (Federal Office Bldg., 230 S. Dearborn); Honolulu (Fed. Bldg., 335 Merchant St.); Los Angeles (Hawthorne Fed. Bldg., 15000 Aviation Blvd., Rm. 2W16, Lawndale, Calif.); Miami (Fed. Bldg., 51 S.W. First Ave.); New Orleans (International Trade Mart, 2 Canal Street); New York (630 Fifth Ave.); Philadelphia, (Federal Bldg., 600 Arch Street); San Francisco (Fed. Bldg., 450 Golden Gate Ave.); Seattle (Federal Bldg., 915 Second Ave.); Washington D.C. (Passport Office, 1425 K St., N.W.)

A passport previously issued to the applicant, or one in which he was included, will be accepted as proof of citizenship in lieu of the following documents. A person born in the United States shall present his birth certificate. To be acceptable, the certificate must show the given name and surname, the date and place of birth and that the birth record was filed shortly after birth. The certificate must also be certified with the registrar's signature and the raised, impressed, embossed, or multi-colored seal of his office. Uncertified copies of birth certificates are not acceptable. A delayed birth certificate (a record filed more than one year after the date of birth) is acceptable provided that it shows that the report of birth was supported by acceptable secondary evidence of birth as described below.

If such primary evidence is not obtainable, a notice from the registrar shall be submitted stating that no birth record exists. The notice shall be accompanied by the best obtainable secondary evidence such as a baptismal certificate, a certificate of circumcision, a hospital birth record, affidavits of persons having personal knowledge of the facts of the birth or other documentary evidence such as early census, school or family bible records, newspaper files and insurance papers. Secondary evidence should be created as close to the time of birth as possible.

A person in the U.S. who has been issued a passport in his own name within the last eight years may obtain a new passport by filling out, signing and mailing a passport by mail application together with his previous passport, two identical signed photographs taken within the last 6 months and the established fee to the nearest Passport Agency or to the Passport Office in Wash., D.C. If, however, an applicant is applying for a passport for the first time, if his prior passport was issued before his 18th birthday, if he wishes to include a person other than himself in the passport, or if he is applying for an official, diplomatic, or other no-fee passport, he must execute a passport application in person before a Passport Agent; a clerk of any Federal court, a clerk of any State court of record or a judge or clerk of any probate court, a postal employee designated by the Postmaster at a Post Office which has been selected to accept passport applications; or a diplomatic or consular officer of the U.S. abroad.

A naturalized citizen should present his naturalization certificate. A person born abroad claiming citizenship through either a native-born or naturalized citizen must submit a certificate of citizenship issued by the Immigration and Naturalization Service; or a Consular Report of Birth or Certification of Birth issued by the Dept. of State. If one of the above documents has not been obtained, he must submit evidence of citizenship of the parent(s) through whom citizenship is claimed and evidence which would establish the parent/child relationship. Additionally, if through birth to one American and one alien parent, an affidavit from parent(s) showing periods and places of residence in the United States and abroad, specifying periods spent abroad in the employment of the U.S. Government, including the Armed Forces, or with certain international organizations; if through naturalization of parents, evidence of admission to the United States for permanent residence.

Under certain conditions, married women must present evidence of marriage. Special laws govern women married prior to Mar. 3, 1931 and should be discussed with the person executing the application.

The applicant shall establish his identity to the satisfaction of the person executing the application. Proof of identity may be established through a personal knowledge of the applicant by the Clerk or Agent or by an item which contains the signature and either a physical description or photograph of the applicant. The following items of identification are acceptable: previous United States Passport; certificate of naturalization; driver's license (not temporary or learner's license); a governmental (Federal, State, Municipal) identification card or pass.

If the applicant is not able to establish his identity by personal knowledge or by presentation of one of the above acceptable documents, he should be accompanied by an identifying witness who has known him for at least 2 years, and who is a U.S. citizen or a permanent resident alien of the United States. The witness shall be required to establish his own identity to the satisfaction of the person executing the application by one of the above means.

The identifying witness shall sign an affidavit in the presence of the same person who executes the passport application. The affidavit shall show:

The witness resides at a specific address:

The witness knows or has reason to believe that the applicant is a citizen of the United States:

The basis of the witness' knowledge concerning the applicant;

The information set forth in the affidavit is true to the best of his knowledge and belief.

A person included in the passport of another may not use the passport for travel unless he is accompanied by the bearer.

Aliens — An alien leaving the U.S. must request passport facilities from his home government. He must have a permit from his local Collector of Internal Revenue, and if he wishes to return he should request a re-entry permit from the Immigration and Naturalization Service if it is required.

Contract Employees — Persons traveling because of a contract with the Government must submit with their applications letters from their employer stating position. destination and purpose of travel and Armed Forces contract number when pertinent.

Photographs and Fees

Photographs — Identical photographs taken within six months, both signed by the applicant and which are a good likeness, must accompany the passport application. A group photograph is preferred if more than one person is included in the passport. Photographs may be in color or in black and white. They must be full face. printed on thin. nonglossy paper on a plain. light background and must be no smaller than 2-1/2 x 2-1/2 inches nor larger than 3 x 3 inches in size. They must also be capable of withstanding a mounting temperature of over 200°F.

Fees — The passport fee is $10. A fee of $3 shall be charged for execution of the application. No execution fee is payable where a passport is applied for by mail. All applicants must pay the passport fee and, where applicable. the execution fee unless specifically exempted by law. If applying in person, service will be expedited by presenting exact fees. An emergency service fee of $10 is charged in addition to all other fees where work must be performed after hours. The only other fees are for special postage. A passport is valid for five years unless otherwise limited.

During the calendar year 1975 the Passport Office, Dept. of State. issued 2,334,359 passports to American citizens.

The loss of a valid passport is a serious matter and should be reported in writing immediately to the Passport Office, Dept. of State, Wash., D.C. 20524, or to the nearest consular office of the U.S. when abroad.

Foreign Regulations

A visa is an endorsement or a notation, usually rubber stamped in a passport by a representative of the country to be visited. It certifies that the bearer of the passport is to be permitted to enter that country for a certain purpose and length of time. With the exception of the Iron Curtain countries, no visas are required for brief tourist travel to Western European countries. Authoritative visa information can be obtained by writing directly to foreign consular officials. The locations of foreign consular offices in the U.S. may be obtained by consulting the Congressional Directory available in most libraries. (Check city telephone directories for complete address.)

Health Information

Smallpox — Smallpox vaccination is required for travel to most countries of the world except Europe. However, in the event of an outbreak of smallpox in any country in Europe. most countries remaining on the itinerary following a visit to the infected country will require a Vaccination Certificate. A Certificate is not required for travel from the United States directly to and from Europe, Canada, Mexico, Australia. and New Zealand. For travel to more than one island in the Caribbean, a Certificate may be required. The United States requires a Certificate upon the traveler's return only if, in the preceding 14 days, he has visited a country reporting smallpox. Currently smallpox is limited to a few areas in Ethiopia.

Yellow Fever — A few African countries require a Vaccination Certificate of all travelers. A number of countries require vaccination if travelers arrive from infected or endemic areas. Vaccination is recommended for travel to infected areas. currently parts of Africa and South America. The United States has no vaccination requirement.

Cholera — A few countries require vaccination if travelers arrive from infected areas. The United States has no vaccination requirement.

Plague — Vaccination is not required by any country as a condition of entry. Selective immunization is advisable for travelers to Vietnam. Cambodia and Laos.

Vaccination Information — Yellow fever vaccine must be obtained at an officially designated Yellow Fever Vaccination Center, and the Certificate. valid for 10 years, must be stamped by the Center. Other vaccinations may be obtained from licensed physicians. and sometimes from local health departments. The Smallpox Certificate, valid for 3 years, and the Cholera Certificate, valid for 6 months, must be stamped by the State or local health department. Vaccinations must be recorded on an approved version of PHS-731, International Certificates of Vaccination. which are available from State and local health departments, passport offices. travel agencies. and the Superintendent of Documents. U.S. Printing Office. Washington, D.C. 20402.

Travelers are advised to contact their local health department 2 weeks prior to departure to obtain the most current information on countries to be visited.

Customs Exemptions and Advice to Travelers

United States residents returning after a stay abroad of at least 48 hours are, generally speaking, granted customs exemptions of $100 each. Each returning resident may bring home free of duty articles totaling $100 in fair retail value in the country of acquisition, subject to limitations on liquors and cigars. These articles must accompany the traveler at the time of his return, must be for his personal or household use, must have been acquired as an incident of his trip, and must be properly declared to Customs. Not more than one quart of alcoholic beverages may be included in the $100 exemption.

If a U. S. resident arrives directly or indirectly from American Samoa, Guam, or the Virgin Islands of the United States, his purchase may be valued up to $200 fair retail value, but not more than $100 of the exemption may be applied to the value of articles acquired elsewhere than in such insular possessions, and one gallon of alcoholic beverages may be included in his exemption, but not more than 1 quart of such beverages may have been acquired elsewhere than in the designated islands.

The exemption for articles acquired in the Virgin Islands of the United States and in Mexico is not conditional upon the 48-hour absence requirement.

In either case, the exemption for alcoholic beverages is accorded only when the returning resident has attained 21 years of age at the time of his arrival. One hundred cigars may be included (except Cuban products) in either exemption.

The $100 or $200 exemption may be granted only if the exemption, or any part of it, has not been used within the preceding 30-day period.

Bona fide gifts costing no more than $10 fair retail value or $20 from American Samoa, Guam, or Virgin Islands. may be mailed to friends at home duty-free; addressee cannot receive in a single day gifts exceeding the $10 limit.

Air Travel

On a first-class trans-Atlantic flight a passenger may carry 66 lbs. of luggage free; a tourist class passenger. 44 lbs. free. A charge is made for extra weight.

Precautions for Travel

In some cases naturalized United States citizens desiring to visit the countries of their birth, and. sometimes their American-born children traveling to those countries. may be subject to military service and other regulations there. The United States Department of State advises such travelers to get specific information from the consulates of the countries concerned before departure.

Service in Foreign Armed Forces

Voluntary service in the armed forces of a foreign state engaged in hostilities against the U. S. is highly persuasive evidence of an intention to relinquish citizenship and will normally result in loss of U. S.

citizenship. Voluntary service in the armed forces of a foreign state not engaged in hostilities against the U. S. does not result in loss of U. S. citizenship unless there is persuasive evidence of an intent to transfer or abandon allegiance by reason of such military service.

U.S. Immigration Law

The national origins quota system disappeared from United States immigration procedures July 1, 1968, as provided by the Act. of Oct. 3, 1965, which amended the Immigration and Nationality Act.

The Immigration and Nationality Act. as amended, provides for numerical limitations on immigration from the Eastern and Western Hemispheres. Not subject to any numerical limitations, however, are immigrants who are spouses or children of U.S. citizens, or parents of citizens who are 21 years of age or older; returning residents; certain former U.S. citizens; ministers of religion; and certain long-term U. S. Government employees.

The Act of Oct. 3, 1965, established new controls to protect the American labor market from an influx of skilled and unskilled foreign labor. The primary responsibility was placed on the would-be immigrant to obtain the Secretary of Labor's clearance, prior to the issuance of a visa, establishing that there are not sufficient workers in the U. S. at the alien's destination who are able, willing and qualified to perform the skilled or unskilled labor; and that the employment of the alien will not adversely affect wages and working conditions of workers in the U. S. similarly employed.

Eastern Hemisphere Immigrants

Persons born in countries of the Eastern Hemisphere and dependent areas thereof are subject to an annual limitation of 170,000. Within this numerical limitation there is an annual limitation of 20,000 for each country and 200 for each dependent area. Applicants are classified as either preference or nonpreference.

The preference visa categories are based on certain relationships to persons in the U. S.; i.e., unmarried sons and daughters of United States citizens, spouses and unmarried sons and daughters of resident aliens, married sons and daughters of U.S. citizens, and brothers and sisters of U. S. citizens (first, 2d, 4th and 5th preference, respectively); certain professions and skills (3d preference); and certain categories of workers which are in short supply in the U. S. (6th preference); refugees (7th preference). Spouses and children of preference applicants are entitled to the same preference if accompanying or following to join such persons.

Except for refugee status, preference status is based upon approved petitions, filed with the Immigration and Naturalization Service, by the appropriate relative or employer (or in the 3rd preference by the alien himself). Visa numbers for qualified preference applicants are made available in the order of the preference classes and, within such classes, in the order of the filing dates of the petitions.

Immigrants not entitled to classification within one of the above-mentioned preference groups are non-preference applicants and receive only those visa numbers not needed by preference applicants.

A prerequisite for nonpreference classification is a labor certification under Section 212 (a) (14) of the Immigration and Nationality Act, or satisfactory evidence that the provisions of that section do not apply to the alien's case. The availability of nonpreference visa numbers is contingent on the level of preference demand and cannot therefore be predicted with real accuracy. However, in some countries and dependent areas the higher preference categories may utilize the entire numerical limitation, which will prevent any visa numbers from becoming available for persons from such countries or areas in the nonpreference category.

Western Hemisphere Immigrants

The act establishes an annual ceiling of 120,000 on immigration by persons born in independent countries of the Western Hemisphere (Canada, Mexico, Central and South America and the Caribbean Area). Within this over-all ceiling there is no numerical limitation set for individual countries, and no preference classes have been established for such applicants. Visas within the 120,000 limitation will be made available to qualified applicants in the chronological order of the priority dates. An applicant's date is the date a labor certification for the applicant is accepted for processing by the Dept. of Labor or the date proof is received by a consular officer that a labor certification is not required.

Excludable Aliens

Aliens who are excludable on medical grounds are those who are mentally retarded, insane, psychopathic, mentally defective, sexual deviates, chronic alcoholics, narcotic addicts, and those who are afflicted with any dangerous contagious disease or who have a physical defect impairing the ability to earn a living. Also excludable are paupers, beggars, illiterates, stowaways, prostitutes, persons engaged in commercial vice, narcotics traffickers, persons convicted of crimes involving moral turpitude, persons who obtain or try to obtain a visa by fraud, or who left the U. S. to avoid military service. Those excludable on security grounds include persons who are anarchists, members or affiliates of certain proscribed organizations, and those who teach or advocate overthrow of the U. S. Government by force or violence.

For more detailed information consult the nearest office of the U. S. Immigration & Naturalization Service, or any U. S. Consul abroad.

Naturalization: How to Become an American Citizen
Source: The Federal Statutes

A person who desires to be naturalized as a citizen of the United States may obtain the necessary application form as well as detailed information from the nearest office of the Immigration and Naturalization Service or from the clerk of a court handling naturalization cases.

There are no racial bars to naturalization. Women have the same right as men to become naturalized.

An applicant must be at least 18 years old. He must have been a lawful resident of the United States continuously for 5 years. For husbands and wives of U.S. citizens the period is 3 years in most instances. Special provisons apply to certain veterans of the Armed Forces.

An applicant must have been physically present in this country for at least half of the required 5 years' residence.

Every applicant for naturalization must:

(1) sign the petition in his own handwriting, if physically able to write.

(2) demonstrate an understanding of the English language, including an ability to read, write, and speak words in ordinary usage in the English language (persons physically unable to do so, and per-

sons who were on December 24, 1952 over 50 years of age and had been residing in the United States for 20 years are excepted.

(3) have been a person of good moral character, attached to the principles of the Constitution, and well disposed to the good order and happiness of the United States for five years just before filing the petition or for whatever other period of residence is required in his case and continue to be such a person until admitted to citizenship; and

(4) demonstrate a knowledge and understanding of the fundamentals of the history, and the principles and form of government, of the U.S.

The petitioner also is obliged to have two credible citizen witnesses. These witnesses must have personal knowledge of the applicant.

A person not of good moral character includes a habitual drunkard, an adulterer, a polygamist, a violator of criminal law, a gambler, one who gave false testimony to obtain a benefit under the immigration law, one in prison for 180 days or more, one convicted of murder.

Naturalization is denied to any person who, within 10 years, has been subversive, including communists and others who favor totalitarian government, and who were members of a proscribed organization, unless the petitioner was under 16 or joined under duress.

A law approved Aug. 20, 1958, provides for the expeditious naturalization of alien spouses and adopted children of U.S. citizens who are missionaries or performing religious duties and are stationed abroad.

When the applicant files his petition he pays the court clerk $25. At the preliminary hearing he may be represented by a lawyer or social service agency. There is a 30-day wait. If action is favorable, there is a final hearing before a judge, who administers the following oath of allegiance:

Oath of Allegiance

I hereby declare, on oath, that I absolutely and entirely renounce and abjure all allegiance and fidelity to any foreign prince, potentate, state or sovereignty, to whom or which I have heretofore been a subject or citizen; that I will support and defend the Constitution and laws of the United States of America against all enemies, foreign and domestic; that I will bear true faith and allegiance to the same; that I will bear arms on behalf of the United States when required by the law; that I will perform noncombatant service in the armed forces of the United States when required by the law; that I will preform work of national importance under civilian direction when required by the law; and that I take this obligation freely without any mental reservation or purpose of evasion; so help me God.

Immigrants Admitted from All Countries

Source: Immigration and Naturalization Service, U.S. Dept. of Justice

Year	Number	Year	Number	Year	Number	Year	Number
1820.	8,385	1881–1890 . . .	5,246,613	1951–1960 . . .	2,515,479	1969	358,579
1821–1830 . . .	143,439	1891–1900 . . .	3,687,564	1962	283,763	1970	373,326
1831–1840 . . .	599,125	1901–1910 . . .	8,795,386	1963	306,360	1971	370,478
1841–1850 . . .	1,713,251	1911–1920 . . .	5,735,811	1964	292,248	1972	384,685
1851–1860 . . .	2,598,214	1921–1930 . . .	4,107,209	1965	296,697	1973	400,063
1861–1870 . . .	2,314,824	1931–1940 . . .	528,431	1966	323,040	1974	394,861
1871–1880 . . .	2,812,191	1941–1950 . . .	1,035,039	1968	454,448	1975	386,194
						1820–1975 . . .	47,098,919

Passports Issued and Renewed

Source: Passport Office, Dept. of State

Passports are actual count; other data based on sample.

Item	1960	1965	1969[6]	1970	1972	1973	1974	1975
New and renewed passports.	853,087	1,330,290	1,820,192	2,219,159	2,728,021	2,729,104	2,415,003	2,334,359
Object of Travel.[1]								
Government.	115,910	119,130	167,562	146,169	136,901	146,494	206,343	210,399
Nongovernment.	737,177	1,139,160	1,652,630	2,072,990	2,591,120	2,582,610	2,208,660	2,123,960
Personal reasons[2].	321,590	487,470	1,475,630	1,791,330	2,042,560	1,245,780	384,930	376,400
Pleasure[3].	350,897	535,150	130,670	216,700	441,010	1,077,240	1,382,100	1,315,600
Business[4].	24,540	76,210	25,180	39,940	68,700	154,820	267,980	273,110
Education.	31,240	31,120	15,490	20,230	33,290	95,240	153,210	132,490
Religion.	6,780	6,780	2,180	3,350	3,980	7,930	16,510	22,450
Health	1,460	500	220	640	800	1,140	1,860	1,510
Other.	670	1,930	3,260	800	780	460	2,070	2,400
First area destination:								
Africa	8,440	19,580	19,760	18,790	29,750	26,420	32,110	32,930
Australia and Oceania.	35,220	50,750	68,190	51,210	78,580	80,670	101,250	96,300
Europe.	669,662	992,800	1,460,212	1,910,169	2,244,161	2,181,114	1,714,613	1,611,410
Far East	55,960	111,320	125,100	116,730	135,230	139,740	162,130	154,660
North Central and South America .	58,935	99,620	91,850	72,410	135,720	189,280	287,260	317,980
Middle-East	24,670	56,070	54,990	48,890	103,870	111,000	117,110	121,010
World Tour	200	150	90	960	710	880	530	60
Mode of Travel — departure:[4]								
Ship	226,245	39,340	2,766	. . . .	. . . .	. . . .	. . . .	. . . .
Air.	626,842	1,290,950	1,817,426	. . . .	. . . .	. . . .	. . . .	. . . .
Sex of Passport Recipients:								
Male.	419,615	700,080	945,520	1,123,620	1,358,530	1,321,050	1,154,940	1,128,050
Female.	433,472	630,210	874,672	1,095,539	1,369,491	1,408,054	1,260,063	1,206,309
Citizenship of Passport Recipients:								
Native	710,172	1,236,797	1,702,320	2,072,560	2,553,750	2,511,266	2,154,920	2,039,690
Naturalized	142,915	93,493	117,872	146,599	174,271	217,838	260,083	294,669

(1). Data not entirely comparable because of changes in classifications in 1961.
(2). Includes "Personal business," "Join husband," "Accompany husband," "Business and pleasure," "Visit family."
(3). Includes "Sightsee," "Vacation," "Visit," and "Tourist."
(4). Includes applicants formerly listed under "Employment" and "Commercial business."
(5). Legislation effective Aug. 26, 1968 eliminated passport renewals.
(6). Data eliminated. Over 99% of passport recipients indicate departure by air.

SPORTS OF 1976
Olympic Games Records

The modern Olympic Games, first held in Athens, Greece, in 1896, were the result of efforts by Baron Pierre de Coubertin, a French educator, to promote interest in education and culture, also to foster better international understanding through the universal medium of youth's love of athletics.

His source of inspiration for the Olympic Games was the ancient Greek Olympic Games, most notable of the four Panhellenic celebrations. The games were combined patriotic, religious, and athletic festivals held every four years. The first such recorded festival was that held in 776 B.C., the date from which the Greeks began to keep their calendar by "Olympiads," or four-year spans between the games.

The first Olympiad is said to have consisted merely of a 200-yard foot race near the small city of Olympia, but the games gained in scope and became demonstrations of national pride. Only Greek citizens — amateurs — were permitted to participate. Winners received laurel, wild olive, and palm wreaths and were accorded many special privileges. Under the Roman emperors, the games deteriorated into professional carnivals and circuses. Emperor Theodosius banned them in 394 A.D.

Baron de Coubertin enlisted 9 nations to send athletes to the first modern Olympics in 1896; now more than 100 nations compete. Winter Olympic Games were started in 1924.

Sites and Unofficial Winners of Games

1896 Athens (U.S.)	**1912** Stockholm (U.S.)	**1936** Berlin (Germany)	**1964** Tokyo (U.S.)
1900 Paris (U.S.)	**1920** Antwerp (U.S.)	**1948** London (U.S.)	**1968** Mexico City (U.S.)
1904 St. Louis (U.S.)	**1924** Paris (U.S.)	**1952** Helsinki (U.S.)	**1972** Munich (USSR)
1906 Athens (U.S.)*	**1928** Amsterdam (U.S.)	**1956** Melbourne (USSR)	**1976** Montreal (USSR)
1908 London (U.S.)	**1932** Los Angeles (U.S.)	**1960** Rome (USSR)	**1980** Moscow (scheduled)

*Games not recognized by International Olympic Committee. Games 6 (1916), 12 (1940), and 13 (1944) were not celebrated.

Olympic Games Champions 1896—1976
*Indicates Olympic Record
Track and Field — Men

60 Meter Run
1900	Alvin Kraenzlein, United States	7s*
1904	Archie Hahn, United States	7s*

100 Meter Run
1896	Thomas Burke, United States	12s
1900	Francis W. Jarvis, United States	10.8s
1904	Archie Hahn, United States	11s
1908	Reginald Walker, South Africa	10.8s
1912	Ralph Craig, United States	10.8s
1920	Charles Paddock, United States	10.8s
1924	Harold Abrahams, Great Britain	10.6s
1928	Percy Williams, Canada	10.8s
1932	Eddie Tolan, United States	10.3s
1936	Jesse Owens, United States	10.3s
1948	Harrison Dillard, United States	10.3s
1952	Lindy Remigino, United States	10.4s
1956	Bobby Morrow, United States	10.5s
1960	Armin Hary, Germany	10.2s
1964	Bob Hayes, United States	10.0s
1968	Jim Hines, United States	9.9s*
1972	Valeri Borzov, USSR	10.14s
1976	Hasely Crawford, Trinidad	10.06s

200 Meter Run
1900	Walter Tewksbury, United States	22.2s
1904	Archie Hahn, United States	21.6s
1908	Robert Kerr, Canada	22.4s
1912	Ralph Craig, United States	21.7s
1920	Allan Woodring, United States	22s
1924	Jackson Scholz, United States	21.6s
1928	Percy Williams, Canada	21.8s
1932	Eddie Tolan, United States	21.2s
1936	Jesse Owens, United States	20.7s
1948	Mel Patton, United States	21.1s
1952	Andrew Stanfield, United States	20.7s
1956	Bobby Morrow, United States	20.6s
1960	Livio Berruti, Italy	20.5s
1964	Henry Carr, United States	20.3s
1968	Tommie Smith, United States	19.8s*
1972	Valeri Borzov, USSR	20.00s
1976	Donald Quarrie, Jamaica	20.23s

400 Meter Run
1896	Thomas Burke, United States	54.2s
1900	Maxey Long, United States	49.4s
1904	Harry Hillman, United States	49.2s
1908	Wyndham Halswelle, Great Britain, walkover.	50s
1912	Charles Reidpath, United States	48.2s
1920	Bevil Rudd, South Africa	49.6s
1924	Eric Liddell, Great Britain	47.6s
1928	Ray Barbuti, United States	47.8s
1932	William Carr, United States	46.2s
1936	Archie Williams, United States	46.5s

(400 Meter Run continued)
1948	Arthur Wint, Jamaica, B.W.I.	46.2s
1952	George Rhoden, Jamaica, B.W.I.	45.9s
1956	Charles Jenkins, United States	46.7s
1960	Otis Davis, United States	44.9s
1964	Michael Larrabee, United States	45.1s
1968	Lee Evans, United States	43.8s*
1972	Vincent Matthews, United States	44.66s
1976	Alberto Juantorena, Cuba	44.26s

800 Meter Run
1896	Edwin Flack, Great Britain	2m. 11s
1900	Alfred Tysoe, Great Britain	2m. 1.4s
1904	James Lightbody, United States	1m. 56s
1908	Mel Sheppard, United States	1m. 52.8s
1912	James Meredith, United States	1m. 51.9s
1920	Albert Hill, Great Britain	1m. 53.4s
1924	Douglas Lowe, Great Britain	1m. 52.4s
1928	Douglas Lowe, Great Britain	1m. 51.8s
1932	Thomas Hampson, Great Britain	1m. 49.8s
1936	John Woodruff, United States	1m. 52.9s
1948	Mal Whitfield, United States	1m .49.2s
1952	Mal Whitfield, United States	1m. 49.2s
1956	Thomas Courtney, United States	1m. 47.7s
1960	Peter Snell, New Zealand	1m. 46.3s
1964	Peter Snell, New Zealand	1m. 45.1s
1968	Ralph Doubell, Australia	1m. 44.3s
1972	Dave Wottle, United States	1m .45.9s
1976	Alberto Juantorena, Cuba	1m. 43.50s*

1,500 Meter Run
1896	Edwin Flack, Great Britain	4m. 33.2s
1900	Charles Bennett, Great Britain	4m. 6s
1904	James Lightbody, United States	4m. 5.4s
1908	Mel Sheppard, United States	4m. 3.4s
1912	Arnold Jarkson, Great Britain	3m. 56.8s
1920	Albert Hill, Great Britain	4m. 1.8s
1924	Paavo Nurmi, Finland	3m. 53.6s
1928	Harry Larva, Finland	3m.53.2s
1932	Luigi Beccali, Italy	3m. 51.2s
1936	Jack Lovelock, New Zealand	3m. 47.8s
1948	Henri Eriksson, Sweden	3m. 49.8s
1952	Joseph Barthel, Luxemburg	3m. 45.2s
1956	Ron Delany, Ireland	3m. 41.2s
1960	Herb Elliott, Australia	3m. 35.6s
1964	Peter Snell, New Zealand	3m. 38.1s
1968	Kipchoge Keino, Kenya	3m. 34.9s*
1972	Pekka Vasala, Finland	3m. 36.3s
1976	John Walker, New Zealand	3m. 39.17s

3,000 Meter Steeplechase
1920	Percy Hodge, Great Britain	10m. 2.4s
1924	Willie Ritola, Finland	9m. 33.6s
1928	Toivo Loukola, Finland	9m. 21.8s

1932	Volnari Iso-Hollo, Finland	10m. 33.4s
	(About 3450 mtrs. extra lap by error)	
1936	Volnari Iso-Hollo, Finland	9m. 3.8s
1948	Thure Sjoestrand, Sweden	9m. 4.6s
1952	Horace Ashenfelter, United States	8m. 45.4s
1956	Chris Brasher, Great Britain	8m. 42.2s
1960	Zdzislaw Krzyszkowiak, Poland	8m. 34.2s
1964	Gaston Roelants, Belgium	8m. 30.8s
1968	Amos Biwott, Kenya	8m. 51s
1972	Kipchoge Keino, Kenya	8m. 23.6s
1976	Anders Garderud, Sweden	8m. 08.2s*

5,000 Meter Run

1912	Hannes Kolehmainen, Finland	14m. 36.6s
1920	Joseph Guillemot, France	14m. 55.6s
1924	Paavo Nurmi, Finland	14m. 31.2s
1928	Willie Ritola, Finland	14m. 38s
1932	Lauri Lehtinen, Finland	14m. 30s
1936	Gunnar Hockert, Finland	14m. 22.2s
1948	Gaston Reiff, Belgium	14m. 17.6s
1952	Emil Zatopek, Czechoslovakia	14m. 6.0s
1956	Vladimir Kuts, USSR	13m. 39.6s
1960	Murray Halberg, New Zealand	13m. 43.4s
1964	Bob Schul, United States	13m. 48.8s
1968	Mohamed Gammoudi, Tunisia	14m. 05.0s
1972	Lasse Viren, Finland	13m. 26.4s
1976	Lasse Viren, Finland	13m. 24.76s*

Cross-Country

1912	Hannes Kolehmainen, Finland	45m. 11.6s

5 Mile Run

1908	Emil Voigt, Great Britain	25m. 11.2s*

10,000 Meter Run

1912	Hannes Kolehmainen, Finland	31m. 20.8s
1920	Paavo Nurmi, Finland	31m. 45.8s
1924	Willie Ritola, Finland	30m. 23.2s
1928	Paavo Nurmi, Finland	30m. 18.8s
1932	Janusz Kusocinski, Poland	30m. 11.4s
1936	Ilmari Salminen, Finland	30m. 15.4s
1948	Emil Zatopek, Czechoslovakia	29m. 59.6s
1952	Emil Zatopek, Czechoslovakia	29m. 17.0s
1956	Vladimir Kuts, USSR	28m. 45.6s
1960	Pytor Bolotnikov, USSR	28m. 32.2s
1964	Billy Mills, United States	28m. 24.4s
1968	Naftali Temu, Kenya	29m. 27.4s
1972	Lasse Viren, Finland	27m. 38.4s*
1976	Lasse Viren, Finland	27m. 40.38s

Marathon

1896	Spyros Loues, Greece	2h. 55m. 20s
1900	Michael Teato, France	2h. 59m. 45s
1904	Thomas Hicks, United States	3h. 28m. 53s
1908	John J. Hayes, United States	2h. 55m. 18.4s
1912	Kenneth McArthur, South Africa	2h. 36. 54.8s
1920	Hannes Kolehmainen, Finland	2h. 32m. 35.8s
1924	Albin Stenroos, Finland	2h. 41m. 22.6s
1928	El Ouafl, France	2h. 32m. 57s
1932	Juan Zabala, Argentina	2h. 31m. 36s
1936	Kitei Son, Japan	2h. 29m. 19.2s
1948	Delfo Cabera, Argentina	2h. 34m. 51.6s
1952	Emil Zatopek, Czechoslovakia	2h. 23m. 03.2s
1956	Alain Mimoun, France	2h. 25m.
1960	Abebe Bikila, Ethiopia	2h. 15m. 15.2s
1964	Abebe Bikila, Ethiopia	2h. 12m. 11.2s
1968	Mamo Wolde, Ethiopia	2h. 20m. 26.4s
1972	Frank Shorter, United States	2h. 12m. 19.8s
1976	Waldemer Cierpinski, E. Germany	2h. 09m. 55s*

10,000 Meter Cross-Country

1920	Paavo Nurmi, Finland	27m. 15s*
1924	Paavo Nurmi, Finland	32m. 54.8s

10,000 Meter Walk

1912	George Goulding, Canada	46m. 28.4s
1920	Ugo Frigerio, Italy	48m. 6.2s
1924	Ugo Frigerio, Italy	47m. 49s
1948	John Mikaelsson, Sweden	45m. 13.2s
1952	John Mikaelsson, Sweden	45m. 02.8s*

20,000 Meter Walk

1956	Leonid Spirine, United States	1h. 31m. 27.4s
1960	Vladimir Golubnichy, USSR	1h. 34m. 7.2s
1964	Kenneth Mathews, Great Britain	1h. 29m. 34.0s
1968	Vladimir Golubnichy, USSR	1h. 35m. 58.4s
1972	Peter Frenkel, E. Germany	1h. 26m. 42.4s
1976	Daniel Bautista, Mexico	1h. 24m. 40.6s*

50,000 Meter Walk

1932	Thomas W. Green, Great Britain	4h. 50m. 10s
1936	Harold Whitlock Great Britain	4h. 30m. 41.4s
1948	John Lundgren, Sweden	4h. 41m. 52s
1952	Giuseppe Bordoni, Italy	4h. 28m. 07.8s
1956	Norman Read, New Zealand	4h. 30m. 42.8s
1960	Donald Thompson, Great Britain	4h. 25m. 30s
1964	Abdon Pamich, Italy	4h. 11m. 11.2s
1968	Christoph Hohne, E. Germany	4h. 20m. 13.6s
1972	Bern Kannenberg, W. Germany	3h. 56m. 11.6s*

110 Meter Hurdles

1896	Thomas Curtis, United States	17.6s
1900	Alvin Kraenzlein, United States	15.4s
1908	Frederick Schule, United States	16s
1908	Forrest Smithson, United States	15s
1912	Frederick Kelly, United States	15.1s
1920	Earl Thomson, Canada	14.8s
1924	Daniel Kinsey, United States	15s
1928	Sydney Atkinson, South Africa	14.8s
1932	George Saling, United States	14.6s
1936	Forrest Towns, United States	14.2s
1948	William Porter, United States	13.9s
1952	Harrison Dillard, United States	13.7s
1956	Lee Calhoun, United States	13.5s
1960	Lee Calhoun, United States	13.8s
1964	Hayes Jones, United States	13.6s
1968	Willie Davenport, United States	13.3s
1972	Rod Milburn, United States	13.24s*
1976	Guy Drut, France	13.30s

200 Meter Hurdles

1900	Alvin Kraenzlein, United States	25.4s
1904	Harry Hillman, United States	24.6s*

400 Meter Hurdles

1900	J. W. B. Tewksbury, United States	57.6s
1904	Harry Hillman, United States	53s
1908	Charles Bacon, United States	55s
1920	Frank Loomis, United States	54s
1924	F. Morgan Taylor, United States	52.6s
1928	Lord Burghley, Great Britain	53.4s
1932	Robert Tisdall, Ireland	51.8s
1936	Glenn Hardin, United States	52.4s
1948	Roy Cochran, United States	51.1s
1952	Charles Moore, United States	50.8s
1956	Glenn Davis, United States	50.1s
1960	Glenn Davis, United States	49.3s
1964	Rex Cawley, United States	49.6s
1968	Dave Hemery, Great Britain	48.1s
1972	John Akii-Bua, Uganda	47.82s
1976	Edwin Moses, United States	47.64s*

Standing High Jump

1900	Ray Ewry, United States	5ft. 5 in.
1904	Ray Ewry, United States	4ft. 11 in.
1908	Ray Ewry, United States	5ft. 2 in.
1912	Platt Adams, United States	5ft. 4 1-4 in.*

Running High Jump

1896	Ellery Clark, United States	5ft. 11 1-4 in.
1900	Irving Baxter, United States	6ft. 2 4-5 in.
1904	Samuel Jones, United States	5ft. 11 in.
1908	Harry Porter, United States	6ft. 3 in.
1912	Almer W. Richards, United States	6ft. 4 in.
1920	Richard Landon, United States	6ft. 4 3-8 in.
1924	Harold Osborn, United States	6ft. 6 in.
1928	Robert W. King, United States	6ft. 4 3-8 in.
1932	Duncan McNaughton, Canada	6ft. 5 5-8 in.
1936	Cornelius Johnson, United States	6ft. 7 15-16 in.
1948	John L. Winter, Australia	6ft. 6 in.
1952	Walter Davis, United States	6ft. 8.32 in.
1956	Charles Dumas, United States	6ft. 11 1-4 in.
1960	Robert Shavlakadze, USSR	7ft. 1in.
1964	Valery Brumel, USSR	7ft. 1 7-8 in.
1968	Dick Fosbury, United States	7ft. 4 1-4 in.
1972	Yuri Tarmak, USSR	7ft. 3 3-4 in.
1976	Jacek Wszola, Poland	7ft. 4 1-2 in.*

Standing Broad Jump

1900	Ray Ewry, United States	10ft. 6 2-5 in.
1904	Ray Ewry, United States	11ft. 4 7-8 in.*
1908	Ray Ewry, United States	10ft. 11 1-4 m.
1912	Constantin Tsicilitras, Greece	11ft. 3-4 in.

Long Jump

1896	Ellery Clark, United States	20ft. 9 3-4 in.
1900	Alvin Kraenzlein, United States	23ft. 6 7-8 in.

1904	Myer Prinstein, United States	24ft. 1in.
1908	Frank Irons, United States	24ft. 6 1-2 in.
1912	Albert Gutterson, United States	24ft. 11 1-4 in.
1920	Wm. Petterssen, Sweden	23ft. 5 1-2 in.
1924	DeHart Hubbard, United States	24ft. 5 1-8 in.
1928	Edward B. Hamm, United States	25ft. 4 3-4 in.
1932	Edward Gordon, United States	25ft. 3-4 in.
1936	Jesse Owens, United States	26ft. 5 5-16 in.
1948	William Steele, United States	25ft. 8 in.
1952	Jerome Biffle, United States	24ft. 10.03 in.
1956	Gregory Bell, United States	25ft. 8 1-4 in.
1960	Ralph Boston, United States	26ft. 7 3-4 in.
1964	Lynn Davies, Great Britain	26ft. 5 3-4 in.
1968	Bob Beamon, United States	29ft. 2 1-2 in.*
1972	Randy Williams, United States	27ft. 1-2 in.
1976	Arnie Robinson, United States	27 ft. 4 1/2 in.

400 Meter Relay

1912	Great Britain	42.4s
1920	United States	42.2s
1924	United States	41s
1928	United States	41s
1932	United States	40s
1936	United States	39.8s
1948	United States	40.3s
1952	United States	40.1s
1956	United States	39.5s
1960	Germany (U.S. disqualified)	39.5s
1964	United States	39.0s
1968	United States	38.2s
1972	United States	38.19s
1976	United States	38.33s

1,600 Meter Relay

1908	United States	3m. 27.2s
1912	United States	3m. 16.6s
1920	Great Britain	3m. 22.2s
1924	United States	3m. 16s
1928	United States	3m. 14.2s
1932	United States	3m. 8.2s
1936	Great Britain	3m. 9s
1948	United States	3m. 10.4s
1952	Jamaica, B.W.I.	3m. 03.9s
1956	United States	3m. 04.8s
1960	United States	3m. 02.2s
1964	United States	3m. 00.7s
1968	United States	2m. 56.1s*
1972	Kenya	2m. 59.8s
1976	United States	2m. 58.65s

Pole Vault

1896	William Hoyt, United States	10ft. 9 3-4 in.
1900	Irving Baxter, United States	10ft. 9.9 in.
1904	Charles Dvorak, United States	11ft. 6 in.
1908	A. C. Gilbert, United States Edward Cook Jr., United States	12ft. 2 in.
1912	Harry Babcock, United States	12ft. 11 1-2 in.
1920	Frank Foss, United States	13ft. 5 in.
1924	Lee Barnes, United States	12ft. 11 1-2 in.
1928	Sabin W. Carr, United States	13ft. 9 1-2 in.
1932	William Miller, United States	14ft. 1 7-8 in.
1936	Earle Meadows, United States	14ft. 3 1-4 in.
1948	Guinn Smith, United States	14ft. 1 1-4 in.
1952	Robert Richards, United States	14ft. 11 1-4 in.
1956	Robert Richards, United States	14ft. 11 1-2 in.
1960	Don Bragg, United States	15ft. 5 1-8 in.
1964	Fred Hansen, United States	16ft. 8 1-2 in.
1968	Bob Seagren, United States	17ft. 8 1-2 in.
1972	Wolfgang Nordwig, E. Germany	18ft. 1-2 in.*
1976	Tadeusz Slusarski, Poland	18ft. 1-2 in.*

16-Lb. Hammer Throw

1900	Jqhn Flannagan, United States	167ft. 4 in.
1904	John Flannagan, United States	168ft. 1 in.
1908	John Flannagan, United States	170ft. 4 1-4 in.
1912	Matt McGrath, United States	179ft. 7 1-8 in.
1920	Pat Ryan, United States	172ft. 5 5-8 in.
1924	Fred Tootell, United States	174ft. 10 1-8 in.
1928	Patrick O'Callaghan, Ireland	168ft. 7 3-8 in.
1932	Patrick O'Callaghan, Ireland	176ft. 11 1-8 in.
1936	Karl Hein, Germany	185ft. 4 3-16 in.
1948	Imre Nemeth, Hungary	183ft. 11 1-2 in.
1952	Jozsef Csermak, Hungary	197ft. 11.67 in.
1956	Harold Connolly, United States	207ft. 3 1-2 in.
1960	Vasily Rudenkov, USSR	220ft. 2 in.
1964	Romuald Klim, USSR	228ft. 9 1-2 in.
1968	Gyula Zsivotsky, Hungary	240ft. 8 in.
1972	Anatoli Bondarchuk, USSR	248ft. 8 in.
1976	Yuri Sedyh, USSR	254ft. 3 3-4 in.*

Discus Throw

1896	Robert Garrett, United States	95ft. 7 1-2 in.
1900	Rudolf Bauer, Hungary	118ft. 2.9-10in.
1904	Martin Sheridan, United States	128ft. 10 1-2 in.
1908	Martin Sheridan, United States	134ft. 2 in.
1912	Armas Taipale, Finland	148ft. 4 in.
	Both hands—Armas Taipale, Finland	271ft. 10 1-4 in.
1920	Elmer Niklander, Finland	146ft. 7 1-4 in.
1924	Clarence Houser, United States	151ft. 5 1-8 in.
1928	Clarence Houser, United States	155ft. 3 in.
1932	John Anderson, United States	162ft. 4 7-8 in.
1936	Ken Carpenter, United States	165ft. 7 3-8 in.
1948	Adolfo Consolini, Italy	173ft. 2 in.
1952	Sim Iness, United States	180ft. 6.85 in.
1956	Al Oerter, United States	184ft. 11 in.
1960	Al Oerter, United States	194ft. 2 in.
1964	Al Oerter, United States	200ft. 1 1-2 in.
1968	Al Oerter, United States	212ft. 6 1-2 in.
1972	Ludik Danek, Czechoslovakia	211 ft. 3 in.
1976	Mac Wilkins, United States	221ft. 5.4 in.*

Standing Hop, Step, and Jump

1900	Ray Ewry, United States	34ft. 8 1-2 in.*
1904	Ray Ewry, United States	34ft. 7 1-4 in.

Triple Jump

1896	James Connolly, United States	45 ft.
1900	Myer Prinstein, United States	47ft. 4 1-4 in.
1904	Myer Prinstein, United States	47 ft.
1908	Timothy Ahearne, Great Britain	48ft. 11 1-4 in.
1912	Gustaf Lindblom, Sweden	48ft. 5 1-8 in.
1920	Vilho Tuulos, Finland	47ft. 7 in.
1924	Archie Winter, Australia	50ft. 11 1-4in.
1928	Mikio Oda, Japan	49ft. 11 in.
1932	Chuhei Nambu, Japan	51ft. 7 in.
1936	Naoto Tajima, Japan	52ft. 5 7-8 in.
1948	Arne Ahman, Sweden	50ft. 6 1-4 in.
1952	Adhemar de Silva, Brazil	53ft. 2.59 in.
1956	Adhemar de Silva, Brazil	53ft. 7 1-2 in.
1960	Jozef Schmidt, Poland	55ft. 1 3-4 in.
1964	Jozef Schmidt, Poland	55ft. 3 1-2 in.
1968	Viktor Saneev, USSR	57ft. 3-4 in.*
1972	Viktor Saneev, USSR	56ft. 11 in.
1976	Viktor Saneev, USSR	56 ft. 8 3-4 in.

16-Lb. Shot Put

1896	Robert Garrett, United States	36ft. 2 in.
1900	Robert Sheldon, United States	46ft. 3 1-8 in.
1904	Ralph Rose, United States	48ft. 7 in.
1908	Ralph Rose, United States	46ft. 7 1-2 in.
1912	Pat McDonald, United States	50ft. 4 in.
	Both hands—Ralph Rose, United States	90ft. 5 1-2 in.
1920	Ville Porhola, Finland	48ft. 7 1-8 in.
1924	Clarence Houser, United States	49ft. 2 3-8 in.
1928	John Kuck, United States	52ft. 3-4 in.
1932	Leo Sexton, United States	52ft. 6 3-16 in.
1936	Hans Woelke, Germany	53ft. 1 13-16 in.
1948	Wilbur Thompson, United States	56ft. 2 in.
1952	Parry O'Brien, United States	57ft. 1.43 in.
1956	Parry O'Brien, United States	60ft. 11 in.
1960	William Nieder, United States	64ft. 6 3-4 in.
1964	Dallas Long, United States	66ft. 8 1-2 in.
1968	Randy Matson, United States	67ft. 4 3-4 in.
1972	Wladyslaw Komar, Poland	69ft. 6 in.
1976	Udo Beyer, E. Germany	69 ft. 6.7 in.*

Discus Throw—Greek Style

1908	Martin Sheridan, United States	124ft. 8 in.*

Javelin Throw

1908	Erik Lemming, Sweden	178ft. 7 1-2 in.
	Held in middle—Erik Lemming, Sweden	179ft. 10 1-2 in.
1912	Erik Lemming, Sweden	198ft. 11 1-4 in.
	Both hands, Julius Saaristo, Finland	358ft. 11 7-8 in.
1920	Jonni Myrra, Finland	215ft. 9 3-4 in.
1924	Jonni Myrra, Finland	206ft. 6 3-4 in.
1928	Eric Lundquist, Sweden	218ft. 6 1-8 in.
1932	Matti Jarvinen, Finland	238ft. 7 in.
1936	Gerhard Stoeck, Germany	235ft. 8 5-16 in.
1948	Kaj T. Rautavaara, Finland	228ft. 10 1-2 in.
1952	Cy Young, United States	242ft. 0.79 in.
1956	Egil Danielsen, Norway	281ft. 2 1-4 in.
1960	Viktor Tsibulenko, USSR	277ft. 8 3-8 in.
1964	Pauli Nevala, Finland	271ft. 2 1-2 in.
1968	Yanis Lusis, USSR	295ft. 7 1-4 in.
1972	Klaus Wolferman, W. Germany	296ft. 10 in.
1976	Miklos Nemeth, Hungary	310 ft. 4 1/2 in.*

Decathlon

1912	Hugo Wieslander, Sweden	7,724.49 pts.
1920	Helge Loveland, Norway	6,804.35 pts.
1924	Harold Osborn, United States	7,710.775 pts.
1928	Paavo Yrjola, Finland	8,056.20 pts.
1932	James Bausch, United States	8,462.23 pts.
1936	Glenn Morris, United States	7,900 pts.
1948	Robert Mathias, United States	7,139 pts.
1952	Robert Mathias, United States	7,887 pts.
1956	Milton Campbell, United States	7,937 pts.
1960	Rafer Johnson, United States	8,392 pts.
1964	Willi Holdorf, Germany	7,887 pts.
1968	Bill Toomey, United States	8,193 pts.
1972	Nikola Avilov, USSR	8,454 pts.
1976	Bruce Jenner, United States	8,618 pts.*

former point systems used prior to 1964.

Track and Field—Women

100 Meter Run

1928	Elizabeth Robinson, United States	12.2s
1932	Stella Walsh, Poland	11.9s
1936	Helen Stephens, United States	11.5s
1948	Francina Blankers-Koen, Netherlands	11.9s
1952	Marjorie Jackson, Australia	11.5s
1956	Betty Cuthbert, Australia	11.5s
1960	Wilma Rudolph, United States	11.0s*
1964	Wyomia Tyus, United States	11.4s
1968	Wyomia Tyus, United States	11.0s*
1972	Renate Stecher, E. Germany	11.07s
1976	Annegret Richter, W. Germany	11.01s*

200 Meter Run

1948	Francina Blankers-Koen, Netherlands	24.4s
1952	Marjorie Jackson, Australia	23.7s
1956	Betty Cuthbert, Australia	23.4s
1960	Wilma Rudolph, United States	24.0s
1964	Edith McGuire, United States	23.0s
1968	Irene Szewinska, Poland	22.5s
1972	Renate Stecher, E. Germany	22.40s
1976	Baerbel Eckert, E. Germany	22.37s*

400 Meter Run

1964	Betty Cuthbert, Australia	52s
1968	Colette Besson, France	52s
1972	Monika Zehrt, E. Germany	51.08s
1976	Irena Szewinska, Poland	49.29s*

800 Meter Run

1928	Linda Radke, Germany	2m. 16.8s
1960	Ludmila Shevcova, USSR	2m. 4.3s
1964	Ann Packer, Great Britain	2m. 1.1s
1968	Madeline Manning, United States	2m. 0.9s
1972	Hildegard Falck, W. Germany	1m. 58.6s
1976	Tatyana Kazankina, USSR	1m. 54.94s*

1500 Meter Run

1972	Lucmila Bragina, USSR	4m. 01.4s*
1976	Tatyana Kazankina, USSR	4m. 05.48s

400 Meter Relay

1928	Canada	48.4s
1932	United States	47.0s
1936	United States	46.9s
1948	Netherlands	47.5s
1952	United States	45.9s
1956	Australia	44.5s
1960	United States	44.5s
1964	Poland	43.6s
1968	United States	42.8s
1972	West Germany	42.81s
1976	East Germany	42.55s*

1,600 Meter Relay

1972	East Germany	3m. 23s
1976	East Germany	3m. 19.23s*

80 Meter Hurdles

1932	Mildred Didrikson, United States	11.7s
1936	Trebisonda Villa, Italy	11.7s
1948	Francina Blankers-Koen, Netherlands	11.2s
1952	Shirley Strickland de la Hunty, Australia	10.9s
1956	Shirley Strickland de la Hunty, Australia	10.7s
1960	Irina Press, USSR	10.8s
1964	Karen Balzer, Germany	10.5s
1968	Maureen Caird, Australia	10.3s*

100 Meter Hurdles

1972	Annelie Ehrhardt, E. Germany	12.59*
1976	Johanna Schaller, E. Germany	12.77s

High Jump

1928	Ethel Catherwood, Canada	5ft. 3 in.
1932	Jean Shiley, United States	5ft. 5 1-4 in.
1936	Ibolya Csak, Hungary	5ft. 3 in.
1948	Alice Coachman, United States	5ft. 6 1-8 in.
1952	Esther Brand, South Africa	5ft. 5 3-4 in.
1956	Mildred L. McDaniel, United States	5ft. 9 1-4 in.
1960	Iolanda Balas, Romania	6ft. 1-4 in.
1964	Iolanda Balas, Romania	6 ft. 2 7-8 in.
1968	Miloslava Reskova, Czechoslovakia	5ft. 11 3-4 in.
1972	Ulrike Meyfarth, W. Germany	6ft. 3 1-4 in.
1976	Rosemarie Ackermann, E. Germany	6ft. 3 3-4 in.*

Discus Throw

1928	Helena Konopacka, Poland	129ft. 11 7-8 in.
1932	Lillian Copeland, United States	133ft. 2 in.
1936	Gisela Mauermayer, Germany	156ft. 3 3-16 in.
1948	Micheline Ostermeyer, France	137ft. 6 1-2 in.
1952	Nina Romaschkova, USSR	168ft. 8 1-2 in.
1956	Olga Fikotova, Czechoslovakia	176ft. 1 1-2 in.
1960	Nina Ponomareva, USSR	180ft. 8 1-4 in.
1964	Tamara Press, USSR	187ft. 10 1-2 in.
1968	Lia Manolin, Romania	191ft. 2 1-2 in.
1972	Faina Melnik, USSR	218 ft. 7 in.
1976	Evelin Schlaak, E. Germany	226 ft. 4 1-2 in. *

Javelin Throw

1932	Mildred Didrikson, United States	143ft. 4 in.
1936	Tilly Fleischer, Germany	148ft. 2 3-4 in.
1948	Herma Bauma, Austria	149ft. 6 in.
1952	Dana Zatopekova, Czechoslovakia	165ft. 7 in.
1956	Inessa Janzeme, USSR	176ft. 8 in.
1960	Elvira Ozolina, USSR	183ft. 8 in.
1964	Mihaela Penes, Romania	198ft. 7 1-2 in.
1968	Angela Nemeth, Hungary	198ft. 1-2 in.
1972	Ruth Fuchs, E. Germany	209 ft. 7 in.
1976	Ruth Fuchs, E. Germany	216ft. 4 in.*

Shot Put

1948	Micheline Ostermeyer, France	45ft. 1 1-2 in.
1952	Galina Zybina, USSR	50ft. 1 1-2 in.
1956	Tamara Tishkyevich, USSR	54ft. 5 in.
1960	Tamara Press, USSR	56ft. 9 7-8 in.
1964	Tamara Press, USSR	59ft. 6 1-4 in.
1968	Margitta Gummel, E. Germany	64ft. 4 in.
1972	Nadezwda Chizova, USSR	69ft.
1976	Ivanka Christova, Bulgaria	69ft. 5 in.*

Long Jump

1948	Olga Gyarmati, Hungary	18ft. 8 1-4 in.
1952	Yvette Williams, New Zealand	20ft. 5 3-4 in.
1956	E. Krzeskinska, Poland	20ft. 9 3-4 in.
1960	Vyera Krepina, USSR	20ft. 10 3-4 in.
1964	Mary Rand, Great Britain	22ft. 2 1-4 in.
1968	V. Viscopoleanu, Romania	22ft. 4 1-2 in.*
1972	Heidemarie Rosendahl, W. Germany	22ft. 3 in.
1976	Angela Voigt, E. Germany	22 ft. 2 1-2 in.

Pentathlon

1964	Irina Press, USSR	5,246 pts.
1968	Ingred Becker, W. Germany	5,098 pts.
1972	Mary Peters, England	4,801 pts.*
1976	Sigrun Siegl, E. Germany	4,745 pts.

Former point system, 1964-1968

Value of Olympic Medals

An Olympic gold medal is basically silver coated with about six grams of fine gold. It is worth $110. The silver medal is pure silver, and its actual value is about $66. The bronze, which is pure bronze, is worth $16.

Swimming-Men

100 Meter Freestyle

1896	Alfred Hajos, Hungary	1:22.2
1904	Zoltan de Halmay, Hungary (100 yards)	1:02.8
1908	Charles Daniels, U.S.	1:05.6
1912	Duke P. Kahanamoku, U.S.	1:03.4
1920	Duke P. Kahanamoku, U.S.	1:01.4
1924	John Weissmuller, U.S.	59.0
1928	John Weissmuller, U.S.	58.6
1932	Yasuji Miyazaki, Japan	58.2
1936	Ferenc Csik, Hungary	57.6
1948	Wally Ris, U.S.	57.3
1952	Clark Scholes, U.S.	57.4
1956	Jon Henricks, Australia	55.4
1960	John Devitt, Australia	55.2
1964	Don Schollander, U.S.	53.4
1968	Mike Wenden, Australia	52.2
1972	Mark Spitz, U.S.	51.22
1976	Jim Montgomery, U.S.	49.99*

200 Meter Freestyle

1968	Mike Wenden, Australia	1:55.2
1972	Mark Spitz, U.S.	1:52.78
1976	Bruce Furniss, U.S.	1:50.29*

400 Meter Freestyle

1904	C. M. Daniels, U.S. (440 yards)	6:16.2
1908	Henry Taylor, Great Britain	5:36.8
1912	George Hodgson, Canada	5:24.4
1920	Norman Ross, U.S.	5:26.8
1924	John Weissmuller, U.S.	5:04.2
1928	Albert Zorilla, Argentina	5:01.6
1932	Clarence Crabbe, U.S.	4:48.4
1936	Jack Medica, U.S.	4:44.5
1948	William Smith, U.S.	4:41.0
1952	Jean Boiteux, France	4:30.7
1956	Murray Rose, Australia	4:27.3
1960	Murray Rose, Australia	4:18.3
1964	Don Schollander, U.S.	4:12.2
1968	Mike Burton, U.S.	4:09.0
1972	Brad Cooper, Australia	4:00.27
1976	Brian Goodell, U.S.	3:51.93*

1,500 Meter Freestyle

1908	Henry Taylor, Great Britain	22:48.4
1912	George Hodgson, Canada	22:00.0
1920	Norman Ross, U.S.	22:23.2
1924	Andrew Charlton, Australia	20:06.6
1928	Arne Borg, Sweden	19:51.8
1932	Kasuo Kitamura, Japan	19:12.4
1936	Noboru Terada, Japan	19:13.7
1948	James P. McClane, U.S.	19:18.5
1952	Ford Konno, U.S.	18:30.0
1956	Murray Rose, Australia	17:58.9
1960	Jon Konrads, Australia	17:19.6
1964	Robert Windle, Australia	17:01.7
1968	Mike Burton, U.S.	16:38.9
1972	Mike Burton, U.S.	15:52.58
1976	Brian Goodell, U.S.	15:02.40*

400 Meter Medley Relay

1960	United States	4:05.4
1964	United States	3:58.4
1968	United States	3:54.9
1972	United States	3:48.16
1976	United States	3:42.22*

400 Meter Freestyle Relay

1964	United States	3:33.2
1968	United States	3:31.7
1972	United States	3:26.4*

800 Meter Freestyle Relay

1908	Great Britain	10:55.6
1912	Australia	10:11.6
1920	United States	10:04.4
1924	United States	9:53.4
1928	United States	9:36.2
1932	Japan	8:58.4
1936	Japan	8:51.5
1948	United States	8:46.0
1952	United States	8:31.1
1956	Australia	8:23.6
1960	United States	8:10.2
1964	United States	7:52.1

1968	United States	7:52.3
1972	United States	7:35.78
1976	United States	7:23.22*

100 Meter Backstroke

1904	Walter Brack, Germany (100 yds.)	1:16.8
1908	Arno Bieberstein, Germany	1:24.6
1912	Harry Hebner, U.S.	1:21.2
1920	Warren Kealoha, U.S.	1:15.2
1924	Warren Kealoha, U.S.	1:13.2
1928	George Kojac, U.S.	1:08.2
1932	Masaji Kiyokawa, Japan	1:08.6
1936	Adolph Kiefer, U.S.	1:05.9
1948	Allen Stack, U.S.	1:06.4
1952	Yoshi Oyokawa, U.S.	1:05.4
1956	David Thiele, Australia	1:02.2
1960	David Thiele, Australia	1:01.9
1968	Roland Matthes, E. Germany	58.7
1972	Roland Matthes, E. Germany	56.58
1976	John Naber, U.S.	55.49*

200 Meter Backstroke

1964	Jed Graef, U.S.	2:10.3
1968	Roland Matthes, E. Germany	2:09.6
1972	Roland Matthes, E. Germany	2:02.82
1976	John Naber, U.S.	1:59.19*

100 Meter Breaststroke

1968	Don McKenzie, U.S.	1:07.7
1972	Nobutaka Taguchi, Japan	1:04.94
1976	John Hencken, U.S.	1:03.11*

200 Meter Breaststroke

1908	Frederick Holman, Great Britain	3:09.2
1912	Walter Bathe, Germany	3:01.8
1920	Haken Malmroth, Sweden	3:04.4
1924	Robert Skelton, U.S.	2:56.6
1928	Yoshiyuki Tsuruta, Japan	2:48.8
1932	Yoshiyuki Tsuruta, Japan	2:45.4
1936	Tetsuo Hamuro, Japan	2:42.5
1948	Joseph Verdeur, U.S.	2:39.3
1952	John Davies, Australia	2:34.4
1956	Masaru Furukawa, Japan	2:34.7
1960	William Mulliken, U.S.	2:37.4
1964	Ian O'Brien, Australia	2:27.8
1968	Felipe Munoz, Mexico	2:28.7
1972	John Hencken, U.S.	2:21.55
1976	David Wilkie, Great Britain	2:15.11*

100 Meter Butterfly

1968	Doug Russell, U.S.	55.9
1972	Mark Spitz, U.S.	54.27*
1976	Matt Vogel, U.S.	54.35

200 Meter Butterfly

1956	William Yorzyk, U.S.	2:18.6
1960	Michael Troy, U.S.	2:12.8
1964	Kevin J. Berry, Australia	2:06.6
1968	Carl Robie, U.S.	2:08.7
1972	Mark Spitz, U.S.	2:00.70
1976	Mike Bruner, U.S.	1:59.23*

200 Meter Individual Medley

1968	Charles Hickcox, U.S.	2:12.0
1972	Gunnar Larsson, Sweden	2:07.2*

400 Meter Individual Medley

1964	Dick Roth, U.S.	4:45.4
1968	Charles Hickcox, U.S.	4:48.4
1972	Gunnar Larsson, Sweden	4.31.98
1976	Rod Strachan, U.S.	4:23.68*

Springboard Diving — Points

1904	Dr. G. E. Sheldon, U.S.	12 2-3
1908	Albert Zuerner, Germany	85.5
1912	Paul Guenther, Germany	6
1920	Louis Kuehn, U.S.	6
1924	Albert White, U.S.	7
1928	Pete Desjardins, U.S.	185.04
1932	Michael Gallitzen, U.S.	161.38
1936	Richard Degener, U.S.	161.57
1948	Bruce Harlan, U.S.	163.64
1952	David Browning, U.S.	205.29

1956	Robert Clothworthy, U.S.	159.56
1960	Gary Tobian, U.S.	170.00
1964	Kenneth Sitzberger, U.S.	159.90
1968	Bernie Wrightson, U.S.	170.15
1972	Vladimir Vasin, USSR	594.09
1976	Phil Boggs, U.S.	619.52

Platform Diving

1928	Pete Desjardins, U.S.	98.74

1932	Harold Smith, U.S.	124.80
1936	Marshall Wayne, U.S.	113.58
1948	Sammy Lee, U.S.	130.05
1952	Sammy Lee, U.S.	156.28
1956	Joaquin Capilla, Mexico	152.44
1960	Robert Webster, U.S.	165.56
1964	Robert Webster, U.S.	148.58
1968	Klaus Dibiasi, Italy	164.18
1972	Klaus Dibiasi, Italy	504.12
1976	Klaus Dibiasi, Italy	600.51

Swimming—Women

100 Meter Freestyle

1912	Fanny Durack, Australia	1:22.2
1920	Ethelda Bleibtrey, U.S.	1:13.6
1924	Ethel Lackie, U.S.	1:12.4
1928	Albina Osipowich, U.S.	1:11.0
1932	Helene Madison, U.S.	1:06.8
1936	Hendrika Mastenbroek, Holland	1:05.9
1948	Greta Anderson, Denmark	1:06.3
1952	Katalin Szoke, Hungary	1:06.3
1956	Dawn Fraser, Australia	1:02.0
1960	Dawn Fraser, Australia	1:01.2
1964	Dawn Fraser, Australia	59.5
1968	Jan Henne, U.S.	1:00.0
1972	Sandra Neilson, U.S.	58.59
1976	Kornelia Ender, E. Germany	55.65*

200 Meter Freestyle

1968	Debbie Meyer, U.S.	2:10.5
1972	Shane Gould, Australia	2:03.56
1976	Kornelia Ender, E. Germany	1:59.26*

400 Meter Freestyle

1924	Martha Norelius, U.S.	6:02.2
1928	Martha Norelius, U.S.	5:42.8
1932	Helene Madison, U.S.	5:28.5
1936	Hendrika Mastenbroek, Netherlands	5:26.4
1948	Ann Curtis, U.S.	5:17.8
1952	Valerie Gyenge, Hungary	5:12.1
1956	Lorraine Crapp, Australia	4:54.6
1960	Susan Chris von Saltza, U.S.	4:50.6
1964	Virginia Duenkel, U.S.	4:43.3
1968	Debbie Meyer, U.S.	4:31.8
1972	Shane Gould, Australia	4:19.04
1976	Petra Thumer, E. Germany	4:09.89*

800 Meter Freestyle

1968	Debbie Meyer, U.S.	9:24.0
1972	Keena Rothhammer, U.S.	8:53.68
1976	Petra Thumer, E. Germany	8:37.14*

100 Meter Backstroke

1924	Sybil Bauer, U.S.	1:23.3
1928	Marie Braun, Netherlands	1:22.0
1932	Eleanor Holm, U.S.	1:19.4
1936	Dina Senff, Netherlands	1:18.9
1948	Karen Harup, Denmark	1:14.4
1952	Joan Harrison, South Africa	1:14.3
1956	Judy Grinham, Great Britain	1:12.9
1960	Lynn Burke, U.S.	1:09.3
1964	Cathy Ferguson, U.S.	1:07.7
1968	Kaye Hall, U.S.	1:06.2
1972	Melissa Belote, U.S.	1:05.78
1976	Ulrike Richter, E. Germany	1:01.83*

200 Meter Backstroke

1968	Pokey Watson, U.S.	2:24.8
1972	Melissa Belote, U.S.	2:19.19
1976	Ulrike Richter, E. German	2:13.43*

100 Meter Breaststroke

1968	Djurdjica Bjedov, Yugoslavia	1:15.8
1972	Cathy Carr, U.S.	1:13.58
1976	Hannelore Anke, E. Germany	1:11.16*

200 Meter Breaststroke

1924	Lucy Morton, Great Britain	3:32.2
1928	Hilde Schrader, Germany	3:12.6
1932	Clare Dennis, Australia	3:06.3
1936	Hideko Maehata, Japan	3:03.6
1948	Nelly Van Vliet, Netherlands	2:57.2
1952	Eva Szekely, Hungary	2:51.7
1956	Ursula Happe, Germany	2:53.1
1960	Anita Lonsbrough, Great Britain	2:49.5
1964	Galina Prozumenschikova, USSR	2:46.4
1968	Sharon Wichman, U.S.	2:44.4

1972	Beverly Whitfield, Australia	2:41.71
1976	Marina Koshevala, USSR	2:33.35*

200 Meter Individual Medley

1968	Claudia Kolb, U.S.	2:24.7
1972	Shane Gould, Australia	2:23.1*

400 Meter Individual Medley

1964	Donna de Varona, U.S.	5:18.7
1968	Claudia Kolb, U.S.	5:08.5
1972	Gail Neall, Australia	5:02.97
1976	Ulrike Tauber, E. Germany	4:42.77*

100 Meter Butterfly

1956	Shelley Mann, U.S.	1:11.0
1960	Carolyn Schuler, U.S.	1:09.5
1964	Sharon Stouder, U.S.	1:04.7
1968	Lynn McClements, Australia	1:05.5
1972	Mayumi Aoki, Japan	1:03.34
1976	Kornelia Ender, E. Germany	1:00.13*

200 Meter Butterfly

1968	Ada Kok, Netherlands	2:24.7
1972	Karen Moe, U.S.	2:15.57
1976	Andrea Pollack, E. Germany	2:11.41*

400 Meter Medley Relay

1960	United States	4:41.1
1964	United States	4:33.9
1968	United States	4:28.3
1972	United States	4:20.7
1976	East Germany	4:07.95*

400 Meter Freestyle Relay

1912	Great Britain	5:52.8
1920	United States	5:11.6
1924	United States	4:58.8
1928	United States	4:47.6
1932	United States	4:38.0
1936	Netherlands	4:36.0
1948	United States	4:29.2
1952	Hungary	4:24.4
1956	Australia	4:17.1
1960	United States	4:08.9
1964	United States	4:03.8
1968	United States	4:02.5
1972	United States	3:55.19
1976	United States	3:44.82*

Springboard Diving

		Points
1920	Aileen Riggin, U.S.	9
1924	Elizabeth Becker, U.S.	8
1928	Helen Meany, U.S.	78.62
1932	Georgia Coleman, U.S.	87.52
1936	Marjorie Gestring, U.S.	89.27
1948	Victoria M. Draves, U.S.	108.74
1952	Patricia McCormick, U.S.	147.30
1956	Patricia McCormick, U.S.	142.36
1960	Ingrid Kramer, Germany	155.81
1964	Ingrid Engel-Kramer, Germany	145.00
1968	Sue Gossick, U.S.	150.77
1972	Micki King, U.S.	450.03
1976	Jenni Chandler, U.S.	506.19

Platform Diving

		Points
1928	Elizabeth B. Pinkston, U.S.	31.60
1932	Dorothy Poynton, U.S.	40.26
1936	Dorothy Poynton Hill, U.S.	33.93
1948	Victoria M. Draves, U.S.	68.87
1952	Patricia McCormick, U.S.	79.37
1956	Patricia McCormick, U.S.	84.85
1960	Ingrid Kramer, Germany	91.28
1964	Lesley Bush, U.S.	99.80
1968	Milena Duchkova, Czech	109.59
1972	Ulrika Knape, Sweden	390.00
1976	Elena Vaytsekhouskaya, USSR	406.59

21st Summer Olympics

Montreal, Quebec, July 17-Aug. 1, 1976

Final Medal Standings

(Nations in alphabetical order)

	Gold	Silver	Bronze	Total		Gold	Silver	Bronze	Total
Australia	0	1	4	5	Mongolia	0	1	0	1
Austria	0	0	1	1	New Zealand	2	1	1	4
Belgium	0	3	3	6	North Korea	1	1	0	2
Bermuda	0	0	1	1	Norway	1	1	0	2
Brazil	0	0	2	2	Pakistan	0	0	1	1
Britain	3	5	5	13	Poland	8	6	11	25
Bulgaria	7	8	9	24	Portugal	0	2	0	2
Canada	0	5	6	11	Puerto Rico	0	0	1	1
Cuba	6	4	3	13	Romania	4	9	14	27
Czechoslovakia	2	2	4	8	South Korea	1	1	4	6
Denmark	1	0	2	3	Soviet Union	47	43	35	125
East Germany	40	25	25	90	Spain	0	2	0	2
Finland	4	2	0	6	Sweden	4	1	0	5
France	2	2	5	9	Switzerland	1	1	2	4
Holland	0	2	3	5	Thailand	0	0	1	1
Hungary	4	5	12	21	Trinidad	1	0	0	1
Iran	0	1	1	2	United States	34	35	25	94
Italy	2	7	4	13	Venezuela	0	1	0	1
Jamaica	1	1	0	2	West Germany	10	12	17	39
Japan	9	6	10	25	Yugoslavia	2	3	3	8
Mexico	1	0	1	2	Duplicate medals awarded in some events			

Olympic Medal Winners

Track and Field — Men

100 Meters — 1. Hasely Crawford, Trinadad; 2. Donald Quarrie, Jamaica; 3. Valery Borzov, USSR. **Time** — 0:10.06.

200 Meters — 1. Donald Quarrie, Jamaica; 2. Millard Hampton, United States; 3. Dwayne Evans, United States. **Time** — 0:20.23.

400 Meters — 1. Alberto Juantorena, Cuba; 2. Fred Newhouse, United States; 3. Herman Frazier, United States. **Time** — 0:44.26.

800 Meters — 1. Alberto Juantorena, Cuba; 2. Ivo Vandamme, Belgium; 3. Rick Wohlhuter, United States. **Time** — 1:43.50.

1,500 Meters — 1. John Walker, New Zealand; 2. Ivo Vandamme, Belgium; 3. Paul Wellmann, W. Germany. **Time** — 3:39.17.

5,000 Meters — 1. Lasse Viren, Finland; 2. Dick Quax, New Zealand; 3. Klaus Hildebrand, W. Germany. **Time** — 13:27.76.

10,000 Meters — 1. Lasse Viren, Finland; 2. Carlos Lopes, Portugal; 3. Brendan Foster, Gt. Britain. **Time** — 27:40.38.

110 Meter Hurdles — 1. Guy Drut, France; 2. Alejandro Casanas, Cuba; 3. Willie Davenport, United States. **Time** — 0:13.30.

400 Meter Hurdles — 1. Edwin Moses, United States; 2. Mike Shine, United States; 3. Evgeny Gavrilenko, USSR. **Time** — 0:47.64.

400 Meter Relay — 1. United States (Glance, Jones, Hampton, Riddick); 2. E. Germany; 3. USSR. **Time** — 0:38.33.

1,600 Meter Relay — 1. United States (Frazier, Brown, Newhouse, Parks); 2. Poland; 3. W. Germany. **Time** — 2:58.65.

3,000 Meter Steeplechase — 1. Anders Garderud, Sweden; 2. Bronislaw Malinowski, Poland; 3. Frank Baumgartl, E. Germany. **Time** — 8:08.2.

20 Km. Walk — Daniel Bautista, Mexico; 2. Hans Reimann, E. Germany; 3. Peter Frenkel, E. Germany. **Time** — 1:24:40.6.

Marathon — 1. Waldemar Cierpinski, E. Germany; 2. Frank Shorter, United States; 3. Karel Lismont, Belgium. **Time** — 2:09:55.

Long Jump — 1. Arnie Robinson, United States; 2. Randy Williams, United States; 3. Frank Wartenberg, E. Germany. **27 ft. ¹/₂ in.**

Triple Jump — 1. Viktor Saneev, USSR; 2. James Butts, United States; 3. Joao de Oliviera, Brazil. **50 ft. 8.7 in.**

High Jump — 1. Jacek Wszola, Poland; 2. Greg Joy, Canada; 3. Dwight Stones, United States. **7 ft. 4¹/₂ in.**

Discus — 1. Mac Wilkins, United States; 2. Wolfgang Schmidt, E. Germany; 3. John Powell, United States. **221 ft. 5.4 in.**

Hammer — 1. Yuri Sedykh, USSR; 2. Alexei Spiridonov, USSR; 3. Anatoli Bondarchuk, USSR. **254 ft. 3⁴/₄ in.**

Javelin — 1. Miklos Nemeth, Hungary; 2. Hannu Sitonen, Finland; 3. Gheorghe Megelea, Romania. **310 ft. 3³/₄ in.**

Shot Put — 1. Udo Beyer, E. Germany; 2. Evgeni Mironov, USSR; 3. Alexandr Barishnikov, USSR. **69 ft. ³/₄ in.**

Pole Vault — 1. Tadeusz Slusraski, Poland; 2. Antti Kalliomaki, Finland; 3. Dave Roberts, United States. **18 ft. ¹/₂ in.**

Decathlon — 1. Bruce Jenner, United States; 2. Guido Kratschmer, W. Germany; 3. Nikoli Avilov, USSR. **8,618 pts.**

Track and Field — Women

100 Meters — 1. Annegret Richter, W. Germany; 2. Renate Stecher, E. Germany; 3. Inge Helten, W. Germany. **Time** — 0:11.01.

200 Meters — 1. Baerbel Eckert, E. Germany; 2. Annegret Richter, W. Germany; 3. Renate Stecher, E. Germany. **Time** — 0:22.37.

400 Meters — 1. Irena Szewinska, Poland; 2. Christina Brehmer, E. Germany; 3. Ellen Streidt, E. Germany. **Time** — 0:49.29.

800 Meters — 1. Tatyana Kazankina, USSR; 2. Nikolina Chiereva, Bulgaria; 3. Elfi Zinn, E. Germany. **Time** — 1:54.94.

1,500 Meters — 1. Tatyana Kazankina, USSR; 2. Gunhilde Hoffmeister, E. Germany; 3. Ulrike Klapezynski, E. Germany. **Time** — 4:05.48.

100 Meter Hurdles — 1. Johanna Schaller, E. Germany; 2. Tatyana Anisimova, USSR; 3. Natalia Lebedeva, USSR. **Time** — 0:12.77.

400 Meter Relay — 1. E. Germany; 2. W. Germany; 3. USSR. **Time** — 0:42.55.

1,600 Meter Relay — 1. E. Germany; 2. United States; 3. USSR. **Time** — 3:19.23.

Long Jump — 1. Angela Voigt, E. Germany; 2. Kathy McMillan, United States; 3. Lidiya Alfeyeva, USSR. **22 ft. 2¹/₄ in.**

High Jump — 1. Rosemarie Ackermann, E. Germany; 2. Sara Simeoni, Italy; 3. Yordanka Blagoyeva, Bulgaria. **6 ft. 3³/₄ in.**

Javelin — 1. Ruth Fuchs, E. Germany; 2. Marion Becker, W. Germany; 3. Kathy Schmidt, United States. **216 ft. 4 in.**

Discus — 1. Evelin Schlaak, E. Germany; 2. Maria Vergova, Bulgaria; 3. Gabriele Hinzmann, E. Germany. **226 ft. 4¹/₂ in.**

Shot Put — 1. Ivanka Khristova, Bulgaria; 2. Nadejda Chizova, USSR; 3. Helena Fibingerova, Czech. **69 ft. 5 in.**

Pentathlon — 1. Sigrun Siegl, E. Germany; 2. Christine Laser, E. Germany; 3. Burlinde Pollak, E. Germany. **4,745 pts.**

Swimming — Men

100 Meter Freestyle — 1. Jim Montgomery, United States; 2. Jack Babashoff, United States; 3. Peter Nocke, W. Germany. **Time** — 0:49.99.

200 Meter Freestyle — 1. Bruce Furniss, United States; 2. John Naber, United States; 3. Jim Montgomery, United States. **Time** — 1:50.29.

400 Meter Freestyle — 1. Brian Goodell, United States; 2. Tim Shaw, United States; 3. Vladimir Raskatov, USSR. **Time** — 3:51.93.

1,500 Meter Freestyle — 1. Brian Goodell, United States; 2. Bobby Hackett, United States; 3. Steve Holland, Australia. **Time** — 15:02.40.

100 Meter Breaststroke — 1. John Hencken, United States; 2. David Wilkie, Scotland; 3. Arvidas Iuozaytis, USSR. **Time** — 1:03.11.

200 Meter Breaststroke — 1. David Wilkie, Scotland; 2. John Hencken, United States; 3. Rick Colella, United States. **Time** — 2:15.11.

100 Meter Butterfly — 1. Matt Vogel, United States; 2. Joe Bottom, United States; 3. Gary Hall, United States. **Time — 0:54.35.**

200 Meter Butterfly — 1. Mike Bruner, United States; 2. Steve Gregg, United States; 3. Bill Forrester, United States. **Time — 1:59.23.**

100 Meter Backstroke — 1. John Naber, United States; 2. Peter Rocca, United States; 3. Roland Matthes, E. Germany. **Time — 0:55.49.**

200 Meter Backstroke — 1. John Naber, United States; 2. Peter Rocca, United States; 3. Dan Harrigan, United States. **Time — 1:59.19.**

400 Meter Individual Medley — 1. Rod Strachan, United States; 2. Tim McKee, United States; 3. Andrey Smirnov, USSR. **Time — 4:23.68.**

400 Meter Medley Relay — 1. United States (Hencken, Naber, Montgomery, Vogel); 2. Canada; 3. W. Germany. **Time — 3:42.22.**

800 Meter Freestyle Relay — 1. United States (Bruner, Furniss, Naber, Montgomery); 2. USSR; 3. Gt. Britain. **Time — 7:23.22.**

Swimming — Women

100 Meter Freestyle — 1. Kornelia Ender, E. Germany; 2. Petra Priemer, E. Germany; 3. Enith Brigitha, Holland. **Time — 0:55.65.**

200 Meter Freestyle — 1. Kornelia Ender, E. Germany; 2. Shirley Babashoff, United States; 3. Enith Brigitha, Holland. **Time — 1:59.26.**

400 Meter Freestyle — 1. Petra Thumer, E. Germany; 2. Shirley Babashoff, United States; 3. Shannon Smith, Canada. **Time — 4:09.89.**

800 Meter Freestyle — 1. Petra Thumer, E. Germany; 2. Shirley Babashoff, United States; 3. Wendy Weinberg, United States. **Time — 8:37.14.**

100 Meter Breaststroke — 1. Hannelore Anke, E. Germany; 2. Liubov Rusanova, USSR; 3. Marina Koshevaia, USSR. **Time — 1:11.16.**

200 Meter Breaststroke — 1. Marina Koshevaia, USSR; 2. Marina Iurchenia, USSR; 3. Liubov Rusanova, USSR. **Time — 2:33.35.**

100 Meter Butterfly — 1. Kornelia Ender, E. Germany; 2. Andrea Pollack, E. Germany; 3. Wendy Boglioli, United States. **Time — 1:00.13.**

200 Meter Butterfly — 1. Andrea Pollack, E. Germany; 2. Ulrike Tauber, E. Germany; 3. Rosemarie Gabriel, E. Germany. **Time — 2:11.41.**

100 Meter Backstroke — 1. Ulrike Richter, E. Germany; 2. Birgit Treiber, E. Germany; 3. Nancy Garapick, Canada. **Time — 1:01.83.**

200 Meter Backstroke — 1. Ulrike Richter, E. Germany; 2. Birgit Treiber, E. Germany; 3. Nancy Garapick, Canada. **Time — 2:13.43.**

400 Meter Individual Medley — 1. Ulrike Tauber, E. Germany; 2. Cheryl Gibson, Canada; 3. Becky Smith, Canada. **Time — 4:42.77.**

400 Meter Freestyle Relay — 1. United States (Peyton, Boglioli, Sterkel, Babashoff); 2. E. Germany; 3. Canada. **Time — 3:44.82.**

400 Meter Medley Relay — 1. E. Germany (Richter, Anke, Pollack, Ender); 2. United States; 3. Canada. **Time — 4:07.95.**

Archery

Men's Individual — 1. Darrell Pace, United States; 2. Hiroshi Michinaga, Japan; 3. Carlo Ferrari, Italy.

Women's Individual — 1. Luann Ryon, United States; 2. Valentina Kovpan, USSR; 3. Zebeniso Rustamova, USSR.

Basketball

Men— 1. United States; 2. Yugoslavia; 3. USSR.
Women — 1. USSR; 2. United States; 3. Bulgaria.

Boxing

Light Flyweight — 1. Jorge Hernandez, Cuba; 2. Byong Uk Li, N. Korea; 3. Pooltarat, Thailand, Malfonado, Puerto Rico.

Flyweight — 1. Leo Randolph, United States; 2. Raymon Duvalon, Cuba; 3. Torosyan, USSR, Bazinski, Poland.

Bantamweight — 1. Yong Jo Gu, No. Korea; 2. Charles Mooney, United States; 3. Cowoell, Gt. Britain, Rybakov, USSR.

Featherweight — 1. Angel Herrera, Cuba; 2. Nowakowski, E. Germany; 3. Kosedowski, Poland, Parades, Mexico.

Lightweight — 1. Howard Davis, United States; 2. Simion Cutov, Romania; 3. Solomin, USSR, Rusevski, Yugoslavia.

Light Welterweight — 1. Ray Leonard, United States; 2. Andres Aldama, Cuba; 3. Kolev, Bulgaria, Szcerba, Poland.

Welterweight — 1. Jochen Bachfeld, E. Germany; 2. Gamarro, Venezuela; 3. Skricek, W. Germany, Zilbermann, Bulgaria.

Light Middleweight — 1. Jerzy Rybicki, Poland; 2. Kacar, Yugoslavia; 3. Savchenko, USSR, Garbey, Cuba.

Middleweight — 1. Mike Spinks, United States; 2. Rufat Riskiev, USSR; 3. Nastac, Romania, L. Martinez, Cuba.

Light Heavyweight — 1. Leon Spinks, United States; 2. Sixto Soria, Cuba; Dafinoiu, Romania, Gortat, Poland.

Heavyweight — 1. Teofilo Stevenson, Cuba; 2. Mircea Simon, Romania; 3. John Tate, United States, Hill, Bermuda.

Canoeing — Men

500 Meter Kayak Singles — 1. Vasile Diba, Romania; 2. Zoltan Szfanity, Hungary; 3. Rudiger Helm, E. Germany.

1,000 Meter Kayak Singles — 1. Rudiger Helm, E. Germany; 2. Czapo, Hungary; 3. Vasile Diba, Romania.

500 Meter Kayak Doubles — 1. E. Germany; 2. USSR; 3. Romania.

1,000 Meter Kayak Doubles — 1. USSR; 2. E. Germany; 3. Hungary.

1,000 Meter Kayak Fours — 1. USSR; 2. Spain; 3. E. Germany.

500 Meter Canadian Singles — 1. Aleksandr Rogov, USSR; 2. John Wood, Canada; 3. Matija Ljubek, Yugoslavia.

1,000 Meter Canadian Singles — 1. Matija Ljubek, Yugoslavia; 2. Urchenko, USSR; 3. Wichmann, Hungary.

500 Meter Canadian Doubles — 1. USSR; 2. Poland; 3. Hungary.

1,000 Meter Canadian Doubles — 1. USSR; 2. Romania; 3. Hungary.

Canoeing — Women

500 Meter Kayak Singles — 1. Carola Zirzow, E. Germany; 2. Tatyana Korshunova, USSR; 3. Klara Rajnai, Hungary.

500 Meter Kayak Doubles — 1. USSR; 2. Hungary; 3. E. Germany.

Cycling

Individual Road Race — 1. Bernt Johansson, Sweden; 2. Giuseppe Martinelli, Italy; 3. Miecsys Nowicki, Poland.

1,000 Meter Time Trial — 1. Klaus-Jurgen Grunke, E. Germany; 2. Michel Vaarten, Belgium; 3. Niels Fredborg, Denmark.

4,000 Meter Individual Pursuit — 1. Gregor Braun, W. Germany; 2. Ponsteen, Holland; 3. Huschke, E. Germany.

4,000 Meter Team Pursuit — 1. W. Germany; 2. USSR; 3. Gt. Britain.

Match Sprint — 1. Anton Tkac, Czech.; 2. Daniel Morelon, France; 3. Geschke, E. Germany.

100 Km. Team — 1. USSR; 2. Poland; 3. Denmark.

Diving — Men

Springboard — 1. Phil Boggs, United States; 2. Franco Cagnotto, Italy; 3. Kosenkov, USSR.

Platform — 1. Klaus Dibiasi, Italy; 2. Greg Louganis, United States; 3. Aleynik, USSR.

Diving — Women

Springboard — 1. Jenni Chandler, United States; 2. Christa Kohler, E. Germany; 3. Cynthia McIngvale, United States.

Platform — 1. Elena Vaytsekhovskaya, USSR; 2. Ulrika Knape, Sweden; 3. Deborah Wilson, United States.

Equestrian

3-Day Individual —1. Tad Coffin, United States; 2. John Plumb, United States; 3. Karl Schultz, W. Germany.

3-Day Team — 1. United States; 2. W. Germany; 3. Australia.

Individual Grand Prix Dressage — 1. Christine Stueckelberger, Switzerland; 2. Harry Boldt, W. Germany; 3. Reiner Klimke, W. Germany.

Individual Grand Prix Jumping — 1. Alwin Schockemoehle, W. Germany; 2. Michel Viaillancourt, Canada; 3. Francois Mathy, Belgium.

Team Dressage — 1. W. Germany; 2. Switzerland; 3. United States.

Team Jumping — 1. France; 2. W. Germany; 3. Belgium.

Fencing — Men

Individual Foil — 1. Fabio Dal Zotto, Italy; 2. Alexandr Romankov, USSR; 3. Bernard Talvard, France.

Team Foil — 1. W. Germany; 2. Italy; 3. France.

Individual Epee — 1. Alexander Pusch, W. Germany; 2. Jurgen Hehn, W. Germany; 3. Gyozo Kulcsar, Hungary.

Team Epee — 1. Sweden; 2. W. Germany; 3. Switzerland.

Individual Saber — 1. Viktor Krovopouskov, USSR; 2. Vládimir Nazlymov, USSR; 3. Viktor Sidyak, USSR.

Team Saber — 1. USSR; 2. Italy; 3. Romania.

Fencing — Women

Individual Foil — 1. Ildiko Schwarczenberger, Hungary; 2. Collino, Italy; 3. Belova, USSR.

Team Foil — 1. USSR; 2. France; 3. Hungary.

Field Hockey

Team Championship — 1. New Zealand; 2. Australia; 3. Pakistan.

Gymnastics — Men

All-Around — 1. Nikolai Andrianov, USSR; 2. Sawao Kato, Japan; 3. Mitsuo Tsukahara, Japan.
Floor Exercise — 1. Nikolai Andrianov, USSR; 2. Vladimir Marchenko, USSR; 3. Peter Kormann, United States.
Pommeled Horse — 1. Zoltan Magyar, Hungary; 2. Elzo Kemmotsu, Japan; 3. Nikolai Andrianov, USSR.
Rings — 1. Nikolai Andrianov, USSR; 2. Alexandr Ditiatin, USSR; 3. Danut Grecu, Romania.
Vault — 1. Nikolai Andrianov, USSR; 2. Mitsuo Tsukahara, Japan; 3. Hiroshi Kajiyama, Japan.
Parallel Bars — 1. Sawao Kato, Japan; 2. Nikolai Andrianov, USSR; 3. Mitsuo Tsukahara, Japan.
Horizontal Bar — 1. Mitsuo Tsukahara, Japan; 2. Elzo Kemmotsu, Japan; 3. Eberhard Gienger, W. Germany.
Team Championship — 1. Japan; 2. USSR; 3. E. Germany.

Gymnastics — Women

All-Around — 1. Nadia Comaneci, Romania; 2. Nelli Kim, USSR; 3. Ludmila Tourischeva, USSR.
Floor Exercise — 1. Nelli Kim, USSR; 2. Ludmila Tourischeva, USSR; 3. Nadia Comaneci, Romania.
Vault — 1. Nelli Kim, USSR; 2. Ludmila Tourishcheva, USSR; 3. Carola Dombeck, E. Germany.
Uneven Parallel Bars — 1. Nadia Comaneci, Romania; 2. Teodora Ungureanu, Romania; 3. Egervari, Hungary.
Balance Beam — 1. Nadia Comaneci, Romania; 2. Olga Korbut, USSR; 3. Teodora Ungureanu, Romania.
Team Championship — 1. USSR; 2. Romania; 3. E. Germany.

Team Handball

Men — 1. USSR; 2. Romania; 3. Poland.
Women — 1. USSR; 2. E. Germany; 3. Hungary.

Judo

Lightweight — 1. Hector Rodriguez, Cuba; 2. Hyung Chang, S. Korea; 3. Felice Mariani, Italy, Jozsef Tuncsik, Hungary.
Light Middleweight — 1. Vladimir Nevzorov, USSR; 2. Koji Kuramoto, Japan; 3. Patrick Vial, France, Marian Talij, Poland.
Middleweight — 1. Isamu Sonoda, Japan; 2. Valeriy Dvoinikov, USSR; 3. Slavko Obadov, Yugoslavia, Park, S. Korea.
Light Heavyweight — 1. Kazuhiro Nimomiya, Japan; 2. Ramaz Harshiladze, USSR; 3. Dave Starbrook, Gt. Britain, Juerg Reohlisberger, Switzerland.
Heavyweight — 1. Sergei Novikov, USSR; 2. Gunther Neureuther, W. Germany; 3. Sumio Endo, Japan, Allen Coage, United States.
Open — 1. Haruki Uemura, Japan; 2. Remfry, Gt. Britain; 3. Chochishvily, USSR; Cho, S. Korea.

Modern Pentathlon

Individual — 1. Janusz Pyciak-Peciak, Poland; 2. Pavel Lednev, USSR; Jan Bartu, Czechoslovakia.
Team — 1. Gt. Britain; 2. Czechoslovakia; 3. Hungary.

Rowing — Men

Single Sculls — 1. Pertti Karppinen, Finland; 2. Peter Kolbe, W. Germany; 3. Joachim Dreifke, E. Germany.
Double Sculls — 1. Norway; 2. Gt. Britain; 3. E. Germany.
Quadruple Sculls — 1. E. Germany; 2. USSR; 3. Czechoslovakia.
Pairs with Coxswain — 1. E. Germany; 2. USSR; 3. Czechoslovakia.
Pairs without Coxswain — 1. E. Germany; 2. United States; 3. W. Germany.
Fours with Coxswain — 1. USSR; 2. E. Germany; 3. W. Germany.
Fours without Coxswain — 1. E. Germany; 2. Norway; 3. USSR.
Eights with Coxswain — 1. E. Germany; 2. Gt. Britain; 3. New Zealand.

Rowing — Women

Single Sculls — 1. Christine Scheiblich, E. Germany; 2. Joan Lind, United States; 3. Elena Antonova, USSR.
Double Sculls — 1. Bulgaria; 2. E. Germany; 3. USSR.
Quadruple Sculls — 1. E. Germany; 2. USSR; 3. Romania.
Pairs without Coxswain — 1. Bulgaria; 2. E. Germany; 3. W. Germany.
Fours with Coxswain — 1. E. Germany; 2. Bulgaria; 3. USSR.
Eights with Coxswain — 1. E. Germany; 2. USSR; 3. United States.

Shooting

Small-bore Rifle Prone — 1. Karlheinz Smieszek, W. Germany; 2. Ulrich Lind, W. Germany; 3. Gennady Lushchikov, USSR.
Small-bore Rifle (3-positions) — 1. Lanny Bassham, United States; 2. Margaret Murdock, United States; 3. Werner Siebold, W. Germany.

Rapid Fire Pistol — 1. Norbert Klaar, E. Germany; 2. Jurgen Wiefel, E. Germany; 3. Roberto Ferraris, Italy.
Free Pistol — 1. Uwe Potteck, E. Germany; 2. Harald Vollimar, E. Germany; 3. Rudolf Dollinger, Austria.
Moving Target — 1. Alexandr Gazov, USSR; 2. Alexandr Kedyarov, USSR; 3. Jerzy Greszkiewicz, Poland.
Trapshooting — 1. Don Haldeman, United States; 2. Armondo Silva-Marquis, Portugal; 3. Ubaldesc Baldi, Italy.
Skeetshooting — 1. Josef Panacek, Czechoslovakia; 2. Swinkles, Holland; 3. Gawlikowski, Poland.

Soccer

Team Championship — 1. E. Germany; 2. Poland; 3. USSR.

Volleyball

Men — 1. Poland; 2. USSR; 3. Cuba.
Women — 1. Japan; 2. USSR; 3. S. Korea.

Water Polo

Team Championship — 1. Hungary; 2. Italy; 3. Holland

Weight Lifting

Flyweight — 1. Alexandr Voronin, USSR; 2. Koszegi, Hungary; 3. Nassiri, Iran.
Bantamweight — 1. Norair Nourikian, Bulgaria; 2. Cziura, Poland; 3. Ando, Japan.
Featherweight — 1. Nikolai Kolesnikov, USSR; 2. Georgi Todorov, Bulgaria; 3. Kazumasa Hiraj, Japan.
Lightweight — 1. Zbigniew Kaczmarek, Poland; 2. Korol, USSR; 3. Senet, France.
Middleweight — 1. Yordan Mitkov, Bulgaria; 2. Vartan Militosyan, USSR; 3. Peter Wenzel, E. Germany.
Light Heavyweight — 1. Valery Shary, USSR; 2. Blagoev, Bulgaria; 3. Stoychev, Bulgaria.
Middle Heavyweight — 1. David Rigert, USSR; 2. Lee James, United States; 3. Atanas Shopov, Bulgaria.
Heavyweight — 1. Valentin Khristov, Bulgaria; 2. Yuri Zaitsev, USSR; 3. Drastlo Semerdjiev, Bulgaria.
Super Heavyweight — 1. Vasily Alexeev, USSR; 2. Gerd Bonk, E. Germany; 3. Helmut Losch, E. Germany.

Wrestling — Freestyle

Paperweight — 1. Khassan Issaev, Bulgaria; 2. Dimitriev, USSR; 3. Kudo, Japan.
Flyweight — 1. Yuji Takada, Japan; 2. Ivanov, USSR; 3. Jeon, S. Korea.
Bantamweight — 1. Vladimir Yumin, USSR; 2. Bruchert, E. Germany; 3. Arai, Japan.
Featherweight — 1. Jung-Mo Yang, S. Korea; 2. Zeveg Oidov, Mongolia; 3. Gene Davis, United States.
Lightweight — 1. Pavel Pinigin, USSR; 2. Lloyd Keaser, United States; 3. Sugawara, Japan.
Welterweight — 1. Date Jiichiro, Japan; 2. Barzegar, Iran; 3. Stan Dziedzic, United States.
Middleweight — 1. John Peterson, United States; 2. Novojilov, USSR; 3. Seger, W. Germany.
Light Heavyweight — 1. Levan Tediashvily, USSR; 2. Ben Peterson, United States; 3. Morcov, Romania.
Heavyweight — 1. Ivan Yarygin, USSR; 2. Russell Hellickson, United States; 3. Kostov, Bulgaria.
Super Heavyweight — 1. Soslan Andiev, USSR; 2. Balla, Hungary; 3. Simon, Romania.

Wrestling — Greco-Roman

Paperweight — 1. Alexey Shumakov, USSR; 2. Berceanu, Romania; 3. Anghelov, Bulgaria.
Flyweight — 1. Vitaly Konstantinov, USSR; 2. Jinga, Romania; 3. Hirayama, Japan.
Bantamweight — 1. Pertti Ukkola, Finland; 2. Frgic, Yugoslavia; 3. Mustafin, USSR.
Featherweight — 1. Kazimer Lipien, Poland; 2. Davidian, USSR; 3. Reczi, Hungary.
Lightweight — 1. Suren Nalbandyan, USSR; 2. Rusu, Romania; 3. Wehling, E. Germany.
Welterweight — 1. Antoly Bykov, USSR; 2. Macha, Czechoslovakia; 3. Helbing, W. Germany.
Middleweight — 1. Momir Petkovic, Yugoslavia; 2. Cheboksarov, USSR; 3. Kolev, Bulgaria.
Light Heavyweight — 1. Valery Rezantsev, USSR; 2. Ivanov, Bulgaria; 3. Kweicinski, Poland.
Heavyweight — 1. Nikolai Balboshin, USSR; 2. Goranov, Bulgaria; Skrzylewski, Poland.
Super Heavyweight — 1. Alexandr Kolchinsky, USSR; 2. Tomov, Bulgaria; 3. Codreanu, Romania.

Yachting

Soling — 1. Denmark; 2. United States; 3. E. Germany.
Tempest — 1. Sweden; 2. USSR; 3. United States.
Flying Dutchman — 1. W. Germany; 2. Gt. Britain; 3. Brazil.
470 Class — 1. W. Germany; 2. Spain; 3. Australia.
Tornado — 1. Gt. Britain; 2. United States; 3. W. Germany.
Finn — 1. E. Germany; 2. USSR; 3. Australia.

Winter Olympic Games Champions, 1924-1976

Sites and Unofficial Winners of Games

1924—Chamonix, France (Norway)
1928—St. Moritz, Switzerland (Norway)
1932—Lake Placid, N.Y. (U.S.)
1936—Garmisch-Partenkirchen (Norway)
1948—St. Moritz (Sweden)

1952—Olso, Norway (Norway)
1956—Cortina d'Ampezzo, Italy (USSR)
1960—Squaw Valley, Cal. (USSR)
1964—Innsbruck, Austria (USSR)

1968—Grenoble, France (Norway)
1972—Sapporo, Japan (USSR)
1976—Innsbruck, Austria, (USSR)
1980—Lake Placid, N.Y. (Scheduled)

Biathlon (20-KM)

		Time
1960—Klas Lestander, Sweden		1:33:21.6
1964—Vladimir Melanin, USSR		1:20:26.8
1968—Magnar Solberg, Norway		1:13:45.9
1972—Magnar Solberg, Norway		1:15:55.50
1976—Nikolai Kruglov, USSR		1:14:12.26

Biathlon Relay (40-KM)

		Time
1968—USSR, Norway, Sweden		2:13.02
1972—USSR, Finland, E. Germany		1:51.44
1976—USSR, Finland, E. Germany		1:57.55.64

Bobsledding

4-Man Bob

	(Driver in parentheses)	Time
1924—Switzerland (Edward Scherrer)		5:45.54
1928—*United States (William Fiske) (A)		3:20.5
1932—United States (William Fiske)		7:53.68
1936—Switzerland (Pierre Musy)		5:19.85
1948—United States (Edward Rimkus)		5:20.1
1952—Germany (Andreas Ostler)		5:07.84
1956—Switzerland (Frank Kapus)		5:10.44
1964—Canada (Victor Emery)		4:14.46
1968—Italy (Eugenio Monti) (A)		2:17.39
1972—Switzerland (Jean Wicki)		4:43.07
1976—E. Germany (Meinhard Nehmer)		3:40.43

*Five-man bobsled (A) 2 races

2-Man Bob

		Time
1932—U.S.A. (Hubert Stevens)		8:14.74
1936—U.S.A. (Ivan Brown)		5:29.29
1948—Switzerland (F. Endrich)		5:29.2
1952—Germany (Andreas Ostler)		5:24.54
1956—Italy (Dalla Costa)		5:30.14
1964—Great Britain (Antony Nash)		4:21.90
1968—Italy (Eugenio Monti)		4:41.54
1972—W. Germany (Wolfgang Zimmerer)		4:47.07
1976—E. Germany (Meinhard Nehmer)		3:40.43

Figure Skating

Men's Singles

1908 Ulrich Sachow, Sweden
1920 Gillis Grafstrom, Sweden
1924 Gillis Grafstrom, Sweden
1928 Gillis Grafstrom, Sweden
1932 Karl Schaefer, Austria
1936 Karl Schaefer, Austria
1948 Richard T. Button, U.S.
1952 Richard T. Button, U.S.
1956 Hayes Alan Jenkins, U.S.
1960 David W. Jenkins, U.S.
1964 Manfred Schnelldorfer, Germany
1968 Wolfgang Schwartz, Austria
1972 Ondrej Nepela, Czechoslovakia
1976 John Curry, Great Britain

Women's Singles

1908 Madge Syers, Great Britain
1920 Magda Julin-Mauroy, Sweden
1924 Mrs. Heima von Szabo-Planck, Austria
1928 Sonja Henie, Norway
1932 Sonja Henie, Norway
1936 Sonja Henie, Norway
1948 Barbara Ann Scott, Canada
1952 Jeanette Altwegg, Great Britain
1956 Tenley Albright, U.S.
1960 Carol Heiss, U.S.
1964 Sjoukje Dijkstra, Netherlands
1968 Peggy Fleming, U.S.
1972 Beatrix Schuba, Austria
1976 Dorothy Hamill, U.S.

Pairs

1908 Anna Hubler & Heinrich Burger, Germany
1920 Ludovika & Walter Jakobsson, Finland
1924 Helene Engelman & Alfred Berger, Austria
1928 Andree Joly & Pierre Brunet, France
1932 Andree Joly & Pierre Brunet, France
1936 Maxie Herber & Ernest Baier, Germany

1948 Micheline Lannoy & Pierre Baugniet, Belgium
1952 Ria and Paul Falk, Germany
1956 Elisabeth Schwarz & Kurt Oppelt, Austria
1960 Barbara Wagner & Robert Paul, Canada
1964 Ludmila Beloussova & Oleg Protopopov, USSR
1968 Ludmila Beloussova & Oleg Protopopov, USSR
1972 Irina Rodnina & Alexei Ulanov, USSR
1976 Irina Rodnina & Aleksandr Zaitzev, USSR

Ice Dancing

1976 Ludmila Pakhomova & Aleksandr Gorschkov, USSR

Alpine Skiing

Men's Downhill

		Time
1948—Henri Oreiller, France		2:55.0
1952—Zeno Colo, Italy		2:30.8
1956—Anton Sailer, Austria		2:52.2
1960—Jean Vuarnet, France		2:06.0
1964—Egon Zimmermann, Austria		2:18.16
1968—Jean Claude Killy, France		1:59.85
1972—Bernhard Russi, Switzerland		1:51.43
1976—Franz Klammer, Austria		1:45.73

Men's Giant Slalom

		Time
1952—Stein Eriksen, Norway		2:25.0
1956—Anton Sailer, Austria		3:00.1
1960—Roger Staub, Switzerland		1:48.3
1964—Francois Bonlieu, France		1:46.7
1968—Jean Claude Killy, France		3:29.28
1972—Gustavo Thoeni, Italy		3:09.62
1976—Heini Hemmi, Switzerland		3:26.97

Men's Slalom

		Time
1948—Edi Reinalter, Switzerland		2:10.3
1952—Othmar Schneider, Austria		2:00.0
1956—Anton Sailer, Austria		194.7 pts.
1960—Ernst Hinterseer, Austria		2:08.9
1964—Josef Stiegler, Austria		2:11.13
1968—Jean Claude Killy, France		1:39.73
1972—Francesco Fernandez Ochoa, Spain		1:49.27
1976—Piero Gros, Italy		2:03.29

Women's Downhill

		Time
1948—Hedi Schlunegger, Switzerland		2:28.3
1952—Trude Jochum-Beiser, Austria		1:47.1
1956—Madeline Bethod, Switzerland		1:40.7
1960—Heidi Biebl, Germany		1:37.6
1964—Christl Haas, Austria		1:55.3
1968—Olga Pall, Austria		1:40.87
1972—Marie Therese Nadig, Switzerland		1:36.68
1976—Rosi Mittermaier, W. Germany		1:46.16

Women's Giant Slalom

		Time
1952—Andrea Mead Lawrence, U.S.		2:06.8
1956—Ossi Reichert, Germany		1:56.5
1960—Yvonne Ruegg, Switzerland		1:39.9
1964—Marielle Goitschel, France		1:52.2
1968—Nancy Greene, Canada		1:51.97
1972—Marie Therese Nadig, Switzerland		1:29.90
1976—Kathy Kreiner, Canada		1:29.13

Women's Slalom

		Time
1948—Gretchen Fraser, U.S.		1:57.2
1952—Andrea Mead Lawrence, U.S.		2:10.6
1956—Renee Colliard, Switzerland		112.3 pts.
1960—Anne Heggtveigt, Canada		1:49.6
1964—Christine Goitschel, France		1:35.11
1968—Marielle Goitschel, France		1:25.86
1972—Barbara Cochran, U.S.		1:31.24
1976—Rosi Mittermaier, W. Germany		1:30.54

Nordic Skiing

Men's Cross-Country Events
15 Kilometers (9.3 miles) or Equivalent

		Time
1924—Thorleif Haug, Norway		1:14:31
1928—Johan Grottumsbraaten, Norway		1:37:01
1932—Sven Utterstrom, Sweden		1:23:07
1936—Erik-August Larsson, Sweden		1:14:38

1948—Martin Lundstrom, Sweden. 1:13:50
1952—Hallgeir Brenden, Norway. 1:01:34
1956—Hallgeir Brenden, Norway. 49:39.0
1960—Haakon Brusveen, Norway. 51:55.0
1964—Eero Mantyranta, Finland 50:54.1
1968—Harald Groenningen, Norway. 47:54.2
1972—Sven-Ake Lundback, Sweden. 45:28.24
1976—Nikolai Bajukov, USSR. 43:58.47
(Note: Approx. 18-kilometer course 1924-1952)

30 Kilometers (18.6 miles)   Time
1956—Veikko Hakulinen, Finland 1:44:06.0
1960—Sixten Jernberg, Sweden. 1:51:03.9
1964—Eero Mantyranta, Finland 1:30:50.7
1968—Franco Nones, Italy. 1:35:39.2
1972—Vyacheslav Vedenin, USSR. 1:36:31.1
1976—Sergei Savaliev, USSR. 1:30:29.38

50 Kilometers (31 miles)   Time
1924—Thorleif Haug, Norway. 3:44:32.0
1928—Per Erik Hedlund, Sweden. 4:52:03.0
1932—Veli Saarinen, Finland. 4:28:00.0
1936—Elis Viklund, Sweden. 3:30:11.0
1948—Nils Karlsson, Sweden. 3:47:48.0
1952—Veikko Hakulinen, Finland 3:33:33.0
1956—Sixten Jernberg, Sweden. 2:50:27.0
1960—Kalevi Hamalainen, Finland. 2:59:06.3
1964—Sixten Jernberg, Sweden. 2:43:52.6
1968—Ole Ellefsaeter, Norway. 2:28:45.8
1972—Paal Tyldum, Norway. 2:43:14.7
1976—Ivar Formo, Norway. 2:37:30.05

40 Kilometer Cross-Country Relay   Time
1936—Finland, Norway, Sweden. 2:41:33.0
1948—Sweden, Finland, Norway. 2:32:08.0
1952—Finland, Norway, Sweden. 2:20:16.0
1956—USSR, Finland, Sweden. 2:15:30.0
1960—Finland, Norway, USSR. 2:18:45.6
1964—Sweden, Finland, USSR 2:18:34.6
1968—Norway, Sweden, Finland. 2:08:33.5
1972—USSR, Norway, Switzerland 2:04:47.94
1976—Finland, Norway, USSR. 2:07:59.72

15 Km. Cross-Country & Jumping   Points
1924—Thorleif Haug, Norway. 453.800
1928—Johan Grottumsbraaten, Norway. 427.800
1932—Johan Grottumsbraaten, Norway. 446.200
1936—Oddbjorn Hagen, Norway 430.300
1948—Heikki Hasu, Finland. 448.800
1952—Simon Slattvik, Norway. 451.621
1956—Sverre Stenersen, Norway. 455.000
1960—Georg Thoma, Germany. 457.952
1964—Tormod Knutsen, Norway 469.280
1968—Franz Keller, W. Germany. 449.040
1972—Ulrich Wehling, E. Germany. 413.340
1976—Ulrich Wehling, E. Germany. 423.390

Ski Jumping (90 Meters)   Points
1924—Jacob T. Thams, Norway 227.5
1928—Alfred Andersen, Norway. 230.5
1932—Birger Ruud, Norway. 228.0
1936—Birger Ruud, Norway 232.0
1948—Petter Hugsted, Norway. 228.1
1952—A. Bergmann, Norway. 226.0
1956—Antti Hyvarinen, Finland. 227.0
1960—Helmut Recknagel, Germany. 227.2
1964—Toralf Engan, Norway. 230.7
1968—Vladimir Beloussov, USSR 231.3
1972—Wojiech Fortuna, Poland 219.9
1976—Karl Schnabl, Austria. 234.8

Ski Jumping (70 Meters)   Points
1964—Veikko Kankkonen, Finland. 229.9
1968—Jiri Raska, Czechoslovakia. 216.5
1972—Yukio Kasaya, Japan. 244.2
1976—Hans Aschenbach, E. Germany. 252.0

Women's Events
5 Kilometers (approx. 3.1 miles)   Time
1964—Claudia Boyarskikh, USSR. 17:50.5
1968—Toini Gustafsson, Sweden. 16:45.2
1972—Galina Koulacova, USSR. 17:00.5
1976—Helena Takalo, Finland. 15:48.69

10 Kilometers (6.2 miles)   Time
1952—Lydia Wideman, Finland. 41:40.0
1956—Lyubov Kosyreva, USSR. 38:11.0
1960—Maria Gusakova, USSR. 39:46.6
1964—Claudia Boyarskikh, USSR. 40:24.3
1968—Toini Gustafsson, Sweden. 36:46.5

1972—Galina Koulacova, USSR. 34:17.82
1976—Raisa Smetanina, USSR. 30:13.41

15 Kilometer Cross-Country Relay   Time
1956—Finland, USSR, Sweden. 1:09:01.0
1960—Sweden, USSR, Finland. 1:04:21.4
1964—USSR, Sweden, Finland. 59:20.2
1968—Norway, Sweden, USSR. 57:30.0
1972—USSR, Finland, Norway. 48:46.1
1976—USSR, Finland, E. Germany. 1:07:49.75
(20-KM in 1976)

Ice Hockey
1920 Canada, U.S. Czechoslovakia
1924 Canada, U.S., Great Britain
1928 Canada, Sweden, Switzerland
1932 Canada, U.S., Germany
1936 Great Britain, Canada, U.S.
1948 Canada, Czechoslovakia, Switzerland
1952 Canada, U.S., Sweden
1956 USSR, U.S., Canada
1960 U.S., Canada, USSR
1964 USSR, Sweden, Czechoslovakia
1968 USSR, Czechoslovakia, Canada
1972 USSR, U.S., Czechoslovakia
1976 USSR, Czechoslovakia, W. Germany

Luge
Men's Singles   Time
1964—Thomas Kohler, Germany. 3:26.77
1968—Manfred Schmid, Austria 2:52.48
1972—Wolfgang Scheidel, E. Germany. 3:27.58
1976—Detlef Guenther, E. Germany 3:27.688

Men's Doubles   Time
1964—Austria. 1.41.62
1968—East Germany. 1:35.85
1972—Italy, E. Germany (tie). 1:28.35
1976—E. Germany. 1:25.604

Women's Singles   Time
1964—Ortun Enderlein, Germany. 3:24.67
1968—Erica Lechner, Italy. 2:28.66
1972—Anna M. Muller, E. Germany. 2:59.18
1976—Margit Schumann, E. Germany. 2:50.621

Speed Skating
Men's Events
500 Meters   Time
1924—Charles Jewtraw, U.S.. . . . . .0:44.0
1928—Clas Thunberg, Finland &
     Bernt Evensen, Norway (tie). 0:43.4
1932—John A. Shea, U.S.. . . . . 0:43.4
1936—Ivar Ballangrud, Norway. 0:43.4
1948—Finn Helgesen, Norway. 0:43.1
1952—Kenneth Henry, U.S.. . . . . 0:43.2
1956—Evgeni Grishin, USSR. 0:40.2
1960—Evgeniy Grishin, USSR. 0:40.2
1964—Terry McDermott, U.S.. . . . . 0:40.1
1968—Erhard Keller, W. Germany. 0:40.3
1972—Erhard Keller, W. Germany. 0:39.44
1976—Evgeny Kulikov, USSR. 0:39.17

1,000 Meters   Time
1976—Peter Mueller, U.S. 1:19.32

1,500 Meters   Time
1924—Clas Thunberg, Finland 2:20.8
1928—Clas Thunberg, Finland 2:21.1
1932—John A. Shea, U.S.. . . . . 2:57.2
1936—Charles Mathiesen, Norway. 2:19.2
1948—Sverre Farstad, Norway. 2:17.6
1952—Hjalmar Anderson, Norway. 2:20.4
1956—Evgeniy Grishin, USSR. 2:08.6
1960—Roald Edgar Aas, Norway &
     Evgeniy Grishin, USSR (tie). 2:10.4
1964—Ants Anston, USSR 2:10.3
1968—Cornelis Verkerk, Netherlands. 2:03.4
1972—Ard Schenk, Netherlands. 2:02.96
1976—Jan Egil Storholt, Norway. 1:59.38

5,000 Meters   Time
1924—Clas Thunberg, Finland 8:39.0
1928—Ivar Ballangrud, Norway. 8:50.5
1932—Irving Jaffee, U.S.. . . . . 9:40.8
1936—Ivar Ballangrud, Norway. 8:19.6
1948—Reidar Liakleb, Norway. 8:29.4
1952—Hjalmar Anderson, Norway. 8:10.6

1956—Boris Shilkov, USSR	7:48.7
1960—Viktor Kosichkin, USSR	7:51.3
1964—Knut Johannesen, Norway	7:38.4
1968—F. Anton Maier, Norway	7:22.4
1972—Ard Schenk, Netherlands	7:23.61
1976—Sten Stensen, Norway	7:24.48

10,000 Meters	Time
1924—Julius Skutnabb, Finland	18:04.8
1928—Event not held, thawing of ice	
1932—Irving Jaffee, U.S.	19:13.6
1936—Ivar Ballangrud, Norway	17:24.3
1948—Ake Seyffarth, Norway	17:26.3
1952—Hjalmar Anderson, Norway	16:45.8
1956—Sigvard Ericsson, Sweden	16:35.9
1960—Knut Johannesen, Norway	15:46.6
1964—Jonny Nilsson, Sweden	15:50.1
1968—Jonny Hoeglin, Sweden	15:23.6
1972—Ard Schenk, Netherlands	15:01.3
1976—Piet Kleine, Netherlands	14:50.59

Women's Events

500 Meters	Time
1960—Helga Haase, Germany	0:45.9
1964—Lydia Skoblikova, USSR	0:45.0

1968—Ludmila Titova, USSR	0:46.1
1972—Anne Henning, U.S.	0:43.44
1976—Sheila Young, U.S.	0:42.76

1,000 Meters	Time
1960—Klara Guseva, USSR	1:34.1
1964—Lydia Skoblikova, USSR	1:33.2
1968—Carolina Geijssen, Netherlands	1:32.6
1972—Monika Pflug, W. Germany	1:31.40
1976—Tatiana Averina, USSR	1:28.43

1,500 Meters	Time
1960—Lydia Skoblikova, USSR	2:52.2
1964—Lydia Skoblikova,USSR	2:22.6
1968—Kaija Mustonen, Finland	2:22.4
1972—Dianne Holum, U.S.	2:20.85
1976—Galina Stepanskaya, USSR	2:16.58

3,000 Meters	Time
1960—Lydia Skoblikova, USSR	5:14.3
1964—Lydia Skoblikova, USSR	5:14.9
1968—Johanna Schut, Netherlands	4:56.2
1972—Stien Baas-Kaiser, Netherlands	4:52.14
1976—Tatiana Averina, USSR	4:45.19

1976 Winter Olympic Medal Winners

Innsbruck, Austria, Feb. 4-15

Final Medal Standing

	Gold	Silver	Bronze	Total
Soviet Union	13	6	8	27
East Germany	7	5	7	19
United States	3	3	4	10
Norway	3	3	1	7
West Germany	2	5	3	10
Finland	2	4	1	7
Austria	2	2	2	6
Switzerland	1	3	1	5
Netherlands	1	2	3	6
Italy	1	2	1	4
Canada	1	1	1	3
Britain	1	0	0	1
Czechoslovakia	0	1	0	1
Liechtenstein	0	0	2	2
Sweden	0	0	2	2
France	0	0	1	1

Alpine Skiing

Men's Downhill—1. Franz Klammer, Austria; 2. Bernhard Russi, Switzerland; 3. Herbert Plank, Italy. **Time—1:45.73.**

Men's Giant Slalom—1. Heini Hemmi, Switzerland; 2. Ernest Good, Switzerland; 3. Ingemar Stenmark, Sweden. **Time—3:26.97.**

Men's Slalom—1. Piero Gros, Italy; 2. Gustavo Thoeni, Italy; 3. Willy Frommelt, Liechtenstein. **Time—2:03.29.**

Women's Downhill—1. Rosi Mittermaier, W. Germany; 2. Brigitte Totschnig, Austria; 3. Cindy Nelson, U.S. **Time—1:46.16.**

Women's Giant Slalom—1. Kathy Kreiner, Canada; 2. Rosi Mittermaier, W. Germany; 3. Danielle Debernard, France. **Time—1:29.13.**

Women's Slalom—1. Rosi Mittermaier, W. Germany; 2. Claudia Giordani, Italy; 3. Hanny Wenzel, Liechtenstein. **Time—1:30.54.**

Nordic Skiing

Men's Combined Cross Country—1. Ulrich Wehling, E. Germany; 2. Urban Hettich, W. Germany; 3. Konrad Winkler, E. Germany. **423.390 pts.**

Men's 15-km Cross Country—1. Nikolai Bajukov, USSR; 2. Evgeny Baliaev, USSR; 3. Arto Koivisto, Finland, **Time — 43:58.47.**

Men's 30-km Cross Country—1. Sergei Savaliev, USSR; 2. Bill Koch, U.S.; 3. Ivan Garanin, USSR. **Time—1:30:29.38.**

Men's 40-km Cross Country Relay—1. Finland; 2. Norway; 3. USSR. **Time—2:07:59.72.**

Men's 50-km Cross Country—1. Ivar Formo, Norway; 2. Gertdietmar Klause, E. Germany; 3. Benny Soedergren, Sweden. **Time—2:37:30.05.**

Women's 5-km Cross Country—1. Helena Takalo, Finland; 2. Raisa Smetanina, USSR; 3. Nina Baldicheava, USSR. **Time—15:48.69.**

Women's 10-km Cross Country—1. Raisa Smetanina, USSR; 2. Helena Takalo, Finland; 3. Galina Kulakova, USSR. **Time—30:13.41.**

Women's 20-km Cross Country Relay—1. USSR; 2. Finland; 3. E. Germany. **Time—1:07:49.75.**

Men's 20-km Biathlon

Men's 20-km Biathlon—1. Nikolai Kruglov, USSR; 2. Heikki Ikola, Finland; 3. Aleksandr Elizarov, USSR. **Time—1:14:12.26.**

Men's 40-km Biathlon Relay—1. USSR; 2. Finland; 3. E. Germany. **Time—1:57:55.64.**

Speed Skating

Men's 500 Meters—1. Evgeny Kulikov, USSR; 2. Valery Muratov, USSR; 3. Dan Immerfall, U.S. **Time—0:39.17.**

Men's 1,000 Meters—1. Peter Mueller, U.S.; 2. Jorn Didricksen, Norway; 3. Valery Muratov, USSR. **Time—1:19.32.**

Men's 1,500 Meters—1. Jan Egil Storholt, Norway; 2. Yuri Kondakov, USSR; 3. Hans Van Helden, Netherlands. **Time—1:59.38.**

Men's 5,000 Meters—1. Sten Stensen, Norway; 2. Piet Kleine, Netherlands; 3. Hans Van Helden, 'etherlands. **Time—7:24.48.**

Men's 10,000 Meters—1. Piet Kleine, Netherlands; 2. Sten Stensen, Norway; 3. Hans Van Helden, Netherlands. **Time — 14:50.59.**

Women's 500 Meters—1. Sheila Young, U.S.; 2. Cathy Priestner, Canada; 3. Tatiana Averina, USSR. **Time—0:42.76.**

Women's 1,000 Meters—1. Tatiana Averina, USSR; 2. Leah Poulos, U.S.; 3. Sheila Young, U.S. **Time—1:28.43.**

Women's 1,500 Meters—1. Galina Stepanskaya, USSR; 2. Sheila Young, U.S.; 3. Tatiana Averina, USSR. **Time—2:16.58.**

Women's 3,000 Meters—1. Tatiana Averina, USSR; 2. Andrea Mitscherlich, E. Germany; 3. Lisbeth Korsmo, Norway. **Time—4:45.19.**

Luge

Men's Single—1. Detlef Guenther, E. Germany; 2. Josef Fendt, W. Germany; 3. Hans Rinn, E. Germany. **Time — 3:27.688.**

Women's Single—1. Margit Schumann, E. Germany; 2. Ute Reuhrold, E. Germany; 3. Elisabeth Demleitner, W. Germany. **Time—2:50.621.**

Men's 2-Man—1. E. Germany; 2. W. Germany; 3. Austria. **Time—1:25.604.**

Ski Jumping

70 Meters—1. Hans Aschenbach, E. Germany; 2. Jochen Dannenberg, E. Germany; 3. Karl Schnabl, Austria. **252 pts.**

90 Meters—1. Karl Schnabl, Austria; 2. Anton Innauer, Austria; 3. Henry Glass, E. Germany. **234.8 pts.**

Figure Skating

Men—1. John Curry, Great Britain; 2. Vladimir Kovalev, USSR; 3. Toller Cranston, Canada.

Women—1. Dorothy Hamill, U.S.; 2. Dianne de Leeuw, Netherlands; 3. Christine Errath, E. Germany.

Pairs—1. Irina Rodnina & Aleksandr Zaitzev, USSR; 2. Romy Kermer & Rolf Oesterreich, E. Germany; 3. Manuela Gross & Uwe Kagelmann, E. Germany.

Ice Dancing—1. Ludmilla Pakhomova & Aleksandr Gorschkov, USSR; 2. Irina Moiseeva & Andrei Minenkov, USSR; 3. Colleen O'Connor & John Millns, U.S.

Hockey in 1975-76
National Hockey League
Final Standings

Clarence Campbell Conference

Lester Patrick Division							Conn Smythe Division					
Club	W.	L.	T.	Pts.	GF	GA	Club	W.	L.	T.	Pts.	GF	GA
Philadelphia	51	13	16	118	348	209	Chicago	32	30	18	82	254	261
N. Y. Islanders	42	21	17	101	297	190	Vancouver	33	32	15	81	271	272
Atlanta	35	33	12	82	262	237	St. Louis	29	37	14	72	249	290
N. Y. Rangers	29	42	9	67	262	333	Minnesota	20	53	7	47	195	303
							Kansas City	12	56	12	36	190	351

Prince of Wales Conference

Charles P. Adams Division							James Norris Division					
Club	W.	L.	T.	Pts.	GF	GA	Club	W.	L.	T.	Pts.	GF	GA
Boston	48	15	17	113	313	237	Montreal	58	11	11	127	337	174
Buffalo	46	21	13	105	339	240	Los Angeles	38	33	9	85	263	265
Toronto	34	31	15	83	294	276	Pittsburgh	35	33	12	82	339	303
California	27	42	11	65	250	278	Detroit	26	44	10	62	226	300
							Washington	11	59	10	32	224	394

Stanley Cup Playoff Results

Buffalo defeated St. Louis 2 games to 1.
N. Y. Islanders defeated Vancouver 2 games to 0.
Toronto defeated Pittsburgh 2 games to 1.
Los Angeles defeated Atlanta 2 games to 0.
Montreal defeated Chicago 4 games to 0.
N. Y. Islanders defeated Buffalo 4 games to 2.

Boston defeated Los Angeles 4 games to 3.
Philadelphia defeated Toronto 4 games to 3.
Montreal defeated N. Y. Islanders 4 games to 1.
Philadelphia defeated Boston 4 games to 1.
Montreal defeated Philadelphia 4 games to 0.

Leading Scorers

Player-Club	G.	Goals	Asts.	Pts.	Player-Club	G.	Goals	Asts.	Pts.
Lafleur, Montreal	80	56	69	125	D. Potvin, Islanders	78	31	66	97
Clarke, Philadelphia	76	30	89	119	Trottier, Islanders	79	32	63	95
Perreault, Buffalo	80	44	69	113	Dionne, Los Angeles	80	40	54	94
Barber, Philadelphia	80	50	62	112	McDonald, Toronto	75	37	56	93
Larouche, Pittsburgh	76	53	58	111	Leach, Philadelphia	80	61	30	91
Ratelle, Boston	80	36	69	105	Robert, Buffalo	72	35	52	87
Mahovlich, Montreal	80	34	71	105	Martin, Buffalo	80	49	37	86
Pronovost, Pittsburgh	80	52	52	104	Gilbert, Rangers	70	36	50	86
Sittler, Toronto	79	41	59	100	Lefley, St. Louis	75	43	42	85
Apps, Pittsburgh	80	32	67	99	Unger, St. Louis	80	39	44	83

Leading Goalies
(25 or more games)

Goalie, Club	G.	Min.	GA	SO	Avg.	Goalie, Club	G.	Min.	GA	SO	Avg.
Ken Dryden, Montreal	62	3,580	121	8	2.03	Cesare Maniago, Minnesota	47	2,704	151	2	3.35
Glenn Resch, N.Y. Islanders	44	2,546	88	7	2.07	Gilles Meloche, California	41	2,440	140	1	3.44
Daniel Bouchard, Atlanta	47	2,671	113	2	2.54	*Ed Giacomin, Detroit	29	1,740	100	2	3.45
Wayne Stephenson, Philadelphia	66	3,819	164	1	2.58	Michel Plasse, Pittsburgh	55	3,096	178	2	3.45
Bill Smith, N.Y. Islanders	39	2,254	98	3	2.61	Phil Myre, Atlanta	37	2,129	123	1	3.47
Gilles Gilbert, Boston	55	3,123	151	2	2.90	Ken Lockett, Vancouver	30	1,436	83	0	3.47
Gerry Desjardins, Buffalo	55	3,280	161	2	2.95	Gary Smith, Vancouver	51	2,864	167	2	3.50
Tony Esposito, Chicago	68	4,003	198	4	2.97	Gary Edwards, Los Angeles	29	1,740	103	0	3.55
Rogie Vachon, Los Angeles	51	3,060	160	5	3.14	Jim Rutherford, Detroit	44	2,640	158	4	3.59
Wayne Thomas, Toronto	64	3,684	196	2	3.19	Ed Johnston, St. Louis	38	2,152	130	1	3.62
Gary Simmons, California	40	2,360	131	3	3.33	*Record with N.Y. Rangers not included.					

Team Penalties

	GP	Min.	Avg.		GP	Min.	Avg.
Philadelphia	80	1980	24.8	Los Angeles	80	1022	12.8
Detroit	80	1922	24.0	Pittsburgh	80	1004	12.6
Toronto	80	1368	17.1	Kansas City	80	984	12.3
N.Y. Islanders	80	1277	16.0	Montreal	80	977	12.2
St. Louis	80	1274	15.9	Washington	80	951	11.9
Boston	80	1195	14.9	Chicago	80	944	11.8
Minnesota	80	1191	14.9	Buffalo	80	943	11.8
Vancouver	80	1122	14.0	Atlanta	80	928	11.6
California	80	1058	13.2	N.Y. Rangers	80	911	11.4

NHL All Star Team, 1976

	First Team	Second Team
Goal	Ken Dryden, Montreal	Glenn Resch, N.Y. Islanders
Defense	Brad Park, Boston	Guy Lapointe, Montreal
Defense	Denis Potvin, N.Y. Islanders	Bjorn Salming, Toronto
Center	Bobby Clarke, Philadelphia	Gilbert Perreault, Buffalo
Right Wing	Guy Lafleur, Montreal	Reggie Leach, Philadelphia
Left Wing	Bill Barber, Philadelphia	Rick Martin, Buffalo

Team Scoring Leaders

Atlanta	GP	G.	A.	Pts.
Tom Lysiak	80	31	51	82
Curt Bennett	80	34	31	65
Bill Clement	77	23	31	54
Hilliard Graves	80	19	30	49
Claude St. Sauveur	79	24	24	48

Montreal	GP	G.	A.	Pts.
Guy Lafleur	80	56	69	125
Pete Mahovlich	80	34	71	105
Steve Shutt	80	45	34	79
Yvan Cournoyer	71	32	36	68
Guy Lapointe	77	21	47	68

Boston	GP	G.	A.	Pts.
Jean Ratelle	80	36	69	105
John Bucyk	77	36	47	83
Gregg Sheppard	70	31	43	74
Wayne Cashman	80	28	43	71
Bobby Schmautz	75	28	34	62

N.Y. Islanders	GP	G.	A.	Pts.
Denis Potvin	78	31	67	98
Bryan Trottier	80	32	63	95
Jean Potvin	78	17	55	72
Billy Harris	80	32	38	70
Jude Drouin	76	21	41	62

Buffalo	GP	G.	A.	Pts.
Gil Perreault	80	44	69	113
Rene Robert	72	35	52	87
Rick Martin	80	49	37	86
Danny Gare	79	50	23	73
Craig Ramsey	80	22	49	71

N.Y. Rangers	GP	G.	A.	Pts.
Rod Gilbert	70	36	50	86
Phil Esposito	74	35	48	83
Steve Vickers	80	30	53	83
Carol Vadnais	76	22	35	57
Rick Middleton	77	24	26	50

California	GP	G.	A.	Pts.
Wayne Merrick	75	32	35	67
Al MacAdam	80	32	31	63
Dennis Maruk	80	30	32	62
Rick Hampton	73	14	37	51
Bob Murdoch	78	22	27	49

Philadelphia	GP	G.	A.	Pts.
Bobby Clarke	76	30	89	119
Bill Barber	80	50	62	112
Reg Leach	80	61	30	91
Orest Kindrachuk	76	26	49	75
Gary Dornhoefer	74	28	35	63

Chicago	GP	G.	A.	Pts.
Pit Martin	80	32	39	71
Dennis Hull	80	27	39	66
Ivan Boldirev	78	28	34	62
Dale Tallon	80	15	47	62
Cliff Korell	80	25	33	58

Pittsburgh	GP	G.	A.	Pts.
Pierre Larouche	76	53	58	111
Jean Pronovost	80	52	52	104
Syl Apps	80	32	67	99
Rick Kehoe	71	29	47	76
Lowell MacDonald	69	30	43	73

Detroit	GP	G.	A.	Pts.
Walt MacKechnie	80	26	56	82
Dan Maloney	77	27	39	66
Dennis Hextall	76	16	44	60
Michel Bergeron	72	32	27	59
Nick Libett	80	20	26	46

St. Louis	GP	G.	A.	Pts.
Chuck Lefley	75	43	42	85
Garry Unger	80	39	44	83
Derek Sanderson	73	24	43	67
Bob MacMillan	80	20	32	52
Red Berenson	72	20	27	47

Kansas City	GP	G.	A.	Pts.
Guy Charron	78	27	44	71
Wilf Paiement	57	21	22	43
Gary Bergman	75	5	33	38
Craig Patrick	80	17	18	35
Chuck Arnason	69	21	13	34

Toronto	GP	G.	A.	Pts.
Darryl Sittler	79	41	59	100
Lanny McDonald	75	37	56	93
Errol Thompson	75	43	37	80
Borje Salming	78	16	41	57
Ian Turnbull	76	20	36	56

Los Angeles	GP	G.	A.	Pts.
Marcel Dionne	80	40	54	94
Butch Goring	80	33	40	73
Mike Murphy	80	26	42	68
Bob Nevin	77	13	42	55
Don Kozak	62	20	24	44

Vancouver	GP	G.	A.	Pts.
Dennis Ververgaert	80	37	34	71
Don Lever	80	25	40	65
Chris Oddleifson	80	16	46	62
John Gould	70	32	27	59
Rick Blight	74	25	31	56

Minnesota	GP	G.	A.	Pts.
Bill Hogaboam	68	28	23	51
Tim Young	63	18	33	51
Dean Talafous	79	18	30	48
Bill Goldsworthy	68	24	22	46
Ernie Hicke	80	23	19	42

Washington	GP	G.	A.	Pts.
Gerry Meehan	80	23	35	58
Nelson Pyatt	77	26	23	49
Hart Monahan	80	17	29	46
Tony White	80	25	17	42
Jean Lemieux	66	10	23	33

Stanley Cup Champions

1928—New York	1940—New York	1952—Detroit	1964—Toronto
1929—Boston	1941—Boston	1953—Montreal	1965—Montreal
1930—Montreal	1942—Toronto	1954—Detroit	1966—Montreal
1931—Montreal	1943—Detroit	1955—Detroit	1967—Toronto
1932—Toronto	1944—Montreal	1956—Montreal	1968—Montreal
1933—New York	1945—Toronto	1957—Montreal	1969—Montreal
1934—Chicago	1946—Montreal	1958—Montreal	1970—Boston
1935—Montreal Maroons	1947—Toronto	1959—Montreal	1971—Montreal
1936—Detroit	1948—Toronto	1960—Montreal	1972—Boston
1937—Detroit	1949—Toronto	1961—Chicago.	1973—Montreal
1938—Chicago	1950—Detroit	1962—Toronto	1974—Philadelphia
1939—Boston	1951—Toronto	1963—Toronto	1975—Philadelphia
			1976—Montreal

Conn Smythe Trophy (MVP in Playoffs)

1965—Jean Beliveau, Montreal	1969—Serge Savard, Montreal	1973—Yvan Cournoyer, Montreal
1966—Roger Crozier, Detroit	1970—Bobby Orr, Boston	1974—Bernie Parent, Philadelphia
1967—Dave Keon, Toronto	1971—Ken Dryden, Montreal	1975—Bernie Parent, Philadelphia
1968—Glenn Hall, St. Louis	1972—Bobby Orr, Boston	1976—Reg Leach, Philadelphia

Hockey Trophy Winners

Ross Trophy Leading Scorer	Norris Trophy Best Defenseman	Calder Trophy Best Rookie
1976—Guy Lafleur, Montreal	Denis Potvin, N.Y. Islanders	Bryan Trottier, N.Y. Islanders
1975—Bobby Orr, Boston	Bobby Orr, Boston	Eric Vail, Atlanta
1974—Phil Esposito, Boston	Bobby Orr, Boston	Denis Potvin, N.Y. Islanders
1973—Phil Esposito, Boston	Bobby Orr, Boston	Steve Vickers, N.Y. Rangers
1972—Phil Esposito, Boston	Bobby Orr, Boston	Ken Dryden, Montreal
1971—Phil Esposito, Boston	Bobby Orr, Boston	Gil Perreault, Buffalo
1970—Bobby Orr, Boston	Bobby Orr, Boston	Tony Esposito, Chicago
1969—Phil Esposito, Boston	Bobby Orr, Boston	Danny Grant, Minn.
1968—Stan Mikita, Chicago	Bobby Orr, Boston	Derek Sanderson, Boston
1967—Stan Mikita, Chicago	Harry Howell, N.Y. Rangers	Bobby Orr, Boston
1966—Bobby Hull, Chicago	Jacques Laperriere, Montreal	Brit Selby, Toronto
1965—Stan Mikita, Chicago	Pierre Pilote, Chicago	Roger Crozier, Detroit
1964—Stan Mikita, Chicago	Pierre Pilote, Chicago	Jacques Laperriere, Montreal

Hart Trophy MVP	Vezina Trophy Leading Goalie	Lady Byng Trophy Sportsmanship
1976—Bobby Clarke, Philadelphia	Ken Dryden, Montreal	Jean Ratelle, Boston
1975—Bobby Clarke, Philadelphia	Bernie Parent, Philadelphia	Marcel Dionne, Detroit
1974—Phil Esposito, Boston	Tony Esposito, Chicago	John Bucyk, Boston
	Bernie Parent, Philadelphia	
1973—Bobby Clarke, Philadelphia	Ken Dryden, Montreal	Gilbert Perreault, Buffalo
1972—Bobby Orr, Boston	Esposito, Smith, Chicago	Jean Ratelle, N.Y. Rangers
1971—Bobby Orr, Boston	Giacomin, Villemure, New York	John Bucyk, Boston
1970—Bobby Orr, Boston	Tony Esposito, Chicago	Phil Goyette, St. Louis
1969—Phil Esposito, Boston	Hall, Plante, St. Louis	Alex Devecchio, Detroit
1968—Stan Mikita, Chicago	Worsley, Vachon, Montreal	Stan Mikita, Chicago
1967—Stan Mikita, Chicago	Hall, De Jordy, Chicago	Stan Mikita, Chicago
1966—Bobby Hull, Chicago	Hodge, Worsley, Montreal	Alex Devecchio, Detroit
1965—Bobby Hull, Chicago	Sawchuck, Bower, Toronto	Bobby Hull, Chicago
1964—Jean Beliveau, Montreal	Charlie Hodge, Montreal	Ken Wharram, Chicago

Players in the Hockey Hall of Fame

Canadian National Exhibition Park, Toronto, Ont.

Sid Abel
John J. (Jack) Adams
C. J. S. (Syl) Apps
George Armstrong
Ace Bailey
Donald Bain
Hobart (Hobey) Baker
Martin (Marty) Barry
Jean Beliveau
Clint (Benny) Benedict
Douglas (Doug) Bentley
Max Bentley
Hector (Toe) Blake
Richard (Dickie) Boon
Emile (Butch) Bouchard
Frank Boucher
George (Buck) Boucher
John Bower
Russell Bowie
Frank Brimsek
H. L. (Punch) Broadbent, M.M
Walter (Turk) Broda
Billy Burch
H. H. (Harry) Cameron
Francis (King) Clancy
Aubrey (Dit) Clapper
Sprague Cleghorn
Neil Colville
Charles Conacher
Alex Connell
William (Bill) Cook
Art Coulter
W. M. (Bill) Cowley
Samuel R. (Rusty) Crawford
John P. (Jack) Darragh
Allan (Scotty) Davidson
Clarence (Hap) Day
Cyril (Cy) Denney

Gordon Drillon
Charles G. Drinkwater
Tommy Dunderdale
William (Bill) Durnan
Mervyn (Red) Dutton
Cecil H. (Babe) Dye
Arthur Farrell
Frank Foyston
Frank Fredrickson
W. A. (Bill) Gadsby
Charles (Chuck) Gardiner
Herbert Gardiner
James H. (Jimmy) Gardner
Bernard (Boom Boom) Geoffrion
Edward (Eddie) Gerard
H. L. (Billy) Gilmour
E. R. (Ebbie) Goodfellow
F.X. (Moose) Goheen
Michael (Mike) Grant
Wilfred (Shorty) Green
Silas (Si) Griffis
George Hainsworth
Glenn Hall
Joseph (Joe) Hall
Doug Harvey
George Hay
W.M. (Riley) Hern
Bryan Hextall
Harry (Hap) Holmes
Thomas (Tom) Hooper
G. R. (Red) Horner
Gordon Howe
Sydney (Syd) Howe
John B. (Bouse) Hutton
Harry Hyland
James Dickenson Irvin
H. (Busher) Jackson
Ernest (Moose) Johnson

I. W. (Ching) Johnson
T. C. (Tom) Johnson
Aurel Joliat
Gordon (Duke) Keats
Leonard (Red) Kelly
Theodore (Teeder) Kennedy
Elmer Lach
Edouard (Newsy) Lalonde
J. B. (Jack) Laviolette
Hugh Lehman
Percy LeSueur
Ted Lindsay
Duncan (Mickey) MacKay
Sylvio Mantha
Joseph Malone
John (Jack) Marshall
Fred (Steamer) Maxwell
Frank McGee
W. G. (Billy) McGimsie
George McNamara
Dickie Moore
Patrick (Paddy) Moran
H. W. (Howie) Morenz
Bill Mosienko
Frank Nighbor
Reginald Noble
Harold (Harry) Oliver
Lester Patrick
Thomas (Tom) Phillips
Pierre Pilote
Didier (Pit) Pitre
Walter (Babe) Pratt
Joseph (Joe) Primeau
Harvey Pulford
Hubert (Bill) Quakenbush
Frank Rankin
Chuck Rayner

Kenneth (Ken) Reardon
Maurice (The Rocket) Richard
George Richardson
Gordon Roberts
Arthur H. Ross
Blair Russell
Ernie Russell
J. D. (Jack) Ruttan
T. G. (Terry) Sawchuk
Fred Scanlan
Milt Schmidt
David (Sweeney) Schriner
Earl Walter Seibert
Oliver Seibert
Edward William Shore
Albert (Babe) Siebert
H. J. (Bullet Joe) Simpson, M.M.
Alfred (Alf) Smith
Reginald (Hooley) Smith
Tommy Smith
Russell (Barney) Stanley
John (Black Jack) Stewart
Nelson Stewart
Bruce Stuart
Horace (Hod) Stuart
Fred (Cyclone) Taylor, OBE
Harry J. Trihey
Cecil (Tiny) Thompson
Georges Vezina
Martin Walsh
John (Jack) Walker
Harry Watson
Harry Westwick
R. C. (Cooney) Weiland
Fred Whitcroft
Gordon (Phat) Wilson
Roy Worters

Super Series '76

Two Soviet touring hockey teams, Central Army and the Soviet Wings, won Super Series '76 by winning 5 games and tieing 1 in an 8 game series against National Hockey League teams. The Stanley Cup champion Philadelphia Flyers defeated the Soviet champion Central Army team 4-1 in the final game of the series and claimed the world championship.

NHL Amateur Draft, 1976
First Round Selections

Team	Player	Position	1975-76 Team
1—Washington	Rick Green	D	London
2—Pittsburgh	Blair Chapman	RW	Saskatoon
3—Minnesota	Glen Sharpley	C	Hull
4—Detroit	Fred Williams	C	Saskatoon
5—California	Bjorn Johansson	D	Orebro IK
6—Rangers	Don Murdoch	RW	Medicine Hat
7—St. Louis	Bernie Federko	C	Saskatoon
8—Atlanta	Dave Shand	D	Peterborough
9—Chicago	Real Cloutier	RW	Quebec
10—Atlanta	Harold Phillipoff	LW	New Westminster
11—Kansas City	Paul Gardner	LW	Oshawa
12—Montreal	Peter Lee	RW	Ottawa
13—Montreal	Rod Schutt	LW	Sudbury
14—Islanders	Alex McKendry	RW	Sudbury
15—Washington	Greg Carroll	C	Medicine Hat
16—Boston	Clay Pachal	LW	New Westminster
17—Philadelphia	Mark Suzor	D	Kingston
18—Montreal	Bruce Baker	RW	Ottawa

1976 Final Standings
American League

North Division

	W.	L.	T.	GF	GA	Pts.
Nova Scotia	48	20	8	326	209	104
Rochester	42	25	9	304	243	93
Providence	34	34	8	294	300	76
Springfield	33	39	4	267	321	70

South Division

	W.	L.	T.	GF	GA	Pts.
Hershey	39	31	6	304	275	84
Richmond	29	39	8	262	297	66
New Haven	29	39	8	261	295	66
Baltimore	21	48	7	238	316	49

Central League

	W.	L.	T.	GF	GA	Pts.
Tulsa	45	21	10	301	228	100
Dallas	41	24	11	282	211	93
Salt Lake	37	35	4	300	299	78

	W.	L.	T.	GF	GA	Pts.
Oklahoma City	32	34	10	256	263	74
Fort Worth	29	31	16	287	271	74
Tucson	14	53	9	242	396	37

Ontario Major League

Emms Division

	W.	L.	T.	GF	GA	Pts.
Hamilton	43	15	8	379	232	94
London	31	26	9	317	256	71
Toronto	26	30	10	278	294	62
Kitchener	26	35	5	298	384	57
St. Catherines	16	40	10	283	366	42
Windsor	12	50	4	251	470	28

Leyden Division

	W.	L.	T.	GF	GA	Pts.
Sudbury	47	11	8	384	224	102
Ottawa	34	23	9	331	291	77
Kingston	33	24	9	357	316	75
Oshawa	31	27	8	312	299	70
Sault	27	26	13	341	319	67
Peterborough	18	37	11	204	284	47

Western Canada League

Eastern Division

	W.	L.	T.	GF	GA	Pts.
Saskatoon	43	19	10	390	269	96
Brandon	34	30	8	341	303	76
Lethbridge	28	35	9	392	352	65
Winnipeg	27	39	6	302	378	60
Regina	22	42	8	278	347	52
Flin Flon	18	44	10	279	441	46

Western Division

	W.	L.	T.	GF	GA	Pts.
New Westminster	54	14	4	463	247	112
Kamloops	40	26	6	365	285	86
Medicine Hat	38	24	10	379	306	86
Victoria	37	28	7	343	320	81
Edmonton	25	42	5	312	400	55
Calgary	22	45	5	284	381	49

World Hockey Association
Final Standings

East Division

Club	W.	L.	T.	Pts.	GF	GA
Indianapolis	35	39	6	76	245	247
Cleveland	35	40	5	75	273	279
New England	33	40	7	73	255	290
Cincinnati	35	44	1	71	285	340

West Division

Club	W.	L.	T.	Pts.	GF	GA
Houston	53	27	0	106	341	263
Phoenix	39	35	6	84	302	287
San Diego	36	38	6	78	303	290
(a)Minnesota	30	25	4	64	211	212

Canadian Division

Club	W.	L.	T.	Pts.	GF	GA
Winnipeg	52	27	2	106	345	254
Quebec	50	27	4	104	371	316
Calgary	41	35	4	86	307	282

Club	W.	L.	T.	Pts.	GF	GA
Edmonton	27	49	5	59	268	345
Toronto	24	52	5	53	335	398
(b) Ottawa	14	26	1	29	134	172

(a)Franchise folded February 28.   (b)Formerly the Denver Spurs; disbanded January 17.

WHA Playoff Results

New England def. Cleveland 3 games to 1.
San Diego def. Phoenix 3 games to 2.
Calgary def. Quebec 4 games to 1.
Winnipeg def. Edmonton 4 games to 0.
New England def. Indianapolis 4 games to 3.

Houston def. San Diego 4 games to 2.
Winnipeg def. Calgary 4 games to 1.
Houston def. New England 4 games to 3.
Winnipeg def. Houston 4 games to 1.

Leading Scorers

Player—Club	G.	Goals	Asts.	Pts.	Player—Club	G.	Goals	Asts.	Pts.
Tardif, Quebec	81	71	77	148	Lawson, Calgary	80	44	52	96
Hull, Winnipeg	80	53	70	123	Napier, Toronto	78	43	50	93
Cloutier, Quebec	80	60	54	114	Hall, Phoenix	80	47	44	91
Nilsson, Winnipeg	78	38	76	114	Adduono, San Diego	80	23	67	90
Ftorek, Phoenix	80	41	72	113	Mahovlich, Toronto	75	34	55	89
Bordeleau, Quebec	74	37	72	109	Tremblay, Quebec	80	12	77	89
Hedberg, Winnipeg	76	50	55	105	Ullman, Edmonton	77	31	56	87
Houle, Quebec	81	51	52	103	Chipperfield, Calgary	75	42	41	83
S. Bernier, Quebec	70	34	68	102	Backstrom, New England	55	33	49	82
G. Howe, Houston	78	32	70	102	Ward, Cleveland	75	32	50	82
Lacroix, San Diego	80	29	72	101	Dudley, Cincinnati	74	43	38	81
Nedomansky, Toronto	81	56	42	98	Kirk, Calgary	77	35	46	81

Leading Goalies

Goalie—Club	G.	GA.	ShO.	Avg.	Goalie—Club	G.	GA	ShO.	Avg.
Dion, Indianapolis	31	85	0	2.74	Garrett, Toronto	61	210	3	3.38
Daley, Winnipeg	62	171	5	2.84	C. Abrahamson, N.E.	41	136	2	3.42
Norris, Phoenix	41	128	1	3.18	McLeod, Calgary	62	204	1	3.47
Wakely, San Diego	67	208	3	3.26	Landon, New England	38	126	0	3.47
Grahame, Houston	57	182	3	3.27	Johnson, Cleveland	42	144	1	3.62

WHA All-Star Team, 1976

Position	First Team	Second Team
Goal	Joe Daley, Winnipeg	Ron Grahame, Houston
Defense	J. C. Tremblay, Quebec	Pat Stapleton, Indianapolis
Defense	Paul Shmyr, Cleveland	Kevin Morrison, San Diego
Center	Ulf Nilsson, Winnipeg	Robbie Ftorek, Phoenix
Right Wing	Anders Hedberg, Winnipeg	Real Cloutier, Quebec
Left Wing	Marc Tardiff, Quebec	Bobby Hull, Winnipeg

NCAA Hockey Champions

1951	Michigan	1957	Colorado College	1964	Michigan	1971	Boston Univ.
1952	Michigan	1958	Denver	1965	Michigan Tech	1972	Boston Univ.
1953	Michigan	1959	North Dakota	1966	Michigan State	1973	Wisconsin
1954	Rensselaer Poly	1960	Denver	1967	Cornell	1974	Minnesota
1955	Michigan	1961	Denver	1968	Denver	1975	Michigan Tech
1956	Michigan	1962	Michigan Tech	1969	Denver	1976	Minnesota
		1963	North Dakota	1970	Cornell		

Canadian Intercollegiate Athletic Union Champions

Basketball

1968	Waterloo Lutheran
1969	Windsor
1970	British Columbia
1971	Acadia
1972	British Columbia
1973	St. Mary's
1974	Guelph
1975	Waterloo
1976	Manitoba

Football

1967	Alberta
1968	Manitoba
1969	Manitoba
1970	Western Ontario
1971	Western Ontario
1972	Alberta
1973	St. Mary's
1974	Western Ontario
1975	Ottawa

Wrestling

1970	Alberta
1971	Alberta
1972	Alberta
1973	Assoc. Champion
1974	Assoc. Champion
1975	Ontario Assoc. Champion
1976	O.U.A.A.

Swimming and Diving

1968	Toronto
1969	Toronto
1970	Toronto
1971	Toronto
1972	McGill
1973	Toronto
1974	Toronto
1975	Toronto
1976	Toronto

Soccer

1972	Alberta
1973	Loyola
1974	British Columbia
1975	Victoria

Hockey

1964	Alberta
1965	Manitoba
1966	Toronto
1967	Toronto
1968	Alberta
1969	Toronto
1970	Toronto
1971	Toronto
1972	Toronto
1973	Toronto
1974	Waterloo
1975	Alberta
1976	Toronto

Volleyball

1969	Winnipeg
1970	Montreal
1971	Winnipeg
1972	Winnipeg
1973	Winnipeg
1974	Winnipeg
1975	Alberta
1976	Sherbrooke

Badminton Championships in 1976

Source: American Badminton Association

U. S. Open Championships

Philadelphia, Pa., April 15-17

Men's Singles—Paul Whetnall, England def. Tom Kihlstrom, Sweden, 17-14, 15-10.

Women's Singles—Gillian Gilks, England def. Lene Koppen, Denmark, 8-11, 11-5, 11-6.

Men's Doubles—Roland Maywald and Willie Braun, W. Germany def. Tom Kihlstrom and Bengt Froman, Sweden, 18-15, 15-12.

Women's Doubles—Sue Whetnall and Gillian Gilks, England def. Pam Bristol and Rosine Lemon, U.S., 15-4, 15-10.

Mixed Doubles—David Eddy and Sue Whetnall, England def. Tom Kihlstrom and Pam Bristol, 15-4, 7-15, 15-3.

U. S. National Championships

Philadelphia, Pa., April 12-14

Men's Singles—Chris Kinard, Pasadena, Cal. def. Ray Park, San Diego, 8-15, 15-10, 15-8.

Women's Singles—Pam Bristol, Flint, Mich. def. Judianne Kelly, Norwalk, Cal., 11-8, 11-7.

Men's Doubles—Don Paup, Vienna, Va. and Bruce Pontow, Chicago def. Bob Dickie and Gary Higgins, Alhambra, Cal. 15-10, 15-11.

Women's Doubles—Pam Bristol and Rosine Lemon, New York, N.Y. def. Diana Oesterhues, Arcadia, Cal. and Janet Wilts, Pasadena, Cal., 15-6, 15-9.

Mixed Doubles—Mike Walker, Manhattan Beach, Cal. and Judianne Kelly def. Jim Poole, Westminster, Cal. and Vickie Toutz, Los Alamitos, Cal., 15-7, 15-10.

Senior Men's Singles—Jim Poole def. Tom Heden, Millwood, N.Y., 15-6, 15-3.

Senior Men's Doubles—Poole and Heden def. Bob Carpenter, Pt. Jervis, N.Y. and Bill Goodman, Wellesley Hills, Mass., 18-14, 15-3.

Senior Women's Doubles—Ethel Marshall and Bea Massman, Buffalo, N.Y. def. Ket Hoffman, Rochester, Mich. and Jean Safford, Bloomfield Hills, Mich., 15-5, 15-2.

Senior Mixed Doubles—Jim Poole and Helen Tibbetts, Torrance, Cal., def. Tom Heden and Ket Hoffman, 15-10, 15-10.

Master Men's Singles—Ed Phillips, Warwick, R.I. def. Charles Thomas, Natchitoches, La., 15-11, 15-7.

Master Men's Doubles—Charles Thomas and Richard Witte, St. Louis def. Ernest Schimmer, Fullerton, Cal. and Don West, Sunnyvale, Cal., 15-11, 15-13.

Master Mixed Doubles—Scott Garman, Lititz, Pa. and Ethel Marshall def. John Cornell, Philadelphia and Ket Hoffman, 15-10, 15-7.

Canadian National Championships

Moncton, New Brunswick

Men's Singles—Bruce Rollick, Vancouver def. John Czick, Kingston, 18-15, 3-15, 15-9.

Women's Singles—Wendy Clarkson, Calgary def. Jane Youngberg, Vancouver, 11-6, 3-11, 11-4.

Men's Doubles—Chanarong Ratanaseangsuang and Raphi Kanchaneraphi, Calgary, Toronto def. Lucio Fabris, Creighton Mine, Ont. and James Muir, Toronto, 15-3, 18-17.

Women's Doubles—Jane Youngberg and Sheri Boyse, Calgary def. Pauline De Lisle and Leslie Harris, Montreal, 15-11, 15-10.

Mixed Doubles—Lucio Fabris and Lillian Cozzarini, Creighton Mine, Ont. def. Raphi Kanchanaraphi and Ann Frickleton, Toronto, 12-15, 15-6, 15-6.

U. S. National Junior Championships

San Diego, Cal., March 10-13

Boys' Singles—Gene Miller, Buffalo def. Geofrey Stensland, Seattle, 15-3, 15-9.

Girls' Singles—Carrie Morrison, Pt. Angeles, Wash. def. Lisa De Rousie, Pt. Angeles, Wash., 11-6, 11-1.

Boys' Doubles—Gene Miller and Paul Rogind, Farmington, Mich. def. Robbie Hankins and Russ Nelson, Pt. Angeles, Wash., 15-2, 15-10.

Girls' Doubles—Carrie Morrison and Lisa De Rousie def. Kathy Bell and Carrie Theis, Manhattan Beach, Cal., 15-5, 15-4.

Mixed Doubles—Russ Nelson and Lisa De Rousie def. Robbie Hankins and Carrie Morrison, 15-10, 15-10.

Skiing in 1976

U.S. National Alpine Championships

Copper Mountain, Col., Feb. 26-28

Men's Downhill — Greg Jones. Time — 1:56.56.
Men's Giant Slalom — Geoff Bruce. Time — 2:29.40.
Men's Slalom — Cary Adgate. Time — 1:11.37.
Men's Combined — Gary Adgate.

Women's Downhill — Susie Patterson. Time — 1:46.17.
Women's Giant Slalom — Lindy Cochran. Time — 1:18.87.
Women's Slalom — Cindy Nelson. Time — 1:08.94.
Women's Combined — Viki Fleckenstein.

U.S. National Cross-Country Championships

Big Sky, Mont., Mar. 8-14

Men's 15 Km — Kevin Swigert. Time — 47.13.30.
Men's 30 Km — Kevin Swigert. Time — 84.16.83.
Men's 50 Km — Stan Kunklee. Time — 168:21.92.

Women's 5 Km — Jana Hlavaty. Time — 18.13.91.
Women's 10 Km — Jana Hlavaty. Time — 36.02.40.
Women's 20 Km — Jana Hlavaty. Time — 81.53.46.

The World Cup Winners

Men	Women	Nation's Cup
1967—Jean Claude Killy, France	1967—Nancy Greene, Canada	1967—France
1968—Jean Claude Killy, France	1968—Nancy Greene, Canada	1968—France
1969—Karl Schranz, Austria	1969—Gertrud Gabl, Austria	1969—Austria
1970—Karl Schranz, Austria	1970—Michele Jacot, France	1970—France
1971—Gustavo Thoeni, Italy	1971—Annemarie Proell, Austria	1971—France
1972—Gustavo Thoeni, Italy	1972—Annemarie Proell, Austria	1972—France
1973—Gustavo Thoeni, Italy	1973—Annemarie Proell, Austria	1973—Austria
1974—Piero Gros, Italy	1974—Annemarie Proell, Austria	1974—Austria
1975—Gustavo Thoeni, Italy	1975—Annemarie Proell, Austria	1975—Austria
1976—Ingemar Stenmark, Sweden	1976—Rose Mittermaier, W. Germany	1976—Italy

National Basketball Association, 1975-76

Final Standings

Eastern Conference
Atlantic Division

Club	W.	L.	Pct.	G.B.
Boston	54	28	.659	......
Philadelphia	46	36	.561	8
Buffalo	46	36	.561	8
New York	38	44	.463	16

Central Division

Club	W.	L.	Pct.	G.B.
Cleveland	49	33	.598	......
Washington	48	34	.585	1
Houston	40	42	.488	9
New Orleans	38	44	.463	11
Atlanta	29	53	.354	20

Western Conference
Midwest Division

Club	W.	L.	Pct.	G.B.
Milwaukee	38	44	.463	......
Detroit	36	46	.439	2
Kansas City	31	51	.378	7
Chicago	24	58	.293	14

Pacific Division

Club	W.	L.	Pct.	G.B.
Golden State	59	23	.720	......
Seattle	43	39	.524	16
Phoenix	42	40	.512	17
Los Angeles	40	42	.488	19
Portland	37	45	.451	22

NBA Playoff Results

Buffalo defeated Philadelphia 2 games to 1.
Detroit defeated Milwaukee 2 games to 1.
Phoenix defeated Seattle 4 games to 2.
Cleveland defeated Washington 4 games to 3.
Golden State defeated Detroit 4 games to 2.

Boston defeated Buffalo 4 games to 2.
Phoenix defeated Golden State 4 games to 3.
Boston defeated Cleveland 4 games to 2.
Boston defeated Phoenix 4 games to 2.

Final Statistics

Individual Scoring Leaders
(Minimum 70 Games Played or 1400 Points)

	G.	FG	FT	Pts.	Avg.
McAdoo, Buff.	78	934	559	2427	31.1
Abdul-Jabbar, L.A.	82	914	447	2275	27.7
Maravich, N.O.	62	604	396	1604	25.9
Archibald, K.C.	78	717	501	1935	24.8
F. Brown, Sea.	76	742	273	1757	23.1
McGinnis, Phil.	77	647	475	1769	23.0
R. Smith, Buff.	82	702	383	1787	21.8
Drew, Atl.	77	586	488	1660	21.6
Dandridge, Mil.	73	650	271	1571	21.5
Barry, G.S.	81	707	287	1701	21.0
Murphy, Hou.	82	675	372	1722	21.0
Collins, Phil.	77	614	372	1600	20.8
Monroe, N.Y.	76	647	280	1574	20.7
Westphal, Phoe.	82	657	365	1679	20.5
P. Smith, G.S.	82	659	323	1641	20.0
Chenier, Wash.	80	654	282	1590	19.9
Haywood, N.Y.	78	605	339	1549	19.9
Hayes, Wash.	80	649	287	1585	19.8
Goodrich, L.A.	75	583	293	1459	19.5
Love, Chi.	76	543	362	1448	19.1

Field Goal Leaders
(Minimum 300 FG Made)

	FGM	FGA	Pct.
Unseld, Washington	318	567	.56085
Shumate, Buffalo	332	592	.56081
McMillian, Buffalo	492	918	.536
Lanier, Detroit	541	1017	.532
Abdul-Jabbar, Los Angeles	914	1728	.529
E. Smith, Milwaukee	498	962	.518
Tomjanovich, Houston	622	1202	.517
Collins, Philadelphia	614	1196	.513
O. Johnson, Kansas City	348	678	.513
Newlin, Houston	569	1123	.507

Free Throw Leaders
(Minimum 125 FT Made)

	FTM	FTA	Pct.
Barry, Golden State	287	311	.923
Murphy, Houston	372	410	.907
C. Russell, Los Angeles	132	148	.892
Bradley, New York	130	148	.878
F. Brown, Seattle	273	314	.869
Newlin, Houston	385	445	.865
J. Walker, Kansas City	231	267	.865
McMillian, Buffalo	188	219	.858
Marin, Chicago	161	188	.856
Erickson, Phoenix	134	157	.854

Rebound Leaders
(Minimum 70 games or 800 rebounds)

	G	Off.	Def.	Tot.	Avg.
Abdul-Jabbar, L.A.	82	272	1111	1383	16.9
Cowens, Bos.	78	335	911	1246	16.0
Unseld, Wash.	78	271	765	1036	13.3
Silas, Bos.	81	365	660	1025	12.7
Lacey, K.C.	81	218	806	1024	12.6
McGinnis, Phil.	77	260	707	967	12.6
McAdoo, Buff.	78	241	724	965	12.4
E. Smith, Mil.	78	201	692	893	11.4
Haywood, N.Y.	78	234	644	878	11.3
Hayes, Wash.	80	210	668	878	11.0

Assists Leaders
(Minimum 70 games or 400 assists)

	G.	No.	Avg.
Watts, Seattle	82	661	8.1
Archibald, Kansas City	78	615	7.9
Murphy, Houston	82	596	7.3
Van Lier, Chicago	76	500	6.6
Barry, Golden State	81	496	6.1
Bing, Washington	82	492	6.0
R. Smith, Buffalo	82	484	5.9
A. Adams, Phoenix	80	450	5.6
Goodrich, Los Angeles	75	421	5.6
Newlin, Houston	82	457	5.6

Blocked Shots Leaders
(Minimum 70 games or 100 blocked shots)

	G.	No.	Avg.
Abdul-Jabbar, Los Angeles	82	338	4.12
E. Smith, Milwaukee	78	238	3.05
Hayes, Washington	80	202	2.53
Catchings, Philadelphia	75	164	2.19
G. Johnson, Golden State	82	174	2.12
McAdoo, Buffalo	78	160	2.05
Burleson, Seattle	82	150	1.83
Moore, New Orleans	81	136	1.68
Lacey, Kansas City	81	134	1.65
Neal, Portland	68	107	1.57

Steals Leaders
(Minimum 70 games or 125 steals)

	G.	No.	Avg.
Watts, Seattle	82	261	3.18
McGinnis, Philadelphia	77	198	2.57
Westphal, Phoenix	82	210	2.56
Barry, Golden State	81	202	2.49
C. Ford, Detroit	82	178	2.17
Steele, Portland	81	170	2.10

NBA Champions 1947-1976

Year	Eastern Conference	Western Conference	Winner	Runner-Up
	Regular Season		**Playoffs**	
1947	Washington	Chicago	Philadelphia	Chicago
1948	Philadelphia	St. Louis	Baltimore	Philadelphia
1949	Washington	Rochester	Minneapolis	Washington
1950	Syracuse	Minneapolis	Minneapolis	Syracuse
1951	Philadelphia	Minneapolis	Rochester	New York
1952	Syracuse	Rochester	Minneapolis	New York
1953	New York	Minneapolis	Minneapolis	New York
1954	New York	Minneapolis	Minneapolis	Syracuse
1955	Syracuse	Ft. Wayne	Syracuse	Ft. Wayne
1956	Philadelphia	Ft. Wayne	Philadelphia	Ft. Wayne
1957	Boston	St. Louis	Boston	St. Louis
1958	Boston	St. Louis	St. Louis	Boston
1959	Boston	St. Louis	Boston	Minneapolis
1960	Boston	St. Louis	Boston	St. Louis
1961	Boston	St. Louis	Boston	St. Louis
1962	Boston	Los Angeles	Boston	Los Angeles
1963	Boston	Los Angeles	Boston	Los Angeles
1964	Boston	San Francisco	Boston	San Francisco
1965	Boston	Los Angeles	Boston	Los Angeles
1966	Philadelphia	Los Angeles	Boston	Los Angeles
1967	Philadelphia	San Francisco	Philadelphia	San Francisco
1968	Philadelphia	St. Louis	Boston	Los Angeles
1969	Baltimore	Los Angeles	Boston	Los Angeles
1970	New York	Atlanta	New York	Los Angeles

Year	Atlantic	Central	Midwest	Pacific	Winner	Runner-Up
1971	New York	Baltimore	Milwaukee	Los Angeles	Milwaukee	Baltimore
1972	Boston	Baltimore	Milwaukee	Los Angeles	Los Angeles	New York
1973	Boston	Baltimore	Milwaukee	Los Angeles	New York	Los Angeles
1974	Boston	Capital	Milwaukee	Los Angeles	Boston	Milwaukee
1975	Boston	Washington	Chicago	Golden State	Golden State	Washington
1976	Boston	Cleveland	Milwaukee	Golden State	Boston	Phoenix

NBA Scoring Leaders

Year	Scoring Champion	Pts.	Avg.
1947	Joe Fulks, Philadelphia	1,389	23.2
1948	Max Zaslofsky, Chicago	1,007	21.0
1949	George Mikan, Minneapolis	1,698	28.3
1950	George Mikan, Minneapolis	1,865	27.4
1951	George Mikan, Minneapolis	1,932	28.4
1952	Paul Arizin, Philadelphia	1,674	25.4
1953	Neil Johnston, Philadelphia	1,564	22.3
1954	Neil Johnston, Philadelphia	1,759	24.4
1955	Neil Johnston, Philadelphia	1,631	22.7
1956	Bob Pettit, St. Louis	1,849	25.7
1957	Paul Arizin, Philadelphia	1,817	25.6
1958	George Yardley, Detroit	2,001	27.8
1959	Bob Pettit, St. Louis	2,105	29.2
1960	Wilt Chamberlain, Philadelphia	2,707	37.9
1961	Wilt Chamberlain, Philadelphia	3,033	38.4
1962	Wilt Chamberlain, Philadelphia	4,029	50.4
1963	Wilt Chamberlain, San Francisco	3,586	44.8
1964	Wilt Chamberlain, San Francisco	2,948	36.5
1965	Wilt Chamberlain, San Fran., Phila.	2,534	34.7
1966	Wilt Chamberlain, Philadelphia	2,649	33.5
1967	Rick Barry, San Francisco	2,775	35.6
1968	Dave Bing, Detroit	2,142	27.1
1969	Elvin Hayes, San Diego	2,327	28.4
1970	Jerry West, Los Angeles	2,309	31.2
1971	Lew Alcindor, Milwaukee	2,596	31.7
1972	Kareem Abdul-Jabbar (Alcindor), Milwaukee	2,822	34.8
1973	Nate Archibald, Kansas City-Omaha	2,719	34.0
1974	Bob McAdoo, Buffalo	2,261	30.6
1975	Bob McAdoo, Buffalo	2,831	34.5
1976	Bob McAdoo, Buffalo	2,427	31.1

NBA All-Star Team, 1976

Position	First Team	Second Team
Forward	Rick Barry, Golden State	John Havlicek, Boston
Forward	George McGinnis, Philadelphia	Elvin Hayes, Washington
Center	Kareem Abdul-Jabbar, Los Angeles	Dave Cowens, Boston
Guard	Pete Maravich, New Orleans	Phil Smith, Golden State
Guard	Nate Archibald, K.C.-Omaha	Randy Smith, Buffalo

NBA All-Defensive Team, 1976

Position	First Team	Second Team
Forward	John Havlicek, Boston	Jim Brewer, Cleveland
Forward	Paul Silas, Boston	Jamaal Wilkes, Golden State
Center	Dave Cowens, Boston	Kareem Abdul-Jabbar, Los Angeles
Guard	Slick Watts, Seattle	Jim Cleamons, Cleveland
Guard	Norm Van Lier, Chicago	Phil Smith, Golden State

1976 NBA Player Draft

The following are the first round picks of the National Basketball Assn.

Houston	John Lucas, Maryland
Chicago	Scott May, Indiana
Kansas City	Richard Washington, UCLA
Detroit	Leon Douglas, Alabama
Portland	Wally Walker, Virginia
Buffalo	Adrian Dantley, Notre Dame
Milwaukee	Quinn Buckner, Indiana
Golden State	Robert Parish, Centenary
Atlanta	Armond Hill, Princeton
Phoenix	Ron Lee, Oregon
Seattle	Bob Wilkerson, Indiana
Philadelphia	Terry Furlow, Michigan State
Washington	Mitch Kupchak, North Carolina
Washington	Larry Wright, Grambling
Cleveland	Chuckie Williams, Kansas State
Boston	Norman Cook, Kansas
Golden State	Sonny Parker, Texas A&M

N. Y. Knickerbockers were denied a first round pick by the NBA Commissioner as a penalty for illegally signing George McGinnis.

Podoloff Cup Winners

Kareem Abdul-Jabbar of the Los Angeles Lakers was selected as the winner of the Maurice Podoloff Cup (named after the former league commissioner) for Most Valuable Player in the NBA for the 1975-76 season.

1956—Bob Pettit, St. Louis
1957—Bob Cousy, Boston
1958—Bill Russell, Boston
1959—Bob Pettit, St. Louis
1960—Wilt Chamberlain, Philadelphia
1961—Bill Russell, Boston
1962—Bill Russell, Boston
1963—Bill Russell, Boston
1964—Oscar Robertson, Cincinnati
1965—Bill Russell, Boston
1966—Wilt Chamberlain, Philadelphia

1967—Wilt Chamberlain, Philadelphia
1968—Wilt Chamberlain, Philadelphia
1969—Wes Unseld, Baltimore
1970—Willis Reed, New York
1971—Lew Alcindor, Milwaukee
1972—Kareem Abdul-Jabbar (Alcindor), Milwaukee
1973—Dave Cowens, Boston
1974—Kareem Abdul-Jabbar, Milwaukee
1975—Bob McAdoo, Buffalo
1976—Kareem Abdul-Jabbar, Los Angeles

NBA Rookie of the Year Awards

1954—Don Meineke, Ft. Wayne
1955—Ray Felix, Baltimore
1956—Maurice Stokes, Rochester
1957—Tom Heinsohn, Boston
1958—Woody Sauldsberry, Philadelphia.
1959—Elgin Baylor, Minnesota
1960—Wilt Chamberlain, Philadelphia
1961—Oscar Robertson, Cincinnati
1962—Walt Bellamy, Chicago
1963—Terry Dischinger, Chicago
1964—Jerry Lucas, Cincinnati
1965—Willis Reed, New York

1966—Rick Barry, San Francisco
1967—Dave Bing, Detroit
1968—Earl Monroe, Baltimore
1969—Wes Unseld, Baltimore
1970—Lew Alcindor, Milwaukee
1971—Dave Cowens, Boston;
         Geoff Petrie, Portland (Tie)
1972—Sidney Wicks, Portland
1973—Bob McAdoo, Buffalo
1974—Ernie DiGregorio, Buffalo
1975—Keith Wilkes, Golden State
1976—Alvan Adams, Phoenix

Sports Arenas

The seating capacity of sports arenas can vary depending on the event being presented. The figures below are the normal seating capacity for basketball. (*) indicates hockey seating capacity.

Name and location	
Allen County Mem., Ft. Wayne	*8,032
Astrohall, Houston	10,000
Atlantic City Audit, Atlantic City, N.J.	40,000
Baltimore Civic Center	13,043-*11,329
Bismarck Coliseum, N. Dakota.	7,000
Boston Garden	15,320-*15,003
Buffalo Memorial Auditorium	17,900-*16,433(a)
Calgary Corral.	*7,000
Capital Center, Landover, Md.	19,035-*18,130
Charlotte Coliseum	11,666-*9,575
Chicago Stadium.	17,374-*18,000
Cincinnati Gardens.	11,650-*10,606
Cleveland Arena.	11,000-*9,300
Cobo Arena, Detroit.	11,147
The Coliseum, Richmond Township, Ohio.	20,074-*18,661
Convention Center, San Antonio.	10,146
Convention Hall, Philadelphia.	9,200-*9,500
Cow Palace, San Francisco.	14,500
Dallas State Fair Coliseum.	7,928
Denver Coliseum.	*9,038
Dorton Arena, Raleigh, N. C.	8,058
Edmonton Coliseum, Alberta.	*15,000
Fairgrounds Coliseum, Indianapolis.	9,479
Freedom Hall, Louisville, Ky.	16,613
Greensboro Coliseum	15,500-*13,280
Hampton Coliseum, Virginia.	10,000-*6,000
Hartford Civic Center	*10,346
Hemis Fair Arena, San Antonio.	10,146
Hershey (Pa.) Sports Arena.	*7,286
Hofheinz Pavilion, Houston.	10,218
International Amphitheatre, Chicago.	9,000
Jacksonville Coliseum	*7,900
Kemper Memorial Arena, Kansas City	16,382-15,994
Kiel Auditorium, St. Louis	10,574
Las Vegas Convention Center.	9,000
Long Beach Arena, Cal.	11,168
Los Angeles Forum	17,505-*16,005
Los Angeles Sports Arena	15,333-*11,325
Louisiana Superdome.	19,203
Lubbock Municipal Coliseum, Texas	10,400
Macon Coliseum	*8,000
Madison Square Garden, New York.	19,694-*17,500
Maple Leaf Gardens, Toronto.	17,000-*16,485(a)
Market Square Arena, Indianapolis.	17,500-*15,872
McNichols Sports Arena, Denver.	17,128-*16,800
Met. Sports Center, Bloomington, Minn.	*15,184

Name and location	
Mid-South Coliseum, Memphis.	11,065
Milwaukee Arena.	10,938
Mobile Municipal Auditorium	13,100
Montreal Forum.	*18,350
Moody Coliseum, Dallas	9,500
Municipal Auditorium, Kansas City.	9,929
Municipal Auditorium, New Orleans.	7,853
Myriad Gardens, Oklahoma City.	*13,399
Nashville Municipal Auditorium.	8,000
Nassau Coliseum, Uniondale, N.Y.	15,934-*14,865
New Orleans Municipal Auditorium.	9,100
Norfolk Scope, Va.	10,600-*9,364
Oakland Alemeda County Coliseum.	12,787-*12,021
Olympia, Detroit.	*16,200 (a)
Olympic Auditorium, Los Angeles.	10,500
Omaha Civic Auditorium.	9,144
The Omni, Atlanta.	16,181-*15,141
Ottawa Civic Center	*9,355
Pacific Coliseum, Vancouver.	*15,569
Penn Palestra, Philadelphia.	*9,200
Philadelphia Civic Center.	*8,155
Pittsburgh Civic Arena.	*16,402
Providence Civic Center	11,619-*10,730
Portland Memorial Coliseum.	11,815-*10,500
Quebec Coliseum	*10,000
Reynolds Coliseum, Raleigh, N.C.	12,400
Richmond Coliseum, Virginia.	10,700-*9,674
Riverfront Coliseum, Cincinnati.	*16,820
Roanoke Civic Center, Virginia.	10,100-*8,372
St. Louis Arena.	*18,006
St. Paul Civic Center, Minn.	*15,705
Salt Palace, Salt Lake City.	12,201-*10,640
Sam Houston Coliseum, Houston.	8,925-*9,300
San Diego Intl. Sports Arena.	14,000-*13,039
Seattle Center Coliseum.	14,090
Spectrum, Philadelphia.	17,920-*17,077
Springfield Civic Center, Mass.	*7,466
The Summit, Houston.	15,600-*14,906
Tarrant County Convention Center, Ft. Worth.	13,500
Tingley Coliseum, Albuquerque.	*12,000
Uline Arena, Washington, D. C.	11,000
Veterans Memorial Audit., Des Moines.	15,000
Veterans Memorial Coliseum, New Haven.	*8,765
Vets Memorial Coliseum, Phoenix.	13,036-*12,800
Winnipeg Arena.	*11,000
Winston-Salem Memorial Coliseum.	9,020-*6,100
(a) includes standees	

American Basketball Association, 1975-76

Final Standings*

Club	W.	L.	Pct.	G.B.	Club	W.	L.	Pct.	G.B.
Denver	60	24	.714	......	Indiana	39	45	.464	21
New York	55	29	.655	5	St. Louis	35	49	.417	25
San Antonio	50	34	.595	10	Virginia	15	68	.181	44½
Kentucky	46	38	.548	14					

*San Diego and Utah disbanded during season.

ABA Playoff Results

Kentucky defeated Indiana 2 games to 1.
New York defeated San Antonio 4 games to 3.

Denver defeated Kentucky 4 games to 3.
New York defeated Denver 4 games to 2.

Final Statistics

Individual Scoring
(Minimum of 900 points)

	G.	FG	FT	Pts.	Avg.
Erving, N.Y.	84	915	530	2462	29.3
Knight, Ind.	70	768	415	1969	28.1
Thompson, Den.	83	804	541	2158	26.0
Gilmore, Ky.	84	773	521	2067	24.6
Barnes, St. Louis	67	678	251	1616	24.1
Silas, S. Ant.	84	718	564	2000	23.8
Issel, Den.	84	751	425	1930	22.9
Boone, St. Louis	78	697	277	1719	22.0
Gervin, S. Ant.	81	692	342	1768	21.8
Burden, Va.	71	553	283	1413	19.9
Kenon, S. Ant.	81	647	221	1515	18.7
Simpson, Den.	84	615	273	1515	18.7
Averitt, Ky.	78	506	266	1398	17.9
Green, Va.	54	385	154	924	17.1
Lucas, Ky.	86	617	217	1460	16.9
Taylor, New York	54	322	164	904	16.7
Paultz, S. Ant.	83	566	238	1370	16.5
Williamson, N.Y.	76	511	187	1233	16.2
B. Jones, Den.	83	510	215	1235	14.8
Lewis, St. Louis	74	372	259	1096	14.8
Elmore, Ind.	76	480	152	1112	14.6
Keller, Ind.	78	287	164	1107	14.1
Robisch, Ind.	87	436	324	1196	13.7

Three-point field goals: Erving 34, Knight 6, Thompson 3, Barnes 3, Issel 1, Boone 16, Gervin 14, Burden 8, Simpson 4, Averitt 40, Lucas 3, Taylor 32, Williamson 8, Lewis 31, Keller 123.

Rebounds
(Minimum of 550)

	G.	Off.	Def.	Tot.	Avg.
Gilmore, Kentucky	84	402	901	1303	15.51
Lucas, Kentucky	86	297	673	970	11.28
C. Jones, St. Louis	76	246	607	853	11.22
Kenon, San Antonio	81	287	610	897	11.07
Erving, New York	84	337	588	925	11.01
Issel, Denver	84	303	620	923	10.99
Barnes, St. Louis	67	263	462	725	10.82
Elmore, Indiana	76	242	577	819	10.78
Paultz, San Antonio	83	210	652	862	10.39
Knight, Indiana	70	294	414	708	10.11
Nater, Virginia	76	229	537	766	10.08
B. Jones, Denver	83	241	550	791	9.53
Hughes, New York	84	341	434	775	9.23
Robisch, Indiana	87	281	513	794	9.13

Two-Point Percentage
(Minimum 220 Made)

	FGM	FGA	Pct.
B. Jones, Denver	510	878	.581
Gilmore, Kentucky	773	1401	.552
Hughes, New York	300	566	.530
Silas, San Antonio	718	1382	.520
Thompson, Denver	804	1548	.519
Simpson, Denver	615	1187	.518
Beck, Denver	329	635	.518
Erving, New York	915	1770	.517
Williams, Denver	339	656	.517
Malone, St. Louis	251	488	.514

Three-Point Percentage
(Minimum 13 Made)

	FGM	FGA	Pct.
Taylor, New York	32	76	.421
Boone, St. Louis	16	43	.372
Dampier, Kentucky	32	87	.368
Keller, Indiana	123	349	.352
Buse, Indiana	72	208	.346
Neumann, Kentucky	71	208	.341
Erving, New York	34	103	.330
Averitt, Kentucky	40	128	.313
Lewis, St. Louis	31	106	.292
Lamar, Indiana	24	86	.279

Free Throws
(Minimum 150 Made)

	FTM	FTA	Pct.
Keller, Indiana	164	183	.896
Eakins, New York	198	223	.888
Calvin, Virginia	253	285	.888
Silas, San Antonio	564	647	.872
Boone, St. Louis	277	318	.871
Gervin, San Antonio	342	399	.857
Robisch, Indiana	324	381	.850
Skinner, New York	203	241	.842
Van Breda Kolff, Kentucky	165	198	.833

Assists
(Minimum of 225)

	G.	No.	Avg.
Buse, Indiana	84	689	8.20
Simpson, Denver	84	597	7.11
Calvin, Virginia	45	271	6.02
Dampier, Kentucky	82	467	5.70
Silas, San Antonio	84	452	5.38
Taylor, Virginia	76	401	5.28
Erving, New York	84	423	5.04
Boone, St. Louis	78	387	4.96
Williams, Denver	79	375	4.75

Blocked Shots
(Minimum of 110)

	G.	No.
Paultz, San Antonio	83	253
C. Jones, St. Louis	76	218
Gilmore, Kentucky	84	205
Elmore, Indiana	76	178
B. Jones, Denver	83	184
Barnes, St. Louis	67	134
Erving, New York	84	160
Gervin, San Antonio	81	119
Hughes, New York	84	120

Steals
(Minimum of 110)

	G.	No.
Buse, Indiana	84	346
Taylor, Virginia	76	206
Erving, New York	84	207
Taylor, New York	54	125
B. Jones, Denver	83	170
Boone, St. Louis	78	154
McClain, New York	73	138
Barnes, St. Louis	67	124
Silas, San Antonio	84	155

ABA Champions

Year	Regular Season		Playoffs	
	Eastern Division	Western Division	Winner	Runner-Up
1968	Pittsburgh	New Orleans	Pittsburgh	New Orleans
1969	Indiana	Oakland	Oakland	Indiana
1970	Indiana	Denver	Indiana	Los Angeles
1971	Virginia	Indiana	Utah	Kentucky
1972	Kentucky	Utah	Indiana	New York
1973	Carolina	Utah	Indiana	Kentucky
1974	New York	Utah	New York	Utah
1975	Kentucky	Denver	Kentucky	Indiana
1976	Denver	New York	Denver	

ABA Most Valuable Player & Rookie of Year

Year	MVP	Rookie
1968	Connie Hawkins, Pittsburgh	Mel Daniels, Indiana
1969	Mel Daniels, Indiana.	Warren Armstrong, Oakland
1970	Spencer Haywood, Denver	Spencer Haywood, Denver
1971	Mel Daniels, Indiana	Dan Issel, Kentucky; Charlie Scott, Virginia (tie)
1972	Artis Gilmore, Kentucky	Artis Gilmore, Kentucky
1973	Billy Cunningham, Carolina	Brian Taylor, New York
1974	Julius Erving, New York	Swen Nater, San Antonio
1975	Julius Erving, New York;	Marvin Barnes, St. Louis
	George McGinnis, Indiana (tie)	
1976	Julius Erving, New York	David Thompson, Denver

ABA Scoring Leaders

Year	Scoring Champion	Pts.	Avg.	Year	Scoring Champion	Pts.	Avg.
1968	Connie Hawkins, Pittsburgh	1,875	26.7	1973	Julius Erving, Virginia.	2,268	31.9
1969	Rick Barry, Oakland	1,190	34.0	1974	Julius Erving, New York	2,299	27.3
1970	Spencer Haywood, Denver	2,519	29.9	1975	George McGinnis, Indiana	2,353	29.7
1971	Dan Issel, Kentucky	2,480	29.8	1976	Julius Erving, New York	2,462	29.3
1972	Charlie Scott, Virginia	2,524	34.5				

ABA All-Star Team, 1976

Position	First Team	Second Team
Forward	Julius Erving, New York	David Thompson, Denver
Forward	Billy Knight, Indiana	Bobby Jones, Denver
Center	Artis Gilmore, Kentucky	Dan Issel, Denver
Guard	James Silas, San Antonio	Don Buse, Indiana
Guard	Ralph Simpson, Denver	George Gervin, San Antonio

Basketball Hall of Fame

Springfield, Mass.

The Naismith Memorial Basketball Hall of Fame was incorporated in 1959 to serve as a memorial to James Naismith, who invented the game of basketball for students of the School for Christian Workers (now Springfield College) in December, 1891, at Springfield, Mass. The following persons have been enshrined in the Basketball Hall of Fame for outstanding contributions to basketball:

Players
Beckman, John
Borgmann, Bennie
Brennan Joseph
Cousy, Robert J.
Davies, Robert
DeBernardi, Forrest
Dehnert, Henry G.
Endacott, Paul
Foster, Harold
Friedman, Max
Gola, Thomas
Gruenig, Robert
Hanson, Victor
Holman, Nat
Hyatt, Charles
Krause, Edward W.
Kurland, Robert
Lapchick, Joe
Luisetti, Angelo
McCracken, Branch
McCracken, Jack
Macauley, C. Edward
Mikan, George L.
Murphy, Charles
Page, H. O. "Pat"
Pettit, Robert L.
Phillip, Andy

Roosma, Col. John S.
Russell, John
Russell, Bill
Schayes, Dolph
Schmidt, Ernie
Schommer, John J.
Sedran, Barney
Sharman, William W.
Steinmetz, Christian
Thompson, John A.
Vandivier, Robert
Wachter, Edward A.
Wooden, John R.

Coaches
Auerbach, Arnold J.
Blood, Ernest A.
Cann, Howard G.
Carlson, Dr. H. Clifford
Carnevale, Ben
Dean, Everett S.
Diddle, Edgar A.
Drake, Bruce
Gill, Amory T.
Hobson, Howard A.
Iba, Henry P.
Julian, Alvin F.
Keaney, Frank W.

Keogan, George E.
Lambert, Ward L.
Litwack, Harrry
Loeffler, Kenneth D.
Lonborg, Arthur
Meanwell, Dr. Walter E.
Rupp, Adolph F.
Sachs, Leonard D.
Wooden, John R.

Contributors
Allen, Dr. Forrest C.
Bee, Clair F.
Brown, Walter A.
Bunn, John W.
Douglas, Robert L.
Fisher, Harry
Gottlieb, Edward
Gulick, Dr. Luther H.
Hickox, Edward J.
Hinkle, Paul D.
Irish, Ned
Jones, R. William
Liston, Emil S.
Mokray, William G.
Morgan, Ralph
Morgenweck, Frank

Naismith, Dr. James
O'Brien, John J.
Olsen, Harold G.
Podoloff, Maurice
Porter, H. V.
Ripley, Elmer
St. John, Lynn W.
Saperstein, Abe
Schabinger, Arthur A.
Stagg, Amos Alonzo
Taylor, Charles H.
Tower, Oswald
Trester, Arthur L.
Wells, W. R. Clifford

Referees
Hepbron, George T.
Hoyt, George
Kennedy, Matthew P.
Quigley, Ernest C.
Tobey, David
Walsh, David H.

Teams
First Team
Original Celtics
Buffalo Germans
Renaissance

UCLA Wins NCAA Volleyball Championship in 1976

UCLA won its 3d consecutive NCAA Volleyball championship, and its 6th in the past 7 years, by defeating Pepperdine 18-16, 15-9, 15-11 in Muncie, Ind. The outstanding player in the tournament was Joe Mica of UCLA.

Figure Skating Champions

National Champions | World Champions

Year	Men	Women	Men	Women
1951	Richard Button	Sonya Klopfer	Richard Button, US.	Jeannette Altwegg, Eng.
1952	Richard Button	Tenley Albright	Richard Button, U.S.	Jacqueline du Bief, France
1953	Hayes Jenkins	Tenley Albright	Hayes Jenkins, U.S.	Tenley Albright, U.S.
1954	Hayes Jenkins	Tenley Albright	Hayes Jenkins, U.S.	Gundi Busch, W. Germany
1955	Hayes Jenkins	Tenley Albright	Hayes Jenkins, U.S.	Tenley Albright, U.S.
1956	Hayes Jenkins	Tenley Albright	Hayes Jenkins, U.S.	Carol Heiss, U.S.
1957	Dave Jenkins	Carol Heiss	Dave Jenkins, U.S.	Carol Heiss, U.S.
1958	Dave Jenkins	Carol Heiss	Dave Jenkins, U.S.	Carol Heiss, U.S.
1959	Dave Jenkins	Carol Heiss	Dave Jenkins, U.S.	Carol Heiss, U.S.
1960	Dave Jenkins	Carol Heiss	Alain Giletti, France	Carol Heiss, U.S.
1961	Bradley Lord	Laurence Owen	none	none
1962	Monty Hoyt	Barbara Roles Pursley	Don Jackson, Canada	Sjoukje Dijkstra, Neth.
1963	Tommy Litz	Lorraine Hanlon	Don McPherson, Canada	Sjoukje Dijkstra, Neth.
1964	Scott Allen	Peggy Fleming	Manfred Schnelldorfer, W. Germany	Sjoukje Dijkstra, Neth.
1965	Gary Visconti	Peggy Fleming	Alain Calmat, France	Petra Burka, Canada
1966	Scott Allen	Peggy Fleming	Emmerich Danzer, Austria	Peggy Fleming, U. S.
1967	Gary Visconti	Peggy Fleming	Emmerich Danzer, Austria	Peggy Fleming, U.S.
1968	Tim Wood	Peggy Fleming	Emmerich Danzer, Austria	Peggy Fleming, U.S.
1969	Tim Wood	Janet Lynn	Tim Wood, U.S.	Gabriele Seyfert, E. Ger.
1970	Tim Wood	Janet Lynn	Tim Wood, U.S.	Gabriele Seyfert, E. Ger.
1971	John Misha Petkevich	Janet Lynn	Ondrej Nepela, Czech.	Beatrix Schuba, Austria
1972	Ken Shelley	Janet Lynn	Ondrej Nepela, Czech.	Beatrix Schuba, Austria
1973	Gordon McKellen Jr.	Janet Lynn	Ondrej Nepela, Czech.	Karen Magnussen, Canada
1974	Gordon McKellen Jr.	Dorothy Hamill	Jan Hoffman, E. Germany	Christine Errath, E. Germany
1975	Gordon McKellen Jr.	Dorothy Hamill	Sergei Volkov, USSR	Dianne de Leeuw, Neth.-U.S.
1976	Charlie Tickner	Dorothy Hamill	John Curry, Gt. Britain	Dorothy Hamill, U.S.

Canadian National Figure Skating Champions

Year	Men	Women	Year	Men	Women
1959	Donald Jackson	Marg. Crosland	1968	Jay Humphrey	Karen Magnussen
1960	Donald Jackson	Wendy Griner	1969	Jay Humphrey	Linda Carbonetto
1961	Donald Jackson	Wendy Griner	1970	David McGillivray	Karen Magnussen
1962	Donald Jackson	Wendy Griner	1971	Toller Cranston	Karen Magnussen
1963	Donald McPherson	Wendy Griner	1972	Toller Cranston	Karen Magnussen
1964	Charles Snelling	Petra Burka	1973	Toller Cranston	Karen Magnussen
1965	Donald Knight	Petra Burka	1974	Toller Cranston	Lynn Nightingale
1966	Donald Knight	Petra Burka	1975	Toller Cranston	Lynn Nightingale
1967	Donald Knight	Valerie Jones	1976	Toller Cranston	Lynn Nightingale

Speed Ice-Skating Championships, 1976

North American Outdoor Championships, Lake Placid, N.Y., Feb. 14-15: Men's Champion: Leigh Barczewski, Wis. Women's Champion: Connie Carpenter, Wis.

National Outdoor Championships, St. Paul, Minn., Jan. 31-Feb. 1. Men's Champion: J. Wurster, N.Y. Women's Champion: Connie Carpenter, Wis.

National Indoor Championships, Lakewood, Ohio, Mar. 13-14. Men's Champion: Allan Rattray, Cal. Women's Champion: Peggy Hartrick, St. Louis, Mo.

North American Indoor Championships, Wyandotte, Mich., Apr. 2-4, Men's Champion: J. Wurster, N.Y. Women's Champion: Peggy Hartrick, St. Louis, Mo.

The America's Cup

Competition for the America's Cup grew out of the first contest to establish a world yachting championship, one of the carnival features of the London Exposition of 1851. The race, open to all classes of yachts from all over the world, covered a 60-mile course around the Isle of Wight; the prize was a cup worth about $500, donated by the Royal Yacht Squadron of England, known as the "America's Cup" because it was first won by the United States yacht America. Successive efforts of British and Australian yachtsmen have failed to win the famous trophy, which remains in the United States.

On Sept. 17, 1974, the 66-foot 12-meter yacht Courageous won a fourth straight victory over the Australian challenger, Southern Cross, to keep the symbol of world sailing supremacy in the United States. In four races, Southern Cross lost to Courageous by a total of 18 minutes 51 seconds. The U.S. yacht was designed by Olin Stephens and skippered by Ted Hood.

Winners of the America's Cup

1851	America
1870	Magic defeated Cambria, England, (1-0)
1871	Columbia (first three races) and Sappho (last two races) defeated Livonia, England, (4-1)
1876	Madeline defeated Countess of Dufferin, Canada, (2-0)
1881	Mischief defeated Atalanta, Canada, (2-0)
1885	Puritan defeated Genesta, England, (2-0)
1886	Mayflower defeated Galatea, England, (2-0)
1887	Volunteer defeated Thistle, Scotland, (2-0)
1893	Vigilant defeated Valkyrie II, England, (3-0)
1895	Defender defeated Valkyrie III, England, (3-0)
1899	Columbia defeated Shamrock, England, (3-0)
1901	Columbia defeated Shamrock II, England, (3-0)
1903	Reliance defeated Shamrock III, England, (3-0)
1920	Resolute defeated Shamrock IV, England, (3-2)
1930	Enterprise defeated Shamrock V, England, (4-0)
1934	Rainbow defeated Endeavour, England, (4-2)
1937	Ranger defeated Endeavour II, England, (4-0)
1958	Columbia defeated Sceptre, England, (4-0)
1962	Weatherly defeated Gretel, Australia, (4-1)
1964	Constellation defeated Sovereign, England, (4-0)
1967	Intrepid defeated Dame Pattie, Australia, (4-0)
1970	Intrepid defeated Gretel II, Australia, (4-1)
1974	Courageous defeated Southern Cross, (4-0)

World Record Fish Caught by Rod and Reel

Source: Saltwater: International Game Fish Association. Freshwater: Field & Stream Magazine.
Records confirmed to June, 1976

Saltwater Fish

The International Game Fish Assn. revised its standards for world records, effective July 1, 1970. Line samples and line tests are now required in order for a world record application to be recognized. Records listed below are based on the new standards.

Species	Weight	Length	Girth	Where caught	Date	Angler
Albacore	74 lbs. 13 oz.	4'2"	34³/₄"	Arguineguin, Canary Is.	Oct. 28, 1973	Olof Idegren
Amberjack	149 lbs.	5'11"	41³/₄"	Bermuda	June 21, 1964	Peter Simons
Barracuda, Great	83 lbs.	6'¹/₄"	29"	Lagos, Nigeria	Jan. 13, 1952	K. J. W. Hackett
Bass, Black Sea	8 lbs.	1'10"	19"	Nantucket Sound, Mass.	May 13, 1951	H. R. Rider
Bass, Giant Sea	563 lbs. 8 oz.	7'5"	72"	Anacaba Island, Cal.	Aug. 20, 1968	James D. McAdam Jr.
Bass, Striped	72 lbs.	4'6¹/₂"	31"	Cuttyhunk, Mass.	Oct. 10, 1969	Edward J. Kirker
Blackfish (or Tautog)	21 lbs. 6 oz.	2'7¹/₂"	23¹/₂"	Cape May, N.J.	June 12, 1954	R. N. Sheafer
Bluefish	31 lbs. 12 oz.	3'11"	23"	Hatteras Inlet, N.C.	Jan. 30, 1972	James M. Hussey
Bonefish	19 lbs.	3'3⁵/₈"	17"	Zululand, S. Africa	May 26, 1962	Brian W. Batchelor
Cobia	110 lbs. 5 oz.	5'3"	34"	Mombasa, Kenya	Sept. 8, 1964	Eric Tinworth
Cod	98 lbs. 12 oz.	5'3"	41"	Isle of Shoals, Mass.	June 8, 1969	Alphonse Bielevich
Dolphin	85 lbs.	5'9"	37¹/₂"	Spanish Wells, Bahamas	May 29, 1968	Richard Seymour
Drum, Black	113 lbs. 1 oz.	4'5¹/₄"	43¹/₂"	Lewes, Delaware	Sept. 15, 1975	Gerald Townsend
Drum, Red	90 lbs.	4'7¹/₂"	38¹/₄"	Rodanthe, N.C.	Nov. 7, 1973	Elvin Hooper
Flounder	30 lbs. 12 oz.	3'2¹/₂"	30¹/₂"	Vina del Mar, Chile	Nov. 1, 1971	Augusto Nunez Moreno
Jewfish	680 lbs.	7'1¹/₂"	66"	Fernandina Beach, Fla.	May 20, 1961	Lynn Joyner
Mackerel, King	90 lbs.	....	....	Key West, Fla.	Feb. 16, 1976	Norton Thornton
Marlin, King	78 lbs. 12 oz.	5'5¹/₂"	30"	La Romana, Dominican Republic	Nov. 26, 1971	Fernando Viyella
Marlin, Black	1,560 lbs.	14'6"	81"	Cabo Blanco, Peru	Aug. 4, 1953	A. C. Glassell Jr.
Marlin, Atlantic Blue	1,142 lbs.	13'9"	80"	Nags Head, N.C.	July 26, 1974	Jack Herrington
Marlin, Pacific Blue	1,153 lbs.	14'8"	73"	Guam	Aug. 21, 1969	Greg Perez
Marlin, Striped	415 lbs.	11'	52"	Cape Brett, N.Z.	Mar. 31, 1964	B. C. Bain
Marlin, White	159 lbs. 8 oz.	9'	36"	Pompano Beach, Fla.	Apr. 25, 1953	W. E. Johnson
Permit	50 lbs. 8 oz.	3'8³/₄"	33³/₄"	Key West, Fla.	Mar. 15, 1971	Marshall Earnest
Pollock	46 lbs. 7 oz.	4'2¹/₂"	30"	Brielle, N.J.	May 26, 1975	John Torres Holton
Runner, Rainbow	30 lbs. 15 oz.	3'11"	22"	Kauai, Hawaii	Apr. 27, 1963	Holbrook Goodale
Roosterfish	114 lbs.	5'4"	33"	La Paz, Mex.	June 1, 1960	Abe Sackheim
Sailfish, Atlantic	128 lbs. 1 oz.	8'10¹/₄"	34¹/₄"	Luanda, Angola	Mar. 27, 1974	Harm Steyn
Sailfish, Pacific	221 lbs.	10'9"	....	Santa Cruz Is.	Feb. 12, 1947	C. W. Stewart
Seabass, White	83 lbs. 12 oz.	5'5¹/₂"	34"	San Felipe, Mex.	Mar. 31, 1953	L.C. Baumgardner
Seatrout, Spotted	15 lbs. 6 oz.	2'9"	23¹/₄"	Jensen Beach, Fla.	May 4, 1969	Michael J. Foremny
Shark, Blue	410 lbs.	11'6"	52"	Rockport, Mass.	Sept. 1, 1960	R.C. Webster
	410 lbs.	11'2"	52¹/₂"	Rockport, Mass.	Aug. 17, 1967	Martha Webster
Shark, Hammerhead	703 lbs.	14'4"	63"	Jacksonville Beach, Fla.	July 5, 1975	H. B. Reasor
Shark, Mako	1,061 lbs.	12'2"	79¹/₂"	Mayor Island, N.Z.	Feb. 17, 1970	James Penwarden
Shark, Man-Eater or White	2,664 lbs.	16'10"	114"	Ceduna, Australia	Apr. 21, 1959	Alfred Dean
Shark, Porbeagle	430 lbs.	8'	63"	Channel Island, Eng.	June 29, 1969	Desmond Bougourd
Shark, Thresher	739 lbs.	8'10"	68"	Tutukaka, N.Z.	Feb. 17, 1975	Brian Galvin
Shark, Tiger	1,780 lbs.	13'10¹/₂"	103"	Cherry Grove, S.C.	June 14, 1964	Walter Maxwell
Snook	52 lbs. 6 oz.	4'1¹/₂"	26"	La Paz, Mexico	Jan. 9, 1963	Jane Haywood
Swordfish	1,182 lbs.	14'11¹/₂"	78"	Iquique, Chile	May 7, 1953	L. Marron
Tanguigue	81 lbs.	5'11¹/₂"	29¹/₄"	Karachi, Pakistan	Aug. 27, 1960	George E. Rusinak
Tarpon	283 lbs.	7'2¹/₂"	....	L. Maracaibo, Venezuela	Mar. 19, 1956	M. Salazar
Tuna, Allison (Yellowfin)	308 lbs.	7'	57"	San Benedicto Isl., Mex.	Jan. 18, 1973	Harold J. Tolson
Tuna, Atlantic Bigeye	355 lbs. 10 oz.	8'4³/₄"	60¹/₂"	Canary Islands	July 11, 1975	Wilhelm Rapp
Tuna, Pacific Bigeye	435 lbs.	7'9"	63¹/₂"	Cabo Blanco, Peru	Apr. 17, 1957	Dr. Russel Lee
Tuna, Blackfin	38 lbs.	3'3¹/₄"	28¹/₄"	Bermuda	June 26, 1970	Archie L. Dickens
	38 lbs.	3'5"	28"	Islamorada, Fla.	May 21, 1973	Elizabeth Jean Wade
Tuna, Bluefin	1,120 lbs.	12'2"	85¹/₂"	P.E.I., Canada	Oct. 19, 1973	Lee Coffin
Tuna, Dog-tooth	153 lbs. 8 oz.	....	....	Cooktown, Aust.	Sept. 25, 1975	William Chapman
Tuna, Longtail	60 lbs.	4'8"	30"	Australia	Mar. 17, 1975	N. Noel Webster
Tuna, Skipjack (Oceanic Bonito)	39 lbs. 15 oz.	3'3"	28"	Walker Cay, Bahamas	Jan 21, 1952	F. Dowley
	40 lbs.	3'2¹/₂"	27¹/₂"	Mauritius	Apr. 19, 1971	Joseph Caboche Jr.
Tunny, Little	21 lbs. 12 oz.	2'9¹/₂"	21¹/₂"	Key Largo, Fla.	June 29, 1976	Paul F. Leader
Wahoo	149 lbs.	6'7³/₄"	37¹/₂"	Cat Cay, Bahamas	June 15, 1962	John Pirovano
Weakfish	19 lbs. 8 oz.	3'1"	23¹/₄"	Trinidad, W. Indies	Apr. 13, 1962	Dennis Hall
Yellowtail	111 lbs.	5'2"	38"	Bay of Islands, N.Z.	June 11, 1961	A.F. Plim

Freshwater Fish

Species	Weight	Length	Girth	Where caught	Date	Angler
Bass, Largemouth	22 lbs. 4 oz.	32¹/₂"	28¹/₂"	Montgomery Lake, Ga.	June 2, 1932	George W. Perry
Bass, Redeye	8 lbs. 8 oz.	23"	18"	Lazer Creek, Ga.	Apr. 9, 1975	Jimmy L. Rogers
Bass, Rock	3 lbs.	13¹/₂"	10³/₄"	York River, Ont.	Aug. 1, 1974	Peter Gulgin
Bass, Smallmouth	11 lbs. 15 oz.	27"	21²/₃"	Dale Hollow Lake, Ky.	July 9, 1955	David L. Hayes
Bass, Spotted	8 lbs. 10¹/₂ oz.	23¹/₂"	19³/₄"	Smith Lake, Ala.	Feb. 25, 1972	Billy Henderson
Bass, White	5 lbs. 5 oz.	19¹/₃"	17"	Ferguson Lake, Cal.	Mar. 8, 1972	Norman W. Mize
Bass, Yellow	2 lbs. 2 oz.	14"	13"	Lake Monona, Wis.	Jan. 18, 1972	James Thrun
Black Bullhead	8 lbs.	24"	17³/₄"	Lake Waccabuc, N.Y.	Aug. 1, 1951	Kani Evans
Bluegill	4 lbs. 12 oz.	15"	18¹/₄"	Ketona Lake, Ala.	Apr. 9, 1950	T.S. Hudson

Species	Weight	Length	Girth	Where caught	Date	Angler
Bowfin	19 lbs. 12 oz.	39″	....	Lake Marion, S.C.	Nov. 5, 1972	M. R. Webster
Buffalo, Bigmouth	47 lbs. 2 oz.	43″	30″	Tippecanoe Lake, Ind.	May 10, 1975	David F. Hulley
Buffalo, Smallmouth	26 lbs. 10 oz.	34¹/₂″	28¹/₄″	Lake Wylie, N.C.	Feb. 19, 1976	J. Gary Hill
Carp	55 lbs. 5 oz.	42″	31″	Clearwater Lake, Minn.	July 10, 1952	Frank J. Ledwein
Catfish, Blue	97 lbs.	57″	37″	Missouri River, S.D.	Sept. 16, 1959	E.B. Elliott
Catfish, Channel	58 lbs.	47¹/₂″	29¹/₈″	Santee-Cooper Res., S.C.	July 7, 1964	W.B. Whaley
Catfish, Flathead	79 lbs. 8 oz.	44″	27″	White River, Ind.	Aug. 13, 1955	Glenn T. Simpson
Char, Arctic	29 lbs. 11 oz.	39³/₄″	26″	Arctic River, N.W.T.	Aug. 21, 1968	Jeanne P. Branson
Crappie, Black	5 lbs.	19¹/₄″	18⁵/₈″	Santee-Cooper Res., S.C.	Mar. 15, 1957	Paul E. Foust
Crappie, White	5 lbs. 3 oz.	21″	19″	Enid Dam, Miss.	July 31, 1957	Fred L. Bright
Dolly Varden	32 lbs.	40¹/₂″	29³/₄″	L. Pend Oreille, Ida.	Oct. 27, 1949	N. L. Higgins
Drum, Freshwater	54 lbs. 8 oz.	31¹/₂″	29″	Nickajack Lake, Tenn.	Apr. 20, 1972	Benny E. Hull
Gar, Alligator	279 lbs.	93″	....	Rio Grande R., Tex.	Dec. 2, 1951	Bill Valverde
Gar, Longnose	50 lbs. 5 oz.	72¹/₄″	22¹/₄″	Trinity River, Tex.	July 30, 1954	Townsend Miller
Grayling, American	5 lbs. 15 oz.	29³/₄″	15¹/₄″	Katseyedie R., N.W.T.	Aug. 16, 1967	Jeanne P. Branson
Kokanee	6 lbs.	24¹/₂″	14¹/₂″	Priest Lake, Idaho	June 9, 1975	Jerry Verge
Muskellunge	69 lbs.	64¹/₂″	31³/₄″	St. Lawrence R., N.Y.	Sept. 22, 1957	Arthur Lawton
Perch, White	4 lbs. 12 oz.	19¹/₂″	13″	Messalonskee Lake, Me.	June 4, 1949	Mrs. Earl Small
Perch, Yellow	4 lbs. 3¹/₂ oz.	....	....	Bordentown, N.J.	May, 1865	Dr. C. C. Abbot
Pickerel, Chain	9 lbs. 6 oz.	31″	14″	Homerville, Ga.	Feb. 17, 1961	Baxley McQuaig Jr.
Pike, Northern	46 lbs. 2 oz.	52¹/₂″	25″	Sacandaga Res., N.Y.	Sept. 15, 1940	Peter Dubuc
Redhorse, Silver	4 lbs. 2 oz.	20¹/₂″	14″	Gasconade River, Mo.	Oct. 5, 1974	C. Larry McKinney
Salmon, Atlantic	79 lbs. 2 oz.	....	....	Tana R., Norway	1928	Henrik Henriksen
Salmon, Chinook	92 lbs.	58¹/₂″	36″	Skeena River, B.C.	July 19, 1959	Heinz Wichmann
Salmon, Chum	24 lbs. 4 oz.	40¹/₂″	22³/₄″	Margarita Bay, Alaska	Aug. 19, 1974	Richard Coleman
Salmon, Landlocked	22 lbs. 8 oz.	36″	est.20″	Sebago Lake, Maine	Aug. 1, 1907	Edward Blakely
Salmon, Silver	31 lbs.	....	....	Cowichan Bay, B.C.	Oct. 11, 1947	Mrs. Lee Hallberg
Sauger	8 lbs. 12 oz.	28″	15″	Lake Sakakawea, N.D.	Oct. 6, 1971	Mike Fischer
Shad, American	9 lbs. 2 oz.	25″	17¹/₂″	Enfield, Conn.	Apr. 28, 1973	Edward P. Nelson
Sturgeon, White	360 lbs.	111″	86″	Snake River, Idaho	Apr. 24, 1956	Willard Cravens
Sunfish, Green	2 lbs. 2 oz.	14³/₄″	14″	Stockton Lake, Mo.	June 18, 1971	Paul M. Dilley
Sunfish, Redear	4 lbs. 8 oz.	16¹/₄″	17³/₄″	Chase City, Va.	June 19, 1970	Maurice E. Ball
Trout, Brook	14¹/₂ lbs.	31¹/₂″	11¹/₂″	Nipigon R., Ontario	July, 1916	Dr. W. J. Cook
Trout, Brown	39¹/₂ lbs.	....	....	Lock Awe, Scotland	1866	W. Muir
Trout, Cutthroat	41 lbs.	39″	....	Pyramid Lake, Nev.	Dec., 1925	J. Skimmerhorn
Trout, Golden	11 lbs.	28″	16″	Cook's Lake, Wyo.	Aug. 5, 1948	Charles S. Reed
Trout, Lake	65 lbs.	52″	38″	Great Bear Lake, N.W.T.	Aug. 8, 1970	Larry Daunis
Trout, Rainbow						
Stlhd. or Kamloops.	42 lbs. 2 oz.	43″	23¹/₂″	Bell Island, Alaska	June 22, 1970	David Robert White
Trout, Sunapee	11 lbs. 8 oz.	33″	17¹/₄″	Lake Sunapee, N.H.	Aug. 1, 1954	Ernest Theoharis
Trout, Tiger	10 lbs.	27″	16³/₄″	Deerskin River, Wis.	May 23, 1974	Charles J. Mattek
Walleye	25 lbs.	41″	29″	Old Hickory Lake, Tenn.	Aug. 1, 1960	Mabry Harper
Warmouth	2 lbs.	12″	12¹/₂″	Sylvania, Ga.	May 4, 1974	Carlton Robbins
Whitefish, Lake	13 lbs.	32¹/₄″	19″	Great Bear Lake, N.W.T.	July 14, 1974	Robert L. Stintsman
Whitefish, Mountain	5 lbs.	19″	14″	Athabasca R., Alberta	June 3, 1963	Orville Welch

Rodeo Championship Standings 1975

Source: Rodeo Cowboys Assn., Inc.

Event	Winner	Money Won	Event	Winner	Money Won
All Around	Leo Camarillo, Oakdale, Cal.	$50,830	Calf Roping	Jeff Copenhaver, Spokane, Wash.	$34,628
Saddle Bronc	Monte Henson, Mesquite, Tex.	29,788	Steer Wrestling	Frank Shepperson, Midwest, Wyo.	34,862
Bareback Bronc	Joe Alexander, Cora, Wyoming	41,184	Team Roping	Leo Camarillo, Oakdale, Cal.	28,101
Bull Riding	Don Gay, Mesquite, Texas	34,850			

Rodeo Cowboy All Around Champions

Year	Winner	Money Won	Year	Winner	Money Won
1960	Harry Tompkins, Dublin, Texas	$32,522	1968	Larry Mahan, Salem, Oregon	$49,129
1961	Benny Reynolds, Melrose, Mont.	31,309	1969	Larry Mahan, Brooks, Oregon	57,726
1962	Tom Nesmith, Bethel, Okla.	32,611	1970	Larry Mahan, Brooks, Oregon	41,493
1963	Dean Oliver, Boise, Idaho.	31,329	1971	Phil Lyne, George West, Texas	49,245
1964	Dean Oliver, Boise, Idaho.	31,150	1972	Phil Lyne, George West, Texas	60,852
1965	Dean Oliver, Boise, Idaho.	33,163	1973	Larry Mahan, Dallas, Texas.	64,447
1966	Larry Mahan, Brooks, Oregon	40,358	1974	Tom Ferguson, Miami, Oklahoma	66,929
1967	Larry Mahan, Brooks, Oregon	51,996	1975	Leo Camarillo, Oakdale, Cal.	50,830

80th Annual Boston Marathon

Jack Fultz of Arlington, Va. covered the traditional distance of 26 miles 385 yards in 2 hours 20 minutes 19 seconds to win the 1976 Boston Marathon. The leading finishers and their times follow:

1—Jack Fultz, Arlington, Va.	2:20.19	
2—Mario Cuevas, Mexico.	2:21.13	
3—Jose de Jesus, Puerto Rico.	2:22.10	
4—Jack Foster, New Zealand.	2:22.30	
5—James Berka, Minneapolis.	2:24.32	
6—Eduardo Pacheco, Puerto Rico.	2:25.11	
7—Michael Burke, Randolph, Mass.	2:26.12	
8—Ron Kurle, Long Beach, Cal.	2:26.22	
9—Donald Slusser, Pittsburgh.	2:26.40	
10—David Fiskin, New Zealand.	2:26.44	
11—Paul Salkington, Summit A.C.	2:27.27	

12—A.J. Burfoot, Middletown, Conn.	2:27.57
13—Rafael Perez, Costa Rica.	2:28.16
14—Norb Sander, Millrose A.A.	2:28.20
15—Tony Wilcox, Sugarloaf Mt. A.C.	2:29.28

Leading Women

1—Kim Merritt, Kenosha, Wis.	2:47.10
2—Miki Gorman, Los Angeles.	2:52.26
3—Dorothy Doolittle, Austin, Tex.	2:56.26
4—Gayle Barron, Atlanta.	2:58.23
5—Nancy Kent, Conshohocken, Pa.	3:00.53

Lacrosse Championships in 1976

Source: Jack Kelly, U.S. Lacrosse Information

NCAA University Champion—Cornell Univ.
NCAA College Champion—Hobart College
National Club Lacrosse Champion—Mt. Washington Club of Baltimore
U.S. Intercollegiate Lacrosse Association Champion—Cornell Univ.
Atlantic Coast Conference Champion—Univ. of Maryland
Ivy League Champion—Cornell Univ.
South Atlantic Division Champion—Univ. of North Carolina
East Coast Conference Division—Univ. of Delaware
Mason Dixon Division—UMBC
New England Intercollegiate Champion—Univ. of Massachusetts
Independent Division—Hobart College
Middle Atlantic Division—Gettysburg
Midwest Division—Ohio Wesleyan
Northern New York Division—Geneseo State
Knickerbocker Division—Dowling College
Snively Division (New England)—Middlebury College
Colonial Division (New England)—Boston State
National Jr. College Champion—Nassau Community (L.I.)

NCAA University Championship
at Brown University—Providence, R.I., May 29; Cornell 16, Maryland 13 (o.t.).

NCAA semi-finals
Maryland 22, Navy 11; Cornell 13, Johns Hopkins 5.

NCAA quarter-finals
Maryland 17, Brown 8; Navy 13, North Carolina 9; Johns Hopkins 11, Massachusetts 9; Cornell 14, Washington & Lee 0.

All-Star College Game
Charlottesville, Va., June 5; North 22, South 17.

NCAA College Championship
at UMBC-Baltimore, Md., May 22; Hobart 18, Adelphi 9.

Junior College Championship
Selden, L.I., May 15; Nassau Community College 9, Suffolk County 6.

U.S. Club Lacrosse Association Championship
White Plains, N.Y., June 19; Mt. Washington 19, Brine L.C. 5.

USILA University All America Team — 1976

Position	Player	College
Goalie	Dan Mackesey	Cornell
Defense	Mike Farrell	Maryland
Defense	Tom Keigler	Washington & Lee
Defense	Rob Lindsey	Washington & Lee
Midfield	Roger Tuck	Maryland
Midfield	Dale Kohler	Johns Hopkins
Midfield	Frank Urso	Maryland
Midfield	Bill Marino	Cornell
Attack	Mike O'Neill	Johns Hopkins
Attack	Ed Mullen	Maryland
Attack	Mike French	Cornell
Attack	Eamon McEneaney	Cornell

USILA University Top Ten Teams — 1976

Rank	University	Rank	University
1	Cornell	6	Massachusetts
2	Maryland	7	Washington & Lee
3	Johns Hopkins	8	Brown
4	Navy	9	Virginia
5	North Carolina	10	Hofstra

USILA College Division All America Team — 1976

Position	Player	College
Goalie	Rick Blick	Hobart
Defense	Gary Clipp	UMBC
Defense	Jim Burke	Cortland State
Defense	John Pirro	Roanoke
Midfield	Mitch Lekas	Towson State
Midfield	David McNaney	Hobart
Midfield	Bob Sargent	Ohio Wesleyan
Attack	Jud Smith	Cortland
Attack	Harold McVey	Adelphi
Attack	John Cheek	Washington College

USILA College Division Top Ten Teams — 1976

Rank	College	Rank	College
1	Hobart	6	Washington College
2	Adelphi	7	Roanoke
3	Ohio Wesleyan (Tie)	8	Baltimore
3	Towson State (Tie)	9	UMBC
5	Cortland State	10	Kutztown

Chess

Chess dates back to antiquity. Its exact origin is unknown. The strongest players of their time, and therefore regarded by later generations as world champions, were Francois Philidor, France; Alexandre Deschappelles, France; Louis de la Bourdonnais, France; Howard Staunton, England; Adolph Anderssen, Germany and Paul Morphy, United States. In 1866 Wilhelm Steinitz of Austria defeated Adolph Anderssen and claimed the title of World Champion. The official world champions, since the title was first used follow:

1866-1894 Wilhelm Steinitz, Vienna	1937-1946 Dr. Alexander A. Alekhine, Paris	1961-1963 Mikhail Botvinnik, USSR
1894-1921 Dr. Emanuel Lasker, Berlin		1963-1969 Tigran Petrosian, USSR
1921-1927 Jose R. Capablanca, Havana	1948-1957 Mikhail Botvinnik, USSR	1969-1972 Boris Spassky, USSR
1927-1935 Dr. Alexander A. Alekhine, Paris	1957-1958 Vassily Smyslov, USSR	1972-1975 Bobby Fischer, U.S. (a)
1935-1937 Dr. Max Euwe, Holland	1958-1959 Mikhail Botvinnik, USSR	1975 Anatoly Karpov, USSR
	1960-1961 Mikhail Tal, USSR	

(a) Defaulted championship after refusal to accept International Chess Federation rules for a championship match, April 1975.

United States Champions

Unofficial champions	Official Champions		
1857-1871 Paul Morphy	1891-1892 Jackson Showalter	1909-1936 Frank Marshall	1961-1962 Larry Evans
1871-1876 George Mackenzie	1892-1894 S. Lipschutz	1936-1944 Samuel Reshevsky	1962-1968 Bobby Fischer
1876-1880 James Mason	1894 Jackson Showalter	1944-1946 Arnold Denker	1968-1969 Larry Evans
1880-1889 George Mackenzie	1894-1895 Albert Hodges	1946-1948 Samuel Reshevsky	1969-1972 Samuel Reshevsky
1889-1890 S. Lipschutz	1895-1897 Jackson Showalter	1948-1951 Herman Steiner	1972-1973 Robert Byrne
1890 Jackson Showalter	1897-1909 Harry Pillsbury	1951-1954 Larry Evans	1973-1974 Lubomir Kavalek & John Grefe
1890-1891 Max Judd		1954-1957 Arthur Bisguier	
		1957-1961 Bobby Fischer	1974 Walter Browne

National Duckpin Bowling Champions, 1976

Men's Singles—Bob Atkins, Baltimore, Md., 501.
Women's Singles—Doris Shortt, Baltimore, Md., 467.
Men's Doubles—Tony Adams-Mike Piersanti, East Haven, Conn., 923.
Women's Doubles—Lorraine Watts-Kathy Cahoon, Willimantic, Conn., 810.

Men's Team—Connecticut Frozen Food, Hamden, Conn., 2125.
Women's Team—Overlea Exxon, Baltimore, Md., 1926.
Men's All Events—Mike Piersanti, New Haven, Conn., 1426.
Women's All Events—Susan Slattery, Baltimore, Md., 1244.
Mixed Doubles—Debbie Nettleton-Dennis Pontes, Manchester, Conn., 955.

World Swimming Records

As of Aug. 1, 1976

Effective June 1, 1969, FINA will recognize only records made over a 50-meter course.

Men's Freestyle

Distance	Time	Holder	Country	Where made	Date
100 Meters	0:49.99	Jim Montgomery	U.S.A.	Montreal	July, 1976
200 Meters	1:50.29	Bruce Furniss	U.S.A.	Montreal	July, 1976
400 Meters	3:51.93	Brian Goodell	U.S.A.	Montreal	July, 1976
800 Meters	8:09.60	Tim Shaw	U.S.A.	Mission Viejo, Cal.	July 12, 1975
1,500 Meters	15:02.40	Brian Goodell	U.S.A.	Montreal	July, 1976

Men's Breaststroke

| 100 Meters | 1:03.11 | John Hencken | U.S.A. | Montreal | July, 1976 |
| 200 Meters | 2:15.11 | David Wilkie | Scotland | Montreal | July, 1976 |

Men's Butterfly

| 100 Meters | 0:54.27 | Mark Spitz | U.S.A. | Munich | Aug. 31, 1972 |
| 200 Meters | 1:59.23 | Mike Bruner | U.S.A. | Montreal | July, 1976 |

Men's Backstroke

| 100 Meters | 0:55.49 | John Naber | U.S.A. | Montreal | July, 1976 |
| 200 Meters | 1:59.19 | John Naber | U.S.A. | Montreal | July, 1976 |

Men's Individual Medley

| 200 Meters | 2:06.08 | Bruce Furniss | U.S.A. | Kansas City, Kan. | Aug. 23, 1975 |
| 400 Meters | 4:23.68 | Rod Strachan | U.S.A. | Montreal | July, 1976 |

Men's Freestyle Relays

| 400 M. (4x100) | 3:24.85 | Nat'l Team (B. Furniss, Coan, Montgomery, Murphy) | U.S.A. | Cali, Colombia | July 23, 1975 |
| 800 M. (4x200) | 7:23.22 | Nat'l Team (Bruner, Furniss, Naber, Montgomery) | U.S.A. | Montreal | July, 1976 |

Men's Medley Relays

| 400 M. (4x100) | 3:42.22 | Nat'l Team (Hencken, Naber, Montgomery, Vogel) | U.S.A. | Montreal | July, 1976 |

Women's Freestyle

100 Meters	0:55.65	Kornelia Ender	E. Germany	Montreal	July, 1976
200 Meters	1:59.26	Kornelia Ender	E. Germany	Montreal	July, 1976
400 Meters	4:09.89	Petra Thumer	E. Germany	Montreal	July, 1976
800 Meters	8:37.14	Petra Thumer	E. Germany	Montreal	July, 1976
1,500 Meters	16:33.94	Jenny Turrall	Australia	Concord, Cal.	Aug. 25, 1974

Women's Breaststroke

| 100 Meters | 1:10.86 | Hannelore Anke | E. Germany | Montreal | July, 1976 |
| 200 Meters | 2:33.35 | Marina Koshevala | USSR | Montreal | July, 1976 |

Women's Butterfly

| 100 Meters | 1:00.13 | Kornelia Ender | E. Germany | E. Berlin | June, 1976 |
| 200 Meters | 2:11.22 | Rosemarie Gabriel | E. Germany | E. Berlin | June, 1976 |

Women's Backstroke

| 100 Meters | 1:01.51 | Ulrike Richter | E. Germany | E. Berlin | June, 1976 |
| 200 Meters | 2:12.47 | Brigit Treiber | E. Germany | E. Berlin | June, 1976 |

Women's Individual Medley

| 200 Meters | 2:17.14 | Kornelia Ender | E. Germany | E. Berlin | June, 1976 |
| 400 Meters | 4:42.77 | Ulrike Tauber | E. Germany | Montreal | July, 1976 |

Women's Freestyle Relays

| 400 M. (4x100) | 3:44.82 | Nat'l Team (Boglioli, Sterkel, Peyton, Babashoff) | U.S.A. | Montreal | July, 1976 |

Women's Medley Relays

| 400 M. (4x100) | 4:07.95 | Nat'l Team (Richter, Anke, Pollack, Ender) | E. Germany | Montreal | July, 1976 |

National AAU Indoor Diving Championships

*Cleveland, Ohio

Men	Women
One-Meter Springboard — Tim Moore.	**One-Meter Springboard** — Cynthia McIngvale.
Three-Meter Springboard — Tim Moore.	**Three-Meter Springboard** — Jennifer Chandler.
Ten-Meter Platform — Tim Moore.	**Ten-Meter Platform** — Melissa Briley.

Swimming Events in 1976

National AAU Short Course Swimming Championships

Long Beach, Cal., Apr. 1-4, 1976

Men

100 Meter Freestyle — James Montgomery, Bloomington, Ind. Time—0:50.77.
200 Meter Freestyle — James Montgomery. Time—1:51.41.
400 Meter Freestyle — Doug Northway, Oasis AC. Time—3:56.48.
1,500 Meter Freestyle — Casey Converse, Mission Viejo Nad. Time—15:40.04.
100 Meter Backstroke — John Naber, USC. Time—0:56.99.
200 Meter Backstroke — John Naber. Time—2:03.25.
100 Meter Breaststroke — David Wilkie, Univ. of Miami. Time—1:04.46.
200 Meter Breaststroke — David Wilkie. Time—2:18.48.
100 Meter Butterfly — Steve Gregg, N.C. State. Time—0:55.49.
200 Meter Butterfly — Mike Bruner, DeAnza. Time—2:02.49.
200 Meter Individual Medley — David Wilkie. Time—2:06.25.
400 Meter Individual Medley — Zoltan Verraszto, Hungary. Time—4:26.
400 Meter Medley Relay — Gatorade SC. Time—3:52.19.
400 Meter Freestyle Relay — Univ. of Tennessee. Time—3:26.97.
800 Meter Freestyle Relay — USC. Time—7:33.53.

Women

100 Meter Freestyle — Kim Peyton, David Douglas ST. Time—0:57.53.
200 Meter Freestyle — Shirley Babashoff, Mission Viejo Nad. Time—2:02.54.
400 Meter Freestyle — Shirley Babashoff. Time—4:15.82.
800 Meter Freestyle — Shannon Smith, Hyack SC. Time—8:46.39.
100 Meter Backstroke — Linda Jezek, Santa Clara SC. Time—1:04.45.
200 Meter Backstroke — Cheryl Gibson, Canadian Dolphin SC. Time—2:18.11.
100 Meter Breaststroke — Christine Jarvis, N. River Yacht Club. Time—1:14.70.
200 Meter Breaststroke — Noel Moran, Santa Clara SC. Time—2:39.39.
100 Meter Butterfly — Wendy Boglioli, Central Jersey AC. Time—1:02.14.
200 Meter Butterfly — Nicole Kramer, Mission Viejo Nad. Time—2:19.01.
200 Meter Individual Medley — Kathy Heddy, Central Jersey AC. Time—2:23.02.
400 Meter Individual Medley — Cheryl Gibson, Canadian Dolphin SC. Time—4:57.20.
400 Meter Medley Relay — Santa Clara SC. Time—4:24.09.
400 Meter Freestyle Relay — El Monte AC. Time—3:56.06.
800 Meter Freestyle Relay — Central Jersey AC. Time — 8:22.98.

U.S. Olympic Trials

Long Beach, Cal., June 16-20, 1976

Men

100 Meter Freestyle—Jim Montgomery. Time—0:50.95.
200 Meter Freestyle—Bruce Furniss. Time—1:50.61.
400 Meter Freestyle—Brian Goodell. Time—3:53.08.
1,500 Meter Freestyle—Brian Goodell. Time—15:06.66.
100 Meter Backstroke—John Naber. Time—0:56.82.
200 Meter Backstroke—John Naber. Time—2:00.64.
100 Meter Breaststroke—John Hencken. Time—1:04.20.
200 Meter Breaststroke—John Hencken. Time—2:19.37.
100 Meter Butterfly—Joe Bottom. Time—0:54.07.
200 Meter Butterfly—Mike Brunner. Time—2:00.03.
400 Meter Individual Medley—Rod Strachan. Time—4:26.79.

Women

100 Meter Freestyle—Shirley Babashoff. Time—0:56.96.
200 Meter Freestyle—Shirley Babashoff. Time—2:00.69.
400 Meter Freestyle—Shirley Babashoff. Time—4:12.85.
800 Meter Freestyle—Shirley Babashoff. Time—8:39.63.
100 Meter Backstroke—Linda Jezek. Time—1:05.17.
200 Meter Backstroke—Maryanne Graham. Time—2:17.39.
100 Meter Breaststroke—Lauri Siering. Time—1:14.46.
200 Meter Breaststroke—Lauri Siering. Time—2:38.75.
100 Meter Butterfly—Camille Wright. Time—1:01.84.
200 Meter Butterfly—Karen Moe Thornton. Time—2:14.23.
400 Meter Individual Medley—Shirley Babashoff. Time—4:57.11.

James E. Sullivan Memorial Trophy Winners

The James E. Sullivan Memorial Trophy, named after the former president of the AAU and inaugurated in 1930, is awarded annually by the AAU to the athlete who "by his or her performance, example and influence as an amateur, has done the most during the year to advance the cause of sportsmanship."

Year	Winner	Sport	Year	Winner	Sport	Year	Winner	Sport
1930	Bobby Jones	Golf	1945	Doc Blanchard	Football	1961	Wilma Rudolph Ward	Track
1931	Barney Berlinger	Track	1946	Arnold Tucker	Football	1962	James Beatty	Track
1932	Jim Bausch	Track	1947	John Kelly Jr.	Rowing	1963	John Pennel	Track
1933	Glenn Cunningham	Track	1948	Robert Mathias	Track	1964	Don Schollander	Swimming
1934	Bill Bonthron	Track	1949	Dick Button	Skating	1965	Bill Bradley	Basketball
1935	Lawson Little	Golf	1950	Fred Wilt	Track	1966	Jim Ryun	Track
1936	Glenn Morris	Track	1951	Rev. Robert Richards	Track	1967	Randy Matson	Track
1937	Don Budge	Tennis	1952	Horace Ashenfelter	Track	1968	Debbie Meyer	Swimming
1938	Don Lash	Track	1953	Dr. Sammy Lee	Diving	1969	Bill Toomey	Track
1939	Joe Burk	Rowing	1954	Mal Whitfield	Track	1970	John Kinsella	Swimming
1940	Greg Rice	Track	1955	Harrison Dillard	Track	1971	Mark Spitz	Swimming
1941	Leslie Mac Mitchell	Track	1956	Patricia McCormick	Diving	1972	Frank Shorter	Track
1942	Cornelius Warmerdam	Track	1957	Bobby Joe Morrow	Track	1973	Bill Walton	Basketball
1943	Gilbert Dodds	Track	1958	Glenn Davis	Track	1974	Rick Wohlhuter	Track
1944	Ann Curtis	Swimming	1959	Parry O'Brien	Track	1975	Tim Shaw	Swimming
			1960	Rafer Johnson	Track			

Intercollegiate Rowing Association Regatta

Onondaga Lake, Syracuse, N.Y. (3 miles)

Year	Winner	Time	Year	Winner	Time	Year	Winner	Time
1956	Cornell	16:22.4	1963	Cornell	17:24.0	1970	Washington (A)	—
1957	Cornell	15:26.6	1964	California (A)	6:31.1	1971	Cornell (A)	6:06.0
1958	Cornell	17:12.1	1965	Navy	16:51.3	1972	Penn (A)	6:22.6
1959	Wisconsin	18:01.7	1966	Wisconsin	16:03.4	1973	Wisconsin (A)	6:21.0
1960	California	15:57.0	1967	Penn	16:15.9	1974	Wisconsin (A)	6:33.0
1961	California	16:49.2	1968	Penn (A)	6:15.6	1975	Wisconsin (A)	6:08.2
1962	Cornell	17:02.9	1969	Penn (A)	6:30.4	1976	California (A)	6:31.0

(A) Race at 2,000 meters.

World Track and Field Records

As of Aug. 7, 1976

*Indicates pending record: a number of new records await confirmation. The International Amateur Athletic Federation, the world body of track and field, announced July 27, 1976, a plan to overhaul the track and field record book. Eliminated are all records in yards except for the mile. Also eliminated are all hand-timed records for distances up to and including 400 meters. The records below meet the new standards except where noted. Records in yards and miles are included although they are no longer officially considered world records.

Men

Running

Event	Record	Holder	Country	Date	Where made
100 yds.	9.0 s.	Ivory Crockett	U.S.A.	May 11, 1974	Knoxville, Tenn.
		Houston McTear	U.S.A.	May 9, 1975	Winter Park, Fla.
220 yds.	19.5 s.	Tommie Smith	U.S.A.	May 7, 1966	San Jose, Cal.
220 yds.	*19.9 s (Turn)	Don Quarrie	Jamaica	June, 1975	Eugene, Ore.
		Steve Williams	U.S.A.	June, 1975	Eugene, Ore.
440 yds.	44.5 s	John Smith	U.S.A.	June 26, 1972	Eugene, Ore.
880 yds.	1 m., 44.1 s.	Rick Wohlhuter	U.S.A.	June 8, 1974	Eugene, Ore.
1 mile	3 m., 49.4 s.	John Walker	New Zealand	Aug. 12, 1975	Goteborg, Sweden
2 miles	8 m., 13.8 s.	Brendon Foster	Gt. Britain	Aug. 27, 1973	London
3 miles	12 m., 47.8 s.	Emiel Puttemans	Belgium	Sept. 20, 1972	Brussels
6 miles	26 m., 47.0 s.	Ron Clarke	Australia	July 14, 1965	Oslo
10 miles	45 m., 57.2 s.	Jos Hermens	Netherlands	Sept. 14, 1975	Netherlands
15 miles	1 hr., 11 min., 52.6 s.	Pekka Paivarinta	Finland	May 15, 1975	Oulu, Finland

Running — Metric Distances

Event	Record	Holder	Country	Date	Where made
100 meters	9.96 s.	Jim Hines	U.S.A.	Oct. 14, 1968	Mexico City
200 meters	19.8 s. (Turn)	Donald Quarrie	Jamaica	Aug. 3, 1971	Cali, Colombia
400 meters	43.9 s.	Lee Evans	U.S.A.	Oct. 18, 1968	Mexico City
800 meters	*1 m., 43.50 s.	Alberto Juantorena	Cuba	July, 1976	Montreal
1,000 meters	2 m., 13.9 s.	Rick Wohlhuter	U.S.A.	July 30, 1974	Oslo
1,500 meters	3 m., 32.2 s.	Filbert Bayi	Tanzania	Feb. 2, 1974	Christchurch, N.Z.
2,000 meters	*4 m., 51.4 s.	John Walker	New Zealand	July, 1976	Oslo
3,000 meters	7 m., 35.2 s.	Brendon Foster	Gt. Britain	Aug. 3, 1974	Gateshead, Eng.
5,000 meters	13 m., 13 s.	Emiel Puttemans	Belgium	Sept. 20, 1972	Brussels
10,000 meters	27 m., 30.8 s.	Dave Bedford	Gr. Britain	July 13, 1973	London
20,000 meters	57 m., 31.6 s.	Jos Hermens	Netherlands	Sept. 28, 1975	Netherlands
25,000 meters	1 hr., 14 m., 16.8 s.	Pekka Paivarinta	Finland	May 15, 1975	Oulu, Finland
30,000 meters	1 hr., 31 m., 30.4 s.	Jim Alder	Gr. Britain	Sept. 5, 1970	London
3,000 meter stpl.	*8 m., 08.2 s.	Anders Garderud	Sweden	July, 1976	Montreal

Hurdles

Event	Record	Holder	Country	Date	Where made
120 yards	13.0 s.	Rod Milburn	U.S.A.	June 25, 1971	Eugene, Ore.
		Rod Milburn	U.S.A.	June 20, 1973	Eugene, Ore.
220 yards	21.9 s.	Don Styron	U.S.A.	Apr. 2, 1960	Baton Rouge
440 yards	48.7 s.	Jim Bolding	U.S.A.	July 24, 1974	Turin, Italy
110 meters	13.2 s.	Rod Milburn	U.S.A.	Sept. 7, 1972	Munich
200 meters	21.9 s. (not ET)	Don Styron	U.S.A.	Apr. 2, 1960	Baton Rouge
200 meters	22.5 s. (not ET) (Turn)	Martin Lauer	W. Germany	July 7, 1959	Zurich
	(not ET)	Glen Davis	U.S.A.	Aug. 20, 1960	Berne
400 meters	*47.64 s.	Edwin Moses	U.S.A.	July, 1976	Montreal

Relay Races

Event	Record	Holder	Country	Date	Where made
440 yds. (4x110) (2 Turns)	38.6 s.	USC (McCullough, Kuller, Simpson, Miller)	U.S.A.	June 17, 1967	Provo, Utah
880 yds. (4x220)	1 m., 21.7 s.	Texas A&M. (Rogers, Woods, M. Mills, C. Mills)	U.S.A.	Apr. 24, 1970	Des Moines
1 mile (4x440)	*3 m., 02.4 s.	National Team (Ray, Taylor, Peoples, Vinson)	U.S.A.	July, 1975	Durham, N.C.
2 miles (4x880)	7 m., 10.4 s.	Chicago TC (Bach, Sparks, Paul, Wohlhuter)	U.S.A.	May 12, 1973	Durham, N.C.
4 miles (4x1) (mile)	16 m., 02.8 s.	Nat'l. Team	New Zealand	Feb. 3, 1972	Auckland, N.Z.

Relay Races—Metric Distances

Event	Record	Holder	Country	Date	Where made
400 mtrs.	38.2 s.	Nat'l. Team (Black, Taylor, Tinker, Hart)	U.S.A.	Sept. 10, 1972	Munich
800 mtrs. (4x200)	1 m., 21.5 s.	Nat'l. Team (Ossola, Abeti, Benedetti, Mennea)	Italy	July 21, 1972	Barletta
1,600 mtrs. (4x400)	2 m., 56.1 s.	Nat'l. Team (Matthews, Freeman, James, Evans)	U.S.A.	Oct. 20, 1968	Mexico City
3,200 mtrs. 4x800)	7 m., 08.6 s.	Nat'l. Team (Kinder, Adams, Bogatzki, Kemper)	W. Germany	Aug. 13, 1966	Wiesbaden

Field Events

High Jump	7 ft., 7 1/4 in.	Dwight Stones	U.S.A.	Aug. 4, 1976	Philadelphia
Long Jump	29 ft., 2¹/₂ in.	Bob Beamon	U.S.A.	Oct. 18, 1968	Mexico City
Triple Jump	58 ft., 8¹/₂ in.	Joad de Oliveira	Brazil	Oct. 15, 1975	Mexico City
Pole Vault	*18 ft., 8¹/₄ in.	Dave Roberts	U.S.A.	June, 1976	Eugene, Ore.
16 lb. shot put	*72 ft., 2¹/₄ in.	Alexander Baryshnikov	USSR	July, 1976	Paris
Discus throw	*232 ft., 6 in.	Mac Wilkins	U.S.A.	Apr. 1976	San Jose, Cal.
Javelin throw	*310 ft., 4 1/2 in.	Miklos Nemeth	Hungary	July, 1976	Montreal
16 lb. hammer throw	*260 ft., 2 in.	Walter Schmidt	W. Germany	Aug., 1975	Frankfurt
Decathlon	*8,618 pts.	Bruce Jenner	U.S.A.	July, 1976	Montreal

Walking

20 miles	2 h., 30 m., 38.6 s.	Gerhard Weidner	W. Germany	May 25, 1974	Hamburg
30 miles	3 h., 51 m., 48.6 s.	Gerhard Weidner	W. Germany	Apr. 8, 1973	Hamburg
16 mi., 1,270 yds.	2 hours	Bernd Kannenberg	W. Germany	May 11, 1974	Kassel, W. Germany
30 km.	2 h., 12 m., 58.0 s.	Bernd Kannenberg	W. Germany	May 11, 1974	Kassel, W. Germany
50 km.	4 hr., 00 m., 27.2 s.	Gerhard Weidner	W. Germany	Apr. 8, 1973	Hamburg

Women   Running

100 yards	10.0 s.	Chi Cheng	Taiwan	June 13, 1970	Portland, Ore.
220 yards	22.6 s.	Chi Cheng	Taiwan	July 3, 1970	Los Angeles
440 yards	52.2 s.	Kathy Hammond	U.S.A.	Aug. 12, 1972	Urbana, Ill.
		Debra Sapenter	U.S.A.	June 29, 1974	Bakersfield, Cal.
880 yards	2 m., 02.0 s.	Judy Pollock	Australia	July 5, 1967	Sweden
		Dixie Willis	Australia	Mar. 3, 1962	Perth, Aust.
1 mile	4 m., 28.5 s.	Francie Larrieu	U.S.A.	Mar., 1975	Richmond, Va.
100 meters	11.01	Annegret Richter	E. Germany	July, 1976	Montreal
200 meters	22.2 s.	Irena Szewinska	Poland	June 13, 1974	Potsdam
400 meters	*49.29 s.	Irena Szewinska	Poland	July, 1976	Montreal
800 meters	*1 m., 54.94 s.	Tatyana Kazankina	USSR	July, 1976	Montreal
500 meters	*3 m., 56 s.	Tatyana Kazankina	USSR	July, 1976	USSR
3000 meters	*8 m., 27.1 s.	Ludmila Bragina	USSR	Aug. 7, 1976	College Park, Md.

Hurdles

100 meters	12.6 s.	Annelie Ehrhardt	E. Germany	Sept. 8, 1972	Munich
400 meters	56.5 s.	Krystyna Kasperczik	Poland	June 13, 1974	W. Germany

Field Events

High jump	6 ft., 5 in.	Rosemarie Witschas	E. Germany	Sept. 8, 1974	Rome
Shot put	*71 ft., 9 in.	Ivanka Khristova	Bulgaria	July, 1976	Sofia
Long jump	*22 ft., 11¹/₄ in.	Sigrun Siegl	E. Germany	May, 1976	Dresden
Discus throw	*230 ft., 4 in.	Faina Melnik	USSR	Aug. 20, 1975	Zurich
Javelin	*226 ft., 9¹/₄ in.	Ruth Fuchs	E. Germany	July, 1976	Paris
Pentathlon	4,932 pts.	Burglinde Pollak	E. Germany	Sept 22, 1973	Bonn

Relay Races

400 mtrs. (4x100)	*42.5 s.	National Team	E. Germany	Sept. 8, 1974	Rome
800 mtrs. (4x200)	1 m., 33.8 s.	Nat'l. Team (Tranter, James, Simpson, Peal)	Gt. Britain	Aug. 24, 1968	London
880 yds. (4x220)	1 m., 35.8 s.	(Hoffman, Boyle, Kilborn, Lamy)	Australia	Nov. 9, 1969	Brisbane, Aust.
1,600 mtrs. (4x400)	3 m., 23.0 s.	Nat'l. Team	E. Germany	Sept. 10, 1972	Munich
1 mile (4x440)	*3 m., 30.3 s.	National Team (Krause, Jost, Weinstein, Barth)	W. Germany	July, 1975	Durham, N.C.

Evolution of the World Record for the One Mile Run

The table below shows how the world record for the one-mile has been lowered in the past 112 years.

Time	Individual	Year	Time	Individual	Year
4:56	Charles Lawes, Britain	1864	4:06.8	Glen Cunningham, U. S.	1934
4:36.5	Richard Webster, Britain	1865	4:06.4	Sydney Wooderson, Britain	1937
4:29	William Chinnery, Britain	1868	4:06.2	Gunder Haegg, Sweden	1942
4:28.8	W. C. Gibbs, Britain	1868	4:06.2	Arne Andersson, Sweden	1942
4:26	Walter Slade, Britain	1874	4:04.6	Gunder Haegg, Sweden	1942
4:24.5	Walter Slade, Britain	1875	4:02.6	Arne Andersson, Sweden	1943
4:23.2	Walter George, Britain	1880	4:01.6	Arne Andersson, Sweden	1944
4:21.4	Walter George, Britain	1882	4:01.4	Gunder Haegg, Sweden	1945
4:19.4	Walter George, Britain	1882	3:59.4	Roger Bannister, Britain	1954
4:18.4	Walter George, Britain	1884	3:58	John Landy, Australia	1954
4:18.2	Fred Bacon, Scotland	1894	3:57.2	Derek Ibbotson, Britain	1957
4:17	Fred Bacon, Scotland	1895	3:54.5	Herb Elliott, Australia	1958
4:15.6	Thomas Conneff, U. S.	1895	3:54.4	Peter Snell, New Zealand	1962
4:15.4	John Paul Jones, U. S.	1911	3:54.1	Peter Snell, New Zealand	1964
4:14.6	John Paul Jones, U. S.	1913	3:53.6	Michel Jazy, France	1965
4:12.6	Norman Taber, U. S.	1915	3:51.3	Jim Ryun, U. S.	1966
4:10.4	Paavo Nurmi, Finland	1923	3:51.1	Jim Ryun, U. S.	1967
4:09.2	Jules Ladoumegue, France	1931	3.51	Filbert Bayi, Tanzania	1975
4:07.6	Jack Lovelock, New Zealand	1933	3:49.4	John Walker, New Zealand	1975

Track and Field Events, 1976

69th Annual Millrose Games
New York, N. Y., Jan. 30, 1976

60 Yds.—Houston McTear, Northwest Florida TC. Time—0:05.9.
60 Yd. High Hurdles—Tom Hill, U. S. Army. Time—0:07.
500 Yds.—Willie Smith, Auburn Univ. Time—0:57.4.
600 Yds.—Fred Sowerby, D. C. Striders. Time—1:10.
880 Yds.—Rick Wohlhuter, Chicago TC. Time—1:52.
1,000 Yds.—Mike Boit, Eastern New Mexico. Time—2:07.4.
One Mile—Paul Cummings, Beverly Hills Striders. Time—3:57.6.

High Jump—Tom Woods, Pacific Coast Club. 7 ft. 4¹/₄ in.
Women's 60 Yds.—Alice Annum, D. C. Striders. Time—0:06.7.
Women's 600 Yds.—Sharon Dabney, Clippers TC. Time—1:23.8.
Women's 800 Yds.—Kathy Weston, Willis Spikettes. Time—2:10.1.
Women's 1,500 Yds.—Jan Merrill. Time—4:15.2.
Women's High Jump—Joni Huntley, Oregon State. 6 ft. 2¹/₂ in.

Toronto Star-Maple Leaf Indoor Games
Toronto, Ont., Feb. 13, 1976

Men
50 Yds.—Hasely Crawford, Philadelphia Pioneers.Time—0:05.1.
50 Yd. High Hurdles—Danny Smith, Bahamas.Time—0:06.
600 Yds.—Stan Vinson, Florida TC.Time—1:10.3.
1,000 Yds.—Rick Wohlhuter, Chicago TC.Time—2:08.1.
One Mile—Eamonn Coghlan, Villanova.Time—3:59.3.
3 Miles—John Ngeno, Washington State.Time—13:19.4.
Pole Vault—Wladyslaw Kozakiewicz, Poland.18 ft. 3¹/₂ in.
High Jump—Dwight Stones, Long Beach State.7 ft. 3 in.

Women
50 Yds.—Patty Loverock, B. C. International. Time—0:05.7.
50 Yd. High Hurdles—Sue Bradley, Univ. of Toronto TC. Time—0:06.6.
300 Meters—Marjorie Bailey, B. C. Internationals. Time—0:39.5.
1,500 Meters—Francie Larrieu, Pacific Coast Club. Time—4:18.5.
High Jump—Julie White, Etobicoke Striders. 6 ft. 1 in.

8th Annual U. S. Olympic Invitational
New York, N. Y., Feb. 20, 1976

Men
50 Meters—Cliff Outlin, Decatur AC. Time—0:05.6.
55 Meter Hurdles—Tom Hill, U. S. Army. Time—0:07.
400 Meters—Evis Jennings, Mississippi State. Time—0:48.2.
800 Meters—Orlando Greene, Seton Hall. Time—1:50.3.
1,500 Meters—Phil Kane, Villanova. Time—3:45.4.
1,500 Meter Walk—Todd Scully, Shore AC. Time—6:09.2.
3,000 Meters—Ron Martin, D. C. Striders, Time—7:59.6.

Pole Vault—Dan Ripley, Pacific Coast Club. 18 ft. 3³/₄ in.
High Jump—Dwight Stones, Long Beach State. 7 ft. 6¹/₄ in.
Women
50 Yds.—Mattline Hander, PAL. Time—0:06.3.
400 Meters—Debra Armstrong, Florida TC. Time—0:55.1.
1,500 Meters—Francie Larrieu, Pacific Coast Club. Time—4:20.1.

AAU Indoor Track and Field Championships
New York, N. Y., Feb. 27, 1976

Men
60 Yds.—Steve Williams, Florida TC. Time—0:06.
60 Yd. High Hurdles—Guy Drut, France. Time—0:07.
600 Yds.—Fred Sowerby, D. C. Striders. Time—1:09.8.
1,000 Yds.—Rick Wholhuter, Chicago TC. Time—2:09.3.
One Mile—Filbert Bayi, Tanzania. Time—3:56.1.
3 Miles—Suleiman Nyambui, Tanzania. Time—13:15.
2 Mile Walk—Ron Laird, New York AC. Time—13:37.
35 Lb. Weight Throw—Larry Hart, New York AC. 67 ft. 9¹/₂ in.
Triple Jump—Tommy Haynes, U. S. Army. 55 ft. 5¹/₂ in.
Long Jump—Larry Myricks, Mississippi Coll. 26 ft. ¹/₂ in.
Shot Put—Terry Albritton, Univ. of Hawaii. 65 ft. 6 in.
Pole Vault—Roland Carter, Gulf Coast TC. 18 ft. ¹/₄ in.
High Jump—Robert Forget, Canada. 7 ft. 3 in.
Team Champion—New York AC.

Women
60 Yds.—Lise Hopkins, Chicago Murcherettes.Time—0:06.7.
60 Yd. Hurdles—Debby Laplante, Belleville, Mich.Time—0:07.7.
220 Yds.—Pamela Jiles, New Orleans Superdames.Time—0:24.
440 Yds.—Lorne Forde, Atorns TC.Time—0:54.6.
880 Yds.—Johanna Forman, Falmouth TC.Time—2:07.9.
One Mile—Jan Merrill. Age Group AA.Time—4:38.5.
2 Miles—Jan Merrill, Age Group AA.Time—9:59.6.
One Mile Walk—Susan Bradock, Rialto Road Runners.Time—7:12.7.
Shot Put—Ann Turbyne, Winslow, Me.51 ft. 5¹/₄ in.
Long Jump—Martha Watson, Lakewood International.20 ft. 9¹/₂ in.
High Jump—Julie White, Canada.6 ft. 1 in.
Team Champion—Atoms TC.

12th Annual NCAA Indoor Track and Field Championships
Detroit, Mich., March 13, 1976. Sponsored by the Detroit News

60 Yds.—Harvey Glance, Auburn. Time—0:06.21.
60 Yd. High Hurdles—Allen Misher, Louisville State. Time—0:07.29.
600 Yds.—Charles Dramiga, New Mexico. Time—1:10.58.
1,000 Yds.—Mark Belger, Villanova. Time—2:07.29.
One Mile—Eamonn Coghlan, Villanova. Time—4:01.48.
2 Miles—Nick Rose, Western Kentucky. Time—8:30.91.

One Mile Relay—Tennessee. Time—3:16.03.
2 Mile Relay—Wisconsin. Time—7:26.79.
Medley Relay—Texas, El Paso. Time—9:43.16.
High Jump—Dwight Stones, Long Beach State. 7 ft. 3 in.
Pole Vault—Earl Bell, Arkansas State. 18 ft. ¹/₄ in.
Team Champion—Texas, El Paso.

55th Annual NCAA Outdoor Track and Field Championships
Philadelphia, Pa., June 3-5, 1976

100 Meters—Harvey Glance, Auburn. Time—0:10.16.
200 Meters—Harvey Glance. Time—0:20.74.
400 Meters—Ken Randle, South Cal. Time—0:45.2.
800 Meters—Tom McLean, Bucknell. Time—1:47.36.
1,500 Meters—Eamon Coghlan, Villanova. Time—3:37.01.
5,000 Meters—Josh Kimeto, Washington State. Time—13:47.84.
400 Meter Intermediate Hurdles—Quentin Wheeler, San Diego St. Time—0:48.55.
3,000 Meter Steeplechase—James Munyala, Texas at El

Paso. Time—8:24.86.
400 Meter Relay—Tennessee. Time—0:39.16.
1,600 Meter Relay—Arizona State. Time—3:03.49.
Javelin—Phil Olsen, Tennessee. 273 ft. 2 in.
Pole Vault—Earl Bell, Arkansas St. 18 ft. 1¹/₄ in.
Discus—Borys Chambul, Washington. 202 ft. 3 in.
High Jump—Dwight Stones, Long Beach St. 7 ft. 7 in.
Triple Jump—Phil Robins, Southern Illinois. 54 ft. 7¹/₄ in.
Team Champion—Southern Cal., 64 pts.

National Interscholastic Outdoor Track and Field Records

Source: National Federation of State High School Associations. Records approved to June, 1975.

Event	Record	Holder	School	Site and year
100 yds.	0:09.0	Houston McTear	Baker H.S. Baker, Fla.	Winter Park, Fla., 1976
220 yds. (straightaway)	0:20.2	Forrest Beaty	Herbert Hoover H.S. Glendale, Cal.	Chaffey, Cal., 1961
220 yds. (full Curve)	0:20.5	Dwayne E. Evans	So. Mountain H.S. Phoenix, Ariz.	Glendale, Ariz., 1976
440 yds.	0:45.8	Ronald E. Ray	Ferguson H.S. Newport News, Va.	Charlottesville, Va., 1972
880 yds.	1:48.8	Richard J. Joyce	Sierra H.S. Whittier, Cal.	Bakersfield, Cal., 1965
1 mile	3:58.3	James Ryun	Wichita East H.S., Wichita, Kan.	Wichita, Kan., 1965
2 mile	8:41.5	Steve Prefontaine	Marshfield H.S. Coos Bay, Ore.	Corvallis, Ore., 1969
120 yd. high hurdles	0:13.2	Michael Robertson	Winter Pk. H.S. Winter Pk., Fla.	Winter Pk., Fla., 1975
		Dedy Cooper	Ells H.S. Richmond, Cal.	San Diego, Cal., 1975
		Gregory Foster	Proviso E. H.S. Maywood, Ill.	Charleston, Ill., 1976
180 yd. low hurdles	0:18.1	Donald Castronovo	Oceanside H.S. Oceanside, N.Y.	Ithaca, N.Y., 1964
		Earl McCullouch	Polytechnic H.S. Long Beach, Cal.	Norwalk, Cal., 1964
High Jump	7 ft. 1³/₄ in.	Mark Wilson	Monte Vista H.S. Danville, Cal.	Fresno, Cal., 1974
Long jump	25 ft. 9¹/₂ in.	Gerald Hardeman	Edison H.S., Fresno, Cal.	Porterville, Cal., 1972
Pole Vault	16 ft. 7 in.	Casey Carringan	Orting H.S. Orting, Wash.	Bellingham, Wash., 1969
		Robert Pullard	Los Angeles H.S., Los Angeles, Cal.	Los Angeles, Cal., 1969
Triple jump	52 ft. 6¹/₄ in.	David Tucker	San Joaquin Mem. H.S. Fresno, Cal.	Bakersfield, Cal., 1970
Shot put (12 lbs.)	72 ft. 3¹/₄ in.	Sam Walker	W. W. Samuell H.S., Dallas, Tex.	Corpus Christi, Tex., 1968
Discus	201 ft. 3 in.	Christopher James Adams	Los Altos H.S., Los Altos, Cal.	Berkeley, Cal., 1970
Javelin	254 ft. 11 in.	Russell Francis	Pleasant Hill H.S. Pleasant Hill, Ore.	Pleasant Hill, Ore., 1971
440 yd. relay	0:40.2	Delley, G. Pouncy, J. Pouncy, Shaw	Lincoln H.S, Dallas, Texas.	Austin, Texas, 1970
880 yd. relay	1:25.4	Jackson, James, Reed, Hill	White Plains (N.Y.) H.S.	Jamaica, N.Y., 1966
1 mile relay	3:11.8	Bouche, Bradley, Brents, Morton	Memorial H.S., Houston, Texas.	Baytown, Texas, 1967
		Anderson, Black, Thompkins, Thompson	Killian H.S. Miami, Fla.	Gainesville, Fla., 1969
2 mile relay	7:41.9	Mentz, Jakosa, Bowman, Grant	Proviso West H.S., Hillside, Ill.	Glen Ellyn, Ill., 1965
Sprint Medley Relay (1 mile)	3:23.3	Corson, Brake, Brents, Morton	Memorial H.S., Houston, Texas.	Houston, Texas, 1967

Table Tennis Championships in 1976

46th U.S. National Open Championship

Philadelphia, Pa., June 10-13, 1976

Men's Singles — Dragutin Surbek, Yugoslavia.
Women's Singles — Kim Soon Ok, South Korea.
Men's Doubles — Milivot Karakasevic & Dragutin Surbek, Yugoslavia.
Women's Doubles — Kim Soon Ok & Son Hye Soon, South Korea.
Mixed Doubles — Desmond Douglas & Jill Mammersley, England.
Senior Men — Houshang Bororgzadeh, Independence, Iowa.

Senior Women — Leah Neuberger, New York, N.Y.
Senior Doubles — George Rocker & Bill Sharpe, Philadelphia, Pa.
Esquire — Frank Dwelly, Natick, Mass.
Veterans — Oliver Nicholas, Apache Junction, Ariz.
Boys Under 17 — Dean Galardi, Torrance, Cal.
Girls Under 17 — Biruta Plucas, Toronto, Ont.
Men's Team — Yugoslavia.
Women's Team — South Korea.

Curling Champions

World Champions

Year	Country & Skip	Year	Country & Skip	Year	Country & Skip
1965	United States (Bud Somerville)	1969	Canada (Ron Northcott)	1973	Sweden (Kjell Oscarius)
1966	Canada (Ron Northcott)	1970	Canada (Don Duguid)	1974	United States (Bud Somerville)
1967	Scotland (Chuck Hay)	1971	Canada (Don Duguid)	1975	Switzerland
1968	Canada (Ron Northcott)	1972	Canada (Orest Melesnuk)	1976	United States (Bruce Roberts)

U.S. National Champions

Year	State & Skip	Year	State & Skip	Year	State & Skip
1965	Wisconsin (Bud Somerville)	1973	Massachusetts (Barry Blanchard)	1969	Wisconsin (Bud Somerville)
1966	North Dakota (Joe Zbacnik)	1974	Wisconsin (Bud Somerville)	1970	North Dakota (Art Tallackson)
1967	Washington (Bruce Roberts)	1975	Washington (Ed Risling)	1971	North Dakota (Dale Dalziel)
1968	Wisconsin (Bud Somerville)	1976	Minnesota (Bruce Roberts)	1972	North Dakota (Bob LaBonte)

Annual Results of Major Bowl Games

Rose Bowl, Pasadena

1902—Michigan 49, Stanford 0
1916—Wash. State 14, Brown 0
1917—Oregon 14, Pennsylvania 0
1918-19—Service Teams
1920—Harvard 7, Oregon 6
1921—California 28, Ohio State 0
1922—Wash. & Jeff. 0, California 0
1923—So. California 14, Penn State 3
1924—Navy 14, Washington 14
1925—Notre Dame 27, Stanford 10
1926—Alabama 20, Washington 19
1927—Alabama 7, Stanford 7
1928—Stanford 7, Pittsburgh 6
1929—Georgia Tech 8, California 7
1930—So. California 47, Pittsburgh 14
1931—Alabama 24, Wash. State 0
1932—So. California 21, Tulane 12
1933—So. California 35, Pittsburgh 0
1934—Columbia 7, Stanford 0
1935—Alabama 29, Stanford 13
1936—Stanford 7, So. Methodist 0

1937—Pittsburgh 21, Washington 0
1938—California 13, Alabama 0
1939—So. California 7, Duke 3
1940—So. California 14, Tennessee 0
1941—Stanford 21, Nebraska 13
1942—Oregon St. 20, Duke 16
(at Durham)
1943—Georgia 9, UCLA 0
1944—So. California 29, Washington 0
1945—So. California 25, Tennessee 0
1946—Alabama 34, So. California 14
1947—Illinois 45, UCLA 14
1948—Michigan 49, So. California 0
1949—Northwestern 20, California 14
1950—Ohio State 17, California 6
1951—Michigan 14, California 6
1952—Illinois 40, Stanford 7
1953—So. California 7, Wisconsin 0
1954—Mich. State 28, UCLA 20
1955—Ohio State 20, So. California 7
1956—Mich. State 17, UCLA 14

1957—Iowa 35, Oregon St. 19
1958—Ohio State 10, Oregon 7
1959—Iowa 38, California 12
1960—Washington 44, Wisconsin 8
1961—Washington 17, Minnesota 7
1962—Minnesota 21, UCLA 3
1963—So. California 42, Wisconsin 37
1964—Illinois 17, Washington 7
1965—Michigan 34, Oregon St. 7
1966—UCLA 14, Mich. State 12
1967—Purdue 14, So. California 13
1968—Southern Cal. 14, Indiana 3
1969—Ohio State 27, Southern Cal 16
1970—Southern Cal 10, Michigan 3
1971—Stanford 27, Ohio State 17
1972—Stanford 13, Michigan 12
1973—So. California 42, Ohio State 17
1974—Ohio State 42, So. California 17
1975—So. California 18, Ohio State 17
1976—UCLA 23, Ohio State 10

Orange Bowl, Miami

1933—Miami (Fla.) 7, Manhattan 0
1934—Duquesne 33, Miami (Fla.) 7
1935—Bucknell 26, Miami (Fla.) 0
1936—Catholic U. 20, Mississippi 19
1937—Duquesne 13, Miss. State 12
1938—Auburn 6, Mich. State 0
1939—Tennessee 17, Oklahoma 0
1940—Georgia Tech 21, Missouri 7
1941—Miss. State 14, Georgetown 7
1942—Georgia 40, TCU 26
1943—Alabama 37, Boston Col. 21
1944—LSU 19, Texas A&M 14
1945—Tulsa 26, Georgia Tech 12
1946—Miami (Fla.) 13, Holy Cross 6
1947—Rice 8, Tennessee 0

1948—Georgia Tech 20, Kansas 14
1949—Texas 41, Georgia 28
1950—Santa Clara 21, Kentucky 13
1951—Clemson 15, Miami (Fla.) 14
1952—Georgia Tech 17, Baylor 14
1953—Alabama 61, Syracuse 6
1954—Oklahoma 7, Maryland 0
1955—Duke 34, Nebraska 7
1956—Oklahoma 20, Maryland 6
1957—Colorado 27, Clemson 21
1958—Oklahoma 48, Duke 21
1959—Oklahoma 21, Syracuse 6
1960—Georgia 14, Missouri 0
1961—Missouri 21, Navy 14
1962—LSU 25, Colorado 7

1963—Alabama 17, Oklahoma 0
1964—Nebraska 13, Auburn 7
1965—Texas 21, Alabama 17
1966—Alabama 39, Nebraska 28
1967—Florida 27, Georgia Tech 12
1968—Oklahoma 26, Tennessee 24
1969—Penn State 15, Kansas 14
1970—Penn State 10, Missouri 3
1971—Nebraska 17, Louisiana St. 12
1972—Nebraska 38, Alabama 6
1973—Nebraska 40, Notre Dame 6
1974—Penn State 16, Louisiana St. 9
1975—Notre Dame 13, Alabama 11
1976—Oklahoma 14, Michigan 6

Sugar Bowl, New Orleans

1935—Tulane 20, Temple 14
1936—TCU, 3, LSU 2
1937—Santa Clara 21, LSU 14
1938—Santa Clara 6, LSU 0
1939—TCU 15, Carnegie Tech 7
1940—Texas A&M 14, Tulane 13
1941—Boston Col. 19, Tennessee 13
1942—Fordham 2, Missouri 0
1943—Tennessee 14, Tulsa 7
1944—Georgia Tech 20, Tulsa 18
1945—Duke 29, Alabama 26
1946—Oklahoma A&M 33, St. Mary's 13
1947—Georgia 20, No. Carolina 10
1948—Texas 27, Alabama 7
1949—Oklahoma 14, No. Carolina 6

1950—Oklahoma 35, LSU 0
1951—Kentucky 13, Oklahoma 7
1952—Maryland 28, Tennessee 13
1953—Georgia Tech. 24, Mississippi 7
1954—Georgia Tech 42, West Virginia 19
1955—Navy 21, Mississippi 0
1956—Georgia Tech 7, Pittsburgh 0
1957—Baylor 13, Tennessee 7
1958—Mississippi 39, Texas 7
1959—LSU 7, Clemson 0
1960—Mississippi 21, LSU 0
1961—Mississippi 14, Rice 6
1962—Alabama 10, Arkansas 3
1963—Mississippi 17, Arkansas 13

1964—Alabama 12, Mississippi 7
1965—LSU 13, Syracuse 10
1966—Missouri 20, Florida 18
1967—Alabama 34, Nebraska 7
1968—LSU 20, Wyoming 13
1969—Arkansas 16, Georgia 2
1970—Mississippi 27, Arkansas 22
1971—Tennessee 34, Air Force 13
1972—Oklahoma 40, Auburn 22
*1972 (Dec.)—Oklahoma 14, Penn State 0
1973—Notre Dame 24, Alabama 23
1974—Nebraska 13, Florida 10
1975—Alabama 13, Penn State 6
*Penn St. awarded game by forfeit

Cotton Bowl, Dallas

1937—TCU 16, Marquette 6
1938—Rice 28, Colorado 14
1939—St. Mary's 20, Texas Tech 13
1940—Clemson 6, Boston Col. 3
1941—Texas A&M 13, Fordham 12
1942—Alabama 29, Texas A&M 21
1943—Texas 14, Georgia Tech 7
1944—Randolph Field 7, Texas 7
1945—Oklahoma A&M 34, TCU 0
1946—Texas 40, Missouri 27
1947—Arkansas 0, LSU 0
1948—So. Methodist 13, Penn State 13
1949—So. Methodist 21, Oregon 13
1950—Rice 27, No. Carolina 13

1951—Tennessee 20, Texas 14
1952—Kentucky 20, TCU 7
1953—Texas 16, Tennessee 0
1954—Rice 28, Alabama 6
1955—Georgia Tech 14, Arkansas 6
1956—Mississippi 14, TCU 13
1957—TCU 28, Syracuse 27
1958—Navy 20, Rice 7
1959—TCU 0, Air Force 0
1960—Syracuse 23, Texas 14
1961—Duke 7, Arkansas 6
1962—Texas 12, Mississippi 7
1963—LSU 13, Texas 0

1964—Texas 28, Navy 6
1965—Arkansas 10, Nebraska 7
1966—LSU 14, Arkansas 7
1967—Georgia 24, So. Methodist 9
1968—Texas A&M 20, Alabama 16
1969—Texas 36, Tennessee 13
1970—Texas 21, Notre Dame 17
1971—Notre Dame 24, Texas 11
1972—Penn State 30, Texas 6
1973—Texas 17, Alabama 13
1974—Nebraska 19, Texas 3
1975—Penn State 41, Baylor 20
1976—Arkansas 31, Georgia 10

Liberty Bowl, Memphis

1959—Penn State 7, Alabama 0
1960—Penn State 41, Oregon 12
1961—Syracuse 15, Miami 14
1962—Oregon 6, Villanova 0
1963—Miss. State 16, N. C. State 12
1964—Utah 32, West Virginia 6

1965—Mississippi 13, Auburn 7 ʼ
1966—Miami (Fla.) 14, Va. Tech 7
1967—N. C. State 14, Georgia 7
1968—Mississippi 34, Va. Tech 17
1969—Colorado 47, Alabama 33
1970—Tulane 17, Colorado 3

1971—Tennessee 14, Arkansas 13
1972—Georgia Tech 31, Iowa State 30
1973—No. Carolina St. 31, Kansas 18
1974—Tennessee 7, Maryland 3
1975—USC 20, Texas A&M 0

Sun Bowl, El Paso

1936—Hardin Simmons 14, New Mex. St. 14
1937—Hardin-Simmons 34, Texas Mines 6
1938—West Virginia 7, Texas Tech 6
1939—Utah 26, New Mexico 0
1940—Catholic U. 0, Arizona St. 0
1941—Western Reserve 26, Arizona St. 13
1942—Tulsa 6, Texas Tech 0
1943—20 Air Force 13, Hardin-Simmons 7
1944—Southwestern (Tex.) 7, New Mexico 0
1945—Southwestern (Tex.) 35, U. of Mex. 0
1946—New Mexico 34, Denver 24
1947—Cincinnati 38, Virginia Tech 6
1948—Miami (O.) 13, Texas Tech 12

1949—West Virginia 21, Texas Mines 12
1950—Texas Western 33, Georgetown 20
1951—West Texas St. 14, Cincinnati 13
1952—Texas Tech 25, Col. Pacific 14
1953—Col. Pacific 26, Miss. Southern 7
1954—Texas Western 37, Miss. Southern 14
1955—Texas Western 47, Florida St. 20
1956—Wyoming 21, Texas Tech 14
1957—Geo. Washington 13, Tex. Western 0
1958—Louisville 34, Drake 20
1959—Wyoming 14, Hardin-Simmons 6
1960—New Mexico St. 28, No. Texas St. 8
1961—New Mexico St. 20, Utah State 13
1962—Villanova 17, Wichita 9

1963—West Texas St. 15, Ohio U. 14
1964—Oregon 21, So. Methodist 14
1965—Georgia 7, Texas Tech 0
1966—Texas Western 13, TCU 12
1967—Wyoming 28, Florida St. 20
1968—UTex El Paso 14, Mississippi 7
1969—Auburn 34, Arizona 10
1969—(Dec. 20) Nebraska 45, Georgia 6
1970—Georgia Tech. 17, Texas Tech. 9
1971—LSU 33, Iowa State 15
1972—North Carolina 32, Texas Tech 28
1973—Missouri 34, Auburn 17
1974—Mississippi St. 26, North Carolina 24
1975—Pittsburgh 33, Kansas 19

Gator Bowl, Jacksonville

1946—Wake Forest 26, So. Carolina 14
1947—Oklahoma 34, N.C. State 13
1948—Maryland 20, Georgia 20
1949—Clemson 24, Missouri 23
1950—Maryland 20, Missouri 7
1951—Wyoming 20, Wash. & Lee 7
1952—Miami (Fla.) 14, Clemson 0
1953—Florida 14, Tulsa 13
1954—Texas Tech 35, Auburn 13
1955—Auburn 33, Baylor 13
1956—Vanderbilt 25, Auburn 13

1957—Georgia Tech 21, Pittsburgh 14
1958—Tennessee 3, Texas A&M 0
1959—Mississippi 7, Florida 3
1960—Arkansas 14, Georgia Tech 7
1961—Florida 13, Baylor 12
1962—Penn State 30, Georgia Tech 15
1963—Florida 17, Penn State 7
1964—No. Carolina 35, Air Force 0
1965—Florida St. 36, Oklahoma 19
1966—Georgia Tech 31, Texas Tech 21

1967—Tennessee 18, Syracuse 12
1968—Penn State 17, Florida St. 17
1969—Missouri 35, Alabama 10
1969—(Dec. 27) Florida 14, Tenn. 13
1971—Auburn 35, Mississippi 28
1972—Georgia 7, N. Carolina 3
1973—Auburn 24, Colorado 3
1973—(Dec.) Tex. Tech. 28, Tenn. 19
1974—Auburn 27, Texas 3
1975—Maryland 13, Florida 0

Bluebonnet Bowl, Houston

1959—Clemson 23, TCU 7
1960—Texas 3, Alabama 3
1961—Kansas 33, Rice 7
1962—Missouri 14, Georgia Tech 10
1963—Baylor 14, LSU 7
1964—Tulsa 14, Mississippi 7

1965—Tennessee 27, Tulsa 6
1966—Texas 19, Mississippi 0
1967—Colorado 31, Miami (Fla.) 21
1968—SMU 28, Oklahoma 27
1969—Houston 36, Auburn 7
1970—Oklahoma 24, Alabama 24

1971—Colorado 29, Houston 17
1972—Tennessee 24, Louisiana St. 17
1973—Houston 47, Tulane 7
1974—N. Carolina St. 31, Houston 31
1975—Texas 38, Colorado 21

Peach Bowl, Atlanta

1968—LSU 31, Florida St. 27
1969—West Virginia 14, S. Carolina 3
1970—Arizona St. 48, N. Carolina 26

1971—Mississippi 41, Georgia Tech. 18
1972—N. Carolina St. 49, W. Va. 13
1973—Georgia 17, Maryland 16

1974—Vanderbilt 6, Texas Tech. 6
1975—West Virginia 13, No. Carolina St. 10

Tangerine Bowl, Orlando

1968—Richmond 49, Ohio 42
1969—Toledo 56, Davidson 33
1970—Toledo 40, William & Mary 12

1971—Toledo 28, Richmond 3
1972—Tampa 21, Kent State 18
1973—Miami, Ohio 16, Florida 7

1974—Miami, Ohio 21, Georgia 10
1975—Miami, Ohio 20, South Carolina 7

Fiesta Bowl, Phoenix

1971—Arizona St. 45, Florida St. 38
1972—Arizona St. 49, Missouri 35

1973—Arizona St. 28, Pittsburgh 7
1974—Okla. St. 16, Brigham Young 6

1975—Arizona St. 17, Nebraska 14

Heisman Trophy Winners

The Heisman Trophy is named after John Heisman, football coach and athletic director of the New York Downtown Athletic Club. Awarded annually to the nation's outstanding college football player.

1935	Jay Berwanger, Chicago, HB
1936	Larry Kelley, Yale, E
1937	Clinton Frank, Yale, QB
1938	David O'Brien, Tex. Christian, QB
1939	Nile Kinnick, Iowa, QB
1940	Tom Harmon, Michigan, HB
1941	Bruce Smith, Minnesota, HB
1942	Frank Sinkwich, Georgia, HB
1943	Angelo Bertelli, Notre Dame, QB
1944	Leslie Horvath, Ohio State, QB
1945	Felix Blanchard, Army, FB
1946	Glenn Davis, Army, HB
1947	John Lujack, Notre Dame, QB
1948	Doak Walker, SMU, HB

1949	Leon Hart, Notre Dame, E
1950	Vic Janowicz, Ohio State, NB
1951	Richard Kazmaier, Princeton, HB
1952	Billy Vessels, Oklahoma, HB
1953	John Lattner, Notre Dame, HB
1954	Alan Ameche, Wisconsin, FB
1955	Howard Cassady, Ohio St., HB
1956	Paul Hornung, Notre Dame, QB
1957	John Crow, Texas A & M, HB
1958	Pete Dawkins, Army, HB
1959	Billy Cannon, La. State, NB
1960	Joe Bellino, Navy, HB
1961	Ernest Davis, Syracuse, HB
1962	Terry Baker, Oregon State, QB

1963	Roger Staubach, Navy, QB
1964	John Huarte, Notre Dame, QB
1965	Mike Garrett, USC, HB
1966	Steve Spurrier, Florida, QB
1967	Gary Beban, UCLA, QB
1968	O. J. Simpson, USC, RB
1969	Steve Owens, Oklahoma, RB
1970	Jim Plunkett, Stanford, QB
1971	Pat Sullivan, Auburn, QB
1972	Johnny Rodgers, Nebraska, RB-R
1973	John Cappelletti, Penn State, RB
1974	Archie Griffin, Ohio State, RB
1975	Archie Griffin, Ohio State, RB

Outland Awards

Honoring the outstanding interior lineman selected by the Football Writers' Association of America.

1946	George Connor, Notre Dame, T
1947	Joe Steffy, Army, G
1948	Bill Fischer, Notre Dame, G
1949	Ed Bagdon, Michigan St., G
1950	Bob Gain, Kentucky, T
1951	Jim Weatherall, Oklahoma, T
1952	Dick Modzelewski, Maryland, T
1953	J. D. Roberts, Oklahoma, G
1954	Bill Brooks, Arkansas, G
1955	Calvin Jones, Iowa, G

1956	Jim Parker, Ohio State, G
1957	Alex Karras, Iowa, T
1958	Zeke Smith, Auburn, G
1959	Mike McGee, Duke, T
1960	Tom Brown, Minnesota, G
1961	Merlin Olsen, Utah State, T
1962	Bobby Bell, Minnesota, T
1963	Scott Appleton, Texas, T
1964	Steve Delong, Tennessee, T
1965	Tommy Nobis, Texas, G

1966	Loyd Phillips, Arkansas, T
1967	Ron Yary, Southern Cal, T
1968	Bill Stanfill, Georgia, T
1969	Mike Reid, Penn State, DT
1970	Jim Stillwagon, Ohio State, LB
1971	Larry Jacobson, Nebraska, DT
1972	Rich Glover, Nebraska, MG
1973	John Hicks, Ohio State, G
1974	Randy White, Maryland, DE
1975	Leroy Selmon, Oklahoma, DT

College Football Conference Champions

Atlantic Coast
1962—Duke
1963—No. Carolina St., No. Carolina
1964—No. Carolina St.
1965—Duke
1966—Clemson
1967—Clemson
1968—No. Carolina St.
1969—So. Carolina
1970—Wake Forest
1971—North Carolina
1972—North Carolina
1973—No. Carolina St.
1974—Maryland
1975—Maryland

Ivy League
1962—Dartmouth
1963—Dartmouth, Princeton

1964—Princeton
1965—Dartmouth
1966—Dartmouth, Harvard, Princeton
1967—Yale
1968—Yale, Harvard
1969—Princeton, Dartmouth, Yale
1970—Dartmouth
1971—Dartmouth, Cornell
1973—Dartmouth
1974—Yale, Harvard
1975—Harvard

Big Eight
1962—Oklahoma
1963—Nebraska

1964—Nebraska
1965—Nebraska
1966—Nebraska
1967—Oklahoma
1968—Kansas, Oklahoma
1969—Missouri, Nebraska
1970—Nebraska
1971—Nebraska
1972—Nebraska
1973—Oklahoma
1974—Oklahoma
1975—Oklahoma, Nebraska

Big Ten
1962—Wisconsin
1963—Illinois

1964—Michigan
1965—Michigan St.
1966—Michigan St.
1967—Indiana, Purdue, Minn.
1968—Ohio State
1969—Michigan, Ohio State
1970—Ohio State
1971—Michigan
1972—Ohio State, Michigan
1973—Ohio State, Michigan
1974—Ohio State, Michigan
1975—Ohio State

Mid-America
1962—Bowling Green
1963—Ohio Univ.
1964—Bowling Green
1965—Bowling Green, Miami
1966—Miami, Western Mich.
1967—Toledo, Ohio Univ.
1968—Ohio Univ.
1969—Toledo
1970—Toledo
1971—Toledo
1972—Kent State
1973—Miami
1974—Miami
1975—Miami

Missouri Valley
1962—Tulsa
1963—Cincinnati, Wichita
1964—Cincinnati
1965—Tulsa
1966—No. Texas, Tulsa
1967—North Texas
1968—Memphis State
1969—Memphis State
1970—Louisville
1971—Memphis State
1972—Louisville, W. Texas, Drake
1973—No. Texas St., Tulsa
1974—Tulsa
1975—Tulsa

Southeastern
1962—Mississippi
1963—Mississippi
1964—Alabama
1965—Alabama
1966—Alabama, Georgia
1967—Tennessee
1968—Georgia
1969—Tennessee
1970—Louisiana State
1971—Alabama
1972—Alabama
1973—Alabama
1974—Alabama
1975—Alabama

Southwest
1962—Texas
1963—Texas
1964—Arkansas
1965—Arkansas
1966—Southern Methodist
1967—Texas A & M
1968—Texas, Arkansas
1969—Texas
1970—Texas
1971—Texas
1972—Texas
1973—Texas
1974—Baylor
1975—Texas A&M, Arkansas, Texas

Pacific Eight
1962—USC
1963—Washington
1964—Oregon St., USC
1965—UCLA
1966—USC
1967—USC
1968—USC
1969—USC
1970—Stanford
1971—Stanford
1972—USC
1973—USC
1974—USC
1975—UCLA, Cal.

Southern
1962—VMI
1963—Virginia Tech
1964—West Virginia
1965—West Virginia
1966—E. Carolina, William & Mary
1967—West Virginia
1968—Richmond
1969—Richmond, Davidson
1970—William & Mary
1971—Richmond
1972—East Carolina
1973—East Carolina
1974—VMI
1975—Richmond

Western Athletic
1962—New Mexico
1963—New Mexico
1964—New Mexico, Arizona, Utah
1965—Brigham Young
1966—Wyoming
1967—Wyoming
1968—Wyoming
1969—Arizona State
1970—Arizona State
1971—Arizona State
1972—Arizona State
1973—Arizona State, Arizona
1974—Brigham Young
1975—Arizona State

Pacific Coast
1969—San Diego State
1970—Long Beach State
1971—Long Beach State
1972—San Diego State
1973—San Diego State
1974—San Diego State
1975—San Diego State

College Football Teams

Division I

Team	Nickname	Team Colors	Conference	Coach	1975 Record (W-L-T)
Air Force	Falcons	Blue & Silver	Independent	Ben Martin	2-8-1
Alabama	Crimson Tide	Crimson & White	Southeastern	Paul Bryant	11-1-0
Appalachian State	Mountaineers	Black & Gold	Southern	Jim Brakefield	8-3-0
Arizona State	Sun Devils	Maroon & Gold	Western Athletic	Frank Kush	12-0-0
Arizona	Wildcats	Red & Blue	Western Athletic	Jim Young	9-2-0
Arkansas	Razorbacks	Cardinal & White	Southwest	Frank Broyles	10-2-0
Arkansas State	Indians	Scarlet & Black	Southland	Bill Davidson	11-0-0
Army	Cadets	Black, Gold, Gray	Independent	Homer Smith	2-9-0
Auburn	Tigers	Orange & Blue	Southeastern	Doug Barfield	3-6-2
Ball State	Cardinals	Cardinal & White	Mid-American	Dave McClain	9-2-0
Baylor	Bears	Green & Gold	Southwest	Grant Teaff	3-6-2
Boston College	Eagles	Maroon & Gold	Independent	Joseph Yukica	7-4-0
Bowling Green	Falcons	Orange & Brown	Mid-American	Don Nehlen	8-3-0
Brigham Young	Cougars	Royal Blue & White	Western Athletic	LaVell Edwards	6-5-0
Brown	Bruins	Brown & Cardinal	Ivy	John Anderson	6-2-1
California	Golden Bears	Blue & Gold	Pacific-8	Mike White	8-3-0
Central Michigan	Chippewas	Maroon & Gold	Mid-American	Roy Kramer	8-2-1
Cincinnati	Bearcats	Red & Black	Independent	Tommy Mason	6-5-0
Citadel	Bulldogs	Blue & White	Southern	Bobby Ross	6-5-0
Clemson	Tigers	Purple & Orange	Atlantic Coast	Jim Parker	2-9-0
Colgate	Red Raiders	Maroon	Independent	Fred Dunlap	6-4-0
Colorado State	Rams	Green & Gold	Western Athletic	Sarkis Arslanian	6-5-0
Colorado	Buffaloes	Silver & Gold	Big Eight	Bill Mallory	9-3-0
Columbia	Lions	Blue & White	Ivy	Bill Campbell	2-7-0
Cornell	Big Red	Carnelian & White	Ivy	George Seifert	1-8-0
Dartmouth	Big Green	Dartmouth Green	Ivy	Jake Crouthamel	5-3-1
Davidson	Wildcats	Red & Black	Southern	Ed Farrell	1-8-0
Dayton	Flyers	Red & Blue	Independent	Ron Marciniak	5-6-0
Drake	Bulldogs	Blue & White	Missouri Valley	Jack Wallace	3-8-0
Duke	Blue Devils	Blue & White	Atlantic Coast	Mike McGee	4-5-2

Team	Nickname	Team Colors	Conference	Coach	1975 Record (W-L-T)
East Carolina	Pirates	Purple & Gold	Southern	Pat Dye	8-3-0
Eastern Michigan	Hurons	Green & White	Mid-America	Ed Chiebek	4-6-0
Florida State	Seminoles	Garnet & Gold	Independent	Bobby Bowden	3-8-0
Florida	Gators	Orange & Blue	Southeastern	Doug Dickey	9-3-0
Fresno State	Bulldogs	Cardinal & Blue	Pacific Coast	Jim Sweeney	3-8-0
Fullerton, Cal. State	Titans	Blue, Orange, White	Pacific Coast	Jim Colletto	2-9-0
Furman	Palidans	Purple & White	Southern	Art Baker	5-5-1
Georgia Tech	Yellow Jackets	Old Gold & White	Independent	Pepper Rodgers	7-4-0
Georgia	Bulldogs	Red & Black	Southeastern	Vince Dooley	9-3-0
Harvard	Crimson	Crimson	Ivy	Joe Restic	7-2-0
Hawaii	Rainbow Warriors	Green & White	Independent	Larry Price	6-5-0
Holy Cross	Crusaders	Royal Purple	Independent	Neil Wheelwright	1-10-0
Houston	Cougars	Scarlet & White	Southwest	Bill Yeoman	2-8-0
Idaho	Vandals	Silver & Gold	Big Sky	Ed Troxel	4-5-2
Illinois State	Redbirds	Red & White	Independent	Gerry Hart	2-7-1
Illinois	Fighting Illini	Orange & Blue	Big Ten	Bob Blackman	5-6-0
Indiana State	Sycamores	Blue & White	Missouri Valley	Tom Harp	5-5-0
Indiana	Fightin' Hoosiers	Cream & Crimson	Big Ten	Lee Corso	2-8-1
Iowa State	Cyclones	Cardinal & Gold	Big Eight	Earle Bruce	4-7-0
Iowa	Hawkeyes	Old Gold & Black	Big Ten	Bo Commings	3-8-0
Kansas State	Wildcats	Purple & White	Big Eight	Ellis Rainsberger	3-8-0
Kansas	Jayhawks	Crimson & Blue	Big Eight	Bud Moore	7-5-0
Kent State	Golden Flashes	Blue & Gold	Mid-American	Dennis Fitzgerald	4-7-0
Kentucky	Wildcats	Blue & White	Southeastern	Fran Curci	2-8-1
Lamar	Cardinals	Red & White	Southland	Bob Frederick	1-10-0
Long Beach State	Forty Niners	Brown & Gold	Pacific Coast	Wayne Howard	9-2-0
Louisiana State	Fighting Tigers	Purple & Gold	Southeastern	Charles McClendon	4-7-0
Louisiana Tech	Bulldogs	Red & Blue	Southland	Maxie Lambright	8-2-0
Louisville	Cardinals	Red, Black, White	Missouri Valley	Vince Gibson	1-10-0
Marshall	Thundering Herd	Green & White	Independent	Frank Ellwood	2-9-0
Maryland	Terps	Red & White	Atlantic Coast	Jerry Claiborne	9-2-1
McNeese State	Cowboys	Blue & Gold	Southland	Jack Doland	7-4-0
Memphis State	Tigers	Blue & Gray	Independent	Richard Williamson	7-4-0
Miami (Fla.)	Hurricanes	Orange, Green, White	Independent	Carl Selmer	2-8-0
Miami (Ohio)	Redskins	Red & White	Mid-American	Dick Crum	11-1-0
Michigan State	Spartans	Green & White	Big Ten	Darryl Rogers	7-4-0
Michigan	Wolverines	Maize & Blue	Big Ten	Bo Schembechler	8-2-2
Minnesota	Gophers	Maroon & Gold	Big Ten	Cal Stoll	6-5-0
Mississippi State	Bulldogs	Maroon & White	Southeastern	Bob Tyler	6-4-1
Mississippi	Rebels	Red & Blue	Southeastern	Ken Cooper	6-5-0
Missouri	Tigers	Old Gold & Black	Big Eight	Al Onofrio	6-5-0
Navy	Midshipmen	Navy Blue & Gold	Independent	George Welsh	7-4-0
Nebraska	Cornhuskers	Scarlet & Cream	Big Eight	Tom Osborne	10-2-0
New Mexico State	Aggies	Crimson & White	Missouri Valley	Jim Bradley	5-6-0
New Mexico	Lobos	Cherry & Silver	Western Athletic	Bill Mondt	6-5-0
North Carolina	Tar Heels	Blue & White	Atlantic Coast	Bill Dooley	3-7-1
North Carolina State	Wolfpack	Red & White	Atlantic Coast	Robert Rein	7-4-1
North Texas State	Eagles, Mean Green	Green & White	Independent	Hayden Fry	7-4-0
Northeast Louisiana	Indians	Maroon & Gold	Independent	John David Crow	4-6-1
Northern Illinois	Huskies	Cardinal & Black	Mid-American	Pat Culpepper	3-8-0
Northwestern	Wildcats	Purple & White	Big Ten	John Pont	3-8-0
Northwestern Louisiana	Demons	Purple & White	Gulf South	A. L. Williams	1-10-0
Notre Dame	Fighting Irish	Gold & Blue	Independent	Dan Devine	8-3-0
Ohio State	Buckeyes	Scarlet & Gray	Big Ten	Woody Hayes	11-1-0
Ohio Univ.	Bobcats	Green & White	Mid-American	Bill Hess	5-5-1
Oklahoma State	Cowboys	Orange & Black	Big Eight	Jim Stanley	7-4-0
Oklahoma	Sooners	Crimson & Cream	Big Eight	Barry Switzer	11-1-0
Oregon State	Beavers	Orange & Black	Pacific-8	Craig Fertig	1-10-0
Oregon	Ducks	Green & Yellow	Pacific-8	Don Read	3-8-0
Pacific	Tigers	Orange & Black	Pacific Coast	Chester Caddas	5-6-0
Penn State	Nittany Lions	Blue & White	Independent	Joe Paterno	9-3-0
Pennsylvania	Red & Blue	Red & Blue	Ivy	Harry Gamble	3-6-0
Pittsburgh	Panthers	Gold & Blue	Independent	John Majors	8-4-0
Princeton	Tigers	Orange & Black	Ivy	Bob Casciola	4-5-0
Purdue	Boilermakers	Old Gold & Black	Big Ten	Alex Agese	4-7-0
Rice	Owls	Blue & Gray	Southwest	Homer Rice	2-9-0
Richmond	Spiders	Red & Blue	Independent	Jim Tait	5-6-0
Rutgers	Scarlet Knights	Scarlet	Independent	Frank Burns	9-2-0
San Diego State	Aztecs	Scarlet & Black	Independent	Claude Gilbert	8-3-0
San Jose State	Spartans	Gold & White	Pacific Coast	Lynn Stiles	9-2-0
South Carolina	Fighting Gamecocks	Garnet & Black	Independent	Jim Carlen	7-5-0
Southern California	Trojans	Cardinal & Gold	Pacific-8	John Robinson	8-4-0
Southern Illinois	Salukis	Maroon & White	Missouri Valley	Rey Dempsey	1-9-1
Southern Methodist	Mustangs	Red & Blue	Southwest	Ron Meyer	4-7-0
Southern Mississippi	Golden Eagles	Black & Gold	Independent	Bobby Collins	7-4-0
Southwestern La.	Ragin' Cajuns	Vermilion	Southland	Augie Tamariello	6-5-0
Stanford	Cardinals	Cardinal & White	Pacific-8	Jack Christiansen	6-4-1
Syracuse	Orangemen	Orange	Independent	Frank Maloney	6-5-0
Temple	Owls	Cherry & White	Independent	Wayne Hardin	6-5-0
Tennessee	Volunteers	Orange & White	Southeastern	Bill Battle	7-5-0
Texas-Arlington	Mavericks	Royal Blue & White	Southland	Bud Elliott	4-7-0
Texas-El Paso	Miners	Orange & White	Western Athletic	Gil Bartosh	1-10-0
Texas A & M.	Aggies	Maroon &White	Southwest	Emory Bellard	10-2-0
Texas Christian	Horned Frogs	Purple & White	Southwest	Jim Shofner	1-10-0
Texas Tech	Red Raiders	Scarlet & Black	Southwest	Steve Sloan	6-5-0
Texas	Longhorns	Orange & White	Southwest	Darrell Royal	10-2-0
Toledo	Rockets	Blue & Gold	Mid-American	Jack Murphy	5-6-0

Team	Nickname	Team Colors	Conference	Coach	1975 Record (W-L-T)
Tulane	Green Wave	Olive Green & Sky Blue	Independent	Larry Smith	4-7-0
Tulsa	Golden Hurricane	Blue, Red, Gold	Missouri Valley	F. A. Dry	7-4-0
UCLA	Bruins	Navy Blue & Gold	Pacific-8	Terry Donahue	9-2-1
Utah State	Aggies	Navy Blue & White	Independent	Bruce Snyder	6-5-0
Utah	Utes	Crimson & White	Western Athletic	Tom Lovat	1-10-0
Vanderbilt	Commodores	Black & Gold	Southeastern	Fred Pancoast	7-4-0
Villanova	Wildcats	Blue & White	Independent	Dick Bedesem	4-7-0
VMI	Keydets	Red, White, Yellow	Southern	Bob Thalman	3-8-0
Virginia Polytech Inst.	Gobblers	Orange & Maroon	Independent	Jimmy Sharpe	8-3-0
Virginia	Cavaliers	Orange & Blue	Atlantic Coast	Dick Bestwick	1-10-0
Wake Forest	Demon Deacons	Old Gold & Black	Atlantic Coast	Chuck Mills	3-8-0
Washington State	Cougars	Crimson & Gray	Pacific-8	Jackie Sherrill	3-8-0
Washington	Huskies	Purple & Gold	Pacific-8	Don James	6-5-0
West Texas State	Buffaloes	Maroon & White	Missouri Valley	Gene Mayfield	5-6-0
West Virginia	Mountaineers	Old Gold & Blue	Independent	Frank Cignetti	9-3-0
Western Michigan	Broncos	Brown & Gold	Mid-American	Elliot Uzelac	1-10-0
Wichita State	Shockers	Gold & Black	Missouri Valley	Jim Wright	3-8-0
William & Mary	Indians	Green, Gold, Silver	Southern	Jim Root	2-9-0
Wisconsin	Badgers	Cardinal & White	Big Ten	John Jardine	4-6-1
Wyoming	Cowboys	Brown & Yellow	Western Athletic	Fred Akers	2-9-0
Yale	Elis	Yale Blue	Ivy	Carmen Cozza	7-2-0

Selected Division 2 and 3 Teams

Team	Nickname	Team Colors	Conference	Coach	Record
Akron	Zips	Blue & Gold	Independent	Jim Dennison	7-4-0
Alabama A & M	Bulldogs	Maroon & White	Southern IAC	Curt Gentry	3-8-0
Alcorn State	Braves	Purple & Gold	Southwestern	Marino Casem	6-3-1
Alma	Scots	Maroon & Cream	Michigan	Phil Brooks	6-3-0
Baldwin-Wallace	Yellow Jackets	Brown & Gold	Ohio	Lee J. Tressel	7-2-0
Boise State	Broncos	Orange & Blue	Big Sky	Jim Criner	9-2-1
Boston Univ.	Terriers	Scarlet & White	Yankee	Paul Kemp	5-6-0
Bucknell	Bisons	Orange & Blue	Independent	Bob Curtis	5-4-0
Butler	Bulldogs	Blue & White	Indiana	Bill Sylvester	9-1-0
Carleton	Carls	Maize & Blue	Midwest	Dale Quist	2-7-0
Case Reserve	Spartans	Blue & Gray	Presidents Athletic	Bob DelRosa	0-8-0
Chico State	Wildcats	Cardinal & White	Far Western	Dick Trimmer	4-6-0
Coast Guard	Cadets	Blue & White	Independent	Bill Hickey	8-2-0
Coe	Kohawks	Crimson & Gold	Midwest	Wayne Phillips	4-5-0
Connecticut	Huskies	Blue & White	Yankee	Larry Naviaux	4-7-0
C.W. Post	Pioneers	Green & Gold	Metropolitan	Dom Anile	9-1-0
Delaware	Fightin' Blue Hens	Blue & Gold	Independent	Harold Raymond	8-3-0
Denison	Big Red	Red & White	Ohio	Keith Piper	5-4-0
De Pauw	Tigers	Old Gold & Black	Indiana	Tom Mont	5-5-0
Doane	Tigers	Orange & Black	Nebraska Inter.	Ray Best	6-4-1
Emory & Henry	Wasps	Blue & Gold	Independent	Jimmy Hughes	2-9-0
Evansville	Purple Aces	Purple & White	Indiana	James Byers	7-3-0
Florida A & M	Rattlers	Orange & Green	Southern IAC	Rudy Hubbard	9-2-0
Grambling	Tigers	Black & Gold	Southwestern	Eddie Robinson	10-2-0
Idaho State	Bengals	Orange & Black	Big Sky	Joe Pascale	7-3-0
Jackson State	Tigers	Red & White	Southwestern	Robert Hill	7-3-0
John Carroll	Blue Streaks	Blue & Gold	Presidents	Jerry Schweickert	4-5-0
Kalamazoo	Hornets	Orange & Black	Michigan	Ed Baker	4-4-0
Kenyon	Lords	Purple & White	Ohio	Philip Morse	3-6-0
Knox	Siwash	Purple & Gold	Midwest	Albert Reilly	4-5-0
Lafayette	Leopards	Maroon & White	Independent	Neil Putnam	5-5-0
Lawrence	Vikings	Navy & White	Midwest	Ron Roberts	8-1-0
Lehigh	Engineers	Brown & White	Independent	John Whitehead	9-3-0
Los Angeles State	Diablos	Black & Gold	Cal. Collegiate	Ron Hull	1-7-1
Maine	Black Bears	Blue & White	Yankee	Jack Bicknell	4-6-0
Massachusetts	Minutemen	Maroon & White	Yankee	Richard MacPherson	8-2-0
Michigan Tech	Huskies	Silver & Gold	Northern	Jim Kapp	7-2-0
Middlebury	Panthers	Blue & White	Independent	Mickey Heinecken	4-4-0
Middle Tenn. St.	Blue Raiders	Blue & White	Ohio Valley	Ben Hurt	4-7-0
Montana State	Bobcats	Blue & Gold	Big Sky	Sonny Holland	5-5-0
Montana	Grizzlies	Copper, Silver, Gold	Big Sky	Jack Swarthout	6-4-0
Moorhead State	Dragons	Scarlet & White	Northern	Ross Fortier	2-7-0
Morgan State	Bears	Blue & Orange	Mid-Eastern	Nathaniel Taylor	4-5-1
Mt. Union	Purple Raiders	Purple & White	Ohio	Ken Wable	7-2-0
Muhlenberg	Mules	Cardinal & Gray	Middle Atlantic	Frank Marino	2-6-2
Nevada-Las Vegas	Rebels	Scarlet & Gray	Independent	Tony Knap	7-4-0
New Hampshire	Wildcats	Blue & White	Yankee	William Bowes	9-3-0
Norfolk State	Spartans	Green & Gold	Central	Dick Price	8-3-0
North Dakota State	Bison	Yellow & Green	North Central	Jim Wacker	2-7-0
North Dakota	Sioux	Green & White	North Central	Jerry Olson	9-1-0
Northern Arizona	Lumberjacks	Blue & Gold	Big Sky	Joe Salem	1-9-0
Northern Iowa	Panthers	Purple & Old Gold	North Central	Stan Sheriff	9-3-0
Northern Michigan	Wildcats	Old Gold & Green	Independent	Gil Krueger	13-1-0
Ohio Northern	Polar Bears	Orange & Black	Ohio	A. Wallace Hood	4-4-1
Ohio Wesleyan	Battling Bishops	Red & Black	Ohio	Jack Fouts	4-5-0
Olivet	Comets	Cardinal & White	Michigan	Douglas Kay	4-5-0
Portland State	Vikings	Green & White	Independent	Darrel Davis	8-3-0
Puget Sound	Loggers	Green, Gold, Blue.	Independent	Paul Wallrof	7-3-1
Redlands	Bulldogs	Maroon & Gray	So. Cal.	Frank Serrao	7-2-1
Rhode Island	Rams	Blue & White	Yankee	Bob Griffin	2-8-0
Ripon	Redmen	Crimson & White	Midwest	William Connor	6-3-0
Rochester	Yellow Jackets	Yellow, Blue	Independent	Peter Stark	5-4-0

Team	Nickname	Team Colors	Conference	Coach	1975 Record (W-L-T)
St. Cloud State	Huskies	Red & Black	Northern	Mike Simpson	7-3-0
St. Lawrence	Saints	Scarlet & Brown	ICAC	Ted Stratford	7-2-0
St. Norbert	Knights	Green & Gold	Independent	Howie Kolstad	5-5-0
St. Olaf	Oles	Black & Gold	Minn. IAC	Tom Porter	5-3-1
Santa Clara	Broncos	Cardinal & White	Independent	Pat Malley	6-5-0
Slippery Rock	Rockets	Green & White	Pennsylvania	Bob Despirito	4-5-0
So. Carolina State	Bulldogs	Garnet & Blue	Mid-Eastern	Willie Jeffries	8-2-1
So. Dakota State	Jackrabbits	Yellow & Blue	North Central	John Gregory	7-4-0
South Dakota	Coyotes	Vermilion & White	North Central	Bernard Cooper	3-8-0
Southern	Jaguars	Blue & Gold	Southwestern	Charlie Bates	9-3-0
Southern Oregon	Red Raiders	Red & Black	Evergreen	Scott Johnson	6-4-0
Swarthmore	Little Quakers	Garnet	Middle Atlantic	Tom Lapinski	1-7-0
Tennessee Tech	Golden Eagles	Purple & Gold	Ohio Valley	Don Wade	8-3-0
Texas Southern	Tigers	Maroon & Grey	Southwestern	Wendell Mosley	4-6-0
Thiel	Tomcats	Blue & Gold	President's Athletic	James McCullough	5-4-0
Trenton State	Lions	Blue & Gold	New Jersey State	Carmen Piccone	5-4-0
Tufts	Jumbos	Blue & Brown	Independent	Paul Pawlak	2-6-0
Upsala	Vikings	Blue & Gray	Middle Atlantic	John Hooper	5-4-0
Valparaiso	Crusaders	Brown & Gold	Indiana	Norn Amundsen	3-6-0
Wash. & Jeff	Presidents	Red & Black	Presidents Athletic	Pat Mondock	6-3-0
Wash. & Lee	Generals	Royal Blue, White	Independent	William McHenry	1-8-1
Wayne State	Tartars	Green & Gold	Great Lakes	Dick Lowry	8-3-0
Weber State	Wildcats	Purple & White	Big Sky	Dick Gwinn	1-9-1
Wesleyan	Cardinals	Red & Black	Little Three	Bill Macdermott	4-3-1
Western Carolina	Catamounts	Purple & Gold	Independent	Bob Waters	3-7-0
Western Illinois	Leathernecks	Purple & Gold	Independent	Bill Shanahan	5-4-1
Western Kentucky	Hilltoppers	Red & White	Ohio Valley	Jimmy Feix	11-2-0
Wilkes	Colonels	Navy & Gold	Middle Atlantic	Roland Schmidt	3-5-0
Williams	Ephmen	Purple	Little Three	Robert Odell	7-0-1
Wittenberg	Tigers	Red & White	Ohio	Dave Maurer	12-1-0
Wooster	Fighting Scots	Black, Gold	Ohio	Don Hunsinger	1-8-0
Youngstown State	Penguins	Red & White	Independent	Bill Narduzzi	5-4-0

National College Football Champions

The NCAA recognizes as unofficial national champion the team selected each year by the AP (poll of writers) and the UPI (poll of coaches). When the polls disagree both teams are listed. The AP poll originated in 1936 and the UPI poll in 1950.

1936 Minnesota	1946 Notre Dame	1956 Oklahoma	1966 Notre Dame
1937 Pittsburgh	1947 Notre Dame	1957 Auburn, Ohio State	1967 Southern Cal.
1938 Texas Christian	1948 Michigan	1958 Louisiana State	1968 Ohio State
1939 Texas A&M	1949 Notre Dame	1959 Syracuse	1969 Texas
1940 Minnesota	1950 Oklahoma	1960 Minnesota	1970 Nebraska, Texas
1941 Minnesota	1951 Tennessee	1961 Alabama	1971 Nebraska
1942 Ohio State	1952 Michigan State	1962 Southern Cal.	1972 Southern Cal.
1943 Notre Dame	1953 Maryland	1963 Texas	1973 Notre Dame, Alabama
1944 Army	1954 Ohio State, UCLA	1964 Alabama	1974 Oklahoma, So. Cal.
1945 Army	1955 Oklahoma	1965 Alabama, Mich. State	1975 Oklahoma

Canadian Football League

1975 Final Standings

Eastern Conference	W.	L.	T.	PF	PA	Pts.
Ottawa	10	5	1	394	280	21
Montreal	9	7	0	353	345	18
Hamilton	5	10	1	284	395	11
Toronto	5	10	1	261	324	11

Western Confernece	W.	L.	T.	PF	PA	Pts.
Edmonton	12	4	0	432	370	24
Saskatchewan	10	5	1	373	309	21
Winnipeg	6	8	2	340	383	14
Calgary	6	10	0	387	363	12
British Columbia	6	10	0	276	331	12

East semifinal—Montreal 35, Hamilton 12
West semifinal—Saskatchewan 42, Winnipeg 24
East final—Montreal 20, Ottawa 10

West final—Edmonton 30, Saskatchewan 18
Championship (Grey Cup)—Edmonton 9, Montreal 8

Canadian Football League (Grey Cup)

Winners of Eastern and Western divisions meet in championship game for Grey Cup (donated by Governor-General Earl Grey in 1909). Canadian football features 3 downs, 110-yard field, and each team can have 12 players on field at one time.

1948—Calgary Stampeders 12, Ottawa Rough Riders 7	1962—Winnipeg Blue Bombers 28, Hamilton Tiger-Cats 27
1949—Montreal Alouettes 28, Calgary Stampeders 15	1963—Hamilton Tiger-Cats 21, British Columbia Lions 10
1950—Toronto Argonauts 13, Winnipeg Blue Bombers 0	1964—British Columbia Lions 34, Hamilton Tiger-Cats 24
1951—Ottawa Rough Riders 21, Saskatchewan Roughriders 14	1965—Hamilton Tiger-Cats 22, Winnipeg Blue Bombers 16
1952—Toronto Argonauts 21, Edmonton Eskimos 11	1966—Saskatchewan Roughriders 29, Ottawa Rough Riders 14
1953—Hamilton Tiger-Cats 12, Winnipeg Blue Bombers 6	1967—Hamilton Tiger-Cats 24, Saskatchewan Roughriders 1
1954—Edmonton Eskimos 26, Montreal Alouettes 25	1968—Ottawa Rough Riders 24, Calgary Stampeders 21
1955—Edmonton Eskimos 34, Montréal Alouettes 19	1969—Ottawa Rough Riders 29, Saskatchewan Roughriders 11
1956—Edmonton Eskimos 50, Montreal Alouettes 27	1970—Montreal Alouettes 23, Calgary Stampeders 10
1957—Hamilton Tiger-Cats 32, Winnipeg Blue Bombers 7	1971—Calgary Stampeders 14, Toronto Argonauts 11
1958—Winnipeg Blue Bombers 35, Hamilton Tiger-Cats 28	1972—Hamilton Tiger-Cats 13, Saskatchewan Rough Riders 10
1959—Winnipeg Blue Bombers 21, Hamilton Tiger-Cats 7	1973—Ottawa Rough Riders 22, Edmonton Eskimos 18
1960—Ottawa Rough Riders 16, Edmonton Eskimos 6	1974—Montreal Alouettes 20, Edmonton Eskimos 7
1961—Winnipeg Blue Bombers 21, Hamilton Tiger-Cats 14	1975—Edmonton Eskimos 9, Montreal Alouettes 8

College Football Stadiums

School	Capacity
Alabama Univ. of (Denny Stad.), University, Ala. . .	59,000
Arizona State Univ. (Sun Devil), Tempe	51,000
Arizona, Univ. of (Arizona Stad.), Tucson	57,000
Arkansas, Univ. of (Razorback Stad.) Fayetteville . .	43,500
Auburn Univ. (Jordan Hare Stad.), Auburn, Ala. . . .	62,291
Baylor Univ. Stad., Waco, Texas	48,000
Boston Coll. (Alumni Stad.), Boston, Mass.	32,000
Bowling Green State Univ. (Doyt Perry Field).	23,272
Brigham Young Univ. Utah.	30,000
Brown Stad., Providence, R. I.	20,000
Butler Univ. (Butler Bowl), Indianapolis, Ind.	19,500
Cal., Univ. of (Memorial Stad.), Berkeley	77,000
Central Mich. Univ. (Shorts Stad.), Mt. Pleasant . .	20,000
Cincinnati, Univ. of (Nippert), Ohio	25,692
Citadel (Johnson Hagood Stadium), Charleston . . .	22,500
Clemson Univ. (Memorial Stad.), S.C.	43,451
Colorado St. Univ. (Hughes Stad.), Ft. Collins	30,000
Colorado, Univ. of (Folsom Field), Boulder	55,000
Columbia Univ. (Baker Field), N.Y., N.Y.	32,000
Cornell (Schoellkopf Crescent), Ithaca, N.Y.	27,000
Dartmouth Coll. (Memorial), Hanover, N.H.	20,816
Delaware, Univ. of (Delaware Stad.), Newark	21,919
Drake Stad., Des Moines, Iowa.	18,000
Duke Univ. (Wade Stad.), Durham, N.C.	44,000
E. Carolina Univ. (Ficklen Stad.), Greenville.	20,000
Eastern Kentucky (Hanger Stadium), Richmond . . .	20,000
Florida State, (Campbell Stad.), Tallahassee	40,500
Florida, Univ. of (Florida Field), Gainesville	62,000
Georgia Inst. of Tech. (Grant Field), Atlanta	58,121
Georgia, Univ. of (Sanford Stad.), Athens.	59,200
Harvard Stad., Boston, Mass.	37,289
Hawaii, Univ. of (Aloha Stad.).	50,000
Holy Cross (Fitton Field), Worcester, Mass.	25,000
Idaho, Univ. of (Kibbie Stad.), Moscow	18,000
Illinois, Univ. of (Memorial Stad.), Urbana	71,229
Indiana St. (Memorial Stad.), Terre Haute	20,500
Indiana Univ. (Memorial Stad.), Bloomington	52,354
Iowa State Univ. (Cyclone Stad.), Ames.	50,000
Iowa, Univ. of (Kinnick Stad.), Iowa City	60,200
Kansas State Univ. Stad., Manhattan	42,000
Kansas, Univ. of (Memorial Stad.), Lawrence	51,500
Kent State Univ. (Dix Stad.), Kent.	28,748
Kentucky, Univ. of (Commonwealth), Lexington . . .	58,000
La. State Univ. (Tiger), Baton Rouge.	67,720
Louisiana Tech. Univ. (Joe Aillet Stad.), Ruston. . .	23,318
Maryland, Univ. of (Byrd), College Park.	45,000
McNeese St. Univ. (Cowboy Stad.), Lake Charles, La.	20,000
Memphis State (Memphis Memorial)	50,164
Michigan State Univ. (Spartan Stadium)	76,000
Michigan, Univ. of (Mich. Stad.), Ann Arbor.	101,701
Minnesota, Univ. of (Memorial Stad.).	56,725
Mississippi St. Univ. (Scott Field)	35,000
Mississippi, Univ. of (Hemingway Stad.).	37,500
Missouri, Univ. of (Faurot Field), Columbia.	55,000
Nebraska, Univ. of (Memorial Stad.), Lincoln.	76,400
New Mexico, Univ. Stad., Albuquerque	30,000

School	Capacity
North Carolina St. U. (Carter Stad.), Raleigh.	44,000
North Carolina, Univ. of (Kenan Stad.).	47,000
North Texas St. Univ. (Fouts Field), Denton	20,200
Northern Illinois Univ. (Huskie Stad.) DeKalb	20,257
Northwestern Univ. (Dyche Stad.), Evanston, Ill. . .	48,500
Notre Dame Stad., South Bend, Ind.	59,075
Ohio State Univ. (Ohio Stad.), Columbus	83,112
Oklahoma State (Lewis Stad.), Stillwater.	51,000
Oklahoma, Univ. of (Owen Field), Norman	70,286
Old Dominion Univ. (Foreman Field), Norfolk.	32,000
Oregon St. Univ. (Parker Stad.), Corvallis.	41,000
Oregon, Univ. of (Autzen Stad.), Eugene	41,097
Pacific, Univ. of the (Pacific Memorial), Calif.	31,895
Penn. State Univ. (Beaver Stad.)	57,538
Penn., Univ. of (Franklin Field), Phila.	60,546
Pittsburgh, Univ. of (Pitt. Stad.), Pa.	56,500
Princeton, (Palmer Stad.), Princeton, N.J.	45,725
Purdue, (Ross-Ade Stad.), Lafayette, Ind.	69,250
Rice Stad., Houston, Texas.	72,000
Rutgers Stad., New Brunswick, N.J.	23,000
San Jose St. Univ. (Spartan Stad.)	18,155
So. Carolina, Univ. of (Williams-Brice), Columbia . .	54,504
So. Illinois Univ. (McAndrew), Carbondale.	20,013
So. Miss., Univ. of (Roberts Stad.), Hattiesburg . . .	36,000
Southwestern La., (Cajun Field), Lafayette, La. . . .	27,000
Stanford Univ., Stanford, Cal.	90,000
Syracuse Univ. (Archbold Stad.).	26,388
Tampa, Univ. of (Tampa Stad.), Fla.	47,000
Tenn., Univ. of (Neyland Stad.), Knoxville	80,290
Texas A. & M. Univ. (Kyle Field).	48,000
Texas Christian Univ. (Carter Stad.), Ft. Worth . . .	46,000
Texas Tech. Univ. (Jones Stad.), Lubbock	47,000
Texas, Univ. of (Memorial), Austin.	80,000
Toledo, Univ. of (Glass Bowl), Ohio	18,210
Trinity Univ. (Alamo Stad.), San Antonio, Tex.	22,500
Tulsa, Univ. of (Skelly), Tulsa, Okla.	40,235
U. S. Air Force Acad. (Falcon Stad.), Col.	49,068
U. S. Military Academy (Michie Stad.)	41,428
U. S. Naval Academy (Navy-Marine Corps Mem. Stad.), Annapolis, Md.	28,000
Utah State Univ. (Romney Stad.), Logan	20,000
Utah, Univ. of (Robert Rice Stad.), Salt Lake City . .	30,000
Vanderbilt, (Dudley Stad.), Nashville.	34,000
Va. Poly Inst. (Lane Stad.), Blacksburg	40,000
Virginia, Univ. of (Scott Stad.), Charlottesville . . .	25,000
Wake Forest (Groves Stad.), Winston-Salem, N.C. . .	31,000
Washington State Univ. (Clarence D. Martin).	28,000
Washington, Univ. of (Husky Stad.), Seattle.	58,946
West Texas State Univ. (Kimbrough), Canyon	20,500
West Virginia Univ. (Mountaineer Field)	37,000
Western Illinois Univ. (Hanson Field), Macomb . . .	18,000
Western Kentucky Univ. (L. T. Smith Stad.).	19,250
Western Mich. Univ. (Waldo Stad.), Kalamazoo . . .	24,500
Wichita State Univ. (Cessna Stadium)	30,500
Wisconsin, Univ. of (Camp Randall).	77,280
Wyoming, Univ. of (Memorial), Laramie	27,000
Yale Bowl, New Haven, Conn.	70,874

National AAU Judo Championships in 1976

Baltimore, Md., Apr. 22-23, 1976

Men

139 Lbs. — George Cozzio, Chicago, Ill.
154 Lbs. — Patrick Burris, Anaheim, Cal.
176 Lbs. — Teimoc Jonston-Ono, New York, N.Y.
205 Lbs. — Irwin Cohen, Chicago, Ill.
Over 205 Lbs. — Dean Sedgwick, River Forest, Ill.
Open Division — Jim Wooley, Houston, Tex.
Overall Champion — Patrick Burris.

Women

110 Lbs. — Lynn Lewis, Revere, Mass.
120 Lbs. — Diane Pierce, Minneapolis, Minn.
130 Lbs. — Becky Tushek, Ft. Lee, N.J.
142 Lbs. — Delores Brodie, Barstow, Cal.
154 Lbs. — Amy Kublin, Sharon, Mass.
166 Lbs. — Frances Watkins, New York, N.Y.
Over 166 Lbs. — Debbie Fisher, Concord, Cal.
Open Division — Maureen Braziel, Brooklyn, N.Y.
Overall Champion — Maureen Braziel.

National AAU Gymnastics Championship in 1976

Philadelphia, Pa., Apr. 29-May 1, 1976

Men

All-Around — Koji Saito, Mobile, Ala.
Floor Exercise — Ron Galimore, Tallahassee, Fla.
Pommel Horse — Ed Paul, National Gymnastic Center.
Rings — (tie) Vic Randazzo, New York AC, and Todd Kouni, Baton Rouge, La.
Vault — Mike Carter, Philadelphia International Gymnastics.
Parallel Bars — Koji Saito.
Horizontal Bars — Koji Saito.

Team Championship — National Gymnastic Center
Horizontal Bar—Tim Shaw, California.

Women

All-Around — Roxanne Pierce, Phil. Gymnastics Center.
Vault — Ann Woods, Alt's Gym Club.
Balance Beam — Roxanne Pierce.
Uneven Bars — Ann Carr, Philadelphia Gymnastics Center.
Floor Exercise — Janice Baker, Syracuse, N.Y.
Team Championship — Philadelphia Gymnastics Center.

National Football League
Final 1975 Standings

National Conference

Eastern Division

	W.	L.	T.	Pct.	PF	PA
St. Louis	11	3	0	.786	356	276
Dallas	10	4	0	.714	350	268
Washington	8	6	0	.571	325	276
N.Y. Giants	5	9	0	.357	216	306
Philadelphia	4	10	0	.286	226	302

Central Division

	W.	L.	T.	Pct.	PF	PA
Minnesota	12	2	0	.857	377	180
Detroit	7	7	0	.500	245	262
Chicago	4	10	0	.286	191	379
Green Bay	4	10	0	.286	226	285

Western Division

	W.	L.	T.	Pct.	PF	PA
Los Angeles	12	2	0	.857	312	135
San Francisco . . .	5	9	0	.357	255	286
Atlanta	4	10	0	.286	240	289
New Orleans	2	12	0	.143	165	360

American Conference

Eastern Division

	W.	L.	T.	Pct.	PF	PA
Baltimore	10	4	0	.714	395	269
Miami	10	4	0	.714	357	222
Buffalo	8	6	0	.571	420	355
N.Y. Jets	3	11	0	.214	258	438
New England	3	11	0	.214	258	358

Central Division

	W.	L.	T.	Pct.	PF	PA
Pittsburgh	12	2	0	.857	373	162
Cincinnati	11	3	0	.786	340	246
Houston	10	4	0	.714	293	226
Cleveland	3	11	0	.214	218	372

Western Division

	W.	L.	T.	Pct.	PF	PA
Oakland	11	3	0	.786	375	255
Denver	6	8	0	.429	254	307
Kansas City	5	9	0	.357	282	341
San Diego	2	12	0	.143	189	345

NFC Playoffs — Dallas 17, Minnesota 14; Los Angeles 35, St. Louis 23; Dallas 37, Los Angeles 7.
AFC Playoffs — Pittsburgh 28, Baltimore 10; Oakland 31, Cincinnati 28; Pittsburgh 16, Oakland 10.
Championship Game — Pittsburgh 21, Dallas 17

Pittsburgh Defeats Dallas in Super Bowl

The Pittsburgh Steelers won their second straight Super Bowl championship by defeating the Dallas Cowboys 21-17 on Jan. 18, 1976 at the Orange Bowl in Miami.

Score by Periods

Dallas	7	3	0	7-17
Pittsburgh	7	0	0	14-21

Scoring

Dallas—D. Pearson 29 pass from Staubach (Fritsch kick).
Pittsburgh—Grossman 7 pass from Bradshaw (Gerela kick).
Dallas—Field goal Fritsch 36.
Pittsburgh—Safety Harrison blocked punt out of end zone.
Pittsburgh—Field goal Gerela 36.
Pittsburgh—Field goal Gerela 18.
Pittsburgh—Swann 64 pass from Bradshaw (kick failed).
Dallas—Howard 34 pass from Staubach (Fritsch kick).

Team Statistics

	Dallas	Pittsburgh
First downs	14	13
Rushes-Yards	31-108	46-149
Passing yards	162	190
Return yards	101	216
Passes	15-24-3	9-19-0
Punts	7-35.0	4-39.8
Fumbles-Lost	4-0	4-0
Penalties-Yards	2-20	0-00
Attendance—80,187.		

Individual Statistics

Dallas rushing — Newhouse, 16 for 56 yards; Staubach, 5 for 22; Dennison, 5 for 16; P. Pearson, 5 for 14.
Pittsburgh rushing — Harris, 27 for 82 yards; Bleier, 15 for 51; Bradshaw, 4 for 16.
Dallas passing — Staubach, 15 of 24 for 204 yards (3 intercepted).

Pittsburgh passing — Bradshaw, 9 of 19 for 209 yards.
Dallas pass receiving — D. Pearson, 2 for 59 yards; P. Pearson, 5 for 53; P. Howard, 1 for 34; Young, 3 for 31; Newhouse, 2 for 12; Fugett, 1 for 9; Dennison, 1 for 6.
Pittsburgh pass receiving — Swann, 4 for 161 yards; Harris, 1 for 26; Stallworth, 2 for 8; L. Brown, 1 for 7; Grossman, 1 for 7.

Super Bowl

Year	Winner	Loser	Site
1967 . . .	Green Bay Packers, 35	Kansas City Chiefs, 10	Los Angeles Coliseum
1968 . . .	Green Bay Packers, 33	Oakland Raiders, 14	Orange Bowl, Miami
1969 . . .	New York Jets, 16	Baltimore Colts, 7	Orange Bowl, Miami
1970 . . .	Kansas City Chiefs, 23	Minnesota Vikings, 7	Tulane Stadium, New Orleans
1971 . . .	Baltimore Colts, 16	Dallas Cowboys, 13	Orange Bowl, Miami
1972 . . .	Dallas Cowboys, 24	Miami Dolphins, 3	Tulane Stadium, New Orleans
1973 . . .	Miami Dolphins, 14	Washington Redskins, 7	Los Angeles Coliseum
1974 . . .	Miami Dolphins, 24	Minnesota Vikings, 7	Rice Stadium, Houston
1975 . . .	Pittsburgh Steelers, 16	Minnesota Vikings, 6	Tulane Stadium, New Orleans
1976 . . .	Pittsburgh Steelers, 21	Dallas Cowboys, 17	Orange Bowl, Miami

Jim Thorpe Trophy Winners

The winner of the Jim Thorpe Trophy, named after the athletic great, is picked by Murray Olderman of Newspaper Enterprise Assn. in a poll of players from the 26 NFL teams. It goes to the most valuable NFL player and is the oldest and highest professional football award.

Year	Player and Team	Year	Player and Team
1955	Harlon Hill, Chicago Bears	1965	Jim Brown, Cleveland Browns
1956	Frank Gifford, N. Y. Giants	1966	Bart Starr, Green Bay Packers
1957	John Unitas, Baltimore Colts	1967	John Unitas, Baltimore Colts
1958	Jim Brown, Cleveland Browns	1968	Earl Morrall, Baltimore Colts
1959	Charley Conerly, N. Y. Giants	1969	Roman Gabriel, Los Angeles Rams
1960	Norm Van Brocklin, Philadelphia Eagles	1970	John Brodie, San Francisco
1961	Y. A. Tittle, N. Y. Giants	1971	Bob Griese, Miami
1962	Jim Taylor, Green Bay Packers	1972	Larry Brown, Washington
1963	(tie) Jim Brown, Cleveland Browns, and	1973	O. J. Simpson, Buffalo
	Y. A. Tittle, N. Y. Giants	1974	Ken Stabler, Oakland
1964	Lenny Moore, Baltimore Colts	1975	Fran Tarkenton, Minnesota

National Football League

Year	Winners (W-L-T) (East)	Winners (W-L-T) (West)	Playoff
1933	New York Giants (11-3-0)	Chicago Bears (10-2-1)	Chicago Bears 23, New York 21
1934	New York Giants (8-5-0)	Chicago Bears (13-0-0)	New York 30, Chicago Bears 13
1935	New York Giants (9-3-0)	Detroit Lions (7-3-2)	Detroit 26, New York 7
1936	Boston Redskins (7-5-0)	Green Bay Packers (10-1-1)	Green Bay 21, Boston 6
1937	Washington Redskins (8-3-0)	Chicago Bears (9-1-1)	Wash. 28, Chicago Bears 21
1938	New York Giants (8-2-1)	Green Bay Packers (8-3-0)	New York 23, Green Bay 17
1939	New York Giants (9-1-1)	Green Bay Packers (9-2-0)	Green Bay 27, New York 0
1940	Washington Redskins (9-2-0)	Chicago Bears (8-3-0)	Chicago Bears 73, Wash. 0
1941	New York Giants (8-3-0)	Chicago Bears (10-1-1) (A)	Chicago Bears 37, New York 9
1942	Wash. Redskins (10-1-1)	Chicago Bears (11-0-0)	Wash. 14, Chicago Bears 6
1943	Wash. Redskins (6-3-1) (A)	Chicago Bears (8-1-1)	Chicago Bears 41, Wash. 21
1944	New York Giants (8-1-1)	Green Bay Packers (8-2-0)	Green Bay 14, New York 7
1945	Wash. Redskins (8-2-0)	Cleveland Rams (9-1-0)	Cleveland 15, Washington 14
1946	New York Giants (7-3-1)	Chicago Bears (8-2-1)	Chicago Bears 24, New York 14
1947	Philadelphia Eagles (8-4-0) (A)	Chicago Cardinals (9-3-0)	Chicago Cardinals 28, Phila. 21
1948	Philadelphia Eagles (9-2-1)	Chicago Cardinals (11-0-0)	Phila. 7, Chicago Cardinals 0
1949	Philadelphia Eagles (11-1-0)	Los Angeles Rams (8-2-2)	Philadelphia 14, Los Angeles 0
1950	Cleveland Browns (10-2-0) (A)	Los Angeles Rams (9-3-0) (A)	Cleveland 30, Los Angeles 28
1951	Cleveland Browns (11-1-0)	Los Angeles Rams (8-4-0)	Los Angeles 24, Cleveland 17
1952	Cleveland Browns (8-4-0)	Detroit Lions (9-3-0) (A)	Detroit 17, Cleveland 7
1953	Cleveland Browns (11-1-0)	Detroit Lions (10-2-0)	Detroit 17, Cleveland 16
1954	Cleveland Browns (9-3-0)	Detroit Lions (9-2-1)	Cleveland 56, Detroit 10
1955	Cleveland Browns (9-2-1)	Los Angeles Rams (8-3-1)	Cleveland 38, Los Angeles 14
1956	New York Giants (8-3-1)	Chicago Bears (9-2-1)	New York 47, Chicago Bears 7
1957	Cleveland Browns (9-2-1)	Detroit Lions (8-4-0) (A)	Detroit 59, Cleveland 14
1958	New York Giants (9-3-0) (A)	Baltimore Colts (9-3-0)	Baltimore 23, New York 17 (B)
1959	New York Giants (10-2-0)	Baltimore Colts (9-3-0)	Baltimore 31, New York 16
1960	Philadelphia Eagles (10-2-0)	Green Bay Packers (8-4-0)	Philadelphia 17, Green Bay 13
1961	New York Giants (10-3-1)	Green Bay Packers (11-3-0)	Green Bay 37, New York 0
1962	New York Giants (12-2-0)	Green Bay Packers (13-1-0)	Green Bay 16, New York 7
1963	New York Giants (11-3-0)	Chicago Bears (11-1-2)	Chicago 14, New York 10
1964	Cleveland Browns (10-3-1)	Baltimore Colts (12-2-0)	Cleveland 27, Baltimore 0
1965	Cleveland Browns (11-3-0)	Green Bay Packers (10-3-1) (A)	Green Bay 23, Cleveland 12
1966	Dallas Cowboys (10-3-1)	Green Bay Packers (12-2-0)	Green Bay 34, Dallas 27

(A) Won divisional playoff. (B) Won at 8:15 sudden death overtime period.

Year	Conference	Division	Winners (W-L-T)	Playoffs
1967	East	Century	Cleveland (9-5-0)	Dallas 52, Cleveland 14
		Capitol	Dallas (9-5-0)	
	West	Central	Green Bay (9-4-1)	Green Bay 28, Los Angeles 7
		Coastal	Los Angeles (11-1-2) (A)	Green Bay 21, Dallas 17
1968	East	Century	Cleveland (10-4-0)	Cleveland 31, Dallas 20
		Capitol	Dallas (12-2-0)	
	West	Central	Minnesota (8-6-0)	Baltimore 24, Minnesota 14
		Coastal	Baltimore (13-1-0)	Baltimore 34, Cleveland 0
1969	East	Century	Cleveland (10-3-1)	Cleveland 38, Dallas 14
		Capitol	Dallas (11-2-1)	
	West	Central	Minnesota (12-2-0)	Minnesota 23, Los Angeles 20
		Coastal	Los Angeles (11-3-0)	Minnesota 27, Cleveland 7
1970	American	Eastern	Baltimore (11-2-1)	Baltimore 17, Cincinnati 0
		Central	Cincinnati (8-6-0)	Oakland 21, Miami 14
		Western	Oakland (8-4-2)	Baltimore 27, Oakland 17
	National	Eastern	Dallas (10-4-0)	Dallas 5, Detroit 0
		Central	Minnesota (12-2-0)	San Francisco 17, Minnesota 14
		Western	San Francisco (10-3-1)	Dallas 17, San Francisco 10
1971	American	Eastern	Miami (10-3-1)	Miami 27, Kansas City 24
		Central	Cleveland (9-5-0)	Baltimore 20, Cleveland 3
		Western	Kansas City (10-3-1)	Miami 21, Baltimore 0
	National	Eastern	Dallas (11-3-0)	Dallas 20, Minnesota 12
		Central	Minnesota (11-3-0)	San Francisco 24, Washington 20
		Western	San Francisco (9-5-0)	Dallas 14, San Francisco 3
1972	American	Eastern	Miami (14-0-0)	Miami 20, Cleveland 14
		Central	Pittsburgh (11-3-0)	Pittsburgh 13, Oakland 7
		Western	Oakland (10-3-1)	Miami 21, Pittsburgh 17
	National	Eastern	Washington (11-3-0)	Washington 16, Green Bay 3
		Central	Green Bay (10-4-0)	Dallas 30, San Francisco 28
		Western	San Francisco (8-5-1)	Washington 26, Dallas 3
1973	American	Eastern	Miami (12-2-0)	Miami 34, Cincinnati 16
		Central	Cincinnati (10-4-0)	Oakland 33, Pittsburgh 14
		Western	Oakland (9-4-1)	Miami 27, Oakland 10
	National	Eastern	Dallas (10-4-0)	Dallas 27, Los Angeles 16
		Central	Minnesota (12-2-0)	Minnesota 27, Washington 20
		Western	Los Angeles (12-2-0)	Minnesota 27, Dallas 10
1974	American	Eastern	Miami (11-3-0)	Oakland 28, Miami 26
		Central	Pittsburgh (10-3-1)	Pittsburgh 32, Buffalo 14
		Western	Oakland (12-2-0)	Pittsburgh 24, Oakland 13
	National	Eastern	St. Louis (10-4-0)	Minnesota 30, St. Louis 14
		Central	Minnesota (10-4-0)	Los Angeles 19, Washington 10
		Western	Los Angeles (10-4-0)	Minnesota 14, Los Angeles 10
1975	American	Eastern	Baltimore (10-4-0)	Pittsburgh 28, Baltimore 10
		Central	Pittsburgh (12-2-0)	Oakland 31, Cincinnati 28
		Western	Oakland (11-3-0)	Pittsburgh 16, Oakland 10
	National	Eastern	St. Louis (11-3-0)	Dallas 17, Minnesota 14
		Central	Minnesota (12-2-0)	Los Angeles 35, St. Louis 23
		Western	Los Angeles (12-2-0)	Dallas 37, Los Angeles 7

American Football League

Year	Eastern Division	Western Division	Playoff
1960	Houston Oilers (10-4-0)	L. A. Chargers (10-4-0)	Houston 24, Los Angeles 16
1961	Houston Oilers (10-3-1)	San Diego Chargers (12-2-0)	Houston 10, San Diego 3
1962	Houston Oilers (11-3-0)	Dallas Texans (11-3-0)	Dallas 20, Houston 17 (b)
1963	Boston Patriots (8-6-1) (a)	San Diego Chargers (11-3-0)	San Diego 51, Boston 10
1964	Buffalo Bills (12-2-0)	San Diego Chargers (8-5-1)	Buffalo 20, San Diego 7
1965	Buffalo Bills (10-3-1)	San Diego Chargers (9-2-3)	Buffalo 23, San Diego 0
1966	Buffalo Bills (9-4-1)	Kansas City Chiefs (11-2-1)	Kansas City 31, Buffalo 7
1967	Houston Oilers (9-4-1)	Oakland Raiders (13-1-0)	Oakland 40, Houston 7
1968	New York Jets (11-3-0)	Oakland Raiders (12-2-0) (a)	New York 27, Oakland 23
1969	New York Jets (10-4-0)	Oakland Raiders (12-1-1)	Kansas City 17, Oakland 7 (c)

(a) won divisional playoff (b) won at 2:45 of second overtime. (c) K. C. def. Jets to make playoffs.

National Football Conference Leaders

(National Football League, 1962-1969)

Passing

Year	Player	Atts.	Com.	YG	TD
1962	Bart Starr, Green Bay	285	178	2,438	9
1963	Y. A. Tittle, N. Y. Giants	367	221	3,145	14
1964	Bart Starr, Green Bay	272	163	2,144	4
1965	Rudy Bukich, Chicago	312	176	2,641	9
1966	Bart Starr, Green Bay	251	156	2,257	3
1967	Sonny Jurgensen, Washington	508	288	3,747	16
1968	Earl Morrall, Baltimore	317	182	2,909	17
1969	Sonny Jurgensen, Washington	422	274	3,102	15
1970	John Brodie, San Francisco	378	223	2,941	24
1971	Roger Staubach, Dallas	211	126	1,882	15
1972	Norm Snead, N. Y. Giants	325	196	2,307	17
1973	Roger Staubach, Dallas	286	179	2,428	23
1974	Sonny Jurgensen, Washington	167	107	1,185	11
1975	Fran Tarkenton, Minnesota	425	273	2,294	25

Pass-Receiving

Year	Player	Ct.	YG	TD
1962	Bobby Mitchell, Washington	72	1,384	11
1963	Bobby Conrad, Cards, St. Louis	73	967	10
1964	Johnny Morris, Chicago	93	1,200	10
1965	Dave Parks, San Francisco	80	1,344	12
1966	Charlie Taylor, Washington	72	1,119	12
1967	Charlie Taylor, Washington	70	990	9
1968	Clifton McNeil, San Francisco	71	944	7
1969	Dan Abramowicz, New Orleans	73	1,015	7
1970	Dick Gordon, Chicago	71	1,026	13
1971	Bob Tucker, Giants	59	791	4
1972	Harold Jackson, Philadelphia	62	1,048	4
1973	Harold Carmichael, Philadelphia	67	1,116	9
1974	Charles Young, Philadelphia	63	696	3
1975	Chuck Foreman, Minnesota	73	691	9

Scoring

Year	Player	TDs	PAT	FG	Pts.
1962	Jim Taylor, Green Bay	19	0	0	114
1963	Don Chandler, New York	0	52	18	106
1964	Lenny Moore, Baltimore	20	0	0	120
1965	Gale Sayers, Chicago	22	0	0	132
1966	Bruce Gossett, Los Angeles	0	29	28	113
1967	Jim Bakken, St. Louis	0	36	27	117
1968	Leroy Kelly, Cleveland	20	0	0	120
1969	Fred Cox, Minnesota	0	43	26	121
1970	Fred Cox, Minnesota	0	35	30	125
1971	Curt Knight, Washington	0	27	29	114
1972	Chester Marcol, Green Bay	0	29	33	128
1973	David Ray, Los Angeles	0	40	30	130
1974	Chester Marcol, Green Bay	0	19	25	94
1975	Chuck Foreman, Minnesota	22	0	0	132

Rushing

Year	Player	YG	Atts.	TD
1962	Jim Taylor, Green Bay	1,474	272	19
1963	Jimmy Brown, Cleveland	1,863	291	12
1964	Jimmy Brown, Cleveland	1,446	280	7
1965	Jimmy Brown, Cleveland	1,544	289	17
1966	Gale Sayers, Chicago	1,231	229	8
1967	Leroy Kelly, Cleveland	1,205	235	11
1968	Leroy Kelly, Cleveland	1,239	248	16
1969	Gale Sayers, Chicago	1,032	236	8
1970	Larry Brown, Washington	1,125	237	5
1971	John Brockington, Green Bay	1,105	216	4
1972	Larry Brown, Washington	1,216	285	8
1973	John Brockington, Green Bay	1,144	265	3
1974	Larry McCutcheon, Los Angeles	1,109	236	3
1975	Jim Otis, St. Louis	1,076	269	5

American Football Conference Leaders

(American Football League, 1962-1969)

Scoring

Year	Player	TD	PAT	FG	Pts.
1962	Gene Mingo, Denver	4	32	27	137
1963	Gino Cappelletti, Boston	2	35	22	113
1964	Gino Cappelletti, Boston	7	36	25	155
1965	Gino Cappelletti, Boston	9	27	17	132
1966	Gino Cappelletti, Boston	6	35	16	119
1967	George Blanda, Oakland	0	56	20	116
1968	Jim Turner, N. Y. Jets	0	43	34	145
1969	Jim Turner, N. Y. Jets	0	33	32	129
1970	Jan Stenerud, Kansas City	0	26	30	116
1971	Garo Yepremian, Miami	0	33	28	117
1972	Bobby Howfield, N. Y. Jets	0	40	27	121
1973	Roy Gerela, Pittsburgh	0	36	29	123
1974	Roy Gerela, Pittsburgh	0	33	20	93
1975	O. J. Simpson, Buffalo	23	0	0	138

Rushing

Year	Player	YG	Atts.	TD
1962	Cookie Gilchrist, Buffalo	1,096	214	13
1963	Clem Daniels, Oakland	1,098	214	3
1964	Cookie Gilchrist, Buffalo	981	230	6
1965	Paul Lowe, San Diego	1,121	222	7
1966	Jim Nance, Boston	1,458	299	11
1967	Jim Nance, Boston	1,216	269	7
1968	Paul Robinson, Cincinnati	1,023	238	8
1969	Dick Post, San Diego	873	182	6
1970	Floyd Little, Denver	901	209	3
1971	Floyd Little, Denver	1,133	284	6
1972	O. J. Simpson, Buffalo	1,251	292	6
1973	O. J. Simpson, Buffalo	2,003	332	12
1974	Otis Armstrong, Denver	1,407	263	9
1975	O. J. Simpson, Buffalo	1,817	329	16

Passing

Year	Player	Atts.	Com.	YG	TD
1962	Len Dawson, Dallas	310	189	2,749	17
1963	Tobin Rote, San Diego	287	170	2,510	17
1964	Len Dawson, Kansas City	354	199	2,879	18
1965	Jack Hadl, San Diego	348	174	2,798	21
1966	Len Dawson, Kansas City	284	159	2,527	10
1967	Daryle Lamonica, Oakland	425	220	3,228	20
1968	Len Dawson, Kansas City	224	131	2,109	9
1969	Greg Cook, Cincinnati	197	106	1,845	11
1970	Daryle Lamonica, Oakland	356	179	2,516	22
1971	Bob Griese, Miami	263	145	2,089	19
1972	Earl Morrall, Miami	150	83	1,360	11
1973	Ken Stabler, Oakland	260	163	1,997	14
1974	Ken Anderson, Cincinnati	328	213	2,667	18
1975	Ken Anderson, Cincinnati	377	228	3,169	21

Pass-Receiving

Year	Player	Ct.	YG	TD
1962	Lionel Taylor, Denver	77	908	4
1963	Lionel Taylor, Denver	78	1,101	10
1964	Charlie Hennigan, Houston	101	1,561	8
1965	Lionel Taylor, Denver	85	1,131	6
1966	Lance Alworth, San Diego	73	1,383	13
1967	George Sauer, N. Y. Jets	75	1,189	6
1968	Lance Alworth, San Diego	68	1,312	10
1969	Lance Alworth, San Diego	64	1,003	4
1970	Marlin Briscoe, Buffalo	57	1,036	8
1971	Fred Biletnikoff, Oakland	61	929	9
1972	Fred Biletnikoff, Oakland	58	802	7
1973	Fred Willis, Houston	57	371	1
1974	Lydell Mitchell, Baltimore	72	544	2
1975	Reggie Rucker, Cleveland	60	770	3
	Lydell Mitchell, Baltimore	60	544	4

1975 NFL Individual Leaders

National Conference

Passing*

	Att.	Comp.	Pct. Comp.	Yards Gained	Avg. Yd. Gained	TD Pass	Int.	Rating
Tarkenton, Minnesota	425	273	64.2	2994	7.04	25	13	91.7
Staubach, Dallas	348	198	56.9	2666	7.66	17	16	78.6
Kilmer, Washington	346	178	51.4	2440	7.05	23	16	77.1
Harris, Los Angeles	285	157	55.1	2148	7.54	14	15	73.7
Snead, San Francisco	189	108	57.1	1337	7.07	9	10	73.1
Hart, St. Louis	345	182	52.8	2507	7.27	19	19	71.8
Gabriel, Philadelphia	292	151	51.7	1644	5.63	13	11	67.8
Morton, New York	363	186	51.2	2359	6.50	11	16	63.5
Spurrier, San Francisco	207	102	49.3	1151	5.56	5	7	60.2
Reed, Detroit	191	86	45.0	1181	6.18	9	10	59.3
Bartkowski, Atlanta	255	115	45.1	1662	6.52	13	15	59.3
Huff, Chicago	205	114	55.6	1083	5.28	3	9	57.1
Hadl, Green Bay	353	191	54.1	2095	5.93	6	21	53.0
Boryla, Philadelphia	166	87	52.4	996	6.00	6	12	52.8
Manning, New Orleans	338	159	47.0	1683	4.98	7	20	44.4

Scorers—Touchdowns

	Tot.	Rush.	Pass.	Ret.	Pts.
Foreman, Minnesota	22	13	9	0	132
Metcalf, St. Louis	13	9	2	2	78
M. Gray, St. Louis	11	0	11	0	66
G. Washington, S.F.	9	0	9	0	54
Brockington, Green Bay	8	7	1	0	48
Grant, Washington	8	0	8	0	48
D. Pearson, Dallas	8	0	8	0	48

Scorers—Kicking

	XP—XPA	FG—FGA	Pts.
Fritsch, Dallas	38—40	22—35	104
Bakken, St. Louis	40—41	19—24	97
Dempsey, Los Angeles	31—36	21—26	94
Cox, Minnesota	46—48	13—17	85
Moseley, Washington	37—39	16—25	85
Muhlmann, Philadelphia	21—24	20—29	81
Mike-Mayer, S.F.	27—31	14—28	69
Mann, Detroit	25—29	14—21	67
Thomas, Chicago	18—22	13—23	57

Pass Receiving

	No.	Yds.	Avg.	TDs.
Foreman, Minnesota	73	691	9.5	9
Payne, Green Bay	58	766	13.2	0
Marinaro, Minnesota	54	462	8.6	3
Taylor, Washington	53	744	14.0	6
Gilliam, Minnesota	50	777	15.5	7
Young, Philadelphia	49	659	13.4	3
Carmichael, Philadelphia	49	639	13.0	7
M. Gray, St. Louis	48	926	19.3	11
D. Pearson, Dallas	46	822	17.9	8
G. Washington, S.F.	44	735	16.7	9

Interceptions

	No.	Yds.	Long	TDs.
Krause, Minnesota	10	201	81	0
Lawrence, Atlanta	9	163	87	1
Thompson, St. Louis	7	141	61	1
Bryant, Minnesota	7	111	41	0
P. Smith, Green Bay	6	97	61	0
Simpson, Los Angeles	6	90	29	0
Jordan, Dallas	6	80	38	0
Wehrli, St. Louis	6	31	31	0

Rushing

	Att.	Yds.	Avg.	TDs.
Otis, St. Louis	269	1076	4.0	
Foreman, Minnesota	280	1070	3.8	
Hampton, Atlanta	250	1002	4.0	
Newhouse, Dallas	209	930	4.4	
M. Thomas, Washington	235	919	3.9	
McCutcheon, Los Angeles	213	911	4.3	
Metcalf, St. Louis	165	816	4.9	
Bussey, Detroit	157	696	4.4	
Payton, Chicago	196	679	3.5	
Strachan, New Orleans	161	668	4.1	

Punting

	No.	Yds.	Avg.	Long
H. Weaver, Detroit	80	3361	42.0	61
Wittum, San Francisco	67	2804	41.9	64
James, Atlanta	89	3696	41.5	75
Clabo, Minnesota	73	2997	41.1	62
Blanchard, New Orleans	92	3776	41.0	61
Jennings, New York	76	3107	40.9	64
Bragg, Washington	72	2924	40.6	63
Jones, Philadelphia	68	2742	40.3	64
Carrell, Los Angeles	73	2874	39.4	57
Hoppes, Dallas	68	2676	39.4	55

Punt Returns

	No.	Yds.	Avg.	TDs.
Metcalf, St. Louis	23	285	12.4	1
Chapman, New Orleans	17	207	12.2	0
Livers, Chicago	42	456	10.9	0
Taylor, San Francisco	16	166	10.4	0
Richards, Dallas	28	288	10.3	1
Marshall, Philadelphia	23	235	10.2	0
Moore, San Francisco	16	160	10.0	0
West, Detroit	22	219	10.0	0

Kickoff Returns

	No.	Yds.	Avg.	TDs.
Payton, Chicago	14	444	31.7	0
Metcalf, St. Louis	35	960	27.4	1
B. Thompson, Detroit	22	565	25.7	0
Marshall, Philadelphia	22	557	25.3	0
Moore, San Francisco	26	650	25.0	0
Odom, Green Bay	42	1034	24.6	1

American Conference

Passing*

	Att.	Comp.	Pct. Comp.	Yards Gained	Avg. Yd. Gained	TD Pass	Int.	Rating
Anderson, Cincinnati	377	228	60.5	3169	8.41	21	11	94.1
Dawson, Kansas City	140	93	66.4	1095	7.82	5	4	89.9
Jones, Baltimore	344	203	59.0	2483	7.22	18	8	89.1
Bradshaw, Pittsburgh	286	165	57.7	2055	7.19	18	9	88.2
Griese, Miami	191	118	61.8	1693	8.86	14	13	86.5
Ferguson, Buffalo	321	169	52.6	2426	7.56	25	17	81.3
Livingston, Kansas City	176	88	50.0	1245	7.07	8	6	74.1
Stabler, Oakland	293	171	58.4	2296	7.84	16	24	67.6
Ramsey, Denver	233	128	54.9	1562	6.70	9	14	63.8
Pastorini, Houston	342	163	47.7	2053	6.00	14	16	60.9
Grogan, New England	274	139	50.7	1976	7.21	11	18	60.2
Fouts, San Diego	195	106	54.4	1396	7.16	2	10	59.3
Namath, New York	326	157	48.2	2286	7.01	15	28	51.0
Phipps, Cleveland	313	162	51.8	1749	5.59	4	19	47.5
Johnson, Denver	142	65	45.8	1021	7.19	5	12	46.5

*At least 140 passes needed to qualify. Leader based on percentage of completions—touchdown passes—interceptions—and average yards.

(AFC leaders cont'd.)

Scorers—Touchdowns

	Tot.	Rush.	Pass.	Ret.	Pts.
Simpson, Buffalo	23	16	7	0	138
Banaszak, Oakland	16	16	0	0	96
Mitchell, Baltimore	15	11	4	0	90
Braxton, Buffalo	13	9	4	0	78
Nottingham, Miami	12	12	0	0	72
Harris, Pittsburgh	11	10	1	0	66
McCauley, Baltimore	11	10	1	0	66
Swann, Pittsburgh	11	0	11	0	66
Bulaich, Miami	10	5	5	0	60
Fritts, Cincinnati	10	8	2	0	60

Rushing

	Att.	Yds.	Avg.	TDs.
Simpson, Buffalo	329	1817	5.5	16
Harris, Pittsburgh	262	1246	4.8	10
Mitchell, Baltimore	289	1193	4.1	11
Pruitt, Cleveland	217	1067	4.9	8
Riggins, New York	238	1005	4.2	8
Morris, Miami	219	875	4.0	4
Braxton, Buffalo	186	823	4.4	9
Coleman, Houston	175	790	4.5	5
Keyworth, Denver	182	725	4.0	3
Nottingham, Miami	168	718	4.3	12

Scorers—Kicking

	XP—XPA	FG—FGA	Pts.
Stenerud, Kan. City	30—31	22—32	96
Gerela, Pittsburgh	44—46	17—21	95
Turner, Denver	23—26	21—28	86
Butler, Houston	31—34	18—30	85
Blanda, Oakland	44—48	13—21	83
Linhart, Baltimore	51—52	10—18	81
Yepremian, Miami	40—46	13—16	79
Leypoldt, Buffalo	51—57	9—16	78
Cockroft, Cleveland	21—24	17—23	72

Punting

	No.	Yds.	Avg.	Long
Guy, Oakland	68	2979	43.8	64
Bateman, Buffalo	61	2536	41.6	74
J. Wilson, Kansas City	54	2233	41.4	64
Cockroft, Cleveland	82	3317	40.5	67
Van Heusen, Denver	63	2515	39.9	64
Lee, Baltimore	86	3402	39.6	62
Pastorini, Houston	62	2447	39.5	68
Walden, Pittsburgh	69	2717	39.4	67
Green, Cincinnati	68	2655	39.0	57

Pass Receiving

	No.	Yds.	Avg.	TDs.
Rucker, Cleveland	60	770	12.8	3
Mitchell, Baltimore	60	544	9.1	4
Chandler, Buffalo	55	746	13.6	6
Burrough, Houston	53	1063	20.1	8
Branch, Oakland	51	893	17.5	9
Swann, Pittsburgh	49	781	15.9	11
Caster, New York	47	820	17.4	4
Vataha, New England	462	720	15.7	6
Curran, San Diego	45	619	13.8	0
Curtis, Cincinnati	44	934	21.2	7

Punt Returns

	No.	Yds.	Avg.	TDs.
Johnson, Houston	40	610	15.3	3
Colzie, Oakland	48	655	13.6	0
Solomon, Miami	26	320	12.3	1
Upchurch, Denver	27	312	11.6	0
Fuller, San Diego	36	410	11.4	1
Stevens, Baltimore	36	396	11.0	0
Edwards, Pittsburgh	25	267	10.7	0
D. Brown, Pittsburgh	20	196	9.8	0
Hayman, Buffalo	25	216	8.6	0

Interceptions

	No.	Yds.	Long	TDs.
Blount, Pittsburgh	11	121	47	0
White, Baltimore	8	135	32	1
Harrison, Buffalo	8	99	40	0
E. Thomas, Kansas City	6	119	36	0
Fletcher, San Diego	6	100	45	0
Thomas, Oakland	6	86	48	0
Green, Buffalo	6	81	37	0
Riley, Kansas City	6	76	30	1

Kickoff Returns

	No.	Yds.	Avg.	TDs.
Hart, Oakland	17	518	30.5	1
Carter, New England	32	879	27.5	1
Upchurch, Denver	40	1084	27.1	0
Washington, Buffalo	35	923	26.4	0
Laird, Baltimore	31	799	25.8	0
Piccone, New York	26	637	24.5	0
Johnson, Houston	33	798	24.2	1
S. Davis, New York	20	483	24.2	0
Collier, Pittsburgh	22	523	23.8	1

1975 NEA All-NFL Team

Offense	First Team	Second Team
Wide Receiver	Cliff Branch, Oakland	Mel Gray, St. Louis
Wide Receiver	Isaac Curtis, Cincinnati	Lynn Swann, Pittsburgh
Tight End	Charles Young, Philadelphia	Riley Odoms, Denver
Tackle	Ron Yary, Minnesota	Dan Dierdorf, St. Louis
Tackle	Rayfield Wright, Dallas	Art Snell, Oakland
Guard	Bob Kuechenberg, Miami	Tom Mack, Los Angeles
Guard	Ed White, Minnesota	Larry Little, Miami
Center	Jim Langer, Miami	Jack Rudnay, Kansas City
Quarterback	Fran Tarkenton, Minnesota	Ken Anderson, Cincinnati
Running Back	O.J. Simpson, Buffalo	Franco Harris, Pittsburgh
Running Back	Chuck Foreman, Minnesota	Terry Metcalf, St. Louis
Placekicker	Jim Bakken, St. Louis	Jan Stenerud, Kansas City

Defense	First Team	Second Team
End	Jack Youngblood, Los Angeles	Elvin Bethea, Houston
End	L.C. Greenwood, Pittsburgh	Cedrick Hardman, San Francisco
Tackle	Curley Culp, Houston	Joe Greene, Pittsburgh
Tackle	Wally Chambers, Chicago	Alan Page, Minnesota
Middle Linebacker	Willie Lanier, Kansas City	Bill Bergey, Philadelphia
Outside Linebacker	Jack Ham, Pittsburgh	Fred Carr, Green Bay
Outside Linebacker	Isiah Robertson, Los Angeles	Chris Hanburger, Washington
Corner Back	Mel Blount, Pittsburgh	Roger Wehrli, St. Louis
Corner Back	Emmitt Thomas, Kansas City	Lemar Parrish, Cincinnati
Strong Safety	Ken Houston, Washington	Dave Elmendorf, Los Angeles
Weak Safety	Cliff Harris, Dallas	Paul Krause, Minnesota
Punter	Ray Guy, Oakland	Jerrel Wilson, Kansas City

George Halas Trophy Winners

The Halas Trophy, named after football coach George Halas, is awarded annually to the outstanding defensive player in football in a poll conducted by Murray Olderman of Newspaper Enterprise Assn.

1966—Larry Wilson, St. Louis
1967—Deacon Jones, Los Angeles
1968—Deacon Jones, Los Angeles
1969—Dick Butkus, Chicago

1970—Dick Butkus, Chicago
1971—Carl Eller, Minnesota
1972—Joe Greene, Pittsburgh

1973—Alan Page, Minnesota
1974—Joe Greene, Pittsburgh
1975—Curley Culp, Houston

All-Time Pro Football Records
(NFL, AFL, and AAFC—All-American Football Conference)
Leading Lifetime Rushers (As of Sept. 11, 1976)

Player	League	Yrs.	Att.	Yards	Avg.	Player	League	Yrs.	Att.	Yards	Avg.
Jim Brown	NFL	9	2,359	12,312	5.2	Steve Van Buren	NFL	8	1,320	5,860	4.3
Joe Perry	AAFC-NFL	16	1,929	9,723	5.0	Bill Brown	NFL	14	1,649	5,838	3.4
Jim Taylor	NFL	10	1,941	8,597	4.4	Larry Brown	NFL	7	1,510	5,819	3.9
O.J. Simpson	AFL-NFL	7	1,707	8,123	4.8	Rick Casares	NFL-AFL	12	1,431	5,797	4.1
Leroy Kelly	NFL	10	1,727	7,274	4.2	Mike Garrett	AFL-NFL	9	1,308	5,481	4.2
John Henry Johnson	NFL-AFL	13	1,571	6,803	4.3	Dick Bass	NFL	10	1,218	5,417	4.4
Floyd Little	AFL-NFL	9	1,641	6,323	3.9	Jim Nance	NFL-AFL	8	1,341	5,401	4.0
Don Perkins	NFL	8	1,500	6,217	4.1	Hugh McElhenny	NFL	13	1,124	5,231	4.7
Ken Willard	NFL	10	1,622	6,105	3.8	Lenny Moore	NFL	12	1,069	5,174	4.8
Larry Csonka	AFL-NFL	7	1,286	5,900	4.6	Ollie Matson	NFL	14	1,170	5,173	4.4

Most Yards Gained, Season — 2,003, O.J. Simpson, Buffalo Bills, 1973.
Most Yards Gained, Game — 250, Orban (Spec) Sanders, New York Yankees vs. Chicago Rockets, Oct. 24, 1947; O. J. Simpson, Buffalo vs. New England, Sept. 16, 1973.
Most Games, 100 Yards or more, Season — 11, O.J. Simpson, Buffalo Bills, 1973.
Most Games, 100 Yards or more, Career — 58, Jim Brown, Cleveland Browns, 1957-1965.
Most Touchdowns Rushing, Career — 106, Jim Brown, Cleveland Browns, 1957-1965.
Most Touchdowns Rushing, Season — 19, Jim Taylor, Green Bay Packers, 1962.
Most Touchdowns Rushing, Game — 6, Ernie Nevers, Chicago Cardinals vs. Chicago Bears, Nov. 8, 1929.
Most Rushing Attempts, Season — 332, O.J. Simpson, Buffalo Bills, 1973.
Most Rushing Attempts, Game — 40, Lydell Mitchell, Baltimore vs. N. Y. Jets, Oct. 4, 1974.
Longest run from Scrimmage — 97 yds., Andy Uram, Green Bay vs. Chicago Cardinals, Oct. 8, 1939; Bob Gage, Pittsburgh vs. Chicago Bears, Dec. 4, 1949. (Both scored touchdown).

Leading Lifetime Passers (Minimum 1,500 attempts)

Player	League	Yrs.	Att.	Comp.	Yds.	Pts.*	Player	League	Yrs.	Att.	Comp.	Yds.	Pts.*
Otto Graham	AAFC-NFL	10	2,626	1,464	23,584	86.8	Roman Gabriel	NFL	14	4,403	2,319	28,953	74.7
Sonny Jurgensen	NFL	18	4,262	2,433	32,224	82.8	Don Meredith	NFL	9	2,308	1,170	17,199	74.7
Len Dawson	NFL-AFL	19	3,741	2,136	28,711	82.6	Y.A. Tittle	AAFC-NFL	17	4,395	2,427	33,070	74.4
Fran Tarkenton	NFL	15	5,225	2,931	38,840	81.4	Earl Morrall	NFL	20	2,663	1,369	20,661	74.3
Bart Starr	NFL	16	3,149	1,808	24,718	80.3	Frank Albert	AAFC-NFL	7	1,564	831	10,795	73.5
Johnny Unitas	NFL	18	5,186	2,830	40,239	78.2	Daryle Lamonica	AFL-NFL	12	2,601	1,288	19,154	72.9
Frank Ryan	NFL	13	2,133	1,090	16,042	77.7	John Brodie	NFL	17	4,491	2,469	31,548	72.3
Norm Van Brocklin	NFL	12	2,895	1,553	23,611	75.3	Billy Wade	NFL	13	2,523	1,370	18,530	72.2
Sid Luckman	NFL	12	1,744	904	14,686	75.3	Bill Kilmer	NFL	13	2,531	1,355	17,740	72.1
Bob Griese	AFL-NFL	9	2,205	1,199	16,002	74.9	Sammy Baugh	NFL	16	2,995	1,693	21,886	72.0

*Rating points based on performances in the following categories: Percentage of completions, percentage of touchdown passes, percentage of interceptions, and average gain per pass attempt.

Most Yards Gained, Season — 4,007, Joe Namath, New York Jets, 1967.
Most Yards Gained Game — 554, Norm Van Brocklin, Los Angeles Rams vs. New York Yankees, Sept. 18, 1951 (27 completions in 41 attempts).
Most Touchdowns Passing, Career — 291, Fran Tarkenton, Minnesota Vikings, 1961-65; N.Y. Giants, 1967-71; Minnesota Vikings, 1972-75.
Most Touchdowns Passing, Season — 36, George Blanda, Houston Oilers, 1961 and Y.A. Tittle, N.Y. Giants, 1963.
Most Touchdowns Passing, Game — 7, Sid Luckman, Chicago Bears vs. New York Giants, Nov. 14, 1943; Adrian Burk, Philadelphia Eagles vs. Washington Redskins Oct. 17, 1954; George Blanda, Houston Oilers vs. New York Titans, Nov. 19, 1961; Y. A. Tittle, New York Giants vs. Washington Redskins, Oct. 28, 1962. Joe Kapp, Minnesota Vikings vs. Baltimore Colts, Sept. 28, 1969.
Most Passing Attempts, Season — 508, Sonny Jurgensen, Washington Redskins, 1967 (288 completions).
Most Passing Attempts, Game — 68, George Blanda, Houston Oilers vs. Buffalo Bills, Nov. 1, 1964 (37 completions).
Most Passes Completed, Season — 288, Sonny Jurgensen, Washington Redskins, 1967 (508 attempts).
Most Passes Completed, Game — 37, George Blanda, Houston Oilers vs. Buffalo Bills, Nov. 1, 1964 (68 attempts).
Most Consecutive Passes Completed — 17, Bert Jones, Baltimore Colts vs. N.Y. Jets, Dec. 15, 1974.

Leading Lifetime Receivers

Player	League	Yrs.	No.	Yds.	Avg.	Player	League	Yrs.	No.	Yds.	Avg.
Charley Taylor	NFL	12	635	8,952	14.1	Art Powell	AFL-NFL	10	479	8,046	16.8
Don Maynard	AFL-NFL	15	633	11,834	18.7	Boyd Dowler	NFL	12	474	7,270	15.4
Ray Berry	NFL	13	631	9,275	14.7	Jackie Smith	NFL	13	472	7,847	16.6
Lionel Taylor	AFL	9	567	7,195	12.7	Pete Retzlaff	NFL	11	452	7,412	16.4
Lance Alworth	AFL-NFL	11	542	10,266	18.9	Carroll Dale	NFL	14	438	8,271	18.9
Bobby Mitchell	NFL	11	521	7,954	15.3	Mike Ditka	NFL	12	427	5,812	13.6
Billy Howton	NFL	12	503	8,459	16.8	Roy Jefferson	NFL	11	424	7,175	16.9
Tom McDonald	NFL	12	495	8,410	17.0	Bobby Joe Conrad	NFL	12	422	5,902	14.0
Fred Biletnikoff	AFL-NFL	11	493	7,692	15.6	Jerry Smith	NFL	11	413	5,415	13.1
Don Hutson	NFL	11	488	7,991	16.4	Charley Hennigan	AFL	7	410	6,823	16.6

Most Yards Gained, Season — 1,746, Charley Hennigan, Houston Oilers, 1961.
Most Yards Gained Game — 303, Jim Benton, Cleveland Rams vs. Detroit Lions, Nov. 22, 1945 (10 receptions).
Most Pass Receptions, Season — 101, Charley Hennigan, Houston Oilers, 1964.
Most Pass Receptions, Game — 18, Tom Fears, Los Angeles Rams vs. Green Bay Packers, Dec. 3, 1950 (189 yards).
Most Consecutive Games, Pass Receptions — 105, Dan Abramowicz, New Orleans Saints, 1967-1973; San Francisco 49ers, 1973-1974.
Most Touchdown Passes, Career — 99, Don Hutson, Green Bay Packers, 1935-1945.
Most Touchdown Passes, Season — 17, Don Hutson, Green Bay Packers, 1942; Elroy Hirsch, Los Angeles Rams, 1951; Bill Groman, Houston Oilers, 1961.
Most Touchdown Passes, Game — 5, Bob Shaw, Chicago Cardinals vs. Baltimore Colts, Oct. 2, 1950.
Most Consecutive Games, Touchdown Passes — 11, Elroy Hirsch, Los Angeles Rams, 1950-1951; Buddy Dial, Pittsburgh, 1959-60.

Leading Lifetime Scorers

Player	League	Yrs.	TD	PAT	FG	Total	Player	League	Yrs.	TD	PAT	FG	Total
George Blanda	NFL-AFL	26	9	943	335	2,002	Bobby Walston	NFL	12	46	365	80	881
Lou Groza	AAFC-NFL	21	1	810	264	1,608	Pete Gogolak	AFL-NFL	10	0	344	173	863
Fred Cox	NFL	13	0	462	255	1,227	Don Hutson	NFL	11	105	172	7	823
Jim Bakken	NFL	14	0	439	244	1,171	Paul Hornung	NFL	9	62	190	66	760
Jim Turner	AFL-NFL	12	0	391	252	1,147	Jim Brown	NFL	9	126	0	0	756
Gino Cappelletti	AFL	11	42	350	176	1,130	Tom Davis	NFL	11	0	348	130	738
Bruce Gossett	NFL	11	0	374	219	1,031	Mike Clark	NFL	10	0	325	133	724
Sam Baker	NFL	15	2	428	179	977	Lenny Moore	NFL	12	113	0	0	678
Lou Michaels	NFL	13	1	386	187	955*	Roy Gerela	AFL-NFL	7	0	227	148	671
Jan Stenerud	AFL-NFL	9	0	287	218	941	Garo Yepremian	AFL-NFL	8	0	227	148	671

*Includes safety.

Most Points, Season — 176, Paul Hornung, Green Bay Packers, 1960 (15 TD's, 41 PAT's, 15 FG's).
Most Points, Game — 40, Ernie Nevers, Chicago Cardinals vs. Chicago Bears, Nov. 28, 1929 (6 TD's, 4 PAT's).
Most Touchdowns, Season — 23, O.J. Simpson, Buffalo Bills, 1975 (16 rushing, 9 pass receptions).
Most Touchdowns, Game — 6, Ernie Nevers, Chicago Cardinals vs. Chicago Bears Nov. 28, 1929 (6 rushing); Dub Jones, Cleveland Browns vs. Chicago Bears, Nov. 25, 1951 (4 rushing, 2 pass receptions); Gale Sayers, Chicago Bears vs. San Francisco 49ers, Dec. 12, 1965 (4 rushing, 1 pass reception, 1 punt return).
Most Points After Touchdown, Season — 64, George Blanda, Houston Oilers, 1961 (65 attempts).
Most Consecutive Points After Touchdown — 234, Tommy Davis, San Francisco 49ers, 1959-1965.
Most Field Goals, Game — 7, Jim Bakken, St. Louis Cardinals vs. Pittsburgh Steelers, Sept. 24, 1967.
Most Field Goals, Season — 34, Jim Turner, New York Jets, 1968 and 1969.
Most Field Goals Attempted, Season — 49, Bruce Gossett, Los Angeles Rams, 1966; Curt Knight, Washington Redskins, 1971.
Most Field Goals Attempted, Game — 9, Jim Bakken, St. Louis Cardinals vs. Pittsburgh Steelers, Sept. 24, 1967 (7 successful).
Most Consecutive Field Goals — 16, Jan Stenerud, Kansas City Chiefs, Nov. 2, 1969-Dec. 7, 1969.
Most Consecutive Games, Field Goal — 31, Fred Cox, Minnesota Vikings, 1968-1969.
Longest Field Goal — 63 yds., Tom Dempsey, New Orleans Saints vs. Detroit Lions, Nov, 8, 1970.
Highest Field Goal Percentage, Career (400 attempts) — 66.7, Jan Stenerud, Kansas City Chiefs, 1967-1975 (218 FG's in 327 attempts).
Highest Field Goal Completion Percentage, Season (20 attempts) — 88.5, Lou Groza, Cleveland Browns, 1953 (23 FG's in 26 attempts).

Pass Interceptions

Most Passes Had Intercepted, Game — 8, Jim Hardy, Chicago Cardinals vs. Philadelphia Eagles, Sept. 24, 1950 (39 ats).
Most Passes Had Intercepted, Season — 42, George Blanda, Houston Oilers, 1962 (418 attempts).
Most Passes Had Intercepted, Career — 277, George Blanda, Chicago Bears, 1949-1958; Houston Oilers, 1960-1966; Oakland Raiders, 1967-1975 (4,000 Attempts).
Most Consecutive Passes Attempted Without Interception — 294, Bart Starr, Green Bay Packers, 1964-1965.
Most Interceptions By, Season — 14, Dick Lane, Los Angeles Rams, 1952.
Most Interceptions By, Career — 79, Emlen Tunnell, New York Giants, 1948-1958: Green Bay Packers, 1959-1961.
Most Consecutive Games, Passes Intercepted By — 8, Tom Morrow, Oakland Raiders, 1962 (4), 1963 (4).
Most Touchdowns Scored via Pass Interceptions, Lifetime — 9, Ken Houston, Houston Oilers, 1967 (2); 1968 (2); 1969; 71 (4).

Punting

Highest Punting Average, Career (300 Punts) — 45.10, Sam Baugh, Washington Redskins, 1937-1952 (338 Punts).
Highest Punting Average, Season (20 Punts) — 51.3, Sam Baugh, Washington Redskins, 1940 (35 Punts).
Highest Punting Average, Game (4 Punts) — 59.4 Sam Baugh, Washington Redskins vs. Detroit Lions, Oct. 27, 1940 (5 punts.
Longest Punt — 98 yds., Steve O'Neal, New York Jets vs. Denver Broncos, Sept. 21, 1969.

Kickoff Returns

Most Yardage Returning Kickoffs, Career — 6,922 Ron Smith, Chicago Bears, 1965; Atlanta Falcons, 1966-67; Los Angeles Rams, 1968-69; Chicago Bears, 1970-72, San Diego Chargers, 1973; Oakland Raiders, 1974.
Most Yardage Returning Kickoffs, Season — 1,317, Bobby Jancik, Houston Oilers, 1963.
Most Yardage Returning Kickoffs, Game — 294, Wally Triplett, Detroit Lions vs. Los Angeles Rams, Oct. 29, 1950 (4 returns).
Most Touchdowns Scored via Kickoff Returns, Career — 6, Ollie Matson, Chicago Cardinals, 1952 (2), 1954, 1956, 1958 (2);Gale Sayers, Chicago Bears, 1965, 1966 (2), 1967 (3); Travis Williams, Green Bay Packers, 1967 (4), 1969; Los Angeles Rams, 1971.
Most Touchdowns Scored via Kickoff Returns, Season — 4, Travis Williams, Green Bay Packers, 1967; Cecil Turner, Chicago Bears, 1970.
Most Touchdowns Scored via Kickoff Returns, Game — 2, Tim Brown, Philadelphia Eagles vs. Dallas Cowboys, Nov. 6, 1966; Travis Williams, Green Bay Packers vs. Cleveland Browns, Nov. 12, 1967.
Most Kickoff Returns, Career — 275, Ron Smith, Chicago Bears, 1965; Atlanta Falcons, 1966-67; Los Angeles Rams, 1968-69 Chicago Bears, 1970-72, San Diego Chargers, 1973; Oakland Raiders, 1974.
Most Kickoff Returns, Season — 47, Odell Barry, Denver Broncos, 1964.
Longest Kickoff Return — 106 yds., Al Carmichael, Green Bay Packers vs. Chicago Bears, October 7, 1956 (scored touchdown); Noland Smith, Kansas City vs. Denver, Dec. 17, 1967 (scored touchdown).

Punt Returns

Most Yardage Returning Punts, Career — 2,209, Emlen Tunnell, New York Giants, 1948-1958; Green Bay Packers, 1959-1961.
Most Yardage Returning Punts, Season — 655, Neal Colzie, Oakland Raiders, 1975.
Most Yardage Returning Punts, Game — 205, George Atkinson, Oakland Raiders vs. Buffalo Bills, Sept. 15, 1968.
Most Touchdowns Scored via Punt Returns, Career — 8, Jack Christiansen, Detroit Lions, 1951 (4), 1952 (2), 1954, 1956.
Most Punt Returns, Career — 258, Emlen Tunnell, New York Giants, 1948-1958; Green Bay Packers, 1959-1961.
Most Punt Returns, Season — 53, Alvin Haymond, L.A. Rams, 1970; Larry Jones, Washington Redskins, 1975.
Most Punt Returns, Game — 9, Rodger Bird, Oakland Raiders vs. Denver Broncos, Sept. 10, 1967.
Longest Punt Return — 98, Gil LeFebvre, Cincinnati Reds vs. Brooklyn Dodgers, Dec. 3, 1933 (scored touchdown); Charles West, Minnesota Vikings vs. Washington Redskins, Nov. 3, 1968 (scored touchdown); Dennis Morgan, Dallas Cowboys vs. St. Louis Cardinals, Oct. 13, 1974 (scored touchdown).

Miscellaneous Records

Most Fumbles, Season — 16, Don Meredith, Dallas Cowboys, 1964.
Most Fumbles, Game — 7, Len Dawson, Kansas City Chiefs vs. San Diego Chargers, Nov. 15, 1964.
Longest Run with Recovered Fumble — 104 yds., Jack Tatum, Oakland Raiders vs. Green Bay Packers, Sept. 24, 1972.
Longest Winning Streak (Regular Season) — 17 games, Chicago Bears, 1933-1934.
Longest Undefeated Streak (Includes Tie Games) — 29 games, Cleveland Browns, 1947-1949 (won 27, tied 2).
Most Seasons, Active Player — 26, George Blanda, Chicago Bears, 1949-1958; Houston Oilers, 1960-1966 and Oakland, 67-75.

NFL Attendance

The National Football League drew 10,213,193 fans for the 182 regular season games in 1975, a decline of 0.2% from the previous year.

Steelers Defeat College All-Stars

The champion Pittsburgh Steelers defeated the College All-Stars 24-0 at Soldier Field, Chicago, July 23, 1976. Rain caused the game to be terminated in the 3d quarter. The annual charity event is sponsored by the Chicago Tribune.

1976 NFL Player Draft

The following are the first round picks of the National Football League

Team	Player	Pos.	College	Team	Player	Pos.	College
1—Tampa Bay	Leroy Selmon	DE	Oklahoma	15—Denver	Tom Glassic	G	Virginia
2—Seattle	Steve Niehaus	DT	Notre Dame	16—Detroit	Larry Gaines	RB	Wyoming
3—New Orleans	Chuck Muncie	RB	California	17—Miami	Larry Gordon	LB	Arizona State
4—San Diego	Joe Washington	RB	Oklahoma	18—Buffalo	Mario Clark	DB	Oregon
5—New England	Mike Haynes	DB	Arizona	19—Miami	Kim Bokamper	LB	San Jose State
6—New York Jets	Richard Todd	QB	Alabama	20—Baltimore	Ken Novak	DT	Purdue
7—Cleveland	Mike Pruitt	RB	Purdue	21—New England	Tim Fox	DB	Ohio State
8—Chicago	Dennis Lick	OT	Wisconsin	22—St. Louis	Mike Dawson	DT	Arizona
9—Atlanta	Bubba Bean	RB	Texas A & M	23—Green Bay	Mark Koncar	OT	Colorado
10—Detroit	James Hunter	DB	Grambling	24—Cincinnati	Archie Griffin	RB	Ohio State
11—Cincinnati	Billy Brooks	WR	Oklahoma	25—Minnesota	James White	DT	Oklahoma State
12—New England	Pete Brock	C	Colorado	26—Los Angeles	Kevin McLain	LB	Colorado State
13—N.Y. Giants	Troy Archer	DE	Colorado	27—Dallas	Aaron Kyle	DB	Wyoming
14—Kansas City	Rod Walters	OT	Iowa	28—Pittsburgh	Bennie Cunningham	TE	Clemson

Pro Football Hall Of Fame, Canton, Ohio

Cliff Battles	Len Ford	Dante Lavelli	Jim Parker
Sammy Baugh	Dr. Daniel Fortmann	Bobby Layne	Joe Perry
Chuck Bednarik	Bill George	Vince Lombardi	Pete Pihos
Bert Bell	Otto Graham	Sid Luckman	Hugh (Shorty) Ray
Raymond Berry	Red Grange	Link Lyman	Dan Reeves
Charles Bidwell	Lou Groza	Tim Mara	Andy Robustelli
Jim Brown	Joe Guyon	Gino Marchetti	Art Rooney
Paul Brown	George Halas	George Marshall	Joe Schmidt
Roosevelt Brown	Ed Healey	Ollie Matson	Ernie Stautner
Tony Canadeo	Mel Hein	George McAfee	Ken Strong
Joe Carr	Pete Henry	Hugh McElhenny	Joe Stydahar
Guy Chamberlin	Arnold Herber	John (Blood) McNally	Jim Taylor
Jack Christiansen	Bill Hewitt	Mike Michalske	Jim Thorpe
Dutch Clark	Clarke Hinkle	Wayne Millner	Y. A. Tittle
George Connor	Elroy Hirsch	Lenny Moore	George Trafton
Jim Conzelman	Cal Hubbard	Marion Motley	Charlie Trippi
Art Donovan	Lamar Hunt	Bronko Nagurski	Emlen Tunnell
Paddy Driscoll	Don Hutson	Greasy Neale	Clyde (Bulldog) Turner
Bill Dudley	Walt Kiesling	Ernie Nevers	Norm Van Brocklin
Turk Edwards	Frank (Bruiser) Kinard	Leo Nomellini	Steve Van Buren
Tom Fears	Curly Lambeau	Steve Owen	Bob Waterfield
Ray Flaherty	Dick (Night Train) Lane	Clarence (Ace) Parker	Alex Wojciechowicz

Stadiums

For stadiums that house a major league baseball team and college stadiums see index.

Name and location	Capacity	Name and location	Capacity
Joseph Albi Memorial Stadium, Spokane	31,820	Legion Field, Birmingham, Ala.	72,000
American Legion Memorial, Charlotte, N.C.	22,315	Long Beach (Cal.) Veterans Memorial	15,000
Arrowhead Stadium, Kansas City, Mo.	78,097	Los Angeles Memorial Coliseum	90,000
Balboa Stadium, San Diego, Calif.	34,500	Louisiana Superdome, New Orleans	74,726
Bowman Grey Stad., Winston-Salem, N.C.	16,841	Memphis Memorial Stadium	50,000
Buffalo War Memorial Stadium	46,206	Mile High Stadium, Denver	63,500
Columbus (Ga.) Memorial Stadium	35,000	Mississippi Memorial Stadium, Jackson	46,000
Cotton Bowl, Dallas, Texas	72,000	Orange Bowl, Miami, Fla.	80,045
Downing Stadium, New York, N.Y.	27,000	Ottawa Stadium, Ottawa, Canada	27,872
Empire Stadium, Vancouver	32,759	Pontiac Metropolitan Stadium, Mich.	80,638
Exhibition Stadium, Toronto	39,485	Portland Civic Stadium	33,000
Franklin Field, Philadelphia	60,658	Rich Stadium, Buffalo, N.Y.	80,020
Gator Bowl, Jacksonville, Fla.	70,000	Richmond (Va.) City Stadium	22,009
Giants Stadium, New Jersey	76,500	Roanoke (Va.) Victory Stadium	30,000
Halawa Stadium, Hawaii	50,000	Roosevelt Stadium, Jersey City	25,000
Honolulu Stadium	25,000	Rose Bowl, Pasadena, Cal.	106,721
John F. Kennedy Stadium, Philadelphia	105,000	Rubber Bowl, Akron, Ohio	35,007
Robert F. Kennedy Memorial Stadium, Wash., D.C.	55,004	Schaefer Stadium, Foxboro, Mass.	61,279
Kentucky Exposition Stadium, Louisville	21,000	Sicks Stadium, Seattle	24,420
Kezar Stadium, San Francisco	59,636	Soldier Field, Chicago	57,455
Kingdome, Seattle	65,000	Sugar Bowl, New Orleans, La.	80,982
Ladd Memorial Stadium, Mobile, Ala.	40,605	Sun Bowl, El Paso, Texas	30,000
Lambeau Field, Green Bay, Wis.	56,267	Tampa Stadium, Tampa, Fla.	71,000
Las Vegas Stadium	16,000	Texas Stadium, Dallas	65,101

Amateur Softball Association Champions in 1976

Division	National Champion	Division	National Champion
Men's Slow Pitch	Levittown Legion, Long Island, N.Y.	Men's Fast Pitch	Neals' Truck Parts, Grand Rapids, Mich.
Women's Slow Pitch	Shamrocks, Winston-Salem, N.C.	16-Inch Slow Pitch	Josef's, Chicago, Ill.

American Bowling Congress Championships, 1976

73d Tournament-Oklahoma City, Okla.

Regular Division

Individual

1. Mike Putzer, Oshkosh, Wis. 279, 258, 221 — 758.
2. Jim Lindquist, Minneapolis, Minn. 277, 268, 212 — 757.
3. Mike Rokita, Quincy, Ill. 215, 249, 279 — 743.

Runners-up — H. B. Childress, Virginia Beach, Va. 741; Wade Smith, Springfield, Ill. 737; Dale Euwer, Topeka, Kan. 732; Tom Donnelly, Milwaukee, Wis. 731; Joe Drusbacky, Port Clinton, Oh. 730; Bob Metz, Dayton, Oh. 728; Mike Dragomir, Massillon, Oh. 724.

All-Events

1. Jim Lindquist, Minneapolis, Minn. 618, 696, 757 — 2071.
2. Mike Putzer, Oshkosh, Wis. 646, 632, 758 — 2036.
3. Ed Hansen, Seattle, Wash. 604, 709, 722 — 2035.

Runners-up — Dale Euwer, Topeka, Kan. 2026; Wade Smith, Springfield, Ill. 1983; Glenn Chesser, Chicago, Ill. 1979; Al Cohn, Chicago, Ill. 1978; Pat Tyler, St. Louis, Mo. 1977; Dave Skillingstad, Minneapolis, Minn., Richard Stephens, St. Joseph, Mo. 1976.

Doubles

1. Fred Willen Sr., St. Louis, Mo. 181, 230, 287 — 698; Gary Voss, St. Louis, Mo. 247, 220, 191 — 658. Aggregate — 1356.
2. Joe Camloh, Cleveland, Oh. 225, 158, 226 — 609; Gary Bush, Cleveland, Oh. 264, 236, 236 — 736. Aggregate — 1345.
3. Malcolm McEwen, Flint, Mich. 194, 208, 247 — 649; Bernie Morgan, Flint, Mich. 226, 215, 247 — 688. Aggregate — 1337.

Teams

1. Andy's Pro Shop, Tucson, Ariz. — John Palko 226, 189, 224 — 639; Dewey Yoho 213, 224, 221 — 658; Bob Vaughn 209, 174, 171 — 554; Richard Zimmerman 233, 190, 201 — 624; Pete Tountas 190, 264, 258 — 712. Aggregate — 3187.
2. Widman's Motorcycles, St. Louis, Mo.—Ray Brand 214, 232, 212—658; Earl Widman 217, 203, 224—664; Bob Brissette 219, 204, 192 — 615; Elvin Mesger 181, 230, 169 — 580; John Wonders 221, 235, 214 — 670. Aggregate — 3167.

Classic Division

Individual

1. Jim Schroeder, Buffalo, N.Y. 258, 247, 245 — 750.
2. Gary Fust, Des Moines, Iowa 258, 217, 268 — 743.
3. Maury Newman, Dallas, Tex. 233, 245, 242 — 720

Runners-up — Bud Horn, Los Angeles, Cal. 717; Bill McCorkle, Columbus, Oh. and Mark Tietjens, St. Louis, Mo. 716; George Pappas, Charlotte, N.C. 713; John Weber, St. Louis, Mo. 709; Jim Godman, Lorain, Oh. 707; Fred Wilson, New Orleans, La. 703.

All-Events

1. Gary Fust, Des Moines, Iowa 622, 685, 743 — 2050.
2. Pete Tountas, Tucson, Ariz. 712, 701, 626 — 2039.
3. Fred Wilson, New Orleans, La. 681, 654, 703 — 2038.

Runners-up: Ernie Schlegel, New York, N.Y. and Jim Stefanich, Joliet, Ill. 1989; Dennis Lane, Kingsport, Tenn. 1983; Paul Colwell, Tucson, Ariz. 1982; Wally Bush, St. Louis, Mo. 1981; Barry Asher, Costa Mesa, Cal. 1976; Glenn Allison, Los Angeles, Cal. 1965.

Doubles

1. Don Johnson, Las Vegas, Nev. 258, 245, 268 — 771; Paul Colwell, Tucson, Ariz. 203, 244, 224 — 671. Aggregate 1442.
2. Les Zikes, Chicago, Ill. 190, 269, 241 — 700; Tommy Hudson, Akron, Oh. 173, 289, 215 — 677. Aggregate — 1377.
3. Mark Keltner, St. Louis, Mo. 226, 258, 199 — 683; Norm Friedmeyer, St. Louis, Mo. 208, 254, 225 — 687. Aggregate — 1370.

Teams

1. Munsingwear No. 2, Minneapolis, Minn. — Roy Buckley 215, 237, 289 — 741; Norm Meyers 212, 177, 249 — 638; Barry Asher 206, 248, 223 — 677; Bud Horn 187, 209, 213 — 609; Nelson Burton Jr. 232, 215, 169 — 616. Aggregate 3281.
2. Cherokee Lanes No. 2, Springfield, Mo. — Roger Wiemer 164, 199, 205— 568; Bill Walden, 192, 209, 179 — 580; Hike Tietjens 210, 221, 245 — 676; Gus Marsala 195, 228, 237 — 660; Ray Orf 213, 235, 192— 640. Aggregate — 3124.

Other Bowling Championships in 1976

6th U.S. Open—Men—Grand Prairie, Tex., Mar. 14-20; Paul Moser, Medford, Pa. Average 212. Prize $10,000. Women — Tulsa, Okla, May 30-June 3; Patty Costello, Scranton, Pa. Average 227. Prize $6,000.

National Intercollegiate Championships — Oklahoma City, Okla. April 5; Doubles — Tom Porwell, Florida State-Ellis Mitchell, Alabama. Singles — Mark Schwabe, U-Wisconsin-

Milwaukee. All-events—Mark Schwabe, U-Wisconsin-Milwaukee.

Invitational Tournament of the Americas — Miami, Fla.-July 11-17; Men's Doubles — Glen Watson and Jean Bernard, Canada; Singles — Tomas Barria, Panama; All-events — Glen Watson, Canada; Women's Doubles — Lyn Carpenter - Ruby Sizemore, United States; Singles — Regina Penaloza, Venezuela; All-events — Cathy Townsend, Canada.

Masters Bowling Tournament Champions

Year	Winner	Runner-up	W.L.	Avg.
1964	Billy Welu, St. Louis, Mo.	Harry Smith, Baltimore, Md.	7-0.	227
1965	Billy Welu, St. Louis, Mo.	Don Ellis, Houston, Tex.	9-1.	202-12
1966	Bob Strampe, Detroit, Mich.	Al Thompson, Cleveland, Ohio.	7-0.	219-8
1967	Lou Scalia, Miami, Fla.	Bill Johnson, New Orleans, La.	7-0.	216-9
1968	Pete Tountas, Tucson, Ariz.	Buzz Fazio, Detroit, Mich.	9-1.	220-15
1969	Jim Chestney, Denver, Col.	Barry Asher, Costa Mesa, Cal.	10-1.	223-2
1970	Don Glover, Bakersfield, Cal.	Bob Strampe, Detroit, Mich.	9-1.	215-10
1971	Jim Godman, Lorain, Ohio.	Don Johnson, Akron, Ohio.	9-1.	229-8
1972	Bill Beach, Sharon, Pa.	Jim Godman, Lorain, Ohio.	8-1.	220-27
1973	Dave Soutar, Gilroy, Cal.	Dick Ritger, Hartford, Wis.	7-0.	218-61
1974	Paul Colwell, Tucson, Ariz.	Steve Neff, Sarasota, Fla.	7-0.	234-17
1975	Ed Ressler Jr., Allentown, Pa.	Sam Flanagan, Parkersburg, W. Va.	9-1.	213-57
1976	Nelson Burton Jr., St. Louis, Mo.	Steve Carson, Oklahoma City, Okla.	7-0.	220-79

All-Time Records for League and Tournament Play

Type of record	Holder of record	Year	Score	Competition
High team total	Budweiser Beer, St. Louis	1958	3,858	League
High team game	Hook Grip Five, Lodi, N.J.	1950	1,342	League
High doubles total	Nelson Burton Jr., Billy Walden, St. Louis.	1970	1,614	Tournament
High doubles game	Jesse Foley and Wendell Cromer, Shreveport, La.	1976	598*	League
High individual total	Albert Brandt, Lockport, N.Y.	1939	886	League
High all events score	Denny Campbell, Chicago, Ill.	1976	2,314	Tournament

*In 4 person league.

Record Averages for Consecutive Tournaments

No. in row	Name of record holder	Span	Games	Average
Two	Jim Godman, Lorain, Ohio	1974-75	18	228.78
Three	Jim Godman, Lorain, Ohio	1974-76	27	222.96
Four	Jim Godman, Lorain, Ohio	1972-76	36	218.41
Five	Bob Strampe, Detroit, Mich.	1964-68	57	215.28
Ten	Bob Strampe, Detroit, Mich.	1961-70	111	211.10

Official Records of Annual ABC Tournaments

Type of record	Holder of record	Year	Score
High team total	Ace Mitchell Shur-Hooks, Akron, Ohio	1966	3,357
High team game	Falstaff Beer, San Antonio, Texas	1958	1,226
High doubles score	John Klares-Steve Nagy, Cleveland, Ohio	1952	1,453
High doubles game	Tommy Hudson, Akron, Ohio-Les Zikes, Chicago, Ill.	1976	558
High singles total	Lee Jouglard, Detroit, Mich.	1951	775
High all events score	Jim Godman, Lorain, Ohio	1974	2,184
High team all events	Falstaff Beer, St. Louis, Mo.	1958	9,608
High life-time pin total	Bill Doehrman, Ft. Wayne, Ind.	1908-1976	106,768

Bowlers With Six or More Sanctioned 300 Games

Elvin Mesger, Sullivan, Mo. — 26	Dave Williams, Sebastopal, Cal. — 9	Don Glover, Bakersfield, Cal. — 7
George Billick, Old Forge, Pa. — 17	Norm Meyers, St. Louis — 9	Salvatore Bivona, Paterson, N.J. — 6
Dick Weber, St. Louis — 16	Tom Hennessey, St. Louis — 9	Lou Campi, Dumont, N.J. — 6
Al Faragalli, Wayne, N.J. — 14	Howard Holmes, Los Angeles — 8	Ed Davis, Milford, N.J. — 6
Dave Soutar, Gilroy, Cal. — 14	Russell Field, San Jose, Cal. — 8	Don Dubro, St. Louis — 6
Ron Graham, Louisville — 14	Roger Fink, Lodi, Cal. — 8	*Bill Flynn, Cleveland — 6
Don Carter, Miami, Fla. — 13	George Pappas, Charlotte, N.C. — 8	Sam Garofalo, St. Louis — 6
Ray Bluth, St. Louis — 12	Dennis Wright, Milwaukee — 8	Joe Joseph, Lansing, Mich. — 6
Walter Ward, Cleveland — 12	Ray Eklund, Milwaukee — 8	Pete Kozloski, Plains, Pa. — 6
Don Johnson, Las Vegas. — 12	Walter King, Detroit, Mich. — 8	Vince Lucci, Trenton, N.J. — 6
*Hank Marino, Milwaukee — 11	Junie McMahon, Lodi, N.J. — 8	Steve Nagy, Cleveland — 6
Frank Clause, Old Forge, Pa. — 11	Bud Horn, Los Angeles. — 8	Frank Pollak, Pittsburgh — 6
Ed Lubanski, Detroit — 11	Joe Donato, Schenectady, N.Y. — 7	Robert Pinkalla, Milwaukee — 6
Pat Patterson, St. Louis. — 11	Eddie Botten, Union City, N.J. — 7	Harold Schaeffer, St. Louis. — 6
Dennis Soper, Tustin, Cal. — 11	Dick Hoover, Akron. — 7	Harry Smith, Rochester, N.Y. — 6
Mike Durbin, Lorain, Ohio. — 10	Ken McKenzie, Dallas — 7	Bob Strampe, Detroit, Mich. — 6
Casey Jones, Plymouth, Wis. — 10	Ray Schanen, Milwaukee — 7	Jerry Tharp, St. Louis — 6
Boss Bosco, Akron, O. — 9	Wayne Pinkalla, Milwaukee. — 7	George Tomek, Plymouth, Pa. — 6
Al Savas, Milwaukee — 9	George Pappas, Charlotte. — 7	Stephen Tomek, Plymouth, Pa. — 6
Lou Foxie, Paterson, N.J. — 9	Bob Ramirez, Los Angeles — 7	William Capleton, Prospect Park, N.J. — 6
Jerry Woji, Stockton, Cal. — 9	Don McCune, Munster, Ind. — 7	Mark Sutter, St. Louis. — 6

*Bowled two 300 games in official 3-game-series.

PBA Winter Tour, 1976

Date	Event	Winner	Winner's Share
Dec. 28-Jan. 3	Ford Open, Arcadia, Cal.	Johnny Guenther	$ 8,000
Jan. 6-10.	ARC Alameda Open, Alameda, Cal.	Roy Buckley	7,500
Jan. 11-17.	Showboat Invitational, Las Vegas	Wayne Zahn	14,000
Jan. 20-24.	Denver Open	Jim Stefanich	7,500
Jan. 27-31.	King Louie Open, Overland Park, Kan.	George Pappas	8,000
Feb. 3-7.	Cleveland Open, No. Olmsted, Ohio.	Tom Hudson	7,500
Feb. 10-14.	Fair Lanes Open, Baltimore	Curt Schmidt	8,000
Feb. 17-21.	AMF Pro Classic, Garden City, N.Y.	Dick Weber	14,000
Feb. 24-28.	Midas Open, Windsor Locks, Conn.	Earl Anthony	14,000
Mar. 2-6.	AMF Dick Weber 5 Star Open, Tamarac, Fla.	Earl Anthony	14,000
Mar. 9-13.	New Orleans Lions Open.	Louis Moore	7,500
Mar. 14-20.	BPAA U. S. Open, Grand Prairie, Tex.	Paul Moser	10,000
Mar. 23-27.	Rolaids Open, St. Louis	Mark Roth	14,000
Mar. 30-Apr. 3.	Miller High Life Open, Milwaukee	Dave Soutar	10,000
Apr. 6-10.	Monro-Matic Open, Toledo	Billy Hardwick	10,000
Apr. 12-17.	Firestone Tournament of Champions, Akron	Marshall Holman	25,000

Leading PBA Averages in 1975
(16 or More Tournaments)

Pos.	Name, City	Tournaments	Games	Pinfall	Average
1.	Earl Anthony, Tacoma, Wash.	30	1,160	254,110	219,060
2.	Mark Roth, Staten Island, N.Y.	24	757	163,430	215,892
3.	Roy Buckley, Columbus, O.	30	1,013	218,299	215,498
4.	Gary Dickinson, Ft. Worth, Tex.	33	923	197,903	214,413
5.	Nelson Burton Jr., St. Louis, Mo.	26	804	172,331	214,342
6.	Johnny Petraglia, Staten Island, N.Y.	20	660	141,323	214,126
7.	Dick Weber, St. Louis, Mo.	16	522	111,268	213,157
8.	Cliff McNealy, San Lorenzo, Cal.	24	727	154,648	212,721
9.	Tommy Hudson, Akron, O.	34	1,006	213,175	212,500
10.	Dave Davis, Atlanta, Ga.	20	573	121,661	212,323
11.	Eddie Ressler Jr., Allentown, Pa.	34	1,053	223,498	212,249
12.	Carmen Salvino, Chicago, Ill.	33	1,079	228,993	212,227
13.	Ed DiTolla, Maywood, N.J.	19	557	117,995	211,840
14.	Don Johnson, Las Vegas, Nev.	26	762	161,069	211,377
15.	George Pappas, Charlotte, N.C.	30	925	195,452	211,299
16.	Jim Frazier, Spokane, Wash.	30	887	187,389	211,262
17.	Larry Laub, San Francisco, Cal.	34	955	201,750	211,257
18.	Jim Godman, Lorain, O.	29	813	171,661	211,145
19.	Jay Robinson, Los Angeles, Cal.	32	930	196,363	211,143
20.	Fred Conner, Mar Vista, Cal.	26	745	157,265	211,094

Firestone Tournament of Champions

This is professional bowling's richest tournament and has been held each year since its inception in 1965, in Akron, Oh., the home of the Professional Bowlers Association. First prize is $25,000.

Year	Winner	Year	Winner	Year	Winner	Year	Winner
1965. . . .	Billy Hardwick	1968. . . .	Dave Davis	1971. . . .	Johnny Petraglia	1974. . . .	Earl Anthony
1966. . . .	Wayne Zahn	1969. . . .	Jim Godman	1972. . . .	Mike Durbin	1975. . . .	Dave Davis
1967. . . .	Jim Stefanich	1970. . . .	Don Johnson	1973. . . .	Jim Godman	1976. . . .	Marshall Holman

Leading PBA Averages by Years

Year	Player	Tour-naments	Average	Year	Player	Tour-naments	Average
1962 —	Don Carter, St. Louis, Mo. . . .	25	212.844	1969 —	Bill Hardwick, Louisville, Ky. . .	33	212.957
1963 —	Billy Hardwick, Louisville, Ky. .	26	210.346	1970 —	Nelson Burton Jr., St. Louis, Mo.	32	214.908
1964 —	Ray Bluth, St. Louis, Mo.	27	210.512	1971 —	Don Johnson, Akron, Oh.	31	213.977
1965 —	Dick Weber, St. Louis, Mo. . . .	19	211.895	1972 —	Don Johnson, Akron, Oh.	30	215.290
1966 —	Wayne Zahn, Atlanta, Ga.	27	208.663	1973 —	Earl Anthony, Tacoma, Wash. .	29	215.799
1967 —	Wayne Zahn, Atlanta, Ga.	29	212.342	1974 —	Earl Anthony, Tacoma, Wash. .	28	219.394
1968 —	Jim Stefanich, Joliet, Ill.	33	211.895	1975 —	Earl Anthony, Tacoma, Wash. .	30	219.060

PBA Leading Money Winners

Total winnings are from PBA, ABC Masters, and BPAA All-Star tournaments only, and do not include numerous other tournaments or earnings from special television shows and matches.

Year	Player	Total	Year	Player	Total	Year	Player	Total
1959	Dick Weber.	$ 7,672	1965	Dick Weber.	$47,674	1971	Johnny Petraglia.	$85,065
1960	Don Carter.	22,525	1966	Wayne Zahn.	54,720	1972	Don Johnson	56,648
1961	Dick Weber.	26,280	1967	Dave Davis.	54,165	1973	Don McCune.	69,000
1962	Don Carter.	49,972	1968	Jim Stefanich.	67,377	1974	Earl Anthony.	99,585
1963	Dick Weber.	46,333	1969	Billy Hardwick.	64,160	1975	Earl Anthony.	107,585
1964	Bob Strampe.	33,592	1970	Mike McGrath.	52,049			

Women's International Bowling Congress Champions

Year	Individual	All Events	2-Woman Teams	5-Woman Teams
1970	Dorothy Fothergill, N. Attleboro, Mass.. **695**	Dorothy Fothergill. . **1,984**	Gloria Bouvia, Portland, Ore.-Judy Cook, Kansas City, Mo. . . **1,256**	Parker-Fothergill Pro Shop, Cranston, R.I.. . . . . **3,034**
1971	Mary Scruggs, Richmond, Va. **698**	Lorrie Koch, Carpentersville, Ill. **1,840**	Dorothy Fothergill, N. Attleboro, Mass.- Mildred Martorella, Rochester, N.Y.. . . **1,263**	Koenig & Strey Real Estate, Wilmette, Ill.. . . . . . **2,891**
1972	D. D. Jacobson, Playa Del Rey, Cal.. **737**	Mildred Martorella, Rochester, N.Y.. . . **1,877**	Judy Roberts- Betty Remmick, Denver, Lakewood, Col.. . . . . **1,247**	Angeltown Creations, Placentia, Cal.. . . . . **2,838**
1973	Bobbie Buffaloe, Costa Mesa, Cal.. . . . **706**	Toni Calvery, Midwest City, Okla.. . . . . **1,910**	Dorothy Fothergill, N. Attleboro, Mass.- Mildred Martorella, Rochester, N.Y.. . **1,238**	Fitzpatrick Chevrolet, Concord, Cal.. . . . . **2,897**
1974	Shirley Garms, Lake Island, Ill.. . . . **702**	Judy Cook Soutar, Kansas City, Mo.. . **1,944**	Jane Leszczynski, Milwaukee-Carol Miller, Waukesha, Wis.. . . . . **1,313**	Kalicak International Construction, Kansas City, Mo. . . **2,973**
1975	Barbara Leicht, Albany, N.Y.. . . . . . . **689**	Virginia Park, Whittier, Cal.. . . . **1,821**	Jennette James, Oyster Bay, Dawn Raddatz, Northport, N.Y.. . . . . **1,234**	Atlanta Bowling Center (Ga.) Buffalo, N.Y.. . . . . . **2,836**
1976	Beverly Shonk, Canton, Ohio. **686**	Betty Morris, Stockton, Cal.. . . . **1,866**	Georgene Cordes-Shirley Stostrom, Bloomington, Minn.; Eloise Vacco- Debbie Rainone, Cleveland Hts., Oh. (tie). **1,232**	PWBA 1, Oklahoma City, Okla.. . . . . **2,839**

Records of 300 Games in WIBC Sanctioned Play

1975-76—Irma Chase, Chico, Cal.; Terry Christianson, Onawa, Iowa; Doris Coburn, Buffalo, N.Y.; Mary Denny, St. Louis, Mo.; Velda Gooden, Richmond, Cal.; Carolyn Grund, Solvay, N.Y.; Norma Hill, Lawton, Okla.; Pamela Johnson, Canoga Park, Cal.; Casandra Kalina, Lynchburg, Va.; Alice King, Victoria, Tex.; Rosia McVea, Stuttgart Area, Germany; Connie Medlin, Niangua, Mo; Betty Morris, Stockton, Cal. (2); Bobbie Nelius, Houston, Tex.; Bev Ortner, Tucson, Ariz. (2); Banky Pearson, Fresno, Cal.; Pat Petersohn, San Jose, Cal.; Ethel Poor, San Jose, Cal.; Rita Resek, Heath, Ohio; Ann Slattery, Salt Lake City, Utah; Mary Smith, Asheville, N.C.; Karen Spero, Aviano, Italy; Robin Sperry, Port Jervis, N.Y.; Lila Swaney, Xenia, Ohio; Judith Van Pelt, East Brunswick, N.J.; Irma Whitney, Ojai, Cal.

1974-75—Mary Altmeyer, St. Louis, Mo. (2); Dianne Bonney, New London, Ohio; Ann Carroll, Fort Worth, Texas; Linda Clayton, Alexandria, La.; Virginia Copeland, Cypress, Cal.; Shirley Davis, Asheville, N.C.; Charlene Grossman, Rothbury, Mich.; Linda Harris, Minot, N.D.; Linda Huffman, Topeka, Kan.; Barbara Leicht, Albany, N.Y.; Joan McCord, Cedar Rapids, Iowa; Myrtie Minster, Irving, Texas; Sharon Pippitt, Liberal, Kan.; Judy Soutar, Grandview, Mo.; Cecilia Straley, Omaha, Neb.; Barbara Urban, St. Paul, Minn.; Barbara Waling, Northville, Mich.; Claudine Walker, Chicago, Ill.; Jean Worthy, Norwalk, Cal.; Patricia Paulson, Mt. Prospect, Ill.; Barbara Cunningham, Waco, Texas.

1973-74—Irene Arslan, Sunnyvale, Cal.; Nancy Bassett, Salina, Kan.; Leemoi Bekey, San Rafael, Cal.; Josephine Borges, Oakland, Cal.; Lydia Brewer, LaMirada, Cal.; Judith Chapman, Littleton, Col.; Ferrie Crawford, Philadelphia, Pa.; Ethel Dezell, Staples, Minn.; Mary Ickes, Woodville, Ohio; Barbara Kaufold, Butler, Pa.; Nell Kleinschmidt, Mt. Carmel, Ill.; Betty Morris, Stockton, Cal.; Lou Lane, Austin, Texas; Patsy Lynn, Spokane, Wash.; Lupe McCabe, Fresno, Cal.; Cindy Pearl, Louisville, Ky.; Roslyn Stewart, Detroit, Mich.; Mel Williams, Fayetteville, N.C.; Jacqueline Kissler, Reading, Pa.

Rifle and Pistol Individual Championships in 1976

Source: National Rifle Association of America

National Rifle & Pistol Championships (Outdoor, Conventional)

Pistol—SFC Bonnie Harmon, USA, Ft. Benning, Ga. 2647-133X
Civilian Pistol—H. B. Bowlin, San Diego, Cal. 2617-113X
Woman Pistol—SP4 Ruby Fox, USAR, Parker, Ariz., 2586-77X
Senior Pistol—Gil Hebard, Knoxville, Ill., 2574-86X
Police Pistol—John Farley, Americus, Ga., 2613-115X
Nat'l Gd. Pistol—Sgt. James Lenardson, Erie, Mich., 2641-123X
Collegiate Pistol—Bradley Tilgner, Severna Park., Md., 2521-82X
USAR Pistol—Sgt. Frank M. Goza, Lookout Mtn., Tenn., 2615-96X
USN Pistol—William Boyd, Poway, Cal. 2621-107X
USNR Pistol—Donald Hamilton, Kingston, Mass., 2633-127X
Smallbore Rifle Prone—David Weaver, Oil City, Pa., 6396-538X
Service Smallbore Rifle Prone—Maj. Lones W. Wigger Jr., USA, Ft. Benning, Ga., 6395-549X
Woman Smallbore Rifle Prone—Mary Stidworthy, NGUS, Prescott, Ariz., 6394-518X
Collegiate Smallbore Rifle Prone—William Lewellen, Canoga Park, Cal., 6388-458X
Senior Smallbore Rifle Prone—Joseph E. Steffey, Paris, Ill., 6384-478X
Junior Smallbore Rifle Prone—Tracy A. Hill, Arlington, Tex., 6383-475X
Smallbore Rifle Position—Lones W. Wigger Jr., 3175-206X
Civilian Smallbore Rifle Position—Calvin Roberts, Beaver Falls, Pa., 3146-163X

Woman Smallbore Rifle Position—Sherri Lewellen, Canoga Park, Cal., 3144-154X
Senior Smallbore Rifle Position—Robert Makielski, Mishawaka, Ind., 3099-133X
Collegiate Smallbore Rifle Position—Shawn McDonnell, Coos Cob, Conn., 3137-150X
High Power Rifle—Gary Anderson, Axtell, Neb., 1990-111X
Match Rifle Senior—Robert Wright, Farmersville, Ohio, 1951-61X
Match Rifle Woman—Nancy Clark, Phoenix, Ariz., 1929-53X
Match Rifle Junior—Randy Ciavarelli, Plymouth, Iowa, 1947-67X
Match Rifle Collegiate—Carl Bernosky, Gordon, Pa., 1963-75X
Service Rifle Champion—Cpt. Boyd Goldsby, USAR, Little Rock, Ark., 1981-87X
Service Rifle Civilian—Bert Rollins, Fairfax, Va., 1955-73X
Service Rifle Woman—Cpl. Jamie Trombley, USMC, Parris Island, S.C., 1935-39X
Service Rifle Junior—Matthew McSheehy, Redding, Mass., 1868-27X
Service Rifle Senior—Gerritt H. Stekeur, Latham, N.Y., 1949-53X
Service Rifle Regular Service—SFC William Lee, USA, Ft. Benning, Ga., 1980-96X
Service Rifle Collegiate—Dale Pierce, Ft. Meade, Md., 1887-30X
Service Rifle Marine—MGYSGT Russell Martin, Quantico, Va., 1973-76X

U.S. NRA International Shooting Championships

English Match—David Ross, Houston, Tex., 1782
Smallbore 3-Position—Lanny Bassham, Columbus, Ga., 3475
Air Rifle—Lanny Bassham, 1166
Junior Air Rifle—Roderick Fitz-Randolph, El Paso, Tex., 1146
Ladies Air Rifle—Karen Monez, San Leandro, Cal., 1136
Ladies Stand. Rifle Prone—Mary Stidworthy, Prescott, Ariz., 1753
Junior Stand. Rifle Prone—Matthew Stark, Alexandria, Va., 1761
Standard Rifle 3-Pos.—David Kimes, Huntington Beach, Cal., 1709
Ladies Stand. Rifle 3-Pos.—Sue Sandusky, Ft. Worth, Tex., 1696
Junior Stand. Rifle 3-Pos.—Roderick Fitz-Randolph, 1682
Free Rifle, 300 Meter—Lones Wigger, Columbus, Ga., 3423
Big Bore Stand. Rifle—Lones Wigger, 1141

Free Pistol—Hershel Anderson, Columbus, Ga., 1672
Air Pistol—Hershel Anderson, 1149
Ladies Air Pistol—Ruby Fox, Parker, Ariz., 1109
Junior Air Pistol—Matthew Nesbitt, San Jose, Cal., 1083
Centerfire Pistol—Hershel Anderson,1774
Rapid Fire Pistol—William McMillan, Delmar, Cal., 1768
Standard Pistol—Francis Higginson, Quantico, Va., 1739
Ladies Smallbore Pistol—Ruby Fox, 1729
Running Boar, Slow & Fast—Louis Theimer, Columbus, Ga., 1679
Running Boar, Mixed—Louis Theimer, 376
Int'l Skeet—Co-Champions—John Satterwhite, Kirkland, Wash., Brad Simmons, Tyler, Tex., 292
Ladies Int'l Skeet—Ila Hill, Troy, Mich. 278
Junior Int'l Skeet—Matt Dryke, Sequim, Wash., 289

National Indoor Rifle & Pistol Champions

Conventional Rifle—Co-Holders: PFC Karen Monez, USAR, San Leandro, Cal., Maj. Lones Wigger Jr., USA, Ft. Benning, Ga., 800
Conventional Rifle Woman—PFC Karen Monez, 800
International Rifle—Lt. Edward Etzel Jr., USA, Ft. Benning, Ga., 1179
International Rifle Woman—SP-4 Sue Ann Sandusky, USAR, Ft. Worth, Tex., 1166
NRA 3-Postion Rifle—Capt. Larry Bassham, USA, Ft. Benning,

Ga., 591
NRA 3-Position Rifle Woman—SP-4 Sue Ann Sandusky, 587
Conventional Pistol—SFC Hershel Anderson, USA, Ft. Benning, Ga., 887
Conventional Pistol Woman—SP-5 Kimberly Dyer, USA, Ft. Benning, Ga., 866
International Pistol—SFC Hershel Anderson, 569
International Pistol Woman—SP-5 Beth Thomas, USA, Ft. Benning, Ga., 525

National Intercollegiate Indoor Rifle & Pistol Championships

NRA 3-Positon Rifle—Wanda Oliver, Eastern Washington State, 292
NRA 3-Position Rifle Woman—Wanda Oliver, 292
NRA 3-Position Rifle ROTC—Wanda Oliver, 292
International Rifle—Linda Baily, East Tenn. State, 576
International Rifle Woman—Linda Baily, 576
International Rifle ROTC—Linda Baily, 576
Conventional Pistol—Stephan Goldstein, MIT, 860
Conventional Pistol Woman—Lynn Buchan, Ohio State, 769

Conventional Pistol ROTC—Peter Daspit, Univ. of Virginia, 851
International Pistol—Stephen Goldstein, 821
International Pistol Woman—Holly Hazlett, Univ. of Texas, 745
International Pistol ROTC—Michael Woodcock, Fayetteville State, 802
Clay Pigeon—Charvin Dixon, Columbus, Ga., 293
Ladies Clay Pigeon—Audrey Grosch, Minneapolis, Minn., 260
Junior Clay Pigeon—Michael Coleman, Ackerly, Tex., 286

National AAU Wrestling Championships, 1976

Cleveland, Ohio

Freestyle	Greco-Roman
105.5 Lbs. — Bill Rosado.	**105.5 Lbs.** — Karoly Kancsar.
114.5 Lbs. — Jim Haines.	**114.5 Lbs.** — Chris Sones.
125.5 Lbs. — Jan Gitcho.	**125.5 Lbs.** — Bruce Thompson.
136.5 Lbs. — Kiyoshi Abe.	**136.5 Lbs.** — Hachiro Oishi.
149.5 Lbs. — Lloyd Keaser.	**149.5 Lbs.** — Larry Morgan.
163 Lbs. — Stan Dziedzic.	**163 Lbs.** — John Matthews.
180.5 Lbs. — Brady Hall.	**180.5 Lbs.** — Dan Chandler.
198 Lbs. — Ben Peterson.	**198 Lbs.** — Williams Williams.
220 Lbs. — Russ Hellickson.	**220 Lbs.** — Brad Rheingans.
Heavyweight — Mike McCready.	**Heavyweight** — Mike McCready.

NCAA Wrestling Champions

Year	Champion	Year	Champion	Year	Champion
1960	Oklahoma	1966	Oklahoma State	1972	Iowa State
1961	Oklahoma State	1967	Michigan State	1973	Iowa State
1962	Oklahoma State	1968	Oklahoma State	1974	Oklahoma
1963	Oklahoma	1969	Iowa State	1975	Iowa
1964	Oklahoma State	1970	Iowa State	1976	Iowa
1965	Iowa State	1971	Oklahoma State		

Contract Bridge Championships in 1975-76

Winners of Major Events at 3 ACBL Championship Tournaments
Fall 1975 — Spring and Summer 1976 and World Championships
Source: American Contract Bridge League, Memphis, Tenn.

Fall Championships
New Orleans, La., November 21-30, 1975; attendance, 11,705 tables

Reisinger Open Teams — Ira Rubin, Paramus, N.J.; Fred Hamilton, Utica, Mich.; Hugh Ross, Oakland, Cal.; Erik Paulsen, Culver City, Cal.

Blue Ribbon Pairs — Kit Woolsey, Arlington, Va. and Steve Robinson, Alexandria, Va.

Life Master Men's Pairs — Steve Sapides, Baltimore, Md. and Walt Walvick, McLean, Va.

Life Master Women's Pairs — Dorothy Moore and Marion Weed, Dallas, Tex.

Mixed Pairs — Barry Crane, Studio City, Cal. and Kerri Shuman, Los Angeles, Cal.

Most Master Points for the Tournament — Walt Walvick, McLean, Va., 170.83 Master Points.

Spring Championships
Kansas City, Mo., March 12-21, 1976; attendance, 8,790 tables

Vanderbilt Knockout Teams — Dr. George Rosenkranz, Mexico City, Mex.; John Gerber, Houston, Tex. (non-playing captain); Dr. Richard Katz, Los Angeles, Cal.; John Mohan, La Jolla, Cal.; Larry Cohen, Chicago, Ill.; Roger Bates, Las Vegas, Nev.

Men's Teams — John Lowenthal, Montvale, N.J.; Paul Heitner, Hartsdale, N.Y.; Mike Smolen, Los Angeles, Cal.; David Ashley, Las Vegas, Nev.

Women's Teams — Dorothy Hayden Truscott, Gail Moss, Jacqui Mitchell, New York, N.Y.; Mary Jane Farell, Beverly Hills,

Cal.; Marilyn Johnson, Houston, Tex.; Emma Jean Hawes, Fort Worth, Tex.

Men's Pairs — Gerald Caravelli, Des Plaines, Ill. and Larry Cohen, Chicago, Ill.

Women's Pairs — Gail Schaab, Omaha, Neb. and Barbara Staton, Beale AFB, Cal.

Open Pairs — Ernest Ivey, Colorado Springs, Col. and Terry Hause, San Jose, Cal.

Most Master Points for the Tournament — Larry Cohen, Chicago, Ill., 225 Master Points.

Summer Championships
Salt Lake City, Utah, July 30-August 8, 1976; attendance, 10,722 tables

Spingold Knockout Teams — Dr. George Rosenkranz, Mexico City, Mex.; John Gerber, Houston, Tex. (non-playing captain); Dr. Richard Katz and Larry Cohen, Los Angeles, Cal; John Mohan, La Jolla, Cal.; Roger Bates, Las Vegas, Nev.

Grand National Teams — John Swanson, Paul Soloway, Billy Eisenberg, Eddie Kantar, Los Angeles, Cal.

Master Mixed Teams — Dr. Richard Katz, Los Angeles, Cal.; Marion Weed, Dallas, Tex.; Carol Sanders, Nashville, Tenn.; Paul Swanson, Morgantown, W. Va.; Fred Hamilton, W. Holly-

wood, Cal., Rhoda Walsh, Los Angeles, Cal.; John & Peggy Sutherlin, San Francisco, Cal.; Peter and Nancy Weichsel, New York, N.Y. (tie).

Life Master Pairs — Neil Silverman, New York, N.Y. and Robert Lipsitz, Potomac, Md.

National Amateur Pairs — John Van Ness, Aspen, Col. and Blair Fedder, Houston, Tex.

Most Master Points for Tournament — Dr. Richard Katz, Los Angeles, Cal. 219.44 Master Points.

1976 World Championship
22d Bermuda Bowl and 2d Venice Trophy, Monte Carlo, Monaco, May 2-8, 1976

World Champion Contract Bridge Team — North America; William Eisenberg, Fred Hamilton, Ira Rubin, Paul Soloway, Hugh Ross, Erik Paulsen. (Dan Morse, non-playing captain).

Champion of Ladies Challenge Match — North America;

Betty Ann Kennedy, Jacqui Mitchell, Gail Moss, Emma Jean Hawes, Carol Sanders, Dorothy Hayden Truscott. (Peter Pender, coach; Ruth McConnell, non-playing captain).

5th World Bridge Team Olympiad
Monte Carlo, Monaco, May 9-22, 1976

Open Champion — Brazil; — Pedro-Apulo Assumpcao, Gabriel Chagas, Christiano Fonseca, Gabino Cintra, Sergio Barbosa, Pedro Branco, (Serge Apoteker, non-playing captain).

Ladies Champion — Italy; — Anna Valenti, Rina Jabes, Maria Robaudo, Lucianna Capodanno, Marisaa D'Andra, Marissa Bianchi. (Giovanni Pelucchi, non-playing captain).

Polo Records

National Open Tournament
1967—Bunntyco-Oak Brook 8, Milwaukee 2.
1968—Midland 9, Milwaukee 0.
1969—Tulsa Green Hill 11, Milwaukee 10.
1970—Tulsa Green Hill 9, Oak Brook 5.
1971—Oak Brook 8, Green Hill Farm 7.
1972—Milwaukee 9, Tulsa 5.
1973—Oak Brook 9, Willow Bend 4.
1974—Milwaukee 7, Houston 6.
1975—Milwaukee 14, Tulsa-Dallas 6.

Silver Cup
1967—Milwaukee 11, Keswick-Blue Ridge 7.
1968—Oak Brook 12, Keswick Sunny Climes 9.
1969—Oak Brook 7, Milwaukee 6.
1970—Oak Brook 9, Tulsa Green Hill 7.
1971—Green Hill Farm 8, Milwaukee 6.
1972—Red Doors Farm 10, Sun Ranch 6.
1973—Houston 6, Willow Bend 4.
1974—Houston 7, Willow Bend 6.
1975—Lone Oak-Bunntyco 8, Tulsa 5.

Intercollegiate Championship
1966—Cornell 12, Yale 10
1967—Yale 12, Cornell 11
1968—Yale 17, Cornell 13
1969—Yale 17, Cornell 16
1970—Yale 22, Cornell 10
1971—Yale 12, Virginia 11
1972—Univ. of Conn. 17, Univ of Virginia 15
1973—Univ. of Conn. 19, Univ. of Virginia 10
1974—Univ. of Conn. 18, Cornell 16
1975—Univ. of Cal.-Davis 15, Yale 12
1976—Xavier Univ. 25, Cornell 12.

Other Tournaments, 1976
Delegate's Cup—Mallet Hill 5, The Tackeria 4.
America Cup—Boca Raton 6, Tennessee 3.
Butler Handicap—Tulsa 10, Milwaukee 5.
Continental Cup—Joy Farm 11, Indianapolis 5.
National Copper Cup—Village Farm 12, Adidas 2.

Westminster Kennel Club

Year	Best-in-show	Breed	Owner
1966	Ch. Zeloy Mooremaides Magic	Wire Fox terrier	Marion G. Bunker
1967	Ch. Bardene Bingo	Scottish terrier	E. H. Stuart
1968	Ch. Stingray of Derryabah	Lakeland terrier	Mr. and Mrs. James A. Farrell Jr.
1969	Ch. Glamoor Good News	Skye terrier	Walter & Mrs. Adele F. Goodman
1970	Ch. Arriba's Prima Donna	Boxer	Dr. & Mrs. P. J. Pagano & Dr. Theodore S. Fickles
1971	Ch. Chinoe's Adamant James	English springer spaniel	Dr. Milton Prickett
1972	Ch. Chinoe's Adamant James	English springer spaniel	Dr. Milton Prickett
1973	Ch. Acadia Command Performance	Poodle	Mrs. Jo Ann Sering & Edward B. Jenner
1974	Ch. Gretchenhof Columbia River	German pointer	Dr. Richard Smith
1975	Ch. Sir Lancelot of Barvan	Old English sheepdog	Mr. and Mrs. Ronald Vanword
1976	Ch. Jo-Ni's Red Baron of Crofton	Lakeland terrier	Virginia Dickson

Leonard Brumby, Sr. Memorial Trophy
Junior Winner at Westminster Kennel Club

1965—Jennifer Sheldon, Massapequa, N. Y. **Breed**—Afghan.
1966—Laura Swyler, Commack, N.Y. **Breed**—Dox.
1967—David L. Brumbaugh, Perry, Ga. **Breed**—Min. Schnauzer.
1968—Cheryl Baker, Kennesaw, Ga. **Breed**—Beagle.
1969—Charles Garvin, Columbus, Ohio. **Breed**—Dalmatian.
1970—Pat Hardy, Cincinnati, Ohio. **Breed**—Golden Retriever.
1971—Heidi Shellenbarger, Costa Mesa, Cal. **Breed**—Whippet.

1972—Deborah Dagny Von Aherns, Edison Township, N. J. **Breed**—Afghan.
1973—Teresa Nail, Ft. Worth, Texas. **Breed**—Doberman Pinscher.
1974—Leslie Church, St. Louis, Mo. **Breed**—Min. Schnauzer.
1975—Virginia Westfield, Huntington, N.Y. **Breed**—Bulldog.
1976—Cathy Hritzo, Hubbard, Ohio. **Breed**—Samoyed.

Pure-Bred Dogs

Six main classes of dogs are recognized: Sporting dogs which include pointers, retrievers, setters, spaniels, welmaraners; the hound group; working dogs which include boxers, collies, doberman pinschers, shepherds, mastiffs; the terrier group; the toy group which includes chihuahuas, toy spaniels, papillions, pekingese, pomeranians, yorkshires; non-sporting group which includes boston terriers, bulldogs, chow chows, dalmatians, poodles. In all, 116 different breeds are recognized and shown in the United States.

Cat Breeds

There are 27 cat breeds recognized: abyssinian, american shorthair, balinese, birman, bombay, burmese, colorpoint shorthair, egyptian mau, exotic shorthair, havana brown, himalayan, japanese bobtail, korat, leopard cat, lilac foreign shorthair, maine coon cat, manx, ocicat, oriental shorthair, persian, rex, russian blue, scottish fold, siamese, sphynx, turkish angora, wirehair shorthair.

World Pocket Billiards Champions

1931—Ralph Greenleaf	1945—Willie Mosconi	1964—Luther Lassiter, Arthur Cranfield
1932—Ralph Greenleaf	1946—Irving Crane	1965—Joe Balsis
1933—Erwin Rudolph	1947—Willie Mosconi	1966—Luther Lassiter
1934—Erwin Rudolph	1948—Willie Mosconi	1967—Luther Lassiter
1935—Andrew Ponzi	1949—James Caras	1968—Irving Crane
1936—James Caras	1950—Willie Mosconi	1969—Ed Kelly
1937—Ralph Greenleaf	1951—Willie Mosconi	1970—Irving Crane
1938—James Caras	1952—Willie Mosconi	1971—Ray Martin
1939—James Caras	1953—Willie Mosconi	1972—Irving Crane
1940—Andrew Ponzi	1954—none	1973—Lou Butera
1941—Willie Mosconi, Erwin Rudolph	1955—Irving Crane,. Willie Mosconi	1974—Ray Martin
1942—Irving Crane	1956-62—none	1975—none
1943—Andrew Ponzi	1963—Luther Lassiter	1976—none
1944—Willie Mosconi		

U.S. Open Pocket Billiards Champions

1966—Irving Crane	1970—Steve Mizerak	1974—Joe Balsis
1967—James Caras	1971—Steve Mizerak	1975—Dallas West
1968—Joe Balsis	1972—Steve Mizerak	1976—Tom Jennings
1969—Luther Lassiter	1973—Steve Mizerak	

Women's Division

Jean Balukas, 17-year-old high school student from Brooklyn, N.Y., won the women's division of the U.S. Open Pocket Billiards Championship for the 5th straight year on Aug. 15, 1976.

Motorcycle Racing
Grand National Champion

Year	Champion	Year	Champion	Year	Champion	Year	Champion
1952	Bobby Hill	1958	Carroll Resweber	1964	Roger Reiman	1970	Gene Romero
1953	Bill Tuman	1959	Carroll Resweber	1965	Bart Markel	1971	Dick Mann
1954	Joe Leonard	1960	Carroll Resweber	1966	Bart Markel	1972	Mark Brelsford
1955	Brad Andres	1961	Carroll Resweber	1967	Gary Nixon	1973	Ken Roberts
1956	Joe Leonard	1962	Bart Markel	1968	Gary Nixon	1974	Ken Roberts
1957	Joe Leonard	1963	Dick Mann	1969	Mert Lawwill	1975	Gary Scott

Professional Sports Directory
Baseball

Commissioner's Office
75 Rockefeller Plaza
New York, N.Y. 10019

National League

National League Office
Mills Bldg.
220 Montgomery St.
San Francisco, Cal. 94104

Atlanta Braves
PO Box 4064
Atlanta, Ga. 30302

Chicago Cubs
Wrigley Field
Chicago, Ill. 60613

Cincinnati Reds
100 Riverfront Stadium
Cincinnati, Ohio 45202

Houston Astros
Astrodome
Houston, Texas 77001

Los Angeles Dodgers
Dodger Stadium
1000 Elysian Park Ave.
Los Angeles, Cal. 90012

Montreal Expos
PO Box 500, Station R
Montreal, Quebec H2S 3G7

New York Mets
William A. Shea Stadium
Roosevelt Ave. & 126th St.
Flushing, N.Y. 11368

Philadelphia Phillies
Philadelphia Veterans Stadium
Broad St. & Pattison Ave.
Philadelphia, Pa. 19148

Pittsburgh Pirates
600 Stadium Circle
Pittsburgh, Pa. 15212

St. Louis Cardinals
Busch Memorial Stadium
250 Stadium Plaza
St. Louis, Mo. 63102

San Diego Padres
San Diego Stadium
9449 Friars Rd.
San Diego, Cal. 92120

San Francisco Giants
Candlestick Park
San Francisco, Cal. 94124

American League

American League Office
280 Park Ave.
New York, N.Y. 10017

Baltimore Orioles
Memorial Stadium
Baltimore, Md. 21218

Boston Red Sox
24 Jersey St.
Boston, Mass. 02215

California Angels
Anaheim Stadium
2000 State College Blvd.
Anaheim, Cal. 92806

Chicago White Sox
Comiskey Park
Dan Ryan & 35th St.
Chicago, Ill. 60616

Cleveland Indians
Municipal Stadium
Cleveland, Ohio 44114

Detroit Tigers
Tiger Stadium
Detroit, Mich. 48216

Kansas City Royals
Harry S. Truman Sports Complex
PO Box 1969
Kansas City, Mo. 64141

Milwaukee Brewers
Milwaukee County Stadium
Milwaukee, Wis. 53214

Minnesota Twins
Metropolitan Stadium
8001 Cedar Ave.
Bloomington, Minn. 55420

New York Yankees
Yankee Stadium
Bronx, N.Y. 10451

Oakland A's
Oakland-Alameda County
Coliseum
Oakland, Cal. 94621

Texas Rangers
Arlington Stadium
PO Box 1111
Arlington, Texas 76010

Hockey

National Hockey League

League Headquarters
*920 Sun Life Bldg.
Montreal, Quebec H3B 2W2

League Services
2 Pennsylvania Plaza
New York, N.Y. 10001

Atlanta Flames
100 Techwood Dr., NW
Atlanta, Ga. 30303

Boston Bruins
150 Causeway St.
Boston, Mass. 02114

Buffalo Sabres
Memorial Auditorium
Buffalo, N.Y. 14202

Chicago Black Hawks
1800 W. Madison St.
Chicago, Ill. 60612

Cleveland Barons
The Coliseum
Richfield Township, Ohio 44286

Colorado Rockies
McNichols Sports Arena
Denver, Col.

Detroit Red Wings
5920 Grand River
Detroit, Mich. 48208

Los Angeles Kings
PO Box 10
Inglewood, Cal. 90306

Minnesota North Stars
7901 Cedar Ave. S.
Bloomington, Minn. 55420

Montreal Canadiens
2313 St. Catherine St., West
Montreal, Quebec H3H 1N2

New York Islanders
1155 Conklin St.
Farmingdale, N.Y. 11735

New York Rangers
Madison Square Garden
4 Pennsylvania Plaza
New York, N.Y. 10001

Philadelphia Flyers
The Spectrum
Pattison Place
Philadelphia, Pa. 19148

Pittsburgh Penguins
Civic Arena
Pittsburgh, Pa. 15219

St. Louis Blues
5700 Oakland Ave.
St. Louis, Mo. 63110

Toronto Maple Leafs
60 Carlton St.
Toronto, Ont. M5B 1L1

Vancouver Canucks
100 North Renfrew St.
Vancouver, B.C. V5K 3N7

Washington Capitals
Capital Centre
Landover, Md. 20786

World Hockey Assn.

League Office
415 Yonge St.
Toronto, Ont. M5B 2E7

Birmingham Bulls
Jefferson Co. Civic Center
Birmingham, Ala. 35203

Calgary Cowboys
1418 McLedd Trail SE
Calgary, Alta. T2G 2N5

Cincinnati Stingers
Riverfront Coliseum
Cincinnati, Ohio 45202

Edmonton Oilers
MacDonald Hotel
Edmonton, Alberta T5J 0N6

Houston Aeros
10 Greenway Plaza
Houston, Texas 77046

Indianapolis Racers
Market Square Arena
Indianapolis, Ind. 46204

Minnesota Fighting Saints
St. Paul Civic Center
St. Paul, Minn. 55102

New England Whalers
1 Civic Center Plaza
Hartford, Conn. 06103

Phoenix Roadrunners
1826 W. McDowell Rd.
Phoenix, Ariz. 85007

Quebec Nordiques
2025 Ave. Du Colisee
Quebec, Quebec. G1L 4W7

San Diego Mariners
3500 Sports Arena Blvd.
San Diego, Cal. 92138

Winnipeg Jets
15-1430 Maroons Rd.
Winnipeg, Man. R3G 0L5

Basketball

National Basketball Assn.

League Office
2 Pennsylvania Plaza
Suite 2010
New York, N.Y. 10001

Atlanta Hawks
100 Techwood Drive
Atlanta, Ga. 30303

Boston Celtics
North Station
Boston, Mass. 02114

Buffalo Braves
Memorial Auditorium
Buffalo, N.Y. 14202

Chicago Bulls
333 North Michigan Ave.
Chicago, Ill. 60601

Cleveland Cavaliers
The Coliseum
2923 Streetsboro Rd.
Richfield Township, Ohio 44286

Denver Nuggets
P.O. Box 16307
Denver, Col. 80216

Detroit Pistons
Cobo Hall
Detroit, Mich. 48226

Golden State Warriors
556 Golden Gate Ave.
San Francisco, Cal. 94102

Houston Rockets
The Summit
Houston, Texas 77046

Indiana Pacers
Market Square Center
151 N. Delaware
Indianapolis, Ind. 46204

Kansas City Kings
1800 Genessee
Kansas City, Mo. 64102

Los Angeles Lakers
The Forum
3900 W. Manchester Blvd.
or PO Box 10
Inglewood, Cal. 90306

Milwaukee Bucks
901 North 4th St.
Milwaukee, Wis. 53203

New Orleans Jazz
Braniff Place Hotel
1500 Canal St.
New Orleans, La. 70140

New York Knickerbockers
Madison Square Garden Center
4 Pennsylvania Plaza
New York, N.Y. 10001

New York Nets
1 Old Country Rd.
Carle Place, N.Y. 11514

Philadelphia 76ers
The Spectrum
Philadelphia, Pa. 19148

Phoenix Suns
PO Box 1369
Phoenix, Ariz. 85001

Portland Trail Blazers
Lloyd Bldg.
700 NE Multnomah St.
Portland, Ore. 97232

San Antonio Spurs
HemisFair Arena
P.O. Box 530
San Antonio, Tex.

Seattle SuperSonics
221 West Harrison St.
Seattle, Wash. 98119

Washington Bullets
Capital Centre
Landover, Md. 20786

Football

National Football League

NFL League Office
410 Park Avenue
New York, N.Y. 10022

Atlanta Falcons
521 Capitol Ave. SW
Atlanta, Ga. 30312

Baltimore Colts
Executive Plaza
Hunt Valley, Md. 21031

Buffalo Bills
1 Bills Drive
Orchard Park, N.Y. 14127

Chicago Bears
55 E. Jackson
Chicago, Ill. 60604

Cincinnati Bengals
200 Riverfront Stadium
Cincinnati, Ohio 45202

Cleveland Browns
Cleveland Stadium
Cleveland, Ohio 44114

Dallas Cowboys
6116 North Central Expressway
Dallas, Texas 75206

Denver Broncos
5700 Logan St.
Denver, Col. 80216

Detroit Lions
1200 Featherstone Rd.
Pontiac, Mich. 48057

Green Bay Packers
1265 Lombardi Ave.
Green Bay, Wis. 54303

Houston Oilers
P.O. Box 1516
Houston, Texas 77021

Kansas City Chiefs
1 Arrowhead Drive
Kansas City, Mo. 64129

Los Angeles Rams
10271 W. Pico Blvd.
Los Angeles, Cal. 90064

Miami Dolphins
330 Biscayne Blvd.
Miami, Fla. 33132

Minnesota Vikings
7110 France Ave. So.
Edina, Minn. 55435

New England Patriots
Schaefer Stadium
Foxboro, Mass. 02035

New Orleans Saints
944 St. Charles
New Orleans, La. 70130

New York Giants
10 Columbus Circle
New York, N.Y. 10019

New York Jets
598 Madison Ave.
New York, N.Y. 10022

Oakland Raiders
7811 Oakport St.
Oakland, Cal. 94621

Philadelphia Eagles
Veterans Stadium
Philadelphia, Pa. 19148

Pittsburgh Steelers
Three Rivers Stadium
Pittsburgh, Pa. 15212

St. Louis Cardinals
200 Stadium Plaza
St. Louis, Mo. 63102

San Diego Chargers
San Diego Stadium
P.O. Box 20666
San Diego, Cal. 92120

San Francisco 49ers
1255 Post St.
San Francisco, Cal. 94109

Seattle Seahawks
1200 Westlake Ave. N.
Seattle, Wash. 98109

Tampa Bay Buccaneers
1 Buccaneer Place
Tampa, Fla. 33607

Washington Redskins
PO Box 17247
Dulles Intl. Airport
Washington, D.C. 20041

U.S. National Squash Racquets Champions

Year	Champion	Year	Champion	Year	Champion
1965	Stephen Vehslage, N.Y., N.Y.	1969	Anil Nayar, Boston, Mass.	1973	Vic Niederhoffer, N.Y., N.Y.
1966	Vic Niederhoffer, N.Y., N.Y.	1970	Anil Nayar, Boston, Mass.	1974	Vic Niederhoffer, N.Y., N.Y.
1967	Samuel Howe 3d, Phil., Pa.	1971	Colin Adair, Canada	1975	Vic Niederhoffer, N.Y., N.Y.
1968	Colin Adair, Canada	1972	Vic Niederhoffer, N.Y., N.Y.	1976	Peter Briggs, N.Y., N.Y.

Ski Jumping

Jim Denny, Duluth, Minn., won the 1976 U. S. National Jumping Championship at Squaw Valley, Cal. on Jan. 11. He had jumps of 305 and 320 feet.

Kentucky Derby, 3 Year Olds

Churchill Downs, Louisville, Ky.

Inaugurated 1875, Distance 1¼ miles; 1½ miles until 1896

Year	Winner	Jockey	Wt.	Second	Winner's Share	Time
1903	Judge Himes	H. Booker	117	Early	$4,850	2:09
1904	Elwood	F. Prior	117	Ed Tierney	4,850	2:08.1-5
1905	Agile	J. Martin	122	Ram's Horn	4,850	2:10.3-4
1906	Sir Huon	R. Troxer	117	Lady Navarre	4,850	2:08.4-5
1907	Pink Star	A. Minder	117	Zal	4,850	2:12.3-5
1908	Stone Street	A. Pickens	117	Sir Cleges	4,850	2:15.1-5
1909	Wintergreen	V. Powers	117	Miami	4,850	2:08.1-5
1910	Donau	F. Herbert	117	Joe Morris	4,850	2:06.2-5
1911	Meridian	G. Archibald	117	Governor Gray	4,850	2:05
1912	Worth	C. H. Shilling	117	Duval	4,850	2:09.2-5
1913	Donerail	R. Goose	117	Ten Point	5,475	2:04.4-5
1914	Old Rosebud	J. McCabe	114	Hodge	9,125	2:03.2-5
1915	Regret*	J. Notter	112	Pebbles	11,450	2:05.2-5
1916	George Smith	J. Loftus	117	Star Hawk	16,600	2:04.3-5
1917	Omar Khayyam	C. Borel	117	Ticket	9,750	2:04
1918	Exterminator	W. Knapp	114	Escoba	14,700	2:10.4-5
1919	Sir Barton	J. Loftus	112	Billy Kelly	20,825	2:09.4-5
1920	Paul Jones	T. Rice	126	Upset	30,375	2:09
1921	Behave Yourself	C. Thompson	126	Black Servant	38,450	2:04.1-5
1922	Morvich	A. Johnson	126	Bet Mosie	46,775	2:04.3-5
1923	Zev	E. Sande	126	Martingale	53,600	2:05.2-5
1924	Black Gold	J. D. Mooney	126	Chilhowee	52,775	2:05.1-5
1925	Flying Ebony	E. Sande	126	Captain Hal	52,950	2:07.3-5
1926	Bubbling Over	A. Johnson	126	Bagenbaggage	50,075	2:03.4-5
1927	Whiskery	L. McAtee	126	Osmand	51,000	2:06
1928	Reigh Count	C. Lang	126	Misstep	55,375	2:10.2-5
1929	Clyde Van Dusen	L. McAtee	126	Naishapur	53,950	2:10.4-5
1930	Gallant Fox	E. Sande	126	Gallant Knight	50,725	2:07.3-5
1931	Twenty Grand	C. Kurtsinger	126	Sweep All	48,725	2:01.4-5
1932	Burgoo King	E. James	126	Economic	52,350	2:05.1-5
1933	Brokers Tip	D. Meade	126	Head Play	48,925	2:06.4-5
1934	Cavalcade	M. Garner	126	Discovery	28,175	2:04
1935	Omaha	W. Saunders	126	Roman Soldier	39,525	2:05
1936	Bold Venture	I. Hanford	126	Brevity	37,725	2:03.3-5
1937	War Admiral	C. Kurtsinger	126	Pompoon	52,050	2:03.1-5
1938	Lawrin	E. Arcaro	126	Dauber	47,050	2:04.4-5
1939	Johnstown	J. Stout	126	Challedon	46,350	2:03.2-5
1940	Gallahadion	C. Bierman	126	Bimelech	60,150	2:05
1941	Whirlaway	E. Arcaro	126	Staretor	61,275	2:01.2-5
1942	Shut Out	W. D. Wright	126	Alsab	64,225	2:04.2-5
1943	Count Fleet	J. Longden	126	Blue Swords	60,275	2:04
1944	Pensive	C. McCreary	126	Broadcloth	64,675	2:04.1-5
1945	Hoop, Jr.	E. Arcaro	126	Pot o' Luck	64,850	2:07
1946	Assault	W. Mehrtens	126	Spy Song	96,400	2:06.3-5
1947	Jet Pilot	E. Guerin	126	Phalanx	92,160	2:06.3-5
1948	Citation	E. Arcaro	126	Coaltown	83,400	2:05.2-5
1949	Ponder	S. Brooks	126	Capot	91,600	2:04.1-5
1950	Middleground	W. Boland	126	Hill Prince	92,650	2:01.3-5
1951	Count Turf	C. McCreary	126	Royal Mustang	98,050	2:02.3-5
1952	Hill Gail	E. Arcaro	126	Sub Fleet	96,300	2:01.3-5
1953	Dark Star	H. Moreno	126	Native Dancer	90,050	2:02
1954	Determine	R. York	126	Hasty Road	102,050	2:03
1955	Swaps	W. Shoemaker	126	Nashua	108,400	2:01.4-5
1956	Needles	D. Erb	126	Fabius	123,450	2:03.2-5
1957	Iron Liege	W. Hartack	126	Gallant Man	107,950	2:02.1-5
1958	Tim Tam	I. Valenzuela	126	Lincoln Road	116,400	2:05
1959	Tomy Lee	W. Shoemaker	126	Sword Dancer	119,650	2:02.1-5
1960	Venetian Way	W. Hartack	126	Bally Ache	114,850	2:02.2-5
1961	Carry Back	J. Sellers	126	Crozier	120,500	2:04
1962	Decidedly	W. Hartack	126	Roman Line	119,650	2:00.2-5
1963	Chateaugay	B. Baeza	126	Never Bend	108,900	2:01.4-5
1964	Northern Dancer	W. Hartack	126	Hill Rise	114,300	2:00
1965	Lucky Debonair	W. Shoemaker	126	Dapper Dan	112,000	2:01.1-5
1966	Kauai King	D. Brumfield	126	Advocator	120,500	2:02
1967	Proud Clarion	R. Ussery	126	Barbs Delight	119,700	2:00.3-5
1968	Dancer's Image (A)	R. Ussery	126	Forward Pass	122,600	2:02.1-5
1969	Majestic Prince	W. Hartack	126	Arts and Letters	113,200	2:01.4-5
1970	Dust Commander	M. Manganello	126	My Dad George	127,800	2:03.2-5
1971	Canonero II	G. Avila	126	Jim French	145,500	2:03.1-5
1972	Riva Ridge	R. Turcotte	126	No Le Hace	140,300	2:01.4-5
1973	Secretariat	R. Turcotte	126	Sham	155,050	1:59.2-5
1974	Cannonade	A. Cordero	126	Hudson County	274,000	2:04
1975	Foolish Pleasure	J. Vasquez	126	Avatar	209,611	2:02
1976	Bold Forbes	A. Cordero	126	Honest Pleasure	165,200	2:01.3-5

(A) Dancer's Image was disqualified from purse money by order of the Churchill Downs stewards after tests disclosed that he had run with a pain-killing drug, phenylbutazone, in his system. All wagers were paid on Dancer's Image. Forward Pass was awarded first place money.

The Kentucky Derby has been won five times by two jockeys, Eddie Arcaro, 1938, 1941, 1945, 1948 and 1952; and Bill Hartack, 1957, 1960, 1962, 1964 and 1969; and three times by each of three jockeys, Isaac Murphy, 1884, 1890 and 1891; Earle Sande, 1923, 1925 and 1930, and Willie Shoemaker, 1955, 1959, 1965. *Regret only filly ever to win the Derby.

Belmont Stakes
Elmont, N.Y. Inaugurated 1867; 1 1/2 miles, 3 year olds

Year	Winner	Jockey	Wt.	Second	Winning Share	Time
1937	War Admiral	C. Kurtsinger	126	Sceneshifter	$38,020	2:28.3-5
1938	Pasteurized	J. Stout	126	Dauber	34,530	2:29.2-5
1939	Johnstown	J. Stout	126	Belay	37,020	2:29.3-5
1940	Bimelech	F. A. Smith	126	Your Chance	35,030	2:29.3-5
1941	Whirlaway	E. Arcaro	126	Robert Morris	39,770	2:31
1942	Shut Out	E. Arcaro	126	Alsab	44,520	2:29.1-5
1943	Count Fleet	J. Longden	126	Fairy Manhurst	35,340	2:28.1-5
1944	Bounding Home	G. L. Smith	126	Pensive	55,000	2:32.1-5
1945	Pavot	E. Arcaro	126	Wildlife	52,675	2:30.1-5
1946	Assault	W. Mehrtens	126	Natchez	75,400	2:30.4-5
1947	Phalanx	R. Donoso	126	Tide Rips	78,900	2:29.2-5
1948	Citation	E. Arcaro	126	Better Self	77,700	2:28.1-5
1949	Capot	T. Atkinson	126	Ponder	60,900	2:30.1-5
1950	Middleground	W. Boland	126	Lights Up	61,350	2:28.3-5
1951	Counterpoint	D. Gorman	125	Battlefield	82,000	2:29
1952	One Count	E. Arcaro	126	Blue Man	82,400	2:30.1-5
1953	Native Dancer	E. Guerin	126	Jamie K.	82,500	2:28.3-5
1954	High Gun	E. Guerin	126	Fisherman	89,000	2:30.4-5
1955	Nashua	E. Arcaro	126	Blazing Count	83,700	2:29
1956	Needles	D. Erb	126	Career Boy	83,600	2:29.4-5
1957	Gallant Man	W. Shoemaker	126	Inside Tract	77,300	2:26.3-5
1958	Cavan	P. Anderson	126	Tim Tam	73,440	2:30.1-5
1959	Sword Dancer	W. Shoemaker	126	Bagdad	93,525	2:28.2-5
1960	Celtic Ash	W. Hartack	126	Venetian Way	96,785	2:29.3-5
1961	Sherluck	B. Baeza	126	Globemaster	104,900	2:29.1-5
1962	Jaipur	W. Shoemaker	126	Admiral's Voyage	109,550	2:28.4-5
1963	Chateaugay	B. Baeza	126	Candy Spots	101,700	2:30.1-5
1964	Quadrangle	M. Ycaza	126	Roman Brother	110,850	2:28.2-5
1965	Hail to All	J. Sellers	126	Tom Rolfe	104,150	2:28.2-5
1966	Amberoid	W. Boland	126	Buffle	117,700	2:29.3-5
1967	Damascus	W. Shoemaker	126	Cool Reception	104,950	2:28.4-5
1968	Stage Door Johnny	H. Gustines	126	Forward Pass	117,700	2:27.1-5
1969	Arts and Letters	B. Baeza	126	Majestic Prince	104,050	2:28.4-5
1970	High Echelon	J. L. Rotz	126	Needles N Pens	115,000	2:34
1971	Pass Catcher	W. Blum	126	Jim French	97,710	2:30.2-5
1972	Riva Ridge	R. Turcotte	126	Ruritania	93,950	2:28
1973	Secretariat	R. Turcotte	126	Twice A Prince	90,120	2:24
1974	Little Current	M. Rivera	126	Jolly Johu	101,970	2:29.1-5
1975	Avatar	W. Shoemaker	126	Foolish Pleasure	116,160	2:28.1-5
1976	Bold Forbes	A. Cordero	126	McKenzie Bridge	116,850	2:29

Preakness
Pimlico, Baltimore, Md.; inaugurated 1873; 1 3-16 miles, 3 year olds

Year	Winner	Jockey	Wt.	Second	Winning Share	Time
1937	War Admiral	C. Kurtsinger	126	Pompoon	$45,600	1:58.2-5
1938	Dauber	M. Peters	126	Cravat	51,875	1:59.4-5
1939	Challedon	G. Seabo	126	Gilded Knight	53,710	1:59.4-5
1940	Bimelech	F. A. Smith	126	Mioland	53,230	1:58.3-5
1941	Whirlaway	E. Arcaro	126	King Cole	49,365	1:58.4-5
1942	Alsab	B. James	126	Requested, Sun Again (tie)	58,175	1:57
1943	Count Fleet	J. Longden	126	Blue Swords	43,190	1:57.2-5
1944	Pensive	C. McCreary	126	Platter	60,075	1:59.1-5
1945	Polynesian	W. D. Wright	126	Hoop Jr.	66,170	1:58.4-5
1946	Assault	W. Mehrtens	126	Lord Boswell	96,620	2:01.2-5
1947	Faultless	D. Dodson	126	On Trust	98,005	1:59
1948	Citation	E. Arcaro	126	Vulcan's Forge	91,870	2:02.2-5
1949	Capot	T. Atkinson	126	Palestinian	79,985	1:56
1950	Hill Prince	E. Arcaro	126	Middleground	56,115	1:59.1-5
1951	Bold	E. Arcaro	126	Counterpoint	83,110	1:56.2-5
1952	Blue Man	C. McCreary	126	Jampol	86,135	1:57.2-5
1953	Native Dancer	E. Guerin	126	Jamie K.	65,200	1:57.4-5
1954	Hasty Road	J. Adams	126	Correlation	91,600	1:57.2-5
1955	Nashua	E. Arcaro	126	Saratoga	67,550	1:54.3-5
1956	Fabius	W. Hartack	126	Needles	84,250	1:58.2-5
1957	Bold Ruler	E. Arcaro	126	Iron Liege	65,200	1:56.1-5
1958	Tim Tam	I. Valenzuela	126	Lincoln Road	97,900	1:57.1-5
1959	Royal Orbit	W. Harmatz	126	Sword Dancer	136,200	1:57
1960	Bally Ache	R. Ussery	126	Victoria Park	121,000	1:57.3-5
1961	Carry Back	J. Sellers	126	Globemaster	126,200	1:57.3-5
1962	Greek Money	J. L. Rotz	126	Ridan	135,800	1:56.1-5
1963	Candy Spots	W. Shoemaker	126	Chateaugay	127,500	1:56.1-5
1964	Northern Dancer	W. Hartack	126	The Scoundrel	124,200	1:56.4-5
1965	Tom Rolfe	R. Turcotte	126	Dapper Dan	128,100	1:56.1-5
1966	Kauai King	D. Brumfield	126	Stupendous	129,000	1:55.2-5
1967	Damascus	W. Shoemaker	126	In Reality	141,500	1:55.1-5
1968	Forward Pass	I. Valenzuela	126	Out of the Way	142,700	1:56.4-5
1969	Majestic Prince	W. Hartack	126	Arts and Letters	129,500	1:55.3-5
1970	Personality	E. Belmonte	126	My Dad George	151,300	1:56.1-5
1971	Canonero II	G. Avila	126	Eastern Fleet	137,400	1:54
1972	Bee Bee Bee	E. Nelson	126	No Le Hace	135,300	1:55.3-5
1973	Secretariat	R. Turcotte	126	Sham	129,900	1:54.2-5
1974	Little Current	M. Rivera	126	Neopolitan Way	156,000	1:56.3-5
1975	Master Derby	D. McHargue	126	Foolish Pleasure	158,100	1:56.2-5
1976	Elocutionist	J. Lively	126	Play the Red	129,700	1:55

Triple Crown Turf Winners, Owners and Jockeys

(Kentucky Derby, Preakness and Belmont Stakes)

Year	Horse	Owner	Jockey	Year	Horse	Owner	Jockey
1919	Sir Barton	J.K.L. Ross	J. Loftus	1943	Count Fleet	Mrs. J. D. Hertz	J. Longden
1930	Gallant Fox	W. Woodward	E. Sande	1946	Assault	R.J. Kleberg	W. Mehrtens
1935	Omaha	W. Woodward	W. Sanders	1948	Citation	Warren Wright	E. Arcaro
1937	War Admiral	S.D. Riddle	C. Kurtsinger	1973	Secretariat	Meadow Stable	R. Turcotte
1941	Whirlaway	Warren Wright	E. Arcaro				

American Thoroughbred Records
Dirt Course

Distance Furlongs	Horse, Age, Weight	Track, State	Date	Time
3	El Macho	Gulfstream, Fla.	Feb. 26, 1974	0:32 1-5
3½	Deep Sun, 7, 120	Shenandoah Downs, W. Va.	July 11, 1959	0:39
	Crying For More, 7, 128	Shenandoah Downs, W. Va.	Mar. 18, 1972	0:39
4 (½ mile)	Tamran's Jet, 2, 118	Sunland Park, N.M.	Mar. 22, 1968	0:44 4-5
	Crimson Saint, 2, 119	Oaklawn Park, Ark.	Apr. 1, 1971	0:44 4-5
	Mighty Mr. A., 3, 116	Sportsman Park, Ill.	Nov. 1, 1971	0:44 4-5
	Thief of Bagdad, 5, 114	Sportsman Park, Ill.	Nov. 5, 1971	0:44 4-5
	Argus Ruler, 5, 114	Cahokia Downs, Ill.	Apr. 25, 1973	0:44 4-5
4½	Kathryn's Doll, 2, 111	Turf Paradise, Ariz.	Apr. 9, 1967	0:50 2-5
	Bold Liz, 2, 118	Sunland Park, N.M.	Mar. 19, 1972	0:50 2-5
	Dear Ethel, 2, 114	Miles Park, Ky.	July 4, 1967	0:50 2-5
5	Zip Pocket, 3, 122	Turf Paradise, Ariz.	Apr. 22, 1967	0:55 2-5
5½	Zip Pocket, 3, 129	Turf Paradise, Ariz.	Nov. 19, 1967	1:01 2-5
6 (¾ mile)	Grey Papa, 6, 116	Longacres, Wash.	Sept. 4, 1972	1:07 1-5
6½	Best Hitter, 4, 114	Longacres, Wash.	Aug. 24, 1973	1:13 4-5
7	Triple Bend, 4, 123	Hollywood, Cal.	May 6, 1972	1:19 4-5
7½	Aurecolt, 3, 122	Churchill Downs, Ky.	Nov. 12, 1957	1:29
8 (1 mile)	Dr. Fager, 4, 134	Arlington, Ill.	Aug. 24, 1968	1:32 1-5
8½	Swaps, 4, 130	Hollywood, Cal.	June 23, 1956	1:39
9	Secretariat, 3, 124	Belmont, N.Y.	Sept. 15, 1973	1:45 2-5
9½	Riva Ridge, 4, 127	Aqueduct, N.Y.	July 4, 1973	1:52 2-5
10	Noor, 5, 127	Golden Gate, Cal.	June 24, 1950	1:58 1-5
	Quack, 3, 115	Hollywood, Cal.	July 15, 1972	1:58 1-5
10½	Tempted, 4, 128	Aqueduct, N.Y.	Oct. 12, 1959	2:09
11	Man o' War, 3, 126	Belmont, N.Y.	June 12, 1920	2:14 1-5
11½	Theoretic, 6, 111	Sportsman Park, Ill.	Oct. 15, 1973	2:24 1-5
12 (1½ miles)	Secretariat, 3, 126	Belmont, N.Y.	June 9, 1973	2:24
13	Swaps, 4, 130	Hollywood, Cal.	July 25, 1956	2:38 1-5
14	Noor, 5, 117	Santa Anita, Cal.	Mar. 4, 1950	2:52 4-5
15	Pharawell, 5, 119	Gulfstream, Fla.	Apr. 8, 1947	3:13 4-5
16 (2 miles)	Kelso, 7, 124	Aqueduct, N.Y.	Oct. 31, 1964	3:19 1-5
18	Fenelon, 4, 119	Belmont, N.Y.	Oct. 4, 1941	3:47
20	Miss Grillo, 6, 118	Pimlico, Md.	Nov. 12, 1948	4:14 3-5

Leading Money-Winning Horses
(As of April 25, 1976.)

Horse, Year Foaled	Sts.	1st	2d	3d	Dollars	Horse, Year Foaled	Sts.	1st	2d	3d	Dollars
Kelso, 1957	63	39	12	2	1,977,896	Damascus, 1964	32	21	7	3	1,176,781
Round Table, 1954	66	43	8	5	1,749,869	Forego, 1970	40	23	6	6	1,163,516
Buckpasser, 1963	31	25	4	1	1,462,014	Cougar, 2nd, 1966	50	20	7	17	1,162,725
Dahlia, 1970	40	13	3	7	1,386,889	Riva Ridge, 1969	30	17	3	1	1,111,497
Allez France, 1970	21	13	3	1	1,386,146	Fort Marcy, 1964	75	21	18	14	1,109,791
Secretariat, 1970	21	16	3	1	1,316,808	Citation, 1945	45	32	10	2	1,085,760
Nashua, 1952	30	22	4	1	1,288,565	Foolish Pleasure, 1972	21	14	4	1	1,045,353
Susan's Girl, 1969	63	29	14	11	1,251,667	Native Diver, 1959	81	37	7	12	1,026,500
Carry Back, 1958	62	21	11	11	1,241,165	Dr. Fager, 1964	22	18	2	1	1,002,642

Annual Leading Jockey—Money Won

Year	Jockey	Dollars	Year	Jockey	Dollars	Year	Jockey	Dollars
1942	Arcaro, E.	481,949	1954	Shoemaker, W.	1,876,760	1965	Baeza, B.	2,582,702
1943	Longden, J.	573,276	1955	Arcaro, E.	1,864,796	1966	Baeza, B.	2,951,022
1944	Atkinson, T.	899,101	1956	Hartack, W.	2,343,955	1967	Baeza, B.	3,088,888
1945	Longden, J.	981,977	1957	Hartack, W.	3,060,501	1968	Baeza, B.	2,835,108
1946	Atkinson, T.	1,036,825	1958	Shoemaker, W.	2,961,693	1969	Valasquez, J.	2,542,315
1947	Dodson, D.	1,429,949	1959	Shoemaker, W.	2,843,133	1970	Pincay, L. Jr.	2,626,526
1948	Arcaro, E.	1,686,230	1960	Shoemaker, W.	2,123,961	1971	Pincay, L. Jr.	3,784,377
1949	Brooks, S.	1,316,817	1961	Shoemaker, W.	2,690,819	1972	Pincay, L. Jr.	3,225,827
1950	Arcaro, E.	1,410,160	1962	Shoemaker, W.	2,916,844	1973	Pincay, L. Jr.	4,093,492
1951	Shoemaker, W.	1,329,890	1963	Shoemaker, W.	2,526,925	1974	Pincay, L. Jr.	4,251,060
1952	Arcaro, E.	1,859,591	1964	Shoemaker, W.	2,649,553	1975	Baeza, B.	3,695,198
1953	Shoemaker, W.	1,784,187						

All-Time Winning Jockeys
(as of Jan. 1, 1976)

Jockey	Wins	Jockey	Wins	Jockey	Wins	Jockey	Wins
Willie Shoemaker	6,953	Walter Blum	4,383	Ralph Neves	3,771	Darrell Madden	2,999
Johnny Longden	6,026	Bill Hartack	4,272	Bobby Ussery	3,611	Ray York	2,910
Eddie Arcaro	4,779	Avelino Gomez	3,854	Robert Lee Baird	3,571	John Rotz	2,908
Steve Brooks	4,447	Ted Atkinson	3,795	Johnny Adams	3,270		

Annual Leading Money-Winning Horses

Year	Horse	Dollars	Year	Horse	Dollars	Year	Horse	Dollars
1942	Shut Out	238,872	1953	Native Dancer	513,425	1965	Buckpasser	568,096
1943	Count Fleet	174,055	1954	Determine	328,700	1966	Buckpasser	669,078
1944	Pavot	179,040	1955	Nashua	752,550	1967	Damascus	817,941
1945	Busher	273,735	1956	Needles	440,850	1968	Forward Pass	546,674
1946	Assault	424,195	1957	Round Table	600,383	1969	Arts and Letters	555,604
1947	Armed	376,325	1958	Round Table	662,780	1970	Personality	444,049
1948	Citation	709,470	1959	Sword Dancer	537,004	1971	Riva Ridge	503,263
1949	Ponder	321,825	1960	Bally Ache	455,045	1972	Droll Roll	471,633
1950	Noor	346,940	1961	Carry Back	565,349	1973	Secretariat	860,404
1951	Counterpoint	250,525	1962	Never Bend	402,969	1974	Chris Evert	551,063
1952	Crafty Admiral	277,255	1963	Candy Spots	604,481	1975	Foolish Pleasure	716,278
			1964	Gun Bow	580,100			

Queen's Plate

The Queen's Plate (known as the King's Plate during reign of male), Canada's most famous thoroughbred race, is the oldest continuously run stakes race in North America. Originated in 1860 over ⅛ miles (now ¼ miles) for 3-year-olds, Canadian-foaled, race is staged under Royal tutelage for trophy and 50 gold sovereigns plus purse. Trophy is not a plate but a foot-high gold cup valued at $5,000. However, race is identified as a plate race because of 17th century English tradition of awarding plates.

Year	Winner, Jockey	Time	Dollars	Year	Winner, Jockey	Time	Dollars
1963	Canebora, M. Ycaza	2:04	54,850	1970	Almoner, S. Hawley	2:04.4-5	57,395
1964	Northern Dancer, W. Hartack	2:02.1-5	49,234	1971	Kennedy Road, S. Hawley	2:03	54,388
1965	Whistling Sea, T. Inouye	2:03.4-5	47,852	1972	Victoria Song, R. Platts	2:02	56,143
1966	Titled Hero, A. Gomez	2:03.3-5	52,173	1973	Royal Chocolate, T. Colangelo	2:08	80,697
1967	Jammed Lovely, J. Fitzsimmons	2:03	51,821	1974	Amber Herod, R. Platts	2:09.1-5	96,541
1968	Merger, W. Harris	2:05.2-5	53,641	1975	L'Enjoleur, S. Hawley	2:02.3-5	95,351
1969	Jumping Joseph, A. Gomez	2:04.1-5	55,022	1976	Norcliffe, J. Fell	2:05	89,716

North American Soccer League, 1976
(Final Standings)

Northern Division	Won	Lost	GF	GA	Bonus Points	Total Points	Western Division	Won	Lost	GF	GA	Bonus Points	Total Points
Chicago	15	9	52	32	42	132	Minnesota	15	9	54	33	48	138
Toronto	15	9	38	30	33	123	Seattle	14	10	40	31	39	123
Rochester	13	11	36	32	36	114	Vancouver	14	10	38	30	36	120
Hartford	12	12	37	56	35	107	Portland	8	16	23	40	23	71
Boston	7	17	35	64	32	74	St. Louis	5	19	28	57	28	58
Eastern Division							**Southern Division**						
Tampa Bay	18	6	58	30	46	154	San Jose	14	10	47	30	39	123
New York	16	8	65	34	52	148	Dallas	13	11	44	45	39	117
Washington	14	10	46	38	42	126	Los Angeles	12	12	43	44	36	108
Philadelphia	8	16	32	49	32	80	San Antonio	12	12	38	32	35	107
Miami	6	18	29	58	27	63	San Diego	9	15	29	47	28	82

Total points: Win-6 pts., Loss-0 pts.; Bonus points — one point is awarded for each goal scored up to a maximum of 3 per team per game. Playoff winner — Toronto.

Leading Scorers

Player-Team	Goals	Assists	Points	Player-Team	Goals	Assists	Points
George Chinaglia—New York	19	11	49	George Best—Los Angeles	15	7	37
Derek Smethurst—Tampa Bay	20	5	45	Ilija Mitic—San Jose	14	9	37
Pele—New York	13	18	44	Ron Futcher—Minnesota	14	6	34
Mike Stojanovic—Rochester	17	7	41	Jeff Bourne—Dallas	15	3	33
Alan Willey—Minnesota	16	6	38	Rodney Marsh—Tampa Bay	11	9	31

Leading Goalkeepers

Player-Team	*Minutes	Goals	Avg.	Player-Team	*Minutes	Goals	Avg.
Tony Chursky—Seattle	1981	20	0.91	Phil Parkes—Vancouver	1836	25	1.23
Mike Hewitt—San Jose	1657	17	0.92	Shep Messing—New York	1728	24	1.25
Paolo Cimpiel—Toronto	2058	22	0.96	Geoff Barnett—Minnesota	1984	28	1.27
Arnold Mausser—Tampa Bay	2161	28	1.17	Bobby Clark—San Antonio	1775	25	1.27
Mervyn Cawston—Chicago	2172	29	1.20	Blasic Tamindic—Rochester	2184	31	1.28

*At least 1365 minutes

NASL All-Star Team, 1976

Position	Player-Team	Position	Player-Team
Goalkeeper	Arnold Mausser (Tampa Bay)	Midfield	Antonio Simoes (Boston, San Jose)
Defender	Bobby Moore (San Antonio)	Midfield	Rodney Marsh (Tampa Bay)
Defender	Mike England (Seattle)	Forward	George Best (Los Angeles)
Defender	Tommy Smith (Tampa Bay)	Forward	Pele (New York)
Defender	Keith Eddy (New York)	Forward	Giorgio Chinaglia (New York)
Midfield	Ramon Mifflin (New York)		

The World Cup

The World Cup, emblematic of international soccer supremacy, was won by West Germany on July 7, 1974, with a 2-1 victory over the Netherlands. By winning the championship, West Germany became the fourth host country to emerge as champion since the trophy was put up in 1930. The next World Cup will be held in 1978 in Argentina. Winners and sites of previous World Cup play follow:

Year	Winner	Site	Year	Winner	Site
1930	Uruguay	Uruguay	1958	Brazil	Sweden
1934	Italy	Italy	1962	Brazil	Chile
1938	Italy	France	1966	England	England
1950	Uruguay	Brazil	1970	Brazil	Mexico City
1954	W. Germany	Switzerland	1974	W. Germany	W. Germany

Sports on Television
Source: Nielsen Sports, 1975

Average Ratings and Viewer Composition

Ages of Men Viewers

	Household Rating	Percent Men	Percent Women	18-34 (U.S.=40%)	35-49 (25%)	50+ (35%)
Football						
NFL Superbowl	42.3	62	38	39%	24%	37%
ABC-NFL	20.2	65	35	38	28	34
CBS-NFL	14.0	65	35	35	26	39
NBC-NFL	14.2	66	34	37	25	38
College Bowl Games	23.4	59	41	32	31	37
College All-Star Games	12.3	67	33	32	23	45
NCAA Reg. Season	13.2	66	34	33	25	42
Baseball						
World Series	28.7	57	43	30	23	47
All Star Game	21.5	61	39	32	22	46
Regular Season	8.0	63	37	29	19	52
Horse Racing						
Kentucky Derby	18.9	49	51	29	17	54
Preakness	12.2	49	51	25	17	58
Basketball						
NBA Regular Season	8.0	64	36	34	25	41
NBA Playoffs	8.1	63	37	40	25	35
NBA All Star Game	12.1	57	43	43	22	35
NBA Championships	10.1	62	38	39	24	37
NCAA Tournaments	15.3	62	38	38	27	35
Bowling						
Pro Bowl Tour	9.1	51	49	28	25	47
Red Crown Bowl	8.2	45	55	24	19	57
Auto Racing	9.9	55	45	33	33	34
Golf						
Tournaments	7.5	57	43	27	24	49
Tennis						
CBS Tennis Classic	3.9	51	49	30	25	45
World Championship	3.3	54	46	39	22	39
World Invitational	4.2	56	44	37	25	38
				18-49		**50+**
Women's Pro	3.9	48	52		50	50
Multi-Sports Series						
American Sportsman	9.6	58	42	40	29	31
ABC WW Sports						
Sat	11.3	58	42	41	25	34
Sun	15.3	56	44	41	27	32
CBS Sports Spectacular						
Sat	5.2	52	48	38	22	40
Sun	7.1	64	36	36	26	38

U.S. National Roller Skating Championship, 1976

American Senior Dance — John LaBriola - Debra Coyne, Fountain Valley, Cal.
American Esquire Dance — Fred and Nancy Doyle, Norwood, Ma.
American Free Dance — Mark Howard-Cindy Smith, Richmond, Va.
International Senior Dance — Kerry Cavazzi - Jane Puracchio, East Meadow, N.Y.
International Junior Dance — Greig Patton - Terry Campbell, Pontiac, Mich.
American Senior Men's Figures — William Combs, Columbus, Ohio.
American Ladies' Figures — Donna Kiker, Decatur, Ga.
American Junior Men's Figures — Greig Patton, Pontiac, Mich.
American Junior Ladies' Figures — Kimberly Campbell, Pontiac, Mich.
American Senior Men's Singles — Paul Jones, Flint, Mich.
American Senior Ladies' Singles — Lisa Bergin, Ft. Worth, Tex.
American Junior Men's Singles — George Podolsky, Cortland, Ohio.
American Junior Ladies' Singles — Robbie Coleman, Memphis, Tenn.
American Senior Pairs — Ron Sabo - Darlene Waters, Columbus, Ohio.
American Junior Pairs — Billy Joe and Rose Marie Carroll, Austin, Tex.

Speed

Senior Men's Speed — Tim Small, Loveland, Ohio.
Senior Ladies' Speed — Marcia Yager, Loveland, Ohio.
Junior Men's Speed — Jeff Couey, Riverdale, Ga.
Junior Ladies' Speed — Gayle Falconer, Olympia, Wash.
Senior Four Man Relay — Peter Deibele, Tim Small, Tom Small, Greg Phillips, Loveland, Ohio.
Senior Four Lady Relay — Brenda Haggard, Marcia Yager, Sandy Hoier, Danna Capozzi, Loveland, Ohio.

Quarter Horse Racing

The richest horse race in the world, the All American Futurity is run each Labor Day at Ruidoso Downs, New Mexico. It is open to 2-year-old Quarter Horses. The distance of the event was 400 yards through 1972; 440 yards starting in 1973.

Year	Winner	Time	Value To Winner	Jockey	Year	Winner	Time	Value To Winner	Jockey
1961	Pokey Bar	20.1	$101,212	K. Chapman	1969	Easy Jet	20.46	$159,840	W. Lovell
1962	Hustling Man	20.3	96,425	C. Detiege	1970	Rocket Wrangler	20.09	178,488	J. Nicodemus
1963	Goetta	20.40	127,500	C. Smith	1971	Mr. Kid Charge	19.65	200,841	J. Cox
1964	Decketta	20.30	134,030	B. Morris	1972	Possumjet	20.04	336,629	P. Herrera
1965	Savannah Jr.	20.30	192,730	J. Wallace	1973	Time To Thinkrich	21.58	330,000	J. Watson
1966	Go Dick Go	20.27	198,300	B. Nesmith	1974	Easy Date	21.60	330,000	D. Knight
1967	Laico Bird	20.11	228,300	B. Harmon	1975	Bugs Alive in 75	21.98	330,000	J. Burgess
1968	Three Oh's	20.06	160,372	J. Nicodemus	1976	Real Wind	21.70	330,000	G. Sumpter

Golf Records
United States Open

Year	Winner	Year	Winner	Year	Winner	Year	Winner
1896	James Foulis	1916	Chick Evans*	1936	Tony Manero	1958	Tommy Bolt
1897	Joe Lloyd	1917-18	(Not played)	1937	Ralph Guldahl	1959	Billy Casper
1898	Fred Herd	1919	Walter Hagen	1938	Ralph Guldahl	1960	Arnold Palmer
1899	Willie Smith	1920	Edward Ray	1939	Byron Nelson	1961	Gene Littler
1900	Harry Vardon	1921	Jim Barnes	1940	Lawson Little	1962	Jack Nicklaus
1901	Willie Anderson	1922	Gene Sarazen	1941	Craig Wood	1963	Julius Boros
1902	L. Auchterlonie	1923	Bob Jones*	1942-45	(Not played)	1964	Ken Venturi
1903	Willie Anderson	1924	Cyril Walker	1946	Lloyd Mangrum	1965	Gary Player
1904	Willie Anderson	1925	Willie MacFarlane	1947	L. Worsham	1966	Billy Casper
1905	Willie Anderson	1926	Bob Jones*	1948	Ben Hogan	1967	Jack Nicklaus
1906	Alex Smith	1927	Tommy Armour	1949	Cary Middlecoff	1968	Lee Trevino
1907	Alex Ross	1928	John Farrell	1950	Ben Hogan	1969	Orville Moody
1908	Fred McLeod	1929	Bob Jones*	1951	Ben Hogan	1970	Tony Jacklin
1909	George Sargent	1930	Bob Jones*	1952	Julius Boros	1971	Lee Trevino
1910	Alex Smith	1931	Wm. Burke	1953	Ben Hogan	1972	Jack Nicklaus
1911	John McDermott	1932	Gene Sarazen	1954	Ed Furgol	1973	Johnny Miller
1912	John McDermott	1933	John Goodman*	1955	Jack Fleck	1974	Hale Irwin
1913	Francis Ouimet*	1934	Olin Dutra	1956	Cary Middlecoff	1975	Lou Graham
1914	Walter Hagen	1935	Sam Parks Jr.	1957	Dick Mayer	1976	Jerry Pate
1915	Jerome Travers*						

*Amateur

U. S. Women's Open Golf Champions

Year	Winner	Year	Winner	Year	Winner	Year	Winner
1948	Mrs. M. D. Zaharias	1956	Mrs. K. Cornelius	1964	Mickey Wright	1971	JoAnne Gunderson Carner
1949	Louise Suggs	1957	Betsy Rawls	1965	Carol Mann		
1950	Mrs. M. D. Zaharias	1958	Mickey Wright	1966	Sandra Spuzich	1972	Susie Maxwell Berning
1951	Betsy Rawls	1959	Mickey Wright	1967	Catherine Lacoste (a)	1973	Susie Maxwell Berning
1952	Louise Suggs	1960	Betsy Rawls	1968	Susie Maxwell Berning	1974	Sandra Haynie
1953	Betsy Rawls	1961	Mickey Wright	1969	Donna Caponi	1975	Sandra Palmer
1954	Mrs. M. D. Zaharias	1962	Murie Lindstrom	1970	Donna Caponi	1976	JoAnne Carner
1955	Fay Crocker	1963	Mary Mills				

(a) Amateur

Professional Golfers' Association Championships

Year	Winner	Year	Winner	Year	Winner	Year	Winner
1919	Jim Barnes	1934	Paul Runyan	1949	Sam Snead	1963	Jack Nicklaus
1920	Jock Hutchison	1935	Johnny Revolta	1950	Chandler Harper	1964	Bob Nichols
1921	Walter Hagen	1936	Denny Shute	1951	Sam Snead	1965	Dave Marr
1922	Gene Sarazen	1937	Denny Shute	1952	James Turnesa	1966	Al Geiberger
1923	Gene Sarazen	1938	Paul Runyan	1953	Walter Burkemo	1967	Don January
1924	Walter Hagen	1939	Henry Picard	1954	Melvin Harbert	1968	Julius Boros
1925	Walter Hagen	1940	Byron Nelson	1955	Doug Ford	1969	Ray Floyd
1926	Walter Hagen	1941	Victor Ghezzi	1956	Jack Burke	1970	Dave Stockton
1927	Walter Hagen	1942	Sam Snead	1957	Lionel Hebert	1971	Jack Nicklaus
1928	Leo Diegel	1944	Bob Hamilton	1958	Dow Finsterwald	1972	Gary Player
1929	Leo Diegel	1945	Byron Nelson	1959	Bob Rosburg	1973	Jack Nicklaus
1930	Tommy Armour	1946	Ben Hogan	1960	Jay Hebert	1974	Lee Trevino
1931	Tom Creavy	1947	Jim Ferrier	1961	Jerry Barber	1975	Jack Nicklaus
1932	Olin Dutra	1948	Ben Hogan	1962	Gary Player	1976	Dave Stockton
1933	Gene Sarazen						

Masters Golf Tournament Champions

Year	Winner	Year	Winner	Year	Winner	Year	Winner
1934	Horton Smith	1947	Jimmy Demaret	1957	Doug Ford	1967	Gay Brewer Jr.
1935	Gene Sarazen	1948	Claude Harmon	1958	Arnold Palmer	1968	Bob Goalby
1936	Horton Smith	1949	Sam Snead	1959	Art Wall Jr.	1969	George Archer
1937	Byron Nelson	1950	Jimmy Demaret	1960	Arnold Palmer	1970	Billy Casper
1938	Henry Picard	1951	Ben Hogan	1961	Gary Player	1971	Charles Coody
1939	Ralph Guldahl	1952	Sam Snead	1962	Arnold Palmer	1972	Jack Nicklaus
1940	Jimmy Demaret	1953	Ben Hogan	1963	Jack Nicklaus	1973	Tommy Aaron
1941	Craig Wood	1954	Sam Snead	1964	Arnold Palmer	1974	Gary Player
1942	Byron Nelson	1955	Cary Middlecoff	1965	Jack Nicklaus	1975	Jack Nicklaus
1943-1945	(Not played)	1956	Jack Burke	1966	Jack Nicklaus	1976	Ray Floyd
1946	Herman Keiser						

Canadian Open Golf Champions

Year	Winner	Year	Winner	Year	Winner	Year	Winner
1942	Craig Wood	1952	John Palmer	1961	Jacky Cupit	1969	Tommy Aaron
1943-44	(Not played)	1953	Dave Douglas	1962	Ted Kroll	1970	Kermit Zarley
1945	Byron Nelson	1954	Pat Fletcher	1963	Doug Ford	1971	Lee Trevino
1946	George Fazio	1955	Arnold Palmer	1964	Kel Nagle	1972	Gay Brewer
1947	Bobby Locke	1956	Doug Sanders	1965	Gene Littler	1973	Tom Weiskopf
1948	C. W. Congdon	1957	George Bayer	1966	Don Massengale	1974	Bobby Nichols
1949	E. J. Harrison	1958	Wes Ellis Jr.	1967	Billy Casper	1975	Tom Weiskopf
1950	Jim Ferrier	1959	Doug Ford	1968	Bob Charles	1976	Jerry Pate
1951	Jim Ferrier	1960	Art Wall, Jr.				

Professional Golf Tournaments in 1976

Date	Event	Winner	Scores	Prize
Jan. 11	Tucson Open	Johnny Miller	274	$40,000
Jan. 18	Phoenix Open	Bob Gilder	268	40,000
Jan. 25	Bing Crosby National Pro-Am, Pebble Beach, Cal.	Ben Crenshaw	283	37,000
Feb. 1	Hawaiian Open, Honolulu	Ben Crenshaw	270	46,000
Feb. 8	Bob Hope Desert Classic, Palm Springs, Cal.	Johnny Miller	344	36,000
Feb. 15	Andy Williams-San Diego Open	J. C. Snead	272	36,000
Feb. 22	Glen Campbell-Los Angeles Open	Hale Irwin	272	37,000
Mar. 1	Tournament Players Championship, Lauderhill, Fla.	Jack Nicklaus	269	60,000
Mar. 8	Florida Citrus Open, Orlando, Fla.	Hale Irwin	*270	40,000
Mar. 14	Doral-Eastern Open, Miami	Hubert Green	270	40,000
Mar. 21	Greater Jacksonville Open	Hubert Green	276	35,000
Mar. 28	Heritage Classic, Hilton Head Island, S.C.	Hubert Green	274	43,000
Apr. 4	Greater Greensboro Open	Al Geiberger	268	46,000
Apr. 11	Masters Tournament, Augusta, Ga.	Ray Floyd	271	40,000
Apr. 18	Tournament of Champions, Carlsbad, Cal.	Don January	277	45,000
Apr. 25	New Orleans Open	Larry Ziegler	274	35,000
May 2	Houston Open	Lee Elder	278	40,000
May 9	Bryon Nelson Classic, Dallas	Mark Hayes	273	40,000
May 16	Colonial Invitational, Ft. Worth, Tex.	Lee Trevino	273	40,000
May 23	Danny Thomas-Memphis Classic	Gibby Gilbert	273	40,000
May 30	Memorial Tournament, Dublin, Ohio	Roger Maltbie	*288	40,000
June 6	Bicentennial Classic, Philadelphia	Tom Kite	*277	40,000
June 13	Kemper Open, Charlotte, N.C.	Joe Inman	277	50,000
June 20	U.S. Open, Duluth, Ga.	Jerry Pate	277	42,000
June 27	Western Open, Oak Brook, Ill.	Al Geiberger	288	40,000
July 4	Greater Milwaukee Open	Dave Hill	270	26,000
July 11	Quad Cities Open, Coal Valley, Ill.	John Lister	268	20,000
July 18	Westchester Classic, Harrison, N.Y.	David Graham	272	60,000
July 25	Canadian Open, Windsor, Ont.	Jerry Pate	267	40,000
Aug. 1	Pleasant Valley Classic, Sutton, Mass.	Bud Allin	277	40,000
Aug. 8	B. C. Open, Endicott, N.Y.	Bob Wynn	271	40,000
Aug. 16	PGA Championship, Bethesda, Md.	Dave Stockton	281	45,000
Aug. 22	Sammy Davis-Greater Hartford Open	Rik Massengale	266	42,000
Aug. 30	American Classic, Akron, Ohio	David Graham	274	40,000
Sept. 5	World Series of Golf, Akron, Ohio	Jack Nicklaus	275	100,000
Sept. 12	World Open, Pinehurst, N.C.	Ray Floyd	*274	40,000
Sept. 19	Ohio Kings Island Open, Mason, Ohio	Ben Crenshaw	271	30,000
Sept. 26	Kaiser International Open, Napa, Cal.	J. C. Snead	274	35,000
Oct. 3	Sahara Invitational, Las Vegas	George Archer	271	27,000

Women

Date	Event	Winner	Scores	Prize
Feb. 15	Orange Blossom Classic, St. Petersburg, Fla.	JoAnne Carner	*209	$ 6,400
Mar. 22	Bent Tree Classic, Sarasota, Fla.	Kathy Whitworth	209	8,500
Apr. 4	Colgate-Dinah Shore-Winners Circle Championship, Palm Springs, Cal.	Judy Rankin	285	32,000
Apr. 18	Karsten-Ping Open, Scottsdale, Ariz.	Judy Rankin	205	14,000
Apr. 25	Birmingham Classic	Jan Stephenson	203	5,700
May 2	Lady Tara Classic, Atlanta	JoAnne Carner	209	7,000
May 9	Women's International, Hilton Head Island, S.C.	Sally Little	281	10,000
May 23	'76 Classic, Jamesburg, N.J.	Amy Alcott	209	14,000
May 30	LPGA Championship, Baltimore	Betty Burfeindt	287	8,000
June 6	Girl Talk Classic, New Rochelle, N.Y.	Pat Bradley	*217	14,000
June 28	Babe Zaharias Invitational, Chagrin Falls, Ohio	Judy Rankin	287	15,000
July 12	U. S. Women's Open, Springfield, Pa.	JoAnne Carner	*292	9,000
July 18	Columbus Classic, Ohio	Judy Rankin	205	10,000
July 25	Lady Keystone Open, Harrisburg, Pa.	Susie Berning	215	7,000
Aug. 15	Wheeling Classic	Jane Blalock	*217	7,000
Aug. 22	Patty Berg Classic, St. Paul, Minn.	Kathy Whitworth	212	8,000
Aug. 30	National Jewish Hospital Open, Denver	Sandra Palmer	206	8,000
Sept. 5	Jerry Lewis Muscular Dystrophy Tournament, Springfield, Ill.	Sandra Palmer	*213	15,000
Sept. 12	Dallas Civitan Women's Open	Jane Blalock	205	8,000
Sept. 19	Portland (Ore.) Classic	Donna Caponi Young	*217	6,400
Sept. 26	Carlton, Calabasas, Cal.	Donna Caponi Young	282	35,000

* Won playoff

British Open Golf Champions

Year	Winner	Year	Winner	Year	Winner	Year	Winner
1908	James Braid	1927	Bob Jones	1947	Fred Daly	1962	Arnold Palmer
1909	J. H. Taylor	1928	Walter Hagen	1948	Henry Cotton	1963	Bob Charles
1910	James Braid	1929	Walter Hagen	1949	Bobby Locke	1964	Tony Lema
1911	Harry Vardon	1930	Bob Jones	1950	Bobby Locke	1965	Peter Thomson
1912	Ted Ray	1931	Tommy Armour	1951	Max Faulkner	1966	Jack Nicklaus
1913	J. H. Taylor	1932	Gene Sarazen	1952	Bobby Locke	1967	Roberto de Vicenzo
1914	Harry Vardon	1933	Denny Shute	1953	Ben Hogan	1968	Gary Player
1915-19	(Not played)	1934	Henry Cotton	1954	Peter Thomson	1969	Tony Jacklin
1920	George Duncan	1935	Alf Perry	1955	Peter Thomson	1970	Jack Nicklaus
1921	Jock Hutchison	1936	Alf Padgham	1956	Peter Thomson	1971	Lee Trevino
1922	Walter Hagen	1937	T. H. Cotton	1957	Bobby Locke	1972	Lee Trevino
1923	Arthur Havers	1938	R. A. Whitcombe	1958	Peter Thomson	1973	Tom Weiskopf
1924	Walter Hagen	1939	Richard Burton	1959	Gary Player	1974	Gary Player
1925	Jim Barnes	1940-45	(Not played)	1960	Ken Nagle	1975	Thomas Watson
1926	Bob Jones	1946	Sam Snead	1961	Arnold Palmer	1976	Johnny Miller

Golf Records

U. S. Amateur

Year	Winner	Year	Winner	Year	Winner	Year	Winner
1901	Walter Travis	1920	Chick Evans Jr.	1938	Willie Turnesa	1959	Jack Nicklaus
1902	Louis James	1921	Jesse Guilford	1939	Bud Ward	1960	Deane Beman
1903	Walter Travis	1922	Jess Sweetser	1940	Dick Chapman	1961	Jack Nicklaus
1904	Chandler Egan	1923	Max Marston	1941	Bud Ward	1962	Labron Harris Jr.
1905	Chandler Egan	1924	Bob Jones	1942-45	(Not Played)	1963	Deane Beman
1906	Eben Byers	1925	Bob Jones .	1946	Ted Bishop	1964	Bill Campbell
1907	Jerome Travers	1926	George Von Elm	1947	Skee Riegel	1965	Robert Murphy Jr.
1908	Jerome Travers	1927	Bob Jones	1948	Willie Turnesa	1966	Gary Cowan
1909	Robert Gardner	1928	Bob Jones	1949	Charles Coe	1967	Bob Dickson
1910	William Fownes Jr.	1929	Harrison Johnston	1950	Sam Urzetta	1968	Bruce Fleisher
1911	Harold Hilton	1930	Bob Jones	1951	Billy Maxwell	1969	Steve Melnyk
1912	Jerome Travers	1931	Francis Ouimet	1952	Jack Westland	1970	Lanny Wadkins
1913	Jerome Travers	1932	Ross Somerville	1953	Gene Littler	1971	Gary Cowan
1914	Francis Ouimet	1933	George Dunlap Jr.	1954	Arnold Palmer	1972	Vinnie Giles
1915	Robert Gardner	1934	Lawson Little	1955	Harvie Ward	1973	Craig Stadler
1916	Chick Evans Jr.	1935	Lawson Little	1956	Harvie Ward	1974	Jerry Pate
1917-18	(Not Played)	1936	John Fischer	1957	Hillman Robbins	1975	Fred Ridley
1919	Davidson Herron	1937	John Goodman	1958	Charles Coe	1976	Bill Sander

Women's U.S. Amateur

Year	Winner	Year	Winner	Year	Winner	Year	Winner
1905	Pauline Mackay	1923	Edith Cummings	1940	Betty Jameson	1960	JoAnne Gunderson
1906	Harriot Curtis	1924	Mrs. D. C. Hurd	1941	Mrs. Frank New	1961	Anne Q. Decker
1907	Margaret Curtis	1925	Glenna Collett	1942-45	(not played)	1962	JoAnne Gunderson
1908	Kate Harley	1926	Mrs. G. Stetson	1946	Babe Zaharias	1963	Anne Q. Welts
1909	Dorothy Campbell	1927	Mrs. M. Horn	1947	Louise Suggs	1964	Barbara McIntire
1910	Dorothy Campbell	1928	Glenna Collett	1948	Grace Lenczyk	1965	Jean Ashley
1911	Margaret Curtis	1929	Glenna Collett	1949	Dorothy Porter	1966	JoAnne Carner
1912	Margaret Curtis	1930	Glenna Collett	1950	Beverly Hanson	1967	Lou Dill
1913	Gladys Raven Scroft	1931	Helen Hicks	1951	Dorothy Kirby	1968	JoAnne Carner
1914	Mrs. H. A. Jackson	1932	Virginia Van Wie	1952	Jackie Pung	1969	Catherine Lacoste
1915	Mrs. C. H. Vanderbeck	1933	Virginia Van Wie	1953	Mary Faulk	1970	Martha Wilkinson
1916	Alexa Stirling	1934	Virginia Van Wie	1954	Barbara Romack	1971	Laura Baugh
1917-18	(not played)	1935	Glenna C. Vare	1955	Pat Lesser	1972	Mary Budke
1919	Alexa Stirling	1936	Pamela Barton	1956	Marlene Stewart	1973	Carol Semple
1920	Alexa Stirling	1937	Mrs. J. A. Page	1957	JoAnne Gunderson	1974	Cynthia Hill
1921	Marion Hollins	1938	Patty Berg	1958	Anne Quast	1975	Beth Daniel
1922	Glenna Collett	1939	Betty Jameson	1959	Barbara McIntire	1976	Donna Horton

British Amateur Golf Champions

Year	Winner	Year	Winner	Year	Winner	Year	Winner
1930	Bobby Jones (U.S.)	1946	James Bruen	1957	Reid Jack	1967	Bob Dickson (U.S.)
1931	E. Martin-Smith	1947	Willie Turnesa	1958	Joseph Carr	1968	Mike Bonallack
1932	J. De Forest	1948	Frank Stranahan (U.S.)	1959	Deane Beman (U.S.)	1969	Mike Bonallack
1933	Michael Scott	1949	Sam McCready	1960	Joseph Carr	1970	Mike Bonallack ·
1934	Lawson Little (U.S.)	1950	Frank Stranahan (U.S.)	1961	Michael Bonallack	1971	Steve Melnyk (U.S.)
1935	Lawson Little (U.S.)	1951	Dick Chapman (U.S.)	1962	Richard Davies (U.S.)	1972	Trevor Homer
1936	H. Thompson	1952	Harvie Ward (U.S.)	1963	Michael Lunt	1973	Dick Siderowe (U.S.)
1937	Robert Sweeny	1953	Joseph Carr	1964	Gordon Clark	1974	Trevor Homer
1938	C. Yates (U.S.)	1954	Doug Bachli	1965	Mike Bonallack	1975	Vinny Giles (U.S.)
1939	Alex Kyle	1955	Joseph Conrad (U.S.)	1966	Bobby Cole	1976	Dick Siderowf (U.S.)
1940-45	(not played)	1956	John Beharrell				

PGA Hall of Fame

Established in 1940 to honor those who have made outstanding contributions to the game by their lifetime playing ability

Anderson, Willie
Armour, Tommy
Barnes, Jim
Boros, Julius
Brady, Mike
Burke, Billy
Burke Jr., Jack
Cooper, Harry
Cruickshank, Bobby
Demaret, Jimmy
Diegel, Leo
Dudley, Edward
Dutra, Olin
Evans, Chick
Farrell, Johnny
Ford, Doug
Ghezzi, Vic
Guldahl, Ralph
Hagen, Walter
Harbert, M. R. (Chick)
Harper, Chandler
Harrison, E. J.
Hogan, Ben
Hutchison Sr., Jock
Jones, Bob
Little, W. Lawson
Mangrum, Lloyd
McDermott, John
McLeod, Fred
Middlecoff, Cary
Nelson, Byron
Ouimet, Francis
Picard, Henry
Revolta, Johnny
Runyan, Paul
Sarazen, Gene
Shute, Denny
Smith, Alex
Smith, Horton
Smith, MacDonald
Snead, Sam
Travers, Jerry
Travis, Walter
Wood, Craig

PGA Leading Money Winners

Year	Player	Dollars	Year	Player	Dollars	Year	Player	Dollars
1945	Byron Nelson	52,511	1956	Ted Kroll	72,835	1966	Billy Casper	121,944
1946	Ben Hogan	42,556	1957	Dick Mayer	65,835	1967	Jack Nicklaus	188,988
1947	Jimmy Demaret	27,936	1958	Arnold Palmer	42,407	1968	Billy Casper	205,168
1948	Ben Hogan	36,812	1959	Art Wall, Jr.	53,167	1969	Frank Beard	175,223
1949	Sam Snead	31,593	1960	Arnold Palmer	75,262	1970	Lee Trevino	157,037
1950	Sam Snead	35,758	1961	Gary Player	64,540	1971	Jack Nicklaus	244,490
1951	Lloyd Mangrum	26,088	1962	Arnold Palmer	81,448	1972	Jack Nicklaus	320,542
1952	Julius Boros	37,032	1963	Arnold Palmer	128,230	1973	Jack Nicklaus	308,362
1953	Lew Worsham	34,002	1964	Jack Nicklaus	113,284	1974	Johnny Miller	353,201
1954	Bob Toski	65,819	1965	Jack Nicklaus	140,752	1975	Jack Nicklaus	323,149
1955	Julius Boros	65,121						

LPGA Leading Money Winners

Year	Winner	Dollars	Year	Winner	Dollars	Year	Winner	Dollars
1952	Betsy Rawls	14,505	1960	Louise Suggs	16,892	1968	Kathy Whitworth	48,379
1953	Louise Suggs	19,816	1961	Mickey Wright	22,236	1969	Carol Mann	49,152
1954	Patty Berg	16,011	1962	Mickey Wright	21,641	1970	Kathy Whitworth	30,235
1955	Patty Berg	16,492	1963	Mickey Wright	31,269	1971	Kathy Whitworth	41,181
1956	Marlene Hagge	20,235	1964	Mickey Wright	29,800	1972	Kathy Whitworth	65,063
1957	Patty Berg	16,272	1965	Kathy Whitworth	28,658	1973	Kathy Whitworth	82,854
1958	Beverly Hanson	12,629	1966	Kathy Whitworth	33,517	1974	JoAnne Carner	87,094
1959	Betsy Rawls	26,774	1967	Kathy Whitworth	32,937	1975	Sandra Palmer	94,805

PGA Career Money Winners

(as of January 1, 1976)

Player	Dollars	Player	Dollars	Player	Dollars
Jack Nicklaus	2,541,772.99	Julius Boros	993,756.10	Al Geiberger	794,505.90
Arnold Palmer	1,723,114.07	Miller Barber	989,702.34	Dan Sikes Jr.	773,233.66
Billy Casper	1,581,606.62	Frank Beard	951,596.54	Doug Sanders	766,844.19
Lee Trevino	1,396,959.44	Johnny Miller	947,152.59	Hale Irwin	760,055.93
Bruce Crampton	1,323,400.33	Dave Hill	922,233.87	Tommy Aaron	744,016.27
Tom Weiskopf	1,224,854.80	Bobby Nichols	906,277.55	Gay Brewer	712,087.75
Gene Littler	1,203,541.74	Dave Stockton	814,483.50	Bob Murphy	708,392.47
Gary Player	1,163,153.49	George Archer	810,020.91	Ray Floyd	697,588.24

Ryder Cup Matches

United States vs. Great Britain Professional (biennial)
Series Standing, United States 17, Great Britain 3, 1 Tie

Series Record	Series Record
1953 United States 6¹/₂; Great Britain 5¹/₂	1965 United States 19¹/₂; Great Britain 12¹/₂
1955 United States 8; Great Britain 4	1967 United States 23¹/₂; Great Britain 8¹/₂
1957 Great Britain 7; United States 4	1969 United States 16; Great Britain 16
1959 United States 8¹/₂; Great Britain 3¹/₂	1971 United States 18¹/₂; Great Britain 13¹/₂
1961 United States 14¹/₂; Great Britain 9¹/₂	1973 United States 19; Great Britain 13
1963 United States 23; Great Britain 9	1975 United States 21; Great Britain 11

International Walker Cup Golf Match

United States vs. Great Britain — Men's Amateur (Biennial)
Series Standing — United States 22, Great Britain 2, 1 Tie

Series Record	Series Record
1953 United States 9; Great Britain 3	1965 United States 11; Great Britain 11
1955 United States 10; Great Britain 2	1967 United States 13; Great Britain 7
1957 United States 8; Great Britain 3	1969 United States 10; Great Britain 8
1959 United States 9; Great Britain 3	1971 Great Britain 13; United States 11
1961 United States 11; Great Britain 1	1973 United States 14; Great Britain 10
1963 United States 9; Great Britain 3	1975 United States 15¹/₂; Great Britain 8¹/₂

International Curtis Cup Golf Match

United States vs. Great Britain — Women's Amateur (Biennial)
Series Standing — United States 15, Great Britain 2, 2 Ties

Series Record	Series Record
1952 Great Britain 5; United States 4	1964 United States 10¹/₂; Great Britain 7¹/₂;
1954 United States 6; Great Britain 3	1966 United States 13; Great Britain 5
1956 Great Britain 5; United States 4	1968 United States 10¹/₂; Great Britain 7¹/₂
1958 Great Britain 4¹/₂; United States 4¹/₂	1970 United States 11¹/₂; Great Britain 6¹/₂
1960 United States 6¹/₂; Great Britain 2¹/₂	1972 United States 10; Great Britain 8
1962 United States 8; Great Britain 1	1974 United States 13; Great Britain 5
	1976 United States 11¹/₂; Great Britain 6¹/₂.

31st Annual National Field Archery Championships

Aurora, Ill., July 21-25, 1976

Freestyle
Professional Men—Ronald Lauhon, Huntington, W. Va.
Professional Women—Liz Colombo, Cal.
Open Men—Kenneth Cranberg, Dallas City, Ill.
Open Woman—Janet Boatman, Alden, N.Y.
Amateur Men—(tie) Barry Velarde, Ft. Knox, Ky. & Phillip Schmidt, Tacoma, Wash.
Amateur Women—Michelle Sanderson, Hastings, Minn.

Freestyle—Limited
Professional Men—Jerry Podratz, Shakopee, Minn.
Open Men—Terry Frazier, Houston, Tex.
Open Women—Millie Foster, Kansas City, Mo.
Amateur Men—Edwin Eliason, Seattle, Wash.
Amateur Women—Valerie Gramzow, Creswell, Ore.

Barebow
Open Men—David Hughes, Irving, Tex.
Open Women—Frozine Greene, Liberal, Kan.
Amateur Men—Donald Morehead, Wheaton, Ill.
Amateur Women—Patricia Kramer, Ft. Lauderdale, Fla.

Bowhunter
Professional Men—Gilbert Smith, Pasadena, Cal.
Open Men—Hugh McConnell, Hiltons, Va.
Open Women—June Hardy, Houston, Tex.
Amateur Men—John Saporiti, Rockford, Ill.

Shuffleboard Championships in 1976

National Singles Championships, St. Petersburg, Fla., Mar. 8-10—Men's Open, Merritt Gordon; Men's Closed, Ed Travis; Women's Open, Mary Eldridge; Women's Closed, Wilma Krieg.
National Doubles Championships, No. Miami, Fla., Jan. 19-21—Men's Division, Austin Sutton and Bob Pearson; Women's Division, Wilma Krieg and Terese Charbonneau.

Summer National Championships, Lakeside, Ohio, July 19-24—Men's Open, Dave Karaska; Men's Closed, Howard Hawkins; Men's Doubles, Clarence Goodman and Bailie Stepp. Women's Open, Dorcas Donelson; Women's Closed, Elsie Hodges; Women's Doubles, Adele Pearson and Elnora Rhoades.

Boxing Champions by Classes

Recognized by Ring Magazine as of Sept. 1, 1976.

Heavyweight . . . . Muhammad Ali, Chicago, Ill.
Light-Heavyweight (175 lbs.) . . vacant
Middleweight (160 lbs.) . . . . . . Carlos Monzon, Argentina
Jr. Middleweight (154 lbs.) . . . . Jose Duran, Spain
Welterweight (147 lbs.) . . . . . . Carlos Palomino, Los Angeles, Cal.

Jr. Welterweight (140 lbs.) . . . . Wilfredo Benitez, Puerto Rico
Lightweight (135 lbs.) . . . . Roberto Duran, Panama
Junior Lightweight (130 lbs.) . . . Ben Villaflor, Philippines
Featherweight (126 lbs.) . . . . . . Alexis Arguello, Nicaragua
Bantamweight (118 lbs.) . . . . . . Alfonso Zamora, Mexico
Flyweight (112 lbs.) . . . . Miguel Canto, Mexico

As of Sept. 1, 1976, the only universally accepted title holders were in the heavyweight and middleweight divisions. The following are the recognized champions of the World Boxing Assn. and the World Boxing Council.

	WBA	WBC
Heavyweight	Muhammad Ali, Chicago, Ill.	Muhammad Ali
Light Heavyweight	Victor Galindez, Argentina	John Conteh, England
Middleweights	Carlos Monzon, Argentina	Carlos Monzon
Jr. Middleweight	Jose Duran, Spain	Eckhart Dagge, W. Germany
Welterweight	Jose Cuevas, Mexico	Carlos Palomino, Los Angeles
Jr. Welterweight	Wilfredo Benitez, Puerto Rico	Miguel Velasquez, Spain
Lightweight	Roberto Duran, Panama	Esteban DeJesus, Puerto Rico
Jr. Lightweight	Ben Villaflor, Philippines	Alfredo Escalera, Puerto Rico
Featherweight	Alexis Arguello, Nicaragua	David Poison Kotey, Ghana
Bantamweight	Alfonso Zamora, Mexico	Carlos Zarate, Mexico
Flyweight	Alfonzo Lopez, Panama	Miguel Canto, Mexico

Ring Champions by Years

*Abandoned title

Heavyweights

1882-1892	John L. Sullivan (A)
1892-1897	James J. Corbett (B)
1897-1899	Robert Fitzsimmons
1899-1905	James J. Jeffries (C)
1905-1906	Marvin Hart
1906-1908	Tommy Burns
1908-1915	Jack Johnson
1915-1919	Jess Willard
1919-1926	Jack Dempsey
1926-1928	Gene Tunney*
1928-1930	Vacant
1930-1932	Max Schmeling
1932	Jack Sharkey
1933	Primo Carnera
1934	Max Baer
1935-1937	James J. Braddock
1937-1949	Joe Louis*
1949-1951	Ezzard Charles
1951-1952	Joe Walcott
1952-1956	Rocky Marciano*
1956-1959	Floyd Patterson
1959	Ingemar Johansson
1960-1962	Floyd Patterson
1962-1964	Sonny Liston
1964-1967	Cassius Clay* (Muhammad Ali) (D)
1970-1973	Joe Frazier
1973-1974	George Foreman
1974	Muhammad Ali

(A) London Prize Ring (bare knuckle champion).
(B) First Marquis of Queensberry Champion.
(C) Jeffries abandoned the title (1905) and designated Marvin Hart and Jack Root as logical contenders and agreed to referee a fight between them, the winner to be declared champion. Hart defeated Root in 12 rounds (1905) and in turn was defeated by Tommy Burns (1906) who immediately laid claim to the title. Jack Johnson defeated Burns (1908) and was recognized as champion. He clinched the title by defeating Jeffries in an attempted comeback (1910).
(D) Title declared vacant by the World Boxing Assn. and other groups in 1967 after Clay's refusal to fulfill his military obligation.

Light Heavyweights

1903	Jack Root, George Gardner
1903-1905	Bob Fitzsimmons
1905-1912	Philadelphia Jack O'Brien*
1912-1916	Jack Dillon
1916-1920	Battling Levinsky
1920-1922	Georges Carpentier
1922-1923	Battling Siki
1923-1925	Mike McTigue
1925-1926	Paul Berlenbach
1926-1927	Jack Delaney*
1927-1929	Tommy Loughran*
1930-1934	Maxey Rosenbloom
1934-1935	Bob Olin

1935-1939	John Henry Lewis*
1939	Melio Bettina
1939-1941	Billy Conn*
1941	Anton Christoforidis (won NBA title)
1941-1948	Gus Lesnevich, Freddie Mills
1948-1950	Freddie Mills
1950-1952	Joey Maxim
1952-1960	Archie Moore
1961-1962	Vacant
1962-1963	Harold Johnson
1963-1965	Willie Pastrano
1965-1966	Jose Torres
1966-1968	Dick Tiger
1968-1974	Bob Foster*

Middleweights

1884-1891	Jack "Nonpareil" Dempsey
1891-1897	Bob Fitzsimmons*
1897-1907	Tommy Ryan*
1907-1908	Stanley Ketchel, Billy Papke
1908-1910	Stanley Ketchel
1911-1913	Vacant
1913	Frank Klaus, George Chip
1914-1917	Al McCoy
1917-1920	Mike O'Dowd
1920-1923	Johnny Wilson
1923-1926	Harry Greb
1926-1931	Tiger Flowers, Mickey Walker
1931-1932	Gorilla Jones (NBA)
1932-1937	Marcel Thil
1938	Al Hostak (NBA), Solly Krieger (NBA)
1939-1940	Al Hostak (NBA)
1941-1947	Tony Zale
1947-1948	Rocky Graziano
1948	Tony Zale, Marcel Cerdan
1949	Marcel Cerdan, Jake LaMotta
1950	Jake LaMotta
1951	Ray Robinson, Randy Turpin, Ray Robinson*
1953-1955	Carl (Bobo) Olson
1955-1957	Ray Robinson
1957	Gene Fullmer, Ray Robinson, Carmen Basilio
1958	Carmen Basilio, Ray Robinson
1959	Gene Fullmer (NBA); Ray Robinson (N.Y.)
1960	Gene Fullmer (NBA); Paul Pender (New York and Mass.)
1961	Gene Fullmer (NBA); Terry Downes (New York, Mass., Europe)
1962	Gene Fullmer, Dick Tiger (NBA); Paul Pender (New York and Mass.)*
1963	Dick Tiger (universal).
1963-1965	Joey Giardello
1965-1966	Dick Tiger
1966-1967	Emile Griffith
1967	Nino Benvenuti
1967-1968	Emile Griffith
1968-1970	Nino Benvenuti
1970	Carlos Monzon

Welterweights

1892-1894	Mysterious Billy Smith
1894-1896	Tommy Ryan
1896	Kid McCoy (outgrew class)
1900	Rube Ferns, Matty Matthews
1901	Matty Matthews, Rube Ferns
1901-1904	Joe Walcott
1904-1906	Dixie Kid, Joe Walcott, Honey Mellody
1907-1911	Mike Sullivan
1911-1915	Vacant
1915-1919	Ted Lewis
1919-1922	Jack Britton
1922-1926	Mickey Walker
1926	Pete Latzo
1927-1929	Joe Dundee
1929	Jackie Fields
1930	Jackie Fields, Jack Thompson, Tommy Freeman
1931	Freeman, Thompson, Lou Brouillard
1932	Jackie Fields
1933	Young Corbett, Jimmy McLarnin
1934	Barney Ross, Jimmy McLarnin
1935-1938	Barney Ross
1938-1940	Henry Armstrong
1940	Fritzie Zivic
1941-1946	Fred Cochrane
1946-1946	Marty Servo*; Ray Robinson (A)
1946-1950	Ray Robinson*
1951	Johnny Bratton (NBA): Kid Gavilan
1951-1954	Kid Gavilan
1954-1955	Johnny Saxton
1955	Tony De Marco, Carmen Basilio
1956	Carmen Basilio, Johnny Saxton, Carmen Basilio
1957	Carmen Basilio*
1958-1960	Virgil Akins, Don Jordan
1960	Benny Paret
1961	Emile Griffith, Benny Paret
1962	Benny Paret, Emile Griffith
1963	Luis Rodriguez, Emile Griffith
1964-1966	Emile Griffith*
1966-1969	Curtis Cokes
1969-1970	Jose Napoles, Billy Backus
1971-1975	Jose Napoles

(A) Robinson gained the title by defeating Tommy Bell in an elimination agreed to by the NY Commission and the N.B.A. Both claimed Robinson waived his title when he won the middleweight crown from LaMotta in 1951. Gavilan defeated Bratton in an elimination to find a successor.

Lightweights

1896-1899	Kid Lavigne
1899-1902	Frank Erne
1902-1908	Joe Gans
1908-1910	Battling Nelson
1910-1912	Ad Wolgast
1912-1914	Willie Ritchie
1914-1917	Freddie Welsh
1917-1925	Benny Leonard*
1925	Jimmy Goodrich, Rocky Kansas
1926-1930	Sammy Mandell
1930	Al Singer, Tony Canzoneri

1930-1933	Tony Canzoneri
1933-1935	Barney Ross*
1935-1936	Tony Canzoneri
1936-1938	Lou Ambers
1938	Henry Armstrong
1939	Lou Ambers
1940	Lew Jenkins
1941-1943	Sammy Angott
1944	S. Angott (NBA), J. Zurita (NBA)
1945-1951	Ike Williams (NBA: later universal)
1951-1952	James Carter
1952	Lauro Salas, James Carter
1953-1954	James Carter
1954	Paddy De Marco; James Carter
1955	James Carter; Bud Smith
1956	Bud Smith, Joe Brown
1956-1962	Joe Brown
1962-1965	Carlos Ortiz
1965	Ismael Laguna
1965-1968	Carlos Ortiz
1968-1969	Teo Cruz
1969-1970	Mando Ramos
1970	Ismael Laguna
1970-1972	Ken Buchanan
1972	Roberto Duran (WBA)

Featherweights

1892-1900	George Dixon (disputed)
1900-1901	Terry McGovern, Young Corbett*
1901-1912	Abe Attell
1912-1923	Johnny Kilbane
1923	Eugene Criqui, Johnny Dundee
1923-1925	Johnny Dundee*
1925-1927	Kid Kaplan*
1927-1928	Benny Bass, Tony Canzoneri
1928-1929	Andre Routis
1929-1932	Battling Battalino*
1932-1934	Tommy Paul (NBA)
1933-1936	Freddie Miller
1936-1937	Petey Sarron
1937-1938	Henry Armstrong*
1938-1940	Joey Archibald (B)
1942-1948	Willie Pep
1948-1949	Sandy Saddler
1949-1950	Willie Pep
1950-1957	Sandy Saddler*
1957-1959	Hogan (Kid) Bassey
1959-1963	Davey Moore
1963-1964	Sugar Ramos
1964-1969	Vicente Saldivar*
1969	John Famechon
1970	Vicente Saldivar
1970-1972	Kuniaki Shibata
1972	Clemente Sanchez*
1974	Ruben Olivares
1975	Alexis Arguello (WBA)

(B) After Petey Scalzo knocked out Archibald (Dec. 5, 1938) in an overweight match and was refused a title bout, the NBA named Scalzo champion. The NBA title succession was: Petey Scalzo, 1938-1941: Richard Lemos, 1941: Jackie Wilson, 1941-1943: Jackie Callura, 1943: Phil Terranova, 1943-1944: Sal Bartolo, 1944-1946.

History of Heavyweight Championship Bouts
*Title Changed Hands

1889—July 8—John L. Sullivan beat Jake Kilrain, 75 rounds, Richburg, Miss. (Last championship bare knuckles bout.)

*1892—Sept. 7—James J. Corbett defeated John L. Sullivan, 21 rounds, New Orleans. (Used big gloves for first time.)

1894—Jan. 25—James J. Corbett knocked out Charley Mitchell, 3 rounds, Jacksonville, Fla.

*1897—March 17—Bob Fitzsimmons defeated James J. Corbett, 14 rounds, Carson City, Nev.

*1899—June 9—James J. Jeffries beat Bob Fitzsimmons, 11 rounds, Coney Island, N.Y.

1899—Nov. 3—James J. Jeffries beat Tom Sharkey, 25 rounds, Coney Island, N.Y.

1900—May 11—James J. Jeffries knocked out James J. Corbett, 23 rounds, Coney Island, N.Y.

1901—Nov. 15—James J. Jeffries, knocked out Gus Ruhlin, 5 rounds, San Francisco.

1902—July 25—James J. Jeffries knocked out Bob Fitzsimmons, 8 rounds, San Francisco.

1903—Aug. 14—James J. Jeffries knocked out James J. Corbett, 10 rounds, San Francisco.

1904—Aug. 26—James J. Jeffries knocked out Jack Monroe, 2 rounds, San Francisco.

*1905—James J. Jeffries retired, July 3—Marvin Hart knocked out Jack Root, 12 rounds, Reno. Jeffries refereed and presented the title to the victor. Jack O'Brien also claimed the title.

*1906—Feb. 23—Tommy Burns defeated Marvin Hart, 20 rounds, Los Angeles.

1906—Nov. 28—Philadelphia Jack O'Brien and Tommy Burns, 20 rounds, draw, Los Angeles.

1907—May 8—Tommy Burns defeated Jack O'Brien, 20 rounds, Los Angeles.

1907—July 4—Tommy Burns knocked out Bill Squires, 1 round, Colma, Cal.

1907—Dec. 2—Tommy Burns knocked out Gunner Moir, 10 rounds, London.

1908—Feb. 10—Tommy Burns knocked out Jack Palmer, 4 rounds, London.

1908—March 17—Tommy Burns knocked out Jem Roche, 1 round, Dublin.

1908—April 18—Tommy Burns knocked out Jewey Smith, 5 rounds, Paris.

1908—June 13—Tommy Burns knocked out Bill Squires, 8 rounds, Paris.

1908—Aug. 24—Tommy Burns knocked out Bill Squires, 13

rounds, Sydney, New South Wales.

1908—Sept. 2—Tommy Burns knocked out Bill Lang, 2 rounds, Melbourne, Australia.

*1908—Dec. 26—Jack Johnson stopped Tommy Burns, 14 rounds, Sydney, Australia. Police halted contest.

1909—May 19—Jack Johnson and Jack O'Brien, 6 rounds, draw, Philadelphia.

1909—June 30—Jack Johnson and Tony Ross, 6 rounds, draw, Pittsburgh, Pa.

1909—Sept. 9—Jack Johnson and Al Kaufman, 10 rounds, no decision, San Francisco.

1909—Oct. 16—Jack Johnson knocked out Stanley Ketchel, 12 rounds, Colma, Cal.

1910—July 4—Jack Johnson knocked out Jim Jeffries, 15 rounds, Reno, Nev. (Jeffries came back from retirement.)

1912—July 4—Jack Johnson won on points from Jim Flynn, 9 rounds, Las Vegas, N.M. (contest stopped by police)

1913—Nov. 28—Jack Johnson knocked out Andre Spaul, 2 rounds, Paris.

1913—Dec. 9—Jack Johnson and Jim Johnson, 10 rounds, draw, Paris. (Bout called a draw when Jack Johnson declared he had broken his arm.)

1914—June 27—Jack Johnson won from Frank Moran, 20 rounds, Paris.

*1915—April 5—Jess Willard knocked out Jack Johnson, 26 rounds, Havana, Cuba.

1916—March 25—Jess Willard and Frank Moran, 10 rounds (no decision), New York City.

*1919—July 4—Jack Dempsey knocked out Jess Willard, Toledo, Oh. (Willard failed to answer bell for fourth round.)

1920—Sept. 6—Jack Dempsey knocked out Billy Miske, 3 rounds, Benton Harbor, Mich.

1920—Dec. 14—Jack Dempsey knocked out Bill Brennan, 12 rounds, New York City.

1921—July 2—Jack Dempsey knocked out George Carpentier, 4 rounds, Boyle's Thirty Acres, Jersey City, N.J. (Carpentier had held the so-called white heavyweight title since July 16, 1914, in a series established in 1913, after Jack Johnson's exile in Europe late in 1912.)

1923—July 4—Jack Dempsey won on points from Tom Gibbons, 15 rounds, Shelby, Mont.

1923—Sept. 14—Jack Dempsey knocked out Luis Firpo, 2 rounds, New York City.

*1926—Sept. 23—Gene Tunney beat Jack Dempsey, 10 rounds, decision, Philadelphia.

1927—Sept. 22—Gene Tunney beat Jack Dempsey, 10 rounds, decision, Chicago.

1928—July 26—Gene Tunney knocked out Tom Heeney, 11 rounds, Yankee Stadium, New York; soon afterward he announced his retirement.

*1930—June 12—Max Schmeling of Germany defeated Jack Sharkey in 4th round when Sharkey fouled Schmeling in a bout which was generally considered to have resulted in the election of a successor to Gene Tunney, New York.

1931—July 3—Max Schmeling knocked out Young Stribling, 15 rounds, Cleveland.

*1932—June 21—Jack Sharkey defeated Max Schmeling, 15 rounds, decision, New York City.

*1933—June 29—Primo Carnera knocked out Jack Sharkey, 6th round, New York City.

1933—Oct. 22—Primo Carnera defeated Paulino Uzcudun, 15 rounds, Rome.

1934—March 1—Primo Carnera defeated Tommy Loughran, 15 rounds, Miami.

*1934—June 14—Max Baer knocked out Primo Carnera, 11 rounds, New York City.

*1935—June 13—James J. Braddock defeated Max Baer, 15 rounds, New York City.

*1937—June 22—Joe Louis knocked out James J. Braddock, 8 rounds, Chicago.

1937—Aug. 30—Joe Louis defeated Tommy Farr, 15 rounds, decision, New York City.

1938—Feb. 23—Joe Louis knocked out Nathan Mann, 3 rounds, New York City.

1938—April 1—Joe Louis knocked out Harry Thomas, 5 rounds, New York City.

1938—June 22—Joe Louis knocked out Max Schmeling, one round, New York City.

1939—Jan. 25—Joe Louis knocked out John H. Lewis, 1 round, New York City.

1939—April 17—Joe Louis knocked out Jack Roper, 1 round, Los Angeles.

1939—June 28—Joe, Louis knocked out Tony Galento, 4 rounds, New York City.

1939—Sept. 20—Joe Louis knocked out Bob Pastor, 11 rounds, Detroit, Mich.

1940—February 9—Joe Louis defeated Arturo Godoy, 15 rounds, decision, New York City.

1940—March 29—Joe Louis knocked out Johnny Paychek, 2 rounds, New York City.

1940—June 20—Joe Louis knocked out Arturo Godoy, 8 rounds, New York City.

1940—Dec. 16—Joe Louis knocked out Al McCoy, 6 rounds, Boston.

1941—Jan. 31—Joe Louis knocked out Red Burman, 5 rounds, New York City.

1941—Feb. 17—Joe Louis knocked out Gus Dorzaio, 2 rounds, Philadelphia.

1941—March 21—Joe Louis knocked out Abe Simon, 13 rounds, Detroit, Mich.

1941—April 8—Joe Louis knocked out Tony Musto, 9 rounds, St. Louis, Mo.

1941—May 23—Joe Louis beat Buddy Baer, 7 rounds, Washington, D. C., on a disqualification.

1941—June 18—Joe Louis knocked out Billy Conn, 13 rounds, New York City.

1941—Sept. 29—Joe Louis knocked out Lou Nova, 6 rounds, New York City.

1942—Jan. 9—Joe Louis knocked out Buddy Baer, 1 round, New York City.

1942—March 27—Joe Louis knocked out Abe Simon, 6 rounds, New York City.

1946—June 19—Joe Louis knocked out Billy Conn, 8 rounds, New York City.

1946—Sept. 18—Joe Louis knocked out Tami Mauriello, 1 round, New York City.

1947—Dec. 5—Joe Louis defeated Joe Walcott in a 15-round bout by a split decision, New York City.

1948—June 25—Joe Louis knocked out Joe Walcott, 11 rounds, New York City.

*1949—June 22—Following Joe Louis' retirement Ezzard Charles defeated Joe Walcott by a unanimous decision, 15 rounds, Chicago, Ill. (N.B.A. recognition only).

1949—Aug. 10—Ezzard Charles knocked out Gus Lesnevich, 7 rounds, New York City.

1949—Oct. 14—Ezzard Charles knocked out Pat Valentino, 8 rounds, San Francisco (clinched American title).

1950—Aug. 15—Ezzard Charles knocked out Freddy Beshore, 14 rounds, Buffalo, N.Y.

1950—Sept. 27—Ezzard Charles defeated Joe Louis in latter's attempted comeback, 15 rounds, New York City (universal recognition).

1950—Dec. 5—Ezzard Charles knocked out Nick Barone, 11th round, Cincinnati, Ohio.

1951—Jan. 12—Ezzard Charles knocked out Lee Oma, 10th round, New York, N.Y.

1951—March 7—Ezzard Charles outpointed Joe Walcott, 15 rounds, Detroit, Mich.

1951—May 30—Ezzard Charles outpointed Joey Maxim, light heavyweight champion, 15 rounds, Chicago.

*1951—July 18—Joe Walcott knocked out Ezzard Charles, 7th round, Pittsburgh, Pa.

1952—June 5—Joe Walcott outpointed Ezzard Charles, 15 rounds, Philadelphia, Pa.

*1952—Sept. 23—Rocky Marciano knocked out Joe Walcott, 13th round, Philadelphia, Pa.

1953—May 15—Rocky Marciano knocked out Joe Walcott, first round, Chicago, Ill.

1953—Sept. 24—Rocky Marciano knocked out Roland LaStarza, 11th round, Polo Grounds, New York, N.Y.

1954—June 17—Rocky Marciano outpointed Ezzard Charles, 15 rounds, Yankee Stadium, New York, N.Y.

1954—Sept. 17—Rocky Marciano knocked out Ezzard Charles, 8th round, Yankee Stadium, New York, N.Y.

1955—May 16—Rocky Marciano knocked out Don Cockell, 9th round, Kezar Stadium, San Francisco.

1955—Sept. 21—Rocky Marciano knocked out Archie Moore, 9th round, Yankee Stadium, N.Y. Marciano retired undefeated, Apr. 27, 1956.

*1956—Nov. 30—Floyd Patterson knocked out Archie Moore, 5th round, Chicago, Ill.

1957—July 29—Floyd Patterson knocked out Hurricane Jackson, 10th round, Polo Grounds, New York, N.Y.

1957—Aug. 22—Floyd Patterson knocked out Pete Rademacher, 6th round, Seattle, Wash.

1958—Aug. 18—Floyd Patterson knocked out Roy Harris, 12th round, Los Angeles.

1959—May 1—Floyd Patterson knocked out Brian London, 11th round, Indianapolis, Ind.

*1959—June 26—Ingemar Johansson knocked out Floyd Patterson, 3rd round, Yankee Stadium, New York City.

*1960—June 20—Floyd Patterson knocked out Ingemar Johansson, 5th round, Polo Grounds, New York, N.Y. (First heavyweight in boxing history to regain title.)

1961—Mar. 13—Floyd Patterson knocked out Ingemar Johansson, 6th round, Convention Hall, Miami Beach, Fla.

1961—Dec. 4—Floyd Patterson knocked out Tom McNeeley, 4th round, Toronto, Ont.

*1962—Sept. 25—Sonny Liston knocked out Floyd Patterson, first round, Comiskey Park, Chicago, Ill.

1963—July 22—Sonny Liston knocked out Floyd Patterson, first round, Las Vegas, Nevada.

*1964—Feb. 25—Cassius Clay knocked out Sonny Liston, 7th round, Miami Beach, Fla.

1965—May 25—Cassius Clay knocked out Sonny Liston, first round, Lewiston, Maine.

1965—Nov. 11—Cassius Clay knocked out Floyd Patterson, 12th round, Las Vegas, Nev.

1966—Mar. 29—Cassius Clay outpointed George Chuvalo, 15 rounds, Toronto, Ont.

1966—May 21—Cassius Clay knocked out Henry Cooper, 6th round, London, Eng.

1966—Aug. 6—Cassius Clay knocked out Brian London, 3rd round, London, Eng.

1966—Sept. 10—Cassius Clay knocked out Karl Mildenberger, 12th round, Frankfurt, Germany.

1966—Nov. 14—Cassius Clay knocked out Cleveland Williams, 3rd round, Houston, Tex.

1967—Feb. 6—Cassius Clay outpointed Ernie Terrell, 15 rounds, Houston, Tex.

1967—Mar. 22—Cassius Clay knocked out Zora Folley, 7th round, New York. Clay was stripped of his title by the WBA and others for refusing military service.

*1970—Feb. 16—Joe Frazier knocked out Jimmy Ellis, 5th round, New York.

1970—Nov. 18—Joe Frazier knocked out Bob Foster, 2nd round, Detroit.

1971—Mar. 8—Joe Frazier outpointed Cassius Clay (Muhammad Ali), 15 rounds, New York, N.Y.

1972—Jan. 15—Joe Frazier knocked out Terry Daniels, fourth round, New Orleans.

1972—May 25—Joe Frazier knocked out Ron Stander, fifth round, Omaha.

*1973—Jan. 22—George Foreman knocked out Joe Frazier, 2nd round, Kingston, Jamaica.

1973—Sept. 1—George Foreman knocked out Joe Roman, first round, Tokyo.

1974—Mar. 3—George Foreman knocked out Ken Norton, 2nd round, Caracas.

*1974—Oct. 30—Muhammad Ali knocked out George Foreman, 8th round, Zaire.

1975—Mar. 24.—Muhammad Ali knocked out Chuck Wepner, 15th round, Cleveland.

1975—May 16—Muhammad Ali knocked out Ron Lyle, 11th round, Las Vegas.

1975—June 30—Muhammad Ali outpointed Joe Bugner, 15 rounds, Malaysia.

1975—Oct. 1—Muhammad Ali knocked out Joe Frazier, 14th round, Manila.

1976—Feb. 20—Muhammad Ali knocked out Jean-Pierre Coopman, 5th round, San Juan.

1976—Apr. 30—Muhammad Ali outpointed Jimmy Young, 15 rounds, Landover, Md.

1976—May 25—Muhammad Ali knocked out Richard Dunn, 5th round, Munich.

1976—Sept. 28—Muhammad Ali outpointed Ken Norton, 15 rounds, New York, N.Y.

National AAU Boxing Championships in 1976
Las Vegas, Nev., May 12-15, 1976

106 Lbs.—Brett Summers, Marysville, Wash.
112 Lbs.—Leo Randolph, Tacoma, Wash.
119 Lbs.—Bernard Raylor, Charlotte, N.C.
125 Lbs.—Davey Armstrong, Puyallup, Wash.
132 Lbs.—Howard Davis, Glen Cove, N.Y.
139 Lbs.—Pete Seward, Columbus, Ohio

147 Lbs.—Clinton Jackson, Nashville, Tenn.
156 Lbs.—J. B. Williamson, Honolulu, Hawaii
165 Lbs.—Keith Broom, Charlotte, N.C.
178 Lbs.—Leon Spinks, St. Louis, Mo.
Heavyweight—Marv Stinson, Philadelphia, Pa.
Team Championship—Pacific Northwest AAU.

Water Ski Champions in 1976
34th Annual National Water Ski Championships
Miami, Fla., Aug. 18-22, 1976

Men's Overall — Chris Redmond, Canton, Ohio, 2,652 points.
Men's Slalom — Bob LaPoint, Castro Valley, Cal., 56'/2 buoys.
Men's Tricks — Tony Krupa, Jackson, Mich. 5,710 points.
Men's Jumping — Bob La Point, 171 feet.
Women's Overall — Cindy Todd, Fla., 2,876 points.
Women's Slalom — Cindy Todd, 56 buoys.
Women's Tricks — Cindy Todd, 4,060 points.
Women's Jumping — Cindy Todd, 120 feet.
Senior Men's Overall — Dr. J.D. Morgan, Norfolk, Va., 3,578 points.
Senior Men's Slalom — Dr. J.D. White, 49 buoys.
Senior Men's Tricks — Jerry Hosner, Fenton, Mich., 4,190 points.
Senior Men's Jumping — Dr. J.D. Morgan, 132 feet.
Senior Women's Overall — Thelma Salmas, Canyon Lake, Cal., 3,455 points.
Senior Women's Slalom — Barbara Cleveland, Hawthorne, Fla., 51'/2 buoys.
Senior Women's Tricks — Artis Price, Libertyville, Ill., 3,030 points.

Senior Women's Jumping — Barbara Cleveland, 101 feet.
Boys' Overall — Sammy Duvall, Greenville, S.C., 3,044 points.
Boys' Slalom — Mike Mellenthin Studio City, Cal., 46'/2 buoys.
Boys' Tricks — Craig Pickos, Kenosha, Wis., 5,180 points.
Boys' Jumping — Joe Cornell, Bethel Island, Cal., 127 feet.
Girls' Overall — Camille Duvall, Greenville, S.C., 3,470 points.
Girls' Slalom — Camille Duvall, 53 buoys.
Girls' Tricks — Pam Folsom, Boynton Beach, Fla., 4,490 points.
Girls' Jumping — Camille Duvall, 113 feet.
Junior Boys' Overall — Carl Roberge, San Diego, Cal., 4,111 points.
Junior Boys' Slalom — Carl Roberge, 50'/2 buoys.
Junior Boys Tricks — Carl Roberge, 5,160 points.
Junior Boys' Jumping — Carl Roberge, 108 feet.
Junior Girls' Overall — Karen Crosier, Keystone Hgts., Fla., 3,994 points.
Junior Girls' Slalom —Karen Crosier, 49 buoys.
Junior Girls' Tricks — Karen Crosier, 3,000 points.
Junior Girls' Jumping — Karen Crosier, 84 feet.

18th Annual Masters Tournament
Callaway Gardens, Ga., July 10-11, 1976

Men's Overall — Carlos Louis Suarez, Venezuela, 2,744 points.
Men's Slalom — Bob LaPoint, Castro Valley, Cal., 52 buoys.
Men's Tricks — Carlos Louis Suarez, 5,500 points.
Men's Jumping — Wayne Grimditch, Hillsboro Beach, Fla., 171 feet.

Women's Overall — Cindy Todd, Pierson, Fla., 2,521.5 points.
Women's Slalom — Cindy Todd, 54 buoys.
Women's Tricks — Camille Duvall, Greenville, S.C., 3,130 points.
Women's Jumping — Linda Giddens, Eastman, Ga., 121 feet.

U.S. National Fencing Champions in 1976

Men's Foil—Edward Donofrio, U.S. Marine Corps.
Men's Epee—George Masin, N.Y. Athletic Club.
Men's Sabre—Thomas Losonczy, N.Y. Athletic Club.
Women's Foil—Ann O'Donnell, Salle Santelli, N.Y.

Men's Foil Team—Wauwatosa Fencing Club, Wis.
Men's Epee Team—N.Y. Athletic Club.
Men's Sabre Team—N.Y. Fencers Club.
Women's Foil Team—Salle D'Asaro, San Jose, Cal.

"Parked Out" Computations

Harness Racing mathematicians have compiled these figures on the added distance in each mile that a horse travels when "parked out" (racing outside another horse, five feet out from the point at which the track is measured).

1/2 mile track (4 turns to mile)...........62.832 feet
5/8 mile track (3 turns to mile)...........47.124 feet

3/4 mile track with chute, and mile track (2 turns to mile)..............................31.416 feet

Trotting and Pacing Records

Source: Philip Pikelny, United States Trotting Association, Records to Sept., 1976

Trotting Records

Asterisk (*) denotes record was made in a race. Times—seconds in fifths.

One Mile Records (Mile Track)

All-age — 1:54.4 — Nevele Pride, Indianapolis, Ind., Aug. 31, 1969.

Two-year-old — *1:58.2 — Nevele Pride, Lexington, Ky., Oct. 4, 1967.

Three-year-old — *1:56.2 — Super Bowl, Du Quoin, Ill., Aug. 30, 1972; Steve Lobell, Du Quoin, Ill., Sept. 4, 1976.

(Half-Mile Track)

All-age — *1:56.4 — Nevele Pride, Saratoga Springs, N.Y., Sept. 6, 1969.

Two-year-old — *2:00.1 — Ayres, Delaware, Ohio, 1963.

Three-year-old Colt — *1:58.3 — Songcan, Delaware, Ohio, 1972.

(Five Eighth-mile Track)

All-Age — *1:57.3 — Dream of Glory, Chicago, Ill., Aug. 21, 1976.

Two-year-old — *2:01 — Starlark Hanover, Wilkes-Barre, Pa., 1973.

Three-year-old — *1:59 — Nevele Pride, Philadelphia, Pa., 1968.

Odd Distances

1-1/16 Miles — *2:05.3 — Senator Frost, Inglewood, Cal., Oct. 17, 1959.

1-1/16 Miles, Half-mile Track — *2:07.2 — Nevele Pride, Westbury, N.Y., 1969.

1-3/16 Miles — *2:22.4 — Scotch Victor, Inglewood, Cal., Nov. 6, 1954.

1¼ Miles — *2:30.3 — Pronto Don, Inglewood, Cal., Nov. 24, 1951.

1¼ Miles, Half-mile Track — *2:31.2 — Speedy Scot, Westbury, N.Y., 1964; Noble Victory, Westbury, N.Y., 1966.

1½ Miles — 3:02.1 — Greyhound, Indianapolis, Ind., Sept. 14, 1937.

1½ Miles, Half-mile Track — *3:05.2 — Snow Speed, Yonkers, N.Y., 1969.

2 Miles — 4:06 — Greyhound, Indianapolis, Ind., Sept. 19, 1939.

2 Miles, Half-mile Track — *4:10.4 — Pronto Don, Westbury, N.Y., Sept. 13, 1951.

Fastest Two Heats — *1:57.2; *1:56.2 — Super Bowl, Du Quoin, Ill., Aug. 29, 1972.

Fastest Two Heats, Half-Mile Track — *1:58.4, *2:00.3 — Speedy Rodney, Goshen, N.Y., 1966. and *2:00.4; *1:58.3, Songcan, Delaware, Ohio, 1972.

Pacing Records

One Mile Records (Mile Track)

All-age — 1:52 — Steady Star, Lexington, Ky., Oct. 1, 1971.

Two-year-old — *1:55 — Striking Image, Springfield, Ill., Aug. 18, 1976.

Three-year-old — 1:54 — Steady Star, Lexington, Ky., Oct. 7, 1970.

(Half-Mile Track)

All-age — 1:55.3 — Adios Butler, Delaware, Ohio, Sept. 21, 1961; Albatross, Delaware, Ohio, 1972.

Two-year-old — *1:58.4 — Columbia George, Yonkers, N.Y., Nov. 8, 1969; J. R. Skipper, Delaware, Ohio, 1972; Armbro Ranger, Delaware, Ohio, 1975.

Three-year-old — 1:56.2 — Keystone Ore, Saratoga Springs, N.Y., July 17; 1976.

(Five Eighth-mile Track)

All-Age — *1:54.3 — Albatross, Chicago, Ill., 1972.

Two-year-old — *1:58.2 — Truluck, Philadelphia, Pa., 1969.

Three-year-old — *1:56 — Armbro Ranger; Keystone, Ore, Meadowlands, Pa., Aug. 14, 1976.

Odd Distances

1¼ Miles — *2:30.2 — Dr. Stanton, Arcadia, Cal., May 15, 1948.

1¼ Miles, Half-mile Track — *2:29.2 — Rambling Willie, Yonkers, N.Y., Aug. 14, 1976.

1-1/16 Miles — *2:03.1 — Adios Vic, Inglewood, Cal., Oct. 23, 1965.

1-1/16 Miles, Half-mile Track — *2:06 — Albatross, Westbury, N.Y., 1972.

1½ miles — *2:09.1 — True Duane, Hollywood Park, 1966.

1½ Miles — *3:05.2 — Right Time, Inglewood, Cal., 1961; and K. D. Senator, E. Boston, Mass., 1963.

1½ Miles, Half-mile Track — *3:01.4 — Handle With Care, Yonkers, N.Y., Aug. 21, 1976.

2 Miles — 4:17 — Dan Patch, Macon, Ga., 1903.

2 Miles, Half-mile Track — *4:08.4 — Irvin Paul, Yonkers, N.Y., June 28, 1962.

Fastest Two Heats — *1:54.4, *1:54.4 — Albatross, Lexington, Ky., Oct. 2, 1971.

The Hambletonian (3-year-old trotters), Du Quoin, Ill.

Year	Winner	Driver	Purse	Year	Winner	Driver	Purse
1941	Bill Gallon	Lee Smith	$38,729	1959	Diller Hanover	Frank Ervin	$125,284
1942	The Ambassador	Ben White	38,954	1960	Blaze Hanover	Joe O'Brien	144,590
1943	Volo Song	Ben White	42,298	1961	Harlan Dean	James Arthur	131,573
1944	Yankee Maid	Henry Thomas	33,577	1962	A.C.Os Viking	Sanders Russell	116,312
1945	Titan Hanover	Harry Pownall Jr.	50,190	1963	Speedy Scot	Ralph Baldwin	115,549
1946	Chestertown	Thomas Berry	50,905	1964	Ayres	John Simpson Sr.	115,281
1947	Hoot Mon	S.F. Palin	46,267	1965	Egyptian Candor	Frank Ervin	122,245
1948	Demon Hanover	Harrison Hoyt	59,941	1966	Kerry Way	Del Cameron	122,540
1949	Miss Tilly	Fred Egan	69,791	1967	Speedy Streak	Del Cameron	122,650
1950	Lusty Song	Del Miller	75,209	1968	Nevele Pride	Stanley Dancer	116,190
1951	Mainliner	Guy Crippen	95,263	1969	Lindy's Pride	Howard Bessinger	124,910
1952	Sharp Note	Bion Shively	87,637	1970	Timothy T.	John Simpson Sr.	143,630
1953	Helicopter	Harry Harvey	117,118	1971	Speedy Crown	Howard Bessinger	128,770
1954	Newport Dream	Del Cameron	106,830	1972	Super Bowl	Stanley Dancer	119,090
1955	Scott Frost	Joe O'Brien	86,863	1973	Flirth	Ralph Baldwin	144,710
1956	The Intruder	Ned Bower	98,591	1974	Christopher T.	Bill Haughton	160,150
1957	Hickory Smoke	John Simpson Sr.	111,126	1975	Bonefish	Stanley Dancer	232,192
1958	Emily's Pride	Flave Nipe	106,719	1976	Steve Lobell	Bill Haughton	263,524

Little Brown Jug (3-year-old pacers)

Year	Winner	Winning Driver	Purse	Year	Winner	Winning Driver	Purse
1953	Keystoner	Frank Ervin	$54,972	1965	Bret Hanover	Frank Ervin	$71,447
1954	Adios Harry	Morris MacDonald	69,332	1966	Romeo Hanover	George Sholty	74,616
1955	Quick Chief	Billy Haughton	66,608	1967	Best of All	James Hackett	84,778
1956	Noble Adios	John Simpson Sr.	52,666	1968	Rum Customer	Billy Haughton	104,226
1957	Torpid	John Simpson Sr.	73,528	1969	Laverne Hanover	Billy Haughton	109,731
1958	Shadow Wave	Joe O'Brien	65,252	1970	Most Happy Fella	Stanley Dancer	100,110
1959	Adios Butler	Clint Hodgins	76,582	1971	Nansemond	Herve Filion	102,944
1960	Bullet Hanover	John Simpson Sr.	66,510	1972	Strike Out	Keith Waples	104,916
1961	Henry T. Adios	Stanley Dancer	70,069	1973	Melvin's Woe	Joe O'Brien	120,000
1962	Lehigh Hanover	Stanley Dancer	75,038	1974	Ambro Omaha	Billy Haughton	132,630
1963	Overtrick	John Patterson Sr.	68,294	1975	Seatrain	Ben Webster	147,813
1964	Vicar Hanover	Billy Haughton	66,590	1976	Keystone Ore	Stanley Dancer	161,485

Leading Drivers

Races Won

Year		Year		Year		Year	
1957 Bill Haughton	156	1962 Bob Farrington	203	1967 Bob Farrington	277	1972 Herve Filion	605
1958 Bill Haughton	176	1963 Donald Busse	201	1968 Herve Filion	407	1973 Herve Filion	445
1959 William Gilmour	165	1964 Bob Farrington	312	1969 Herve Filion	394	1974 Herve Filion	637
1960 Del Insko	156	1965 Bob Farrington	310	1970 Herve Filion	486	1975 Daryl Buse	360
1961 Bob Farrington	201	1966 Bob Farrington	283	1971 Herve Filion	543		

Money Won

Year	Dollars	Year	Dollars	Year	Dollars
1957 Bill Haughton	586,950	1964 Stanley Dancer	1,051,538	1970 Herve Filion	1,647,837
1958 Bill Haughton	816,659	1965 Bill Haughton	889,943	1971 Herve Filion	1,915,945
1959 Bill Haughton	711,435	1966 Stanley Dancer	1,218,403	1972 Herve Filion	2,473,265
1960 Del Miller	567,282	1967 Bill Haughton	1,305,773	1973 Herve Filion	2,233,302
1961 Stanley Dancer	674,723	1968 Bill Haughton	1,654,172	1974 Herve Filion	3,474,315
1962 Stanley Dancer	760,343	1969 Del Insko	1,635,463	1975 Carmine Abbatiello	2,275,093
1963 Bill Haughton	790,086				

Harness Horse of the Year

1948 — Rodney	1955 — Scott Frost	1962 — Su Mac Lad	1969 — Nevele Pride
1949 — Good Time	1956 — Scott Frost	1963 — Speedy Scot	1970 — Fresh Yankee
1950 — Proximity	1957 — Torpid	1964 — Bret Hanover	1971 — Albatross
1951 — Pronto Don	1958 — Emily's Pride	1965 — Bret Hanover	1972 — Albatross
1952 — Good Time	1959 — Bye Bye Byrd	1966 — Bret Hanover	1973 — Sir Dalrae
1953 — Hi Lo's Forbes	1960 — Adios Butler	1967 — Nevele Pride	1974 — Delmonica Hanover
1954 — Stenographer	1961 — Adios Butler	1968 — Nevele Pride	1975 — Savior

National Amateur Bicycle Championships in 1976
Louisville, Ky. (Road): Carrollton, Ky. (Time Trial): North Brook, Ill. (Track)

Road

Senior Men—Wayne Stetina, Indiana
Senior Women—Connie Carpenter, Wisconsin
Veterans—Jim Meyers, California
Junior Men—Larry Shields, California
Junior Women—Francesca Saveri, California
Intermediate Boys—Jeff Bradley, Iowa
Intermediate Girls—Jacque Bradley, Iowa
Midget Boys—Grant Foster, California

Time Trial

Senior Men—John Howard, Missouri
Senior Women—Lyn Lemaire, Massachusetts
Veterans—Nick Farac Ban, California
Junior Men—Andy Weaver, Florida

Track

Kilometer—Bob Vehe, Illinois
Senior Men's Sprints—Leigh Barczewski, Wisconsin
Senior Men's Pursuit—Leonard Nitz, California
Team Pursuit—Southern California (Kevin Lutz, Ron Skarin, Paul Murray, Paul Deem)
Ten Mile—Ron Skarin, California
Women's Sprint—Sheila Young, Michigan
Women's Pursuit—Connie Carpenter, Wisconsin
Junior Men—Chris Springer, California
Junior Women—Jane Brennan, Michigan
Intermediate Boys—Jeff Bradley, Iowa
Intermediate Girls—Connie Paraskevin, Michigan
Midget Boys—Guillermo Lopez, New York
Midget Girls—Kirstie Walz, New Jersey

Members of National Baseball Hall of Fame and Museum
The shrine of organized baseball, dedicated June 12, 1939, is located in Cooperstown, N.Y.

Alexander, Grover Cleveland	Combs, Earle	Griffith, Clark	Landis, Kenesaw M.	Roush, Edd
Anson, Cap	Comiskey, Charles A.	Grimes, Burleigh	Lemon, Bob	Ruffing, Red
Averill, Earl	Conlan, Jocko	Grove, Lefty	Leonard, Buck	Ruth, Babe
Appling, Luke	Connolly, Thomas H.	Hafey, Chick	Lindstrom, Fred	Schalk, Ray
Baker, Home Run	Connor, Roger	Haines, Jessee	Lyons, Ted	Simmons, Al
Bancroft, Dave	Coveleski, Stan	Hamilton, Bill	Mack, Connie	Sisler, George
Barrow, Edward G.	Crawford, Sam	Harridge, Will	Mantle, Mickey	Spahn, Warren
Beckley, Jake	Cronin, Joe	Harris, Bucky	Manush, Henry	Spalding, Albert
Bell, Cool Papa	Cummings, Candy	Hartnett, Gabby	Maranville, Rabbit	Speaker, Tris
Bender, Chief	Cuyler, Kiki	Heilmann, Harry	Marquard, Rube	Stengel, Casey
Berra, Yogi	Dean, Dizzy	Herman, Billy	Mathewson, Christy	Terry, Bill
Bottomley, Jim	Delahanty, Ed	Hooper, Harry	McCarthy, Joe	Thompson, Sam
Boudreau, Lou	Dickey, Bill	Hornsby, Rogers	McCarthy, Thomas	Tinker, Joe
Bresnahan, Roger	DiMaggio, Joe	Hoyt, Waite	McGinnity, Joe	Traynor (Pie), Harold J.
Brouthers, Dan	Duffy, Hugh	Hubbard, Cal	McGraw, John	Vance, Dazzy
Brown (Three Finger), Mordecai	Evans, Billy	Hubbell, Carl	McKechnie, Bill	Waddell, Rube
Bulkeley, Morgan C.	Evers, John	Huggins, Miller	Medwick, Joe	Wagner, Honus
Burkett, Jesse C.	Ewing, Buck	Irvin, Monte	Musial, Stan	Wallace, Roderick
Campanella, Roy	Faber, Urban	Jennings, Hugh	Nichols, Kid	Walsh, Ed
Carey, Max	Feller, Bob	Johnson, Byron	O'Rourke, James	Waner, Lloyd
Cartwright, Alexander	Flick, Elmer H.	Johnson, William (Rudy)	Ott, Mel	Waner, Paul
Chadwick, Henry	Ford, Whitey	Johnson, Walter	Paige, Satchel	Ward, John
Chance, Frank	Foxx, James E.	Keefe, Timothy	Pennock, Herb	Weiss, George
Charleston, Oscar	Frick, Ford	Keeler, William	Plank, Ed	Welch, Mickey
Chesbro, John	Frisch, Frank	Kelley, Joe	Radbourne, Charlie	Wheat, Zach
Clarke, Fred	Galvin, Pud	Kelly, George	Rice, Sam	Williams, Ted
Clarkson, John	Gehrig, Lou	Kelly, King	Rickey, Branch	Wright, George
Clemente, Roberto	Gehringer, Charles	Kiner, Ralph	Rixey, Eppa	Wright, Harry
Cobb, Ty	Gibson, Josh	Klem, Bill	Roberts, Robin	Wynn, Early
Cochrane, Mickey	Gomez, Lefty	Koufax, Sandy	Robinson, Jackie	Young, Cy
Collins, Edward T.	Goslin, Goose	Lajoie, Napoleon	Robinson, Wilbert	Youngs, Ross
Collins, James	Greenberg, Hank			

Major League Pennant Winners, 1901-1976

National League / American League

Year	Winner	Won	Lost	Pct.	Manager		Year	Winner	Won	Lost	Pct.	Manager
1901	Pittsburgh	90	49	.647	Clarke		1901	Chicago	83	53	.610	Griffith
1902	Pittsburgh	103	36	.741	Clarke		1902	Philadelphia	83	53	.610	Mack
1903	Pittsburgh	91	49	.650	Clarke		1903	Boston	91	47	.659	Collins
1904	New York	106	47	.693	McGraw		1904	Boston	95	59	.617	Collins
1905	New York	105	48	.686	McGraw		1905	Philadelphia	92	56	.622	Mack
1906	Chicago	116	36	.763	Chance		1906	Chicago	93	58	.616	Jones
1907	Chicago	107	45	.704	Chance		1907	Detroit	92	58	.613	Jennings
1908	Chicago	99	55	.643	Chance		1908	Detroit	90	63	.588	Jennings
1909	Pittsburgh	110	42	.724	Clarke		1909	Detroit	98	54	.645	Jennings
1910	Chicago	104	50	.675	Chance		1910	Philadelphia	102	48	.680	Mack
1911	New York	99	54	.647	McGraw		1911	Philadelphia	101	50	.669	Mack
1912	New York	103	48	.682	McGraw		1912	Boston	105	47	.691	Stahl
1913	New York	101	51	.664	McGraw		1913	Philadelphia	96	57	.627	Mack
1914	Boston	94	59	.614	Stallings		1914	Philadelphia	99	53	.651	Mack
1915	Philadelphia	90	62	.592	Moran		1915	Boston	101	50	.669	Carrigan
1916	Brooklyn	94	60	.610	Robinson		1916	Boston	91	63	.591	Carrigan
1917	New York	98	56	.636	McGraw		1917	Chicago	100	54	.649	Rowland
1918	Chicago	84	45	.651	Mitchell		1918	Boston	75	51	.595	Barrow
1919	Cincinnati	96	44	.686	Moran		1919	Chicago	88	52	.629	Gleason
1920	Brooklyn	93	60	.604	Robinson		1920	Cleveland	98	56	.636	Speaker
1921	New York	94	59	.614	McGraw		1921	New York	98	55	.641	Huggins
1922	New York	93	61	.604	McGraw		1922	New York	94	60	.610	Huggins
1923	New York	95	58	.621	McGraw		1923	New York	98	54	.645	Huggins
1924	New York	93	60	.608	McGraw		1924	Washington	92	62	.597	Harris
1925	Pittsburgh	95	58	.621	McKechnie		1925	Washington	96	55	.636	Harris
1926	St. Louis	89	65	.578	Hornsby		1926	New York	91	63	.591	Huggins
1927	Pittsburgh	94	60	.610	Bush		1927	New York	110	44	.714	Huggins
1928	St. Louis	95	59	.617	McKechnie		1928	New York	101	53	.656	Huggins
1929	Chicago	98	54	.645	McCarthy		1929	Philadelphia	104	46	.693	Mack
1930	St. Louis	92	62	.597	Street		1930	Philadelphia	102	52	.622	Mack
1931	St. Louis	101	53	.656	Street		1931	Philadelphia	107	45	.704	Mack
1932	Chicago	90	64	.584	Grimm		1932	New York	107	47	.695	McCarthy
1933	New York	91	61	.599	Terry		1933	Washington	99	53	.651	Cronin
1934	St. Louis	95	58	.621	Frisch		1934	Detroit	101	53	.656	Cochrane
1935	Chicago	100	54	.649	Grimm		1935	Detroit	93	58	.616	Cochrane
1936	New York	91	62	.597	Terry		1936	New York	102	51	.667	McCarthy
1937	New York	95	57	.625	Terry		1937	New York	102	52	.662	McCarthy
1938	Chicago	89	63	.586	Hartnett		1938	New York	99	53	.651	McCarthy
1939	Cincinnati	97	57	.630	McKechnie		1939	New York	106	45	.702	McCarthy
1940	Cincinnati	100	53	.654	McKechnie		1940	Detroit	90	64	.584	Baker
1941	Brooklyn	100	54	.649	Durocher		1941	New York	101	53	.656	McCarthy
1942	St. Louis	106	48	.688	Southworth		1942	New York	103	51	.669	McCarthy
1943	St. Louis	105	49	.682	Southworth		1943	New York	98	56	.636	McCarthy
1944	St. Louis	105	49	.682	Southworth		1944	St. Louis	89	65	.578	Sewell
1945	Chicago	98	56	.636	Grimm		1945	Detroit	88	65	.575	O'Neill
1946	St. Louis	98	58	.628	Dyer		1946	Boston	104	50	.675	Cronin
1947	Brooklyn	94	60	.610	Shotton		1947	New York	97	57	.630	Harris
1948	Boston	91	62	.595	Southworth		1948	Cleveland	97	58	.626	Boudreau
1949	Brooklyn	97	57	.630	Shotton		1949	New York	97	57	.630	Stengel
1950	Philadelphia	91	63	.591	Sawyer		1950	New York	98	56	.636	Stengel
1951	New York	98	59	.624	Durocher		1951	New York	98	56	.636	Stengel
1952	Brooklyn	96	57	.627	Dressen		1952	New York	95	59	.617	Stengel
1953	Brooklyn	105	49	.682	Dressen		1953	New York	99	52	.656	Stengel
1954	New York	97	57	.630	Durocher		1954	Cleveland	111	43	.721	Lopez
1955	Brooklyn	98	55	.641	Alston		1955	New York	96	58	.623	Stengel
1956	Brooklyn	93	61	.604	Alston		1956	New York	97	57	.630	Stengel
1957	Milwaukee	95	59	.617	Haney		1957	New York	98	56	.636	Stengel
1958	Milwaukee	92	62	.597	Haney		1958	New York	92	62	.597	Stengel
1959	Los Angeles	88	68	.564	Alston		1959	Chicago	94	60	.610	Lopez
1960	Pittsburgh	95	59	.617	Murtaugh		1960	New York	97	57	.630	Stengel
1961	Cincinnati	93	61	.604	Hutchinson		1961	New York	109	53	.673	Houk
1962	San Francisco	103	62	.624	Dark		1962	New York	96	66	.593	Houk
1963	Los Angeles	99	63	.611	Alston		1963	New York	104	57	.646	Houk
1964	St. Louis	93	69	.574	Keane		1964	New York	99	63	.611	Berra
1965	Los Angeles	97	65	.599	Alston		1965	Minnesota	102	60	.630	Mele
1966	Los Angeles	95	67	.586	Alston		1966	Baltimore	97	63	.606	Bauer
1967	St. Louis	101	60	.627	Schoendienst		1967	Boston	92	70	.568	Williams
1968	St. Louis	97	65	.599	Schoendienst		1968	Detroit	103	59	.636	Smith

National League

	East						West						Playoff
Year	Winner	W.	L.	Pct.	Manager	Winner	W.	L.	Pct.	Manager		Winner
1969	N.Y. Mets	100	62	.617	Hodges	Atlanta	93	69	.574	Harris		New York
1970	Pittsburgh	89	73	.549	Murtaugh	Cincinnati	102	60	.630	Anderson		Cincinnati
1971	Pittsburgh	97	65	.599	Murtaugh	San Francisco	90	72	.556	Fox		Pittsburgh
1972	Pittsburgh	96	59	.619	Virdon	Cincinnati	95	59	.617	Anderson		Cincinnati
1973	N.Y. Mets	82	79	.509	Berra	Cincinnati	99	63	.611	Anderson		New York
1974	Pittsburgh	88	82	.543	Murtaugh	Los Angeles	102	60	.630	Alston		Los Angeles
1975	Pittsburgh	92	69	.571	Murtaugh	Cincinnati	108	54	.667	Anderson		Cincinnati
1976	Philadelphia	101	61	.623	Ozark	Cincinnati	102	60	.630	Anderson		Cincinnati

American League

	East					West				
Year	Winner	W.	L.	Pct.	Manager	Winner	W.	L.	Pct.	Manager	Playoff Winner
1969	Baltimore.......	109	53	.673	Weaver	Minnesota......	97	65	.599	Martin	Baltimore
1970	Baltimore.......	108	54	.677	Weaver	Minnesota......	98	64	.605	Rigney	Baltimore
1971	Baltimore.......	101	57	.639	Weaver	Oakland........	101	60	.627	Williams	Baltimore
1972	Detroit.........	86	70	.551	Martin	Oakland........	93	72	.600	Williams	Oakland
1973	Baltimore.......	97	65	.599	Weaver	Oakland........	94	68	.580	Williams	Oakland
1974	Baltimore.......	91	71	.562	Weaver	Oakland........	90	72	.556	Dark	Oakland
1975	Boston..........	95	65	.594	Johnson	Oakland........	98	64	.605	Dark	Boston
1976	New York......	97	62	.610	Martin	Kansas City.....	90	72	.556	Herzog	New York

All-Star Baseball Games, 1933-1976

Year	Winner	Score	Location	Year	Winner	Score	Location
1933	American	4-2	Chicago	1957	American	6-5	St. Louis
1934	American	9-7	New York	1958	American	4-3	Baltimore
1935	American	4-1	Cleveland	1959	National	5-4	Pittsburgh
1936	National	4-3	Boston	1959	American	5-3	Los Angeles
1937	American	8-3	Washington	1960	National	5-3	Kansas City
1938	National	4-1	Cincinnati	1960	National	6-0	New York
1939	American	3-1	New York	1961	National(3)	5-4	San Francisco
1940	National	4-0	St. Louis	1961	Called-Rain	1-1	Boston
1941	American	7-5	Detroit	1962	National(3)	3-1	Washington
1942	American	3-1	New York	1962	American	9-4	Chicago
1943*	American	5-3	Philadelphia	1963	National	5-3	Cleveland
1944*	National	7-1	Pittsburgh	1964	National	7-4	New York
1945	(not played)			1965	National	6-5	Minnesota
1946.	American	12-0	Boston	1966	National(3)	2-1	St. Louis
1947	American	2-1	Chicago	1967	National(4)	2-1	Anaheim
1948	American	5-2	St. Louis	1968*	National	1-0	Houston
1949	American	11-7	New York	1969	National	9-3	Washington
1950	National (1)	4-3	Chicago	1970*	National(2)	5-4	Cincinnati
1951	National	8-3	Detroit	1971*	American	6-4	Detroit
1952	National	3-2	Philadelphia	1972*	National	4-3	Atlanta
1953	National	5-1	Cincinnati	1973*	National	7-1	Kansas City
1954	American	11-9	Cleveland	1974*	National	7-2	Pittsburgh
1955	National(2)	6-5	Milwaukee	1975*	National	6-3	Milwaukee
1956	National	7-3	Washington	1976*	National	7-1	Philadelphia

(1.) 14 innings. (2.) 12 innings. (3.) 10 innings. (4.) 15 innings. *Night game.

Cy Young Award Winners

Year	Player, Club	Year	Player, Club	Year	Player, Club
1956	Don Newcombe, Dodgers	1967	(NL) Mike McCormick, Giants	1972	(NL) Steve Carlton, Phillies
1957	Warren Spahn, Braves		(AL) Jim Lonborg, Red Sox		(AL) Gaylord Perry, Indians
1958	Bob Turley, Yankees	1968	(NL) Bob Gibson, Cardinals	1973	(NL) Tom Seaver, Mets
1959	Early Wynn, White Sox		(AL) Dennis McLain, Tigers		(AL) Jim Palmer, Orioles
1960	Vernon Law, Pirates	1969	(NL) Tom Seaver, Mets	1974	(NL) Mike Marshall, Dodgers
1961	Whitey Ford, Yankees		(AL) (tie) Dennis McLain, Tigers		(AL) Jim (Catfish) Hunter, A's
1962	Don Drysdale, Dodgers		Mike Cuellar, Orioles	1975	(NL) Tom Seaver, Mets
1963	Sandy Koufax, Dodgers	1970	(NL) Bob Gibson, Cardinals		(AL) Jim Palmer, Orioles
1964	Dean Chance, Angels		(AL) Jim Perry, Twins		
1965	Sandy Koufax, Dodgers	1971	(NL) Ferguson Jenkins, Cubs		
1966	Sandy Koufax, Dodgers		(AL) Vida Blue, A's		

Baseball Stadiums
National League

		Home Run Distances (in ft.)			Seating
Team	Stadium	LF	Center	RF	Capacity
Atlanta Braves...............	Atlanta-Fulton County Stadium...........	330	402	330	51,556
Chicago Cubs................	Wrigley Field...................	355	400	353	37,741
Cincinnati Reds..............	Riverfront Stadium...............	330	404	330	51,786
Houston Astros..............	Astrodome..................	330	400	330	45,000
Los Angeles Dodgers.........	Dodger Stadium................	330	395	330	56,000
Montreal Expos..............	Jarry Park...................	340	420	340	28,000
New York Mets..............	Shea Stadium..................	341	410	341	55,300
Philadelphia Phillies..........	Veterans Stadium...............	330	408	330	56,581
Pittsburgh Pirates............	Three Rivers Stadium............	335	400	335	50,235
St. Louis Cardinals...........	Busch Memorial Stadium..........	330	404	330	50,126
San Diego Padres............	San Diego Stadium..............	330	410	330	47,491
San Francisco Giants.........	Candlestick Park...............	335	410	335	58,000

American League

Team	Stadium	LF	Center	RF	Seating Capacity
Baltimore Orioles.............	Memorial Stadium...............	309	405	309	52,137
Boston Red Sox..............	Fenway Park..................	315	420	302	33,437
California Angels.............	Anaheim Stadium...............	333	404	333	43,204
Chicago White Sox...........	Comiskey Park................	352	440	352	44,492
Cleveland Indians............	Cleveland Stadium..............	320	400	320	76,713
Detroit Tigers...............	Tiger Stadium.................	340	440	325	54,226
Kansas City Royals...........	Royals Stadium................	330	410	330	40,762
Milwaukee Brewers...........	Milwaukee County Stadium........	320	402	315	52,293
Minnesota Twins.............	Metropolitan Stadium............	330	410	330	45,919
New York Yankees...........	Yankee Stadium................	312	417	310	54,028
Oakland A's................	Oakland-Alameda County Coliseum......	330	400	330	50,000
Texas Rangers..............	Arlington Stadium..............	330	400	330	35,698

Most Valuable Player Awards

Source: Baseball Writers' Association

National League

Year	Player	Club	Year	Player	Club	Year	Player	Club
1931	Frank Frisch	St. Louis	1946	Stan Musial	St. Louis	1961	Frank Robinson	Cincinnati
1932	Charles Klein	Philadelphia	1947	Bob Elliott	Boston	1962	Maury Wills	Los Angeles
1933	Carl Hubbell	New York	1948	Stan Musial	St. Louis	1963	Sandy Koufax	Los Angeles
1934	Dizzy Dean	St. Louis	1949	Jackie Robinson	Brooklyn	1964	Ken Boyer	St. Louis
1935	Gabby Hartnett	Chicago	1950	Jim Konstanty	Philadelphia	1965	Willie Mays	San Francisco
1936	Carl Hubbell	New York	1951	Roy Campanella	Brooklyn	1966	Roberto Clemente	Pittsburgh
1937	Joe Medwick	St. Louis	1952	Hank Sauer	Chicago	1967	Orlando Cepeda	St. Louis
1938	Ernie Lombardi	Cincinnati	1953	Roy Campanella	Brooklyn	1968	Bob Gibson	St. Louis
1939	Bucky Walters	Cincinnati	1954	Willie Mays	New York	1969	Willie McCovey	San Francisco
1940	Frank McCormick	Cincinnati	1955	Roy Campanella	Brooklyn	1970	Johnny Bench	Cincinnati
1941	Dolph Camilli	Brooklyn	1956	Don Newcombe	Brooklyn	1971	Joe Torre	St. Louis
1942	Mort Cooper	St. Louis	1957	Henry Aaron	Milwaukee	1972	Johnny Bench	Cincinnati
1943	Stan Musial	St. Louis	1958	Ernie Banks	Chicago	1973	Pete Rose	Cincinnati
1944	Martin Marion	St. Louis	1959	Ernie Banks	Chicago	1974	Steve Garvey	Los Angeles
1945	Phil Cavarretta	Chicago	1960	Dick Groat	Pittsburgh	1975	Joe Morgan	Cincinnati

American League

Year	Player	Club	Year	Player	Club	Year	Player	Club
1931	Lefty Grove	Philadelphia	1946	Ted Williams	Boston	1961	Roger Maris	New York
1932	Jimmy Foxx	Philadelphia	1947	Joe DiMaggio	New York	1962	Mickey Mantle	New York
1933	Jimmy Foxx	Philadelphia	1948	Lou Boudreau	Cleveland	1963	Elston Howard	New York
1934	Mickey Cochrane	Detroit	1949	Ted Williams	Boston	1964	Brooks Robinson	Baltimore
1935	Henry Greenberg	Detroit	1950	Phil Rizzuto	New York	1965	Zoilo Versalles	Minnesota
1936	Lou Gehrig	New York	1951	Yogi Berra	New York	1966	Frank Robinson	Baltimore
1937	Charley Gehringer	Detroit	1952	Bobby Shantz	Philadelphia	1967	Carl Yastrzemski	Boston
1938	Jimmy Foxx	Boston	1953	Al Rosen	Cleveland	1968	Denny McLain	Detroit
1939	Joe DiMaggio	New York	1954	Yogi Berra	New York	1969	Harmon Killebrew	Minnesota
1940	Hank Greenberg	Detroit	1955	Yogi Berra	New York	1970	John (Boog) Powell	Baltimore
1941	Joe DiMaggio	New York	1956	Mickey Mantle	New York	1971	Vida Blue	Oakland
1942	Joe Gordon	New York	1957	Mickey Mantle	New York	1972	Dick Allen	Chicago
1943	Spurgeon Chandler	New York	1958	Jackie Jensen	Boston	1973	Reggie Jackson	Oakland
1944	Hal Newhouser	Detroit	1959	Nellie Fox	Chicago	1974	Jeff Burroughs	Texas
1945	Hal Newhouser	Detroit	1960	Roger Maris	New York	1975	Fred Lynn	Boston

Rookie of the Year Award (Baseball Writers Assn.)

1947—Combined Selection—Jackie Robinson, Brooklyn, 1b
1948—Combined Selection—Alvin Dark, Boston, N. L. ss

National League

Year	Winner	Year	Winner	Year	Winner
1949	Don Newcombe, Brooklyn, p	1958	Orlando Cepeda, S. F., 1b	1967	Tom Seaver, N. Y., p
1950	Sam Jethroe, Boston, of	1959	Willie McCovey, S. F., 1b	1968	Johnny Bench, Cinn., c
1951	Willie Mays, N. Y., of	1960	Frank Howard, Los Angeles, of	1969	Ted Sizemore, L. A., 2b
1952	Joe Black, Brooklyn, p	1961	Billy Williams, Chicago, of	1970	Carl Morton, Mont., p
1953	Jim Gilliam, Brooklyn, 2b	1962	Ken Hubbs, Chicago, 2b	1971	Earl Williams, Atl., c
1954	Wally Moon, St. Louis, of	1963	Pete Rose, Cinn., 2b	1972	Jon Matlack, N. Y., p
1955	Bill Virdon, St. Louis, of	1964	Richie Allen, Phil., 3b	1973	Gary Matthews, S. F., of
1956	Frank Robinson, Cinn., of	1965	Jim Lefebvre, L. A., 2b	1974	Bake McBride, S. L., of
1957	Jack Sanford, Phil., p	1966	Tommy Helms, Cinn., 2b	1975	John Montefusco, S.F., p

American League

Year	Winner	Year	Winner	Year	Winner
1949	Roy Sievers, St. Louis, of	1958	Albie Pearson, Wash., of	1967	Rod Carew, Minn., 2b
1950	Walt Dropo, Boston, 1b	1959	Bob Allison, Wash., of	1968	Stan Bahnsen, N. Y., p
1951	Gil McDougald, N. Y., 3b	1960	Ron Hansen, Balt., ss	1969	Lou Piniella, K. C., of
1952	Harry Byrd, Phil., p	1961	Don Schwall, Boston, p	1970	Thurman Munson, N. Y., c
1953	Harvey Kuenn, Detroit, ss	1962	Tom Tresh, N. Y., if-of	1971	Chris Chambliss, Cleve., 1b
1954	Bob Grim, N. Y., p	1963	Gary Peters, Chicago, p	1972	Carlton Fisk, Bos., c
1955	Herb Score, Cleveland, p	1964	Tony Oliva, Minn., of	1973	Al Bumbry, Balt., of
1956	Luis Aparicio, Chicago, ss	1965	Curt Blefary, Balt., of	1974	Mike Hargrove, Texas, 1b
1957	Tony Kubek, N. Y., if-of	1966	Tommie Agee, Chicago, of	1975	Fred Lynn, Boston, of

Triple Crown Winners

Players leading league in batting, runs batted in and homers

Year	Player & Team	Year	Player & Team
1909	Ty Cobb, Detroit Tigers	1937	Joe Medwick, St. Louis Cardinals
1912	Heinie Zimmerman, Chicago Cubs (a)	1942	Ted Williams, Boston Red Sox
1922	Rogers Hornsby, St. Louis Cardinals	1947	Ted Williams, Boston Red Sox
1925	Rogers Hornsby, St. Louis Cardinals	1956	Mickey Mantle, New York Yankees
1933	Jimmy Foxx, Philadelphia Athletics	1966	Frank Robinson, Baltimore Orioles
1933	Chuck Klein, Philadelphia Phillies	1967	Carl Yastrzemski, Boston Red Sox
1934	Lou Gehrig, New York Yankees		

(a) A recent review of baseball statistics indicates that Heinie Zimmerman did not lead the NL in RBIs in 1912.

Home Run Leaders

Year	National League	HR.	Year	American League	HR.
1920	Cy Williams, Philadelphia	15	1920	Babe Ruth, New York	54
1921	George Kelly, New York	23	1921	Babe Ruth, New York	59
1922	Rogers Hornsby, St. Louis	42	1922	Ken Williams, St. Louis	39
1923	Cy Williams, Philadelphia	41	1923	Babe Ruth, New York	41
1924	Jacques Fournier, Brooklyn	27	1924	Babe Ruth, New York	46
1925	Rogers Hornsby, St. Louis	39	1925	Bob Meusel, New York	33
1926	Hack Wilson, Chicago	21	1926	Babe Ruth, New York	47
1927	Hack Wilson, Chi; Cy Williams, Phil.	30	1927	Babe Ruth, New York	60
1928	Hack Wilson, Chi.; Jim Bottomley, S.L.	31	1928	Babe Ruth, New York	54
1929	Charles Klein, Philadelphia	43	1929	Babe Ruth, New York	46
1930	Hack Wilson, Chicago	56	1930	Babe Ruth, New York	49
1931	Charles Klein, Philadelphia	31	1931	Babe Ruth, Lou Gehrig, New York	46
1932	Charles Klein, Philadelphia, Mel Ott, N.Y.	38	1932	Jimmy Foxx, Philadelphia	58
1933	Charles Klein, Philadelphia	28	1933	Jimmy Foxx, Philadelphia	48
1934	Collins, S.L.; Mel Ott, N.Y.	35	1934	Lou Gehrig, New York	49
1935	Walter Berger, Boston	34	1935	Jimmy Foxx, Phil., Hank Greenberg, Det.	36
1936	Mel Ott, New York	33	1936	Lou Gehrig, New York	46
1937	Mel Ott, N.Y.; Joe Medwick, S.L.	31	1937	Joe DiMaggio, New York	46
1938	Mel Ott, New York	36	1938	Hank Greenberg, Detroit	58
1939	John Mize, St. Louis	28	1939	Jimmy Foxx, Boston	35
1940	John Mize, St. Louis	43	1940	Hank Greenberg, Detroit	41
1941	Dolph Camilli, Brooklyn	34	1941	Ted Williams, Boston	37
1942	Mel Ott, New York	30	1942	Ted Williams, Boston	36
1943	Bill Nicholson, Chicago	29	1943	Rudy York, Detroit	34
1944	Bill Nicholson, Chicago	33	1944	Nick Etten, New York	22
1945	Tommy Holmes, Boston	28	1945	Vern Stephens, St. Louis	24
1946	Ralph Kiner, Pittsburgh	23	1946	Hank Greenberg, Detroit	44
1947	Ralph Kiner, Pitts.; John Mize, N.Y.	51	1947	Ted Williams, Boston	32
1948	Ralph Kiner, Pitts.; John Mize, N.Y.	40	1948	Joe DiMaggio, New York	39
1949	Ralph Kiner, Pittsburgh	54	1949	Ted Williams, Boston	43
1950	Ralph Kiner, Pittsburgh	47	1950	Al Rosen, Cleveland	37
1951	Ralph Kiner, Pittsburgh	42	1951	Gus Zernial, Chicago-Philadelphia	33
1952	Ralph Kiner, Pittsburgh; Hank Sauer, Chicago.	37	1952	Larry Doby, Cleveland	32
1953	Ed Mathews, Milwaukee	47	1953	Al Rosen, Cleveland	43
1954	Ted Kluszewski, Cincinnati	49	1954	Larry Doby, Cleveland	32
1955	Willie Mays, New York	51	1955	Mickey Mantle, New York	37
1956	Duke Snider, Brooklyn	43	1956	Mickey Mantle, New York	52
1957	Hank Aaron, Milwaukee	44	1957	Roy Sievers, Washington	42
1958	Ernie Banks, Chicago	47	1958	Mickey Mantle, New York	42
1959	Ed Mathews, Milwaukee	46	1959	Rocky Colavito, Cleveland, Harmon Killebrew, Washington	42
1960	Ernie Banks, Chicago	41	1960	Mickey Mantle, New York	40
1961	Orlando Cepeda, San Francisco	46	1961	Roger Maris, New York	61
1962	Willie Mays, San Francisco	49	1962	Harmon Killebrew, Minnesota	48
1963	Hank Aaron, Milwaukee, Willie McCovey, San Francisco	44	1963	Harmon Killebrew, Minnesota	45
1964	Willie Mays, San Francisco	47	1964	Harmon Killebrew, Minnesota	49
1965	Willie Mays, San Francisco	52	1965	Tony Conigliaro, Boston	32
1966	Hank Aaron, Atlanta, Willie McCovey, San Francisco	44	1966	Frank Robinson, Baltimore	49
1967	Hank Aaron, Atlanta	39	1967	Carl Yastrzemski, Boston, Harmon Killebrew, Minnesota	44
1968	Willie McCovey, San Francisco	36	1968	Frank Howard, Washington	44
1969	Willie McCovey, San Francisco	45	1969	Harmon Killebrew, Minnesota	49
1970	Johnny Bench, Cincinnati	45	1970	Frank Howard, Washington	44
1971	Willie Stargell, Pittsburgh	48	1971	Bill Melton, Chicago	33
1972	Johnny Bench, Cincinnati	40	1972	Dick Allen, Chicago	37
1973	Willie Stargell, Pittsburgh	44	1973	Reggie Jackson, Oakland	32
1974	Mike Schmidt, Philadelphia	36	1974	Dick Allen, Chicago	32
1975	Mike Schmidt, Philadelphia	38	1975	George Scott, Milwaukee; Reggie Jackson, Oak.	36
1976	Mike Schmidt, Philadelphia	38	1976	Graig Nettles, New York	32

All-time Major League Record (154-game Season)—60—Babe Ruth, New York Yankees (A), 1927. **(162-game Season)—61—**Roger Maris, New York Yankees, 1961. Prior to the 1931 season a batted ball that bounced into the stands was a home run (now a ground-rule double). None of Babe Ruth's record 60 homers bounced into the stands.

Runs Batted In Leaders

Year	National League	RBI	Year	American League	RBI
1939	Frank McCormick, Cinn.	128	1939	Ted Williams, Boxton	145
1940	John Mize, St. Louis	137	1940	Hank Greenberg, Detroit	150
1941	Dolph Camilli, Brooklyn	120	1941	Joe DiMaggio, New York	125
1942	John Mize, New York	137	1942	Ted Williams, Boston	137
1943	Bill Nicholson, Chi.	128	1943	Rudy York, Detroit	118
1944	Bill Nicholson, Chi.	122	1944	Vern Stephens, St. Louis	109
1945	Dixie Walker, Brooklyn	124	1945	Nick Etten, New York	111
1946	Enos Slaughter, St. Louis	130	1946	Hank Greenberg, Detroit	127
1947	John Mize, New York	138	1947	Ted Williams, Boston	114
1948	Stan Musial, St. Louis	131	1948	Joe DiMaggio, New York	155
1949	Ralph Kiner, Pittsburgh	127	1949	Ted Williams, Vern Stephens, Boston	159
1950	Del Ennis, Philadelphia	126	1950	Walt Dropo, Vern Stephens, Boston	144
1951	Monte Irvin, New York	121	1951	Gus Zernial, Chi.-Phila.	129
1952	Hank Sauer, Chicago	121	1952	Al Rosen, Cleveland	105
1953	Roy Campanella, Brooklyn	142	1953	Al Rosen, Cleveland	145
1954	Ted Kluszewski, Cincinnati	141	1954	Larry Doby, Cleveland	126
1955	Duke Snider, Brooklyn	136	1955	Ray Boone, Detroit, Jack Jensen, Boston	116
1956	Stan Musial, St. Louis	109	1956	Mickey Mantle, New York	130
1957	Hank Aaron, Milwaukee	132	1957	Roy Sievers, Washington	114
1958	Ernie Banks, Chicago	129	1958	Jack Jensen, Boston	122

Year	Player, Club	RBI		Year	Player, Club	RBI
1959	Ernie Banks, Chicago	143		1959	Jack Jensen, Boston	112
1960	Hank Aaron, Milwaukee	126		1960	Roger Maris, New York	112
1961	Orlando Cepeda, San Francisco	142		1961	Roger Maris, New York	142
1962	Tommy Davis, Los Angeles	153		1962	Harmon Killebrew, Minn.	126
1963	Hank Aaron, Milwaukee	130		1963	Dick Stuart, Boston	118
1964	Ken Boyer, St. Louis	119		1964	Brooks Robinson, Baltimore	118
1965	Deron Johnson, Cincinnati	130		1965	Rocky Colavito, Cleveland	108
1966	Hank Aaron, Atlanta	127		1966	Frank Robinson, Baltimore	122
1967	Orlando Cepeda, St. Louis	111		1967	Carl Yastrzemski, Boston	121
1968	Willie McCovey, San Francisco	105		1968	Ken Harrelson, Boston	109
1969	Willie McCovey, San Francisco	126		1969	Harmon Killebrew, Minn.	140
1970	Johnny Bench, Cincinnati	148		1970	Frank Howard, Wash.	126
1971	Joe Torre, St. Louis	137		1971	Harmon Killebrew, Minn.	119
1972	Johnny Bench, Cincinnati	125		1972	Dick Allen, Chicago	113
1973	Willie Stargell, Pittsburgh	119		1973	Reggie Jackson, Oakland	117
1974	Johnny Bench, Cincinnati	129		1974	Jeff Burroughs, Texas	118
1975	Greg Luzinski, Philadelphia	120		1975	George Scott, Milwaukee	109
1976	George Foster, Cincinnati	121		1976	Lee May, Baltimore	109

Batting Champions

	National League				American League		
Year	Player	Club	Pct.	Year	Player	Club	Pct.
1910	Sherwood Magee	Philadelphia	.331	1910	Ty Cobb	Detroit	.385
1911	Honus Wagner	Pittsburgh	.334	1911	Ty Cobb	Detroit	.420
1912	Henry Zimmerman	Chicago	.372	1912	Ty Cobb	Detroit	.410
1913	Jacob Daubert	Brooklyn	.350	1913	Ty Cobb	Detroit	.390
1914	Jacob Daubert	Brooklyn	.329	1914	Ty Cobb	Detroit	.368
1915	Larry Doyle	New York	.320	1915	Ty Cobb	Detroit	.369
1916	Hal Chase	Cincinnati	.339	1916	Tris Speaker	Cleveland	.386
1917	Edd Roush	Cincinnati	.341	1917	Ty Cobb	Detroit	.383
1918	Zack Wheat	Brooklyn	.335	1918	Ty Cobb	Detroit	.382
1919	Edd Roush	Cincinnati	.321	1919	Ty Cobb	Detroit	.384
1920	Rogers Hornsby	St. Louis	.370	1920	George Sisler	St. Louis	.407
1921	Rogers Hornsby	St. Louis	.397	1921	Harry Heilmann	Detroit	.394
1922	Rogers Hornsby	St. Louis	.401	1922	George Sisler	St. Louis	.420
1923	Rogers Hornsby	St. Louis	.384	1923	Harry Heilmann	Detroit	.403
1924	Rogers Hornsby	St. Louis	.424	1924	Babe Ruth	New York	.378
1925	Rogers Hornsby	St. Louis	.403	1925	Harry Heilmann	Detroit	.393
1926	Eugene Hargrave	Cincinnati	.353	1926	Henry Manush	Detroit	.378
1927	Paul Waner	Pittsburgh	.380	1927	Harry Heilmann	Detroit	.398
1928	Rogers Hornsby	Boston	.387	1928	Goose Goslin	Washington	.379
1929	Lefty O'Doul	Philadelphia	.398	1929	Lew Fonseca	Cleveland	.369
1930	Bill Terry	New York	.401	1930	Al Simmons	Philadelphia	.381
1931	Chick Hafey	St. Louis	.349	1931	Al Simmons	Philadelphia	.390
1932	Lefty O'Doul	Brooklyn	.368	1932	Dale Alexander	Det.-Bos.	.367
1933	Charles Klein	Philadelphia	.368	1933	Jimmy Foxx	Philadelphia	.356
1934	Paul Waner	Pittsburgh	.362	1934	Lou Gehrig	New York	.363
1935	Arky Vaughan	Pittsburgh	.385	1935	Buddy Myer	Washington	.349
1936	Paul Waner	Pittsburgh	.373	1936	Luke Appling	Chicago	.388
1937	Joe Medwick	St. Louis	.374	1937	Charlie Gehringer	Detroit	.371
1938	Ernie Lombardi	Cincinnati	.342	1938	Jimmy Foxx	Boston	.349
1939	John Mize	St. Louis	.349	1939	Joe DiMaggio	New York	.381
1940	Debs Garms	Pittsburgh	.355	1940	Joe DiMaggio	New York	.352
1941	Pete Reiser	Brooklyn	.343	1941	Ted Williams	Boston	.406
1942	Ernie Lombardi	Boston	.330	1942	Ted Williams	Boston	.356
1943	Stan Musial	St. Louis	.357	1943	Luke Appling	Chicago	.328
1944	Dixie Walker	Brooklyn	.357	1944	Lou Boudreau	Cleveland	.327
1945	Phil Cavarretta	Chicago	.355	1945	George Stirnweiss	New York	.309
1946	Stan Musial	St. Louis	.365	1946	Mickey Vernon	Washington	.353
1947	Harry Walker	Philadelphia	.363	1947	Ted Williams	Boston	.343
1948	Stan Musial	St. Louis	.376	1948	Ted Williams	Boston	.369
1949	Jackie Robinson	Brooklyn	.342	1949	George Kell	Detroit	.343
1950	Stan Musial	St. Louis	.346	1950	Billy Goodman	Boston	.354
1951	Stan Musial	St. Louis	.355	1951	Ferris Fain	Philadelphia	.344
1952	Stan Musial	St. Louis	.336	1952	Ferris Fain	Philadelphia	.327
1953	Carl Furillo	Brooklyn	.344	1953	Mickey Vernon	Washington	.337
1954	Willie Mays	New York	.345	1954	Roberto Avila	Cleveland	.341
1955	Richie Ashburn	Philadelphia	.338	1955	Al Kaline	Detroit	.340
1956	Hank Aaron	Milwaukee	.328	1956	Mickey Mantle	New York	.353
1957	Stan Musial	St. Louis	.351	1957	Ted Williams	Boston	.388
1958	Richie Ashburn	Philadelphia	.350	1958	Ted Williams	Boston	.328
1959	Hank Aaron	Milwaukee	.355	1959	Harvey Kuenn	Detroit	.353
1960	Dick Groat	Pittsburgh	.325	1960	Pete Runnels	Boston	.320
1961	Roberto Clemente	Pittsburgh	.351	1961	Norm Cash	Detroit	.361
1962	Tommy Davis	Los Angeles	.346	1962	Pete Runnels	Boston	.326
1963	Tommy Davis	Los Angeles	.326	1963	Carl Yastrzemski	Boston	.321
1964	Roberto Clemente	Pittsburgh	.339	1964	Tony Oliva	Minnesota	.323
1965	Roberto Clemente	Pittsburgh	.329	1965	Tony Oliva	Minnesota	.321
1966	Matty Alou	Pittsburgh	.342	1966	Frank Robinson	Baltimore	.316
1967	Roberto Clemente	Pittsburgh	.357	1967	Carl Yastrzemski	Boston	.326
1968	Pete Rose	Cincinnati	.335	1968	Carl Yastrzemski	Boston	.301
1969	Pete Rose	Cincinnati	.348	1969	Rod Carew	Minnesota	.332
1970	Rico Carty	Atlanta	.366	1970	Alex Johnson	California	.328
1971	Joe Torre	St. Louis	.363	1971	Tony Oliva	Minnesota	.337
1972	Billy Williams	Chicago	.333	1972	Rod Carew	Minnesota	.318
1973	Pete Rose	Cincinnati	.338	1973	Rod Carew	Minnesota	.350
1974	Ralph Garr	Atlanta	.353	1974	Rod Carew	Minnesota	.364
1975	Bill Madlock	Chicago	.354	1975	Rod Carew	Minnesota	.359
1976	Bill Madlock	Chicago	.339	1976	George Brett	Kansas City	.333

American League Records, 1976

Final Standings

Eastern Division

Club	W.	L.	Pct.	G.B.
New York	97	62	.610	—
Baltimore	88	74	.543	10½
Boston	83	79	.512	15½
Cleveland	81	78	.509	16
Detroit	74	87	.460	24
Milwaukee	66	95	.410	32

Western Division

Club	W.	L.	Pct.	G.B.
Kansas City	90	72	.556	—
Oakland	87	74	.540	2½
Minnesota	85	77	.525	5
California	76	86	.469	14
Texas	76	86	.469	14
Chicago	64	97	.398	25½

American League Playoffs

Oct. 9 — New York 4, Kansas City 1
Oct. 10 — Kansas City 7, New York 3
Oct. 12 — New York 5, Kansas City 3

Oct. 13 — Kansas City 7, New York 4
Oct. 14 — New York 7, Kansas City 6

Club Batting

Club	Pct.	AB	R.	H.	HR	SB
Minnesota	.274	5574	743	1526	81	146
New York	.269	5555	730	1496	120	163
Kansas City	.269	5540	713	1490	65	218
Cleveland	.263	5412	615	1423	85	75
Boston	.263	5511	716	1448	134	95
Detroit	.257	5441	609	1401	101	107
Chicago	.255	5532	586	1410	73	120
Texas	.250	5555	616	1390	80	87
Oakland	.246	5353	686	1319	113	341
Milwaukee	.246	5396	570	1326	88	62
Baltimore	.243	5457	619	1326	119	150
California	.235	5385	550	1265	63	126

Club Pitching

Club	ERA	CG.	IP	H.	R.	BB	SO
New York	3.19	62	1455	1300	575	448	674
Kansas City	3.21	41	1472	1356	611	492	735
Oakland	3.26	39	1459	1412	598	415	711
Baltimore	3.31	59	1469	1396	598	489	678
California	3.36	64	1477	1323	631	553	992
Texas	3.45	63	1472	1464	652	461	773
Cleveland	3.47	30	1432	1361	615	533	928
Boston	3.52	49	1458	1495	660	409	673
Milwaukee	3.64	45	1435	1406	655	567	677
Minnesota	3.69	29	1459	1421	704	610	762
Detroit	3.87	55	1431	1426	709	550	737
Chicago	4.25	54	1448	1460	745	600	802

Individual Batting

Leaders — 450 or More At Bats

Player—Club	Pct.	AB	R.	H.	HR	RBI	SB
Brett, Kansas City†	.333	645	94	215	7	67	21
McRae, Kansas City	.332	527	75	175	8	73	22
Carew, Minnesota†	.331	605	97	200	9	90	49
Bostock, Minnesota†	.323	474	75	153	4	60	12
LeFlore, Detroit	.316	544	93	172	4	39	58
Lynn, Boston†	.314	507	76	159	10	65	14
Carty, Cleveland	.310	552	67	171	13	83	1
Rivers, New York†	.312	590	95	184	8	67	43
Munson, New York	.302	616	79	186	17	105	14
Garr, Chicago†	.300	527	63	158	4	36	14

Individual Pitching

Leaders — 162 or More Innings

Pitcher—Club	W.	L.	ERA	G.	IP	H.	BB	SO
*Fidrych, Detroit	19	9	2.34	31	250	217	53	97
Blue, Oakland†	18	13	2.36	37	298	268	63	166
Tanana, California†	19	10	2.44	34	288	212	73	261
Torrez, Oakland	16	12	2.50	39	266	231	87	115
Palmer, Baltimore	22	13	2.51	40	315	255	84	159
Garland, Baltimore	20	7	2.68	38	232	224	64	113
*Hartzell, California	7	4	2.77	37	166	166	43	51
Travers, Milwaukee†	15	16	2.81	34	240	211	95	120
Blyleven, Texas	13	16	2.87	36	298	283	81	219
Ross, California	8	16	3.00	34	225	224	58	100
Campbell, Minnesota	17	5	3.00	78	168	145	62	115

*Rookie   †Bats — Pitches Lefthanded   ‡Switch Hitter

Individual Batting (over 100 at-bats) Individual Pitching (over 50 innings)

Milwaukee Brewers

BATTING	Pct.	G.	AB	R.	H.	HR	RBI	SB
Lezcano	.285	145	513	53	146	7	56	14
*D. Thomas	.276	32	105	13	29	4	15	1
Johnson†	.275	105	273	25	75	0	14	4
Scott	.274	156	606	73	166	18	77	0
Joshua†	.267	107	423	44	113	5	28	8
Money	.267	117	439	51	117	12	62	6
Yount	.252	161	638	59	161	2	54	16
Hegan†	.248	80	218	30	54	5	31	0
Sharp†	.244	78	180	16	44	0	11	1
Carbo†	.235	86	238	25	56	5	21	2
Aaron	.229	85	271	22	62	10	35	0
Heidemann	.219	69	146	11	32	2	10	1
Sutherland	.211	101	232	19	49	1	15	0
Porter†	.208	119	389	43	81	5	32	2
G. Thomas	.198	99	227	27	45	8	36	2
Moore	.191	87	241	33	46	3	16	1

PITCHING	W.	L.	ERA	G.	IP	H.	BB	SO
Travers†	15	16	2.81	34	240	211	95	120
*Augustine†	9	12	3.30	39	172	167	56	59
Slaton	14	15	3.44	38	293	287	94	138
Castro	4	6	3.47	39	70	70	19	23
Rodriguez	5	13	3.64	45	136	124	65	77
Colborn	9	15	3.70	32	226	232	54	101
Broberg	1	7	4.99	20	92	99	72	28

Cleveland Indians

BATTING	Pct.	G.	AB	R.	H.	HR	RBI	SB
Carty	.310	152	552	67	171	13	83	1
Fosse	.301	90	276	26	83	2	30	1
Manning†	.292	138	552	73	161	6	43	16
Bell	.281	159	604	75	170	7	60	3
Blanks	.280	104	328	45	92	5	41	1
Hendrick	.265	149	551	72	146	25	81	4
Kuiper†	.263	135	506	47	133	0	37	10
*Smith†	.256	55	164	17	42	2	12	8
Ashby‡	.239	89	247	26	59	4	32	0
Spikes	.237	101	334	34	79	3	31	5
Powell†	.215	95	293	29	63	9	33	1
Duffy	.212	133	392	38	83	2	30	10
Lowenstein†	.205	93	229	33	47	2	14	11

PITCHING	W.	L.	ERA	G.	IP	H.	BB	SO
LaRoche†	1	4	2.25	61	96	57	49	104
Thomas	4	4	2.29	37	106	88	41	54
Kern	10	7	2.36	50	118	91	50	111
Bibby	13	7	3.20	34	163	162	56	84
Eckersley	13	12	3.44	36	199	155	78	200
Dobson	16	12	3.48	35	217	226	65	117
Buskey	5	4	3.64	39	94	88	34	32
Waits†	7	9	3.99	26	124	143	54	65
Brown	9	11	4.25	32	180	193	55	104
Hood†	3	5	4.85	33	78	89	41	32

Minnesota Twins

BATTING	Pct.	G.	AB	R.	H.	HR	RBI	SB
Carew†	.331	156	605	97	200	9	90	49
Bostock†	.323	128	474	15	153	4	60	12
Braun†	.288	122	417	73	120	3	61	12
Hisle	.272	155	581	81	158	14	96	31
*Randall	.267	153	475	55	127	1	34	3
Ford	.267	145	514	87	137	20	86	17
Brye	.264	87	258	33	68	2	23	1
*Wynegar‡	.260	149	534	58	139	10	69	0
Kusick	.259	109	266	33	69	11	36	5
Smalley†	.259	144	513	61	133	3	44	2
Cubbage†	.257	118	374	42	96	3	49	1
Terrell	.246	89	171	29	42	0	8	11
Oliva†	.211	67	123	3	26	1	16	0
*McKay	.203	45	138	8	28	0	8	1

PITCHING	W.	L.	ERA	G.	IP	H.	BB	SO
Burgmeier†	8	1	2.50	57	115	95	29	45
Campbell	17	5	3.00	78	168	145	62	115
Goltz	14	14	3.36	36	249	239	91	133
*Redfern	8	8	3.51	23	118	105	63	74
Albury†	3	1	3.60	23	50	51	24	23
Singer	13	10	3.68	36	237	233	96	97
Luebber	4	5	4.01	38	119	109	62	45
Hughes	9	14	4.98	37	177	190	73	87
Bane†	4	7	5.13	17	79	92	39	24
Decker	2	7	5.28	13	58	60	51	35

Detroit Tigers

BATTING	Pct.	G.	AB	R.	H.	HR	RBI	SB
LeFlore	.316	135	544	93	172	4	39	58
Staub†	.299	161	589	73	176	15	96	3
Oglivie†	.285	115	305	36	87	15	47	9
Freehan	.270	71	237	22	64	5	27	0
Johnson	.268	125	429	41	115	6	45	14
*Kimm	.263	63	152	13	40	1	6	4
Horton	.262	114	401	40	105	14	56	0
*Wagner	.261	39	115	9	30	0	12	0
Stanley	.257	84	214	34	55	4	29	2
Meyer†	.252	105	294	37	74	2	16	10
Rodriguez	.240	128	480	40	115	8	50	0
Veryzer	.234	97	354	31	83	1	25	1
Wockenfuss	.222	60	144	18	32	3	10	0
*Scrivener	.221	80	222	28	49	2	16	1
*Thompson†	.218	123	412	45	90	17	54	2
Garcia	.204	118	333	33	68	4	29	4

PITCHING	W.	L.	ERA	G.	IP	H.	BB	SO
*Fidrych	19	9	2.34	31	250	217	53	97
Hiller†	12	8	2.38	56	121	93	67	117
Ruhle	9	12	3.92	32	200	227	59	88
Roberts†	16	17	4.00	36	252	254	63	79
Laxton†	0	5	4.07	26	95	77	51	74
Crawford†	1	8	4.54	32	109	115	43	68
Bare	7	8	4.63	30	134	157	51	59
*Grilli	3	1	4.64	36	66	63	41	36
Coleman	2	5	4.84	12	67	80	34	38
Lemanczyk	4	6	5.11	20	81	86	34	51

New York Yankees

BATTING	Pct.	G.	AB	R.	H.	HR	RBI	SB
Rivers†	.312	137	590	95	184	8	67	43
Munson	.302	152	616	79	186	17	105	14
Chambliss†	.293	156	641	79	188	17	96	1
White‡	.286	156	626	104	179	14	65	31
Piniella	.281	100	327	36	92	3	38	0
*Randolph	.267	125	430	59	115	1	40	37
May†	.259	107	351	45	91	3	43	5
Nettles†	.254	158	583	88	148	32	93	11
Healy	.243	54	144	12	35	0	10	5
Alomar‡	.239	67	163	20	39	1	10	12
Stanley	.238	110	260	32	62	1	20	1
Gamble†	.232	110	340	43	79	17	57	5
Mason†	.180	93	217	17	39	1	14	0
Hendricks†	.174	54	132	8	23	4	9	0

PITCHING	W.	L.	ERA	G.	IP	H.	BB	SO
Lyle†	7	8	2.26	64	104	82	42	61
Jackson†	7	1	2.54	34	78	57	25	39
Tidrow	4	5	2.64	47	92	80	24	65
Figueroa	19	10	3.01	34	257	237	94	119
Ellis	17	8	3.18	32	212	195	76	65
Alexander	13	9	3.36	30	201	172	63	58
Hunter	17	15	3.52	36	299	268	68	173
Holtzman†	14	11	3.64	30	247	265	70	66

Texas Rangers

BATTING	Pct.	G.	AB	R.	H.	HR	RBI	SB
Hargrove†	.287	151	541	80	155	7	58	2
Clines	.276	116	446	52	123	0	38	11
Harrah	.260	155	584	64	152	15	67	8
Beniquez	.255	145	478	49	122	0	33	17
Grieve	.255	149	546	57	139	20	81	4
Howell†	.253	140	491	55	124	8	53	1
Moates†	.241	85	137	21	33	0	13	6
Burroughs	.237	158	604	71	143	18	86	0
Fregosi	.233	58	133	17	31	2	12	2
Sundberg	.228	140	448	33	102	3	34	0
Randle‡	.224	142	539	53	121	1	51	30
Thompson	.222	98	320	21	71	1	19	3
Lahoud†	.200	80	185	18	37	1	9	1

PITCHING	W.	L.	ERA	G.	IP	H.	BB	SO
Terpko	3	3	2.38	32	53	42	29	24
Blyleven	13	16	2.87	36	298	283	81	219
Umbarger†	10	12	3.15	30	197	208	54	105
Perry	15	14	3.24	32	250	232	52	143
Briles	11	9	3.26	32	210	224	47	98
Foucault	8	8	3.32	46	76	68	25	41
*Boggs	1	7	3.50	13	90	87	34	36
Hargan	8	8	3.63	35	124	127	38	63
*Bacsik	3	2	4.25	23	55	66	26	21
Peterson†	1	3	5.08	13	62	80	17	23
*Barr†	2	6	5.56	20	68	70	44	27

Chicago White Sox

BATTING	Pct.	G.	AB	R.	H.	HR	RBI	SB
*L. Johnson	.320	82	222	29	71	4	33	2
Garr†	.300	136	527	63	158	4	36	14
Orta†	.274	158	636	74	174	14	72	24
Stein	.268	117	392	32	105	4	36	4
Downing	.256	104	317	38	81	3	30	7
Kelly†	.254	107	311	42	79	5	34	15
Spencer†	.253	150	518	53	131	14	70	6
Brohamer	.251	119	354	33	89	7	40	1
Bannister	.248	73	145	19	36	0	8	12
*Bell	.248	68	230	24	57	5	20	2
Essian	.246	78	199	20	49	0	21	2
*Lemon	.246	132	451	46	111	4	38	13
Dent	.246	158	562	44	138	2	52	3
Hairston‡	.227	44	119	20	27	0	10	1
Bradford	.219	55	160	20	35	4	14	6
Coggins†	.160	39	100	5	16	0	6	4

PITCHING	W.	L.	ERA	G.	IP	H.	BB	SO
Wood†	4	3	2.25	7	56	51	11	31
Carroll	4	4	2.57	29	77	67	24	38
Brett†	10	12	3.28	29	203	173	76	92
Hamilton†	6	6	3.60	45	90	81	45	62
Gossage	9	17	3.94	31	224	214	90	135
*Barrios	5	9	4.31	35	142	136	46	81
Forster†	2	12	4.38	29	111	126	41	70
*Vuckovich	7	4	4.66	33	110	122	60	62
B. Johnson	9	16	4.73	32	211	231	62	91
*Knapp	3	1	4.85	11	52	54	32	41
*Kravec†	1	5	4.86	9	50	49	32	38
Jefferson	2	3	8.56	19	62	86	42	30

Baltimore Orioles

BATTING	Pct.	G.	AB	R.	H.	HR	RBI	SB
Singleton‡	.278	154	544	62	151	13	70	2
Jackson†	.277	134	498	84	138	27	91	28
Belanger	.270	153	522	66	141	1	40	27
Grich	.266	144	518	93	138	13	54	14
L. May	.258	148	530	61	137	25	109	4
Bumbry†	.251	133	450	71	113	9	36	42
DeCinces	.234	129	440	36	103	11	42	8
Muser†	.227	136	326	25	74	1	30	1
*Mora	.218	73	220	18	48	6	25	1
Robinson	.211	71	218	16	46	3	11	0
Duncan	.204	93	284	20	58	4	17	0
Blair	.197	145	375	29	74	3	16	15
Dempsey	.194	80	216	12	42	0	12	1

PITCHING	W.	L.	ERA	G.	IP	H.	BB	SO
F. Martinez†	5	1	2.31	39	70	50	42	45
Palmer	22	13	2.51	40	315	255	84	159
Garland	20	7	2.68	38	232	224	64	113
Miller	2	4	2.93	49	89	79	36	37
R. May†	15	10	3.72	35	220	205	70	109
Grimsley†	8	7	3.94	28	137	143	35	41
*Flanagan†	3	5	4.13	20	85	83	33	56
Pagan	2	5	4.76	27	70	72	27	47
Cuellar†	4	13	4.96	26	107	129	50	32

California Angels

BATTING	Pct.	G.	AB	R.	H.	HR	RBI	SB
Guerrero......	.284	83	268	24	76	1	18	0
Bonds.........	.265	99	378	48	100	10	54	30
Collins‡......	.263	99	365	45	96	4	28	32
Remy†.......	.263	143	502	64	132	0	28	35
Solaita†......	.261	94	283	29	74	9	42	1
Bochte†......	.258	146	466	53	120	2	49	4
Humphrey.....	.245	71	196	17	48	1	19	0
*Jackson.....	.227	127	410	44	93	8	40	5
Etchebarren...	.227	103	247	15	56	0	21	0
Chalk........	.217	142	438	39	95	0	33	0
*Briggs‡.....	.214	77	248	19	53	1	14	0
*Jones‡......	.211	78	166	22	35	6	17	3
Melton.......	.208	118	341	31	71	6	42	2
Torres‡......	.205	120	264	37	54	6	27	4
Stanton.......	.190	93	231	12	44	2	25	2

PITCHING	W.	L.	ERA	G.	IP	H.	BB	SO
Tanana†......	19	10	2.44	34	288	212	73	261
*Hartzell.....	7	4	2.77	37	166	166	43	51
Ross........	8	16	3.00	34	225	224	58	100
*Monge†.....	6	7	3.36	32	118	108	49	53
Ryan........	17	18	3.36	39	284	193	183	327
Drago........	7	8	4.44	43	79	80	31	43
Kirkwood.....	6	12	4.61	28	158	167	57	78

Boston Red Sox

BATTING	Pct.	G.	AB	R.	H.	HR	RBI	SB
Lynn†........	.314	132	507	76	159	10	65	14
Burleson.....	.291	152	540	75	157	7	42	14
Miller†.......	.283	105	269	40	76	0	27	11
Rice........	.282	153	581	75	164	25	85	8
Cooper†......	.282	123	451	66	127	15	78	7
*Dillard......	.275	57	167	22	46	1	15	6
Yastrzemski†..	.267	155	546	71	146	21	102	5
Fisk.........	.255	134	487	76	124	17	58	12
Doyle†.......	.250	117	432	51	108	0	26	8
Evans.......	.242	146	501	61	121	17	62	6
*Hobson.....	.234	76	269	34	63	8	34	0
Petrocelli....	.213	85	240	17	51	3	24	0
Darwin.......	.207	68	179	15	37	4	18	1
Griffin.......	.189	49	127	14	24	0	4	2

PITCHING	W.	L.	ERA	G.	IP	H.	BB	SO
Willoughby....	3	12	2.82	54	99	94	31	37
Tiant.........	21	12	3.06	38	279	274	64	131
Cleveland.....	10	9	3.07	41	170	159	61	76
Jenkins......	12	11	3.27	30	209	201	43	142
*Jones†......	5	3	3.38	24	104	133	26	45
Wise........	14	11	3.54	34	224	218	48	93
Murphy.......	4	6	4.18	52	99	116	34	39
Pole.........	6	5	4.31	31	121	131	48	49
Lee†.........	5	7	5.63	24	96	124	28	29

Kansas City Royals

BATTING	Pct.	G.	AB	R.	H.	HR	RBI	SB
Brett†........	.333	159	645	94	215	7	67	21
McRae.......	.332	149	527	75	175	8	73	22
*Poquette†....	.302	104	344	43	104	2	34	6
Otis.........	.279	153	592	93	165	18	86	26
Cowens......	.265	152	581	71	154	3	59	23
Davis........	.265	80	238	17	63	3	26	0
Stinson†......	.263	79	209	26	55	2	25	3
Wohlford.....	.249	107	293	47	73	1	24	22
*Quirk†......	.246	64	114	11	28	1	15	0
Rojas........	.242	63	132	11	32	0	16	2
Patek........	.241	144	432	58	104	1	43	51
D. Nelson.....	.235	78	153	24	36	1	17	15
Mayberry†.....	.232	161	594	76	138	13	95	3
White........	.229	152	446	39	102	2	46	20
Martinez......	.228	95	267	24	61	5	34	0

PITCHING	W.	L.	ERA	G.	IP	H.	BB	SO
Littell........	8	4	2.08	60	104	68	60	92
Gurat........	4	0	2.29	20	63	47	20	22
Mingori†......	5	5	2.33	55	85	73	24	38
Pattin........	8	14	2.49	44	141	114	38	65
Fitzmorris.....	15	11	3.07	35	220	227	56	80
Bird.........	12	10	3.36	39	198	191	31	107
Leonard......	17	10	3.51	35	259	247	70	150
Hassler†.....	5	12	3.61	33	147	139	56	61
Splittorff††....	11	8	3.96	26	159	169	59	59
Busby........	3	3	4.38	13	72	58	49	29

Oakland A's

BATTING	Pct.	G.	AB	R.	H.	HR	RBI	SB
North†........	.276	154	590	91	163	2	31	75
Rudi.........	.270	130	500	54	135	13	94	6
Garner.......	.261	159	555	54	145	8	74	35
Washington†...	.257	134	490	65	126	5	53	37
Campaneris...	.256	149	536	67	137	1	52	54
Tenace.......	.249	128	417	64	104	22	66	5
Baylor.......	.247	157	595	85	147	15	68	52
Bando.......	.240	158	550	75	132	27	84	20
Haney.......	.226	88	177	12	40	0	10	0
McMullen.....	.220	98	186	20	41	5	23	1
Williams†.....	.211	120	351	36	74	11	41	4

PITCHING	W.	L.	ERA	G.	IP	H.	BB	SO
Blue†........	18	13	2.39	37	298	268	63	166
Torrez.......	16	12	2.50	39	266	231	87	115
Fingers......	13	11	2.53	70	135	118	40	113
Lindblad†.....	6	5	2.97	65	115	111	24	37
Bahnsen.....	8	7	3.34	35	143	124	43	82
Todd........	7	8	3.80	49	83	87	34	22
Bosman......	4	2	4.10	27	112	118	19	34
P. Mitchell....	9	7	4.25	26	142	169	30	67
*Norris......	4	5	4.78	24	96	91	56	44
Abbott.......	2	4	5.52	19	62	87	16	27

Leading Pitchers, Earned-Run Average

Based on 10 complete games through 1950, then 154 innings until A.L. expanded in '61, N.L. in '62, then 162 innings.

National League

Year	Pitcher, Club	G	IP	ERA
1957	Johnny Podres, Brooklyn......	31	196	2.66
1958	Stu Miller, San Francisco......	41	182	2.47
1959	Sam Jones, San Francisco....	50	271	2.82
1960	Mike McCormick, San Fran....	40	253	2.70
1961	Warren Spahn, Milwaukee....	38	263	3.01
1962	Sandy Koufax, Los Angeles....	28	184	2.54
1963	Sandy Koufax, Los Angeles....	40	311	1.88
1964	Sandy Koufax, Los Angeles....	29	223	1.74
1965	Sandy Koufax, Los Angeles....	43	336	2.04
1966	Sandy Koufax, Los Angeles....	41	323	1.73
1967	Phil Niekro, Atlanta..........	46	207	1.87
1968	Bob Gibson, St. Louis........	34	305	1.12
1969	Juan Marichal, San Francisco..	37	300	2.10
1970	Tom Seaver, New York.......	37	291	2.81
1971	Tom Seaver, New York.......	36	286	1.76
1972	Steve Carlton, Philadelphia...	41	346	1.98
1973	Tom Seaver, New York.......	36	290	2.07
1974	Buzz Capra, Atlanta..........	39	217	2.28
1975	Randy Jones, San Diego.......	37	285	2.24
1976	John Denny, St. Louis........	30	207	2.52

American League

Year	Pitcher, Club	G	IP	ERA
1957	Bobby Shantz, New York......	30	173	2.01
1958	Whitey Ford, New York.......	30	219	2.01
1959	Hoyt Wilhelm, Baltimore......	32	226	2.19
1960	Frank Baumann, Chicago......	47	185	2.68
1961	Dick Donovan, Washington....	23	169	2.40
1962	Hank Aquirre, Detroit........	42	216	2.21
1963	Gary Peters, Chicago........	41	243	2.33
1964	Dean Chance, Los Angeles....	46	278	1.56
1965	Sam McDowell, Cleveland.....	42	274	2.17
1966	Gary Peters, Chicago........	29	204	2.03
1967	Joe Horlen, Chicago.........	35	258	2.06
1968	Luis Tiant, Cleveland........	34	258	1.60
1969	Dick Bosman, Washington....	31	193	2.19
1970	Diego Segui, Oakland........	47	162	2.56
1971	Vida Blue, Oakland..........	39	312	1.82
1972	Luis Tiant, Boston..........	43	179	1.91
1973	Jim Palmer, Baltimore.......	38	296	2.40
1974	Catfish Hunter, Oakland......	41	318	2.49
1975	Jim Palmer, Baltimore.......	39	323	2.09
1976	Mark Fidrych, Detroit........	31	250	2.34

ERA is computed by multiplying the number of earned runs allowed by 9, then dividing by the number of innings pitched.

National League Records, 1976

Final Standings

Eastern Division

Club	W.	L.	Pct.	G.B.
Philadelphia	101	61	.623	—
Pittsburgh	92	70	.568	9
New York	86	76	.531	15
Chicago	75	87	.463	26
St. Louis	72	90	.444	29
Montreal	55	107	.340	46

Western Division

Club	W.	L.	Pct.	G.B.
Cincinnati	102	60	.630	—
Los Angeles	92	70	.568	10
Houston	80	82	.494	22
San Francisco	74	88	.457	28
San Diego	73	89	.451	29
Atlanta	70	92	.432	32

National League Playoffs

Oct. 9—Cincinnati 6, Philadelphia 2.
Oct. 10—Cincinnati 6, Philadelphia 2.

Oct. 12—Cincinnati 7, Philadelphia 6.

Club Batting

Club	Pct.	AB	R.	H.	HR	SB
Cincinnati	.280	5702	857	1599	141	210
Philadelphia	.272	5528	770	1505	110	127
Pittsburgh	.267	5604	708	1499	110	130
St. Louis	.260	5516	629	1432	63	123
Houston	.256	5464	625	1401	66	150
Chicago	.251	5519	611	1386	105	74
Los Angeles	.251	5472	608	1371	91	144
San Diego	.247	5369	570	1327	64	92
New York	.246	5415	615	1334	102	66
San Francisco	.246	5452	595	1340	85	88
Atlanta	.245	5345	620	1309	82	74
Montreal	.235	5428	531	1275	94	86

Club Pitching

Club	ERA	CG.	IP	H.	R.	BB	SO
New York	2.94	53	1449	1248	538	419	1025
Los Angeles	3.02	47	1471	1330	543	479	747
Philadelphia	3.08	34	1459	1377	557	397	918
Pittsburgh	3.36	45	1466	1402	630	460	762
Cincinnati	3.51	33	1471	1436	633	491	790
San Francisco	3.53	27	1462	1464	686	518	746
Houston	3.56	42	1444	1349	657	662	780
St. Louis	3.60	35	1454	1416	671	581	731
San Diego	3.65	47	1432	1368	662	543	651
Atlanta	3.86	33	1438	1435	700	564	818
Chicago	3.93	27	1471	1511	728	490	850
Montreal	3.99	26	1440	1442	734	659	783

Individual Batting

Leaders—450 or More At Bats

Player—Club	Pct.	AB	R.	H.	HR	RBI	SB
Madlock, Chicago	.339	514	68	174	15	84	15
Griffey, Cincinnati†	.336	562	111	189	6	74	34
Maddox, Philadelphia	.330	531	75	175	6	68	29
Rose, Cincinnati‡	.323	665	130	215	10	63	9
Morgan, Cincinnati†	.320	472	113	151	27	111	60
Garvey, Los Angeles	.317	631	85	200	13	80	19
Montanez, Atlanta†	.317	650	74	206	11	84	2
Parker, Pittsburgh†	.313	537	82	168	13	90	19
Watson, Houston	.313	585	76	183	16	102	3
Geronimo, Cincinnati†	.307	486	59	149	2	49	22
Foster, Cincinnati	.306	562	86	172	29	121	17

Individual Pitching

Leaders—162 or More Innings

Pitcher—Club	W.	L.	ERA	G.	IP	H.	BB	SO
Denny, St. Louis	11	9	2.52	30	207	189	74	74
Rau, Los Angeles	16	12	2.57	34	231	221	69	98
Seaver, New York	14	11	2.59	35	271	211	77	235
Koosman, New York†	21	10	2.70	34	247	205	66	200
*Zachry, Cincinnati	14	7	2.74	38	204	170	83	143
Jones, San Diego†	22	14	2.74	40	315	274	50	93
Richard, Houston	20	15	2.75	39	291	221	151	214
Montefusco, S. Fran.	16	14	2.85	37	253	224	74	172
Barr, San Francisco	15	12	2.89	37	252	260	60	75
Matlack, New York†	17	10	2.95	35	262	236	57	153
Rhoden, Los Angeles	12	3	2.98	27	181	165	53	77

*Rookie   † Bats — Pitches Lefthanded   ‡Switch Hitter

Individual Batting (over 100 at-bats) Individual Pitching (over 50 innings)

Houston Astros

BATTING	Pct.	G.	AB	R.	H.	HR	RBI	SB
Watson	.313	157	585	76	183	16	102	3
Cruz†	.303	133	439	49	133	4	61	28
Cedeno	.297	150	575	89	171	18	83	58
DaVanon	.290	61	107	19	31	1	20	0
Roberts	.289	87	235	31	68	7	33	1
Gross†	.286	128	426	52	122	0	27	2
Cabell	.273	144	586	85	160	2	43	35
Boswell†	.262	91	126	12	33	0	18	1
Andrews	.256	109	410	42	105	0	23	7
Milbourne†	.248	59	145	22	36	0	7	6
Johnson	.226	108	318	36	72	10	49	0
Howard†	.220	94	191	26	42	1	18	7
Metzger†	.210	152	481	37	101	0	29	1
Herrmann†	.204	79	265	14	54	3	25	0

PITCHING	W.	L.	ERA	G.	IP	H.	BB	SO
Forsch	4	3	2.15	52	92	76	26	49
Richard	20	15	2.75	39	291	221	151	214
*McLaughlin	4	5	2.85	17	79	71	17	32
*Pentz	3	3	2.95	40	64	62	31	36
*Larson	5	8	3.03	13	92	81	28	42
Niekro	4	8	3.36	36	118	107	56	77
*Sambito†	3	2	3.57	20	53	45	14	26
*Andujar	9	10	3.61	28	172	163	75	59
Dierker	13	14	3.69	28	188	171	72	112
Cosgrove†	3	4	5.50	22	90	106	58	34
*Rondon	2	2	5.67	19	54	70	39	21

Montreal Expos

BATTING	Pct.	G.	AB	R.	H.	HR	RBI	SB
Morales	.316	104	158	12	50	4	37	0
*Valentine	.279	94	305	36	85	7	39	14
*Rivera	.276	68	185	22	51	2	19	1
Foli	.264	149	546	41	144	6	54	6
Jorgensen†	.254	125	343	36	87	6	23	7
Frias	.248	76	113	7	28	0	8	1
*White‡	.245	114	278	32	68	2	21	15
Foote	.234	105	350	32	82	7	27	2
Parrish	.232	154	543	65	126	11	61	2
Garrett†	.231	139	428	51	99	6	37	9
Unser†	.228	146	496	57	113	12	40	7
Williams	.225	122	374	35	84	17	55	0
Mackanin	.224	114	380	36	85	8	33	6
Carter	.219	91	311	31	68	6	38	0
Thornton	.194	96	268	28	52	11	38	4

PITCHING	W.	L.	ERA	G.	IP	H.	BB	SO
Rogers	7	17	3.21	33	230	212	69	150
Murray	4	9	3.27	81	113	117	37	35
Fryman†	13	13	3.38	34	216	218	76	123
Stanhouse	9	12	3.77	34	184	182	92	79
*Kerrigan	2	6	3.79	38	57	63	23	22
Dunning	2	6	4.15	32	91	93	33	72
*Lang	1	3	4.21	29	62	56	34	30
Carrithers	6	12	4.44	34	140	153	78	71
Warthen†	2	10	5.30	23	90	76	66	67
Kirby	1	8	5.70	22	79	81	63	51

Cincinnati Reds

BATTING	Pct.	G.	AB	R.	H.	HR	RBI	SB
Griffey†	.336	148	562	111	189	6	74	34
Rose†	.323	162	665	130	215	10	63	9
Morgan†	.320	141	472	113	151	27	111	60
Geronimo†	.307	149	486	59	149	2	49	22
Foster	.306	144	562	86	172	29	121	17
Bailey	.298	69	124	17	37	6	23	0
Flynn	.283	93	219	20	62	1	20	2
Concepcion	.281	152	576	74	162	9	69	21
Perez	.260	139	527	77	137	19	91	10
Plummer	.248	56	153	16	38	4	19	0
Driessen†	.247	98	219	32	54	7	44	14
Bench	.234	135	465	62	109	16	74	13
Lum†	.228	84	136	15	31	3	20	0

PITCHING	W.	L.	ERA	G.	IP	H.	BB	SO
Eastwick	11	5	2.08	71	108	93	27	70
*Zachry	14	7	2.74	38	204	170	83	143
Gullett†	11	3	3.00	23	126	119	48	64
Norman†	12	7	3.10	33	180	153	70	126
Borbon	4	3	3.35	69	121	135	31	53
Nolan	15	9	3.46	34	239	232	27	113
Billingham	12	10	4.32	34	177	190	62	76
*Alcala	11	4	4.70	30	132	131	67	67
McEnaney†	2	6	4.88	55	72	97	23	28

Chicago Cubs

BATTING	Pct.	G.	AB	R.	H.	HR	RBI	SB
Madlock	339	142	514	68	174	15	84	15
Cardenal	.299	136	521	64	156	8	47	23
Morales	.274	140	537	66	147	16	67	3
Monday†	.272	137	534	107	145	32	77	5
*Wallis†	.254	121	338	51	86	5	21	3
Rosello	.242	91	227	27	55	1	11	1
Trillo	.239	158	582	42	139	4	59	17
Bittner†	.237	89	224	23	53	0	18	0
Swisher	.236	109	377	25	89	5	42	2
Kelleher	.228	124	337	28	77	0	22	0
LaCock†	.221	106	244	34	54	8	28	1
Mitterwald	.215	101	303	19	65	5	28	1
Summers†	.206	83	126	11	26	3	13	1

PITCHING	W.	L.	ERA	G.	IP	H.	BB	SO
*Sutter	6	3	2.71	52	83	63	26	73
Knowles†	5	7	2.88	58	72	61	22	39
Burris	15	13	3.11	37	249	251	70	112
R. Reuschel	14	12	3.46	38	260	260	64	146
Renko	8	12	3.99	33	176	179	46	116
Stone	3	6	4.08	17	75	70	21	33
Coleman	2	8	4.10	39	79	72	35	66
Bonham	9	13	4.27	32	196	215	96	110
*P. Reuschel	4	2	4.55	50	87	94	33	55
Garman	2	4	4.97	47	76	79	35	37
Zamora	5	3	5.24	40	55	70	17	27

Los Angeles Dodgers

BATTING	Pct.	G.	AB	R.	H.	HR	RBI	SB
Garvey	.317	162	631	85	200	13	80	19
Buckner†	.301	154	642	76	193	7	60	28
Cey	.277	145	502	69	139	23	80	0
Russell	.274	149	554	53	152	5	65	15
Lacy	.269	103	338	42	91	3	34	3
Smith†	.253	112	395	55	100	18	49	3
Lyttle†	.248	65	153	9	38	1	13	0
Baker	.242	112	384	36	93	4	39	2
Lopes	.241	117	427	72	103	4	20	63
Sizemore	.241	84	266	18	64	0	18	2
Goodson†	.229	83	118	8	27	3	17	0
Yeager	.214	117	359	42	77	11	35	3

PITCHING	W.	L.	ERA	G.	IP	H.	BB	SO
Hough	12	8	2.20	77	143	102	77	81
Rau†	16	12	2.57	34	231	221	69	98
Rhoden	12	3	2.98	27	181	165	53	77
Sutton	21	10	3.06	35	268	231	82	161
John†	10	10	3.09	31	207	207	61	91
Hooton	11	15	3.25	33	227	203	60	116
*Wall†	2	2	3.60	31	50	50	15	27
Sosa	6	8	4.43	45	69	71	25	52

New York Mets

BATTING	Pct.	G.	AB	R.	H.	HR	RBI	SB
Torre	.306	114	310	36	95	5	31	1
Kranepool†	.292	123	415	47	121	10	49	1
*Boisclair†	.287	110	286	42	82	2	13	9
Millan	.282	139	531	55	150	1	35	2
Grote	.272	101	323	30	88	4	28	1
Milner†	.271	127	443	56	120	15	78	0
Stearns	.262	32	103	13	27	2	10	1
Phillips†	.256	87	262	30	67	4	29	2
Kingman	.238	123	474	70	113	37	86	7
Mangual	.237	107	317	49	75	4	25	24
Harrelson‡	.234	118	359	34	84	1	26	9
Hodges†	.226	56	155	21	35	4	24	2
*Staiger	.220	95	304	23	67	2	26	3
Vail	.217	53	143	8	31	0	9	0
Dwyer†	.181	61	105	9	19	0	5	0

PITCHING	W.	L.	ERA	G.	IP	H.	BB	SO
Seaver	14	11	2.59	35	271	211	77	235
Lockwood	10	7	2.68	56	94	62	34	108
Koosman†	21	10	2.70	34	247	205	66	200
Apodaca	3	7	2.80	43	90	71	29	45
Matlack‡	17	10	2.95	35	262	236	57	153
Lolich†	8	13	3.22	31	193	184	52	120
Swan	6	9	3.55	23	132	129	44	89

San Diego Padres

BATTING	Pct.	G.	AB	R.	H.	HR	RBI	SB
Ivie	.291	140	405	51	118	7	70	6
Grubb†	.284	109	384	54	109	5	27	1
Winfield	.283	137	492	81	139	13	69	26
W. Davis†	.268	141	493	61	132	5	46	14
*Turner†	.266	105	282	40	75	5	37	12
Fuentes‡	.263	135	520	48	137	2	36	5
Rader	.257	139	471	45	121	9	55	3
Hernandez	.256	113	340	31	87	1	24	12
Kendall	.246	146	455	30	112	2	39	1
Kubiak‡	.236	96	212	16	50	0	26	0
Rettenmund	.229	86	140	16	32	2	11	4
Melendez	.224	92	143	15	32	0	5	1
McCovey†	.203	71	202	20	41	7	36	0
Torres	.195	74	215	8	42	4	15	2

PITCHING	W.	L.	ERA	G.	IP	H.	BB	SO
*Sawyer	5	3	2.52	13	82	84	38	32
Jones‡	22	14	2.74	40	315	274	50	93
Tomlin†	0	1	2.84	49	73	62	20	43
*Metzger	11	4	2.93	77	123	119	52	89
Foster	3	6	3.21	26	87	75	35	22
Strom†	12	16	3.28	36	211	188	73	103
Freisleben	10	13	3.51	34	172	163	66	81
Griffin	9	6	4.10	31	112	100	79	69
Spillner	2	11	5.05	32	107	120	55	57
Folkers†	2	3	5.25	33	60	67	25	26

San Francisco Giants

BATTING	Pct.	G.	AB	R.	H.	HR	RBI	SB
*Herndon	.288	115	337	42	97	2	23	12
Matthews	.279	156	587	79	164	20	84	12
Reitz	.267	155	577	40	154	5	66	5
Joshua†	.263	42	156	13	41	0	2	1
Rader†	.263	88	255	25	67	1	22	2
Thomasson†	.259	103	328	45	85	8	38	8
Murcer†	.259	147	533	73	138	23	90	12
Perez	.257	124	428	49	110	3	32	3
Thomas‡	.232	81	272	38	63	2	19	10
Speier	.226	145	495	51	112	3	40	2
*Clark	.225	26	102	14	23	2	10	6
*LeMaster	.210	33	100	9	21	0	9	2
Evans†	.205	136	396	53	81	11	46	9
Hill	.183	54	131	11	24	3	15	0

PITCHING	W.	L.	ERA	G.	IP	H.	BB	SO
Moffitt	6	6	2.27	58	103	92	35	50
Lavelle‡	10	6	2.70	65	110	102	52	71
Montefusco	16	14	2.85	37	253	224	74	172
Barr	15	12	2.89	37	252	260	60	75
Williams	2	0	2.96	48	85	80	39	34
Halicki	12	14	3.63	32	186	171	61	130
*Dressler	3	10	4.42	25	108	125	35	33
Heaverlo	4	4	4.44	61	75	85	15	40
Caldwell†	1	7	4.88	50	107	145	20	55
D'Acquisto	3	8	5.35	28	106	93	102	53

Pittsburgh Pirates

BATTING	Pct.	G.	AB	R.	H.	HF:	RBI	SB
Oliver†	.323	121	443	62	143	12	61	6
Parker†	.313	138	537	82	168	13	90	19
Robinson	.303	122	393	55	119	21	64	2
Sanguillen	.290	114	389	52	113	2	36	2
Zisk	.289	155	581	91	168	21	89	1
*Moreno†	.270	48	122	24	33	2	12	15
Taveras	.258	144	519	76	134	0	24	58
Stargell†	.257	117	428	54	110	20	65	2
Stennett	.257	157	654	59	168	2	60	18
Hebner†	.249	132	434	60	108	8	51	1
Kirkpatrick†	.233	83	146	14	34	0	16	1
Dyer	.223	69	184	12	41	3	9	0
Robertson	.217	61	129	10	28	2	25	0

PITCHING	W.	L.	ERA	G.	IP	H.	BB	SO
Tekulve	5	3	2.45	64	103	91	25	68
Kison	14	9	3.08	31	193	180	52	98
Candelaria†	16	7	3.15	32	220	173	60	138
Demery	10	7	3.17	36	145	123	58	72
Rooker†	15	8	3.35	30	199	201	72	92
Medich	8	11	3.52	29	179	193	48	86
Reuss†	14	9	3.53	31	209	209	51	108
Moose	3	9	3.68	53	88	100	32	38
Giusti	5	4	4.34	40	58	59	27	24

Atlanta Braves

BATTING	Pct.	G.	AB	R.	H.	HR	RBI	SB
Montanez†	.317	163	650	74	206	11	84	2
Gaston	.291	69	134	15	39	4	25	1
Paciorek	.290	111	324	39	94	4	36	2
Office†	.281	99	359	51	101	4	34	2
Henderson†	.262	133	435	52	114	13	61	5
Chaney†	.252	153	496	42	125	1	50	5
Gilbreath	.251	116	383	57	96	1	32	7
*Royster	.248	149	533	65	132	5	45	24
Pocoroba†	.241	54	174	16	42	0	14	1
Correll	.225	69	200	26	45	5	16	0
May†	.215	105	214	27	46	3	23	5
Wynn	.207	148	449	75	93	17	66	16

PITCHING	W.	L.	ERA	G.	IP	H.	BB	SO
Messersmith	11	11	3.04	29	207	166	74	135
Devine	5	6	3.21	48	73	72	26	48
Niekro	17	11	3.29	38	271	249	101	173
*Torrealba†	0	2	3.57	36	53	67	22	33
Dal Canton	3	5	3.58	42	73	67	42	36
Marshall	6	4	4.00	54	99	99	39	56
Morton	4	9	4.18	26	140	172	45	42
Ruthven	14	17	4.20	36	240	255	90	142
*LaCorte	3	12	4.71	19	105	97	53	79
Moret†	3	5	5.03	27	77	84	27	30

Philadelphia Phillies

BATTING	Pct.	G.	AB	R.	H.	HR	RBI	SB
Maddox	.330	146	531	75	175	6	68	29
Johnstone†	.318	129	440	62	140	5	53	5
Luzinski	.304	149	533	74	162	21	95	1
Cash	.284	160	666	92	189	1	56	10
McCarver†	.277	90	155	26	43	3	29	2
Boone	.271	121	361	40	98	4	54	2
Allen	.268	85	298	52	80	15	49	11
Schmidt	.262	160	584	112	153	38	107	14
Tolan†	.261	110	272	32	71	5	35	10
Brown	.254	92	209	30	53	5	30	2
Bowa‡	.248	156	624	71	155	0	49	30
Martin	.248	130	121	30	30	2	15	3
Hutton†	.202	95	124	15	25	1	13	1

PITCHING	W.	L.	ERA	G.	IP	H.	BB	SO
Twitchell	3	1	1.74	26	62	55	18	67
Reed	8	7	2.46	59	128	88	32	96
McGraw†	7	6	2.51	58	97	81	42	76
Garber	9	3	2.81	59	93	78	30	92
Schueler	1	0	2.88	35	50	44	16	43
Lonborg	18	10	3.08	33	222	210	50	118
Carlton†	20	7	3.13	35	253	224	72	195
Kaat†	12	14	3.47	38	228	241	32	83
Underwood†	10	5	3.52	33	156	154	63	94
Christenson	13	8	3.67	32	169	199	42	54

St. Louis Cardinals

BATTING	Pct.	G.	AB	R.	H.	HR	RBI	SB
McBride†	.335	72	272	40	91	3	24	10
Crawford†	.304	120	392	49	119	9	50	2
Brock†	.301	133	498	73	150	4	67	56
Anderson	.291	86	199	17	58	1	12	1
Simmons‡	.291	150	546	60	159	5	75	0
*Templeton‡	.291	53	213	32	62	1	17	11
Hernandez†	.289	129	374	54	108	7	46	4
Tyson	.286	76	245	26	70	3	28	3
Fairly†	.264	73	110	13	29	0	21	0
*Mumphrey‡	.258	112	384	51	99	1	26	22
Kessinger‡	.239	145	502	55	120	1	40	3
*Cruz	.228	151	526	54	120	13	71	1
Harris‡	.228	97	259	21	59	1	19	1
Ferguson	.211	125	374	46	79	10	39	6

PITCHING	W.	L.	ERA	G.	IP	H.	BB	SO
Denny	11	9	2.52	30	207	189	74	74
Falcone†	12	16	3.23	32	212	173	93	138
Hrabosky†	8	6	3.32	68	95	89	39	73
Rasmussen	6	12	3.54	43	150	139	54	76
McGlothen	13	15	3.91	33	205	209	68	106
Forsch	8	10	3.94	33	194	209	71	76
Wallace†	3	2	4.09	49	66	66	39	40
Curtis†	6	11	4.50	37	134	139	65	52
Greif	2	8	5.26	52	77	87	37	37

Major League Baseball Attendance

Club	American League 1976	1975	Increase Decrease
Baltimore	1,058,609	1,002,157	+ 56,452
Boston	1,895,344	1,748,587	+ 146,757
California	1,006,764	1,058,163	− 51,459
Chicago	917,773	750,802	+ 166,971
Cleveland	948,776	977,039	− 28,263
Detroit	1,467,020	1,058,836	+ 408,184
Kansas City	1,680,256	1,151,836	+ 528,420
Milwaukee	1,012,065	1,213,357	− 201,292
Minnesota	715,394	737,156	− 21,762
New York	2,012,434	1,288,048	+ 724,386
Oakland	780,585	1,075,518	− 294,933
Texas	1,164,986	1,127,924	+ 37,062
Totals	**14,660,006**	**13,189,423**	**+1,470,583**

Club	National League 1976	1975	Increase Decrease
Atlanta	818,179	534,672	+ 283,507
Chicago	1,026,217	1,034,819	− 8,602
Cincinnati	2,629,708	2,315,603	+ 314,105
Houston	886,146	858,004	+ 28,142
Los Angeles	2,386,301	2,539,349	− 153,048
Montreal	646,704	908,292	− 261,588
New York	1,468,754	1,730,566	− 261,812
Philadelphia	2,480,150	1,909,233	+ 570,917
Pittsburgh	1,025,945	1,270,018	− 244,973
St. Louis	1,207,136	1,695,394	− 488,258
San Diego	1,458,478	1,281,747	+ 176,731
San Francisco	626,868	522,925	+ 103,943
Totals	**16,660,586**	**16,600,622**	**+ 59,964**

Major League Attendance Records

All-time Season Records, Both Leagues—31,320,592 in 1976
All-time Season Record, One Club—2,755,184—Los Angeles Dodgers, 1962.
Record Attendance, World Series—420,784—1959 Series between Los Angeles Dodgers and Chicago White Sox.
Record Attendance, World Series Game—92,706—fifth game, 1959 Series, Los Angeles, Oct. 6.
Record Attendance, Regular Season Game—84,587—Municipal Stadium, Cleveland, Sept. 12, 1954, in doubleheader between the Indians and Yankees. (Not including pass list of 1,976.)
Attendance, Regular-Season Single Game—78,672—Los Angeles Memorial Coliseum, April 18, 1958, in opening game between Los Angeles Dodgers and San Francisco Giants.

World Series, 1976

Composite Box Scores

Cincinnati Reds

	G.	AB	R.	H.	2B	3B	HR	RBI	SO	BB	BA	PO	A.	E.	FA
Pete Rose, 3b	4	16	1	3	1	0	0	1	2	2	.188	6	3	0	1.000
Ken Griffey, rf	4	17	2	1	0	0	0	1	1	0	.059	5	0	0	1.000
Joe Morgan, 2b	4	15	3	5	1	1	1	2	2	2	.333	13	11	2	.923
Tony Perez, 1b	4	16	1	5	1	0	0	2	2	1	.313	32	4	0	1.000
Dan Driessen, dh	4	14	4	5	2	0	1	1	0	2	.357	0	0	0	.000
George Foster, lf	4	14	3	6	1	0	0	4	3	2	.429	14	0	0	1.000
Johnny Bench, c	4	15	4	8	1	1	2	6	1	0	.533	18	2	0	1.000
Cesar Geronimo, cf	4	13	3	4	2	0	0	1	2	2	.308	12	0	1	.923
Dave Concepcion, ss	4	14	1	5	1	1	0	3	3	1	.357	6	10	1	.941
Don Gullett, p	1	0	0	0	0	0	0	0	0	0	.000	0	1	0	1.000
Pedro Borbon, p	1	0	0	0	0	0	0	0	0	0	.000	0	1	0	1.000
Fred Norman, p	1	0	0	0	0	0	0	0	0	0	.000	0	1	0	1.000
Jack Billingham, p	1	0	0	0	0	0	0	0	0	0	.000	1	0	0	1.000
Pat Zachry, p	1	0	0	0	0	0	0	0	0	0	.000	0	1	1	.500
Will McEnaney, p	2	0	0	0	0	0	0	0.	0	0	.000	1	0	0	1.000
Gary Nolan, p	1	0	0	0	0	0	0	0	0	0	.000	0	1	0	1.000
Total	4	134	22	42	10	3	4	21	16	12	.313	108	35	5	.976

New York Yankees

	G.	AB	R.	H.	2B	3B	HR	RBI	SO	BB	BA	PO	A.	E.	FA
Mickey Rivers, cf	4	18	1	3	0	0	0	0	2	1	.167	14	0	0	1.000
Roy White, lf	4	15	0	2	0	0	0	0	0	3	.133	13	0	0	1.000
Thurman Munson, c	4	17	2	9	0	0	0	2	1	0	.529	21	7	0	1.000
Lou Piniella, dh-rf	4	9	1	3	1	0	0	0	0	0	.333	1	0	0	1.000
Carlos May, dh	4	9	0	0	0	0	0	0	1	0	.000	0	0	0	.000
Chris Chambliss, 1b	4	16	1	5	1	0	0	1	2	0	.313	26	3	1	.967
Graig Nettles, 3b	4	12	0	0	0	0	0	2	1	3	.250	8	8	0	1.000
Elliott Maddox, rf-dh	2	5	0	1	0	1	0	0	2	1	.200	0	0	0	1.000
Oscar Gamble, ph-rf	3	8	0	1	0	0	0	1	0	0	.125	3	0	0	1.000
Willie Randolph, 2b	4	14	1	1	0	0	0	0	3	1	.071	13	8	0	1.000
Fred Stanley, ss	4	6	1	1	1	0	0	1	1	3	.167	4	7	1	.917
Otto Velez, ph	3	3	0	0	0	0	0	0	3	0	.000	0	0	0	.000
Jim Mason, ss	3	1	1	1	0	0	1	.1	0	0	1.000	1	2	0	1.000
Elrod Hendricks, ph	2	2	0	0	0	0	0	0	0	0	.000	0	0	0	.000
Doyle Alexander, p	1	0	0	0	0	0	0	0	0	0	.000	0	1	0	.000
Sparky Lyle, p	2	0	0	0	0	0	0	0	0	0	.000	0	0	0	.000
Catfish Hunter, p	1	0	0	0	0	0	0	0	0	0	.000	0	1	0	1.000
Dock Ellis, p	1	0	0	0	0	0	0	0	0	0	.000	0	0	0	.000
Grant Jackson, p	1	0	0	0	0	0	0	0	0	0	.000	0	2	0	1.000
Dick Tidrow, p	2	0	0	0	0	0	0	0	0	0	.000	0	0	0	.000
Ed Figueroa, p	1	0	0	0	0	0	0	0	0	0	.000	0	1	0	1.000
Total	4	135	8	30	3	1	1	8	16	12	.222	104	40	2	.986

Pitching Summary
Cincinnati

	G.	CG	IP	H.	R.	BB	SO	HB	WP	W.	L.	Pct.	ER	ERA
Don Gullett	1	0	7 1/3	5	1	3	4	1	0	1	0	1.000	1	1.29
Pedro Borbon	1	0	1 2/3	0	0	0	0	0	0	0	0	.000	0	0.00
Fred Norman	1	0	6 1/3	9	3	2	2	0	0	0	0	.000	3	4.50
Jack Billingham	1	0	2 2/3	0	0	0	1	0	0	1	0	1.000	0	0.00
Pat Zachry	1	0	6 2/3	6	2	5	6	0	0	1	0	1.000	2	2.57
Will McEnaney	2	0	4 2/3	2	0	1	2	0	0	0	0	.000	0	0.00
Gary Nolan	1	0	6 2/3	8	2	1	1	0	0	1	0	1.000	2	2.57
Total	4	0	36	30	8	12	16	1	0	4	0	1.000	8	2.00

New York

	G.	CG	IP	H.	R.	BB	SO	HB	WP	W.	L.	Pct.	ER	ERA
Doyle Alexander	1	0	6	9	5	2	1	0	0	0	1	.000	5	7.50
Sparky Lyle	2	0	2 2/3	1	0	0	3	0	1	0	0	.000	0	0.00
Catfish Hunter	1	1	8 1/3	10	4	4	5	0	0	0	1	.000	3	3.00
Dock Ellis	1	0	3 1/3	7	4	0	1	0	0	0	1	.000	4	12.00
Grant Jackson	1	0	3 1/3	4	2	0	3	0	0	0	0	.000	2	4.50
Dick Tidrow	2	0	2 1/3	5	2	1	1	0	0	0	0	.000	2	9.00
Ed Figueroa	1	0	8	6	5	5	2	0	1	0	1	.000	5	5.63
Total	4	1	34 2/3	42	22	12	16	0	2	0	4	.000	21	5.40

Composite Score By Inning

Cincinnati Reds	1	6	1	4	0	1	2	2	5—22		
New York Yankees	1	1	0	2	1	0	3	0	0—8		

Reds Sweep Yankees in 4 Straight

The Cincinnati Reds defeated the New York Yankees in 4 straight games to win the 1976 world series. Johnny Bench was voted the outstanding player in the series.

1976 World Series Box Scores

First Game

Riverfront Stadium, Cincinnati, Oct. 16

New York	ab	r	h	bi
Rivers, cf	4	0	0	0
White, lf	4	0	1	0
Munson, c	4	0	1	0
Piniella, dh	3	1	1	0
May, dh	1	0	0	0
Chambliss, 1b	3	0	1	0
Nettles, 3b	3	0	0	1
Maddox, rf	2	0	1	0
Gamble, ph	1	0	0	0
Randolph, 2b	2	0	0	0
Stanley, ss	1	0	0	0
Velez, ph	1	0	0	0
Mason, ss	0	0	0	0
Alexander p	0	0	0	0
Lyle, p	0	0	0	0
Total	29	1	5	1

Cincinnati	ab	r	h	bi
Rose, 3b	2	0	0	1
Griffey, rf	4	1	0	0
Morgan, 2b	4	1	1	1
Perez, 1b	4	0	3	1
Driessen, dh	4	0	0	0
Foster, lf	3	1	2	0
Bench, c	3	1	2	0
Geronimo, cf	3	0	1	0
Concepcion, ss	3	1	1	0
Gullett, p	0	0	0	0
Borbon, p	0	0	0	0
Total	30	5	10	4

Errors—Geronimo, Chambliss. Double plays—Yankees 2, Cincinnati 2. Left on base—Yankees 6, Cincinnati 4. Two base hits—Piniella, Perez, Geronimo. Three base hits—Concepcion, Maddox, Bench. Home run—Morgan (1). Stolen base—Griffey. Sacrifice fly—Nettles, Rose.

	ip	h	r	er	bb	so
Alexander (L, 0-1)	6	9	5	5	2	1
Lyle	2	1	0	0	0	3
Gullett (W, 1-0)	7 1/3	5	1	1	3	4
Borbon	1 2/3	0	0	0	0	0

Hit by pitch—by Gullett (Chambliss). Wild pitch—Lyle. Time of game—2:10. Attendance—54,826.

How runs were scored—One in Reds first: Morgan hit a home run.

One in Yankees second: Piniella doubled. Piniella went to third on a ground out. Nettles hit a sacrifice fly, scoring Piniella.

One in Reds third: Concepcion tripled. Rose hit a sacrifice fly, scoring Concepcion.

One in Reds sixth: Rose walked. Griffey forced Rose at second. Griffey stole second. Perez singled, scoring Griffey.

Two in Reds seventh: Foster singled. Bench tripled, scoring Foster. Bench scored on a wild pitch.

Yankees ... 010 000 000—1
Cincinnati ... 101 001 20x—5

Second Game

Riverfront Stadium, Cincinnati, Oct. 17

New York	ab	r	h	bi
Rivers, cf	5	0	0	0
White, lf	3	0	1	0
Munson, c	4	1	1	1
Piniella, dh	4	0	2	0
Chambliss, 1b	4	0	2	0
Nettles, 3b	4	0	1	1
Maddox, dh	3	0	0	0
May, dh	1	0	0	0
Randolph, 2b	4	1	1	0
Stanley, ss	3	1	1	1
Hunter, p	0	0	0	0
Total	35	3	9	3

Cincinnati	ab	r	h	bi
Rose, 3b	4	0	0	0
Griffey, rf	4	1	0	1
Morgan, 2b	4	0	2	0
Perez, 1b	5	0	2	1
Driessen, dh	4	1	2	0
Foster, lf	4	0	1	1
Bench, c	4	1	2	0
Geronimo, cf	2	1	0	0
Concepcion, ss	4	0	1	1
Norman, p	0	0	0	0
Billingham, p	0	0	0	0
Total	35	4	10	4

Errors—Stanley. Double plays—Cincinnati 1. Left on base—Yankees 7, Cincinnati 10. Two base hits—Stanley, Driessen, Bench. Three base hits—Morgan. Stolen base—Morgan. Sacrifice fly—Griffey.

	ip	h	r	er	bb	so
Hunter (L, 0-1)	8 2/3	10	4	3	4	5
Norman	6 1/3	9	3	3	2	2
Billingham (W, 1-0)	2 2/3	0	0	0	0	1

Time of game—2:33. Attendance—54,816.

How runs were scored—Three in Reds second: Driessen doubled. Foster singled, scoring Driessen. Foster was caught stealing. Bench doubled. Geronimo walked. Concepcion singled, scoring Bench. Rose walked. Griffey hit a sacrifice fly, scoring Geronimo.

One in Yankees fourth: Munson and Chambliss singled. Nettles singled, scoring Munson.

Two in Yankees seventh: Randolph singled. Stanley doubled, scoring Randolph. Stanley went to third on a single, and scored as Munson grounded out.

One in Reds ninth: Griffey reached second on an error. Perez singled, scoring Griffey.

Yankees ... 000 100 200—3
Cincinnati ... 030 000 001—4

Third Game

Yankee Stadium, New York, Oct. 19, 1976

Cincinnati	ab	r	h	bi
Rose, 3b	5	1	2	0
Griffey, rf	4	0	1	0
Morgan, 2b	4	1	1	1
Perez, 1b	4	0	0	0
Driessen, dh	3	2	3	1
Foster, lf	4	1	2	2
Bench, c	4	0	2	0
Geronimo, cf	4	1	1	1
Concepcion, ss	4	0	1	1
Zachry, p	0	0	0	0
McEnany, p	0	0	0	0
Total	36	6	13	6

New York	ab	r	h	bi
Rivers, cf	4	0	2	0
White, lf	3	0	0	0
Munson, c	5	0	3	0
Chambliss, 1b	5	1	1	0
May, dh	4	0	0	0
Nettles, 3b	2	0	0	0
Gamble, ph	3	0	1	1
Piniella, rf	1	0	0	0
Randolph, 2b	4	0	0	0
Stanley, ss	1	0	0	0
Hendrcks, ph	1	0	0	0
Mason, ss	1	1	1	1
Velez, ph	1	0	0	0
Ellis, p	0	0	0	0
Jackson, p	0	0	0	0
Tidrow, p	0	0	0	0
Total	35	2	8	2

Cincinnati ... 030 100 020—6
New York ... 000 100 100—2

Errors—T. Perez, Morgan. Double plays—Cincinnati 1, New York 3. Left on base—Cincinnati 4, New York 11. Two base hits —G. Foster, Driessen, Morgan. Home runs—Driessen (1), Mason (1). Stolen bases—Driessen, Geronimo.

	ip	h	r	er	bb	so
Zachry (W, 1-0)	6 2/3	6	2	2	5	6
McEnany	2 1/3	2	0	0	0	1
Ellis (L, 0-1)	3 1/3	7	4	4	0	1
Jackson	3 2/3	4	2	2	0	3
Tidrow	2	0	0	0	1	1

Save—McEnany (1). Time 2:42. Attendance 56,667.

How runs were scored—Three in Reds second: Driessen singled and stole second. Foster doubled, scoring Driessen. Bench singled, Foster stopping at third. Geronimo forced Bench at second, Foster scoring. Geronimo stole second. Concepcion singled, scoring Geronimo.

One in Reds fourth: Driessen hit a home run.

One in Yankees fourth: Chambliss singled. Nettles walked. Gamble singled, scoring Chambliss.

One in Yankees seventh: Mason hit a home run.

Two in Reds eighth: Rose singled. Griffey singled. Morgan doubled, scoring Rose. Griffey was out at home on Perez's grounder. Driessen walked. Foster singled, scoring Morgan.

Fourth Game
Yankee Stadium, New York, Oct. 21

Cincinnati	ab	r	h	bi		New York	ab	r	h	bi
Rose, 3b	5	0	1	0		Rivers, cf	5	1	1	0
Griffey, rf	5	0	0	0		White, lf	5	0	0	0
Morgan, 2b	3	1	1	0		Munson, c	4	1	4	1
Perez, 1b	3	1	0	0		Chambliss, 1b	4	0	1	1
Driessen, dh	3	1	0	0		May, dh	3	0	0	0
Foster, lf	3	1	1	1		Piniella, dh	1	0	0	0
Bench, c	4	2	2	5		Nettles, 3b	3	0	2	0
Geronimo, cf	4	1	2	0		Gamble, rf	4	0	0	0
Concepcion, ss	3	0	2	1		Randolph, 2b	4	0	0	0
Nolan, p	0	0	0	0		Stanley, ss	1	0	0	0
McEnany, p	0	0	0	0		Hendricks, ph	1	0	0	0
						Mason, ss	0	0	0	0
						Velez, ph	1	0	0	0
						Figueroa, p	0	0	0	0
						Tidrow, p	0	0	0	0
						Lyle, p	0	0	0	0
Total	**33**	**7**	**9**	**7**		**Total**	**36**	**2**	**8**	**2**

Cincinnati . . . . 0 0 0 3 0 0 0 0 4—7
Yankees . . . . 1 0 0 0 1 0 0 0 0—2

Errors—Morgan, Concepcion. Double plays—Yankees 1. Left on base—Cincinnati 4, Yankees 9. Two base hits—Rose, Chambliss, Geronimo, Concepcion. Home runs—Bench 2 (3). Stolen bases—Geronimo, Morgan, Rivers.

	ip	h	r	er	bb	so
Nolan (W, 1-0)	6²/₃	8	2	2	1	1
McEnaney	2¹/₃	0	0	0	1	1
Figueroa (L, 0-1)	8	6	5	5	5	2
Tidrow	¹/₃	3	2	2	0	0
Lyle	²/₃	0	0	0	0	0

Save—McEnaney (2). Wild pitch—Figueroa. Time of game—2:36. Attendance—56,700.

How runs were scored—One in Yankees first: Munson singled. Chambliss doubled, scoring Munson.

Three in Reds fourth: Morgan walked and stole second. Foster singled, scoring Morgan. Bench hit a home run.

One in Yankees fifth: Rivers walked and stole second. Munson singled, scoring Rivers.

Four in Reds ninth: Perez and Driessen walked. Bench hit a home run. Geronimo doubled. Concepcion doubled, scoring Geronimo.

World Series Results, 1903-1976

1903 Boston AL 5, Pittsburgh NL 3
1904 No Series
1905 New York NL 4, Philadelphia AL 1
1906 Chicago AL 4, Chicago NL 2
1907 Chicago NL 4, Detroit AL 0, 1 tie
1908 Chicago NL 4, Detroit AL 1
1909 Pittsburgh NL 4, Detroit AL 3
1910 Philadelphia AL 4, Chicago NL 1
1911 Philadelphia AL 4, New York NL 2
1912 Boston AL 4, New York NL 3, 1 tie
1913 Philadelphia AL 4, New York NL 1
1914 Boston NL 4, Philadelphia AL 0
1915 Boston AL 4, Philadelphia NL 1
1916 Boston AL 4, Brooklyn NL 1
1917 Chicago AL 4, New York NL 2
1918 Boston AL 4, Chicago NL 2
1919 Cincinnati NL 5, Chicago AL 3
1920 Cleveland AL 5, Brooklyn NL 2
1921 New York NL 5, New York AL 3
1922 New York NL 4, New York AL 0, 1 tie
1923 New York AL 4, New York NL 2
1924 Washington AL 4, New York NL 3
1925 Pittsburgh NL 4, Washington AL 3
1926 St. Louis NL 4, New York AL 3
1927 New York AL 4, Pittsburgh NL 0

1928 New York AL 4, St. Louis NL 0
1929 Philadelphia AL 4, Chicago NL 1
1930 Philadelphia AL 4, St. Louis NL 2
1931 St. Louis NL 4, Philadelphia AL 3
1932 New York AL 4, Chicago NL 0
1933 New York NL 4, Washington AL 1
1934 St. Louis NL 4, Detroit AL 3
1935 Detroit AL 4, Chicago NL 2
1936 New York AL 4, New York NL 2
1937 New York AL 4, New York NL 1
1938 New York AL 4, Chicago NL 0
1939 New York AL 4, Cincinnati NL 0
1940 Cincinnati NL 4, Detroit AL 3
1941 New York AL 4, Brooklyn NL 1
1942 St. Louis NL 4, New York AL 1
1943 New York AL 4, St. Louis NL 1
1944 St. Louis NL 4, St. Louis AL 2
1945 Detroit AL 4, Chicago NL 3
1946 St. Louis NL 4, Boston AL 3
1947 New York AL 4, Brooklyn NL 3
1948 Cleveland AL 4, Boston NL 2
1949 New York AL 4, Brooklyn NL 1
1950 New York AL 4, Philadelphia NL 0
1951 New York AL 4, New York NL 2
1952 New York AL 4, Brooklyn NL 3

1953 New York AL 4, Brooklyn NL 2
1954 New York NL 4, Cleveland AL 0
1955 Brooklyn NL 4, New York AL 3
1956 New York AL 4, Brooklyn NL 3
1957 Milwaukee NL 4, New York AL 3
1958 New York AL 4, Milwaukee NL 3
1959 Los Angeles NL 4, Chicago AL 2
1960 Pittsburgh NL 4, New York AL 3
1961 New York AL 4, Cincinnati NL 1
1962 New York AL 4, San Francisco NL 3
1963 Los Angeles NL 4, New York AL 0
1964 St. Louis NL 4, New York AL 3
1965 Los Angeles NL 4, Minnesota AL 3
1966 Baltimore AL 4, Los Angeles NL 0
1967 St. Louis NL 4, Boston AL 3
1968 Detroit AL 4, St. Louis NL 3
1969 New York NL 4, Baltimore AL 1
1970 Baltimore AL 4, Cincinnati NL 1
1971 Pittsburgh NL 4, Baltimore AL 3
1972 Oakland AL 4, Cincinnati NL 3
1973 Oakland AL 4, New York NL 3
1974 Oakland AL 4, Los Angeles NL 1
1975 Cincinnati NL 4, Boston AL 3
1976 Cincinnati NL 4, New York AL 0

All-Time Home Run Leaders

Player	HR	Player	HR	Player	HR	Player	HR
Hank Aaron	755	Al Kaline	399	Hank Greenberg	331	Lee May	273
Babe Ruth	714	Willie Stargell	388	Roy Sievers	318	Brooks Robinson	267
Willie Mays	660	Frank Howard	382	Al Simmons	307	Vic Wertz	266
Frank Robinson	586	Orlando Cepeda	379	Rogers Hornsby	302	Bobby Thomson	264
Harmon Killebrew	573	Norm Cash	377	Chuck Klein	300	Willie Horton	262
Mickey Mantle	536	Rocco Colavito	374	Jim Wynn	290	Johnny Bench	256
Jimmy Foxx	534	Gil Hodges	370	Robert Johnson	288	Bob Allison	256
Ted Williams	521	Ralph Kiner	369	Hank Sauer	288	Vada Pinson	256
Ed Mathews	512	Joe DiMaggio	361	Del Ennis	288	Joe Gordon	253
Ernie Banks	512	John Mize	359	Frank Thomas	286	Larry Doby	253
Mel Ott	511	Yogi Berra	358	Ken Boyer	282	Joe Torre	251
Lou Gehrig	493	Dick Allen	346	Reggie Jackson	281	Fred (Cy) Williams	251
Stan Musial	475	Ron Santo	342	Ted Kluszewski	279	Leon Goslin	248
Willie McCovey	465	John (Boog) Powell	339	Tony Perez	277	Vernon Stephens	247
Billy Williams	426	Carl Yastrzemski	338	Rudy York	277	Deron Johnson	245
Duke Snider	407	Joe Adcock	336	Roger Maris	275	Hack Wilson	244

Major League Perfect Games

Year	Player	Clubs	Score	Year	Player	Clubs	Score
1904	Cy Young	Boston vs. Phil. (AL)	3-0	1956	Don Larson (b)	N.Y. Yankees vs. Brooklyn	2-0
1908	Addie Joss	Cleveland vs. Chicago (AL)	1-0	1964	Jim Bunning	Phil. vs. N.Y. Mets (NL)	6-0
1971	Ernie Shore (a)	Boston vs. Wash. (AL)	4-0	1965	Sandy Koufax	Los Angeles vs. Chic. (NL)	1-0
1922	Charles Robertson	Chicago vs. Detroit (AL)	2-0	1968	Jim Hunter	Oakland vs. Minn. (AL)	4-0

(a) Babe Ruth, the starting pitcher, was ejected from the game after walking the first batter. Shore replaced him, and the base-runner was out stealing. Shore retired the next 26 batters. (b) World Series.

College World Series
Arizona won the 1976 College World Series by defeating Eastern Michigan 7-1 at Omaha, Neb.

Selected Major League Baseball Records
(After 1900)

Highest batting average, lifetime—.367—Ty Cobb.

Most seasons leading league in batting average—12—Ty Cobb.

Highest slugging average, lifetime—.690—Babe Ruth.

Most consecutive games played, lifetime—2,130—Lou Gehrig.

Most hits, lifetime—4,191—Ty Cobb.

Most hits, season—257—George Sisler, St. Louis AL, 1920.

Most hits, game (nine innings)—7—Rennie Stennett, Pittsburgh NL, Sept. 16, 1975

Longest consecutive game hitting streak—56—Joe DiMaggio, New York AL, May 15-July 16, 1941.

Most two base hits, lifetime—793—Tris Speaker.

Most two base hits, season—67—Earl Webb, Boston AL, 1931.

Most three base hits, lifetime—312—Sam Crawford.

Most three base hits, season—36—Owen Wilson, Pittsburgh, 1912.

Most seasons leading major leagues in home runs—11—Babe Ruth.

Most consecutive seasons leading major leagues in home runs—6—Ralph Kiner, Pittsburgh 1947-52.

Most home runs, lifetime—755—Henry Aaron.

Most home runs, season—61—Roger Maris, New York AL, 1961.

Most home runs, game, nine innings—4—Gil Hodges, Brooklyn, August 31, 1950
Joe Adcock, Milwaukee, July 31, 1954
Willie Mays, San Francisco, April 30, 1961
Lou Gehrig, New York AL, June 3, 1932
Rocky Colavito, Cleveland, June 10, 1959

Most grand slam home runs, lifetime—23—Lou Gehrig.

Most runs batted in season—190—Hack Wilson, Chicago NL, 1930.

Most stolen bases, season—118—Lou Brock, St. Louis NL 1974

Most steals of home, season—7—Pete Reiser, Brooklyn, 1946
Rod Carew, Minnesota, 1969

Most shutouts, lifetime—113—Walter Johnson, Washington, 1907-27.

Most shutouts, season—16—Grover Cleveland Alexander, Philadelphia NL, 1916

Most consecutive shutouts, season—6—Don Drysdale, Los Angeles, 1968.

Most consecutive scoreless innings, season—58—Don Drysdale, Los Angeles, May 14-June 8, 1968.

Most no-hit games, lifetime—4—Sandy Koufax, Nolan Ryan.

Most no-hit games, season—2—Johnny Vander Meer, Cincinnati, 1938 (consecutive), Allie Reynolds, New York AL, 1951, Nolan Ryan, California, 1973, Virgil Trucks, Detroit, 1952

Lowest earned run average, season—1.01—Hub Leonard, Boston AL, 1914.

Most games won, lifetime—511—Cy Young,.

Most seasons leading league in strikeouts—12—Walter Johnson.

Most strikeouts season—383—Nolan Ryan, California, 1973.

Most strikeouts, game—19—Steve Carlton, St. Louis NL, 1969; Tom Seaver, New York NL, 1970; Nolan Ryan, California, 1974.

Most consecutive strikeouts game—10—Tom Seaver, New York NL April 22, 1970 vs. San Diego.

National Skeet Shooting Assn. Championship, 1976

All-Around Championship—550 Targets

Champion—Charles Parks, Homeworth, Ohio, 550.
Women—Valeire Johnson, San Antonio, Tex., 539.
Industry—Jimmy Prall, Tulsa, Okla., 547
Veteran—Tom Sanfilipo, Fairfield, Cal., 532
Senior—Tom Hanzel, San Antonio, Tex., 534
Junior—Alan Clark, Delmar, Cal., 540.
Collegiate—Tito Killian, San Antonio, Tex., 547.

12 Gauge—250 Targets

Champion—Martin Wood, Dallas, Tex., 250.
Women—Karla Roberts, Bridgeton, Mo., 248.
Industry—Jimmy Prall, Tulsa, Okla., 250.
Veteran—Tom Sanfilipo, Fairfield, Cal., 245.
Senior—Barbee Ponder, Amite, Ia., 248.
Junior—Mack Morrison, Goldsmith, Tex., 250.
Collegiate—Tom Tomlinson, Washington, Mich.

20 Gauge—100 Targets

Champion—Tito Killian, San Antonio, Tex., 100.
Women—Cathy Kaufman, San Antonio, Tex., 100.
Industry—Jimmy Prall, Tulsa, Okla., 100.

Veteran—George Vicknair, Baton Rouge, La., 98.
Senior—Tom Hanzel, San Antonio, Tex., 99.
Junior—Alan Clark, Delmar, Cal., 100.
Collegiate—Tito Killian, 100.

28 Gauge—100 Targets

Champion—Ricky Pope, San Antonio, Tex., 100.
Women—Cathy Kaufman, San Antonio, Tex., 99.
Industry—J.P. Stotts, East Alton, Ill., 99.
Veteran—Richard Edge, Dallas, Tex., 97.
Senior—K.E. Pletcher, Bellevue, Neb., 98.
Junior—Tony West, Wellsville, Kan., 100.
Collegiate—Ricky Pope, 100.

410 Gauge—100 Targets

Champion—Charles Parks, Homeworth, Ohio, 100.
Industry—Jimmy Prall, Tulsa, Okla., 100
Veteran—Tom Sanfilipo, Fairfield, Cal., 94.
Senior—M.E. Kidd, Monroe, La., 96.
Junior—Todd Bender, Fountain Valley, Cal., 97.
Collegiate—Ed Simmons, Houston, Tex., 99.

Ten Most Dramatic Sports Events, Nov. 1975-Oct. 1976
Selected by The World Almanac Sports Staff

—Roger Staubach's 50-yard touchdown pass to Drew Pearson with 24 seconds remaining in the game against Minnesota in the NFL playoffs. The toss gave Dallas a 17-14 victory.

—The controversial decision on the Ali-Norton fight. Ali retained his heavyweight title in the 15-round bout.

—UCLA's upset of Ohio State in the Rose Bowl. The defeat deprived Ohio State of a perfect season and #1 national ranking.

—The Stanley Cup champion Philadelphia Flyers defeat of the Soviet Central Army team in the final game of the Soviet tour. Two Soviet touring teams had previously lost only 1 of 7 games to NHL teams.

—Mac Wilkins breaking world records the first 3 times he threw the discus at the San Jose Invitational. His tosses were 229 ft., 230.5 ft., and 232.6 ft.

—Nadia Comaneci awarded the first perfect gymnastic score in Olympic history. The 14-year-old from Romania eventually earned 7 perfect scores.

—Forego winning the 1 1/4-mile, $283,700 Marlboro Cup race carrying 137 lbs. The 6-year-old gelding clinched his 3d straight Horse of the Year award.

— Ray Floyd's overwhelming victory in the Masters. His score of 271, 17 under par, tied a Masters record held by Jack Nicklaus.

—Indiana's second-half victory over Michigan in the NCAA basketball championship. The 86-68 victory completed a perfect season.

—Chris Chambliss's home run in the 9th inning of the final playoff game against Kansas City. The blow gave the Yankees a 7-6 victory and the American League pennant.

Olympic Information

Olympic Symbol: Five rings or circles, linked together to represent the sporting friendship of all peoples. The rings also symbolize the 5 continents — Europe, Asia, Africa, Australia, and America. Each ring is a different color — blue, yellow, black, green, and red.

Olympic Flag: The symbol of the 5 rings on a plain white background.

Olympic Motto: "Citius, Altius, Fortuis," Latin meaning "faster, higher, braver", or the modern interpretation "swifter, higher, stronger". The motto was coined by Father Didon, a French educator, in 1895.

Olympic Creed: "The most important thing in the Olympic Games is not to win but to take part, just as the most important thing in life is not the triumph but the struggle. The essential thing is not to have conquered but to have fought well."

Olympic Oath: An athlete of the host country recites the following at the opening ceremony. "In the name of all competitors I promise that we will take part in these Olympic Games, respecting and abiding by the rules which govern them, in the true spirit of sportsmanship for the glory of sport and the honor of our teams." Both the oath and the creed were composed by Pierre de Coubertin, the founder of the modern Games.

Olympic Flame: Symbolizes the continuity between the ancient and modern Games. The modern version of the flame was adopted in 1936. The torch used to kindle the flame is first lit by the sun's rays at Olympia, Greece, and then carried to the site of the Games by relays of runners. Ships and planes are used when necessary.

World Horseshoe Pitching Champions

Year	Champion	W.	L.	Ringer %	Year	Champion	W.	L.	Ringer %
1965	Elmer Hohl, Wellesley, Ont.	32	3	84.6	1971	Curt Day, Frankfort, Ind.	35	0	85.0
1966	Curt Day, Frankfort, Ind.	26	2	86.6	1972	Elmer Hohl, Wellesley, Ont.	33	2	86.0
1967	Dan Kuchcinski, Erie, Pa.	34	1	84.4	1973	Elmer Hohl, Wellesley, Ont.	32	3	83.5
1968	Elmer Hohl, Wellesley, Ont.	35	0	88.5	1974	Curt Day, Frankfort, Ind.	32	3	81.8
1969	Dan Kuchcinski, Erie, Pa.	35	0	84.7	1975	Elmer Hohl, Wellesley, Ont.	33	2	84.5
1970	Dan Kuchcinski, Erie, Pa.	34	1	84.9	1976	Carl Steinfeldt, Rochester, N.Y.	33	2	82.6

Year	Ladies Champion	Ringer %	Junior Champion	Ringer %
1969	Vicki Winston, Lamonte, Mo.	79.6	Mark Seibold, Huntington, Ind.	83.7
1970	Ruth Hangen, Buffalo, N.Y.	72.0	Bill Holland, Indianapolis, Ind.	79.2
1971	Ruth Hangen, Buffalo, N.Y.	73.4	Walter Ray Williams, Eureka, Cal.	86.7
1972	Ruth Hangen, Buffalo, N.Y.	76.6	Walter Ray Williams, Eureka, Cal.	89.2
1973	Ruth Hangen, Getzville, N.Y.	79.6	Jeffrey Williams, Eureka, Cal.	85.5
1974	Lorraine Thomas, Lockport, N.Y.	80.2	Doug Kienia, Kittery, Me.	81.2
1975	Vicki Winston, Lamonte, Mo.	73.5	Walter Ray Williams, Auburn Cal.	86.6
1976	Ruth Hangen, Getzville, N.Y.	75.6	Jeffrey Williams, Auburn, Cal.	86.2

American Casting Assn. Combined Championships in 1976
Lexington, Ky., Aug. 9-14, 1976

(Distance plugs includes the 3 longest casts in 3 separate events — 3/8 oz. plug, 5/8 oz. plug, and 1 ounce plug. The 9 casts are added to determine the champion.

Men

Grand All Around — Steve Rajeff, San Francisco, Cal.
Anglers All Around — Steve Rajeff
All Accuracy — Steve Rajeff, 591 pts.
Distance Plugs — Terry Schneider, Jeffersonville, Ind., 3,682 ft.
Distance Flies — Steve Rajeff, 1,681 ft.
Accuracy Plugs — Steve Rajeff, 295 pts.
Accuracy Flies — Steve Rajeff, 296 pts.

Accuracy Flies — (tie) Pauline Cathcart, La Canada, Cal. and Molly Light, 273 pts.

Intermediates

All Accuracy — Bruce Rogers, St. Louis, Mo., 535 pts.
Accuracy Plugs — Bruce Rogers, 269 pts.
Accuracy Flies — Baker Burke, Jackson, Ky. 281 pts.

Women

All Accuracy — Molly Light, New Albany, Ind., 541 pts.
Accuracy Plugs — Molly Light, 268 pts.

Juniors

Accuracy Plugs — (tie) Devin Light, New Albany, Ind. and Mike Beck, St. Louis, Mo., 268 pts.

Power Boat Racing Champions
APBA Gold Cup Race

Year	Boat	Owner	Driver	Winner's fastest Heat	Site
1964	Miss Bardahl	Ole Bardahl	Ron Musson	108.104	Detroit, Mich.
1965	Miss Bardahl	Ole Bardahl	Ron Musson	110.655	Seattle, Wash.
1966	Tahoe Miss	Harrah's	Mira Slovak	97.861	Detroit, Mich.
1967	Miss Bardahl	Ole Bardahl	Bill Schumacher	104.691	Seattle, Wash.
1968	Miss Bardahl	Ole Bardahl	Bill Schumacher		Detroit, Mich.
1969	Miss Budweiser	Bernard Little & Tom Friedkin	Bill Sterett	103.587	San Diego, Cal.
1970	Miss Budweiser	Hydroplanes, Inc.	Dean Chenoweth	101.848	San Diego, Cal.
1971	Miss Madison	Miss Madison, Inc.	Jim McCormick	101.522	Madison, Ind.
1972	Atlas Van Lines	Atlas Van Lines	Bill Muncey	103.547	Detroit, Mich.
1973	Miss Budweiser	Hydroplanes, Inc.	Dean Chenoweth	104.046	Tri-Cities, Wash.
1974	Pay'N Pak	David J. Heerensperger	George Henley	112.056	Seattle, Wash.
1975	Pay 'N Pak	David J. Heerensperger	George Henley	113.350	Tri-Cities, Wash.
1976	Miss U.S.	U.S. Racing Team, Inc.	Tom D'Eath	108.021	Detroit, Mich.

1976 Little League World Series
Japan won the 1976 Little League World Series by defeating Campbell (Cal.) 10-3, at Williamsport, Pa.

College Basketball

National Invitation Tournament Champions

Year Champion	Year Champion	Year Champion	Year Champion
1938—Temple	1948—St. Louis	1958—Xavier (Ohio)	1968—Dayton
1939—Long Island Univ.	1949—San Francisco	1959—St. John's	1969—Temple
1940—Colorado	1950—CCNY	1960—Bradley	1970—Marquette
1941—Long Island Univ.	1951—Brigham Young	1961—Providence	1971—North Carolina
1942—West Virginia	1952—LaSalle	1962—Dayton	1972—Maryland
1943—St. John's	1953—Seton Hall	1963—Providence	1973—Virginia Tech
1944—St. John's	1954—Holy Cross	1964—Bradley	1974—Purdue
1945—DePaul	1955—Duquesne	1965—St. John's	1975—Princeton
1946—Kentucky	1956—Louisville	1966—Brigham Young	1976—Kentucky
1947—Utah	1957—Bradley	1967—Southern Illinois	

NCAA Division I Basketball Champions

Year Champion	Year Champion	Year Champion	Year Champion
1939—Oregon	1949—Kentucky	1958—Kentucky	1967—UCLA
1940—Indiana	1950—CCNY	1959—California	1968—UCLA
1941—Wisconsin	1951—Kentucky	1960—Ohio State	1969—UCLA
1942—Stanford	1952—Kansas	1961—Cincinnati	1970—UCLA
1943—Wyoming	1953—Indiana	1962—Cincinnati	1971—UCLA
1944—Utah	1954—La Salle	1963—Loyola (Chi.)	1972—UCLA
1945—Oklahoma A&M	1955—San Francisco	1964—UCLA	1973—UCLA
1946—Oklahoma A&M	1956—San Francisco	1965—UCLA	1974—No. Carolina State
1947—Holy Cross	1957—North Carolina	1966—Texas Western	1975—UCLA
1948—Kentucky			1976—Indiana

NCAA Division II Basketball Champions

Year Champion	Year Champion	Year Champion	Year Champion
1957—Wheaton	1962—Mt. St. Mary's	1967—Winston-Salem	1972—Roanoke
1958—South Dakota	1963—South Dakota St.	1968—Kentucky Wesleyan	1973—Kentucky Wesleyan
1959—Evansville	1964—Evansville	1969—Kentucky Wesleyan	1974—Morgan State
1960—Evansville	1965—Evansville	1970—Philadelphia Textile	1975—Old Dominion
1961—Wittenberg	1966—Kentucky Wesleyan	1971—Evansville	1976—Puget Sound

Major-College Records

(Restricted to games between four-year colleges.)

Career Scoring Averages

Player, Team	Last Year	Games	FG	FT	Pts.	Avg.
Pete Maravich, LSU	1970	83	1,387	893	3,667	44.2
Austin Carr, Notre Dame	1971	74	1,017	526	2,560	34.6
Oscar Robertson, Cincinnati	1960	88	1,052	869	2,973	33.8
Calvin Murphy, Niagara	1970	77	974	654	2,548	33.1
Frank Selvy, Furman	1954	78	922	694	2,538	32.5
Rick Mount, Purdue	1970	72	910	503	2,323	32.3
Darrell Floyd, Furman	1956	71	868	545	2,281	32.1
Nick Werkman, Seton Hall	1964	71	812	649	2,273	32.0
Willie Humes, Idaho St.	1971	48	565	380	1,510	31.5
Elgin Baylor, Col. Idaho-Seattle	1958	80	956	588	2,500	31.3
William Averitt, Pepperdine	1973	49	615	311	1,541	31.4
Dwight Lamar, SW Louisiana	1973	112	1,445	603	3,493	31.2
Elvin Hayes, Houston	1968	93	1,215	454	2,884	31.0
Bill Bradley, Princeton	1965	83	856	791	2,503	30.2

Season Averages

Player, Team	Year	Games	FG	FT	Pts.	Avg.
Pete Maravich, LSU	1970	31	522	337	1,381	44.5
Pete Maravich, LSU	1969	26	433	282	1,148	44.2
Pete Maravich, LSU	1968	26	432	274	1,138	43.8
Frank Selvy, Furman	1954	29	427	355	1,209	41.7
Johnny Neumann, Mississippi	1971	23	366	191	923	40.1
Billy McGill, Utah	1962	26	394	221	1,009	38.8
Calvin Murphy, Niagara	1968	24	337	242	916	38.2
Austin Carr, Notre Dame	1970	29	444	218	1,106	38.1
Austin Carr, Notre Dame	1971	29	430	241	1,101	38.0
Rick Barry, Miami (Fla.)	1965	26	340	293	973	37.4

Single-Game Scoring

Player, Team (Opponent)	Year	Pts.	Player, Team (Opponent)	Year	Pts.
Selvy, Furman (Newberry)	1954	100	Floyd, Furman (Morehead St.)	1955	67
Mlkvy, Temple (Wilkes)	1951	73	Maravich, LSU (Tulane)	1969	66
Maravich, LSU (Alabama)	1970	69	Handlan, W. & Lee (Furman)	1951	66
Murphy, Niagara (Syracuse)	1969	68	Zawoluk, St. John's (St. Peter's)	1950	65

Individual Records, Season

Field Goal Percentage	Alcindor, UCLA, 1967	.667	Rebounds Per Game	Slack, Marshall, 1955	25.6
	Martens, Ab. Christian, 1972	.667	Rebounds	Dukes, Seton Hall, 1953	734
	Fleming, Airzona, 1974	.667	Field Goals Attempted	Maravich, LSU, 1970	1,168
Free Throw Percentage	Boyer, Arkansas, 1962	.993	Free Throws Attempted	Selvy, Furman, 1954	444

Auto Racing
Indianapolis 500 Winners

Year	Winner	Chassis	Engine	MPH	Gross	Runner up
1946	George Robson	Adams	Sparks	114,820	$115,450	Jimmy Jackson
1947	Mauri Rose	Deidt	Offenhauser	116.338	137,425	Bill Holland
1948	Mauri Rose	Deidt	Offenhauser	119.814	171,075	Bill Holland
1949	Bill Holland	Deidt	Offenhauser	121.327	179,050	Johnnie Parsons
1950	Johnnie Parsons	Kurtis Kraft	Offenhauser	124.002(a)	201,135	Bill Holland
1951	Lee Wallard	Kurtis Kraft	Offenhauser	126.244	207,650	Mike Nazaruk
1952	Troy Ruttman	Kuzma	Offenhauser	128.922	230,100	Jim Rathmann
1953	Bill Vukovich	Kurtis Kraft 500A	Offenhauser	128.740	246,300	Art Cross
1954	Bill Vukovich	Kurtis Kraft 500A	Offenhauser	130.840	269,375	Jim Bryan
1955	Bob Sweikert	Kurtis Kraft 500C	Offenhauser	128.209	270,400	Tony Bettenhausen
1956	Pat Flaherty	Watson	Offenhauser	128.490	282,052	Sam Hanks
1957	Sam Hanks	Epperly	Offenhauser	135.601	300,252	Jim Rathmann
1958	Jimmy Bryan	Epperly	Offenhauser	133.791	305,217	George Amick
1959	Rodger Ward	Watson	Offenhauser	135.857	338,100	Jim Rathmann
1960	Jim Rathmann	Watson	Offenhauser	138.767	369,150	Rodger Ward
1961	A. J. Foyt	Watson	Offenhauser	139.130	400,000	Eddie Sachs
1962	Rodger Ward	Watson	Offenhauser	140.293	426,152	Len Sutton
1963	Parnelli Jones	Watson	Offenhauser	143.137	494,031	Jim Clark
1964	A. J. Foyt	Watson	Offenhauser	147.350	506,625	Rodger Ward
1965	Jim Clark	Lotus	Ford	151.388	628,399	Parnelli Jones
1966	Graham Hill	Lola	Ford	144.317	691,809	Jim Clark
1967	A. J. Foyt	Coyote	Ford	151.207	737,109	Al Unser
1968	Bobby Unser	Eagle	Offenhauser	152.882	809,627	Dan Gurney
1969	Mario Andretti	Hawk	Ford	156.867	805,127	Dan Gurney
1970	Al Unser	P. J. Colt	Ford	155.749	1,000,002	Mark Donohue
1971	Al Unser	P. J. Colt	Ford	157.735	1,001,604	Peter Revson
1972	Mark Donohue	McLaren	Offenhauser	163.465	1,011,846	Al Unser
1973	Gordon Johncock	Eagle	Offenhauser	159.014 (b)	1,011,846	Billy Vukovich
1974	Johnny Rutherford	McLaren	Offenhauser	158.589	1,015,686	Bobby Unser
1975	Bobby Unser	Eagle	Offenhauser	149.213(c)	1,101,322	Johnny Rutherford
1976	Johnny Rutherford	McLaren	Offenhauser	148.725 (d)	1,037,775	A.J. Foyt

(a) 345 miles. (b) 332.5 miles. (c) 435 miles. (d) 255 miles. Race Record—163.465 MPH, Mark Donohue, 1972.

1976 Indianapolis 500 Final Standings

1—Johnny Rutherford, Fort Worth, Tex., McLaren-Offy, 102 laps, 148.725 miles per hour.

2—A. J. Foyt Jr., Houston Tex., Coyote-Foyt, 102 laps, 148.354.

3—Gordon Johncock, Phoenix, Ariz., Wildcat-DGS, 102 laps, 146.238.

4—Wally Dallenbach, Basalt, Col., Wildcat-DGS, 101 laps, 147.156.

5—Duane Pancho Carter, Brownsburg, Ind., Eagle-Offy, 101 laps, 147.134.

6—Tom Sneva, Spokane, Wash., McLaren-Offy, 101 laps, 146.830.

7—Al Unser, Albuquerque, N.M., Parnelli-Cosworth, 101 laps, 145.578.

8—Mario Andretti, Nazareth, Pa., McLaren-Offy, 101 laps, 144.652.

9—Salt Walther, Dayton, Ohio, McLaren-Offy, 100 laps, 144.492.

10—Bobby Unser, Albuquerque, N.M., Eagle-Offy, 100 laps, 144.235.

World's Land Speed Records—Evolution of the Mile Record

Date	Driver	Car	MPH	Date	Driver	Car	MPH
12/18/98	Chassenloup-Laubat	Jeantaud	39.24	4/22/28	Keech	White Triplex	207.552
4/29/99	Jenatzy	Jamais Contente Jenatzy	65.79	3/11/29	Seagrave	Irving-Napier	231.446
				2/ 5/31	Campbell	Napier-Campbell	246.086
11/17/02	Augieres	Mars	77.13	2/24/32	Campbell	Napier-Campbell	253.96
11/ 5/03	Duray	Gabron-Brillie	84.73	2/22/33	Campbell	Napier-Campbell	272.109
12/30/04	Barras	Darracq	109.65	9/ 3/35	Campbell	Bluebird Spl.	301.13
1/25/05	Bowden	Mercedes	109.75	11/19/37	Eyston	Thunderbolt 1	311.42
1/26/06	Marriott	Stanley (Steam)	127.659	9/16/38	Eyston	Thunderbolt 1	357.5
3/16/10	Oldfield	Benz	131.724	8/23/39	Cobb	Railton	368.9
4/23/11	Burman	Benz	141.732	9/16/47	Cobb	Railton-Mobil	394.2
2/12/19	DePalma	Packard	149.875	8/ 5/63	Breedlove	Spirit of America	407.45
4/27/20	Milton	Dusenberg	155.046	10/27/64	Arfons	Green Monster	536.71
4/28/26	Parry-Thomas	Thomas Spl.	170.624	11/15/65	Breedlove	Spirit of America	600.601
3/29/27	Seagrave	Sunbeam	203.790	10/23/70	Gary Gabelich	Blue Flame	622.407

World Grand Prix Champions

Year	Driver	Year	Driver	Year	Driver
1950	Nino Farina, Italy	1959	Jack Brabham, Australia	1967	Denis Hulme, New Zealand
1951	Juan Fangio, Argentina	1960	Jack Brabham, Australia	1968	Graham Hill, England
1952	Alberto Ascari, Italy	1961	Phil Hill, United States	1969	Jackie Stewart, Scotland
1953	Alberto Ascari, Italy	1962	Graham Hill, England	1970	Jochen Rindt, Austria
1954	Juan Fangio, Argentina	1963	Jim Clark, Scotland	1971	Jackie Stewart, Scotland
1955	Juan Fangio, Argentina	1964	John Surtees, England	1972	Emerson Fittipaldi, Brazil
1956	Juan Fangio, Argentina	1965	Jim Clark, Scotland	1973	Jackie Stewart, Scotland
1957	Juan Fangio, Argentina	1966	Jack Brabham, Australia	1974	Emerson Fittipaldi, Brazil
1958	Mike Hawthorne, England			1975	Nicki Lauda, Austria

U.S. Auto Club National Champions

Year	Driver	Year	Driver	Year	Driver	Year	Driver
1952	Chuck Stevenson	1958	Tony Bettenhausen	1964	A. J. Foyt	1970	Al Unser
1953	Sam Hawks	1959	Rodger Ward	1965	Mario Andretti	1971	Joe Leonard
1954	Jimmy Bryan	1960	A. J. Foyt	1966	Mario Andretti	1972	Joe Leonard
1955	Bob Sweikert	1961	A. J. Foyt	1967	A. J. Foyt	1973	Roger McCluskey
1956	Jimmy Bryan	1962	Rodger Ward	1968	Bobby Unser	1974	Bobby Unser
1957	Jimmy Bryan	1963	A. J. Foyt	1969	Mario Andretti	1975	A. J. Foyt

Grand Prix for Formula 1 Cars, 1976

Grand Prix	Winner, Car	Grand Prix	Winner, Car
Austrian	John Watson, Penske	Monte Carlo	Niki Lauda, Ferrari
Belgian	Niki Lauda, Ferrari	South African	Niki Lauda, Ferrari
British	Niki Lauda, Ferrari	Spanish	James Hunt, McLaren
Brazilian	Niki Lauda, Ferrari	Swedish	Jody Scheckter, Tyrrell
Dutch	James Hunt, McLaren	United States	James Hunt, McLaren
French	James Hunt, McLaren	United States (west)	Clay Regazzoni, Ferrari
Italian	Ronnie Peterson, March Ford	West German	James Hunt, McLaren

NASCAR Racing in 1976

Winston Cup Grand National Races

Date	Race and Site	Winner	Car	Money Won
Jan. 18	Winston Western 500, Riverside, Cal.	David Pearson	Mercury	$17,295
Feb. 15	Daytona 500, Daytona Beach, Fla.	David Pearson	Mercury	46,800
Feb. 29	Carolina 500, Rockingham, N.C.	Richard Petty	Dodge	19,915
Mar. 7	Richmond 400, Richmond, Va.	Dave Marcis	Dodge	9,300
Mar. 14	Southeastern 400, Bristol, Tenn.	Cale Yarborough	Chevrolet	18,070
Mar. 21	Atlanta 500, Atlanta, Ga.	David Pearson	Mercury	11,700
Apr. 4	Gwyn Staley 400, N. Wilkesboro, N.C.	Cale Yarborough	Chevrolet	10,075
Apr. 11	Rebel 500, Darlington, S.C.	David Pearson	Mercury	11,670
Apr. 25	Virginia 500, Martinsville, Va.	Darrell Waltrip	Chevrolet	20,950
May 2	Winston 500, Talladega, Ala.	Buddy Baker	Ford	25,285
May 8	Music City USA 420, Nashville, Tenn.	Cale Yarborough	Chevrolet	7,365
May 16	Mason-Dixon 500, Dover, Del.	Benny Parsons	Chevrolet	14,015
May 30	World 600, Charlotte, N.C.	David Pearson	Mercury	42,390
June 13	Riverside 400, Riverside, Cal.	David Pearson	Mercury	11,820
June 20	Cam2 Motor Oil 400, Brooklyn, Mich.	David Pearson	Mercury	11,295
July 4	Firecracker 400, Daytona Beach, Fla.	Cale Yarborough	Chevrolet	14,715
July 17	Nashville 420, Nashville, Tenn.	Benny Parsons	Chevrolet	7,217
Aug. 1	Purolator 500, Mt. Pocono, Pa.	Richard Petty	Dodge	15,290
Aug. 8	Talladega 500, Talladega, Ala.	Dave Marcis	Dodge	21,310
Aug. 22	Champion Spark Plug 400, Brooklyn, Mich.	David Pearson	Mercury	11,950
Aug. 29	Volunteer 400, Bristol, Tenn.	Cale Yarborough	Chevrolet	8,950
Sept. 6	Southern 500, Darlington, S.C.	David Pearson	Mercury	16,155
Sept. 12	Capital City 400, Richmond, Va.	Cale Yarborough	Chevrolet	9,250
Sept. 19	Delaware 500, Dover, Del.	Cale Yarborough	Chevrolet	14,300

Daytona 500 Winners

Year	Driver (Car)	Avg. MPH	Year	Driver (Car)	Avg. MPH
1961	Marvin Panch (Pontiac)	149.601	1969	Lee Roy Yarborough (Ford)	160.875
1962	Fireball Roberts (Pontiac)	152.529	1970	Pete Hamilton (Plymouth)	149.601
1963	Tiny Lund (Ford)	151.566	1971	Richard Petty (Plymouth)	144.456
1964	Richard Petty (Plymouth)	154.334	1972	A. J. Foyt (Mercury)	161.550
(a) 1965	Fred Lorenzen (Ford)	141.539	1973	Richard Petty (Dodge)	157.205
(b) 1966	Richard Petty (Plymouth)	160.627	(c) 1974	Richard Petty (Dodge)	140.894
1967	Mario Andretti (Ford)	146.926	1975	Benny Parsons (Chevrolet)	153.649
1968	Cale Yarborough (Mercury)	143.251	1976	David Pearson (Mercury)	152.181

(a)322.5 miles because of rain. (b)495 miles because of rain.(c)450 miles.

1976 Leading Daytona 500 Finishers

Driver, Car	Laps	Purse	Driver, Car	Laps	Purse
1—David Pearson, Mercury	200	$46,800	5—Neil Bonnett, Chevrolet	197	$14,000
2—Richard Petty, Dodge	199	35,750	6—Terry Ryan, Chevrolet	196	13,800
3—Benny Parsons, Chevrolet	199	23,680	7—J. D. McDuffie, Chevrolet	193	11,260
4—Lennie Pond, Chevrolet	198	16,890	8—Terry Bivins, Chevrolet	193	9,665

Grand National Champions (NASCAR)

Year	Driver	Year	Driver	Year	Driver	Year	Driver
1951	Herb Thomas	1958	Lee Petty	1964	Richard Petty	1970	Bobby Isaac
1952	Tim Flock	1959	Lee Petty	1965	Ned Jarrett	1971	Richard Petty
1953	Herb Thomas	1960	Rex White	1966	David Pearson	1972	Richard Petty
1954	Lee Petty	1961	Ned Jarrett	1967	Richard Petty	1973	Benny Parsons
1955	Tim Flock	1962	Joe Weatherly	1968	David Pearson	1974	Richard Petty
1956	Buck Baker	1963	Joe Weatherly	1969	David Pearson	1975	Richard Petty
1957	Buck Baker						

World Team Tennis

Final Standings

Eastern Division	W.	L.	Pct.	GB	Western Division	W.	L.	Pct.	GB
New York	33	10	.767	—	Phoenix	30	14	.682	—
Pittsburgh	24	20	.545	9 1/2	Golden Gaters	28	16	.636	2
Cleveland	20	24	.455	13 1/2	Los Angeles	22	22	.500	8
Indiana	19	25	.432	14 1/2	San Diego	13	31	.295	17
Boston	18	25	.419	15	Hawaii	12	32	.273	18

Playoff Winner — New York.

USTA National Champions

Men's Singles

Year	Champion	Final Opponent	Year	Champion	Final Opponent
1920	Bill Tilden	William Johnston	1949	Pancho Gonzales	F. R. Schroeder Jr.
1921	Bill Tilden	Wallace Johnston	1950	Arthur Larsen	Herbert Flam
1922	Bill Tilden	William Johnston	1951	Frank Sedgman	E. Victor Seixas Jr.
1923	Bill Tilden	William Johnston	1952	Frank Sedgman	Gardnar Mulloy
1924	Bill Tilden	William Johnston	1953	Tony Trabert	E. Victor Seixas Jr.
1925	Bill Tilden	William Johnston	1954	E. Victor Seixas, Jr.	Rex Hartwig
1926	Rene Lacoste	Jean Borotra	1955	Tony Trabert	Ken Rosewall
1927	Rene Lacoste	Bill Tilden	1956	Kenneth Rosewall	Lewis Hoad
1928	Henri Cochet	Francis Hunter	1957	Malcolm Anderson	Ashley Cooper
1929	Bill Tilden	Francis Hunter	1958	Ashley Cooper	Malcolm Anderson
1930	John Doeg	Francis Shields	1959	Neale A. Fraser	Alejandro Olmedo
1931	H. Ellsworth Vines	George Lott	1960	Neale A. Fraser	Rod Laver
1932	H. Ellsworth Vines	Henri Cochet	1961	Roy Emerson	Rod Laver
1933	Fred Perry	John Crawford	1962	Rod Laver	Roy Emerson
1934	Fred Perry	Wilmer Allison	1963	Rafael Osuna	F. A. Froehling 3d
1935	Wilmer Allison	Sidney Wood	1964	Roy Emerson	Fred Stolle
1936	Fred Perry	Don Budge	1965	Manuel Santana	Cliff Drysdale
1937	Don Budge	Baron G. von Cramm	1966	Fred Stolle	John Newcombe
1938	Don Budge	C. Gene Mako	1967	John Newcombe	Clark Graebner
1939	Robert Riggs	S. Welby Van Horn	1968	Arthur Ashe	Tom Okker
1940	Don McNeill	Robert Riggs	1969	Rod Laver	Tony Roche
1941	Robert Riggs	F. L. Kovacs	1970	Ken Rosewall	Tony Roche
1942	F. R. Schroeder Jr.	Frank Parker	1971	Stan Smith	Jan Kodes
1943	Joseph Hunt	Jack Kramer	1972	Ilie Nastase	Arthur Ashe
1944	Frank Parker	William Talbert	1973	John Newcombe	Jan Kodes
1945	Frank Parker	William Talbert	1974	Jimmy Connors	Ken Rosewall
1946	Jack Kramer	Thomas Brown Jr.	1975	Manuel Orantes	Jimmy Connors
1947	Jack Kramer	Frank Parker	1976	Jimmy Connors	Bjorn Borg
1948	Pancho Gonzales	Eric Sturgess			

Men's Doubles

Year	Doubles Champions	Year	Doubles Champions
1920	William Johnston and Clarence Griffin	1949	John Bromwich and William Sidwell
1921	Bill Tilden and Vincent Richards	1950	John Bromwich and Frank Sedgman
1922	Bill Tilden and Vincent Richards	1951	Frank Sedgman and Kenneth McGregor
1923	Bill Tilden and Brian Norton	1952	Mervyn Rose and E. Victor Seixas Jr.
1924	Howard Kinsey and Robert Kinsey	1953	Rex Hartwig and Mervyn Rose
1925	R. Norris Williams and Vincent Richards	1954	E. Victor Seixas, Jr. and Tony Trabert
1926	R. Norris Williams and Vincent Richards	1955	Kosei Kamo and Atsushi Miyagi
1927	Bill Tilden and Francis Hunter	1956	Lewis Hoad and Kenneth Rosewall
1928	George Lott and John Hennessey	1957	Ashley Cooper and Neale Fraser
1929	George Lott and John Doeg	1958	Hamilton Richardson and Alejandro Olmedo
1930	George Lott and John Doeg	1959	Neale A. Fraser and Roy Emerson
1931	Wilmer Allison and John Van Ryn	1960	Neale A. Fraser and Roy Emerson
1932	H. Ellsworth Vines and Keith Gledhill	1961	Dennis Ralston and Chuck McKinley
1933	George Lott and Lester Stoefen	1962	Rafael Osuna and Antonio Palafox
1934	George Lott and Lester Stoefen	1963	Dennis Ralston and Chuck McKinley
1935	Wilmer Allison and John Van Ryn	1964	Dennis Ralston and Chuck McKinley
1936	Don Budge and C. Gene Mako	1965	Roy Emerson and Fred Stolle
1937	Baron G. von Cramm and Henner Henkel	1966	Roy Emerson and Fred Stolle
1938	Don Budge and C. Gene Mako	1967	John Newcombe and Tony Roche
1939	Adrian Quist and John Bromwich	1968	Robert Lutz and Stan Smith
1940	Jack Kramer and Frederick Schroeder Jr.	1969	Fred Stolle and Ken Rosewall
1941	Jack Kramer and Frederick Schroeder Jr.	1970	Pierre Barthes and Nicki Pilic
1942	Gardnar Mulloy and William Talbert	1971	John Newcombe and Roger Taylor
1943	Jack Kramer and Frank Parker	1972	Cliff Drysdale and Roger Taylor
1944	Don McNeill and Robert Falkenburg	1973	John Newcombe and Owen Davidson
1945	Gardnar Mulloy and William Talbert	1974	Bob Lutz and Stan Smith
1946	Gardnar Mulloy and William Talbert	1975	Jimmy Connors and Ilie Nastase
1947	Jack Kramer and Frederick Schroeder Jr.	1976	Marty Riessen and Tom Okker
1948	Gardnar Mulloy and William Talbert		

Mens Indoor Champions

Year	Singles	Doubles	Year	Singles	Doubles
1965	Jan Erik Lundquist	D. Ralston-C. McKinley	1971	Clark Graebner	Juan Gisbert-Manuel Orantes
1966	Charles Pasarell	Robert Lutz-Stan Smith	1972	Stan Smith	Andres Gimeno-Manuel Orantes
1967	Charles Pasarell	Arthur Ashe-Charles Pasarell	1973	Jimmy Connors	Juan Gisbert-Jurgen Fassbender
1968	Cliff Richey	Thomas Koch-Tom Okker	1974	Jimmy Connors	Jimmy Connors-Frew McMillan
1969	Stan Smith	Stan Smith-Robert Lutz	1975	Jimmy Connors	Jimmy Connors-Ilie Nastase
1970	Ilie Nastase	Stan Smith-Arthur Ashe	1976	Ilie Nastase	Sherwood Stewart-Fred McNair

Women's Indoor Champions

Year	Singles	Doubles	Year	Singles	Doubles
1963	Carol Hanks	Carol Hanks & Mary Ann Eisel	1969	Mary Ann E. Curtis	Mary Ann Eisel & Valerie Ziegenfuss
1964	Mary Ann Eisel	Mary Ann Eisel & Katharine Hubbell			
1965	Nancy Richey	Carol Hanks Aucamp & Mary Ann Eisel	1970	Mary Ann E. Curtis	Peaches Bartkowicz & Nancy Richey
1966	Billie Jean King	Billlie Jean King & Rosemary Casals	1971	Billie Jean King	Billie Jean King & Rosemary Casals
			1972	Virginia Wade	Rosemary Casals & Virginia Wade
1967	Billie Jean King	Carol Hanks Aucamp & Mary Ann Eisel	1973	Evonne Goolagong	Olga Morozova & Marina Kroskina
			1974	Billie Jean King	None
1968	Billie Jean King	Billie Jean King & Rosemary Casals	1975	Martina Nauratilova	Billie Jean King & Rosemary Casals
			1976	Virginia Wade	Francoise Durr & Rosemary Casals

Women's Singles, Doubles, Mixed Doubles

Year	Singles Champions	Doubles Champions	Mixed Doubles Champions
1935	Helen Jacobs	Helen Jacobs & Mrs. Sarah P. Fabyan	Mrs. Sarah P. Fabyan & Enrique Maier
1936	Alice Marble	Mrs. M. G. Van Ryn & Carolin Babcock	Alice Marble & C. Gene Mako
1937	Anita Lizana	Mrs. Sarah P. Fabyan & Alice Marble	Mrs. Sarah P. Fabyan & Don Budge
1938	Alice Marble	Alice Marble & Mrs. Sarah P. Fabyan	Alice Marble & Don Budge
1939	Alice Marble	Alice Marble & Mrs. Sarah P. Fabyan	Alice Marble & Harry Hopman
1940	Alice Marble	Alice Marble & Mrs. Sarah P. Fabyan	Alice Marble & Robert Riggs
1941	Mrs. Sarah P. Cooke	Mrs. S. P. Cooke & Margaret Osborne	Mrs. Sarah P. Cooke & Jack Kramer
1942	Pauline Betz	A. Louise Brough & Margaret Osborne	A. Louise Brough & Frederick Schroeder
1943	Pauline Betz	A. Louise Brough & Margaret Osborne	Margaret Osborne & William Talbert
1944	Pauline Betz	A. Louise Brough & Margaret Osborne	Margaret Osborne & William Talbert
1945	Sarah P. Cooke	A. Louise Brough & Margaret Osborne	Margaret Osborne & William Talbert
1946	Pauline Betz	A. Louise Brough & Margaret Osborne	Margaret Osborne & William Talbert
1947	A. Louise Brough	A. Louise Brough & Margaret Osborne	A. Louise Brough & John Bromwich
1948	Mrs. Margaret O. du Pont	A. Louise Brough & Mrs. M. O. du Pont	A. Louise Brough & Thomas Brown Jr.
1949	Mrs. Margaret O. du Pont	A. Louise Brough & Mrs. M. O. du Pont	A. Louise Brough & Eric Sturgess
1950	Mrs. Margaret O. du Pont	A. Louise Brough & Mrs. M. O. du Pont	Mrs. M. O. du Pont & Kenneth MacGregor
1951	Maureen Connolly	Doris Hart & Shirley Fry	Doris Hart & Frank Sedgman
1952	Maureen Connolly	Doris Hart & Shirley Fry	Doris Hart & Frank Sedgman
1953	Maureen Connolly	Doris Hart & Shirley Fry	Doris Hart & E. Victor Seixas Jr.
1954	Doris Hart	Doris Hart & Shirley Fry	Doris Hart & E. Victor Seixas Jr.
1955	Doris Hart	A. Louise Brough & Mrs. M. O. du Pont	Doris Hart & E. Victor Seixas Jr.
1956	Shirley J. Fry	A. Louise Brough & Mrs. M. O. du Pont	Mrs. M. O. du Pont & Kenneth Rosewall
1957	Althea Gibson	A. Louise Brough & Mrs. M. O. du Pont	Althea Gibson and Kurt Nielsen
1958	Althea Gibson	Darlene Hard & Jeanne Arth	Mrs. M. O. du Pont & Neale Fraser
1959	Maria Bueno	Darlene Hard & Jeanne Arth	Mrs. M. O. du Pont & Neale Fraser
1960	Darlene Hard	Darlene Hard & Maria Bueno	Mrs. M. O. du Pont & Neale Fraser
1961	Darlene Hard	Darlene Hard & Lesley Turner	Margaret Smith & Robert Mark
1962	Margaret Smith	Maria Bueno & Darlene Hard	Margaret Smith & Fred Stolle
1963	Maria Bueno	Margaret Smith & Robyn Ebbern	Margaret Smith & Kenneth Fletcher
1964	Maria Bueno	Billie Jean Moffit & Karen Susman	Margaret Smith & John Newcombe
1965	Margaret Smith	Carole C. Graebner & Nancy Richey	Margaret Smith & Fred Stolle
1966	Maria Bueno	Maria Bueno & Nancy Richey	Donna Floyd Fales & Owen Davidson
1967	Billie Jean King	Rosemary Casals & Billie Jean King	Billie Jean King & Owen Davidson
1968	Virginia Wade	Maria Bueno & Margaret S. Court	Mary Ann Eisel & Peter Curtis
1969	Margaret Smith Court	Francoise Durr & Darlene Hard	Margaret S. Court & Marty Riessen
1970	Margaret Smith Court	M. S. Court & Judy Tegart Dalton	Margaret S. Court & Marty Riessen
1971	Billie Jean King	Rosemary Casals & Judy Tegart Dalton	Billie Jean King & Owen Davidson
1972	Billie Jean King	Francoise Durr & Betty Stove	Margaret S. Court & Marty Riessen
1973	Margaret Smith Court	Margaret S. Court & Virginia Wade	Billie Jean King & Owen Davidson
1974	Billie Jean King	Billie Jean King & Rosemary Casals	Pam Teeguarden & Geoff Masters
1975	Chris Evert	Margaret Court & Virginia Wade	Rosemary Casals & Dick Stockton
1976	Chris Evert	Linky Boshoff & Ilana Kloss	Billie Jean King & Phil Dent

NCAA Tennis Champions

Year	Singles	College	Doubles	College
1966	Charles Pasarell	UCLA	Charles Pasarell & Ian Crookenden	UCLA
1967	Bob Lutz	USC	Stan Smith & Bob Lutz	USC
1968	Stan Smith	USC	Stan Smith & Bob Lutz	USC
1969	Joaquin Loyo Mayo	USC	Joaquin Loyo Mayo & Marcelo Lara	USC
1970	Jeff Borowiak	UCLA	Pat Cramer & Luis Garcia	Miami (Fla.)
1971	Jimmy Connors	UCLA	Jeff Borowiak & Haroon Rahim	UCLA
1972	Dick Stockton	Trinity (Tex.)	Sandy Mayer & Roscoe Tanner	Stanford
1973	Sandy Mayer	Stanford	Sandy Mayer & Jim Delaney	Stanford
1974	John Whitlinger	Stanford	John Whitlinger & Jim Delaney	Stanford
1975	Billy Martin	UCLA	Butch Walts & Bruce Manson	USC
1976	Bill Scanlon	Trinity	Peter Fleming & Ferdi Taygan	UCLA

Clay Court Champions

Year	Champion	Year	Champion	Year	Champion	Year	Champion
1953	E. Vic Seixas Jr.	1959	Bernard Bartzen	1965	Dennis Ralston	1971	Zeljko Franulovic
1954	Bernard Bartzen	1960	Barry MacKay	1966	Cliff Richey	1972	Bob Hewitt
1955	Tony Trabert	1961	Bernard Bartzen	1967	Arthur Ashe	1973	Manuel Orantes
1956	Herbert Flam	1962	Chuck McKinley	1968	Clark Graebner	1974	Jimmy Connors
1957	E. Victor Seixas, Jr.	1963	Chuck McKinley	1969	Zeljko Franulovic	1975	Manuel Orantes
1958	Bernard Bartzen	1964	Dennis Ralston	1970	Cliff Richey	1976	Jimmy Connors

British (Wimbledon) Champions
Inaugurated 1877

Year	Men's Singles	Women's Singles	Year	Men's Singles	Women's Singles
1946	Yvon Petra	Pauline Betz	1962	Rod Laver	Karen Hantze Susman
1947	Jack Kramer	Margaret Osborne	1963	Chuck McKinley	Margaret Smith
1948	Bob Falkenburg	A. Louise Brough	1964	Roy Emerson	Maria Bueno
1949	Fred R. Schroeder	A. Louise Brough	1965	Roy Emerson	Margaret Smith
1950	Budge Patty	A. Louise Brough	1966	Manuel Santana	Billie Jean King
1951	Dick Savitt	Doris Hart	1967	John Newcombe	Billie Jean King
1952	Frank Sedgman	Maureen Connolly	1968	Rod Laver	Billie Jean King
1953	Victor Seixas	Maureen Connolly	1969	Rod Laver	Ann Jones
1954	Jaroslav Drobny	Maureen Connolly	1970	John Newcombe	Margaret S. Court
1955	Tony Trabert	A. Louise Brough	1971	John Newcombe	Evonne Goolagong
1956	Lewis Hoad	Shirley Fry	1972	Stan Smith	Billie Jean King
1957	Lewis Hoad	Althea Gibson	1973	Jan Kodes	Billie Jean King
1958	Ashley Cooper	Althea Gibson	1974	Jimmy Connors	Chris Evert
1959	Alex Olmedo	Maria Bueno	1975	Arthur Ashe	Billie Jean King
1960	Neale Fraser	Maria Bueno	1976	Bjorn Borg	Chris Evert
1961	Rod Laver	Angela Mortimer			

Davis Cup International Tennis—Challenge Round

Year	Winner	Loser	Score	Year	Winner	Loser	Score	Year	Winner	Loser	Score
1900	U.S.	Brit. Isles	3-0	1928	France	U.S.	4-1	1954	U.S.	Australia	3-2
1902	U.S.	Brit. Isles	3-2	1929	France	U.S.	3-2	1955	Australia	U.S.	5-0
1903	British	U.S.	4-1	1930	France	U.S.	4-1	1956	Australia	U.S.	5-0
1904	British	Belgium	5-0	1931	France	Gt. Britain	3-2	1957	Australia	U.S.	3-2
1905	British	U.S.	5-0	1932	France	U.S.	3-2	1958	U.S.	Australia	3-2
1906	British	U.S.	5-0	1933	Gt. Britain	France	3-2	1959	Australia	U.S.	3-2
1907	Australasia	British	3-2	1934	Gt. Britain	U.S.	4-1	1960	Australia	Italy	4-1
1908	Australasia	U.S.	3-2	1935	Gt. Britain	U.S.	5-0	1961	Australia	Italy	5-0
1909	Australasia	U.S.	5-0	1936	Gt. Britain	Australia	3-2	1962	Australia	Mexico	5-0
1911	Australasia	U.S.	5-0	1937	U.S.	Gt. Britain	4-1	1963	U.S.	Australia	3-2
1912	British	Australasia	3-2	1938	U.S.	Australia	3-2	1964	Australia	U.S.	3-2
1913	U.S.	British	3-2	1939	Australia	U.S.	3-2	1965	Australia	Spain	4-1
1914	Australasia	U.S.	3-2	1940-1945 (Not played)				1966	Australia	India	4-1
1919	Australasia	British	4-1	1946	U.S.	Australia	5-0	1967	Australia	Spain	4-1
1920	U.S.	Australasia	5-0	1947	U.S.	Australia	4-1	1968	U.S.	Australia	4-1
1921	U.S.	Japan	5-0	1948	U.S.	Australia	5-0	1969	U.S.	Romania	5-0
1922	U.S.	Australasia	4-1	1949	U.S.	Australia	4-1	1970	U.S.	W. Germany	5-0
1923	U.S.	Australasia	4-1	1950	Australia	U.S.	4-1	1971	U.S.	Romania	3-2
1924	U.S.	Australasia	5-0	1951	Australia	U.S.	3-2	1972	U.S.	Romania	3-2
1925	U.S.	France	5-0	1952	Australia	U.S.	4-1	1973	Australia	U.S.	5-0
1926	U.S.	France	4-1	1953	Australia	U.S.	3-2	1974	S. Africa	India (default)	
1927	France	U.S.	3-2					1975	Sweden	Czech.	3-2

National Junior Tennis Champions

Boys' 18 Singles
1970	Brian Gottfried
1971	Raul Ramirez
1972	Patrick DuPre
1973	Billy Martin
1974	Ferd Taygan
1975	Howard Schoenfield
1976	Larry Gottfried

Girls' 18 Singles
1970	Sharon Walsh
1971	Chris Evert
1972	Ann Kiyomura
1973	Carrie Fleming
1974	Rayni Fox
1975	Beth Norton
1976	Lynn Epstein

Boys' 18 Doubles
1970	Brian Gottfried and Alex Mayer, Jr.
1971	Jim Delaney and Chip Fisher
1972	Steve Mott and Brian Teachar
1973	Billy Martin and Trey Waitke
1974	Francisco Gonzalez and Rocky Maguire
1975	Larry Gottfried and John McEnroe
1976	Larry Gottfried and John McEnroe

Girls' 18 Doubles
1970	Kristien Kemmer and Nancy Ornstein
1971	Janet Newberry and Eliza Pande
1972	Marita Redondo and Laurie Tenney
1973	Susan Boyle and Kathy May
1974	Anne Bruning and Barbara Hallquist
1975	Lea Antonoplis and Berta McCallum
1976	Sherry Acker and Anne Smith

Boys' 16 Singles
1970	Freddy DeJesus
1971	Billy Martin
1972	Bill Maze
1973	Ben McKnown
1974	Walter Redondo
1975	Larry Gottfried
1976	Tim Wilkison

Girls' 16 Singles
1970	Chris Evert
1971	Carrie Fleming
1972	Marita Redondo
1973	Betsy Nagelson
1974	Zenda Leiss
1975	Lea Antonoplis
1976	Peanut Louie

Boys' 16 Doubles
1970	Freddy DeJesus and John Whitinger
1971	Billy Martin and Trey Waitke
1972	Bruce Manson and Perry Wright
1973	Nial Brash and Matt Mitchell
1974	Jeff Robbins and Van Winitsky
1975	Tony Giammalua and Billy Scanlon
1976	Murray Robinson and Tim Wilkison

Girls' 16 Doubles
1970	Barbara Downs and Ann Kiyomura
1971	Ann Kiyomura and Marita Redondo
1972	Jeanne Evert and Kathy Kendall
1973	Susan Mehmedbasich and Robin Tenney
1974	Sherry Acker and Anne Smith
1975	Lea Antonoplis and Berta McCallum
1976	Lucia Fernandez and Trey Lewis

Tennis Championships in 1976

Australian Open (Melbourne) — Men's Singles: Mark Edmondson d. John Newcombe 6-7, 6-3, 7-6, 6-1; Men's Doubles: Newcombe-Roche d. Case-Masters 7-6, 6-4; Women's Singles: Evonne Goolagong d. Renata Tomanova 6-2, 6-2; Women's Doubles: Goolagong-Gourlay d. Tomanova-Bowrey 8-1 (pro set).

Italian Open (Rome) — Men's Singles: Adriano Panatta d. Guillermo Vilas 2-6, 7-6, 6-2, 7-6; Men's Doubles: Gottfried-Ramirez vs. Masters-Newcombe 7-6, 5-7, 6-3, 3-6: Match abandoned and title divided. Women's Singles: Mima Jausovec d. Lesley Hunt 6-1, 6-3; Women's Doubles: Boshoff-Kloss d. Ruzici-Simionescu 6-1, 6-2.

French Open (Paris) — Men's Singles: Adriano Panatta d. Harold Solomon 6-1, 6-4, 4-6, 7-6; Men's Doubles: Fred McNair-Sherwood d. Brian Gottfried-Raul Ramirez 7-6, 6-3, 6-1; Women's Singles: Sue Barker d. Renata Tomanova 6-3, 1-6, 6-2; Women's Doubles: Fiorella Bonicelli-Gail Lovera d. Kathy Harter-Helga Masthoff 6-4, 1-6, 6-3.

Women's Collegiates — Singles: Barbara Hallquist (USC); Doubles: Linda Mitchell-Karen Meares (Tex-Perm Basin).

Leading Tennis Money Winners, 1975

Men
(Tournament Winnings & Bonus Money)
1.	Arthur Ashe, United States	$306,712
2.	Manuel Orantes, Spain	270,166
3.	Guillermo Vilas, Argentina	247,372
4.	Bjorn Borg, Sweden	219,875
5.	Jimmy Connors, United States	200,273
6.	Raul Ramirex, Mexico	195,850
7.	Ilie Nastase, Romania	193,293
8.	Brian Gottfried, United States	159,055

Women
(Tournament Winnings)
1.	Chris Evert, United States	$323,977
2.	Martina Navratilova, Czechoslovakia	180,318
3.	Virginia Wade, G. Britain	138,576
4.	Evonne Goolagong, Australia	132,754
5.	Margaret Court, Australia	105,646
6.	Billie Jean King, United States	99,900
7.	Francoise Durr, France	78,602
8.	Olga Morozova, USSR	64,527

World Championship Tennis, 1976

Date	Event-City	Singles Winner	Doubles Winner
Jan. 5-10	Copa International Serfin, Monterrey, Mexico	Eddie Dibbs	Brian Gottfried-Raul Ramirez
Jan. 7-11	WCT-Dispatch Charities, Columbus, Ohio	Arthur Ashe	Bob Hewitt-Frew McMillan
Jan. 12-19	Merchants Bank Classic, Indianapolis	Arthur Ashe	Bob Lutz-Stan Smith
Jan. 14-19	WCT-Phoenix Cup, Atlanta	Ilie Nastase	John Alexander-Phil Dent
Jan. 26-Feb. 1	U.S. Pro Indoor Championships, Philadelphia	Jimmy Connors	Rod Laver-Dennis Ralston
Feb. 2-7	Floid Banca Catalana Classic, Barcelona	Eddie Dibbs	Bob Lutz-Stan Smith
Feb. 4-8	United Virginia Bank Tennis Classic, Richmond	Arthur Ashe	Brian Gottfried-Raul Ramirez
Feb. 10-15	Rothmans International Tennis Tournament, Toronto	Bjorn Borg	Jaime Fillol-Frew McMillan
Feb. 10-15	Lagos Tennis Classic, Lagos, Nigeria	Dick Stockton	Uncompleted
Feb. 17-22	St. Louis Tennis Classic, St. Louis	Guillermo Vilas	Brian Gottfried-Raul Ramirez
Feb. 17-22	Coppa Puma, Rome	Arthur Ashe	Bob Lutz-Stan Smith
Feb. 23-29	ABN World Tennis, Rotterdam	Arthur Ashe	Rod Laver-Frew McMillan
Feb. 24-29	Robintech Tennis Classic, Fort Worth	Guillermo Vilas	Vitas Gerulaitis-Alex Mayer
Mar. 9-14	II Campeonato Internacional Old Spice de Tenis Mexico City	Raul Ramirez	Brian Gottfried-Raul Ramirez
Mar. 9-14	Racquet Club Classic, Memphis	Vijay Amritraj	Anand Amritraj-Vijay Amritraj
Mar. 15-21	Volvo Classic, Washington, D. C.	Harold Solomon	Eddie Dibbs-Harold Solomon
Mar. 17-21	Tennis South Invitational, Jackson, Miss.	Ken Rosewall	Brian Gottfried-Raul Ramirez
Mar. 29-Apr. 4	WCT-Copersucar Uniao, Sao Paulo	Bjorn Borg	Ross Case-Geoff Masters
Mar. 30-Apr. 4	XXI Torneo Internacional de Tenis, Caracas	Raul Ramirez	Brian Gottfried-Raul Ramirez
Apr. 5-10	Clows Classic, Johannesburg	Onny Parun	Marty Riessen-Roscoe Tanner
Apr. 5-11	River Oaks/Mid-American Oil Tennis Tournament, Houston	Harold Solomon	Rod Laver-Ken Rosewall
Apr. 12-19	WCT-Marlboro Classic, Monte Carlo	Guillermo Vilas	Wojtek Fibak-Karl Meiler
Apr. 13-18	NCNB Tennis Classic, Charlotte	Tony Roche	John Newcombe-Tony Roche
Apr. 19-25	United Bank Tennis Classic, Denver	Jimmy Connors	John Alexander-Phil Dent
Apr. 19-26	Opel Tennis Cup, Stockholm	Wojtek Fibak	Alex Metreveli-Ilie Nastase

WCT Final Championship Summaries

Singles Quarterfinals

Solomon defeated Ashe 7-5, 3-6, 6-1, 6-3.
Borg defeated Dibbs 3-6, 6-3, 6-4, 6-2
Stockton defeated Ramirez 6-3, 7-6, 7-6.
Vilas defeated Lutz 5-7, 6-1, 6-1, 6-2.

Semifinals

Borg defeated Solomon 7-5, 6-0, 6-3.
Vilas defeated Stockton 7-5, 6-4, 6-1.

Third-Place

Solomon defeated Stockton 6-7, 6-3, 6-2.

WCT Final

Borg defeated Vilas 1-6, 6-1, 7-5, 6-1.

WCT World Doubles Championship Quarterfinals *

Gottfried-Ramirez def. Amritraj-Amritraj 6-2, 7-6, 4-6, 6-4.
Fibak-Meiler def. Case-Masters 7-6, 7-6, 7-5
Ashe-Okker def. Alexander-Dent 4-6,6-3, 6-4, 7-6.
Lutz-Smith def. Dibbs-Solomon 6-1, 6-3, 6-4.

Semifinals

Fibak-Meiler def. Gottfried-Ramirez 6-4, 6-4, 4-6, 4-6, 6-4
Lutz-Smith def. Ashe-Okker 6-2, 7-6, 2-6, 7-6

Third-Place

Ashe-Okker def. Gottfried-Ramirez 6-3, 3-6, 6-1

SCT Final

Fibak-Meiler def. Lutz-Smith 6-3, 2-6, 3-6, 6-3, 6-4

1976 WCT-Avis Challenge Cup

Round Robin, $10,000 Winner-Take-All

Arthur Ashe def. Raul Ramirez 6-2, 7-6, 6-1
Ken Rosewall def. Rod Laver 6-4, 6-1, 6-3
Bjorn Borg def. John Newcombe 2-6, 7-5, 6-2, 6-4.
Ilie Nastase def. Ken Rosewall 6-0, 6-2, 6-2.
Bjorn Borg def. Raul Ramirez 6-3, 4-6, 6-0, 3-0, ret.
Rod Laver def. John Alexander 6-1, 1-6, 7-6, 6-2.

Arthur Ashe def. Bjorn Borg 6-4, 7-6, 6-3.
Ken Rosewall def. John Alexander 3-6, 7-5, 7-6, 7-6.
John Newcombe def. Raul Ramirez 6-4, 6-1, 3-6, 5-7, 3-2, ret.
Ilie Nastase def. John Alexander 6-3, 6-4, 7-6.
Ilie Nastase def. Rod Laver 7-6, 6-1, 4-6, 6-3.
Arthur Ashe def. John Newcombe 3-6, 6-2, 6-3, 7-5.

Semifinals, $50,000 Winner-Take-All

Ilie Nastase def. Bjorn Borg 6-1, 3-6, 0-6, 6-3, 6-4.
Arthur Ashe def. Ken Rosewall 2-6, 6-4, 6-2, 6-2.

Final, $100,000 Winner-Take-All

Ilie Nastase def. Arthur Ashe 6-3, 1-6, 6-7, 6-3, 6-1.

Trapshooting Championship in 1976

Source: Trap & Field Magazine

77th Grand American Tournament
Vandalia, Ohio, Aug. 14-21, 1976

Grand American Handicap

Men—Frank Crevatin, Tucernseh, Ont.
Women—Judith Whittenberger, Ft. Wayne, Ind.
Juniors—James Linke, Woonsocket, S.D.
Sub-Juniors—Robert Mathisen, Duluth, Minn.
Veterans—Ronald Cornwell, Washington Court House, Ohio
Industry—Arthur Wheaton, Edina, Minn.
Past Trophy Winner—Wayne Hegwood, Jackson, Miss.
Jimmy Robinson Trophy to High Canadian—Frank Crevatin.

Clay Target Championship

Men—Ray Stafford, Denver, Col.
Women—Anna Mae Eberle, Pittsburgh, Pa.
Juniors—Michael Ogorzalek, Kewauke, Ill.
Sub-Juniors—Gene Davidson, Devils Lake, Minn.
Veterans—Sam Knott, Prairie Village, Mo.
Industry—Art Wheaton, Edina, Minn.

Champion of Champions

Men—B. E. Morrissey, Blair, Neb.
Women—Susan Nattrass, Hamilton, Ont.
Junior—Martin Wilbur, Salinas, Kan.

High-Over-All

Men—Gene Sears, El Reno, Okla.
Women—Susan Nattrass, Hamilton, Ont.
Juniors—Jeffrey Heino, Dunlevy, Pa.
Sub-Juniors—Robert Mathisen, Duluth, Minn.
Veterans—A. J. Zebehazy, Painesville, Ohio
Industry—Bob Oxsen, Livermore, Cal.

All-Around Championship

Men—Frank Little, Mechanicsburg, Pa.
Women—Susan Nattrass, Hamilton, Ont.
Junior—Ken Scott, Racine, Wis.
Sub-Juniors—David Craite, Grosse Point Farms, Mich.
Veteran—R. H. Sailer, Oklahoma City, Okla.
Industry—Cecil Trammell, Brooks, Ga.

CHRONOLOGY OF THE YEAR'S EVENTS

Reported Month by Month in 3 Categories: National, International, and General — Nov. 1, 1975, to Nov. 1, 1976

NOVEMBER 1975
National

Ford Reshuffles Cabinet; Rockefeller Out in '76—In the midst of a major cabinet shake-up, Vice President Nelson A. Rockefeller, **Nov. 3**, announced that he would not run as Pres. Gerald R. Ford's vice president in 1976. He did not give any reason for the decision. Ford, at a nationally-televised press conference, said he had not requested Rockefeller's decision and confirmed major changes in his cabinet which had been widely reported **Nov. 2**. White House chief of Staff Donald H. Rumsfeld was named to replace Defense Secretary James R. Schlesinger. George Bush, head of the U. S. liasion office in Peking, China, was chosen to replace CIA Director William E. Colby. Ford also announced that he would nominate Elliot L. Richardson, the recently named ambassador to Great Britain, to replace Rogers C. B. Morton as secretary of commerce. Morton had expressed a desire to return to private life. Air Force Lt. Gen. Brent Scowcroft was named to succeed Henry A. Kissinger as White House adviser on national security. Kissinger would retain his post as secretary of state. Ford stressed that Kissinger would continue to "have the dominant role" in the formulation of foreign policy. In response to suggestions that the changes had been made to eliminate friction over policy between Schlesinger and Kissinger, Ford asserted that the decision was totally his own. Republican conservatives were sharply critical of the Schlesinger dismissal and Republican presidential hopeful Ronald Reagan stated that he was "shocked." The Bush appointment also came under immediate criticism. Senator Frank Church (D. Ida.) stated that he knew of no reason why the former chairman of the Republican National Committee was qualified to head the agency that was "the least political and most sensitive in government." In a **Nov. 9** appearance on "Meet the Press," Ford acknowledged that "growing tension" in the cabinet over defense policy had influenced his decision to dismiss Schlesinger. Schlesinger, **Nov. 23**, in his first public appearance since his dismissal, stated plainly that he believed his objections to administration attempts to restrict growth in the defense budget had been the "chief substantive issue" in his removal from office. The Senate, **Nov. 18**, confirmed Rumsfeld as defense secretary in a 95-2 vote. Richardson was confirmed, **Dec. 11**, by a voice vote in the Senate. Bush, whose confirmation as CIA director was delayed until Ford excluded him as a potential vice presidential running mate, was confirmed, **Jan. 27**, by a Senate vote of 64-27.

Douglas Retires; Stevens Nominated—Supreme Court Associate Justice William O. Douglas, one of the most adamant defenders of the liberal view of the Constitution, **Nov. 12**, retired from the court, citing failing health. The 77-year-old justice had taken his seat on the court 36 1/2 years earlier during the administration of Pres. Franklin D. Roosevelt. Douglas had been in poor health since he suffered a stroke the previous New Year's Eve. Pres. Gerald R. Ford, who as a congressman had led the last of 3 abortive attempts to impeach Douglas in 1971, stated that Douglas' "distinguished years of service are unequaled in all the history of the Court." Associate Justice Potter Stewart also paid tribute to Douglas, " . . . I

have long admired his intellect, his independence, his energy and his vision. I salute him now as a man of extraordinary courage." Amid rumors that Ford would nominate a woman to replace Douglas, the president, **Nov. 28**, selected John Paul Stevens, 55, a Chicago, Ill., federal appeals court judge. Stevens, regarded as a centrist, was confirmed, **Dec. 17**, by a Senate vote of 98-0. Supreme Court Chief Justice Warren E. Burger, **Dec. 19**, swore Stevens into office.

Wallace Enters Presidential Race—Alabama Gov. George C. Wallace, **Nov. 12**, announced in Montgomery, Ala., that he would wage his third campaign for the Democratic presidential nomination.

Senate Issues CIA Assassination Report—The bipartisan Senate Select Committee to Study Government Operations with Respect to Intelligence Activities, **Nov. 21**, issued a 347-page report which stated officials of the U. S. government had instigated assassination plots against 2 foreign leaders and had become involved in plotting that led to the deaths of 3 other leaders. The report was released over the objection of Pres. Gerald R. Ford and following 4 hours of closed Senate debate on a resolution to keep the report secret. The Senate refused to vote, thus permitting the release of the report. Specifically, the report stated that the CIA had initiated and furthered death plots aimed at Cuban Premier Fidel Castro and Patrice Lumumba of the Congo, now Zaire. The 3 other leaders were South Vietnamese Pres. Ngo Dinh Diem, Dominican dictator Rafael Leonidas Trujillo, and Gen. Rene Schneider, chief of Chile's general staff. Although all except Castro were assassinated, the committee found no evidence any of the killings resulted from the plots initiated by U. S. officials.

Moore Mentally Fit for Trial—Judge Samuel Conti, **Nov. 17**, in San Francisco, Calif., found Sara Jane Moore, accused of attempting to assassinate Pres. Gerald R. Ford on Sept. 22, competent to stand trial. Moore, 45, had been hospitalized 7 times for mental treatment during the past 25 years.

Reagan to Seek Republican Nomination—Former California Gov. Ronald Reagan, **Nov. 21**, announced that he would challenge Pres. Gerald R. Ford for the Republican presidential nomination. Reagan stated that his chief target was not Pres. Ford but the philosophy of governmental spending that had caused many of the nation's economic problems.

Fromme Convicted in Assassination Attempt—A Sacramento, Calif., federal jury of 8 women and 4 men, **Nov. 26**, convicted Lynette Alice Fromme of attempting to kill Pres. Gerald R. Ford on Sept. 5. In the decision, the jury, which had deliberated for more than 19 hours, threw out a lesser charge of assault. Fromme, who had refused to testify in her own defense, listened to the verdict over closed-circuit television in her cell. Fromme's defense attorney John E. Virga had argued that Fromme had not intended to kill Ford, but had drawn the gun in order to publicize the attempts of convicted murderer Charles M. Manson to get a new trial and symbolically to inform environmental polluters that their actions would destroy the world. For the first 4 days of the 3-week trial, Fromme had conducted her own defense, but was then barred from the court by Judge Thomas J. MacBride because of her outbursts and disruptions. The highlight of the trial was the videotape testimony of Pres. Ford, who testified that he had never seen her hand on the trigger of the gun nor heard any metallic clicks. In a private statement submitted to the court following the trial, Fromme stated publicly for the first time that she did not intend to shoot Ford, and had engaged the safety catch and removed the cartridge from the firing chamber before the confrontation. MacBride, however, said that the statement had come too late. On **Dec. 17**, MacBride, sentenced Fromme to life in prison; she would be eligible for parole in 15 years. He said he was convinced that she "would murder or cause another to commit murder in the false and distorted belief that only terror and violence can save our environment and natural resources."

International

Bangladesh President Forced to Resign—After a 3-day power struggle with the military, Bangladesh Pres. Khandaker Moshtaque Ahmed, **Nov. 6**, was forced to resign. He had assumed office 10 weeks previously following the **Aug. 15** coup that overthrew Pres. Sheik Mujibur Rahman. Supreme Court Chief Justice Abu Sadat Mohammed Sayem was sworn in as president and stated he would conduct a "neutral, nonpartisan and interim" government. On **Nov. 7**, Sayem said he would remain as martial law administrator, but would be assisted by a council of 3 armed services commanding officers. Ahmed, the dismissed president, announced support for Sayem, stating that he had stepped down from office because Bangladesh needed "a nonpolitical and independent person to take the reigns at this hour of crisis."

Conviction of Indian Prime Minister Overturned—The Indian Supreme Court, **Nov. 7**, unanimously overturned the June 1975 conviction of Indian Prime Minister Indira Gandhi for 2 electoral offenses in the 1971 parliamentary campaign. The move ended any threat that Gandhi would be forced to resign from office. In August, the parliament, which is dominated by Gandhi's Congress party, had retroactively amended the election law using language tailored specifically to suit her case — a change the court upheld in its ruling.

Hassan Calls off March into Spanish Sahara—Moroccan King Hassan II, **Nov. 9**, called off his nation's civilian march to annex Spanish-controlled Spanish Sahara. Some 350,000 Moroccans had begun the march **Nov. 6**. On **Nov. 14**, following 3 days of trilateral negotiations, Spain agreed to abandon Spanish Sahara by the end of February and to share the interim administration of the territory with Morocco and Mauritania.

Portuguese Leave Angola in State of Civil War—The Portuguese, **Nov. 10**, formally withdrew from civil war-torn Angola, the nation's first and last colony in Africa. On **Nov. 11**, 2 rival governments were proclaimed in Angola. Dr. Agostinho Neto, the leader of the Soviet-backed Popular Movement for the Liberation of Angola, was proclaimed head of the People's Republic of Angola in Luanda. Meanwhile, the Western-backed National Union for the Total Independence of Angola joined with the National Front for the Liberation of Angola, backed by China and Zaire, to form the Democratic People's Republic with interim headquarters at Nova Lisboa, immediately renamed Huambo. The Huambo government vowed that it would recapture Luanda and move its capital there. On **Nov. 20**, U.S. government officials reported that Cuba had sent 3,000 fighting men and advisers to Angola and that the Soviet Union had shipped large quantities of arms. U.S. Secretary of State Henry A. Kissinger, **Nov. 24**, warned that the U.S. could not remain "indifferent" to Soviet and Cuban intervention in the Angolan civil war. He also asserted that their intervention could have conse-

quences for East-West detente. However, Kissinger also stated, **Nov. 28** that "the United States will not intervene militarily in Angola."

UN General Assembly Calls Zionism "Racism"—In a highly tense atmosphere, the United Nations General Assembly, **Nov. 10**, adopted an Arab-backed resolution that defined Zionism as "a form of racism and racial discrimination." The vote was 72 to 35, with 32 abstentions and 3 delegates absent. Backers of the resolution included the Arab and other Islamic countries, communist nations, Brazil, Mexico, and many 3rd world nations. The United States, Canada, Israel, the 9 European Community nations, Australia, New Zealand, and several Latin American nations opposed the resolution. Chief U.S. Delegate, Daniel P. Moynihan declared that the U.S. "does not acknowledge it, will not abide by it, it will never acquiesce in this infamous act." Earlier, the general assembly had adopted by an overwhelming majority 2 other resolutions, one calling for the participation of the Palestine Liberation Organization in all peace efforts in the Middle East and another that would set up a procedure to allow the Palestinians to present their demands in the UN. The United States and Israel opposed both resolutions. In reaction to the vote, the U.S. Senate and House of Representatives, **Nov. 11**, passed nearly identical resolutions, calling for reassessment of the U.S. relationship to the UN and condemning the anti-Zionist resolution.

Whitlam Removed as Australian PM—In a move unprecedented in the 75-year history of the Australian confederation, Governor-General Sir John Kerr, **Nov. 11**, removed Prime Minister Gough Whitlam from office. Whitlam, a Laborite, had been unable to move the 1975-76 budget through the opposition-controlled Senate, leading to a 28-day money crisis. Kerr asked opposition leader Malcolm Fraser to form a caretaker government pending new parliamentary elections for both the Senate and House in December.

Sakharov Denied Visa—The Soviet government, **Nov. 12**, denied physicist and human rights advocate Andrei D. Sakharov permission to travel to Oslo, Norway, in December to receive the Nobel Peace Prize.

French, Italian Communists Back Democracy—Europe's 2 largest communist parties, the French and Italian, **Nov. 15**, in Rome, Italy, issued a joint statement asserting that the road to power was through the democratic systems in their countries. French Communist leader George Marchais termed the statement a "historic document" and Italian Communist party leader Enrico Berlinguer asserted that the document charted a "democratic path to socialism." The 2 parties declared their opposition to "all foreign interference," specifically by "American imperialism" and, by implication, the Soviet Union.

Franco Dies; Juan Carlos Takes Oath as King—For 36 years the dictator of Spain, Generalissimo Francisco Franco died, **Nov. 20**, at the age of 82. Franco had ruled Spain with an iron hand since he had led the rightist military forces to victory in the Spanish Civil War. After a 5-week battle against death, Franco died in Madrid's La Paz hospital. Franco's body was taken to the Pardo Palace on the outskirts of Madrid to lie in state. Juan Carlos, **Nov. 22**, after swearing fidelity to the principles of the Spanish regime and promising to stimulate "profound improvements," was proclaimed king in a short parliamentary ceremony. King Juan Carlos I, in the uniform of captain general of the army, **Nov. 23**, presided as Franco was buried in a vast crypt inside a mountain in the Valley of the Fallen.

Leftist Military Rebellion Crushed in Portugal—Loyalist military forces, **Nov. 25-26**, crushed a leftist military revolt against the Portuguese government.

The rebellion began early **Nov. 25**, when paratroopers and other regiments seized the air force command and 4 air force bases. Other leftist commandos seized the national television station and broadcast anti-government messages throughout the day. The rebellion was seen as part of a drive by the Communist party and other extremist factions to seize power from Prime Minister Adm. Jose Pinheiro de Azevedo. By **Nov. 26**, government authorities announced they had regained control of 3 air force bases and the air command. Gen. Otelo Saraiva de Carvalho, the leftist military security chief, was deposed and his command was dissolved. The real death blow to the rebellion came when the Communist party released a statement acknowledging serious errors and called for a political solution to the crisis. On **Nov. 27**, Pres. Francisco da Costa Gomez stated that a coup of vast proportions had been crushed and attributed the abortive rebellion to a false left which had tried to manipulate the people. He pledged to defend multiparty democracy in Portugal. On **Nov. 28**, authorities arrested at least 77 military officers. The ruling High Council of the Revolution dismissed the management and editorial employees of 8 Lisbon daily newspapers and suspended publication pending their replacement. The dismissals came in the wake of accusations by several military leaders that the leftist papers had instigated the coup through their anti-government campaigns.

Franjieh, Karami Press for Lebanese Accord—As fierce fighting obliterated the current Lebanese cease-fire, long-time political rivals Pres. Suleiman Franjieh and Prime Minister Rashid Karami, **Nov. 30**, agreed in principle on a political and economic solution to end the civil strife and pleaded for an end to the fighting. Karami called the basis of the agreement "necessary readjustments" in Lebanon's sectarian political systems while providing "necessary guarantees" for the various religious communities. The agreement implied that the Christian Maronite community, long politically and economically dominant, would make political concessions to the Moslem majority.

General

Cleaver Arrested Upon Return from Exile— Former Black Panther leader Eldridge Cleaver, **Nov. 17**, returned to the U.S., after spending 7 years in exile. Upon his arrival at John F. Kennedy International Airport in New York City, Cleaver was arrested on a federal warrant for flight to avoid confinement. Cleaver faced murder charges in connection with the April 1968 Oakland, Calif., shootout between Black Panthers and police. He also faced parole violation charges. On **Nov. 19**, Cleaver was flown to San Diego, Calif., where he was placed in a federal correctional facility. Cleaver, who had lived in Cuba, Guinea, Algeria, North Korea, and France, stated that he was tired of exile outside of America and now had "confidence in the American system of justice" and expected a "fair and objective trial." He also stated that "the status of blacks has undergone fundamental changes and Watergate developed a new look at institutions by the American public."

Ford Agrees to Federal Aid for NYC—Following an 8-month campaign by New York State and New York City officials, Pres. Gerald R. Ford, **Nov. 26**, agreed to give federal aid to New York City to help meet its seasonal cash flow needs and avert default. At a nationally televised press conference, Ford asked Congress to approve legislation authorizing up to $2.3 billion annually in federal short-term loans to New York City until June 1978. The loans would be administered by Treasury Secretary William E. Simon. Ford's decision came one day after the New York

State legislature, **Nov. 25**, had passed a $200-million tax package, part of a complicated $6.6 billion finance package geared to enable New York City to meet its immediate cash needs for December and to refinance the city's debt over the next 3 years. The $200-million tax package included an average 25% tax increase for New York City residents, a 50% surcharge on estate tax, and tax increases on banks, cigarettes, and various personal services. On **Nov. 24**, following protracted negotiations, New York City's major banks and the teachers' union, the last remaining holdouts, had agreed to join in the elaborate 3-year finance plan, paving the way for the legislative action. Ford, who, **Oct. 29**, had said he would veto any federal "bailout" passed by Congress to avert New York City default through a federal guarantee of funds for the city, denied that he had reversed his position. "New York City," Ford stated, "by what they have done in conjunction with New York State, in conjunction with the noteholders, pension fund people, they have bailed themselves out." Following House approval, **Dec. 2**, in a 213-203 vote and Senate acceptance, **Dec. 6**, in 57-30 vote, Ford, **Dec. 9**, signed legislation authorizing the loans.

Guinness Book Editor Slain—Ross McWhirter, 50 years old, who with his twin brother, Norris, edited The Guinness Book of World Records, was killed, **Nov. 27**, by two gunmen on the doorstep of his London, England, home. On **Nov. 4**, McWhirter had offered a $100,000 reward for information leading to the arrest of those responsible for London bombings that had claimed the lives of 8 people and injured some 200 persons since August. McWhirter had headed Self-Help, an organization that demands the death penalty for all terrorists and registration of all citizens of the Irish Republic in Britain. The shooting prompted a public outcry and the support of Conservative party leader Margaret Thatcher for restoration of the death penalty, abolished 10 years previously.

DECEMBER
National

Senate Panel Clears CIA of Direct Chile Role—The staff of the Senate Select Committee on Intelligence, **Dec. 4**, in a 62-page report, stated that it had established no direct involvement of the CIA or the American Embassy in the 1973 overthrow of Chilean Pres. Salvador Allende Gossens. The panel, however, did find that the U.S. had encouraged and "created the atmosphere" for the overthrow of the "democratically elected" Allende government. The staff had listened to the testimony of CIA officials and other government officials, including Secretary of State Henry A. Kissinger, and had gained access to secret CIA, National Security Council, and state department documents.

Moore Guilty Plea Accepted—Federal District Court Judge Samuel Conti, **Dec. 16**, in a San Francisco, Calif., courtroom, accepted Sara Jane Moore's plea of guilty of attempting to assassinate Pres. Gerald R. Ford on **Sept. 22** in San Francisco. He ruled that a jury of reasonable minds could find Moore guilty as charged and that there was factual cause for accepting the plea. Moore, **Dec. 12**, had read a 500-word statement declaring her willful and knowing attempt to kill Ford. In her statement, Moore declared: "When any government uses assassination, whether of political leaders in other countries or its own citizens, to put down dissent or to hide its own repressive actions, it must expect that tool to be turned back against it." Judge Conti, **Jan. 15**, sentenced Moore to life in prison; eligible for parole in 15 years. Conti called Moore a "product of a permissive society" who would not have tried to kill Ford "if we had in this country any effective capital punishment law."

Senator Denies Cover-up of Kennedy-Mafia Link— Sen. Frank Church, chairman of the Senate Select Committee on Intelligence Operations, **Dec. 15,** denied published assertions his committee had covered up information linking former Pres. John F. Kennedy with a woman who had a close friendship with 2 organized crime leaders. He acknowledged, however, that, in the course of the committee's inquiry into Mafia involvement in CIA plots to kill Cuban Premier Fidel Castro, the committee had discovered that Kennedy had had a friendship with a woman who was involved with 2 Mafia figures who were involved in assassination plots during the same period. Church asserted that the details of the relationship, which was mentioned briefly in the committee's report released the previous month, were withheld because they were irrelevant to the matter at hand, according to the unanimous agreement of the committee's 11 senators. The committee, according to Church, had concluded that the woman had had no knowledge of the assassination activities. The woman, Judith Campbell Exner, had been extensively interviewed by the committee.

Ford Vetoes Tax-Cut Bill, Compromise Passed— Pres. Gerald R. Ford, **Dec. 17,** immediately following its passage by Congress, vetoed an extension of the 1975 tax reductions for individuals and businesses because it was not linked to a ceiling on government spending. Ford declared that the nation would "risk a new round of double-digit inflation" if the growth rate of federal spending was not eased. After the House, **Dec. 18,** in a 265-157 vote, failed to override Ford's veto, Congress, **Dec. 19,** in a last-minute action before adjournment, passed compromise tax-cut legislation that incorporated a nonbinding commitment to control government spending. Although the bill's language was nonexplicit, Ford stated that the revised legislation would be acceptable. With some significant modifications and expansions, the final bill extended the 1975 individual and corporate tax reductions through June of 1976.

West Virginia Governor Indicted—A West Virginia federal grand jury, **Dec. 18,** in Charleston, indicted Republican Gov. Arch A. Moore Jr., on charges of extorting $25,000 from a financier who had sought a state bank charter. The indictment stated that in the fall of 1972, Moore had "induced and obtained" the payment "by wrongful use of fear and economic harm and under color of official right." The financier had pleaded guilty to federal fraud charges and was cooperating with the prosecution. At a news conference called immediately after the indictment, Moore declared his innocence and announced that he would run for a 3rd term as governor.

Ford Signs Energy Bill—Ending a year-long Congress-administration stalemate over energy policy, Pres. Gerald R. Ford, **Dec. 22,** signed the Energy Policy and Conservation Act which would immediately roll back the price of crude oil. The House of Representatives, **Dec. 15,** passed the legislation in a 236-160 vote and the Senate, **Dec. 17,** approved the bill by a 58-40 vote. Also effective **Dec. 22,** Ford removed a $2-a-barrel import fee on crude oil which he had imposed earlier in the year to discourage imports. Under the new legislation, oil prices could rise by a maximum of 10% per year at the discretion of the president. However, upon expiration of the legislation in Feb. 1977, the Congress would have authority to stop any increase in fuel prices which exceeded the inflation rate for the economy as a whole.

International

Ford Travels to China; Announces Pacific Doctrine —U.S. Pres. Gerald R. Ford, **Dec. 1-5,** conferred with Chinese leaders, including Chairman Mao Tse-tung, in Peking, and then traveled to Indonesia and the Philippines before completing his Pacific tour with a stop in Honolulu, Hawaii. At the **Dec. 1** dinner marking Ford's arrival in Peking, Deputy Prime Minister Teng Hsiao-ping stated that "rhetoric about 'detente' cannot cover up the stark reality of the growing danger of war" posed by appeasement of the Soviet Union. Ford responded that the U.S. would pursue detente, balancing "strength, vigilance, and firmness" with continued exploration of "new opportunities for peace without illusions." On **Dec. 2,** Ford met with Mao for one hour and 50 minutes in what was termed a "significant conversation" about international issues, including Chinese-American relations. After Ford met with Indonesian Pres. Suharto, **Dec. 6,** the 2 leaders issued a joint communique stating "the intention of the United States to continue to provide substantial aid to Indonesia in support of Indonesia's development efforts." On **Dec. 7,** Philippine Pres. Ferdinand E. Marcos and Ford agreed to complete negotiations to provide "clear recognition of Philippine sovereignty" over Clark Air Force Base and the Subic Navy Base, both strategic U.S. installations in the Western Pacific.

South Moluccan Terrorists Stage 2 Dutch Attacks— Two bands of armed South Moluccan terrorists, seeking independence from Indonesia for their homeland, **Dec. 2** and **Dec. 4,** staged attacks in the Netherlands. On **Dec. 2,** 7 terrorists seized a train near the northern town of Beilen, killing 2 people and taking 50 hostages. On **Dec. 4,** another band of 7 armed terrorists beseiged the Indonesian consulate in Amsterdam, taking 30 hostages, including 16 children. The South Moluccan radicals hold the Dutch responsible for failing to fulfill alleged promises of independence when the Netherlands allowed Indonesia to take over the South Molucca Islands, formerly the Spice Islands, in 1950. The leaders of the community of 35,000 South Moluccans living in the Netherlands condemned the acts and assisted in mediation efforts. Throughout both sieges, as both groups of terrorists continued to release hostages, the Dutch government refused to make any concessions. On **Dec. 14,** 12 days after the original attack, the 7 terrorists who had seized the train released the remaining hostages and surrendered peacefully. On **Dec. 19,** the 2nd band of terrorists ended their 16-day siege at the Indonesian consulate, freeing their hostages.

Laotian Coalition Dissolved—According to a Vientiane radio announcement, the Communist-led Pathet Lao, **Dec. 3,** abolished the 19-month-old Laotian coalition government and established a People's Democratic Republic. The Lao Patriotic Front, the official name of the Pathet Lao organization, thereby took full control of Laos. The decision was made by a people's congress, convened **Dec. 1-2,** by the central committee of the Pathet Lao. According to the broadcast, the congress also abolished the 600-year-old monarchy, and King Savang Vatthana gave up the throne. The congress named Prince Souphanouvong, the titular head of the Pathet Lao, as president and Kaysone Phoumvihan, the secretary-general of the Pathet Lao, as prime minister. The congress also accepted the resignation of Prime Minister Souvanna Phouma, the 74-year-old neutralist who led the coalition of leftists, rightists, and neutralists.

U.S. Vetoes Israeli Censure — The U.S., **Dec. 8,** in the United Nations Security Council, vetoed an Arab-instigated resolution condemning Israel for its "premeditated air attacks" **Dec. 2** on Palestinian refugee camps in Lebanon. Chief U.S. Delegate Daniel P. Moynihan stated that the U.S. "strongly deplores" the attacks, but wanted the resolution to also cite Arab violence against Israel. On **Dec. 2**, Israeli jets had attacked Palestinian camps in northern and southern Lebanon, killing 57 persons and injuring 110, the highest death toll in such attacks in a year and a half. Palestinian sources viewed the "criminal attack against innocent civilians a desperate Zionist act in retaliation for Palestinian victories in the UN." Israel, who claimed it had launched the attack against various Palestinian terrorist organizations, **Dec. 1**, had announced it would boycott the upcoming UN Security Council debate on the Middle East.

Quasi-Liberal Cabinet Named in Spain — Spanish Prime Minister Carlos Arias Navarro, a hold-over from the Franco regime, **Dec. 11**, named a new cabinet that was liberal by Spanish standards. King Juan Carlos I, **Dec. 5**, had decided to retain Navarro as prime minister, a move that had disturbed liberals and leftists. The new cabinet, which included only 3 ministers from the Franco regime, was expected to follow a program of cautious political reform. In its first policy statement, **Dec. 15**, the new cabinet promised to place high priority on broadening civil liberties and on drawing Spain closer to the Western community.

Coalition Sweeps Australian Elections — In nationwide parliamentary elections, caretaker Prime Minister Malcolm Fraser's conservative-oriented Liberal-National Country party coalition, **Dec. 13**, won the biggest coalition majority in the 75-year history of the Australian confederation. The swing to the right was interpreted as a reaction to recession and unemployment during Gough Whitlam's 3-year Labor government.

Soviet 5-Year Plan Sets Slower Growth Goal—The Central Committee of the Soviet Communist party, **Dec. 14**, publicly outlined its new 5-year plan for 1976-80, setting more modest goals for economic growth. In December 1974, the Soviet Union had recognized the failure of the 1971-75 plan to raise living standards substantially. The new plan, marked by emphasis on heavy industry and agriculture, indicated the Soviet Union was scrapping its decade-long effort to redirect the economy in favor of the consumer. The plan called for a 38%-42% growth rate in heavy industry in contrast to a growth rate of 30%-32% in the production of consumer goods. The new plan called for a rise in overall industrial production of 35% to 39%, substantially less than the 43% achieved during the previous plan and the 47% initially planned. The plan also called for an increase of nearly 1/3 in agricultural expenditures. This indirectly confirmed earlier reports of a 1975 harvest disaster.

Brandt Aide Convicted of Treason—Gunter Guillaume, an aide to former West German Chancellor Willy Brandt, **Dec. 15**, was convicted of treason by a 5-judge court in Dusseldorf. Guillaume was sentenced to 13 years in prison. His wife, Christel, was found guilty of complicity and sentenced to 8 years in prison. The arrest of the couple as spies for East Germany in April 1974 had lead to the resignation of Brandt.

U.S. Senate Bars Further Covert Aid to Angola— The U.S. Senate, **Dec. 19**, in an overwhelming 54-22 vote, supported a cut-off of funds for covert military support for the U.S.-backed factions in the Angolan civil war. The vote came on an amendment to the 1976 defense appropriations bill. U.S. Pres. Gerald R. Ford called the vote "a deep tragedy for all countries whose security" depends on the U.S. Secretary of State Henry A. Kissinger, **Dec. 23**, warned that, although Soviet-American tensions may heighten, the Ford administration would use $9 million for military aid and take other steps to oppose Soviet expansion in Angola. Kissinger was referring to the funds still in the pipeline for covert aid. The Senate action grew out of a revelation, **Dec. 11**, by a high-ranking government official, that the U.S. had sent $25 million in arms and support to Angola over the past 3 months and planned to send another $25 million in aid.

Terrorists Attack Vienna OPEC Meeting—Six armed pro-Palestinian terrorists, **Dec. 21**, raided the Vienna, Austria, conference of the Organization of Petroleum Exporting Countries and shot to death 3 persons and wounded 6 others. The terrorists also seized 81 hostages, including Saudi Arabian oil minister Shiek Ahmed Zaki Yamani and 10 other OPEC ministers. Early **Dec. 22**, Austrian Chancellor Bruno Kreisky announced that his government would provide the guerrillas with a jetliner to fly the hostages to Algeria. The guerrillas then freed all 41 Austrian hostages and flew to Algiers where they released several more hostages. The terrorists continued to Tripoli, Libya, where they freed more captives and, **Dec. 23**, returned to Algiers and freed the remaining hostages. The terrorists then surrendered to Algerian authorities. The terrorists, **Dec. 22**, had identified themselves as the Arm of the Arab Revolution and termed the raid "an act of political contestation" aimed at "the alliance between American imperialism and the capitulating reactionary forces in the Arab homeland."

General

Boston School Placed Under Federal Supervision— Federal District Court Judge W. Arthur Garrity Jr., **Dec. 9**, placed the racially troubled South Boston High School under federal receivership, thereby stripping the Boston School Committee of much of its control over the school. Garrity's decision followed 2 weeks of testimony, during which black students stated they had been harassed and beaten by white students and ignored by administrators and teachers. Garrity, who placed the school under the direction of a court officer directly responsible to him, accused the school committee of dragging its feet in implementing his June 1974 desegregation order.

Attica Report Cites Poor Judgment—Special State Investigator Bernard S. Meyer, a former New York State Supreme Court Justice, **Dec. 22**, in his 130-page report on the Attica prosecution, concluded that "serious errors in judgment" were made in the investigation of the 1971 riot. However, he found no evidence of an "intentional coverup in the Attica prosecution." Based on a recommendation in the report, New York State Gov. Hugh L. Carey and Attorney General Louis J. Lefkowitz appointed Alfred J. Scotti, a former chief assistant district attorney in New York City, as the new special prosecutor in the Attica case. Scotti would determine whether indictments should be sought against law enforcement officers who took part in the retaking of Attica prison. He would also review the indictments and convictions already obtained against inmates and would have the authority to recommend dismissal or executive clemency if he felt it were warranted.

Disasters—Fire swept through a tent camp at Mina, a few miles distant from Mecca, Saudi Arabia, **Dec. 12**, killing 138 Moslem pilgrims and injuring 151 other pilgrims. The dead and injured were part of reported 2,000,000 Moslems who had gathered to celebrate the annual feast of Id al-Adha, the sacred festival marking Abraham's sacrifice of the lamb. . . An explosion, **Dec. 27**, in a major coal mine in northeastern India near Dhanbad, Bihar, some 160 miles northwest of Calcutta, set off flooding from a nearby reservoir that trapped and killed 372 miners. . . A bomb hidden in a locker in the baggage claim area at New York City's LaGuardia Airport exploded. **Dec. 29**, killing 11 and injuring 70 holiday travelers.

JANUARY

National

Byrd Enters Democratic Race, Sanford Quits—Senate Majority Leader Robert C. Byrd (D. W.Va.), **Jan. 9**, joined the ranks of candidates for the 1976 Democratic presidential nomination. The 11th Democrat in the race, Byrd said he was entering the race to give his state a "greater impact" at the party's nominating convention in July. Byrd said he would also seek re-election to his 4th term in the Senate. On **Jan. 23**, Duke University Pres. Terry Sanford withdrew from the race.

Ford Names Morton to Cabinet-Level Post—Pres. Gerald R. Ford, **Jan. 13**, named former Commerce Secretary Rogers C. B. Morton as a cabinet-rank adviser on economic and domestic policy matters. White House Press Secretary Ron Nessen stated that Morton would devote only "incidental" attention to the 1976 election campaign. National Democratic Committee Chairman Robert S. Strauss, **Jan. 14**, however, shunted aside Nessen's assertion and declared it was "disgraceful, shameful" for the administration to try to disguise what he claimed was a political role for Morton and place him on the public payroll.

Dunlop, Labor Leaders Defect—In the aftermath of Pres. Gerald R. Ford's **Jan. 2** veto of the construction site picketing bill, Labor Secretary John T. Dunlop, **Jan. 14**, resigned effective Feb. 1. At a news conference, Dunlop said his resignation was a direct consequence of the veto. Dunlop, who was the chief architect of the bill, had told Ford privately, **Jan. 13**, that "the requisite communications, confidence and trust" among labor, management, and government were "no longer possible," at least in his case. The bill would have allowed a union in dispute with one subcontractor to picket an entire building site. In a prelude to Dunlop's resignation, 9 labor leaders, including International Brotherhood of Teamsters Pres. Frank E. Fitzsimmons, **Jan. 8**, had quit Ford's Collective Bargaining Committee in Construction, charging Ford had "double-crossed" them. Ford had originally promised to sign the bill, but heavy pressure from the conservative wing of the Republican party had forced him to change his mind. Ford, **Jan. 22**, named W. J. Usery Jr., head of the independent Federal Mediation and Conciliation Service, to succeed Dunlop. The Senate, **Feb. 4**, confirmed the nomination in a 79-9 vote.

Ford's State of Union Stresses "New Realism"—Advocating the need for "common sense" and a "new realism," Pres. Gerald R. Ford, **Jan. 19**, in the annual State of the Union message to Congress, told the nation the state of the union "is better . . . but still not good enough." "The time has come," Ford declared, "for a fundamentally different approach, for a new realism that is true to the great principles on which this nation is founded." Consequently, he asked Congress to show restraint and forego massive, expensive new programs and search instead for a "new realism" in relations between government and the governed. Specifically, in outlining his program for 1976, Ford asked Congress to hold fiscal spending to $394.2 billion in order to stop inflation "cold." To spur the recovery from recession, Ford asked for $10 billion more in federal income tax reductions. Ford also called for business incentives to create jobs by accelerating tax write-offs for plant expansion in high-unemployment areas. He further asked for tax breaks for middle-income families that invested in corporate stocks and a change in estate tax laws to enhance the likelihood small businesses and farms would be passed from generation to generation. Ford also called for an increase in the social security tax rate and wage base because the program was "headed for trouble." In the area of foreign policy, Ford asked Congress for more flexibility in conducting diplomacy and warned Congress to resist temptation to legislate "crippling" and dangerous shackles on the intelligence community.

Carter Wins in Iowa, Wallace Takes Mississippi—In the year's first test of Democratic presidential candidate strength, former Georgia Gov. Jimmy Carter, **Jan. 19**, scored an impressive victory in the Iowa precinct caucuses. His 2-to-1 margin over this closest rival, Indiana Sen. Birch Bayh, led many political observers, **Jan. 20**, to consider Carter a major contender for the Democratic presidential nomination. Carter's support in Iowa came from farmers and urban voters, including Roman Catholics, Protestants, blacks, and both blue and white-collar workers. However, on **Jan. 24**, Alabama Gov. George C. Wallace topped Carter 3-1 in the Mississippi precinct caucuses, amassing 44% of the vote. Wallace campaign strategists claimed that the victory proved they had mastered the intricacies of caucuses which had baffled them in 1972.

House Intelligence Committee Report Leaked—According to reports in The New York Times and Washington Post beginning **Jan. 20**, the House Select Committee on Intelligence, in its unreleased 338-page final report, concluded that federal intelligence agencies currently operate in such secret ways that they are "beyond the scrutiny" of Congress. The committee, despite CIA concern that report would disclose classified and sensitive information, had voted, 9 to 4, **Jan. 23**, to publish the report at the end of the month. On **Jan. 26**, Presidential Press Secretary Ron Nessen and CIA Director William E. Colby charged the leaks of the report had violated a security agreement between the committee and the executive branch. Colby, who had seen a preliminary draft of the report, said it was "biased and irresponsible." Under pressure from Pres. Gerald R. Ford and intelligence agency officials, the House, **Jan. 29**, voted, 246-124, to withhold publication of the final report until it had been censored by the executive branch. Otis G. Pike (D. N.Y.), chairman of the House intelligence committee, attacked the vote as "a complete travesty of the whole doctrine of separation of powers." The final report, as reported in The New York Times Jan. 26, revealed an apparent violation by the CIA of a 1967 presidential directive barring secret financial assistance to the nation's education institutions. The report also concluded that federal intelligence agency budgets were 3 or 4 times greater than the secret figures given to Congress. The report also stated that the National Security Agency had listened illegally to overseas conversations of American citizens whose names and addresses had been provided by "another government agency." The committee also found that thousands, perhaps millions, of dollars in unwarranted markups had added to the cost of bugging equipment bought by the FBI from a private company whose president was a close friend of high FBI officials.

Ford Presents Restraint Budget—As promised in his State of the Union message, Pres. Gerald R. Ford, **Jan. 21**, presented to Congress a budget based on economic restraint for fiscal year 1977. The budget called for estimated spending at $394.2 billion. This estimate incorporated Ford proposals for a spending reduction of $20 billion for federal programs. If Congress accepted his plan, Ford promised additional tax reductions. The combination of tax and spending changes, according to Ford, would lead to a balanced budget within 3 years and would improve prospects for sustained economic growth. Ford projected that in fiscal year 1977 receipts would be $351.3 billion, leaving a deficit of about $43 billion. The largest budget increases were in the areas of defense spending — a $10-billion increase — and energy research. Ford also called for increased funds for mass transit and water pollution control. Most of the spending reductions proposed by Ford, i.e. social security, food stamps, housing subsidies, child nutrition, and veterans benefits, would require Congressional action to change existing law.

Moynihan Scores State Department—Chief United Nations Delegate Daniel P. Moynihan, it was reported Jan. 27, sent a cablegram to Secretary of State Henry A. Kissinger and all U.S. embassies, accusing the State Department of failing to support his efforts in the UN. In the cablegram, entitled "The Blocs Are Breaking Up," Moynihan asserted that he was succeeding in breaking up the anti-American voting bloc in the UN, but the State Department failed to see this and was not supporting him. He cited many examples where his threats and tough talk tactics had produced results toward the U.S.'s "basic foreign policy goal" of breaking up the large bloc of "mostly new nations." He stated further that "the conventional wisdom" in the State Department predicted his efforts would fail and was now determined to prove his tactics were a failure. On Jan. 28, Presidential Press Secretary Ron Nessen stated that Moynihan "is supported by the President, the Secretary of State and top officials of the State Department." Kissinger acknowledged there was criticism of Moynihan in the State Department, but attributed it to bureaucratic "backbiting."

Congress Overrides Social Funds Veto—The House, Jan. 27, in a 310-113 vote, and the Senate, Jan. 28, in a 70-24 vote, overrode Pres. Gerald R. Ford's veto of a $45-billion appropriation for health, welfare, and manpower programs. The votes represented a challenge to Ford's policy of fiscal restraint. Ford had vetoed the bill because it would add almost $1 billion to the current budget deficit and nearly $2 billion in the deficit projected for fiscal year 1977.

Supreme Court Rules on Election Campaign Law— In a landmark decision, the Supreme Court, Jan. 30, struck down certain provisions in the 1974 Federal Election Campaign Act, but retained others. The court upheld public financing for presidential campaigns, limits on individual contributions to candidates in federal election races, and strict requirements for reporting of contributions and expenditures. The court, however, ruled as unconstitutional all limits on spending by the candidate or in his behalf in Congressional campaigns and almost all limits on spending in presidential campaigns. In the latter, court did rule that presidential candidates who accept federal financing must abide by limits on expenditures. The court also ruled that the Federal Election Commission, which had been created to implement the legislation, must be restructured or cease to exercise all but a few of its powers within 30 days. According to the court, many of the commission's powers, particularly initiating civil suits to enforce the law, were executive duties and, according to the doctrine of separation of powers, should be exercised by officers appointed by the executive branch. The 1974 law had delegated the power to appoint the majority of the officers on the commission to Congress. The court found portions of the election campaign law, particularly the limits on spending and contributions, posed possible conflicts with the first amendment.

International

Italian Government Resigns—Following the sudden withdrawal of Socialist party support, the Italian cabinet, led by Prime Minister Aldo Moro, Jan. 7, resigned from office. Although the Socialists were not part of the Christian Democrat-dominated government, they had provided the Moro government with a parliamentary majority. The Socialists charged that their views had been ignored by the government. The cabinet crisis raised the possibility of national elections in which the Italian Communists were expected to gain strength. The cabinet crisis came in the wake of reports, Jan. 6 from well-placed U.S. government officials, that the CIA had channeled some $6 million in secret cash payments since Dec. 8 to anti-communist Italian political leaders to prevent further gains by the Communist party in national elections. The sources stated that U.S. Pres. Gerald R. Ford strongly supported by Secretary of State Henry A. Kissinger, had approved the payment, Dec. 8. On Jan. 7, spokesmen for the Italian Christian Democrats, Socialists, Liberals, and Republicans all denied any of their leaders had received funds through the CIA.

Chou En-lai Dies—Following a long illness, Chinese Prime Minister Chou En-lai, 78, died, Jan. 8, of cancer. The official announcement released by Hsinhua, the Chinese news agency, called Chou's death a "gigantic" loss to the Communist party, the army, and people, as well as the cause of international communism. Chou had been the Chinese premier since 1949 when the Communists assumed power in China.

Ecuadorian President Overthrown—The commanders of Ecuador's 3 armed forces, Jan. 11, took over the government in a bloodless coup, forcing Pres. Guillermo Rodriguez Lara to resign. Rodriguez had seized power in 1972, in one of more than 50 coups in Ecuador in the past 146 years. The new junta, led by Navy Vice Admiral Alfredo Povedo Burbano, promised to turn the government over to the people by the end of 1977. On Jan. 12, the junta said it would form a mostly military government which would rule for 2 years, after which there **Thai Prime Minister Resigns**—Thailand's Prime

Thai Prime Minister Resigns—Thailand's Prime Minister Kukrit Pramoj, Jan. 12, resigned, bringing about the collapse of his coalition cabinet. King Phumiphol Adudet immediately dissolved parliament, ending the nation's first democratically elected government, and called for new elections in April. Kukrit, who agreed to stay on as caretaker prime minister until elections could be held, appealed for calm and blamed his resignation on the opposition's "pressuring the government" for "some benefits that were not in the public interest." The most recent demands, instigated by a coalition of the Democratic party, headed by the prime minister's brother Seni Pramoj, and the Socialist party, had called for a 12-point program that included nationalization of banks and businesses, land reform, and reinstatement of the banned Thai Communist party.

Progress in Moscow SALT Talks—U.S. Secretary of State Henry A. Kissinger, Jan. 21-22, conducted high-level arms control negotiations in Moscow with Soviet Communist Party chief Leonid Brezhnev, Foreign Minister Andrei Gromyko, and other Soviet officials, on a new Strategic Arms Limitation Talk (SALT II) agreement. Kissinger, Jan. 23, stated that "significant progress" had been achieved, although he had failed to attain his maximum goal — an agreement in principle on all outstanding issues. Kissinger, however, according to sources, had brought back a new Soviet proposal to settle the issues still holding up the treaty, which would limit the number of strategic bombers and missile forces maintained by the U.S. and Soviet Union. The Soviet plan tackled one of the most controversial outstanding problems — whether the Backfire, the new Soviet bomber, should be counted in the overall force level of 2,400 missiles and strategic bombers agreed on at Vladivostok in 1974. The Soviet Union which does not consider the Backfire to be a strategic bomber, suggested that the maximum force level be reduced to 2,100 or 2,200 strategic bombers and missiles. The Backfire then would not be counted among them.

Syria-mediated Truce Set in Lebanon—Following the **Jan. 21** arrival of a high-level 3-man meditation team from Syria, Lebanese Pres. Suleiman Franjieh, **Jan. 22**, announced the 24th cease-fire in the Lebanese civil war and stated that all parties had agreed to an "all-embracing political settlement." The truce followed a week marked by the severest political crisis and most violent fighting since April 1975. Although details were not announced, it appeared that the accord would grant some Moslem demands for greater participation in political power while preserving the position of the Christian community. The cornerstone of the accord was the newly formed Higher Military Committee, composed of Lebanese, Palestinian, and Syrian officers, which would be charged with enforcing the cease-fire. Palestine Liberation Army troops from Syria, which had entered Lebanon just before the truce, and other Palestinian units, **Jan. 23**, began to patrol Beirut to enforce the cease-fire.

U.S. Vetoes UN Middle East Plan—The U.S., **Jan. 26**, vetoed a United Nations Security Council resolution calling for the establishment of an independent Palestinian state and total Israeli withdrawal from territories occupied during the 1967 Arab-Israeli war. The resolution was drafted by a group of delegates from Arab nations. U.S. delegate Daniel P. Moynihan declared that the resolution would have been "seriously harmful to the future of the peace-making process" in the Middle East. In the debate preceding the vote, the United States had been nearly isolated in its demands that no changes be made in the basis for Middle East talks. At the beginning of the debate, the U.S., **Jan. 12**, had been the only Security Council member to oppose a procedural resolution to allow the Palestine Liberation Organization to participate in the debate with the rights of a member nation.

Western-Backed Angola Faction Abandons Capital —Under heavy military pressure from the communist-backed Popular Movement for the Liberation of Angola (MPLA), the western-backed National Union for the Total Independence of Angola (Unita), **jan. 27**, abandoned Huambo, the provisional capital of its coalition government with the National Front for the Liberation of Angola. Unita announced that it was shifting its administrative facilities to Silva Porto, the movement's military headquarters. Despite the entry of South African forces, reported **Jan. 20**, in support of Unita troops, the MPLA, heavily supported by Cuban troops, had advanced 140 miles during the preceding 10 days, and threatened Huambo. South African forces, however, pulled back, **Jan. 25**, in an apparent attempt to encourage a similar move on the part of the Cuban troops. The South African forces did not leave Angola, but remained on alert in a non-operational area.

Strikes Spread in Spain, Elections Delayed—As strikes spread through Spain, the government stiffened its attitude toward unrest. King Juan Carlos I issued a decree, **Jan. 27**, postponing new parliamentary elections for at least one year. According to the decree, parliament was extended to allow time for the government to draw up a new electoral law and institute other reforms for legislative election by free universal suffrage. Popular protests had begun, **Jan. 1**, when Rev. Luis Maria Xirinachs, one of the nation's most militant Roman Catholic priests, led a parade of 500 people around Barcelona's main prison in a demand for a general amnesty. In an unexpected turn of events, the Barcelona police helped clear a path for the protestors. Illegal strikes, generally in protest of a government freeze on wages, also began to spread. By **Jan. 14**, when the government drafted several thousand postal workers to end a 2-day halt in mail deliveries, it was estimated that some 150,000 workers in the Madrid area had gone out on strike. In their first public announcement, Spain's 2 major opposition parties, the Communist-dominated Democratic Junta and, the Socialist Workers party-led Democratic Platform, presented the strike movement as a direct political and economic challenge to the government. On **Jan. 15**, the cabinet warned, in a communique, that extremist groups which tried to disrupt reform would only discredit themselves. In evidence of a stiffer attitude toward the spreading protest, on **Jan. 16**, 120 persons were arrested in Madrid and charged with planning a general political strike. On **Jan. 18**, also in Madrid, 22 lawyers and 33 professional people were arrested at what police called "an unauthorized political gathering." And, on **Jan. 19**, the government drafted 70,000 railroad workers, after strike waves had begun to disrupt train service.

Morocco Defeats Algeria in Sahara—Morocco reported, **Jan. 29**, that, following 3 days of intense fighting, it had defeated Algerian soldiers and members of the Algerian-backed Saharan independence movement, the Polisario Front, in Spanish Sahara. Morocco reported that all Algerian forces were being withdrawn from the area and that they had captured more than 100 Algerian soldiers. Although Algeria made no direct claim to Spanish Sahara, it had contested the arrangement made in November in which Spain ceded control over the territory to Morocco and Mauritania.

General

Marion Javits Resigns PR Post—Marion Javits, the wife of Sen. Jacob K. Javits (R. N.Y.), **Jan. 27**, resigned her job as a $67,500 per year consultant to Iran Air, Iran's national airline, and gave up her post as senior vice president at Ruder and Finn, a New York City public relations firm. She stated that her primary concern was the "unjustifiable criticism that has been leveled at my husband because of the appearance of possible conflict."

Disasters—A Lebanese Middle East Airline Boeing 707 enroute from Beirut to Dubai and the Persian Gulf sultanate of Oman, **Jan. 1**, crashed in the Saudi Arabian desert, killing all 82 persons aboard . . . A Soviet TU-134 carrying 56 passengers crashed on take-off at Vnukovo Airport near Moscow, **Jan. 3**, killing all aboard.

FEBRUARY

National

Moynihan Resigns UN Post, Scranton Named— Daniel P. Moynihan, **Feb. 2**, resigned his position as the U.S. delegate to the United Nations. In a letter to Pres. Gerald R. Ford, Moynihan wrote he had been forced by circumstance to choose, "with a heavy and still divided heart," between remaining in the post or returning to the Harvard University faculty. Moynihan made no mention of having insufficient support from the State Department for his attempt to break up the UN's anti-American voting bloc, a charge he made the previous month. Ford regretfully accepted the resignation, stating Moynihan had "elevated public disclosure by puncturing pretense and eloquently advocating the cause of reason." On Feb. 11, Ford who had vowed previously that Moynihan's successor would follow the same policy of challenging 3rd and 4th world powers, asked former Pennsylvania Gov. William W. Scranton to take the UN post. Scranton accepted Feb. 18, and was confirmed by the Senate Mar. 3.

Ford States Abortion Position—Pres. Gerald R. Ford, **Feb. 3**, in a television interview with Walter Cronkite, declared that the Supreme Court had gone "too far" in striking down anti-abortion laws. Ford, however, stated that he opposed a nation-wide restoration of abortion limits through a constitutional amendment. Although Ford said he was opposed to "abortion on demand," he explained that there are cases, including threat to the life of a pregnant woman and rape, when abortions should be allowed. Ford asserted that redefinition of abortion limits should be left to individual states.

Lockheed Payments Abroad Revealed—The Senate subcommittee on multinational corporations, **Feb. 4**, disclosed that the Lockheed Aircraft Corporation had paid $7 million to Yoshio Kodama, a powerful Japanese rightist, part of a total of $12.6 million in payoffs in Japan, to sell its airplanes. Lockheed had admitted previously that it had paid $22 million in bribes overseas, but had not revealed the names of the recipients or the countries involved. The subcommittee also revealed that Lockheed had made payments to Italian politicians, provided "gifts" in Turkey, lobbied in West Germany, and purchased industrial intelligence from European airline officials. The subcommittee released documents with specific information detailing, often in Lockheed's own words, a corporate pattern of influence buying in Western Europe, the Middle East, and the Far East. In testimony before the committee, Lockheed Pres. A.C. Kotchian, **Feb. 6**, stated that, in addition to the payments in Japan, Turkey, and Italy, Lockheed had paid $1.1 million to a high Dutch official. The Dutch cabinet, **Feb. 8**, identified the Dutch official as Queen Juliana's husband, Prince Bernhard, who is also inspector general of the Dutch armed forces.

Concorde Flights O.K.'d on Trial Basis—Transportation Secretary William T. Coleman, **Feb. 4**, granted France and Great Britain limited operation of the Concorde supersonic jet airliner to New York City and Washington, D.C., on a 16-month trial basis. With the long-awaited go-ahead, Concorde flights to Washington's federally-owned Dulles Airport could begin by April. However, the service to New York City's JFK International Airport would require the permission of the Port Authority of New York and New Jersey which operates the airport. In the 61-page opinion, Coleman specifically approved the requests of Air France and British Airways for 2 flights daily to JFK and one flight daily to Dulles. Coleman stated that he had weighed the economic and environmental drawbacks, but felt the advantages outweighed the disadvantages. Concorde opponents had argued, in part, that the planes were too noisy and also posed the peril of increasing incidence of a nonfatal form of skin cancer. Coleman stated that the limited test operation could be cancelled forthwith for safety or other overriding reasons. As advantages, Coleman stated the test flights would help determine whether the SST is commercially viable and would make possible a more intelligent and reasonable judgment of the noise problem. Although Pres. Gerald R. Ford stated he would "stand behind" Coleman's decision, much public dismay at the decision was voiced. The

Environmental Defense Fund immediately filed a suit contesting the decision in the U.S. Court of Appeals in Washington, D.C. New York Gov. Hugh L. Carey, who had previously expressed opposition to the SST flights, stated that he would ask the Port Authority to bar operation of the Concorde at New York airports. On **Feb. 22**, a motorcade of 1,500 cars slowed traffic on the main roads to JFK for 2 1/2 hours. The protestors represented various civic associations from the surrounding vicinity. On **Feb. 23**, the New York State legislature passed a bill limiting the noise level of planes landing and taking off at New York's publically-operated airports. The bill would, in effect, be the first step toward banning SST flights at JFK.

Employment Leads Economic Recovery—The Labor Department, **Feb. 6**, reported that during the month of January national employment had increased by 800,000 jobs. The decrease in unemployment from 8.3% of the labor force in December to 7.8% in January was the largest monthly decline since late 1959. Although the decrease reflected, in part, an unmeasurable "fluke" of seasonal adjustment, government economists felt the improvement was real and substantial. Pres. Gerald R. Ford stated that virtually "all the jobs lost during the recession have now been recovered."

Bentsen Quits Presidential Race—Texas Sen. Lloyd Bentsen, a moderate, **Feb. 10**, withdrew from the race for the 1976 Democratic presidential nomination, citing his poor showing in early caucuses. Bentsen blamed his lack of success on ideological extremism that made it "pretty tough" for a moderate to win in the current political situation.

Ford Announces Sweeping Intelligence Reforms—Pres. Gerald R. Ford, at a **Feb. 17** news conference, announced the most dramatic reform and reorganization of U.S. intelligence agencies since 1947. Ford explained that he had created new powers for the director of the CIA, a new apparatus for improved oversight by the executive branch, and new rigid operating guidelines for intelligence agencies that would protect the rights of American citizens. CIA Director George Bush, Ford stated, would chair a new committee which would conduct the "management of intelligence," with power to prepare intelligence agency budgets and allocate their resources. Ford also would create a 3-man "independent oversight board" charged with monitoring "the performance of the country's intelligence systems." The oversight committee would be headed by Robert D. Murphy, a former undersecretary of state, who recently had conducted a study of U.S. intelligence systems. Stephen Ailes, secretary of the army under the Johnson administration, and Leo Cherne, a publisher of business books and a leader in private movements to rescue persons from totalitarian nations, would complete the oversight board. To improve the performance of intelligence agencies and restore public confidence in their operations, Ford said he would issue a "comprehensive set of public guidelines" which would function as "legally binding charters for our intelligence agencies." Ford also announced that he would send to Congress the next day "special legislation to safeguard critical intelligence secrets." Ford, **Feb. 18**, submitted to Congress legislation which, if passed, would make a serious crime of any disclosure by government employees of the ways the CIA and other agencies collect and evaluate their information. Ford also asked Congress to pass legislation specifically to permit, with a judge's approval, electronic surveillance within the U.S. for foreign intelligence purposes. In the last phase of his overhaul of intelligence activities, Ford issued a 36-page executive order, effective Mar. 1, that sharply restricted the power of intelligence agencies to intrude upon the lives and activities of U.S. citizens. The order limited both physical and electronic surveillance of Americans and set tight regulations on the collection and dissemination of information about Americans. Ford, in the order, also barred burglaries, drug tests on unsuspecting humans, and illegal use of tax return information. Ford also restricted infiltration of any group, be it for intelligence purposes or for influencing its activities to those made up of largely foreign nationals or directly controlled by a foreign government.

Schorr Relieved of Duties Pending Investigation— CBS News announced, **Feb. 23**, that its Washington correspondent Daniel Schorr would be relieved of all duties "for an indefinite period" pending Congressional investigation. Schorr had admitted, **Feb. 12**, that he had leaked a copy of the House Intelligence Committee report to The Village Voice, a weekly New York City newspaper. The House of Representatives, **Feb. 19**, in a 269-115 vote, had decided that its ethics committee should investigate the circumstances surrounding the publication of the material.

Ford, Carter Take New Hampshire Primary—Pres. Gerald R. Ford, **Feb. 24** won a narrow victory over Ronald Reagan in the Republican New Hampshire non-binding preferential primary. Former Georgia Gov. Jimmy Carter, benefiting from a wide split of the liberal vote, won the Democratic primary. When the final ballots were counted, Ford had won the so-called "beauty contest" by a 51%-49% vote. In a separate race for delegates to the Republican convention, Ford fared better, taking at least 17 of 21 delegates. Although most analysts said the race was too close to garner an advantage for either candidate, Reagan, **Feb. 25**, campaigning in Illinois, called the result a "virtual tie" that proved the "viability" of his campaign against an incumbent president. In the Democratic "beauty contest," Carter led 4 others with 29% of the vote. Arizona Rep. Morris K. Udall took 24% of the vote, Indiana Sen. Birch Bayh 18%, Fred R. Harris of Oklahoma 11%, and Sargent Shriver of Massachusetts trailed with 9% of the vote. In the separate race for delegates to the Democratic convention in July, Carter won 15 of the 17 delegates, with the remainder going to Udall.

International

Earthquake Devastates Guatemala—A major earthquake, **Feb. 4**, struck Guatemala and neighboring Honduras, causing the most massive destruction in Guatemala where, in the final count, 22,836 persons lost their lives. Severe damage occurred in Honduras, but no one died. The quake's tremors were also felt in El Salvador and parts of Mexico. Powerful aftershocks hit Guatemala through **Feb. 9**, causing more damage but no further casualties. The epicenter of the earthquake, which registered 7.5 on the Richter scale, was placed 30 miles southwest of Guatemala City. In Guatemala, the earthquake caused serious damage in the provinces, destroying entire villages, and in Guatemala City where the slum areas in the old part of the city were hardest hit. The most severely damaged area was a 100-mile arc to the north and west of Guatemala City. Immediate aid was sent by the U.S., Venezuela, the United Nations Disaster Relief Office, and the Organization of American States. Help began to reach many victims, **Feb. 7**, but scores of outlying villages, blocked by landslides, remained without food, water, and medical attention. On **Feb. 9** and **10**, as emergency relief by airlift gained momentum, the devastated areas north of the capital began to receive food and medi-

cal supplies. According to Guatemala's National Emergency Committee, **Feb. 25**, some 76,504 persons were injured in the quake and aftereffects and some 1.5 million were left homeless.

Hua Named Chinese Premier, Rightists Attacked— In a surprise move, Hua Kuo-feng, a relatively unknown deputy prime minister and minister of public security, **Feb. 7**, was named China's acting prime minister to succeed Chou En-lai. Shortly thereafter, an ideological campaign against alleged rightist party officials, including senior Deputy Prime Minister Teng Hsiao-ping, who had widely been expected to succeed Chou, began to spread through China. It was reported, **Feb. 12**, that 2 days previously a wall-poster campaign against Teng had begun at Peking University amid signs of increasing strain within the Chinese leadership. Reports **Feb. 13** stated the campaign was intensifying and spreading throughout the provinces. Jenmin Jih Pao, China's official daily paper, **Feb. 17**, attacked unnamed "capitalist roaders within the party" who, during the past year, had distorted an important instruction from Mao. The newspaper charged the capitalist roaders had called for unity, stability, and economic growth, a policy closely associated with both Chou En-lai and Teng Hsiao-ping. In a further intensification of the anti-rightist campaign, Mao, **Feb. 24**, in Jenmin Jih Pao, was directly quoted as personally indignant at the rightists, and, **Feb. 27**, Teng was attacked directly by name on wall posters appearing in Peking.

Minority Government Resolves Italian Crisis—Five weeks after the fall of the Italian government, Aldo Moro, prime minister in the previous government, **Feb. 10**, announced that he had formed a one-party minority government of only Christian Democrats. Moro's decision came after he had failed to put together a variety of coalition cabinets. The fragile minority government was viewed as a last resort to avoid national elections in which the Italian Communists were expected to make large gains.

Nigerian Leader Killed in Abortive Coup—Nigerian head of state Gen. Murtala Ramat Mohammed was assassinated, **Feb. 13**, by a small group of young Nigerians calling themselves "young revolutionaries." The revolutionaries, led by Lt. Col. B.S. Dimka, ambushed Mohammed's car on Ikoyi Island, where the nation's military headquarters are located, and then seized Nigeria's radio station. They held the station for 6 1/2 hours, broadcasting in Lagos and in Ibadan, Nigeria's 2d largest city, that they had taken control of the country. However, as divisional commanders throughout the country dissociated themselves from the coup throughout the day, the coup was crushed by evening. Dimka escaped. The 20-member Supreme Military Council, **Feb. 14**, announced that it had unanimously chosen armed forces chief of staff Lt. Gen. Olusegan Obasanjo to succeed Mohammed. It was reported, **Feb. 16**, that Dimka, after Mohammed's assassination, had gone to the British High Commissioner's office, in an attempt to telephone former Nigerian head of state Gen. Yakubu Gowon, a student at Warwick University in England. He was turned away by British authorities. On **Feb. 17**, several hundred Nigerian students stormed the U.S. Embassy and the British High Commission, charging complicity in the attempted coup. The Nigerian government, **Feb. 18**, declared "there was ample evidence Gowon knew and by implication approved of the plot" to restore him to power.

Plan for New Lebanon Announced—Lebanese Pres. Suleiman Franjieh, **Feb. 14**, detailed a "new foundation" for the nation's political and economic system which would end Lebanon's 10-month civil war. The proposal, the product of Syrian mediation and support. would be submitted to parliament for approval. In general. the plan readjusted Lebanon's sectarian political arrangement to give the Moslem majority a greater share of power. while protecting the position of the Christian minority.

U.S., Brazil Agree to Consult—The U.S. and Brazil, **Feb. 21,** agreed to consult with each other on all important economic and political matters involving both nations and their relations with the rest of the world. The agreement signed by U.S. Secretary of State Henry A. Kissinger and Brazilian Foreign Minister Antonio Azeredo da Silveira was the high point of Kissinger's 6-nation tour of South America. It was agreed that the 2 nations would hold semi-annual consultations and that the U.S. Secretary of State would travel to Brazil once a year to consult with the Brazilian foreign minister.

Nixon Returns to China—Former U.S. Pres. Richard M. Nixon and his wife. Pat. **Feb. 21.** returned to China. 4 years after their historic trip. for a "strictly private" visit at the invitation of the Chinese government. When the trip had been announced, **Feb. 6,** U.S. Pres. Gerald R. Ford had been reported irritated at the timing of the visit. just 3 days before the New Hampshire primary.

East-West Rift Marks Soviet Party Congress—The emerging independence of western communist parties from Soviet domination highlighted the 25th Soviet Communist Party Congress held in Moscow **Feb. 24-Mar. 5.** Italian Communist party leader Enrico Berlinguer, **Feb. 27,** in an address to the congress, stated that his party supported Italy's membership in NATO, would seek to cooperate with diverse ideologies at home, and favored a "pluralistic and democratic system." Although Berlinguer did not directly criticize the Soviet Union, he drew a clear independent line, stressing the Italian party's support for individual liberties in religion and the arts.

On the same day, Stane Dolanc, the secretary of the Yugoslav Communist party, calling for each party to follow its own road commensurate with its own local culture and conditions, declared the need "for equality, independence and responsibility of each movement before its own working class and peoples." The French delegate, Gaston Plissonier, **Feb. 28,** stated his party would build a "socialism in the colors of France," explaining that, for the French, Lenin's belief that democracy was necessary "right to the end" implied "the guarantee of all individual and collective liberties." Plissonier spoke in place of French Communist party leader Goerges Marchais who had boycotted the congress because of his differences with Moscow. On **Feb. 5,** at the French Communist party congress in Paris, the delegates had endorsed a proposal to seek power through democratic means and to drop the key Marxist doctrine calling for dictatorship of the proletariat.

Portuguese Military to Surrender Power—Portugal's 5 main parties and armed forces leaders, **Feb. 26,** in Lisbon, signed an agreement which would end military rule and establish a democratic system in Portugal. Under the agreement, the ruling military Council of the Revolution would surrender its power to a president and legislature to be chosen in the nation's first free elections in 50 years. Under the democratic system, the Council of the Revolution would have a consultative role and act as a guarantor of democratic institutions.

Soviets Beam Microwaves on U.S. Embassy—According to a **Feb. 26** report in The New York Times, Soviet authorities had conceded in private that they had beamed microwaves at the U.S. Embassy in Moscow. However, the Soviets denied the waves were linked with Soviet devices to bug conversations at the embassy but rather used to jam American listening devices on the roof of the embassy. The Americans

---

MPLA Claims Victory in Angolan Civil War; Western-backed Factions Begin Guerrilla War

In control of almost all of civil-war torn Angola, the Soviet-backed Popular Movement for the Liberation of Angola (MPLA). in a **Feb. 12** broadcast, stated that it had won the civil war and claimed that the opposing forces were fleeing over the South-West African border. At the same time. it was reported that the western-backed Angolan national factions had decided to abandon the major towns still in their control and prepare for guerrilla warfare.

On **Feb. 11,** the secretariat of the Organization of African Unity had recognized the People's Republic of Angola. the Luanda-based government of the MPLA. as its 47th member. The organization's decision followed a rapid deterioration in the military position of the western-backed factions.

On **Feb. 9,** Jorge Sangumba. the secretary of foreign affairs of the western-supported National Union for the Total Independence of Angola (Unita) had announced the fall of Huambo to the MPLA, strongly aided by Cuban forces. Huambo was the capital of Unita's coalition government with the National Front for the Liberation of Angola (FLNA). On **Feb. 10** the MPLA had taken the strategic Atlantic seaports of Benguela and Lobito. giving it almost total control of the strategically situated Benguela railroad. On **Feb. 11,** in its continued offensive through the center of Angola. the MPLA took Silva Porto. the new Unita headquarters. Unita announced that it would establish new headquarters at Serpa Pinto in the south. The MPLA forces. however. were already moving into the area and it appeared that Unita was holding

only one major town. Luso. near the eastern end of the Benguela railroad. Reports from the north stated that FLNA forces. with the fall. **Feb. 9.** of Sao Salvador. a major stronghold. were virtually crushed. On **Feb. 14,** MPLA forces were reported to be moving deep into southern Angola and meeting virtually no resistance.

Unita. in its **Feb. 12** statement announcing the preparation for guerrilla warfare. declared: "For our liberty and our country. we are determined to continue our struggle in the forests. mountains. and valleys. to conquer the Russian. Cuban and Czech invaders, who know in the long run they face the same destiny as the Portuguese colonialists in Africa." Sangumba claimed Unita had sufficient guns to wage a 10-year guerrilla campaign. but could not fight the Russian tanks that supported the MPLA. On **Feb. 16,** in a statement recorded somewhere in eastern Angola's bush country. Unita Pres. Jonas Savimbi announced the beginning of guerrilla attacks against Cuban soldiers. Unita claimed to have between 15.000 to 20.000 soldiers in the bush country.

France. **Feb. 17,** became the first major Western European nation to recognize the MPLA government. Great Britain. Canada. Denmark. Ireland. Italy. the Netherlands. Norway. Sweden. and Switzerland followed suit **Feb. 19.** Portugal. which. **Feb. 11.** had suspended its agreement with Angola's 3 warring factions. recognizing all 3 as legitimate representatives of the Angola people. recognized the MPLA on **Feb. 22.**

accepted the Soviet contentions. The American devices were used to eavesdrop on Soviet officials riding in limousines and to monitor Soviet radio frequencies. A controversy over microwave emission had arisen, **Feb. 8,** when U.S. diplomatic sources had reported microwaves emanating from Soviet bugging devices placed in the U.S. Embassy posed a potential health hazard. On **Feb. 29,** the medical division of the U.S. State Department asserted that they discovered "no medical problems" related to the presence of microwave emissions.

General

EPA Bans Mercury Pesticides—The Environmental Protection Agency, **Feb. 18,** banned the production of almost all pesticides containing mercury. The ban would bar production of all mercurial pesticides used as bacteriacides or fungicides in paints, varnishes, and lacquers. The ban would also halt use of pesticides on golf course greens and in the treatment of seeds. EPA head Russell E. Train cited as evidence of hazards presented by the unchecked use of such products cases of nervous system disorders caused by mercury poisoning in Japan, Iran, and the U.S. According to the EPA, the ban would reduce the amount of mercury entering the environment by 98.5%.

Swine Flu Danger Cited—The federal government's Center for Disease Control in Atlanta, Ga., **Feb. 19,** alerted all state health department and the World Health Organization to watch for a flu virus that might be related to the virus that caused the great flu pandemic of 1918-19. The basis for the alert was the discovery at Ft. Dix, N. J., of an unusual hybrid flu virus combining the characteristics of human Asian flu virus with one that caused flu-like illness in swine. One of the 4 recruits at Ft. Dix infected with the virus had died.

Marianas Gain Commonwealth Status—The Senate, **Feb. 24,** voted, 67 to 72, to grant commonwealth status to the northern Mariana Islands, leading toward the first U.S. territorial expansion since 1924. The Marianas, comprising 21 islands, stretch for 500 miles in a north-south direction in the Pacific Ocean over 3,500 miles west of Hawaii. In July, the House of Representatives had approved a covenant to establish a political union between the Marianas and the U.S., thereby making the Mariana's 14,500 population U.S. citizens.

Scotti Cites Uneven Justice in Attica Prosecution—Alfred J. Scotti, special New York State prosecutor in the Attica case, **Feb. 26,** declared that the state Attica investigation had "amply demonstrated lack of firmness and evenhandedness." Consequently, Scotti requested that "in the interests of justice" all but one of the remaining indictments arising from the 1971 uprising be dismissed. Scotti stated, "the name 'Attica' should be a symbol, not only of riot and death, but also the capacity of our system of criminal justice to redress its own wrongs."

MARCH
National

Ford Leads Reagan, Carter Gains Momentum — In early Republican presidential primaries, Pres. Gerald R. Ford topped Ronald Reagan 4 times in a row until he lost the North Carolina primary to Reagan on **Mar. 23.** In the **Mar. 2** Massachusetts Democratic preferential primary, Washington Sen. Henry M. Jackson topped 7 opponents, winning 23% of the vote and 30 convention delegates. Alabama Gov. George Wallace, who carried Boston, won 17% of the preferential vote and 21 delegates. Udall, who said his showing indicated he was "the only horse to ride" for party "progressives," placed 3d with 18% of the vote. Former Georgia Gov. Jimmy Carter was 4th with

14% and 16 delegates. In the Republican preferential primary, in which neither candidate had actively campaigned, Ford easily won 62% of the vote and took 27 delegates. Reagan won 35% of the preferential vote and 15 convention delegates. In the Vermont Democratic preferential primary, also on **Mar. 2,** Carter easily topped a 5-candidate field with 46% of the vote. Ford, who was the only candidate on the Republican ballot, won 84% of the vote. The next week, in Florida, Ford, **Mar. 9,** won his 4th victory in 4 primaries over Reagan, winning 53% of the preferential vote to Reagan's 47%. Ford won 43 delegates and Reagan captured 23. Carter beat Wallace in Florida. Wallace placed 2d with 26% of the vote to Carter's 34%. Jackson was 3d with 24%. Carter took 34 delegates, Wallace 26, and Jackson 21. On **Mar. 16,** in Illinois, Ford, with 59% of the preferential vote and 70 delegates, again won a decisive victory over Reagan who won 40% of the vote and 13 delegates. Carter amassed 48% of the preferential vote and 53 delegates in the Democratic primary in Illinois. Wallace won 28% of the vote and 3 delegates. Finally, on **Mar. 23,** in the conservative state of North Carolina, Reagan defeated Ford for the first time, winning 52% of the preferential vote, 28 delegates, and the impetus to stay in the race. Ford won 46% of the vote and 25 delegates. In the Democratic preferential primary, Carter, with 54% of the vote, again beat Wallace who won 35%. Carter also won 35 convention delegates to Wallace's 24.

Bayh, Shapp, Shriver Bow Out — Lacking in both funds and votes, Indiana Sen. Birch Bayh, **Mar. 4,** stated he was "suspending" his campaign for the Democratic nomination for president. Bayh suspended rather than closed his campaign in order not to jeopardize the federal campaign funds still due to him, but conceded "the possibility of resurrecting a suspended candidacy is not great." On **Mar. 12,** Pennsylvania Gov. Milton J. Shapp also withdrew from the race. On **Mar. 22,** Sargent Shriver of Massachusetts became the 5th candidate to withdraw from the race. None of the former candidates endorsed anyone else.

New York Bans SST — The Port Authority of New York and New Jersey, **Mar. 11,** banned any Concorde supersonic airliner flights in the New York City area. The ban would remain in effect until after evaluation of at least 6 months of SST operations elsewhere. The action followed the notification by Air France and British Airways of their intention to begin passenger service to JFK International Airport Apr. 10.

Church Enters Democratic Race — Idaho Sen. Frank Church, **Mar. 18,** in Idaho City, announced that he was making a late entry into the race for the Democratic presidential nomination because he believed "the most important issues are being ignored." Church had delayed his announcement because of his involvement with the Senate investigation of intelligence activities. Church said he would seek the "restoration of the Federal government to legitimacy in the eyes of the people" and would strive toward "better, not bigger, government."

Supreme Court Backs Seniority for Blacks — In a landmark civil rights decision, the Supreme Court, **Mar. 24,** ruled 5-to-3 that blacks who were denied jobs in violation of the Civil Rights Act of 1964 must be rewarded retroactive seniority. Under the decision, which apparently would also extend to sex, ethnic, and religious discrimination, blacks, once they succeeded in getting jobs, would receive seniority as if they had been hired on first applying, if they could prove that racial discrimination was behind the original denial of employment. In the event of layoffs, such persons would also have better job security than those workers with less seniority. As a result of the ruling, some white employees — those hired after the blacks' initial applications were denied but before the blacks were finally put on the job — would have less seniority and job protection than they previously possessed.

Ford Asks National Anti-Flu Campaign — Pres. Gerald R. Ford, **Mar. 24**, asked for a government-supported campaign to vaccinate the entire U.S. population against a new virus closely related to the swine influenza that killed more than 500,000 Americans during the great pandemic of 1918-19. In order to bar possible epidemics during the coming fall and winter, Ford asked Congress to appropriate $135 million to produce the vaccine. Ford, who also asked "each and every American to receive an innoculation" in the fall, said the campaign would be a cooperative effort of federal, state, and local public health forces, as well as private groups and individuals. Ford directed HEW Secretary F. David Mathews and Assistant Secretary of Health Theodore Cooper to develop a program for mass innoculation.

FBI Burglarized Socialist Party — Official FBI reports made public **Mar. 28**, disclosed that on at least 92 occasions, from 1960 to 1966, the FBI burglarized the New York City offices of the Socialist Workers party and its affiliated organizations. The reports, which directly contradicted a Justice Department assertion that the Socialist Workers party had never been an FBI target, were obtained by the party during the course of a civil suit against the government. According to the FBI reports, specially-trained teams had made early morning raids on an average of once every 3 weeks during the 6 1/2-year period. The raids had produced some 10,000 photographs of documents and correspondence relating to almost all aspects of the party's business, including legal strategies of members involved in federal proceedings.

Callaway Quits Ford Campaign — Pres. Gerald R.

Ford's national campaign manager, former Army Secretary Howard H. Callaway, **Mar. 30**, quit the Ford campaign amidst accusations he had misused his influence. Ford named former Commerce Secretary Rogers C. B. Morton to succeed Callaway. Callaway, **Mar. 13**, had taken a "temporary leave" as national campaign manager pending investigation of charges he had intervened with agriculture department officials to obtain approval of the development of a ski resort he controlled on federal land in Crested Butte, Col. Ford, **Mar. 30**, stated he was "absolutely sure" Callaway would be cleared of all charges.

International

Polyansky Dropped From Top Positions — At the closing of the 25th Communist Party Congress, Soviet Minister of Agriculture Dmitri S. Polyansky, **Mar. 5**, was dropped from the Politburo, the ruling body of the Soviet Communist Party Central Committee. Polyansky had been severely criticized at the congress for the past year's disastrous grain failure. On **Mar. 6**, it was announced that Polyansky had been allowed to retain his seat on the Central Committee. However, Polyansky was later dismissed as minister of agriculture and replaced by Valentin K. Meyats, a relatively unknown 2d secretary of the Central Asian republic of Kazakhstan.

Britain to Rule in Ulster — Merlyn Rees, the British secretary of state for Northern Ireland, **Mar. 5**, told the House of Commons that Great Britain would rule Ulster "for some time to come." He said that the 78-member Northern Ireland Convention, elected the previous May to work out a political arrangement among Northern Ireland's Protestants and Roman Catholics, would be dissolved at midnight. The Protestant majority in the convention had refused to share power with the Roman Catholics in any future Ulster government.

Patricia Hearst Convicted of Armed Robbery; Sentencing Delayed Pending Psychiatric Tests

A San Francisco, Cal., federal court jury, **Mar. 20**, convicted Patricia Hearst, 22, on charges of armed robbery. After the verdict was read, the pale, shaken defendant whispered to her chief defense attorney, F. Lee Bailey, "I wonder if I ever had a chance." Although Hearst had testified that she had helped the Symbionese Liberation Army rob the Sunset Branch of the Hibernia Bank on April 15, 1974, she had contended she had acted only under the threat of death.

On **Apr. 12**, U.S. District Judge Oliver J. Carter, at the request of the defense, postponed final sentencing and sent Hearst to a federal institution for a 90-day period of medical and psychiatric diagnostic study. However, as required by law, he imposed the maximum sentence of 25 years in prison, pending the results of the examinations.

During the 39-day trial, the jury heard 66 witnesses and examined almost 1,000 exhibits, including the apartment and closet where Hearst had allegedly been imprisoned. During the course of the trial, the prosecution, led by U.S. Attorney James L. Browning, and the defense fought several legal battles over the admission of evidence. In a major prosecution victory, Judge Carter, **Feb. 11**, had ruled the evidence concerning events after the robbery was admissible. This evidence included tapes made by Hearst in which she stated she had willingly joined the SLA and taken part in the robbery.

Hearst, in her own testimony, described countless threats of death if she did not cooperate with the SLA. She also described in detail her alleged mis-

treatment — her incarceration in narrow closets and forced intercourse with SLA leader Donald DeFreeze and SLA member William Wolfe — during the period after her kidnaping. On **Feb. 23**, after Carter ruled Hearst could be questioned about her activities preceding her arrest in Sept. 1975, Hearst took the Fifth Amendment 42 times.

The defense called 3 expert witnesses to testify on Hearst's state of mind during her captivity. Dr. Louis J. West, a psychiatry professor at the University of California at Los Angeles, **Feb. 23**, testified that his examinations of Hearst after her arrest indicated "it was clear that this was a person terrorized." Two other psychiatrists, Dr. Robert J. Lifton of Yale University and Dr. Martin T. Orne of the University of Pennsylvania, **Feb. 25-27**, supported West's testimony. In rebuttal, the prosecution called Dr. Joel Fort and Dr. Harry Kozol as witnesses. Fort, **Mar. 8**, depicted Hearst as "rebellious, bored with conventional life," and "tending to be dogmatic" and stated that she had voluntarily taken part in the robbery. In similar testimony, Kozol described Hearst as "a rebel in search of a cause." Hearst's mother, **Mar. 17**, testified that, on the contrary, Hearst had been a "very warm and loving girl."

In the closing statements, **Mar. 18**, Browning, the chief prosecutor, told the jury that Hearst's testimony was "too big a pill to swallow." Bailey told the jury, "this is a case about dying or surviving . . . You know in your hearts to be undisputed . . . that there was talk about dying — and she wanted to survive."

Lebanese Civil War Resumes — The Syrian-mediated cease-fire that stopped Lebanese fighting in January, collapsed in March as Lebanese Moslem soldiers went into open revolt, **Mar. 8-10**, precipitating renewed civil strife in Beirut and other sections of Lebanon. Beginning **Mar. 8**, large numbers of Moslem deserters from the Lebanese army, who in recent weeks had formed themselves into the Lebanese Arab army, revolted against their commanders and took over several garrisons throughout Lebanon. On **Mar. 10**, Christian army head Gen. Hanna Saed proclaimed a general amnesty for deserters in an attempt to head off the disintegration of the Lebanese army. Joining the rebellion, Brig. Gen. Abdel Aziz al-Ahdab, a Sunni Moslem and commander of the Beirut military garrison, **Mar. 11**, proclaimed himself military governor of Lebanon. He demanded that both Lebanese Pres. Suleiman Franjieh and Prime Minister Rashid Karami resign within 24 hours and asked the parliament to meet in 7 days to elect a new president. Franjieh immediately denounced the military intervention and refused to resign. On **Mar. 12**, Franjieh refused a formal petition by two-thirds of the parliament that he resign. However, on **Mar. 14**, parliament rejected a call from Ahdab to elect a successor to Franjieh, who remained defiant in his heavily-guarded palace. On **Mar. 15**, 2 armored columns moved close to Franjieh's palace in an attempt to force him to flee. In renewed fighting between leftist Moslem gunmen and right-wing Phalangists, the latter, **Mar. 21**, were driven from their stronghold in the Beirut Holiday Inn. On **Mar. 25**, Franjieh, who still refused to step down, was forced by heavy artillery attacks to abandon his palace to take refuge in a Christian stronghold 13 miles north of Beirut.

Egypt Ends Treaty with USSR — Pres. Anwar Sadat, **Mar. 14**, asked the Egyptian People's Assembly to end immediately their nation's Treaty of Friendship and Cooperation with the Soviet Union, in effect since 1971. The assembly approved the legislation formalizing the break, **Mar. 15**, in a 307-2 vote. An official Soviet statement, released **Mar. 16**, termed the action "a new manifestation of the unfriendly policy in regard to the Soviet Union" that Egypt had been pursuing for a long time and warned Egypt that it would be responsible for any consequences. Prior to the official cancellation of the treaty, Sadat had been seeking financial and political support and military equipment from western countries. U.S. Pres. Gerald R. Ford, **Mar. 3**, much to the dismay of Israel supporters, had told key Congressmen that, in order to encourage Egypt on a moderate path, his administration would like to lift the long-standing embargo on military sales to Egypt. The administration proposed to begin by selling 6 C-130 military transport planes to Egypt at a cost of about $40 million. Despite the protests from American Jewish leaders, Ford, **Mar. 17**, said he would proceed with the sale, calling Sadat a "courageous" leader in moving his nation toward the West.

Wilson Resigns as British Prime Minister — In a move that stunned both his party and the United Kingdom, Labor party leader Harold Wilson, **Mar. 16**, resigned as prime minister. The resignation would take effect as soon as the Labor party in the House of Commons agreed on a successor. Over the long span of his career in British politics, Wilson had served as prime minister for 8 years and as Labor party leader for 13 years. Wilson stated that in March 1974, when he had assumed office again as prime minister, he had made an "irrevocable" decision to remain in office for no more than 2 years. Among the reasons for his departure from office, Wilson cited his desire to give his successor sufficient time to establish his own style and authority before the end of the current parliament in 1979. Wilson's resignation at a critical time in his government's efforts to contain inflation and restore the nation's faltering economy raised a great deal of speculation about the prime minister's motives and sense of timing.

Thais Close Remaining U.S. Bases — The Thai government, **Mar. 20**, ending a year-long deadlock, ordered the U.S. to close all of its military installations in Thailand and to withdraw all remaining military personnel, except 270 military aid advisers, within the next 4 months. The forces in Thailand were the last U.S. forces in Southeast Asia. The remaining Americans would administer the U.S. military assistance program which was expected to cost $54.1 million in the next year. On **Mar. 21**, at least 4 persons were killed and some 70 injured when thousands of Thai students demonstrated in front of the U.S. Embassy in Bangkok in protest against a 4-month extension of the U.S. presence.

Britain Proposes Rhodesian Plan — In an attempt to end the Rhodesian crisis, Great Britain, **Mar. 22**, proposed a new plan for majority rule and offered financial help to insure an orderly transition to a multiracial society. However, British Foreign Minister James Callaghan stated that such aid would not be available unless Rhodesian Prime Minister Ian D. Smith agreed to accept the principle of majority rule and to hold democratic elections within 18 months to 2 years. The British proposal followed the **Mar. 19** break-off of negotiations between Smith and Rhodesian black nationalists on a constitutional settlement that would lead to majority rule in Rhodesia. Smith, **Mar. 23**, rejected the British plan, stating that Callaghan had "chosen to disregard the realities and had come forward with proposals no less extreme than those of the African National Council." The African National Council, the majority black nationalist faction with which Smith had been negotiating, had demanded the immediate resignation of the Rhodesian government, dissolution of the parliament, and a lowering of franchise qualifications.

Military Ousts Peron in Argentina — In a smooth, well-planned coup, the Argentine armed forces, **Mar. 24**, overthrew the Peronist government of Isabel Martinez de Peron. Ten hours later, a 3-man military junta headed by army commander Gen. Jorge Rafael Videla was installed in office. Buenos Aries remained calm indicating acceptance of the overthrow by the majority of Argentines. Since Peron had taken power after the death of her husband, Juan Peron, some 20 months before, Argentina had been in a state of almost perpetual crisis, wracked by severe inflation, labor unrest, and terrorism. According to an official communique, Peron was flown to the resort center of La Angostura and held in "protective custody." The junta proclaimed martial law and threatened terrorists and saboteurs with death. A number of Peronist union and political officials were arrested in Buenos Aries and Cordoba. The General Confederation of Labor and all affiliated unions were placed under military control. Gen. Videla, considered a moderate in the military, was chosen president of the 3-man junta. Videla and the other 2 junta members, navy commander Adm. Emilio Massera and air force commander Brig. Gen. Orlando R. Agosti, would serve for 3 years. The junta, **Mar. 28**, named an 8-member cabinet, including 2 civilians and 2 officers each for the army, navy, and air force.

U.S. Vetoes Anti-Israel Resolution in UN — The U.S., **Mar. 25**, vetoed an United National Security Council resolution deploring Israeli policies in Jerusalem and occupied areas of the West Bank, following 2 weeks of Arab demonstrations and strikes on the Israeli-occupied West Bank area of the Jordan. The outbreak of violence, **Mar. 7-23,** which was the worst since the territory came under Israeli control in 1967, was linked to a Moslem-Jewish controversy over the Temple Mount in Jerusalem and to tension arising from upcoming local elections on the West Bank and from the Israeli occupation in general. On **Mar. 16,** violence had spread to the Old City of Jerusalem as some 200 Arabs marched on the Temple Mount, shouting anti-Israeli slogans. On **Mar. 28,** Israel deported 2 Arab mayoral candidates on charges of having incited the recent wave of riots in their cities. Further Arab violence within Israel, the worst in the nation's 28-year history, erupted **Mar. 29-30,** in more than a dozen northern Israeli villages as Rakah, the Arab-dominated Israeli Communist party, called for a general strike. On **Mar. 31,** Israeli Prime Minister Itzhak Rabin claimed that the riots, in which 6 Arabs died, were part of a campaign encouraged by the Arab world to damage the relations that had developed between Jews and Israeli Arabs.

U.S., Turkey Reach New Accord on Aid and Bases — The U.S. and Turkey, **Mar. 26,** agreed on a new 4-year accord under which American military installations in Turkey would be reopened in exchange for a pledge of about $1 billion in U.S. grants and loans. The accord followed 3 days of talks between U.S. Secretary of State Henry A. Kissinger and Turkish foreign Minister Ihsan S. Caglayangil and months of negotiations. In February 1975, Congress, in reaction to Turkey's 1974 invasion of Cyprus and occupation of many Greek Cypriot areas, had voted an embargo on military aid to Turkey. In retaliation, Turkey, in July 1975, had closed 25 bases in Turkey, including several intelligence gathering installations. Congress, in October 1975, had partially lifted the embargo on military aid, leading to the current round of negotiations. Kissinger, **Mar. 29,** on Capitol Hill, acknowledged the new accord would have "very rough sledding" in Congress. Although he admitted Turkey had made no concessions on the Cyprus issue, Kissinger told the House International Relations Committee that an attempt by Congress to link Cyprus negotiations to Turkish-American military relations "would lead to disastrous consequences that would last for decades."

General

Dow Jones Tops 1,000—Capping an exceptionally strong 3 months on Wall Street, the Dow Jones industrial average, **Mar. 11,** closed above the psychologically - important 1,000-mark in trading on the New York Stock Exchange. The Dow, the barometer of stock activities of 30 major "blue chip" companies, rose 8.03 points during the session to close at 1003.31, the highest closing level since Jan. 26, 1973. The event strengthened a chain of promising economic indicators, including a rise in industrial production and retail sales, expansion of consumer installment credit, and signs of slowing in the inflation rate. Earlier, as the Dow had climbed steadily, 44.51 million shares were traded on Feb. 20, the largest trading volume in the history of Wall Street. Brokers had attributed the trading surge to a growing speculative interest by individual investors.

New Trial Ordered for Carter and Artis—In a unanimous ruling, the New Jersey Supreme Court, **Mar. 18,** ordered a new trial for Rubin "Hurricane" Carter and John Artis. Both Carter and Artis had been convicted and condemned to life imprisonment in a 1967 triple murder in Paterson, N. J. The Court ruled that in the original trial, the Passaic County Prosecutor's office had "substantially prejudiced" a fair trial by suppressing evidence. The suppressed evidence included promises of leniency given to 2

important prosecution witnesses in connection with unrelated criminal matters. On **Mar. 19,** a joint bail set by the court at $35,000 was immediately paid by heavyweight boxing champion Muhammad Ali and a Carter-Artis defense committee. Carter and Artis, **Mar. 20,** were released from prison.

Princess Margaret, Lord Snowdon Separate—In a brief announcement from Kensington Palace, it was announced, **Mar. 19,** that Great Britain's Princess Margaret and her husband, Antony Armstrong-Jones, Lord Snowdon, had agreed to live apart. The statement, which came at the end of a week filled with speculation about the reported dissolution of the couple's marriage, said there were no plans for divorce. A spokesman for Queen Elizabeth II said the queen was "naturally very sad at what has happened."

Supreme Court Rules on Homosexuality—The U.S. Supreme Court, **Mar. 29,** in a 6-3 decision, ruled that individual states could prosecute and imprison persons for committing homosexual acts, even if the acts were performed in private and between consenting adults. The court had not heard oral arguments nor did it issue an opinion, but simply affirmed a Virginia lower court ruling which had rejected a challenge to the state's law prohibiting consensual sodomy. The Virginia court had ruled that the law did not violate the right to privacy or other constitutional protections, including freedom of expression and the ban against cruel and unusual punishment. The Supreme Court ruling departed from a 10-year trend expanding the constitutional right to privacy. The decision, however, did not require states that have repealed the sodomy prohibition — 10 states according to the National Gay Task Force — to reinstitute it. Both civil liberties groups and homosexual organizations expressed astonishment and dismay at the high court's ruling.

Court Rules Quinlan Has Right to Die—The New Jersey Supreme Court, in an unanimous decision, **Mar. 31,** ruled that the mechanical respirator that had been keeping Karen Anne Quinlan, 22, alive since April 1975 might be disconnected. However, the ruling, which reversed a lower court decision, specified that Quinlan's attending physicians and a panel of hospital officials must first agree there was "no reasonable possibility" that she would recover. The court also ruled that there would be no civil or criminal liability if the respirator were disconnected in accordance with the guidelines established in its 59-page opinion. The court appointed Karen's father, Joseph Quinlan, her guardian and empowered him to find physicians and hospital officials who would agree to remove the respirator. Joseph Quinlan, along with his wife, had petitioned that Karen might be allowed to die "with grace and dignity."

Disasters—In Europe's worst ski-lift disaster, a cable car returning to Cavalese, a ski resort in the Italian Dolomites, **Mar. 9,** plunged 200 feet to the ground, killing 42 of its 43 passengers, most of them West Germans. . . . At least 45 wedding guests were killed, **Mar. 26,** in Pune, India, when the tractor-drawn wagon they were riding plunged into a canal.

APRIL
National

Teamsters Pact Ends Strike — Labor Secretary W. J. Usery, **Apr. 3,** announced that the teamsters union and the trucking industry had agreed on a new 3-year contract, ending a strike that began **Apr. 1.** The agreement provided an hourly raise of $1.65 over 3 years, an open-ended cost-of-living formula, an increase in pension and health benefits of $17 per week over the 3-year period, and air-conditioned truck cabs. Pres. Gerald R. Ford said he was "delighted" and pleased that the settlement was reached through the collective-bargaining process.

Calley Case Closed — The Supreme Court, **Apr. 5,** refused to review the court martial conviction of Lt. William J. Calley, closing one of the most bitter chapters of the Vietnam war. Calley had been convicted of murdering 28 civilians at Mylai in 1968. The army announced immediately that Calley would be "transferred to parole status" and released to a federal parole officer as soon as all legal technicalities were completed. Calley, free on bail since 1974 after he had served little more than 3 years of his original life sentence, would not be required to return to confinement.

Jackson Wins in NY, Carter Rebounds in Pennsylvania — Winning support for his strategy of building a coalition of northern industrial states, Sen. Henry M. Jackson, **Apr. 6,** won the New York Democratic presidential primary, but, **Apr. 27,** in a severe setback, lost the pivotal Pennsylvania primary to Jimmy Carter. In the New York delegate primary, where Jackson had predicted a landslide victory, he won 104 delegates (38%) of the 206 to be selected that day. Arizona Rep. Morris K. Udall won 70 delegates (25.5%) and Jimmy Carter won 35 delegates (12.8%). Of the 65 uncommitted delegates, 10 were considered favorable to Jackson and 16 to Sen. Hubert H. Humphrey. The remaining 68 New York delegates would be chosen by the state Democratic committee in proportion to the primary results. In Wisconsin, on **Apr. 6,** Carter, with 37% of the vote, beat Udall by a narrow margin. Udall had earlier been proclaimed the winner by 2 televison networks and several newspapers on the basis of computer projections. Wallace placed 3d with 13% and Jackson was 4th with 7%, followed by anti-abortion candidate Ellen McCormack who had 4%. In the delegate race, Carter won 26, Udall 25, Wallace 10, Jackson 6, and McCormack 1. In the Republican primary, Pres. Gerald R. Ford won 55% of the vote and all 45 convention delegates, defeating Ronald Reagan who took 45% of the vote. In Pennsylvania, **Apr. 27,** Carter won his 7th primary in 9 contests, his first in a northern industrial state. Jackson came in 2d with 25% of the vote, Udall 3d with 19%, and Wallace was 4th with 11%. Both anti-abortion candidate Ellen McCormack and Pennsylvania Gov. Milton J. Shapp, who was no longer a candidate, received 3%. In the separate delegate race, Carter won 64, Udall 22, Jackson 19, Shapp 17, Wallace 3, and 46 were designated uncommitted.

Harris Quits Presidential Campaign — Former Oklahoma Sen. Fred Harris, **Apr. 8,** announced that he would end his "national effort" in the presidential primaries to win the Democratic nomination for president. He said that he was still a candidate, but it was "very unlikely" that he could win the nomination. He stated that he would concentrate his efforts on influencing the platform or possibly the selection of a nominee.

Economic Recovery on Upswing—The Commerce Department reported, **Apr. 19,** that the recovery of the nation's economy had speeded up during the first quarter of 1976 with a 7.5% "real" rise in gross national product. As measured by the G.N.P. Price Index, known as the "deflator," inflation during the January-March period had run at 3.7%, the lowest since the 3d quarter of 1972. The Labor Department, **Apr. 21,** confirmed the good news on inflation, announcing consumer prices for the first quarter had risen at an annual rate of 2.9%, the lowest quarterly rise since the 2d quarter of 1972. Earlier in the month, the Labor Department, **Apr. 2,** had reported that unemployment had fallen for the 5th month in a row to 7.5% of the labor force. Jobs in March had

risen by 375,000 to a record 86.7 million. The fast rate of economic recovery was attributed chiefly to a rise in consumer spending, particularly for automobiles and other durable goods, and the re-accumulation of inventories by businesses.

Senate Issues Intelligence Reports—Concluding its 15-month investigation, the Senate Select Committee on Intelligence Activities, **Apr. 26,** issued a 474-page report on foreign and military intelligence, and, **Apr. 28,** a 341-page report on domestic intelligence activities. The first report, which had been heavily censored at the request of intelligence agencies, urged Congress to adopt a new, omnibus law dealing with foreign and military intelligence gathering. The law would create charters for the major intelligence agencies and sharply limit the use of covert action as a foreign policy tool. The new law was needed, the committee reported, because "Congress had failed to provide the necessary statutory guidelines to insure that intelligence agencies carry out their missions in accord with constitutional processes." The charters would define the roles of each intelligence agency and "set forth the basic purposes of national intelligence agencies." The committee also recommended that a permanent oversight committee be created in the Senate which would have authority over the budgets of intelligence agencies and receive prior notification of planned covert activities. Although the report made few new disclosures, the committee reported that the U.S. had conducted some 900 major or sensitive covert operations over the preceeding 15 years. The committee also made 87 separate recommendations in areas ranging from drug tests on humans to covert operations in Chile. In the domestic intelligence report, the committee sharply criticized several agencies, especially the FBI, charging they had knowingly and repeatedly violated laws and the Constitution in their investigations of the political activities of hundreds of thousands of law-abiding U.S. citizens. The committee found that the agencies had investigated too many people and at many times for the wrong reasons or no reason at all. Acting largely without the knowledge of presidents or attorneys general, the agencies, as a matter of course, had used "illegal" or "questionable" methods, including burglary, mail opening, electronic surveillance, and informers. This kind of conduct, the committee reported, had been neither partisan nor the product of a "few willful men," but rather the inevitable product of the "excessive growth of executive power unchecked by Congress." Such activities, the committee concluded, demanded a "fundamental reform" of the domestic intelligence community. In broad terms, the committee recommended that no federal agency be allowed to undertake any activity not explicitly authorized by law. Court approval, the committee stated, should be obtained in advance for such activities as wiretapping, the opening of first class mail, and unauthorized break-ins by federal agents. In specific recommendations, of which there were 96 in the report, the committee proposed that all noncriminal investigations be concentrated in the FBI where they could be closely watched by Congress and conducted under new stringent safeguards designed to protect civil liberties. The committee also proposed that the IRS deal only with tax matters, that military security domestic investigations be sharply reduced, and that the CIA be banned from using electronic surveillance, unauthorized entries, or mail opening inside the U.S.

Humphrey Rejects 4th Presidential Campaign— Minnesota Sen. Hubert H. Humphrey, **Apr. 29,** tearfully announced that he would reject the pleas of his friends to wage a 4th campaign for the Democratic presidential nomination. On **Apr. 28**, Humphrey had hinted on a national television program that he might form a committee to seek the support of uncommitted delegates pending a decision to enter the race after the last primary on June 8. Instead, Humphrey said he would not enter the New Jersey primary or authorize such a committee to solicit delegate support on his behalf. Humphrey, however, did assure his supporters that, in the "unlikely event" of a deadlocked convention, he would be willing to accept the nomination. Shortly after Humphrey's announcement, New Jersey Gov. Brendan Byrne announced his support for Jimmy Carter and urged the nation's 36 other Democratic governors to rally behind Carter in a demonstration of national unity.

International

New Truce Set, Syrian Army Enters Lebanon—Lebanon's warring factions, **Apr. 1**, agreed to a 10-day truce, mediated by Syria and the Palestine Liberation Organization, to give parliament time to select a successor to Pres. Suleiman Franjieh and open the way for a political settlement. Despite heavy pressure from the army and parliament, Franjieh had refused to resign. The truce agreement resulted from a compromise in which Kamal Jumblat, the leader of the leftist-Moslem alliance, had agreed to drop his demand for Franjieh's immediate resignation and Syria had expressed a willingness to drop its support of Franjieh. Buoyed by leftist-Moslem military gains in late March, Jumblat had previously resisted such a compromise. The truce was renewed **Apr. 11**. As Syrian troops began to move into Lebanon **Apr. 9**, Syrian Pres. Hafez al-Assad, **Apr. 13**, warned Palestinian and Lebanese leaders that Syria would take any step to prevent further bloodshed in Lebanon. Following a fresh outbreak of fighting in Beirut **Apr. 15**, Syria and the Palestine Liberation guerrilla movement, **Apr. 16**, announced a 7-point agreement on moves to end the civil war under which they would take "a unified stand against any party that resumes military operations." The agreement also called for re-establishment of a Syrian-Palestinian Higher Military Committee and a new truce, effective **Apr. 20**, as well as resistance to partition in any forms, and opposition to both "arabization" and internationalization of the conflict.

Kukrit Ousted in Thai Elections—Losing re-election to the National Assembly, Thai Prime Minister Kukrit Pramoj, **Apr. 4**, lost his office as head of his 17-party governing coalition. His brother, Seni Pramoj, whose Democratic party won a plurality in the elections, formed a new 4-party coalition, **Apr. 22**, with the Thai Nation, Social Justice, and Social Nationalist parties. Kukrit's defeat was attributed to the army's dissatisfaction with his government's decision to order all U.S. personnel, with the exception of 270 military advisers, out of Thailand within 4 months. On **Apr. 5**, Seni had stated he would consider renegotiation of an agreement with the U.S.

Callaghan Chosen British Prime Minister—In the 3d and final round of balloting, the British Labor party in the House of Commons, **Apr. 5**, selected Foreign Secretary James Callaghan as their party leader. Callaghan won by a comfortable margin. On **Apr. 6**, in his first official act, Callaghan announced a new budget and enunciated his commitment to former prime minister Wilson's anti-inflation policies. The budget focused directly on the revival of the nation's ailing mills and factories, rather than on public services and social welfare, the traditional hallmarks of Labor government policy. In a surprise move, Callaghan, **Apr. 8**, named as foreign secretary Anthony Crosland, a moderate intellectual who had been

secretary of state for the environment. Michael Foot, the champion of the party's left wing and Callaghan's major rival for the party leader spot, was given the pivotal job of lord president of the council or leader of the House of Commons.

Hua Named Chinese Premier, Teng Ousted—The Chinese Communist leadership, **Apr. 7**, named acting Prime Minister Hua Kuo-feng prime minister and first deputy chairman of the Communist party and deposed Teng Hsiao-ping as deputy chairman of the party and first deputy prime minister, and as chief of staff of the armed forces. In the move, Hua emerged as the leading potential successor to party chairman Mao Tse-tung, a position previously attributed to Teng. The Communist party linked Teng's dismissal to violent demonstration, **Apr. 5**, in Peking, in support of former Prime Minister Chou En-lai and his associates, including Teng. Chou's death in January had prompted an anti-rightist campaign aimed primarily at Teng, Chou's logical successor. Some 100,000 people, **Apr. 8**, marched in Peking's Tien An Men Square in an organized display of support for the leadership changes. On **Apr. 9**, Foreign Minister Chiao Kuanhua and other senior officials joined the street demonstrators in an apparent attempt to prevent any further outbreak of unrest. An ambiguously-worded **Apr. 10** editorial in Jenmin Jih Pao, the Communist party newspaper, stated that the anti-rightist campaign should now concentrate on criticizing Teng. Political observers concluded that this apparent suggestion that the campaign not be immediately expanded to other rightists reflected the severe shock and concern of the Peking leadership at the violent demonstrations in support of Chou.

West Bank Riots Resume After Election Gains—Palestinian nationalists and Arab radicals, **Apr. 12**, made large gains in local elections on the Israeli-occupied West Bank of the Jordan River. Generally more radical mayors — communists, Syrian Baathists, and those sympathetic to the Palestine Liberation Movement — were selected in 10 of 24 towns involved in the elections. Arab leaders viewed the victories as a demonstration that the residents preferred an independent Palestinian state on the West Bank. Israeli Defense Minister Shimon Peres, at an **Apr. 13** news conference, denied it was "a day of mourning for Israel," but rather "a national challenge with which we will now have to grapple." From **Apr. 17** to **Apr. 21**, anti-Israeli rioting, similar to that which preceded the elections, broke out anew on the West Bank. Much of the violence was aimed against a march through the West Bank to Jericho staged by some 30,000 Israeli nationalists to dramatize their claim to the territory and to demand the right to settle there. On **Apr. 19**, Israeli soldiers shot and killed one Arab and wounded 3 others who stoned Israeli marchers in Nablus.

Amalrik Accepts Exile—Soviet dissident writer Andrei Amalrik, who had spent many years in prison and in Siberian exile, and his wife, **Apr. 12**, agreed to go into exile abroad. Although not Jewish, they yielded to a relentless police harassment campaign to apply for emigration to Israel. Amalrik stated, "This is not a decision taken freely. . . When a man is born in a country and is a writer, he does not want to leave — not ever."

Kissinger Warns Against Italian Communist Gains —U.S. Secretary of State Henry A. Kissinger, **Apr. 13**, told the American Society of Newspaper Editors in Washington, D.C., that the entry of the Italian Communist party into that nation's government would be a long-term dangerous trend because other European countries would "also be tempted to move in the same direction." He warned that the U.S. must not create "the impression it would be indifferent to such developments."

India Moves to Ease Foreign Relations—In April, the Indian government moved to improve relations with both China and Pakistan. External Affairs Minister Y.B. Chavan, **Apr. 15**, announced, amid cheers from parliament, that for the first time in 15 years, India would send an ambassador to Peking. Chavan said the move to ease the hostility separating the 2 largest nations in Asia was part of an "endeavor to develop amicable relations with all countries." On **Apr. 19**, the government announced that Prime Minister Indira Gandhi, in a letter to Pakistani Prime Minister Zulfikar Ali Bhutto, had offered to resume discussion on matters such as air and surface communications and even "to discuss measures for the restoration of diplomatic relations." In Dec. 1971, in the midst of the Bangladesh war, India and Pakistan had severed diplomatic and virtually all other links.

U.S., Greece Renew Military Agreement—The U.S. and Greece, **Apr. 15**, signed a 4-year agreement in principle that would allow the U.S. to continue to use 4 military facilities in Greece. In return, according to the agreement, the U.S. would give Greece $700 million in military aid over the span of the agreement. Like the recent U.S.-Turkish military accord, the agreement needed approval in both houses of the U.S. congress.

Egypt, China Sign Military Protocol—Egypt and China, **Apr. 21**, in Peking, signed a military protocol and heralded a new phase in relations between the 2 countries. Although details of the protocol were not announced, it was understood that China would provide spare parts for Egypt's Soviet-supplied MIG fighters. Arab diplomats in Egypt, **Apr. 22**, termed the protocol the first breakthrough for the Chinese in relations with a major Arab nation. Egyptian sources indicated that Egyptian Pres. Anwar Sadat's need to enter into a permanent military-supply relationship with China had prompted the abrogation of Egypt's treaty with the Soviet Union in March.

Socialists Lead Portuguese Elections—In Portugal's first free parliamentary elections in 50 years, the Socialist party, **Apr. 25**, won a plurality of the 263 seats in the National Assembly. However, the official results, announced **Apr. 27**, showed that no party had won a clearcut majority. The Socialists had won 34.9% of the vote, giving them 107 seats, 25 short of a majority. The centrist Popular Democratic party won 24.03%, the conservative Social Democratic Center 15.91%, and the Communist party won 14.56% of the vote. Socialist party leader Mario Soares, **Apr. 26**, had termed the balloting an "indisputable victory" for his party and vowed to honor his campaign pledge to form a minority government if called upon. He rejected an alliance with either the communists or any centrist or conservative group.

Kissinger Sets Rhodesian Program—In the major policy speech of his 7-nation African tour, U.S. Secretary of State Henry A. Kissinger, **Apr. 27**, in Lusaka, Zambia, outlined a program of American actions designed to force Rhodesia's white minority government to accept majority rule. Kissinger stated that he would ask the U.S. Congress to repeal the Byrd Amendment which had made it possible for the U.S. to import Rhodesian chrome in contravention of United Nations sanctions. Kissinger also pledged U.S. economic and educational assistance to the Rhodesian people as "they make the peaceful transition to majority rule and independence." Kissinger further stated that the U.S. government would advise its citizens against visiting Rhodesia and would urge those

living there to leave. Rhodesian Prime Minister Ian D. Smith announced, on the same day, a "new initiative" to include blacks in his minority government for the first time. He stated that 4 black tribal chiefs would be sworn in, **Apr. 28**, as cabinet ministers and 6 other blacks would be made deputy ministers. Black nationalist leaders denounced the initiative as "irrelevant" because the 4 chiefs were already receiving government salaries and it seemed unlikely that any of the others would represent the black nationalists who are demanding immediate majority rule.

General

Howard Hughes Dies—The reclusive 70-year-old billionaire Howard R. Hughes, **Apr. 5**, died over south Texas while enroute to Houston, Tex. Hughes had been traveling from seclusion in Acapulco, Mex., to Houston's Methodist Hospital for emergency treatment. According to the official autopsy, released **Apr. 6**, Hughes died of kidney failure due to chronic renal disease. Concern over disbursement of Hughes' $1.5 billion estate grew **Apr. 7** as knowledgeable Hughes associates failed to establish the existence of a will. On **Apr. 29**, officials of the Mormon Church disclosed the discovery of a handwritten will allegedly made by Hughes 6 years previously. The church, however, did not vouch for the authenticity of the will which gave 1/16 of the estate — possibly as much as $100 million — to the church.

50 Convicted in USMA Cheating Scandal—According to army officials, **Apr. 22**, the cadet honor boards at the U.S. Military Academy at West Point, N.Y., convicted 50 3d-year cadets of cheating on a take-home electrical engineering exam. The board acquitted 49 other cadets, and 2 resigned before the charges could be pressed. A conviction under the cadet honor code entailed expulsion from the Academy and, in the case of 3d and 4th year students, 2 years service in the army as enlisted men. A New York Times report, **Apr. 23**, based on information from cadets, stated that the Academy had covered up the fact that the number of cadets who cheated was actually much higher. Army officials denied the report.

Bergman Leaves Sweden—Internationally-renowned film director Ingmar Bergman, **Apr. 22**, announced that he would leave his native Sweden and would continue his film work abroad. In a bitter, open letter published in a widely circulated Swedish newspaper, Bergman wrote that harassment and humiliation by public tax officials made it impossible to live in Sweden. Although Bergman had been cleared of fraud charges connected with a Swiss company he had established and owned, he had suffered a nervous breakdown in the process.

Soliah Acquitted—A Sacramento, Calif., federal jury, **Apr. 27**, acquitted Steven Soliah, a 27-year-old house painter, of a $15,000 bank robbery in which a woman was killed. During the 7-week trial, Soliah, a former boy friend of Patricia Hearst, admitted he had harbored Hearst and SLA members William and Emily Harris, helped them find a house in Sacramento, and given them money. Although 2 bank employes had identified Soliah as one of the 4 bank robbers, the defense had contended Soliah could have been mistaken for a look-alike who had entered the bank at the time of the robbery.

Disasters—All 37 persons aboard died, **Apr. 14**, when a plane owned by the Argentine state oil company crashed in Neuquen province in southern Argentina. . . An American Airlines jet, beset by engine trouble, **Apr. 27**, crashed on landing at Charlotte Amalie in the U.S. Virgin Islands, killing 37 of the 88 persons aboard.

MAY
National

Reagan Threatens Ford Nomination Bid—Winning several important Republican primaries in March, former California Gov. Ronald Reagan built up an early delegate lead against Pres. Gerald R. Ford. However, **May 24**, Ford received the endorsement of 119 New York Republican convention delegates and regained the lead. In Texas, on **May 1**, Reagan, aided by a Democratic crossover vote, soundly beat Ford. Reagan won by a 2-to-1 margin in virtually every district and took all of the state's 96 delegates. In the Democratic primary, Jimmy Carter, taking 92 delegates, won impressively over the favorite son, Sen. Lloyd M. Bentsen, who won 6 delegates. On **May 4**, Reagan won another major, although narrow, victory (51% to 49%) over Ford in Indiana, again aided by a Democratic crossover vote. Adding victories in Alabama and Georgia, Reagan, according to an unofficial New York Times estimate **May 5**, led Ford 357 to 297 in the delegate tally. Carter, **May 4**, also won soundly in Indiana (68%) and Georgia (84%), but, in Alabama, lost to Gov. George Wallace. Over the **May 8-9** weekend, Reagan picked up 30 delegates in Oklahoma, Louisiana, and Kansas, while Ford added 17 delegates from Kansas, Missouri, and Minnesota. In the **May 11** Republican primary in Nebraska, Reagan won 55% of the vote and 18 delegates, beating Ford for the 5th time in 10 days. In the Democratic primary, Idaho Sen. Frank Church, with 39% of the vote, edged out Carter with 38%. The remaining 23% was split among 9 candidates. In West Virginia, Ford beat Reagan, 57% to 43% of the vote. Among the Democrats, favorite-son Sen. Robert C. Byrd swept the primary, with 89% to Wallace's 11% of the vote. Carter had not entered the race. In Connecticut, Carter narrowly beat Arizona Rep. Morris K. Udall, 33% to 31%. Jackson, who was strongly supported by Gov. Ella Grasso, ran 3d with 18%. Ford, **May 18**, revived his campaign hopes in his home-state of Michigan with a 65% to 34% victory over Reagan. Ford took 55 delegates and Reagan 29. Carter again won a narrow victory (44% to 43%) over Udall, who had made a major effort in an attempt to stop the Carter bandwagon. In the Maryland Democratic primary, California Gov. Edmund G. Brown, who had entered the contest late, turned a 20-day blitz campaign into a 49%-to-37% preferential victory over Carter. However, because Brown had not entered any delegate slates, Carter won 32 delegates, Jackson 10, and Udall 7. On **May 25**, the busiest day of the primary schedule, Ford upset Reagan in Kentucky and also won in Tennessee and Oregon. Reagan won in Arkansas, Idaho, and Nevada. Although Reagan picked up 24 more delegates than Ford, the president's 76 delegates, plus the support from the New York delegation was enough to protect Ford's lead of 771 delegates to 643, of the 1,130 needed for the nomination. In the Democratic races, Carter won landslide victories in Tennessee, Arkansas, and Kentucky, but lost to Church in Idaho and Oregon and to Brown in Nevada. Carter's victories gave him 879 delegates, well over half the 1,505 needed to win the nomination.

Jackson Ends Active Campaign—Washington Sen. Henry M. Jackson, **May 1**, told his supporters that he would end his "active pursuit" of the Democratic presidential nomination. Jackson stated that he would not endorse another candidate and that he believed the nomination was still open although Jimmy Carter "quite clearly has a commanding lead."

Override of Day Care Veto Fails—The Senate, **May 5**, failed by 3 votes to override a presidential veto of a $125-million child day-care bill which would have supplied federally-supported centers with sufficient funds to meet unenforced staffing and safety standards. The House of Representatives, **May 4**, in a 301-101 vote, had overridden the veto. Pres. Gerald R. Ford, **Apr. 6**, had vetoed the bill because he felt it cost too much, failed to expand services, and intruded into the ability of states to run their programs. The bill would have postponed until July 1 enforcement of federal staffing and safety standards. Failure to comply would mean a retroactive loss of federal funds, which threatened to cause mass closings of day-care centers.

Moore acquitted of Extortion Charges—A Charleston, W. Va., jury, **May 5**, found Gov. Arch A. Moore Jr. not guilty of charges that he conspired to extort $25,-000 from a businessman who was seeking a state bank charter. Moore and his former administrative assistant William Loy, who was also acquitted, had faced a $10,000-fine and 20 years in prison. Moore had charged that the indictment and investigation of his affairs were a political vendetta by the prosecutor conducted in association with an anti-Moore Republican faction. The governor's political future, however, was still unclear because he had recently lost a separate court fight to become eligible for a 3d gubernatorial term.

Ford Vetoes Foreign Aid Bill—Pres. Gerald R. Ford, **May 7**, exercised his 49th veto since assuming the presidency on a $4.4 billion foreign aid authorization bill because "unprecedented restrictions" in the measure would "seriously inhibit my ability to implement a coherent and consistent foreign policy." The bill had authorized economic and military aid, much of it for the middle East, for both the fiscal year ending June 30 and the 3-month transition period before fiscal year 1977 would begin on Oct. 1. The Congress, lacking the 2/3's necessary to override the veto, did not attempt to challenge the president's decision. The objectionable restrictions had been deliberately written into the legislation to give Congress more influence over controversial areas such as the sale of military equipment, aid to countries violating human rights, and the granting of direct military gifts as distinct from credits for purchase of military items. Sen. Hubert H. Humphrey (D, Minn.) and Sen. Thomas E. Morgan (D, Pa.) called the veto an act of bad faith, charging Ford had acted at the last minute, against advice from the departments of state and defense.

Ehrlichman Conviction Upheld—The U.S. Court of Appeals in Washington, D.C., **May 17**, in a unanimous decision, upheld the conviction of John D. Ehrlichman, former Pres. Richard M. Nixon's chief adviser for domestic affairs, for his part in the 1971 White House "plumbers" break-in of the office of Dr. Lewis Fielding, psychiatrist to Daniel Ellsberg. The court also upheld the conviction of Ehrlichman's co-defendant G. Gordon Liddy, who had worked for both the White House and the Committee to Re-elect the President. The court, however, reversed the convictions of 2 other White House plumbers, Bernard L. Barker and Eugenio L. Martinez, who had carried out the break-in instructions. The court agreed that U.S. District Judge Gerhard A. Gesell had been mistaken in refusing the jury the right to consider the "mistake-of-law" defense offered by the 2 men.

Senate Votes Intelligence Oversight Committee—The Senate, **May 19**, in a 72-22 vote, created a permanent 15-member Select Committee on Intelligence with exclusive authority to oversee CIA activities and authorize funds for CIA operations. The committee, along with existing committees, would share jurisdiction over other intelligence agencies, such as the FBI.

Federal Election Commission Re-activated—The Federal Election Commission, inactive by Supreme Court order since March, was revived, **May 21**, and immediately began disbursement of a $3.2-billion backlog in matching funds to 9 presidential candidates. Pres. Gerald R. Ford, May 11, had signed legislation reconstituting the commission to conform to the requirements of the Supreme Court.

Supersonics Begin Transatlantic Flights—Air France and British Airways Concordes, May 24, made their first transatlantic flights to Dulles Airport in Washington, D.C., from Paris and London respectively. The flights took a little less than 4 hours, about half the flight time of conventional subsonic jets. On landing, the Air France SST, according to Federal Aviation Agency measuring equipment, makes less noise than a Boeing 707 and 727 monitored during the same period. The British Airways SST was quieter than the 707 but louder than the 727. However, on takeoff for the return flight May 28, the French plane was monitored at a thundering 129 perceived decibels, twice the maximum noise output the supersonics would be allowed if they were ever permitted to fly to New York's JFK International Airport. A noise meter was not in place on the runway used by the British Airways pilot.

Hays Admits Affair with Ray—Rep. Wayne L. Hays (D, Oh.), May 25, told the House of Representatives, in an emotional speech, that he had conducted a "personal relationship" with Elizabeth Ray, a staff aide for the House Administration Committee, of which Hays was chairman. Hays admitted that he had "committed a grievous error in not presenting all the facts." He denied, however, that he had hired Ray to be his mistress and asserted that she had done sufficient work to merit her $14,000 yearly salary. Ray, in charges published, May 23, in The Washington Post, had alleged she had hardly ever gone to her private office and could not type or adequately answer the telephones, but about twice weekly had been invited by Hays on dinner dates which ended in her Arlington, Va. apartment. Federal officials, May 24, had disclosed that the justice department was investigating the charges against Hays. On May 26, Hays asserted that Ray, by threatening to reveal the details of their relationship, had extorted more than $1,000 from him over the preceding 5 weeks. By the end of the month, several members of the House were beginning a drive to oust Hays from his chairmanship of 4 house committees.

International

Italian Elections Set—The Italian government, May 3, called for national elections to be held June 20-21. The elections, in which the Communist party was expected to make substantial gains, were set following the Apr. 30 resignation of Prime Minister Aldo Moro's 11-week minority government. The government had resigned when the Socialists withdrew their tacit support of it in a dispute over the adoption of a liberal or restrictive abortion bill.

Kissinger Gives UNCTAD Economic Program—In an address to the United Nations Conference on Trade and Development in Nairobi, Kenya, U.S. Secretary of State Henry A. Kissinger, May 6, introduced a complicated, comprehensive U.S. program for relations between rich and poor nations. Laying strong emphasis on free enterprise and private initiative, Kissinger urged the delegates to lay aside slogans and build economic institutions that would fairly allocate the benefits of growth and technology. The centerpiece of the program was an International Resources Bank which "would promote more rational, systematic and equitable development of resources in developing nations." The bank would mediate between countries and foreign investors in negotiating the share of profits from the development of primary resources and in other key agreements. The bank would be capitalized at about $1 billion, provided chiefly by industrialized and oil-producing countries. Kissinger also underlined American acceptance of the concept of maintaining buffer stocks of certain commodities. Such stocks could be released into the free market when necessary to maintain price stability and protect the producer countries from critical price fluctuations in their primary sources of foreign exchange. Kissinger also emphasized the importance of creating technologies suitable to developing countries and the need to stem the emigration of the most skilled and trained people from developing countries. The delegates from developing countries, May 7, generally agreed that, although Kissinger had not fully met their demands, he had gone farther than anticipated.

Lebanese President Chosen—Under a barrage of mortar shells and small arms fire, 68 members of the Lebanese parliament, May 8, elected Elias Sarkis, a Christian and a conservative banker and civil servant, to succeed Pres. Suleiman Franjieh, who still had not resigned. The 29 other members of parliament, who had supported Raymond Edde, boycotted the session, charging that Syria had interfered politically and militarily in support of Sarkis. It was a crushing defeat for the leftist-Moslem alliance and its leader Kamal Jumblat, who, May 7, recognizing he lacked the votes to win, had called for a general strike and resistence by "popular organizations." In a statement, issued May 11, Jumblat's loose coalition offered to cooperate with Sarkis if he kept Syria out of Lebanon's internal affairs and protected the presence of the Palestinian guerrilla movement in Lebanon. However, it was clear Sarkis could not meet the demands, thus making any political negotiations between Christians and Moslems extremely difficult.

British Liberal Party Leader Resigns—Pressured by allegations of homosexuality, Jeremy Thorpe, May 10, resigned as leader of the small, but influential, British Liberal party. Thorpe charged that over the preceding 3 months British newspapers had conducted a "sustained witch hunt" which could ruin the party. The newspapers, in what became known as the "Thorpe Affair," had made allegations of homosexuality, blackmail, and financial improprieties. Thorpe again denied the allegations of Norman Scott, a former model who claimed to have had a homosexual relationship with Thorpe. On May 12, Jo Grimond, the former leader of the Liberals, accepted a caretaker role as party leader, but refused to serve on a permanent basis.

India, Pakistan To Resume Relations—Following 3 days of negotiations in Islamabad, Pakistan, the foreign ministers of India and Pakistan, May 14, agreed to resume diplomatic relations "within a short period of time." The decision to end the 4 1/2-year rift between the 2 nations was part of an agreement to resume airline and railroad communications and other links as soon as possible.

NATO Warns of Dangers to Detente—Concluding a 2-day conference in Oslo, Norway, the 15 NATO foreign ministers, May 21, warned that continuing Soviet military buildup in Central Europe and lack of restraint in other parts of the world presented serious dangers to detente. Should "sustained growth in the Warsaw Pact countries' military power beyond levels apparently justified for defensive purposes" continue, the NATO minister warned, "it could lead to an arms race of dangerous dimensions."

U.S., USSR Sign Underground A-Pact—U.S. Pres. Gerald R. Ford, in Washington, D.C., and Soviet Communist party leader Leonid I. Brezhnev, in Moscow, May 28, signed a 5-year treaty limiting the size of underground nuclear explosions set off for peaceful purposes. The agreement also provided for U.S. on-site inspection of Soviet tests. The treaty was signed after a 2-week delay by the U.S. According to administration sources in Washington, the delay, which came after Ford's defeat in the Nebraska primary, had been aimed at averting further criticism of Ford from the conservative camp of his opponent, Ronald Reagan.

OPEC Continues Oil Price Freeze—The Organization of Petroleum Exporting Countries, meeting in Buta Beach, Bali, Indonesia, **May 28**, decided to extend their 9-month-old freeze on world petroleum prices "for the present." The decision was widely viewed as a reflection of a lack of unanimity among OPEC members on how, if at all, to raise prices and an understanding that the recovery from worldwide recession had not progressed far enough to sustain higher prices. U.S. Pres. Gerald R. Ford hailed the decision as a "responsible one for the world's economy which is just beginning to recover from recession and adjusting to existing high oil prices."

General

New Jersey Doctor Indicted—A Bergen County, N.J., grand jury, **May 19**, indicted Dr. Mario E. Jascalevich, a 46-year-old surgeon, on charges of murdering 5 patients 10 years previously while he was head surgeon at Riverdell Hospital in Oradell, N.J. According to the indictment, he had used overdoses or curare, a muscle relaxant, to kill the patients. The New Jersey Board of Medical Examiners, **May 21**, filed malpractice charges against the surgeon. Jascalevich, **May 28**, voluntarily surrendered his medical license.

USMA Cheating Scandal Inquiry Widens—Lt. Gen. Sidney Berry, the superintendent of the U.S. Military Academy at West Point, N.Y., **May 23**, acknowledged that cheating at the academy had been more widespread than previously reported. He stated that an internal review panel of officers and cadets had been formed to investigate "new evidence" that had developed recently. On **May 24**, Berry announced that the panel was investigating some 70 to 90 new cases of suspected cheating.

Disasters—An earthquake, registering 6.5 on the Richter scale, **May 6**, struck northeastern Italy, collapsing entire sections of towns northeast of Venice, near the Yugoslav border. Some 900 bodies were recovered. 400 people were reported missing, and 2,000 persons were injured in the quake. Fifty aftershocks struck **May 7-11**, damaging 19 towns and villages and leaving some 150,000 people homeless. . . . On **May 20**, an earthquake struck the Soviet republic of Uzbek in Central Asia, leaving some 10,000 persons homeless, killing 6 and injuring 106 persons. Hardest hit in the quake, which registered 7.3 on the Richter scale, was the Kyzyl Kum desert. . . . Typhoon Olga, **May 20**, struck the northern Philippines, causing 4 days of torrential rains and flooding which claimed 215 lives and left 630,000 persons homeless. . . . A school bus carrying members of the Yuba City, Cal., High School choir, crashed, **May 21**, in Martinez, Cal., killing 28 students and injuring more than 20 others.

JUNE
National

Jobless Rate Hits New Low—The labor department, **June 4**, reported that unemployment during May had fallen to 7.3% of the labor force, the lowest in 17 months. The number of people working had increased by 300,000 to a record 87.7 million. However, sounding a more dismal note, AFL-CIO Pres. George Meany stated that "the nation must not be misled into believing the economy is in good shape." He indicat-

ed that the true rate of unemployment was actually 10.1% of the labor force. The 10.1% rate, as calculated by the labor federation and other organizations, such as the Urban League, included those people who want jobs but have stopped searching because none are available and also half of those employed part-time who want to find full-time work.

Carter Bandwagon Rolls, Ford and Reagan Almost Even—Following the last presidential primaries June 8, former Georgia Gov. Jimmy Carter seemed virtually assured of the Democratic nomination, but Pres. Gerald R. Ford and former California Gov. Ronald Reagan were running neck-and-neck for the Republican nomination. On **June 1**, Carter soundly beat Arizona Rep. Morris K. Udall to take the South Dakota primary, but lost Montana to Idaho Sen. Frank Church and Rhode Island to an uncommitted slate supported by California Gov. Edmund G. Brown Jr. Because Brown had entered the presidential campaign at a late date, his name did not even appear on the Rhode Island ballot. Ford won a landslide victory over Reagan in the **June 1** Rhode Island primary, taking all 19 delegates, but lost to Reagan in South Dakota and Montana, where Reagan accumulated 11 delegates to Ford's 9. On **June 8**, the last day on the primary schedule, Carter won a major victory in Ohio, capturing 126 delegates. Although Carter lost to Brown in California and to an uncommitted slate of delegates in New Jersey that supported Humphrey and Brown, he amassed another 100 delegates. On June 9, opposition to the Carter nomination began to crumble as Carter was endorsed by Alabama Gov. George Wallace, Chicago Mayor Richard J. Daley, and received a promise of support from Sen. Henry M. Jackson. The results of the **June 8** Republican primaries were inconclusive. Ford won a convincing 55% to 45% victory over Reagan in Ohio, and got the support of all of New Jersey's uncommitted delegates, but he lost decisively to Reagan in California by a 60%-to-45% margin.

Hays Cedes One Chairmanship—Under heavy pressure from his colleagues in the House of Representatives, Wayne L. Hays (D, Oh.), **June 18**, resigned as chairman of the House Administration Committee, the committee he had used to exert great power in Congress. Hays, the object of a sex scandal, was recovering from a coma he had suffered, **June 10**, due to an overdose of sleeping pills. Hays' personal physician had stated, **June 11**, that laboratory tests had shown Hays had taken more than 10 times the prescribed amount.

Supreme Court Rules in 2 Civil Rights Cases—In a 7-2 decision, the Supreme Court ruled, **June 25**, that private nonsectarian schools could not exclude black children because of their race. The ruling came in suits against 2 segregated private academies which had been established following the historic 1954 Brown decision in which the Supreme Court had ordered desegregation of public schools. It was not clear, however, whether the ruling extended to private religious schools as well. In another 7-2 decision, the court ruled that a major Reconstruction civil rights law, the 1866 Civil Rights Act known as Section 1981, protects whites, as well as blacks, against racial discrimination. In an unanimous ruling, the court also decided that Title VII of the 1964 Civil Rights Act barred employers from racially discriminating against blacks on the basis of their race. The last 2 rulings were handed down in a case brought by 2 men who contended they had been discriminated against when their employers fired them for an alleged misdeed but did not fire a black man also implicated in the matter.

Supreme Court Rules Against Gag Orders—The Supreme Court, **June 30**, ruled that, in most instances, judges may not forbid the press to publish information about criminal cases. The ruling extended to cases in which a judge deemed such an order would help assure the defense of a fair trial by preventing prejudicial publicity. While all 9 justices agreed that in almost every case a gag order would contravene the First Amendment, 3 justices felt all gag orders were an unconstitutional violation of the First Amendment's guarantee of freedom of the press.

International

Britain Offered Credit to Buoy Pound—The Group of 10, the world's largest industrial countries, together with Switzerland and the Bank for International Settlements, **June 7**, provided Great Britain with a $5.3 billion short-term credit to bolster the depreciating pound. Following the agreement, the pound immediately rose on foreign exchange markets, ending at $1.7590 on the London market.

Spain Legalizes Political Parties—The Spanish parliament, **June 9**, in a 338-91 vote, legalized political parties. Parties had been banned since 1939. However, restrictions written into the law could give the government the power to accept or reject a particular party. The government had already indicated that it would use this power against the Communists.

Uruguayan President Ousted—The Uruguayan armed forces, **June 12**, removed Pres. Juan M. Bordaberry from office because of "irreconcilable differences" over the future of democratic institutions in the country. Bordaberry, who had ruled under the thumb of the military since 1973 when he dissolved congress in a military power play, was replaced by the 80-year-old vice president Alberto Demicheli. Demicheli would remain in office for 60 days until a special electoral council selected a new president. The military had reportedly disagreed with Bordaberry's plans to abolish political parties and to institute a corporate state structure with the participation of the armed forces written into law. The armed forces wanted to maintain the status quo with a gradual return to democratic policies.

Black Rioting Breaks Out in South Africa—Racial violence, the worst in South Africa's history, broke out, **June 16**, when a 10,000-strong student protest turned into a riot in Soweto, short for the all-black South West Township 10 miles from Johannesburg. The students had gathered to protest a government requirement that Afrikaans, the language of South Africa's ruling Nationalist party, be used for instruction in some subjects in the township's schools. Police anti-terrorist squads and army reinforcements were called in to stem the rioting which continued **June 17** and, **June 18**, spread to 7 other black townships around Johannesburg. As the rioting spread, it was accompanied by arson and looting. Some 100 persons, nearly all blacks, were unofficially reported dead by **June 18**, and some 1,000 were injured. On **June 21**, new rioting broke out in black townships around Pretoria. At least 10 persons were reported dead and scores injured. The almost simultaneous flaring of violence in 3 separate black enclaves gave support to the official contention that the riots had been planned and coordinated. South African police, **June 21**, disclosed the official casualty count in the Johannesburg rioting was 128 dead and 1,112 injured. The police set damages at $34.5 million, some $10 million sustained by government liquor stores alone.

U.S. To Sell Planes to Kenya—In one of the single largest U.S. arms deals in Africa, the U.S., **June 16**, agreed to sell 12 F-5 jet fighter planes to Kenya. The sale, which awaited Congressional approval, was estimated at $70-$75 million dollars.

Communists Score Gains in Italian Elections—Although the Christian Democrats retained a plurality in the **June 20-21** Italian national elections, the Communist party made impressive gains in both the Senate and Chamber of Deputies. In balloting for the

---

U.S. Ambassador, Aide, and Chauffeur Slain in Beirut; Arab Peace-Keeping Force Set after Syrian Troop Entry

Unidentified gunmen, **June 16**, kidnaped and shot to death in Beirut the newly-appointed U.S. ambassador, Francis E. Meloy Jr., his economic counselor, Robert O. Waring, and the Lebanese U.S. Embassy driver. The 3 men were captured while enroute through the combat sector to a meeting with Elias Sarkis, the Lebanese president-elect. U.S. Pres. Gerald R. Ford expressed "shock and revulsion" at the killings, but declared that the "United States will not be deterred from its search for peace by these murders."

Wafa, the Palestinian news agency, announced, **June 17**, that Al Fatah agents had seized 3 Lebanese who confessed to the killings. They were not associated with any identifiable political organization, Wafa stated, and would be turned over to the Arab League peace-keeping force when it arrived.

An agreement to introduce a token Arab peace-keeping force, including Syrian troops, had been negotiated, **June 10**, in Cairo, by Syria and 19 other Arab League countries. The Arab force, including troops from Algeria, Libya, Saudi Arabia, and Sudan, would "replace" the large Syrian force that had entered the beleaguered country May 31. By **June 1**, Syrian tanks had advanced deep into Lebanon along the Damascus-Beirut highway and turned north to relieve rightist Christian forces which had been besieged by Palestinian guerrillas and Lebanese Moslems for several months.

The U.S., **June 1**, gave tacit approval to Syria's troop entry, but warned Damascus not to increase its forces beyond Israel's tolerance. Both the PLO and the Lebanese leftist-Moslem alliance appealed for outside political assistance to prevent an escalation of Syrian military intervention. By the eve of the agreement, the main Syrian force had closed in on Beirut, holding it in a state of siege. The Syrians held Beirut airport and a major road junction south of the air field.

On **June 20**, before the arrival of the Arab League force, the U.S. Navy began an evacuation of the U.S. and other citizens from Beirut. In view of the triple slaying and the closing of Beirut airport, the U.S. government had "strongly urged" all remaining Americans to evacuate. However, according to an unofficial count, only a tenth of the 1,400 U.S. citizens remaining in Beirut left by sea. The others preferred to make their way by road to Damascus or chose to stay in Lebanon.

On **June 21**, the vanguard of the Arab League peace-keeping force entered Beirut overland from Damascus to take up positions around the Beirut airport as a new cease-fire went into effect. Moslem and Christian fighting, not covered under the cease-fire, resumed **June 22**, and centered around Palestinian refugee camps in the Beirut area. Heavy fighting in the area continued through **June 29**, as Christian forces intensified their efforts to capture the Palestinian camps at Tell Zatar and Jisr el-Pasha.

315-seat Senate, for which voters 25 and older were eligible, the Christian Democrats won 38.9% of the vote to maintain their strength at 135 seats. The Communists, who took 33.8%, won 116 seats, an increase of 23. In the election for the 630-member Chamber of Deputies, open to voters 18 and over, the Communists, with 34.5% of the vote, won 49 new seats, bringing their total to 228. The Christian Democrats, although winning a plurality at 38.8%, lost 3 seats for a total of 263. The losers in the elections were the Socialists who had provoked the elections on the assumption they would gain ground. In the Senate, the Socialists, with 10.2% of the vote, lost 4 seats; they also lost 4 in the Chamber of Deputies where they polled 9.6% of the vote. In view of the poor showing, Socialist party deputy secretary Giovanni Mosca, June 21, resigned and called for a critical debate in the party leadership. On June 23, staving off fears of a new crisis over the formation of a government, Communist party officials said they would forego demands for immediate cabinet seats in exchange for a more formal role in policy development. A senior official stated "our policy is not all or nothing," but indicated that the Communists had not given up their long-range goal of joining in a coalition government with the Christian Democrats and other parties. On July 3, in a major victory for the Communists, the major party leaders agreed to give the Communists the presidency of the Chamber of Deputies, their most important parliamentary post in the history of the Italian Republic. Pietro Ingrao, July 5, was elected to the post.

Riots Force Poland to Drop Food Price Rises— Workers' riots forced the Polish government, June 25, to cancel a plan, announced June 24, to raise food prices drastically. Prime Minister Piotr Jaroszewicz, in a one-minute television address, stated that, although most workers had understood the need for the higher prices, there were some proposals that "deserve close analysis," a process which would take several months "to work out a proper solution." The rioting was most severe at Plock, Radom, and Ursus, a suburb of Warsaw. Striking workers had torn up railroad tracks outside of Warsaw, halting both local and international trains. Some 700 workers struck the Ursus Tractor Factory, refusing to work until the price rise was recalled. On June 26, Polish television reported that many factories and shops had also been looted and plundered by "hooligans" before the government withdrew the price hike.

Army Chief Wins Portuguese Elections—Army Chief of Staff Gen. Antonio Ramalho Eanes, June 27, won a landslide victory in Portugal's first presidential elections in 50 years. Backed by the army and Portugal's 3 largest noncommunist parties, Ramalho captured 61.54% of the vote. The radical leftist candidate Maj. Otelo Saraiva de Carvalho, the former military security chief, received 16.52% and Prime Minister Jose Pinheiro de Azevedo, who had suffered a heart attack during the campaign, won a strong sympathy vote of 14.36%. The Communist party candidate, Octavio Pato won 7.58%, a setback following a 14.42% vote for the Communist party in the national legislative elections 2 months previously.

Industrial Nations Hold Economic Parley— Concluding a 2-day economic summit, in Puerto Rico, the 7 major industrial nations, June 28, agreed on a go-slow policy of economic growth that would guard against a revival of worldwide inflation. In a joint statement, the U.S., Canada, West Germany, Japan, Great Britain, France, and Italy also agreed to consider the creation of a new multinational credit facility, perhaps as part of the International Monetary Fund, to help Italy and other developed nations which temporarily experience international payments problems.

European Communists Support Autonomy—The long-delayed conference of the leaders of the 29 West and East European Communist parties, June 30, in East Berlin, issued a joint-declaration endorsing the independence of each party to find its own road to Socialism. The document, which had taken 2 years to write, made no mention of "proletarian internationalism," the Marxist concept which had come to mean Soviet domination of the international Communist movement. In perhaps the sharpest attack on the Soviet Union, Italian Communist party leader Enrico Berlinguer stated that the Russian Bolsheviks, although they had opened a "completely new road" for humanity with the revolution of 1917, had made many mistakes along the road to building Socialism. Berlinguer criticized the Soviet invasion of Czechoslovakia, endorsed pluralistic political structures, and supported frank discussion within the Communist movement.

General

Teton Dam Burst Leaves Thousands Homeless— Idaho's Teton, a 310-foot earth-fill structure, June 5, burst, flooding the upper Snake River Valley and forcing some 30,000 persons to evacuate their homes in 6 downstream towns. Aerial surveys reported that Teton and Sugar City were underwater and a 10-foot wall of water was moving toward Idaho Falls. Pres. Gerald R. Ford, June 6, declared the area a disaster area, making the residents eligible for low-cost loans to restore property and businesses. Flood waters continued, June 6-7, inundating 2 more towns and an area of 300 square miles, including 50,000 acres of farmland. By June 8, when flood waters began to recede, at least 9 persons were reported dead, some 30 persons missing, and 4,000 homes and businesses destroyed. The Teton Dam project, which had begun in 1971, had been challenged by geologists and environmentalists who had claimed the site was on particularly porous rock in an earthquake zone.

Quinlan Transferred, Will be Allowed to Die—The ethics committee at Morris View Nursing Home in Morris Plains, N.J., June 10, decided unanimously that Karen Anne Quinlan was in an irreversible coma and there was no reasonable possibility that she would return to a "cognitive, sapient state." The committee's decision set the stage for the withholding of extraordinary care in the event of a major medical crisis, a move that would allow her to die. Quinlan's parents, June 9, had transferred their daughter to Morris View from St. Clare's Hospital in Denville, N.J., because they believed that St. Clare's, despite a New Jersey Supreme Court ruling, would do all they could to keep Karen Quinlan alive. Although St. Clare's doctors, after removing Quinlan, May 22, from the mechanical respirator that had been keeping her alive, had indicated, June 3, that her condition was stable, they had said they would put her back on the respirator if necessary.

Disasters—Following take-off from Guam International Airport in Agana, an Air Manila propeller jet, June 4, crashed and collided with a truck, killing all 45 persons aboard the plane and the driver of the truck. . . A landslide, June 4, swept over the Nepalese village of Pahire Phedi, 90 miles west of Katmandu, killing some 150 persons. . . An earthquake registering 7.2 on the Richter scale, June 26, struck the remote western New Guinean province of Irian Jaya, with subsequent mudslides wiping out some 20 communities. Casualty reports stated 443 persons had died and some 3,000 were missing.

JULY
National

Unemployment Up—The labor department reported, **July 2,** that unemployment in June, following a May decrease, had risen from 7.3% to 7.5% of the labor force. The number of persons employed also had fallen by 197,000 to an adjusted total of 87.5 million.

Supreme Court Supports Death Penalty—The Supreme Court, **July 2,** in a 7-2 decision, ruled that the death penalty is not inherently cruel or unusual punishment and, therefore, is a constitutionally acceptable form of punishment in certain cases. As a result of the decision, about one-half of the 600 inmates currently on death row would face execution In 1972, the court had decided that capital punishment, as then practiced, violated the 8th Amendment ban on cruel and unusual punishment. The court had cited the arbitrary and "freakish" way in which some defendants were sentenced to die while others were allowed to live. However, in the new decision, which came in a review of 5 state statutes passed to meet the objections of the 1972 ruling, the court stated that judges and juries could impose the death penalty as long as they first received adequate information and guidance for determining whether the sentence was appropriate in a given case. In a separate ruling, the court, 5 to 4, decided that states may not impose "mandatory" capital punishment laws requiring the death penalty for every defendant convicted of murder. However, in light of the first ruling and the opinions handed down in the case, it was apparent statutes close to being mandatory would be permitted.

America Celebrates 200 Years as a Nation—Americans across the United States, **July 4,** held festivals and parades to celebrate the U.S. Bicentennial. Pres. Gerald R. Ford traveled from Valley Forge, Pa., to Philadelphia, where some one million people had gathered for the centerpiece of bicentennial celebrations in the nation's first capital. Speaking at Independence Hall, Ford recalled the first 4th of July as "the beginning of a continuing adventure" that was yet unfulfilled, unfinished, but still unchallenged as a model of social and political achievement. Ford then traveled to New York City where the day's largest crowd, some 6 million people, had gathered for Operation Sail. The most spectacular of the nation's many observances, Operation Sail included hundreds of sailing boats, including a unique armada of 16 tall ships from all over the world. A massive fireworks display over lower Manhattan ended the celebration. In addition to the official celebrations, protesters gathered in Washington, D.C., and Philadelphia to hold their own peaceful celebrations. In honor of the bicentennial, Queen Elizabeth II of England arrived, **July 6,** for a 6-day visit. On **July 7,** in Washington, D.C., she was entertained by the president at a state dinner in the Rose Garden of the White House.

New York Court Disbars Nixon—The Appellate Division of the New York State Supreme Court for the First Department, **July 8,** in a 4-to-1 decision, disbarred former Pres. Richard M. Nixon for actions relating to the Watergate scandal. The ruling marked the first instance in which Nixon had been found guilty by an official body. The court found Nixon guilty of 5 charges of obstruction of "the due administration of justice" and, consequently, in violation of the Code of Professional Responsibility, the code that all lawyers are required to observe. The charges, brought by the Association of the Bar of the City of New York, resembled the Articles of Impeachment drafted by the House Judiciary Committee. Although

Nixon had previously tried to resign from the New York bar, he had been refused on the grounds that he had not acknowledged that he could not successfully defend himself against the charges.

Democrats Nominate Carter, Mondale—The 37th Democratic National Convention, meeting in New York City, **July 12-15,** nominated former Georgia Gov. Jimmy Carter and Minnesota Sen. Walter F. Mondale to run for president and vice president on the Democratic ticket in the 1976 election. (See Convention.)

Congress Overrides Veto of Jobs Bill—The Senate, **July 21,** 73-24, and the House of Representatives, **July 22,** in a 310-96 vote, overrode Pres. Gerald R. Ford's veto of a $3.95-billion bill to provide public works jobs. Ford, **July 6,** had vetoed the bill because, he said, it would not provide the 300,000 jobs predicted by its Democratic sponsors, but would, instead, lead to "larger deficits, higher taxes, higher inflation, and, ultimately, higher unemployment." The bill was a scaled-down version of a $6-billion program which Ford had also vetoed. The Senate had failed in an attempt to override his veto of the earlier bill.

Howe Found Guilty on Sex Charges—Rep. Allan Turner Howe (D, Ut.), **July 23,** in Salt Lake City, was found guilty of offering money to 2 policewomen decoys for "the performance of sex acts for hire." Howe had denied the charges, asserting that he was the "target of some trap or setup." Howe was sentenced to 30 days in jail and fined $150, with the sentence to be suspended upon payment of the fine. Despite heavy pressure to end his campaign for re-election, Howe iterated his intention to continue to run for Congress.

Reagan Names Schweiker as Running Mate—Breaking political tradition, Republican presidential hopeful Ronald Reagan, **July 26,** named Pennsylvania Sen. Richard S. Schweiker, a staunch liberal and pro-labor voice in the Senate, as his running mate should he win the nomination. The announcement, which stunned party conservatives, was seen as an attempt to broaden the conservative Reagan's appeal in the struggle for uncommitted delegates, particularly in the Pennsylvania delegation which had been aligned with Pres. Gerald R. Ford. On **July 20,** the New York Times had reported that Ford was only 18 votes short of a first-ballot nomination at the Republican convention in August. A conservative rebellion to Reagan's choice of a liberal running mate developed and, **July 27,** it was apparent that Reagan's gamble would probably fail.

International

Spanish Prime Minister Resigns—Spanish Prime Minister Carlos Arias Navarro and his cabinet resigned unexpectedly, **July 1.** Tensions in the cabinet over proposals leading to democratic change in Spain had apparently forced King Juan Carlos I to dismiss the prime minister. On **July 3,** Adolfo Suarez Gonzalez, a personal friend of the king, was named prime minister. Liberals and leftists immediately protested the appointment, citing Suarez' inexperience in government and his ties with the fascist National Movement.

Vietnam Officially Re-united—Following almost 20 years of continuous warfare, North and South Vietnam, **July 2,** were officially re-united into one nation. Hanoi was declared the official capital and the former North Vietnamese flag, anthem, and emblems were approved as official symbols of the new nation. According to a radio Hanoi announcement, the leaders of the Socialist Republic of Vietnam had been selected by secret ballot in the National Assembly. All but one high government office went to former leaders of North Vietnam. Ton Duc Thang, the 88-year-old former North Vietnamese chief of state was elected president and North Vietnamese Prime Minister Pham Van Dong became prime minister in the new government. On **July 12**, in a major policy switch, Vietnam announced that it had agreed to establish ties with the Philippines and that a Thai delegation would arrive the next month to discuss normalization of relations between the 2 countries.

South African Language Dispute Settled—The language dispute that precipitated the worst riots in South Africa's history was settled, **July 6**, when the government bowed to demands for the end of compulsory use of Afrikaans in black schools.

British Envoy Killed in Dublin—Christopher T.E. Ewart-Biggs, the newly appointed British Ambassador to Ireland, was killed, **July 21**, when a mine exploded beneath his car near his official residence on the outskirts of Dublin. His 26-year-old secretary was also killed and 2 other passengers were seriously injured.

New Portuguese Government Sworn In—Socialist party leader Mario Soares, **July 23**, was sworn in as prime minister of Portugal's first constitutional government since the 1974 overthrow of the rightist dictatorship. The cabinet was made up, in large part, of moderate socialists and several independents and military officers. Despite pressure from the Communists, liberals, and conservatives to form a governmental alliance, Soares had refused, arguing that Portugal needed a strong, cohesive government to restore national confidence. Soares, **July 19**, had outlined his foreign policy aims, stressing a more active role in the Atlantic alliance and the integration of Portugal into "all European institutions."

Italian CP Makes Gains, New Government Named —For the first time in the history of the Italian Republic, the Communist party, **July 26**, won the chairmanships of 4 parliamentary committees, reflecting strength gained in the last national elections. However, the new cabinet, led by Giulio Andreotti, the former budget minister, and sworn in, **July 30**, was formed entirely of members of the Christian Democratic party. Arnaldo Forlani, the new foreign minister, warned that giving the Communists influence over the government was "full of risks" for Italy, but acknowledged that the party's growing strength precluded any other course. Earlier in the month, the U.S., West Germany, France, and Great Britain had announced an informal understanding to bar further loans to Italy if the Communists received cabinet posts. However, according to the understanding, anything short of Communist participation in the cabinet would not be an obstacle to further financial aid.

China Hit by Severe Earthquakes—Two powerful earthquakes struck heavily populated areas of Northern China, **July 28**, causing severe damage and claiming an estimated 100,000 lives. The first quake,

---

Israeli Strike Force Frees 103 Hostages Held in Uganda

Israeli airborne commandos, **July 3**, raided Entebbe Airport in Uganda and freed 103 hostages, many of them Israelis. The hostages were part of some 250 passengers and 12 crewmen aboard an Air France airbus seized, **June 27**, by 7 pro-Palestinian guerrillas.

In skirmishes accompanying the raid, 3 Israeli hostages, one Israeli officer, all 7 hijackers, and 20 Ugandan soldiers were killed. The success of the raid electrified Israel. Prime Minister Itzhak Rabin told a special session of parliament: "This operation will become a legend. It is Israel's contribution to the fight against terrorism, a fight that has not yet ended."

The drama began to unroll **June 27**, when the hijackers, who identified themselves as members of the Popular Front for the Liberation of Palestine, seized the plane after take-off from Athens, where it had stopped enroute from Tel Aviv to Paris. The hijackers forced the plane to refuel at Benghazi, Libya, and then flew it to Entebbe Airport in Uganda.

On **June 28**, apparently in response to demands by negotiators led by Ugandan leader Idi Amin and French Ambassador Pierre Renaud, the hijackers allowed the hostages to leave the plane, but held them in custody at the airport. The guerrillas threatened to blow up the planes unless their demands were met. In a statement broadcast over Ugandan radio, the hijackers condemned France as a tool of U.S. "imperialism," attacked Israel, denounced the reactionary regimes in Egypt and Syria, and called revolutionaries everywhere to unite and free the world.

The hijackers' demands, made public **June 29**, called for the release of 53 Palestinians and pro-Palestinians imprisoned in Israel and several other countries. Unless the prisoners were flown to Entebbe in exchange for the hostages, the guerrillas said, "severe and heavy penalties" would follow. On **June 30**, the hijackers released 47 hostages, mostly women, children, and ailing and elderly passengers, but said they would blow up the plane and the remaining hostages unless their demands were met by July 1.

On **July 1**, as negotiations over the demands were deadlocked, Israel announced that, contrary to its longstanding policy, it would negotiate the release of an unspecified number of Arab prisoners. Soon afterwards, the hijackers released 100 more passengers and extended the deadline for their demands.

On **July 3**, while negotiations were continuing without apparent success, 3 Israeli C-130 Hercules transports flew to Uganda under cover of darkness. Firing machine guns and hurling grenades, the strike force rushed the terminal and cut down the 7 hijackers before rushing the hostages into planes and flying them to Tel Aviv.

In Paris, officials and the previously released hostages stated there was substantial evidence Amin had acted in collusion with the hijackers in the seizure of the plane and afterwards. It was disclosed that 5 prisoners whose release had been demanded and who were allegedly being held in Kenya were Ugandans. Israeli Defense Minister Shimon Peres charged that Uganda deserved a major share of the blame for the hijacking: "It is the first time in history that a state and its President, Field Marshal Idi Amin Dada, and its army cooperated with a group of hijackers to blackmail another country by threatening the lives of innocent passengers on an international aircraft." Amin, **July 5**, stated that he had only become involved with the hijackers when they requested permission to land and announced that Uganda reserved the right to retaliate in any way to redress Israeli aggression against it in the raid.

On **July 6**, prompted by Amin, African members at the United Nations asked for an urgent Security Council meeting to consider Israel's "wanton act of aggression." However, **July 14**, the Security Council ended 4 days of inconclusive debate without condemning Israel or approving a rival resolution against hijacking and terrorism.

according to the U.S. Geological Survey, registered 8.2 on the Richter scale, making it the strongest earthquake in 12 years. The quake was centered near Tientsin, 90 miles southeast of Peking. The 2d tremor, which followed 16 hours later, registered 7.9 on the Richter scale and was centered about 60 miles east of Peking. Tangshan City, an industrial city of about one million people located near the center of the quakes some 100 miles southeast of Peking, suffered particularly serious losses and damages. A group of French survivors in Tangshan reported that the city was 100% ruined. Although damage and casualties in Peking were reported to be light, some buildings suffered extensive damage and the streets were littered with rubble.

Syria, PLO Sign Agreement—Following 9 days of negotiations, Syria and the Palestine Liberation Organization, **July 29**, signed an agreement providing for a cease-fire in the Lebanese civil war. Many Lebanese politicians called the agreement, which would allow Syria to keep some 15,000 troops in Lebanon, a "capitulation" by the Palestinians. On the military front, rightist Christian forces, **June 30**, had overrun Jisr el-Pasha, a Palestinian refugee camp on the outskirts of Beirut, and, **July 2**, had overrun the outer defenses of Tell Zaatar, another refugee camp in the area. On **July 26**, the PLO announced that the rightist Christian forces had cut off the water supply to Tell Zaatar and continued to hamper rescue efforts, particularly for some 400 persons, mostly women, children, and old men, believed to be trapped under a collapsed underground shelter. On **July 27**, the U.S. Navy evacuated another 308 foreigners, including 160 U.S. citizens. Approximately 1,000 U.S. citizens remained in Lebanon.

General

Chowchilla School Children Escape—Twenty-six Chowchilla, Calif., school children and their bus driver, **July 17**, dug their way out of a makeshift prison in a quarry near Livermore, Calif., after being kidnaped by 3 masked gunmen. The children, while returning home following a summer school session, and the bus driver had mysteriously disappeared, **July 15**. According to the testimony of the kidnap victims, the gunmen had stopped the bus, herded the children and the driver into 2 vans, and driven them about 100 miles to the quarry where they were placed into an underground makeshift cell. The children, 19 girls and 7 boys aged 6 to 14 years, then dug their way out and one boy raced for help. During a 12-day search, 3 men were finally arrested and charged with kidnaping. Richard Schoenfeld, the son of a prominent Atherton, Calif., podiatrist, surrendered to authorities, **July 23**. On **July 29**, in Vancouver, B.C. authorities arrested Fred Newhall Woods, son of Fred N. Woods 3d, the president of the California Rock and Gravel Co. and owner of the quarry. James Schoenfeld, Richard's brother, was also arrested **July 29**, near his Atherton home. The 3 suspects were held on a bail of $1 million each.

Boycott Mars Olympics—The Summer Olympics, **July 17**, opened in Montreal, Canada, under the shadow of 2 political protests that eventually led to the departure of some 700 athletes from 32 nations. The first dispute began **July 9**, when Tanzania said it would boycott the games because one of the participants, New Zealand, had sent a rugby team to tour South Africa despite the nation's racial discriminatory policy of apartheid. By **July 21**, after a failure to win concessions from New Zealand, 30 nations, including virtually all of Africa, had withdrawn their athletes from competition in support of Tanzania. In the 2d dispute, which culminated **July 16**, Taiwan withdrew its athletes from Olympics because they would not be allowed to call themselves representatives of the Republic of China. The withdrawal came despite a last-minute proposal by the Canadian government, approved by the U.S. and the International Olympic Committee, that would have allowed the 42 athletes to participate under their own flag and anthem, but not as representatives of the Republic of China.

Viking I Makes Successful Landing on Mars—On the 7th anniversary of man's first walk on the moon, the robot craft Viking I, **July 20**, made the first successful landing on Mars and transmitted black-and-white photographs. The journey, covering almost one billion miles, had taken 11 months to complete. The robot craft's descent from the mother ship to the rocky wind-scoured Chryse Plain, took 3 hours and 13 minutes. The first photographs showed a plain strewn with light and dark-colored rocks, some round and others sharp-edged as if they had undergone little erosion. A panoramic view disclosed sand dunes, a depression that might be an eroded crater, patches of sand, rocks partially covered by drifting sand, low ridges, and a distant ridge which scientists said could be the rim of an impact crater. After an initial examination, most project scientists agreed the primary material in the area was probably volcanic in origin, modified by the impact of meteors, winds of the thin Martian atmosphere, and possibly water erosion. The first color photographs, transmitted **July 21**, revealed light blue skies above a reddish soil and rocks of apparently varied chemical makeup. According to project scientists, the color of the sky indicated the presence of a large number of particles, presumably dust and water vapor, in the air. The reddish color of the soil indicated oxidation had changed the Martian surface. These discoveries, together with a previous detection of nitrogen in the air, made the scientists eager to initiate the robot craft's life detection laboratory. However, an apparent malfunction in the craft's scooper arm, discovered **July 22**, temporarily set back plans to gather soil for biological examination. On **July 26**, an atmospheric "sniffer" detected between 2% and 3% nitrogen in the atmosphere, offering further encouragement to the search for life on Mars. On **July 28**, the robot arm, now functioning, scooped up its first samples of soil. On **July 30**, project scientists indicated the first inorganic samples showed Mars to be a rather primitive planet that had not undergone the continental upheavals that the earth has. The soil was found to contain iron oxide, iron, calcium, silicon, titanium, and aluminum, all common on earth, but lacked other trace elements typical to earth. On **July 31**, scientists discovered an unexpected abundance of oxygen and chemical activity in Martian soil. The "exciting and interesting and surprising" discovery, scientists said, could be either the first evidence of Martian life or a sign of an unusually active oxidation process. A further soil test, a radioactivity reading from a pyrolytic release experiment, **Aug. 7**, turned up the strongest evidence to date of biological activity. Optimism, however, diminished for lack of any detectable level of complex carbon-containing molecules that might be produced by microbes. On **Aug. 23**, a gas chromatograph mass spectrometer confirmed an earlier test that had found no signs to suggest the existence of life forms. However, a 2d-round of tests with the pyrolytic release experiment, **Aug. 26**, again gave evidence supporting the possibility of life.

Disasters—More than 500 persons died and some 3,400 were injured, **July 14**, when an earthquake registering 5.6 on the Richter scale leveled the town of Seririt on the Indonesian island of Bali . . . A

Czechoslovak airliner on approach to Bratislava, Czechoslovakia, **July 28**, crashed into a recreation lake, killing 70 of the 76 persons aboard.

AUGUST
National

Unemployment Rises Sharply—Despite a large increase in the number of jobs, the unemployment rate in July rose from 7.5% to 7.8%, the labor department reported **Aug. 6**. The rapid growth in the number of people seeking jobs had outpaced the month's jump in employment, which rose to 87.9 million.

Roselli Found Dead in Miami—The body of crime figure John Roselli, **Aug. 7**, was found floating in Miami's Biscayne Bay. Roselli, along with slain Chicago mobster Sam Giancana, had been key figures in the CIA plot to assassinate Cuba's Fidel Castro. Roselli had testified before the Senate Select Committee on Intelligence in 1975. Attorney General Edward H. Levi, **Aug. 13**, asked the FBI to determine whether Roselli had been slain as a result of his Senate testimony or to prevent future testimony before a Congressional committee.

Harrises Convicted—A Los Angeles Superior Court jury, **Aug. 9**, convicted SLA members William and Emily Harris of kidnaping, armed robbery, and auto theft. They were acquitted of other charges, including assault with a deadly weapon. The jury rejected the major charge against the Harrises, kidnaping for the purpose of robbery, which carries a mandatory life sentence. The charges stemmed from a 1974 shoplifting incident at a sporting goods store. Convicted bank robber Patricia Hearst had accompanied the Harrises and opened fire on the store when she saw the Harrises were in trouble, permitting them to escape. The prosecution had alleged that, after fleeing from the store, the Harrises, along with Hearst, kidnaped 2 men along with their vehicles. Although the defense had accepted many of the prosecution's facts, it had contended that the charges in the state's 11-count indictment were excessive. In the end, the jury either rejected or reduced 9 of 11 counts. Brandler, **Aug. 31**, sentenced the Harrises to 11 years to life in prison, the 11 years for armed robbery and the life sentence for kidnaping.

Kelley Announced FBI Restructuring—Following wide publicity of misconduct by FBI agents investigating domestic groups during the 1970s, FBI Director Clarence M. Kelley, **Aug. 11**, announced the most extensive internal reorganization of the bureau since the beginning of World War II. Kelley, **Aug. 8**, had admitted that he had been deliberately "deceived" by aides who had withheld information about a number of illegal burglaries carried out by bureau agents during the 1970s. The disclosures of the burglaries, apparently aimed primarily against the radical Weatherman organization, had become public in a suit filed against the FBI by the Socialist Workers' party. Under the restructuring, domestic intelligence investigations would be moved to the general investigative division "for the express purpose that they be managed like all other criminal cases in that division."

Republicans Nominate Ford, Dole—The 31st Republican National Convention, meeting **Aug. 16-19** in Kansas City, Kansas, nominated Pres. Gerald R. Ford and Kansas Sen. Robert J. Dole as the presidential and vice presidential candidates in the 1976 national election. (See Convention.)

Conservatives Nominate Maddox—The American Independent Party, **Aug. 27**, in Chicago, nominated former Georgia Gov. Lester G. Maddox, an avowed segregationist, as their 1976 presidential candidate. On **Aug. 28**, the conservatives nominated one-time Madison, Wis., mayor William E. Dyke as the vice-

presidential nominee. Maddox and Dyke would run on a platform calling for repeal of the federal income tax and opposition to busing, abortion, public housing, gun control, and the equal rights amendment.

Senate Study Scores Medicaid—A Senate committee investigation of the 10-year-old Medicaid program, made public **Aug. 30**, concluded that from $4 billion to $7.5 billion of the $15 billion annual Medicaid payout was being wasted through fraud, the poor quality of care, and provision of services to ineligible persons. The study of the health program in 8 cities found rampant abuses by both providers and recipients. The study concluded that federal action was needed to correct the program's "abysmal" administration at all levels. One of the most dramatic findings revealed the nature of the so-called "Medicaid mills." According to the investigation, greed had induced health professionals, including doctors, dentists, podiatrists, optometrists, and chiropractors, to establish quasi clinics which dispensed a variety of substandard and often unnecessary services. It was estimated about two-thirds of the $2.225 billion available annually for such clinics was wasted. During the course of the investigation, committee chairman Frank E. Moss (D, Ut.) and 6 aides had posed as patients and personally visited over 200 facilities dispensing Medicaid services. In Congressional hearings on the Medicaid program, 2 chiropractors, convicted of Medicaid fraud, **Aug. 31**, testified that they had taken advantage of the Medicaid system because Medicaid officials ignored fraud and deception.

U.S. Steel Drops Price Rise—In an unusual move, the U.S. Steel Company, **Aug. 30**, bowed to competitive and consumer pressure and dropped a 4.5% price increase scheduled to go into effect Oct. 1. Bethlehem Steel and Inland Steel followed suit immediately and other steel makers indicated that they would do the same.

International

Unrest Resumes in South Africa—Between 35 to 40 persons were killed, **Aug. 4-12**, when new racial disturbances erupted in the South African black township of Soweto and other areas. The rioting in Soweto was aimed primarily against the continued detention of persons held in connection with the June riots and in support of a job boycott by blacks working for white employers in Johannesburg. On **Aug. 18-19**, rioting spread to 3 black townships near the east coast seaside resort of Port Elizabeth. Representatives of 7 of South Africa's 9 tribal homelands, considered by the government to be the authentic representatives of the blacks, **Aug. 21**, strongly condemned apartheid. The Vorster government's reaction to black unrest, the leaders stated, showed that the only language the government was prepared to listen to was violence. Blacks demonstrating in Soweto in support of a national strike by black workers, **Aug. 24-25**, clashed violently with Zulu vigilante groups armed with clubs and knives. The Zulu backlash against the harassment campaign against black workers had been openly encouraged by white officials. The death toll during the clashes was placed at 35.

98 Executed in Sudan for Coup Attempt—Sudan executed 81 persons, **Aug. 4**, and 17 persons, **Aug. 5**, following their conviction on charges of plotting an unsuccessful coup, July 2, against Pres. Gaafar al-Nimeiry. Those executed included Brig. Gen. Mohammed Nur Saeed who allegedly had confessed to being the military leader of the coup which had been planned in London with 2 exiled Sudanese politicians. Saeed and the other defendants allegedly also confessed that the Libyan government had provided training for the insurgents. From London, former Sudanese Prime Minister Sadik al-Mahdi, **Aug. 4**, admitted that he had planned the coup. On **Aug. 9,** Pres. al-Nimeiry hinted that the USSR, which is a major arms supplier to Libya, had been behind the unsuccessful overthrow attempt.

U.S., Iran Announce $10-Billion Military Deal— U.S. and Irani officials, after meeting in Teheran, announced, **Aug. 7,** that Iran would spend $10 billion for military purchases in the U.S. The purchases would be part of the mounting trade between the 2 countries estimated to total $50 billion between 1975 and 1980. The agreement came despite a recent Senate foreign relations subcommittee study which had charged the $10 billion in arms sold to Iran in recent years was excessive, not well used, and required the employment of too many Americans to operate the arms systems. Shah Mohammed Reza Pahlavi, **Aug. 6,** had denied the charges, arguing that the U.S. must continue arms sales to Iran or risk instability and war in his area of the world. On **Aug. 27,** Secretary of State Henry A. Kissinger, who had negotiated the $10-billion agreement, told the Senate foreign relations subcommittee that the U.S. would sell Iran 160 F-16 fighters at a cost of about $3.4 billion.

Tell Zaatar Falls to Christians— Under siege since mid-June, the Palestinian refugee camp at Tell Zaatar, **Aug. 12,** fell to rightist Christian forces, ending almost all possibility of a negotiated settlement in the Lebanese civil war. As thousands of civilians fled the camp, Palestinian sources accused the rightists of reneging on promises to allow a peaceful evacuation of the camp. Some 300 civilians, evacuated **Aug. 3** and **4** by the International Red Cross, had told horrifying stories of suffering and endurance. Firing from Christian positions had stopped the evacuation **Aug. 6.** The death toll during the long siege of Tell Zaatar, **Aug. 13,** was placed at 1,600 persons dead and 4,000 wounded.

Tanaka Indicted, Miki Ouster Urged— Former Japanese Prime Minister Kakuei Tanaka, **Aug. 16,** was indicted on charges of accepting bribes of $1.6 million to arrange the purchase of Lockheed aircraft by All-Nippon, Japan's largest airline. Also indicted were 3 Japanese executives with Marubeni Trading Corp., Lockheed's sales agent in Japan. According to the indictment, Tanaka had used his office, which included jurisdiction over the transport ministry, to arrange the sales. Former Transportation Minister Tomisaburo Hashimoto, **Aug. 21,** was arrested and also charged with accepting a Lockheed bribe, $14,000 in this case, to influence All-Nippon to buy Lockheed planes. In the wake of the latest developments in the Lockheed bribery scandal, a majority of Prime Minister **Takeo Miki**'s ruling Liberal-Democratic party, **Aug. 24,** called for his ouster, charging he had lost the capacity to govern. Miki, who had come under fire for his dogged insistence on carrying through a thorough Lockheed investigation, refused to quit.

Developing Nations Parley Warns Rich Nations— Representatives of 85 nonaligned nations concluded, **Aug. 20,** their 5th formal conference since 1961 with a stern warning that rich nations must give up some of their privileges to create a new and just world economic order. The final communique, issued from the conference site, Colombo, Sri Lanka, declared that economic problems were the most acute problems in international relations and stated that nothing short of a complete rearrangement of international economic relations would enable developing countries to reach an acceptable level of development. Covering a wide range of topics, the communique called for an oil embargo against France and Israel to punish them for arms deals with South Africa, deplored U.S. "imperialist aggression" in Korea, welcomed Soviet-U.S. detente, called for the independence of Puerto Rico, and hailed the "historic and total victory achieved by the people of Vietnam in their struggle against aggressive United States imperialism."

Namibian Independence Set — A South-West African constitutional committee, **Aug. 8** in Windhoek, announced plans for a multiracial govern-

---

U.S. Conducts Major Show of Force In Korea
After North Koreans Kill 2 American Officers

The U.S., **Aug. 21,** conducted a major show of force in a dispute over the **Aug. 18** slaying of 2 U.S. officers in the Korean demilitarized zone.

B-52 strategic bombers from Guam, F-4 Phantom and F-111 fighter bombers, helicopters, and about 300 armed U.S. and South Korean soldiers went on alert while American and South Korean personnel chopped down the tree that was the center of the controversy. The U.S. and North Korea both had alerted their forces **Aug. 19.** The U.S. had also cancelled leaves for forces in the area and, **Aug. 20,** had ordered the aircraft carrier Midway to sail to Yokosuka with an accompanying task force of destroyers, cruisers, and frigates.

According to the United Nations Command, a U.S.-South Korean group on a routine tree-pruning mission to improve surveillance at the Panmunjom truce site had been attacked by North Korean soldiers wielding axes and metal pikes, **Aug. 18.** The North Koreans killed 2 American officers and wounded 4 U.S. enlisted men and 5 South Korean soldiers. U.S. Pres. Gerald R. Ford had condemned the attack as "brutal and cowardly" and warned the North Korean government that it would be responsible for "the consequences." North Korea had claimed "U.S. imperialist troops" armed with lethal weapons had attacked the North Koreans when they protested the trimming of a tree in an area under North Korean control.

U.S. Secretary of State Henry A. Kissinger, **Aug. 20,** demanded "explanations and reparation," stating the U.S. "absolutely cannot and will not accept the premeditated act of murder." Following the show of force, North Korean Pres. Kim Il Sung called the **Aug. 18** incident "regretful." The U.S. state department asserted that the statement was not acceptable because it did not admit responsibility.

However, on **Aug. 23,** after the display of force and the removal of the offending tree, the state department softened its reaction and called the North Korean president's statement "a positive step." The department also announced that the U.S. was calling for a meeting of the Korean Military Armistice Commission to demand assurances from North Korea for the safety of U.S. personnel in the demilitarized zone.

The U.S.-led United Nations Command and North Korea, **Sept. 6,** signed an agreement on new security arrangements designed to prevent future clashes in the demilitarized zone. Under the accord, which amended the 1953 truce accord that ended the Korean war, the joint security area at Panmunjom would be partitioned. North Korea would remove 4 guard posts in the southern part where the Aug. 18 clash occurred. The agreement called for elimination of contact between North Korean and UN military units. Nonmilitary personnel, such as work details, tourists, and journalists, would have free movement through the area.

ment to lead the South African trust territory of Namibia to independence by the end of 1978. The conference was immediately attacked by the United Nations, black African leaders, and the U.S. because it failed to take into account the South-West African People's Organization (SWAPO), the group recognized by the UN as the representative of the 800,000 inhabitants of Namibia. The UN Council for Namibia, **Aug. 20**, rejected the plan because it failed to comply with a UN Security Council ultimatum calling for the withdrawal of South African troops from Namibia and the holding of UN-supervised elections. The UN Council, terming the plan an "ambiguous and equivocal" blueprint, asked the Security Council to consider taking appropriate measures under the UN charter against South Africa because it had failed to comply with the UN ultimatum.

French Prime Minister Resigns—French Prime Minister and leader of the Gaullist party, Jacques Chirac, **Aug. 25**, resigned, charging Pres. Valery Giscard d'Estaing had not given him sufficient authority to deal with France's problems. Chirac was replaced by Foreign Trade Minister Raymond Barre, a professor of economics with no party affiliation. Barre, **Aug. 27**, announced a new government coalition, markedly broader than the previous government. Five ministries went to the Gaullist party, 4 to Giscard d'Estaing's small Independent Republican party, 3 to the Radical party, and 4 to persons without party affiliations.

Bernhard Resigns Military, Business Posts—Dutch Prince Bernhard, consort to Queen Juliana, **Aug. 26**, gave up virtually all his military and business positions in face of official criticism of his involvement with the Lockheed Aircraft Corp. A 6-month investigation by a 3-man government commission had failed to find firm evidence supporting allegations the prince had accepted bribes of $1.1 million from Lockheed officials, but the study had concluded he "showed himself open to dishonorable requests and offers." Bernhard, in his resignation statement, admitted that he had "not observed the caution in this matter which is required in my vulnerable position as consort of the Queen and Prince of the Netherlands." Prime Minister Joop M. den Uyl, who released the report and resignation statement to parliament, made it clear that there was no possibility of criminal prosecution. On **Aug. 30**, a left-wing attempt to demand criminal prosecution of Bernhard was defeated in parliament in a 142-to-2 vote.

General

Flash Flood Rages Through Colorado Canyon—A flash flood caused by heavy rains the previous night, **Aug. 1**, raged through Colorado's Big Thompson Canyon, 50 miles north of Denver. The swollen waters of the Big Thompson River drowned motorists, fishermen, campers, and residents in the recreation area located between Loveland and the vacation town of Estes Park. Pres. Gerald R. Ford, **Aug. 2**, declared the region a disaster area, as ground search helicopters evacuated survivors. By **Oct. 3**, the death toll was officially set at 139 persons, with 6 people still listed as missing.

"San Quentin Six" Verdict Handed Down—Following a 16-month trial, a Marin County (Calif.) Superior Court jury, **Aug. 12**, acquitted 3 members of the "San Quentin Six" of murder, conspiracy and assault in an escape attempt from the prison in 1971. One member was convicted of murder and conspiracy and 2 others were found guilty of lesser charges. Black revolutionary writer George Jackson, 3 guards, and 2 inmate trusties had been killed on the day of the escape. The prosecution had contended that all the defendants, 5 black and Hispanic inmates and a former black

prisoner, had participated in a conspiracy to escape from prison. The defense had argued that state authorities had created a "counterconspiracy" to assassinate Jackson. The question of how Jackson was killed was not resolved.

GM Raises Prices on '77 Models—The General Motors Corp., **Aug. 25**, announced the average retail price of 1977 model cars would rise by 5.9%, or $338 per car, bringing the average "sticker price" of a GM car above $6,000 for the first time. Thomas A. Murphy, the chairman of GM, traditionally the price leader among American automobile companies, said GM felt that the American consumer would "recognize this G.M. price as moderate in light of the value which these new 1977 models represent." On **Aug. 26**, GM unveiled its 1977 Buick models, the first installment of a long-heralded array of scaled-down cars. GM stated that the cars, which were built to get 3 to 4 more miles per gallon, were designed to meet the demands of an age of scarce and expensive energy.

Mysterious Ailment Kills 28—By **Aug. 31**, 28 persons who had attended an American Legion convention in Philadelphia, Pa., **July 21-24**, or stayed at Philadelphia's Bellevue Stratford Motel since July 1, had died, victims of a mysterious flu-like ailment. Altogether, 179 cases of the so-called "legion fever" had been reported. Under criteria established **Aug. 6** by the Center for Disease Control's Bureau of Epidemiology, official cases included persons with a fever and x-ray evidence of pneumonia. The victims included 26 persons who had attended the legionnaires' convention, headquartered at the Bellevue Stratford, and 2 men who had attended the Eucharistic Conference, **Aug. 1-8**. U.S. Public Health Service and Pennsylvania State Health Department epidemiologists, **Aug. 2**, began an investigation of the mysterious disease when the deaths of at least 6 legionnaires who had attended the convention had been reported. By **Aug. 12**, health officials had ruled out bacteria and food or water contaminants, swine flu, and 17 toxic metals as probable causes. On **Aug. 25**, the results of tests on tissue specimens from victims suggested the cause might be nickel carbonyl, a highly toxic substance. The tests, however, were not considered conclusive.

Disasters—More than 150 persons died and 140,000 were left homeless when rain-swollen rivers flooded Northern Pakistan, it was reported **Aug. 10**. More than 5 million acres of land were flooded and some 53,000 homes collapsed or were washed away. . . . An earthquake registering 7.8 on the Richter scale and centered in the Gulf of Moro, **Aug. 18**, struck the southern Philippine island of Mindanao. Philippine Pres. Ferdinand E. Marcos, **Aug. 22**, reported that the quake and resulting tidal wave caused 4,000 fatalities with another 4,000 persons missing and presumed dead. Damage was set at $130 million and 35,138 persons were left homeless.

SEPTEMBER
National

Hays Resigns From House — Veteran Rep. Wayne L. Hays (D, O.), **Sept. 1**, resigned the seat he had held for 28 years in the House of Representatives. His decision followed an unanimous vote, **Aug. 30**, in the House ethics committee to hold public hearings into allegations of improper and illegal conduct by Hays in association with a widely publicized sex scandal. On **Aug. 14**, Hays had announced that he would not seek re-election. Hays failed to secure a House pledge to take no further action against him after his resignation. •

Unemployment Continues to Rise — For the 3d month in a row, the labor department reported, **Sept. 3**, that unemployment had risen. The rise, to 7.9% of the labor force in August, was a blow to the White House, forcing it to retreat from its long-held forecast that the jobless rate would fall below 7% by the end of 1976. Council of Economic Advisers head Alan Greenspan, admitting unemployment might not decline to 7% before January or February 1977, attributed the rise to the continuing "extremely abnormal" growth in the number of persons seeking work. Democratic presidential hopeful Jimmy Carter, however, immediately charged the economic news was evidence of the White House's lack of leadership in dealing with unemployment.

Ford Decides to Keep Kelley — After studying a justice department report on allegations FBI Director Clarence M. Kelley had misused government services and property and accepted expensive gifts from subordinates, Pres. Gerald R. Ford, **Sept. 4,** concluded there was "no adequate justification" for asking Kelley to resign. The justice department, in a report delivered **Sept. 3** by Attorney General Edward H. Levi, had concluded gifts Kelley had received from subordinates were permissable under pertinent federal regulations and that Kelley should be allowed to reimburse the government for any goods and services applied to his suburban apartment "about which there is the slightest question."

Croatian Nationalists Hijack Airliner — Five proponents of Croatian independence from Yugoslavia, brandishing fake bombs, **Sept. 10,** seized a TWA jetliner with 92 persons aboard enroute from New York City to Chicago, forced it to Montreal and then, with stops in Newfoundland and Iceland, across the Atlantic Ocean. After a 30-hour flight to Paris's Charles de Gaulle airport, the hijackers finally surrendered, **Sept. 12,** in the face of a tough French government ultimatum either to surrender to be expelled or face execution in France. Upon their return to New York, the 4 men and one woman were arraigned, **Sept. 13,** on federal air piracy charges and also faced a state murder charge in the death of a New York City policeman. The officer had died, **Sept. 11,** while working to dismantle a bomb apparently placed by the hijackers in a locker in Grand Central Station. The hijackers, **Sept. 10,** had relayed instructions from Montreal concerning the location of the bomb and 2 statements appealing for U.S. support for their cause. The hijackers had stated that a bomb planted "somewhere in the United States" would be set off unless 5 major newspapers printed the statements. This demand was essentially met **Sept. 11.** To further publicize their cause, the hijackers, **Sept. 11,** released 35 hostages in Gander, Newfoundland in return for an agreement that TWA would drop propaganda leaflets on Chicago, Montreal, and New York City. This was also done **Sept. 11.** The hijacked plane, **Sept. 11,** also dropped thousands of propaganda leaflets over London and Paris. The Yugoslav government, **Sept. 13,** said the U.S. had committed an "unfriendly act" and complained that the FBI had failed to stop the terrorists and had complied with their demands to publish anti-Belgrade statements. On **Sept. 17,** Zvonko Busic, the leader of the hijackers, told investigators that he alone had planned the seizure and was responsible for the planting of the bomb. However, all 5, **Sept. 21,** were indicted for air piracy and causing the death of the New York City police officer. The 5 hijackers, **Sept. 25,** pleaded not guilty.

Schorr Refuses to Disclose Source — In testimony before the House ethics committee, CBS news correspondent Daniel Schorr, **Sept. 15,** refused on 9 occasions to reveal details of how he had obtained a copy of a House committee report on intelligence activities. Schorr also refused to hand over subpoenaed documents in his possession, including copies of the intelligence report. In his opening statement, Schorr told the ethics committee, "I appear before this committee today, under protest, in response to a subpoena whose issuance I deeply deplore." As protection for his refusal to reveal his source, Schorr cited the freedom of the press under the First Amendment. Despite Schorr's refusal, it became apparent after the testimony that, lacking majority support, the ethics committee would not cite Schorr for contempt of Congress.

Ford, Carter Debate Domestic Issues — Under the auspices of the League of Women Voters, Pres. Gerald R. Ford, **Sept. 23,** met presidential rival Jimmy Carter in Philadelphia in a nationally-televised debate on domestic issues. It was estimated that a television audience of more than 90 million persons watched the first of 3 scheduled debates. Liberally sprinkled with confusing, often contradictory statistics and details, the debate's highlight was a mysterious technical failure which cut off the sound for 27 minutes before the closing statements. The consensus of polls taken following the verbal contest gave the winning edge to Ford. The New York Times, **Sept. 27,** cited the debate as a factor in a major upsurge in Ford's position in the presidential contest.

Congress Overrides Social Services Veto — Conservatives in both parties joined liberal Democrats in Congress, **Sept. 30,** to override Pres. Gerald R. Ford's veto of a $56-billion appropriations bill for social services. Ford, **Sept. 29,** had vetoed the bill to fund manpower, health, education, and welfare programs "purely and simply on the issue of fiscal integrity." Ford had said, while he agreed with most the programs and a provision that restricted federal funds for abortions to cases where the life of the mother would be endangered, the bill appropriated too much money.

Ford Denies Misuse of Campaign Funds, Golf Trips — Answering a campaign challenge from Gov. Jimmy Carter, Pres. Gerald R. Ford, **Sept. 30,** stated that he had never diverted any campaign funds for personal use and that he was confident the current investigation into the matter by the Watergate special prosecutor Charles H. Ruff would prove him to be "free of allegations." In response to another allegation, Ford conceded he may have discussed government business with corporate officials while their guest on golfing trips, but asserted that no impropriety had been involved. Carter, **Sept. 30,** accepted Ford's response, stating, "I don't have any reason to think President Ford is misleading the American people."

International

Racial Unrest Hits South African Colored Townships — Some 3,000 colored (mixed race) and black demonstrators, **Sept. 2,** battled with riot police in downtown Cape Town, South Africa, in the first racial disturbances to reach a white area. The disturbances in the area continued through **Sept. 10,** hitting a peak on **Sept. 9,** when at least 16 nonwhites were killed as protests against apartheid exploded in a ring of nonwhite townships around Cape Town. The colored protest against apartheid reflected long-standing pressure, even inside South Africa's ruling Nationalist party, for reforms which whould bind the nation's 2.3 million colored in a firm alliance with South Africa's 4.2 million whites. However, Prime Minister John Vorster, **Sept. 8,** iterated his government's long-standing opposition to the integration of "colored people" into a parliament which is reserved for whites. This integration, the principle recommendation of a government-appointed inquiry into the status of the colored, had been rejected by the government in June.

Soviet Pilot Seeks Asylum in U. S. — Soviet Air Force pilot Viktor I. Belenko, **Sept. 6**, flew his MiG-25, one of the most advanced Soviet jet fighters, to Hakodate on the northern Japanese island of Hokkaido. Upon landing, Belenko told Japanese officials that he was seeking refuge in the U. S. The U. S. government, **Sept. 7**, in a personal decision by U.S. Pres. Gerald R. Ford, informed Japan it would grant political asylum to the pilot, but would leave to Japan the decision on disposition of the plane. Belenko, **Sept. 9**, after meeting with Soviet officials who urged him to return to the USSR, was flown to the U. S. CIA Director George Bush, **Sept. 19**, said the defection was "probably a major intelligence bonanza" for the West and asserted that Belenko's debriefing was going well. Japanese and American specialists examining the MiG-25 indicated, **Sept. 21**, that the plane was not as sophisticated as had been assumed.

Mao Dies at 82 — Chinese Communist Party Chairman Mao Tse-tung died, **Sept. 9**, in Peking, at the age of 82, following a long illness. The fact that Mao, who had led China since 1949, left no designated heir, left China's already uncertain political situation even murkier. The official death announcement, which was delayed 16 hours, appealed to the Chinese people to uphold the unity of the party and to "continue to carry out Chairman Mao's revolutionary line and policies in foreign affairs resolutely." The announcement also urged the Chinese people to "deepen criticism" of former Deputy Premier Teng Hsiao-ping, who had lost his position to Hua Kuo-feng in the January power struggle. An 8-day period of mourning began **Sept. 11**. On the final day of the mourning period, some 750,000 people gathered in an austere memorial to Mao. Prime Minister Hua Kuo-feng, in his memorial speech, called on the party, army, and people to "carry out the cause left behind by Chairman Mao."

Social Democrats Ousted in Swedish Elections — Ending more than 4 decades of Social Democratic rule, the Swedish electorate, **Sept. 20**, gave a narrow victory to a coalition of 3 non-Socialist parties. Despite predictions of a close race, the outcome stunned civil servants, businessmen, journalists, and office workers. Following his party's defeat, Prime Minister Olof Palme, obviously shaken by the results, resigned. The official results gave the non-Socialist bloc 180 seats in parliament to 169 seats for the Social Democrats and the Communists, their unofficial legislative partners. The new prime minister was expected to be Thorbjorn Falldin, the 50-year-old leader of the Center party. The non-Socialists had decried the long period of Social Democratic rule, high taxes, the growth of bureaucratic power, the centralization of the government, and the growing leverage of labor unions. The new party leaders, however, indicated that they would make no attempt to dismantle the advanced social welfare programs shaped under Social Democratic rule. A major issue in the last weeks of the campaign had been Falldin's pledge to close Sweden's 5 nuclear power plants and to abandon the government's plans to build another 8 plants by 1985. In a **Sept. 23** interview, Palme indicated that he believed the nuclear plant issue had been crucial to the outcome of the election in which the opposition had conducted a "scare" campaign about "the so-called terrible things we were about to do."

South Africa Allows Multiracial Sports — Reversing a much criticized policy, Minister of Sport Piet W. Koornhof, **Sept. 23**, announced that the South African government would sanction multiracial games at all levels as well as mixed racial teams in international athletic competition. The decision was widely acclaimed as "sensational" by sports commentators.

Smith Yields on Rhodesia After Talks With Kissinger — Following talks, **Sept. 19**, with U. S. Secretary of State Henry A. Kissinger and South African Prime Minister John Vorser, in Pretoria, South Africa, Rhodesian Prime Minister Ian Smith, **Sept. 24**, announced that he had accepted Kissinger's proposal for an immediate biracial government in Rhodesia and black majority rule within 2 years. Smith stated, "It was made abundantly clear to me that as long as the present circumstances in Rhodesia prevailed, we could expect no help or support of any kind from the free world." Smith's decision followed secret high-level talks with his cabinet **Sept. 21-22**. The U. S.-British plan which Smith accepted called for an immediate meeting between representatives of the Rhodesian government and black leaders to form a temporary biracial council of state and council of ministers. Majority rule would be achieved through a new constitution and elections. The plan also stipulated that, with the establishment of the temporary government, international economic sanctions against Rhodesia would be lifted and the guerrilla war being waged by black nationalist factions would end. Despite an initial welcome of Smith's move, 5 presidents of neighboring African countries, **Sept. 26**, refused to accept the British-American plan and called on Britain, as "the colonial authority" over Rhodesia, to convene a conference to work out a substitute plan. Although not implicitly stated, it was widely known that the chief objection lay in the structure and racial composition of the interim government in which the real power would lie in the white-led council. The African statement strongly indicated that the guerrilla war against Rhodesia would continue.

Britain Asks IMF Support for Battered Pound — As the British pound, once the world's strongest currency, continued to suffer sharp losses, Great Britain, **Sept. 29**, asked the International Monetary Fund for a standby loan of $3.9 billion, the limit on its borrowing from the IMF. The pound, **Sept. 28**, had plunged 4 cents to $1.64, throwing the government deeper into economic crisis. The IMF credit would be the 4th, and most painful, large credit undertaken by the British in less than a year. The new loan immediately buoyed the pound which rose to $1.67 by the close of the business day, **Sept. 29**.

Syrians Launch Offensive on PLO in Lebanon — Syrian forces, supported by Lebanese rightist Christian militia forces, **Sept. 29**, dislodged Palestine Liberation Organization forces from most of the key positions in the wide mountain area east of Beirut. Palestinian, Syrian, and Lebanese attempts to reach a cease-fire prior to Pres. Elias Sarkis' inauguration **Sept. 23**, had reached an impasse, **Sept. 19**, over PLO leader Yasir Arafat's refusal to withdraw Palestinian and leftist Moslem military from the strategic mountain area.

General

Viking II Lands on Mars — The Viking II lander, **Sept. 3**, descended to the Utopia Plains on Mars. Although a breakdown in the lander's communications system prevented detailed monitoring of the descent, signals from the orbiting mother ship confirmed shortly after the landing that it was receiving the first surface photographs. Panoramic photographs transmitted **Sept. 4** showed a largely level surface of sand and small stones strewn with boulders, superficially not unlike the Chryse Plain where the Viking I lander had descended. Project scientists reported, **Sept. 22**, that the Viking II spacecraft had discovered that Mars' permanent northern polar cap was composed entirely of frozen water, indicating that Mars had more water than had been expected. The scientists also announced that Viking instruments had detected the presence of rare gases — krypton and xenon, in Mars' atmosphere. This discovery provided the first solid and direct confirmation that Mars once must have had a considerably denser atmosphere.

More Widespread Cheating at USMA Alleged — Sworn statements by 65 West Point Military Academy cadets, made available **Sept. 8** to several Congressmen, alleged that some 700 of their classmates had engaged in the practices that violated the academy honor code. The 65 cadets, all accused of cheating in the scandal that had recently rocked the academy, stated that their colleagues, many of them high-ranking students and athletic team captains, had cheated in academic courses, lied to officers, and even "fixed" student honor boards to obtain not-guilty verdicts. The affidavits presented a picture of pervasive cheating and other dishonest practices far more widespread than had been previously disclosed. However, Army Secretary Martin R. Hoffman, **Sept. 10,** stated that he believed "the overwhelming majority of violators" in the cheating scandal had been found and punished. According to his status report, 134 cadets had been found guilty or resigned in the face of charges of violation of the honor code, and 12 cases were still pending. Hoffman termed the affidavits, which had not been formally presented, "hearsay" evidence as far as the army was concerned.

Episcopal Church Approves Ordination of Women — The House of Deputies of the Episcopal Church, a lay and clerical body, **Sept. 16,** in Minneapolis, Minn., approved the ordination of women as priests and bishops in the church.

Fresno Bee Newsmen Freed From Jail — Superior Court Judge Hollis G. Best, **Sept. 17,** in Fresno, Cal., freed from jail 4 Fresno Bee newsmen who had been convicted of contempt of court for refusing to identify their source for a series of articles written in 1975. Best, in freeing the newsmen, argued that it was pointless to keep them in jail because in their testimony they had made it clear that they would not reveal the source. The 4 newsmen had entered jail, **Sept. 3,** stating they were "firmly proud" of "defending one of our basic freedoms."

Disasters — A Venezuelan air force transport, carrying members of the Central University of Venezuela choir to Spain, **Sept. 4,** crashed while attempting to land during a hurricane at the U.S. air force base in the Azores, killing all 68 persons aboard. . . . In "one of the worst" train disasters in South African history, a South African commuter train, **Sept. 6,** collided with a Mozambique-bound express train east of Johannesburg, killing at least 31 persons and injuring more than 70 persons. . . . A British Airways Trident enroute from London to Istanbul, **Sept. 10,** collided head on near Zagreb, Yugoslavia, with a Yugoslav charter DC-9, carrying mostly West German tourists from Split to Cologne, in the worst collision in aviation history. All 176 persons aboard both planes were killed. . . . Heavy rains and a typhoon that roared ashore on the southern Japanese island of Kyushu, **Sept. 13,** left 104 persons known dead, 57 missing, and at least 290 injured. The heavy rains and storm left nearly 325,000 persons homeless. . . . All 155 persons aboard died, **Sept. 19,** when a Turkish Airlines Boeing 727 crashed into Karakaya Mountain in southwestern Turkey and exploded into flames.

OCTOBER
National

Butz Resigns Under Pressure — Secretary of Agriculture Earl L. Butz, **Oct. 4,** resigned from office, apologizing for the "gross indiscretion" of making a racist remark. Disclosure of his remark about blacks, described as derogatory, obscene, and scatalogical had provoked a political storm and numerous demands for the secretary's resignation. Although Pres. Gerald R. Ford, **Oct. 1,** had summoned Butz to the White House for a "severe reprimand" for the "highly offensive" remarks, the criticism of Butz had continued to grow. In resigning, Butz stated that he hoped his resignation would "remove even the appearance of racism as an issue in the Ford campaign." Despite general praise for the resignation, Sen. Robert C. Byrd (D. W. Va.) and others attacked Ford for "trying to ride out the storm" rather than demanding Butz's resignation.

Economic Recovery Lagging — Government economic statistics released in October painted a picture of a lagging economy still plagued by high unemployment and inflation. On **Oct. 7,** the labor department reported that wholesale prices in September had increased by 0.9%, the largest rise in nearly a year. On **Oct. 8,** the labor department disclosed, in the last report before the presidential election, that unemployment had eased slightly in September from 7.9% of the labor force to 7.8%, but the total number of jobs had also declined. The commerce department, **Oct. 19,** reported that the GNP growth rate, the broadest gauge of U.S. economic performance, had slowed during the 3d quarter of 1976 to 4%, far below the rate projected by the administration and private economists. The report, however, included an optimistic note in indicating housing starts had shown a sharp rise of 17.6% during September to an annual rate of 1.81 million, the highest monthly level since February 1974. Completing the economic picture, the labor department, **Oct. 21,** stated that, although consumer prices had eased slightly during September, the real buying power of the typical worker had continued to decline.

Presidential, VP Candidates Debate — Changing tactics, Jimmy Carter went on the attack in San Francisco, **Oct. 7,** as he met Pres. Gerald R. Ford for the 2d presidential debate covering foreign policy issues. Carter charged the U.S. was neither strong or respected, while Ford countered that it was. In the most publicized moment of the debate, Ford, committing an apparent political gaffe, stated that there was "no Soviet domination of Eastern Europe and there never will be under a Ford administration." The remark, **Oct. 8,** provoked astonishment and derision from Eastern European ethnic groups across the country, and public opinion polls gave the victory in the debate to Carter. Back on the campaign stump, Carter, **Oct. 8,** variously attacked Ford as being "brainwashed" and lacking "common sense and knowledge" on foreign policy. Following numerous apologies for his remarks on East Europe, Ford, **Oct. 13,** finally admitted he had made a mistake and charged Carter with "moral conceit" in his criticism on the subject. In contrast to their campaign attacks, both Carter and Ford, **Oct. 22,** assumed a conciliatory and subdued tone in their last debate in Williamsburg, Va. They both promised to emphasize issues rather than personalities in the final week of the campaign with a hope of awakening interest among disillusioned voters. Both admitted that they had made mistakes in the campaign. Neither candidate committed any gaffes and the polls generally termed the debate a tossup. The vice presidential candidates, Sen. Walter F. Mondale and Sen. Robert J. Dole, **Oct. 15,** in Houston, met in a spirited, sometimes sharp debate, stressing their differing views on the economy.

Mardian Conviction Overturned — A Washington, D.C., federal appeals court, **Oct. 12,** reversed the conviction of former Assistant Attorney General Robert

C. Mardian for conspiring to cover up the Watergate break-in. He had been found guilty 21 months previously along with former Attorney General John N. Mitchell and former Nixon aides H. R. Haldeman and John D. Ehrlichman, whose convictions were upheld in a separate opinion. The 3-judge appeals court stated that Judge John J. Sirica had erred in failing to grant Mardian's request for a separate trial. Mardian had argued that because his role was a marginal one, there was a danger the government's evidence against the other 3 defendants might taint his own defense.

Deaths Force Temporary Halt of Swine-Flu Shots — Nine states and the Pittsburgh, Pa., area, **Oct. 12**, suspended administration of swine-flu vaccinations, following the deaths of 3 elderly persons who had received shots in a Pittsburgh clinic. Although federal and Pennsylvania officials asserted there was no evidence linking the deaths with the shots, they stated that the unusual circumstances of the deaths of 3 patients at one clinic called for investigation. On **Oct. 13**, after some 11 states had suspended their programs, the Disease Control Center reported that 14 persons in 9 states had died within 48 hours after receiving the swine-flu vaccine. However, **Oct. 14**, when no evidence linking the deaths and the vaccine had been discovered, most states had resumed or planned to resume the swine-flu vaccination program.

Arab Boycott Participation Disclosed — The commerce department, **Oct. 18**, released for public scrutiny 59 reports, all filed after Oct. 6, from companies stating they had been asked to comply with the Arab boycott of Israel. According to the reports, none of the companies, which included manufacturers, freight forwarders, and banks, stated they would refuse to comply. The disclosure stemmed from an **Oct. 7** order by Pres. Gerald R. Ford to make available for inspection all "future" reports filed in connection with the Arab boycott. The commerce department, in contradiction of a Ford debate pledge, had declined to disclose the names of U.S. companies participating in the boycott because the reports had been submitted under a promise of confidentiality.

Brown Forced to Clarify Controversial Remarks — In a rare public occurence, Jt. Chiefs of Staff head Air Force Gen. George S. Brown, **Oct. 18**, clarified controversial remarks he had made about Israel, Britain, and Iran in an interview. Clarifying a suggestion that Israel was becoming a military burden to the U.S., Brown emphasized his "personal commitment" to a policy of protecting the security and survival of Israel. He further stated that the Shah of Iran, to whom Brown had attributed "visions of a Persian Empire," was an able leader who contributed to the stability of his region of the world. Brown also explained that "compassion" had spurred him to describe Britain and its military forces as a "pathetic sight." The remarks, made in an interview with Newsweek, had prompted a storm of criticism and demands for Brown's resignation. However, both Pres. Gerald R. Ford and Defense Secretary Donald H. Rumsfeld, **Oct. 18**, gave no indication Brown should resign, stating Brown was a "fine officer" and the "proper thing" for him to do was to put his remarks in perspective.

Court Voids Medicaid Abortion Curb — Federal District Court Judge John F. Dooling, **Oct. 22**, in New York City, held unconstitutional a federal bar against Medicaid reimbursement for most abortions. The federal curb, the Hyde Amendment to a $65-billion social services appropriations bill passed **Sept. 30** over a presidential veto, limited Medicaid reimbursement to abortions in which the life of the mother was endangered. Although Federal District Court Judge John J. Sirica, **Oct. 21**, in Washington, D.C., had refused to overturn the ban, Dooling stated that his ruling would, in effect, nullify the Hyde Amendment in all 50 states.

International

Schmidt Wins Close West German Election — Barely staving off his conservative challenger Helmut Kohl, West German Chancellor Helmut Schmidt, **Oct. 3**, won a precariously small parliamentary majority in national elections. The majority held by Schmidt's Social Democratic party and its governing partner, the Free-Democratic party, in the 496-seat lower house of parliament, was reduced to 8 seats. Kohl, the governor of the Rhineland-Palatinate, described himself as the "moral victor of this election." His Christian Democrat Union, which had polled 48.6% of the vote to 42.6% for the Social Democrats, would have a plurality in the lower house of parliament. Kohl had campaigned on the slogan of "Freedom Instead of Socialism," criticizing Schmidt's deficit budgets and casting doubt on the soundness of a welfare state after 7 years of Social Democratic rule. On **Oct. 5**, Foreign Minister Hans-Dietrich Genscher, head of the Free Democrats, formally confirmed that his party would support the Chancellor.

Military Seizes Power in Thailand — Following a violent battle between leftist university students and police, the military, **Oct. 6**, seized control of the government in Thailand. Defense Minister Admiral Sagnad Chaloryu announced Thailand would be ruled by an Administrative Reform Committee which he would head. Adm. Sa-gnad also announced that the 1974 constitution had been abolished, all newspapers and periodicals would be banned, and a midnight-to-5 a.m. curfew would be enforced. The events leading to the take-over began **Oct. 4**, when some 2,000 students barricaded themselves in Thammasat University, demanding deportation of former strongman Field Marshal Thamon Kittikachorn and punishment of policemen who had garroted 2 leftist students. Marshal Thamon had returned from exile 3 weeks previously and had entered a Buddhist monastary. On **Oct. 6**, a sniping incident turned the protest into a battle between the students and the 1,500 armed policemen sent in to keep peace. At least 30 students were killed, hundreds wounded, and more than 1,700 students arrested in the ensuing bloodbath. On **Oct. 9**, King Phumiphol Aduldet named a civilian, Supreme Court Chief Justice Thanin Kraivichen, as the new prime minister. Thanin stated it would be at least 4 years before democratic elections would be held and perhaps a decade before full democratic rule might be restored. On **Oct. 16**, under "order number 22," the junta began a nationwide roundup of leftist writers, professors, and intellectuals as suspected Communists. The new directive allowed detention for up to 30 days without arraignment or bail. On **Oct. 20**, the junta disclosed that, since the coup, it had arrested more than 4,000 persons on suspicion of being Communist subversives.

South African Mixed Sports Policy Narrowed — Despite a ruling 3 weeks previously sanctioning multiracial sports, the South African government, **Oct. 12**, threatened to prosecute 8 white and 22 black rugby players who had played on the same team in a club match **Oct. 11**. Sports Minister Piet G. Koornhof asserted that multiracial teams would not be allowed at the club level, where most sports are played. His statement made it clear that, although the new policy would allow white teams to play black teams at the club level, mixed teams would be sanctioned only in international competition.

Vorster Rules Out Major Role for Blacks — In an interview in Pretoria, South Africa, Prime Minister John Vorster, **Oct. 18**, stated that he could not "foresee such a day" when his nation's 4.2 million ruling whites would cede power to South Africa's 18 million blacks. Vorster stated unequivocally that his government would continue to exclude blacks from participation in the mainstream of South Africa's political life. Stressing that his government had done more than any other to ease apartheid, Vorster pledged that all discriminatory measures that served no purpose would be scrapped.

Saudi Arabia Intervenes to Force Lebanon Pact — Six Arab leaders, meeting in Riyadh, Saudi Arabia, **Oct. 18**, signed a peace plan to end civil strife in Lebanon. The agreement followed a Saudi Arabian request, its first intervention in Lebanon, **Oct. 16**, for both Syria and the Palestine Liberation Organization to accept a cease-fire. The order came as Syrian tanks and artillery, in a 3-day offensive, broke through Palestinian positions both east and south of Beirut, virtually cutting off the predominantly Moslem part of the city from the rest of the country. Both Syrian Pres. Hafez al-Assad and PLO leader Yasir Arafat accepted the Saudi request and immediately proceeded to Riyadh. The plan approved in Riyadh, after a 2-day summit, called for a cease-fire beginning **Oct. 21** and the creation of an expanded Arab peacekeeping force, from the existing 2,300 to 30,000. After the cease-fire, the combatants would withdraw to positions held before the civil war broke out in April 1975. The peace-keeping force, under the command of Lebanese Pres. Elias Sarkis would separate the warring factions, confiscate all heavy weapons, arrest truce violators, and help the Lebanese government to restore public utilities and protect military installations. As generally interpreted, the accord gave Syria a mandate to continue its political and military intervention under the supervision of other Arab powers, but saved the Palestinian leadership from a Syrian imposed shake-up. On **Oct. 25**, a conference of Arab heads of state and government, in a 19-2 vote, approved the peace plan. However, the conference ended **Oct. 26** without final agreement on arrangements for the peace-keeping forces and the role of Syria's forces in it. It appeared, nevertheless, that Syrian forces already in Lebanon would dominate it. With the exception of continued fighting in the south near the Israeli border between Israeli-equipped Christian forces and leftist-Moslem alliance forces, the cease-fire seemed to be effective, for the most part, in Beirut and the remainder of Lebanon.

South African Arms Embargo Vetoed in UN — The U.S., Great Britain, and France, **Oct. 19**, voted against a United Nations Security Council resolution to impose an embargo on arms shipments to South Africa. The resolution had been aimed to force South Africa to relinquish its control of South-West Africa and to accede to free elections in the territory. The 3 nations opposed the resolution on the grounds that it would upset diplomatic efforts by U.S. Secretary of State Henry A. Kissinger to induce South Africa to accept terms for a conference on the independence of Namibia, as the territory is called.

Hua Named Chairman, Radicals Purged — Hsinhua, the official Chinese press agency, announced, Oct. 22, that the Communist Party Central Committee under the leadership of Chairman Hua had "shattered" an attempt by 4 senior radicals, including Mao's widow Chian Ching, to "usurp party and state power." The announcement was the first official report to the Chinese people of Hua's elevation to chairman and the downfall of the radicals, confirming reports circulating for several weeks. Beginning

Oct. 21, millions of Chinese marched in the streets of Peking, Shanghai, Tientsin, and Canton to celebrate the fall of the "anti-party clique." The mass demonstrations culminated, **Oct. 24**, in a vast rally of one million Chinese in Peking to acclaim Hua as the new party chairman. On **Oct. 12**, reports had begun to circulate to the Chinese people that Chiang and 3 leading Shanghai radicals had been purged from their party positions, arrested, and charged with plotting a coup. Although these reports received an official "no comment," an official spokesman had confirmed that Hua now held 3 top posts, chairman, military commission head, and prime minister. Indications that China's new leadership was preparing a campaign to discredit so-called leftist leaders had escalated **Oct. 16**, as crowds in Shanghai had carried effigies of Chiang and reports had circulated that more leftists had lost their jobs or been arrested.

UN Bars Dealings with Transkei — The United Nations General Assembly, **Oct. 26**, in a 134-0 vote with the U.S. abstaining, approved a resolution calling on all member nations to prohibit all "contacts" with Transkei. The action came on the day Transkei became the first of the South African black homelands to gain independence. The General Assembly asserted that Transkei's independence was merely an extension of South Africa's policy of apartheid. The U.S., which had stated previously that it would not recognize Transkei, abstained because it felt some of the sanctions involved in the resolution could only be invoked by the Security Council.

Allied Chemical Fined $13 Million for Polluting — Judge Robert Merhige Jr., **Oct. 5**, in a Richmond, Va., federal district court, fined the Allied Chemical Corp. the maximum fine of $13,375,000 for polluting the James River. The company, **Sept. 30**, had been found guilty of polluting the river from their Hopewell, Va., chemical plant with highly toxic insecticide Kepone over a period of nearly 4 years.

Ford-UAW Contract Approved — Ford Motor Company workers, **Oct. 12**, narrowly approved a new national 3-year labor contract, ending a UAW strike against Ford that had begun **Sept. 15**. The contract, considered by union officials to be a modest building block toward a 4-day week, had been negotiated between the United Automobile Workers and Ford **Oct. 5**. In addition to a 3 per cent per year wage increase over the life of the contract and automatic cost-of-living increases, the contract guaranteed workers 12 more paid days off, besides regularly scheduled holidays, during the 3-year period.

Disasters — Hurricane Liza, **Oct. 1**, with winds up to 130 miles per hour, struck Baja California, Mexico, killing at least 630 persons and perhaps as many as 1,000. The storm, which caused the worst damage at the resort city of La Paz, also injured some 14,000 persons and left 70,000 homeless. . . . When rain-swollen waters broke on a dike on the outskirts of Pereira, Colombia, **Oct. 6**, flood waters claimed the lives of at least 47 persons and injured 26. . . . All 78 aboard perished, **Oct. 6**, when a Cuban passenger jet crashed into the sea near Barbados. The plane was attempting to return to Barbados following an explosion on the plane. . . . Shortly after take-off, an Indian Airlines Caravelle jet crashed in flames, **Oct. 12**, at Bombay, India's Santa Cruz Airport, killing 95 persons. . . . An estimated 100 persons died, **Oct. 13**, when a Miami-bound cargo jet crashed into a main downtown avenue of Santa Cruz, Bolivia, leaving a 300-yard path of destruction. . . . At least 58 persons were known dead and 44 missing, **Oct. 20**, when a Norwegian tanker collided with the ferry George Prince on the Mississippi River at Luling, La. . . . At least 133 died on Oct. 29 in West Irian, Indonesia earthquake.

Deaths, Nov. 1, 1975-Nov. 1, 1976

A

Aalto, Alvar, 78; Finnish architect; Helsinki, May 11.

Albers, Josef, 88; artist, art teacher, and color theorist; New Haven, Conn., Mar. 25.

Anda, Geza, 54; Swiss pianist and conductor; Zurich, June 13.

Anderson, Sen. Clinton P.; 80; former senator from New Mexico; Secretary of Agriculture in the Truman administration; Albuquerque, Nov. 11.

Arendt, Hannah, 69; political philosopher; New York, Dec. 4.

Arlen, Richard, 75; actor appeared in some 250 films; starred in "Wings" in 1927, the first film to win an academy award; No. Hollywood, Cal., Mar. 28.

Auchincloss, Rep. James C., 91; New Jersey Republican served 11 terms in the House; Alexandria, Va., Oct. 3.

August, Jan, 71; pianist whose records sold in the millions; New York, Jan. 18.

B

Bachauer, Gina, 63; concert pianist; Greece, Aug. 22.

Baddeley, Angela, 71; British actress played the cook in TVs "Upstairs, Downstairs"; Essex, Eng., Feb. 22.

Ballard, Florence, 32; original member of the "Supremes" singing trio; Detroit, Feb. 22.

Bankhead, Dan, 54; first black pitcher in major league baseball, 1947; Houston, May 2.

Barrett, Rep. William, 79; Philadelphia congressman served in house since 49; Philadelphia, Apr. 12.

Baukhage, Hilmar R., 87; radio commentator made first live news broadcast from the White House in 1941; Washington, D.C., Feb. 1.

Beecher, Henry K., 72; physician helped make anesthesiology a specialized field of medicine; Boston, July 25.

Berkeley, Busby, 80; choreographer famed for imaginative and extravagant movie musicals, "Gold Diggers of 1935", "Footlight Parade"; Palm Springs, Cal., Mar. 14.

Beyen, Johan Willem, 78; Dutch economist, a founder of the World Bank and International Monetary Fund; The Hague, Apr. 29.

Blair, David, 43; British dancer; choreographer for American Ballet Theater; London, Apr. 1.

Bloomgarden, Kermit, 71; Broadway producer, "Death of a Salesman", "The Music Man"; New York, Sept. 20.

Bolles, Don, 47; reporter for The Arizona Republic whose car was bombed while he was working on an article about the Mafia; Phoenix, June 13.

Bonavena, Oscar, 33; heavyweight boxer; nr. Reno, Nev., May 22.

Bosco, Henri, 87; French poet and novelist; Nice, May 4.

Boswell, Connee, 68; popular singer whose recordings sold 75 million copies; New York, Oct. 11.

Brailowsky, Alexander, 80; Russianborn concert pianist; New York, Apr. 25.

Bronk, Detlev W., 78; scientist and educator; New York, Nov. 17.

Brown, Joe David, 60; author and journalist; Mayfield, Ga., Apr. 22.

Bullock, Wynn, 73; photographer of nature scenes; Monterey, Cal., Nov. 16.

Burnett, Chester (Howlin' Wolf), blues singer, guitarist; Chicago, Jan. 10.

C

Canaday, Ward, 90; developer of the military jeep used during WW2; Toledo, Ohio, Feb. 28.

Carey, Max, 86; baseball hall of famer noted for base stealing; Miami Beach, Fla., May 30.

Carter, Judge Oliver, 65; presided over the Patricia Hearst bank-robbery trial; San Francisco, June 14.

Case, Nelson, 66; announcer in radio and TV for 50 years; Doylestown, Pa., Mar. 24.

Cassin, Rene, 88; French jurist won the 1968 Nobel peace prize; Paris, Feb.)?.

Chamberlin, Clarence, 83; first American pilot to fly a passenger across the Atlantic, 1927; Shelton, Conn., Oct. 30.

Chapman, Charles, 95; author of the boatman's bible "Piloting, Seamanship and Small Boat Handling"; Essex, Conn., Mar. 21.

Charlton, Andrew (Boy), 68; Australian swimmer won gold medal in 1924 Olympic games; Sydney, Aust., Dec. 11.

Chou En-lai, 78; prime minister of China since 1949; Peking, Jan. 8.

Christie, Agatha, 85; British author of detective novels and plays; created Hercule Poirot, Jane Marble; Wallingford, Eng., Jan. 12.

Chu Teh, 89; Chinese military leader led the historic, "Long March," in 1934; Peking, July 6.

Cloete, Stuart, 78; author known for his books about South Africa; Cape Town, South Africa, Mar. 19.

Cobb, Lee J., 64; actor starred on stage, screen, and TV; created role of Willy Loman in "Death of a Salesman" on stage; Woodland Hills, Cal., Feb. 11.

Cohen, Mickey, 62; former leader of West Coast rackets; Los Angeles, July 29.

Combs, Earle, 77; baseball hall of famer had a career batting average of .325; Richmond, Ky., July 21.

Costello, John A., 84; former prime minister of Ireland; Dublin, Jan. 5.

Crawford, John, 60; contract bridge and backgammon champion; New York, Feb. 14.

Cunningham, Imogen, 93; photographer; San Francisco, June 24.

D

Dam, Henrik, 81; Danish biochemist discovered vitamin K; won Nobel prize in 1943; Copenhagen, Apr. 17.

Davis, Meyer, 81; society orchestra leader; New York, Apr. 5.

Deschler, Lewis, 71; parliamentarian of the House of Representatives for 46 years; Bethesda, Md., July 12.

Disney, Doris Miles, 68; mystery novelist; Fredericksburg, Va., Mar. 8.

Dobzhansky, Theodosius, 75; geneticist; Davis, Cal., Dec. 19.

Douglas, Sen. Paul, 84; Illinois Democrat championed liberal causes in the Senate for 18 years; Washington, D.C., Sept. 24.

Dowling, Eddie, 81; playwright, actor, director; Smithfield, R.I., Feb. 18.

Dwyer, Florence, 73; New Jersey Congresswoman served 8 terms in the House; Elizabeth, N.J., Feb. 29.

Dykes, Jimmy, 79; baseball player and manager whose career spanned 50 years; Philadelphia, June 15.

E

Elazar, Gen. David, 50; commander of Israeli forces during the 1973 October war; Tel Aviv, Apr. 15.

Ernst, Max, 84; surrealist painter and sculptor; Paris, Apr. 1.

Ernst, Morris, 87; lawyer won landmark federal court case in 1933 exonerating Joyce's "Ulysses" from charges of obscenity; New York, May 21.

Evans, Dame Edith, 88; British stage actress; Kent, Eng., Oct. 14.

F

Faber, Urban (Red), 88; Hall of Fame pitcher won 254 major league games; Chicago, Sept. 25.

Faith, Percy, 67; orchestra conductor and arranger; Los Angeles, Feb. 9.

Farley, James A., 88; major Democratic party figure during the administration of FDR; former postmaster general; New York, June 9.

Feather, Victor, 68; British labor leader; London, July 28.

Fishbein, Harry J., 78; bridge champion won 16 national titles; New York, Feb. 19.

Fishbein, Dr. Morris, 87; former editor of the Journal of the American Medical Assn.; Chicago, Sept. 27.

Flavin, James, 69; veteran supporting actor in over 400 films and TV programs; Los Angeles, Apr. 23.

Folsom, Marion B., 82; chief drafter in the 30s of the nation's Social Security laws; secy. of HEW in the Eisenhower administration; Rochester, N.Y., Sept. 28.

Ford, Eleanor Clay, 80; widow of Edsel Ford, mother of Henry Ford 2d; Detroit, Oct. 19.

Ford, Paul, 74; character actor on stage and television; Mineola, N.Y., Apr. 12.

Fox, Nellie, 47; former star second baseman for the Chicago White Sox; American League MVP in 1959; Baltimore, Dec. 1.

Franco, Generalissimo Francisco, 82; ruler of Spain for 36 years; Madrid, Nov. 20.

Franklin, Sidney, 72; Brooklyn-born bullfighter; New York, Apr. 26.

Fuchida, Mitsuo, 73; Japanese navy commander led attack on Pearl Harbor in 1941; Kashiwara, Japan, May 30.

Fulks, Joe, 54; basketball player led the NBA in scoring in 1947; Eddyville, Ky., Mar. 21.

G

Gabl, Gertrud, 27; Austrian skier won the World Cup in alpine skiing in 1969; St. Anton, Austria, Jan. 18.

Gabrielson, Guy, 84; GOP national chairman, 1949-52; Point Pleasant, N.J., May 1.

Gallico, Paul, 78; Sportswriter and author, "The Snow Goose", "The Poseidon Adventure"; Monaco, July 15.

Gambino, Carlo, 74; organized crime leader; Massapequa, N.Y., Oct. 15.

Garrison, Candace Mossler, 55; acquitted in the death of her millionaire husband in sensational murder trial in the 60's; Miami Beach, Oct. 26.

Getty, J. Paul, 83; oil billionaire reputed to be the world's wealthiest man; Surrey, England, June 6.

Ghezzi, Vic, 65; golfer won PGA championship in 1941; Miami Beach, Fla., May 30.

Gibbons, Euell, 64; author of books on natural foods; Sunbury, Pa., Dec. 29.

Gilbert, Edwin, 69; dramatist, scriptwriter, and novelist; Cannes, France, Aug. 28.

Gilbert, Ray, 63; song writer, "Zip-a-Dii-Doo-Dah"; Los Angeles, Mar. 3.

Goldfinger, Nathaniel, 59; chief economist of the AFL-CIO; Silver Springs, Md., July 22.

Granger, Lester, 79; executive director of National Urban League, 1941-61; Alexandria, La., Jan. 9.

Gray, Jerry, 61; band leader and composer, "String of Pearls," "Pennsylvania 6-5000"; Dallas, Aug. 10.

Grechko, Marshal Andrei Antonovich, 72; Soviet minister of defense whose career spanned 50 years; USSR, Apr. 26.

Green, Constance McLaughlin, 78; historian won Pulitzer prize in 1963; Annapolis, Md., Dec. 5.

H

Hackett, Bobby, 61; cornetist whose style was popular with both jazz and pop music audiences; Chatham, Mass., June 7.

Halsted, Anna Roosevelt, 69; only daughter of FDR; New York, Dec. 1.

Hannah, Dick, 70; public relations executive represented Howard Hughes; Los Angeles, Jan. 15.

Hansburg, George B., 88; inventor of the pogo stick; Miami, Dec. 3.

Heidegger, Martin, 86; German philosopher affected many fields ranging from physics to literary criticism; Messkirch, W. Germany, May 26.

Heisenberg, Dr. Werner Carl, 74; German nuclear physicist won Nobel prize in 1932; Munich, Feb. 1.

Henabery, Joseph, 88; film director and silent-film actor; Woodland Hills, Cal.

Henderson, Vivian, 52; educator, labor economist pioneered studies in the labor market for blacks; Atlanta, Jan. 28.

Herrmann, Bernard, 64; composer of film scores, "Citizen Kane," "Psycho"; Los Angeles, Dec. 24.

Hill, Graham, 46; twice world champion auto racer; No. London, Eng., Nov. 30.

Hole, Mike, 35; English-born jockey rode mostly in New York; Long Island, N. Y., Apr. 22.

Howe, James Wong, 76; pioneering cinematographer won 2 Oscars; Hollywood, Cal., July 12.

Hsu Chin-chiang, 61; major figure in the development of China's petroleum, chemical, and coal industries; Peking, July 21.

Hubbard, DeHart, 72; track star won Olympic broad jump title;in 1924 becoming the first black American to win a gold medal; Cleveland, June 23.

Hughes, Howard, 70; reclusive billionaire industrialist; film maker; on airplane over Texas; Apr. 5.

Hughes, Richard, 76; British novelist, "A High Wind in Jamaica"; Merioeth, Wales, Apr. 28.

I

Ingersoll, Adm. Royal, 92; commander

of the Atlantic Fleet during WW 2; Bethesda, Md., May 20.

J

Johnson, Malcom, 71; journalist won Pulitzer prize in 1949; Middletown, Conn.

Johnson, Mordecai Wyatt, 86; president of Howard Univ. for 34 years; Washington, D. C., Sept. 10.

Jones, Mary Anissa, 18; actress portrayed Buffy in TV series, "Family Affair"; Oceanside, Cal., Aug. 28.

K

Kahn, Ben, 89; leading furrier and figure in the fashion world; New York, Feb. 5.

Kempe, Rudolf, 65; German conductor associated with the London and Munich philharmonic orchestras, Zurich, May 11.

Kenny, Nick, 80; former columnist for the N. Y. Mirror wrote verses and lyrics; Sarasota, Fla., Dec. 1.

Kenny, Robert W., 74; lawyer helped found the National Lawyers Guild; La Jolla, Cal., July 20.

Kern, Harold G., 77; publisher of the Boston Herald-American and Sunday Herald Advertiser for 37 years; Boston, Feb. 10.

Kerner, Otto, 67; former Illinois governor; Chicago, May 9.

Kohler, Walter J., 71; former governor of Wisconsin; Sheboygan, Wis., Mar. 21.

Konstanty, Jim, 59; baseball relief pitcher was the National League MVP in 1950; Oneonta, N. Y., June 11.

Koslo, Dave, 55; former pitcher for the N. Y. Giants; Nebasgam, Wis., Dec. 1.

Kubitschek, Juscelino, 73; president of Brazil, 1956-61; Rio de Janeiro, Aug. 22.

Kulski, Julian S., 83; president (mayor) of Poland, 1939-44; wrote books and articles on Polish wartime history; Warsaw, Aug. 18.

L

Lang, Fritz, 85; film director, "M"; Los Angeles, Aug. 2.

Lee, Rowland, 84; producer and director of some 60 films, "Bridge of San Luis Rey"; Palm Desert, Cal., Dec. 21.

Lehmann, Lotte, 88; operatic soprano and lieder singer; Santa Barbara, Cal.

Leighton, Margaret, 53; British actress of films and stage; won 2 Tony awards; Chichester, Eng., Jan. 13.

Lercaro, Giacomo Cardinal, 84; major force behind the Vatican's liturgical reforms; Bologna, Italy, Oct. 18.

Leslie, Edgar, 90; lyricist wrote "Moon Over Miami", "For Me and My Gal"; a founder of ASCAP; New York, Jan. 22.

Leventhal, Albert Rice, 68; book publisher developed Little Golden Books series for children; New York, Jan. 6.

Lin Yutang, 80; Chinese historian, philosopher, and novelist; Hong Kong, Mar. 26.

Lippisch, Alexander, 81; aeronautics pioneer designed Germany's early Dornier and Messerschmidt aircraft; Cedar Rapids, Iowa, Feb. 11.

Livesey, Roger, 69; veteran character actor of stage and screen; Watford, Eng., Feb. 5.

Loening, Grover C., 87; aviation pio-

neer; Key Biscayne, Fla., Feb. 29.

Loftus, John, 80; first jockey to win racing's triple crown, on Sir Barton in 1919; Carlsbad, Cal., Mar. 23.

Losch, Tilly, 70's; a leading dancer of the 20's and 30's; New York, Dec. 24.

Lundigan, William, 61; actor appeared in over 125 films; Los Angeles, Dec. 21.

Lundin, Earl H., 74; architect designed many New York City buildings including Exxon and Sinclair bldgs.; Naples, Fla., Mar. 1.

Lyons, Leonard, 70; Broadway columnist whose "The Lyons Den", appeared in scores of newspapers for 40 years; New York, Oct. 7.

M

Macdonald, Rep. Torbert, 58; Massachusetts Democrat served 11 terms in the House; Bethesda, Md., May 21.

Mack, Ted, 72; host of the Original Amateur Hour on TV for 22 years; No. Tarrytown, N. Y., July 12.

MacMillan, H. R., 90; Canadian lumberman and philanthropist; Vancouver, B. C., Feb. 9.

Mao Tse-tung, 82; leader of China since 1949; China, Sept. 9.

Martinon, Jean, 66; conductor specialized in early 20th-century French music; Paris, Mar. 1.

Maserati, Ernesto, 77; Italian auto maker founded the luxury auto company; Bologna, Italy, Dec. 1.

Mauze, Abby Rockefeller, 72; philanthropist, only daughter of John D. Rockefeller Jr.; New York, May 27.

May, Marty, 77; comedian in vaudeville, theater, and radio; Las Vegas, Nov. 11.

May, Robert L., 71; creator of Rudolph the Red-Nosed Reindeer; Evanston, Ill., Aug. 11.

McBride, Mary Margaret, 76; radio talk show hostess for over 20 years; West Shokun, N. Y., Apr. 7.

McKelway, Benjamin M., 80; former president of the Associated Press and editor of the Washington Star; Washington, D. C., Aug. 30.

McWhirter, Ross, 50; co-editor of the "Guinness Book of World Records"; London, Nov. 27.

Meilziner, Jo, 74; designer created settings for over 300 dramas, musicals, operas, and ballets; New York, Mar. 15.

Menshikov, Mikhail, 73; Soviet ambassador in Washington during Eisenhower and Kennedy administrations; Moscow, July 21.

Mercer, Johnny, 66; songwriter, "Moon River", "That Old Black Magic"; Bel Air, Cal., June 25.

Meyer, Gen. John, 56; World War II flying ace; former SAC commander; Los Angeles, Dec. 2.

Mineo, Sal, 37; stage, screen, and TV actor; Hollywood, Cal., Feb. 12.

Mitchell, Martha, 57; outspoken estranged wife of former Attorney General John Mitchell; New York, May 31.

Monod, Jacques, 66; French biologist shared Nobel prize in 1965; Cannes, May 31.

Montgomery, Viscount Bernard Law, 88; British field marshall defeated the Germans and Italians at El Alamein in 1942 in a major and historic battle; Isington, Eng., Mar. 24.

Moose, Bob, 29; pitcher for the Pittsburgh Pirates baseball team; Martin's Ferry, Ohio, Oct. 9.

Morison, Samuel Eliot, 88; historian

chronologized voyages of early explorers; won 2 Pulitzer prizes; wrote "The Oxford History of the American People"; Boston, May 15.

Morton, Louis, 61; military historian; Burlington, Vt., Feb. 12

Moss, Rev. Robert V. Jr., 54; president of the United Church of Christ; Montclair, N.J., Oct. 25.

Mueller, Frederick, 82; secretary of commerce in the Eisenhower administration; Sarasota, Fla., Aug. 31.

N

Nevers, Ernie, 73; football star elected to both college and professional hall of fame; San Rafael, Cal., May 3.

O

Ochs, Phil, 35; folk singer and lyricist of the 60's; Far Rockaway, N.Y., Apr. 9.

Odlum, Floyd B., 84; financier; Indio, Cal., June 17.

Onsager, Lars, 72; chemist won Nobel prize in 1968; Coral Gables, Fla., Oct. 5.

Ortega, Santos, 76; veteran radio and TV actor, "As the World Turns"; Ft. Lauderdale, Fla., Apr. 10.

P

Pasolini, Pier Paolo, 53; Italian film director, poet and novelist; Ostia, Italy, Nov. 2.

Patman, Rep. Wright, 82; Texas Democrat served in the House since 1929; Bethesda, Md., Mar.7.

Patterson, Mary King, 90; former women's editor of N.Y. Daily News; New York, Dec. 27.

Penfield, Dr. Wilder G., 85; neurologist refined techniques for treating epilepsy; Montreal, Apr. 5.

Petty, Mary, 77; cartoonist for the New Yorker magazine for 39 years; Paramus, N.J., Mar. 6.

Phillips, Cabell, 70; newsman and author; Savannah, Ga., Nov. 14.

Phillips, Dr. Robert Allan, 70; public health leader led fight against Cholera; The Phillippines, Sept. 20.

Piatigorsky, Gregor, 73; Russian-born cellist; Los Angeles, Aug. 6.

Polanyi, Michael, 84; physical chemist and philosopher; Northampton, Eng., Feb. 22.

Pons, Lily, 71; French-born coloratura soprano starred at the Metropolitan Opera for over 25 years; Dallas, Tex., Feb. 13.

Q

Queneau, Raymond, 73; French novelist and literary figure; Paris, Oct. 25.

Quinn, John, 68; baseball executive headed the Boston-Milwaukee Braves and the Philadelphia Phillies; Stanton, Cal., Sept.

R

Razak, Abdul, 53; prime minister of Malaysia; London, Jan. 14.

Red Fox, Chief William, 105; Sioux whose memoirs of Little Big Horn and Wounded Knee stirred controversy; Corpus Christi, Tex., Mar. 1.

Reed, Sir Carol, 69; British film director, "The Third Man", "The Fallen Idol"; London, Apr. 25.

Rethberg, Elisabeth, 81; lyric-dramatic soprano starred at the Metropolitan Opera during the 20s and 30s; Yorktown Heights, N.Y., June 6.

Reynolds, Milton, 84; popularized the ball point pen; Mexico City, Jan. 23.

Reznikoff, Charles, 81; a founding member of the objectivist school of poetry; New York, Jan. 22

Richter, Hans, 87; artist and film director; Locarno, Switz., Feb. 1.

Ritz, Charles, 84; director of famed Paris hotel; Paris, July 11.

Robeson, Paul, 77; actor, singer, and black activist; Philadelphia, Jan. 23.

Rosenbloom, Maxie, 71; former light-heavyweight boxing champion, actor; South Pasadena, Cal., Mar. 6.

Russo, Paul, 62; auto race driver appeared in 15 Indianapolis 500s; Daytona Beach, Fla., Feb. 15.

Ruth, Claire (Mrs. Babe), 76; widow of the baseball immortal; New York, Oct. 25.

Ruzicka, Dr. Leopold, 89; Swiss chemist won Nobel prize in 1939; Zurich, Sept.

Ryle, Gilbert, 76; British philosopher; Yorkshire, Eng., Oct. 6.

S

Schmertz, Fred, 87; director for 41 years of the Millrose games, the oldest invitational track meet; Baton Rouge, La., Mar. 25.

Schoene, Lester P., 68; attorney represented the nation's railway unions for over 30 years; Waterford, Va., July 19.

Schoonmaker, Frank, 70; writer and authority on wines; New York, Jan. 11.

Shepard, Ernest, 96; illustrator drew Winnie-the-Pooh in the classic stories for children; Lodsworth, Eng., Mar. 24.

Sheriff, Robert C., 79; British playwright, "Journey's End"; London, Nov. 13.

Shimada, Adm. Shigetaro, 92; Japanese navy minister during WW2; Tokyo, June 7.

Sim, Alastair, 75; British actor of stage and screen; London, Aug. 19.

Sissle, Noble, 86; orchestra leader and song writer, "You Were Meant For Me"; Tampa, Dec. 17.

Sissman, L.E. 48; poet and essayist; Still River, Mass. Mar. 10.

Skaggs, Marion B., 88; founder of Safeway Stores, the nation's largest supermarket chain; Oakland, Cal., May 8.

Slonim, Marc, 82; American critic and author; expert on European literature; Beaulieu-sur-Mer, France, May 8.

Smith, David Frederick, 86; created Newscasting and the March of Time radio newsreel programs; New York, Aug. 14.

Smith, Gerald L. K., 78; right-wing crusader; Glendale, Cal., Apr. 15.

Smith, H. Allen, 68; best-selling humorist, "Low Man on a Totem Pole"; San Francisco, Feb. 23.

Smith, Rep. Howard W., 93; Virginia Democrat served 36 years in the House; headed House Rules Committee"; Alexandria, Va., Oct. 3.

Snyder, Jerome, 60; illustrator and graphic designer, co-author of the Underground Gourmet column in New York magazine; New York, May 2.

Strand, Paul, 85; photographer and film maker; Oregeval, France, Mar. 31.

Streeter, Edward, 84; humorist and author, "Father of the Bride"; New York, Mar.

Strode, Hudson, 83; travel writer, biographer; Tuscaloosa, Ala., Sept. 22.

Sullivan, Annette Kellerman, 87; swimmer and entertainer; shocked Boston in 1907 with her daring one-piece bathing suit; Southport, Australia, Nov. 5.

Sullivan, Frank, 83; humorist; Saratoga Springs, N.Y., Feb. 19.

T

Taylor, Phoebe Atwood, 66; author of Cape Cod mystery tales; Boston, Jan. 9.

Thomas, James T., 82; British eye surgeon helped found the world's first eye bank; Cardiff, Wales, Jan. 23.

Thomson, Lord Roy, 82; Canadian built a vast and influential publishing empire; London, Aug. 4.

Thorndike, Dame Sybil, 93; British actress whose career spanned 7 decades; London, June 9.

Tobey, Mark, 85; American abstract painter; Basel, Switzerland, Apr. 24.

Treacher, Arthur, 81; British-born actor specialized in crusty butler parts in films, plays, and TV; Manhasset, N.Y., Dec. 14.

Trilling, Lionel, 70; literary critic and essayist; New York, Nov. 5.

Trumbo, Dalton, 70; Hollywood screen writer who while blacklisted won an Academy Award under a pseudonym in 1957, "The Brave One"; Los Angeles, Sept. 10.

V

Visconti, Luchino, 69; Italian film director, "Rocco and His Brothers"; Rome, Mar.

W

Wallace, Ed. 70; newsman and feature writer for New York newspapers for 35 years; New York, Oct. 10.

Warneke M Lon, 67; former major league pitcher and umpire; Hot Springs, Ark., June 23.

Warner, Roger Sherman Jr., 69; engineer participted in the development of the atomic and hydrogen bombs; Washington, D.C., Aug. 3.

Weil, Joseph, 100; confidence man known as the "Yellow Kid"; Chicago, Feb. 26.

Wellman, William A., 79; director of 82 films; "Wings", "The Ox-Bow Incident"; "Public Enemy"; "A Star is Born"; Los Angeles, Dec. 9.

Wheeler, Gen. Earle, 67; former chairman of the joint chiefs of staff; Frederick, Md., Dec. 18.

Wheeler, Sir Mortimer, 85; British archeologist discovered relics believed to be from King Arthur's Camelot; England, July 22

Whipple, Dr. George H., 97; pathologist won Nobel prize in 1934; Rochester, N.Y., Feb. 1.

White, Minor, 67; photographer; Boston, June 24.

Wilder, Thornton, 78; novelist and playwright; won 3 Pulitzer prizes; Hamden Conn., Dec. 7.

Wolfgang, Myra K., 61; pioneer in the battle for working women's rights; Detroit, Apr. 12.

Y

Yawkey, Tom, 73; owner of the Boston Red Sox baseball team; Boston, July 9.

Z

Zeckendorf, William, 71; real estate developer; New York, Oct. 1

Zukor, Adolph, 103; film executive offered first feature-length film in U.S. in 1912; built Paramount movie empire; Los Angeles, June 10.

Laws Passed, Bills Vetoed During 94th Congress, 2d Session (1976)

The 94th Congress convened its Second Session Jan. 19, 1976, and adjourned Oct. 2, 1976.

The heavily Democratic Congress continued its long struggle with Republican Pres. Ford; Congress blocked his efforts to cut back on federal spending and revise social legislation; Ford prevented Congress from realizing its promises to expand government services.

Ford vetoed a total of 66 bills in the First and Second Session; Congress overrode 12 of the vetoes. The 2-year battle, in the opinion of many, ended in a draw.

Major bills passed and signed, and other actions taken during the Second Session, included:

Railroad Aid. A scaled-down bill, passed after Ford threatened to veto an earlier version, provided for loans to modernize bankrupt Northeastern railroads, help roads avoid bankruptcy, and improve Boston-Washington, D. C., service (signed by Ford Feb. 5).

Defense Funds — Angolan Aid Ban. An amendment banning further aid to any faction in the Angolan Civil War was attached by Congress to a $112.3 billion defense appropriation bill; Ford called it a serious mistake, but signed it (Feb. 10).

Drug Abuse Office. Authorized funds to establish a White House Office of Drug Abuse Policy plus grants for programs and research (signed Mar. 30).

Consumer Bills

Consumer Leasing Protection. Protected leasers of cars, appliances, etc., from misleading advertising and unfair charges (signed Mar. 23).

Credit Discrimination Ban. Prohibited firms providing credit from discriminating because of age, race, color, religion, or national origin, extending a law which banned sex discrimination (signed Mar. 23).

Conrail Aid. Provided for $2 billion aid for Conrail over 4 years (signed Mar. 30).

Swine Flu Program. Appropriated $135 million for vaccinating 200 million Americans (signed Apr. 15).

Foreign Military Aid. Authorized $6.9 billion in military aid for fiscal 1976-77, replacing an earlier bill vetoed by Ford; it expanded the role of Congress in oversight of foreign arms aid, but not as much as the vetoed bill (signed June 30).

Agriculture, Food Stamp funds. Appropriated $11.5 billion for fiscal 1977 for the Dept. of Agriculture, including $4.79 billion for the food stamp program (signed July 12).

Energy Funds. Appropriated $5.7 billion for fiscal 1977 for programs of the Energy Research and Development Administration including solar, nuclear fusion and fission, geothermal, etc. systems (signed July 12).

Airport, Aviation Aid. Authorized $5.6 billion for capital improvement of airports and for air navigation and research programs (signed July 12).

Aid to Coastal States. Authorized $1.6 billion to help cope with problems arising from exploitation of offshore oil and gas reserves, including loans to municipalities (signed July 26).

Housing Programs. Appropriated $15.6 billion for housing programs as part of funds for several agencies (signed Aug. 9).

Oil Prices Raised

Domestic Oil Prices Upped. Authorized a 10% annual increase in domestic oil prices; ended price ceilings on oil from "stripper" wells (those producing less than 12 barrels a day — accounting for 12% of domestic production); provided pilot loans and grants program for persons insulating their homes (signed Aug. 14).

Congress Pay Boost Rejected. Both houses rejected in Sept. cost-of-living pay increases which were scheduled to take effect automatically Oct. 1 for senators and representatives.

"Government in Sunshine." Required about 50 executive agencies to open their meetings to press and public except when subjects require confidentiality (signed Sept. 13).

Curb on Presidential Powers. Provided for regular Congressional review (every 6 months) of states of national emergency declared by the president; terminations of such states, ordered by Congress, would take 2 years to take effect (signed Sept. 14).

Taxes. Continued $18 billion in income tax cuts previously in effect, increased government revenues by $1.6 billion, raised the minimum tax on some wealthy persons from 10% to 15%, and reduced taxes on airlines, railroads, insurance companies, and certain other businesses; it also denied certain tax benefits to U. S. companies complying with the Arab boycott of Israel (signed Oct. 4).

Defense Funds. Appropriated $104.3 billion for defense in fiscal 1977, $14 billion more than in fiscal 1976 but $3.6 billion less than asked by the Pentagon; largest items were for Trident missiles, attack subs, missile frigates, and F-14 and F-15 fighter planes (signed Sept. 22).

Toxic Substances. Required pre-release testing of chemicals potentially dangerous to humans or the environment by manufacturers, and gave the Environmental Protection Agency the power to ban the chemicals (signed Oct. 12).

Vetoes Sustained During 2d Session

Milk Price Bill. Increased federal price supports for milk; Ford vetoed it saying it would increase consumer prices (Jan. 30).

Public Works Bill. Provided $6.1 billion to create jobs; Ford called it "little more than an election year pork barrel" and vetoed it (Feb. 13).

Funds for Day Care. Provided $125 million to states to help centers meet new federal standards; Ford said the states, not the federal government, should provide standards and vetoed it (Apr. 6).

Hatch Act Revision. Lifted ban against partisan political activity by federal employees; Ford vetoed it saying "politicizing the civil service is intolerable (Apr. 12).

Foreign Aid Bill. Authorized $4.4 billion for foreign aid; Ford vetoed it saying it contained restrictions on presidential authority (May 7).

Defense Construction Funds. Provided $3.3 billion for military construction projects; it also would have enforced delays of one year in closing any military base in the U.S., which Ford objected to in his veto (July 2).

Congressional Tax Exemption. Exempted members of Congress from Maryland from Maryland's state income tax; Ford vetoed it calling it federal interference in state affairs (Aug. 3).

Pesticide Bill. Authorized $19.7 million for Environmental Protection Agency pesticide programs; Ford vetoed it saying it also provided for Congressional vetoes of any EPA regulation (Aug. 13).

Vetoes Overridden in 2d Session

Public Works Jobs. Congress July 22 enacted over Ford's veto a $3.95 billion authorization for public works jobs (in February the Senate had sustained Ford's veto of another bill providing $6 billion for similar purposes); included was $700 million for water-pollution-control plants.

Coal Land Leases. Revised federal regulations for leasing federal coal lands and increased states' shares of royalties from the leases; Ford vetoed it July 3 saying it would cut coal production; congress overrode the veto Aug. 4.

Electric Autos. Congress Sept. 17 overrode Ford's Sept. 13 veto of this bill to authorize $220 million to develop a mass-producible electric car.

Funds for HEW. Congress Sept. 30 overrode Ford's Sept. 29 veto of this bill appropriating $45.12 billion for various programs of the Health, Education, and Welfare Dept. and $11.49 billion for the Labor Dept.; the bill also barred use of federal Medicaid funds for most abortions (a section praised by Ford).

Major Decisions of the U.S. Supreme Court, 1976

Notable decisions of the U.S. Supreme Court in 1976 included the following actions:

Let stand a lower court ruling that found the Denver school system segregated black and Chicano children from whites, and ordered broad reassignment of children systemwide (Jan. 12).

Unanimously upheld a lower court ruling declaring unconstitutional sections of New York State's election fair practices code which prohibited attacks on candidates based on racial, religious, or ethnic backgrounds, or on deliberate misrepresentation; the court said the rules violated freedom of speech (Jan. 12).

Let stand a lower court decision that the Marine Corps has the right to require Marine Reservists to wear their hair short. Three men had charged discrimination because women marines were allowed long hair; the Marine Corps argued men had to wear gas masks in combat (Jan. 19).

'Probable Cause' Upheld

Held 6-2 that police may make arrests in public places without a warrant but just on "probable cause" — the belief a felony had been committed — even though there was adequate time to have obtained a warrant (Jan. 26).

Let stand a lower court decision that it was unconstitutional for Missouri to deny Medicaid payments for abortions while providing Medicaid payments to those who chose to give birth (Jan. 26).

Upheld, by varying majorities, parts of the federal election laws, and struck down other parts; it upheld public financing for presidential contests, limits on how much an individual may contribute directly to a candidate for federal office, and strict requirements for reporting contributions and expenditures; but it called unconstitutional limits on spending by candidates, terming these a restraint on freedom of speech, and ruled the Federal Election Commission must be restructured because some of its members were appointable by Congress but did administration work, terming this a violation of the separation of powers doctrine; it further held that candidates who accept federal financing must abide by the limits on expenditures (Jan. 30).

Let stand a lower court decision that the ABC-TV network did not have to give the Polish-American Congress equal air time to respond to a Dick Cavett show on which derogatory "Polish jokes" were told (Feb. 23).

Held unanimously that state prosecutors are immune from civil damage suits even if they deliberately violate the civil rights of defendants, as in this Los Angeles case in which a deputy district attorney knowingly used perjured testimony in a murder trial; the court said it decided in the public interest (Mar. 2).

Ruled 6-2 that striking union members do not have the right to picket in front of a store leased by their employer in a privately owned shopping center; this contradicted a 1968 decision of the court (Mar. 3).

Decided 6-2 that black defendants in a state court do not have the right to quiz prospective jurors about possible racial prejudice unless racial issues are part of the case (Mar. 3).

Let stand a lower court ruling that a Roman Catholic lawyer-priest could not wear clerical garb while appearing as a criminal defense lawyer before a jury (Mar. 22).

Residence Law Upheld

Upheld in a Philadelphia case the right of cities to require municipal employees to reside within the city (Mar. 22).

Held 6-3 that states may prosecute and sentence people for homosexual acts even though both parties are consenting adults and the acts are committed in private in their own homes (Mar. 29).

Let stand an appeals court decision that former Army Lt. William L. Calley Jr. was properly convicted by a court-martial for the 1968 murder of 22 civilians at My Lai, South Vietnam (Apr. 5).

Ruled 6-2 in a Suffolk County, N.Y., case that police departments have the right to order policemen to wear short haircuts and no beards "where there is "a rational basis" for such regulations (Apr. 5).

Upheld a lower court ruling that a husband does not have a constitutional right to be in the delivery room when his wife is giving birth (Apr. 5).

Affirmed a lower court decision upholding the right of the Highway Traffic Safety Administration to impose civil penalties on a car manufacturer who failed to remedy, when ordered, a safety-related defect (Apr. 19).

In a landmark case, held 8-0 that federal courts can order the U.S. Dept. of Housing and Urban Development to create low-cost public housing for minorities in the white suburbs of a city where the federal government, through public housing programs, contributed to segregation within the city (Apr. 20).

Defendants' Rights Limited

Decided 6-2 that, while a defendant held in jail should not be forced to wear his jail uniform to trial, the defendant must have objected to the trial judge if he later wants the trial declared unconstitutional (May 3).

Similarly, held 6-1 that failure of a defendant in a state court to make a "timely" objection to the lack of blacks on the grand jury that indicted him precludes the defendant from seeking relief in a federal court (May 3).

Overruled by 8-0 a lower court decision that suspects called to testify before a grand jury must be told of their right to remain silent and to have a lawyer (May 19).

Decided 7-1, in a Virginia case, that states may not prohibit pharmacists from advertising prices of their prescription drugs (May 24).

Declared unconstitutional, by 5-4 vote, the Civil Service Commission practice of barring aliens from most federal jobs (June 2).

But ruled unanimously it is constitutional for the government to deny supplemental Medicare benefits to aliens unless they have been admitted for permanent residence and have been in the U.S. at least 5 years (June 1).

Let stand a state court order closing New Jersey's public schools unless the state Legislature approved a legal method of school financing (June 10).

Struck down as unconstitutional state laws requiring a woman to obtain her husband's consent to an abortion (by 6-3 vote), or, in the case of an unwed minor, permission of parents (by 5-4 vote) (July 1).

Unanimously upheld the 1972 Coal Mine Safety Act requiring coal mine operators to pay benefits to miners suffering from advanced black lung disease (July 1).

Upheld the death penalty, 7-2, under the laws of Georgia, Texas, and Florida, but struck down, 5-4, the capital punishment laws of North Carolina and Louisiana because they made the death penalty mandatory in certain crimes (July 2).

The Rules of Evidence

Approved, 5-4, use of evidence obtained by police in a warrantless search of a car's glove compartment while making an inventory of the contents of a car legally impounded (July 6).

Declared the 4th Amendment is not violated when evidence seized illegally by state police in a criminal case is used by the Internal Revenue Service to collect back taxes from illegal gambling (July 6).

Ruled 6-3 a defendant has no constitutional right to appeal a state court conviction to federal courts on the grounds that police illegally seized evidence used against him — thus overriding a 1961 Supreme Court decision (July 6).

Declined to review a Texas court decision which held that a juvenile committed a delinquent act even though the evidence would not have been sufficient for conviction of an adult (Oct. 4).

VITAL STATISTICS

Source: Division of Vital Statistics, National Center for Health Statistics, Public Health Service

First Half-Year, January-June 1976

Births

There were 1,508,000 births during the first half of 1976, almost 2% fewer than for the same period in 1975. The birth rate for this period was 14.2 per 1,000 population, compared with 14.5 for the corresponding period in 1975. The fertility rate was 63.3 births per 1,000 women 15-44 years of age, 4% lower when compared with the 1975 rate of 65.8.

Marriages

Provisional data for the first half of 1976 indicate a maintenance of the marriage rate as reported for the similar period of 1975.

In the first half of 1976, 987,000 marriages were reported, higher by 7,000 than the total for the first 6 months in 1975. The marriage rate for the first half of the year was the same as that a year earlier, 9.3 per 1,000 population.

Divorces

The number of divorces granted during the 6 months ending with June was 538,000, a 9% increase over the total for the first half of 1975. The divorce rate was 5.0 per 1,000 population, 6% higher than that of the corresponding period in 1975.

Deaths

The cumulative death rate for January-May 1976 was 9.5 per 1,000 population, the same as that for the corresponding period of 1975.

This identical rate occurred despite the fact that there was a severe influenza epidemic during the first part of 1976. The cumulative death rate for influenza and pneumonia for January-May 1976 was 40.8 deaths per 100,000, about 17% higher than that for the corresponding 5-month period of 1975. The effect on the death rate of this epidemic was offset by the continuing downturn in the death rate for a number of causes.

Provisional Statistics
12 months ending with June 1976

| | Number | | Rate* | |
	1976	1975	1976	1975
Live births	3,126,000	3,187,000	14.6	15.0
Deaths	1,912,000	1,936,000	8.9	9.1
Natural increase	1,214,000	1,251,000	5.7	5.9
Marriages	2,132,000	2,182,000	10.0	10.3
Divorces	1,072,000	987,000	5.0	4.6
Infant deaths . . .	48,700	52,200	15.6	16.4
Population base (in millions)			214.0	212.3

*Per 1,000 population

Annual Report for the Year 1975 (Provisional Statistics)

Births

During 1975 the number of live births in the United States totaled an estimated 3,149,000, resulting in a provisional birth rate of 14.8 births per 1,000 population. The fertility rate continued to decline to an estimated 66.7 births per 1,000 women 15-44 years of age, reaching an all-time low for the 4th consecutive year. The rate for 1975 was two-tenths of a percent lower than the final rate recorded for 1974 (67.7).

Between 1974 and 1975 the number of women in the childbearing ages (assumed to be 15-44 years) increased 2 percent and, according to projections from the U.S. Bureau of the Census, it will increase another 10 percent by 1980.

During 1975 growth of the population due to natural increase (the excess of births over deaths) amounted to 1,239,000 persons. The provisional rate of natural increase was 5.8 persons per 1,000 population compared with the final rate of 5.7 for 1974. The increase in this rate can be attributed entirely to the decline in the death rate.

Deaths

An estimated 1,910,000 deaths occurred in the U.S. during 1975. The provisional death rate was 9.0 per 1,000 population, a reduction of 2.2 percent from the final rate of 9.2 for 1974.

In 1975 there were approximately 50,000 infant deaths resulting in an estimated infant mortality rate of 16.1 per 1,000 live births. This was the lowest annu-

al rate ever recorded in the United States and represents a decrease of 3.6 percent from the final rate of 16.7 for 1974. Both the neonatal (under 28 days) and the postneonatal (28 days to 11 months) mortality rates declined in 1975 with the neonatal rate showing a proportionately greater decline than the postneonatal rate.

Marriages and Divorces

In 1975 marriages declined for the 2d year from the 27-year high reached in 1973. Provisional reports indicate that 2,126,000 marriages were performed in 1975, about 104,000 fewer than the final number for 1974. The number of marriages was lower in 1975 than in any year since 1968. The marriage rate dropped from 10.5 per 1,000 population in 1974 to 10.0 in 1975, a decline of 4.8 percent. The marriage rate was lower for 1975 than for any year since 1967.

In 1975 the number of divorces in the United States exceeded one million for the first time in history. An estimated 1,026,000 divorces were granted. The number of divorces has increased every year since 1962 and has more than doubled from 1966 to 1975. The provisional divorce rate for 1975 was 4.8 per 1,000 population, up from 4.6 in 1974. The rate has increased every year since 1966. The rise was very rapid in the late sixties but the rate of increase tapered off in the early seventies. The increase from 1974 to 1975 was 4.3 percent, the smallest annual increase since 1967.

Births and Deaths in the U.S.

Refers only to events occurring within the U.S., including Alaska beginning in 1959 and Hawaii in 1960. Excludes fetal deaths. Rates per 1,000 population enumerated as of April 1 for 1955, and 1960; estimated as of July 1 for all other years. (P) Provisional.

| | Births | | | | Deaths | | | |
Year	Males	Females	Total Number	Rate	Males	Females	Total Number	Rate
1955	2,073,719	1,973,576	4,047,295	24.6	872,638	656,079	1,528,717	9.3
1960	2,179,708	2,078,142	4,257,850	23.7	975,648	736,334	1,711,982	9.5
1965	1,927,054	1,833,304	3,760,358	19.4	1,035,200	792,936	1,828,136	9.4
1970	1,915,378	1,816,008	3,731,386	18.4	1,078,478	842,553	1,921,031	9.5
1973	1,608,326	1,528,639	3,136,965	14.9	1,096,795	876,208	1,973,003	9.4
1974	1,622,114	1,537,844	3,159,958	14.9	1,071,627	862,761	1,934,388	9.2
1975(P)	NA	NA	3,149,000	14.8	NA	NA	1,910,000	9.0

Births and Deaths by States

Source: Division of Vital Statistics, National Center for Health Statistics.

States	Births 1975ᵖ	1974	Deaths 1975ᵖ	1974	States	Births 1975ᵖ	1974	Deaths 1975ᵖ	1974
Alabama	58,182	58,926	34,041	34,600	Nebraska	23,767	23,962	14,704	15,107
Alaska	7,350	7,014	1,587	1,491	Nevada	8,673	8,782	4,743	4,656
Arizona	39,465	39,846	17,543	17,396	New Hampshire	10,918	11,428	7,070	7,673
Arkansas	33,852	33,856	21,681	21,915	New Jersey	88,205	91,866	64,630	65,786
California	314,311	312,034	171,121	170,672	New Mexico	20,413	20,112	7,877	8,029
Colorado	40,270	39,815	17,634	18,449	New York	237,116	241,016	169,274	176,007
Connecticut	35,166	36,382	25,921	26,194	North Carolina	80,868	84,294	46,069	46,366
Delaware	8,416	8,432	4,904	5,191	North Dakota	11,275	10,716	5,673	5,928
Dist. of Col.	19,438	19,866	9,522	9,759	Ohio	161,191	160,848	96,834	98,964
Florida	106,031	109,780	88,859	89,495	Oklahoma	41,441	40,954	26,729	26,440
Georgia	81,161	84,696	43,084	43,550	Oregon	34,271	33,438	20,253	20,363
Hawaii	15,838	15,514	4,579	4,599	Pennsylvania	150,058	152,572	120,323	122,793
Idaho	15,743	15,160	6,219	6,239	Rhode Island	10,968	11,696	9,009	9,155
Illinois	167,342	166,532	100,816	105,542	South Carolina	45,247	47,005	23,142	23,766
Indiana	83,837	83,432	47,107	48,256	South Dakota	11,126	10,962	6,327	6,525
Iowa	41,514	40,562	28,936	28,615	Tennessee	67,035	67,988	41,757	41,822
Kansas	32,386	31,295	21,176	21,686	Texas	222,988	221,264	100,325	100,981
Kentucky	56,188	54,388	33,197	33,238	Utah	32,641	30,648	7,871	7,705
Louisiana	67,394	65,988	33,597	33,895	Vermont	5,999	6,550	4,080	4,427
Maine	14,408	14,753	10,275	10,711	Virginia	68,122	67,974	39,677	39,725
Maryland	45,501	46,724	31,203	32,129	Washington	50,132	49,672	30,256	30,051
Massachusetts	68,907	71,900	55,791	56,388	West Virginia	27,686	27,726	19,746	19,652
Michigan	132,754	136,452	73,668	75,364	Wisconsin	64,634	65,114	39,931	41,027
Minnesota	56,983	55,856	33,701	34,154	Wyoming	6,453	6,298	3,017	3.090
Mississippi	42,846	43,568	25,103	22,728					
Missouri	71,701	71,915	50,558	51,672	Total	3,149,000	3,159,958	1,910,000	1,934,388
Montana	11,781	12,084	6,493	6,500	(p) Provisional.				

Marriages, Divorces, and Rates in the U. S.

Source: Division of Vital Statistics, National Center for Health Statistics.

Data refer only to events occurring within the United States, including Alaska beginning with 1959 and Hawaii with 1960. Rates per 1,000 population.

Year	Marriages[1] No.	Rate	Divorces[2] No.	Rate	Year	Marriages[1] No.	Rate	Divorces[2] No.	Rate
1890	570,000	9.0	33,461	0.5	1940	1,595,879	12.1	264,000	2.0
1895	620,000	8.9	40,387	0.6	1945	1,612,992	12.2	485,000	3.5ᵖ
1900	709,000	9.3	55,751	0.7	1950	1,667,231	11.1	385,144	2.6
1905	842,000	10.0	67,976	0.8	1955	1,531,000	9.3	377,000	2.3
1910	948,166	10.3	83,045	0.9	1960	1,523,000	8.5	393,000	2.2
1915	1,007,595	10.0	104,298	1.0	1965	1,800,000	9.3	479,000	2.5
1920	1,274,476	12.0	170,505	1.6	1970	2,158,802	10.6	708,000	3.5
1925	1,188,334	10.3	175,449	1.5	1973	2,277,000	10.9	915,000	4.4
1930	1,126,856	9.2	195,961	1.6	1974	2,229,667	10.5	977,000	4.6
1935	1,327,000	10.4	218,000	1.7	1975(p)	2,126,000	10.0	1,026,000	4.8

(1) Includes estimates and marriage licenses for some states for all years. (2) Includes reported annulments. (3)Divorce rates for 1945, based on population including armed forces overseas. (p) Provisional.

Marriages and Divorces by States 1975[1]

Source: Division of Vital Statistics, National Center for Health Statistics
(Divorces include reported annulments)

State	Marriages	Divorces	State	Marriages	Divorces	State	Marriages	Divorces
Alabama	44,734	22,260	Louisiana	36,789	NA	Oklahoma	39,001	20,104
Alaska	4,789	2,890	Maine	11,189	5,447	Oregon	18,682	15,453
Arizona	27,963	NA	Maryland	44,667	14,909	Pennsylvania	89,313	32,384
Arkansas	23,069	15,562	Massachusetts	42,085	16,164	Rhode Island	6,697	2,657
California	159,698	129,144	Michigan	81,356	41,249	South Carolina	49,944	9,158
Colorado	27,220	15,613	Minnesota	30,457	12,473	South Dakota	11,075	2,233
Connecticut	22,887	11,957	Mississippi	26,451	12,671	Tennessee	51,673	24,507
Delaware	3,947	2,745	Missouri	45,618	25,455	Texas	153,826	77,438
Dist. of Col.	5,033	2,508	Montana	7,318	4,307	Utah	13,899	6,160
Florida	86,152	63,267	Nebraska	13,153	5,573	Vermont	4,351	1,866
Georgia	60,116	28,187	Nevada	98,469	9,906	Virginia	55,666	19,412
Hawaii	9,686	4,264	New Hampshire	8,597	4,507	Washington	43,361	25,065
Idaho	12,794	5,223	New Jersey	50,345	18,768	West Virginia	17,002	8,427
Illinois	111,342	51,899	New Mexico	13,505	7,223	Wisconsin	35,862	14,840
Indiana	55,844	NA	New York	141,973	55,502	Wyoming	5,705	2.809
Iowa	25,620	10,387	North Carolina	42,514	22,182			
Kansas	23,887	12,565	North Dakota	6,055	1,737	Total	2,126,000	1,026,000
Kentucky	33,788	15,118	Ohio	101,380	51,367	¹Provisional.		

Wedding Anniversaries

The traditional names for wedding anniversaries go back many years in social usage. As such names as wooden, crystal, silver, and golden were applied it was considered proper to present the married pair with gifts made of these products or of something related. While the list of permissible gifts is extensive, gifts are most appropriate when retaining a suggestion of the originals. Thus the wooden anniversary may call for anything of wood, including furniture, but as the years mount the gifts become more valuable until the 60th or diamond anniversary, calls for diamonds. The traditional list follows, with a few allowable revisions in parentheses.

1st—Paper	6th—Iron	11th—Steel	20th—China	45th—Sapphire
2d—Cotton	7th—Wool, copper	12th—Silk	25th—Silver	50th—Gold
3d—Leather	8th—Bronze	13th—Lace	30th—Pearl	55th—Emerald
4th—Linen, (silk)	9th—Pottery, (china)	14th—Ivory	35th—Coral	60th—Diamond
5th—Wood	10th—Tin, (aluminum)	15th—Crystal	40th—Ruby	

Deaths and Death Rates for Selected Causes*

Source: Division of Vital Statistics, National Center for Health Statistics.
Rates per 100,000 population

1975* Cause of death	Number	Rate	1975* Cause of death	Number	Rate
All causes....................	1,910,000	896.1	Acute bronchitis and bronchiolitis........	820	0.4
Enteritis and other diarrheal diseases.....	1,920	0.9	Influenza and pneumonia..............	57,520	27.0
Tuberculosis, all forms...............	3,300	1.5	Influenza.......................	4,780	2.2
Syphilis and its sequelae.............	360	0.2	Pneumonia......................	52,740	24.7
Other infective and parasitic diseases....	3,630	1.7	Bronchitis, emphysema, and asthma.....	25,300	11.9
Malignant neoplasms, including			Chronic and unqualified bronchitis.....	4,850	2.3
neoplasms of lymphatic and			Emphysema......................	18,410	8.6
hematopoietic tissues..............	371,660	174.4	Asthma.........................	2,040	1.0
Diabetes mellitus...................	35,890	16.8	Peptic ulcer.....................	6,840	3.2
Meningitis.......................	1,820	0.9	Hernia and intestinal obstruction........	6,440	3.0
Major cardiovascular diseases.........	979,180	459.4	Cirrhosis of liver..................	32,080	15.1
Diseases of heart..................	722,570	339.0	Cholelithiasis, cholecystitis and cholangitis	3,000	1.4
Active rheumatic fever and chronic			Nephritis and nephrosis..............	8,410	3.9
rheumatic heart disease..........	12,460	5.8	Infections of kidney................	4,420	2.1
Hypertensive heart disease with or			Hyperplasia of prostate..............	1,290	0.6
without renal disease............	11,200	5.2	Congenital anomalies................	14,380	6.7
Ischemic heart disease.............	648,540	304.3	Certain causes of mortality in early infancy.	27,350	12.8
Chronic disease of endocardium and			Symptoms and ill-defined conditions.....	32,610	15.3
other myocardial insufficiency.....	4,720	2.2	All other diseases..................	119,090	55.9
All other forms of heart disease......	45,650	21.4	Accidents.......................	101,400	47.6
Hypertension.....................	6,370	3.0	Motor vehicle accidents............	44,570	20.9
Cerebrovascular diseases............	195,630	91.8	All other accidents.............	56,830	26.7
Arteriosclerosis...................	29,230	13.7	Suicide.........................	26,960	12.6
Other diseases of arteries			Homicide.......................	21,730	10.2
arterioles, and capillaries..........	25,380	11.9	All other external causes.............	4,940	2.3

Due to rounding estimates of death, figures may not add to total. *Provisional.
Data based on a 10% sampling of all death certificates for a 12-month (Jan.-Dec.) period.

Principal Types of Accidental Deaths

Source: Division of Vital Statistics, National Center for Health Statistics,

Year	All types	Motor vehicle	Falls	Burns	Drowning	Firearms	Machinery	Poison gases	Other poisons
1960......	93,806	38,137	19,023	7,645	6,529	2,334	1,951	1,253	1,679
1965......	108,004	49,163	19,984	7,347	6,799	2,344	2,054	1,526	2,110
1970......	114,638	54,633	16,926	6,718	6,391	2,406	....	1,620	3,679
1972......	115,448	56,278	16,744	6,714	6,196	2,442	....	1,690	3,728
1973......	115,821	55,511	16,506	6,503	7,152	2,618	....	1,652	3,683
1974......	104,622	46,402	16,339	6,236	6,463	2,513	....	1,518	4,016
1975......	101,400	44,570	NA	NA	NA	NA	NA	NA	NA

Death Rates per 100,000 Population

1960......	52.1	21.2	10.6	4.2	3.6	1.3	1.1	0.7	0.9
1965......	55.7	25.4	10.3	3.8	3.5	1.2	1.1	0.8	0.1
1970......	56.4	26.9	8.3	3.3	3.1	1.2	....	0.8	1.8
1972......	55.4	27.0	8.0	3.2	3.0	1.2	....	0.8	1.8
1973......	55.2	26.5	7.9	3.1	3.4	1.2	....	0.8	1.7
1974......	49.5	22.0	7.7	2.9	3.1	1.2	....	0.7	1.9
1975......	47.6	20.9	NA	NA	NA	NA	NA	NA	NA

Accidental Injuries by Severity of Injury

Source: National Safety Council

1975 Severity of Injury	Total*	Motor-Vehicle	Work	Home	Public Non-Motor-Vehicle
All Injuries*.................	10,800,000	1,850,000	2,200,000	4,050,000	2,800,000
Deaths......................	102,500	46,000	12,600	25,500	22,500
Nonfatal injuries................	10,700,000	1,800,000	2,200,000	4,000,000	2,800,000
Permanent impairments........	380,000	150,000	80,000	100,000	70,000
Temporary total disabilities.....	10,300,000	1,650,000	2,100,000	3,900,000	2,700,000

Certain Costs of Accidental Injuries, 1975 ($ billions)

Total*........................	$47.1	$21.2	$16.0	$6.0	$4.8
Wage loss....................	15.4	7.1	3.4	2.8	2.9
Medical expense................	6.2	1.9	1.7	1.6	1.1
Insurance admin., costs..........	6.3	4.2	1.9	0.1	0.1

*Duplication between motor-vehicle, work and home are eliminated in the Total column.

Birth Stones

Source: Retail Jewelers of America, Inc.

Month	Ancient	Modern	Month	Ancient	Modern	Month	Ancient	Modern
January...	Garnet...	Garnet	May...	Agate...	Emerald	September	Chrysolite	Sapphire
February...	Amethyst...	Amethyst	June...	Emerald	Pearl, Moonstone	October...	Aquamarine	Opal or
March.....	Jasper.....	Bloodstone			or			Tourmaline
		or			Alexandrite	November.	Topaz.....	Topaz
		Aquamarine	July...	Onyx...	Ruby	December.	Ruby......	Turquoise
April.....	Sapphire...	Diamond	August	Carnelian.....	Sardonyx or Peridot			or Zircon

The term precious stones actually applies only to diamonds, rubies, sapphires, and emeralds. All others are semiprecious. Precious gems are minerals brought to perfection by the lapidary's art. The pearl, often a gem of great value, is not a precious stone.

Motor Vehicle Traffic Deaths by States

Source: State traffic authorities

Place of accidents	Number 1975	Number 1974	Mil. death rate* 1975	Mil. death rate* 1974	Place of accidents	Number 1975	Number 1974	Mil. death rate* 1975	Mil. death rate* 1974
Total U.S.†	46,000	...	3.5	3.6	Missouri	1,073	1,046	3.5	3.5
Alabama	975	976	3.9	4.1	Montana	298	299	5.2	5.1
Alaska	114	85	4.5	4.1	Nebraska	376	388	3.4	3.5
Arizona	676	748	4.2	4.8	Nevada	220	216	4.9	5.1
Arkansas	566	527	4.1	3.9	New Hampshire	151	166	2.9	3.3
California	4,189	4,019	3.2	3.1	New Jersey	1,080	1,112	2.2	2.4
Colorado	591	615	3.6	3.8	New Mexico	568	540	5.7	5.7
Connecticut	395	398	2.2	2.2	New York	2,459	2,633	3.8	4.0
Delaware	125	113	3.4	3.3	North Carolina	1,518	1,585	4.2	4.5
Dist of Col.	74	78	2.4	2.6	North Dakota	169	162	3.8	3.7
Florida	2,040	2,270	3.2	3.7	Ohio	1,809	1,900	2.8	3.0
Georgia	1,387	1,557	3.5	4.4	Oklahoma	762	751	3.4	3.5
Hawaii	146	129	3.5	3.3	Oregon	571	672	3.6	4.4
Idaho	283	327	4.9	6.0	Pennsylvania	2,082	2,155	3.3	3.2
Illinois	2,084	2,007	3.4	3.4	Rhode Island	111	98	1.9	1.8
Indiana	1,133	1,244	3.0	3.4	South Carolina	821	873	4.0	4.4
Iowa	674	685	3.4	3.4	South Dakota	198	229	3.9	4.5
Kansas	517	519	3.3	3.6	Tennessee	1,145	1,274	3.5	4.1
Kentucky	882	795	3.6	3.3	Texas	3,429	3,046	4.1	3.9
Louisiana	940	864	4.6	4.4	Utah	275	229	3.5	3.1
Maine	226	217	3.3	3.3	Vermont	143	127	4.3	4.2
Maryland	691	737	2.7	3.1	Virginia	1,030	1,050	3.0	3.1
Massachusetts	883	961	3.0	3.4	Washington	771	761	3.2	3.4
Michigan	1,812	1,875	3.1	3.4	West Virginia	486	449	4.6	4.4
Minnesota	777	852	3.0	3.5	Wisconsin	940	912	3.3	3.3
Mississippi	612	643	4.3	4.7	Wyoming	213	195	5.8	5.6
					Puerto Rico	490	565	...	7.7

*The mileage death rate is the number of deaths per 100 million vehicle miles. †Includes both traffic and nontraffic motor vehicle deaths.

Deaths in Civil Aviation Accidents

Source: National Safety Council

Year	Total Deaths*	Scheduled Flights (passengers)				General aviation†	
		Domestic No.	Rate**	International No.	Rate**	No.	Rate**
1960	1,286	297	0.93	10	0.12	787	24
1965	1,279	205	0.38	21	0.12	1,029	21
1970	1,454	0	0.00	2	0.01	1,310	20
1973	1,639	128	0.10	69	0.18	1,412	19
1974	1,905	158	0.12	262	0.51	1,438	18
1975	1,448	113	0.09	0	0.00	1,324	16

*Includes some deaths not shown separately—crew members in scheduled operations and persons not in planes killed in airplane accidents. Excludes deaths in military plane accidents.
**Rates are the number of deaths per 100,000 passenger miles (NSC estimate), (1) Pilots and other crew members are considered passengers for general aviation only.

Accidental Deaths by Age, Sex, and Type

Source: National Safety Council (1974)

Age and Sex	All Types	Motor-Vehicle	Falls	Drown-ing	Fires, Burns	Ingest. of Food, Object	Fire-arms	Poison (solid, liquid)	Poison by Gas	% Male All Types
All Ages	104,622	46,402	16,339	7,876	6,236	2,991	2,513	4,016	1,518	70%
Under 5	5,335	1,546	246	920	790	605	85	135	43	60%
5 to 14	7,037	3,332	172	1,320	569	105	447	44	64	70%
15 to 24	24,200	15,905	504	2,390	519	235	832	1,088	404	81%
25 to 34	13,436	7,504	501	1,010	455	193	407	914	246	81%
35 to 44	9,111	4,330	600	640	510	233	229	511	177	77%
45 to 54	10,353	4,357	1,104	620	712	356	227	524	230	74%
55 to 64	9,981	3,802	1,512	480	873	424	161	390	162	71%
65 to 74	9,323	3,071	2,384	316	893	387	87	226	116	63%
75 & over	15,846	2,555	9,316	180	915	462	38	184	76	45%
Sex										
Male	73,209	34,133	8,369	6,678	3,821	1,782	2,127	2,595	1,158	
Female	31,413	12,269	7,970	1,198	2,415	1,209	386	1,421	360	
Per cent male	70%	74%	51%	85%	61%	60%	85%	65%	76%	

Accidental Deaths by Month and Type, 1974 and 1975

1974 Details by Type

Month	1975 Totals	All Types	Motor-Vehicle	Falls	Drown-ing†	Fires, Burns*	Ingest. of Food, Object	Fire-arms	Poison (solid, liquid)	Poison by Gas
All Months	102,500	104,622	46,402	16,339	7,876	6,236	2,991	2,513	4,016	1,518
January	7,800	7,750	3,020	1,521	256	688	263	194	311	228
February	7,500	6,981	2,699	1,315	270	660	250	141	317	159
March	8,000	8,038	3,311	1,414	420	637	272	180	375	140
April	7,850	8,422	3,425	1,397	590	513	226	179	344	121
May	9,000	8,714	3,678	1,283	1,020	437	233	149	343	110
June	9,600	9,512	4,243	1,318	1,360	374	218	189	311	56
July	10,000	10,120	4,401	1,336	1,660	319	202	198	361	50
August	9,650	9,823	4,718	1,382	990	360	258	194	337	59
September	8,150	8,743	4,256	1,280	530	337	225	224	324	110
October	8,600	9,129	4,465	1,386	310	512	253	256	327	112
November	8,250	8,710	4,273	1,343	250	608	257	328	304	173
December	8,100	8,680	3,913	1,364	220	791	282	281	362	200
Average	8,540	8,719	3,867	1,362	666	520	249	209	335	127

Source: NCHS and NSC. *Includes deaths resulting from conflagration regardless of nature of injury. †Includes drowning in water transport accidents. Some totals partly estimated.

Average Future Lifetime in U.S.

Source: Division of Vital Statistics, National Center for
Health Statistics, 1975 Data

Average remaining lifetime[2]

Age Interval	Number Living[1]	Avg. Life Expect.	White Male	White Female	All Others Male	All Others Female
0-1	100,000	72.4	69.3	77.0	63.6	72.5
1-5	98,387	72.6	69.4	77.0	64.2	73.1
5-10	98,104	68.6	65.6	73.2	60.5	69.3
10-15	97,930	63.9	60.8	68.3	55.6	64.5
15-20	97,747	59.0	55.9	63.4	50.8	59.5
20-25	97,251	54.3	51.3	58.6	46.2	54.7
25-30	96,572	49.7	46.8	53.7	42.0	50.0
30-35	95,902	45.0	42.1	48.9	37.8	45.3
35-40	95,186	40.3	37.5	44.1	33.7	40.7
40-45	94,164	35.7	32.9	39.3	29.7	36.3
45-50	92,643	31.3	28.4	34.7	25.9	32.0
50-55	90,335	27.0	24.2	30.2	22.3	27.9
55-60	86,855	23.0	20.3	25.9	19.0	24.1
60-65	81,778	19.3	16.7	21.8	16.1	20.7
65-70	74,502	15.9	13.6	18.0	13.6	17.5
70-75	65,367	12.7	10.8	14.3	11.2	14.3
75-80	58,151	10.1	8.5	11.1	9.6	12.5
80-85	38,694	7.9	6.6	8.5	8.5	11.0
85 and up	24,137	6.2	5.2	6.5	7.1	9.4

(1) Of 100,000 born alive, number living at beginning of age interval. (2) Average number of years of life remaining at beginning of age interval.

Years of Life Expected at Birth

Year	Total	Male	Female	Year	Total	Male	Female
1975[1]	72.4	68.5	76.4	1960	69.7	66.6	73.1
1974	71.9	68.1	75.8	1950	68.2	65.6	71.1
1973	71.3	67.6	75.3	1940	62.9	60.8	65.2
1972	71.1	67.4	75.1	1930	59.7	58.1	61.6
1970	70.8	67.1	74.6	1920	54.1	53.6	54.6
1965	70.2	66.8	73.7	1910	47.3	46.3	48.3

Based on Death-Registration States 1900-1925, and United States 1930-1974. (1) Provisional.

Purchases and Ownership of Life Insurance in U.S. and Assets of U.S. Life Insurance Companies

Legal Reserve Life Insurance Companies
Source: Statistical Services, Institute of Life Insurance

In millions of dollars.

Year	Purchases of Life Insurance Ordinary	Group	Industrial	Total	Insurance in Force Ordinary	Group	Industrial	Credit	Total	Assets
1940	7,022	747	3,318	1,087	79,346	14,938	20,866	380	115,530	30,802
1950	18,260	6,237	5,492	29,989	149,116	47,793	33,415	3,844	234,168	64,020
1960	56,183	15,328	6,906	78,417	341,881	175,903	39,563	29,101	586,448	119,576
1965	89,643	52,867*	7,302	149,812*	499,638	308,078	39,818	53,020	900,554	158,884
1970	138,356	68,939*	6,612	213,907*	734,730	551,357	38,644	77,392	1,402,123	207,254
1972	156,859	59,953	7,394	224,206	853,911	640,689	39,975	93,410	1,627,985	239,730
1973	173,049	67,100*	7,224	247,373*	928,192	708,322	40,632	101,154	1,778,300	252,436
1974	195,465	117,054*	6,680	319,199*	1,009,038	827,018	39,441	109,623	1,985,120	263,349
1975	209,071	103,871*	6,741	319,683*	1,083,421	904,695	39,423	112,032	2,139,571	289,304

*Includes Servicemen's Group Life Insurance $27.4 billion in 1965, $16.8 billion in 1970, $28.8 billion in 1974, and $1.7 billion in 1975.

Home Accident Deaths

Source: National Safety Council

Year	Total Home	Falls	Fires, Burns[B]	Suffo.-Ingested Object	Suffo.-Mechanical	Poison (solid, liquid)	Poison by Gas	Fire-arms	Other
1950	29,000	14,800	5,000	A	1,600	1,300	1,250	950	4,100
1955	28,500	14,100	5,400	A	1,250	1,150	900	1,100	4,600
1960	28,000	12,300	6,350	1,850	1,500	1,350	900	1,200	2,550
1962	28,500	12,600	6,200	1,400*	1,400	1,400	1,000	1,000	3,500
1964	28,000	11,400	6,200	1,400	1,300	1,700	900	1,200	3,900
1965	28,500	11,700	6,100	1,300	1,200	1,700	1,100	1,300	4,100
1966	29,500	11,900	6,800	1,300	1,100	1,800	1,200	1,400	4,000
1967	29,000	12,000	6,200	1,300	900	2,000	1,100	1,600	3,900
1968	28,000	10,800	6,100	2,000*	1,200*	2,100	1,100	1,300*	3,400*
1969	27,500	10,300	6,000	2,400	1,100	2,400	1,100	1,300	2,900
1970	27,000	9,700	5,600	1,800	1,100	3,000	1,100	1,400	3,300
1971	26,500	9,300	5,600	1,900	1,000	3,000	1,000	1,300	3,400
1972	26,500	9,300	5,500	1,800	900	3,000	1,000	1,400	3,600
1973	26,500	9,200	5,300	1,900	1,100	3,000	1,000	1,500	3,500
1974	26,000	9,000	5,100	1,800	900	3,200	900	1,400	3,700
1975	25,500	8,400	5,100	1,900	800	3,300	1,000	1,400	3,600

*Data for this year and subsequent years not comparable with previous years due to classification changes. (A) Included in Other. (B) Includes deaths resulting from conflagration, regardless of nature of injury.

Physical Growth Range for Children from 1 to 18 Years*

Source: U.S. Public Health Service, H.E.W.

Age	Shortest 5%	Median Height	Tallest 5%	Lightest 5%	Median Weight	Heaviest 5%
Boys						
1	28.4	30.2	32.0	18.7	23.3	27.8
2	32.1	34.6	37.1	23.3	28.3	33.3
3	35.3	37.8	40.3	27.1	32.5	37.9
4	38.3	40.8	43.3	30.0	36.1	42.2
5	40.3	43.4	46.4	33.0	40.3	47.6
6	42.8	45.9	49.0	36.0	44.7	53.4
7	44.8	48.1	51.4	40.3	50.9	61.5
8	46.9	50.5	54.1	44.4	57.4	70.4
9	48.8	52.8	56.8	48.0	64.4	80.4
10	50.6	54.3	59.2	51.4	71.4	91.4
11	51.9	56.4	60.9	53.3	78.9	102.5
12	53.5	58.6	63.7	60.0	86.0	113.5
13	55.2	61.3	67.4	65.3	98.6	131.9
14	57.5	64.1	70.7	75.5	111.8	148.1
15	61.0	66.9	72.8	88.0	124.3	160.6
16	63.8	68.9	74.0	97.8	133.8	169.8
17	65.2	69.8	74.4	106.5	139.8	174.0
18	65.9	70.2	74.5	110.3	144.8	179.3
Girls						
1	27.6	29.4	31.2	17.4	21.7	26.0
2	31.6	33.8	36.0	22.3	27.1	31.9
3	35.3	37.5	39.7	26.3	32.3	38.3
4	38.1	40.7	43.3	28.8	36.1	43.4
5	40.6	43.4	46.2	32.2	40.9	49.6
6	42.8	45.9	49.0	35.5	45.7	55.9
7	44.5	47.8	51.1	38.3	51.0	63.7
8	46.4	50.0	53.6	42.0	57.2	72.4
9	48.2	52.2	56.2	45.1	63.6	82.1
10	49.9	54.5	59.1	48.2	71.0	95.0
11	51.9	57.0	62.1	55.4	82.0	108.6
12	54.1	59.5	64.9	63.9	94.4	124.9
13	57.1	62.2	66.8	72.8	105.5	138.2
14	58.5	63.1	67.7	83.0	113.0	144.0
15	59.5	63.8	68.1	89.5	120.0	150.5
16	59.8	64.1	68.4	95.1	123.0	150.1
17	60.1	64.2	68.3	97.9	125.8	153.7
18	60.1	64.4	68.7	96.0	126.2	156.4

*This table simply gives a general picture for American children. When used as a standard, the individual variation in children's growth should not be overlooked. In most cases the height-weight relationship is probably a more valid index of weight status than a weight-for-age assessment.

Average Weight of Americans by Height and Age

Source: Society of Actuaries; based on a 4-year study of 5,000,000 persons
The figures represent weights in ordinary indoor clothing and shoes, and heights with shoes.

Height	MEN 20-24	25-29	30-39	40-49	50-59	Height	WOMEN 20-24	25-29	30-39	40-49	50-59
5′0″	122	128	131	134	136	4′10″	102	107	115	122	125
5′1″	125	131	134	137	139	4′11″	105	110	117	124	127
5′2″	128	134	137	140	142	5′0″	108	113	120	127	130
5′3″	132	138	141	144	145	5′1″	112	116	123	130	133
5′4″	136	141	145	148	149	5′2″	115	119	126	133	136
5′5″	139	144	149	152	153	5′3″	118	122	129	136	140
5′6″	142	148	153	156	157	5′4″	121	125	132	140	141
5′7″	145	151	157	161	162	5′5″	125	129	135	143	148
5′8″	149	155	161	165	166	5′6″	129	133	139	147	152
5′9″	153	159	165	169	170	5′7″	132	136	142	151	156
5′10″	157	163	170	174	175	5′8″	136	140	146	155	160
5′11″	161	167	174	178	180	5′9″	140	144	150	159	164
6′0″	166	172	179	183	185	5′10″	144	148	154	164	169
6′1″	170	177	183	187	189	5′11″	149	153	159	169	174
6′2″	174	182	188	192	194	6′0″	154	158	164	174	180
6′3″	178	186	193	197	199						
6′4″	181	190	199	203	205						

Pedalcycle Accidents

Since 1935, the number of pedalcycle-motor-vehicle deaths has more than doubled. The number of pedalcycles in use is 27 times the number in 1935; so the death rate in 1975 was about one-twelfth the rate in 1935. The proportion of deaths occuring to young adults and adults has steadily increased since 1960. Persons 15 years of age and older accounted for more than one-half the deaths in 1975 compared to one-fifth in 1960.

Fitness Tests for Children

These standards were developed by nationwide testing of a sample of 7,600 girls and boys in public schools in a study funded by the U. S. Office of Education.

Girls
Boys

Standing Long Jump
(in feet and inches)

Age	10	11	12	13	14	15	16	17		10	11	12	13	14	15	16	17
Excellent	5-8	5-9	6-0	6-2	6-5	6-3	6-3	6-6		5-10	6-0	6-3	6-10	7-2	7-7	7-11	8-2
Good	5-2	5-5	5-8	5-10	6-0	6-0	5-11	6-2		5-6	5-9	6-0	6-5	6-10	7-3	7-6	7-10
Satisfactory	4-10	5-1	5-2	5-5	5-7	5-6	5-6	5-9		5-1	5-5	5-7	6-0	6-4	6-10	7-2	7-5
Poor	4-6	4-8	4-10	5-1	5-2	5-2	5-1	5-3		4-9	5-0	5-3	5-6	5-11	6-5	6-9	7-0

50-yard Dash
(time in seconds)

Age	10	11	12	13	14	15	16	17		10	11	12	13	14	15	16	17
Excellent	7.5	7.5	7.2	7.0	7.0	7.0	7.1	7.0		7.5	7.2	7.0	6.7	6.4	6.2	6.2	6.0
Good	8.0	7.8	7.5	7.3	7.2	7.2	7.4	7.3		7.8	7.5	7.3	7.0	6.6	6.4	6.4	6.3
Satisfactory	8.4	8.1	8.0	7.7	7.6	7.6	7.7	7.6		8.0	7.9	7.6	7.3	7.0	6.8	6.6	6.5
Poor	8.9	8.5	8.3	8.1	8.0	8.0	8.0	8.0		8.6	8.3	8.0	7.6	7.4	7.0	6.8	6.8

Sit-ups
(number in 60 seconds)

Age	10	11	12	13	14	15	16	17		10	11	12	13	14	15	16	17
Excellent	40	40	40	41	43	42	40	41		44	45	48	50	52	52	52	51
Good	35	36	37	38	39	38	36	38		40	41	43	47	48	49	49	47
Satisfactory	30	31	32	32	33	33	32	32		35	37	38	41	43	44	43	42
Poor	24	26	27	27	29	29	27	28		29	31	33	35	38	40	40	39

Flexed-arm Hang
(score in seconds)

Pull-ups
(number)

Age	10	11	12	13	14	15	16	17		10	11	12	13	14	15	16	17
Excellent	29	30	27	25	29	28	24	28		7	6	7	9	10	12	12	13
Good	21	21	21	20	23	21	17	19		4	5	5	6	8	10	10	11
Satisfactory	12	13	12	11	13	12	10	10		2	3	3	4	5	7	8	8
Poor	6	7	6	6	7	7	5	6		1	1	1	2	3	5	6	6

600-yard Run
(time in minutes and seconds)

Age	10	11	12	13	14	15	16	17		10	11	12	13	14	15	16	17
Excellent	2-26	2-21	2-14	2-12	2-7	2-10	2-15	2-10		2-9	2-6	1-57	1-50	1-44	1-40	1-38	1-35
Good	2-33	2-30	2-23	2-20	2-15	2-18	2-21	2-20		2-15	2-12	2-4	1-57	1-50	1-45	1-42	1-41
Satisfactory	2-48	2-45	2-39	2-34	2-32	2-30	2-36	2-35		2-30	2-22	2-14	2-5	1-58	1-52	1-49	1-49
Poor	3-1	2-59	2-56	2-49	2-47	2-45	2-49	2-48		2-40	2-34	2-24	2-15	2-7	1-59	1-56	1-56

Pedalcycle Accident Deaths
Source: National Safety Council

Year	Pedalcycles* (millions)	Deaths	Death Rate**	Per Cent of Deaths by Age			
				All Ages	0-14	15-24	25 & Over
1935........	3.5	450	12.80	100%	57	29	14
1940........	7.8	750	9.59	100%	48	39	13
1945........	9.0	500	5.55	100%	56	22	22
1950........	13.8	440	3.18	100%	82	9	9
1955........	23.1	410	1.78	100%	71	12	17
1960........	28.2	460	1.63	100%	78	9	13
1965........	38.8	680	1.75	100%	64	18	18
1970........	56.5	780	1.38	100%	66	15	19
1972........	71.4	1,000	1.40	100%	50	27	23
1973........	80.0	1,000	1.25	100%	49	30	21
1974........	90.0	1,000	1.11	100%	47	31	22
1975........	95.0	1,000	1.05	100%	49	28	23

*Pedalcycles in use for a given year is the ten-year total (that year and the previous nine years) of domestic production plus imports less exports. **Deaths per 100,000 pedalcycles in use.

The Nation's Hospitals

Source: American Hospital Association

In 1975, there were 7,156 hospitals in the United States registered by the American Hospital Association. These institutions had about 1.47 million beds and reported admitting some 36.2 million inpatients. About $48.7 billion was spent to provide services for both inpatients and outpatients, or a cost of $229 per resident of the nation.

	Hospitals		Beds		Average Daily Census		Admissions		Expenses ($1,000)	
	Fed.	Non-Fed.	Fed.	Non-Fed.	Fed.	Non-Fed.	Fed.	Non-Fed.	Fed.	Non-Fed.
Ala.	8	139	2,746	22,651	2,179	16,815	37,870	640,809	77,703	583,914
Alask.	9	16	649	944	398	595	18,259	35,540	30,508	43,398
Ariz.	17	61	1,630	9,287	1,226	6,766	49,335	299,607	76,292	402,538
Ark.	4	92	1,952	9,744	1,712	7,069	24,314	383,431	54,231	263,463
Cal.	32	606	11,832	111,258	8,875	76,544	211,836	3,091,482	527,097	4,776,852
Col.	7	94	2,031	12,581	1,688	9,166	40,331	426,918	77,841	471,055
Conn.	6	63	1,217	18,846	866	15,177	21,654	435,326	51,723	720,348
Del.	2	13	386	4,249	294	3,749	6,713	74,423	12,747	127,040
D. C.	4	16	5,224	5,826	4,439	4,695	37,395	181,707	167,190	311,404
Fla.	14	225	4,306	50,717	3,557	37,617	96,227	1,375,992	201,340	1,653,058
Ga.	10	172	3,170	28,114	2,367	20,998	48,655	832,150	107,097	813,023
Ha.	1	28	621	4,105	457	3,076	21,206	91,788	29,348	119,418
Ida.	2	50	195	3,466	166	2,394	4,395	125,494	6,786	100,783
Ill.	10	279	6,578	71,817	5,557	56,005	74,947	1,939,820	206,671	2,729,387
Ind.	6	132	2,153	33,016	1,873	25,645	21,115	842,534	53,263	929,610
Ia.	3	141	1,654	20,237	1,247	14,011	16,769	543,155	51,616	494,953
Kan.	7	159	2,141	16,390	1,648	11,777	24,164	426,972	63,561	422,163
Ky.	5	122	1,992	17,704	1,659	13,793	36,964	586,079	69,947	489,081
La.	8	148	2,544	22,088	1,906	15,808	47,557	677,649	84,463	645,748
Me.	2	53	805	6,824	648	4,949	7,233	171,731	18,202	197,728
Md.	11	71	3,504	25,131	2,759	20,563	48,874	474,593	151,431	842,233
Mass.	7	188	3,812	46,013	3,266	36,761	27,328	938,170	104,316	1,855,869
Mich.	9	245	2,879	51,279	2,252	40,962	32,048	1,413,728	86,467	2,104,711
Minn.	5	187	1,927	29,933	1,607	21,623	20,766	704,104	60,722	807,241
Miss.	5	110	1,731	15,692	1,475	11,723	27,259	419,352	54,431	313,103
Mo.	8	163	3,170	31,979	2,559	24,125	54,388	888,619	134,079	1,009,297
Mont.	6	59	391	3,967	300	2,443	9,434	135,800	13,472	98,534
Neb.	5	104	951	10,532	724	6,949	20,993	281,597	35,100	280,984
Nev.	4	19	277	2,879	207	1,946	6,876	93,627	13,440	115,649
N. H.	1	33	188	5,895	185	4,368	3,251	126,868	8,882	135,216
N. J.	4	142	3,149	45,924	2,538	37,159	28,084	1,031,701	81,201	1,461,513
N. M.	11	43	1,031	5,453	716	3,653	30,899	149,938	40,017	144,356
N. Y.	16	391	10,246	149,135	8,675	124,986	93,540	2,716,922	312,474	5,870,250
N. C.	9	152	3,263	31,178	2,812	24,154	54,332	832,049	107,937	814,422
N. D.	5	55	419	5,373	296	3,782	11,688	130,057	15,332	115,596
Oh.	6	245	4,734	68,187	4,001	55,084	41,872	1,784,542	127,607	2,212,582
Okla.	12	135	1,346	16,160	911	11,581	38,095	464,478	58,531	433,805
Ore.	2	85	966	10,922	833	7,430	14,776	343,757	32,964	357,809
Pa.	12	308	6,958	87,740	5,922	68,739	49,989	1,856,660	188,620	2,680,487
R. I.	2	20	553	7,119	385	6,043	10,157	140,487	24,246	246,317
S. C.	7	81	1,945	16,308	1,531	12,553	46,167	405,515	78,236	377,234
S. D.	10	60	1,252	4,691	999	3,092	19,683	124,972	33,082	92,568
Tenn.	5	153	3,003	27,338	2,591	21,296	38,157	795,628	84,718	736,810
Tex.	26	545	8,990	69,619	7,301	49,755	162,728	2,108,620	311,852	1,962,735
Ut.	2	37	541	4,302	403	3,258	11,587	181,724	24,069	161,450
Vt.	1	20	224	3,615	190	2,800	3,630	76,749	9,527	92,258
Va.	11	118	3,930	28,384	2,914	22,525	67,929	700,904	152,305	754,765
Wash.	11	116	2,630	13,678	2,022	9,366	48,037	530,042	99,376	526,345
W. V.	6	80	1,328	14,656	1,095	11,290	17,064	378,554	41,486	341,344
Wis.	3	173	2,227	28,849	1,842	20,449	21,273	767,996	72,568	881,046
Wy.	3	27	555	2,087	472	1,225	5,384	62,929	13,737	44,813
Total	**382**	**6,774**	**131,946**	**1,333,882**	**106,545**	**1,018,332**	**1,913,227**	**34,243,289**	**4,539,851**	**44,166,306**

Canadian General and Allied Special Hospitals

1974	Hospitals			Beds			Admissions			Expenses ($1,000)
	Pub.	Prop.*	Fed.	Pub.	Prop.	Fed.	Pub.	Prop.	Fed.	Pub.
Canada	1,043	99	99	147,167	3,976	6,091	3,707,699	32,325	53,133	3,871,142
Nfld.	47	—	—	3,143	—	—	90,976	—	—	83,119
P. E. I.	9	—	—	751	—	—	24,389	—	—	12,858
N. S.	47	—	2	4,762	—	522	133,254	—	4,011	123,370
N. B.	38	—	—	4,348	—	—	122,468	—	—	102,441
Que.	186	44	10	38,629	2,625	1,618	800,056	18,247	4,587	1,155,124
Ont.	233	51	13	50,669	1,292	1,811	1,389,340	13,541	13,584	1,428,300
Man.	81	1	16	6,545	40	647	170,708	359	6,377	155,486
Sask.	135	—	3	7,733	—	110	201,541	—	2,648	139,657
Alta.	146	—	8	14,214	—	902	356,526	—	11,975	283,611
B. C.	117	2	1	16,217	16	60	414,326	149	1,129	384,029
Yukon	—	1	6	—	3	160	—	29	4,283	—
N.W.T.	4	—	40	156	—	261	4,115	—	4,539	3,147

*Proprietary

How to Obtain Birth, Marriage, Death Records

The United States Government has published a series of inexpensive booklets entitled Where to Write for Birth & Death Records; Where to Write for Marriage Records; Where to Write for Divorce Records; Where to Write for Birth and Death Records of U. S. Citizens who were born or died outside of the U. S. and birth certifications for alien children adopted by U. S. citizens; You May Save Time Proving Your Age and Other Birth Facts. They tell where to write to get a certified copy of an original vital record. Supt. of Documents, Government Printing Office, Washington, D. C. 20402.

Nursing Care Homes in U.S.

Source: Division of Health Manpower and Facilities Statistics, National Center for Health Statistics

State	Nursing care homes				Personal care homes	
	Homes	Beds	Residents	Full-time Personnel	Homes	Beds
Total	14,873	1,107,358	1,011,092	559,684	6,961	220,346
Alabama	188	13,997	13,350	8,320	9	847
Alaska	8	606	477	238	—	—
Arizona	75	5,969	5,332	3,189	13	461
Arkansas	199	17,070	15,404	7,933	12	882
California	1,618	115,560	100,742	56,159	2,527	35,396
Colorado	179	15,126	13,783	7,425	35	1,544
Connecticut	261	19,438	18,553	9,320	104	3,856
Delaware	34	2,199	2,071	1,472	2	14
District of Columbia	43	2,825	2,434	1,546	29	322
Florida	297	29,304	25,069	16,251	63	5,652
Georgia	285	24,340	23,174	12,759	21	1,596
Hawaii	41	2,105	1,967	1,313	6	143
Idaho	58	4,047	3,693	2,031	253	12,922
Illinois	786	67,229	60,998	30,030	78	4,446
Indiana	417	29,801	26,798	14,892	214	8,418
Iowa	464	26,734	24,591	10,978	163	5,068
Kansas	305	17,821	16,460	7,856	125	5,059
Kentucky	187	13,118	11,865	6,292	10	454
Louisiana	202	16,550	15,666	7,919	173	1,560
Maine	168	7,667	7,315	4,487	29	1,556
Maryland	175	16,199	15,187	9,315	191	7,788
Massachusetts	754	46,070	43,271	21,548	133	9,832
Michigan	444	38,735	36,860	24,117	148	6,958
Minnesota	441	37,703	34,786	13,775	17	392
Mississippi	126	7,494	7,086	4,180	87	4,453
Missouri	415	29,191	26,827	15,001	26	782
Montana	79	3,977	3,765	2,000	56	2,686
Nebraska	195	14,710	13,325	5,763	18	281
Nevada	23	1,201	1,031	763	24	659
New Hampshire	106	5,214	4,925	2,709	193	6,256
New Jersey	356	28,174	25,857	16,634	23	696
New Mexico	43	2,649	2,268	1,509	392	24,864
New York	691	68,024	63,439	45,461	607	8,255
North Carolina	231	13,890	12,693	6,983	44	2,068
North Dakota	63	4,563	4,338	1,802	148	6,945
Ohio	1,015	58,189	53,305	29,446	31	1,299
Oklahoma	386	28,213	25,270	12,953	94	4,149
Oregon	218	14,157	13,135	6,776	102	7,733
Pennsylvania	666	58,230	53,724	34,471	46	924
Rhode Island	113	5,569	5,326	2,357	13	621
South Carolina	110	7,510	7,062	4,468	46	1,161
South Dakota	114	6,634	6,212	2,633	31	2,084
Tennessee	213	12,473	11,997	7,162	94	6,080
Texas	873	74,430	65,882	35,138	28	615
Utah	92	3,941	3,674	1,698	30	533
Vermont	71	3,369	2,974	1,923	150	2,796
Virginia	198	13,936	12,479	7,755	55	3,193
Washington	327	27,954	25,475	12,151	62	1,243
West Virginia	75	3,510	3,290	2,153	95	13,856
Wisconsin	421	38,104	34,484	15,949	10	327
Wyoming	24	1,569	1,403	681		

Active Federal And Non-Federal Doctors (M.D.s) by States

(as of Dec. 31, 1974)

Source: Division of Health Manpower and Facilities Statistics, National Center for Health Statistics

State	Total	Non-fed.	Fed.	State	Total	Non-fed.	Fed.	State	Total	Non-fed.	Fed.
All areas	[1]350,609	323,993	26,616	Kansas	3,038	2,798	240	North Dakota	675	600	75
United States	345,659	321,089	24,570	Kentucky	3,957	3,698	259	Ohio	15,208	14,633	575
Alabama	3,579	3,333	246	Louisiana	4,963	4,596	367	Oklahoma	2,986	2,728	258
Alaska	426	288	138	Maine	1,304	1,210	103	Oregon	3,653	3,458	195
Arizona	3,661	3,260	401	Maryland	10,333	8,130	2,203	Pennsylvania	19,116	18,347	769
Arkansas	2,069	1,892	177	Mass.	13,249	12,546	703	Rhode Island	1,710	1,610	100
California	44,223	40,526	3,697	Michigan	12,367	11,987	380	South Carolina	3,118	2,803	315
Colorado	4,731	4,215	516	Minnesota	6,529	6,166	363	South Dakota	609	529	80
Connecticut	6,476	6,230	246	Mississippi	2,252	2,007	245	Tennessee	5,589	5,244	345
Delaware	843	794	49	Missouri	6,751	6,408	343	Texas	16,546	14,616	1,930
D.C.	4,031	3,103	928	Montana	849	767	82	Utah	1,829	1,697	132
Florida	12,801	11,789	1,012	Nebraska	1,971	1,840	131	Vermont	884	839	45
Georgia	6,255	5,652	603	Nevada	696	643	53	Virginia	7,440	6,426	1,014
Hawaii	1,386	1,310	76	N.H.	1,205	1,135	70	Washington	5,869	5,295	574
Idaho	784	738	46	New Jersey	11,963	11,448	515	West Virginia	2,109	1,991	118
Illinois	17,759	16,835	924	New Mexico	1,502	1,280	222	Wisconsin	6,019	5,713	306
Indiana	5,761	5,586	175	New York	44,390	42,830	1,560	Wyoming	390	347	43
Iowa	3,079	2,942	137	North Carolina	6,726	6,240	486	Puerto Rico	2,913	2,745	168
								Outlying areas	2,037	159	1,878

(1) Excludes 7,525 physicians with addresses unknown.

Transportation Accident Death Rates

Source: National Safety Council

Kind of Transportation Passenger Deaths in 1975	Passenger Miles (in millions)	Passenger Deaths	Rate Per 100,000,000 Pass. Miles	1973-1975 Aver. Death Rate
Passenger automobiles and taxis[1]	1,940.0	27,200	1.40	1.50
Passenger automobiles on turnpikes	47.0	320	0.70	0.80
Buses	73.0	110	0.15	0.20
Intercity buses[2]	18.1	3	0.02	0.08
Railroad passenger trains	9.6	8	0.08	0.07
Scheduled air transport (domestic)	131.0	113	0.09	0.10

(1) Drivers of passenger automobile are considered passengers. (2) Class 1 only, representing 70 per cent of total intercity bus passenger mileage.

Selected Statistics on State and County Mental Hospitals

Source: National Institute of Mental Health

Year	Total Admitted[1]	Net Releases[2]	Deaths in Hospital	Residents End of Year	Expense Per Patient[3]
1955	178,003	NA	44,384	558,922	$1,116.59
1960	234,791	NA	49,748	535,540	1,702.41
1970	393,174	394,627	30,804	338,592	5,435.38
1973	377,020*	386,962	19,899	248,562	9,207.92
1974	374,554*	389,094	16,597	215,573	11,277.23
1975	376,156	391,345	13,401	193,436	13,634.53

*Includes estimates. NA Not Available. (1) Excludes transfers.
(2) Net releases alive from hospital is computed by subtracting returns from long-term leave from the total discontinuations.
(3) Per average daily resident patient population.

Patients in State and County Mental Hospitals

Source: National Institute of Mental Health. Average Daily Census 1975

State	Number	State	Number	State	Number	State	Number
United States Total	193,721	Idaho	228	Missouri	3,214	Pennsylvania	15,126
Alabama	2,735	Illinois	7,183	Montana	954	Rhode Island	1,530
Alaska	123	Indiana	4,374	Nebraska	696	South Carolina	4,272
Arizona	640	Iowa	1,168	Nevada	317	South Dakota	663
Arkansas	408	Kansas	1,283	New Hampshire	1,162	Tennessee	4,111
California	8,727	Kentucky	717	New Jersey	9,606	Texas	7,733
Colorado	1,078	Louisiana	2,712	New Mexico	581	Utah	313
Connecticut	3,093	Maine	812	New York	36,297	Vermont	453
Delaware	903	Maryland	5,093	North Carolina	4,508	Virginia	6,511
District of Columbia	2,735	Massachusetts	5,702	North Dakota	605	Washington	1,227
Florida	6,307	Michigan	5,509	Ohio	9,889	West Virginia	2,801
Georgia	6,922	Minnesota	3,829	Oklahoma	2,316	Wisconsin	1,155
Hawaii	203	Mississippi	3,777	Oregon	1,138	Wyoming	286

The above data was based on reports of the 313 state and county hospitals. The full-time personnel was estimated at 211,899 and the expenditures $2,641,295,000. The average daily expenditures per patient based on the resident patient population of hospitals reporting expenditures was $37.54.

Patient Care Episodes in Mental Health Facilities

Source: National Institute of Mental Health

Year	Total All Facilities	Inpatient Services					Outpatient Services		
		State & County Mental Hospitals	Private Mental[1] Hospitals	Gen. Hosp. Psychiatric Service (non-VA)	VA Psychiatric Inpatient Services	Federally Assisted Comm. Men. Health Cen.	Federally Assisted Comm. Men. Health Cen.	Other	
1973	5,248,832	651,857	151,941	475,448	208,416	191,946	982,552	2,586,672	
1971	4,038,143	745,259	126,600	542,642	176,800	130,088	622,906	1,693,848	
1969	3,572,822	767,115	123,850	535,493	186,913	65,000	291,148	1,603,303	
1965	2,636,525	804,926	125,428	519,328	115,843	—	—	1,071,000	
1955	1,675,352	818,832	123,231	265,934	88,355	—	—	379,000	

(1) In order to present trends on the same set of facilities over this interval, it has been necessary to exclude from this table the following: private psychiatric office practice; psychiatric service modes of all types in hospitals or outpatient clinics of federal agencies other than the VA (e.g., Public Health Service, Indian Health Service, Department of Defense Bureau of Prisons, etc.); inpatient service modes of multiservice facilities not shown in this table; all partial care episodes, and outpatient episodes of VA hospitals. (2) Includes estimates of episodes of care in residential treatment centers for emotionally disturbed children.

Patients in Canadian Mental Hospitals

Average Patients Per Day, 1974

	Public Hospitals					Total Private	Total Mental Hospital
	Mental	Psychiatric	Retardates	Emotionally Disturbed Children	Other		
Canada	24,721	1,183	14,696	142	1,853	963	43,558
Newfoundland	460	—	—	—	—	—	460
Prince Edward Island	275	—	21	—	—	—	296
Nova Scotia	787	519	—	—	—	—	1,305
New Brunswick	1,027	—	160	—	—	—	1,188
Quebec	11,705	147	1,554	—	367	—	13,773
Ontario	5,900	358	7,036	142	127	889	14,452
Manitoba	952	34	1,155	—	—	—	2,141
Saskatchewan	347	65	938	—	—	—	1,350
Alberta	1,519	—	2,095	—	372	—	3,986
British Columbia	1,749	61	1,736	—	987	74	4,607

Annual Fire Losses in the U.S.

Source: Insurance Services Office

Year	Loss	Year	Loss	Year	Loss	Year	Loss
1940	$285,878,697	1960	1,107,824,000	1971	2,316,000,000	1974	3,190,000,000
1945	484,274,000	1965	1,455,631,000	1972	2,304,000,000	1975	3,560,000,000
1955	885,218,000	1970	2,264,000,000	1973	2,639,000,000	1976, 6 mos.	1,869,000,000

Marriage Information

Source: Compiled by William E. Mariano: Council on Marriage Relations, Inc.,
110 East 42 St., New York, N. Y. 10017 (as of Oct. 1, 1976)

Marriageable age, by states, for both males and females with and without consent of parents or guardians. But in most states, the court has authority, in an emergency, to marry young couples below the ordinary age of consent, where due regard for their morals and welfare so requires. In many states, under special circumstances, blood test and waiting period may be waived.

State	With consent		Without consent		Blood test		Wait for license	Wait after license
	Men	Women	Men	Women	Required	Other state accepted*		
Alabama (b)	17	14	21	18	Yes	Yes	None	None
Alaska	18	16	19	18	Yes	No	3 days	None
Arizona	16²	16	18	18	Yes	Yes	None	None
Arkansas	17	16⁴	18	18	Yes	No	3 days	None
California	—²	—²	18	18	Yes	Yes	None	None
Colorado	16	16	18	18	Yes	. . .	None.	None
Connecticut	16	16(q)	18	18	Yes	Yes	4 days	None
Delaware	—(q)	16⁴	18	18	Yes	Yes	None	24 hrs. (c)
District of Columbia	18	16	21	18	Yes	Yes	3 days	None
Florida	18	16	21	21	Yes	Yes	3 days	None
Georgia	18	16	18	18	Yes	Yes	None (b)	None (o)
Hawaii	16	16	18	18	Yes	Yes	None	None
Idaho	16	16	18	18	Yes	Yes	None (p)	None
Illinois (a)	—(e)	15(e)	18	18	Yes	Yes	None	None
Indiana	17	17	18	18	Yes	No	3 days	None
Iowa	16(e)	16(e)	18	18	Yes	Yes	3 days	None
Kansas	—(e)²	—(e)²	18	18	Yes	Yes	3 days	None
Kentucky	18	16	18	18	Yes	No	3 days	None
Louisiana (a)	18	16	18	18	Yes	No	None	72 hours
Maine	16	16	18	18	No	No	5 days	None
Maryland	18	16	21	18	None	None	48 hours	None
Massachusetts	—²	—²	18	18	Yes	Yes	3 days	None
Michigan (a)	—	16	18	18	Yes	No	3 days	None
Minnesota	—	16(e)	18	18	None	. . .	5 days	None
Mississippi (b)	17	15	21	21	Yes	. . .	3 days	None
Missouri	15	15	18	18	Yes	Yes	3 days	None
Montana	—²	—²	18	18	Yes	Yes	5 days	None
Nebraska	18	16	18	18	Yes	Yes	5 days	None
Nevada	18	16	21	18	None	None	None	None
New Hampshire (a)	14(e)	13(e)	18	18	Yes	Yes	5 days	None
New Jersey (a)	—	16	18	18	Yes	Yes	72 hours	None
New Mexico	16	16	21	21	Yes	Yes	None	None
New York	16	14	18	18	Yes	No	None	24 hrs.(h)
North Carolina (a)	16	16	18	18	Yes	Yes	None	None
North Dakota (a)	—²	15	18	18	Yes	. . .	None	None
Ohio (a)	18	16	18	18	Yes	Yes	5 days	None
Oklahoma	16	16	18	18	Yes	No	None (f)	. . .
Oregon	18 (e)	15 (e)	18	18	Yes	No	7 days	None
Pennsylvania	16	16	18	18	Yes	Yes	3 days	None
Rhode Island (a) (b)	18	16	18	18	Yes	No	None	None
South Carolina	16	14	18	18	None	None	24 hrs.	None
South Dakota	18	16	18	18	Yes	Yes	None	None
Tennessee (b)	16	16	21	21	Yes	Yes	3 days	None
Texas	16	16	18	18	Yes	Yes	None	None
Utah (a)	16	14	21	18	Yes	Yes	None	None
Vermont (a)	18	16	18	18	Yes	. . .	None	5 days
Virginia (a)	16	16	18	18	Yes	Yes (r)	None	None
Washington	17	17	18	18	(d)	. . .	3 days	None
West Virginia	18²	16	18	18	Yes	No	3 days	None
Wisconsin	18	16	18	18	Yes	Yes	5 days	None
Wyoming	18	16	21	21	Yes	Yes	None	None
Puerto Rico	16	16	21	21	(f)	None	None	None
Virgin Islands	16	14	21	18	None	None	8 days	None

Many states have additional special requirements; contact individual state.
(a) Special laws applicable to non-residents. (b) Special laws applicable to those under 21 years; Alabama: bond required if male is under 21, female under 18. (c) 24 hours if one or both parties resident of state; 96 hours if both parties are non-residents. (d) None, but male must file affidavit. (e) Parental consent plus Court's consent required. (f) None, but a medical certificate is required. (g) Wait for license from time blood test is taken; Arizona, 48 hours. (h) Marriage may not be solemnized within 10 days from date of blood test. (j) If either under 21; Idaho, 3 days; Oklahoma, 72 hrs. (x) May be waived. (1) 3 days if both applicants are under 18 or female is pregnant. (2) Statute provides for obtaining license with parental or court consent with no state minimum age. (3) If either party is under 18, 3 days. (4) Under 16, with parental and court consent. Delaware; Female under 18. (o) All those between 19-21 cannot waive 3 day waiting period. (p) If either under 18—wait full 3 days. (q) If under stated age court consent required. (r) Virginia blood test form must be used.

Grounds for Divorce

Source: Compiled by William E. Mariano, Council on Marriage Relations, Inc., 110 East 42nd Street, New York, N.Y. 10017 (as of Oct. 1, 1976). Persons contemplating divorce should study latest decisions or secure legal advice before initiating proceedings since different interpretations or exceptions in each case can change the conclusion reached.

*Exceptions are to be noted.

State	Cruelty	Desertion	Non-support	Alcohol	Felony	Impotency	Pregnancy at marriage	Drug addiction	Fraudulent contract	Other causes	Residence time	Time between interlocut'y and final decrees
Alabama	X	X	X	X	X	X		X		Q-K-W-F-MM	1 year*	None-R
Alaska	X	X		X	X	X		X		F-K-B	1 year	None
Arizona								X		QQ	1 year	None
Arkansas	X		X	X	X	X				B-Y-K-DD	90 days	None
California	X									K-KK	3 months*	None
Colorado										QQ	6 months	6 months
Connecticut	X	X		X	X				X	K-F-QQ	1 year*	None
Delaware		X				X				QQ	2 years	3 months
Dist. of Columbia		X			X				X	Y-Z	1 year	None
Florida										QQ-K	6 months	None
Georgia	X	X	X	X	X	X	X	X		K-M-AA-QQ	6 months	None
Hawaii										QQ	1 year	'
Idaho	X	X	X	X	X	X		X		X-K	6 weeks	None
Illinois	X	X		X	X	X		X		DD	6 months*	None
Indiana					X					K-QQ	6 months	None
Iowa										MM	1 year*	None-S
Kansas	X		X	X	X	X	X			K-CC-DD	60 days	None-T
Kentucky										QQ	180 days	None
Louisiana					X					X-Z	1 year*	None
Maine	X		X	X	X	X		X		X-KK	6 months	None
Maryland		X			X					Y-K	1 year	None
Massachusetts	X		X	X	X	X		X		LL	2 years*	6 mos.
Michigan										MM	1 year*	None
Minnesota								X		K-W-OO-QQ	1 year*	None-T
Mississippi	X	X		X	X	X	X	X		K-M-DD	1 year*	None-U
Missouri	X	X	X	X	X	X	X			B-J	1 year	None
Montana	X	X	X	X	X					K-KK	1 year	None*
Nebraska										QQ	1 year	6 months
Nevada										K-Y-F	6 weeks	None
New Hampshire	X	X	X	X	X					D-GG-HH-II-KK	1 year*	None
New Jersey	X	X		X	X			X		NN-K-Y	1 year*	None
New Mexico	X	X		X						F	6 months	None
New York	X	X								X-Z*	1 year	
North Carolina										Q-K-X	6 months	None
North Dakota	X	X	X	X	X					K-KK	1 year	None
Ohio	X	X	X		X				X	BB-CC-DD	6 months	None
Oklahoma	X	X	X	X	X	X			X	F-K-BB-CC	6 months	None
Oregon									X	KK	6 months*	90 days
Pennsylvania	X	X		X	X				X	B-M-DD-K-Y	1 year*	None
Rhode Island	X	X	X	X	X			X		H-X	2 years*	6 months
South Carolina	X	X	X	X						Y	1 year	None
South Dakota	X	X	X	X	X						1 year*	None
Tennessee	X	X	X	X	X	X		X		A-DD-EE	6 months*	None
Texas	X	X	X		X					K-X-F-PP	1 year	None-T
Utah	X	X	X	X	X					W-K	3 months	3 mos.*
Vermont	X	X	X	X	X					Y-K	6 months	3 mos.-O*
Virginia		X			X			X		B-X	1 year	None-U*
Washington									X	QQ	6 months	None
West Virginia	X	X	X	X	X					X-K	2 years*²	None
Wisconsin	X	X	X	X	X					Y-Z-K	6 months	None-T
Wyoming	X	X	X	X	X	X	X	X		B-J-K	60 days	None

(1.) Determined by court order. (2.) No minimum residence required in adultery cases. (A) Violence. (B) Indignities. (D) Joining religious order disbelieving in marriage. (E) unchaste behavior after marriage. (F) Incompatibility. (H) Any gross misbehavior or wickedness. (I) Wife being a prostitute. (J) Husband being a vagrant. (K) 5-yrs. insanity; permanent insanity in Utah; incurable insanity in Calif. Exceptions 1 yr. Wis.; 18 mos. Alaska; 2 yrs. Ga., Ha., Ind., N.J., Nev., Ore., Wash., and Wyo.; 3 yrs. Ark., N.C., Fla., Tex., Minn., Colo., Kan., Hawaii, Md., Miss., W. Va.; 6 yrs. Idaho. (M) Consanguinity. (N) In cruelty cases, one yr. to remarry. (O) Plaintiff, 6 mos.; defendant 2 yrs. to remarry. (P) If guilty spouse is sentenced to infamous punishment. (Q) Crime against nature. (R) Sixty days to remarry. (S) One year to remarry; Hawaii one year with minor child. Except Iowa, 90 days. (T) Six months to remarry; in Kan. 60 days. (U) Adultery cases, remarriage in discretion of court. (W) Separation for 2 yrs. after decree for same in Ala. and Minn.; 3 yrs. in Utah; 4 yrs. in N.J.; 18 mos. in N.H.; 5 yrs. in Md. (X) Separation, no cohabitation—5 yrs. Exceptions La., Va., Wyo., W. Va. 2 yrs.; Tex. and Maine 3 yrs.; Nev. and N.C. 1 yr. and R.I. 10 yrs. (Y) Separation, no cohabitation—3 years. Exceptions: Vt., Wash., 2 yrs.; Del., Mo., and N.J. 18 mos.; N.Y., Nev., Va., D.C. and Wis. 1 yr.; (Z) Separation for 2 yrs. after decree for Dist. of Col.; 1 yr. for N.Y., Wis. and La., per decree in Ha. (AA) Mental incapacity at time of marriage. (BB) Procurement of out-of-state divorce. (CC) Gross neglect of duty. (DD) Bigamy. (EE) Attempted homicide. (FF) Plaintiff under age at time of marriage. (GG) Treatment which injures health or endangers reason. (HH) Wife without state for 10 yrs. (II) Wife in state 2 yrs.; husband never in state and has intent to become citizen of foreign country. (JJ) Seven years absence. (KK) Irreconcilable differences. (LL) Life sentence dissolves marriage. (MM) Breakdown of marriage with no reasonable likelihood of preservation. (NN) Deviate sexual conduct. (OO) Course of conduct detrimental to the marriage relationship of party seeking divorce. (PP) Incompatibility without regard to fault. (QQ) Marriage irretrievably broken.

Adultery is either grounds for divorce or evidence of irreconcilable differences and a breakdown of the marriage, in all states. The plaintiff can invariably remarry in the same state where he or she procured a decree of divorce or annulment. Not so the defendant, who is barred in certain states for some offenses. After a period of time has elapsed even the offender can apply for special permission. The U.S. Supreme Court in a 5 to 4 opinion ruled April 18, 1949, that one-sided quick divorces could be challenged as illegal if notice of the action was not served on the divorced partner within the divorcing states, excepting where the partner was represented at the proceedings. **Enoch Arden Laws.** Disappearance and unknown to be alive—Conn. 7 years absence; N. H., 2 years; N. Y., 5 years (called dissolution); Vt., 7 years.

Marriage Information—Canada

Source: Compiled from information provided by the various Provincial Government departments and agencies concerned. (As of June, 1975)

Marriageable age, by provinces, for both males and females with and without consent of parents or guardians. In some provinces, the court has authority, given special circumstances, to marry young couples below the minimum age. Most provinces waive the blood test requirement and the waiting period varies across the provinces.

Province	With consent Men	With consent Women	Without consent Men	Without consent Women	Blood Test Other Province Required	Blood Test Other Province Accepted	Wait for License	Wait after License
Newfoundland.....	—	—	19	19	—	—	—	—
Prince Edward Island	16	16	18	18	Yes	Yes	5 days	None
Nova Scotia.......	(1)	(1)	19	19	None	None	5 days	None
New Brunswick.....	14-18	14-18	18+	18+	None	None	5 days	None
Quebec..........	14	12	18	18	None	—	—	None
Ontario....:......	14	14[2]	18	18	None	—	None[3]	3 days
Manitoba.........	16	16	18	18	Yes	Yes	None	24 hours
Saskatchewan.....	15	15	18	18	Yes	Yes	5 days	None
Alberta..........	18−	18−	18+	18+	Yes[4]	Yes[5]	None[6]	None
British Columbia....	16[7]	16[7]	19	19	None	None	2 days[8]	None
Yukon Territory.....	15	15	19	19	None	None	None	24 hours
Northwest Territories	15	15	19	19	None	Yes	None	None

(1) There is no statutory minimum age in the Province. Anyone under the age of 19 years must have consent for marriage and no person under the age of 16 years may be married without authorization of a Family Court Judge and in addition must have the necessary consent of the parent or guardian. (2) Women under 14 years also require a medical certificate as to necessity of marriage to prevent illegitimacy of offspring. (3) Special requirements applicable to non-residents. (4) Applies only to applicants under 60 years of age. (5) This is upon filing of negative lab report indicating blood test was taken within 14 days preceding date of application for license. (6) Exception where consent is required by mail; depending receipt of divorce documents, etc. (7) Persons under 16 years of age (no minimum age specified) may also be married if they have obtained, in addition to the usual consent from parents or guardian, an Order from a Judge of the Supreme or County Court in this Province. (8) Including day of application, e.g., a license applied for on a Monday cannot be issued until Wednesday.

Grounds for Divorce in Canada

Source: Government of Canada Divorce Act

The grounds for divorce in Canada are the same for all the provinces and its territories. There are two categories of offence.

A. Marital Offence:
Adultery
Sodomy
Bestiality
Rape
Homosexual act
Subsequent marriage
Physical cruelty
Mental cruelty

B. Marriage Breakdown by Reason of:

Imprisonment for aggregate period of not less than 3 years
Imprisonment for not less than 2 years on sentence of death or sentence of 10 years or more
Addiction to alcohol
Addiction to narcotics
Whereabouts of spouse unknown
Non-consummation
Separation for not less than 3 years
Desertion by Petitioner for not less than 5 years
Residence time: Domicile in Canada
Time between interlocutory and final decree:
    normally 3 months before final can be applied for.

Number of Active Civilian Physicians, and Population per Physician, Canada

Source: Health Programs Branch, Health and Welfare Canada, December 31, 1975

Province	Number[1]	Population per Physician[1]	Province	Number[1]	Population per Physician[1]
Newfoundland....................	732	757	Alberta........................	2,732	660
Prince Edward Island...............	120	1,000	British Columbia..................	4,309	576
Nova Scotia......................	1,351	614	Yukon........................	23	913
New Brunswick...................	744	919	Northwest Territories...............	30	1,267
Quebec........................	10,752	579	Not Specified....................	1	—
Ontario........................	14,871	557			
Manitoba.......................	1,738	589	Canada........................	38,666	595
Saskatchewan...................	1,263	736	(1) Preliminary		

Canadian Motor Vehicle Traffic Deaths

Source: Statistics Canada

Province	Number 1974	Number 1973	Province	Number 1974	Number 1973
TOTAL..........	**6,290**	**6,706**	Ontario........................	1,748	1,959
Newfoundland..................	117	98	Manitoba.......................	201	231
Prince Edward Island.............	42	43	Saskatchewan..................	306	251
Nova Scotia....................	268	277	Alberta.......................	573	511
New Brunswick.................	287	265	British Columbia................	844	825
Quebec.......................	1,882	2,209	Yukon........................	8	19
			Northwest Terr.................	14	18

U.S. Building Fire Losses By Causes

Source: National Fire Protection Assn. Copyright 1975

These estimated figures are intended to show the relative order of magnitude of fire losses by cause, and to indicate year-to-year trends. While they are reasonable approximations based on experience in typical states, they should not be taken as exact records for each class. The figures by themselves do not show the relative safety in use of various types of materials, devices, fuels, or services, and they should not be used for that purpose.

Cause	No. of Fires	Estimated Loss
Heating and Cooking Equipment.	160,000	$ 199,300,000
Defective or misused equipment.	93,300	$137,300,000
Chimneys and flues	14,000	19,300,000
Hot ashes and coals.	12,600	2,000,000
Combustibles near heaters and stoves.	40,100	40,700,000
Smoking-Related.	121,600	136,300,000
Electrical.	165,000	363,500,000
Wiring distribution equipment.	112,200	253,300,000
Motors and appliances[1].	52,800	110,200,000
Trash Burning.	177,000	5,000,000
Flammable Liquids[1].	56,100	53,200,000
Open Flames and Sparks[1].	77,500	147,600,000
Sparks and embers.	13,300	7,900,000
Welding and cutting.	11,600	48,900,000
Friction, sparks from machinery.	11,900	19,100,000
Thawing pipes.	5,800	15,300,000
Other open flames	34,900	56,400,000
Lightning.	16,600	39,100,000
Children and Fire.	59,600	100,100,000
Exposure	44,200	26,200,000
Incendiary and Suspicious.	114,400	563,000,000
Spontaneous Ignition.	11,000	41,200,000
Gas Fires and Explosions[1].	11,900	41,900,000
Fireworks and Explosives	4,200	38,100,000
Miscellaneous Known Causes.	91,700	268,500,000
Unknown Causes.	159,200	1,237,000,000
TOTAL BUILDING FIRES.	1,270,000	$3,260,000,000

[1]Does not include fires originating in heating and cooking equipment.

INTERPOL (International Criminal Police Organization)

The United States is one of 120 countries that are members of INTERPOL, the International Criminal Police Organization. United States participation in INTERPOL was authorized by Congress in 1938. Because of the Treasury Dept.'s activities in the suppression of counterfeiting, smuggling and the narcotics traffic, all of which have international ramifications, that department was designated as U.S. representative to INTERPOL in 1958.

Each member nation has one vote at a general assembly of INTERPOL held annually at a site chosen by the delegates at the previous year's assembly. The chairman of the U.S. delegation attending such meetings is the Assistant Secretary of the Treasury (Enforcement and Operations).

INTERPOL dates from 1914, but World War I brought suspension of all its activities until 1923. The organization's first constitution was drawn up in that year. Files on international criminals were built up gradually to a point where their value to the police of member nations became apparent. During World War II the files disappeared from Vienna, where the General Secretariat of INTERPOL was located.

The organization was reconstituted at the end of World War II. The General Secretariat was moved to Paris and is now located in the Parisian suburb of Saint-Cloud. The Secretariat functions as a central depository for fingerprints, photographs and other records of international criminals. It also operates an international radio network to 54 of the member countries.

Interpol does not employ any investigators as such. Foreign requirements for investigation are referred to the National Central Bureaus, the offices established in each country to handle INTERPOL coordination. Scotland Yard is the National Central Bureau for the United Kingdom; the Surete in France, the Italiano Di Polizia in Italy, and the Canberra Commonwealth police in Australia serve as the National Central Bureaus for those countries.

In the United States the U.S. National Central Bureau is staffed by U.S. Federal Law Enforcement Agents on loan from the Secret Service, Customs Service, Bureau of Alcohol, Tobacco, and Firearms, and the Drug Enforcement Administration. All inquiries, both domestic and foreign, are channeled through the National Central Bureau at the Treasury Dept. in Washington. Unless foreign requirements for investigation in the United States involve federal jurisdiction or interest, they are referred to local and state police agencies for investigation. All U.S. enforcement agencies may call upon Interpol Washington for investigation in other member countries.

Locations of Federal Detention Areas

Source: U.S. Bureau of Prisons

Penitentiaries; Atlanta, Ga.; Leavenworth, Kan.; Lewisburg, Pa.; McNeil Island, Wash.; Marion, Ill.; Terre Haute, Ind. **Reformatories:** El Reno, Okla.; Petersburg, Va.; Women, Alderson, W.Va. **Medical center:** Springfield, Mo.; Hospital; Maintenance unit. **Prison camps:** Eglin Air Force Base, Florida; Montgomery, Ala.; Safford, Ariz.; Allenwood, Pa. **Correctional Institutions:** Danbury, Conn.; La Tuna, Tex.; Lompoc, Cal.; Texarkana, Tex.; Milan, Mich.; Tallahassee, Fla; Seagoville, Tex.; Terminal Island, Cal.; Sandstone, Minn.; Ft. Worth, Tex. **Detention headquarters center:** Florence, Ariz. **Institutions for juvenile and youth offenders:** Ashland, Ky.; Englewood, Col.; Morgantown, W. Va.; Pleasonton, Cal. **Community reament Centers:** Detroit, Mich.; Chicago, Ill.; Los Angeles, Cal.; Kansas City, Mo.; Atlanta, Ga.; Houston, Tex.; Oakland, Cal.; New York City.; Dallas, Tex.; Phonix, Ariz.

Federal Bureau of Investigation

The Federal Bureau of Investigation (FBI) is the investigative arm of the Department of Justice, and is located at 9th St. and Pennsylvania Ave., Washington, D. C., 20535. It investigates all violations of Federal laws except those specifically assigned to some other agency by legislative action, such violations including counterfeiting, and internal revenue, postal, and customs violations. It also investigates espionage, sabotage, treason, and other matters affecting internal security, as well as kidnaping, transportation of stolen goods across state lines, interstate traffic in prostitution, and violations of the Federal bank and atomic energy laws.

The FBI collects and classifies police and crime reports for the nation. While this division is of great usefulness in detecting criminals, it serves a wider purpose in recording the fingerprints of many other citizens who voluntarily make this record.

The FBI has 59 field divisions in the principal cities of the country. *Consult telephone directories for location and phone numbers.*

An applicant for the position of Special Agent of the FBI must be a citizen of the U.S. at least 23 and under 35 years old and graduate of a state-accredited resident law school or from a resident four-year college with a major in accounting with at least one year of practical accounting and/

or auditing experience. In addition, applicants with a four-year resident college degree with a major in certain areas or 3 years specialized experience of a professional, executive, or complex investigative nature are presently being considered on a limited basis. An agent gets 15 weeks of training, during which he learns techniques of investigation and arrest and recognition of evidence.

Clarence M. Kelley, former FBI agent and professional law enforcement officer, became Director on July 9, 1973.

U. S. Govt. Crime Reports

Source: Federal Bureau of Investigation

Offense	1975 est.	Percent over[1] 1974	1970
Murder	20,510	−1.0	+28.2
Forcible rape	56,090	+1.3	+47.6
Robbery	464,970	+5.1	+32.9
Aggravated assault	484,710	+6.2	+44.7
Burglary	3,252,100	+7.0	+47.5
Larceny-theft	5,977,700	+13.6	+41.5
Auto theft	1,000,500	+2.4	+7.8
Total	11,256,600	+9.8	+39.0

[1] Percent by which the rate of crime per 100,000 population increased in 1975 over 1974 and 1970.

Crime in the U.S. Increases 10% in 1975

Crime in the U.S., as measured by the Crime Index offenses, increased by 10% in 1975 over 1974. Violent crimes were up 5%, with forcible rape reports up 1% and aggravated assault (assault with a dangerous weapon, including the fists) was up 6%. Murders decreased 1% but robberies were up 5%. Property crimes went up 10%, with burglaries increasing by 7%, larceny-theft up 14%, and auto theft up 2%. Serious crime in cities of 250,000 or more people was up 7%, while crime in suburban areas grew by 10%.

Reported Crime, 1974-75, by Size of Place

Source: Federal Bureau of Investigation, Uniform Crime Reports - 1975

Population group (1975 estimates)	Crime Index total	Violent crime[1]	Property crime[2]	Murder and non-negligent man-slaughter	Forcible rape	Robbery	Aggra-vated assault	Burglary-breaking or entering	Motor vehicle theft
Total All Agencies: 8,523 agencies; total population 187,273,000:									
1974	9,437,431	912,779	8,524,652	19,006	51,723	425,528	416,522	2,782,613	911,470
1975	10,255,038	953,993	9,301,045	18,830	52,350	445,035	437,778	2,948,906	924,739
Percent change	+8.7	+4.5	+9.1	−.9	+1.2	+4.6	+5.1	+6.0	+1.5
Total Cities: 6,410 cities; total population 133,051,000:									
1974	7,779,483	782,327	6,997,156	14,993	40,976	393,233	333,125	2,193,784	790,976
1975	8,440,481	814,694	7,625,787	14,764	41,560	410,426	347,944	2,318,535	804,080
Percent change	+8.5	+4.1	+9.0	−1.5	+1.4	+4.4	+4.4	+5.7	+1.7
58 cities over 250,000; population 42,209,000:									
1974	3,198,814	472,312	2,726,502	9,212	23,761	276,481	162,858	959,060	418,738
1975	3,438,521	485,650	2,952,871	9,015	23,450	286,097	167,088	999,657	428,503
Percent change	+7.5	+2.8	+8.3	−2.1	−1.3	+3.5	+2.6	+4.2	+2.3
101 cities, 100,000 to 250,000; population 14,505,000:									
1974	1,000,847	83,711	917,136	1,832	4,857	38,101	38,921	292,781	102,512
1975	1,076,447	86,470	989,977	1,715	5,047	39,808	39,900	306,020	98,074
Percent change	+7.6	+3.3	+7.9	−6.4	+3.9	+4.5	+2.5	+4.5	−4.3
267 cities, 50,000 to 100,000; population 18,464,000:									
1974	1,065,072	76,250	988,822	1,241	4,291	31,680	-39,038	291,622	95,392
1975	1,160,760	82,222	1,078,538	1,314	4,718	34,167	42,023	315,273	96,090
Percent change	+9.0	+7.8	+9.1	+5.9	+10.0	+7.9	+7.6	+8.1	+.7
571 cities, 25,000 to 50,000; population 19,857,000:									
1974	1,011,702	64,664	947,038	1,123	3,457	24,087	35,997	262,090	80,470
1975	1,100,892	·67,505	1,033,387	1,152	3,697	25,266	37,390	279,428	83,933
Percent change	+8.8	+4.4	+9.1	+2.6	+6.9	+4.9	+3.9	+6.6	+4.3
1,357 cities, 10,000 to 25,000; population 21,365,000:									
1974	907,527	51,044	856,483	955	2,794	15,578	31,717	234,704	60,376
1975	1,002,637	55,794	946,843	925	2,827	17,006	35,036	252,504	63,319
Percent change	+10.5	+9.3	+10.6	−3.1	+1.2	+9.2	+10.5	+7.6	+4.9
4,056 cities under 10,000; population 16,650,000:									
1974	595,521	34,346	561,175	630	1,816	7,306	24,594	153,527	33,488
1975	661,224	37,053	624,171	643	1,821	8,082	26,507	165,653	34,161
Percent change	+11.0	+7.9	+11.2	+2.1	- +.3	+10.6	+7.8	+7.9	+2.0
Suburban Area: 3,719 agencies; population 66,474,000:									
1974	2,762,295	182,651	2,579,644	3,665	12,615	59,019	107,352	815,109	220,108
1975	3,029,127	194,958	2,834,169	3,656	12,948	63,183	115,171	874,020	224,349
Percent change	+9.7	+6.7	+9.9	−.2	+2.6	+7.1	+7.3	+7.2	+1.9
Rural Area: 1,640 agencies; population 23,013,000:									
1974	452,866	37,122	415,744	1,750	2,953	5,150	27,269	178,680	23,268
1975	488,895	38,986	449,909	1,821	2,891	5,523	28,751	190,619	24,548
Percent change	+8.0	+5.0	+8.2	+4.1	−2.1	+7.2	+5.4	+6.7	+5.5

Reported Crime in Metropolitan Areas, 1975

Source: Federal Bureau of Investigation, Uniform Crime Reports—1975

The 27 Standard Metropolitan Statistical Areas listed below are those which appear most frequently among the top 30 cities in per capita reported crime rate for each of 7 kinds of major crime: the 5 listed below plus forcible rape and aggravated assault.

The rates are for reported crimes only; they are not an accurate index of crimes actually committed. In many metropolitan areas an unknown number of crimes go unreported by victims. This is especially true of the crimes of rape, burglary, and larceny. Additionally, figures are often distorted for political reasons.

The number in parentheses following the city name indicates the number of categories (including forcible rape and aggravated assault) in which the city appears among the top 30.

The numbers in parentheses following crime rate figures give that city's rank in that category of crime. If no number appears, the city is not among the top 30 in that category. The cities are listed in order of the diversity and violence of criminal activity.

Rate per 100,000 population

Metropolitan Areas	Total[1]	Violent[2]	Property[3]	Murder[4]	Robbery	Burglary	Larceny	Auto Theft
Las Vegas, Nev. (7)	10,286.4 (1)	988.8 (6)	9,297.7 (2)	15.8(24)	466.6 (5)	3,319.2 (1)	5,292.9 (5)	685.6(20)
Miami, Fla. (6).............	9,482.1 (4)	1,158.1 (2)	8,323.9 (6)	18.3(10)	457.0 (6)	2,855.8 (6)	4,772.9(13)	695.2(18)
Little Rock-N. Lit. Rock, Ark. (5).	8,442.4(10)	798.2(12)	7,644.3(12)	17.5(18)	319.7(20)	2,397.8(17)	4,797.6(12)	448.8
Fayetteville, N.C. (5).........	5,995.6	964.4 (8)	5,031.1	18.0(12)	284.8(28)	2,358.4(21)	2,247.9	.424.8
Los Angeles-Long Beach, Cal. (5)........	7,201.5	927.1 (9)	6,274.4	14.3	421.2 (8)	2,332.9(24)	3,078.6	863.0(12)
Orlando, Fla. (4).............	8,326.7(12)	724.7(25)	7,601.9(13)	15.1	189.8	2,759.9 (7)	4,358.7(30)	483.3
Saginaw, Mich. (4)..........	7,710.7(25)	1,008.1 (4)	6,702.6	20.5 (5)	392.2(10)	2,226.0	4,239.2	237.3
New York, N.Y. (4)..........	6,967.3	1,423.2 (1)	5,544.1	18.0(12)	889.4 (1)	2,081.0	2,514.0	949.1 (8)
Savannah, Ga. (4)..........	7,188.5	789.3(13)	6,399.2	21.1 (3)	267.8	2,492.8(13)	3,559.2	347.2
Memphis, Tenn. (4).........	7,055.0	704.1(27)	6,350.9	15.5(30)	362.9(16)	2,339.8(23)	3,493.7	517.4
W. Palm Beach-Boca-Raton, Fla. (3)........	8,645.6 (7)	763.2(16)	7,882.4 (9)	7.7	202.1	2,507.6(11)	5,003.3 (8)	371.5
Albuquerque, N.M. (3).......	7,861.1(20)	732.3(20)	7,128.8(23)	10.9	233.2	2,479.8(14)	4,220.6	428.4
Daytona Beach, Fla. (3).....	10,056.1 (2)	726.1(24)	9,330.0 (1)	11.5	273.9	3,266.1 (2)	5,603.1 (1)	460.8
Flint, Mich. (3).............	7,583.9(28)	768.8(15)	6,815.2	10.8	225.2	1,994.9	4,446.3(28)	374.0
Pensacola, Fla. (3)..........	7,928.2(18)	673.9	7,254.3(18)	11.2	184.9	2,536.3 (9)	4,205.1	512.9
Fresno, Cal. (3).............	8,415.9(11)	612.5	7,803.4(10)	12.7	207.7	2,963.1 (4)	4,142.0	698.4(17)
Tucson, Ariz. (3)............	9,224.7 (5)	594.9	8,629.8 (5)	8.0	198.2	3,051.4 (3)	5,009.3 (7)	569.1
Portland, Oreg. (3)..........	7,776.0(24)	571.0	7,205.0(22)	6.9	221.1	2,382.3(19)	4,185.1	637.6(26)
Denver-Boulder, Colo. (3).....	7,806.5(22)	570.2	7,236.3(20)	8.1	249.9	2,448.3(15)	4,179.2	608.8(30)
Tyler, Tex. (3).............	6,112.5	1,066.1 (3)	5,046.4	19.6 (6)	306.6(23)	1,981.3	2,691.4	373.7
Baltimore, Md. (3)..........	6,606.4	965.2 (7)	5,641.2	14.8	492.1 (3)	1,542.4	3,474.8	624.0(28)
Jacksonville, Fla. (3)........	7,362.6	733.7(19)	6,628.8	15.5(30)	270.9	2,255.9	3,971.0	402.0
St. Louis, Mo. (3)..........	7,103.0	719.7(26)	6,383.3	161.1(23)	385.2(11)	2,019.0	3,612.1	752.2(14)
New Orleans, La. (3)........	5,453.4	702.3(29)	4,751.1	18.2(11)	371.6(15)	1,440.9	2,607.1	703.1(16)

[1]Other metro areas among the top 30 in total reported crime (predominantly property crime): Phoenix, Ariz. (3); Fort Lauderdale-Hollywood, Fla. (6); Gainesville, Fla. (8); Bakersfield, Cal. (9); Stockton, Cal. (13); Sacramento, Cal. (16); Modesto, Cal. (17); Tallahassee, Fla. (21); Ann Arbor, Mich. (23); Yakima, Wash. (26); Kalamazoo, Mich. (27); Kenosha, Wis. (29); and Dallas-Ft. Worth, Tex. (30).

[2]Violent crime includes murder and non-negligent manslaughter, forcible rape, robbery, and aggravated assault. Other metro areas in the top 30 in violent crime are: Lafayette, La. (1); Baton Rouge, La. (14); Washington, D.C. (18); Charleston, S.C. (21); Albany, Ga. (22); Kansas City, Mo. (23); Galveston-Texas City, Tex. (28); and Chicago, Ill. (30).

[3]Property crime includes burglary, larceny and auto theft. Other metro areas in the top 30 in reported property crime are: Phoenix, Ariz. (3); Fort Lauderdale-Hollywood, Fla. (4); Gainesville, Fla. (7); Bakersfield, Cal. (8); Stockton, Cal. (11); Modesto, Cal. (14); Kenosha, Wis. (16); Ann Arbor, Mich. (19); Tallahassee, Fla. (21); Dallas-Ft. Worth, Tex. (24); Lubbock, Tex. (25); Yakima, Wash. (26); Kalamazoo, Mich. (27); Eugene, Ore. (28); and San Jose, Cal. (30).

[4]Of the top 30 cities in murder, all but 5 are in the South.

Crime Rates by States

Source: Federal Bureau of Investigation, Uniform Crime Reports — 1975
(Rates per 100,000 population)

State	Total	Violent	Property	Murder	Rape	Robbery	Assault	Burglary	Larceny	Auto Theft
Alabama...........	3,472.5	392.9	3,079.6	16.0	20.4	123.0	233.5	1,163.8	1,645.5	270.3
Alaska............	6,196.6	539.8	5,656.8	12.2	44.6	129.5	353.4	1,214.5	3,522.4	919.9
Arizona...........	8,341.5	547.8	7,793.7	8.6	35.5	170.0	333.8	2,529.9	4,747.7	516.1
Arkansas..........	3,540.1	348.3	3,191.9	10.1	25.9	87.6	224.7	1,077.1	1,947.0	167.8
California..........	7,204.6	655.4	6,549.2	10.4	41.6	282.4	321.0	2,217.3	3,703.7	628.2
Colorado..........	6,675.5	463.1	6,212.4	7.4	41.5	174.1	240.1	2,001.2	3,744.0	467.2
Connecticut........	4,957.0	268.4	4,688.6	3.9	12.4	131.5	120.6	1,512.6	2,603.6	572.4
Delaware..........	6,668.2	392.1	6,276.2	7.3	18.1	157.2	209.5	1,826.3	3,926.9	523.0
Florida............	7,721.2	688.5	7,032.7	13.5	35.7	239.7	399.6	2,349.6	4,240.4	442.6
Georgia...........	4,625.9	459.0	4,167.0	14.4	25.4	166.5	252.6	1,580.7	2,248.5	337.7
Hawaii............	6,026.6	218.4	5,808.2	7.7	24.7	127.6	58.3	1,826.8	3,457.7	523.7
Idaho.............	4,141.1	203.7	3,937.4	5.2	16.1	42.0	140.4	1,063.0	2,651.3	223.0
Illinois............	5,382.0	549.7	4,832.3	10.6	25.7	276.2	237.2	1,291.1	3,030.0	511.1
Indiana...........	4,911.4	332.8	4,578.6	8.5	24.3	156.8	143.3	1,376.4	2,813.9	388.3
Iowa..............	3,908.7	140.7	3,768.0	2.5	10.3	53.5	74.4	818.5	2,719.8	229.7
Kansas...........	4,747.0	278.2	4,468.8	5.4	17.2	92.8	162.8	1,369.5	2,862.8	236.4

continued

State	Total	Violent	Property	Murder	Rape	Robbery	Assault	Burglary	Larceny	Auto Theft
Kentucky	3,264.4	264.0	3,000.3	10.2	15.4	103.2	135.3	962.8	1,774.2	263.4
Louisiana	4,123.4	478.4	3,645.0	12.6	23.7	153.1	289.0	1,114.6	2,191.8	338.5
Maine	3,959.6	219.5	3,740.1	2.8	10.4	36.4	169.8	1,361.5	2,167.9	210.8
Maryland	5,907.5	709.8	5,197.7	10.7	31.5	344.2	323.4	1,413.2	3,267.6	516.9
Massachusetts	6,077.8	442.6	5,635.3	4.2	19.2	227.0	192.2	1,712.5	2,351.7	1,571.1
Michigan	6,800.3	685.7	6,114.6	11.9	38.1	353.1	282.7	1,891.8	3,572.9	649.9
Minnesota	4,298.7	207.0	4,091.7	3.3	18.6	103.6	81.4	1,193.1	2,516.1	382.5
Mississippi	2,410.7	315.9	2,094.8	13.9	16.5	54.6	230.9	784.2	1,181.3	129.3
Missouri	5,397.8	493.8	4,904.0	10.6	25.2	244.7	213.3	1,512.6	2,924.7	466.7
Montana	4,188.9	189.6	3,999.3	5.2	14.3	41.4	128.6	875.1	2,814.8	309.4
Nebraska	3,614.0	257.8	3,356.2	4.3	19.2	90.4	143.9	760.2	2,365.0	231.0
Nevada	8,152.9	678.7	7,474.2	13.0	47.1	302.5	316.0	2,447.1	4,517.1	510.0
New Hampshire	3,346.6	99.8	3,246.8	2.9	8.7	28.9	59.3	583.1	2,135.7	258.1
New Jersey	5,144.3	413.0	4,731.3	6.8	18.9	222.6	164.6	1,521.2	2,672.5	537.7
New Mexico	5,839.4	534.8	5,304.6	13.3	41.0	126.7	353.8	1,728.7	3,258.8	317.2
New York	5,635.7	856.4	4,779.3	11.0	28.1	516.0	301.3	1,666.6	2,471.0	641.7
North Carolina	3,816.7	436.5	3,380.3	12.4	16.2	82.2	325.6	1,285.1	1,909.2	186.0
North Dakota	2,337.2	53.1	2,284.1	0.8	5.8	14.3	32.1	539.2	1,614.3	130.6
Ohio	4,914.4	408.0	4,506.4	8.1	25.3	220.0	154.6	1,271.4	2,808.6	426.4
Oklahoma	4,578.1	303.3	4,274.8	9.4	27.2	90.2	176.5	1,551.8	2,375.0	348.0
Oregon	6,752.2	438.5	6,313.7	6.2	32.6	130.3	269.4	1,911.6	3,935.9	466.2
Pennsylvania	3,349.4	329.2	3,020.3	6.8	17.4	168.6	136.5	983.3	1,670.0	367.0
Rhode Island	5,643.8	302.3	5,341.5	3.0	10.9	95.9	192.4	1,446.3	2,878.4	1,016.8
South Carolina	4,641.5	511.4	4,130.1	14.7	26.5	110.9	359.3	1,714.2	2,156.3	259.6
South Dakota	2,738.9	205.3	2,533.7	3.7	16.5	31.0	154.0	667.8	1,698.0	167.9
Tennessee	4,270.5	397.0	3,873.5	11.4	26.1	166.8	192.6	1,379.3	2,129.5	364.7
Texas	5,407.2	390.6	5,016.5	13.4	28.0	164.1	185.2	1,665.6	2,963.7	387.2
Utah	5,112.6	231.8	4,880.8	2.7	20.9	79.0	129.2	1,187.8	3,372.6	320.5
Vermont	3,481.1	95.1	3,386.0	2.1	14.6	15.7	62.6	1,100.0	2,112.1	173.9
Virginia	4,546.4	380.9	4,165.6	11.5	24.0	138.5	206.9	1,165.7	2,730.7	269.2
Washington	6,104.9	390.8	5,750.1	5.7	32.7	124.0	228.4	1,723.1	3,641.6	385.4
West Virginia	2,107.8	161.7	1,946.1	7.4	9.3	45.5	99.5	591.0	1,228.7	126.4
Wisconsin	3,975.6	151.8	3,823.9	3.3	10.6	73.4	64.5	918.5	2,665.4	239.9
Wyoming	4,155.9	204.3	3,951.6	10.2	17.1	49.5	127.5	863.4	2,810.7	277.5

Total Arrest Trends by Sex — 1974-75

Source: Federal Bureau of Investigation, Uniform Crime Reports — 1975

Offense charged	Males				Females			
	Total		Under 18		Total		Under 18	
	1975	Percent change 1974-75	1975	Percent change 1974-75	1975	Percent change 1974-75	1975	Percent change 1974-75
Total[1]	5,521,491	+2.0	1,409,358	+1.4	1,071,747	+4.4	380,067	+2.8
Murder and non-negligent manslaughter	12,055	—1.1	1,235	—5.9	2,214	+5.3	138	+27.8
Manslaughter by negligence	2,195	—.3	244	+11.9	286	—9.5	47	+51.6
Forcible rape	18,829	+.9	3,345	—9.5	189	+18.1	49	—18.3
Robbery	108,257	+6.6	37,763	+10.4	8,164	+9.6	3,033	+19.2
Aggravated assault	147,912	+5.2	25,966	+13.1	22,571	+3.1	4,892	+11.6
Burglary—breaking or entering	362,148	+7.3	191,202	+5.6	20,352	+7.1	10,367	+4.7
Larceny—theft	564,272	+6.7	269,415	+1.0	263.471	+10.4	109,298	+3.2
Motor vehicle theft	97,195	—5.3	52,734	—8.1	7,186	+.8	4,192	+1.8
Other assaults	260,253	+7.9	48,411	+11.3	42,219	+9.0	13,129	+13.7
Arson	10,968	+8.6	6,005	+1.8	1,446	+19.2	636	+2.9
Forgery and counterfeiting	34,618	+9.8	4,424	+8.3	14,187	+12.9	1,843	+7.2
Fraud	74,577	+13.9	2,905	+14.1	39,655	+18.0	1,104	+8.1
Embezzlement	4,459	—5.3	451	+24.6	1,497	—8.6	119	+8.2
Stolen property offenses	77,967	+7.4	26,233	+4.3	9,302	+10.8	2,423	+4.2
Vandalism	141,902	+4.1	93,325	—1.4	12,525	+6.8	7,617	+2.1
Weapons: carrying, possessing, etc.	105,148	—2.3	17,729	—1.6	9,099	—1.9	1,196	+12.1
Prostitution and commercialized vice	11,677	—.5	505	—17.6	33,306	—.3	1,525	+12.4
Sex offenses (except forcible rape and prostitution)	41,026	—.2	8,398	—4.2	3,453	—1.8	1,019	—17.6
Narcotic drug laws	366,392	—6.2	86,323	—11.8	59,050	—7.4	16,929	—15.0
Gambling	41,698	+1.8	1,502	—1.3	3,702	—4.6	81	+12.5
Offenses against family, children	38,498	+13.4	3,366	+24.8	5,158	+9.7	2,037	+26.7
Driving under the influence	680,272	+11.6	12,678	+45.7	62,880	+20.5	1,092	+55.1
Liquor laws	190,087	+10.3	72,532	+9.6	32,519	+6.4	18,838	+14.4
Drunkenness	851,599	—8.8	28,311	+6.9	67,725	—7.0	4,438	+9.0
Disorderly conduct	375,178	—.9	84,159	—7.7	98,721	—8.2	16,901	—9.1
Vagrancy	25,670	—13.5	3,880	—14.0	5,605	+6.3	659	—16.3
All other offenses (except traffic)	729,245	+3.4	178,923	+2.6	135,099	+3.4	46,299	—3.0

[1]Totals will not add due to deletion of several minor arrest categories.

Police Roster

Police officers and civilian employees in large cities as of Oct. 31. 1975

City	Officers	Civilian	City	Officers	Civilian	City	Officers	Civilian
Anchorage, Alas....	119	53	Indianapolis, Ind....	1,078	256	Philadelphia, Pa....	8,085	942
Atlanta, Ga........	1,415	453	Jacksonville, Fla....	935	601	Phoenix, Ariz.......	1,527	374
Baltimore, Md......	3,377	570	Jersey City, N.J.....	981	37	Pittsburgh, Pa......	1,411	23
Birmingham, Ala....	644	137	Kansas City, Mo.....	1,246	461	Portland, Ore.......	720	192
Boston, Mass......	2,425	395	Little Rock, Ark.....	278	64	Rochester, N.Y.....	639	137
Bridgeport, Conn...	480.	9	Los Angeles, Cal...	7,532	3,020	Sacramento, Cal....	522	153
Buffalo, N.Y.......	1,288	168	Louisville, Ky.......	799	232	St. Louis, Mo.......	2,173	590
Chicago, Ill.......	13,039	1,795	Memphis, Tenn.....	1,316	319	St. Petersburg, Fla..	480	211
Cincinnati, Ohio....	1,169	134	Miami, Fla.........	645	460	San Antonio, Tex....	1,175	267
Cleveland, Ohio....	1,211	105	Milwaukee, Wisc....	2,128	208	San Bernardino, Cal.	192	61
Columbus, Ohio....	1,145	242	Minneapolis, Minn..	840	114	San Diego, Cal.....	1,070	319
Dallas, Tex.......	1,968	594	Nashville, Tenn.....	874	198	San Francisco, Cal..	1,795	440
Denver, Col.......	1,382	310	Newark, N.J.......	1,565	289	San Jose, Cal......	723	167
Detroit, Mich......	5,404	613	New Orleans, La....	1,647	289	Santa Ana, Cal.....	311	110
Ft. Worth, Tex......	686	139	New York, N.Y......		33,401	Seattle, Wash......	1,085	288
Fresno, Cal.......	304	94	Norfolk, Va........	553	117	Stockton, Cal......	216	81
Gary, Ind.........	359	61	Oakland, Cal.......	697	326	Tampa, Fla........	571	241
Hartford, Conn.....	505	102	Oklahoma City, Okl.	598	122	Toledo, Ohio.......	704	119
Honolulu, Hawaii ...	1,496	337	Omaha, Nebr.......	571	125	Tucson, Ariz.......	506	170
Houston, Tex......	2,598	447	Pasadena, Cal.....	188	90	Washington, D.C....	4,583	808

1,023 Law Enforcement Officers Killed 1966-1975

Source: Uniform Crime Reports (FBI)

Responding to disturbance calls......................	157
Burglaries in progress or pursuing suspect...........	65
Robberies in progress or pursuing suspect...........	205
Attempting other arrests...........................	239
Civil disorders...................................	12
Handling, transporting, custody of prisoners............	47
Investigating suspicious persons and circumstances......	73
Ambush..	82
Mentally deranged...............................	38
Traffic stops....................................	105

Geographically for the period of 1966-1975 the 1,023 officers who were slain in the line of duty were divided in this fashion: Northeast 149; North Central 262; South 412; and West 179. Another 21 officers were killed in outlying territories.

Crime Index Trends by Geographic Region 1975 over 1974

(rates per 100,000 population)

Region[1]	Total	Violent	Property	Murder	Forcible Rape	Robbery	Assault	Burglary	Larceny	Auto Theft
Northeast	+11.0	+7.1	+11.5	+2.7	+0.5	+7.5	+7.5	+9.1	+14.1	+8.1
North Central	+ 9.0	+1.8	+ 9.7	−4.7	−0.4	+2.7	+1.3	+4.3	+13.7	+1.6
South	+10.2	+2.1	+11.2	−5.2	−1.5	−0.5	+4.8	+5.9	+16.6	−2.5
West	+ 5.0	+7.9	+ 4.7	+8.4	+3.6	+8.6	+7.9	+5.2	+ 5.7	−3.1

[1]Northeast includes New England, New Jersey, New York, and Pennsylvania; North Central extends west through Nebraska and includes Missouri; South extends from Delaware, Maryland, and West Virginia to Oklahoma and Texas.

Canada: Criminal Offenses and Crime Rate

Source: Statistics Canada

	1974 Actual Offenses	1974 Rate	1975 Actual Offenses	1975 Rate	Percent change in rate
Murder.......................................	7	.03	4	.02	-33.2
Murder, Non-capital...........................	538	2.40	616	2.70	12.5
Manslaughter................................	53	.24	66	.29	20.8
Infanticide...................................	4	.02	4	.02	.0
Attempted murder.............................	521	2.32	642	2.82	21.6
Total-Homicide.........................	**1,123**	**5.00**	**1,332**	**5.84**	**16.8**
Rape..	1,823	8.12	1,852	8.12	.0
Indecent Assault-Female.......................	5,358	23.87	5,106	22.39	-6.1
Indecent Assault-Male.........................	1,167	5.20	1,155	5.07	-2.4
Other Sexual Offenses.........................	2,763	12.31	2,805	12.30	.0
Total-Sexual Offenses...................	**11,111**	**49.50**	**10,918**	**47.89**	**-3.2**
Assaults (Not Indecent).......................	96,864	431.54	102,194	448.22	3.9
Robbery.....................................	16,953	75.53	21,310	93.46	23.7
Total-Crimes of Violence................	**126,051**	**561.57**	**135,754**	**595.41**	**6.0**
Breaking and Entering.........................	233,360	1,039.64	261,287	1,146.00	10.2
Theft-Motor Vehicle...........................	83,305	371.13	90,914	398.75	7.4
Theft Over $200	79,743	355.26	95,102	417.11	17.4
Theft $200 and under..........................	459,192	2,045.74	494,777	2,170.07	6.1
Have Stolen Goods............................	15,312	68.22	16,254	71.29	4.5
Frauds......................................	75,873	338.02	86,140	377.81	11.8
Total-Property Crimes..................	**946,785**	**4,218.01**	**1,044,474**	**4,581.03**	**8.6**
Prostitution..................................	3,249	14.47	3,409	14.95	3.3
Gaming and Betting...........................	3,264	14.54	3,626	15.90	9.4
Offensive Weapons...........................	10,812	48.17	12,610	55.31	14.8
Other Criminal Code...........................	366,708	1,633.71	391,185	1,715.72	5.0
Total-Other Crimes.....................	**384,033**	**1,710.89**	**410,830**	**1,801.88**	**5.3**
Total-Criminal Code....................	**1,456,869**	**6,490.47**	**1,591,058**	**6,978.32**	**7.5**
Federal Statutes-Drugs........................	58,585	261.00	55,616	243.93	-6.4
Federal Statutes-Other........................	44,394	197.78	44,991	197.33	-.1
Provincial Statutes	368,716	1,642.66	382,480	1,677.54	2.1
Municipal By-Laws............................	81,306	362.22	65,105	285.55	-21.1
Total-All Offenses......................	**2,009.870**	**8,954.13**	**2,139,250**	**9,382.67**	**4.8**

POSTAL INFORMATION
United States Postal Service

The Postal Reorganization Act, creating a government-owned postal service under the executive branch and replacing the old Post Office Department, was signed into law by President Nixon on Aug. 12, 1970. The service officially came into being on July 1, 1971.

The new U.S. Postal Service is governed by an 11-man Board of Governors. Nine members are appointed to 9-year terms by the President with Senate approval. These 9, in turn, choose a Postmaster General, who is no longer a member of the Presi-

dent's Cabinet. The Governors and the new Postmaster General choose the 11th member, who serves as Deputy Postmaster General. A new Postal Rate Commission of 5 members, appointed by the President, recommends postal rates to the governors for their approval.

The first Postmaster General under the new system was Winton M. Blount. He resigned Oct. 29, 1971, and was replaced by his deputy, E. T. Klassen, Dec. 7, 1971. Benjamin F. Bailar succeeded him Feb. 16 1975.

U.S. Domestic Rates (effective Dec. 28, 1975)

First Class

Letters written, and matter sealed against inspection, 13c for 1st ounce or fraction, 11c for each additional ounce or fraction.

U.S. Postal cards; single 9c; double 18c; private post cards, same.

First class includes written matter, namely letters, postal cards, post cards (private mailing cards) and all other matter wholly or partly in writing, whether sealed or unsealed, except manuscripts for books, periodical articles and music, manuscript copy accompanying proofsheets or corrected proofsheets of the same and the writing authorized by law on matter of other classes. Also matter sealed or closed against inspection, bills and statements of accounts.

Greeting Cards

May be sent first class or single piece third class.

Airmail

At the present time first class mail receives the same service as airmail, as a result of the Postal Service's First Class Mail Service Improvement Program.

Second Class

Single copy mailings by general public 10c for first 2 ounces and 4c for each additional ounce or the 4th class rate, whichever is lower. There are special rates for publications, newspapers, and bulk mailing, consult local postmasters for rates and permit.

Third Class

Third Class (limit up to but not including 16 ounces): Mailable matter not in 1st and 2d classes.

Single mailing: Greeting cards (sealed or unsealed), small parcels, printed matter, booklets and catalogs. 14c the first 2 ounces plus 14c for the next 2 ounces, plus 11c for each additional 2 ounces through 15.9 ounces.

Bulk material: books, catalogs of 24 pages or more, seeds, cuttings, bulbs, roots, scions, and plants; subject to a minimum rate, consult postmaster.

Other matter: newsletters, shoppers' guides, advertising circulars. Subject to a minimum rate for which Post Office should be consulted. Separate rates for some nonprofit organizations. Bulk mailing fee, $40 per calendar year. Apply to postmaster for permit. One-time fee for permit, $20.

Parcel Post—Fourth Class

Fourth Class or Parcel Post (16 ounces and over): Merchandise, printed matter, etc., may be sealed,

subject to inspection.

On parcels weighing less than 15 lbs. and measuring more than 84 inches, but not more than 100 inches in length and girth combined, the minimum postal charge shall be the zone charge applicable to a 15-pound parcel.

Priority Mail

First-class mail of more than 13 ounces and airmail of more than 10 ounces have been merged into a "Priority Mail (Heavy Pieces)" service. The most expeditious handling and transportation available will be used for fastest delivery.

Forwarding Addresses

The mailer, in order to obtain a forwarding address, must endorse the envelope or cover "Address Correction Requested." The destination post office then will determine whether a forwarding address has been left on file and provide it for a fee.

Special Handling

Third and Fourth Class parcels will be handled and delivered as expeditiously as practicable (but not special delivery) upon payment, in addition to the regular postage: up to 2 lbs., 50c; over 2 lbs. and up to 10 lbs., 70c; over 10 lbs., $1.00. Such parcels must be endorsed, Special Handling.

Special Delivery

First class mail up to 2 lbs. $1.25, over 2 lbs. and up to 10 lbs. $1.50; over 10 lbs. $1.75. All other classes up to 2 lbs. $1.75, over 2 and up to 10 lbs. $1.85, over 10 lbs. $2.15.

Priority Mail

Air Parcel Post (over 10 ounces to 70 lbs.): packages not to exceed 100 inches in length and girth combined, including written and other matter of the first class, whether sealed or unsealed, fractions of a pound being charged as a full pound, except in the 1 to 5 pound weight category where half-pound weight increments apply.

Rates according to zone apply between the U.S. and Puerto Rico and Virgin Islands.

Parcels weighing less than 15 pounds, measuring over 84 inches but not exceeding 100 inches in length and girth combined are chargeable with a minimum rate equal to that for a 15 pound parcel for the zone to which addressed.

Zones	To 1 lb.	1½	2	2½	3	3½	4	4½	5
1, 2, 3	$1.56	$1.73	$1.89	$2.05	$2.21	$2.37	$2.53	$2.68	$2.83
4	1.58	1.77	1.96	2.15	2.33	2.51	2.69	2.86	3.03
5	1.60	1.84	2.07	2.29	2.50	2.70	2.90	3.09	3.27
6	1.62	1.90	2.18	2.43	2.68	2.91	3.14	3.35	3.56
7	1.64	1.97	2.29	2.59	2.88	3.15	3.41	3.65	3.88
8	1.67	2.07	2.46	2.78	3.09	3.38	3.67	3.94	4.20

Postal Union Mail Special Services

Registration — Available to practically all countries. Fee $2.10. The maximum indemnity payable — generally only in case of complete loss (of both contents and wrapper) — is $15.76. To Canada only the fees are $2.10 and $2.30, providing indemnity for loss up to $100 to $200, respectively.

Return receipt — Fee is 32c.

Special delivery — Available to most countries. Consult post office. Fees: for post cards, letter mail, and airmail "other articles," $1.25 up to 2 pounds; over 2 to 10 pounds, $1.50; over 10 pounds, $1.75. For surface "other articles," $1.75, $1.85, and $2.15, respectively.

Marking — An article intended for special delivery service must have affixed to the cover near the name of the country of destination "EXPRESS" (Special Delivery) label, obtainable at the post office, or it may be marked on the cover boldly in red "EXPRESS" (Special Delivery).

Special handling — Entitles AO *surface* packages to priority handling between mailing point and U.S. point of dispatch. Fees: 50c for packages to 2 pounds, 70c for packages over 2 pounds to 10 pounds, and $1.00 for packages over 10 pounds.

Airmail — There is daily air service to practically all countries.

Prepayment of replies from other countries — A mailer who wishes to prepay a reply by letter from another country may do so by sending his correspondent one or more international reply coupons, which may be purchased at United States post offices. One coupon should be accepted in any country in exchange for stamps to prepay a surface letter of the first unit of weight to the U.S.

Domestic Mail Special Services

Registry — All mailable matter prepaid with postage at the first-class or airmail rate may be registered. The mailer is required to declare the value of mail presented for registration.

Insurance — Is applicable to 3d and 4th class matter. Matter for sale addressed to prospective purchasers who have not ordered it or authorized its sending will not be insured.

C.O.D.: Unregistered — Is applicable to 3d and 4th class matter and sealed domestic mail of any class bearing postage at the 1st class rate. Such mail must be based on bona fide orders or be in conformity with agreements between senders and addressees. **Registered** — for details consult postmaster.

Certified mail — service is available for any matter having no intrinsic value on which 1st class or air mail postage is paid. Receipt is furnished at time of mailing and evidence of delivery obtained. The fee is 60c in addition to postage. Return receipt, restricted delivery and special delivery are available upon payment of additional fees. No indemnity.

Individual Piece Mailings
(Fourth Class Catalogs)

Weight lbs.	Local	1&2	3	4	5	6	7	8
				Zones				
1.5	$0.45	.54	.56	.58	.61	.64	.68	.73
2	.46	.57	.58	.62	.65	.69	.74	.81
2.5	.48	.60	.61	.66	.70	.74	.81	.89
3	.50	.62	.65	.69	.74	.81	.88	.97
3.5	.52	.65	.68	.73	.80	.86	.94	1.05
4	.53	.68	.70	.77	.84	.92	1.02	1.14
4.5	.54	.69	.73	.81	.88	.97	1.09	1.22
5	.56	.72	.76	.84	.93	1.02	1.15	1.30
6	.60	.77	.82	.92	1.02	1.14	1.29	1.46
7	.62	.82	.88	.98	1.10	1.25	1.42	1.62
8	.66	.88	.94	1.06	1.20	1.37	1.56	1.78
9	.69	.93	1.00	1.13	1.29	1.48	1.70	1.96
10	.72	.97	1.05	1.21	1.38	1.58	1.84	2.12

Zone Mileage

1... Up to 50	3...150-300	5... 600-1,000	7...1,400-1,800
2.... 50-150	4...300-600	6... 1,000-1,400	8...over, 1,800

Registered Mail

Indemnity to $100	$2.10
100.01 to 200	2.30
200.01 to 400	2.60
400.01 to 600	2.90
600.01 to 800	3.20
800.01 to 1,000	3.50
1,000.01 to 2,000	3.80
2,000.01 to 3,000	4.10
3,000.01 to 4,000	4.40
4,000.01 to 5,000	4.70
5,000.01 to 6,000	5.00
6,000.01 to 7,000	5.30
7,000.01 to 8,000	5.60
8,000.01 to 9,000	5.90
9,000.01 to 10,000	6.20

Consult postmaster for registry rates above $10,000.

Insured Mail

$0.01 to $15	$0.40
15.01 to 50	.60
50.01 to 100	.80
100.01 to 150	1.00
150.01 to 200	1.20

Liability for insured mail is limited to $200.

C.O.D. Mail

Consult postmaster for fees and conditions of mailing.

Parcel Post Rate Schedule

1 lb., not exceeding	Local	1 & 2	3	4	5	6	7	8
				Zones				
2	$0.77	$0.90	$0.93	$1.04	$1.15	$1.28	$1.40	$1.48
3	.82	.97	1.02	1.15	1.29	1.46	1.62	1.74
4	.86	1.04	1.10	1.25	1.42	1.63	1.84	2.00
5	.91	1.11	1.19	1.36	1.56	1.81	2.06	2.26
6	.95	1.18	1.27	1.46	1.69	1.98	2.28	2.52
7	1.00	1.25	1.36	1.57	1.83	2.16	2.50	2.78
8	1.04	1.32	1.44	1.67	1.96	2.33	2.72	3.04
9	1.09	1.39	1.53	1.78	2.10	2.51	2.94	3.30
10	1.13	1.46	1.61	1.88	2.23	2.68	3.16	3.56
11	1.18	1.53	1.70	1.99	2.37	2.86	3.38	3.82
12	1.22	1.60	1.78	2.09	2.50	3.03	3.60	4.08
13	1.27	1.67	1.87	2.20	2.64	3.21	3.82	4.34
14	1.31	1.74	1.95	2.30	2.77	3.38	4.04	4.60
15	1.36	1.81	2.04	2.41	2.91	3.56	4.26	4.86
16	1.40	1.88	2.12	2.51	3.04	3.73	4.48	5.12
17	1.45	1.95	2.21	2.62	3.18	3.91	4.70	5.38
18	1.49	2.02	2.29	2.72	3.31	4.08	4.92	5.64
19	1.54	2.09	2.38	2.83	3.45	4.26	5.14	5.90
20	1.58	2.16	2.46	2.93	3.58	4.43	5.36	6.16

(Consult postmaster for parcels over 20 pounds or measuring more than 72 inches, length and girth.)

Special Fourth-Class Rate
(limit 70 lbs.)

First pound or fraction, 25c (23.9c if special rate matter is presorted to 5 digit ZIP code or 24.2c if presorted to 3 digits); each additional pound or fraction through 7 pounds,' 10c; each additional pound, 8c. Only following specific articles: books 24 pages or more, at least 22 of which are printed consisting wholly of reading matter or scholarly bibliography containing no advertisement other than incidental announcements of books; 16 millimeter films in final form (except when mailed to or from commercial theaters); printed music in bound or sheet form; printed objective test materials; sound recordings, playscripts and manuscripts for books, periodicals and music; printed educational reference charts; loose-leaf pages and binders therefor consisting of medical information for distribution to doctors, hospitals, medical schools and medical students. Package must be marked "Special 4th-Class Rate" stating item contained.

Library Rate (limit 70 lbs.)

First pound or fraction 9c, each additional pound or fraction 4c. Books when loaned or exchanged between schools, colleges, public libraries, and certain non-profit organizations; books, printed music, bound academic theses, periodicals, sound recordings, other library materials, museum materials (specimens, collections), scientific or mathematical kits, instruments or other devices; also catalogs, guides or scripts for some of these materials. Must be marked "Library Rate".

Post Office-Authorized 2-Letter State Abbreviations

Gradually replacing the traditional abbreviations for the states of the United States are the two-letter ones approved by the Post Office Department when it introduced the ZIP Code in 1963. The official list follows, including the District of Columbia, Guan, Puerto Rico, the Canal Zone, and the Virgin Islands (all capital letters are used):

State		State		State	
Alabama	AL	Kentucky	KY	Ohio	OH
Alaska	AK	Louisiana	LA	Oklahoma	OK
Arizona	AZ	Maine	ME	Oregon	OR
Arkansas	AR	Maryland	MD	Pennsylvania	PA
California	CA	Massachusetts	MA	Puerto Rico	PR
Canal Zone	CZ				
Colorado	CO	Michigan	MI	Rhode Island	RI
Connecticut	CT	Minnesota	MN	South Carolina	SC
Delaware	DE	Mississippi	MS	South Dakota	SD
Dist. of Col.	DC	Missouri	MO	Tennessee	TN
Florida	FL	Montana	MT	Texas	TX
Georgia	GA	Nebraska	NE	Utah	UT
Guam	GU	Nevada	NV	Vermont	VT
Hawaii	HI	New Hampshire	NH	Virginia	VA
Idaho	ID	New Jersey	NJ	Virgin Islands	VI
Illinois	IL	New Mexico	NM	Washington	WA
Indiana	IN	New York	NY	West Virginia	WV
Iowa	IA	North Carolina	NC	Wisconsin	WI
Kansas	KS	North Dakota	ND	Wyoming	WY

Commemorative Stamps and Regular Postal Issues 1976

Date		Commemorative Stamp	Value	From
Jan.	1	Spirit of '76	13c	Pasadena, CA
Jan.	2	International Airmail	25c	Honolulu, HI
Jan	2	International Airmail	31c	Honolulu, HI
Jan.	16	Aerogramme	22c	Tempe, AZ
Jan.	17	Interphil 76	13c	Philadelphia, PA
Feb.	2	Homemaker Embossed Envelope	13c	Biloxi, MS
Feb.	23	50 State Flags	13c	Washington, DC
Mar.	5	Freedom to Assemble (coil)	9c	Milwaukee, WI
Mar.	10	Telephone	13c	Boston, MA
Mar.	15	Farmer Embossed Envelope	13c	New Orleans, LA
Mar.	19	Commercial Aviation	13c	Chicago, IL
Apr.	2	Liberty Bell Book	13c	Liberty, MO
Apr.	6	Chemistry	13c	New York, NY
Apr.	23	Drum "Americana Series" (coil)	7.9c	Miami, FL
May	29	Surrender of Cornwallis at Yorktown	13c	Philadelphia, PA
May	29	Signing Declaration of Independence	18c	Philadelphia, PA
May	29	Washington Crossing the Delaware	24c	Philadelphia, PA
May	29	Washington at Valley Forge	31c	Philadelphia, PA
June	1	Benjamin Franklin	13c	Philadelphia, PA
June	30	Doctor Embossed Envelope	13c	Dallas, TX
July	1	Caesar Rodney Postal Card	9c	Dover, DE
July	4	Signing Declaration of Independence (4 stamps)	13c	Philadelphia, PA
July	16	Olympic Games (4 stamps)	13c	Lake Placid, NY
Aug.	6	Craftsman Embossed Envelope	13c	Hancock, MA
Aug.	18	Clara Maass	13c	Belleville, NJ
Sept.	10	Nonprofit Embossed Envelope	2c	Hempstead, NY
Sept.	18	Adolph S. Ochs	13c	New York, NY
Oct.	15	Centennial Embossed Envelope	13c	Los Angeles, CA
Oct.	27	Christmas — Copley	13c	Boston, MA
Oct.	27	Christmas — Currier	13c	Boston, MA

Postal Receipts at Large Cities

Fiscal Year	Boston	Chicago	Detroit	L.A.	New York	Phil.	St Louis	Wash., D.C.
1971	96,205,407	292,558,518	70,256,324	149,063,344	359,170,452	107,122,556	65,104,974	84,053,982
1972	109,178,539	332,951,729	85,997,396	172,644,940	395,523,484	120,055,844	73,246,822	99,980,611
1973	114,159,472	339,770,450	84,358,518	172,365,582	392,348,195	120,173,378	75,342,257	103,152,177
1974	123,164,661	347,561,637	87,784,811	176,847,940	409,392,651	130,655,216	79,412,843	133,458,807
1975	136,453,079	365,378,795	84,338,282	193,229,077	453,905,277	134,571,376	85,591,774	115,489,343

Other cities for fiscal year 1975: Atlanta, $113,262,174; Baltimore, $79,662,340; Cincinnati, $54,599,716; Cleveland, $82,797,098; Columbus, $60,879,274; Dallas, $109,882,677; Denver, $63,226,335; Houston, $92,854,755; Indianapolis, $63,383,916; Kanss City, $68,068,048; Minneapolis, $86,135,949; Pittsburgh, $67,224,943; San Francisco, $99,134,080; Seattle, $55,855,660.

Post Offices in the United States

As of June 30, 1975, there was a total of 30,754 post offices throughout the U.S. and possessions. Of this number 5,477 were First Class; 7,396 Second Class; 12,191 Third Class; and 5,690 Fourth Class.

Air Mail, Parcel Post International Rates

Aerogrammes — 22 cents each to all countries.
Air Mail Post Cards (single) — 21 cents to all countries except Canada and Mexico (14c).

Country	Letters and letter pkgs. per ¹/₂ oz. thru 2 oz.	per ¹/₂ oz. over 2 oz.	Other Articles First 2 oz.	Each add'l. 2 oz. or fraction	Parcel Post First 4 oz.	Each add'l. 4 oz. or fraction	Surface Parcel Post First 2 lbs.	Each add'l. pound or fraction	Max. wt. for parcel post (surface or air) lbs.
Afghanistan	.31	.26	.86	.42	3.14	1.20	1.90	.57	22
Albania	.31	.26	.73	.29	3.33	.79	1.90	.57	22
Algeria	.31	.26	.73	.29	2.71	.80	1.90	.57	44
Andorra	.31	.26	.73	.29	2.79	.70	1.90	.57	44
Angola	.31	.26	.86	.42	2.93	1.01	1.90	.57	22
Anguilla	.25	.25	.60	.16	1.78	.36	1.90	.57	22
Antigua	.25	.25	.60	.16	1.78	.36	1.90	.57	22
Argentina	.31	.26	.73	.29	2.46	1.07	1.75	.50	22
Aruba	.25	.25	.60	.16	2.08	.45	1.75	.50	44
Ascension Isl.	.25	.25	.73	.29	(4)	—	1.90	.57	22
Australia[3]	.31	.26	.86	.42	2.62	1.21	1.90	.57	44
Austria	.31	.26	.73	.29	2.70	.74	1.90	.57	44
Azores	.31	.26	.73	.29	1.95	.56	1.90	.57	22
Bahamas	.25	.25	.60	.16	2.19	.27	1.75	.50	22
Bahrian	.31	.26	.86	.42	2.42	1.03	1.90	.57	22
Bangladesh	.31	.26	.86	.42	3.46	1.22	1.90	.57	22
Barbados	.25	.25	.60	.16	1.90	.51	1.75	.50	22
Barbuda	.25	.25	.60	.16	1.78	.36	1.75	.50	22
Belgium	.31	.26	.73	.29	2.41	.66	1.90	.57	44
Belize	.25	.25	.60	.16	2.14	.46	1.90	.57	44
Benin	.31	.26	.86	.42	2.36	.85	1.90	.57	44
Bermuda	.25	.25	.60	.16	1.77	.35	1.75	.50	33
Bhutan	.31	.26	.86	.42	(4)	—	....	....	(5)
Bolivia[3]	.31	.26	.73	.29	2.47	.69	1.90	.57	44
Bonaire	.25	.25	.60	.16	2.08	.45	1.75	.50	44
Botswana	.31	.26	.86	.42	2.66	1.27	1.90	.57	22
Brazil	.25	.25	.73	.29	2.94	.79	1.90	.57	44
Br. Virgin Isl.	.25	.25	.60	.16	1.78	.36	1.75	.50	22
Brunei	.31	.26	.86	.42	3.01	1.47	1.90	.57	22
Bulgaria	.31	.26	.73	.29	2.15	.75	1.90	.57	22
Burma[3]	.31	.26	.86	.42	3.30	1.43	1.90	.57	22
Burundi	.31	.26	.86	.42	2.76	1.07	1.90	.57	22
Cameroon	.31	.26	.86	.42	2.79	.92	1.90	.57	22
Canada[3]	(oz.) .17	(addl. oz.) .15	(6)	—	(6)	—	1.75	.50	35
Cape Verde	.31	.26	.86	.42	2.72	.81	1.90	.57	22
Cen. Africa Rep.	.31	.26	.86	.42	2.76	1.07	1.90	.57	44
Chad	.31	.26	.86	.42	2.76	1.07	1.90	.57	44
Chile[3]	.31	.26	.73	.29	2.92	.89	1.90	.57	22
China Rep.	.31	.26	.86	.42	2.46	1.05	1.90	.57	44
China, People's Rep.	.31	.26	.86	.42	3.08	1.37	1.90	.57	44
Colombia	.31	.26	.60	.16	2.86	.50	1.90	.57	44
Comoro Isl.	.31	.26	.86	.42	3.13	1.43	1.90	.57	44
Congo (Brazza.)	.31	.26	.86	.42	2.76	1.07	1.90	.57	44
Corsica	.31	.26	.73	.29	2.98	.66	1.90	.57	44
Costa Rica	.25	.25	.60	.16	2.06	.43	1.75	.50	44
Cuba	.25	.25	.60	.16	(4)	—	....	....	(5)
Curacao	.25	.25	.60	.16	2.08	.45	1.75	.50	44
Cyprus	.31	.26	.73	.29	2.88	.85	1.90	.57	22
Czechoslovakia	.31	.26	.73	.29	2.17	.76	1.90	.57	44
Denmark	.31	.26	.73	.29	2.14	.72	1.90	.57	44
Dominica	.25	.25	.60	.16	2.39	.48	1.75	.50	22
Dominican Rep.	.25	.25	.60	.16	2.24	.36	1.75	.50	44
Ecuador	.31	.26	.73	.29	2.78	.48	1.90	.57	44
Egypt	.31	.26	.73	.29	2.32	.92	1.90	.57	44
El Salvador	.25	.25	.60	.16	2.21	.44	1.75	.50	44
Equatorial Guinea	.31	.26	.86	.42	2.82	1.22	1.90	.57	44
Estonia[2]	.31	.26	.86	.42	2.84	.95	1.90	.57	44
Ethiopia	.31	.26	.86	.42	2.83	1.10	1.90	.57	44
Faeroe Isl.	.31	.26	.73	.29	2.14	.72	1.90	.57	44
Falkland Isl.	.31	.26	.73	.29	2.99	.85	1.90	.57	22
Fiji Islands	.31	.26	.86	.42	2.79	.90	1.90	.57	22
Finland	.31	.26	.73	.29	2.17	.79	1.90	.57	44
France incl. Monaco	.31	.26	.73	.29	2.98	.66	1.90	.57	44
French Guiana	.31	.26	.73	.29	2.19	.56	1.90	.57	44
Fr. Polynesia	.31	.26	.86	.42	2.70	.76	1.90	.57	44
Fr. Ter. Afars, Issas	.31	.26	.86	.42	2.89	1.03	1.90	.57	44
Gabon Rep.	.31	.26	.86	.42	2.76	1.07	1.90	.57	44
Gambia	.31	.26	.86	.42	2.39	.76	1.90	.57	22
Germany, incl. Saar.	.31	.26	.73	.29	2.10	.70	1.90	.57	44
Ghana	.31	.26	.86	.42	2.92	.92	1.90	.57	44
Gilbraltar	.31	.26	.73	.29	2.16	.75	1.90	.57	22
Gilbert & Ellice	.31	.26	.86	.42	2.66	1.00	1.90	.57	22
Great Britain	.31	.26	.73	.29	2.08	.66	1.90	.57	44
Greece	.31	.26	.73	.29	2.62	.84	1.90	.57	44
Greenland	.31	.26	.73	.29	2.35	.93	1.90	.57	44
Grenada	.25	.25	.60	.16	2.39	.48	1.75	.50	22
Guadeloupe	.25	.25	.60	.16	2.00	.36	1.75	.50	44

Country	Letters and letter pkgs. per ½ oz. thru 2 oz.	per ½ oz. over 2 oz.	Other Articles First 2 oz.	Each add'l. 2 oz. or fraction	Parcel Post First 4 oz.	Each add'l. 4 oz. or fraction	Surface Parcel Post First 2 lbs.	Each add'l. pound or fraction	Max. wt. for parcel post (surface or air) lbs.
Guatemala	.25	.25	.60	.16	2.51	.46	1.75	.50	44
Guinea, Rep. of	.31	.26	.86	.42	2.46	.96	1.90	.57	44
Guinea-Bissau	.31	.26	.86	.42	2.93	1.01	1.90	.57	22
Guyana	.31	.26	.73	.29	2.42	.50	1.90	.57	22
Haiti	.25	.25	.60	.16	2.25	.35	1.75	.50	44
Honduras	.25	.25	.60	.16	2.14	.46	1.75	.50	¹44
Hong Kong	.31	.26	.86	.42	2.65	1.24	1.90	.57	22
Hungary	.31	.26	.73	.29	2.16	.76	1.90	.57	44
Iceland	.31	.26	.73	.29	2.66	.56	1.90	.57	44
India	.31	.26	.86	.42	2.67	1.27	1.90	.57	¹44
Indonesia	.31	.26	.86	.42	3.48	1.52	1.90	.57	22
Iran	.31	.26	.86	.42	2.67	.96	1.90	.57	44
Iraq	.31	.26	.86	.42	2.98	.95	1.90	.57	44
Ireland (Eire)	.31	.26	.73	.29	2.06	.66	1.90	.57	22
Israel	.31	.26	.86	.42	2.93	.91	1.90	.57	44
Italy	.31	.26	.73	.29	2.63	.79	1.90	.57	44
Ivory Coast	.31	.26	.86	.42	2.46	.95	1.90	.57	44
Jamaica	.25	.25	.60	.16	2.36	.33	1.75	.50	22
Japan	.31	.26	.86	.42	2.19	.80	1.90	.57	22
Jordan	.31	.26	.86	.42	2.72	.90	1.90	.57	22
Kampuchea (Cambodia)	.31	.26	.86	.42	(4)	—	1.90	.57	(5)
Kenya	.31	.26	.86	.42	2.93	1.10	1.90	.57	22
Korea (Rep. of)	.31	.26	.86	.42	2.25	.85	1.90	.57	22
No. Korea¹	.31	.26	.86	.42	(4)	—	—	—	(5)
Kuwait	.31	.26	.86	.42	2.39	1.00	1.90	.57	44
Laos	.31	.26	.86	.42	3.35	1.37	1.90	.57	22
Latvia²	.31	.26	.86	.42	2.84	.95	1.90	.57	44
Lebanon	.31	.26	.86	.42	2.72	.90	1.90	.57	¹44
Leeward Islands	.25	.25	.60	.16	1.78	.36	1.75	.50	44
Lesotho	.31	.26	.86	.42	2.66	1.27	1.90	.57	22
Liberia	.31	.26	.86	.42	2.24	.84	1.90	.57	22
Libya	.31	.26	.73	.29	2.70	.85	1.90	.57	44
Liechtenstein	.31	.26	.73	.29	2.39	.67	1.90	.57	44
Lithuania²	.31	.26	.86	.42	2.84	.95	1.90	.57	44
Luxembourg	.31	.26	.73	.29	2.47	.65	1.90	.57	44
Macao	.31	.26	.86	.42	3.20	1.24	1.90	.57	22
Madagascar	.31	.26	.86	.42	3.09	1.22	1.90	.57	44
Madeira Isl.	.31	.26	.73	.29	2.10	.72	1.90	.57	22
Malawi	.31	.26	.86	.42	2.66	1.24	1.90	.57	22
Malaysia	.31	.26	.86	.42	3.23	1.42	1.90	.57	22
Maldives, Rep. of	.31	.26	.86	.42	3.59	1.29	1.90	.57	22
Mali	.31	.26	.86	.42	3.46	.82	1.90	.57	22
Malta	.31	.26	.73	.29	2.61	.79	1.90	.57	44
Martinique	.25	.25	.60	.16	2.00	.36	1.75	.50	44
Mauritania	.31	.26	.86	.42	2.36	.79	1.90	.57	44
Mauritius	.31	.26	.86	.42	3.01	1.29	1.90	.57	22
Mexico	(oz.) .17	(add'l. oz.) .15	.60	.16	1.77	.35	1.75	.50	44
Montserrat	.25	.25	.60	.16	1.78	.36	1.90	.57	22
Morocco	.31	.26	.73	.29	2.63	.79	1.90	.57	44
Mozambique	.31	.26	.86	.42	3.43	1.28	1.90	.57	22
Namibia (SW Africa)	.31	.26	.86	.42	2.66	1.27	1.90	.57	22
Nauru (Rep.)	.31	.26	.86	.42	2.62	1.21	1.90	.57	22
Nepal	.31	.26	.86	.42	2.66	1.27	1.90	.57	44
Netherlands	.31	.26	.73	.29	2.36	.66	1.90	.57	44
Neth. Antilles	.25	.25	.60	.16	2.08	.45	1.75	.50	44
Nevis	.25	.25	.60	.16	1.78	.36	1.75	.50	44
New Caledonia	.31	.26	.86	.42	2.81	.93	1.90	.57	44
New Guinea, Terr. of	.31	.26	.86	.42	2.72	1.32	1.90	.57	22
New Hebrides	.31	.26	.86	.42	2.65	.93	1.90	.57	44
New Zealand	.31	.26	.86	.42	2.98	1.07	1.90	.57	22
Nicaragua	.25	.25	.60	.16	2.08	.43	1.75	.50	44
Niger	.31	.26	.86	.42	3.45	.80	1.90	.57	44
Nigeria	.31	.26	.86	.42	3.14	.93	1.90	.57	22
Norway	.31	.26	.73	.29	2.14	.72	1.90	.57	44
Oman, Sultanate of	.31	.26	.86	.42	2.42	1.03	1.90	.57	22
Outer Mongolia	.31	.26	.86	.42	(4)	—	1.90	.57	(5)
Pakistan	.31	.26	.86	.42	3.46	1.22	1.90	.57	22
Panama	.25	.25	.60	.16	2.50	.45	1.75	.50	¹70
Papua - New Guinea	.31	.26	.86	.42	2.72	1.32	1.90	.57	22
Paraguay	.31	.26	.73	.29	2.47	.67	1.90	.57	44
Peru	.31	.26	.73	.29	2.88	.60	1.90	.57	44
Philippines	.31	.26	.86	.42	3.03	1.17	1.90	.57	¹44
Pitcairn	.31	.26	.86	.42	2.89	1.03	1.90	.57	22
Poland	.31	.26	.73	.29	2.61	.75	1.90	.57	44
Portugal	.31	.26	.73	.29	2.05	.64	1.90	.57	22
Portuguese Timor	.31	.26	.86	.42	3.64	1.72	1.90	.57	22
" W. Africa	.31	.26	.86	.42	2.93	1.01	1.90	.57	22
Qatar	.31	.26	.86	.42	2.42	1.03	1.90	.57	22
Reunion	.31	.26	.86	.42	2.89	1.27	1.90	.57	44
Rhodesia	.31	.26	.86	.42	2.66	1.24	1.90	.57	22
Romania	.31	.26	.73	.29	2.42	.79	1.90	.57	22

| | Air Service | | | | | | Surface Parcel Post | | |
| | Letters and letter pkgs. | | Other Articles | | Parcel Post | | | | Max. wt. for parcel post (surface or air) lbs. |
Country	Per ½ oz. thru 2 oz.	Per ½ oz. over 2 oz.	First 2 oz.	Each add'l. 2 oz. or fraction	First 4 oz.	Each add'l. 4 oz. or fraction	First 2 lbs.	Each add'l. pound or fraction	
Rwanda	.31	.26	.86	.42	2.76	1.07	1.90	.57	22
Ryukyu	.31	.26	.86	.42	2.19	.80	1.90	.57	22
Sabah	.25	.25	.60	.16	2.08	.45	1.90	.57	44
St. Christopher	.25	.25	.60	.16	2.39	.48	1.75	.50	22
St. Eustatius	.25	.25	.60	.16	2.08	.45	1.75	.50	44
St. Helena	.31	.26	.86	.42	3.01	1.22	1.90	.57	22
St. Lucia	.25	.25	.60	.16	2.39	.48	1.75	.50	22
St. Pierre, Miquelon	.25	.25	.60	.16	1.72	.35	1.75	.50	44
St. Vincent	.25	.25	.60	.16	2.39	.48	1.75	.50	22
Santa Cruz Isl	.31	.26	.86	.42	3.10	1.39	1.90	.57	22
Sao Tome & Principe	.31	.26	.86	.42	2.93	1.01	1.90	.57	22
Saudi Arabia	.31	.26	.86	.42	3.10	1.00	1.90	.57	22
Senegal	.31	.26	.86	.42	2.34	.75	1.90	.57	44
Seychelles	.31	.26	.86	.42	2.53	1.12	1.90	.57	22
Sierra Leone	.31	.26	.86	.42	3.09	.81	1.90	.57	22
Singapore	.31	.26	.86	.42	3.23	1.42	1.90	.57	22
Solomon Isl	.31	.26	.86	.42	3.12	1.39	1.90	.57	22
Somali Rep	.31	.26	.86	.42	3.23	1.13	1.90	.57	22
South Africa	.31	.26	.86	.42	2.66	1.27	1.90	.57	22
Spain	.31	.26	.73	.29	2.79	.70	1.90	.57	44
Sp. W. Africa	.31	.26	.86	.42	2.81	.81	1.90	.57	44
Sri Lanka (Ceylon)	.31	.26	.86	.42	3.33	1.28	1.90	.57	22
Sudan	.31	.26	.86	.42	3.13	1.01	1.90	.57	22
Surinam	.31	.26	.73	.29	2.24	.53	1.90	.57	44
Swaziland	.31	.26	.86	.42	2.66	1.27	1.90	.57	44
Sweden	.31	.26	.73	.29	2.14	.72	1.90	.57	44
Switzerland	.31	.26	.73	.29	2.39	.67	1.90	.57	44
Syria	.31	.26	.86	.42	2.47	.92	1.90	.57	44
Tanzania	.31	.26	.86	.42	2.99	1.15	1.90	.57	22
Thailand	.31	.26	.86	.42	3.28	1.17	1.90	.57	22
Togo	.31	.26	.86	.42	2.57	.95	1.90	.57	44
Tonga	.31	.26	.86	.42	2.34	.93	1.90	.57	22
Trinidad, Tobago	.31	.26	.60	.16	2.37	.45	1.75	.50	22
Tristan da Cunha	.31	.26	.86	.42	2.83	1.21	1.90	.57	22
Tunisia	.31	.26	.73	.29	2.62	.75	1.90	.57	44
Turkey	.31	.26	.73	.29	2.26	.85	1.90	.57	44
Turks Islands	.25	.25	.60	.16	2.25	.33	1.75	.50	22
Uganda	.31	.26	.86	.42	2.93	1.10	1.90	.57	22
USSR[2]	.31	.26	.86	.42	2.84	.95	1.90	.57	44
United Arab Emir	.31	.26	.86	.42	2.42	1.03	1.90	.57	44
Upper Volta	.31	.26	.86	.42	2.72	.89	1.90	.57	44
Uruguay	.31	.26	.73	.29	2.93	.90	1.90	.57	44
Vatican City	.31	.26	.73	.29	2.42	.74	1.90	.57	44
Venezuela	.25	.25	.60	.16	2.71	.43	1.90	.57	44
Vietnam	.31	.26	.86	.42	(4)	....	....	....	(5)
Western Samoa	.31	.26	.86	.42	2.71	.80	1.90	.57	22
Windward Isl	.25	.25	.60	.16	2.39	.48	1.75	.50	22
Yemen (Aden)	.31	.26	.86	.42	2.81	1.10	....	....	44
Yemen (Sanaa)	.31	.26	.86	.42	3.04	1.55	1.90	.57	44
Yugoslavia	.31	.26	.73	.29	2.17	.79	1.90	.57	44
Zaire	.31	.26	.86	.42	2.76	1.07	1.90	.57	44
Zambia	.31	.26	.86	.42	2.66	1.24	1.90	.57	44

(1.) Restrictions apply; consult post office. (2.) To facilitate distribution and delivery, include "Union of Soviet Socialist Republics" or "USSR" as part of the address. (3.) Small packets weight limit one pound. (4.) No air parcel post service. (5.) No surface parcel post service. (6.) No airmail AO or parcel post to Canada; prepare and prepay all airmail packages as letter mail. (7.) The Continental Cina Postal authorities will not deliver articles unless addressed to show name of the country as "People's Republic of China"; also, acceptable spelling of capital is "Peking."

International Mails
Weight and Dimensional Limits and Surface Rates

For air rates and parcel post see pages 972-974

Letters and letter packages: All written matter or correspondence recordings, must be sent as letter mail. Weight limit: 4 lbs. to all countries except Canada, which is 60 lbs. Surface rates: Canada and Mexico, 13c first ounce; 11c each additional ounce or fraction up to 13 ounces; eighth-zone priority rates for heavier weights. Countries other than Canada and Mexico, 1 ounce, 18c; over 1 to 2 ounces, 31c; over 2 to 4 ounces, 41c; over 4 to 8 ounces, 82c; over 8 ounces to 1 pound, $1.58; over 1 to 2 pounds, $2.75; and over 2 to 4 pounds, $4.46. Air rates: Canada and Mexico, 17c first ounce; 15c each additional ounce or fraction. Central America, Colombia, Venezuela, the Caribbean Islands, Bahamas, Bermuda and St. Pierre and Miquelon, 25c per half ounce up to and including 2 ounces; 21c each additional half ounce or fraction. All other countries, 31c per half ounce up to and including 2 ounces; 26c each additional half ounce or fraction. Aerogrammes, which can be folded into the form of an envelope and sent by air to all countries, are available at post offices for 22c each.

NOTE. Mail to Canada bearing postage paid at the surface letter rate will receive airmail service in both the U.S. and Canada during the Postal Service First Class Mail Service Improvement Program.

Post cards. Surface rates to Canada and Mexico, 9c; to all other countries, 12c. By air, Canada and Mexico, 14c; to all other countries, 21c. Maximum size permitted, 6 x 4 1/4 in.; minimum, 5 1/2 x 3 1/2.

Printed matter. To Canada and Mexico, 14c the first 2 ounces, 14c for the next two ounces, plus 11c each add'l. 2 ounces or fraction through 1 pound; $1.15 for 1 to 2 pounds, $1.44 for 2 to 4 pounds. To other countries, 14c the first 2 ounces, 28c 2 to 4 ounces, 50c 4 to 8 ounces, 83c 8 to 16 ounces, $1.15 1 to 2 pounds, $1.44 2 to 4 pounds. To countries admitting regular prints over 4 lbs. 72c for each additional 2 lbs. or fraction. (Consult post office for rates and conditions applying to certain publications mailed by the publishers or by registered news agents.) Book weight limits for most countries is 11 lbs; for exceptions see below. Consult post office for book rates.

Exceptional weight limits for printed matter. Printed matter may weigh up to 22 lbs. to Argentina, Bolivia, Brazil, Chile, Colombia, Costa Rica, Cuba, Dominican Republic, Ecuador, El Salvador, Guatemala, Haiti, Honduras, Mexico, Nicaragua, Panama, Paraguay, Peru, Spain (including Balearic Islands, Canary Islands and offices in Northern Africa), Uruguay, and Venezuela. For other countries, limit for books is 11 lbs., all other prints. 4 lbs.

Matter for the blind. Surface rate free; air rates to Canada

17c per oz. (For all other countries, consult postmaster.) Weight limit 15 lbs.

Small packets. Postage rates for small items of merchandise and samples are lower than for letter packages or parcel post; consult post office for weight limits and requirements for customs declarations. Surface rates: Canada and Mexico, 14c the first 2 oz., 14c for the next 2 oz., plus 11c for each add'l 2 oz. or fraction. All other countries, for 4 oz. or less 28c; 4 to 8 oz. 50c; 8 oz. to 1 lb. 83c; 1 to 2 lbs. $1.15. For other rates, see schedule "Air Service Other Articles" under heading of International Rates for Air Mail and Surface Parcel Post, pages 972-974.

Canadian Postal Rates
(effective Sept. 1, 1976)

Letter Mail and Postcards.
Up to 1 oz. $.10, over 1 and up to 2 oz. $.18, over 2 and up to 4 oz. $.25, plus $.10 for each additional 2 oz. up to 16 oz.

Parcels (over 1 lb.)
First class (maximum 66 lb.) parcels receive priority air service.
Fourth class (maximum 35 lb.) parcels receive surface transmission.
The charges given below are for local (short haul) deliveries. A chart showing the cost for deliveries to all other postal zones may be obtained from your local postmaster.

over up to	1 lb. 2 lb.	2 3	3 4	4 5	5 6	6 7	7 8	8 9	9 10	10 15
1st 4th	$1.25 .60	1.55 .75	1.80 .90	2.10 1.05	2.40 1.15	2.65 1.30	2.95 1.45	3.20 1.60	3.50 1.75	4.05 1.95
over up to	15 lb. 20 lb.	20 25	25 30	30 35	35 40	40 45	45 50	50 55	55 60	60 66
1st 4th	4.65 2.15	5.20 2.35	5.75 2.55	6.30 2.75	6.85	7.45	8.00	8.55	9.15	9.70

Third Class. Standard addressed rates (includes greeting cards).
Up to 2 oz. $.08, plus $.04 for each additional 2 oz. up to a maximum of 1 lb.

Premium Services. Certified mail - (proof of delivery service) $.40 plus postage. Special Delivery on 1st class mail only $.60 plus 1st class postage. Money order fee (maximum $200) - $.25.

To U.S.A. its Territories and Possessions

Airmail letters and postcards, up to and including 1 oz. $.10 plus $.09 for each additional oz. up to 1 lb. Over 1 lb. up to and including 2 lbs. $2.50 plus $.65 for each additional lb. up to a maximum of 66 lbs.

Surface parcel post. Up to and including 2 lbs. $1.50 plus $.40 for each additional lb. up to a maximum of 35 lbs.

International Parcel Post
For rates see pages 972-974

General dimensional limits — Greatest length, 3 1/2 feet; greatest length and girth combined, 6 feet.

Prohibited articles. Before sending goods abroad the mailer should satisfy himself that they will not be confiscated or returned because their importation is prohibited or restricted by the country of address.

Packing. Parcels for transmission overseas should be even more carefully packed than those intended for delivery within the continental United States. Containers should be used which will be strong enough to protect the contents from the weight of

other mails, from pressure and friction, climatic changes, and repeated handlings.

Sealing. Registered or insured parcels must be sealed. To some countries the sealing of ordinary (unregistered and uninsured) parcels is optional, and to others compulsory. Consult post office.

Customs declarations, and other forms. A parcel post sticker, and at least one customs declaration giving a complete description of the contents, are required for each parcel mailed to another country.

United Nations Postage Stamps Issued in 1975

UN stamps in United States denominations, valid for postage only on mail deposited at UN Headquarters, New York, and UN stamps in Swiss denominations, valid for postage only on mail deposited at the United Nations Office, Geneva, are available at face value from the U.N. Postal Administration in New York and Geneva and through sales agencies around the world. They may be obtained by mail or automatically through the Customer Deposit Account service, both in New York and Geneva. Revenue from the sale of UN stamps for postage purposes goes to the U.S. Postal Service and the Swiss PTT, respectively; from

philatelic sales, revenue goes to the UN.

Date	Stamp	Value
9 Jan.	Definitives	3c, 4c, 30c, 50c
12 Mar.	World Federation of U.N. Associations	13c, 26c
23 Apr.	UNCTAD	13c, 31c
28 May	Human Settlements	13c, 25c
8 Oct.	UNPA 25th Anniversary	13c, 31c
19 Nov.	World Food Council	13c
"	Definitive	9c

QUICK REFERENCE INDEX

First Class Postal Rates in Brief

(Effective Dec. 28, 1975)

United States Domestic

Letters—13c first ounce, 11c each additional ounce.
Postal Cards—9c each (up to 4 1/2 x 6 in.). Double cards, 18c. Private cards, 18c.

United States International

Letters—(1) Canada and Mexico, 13c first ounce, 11c each addl. ounce to 13 ounces; over 12 ounces to 1 pound, $1.67; over 1 pound to 1 1/2 pounds, $2.07; over 1 1/2 to 2 pounds, $2.46; over 2 to 2 1/2 pounds, $2.78; over 2 1/2 to 3 pounds, $3.09; over 3 to 3 1/2 pounds, $3.38; over 3 1/2 to 4 pounds, $3.67; over 4 to 4 1/2 pounds, $3.94; over 4 1/2 to 5 pounds, $4.20; over 5 pounds, 52c each additional pound or fraction.
(2) Countries other than Canada and Mexico, 1 ounce, 18c; over 1 to 2 ounces, 31c; over 2 to 4 ounces, 41c; over 4 to 8 ounces, 82c; over 8 ounces to 1 pound, $1.58; over 1 to 2 pounds, $2.75; and over 2 to 4 pounds, $4.46.
Air Mail Letters—(1) Canada and Mexico, 17c per ounce. (2). Cen. America, S. America, the Caribbean Is., Bahamas, Bermuda and St. Pierre and Miquelon, 25c per half ounce. (3) All other countries, 31c per half ounce.
Aerogrammes—To all countries, 18c each.
Postal cards—To Canada and Mexico 9c each. To all other countries, 12c each.
Air mail post cards—To Canada and Mexico 14c each, to other countries 21c each.

Canada

Domestic—1 oz., 10c; 1-2 oz., 18c; 2-4 oz., 25c; each additional 2 oz., 10c.
International—Letters to U.S. by air, 10c for 1st oz.; 9c each additional oz. to 1 lb.; 1-2 lbs., $2.50, and 65c each additional oz.
Postcards 10c.
Aerogrammes 15c.